Collins | COBUILD
ADVANCED AMERICAN ENGLISH DICTIONARY

HarperCollins Publishers
Westerhill Road
Bishopbriggs
Glasgow
G64 2QT

HarperCollins Publishers
Macken House
39/40 Mayor Street Upper
Dublin 1, D01 C9W8, Ireland

Third edition 2023

10 9 8 7 6 5 4 3 2 1

© HarperCollins Publishers 2006, 2016, 2023

ISBN 978-0-00-860778-4

Collins® and COBUILD® are registered trademarks of HarperCollins Publishers Limited

www.collinsdictionary.com/cobuild
www.collins.co.uk/elt

A catalogue record for this book is available from the British Library

Printed in India

Typeset by Davidson Publishing Solutions, Glasgow, Scotland

All rights reserved. No part of this book may be reproduced, stored in a retrieval system, or transmitted in any form or by any means, electronic, mechanical, photocopying, recording or otherwise, without the prior permission in writing of the Publisher. This book is sold subject to the conditions that it shall not, by way of trade or otherwise, be lent, re-sold, hired out or otherwise circulated without the Publisher's prior consent in any form of binding or cover other than that in which it is published and without a similar condition including this condition being imposed on the subsequent purchaser.

HarperCollins does not warrant that www.collinsdictionary.com and www.collins.co.uk/elt or any other website mentioned in this title will be provided uninterrupted, that any website will be error free, that defects will be corrected, or that the website or the server that makes it available are free of viruses or bugs. For full terms and conditions please refer to the site terms provided on the website.

Entered words that we have reason to believe constitute trademarks have been designated as such. However, neither the presence nor absence of such designation should be regarded as affecting the legal status of any trademark.

If you would like to comment on any aspect of this book, please contact us at the given address or online.
Email: dictionaries@harpercollins.co.uk
facebook.com/collinselt
@CollinsELT

Acknowledgments
We would like to thank those authors and publishers who kindly gave permission for copyright material to be used in the Collins Corpus. We would also like to thank Times Newspapers Ltd for providing valuable data.

Founding Editor-in-Chief
John Sinclair

For the Publisher
Maree Airlie, Gillian Bowman, Kerry Ferguson, Janice McNeillie, Anna Stevenson, Lisa Todd

Contributors
Ian Brookes, Alice Grandison, Susan Iannuzzi, Maggie Seaton

This book is produced from independently certified FSC™ paper to ensure responsible forest management.

For more information visit: www.harpercollins.co.uk/green

Contents

About COBUILD dictionaries	v
Acknowledgements	vi
Guide to dictionary entries	viii
Guide to dictionary features	x
Introduction	xiii
Guide to definitions	xiv
Pronunciation	xvii
IPA symbols	xvii
List of grammatical notations	xx
Explanation of grammatical terms	xxii
Irregular verbs	xxxiv

Dictionary A–Z   1–1500

Writing style guide	1505
Special information	1520
Language in use	1524
General grammar guide	1549
Business English grammar	1567
Academic English grammar	1577
Glossary of grammatical terms	1595
Frequent words	1607
Academic Word List	1620
Credits	1627

Visual Dictionary:

This supplement is in the middle of the book between letters L and M.

Contents

About COBUILD dictionaries   iv
Acknowledgements   v
Guide to dictionary entries   vii
Guide to dictionary features   ix
Introduction   xiii
Guide to definitions   xiv
Pronunciation   xvi
IPA symbols   xviii
List of grammatical notations   xix
Explanation of grammatical terms   xxi
Irregular verbs   xxiv

Dictionary A–Z   1–1500

Writing style guide   1503
Spelling information   1509
Language in use   1521
General maths guide   1540
Business English grammar   1567
Academic English grammar   1577
Glossary of grammatical terms   1595
Frequent words   1607
Academic Word List   1620
Credits   1627

Visual Dictionary

This supplement is in the middle of the book between letters L and M.

About COBUILD dictionaries

When the first COBUILD dictionary was published in 1987, it revolutionized dictionaries for learners. It was the first of a new generation of dictionaries that were based on actual evidence of how English was used, rather than lexicographer intuition.

Collins and the University of Birmingham, led by the outstanding linguist John Sinclair, developed an electronic corpus in the 1980s, called the Collins Birmingham University International Language Database (COBUILD). This corpus, which is also known as the Collins Corpus, became the largest collection of English data in the world, and COBUILD dictionary editors use the corpus to analyze the way that people really use the language.

The Collins Corpus contains over 20 billion words taken from websites, newspapers, magazines, and books published around the world, and from spoken material from radio, TV, and everyday conversations. New data is added to the corpus every month to help COBUILD editors identify new words and meanings from the moment they are first used.

All COBUILD dictionaries are based on the information our editors find in the Collins Corpus. Because the corpus is so large, our editors can look at lots of examples of how people really use words. The data tells us how words are used; what they mean; which words are used together; and how often words are used.

This information helps us decide which words to include in COBUILD dictionaries. Did you know, for example, that around 90% of English speech and writing is made up of approximately 3,500 words? The corpus tells us which words these are, and helps us ensure that when you use a COBUILD dictionary, you can be sure that you are learning the words you really want to know.

All of the examples in COBUILD dictionaries are examples of real English taken from the Collins Corpus. The examples have been carefully chosen to demonstrate typical grammatical patterns, typical vocabulary, and typical contexts for each word.

The corpus lies at the heart of COBUILD, and you can be confident that COBUILD will show you what you need to know to be able to communicate easily and accurately in English.

Acknowledgements

The publishers would like to acknowledge the following for their invaluable contribution to the original COBUILD concept:

John Sinclair   Patrick Hanks   Gwyneth Fox   Richard Thomas

Stephen Bullon, Jeremy Clear, Rosalind Combley, Susan Hunston, Ramesh Krishnamurthy, Rosamund Moon, Elizabeth Potter

Jane Bradbury, Joanna Channell, Alice Deignan, Andrew Delahunty, Sheila Dignen, Gill Francis, Helen Liebeck, Elizabeth Manning, Carole Murphy, Michael Murphy, Jonathan Payne, Elaine Pollard, Christina Rammell, Penny Stock, John Todd, Jenny Watson, Laura Wedgeworth, John Williams

The publishers would also like to acknowledge the following for their contribution to the first edition:

Carol Braham, Carol-June Cassidy, Pat Cook, Robert Grossmith, Orin Hargraves, Dana Darby Johnson, Cindy Mitchell, Marianne Noble, Susan Norton, Sue Ogden, Enid Pearsons, Maggie Seaton

We would like to acknowledge the assistance of the many hundreds of individuals and companies who have kindly given permission for copyright material to be used in the Collins Corpus. The written sources include many national and regional newspapers in Britain and overseas; magazines and periodical publishers; and book publishers in Britain, the United States, and Australia. Extensive spoken data has been provided by radio and television broadcasting companies; research workers at many universities and other institutions; and numerous individual contributors. We are grateful to them all.

Consultant
Paul Nation

Editors
Arline Burgmeier
John Chapman
Orin Hargraves
Robert Harris

Candace-Lynch Thompson
Len Neufeld
Enid Pearsons

Reviewers — International
Hirosada
Foreign Language Center
University of Tsukuba, Japan

Yoshiro Kaji
Hibiya High School, Tokyo, Japan

Kazumi Aizawa
Tokyo Denki University, Japan

Tim Knight
Musashino University

Tokyo Women's University

Japan Tsuda Juku University

Hidai Shigeyuki
Setagaya Junior High School
Tokyo, Japan

Kosuge Atsuko
Setagaya Junior High School
Tokyo, Japan

Kevin Kornburger
Kanda University of International Studies (KUIS)
Muhuhari, Japan

Kevin Miller
Shikoku University, Tokushima City, Japan

Tim Budden
Taipei European School British Section
Taiwan

Reviewers — USA

Sarah Bickle
Jasper High School
Plano, Texas

Donna Biscay
Shoreline Community College
Seattle, Washington

Dawn (Missey) Chavez
Denton ISD
Denton, Texas

Mary Diaz
Broward Community College
Fort Lauderdale, Florida

Sally Gearhart
Santa Rosa Junior College
Santa Rosa, California

Jacqueline George
Seattle Community College
Seattle, Washington

Judith Gex
La Guardia Community College
Long Island City, New York

Sarah Guedry
McMath Middle School
Denton, Texas

Dale Keith
Miami-Dade County Public Schools
Miami, Florida

Kathleen Krokar
Truman College
Chicago, Illinois

Wendalyn Nichols
New York, New York

Helen Roland
Miami Dade College
Miami, Florida

Eric Rosenbaum
BEGIN Managed Programs
New York, New York

Marilyn Santos
Valencia Community College
Orlando, Florida

Miriam Snyder
Westchester Community College
Valhalla, New York

Stephanie Steussel
Bunker Hill Community College
Charlestown, Massachusetts

Betty Stone
Somerville Center for Adult Learning
Somerville, Massachusetts

Yilin Sun
Seattle Central Community College
Seattle, Washington

Evelyn Trottier
Seattle Central Community College
Seattle, Washington

Denise Vaughn
Seattle Central Community College
Seattle, Washington

Donald Weasenforth
Collin County Community College
Plano, Texas

John Whitney
Chemeketa Community College
Salem, Oregon

Guide to dictionary entries

Bold headwords → **after|noon tea** (afternoon teas) N-VAR **Afternoon tea** is a small meal you can have in the afternoon. It includes a cup of tea and food such as sandwiches and cakes. [BRIT]

- **Geographical labels**
- **Plural forms**

Hyphenation points show where a word may be split across lines.

after|shock /æftərʃɒk/ (aftershocks) **1** N-COUNT **Aftershocks** are smaller earthquakes that occur after a large earthquake. **2** N-COUNT [usu with supp] People sometimes refer to the effects of an important event, especially a bad one, as the **aftershock**. [mainly JOURNALISM] ❑ *They were already under stress, thanks to the aftershock of last year's drought.*

Authentic examples from the Collins Corpus

after|taste /æftərteɪst/ also **after-taste** N-SING An **aftertaste** is a taste that remains in your mouth after you have finished eating or drinking something.

- **Full-sentence definitions show the ways in which the headword is used.**
- **Alternative spellings of headwords**

Pronunciation

around ◆◆◆ /əraʊnd/

Frequency information indicates which words are the most common.

> **Around** is an adverb and a preposition. In British English, the word 'round' is often used instead. **Around** is often used with verbs of movement, such as 'walk' and 'drive,' and also in phrasal verbs such as 'get around' and 'turn around.'

CEFR level shows which level each meaning fits into, from A1 to B2.

1 PREP To be positioned **around** a place or object means to surround it or be on all sides of it. To move **around** a place means to go along its edge, back to your starting point. ❑ *She looked at the papers around her.* ❑ *Today she wore her hair down around her shoulders.* • ADV [n ADV] **Around** is also an adverb. ❑ *...a village with a rocky river, a ruined castle and hills all around.* **2** PREP If you move **around** a corner or obstacle, you move to

Language notes provide more information on how to use the word correctly.

Stress markers for compound headwords

black pep|per N-UNCOUNT **Black pepper** is pepper which is dark in color and has been made from the dried berries of the pepper plant, including their black outer cases.

Important grammatical structures are shown in bold within definitions.

ocean ◆◆◆ /oʊʃən/ (oceans) **1** N-SING **The ocean** is the sea. ❑ *There were few sights as beautiful as the calm ocean on a warm night.* **2** N-COUNT An **ocean** is one of the five very large areas of sea on the Earth's surface. ❑ *They spent many days cruising the northern Pacific Ocean.* **3** N-COUNT If you say that there is an **ocean of** something, you are emphasizing that there is a very large amount of it. [INFORMAL, EMPHASIS] ❑ *I had cried oceans of tears.* **4** PHRASE If you say that something is **a drop in the ocean**, you mean that it is a very small amount which is unimportant compared to the cost of other things or is so small that it has very little effect on something. [EMPHASIS] ❑ *His fee is a drop in the ocean compared with the real cost of broadcasting.* **5** → See feature box at **water**

Pragmatics labels give you information about additional ideas or emotions that a word expresses.

Style labels indicate words that are used in formal and informal language, and in certain areas such as business or computing.

Cross-references to other relevant entries and to illustrated features

per|mit ◆◆◇ (permits, permitting, permitted)

Verb forms

> The verb is pronounced /pərmɪt/. The noun is pronounced /pɜrmɪt/.

Meaning splits

1 V-T If someone **permits** something, they allow it to happen. If they **permit** you to do something, they allow you to do it. [FORMAL] ❑ *He can let the court's decision stand and permit the extradition.* ❑ *The guards permitted me to bring my camera.* **2** N-COUNT A **permit** is an official document which says that you may do something. For example, you usually need a **permit** to work in a foreign country. ❑ *He has to apply for a permit, and we have to find him a job.* **3** V-T/V-I If a situation **permits** something, it makes it possible for that thing to exist, happen, or be done or it provides the opportunity for it. [FORMAL] ❑ *Try to go out for a walk at lunchtime, if the weather permits.* ❑ *This method of cooking also permits heat to penetrate evenly*

Pronunciation notes provide information on how to pronounce words correctly.

Word classes

pret|ty ♦♦◇ /prɪti/ (prettier, prettiest) **1** ADJ If you describe someone as **pretty**, you mean that they are attractive. ❏ *She's a very charming and very pretty girl.* ● **pret|ti|ly** /prɪtɪli/ ADV ❏ *She smiled again, prettily.* **2** ADJ A place or a thing that is **pretty** is attractive and pleasant, in a charming but not particularly unusual way. ❏ *...a very pretty little town.* ● **pret|ti|ly** ADV ❏ *The living-room was prettily decorated.* **3** ADV [ADV adj/adv] You can use **pretty** before an adjective or adverb to slightly lessen its force. [INFORMAL] ❏ *I had a pretty good idea what she was going to do.*

STILL

① ADVERB USES
② NOT MOVING OR MAKING A NOISE
③ EQUIPMENT

---

① **still** ♦♦♦ /stɪl/ **1** ADV If a situation that used to exist **still** exists, it has continued and exists now. ❏ *I still dream of home.* ❏ *Brian's toe is still badly swollen and he cannot put on his shoe.* **2** ADV [ADV before v] If something that has not yet happened could **still** happen, it is possible that it will happen. If something that has not yet happened is **still** to happen, it will happen at a later time. ❏ *Big money could still be made if the crisis keeps oil prices high.* ❏ *We could still make it, but we won't get there till three.* **3** ADV [be ADV n] If you say that there **is still** an amount of something left, you are emphasizing that there is that amount left. ❏ *There are still some outstanding problems.* **4** ADV [ADV before v] You use **still** to emphasize that something remains the case or is true in spite of what you have just said. ❏ *I'm average for my height. But I still feel I'm fatter than I should be.* **5** ADV [ADV with cl] You use **still** to indicate that a problem or difficulty is not really worth worrying about. ❏ *Their luck had simply run out. Still, never fear.* **6** ADV [ADV n/adv] You use **still** in expressions such as **still further, still another,** and **still more** to show that you find the number or quantity of things you are referring to surprising or excessive. [EMPHASIS] ❏ *We look forward to strengthening still further our already close co-operation with the police.* **7** ADV [ADV with compar] You use **still** with comparatives to indicate that something has even more of a quality than something else. [EMPHASIS] ❏ *Formula One motor car racing is supposed to be dangerous. "Indycar" racing is supposed to be more dangerous still.*

② **still** ♦♦♦ /stɪl/ (stiller, stillest, stills) **1** ADJ [ADJ after v] If you stay **still**, you stay in the same position and do not move. ❏ *David had been dancing about like a child, but suddenly he stood still and looked at Brad.* **2** ADJ If air or water is **still**, it is not moving. ❏ *The night air was very still.* **3** ADJ If a place is **still**, it is quiet and shows no sign of activity. ❏ *In the room it was very still.* ● **still|ness** N-UNCOUNT ❏ *Four deafening explosions shattered the stillness of the night air.* **4** ADJ Drinks that are **still** do not contain any bubbles of carbon dioxide. ❏ *...a glass of still water.* **5** N-COUNT A **still** is a photograph taken from a movie which is used for publicity purposes. ❏ *...stills from the James Bond movie series.*
③ **still** /stɪl/ (stills) N-COUNT A **still** is a piece of equipment used to make strong alcoholic drinks by a process called distilling.

Guide to dictionary features

Several special features in this dictionary help you to build your vocabulary in interesting and effective ways. These features help you to see how vocabulary items are used in real texts, how words are built, which words commonly go together, and which words have similar meanings. They help you to avoid common mistakes and to understand more about how certain words came into the language and how they got their meaning. You can read about all these features in more detail below.

Vocabulary in Context panels present related words in a typical context. For example, vocabulary relating to the science laboratory is shown through an explanation of how to carry out an experiment, words relating to restaurants can be found in a restaurant review, and vocabulary relating to nutrition and cooking is in a magazine-style article about healthy eating for vegans. The key words shown in bold can be found in the dictionary. These texts are a great way to experience English as it is used in the real world, in both everyday and academic contexts.

VOCABULARY IN CONTEXT

Experiment

What do you think happens when you heat a **saline solution**? Before beginning your experiment, write your **hypothesis** down. To carry out the experiment, first make a saline solution by mixing 10g of salt into 10ml of water in a **beaker**. Stir the mixture well to ensure all the salt has **dissolved**; then pour the solution into an evaporating dish. Before the next step, make sure you put on your safety **goggles**. Set up a **tripod** over a Bunsen burner and put a **wire mesh** on top of the tripod. Then place the evaporating dish on the wire mesh. Remember not to light the Bunsen burner until you have put your evaporating dish in place! As the solution is heated, the water will **evaporate**, leaving solid **salt crystals** behind in the dish. Was your hypothesis correct?

VOCABULARY IN CONTEXT

Nutrition: is a vegan diet healthy?

The answer to this question depends on whether you are following a **balanced diet**. A vegan diet is naturally low in certain **minerals** and vitamins, so it's important to consider the **nutritional** value of what you eat. Provided you do this, vegan food can be both **nourishing** and cheap.

Dieticians recommend that nuts, **legumes**, and **soya** should be included in a vegan diet. Nuts contain **protein** and **fiber**. Although they are **fatty**, and therefore highly **calorific**, they are **high** in so-called 'good fats,' which, unlike trans fats, are actually good for you. Legumes have the effect of lowering **cholesterol**, and soya is an excellent substitute for both meat and **dairy** products.

Synonyms are shown at key entries, each with a lively, up-to-date example, taken from the Collins Corpus. The example will give you a clear idea of the context in which that particular synonym typically appears in English. The numbers refer to the particular meaning within the main entry. To find out more about each synonym, go to that word in the dictionary. The synonyms feature allows you to browse the dictionary, expanding your vocabulary as you go.

SYNONYMS
bite
VERB **1**
nibble: *He started to nibble his biscuit.*
gnaw: *Woodlice attack living plants and gnaw at the stems.*
chew: *Be certain to eat slowly and chew your food extremely well.*
crunch: *Richard crunched into the apple.*

SYNONYMS
career
NOUN **1**
occupation: *I was looking for an occupation which would be an adventure.*
employment: *She was unable to find employment.*
vocation: *It could well be that he has a real vocation.*
livelihood: *...fishermen who depend on the seas for their livelihood.*
profession: *Harper was a teacher by profession.*

Collocations panels show you which words are typically used together. For example, we might talk about 'glorious weather' or 'lovely weather', but if the noun we want to use is 'experience', we would be more likely to talk about a 'memorable experience' or a 'rewarding experience.' The numbers refer to the particular meaning within the main entry. A knowledge of collocations will help you to sound natural and fluent when you are speaking and writing in English.

COLLOCATIONS
building
NOUN
*noun + **building**:* farm, government, office, school
*adjective + **building**:* derelict, historic, Victorian; high-rise, public, residential, tall; brick, stone
*verb + **building**:* construct, erect, renovate; demolish, destroy; evacuate, occupy

---
COLLOCATIONS
subject
NOUN
1
*adjective + **subject**:* controversial, difficult, sensitive, taboo
*verb + **subject**:* address, broach, discuss, raise
3
*noun + **subject**:* degree; art, science
*adjective + **subject**:* academic, compulsory, core, vocational; favorite, specialist
*verb + **subject**:* research, study, teach

Usage notes give tips on avoiding common learner errors in grammar, vocabulary, and pronunciation. These include uncountable nouns that learners often mistakenly use as if they were countable, typical preposition errors, and commonly confused words. Browse the dictionary for these invaluable notes and find out how to avoid all the most frequent mistakes in English.

USAGE
fruit
Don't use 'fruits' to talk about several oranges, bananas, etc. Use **some fruit**. For example, don't say '~~I'm going to the market to buy some fruits.~~' Say 'I'm going to the market to buy **some fruit**.' *...a table with **some fruit** on it.*

USAGE
wish
Don't use 'wish' with a clause to say that you hope something good will happen to someone. Don't say, for example, '~~I wish you'll have a nice time in Finland.~~' Say 'I **hope** you'll **have** a nice time in Finland' or 'I **hope** you **have** a nice time in Finland.' *I **hope** you **like** this village.*

Prefixes and suffixes are parts of words that help to give them their specific meaning. For example, words that start with the prefix *poly-* usually have 'many' as part of their meaning, and words that end in *-ly* are often adverbs that indicate how something is done. Knowing a range of prefixes and suffixes will help you to work out the meanings of words by yourself, without always having to look the word up.

PREFIX
astro-
is used to form words which refer to things relating to the stars or to outer space. *For example, **astronomy** is the scientific study of the stars, the planets and other objects in space.*

SUFFIX
-less
forms adjectives that indicate that someone or something does not have a particular thing. *For example, someone who is **jobless** does not have a job.*

Word histories tell you where certain words come from and how they have changed in meaning over the years. For example, did you know that the word 'slogan' comes from a Gaelic word meaning 'war cry'? Or that the word 'hippopotamus' comes from the Greek for 'river horse'? Finding out the history of a word can be fascinating and sometimes surprising, and the images and ideas formed in our minds can help us to remember the word we have learned about.

WORD HISTORY

hamburger
Hamburgers are named after their city of origin, Hamburg in Germany. The word 'hamburger' has nothing to do with ham, but the 'burger' part has now been taken as a noun in its own right, on the basis of which we now have veggieburgers, cheeseburgers, and so on.

WORD HISTORY

shampoo
A **shampoo** was originally a massage rather than a wash. The word 'shampoo' comes from the Hindi verb *chāmpnā*, meaning 'press,' 'knead,' or 'massage.'

Visual Dictionary panels are presented in a full-color supplement in the middle of the dictionary and show you images of things that are defined in the dictionary. Sometimes it's much easier to understand the meaning of a word if someone shows you a picture of it. Certain Visual Dictionary panels show 'types of' a particular area of vocabulary, for example, 'boats' or 'devices.' Others show 'parts of' something, for example, 'parts of a bicycle' or 'parts of the skeleton.' Browse the supplement containing these images: learning vocabulary sets through images can be particularly helpful for memorizing words.

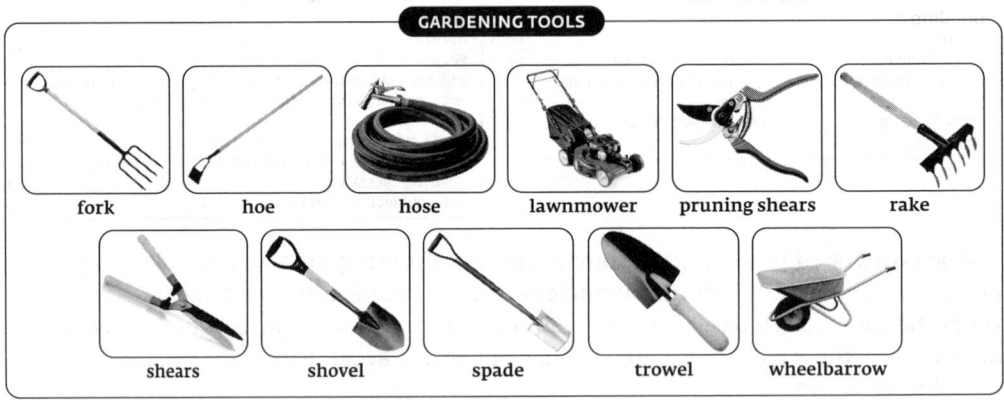

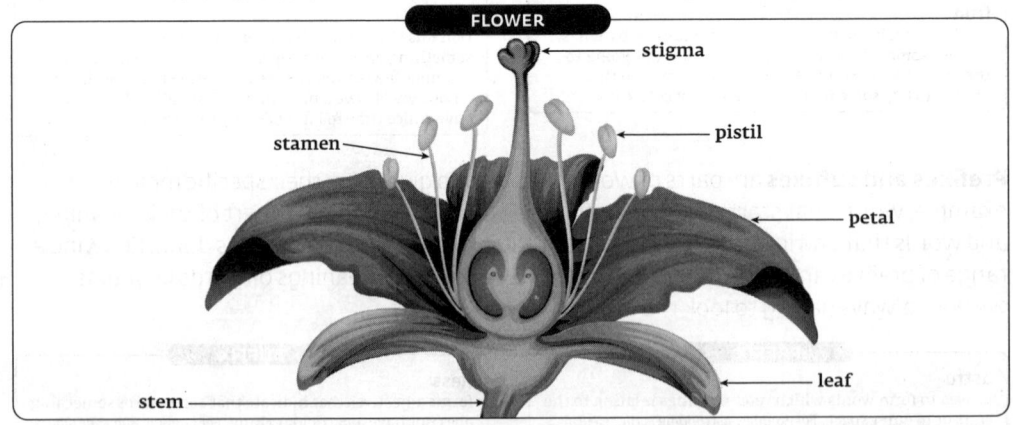

Introduction

Welcome to the third edition of the *Collins COBUILD Advanced American English Dictionary*.

In keeping with COBUILD's long-established, user-friendly tradition, this new edition will help you to understand not only the meanings of words, but also how to use them properly in context. The inclusion of a wealth of new words and meanings taken from areas such as social media, technology, and popular culture means that the *Collins COBUILD Advanced American English Dictionary* continues to reflect today's English. The thousands of example sentences taken from the Collins Corpus ensure that language is shown in a meaningful context.

For this edition, we have updated and included hundreds of interesting and informative language features which will help you to acquire an even better understanding of how real English works. These features include detailed information about collocation, word history, and usage – you can find out more in the 'Guide to dictionary features' on pages x-xii.

As well as checking and explaining the meanings of thousands of existing words, COBUILD's lexicographers have continued to ensure that our 20-billion-word database – the Collins Corpus – is kept up to date. The corpus contains English language material from thousands of different written and spoken sources, both online and in print.

The corpus lies at the heart of each entry. Corpus research helps lexicographers to make confident and accurate decisions about the different senses of a word. It also informs the choice of words that are suitable for the dictionary (based on word frequency), the language used in the full-sentence definitions, the choice of examples, and the grammatical information given. Finally, it helps us to provide accurate information relating to the connotations of particular words – whether they express approval, disapproval, a particular emotion, or politeness, for example.

New to this edition is a full-color Visual Dictionary section, as well as several supplementary sections which will help you to use English accurately and appropriately. The new 'Writing style guide' and 'Language in use' sections help you to choose the right language for both written and spoken communication in a range of everyday situations. In addition, the 'Grammar guide' gives you the information you need to be able to write in a way which is appropriate for academic and business contexts.

Finally, we are pleased to announce that the full dictionary text is available both for Kindle™ and online, so that COBUILD is always available to you, wherever you are. Set it as your default Kindle™ dictionary, or just go to www.collinsdictionary.com for free online access.

We hope you will find this new edition of the *Collins COBUILD Advanced American English Dictionary* a valuable resource that complements and enhances all areas of language study.

Guide to definitions

Definitions
One of the features of the *Collins COBUILD Advanced American English Dictionary* is that the definitions are written in full sentences, using vocabulary and grammatical structures that occur naturally with the word being explained. These definitions give you much more than the meaning of the word you are looking up, and also contain information on usage, register, typical context, and syntax. Whenever possible, words are explained using simpler and more common words. This gives us a natural defining vocabulary, with most words in our definitions being among the 2,500 most common words in English.

Information about collocates and structure
In our definitions, we show the typical collocates of a word: that is, the other words that are used with the word we are defining. For example, the definition of meaning 1 of the adjective **savory** says:

> **Savory** food has a salty or spicy flavor rather than a sweet one.

This shows that you use the adjective **savory** to describe food, rather than other things.

Meaning 1 of the verb **wag** says:

> When a dog **wags** its tail, it repeatedly waves its tail from side to side.

This shows that the subject of meaning 1 of **wag** refers to a dog, and the object of the verb is "tail."

Information about grammar
The definitions also give information about the grammatical structures in which a word is used. For example, meaning 1 of the adjective **candid** says:

> When you are **candid** about something or with someone, you speak honestly.

This shows that you use **candid** with the preposition "about" with something and "with" with someone.

Other definitions show other kinds of structure. Meaning 1 of the verb **soften** says:

> If you **soften** something or if it **softens**, it becomes less hard, stiff, or firm.

This shows that the verb is used both transitively and intransitively. In the transitive use, you have a human subject and a non-human object. In the intransitive use, you have a non-human subject.

Finally, meaning 1 of **compel** says:

> If a situation, a rule, or a person **compels** you to do something, they force you to do it.

This shows you what kinds of subject and object to use with **compel**, and it also shows that you typically use the verb in a structure with a to-infinitive.

Information about context and usage

In addition to information about collocation and grammar, definitions also can be used to convey your evaluation of something, for example to express your approval or disapproval. For example, here is the definition of **unhelpful**:

> If you say that someone or something is **unhelpful**, you mean that they do not help you or improve a situation, and may even make things worse.

In this definition, the expressions "if you say that" and "you mean that" indicate that these words are used subjectively, rather than objectively.

Other kinds of definition

We sometimes explain grammatical words and other function words by paraphrasing the word in context. For example, meaning 3 of **through** says:

> To go **through** a town, area, or country means to travel across it or in it.

In many cases, it is impossible to paraphrase the word, and so we explain its function instead. For example, the definition of **unfortunately** says:

> You can use **unfortunately** to introduce or refer to a statement when you consider that it is sad or disappointing, or when you want to express regret.

Lastly, some definitions are expressed as if they are cross-references. For example:

> **rd**. is a written abbreviation for **road**.
> **e-commerce** is the same as **e-business**.

If you need to know more about the words **road** or **e-business**, you look at those entries.

Style and usage

Some words or meanings are used mainly by particular groups of people, or in particular social contexts. In this dictionary, where relevant, the definitions also give information about the kind of people who are likely to use a word or expression, and the type of social situation in which it is used.

In terms of geographical diversity, this dictionary focuses on American and British English using evidence from the Collins Corpus. Where relevant, the American or British form is shown at its equivalent word or meaning.

This information is usually placed at the end of the definition, in small capitals and within square brackets. If more than one type of information is provided, they are given in a list.

Geographical labels

AM: used mainly by speakers and writers in the U.S., and in other places where American English is used or taught. Where relevant the British equivalent is provided.

BRIT: used mainly by speakers and writers in Britain, and in other places where British English is used or taught. Where relevant the American equivalent is provided.

Other geographical labels are used in the text to refer to English as it is spoken in other parts of the world, e.g., SCOTTISH.

Style labels

BUSINESS: used mainly when talking about the field of business, e.g., **annuity**

COMPUTING: used mainly when talking about the field of computing, e.g., **chat room**

DIALECT: used in some dialects of English, e.g., **ain't**

FORMAL: used mainly in official situations, or by political and business organizations, or when speaking or writing to people in authority, e.g., **gracious**

HUMOROUS: used mainly to indicate that a word or expression is used in a humorous way, e.g., **mustachioed**

INFORMAL: used mainly in informal situations, conversations, and personal letters, e.g., **pep talk**

JOURNALISM: used mainly in journalism, e.g., **glass ceiling**

LEGAL: used mainly in legal documents, in law courts, and by the police in official situations, e.g., **manslaughter**

LITERARY: used mainly in novels, poetry, and other forms of literature, e.g., **plaintive**

MEDICAL: used mainly in medical texts, and by doctors in official situations, e.g., **psychosis**

MILITARY: used mainly when talking or writing about military terms, e.g., **armor**

OFFENSIVE: likely to offend people, or to insult them; these words should therefore usually be avoided, e.g., **cripple**

OLD-FASHIONED: generally considered to be old-fashioned, and no longer in common use, e.g., **dashing**

SPOKEN: used mainly in speech rather than in writing, e.g., **pardon**

TECHNICAL: used mainly when talking or writing about objects, events, or processes in a specialist subject, such as business, science, or music, e.g., **biotechnology**

TRADEMARK: used to show a designated trademark, e.g., **Biro**

VULGAR: used mainly to describe words which could be considered taboo by some people; these words should therefore usually be avoided, e.g., **piss**

WRITTEN: used mainly in writing rather than in speech, e.g., **avail**

Pragmatics labels

People use words to do many things: give invitations, express their feelings, emphasize what they are saying, and so on. The study and description of the way in which people use language to do these things is called pragmatics.

In the dictionary, we draw attention to certain pragmatic aspects of words and phrases of English, paying special attention to those that, for cultural and linguistic reasons, we feel may be confusing to learners. The following labels are used:

APPROVAL: used to show that you approve of the person or thing you are talking about, e.g., **angelic**

DISAPPROVAL: used to show that you disapprove of the person or thing you are talking about, e.g., **brat**

EMPHASIS: used to emphasize the point you are making, e.g., **never-ending**

FEELINGS: used to express your feelings about something, or towards someone, e.g., **unfortunately**

FORMULAE: used in particular situations such as greeting and thanking people, or acknowledging something, e.g., **hi, congratulations**

POLITENESS: used to express politeness, sometimes even to the point of being euphemistic, e.g., **mature**

VAGUENESS: used to show how certain you are about the truth or validity of your statements; this is sometimes called "hedging" or "modality", e.g., **presumably**

Pronunciation

The basic principle underlying the suggested pronunciations is "If you pronounce it like this, most people will understand you." The pronunciations are therefore broadly based on the two most widely taught accents of English, GenAm or General American for American English, and RP or Received Pronunciation for British English.

For the majority of words, a single pronunciation is given, as most differences between American and British pronunciation are systematic. Where the usual British pronunciation differs from the usual American pronunciation more significantly, a separate transcription is given after the code BRIT. Where more than one pronunciation is common in either American or British English, alternative pronunciations are given.

The pronunciations are the result of a program of monitoring spoken English and consulting leading reference works. The transcription system has developed from original work by Dr. David Brazil for the *Collins COBUILD English Language Dictionary*. The symbols used in the dictionary are adapted from those of the International Phonetic Alphabet (IPA), as standardized in the *English Pronouncing Dictionary* by Daniel Jones (14th Edition, revised by A.C. Gimson and S.M. Ramsaran 1988).

IPA symbols

Vowel sounds

ɑ	c**a**lm, **ah**
æ	**a**ct, m**a**ss
aɪ	d**i**ve, cr**y**
aʊ	**ou**t, d**ow**n
ɛ	m**e**t, l**e**nd, p**e**n
eɪ	s**ay**, w**eigh**t
ɛə	ch**air**, th**eir**, c**are**
ɜ	ch**ir**p, h**er**b, w**or**k
ɪ	f**i**t, w**i**n
i	f**ee**d, m**e**
ə	d**ear**, **e**ra, w**eir**d
ɒ	l**o**t, sp**o**t
oʊ	n**o**te, c**oa**t
ɔ	cl**aw**, m**au**l
ɔɪ	b**oy**, j**oi**nt
ʊ	c**ou**ld, st**oo**d
u	y**ou**, **u**se, act**u**al
ʌ	f**u**nd, m**u**st
ə	*the first vowel in* **a**bout

Consonant sounds

b	**b**ed, ru**b**
d	**d**one, re**d**
f	**f**it, i**f**
g	**g**ood, do**g**
h	**h**at, **h**orse
y	**y**ellow, **y**ou
k	**k**ing, pi**ck**
l	**l**ip, bi**ll**
ᵊl	hand**le**, pane**l**
m	**m**at, ra**m**
n	**n**ot, ti**n**
ᵊn	hidd**en**, writt**en**
p	**p**ay, li**p**
r	**r**un, **r**ead
s	**s**oon, bu**s**
t	**t**alk, be**t**
v	**v**an, lo**v**e
w	**w**in, **w**ool
x	lo**ch**
z	**z**oo, bu**zz**
ʃ	**sh**ip, wi**sh**
ʒ	mea**s**ure, lei**s**ure
ŋ	si**ng**, worki**ng**
tʃ	**ch**eap, wit**ch**
θ	**th**in, my**th**
ð	**th**en, ba**the**
dʒ	**j**oy, bri**dge**

Notes

/æ/ or /ɑ/

There are a number of words which use the /æ/ sound in GenAm and in most accents of English, but /ɑ/ in RP, such as "bath" which is pronounced /bæθ/ in GenAm and /bɑθ/ in RP. This affects some words in which this vowel is followed by the sounds /f/, /nd/, /ns/, /nt/, /ntʃ/, /s/, /θ/. For example, "graph", "command", "can't", "ranch", "class", and "bath" are pronounced /græf/, /kəmænd/, /kænt/, /ræntʃ/, /klæs/, and /bæθ/ in GenAm, but /grɑf/, /kəmɑnd/, /kɑnt/, /rɑntʃ/, /klɑs/, and /bɑθ/ in RP.

/r/

In most accents of English, including GenAm, "r" is always pronounced. One of the main ways in which RP differs is that "r" is only pronounced as /r/ when the next sound is a vowel. Thus, in RP, "far gone" is pronounced /fɑ gɒn/ but "far out" is pronounced /fɑr aʊt/. Similarly, "fire", "flour", "fair", "near", and "pure" are pronounced /faɪər/, /flaʊər/, /fɛər/, /nɪər/, and /pyʊər/ in GenAm, but /faɪə/, /flaʊə/, /fɛə/, /nɪə/, and /pyʊə/ in RP.

/oʊ/

This symbol is used to represent the sound /oʊ/ in GenAm, and also the sound /əʊ/ in RP, as these sounds are almost entirely equivalent.

/əl/ and /ən/

These show that /l/ and /n/ are pronounced as separate syllables:

handle /hændəl/
hidden /hɪdən/

Stress

Stress is shown by underlining the vowel in the stressed syllable:

two /tu̲/
result /rɪzʌ̲lt/
disappointing /dɪ̲səpɔɪ̲ntɪŋ/

When a word is spoken in isolation, stress falls on the syllables which have vowels which are underlined. If there is one syllable underlined, it will have primary stress.

"TWO"
"reSULT"

If two syllables are underlined, the first will have secondary stress, and the second will have primary stress:

"DISapPOINTing"

A few words are shown with three underlined syllables, for example "disqualification" /dɪ̲skwɒ̲lɪfɪke̲ɪʃən/. In this case, the third underlined syllable will have primary stress, while the secondary stress may be on the first or second syllable:

"DISqualifiCAtion" or "disQUALifiCAtion"

GenAm usually prefers "dis-", while RP tends to prefer "DIS-."

In the case of compound words, where the pronunciation of each part is given separately, the stress pattern is shown by underlining the headword: "o̲ff-pe̲ak", "fi̲rst-cla̲ss", but "ca̲ke pan."

Stressed syllables

When words are used in context, the way in which they are pronounced depends upon the information units that are constructed by the speaker. For example, a speaker could say:

1. "the reSULT was disapPOINTing"
2. "it was a DISappointing reSULT"
3. "it was VERy disappointing inDEED"

In (3), neither of the two underlined syllables in disappointing /dɪsəpɔɪntɪŋ/ receives either primary or secondary stress. This shows that it is not possible for a dictionary to predict whether a particular syllable will be stressed in context.

It should be noted, however, that in the case of adjectives with two stressed syllables, the second syllable often loses its stress when it is used before a noun:

"an OFF-peak FARE"
"a FIRST-class SEAT"

Two things should be noted about the marked syllables:

1. They can take primary or secondary stress in a way that is not shared by the other syllables.
2. Whether they are stressed or not, the vowel must be pronounced distinctly; it cannot be weakened to /ə/, /ɪ/, or /ʊ/.

These features are shared by most of the one-syllable words in English, which are therefore transcribed in this dictionary as stressed syllables:

two /tu/
inn /ɪn/
tree /tri/

Unstressed syllables

It is an important characteristic of English that vowels in unstressed syllables tend not to be pronounced clearly. Many unstressed syllables contain the vowel /ə/, a neutral vowel which is not found in stressed syllables. The vowels /ɪ/ or /ʊ/, which are relatively neutral in quality, are also common in unstressed syllables.

Single-syllable grammatical words such as "shall" and "at" are often pronounced with a weak vowel such as /ə/. However, some of them are pronounced with a more distinct vowel under certain circumstances, for example when they occur at the end of a sentence. This distinct pronunciation is generally referred to as the strong form, and is given in this dictionary after the word STRONG.

shall /ʃəl, STRONG ʃæl/
at /ət, STRONG æt/

List of grammatical notations

Word classes

ADJ	adjective	PREDET	predeterminer
ADV	adverb	PREFIX	prefix
AUX	auxiliary verb	PREP	preposition
COLOR	color word	PRON	pronoun
COMB	combining form	PRON-EMPH	emphatic pronoun
CONJ	conjunction	PRON-INDEF	indefinite pronoun
CONVENTION	convention	PRON-INDEF-NEG	negative indefinite pronoun
DET	determiner	PRON-NEG	negative pronoun
EXCLAM	exclamation	PRON-PLURAL	plural pronoun
FRACTION	fraction	PRON-POSS	possessive pronoun
MODAL	modal verb	PRON-RECIP	reciprocal pronoun
N-COUNT	count noun	PRON-REFL	reflexive pronoun
N-COUNT-COLL	collective count noun	PRON-REFL-EMPH	emphatic reflexive pronoun
N-FAMILY	family noun	PRON-REL	relative pronoun
N-IN-NAMES	noun in names	PRON-SING	singular pronoun
N-MASS	mass noun	QUANT	quantifier
N-PLURAL	plural noun	QUANT-NEG	negative quantifier
N-PROPER	proper noun	QUANT-PLURAL	plural quantifier
N-PROPER-COLL	collective proper noun	QUEST	question word
N-PROPER-PLURAL	plural proper noun	SOUND	sound word
N-SING	singular noun	SUFFIX	suffix
N-SING-COLL	collective singular noun	V-ERG	ergative verb
N-TITLE	title noun	V-I	intransitive verb
N-UNCOUNT	uncount noun	V-LINK	link verb
N-UNCOUNT-COLL	collective uncount noun	V-PASSIVE	passive verb
N-VAR	variable noun	V-RECIP	reciprocal verb
N-VAR-COLL	collective variable noun	V-RECIP-PASSIVE	passive reciprocal verb
N-VOC	vocative noun	V-T	transitive verb
NEG	negative	V-T PASSIVE	passive transitive verb
NUM	number	V-T/V-I	intransitive or transitive verb
ORD	ordinal		
PHRASAL VERB	phrasal verb		
PHRASE	phrase		

Words and abbreviations used in patterns

adj	adjective group	**ord**	ordinal
adj-superl	superlative form	**P**	particle, part of a phrasal verb
adv	adverb group		
amount	word or phrase indicating an amount of something	**passive**	passive voice
		pl	plural
brd-neg	broad negative	**pl-n**	noun in the plural, plural noun group, co-ordinated noun group
cl	clause		
color	color word		
compar	comparative form	**pl-num**	plural number
cont	continuous	**poss**	possessive
def-n	definite noun group	**prep**	prepositional phrase or preposition
def-pl-n	definite noun group with a noun in the plural	**pron**	pronoun
det	determiner	**pron-indef**	indefinite pronoun
-ed	past participle of a verb	**pron-refl**	reflexive pronoun
group	noun group, adjective, adverb, or prepositional phrase	**quest**	question word
		sing	singular
		sing-n	noun in the singular
imper	imperative	**superl**	superlative form
inf	infinitive form of a verb	**supp**	supplementary information accompanying a noun
-ing	present participle of a verb		
interrog	interrogative	**that**	'that'-clause
n	noun or noun group	**to-inf**	the to-infinitive form of a verb
names	names of places or institutions	**usu**	usually
neg	negative word	**v**	verb or verb group
n-proper	proper noun	**v-cont**	continuous verb
num	number	**v-link**	link verb
n-uncount	uncount noun or noun group with an uncount noun	**wh**	wh-word, clause beginning with a wh-word
oft	often		

Explanation of grammatical terms

Introduction

For each use of each word in this dictionary, grammar information is provided. For a very few words, such as abbreviations, contractions and some words of foreign origin, no grammar is given, because the words do not belong to any word class, or are used so freely that every example could be given a different word class, e.g., AD, ditto, must've.

The grammar information that is given is of three types:

1. the word class of the word: e.g., PHRASAL VERB, N-COUNT, ADJ, QUANT
2. restrictions or extensions to its behavior, compared to other words of that word class: e.g., **usu passive, usu sing, also no det**
3. the patterns that the word most frequently occurs in: e.g., **N of n, ADJ that, ADV with v**

For all word classes, the patterns are given immediately before the definitions they accompany.

The word class of the word being explained is in small CAPITAL LETTERS. The order of items in a pattern is the order in which they normally occur in a sentence. Words in *italics* are words (not word classes) that occur in the pattern. Alternatives are separated by a slash (/).

Word classes

ADJ

An **adjective** can be graded or ungraded, or be in the comparative or the superlative form, e.g., He has been <u>absent</u> from his desk for two weeks ... the most <u>accurate</u> description of the killer to date ... The <u>eldest</u> child was a daughter called Fatiha.

Adjective patterns

ADJ n The adjective is always used before a noun, e.g., ... a <u>governmental</u> agency.

usu ADJ n The adjective is usually used before a noun. It is sometimes used after a link verb.

v-link ADJ The adjective is used after a link verb such as *be* or *feel*, e.g., He felt <u>unwell</u>. Adjectives with this label are sometimes used in other positions such as after the object of a verb such as *make* or *keep*, but never before a noun.

usu v-link ADJ The adjective is usually used after a link verb. It is sometimes used before a noun.

ADJ after v The adjective is used after a verb that is not a link verb, e.g., The lieutenant stopped and stood <u>stock-still</u>.

n ADJ The adjective comes immediately after a noun, e.g., between archaeology <u>proper</u> and science-based archaeology.

det ADJ The adjective comes immediately after a determiner and before any other adjectives, and sometimes comes before numbers, e.g., You owe a <u>certain</u> person a sum of money.

If the dictionary does not show that an adjective is used only or mainly in the pattern **ADJ n** and **v-link ADJ**, this means that the adjective is used freely in both patterns.

These main adjective patterns are sometimes combined with other patterns.

ADV
An **adverb** can be graded or ungraded, or be in the comparative or the superlative form, e.g., *Much of our behavior is biologically determined ... I'll work hard ... Inflation is below 5% and set to fall further ... those areas furthest from the coast.*

AUX
An **auxiliary verb** is used with another verb to add particular meanings to that verb, for example, to form the continuous aspect or the passive voice, or to form negatives and interrogatives. The verbs *be, do, get*, and *have* have some senses in which they are auxiliary verbs.

COLOR
A **color word** refers to a color. It is like an adjective, e.g., *the blue sky ... The sky was blue*, and also like a noun, e.g., *She was dressed in red ... several shades of yellow.*

COMB
A **combining form** is a word which is joined with another word, usually with a hyphen, to form compounds, e.g., *strawberry-flavored, business-speak*. The word class of the compound is also given, e.g., COMB in ADJ, COMB in N-UNCOUNT.

CONJ
A **conjunction** usually links elements of the same grammatical type, such as two words or two clauses, e.g., *She and Simon had already gone ... I sat on the chair to unwrap the package while he stood by.*

CONVENTION
A **convention** is a word or a fixed phrase which is used in conversation, for example when greeting someone, apologizing, or replying, e.g., *hello, sorry, no comment.*

DET
A **determiner** is a word that is used at the beginning of a noun group, e.g., *a tray, more time, some books, this amount*. It can also be used to say who or what something belongs or relates to, e.g., *his face, my house*, or to begin a question, e.g., *Whose car were they in?*

EXCLAM
An **exclamation** is a word or phrase which is spoken suddenly, loudly, or emphatically in order to express a strong emotion such as shock or anger. Exclamations are often followed by exclamation points, e.g., *Good heavens! Ouch!*

FRACTION
A **fraction** is used in numbers, e.g., *five and a half, two and two thirds*; before *of* and a noun group, e.g., *half of the money, a third of the children, an eighth of Russia's grain*; after *in* or *into*, e.g., *in half, into thirds*. A fraction is also used like a count noun, e.g., *two halves, the first quarter of the year.*

MODAL
A **modal** is used before the infinitive form of a verb, e.g., *You may go*. In questions, it comes before the subject, e.g., *Must you speak?* In negatives, it comes before the negative word, e.g., *They would not like this.* It does not inflect, for example, it does not take an *-s* in the third person singular, e.g., *She can swim.*

N-COUNT
A **count noun** has a plural form, usually made by adding -s. When it is singular, it must have a determiner in front of it, such as *the, her,* or *such,* e.g., *My cat is getting fatter ... She's a good friend.*

N-COUNT-COLL
A **collective count noun** is a count noun which refers to a group of people or things. It behaves like a count noun, and when it is in the singular form it is generally used with a singular verb, e.g., *The British audience has a huge appetite for serials ... Audiences are becoming more selective.*

N-FAMILY
A **family noun** refers to a member of a family, e.g., *father, mommy,* and *granny.* Family nouns are count nouns which are typically used in the singular, and usually follow a possessive determiner. They are also vocative nouns. They are also proper nouns, used with no determiner, e.g., *My mommy likes marzipan ... Tell them I didn't do it, Mommy ... Mommy's always telling me I'm too old for dolls.*

N-IN-NAMES
The **noun** occurs **in names** of people, things, or institutions, e.g., *the Federal Bureau of Investigation.*

N-MASS
A **mass noun** typically combines the behavior of both count and uncount nouns in the same sense. It is used like an uncount noun to refer to a substance. It is used like a count noun to refer to a brand or type, e.g., *Rinse in cold water to remove any remaining detergent ... Wash it in hot water with a good detergent ... We used several different detergents in our stain-removal tests.*

N-PLURAL
A **plural noun** is always plural, and is used with plural verbs. If a pronoun is used to stand for the noun, it is a plural pronoun such as *they* or *them,* e.g., *These clothes are ready to wear ... He expressed his condolences to the families of people who died in the incident.* If they refer to a single object which has two main parts, such as *jeans* and *glasses,* the expression *a pair of* is sometimes used, e.g., *a pair of jeans.* This is shown as: [also *a pair of* N].

N-PROPER
A **proper noun** refers to one person, place, thing, or institution, and begins with a capital letter. Many proper nouns are used without a determiner, e.g., *... Earth;* some must be used with *the,* and this can be indicated as: [*the* N], e.g., *the U.S.*

N-PROPER-COLL
A **collective proper noun** is a proper noun which refers to a group of people or things. It is generally used with a singular verb, e.g., *The Senate is expected to pass the bill shortly.*

N-SING
A **singular noun** is always singular, and needs a determiner, e.g., *... to respect the environment ... Maureen was the epitome of sophistication.* When only *a* or *the* is used, this is indicated as: [*a* N] or [*the* N], e.g., *The traffic slowed to a crawl ... We dropped to the ground.*

N-SING-COLL
A **collective singular noun** is a singular noun which refers to a group of people or things. It behaves like a singular noun, and is generally used with a singular verb, e.g., *Their defense has now conceded 12 goals in six games.*

N-TITLE
A **title noun** is used to refer to someone who has a particular role or position. Titles come before the name of the person and begin with a capital letter, e.g., *the Secretary of State.*

N-UNCOUNT
An **uncount noun** refers to things that are not normally counted or considered to be individual items. Uncount nouns do not have a plural form, and are used with a singular verb. They do not need determiners, e.g., *an area of outstanding natural beauty.*

N-UNCOUNT-COLL
A **collective uncount noun** is an uncount noun which refers to a group of people or things. It behaves like an uncount noun, and is generally used with a singular verb, e.g., *Hearts is one of the four suits in a pack of playing cards.*

N-VAR
A **variable noun** typically combines the behavior of both count and uncount nouns in the same sense (see **N-COUNT, N-UNCOUNT**). The singular form occurs freely both with and without determiners. Variable nouns also have a plural form, usually made by adding -s. Some variable nouns when used like uncount nouns refer to abstract things like *hardship* and *technology*, and when used like count nouns refer to individual examples or instances of that thing, e.g., *Technology is changing fast ... They should be allowed to wait for cheaper technologies to be developed.* Others refer to objects which can be mentioned either individually or generally, like *potato* and *salad*: you can talk about *a potato, potatoes,* or *potato.*

N-VAR-COLL
A **collective variable noun** is a variable noun which refers to a group of people or things. It behaves like a variable noun, but when it is singular it is generally used with a singular verb, e.g., *The management is doing its best to improve the situation.*

N-VOC
A **vocative noun** is used when speaking directly to someone or writing to them.

Vocative nouns do not need a determiner, but some may be used with a possessive determiner, e.g., *Thank you, darling ... How are you, my darling?*

NEG see PRON-INDEF-NEG, PRON-NEG, QUANT-NEG

NUM
A **number** is a word such as *three* and *hundred*. Numbers such as *one, two, three* are used like determiners, e.g., *three bears*; like adjectives, e.g., *the four horsemen*; like pronouns, e.g., *She has three cases and I have two*; and like quantifiers, e.g., *Six of the boys stayed behind.* Numbers such as *hundred, thousand, million* always follow a determiner or another number, e.g., *two hundred people ... the thousand horsemen ... She has a thousand dollars and I have a million ... A hundred of the boys stayed behind.*

ORD
An **ordinal** is a type of number. Ordinals are used like adjectives, e.g., *He was the third victim*; like pronouns, e.g., *the second of the two teams*; like adverbs, e.g., *The other team came first*; and like determiners, e.g., *Fourth place goes to Timmy*.

PHRASAL VERB
A **phrasal verb** consists of a verb and one or more particles, e.g., *look after, look back, look down on*. Some phrasal verbs are reciprocal, link, or passive verbs.

PHRASE
Phrases are groups of words which are used together with little variation and which have a meaning of their own, e.g., *The emergency services were working against the clock*.

PREDET
A **predeterminer** is used in a noun group before *a*, *the*, or another determiner, e.g., *What a terrific idea! ... both the children ... all his life*.

PREFIX
A **prefix** is a letter or group of letters, such as *un-* or *multi-*, which is added to the beginning of a word in order to form another word. For example, the prefix *un-* is added to *happy* to form *unhappy*.

PREP
A **preposition** begins a prepositional phrase and is followed by a noun group or a present participle. Patterns for prepositions are shown in the dictionary only if they are restricted in some way. For example, if a preposition occurs only before a present participle, it is shown as PREP *-ing*.

PREP-PHRASE
A **phrasal preposition** is a phrase which behaves like a preposition, e.g., *Unbeknownst to her father, she began taking dancing lessons*.

PRON
Pronouns are used like noun groups, to refer to someone or something that has already been mentioned or whose identity is known, e.g., *They produced their own shampoos and hair-care products, all based on herbal recipes ... two bedrooms, each with three beds*. Some pronouns are further classified, for example as PRON-EMPH, PRON-INDEF, and so on.

PRON-EMPH
Emphatic pronouns are words like *all*, *both*, and *each*, when they are used to emphasize another noun or pronoun, e.g., *We each have different needs and interests ... I wish you both a good trip*.

PRON-INDEF
Indefinite pronouns are words like *anyone*, *anything*, *everyone*, and *something*, e.g., *Why would anyone want that job? ... after everything else in his life had changed*.

PRON-INDEF-NEG
Negative indefinite pronouns are words like *none*, *no-one*, and *nothing*, e.g., *He searched for a sign of recognition on her face, but there was none ... Do our years together mean nothing?*

PRON-NEG
Negative pronouns are words like *neither*, e.g., *Neither seemed likely to be aware of my absence for long.*

PRON-PLURAL
Plural pronouns are the plural personal pronouns, which include *we, us, they*, and *them*, e.g., *Neither of us forgot about it.*

PRON-POSS
A **possessive pronoun** is used to say who or what something belongs to or relates to. The possessive pronouns are *mine, yours, his, hers, ours*, and *theirs*, e.g., *That wasn't his fault, it was mine ... The author can report other people's results which more or less agree with hers.*

PRON-RECIP
The **reciprocal pronouns** are *each other* and *one another*, e.g., *We looked at each other in silence.*

PRON-REFL
Reflexive pronouns are pronouns which are used as the object of a verb or preposition when they refer to the same person or thing as the subject of the verb. They are used in the same positions as other pronouns. The reflexive pronouns are *myself, yourself, himself, herself, itself, oneself, ourselves, yourselves*, and *themselves*, e.g., *I asked myself what I would have done in such a situation ... One must apply oneself to the present.*

PRON-REFL-EMPH
Emphatic reflexive pronouns are reflexive pronouns which are used for emphasis, often after another pronoun or at the end of a clause, e.g., *A wealthy man like yourself is bound to make an enemy or two along the way ... The president himself is on a visit to Beijing ... I made it myself.*

PRON-REL
Relative pronouns are words like *which* and *who*, that introduce relative clauses. They are the subject or object of the verb in the relative clause, or the object of a preposition, e.g., *... those who eat out for a special occasion ... The largest asteroid is Ceres, which is about a quarter the size of the moon.*

PRON-SING
Singular pronouns are the singular personal pronouns, which include *I, me, he, him, she, her, it*, and *one*, e.g., *He didn't mean to be cruel but I cried my eyes out.*

QUANT
A **quantifier** comes before *of* and a noun group, e.g., *most of the house* If there are any restrictions on the type of noun group, this is indicated as: [QUANT *of* **def-n**] meaning that the quantifier occurs before *of* and a definite noun group, e.g., *Most of the kids have never seen the ocean.*

QUANT-NEG
Negative quantifiers are words like *neither*, e.g., *Neither of us felt like going out.*

QUANT-PLURAL
Plural quantifiers are words like *billions* and *millions* which are followed by *of* and a noun group, e.g., *... for billions of years.*

QUEST
A **question word** is a word that is used to begin a question, for example, a wh-word, e.g., *Why didn't he stop me?*

SOUND
Sound words are used before or after verbs such as *go* and *say*, e.g., *My head was going thrum thrum thrum*.

SUFFIX
A **suffix** is a letter or group of letters such as *–ly* or *–ness*, which is added to the end of a word in order to form a new word, usually of a different word class, e.g., *quick, quickly*.

V-I
An **intransitive verb** is one which takes an indirect object or no object, e.g., *The problems generally fall into two categories ... As darkness fell outside, they sat down to eat.*

V-LINK
A **link verb** connects a subject and a complement. Most link verbs do not occur in the passive voice, e.g., *be, become, taste, feel*.

V-RECIP
Reciprocal verbs describe processes in which two or more people, groups, or things interact mutually: they do the same thing to each other, or participate jointly in the same action or event. Reciprocal verbs are used where the subject is both participants, e.g., *Fred and Sally met*. The participants can also be referred to separately, e.g., *Fred met Sally ... Fred argued with Sally*. These patterns are reciprocal because they also mean that *Sally met Fred* and *Sally argued with Fred*. Note that many reciprocal verbs can also be used in a way that is not reciprocal. For example, *Fred and Sally kissed* is reciprocal, but *Fred kissed Sally* is not reciprocal (because it does not mean that Sally also kissed Fred).

V-RECIP-PASSIVE
A **passive reciprocal verb** behaves like both a passive verb and a reciprocal verb, e.g., *He never believed he and Susan would be reconciled*.

V-T
A **transitive verb** is one which takes a direct object, e.g., *He mailed me the contract.*

V-T PASSIVE
A **passive verb** occurs in the passive voice only, e.g., *The company is rumored to be a takeover target.*

V-T/V-I
Some verbs may be **transitive** or **intransitive** depending on how they are used, e.g., *He opened the window and looked out ... The flower opens to reveal a bee.*

Words and abbreviations used in patterns

In a pattern, the element in small capital letters represents the word in the entry. All the other elements are in small letters. Items in *italics* show the actual word that is used, such as *of*. Items in roman print show the word class or type of clause that is used. For example:

> N *of* n means that the word being explained is a noun (N), and it is followed in the sentence by the word *of* and another noun or noun group (n).
>
> ADV adj/adv means that the word being explained is an adverb (ADV), and it is followed in the sentence by an adjective (adj) or (/) another adverb (adv).

When the word in the entry occurs in a pattern, the element in small capital letters is N for any kind of noun, ADJ for any kind of adjective, and so on. PHR is used for a phrase, and N is used to represent a noun in a phrase.

Words used to structure information in patterns

after: **after v** means after a verb. The word is used either immediately after the verb, or after the verb and another word or phrase, or in a marked position at the beginning of the clause. For example, the adverb **carefully** is used:

> immediately after a verb: *Have a nice time, dear, and drive carefully*.
> after a verb and its object: *Use a flash and position the camera carefully*.
> at the beginning of a clause: *Carefully make a cut with a small knife*.

The phrase **on hold** is used:

> immediately after a verb: *Everything is on hold until we know more*.
> after a verb and its object: *He put his retirement on hold*.

also: used with some nouns to show that the word is used in a way that is not typical of that type of noun. For example, **also N in pl** means that unlike most uncount nouns, this noun also has a plural form and use. **Also** is used with some adverbs and adjectives to show a pattern that is less common than the other patterns mentioned. For example, **usu ADV with v**, **also ADV adj** means that the adverb is usually used with a verb but is also used before an adjective.

before: **before v** means before a verb. The word is used before the main element in a verb group. For example, the adverb **already** is used:

> before the whole verb group: *those who already know of the delights of skiing*.
> immediately before the main element in the group: *They had already voted for him at the first ballot*.

no: used to indicate that a verb is not used in a particular way, for example **no passive**, or that a singular noun is also used without a determiner: **also no det**.

oft: used to indicate that a word or phrase often occurs in a particular pattern or behaves in a particular way.

only: used to indicate that a verb is always used in a particular way, for example **only cont**.

usu: used to indicate that a word or phrase usually occurs in a particular pattern or behaves in a particular way.

with: **with** is used when the position of a word or phrase is not fixed. This means that the word or phrase sometimes comes before the named word class and sometimes comes after it. For example, **quickly** at **quick 1** has the pattern ADV *with* V. It occurs:

>after the verb: *Cussane worked <u>quickly</u> and methodically.*
>before the verb: *She <u>quickly</u> looked away and stared down at her hands.*

In addition, **with cl** is used when the word sometimes occurs at the beginning of the clause, sometimes at the end, and sometimes in the middle. For example, **seriously** has the pattern ADV *with* cl. It occurs:

>at the beginning of the clause: *<u>Seriously</u>, I only watch TV in the evenings.*
>at the end of the clause: *All of us react favorably to those who take our views <u>seriously</u>.*
>in the middle of the clause: *This approach is now <u>seriously</u> out of step with the times.*

Elements used in patterns

adj: stands for **adjective group**. This may be one word, such as "happy", or a group of words, such as "very happy" or "as happy as I have ever been."

>e.g., **adj N: read** 8 ... *Ben Okri's latest novel is a good read.*

adj-superl: stands for **superlative adjective**. It is used to indicate an adjective group with the superlative form of the adjective.

>e.g., ADV **adj-superl: positively** 1 ... *This is positively the last chance for the industry to establish such a system.*
>e.g., ORD **adj-superl: second** 2 ... *the party is still the second strongest in Italy.*

adv: stands for **adverb group**. This may be one word, such as "slowly", or a group of words, such as "extremely slowly" or "more slowly than ever."

>e.g., **adv ADV: else** 1 ... *I never wanted to live anywhere else.*

amount: means **word or phrase indicating an amount of something**, such as "a lot", "nothing", "three percent", "four hundred pounds", "more", or "much."

>e.g., **amount** and ADV: **above** 2 ... *Banks have been charging 25 percent and above for unsecured loans.*

brd-neg: stands for **broad negative**, that is, a clause which is negative in meaning. It may contain a negative element such as "no-one", "never", or "hardly", or may show that it is negative in some other way.

>e.g., **oft with brd-neg: approve** 1 ... *Not everyone approves of the festival.*

cl: stands for **clause**.

>e.g., **cl ADV: anyway** 4 ... *What do you want from me, anyway?*

color: means **color word**, such as "red", "green", or "blue."

>e.g., ADJ **color: pastel** ... *pastel pink, blue, peach, and green.*

compar: stands for **comparative form of an adjective or adverb**.

>e.g., ADV **compar: even** 2 ... *On television he made an even stronger impact as an interviewer.*

cont: stands for **continuous**. It is used when indicating that a verb is always, usually, or never used in the continuous.

e.g., **only cont: die** 4 ... *I'm dying for a breath of fresh air.*
no cont: adore 1 ... *She adored her parents and would do anything to please them.*

def-n: stands for **definite noun group**. A definite noun group is a noun group that refers to a specific person or thing, or a specific group of people or things, that is known and identified.

e.g., QUANT *of* **def-n: whole** 1 ... *I was cold throughout the whole of my body.*

def-pl-n: stands for **definite noun group with a noun in the plural**.

e.g., QUANT *of* **def-pl-n: many** 1 ... *It seems there are not very many of them left in the sea.*

det: stands for **determiner**. A determiner is a word that comes at the beginning of a noun group, such as "the", "her", or "those."

e.g., **det** ADJ**: following** 2 ... *We went to dinner the following Monday evening.*

-ed: stands for **past participle of a verb**, such as "decided", "gone", or "taken."

e.g., ADV **-ed: freshly** ... *freshly baked bread.*

group: stands for **noun group, adjective, adverb, or prepositional phrase**.

e.g., ADV **group: strictly** ... *He seemed fond of her in a strictly professional way.*

imper: stands for **imperative**. It is used when indicating that a verb is always or usually used in the imperative.

e.g., **only imper** and **inf: beware** ... *Beware of being too impatient with others.*

inf: stands for **infinitive form of a verb**, such as "decide", "go", or "sit."

e.g., **v-link** ADJ **to-inf: duty-bound** ... *I felt duty-bound to help.*
ADV **to-inf: yet** 7: ... *She has yet to spend a Christmas with her husband.*

-ing: stands for **present participle of a verb**, such as "deciding", "going", or "taking."

e.g., PREP **-ing: before** 2 ... *He spent his early life in Sri Lanka before moving to Canada.*

it: means an "introductory" or "dummy" *it*. It does not refer to anything in a previous sentence or in the world; it may refer to what is coming later in the clause or it may refer to things in general.

e.g., *it* **v-link** ADJ **to-inf: nice** 7 ... *It's nice to meet you.*

n: stands for **noun** or **noun group**. If the **n** element occurs in a pattern with something that is part of a noun group, such as an adjective or another noun, it represents a noun. If the **n** element occurs in a pattern with something that is not part of a noun group, such as a verb or preposition, it represents a noun group. The noun group can be of any kind, including a pronoun.

e.g., ADJ **n: abiding:** ... *He has a genuine and abiding love of the craft.*

names: means **names of places or institutions**.

e.g., **oft in names: requiem** 2 ... *a performance of Verdi's Requiem.*

neg: stands for **negative words**, such as "not" or "never."

    e.g., **with neg: dream** 6 ... *I wouldn't dream of making fun of you.*

n-proper: stands for **proper noun**. A proper noun is the name of a particular person or thing.

    e.g., **usu n-proper N: lookalike** ... *a Marilyn Monroe lookalike.*

num: stands for **number**.

    e.g., **num ADV: odd** 3 ... *How many pages was it, 500 odd?*

n-uncount: stands for **uncount noun** or **noun group with an uncount noun**. An uncount noun is a noun which has no plural form and which is sometimes used with no determiner.

    e.g., **QUANT** of **n-uncount: touch** 13 ... *She thought she just had a touch of the flu.*

ord: stands for **ordinal**, such as "first" or "second."

    e.g., **ord ADJ N: generation** 4 ... *second generation Jamaicans in New York.*

passive: stands for **passive voice**. It is used when indicating that a verb usually or never occurs in the passive voice.

    e.g., **usu passive: expel** 1 ... *More than five thousand high school students have been expelled for cheating.*

pl: stands for **plural**.

pl-n: stands for **noun in the plural**, **plural noun group**, or **co-ordinate noun group** (two or more noun groups joined by a co-ordinating conjunction).

    e.g., **PREP pl-n: between** 2 ... *I spent a lot of time in the early Eighties travelling between Waco and El Paso.*

pl-num: stands for **plural number**. A plural number is a number which is used only in the plural.

    e.g., **PREP poss pl-num: in** 5 ... *young people in their twenties.*

poss: stands for **possessive**. Possessives which come before the noun may be a possessive determiner, such as "my", "her", or "their", or a possessive formed from a noun group, such as "the horse's." Possessives which come after the noun are of the form "*of* n", such as "of the horse."

    e.g., **usu pl, with poss: ancestor** 1 ... *our daily lives, so different from those of our ancestors.*

prep: stands for **prepositional phrase** or **preposition**.

    prep PRON: him 1 ... *Is Sam there? Let me talk to him.*

pron: stands for **pronoun**. A pronoun is a word such as "I", "it", or "them" which is used like a noun group. It refers to someone or something that has already been mentioned or whose identity is known.

    e.g., **PREP pron: before** 12 ... *Everyone in the room knew it was the single hardest task before them.*

pron-indef: stands for **indefinite pronoun**. An indefinite pronoun is a word like *anyone*, *anything*, *everyone*, and *something*.

    e.g., **pron-indef ADJ: else** 2 ... *I expect everyone else to be truthful.*

pron-refl: stands for **reflexive pronoun**, such as "yourself", "herself", or "ourselves."

    e.g., **PREP pron-refl: among** 9 ... *The girls stood aside, talking among themselves.*

quest: stands for **question word**. A question word is a wh-word such as "what", "how", or "why" which is used to begin a question.

    e.g., **quest ADV: ever** 6 ... *Why ever didn't you tell me?*

sing: stands for **singular**.

sing-n: stands for **noun in the singular**.

    e.g., **PREDET det sing-n: all** 2 ... *She's worked all her life.*

supp: stands for **supplementary information accompanying a noun**. Supplementary information that comes before a noun may be given by a determiner, possessive, adjective, or noun modifier. Supplementary information that comes after the noun may be given by a prepositional phrase or a clause.

    e.g., **supp N: park** 2 ... *a science and technology park.*

that: stands for **"that"-clause**. The clause may begin with the word "that", but does not necessarily do so.

    e.g., **usu N that: conviction** 1 ... *It is our conviction that a step forward has been taken.*

to-inf: stands for **to-infinitive form of a verb**.

    e.g., **v-link ADJ to-inf: inclined** 2 ... *I am inclined to agree with Alan.*

v: stands for **verb or verb group**. It is not used to represent a link verb. See also the explanations of **after**, **before**, and **with**.

    e.g., **V PRON: her** 1 ... *I told her I had something to say.*
        V PREP n: at 10 ... *She opened the door and stood there, frowning at me.*

v-link: stands for **link verb**. A link verb is a verb such as "be" which connects a subject and a complement.

    e.g., **v-link ADJ: down** 3 ... *The computer's down again.*

wh: stands for **wh-word**, or **clause beginning with a wh-word**, such as "what", "why", "when", "how", "if", or "whether."

    e.g., **oft ADJ** *about* **n/wh: tight-lipped** 1 ... *Military officials are still tight-lipped about when their forces will launch a ground offensive.*

Irregular verbs

Infinitive	Past tense	Past participle
arise	arose	arisen
be	was, were	been
beat	beat	beaten
become	became	become
begin	began	begun
bend	bent	bent
bet	bet	bet
bind	bound	bound
bite	bit	bitten
bleed	bled	bled
blow	blew	blown
break	broke	broken
bring	brought	brought
build	built	built
burn	burned	burned
burst	burst	burst
buy	bought	bought
can	could	–
cast	cast	cast
catch	caught	caught
choose	chose	chosen
cling	clung	clung
come	came	come
cost	cost *or* costed	cost *or* costed
creep	crept	crept
cut	cut	cut
deal	dealt	dealt
dig	dug	dug
dive	dove, [BRIT] dived	dived
do	did	done
draw	drew	drawn
dream	dreamed	dreamed
drink	drank	drunk
drive	drove	driven
eat	ate	eaten
fall	fell	fallen
feed	fed	fed
feel	felt	felt
fight	fought	fought
find	found	found
fly	flew	flown
forbid	forbade	forbidden
forget	forgot	forgotten
freeze	froze	frozen
get	got	gotten, [BRIT] got
give	gave	given
go	went	gone
grind	ground	ground
grow	grew	grown
hang	hung *or* hanged	hung *or* hanged
have	had	had
hear	heard	heard
hide	hid	hidden
hit	hit	hit
hold	held	held
hurt	hurt	hurt
keep	kept	kept
kneel	kneeled *or* knelt	kneeled *or* knelt
know	knew	known
lay	laid	laid
lead	led	led
lean	leaned	leaned
leap	leaped *or* leapt	leaped *or* leapt
learn	learned	learned
leave	left	left
lend	lent	lent
let	let	let
lie	lay	lain
light	lit	lit
lose	lost	lost
make	made	made
may	might	–
mean	meant	meant
meet	met	met

Infinitive	Past tense	Past participle	Infinitive	Past tense	Past participle
pay	paid	paid	**speed**	sped	sped
put	put	put	**spell**	spelled	spelled
quit	quit	quit	**spend**	spent	spent
read	read	read	**spill**	spilled	spilled
rid	rid	rid	**spit**	spat	spat
ride	rode	ridden	**spoil**	spoiled	spoiled
ring	rang	rung	**spread**	spread	spread
rise	rose	risen	**spring**	sprang	sprung
run	ran	run	**stand**	stood	stood
say	said	said	**steal**	stole	stolen
see	saw	seen	**stick**	stuck	stuck
seek	sought	sought	**sting**	stung	stung
sell	sold	sold	**stink**	stank	stunk
send	sent	sent	**strike**	struck	struck or stricken
set	set	set			
shake	shook	shaken	**swear**	swore	sworn
shed	shed	shed	**sweep**	swept	swept
shine	shone or shined	shone or shined	**swell**	swelled	swollen
			swim	swam	swum
shoe	shod	shod	**swing**	swung	swung
shoot	shot	shot	**take**	took	taken
show	showed	shown	**teach**	taught	taught
shrink	shrank	shrunk	**tear**	tore	torn
shut	shut	shut	**tell**	told	told
sing	sang	sung	**think**	thought	thought
sink	sank	sunk	**throw**	threw	thrown
sit	sat	sat	**wake**	woke	woken
sleep	slept	slept	**wear**	wore	worn
slide	slid	slid	**weep**	wept	wept
smell	smelled	smelled	**win**	won	won
sneak	sneaked or snuck	sneaked or snuck	**wind**	wound	wound
speak	spoke	spoken	**write**	wrote	written

Aa

A also **a** /eɪ/ (**A's**, **a's**) N-VAR **A** is the first letter of the English alphabet.

a ♦♦♦ /ə, STRONG eɪ/ also **an** /ən, STRONG æn/

A or **an** is the indefinite article. It is used at the beginning of noun groups that refer to only one person or thing. The form **an** is used in front of words that begin with vowel sounds.

1 DET You use **a** or **an** when you are referring to someone or something for the first time or when people may not know which particular person or thing you are talking about. ❑ *A waiter entered with a tray bearing a glass and a bottle of whiskey.* ❑ *He started eating an apple.* **2** DET You use **a** or **an** when you are referring to any person or thing of a particular type and do not want to be specific. ❑ *I suggest you leave it to an expert.* ❑ *Bring a sleeping bag.* **3** DET You use **a** or **an** in front of an uncount noun when that noun follows an adjective, or when the noun is followed by words that describe it more fully. ❑ *The islanders exhibit a constant happiness with life.* **4** DET You use **a** or **an** in front of a mass noun when you want to refer to a single type or make of something. ❑ *Bollinger "RD" is a rare, highly prized wine.* **5** DET You use **a** in quantifiers such as **a lot**, **a little**, and **a bit**. ❑ *I spend a lot on expensive jewelry and clothing.* **6** DET You use **a** or **an** to refer to someone or something as a typical member of a group, class, or type. ❑ *Some parents believe a boy must learn to stand up and fight like a man.* **7** DET You use **a** or **an** in front of the names of days, months, or festivals when you are referring to one particular instance of that day, month, or festival. ❑ *The interview took place on a Friday afternoon.* **8** DET You use **a** or **an** when you are saying what someone is or what job they have. ❑ *I explained that I was an artist.* **9** DET You use **a** or **an** instead of the number 'one,' especially with words of measurement such as 'hundred,' 'hour,' and 'meter,' and with fractions such as 'half,' 'quarter,' and 'third.' ❑ *...more than a thousand acres of land.* **10** DET You use **a** or **an** in expressions such as **$15.95 a day** to express a rate or ratio. ❑ *Prices start at $13.95 a yard for printed cotton.*

PREFIX

a-
is added to the beginning of some adjectives in order to form adjectives that describe someone or something that does not have the feature or quality indicated by the original word. *For example, an* **apolitical** *person is someone who is not interested in politics or who does not support any political party.*

aah /ɑ/ → see ah

A & E /eɪ ən i/ N-UNCOUNT **A & E** is the same as the **ER**. [BRIT]

AB /eɪ bi/ (**ABs**) N-COUNT In some American colleges and universities, an **AB** is the same as a **BA**.

aback /əbæk/ PHRASE If you are **taken aback** by something, you are surprised or shocked by it and you cannot respond at once. ❑ *Roland was taken aback by our strength of feeling.*

aba|cus /æbəkəs/ (**abacuses**) N-COUNT An **abacus** is a frame used for counting. It has rods with sliding beads on them.

aba|lo|ne /æbəlouni/ (**abalones**) N-VAR **Abalone** is a shellfish that you can eat and that has a shiny substance called mother-of-pearl inside its shell.

aban|don ♦⃝ /əbændən/ (**abandons**, **abandoning**, **abandoned**) **1** V-T If you **abandon** a place, thing, or person, you leave the place, thing, or person permanently or for a long time, especially when you should not do so. ❑ *He claimed that his parents had abandoned him.* **2** V-T If you **abandon** an activity or piece of work, you stop doing it before it is finished. ❑ *The authorities have abandoned any attempt to distribute food in an orderly fashion.* **3** V-T If you **abandon** an idea or way of thinking, you stop having that idea or thinking in that way. ❑ *Logic had prevailed and he had abandoned the idea.* **4** N-UNCOUNT [usu *with* N] If you say that someone does something with **abandon**, you mean that they behave in a wild, uncontrolled way and do not think or care about how they should behave. [DISAPPROVAL] ❑ *He approached life with reckless abandon–I don't think he himself knew what he was going to do next.* **5** → see also **abandoned** **6** PHRASE If people **abandon ship**, they get off a ship because it is sinking. ❑ *At the captain's order, they abandoned ship.*

aban|doned ♦⃝ /əbændənd/ ADJ An **abandoned** place or building is no longer used or occupied. ❑ *The digging had left a network of abandoned mines and tunnels.*

aban|don|ment /əbændənmənt/ **1** N-UNCOUNT The **abandonment** of a place, thing, or person is the act of leaving it permanently or for a long time, especially when you should not do so. ❑ *...memories of her father's complete abandonment of her.* **2** N-UNCOUNT The **abandonment** of a piece of work or activity is the act of stopping doing it before it is finished. ❑ *Constant rain forced the abandonment of the next day's competitions.*

abashed /əbæʃt/ ADJ [usu v-link ADJ] If you are **abashed**, you feel embarrassed and ashamed. [WRITTEN] ❑ *He looked abashed and uncomfortable.*

abate /əbeɪt/ (**abates**, **abating**, **abated**) V-I If something bad or undesirable **abates**, it becomes much less strong or severe. [FORMAL] ❑ *The storms had abated by the time they rounded Cape Horn.*

abate|ment /əbeɪtmənt/ N-UNCOUNT [also *a* N] **Abatement** means a reduction in the strength or power of something or the reduction of it. [FORMAL] ❑ *...the abatement of carbon dioxide emissions.* ❑ *...noise abatement.*

ab|at|toir /æbətwɑr/ (**abattoirs**) N-COUNT An **abattoir** is the same as a **slaughterhouse**. [mainly BRIT]

ab|bess /æbɪs/ (**abbesses**) N-COUNT An **abbess** is the nun who is in charge of the other nuns in a convent.

ab|bey /æbi/ (**abbeys**) N-COUNT An **abbey** is a church with buildings attached to it in which monks or nuns live or used to live.

ab|bot /æbət/ (**abbots**) N-COUNT An **abbot** is the monk who is in charge of the other monks in a monastery or abbey.

ab|bre|vi|ate /əbriviert/ (**abbreviates**, **abbreviating**, **abbreviated**) V-T If you **abbreviate** something, especially a word or a piece of writing, you make it shorter. ❑ *The creators of the original X-Men abbreviated the title of its sequel to simply X2.*

ab|bre|via|tion /əbrivieɪʃᵊn/ (**abbreviations**) N-COUNT An **abbreviation** is a short form of a word or phrase, made by leaving out some of the letters or by using only the first letter of each word. ❑ *The abbreviation for Kansas is KS.*

ABCs /eɪ bi siz/ **1** N-PLURAL [N *of* N] The **ABCs** of a subject or activity are the parts of it that you have to learn first because they are the most important and basic. ❑ *...the ABCs of cooking.* **2** N-PLURAL [poss N] Children who have learned their **ABCs** have learned to recognize, write, or say the alphabet. [mainly AM, INFORMAL]

ab|di|cate /æbdɪkeɪt/ (**abdicates**, **abdicating**, **abdicated**) **1** V-I If a king or queen **abdicates**, he or she gives up being

abdomen

king or queen. ☐ *The last French king was Louis Philippe, who abdicated in 1848.* • **ab|di|ca|tion** /æbdɪkeɪʃᵊn/ N-UNCOUNT ☐ *...the most serious royal crisis since the abdication of Edward VIII.* **2** V-T If you say that someone has **abdicated** responsibility for something, you disapprove of them because they have refused to accept responsibility for it any longer. [FORMAL, DISAPPROVAL] ☐ *Many parents simply abdicate all responsibility for their children.* • **ab|di|ca|tion** N-UNCOUNT ☐ *There had been a complete abdication of responsibility.*

ab|do|men /æbdoʊmən/ (abdomens) **1** N-COUNT Your **abdomen** is the part of your body below your chest where your stomach and intestines are. [FORMAL] ☐ *He went into the hospital to undergo tests for a pain in his abdomen.* **2** → See also color supplement

ab|domi|nal /æbdɒmɪnᵊl/ ADJ [ADJ n] **Abdominal** is used to describe something that is situated in the abdomen or forms part of it. [FORMAL] ☐ *...vomiting, diarrhea, and abdominal pain.*

ab|domi|nals /æbdɒmɪnᵊlz/ N-PLURAL You can refer to your abdominal muscles as your **abdominals** when you are talking about exercise.

ab|duct /æbdʌkt/ (abducts, abducting, abducted) V-T If someone **is abducted** by another person, he or she is taken away illegally, usually using force. ☐ *He was on his way to the airport when his car was held up and he was abducted by four gunmen.* • **ab|duc|tion** /æbdʌkʃᵊn/ (abductions) N-VAR ☐ *The U. N. World Food Program confirmed the abduction of eight of its workers in northern Darfur.*

ab|er|rant /əbɛrənt, æbər-/ ADJ [usu ADJ n] **Aberrant** means unusual and not socially acceptable. [FORMAL] ☐ *Ian's rages and aberrant behavior worsened.*

ab|er|ra|tion /æbəreɪʃᵊn/ (aberrations) N-VAR An **aberration** is an incident or way of behaving that is not typical. [FORMAL] ☐ *It became very clear that the incident was not just an aberration; it was not just a single incident.*

abet /əbɛt/ (abets, abetting, abetted) V-T If one person **abets** another, they help or encourage them to do something criminal or wrong. **Abet** is often used in the legal expression 'aid and abet.' [FORMAL, LEGAL] ☐ *His wife was sentenced to seven years imprisonment for aiding and abetting him.*

abey|ance /əbeɪəns/ PHRASE If something is **in abeyance**, it is not operating or being used at the present time. [FORMAL] ☐ *The threat is, at the least, in abeyance.*

ab|hor /æbhɔr/ (abhors, abhorring, abhorred) V-T If you **abhor** something, you hate it very much, especially for moral reasons. [FORMAL] ☐ *He was a man who abhorred violence and was deeply committed to reconciliation.*

ab|hor|rence /æbhɔrəns/ N-UNCOUNT Someone's **abhorrence** of something is their strong hatred of it. [FORMAL] ☐ *They are anxious to show their abhorrence of racism.*

ab|hor|rent /æbhɔrənt/ ADJ If something is **abhorrent** to you, you hate it very much or consider it completely unacceptable. [FORMAL] ☐ *Racial discrimination is abhorrent to my council and our staff.*

abide /əbaɪd/ (abides, abiding, abided) **1** PHRASE If you **can't abide** someone or something, you dislike them very much. ☐ *I can't abide people who can't make up their minds.* **2** → see also abiding, law-abiding
▶ **abide by** PHRASAL VERB If you **abide by** a law, agreement, or decision, you do what it says you should do. ☐ *They have got to abide by the rules.*

abid|ing /əbaɪdɪŋ/ ADJ [ADJ n] An **abiding** feeling, memory, or interest is one that you have for a very long time. ☐ *He has a genuine and abiding love of the craft.*

abil|ity /əbɪlɪti/ (abilities) **1** N-SING Your **ability** to do something is the fact that you can do it. ☐ *The public never had faith in his ability to handle the job.* **2** N-VAR Your **ability** is the quality or skill that you have which makes it possible for you to do something. ☐ *Her drama teacher spotted her ability.* ☐ *Does the school cater to all abilities?* **3** PHRASE If you do something **to the best of** your **abilities** or **to the best of** your **ability**, you do it as well as you can. ☐ *I take care of them to the best of my abilities.* **4** → See feature box at challenge

abolish

SUFFIX

-ability
replaces -able at the end of adjectives to form nouns that refer to a particular state or quality. *For example, reliability is the state or quality of being reliable.*

---

ab|ject /æbdʒɛkt/ ADJ You use **abject** to emphasize that a situation or quality is extremely bad. [EMPHASIS] ☐ *Both of them died in abject poverty.*

ab|jure /æbdʒʊər/ (abjures, abjuring, abjured) V-T If you **abjure** something such as a belief or way of life, you state publicly that you will give it up or that you reject it. [FORMAL] ☐ *...a formal statement abjuring military action.*

ablaze /əbleɪz/ **1** ADJ [v n ADJ, v-link ADJ] Something that is **ablaze** is burning very fiercely. ☐ *Stores, houses, and vehicles were set ablaze.* **2** ADJ [v-link ADJ] If a place is **ablaze** with lights or colors, it is very bright because of them. ☐ *The chamber was ablaze with light.*

able ♦♦♦ /eɪbᵊl/ (abler /eɪblər/, ablest /eɪblɪst/) **1** PHRASE If you **are able to** do something, you have skills or qualities which make it possible for you to do it. ☐ *The older child should be able to prepare a simple meal.* ☐ *The company says they're able to keep pricing competitive.* **2** PHRASE If you **are able to** do something, you have enough freedom, power, time, or money to do it. ☐ *You'll be able to read in peace.* ☐ *Have you been able to have any kind of contact?* **3** ADJ Someone who is **able** is very intelligent or very good at doing something. ☐ *...one of the brightest and ablest members of the government.*

SYNONYMS

able
ADJ **3**
capable: *She's a very capable speaker.*
experienced: *It's a team packed with experienced and mature professionals.*
skilled: *New industries demanded skilled labor not available locally.*
competent: *He was a loyal, distinguished, and very competent civil servant.*

SUFFIX

-able
forms adjectives that indicate what someone or something can have done to them. *For example, if something is movable, it is possible to move it.*

---

able-bodied /eɪbᵊl bɒdid/ ADJ An **able-bodied** person is physically strong and healthy, rather than being weak or having a disability. ☐ *The gym can be used by both able bodied and disabled people.*

ab|lu|tions /əbluʃᵊnz/ N-PLURAL [oft poss N] Someone's **ablutions** are all the activities that are involved in washing himself or herself. [FORMAL or HUMOROUS]

ably /eɪbli/ ADV [ADV with v] **Ably** means skillfully and successfully. ☐ *He was ably assisted by a number of members from other branches.*

ab|nor|mal /æbnɔrmᵊl/ ADJ Someone or something that is **abnormal** is unusual, especially in a way that is troublesome. [FORMAL] ☐ *...abnormal heart rhythms and high anxiety levels.* • **ab|nor|mal|ly** ADV ☐ *...abnormally high levels of glucose.*

ab|nor|mal|ity /æbnɔrmælɪti/ (abnormalities) N-VAR An **abnormality** in something, especially in a person's body or behavior, is an unusual part or feature of it that may be worrying or dangerous. [FORMAL] ☐ *Further scans are required to confirm the diagnosis of an abnormality.*

aboard /əbɔrd/ **1** PREP If you are **aboard** a ship or plane, you are on it or in it. ☐ *She invited 750 people aboard the luxury yacht, the Savarona.* • ADV [ADV after v] **Aboard** is also an adverb. ☐ *It had taken two hours to load all the people aboard.* **2** → See feature box at travel

abode /əboʊd/ (abodes) **1** N-COUNT Your **abode** is the place where you live. [FORMAL] ☐ *She lives in a grand abode overlooking Lake Michigan on the North Shore.* **2** PHRASE [oft of PHR] If someone is **of no fixed abode**, they are homeless. [LEGAL] ☐ *30 percent of the clinic's patients are of no fixed abode.*

abol|ish /əbɒlɪʃ/ (abolishes, abolishing, abolished) V-T If someone in authority **abolishes** a system or practice, they

abolition

formally put an end to it. ❑ *An Illinois House committee voted Thursday to abolish the death penalty.*

abo|li|tion /æbəlɪʃᵊn/ N-UNCOUNT The **abolition** of something such as a system or practice is its formal ending. ❑ *The abolition of slavery in Brazil and the Caribbean closely followed the pattern of the United States.*

abo|li|tion|ist /æbəlɪʃᵊnɪst/ (**abolitionists**) N-COUNT [oft N n] An **abolitionist** is someone who campaigns for the abolition of a particular system or practice. ❑ *He was a national leader in the abolitionist movement.*

A-bomb (**A-bombs**) N-COUNT An **A-bomb** is an atomic bomb.

abomi|nable /əbɒmɪnəbᵊl/ ADJ Something that is **abominable** is very unpleasant or bad. ❑ *The president described the killings as an abominable crime.*

abom|ina|tion /əbɒmɪneɪʃᵊn/ (**abominations**) N-COUNT If you say that something is an **abomination**, you think that it is completely unacceptable. [FORMAL, DISAPPROVAL]

Abo|rigi|nal /æbərɪdʒɪnᵊl/ also **aboriginal**
■ N-COUNT An **Aboriginal** is an Australian Aborigine. ❑ *He remained fascinated by the Aboriginals' tales.* ■ ADJ [ADJ n] **Aboriginal** means belonging or relating to the Australian Aborigines. ❑ *...Aboriginal art.*

Abo|rigi|ne /æbərɪdʒɪni/ (**Aborigines**) N-COUNT **Aborigines** are members of the tribes that were living in Australia when Europeans arrived there. ❑ *...Bigge Island, an area sacred to Aborigines for more than 20,000 years.*

abort /əbɔːrt/ (**aborts**, **aborting**, **aborted**) ■ V-T If an unborn baby **is aborted**, the pregnancy is ended deliberately and the baby is not born alive. ❑ *Her lover walked out on her after she had aborted their child.* ■ V-T If someone **aborts** a process, plan, or activity, they stop it before it has been completed. ❑ *When the decision was made to abort the mission, there was great confusion.*

abor|tion ✦✧ /əbɔːrʃᵊn/ (**abortions**) N-VAR An **abortion** is when a pregnancy is deliberately terminated at an early stage. ❑ *She had an abortion.*

abor|tion|ist /əbɔːrʃᵊnɪst/ (**abortionists**) ■ N-COUNT An **abortionist** is someone who performs abortions, usually illegally. ■ → see also **antiabortionist**

abor|tive /əbɔːrtɪv/ ADJ An **abortive** attempt or action is unsuccessful. [FORMAL] ❑ *...an abortive attempt to prevent the current president from taking office.*

abound /əbaʊnd/ (**abounds**, **abounding**, **abounded**) V-I If things **abound**, or if a place **abounds** with things, there are very large numbers of them. [FORMAL] ❑ *Stories abound about when he was in charge.*

about ✦✦✦ /əbaʊt/

In addition to the uses shown below, **about** is used after some verbs, nouns, and adjectives to introduce extra information. **About** is also often used after verbs of movement, such as 'walk' and 'drive,' especially in British English, and in phrasal verbs such as 'set about.'

■ PREP You use **about** to introduce what or what something relates to or concerns. ❑ *She knew a lot about food.* ❑ *He never complains about his neighbour.* ■ PREP When you mention the things that an activity or institution is **about**, you are saying what it involves or what its aims are. ❑ *Leadership is about the ability to implement change.* ■ PREP You use **about** after some adjectives to indicate the person or thing that a feeling or state of mind relates to. ❑ *"I'm sorry about Patrick," she said.* ■ PREP If you do something **about** a problem, you take action in order to solve it. ❑ *Rachel was going to do something about Jacob.* ■ PREP When you say that there is a particular quality **about** someone or something, you mean that they have this quality. ❑ *There was a warmth and passion about him I never knew existed.* ■ PREP If you put something **about** a person or thing, you put it around them. [mainly BRIT]

in AM, usually use **around**

■ ADV [ADV num] **About** is used in front of a number to show that the number is not exact. ❑ *The rate of inflation is running at about 2.7 percent.* ■ ADV [ADV after v] If someone or something moves **about**, they keep moving in different directions. [mainly BRIT]

in AM, usually use **around**

• PREP [v PREP n] **About** is also a preposition. [mainly BRIT]

in AM, usually use **around**

■ ADJ [v-link ADJ] If someone or something is **about**, they are present or available. [mainly BRIT]

in AM, usually use **around**

■ ADJ [v-link ADJ to-inf] If you are **about** to do something, you are going to do it very soon. If something is **about** to happen, it will happen very soon. ❑ *I think he's about to leave.* ❑ *Argentina has lifted all restrictions on trade and visas are about to be abolished.* ■ how about → see how ■ what about → see what ■ just about → see just ① ■ PHRASE If someone is **out and about**, they are going out and doing things, especially after they have been unable to for a while. ❑ *Despite considerable pain she has been getting out and about almost as normal.*

USAGE

about
Don't use an *-ing* form in '**about to**' sentences. Don't say, for example, 'You are about to crossing the River Jordan.' Say 'You are **about to cross** the River Jordan.' *I was about to go home.*

about-face (**about-faces**) N-COUNT An **about-face** is a complete change of attitude or opinion. ❑ *Few observers believe the president will do an about-face and start spending more.*

about-turn (**about-turns**) N-COUNT An **about-turn** is the same as an **about-face**. [BRIT]

above ✦✦✧ /əbʌv/ ■ PREP If one thing is **above** another one, it is directly over it or higher than it. ❑ *He lifted his hands above his head.* ❑ *Apartment 46 was a quiet apartment, unlike the one above it.* • ADV **Above** is also an adverb. ❑ *A long scream sounded from somewhere above.* ❑ *...a picture of the new plane as seen from above.* ■ PREP If an amount or measurement is **above** a particular level, it is greater than that level. ❑ *The temperature crept up to just above 40 degrees.* ❑ *Victoria Falls has had above average levels of rainfall this year.* • ADV [amount and ADV] **Above** is also an adverb. ❑ *Banks have been charging 25 percent and above for unsecured loans.* ■ PREP If you hear one sound **above** another, it is louder or clearer than the second one. ❑ *Then there was a woman's voice, rising shrilly above the barking.* ■ PREP If someone is **above** you, they are in a higher social position than you or in a position of authority over you. ❑ *I married above myself.* • ADV [from ADV] **Above** is also an adverb. ❑ *The police officers admitted arresting the student, but said they were acting on orders from above.* ■ PREP If you say that someone thinks they are **above** something, you mean that they act as if they are too good or important for it. [DISAPPROVAL] ❑ *This was clearly a failure by someone who thought he was above failure.* ■ PREP [v-link PREP n] If someone is **above** criticism or suspicion, they cannot be criticized or suspected because of their good qualities or their position. ❑ *He was a respected academic and above suspicion.* ■ PREP If you value one person or thing **above** any other, you value them more or consider that they are more important. ❑ *...his tendency to put the team above everything.* ■ **over and above** → see **over** ② ■ **above the law** → see **law** ⑩ ■ → see also **aboveboard** ■ ADV In writing, you use **above** to refer to something that has already been mentioned or discussed. ❑ *Several conclusions could be drawn from the results described above.* • N-SING-COLL **Above** is also a noun. ❑ *For additional information, contact any of the above.* • ADJ [ADJ n] **Above** is also an adjective. ❑ *For a copy of their brochure, write to the above address.*

USAGE

above
Don't use '**above**' in front of a number when you are talking about a quantity or number of things or people. For example, don't say 'She had above thirty pairs of shoes.' Say 'She had **over** thirty pairs of shoes' or 'She had **more than** thirty pairs of shoes.' *It cost **over** 3 million dollars. He saw **more than** 800 children there.*

above|board /əbʌvbɔːrd/ also **above board**, **above-board** ADJ [v-link ADJ] An arrangement or deal that is **aboveboard** is legal and is being carried out openly and honestly. A person who is **aboveboard** is open and honest about what they are doing. ▫ *His business dealings were aboveboard.* ▫ *If there was one thing she prided herself on, it was being open and aboveboard.*

ab|ra|ca|dab|ra /æbrəkədæbrə/ EXCLAM **Abracadabra** is a word that someone says when they are performing a magic trick in order to make the magic happen.

abrade /əbreɪd/ (**abrades**, **abrading**, **abraded**) V-T To **abrade** something means to scrape or wear down its surface by rubbing it. [FORMAL] ▫ *My skin was abraded and very tender.*

abra|sion /əbreɪʒ³n/ (**abrasions**) N-COUNT An **abrasion** is an area on a person's body where the skin has been scraped. [FORMAL] ▫ *He had severe abrasions to his right cheek.*

abra|sive /əbreɪsɪv/ **1** ADJ Someone who has an **abrasive** manner is unkind and rude. ▫ *His abrasive manner has won him an unenviable notoriety.* **2** ADJ An **abrasive** substance is rough and can be used to clean hard surfaces. ▫ *...a new all-purpose, non-abrasive cleaner that cleans and polishes all metals.*

abreast /əbrɛst/ **1** ADV If people or things walk or move **abreast**, they are next to each other, side by side, and facing in the same direction. ▫ *The steep sidewalk was too narrow for them to walk abreast.* **2** PHRASE If you keep **abreast of** a subject, you know all the most recent facts about it. ▫ *He will be keeping abreast of the news.*

abridged /əbrɪdʒd/ ADJ [usu ADJ n] An **abridged** book or play has been made shorter by removing some parts of it. ▫ *This is an abridged version of her new novel "The Queen and I."*

abroad ✦◇◇ /əbrɔd/ ADV If you go **abroad**, you go to a foreign country, usually one that is separated from the country where you live by an ocean or a sea. ▫ *I would love to go abroad this year, perhaps to the South of France.* ▫ *He will stand in for Mr. Goh when he is abroad.*

SYNONYMS

abroad
ADV
overseas: *Her only relatives live overseas.*
away: *Sophia was away on a business trip.*

ab|ro|gate /æbrəgeɪt/ (**abrogates**, **abrogating**, **abrogated**) V-T If someone in a position of authority **abrogates** something such as a law, agreement, or practice, they put an end to it. [FORMAL] ▫ *The next president could abrogate the treaty.*

ab|rupt /əbrʌpt/ **1** ADJ An **abrupt** change or action is very sudden, often in a way that is unpleasant. ▫ *Rosie's idyllic world came to an abrupt end when her parents' marriage broke up.* • **ab|rupt|ly** ADV [ADV with v] ▫ *He stopped abruptly and looked my way.* **2** ADJ Someone who is **abrupt** speaks in a rude, unfriendly way. ▫ *He was abrupt to the point of rudeness.* • **ab|rupt|ly** ADV ▫ *"Good night, then," she said abruptly.*

abs /æbz/ N-PLURAL **Abs** are the same as **abdominals**. [INFORMAL] ▫ *Throughout the exercise, focus on keeping your abs tight.*

ab|scess /æbsɛs/ (**abscesses**) N-COUNT An **abscess** is a painful swelling containing pus.

ab|scond /æbskɒnd/ (**absconds**, **absconding**, **absconded**) **1** V-I If someone **absconds** from somewhere such as a prison, they escape from it or leave it without permission. [FORMAL] ▫ *He was ordered to appear the following day, but absconded.* ▫ *A dozen inmates have absconded from the jail in the past year.* **2** V-I If someone **absconds** with something, they leave and take it with them, although it does not belong to them. [FORMAL] ▫ *Unfortunately, his partners were crooks and absconded with the funds.*

ab|seil /æbseɪl/ (**abseils**, **abseiling**, **abseiled**) V-I To **abseil** down a cliff or rock face means to slide down it in a controlled way using a rope, with your feet against the cliff or rock. [BRIT]

in AM, use **rappel**

ab|sence ✦◇◇ /æbsəns/ (**absences**) **1** N-VAR Someone's **absence** from a place is the fact that they are not there. ▫ *...a bundle of letters which had arrived for me in my absence.* **2** N-SING The **absence** of something from a place is the fact that it is not there or does not exist. ▫ *The presence or absence of clouds can have an important impact on temperature.*

SYNONYMS

absence
NOUN
1
time off: *She has hardly had any time off for the last four years.*
leave: *He's been on paternity leave since the birth of his daughter.*
2
lack: *Despite his lack of experience, he got the job.*
deficiency: *They did blood tests on him for signs of a vitamin deficiency.*
shortage: *There is no shortage of suggestions.*
want: *The men were daily becoming weaker from want of rest.*

ab|sent /æbsənt/ **1** ADJ If someone or something is **absent** from a place or situation where they should be or where they usually are, they are not there. ▫ *He has been absent from his desk for two weeks.* ▫ *The pictures, too, were absent from the walls.* **2** ADJ If someone appears **absent**, they are not paying attention because they are thinking about something else. ▫ *"Nothing," Rosie said in an absent way.* • **ab|sent|ly** /æbsəntli/ ADV ▫ *He nodded absently.* **3** ADJ [ADJ n] An **absent** parent does not live with his or her children. ▫ *...absent fathers who fail to pay toward the costs of looking after their children.* **4** PREP If you say that **absent** one thing, another thing will happen, you mean that if the first thing does not happen, the second thing will happen. [AM, FORMAL] ▫ *Absent a solution, people like Sue Godfrey will just keep on fighting.*

ab|sen|tee /æbsənti/ (**absentees**) **1** N-COUNT An **absentee** is a person who is expected to be in a particular place but who is not there. ▫ *At least two of the three other absentees also had justifiable reasons for being away.* **2** ADJ [ADJ n] **Absentee** is used to describe someone who is not there to do a particular job in person. ▫ *Absentee fathers will be forced to pay child support.* **3** ADJ [ADJ n] In elections in the United States, if you vote by **absentee** ballot or if you are an **absentee** voter, you vote in advance because you will be unable to go to the polling place. [AM] ▫ *He has already voted by absentee ballot.*

ab|sen|tee|ism /æbsəntiɪzəm/ N-UNCOUNT **Absenteeism** is the fact or habit of frequently being away from work or school, usually without a good reason.

ab|sen|tia /æbsɛnʃə/ PHRASE [PHR after v] If something is done to you **in absentia**, it is done to you when you are not present. [FORMAL] ▫ *He was tried in absentia and sentenced to seven years in prison.*

absent-minded ADJ Someone who is **absent-minded** forgets things or does not pay attention to what they are doing, often because they are thinking about something else. ▫ *In his later life he became even more absent-minded.* • **absent-mindedly** ADV [ADV with v] ▫ *Elizabeth absent-mindedly picked a thread from his lapel.*

ab|sinthe /æbsɪnθ/ N-UNCOUNT **Absinthe** is a very strong alcoholic drink that is green and tastes bitter.

ab|so|lute ✦◇◇ /æbsəlut/ (**absolutes**) **1** ADJ **Absolute** means total and complete. ▫ *It's not really suited to absolute beginners.* **2** ADJ [ADJ n] You use **absolute** to emphasize something that you are saying. [EMPHASIS] ▫ *About 12 inches wide is the absolute minimum you should consider.* **3** ADJ [ADJ n] An **absolute** ruler has complete power and authority over his or her country. ▫ *He ruled with absolute power.* **4** ADJ **Absolute** is used to say that something is definite and will not change even if circumstances change. ▫ *John brought the absolute proof that we needed.* **5** ADJ [ADJ n] An amount that is expressed in **absolute** terms is expressed as a fixed amount rather than referring to variable factors such as what you earn or the effects of inflation. ▫ *In absolute terms their wages remain low by national standards.* **6** ADJ **Absolute** rules and principles are believed to be true, right, or relevant in all situations. ▫ *There are no absolute rules.* **7** N-COUNT An **absolute** is a rule or principle that is believed to be true, right, or relevant in all situations. ▫ *This is one of the few absolutes in U.S. constitutional law.*

SYNONYMS

absolute
ADJ **1**
complete: *It shows a complete lack of understanding by management.*
total: *There was an almost total lack of management control.*
sheer: *His music is sheer delight.*
unalloyed: *...an occasion of unalloyed joy.*

ab|so|lute|ly ✦✦◇ /ˈæbsəlutli/ **1** ADV **Absolutely** means totally and completely. [EMPHASIS] ❑ *Joan is absolutely right.* ❑ *I absolutely refuse to get married.* **2** ADV [ADV as reply] Some people say **absolutely** as an emphatic way of saying yes or of agreeing with someone. They say **absolutely not** as an emphatic way of saying no or of disagreeing with someone. [EMPHASIS] ❑ *"It's worrying that they're doing things without training though, isn't it?"—"Absolutely."*

SYNONYMS

absolutely
ADV **1**
completely: *Dozens of homes had been completely destroyed.*
totally: *Young people want something totally different from the old ways.*
fully: *I don't fully agree with that.*
wholly: *For urban areas, this approach was wholly inadequate.*
utterly: *Such an allegation is utterly without foundation.*

---

ab|so|lute ma|jor|ity (absolute majorities) N-COUNT [usu sing] If a political party wins an **absolute majority**, they obtain more seats or votes than the total number of seats or votes gained by their opponents in an election.

ab|so|lute zero N-UNCOUNT **Absolute zero** is a theoretical temperature that is thought to be the lowest possible temperature.

ab|so|lu|tion /ˌæbsəˈluʃən/ N-UNCOUNT If someone is given **absolution**, they are forgiven for something wrong that they have done. [FORMAL] ❑ *She felt as if his words had granted her absolution.*

ab|so|lut|ism /ˈæbsəlutɪzəm/ **1** N-UNCOUNT **Absolutism** is a political system in which one ruler or leader has complete power and authority over a country. ❑ *...royal absolutism.* **2** N-UNCOUNT You can refer to someone's beliefs as **absolutism** if they think that their beliefs are true, right, or relevant in all situations, especially if you think they are wrong to behave in this way. [DISAPPROVAL] • **ab|so|lut|ist** ADJ ❑ *This absolutist belief is replaced by an appreciation that rules can vary.*

ab|solve /æbˈzɒlv/ (absolves, absolving, absolved) V-T If a report or investigation **absolves** someone of blame or responsibility, it formally states that he or she is not guilty or is not to blame. ❑ *A police investigation yesterday absolved the police of all blame in the incident.* ❑ *...the inquiry which absolved the soldiers.*

ab|sorb /əbˈsɔrb, -ˈzɔrb/ (absorbs, absorbing, absorbed) **1** V-T If something **absorbs** a liquid, gas, or other substance, it soaks it up or takes it in. ❑ *Plants absorb carbon dioxide from the air and moisture from the soil.* **2** V-T If something **absorbs** light, heat, or another form of energy, it takes it in. ❑ *A household radiator absorbs energy in the form of electric current and releases it in the form of heat.* **3** V-T If a group **is absorbed** into a larger group, it becomes part of the larger group. ❑ *City schools were absorbed into the countywide school district.* **4** V-T If something **absorbs** a force or shock, it reduces its effect. ❑ *...footwear which does not absorb the impact of the foot striking the ground.* **5** V-T If a system or society **absorbs** changes, effects, or costs, it is able to deal with them. ❑ *The banks would be forced to absorb large losses.* **6** V-T If something **absorbs** something valuable such as money, space, or time, it uses up a great deal of it. ❑ *It absorbed vast amounts of capital that could have been used for investment.* **7** V-T If you **absorb** information, you learn and understand it. ❑ *Too often he only absorbs half the information in the manual.* **8** V-T If something **absorbs** you, it interests you a great deal and takes up all your attention and energy. ❑ *...a second career which absorbed her more completely than her acting ever had.* **9** → see also **absorbed, absorbing**

ab|sorbed /əbˈsɔrbd, -ˈzɔrbd/ ADJ [v-link ADJ] If you are **absorbed** in something or someone, you are very interested in them and they take up all your attention and energy. ❑ *They were completely absorbed in each other.*

ab|sor|bent /əbˈsɔrbənt, -ˈzɔrbənt/ ADJ **Absorbent** material soaks up liquid easily. ❑ *The towels are highly absorbent.*

ab|sorb|er /əbˈsɔrbər, -ˈzɔrbər/ → see **shock absorber**

ab|sorb|ing /əbˈsɔrbɪŋ, -ˈzɔrbɪŋ/ ADJ An **absorbing** task or activity interests you a great deal and takes up all your attention and energy. ❑ *"Two Sisters" is an absorbing read.*

ab|sorp|tion /əbˈsɔrpʃən, -ˈzɔrpʃən/ **1** N-UNCOUNT The **absorption** of a liquid, gas, or other substance is the process of it being soaked up or taken in. ❑ *This controls the absorption of liquids.* **2** N-UNCOUNT The **absorption** of a group into a larger group is the process of it becoming part of the larger group. ❑ *...Serbia's absorption into the Ottoman Empire.*

ab|stain /æbˈsteɪn/ (abstains, abstaining, abstained) **1** V-I If you **abstain** from something, usually something you want to do, you deliberately do not do it. [FORMAL] ❑ *Abstain from sex or use condoms.* **2** V-I If you **abstain** during a vote, you do not use your vote. ❑ *Three countries abstained in the vote.*

ab|ste|mi|ous /æbˈstimiəs/ ADJ Someone who is **abstemious** avoids doing too much of something enjoyable such as eating or drinking. [FORMAL]

ab|sten|tion /æbˈstɛnʃən/ (abstentions) N-VAR **Abstention** is a formal act of not voting either for or against a proposal. ❑ *...a vote of sixteen in favor, three against, and one abstention.*

ab|sti|nence /ˈæbstɪnəns/ N-UNCOUNT **Abstinence** is the practice of abstaining from something such as alcoholic drink or sex, often for health or religious reasons. ❑ *...six months of abstinence.*

ab|stract /ˈæbstrækt/ (abstracts) **1** ADJ An **abstract** idea or way of thinking is based on general ideas rather than on real things and events. ❑ *...starting with a few abstract principles.* ❑ *It's not a question of some abstract concept of justice.* **2** ADJ [ADJ n] In grammar, an **abstract** noun refers to a quality or idea rather than to a physical object. ❑ *...abstract words such as glory, honor, and courage.* **3** ADJ **Abstract** art makes use of shapes and patterns rather than showing people or things. ❑ *A modern abstract painting takes over one complete wall.* **4** PHRASE When you talk or think about something **in the abstract**, you talk or think about it in a general way, rather than considering particular things or events. ❑ *Money was a commodity she never thought about except in the abstract.* **5** N-COUNT An **abstract** is an abstract work of art. ❑ *His abstracts are held in numerous collections.* **6** N-COUNT An **abstract** of an article, document, or speech is a short piece of writing that gives the main points of it. ❑ *It might also be necessary to supply an abstract of the review of the literature as well.* **7** → See feature box at **fine art**

ab|stract|ed /æbˈstræktɪd/ ADJ Someone who is **abstracted** is thinking so deeply that they are not fully aware of what is happening around them. [WRITTEN] ❑ *The same abstracted look was still on his face.* • **ab|stract|ed|ly** ADV [ADV with v] ❑ *She nodded abstractedly.*

ab|strac|tion /æbˈstrækʃən/ (abstractions) N-VAR An **abstraction** is a general idea rather than one relating to a particular object, person, or situation. [FORMAL] ❑ *Is it worth fighting a big war, in the name of an abstraction like sovereignty?*

ab|struse /æbˈstrus/ ADJ GRADED; ADJ You can describe something as **abstruse** if you find it difficult to understand, especially when you think it could be explained more simply. [FORMAL, DISAPPROVAL] ❑ *...fruitless discussions about abstruse resolutions.*

ab|surd /æbˈsɜrd, -ˈzɜrd/ ADJ If you say that something is **absurd**, you are criticizing it because you think that it is ridiculous or that it does not make sense. [DISAPPROVAL] ❑ *That's absurd.* ❑ *It's absurd to suggest that they knew what was going on but did nothing.* • N-SING [the N] **The absurd** is something that is absurd. [FORMAL] ❑ *Connie had a sharp eye for the absurd.* • **ab|surd|ly** ADV ❑ *Prices were still absurdly low, in his opinion.* • **ab|surd|ity** /æbˈsɜrdɪti, -ˈzɜrd-/ (absurdities) N-VAR ❑ *I find myself growing increasingly angry at the absurdity of the situation.*

ab|surd|ist /æbˈsɜrdɪst, -ˈzɜrd-/ ADJ [usu ADJ n] An **absurdist** play or other work shows how absurd some aspect of society or human behavior is.

abun|dance /əˈbʌndəns/ **1** N-SING-COLL [usu N of n, also in N] An **abundance** of something is a large quantity of it. ❑ *This area of Mexico has an abundance of safe beaches and a pleasing climate.* **2** → See feature box at **water**

abun|dant /əˈbʌndənt/ ADJ Something that is **abundant** is present in large quantities. ❑ *There is an abundant supply of cheap labor.*

abun|dant|ly /əˈbʌndəntli/ **1** ADV [ADV adj] If something is **abundantly** clear, it is extremely obvious. ❑ *He made it abundantly clear that anybody who disagrees with his policies will not last long.*

2 ADV Something that occurs **abundantly** is present in large quantities. ❑ *...a plant that grows abundantly in the United States.*

abuse ♦♦◇ (abuses, abusing, abused)

The noun is pronounced /əbyus/. The verb is pronounced /əbyuz/.

1 N-UNCOUNT [also N in pl] **Abuse** of someone is cruel and violent treatment of them. ❑ *...investigation of alleged child abuse.* ❑ *...victims of sexual and physical abuse.* **2** N-UNCOUNT **Abuse** is extremely rude and insulting things that people say when they are angry. ❑ *I was left shouting abuse as the car sped off.* **3** N-VAR [with supp] **Abuse** of something is the use of it in a wrong way or for a bad purpose. ❑ *What went on here was an abuse of power.* **4** V-T If someone **is abused**, they are treated cruelly and violently. ❑ *The charity provides help for women who have been abused.* ❑ *...parents who feel they cannot cope or might abuse their children.* **5** V-T You can say that someone **is abused** if extremely rude and insulting things are said to them. ❑ *He alleged that he was verbally abused by other soldiers.* **6** V-T If you **abuse** something, you use it in a wrong way or for a bad purpose. ❑ *He showed how the rich and powerful can abuse their position.*

--- SYNONYMS ---
abuse
NOUN **1**
ill-treatment: *Ill-treatment of animals is now much less common.*
injury: *She was awarded $3,500 for injury to her feelings.*
maltreatment: *2,000 prisoners died as a result of torture and maltreatment.*
VERB **4**
ill-treat: *They were not ill-treated, but their time in captivity was miserable.*
maltreat: *He said that he was not tortured or maltreated during his detention.*
---

abu|sive /əbyusɪv/ **1** ADJ Someone who is **abusive** behaves in a cruel and violent way toward other people. ❑ *He became violent and abusive toward Ben's mother.* **2** ADJ **Abusive** language is extremely rude and insulting. ❑ *I did not use any foul or abusive language.* **3** → See feature box at **poverty**

abut /əbʌt/ (abuts, abutting, abutted) V-T/V-I When land or a building **abuts** something or **abuts on** something, it is next to it. [FORMAL]

abuzz /əbʌz/ ADJ [v-link ADJ] If someone says that a place is **abuzz** with rumors or plans, they mean that everyone there is excited about them. [JOURNALISM]

abys|mal /əbɪzmᵊl/ ADJ If you describe a situation or the condition of something as **abysmal**, you think that it is very bad or poor in quality. ❑ *The general standard of racing was abysmal.* ● **abys|mal|ly** ADV ❑ *The group for the most part found the standard of education abysmally low.*

abyss /əbɪs/ (abysses) **1** N-COUNT An **abyss** is a very deep hole in the ground. [LITERARY] ❑ *The torrent, swollen by the melting snow, plunges into a tremendous abyss.* **2** N-COUNT If someone is on the edge or brink of an **abyss**, they are about to enter into a very frightening or threatening situation. [LITERARY] ❑ *The economic life of the whole society is being brought to the brink of an abyss.*

AC /eɪ si/ N-UNCOUNT [oft N n] **AC** is used to refer to an electric current that continually changes direction as it flows. **AC** is an abbreviation for **alternating current**.

a/c also **A/C** N-UNCOUNT **a/c** is an abbreviation for **air-conditioning**. ❑ *Keep your windows up and the a/c on high.* ❑ *60 Motel Units. All Units A/C, Heat, Cable TV.*

aca|cia /əkeɪʃə/ (acacias or acacia) N-COUNT An **acacia** or an **acacia tree** is a tree that grows in warm countries and which usually has small yellow or white flowers.

aca|deme /ækədim/ N-UNCOUNT The academic world of colleges and universities is sometimes referred to as **academe**. [FORMAL]

aca|demia /ækədimiə/ N-UNCOUNT **Academia** refers to all the academics in a particular country or region, the institutions they work in, and their work. ❑ *...the importance of strong links between industry and academia.*

aca|dem|ic ♦◇◇ /ækədɛmɪk/ (academics) **1** ADJ [ADJ n] **Academic** is used to describe things that relate to the work done in schools, colleges, and universities, especially work that involves studying and reasoning rather than practical or technical skills. ❑ *Their academic standards are high.* ● **aca|dem|ical|ly** /ækədɛmɪkli/ ADV ❑ *He is academically gifted.* **2** ADJ [ADJ n] **Academic** is used to describe things that relate to schools, colleges, and universities. ❑ *...the start of the last academic year.* **3** ADJ **Academic** is used to describe work, or a school, college, or university, that places emphasis on studying and reasoning rather than on practical or technical skills. ❑ *The author has settled for a more academic approach.* **4** ADJ Someone who is **academic** is good at studying. ❑ *The system is failing most disastrously among less academic children.* **5** ADJ You can say that a discussion or situation is **academic** if you think it is not important because it has no real effect or cannot happen. ❑ *Who wants to hear about contracts and deadlines that are purely academic?* **6** N-COUNT An **academic** is a member of a university or college who teaches or does research. ❑ *A group of academics say they can predict house prices through a computer program.* **7** → See feature box at **research**, **university**

--- SYNONYMS ---
academic
ADJ **4**
scholarly: *He was an intellectual, scholarly man.*
intellectual: *He belonged to the intellectual elite.*
learned: *She is a serious scholar, a genuinely learned woman.*
erudite: *Maria was never dull, always erudite and well-informed.*
well-read: *He was clever, well-read, and interested in the arts.*
---

acad|emi|cian /ækədəmɪʃᵊn, əkædəmɪʃᵊn/ (academicians) N-COUNT An **academician** is a member of an academy, usually one that has been formed to improve or maintain standards in a particular field.

acad|emy /əkædəmi/ (academies) **1** N-COUNT **Academy** is sometimes used in the names of schools and colleges, especially those specializing in particular subjects or skills, or private high schools in the United States. ❑ *He is an English teacher at the Seattle Academy for Arts and Sciences.* **2** N-IN-NAMES **Academy** appears in the names of some societies formed to improve or maintain standards in a particular field. ❑ *...the American Academy of Psychotherapists.*

ac|cede /æksid/ (accedes, acceding, acceded) **1** V-I If you **accede to** someone's request or demands, you do what they ask. ❑ *I never understood why he didn't just accede to our demands at the outset.* **2** V-I When a member of a royal family **accedes to** the throne, they become king or queen. [FORMAL]

ac|cel|er|ate /æksɛləreɪt/ (accelerates, accelerating, accelerated) **1** V-T/V-I If the process or rate of something **accelerates** or if something **accelerates** it, it gets faster and faster. ❑ *Growth will accelerate to 2.9 percent next year.* **2** V-I When a moving vehicle **accelerates**, it goes faster and faster. ❑ *Suddenly the car accelerated.* **3** → See feature box at **global warming**, **travel**

ac|cel|era|tion /æksɛləreɪʃᵊn/ **1** N-UNCOUNT The **acceleration** of a process or change is the fact that it is getting faster and faster. ❑ *He has also called for an acceleration of political reforms.* **2** N-UNCOUNT **Acceleration** is the rate at which a car or other vehicle can increase its speed, often seen in terms of the time that it takes to reach a particular speed. ❑ *Acceleration to 60 mph takes a mere 5.7 seconds.* **3** N-UNCOUNT **Acceleration** is the rate at which the speed of an object increases. [TECHNICAL]

ac|cel|era|tor /æksɛləreɪtər/ (accelerators) N-COUNT The **accelerator** in a car or other vehicle is the pedal that you press with your foot in order to make the vehicle go faster. ❑ *He eased his foot off the accelerator.*

ac|cent /æksɛnt/ (accents) **1** N-COUNT Someone who speaks with a particular **accent** pronounces the words of a language in a distinctive way that shows which country, region, or background they come from. ❑ *He had developed a slight southern accent.* **2** N-COUNT An **accent** is a short line or other mark which is written above certain letters in some languages and which indicates the way those letters are pronounced. ❑ *...an acute accent.*

ac|cent|ed /æksɛntɪd, æksɛntɪd/ ADJ Language or speech that is **accented** is spoken with a particular accent. ❑ *I spoke good, but heavily accented English.*

ac|cen|tu|ate /æksɛntʃueɪt/ (**accentuates, accentuating, accentuated**) V-T To **accentuate** something means to emphasize it or make it more noticeable. ◻ *His shaven head accentuates his large round face.*

ac|cept ♦♦♦ /æksɛpt/ (**accepts, accepting, accepted**) **1** V-T/V-I If you **accept** something that you have been offered, you say yes to it or agree to take it. ◻ *Eventually Esteban persuaded her to accept an offer of marriage.* ◻ *All those invited to next week's peace conference have accepted.* **2** V-T If you **accept** an idea, statement, or fact, you believe that it is true or valid. ◻ *I do not accept that there is any kind of crisis in American science.* ◻ *I don't think they would accept that view.* **3** V-T If you **accept** a plan or an intended action, you agree to it and allow it to happen. ◻ *The Council will meet to decide if it should accept his resignation.* **4** V-T If you **accept** an unpleasant fact or situation, you get used to it or recognize that it is necessary or cannot be changed. ◻ *Some people can accept suffering that can be shown to lead to a greater good.* ◻ *Urban dwellers often accept noise as part of city life.* **5** V-T If a person, company, or organization **accepts** something such as a document, they recognize that it is genuine, correct, or satisfactory and agree to consider it or handle it. ◻ *We took the unusual step of contacting newspapers to advise them not to accept the advertising.* **6** V-T If an organization or person **accepts** you, you are allowed to join the organization or use the services that are offered. ◻ *All-male groups will not be accepted.* **7** V-T If a person or a group of people **accepts** you, they begin to be friendly toward you and are happy with who you are or what you do. ◻ *As far as my grandparents were concerned, they've never had a problem accepting me.* ◻ *Many men still have difficulty accepting a woman as a business partner.* **8** V-T If you **accept** the responsibility or blame for something, you recognize that you are responsible for it. ◻ *The company cannot accept responsibility for loss or damage.* **9** V-T If you **accept** someone's advice or suggestion, you agree to do what they say. ◻ *The army refused to accept orders from the political leadership.* **10** V-T If a machine **accepts** a particular kind of thing, it is designed to take it and deal with it or process it. ◻ *The new parking meters don't accept dollar bills.* **11** → see also **accepted**

▶ **SYNONYMS** ◀

accept
VERB
1
take: *When I took the job, I thought I could change the system.*
take on: *Don't take on more responsibilities than you can handle.*
undertake: *She undertook the very difficult task of monitoring the elections.*
2
acknowledge: *Belatedly, the government has acknowledged the problem.*
admit: *I am willing to admit that I do make mistakes.*
allow: *Warren allows that the policy may sometimes result in increased social inequality.*
4
take: *Harry's rudeness to everyone was becoming hard to take.*
stand: *Stoddart can stand any amount of personal criticism.*
put up with: *They had put up with terrible behavior from their son.*
tolerate: *She can no longer tolerate the position that she's in.*
bear: *They will have to bear the misery of living in constant fear of war.*

▶ **USAGE** ◀

accept
Don't say that you 'accept to do' what someone suggests. You say that you **agree** to do it. *The princess agreed to go on television.*

ac|cept|able ♦◇◇ /æksɛptəbəl/ **1** ADJ **Acceptable** activities and situations are those that most people approve of or consider to be normal. ◻ *It is becoming more acceptable to talk more openly about our mental health.* ● **ac|cept|abil|ity** /æksɛptəbɪlɪti/ N-UNCOUNT ◻ *This assumption played a considerable part in increasing the social acceptability of divorce.* ● **ac|cept|ably** /æksɛptəbli/ ADV ◻ *The aim of discipline is to teach children to behave acceptably.* **2** ADJ If something is **acceptable** to someone, they agree to consider it, use it, or allow it to happen. ◻ *They have thrashed out a compromise formula acceptable to Moscow.* **3** ADJ If you describe something as **acceptable**, you mean that it is good enough or fairly good. ◻ *On the far side of the street was a restaurant that looked acceptable.* ● **ac|cept|ably** ADV ◻ *...a method that provides an acceptably accurate solution to a problem.*

▶ **SYNONYMS** ◀

acceptable
ADJ **3**
all right: *'How was school?'—'It was all right.'*
satisfactory: *Neither solution seemed satisfactory.*
fine: *The skiing is fine.*
adequate: *The western diet should be perfectly adequate for most people.*
passable: *She speaks passable French.*

ac|cept|ance /æksɛptəns/ (**acceptances**) **1** N-VAR **Acceptance** of an offer or a proposal is the act of saying yes to it or agreeing to it. ◻ *The Party is being degraded by its acceptance of secret donations.* ◻ *...his acceptance speech for the Nobel Peace Prize.* **2** N-UNCOUNT If there is **acceptance** of an idea, most people believe or agree that it is true. ◻ *...a theory that is steadily gaining acceptance.* **3** N-UNCOUNT Your **acceptance** of a situation, especially an unpleasant or difficult one, is an attitude or feeling that you cannot change it and that you must get used to it. ◻ *The most impressive thing about him is his calm acceptance of whatever comes his way.* **4** N-UNCOUNT **Acceptance** of someone into a group means beginning to think of them as part of the group and to act in a friendly way toward them. ◻ *A very determined effort by society will ensure that people with disabilities achieve real acceptance and integration.*

ac|cept|ed ♦◇◇ /æksɛptɪd/ **1** ADJ **Accepted** ideas are agreed by most people to be correct or reasonable. ◻ *There is no generally accepted definition of life.* **2** → see also **accept**

ac|cess ♦◇◇ /æksɛs/ (**accesses, accessing, accessed**) **1** N-UNCOUNT If you have **access** to a building or other place, you are able or allowed to go into it. ◻ *The facilities have been adapted to give access to wheelchair users.* ◻ *For logistical and political reasons, scientists have only recently been able to gain access to the area.* **2** N-UNCOUNT If you have **access** to something such as information or equipment, you have the opportunity or right to see it or use it. ◻ *...a Code of Practice that would give patients access to their medical records.* **3** N-UNCOUNT If you have **access** to a person, you have the opportunity or right to see them or meet them. ◻ *He was not allowed access to a lawyer.* **4** V-T If you **access** something, especially information held on a computer, you succeed in finding or obtaining it. ◻ *You've illegally accessed and misused confidential security files.*

▶ **SYNONYMS** ◀

access
NOUN **1**
admission: *There have been increases in hospital admissions of children.*
entry: *Entry to the museum is free.*
admittance: *We had not been able to gain admittance to the apartment.*
VERB **4**
acquire: *I recently acquired some wood from a holly tree.*
get: *I asked him to get me some information.*
gather: *...a private detective using a hidden microphone to gather information.*
obtain: *Evans was trying to obtain a false passport and other documents.*

▶ **COLLOCATIONS** ◀

access
NOUN
1
verb + **access**: allow, grant; deny, restrict; gain
2
adjective + **access**: unlimited, unfettered, unrestricted
VERB **4**
access + noun: the internet, the Web

ac|ces|sible /æksɛsɪbəl/ **1** ADJ If a place or building is **accessible** to people, it is easy for them to reach or get into it. If an object is **accessible**, it is easy to reach. ◻ *The center is easily accessible to the general public.* ● **ac|ces|sibil|ity** /æksɛsɪbɪlɪti/ N-UNCOUNT ◻ *...the easy accessibility of the area.* **2** ADJ If something is **accessible** to people, they can easily use

accession · accommodate

it or obtain it. ▫ *The aim of any reform of legal aid should be to make the system accessible to more people.* • **ac|ces|sibil|ity** N-UNCOUNT ▫ *...growing public concern about the cost, quality and accessibility of health care.* **3** ADJ If you describe a book, painting, or other work of art as **accessible**, you think it is good because it is simple enough for people to understand and appreciate easily. [APPROVAL] ▫ *Both say they want to write literary books that are accessible to a general audience.* • **ac|ces|sibil|ity** N-UNCOUNT ▫ *Seminar topics are chosen for their accessibility to a general audience.*

ac|ces|sion /ækse̱ʃən/ N-UNCOUNT [with poss, oft N *to* n] **Accession** is the act of taking up a position as the ruler of a country. [FORMAL] ▫ *...the anniversary of the king's accession to the throne.*

ac|ces|so|rize /æksesəraɪz/ (**accessorizes**, **accessorizing**, **accessorized**)

in BRIT, also use **accessorise**

V-T To **accessorize** something such as a set of furniture or clothing means to add other things to it in order to make it look more attractive. ▫ *Use a belt to accessorize a plain dress.*

ac|ces|so|ry /æksesəri/ (**accessories**) **1** N-COUNT **Accessories** are items of equipment that are not usually essential, but can be used with or added to something else in order to make it more efficient, useful, or decorative. ▫ *...an exclusive range of hand-made bedroom and bathroom accessories.* **2** N-COUNT **Accessories** are articles such as belts and scarves which you wear or carry but which are not part of your main clothing. ▫ *It also has a good range of accessories, including sunglasses, handbags and belts.* **3** N-COUNT If someone is guilty of being an **accessory** to a crime, they helped the person who committed it, or knew it was being committed but did not tell the police. [LEGAL] ▫ *She had been charged with being an accessory to the embezzlement of funds from a cooperative farm.*

ac|cess road (**access roads**) N-COUNT An **access road** is a road which enables traffic to reach a particular place or area. ▫ *...the access road to the airport.*

ac|cess time (**access times**) N-COUNT **Access time** is the time that is needed to get information that is stored in a computer. [COMPUTING] ▫ *This system helps speed up access times.*

VOCABULARY IN CONTEXT

Accidents

Statistics show that we're more likely than ever to be involved in a **car crash**. Globally, **traffic accidents** account for 1.3 million **fatalities** a year. That makes them the ninth highest cause of death – and that's predicted to rise to fifth highest by 2030. The most likely result of being in a **collision** is still **whiplash**, not death. Even passengers involved in a **head-on collision** may walk away injury-free, despite the car being completely **written off**. Self-driving cars may eventually signal the end of car accidents, as cars will automatically **swerve** to avoid obstacles, and it will be impossible for them to commit common driving errors like **hitting** another vehicle at an intersection or **slamming into** oncoming traffic due to the driver falling asleep at the wheel. Self-driving cars will also presumably be better at getting themselves out of uncontroled **skids** on mud or ice, as they won't panic like human drivers.

ac|ci|dent ✦✧✧ /æksɪdənt/ (**accidents**) **1** N-COUNT An **accident** happens when a vehicle hits a person, an object, or another vehicle, causing injury or damage. ▫ *She was involved in a serious car accident last week.* **2** N-COUNT If someone has an **accident**, something unpleasant happens to them that was not intended, sometimes causing injury or death. ▫ *5,000 people die every year because of accidents in the home.* **3** N-VAR If something happens by **accident**, it happens completely by chance. ▫ *She discovered the problem by accident during a visit to a nearby school.*

COLLOCATIONS

accident
NOUN
1
noun + **accident**: car, motorcycle, road, traffic; riding, skiing
adjective + **accident**: fatal, serious; minor
verb + **accident**: investigate, report, witness; survive
2
noun + **accident**: workplace
adjective + **accident**: freak, horrific, tragic, unfortunate; industrial, nuclear; minor
verb + **accident**: avoid, prevent; cause

ac|ci|den|tal /æksɪdentəl/ ADJ An **accidental** event happens by chance or as the result of an accident, and is not intended. ▫ *...the tragic accidental shooting of his younger brother.* • **ac|ci|den|tal|ly** /æksɪdentli/ ADV [ADV with v] ▫ *A policeman accidentally killed his two best friends with a single bullet.*

ac|ci|dent and emer|gen|cy (**accident and emergencies**) N-COUNT **Accident and emergency** is the same as **emergency room**. [BRIT]

ac|ci|dent prone also **accident-prone** ADJ If you describe someone or something as **accident prone**, you mean that a lot of accidents or other unpleasant things happen to them.

ac|claim /əkleɪm/ (**acclaims**, **acclaiming**, **acclaimed**) **1** V-T [usu passive] If someone or something **is acclaimed**, they are praised enthusiastically. [FORMAL] ▫ *The restaurant has been widely acclaimed for its excellent French cuisine.* ▫ *He was acclaimed as America's greatest filmmaker.* • **ac|claimed** ADJ ▫ *She has published six highly acclaimed novels.* **2** N-UNCOUNT **Acclaim** is public praise for someone or something. [FORMAL] ▫ *Angela Bassett has won critical acclaim for her excellent performance.*

ac|cla|ma|tion /ækləmeɪʃən/ **1** N-UNCOUNT **Acclamation** is a noisy or enthusiastic expression of approval for someone or something. [FORMAL] ▫ *The news was greeted with considerable popular acclamation.* **2** N-UNCOUNT If someone is chosen or elected by **acclamation**, they are elected without a written vote. [FORMAL] ▫ *At first it looked like I was going to win by acclamation.*

ac|cli|mate /æklɪmeɪt, əklaɪmɪt/ (**acclimates**, **acclimating**, **acclimated**) V-T/V-I When you **acclimate** or **are acclimated** to a new situation, place, or climate, you become used to it. [AM] ▫ *I help them acclimate to living in the U.S.* ▫ *I hadn't had any time to acclimate myself.* ▫ *It does take time to acclimate, especially for guys who haven't grown up in an urban environment.* ▫ *The animals have become acclimated to the presence of humans.* • **ac|cli|ma|tion** /ækləmeɪʃən/ N-UNCOUNT ▫ *...gradual acclimation to strenuous exercise.*

ac|cli|ma|tize /əklaɪmətaɪz/ (**acclimatizes**, **acclimatizing**, **acclimatized**)

in BRIT, also use **acclimatise**

V-T/V-I **Acclimatize** means the same as **acclimate**. [FORMAL] ▫ *The athletes are acclimatizing to the heat by staying in Monte Carlo.* ▫ *This year he has left for St. Louis early to acclimatize himself.*

ac|co|lade /ækəleɪd/ (**accolades**) N-COUNT If someone is given an **accolade**, something is done or said about them which shows how much people admire them. [FORMAL] ▫ *The Nobel Prize has become the ultimate accolade in the sciences.* ▫ *He won accolades as one of America's top test pilots.*

ac|com|mo|date /əkɒmədeɪt/ (**accommodates**, **accommodating**, **accommodated**) **1** V-T [no cont] If a building or space can **accommodate** someone or something, it has enough room for them. ▫ *The school was not big enough to accommodate all the children.* **2** V-T To **accommodate** someone means to provide them with a place to live or stay. ▫ *...a hotel built to accommodate guests for the wedding of King Alfonso.*

accommodating

❸ V-T If something is planned or changed to **accommodate** a particular situation, it is planned or changed so that it takes this situation into account. [FORMAL] ❏ *The roads are built to accommodate gradual temperature changes.*

ac|com|mo|dat|ing /əkɒmədeɪtɪŋ/ ADJ If you describe someone as **accommodating**, you like the fact that they are willing to do things in order to please you or help you. [APPROVAL] ❏ *Eddie was among the most approachable athletes on the team, always very accommodating to me.*

ac|com|mo|da|tion /əkɒmədeɪʃən/ (**accommodations**)
❶ N-PLURAL **Accommodations** are buildings or rooms where people live or stay. [AM] ❏ *The government will provide temporary accommodations for up to three thousand homeless people.*

in BRIT, use **accommodation**

❷ N-UNCOUNT **Accommodation** is space in buildings or vehicles that is available for certain things, people, or activities. [FORMAL] ❏ *Their offices are housed in rented accommodation in a modernized wing of the Mathematics Institute.*

USAGE

accommodation
In American English, **accommodation** is usually a countable noun. *The motel provides cheap **accommodations** and good steaks.*

SYNONYMS

accommodation
NOUN ❶
housing: *...a shortage of affordable housing.*
board: *Free room and board are provided for all hotel staff.*
lodging: *He was given free lodging in a three-bedroom apartment.*
dwelling: *Some 3,500 new dwellings are planned for the area.*

COLLOCATIONS

accommodation
NOUN
❶
noun + **accommodation**: hotel, student; emergency
adjective + **accommodation**: overnight, rental, sheltered, temporary; affordable, cheap, comfortable, suitable
verb + **accommodation**: include, offer, provide; book, find
❷
noun + **accommodation**: office

ac|com|pa|ni|ment /əkʌmpənɪmənt/ (**accompaniments**)
❶ N-COUNT The **accompaniment** to a song or tune is the music that is played at the same time as it and forms a background to it. ❏ *He sang "My Funny Valentine" and "Wanted" to musical director Jim Steffan's piano accompaniment.* ❷ N-COUNT An **accompaniment** is something that goes with another thing. ❏ *This recipe makes a good accompaniment to ice cream.* • PHRASE If one thing happens **to the accompaniment of** another, they happen at the same time.

ac|com|pa|nist /əkʌmpənɪst/ (**accompanists**) N-COUNT An **accompanist** is a musician, especially a pianist, who plays one part of a piece of music while someone else sings or plays the main tune.

ac|com|pa|ny ◆◇◇ /əkʌmpəni/ (**accompanies, accompanying, accompanied**) ❶ V-T If you **accompany** someone, you go somewhere with them. [FORMAL] ❏ *Ken agreed to accompany me on a trip to Africa.* ❏ *She was accompanied by her younger brother.* ❷ V-T If one thing **accompanies** another, it happens or exists at the same time, or as a result of it. [FORMAL] ❏ *This volume of essays was designed to accompany an exhibition in Seattle.* ❸ V-T If you **accompany** a singer or a musician, you play one part of a piece of music while they sing or play the main tune. ❏ *On Meredith's new recording, Eddie Higgins accompanies her on all but one song.*

SYNONYMS

accompany
VERB ❶
escort: *I escorted him to the door.*
guide: *He took the bewildered Elliott by the arm and guided him out.*
lead: *He took Dickon by the hand to lead him into the house.*
usher: *I ushered him into the office.*

ac|com|pli /ækɒmpli/ → see **fait accompli**

ac|com|plice /əkɒmplɪs/ (**accomplices**) N-COUNT Someone's **accomplice** is a person who helps them to commit a crime. ❏ *Witnesses said the gunman immediately ran to a motorcycle being ridden by an accomplice.*

ac|com|plish /əkɒmplɪʃ/ (**accomplishes, accomplishing, accomplished**) ❶ V-T If you **accomplish** something, you succeed in doing it. ❏ *If we'd all work together, I think we could accomplish our goal.* ❷ → See feature box at **success**

ac|com|plished /əkɒmplɪʃt/ ADJ If someone is **accomplished** at something, they are very good at it. [FORMAL] ❏ *She is an accomplished painter and a prolific author of stories for children.*

ac|com|plish|ment /əkɒmplɪʃmənt/ (**accomplishments**) N-COUNT An **accomplishment** is something remarkable that has been done or achieved. ❏ *For a novelist, that's quite an accomplishment.*

ac|cord ◆◆◆ /əkɔrd/ (**accords, according, accorded**)
❶ N-COUNT An **accord** between countries or groups of people is a formal agreement, for example, to end a war. ❏ *When the peace accords were signed, all parties agreed to investigate these deals.* ❷ V-T If you **are accorded** a particular kind of treatment, people act toward you or treat you in that way. [FORMAL] ❏ *His predecessor was accorded an equally tumultuous welcome.* ❏ *On his return home, the government accorded him the rank of Colonel.* ❸ → see also **according to** ❹ PHRASE If something happens **of its own accord**, it seems to happen by itself, without anyone making it happen. ❏ *In many cases the disease will clear up of its own accord.* ❺ PHRASE If you do something **of your own accord**, you do it because you want to, without being asked or forced. ❏ *He did not quit as France's prime minister of his own accord.*

SYNONYMS

accord
NOUN ❶
agreement: *The two countries signed an agreement to jointly launch satellites.*
treaty: *...negotiations over a 1992 treaty on global warming.*
pact: *Last month, he signed a new non-aggression pact with Germany.*

ac|cord|ance /əkɔrdəns/ PHRASE If something is done **in accordance with** a particular rule or system, it is done in the way that the rule or system says that it should be done. ❏ *Entries which are illegible or otherwise not in accordance with the rules will be disqualified.*

ac|cord|ing|ly /əkɔrdɪŋli/ ❶ ADV You use **accordingly** to introduce a fact or situation that is a result or consequence of something that you have just referred to. ❏ *We have a different background, a different history. Accordingly, we have the right to different futures.* ❷ ADV [ADV after v] If you consider a situation and then act **accordingly**, the way you act depends on the nature of the situation. ❏ *It is a difficult job and they should be paid accordingly.*

ac|cord|ing to ◆◆◆ ❶ PHRASE If someone says that something is true **according to** a particular person, book, or other source of information, they are indicating where they got their information. ❏ *The van raced away, according to police reports, and police gave chase.* ❷ PHRASE If something is done **according to** a particular set of principles, these principles are used as a basis for the way it is done. ❏ *They both played the game according to the rules.* ❸ PHRASE If something varies **according to** a changing factor, it varies in a way that is determined by this factor. ❏ *Prices vary according to the quantity ordered.* ❹ PHRASE If something happens **according to plan**, it happens in exactly the way that it was intended to happen. ❏ *If all goes according to plan, the first concert will be Tuesday evening.*

USAGE

according to
Don't say '*according to me.*' If you want to say what your opinion is, you can say **in my opinion**. *In my opinion, all children should learn to swim.*

ac|cor|di|on /əkɔrdiən/ (**accordions**) N-COUNT An **accordion** is a musical instrument in the shape of a fairly large box which you hold in your hands. You play the accordion by pressing keys or buttons on either side while moving the two sides together and apart. Accordions are used especially to play traditional popular music.

ac|cost /əkɒst/ (**accosts, accosting, accosted**) V-T If someone **accosts** another person, especially a stranger, they stop them or go up to them and speak to them in a way that seems rude or threatening. [FORMAL, DISAPPROVAL] ❑ *A man had accosted me in the street.*

ac|count ✦✦✦ /əkaʊnt/ (**accounts, accounting, accounted**)
1 N-COUNT If you have an **account** with a bank or a similar organization, you have an arrangement to leave your money there and take some out when you need it. ❑ *Some banks make it difficult to open an account.* **2** N-COUNT In business, a regular customer of a company can be referred to as an **account**, especially when the customer is another company. [BUSINESS] ❑ *All three Internet agencies boast they've won major accounts.* **3** N-COUNT **Accounts** are detailed records of all the money that a person or business receives and spends. [BUSINESS] ❑ *He kept detailed accounts.* **4** N-COUNT An **account** is a written or spoken report of something that has happened. ❑ *He gave a detailed account of what happened on the fateful night.* **5** → see also **accounting, bank account, checking account, deposit account** **6** PHRASE If you say that something is true **by all accounts** or **from all accounts**, you believe it is true because other people say so. ❑ *He is, by all accounts, a superb teacher.* **7** PHRASE If you say that something is **of no account** or **of little account**, you mean that it is very unimportant and is not worth considering. [FORMAL] ❑ *These obscure groups were of little account in either national or international politics.* **8** PHRASE If you buy or pay for something **on account**, you pay nothing or only part of the cost at first, and pay the rest later. ❑ *He was ordered to pay the company $500,000 on account pending a final assessment of his liability.* **9** PHRASE You use **on account of** to introduce the reason or explanation for something. ❑ *The president declined to deliver the speech himself, on account of a sore throat.* **10** PHRASE Your feelings **on** someone's **account** are the feelings you have about what they have experienced or might experience, especially when you imagine yourself to be in their situation. ❑ *Mollie told me what she'd done and I was really scared on her account.* **11** PHRASE If you tell someone not to do something **on** your **account**, you mean that they should do it only if they want to, and not because they think it will please you. [SPOKEN] ❑ *Don't leave on my account.* **12** PHRASE If you say that something should **on no account** be done, you are emphasizing that it should not be done under any circumstances. [EMPHASIS] ❑ *On no account should the mixture come near boiling.* **13** PHRASE If you do something **on** your **own account**, you do it because you want to and without being asked, and you take responsibility for your own action. ❑ *I told him if he withdrew it was on his own account.* **14** PHRASE If you **take** something **into account**, or **take account of** something, you consider it when you are thinking about a situation or deciding what to do. ❑ *The defendant asked for 21 similar offenses to be taken into account.* **15** PHRASE If someone **is called, held,** or **brought to account** for something they have done wrong, they are made to explain why they did it, and are often criticized or punished for it. ❑ *Individuals who repeatedly provide false information should be called to account for their actions.* **16** PHRASE If you say that someone **gave a good account of** themselves in a particular situation, you mean that they performed well, although they may not have been completely successful. [BRIT] ❑ *We have been hindered by our lack of preparation, but I'm sure we will give a good account of ourselves.*
▶ **account for** **1** PHRASAL VERB If a particular thing **accounts for** a part or proportion of something, that part or proportion consists of that thing, or is used or produced by it. ❑ *Computers account for 5% of the country's commercial electricity consumption.* **2** PHRASAL VERB If something **accounts for** a particular fact or situation, it causes or explains it. ❑ *The gene they discovered today doesn't account for all those cases.* **3** PHRASAL VERB If you can **account for** something, you can explain it or give the necessary information about it. ❑ *How do you account for the company's alarmingly high staff turnover?* **4** PHRASAL VERB If someone has to **account for** an action or policy, they are responsible for it, and may be required to explain it to other people or be punished if it fails. ❑ *The president and the president alone must account for his government's reforms.* **5** PHRASAL VERB If a sum of money **is accounted for** in a budget, it has been included in that budget for a particular purpose. ❑ *The really heavy costs have been accounted for.*

COLLOCATIONS

account
NOUN
1
noun + **account**: retirement, savings
adjective + **account**: checking; joint; offshore
verb + **account**: open; close
4
noun + **account**: eyewitness
adjective + **account**: detailed, first-hand, full
verb + **account**: give, provide

SYNONYMS

account
NOUN **4**
description: *Police have issued a description of the man who was aged between fifty and sixty.*
report: *With a report on these developments, here's Jim Fish in Belgrade.*
record: *There's no record of any marriage or children.*
story: *The parents all shared interesting stories about their children.*
version: *There are widely differing versions in the newspapers about the prison siege.*

---

ac|count|able /əkaʊntəbəl/ ADJ If you are **accountable** to someone for something that you do, you are responsible for it and must be prepared to justify your actions to that person. ❑ *Public officials can finally be held accountable for their actions.* • **ac|count|abil|ity** /əkaʊntəbɪlɪti/ N-UNCOUNT ❑ *...a drive toward democracy and greater accountability.*

ac|count|an|cy /əkaʊntənsi/ N-UNCOUNT **Accountancy** is the theory or practice of keeping financial accounts. [BRIT]

in AM, use **accounting**

ac|count|ant /əkaʊntənt/ (**accountants**) N-COUNT An **accountant** is a person whose job is to keep financial accounts.

ac|count|ing /əkaʊntɪŋ/ **1** N-UNCOUNT **Accounting** is the activity of keeping detailed records of the amounts of money a business or person receives and spends. ❑ *...the accounting firm of Leventhal & Horwath.* **2** → see also **account**

ac|cou|tre|ment /əkuːtrəmənt, -tər-/ (**accoutrements**) also **accouterment** N-COUNT **Accoutrements** are all the things you have with you when you travel or when you take part in a particular activity. [HUMOROUS OR OLD-FASHIONED]

ac|cred|it /əkrɛdɪt/ (**accredits, accrediting, accredited**) V-T [usu passive] If an educational qualification or institution **is accredited**, it is officially declared to be of an approved standard. [FORMAL] ❑ *This degree program is fully accredited by the Institution of Electrical Engineers.* ❑ *...a list of accredited medical schools in the U.S. and Canada.* • **ac|credi|ta|tion** /əkrɛdɪteɪʃən/ N-UNCOUNT ❑ *The university's law school failed to win full accreditation from the American Bar Association.*

ac|cre|tion /əkriːʃən/ (**accretions**) **1** N-COUNT An **accretion** is an addition to something, usually one that has been added over a period of time. [FORMAL] ❑ *The script has been gathering editorial accretions for years.* **2** N-UNCOUNT **Accretion** is the process of new layers or parts being added to something so that it increases in size. [FORMAL] ❑ *A coral reef is built by the accretion of tiny, identical organisms.*

ac|cru|al /əkruːəl/ (**accruals**) N-COUNT In finance, the **accrual** of something such as interest or investments is the adding together of interest or different investments over a period of time. [BUSINESS] ❑ *After an employee has 25 years of service, there is no further accrual of benefits.*

ac|crue /əkruː/ (**accrues, accruing, accrued**) V-T/V-I If money or interest **accrues**, it gradually increases in amount over a period of time. [BUSINESS] ❑ *I owed $5,000 – part of this was accrued interest.* ❑ *If you do not pay within 28 days, interest will accrue.*

ac|cu|mu|late /əkyuməleɪt/ (accumulates, accumulating, accumulated) V-T/V-I When you **accumulate** things or when they **accumulate**, they collect or are gathered over a period of time. ☐ *Lead can accumulate in the body until toxic levels are reached.*

ac|cu|mu|la|tion /əkyuməleɪʃən/ (accumulations) **1** N-COUNT An **accumulation** of something is a large number of things that have been collected together or acquired over a period of time. ☐ *...an accumulation of experience and knowledge.* **2** N-UNCOUNT **Accumulation** is the collecting together of things over a period of time. ☐ *...the accumulation of capital and the distribution of income.* **3** → See feature box at **global warming**

ac|cu|mu|la|tive /əkyuməleɪtɪv, -yələtɪv/ ADJ If something is **accumulative**, it becomes greater in amount, number, or intensity over a period of time. ☐ *The consensus is that risk factors have an accumulative effect.*

ac|cu|ra|cy /ækyərəsi/ **1** N-UNCOUNT The **accuracy** of information or measurements is their quality of being true or correct, even in small details. ☐ *Every care has been taken to ensure the accuracy of all information given in this leaflet.* **2** N-UNCOUNT If someone or something performs a task, for example, hitting a target, with **accuracy**, they do it in an exact way without making a mistake. ☐ *...weapons that could fire with accuracy at targets 3,000 yards away.*

ac|cu|rate ♦◇◇ /ækyərɪt/ **1** ADJ **Accurate** information, measurements, and statistics are correct to a very detailed level. An **accurate** instrument is able to give you information of this kind. ☐ *Police have stressed that this is the most accurate description of the killer to date.* ● **ac|cu|rate|ly** ADV ☐ *The test can accurately predict what a bigger explosion would do.* **2** ADJ An **accurate** statement or account gives a true or fair judgment of something. ☐ *Stalin gave an accurate assessment of the utility of nuclear weapons.* ● **ac|cu|rate|ly** ADV [ADV with v] ☐ *What many people mean by the word "power" could be more accurately described as "control."* **3** ADJ You can use **accurate** to describe the results of someone's actions when they do or copy something correctly or exactly. ☐ *We require grammar and spelling to be accurate.* **4** ADJ An **accurate** weapon or throw reaches the exact point or target that it was intended to reach. You can also describe a person as **accurate** if they fire a weapon or throw something in this way. ☐ *His throws were long, hard and accurate, as always.* ● **ac|cu|rate|ly** ADV [ADV with v] ☐ *He hit the golf ball powerfully and accurately.*

ac|curs|ed /əkɜrsɪd, əkɜrst/ **1** ADJ [ADJ n] Some people use **accursed** to describe something that they are very annoyed about. [OLD-FASHIONED, FEELINGS] **2** ADJ [v-link ADJ] If a person is **accursed**, they have been cursed. [LITERARY]

ac|cu|sa|tion /ækyuzeɪʃən/ (accusations) **1** N-VAR If you make an **accusation** against someone, you criticize them or express the belief that they have done something wrong. ☐ *Kim rejects accusations that country music is oversentimental.* **2** N-COUNT An **accusation** is a statement or claim by a witness or someone in authority that a particular person has committed a crime, although this has not yet been proved. ☐ *...people who have made public accusations of rape.*

ac|cu|sa|tive /əkyuzətɪv/ N-SING [the N] In the grammar of some languages, **the accusative**, or **the accusative case**, is the case used for a noun when it is the direct object of a verb, or the object of some prepositions. In English, only the pronouns 'me,' 'him,' 'her,' 'us,' and 'them' are in the accusative. Compare **nominative**.

ac|cu|sa|tory /əkyuzətɔri/ ADJ An **accusatory** look, remark, or tone of voice suggests blame or criticism. [WRITTEN] ☐ *...the accusatory tone of the questions.*

ac|cuse ♦◆◇ /əkyuz/ (accuses, accusing, accused) **1** V-T If you **accuse** someone of doing something wrong or dishonest, you say or tell them that you believe that they did it. ☐ *My mom was really upset because he was accusing her of having an affair with another man.* **2** V-T If you **are accused** of a crime, a witness or someone in authority states or claims that you did it, and you may be formally charged with it and put on trial. ☐ *Her assistant was accused of theft and fraud by the police.* ☐ *He faced a total of seven charges, all accusing him of lying in his testimony.* **3** → see also **accused** **4** PHRASE If someone **stands accused** of something, they have been accused of it. ☐ *The candidate stands accused of breaking promises even before he's in office.*

┌─ SYNONYMS ─┐

accuse
VERB
1
blame: *If it wasn't Sam's fault, why was I blaming him?*
allege: *It was alleged that he had deliberately tried to run someone over.*
denounce: *Some 25,000 demonstrators denounced him as a traitor.*
2
charge: *Police have charged Mr Bell with murder.*
indict: *He was later indicted on corruption charges.*
impeach: *...an opposition move to impeach the President.*

ac|cused /əkyuzd/ (accused)

Accused is both the singular and the plural form.

N-COUNT You can use **the accused** to refer to a person or a group of people charged with a crime or on trial for it. [LEGAL] ☐ *The accused is alleged to be a member of a right-wing gang.*

ac|cus|er /əkyuzər/ (accusers) N-COUNT [usu poss N] An **accuser** is a person who says that another person has done something wrong, especially that he or she has committed a crime. ☐ *...a criminal proceeding where defendants have the right to confront their accusers.*

ac|cus|ing /əkyuzɪŋ/ **1** ADJ If you look at someone with an **accusing** expression or speak to them in an **accusing** tone of voice, you are showing that you think they have done something wrong. ☐ *The accusing look in her eyes conveyed her sense of betrayal.* ● **ac|cus|ing|ly** ADV [ADV after v] ☐ *"Where have you been?" he asked Bob accusingly.* **2** → see also **accuse**

ac|cus|tom /əkʌstəm/ (accustoms, accustoming, accustomed) **1** V-T If you **accustom** yourself or another person to something, you make yourself or them become used to it. [FORMAL] ☐ *She tried to accustom herself to the tight bandages.* **2** → see also **accustomed**

ac|cus|tomed /əkʌstəmd/ **1** ADJ [v-link ADJ to n/-ing] If you are **accustomed to** something, you know it so well or have experienced it so often that it seems natural, unsurprising, or easy to deal with. ☐ *I was accustomed to being the only child at a table full of adults.* **2** ADJ [v-link ADJ to n] When your eyes become **accustomed** to darkness or bright light, they adjust so that you start to be able to see things, after not being able to see properly at first. ☐ *My eyes were becoming accustomed to the gloom and I was able to make out a door at one side of the room.*

┌─ USAGE ─┐

accustomed
Don't say that someone is '~~accustomed to do~~' something or '~~used to do~~' something. You can say that someone is **accustomed to doing** something or **used to doing** something. *The manager is accustomed to working late. I'm used to getting up early.*

ace /eɪs/ (aces) **1** N-COUNT An **ace** is a playing card with a single symbol on it. In most card games, the ace of a particular suit has either the highest or the lowest value of the cards in that suit. ☐ *...the ace of hearts.* **2** N-COUNT If you describe someone such as a sports player as an **ace**, you mean that they are very good at what they do. [JOURNALISM] ☐ *Despite the loss of their ace early in the game, Seattle beat the Brewers 6-5.* ● ADJ [ADJ n] **Ace** is also an adjective. ☐ *...ace horror-film producer Lawrence Woolsey.* **3** N-COUNT In tennis, an **ace** is a serve which is so fast that the other player cannot reach the ball. ☐ *Agassi believed he had served an ace at 5-3 (40-30) in the deciding set.* **4** PHRASE [v-link PHR, PHR after v] Something that is an **ace in the hole** is an advantage which you have over an opponent or rival, and which you can use if necessary. ☐ *Our superior technology is our ace in the hole.*

acer|bic /əsɜrbɪk/ ADJ **Acerbic** humor is critical and direct. [FORMAL] ☐ *He was acclaimed for his acerbic wit and repartee.*

acer|bity /əsɜrbɪti/ N-UNCOUNT **Acerbity** is a kind of bitter, critical humor. [FORMAL]

ac|etate /æsɪteɪt/ N-UNCOUNT **Acetate** is a shiny artificial material, sometimes used for making clothes.

acetic acid /əsitɪk æsɪd/ N-UNCOUNT **Acetic acid** is a colorless acid. It is the main substance in vinegar.

ac|etone /æsɪtoʊn/ N-UNCOUNT **Acetone** is a type of solvent.

acety|lene /əsetɪlin/ N-UNCOUNT [oft N n] **Acetylene** is a colorless gas that burns with a very hot bright flame. It is often used in lamps and for cutting and welding metal.

ache /eɪk/ (aches, aching, ached) **1** V-I If you **ache** or a part of your body **aches**, you feel a steady, fairly strong pain. ❏ *The glands in her neck were swollen, her head was throbbing and she ached all over.* ❏ *My leg is giving me much less pain but still aches when I sit down.* **2** N-COUNT An **ache** is a steady, fairly strong pain in a part of your body. ❏ *You feel nausea and aches in your muscles.* **3** PHRASE You can use **aches and pains** to refer in a general way to any minor pains that you feel in your body. ❏ *It seems to ease all the aches and pains of a hectic and tiring day.* **4** → see also **headache, heartache, stomach ache**

achiev|able /ətʃivəbəl/ ADJ If you say that something you are trying to do is **achievable**, you mean that it is possible for you to succeed in doing it. ❏ *A 50% market share is achievable.* ❏ *It is often a good idea to start with smaller, easily achievable goals.*

achieve ♦◇◇ /ətʃiv/ (achieves, achieving, achieved) V-T If you **achieve** a particular aim or effect, you succeed in doing it or causing it to happen, usually after a lot of effort. ❏ *There are many who will work hard to achieve these goals.*

────── **COLLOCATIONS** ──────

achieve
VERB
achieve + noun: goal, objective, result, success; feat, grade, growth; fame, status
noun + **achieve**: student; company
achieve + adverb: consistently, easily

achieve|ment ♦◇◇ /ətʃivmənt/ (achievements) **1** N-COUNT An **achievement** is something that someone has succeeded in doing, especially after a lot of effort. ❏ *It was a great achievement that a month later a global agreement was reached.* **2** N-UNCOUNT **Achievement** is the process of achieving something. ❏ *It is only the achievement of these goals that will finally bring lasting peace.* **3** → See feature box at **success**

────── **COLLOCATIONS** ──────

achievement
NOUN **1**
noun + **achievement**: career, lifetime; landmark
adjective + **achievement**: major, notable, outstanding, remarkable; academic, educational, sporting; crowning, personal, proud
verb + **achievement**: celebrate, honor; acknowledge, recognize

────── **SYNONYMS** ──────

achievement
NOUN **1**
accomplishment: *By any standards, the accomplishments of the past year are extraordinary.*
feat: *A race car is an extraordinary feat of engineering.*
coup: *The sale is a big coup for the auction house.*

achiev|er /ətʃivər/ (achievers) N-COUNT A high **achiever** is someone who is successful in their studies or their work, usually as a result of their efforts. A low **achiever** is someone who achieves less than those around them. ❏ *High achievers at the company are in line for cash bonuses.*

Achilles heel /əkɪliz hil/ N-SING [usu poss N] Someone's **Achilles heel** is the weakest point in their character or nature, where it is easiest for other people to attack or criticize them. ❏ *Horton's Achilles heel was that he could not delegate.*

Achilles ten|don /əkɪliz tɛndən/ (Achilles tendons) N-COUNT Your **Achilles tendon** or your **Achilles** is the tendon inside the back of your leg just above your heel.

ach|ing|ly /eɪkɪŋli/ ADV [ADV adj/adv] You can use **achingly** for emphasis when you are referring to things that create feelings of wanting something very much, but of not being able to have it. [WRITTEN, EMPHASIS] ❏ *...three achingly beautiful ballads.*

achoo /ɑtʃu/ **Achoo** is used, especially in writing, to represent the sound that you make when you sneeze.

achy /eɪki/ ADJ [usu v-link ADJ] If you feel **achy**, your body hurts. [INFORMAL, SPOKEN] ❏ *I feel achy all over.*

acid ♦◇◇ /æsɪd/ (acids) **1** N-MASS An **acid** is a chemical substance, usually a liquid, which contains hydrogen and can react with other substances to form salts. Some acids burn or dissolve other substances that they come into contact with. ❏ *...citric acid.* **2** ADJ An **acid** substance contains acid. ❏ *These shrubs must have an acid, lime-free soil.* ● **acid|ity** /əsɪdɪti/ N-UNCOUNT [oft N of n] ❏ *...the acidity of rainwater.*

acid house N-UNCOUNT **Acid house** is a type of electronic dance music with a strong, repeated rhythm.

acid|ic /əsɪdɪk/ ADJ **Acidic** substances contain acid. ❏ *Dissolved carbon dioxide makes the water more acidic.*

acid rain N-UNCOUNT **Acid rain** is rain polluted by acid that has been released into the atmosphere from factories and other industrial processes. Acid rain is harmful to the environment.

acid test N-SING [the N] The **acid test** of something is an important aspect or result that it might have, which allows you to decide whether it is true or successful. ❏ *The acid test of a school is "would you send your own children there?"*

ac|knowl|edge ♦◇◇ /æknɒlɪdʒ/ (acknowledges, acknowledging, acknowledged) **1** V-T If you **acknowledge** a fact or a situation, you accept or admit that it is true or that it exists. [FORMAL] ❏ *Naylor acknowledged, in a letter to the judge, that he was a drug addict.* ❏ *Belatedly, the government has acknowledged the problem.* **2** V-T If someone's achievements, status, or qualities **are acknowledged,** they are known about and recognized by a lot of people, or by a particular group of people. ❏ *He is also acknowledged as an excellent goalkeeper.* **3** V-T If you **acknowledge** a message or letter, you write to the person who sent it in order to say that you have received it. ❏ *The army sent me a postcard acknowledging my request.* **4** V-T If you **acknowledge** someone, for example, by moving your head or smiling, you show that you have seen and recognized them. ❏ *He saw her but refused to even acknowledge her.*

ac|knowl|edg|ment /æknɒlɪdʒmənt/ (acknowledgments) also **acknowledgement** **1** N-SING [also no det] An **acknowledgment** is a statement or action which recognizes that something exists or is true. ❏ *The president's resignation appears to be an acknowledgment that he has lost all hope of keeping the country together.* **2** N-PLURAL The **acknowledgments** in a book are the section in which the author thanks all the people who have helped him or her. ❏ *...two whole pages of acknowledgments.* **3** N-UNCOUNT [also a N] A gesture of **acknowledgment**, such as a smile, shows someone that you have seen and recognized them. ❏ *Farling smiled in acknowledgment and gave a bow.*

acme /ækmi/ N-SING [usu the N of n] The **acme** of something is its highest point of achievement or excellence. [FORMAL] ❏ *His work is considered the acme of cinematic art.*

acne /ækni/ N-UNCOUNT If someone has **acne**, they have a skin condition which causes a lot of pimples on their face and neck. ❏ *I used to have acne as a teenager.*

aco|lyte /ækəlaɪt/ (acolytes) N-COUNT An **acolyte** is a follower or assistant of an important person. [FORMAL] ❏ *To his acolytes, he is known simply as "the Boss."*

acorn /eɪkɔrn/ (acorns) N-COUNT An **acorn** is a pale oval nut that is the fruit of an oak tree.

acous|tic /əkustɪk/ (acoustics) **1** ADJ [ADJ n] An **acoustic** guitar or other instrument is one whose sound is produced without any electrical equipment. **2** N-COUNT If you refer to the **acoustics** of a space, you are referring to the structural features which determine how well you can hear music or speech in it. ❏ *In this performance, Rattle had the acoustics of the Symphony Hall on his side.* **3** N-UNCOUNT **Acoustics** is the scientific study of sound. ❏ *...his work in acoustics.*

ac|quaint /əkweɪnt/ (acquaints, acquainting, acquainted) **1** V-T If you **acquaint** someone with something, you tell them about it so that they know it. If you **acquaint** yourself with something, you learn about it. [FORMAL] ❏ *Have steps been taken to acquaint breeders with their right to apply for licenses?* **2** → see also **acquainted**

acquaintance | act

ac|quaint|ance /əkweɪntəns/ (acquaintances) **1** N-COUNT An **acquaintance** is someone who you have met and know slightly, but not well. ❑ *He exchanged a few words with the proprietor, an old acquaintance of his.* **2** N-VAR If you have an **acquaintance** with someone, you have met them and you know them. ❑ *...a writer who becomes involved in a real murder mystery through his acquaintance with a police officer.* **3** PHRASE When you **make** someone's **acquaintance**, you meet them for the first time and get to know them a little. [FORMAL] ❑ *I first made his acquaintance in the early 1960s.*

ac|quaint|ed /əkweɪntɪd/ **1** ADJ [v-link ADJ with n] If you are **acquainted** with something, you know about it because you have learned it or experienced it. [FORMAL] ❑ *He was well acquainted with the literature of Latin America.* **2** ADJ [v-link ADJ] If you get or become **acquainted** with someone that you do not know, you talk to each other or do something together so that you get to know each other. You can also say that two people get or become **acquainted**. ❑ *At first the meetings were a way to get acquainted with each other.* **3** → see also **acquaint**

ac|qui|esce /ˌækwiˈɛs/ (acquiesces, acquiescing, acquiesced) V-I If you **acquiesce** in something, you agree to do what someone wants or to accept what they do. [FORMAL] ❑ *Steve seemed to acquiesce in the decision.* ❑ *When her mother suggested that she stay, Alice willingly acquiesced.*

ac|qui|es|cence /ˌækwiˈɛsəns/ N-UNCOUNT [with supp] **Acquiescence** is agreement to do what someone wants, or acceptance of what they do even though you do not agree with it. [FORMAL] ❑ *Caitlin smiled her acquiescence.*

ac|qui|es|cent /ˌækwiˈɛsənt/ ADJ Someone who is **acquiescent** is ready to agree to do what someone wants, or to accept what they do. [FORMAL] ❑ *Perhaps you are too acquiescent.*

ac|quire ♦♢♢ /əkwaɪər/ (acquires, acquiring, acquired) **1** V-T If you **acquire** something, you buy or obtain it for yourself, or someone gives it to you. [FORMAL] ❑ *General Motors acquired a 50% stake in Saab for about $400m.* **2** V-T If you **acquire** something such as a skill or a habit, you learn it, or develop it through your daily life or experience. ❑ *I've never acquired a taste for wine.* **3** V-T If someone or something **acquires** a certain reputation, they start to have that reputation. ❑ *During her film career, she acquired a reputation as a strong-willed, outspoken woman.*

SYNONYMS

acquire
VERB **1**
get: *I'm getting a bike for my birthday.*
receive: *They will receive their awards at a ceremony in Stockholm.*
obtain: *Evans was trying to obtain a false passport and other documents.*

ac|quired im|mune de|fi|cien|cy syn|drome N-UNCOUNT **Acquired immune deficiency syndrome** is the same as AIDS.

ac|quir|er /əkwaɪərər/ (acquirers) N-COUNT In business, an **acquirer** is a company or person who buys another company. [BUSINESS] ❑ *...the ability of corporate acquirers to finance large takeovers.*

ac|qui|si|tion ♦♢♢ /ˌækwɪˈzɪʃən/ (acquisitions) **1** N-VAR If a company or business person makes an **acquisition**, they buy another company or part of a company. [BUSINESS] ❑ *...the acquisition of a profitable paper recycling company.* **2** N-COUNT If you make an **acquisition**, you buy or obtain something, often to add to things that you already have. ❑ *How did you go about making this marvelous acquisition then?* **3** N-UNCOUNT The **acquisition** of a skill or a particular type of knowledge is the process of learning it or developing it. ❑ *...language acquisition.*

ac|quisi|tive /əkwɪzɪtɪv/ ADJ [usu ADJ n] If you describe a person or an organization as **acquisitive**, you do not approve of them because you think they are too concerned with getting new possessions. [DISAPPROVAL] ❑ *We live in an acquisitive society.*

ac|quit /əkwɪt/ (acquits, acquitting, acquitted) **1** V-T [usu passive] If someone **is acquitted** of a crime in a court of law, they are formally declared not to have committed the crime. ❑ *Mr. Castorina was acquitted of attempted murder.* **2** → See feature box at **legal**

ac|quit|tal /əkwɪtəl/ (acquittals) N-VAR **Acquittal** is a formal declaration in a court of law that someone who has been accused of a crime is innocent. ❑ *...the acquittal of six police officers charged with perverting the course of justice.* ❑ *The jury voted 8-to-4 in favor of acquittal.*

acre ♦♢♢ /eɪkər/ (acres) N-COUNT An **acre** is an area of land measuring around 4,840 square yards or 4,047 square meters. ❑ *The property consists of two acres of land.*

acre|age /eɪkərɪdʒ/ (acreages) N-VAR **Acreage** is a large area of farm land. [FORMAL] ❑ *He has sown coffee on part of his acreage.* ❑ *Enormous acreages of soy beans are grown in the United States.*

ac|rid /ækrɪd/ ADJ [usu ADJ n] An **acrid** smell or taste is strong and sharp, and usually unpleasant. ❑ *The room filled with the acrid smell of tobacco.*

ac|ri|mo|ni|ous /ˌækrɪˈmoʊniəs/ ADJ **Acrimonious** words or quarrels are bitter and angry. [FORMAL] ❑ *The acrimonious debate on the agenda ended indecisively.*

ac|ri|mo|ny /ækrɪmoʊni/ N-UNCOUNT **Acrimony** is bitter and angry words or quarrels. [FORMAL] ❑ *The council's first meeting ended in acrimony.*

ac|ro|bat /ækrəbæt/ (acrobats) N-COUNT An **acrobat** is an entertainer who performs difficult physical acts such as jumping and balancing, especially in a circus.

ac|ro|bat|ic /ˌækrəˈbætɪk/ ADJ [usu ADJ n] An **acrobatic** movement or display involves difficult physical acts such as jumping and balancing, especially in a circus.

ac|ro|bat|ics /ˌækrəˈbætɪks/ N-PLURAL **Acrobatics** are acrobatic movements.

ac|ro|nym /ækrənɪm/ (acronyms) N-COUNT An **acronym** is a word composed of the first letters of the words in a phrase, especially when this is used as a name. An example of an acronym is NATO which is made up of the first letters of the 'North Atlantic Treaty Organization.'

across ♦♦♢ /əkrɔs/

In addition to the uses shown below, **across** is used in phrasal verbs such as 'come across,' 'get across,' and 'put across.'

1 PREP If someone or something goes **across** a place or a boundary, they go from one side of it to the other. ❑ *She walked across the floor and lay down on the bed.* ❑ *He watched Karl run across the street to Tommy.* • ADV [ADV after v] **Across** is also an adverb. ❑ *Richard stood up and walked across to the window.* **2** PREP If something is situated or stretched **across** something else, it is situated or stretched from one side of it to the other. ❑ *...the floating bridge across Lake Washington in Seattle.* ❑ *He scrawled his name across the hill.* • ADV [ADV after v] **Across** is also an adverb. ❑ *Trim toenails straight across using nail clippers.* **3** PREP If something is lying **across** an object or place, it is resting on it and partly covering it. ❑ *She found her clothes lying across the chair.* **4** PREP Something that is **across** something such as a street, river, or area is on the other side of it. ❑ *Anyone from the houses across the road could see him.* • ADV **Across** is also an adverb. ❑ *They parked across from the Castro Theater.* **5** PREP You use **across** to say that a particular expression is shown on someone's face. ❑ *An enormous grin spread across his face.* **6** PREP If someone hits you **across** the face or head, they hit you on that part. ❑ *Graham hit him across the face with the gun, then pushed him against the wall.* **7** PREP When something happens **across** a place or organization, it happens equally everywhere within it. ❑ *The movie opens across the country on December 11.* **8** PREP When something happens **across** a political, religious, or social barrier, it involves people in different groups. ❑ *...parties competing across the political spectrum.* **9 across the board** → see **board 10** ADV If you look **across** at a place, person, or thing, you look toward them. ❑ *He glanced across at his sleeping wife.* ❑ *She rose from the chair and gazed across at him.* **11** ADV [amount ADV] **Across** is used in measurements to show the width of something. ❑ *This hand-decorated plate measures 14 inches across.*

acryl|ic /əkrɪlɪk/ N-UNCOUNT **Acrylic** material is artificial and is manufactured by a chemical process. ❑ *...her pink acrylic sweater.*

act ♦♦♦ /ækt/ (acts, acting, acted) **1** V-T/V-I When you **act**, you do something for a particular purpose. ❑ *The deaths* occurred when police acted to stop widespread looting and vandalism. **2** V-I If you **act on** advice or information, you do what has been advised or suggested. ◻ *A patient will usually listen to the doctor's advice and act on it.* **3** V-I If someone **acts** in a particular way, they behave in that way. ◻ *...a gang of youths who were acting suspiciously.* ◻ *He acted as if he hadn't heard any of it.* **4** V-I If someone or something **acts as** a particular thing, they have that role or function. ◻ *Among his other duties, he acted both as the ship's surgeon and as chaplain for the men.* **5** V-I If someone **acts** in a particular way, they pretend to be something that they are not. ◻ *Chris acted astonished as he examined the note.* **6** V-I When professionals such as lawyers **act for** you, or **act on** your **behalf**, they are employed by you to deal with a particular matter. ◻ *Lawyers acting for the families of the victims ...* **7** V-I If a force or substance **acts on** someone or something, it has a certain effect on them. ◻ *He's taking a dangerous drug: it acts very fast on the central nervous system.* **8** V-I If you **act** in a play or film, you have a part in it. ◻ *She confessed to her parents her desire to act.* **9** N-COUNT [oft N *of* n] An **act** is a single thing that someone does. [FORMAL] ◻ *Language interpretation is the whole point of the act of reading.* **10** N-COUNT An **Act** is a law passed by the government. ◻ *...an Act of Congress.* **11** N-COUNT [oft N num] An **act** in a play, opera, or ballet is one of the main parts into which it is divided. ◻ *Act II contained one of the funniest scenes I have ever witnessed.* **12** N-COUNT An **act** in a show is a short performance which is one of several in the show. ◻ *This year numerous bands are playing, as well as comedy acts.* **13** N-SING If you say that someone's behavior is an **act**, you mean that it does not express their real feelings. ◻ *His anger was real. It wasn't an act.* **14** PHRASE If you **catch** someone **in the act**, you discover them doing something wrong or committing a crime. ◻ *The men were caught in the act of digging up buried explosives.* **15** PHRASE If someone who has been behaving badly **cleans up** their **act**, they start to behave in a more acceptable or responsible way. [INFORMAL] ◻ *The nation's advertisers need to clean up their act.* **16** PHRASE If you **get in on the act**, you take part in or take advantage of something that was started by someone else. [INFORMAL] ◻ *In the 1970s Kodak, anxious to get in on the act, launched its own instant camera.* **17** PHRASE You say that someone is **in the act of** doing something to indicate what they were doing when they were seen or interrupted. ◻ *Ken was in the act of paying his bill when Neil came up behind him.* **18** PHRASE If you **get** your **act together**, you organize your life or your affairs so that you are able to achieve what you want or to deal with something effectively. [INFORMAL] ◻ *The government should get its act together.* **19 to act the fool** → see **fool**

act|ing /ˈæktɪŋ/ **1** N-UNCOUNT [oft N n] **Acting** is the activity or profession of performing in plays or films. ◻ *She returned to London to pursue her acting career.* **2** ADJ [ADJ n] You use **acting** before the title of a job to indicate that someone is doing that job temporarily. ◻ *The new acting president has a reputation of being someone who is independent.*

ac|tion ♦♦♦ /ˈækʃ°n/ (**actions, actioning, actioned**) **1** N-UNCOUNT **Action** is doing something for a particular purpose. ◻ *The government is taking emergency action to deal with a housing crisis.* **2** N-UNCOUNT The fighting which takes place in a war can be referred to as **action**. ◻ *Our leaders have generally supported military action if it proves necessary.* **3** N-COUNT An **action** is something that you do on a particular occasion. ◻ *As always, Peter had a reason for his action.* **4** N-VAR To take legal **action** or to bring a legal **action** against someone means to bring a case against them in a court of law. [LEGAL] ◻ *Two leading law firms are to prepare legal actions against tobacco companies.* **5** ADJ [ADJ n] An **action** movie is a film in which a lot of dangerous and exciting things happen. An **action** hero is the main character in one of these films. **6** V-T [usu passive] If you **action** something that needs to be done, you deal with it. [BUSINESS] ◻ *Documents can be actioned, or filed immediately.* **7** PHRASE If someone or something is **out of action**, they are injured or damaged and cannot work or be used. ◻ *He's been out of action for 16 months with a serious knee injury.* **8** PHRASE If someone wants to have **a piece of the action** or **a slice of the action**, they want to take part in an exciting activity or situation, usually in order to make money or become more important. ◻ *In the late 1990s, investors big and small wanted a piece of the dot.com action.* **9** PHRASE If you **put** an idea or policy **into action**, you begin to use it or cause it to operate. ◻ *They have excelled in learning the lessons of business management theory, and putting them into action.*

COLLOCATIONS

action
NOUN
1
adjective + **action**: appropriate, decisive, drastic; emergency, immediate, urgent; disciplinary, legal, military
verb + **action**: take; defend, justify, support; demand
4
verb + **action**: bring, initiate, launch, pursue; threaten

SYNONYMS

action
NOUN
1
measure: *He said stern measures would be taken against the killers.*
step: *He greeted the agreement as the first step towards peace.*
maneuver: *...maneuvers to block the electoral process.*
3
deed: *His heroic deeds were celebrated in every corner of India.*
move: *It may also be a good move to suggest she talks things over.*
act: *My insurance excludes acts of sabotage and damage done by weapons of war.*

---

ac|tion|able /ˈækʃənəbəl/ ADJ [usu v-link ADJ] If something that you do or say to someone is **actionable**, it gives them a valid reason for bringing a legal case against you.

ac|tion re|play (**action replays**) N-COUNT An **action replay** is a repeated showing, usually in slow motion, of an event that has just been on television. [BRIT]

In AM, use **instant replay**

ac|ti|vate /ˈæktɪveɪt/ (**activates, activating, activated**) **1** V-T [usu passive] If a device or process is **activated**, something causes it to start working. ◻ *Video cameras with night vision can be activated by movement.* **2** → See feature box at **technology**

ac|tive ♦♦◇ /ˈæktɪv/ **1** ADJ Someone who is **active** moves around a lot or does a lot of things. ◻ *With three active little kids running around, there was plenty to keep me busy.* **2** ADJ If you have an **active** mind or imagination, you are always thinking of new things. ◻ *...the tragedy of an active mind trapped by failing physical health.* **3** ADJ If someone is **active** in an organization, cause, or campaign, they do things for it rather than just giving it their support. ◻ *We should play an active role in politics, both at the national and local level.* • **ac|tive|ly** ADV ◻ *They actively campaigned for the vote.* **4** ADJ [ADJ n] **Active** is used to emphasize that someone is taking action in order to achieve something, rather than just hoping for it or achieving it in an indirect way. [EMPHASIS] ◻ *Companies need to take active steps to increase exports.* • **ac|tive|ly** ADV ◻ *They have never been actively encouraged to take such risks.* **5** ADJ If you say that a person or animal is **active** in a particular place or at a particular time, you mean that they are performing their usual activities or performing a particular activity. ◻ *Guerrilla groups are active in the province.* **6** ADJ An **active** volcano has erupted recently or is expected to erupt soon. ◻ *...molten lava from an active volcano.* **7** ADJ An **active** substance has a chemical or biological effect on things. ◻ *The active ingredient in some of the mouthwashes was simply detergent.* **8** N-SING In grammar, **the active** or **the active voice** means the forms of a verb which are used when the subject refers to a person or thing that does something. For example, in 'I saw her yesterday,' the verb is in the active. Compare **passive**. **9** → See feature box at **research, study**

SYNONYMS

active
ADJ **1**
busy: *Phil Martin is an exceptionally busy man.*
lively: *Josephine was bright, lively, and cheerful.*
energetic: *Blackwell is 59, strong-looking, and enormously energetic.*
sprightly: *...the sprightly 85-year-old President.*

---

ac|tive duty N-UNCOUNT [oft *on* N] Someone who is on **active duty** is taking part in a war as a member of the armed forces. [mainly AM]

ac|tiv|ism /ǽktɪvɪzəm/ N-UNCOUNT **Activism** is the process of campaigning in public or working for an organization in order to bring about political or social change.

ac|tiv|ist ♦◇◇ /ǽktɪvɪst/ (**activists**) N-COUNT An **activist** is a person who works to bring about political or social changes by campaigning in public or working for an organization. ☐ *A number of Arctic foxes were released from a fur farm by animal rights activists.* ☐ *...a local activist group which organizes protests.*

COLLOCATIONS

activist
NOUN
noun + **activist**: community, party; human rights, peace
adjective + **activist**: environmental, political; anti-apartheid, Black, gay, left-wing
verb + **activist**: arrest, detain; anger

ac|tiv|ity ♦♦◇ /æktɪ́vɪti/ (**activities**) **1** N-UNCOUNT **Activity** is a situation in which a lot of things are happening or being done. ☐ *Changes in the money supply affect the level of economic activity and the interest rate.* ☐ *Children are supposed to get 60 minutes of physical activity every day.* **2** N-COUNT An **activity** is something that you spend time doing. ☐ *For lovers of the great outdoors, activities range from canoeing to bird watching.* **3** N-PLURAL The **activities** of a group are the things that they do in order to achieve their aims. ☐ *...a jail term for terrorist activities.*

COLLOCATIONS

activity
NOUN
1
noun + **activities**: brain; business
adjective + **activity**: electrical, planetary, volcanic; economic, physical; frantic, heightened, intense
verb + **activity**: stimulate; monitor
2
noun + **activity**: holiday, leisure, sporting
adjective + **activity**: daily, everyday, extracurricular; criminal, suspicious
3
noun + **activity**: fundraising, government, terrorist
adjective + **activity**: military
verb + **activity**: coordinate, monitor, organize, undertake; suspend

SYNONYMS

activity
NOUN
1
action: *Hollywood is where the action is now.*
bustle: *There was a good deal of cheerful bustle.*
commotion: *Sounds of voices and commotion could be heard downstairs now.*
2
pursuit: *His favorite childhood pursuits were sailing, swimming, and cycling.*
hobby: *My hobbies are letter writing, football, music, photography, and tennis.*
pastime: *His favorite pastime is golf.*

act of God (**acts of God**) N-COUNT An **act of God** is an event that is beyond human control, especially one in which something is damaged or someone is hurt.

ac|tor ♦◇◇ /ǽktər/ (**actors**) N-COUNT An **actor** is someone whose job is acting in plays or films. 'Actor' in the singular usually refers to a man, but some women who act prefer to be called 'actors' rather than 'actresses.' ☐ *His father was an actor in the Cantonese Opera Company.*

ac|tress ♦◇◇ /ǽktrɪs/ (**actresses**) N-COUNT An **actress** is a woman whose job is acting in plays or films. Some women who act prefer to be called 'actors' rather than 'actresses.' ☐ *She's not only a great dramatic actress but she's also very funny.*

ac|tual ♦◇◇ /ǽktʃuəl/ **1** ADJ [ADJ n] You use **actual** to emphasize that you are referring to something real or genuine. [EMPHASIS] ☐ *The segments are filmed using either local actors or the actual people involved.* **2** ADJ [ADJ n] You use **actual** to contrast the important aspect of something with a less important aspect. [EMPHASIS] ☐ *She had compiled pages of notes, but she had not yet gotten down to doing the actual writing.*

SYNONYMS

actual
ADJ **1**
genuine: *There was a risk of genuine refugees being returned to Vietnam.*
real: *Who's to know if they're real guns or not?*
true: *I think he's a true genius.*
authentic: *She has authentic charm, whereas most people simply have nice manners.*

ac|tu|al|ity /æktʃuǽlɪti/ **1** PHRASE [PHR with cl] You can use **in actuality** to emphasize that what you are saying is true, when it contradicts or contrasts with what you have previously said. [WRITTEN, EMPHASIS] ☐ *In actuality, Ted did not have a disorder but merely a difficult temperament.* **2** N-UNCOUNT **Actuality** is the state of really existing rather than being imagined. ☐ *It exists in dreams rather than actuality.*

ac|tu|al|ly ♦♦◇ /ǽktʃuəli/ **1** ADV You use **actually** to indicate that a situation exists or happened, or to emphasize that it is true. [EMPHASIS] ☐ *One afternoon, I got bored and actually fell asleep for a few minutes.* **2** ADV [ADV with cl] You use **actually** when you are correcting or contradicting someone. [EMPHASIS] ☐ *No, I'm not a student. I'm a doctor, actually.* **3** ADV [ADV with cl] You can use **actually** when you are politely expressing an opinion that other people might not have expected from you. [POLITENESS] ☐ *"Do you think it's a good idea to socialize with one's patients?"—"Actually, I do, I think it's a great idea."* **4** ADV [ADV with cl] You use **actually** to introduce a new topic into a conversation. ☐ *Well actually, John, I called you for some advice.*

SYNONYMS

actually
ADV **1**
really: *What was really going on?*
indeed: *He did indeed keep important documents inside his hat.*
in fact: *We've had a pretty bad time while you were away. In fact, we very nearly split up this time.*
genuinely: *He was genuinely surprised.*

USAGE

actually
Don't use **actually** when you want to say that something is happening now. Use **at the present time**, **at the moment**, or **right now**. *He's in a meeting at the moment*.

ac|tu|ari|al /æktʃuέəriəl/ ADJ [ADJ n] **Actuarial** means relating to the work of an actuary. ☐ *The company's actuarial report is available on demand.*

ac|tu|ary /ǽktʃuɛri/ (**actuaries**) N-COUNT An **actuary** is a person who is employed by insurance companies to calculate how much they should charge their clients for insurance.

ac|tu|ate /ǽktʃueɪt/ (**actuates, actuating, actuated**) V-T If something **actuates** a device, the device starts working. If a person is **actuated** by an emotion, that emotion makes them act in a certain way. ☐ *The flow of current actuates the signal.* ☐ *They were actuated by desire.*

acu|ity /əkyúɪti/ N-UNCOUNT **Acuity** is sharpness of vision or hearing, or quickness of thought. [FORMAL] ☐ *We work on improving visual acuity.*

acu|men /ǽkyumən/ N-UNCOUNT **Acumen** is the ability to make good judgments and quick decisions.

acu|pres|sure /ǽkyuprɛʃər/ N-UNCOUNT **Acupressure** is the treatment of pain by a type of massage in which pressure is put on certain areas of a person's body.

acu|punc|ture /ǽkyupʌŋktʃər/ N-UNCOUNT **Acupuncture** is the treatment of a person's illness or pain by sticking small needles into their body at certain places. ☐ *I had acupuncture in my lower back.*

acu|punc|tur|ist /ǽkyupʌŋktʃərɪst/ (**acupuncturists**) N-COUNT An **acupuncturist** is a person who performs acupuncture.

acute /əkyúːt/ **1** ADJ You can use **acute** to indicate that an undesirable situation or feeling is very severe or intense.

❑ *The war has aggravated an acute economic crisis.* ❑ *The report has caused acute embarrassment to the government.* ❷ ADJ [ADJ n] An **acute** illness is one that becomes severe very quickly but does not last very long. Compare **chronic**. [MEDICAL] ❑ *...a patient with acute rheumatoid arthritis.* ❸ ADJ If a person's or animal's sight, hearing, or sense of smell is **acute**, it is sensitive and powerful. ❑ *When she lost her sight, her other senses grew more acute.* ❹ ADJ An **acute** angle is less than 90°. Compare **obtuse** angle. ❺ ADJ [ADJ n, n ADJ] An **acute** accent is a symbol that is placed over vowels in some languages in order to indicate how that vowel is pronounced or over one letter in a word to indicate where it is stressed. You refer to a letter with this accent as, for example, e **acute**. For example, there is an acute accent over the letter 'e' in the French word 'café.'

acute|ly /əkyutli/ ADV If you feel or notice something **acutely**, you feel or notice it very strongly. ❑ *He was acutely aware of the odor of cooking oil.*

ad ✦✧✧ /æd/ (**ads**) N-COUNT An **ad** is an advertisement. [INFORMAL] ❑ *She replied to a lonely hearts ad she spotted in the New York Times.*

AD /eɪ di/ You use **AD** in dates to indicate the number of years or centuries that have passed since the year in which Jesus Christ is believed to have been born. Compare **BC**, **BCE**. ❑ *The original castle was probably built about AD 860.* ❑ *The cathedral was destroyed by the Great Fire of 1136 AD.*

ad|age /ædɪdʒ/ (**adages**) N-COUNT An **adage** is something that people often say and that expresses a general truth about some aspect of life. [OLD-FASHIONED] ❑ *...the old adage, "Every baby brings its own love."*

ad agen|cy (**ad agencies**) N-COUNT An **ad agency** is a company whose business is to create advertisements for other companies or organizations.

ada|gio /ədɑdʒoʊ/ (**adagios**) ❶ ADV [ADV after v] **Adagio** written above a piece of music means that it should be played slowly. ❷ N-COUNT [usu sing] An **adagio** is a piece of music that is played slowly. ❑ *...Samuel Barber's Adagio For Strings.* ❑ *...the adagio movement of his Sixth Symphony.*

ada|mant /ædəmənt/ ADJ If someone is **adamant** about something, they are determined not to change their mind about it. ❑ *The president is adamant that he will not resign.* • **ada|mant|ly** ADV ❑ *She was adamantly opposed to her husband taking this trip.*

Adam's ap|ple /ædəmz æpəl/ (**Adam's apples**) N-COUNT Your **Adam's apple** is the lump that sticks out of the front of your neck below your throat.

adapt /ədæpt/ (**adapts, adapting, adapted**) ❶ V-T/V-I If you **adapt** to a new situation or **adapt** yourself to it, you change your ideas or behavior in order to deal with it successfully. ❑ *The world will be different, and we will have to be prepared to adapt to the change.* ❷ V-T If you **adapt** something, you change it to make it suitable for a new purpose or situation. ❑ *Shelves were built to adapt the library for use as an office.* ❸ → see also **adapted**

adapt|able /ədæptəbəl/ ADJ If you describe a person or animal as **adaptable**, you mean that they are able to change their ideas or behavior in order to deal with new situations. ❑ *By making the workforce more adaptable and skilled, he hopes to attract foreign investment.* • **adapt|abil|ity** /ədæptəbɪlɪti/ N-UNCOUNT ❑ *The adaptability of wool is one of its great attractions.*

ad|ap|ta|tion /ædæpteɪʃən/ (**adaptations**) ❶ N-COUNT An **adaptation** of a book or play is a film or a television program that is based on it. ❑ *Branagh won two awards for his screen adaptation of Shakespeare's Henry the Fifth.* ❷ N-UNCOUNT **Adaptation** is the act of changing something or changing your behavior to make it suitable for a new purpose or situation. ❑ *Most living creatures are capable of adaptation when compelled to do so.*

adapt|ed /ədæptɪd/ ADJ [v-link ADJ to/for n] If something is **adapted** to a particular situation or purpose, it is especially suitable for it. ❑ *The camel's feet, well adapted for dry sand, are useless on mud.*

adap|tion /ədæpʃən/ (**adaptions**) N-VAR **Adaption** means the same as **adaptation**.

adap|tive /ədæptɪv/ ADJ **Adaptive** means having the ability or tendency to adapt to different situations. [FORMAL] ❑ *Societies need to develop highly adaptive behavioral rules for survival.*

adap|tor /ədæptər/ (**adaptors**) also **adapter** ❶ N-COUNT An **adaptor** is a special device for connecting electrical equipment to a power supply, or for connecting different pieces of electrical or electronic equipment together. ❷ N-COUNT The **adaptor** of a book or play is the person who rewrites it for a film or a television program.

ad cam|paign (**ad campaigns**) N-COUNT An **ad campaign** is a planned series of advertisements. ❑ *...a $50 million government ad campaign to inform users of its benefits.*

add ✦✦✦ /æd/ (**adds, adding, added**) ❶ V-T If you **add** one thing to another, you put it in or on the other thing, to increase, complete, or improve it. ❑ *Add the grated cheese to the sauce.* ❑ *Since 1908, chlorine has been added to drinking water.* ❷ V-T If you **add** numbers or amounts together, you calculate their total. ❑ *Banks add all the interest and other charges together.* ❸ V-I If one thing **adds** to another, it makes the other thing greater in degree or amount. ❑ *This latest incident will add to the pressure on the White House.* ❹ V-T To **add** a particular quality to something means to cause it to have that quality. ❑ *The generous amount of garlic adds flavor.* ❺ V-T If you **add** something when you are speaking, you say something more. ❑ *"You can tell that he is extremely embarrassed," Mr. Montoya added.* ❻ V-I If you can **add**, you are able to calculate the total of numbers or amounts. [AM] ❑ *More than a quarter of seven-year-olds cannot add properly.*

in BRIT, usually use **add up**

▶ **add in** PHRASAL VERB If you **add in** something, you include it as a part of something else. ❑ *Once the vegetables start to cook add in a couple of tablespoons of water.*

▶ **add on** ❶ PHRASAL VERB If one thing **is added on** to another, it is attached to the other thing, or is made a part of it. ❑ *Vacationers can also add on a week in Florida before or after the cruise.* ❷ PHRASAL VERB If you **add on** an extra amount or item to a list or total, you include it. ❑ *Many loan application forms automatically add on insurance.* ❸ PHRASAL VERB If you **add on**, you increase the size of a house or other building by constructing one or more extra rooms. [AM] ❑ *Investors who cannot afford a larger property now can add on when they have more money.*

▶ **add up** ❶ PHRASAL VERB If you **add up** numbers or amounts, or if you **add** them **up**, you calculate their total. ❑ *Add up the total of those six games.* ❑ *We just added all the numbers up and divided one by the other.* ❷ PHRASAL VERB If facts or events do not **add up**, they make you confused about a situation because they do not seem to be consistent. If something that someone has said or done **adds up**, it is reasonable and sensible. ❑ *Police said they arrested Olivia because her statements did not add up.* ❸ PHRASAL VERB If small amounts of something **add up**, they gradually increase. ❑ *Even small savings, 5 cents here or 10 cents there, can add up.*

▶ **add up to** PHRASAL VERB If amounts **add up to** a particular total, they result in that total when they are put together. ❑ *For a hit show, profits can add up to millions of dollars.*

─── **SYNONYMS** ───

add
VERB
❶
include: *The President is expected to include this idea in his education plan.*
attach: *The gadget can be attached to any vertical surface.*
supplement: *I suggest supplementing your diet with vitamins E and A.*
append: *Violet appended a note at the end of the letter.*
❷
count: *I counted 34 wild goats grazing.*
calculate: *From this you can calculate the total mass in the galaxy.*
total: *They haven't totaled the exact figures.*

ADD /eɪ di di/ **ADD** is an abbreviation for **attention deficit disorder**.

add|ed /ædɪd/ ADJ [ADJ n] You use **added** to say that something has more of a particular thing or quality. ❑ *For added protection choose moisturizing lipsticks with a sunscreen.*

add|ed value N-UNCOUNT In marketing, **added value** is something that makes a product more appealing to customers. [BUSINESS] ❑ *We can create significant added value by pushing the brand into other areas.*

ad|den|dum /ədɛndəm/ (**addenda** /ədɛndə/) N-COUNT An **addendum** is an additional section at the end of a book or document.

add|er /ædər/ (**adders**) N-COUNT In North America, a number of different poisonous and non-poisonous snakes are called **adders**. In Europe and Asia, an **adder** is a small poisonous snake that has a black pattern on its back.

ad|dict /ædɪkt/ (**addicts**) ◼ N-COUNT An **addict** is someone who takes harmful drugs and cannot stop taking them. ☐ *He's only 24 years old and a drug addict.* ◼ N-COUNT If you say that someone is an **addict**, you mean that they like a particular activity very much and spend as much time doing it as they can. ☐ *She is a TV addict and watches as much as she can.*

ad|dict|ed /ədɪktɪd/ ◼ ADJ Someone who is **addicted** to a harmful drug cannot stop taking it. ☐ *Many of the women are addicted to heroin and cocaine.* ◼ ADJ If you say that someone is **addicted** to something, you mean that they like it very much and want to spend as much time doing it as possible. ☐ *She had become addicted to golf.*

ad|dic|tion /ədɪkʃən/ (**addictions**) ◼ N-VAR **Addiction** is the condition of taking harmful drugs and being unable to stop taking them. ☐ *She helped him fight his drug addiction.* ◼ N-VAR An **addiction** to something is a very strong desire or need for it. ☐ *He needed money to feed his addiction to gambling.*

ad|dic|tive /ədɪktɪv/ ◼ ADJ If a drug is **addictive**, people who take it cannot stop taking it. ☐ *Cigarettes are highly addictive.* ◼ ADJ Something that is **addictive** is so enjoyable that it makes you want to do it or have it a lot. ☐ *Be warned jogging can become addictive!*

ad|di|tion ♦♦◇ /ədɪʃən/ (**additions**) ◼ PHRASE You use **in addition** when you want to mention another item connected with the subject you are discussing. ☐ *The web site provides regional weather reports, a shipping forecast and gale warnings. In addition, visitors can download satellite images of the U.S.* ◼ N-COUNT An **addition** to something is a thing which is added to it. ☐ *This is a fine book; a worthy addition to the series.* ◼ N-COUNT [oft N to n] An **addition** is a new room or building which is added to an existing building or group of buildings. [AM] ☐ *The couple said they spent $20,000 on building an addition to their kitchen.* ◼ N-UNCOUNT The **addition** of something is the fact that it is added to something else. ☐ *It was completely refurbished, with the addition of a picnic site.* ◼ N-UNCOUNT **Addition** is the process of calculating the total of two or more numbers. ☐ *...simple addition and subtraction problems using whole numbers.*

ad|di|tion|al ♦◇◇ /ədɪʃənəl/ ADJ **Additional** things are extra things apart from the ones already present. ☐ *The U.S. is sending additional troops to the region.*

---SYNONYMS---

additional
ADJ
extra: *Extra staff have been hired to cover busy periods.*
further: *They believed there were likely to be further attacks.*
supplementary: *Provide them with additional background or with supplementary information.*
spare: *Don't forget to take a few spare batteries.*

ad|di|tion|al|ly /ədɪʃənəli/ ADV [ADV with cl] You use **additionally** to introduce something extra such as an extra fact or reason. ☐ *All teachers are qualified to teach their native language. Additionally, we select our teachers for their engaging personalities.*

ad|di|tive /ædɪtɪv/ (**additives**) N-COUNT An **additive** is a substance which is added in small amounts to foods or other things in order to improve them or to make them last longer. ☐ *Strict safety tests are carried out on food additives.*

ad|dle /æd°l/ (**addles, addling, addled**) V-T If something **addles** someone's mind or brain, they become confused and unable to think properly. ☐ *I suppose the shock had addled his poor old brain.*

ad|dled /æd°ld/ ADJ [usu ADJ n] If you describe someone as **addled**, you mean that they are confused or unable to think properly. ☐ *You're talking like an addled romantic.*

add-on (**add-ons**) N-COUNT An **add-on** is an extra piece of equipment, especially computer equipment, that can be added to a larger one which you already own in order to improve its performance or its usefulness. ☐ *To use this software, you don't need a CD-ROM drive or any expensive add-ons for your computer.*

ad|dress ♦♦◇ (**addresses, addressing, addressed**)

The noun is pronounced /ədrɛs/ or /ædrɛs/. The verb is pronounced /ədrɛs/.

◼ N-COUNT Your **address** is the number of the house or apartment and the name of the street and the town where you live or work. ☐ *The address is 2025 M Street, NW, Washington, DC, 20036.* ◼ N-COUNT The **address** of a website is its location on the internet, for example, http://www.collinsdictionary.com. [COMPUTING] ☐ *Full details, including the website address to log on to, are at the bottom of this page.* ◼ V-T [usu passive] If a letter, envelope, or parcel **is addressed** to you, your name and address have been written on it. ☐ *Applications should be addressed to: The business affairs editor.* ◼ V-T If you **address** a group of people, you give a speech to them. ☐ *He is due to address a conference on human rights next week.* • N-COUNT **Address** is also a noun. ☐ *He had scheduled an address to the American people for the evening of May 27.*

---COLLOCATIONS---

address
VERB ◼
address + noun: audience, crowd, gathering, rally; conference, meeting

ad|dress book (**address books**) ◼ N-COUNT An **address book** is a book in which you write people's names and addresses. ◼ N-COUNT An **address book** is a computer file which contains a list of email addresses. [COMPUTING]

ad|dressee /ædrɛsi/ (**addressees**) N-COUNT [usu the N in sing] The **addressee** of a letter or parcel is the person or company that it is addressed to. [FORMAL]

ad|duce /ædjus/ (**adduces, adducing, adduced**) VERB If you **adduce** something such as a fact or reason, you mention it in order to support an argument. [FORMAL] ☐ *We can adduce evidence to support the claim.*

ad|enoids /ædənɔɪdz/ N-PLURAL **Adenoids** are soft lumps of flesh at the back and top of a person's throat that sometimes become swollen and have to be removed.

adept /ædɛpt/ ADJ Someone who is **adept** at something can do it skillfully. ☐ *He's usually very adept at keeping his private life out of the media.*

ad|equa|cy /ædɪkwəsi/ N-UNCOUNT **Adequacy** is the quality of being good enough or great enough in amount to be acceptable. ☐ *There are questions to be raised about the adequacy of the inmates' legal representation.*

ad|equate ♦◇◇ /ædɪkwɪt/ ADJ If something is **adequate**, there is enough of it or it is good enough to be used or accepted. ☐ *One in four people worldwide are without adequate homes.* ☐ *She is prepared to offer me an amount adequate to purchase another house.* • **ad|equate|ly** ADV [ADV with v] ☐ *Many students are not adequately prepared for higher education.*

ADHD /eɪ di eɪtʃ di/ **ADHD** is an abbreviation for **attention deficit hyperactivity disorder.**

ad|here /ædhɪər/ (**adheres, adhering, adhered**) ◼ V-I If you **adhere** to a rule or agreement, you act in the way that it says you should. ☐ *All members of the association adhere to a strict code of practice.* ◼ V-I If something **adheres** to something else, it sticks firmly to it. ☐ *Small particles adhere to the seed.*

ad|her|ence /ædhɪərəns/ N-UNCOUNT [usu N to n] **Adherence** is the fact of adhering to a particular rule, agreement, or belief. ☐ *...strict adherence to the constitution.*

ad|her|ent /ædhɪərənt/ (**adherents**) N-COUNT An **adherent** is someone who holds a particular belief or supports a particular person or group. ☐ *This idea is gaining adherents.*

ad|he|sion /ædhiʒən/ N-UNCOUNT **Adhesion** is the ability of one thing to stick firmly to another. [FORMAL] ☐ *Better driving equipment will improve track adhesion in slippery conditions.*

ad|he|sive /ædhisɪv/ (**adhesives**) ◼ N-MASS An **adhesive** is a substance such as glue, which is used to make things stick firmly together. ☐ *Glue the mirror in with a strong adhesive.*

2 ADJ An **adhesive** substance is able to stick firmly to something else. ☐ ...*adhesive tape.*

ad hoc /ˌæd hɒk/ ADJ An **ad hoc** activity or organization is not planned in advance, but is done or formed only because a particular situation has made it necessary. ☐ *"I would accept opportunities in TV on an ad hoc basis," he said.*

adieu /ədjuː/ (**adieus**) CONVENTION **Adieu** means the same as **goodbye**. [LITERARY, OLD-FASHIONED]

ad in|fi|ni|tum /ˌæd ɪnfɪnaɪtəm/ ADV [ADV after v] If something happens **ad infinitum**, it is repeated again and again in the same way. ☐ *This cycle repeats itself ad infinitum.*

adj. Adj. is a written abbreviation for **adjective**.

ad|ja|cent /ədʒeɪsənt/ ADJ If one thing is **adjacent** to another, the two things are next to each other. ☐ *He sat in an adjacent room and waited.* ☐ *The schools were adjacent but there were separate doors.*

ad|jec|ti|val /ˌædʒɪktaɪvəl/ ADJ [usu ADJ n] **Adjectival** means relating to adjectives or like an adjective. ☐ *...an adjectival phrase.*

ad|jec|tive /ˈædʒɪktɪv/ (**adjectives**) N-COUNT An **adjective** is a word such as 'big,' 'dead,' or 'financial' that describes a person or thing, or gives extra information about them. Adjectives usually come before nouns or after linking verbs.

ad|jec|tive group (**adjective groups**) N-COUNT An **adjective group** or **adjectival group** is a group of words based on an adjective, such as 'very nice' or 'interested in football.' An adjective group can also consist simply of an adjective.

ad|jec|tive phrase (**adjective phrases**) N-COUNT An **adjective phrase** or **adjectival phrase** is a group of words based on an adjective, such as 'very nice' or 'interested in football.' An adjective phrase can also consist simply of an adjective.

ad|join /ədʒɔɪn/ (**adjoins, adjoining, adjoined**) V-T If one room, place, or object **adjoins** another, they are next to each other. [FORMAL] ☐ *The doctor's bedroom adjoined his wife's and the door between the rooms was always open.*

ad|journ /ədʒɜːrn/ (**adjourns, adjourning, adjourned**) V-T/V-I If a meeting or trial **is adjourned** or if it **adjourns**, it is stopped for a short time. ☐ *The proceedings have now been adjourned until next week.*

ad|journ|ment /ədʒɜːrnmənt/ (**adjournments**) N-COUNT An **adjournment** is a temporary stopping of a trial, inquiry, or other meeting. ☐ *The court ordered a four month adjournment.*

ad|judge /ədʒʌdʒ/ (**adjudges, adjudging, adjudged**) V-T [usu passive] If someone **is adjudged** to be something, they are judged or considered to be that thing. [FORMAL] ☐ *He was adjudged to be guilty.* ☐ *He was adjudged the winner by 54 votes to 3.*

ad|ju|di|cate /ədʒuːdɪkeɪt/ (**adjudicates, adjudicating, adjudicated**) V-T/V-I If you **adjudicate** on a dispute or problem, you make an official judgment or decision about it. [FORMAL] ☐ *...a commissioner to adjudicate on legal rights.* ☐ *The international court of justice might be a suitable place to adjudicate claims.*
• **ad|ju|di|ca|tion** /ədʒuːdɪkeɪʃən/ (**adjudications**) N-VAR ☐ *...a range of UN capabilities, including mediation and adjudication of disputes.* • **ad|ju|di|ca|tor** /ədʒuːdɪkeɪtər/ (**adjudicators**) N-COUNT ☐ *...an independent adjudicator.*

ad|junct /ˈædʒʌŋkt/ (**adjuncts**) **1** N-COUNT [oft N to/of n] Something that is an **adjunct** to something larger or more important is connected with it or helps to perform the same task. ☐ *Physical therapy is an important adjunct to drug treatments.* **2** N-COUNT In grammar, an **adjunct** is a word or group of words which indicates the circumstances of an action, event, or situation. An adjunct is usually a prepositional phrase or an adverb phrase.

ad|just ♦◇◇ /ədʒʌst/ (**adjusts, adjusting, adjusted**) **1** V-T/V-I When you **adjust** to a new situation, you get used to it by changing your behavior or your ideas. ☐ *We have been preparing our fighters to adjust themselves to civil society.* ☐ *I felt I had adjusted to the idea of being a mother very well.* **2** V-T If you **adjust** something, you change it so that it is more effective or appropriate. ☐ *To attract investors, Panama has adjusted its tax and labor laws.* **3** V-T If you **adjust** something such as your clothing or a machine, you correct or alter its position or setting. ☐ *Liz adjusted her mirror and then edged the car out of its parking space.* **4** V-T/V-I If you **adjust** your vision or if your vision **adjusts**, the muscles of your eye or the pupils alter to cope with changes in light or distance. ☐ *He stopped to try to adjust his vision to the faint starlight.*

SYNONYMS
---

adjust
VERB
1
adapt: *They have had to adapt themselves to a war economy.*
accommodate: *Some animal and plant species cannot accommodate to the rapidly changing conditions.*
get used to: *This is how we do things here. You'll soon get used to it.*
accustom: *The team has accustomed itself to the pace of Division 1 rugby.*
3
alter: *They have never altered their programs by a single day.*
adapt: *Shelves were built to adapt the library for use as an office.*
revise: *The staff should work together to revise the school curriculum.*
modify: *The club members did agree to modify their recruitment policy.*
amend: *The president agreed to amend the constitution and allow multi-party elections.*

---

ad|just|able /ədʒʌstəbəl/ ADJ If something is **adjustable**, it can be changed to different positions or sizes. ☐ *The bags have adjustable shoulder straps.*

ad|just|er /ədʒʌstər/ (**adjusters**) also **adjustor** **1** N-COUNT An **adjuster** is a device that allows you to alter a piece of equipment's position or setting. ☐ *...a seat belt adjuster.*
2 → see also **loss adjuster**

ad|just|ment /ədʒʌstmənt/ (**adjustments**) **1** N-COUNT An **adjustment** is a small change that is made to something such as a machine or a way of doing something. ☐ *Compensation could be made by adjustments to taxation.* ☐ *Investment is up by 5.7% after adjustment for inflation.* **2** N-COUNT An **adjustment** is a change in a person's behavior or thinking. ☐ *He will have to make major adjustments to his thinking if he is to survive in office.*

ad|ju|tant /ˈædʒətənt/ (**adjutants**) N-COUNT An **adjutant** is an officer in the army who deals with administrative work.

ad-lib (**ad-libs, ad-libbing, ad-libbed**) also **ad lib** **1** V-T If you **ad-lib** something in a play or a speech, you say something that has not been planned or written beforehand. ☐ *He began comically ad-libbing a script.* ☐ *...ad-libbed phrases.* **2** N-COUNT An **ad-lib** is something that is said without having been planned or written beforehand. ☐ *Every time I fluffed a line Lenny got me out of trouble with a brilliant ad-lib.* • ADV [ADV after v] **Ad lib** is also an adverb. ☐ *I spoke from the pulpit ad lib.*

ad|man /ˈædmæn/ (**admen**) N-COUNT An **adman** is a man who works in advertising. [INFORMAL] ☐ *He was the most brilliant adman that any of us knew.*

ad|min /ˈædmɪn/ **1** ADJ **Admin** is an abbreviation of **administrative**. **2** N-UNCOUNT **Admin** is the activity or process of organizing an institution or organization. **Admin** is an abbreviation of **administration**. [BRIT, INFORMAL]

ad|min|is|ter /ədmɪnɪstər/ (**administers, administering, administered**) **1** V-T If someone **administers** something such as a country, the law, or a test, they take responsibility for organizing and supervising it. ☐ *The plan calls for the UN to administer the country until elections can be held.* **2** V-T If a doctor or a nurse **administers** a drug, they give it to a patient. [FORMAL] ☐ *The physician may prescribe but not administer the drug.*

ad|min|is|tra|tion ♦♦◇ /ədmɪnɪstreɪʃən/ (**administrations**)
1 N-UNCOUNT **Administration** is the range of activities connected with organizing and supervising the way that an organization or institution functions. ☐ *Too much time is spent on administration.* **2** N-UNCOUNT The **administration** of something is the process of organizing and supervising it. ☐ *Standards in the administration of justice have degenerated.* **3** N-SING The **administration** of a company or institution is the group of people who organize and supervise it. ☐ *They would like the college administration to exert more control over the fraternity.* **4** N-COUNT You can refer to a country's government as the **administration**; used especially in the United States. ☐ *O'Leary served in federal energy posts in both the Ford and Carter administrations.*

administrative

> **SYNONYMS**
>
> **administration**
> NOUN **2**
> **management:** *The dispute is about the management of the mining industry.*
> **government:** *The first four years of the new government were completely disastrous.*
> **control:** *The restructuring involves Mr Ronson giving up control of the company.*
> **running:** *...the committee in charge of the day-to-day running of the party.*

ad|min|is|tra|tive /ædmɪnɪstreɪtɪv/ ADJ **Administrative** work involves organizing and supervising an organization or institution. ❑ *Other industries have had to sack managers to reduce administrative costs.*

ad|min|is|tra|tor /ædmɪnɪstreɪtər/ (**administrators**) N-COUNT An **administrator** is a person whose job involves helping to organize and supervise the way that an organization or institution functions. ❑ *On Friday the company's administrators sought permission from a Melbourne court to keep operating.*

ad|mi|rable /ædmɪrəbəl/ ADJ An **admirable** quality or action is one that deserves to be praised and admired. ❑ *She did an admirable job of holding the audience's attention.* • **ad|mi|rably** /ædmɪrəbli/ ADV ❑ *Peter had dealt admirably with the sudden questions about Keith.*

ad|mi|ral /ædmərəl/ (**admirals**) N-COUNT; N-TITLE An **admiral** is a very senior officer who commands a navy. ❑ *...Admiral Hodges.*

ad|mi|ra|tion /ædmɪreɪʃən/ N-UNCOUNT **Admiration** is a feeling of great liking and respect for a person or thing. ❑ *I have always had the greatest admiration for him.*

ad|mire♦◇◇ /ædmaɪər/ (**admires, admiring, admired**) **1** V-T If you **admire** someone or something, you like and respect them very much. ❑ *I admired her when I first met her and I still think she's marvelous.* ❑ *He admired the way she had coped with life.* **2** V-T If you **admire** someone or something, you look at them with pleasure. ❑ *We took time to stop and admire the view.*

> **SYNONYMS**
>
> **admire**
> VERB **1**
> **respect:** *I want him to respect me as a career woman.*
> **look up to:** *You're a popular girl, Grace, and a lot of the younger ones look up to you.*
> **revere:** *Today, he's still revered as the father of the nation.*

ad|mir|er /ædmaɪərər/ (**admirers**) N-COUNT If you are an **admirer** of someone, you like and respect them or their work very much. ❑ *He was an admirer of her grandfather's paintings.*

ad|mir|ing /ædmaɪərɪŋ/ ADJ [usu ADJ n] An **admiring** expression shows that you like or respect someone or something. ❑ *He cast her an admiring glance.*

ad|mis|sible /ædmɪsɪbəl/ ADJ [usu v-link ADJ] If evidence is **admissible**, it is allowed in a court of law. ❑ *Convictions will rise steeply now that photographic evidence is admissible.*

ad|mis|sion /ædmɪʃən/ (**admissions**) **1** N-VAR **Admission** is permission given to a person to enter a place, or permission given to a country to enter an organization. **Admission** is also the act of entering a place. ❑ *Students apply for admission to a particular college.* **2** N-VAR An **admission** is a statement that something bad, unpleasant, or embarrassing is true. ❑ *By his own admission, he is not playing well.* **3** N-PLURAL **Admissions** to a place such as a school or university are the people who are allowed to enter or join it. ❑ *Each school sets its own admissions policy.* **4** N-UNCOUNT **Admission** at a park, museum, or other place is the amount of money that you pay to enter it. ❑ *Gates open at 10:30 a.m. and admission is free.* • N-UNCOUNT **Admission** is also used before a noun. ❑ *The admission price is $8 for adults.*

ad|mit♦♦◇ /ædmɪt/ (**admits, admitting, admitted**) **1** V-T/V-I If you **admit** that something bad, unpleasant, or embarrassing is true, you agree, often unwillingly, that it is true. ❑ *I am willing to admit that I do make mistakes.* ❑ *Up to two-thirds of drivers admit to driving while feeling tired.* ❑ *None of these people will admit responsibility for their actions.* **2** V-T If someone **is admitted** to a hospital, they are taken into the hospital for treatment and kept there until they are well enough to go home. ❑ *She was admitted to the hospital with a soaring temperature.* **3** V-T If someone **is admitted** to an organization or group, they are allowed to join it. ❑ *He was admitted to the Académie Culinaire de France.* **4** V-T To **admit** someone to a place means to allow them to enter it. ❑ *Embassy security personnel refused to admit him or his wife.*

> **SYNONYMS**
>
> **admit**
> VERB **1**
> **confess:** *He had confessed to seventeen murders.*
> **own up:** *The principal is waiting for someone to own up.*
> **allow:** *Warren also allows that capitalist development may result in increased social inequality.*

> **COLLOCATIONS**
>
> **admit**
> VERB **1**
> **admit + noun:** guilt, liability, responsibility, wrongdoing; defeat; error, mistake; charge, offense; assault, fraud, manslaughter, murder, theft
> **admit + adverb:** privately, publicly; candidly, cheerfully, freely, openly, readily; grudgingly, reluctantly, ruefully, sheepishly

ad|mit|tance /ædmɪtəns/ N-UNCOUNT [oft N into/to n] **Admittance** is the act of entering a place or institution or the right to enter it. [mainly BRIT] ❑ *We had not been able to gain admittance to the flat.*

ad|mit|ted|ly /ædmɪtɪdli/ ADV [ADV with cl/group] You use **admittedly** when you are saying something that weakens the importance or force of your statement. ❑ *It's only a theory, admittedly, but the pieces fit together.*

ad|mix|ture /ædmɪkstʃər/ N-SING [usu N of n] **Admixture** means the same as **mixture**. [FORMAL] ❑ *...an admixture of fact and fantasy.*

ad|mon|ish /ædmɒnɪʃ/ (**admonishes, admonishing, admonished**) V-T If you **admonish** someone, you tell them very seriously that they have done something wrong. [FORMAL] ❑ *They admonished me for taking risks with my health.* • **ad|mon|ish|ment** (**admonishments**) N-VAR ❑ *Sometimes he gave them a severe admonishment.*

ad|moni|tion /ædmənɪʃən/ (**admonitions**) N-VAR An **admonition** is a warning or criticism about someone's behavior. [FORMAL] ❑ *She ignored the admonitions of her mother.*

ad nau|seam /æd nɔziæm/ PHRASE [PHR after v] If someone does something **ad nauseam**, they do it repeatedly and over a long period of time so that it becomes annoying or boring. ❑ *We discussed it ad nauseam.*

ado /ædu/ PHRASE [PHR with v] If you do something **without further ado** or **without more ado**, you do it at once and do not discuss or delay it any longer. [OLD-FASHIONED] ❑ *"And now, without further ado, let me introduce our benefactor."*

ado|be /ædoʊbi/ N-UNCOUNT [usu N n] **Adobe** is a mixture of mud and straw that is dried into bricks in the sun and used for building, especially in hot countries. ❑ *...a few blocks of adobe houses.*

ado|les|cence /ædəlɛsəns/ N-UNCOUNT **Adolescence** is the period of your life in which you develop from being a child into being an adult. ❑ *Some young people suddenly become self-conscious and tongue-tied in early adolescence.*

ado|les|cent /ædəlɛsənt/ (**adolescents**) ADJ **Adolescent** is used to describe young people who are no longer children but who have not yet become adults. It also refers to their behavior. ❑ *It is important that an adolescent boy should have an adult in whom he can confide.* • N-COUNT An **adolescent** is an adolescent boy or girl. ❑ *Young adolescents are happiest with small groups of close friends.*

adopt♦♦◇ /ædɒpt/ (**adopts, adopting, adopted**) **1** V-T If you **adopt** a new attitude, plan, or way of behaving, you begin to have it. ❑ *The United Nations General Assembly has adopted a resolution calling on all parties in the conflict to seek a political settlement.* • **adop|tion** /ædɒpʃən/ N-UNCOUNT ❑ *The group is working to promote the adoption of broadband wireless access over long* distances. **2** V-T/V-I If you **adopt** someone else's child, you take it into your own family and make it legally your son or daughter. ☐ *There are hundreds of people desperate to adopt a child.* • **adop|tion** (**adoptions**) N-VAR ☐ *They gave their babies up for adoption.* **3** → See feature box at **family**

SYNONYMS

adopt
VERB
1
take on: *Don't take on more responsibilities than you can handle.*
embrace: *The new rules have been embraced by government watchdog organizations.*
assume: *He contented himself by assuming an air of superiority.*
2
take in: *The monastery has taken in 26 refugees.*
foster: *She has since gone on to find happiness by fostering more than 100 children.*

---

adop|tive /ədɒptɪv/ ADJ [ADJ n] Someone's **adoptive** family is the family that adopted them. ☐ *He was brought up by adoptive parents in Kentucky.*

ador|able /ədɔːrəbəl/ ADJ If you say that someone or something is **adorable**, you are emphasizing that they are very attractive and you feel great affection for them. [EMPHASIS] ☐ *By the time I was 30, we had three adorable children.*

ado|ra|tion /ædəreɪʃən/ N-UNCOUNT **Adoration** is a feeling of great admiration and love for someone or something. ☐ *She needs and wants to be loved with overwhelming passion and adoration.*

adore /ədɔːr/ (**adores, adoring, adored**) **1** V-T [no cont] If you **adore** someone, you feel great love and admiration for them. ☐ *She adored her parents and would do anything to please them.* **2** V-T [no cont] If you **adore** something, you like it very much. [INFORMAL] ☐ *My mother adores bananas and eats two a day.*

ador|ing /ədɔːrɪŋ/ ADJ An **adoring** person is someone who loves and admires another person very much. ☐ *She can still pull in adoring audiences.* • **ador|ing|ly** ADV ☐ *...gazing adoringly at him.*

adorn /ədɔːrn/ (**adorns, adorning, adorned**) V-T If something **adorns** a place or an object, it makes it look more beautiful. ☐ *His watercolor designs adorn a wide range of books.*

adorn|ment /ədɔːrnmənt/ (**adornments**) **1** N-VAR An **adornment** is something that is used to make a person or thing more beautiful. ☐ *It was a building without any adornment or decoration.* **2** N-UNCOUNT **Adornment** is the process of making something more beautiful by adding something to it. ☐ *Cosmetics are used for adornment.*

adrena|lin /ədrɛnəlɪn/ also **adrenaline** N-UNCOUNT **Adrenalin** is a substance which your body produces when you are angry, scared, or excited. It makes your heart beat faster and gives you more energy. ☐ *That was my first big game in months and the adrenalin was going.*

adrift /ədrɪft/ **1** ADJ [v-link ADJ, v n ADJ] If a boat is **adrift**, it is floating on the water and is not tied to anything or controlled by anyone. ☐ *They were spotted after three hours adrift in a dinghy.* **2** ADJ [v-link ADJ, v n ADJ] If someone is **adrift**, they feel alone with no clear idea of what they should do. ☐ *Amy had the growing sense that she was adrift and isolated.*

adroit /ədrɔɪt/ ADJ Someone who is **adroit** is quick and skillful in their thoughts, behavior, or actions. ☐ *She is a remarkably adroit and determined politician.*

ADSL /eɪ diː ɛs ɛl/ [BRIT] → see **DSL**

adu|la|tion /ædʒʊleɪʃən/ N-UNCOUNT **Adulation** is uncritical admiration and praise of someone or something. ☐ *The book was received with adulation by the public.*

adu|la|tory /ædʒʊleɪtəri/ ADJ [usu ADJ n] If someone makes an **adulatory** comment about someone, they praise them and show their admiration for them. ☐ *...adulatory reviews.*

adult ♦♦◇ /ədʌlt/ (**adults**) **1** N-COUNT An **adult** is a mature, fully developed person. An adult has reached the age when they are legally responsible for their actions. ☐ *Becoming a father signified that he was now an adult.* **2** N-COUNT An **adult** is a fully developed animal. ☐ *...a pair of adult birds.* **3** ADJ [ADJ n] **Adult** means relating to the time when you are an adult,

or typical of adult people. ☐ *I've lived most of my adult life in Arizona.* **4** ADJ You can describe things such as films or books as **adult** when they deal with sex in a very clear and open way. ☐ *...an adult movie.*

SYNONYMS

adult
ADJ **3**
grown-up: *I have grown-up children who are doing well.*
mature: *He was a man of mature years.*

---

adult edu|ca|tion N-UNCOUNT **Adult education** is education for adults in a variety of subjects, most of which are practical, not academic. Classes are often held in the evenings. ☐ *Most adult education centers offer computer courses.*

adul|ter|ate /ədʌltəreɪt/ (**adulterates, adulterating, adulterated**) V-T [usu passive] If something such as food or drink **is adulterated**, someone has made its quality worse by adding water or cheaper products to it. ☐ *The food had been adulterated to increase its weight.*

adul|ter|er /ədʌltərər/ (**adulterers**) N-COUNT An **adulterer** is someone who commits adultery.

adul|ter|ess /ədʌltrɪs/ (**adulteresses**) N-COUNT An **adulteress** is a woman who commits adultery. [OLD-FASHIONED]

adul|ter|ous /ədʌltərəs/ ADJ [usu ADJ n] An **adulterous** relationship is a sexual relationship between a married person and someone they are not married to. An **adulterous** person is someone who commits adultery.

adul|tery /ədʌltəri/ N-UNCOUNT If a married person commits **adultery**, they have sex with someone that they are not married to. ☐ *She is going to divorce him on the grounds of adultery.*

adult|hood /ədʌlthʊd/ N-UNCOUNT **Adulthood** is the state of being an adult. ☐ *Few people nowadays are able to maintain friendships into adulthood.*

adv. Adv. is a written abbreviation for **adverb**.

ad|vance ♦♦◇ /ædvæns/ (**advances, advancing, advanced**) **1** V-I To **advance** means to move forward, often in order to attack someone. ☐ *Reports from Chad suggest that rebel forces are advancing on the capital.* ☐ *According to one report, the water is advancing at a rate of between 8 and 10 inches a day.* **2** V-I To **advance** means to make progress, especially in your knowledge of something. ☐ *Medical technology has advanced considerably.* **3** → see also **advanced** **4** V-T If you **advance** someone a sum of money, you lend it to them, or pay it to them earlier than arranged. ☐ *I advanced him some money, which he would repay on our way home.* **5** V-T To **advance** an event, or the time or date of an event, means to bring it forward to an earlier time or date. ☐ *Too much protein in the diet may advance the aging process.* **6** V-T If you **advance** a cause, interest, or claim, you support it and help to make it successful. ☐ *When not producing art of his own, Oliver was busy advancing the work of others.* **7** N-COUNT An **advance** is money lent or paid to someone before they would normally receive it. ☐ *She was paid a $100,000 advance for her next two novels.* **8** N-VAR An **advance** is a forward movement of people or vehicles, usually as part of a military operation. ☐ *In an exercise designed to be as real as possible, they simulated an advance on enemy positions.* **9** N-VAR An **advance** in a particular subject or activity is progress in understanding it or in doing it well. ☐ *Air safety has not improved since the dramatic advances of the 1970s.* **10** N-SING [usu a N on n] If something is an **advance** on what was previously available or done, it is better in some way. ☐ *This could be an advance on the present situation.* **11** ADJ [ADJ n] **Advance** booking, notice, or warning is done or given before an event happens. ☐ *They don't normally give any advance notice about which building they're going to inspect.* **12** PHRASE If you do something **in advance**, you do it before a particular date or event. ☐ *The subject of the talk is announced a week in advance.*

ad|vanced ♦♦◇ /ædvænst/ **1** ADJ An **advanced** system, method, or design is modern and has been developed from an earlier version of the same thing. ☐ *...a superpower equipped with the most advanced military technology in the world.* **2** ADJ A country that is **advanced** has reached a high level of industrial or technological development. ☐ *Agricultural productivity remained low by comparison with advanced countries*

advancement / advertise

like the United States. **3** ADJ An **advanced** student has already learned the basic facts of a subject and is doing more difficult work. An **advanced** course of study is designed for such students. ❏ *The course is suitable for beginners and advanced students.* **4** ADJ Something that is at an **advanced** stage or level is at a late stage of development. ❏ *Medicare is available to victims of advanced kidney disease.*

SYNONYMS
advanced
ADJ **1**
sophisticated: *...a large and sophisticated new British telescope.*
up-to-date: *This is Germany's most up-to-date electric power station.*
state-of-the-art: *...the production of state-of-the-art military equipment.*
latest: *I got to drive the latest model.*

ad|vance|ment /ædvænsmənt/ (advancements)
1 N-UNCOUNT **Advancement** is progress in your job or in your social position. ❏ *He cared little for social advancement.* **2** N-VAR The **advancement** of something is the process of helping it to progress or the result of its progress. ❏ *Her work for the advancement of the status of women in India was recognized by the whole nation.*

ad|van|tage ✦✦◇ /ædvɑ̱ntɪdʒ, -væn-/ (advantages)
1 N-COUNT An **advantage** is something that puts you in a better position than other people. ❏ *They are breaking the law in order to obtain an advantage over their competitors.* **2** N-COUNT An **advantage** is a way in which one thing is better than another. ❏ *The great advantage of home-grown oranges is their magnificent flavor.* **3** N-UNCOUNT **Advantage** is the state of being in a better position than others who are competing against you. ❏ *The family hold a position of social and economic advantage in the region.* **4** PHRASE If you **take advantage of** something, you make good use of it while you can. ❏ *I intend to take full advantage of this trip to do the things we need.* **5** PHRASE If someone **takes advantage of** you, they treat you unfairly for their own benefit, especially when you are trying to be kind or to help them. ❏ *She took advantage of him even after they were divorced.* **6** PHRASE If you use or turn something **to your advantage**, you use it in order to benefit from it, especially when it might be expected to harm or damage you. ❏ *The government has not been able to turn today's demonstration to its advantage.*

SYNONYMS
advantage
NOUN **2**
benefit: *I'm a great believer in the benefits of this form of therapy.*
asset: *Her leadership qualities were the greatest asset of the Conservative Party.*
perk: *One of the perks of being a student is cheap travel.*
plus: *Experience in any career in sales is a big plus.*

ad|van|taged /ædvɑ̱ntɪdʒd/ ADJ A person or place that is **advantaged** is in a better social or financial position than other people or places. ❏ *Some cities are always going to be more advantaged.*

ad|van|ta|geous /æ̱dvənteɪdʒəs/ ADJ If something is **advantageous** to you, it is likely to benefit you. ❏ *Free exchange of goods was advantageous to all.*

ad|vent /æ̱dvent/ N-UNCOUNT The **advent** of an important event, invention, or situation is the fact of it starting or coming into existence. [FORMAL] ❏ *The advent of the computer has brought this sort of task within the bounds of possibility.*

Ad|vent N-UNCOUNT In the Christian church, **Advent** is the period beginning four Sundays before Christmas Day.

ad|ven|ture /ædve̱ntʃər/ (adventures) **1** N-COUNT If someone has an **adventure**, they become involved in an unusual, exciting, and sometimes dangerous trip or series of events. ❏ *I set off for a new adventure in Alaska on the first day of the new year.* **2** N-UNCOUNT **Adventure** is excitement and willingness to do new, unusual, or somewhat dangerous things. ❏ *Their cultural backgrounds gave them a spirit of adventure.*

ad|ven|tur|er /ædve̱ntʃərər/ (adventurers) N-COUNT An **adventurer** is a person who enjoys going to new, unusual, and exciting places.

ad|ven|ture|some /ædve̱ntʃərsəm/ ADJ **Adventuresome** means the same as **adventurous**. [AM] ❏ *Every day was exciting and adventuresome.*

ad|ven|tur|ism /ædve̱ntʃərɪzəm/ N-UNCOUNT **Adventurism** is a willingness to take risks, especially in order to obtain an unfair advantage in politics or business. [DISAPPROVAL] ❏ *Lenin dismissed guerrilla warfare as "adventurism."*

ad|ven|tur|ist /ædve̱ntʃərɪst/ (adventurists) ADJ If you describe someone or something as **adventurist**, you disapprove of them because they are willing to take risks in order to gain an unfair advantage in business or politics. [DISAPPROVAL] ❏ *...aggressive and adventurist foreign policy.* • N-COUNT An **adventurist** is someone who behaves in an adventurist way. ❏ *...political adventurists.*

ad|ven|tur|ous /ædve̱ntʃərəs/ **1** ADJ Someone who is **adventurous** is willing to take risks and to try new methods. Something that is **adventurous** involves new things or ideas. ❏ *Warren was an adventurous businessman.* **2** ADJ Someone who is **adventurous** is eager to visit new places and have new experiences. ❏ *He had always wanted an adventurous life in the tropics.*

ad|verb /æ̱dvɜrb/ (adverbs) N-COUNT An **adverb** is a word such as 'slowly,' 'now,' 'very,' 'politically,' or 'fortunately' which adds information about the action, event, or situation mentioned in a clause.

ad|verb group (adverb groups) N-COUNT An **adverb group** or **adverbial group** is a group of words based on an adverb, such as 'very slowly' or 'fortunately for us.' An adverb group can also consist simply of an adverb.

ad|ver|bial /ædvɜ̱rbiəl/ ADJ [usu ADJ n] **Adverbial** means relating to adverbs or like an adverb. ❏ *...an adverbial expression.*

ad|verb phrase (adverb phrases) N-COUNT An **adverb phrase** or **adverbial phrase** is a group of words based on an adverb, such as 'very slowly' or 'fortunately for us.' An adverb phrase can also consist simply of an adverb.

ad|ver|sar|ial /æ̱dvərse͟əriəl/ ADJ If you describe something as **adversarial**, you mean that it involves two or more people or organizations who are opposing each other. [FORMAL] ❏ *In our country there is an adversarial relationship between government and business.*

ad|ver|sary /æ̱dvərseri/ (adversaries) N-COUNT Your **adversary** is someone you are competing with, or arguing or fighting against. ❏ *His political adversaries would like to discredit him.*

ad|verse /ædvɜ̱rs/ ADJ **Adverse** decisions, conditions, or effects are unfavorable to you. ❏ *The police said Mr. Hadfield's decision would have no adverse effect on the progress of the investigation.* • **ad|verse|ly** ADV [ADV with v] ❏ *Price changes must not adversely affect the living standards of the people.*

ad|ver|sity /ædvɜ̱rsɪti/ (adversities) **1** N-VAR **Adversity** is a very difficult or unfavorable situation. ❏ *He showed courage in adversity.* **2** → See feature box at **challenge**

ad|vert /æ̱dvɜrt/ (adverts) N-COUNT An **advert** is an announcement in a newspaper, on television, or on a poster about something such as a product, event, or job. [BRIT]

in AM, use **ad**

ad|ver|tise ✦◇◇ /æ̱dvərtaɪz/ (advertises, advertising, advertised) **1** V-T/V-I If you **advertise** something such as a product, an event, or a job, you tell people about it in newspapers, on television, or on posters in order to encourage them to buy the product, go to the event, or apply for the job. ❏ *The company is spending heavily to advertise its strongest brands.* ❏ *In 2011, the house was advertised for sale at $490,000.* **2** V-I If you **advertise** for someone to do something for you, for example, to work for you or share your accommodation, you announce it in a newspaper, on television, or on a bulletin board. ❏ *We advertised for staff in a local newspaper.* **3** V-T [usu with brd-neg] If you do not **advertise** the fact that something is the case, you try not to let other people know about it. ❏ *There is no need to advertise the fact that you are a single woman.* **4** → see also **advertising**

advertisement | aerial

SYNONYMS
advertise
VERB **1**
publicize: *The author appeared on television to publicize her latest book.*
promote: *Weller has announced a full British tour to promote his second solo album.*
plug: *They're on the show just to plug their book or movie.*

ad|ver|tise|ment /ædvɜːtaɪzmənt/ (**advertisements**) **1** N-COUNT An **advertisement** is an announcement online, or in a newspaper, on television, or on a poster about something such as a product, event, or job. [WRITTEN] ❑ *Miss Parrish recently placed an advertisement in the local newspaper.* **2** N-COUNT If you say that an example of something is an **advertisement** for that thing in general, you mean that it shows how good that thing is. ❑ *The Treviso team was an effective advertisement for the improving state of Italian club rugby.*

ad|ver|tis|er /ædvɜːtaɪzər/ (**advertisers**) N-COUNT An **advertiser** is a person or company that pays for a product, event, or job to be advertised in a newspaper, on television, or on a poster. ❑ *When will advertisers stop bombarding women with images of unattainable beauty?*

ad|ver|tis|ing /ædvɜːtaɪzɪŋ/ N-UNCOUNT **Advertising** is the activity of creating advertisements and making sure people see them. ❑ *I work in advertising.*

ad|ver|tis|ing agen|cy [BRIT] → see **ad agency**
ad|ver|tis|ing cam|paign [BRIT] → see **ad campaign**
ad|vice ✦✧✧ /ædvaɪs/ N-UNCOUNT If you give someone **advice**, you tell them what you think they should do in a particular situation. ❑ *Don't be afraid to ask for advice about ordering the meal.* ❑ *Take my advice and stay away from him!*

USAGE
advice
Advice is an uncountable noun. Don't say ~~advices~~ or ~~an advice~~. You can say **a piece of advice**. *Could I give you a piece of advice?*

COLLOCATIONS
advice
NOUN
noun + **advice**: career, diet, investment, lifestyle, travel; parenting, relationship
adjective + **advice**: dietary, legal, medical, professional; expert, impartial, independent, specialist; helpful, practical, sage, sound
verb + **advice**: dispense, give, offer, provide; obtain, seek; follow, heed; ignore, reject

ad|vice col|umn (**advice columns**) N-COUNT In a newspaper or magazine, the **advice column** contains letters from readers about their personal problems, and advice on what to do about them. [AM]

in BRIT, use **agony column**

ad|vice col|umn|ist (**advice columnists**) N-COUNT An **advice columnist** is a person who writes a column in a newspaper or magazine in which they reply to readers who have written to them for advice on their personal problems. [AM] ❑ *...the advice columnist at the local paper.*

in BRIT, use **agony aunt**

ad|vice line (**advice lines**) N-COUNT An **advice line** is the same as a **help line**. [BRIT]

ad|vis|able /ædvaɪzəbəl/ ADJ [v-link ADJ] If you tell someone that it is **advisable** to do something, you are suggesting that they should do it, because it is sensible or is likely to achieve the result they want. [FORMAL] ❑ *Because of the popularity of the region, it is advisable to book hotels or camp sites in advance.*

ad|vise ✦✧✧ /ædvaɪz/ (**advises, advising, advised**) **1** V-T If you **advise** someone to do something, you tell them what you think they should do. ❑ *The minister advised him to leave as soon as possible.* ❑ *I would strongly advise against it.* **2** V-T If an expert **advises** people on a particular subject, he or she gives them help and information on that subject. ❑ *...an officer who advises undergraduates from the University on money matters.*

ad|vis|ed|ly /ædvaɪzɪdli/ ADV [ADV after v] If you say that you are using a word or expression **advisedly**, you mean that you have deliberately chosen to use it, even though it may sound unusual, wrong, or offensive, because it draws attention to what you are saying. ❑ *I say "boys" advisedly because we are talking almost entirely about male behavior.* ❑ *What a crazy scheme, and I use that term advisedly.*

ad|vise|ment /ædvaɪzmənt/ PHRASE If someone in authority takes a matter **under advisement**, they decide that the matter needs to be considered more carefully, often by experts. [AM, FORMAL] ❑ *I will take the suggestion under advisement, and refer it to the board.*

ad|vis|er ✦✧✧ /ædvaɪzər/ (**advisers**) also **advisor** N-COUNT An **adviser** is an expert whose job is to give advice to another person or to a group of people. ❑ *In Washington, the president and his advisers spent the day in meetings.*

ad|vi|so|ry /ædvaɪzəri/ (**advisories**) **1** N-COUNT An **advisory** is an official announcement or report that warns people about bad weather, diseases, or other dangers or problems. [AM] ❑ *26 states have issued health advisories.* **2** ADJ An **advisory** group regularly gives suggestions and help to people or organizations, especially about a particular subject or area of activity. [FORMAL] ❑ *...members of the advisory committee on the safety of nuclear installations.*

ad|vo|ca|cy /ædvəkəsi/ **1** N-SING Someone's **advocacy** of a particular action or plan is their act of recommending it publicly. [FORMAL] ❑ *I support your advocacy of free trade.* **2** N-UNCOUNT An **advocacy** group or organization is one that tries to influence the decisions of a government or other authority. [AM] ❑ *Consumer advocacy groups are not so enthusiastic about removing restrictions on the telephone companies.*

ad|vo|cate ✦✧✧ (**advocates, advocating, advocated**)

The verb is pronounced /ædvəkeɪt/. The noun is pronounced /ædvəkɪt/.

1 V-T If you **advocate** a particular action or plan, you recommend it publicly. [FORMAL] ❑ *Mr. Williams is a conservative who advocates fewer government controls on business.* **2** N-COUNT An **advocate** of a particular action or plan is someone who recommends it publicly. [FORMAL] ❑ *He was a strong advocate of free market policies and a multi-party system.* **3** N-COUNT An **advocate** for a particular group is a person who works for the interests of that group. [AM] ❑ *...advocates for the charity.* **4** N-COUNT An **advocate** is a lawyer who speaks in favor of someone or defends them in a court of law. [LEGAL]

SYNONYMS
advocate
VERB **1**
recommend: *We strongly recommend reporting the incident to the police.*
support: *They support a total ban on imported coal*
champion: *The amendments had been championed by pro-democracy activists.*
encourage: *Their task is to help encourage private investment in Russia.*
NOUN **2**
supporter: *Bradley was a major supporter of the 1986 tax reform plan.*
champion: *He was once known as a champion of social reform.*
proponent: *Halsey was a leading proponent of the values of progressive education.*

ad|woman /ædwʊmən/ (**adwomen**) N-COUNT An **adwoman** is a woman who works in advertising. [INFORMAL]

aegis /iːdʒɪs/ PREP-PHRASE Something that is done **under the aegis of** a person or organization is done with their official support and backing. [FORMAL] ❑ *The space program will continue under the aegis of the armed forces.*

aeon /iːɒn/ [BRIT] → see **eon**

aer|ate /eəreɪt/ (**aerates, aerating, aerated**) V-T To **aerate** a substance means to cause air or gas to pass through it. ❑ *Aerate your lawn to allow it to breathe and absorb water better.*

aer|ial /eəriəl/ (**aerials**) **1** ADJ [ADJ n] You talk about **aerial** attacks and **aerial** photographs to indicate that people or things on the ground are attacked or photographed by people in airplanes. ❑ *Weeks of aerial bombardment had destroyed factories and highways.* ❑ *Patterns that are invisible on the ground can be the most striking part of an aerial photograph.* ◨2 N-COUNT An **aerial** is a device that receives television or radio signals. [mainly BRIT]

> in AM, usually use **antenna**

aerie /ɛəri, ɪəri/ (aeries) ◨1 N-COUNT An **aerie** is the nest of a bird of prey such as an eagle, and is usually built high up in the mountains. ◨2 N-COUNT If you refer to a place such as a house or a castle as an **aerie**, you mean it is built high up and is difficult to reach. [mainly BRIT, LITERARY]

PREFIX

aero-
is used at the beginning of words, especially nouns, that refer to things or activities connected with air or movement through the air. *For example,* **aerodynamics** *is the science of how objects move through the air.*

aero|bat|ics /ɛərəbætɪks/

> The form **aerobatic** is used as a modifier.

N-PLURAL **Aerobatics** are skillful displays of flying, usually to entertain people watching from the ground.

aero|bic /ɛəroʊbɪk/ ADJ [usu ADJ n] **Aerobic** activity exercises and strengthens your heart and lungs. ❑ *Aerobic exercise gets the heart pumping and helps you to burn fat.*

aero|bics /ɛəroʊbɪks/ N-UNCOUNT [oft N n] **Aerobics** is a form of exercise which increases the amount of oxygen in your blood, and strengthens your heart and lungs. The verb that follows **aerobics** may be either singular or plural. ❑ *I'd like to join an aerobics class to improve my fitness.*

aero|drome /ɛərədroʊm/ [BRIT] → see **airdrome**

aero|dy|nam|ic /ɛəroʊdaɪnæmɪk/ ADJ If something such as a car has an **aerodynamic** shape or design, it goes faster and uses less fuel than other cars because the air passes over it more easily. ❑ *The secret of the machine lies in the aerodynamic shape of the one-piece, carbon-fiber frame.*

aero|dy|nam|ics /ɛəroʊdaɪnæmɪks/

> The form **aerodynamic** is used as a modifier.

N-UNCOUNT **Aerodynamics** is the study of the way in which objects move through the air.

aero|nau|ti|cal /ɛərənɔtɪkəl/ ADJ [ADJ n] **Aeronautical** means involving or relating to the design and construction of airplanes. ❑ *...the biggest aeronautical research laboratory in the world.*

aero|naut|ics /ɛərənɔtɪks/ N-UNCOUNT **Aeronautics** is the science of designing and building airplanes.

aero|plane /ɛərəpleɪn/ (aeroplanes) N-COUNT An **aeroplane** is a vehicle with wings and one or more engines that enable it to fly through the air. [BRIT]

> in AM, use **airplane**

aero|sol /ɛərəsɔl/ (aerosols) N-COUNT [usu N n] An **aerosol** can or spray is a small container in which a liquid such as paint or deodorant is kept under pressure. When you press a button, the liquid is forced out as a fine spray or foam. ❑ *...an aerosol can of insecticide.*

aero|space /ɛərəspeɪs/ N-UNCOUNT [usu N n] **Aerospace** companies are involved in developing and making aircraft, rockets, missiles, space vehicles, and related equipment. ❑ *...the U.S. aerospace industry.*

aes|thete /ɛsθit/ (aesthetes) also **esthete** N-COUNT An **aesthete** is someone who loves and appreciates works of art and beautiful things.

aes|thet|ic /ɛsθɛtɪk/ also **esthetic** ◨1 ADJ **Aesthetic** is used to talk about beauty or art, and people's appreciation of beautiful things. ❑ *...products chosen for their aesthetic appeal as well as their durability and quality.* • N-SING The **aesthetic** of a work of art is its aesthetic quality. ❑ *He responded very strongly to the aesthetic of this particular work.* • **aes|theti|cal|ly** /ɛsθɛtɪkli/ ADV ❑ *A statue which is aesthetically pleasing to one person, however, may be repulsive to another.* ◨2 → See feature box at **fine art**

aes|thet|ics /ɛsθɛtɪks/ also **esthetics** N-UNCOUNT **Aesthetics** is a branch of philosophy concerned with the study of the idea of beauty.

aeti|ol|ogy /itiɪlɒdʒi/ (aetiologies) → see **etiology**

afar /əfɑr/ ADV **Afar** means a long way away. [LITERARY] ❑ *Seen from afar, its towering buildings beckon the visitor in.*

af|fable /æfəbəl/ ADJ Someone who is **affable** is pleasant and friendly. ❑ *Mr. Brooke is an extremely affable and approachable man.*

af|fair ♦♦◇ /əfɛər/ (affairs) ◨1 N-SING If an event or a series of events has been mentioned and you want to talk about it again, you can refer to it as the **affair**. ❑ *The administration has mishandled the whole affair.* ◨2 N-SING You can refer to an important or interesting event or situation as 'the ... **affair**.' [mainly JOURNALISM] ❑ *...the damage caused to the CIA and FBI in the aftermath of the Watergate affair.* ◨3 N-SING You can describe the main quality of an event by saying that it is a particular kind of **affair**. ❑ *Michael said that his planned 10-day visit would be a purely private affair.* ◨4 N-COUNT If two people who are married, but who are not married to each other have an **affair**, they have a sexual relationship. ❑ *Married male supervisors were carrying on affairs with female subordinates in the office.* ◨5 → see also **love affair** ◨6 N-PLURAL You can use **affairs** to refer to all the important facts or activities that are connected with a particular subject. ❑ *He does not want to interfere in the internal affairs of another country.* ◨7 → see also **current affairs**, **state of affairs** ◨8 N-PLURAL Your **affairs** are all the matters connected with your life that you consider to be private and normally deal with yourself. ❑ *The unexpectedness of my father's death meant that his affairs were not entirely in order.*

af|fect ♦♦◇ /əfɛkt/ (affects, affecting, affected) ◨1 V-T If something **affects** a person or thing, it influences them or causes them to change in some way. ❑ *Nicotine adversely affects the functioning of the heart and arteries.* ❑ *More than seven million people have been affected by drought.* ◨2 V-T If a disease **affects** someone, it causes them to become ill. ❑ *Arthritis is a crippling disease which affects people all over the world.* ◨3 V-T If something or someone **affects** you, they make you feel a strong emotion, especially sadness or pity. ❑ *If Jim had been more independent, the divorce would not have affected him as deeply.*

SYNONYMS

affect
VERB ◨1
influence: *They still influence what's played on the radio.*
impact: *Such schemes mean little unless they impact people.*
alter: *They have never altered their programs by a single day.*

af|fec|ta|tion /æfɛkteɪʃən/ (affectations) N-VAR If you say that someone's attitude or behavior is an **affectation**, you disapprove of the fact that it is not genuine or natural, but is intended to impress other people. [DISAPPROVAL] ❑ *I wore sunglasses all the time and people thought it was an affectation.*

af|fect|ed /əfɛktɪd/ ADJ [usu ADJ n] If you describe someone's behavior as **affected**, you disapprove of the fact that they behave in an unnatural way that is intended to impress other people. [DISAPPROVAL] ❑ *She had an affected air and a disdainful look.*

af|fect|ing /əfɛktɪŋ/ ADJ If you describe something such as a story or a piece of music as **affecting**, you think it is good because it makes you feel a strong emotion, especially sadness or pity. [LITERARY, APPROVAL] ❑ *...an affecting drama about a woman with a terminal illness.*

af|fec|tion /əfɛkʃən/ (affections) ◨1 N-UNCOUNT If you regard someone or something with **affection**, you like them and are fond of them. ❑ *She thought of him with affection.* ◨2 N-PLURAL Your **affections** are your feelings of love or fondness for someone. ❑ *Caroline is the object of his affections.*

af|fec|tion|ate /əfɛkʃənɪt/ ADJ If you are **affectionate**, you show your love or fondness for another person in the way that you behave toward them. ❑ *They seemed devoted to each other and were openly affectionate.* • **af|fec|tion|ate|ly** ADV [ADV with v] ❑ *He looked affectionately at his niece.*

af|fi|da|vit /æfɪdeɪvɪt/ (affidavits) N-COUNT An **affidavit** is a written statement that you swear is true and that may be used as evidence in a court of law. [LEGAL] ❑ *In his sworn affidavit, Roche outlined a history of actions against him by the church.*

af|fili|ate (affiliates, affiliating, affiliated)
The noun is pronounced /əfɪliɪt/. The verb is pronounced /əfɪlieɪt/.

1 N-COUNT An **affiliate** is an organization which is officially connected with another, larger organization or is a member of it. [FORMAL] ❑ *The World Chess Federation has affiliates in around 120 countries.* **2** V-I If an organization **affiliates with** another larger organization, it forms a close connection with the larger organization or becomes a member of it. [FORMAL] ❑ *He wanted to affiliate with a U.S. firm because he needed expert advice in legal affairs.*

af|fili|at|ed /əfɪlieɪtɪd/ **1** ADJ [v-link ADJ with n, ADJ n] If an organization is **affiliated** with another larger organization, it is officially connected with the larger organization or is a member of it. [FORMAL] ❑ *The consortium is a nonprofit group affiliated with the University of Chicago.* **2** ADJ [v-link ADJ with/to n, ADJ n] If a professional person, such as a lawyer or doctor, is **affiliated** with an organization, they are officially connected with that organization or do some official work for it. [FORMAL] ❑ *He will remain affiliated with the firm as a special associate director.* ❑ *...our affiliated members.*

af|filia|tion /əfɪlieɪʃən/ (**affiliations**) N-VAR If one group has an **affiliation** with another group, it has a close or official connection with it. [FORMAL] ❑ *The kidnappers had no affiliation with any militant group.*

af|fin|ity /əfɪnɪti/ N-SING If you have an **affinity** with someone or something, you feel that you are similar to them or that you know and understand them very well. ❑ *He has a close affinity with the landscape and people he knew when he was growing up.*

af|fin|ity card (**affinity cards**) N-COUNT An **affinity card** is a type of credit card. The bank which issues the card gives a small amount of money to a charity or institution each time the customer spends a certain amount with their card.

af|firm /əfɜrm/ (**affirms, affirming, affirmed**) **1** V-T If you **affirm** that something is true or that something exists, you state firmly and publicly that it is true or exists. [FORMAL] ❑ *The court affirmed that the information can be made public under the Freedom of Information Act.* ❑ *...a speech in which he affirmed a commitment to lower taxes.* ● **af|fir|ma|tion** /æfərmeɪʃən/ (**affirmations**) N-VAR ❑ *The North Atlantic Treaty begins with the affirmation that its parties "reaffirm their faith in the purposes and principles of the Charter of the United Nations."* **2** V-T If an event **affirms** something, it shows that it is true or exists. [FORMAL] ❑ *Everything I had accomplished seemed to affirm that opinion.* ● **af|fir|ma|tion** N-UNCOUNT [also a N] ❑ *The ruling was a welcome affirmation of the constitutional right to free speech.*

af|firma|tive /əfɜrmətɪv/ **1** ADJ An **affirmative** word or gesture indicates that you agree with what someone has said or that the answer to a question is 'yes.' [FORMAL] ❑ *Haig was desperately eager for an affirmative answer.* **2** ADJ In grammar, an **affirmative** clause is positive and does not contain a negative word. **3** PHRASE If you reply to a question **in the affirmative,** you say 'yes' or make a gesture that means 'yes.' [FORMAL] ❑ *He asked me if I was ready. I answered in the affirmative.*

af|firma|tive ac|tion N-UNCOUNT **Affirmative action** is the policy of making sure that people such as women, members of smaller racial groups, and people with disabilities get a fair share of the opportunities available. [AM] ❑ *Despite nearly a decade of affirmative action since apartheid was dismantled, few Black sportsmen have reached the top level.*

in BRIT, use **positive discrimination**

af|fix /æfɪks/ (**affixes**) N-COUNT An **affix** is a letter or group of letters, for example, 'un-' or '-y,' which is added to either the beginning or the end of a word to form a different word with a different meaning. For example, 'un-' is added to 'kind' to form 'unkind.' Compare **prefix** and **suffix**.

af|flict /əflɪkt/ (**afflicts, afflicting, afflicted**) V-T If you are **afflicted** by pain, illness, or disaster, it affects you badly and makes you suffer. [FORMAL] ❑ *The organization has been afflicted by political corruption for decades.* ❑ *There are two main problems which afflict people with hearing impairments.*

af|flic|tion /əflɪkʃən/ (**afflictions**) N-VAR An **affliction** is something that causes physical or mental suffering. [FORMAL] ❑ *Hay fever is an affliction that arrives at an early age.*

af|flu|ence /æfluəns/ N-UNCOUNT **Affluence** is the state of having a lot of money or a high standard of living. [FORMAL] ❑ *The postwar era was one of new affluence for the working class.*

af|flu|ent /æfluənt/ ADJ If you are **affluent**, you have a lot of money. ❑ *He found himself among some very affluent people at the event.* ● N-PLURAL **The affluent** are people who are affluent. ❑ *The diet of the affluent has not changed much over the decades.*

af|ford ✦✧ /əfɔrd/ (**affords, affording, afforded**) **1** V-T If you cannot **afford** something, you do not have enough money to pay for it. ❑ *My parents can't even afford a new refrigerator.* ❑ *The arts should be available to more people at prices they can afford.* **2** V-T If you say that you cannot **afford** to do something or allow it to happen, you mean that you must not do it or must prevent it from happening because it would be harmful or embarrassing to you. ❑ *We can't afford to wait.*

USAGE

afford
You use **afford** with **can**, **could**, or **be able to**. Don't say that someone 'affords' something. *It's too expensive – we can't afford it. When will we be able to afford a new TV?*

---

af|ford|able /əfɔrdəbəl/ **1** ADJ If something is **affordable**, most people have enough money to buy it. ❑ *...the availability of affordable housing.* **2** → See feature box at **town**

af|for|esta|tion /æfɔrɪsteɪʃən/ N-UNCOUNT **Afforestation** is the process of planting large numbers of trees on land that has few or no trees on it. ❑ *Since the Sixties, afforestation has completely changed the countryside.*

af|front /əfrʌnt/ (**affronts, affronting, affronted**) **1** V-T If something **affronts** you, you feel insulted and hurt because of it. [FORMAL] ❑ *One recent example, which particularly affronted Kasparov, was at the European team championship in Hungary.* **2** N-COUNT If something is an **affront** to you, it is an obvious insult to you. ❑ *It's an affront to human dignity to treat people so poorly.*

Af|ghan /æfgæn/ (**Afghans**) ADJ **Afghan** means belonging or relating to Afghanistan, or to its people or language. ❑ *...the Afghan capital, Kabul.* ● N-COUNT An **Afghan** is a person who comes from Afghanistan.

afi|cio|na|do /əfɪʃiənɑdoʊ/ (**aficionados**) N-COUNT If someone is an **aficionado** of something, they like it and know a lot about it. ❑ *I happen to be an aficionado of the opera, and I love art museums.* ❑ *...a jazz aficionado.*

afield /əfild/ PHRASE **Further afield** or **farther afield** means in places or areas other than the nearest or most obvious one. ❑ *They enjoy participating in a wide variety of activities, both locally and further afield.*

afire /əfaɪər/ ADJ [v-link ADJ, v n ADJ] If something is **afire** or is set **afire**, it is on fire or looks as if it is on fire.

aflame /əfleɪm/ ADJ [v-link ADJ, v n ADJ] If something is on fire, you can say it is **aflame**. [LITERARY]

afloat /əfloʊt/ **1** ADJ If someone or something is **afloat**, they remain partly above the surface of water and do not sink. ❑ *They talked modestly of their valiant efforts to keep the tanker afloat.* **2** ADJ If a person, business, or country stays **afloat** or is kept **afloat**, they have just enough money to pay their debts and continue operating. [BUSINESS] ❑ *A number of efforts were being made to keep the company afloat.*

afoot /əfʊt/ ADJ [v-link ADJ] If you say that a plan or scheme is **afoot**, it is already happening or being planned, but you do not know much about it. ❑ *Everybody knew that something awful was afoot.*

afore|men|tioned /əfɔrmɛnʃənd/ ADJ [det ADJ, usu the ADJ n] If you refer to **the aforementioned** person or subject, you mean the person or subject that has already been mentioned. [FORMAL] ❑ *This is the draft of a declaration that will be issued at the end of the aforementioned U.N. conference.*

afore|said /əfɔrsɛd/ ADJ [det ADJ, usu the ADJ n] **Aforesaid** means the same as **aforementioned**. [FORMAL] ❑ *...the aforesaid organizations and institutions.*

afoul /əfaʊl/ PHRASE [PHR n] If you **run afoul of** someone or something, you do something that causes problems with them. [AM] ❑ *All of them had run afoul of the law at some time or other.*

afraid /əfreɪd/ **1** ADJ [v-link ADJ] If you are **afraid** of someone or **afraid** to do something, you are frightened because you think that something very unpleasant is going to happen to you. ❏ *She did not seem at all afraid.* ❏ *I was afraid of the other boys.* **2** ADJ [v-link ADJ] If you are **afraid** for someone else, you are worried that something horrible is going to happen to them. ❏ *She's afraid for her family in Somalia.* **3** ADJ [v-link ADJ] If you are **afraid** that something unpleasant will happen, you are worried that it may happen and you want to avoid it. ❏ *I was afraid that nobody would believe me.* **4** PHRASE If you want to apologize to someone or to disagree with them in a polite way, you can say **I'm afraid.** [SPOKEN, POLITENESS] ❏ *We don't have anything like that, I'm afraid.*

USAGE

afraid
Don't use 'afraid' in front of a noun. For example, don't say 'an afraid boy.' Say 'a frightened boy.' What's the best way to comfort a **frightened child**?

---

afresh /əfrɛʃ/ ADV [ADV after v] If you do something **afresh**, you do it again in a different way. ❏ *They believe that the only hope for the French left is to start afresh.*

Af|ri|can /ˈæfrɪkən/ (**Africans**) **1** ADJ **African** means belonging or relating to the continent of Africa, or to its countries or people. ❏ *...the African continent.* ❏ *...African countries.* **2** ADJ **African** means belonging or relating to Black people who come from Africa. ❏ *...traditional African culture.* ❏ *...dance music with African roots.* **3** ADJ **African** is used to describe someone, usually a Black person, who comes from Africa. ❏ *...African women.* • N-COUNT An **African** is someone who is African. ❏ *Fish is a staple in the diet of many Africans.*

African-American (**African-Americans**) N-COUNT **African-Americans** are Black people living in the United States who are descended from families that originally came from Africa. ❏ *Today African-Americans are 12 percent of the population.* • ADJ **African-American** is also an adjective. ❏ *...a group of African-American community leaders.*

African-Caribbean (**African-Caribbeans**) ADJ [usu ADJ n] **African-Caribbean** refers to people from the Caribbean whose ancestors came from Africa. ❏ *...modern African-Caribbean culture.* • N-COUNT An **African-Caribbean** is someone who is African-Caribbean.

Af|ri|kaans /ˌæfrɪˈkɑːns/ N-UNCOUNT [oft N n] **Afrikaans** is one of the official languages of South Africa. ❏ *...a radical Afrikaans newspaper.*

Af|ri|kan|er /ˌæfrɪˈkɑːnər/ (**Afrikaners**) ADJ **Afrikaner** means belonging or relating to the White people in South Africa whose ancestors were Dutch. • N-COUNT An **Afrikaner** is someone who is Afrikaner.

Afro /ˈæfroʊ/ (**Afros**) **1** ADJ [usu ADJ n] **Afro** is used to describe something that is associated with African people or culture. **2** ADJ An **Afro** hairstyle is curled and has a full rounded shape. **3** N-COUNT An **Afro** is an Afro hairstyle.

Afro- /ˈæfroʊ-/ COMB IN ADJ; N-COUNT **Afro-** is used to form adjectives and nouns that describe something that is connected with Africa. ❏ *...a very well known Afro-American family.* ❏ *...an Afro-centric fashion show.*

Afro-Caribbean (**Afro-Caribbeans**) ADJ **Afro-Caribbean** means the same as **African-Caribbean**.

aft /æft/ ADV If you go **aft** in a boat or plane, you go to the back of it. If you are **aft**, you are in the back. ❏ *I went aft to take my turn at the helm.*

af|ter /ˈæftər/

In addition to the uses shown below, **after** is used in phrasal verbs such as 'ask after,' 'look after,' and 'take after.'

1 PREP If something happens **after** a particular date or event, it happens during the period of time that follows that date or event. ❏ *After May 19, strikes were occurring on a daily basis.* ❏ *After breakfast Amy took a taxi to the station.* • CONJ **After** is also a conjunction. ❏ *After Don told me this, he spoke of his mother.* **2** PREP [PREP -ing] If you do one thing **after** doing another, you do it during the period of time that follows the other thing. ❏ *After completing and signing it, please return the form to us in the envelope provided.* **3** PREP [n PREP n] You use **after** when you are talking about time. For example, if something is going to happen during **the day after** or **the weekend after** a particular time, it is going to happen during the following day or during the following weekend. ❏ *She's leaving the day after tomorrow.* • ADV [ADV after v] **After** is also an adverb. ❏ *Tomorrow. Or the day after.* **4** PREP If you go **after** someone, you follow or chase them. ❏ *Alice said to Gina, "Why don't you go after him, he's your son."* **5** PREP If you are **after** something, you are trying to get it. ❏ *They were after the money.* **6** PREP If you call, shout, or stare **after** someone, you call, shout, or stare at them as they move away from you. ❏ *"Come back!" he called after me.* **7** PREP If you tell someone that one place is a particular distance **after** another, you mean that it is situated beyond the other place and further away from you. ❏ *...a station 134 miles after the train starts its journey.* **8** PREP If one thing is written **after** another thing on a page, it is written following it or underneath it. ❏ *I wrote my name after Penny's at the bottom of the page.* **9** PREP You use **after** in order to give the most important aspect of something when comparing it with another aspect. ❏ *After Germany, America is Britain's second-biggest customer.* **10** PREP To be named **after** someone means to be given the same name as them. ❏ *He persuaded Virginia to name the baby after him.* **11** PREP **After** is used when telling the time. If it is, for example, **ten after six**, the time is ten minutes past six. [AM] **12** CONVENTION If you say '**after you**' to someone, you are being polite and allowing them to go in front of you or through a doorway before you do. [POLITENESS] **13** **after all** → see all ③ **14** PHRASE If you do something to several things **one after the other** or **one after another**, you do it to one, then the next, and so on, with no break between your actions ❏ *...a lawyer who wins three cases, one after another.* **15** PHRASE If something happens **day after day** or **year after year**, it happens every day or every year, for a long time. ❏ *...people who'd been coming here year after year.*

after- /ˈæftər-/ COMB IN ADJ [ADJ n] **After-** is added to nouns to form adjectives which indicate that something takes place or exists after an event or process. ❏ *...an after-dinner speech.*

after|care /ˈæftərkɛər/

in BRIT, also use **after-care**

N-UNCOUNT **Aftercare** is the nursing and care of people who have been treated in a hospital, and who are now recovering. ❏ *Individualized aftercare is given to each patient.* ❏ *...a 14-week aftercare program.*

after|effect /ˈæftərɪfɛkt/ (**aftereffects**) N-COUNT [usu pl] The **aftereffects** of an event, experience, or substance are the conditions which result from it. ❏ *...people still suffering from the aftereffects of the world's worst nuclear accident.*

in BRIT, use **after-effect**

after|glow /ˈæftərɡloʊ/ **1** N-UNCOUNT [oft with poss] The **afterglow** is the glow that remains after a light has gone, for example, after the sun has gone down. [LITERARY] ❏ *...the light of the sunset's afterglow.* **2** N-UNCOUNT [oft N of n] You can refer to the good feeling or effects that remain after an event as the **afterglow**. ❏ *Ferguson should be basking in the afterglow of his successes.*

after-hours ADJ [ADJ n] You use **after-hours** to describe activities that happen after the end of the usual time for them. ❏ *...an after-hours club in the Boulevard Park area.*

after|life /ˈæftərlaɪf/ (**afterlives**) also **after-life** N-COUNT [usu sing] The **afterlife** is a life that some people believe begins when you die, for example, a life in heaven or as another person or animal.

after|market /ˈæftərmɑrkɪt/ **1** N-SING The **aftermarket** is all the related products that are sold after an item, especially a car, has been bought. [BUSINESS] ❏ *The company serves the national automotive aftermarket with a broad range of accessory and recreational-vehicle products.* **2** N-SING The **aftermarket** in stocks and bonds is the buying and selling of them after they have been issued. [BUSINESS] ❏ *It's illegal to get into a formal agreement with investors that they'll buy in the aftermarket.*

after|math /ˈæftərmæθ/ N-SING The **aftermath** of an important event, especially a harmful one, is the situation that results from it. ❏ *In the aftermath of the coup, the troops opened fire on the demonstrators.*

after|noon /ˈæftərnuːn/ (**afternoons**) N-VAR The **afternoon** is the part of each day that begins at lunchtime and ends at about six o'clock. ❑ *He's arriving in the afternoon.* ❑ *He had stayed in his room all afternoon.*

after|noon tea (**afternoon teas**) N-VAR **Afternoon tea** is a small meal you can have in the afternoon. It includes a cup of tea and food such as sandwiches and cakes. [BRIT]

after-party (**after-parties**) N-COUNT An **after-party** is a small party held after a larger event, to which only a small group of guests is invited. ❑ *He met her at a fashion-show after-party.*

after-sales ser|vice (**after-sales services**) N-VAR A company's **after-sales service** is all the help and information that it provides to customers after they have bought a particular product. [BUSINESS] ❑ *...a local retailer who offers a good after-sales service.* ❑ *They are also attempting to keep the car buyer as a long-term customer by offering after-sales service.*

after-school ADJ [ADJ n] **After-school** activities are those that are organized for children in the afternoon or evening after they have finished school. ❑ *...an after-school program for advanced students.*

after|shave /ˈæftərʃeɪv/ (**aftershaves**) also **after-shave** N-MASS **Aftershave** is a liquid with a pleasant smell that men sometimes put on their faces after shaving. ❑ *...a bottle of aftershave.*

after|shock /ˈæftərʃɒk/ (**aftershocks**) ◼ N-COUNT **Aftershocks** are smaller earthquakes that occur after a large earthquake. ◼ N-COUNT [usu with supp] People sometimes refer to the effects of an important event, especially a bad one, as the **aftershock**. [mainly JOURNALISM] ❑ *They were already under stress, thanks to the aftershock of last year's drought.*

after|taste /ˈæftərteɪst/ also **after-taste** N-SING An **aftertaste** is a taste that remains in your mouth after you have finished eating or drinking something.

after|thought /ˈæftərθɔːt/ (**afterthoughts**) N-COUNT [usu sing, usu a N] If you do or say something as an **afterthought**, you do or say it after something else as an addition, perhaps without careful thought. ❑ *Almost as an afterthought he added that he missed her.*

after|ward /ˈæftərwərd/ also **afterwards** ADV [ADV with cl] If you do something or if something happens **afterward**, you do it or it happens after a particular event or time that has already been mentioned. ❑ *Shortly afterward, police arrested four suspects.*

after|word /ˈɑːftərwɜːrd/ N-SING An **afterword** is a short essay at the end of a book, usually written by the author.

again /əˈɡɛn, əˈɡeɪn/ ◼ ADV You use **again** to indicate that something happens a second time, or after it has already happened before. ❑ *He kissed her again.* ❑ *Again there was a short silence.* ◼ ADV [ADV after v] You use **again** to indicate that something is now in a particular state or place that it used to be in. ❑ *He opened his attaché case, removed a folder, then closed it again.* ◼ ADV [ADV cl] You can use **again** when you want to point out that there is a similarity between the subject that you are talking about now and a previous subject. ❑ *Again the pregnancy was very similar to my previous two.* ◼ ADV [ADV with cl] You can use **again** in expressions such as **but again**, **then again**, and **there again** when you want to introduce a remark that contrasts with or weakens something that you have just said. ❑ *You may be happy to buy imitation leather, and then again, you may wonder what you're getting for your money.* ◼ ADV [cl ADV] You can add **again** to the end of your question when you are asking someone to tell you something that you have forgotten or that they have already told you. [SPOKEN] ❑ *Sorry, what's your name again?.* ◼ ADV [amount ADV] You use **again** in expressions such as **half as much again** when you are indicating how much greater one amount is than another amount that you have just mentioned or are about to mention. [BRIT] ❑ *A similar wine from France would cost you half as much again.* ◼ PHRASE You can use **again and again** or **time and again** to emphasize that something happens many times. [EMPHASIS] ❑ *He would go over his work again and again until he felt he had it right.* ◼ **now and again** → see **now** ◼ **once again** → see **once**

against /əˈɡɛnst, əˈɡeɪnst/

In addition to the uses shown below, **against** is used in phrasal verbs such as 'come up against,' 'guard against,' and 'hold against.'

◼ PREP If one thing is leaning or pressing **against** another, it is touching it. ❑ *She leaned against him.* ❑ *On a table pushed against a wall there were bottles of beer and wine.* ◼ PREP If you are **against** something such as a plan, policy, or system, you think it is wrong, bad, or stupid. ❑ *Taxes are unpopular – it is understandable that voters are against them.* ❑ *Joan was very much against commencing drug treatment.* • ADV [ADV after v] **Against** is also an adverb. ❑ *The vote for the suspension of the party was 283 in favor with 29 against.* ◼ PREP If you compete **against** someone in a game, you try to beat them. ❑ *This is the first of two games against Denver in the next five days.* ◼ PREP If you take action **against** someone or something, you try to harm them. ❑ *Security forces are still using violence against opponents of the government.* ◼ PREP If you take action **against** a possible future event, you try to prevent it. ❑ *Experts have been discussing how to improve the fight against crime.* ◼ PREP If you do something **against** someone's wishes, advice, or orders, you do not do what they want you to do or tell you to do. ❑ *He discharged himself from the hospital against the advice of doctors.* ◼ PREP If you do something in order to protect yourself **against** something unpleasant or harmful, you do something that will make its effects on you less serious if it happens. ❑ *Any business needs insurance against ordinary risks such as fire, flood, and breakage.* ◼ PREP If something is **against** the law or **against** the rules, there is a law or a rule which says that you must not do it. ❑ *It is against the law to detain you against your will for any length of time.* ◼ PREP If you are moving **against** a current, tide, or wind, you are moving in the opposite direction to it. ❑ *...swimming upstream against the current.* ◼ PREP If something happens or is considered **against** a particular background of events, it is considered in relation to those events, because those events are relevant to it. ❑ *The profits rise was achieved against a backdrop of falling metal prices.* ◼ PREP If something is measured or valued **against** something else, it is measured or valued by comparing it with the other thing. ❑ *Our policies have to be judged against a clear test: will it improve the standard of education?* ◼ PREP [n PREP] The odds **against** something happening are the chances or odds that it will not happen. ❑ *The odds against him surviving are incredible.* • ADV [n ADV] **Against** is also an adverb. ❑ *What were the odds against?* ◼ PHRASE If you **have** something **against** someone or something, you dislike them. ❑ *Have you got something against women, Les?* ◼ **up against** → see **up** ② ◼ **against the clock** → see **clock**

agape /əˈɡeɪp/ ADJ [v-link ADJ] If you describe someone as having their mouth **agape**, their mouth is open very wide, often because they are very surprised by something. [WRITTEN] ❑ *She stood looking at Carmen with her mouth agape.*

ag|ate /ˈæɡɪt/ (**agates**) N-VAR **Agate** is a very hard stone which is used to make jewelry.

age /eɪdʒ/ (**ages, aging** or **ageing, aged**) ◼ N-VAR Your **age** is the number of years that you have lived. ❑ *She has a nephew who is just ten years of age.* ❑ *At the age of sixteen he qualified for a place at the University of North Carolina.* ◼ N-VAR The **age** of a thing is the number of years since it was made. ❑ *Everything in the room looks in keeping with the age of the building.* ◼ N-UNCOUNT **Age** is the state of being old or the process of becoming older. ❑ *Perhaps he has grown wiser with age.* ❑ *This cologne, like wine, improves with age.* ◼ V-T/V-I When someone **ages**, or when something **ages** them, they seem much older and less strong or less alert. ❑ *He had always looked so young, but he seemed to have aged in the last few months.* ◼ N-COUNT An **age** is a period in history. ❑ *...the age of steam and steel.* ◼ N-COUNT You can say **an age** or **ages** to mean a very long time. [INFORMAL] ❑ *He waited what seemed an age.* ◼ → see also **aged, aging, middle age** ◼ → See feature box at **appearance**

───── SYNONYMS ─────

age
NOUN ◼
time: *We are in one of the most severe recessions in modern times.*
era: *It was an era of austerity.*
period: *No reference to their existence appears in any literature of the period.*
epoch: *This marked an epoch in the social history of the city.*

age-appropriate ADJ Something that is **age-appropriate** is suitable for the age that a person is. ❑ *That outfit isn't really age-appropriate.*

aged

Pronounced /eɪdʒd/ for meaning 1, and /eɪdʒɪd/ for meanings 2 and 3.

1 ADJ You use **aged** followed by a number to say how old someone is. ❑ *Alan has two children, aged eleven and nine.* **2** ADJ [ADJ n] **Aged** means very old. ❑ *She has an aged parent who's capable of being very difficult.* **3** N-PLURAL You can refer to all people who are very old as **the aged**. This use could cause offense. [OLD-FASHIONED] ❑ *The American Society on Aging provides resource services to those dealing with the aged.* **4** → see also **middle-aged**

age group (age groups) N-COUNT An **age group** is the people in a place or organization who were born during a particular period of time, for example, all the people aged between 18 and 25. ❑ *...a style that would appeal to all age groups.*

age|ing [BRIT] → see **age**, **aging**

age|ism /eɪdʒɪzəm/ N-UNCOUNT **Ageism** is unacceptable behavior that occurs as a result of the belief that older people are of less value than younger people. [DISAPPROVAL]

age|ist /eɪdʒɪst/ ADJ **Ageist** behavior is unacceptable behavior based on the belief that older people are of less value than younger people. [DISAPPROVAL] ❑ *...ageist bias from employers.*

age|less /eɪdʒlɪs/ **1** ADJ If you describe someone as **ageless**, you mean that they never seem to look any older. [LITERARY] ❑ *She was rich, beautiful and seemingly ageless.* **2** ADJ If you describe something as **ageless**, you mean that it is impossible to tell how old it is, or that it seems to have existed for ever. [LITERARY] ❑ *...the ageless oceans.*

age lim|it (age limits) N-COUNT An **age limit** is the oldest or youngest age at which you are allowed under particular regulations to do something. ❑ *In some cases there is a minimum age limit.*

agen|cy ✦✧✧ /eɪdʒənsi/ (agencies) **1** N-COUNT An **agency** is a business that provides a service on behalf of other businesses. [BUSINESS] ❑ *We had to hire maids through an agency.* **2** → see also **ad agency**, **employment agency** **3** N-COUNT An **agency** is a government organization responsible for a certain area of administration. ❑ *She is calling for a collaboration of local, state and federal agencies to deal with the problem.*

COLLOCATIONS

agency
NOUN
1
noun + **agency**: advertising, marketing; employment, recruitment; news
3
noun + **agency**: aid, development, funding; intelligence, security

agen|da ✦✧✧ /ədʒɛndə/ (agendas) **1** N-COUNT You can refer to the political issues that are important at a particular time as an **agenda**. ❑ *Does television set the agenda on foreign policy?* **2** → see also **hidden agenda** **3** N-COUNT An **agenda** is a list of the items that have to be discussed at a meeting. ❑ *This is sure to be an item on the agenda next week.*

agent ✦✦✧ /eɪdʒənt/ (agents) **1** N-COUNT An **agent** is a person who looks after someone else's business affairs or does business on their behalf. [BUSINESS] ❑ *You are buying direct, rather than through an agent.* **2** → see also **travel agent** **3** N-COUNT An **agent** in the arts world is a person who gets work for an actor or musician, or who sells the work of a writer to publishers. ❑ *My literary agent thinks it is not unreasonable to expect $500,000 in total.* **4** N-COUNT An **agent** is a person who works for a country's secret service. ❑ *All these years he's been an agent for the East.* **5** N-COUNT A chemical that has a particular effect or is used for a particular purpose can be referred to as a particular kind of **agent**. ❑ *...the bleaching agent in white flour.*

agent pro|vo|ca|teur /æʒɒn prɒvɒkətɜr/ (agents provocateurs) N-COUNT An **agent provocateur** is a person who is employed by the government or the police to encourage certain groups of people to break the law, so they can arrest them or make them lose public support. ❑ *Agents provocateurs may seek to discredit the opposition.*

age of con|sent N-SING [the N] The **age of consent** is the age at which a person can legally agree to having a sexual relationship. ❑ *He was under the age of consent.*

age-old ADJ An **age-old** story, tradition, or problem has existed for many generations or centuries. [WRITTEN] ❑ *This age-old struggle for control had led to untold bloody wars.*

ag|glom|era|tion /əglɒməreɪʃ°n/ (agglomerations) N-VAR [usu with supp] An **agglomeration** of things is a lot of different things gathered together, often in no particular order or arrangement. [FORMAL]

ag|gran|dize /əgrændaɪz/ (aggrandizes, aggrandizing, aggrandized)

in BRIT, also use **aggrandise**

V-T To **aggrandize** someone means to make them seem richer, more powerful, and more important than they really are. To **aggrandize** a building means to make it more impressive. [DISAPPROVAL] ❑ *At the dinner table, my father would go on and on, showing off, aggrandizing himself.* ❑ *...plans to aggrandize the building.*

ag|gran|dize|ment /əgrændɪzmənt/

in BRIT, also use **aggrandisement**

1 N-UNCOUNT [usu with supp] If someone does something for **aggrandizement**, they do it in order to get power, wealth, and importance for themselves. [FORMAL, DISAPPROVAL] ❑ *It would be the first time in human history that economic necessity has prevailed over military aggrandizement.* **2** → see also **self-aggrandizement**

ag|gra|vate /ægrəveɪt/ (aggravates, aggravating, aggravated) **1** V-T If someone or something **aggravates** a situation, they make it worse. ❑ *Stress and lack of sleep can aggravate the situation.* **2** V-T If someone or something **aggravates** you, they make you annoyed. [INFORMAL] ❑ *What aggravates you most about this country?* ● **ag|gra|vat|ing** ADJ ❑ *You don't realize how aggravating you can be.* ● **ag|gra|va|tion** /ægrəveɪʃ°n/ (aggravations) N-VAR ❑ *I just couldn't take the aggravation.*

ag|gra|vat|ed /ægrəveɪtɪd/ ADJ [ADJ n] **Aggravated** is used to describe a serious crime that involves violence. [LEGAL] ❑ *He was jailed for aggravated assault.*

ag|gre|gate /ægrɪgɪt/ ADJ [ADJ n] An **aggregate** amount or score is made up of several smaller amounts or scores added together. ❑ *The rate of growth of GNP will depend upon the rate of growth of aggregate demand.*

ag|gres|sion /əgrɛʃ°n/ (aggressions) **1** N-UNCOUNT **Aggression** is a quality of anger and determination that makes you ready to attack other people. ❑ *Aggression is by no means a male-only trait.* **2** N-VAR **Aggression** is violent and attacking behavior. ❑ *...the threat of massive military aggression.*

ag|gres|sive ✦✧✧ /əgrɛsɪv/ **1** ADJ An **aggressive** person or animal has a quality of anger and determination that makes them ready to attack other people. ❑ *Some children are much more aggressive than others.* ❑ *These fish are very aggressive.* ● **ag|gres|sive|ly** ADV ❑ *They'll react aggressively.* **2** ADJ People who are **aggressive** in their work or other activities behave in a forceful way because they are very eager to succeed. ❑ *He is respected as a very aggressive and competitive executive.* ● **ag|gres|sive|ly** ADV ❑ *...countries noted for aggressively pursuing energy efficiency.* **3** → See feature box at **drive**

ag|gres|sor /əgrɛsər/ (aggressors) N-COUNT The **aggressor** in a fight or battle is the person, group, or country that starts it. ❑ *They have been the aggressors in this conflict.*

ag|grieved /əgriːvd/ ADJ If you feel **aggrieved**, you feel upset and angry because of the way in which you have been treated. ❑ *I really feel aggrieved at this sort of thing.*

aghast /əgæst/ ADJ [ADJ after v] If you are **aghast**, you are filled with horror and surprise. [FORMAL] ❑ *While she watched, aghast, his eyes glazed over as his life flowed away.*

ag|ile /ædʒ°l/ **1** ADJ Someone who is **agile** can move quickly and easily. ❑ *At 20 years old he was not as strong, as fast, as agile as he is now.* ● **agil|ity** /ədʒɪlɪti/ N-UNCOUNT ❑ *She blinked in surprise at his agility.* **2** ADJ If you have an **agile** mind, you think quickly and intelligently. ❑ *She was quick-witted and had an extraordinarily agile mind.* ● **agil|ity** N-UNCOUNT ❑ *His intellect and mental agility have never been in doubt.*

ag|ing /eɪdʒɪŋ/ also **ageing** **1** ADJ Someone or something that is **aging** is becoming older and less healthy or efficient.

☐ John lives with his aging mother. **2** N-UNCOUNT **Aging** is the process of becoming old or becoming worn out. ☐ The only signs of aging are the flecks of gray that speckle his dark hair.

agi|tate /ˈædʒɪteɪt/ (**agitates**, **agitating**, **agitated**) **1** V-I If people **agitate** for something, they protest or take part in political activity in order to get it. ☐ The women who worked in these mills had begun to agitate for better conditions. **2** V-T If you **agitate** something, you shake it so that it moves about. [FORMAL] ☐ All you need to do is gently agitate the water with a finger or paintbrush. **3** V-T If something **agitates** you, it worries you and makes you unable to think clearly or calmly. ☐ Carl and Martin may inherit their grandmother's possessions when she dies. The thought agitates her.

agi|tat|ed /ˈædʒɪteɪtɪd/ ADJ If someone is **agitated**, they are very worried or upset, and show this in their behavior, movements, or voice. ☐ Susan seemed agitated about something.

agi|ta|tion /ˌædʒɪˈteɪʃən/ N-UNCOUNT If someone is in a state of **agitation**, they are very worried or upset, and show this in their behavior, movements, or voice. ☐ Danny returned to Father's house in a state of intense agitation.

agi|ta|tor /ˈædʒɪteɪtər/ (**agitators**) N-COUNT [oft supp N] If you describe someone involved in politics as an **agitator**, you disapprove of them because of the trouble they cause in organizing campaigns and protests. [DISAPPROVAL] ☐ ...a famous actress who was accused of being a political agitator.

agit|prop /ˈædʒɪtprɒp/ also **agit-prop** N-UNCOUNT **Agitprop** is the use of artistic forms such as drama or posters to further political aims.

aglow /əˈgloʊ/ **1** ADJ [v-link ADJ] If something is **aglow**, it is shining and bright with a soft, warm light. [LITERARY] ☐ The night skies will be aglow with fireworks. **2** ADJ [v-link ADJ] If someone is **aglow** or if their face is **aglow**, they look excited. [LITERARY] ☐ "It was incredible," Kurt says, suddenly aglow.

ag|nos|tic /ægˈnɒstɪk/ (**agnostics**) N-COUNT An **agnostic** believes that it is not possible to know whether God exists or not. Compare **atheist**. ☐ For the last twenty-three or twenty-four years I have been an agnostic.

ag|nos|ti|cism /ægˈnɒstɪsɪzəm/ N-UNCOUNT **Agnosticism** is the belief that it is not possible to say definitely whether or not there is a God. Compare **atheism**.

ago ♦♦♦ /əˈgoʊ/ ADV You use **ago** when you are referring to past time. For example, if something happened one year **ago**, it is one year since it happened. If it happened a long time **ago**, it is a long time since it happened. ☐ He was killed a few days ago in a skiing accident. ☐ The meeting is the first ever between the two sides since the war there began 14 years ago.

■ USAGE ■

ago
Don't use **ago** and **since** together. Don't say, for example, 'It's been three years ago since it happened.' Say 'It happened three years ago' or 'It has been three years since it happened.' It's been two weeks **since** I wrote to you.

agog /əˈgɒg/ ADJ [usu v-link ADJ, oft ADJ prep] If you are **agog**, you are excited about something, and eager to know more about it.

ago|nize /ˈægənaɪz/ (**agonizes**, **agonizing**, **agonized**)

in BRIT, also use **agonise**

V-I If you **agonize** over something, you feel very anxious about it and spend a long time thinking about it. ☐ Perhaps he was agonizing over the moral issues involved.

ago|nized /ˈægənaɪzd/

in BRIT, also use **agonised**

ADJ [usu ADJ n] **Agonized** describes something that you say or do when you are in great physical or mental pain. ☐ ...the agonized look on his face.

ago|niz|ing /ˈægənaɪzɪŋ/

in BRIT, also use **agonising**

1 ADJ Something that is **agonizing** causes you to feel great physical or mental pain. ☐ He did not wish to die the agonizing death of his mother and brother. **2** ADJ **Agonizing** decisions and choices are very difficult to make. ☐ He now faced an agonizing decision about his immediate future.

ago|ny /ˈægəni/ N-UNCOUNT **Agony** is great physical or mental pain. ☐ A new machine may save thousands of animals from the agony of drug tests.

ago|ny aunt [BRIT] → see **advice columnist**

ago|ny col|umn [BRIT] → see **advice column**

ago|ra|pho|bia /ˌægərəˈfoʊbiə/ N-UNCOUNT **Agoraphobia** is the fear of open or public places.

ago|ra|pho|bic /ˌægərəˈfoʊbɪk/ (**agoraphobics**) ADJ Someone who is **agoraphobic** has agoraphobia. • N-COUNT An **agoraphobic** is someone who has agoraphobia.

agrar|ian /əˈgrɛəriən/ ADJ [usu ADJ n] **Agrarian** means relating to the ownership and use of land, especially farmland, or relating to the part of a society or economy that is concerned with agriculture. [TECHNICAL]

agree ♦♦♦ /əˈgri/ (**agrees**, **agreeing**, **agreed**) **1** V-RECIP If people **agree** with each other about something, they have the same opinion about it or say that they have the same opinion. ☐ Both have agreed on the need for the money. ☐ So we both agree there's a problem? ☐ I agree with you that the open system is by far the best. ☐ "It's appalling."—"It is. I agree." ☐ I agree with every word you've just said. **2** V-RECIP If people **agree** on something, they all decide to accept or do something. ☐ The warring sides have agreed on an unconditional ceasefire. **3** V-RECIP [v with n, pl-n v] In grammar, if a word **agrees** with a noun or pronoun, it has a form that is appropriate to the number or gender of the noun or pronoun. For example, in 'He hates it,' the singular verb agrees with the singular pronoun 'he.' **4** V-T/V-I If you **agree** to do something, you say that you will do it. If you **agree** to a proposal, you accept it. ☐ He agreed to pay me for the drawings. **5** V-I If you **agree** with an action or suggestion, you approve of it. ☐ You didn't want to ask anybody whether they agreed with what you were doing. **6** V-RECIP If one account of an event or one set of figures **agrees** with another, the two accounts or sets of figures are the same or are consistent with each other. ☐ His second statement agrees with facts as stated by the other witnesses. **7** PHRASE If two people who are arguing about something **agree to disagree** or **agree to differ**, they decide to stop arguing because neither of them is going to change their opinion. ☐ You and I are going to have to agree to disagree then. **8** → see also **agreed**

■ USAGE ■

agree
Don't say that you 'agree' something, or that you 'are agreed with it.' Also, when you use 'agree' in this sense, don't use progressive forms. Don't say 'I am agreeing with Mark.' I agree with Mark. He agreed with my idea.

agree|able /əˈgriəbəl/ **1** ADJ If something is **agreeable**, it is pleasant and you enjoy it. ☐ ...workers in more agreeable and better paid occupations. **2** ADJ If someone is **agreeable**, they are pleasant and try to please people. ☐ ...sharing a bottle of wine with an agreeable companion.

agreed /əˈgrid/ **1** ADJ [v-link ADJ] If people are **agreed** on something, they have reached a joint decision on it or have the same opinion about it. ☐ Okay, so are we agreed on going north? **2** → see also **agree**

agree|ment ♦♦◇ /əˈgrimənt/ (**agreements**) **1** N-COUNT An **agreement** is a formal decision about future action that is made by two or more countries, groups, or people. ☐ It looks as though a compromise agreement has now been reached. **2** N-UNCOUNT **Agreement** on something is a joint decision that a particular course of action should be taken. ☐ A spokesman said, however, that the two men had not reached agreement on the issues discussed. **3** N-UNCOUNT **Agreement** with someone means having the same opinion as they have. ☐ The judge kept nodding in agreement. • PHRASE If you are **in agreement** with someone, you have the same opinion as they have. **4** N-UNCOUNT **Agreement** to a course of action means allowing it to happen or giving it your approval. ☐ The clinic doctor will then write to your doctor to get his agreement. • PHRASE If you are **in agreement** with a plan or proposal, you approve of it.

agribusiness

COLLOCATIONS

agreement
NOUN **1**
noun + **agreement**: free trade, loan, peace, tenancy; confidentiality, non-disclosure
adjective + **agreement**: binding, enforceable, unenforceable, voluntary; bilateral, formal, mutual; verbal, written
verb + **agreement**: negotiate; come to, reach; sign

SYNONYMS

agreement
NOUN
1
treaty: ...negotiations over a 1992 treaty on global warming.
arrangement: The caves could be visited only by prior arrangement.
deal: Japan will have to do a deal with America on rice imports.
settlement: Our objective must be to secure a peace settlement.
4
assent: Without their assent a political settlement cannot be reached.
consent: At approximately 11:30 p.m., Pollard finally gave his consent to the search.

ag|ri|busi|ness /ˈæɡrɪbɪznɪs/ N-UNCOUNT **Agribusiness** is the various businesses that produce, sell, and distribute farm products, especially on a large scale. [BUSINESS] ❏ Many of the old agricultural collectives are now being turned into agribusiness corporations.

ag|ri|cul|tur|al ♦◇◇ /ˌæɡrɪˈkʌltʃərəl/ **1** ADJ **Agricultural** means involving or relating to agriculture. ❏ Farmers struggling for survival strip the forests for agricultural land. **2** → See feature box at **farming**

ag|ri|cul|tur|al|ist /ˌæɡrɪˈkʌltʃərəlɪst/ (**agriculturalists**) N-COUNT An **agriculturalist** is someone who is an expert on agriculture and who advises farmers.

ag|ri|cul|ture ♦◇◇ /ˈæɡrɪkʌltʃər/ N-UNCOUNT **Agriculture** is farming and the methods that are used to raise and take care of crops and animals. ❏ Strong both in industry and agriculture, Ukraine produces much of the grain for the nation.

SYNONYMS

agriculture
NOUN
farming: Modern intensive farming is subsidised by cheap oil.
husbandry: ...soil-conserving methods of good husbandry.

PREFIX

agro-
is used to form nouns and adjectives which refer to things relating to agriculture, or to agriculture combined with another activity. For example, **agronomics** is the branch of economics that studies how land is used in farming.

agrono|mist /əˈɡrɒnəmɪst/ (**agronomists**) N-COUNT An **agronomist** is someone who studies the growing and harvesting of crops.

aground /əˈɡraʊnd/ ADV [ADV after v] If a ship runs **aground**, it touches the ground in a shallow part of a river, lake, or the sea, and gets stuck. ❏ The ship ran aground where there should have been a depth of 35 ft.

ah ♦◇◇ /ɑː/ EXCLAM **Ah** is used in writing to represent a noise that people make in conversation, for example, to acknowledge or draw attention to something, or to express surprise, relief, or disappointment. [FEELINGS] ❏ Ah, so many questions, so little time.

aha /ɑːˈhɑː/ EXCLAM **Aha** is used in writing to represent a noise that people make in conversation, for example, to express satisfaction or surprise. [FEELINGS] ❏ Aha! Here at last, the answer to my question.

AHEAD

① ADVERB USES
② PREPOSITION USES

① **ahead** ♦♦◇ /əˈhɛd/

In addition to the uses shown below, **ahead** is used in phrasal verbs such as 'get ahead,' 'go ahead,' and 'press ahead.'

1 ADV Something that is **ahead** is in front of you. If you look **ahead**, you look directly in front of you. ❏ Brett looked straight ahead. ❏ The road ahead was now blocked solid. **2** ADV [ADV after v] You use **ahead** with verbs such as 'push,' 'move,' and 'forge' to indicate that a plan, program, or organization is making fast progress. ❏ Western countries were moving ahead with plans to send financial aid to all of the former Soviet republics. **3** ADV If you are **ahead** in your work or achievements, you have made more progress than you expected to and are performing well. ❏ First half profits have charged ahead from $127.6m to $134.2m. **4** ADV If a person or a team is **ahead** in a competition, they are winning. ❏ Australia was ahead throughout the game. ❏ The party is comfortably ahead in the opinion polls. **5** ADV **Ahead** also means in the future. ❏ A much bigger battle is ahead for the president. **6** ADV [ADV after v] If you prepare or plan something **ahead**, you do it some time before a future event so that everything is ready for that event to take place. ❏ The government wants figures that help it to administer its policies and plan ahead. **7** ADV [ADV after v] If you go **ahead**, or if you go on **ahead**, you go in front of someone who is going to the same place so that you arrive there some time before they do. ❏ I went ahead and waited for Sean.

② **ahead** ♦◇◇ /əˈhɛd/

→ Please look at meanings **6** and **7** to see if the expression you are looking for is shown under another headword.

1 PHRASE If someone is **ahead of** you, they are directly in front of you. If someone is moving **ahead of** you, they are in front of you and moving in the same direction. ❏ I saw a man in a blue jacket thirty yards ahead of me. **2** PHRASE If an event or period of time lies **ahead of** you, it is going to happen or take place soon or in the future. ❏ I tried to think about all the problems that were ahead of me tomorrow. ❏ Heather had been awake all night thinking about the future that lay ahead of her. **3** PHRASE In a competition, if a person or team does something **ahead of** someone else, they do it before the second person or team. ❏ Robert Millar finished 1 minute and 35 seconds ahead of the Frenchman. **4** PHRASE If something happens **ahead of** schedule or **ahead of** time, it happens earlier than was planned. ❏ The election was held six months ahead of schedule. **5** PHRASE If someone is **ahead of** someone else, they have made more progress and are more advanced in what they are doing. ❏ Henry generally stayed ahead of the others in the academic subjects. **6 one step ahead of someone or something** → see **step** **7 ahead of your time** → see **time** ③

ahem /əˈhɛm/ CONVENTION In writing, **ahem** is used to show that someone is being ironic. **Ahem** is also used to show that someone wants to get another person's attention. ❏ I'd say the shows look like being - ahem - a roaring success. ❏ It is not unknown for valuable display items to go, ahem, missing.

ahold /əˈhoʊld/ **1** PHRASE [PHR n] If you **get ahold of** someone or something, you manage to contact, find, or get them. [AM, INFORMAL] ❏ I tried again to get ahold of my cousin Joan. **2** PHRASE [PHR pron-refl] If you **get ahold of** yourself, you force yourself to become calm and sensible after a shock or in a difficult situation. [AM, INFORMAL] ❏ I'm going to have to get ahold of myself.

ahoy /əˈhɔɪ/ EXCLAM **Ahoy** is something that people in boats shout in order to attract attention. ❏ Ahoy there! ❏ Ship ahoy!

AI /ˌeɪ ˈaɪ/ N-UNCOUNT **AI** is an abbreviation for **artificial intelligence**, or **artificial insemination**.

aid ♦♦♦ /eɪd/ (**aids, aiding, aided**) **1** N-UNCOUNT **Aid** is money, equipment, or services that are provided for people, countries, or organizations who need them but cannot provide them for themselves. ❏ ...regular flights carrying humanitarian aid to Cambodia. ❏ They have already pledged billions of dollars in aid. **2** N-UNCOUNT If you perform a task with the **aid** of something, you need or use that thing to perform that task. ❏ He succeeded with the aid of a completely new method he discovered. **3** V-T To **aid** a country, organization, or person means to provide them with money, equipment, or services that they need. ❏ ...U.S. efforts to aid Kurdish refugees. • **-aided** COMB IN ADJ ❏ ...government-aided research. **4** V-T To **aid** something means to help or assist them. [WRITTEN] ❏ ...a software system to aid managers in advanced decision-making. • N-UNCOUNT **Aid** is also a noun. ❏ He was forced to turn for aid to his former enemy. **5** V-T/V-I If something **aids** a process, it makes it easier or more likely to happen. ❏ The survey suggests that the export sector will continue to aid the economic recovery. ❏ Calcium may aid in the prevention of colon cancer. **6** N-COUNT An **aid** is an object, device, or technique that makes something easier to do. ❑ *The book is an invaluable aid to teachers of literature.* **7** → see also **first aid** **8** PHRASE If you **come** or **go to** someone's **aid**, you try to help them when they are in danger or difficulty. ❑ *Dr. Fox went to the aid of the dying man despite having been injured in the crash.*

COLLOCATIONS

aid
NOUN
1
noun + **aid**: development, food; government, state
adjective + **aid**: humanitarian, legal, medical, military; foreign, international, overseas; economic, financial
verb + **aid**: deliver, distribute, pledge, provide; cut, increase, suspend, withdraw; need, receive
2
verb + **aid**: enlist
6
noun + **aid**: buoyancy, hearing, mobility, teaching
adjective + **aid**: electronic, navigational, visual
VERB
4
aid + noun: refugees; economy, research
5
aid + noun: digestion, identification, understanding

SYNONYMS

aid
NOUN
1
handout: *Soldiers oversee the food handouts.*
relief: *...famine relief.*
support: *...the government's proposal to cut agricultural support by only about 15%.*
charity: *Her husband is unemployed, and the family depends on charity.*
assistance: *We can offer you assistance with legal expenses up to $5,000.*
4
backing: *He said the president had the full backing of his government to negotiate a deal.*
support: *The prime minister gave his full support to the government's reforms.*
assistance: *Since 1976, he has been operating the store with the assistance of volunteers.*

---

aide /eɪd/ (aides) **1** N-COUNT An **aide** is an assistant to someone who has an important job, especially in government or in the armed forces. ❑ *A close aide to the prime minister repeated that they would never accept it.* **2** → see also **teacher's aide**

aide-de-camp /eɪd də kɒmp/ (aides-de-camp) N-COUNT An **aide-de-camp** is an officer in the armed forces who helps an officer of higher rank. ❑ *...a colonel who had been aide-de-camp to the king.*

aide-memoire /eɪd mɛmwɑr/ (aide-memoires) also **aide-mémoire** N-COUNT An **aide-memoire** is something such as a list that you use to remind you of something.

AIDS ✦✧ /eɪdz/ N-UNCOUNT **AIDS** is a disease that destroys the natural system of protection that the body has against other diseases. **AIDS** is an abbreviation for **acquired immune deficiency syndrome**. ❑ *...people suffering from AIDS.*

ail /eɪl/ (ails, ailing, ailed) V-T If something **ails** a group or area of activity, it is a problem or source of trouble for that group or for people involved in that activity. ❑ *A full-scale debate is under way on what ails the industry.*

aileron /eɪlərɒn/ (ailerons) N-COUNT An **aileron** is a section on the back edge of the wing of an aircraft that can be raised or lowered in order to control the aircraft's movement.

ailing /eɪlɪŋ/ ADJ An **ailing** organization or society is in difficulty and is becoming weaker. ❑ *The rise in overseas sales is good news for the ailing American economy.*

ailment /eɪlmənt/ (ailments) N-COUNT An **ailment** is an illness, especially one that is not very serious. ❑ *The pharmacist can assist you with the treatment of common ailments.*

aim ✦✦✧ /eɪm/ (aims, aiming, aimed) **1** V-T/V-I If you **aim** for something or **aim** to do something, you plan or hope to achieve it. ❑ *He said he would aim for the 100 meter world record at the world championships in August.* ❑ *Businesses will have to aim at long-term growth.* ❑ *The program aims to educate and prepare students for a challenging career.* **2** V-T/V-I If you **aim** to do something, you decide or want to do it. [AM, INFORMAL] ❑ *I didn't aim to get caught.* **3** V-T [usu passive] If your actions or remarks are **aimed** at a particular person or group, you intend that the person or group should notice them and be influenced by them. ❑ *His message was aimed at the undecided middle ground of Israeli politics.* **4** V-T/V-I If you **aim at** someone or something, or **aim** a weapon or object **at** them, you point it toward them before firing or throwing it. ❑ *When he appeared again, he was aiming the rifle at Wade.* ❑ *...a missile aimed at the arms factory.* **5** V-T If you **aim** a kick or punch at someone, you try to kick or punch them. ❑ *They aimed kicks at his shins.* **6** N-COUNT The **aim** of something that you do is the purpose for which you do it or the result that it is intended to achieve. ❑ *The aim of the festival is to increase awareness of Hindu culture and traditions.* **7** V-T If an action or plan **is aimed** at achieving something, it is intended or planned to achieve it. ❑ *The new measures are aimed at tightening existing sanctions.* **8** N-SING Your **aim** is your skill or action in pointing a weapon or other object at its target. ❑ *He stood with the gun gripped in his right hand and his left hand steadying his aim.* **9** PHRASE When you **take aim**, you point a weapon or object at someone or something, before firing or throwing it. ❑ *She had spotted a man with a shotgun taking aim.* **10** → See feature box at **success**

aimless /eɪmlɪs/ ADJ A person or activity that is **aimless** has no clear purpose or plan. ❑ *After several hours of aimless searching they were getting low on fuel.* ● **aimlessly** ADV [ADV after v] ❑ *I wandered around aimlessly.*

ain't /eɪnt/ People sometimes use **ain't** instead of 'am not,' 'aren't,' 'isn't,' 'haven't,' and 'hasn't.' Many people consider this use to be incorrect. [DIALECT, SPOKEN] ❑ *Well, it's obvious, ain't it?*

air ✦✦✦ /ɛər/ (airs, airing, aired) **1** N-UNCOUNT **Air** is the mixture of gases that forms the Earth's atmosphere and that we breathe. ❑ *Drafts help to circulate air.* ❑ *Keith opened the window and leaned out into the cold air.* **2** N-UNCOUNT **Air** is used to refer to travel in aircraft. ❑ *Air travel will continue to grow at about 6% per year.* **3** N-SING The **air** is the space around things or above the ground. ❑ *Government troops broke up the protest by firing their guns in the air.* **4** V-T If a broadcasting company **airs** a television or radio program, they show it on television or broadcast it on the radio. [mainly AM] ❑ *Tonight PBS will air a documentary called "Democracy In Action."* ● **airing** N-SING ❑ *...the airing of a new television commercial that attacked the president's war record.* **5** V-T If you **air** a room or building, you let fresh air into it. ❑ *One day a week her mother cleaned and aired each room.* **6** PHRASE If you do something to **clear the air**, you do it in order to resolve any problems or disagreements that there might be. ❑ *...an inquiry just to clear the air and settle the facts of the case.* **7** PHRASE If something is **in the air** it is felt to be present, but it is not talked about. ❑ *There was great excitement in the air.* **8** PHRASE If someone is **on the air**, they are broadcasting on radio or television. If a program is **on the air**, it is being broadcast on radio or television. If it is **off the air**, it is not being broadcast. ❑ *We go on the air, live, at 11:30 a.m.* **9** PHRASE If someone or something disappears **into thin air**, they disappear completely. If someone or something appears **out of thin air**, they appear suddenly and mysteriously. ❑ *He had materialized out of thin air; I had not seen or heard him coming.*

air ambulance (air ambulances) N-COUNT [also by N] An **air ambulance** is a helicopter or plane that is used for taking people to a hospital.

airbag /ɛərbæɡ/ (airbags) also **air bag** N-COUNT An **airbag** is a safety device in a car that automatically fills with air if the car crashes, and is designed to protect the people in the car when they are thrown forward in the crash.

air base (air bases) also **airbase** N-COUNT An **air base** is a center where military aircraft take off or land and are serviced, and where many of the center's staff live. ❑ *...the largest U.S. air base in Saudi Arabia.*

airbed /ɛərbɛd/ (airbeds) also **air bed** **1** N-COUNT An **airbed** is a plastic or rubber mattress that can be folded or stored flat and that you fill with air before you use it. **2** → See also color supplement

air|borne /ɛərbɔrn/ **1** ADJ [v-link ADJ] If an aircraft is **airborne**, it is in the air and flying. ❑ *The pilot did manage to get airborne.* **2** ADJ [ADJ n] **Airborne** troops use parachutes to get into enemy territory. ❑ *The allies landed thousands of airborne troops.* **3** ADJ **Airborne** means in the air or carried in the air. ❑ *Many people are allergic to airborne pollutants such as pollen.*

air brake (air brakes) N-COUNT **Air brakes** are brakes that are used on heavy vehicles such as buses and trains and that are operated by means of compressed air.

air|brush /ɛərbrʌʃ/ (airbrushes, airbrushing, airbrushed) **1** N-COUNT An **airbrush** is an artist's tool which sprays paint onto a surface. **2** V-T To **airbrush** a photograph or other image means to change it using an airbrush, especially to make it more beautiful or perfect. ❑ *...bits of photographs cut, pasted and then airbrushed to create a convincing whole.*

Air|bus /ɛərbʌs/ (Airbuses) N-COUNT An **Airbus** is an airplane that is designed to carry a large number of passengers for fairly short distances. [TRADEMARK]

air-conditioned ADJ If a room or vehicle is **air-conditioned**, the air in it is kept cool and dry by means of a special machine. ❑ *...our new air-conditioned trains.*

air con|di|tion|er (air conditioners) N-COUNT An **air conditioner** is a machine that keeps the air in a building cool and dry.

air-conditioning N-UNCOUNT **Air-conditioning** is a method of providing buildings and vehicles with cool dry air.

air-cooled ADJ [usu ADJ n] An **air-cooled** engine is prevented from getting too hot when it is running by cool air that passes over it, rather than being cooled by a liquid. ❑ *The car was powered by a four cylinder air-cooled engine.*

air|craft ♦♦◇ /ɛərkræft/ (aircraft)

Aircraft is both the singular and the plural form.

N-COUNT An **aircraft** is a vehicle that can fly, for example, an airplane or a helicopter. ❑ *The return flight of the aircraft was delayed.*

━━━━ COLLOCATIONS ━━━━

aircraft
NOUN
noun + **aircraft**: combat, enemy, fighter, reconnaissance, surveillance; passenger, transport
adjective + **aircraft**: commercial, military; pilotless, unmanned; light
verb + **aircraft**: fly

air|craft car|ri|er (aircraft carriers) **1** N-COUNT An **aircraft carrier** is a warship with a long, flat deck where aircraft can take off and land. **2** → See also color supplement

air|crew /ɛərkru/ (aircrews) also **air crew** N-COUNT-COLL The **aircrew** on a plane are the pilot and other people who are responsible for flying it and for taking care of any passengers who are on it.

air|drome /ɛərdroʊm/ (airdromes) N-COUNT An **airdrome** is a place or area where small aircraft can land and take off. [AM]

in BRIT, use **aerodrome**

air drop (air drops, air dropping, air dropped) also **airdrop**, **air-drop** **1** N-COUNT An **air drop** is a delivery of supplies by aircraft to an area that is hard to get to. The supplies are dropped from the aircraft on parachutes. **2** V-T If a country or organization **air drops** supplies to a place, it drops supplies there from aircraft.

air|fare /ɛərfɛər/ (airfares) N-COUNT The **airfare** to a place is the amount it costs to fly there.

air|field /ɛərfild/ (airfields) N-COUNT An **airfield** is an area of ground where aircraft take off and land. It is smaller than an airport.

air|flow /ɛərfloʊ/ N-UNCOUNT The **airflow** around an object or vehicle is the way that the air flows around it.

air force ♦♦◇ (air forces) N-COUNT The **air force** is the part of a country's armed forces that is concerned with fighting in the air. ❑ *...the United States Air Force.*

air fresh|en|er /ɛər frɛʃənər/ (air fresheners) N-VAR An **air freshener** is a product people can buy that is meant to make rooms smell pleasant.

air|gun /ɛərgʌn/ (airguns) also **air gun** N-COUNT An **airgun** is a gun which is fired by means of air pressure.

air|head /ɛərhɛd/ (airheads) N-COUNT If you describe someone as an **airhead**, you are critical of them because you think they are not at all intelligent and are interested only in unimportant things. [INFORMAL, DISAPPROVAL]

air|less /ɛərlɪs/ ADJ If a place is **airless**, there is no fresh air in it. ❑ *...a dark, airless room.*

air|lift /ɛərlɪft/ (airlifts, airlifting, airlifted) **1** N-COUNT An **airlift** is an operation to move people, troops, or goods by air, especially in a war or when land routes are closed. ❑ *President Garcia has ordered an airlift of food, medicines and blankets.* **2** V-T If people, troops, or goods **are airlifted** somewhere, they are carried by air, especially in a war or when land routes are closed. ❑ *The injured were airlifted to a hospital in Dayton.*

air|line ♦♦◇ /ɛərlaɪn/ (airlines) **1** N-COUNT An **airline** is a company that provides regular services carrying people or goods in airplanes. ❑ *...the world's largest discount airline.* **2** → See feature box at **tourism**

air|lin|er /ɛərlaɪnər/ (airliners) N-COUNT An **airliner** is a large airplane that is used for carrying passengers.

air|lock /ɛərlɒk/ (airlocks) also **air lock** **1** N-COUNT An **airlock** is a small room that is used to move between areas which do not have the same air pressure, for example, in a spacecraft or submarine. **2** N-COUNT An **airlock** is a bubble of air in a pipe that prevents liquid from flowing through.

air|mail /ɛərmeɪl/ N-UNCOUNT **Airmail** is the system of sending letters, parcels, and goods by air. ❑ *...an airmail letter.*

air|man /ɛərmən/ (airmen) N-COUNT An **airman** is a man who flies aircraft, especially one who serves in his country's air force. ❑ *...an American airman.*

air miles N-PLURAL **Air miles** are points that you collect when you buy certain goods or services and that you can use to pay for air travel.

air pis|tol (air pistols) N-COUNT An **air pistol** is a small gun which is fired by means of air pressure.

air|plane /ɛərpleɪn/ (airplanes) **1** N-COUNT An **airplane** is a vehicle with wings and one or more engines that enable it to fly through the air. [AM]

in BRIT, use **aeroplane**

2 → See also color supplement

air|play /ɛərpleɪ/ N-UNCOUNT [oft supp N] The **airplay** which a piece of popular music receives is the number of times it is played on the radio. ❑ *Our first single got a lot of airplay.*

air|port ♦♦◇ /ɛərpɔrt/ (airports) N-COUNT An **airport** is a place where aircraft land and take off, and that has buildings and facilities for passengers. ❑ *...one of the world's busiest international airports.*

air|port tax (airport taxes) N-VAR **Airport tax** is a tax that airline passengers have to pay in order to use an airport. ❑ *Overnight return flights cost from $349 including airport taxes.*

air pow|er also **airpower** N-UNCOUNT A nation's **air power** is the strength of its air force. ❑ *We will use air power to protect UN peacekeepers if necessary.*

air rage N-UNCOUNT **Air rage** is aggressive or violent behavior by airline passengers. ❑ *Most air rage incidents involve heavy drinking.*

air raid (air raids) N-COUNT An **air raid** is an attack by military aircraft in which bombs are dropped. ❑ *The war began with overnight air raids on various cities.*

air ri|fle (air rifles) N-COUNT An **air rifle** is a rifle that is fired by means of air pressure.

air|ship /ɛərʃɪp/ (airships) N-COUNT An **airship** is an aircraft that consists of a large balloon that is filled with gas and is powered by an engine. It has a section underneath for passengers.

air|show /ɛərʃoʊ/ (airshows) also **air show** N-COUNT An **airshow** is an event at which airplane pilots entertain the public by performing very skillful and complicated movements with the aircraft in the sky.

air|sick /ɛərsɪk/ also **air sick, air-sick** ADJ If you are **airsick** when you are traveling on an aircraft, you experience nausea as a result of the aircraft's motion. ❑ *I was violently airsick all the*

airspace | alarm

way. • **air|sick|ness** /ˈɛərsɪknɪs/ N-UNCOUNT ❏ *A few suffered airsickness on the connecting flight.*

air|space /ˈɛərspeɪs/ also **air space** N-UNCOUNT A country's **airspace** is the part of the sky that is over that country and is considered to belong to it. ❏ *Forty minutes later, they left Colombian airspace.*

air|speed /ˈɛərspid/ (airspeeds) also **air speed** N-COUNT An aircraft's **airspeed** is the speed at which it travels through the air.

air strike (air strikes) also **airstrike** N-COUNT An **air strike** is an attack by military aircraft in which bombs are dropped. ❏ *A senior defense official said last night that they would continue the air strikes.*

air|strip /ˈɛərstrɪp/ (airstrips) N-COUNT An **airstrip** is a stretch of land that has been cleared so that aircraft can take off and land. ❏ *We landed on a grass airstrip, fifteen minutes after leaving Mahe.*

air ter|mi|nal (air terminals) N-COUNT An **air terminal** is a building where passengers wait before they get on an airplane. [mainly BRIT]

air|tight /ˈɛərtaɪt/ also **air-tight** ◼ ADJ If a container is **airtight**, its lid fits so tightly that no air can get in or out. ❏ *Store the cookies in an airtight container.* ◼ ADJ An **airtight** alibi, case, argument, or agreement is one that has been so carefully put together that nobody will be able to find a fault in it. [AM] ❏ *If she could just establish the time the picture had been taken, Mick would have an airtight alibi.*

in BRIT, use **watertight**

air time also **airtime** N-UNCOUNT The **air time** that something gets is the amount of time taken up with broadcasts about it. ❏ *Some argue that women's sport gets too little air time.*

air-to-air ADJ [ADJ n] **Air-to-air** combat is a battle between military airplanes where rockets or bullets are fired at one airplane from another. ❏ *...air-to-air missiles.*

air traf|fic con|trol ◼ N-UNCOUNT [oft N n] **Air traffic control** is the activity of organizing the routes that aircraft should follow, and telling pilots by radio which routes they should take. ❏ *...the nation's overburdened air-traffic-control system.* ◼ N-UNCOUNT-COLL **Air traffic control** is the group of people who organize the routes aircraft take. ❏ *They have to wait for clearance from air traffic control.*

air traf|fic con|trol|ler (air traffic controllers) N-COUNT An **air traffic controller** is someone whose job is to organize the routes that aircraft should follow, and to tell pilots by radio which routes they should take.

air|waves /ˈɛərweɪvz/ also **air waves** N-PLURAL The **airwaves** is used to refer to the activity of broadcasting on radio and television. For example, if someone says something over **the airwaves**, they say it on the radio or television. [JOURNALISM] ❏ *The election campaign has been fought not in street rallies but on the airwaves.*

air|way /ˈɛərweɪ/ (airways) ◼ N-COUNT A person's **airways** are the passages from their nose and mouth down to their lungs, through which air enters and leaves their body. ❏ *...an inflammation of the airways.* ◼ N-PLURAL [usu the N] The **airways** are all the routes that planes can travel along. ❏ *How does a private pilot get access to the airways?* ◼ N-PLURAL [usu the N] **Airways** means the same as **airwaves**. ❏ *The interview went out over the airways.*

air|woman /ˈɛərwʊmən/ (airwomen) N-COUNT An **airwoman** is a woman who flies aircraft, especially one who serves in her country's air force.

air|worthy /ˈɛərwɜrði/ ADJ If an aircraft is **airworthy**, it is safe to fly. ❏ *The mechanics work hard to keep the helicopters airworthy.* • **air|worthiness** N-UNCOUNT ❏ *All our aircraft have certificates of airworthiness.*

airy /ˈɛəri/ (airier, airiest) ADJ If a building or room is **airy**, it has a lot of fresh air inside, usually because it is large. ❏ *The bathroom has a light and airy feel.*

aisle /aɪl/ (aisles) N-COUNT An **aisle** is a long narrow gap that people can walk along between rows of seats in a public building such as a church or between rows of shelves in a supermarket. ❏ *...the frozen food aisle.*

ajar /əˈdʒɑr/ ADJ [v-link ADJ] If a door is **ajar**, it is slightly open. ❏ *He left the door ajar in case I needed him.*

a.k.a. /eɪ keɪ eɪ/ also **aka a.k.a.** is an abbreviation for 'also known as.' **a.k.a.** is used especially when referring to someone's nickname or stage name. ❏ *From the very beginning, Stuart Leslie Goddard, a.k.a. Adam Ant, knew he was going to be a star.*

akim|bo /əˈkɪmboʊ/ PHRASE [usu PHR after v] If you stand **arms akimbo** or **with arms akimbo**, you stand with your hands on your hips and your elbows pointing outward. [OLD-FASHIONED]

akin /əˈkɪn/ ADJ [v-link ADJ to n] If one thing is **akin** to another, it is similar to it in some way. [FORMAL] ❏ *Listening to his life story is akin to reading a good adventure novel.*

┌─────────── SUFFIX ───────────┐

-al
forms adjectives that indicate what something is connected with. For example, **environmental** problems are problems connected with the environment.

└──────────────────────────────┘

à la /ɑ lɑ/ PREP-PHRASE [PREP n-proper] If you do something **à la** a particular person, you do it in the same style or in the same way that they would do it. ❏ *...a crisp, tailored dress à la Audrey Hepburn.*

ala|bas|ter /ˈæləbæstər/ N-UNCOUNT [usu N n] **Alabaster** is a white stone that is used for making statues, vases, and ornaments.

à la carte /ɑ lə kɑrt/ ADJ [ADJ n] An **à la carte** menu in a restaurant offers you a choice of individually priced dishes for each course. ❏ *You could choose as much or as little as you wanted from an à la carte menu.* • ADV [ADV after v] **à la carte** is also an adverb. ❏ *A set meal is 35 dollars, or you can eat à la carte.*

alac|rity /əˈlækrɪti/ N-UNCOUNT [usu with N] If you do something with **alacrity**, you do it quickly and eagerly. [FORMAL]

à la mode /ɑ lə moʊd/ also **a la mode** ADJ [n ADJ] A dessert **à la mode** is served with ice cream. [AM] ❏ *...apple pie à la mode.* • ADV [ADV after v] **à la mode** is also used as an adverb. ❏ *...served à la mode with vanilla ice cream.*

alarm ◆◇◇ /əˈlɑrm/ (alarms, alarming, alarmed) ◼ N-UNCOUNT **Alarm** is a feeling of fear or anxiety that something unpleasant or dangerous might happen. ❏ *The news was greeted with alarm by senators.* ◼ V-T If something **alarms** you, it makes you afraid or anxious that something unpleasant or dangerous might happen. ❏ *We could not see what had alarmed him.* ◼ N-COUNT An **alarm** is an automatic device that warns you of danger, for example, by ringing a bell. ❏ *He heard the alarm go off.* ◼ N-COUNT An **alarm** is the same as an **alarm clock**. ❏ *Dad set the alarm for eight the next day.* ◼ → see also **alarmed, alarming, car alarm, false alarm, fire alarm** ◼ PHRASE If you say that something sets **alarm bells** ringing, you mean that it makes people feel worried or concerned about something. ❏ *This has set the alarm bells ringing in Moscow.* ◼ PHRASE If you **raise the alarm** or **sound the alarm**, you warn people of danger. ❏ *His family raised the alarm when he had not come home by 9 p.m.*

┌─────────── SYNONYMS ───────────┐

alarm
NOUN ◼

fear: *I was sitting on the floor, shivering with fear.*
panic: *An earthquake hit the capital, causing panic among the population.*
anxiety: *They could feel only great anxiety about the future.*
dread: *She thought with dread of the cold winters to come.*
VERB ◼
frighten: *Most children are frightened by the sight of blood.*
scare: *You're scaring me.*
startle: *The telephone startled him.*

└───────────────────────────────┘

┌─────────── COLLOCATIONS ───────────┐

alarm
NOUN
◼
adjective + **alarm**: unnecessary, widespread
verb + **alarm**: cause, express
◼
noun + **alarm**: intruder, panic, rape, security
verb + **alarm**: activate, set, sound, trigger; fit, install

└───────────────────────────────────┘

alarm clock (alarm clocks) N-COUNT An **alarm clock** is a clock that you can set to make a noise so that it wakes you up at a particular time. ❑ *I set my alarm clock for 4:30.*

alarmed /əlɑrmd/ ADJ If someone is **alarmed**, they feel afraid or anxious that something unpleasant or dangerous might happen. ❑ *They should not be too alarmed by the press reports.*

alarm|ing /əlɑrmɪŋ/ **1** ADJ Something that is **alarming** makes you feel afraid or anxious that something unpleasant or dangerous might happen. ● **alarm|ing|ly** ADV ❑ *...the alarmingly high rate of heart disease.* **2** → See feature box at **global warming**

alarm|ist /əlɑrmɪst/ ADJ Someone or something that is **alarmist** causes unnecessary fear or anxiety that something unpleasant or dangerous is going to happen. ❑ *Contrary to the more alarmist reports, he is not going to die.*

alas /əlæs/ ADV [ADV with cl] You use **alas** to say that you think that the facts you are talking about are sad or unfortunate. [FORMAL, FEELINGS] ❑ *Such scandals have not, alas, been absent.*

Al|ba|nian /ælbeɪniən/ (Albanians) **1** ADJ **Albanian** means belonging or relating to Albania, its people, language, or culture. ❑ *Her parents were Albanian.* ❑ *...the Albanian coast.* **2** N-COUNT An **Albanian** is an Albanian citizen or a person of Albanian origin. **3** N-UNCOUNT **Albanian** is the language spoken by people who live in Albania.

al|ba|tross /ælbətrɔs/ (albatrosses) **1** N-COUNT An **albatross** is a very large white seabird. **2** N-COUNT [usu with supp] If you describe something or someone as an **albatross** around your neck, you mean that they cause you great problems from which you cannot escape, or they prevent you from doing what you want to do. [DISAPPROVAL] ❑ *Privatization could become a political albatross for the ruling party.*

al|be|it /ɔlbiɪt/ ADV [ADV with cl/group] You use **albeit** to introduce a fact or comment that reduces the force or significance of what you have just said. [FORMAL] ❑ *Charles's letter was indeed published, albeit in a somewhat abbreviated form.*

al|bi|no /ælbaɪnoʊ/ (albinos) N-COUNT An **albino** is a person or animal with very white skin, white hair, and pink eyes. ● ADJ [ADJ n] **Albino** is also an adjective. ❑ *...an albino rabbit.*

al|bum ♦⬦⬦ /ælbəm/ (albums) **1** N-COUNT An **album** is a collection of songs that is available on a CD, record, or cassette. ❑ *Chris likes music and has a large collection of albums and cassettes.* ❑ *Oasis release their new album on July 1.* **2** N-COUNT An **album** is a book in which you keep things such as photographs or stamps that you have collected. ❑ *Theresa showed me her photo album.*

▶ **COLLOCATIONS**

album
NOUN
1
noun + **album**: concept, compilation, solo, tribute; debut; comeback
adjective + **album**: forthcoming, upcoming; acclaimed, best-selling, platinum, well-received; new, latest
verb + **album**: produce, record; promote, release
2
noun + **album**: photo

al|bu|men /ælbyumən/ N-UNCOUNT **Albumen** is the white of an egg.

al|bu|min /ælbyumɪn/ N-UNCOUNT **Albumin** is a protein that is found in blood plasma, egg whites, and some other substances.

al|chemi|cal /ælkɛmɪkəl/ ADJ [ADJ n] **Alchemical** means relating to the science of alchemy. ❑ *...alchemical experiments.*

al|che|mist /ælkəmɪst/ (alchemists) N-COUNT An **alchemist** was a scientist in the Middle Ages who tried to discover how to change ordinary metals into gold.

al|che|my /ælkəmi/ N-UNCOUNT **Alchemy** was a form of chemistry studied in the Middle Ages, that was concerned with trying to discover ways to change ordinary metals into gold.

al|co|hol ♦⬦⬦ /ælkəhɔl/ (alcohols) **1** N-UNCOUNT Drinks that can make people drunk, such as beer, wine, and whiskey, can be referred to as **alcohol**. ❑ *Do either of you smoke cigarettes or drink alcohol?* **2** N-MASS **Alcohol** is a colorless liquid that is found in drinks such as beer, wine, and whiskey. It is also used in products such as perfumes and cleaning fluids. ❑ *...low-alcohol beer.*

al|co|hol|ic /ælkəhɔlɪk/ (alcoholics) **1** N-COUNT An **alcoholic** is someone who cannot stop drinking large amounts of alcohol, even when this is making them ill. ❑ *He showed great courage by admitting on television that he is an alcoholic.* **2** ADJ **Alcoholic** drinks are drinks that contain alcohol. ❑ *The serving of alcoholic drinks was forbidden after six o'clock.*

al|co|hol|ism /ælkəhɔlɪzəm/ N-UNCOUNT People who suffer from **alcoholism** cannot stop drinking large quantities of alcohol. ❑ *...a physician who specialized in the problems of alcoholism.*

al|co|pop /ælkəpɒp/ (alcopops) N-COUNT **Alcopops** are alcoholic drinks that are made to taste sweet and easy to drink, like soft drinks. ❑ *Most young drinkers at the club are either drinking water or alcopops.*

al|cove /ælkoʊv/ (alcoves) N-COUNT An **alcove** is a small area of a room that is formed by one part of a wall being built further back than the rest of the wall. ❑ *In the alcoves on either side of the fire were bookshelves.*

al den|te /æl dɛnteɪ/ ADJ [usu v-link ADJ] If you cook pasta or a vegetable until it is **al dente**, you cook it just long enough so that it is neither hard nor soft but is firm and slightly chewy.

al|der /ɔldər/ (alders) N-VAR An **alder** is a species of tree or shrub that grows especially in cool, damp places and loses its leaves in winter.

al|der|man /ɔldərmən/ (aldermen) N-COUNT; N-TITLE In some parts of the United States and Canada, an **alderman** is a man who is a member of the governing body of a city.

al|der|woman /ɔldərwʊmən/ (alderwomen) N-COUNT; N-TITLE In some parts of the United States and Canada, an **alderwoman** is a woman who is a member of the governing body of a city.

ale /eɪl/ (ales) N-MASS **Ale** is a kind of strong beer. ❑ *our selection of ales and spirits.*

aleck /ælɪk/ also **alec** → see **smart aleck**

alert ♦⬦⬦ /əlɜrt/ (alerts, alerting, alerted) **1** ADJ If you are **alert**, you are paying full attention to things around you and are able to deal with anything that might happen. ❑ *We all have to stay alert.* ● **alert|ness** N-UNCOUNT ❑ *The drug improved mental alertness.* **2** ADJ [v-link ADJ to n] If you are **alert** to something, you are fully aware of it. ❑ *The bank is alert to the danger.* **3** N-COUNT An **alert** is a situation in which people prepare themselves for something dangerous that might happen soon. ❑ *There has been criticism of how his administration handled last week's terrorism alert.* **4** V-T If you **alert** someone to a situation, especially a dangerous or unpleasant situation, you tell them about it. ❑ *He wanted to alert people to the activities of the group.* **5** PHRASE If you are **on the alert** for something, you are ready to deal with it if it happens. ❑ *They want to be on the alert for similar buying opportunities.*

al|fal|fa /ælfælfə/ N-UNCOUNT **Alfalfa** is a plant that is used for feeding farm animals. The shoots that develop from its seeds are sometimes eaten as a vegetable.

al|fres|co /ælfrɛskoʊ/ also **al fresco** ADJ [ADJ n] An **alfresco** activity, especially a meal, is one that takes place in the open air. ❑ *...an al fresco breakfast of fresh fruit.* ● ADV [ADV after v] **Alfresco** is also an adverb. ❑ *He came across the man shaving alfresco.*

al|gae /ældʒi, ælgaɪ/ N-PLURAL **Algae** are plants with no stems or leaves that grow in water or on damp surfaces. ❑ *...an effort to control toxic algae in Green Lake.*

al|gal /ælgəl/ ADJ [ADJ n] **Algal** means relating to algae. ❑ *Sewage nutrients do increase algal growth in the harbor.*

al|ge|bra /ældʒɪbrə/ N-UNCOUNT **Algebra** is a type of mathematics in which letters are used to represent possible quantities.

▶ **WORD HISTORY**

algebra
The term *al-jabr* is taken from the title of a ninth-century Arabic book on mathematics. In Arabic, *al-jabr* means 'reunion' or 'integration.' When the book was later translated into Latin, *al-jabr* became **algebra**.

al|ge|bra|ic /ˌældʒɪˈbreɪɪk/ ADJ [ADJ n] **Algebraic** equations, expressions, and principles are based on or use algebra.

Al|ge|rian ✦✧✧ /ælˈdʒɪəriən/ (**Algerians**) **1** ADJ **Algerian** means belonging or relating to Algeria, or its people or culture. ❑ *...the Algerian desert.* ❑ *...a young Algerian actor.* **2** N-COUNT An **Algerian** is an Algerian citizen or a person of Algerian origin.

al|go|rithm /ˈælɡərɪðəm/ (**algorithms**) N-COUNT An **algorithm** is a series of mathematical steps, especially in a computer program, which will give you the answer to a particular kind of problem or question.

alia /ˈeɪliə/ → see **inter alia**

ali|as /ˈeɪliəs/ (**aliases**) **1** N-COUNT An **alias** is a false name, especially one used by a criminal. ❑ *Using an alias, he had rented a house in Des Moines.* **2** PREP You use **alias** when you are mentioning another name that someone, especially a criminal or an actor, is known by. ❑ *Richard Thorp, alias Alan Turner, said yesterday: "It is a sad time for both of us."*

ali|bi /ˈælɪbaɪ/ (**alibis**) N-COUNT If you have an **alibi**, you can prove that you were somewhere else when a crime was committed. ❑ *He manages to persuade both his wife and girlfriend to provide him with an alibi.*

al|ien /ˈeɪliən/ (**aliens**) **1** ADJ **Alien** means belonging to a different country, race, or group, usually one you do not like or are frightened of. [FORMAL, DISAPPROVAL] ❑ *Such an attitude is alien to many businesspeople.* **2** ADJ [v-link ADJ to n] If something is **alien** to you or to your normal feelings or behavior, it is not the way you would normally feel or behave. [FORMAL] ❑ *Such an attitude is alien to most businessmen.* **3** N-COUNT An **alien** is someone who is not a legal citizen of the country in which they live. [LEGAL] ❑ *Both women had hired illegal aliens for child care.* **4** N-COUNT In science fiction, an **alien** is a creature from outer space. ❑ *...aliens from another planet.*

al|ien|ate /ˈeɪliəneɪt/ (**alienates, alienating, alienated**) **1** V-T If you **alienate** someone, you make them become unfriendly or unsympathetic toward you. ❑ *The government cannot afford to alienate either group.* **2** V-T To **alienate** a person from someone or something that they are normally linked with means to cause them to be emotionally or intellectually separated from them. ❑ *His second wife, Alice, was determined to alienate him from his two boys.*

alight /əˈlaɪt/ (**alights, alighting, alighted**) **1** ADJ [v n ADJ, v-link ADJ] If something is **alight**, it is burning. ❑ *Several buildings were set alight.* **2** ADJ [v-link ADJ] If someone's eyes are **alight** or if their face is **alight**, the expression in their eyes or on their face shows that they are feeling a strong emotion such as excitement or happiness. [LITERARY] ❑ *She paused and turned, her face alight with happiness.* **3** V-I If a bird or insect **alights** somewhere, it lands there. [LITERARY] ❑ *A thrush alighted on a branch of the pine tree.* **4** V-I When you **alight** from a train, bus, or other vehicle, you get out of it after a trip. [FORMAL]

align /əˈlaɪn/ (**aligns, aligning, aligned**) **1** V-T If you **align** yourself with a particular group, you support them because you have the same political aim. ❑ *When war broke out, they aligned themselves with the rebel forces.* **2** V-T If you **align** something, you place it in a certain position in relation to something else, usually parallel to it. ❑ *A tripod will be useful to align and steady the camera.*

align|ment /əˈlaɪnmənt/ (**alignments**) **1** N-VAR An **alignment** is support for a particular group, especially in politics, or for a side in a quarrel or struggle. ❑ *The church should have no political alignment.* **2** N-UNCOUNT The **alignment** of something is its position in relation to something else or to its correct position. ❑ *They shunned the belief that there is a link between the alignment of the planets and events on the Earth.*

alike /əˈlaɪk/ **1** ADJ [v-link ADJ] If two or more things are **alike**, they are similar in some way. ❑ *We looked very alike.* **2** ADV [ADV after v] **Alike** means in a similar way. ❑ *They even dressed alike.*

───── USAGE ─────

alike

Don't use 'alike' in front of a noun. Don't say, for example, 'They wore alike hats.' You say 'They wore similar hats.' *The two companies sell similar products.*

─────────────────

ali|men|ta|ry ca|nal /ˌælɪmentəri kənæl/ (**alimentary canals**) N-COUNT The **alimentary canal** in a person or animal is the passage in their body through which food passes from their mouth to their anus.

ali|mo|ny /ˈælɪmoʊni/ N-UNCOUNT **Alimony** is money that a court of law orders someone to pay regularly to their former wife or husband after they have gotten divorced. Compare **palimony**.

A-list 1 ADJ [usu ADJ n] An **A-list** celebrity is a celebrity who is very famous. ❑ *...an A-list Hollywood actress.* ❑ *Quinn's connections are strictly A-list.* **2** N-SING [the/a n] An **A-list** of celebrities is a group of celebrities who are very famous. ❑ *...the A-list of Hollywood stars.*

alive ✦✧✧ /əˈlaɪv/ **1** ADJ [v-link ADJ] If people or animals are **alive**, they are not dead. ❑ *She does not know if he is alive or dead.* **2** ADJ If you say that someone seems **alive**, you mean that they seem to be very lively and to enjoy everything that they do. ❑ *She seemed more alive and looked forward to getting up in the morning.* **3** ADJ [v-link ADJ, keep n ADJ] If an activity, organization, or situation is **alive**, it continues to exist or function. ❑ *The big factories are trying to stay alive by cutting costs.* **4** ADJ [v-link ADJ] If a place is **alive** with something, there are a lot of people or things there and it seems busy or exciting. ❑ *The river was alive with birds.* **5** PHRASE If people, places, or events **come alive**, they start to be lively again after a quiet period. If someone or something **brings** them **alive**, they cause them to come alive. ❑ *The doctor's voice had come alive and his small eyes shone.* **6** PHRASE If a story or description **comes alive**, it becomes interesting, lively, or realistic. If someone or something **brings** it **alive**, they make it seem more interesting, lively, or realistic. ❑ *She made history come alive with tales from her own memories.*

───── USAGE ─────

alive

Don't use 'alive' in front of a noun. Don't say, for example, 'I have no alive relatives' or 'They export alive animals.' Instead you use **living** to talk about people, or **live** /laɪv/ to talk about animals. *I have no living relatives. They export live animals.*

─────────────────

al|ka|li /ˈælkəlaɪ/ (**alkalis**) N-MASS An **alkali** is a substance with a pH value of more than 7. Alkalis form chemical salts when they are combined with acids.

al|ka|line /ˈælkəlaɪn/ ADJ Something that is **alkaline** contains an alkali or has a pH value of more than 7. ❑ *Some soils are actually too alkaline for certain plant life.* • **al|ka|lin|ity** /ˌælkəˈlɪnɪti/ N-UNCOUNT ❑ *A pH test measures the acidity or alkalinity of a substance.*

───── ALL ─────

① EVERYTHING, THE WHOLE OF SOMETHING
② EMPHASIS
③ OTHER PHRASES

─────────────────

① **all** ✦✦✦ /ɔːl/ **1** PREDET You use **all** to indicate that you are referring to the whole of a particular group or thing or to everyone or everything of a particular kind. ❑ *...the restaurant that Hugh and all his friends go to.* • DET **All** is also a determiner. ❑ *There is built-in storage space in all bedrooms.* ❑ *He was passionate about all literature.* • QUANT **All** is also a quantifier. ❑ *He was told to pack up all of his letters and personal belongings.* • PRON **All** is also a pronoun. ❑ *The salon produces its own shampoos and hair-care products, all based on herbal recipes.* • PRON-EMPH [n PRON v] **All** is also an emphasizing pronoun. ❑ *Milk, oily fish and eggs all contain vitamin D.* **2** DET You use **all** to refer to the whole of a particular period of time. ❑ *George had to cut grass all afternoon.* • PREDET [PREDET det sing-n] **All** is also a predeterminer. ❑ *She's worked all her life.* • QUANT [QUANT of def-n] **All** is also a quantifier. ❑ *He spent all of that afternoon polishing the silver.* **3** PRON You use **all** to refer to a situation or to life in general. ❑ *All is silent on the island now.* **4** PHRASE **All but** a particular person or thing means everyone or everything except that person or thing. ❑ *The general was an unattractive man to all but his most ardent admirers.* **5** PHRASE You use **all but** to say that something is almost the case. ❑ *The concrete wall that used to divide this city has now all but gone.* **6** PHRASE **In all** means in total. ❑ *There was evidence that*

thirteen people in all had taken part in planning the murder. ◼7 PHRASE You use **all in all** to introduce a summary or general statement. ◻ *We both thought that all in all it might not be a bad idea.*
② **all** ◆◆◆ /ɔl/ ◼1 DET You use **all** in expressions such as **in all sincerity** and **in all probability** to emphasize that you are being sincere or that something is very likely. [EMPHASIS] ◻ *In all fairness he had to admit that she was neither dishonest nor lazy.* ◼2 PRON You use **all** at the beginning of a clause when you are emphasizing that something is the only thing that is important. [EMPHASIS] ◻ *He said all that remained was to agree to a time and venue.* ◻ *All you ever want to do is go shopping!* ◼3 ADV [ADV prep/adv] You use **all** to emphasize that something is completely true, or happens everywhere or always, or on every occasion. [EMPHASIS] ◻ *He loves animals and he knows all about them.* ◻ *He was doing it all by himself.* ◼4 ADV **All** is used in structures such as **all the more** or **all the better** to mean even more or even better than before. ◻ *The living room is decorated in pale colors that make it all the more airy.* ◼5 PRON-EMPH You use **all** in expressions such as **seen it all** and **done it all** to emphasize that someone has had a lot of experience of something. [EMPHASIS] ◻ *They've seen it all, so it takes a lot to rattle them.* ◼6 PHRASE You say **above all** to indicate that the thing you are mentioning is the most important point. [EMPHASIS] ◻ *Above all, chairs should be comfortable.* ◼7 PHRASE You use **and all** when you want to emphasize that what you are talking about includes the thing mentioned, especially when this is surprising or unusual. [EMPHASIS] ◻ *He dropped his hot dog on the pavement and someone's dog ate it, mustard and all.* ◼8 PHRASE You use **at all** at the end of a clause to give emphasis to negative statements, conditional clauses, and questions. [EMPHASIS] ◻ *Robin never really liked him at all.* ◼9 PHRASE You use **for all** in phrases such as **for all I know**, and **for all he cares**, to emphasize that you do not know something or that someone does not care about something. [EMPHASIS] ◻ *For all we know, he may not even be in this country.* ◼10 PHRASE You use **of all** to emphasize the words 'first' or 'last', or a superlative adjective or adverb. [EMPHASIS] ◻ *First of all, answer these questions.* ◼11 PHRASE You use **of all** in expressions such as **of all people** or **of all things** when you want to emphasize someone or something surprising. [EMPHASIS] ◻ *One group of women, sitting on the ground, was singing, of all things, "Greensleeves."* ◼12 PHRASE You use **of all** in expressions like **of all the nerve** or **of all the luck** to emphasize how angry or surprised you are at what someone else has done or said. [FEELINGS] ◻ *Of all the lazy, indifferent, unbusinesslike attitudes to have!* ◼13 PHRASE You use **all of** before a number to emphasize how small or large an amount is. [EMPHASIS] ◻ *It took him all of 41 minutes to score his first goal.*
③ **all** ◆◆◆ /ɔl/ ◼1 ADV [amount ADV] You use **all** when you are talking about an equal score in a game. For example, if the score is three **all**, both players or teams have three points. ◼2 PHRASE You use **after all** when introducing a statement that supports or helps explain something you have just said. ◻ *I thought you might know somebody. After all, you're the man with connections.* ◼3 PHRASE You use **after all** when you are saying that something that you thought might not be the case is in fact the case. ◻ *I came out here on the chance of finding you at home after all.* ◼4 PHRASE You use **for all** to indicate that the thing mentioned does not affect or contradict the truth of what you are saying. ◻ *For all its beauty, Prague could soon lose some of the individuality that the communist years helped to preserve.* ◼5 PHRASE You use **all that** in statements with negative meaning when you want to weaken the force of what you are saying. [SPOKEN, VAGUENESS] ◻ *He wasn't all that much older than we were.* ◼6 PHRASE You can say **that's all** at the end of a sentence when you are explaining something and want to emphasize that nothing more happens or is the case. ◻ *"Why do you want to know that? he demanded.—"Just curious, that's all."* ◼7 PHRASE You use **all very well** to suggest that you do not really approve of something or you think that it is unreasonable. [DISAPPROVAL] ◻ *It is all very well to urge people to give more to charity when they have less, but is it really fair?*

USAGE

after all
Don't use 'after all' when you want to introduce a final point, question, or topic. Instead you use **finally** or **lastly**. *Finally, I want to thank you all for coming.*

all- /ɔl-/ ◼1 COMB IN ADJ [usu ADJ n] **All-** is added to nouns or adjectives in order to form adjectives that describe something as consisting only of the thing mentioned or as having only the quality indicated. ◻ *The all-star cast includes Jeremy Irons.* ◼2 COMB IN ADJ [usu ADJ n] **All-** is added to present participles or adjectives in order to form adjectives that describe something as including or affecting everything or everyone. ◻ *Nursing a demented person is an all-consuming task.* ◼3 COMB IN ADJ [usu ADJ n] **All-** is added to nouns in order to form adjectives that describe something as being suitable for or including all types of a particular thing. ◻ *He wanted to form an all-party government of national unity.*

Allah /ˈælə, ˈælɑ/ N-PROPER **Allah** is the name of God in Islam. ◻ *Allah be praised!*

all-American ADJ [ADJ n] If you describe someone as an **all-American** boy or girl, you mean that they seem to have all the typical qualities that are valued by ordinary Americans, such as good looks and love of their country.

all-around ◼1 ADJ [ADJ n] An **all-around** person is good at a lot of different skills, academic subjects, or sports. ◻ *He is a great all-around player.* ◼2 ADJ [ADJ n] **All-around** means doing or relating to all aspects of a job or activity. ◻ *He demonstrated the all-around skills of a quarterback.*

al|lay /əˈleɪ/ (**allays, allaying, allayed**) V-T If you **allay** someone's fears or doubts, you stop them feeling afraid or doubtful. [FORMAL] ◻ *He did what he could to allay his wife's myriad fears.*

all clear ◼1 N-SING [the N] **The all clear** is a signal that a dangerous situation, for example, an air raid, has ended. ◻ *The all clear was sounded about 10 minutes after the alert was given.* ◼2 N-SING [the N] If someone in authority gives you **the all clear**, they give you permission to continue with a plan or activity, usually after a problem has been sorted out. ◻ *I was given the all clear by the doctor to resume playing.*

all-comers also **all comers** N-PLURAL You use **all-comers** to refer to everyone who wants to take part in an activity, especially in a competition. ◻ *This is her second season offering residential courses for all-comers.*

al|le|ga|tion ◆◇◇ /ˌæləˈɡeɪʃən/ (**allegations**) N-COUNT An **allegation** is a statement saying that someone has done something wrong. ◻ *The company has denied the allegations.*

COLLOCATIONS

allegation
NOUN
noun + **allegation**: abuse, assault, harassment, racism, rape; bribery, corruption, doping, fraud
adjective + **allegation**: baseless, false, unfounded, unsubstantiated, untrue; credible, true; unproven; lurid
verb + **allegation**: deny, dismiss, refute, reject; investigate; make

al|lege /əˈlɛdʒ/ (**alleges, alleging, alleged**) V-T If you **allege** that something bad is true, you say it but do not prove it. [FORMAL] ◻ *She alleged that there was rampant drug use among the male members of the group.* ◻ *The accused is alleged to have killed a man.*

al|leged ◆◇◇ /əˈlɛdʒd/ ADJ [ADJ n] An **alleged** fact has been stated but has not been proved to be true. [FORMAL] ◻ *They have begun a hunger strike in protest at the alleged beating.*
• **al|leg|ed|ly** /əˈlɛdʒɪdli/ ADV ◻ *His van allegedly struck the two as they were crossing a street.*

SYNONYMS

alleged
ADJ
apparent: *There is at last an apparent end to the destructive price war.*
ostensible: *The ostensible purpose of these meetings was to gather information.*
supposed: *...when the rule of law is broken by its supposed guardians.*
putative: *...a putative father.*

al|le|giance /əˈliːdʒəns/ (**allegiances**) N-VAR Your **allegiance** is your support for and loyalty to a particular group, person, or belief. ◻ *My allegiance to Kendall and his company ran deep.*

allegorical — allowable

al|le|gori|cal /ˌælɪgɔrɪkᵊl/ ADJ An **allegorical** story, poem, or painting uses allegory. ☐ *Every Russian knows the allegorical novel The Master And Margarita.*

al|le|go|ry /ˈælɪgɔri/ (allegories) **1** N-COUNT [oft N *of* n] An **allegory** is a story, poem, or painting in which the characters and events are symbols of something else. Allegories are often moral, religious, or political. ☐ *The book is a kind of allegory of Latin American history.* **2** N-UNCOUNT **Allegory** is the use of characters and events in a story, poem, or painting to represent other things. ☐ *The poem's comic allegory was transparent.*

al|le|gro /əˈlɛgroʊ/ (allegros) **1** N-COUNT [oft in names] An **allegro** is a piece of classical music that should be played quickly and in a lively way. **2** ADV **Allegro** written above a piece of music means that it should be played quickly and in a lively way.

all-embracing ADJ Something that is **all-embracing** includes or affects everyone or everything. ☐ *His hospitality was instantaneous and all-embracing.*

al|ler|gen /ˈælərdʒən, -dʒen/ (allergens) N-COUNT An **allergen** is a substance that causes an allergic reaction in someone. [TECHNICAL]

al|ler|gic /əˈlɜrdʒɪk/ **1** ADJ [v-link ADJ *to* n] If you are **allergic** to something, you become ill or get a rash when you eat it, smell it, or touch it. ☐ *I'm allergic to cats.* **2** ADJ [ADJ n] If you have an **allergic** reaction to something, you become ill or get a rash when you eat it, smell it, or touch it. ☐ *Soy milk can cause allergic reactions in some children.* **3** → See feature box at **illness**

al|ler|gist /ˈælərdʒɪst/ (allergists) N-COUNT An **allergist** is a doctor who specializes in treating people with allergies.

al|ler|gy /ˈælərdʒi/ (allergies) N-VAR If you have a particular **allergy**, you become ill or get a rash when you eat, smell, or touch something that does not normally make people ill. ☐ *Food allergies can result in an enormous variety of different symptoms.*

al|le|vi|ate /əˈliviˌeɪt/ (alleviates, alleviating, alleviated) V-T If you **alleviate** pain, suffering, or an unpleasant condition, you make it less intense or severe. [FORMAL] ☐ *Nowadays, a great deal can be done to alleviate back pain.* • **al|le|via|tion** /əˌliviˈeɪʃᵊn/ N-UNCOUNT [usu N *of* n] ☐ *Their energies were focused on the alleviation of the refugees' misery.*

al|ley /ˈæli/ (alleys) N-COUNT An **alley** is a narrow passage or street with buildings or walls on both sides.

al|ley cat (alley cats) N-COUNT An **alley cat** is a cat that lives in the streets of a town, and is usually not owned by anyone.

alley|way /ˈæliweɪ/ (alleyways) also **alley-way** N-COUNT An **alleyway** is the same as an **alley**.

al|li|ance ♦♢♢ /əˈlaɪəns/ (alliances) **1** N-COUNT An **alliance** is a group of countries or political parties that are formally united and working together because they have similar aims. ☐ *The two parties were still too much apart to form an alliance.* **2** N-COUNT [oft N *with/between* n] An **alliance** is a relationship in which two countries, political parties, or organizations work together for some purpose. ☐ *The Socialists' electoral strategy has been based on a tactical alliance with the Communists.*

al|lied ♦♢♢ /əˈlaɪd/ **1** ADJ [ADJ n] **Allied** forces or troops are armies from different countries who are fighting on the same side in a war. ☐ *...the approaching Allied forces.* **2** ADJ [ADJ n, v-link ADJ *to* n] **Allied** countries, troops, or political parties are united by a political or military agreement. ☐ *...forces from three allied nations.* **3** ADJ [v-link ADJ *to/with* n, ADJ n] If one thing or group is **allied** to another, it is related to it because the two things have particular qualities or characteristics in common. ☐ *...lectures on subjects allied to health, beauty and fitness.*

al|li|ga|tor /ˈælɪgeɪtər/ (alligators) N-COUNT An **alligator** is a large reptile with short legs, a long tail, and very powerful jaws. ☐ *There are numerous signs warning people not to feed the alligators in the area.*

WORD HISTORY

alligator
The word **alligator** comes from Spanish *el lagarto*, meaning 'the lizard.'

---

all-inclusive **1** ADJ [usu ADJ n] **All-inclusive** is used to indicate that a price, especially the price of a vacation, includes all the charges and all the services offered. ☐ *An all-inclusive, two-week vacation costs around $2880 per person.* **2** → See feature box at **tourism**

all-in-one **1** ADJ [ADJ n] **All-in-one** means having several different parts or several different functions. ☐ *...the X85, an all-in-one printer that's also a scanner, fax and copier.* ☐ *These funds are an all-in-one approach to investing. They contain a blend of stocks and bonds.* **2** → see also **one** ①

al|lit|era|tion /əˌlɪtəˈreɪʃᵊn/ (alliterations) N-VAR **Alliteration** is the use in speech or writing of several words close together that all begin with the same letter or sound. [TECHNICAL]

al|lit|era|tive /əˈlɪtəreɪtɪv, -ərətɪv/ ADJ **Alliterative** means relating to or connected with alliteration. [TECHNICAL] ☐ *Her campaign slogan, "a president for the people," was pleasantly alliterative but empty.*

al|lo|cate /ˈæləkeɪt/ (allocates, allocating, allocated) V-T If one item or share of something **is allocated** to a particular person or for a particular purpose, it is given to that person or used for that purpose. ☐ *Tickets are limited and will be allocated to those who apply first.* ☐ *The federal budget allocated $7.3 billion for development programs.*

al|lo|ca|tion /ˌæləˈkeɪʃᵊn/ (allocations) **1** N-COUNT An **allocation** is an amount of something, especially money, that is given to a particular person or used for a particular purpose. ☐ *A State Department spokeswoman said that the aid allocation for Pakistan was still under review.* **2** N-UNCOUNT The **allocation** of something is the decision that it should be given to a particular person or used for a particular purpose. ☐ *Town planning and land allocation had to be coordinated.*

al|lot /əˈlɒt/ (allots, allotting, allotted) V-T [usu passive] If something **is allotted** to someone, it is given to them as their share. ☐ *The seats are allotted to the candidates who have won the most votes.*

al|lot|ment /əˈlɒtmənt/ (allotments) N-COUNT [oft N *of* n] An **allotment** of something is a share or amount of it that is given to someone. ☐ *His meager allotment of gas had to be saved for emergencies.*

all-out also **all out** ADJ [ADJ n] You use **all-out** to describe actions that are carried out in a very energetic and determined way, using all the resources available. ☐ *He launched an all-out attack on his critics.*

all-over ADJ [ADJ n] You can use **all-over** to describe something that covers an entire surface. ☐ *They got great all-over tans.* ☐ *...an all-over body scrub and massage.* ☐ *Go for a bold, all-over pattern such as stripes.*

al|low ♦♦♦ /əˈlaʊ/ (allows, allowing, allowed) **1** V-T If someone **is allowed** to do something, it is all right for them to do it and they will not get into trouble. ☐ *The children are allowed to watch TV after school.* ☐ *Smoking will not be allowed.* **2** V-T If you are **allowed** something, you are given permission to have it or are given it. ☐ *Gifts like chocolates or flowers are allowed.* **3** V-T If you **allow** something to happen, you do not prevent it. ☐ *He won't allow himself to fail.* **4** V-T If one thing **allows** another thing to happen, the first thing creates the opportunity for the second thing to happen. ☐ *The compromise will allow him to continue his free market reforms.* ☐ *...an attempt to allow the majority a greater share of power.* **5** V-T If you **allow** a particular length of time or a particular amount of something for a particular purpose, you include it in your planning. ☐ *Please allow 28 days for delivery.* ▶ **allow for** PHRASAL VERB If you **allow for** certain problems or expenses, you include some extra time or money in your planning so that you can deal with them if they occur. ☐ *You have to allow for a certain amount of error.*

SYNONYMS

allow
VERB **1**
permit: *The guards permitted me to bring my camera and tape recorder.*
authorize: *We are willing to authorize the president to use force, if necessary.*
sanction: *He may now be ready to sanction the use of force.*
let: *I love sweets but Mom doesn't let me have them very often.*

---

al|low|able /əˈlaʊəbᵊl/ **1** ADJ If people decide that something is **allowable**, they let it happen without trying to stop it.

allowance / almanac

❑ *Retaking the test is allowable only under certain circumstances.* **2** ADJ **Allowable** costs or expenses are amounts of money that you do not have to pay tax on. [BUSINESS]

al|low|ance /əlaʊəns/ (**allowances**) **1** N-COUNT An **allowance** is money that is given to someone, usually on a regular basis, in order to help them pay for the things that they need. ❑ *She gets an allowance for taking care of Amy.* **2** N-COUNT A child's **allowance** is money that is given to him or her every week or every month by his or her parents. [mainly AM] ❑ *When you give kids an allowance make sure they save some of it.*

> in BRIT, use **pocket money**

3 N-COUNT A particular type of **allowance** is an amount of something that you are allowed in particular circumstances. ❑ *Most of our flights have a baggage allowance of 44 lbs per passenger.* **4** N-COUNT Your tax **allowance** is the amount of money that you are allowed to earn before you have to start paying income tax. [BRIT]

> in AM, use **personal exemption**

5 PHRASE If you **make allowances** for something, you take it into account in your decisions, plans, or actions. ❑ *They'll make allowances for the fact it's affecting our performance.* ❑ *She tried to make allowances for his age.* **6** PHRASE If you **make allowances** for someone, you accept behavior from them that you would not normally accept, because of a problem that they have. ❑ *He's tired so I'll make allowances for him.*

al|loy /ælɔɪ/ (**alloys**) N-MASS An **alloy** is a metal that is made by mixing two or more types of metal together. ❑ *Bronze is an alloy of copper and tin.*

all-points bul|letin (**all-points bulletins**) N-COUNT An **all-points bulletin** is a message sent by a police force to all its officers. The abbreviation **APB** is also used. [AM] ❑ *His capture comes just eight hours after the FBI issued an all-points bulletin for Helder.*

all-powerful ADJ An **all-powerful** person or organization has the power to do anything they want. ❑ *...the all-powerful labor unions.*

all-purpose ADJ [ADJ n] You use **all-purpose** to refer to things that have lots of different uses or can be used in lots of different situations. ❑ *...a biodegradable, all-purpose cleaner for general stain removal.*

all-purpose flour N-UNCOUNT **All-purpose flour** is flour that does not make cakes and cookies rise when they are baked because it has no chemicals added to it. [AM] ❑ *You can substitute all-purpose flour if you cannot find pastry flour.*

> in BRIT, use **plain flour**

all right ♦♦◊

> in BRIT, also use **alright**

1 ADJ [v-link ADJ] If you say that someone or something is **all right**, you mean that you find them satisfactory or acceptable. ❑ *I consider you a good friend, and if it's all right with you, I'd like to keep it that way.* • ADJ [ADJ n] **All right** is also used before a noun. [INFORMAL] ❑ *He's an all right kind of guy really.* **2** ADJ [v-link ADJ] If someone or something is **all right**, they are well or safe. ❑ *All she's worried about is whether he is all right.* **3** ADV [ADV after v] If you say that something happens or goes **all right**, you mean that it happens in a satisfactory or acceptable manner. ❑ *Things have thankfully worked out all right.* **4** CONVENTION You say '**all right**' when you are agreeing to something. [FORMULAE] ❑ *"I think you should go now."—"All right."* **5** CONVENTION You say '**all right?**' after you have given an instruction or explanation to someone when you are checking that they have understood what you have just said, or checking that they agree with or accept what you have just said. ❑ *Peter, you get half the fees. All right?* **6** CONVENTION If someone in a position of authority says '**all right**,' and suggests talking about or doing something else, they are indicating that they want you to end one activity and start another. ❑ *All right, Bob. You can go now.* **7** CONVENTION You say '**all right**' during a discussion to show that you understand something that someone has just said, and to introduce a statement that relates to it. ❑ *I said there was no room in my mother's house, and he said, "All right, come to my studio and paint."* **8** CONVENTION You say **all right** before a statement

or question to indicate that you are challenging or threatening someone. ❑ *All right, who are you and what are you doing in my office?*

all-round [BRIT] → see **all-around**

all|spice /ɔːlspaɪs/ N-UNCOUNT **Allspice** is a powder used as a spice in cooking, made from the berries of a tropical American tree.

all-star ADJ [ADJ n] An **all-star** cast, performance, or game is one which contains only famous or extremely good performers or players.

all-time ADJ [ADJ n] You use **all-time** when you are comparing all the things of a particular type that there have ever been. For example, if you say that something is the **all-time** best, you mean that it is the best thing of its type that there has ever been. ❑ *The president's popularity nationally is at an all-time low.*

al|lude /əluːd/ (**alludes, alluding, alluded**) V-I If you **allude to** something, you mention it in an indirect way. [FORMAL] ❑ *With friends, she sometimes alluded to a feeling that she herself was to blame for her son's predicament.*

al|lure /əlʊər/ N-UNCOUNT The **allure** of something or someone is the pleasing or exciting quality that they have. ❑ *It's a game that has really lost its allure.*

al|lur|ing /əlʊərɪŋ/ ADJ Someone or something that is **alluring** is very attractive. ❑ *...the most alluring city in Southeast Asia.*

al|lu|sion /əluːʒən/ (**allusions**) N-VAR An **allusion** is an indirect reference to someone or something. ❑ *This last point was understood to be an allusion to the long-standing hostility between the two leaders.*

al|lu|sive /əluːsɪv/ ADJ **Allusive** speech, writing, or art is full of indirect references to people or things. ❑ *His new play, Arcadia, is as intricate, elaborate and allusive as anything he has yet written.*

al|lu|vial /əluːviəl/ ADJ **Alluvial** soils are soils which consist of earth and sand left behind on land which has been flooded or where a river once flowed. [TECHNICAL]

all-weather ADJ [ADJ n] **All-weather** sports take place on an artificial surface instead of on grass. ❑ *...all-weather racing.* ❑ *...an all-weather tennis court.*

ally ♦♦◊ (**allies, allying, allied**)

> The noun is pronounced /ælaɪ/. The verb is pronounced /əlaɪ/.

1 N-COUNT A country's **ally** is another country that has an agreement to support it, especially in war. ❑ *Washington would not take such a step without its allies' approval.* **2** N-COUNT If you describe someone as your **ally**, you mean that they help and support you, especially when other people are opposing you. ❑ *He is a close ally of the president.* **3** N-PLURAL **The Allies** were the armed forces that fought against Germany and Japan in World War II. ❑ *...Germany's surrender to the Allies.* **4** V-T If you **ally** yourself with someone or something, you give your support to them. ❑ *He will have no choice but to ally himself with the new movement.* **5** → see also **allied**

SUFFIX

-ally
is added to adjectives ending in *-ic* to form adverbs that indicate how something is done or what something relates to. For example, if something is done **enthusiastically**, it is done in an enthusiastic way.

all-you-can-eat ADJ [usu ADJ n] An **all-you-can-eat** buffet or restaurant is a buffet or restaurant at which you pay a fixed price, no matter how much or how little you eat. [mainly AM] ❑ *...an all-you-can-eat Chinese restaurant.*

alma ma|ter /ælmə mɑːtər, - meɪtər/ (**alma maters**) **1** N-COUNT [usu sing, usu with poss] Your **alma mater** is the school, college, or university that you went to. [FORMAL] **2** N-SING A school, college, or university's **alma mater** is its official song. [AM]

al|ma|nac /ɔːlmənæk/ (**almanacs**) also **almanack** **1** N-COUNT [oft in names] An **almanac** is a book published every year that contains information about the movements of the planets, the changes of the moon and the tides, and the dates of important anniversaries. **2** N-COUNT [oft in names] An **almanac** is a book published every year that contains

al|mighty /ɔlmaɪti/ **1** N-PROPER **The Almighty** is another name for God. You can also refer to **Almighty God**. ☐ *Adam sought guidance from the Almighty.* **2** EXCLAM People sometimes say **God Almighty** or **Christ Almighty** to express their surprise, anger, or horror. These expressions could cause offense. [FEELINGS]

al|mond /ɑmənd, æm-, ælm-/ (almonds) **1** N-VAR **Almonds** are pale oval nuts. They are often used in cooking. ☐ *...sponge cake flavored with almonds.* **2** N-VAR An **almond** or an **almond tree** is a tree on which almonds grow. ☐ *On the left was a plantation of almond trees.* **3** → See also color supplement

al|most ♦♦♦ /ɔlmoʊst/ ADV You use **almost** to indicate that something is not completely the case but is nearly the case. ☐ *The couple had been dating for almost three years.* ☐ *The effect is almost impossible to describe.* ☐ *He contracted Spanish flu, which almost killed him.*

alms /ɑmz/ N-PLURAL **Alms** are gifts of money, clothes, or food to poor people. [OLD-FASHIONED]

aloe vera /ˌæloʊ vɪərə/ N-UNCOUNT [oft N n] **Aloe vera** is a substance that contains vitamins and minerals and is often used in cosmetics. **Aloe vera** is also the name of the plant from which this substance is extracted.

aloft /əlɔft/ ADV [ADV after v, be ADV] Something that is **aloft** is in the air or off the ground. [LITERARY] ☐ *He held the trophy proudly aloft.*

alone ♦♦◊ /əloʊn/ **1** ADJ [v-link ADJ] When you are **alone**, you are not with any other people. ☐ *There is nothing so fearful as to be alone in a combat situation.* • ADV [ADV after v] **Alone** is also an adverb. ☐ *She has lived alone in this house for almost five years now.* **2** ADJ [v-link ADJ] If one person is **alone** with another person, or if two or more people are **alone**, they are together, without anyone else present. ☐ *I couldn't imagine why he would want to be alone with me.* **3** ADJ [v-link ADJ] If you say that you are **alone** or feel **alone**, you mean that nobody who is with you, or nobody at all, cares about you. ☐ *Never in her life had she felt so alone, so abandoned.* **4** ADJ [v-link ADJ] If someone is **alone** in doing something, they are the only person doing it, and so are different from other people. ☐ *Am I alone in recognizing that these two statistics have quite different implications?* • ADV **Alone** is also an adverb. ☐ *I alone was sane, I thought, in a world of crazy people.* **5** ADV [n ADV] You say that one person or thing **alone** does something when you are emphasizing that only one person or thing is involved. [EMPHASIS] ☐ *You alone should determine what is right for you.* **6** ADV [n ADV] If you say that one person or thing **alone** is responsible for part of an amount, you are emphasizing the size of that part and the size of the total amount. [EMPHASIS] ☐ *CNN alone is sending 300 technicians, directors and commentators.* **7** ADV [ADV after v] When someone does something **alone**, they do it without help from other people. ☐ *Bringing up a child alone should give you a sense of achievement.* **8** PHRASE If you **go it alone**, you do something without any help from other people. [INFORMAL] ☐ *I missed the stimulation of working with others when I tried to go it alone.* **9 to leave someone or something alone** → see **leave** ③ **10 let alone** → see **let**

USAGE

alone
Don't use 'alone' in front of a noun. For example, don't talk about 'an alone woman.' Instead, say 'a woman on her own.' *These vacations are popular with people on their own.*

---

along ♦♦♦ /əlɔŋ/

In addition to the uses shown below, **along** is used in phrasal verbs such as 'go along with,' 'play along,' and 'string along.'

1 PREP If you move or look **along** something such as a road, you move or look toward one end of it. ☐ *Pedro walked along the street alone.* ☐ *The young man led Mark Ryle along a corridor.* **2** PREP If something is situated **along** a road, river, or corridor, it is situated in it or beside it. ☐ *...enormous traffic jams all along the roads.* **3** ADV [ADV after v] When someone or something moves **along**, they keep moving in a particular direction. ☐ *She skipped and danced along.* ☐ *He raised his voice a little, talking into the wind as they walked along.* **4** ADV [ADV after v] If you say that something is going **along** in a particular way, you mean that it is progressing in that way. ☐ *...the negotiations which have been dragging along interminably.* **5** ADV [ADV after v] If you take someone or something **along** when you go somewhere, you take them with you. ☐ *This is open to women of all ages, so bring along your friends and colleagues.* **6** ADV [ADV after v] If someone or something is coming **along** or is sent **along**, they are coming or being sent to a particular place. ☐ *She invited everyone she knew to come along.* **7** PHRASE You use **along with** to mention someone or something else that is also involved in an action or situation. ☐ *The baby's mother escaped from the fire along with two other children.* **8** PHRASE If something has been true or been present **all along**, it has been true or been present throughout a period of time. ☐ *I've been fooling myself all along.* **9 along the way** → see **way** ④

along|side ♦♦◊ /əlɔŋsaɪd/ **1** PREP If one thing is **alongside** another thing, the first thing is next to the second. ☐ *He crossed the street and walked alongside Central Park.* • ADV [ADV after v] **Alongside** is also an adverb. ☐ *He waited several minutes for a car to pull up alongside.* **2** PREP If you work **alongside** other people, you all work together in the same place. ☐ *He had worked alongside Frank and Mark and they had become friends.*

aloof /əluːf/ ADJ Someone who is **aloof** is not very friendly and does not like to spend time with other people. [DISAPPROVAL] ☐ *He seemed aloof and detached.*

aloud /əlaʊd/ **1** ADV [ADV after v] When you say something, read, or laugh **aloud**, you speak or laugh so that other people can hear you. ☐ *When we were children, our father read aloud to us.* **2** PHRASE If you **think aloud**, you express your thoughts as they occur to you, rather than thinking first and then speaking. ☐ *He really must be careful about thinking aloud. Who knew what he might say?*

al|paca /ælpækə/ (alpacas) **1** N-UNCOUNT [oft N n] **Alpaca** is a type of soft wool. ☐ *...a light-gray alpaca suit.* **2** N-COUNT **Alpacas** are South American animals similar to llamas. Their hair is the source of alpaca wool.

al|pha|bet /ælfəbɛt, -bɪt/ (alphabets) N-COUNT An **alphabet** is a set of letters usually presented in a fixed order which is used for writing the words of a particular language or group of languages. ☐ *The modern Russian alphabet has 31 letters.*

al|pha|beti|cal /ˌælfəbɛtɪkəl/ ADJ [ADJ n] **Alphabetical** means arranged according to the normal order of the letters in the alphabet. ☐ *Their herbs and spices are arranged in alphabetical order on narrow open shelves.*

al|pine /ælpaɪn/ ADJ **Alpine** means existing in or relating to mountains, especially the ones in Switzerland. ☐ *...grassy, alpine meadows.*

al|ready ♦♦♦ /ɔlrɛdi/ **1** ADV You use **already** to show that something has happened, or that something had happened before the moment you are referring to. Some speakers use **already** with the simple past tense of the verb instead of a perfect tense. ☐ *They had already voted for him at the first ballot.* ☐ *She says she already told the neighbors not to come over for a couple of days.* **2** ADV You use **already** to show that a situation exists at this present moment or that it exists at an earlier time than expected. You use **already** after the verb 'be' or an auxiliary verb, or before a verb if there is no auxiliary. When you want to add emphasis, you can put **already** at the beginning of a sentence. ☐ *The authorities believe those security measures are already paying off.* ☐ *He was already rich.* ☐ *Already, she is thinking ahead.*

USAGE

already
Don't confuse **already** with **still** or **yet**. Use **still** when something that existed in the past continued and exists now. Use **yet** when something has not happened, although it probably will happen in the future. *Donald is 89, and he is still teaching. They haven't finished yet.*

---

al|right /ɔlraɪt/ [BRIT] → see **all right**

Al|sa|tian /ælseɪʃən/ (Alsatians) N-COUNT An **Alsatian** is a large, usually fierce dog that is often used to guard buildings or by the police to help them find criminals. [BRIT]

in AM, use **German shepherd**

also /ˈɔlsoʊ/ **1** ADV You can use **also** to give more information about a person or thing, or to add another relevant fact. ❑ *The book also includes an appendix with a listing of all U.S. presidents.* ❑ *He is an asthmatic who is also anemic.* **2** ADV You can use **also** to indicate that something you have just said about one person or thing is true of another person or thing. ❑ *The general was a survivor. His father, also a top-ranking officer, had perished during the war.* ❑ *This rule has also been applied in the case of a purchase of used tires and tubes.*

also-ran (also-rans) N-COUNT If you describe someone as an **also-ran**, you mean that they have been or are likely to be unsuccessful in a contest.

al|tar /ˈɔltər/ (altars) N-COUNT An **altar** is a holy table in a church or temple. ❑ *...the high altar of the cathedral.*

al|tar boy (altar boys) N-COUNT In the Roman Catholic church, an **altar boy** is a boy who helps the priest during Mass.

al|tar girl (altar girls) N-COUNT In the Roman Catholic church, an **altar girl** is a girl who helps the priest during Mass.

altar|piece /ˈɔltərpis/ (altarpieces) N-COUNT An **altarpiece** is a work of art behind the altar in a church.

al|ter /ˈɔltər/ (alters, altering, altered) V-T/V-I If something **alters** or if you **alter** it, it changes. ❑ *Nothing has altered and the deadline still stands.*

SYNONYMS

alter
VERB
modify: *The club members did agree to modify their recruitment policy.*
change: *They should change the law to make it illegal to own replica weapons.*
adjust: *To attract investors, Panama has adjusted its tax and labor laws.*
amend: *The president agreed to amend the constitution and allow multi-party elections.*
tweak: *The system will get even better as the engineers tweak its performance.*

---

al|tera|tion /ˌɔltəˈreɪʃən/ (alterations) **1** N-COUNT An **alteration** is a change in or to something. ❑ *Making some simple alterations to your diet will make you feel fitter.* **2** N-UNCOUNT The **alteration** of something is the process of changing it. ❑ *Her jacket was at the boutique waiting for alteration.* **3** → See feature box at **sewing**

al|ter|ca|tion /ˌɔltərˈkeɪʃən/ (altercations) N-COUNT [oft N with/between n] An **altercation** is a noisy argument or disagreement. [FORMAL] ❑ *I had a slight altercation with some people who objected to our filming.*

al|ter ego (alter egos) **1** N-COUNT [usu with supp] Your **alter ego** is the other side of your personality from the one that people normally see. **2** N-COUNT [usu with supp] You can describe the character that an actor usually plays on television or in films as their **alter ego**. ❑ *Barry Humphries's alter ego Dame Edna took the U.S. by storm.*

al|ter|nate (alternates, alternating, alternated)

The verb is pronounced /ˈɔltərneɪt/. The adjective and noun are pronounced /ˈɔltɜrnɪt/.

1 V-RECIP When you **alternate** two things, you keep using one then the other. When one thing **alternates** with another, the first regularly occurs after the other. ❑ *Her aggressive moods alternated with gentle or more cooperative states.* ❑ *Now you just alternate layers of that mixture and eggplant.* **2** ADJ [ADJ n] **Alternate** actions, events, or processes regularly occur after each other. ❑ *They were streaked with alternate bands of color.* ● **al|ter|nate|ly** ADV ❑ *He could alternately bully and charm people.* **3** ADJ [ADJ n] If something happens on **alternate** days, it happens on one day, then happens on every second day after that. In the same way, something can happen in **alternate** weeks, years, or other periods of time. ❑ *Lesley had agreed to Jim going skiing in alternate years.* **4** ADJ [ADJ n] You use **alternate** to describe a plan, idea, or system which is different from the one already in operation and can be used instead of it. ❑ *His group was forced to turn back and take an alternate route.* **5** N-COUNT An **alternate** is a person or thing that replaces another, and can act or be used instead of them. [AM] ❑ *In most jurisdictions, twelve jurors and two alternates are chosen.*

al|ter|nat|ing cur|rent (alternating currents) N-VAR An **alternating current** is an electric current that continually changes direction as it flows. The abbreviation **AC** is also used.

al|ter|na|tive /ɔlˈtɜrnətɪv/ (alternatives) **1** N-COUNT If one thing is an **alternative** to another, the first can be found, used, or done instead of the second. ❑ *New ways to treat arthritis may provide an alternative to painkillers.* **2** ADJ [ADJ n] An **alternative** plan or offer is different from the one that you already have, and can be done or used instead. ❑ *There were alternative methods of travel available.* **3** ADJ [ADJ n] **Alternative** is used to describe something that is different from the usual things of its kind, or the usual ways of doing something, in modern Western society. For example, an **alternative** lifestyle does not follow conventional ways of living and working. ❑ *...unconventional parents who embraced the alternative lifestyle of the Sixties.* **4** ADJ [ADJ n] **Alternative** medicine uses traditional ways of curing people, such as medicines made from plants, massage, and acupuncture. ❑ *...alternative health care.* **5** ADJ [ADJ n] **Alternative** energy uses natural sources of energy such as the sun, wind, or water for power and fuel, rather than oil, coal, or nuclear power.

SYNONYMS

alternative
NOUN **1**
substitute: *Biofuels are petrol substitutes made from renewable products such as ethanol.*
option: *What other options do you have?*
ADJ **2**
other: *He would have to accept it; there was no other way.*
alternate: *His group was forced to turn back and take an alternate route.*

---

al|ter|na|tive|ly /ɔlˈtɜrnətɪvli/ ADV [ADV with cl] You use **alternatively** to introduce a suggestion or to mention something different from what has just been stated. ❑ *Hotels are generally of a good standard and not too expensive. Alternatively you could stay in an apartment.*

al|ter|na|tor /ˈɔltərneɪtər/ (alternators) N-COUNT An **alternator** is a device, used especially in a car, that creates an electrical current that changes direction as it flows.

al|though /ɔlˈðoʊ/ **1** CONJ You use **although** to introduce a subordinate clause which contains a statement that contrasts with the statement in the main clause. ❑ *Although he is known to only a few, his reputation among them is very great.* **2** CONJ You use **although** to introduce a subordinate clause which contains a statement that makes the main clause of the sentence seem surprising or unexpected. ❑ *Although I was only six, I can remember seeing it on TV.* **3** CONJ You use **although** to introduce a subordinate clause which gives some information that is relevant to the main clause but modifies the strength of that statement. ❑ *He was in love with her, although he did not put that name to it.* **4** CONJ You use **although** when admitting a fact about something that you regard as less important than a contrasting fact. ❑ *Although they're expensive, they last forever and never go out of style.*

USAGE

although
When a sentence begins with **although** or **though**, don't use 'but' or 'yet' to introduce the main clause. Don't say, for example, 'Although he was late, yet he stopped to buy a sandwich.' You say 'Although he was late, **he stopped** to buy a sandwich.' *Although he was English, **he spoke** fluent French.*

SYNONYMS

although
CONJ **1**
though: *He's very engaging, though he is a little shy.*
while: *While the numbers are relatively small, the potential market is large.*
even though: *Even though I work alone, there are people who I can interact with.*

al|time|ter /ˈæltɪmɪtər/ (altimeters) N-COUNT An **altimeter** is an instrument in an aircraft that shows the height of the aircraft above the ground.

al|ti|tude /ˈæltɪtud/ (altitudes) N-VAR If something is at a particular **altitude**, it is at that height above sea level. ❑ *The aircraft had reached its cruising altitude of about 39,000 feet.*

alto /ˈæltoʊ/ (altos) **1** N-COUNT [oft N n] An **alto** is a woman who has a low singing voice. **2** N-COUNT An **alto** or **male alto** is a man who has the highest male singing voice. **3** ADJ [ADJ n] An **alto** musical instrument has a range of notes of medium pitch.

al|to|geth|er ✦✧✧ /ˌɔltəˈgɛðər/ **1** ADV [ADV after v] You use **altogether** to emphasize that something has stopped, been done, or finished completely. [EMPHASIS] ❑ *When Artie stopped calling altogether, Julie found a new man.* **2** ADV [ADV adj/adv] You use **altogether** in front of an adjective or adverb to emphasize a quality that someone or something has. [EMPHASIS] ❑ *The choice of language is altogether different.* **3** ADV You use **altogether** to modify a negative statement and make it less forceful. ❑ *We were not altogether sure that the comet would miss the Earth.* **4** ADV [ADV with cl] You can use **altogether** to introduce a summary of what you have been saying. ❑ *Altogether, it was a delightful town garden, peaceful and secluded.* **5** ADV [ADV with amount] If several amounts add up to a particular amount **altogether**, that amount is their total. ❑ *Brando received eight Oscar nominations altogether.*

al|to|stra|tus /ˌæltoʊˈstreɪtəs, -ˈstræt-/ (altostrati) N-VAR **Altostratus** is a type of thick gray cloud that forms at intermediate altitudes. [TECHNICAL]

alt-right /ˌɔltˈraɪt/ N-SING [oft N n] **The alt-right** refers to a group of people with extreme right-wing views, including extreme views on race, who use the internet rather than traditional politics to organize and to share opinions. ❑ *...alt-right websites.*

al|tru|ism /ˈæltruɪzəm/ N-UNCOUNT **Altruism** is unselfish concern for other people's happiness and welfare. ❑ *Fortunately, volunteers are not motivated by self-interest, but by altruism.*

al|tru|is|tic /ˌæltruˈɪstɪk/ ADJ If your behavior or motives are **altruistic**, you show concern for the happiness and welfare of other people rather than for yourself.

alum /əˈlʌm/ (alums) N-COUNT An **alum** is the same as an **alumnus**. [AM, INFORMAL] ❑ *...a University of Chicago alum.*

alu|min|ium /ˌæljuˈmɪniəm/ [BRIT] → see **aluminum**

alu|mi|num /əˈlumɪnəm/ **1** N-UNCOUNT **Aluminum** is a lightweight metal used, for example, for making cooking equipment and aircraft parts. [AM] ❑ *...aluminum cans.* **2** → See also color supplement

alum|nus /əˈlʌmnəs/ (alumni /əˈlʌmnaɪ/) N-COUNT The **alumni** of a school, college, or university are the people who used to be students there. [AM]

al|ways ✦✦✦ /ˈɔlweɪz/ **1** ADV [ADV before v] If you **always** do something, you do it whenever a particular situation occurs. If you **always** did something, you did it whenever a particular situation occurred. ❑ *She's always late for everything.* ❑ *Always lock your garage.* **2** ADV If something is **always** the case, was **always** the case, or will **always** be the case, it is, was, or will be the case all the time, continuously. ❑ *We will always remember his generous hospitality.* ❑ *He has always been the family solicitor.* **3** ADV [ADV before v-cont] If you say that something is **always** happening, especially something that annoys you, you mean that it happens repeatedly. ❑ *She was always moving things around.* **4** ADV [can/could ADV inf] You use **always** in expressions such as **can always** or **could always** when you are making suggestions or suggesting an alternative approach or method. ❑ *If you can't find any decent apples, you can always try growing them yourself.* **5** ADV [ADV before v] You can say that someone **always** was, for example, awkward or lucky to indicate that you are not surprised about what they are doing or have just done. ❑ *She's going to be fine. She always was pretty strong.*

Alzheimer's dis|ease /ˈæltshaɪmərz dɪziz, ˈɔlts-/ also **Alzheimer's** N-UNCOUNT **Alzheimer's disease** is a condition in which a person's thinking ability and memory gradually decline.

am /əm, STRONG æm/ **Am** is the first person singular of the present tense of **be**. **Am** is often shortened to **'m** in spoken English. The negative forms are 'I am not' and 'I'm not.' In questions and tags in spoken English, these are usually changed to 'aren't I.'

AM /ˌeɪ ˈɛm/ **AM** is a method of transmitting radio waves that can be used to broadcast sound. **AM** is an abbreviation for 'amplitude modulation.'

Am. Am. is a written abbreviation for **American**.

a.m. /ˌeɪ ˈɛm/ also **am a.m.** is used after a number to show that you are referring to a particular time between midnight and noon. Compare **p.m.** ❑ *The program starts at 9 a.m.*

amal|gam /əˈmælgəm/ (amalgams) N-COUNT [oft N of pl-n] Something that is an **amalgam** of two or more things is a mixture of them.

amal|gam|ate /əˈmælgəmeɪt/ (amalgamates, amalgamating, amalgamated) V-RECIP When two or more things, especially organizations, **amalgamate** or are **amalgamated**, they become one large thing. ❑ *The firm has amalgamated with another company.* ❑ *The chemical companies had amalgamated into a vast conglomerate.* • **amal|gama|tion** /əˌmælgəˈmeɪʃ°n/ (amalgamations) N-VAR ❑ *Athletics South Africa was formed by an amalgamation of two organizations.*

amass /əˈmæs/ (amasses, amassing, amassed) V-T If you **amass** something such as money or information, you gradually get a lot of it. ❑ *How had he amassed his fortune?*

ama|teur ✦✧✧ /ˈæmətʃər, -tʃʊər/ (amateurs) **1** N-COUNT An **amateur** is someone who does something as a hobby and not as a job. ❑ *Jerry is an amateur who dances because he feels like it.* **2** ADJ [ADJ n] **Amateur** sports or activities are done by people as a hobby and not as a job. ❑ *...professional athletes and amateur runners.*

ama|teur|ish /ˈæmətʃərɪʃ, -tʃʊərɪʃ/ ADJ If you describe something as **amateurish**, you think that it is not skillfully made or done. [DISAPPROVAL] ❑ *The paintings looked amateurish.*

ama|teur|ism /ˈæmətʃərɪzəm, -tʃʊərɪzəm/ N-UNCOUNT **Amateurism** is the belief that people should take part in sports and other activities as a hobby, for pleasure, rather than as a job, for money. ❑ *He is a staunch supporter of amateurism in intercollegiate athletics.*

amaze /əˈmeɪz/ (amazes, amazing, amazed) V-T/V-I If something **amazes** you, it surprises you very much. ❑ *He amazed us by his knowledge of Colorado history.* ❑ *The "Riverside" restaurant promises a variety of food that never ceases to amaze!* • **amazed** ADJ ❑ *Most of the cast was amazed by the play's success.*

amaze|ment /əˈmeɪzmənt/ N-UNCOUNT [oft in N] **Amazement** is the feeling you have when something surprises you very much. ❑ *I stared at her in amazement.*

amaz|ing ✦✧✧ /əˈmeɪzɪŋ/ ADJ You say that something is **amazing** when it is very surprising and makes you feel pleasure, approval, or wonder. ❑ *It's amazing what we can remember with a little prompting.* • **amaz|ing|ly** ADV ❑ *She was an amazingly good cook.*

SYNONYMS

amazing
ADJ
astonishing: *...an astonishing display of physical strength.*
surprising: *A surprising number of customers order the same sandwich every day.*
astounding: *The results are quite astounding.*
breathtaking: *The house has breathtaking views from every room.*

Ama|zon /ˈæməzɒn, -zən/ (Amazons) **1** N-COUNT [usu pl] In Greek mythology, the **Amazons** were a tribe of women who were very good at fighting. **2** N-COUNT People sometimes refer to a tall, strong woman as an **Amazon**.

Ama|zo|nian /ˌæməˈzoʊniən/ **1** ADJ [usu ADJ n] **Amazonian** means related to the area around the river Amazon. ❑ *...the Amazonian rainforest.* **2** ADJ [usu ADJ n] People sometimes describe a tall, strong woman as **Amazonian**. ❑ *...an Amazonian swimmer.* **3** ADJ [usu ADJ n] **Amazonian** means belonging to or connected with the Amazons in Greek mythology. ❑ *...Amazonian queens.*

am|bas|sa|dor /æmbæsədər/ (ambassadors) N-COUNT
An **ambassador** is an important official who lives in a foreign country and represents his or her own country's interests there. ☐ ...the German ambassador to Poland.

am|bas|sa|dor|ial /æmbæsədɔriəl/ ADJ [ADJ n]
Ambassadorial means belonging or relating to an ambassador. ☐ ...an ambassadorial post.

am|ber /æmbər/ **1** N-UNCOUNT [usu N n] **Amber** is a hard yellowish-brown substance used for making jewelry. ☐ ...an amber choker with matching earrings. **2** COLOR **Amber** is used to describe things that are yellowish-brown in color. ☐ A burst of sunshine sent a beam of amber light through the window. **3** COLOR An **amber** traffic light is yellow. ☐ Cars did not stop when the lights were on amber.

am|bi|ance /æmbiəns/ → see ambience

am|bi|dex|trous /æmbidɛkstrəs/ ADJ [usu v-link ADJ]
Someone who is **ambidextrous** can use both their right hand and their left hand equally skillfully.

am|bi|ence /æmbiəns/ also **ambiance** N-SING The **ambience** of a place is the character and atmosphere that it seems to have. [LITERARY] ☐ The overall ambience of the room is cozy.

am|bi|ent /æmbiənt/ **1** ADJ [ADJ n] The **ambient** temperature is the temperature of the air above the ground in a particular place. [TECHNICAL] **2** ADJ [usu ADJ n] **Ambient** sound or light is the sound or light which is all around you. [TECHNICAL] ☐ ...ambient sounds of children in the background.

am|bi|gu|ity /æmbɪgyuɪti/ (ambiguities) N-VAR If you say that there is **ambiguity** in something, you mean that it is unclear or confusing, or it can be understood in more than one way. ☐ There is considerable ambiguity about what this part of the agreement actually means.

am|bigu|ous /æmbɪgyuəs/ ADJ If you describe something as **ambiguous**, you mean that it is unclear or confusing because it can be understood in more than one way. ☐ This agreement is very ambiguous and open to various interpretations. • **am|bigu|ous|ly** ADV ☐ The national conference on democracy ended ambiguously.

am|bit /æmbɪt/ N-SING [usu with poss] The **ambit** of something is its range or extent. [FORMAL] ☐ Her case falls within the ambit of moral law.

am|bi|tion /æmbɪʃən/ (ambitions) **1** N-COUNT If you have an **ambition** to do or achieve something, you want very much to do it or achieve it. ☐ His ambition is to sail around the world.
2 N-UNCOUNT **Ambition** is the desire to be successful, rich, or powerful. ☐ Even when I was young I never had any ambition.
3 → See feature box at challenge

SYNONYMS
ambition
NOUN **1**
goal: The goal is to raise as much money as possible.
aim: ...a research program that has largely failed to achieve its principal aims.
target: He's won back his position too late to achieve his target of 20 goals this season.
objective: His objective was to play golf and win.

am|bi|tious /æmbɪʃəs/ **1** ADJ Someone who is **ambitious** has a strong desire to be successful, rich, or powerful. ☐ Chris is so ambitious, so determined to do it all. **2** ADJ An **ambitious** idea or plan is on a large scale and needs a lot of work to be carried out successfully. ☐ The ambitious project was completed in only nine months.

am|biva|lent /æmbɪvələnt/ ADJ If you say that someone is **ambivalent** about something, they seem to be uncertain whether they really want it, or whether they really approve of it. ☐ She remained ambivalent about her marriage.

am|ble /æmbəl/ (ambles, ambling, ambled) V-I When you **amble**, you walk slowly in a relaxed manner. ☐ Slowly they ambled back to the car.

am|bro|sia /æmbroʊʒə/ N-UNCOUNT In Greek mythology, **ambrosia** is the food of the gods.

am|bu|lance /æmbyələns/ (ambulances) N-COUNT [also by N] An **ambulance** is a vehicle for taking people to and from a hospital.

am|bush /æmbʊʃ/ (ambushes, ambushing, ambushed) **1** V-T If a group of people **ambush** their enemies, they attack them after hiding and waiting for them. ☐ The army says rebels ambushed and killed 10 patrolmen. **2** N-VAR An **ambush** is an attack on someone by people who have been hiding and waiting for them. ☐ Three civilians were killed in guerrilla ambushes.

ame|ba /əmibə/ (amebae /əmibi/ or amebas) N-COUNT An **ameba** is the smallest kind of living creature. Amebae consist of only one cell, and are found in water or soil.

ame|lio|rate /əmilyəreɪt/ (ameliorates, ameliorating, ameliorated) V-T If someone or something **ameliorates** a situation, they make it better or easier in some way. [FORMAL]

amen /ɑmɛn, eɪ-/ CONVENTION **Amen** is said by Christians at the end of a prayer. ☐ In the name of the Father and of the Son and of the Holy Ghost, amen.

ame|nable /əminəbəl, əmɛnə-/ ADJ If you are **amenable** to something, you are willing to do it or accept it. ☐ The Jordanian leader seemed amenable to attending a conference.

amend /əmɛnd/ (amends, amending, amended) **1** V-T If you **amend** something that has been written such as a law, or something that is said, you change it in order to improve it or make it more accurate. ☐ The president agreed to amend the constitution and allow multi-party elections. **2** PHRASE If you **make amends** when you have harmed someone, you show that you are sorry by doing something to please them. ☐ He wanted to make amends for causing their marriage to fail.

amend|ment /əmɛndmənt/ (amendments) **1** N-VAR An **amendment** is a section that is added to a law or rule in order to change it. ☐ an amendment to the defense bill. **2** N-COUNT An **amendment** is a change that is made to a piece of writing.

SYNONYMS
amendment
NOUN **1**
adjustment: Compensation could be made by adjustments to tax rates.
revision: An addition to earlier revisions of the questionnaire is the job requirement exercise.

amen|ity /əmɛnɪti/ (amenities) **1** N-COUNT [usu pl]
Amenities are things such as shopping centers or sports facilities that are provided for people's convenience, enjoyment, or comfort. ☐ The hotel amenities include health clubs, conference facilities, and banqueting rooms. **2** → See feature box at working

Am|er|asian /æməreɪʒən/ (Amerasians) N-COUNT People who have one American parent and one Asian parent are sometimes referred to as **Amerasians**. ☐ ...discrimination against Amerasians in Vietnam. • ADJ **Amerasian** is also an adjective. ☐ ...an Amerasian boy.

Ameri|can /əmɛrɪkən/ (Americans) **1** ADJ An **American** person or thing belongs to or comes from the United States of America. ☐ ...the American ambassador at the United Nations. ☐ ...the influence of American television and movies. **2** → see also **Latin American** **3** N-COUNT An **American** is someone who is American. ☐ The 1990 Nobel Prize for medicine was won by two Americans.

Ameri|ca|na /əmɛrɪkɑnə/ N-UNCOUNT Objects that come from or relate to America are referred to as **Americana**, especially when they are in a collection. ☐ 1950s Americana.

Ameri|can foot|ball (American footballs) **1** N-UNCOUNT **American football** is a game that is played by two teams of eleven players using an oval-shaped ball. Players try to score points by passing or carrying the ball to their opponents' end of the field, or by kicking it over a bar fixed between two posts. [BRIT]

in AM, use **football**

2 N-COUNT An **American football** is an oval-shaped ball used for playing American football. [BRIT]

in AM, use **football**

Ameri|can In|dian (American Indians) N-COUNT **American Indians** are people who belong to or come from one of the native peoples of America, especially those native to the continental United States. [mainly BRIT] • ADJ [usu ADJ n] **American Indian** is also an adjective.

Ameri|can|ism /əmɛrɪkənɪzəm/ (**Americanisms**) N-COUNT An **Americanism** is an expression that is typical of people living in the United States.

Ameri|cani|za|tion /əmɛrɪkənaɪzeɪʃᵊn/

in BRIT, also use **Americanisation**

N-UNCOUNT **Americanization** is the process by which people or countries become more and more similar to Americans and the United States. ◻ ...the Americanization of French culture.

Ameri|can|ized /əmɛrɪkənaɪzd/

in BRIT, also use **Americanised**

ADJ If someone is **Americanized**, they do things in a way that is typical of the United States. ◻ He is getting much too Americanized.

Ameri|ca|no /əmɛrɪkɑnoʊ/ (**Americanos**) also **americano** N-UNCOUNT **Americano** is strong coffee with hot water added. • N-COUNT An **Americano** is a cup of Americano.

Ameri|cas /əmɛrɪkəz/ N-PROPER-PLURAL [the N] People sometimes refer to North America, Central America, and South America collectively as the **Americas**. ◻ They're found all over the Far East and the Americas.

Am|er|in|dian /æmərɪndiən/ (**Amerindians**) N-COUNT **Amerindian** means the same as **American Indian**.

am|ethyst /æməθɪst/ (**amethysts**) **1** N-VAR **Amethysts** are clear purple stones, sometimes used to make jewelry. ◻ The necklace consisted of amethysts set in gold. ◻ ...rows of amethyst beads. **2** COLOR **Amethyst** is used to describe things that are pale purple in color. ◻ The colors changed from green to amethyst. ◻ ...amethyst glass. **3** → See also color supplement

WORD HISTORY

amethyst
Amethyst comes from Greek *amethustos* meaning 'not drunk.' It was thought in ancient times that anyone wearing or touching an amethyst would not become drunk. Wine goblets were sometimes carved from amethyst.

ami|abil|ity /eɪmiəbɪlɪti/ N-UNCOUNT **Amiability** is the quality of being friendly and pleasant. [WRITTEN] ◻ I found his amiability charming.

ami|able /eɪmiəbᵊl/ ADJ Someone who is **amiable** is friendly and pleasant to be with. [WRITTEN] ◻ She had been surprised at how amiable and polite he had been. • **ami|ably** ADV [ADV with v] ◻ We chatted amiably about old friends.

ami|cable /æmɪkəbᵊl/ ADJ When people have an **amicable** relationship, they are pleasant to each other and solve their problems without quarreling. ◻ The meeting ended on reasonably amicable terms. • **ami|cably** /æmɪkəbli/ ADV [ADV with v] ◻ He hoped the dispute could be settled amicably.

amid ◆◇◇ /əmɪd/

The form **amidst** is also used, but is old-fashioned.

PREP If something happens **amid** noises or events of some kind, it happens while the other things are happening. ◻ Workers are sifting through the wreckage of the airliners amid growing evidence that the disasters were the work of terrorists.

amid|ships /əmɪdʃɪps/ ADV [ADV after v] **Amidships** means halfway along the length of a ship. ◻ The ferry hit us amidships.

amidst /əmɪdst/ PREP **Amidst** means the same as **amid**. [OLD-FASHIONED]

ami|no acid /əmiːnoʊ æsɪd, əmaɪnoʊ/ (**amino acids**) N-COUNT [usu pl] **Amino acids** are substances containing nitrogen and hydrogen that are found in proteins. Amino acids occur naturally in the body.

Amish /ɑmɪʃ/ **1** N-PLURAL [the N] The **Amish** are members of a Protestant sect whose rural way of life is simple and strict. ◻ ...groups like the Amish who lack conventional medical insurance. **2** ADJ [usu ADJ n] **Amish** means relating to the Amish people or their religion. ◻ ...an Amish community.

amiss /əmɪs/ ADJ [v-link ADJ] If you say that something is **amiss**, you mean there is something wrong. ◻ Their instincts warned them something was amiss.

am|ity /æmɪti/ N-UNCOUNT **Amity** is peaceful, friendly relations between people or countries. [FORMAL] ◻ He wished to live in amity with his neighbor.

ammo /æmoʊ/ N-UNCOUNT **Ammo** is ammunition for guns and other weapons. [INFORMAL]

am|mo|nia /əmoʊniə/ N-UNCOUNT **Ammonia** is a colorless liquid or gas with a strong, sharp smell. It is used in making household cleaning substances.

am|mu|ni|tion /æmjʊnɪʃᵊn/ **1** N-UNCOUNT **Ammunition** is bullets and rockets that are made to be fired from weapons. ◻ He had only seven rounds of ammunition for the revolver. **2** N-UNCOUNT You can describe information that you can use against someone in an argument or discussion as **ammunition**. ◻ The improved trade figures have given the government fresh ammunition.

am|ne|sia /æmniːʒə/ N-UNCOUNT If someone has **amnesia**, they have lost their memory. ◻ People with amnesia don't forget their general knowledge of objects.

am|ne|si|ac /æmniːziæk/ (**amnesiacs**) ADJ Someone who is **amnesiac** has lost their memory. ◻ She was taken to a hospital, apparently amnesiac and shocked. • N-COUNT An **amnesiac** is someone who is amnesiac. ◻ Even profound amnesiacs can usually recall how to perform daily activities.

am|nes|ty /æmnɪsti/ (**amnesties**) **1** N-VAR An **amnesty** is an official pardon granted to a group of prisoners by the state. ◻ Activists who were involved in crimes of violence will not automatically be granted amnesty. **2** N-COUNT An **amnesty** is a period of time during which people can admit to a crime or give up weapons without being punished. ◻ The government has announced an immediate amnesty for rebel fighters.

am|nio|cen|tesis /æmnioʊsɛntiːsɪs/ (**amnioceneses** /æmnioʊsɛntiːsiː/) N-VAR If a pregnant woman has an **amniocentesis**, fluid is removed from her womb in order to check that her unborn baby is not affected by certain genetic disorders.

amoe|ba /əmiːbə/ [BRIT] → see **ameba**

amok /əmʌk, əmɒk/ PHRASE If a person or animal **runs amok**, they behave in a violent and uncontrolled way. ◻ A soldier was arrested after running amok with a vehicle through Berlin.

among ◆◆◆ /əmʌŋ/

The form **amongst** is also used, but is more old-fashioned.

1 PREP Someone or something that is situated or moving **among** a group of things or people is surrounded by them. ◻ ...youths in their late teens sitting among adults. ◻ They walked among the crowds in Red Square. **2** PREP If you are **among** people of a particular kind, you are with them and having contact with them. ◻ Things weren't so bad, after all. I was among friends again. **3** PREP If someone or something is **among** a group, they are a member of that group and share its characteristics. ◻ A fifteen year old girl was among the injured. **4** PREP If you want to focus on something that is happening within a particular group of people, you can say that it is happening **among** that group. ◻ Homicide is the leading cause of death among Black men. **5** PREP If something happens **among** a group of people, it happens within the whole of that group or between the members of that group. ◻ The calls for reform come as intense debate continues among the leadership over the next five-year economic plan. **6** PREP If something such as a feeling, opinion, or situation exists **among** a group of people, most of them have it or experience it. ◻ There was some concern among book and magazine retailers after last Wednesday's news. **7** PREP If something applies to a particular person or thing **among** others, it also applies to other people or things. ◻ ...a news conference attended among others by our foreign affairs correspondent. **8** PREP If something is shared **among** a number of people, some of it is given to all of them. ◻ Most of the furniture was left to the neighbors or distributed among friends. **9** PREP [PREP pron-refl] If people talk, fight, or agree **among** themselves, they do it together, without involving anyone else. ◻ The girls stood aside, talking among themselves, looking over their shoulders at the boys.

amongst /əmʌŋst/ PREP **Amongst** means the same as **among**. [OLD-FASHIONED]

amoral / anabolic steroid

amor|al /eɪmɔ́rəl/ ADJ If you describe someone as **amoral**, you do not like the way they behave because they do not seem to care whether what they do is right or wrong. [DISAPPROVAL] ❑ *I strongly disagree with this amoral approach to politics.*

amo|rous /ǽmərəs/ ADJ [usu ADJ n] If you describe someone's feelings or actions as **amorous**, you mean that they involve sexual desire.

amor|phous /əmɔ́rfəs/ ADJ [usu ADJ n] Something that is **amorphous** has no clear shape or structure. [FORMAL] ❑ *A dark, strangely amorphous shadow filled the room.* ❑ *...the amorphous mass of the crowd.*

amor|tize /ǽmərtaɪz/ (amortizes, amortizing, amortized)

in BRIT, also use **amortise**

V-T In finance, if you **amortize** a debt, you pay it back in regular payments. [BUSINESS] ❑ *There's little advantage to amortizing the loan, especially on a 30 or 40-year basis.*

amount ✦✦◊ /əmáʊnt/ (amounts, amounting, amounted) ◼ N-VAR The **amount** of something is how much there is, or how much you have, need, or get. ❑ *He needs that amount of money to survive.* ❑ *I still do a certain amount of work for them.* ◼ V-I If something **amounts** to a particular total, all the parts of it add up to that total. ❑ *Consumer spending on sports-related items amounted to $9.75 billion.*
▶ **amount to** PHRASAL VERB If you say that one thing **amounts to** something else, you consider the first thing to be the same as the second thing. ❑ *The banks have what amounts to a monopoly.*

COLLOCATIONS

amount
NOUN ◼
adjective + **amount**: certain, considerable, fair, significant, substantial; enormous, huge, large, tremendous, vast; maximum, minimum; total
verb + **amount**: invest, pay, spend; increase, reduce

---

amour /æmʊ́ər/ (amours) N-COUNT An **amour** is a love affair, especially one that is kept secret. [LITERARY OR OLD-FASHIONED]

amp /ǽmp/ (amps) ◼ N-COUNT An **amp** is the same as an **ampere**. ❑ *Use a 3 amp fuse for equipment up to 720 watts.* ◼ N-COUNT An **amp** is the same as an **amplifier**. [INFORMAL]

am|pere /ǽmpɪər, æmpɪ́ər/ (amperes)

in BRIT, also use **ampère**

N-COUNT An **ampere** is a unit used for measuring electric current. The abbreviation **amp** is also used.

am|per|sand /ǽmpərsænd/ (ampersands) N-COUNT An **ampersand** is the sign &, used to represent the word 'and.'

am|pheta|mine /æmfɛ́təmin/ (amphetamines) N-MASS **Amphetamine** is a drug that increases people's energy, makes them excited, and reduces their desire for food.

am|phib|ian /æmfɪ́biən/ (amphibians) ◼ N-COUNT **Amphibians** are animals such as frogs and toads that can live both on land and in water. ◼ N-COUNT An **amphibian** is a vehicle that is able to move on both land and water, or an airplane that can land on both land and water.

am|phibi|ous /æmfɪ́biəs/ ◼ ADJ [ADJ n] In an **amphibious** military operation, army and navy forces attack a place from the sea. ❑ *A third brigade is at sea, ready for an amphibious assault.* ◼ ADJ [ADJ n] An **amphibious** vehicle is able to move on both land and water. ◼ ADJ **Amphibious** animals are animals such as frogs and toads that can live both on land and in water.

am|phi|thea|ter /ǽmfɪθiətər/ (amphitheaters)

in BRIT, use **amphitheatre**

N-COUNT An **amphitheater** is a large open area surrounded by rows of seats sloping upward. Amphitheaters were built mainly in Greek and Roman times for the performance of plays.

am|ple /ǽmpəl/ (ampler, amplest) ADJ If there is an **ample** amount of something, there is enough of it and usually some extra. ❑ *There'll be ample opportunity to relax, swim and soak up some sun.* • **am|ply** ADV ❑ *This collection of his essays and journalism amply demonstrates his commitment to democracy.*

am|pli|fi|er /ǽmplɪfaɪər/ (amplifiers) N-COUNT An **amplifier** is an electronic device in a radio or stereo system that causes sounds or signals to get louder.

am|pli|fy /ǽmplɪfaɪ/ (amplifies, amplifying, amplified) ◼ V-T If you **amplify** a sound, you make it louder, usually by using electronic equipment. ❑ *This landscape seemed to trap and amplify sounds.* ❑ *The music was amplified with microphones.* • **am|pli|fi|ca|tion** /ǽmplɪfɪkeɪʃən/ N-UNCOUNT ❑ *...a voice that needed no amplification.* ◼ V-T To **amplify** something means to increase its strength or intensity. ❑ *The mist had been replaced by a kind of haze that seemed to amplify the heat.*

am|pli|tude /ǽmplɪtud/ (amplitudes) N-VAR In physics, the **amplitude** of a sound wave or electrical signal is its strength. [TECHNICAL]

am|pule /ǽmpyul, -pul/ (ampules)

in BRIT, use **ampoule**

N-COUNT An **ampule** is a small container, usually made of glass, that contains a drug that will be injected into someone.

am|pu|tate /ǽmpyuteɪt/ (amputates, amputating, amputated) V-T To **amputate** someone's arm or leg means to cut all or part of it off in an operation because it is diseased or badly damaged. ❑ *To save his life, doctors amputated his legs.* • **am|pu|ta|tion** /ǽmpyuteɪʃən/ (amputations) N-VAR ❑ *He lived only hours after the amputation.*

am|pu|tee /ǽmpyuti/ (amputees) N-COUNT An **amputee** is someone who has had all or part of an arm or a leg amputated.

amu|let /ǽmyəlɪt/ (amulets) N-COUNT An **amulet** is a small object that you wear or carry because you think it will bring you good luck and protect you from evil or injury.

amuse /əmyúz/ (amuses, amusing, amused) ◼ V-T If something **amuses** you, it makes you want to laugh or smile. ❑ *The thought seemed to amuse him.* ◼ V-T If you **amuse** yourself, you do something in order to pass the time and not become bored. ❑ *I need distractions. I need to amuse myself so I won't keep thinking about things.* ◼ → see also **amused**, **amusing** ◼ → See feature box at **humor**

amused /əmyúzd/ ADJ If you are **amused** by something, it makes you want to laugh or smile. ❑ *Sara was not amused by Franklin's teasing.*

amuse|ment /əmyúzmənt/ (amusements) ◼ N-UNCOUNT **Amusement** is the feeling that you have when you think that something is funny or amusing. ❑ *He stopped and watched with amusement to see the child so absorbed.* ◼ N-UNCOUNT **Amusement** is the pleasure that you get from being entertained or from doing something interesting. ❑ *I stumbled sideways before landing flat on my back, much to the amusement of the rest of the guys.* ◼ N-COUNT **Amusements** are ways of passing the time pleasantly. ❑ *People had very few amusements to choose from. There was no radio, or television.* ◼ N-PLURAL **Amusements** are games, rides, and other things that you can enjoy, for example, at an amusement park or resort. ❑ *...a place full of swings and amusements.*

amuse|ment ar|cade (amusement arcades) N-COUNT An **amusement arcade** is a place where you can play games on machines which work when you put money in them.

amuse|ment park (amusement parks) N-COUNT An **amusement park** is a place where people pay to ride on various machines for amusement or try to win prizes in games. [mainly AM]

amus|ing /əmyúzɪŋ/ ADJ Someone or something that is **amusing** makes you laugh or smile. ❑ *He had a terrific sense of humor and could be very amusing.* • **amus|ing|ly** ADV ❑ *The article must be amusingly written.*

an /ən, STRONG æn/ DET **An** is used instead of 'a,' the indefinite article, in front of words that begin with vowel sounds.

SUFFIX

-an
is added to the names of some places in order to form adjectives or nouns that refer to people or things which come from that place. For example, the **Australian** Ambassador is the ambassador from Australia.

---

ana|bol|ic ster|oid /ǽnəbɒlɪk stɛ́rɔɪd, stɪ́ər-/ (anabolic steroids) N-COUNT **Anabolic steroids** are drugs that people, especially athletes, take to make their muscles bigger and to give them more strength.

anach|ro|nism /ənækrənɪzəm/ (**anachronisms**) **1** N-COUNT You say that something is an **anachronism** when you think that it is out of date or old-fashioned. ❏ *The president tended to regard the Church as an anachronism.* **2** N-COUNT An **anachronism** is something in a book, play, or film that is wrong because it did not exist at the time the book, play, or film is set. ❏ *The last paragraph contains an anachronism. The Holy Office no longer existed at that time.*

anach|ro|nis|tic /ənækrənɪstɪk/ ADJ You say that something is **anachronistic** when you think that it is out of date or old-fashioned. ❏ *Many of its practices seem anachronistic.*

anaemia /ənimiə/ [BRIT] → see **anemia**

anaemic /ənimɪk/ [BRIT] → see **anemic**

an|aero|bic /ænəroʊbɪk/ **1** ADJ **Anaerobic** creatures or processes do not need oxygen in order to function or survive. **2** ADJ **Anaerobic** exercise is exercise such as weight training that improves your strength but does not raise your heart rate.

an|aes|the|sia /ænɪsθiʒə/ [BRIT] → see **anesthesia**

an|aes|thet|ic /ænɪsθɛtɪk/ [BRIT] → see **anesthetic**

anaes|the|tist /ənɡsθətɪst/ (**anaesthetists**) N-COUNT An **anaesthetist** is a doctor who specializes in giving anesthetics to patients. [BRIT]

in AM, use **anesthesiologist**

anaes|the|tize /ənɡsθətaɪz/ [BRIT] → see **anesthetize**

ana|gram /ænəɡræm/ (**anagrams**) N-COUNT An **anagram** is a word or phrase formed by changing the order of the letters in another word or phrase. For example, 'triangle' is an anagram of 'integral.'

anal /eɪnəl/ ADJ **Anal** means relating to the anus of a person or animal. ❏ *...anal injuries.*

an|alge|sic /ænəldʒizɪk/ ADJ [usu ADJ n] An **analgesic** drug reduces the effect of pain. [FORMAL]

ana|log /ænəlɔɡ/ (**analogs**)

in BRIT, use **analogue**

1 ADJ **Analog** technology involves measuring, storing, or recording an infinitely variable amount of information by using physical quantities such as voltage. ❏ *The analog signals are converted into digital code.* **2** ADJ An **analog** watch or clock shows what it is measuring with a pointer on a dial rather than with a number display. Compare **digital**. **3** ADJ If one thing is an **analog** of another, it is similar in some way. [FORMAL] ❏ *No model can ever be a perfect analog of nature itself.*

analo|gous /ənæləɡəs/ ADJ If one thing is **analogous** to another, the two things are similar in some way. [FORMAL] ❏ *Marine construction technology like this is very complex, somewhat analogous to trying to build a bridge under water.*

anal|ogy /ənælədʒi/ (**analogies**) N-COUNT If you make or draw an **analogy** between two things, you show that they are similar in some way. ❏ *The analogy between music and fragrance has stuck.*

ana|lyse /ænəlaɪz/ [BRIT] → see **analyze**

ana|lys|er /ænəlaɪzər/ [BRIT] → see **analyzer**

analy|sis ♦♦◇ /ənæləsɪs/ (**analyses** /ənæləsiz/) **1** N-VAR **Analysis** is the process of considering something carefully or using statistical methods in order to understand it or explain it. ❏ *Sporting greatness defies analysis – but we know it when we see it.* **2** N-VAR **Analysis** is the scientific process of examining something in order to find out what it consists of. ❏ *They collect blood samples for analysis at a national laboratory.* **3** N-COUNT An **analysis** is an explanation or description that results from considering something carefully. ❏ *Coming up after the newscast, an analysis of the president's domestic policy.*

---SYNONYMS---

analysis
NOUN
1
interpretation: *Analysis and interpretation is a very personal thing.*
evaluation: *They announced that an inspection team was conducting an evaluation of the building site.*
scrutiny: *The President promised a government open to public scrutiny.*

3
examination: *A post-mortem examination will check for any traces of drug use.*
study: *...the first study of English children's attitudes.*
test: *X-rays and blood tests will also be used to aid diagnosis.*
diagnosis: *Symptoms may not appear for some weeks, so diagnosis can be difficult.*

ana|lyst ♦♦◇ /ænəlɪst/ (**analysts**) **1** N-COUNT An **analyst** is a person whose job is to analyze a subject and give opinions about it. ❏ *...a political analyst.* **2** N-COUNT An **analyst** is someone, usually a doctor, who examines and treats people who have emotional problems. ❏ *My analyst warned me that I liked married men too much.*

ana|lyt|ic /ænəlɪtɪk/ ADJ **Analytic** means the same as **analytical**. [mainly AM]

ana|lyti|cal /ænəlɪtɪkəl/ ADJ An **analytical** way of doing something involves the use of logical reasoning. ❏ *I have an analytical approach to every survey.*

ana|lyze /ænəlaɪz/ (**analyzes, analyzing, analyzed**)

in BRIT, also use **analyse**

1 V-T If you **analyze** something, you consider it carefully or use statistical methods in order to fully understand it. ❏ *McCarthy was asked to analyze the data from the first phase of trials of the vaccine.* **2** V-T If you **analyze** something, you examine it using scientific methods in order to find out what it consists of. ❏ *We haven't had time to analyze those samples yet.*

ana|lyz|er /ænəlaɪzər/ (**analyzers**)

in BRIT, also use **analyser**

1 N-COUNT [usu n N] An **analyzer** is a piece of equipment used to analyze the substances that are present in something such as a gas. ❏ *...an oxygen analyzer.* **2** N-COUNT An **analyzer** is someone who analyzes information.

an|ar|chic /ænɑrkɪk/ ADJ If you describe someone or something as **anarchic**, you disapprove of them because they do not recognize or obey any rules or laws. [DISAPPROVAL] ❏ *...anarchic attitudes and complete disrespect for authority.*

an|ar|chism /ænərkɪzəm/ N-UNCOUNT **Anarchism** is the belief that the laws and power of governments should be replaced by people working together freely. ❏ *He advocated anarchism as the answer to social problems.*

an|ar|chist /ænərkɪst/ (**anarchists**) **1** N-COUNT [oft N n] An **anarchist** is a person who believes in anarchism. ❏ *West Berlin always had a large anarchist community.* **2** ADJ [ADJ n] If someone has **anarchist** beliefs or views, they believe in anarchism. ❏ *He was apparently quite converted from his anarchist views.*

an|ar|chis|tic /ænərkɪstɪk/ **1** ADJ [usu ADJ n] An **anarchistic** person believes in anarchism. **Anarchistic** activity or literature promotes anarchism. ❏ *...an anarchistic revolutionary movement.* **2** ADJ [usu ADJ n] If you describe someone as **anarchistic**, you disapprove of them because they pay no attention to the rules or laws that everyone else obeys. [DISAPPROVAL] ❏ *The Hell's Angels were once the most notorious and anarchistic of motorbike gangs.*

anarcho- /ænɑrkoʊ-/ COMB IN ADJ; N **Anarcho-** combines with nouns and adjectives to form words indicating that something is both anarchistic and the other thing that is mentioned. ❏ *They were extreme anarcho-pacifists who believed in a pure form of nonviolent resistance.*

an|ar|chy /ænərki/ N-UNCOUNT If you describe a situation as **anarchy**, you mean that nobody seems to be paying any attention to rules or laws. [DISAPPROVAL] ❏ *The school's liberal, individualistic traditions were in danger of slipping into anarchy.*

anath|ema /ənæθəmə/ N-UNCOUNT [usu N to n] If something is **anathema** to you, you strongly dislike it. ❏ *Violence was anathema to them.*

ana|tomi|cal /ænətɒmɪkəl/ ADJ **Anatomical** means relating to the structure of the bodies of people and animals. ❏ *...minute anatomical differences between insects.*

anato|mist /ənætəmɪst/ (**anatomists**) N-COUNT An **anatomist** is an expert in anatomy.

anato|mize /ənǽtəmaɪz/ (anatomizes, anatomizing, anatomized)

> in BRIT, also use **anatomise**

V-T If you **anatomize** a subject or an issue, you examine it in great detail. [FORMAL] ▫ *The magazine is devoted to anatomizing the inadequacies of liberalism.*

anato|my /ənǽtəmi/ **1** N-UNCOUNT **Anatomy** is the study of the structure of the bodies of people or animals. ▫ *...a course in anatomy.* **2** N-COUNT You can refer to your body as your **anatomy**. [HUMOROUS] ▫ *The ball hit him in the most sensitive part of his anatomy.*

SUFFIX

-ance
forms nouns that refer to a particular action, state, or quality. *For example,* **brilliance** *is the state or quality of being brilliant, and* **appearance** *is the action of appearing.*

an|ces|tor /ǽnsɛstər/ (ancestors) **1** N-COUNT [usu pl, with poss] Your **ancestors** are the people from whom you are descended. ▫ *...our daily lives, so different from those of our ancestors.* **2** N-COUNT An **ancestor** of something modern is an earlier thing from which it developed. ▫ *The direct ancestor of the modern cat was the Kaffir cat of ancient Egypt.* **3** → See feature box at **animal**

an|ces|tral /ænsɛ́strəl/ ADJ You use **ancestral** to refer to a person's family in former times, especially when the family is important and has property or land that they have had for a long time. ▫ *...the family's ancestral home in southern Germany.*

an|ces|try /ǽnsɛstri/ (ancestries) N-COUNT Your **ancestry** is the fact that you are descended from certain people. ▫ *...a family who could trace their ancestry back to the sixteenth century.*

an|chor /ǽŋkər/ (anchors, anchoring, anchored) **1** N-COUNT An **anchor** is a heavy hooked object that is dropped from a boat into the water at the end of a chain in order to make the boat stay in one place. **2** N-COUNT The **anchor** on a television or radio program, especially a news program, is the person who presents it. [mainly AM] ▫ *He worked in the news division of ABC – he was the anchor of its 15-minute evening newscast.* **3** V-T/V-I When a boat **anchors** or when you **anchor** it, its anchor is dropped into the water in order to make it stay in one place. ▫ *We could anchor off the pier.* **4** V-T If an object **is anchored** somewhere, it is fixed to something to prevent it moving from that place. ▫ *The roots anchor the plant in the earth.* **5** V-T The person who **anchors** a television or radio program, especially a news program, is the person who presents it and acts as a link between interviews and reports that come from other places or studios. [mainly AM] ▫ *Viewers saw him anchoring a five-minute summary of regional news.* **6** N-COUNT An **anchor** is the main store in a mall or shopping center. [AM] ▫ *A clothing store is to be a key anchor in a new development planned on the vacant lot.* **7** PHRASE If a boat is **at anchor**, it is floating in a particular place and is prevented from moving by its anchor. ▫ *Sailboats lay at anchor in the narrow waterway.* **8** → See also color supplement

an|chor|age /ǽŋkərɪdʒ/ (anchorages) N-VAR An **anchorage** is a place where a boat can anchor safely. ▫ *The nearest safe anchorage was in Halifax, Nova Scotia.* ▫ *The vessel yesterday reached anchorage off Dubai.*

anchor|man /ǽŋkərmæn/ (anchormen) N-COUNT The **anchorman** on a television or radio program, especially a news program, is the man who presents it.

anchor|woman /ǽŋkərwʊmən/ (anchorwomen) N-COUNT The **anchorwoman** on a television or radio program, especially a news program, is the woman who presents it.

an|cho|vy /ǽntʃoʊvi/ (anchovies) N-VAR [oft N n] **Anchovies** are small fish that live in the sea. They are often eaten salted.

an|cient ♦♦◇ /éɪnʃənt/ **1** ADJ [ADJ n] **Ancient** means belonging to the distant past, especially to the period in history before the end of the Roman Empire. ▫ *They believed ancient Greece and Rome were vital sources of learning.* **2** ADJ **Ancient** means very old, or having existed for a long time. ▫ *...ancient Jewish tradition.* **3** → See feature box at **Olympic Games**

an|cient his|to|ry N-UNCOUNT **Ancient history** is the history of ancient civilizations.

an|cil|lary /ǽnsəlɛri/ ADJ [ADJ n] The **ancillary** workers in an institution are the people such as cleaners and cooks whose work supports the main work of the institution. ▫ *...ancillary staff.*

and ♦♦♦ /ənd, STRONG ænd/ **1** CONJ You use **and** to link two or more words, groups, or clauses. ▫ *When he returned, she and Simon had already gone.* **2** CONJ You use **and** to link two words or phrases that are the same in order to emphasize the degree of something, or to suggest that something continues or increases over a period of time. [EMPHASIS] ▫ *Learning becomes more and more difficult as we get older.* ▫ *We talked for hours and hours.* **3** CONJ You use **and** to link two statements about events when one of the events follows the other. ▫ *I waved goodbye and went down the stone harbor steps.* **4** CONJ You use **and** to link two statements when the second statement continues the point that has been made in the first statement. ▫ *You could only really tell the effects of the disease in the long term, and five years wasn't long enough.* **5** CONJ You use **and** to link two clauses when the second clause is a result of the first clause. ▫ *All through the day crowds arrived and by midnight thousands of people packed the square.* **6** CONJ You use **and** to interrupt yourself in order to make a comment on what you are saying. ▫ *Danielle was among the last to find out, and as often happens, too, she learned of it only by chance.* **7** CONJ You use **and** at the beginning of a sentence to introduce something else that you want to add to what you have just said. Some people think that starting a sentence with **and** is ungrammatical, but it is now quite common in both spoken and written English. ▫ *Commuter airlines fly to out-of-the-way places. And business travelers are the ones who go to those locations.* **8** CONJ You use **and** to introduce a question that follows logically from what someone has just said. ▫ *"He used to be so handsome."—"And now?"* **9** CONJ **And** is used by broadcasters and people making announcements to change a topic or to start talking about a topic they have just mentioned. ▫ *And now the drought in Sudan.* **10** CONJ You use **and** to indicate that two numbers are to be added together. ▫ *What does two and two make?* **11** CONJ **And** is used before a fraction that comes after a whole number. ▫ *She has spent five and a half years as the CEO.* **12** CONJ You use **and** in numbers larger than one hundred, after the words 'hundred' or 'thousand' and before other numbers. ▫ *We printed two hundred and fifty invitations.*

an|dan|te /ɑndɑ́nteɪ/ (andantes) **1** ADV [ADV after v] **Andante** written above a piece of music means that it should be played fairly slowly. **2** N-COUNT [usu sing] An **andante** is a piece of music that is played fairly slowly. ▫ *...the lovely central andante.* ▫ *...the violas' andante theme.*

an|drogy|nous /ændrɒ́dʒɪnəs/ **1** ADJ [usu ADJ n] In biology, an **androgynous** person, animal, or plant has both male and female sexual characteristics. [TECHNICAL] **2** ADJ [usu ADJ n] If you describe someone as **androgynous**, you mean that they are not distinctly masculine or feminine in appearance or in behavior.

an|drogy|ny /ændrɒ́dʒɪni/ N-UNCOUNT **Androgyny** is the state of being neither distinctly masculine nor distinctly feminine.

an|droid /ǽndrɔɪd/ (androids) N-COUNT In science fiction books and films, an **android** is a robot that looks like a human being.

an|ec|do|tal /ǽnɪkdoʊt^əl/ ADJ **Anecdotal** evidence is based on individual accounts, rather than on reliable research or statistics, and so may not be valid. ▫ *Anecdotal evidence suggests that sales in the Southwest have slipped.*

an|ec|dote /ǽnɪkdoʊt/ (anecdotes) N-VAR An **anecdote** is a short, amusing account of something that has happened. ▫ *Pete was telling them an anecdote about their mother.*

anemia /ənímiə/

> in BRIT, use **anaemia**

N-UNCOUNT **Anemia** is a medical condition in which there are too few red cells in your blood, causing you to feel tired and look pale. ▫ *She suffered from anemia and even required blood transfusions.*

anemic /əníˈmɪk/

in BRIT, use **anaemic**

ADJ Someone who is **anemic** has anemia. ❑ *Tests showed that she was very anemic.*

anemo|ne /ənɛ́məni/ (anemones) **1** N-COUNT An **anemone** is a garden plant with red, purple, or white flowers. **2** N-COUNT An **anemone** or a **sea anemone** is a small creature with brightly-colored tentacles that lives at the bottom of the sea.

an|es|the|sia /ænɪsθíːʒə/

in BRIT, use **anaesthesia**

N-UNCOUNT **Anesthesia** is the use of anesthetics in medicine and surgery.

an|es|thesi|olo|gist /ænɪsθiːziɒ́lədʒɪst/ (anesthesiologists) N-COUNT An **anesthesiologist** is a doctor who specializes in giving anesthetics to patients.

in BRIT, use **anaesthetist**

an|es|thet|ic /ænɪsθɛ́tɪk/ (anesthetics)

in BRIT, use **anaesthetic**

N-MASS **Anesthetic** is a substance that doctors use to stop you feeling pain during an operation, either in the whole of your body when you are unconscious, or in a part of your body when you are awake. ❑ *The operation is carried out under a general anesthetic.*

anes|the|tist /ənɛ́sθətɪst/ (anesthetists)

in BRIT, use **anaesthetist**

N-COUNT An **anesthetist** is a nurse or other person who gives an anesthetic to a patient.

anes|the|tize /ənɛ́sθətaɪz/ (anesthetizes, anesthetizing, anesthetized)

in BRIT, use **anaesthetize**

1 V-T When a doctor or other trained person **anesthetizes** a patient, they make the patient unconscious or unable to feel pain by giving them an anesthetic. **2** V-T If something such as a drug **anesthetizes** part or all of your body, it makes you unable to feel anything in that part of your body.

anew /ənúː/ ADV [ADV after v] If you do something **anew**, you do it again, often in a different way from before. [WRITTEN] ❑ *She's ready to start anew.*

an|gel /éɪndʒəl/ (angels) **1** N-COUNT **Angels** are spiritual beings that some people believe are God's servants in heaven. ❑ *The artist usually painted his angels with multi-colored wings.* **2** N-COUNT You can call someone you like very much an **angel** in order to show affection, especially when they have been kind to you or done you a favor. [FEELINGS] ❑ *Thank you a thousand times, you're an angel.* **3** N-COUNT If you describe someone as an **angel**, you mean that they seem to be very kind and good. [APPROVAL] ❑ *Papa thought her an angel.*

an|gel|ic /ændʒɛ́lɪk/ **1** ADJ You can describe someone as **angelic** if they are, or seem to be, very good, kind, and gentle. [APPROVAL] ❑ *…an angelic face.* **2** ADJ [ADJ n] **Angelic** means like angels or relating to angels. ❑ *…angelic choirs.*

an|gel|ica /ændʒɛ́lɪkə/ N-UNCOUNT **Angelica** is the candied stems of the angelica plant which can be used in making cakes or candy.

an|ger ◆◇◇ /ǽŋɡər/ (angers, angering, angered) **1** N-UNCOUNT **Anger** is the strong emotion that you feel when you think that someone has behaved in an unfair, cruel, or unacceptable way. ❑ *He cried with anger and frustration.* **2** V-T If something **angers** you, it makes you feel angry. ❑ *The decision to allow more offshore oil drilling angered some Californians.*

COLLOCATIONS

anger
NOUN **1**
adjective + **anger**: growing, mounting, widespread; pent-up, righteous
anger + be + adjective: palpable, understandable
verb + **anger**: express, vent, voice; arouse, provoke, spark; control, suppress
VERB **2**
anger + noun: fans, residents, voters
anger + adverb: deeply

---

an|ger man|age|ment N-UNCOUNT [oft N n] **Anger management** is a set of guidelines that are designed to help people control their anger. ❑ *…anger management courses.*

an|gi|na /ændʒáɪnə/ N-UNCOUNT **Angina** is severe pain in the chest and left arm, caused by heart disease.

an|gle ◆◇◇ /ǽŋɡəl/ (angles) **1** N-COUNT An **angle** is the difference in direction between two lines or surfaces. Angles are measured in degrees. ❑ *The boat is now leaning at a 30 degree angle.* **2** → see also **right angle** **3** N-COUNT An **angle** is the shape that is created where two lines or surfaces join together. ❑ *…the angle of the blade.* **4** N-COUNT An **angle** is the direction from which you look at something. ❑ *Thanks to the angle at which he stood, he could just see the sunset.* **5** N-COUNT You can refer to a way of presenting something or thinking about it as a particular **angle**. ❑ *He was considering the idea from all angles.* **6** PHRASE If something is **at an angle**, it is leaning in a particular direction so that it is not straight, horizontal, or vertical. ❑ *An iron bar stuck out at an angle.*

an|gler /ǽŋɡlər/ (anglers) N-COUNT An **angler** is someone who fishes with a fishing rod as a hobby.

An|gli|can /ǽŋɡlɪkən/ (Anglicans) **1** ADJ [usu ADJ n] **Anglican** means belonging or relating to the Church of England, or to the churches related to it. ❑ *…the Anglican Church.* ❑ *…an Anglican priest.* **2** N-COUNT An **Anglican** is a Christian who is a member of the Church of England, or of one of the churches related to it.

An|gli|can|ism /ǽŋɡlɪkənɪzəm/ N-UNCOUNT **Anglicanism** is the beliefs and practices of the Church of England, and of the churches related to it.

an|gli|cize /ǽŋɡlɪsaɪz/ (anglicizes, anglicizing, anglicized)

in BRIT, also use **anglicise**

V-T If you **anglicize** something, you change it so that it resembles or becomes part of the English language or English culture. ❑ *He had anglicized his surname.* • **an|gli|cized** ADJ ❑ *…anglicized French words such as cafe.*

an|gling /ǽŋɡlɪŋ/ N-UNCOUNT **Angling** is the activity or sport of fishing with a fishing rod.

Anglo- /ǽŋɡloʊ-/ **1** COMB IN ADJ [ADJ n] **Anglo-** combines with adjectives indicating nationality to form adjectives that describe something connected with relations between Britain and another country. ❑ *…the Anglo-Irish Agreement.* **2** COMB IN ADJ [ADJ n] **Anglo-** combines with adjectives indicating nationality to form adjectives that describe a person who has one British parent and one non-British parent. ❑ *He was born of Anglo-American parentage.*

Anglo-Catholic (Anglo-Catholics) **1** ADJ [ADJ n] The **Anglo-Catholic** part of the Church of England, or of the churches related to it, is the part whose beliefs and practices are similar to those of the Catholic Church. ❑ *…a parish in the Anglo-Catholic tradition.* **2** N-COUNT An **Anglo-Catholic** is a Christian who belongs to the Anglo-Catholic section of the Church of England, or to the churches related to it.

An|glo|phile /ǽŋɡləfaɪl/ (anglophiles) ADJ If you describe a non-British person as **Anglophile**, you mean that they admire Britain and British culture. ❑ *…a Shakespeare sonnet taught to him by his Anglophile uncle.* • N-COUNT **Anglophile** is also a noun. ❑ *He became a fanatical Anglophile.*

An|glo|phone /ǽŋɡləfoʊn/ (anglophones) **1** ADJ [ADJ n] **Anglophone** communities are English-speaking communities in areas where more than one language is commonly spoken. ❑ *…anglophone Canadians.* ❑ *…anglophone Africa.* **2** N-COUNT [usu pl] **Anglophones** are people whose native language is English or who speak English because they live in a country where English is one of the official languages.

Anglo-Saxon (Anglo-Saxons) **1** ADJ [usu ADJ n] The **Anglo-Saxon** period is the period of English history from the fifth century AD to the Norman Conquest in 1066. ❑ *…the grave of an early Anglo-Saxon king.* • N-COUNT An **Anglo-Saxon** was someone who was Anglo-Saxon. ❑ *…the mighty sea power of the Anglo-Saxons.* **2** ADJ **Anglo-Saxon** people are members of or are descended from the English race. ❑ *…White Anglo-Saxon Protestant men.* • N-COUNT **Anglo-Saxon** is also a noun. ❑ *The difference is, you are Anglo-Saxons, we are Latins.* **3** ADJ [usu ADJ n] **Anglo-Saxon** attitudes or ideas have been strongly influenced by English culture. ❑ *Debilly had no Anglo-Saxon shyness about discussing money.* **4** N-UNCOUNT **Anglo-Saxon** is the language that was spoken in England between the fifth century AD and the Norman Conquest in 1066.

An|go|lan /æŋgoʊlᵊn/ (**Angolans**) **1** ADJ [usu ADJ n] **Angolan** means belonging or relating to Angola or its people. ❑ *...the Angolan government.* **2** N-COUNT An **Angolan** is someone who comes from Angola.

an|go|ra /æŋgɔːrə/ **1** ADJ [ADJ n] An **angora** goat or rabbit is a particular breed that has long silky hair. **2** N-UNCOUNT [usu N n] **Angora** cloth or clothing is made from the hair of the angora goat or rabbit. ❑ *...an angora sweater.*

an|gry ♦◇◇ /æŋgri/ (**angrier**, **angriest**) ADJ When you are **angry**, you feel strong dislike or impatience about something. ❑ *Are you angry with me for some reason?* ❑ *I was angry about the rumors.* ❑ *An angry mob gathered outside the courthouse.* • **an|gri|ly** /æŋgrɪli/ ADV [ADV with v] ❑ *Officials reacted angrily to those charges.*

angst /æŋst/ N-UNCOUNT **Angst** is a feeling of anxiety and worry. [JOURNALISM] ❑ *Many kids suffer from acne and angst.*

an|guish /æŋgwɪʃ/ N-UNCOUNT **Anguish** is great mental suffering or physical pain. ❑ *Mark looked at him in anguish.*

an|guished /æŋgwɪʃt/ ADJ **Anguished** means showing or feeling great mental suffering or physical pain. [WRITTEN] ❑ *She let out an anguished cry.*

an|gu|lar /æŋgyʊlər/ ADJ **Angular** things have shapes that seem to contain a lot of straight lines and sharp points. ❑ *He had an angular face with prominent cheekbones.*

ani|mal ♦◇◇ /ænɪmᵊl/ (**animals**) **1** N-COUNT An **animal** is a living creature such as a dog, lion, or rabbit, rather than a bird, fish, insect, or human being. ❑ *He was attacked by wild animals.* **2** N-COUNT Any living creature other than a human being can be referred to as an **animal**. ❑ *Language is something that fundamentally distinguishes humans from animals.* **3** N-COUNT Any living creature, including a human being, can be referred to as an **animal**. ❑ *Watch any young human being, or any other young animal.* **4** ADJ **Animal** products come from animals rather than from plants. ❑ *...food high in animal fats such as red meat and dairy products.*

VOCABULARY IN CONTEXT

Animal features and families

Animals with a **common ancestor** are said to belong to the same family or **genus**. However, in many cases, animals that share common **features** don't belong to the same family. Take for example the tapir. The tapir looks like a pig, but it has a prehensile nose like an elephant, albeit a little shorter. But, it isn't related to the pig or the elephant at all. The tapir actually belongs to the same family as the **rhino**. The elephant is another **anomaly**. Its big ears, large trunk, and tusks are not **common to** any other animal, and its closest relative is not even a **land animal** at all! It's a manatee, otherwise known as a sea-cow. Another large, African **mammal** is the **hippopotamus**. The hippo's name is **derived from** the Greek for river horse, but hippos and horses are not related. The hippo's closest relatives are in fact **dolphins**, **whales**, and **porpoises**.

ani|mal|istic /ænɪməlɪstɪk/ ADJ If you describe a person or their behavior as **animalistic**, you mean that they do not try to hide or control their basic feelings and physical needs. ❑ *The two teams were matched in a ferocious, almost animalistic battle.* ❑ *...her animalistic instincts for survival.*

ani|mal rights N-UNCOUNT [oft N n] People who are concerned with **animal rights** believe very strongly that animals should not be exploited or harmed by humans.

ani|mal test|ing N-UNCOUNT **Animal testing** involves doing scientific tests on animals when developing new products or drugs.

ani|mate (**animates**, **animating**, **animated**)

> The adjective is pronounced /ænɪmət/. The verb is pronounced /ænɪmeɪt/.

1 ADJ Something that is **animate** has life, in contrast to things like stones and machines which do not. ❑ *Natural philosophy involved the study of all aspects of the material world, animate and inanimate.* **2** V-T To **animate** something means to make it lively or more cheerful. ❑ *There was precious little about the cricket to animate the crowd.*

ani|mat|ed /ænɪmeɪtɪd/ **1** ADJ Someone who is **animated** or who is having an **animated** conversation is lively and is showing their feelings. ❑ *She was seen in animated conversation with the singer.* • **ani|mat|ed|ly** ADV [ADV with v] ❑ *Sammy was talking animatedly with Ned.* **2** ADJ [ADJ n] An **animated** film is one in which puppets or drawings appear to move. ❑ *The filmmakers have returned to what they do best: making full-length animated feature films.*

ani|ma|tion /ænɪmeɪʃᵊn/ (**animations**) **1** N-UNCOUNT **Animation** is the process of making films in which drawings or puppets appear to move. ❑ *The films are a mix of animation and full-length features.* **2** N-COUNT An **animation** is a film in which drawings or puppets appear to move. ❑ *This film is the first British animation sold to an American network.*

ani|ma|tor /ænɪmeɪtər/ (**animators**) N-COUNT An **animator** is a person who makes films by means of animation.

ani|ma|tron|ic /ænɪmətrɒnɪk/ **1** ADJ **Animatronic** models are made to move in a natural way by means of computers. ❑ *You can take a train ride past animatronic dinosaurs.* ❑ *...an animatronic puppet.* **2** N-UNCOUNT **Animatronics** is the use of computers to make models move in a natural way. ❑ *He is a graphic designer with 20 years' experience in puppets and animatronics for film and TV.*

an|ime /ænɪmeɪ/ N-UNCOUNT **Anime** is a style of Japanese animated movie that often contains scenes that are intended for adults. ❑ *Japanese anime is usually richer and more artistically dynamic than Hollywood's cartoons for kids.*

ani|mos|ity /ænɪmɒsɪti/ (**animosities**) N-VAR [also N in pl] **Animosity** is a strong feeling of dislike and anger. **Animosities** are feelings of this kind. ❑ *There's a long history of animosity between the two nations.*

ani|mus /ænɪməs/ N-UNCOUNT [usu N prep] If a person has an **animus** against someone, they have a strong feeling of dislike for them, even when there is no good reason for it. [FORMAL] ❑ *Your animus toward him suggests that you are the wrong man for the job.*

an|ise /ænɪs/ N-UNCOUNT **Anise** is a plant with seeds that have a strong smell and taste. It is often made into an alcoholic drink.

ani|seed /ænɪsid/ N-UNCOUNT **Aniseed** is a substance made from the seeds of the anise plant. It is used as a flavoring in sweets, drinks, and medicine.

an|kle /æŋkᵊl/ (**ankles**) N-COUNT Your **ankle** is the joint where your foot joins your leg. ❑ *John twisted his ankle badly.*

an|nals /ænᵊlz/ N-PLURAL [usu in the N of n] If something is in the **annals** of a nation or field of activity, it is recorded as part of its history. ❑ *He has become a legend in the annals of military history.*

an|nex (**annexes**, **annexing**, **annexed**)

> The verb is pronounced /æneks/. The noun is pronounced /æneks/.

1 V-T If a country **annexes** another country or an area of land, it seizes it and takes control of it. ❑ *Rome annexed the Nabatean kingdom in AD 106.* • **an|nexa|tion** /æneks**eɪ**ʃᵊn/ (**annexations**) N-COUNT ❑ *The annexation of the territory never won the acceptance of the United Nations.* **2** N-COUNT An **annex** is a building joined to or next to a larger main building. [AM] ❑ *...setting up a museum in an annex to the theater.*

> in BRIT, use **annexe**

an|ni|hi|late /ənaɪɪleɪt/ (annihilates, annihilating, annihilated) ◼ V-T To **annihilate** something means to destroy it completely. ▫ *There are lots of ways of annihilating the planet.* • **an|ni|hi|la|tion** /ənaɪɪleɪʃᵊn/ N-UNCOUNT ▫ *...the threat of nuclear war and annihilation of the human race.* ◼ V-T If you **annihilate** someone in a contest or argument, you totally defeat them. ▫ *The Dutch annihilated the Olympic champions 5-0.*

an|ni|ver|sa|ry ✦✧✧ /ænɪvɜrsəri/ (anniversaries) N-COUNT An **anniversary** is a date that is remembered or celebrated because a special event happened on that date in a previous year. ▫ *Vietnam is celebrating the one hundredth anniversary of the birth of Ho Chi Minh.*

an|no|tate /ænoʊteɪt/ (annotates, annotating, annotated) V-T If you **annotate** written work or a diagram, you add notes to it, especially in order to explain it. ▫ *Historians annotate, check and interpret the diary selections.*

an|no|ta|tion /ænoʊteɪʃᵊn/ (annotations) ◼ N-UNCOUNT **Annotation** is the activity of annotating something. ▫ *She retained a number of copies for further annotation.* ◼ N-COUNT [usu pl] An **annotation** is a note that is added to a text or diagram, often in order to explain it. ▫ *He supplied annotations to nearly 15,000 musical works.*

an|nounce ✦✧✧ /ənaʊns/ (announces, announcing, announced) ◼ V-T If you **announce** something, you tell people about it publicly or officially. ▫ *He will announce tonight that he is resigning from office.* ▫ *She was planning to announce her engagement to Peter.* ◼ V-T If you **announce** a piece of news or an intention, especially something that people may not like, you say it loudly and clearly, so that everyone you are with can hear it. ▫ *Peter announced that he had no intention of wasting his time at any university.* ◼ V-T If an airport or rail employee **announces** something, they tell the public about it by means of a loudspeaker system. ▫ *The loudspeaker announced the arrival of the train.*

an|nounce|ment ✦✧✧ /ənaʊnsmənt/ (announcements) ◼ N-COUNT An **announcement** is a statement made to the public or to the media that gives information about something that has happened or that will happen. ▫ *She made her announcement after talks with the president.* ◼ N-COUNT An **announcement** in a public place, such as a newspaper or the window of a store, is a short piece of writing telling people about something or asking for something. ▫ *The Seattle Times publishes brief announcements of religious events every Saturday.* ◼ N-SING The **announcement** of something that has happened is the act of telling people about it. ▫ *...the announcement of their engagement.*

> **SYNONYMS**
> **announcement**
> NOUN ◼
> **statement:** *The statement by the military denied any involvement in last night's attack.*
> **declaration:** *The opening speeches sounded more like declarations of war than offerings of peace.*
> **bulletin:** *A bulletin was released announcing that the president was out of danger.*
> **communication:** *The ambassador has brought with him a communication from the president.*
> **communiqué:** *The communiqué said military targets had been hit.*

an|nounc|er /ənaʊnsər/ (announcers) ◼ N-COUNT An **announcer** is someone who introduces programs on radio or television or who reads the text of a radio or television advertisement. ▫ *The radio announcer said it was nine o'clock.* ◼ N-COUNT The **announcer** at a train station or airport is the person who makes the announcements. ▫ *The announcer apologized for the delay.*

an|noy /ənɔɪ/ (annoys, annoying, annoyed) ◼ V-T If someone or something **annoys** you, it makes you fairly angry and impatient. ▫ *It annoyed me that I didn't have time to do more ironing.* ◼ → see also **annoyed, annoying**

an|noy|ance /ənɔɪəns/ (annoyances) ◼ N-UNCOUNT **Annoyance** is the feeling that you get when someone makes you feel fairly angry or impatient. ▫ *To her annoyance the stranger did not go away.* ◼ N-COUNT An **annoyance** is something that makes you feel angry or impatient. ▫ *Snoring can be more than an annoyance.*

an|noyed /ənɔɪd/ ◼ ADJ If you are **annoyed**, you are fairly angry about something. ▫ *She is hurt and annoyed that the authorities have banned her from working with children.* ◼ → see also **annoy**

an|noy|ing /ənɔɪɪŋ/ ADJ Someone or something that is **annoying** makes you feel fairly angry and impatient. ▫ *You must have found my attitude annoying.*

an|nual ✦✦✧ /ænyuəl/ (annuals) ◼ ADJ [ADJ n] **Annual** events happen once every year. ▫ *The issues will be voted on at the company's annual meeting on April 21 in Wilmington.* • **an|nual|ly** ADV [ADV with v] ▫ *Companies report to their shareholders annually.* ◼ ADJ [ADJ n] **Annual** quantities or rates relate to a period of one year. ▫ *The electronic and printing unit has annual sales of about $80 million.* • **an|nual|ly** ADV ▫ *El Salvador produces 100,000 tons of refined copper annually.* ◼ N-COUNT An **annual** is a book or magazine that is published once a year. ▫ *I looked for Wyman's picture in my high-school annual.* ◼ N-COUNT An **annual** is a plant that grows and dies within one year. ▫ *Maybe this year I'll sow brilliant annuals everywhere.* ◼ → See feature box at **population, weather**

> **SYNONYMS**
> **annual**
> ADJ ◼
> **yearly:** *...the yearly increase in the cost of raw materials.*

an|nu|ity /ənuɪti/ (annuities) N-COUNT An **annuity** is an investment or insurance policy that pays someone a fixed sum of money each year. [BUSINESS] ▫ *He received a paltry annuity of $100.*

an|nul /ənʌl/ (annuls, annulling, annulled) V-T [usu passive] If an election or a contract **is annulled**, it is declared invalid, so that legally it is considered never to have existed. ▫ *Opposition party leaders are now pressing for the entire election to be annulled.*

an|nul|ment /ənʌlmənt/ (annulments) N-VAR The **annulment** of a contract or marriage is an official declaration that it is invalid, so that legally it is considered never to have existed. ▫ *...the annulment of the elections.*

an|num /ænəm/ → see **per annum**

An|nun|cia|tion /ənʌnsieɪʃᵊn/ N-PROPER [the N] In Christianity, the **Annunciation** was the announcement by the Archangel Gabriel to the Virgin Mary that she was going to give birth to the son of God.

an|ode /ænoʊd/ (anodes) N-COUNT In electronics, an **anode** is the positive electrode in a cell such as a battery. Compare **cathode**. [TECHNICAL]

ano|dyne /ænədaɪn/ ADJ If you describe something as **anodyne**, you are criticizing it because it has no strong characteristics and is not likely to excite, interest, or upset anyone. [mainly BRIT, FORMAL, DISAPPROVAL] ▫ *Their quarterly meetings were anodyne affairs.*

anoint /ənɔɪnt/ (anoints, anointing, anointed) ◼ V-T To **anoint** someone means to put oil or water on a part of their body, usually for religious reasons. ▫ *He anointed my forehead.* ▫ *The Pope has anointed him as Archbishop.* ▫ *...the anointed king.* ◼ V-T If a person in a position of authority **anoints** someone, they choose them to do a particular important job. [JOURNALISM] ▫ *The populist party anointed him as its candidate.* ▫ *Mr. Olsen has always avoided anointing any successor.*

anoma|lous /ənɒmələs/ ADJ Something that is **anomalous** is different from what is usual or expected. [FORMAL] ▫ *For years this anomalous behavior has baffled scientists.*

anoma|ly /ənɒməli/ (anomalies) ◼ N-COUNT If something is an **anomaly**, it is different from what is usual or expected. [FORMAL] ▫ *The space shuttle had stopped transmitting data, a very serious anomaly for the mission.* ◼ → See feature box at **animal**

anon /ənɒn/ ADV [ADV after v] **Anon** means quite soon. [LITERARY] ▫ *You shall see him anon.*

anon. **Anon.** is often written after poems or other writing to indicate that the author is not known. **Anon.** is an abbreviation for **anonymous**.

anony|mous /ənɒnɪməs/ **1** ADJ If you remain **anonymous** when you do something, you do not let people know that you were the person who did it. ❑ *You can remain anonymous if you wish.* ❑ *An anonymous benefactor stepped in to provide the prize money.* • **ano|nym|ity** /ænɒnɪmɪti/ N-UNCOUNT ❑ *Both mother and daughter, who have requested anonymity, are doing fine.* • **anony|mous|ly** ADV ❑ *The latest photographs were sent anonymously to the magazine's headquarters.* **2** ADJ Something that is **anonymous** does not reveal who you are. ❑ *Of course, that would have to be by anonymous vote.* • **ano|nym|ity** N-UNCOUNT ❑ *He claims many more people would support him in the anonymity of a voting booth.*

ano|rak /ænəræk/ (anoraks) N-COUNT An **anorak** is a warm waterproof jacket, usually with a hood. [mainly BRIT]

ano|rexia /ænərɛksiə/ N-UNCOUNT **Anorexia** or **anorexia nervosa** is an illness in which a person has an overwhelming fear of becoming fat, and so refuses to eat enough and becomes thinner and thinner.

ano|rex|ic /ænərɛksɪk/ (anorexics) ADJ If someone is **anorexic**, they have anorexia and so are very thin. ❑ *Claire had been anorexic for three years.* • N-COUNT An **anorexic** is someone who is anorexic. ❑ *Not eating makes an anorexic feel in control.*

an|oth|er ♦♦♦ /ənʌðər/ **1** DET **Another** thing or person means an additional thing or person of the same type as one that already exists. ❑ *Divers this morning found the body of another American sailor drowned during yesterday's ferry disaster.* • PRON-SING **Another** is also a pronoun. ❑ *The demand generated by one factory required the construction of another.* **2** DET You use **another** when you want to emphasize that an additional thing or person is different from one that already exists. ❑ *I think he's just going to deal with this problem another day.* • PRON-SING **Another** is also a pronoun. ❑ *He didn't really believe that any human being could read another's mind.* **3** DET You use **another** at the beginning of a statement to link it to a previous statement. ❑ *Another time of great excitement for us boys was when war broke out.* **4** DET You use **another** before a word referring to a distance, length of time, or other amount, to indicate an additional amount. ❑ *Continue down the same road for another 2 miles until you reach the church of Santa Maria.* **5** PRON-RECIP [V PRON, prep PRON] You use **one another** to indicate that each member of a group does something to or for the other members. ❑ *...young people learning to help themselves and one another.* **6** PHRASE If you talk about **one thing after another**, you are referring to a series of repeated or continuous events. ❑ *They had faced one difficulty after another with bravery and dedication.* **7** PHRASE You use **or another** in expressions such as **one kind or another** when you do not want to be precise about which of several alternatives or possibilities you are referring to. ❑ *...family members and visiting artists of one kind or another crowding the huge kitchen.*

USAGE
another
Don't use 'another' in front of a plural noun or an uncountable noun. Don't say, for example, 'They arrange things better in another countries.' Say 'They arrange things better in **other** countries.' *Other people had the same idea.*

an|swer ♦♦♦ /ænsər/ (answers, answering, answered) **1** V-T/V-I When you **answer** someone who has asked you something, you say something back to them. ❑ *Just answer the question.* ❑ *He paused before answering.* ❑ *Williams answered that he had no specific proposals yet.* **2** V-T/V-I If you **answer** a letter or advertisement, you write to the person who wrote it. ❑ *Did he answer your letter?* **3** V-T/V-I When you **answer** the telephone, you pick it up when it rings. When you **answer** the door, you open it when you hear a knock or the bell. ❑ *She answered her phone on the first ring.* • N-COUNT **Answer** is also a noun. ❑ *I knocked at the front door and there was no answer.* **4** V-T When you **answer** a question in a test or quiz, you write or say something in an attempt to give the facts that are asked for. ❑ *Always read an exam all the way through at least once before you start to answer any questions.* **5** V-T/V-I If someone or something **answers** a particular description or **answers to** it, they have the characteristics described. ❑ *Two men answering the description of the suspects tried to enter Switzerland.* **6** N-COUNT [also *in* N *to* n] An **answer** is something that you say when you answer someone. ❑ *Without waiting for an answer, he turned and went in through the door.* **7** N-COUNT [also *in* N *to* n] An **answer** is a letter that you write to someone who has written to you. ❑ *I wrote to him but I never had an answer back.* **8** N-COUNT An **answer** to a problem is a solution to it. ❑ *There are no easy answers to the problems facing the economy.* **9** N-COUNT Someone's **answer** to a question in a test or quiz is what they write or say in an attempt to give the facts that are asked for. The **answer** to a question is the fact that was asked for. ❑ *Simply marking an answer wrong will not help the student to get future examples correct.* **10** N-COUNT [also *in* N *to* n] Your **answer** to something that someone has said or done is what you say or do in response to it or in defense of yourself. ❑ *In answer to speculation that she wouldn't finish the race, she boldly declared her intention of winning it.* **11** PHRASE If you say that someone will not **take no for an answer**, you mean that they go on trying to make you agree to something even after you have refused. ❑ *She is tough, unwilling to take no for an answer.*

▶ **answer back** PHRASAL VERB If someone, especially a child, **answers back**, they speak rudely to you when you speak to them. [BRIT] ❑ *My youngest child is eight and she has started answering back too.*

▶ **answer for** **1** PHRASAL VERB If you have to **answer for** something bad or wrong you have done, you are punished for it. ❑ *He must be made to answer for his terrible crimes.* **2** PHRASE [have inflects] If you say that someone **has a lot to answer for**, you are saying that their actions have led to problems which you think they are responsible for.

an|swer|able /ænsərəbəl/ **1** ADJ [v-link ADJ *to* n] If you are **answerable** to someone, you have to report to them and explain your actions. ❑ *Councils should be answerable to the people who elect them.* **2** ADJ [v-link ADJ] If you are **answerable** for your actions or for someone else's actions, you are considered to be responsible for them and if necessary must accept punishment for them. ❑ *He must be made answerable for these terrible crimes.*

an|swer|ing ma|chine (answering machines) **1** N-COUNT An **answering machine** is a device that you connect to your telephone to record telephone calls while you are out.
2 → See feature box at **telephone**

ant /ænt/ (ants) N-COUNT **Ants** are small crawling insects that live in large groups. ❑ *Ants swarmed up out of the ground and covered her shoes and legs.*

ant|acid /æntæsɪd/ (antacids) N-MASS **Antacid** is a substance that reduces the level of acid in the stomach.

an|tago|nism /æntægənɪzəm/ (antagonisms) N-VAR [also N in pl] **Antagonism** between people is hatred or dislike between them. **Antagonisms** are instances of this. ❑ *There is still much antagonism between environmental groups and the oil companies.*

an|tago|nist /æntægənɪst/ (antagonists) N-COUNT Your **antagonist** is your opponent or enemy. ❑ *Spassky had never previously lost to his antagonist.*

an|tago|nis|tic /æntægənɪstɪk/ ADJ If a person is **antagonistic** to someone or something, they show hatred or dislike toward them. ❑ *Nearly all the women I interviewed were aggressively antagonistic to the idea.*

an|tago|nize /æntægənaɪz/ (antagonizes, antagonizing, antagonized)

in BRIT, also use **antagonise**

V-T If you **antagonize** someone, you make them feel angry or hostile toward you. ❑ *He didn't want to antagonize her.*

Ant|arc|tic /æntɑrktɪk/ N-PROPER The **Antarctic** is the area around the South Pole.

ante /ænti/ **1** N-SING In card games such as poker, the **ante** is the sum of money staked by the players before the cards are dealt. **2** PHRASE If you **up the ante** or **raise the ante**, you increase your demands when you are in dispute or fighting for something. [JOURNALISM] ❑ *Whenever they reached their goal, they upped the ante, setting increasingly complex challenges for themselves.*

ant|eater /æntiːtər/ (anteaters) also **ant-eater** N-COUNT An **anteater** is an animal with a long nose that eats termites or ants. Anteaters live in warm countries.

ante|ced|ent /ˈæntɪsiːdᵊnt/ (antecedents) N-COUNT [usu with supp] An **antecedent** of something happened or existed before it and was similar to it in some way. [FORMAL] ❑ *We shall first look briefly at the historical antecedents of this theory.*

ante|cham|ber /ˈæntɪtʃeɪmbər/ (antechambers) N-COUNT An **antechamber** is a small room leading into a larger room. [OLD-FASHIONED]

in BRIT, also use **ante-chamber**

ante|di|lu|vian /ˌæntɪdɪˈluːviən/ ADJ **Antediluvian** things are old or old-fashioned. [HUMOROUS] ❑ *...antediluvian attitudes to women.*

ante|lope /ˈæntɪloʊp/ (antelopes or antelope) N-COUNT An **antelope** is an animal like a deer, with long legs and horns, that lives in Africa or Asia. Antelopes are graceful and can run fast. There are many different types of antelope.

ante|na|tal /ˌæntɪˈneɪtᵊl/ ADJ [ADJ n] **Antenatal** is the same as **prenatal**.

an|ten|na /ænˈtɛnə/ (antennae /ænˈtɛni/ or antennas)

antennae is the usual plural form for meaning **1** and **antennas** is the usual plural form for meaning **2**.

1 N-COUNT The **antennae** of something such as an insect or crustacean are the two long, thin parts attached to its head that it uses to feel things with. **2** N-COUNT An **antenna** is a device or a piece of wire that sends and receives television or radio signals and is usually attached to a radio, television, car, or building. **3** → See also color supplement

ante|ri|or /ænˈtɪəriər/ ADJ [usu ADJ n] **Anterior** describes a part of the body that is situated at or toward the front of another part. [MEDICAL] ❑ *...the left anterior descending artery.*

ante|room /ˈæntɪruːm/ (anterooms) also **ante-room** N-COUNT An **anteroom** is a small room leading into a larger room. [OLD-FASHIONED] ❑ *He had been patiently waiting in the anteroom for an hour.*

an|them /ˈænθəm/ (anthems) N-COUNT An **anthem** is a song that is used to represent a particular nation, society, or group and that is sung on special occasions. ❑ *The band played the Czech anthem.*

ant|hill /ˈænthɪl/ (anthills) also **ant-hill** N-COUNT An **anthill** is a pile of earth formed by ants when they are making a nest.

an|thol|ogy /ænˈθɒlədʒi/ (anthologies) **1** N-COUNT An **anthology** is a collection of writings by different writers published together in one book. ❑ *...an anthology of poetry.* **2** → See feature box at **book**

an|thra|cite /ˈænθrəsaɪt/ N-UNCOUNT **Anthracite** is a type of very hard coal that burns slowly, producing a lot of heat and very little smoke.

an|thrax /ˈænθræks/ N-UNCOUNT **Anthrax** is a disease of cattle and sheep, in which they get painful sores and a fever. Anthrax can be used in biological weapons.

an|thro|pol|ogy /ˌænθrəˈpɒlədʒi/ N-UNCOUNT **Anthropology** is the scientific study of people, society, and culture.
• **an|thro|polo|gist** /ˌænθrəˈpɒlədʒɪst/ (anthropologists) N-COUNT ❑ *...an anthropologist who had been in China for three years.*

an|thro|po|mor|phic /ˌænθrəpəˈmɔːrfɪk/ ADJ **Anthropomorphic** means relating to the idea that an animal, a god, or an object has feelings or characteristics like those of a human being. ❑ *...the anthropomorphic attitude to animals.*

an|thro|po|mor|phism /ˌænθrəpəˈmɔːrfɪzəm/ N-UNCOUNT **Anthropomorphism** is the idea that an animal, a god, or an object has feelings or characteristics like those of a human being.

anti /ˈænti, -taɪ/ ADJ [v-link ADJ] If someone is opposed to something you can say that they are **anti** it. [INFORMAL, SPOKEN] ❑ *That's why you're so anti other people smoking.*

PREFIX

anti-
forms nouns and adjectives that refer to some sort of opposition. *For example,* **anti-virus** *software protects a computer from attack by viruses.*

anti|abor|tion|ist /ˌæntiəˈbɔːrʃənɪst, -taɪ-/ (antiabortionists) N-COUNT An **antiabortionist** is someone who wants to limit or prevent the legal availability of abortions.

anti|bac|te|rial /ˌæntibækˈtɪəriəl, -taɪ-/ ADJ [ADJ n] **Antibacterial** substances or products kill bacteria. ❑ *Should people buy antibacterial cleaners?* ❑ *Garlic is said to be especially beneficial for its antibacterial properties.*

anti|bi|ot|ic /ˌæntibaɪˈɒtɪk, -taɪ-/ (antibiotics) N-COUNT **Antibiotics** are medical drugs used to kill bacteria and treat infections. ❑ *Your doctor may prescribe antibiotics.*

anti|body /ˈæntibɒdi, ˈæntaɪ-/ (antibodies) N-COUNT **Antibodies** are substances that a person's or an animal's blood produces in their blood in order to destroy substances that carry disease. ❑ *Such women carry antibodies which make their blood more likely to clot during pregnancy.*

an|tici|pate /ænˈtɪsɪpeɪt/ (anticipates, anticipating, anticipated) **1** V-T If you **anticipate** an event, you realize in advance that it may happen and you are prepared for it. ❑ *At the time we couldn't have anticipated the result of our campaigning.* ❑ *It is anticipated that the equivalent of 192 full-time jobs will be lost.* **2** V-T If you **anticipate** a question, request, or need, you do what is necessary or required before the question, request, or need occurs. ❑ *What Jeff did was to anticipate my next question.*

an|tici|pat|ed /ænˈtɪsɪpeɪtɪd/ ADJ If an event, especially a cultural event, is eagerly **anticipated**, people expect that it will be very good, exciting, or interesting. ❑ *...the most eagerly anticipated rock event of the year.* ❑ *...one of the conference's most keenly anticipated debates.*

an|tici|pa|tion /ænˌtɪsɪˈpeɪʃᵊn/ **1** N-UNCOUNT **Anticipation** is a feeling of excitement about something pleasant or exciting that you know is going to happen. ❑ *There's been an atmosphere of anticipation around here for a few days now.* **2** PHRASE If something is done **in anticipation of** an event, it is done because people believe that event is going to happen. ❑ *Troops in the Philippines have been put on full alert in anticipation of trouble during a planned general strike.*

an|tici|pa|tory /ænˈtɪsɪpətɔːri/ ADJ [usu ADJ n] An **anticipatory** feeling or action is one that you have or do because you are expecting something to happen soon. [FORMAL] ❑ *...an anticipatory smile.*

anti|cli|max /ˌæntiˈklaɪmæks, ˌæntaɪ-/ (anticlimaxes) N-VAR You can describe something as an **anticlimax** if it disappoints you because it happens after something that was very exciting, or because it is not as exciting as you expected. ❑ *After the marvelous display of Saturday morning, the remaining ceremonies were something of an anticlimax.*

anti|clock|wise /ˌæntiˈklɒkwaɪz, ˌæntaɪ-/ ADV also **anti-clockwise** ADV If something is moving **anticlockwise**, it is moving in the opposite direction to the direction in which the hands of a clock move. [BRIT]

in AM, use **counterclockwise**

• ADJ [ADJ n] **Anticlockwise** is also an adjective. ❑ *...an anticlockwise route around the coast.*

an|tics /ˈæntɪks/ N-PLURAL **Antics** are funny, silly, or unusual ways of behaving. ❑ *Elizabeth tolerated Sarah's antics.*

anti|cy|clone /ˌæntiˈsaɪkloʊn, ˌæntaɪ-/ (anticyclones) N-COUNT An **anticyclone** is an area of high atmospheric pressure which causes settled weather conditions and, in summer, clear skies and high temperatures.

anti|de|press|ant /ˌæntidɪˈpresᵊnt, ˌæntaɪ-/ (antidepressants) N-COUNT An **antidepressant** is a drug which is used to treat people who have depression.

in BRIT, also use **anti-depressant**

anti|dote /ˈæntidoʊt/ (antidotes) **1** N-COUNT An **antidote** is a chemical substance that stops or controls the effect of a poison. ❑ *When he returned, he noticed their sickness and prepared an antidote.* **2** N-COUNT Something that is an **antidote** to a difficult or unpleasant situation helps you to overcome the situation. ❑ *Massage is a wonderful antidote to stress.*

anti|freeze /ˈæntifriːz, ˈæntaɪ-/ N-UNCOUNT [also a N] **Antifreeze** is a liquid that is added to water to stop it from freezing. It is used in car radiators in cold weather.

anti|gen /ˈæntɪdʒən/ (antigens) N-COUNT An **antigen** is a substance that helps the production of antibodies.

anti|hero /ǽntihɪərou, ǽntaɪ-/ (**antiheroes**) N-COUNT An **antihero** is the main character in a novel, play, or film who is not morally good and does not behave like a typical hero.

in BRIT, also use **anti-hero**

anti|his|ta|mine /ǽntihɪstəmɪn, ǽntaɪ-/ (**antihistamines**) N-COUNT An **antihistamine** is a drug that is used to treat allergies.

anti|mat|ter /ǽntimætər, ǽntaɪ-/ N-UNCOUNT In science, **antimatter** is a form of matter whose particles have characteristics and properties opposite to those of ordinary matter. [TECHNICAL]

anti|oxi|dant /ǽntipksɪdənt, ǽntaɪ-/ (**antioxidants**) N-COUNT An **antioxidant** is a substance that slows down the damage that can be caused to other substances by the effects of oxygen. Foods that contain antioxidants are thought to be very good for you.

anti|pas|to /ǽntipɑstoʊ/ (**antipasti**) N-VAR **Antipasto** is the sort of food that is often served at the beginning of an Italian meal, for example, cold meats and vegetables in olive oil.

an|tipa|thy /æntɪpəθi/ N-UNCOUNT **Antipathy** is a strong feeling of dislike or hostility toward someone or something. [FORMAL] ❏ ...the voting public's antipathy toward the president.

anti|per|spi|rant /ǽntipɜrspɪrənt, ǽntaɪ-/ (**antiperspirants**) N-VAR **Antiperspirant** is a substance that you can use on your body, especially under your arms, to prevent or reduce sweating. ❏ ...a different brand of antiperspirant. ❏ ...an antiperspirant for sensitive skins. • ADJ **Antiperspirant** is also used as an adjective. ❏ ...a number of deodorants available that do not have an antiperspirant effect.

anti|quar|ian /ǽntɪkwɛəriən/ (**antiquarians**) ❶ ADJ [ADJ n] **Antiquarian** means concerned with old and rare objects. ❏ ...an antiquarian bookseller. ❏ ...antiquarian and secondhand books. ❷ N-COUNT An **antiquarian** is the same as an **antiquary**.

anti|quary /ǽntɪkweri/ (**antiquaries**) N-COUNT An **antiquary** is a person who studies the past, or who collects or buys and sells old and valuable objects.

anti|quat|ed /ǽntɪkweɪtɪd/ ADJ If you describe something as **antiquated**, you are criticizing it because it is very old or old-fashioned. [DISAPPROVAL] ❏ Many factories are so antiquated they are not worth saving.

an|tique ✦◇◇ /æntíːk/ (**antiques**) ❶ N-COUNT An **antique** is an old object such as a piece of china or furniture that is valuable because of its beauty or rarity. ❏ ...a genuine antique. ❷ → See feature box at **upcycle**

an|tiqued /æntíːkt/ ADJ An **antiqued** object is modern but has been made to look like an antique. ❏ Both rooms have antiqued pine furniture.

an|tiq|uity /æntɪ́kwɪti/ (**antiquities**) ❶ N-UNCOUNT **Antiquity** is the distant past, especially the time of the ancient Egyptians, Greeks, and Romans. ❏ ...famous monuments of classical antiquity. ❷ N-COUNT **Antiquities** are things such as buildings, statues, or coins that were made in ancient times and have survived to the present day. ❏ ...collectors of Roman antiquities.

anti-Semite /ǽntisɛmaɪt, ǽntaɪ-/ (**anti-Semites**) N-COUNT An **anti-Semite** is someone who strongly dislikes and is prejudiced against Jewish people.

anti-Semitic ADJ Someone or something that is **anti-Semitic** is hostile to or prejudiced against Jewish people.

anti-Semitism /ǽntisɛmɪtɪzəm, ǽntaɪ-/ N-UNCOUNT **Anti-Semitism** is hostility to and prejudice against Jewish people.

anti|sep|tic /ǽntəsɛptɪk/ (**antiseptics**) N-MASS **Antiseptic** is a substance that kills germs and harmful bacteria. ❏ She bathed the cut with antiseptic.

anti|so|cial /ǽntisoʊʃəl, ǽntaɪ-/ ADJ Someone who is **antisocial** is unwilling to meet and be friendly with other people. ❏ ...a generation of teenagers who will become aggressive and antisocial.

an|tith|esis /æntɪ́θəsɪs/ (**antitheses** /æntɪ́θəsiːz/) N-COUNT The **antithesis** of something is its exact opposite. [FORMAL] ❏ The little black dress is the antithesis of fussy dressing.

anti|theti|cal /ǽntiθɛtɪkəl/ ADJ [usu v-link ADJ to n] Something that is **antithetical** to something else is the opposite of it and is unable to exist with it. [WRITTEN] ❏ Their priorities are antithetical to those of environmentalists.

anti|trust /ǽntitrʌst, ǽntaɪ-/ ADJ [ADJ n] In the United States, **antitrust** laws are intended to stop big companies taking over their competitors, fixing prices with their competitors, or interfering with free competition in any way. ❏ The jury found that the NFL had violated antitrust laws.

anti-virus also **antivirus** ADJ [ADJ n] **Anti-virus** software is software that protects a computer against viruses.

ant|ler /ǽntlər/ (**antlers**) N-COUNT A male deer's **antlers** are the branched horns on its head.

an|to|nym /ǽntənɪm/ (**antonyms**) N-COUNT The **antonym** of a word is a word that means the opposite. [FORMAL]

antsy /ǽntsi/ ADJ [usu v-link ADJ] If someone is **antsy**, they are nervous or impatient. [AM, INFORMAL] ❏ This is the end of a tour so I'm a little antsy, I guess.

anus /éɪnəs/ (**anuses**) N-COUNT A person's **anus** is the hole from which feces leaves their body. [MEDICAL]

an|vil /ǽnvɪl/ (**anvils**) ❶ N-COUNT An **anvil** is a heavy iron block on which hot metals are beaten into shape. ❷ N-COUNT The **anvil** is the middle bone of the three small bones in the ear of mammals. ❸ → See also color supplement

anxi|ety ✦◇◇ /æŋzáɪɪti/ (**anxieties**) N-VAR [also N in pl] **Anxiety** is a feeling of nervousness or worry. ❏ Her voice was full of anxiety.

SYNONYMS

anxiety
NOUN
unease: Garland tried to appear casual, but he couldn't conquer his unease.
worry: His wife Cheryl said she had no worries about his health.
tension: Smiling and laughing has actually been shown to relieve tension and stress.
apprehension: It reflects real anger and apprehension about the future.
nervousness: I smiled warmly so he wouldn't see my nervousness.

---

anx|ious ✦◇◇ /ǽŋkʃəs/ ❶ ADJ [v-link ADJ] If you are **anxious** to do something or **anxious** that something should happen, you very much want to do it or very much want it to happen. ❏ Both the Americans and the Russians are anxious to avoid conflict in South Asia. ❏ He is anxious that there should be no delay. ❷ ADJ If you are **anxious**, you are nervous or worried about something. ❏ The foreign minister admitted he was still anxious about the situation in the country. • **anxiously** ADV [ADV with v] ❏ They are waiting anxiously to see who will succeed him.

SYNONYMS

anxious
ADJ
❶
eager: Robert was eager to talk about life in the Army.
keen: She's still keen to keep in touch.
impatient: He was impatient to get home.
❷
uneasy: I had an uneasy feeling that he was going to spoil it.
concerned: I've been concerned about you lately.
worried: He seemed very worried.
nervous: She described Mr Hutchinson as nervous and jumpy after his wife's disappearance.
tense: There was a tense silence.

---

any ✦✦✦ /ɛ́ni/ ❶ DET You use **any** in statements with negative meaning to indicate that no thing or person of a particular type exists, is present, or is involved in a situation. ❏ I'm not making any promises. ❏ We are doing this all without any support from the hospital. ❏ It is too early to say what effect, if any, there will be on the workforce. • QUANT **Any** is also a quantifier. ❏ You don't know any of my friends. • PRON [PRON after v] **Any** is also a pronoun. ❏ The children needed new school clothes and Kim couldn't afford any. ❷ DET You use **any** in questions and conditional clauses to ask whether there is some of a particular thing or some of a particular group of people, or to suggest that there might be. ❏ Do you speak any foreign languages? • QUANT **Any** is also a

anybody

quantifier. ❑ *Introduce foods one at a time and notice if you feel uncomfortable with any of them.* • PRON [PRON after v] **Any** is also a pronoun. ❑ *If any bright thoughts occur to you pass them straight to me. Have you got any?* **3** DET You use **any** in positive statements when you are referring to someone or something of a particular kind that might exist, occur, or be involved in a situation, when their exact identity or nature is not important. ❑ *Any actor will tell you that it is easier to perform than to be themselves.* • QUANT **Any** is also a quantifier. ❑ *Nealy disappeared two days ago, several miles away from any of the fighting.* • PRON **Any** is also a pronoun. ❑ *Clean the mussels and discard any that do not close.* **4** ADV [ADV compar] You can also use **any** to emphasize a comparative adjective or adverb in a negative statement. [EMPHASIS] ❑ *I can't see things getting any easier for graduates.* **5** PHRASE If you say that someone or something is **not just any** person or thing, you mean that they are special in some way. ❑ *Finzer is not just any East Coast businessman.* **6** PHRASE If something does not happen or is not true **any longer**, it has stopped happening or is no longer true. ❑ *I couldn't keep the tears hidden any longer.* **7 in any case** → see **case** ① **8 by any chance** → see **chance** **9 in any event** → see **event** **10 any old** → see **old** **11 at any rate** → see **rate**

any|body ◆◇◇ /ˈɛnibɒdi, -bʌdi/ PRON-INDEF **Anybody** means the same as **anyone**.

any|how /ˈɛnihaʊ/ **1** ADV **Anyhow** means the same as **anyway**. **2** ADV [ADV after v] If you do something **anyhow**, you do it in a careless or untidy way. ❑ *Her discarded books were piled up just anyhow.*

any|more ◆◆◇ /ˌɛniˈmɔːr/ also **any more** ADV [ADV after v] If something does not happen or is not true **anymore**, it has stopped happening or is no longer true. ❑ *I don't ride my motorbike much anymore.* ❑ *I couldn't trust him anymore.*

any|one ◆◆◇ /ˈɛniwʌn/

The form **anybody** is also used.

1 PRON-INDEF You use **anyone** or **anybody** in statements with negative meaning to indicate in a general way that nobody is present or involved in an action. ❑ *I won't tell anyone I saw you here.* ❑ *You needn't talk to anyone if you don't want to.* **2** PRON-INDEF You use **anyone** or **anybody** in questions and conditional clauses to ask or talk about whether someone is present or doing something. ❑ *Why would anyone want that job?* ❑ *How can anyone look sad at an occasion like this?* **3** PRON-INDEF [PRON cl/group] You use **anyone** or **anybody** before words that indicate the kind of person you are talking about. ❑ *I always had been the person who achieved things before anyone else at my age.* ❑ *It's not a job for anyone who is slow with numbers.* **4** PRON-INDEF You use **anyone** or **anybody** to refer to a person when you are emphasizing that it could be any person out of a very large number of people. [EMPHASIS] ❑ *Anyone could be doing what I'm doing.* **5** PHRASE You use **anyone who is anyone** and **anybody who is anybody** to refer to people who are important or influential. ❑ *It seems anyone who's anyone in business is going to the conference.*

any|place /ˈɛnipleɪs/ ADV [ADV after v] **Anyplace** means the same as **anywhere**. [AM, INFORMAL] ❑ *She didn't have anyplace to go.*

any|thing ◆◆◇ /ˈɛniθɪŋ/ **1** PRON-INDEF You use **anything** in statements with negative meaning to indicate in a general way that nothing is present or that an action or event does not or cannot happen. ❑ *We can't do anything.* ❑ *She couldn't see or hear anything at all.* **2** PRON-INDEF You use **anything** in questions and conditional clauses to ask or talk about whether something is present or happening. ❑ *What happened, is anything wrong?* ❑ *Did you find anything?* **3** PRON-INDEF [PRON cl/group] You can use **anything** before words that indicate the kind of thing you are talking about. ❑ *More than anything else, he wanted to become a teacher.* ❑ *Anything that's cheap this year will be even cheaper next year.* **4** PRON-INDEF You use **anything** to emphasize a possible thing, event, or situation, when you are saying that it could be any one of a very large number of things. [EMPHASIS] ❑ *He is young, fresh, and ready for anything.* **5** PRON-INDEF [PRON prep] You use **anything** in expressions such as **anything near**, **anything close to** and **anything like** to emphasize a statement that you are making. [EMPHASIS] ❑ *Doctors have decided the only way he can live anything near a normal life is to give him an operation.* **6** PRON-INDEF [PRON from n to n, PRON between n and n] When you do not want to be exact, you use **anything** to talk about a particular range of things or quantities. ❑ *…Chinese herbs that have cured anything from colds to broken bones.* **7** PHRASE You use **anything but** in expressions such as **anything but quiet** and **anything but attractive** to emphasize that something is not the case. [EMPHASIS] ❑ *There's no evidence that Christopher told anyone to say anything but the truth.* **8** PHRASE You can say that you **would not** do something **for anything** to emphasize that you definitely would not want to do or be a particular thing. [INFORMAL, SPOKEN, EMPHASIS] ❑ *I wouldn't want to move for anything in the world.* **9** PHRASE You use **if anything**, especially after a negative statement, to introduce a statement that adds to what you have just said. ❑ *I never had to clean up after the lodgers. If anything, they did most of the cleaning.* **10** PHRASE You can add **or anything** to the end of a clause or sentence in order to refer vaguely to other things that are or may be similar to what you just mentioned. [INFORMAL, SPOKEN, VAGUENESS] ❑ *Listen, if you talk to Elizabeth or anything make sure you let everyone know, will you.*

any|time /ˈɛnitaɪm/ ADV You use **anytime** to mean a point in time that is not fixed or set. ❑ *The college admits students anytime during the year.* ❑ *He can leave anytime he wants.*

any|way ◆◆◇ /ˈɛniweɪ/

The form **anyhow** is also used.

1 ADV [ADV with cl] You use **anyway** or **anyhow** to indicate that a statement explains or supports a previous point. ❑ *I'm certain David's told you his business troubles. Anyway, it's no secret that he owes money.* **2** ADV [ADV with cl] You use **anyway** or **anyhow** to suggest that a statement is true or relevant in spite of other things that have been said. ❑ *I don't know why I settled on Miami, but anyway I did.* **3** ADV [cl/group ADV] You use **anyway** or **anyhow** to correct or modify a statement, for example, to limit it to what you definitely know to be true. ❑ *Mary Ann doesn't want to have children. Not right now, anyway.* **4** ADV [cl ADV] You use **anyway** or **anyhow** to indicate that you are asking what the real situation is or what the real reason for something is. ❑ *What do you want from me, anyway?* **5** ADV [ADV with cl] You use **anyway** or **anyhow** to indicate that you are leaving out some details in a story and are passing on to the next main point or event. ❑ *I was told to go to Denver for this interview. It was a very amusing affair. Anyhow, I got the job.* **6** ADV [ADV cl] You use **anyway** or **anyhow** to change the topic or return to a previous topic. ❑ *"I've got a terrible cold."—"Have you? Oh dear. Anyway, so you're not going to go away this weekend?"* **7** ADV [ADV cl] You use **anyway** or **anyhow** to indicate that you want to end the conversation. ❑ *"Anyway, I'd better let you have your dinner. Bye."*

any|ways /ˈɛniweɪz/ ADV **Anyways** is a nonstandard or dialectal form of **anyway**. [AM, SPOKEN] ❑ *Well, anyways, she said it wasn't safe.*

any|where ◆◆◇ /ˈɛniweər/ **1** ADV You use **anywhere** in statements with negative meaning to indicate that a place does not exist. ❑ *I haven't got anywhere to live.* **2** ADV You use **anywhere** in questions and conditional clauses to ask or talk about a place without saying exactly where you mean. ❑ *Did you try to get help from anywhere?* **3** ADV [ADV cl/group] You use **anywhere** before words that indicate the kind of place you are talking about. ❑ *He'll meet you anywhere you want.* **4** ADV You use **anywhere** to refer to a place when you are emphasizing that it could be any of a large number of places. [EMPHASIS] ❑ *…jokes that are so funny they always work anywhere.* **5** ADV When you do not want to be exact, you use **anywhere** to refer to a particular range of things. ❑ *His shoes cost anywhere from $200 up.* **6** ADV [ADV adj/adv] You use **anywhere** in expressions such as **anywhere near** and **anywhere close to** to emphasize a statement that you are making. [EMPHASIS] ❑ *There weren't anywhere near enough empty boxes.*

aor|ta /eɪˈɔːrtə/ (**aortas**) **1** N-COUNT The **aorta** is the main artery through which blood leaves your heart before it flows through the rest of your body. **2** → See also color supplement

apace /əˈpeɪs/ ADV [ADV after v] If something develops or continues **apace**, it is developing or continuing quickly. [FORMAL]

apart

APART
① POSITIONS AND STATES
② INDICATING EXCEPTIONS AND FOCUSING

① **apart** ♦♦◊ /əpɑ́ːrt/

In addition to the uses shown below, **apart** is used in phrasal verbs such as 'grow apart' and 'take apart.'

1 ADV When people or things are **apart**, they are some distance from each other. ❑ *He was standing a bit apart from the rest of us, watching us.* ❑ *Ray and sister Renee lived just 25 miles apart from each other.* **2** ADV [ADV after v] If two people or things move **apart** or are pulled **apart**, they move away from each other. ❑ *John and Isabelle moved apart, back into the sun.* **3** ADV If two people are **apart**, they are no longer living together or spending time together, either permanently or just for a short time. ❑ *It was the first time Jane and I had been apart for more than a few days.* **4** ADV [ADV after v] If you take something **apart**, you separate it into the pieces that it is made of. If it comes or falls **apart**, its parts separate from each other. ❑ *When the clock stopped he took it apart, found what was wrong, and put the whole thing together again.* **5** ADV [ADV after v] If something such as an organization or relationship falls **apart**, or if something tears it **apart**, it can no longer continue because it has serious difficulties. ❑ *Any manager knows that his company will start falling apart if his attention wanders.* **6** ADV If something sets someone or something **apart**, it makes them different from other people or things. ❑ *What really sets them apart is great design and exceptional functionality.* **7** ADJ [v-link amount ADJ, oft ADJ on n] If people or groups are a long way **apart** on a particular topic or issue, they have completely different views and disagree about it. ❑ *Their concept of a performance and our concept were miles apart.* **8** PHRASE If you can't **tell** two people or things **apart**, they look exactly the same to you. ❑ *I can still only tell Mark and Dave apart by the color of their shoes!*

② **apart** ♦◊◊ /əpɑ́ːrt/ **1** PHRASE **Apart from** means the same as **aside from**. **2** ADV [n ADV] You use **apart** when you are making an exception to a general statement. ❑ *This was, New York apart, the first American city I had ever been in where people actually lived downtown.*

apart|heid /əpɑ́ːrthaɪt/ N-UNCOUNT **Apartheid** was a political system in South Africa in which people were divided into racial groups and kept apart by law. ❑ *He praised her role in the struggle against apartheid.*

apart|ment ♦◊◊ /əpɑ́ːrtmənt/ (**apartments**) **1** N-COUNT An **apartment** is a separate set of rooms for living in, in a house or a building with other apartments. [mainly AM] ❑ *Christina has her own apartment, with her own car.*

in BRIT, usually use **flat**

2 → See also color supplement

COLLOCATIONS

apartment
NOUN
noun + **apartment**: basement, studio
adjective + **apartment**: high-rise, self-contained, two-bedroom; empty, furnished
verb + **apartment**: buy, let, rent, sublet

apart|ment build|ing (**apartment buildings**) also **apartment house** N-COUNT An **apartment building** or **apartment house** is a tall building that contains different apartments. [AM] ❑ *...the Manhattan apartment house where they live.*

in BRIT, use **block of flats**

apart|ment com|plex (**apartment complexes**) N-COUNT An **apartment complex** is a group of buildings that contain apartments and are managed by the same company. [AM] ❑ *...the 10-story apartment complex where the jet crashed.*

apa|thet|ic /æpəθétɪk/ ADJ If you describe someone as **apathetic**, you are criticizing them because they do not seem to be interested in or enthusiastic about doing anything. [DISAPPROVAL] ❑ *Even the most apathetic students are beginning to sit up and listen.*

apologetic

apa|thy /æpəθi/ N-UNCOUNT You can use **apathy** to talk about someone's state of mind if you are criticizing them because they do not seem to be interested in or enthusiastic about anything. [DISAPPROVAL] ❑ *They told me about isolation and public apathy.*

APB /eɪ pi bi/ (**APBs**) N-COUNT **APB** is an abbreviation for **all-points bulletin**. [AM]

ape /eɪp/ (**apes, aping, aped**) **1** N-COUNT **Apes** are chimpanzees, gorillas, and other animals in the same family. ❑ *...chimpanzees and other apes.* **2** V-T If you **ape** someone's speech or behavior, you imitate it. ❑ *Modeling yourself on someone you admire is not the same as aping all they say or do.*

ape|ri|tif /əpèrɪtíːf/ (**aperitifs**) N-COUNT An **aperitif** is an alcoholic drink that you have before a meal.

ap|er|ture /æpərtʃər/ (**apertures**) **1** N-COUNT An **aperture** is a narrow hole or gap. [FORMAL] ❑ *Through the aperture he could see daylight.* **2** N-COUNT In photography, the **aperture** of a camera is the size of the hole through which light passes to reach the film. ❑ *Use a small aperture and position the camera carefully.*

apex /eɪpeks/ (**apexes**) **1** N-SING The **apex** of an organization or system is the highest and most important position in it. ❑ *At the apex of the party was its central committee.* **2** N-COUNT The **apex** of something is its pointed top or end. ❑ *The hangar is 103 feet high at the apex of its roof.*

apha|sia /əfeɪʒə/ N-UNCOUNT **Aphasia** is a mental condition in which people are often unable to remember simple words or communicate. [MEDICAL]

aphid /eɪfɪd, æt-/ (**aphids**) N-COUNT [usu pl] **Aphids** are very small insects that live on plants and suck their juices.

apho|rism /æfərɪzəm/ (**aphorisms**) N-COUNT An **aphorism** is a short witty sentence which expresses a general truth or comment. [FORMAL]

aph|ro|disi|ac /æfrədíziæk, -dɪzi-/ (**aphrodisiacs**) N-COUNT An **aphrodisiac** is a food, drink, or drug that is said to make people want to have sex. ❑ *Asparagus is reputed to be an aphrodisiac.*

apiece /əpíːs/ **1** ADV [amount ADV] If people have a particular number of things **apiece**, they have that number each. ❑ *He and I had two fish apiece.* **2** ADV [amount ADV] If a number of similar things are for sale at a certain price **apiece**, that is the price for each one of them. ❑ *Entire roast chickens were sixty cents apiece.*

aplen|ty /əplénti/ ADV [n ADV] If you have something **aplenty**, you have a lot of it. [LITERARY] ❑ *There were problems aplenty at work.*

aplomb /əplɒm, əplʌm/ N-UNCOUNT [usu with N] If you do something with **aplomb**, you do it with confidence in a relaxed way. [FORMAL]

apoca|lypse /əpɒkəlɪps/ N-SING [usu the N] The **apocalypse** is the total destruction and end of the world.

apoca|lyp|tic /əpɒkəlɪptɪk/ **1** ADJ [usu ADJ n] **Apocalyptic** means relating to the total destruction of something, especially of the world. ❑ *...the reformer's apocalyptic warnings that the nation was running out of natural resources.* **2** ADJ [usu ADJ n] **Apocalyptic** means relating to or involving predictions about future disasters and the destruction of the world. ❑ *...a gloomy and apocalyptic vision of a world hastening toward ruin.*

apoc|ry|phal /əpɒkrɪfəl/ ADJ An **apocryphal** story is one that is probably not true or did not happen, but that may give a true picture of someone or something.

apo|gee /æpədʒi/ N-SING [with supp] The **apogee** of something such as a culture or a business is its highest or its greatest point. [FORMAL]

apo|liti|cal /eɪpəlítɪkəl/ **1** ADJ Someone who is **apolitical** is not interested in politics. ❑ *As a musician, you cannot be apolitical.* **2** ADJ If you describe an organization or an activity as **apolitical**, you mean that it is not linked to a particular political party. ❑ *These institutions have to be apolitical in order to function and to perform effectively.*

apolo|get|ic /əpɒlədʒétɪk/ ADJ If you are **apologetic**, you show or say that you are sorry for causing trouble for someone, for hurting them, or for disappointing them. ❑ *The hospital staff were very apologetic but that couldn't really compensate.*

apologia

• **apolo|geti|cal|ly** /əppləd͡ʒɛtɪkli/ ADV [ADV with v] □ *"It's of no great literary merit," he said, almost apologetically.*

apo|lo|gia /æpəlo͡ʊd͡ʒiə/ (**apologias**) N-COUNT [usu sing] An **apologia** is a statement in which you defend something that you strongly believe in, for example, a way of life, a person's behavior, or a philosophy. [FORMAL] □ *The left have seen the work as an apologia for privilege and property.*

apolo|gist /əpplədʒɪst/ (**apologists**) N-COUNT An **apologist** is a person who writes or speaks in defense of a belief, a cause, or a person's life. [FORMAL] □ *"I am no apologist for Hitler," observed Pyat.*

apolo|gize /əpplədʒaɪz/ (**apologizes, apologizing, apologized**)

in BRIT, also use **apologise**

V-I When you **apologize** to someone, you say that you are sorry that you have hurt them or caused trouble for them. You can say 'I apologize' as a formal way of saying sorry. □ *I apologize for being late, but I have just had a message from the hospital.* □ *He apologized to the people who had been affected.*

apol|ogy /əpplədʒi/ (**apologies**) ◼ N-VAR An **apology** is something that you say or write in order to tell someone that you are sorry that you have hurt them or caused trouble for them. □ *I didn't get an apology.* □ *We received a letter of apology.* ◼ N-PLURAL If you offer or make your **apologies**, you apologize. [FORMAL] □ *When Mary finally appeared, she made her apologies to Mrs. Velasquez.*

apo|plec|tic /æpəplɛktɪk/ ADJ If someone is **apoplectic**, they are extremely angry about something. [FORMAL]

apo|plexy /æpəplɛksi/ ◼ N-UNCOUNT **Apoplexy** is a stroke. [OLD-FASHIONED] ◼ N-UNCOUNT **Apoplexy** is extreme anger. [FORMAL] □ *He has already caused apoplexy with his books on class and on war.*

apos|ta|sy /əpɒstəsi/ N-UNCOUNT If someone is accused of **apostasy**, they are accused of abandoning their religious faith, political loyalties, or principles. [FORMAL] □ *...a charge of apostasy.*

apos|tate /əpɒsteɪt/ (**apostates**) N-COUNT An **apostate** is someone who has abandoned their religious faith, political loyalties, or principles. [FORMAL]

apos|tle /əpɒsəl/ (**apostles**) ◼ N-COUNT The **apostles** were the followers of Jesus Christ who went from place to place telling people about him and trying to persuade them to become Christians. ◼ N-COUNT [usu N of n] An **apostle** of a particular philosophy, policy, or cause is someone who strongly believes in it and works hard to promote it. □ *Her mother was a dedicated apostle of healthy eating.*

Ap|os|tol|ic /æpəstɒlɪk/ also **apostolic** ◼ ADJ **Apostolic** means belonging or relating to a Christian religious leader, especially the Pope. □ *He was appointed Apostolic Administrator of Minsk by Pope John Paul II.* ◼ ADJ **Apostolic** means belonging or relating to the early followers of Jesus Christ and to their teaching. □ *He saw his vocation as one of prayer and apostolic work.*

apos|tro|phe /əpɒstrəfi/ (**apostrophes**) N-COUNT An **apostrophe** is the mark ' when it is written to indicate that one or more letters have been left out of a word, as in 'isn't' and 'we'll.' It is also added to nouns to form possessives, as in 'Mike's car.'

apoth|ecary /əpɒθɪkɛri/ (**apothecaries**) N-COUNT An **apothecary** was a person who prepared medicines for people. [OLD-FASHIONED]

apoth|eo|sis /əpɒθio͡ʊsɪs, æpəθiəsɪs/ ◼ N-SING [oft N of n] If something is the **apotheosis** of something else, it is an ideal or typical example of it. [FORMAL] □ *The Oriental in Bangkok is the apotheosis of the grand hotel.* ◼ N-SING [with poss] If you describe an event or a time as someone's **apotheosis**, you mean that it was the high point in their career or their life. [FORMAL] □ *That night was Richard's apotheosis.*

app /æp/ (**apps**) ◼ N-COUNT An **app** is a computer program that is written and designed for a specific purpose. [COMPUTING] □ *...a basic picture-editing app.* ◼ N-COUNT An **app** is a computer program that is designed for use on a mobile digital device. [COMPUTING] □ *The company recently launched a free phone app that translates conversations while you speak.*

appeal

ap|pall /əpɔl/ (**appalls, appalling, appalled**)

in BRIT, use **appal**

V-T If something **appalls** you, it disgusts you because it seems so bad or unpleasant. □ *The new-found strength of local militancy appalls many observers.*

ap|palled /əpɔld/ ADJ If you are **appalled** by something, you are shocked or disgusted because it is so bad or unpleasant. □ *She said that the Americans are appalled at the statements made at the conference.*

ap|pal|ling /əpɔlɪŋ/ ◼ ADJ Something that is **appalling** is so bad or unpleasant that it shocks you. □ *They have been living under the most appalling conditions for two months.* • **ap|pal|ling|ly** ADV □ *He says that he understands why they behaved so appallingly.* ◼ ADJ You can use **appalling** to emphasize that something is very extreme or severe. [EMPHASIS] □ *I developed an appalling headache.* • **ap|pal|ling|ly** ADV □ *It's been an appallingly busy morning.* ◼ → see also appall ◼ → See feature box at review

ap|pa|rat|chik /æpəræt͡ʃɪk/ (**apparatchiks**) N-COUNT An **apparatchik** is someone who works for a government or a political party and who always obeys orders. [FORMAL, DISAPPROVAL]

ap|pa|rat|us /æpəræt̬əs, -reɪ-/ (**apparatuses**) ◼ N-VAR The **apparatus** of an organization or system is its structure and method of operation. □ *For many years, the country had been buried under the apparatus of the regime.* ◼ N-VAR **Apparatus** is the equipment, such as tools and machines, which is used to do a particular job or activity. □ *One of the boys had to be rescued by firemen wearing breathing apparatus.*

ap|par|el /əpærəl/ N-UNCOUNT **Apparel** means clothes, especially formal clothes worn on an important occasion. [mainly AM, FORMAL] □ *Women's apparel is offered in petite, regular, and tall sizes.*

ap|par|ent ✦✧✧ /əpærənt/ ◼ ADJ [ADJ n] An **apparent** situation, quality, or feeling seems to exist, although you cannot be certain that it does exist. □ *I was a bit depressed by our apparent lack of progress.* ◼ ADJ [v-link ADJ] If something is **apparent** to you, it is clear and obvious to you. □ *It has been apparent that in other areas standards have held up well.* ◼ PHRASE If you say that something happens **for no apparent reason**, you cannot understand why it happens. □ *The person may become dizzy for no apparent reason.*

ap|par|ent|ly ✦✦✧ /əpærəntli/ ◼ ADV You use **apparently** to indicate that the information you are giving is something that you have heard, but you are not certain that it is true. [VAGUENESS] □ *Apparently the girls are not at all amused by the whole business.* ◼ ADV You use **apparently** to refer to something that seems to be true, although you are not sure whether it is or not. □ *The recent deterioration has been caused by an apparently endless recession.*

SYNONYMS

apparently
ADV ◼
seemingly: *He is a man with seemingly not an ounce of malice in him.*
outwardly: *Outwardly, this looked like the beginning of a terrific program.*
ostensibly: *He gave an interview ostensibly to talk about the economy.*

---

ap|pa|ri|tion /æpərɪʃən/ (**apparitions**) N-COUNT An **apparition** is someone you see or think you see but who is not really there as a physical being. [FORMAL]

ap|peal ✦✦✧ /əpil/ (**appeals, appealing, appealed**) ◼ V-I If you **appeal** to someone to do something, you make a serious and urgent request to them. □ *He appealed to voters to go to the polls tomorrow.* □ *He will appeal to the state for an extension of unemployment benefits.* ◼ V-T If you **appeal** a decision to someone in authority, you formally ask them to change it. □ *We intend to appeal the verdict.* ◼ V-I If something **appeals** to you, you find it attractive or interesting. □ *On the other hand, the idea appealed to him.* ◼ N-COUNT An **appeal** is a serious and urgent request. □ *He has a message from King Fahd, believed to be an appeal for Arab unity.* ◼ N-COUNT An **appeal** is an attempt to raise money for a charity or for a good cause. □ *...an appeal to save a library* containing priceless manuscripts. **6** N-VAR An **appeal** is a formal request for a decision to be changed. ❏ *They took their appeal to the Supreme Court.* **7** N-UNCOUNT The **appeal** of something is a quality that people find attractive or interesting. ❏ *Its new title was meant to give the party greater public appeal.* **8** → see also **appealing**

SYNONYMS

appeal
VERB **1**
beg: *I begged to be allowed to leave.*
request: *They requested that he leave.*
plead: *The lady pleaded with her daughter to come back home.*
implore: *Opposition leaders this week implored the president to break the deadlock.*
NOUN **4**
plea: *...an impassioned plea to mankind to act to save the planet.*
call: *There have been calls for a new kind of security arrangement.*
request: *Vietnam made an official request that the meeting be postponed.*

ap|peal court (appeal courts) N-COUNT An **appeal court** is the same as a **Court of Appeals**.

ap|peal|ing /əpiːlɪŋ/ **1** ADJ Someone or something that is **appealing** is pleasing and attractive. ❏ *There was a sense of humor to what he did that I found very appealing.* **2** ADJ An **appealing** expression or tone of voice indicates to someone that you want help, advice, or approval. ❏ *She gave him a soft appealing look that would have melted solid ice.* **3** → see also **appeal**

ap|peals court (appeals courts) N-COUNT An **appeals court** is the same as an **appellate court**.

in BRIT, use **Court of Appeal**

ap|pear ♦♦♦ /əpɪər/ (appears, appearing, appeared) **1** V-LINK [no cont] If you say that something **appears** to be the way you describe it, you are reporting what you believe or what you have been told, though you cannot be sure it is true. [VAGUENESS] ❏ *There appears to be increasing support for the leadership to take a more aggressive stance.* **2** V-LINK [no cont] If someone or something **appears** to have a particular quality or characteristic, they give the impression of having that quality or characteristic. ❏ *She did her best to appear more self-assured than she felt.* ❏ *He is anxious to appear a gentleman.* **3** V-I When someone or something **appears**, they move into a position where you can see them. ❏ *A woman appeared at the far end of the street.* **4** V-I When something new **appears**, it begins to exist or reaches a stage of development where its existence can be noticed. ❏ *...small white flowers which appear in early summer.* **5** V-I When something such as a book **appears**, it is published or becomes available for people to buy. ❏ *I could hardly wait for "Boys' Life" to appear each month.* **6** V-I When someone **appears** in something such as a play, a show, or a television program, they take part in it. ❏ *Jill Bennett became John Osborne's fourth wife, and appeared in several of his plays.* **7** V-I When someone **appears** before a court of law or before an official committee, they go there in order to answer charges or to give information as a witness. ❏ *The defendants are expected to appear in federal court today.*

ap|pear|ance ♦♦ /əpɪərəns/ (appearances) **1** N-COUNT When someone makes an **appearance** at a public event or in a broadcast, they take part in it. ❏ *It was the president's second public appearance to date.* **2** N-SING Someone's or something's **appearance** is the way that they look. ❏ *She used to be so fussy about her appearance.* **3** N-SING The **appearance** of someone or something in a place is their arrival there, especially when it is unexpected. ❏ *The sudden appearance of a few bags of rice could start a riot.* **4** N-SING The **appearance** of something new is its coming into existence or use. ❏ *Flowering plants were making their first appearance, but were still a rarity.* **5** N-SING If something has the **appearance** of a quality, it seems to have that quality. ❏ *We tried to meet both children's needs without the appearance of favoritism or unfairness.* **6** PHRASE If something is true **by all appearances**, **from all appearances**, or **to all appearances**, it seems from what you observe or know about it that it is true. ❏ *He was a small and by all appearances an unassuming man.*

SYNONYMS

appearance
NOUN
2
looks: *I never chose people just because of their looks.*
look: *When he came to decorate the kitchen, Kenneth opted for a friendly rustic look.*
4
arrival: *The coronation broadcast marked the arrival of television.*
advent: *The advent of war led to greater austerity.*
emergence: *...the emergence of new democracies in East and Central Europe.*
onset: *With the onset of war, oil prices climbed above $30 a barrel.*

VOCABULARY IN CONTEXT

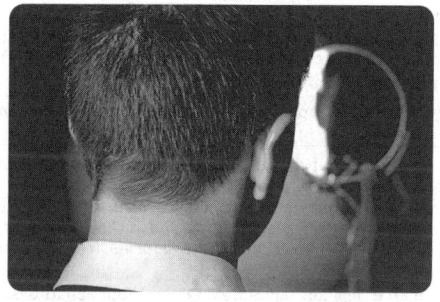

Physical appearance

Our **physical appearance** is the first thing others notice about us. This may explain why many people are preoccupied with their **looks**, from the insecurity of those who dislike their **build** or appearance to the vanity of the **good-looking**. Fashion magazines and the current obsession with selfies don't help. It's unfortunate because our appearance and any **distinguishing features** are programmed into our DNA; we don't earn or choose them. It's not your fault if you don't have a perfect **complexion** or **chiseled jaw** or **high cheekbones**. In fact, historically and culturally, what is perceived as **attractive** differs. For example, someone **slender** or **willowy** might be overlooked for a **heavyset** or **chubby** person whose appearance denotes strength and good health. People don't seem to want to **look their age**. Women fret about **going gray**, men about **receding hairlines**. Life is much easier when we accept ourselves and focus on being happy.

ap|pear|ance fee (appearance fees) N-COUNT An **appearance fee** is money paid to a famous person such as a sports star or movie star for taking part in a public event.

ap|pease /əpiːz/ (appeases, appeasing, appeased) V-T If you try to **appease** someone, you try to stop them from being angry by giving them what they want. [DISAPPROVAL] ❏ *Gandhi was accused by some of trying to appease both factions of the electorate.*

ap|pease|ment /əpiːzmənt/ N-UNCOUNT **Appeasement** means giving people what they want to prevent them from harming you or being angry with you. [FORMAL, DISAPPROVAL] ❏ *He denied there is a policy of appeasement.*

ap|pel|lant /əpɛlənt/ (appellants) N-COUNT An **appellant** is someone who is appealing a court's decision after they have been judged guilty of a crime. [LEGAL] ❏ *The Court of Appeal upheld the appellants' convictions.*

ap|pel|late court /əpɛlɪt kɔːrt/ (appellate courts) N-COUNT In the United States, an **appellate court** is a special court where people who have been convicted of a crime can appeal their conviction. [AM]

in BRIT, use **Court of Appeal**

appellation

ap|pel|la|tion /æpəleɪʃᵊn/ (appellations) N-COUNT An **appellation** is a name or title that a person, place, or thing is given. [FORMAL] ☐ *He earned the appellation "rebel priest."*

ap|pend /əpɛnd/ (appends, appending, appended) V-T When you **append** something to something else, especially a piece of writing, you attach it or add it to the end of it. [FORMAL] ☐ *She appended a note at the end of the letter.* ☐ *It was a relief that his real name hadn't been appended to the manuscript.*

ap|pend|age /əpɛndɪdʒ/ (appendages) **1** N-COUNT [oft N of/to n] An **appendage** is something that is joined to or connected with something larger or more important. [FORMAL] ☐ *Will the new party be more than just an appendage of government?* **2** N-COUNT [usu pl] An **appendage** is a part of the body of a person or animal, for example a leg or a wing, that sticks out from the central part of the body. [FORMAL] ☐ *Their bodies have appendages which look like wings.*

ap|pen|di|ces /əpɛndɪsiz/ **Appendices** is a plural form of **appendix**.

ap|pen|di|ci|tis /əpɛndɪsaɪtɪs/ N-UNCOUNT **Appendicitis** is an illness in which a person's appendix is infected and painful.

ap|pen|dix /əpɛndɪks/ (appendixes)

The plural form **appendices** /əpɛndɪsiz/ is usually used for meaning **2**.

1 N-COUNT Your **appendix** is a small closed tube inside your body that is attached to your digestive system. ☐ *...a burst appendix.* **2** N-COUNT An **appendix** to a book is extra information that is placed after the end of the main text. ☐ *The survey results are published in full as an appendix to Mr. Barton's discussion paper.*

ap|pe|tite /æpɪtaɪt/ (appetites) **1** N-VAR Your **appetite** is your desire to eat. ☐ *He has a healthy appetite.* **2** N-COUNT Someone's **appetite** for something is their strong desire for it. ☐ *...his appetite for success.*

ap|pe|tiz|er /æpɪtaɪzər/ (appetizers)

in BRIT, also use **appetiser**

N-COUNT An **appetizer** is the first course of a meal. It consists of a small amount of food.

ap|pe|tiz|ing /æpɪtaɪzɪŋ/

in BRIT, also use **appetising**

ADJ **Appetizing** food looks and smells good, so that you want to eat it. ☐ *...the appetizing smell of freshly baked bread.*

ap|plaud /əplɔd/ (applauds, applauding, applauded) **1** V-T/V-I When a group of people **applaud**, they clap their hands in order to show approval, for example, when they have enjoyed a play or concert. ☐ *The audience laughed and applauded.* **2** V-T When an attitude or action **is applauded**, people praise it. ☐ *He should be applauded for his courage.* ☐ *This last move can only be applauded.*

ap|plause /əplɔz/ N-UNCOUNT **Applause** is the noise made by a group of people clapping their hands to show approval. ☐ *They greeted him with thunderous applause.*

ap|ple ♦◇◇ /æpᵊl/ (apples) N-VAR An **apple** is a round fruit with smooth red, yellow, or green skin and firm white flesh. ☐ *I want an apple.* ☐ *...his ongoing search for the finest varieties of apple.*

apple|cart /æpᵊlkɑrt/ PHRASE If you **upset the applecart**, you do something that causes a plan, system, or arrangement to go wrong. ☐ *They may also be friends of the chairman, so they are reluctant to upset the applecart.*

ap|ple pie (apple pies) **1** N-COUNT An **apple pie** is a kind of pie made with apples. **2** PHRASE [v-link PHR] If you say that something is **as American as apple pie**, you mean that it is typically American. ☐ *Jeans are as American as apple pie.*

ap|ple sauce N-UNCOUNT **Apple sauce** is a type of sauce made from puréed cooked apples.

ap|plet /æplɪt/ (applets) N-COUNT An **applet** is a computer program contained within a page on the World Wide Web that transfers itself to your computer and runs automatically while you are looking at that Web page.

ap|pli|ance /əplaɪəns/ (appliances) **1** N-COUNT An **appliance** is a device or machine in your home that you use to do a job such as cleaning or cooking. Appliances are often electrical.

apply

[FORMAL] ☐ *He could also learn to use the vacuum cleaner, the washing machine and other household appliances.* **2** → See feature box at **household, housework**

ap|pli|cable /æplɪkəbᵊl, əplɪkə-/ ADJ Something that is **applicable** to a particular situation is relevant to it or can be applied to it. ☐ *What is a reasonable standard for one family is not applicable for another.*

ap|pli|cant /æplɪkənt/ (applicants) N-COUNT An **applicant** for something such as a job or a college is someone who makes a formal written request to be considered for it. ☐ *We have had lots of applicants for these positions.*

ap|pli|ca|tion ♦◇◇ /æplɪkeɪʃᵊn/ (applications) **1** N-COUNT An **application** for something such as a job or membership of an organization is a formal written request for it. ☐ *His application for membership of the organization was rejected.* **2** N-COUNT In computing, an **application** is a piece of software designed to carry out a particular task. ☐ *The service works as a software application that is accessed via the internet.* **3** N-VAR The **application** of a rule or piece of knowledge is the use of it in a particular situation. ☐ *Students learned the practical application of the theory they had learned in the classroom.* **4** N-UNCOUNT **Application** is hard work and concentration on what you are doing over a period of time. ☐ *...his immense talent, boundless energy and unremitting application.*

─── **COLLOCATIONS** ───

application
NOUN
1
noun + **application**: job, license, mortgage, patent; asylum, passport, visa; bail
adjective + **application**: online, postal, written; formal
application + be + adjective: successful, unsuccessful
verb + **application**: lodge, make, submit; dismiss, refuse, reject; approve, process, support
2
noun + **application**: software, web
verb + **application**: develop; run
3
adjective + **application**: clinical, industrial, practical; broad, general, wide

─── **SYNONYMS** ───

application
NOUN **1**
request: *France had agreed to his request for political asylum.*
claim: *Rival claims to Macedonian territory caused conflict in the Balkans.*
demand: *They consistently rejected the demand to remove U.S. troops.*
appeal: *Romania's government issued a last-minute appeal to him to call off his trip.*

ap|pli|ca|tor /æplɪkeɪtər/ (applicators) N-COUNT An **applicator** is a device that you use to put something on a surface when you do not want to touch it or do it with your hands.

ap|plied /əplaɪd/ **1** ADJ [ADJ n] An **applied** subject of study has a practical use, rather than being concerned only with theory. ☐ *...applied physics.* **2** → See feature box at **fine art**

ap|pli|que /æplɪkeɪ/ also **appliqué** N-UNCOUNT **Applique** is the craft of sewing fabric shapes onto larger pieces of cloth. You can also use applique to refer to things you make using this craft.

ap|pli|qued /æplɪkeɪd/ also **appliquéd** ADJ **Appliqued** shapes or fabric are formed from pieces of fabric which are stitched on to clothes or larger pieces of cloth. ☐ *...a magnificent appliqued bedspread.*

ap|ply ♦♦◇ /əplaɪ/ (applies, applying, applied) **1** V-T/V-I If you **apply** for something such as a job or membership of an organization, you write a letter or fill out a form in order to ask formally for it. ☐ *I am continuing to apply for jobs.* ☐ *They may apply to join the organization.* **2** V-T If you **apply yourself to** something or **apply** your mind to something, you concentrate hard on doing it or on thinking about it. ☐ *Scymanski has applied himself to this task with considerable energy.* **3** V-I [no cont]

If something such as a rule or a remark **applies** to a person or in a situation, it is relevant to the person or the situation. ◻ *The convention does not apply to us.* ◻ *The rule applies where a person owns stock in a corporation.* ◢ V-T If you **apply** something such as a rule, system, or skill, you use it in a situation or activity. ◻ *The government appears to be applying the same principle.* ◣ V-T A name that **is applied** to someone or something is used to refer to them. ◻ *...a biological term that cannot be applied to a whole culture.* ◤ V-T If you **apply** something to a surface, you put it on or rub it into the surface. ◻ *The right thing would be to apply direct pressure to the wound.* ◥ → see also **applied**

---- COLLOCATIONS ----

apply
VERB
◢
apply + noun: criterion, method, principle, rule, technique
noun + **apply**: conditions, principles, restrictions, rules; charges, costs, discount, terms
◤
apply + noun: dye, fertilizer, makeup, paint, sunscreen; coat, layer; force, pressure

---- SYNONYMS ----

apply
VERB ◼
request: *Mr Dennis said he had requested access to a telephone.*
solicit: *He's already solicited their support on health care reform.*
appeal: *The United Nations has appealed for help from the international community.*

ap|point ♦◊◊ /əpɔɪnt/ (**appoints**, **appointing**, **appointed**) ◼ V-T If you **appoint** someone to a job or official position, you formally choose them for it. ◻ *It made sense to appoint a banker to this job.* ◻ *The president has appointed a civilian as defense secretary.* ◢ → see also **appointed**

ap|point|ed /əpɔɪntɪd/ ADJ [ADJ n] If something happens at the **appointed** time, it happens at the time that was decided in advance. [FORMAL] ◻ *The appointed hour of the ceremony was drawing nearer.*

-appointed /-əpɔɪntɪd/ ◼ COMB IN ADJ **-appointed** combines with adverbs to form adjectives such as **well-appointed** that describe a building or room that is equipped or furnished in the way that is mentioned. [WRITTEN] ◻ *...the well-appointed kitchen.* ◢ → see also **self-appointed**

ap|poin|tee /əpɔɪntiː/ (**appointees**) N-COUNT An **appointee** is someone who has been chosen for a particular job or position of responsibility. [FORMAL] ◻ *...Becket, a recent appointee to the Supreme Court.*

ap|point|ment ♦◊◊ /əpɔɪntmənt/ (**appointments**) ◼ N-VAR The **appointment** of a person to a particular job is the choice of that person to do it. ◻ *His appointment to the cabinet would please the right wing.* ◢ N-COUNT An **appointment** is a job or position of responsibility. ◻ *Mr. Fay is to take up an appointment as a researcher.* ◣ N-COUNT If you have an **appointment** with someone, you have arranged to see them at a particular time, usually in connection with their work or for a serious purpose. ◻ *She has an appointment with her accountant.* ◤ PHRASE If something can be done **by appointment**, people can arrange in advance to do it at a particular time. ◻ *Viewing is by appointment only.*

ap|por|tion /əpɔːrʃən/ (**apportions**, **apportioning**, **apportioned**) V-T When you **apportion** something such as blame, you decide how much of it different people deserve or should be given. [FORMAL] ◻ *The purpose of this exercise is not to apportion blame but to solve problems.*

ap|po|site /æpəzɪt/ ADJ Something that is **apposite** is suitable for or appropriate to what is happening or being discussed. [FORMAL] ◻ *Recent events have made his central theme even more apposite.*

ap|po|si|tion /æpəzɪʃən/ N-UNCOUNT [usu in N] If two noun groups referring to the same person or thing are in **apposition**, one is placed immediately after the other, with no conjunction joining them, as in 'Her father, Jerry, left home three months ago.'

ap|prais|al /əpreɪzəl/ (**appraisals**) ◼ N-VAR If you make an **appraisal** of something, you consider it carefully and form an opinion about it. ◻ *What is needed in such cases is a calm appraisal of the situation.* ◢ N-VAR **Appraisal** is the official or formal assessment of the strengths and weaknesses of someone or something. Appraisal often involves observation or some kind of testing. ◻ *One of the most important tools for organizational improvement is the performance appraisal.* ◣ N-COUNT An **appraisal** is a judgement that someone makes about how much money something such as a house or a company is worth. [AM] ◻ *It may also be necessary to get a new appraisal of the property.*

ap|praise /əpreɪz/ (**appraises**, **appraising**, **appraised**) ◼ V-T If you **appraise** something or someone, you consider them carefully and form an opinion about them. [FORMAL] ◻ *This prompted many employers to appraise their selection and recruitment policies.* ◢ V-T When experts **appraise** something, they decide how much money it is worth. [AM] ◻ *His estate is now appraised at a figure near $1,000,000.*

ap|prais|er /əpreɪzər/ (**appraisers**) N-COUNT An **appraiser** is someone whose job is to estimate the cost or value of something such as property. [AM]

in BRIT, use **valuer**

ap|pre|ci|able /əpriːʃəbəl, -ʃəbəl/ ADJ [usu ADJ n] An **appreciable** amount or effect is large enough to be important or clearly noticed. [FORMAL]

ap|pre|ci|ate ♦◊◊ /əpriːʃieɪt/ (**appreciates**, **appreciating**, **appreciated**) ◼ V-T If you **appreciate** something, for example, a piece of music or good food, you like it because you recognize its good qualities. ◻ *Anyone can appreciate our music.* ◢ V-T If you **appreciate** a situation or problem, you understand it and know what it involves. ◻ *She never really appreciated the depth and bitterness of the family's conflict.* ◣ V-T If you **appreciate** something that someone has done for you or is going to do for you, you are grateful for it. ◻ *Peter stood by me when I most needed it. I'll always appreciate that.* ◤ V-I If something that you own **appreciates** over a period of time, its value increases. ◻ *They don't have any confidence that houses will appreciate in value.*

ap|pre|cia|tion /əpriːʃieɪʃən/ ◼ N-SING [also no det, oft N of n] **Appreciation** of something is the recognition and enjoyment of its good qualities. ◻ *...an investigation into children's understanding and appreciation of art.* ◢ N-SING [also no det] Your **appreciation** for something that someone does for you is your gratitude for it. ◻ *He expressed his appreciation for what he called Saudi Arabia's moderate and realistic oil policies.* ◣ N-SING [also no det] An **appreciation** of a situation or problem is an understanding of what it involves. ◻ *They have a stronger appreciation of the importance of economic incentives.* ◤ N-UNCOUNT **Appreciation** in the value of something is an increase in its value over a period of time. ◻ *You have to take capital appreciation of the property into account.*

ap|pre|cia|tive /əpriːʃiətɪv, -ʃətɪv/ ◼ ADJ An **appreciative** reaction or comment shows the enjoyment that you are getting from something. ◻ *There is a murmur of appreciative laughter.* ◢ ADJ If you are **appreciative** of something, you are grateful for it. ◻ *We have been very appreciative of their support.*

ap|pre|hend /æprɪhɛnd/ (**apprehends**, **apprehending**, **apprehended**) V-T If the police **apprehend** someone, they catch them and arrest them. [FORMAL] ◻ *Police have not apprehended her killer.*

ap|pre|hen|sion /æprɪhɛnʃən/ (**apprehensions**) N-VAR **Apprehension** is a feeling of fear that something bad may happen. [FORMAL] ◻ *It reflects real anger and apprehension about the future.*

ap|pre|hen|sive /æprɪhɛnsɪv/ ADJ Someone who is **apprehensive** is afraid that something bad may happen. ◻ *People are still terribly apprehensive about the future.*

ap|pren|tice /əprɛntɪs/ (**apprentices**, **apprenticing**, **apprenticed**) ◼ N-COUNT An **apprentice** is a young person who works for someone in order to learn their skill. ◻ *I started off as an apprentice and worked my way up.* ◢ V-T [usu passive] If a young person **is apprenticed** to someone, they go to work for them in order to learn their skill. ◻ *I was apprenticed to a plumber when I was fourteen.*

ap|pren|tice|ship /əprɛntɪsʃɪp/ (**apprenticeships**) N-VAR Someone who has an **apprenticeship** works for a fixed period

apprise

of time for a person who has a particular skill in order to learn the skill. **Apprenticeship** is the system of learning a skill like this. ◻ *After serving his apprenticeship as a toolmaker, he became a manager.*

ap|prise /əpraɪz/ (apprises, apprising, apprised) V-T When you **are apprised** of something, someone tells you about it. [FORMAL] ◻ *Have customers been fully apprised of the advantages?* ◻ *We must apprise them of the dangers that may be involved.*

ap|proach ✦✧ /əproʊtʃ/ (approaches, approaching, approached) **1** V-T/V-I When you **approach** something, you get closer to it. ◻ *He didn't approach the front door at once.* ◻ *When I approached, they grew silent.* • N-COUNT **Approach** is also a noun. ◻ *At their approach the little boy ran away and hid.* **2** V-T [no cont] If you **approach** someone about something, you speak to them about it for the first time, often making an offer or request. ◻ *When Brown approached me about the job, my first reaction was of disbelief.* ◻ *He approached me to create and design the restaurant.* • N-COUNT **Approach** is also a noun. ◻ *There had already been approaches from buyers interested in the whole of the group.* **3** V-T When you **approach** a task, problem, or situation in a particular way, you deal with it or think about it in that way. ◻ *The Bank has approached the issue in a practical way.* **4** V-I As a future time or event **approaches**, it gradually gets nearer as time passes. ◻ *As autumn approached, the plants and colors in the garden changed.* • N-SING **Approach** is also a noun. ◻ *...the festive spirit that permeated the house with the approach of Christmas.* **5** V-T As you **approach** a future time or event, time passes so that you get gradually nearer to it. ◻ *There is a need for understanding and cooperation as we approach the summit.* **6** V-T If something **approaches** a particular level or state, it almost reaches that level or state. ◻ *Oil prices have approached their highest level for almost ten years.* **7** N-COUNT An **approach** to a place is a road, path, or other route that leads to it. ◻ *The path serves as an approach to the boathouse.* **8** N-COUNT Your **approach** to a task, problem, or situation is the way you deal with it or think about it. ◻ *We will be exploring different approaches to gathering information.*

COLLOCATIONS

approach
NOUN **8**
adjective + **approach**: different, fresh, innovative, positive; balanced, cautious, conservative, traditional
verb + **approach**: consider, favor, suggest, try; adopt; require
VERB
1
approach + noun: vehicle
approach + adverb: cautiously, gingerly
2
approach + noun: council
approach + adverb: directly, formally, tentatively
3
approach + noun: subject, task
4
noun + **approach**: deadline, election, holiday, summer; storm
5
approach + noun: age, retirement

SYNONYMS

approach
NOUN **8**
method: *...new teaching methods.*
way: *Another way of making new friends is to go to an evening class.*
technique: *...tests performed using a new technique.*
mode: *...the capitalist mode of production.*
VERB
1
near: *As he neared the stable, he slowed the horse and patted it.*
3
deal with: *...the way that credit unions deal with complaints.*
tackle: *The first reason to tackle these problems is to save children's lives.*
handle: *She admitted to herself she didn't know how to handle the problem.*

---

ap|proach|able /əproʊtʃəbəl/ ADJ If you describe someone as **approachable**, you think that they are friendly and easy to talk to. [APPROVAL]

ap|pro|ba|tion /æprəbeɪʃən/ N-UNCOUNT **Approbation** is approval of something or agreement to it. [FORMAL]

ap|pro|pri|ate ✦✧ /əproʊpriɪt/ ADJ Something that is **appropriate** is suitable or acceptable for a particular situation. ◻ *It is appropriate that Hispanic names dominate the list.* ◻ *Dress neatly and attractively in an outfit appropriate to the job.* • **ap|pro|pri|ate|ly** ADV ◻ *Behave appropriately and ask intelligent questions.*

SYNONYMS

appropriate
ADJ
suitable: *She had no other dress suitable for the occasion.*
right: *She'd made the right choice in leaving New York.*
fitting: *The President's address was a fitting end to a bitter campaign.*
proper: *The Supreme Court will ensure that the proper procedures have been followed.*
apt: *...an apt description of the situation.*

---

ap|pro|pria|tion /əproʊprieɪʃən/ (appropriations) **1** N-COUNT [usu with supp] An **appropriation** is an amount of money that a government or organization reserves for a particular purpose. [FORMAL] ◻ *The government raised defense appropriations by 12 percent.* **2** N-UNCOUNT [also a N, usu N of n] **Appropriation** of something that belongs to someone else is the act of taking it, usually without having the right to do so. [FORMAL] ◻ *Other charges include fraud and illegal appropriation of land.*

ap|prov|al ✦✧ /əpruːvəl/ (approvals) **1** N-UNCOUNT If you win someone's **approval** for something that you ask for or suggest, they agree to it. ◻ *...efforts to win congressional approval for an aid package for Moscow.* ◻ *The chairman has also given his approval for an investigation into the case.* **2** N-UNCOUNT If someone or something has your **approval**, you like and admire them. ◻ *His son had an obsessive drive to gain his father's approval.* **3** N-VAR **Approval** is a formal or official statement that something is acceptable. ◻ *The testing and approval of new drugs will be speeded up.*

ap|prove ✦✧ /əpruːv/ (approves, approving, approved) **1** V-I [oft with brd-neg] If you **approve of** an action, event, or suggestion, you like it or are pleased about it. ◻ *Not everyone approves of the festival.* **2** V-I [oft with brd-neg] If you **approve of** someone or something, you like and admire them. ◻ *You've never approved of Henry, have you?* **3** V-T If someone in a position of authority **approves** a plan or idea, they formally agree to it and say that it can happen. ◻ *The Russian Parliament has approved a program of radical economic reforms.* **4** → see also **approved**

ap|proved /əpruːvd/ ADJ An **approved** method or course of action is officially accepted as appropriate in a particular situation. ◻ *The approved method of cleaning is industrial sand-blasting.* ◻ *Approved methods of gathering shellfish from the wild must be used.*

ap|prov|ing /əpruːvɪŋ/ ADJ [usu ADJ n] An **approving** reaction or remark shows support for something, or satisfaction with it. ◻ *His mother leaned forward and gave him an approving look.* • **ap|prov|ing|ly** ADV ◻ *He nodded approvingly.*

approx. **Approx.** is a written abbreviation for **approximately**. ◻ *Group Size: Approx. 12 to 16.*

ap|proxi|mate (approximates, approximating, approximated)

The adjective is pronounced /əprɒksɪmət/. The verb is pronounced /əprɒksɪmeɪt/.

1 ADJ An **approximate** number, time, or position is close to the correct number, time, or position, but is not exact. ◻ *The approximate cost varies from around $150 to $200.* • **ap|proxi|mate|ly** ADV [ADV num] ◻ *Approximately $150 million is to be spent on improvements.* **2** ADJ An idea or description that is **approximate** is not intended to be precise or accurate, but to give some indication of what something is like. ◻ *They did not have even an approximate idea what the Germans really wanted.* **3** V-T If something **approximates** something else, it is similar to it but is not exactly the same. ❏ *The mixture described below will approximate it, but is not exactly the same.*

ap|proxi|ma|tion /əprɒksɪmeɪʃ°n/ (**approximations**) **1** N-COUNT An **approximation** is a fact, object, or description which is similar to something else, but which is not exactly the same. ❏ *That is a fair approximation of the way in which the next boss is being chosen.* **2** N-COUNT An **approximation** is a number, calculation, or position that is close to a correct number, time, or position, but is not exact. ❏ *Clearly that's an approximation, but my guess is there'll be a reasonable balance.* ❏ *As we know, 365.25 is only an approximation.*

appt. Appt. is a written abbreviation for **appointment**.

Apr. Apr. is a written abbreviation for **April**.

apres-ski /ɑpreɪ ski, æpreɪ/ also **après-ski** N-UNCOUNT [oft N n] **Apres-ski** is evening entertainment and social activities in places where people go skiing.

apri|cot /eɪprɪkɒt/ (**apricots**) **1** N-VAR An **apricot** is a small, soft, round fruit with yellowish-orange flesh and a large seed inside. ❏ *...12 oz apricots, halved and pitted.* **2** COLOR **Apricot** is used to describe things that are yellowish-orange in color. ❏ *The bridesmaids wore apricot and white organza.*

April ♦♦♦ /eɪprɪl/ (**Aprils**) N-VAR **April** is the fourth month of the year in the Western calendar. ❏ *The changes will be introduced in April.*

April Fool (**April Fools**) N-COUNT An **April Fool** is a trick that is played on April Fool's Day.

April Fool's Day N-UNCOUNT **April Fool's Day** is the 1st of April, the day on which people traditionally play tricks on each other.

a prio|ri /eɪ praɪɔraɪ/ ADJ [usu ADJ n] An **a priori** argument, reason, or probability is based on an assumed principle or fact, rather than on actual observed facts. • ADV **A priori** is also an adverb. ❏ *One assumes, a priori, that a parent would be better at dealing with problems.*

apron /eɪprən/ (**aprons**) N-COUNT An **apron** is a piece of clothing that you put on over the front of your normal clothes and tie around your waist, especially when you are cooking, in order to prevent your clothes from getting dirty.

ap|ro|pos /æprəpoʊ/ **1** PREP Something that is **apropos**, or **apropos of**, a subject or event, is connected with it or relevant to it. [FORMAL] ❏ *All my suggestions apropos the script were accepted.* **2** PREP **Apropos** or **apropos of** is used to introduce something that you are going to say that is related to the subject you have just been talking about. [FORMAL] ❏ *She was no longer sure of her position. Apropos of that, it was clearly time for more persuasion.*

apt /æpt/ **1** ADJ An **apt** remark, description, or choice is especially suitable. ❏ *The words of this report are as apt today as in 1929.* • **apt|ly** ADV ❏ *...the beach in the aptly named town of Oceanside.* **2** ADJ [v-link ADJ to-inf] If someone is **apt** to do something, they often do it and so it is likely that they will do it again. ❏ *She was apt to raise her voice and wave her hands about.* **3** ADJ [ADJ n] An **apt** student is intelligent and able to understand things easily. ❏ *She had taught him French and he had been an apt student.*

apt. Apt. is a written abbreviation for **apartment**.

ap|ti|tude /æptɪtud/ (**aptitudes**) N-VAR Someone's **aptitude** for a particular kind of work or activity is their ability to learn it quickly and to do it well. ❏ *He drifted into publishing and discovered an aptitude for working with accounts.*

ap|ti|tude test (**aptitude tests**) N-COUNT An **aptitude test** is a test that is specially designed to find out how easily and how well you can do something.

aqua /ækwə/ COLOR **Aqua** is the same as the color **aquamarine**. ❏ *...floor-length curtains in restful aqua and lavender colors.*

aqua|marine /ækwəmərin/ (**aquamarines**) **1** N-VAR **Aquamarines** are clear, greenish-blue stones, sometimes used to make jewelry. ❏ *A necklace set with aquamarines.* ❏ *...a large aquamarine ring.* **2** COLOR **Aquamarine** is used to describe things that are greenish-blue in color. ❏ *...warm aquamarine seas and white beaches.*

aqua|pon|ics /ækwəpɒnɪks/ N-UNCOUNT **Aquaponics** is a food production system in which fish are raised in tanks of water where plants are also grown, so that the waste from the fish provides food for the plants and the plants keep the water clean. ❏ *Aquaponics is building a sustainable system to breed fish and plants in the same system.* ❏ *I'm going to build an aquaponics farm.*

aquar|ium /əkwɛəriəm/ (**aquariums** or **aquaria** /əkwɛəriə/) **1** N-COUNT An **aquarium** is a building, often in a zoo, where fish and underwater animals are kept. **2** N-COUNT An **aquarium** is a glass tank filled with water, in which people keep fish.

Aquar|ius /əkwɛəriəs/ **1** N-UNCOUNT **Aquarius** is one of the twelve signs of the zodiac. Its symbol is a person pouring water. People who are born approximately between January 20th and February 18th come under this sign. **2** N-SING [a n] An **Aquarius** is a person whose sign of the zodiac is Aquarius.

aquat|ic /əkwætɪk/ **1** ADJ An **aquatic** animal or plant lives or grows on or in water. ❏ *The pond is small but can support many aquatic plants and fish.* **2** ADJ **Aquatic** means relating to water. ❏ *...our aquatic resources.* **3** → See feature box at **water**

aque|duct /ækwɪdʌkt/ (**aqueducts**) **1** N-COUNT An **aqueduct** is a long bridge with many arches that carries a water supply or a canal over a valley. ❏ *...an old Roman aqueduct.* **2** N-COUNT An **aqueduct** is a large pipe or canal that carries a water supply to a city or a farming area. ❏ *...a nationwide system of aqueducts to carry water to the arid parts of this country.*

aque|ous /eɪkwiəs, ækwi-/ ADJ [ADJ n] In chemistry, an **aqueous** solution or cream has water as its base. [TECHNICAL] ❏ *...an aqueous solution containing various sodium salts.*

aqui|fer /ækwɪfər/ (**aquifers**) **1** N-COUNT In geology, an **aquifer** is an area of rock underneath the surface of the earth which absorbs and holds water. [TECHNICAL] **2** → See feature box at **water**

aqui|line /ækwɪlaɪn/ ADJ [usu ADJ n] If someone has an **aquiline** nose or profile, their nose is large, thin, and usually curved. [FORMAL] ❏ *He had a thin aquiline nose and deep-set brown eyes.*

Arab /ærəb/ (**Arabs**) **1** N-COUNT **Arabs** are people who speak Arabic and who come from the Middle East and parts of North Africa. **2** ADJ **Arab** means belonging or relating to Arabs or to their countries or customs. ❏ *On the surface, it appears little has changed in the Arab world.*

ara|besque /ærəbɛsk/ (**arabesques**) N-COUNT An **arabesque** is a position in ballet dancing. The dancer stands on one leg with their other leg lifted and stretched out backwards, and their arms stretched out in front of them.

Ara|bian /əreɪbiən/ ADJ **Arabian** means belonging or relating to Arabia, especially to Saudi Arabia. ❏ *...the Arabian Peninsula.*

Ara|bic /ærəbɪk/ **1** N-UNCOUNT **Arabic** is a language that is spoken in the Middle East and in parts of North Africa. **2** ADJ Something that is **Arabic** belongs or relates to the language, writing, or culture of the Arabs. ❏ *...the development of modern Arabic literature.* ❏ *...Arabic music.* **3** ADJ [ADJ n] An **Arabic** numeral is one of the written figures such as 1, 2, 3, or 4.

Ar|ab|ist /ærəbɪst/ (**Arabists**) N-COUNT An **Arabist** is a person who supports Arab interests or knows a lot about the Arabic language.

ar|able /ærəb°l/ ADJ **Arable** farming involves growing crops such as wheat and barley rather than keeping animals or growing fruit and vegetables. **Arable** land is land that is used for arable farming. ❏ *...arable farmers.*

Arab Spring N-PROPER The **Arab Spring** is a period of time in and around 2011 to 2012 during which people in the Middle East and Africa tried to achieve democratic reforms. ❏ *Social networking sites played an important role in the events of the Arab Spring.*

ar|bi|ter /ɑrbɪtər/ (**arbiters**) **1** N-COUNT An **arbiter** is a person or institution that judges and settles a quarrel between two other people or groups. [FORMAL] ❏ *He was the ultimate arbiter on both theological and political matters.* **2** N-COUNT [usu N of n] An **arbiter** of taste or style is someone who has a lot of influence in deciding what is fashionable or socially desirable. [FORMAL]

ar|bi|trage /ɑrbɪtrɑʒ/ N-UNCOUNT In finance, **arbitrage** is the activity of buying securities or currency in one financial market and selling it at a profit in another. [BUSINESS] ❏ *Astute Singaporeans quickly spotted an arbitrage opportunity.*

ar|bi|tra|ger /ɑrbɪtrɑʒər/ (**arbitragers**) also **arbitrageur** N-COUNT In finance, an **arbitrager** is someone who buys currencies, securities, or commodities on one country's market in order to make money by immediately selling them at a profit on another country's market. [BUSINESS]

ar|bi|trary /ɑrbɪtreri/ ADJ If you describe an action, rule, or decision as **arbitrary**, you think that it is not based on any principle, plan, or system. It often seems unfair because of this. [DISAPPROVAL] ❑ *Arbitrary arrests and detention without trial were common.* ● **ar|bi|trari|ly** /ɑrbɪtrɛərɪli/ ADV [ADV with v] ❑ *The victims were not chosen arbitrarily.*

ar|bi|trate /ɑrbɪtreɪt/ (**arbitrates, arbitrating, arbitrated**) V-I When someone in authority **arbitrates** between two people or groups who are in dispute, they consider all the facts and make an official decision about who is right. ❑ *He arbitrates between investors and members of the association.*

ar|bi|tra|tion /ɑrbɪtreɪʃən/ N-UNCOUNT **Arbitration** is the judging of a dispute between people or groups by someone who is not involved. ❑ *The matter is likely to go to arbitration.*

ar|bor /ɑrbər/ (**arbors**)

> in BRIT, use **arbour**

N-COUNT An **arbor** is a shelter in a garden which is formed by leaves and stems of plants growing close together over a light framework.

ar|bor|eal /ɑrbɔriəl/ **1** ADJ [usu ADJ n] **Arboreal** animals live in trees. [TECHNICAL] ❑ *...arboreal marsupials which resemble monkeys.* **2** ADJ [usu ADJ n] **Arboreal** means relating to trees. [FORMAL] ❑ *...the arboreal splendor of the valley.*

ar|bo|retum /ɑrbəritəm/ (**arboreta** /ɑrbəritə/ or **arboretums**) N-COUNT An **arboretum** is a specially designed garden of different types of trees.

arc /ɑrk/ (**arcs**) **1** N-COUNT An **arc** is a smoothly curving line or movement. ❑ *The helicopter made a slow arc, passing over the mound but not stopping.* **2** N-COUNT In geometry, an **arc** is a part of the line that forms the outside of a circle. [TECHNICAL]

ar|cade /ɑrkeɪd/ (**arcades**) **1** N-COUNT An **arcade** is a place where you can play games on machines which work when you put money in them. **2** → see also **video arcade** **3** N-COUNT An **arcade** is a covered passage where there are stores or market stalls. [mainly BRIT] ❑ *...a shopping arcade.*

ar|cade game (**arcade games**) N-COUNT An **arcade game** is a game, especially a computer game, of the type that is often played in arcades.

ar|cane /ɑrkeɪn/ ADJ Something that is **arcane** is secret or mysterious. [FORMAL] ❑ *Until a few months ago few people outside the arcane world of contemporary music had heard of Gorecki.*

arch /ɑrtʃ/ (**arches, arching, arched**) **1** N-COUNT An **arch** is a structure that is curved at the top and is supported on either side by a pillar, post, or wall. ❑ *When she passed under the arch leading out of the park, Mira whooped with delight.* **2** N-COUNT An **arch** is a curved line or movement. ❑ *...the arch of the fishing rods.* **3** N-COUNT The **arch** of your foot is the curved section at the bottom in the middle. ❑ *"Good girl," said Frank, winding the bandages around the arch of her foot.* **4** → see also **arched** **5** V-T/V-I If you **arch** a part of your body such as your back or if it **arches**, you bend it so that it forms a curve. ❑ *Don't arch your back, keep your spine straight.*

arch- /ɑrtʃ-/ COMB IN N-COUNT **Arch-** combines with nouns referring to people to form new nouns that refer to people who are extreme examples of something. For example, your **archrival** is the rival you most want to beat. ❑ *Neither he nor his archrival, Giuseppe De Rita, won.*

ar|chae|ol|ogy /ɑrkiɒlədʒi/ also **archeology** N-UNCOUNT **Archaeology** is the study of the societies and peoples of the past by examining the remains of their buildings, tools, and other objects. ● **ar|chaeo|logi|cal** /ɑrkiəlɒdʒɪkəl/ ADJ [ADJ n] ❑ *...one of the region's most important archaeological sites.* ● **ar|chae|olo|gist** /ɑrkiɒlədʒɪst/ (**archaeologists**) N-COUNT ❑ *The archaeologists found a house built around 300 BC, with a basement and attic.*

ar|cha|ic /ɑrkeɪɪk/ ADJ **Archaic** means extremely old or extremely old-fashioned. ❑ *...archaic laws that are very seldom used.*

arch|angel /ɑrkeɪndʒəl/ (**archangels**) N-COUNT In the Jewish, Christian, and Muslim religions, an **archangel** is an angel of the highest rank.

arch|bishop /ɑrtʃbɪʃəp/ (**archbishops**) N-COUNT; N-TITLE In the Roman Catholic, Orthodox, and Anglican Churches, an **archbishop** is a bishop of the highest rank, who is in charge of all the bishops and priests in a particular country or region. ❑ *...the Roman Catholic archbishop of Colorado Springs.*

arch|deacon /ɑrtʃdikən/ (**archdeacons**) N-COUNT; N-TITLE An **archdeacon** is a high-ranking member of the clergy who works as an assistant to a bishop, especially in the Anglican church.

arch|diocese /ɑrtʃdaɪəsɪs/ (**archdioceses** /ɑrtʃdaɪəsiz/) N-COUNT An **archdiocese** is the area over which an archbishop has control.

arched /ɑrtʃt/ **1** ADJ An **arched** roof, window, or doorway is curved at the top. ❑ *From the television room an arched doorway leads into the hall.* **2** ADJ An **arched** bridge has arches as part of its structure. ❑ *She led them up some stairs and across a little arched stone bridge.*

ar|che|ol|ogy /ɑrkiɒlədʒi/ → see **archaeology**

arch|er /ɑrtʃər/ (**archers**) N-COUNT An **archer** is someone who shoots arrows using a bow.

ar|chery /ɑrtʃəri/ N-UNCOUNT **Archery** is a sport in which people shoot arrows at a target using a bow.

ar|che|typ|al /ɑrkɪtaɪpəl/ ADJ Someone or something that is **archetypal** has all the most important characteristics of a particular kind of person or thing and is a perfect example of it. [FORMAL] ❑ *...the archetypal American middle-class family living in the suburbs.*

ar|che|type /ɑrkɪtaɪp/ (**archetypes**) N-COUNT An **archetype** is something that is considered to be a perfect or typical example of a particular kind of person or thing, because it has all their most important characteristics. [FORMAL] ❑ *He came to this country 20 years ago and is the archetype of the successful Asian businessman.*

ar|che|typi|cal /ɑrkɪtɪpɪkəl/ ADJ [usu ADJ n] **Archetypical** means the same as **archetypal**.

archi|pela|go /ɑrkɪpɛləgoʊ/ (**archipelagos** or **archipelagoes**) N-COUNT An **archipelago** is a group of islands, especially small islands.

archi|tect /ɑrkɪtɛkt/ (**architects**) **1** N-COUNT An **architect** is a person who designs buildings. **2** N-COUNT [oft N of n] The **architect** of an idea, event, or institution is the person who invented it or made it happen. ❑ *James Madison was the principal architect of the constitution.*

archi|tec|tur|al /ɑrkɪtɛktʃərəl/ ADJ **Architectural** means relating to the design and construction of buildings. ❑ *...Tibet's architectural heritage.* ● **archi|tec|tur|al|ly** ADV ❑ *The old city center is architecturally rich.*

archi|tec|ture /ɑrkɪtɛktʃər/ **1** N-UNCOUNT **Architecture** is the art of planning, designing, and constructing buildings. ❑ *He studied classical architecture and design in Rome.* **2** N-UNCOUNT The **architecture** of a building is the style in which it is designed and constructed. ❑ *...modern architecture.* **3** → See also color supplement

ar|chiv|al /ɑrkaɪvəl/ ADJ [usu ADJ n] **Archival** means belonging or relating to archives. ❑ *...his extensive use of archival material.*

ar|chive /ɑrkaɪv/ (**archives, archiving, archived**) **1** N-COUNT **Archives** are a collection of documents and records that contain historical information. You can also use **archives** to refer to the place where archives are stored. ❑ *...the State Library's archives.* **2** ADJ [ADJ n] **Archive** material is information that comes from archives. ❑ *...archive material.* **3** V-T If you **archive** material such as documents or data, you store it in an archive. ❑ *The system will archive the information so agencies can review it in detail.*

ar|chi|vist /ɑrkɪvɪst, -kaɪv-/ (**archivists**) N-COUNT An **archivist** is a person whose job is to collect, sort, and care for historical documents and records.

arch|way /ɑrtʃweɪ/ (**archways**) N-COUNT An **archway** is a passage or entrance that has a curved roof. ❑ *Access was via a narrow archway.*

arc light (**arc lights**) N-COUNT [usu pl] **Arc lights** are a type of very bright electric light. ❑ *...the brilliant glare of the arc lights.*

arc|tic /ɑrktɪk/ **1** N-PROPER The **Arctic** is the area of the world around the North Pole. It is extremely cold and there is very little light in winter and very little darkness in summer. ☐ ...winter in the Arctic. **2** ADJ If you describe a place or the weather as **arctic**, you are emphasizing that it is extremely cold. [INFORMAL, EMPHASIS] ☐ The bathroom, with its spartan pre-war facilities, is positively arctic.

Arc|tic Cir|cle N-PROPER [the N] **The Arctic Circle** is an imaginary line drawn around the northern part of the world at approximately 66° North.

ar|dent /ˈɑrdənt/ ADJ **Ardent** is used to describe someone who has extremely strong feelings about something or someone. ☐ He's been one of the most ardent supporters of the administration's policy.

ar|dor /ˈɑrdər/

in BRIT, use **ardour**

N-UNCOUNT **Ardor** is a strong, intense feeling of love or enthusiasm for someone or something. [LITERARY] ☐ ...songs of genuine passion and ardor.

ar|du|ous /ˈɑrdʒuəs/ **1** ADJ Something that is **arduous** is difficult and tiring, and involves a lot of effort. ☐ ...a long, hot and arduous trip. **2** → See feature box at **challenge**

are /ər, STRONG ɑr/ **Are** is the plural and the second person singular of the present tense of the verb **be** ①. **Are** is often shortened to **-'re** after pronouns in spoken English.

area ✦✦✦ /ˈɛəriə/ (**areas**) **1** N-COUNT An **area** is a particular part of a town, a country, a region, or the world. ☐ ...the large number of community groups in the area. ☐ The survey was carried out in both urban and rural areas. **2** N-COUNT Your **area** is the part of a town, country, or region where you live. An organization's **area** is the part of a town, country, or region that it is responsible for. ☐ Local authorities have been responsible for the running of schools in their areas. **3** N-COUNT A particular **area** is a piece of land or part of a building that is used for a particular activity. ☐ ...a picnic area. **4** N-COUNT An **area** is a particular place on a surface or object, for example, on your body. ☐ You will notice that your baby has two soft areas on the top of his head. **5** N-COUNT You can use **area** to refer to a particular subject or topic, or to a particular part of a larger, more general situation or activity. ☐ ...the politically sensitive area of social security. **6** N-VAR The **area** of a surface such as a piece of land is the amount of flat space or ground that it covers, measured in square units. ☐ The islands cover a total area of 400 square miles. **7** → see also **gray area**

---- COLLOCATIONS ----

area
NOUN **1**
adjective + **area**: residential, rural, urban; isolated, remote; deprived, disadvantaged; huge, large, vast, wide

area code (**area codes**) N-COUNT The **area code** for a particular place is the series of numbers that you have to dial before someone's personal number if you are making a telephone call to that place from a different area. [mainly AM] ☐ The area code for western Pennsylvania is 412.

in BRIT, use **dialling code**

area rug (**area rugs**) N-COUNT An **area rug** is a rug that covers only part of a floor. [AM] ☐ A different area rug was brought in and placed under the furniture.

arena /əˈriːnə/ (**arenas**) **1** N-COUNT An **arena** is a place where sports, entertainments, and other public events take place. It has seats around it where people sit and watch. ☐ ...the largest indoor sports arena in the world. **2** N-COUNT You can refer to a field of activity, especially one where there is a lot of conflict or action, as an **arena** of a particular kind. ☐ He made it clear he had no intention of withdrawing from the political arena.

aren't ✦✦ /ɑrnt, ˈɑrənt/ **1 Aren't** is the usual spoken form of 'are not.' **2 Aren't** is the form of 'am not' that is used in questions or tags in spoken English.

Ar|gen|tine /ˈɑrdʒəntiːn, -taɪn/ (**Argentines**) ADJ **Argentine** means the same as **Argentinian**. ☐ ...Argentine agricultural products. • N-COUNT An **Argentine** is the same as an **Argentinian**.

Ar|gen|tin|ian /ˌɑrdʒənˈtɪniən/ (**Argentinians**) ADJ **Argentinian** means belonging or relating to Argentina or its people. ☐ ...the Argentinian capital, Buenos Aires. • N-COUNT An **Argentinian** is someone who comes from Argentina.

ar|gon /ˈɑrgɒn/ N-UNCOUNT **Argon** is an inert gas which exists in very small amounts in the atmosphere. It is used in electric lights.

ar|got /ˈɑrgoʊ, ˈɑrgət/ (**argots**) N-VAR [usu with supp] An **argot** is a special language used by a particular group of people, which other people find difficult to understand. [FORMAL] ☐ ...the argot of teenagers.

ar|gu|able /ˈɑrgjuəbəl/ **1** ADJ If you say that it is **arguable** that something is true, you believe that it can be supported by evidence and that many people would agree with it. [FORMAL] ☐ It is arguable that this was not as grave a handicap as it might appear. **2** ADJ An idea, point, or comment that is **arguable** is not obviously true or correct and should be questioned. [FORMAL] ☐ It is arguable whether he ever had much control over the real economic power.

ar|gu|ably /ˈɑrgjuəbli/ ADV You can use **arguably** when you are stating your opinion or belief, as a way of giving more authority to it. ☐ They are arguably the most important band since The Rolling Stones.

ar|gue ✦✦◊ /ˈɑrgju/ (**argues, arguing, argued**) **1** V-RECIP If one person **argues** with another, they speak angrily to each other about something that they disagree about. You can also say that two people **argue**. ☐ The committee is concerned about players' behavior, especially arguing with referees. **2** V-RECIP If you **argue** with someone about something, you discuss it with them, with each of you giving your different opinions. ☐ He was arguing with the king about the need to maintain the cavalry at full strength. ☐ They are arguing over foreign policy. **3** V-I [usu imper with neg] If you tell someone not to **argue** with you, you want them to do or believe what you say without protest or disagreement. ☐ Don't argue with me. **4** V-T If you **argue** that something is true, you state it and give the reasons why you think it is true. ☐ His lawyers are arguing that he is unfit to stand trial. **5** V-I If you **argue for** something, you say why you agree with it, in order to persuade people that it is right. If you **argue against** something, you say why you disagree with it, in order to persuade people that it is wrong. ☐ The report argues against tax increases. **6** → See feature box at **relationship**

---- SYNONYMS ----

argue
VERB
1
disagree: The two men had disagreed about reincarnation.
quarrel: At one point we quarrelled, over something silly.
clash: A group of 400 demonstrators clashed with police.
squabble: My four-year-old squabbles with his friends.
fight: Mostly, they fight about paying bills.
2
discuss: The cabinet met today to discuss how to respond to the ultimatum.
debate: The United Nations Security Council will debate the issue today.
thrash out: ...a sincere effort by two people to thrash out differences.
dispute: Some economists disputed whether consumer spending is as strong as the figures suggest.

ar|gu|ment ✦✦◊ /ˈɑrgjəmənt/ (**arguments**) **1** N-VAR An **argument** is a statement or set of statements that you use in order to try to convince people that your opinion about something is correct. ☐ There's a strong argument for lowering the price. ☐ The doctors have set out their arguments against the proposals. **2** N-VAR An **argument** is a discussion or debate in which a number of people put forward different or opposing opinions. ☐ The incident has triggered fresh arguments about the role of the extreme right in U.S. politics. **3** N-COUNT An **argument** is a conversation in which people disagree with each other angrily or noisily. ☐ Anny described how she got into an argument with one of the marchers. **4** N-UNCOUNT If you accept something without **argument**, you do not question it or disagree with it. ☐ He complied without argument.

---- SYNONYMS ----

argument
NOUN
1
case: Both these facts strengthen the case against fracking.
justification: To me, the only justification for a zoo is educational.
rationale: However, the rationale for such initiatives is not, of course, solely economic.

argumentation

3
quarrel: *I had a terrible quarrel with my other brothers.*
fight: *He had a big fight with his dad the night before.*
clash: *There were clashes between police in riot gear and demonstrators.*
feud: *...a long and bitter feud between the state government and the villagers.*

ar|gu|men|ta|tion /ɑrgyəmɛnteɪʃ³n/ N-UNCOUNT **Argumentation** is the process of arguing in an organized or logical way, for example, in philosophy. [FORMAL]

ar|gu|men|ta|tive /ɑrgyəmɛntətɪv/ ADJ Someone who is **argumentative** is always ready to disagree or start arguing with other people. [DISAPPROVAL] ❏ *You're in an argumentative mood today!*

aria /ɑriə/ (**arias**) N-COUNT An **aria** is a song for one of the leading singers in an opera or choral work.

arid /ærɪd/ **1** ADJ **Arid** land is so dry that very few plants can grow on it. ❏ *...new strains of crops that can withstand arid conditions.* **2** → See feature box at **ecosystem**

Aries /ɛəriz/ **1** N-UNCOUNT **Aries** is one of the twelve signs of the zodiac. Its symbol is a ram. People who are born approximately between March 21st and April 19th come under this sign. **2** N-SING [*a* N] An **Aries** is a person whose sign of the zodiac is Aries.

arise ✦◇◇ /əraɪz/ (**arises, arising, arose, arisen** /ərɪzən/) **1** V-I If a situation or problem **arises**, it begins to exist or people start to become aware of it. ❏ *...if a problem arises later in the pregnancy.* **2** V-I If something **arises from** a particular situation, or **arises out of** it, it is created or caused by the situation. ❏ *This serenity arose in part from Rachel's religious beliefs.*

SYNONYMS

arise
VERB **1**
develop: *A disagreement has developed about the pollution emanating from a chemical plant.*
occur: *If headaches occur at night, lack of fresh air may be the cause.*
result: *Many hair problems result from what you eat.*
stem from: *Much of the instability stems from the economic effects of the war.*

ar|is|toc|ra|cy /ærɪstɒkrəsi/ (**aristocracies**) N-COUNT-COLL The **aristocracy** is a class of people in some countries who have a high social rank and special titles. ❏ *...a member of the aristocracy.*

aris|to|crat /ærɪstəkræt, ərɪst-/ (**aristocrats**) N-COUNT An **aristocrat** is someone whose family has a high social rank, especially someone who has a title. ❏ *...a wealthy southern aristocrat.*

aris|to|crat|ic /ærɪstəkrætɪk/ ADJ **Aristocratic** means belonging to or typical of the aristocracy. ❏ *...a wealthy, aristocratic family.*

arith|me|tic /ərɪθmɪtɪk/ **1** N-UNCOUNT **Arithmetic** is the part of mathematics that is concerned with the addition, subtraction, multiplication, and division of numbers. ❏ *...teaching the basics of reading, writing and arithmetic.* **2** N-UNCOUNT You can use **arithmetic** to refer to the process of doing a particular sum or calculation. ❏ *4,000 women put in ten rupees each, which if my arithmetic is right adds up to 40,000 rupees.* **3** N-UNCOUNT If you refer to the **arithmetic** of a situation, you are concerned with those aspects of it that can be expressed in numbers, and how they affect the situation. ❏ *The arithmetic was discouraging. In less than two months, they had used up six months' worth of food.*

arith|meti|cal /ærɪθmɛtɪkᵊl/ ADJ [usu ADJ n] **Arithmetical** calculations, processes, or skills involve the addition, subtraction, multiplication, or division of numbers.

ark /ɑrk/ N-SING [usu *the* N] In the Bible, the **ark** was a large boat that Noah built in order to save his family and two of every kind of animal from the Flood.

ARM
① PART OF YOUR BODY OR OF SOMETHING ELSE
② WEAPONS

armaments

① **arm** ✦✦✦ /ɑrm/ (**arms**) **1** N-COUNT Your **arms** are the two long parts of your body that are attached to your shoulders and that have your hands at the end. ❏ *She stretched her arms out.* **2** N-COUNT The **arm** of a chair is the part on which you rest your arm when you are sitting down. ❏ *Mack gripped the arms of the chair.* **3** N-COUNT An **arm** of an object is a long thin part of it that sticks out from the main part. ❏ *...the lever arm of the machine.* **4** N-COUNT An **arm** of land or water is a long thin area of it that is joined to a broader area. ❏ *...a small area of woodland between two arms of a small stream.* **5** N-COUNT An **arm** of an organization is a section of it that operates in a particular country or that deals with a particular activity. ❏ *The agency is the central research and development arm of the Department of Defense.* **6** N-COUNT The **arm** of a piece of clothing is the part of it that covers your arm. ❏ *...coats that were short in the arms.* **7** PHRASE If two people are walking **arm in arm**, they are walking together with their arms linked. ❏ *He walked from the court arm in arm with his wife.* **8** PHRASE If you hold something **at arm's length**, you hold it away from your body with your arm straight. ❏ *He struck a match, and held it at arm's length.* **9** PHRASE If you **keep** someone **at arm's length**, you avoid becoming too friendly or involved with them. ❏ *She had always kept the family at arm's length.* **10** PHRASE If you welcome some action or change **with open arms**, you are very pleased about it. If you welcome a person **with open arms**, you are very pleased about their arrival. [APPROVAL] ❏ *They would no doubt welcome the action with open arms.* **11** PHRASE If you **twist** someone's **arm**, you persuade them to do something. [INFORMAL] ❏ *She had twisted his arm to get him to invite her.*

② **arm** ✦✦✦ /ɑrm/ (**arms, arming, armed**) **1** N-PLURAL **Arms** are weapons, especially bombs and guns. [FORMAL] ❏ *Soldiers searched their house for illegal arms.* **2** V-T If you **arm** someone with a weapon, you provide them with a weapon. ❏ *She'd been so terrified that she had armed herself with a loaded rifle.* **3** V-T If you **arm** someone with something that will be useful in a particular situation, you provide them with it. ❏ *She thought that if she armed herself with all the knowledge she could gather she could handle anything.* **4** → see also **armed** **5** PHRASE If a person **bears arms**, they own and use guns as a means of defense. ❏ *...a country where the right to bear arms is enshrined in the constitution.* **6** PHRASE If one group or country **takes up arms** against another, they prepare to attack and fight them. ❏ *They threatened to take up arms against the government if their demands were not met.* **7** PHRASE If people are **up in arms** about something, they are very angry about it and are protesting strongly against it. ❏ *Patient advocates are up in arms over the possible closure of the psychiatric hospital.*

COLLOCATIONS

arm
NOUN
① **1**
adjective + **arm**: left, right, upper; bare, muscular, prosthetic; folded, open, outstretched
verb + **arm**: cross, fold, link; raise, wave; break
① **5**
noun + **arm**: finance, investment, management, research
adjective + **arm**: charitable, commercial, investigative
② **1**
adjective + **arms**: nuclear; illegal
verb + **arms**: bear, carry; smuggle, supply

ar|ma|da /ɑrmɑdə/ (**armadas**) N-COUNT [oft N *of* n] An **armada** is a large group of warships.

ar|ma|dil|lo /ɑrmədɪloʊ/ (**armadillos**) N-COUNT An **armadillo** is a small animal whose body is covered with large bony scales and that rolls itself into a ball when it is attacked. Armadillos are mainly found in Texas and in South and Central America.

Ar|ma|ged|don /ɑrməgɛdᵊn/ N-UNCOUNT **Armageddon** is a terrible battle or war that some people think will lead to the total destruction of the world or the human race.

Ar|ma|gnac /ɑrmənyæk/ (**Armagnacs**) N-MASS **Armagnac** is a type of brandy made in southwest France.

ar|ma|ments /ɑrməmənts/ N-PLURAL **Armaments** are weapons and military equipment belonging to an army or country. ❏ *...global efforts to reduce nuclear and other armaments.*

arm|band /ɑrmbænd/ (armbands) **1** N-COUNT An **armband** is a band of fabric that you wear around your upper arm in order to show that you have an official position or belong to a particular group. Some people wear a black armband as a symbol of mourning or protest. **2** N-COUNT **Armbands** are the same as **water wings**. [BRIT]

arm|chair /ɑrmtʃɛər/ (armchairs) **1** N-COUNT An **armchair** is a big comfortable chair that has a support on each side for your arms. ❑ *She was sitting in an armchair with blankets wrapped around her.* **2** ADJ [ADJ n] An **armchair** critic, fan, or traveler knows about a particular subject from reading or hearing about it rather than from practical experience. ❑ *This great book is ideal for both the traveling supporter and the armchair fan.* **3** → See also color supplement

armed ♦♦◊ /ɑrmd/ **1** ADJ Someone who is **armed** is carrying a weapon, usually a gun. ❑ *City police said the man was armed with a revolver.* ❑ *...a barbed-wire fence patrolled by armed guards.* **2** ADJ [ADJ n] An **armed** attack or conflict involves people fighting with guns or carrying weapons. ❑ *They had been found guilty of armed robbery.* **3** → see also **arm** ②

-armed /-ɑrmd/ **1** COMB IN ADJ **-armed** is used with adjectives to indicate what kind of arms someone has. ❑ *...plump-armed women in cotton dresses.* **2** COMB IN ADJ **-armed** is used with adjectives such as 'nuclear' and nouns such as 'missile' to form adjectives that indicate what kind of weapons an army or person has. ❑ *...nuclear-armed navy vessels.* **3** → see also **armed**

armed forces ♦◊◊ N-PLURAL The **armed forces** or the **armed services** of a country are its military forces, usually the army, navy, marines, and air force. ❑ *Every member of the armed forces is a hero.*

arm|ful /ɑrmfʊl/ (armfuls) N-COUNT [usu N of n] An **armful** of something is the amount of it that you can carry fairly easily. ❑ *He hurried out with an armful of brochures.*

arm|hole /ɑrmhoʊl/ (armholes) N-COUNT The **armholes** of something such as a shirt or dress are the openings through which you put your arms, or the places where the sleeves are attached.

ar|mi|stice /ɑrmɪstɪs/ N-SING An **armistice** is an agreement between countries who are at war with one another to stop fighting and to discuss ways of making peace. ❑ *Finally, the Bolsheviks signed an armistice with Germany.*

arm|load /ɑrmloʊd/ (armloads) N-COUNT [usu N of n] An **armload** of something is the same as an **armful** of something. ❑ *...an armload of books.*

ar|mor /ɑrmər/

in BRIT, use **armour**

1 N-UNCOUNT In former times, **armor** was special metal clothing that soldiers wore for protection in battle. ❑ *...knights in armor.* **2** N-UNCOUNT **Armor** consists of tanks and other military vehicles used in battle. [MILITARY] ❑ *U.S. Army troops and armor blocked access to the main palace grounds.* **3** N-UNCOUNT **Armor** is a hard, metal covering that protects a vehicle against attack. ❑ *...a formidable warhead that can penetrate the armor of most tanks.* **4** **knight in shining armor** → see **knight**

ar|mored /ɑrmərd/

in BRIT, use **armoured**

1 ADJ **Armored** vehicles are equipped with a hard metal covering in order to protect them from gunfire and other missiles. ❑ *More than forty armored vehicles carrying troops have been sent into the area.* **2** ADJ **Armored** troops are troops in armored vehicles. ❑ *These front-line defenses are backed up by armored units in reserve.*

ar|mor|er /ɑrmərər/ (armorers)

in BRIT, use **armourer**

N-COUNT An **armorer** is someone who makes or supplies weapons.

armor-plated

in BRIT, use **armour-plated**

ADJ [usu ADJ n] An **armor-plated** vehicle or building has a hard metal covering in order to protect it from gunfire and other missiles. ❑ *He has taken to traveling in an armor-plated car.*

armor-plating

in BRIT, use **armour-plating**

N-UNCOUNT The **armor-plating** on a vehicle or building is the hard metal covering that is intended to protect it from gunfire and other missiles.

ar|mory /ɑrməri/ (armories)

in BRIT, use **armoury**

1 N-COUNT A country's **armory** is all the weapons and military equipment that it has. ❑ *Nuclear weapons will play a less prominent part in NATO's armory in the future.* **2** N-COUNT An **armory** is a place where weapons, bombs, and other military equipment are stored. ❑ *...a failed attempt to steal weapons from an armory.* **3** N-COUNT In the United States, an **armory** is a building used by the National Guard or Army Reserve for meetings and training. ❑ *The National Guard says an armory in Fairmont has opened to shelter stranded motorists.*

ar|mour /ɑrmər/ [BRIT] → see **armor**

arm|pit /ɑrmpɪt/ (armpits) N-COUNT Your **armpits** are the areas of your body under your arms where your arms join your shoulders. ❑ *I shave my armpits every couple of days.*

arm|rest /ɑrmrɛst/ (armrests) also **arm rest** N-COUNT The **armrests** on a chair are the two pieces on either side that support your arms when you are sitting down.

arms race N-SING An **arms race** is a situation in which two countries or groups of countries are continually trying to get more and better weapons than each other.

army ♦♦♦ /ɑrmi/ (armies) **1** N-COUNT-COLL An **army** is a large organized group of people who are armed and trained to fight on land in a war. Most armies are organized and controlled by governments. ❑ *Perkins joined the Army in 1990.* **2** N-COUNT-COLL An **army** of people, animals, or things is a large number of them, especially when they are regarded as a force of some kind. ❑ *...data collected by an army of volunteers.*

COLLOCATIONS

army
NOUN
1
noun + **army**: guerrilla, rebel; reserve, volunteer
adjective + **army**: regular; advancing, invading, retreating
verb + **army**: command, deploy, lead, mobilize; join; defeat
2
adjective + **army**: growing, small, vast

---

aro|ma /əroʊmə/ (aromas) N-COUNT An **aroma** is a strong, pleasant smell. ❑ *...the wonderful aroma of freshly baked bread.*

aroma|thera|pist /əroʊməθɛrəpɪst/ (aromatherapists) N-COUNT An **aromatherapist** is a person who is qualified to practice aromatherapy.

aroma|thera|py /əroʊməθɛrəpi/ N-UNCOUNT **Aromatherapy** is a type of treatment which involves massaging the body with special fragrant oils.

aro|mat|ic /ærəmætɪk/ ADJ An **aromatic** plant or food has a strong, pleasant smell of herbs or spices. ❑ *...an evergreen shrub with deep green, aromatic leaves.*

arose /əroʊz/ **Arose** is the past tense of **arise**.

around ♦♦♦ /əraʊnd/

Around is an adverb and a preposition. In British English, the word 'round' is often used instead. **Around** is often used with verbs of movement, such as 'walk' and 'drive,' and also in phrasal verbs such as 'get around' and 'turn around.'

1 PREP To be positioned **around** a place or object means to surround it or be on all sides of it. To move **around** a place means to go along its edge, back to your starting point. ❑ *She looked at the papers around her.* ❑ *Today she wore her hair down around her shoulders.* • ADV [n ADV] **Around** is also an adverb. ❑ *...a village with a rocky river, a ruined castle and hills all around.* **2** PREP If you move **around** a corner or obstacle, you move to the other side of it. If you look **around** a corner or obstacle, you look to see what is on the other side. ❑ *The photographer stopped clicking and hurried around the corner.* **3** PREP If you move **around** a place, you travel through it, going to most of its parts. If you look **around** a place, you look at every part of it. ❑ *I've been walking around Moscow and the town is terribly quiet.* • ADV [ADV after v] **Around** is also an adverb. ❑ *He backed away from the edge, looking all around at the flat horizon.* ◳ PREP If someone moves **around** a place, they move through various parts of that place without having any particular destination. ❑ *These days much of my time is spent weaving my way around cocktail parties.* • ADV [ADV after v] **Around** is also an adverb. ❑ *My mornings are spent rushing around after him.* ◳ PREP You use **around** to say that something happens in different parts of a place or area. ❑ *Police in South Africa say ten people have died in scattered violence around the country.* ❑ *Elephants were often to be found in swamp in eastern Kenya around the Tana River.* • ADV **Around** is also an adverb. ❑ *What the hell do you think you're doing following me around?* ◳ PREP The people **around** you are the people whom you come into contact with, especially your friends and relatives, and the people you work with. ❑ *We change our behavior by observing the behavior of those around us.* ◳ PREP If something such as a film, a discussion, or a plan is based **around** something, that thing is its main theme. ❑ *The novel is a political thriller loosely based around current political issues.* ◳ PREP When you are giving measurements, you can use **around** to talk about the distance along the edge of something round. ❑ *She was 5 foot 4 inches, 38 around the chest, 28 around the waist and 40 around the hips.* ◳ ADV [ADV after v] If you turn **around**, you turn so that you are facing in the opposite direction. ❑ *I turned around and wrote the title on the blackboard.* ◳ ADV [ADV after v] If you go **around** to someone's house, you visit them. ❑ *She helped me unpack my things and then we went around to see the other girls.* ◳ ADV [ADV after v] You use **around** in expressions such as **sit around** and **hang around** when you are saying that someone is spending time in a place and not doing anything very important. ❑ *I'm just going to be hanging around twiddling my thumbs.* • PREP **Around** is also a preposition. ❑ *He used to skip lessons and hang around the harbor with some other boys.* ◳ ADV [ADV after v] If you move things **around**, you move them so that they are in different places. ❑ *Furniture in the classroom should not be changed around without warning the blind child.* ◳ ADV [ADV after v] If a wheel or object turns **around**, it turns. ❑ *The boat started to spin around in the water.* ◳ ADV If someone or something is **around**, they exist or are present in a place. ❑ *You haven't seen my publisher anywhere around, have you?* ◳ ADV You use **around** in expressions such as **this time around** or **to come around** when you are describing something that has happened before or things that happen regularly. ❑ *Senator Bentsen has declined to get involved this time around.* ◳ ADV **Around** means approximately. ❑ *My salary was around $45,000 plus a car and expenses.* • PREP **Around** is also a preposition. ❑ *He expects the elections to be held around November.* ◳ PHRASE **Around about** means approximately. [SPOKEN] ❑ *There is an outright separatist party but it only scored around about 10 percent in the vote.* ◳ **the other way around** → see **way** ⑤

around-the-clock → see **clock**

arous|al /əraʊzᵊl/ ◳ N-UNCOUNT **Arousal** is the state of being sexually excited. ❑ *...sexual arousal.* ◳ N-UNCOUNT **Arousal** is a state in which you feel excited or very alert, for example, as a result of fear, stress, or anger. ❑ *Thinking angry thoughts can provoke strong physiological arousal.*

arouse /əraʊz/ (**arouses, arousing, aroused**) ◳ V-T If something **arouses** a particular reaction or attitude in people, it causes them to have that reaction or attitude. ❑ *His revolutionary work in linguistics has aroused intense scholarly interest.* ◳ V-T If something **arouses** a particular feeling or instinct that exists in someone, it causes them to experience that feeling or instinct strongly. ❑ *The smell of frying onions aroused his hunger.* ◳ V-T [usu passive] If you **are aroused** by something, it makes you feel sexually excited. ❑ *Some people are aroused when their partner says erotic words to them.*

arr. ◳ **Arr.** is a written abbreviation for **arrives**. It is used on timetables to indicate what time a bus, train, or plane will reach a place. ❑ *...7.11 p.m. arr. Denver.* ◳ **Arr.** is a written abbreviation for **arranged**. It is used to show that a piece of music written by one person has been rewritten in a different way or for different instruments by another person. ❑ *"A Good New Year," sung by Kenneth McKellar (Trad., Arr. Knight).*

ar|raign /əreɪn/ (**arraigns, arraigning, arraigned**) V-T [usu passive] If someone **is arraigned** on a particular charge, they are brought before a court of law to answer that charge. [LEGAL] ❑ *He was arraigned for criminally abetting a traitor.*

ar|raign|ment /əreɪnmənt/ (**arraignments**) N-VAR **Arraignment** is when someone is brought before a court of law to answer a particular charge. [LEGAL] ❑ *They are scheduled for arraignment October 5th.* ❑ *Crowds appeared at the arraignments, clashing with security forces.*

ar|range ♦◇◇ /əreɪndʒ/ (**arranges, arranging, arranged**) ◳ V-T If you **arrange** an event or meeting, you make plans for it to happen. ❑ *She arranged an appointment for Friday afternoon at four-fifteen.* ◳ V-T/V-I If you **arrange** with someone to do something, you make plans with them to do it. ❑ *I've arranged to see him on Friday morning.* ❑ *It was arranged that the party would gather for lunch in Grant Park.* ❑ *The city had arranged for the National Guard to be brought in.* ◳ V-T/V-I If you **arrange** something for someone, you make it possible for them to have it or to do it. ❑ *I will arrange for someone to take you around.* ❑ *The hotel manager will arrange for a babysitter.* ❑ *Mr. Dambar had arranged a dinner for the three of them.* ◳ V-T If you **arrange** things somewhere, you place them in a particular position, usually in order to make them look attractive or neat. ❑ *When she has a little spare time she enjoys arranging dried flowers.* ◳ V-T [usu passive] If a piece of music **is arranged** by someone, it is changed or adapted so that it is suitable for particular instruments or voices, or for a particular performance. ❑ *The songs were arranged by another well-known bass player, Ron Carter.*

──── SYNONYMS ────

arrange
VERB ◳
plan: *I had been planning a trip to the West Coast.*
prepare: *The Party leadership is preparing for the next election.*
organize: *In the end, we all decided to organize a concert for Easter.*
devise: *We devised a scheme to help him.*

ar|ranged /əreɪndʒd/ ADJ If you say how things are **arranged**, you are talking about their position in relation to each other or to something else. ❑ *The house itself is three stories high and arranged around a courtyard.*

ar|ranged mar|riage (**arranged marriages**) N-COUNT In an **arranged marriage**, the parents choose the person who their son or daughter will marry.

ar|range|ment ♦◇◇ /əreɪndʒmənt/ (**arrangements**) ◳ N-COUNT **Arrangements** are plans and preparations that you make so that something will happen or be possible. ❑ *The staff is working frantically on final arrangements for the summit.* ❑ *She telephoned Ellen, but made no arrangements to see her.* ◳ N-COUNT [also by N] An **arrangement** is an agreement that you make with someone to do something. ❑ *The caves can be visited only by prior arrangement.* ◳ N-COUNT An **arrangement** of things, for example, flowers or furniture, is a group of them displayed in a particular way. ❑ *The house was always decorated with imaginative flower arrangements.* ◳ N-COUNT If someone makes an **arrangement** of a piece of music, they change it so that it is suitable for particular voices or instruments, or for a particular performance. ❑ *...an arrangement of a well-known piece by Mozart.*

──── SYNONYMS ────

arrangement
NOUN
◳
plan: *We're making plans for a trip to Mexico.*
preparation: *Behind any successful event are months of preparations.*
◳
agreement: *It looks as though a compromise agreement has now been reached.*
settlement: *They are not optimistic about a settlement of the eleven-year conflict.*
deal: *The two sides tried and failed to come to a deal.*

ar|rang|er /əreɪndʒər/ (**arrangers**) ◳ N-COUNT An **arranger** is a musician who arranges music by other composers, either for particular instruments or voices, or for a particular performance. ◳ N-COUNT An **arranger** is a person who arranges things for other people. ❑ *...a loan arranger.*

ar|rant /ǽrənt/ ADJ [ADJ n] **Arrant** is used to emphasize that something or someone is very bad in some way. [FORMAL, EMPHASIS] ❑ *That's arrant nonsense.* ❑ *...an arrant coward.*

ar|ray /əréɪ/ (arrays) **1** N-COUNT-COLL An **array** of different things or people is a large number or wide range of them. ❑ *As the deadline approached she experienced a bewildering array of emotions.* **2** N-COUNT An **array** of objects is a collection of them that is displayed or arranged in a particular way. ❑ *We visited the local markets and saw wonderful arrays of fruit and vegetables.*

ar|rayed /əréɪd/ **1** ADJ [v-link ADJ] If things are **arrayed** in a particular way, they are arranged or displayed in that way. [FORMAL] ❑ *Cartons of Chinese food were arrayed on a large oak table.* **2** ADJ [v-link ADJ **against** n] If something such as a military force is **arrayed against** someone, it is ready and able to be used against them. [FORMAL]

ar|rears /ərɪ́ərz/ **1** N-PLURAL **Arrears** are amounts of money that you owe, especially regular payments that you should have made earlier. ❑ *They have promised to pay the arrears over the next five years.* **2** PHRASE If someone is **in arrears** with their payments, or falls **into arrears**, they have not paid the regular amounts of money that they should have paid. ❑ *...the 300,000 households who are more than six months in arrears with their mortgages.* **3** PHRASE If sums of money such as wages or taxes are paid **in arrears**, they are paid at the end of the period of time to which they relate, for example, after a job has been done and the wages have been earned. ❑ *Interest is paid in arrears after you use the money.*

ar|rest ♦♦◊ /ərést/ (arrests, arresting, arrested) **1** V-T If the police **arrest** you, they take charge of you and take you to a police station, because they believe you may have committed a crime. ❑ *Police arrested five young men in connection with one of the attacks.* • N-VAR **Arrest** is also a noun. ❑ *...a substantial reward for information leading to the arrest of the bombers.* ❑ *Police chased the fleeing terrorists and later made two arrests.* **2** V-T If something or someone **arrests** a process, they stop it from continuing. [FORMAL] ❑ *A quarantine was put in place to arrest the spread of the disease.* **3** → see also **house arrest**

SYNONYMS

arrest
VERB **1**
capture: *The guerrillas shot down one airplane and captured the pilot.*
catch: *Police say they are confident about catching the gunman.*
detain: *He was detained for questioning.*

---

ar|rest|able /ərésṭəbəl/ ADJ [usu ADJ n] An **arrestable** offense is an offense that you can be arrested for. ❑ *Possession of cannabis will no longer be an arrestable offense.*

ar|ri|val ♦♦◊ /əráɪvəl/ (arrivals) **1** N-VAR When a person or vehicle arrives at a place, you can refer to their **arrival**. ❑ *...the day after his arrival in Wichita.* ❑ *He was dead on arrival at the nearby hospital.* **2** N-VAR When someone starts a new job, you can refer to their **arrival** in that job. ❑ *...the power vacuum created by the arrival of a new president.* **3** N-SING When something is brought to you or becomes available, you can refer to its **arrival**. ❑ *I was flicking idly through a newspaper while awaiting the arrival of orange juice and coffee.* **4** N-SING When a particular time comes or a particular event happens, you can refer to its **arrival**. ❑ *He celebrated the arrival of the New Year with a bout of drinking that nearly killed him.* **5** N-COUNT You can refer to someone who has just arrived at a place as a new **arrival**. ❑ *A high proportion of the new arrivals are skilled professionals.*

ar|rive ♦♦◊ /əráɪv/ (arrives, arriving, arrived) **1** V-I When a person or vehicle **arrives** at a place, they come to it from somewhere else. ❑ *Fresh groups of guests arrived.* ❑ *...a small group of commuters waiting for their train, which arrived on time.* **2** V-I When you **arrive** at a place, you come to it for the first time in order to stay, live, or work there. ❑ *...in the old days before the European settlers arrived in the country.* **3** V-I When something such as **a letter** or meal **arrives**, it is brought or delivered to you. ❑ *Breakfast arrived while he was in the bathroom.* **4** V-I When something such as a new product or invention **arrives**, it becomes available. ❑ *Several long-awaited movies will finally arrive in the stores this month.* **5** V-I When a particular moment or event **arrives**, it happens, especially after you have been waiting for it or expecting it. ❑ *The time has arrived when I need to give up smoking.* **6** V-I When you **arrive at** something such as a decision, you decide something after thinking about it or discussing it. ❑ *...if the jury cannot arrive at a unanimous decision.*

ar|ri|viste /ǽrivíːst/ (arrivistes) N-COUNT You describe someone as an **arriviste** when you are criticizing them because they are trying very hard to belong to an influential or important social group which you feel they have no right to belong to. [FORMAL, DISAPPROVAL] ❑ *...political arrivistes.*

ar|ro|gant /ǽrəgənt/ ADJ Someone who is **arrogant** behaves in a proud, unpleasant way toward other people because they believe that they are more important than others. [DISAPPROVAL] ❑ *He was so arrogant.* ❑ *That sounds arrogant, doesn't it?* • **ar|ro|gance** N-UNCOUNT ❑ *At times the arrogance of those in power is quite blatant.*

ar|ro|gate /ǽrəgeɪt/ (arrogates, arrogating, arrogated) V-T/V-I If someone **arrogates** to themselves something such as a responsibility or privilege, they claim or take it even though they have no right to do so. [FORMAL, DISAPPROVAL] ❑ *The assembly arrogated to itself the right to make changes.* ❑ *He arrogated the privilege to himself alone.*

ar|row /ǽroʊ/ (arrows) **1** N-COUNT An **arrow** is a long thin weapon that is sharp and pointed at one end and that often has feathers at the other end. An arrow is shot from a bow. ❑ *Warriors armed with bows and arrows and spears have invaded their villages.* **2** N-COUNT An **arrow** is a written or printed sign that consists of a straight line with another line bent at a sharp angle at one end. This is a printed arrow: →. The arrow points in a particular direction to indicate where something is. ❑ *A series of arrows points the way to the modest grave of Andrei Sakharov.*

arrow|head /ǽroʊhed/ (arrowheads) N-COUNT An **arrowhead** is the sharp, pointed part of an arrow.

in BRIT, also use **arrow-head**

arrow|root /ǽroʊruːt/ N-UNCOUNT **Arrowroot** is a substance obtained from a West Indian plant. It is used in cooking, for example, for thickening sauces or in making cookies.

ar|roy|o /əróɪoʊ/ (arroyos) N-COUNT An **arroyo** is a dry stream bed with steep sides. [mainly AM] ❑ *He checked the sandy areas of the arroyo for any tracks.*

arse /ɑːrs/ (arses) N-COUNT Your **arse** is your buttocks. [BRIT, INFORMAL, VULGAR]

arse|hole /ɑːrshoʊl/ (arseholes) [BRIT, INFORMAL, VULGAR] → see **asshole**

ar|senal /ɑ́ːrsənəl/ (arsenals) **1** N-COUNT An **arsenal** is a large collection of weapons and military equipment held by a country, group, or person. ❑ *These countries are committed to destroying most of their nuclear arsenals.* **2** N-COUNT An **arsenal** is a building where weapons and military equipment are stored.

ar|senic /ɑ́ːrsənɪk/ N-UNCOUNT **Arsenic** is a very strong poison that can kill people.

ar|son /ɑ́ːrsən/ N-UNCOUNT **Arson** is the crime of deliberately setting fire to a building or vehicle. ❑ *...a terrible wave of rioting, theft and arson.*

ar|son|ist /ɑ́ːrsənɪst/ (arsonists) N-COUNT An **arsonist** is a person who deliberately sets fire to a building or vehicle.

art ♦♦♦ /ɑːrt/ (arts) **1** N-UNCOUNT **Art** consists of paintings, sculpture, and other pictures or objects that are created for people to look at and admire or think deeply about. ❑ *...the first exhibition of such art in the West.* ❑ *...contemporary and modern American art.* **2** N-UNCOUNT **Art** is the activity or educational subject that consists of creating paintings, sculptures, and other pictures or objects for people to look at and admire or think deeply about. ❑ *...a painter, content to be left alone with her all-absorbing art.* ❑ *...Savannah College of Art and Design.* **3** N-VAR The **arts** are activities such as music, painting, literature, film, and dance, which people can take part in for enjoyment, or to create works that express certain meanings or ideas of beauty. ❑ *Catherine the Great was a patron of the arts and sciences.* **4** N-PLURAL At a university or college, **arts** are subjects such as history, literature, or languages in contrast to scientific subjects. ❑ *...arts and social science graduates.* **5** ADJ [ADJ n] **Arts** or **art** is used to describe theaters that show plays or films that are intended to make the audience think deeply about the content, and not simply to entertain them. ❏ ...*a lower Manhattan art theater.* **6** N-COUNT If you describe an activity as an **art**, you mean that it requires skill and that people learn to do it by instinct or experience, rather than by learning facts or rules. ❏ ...*pioneers who transformed clinical medicine from an art to a science.* **7** → see also **fine art**, **martial art**, **state-of-the-art**, **work of art** **8** → See feature box at **fine art**

COLLOCATIONS

art
NOUN **1**
adjective + **art**: contemporary, modern; abstract, conceptual

Art Deco /ɑːt deɪkoʊ/ also **art deco** N-UNCOUNT [oft N n] **Art Deco** is a style of decoration and architecture that was common in the 1920s and 30s. It uses simple, bold designs on materials such as plastic and glass. ❏ ...*art deco lamps.*

ar|te|fact /ɑːtɪfækt/ [mainly BRIT] → see **artifact**

ar|te|rial /ɑːtɪəriəl/ **1** ADJ [ADJ n] **Arterial** means involving or relating to your arteries and the movement of blood through your body. ❏ ...*people with arterial disease.* **2** ADJ [ADJ n] An **arterial** road or railroad is a main road or railroad within a complex road or rail system.

ar|te|rio|scle|ro|sis /ɑːtɪəriəʊsklɪərəʊsɪs/ N-UNCOUNT **Arteriosclerosis** is a medical condition in which the walls of your arteries become hard and thick, so your blood cannot flow through them properly. [MEDICAL]

ar|tery /ɑːtəri/ (arteries) **1** N-COUNT **Arteries** are the tubes in your body that carry blood from your heart to the rest of your body. Compare **vein**. ❏ ...*patients suffering from blocked arteries.* **2** N-COUNT You can refer to an important main route within a complex road, railroad, or river system as an **artery**. ❏ ...*Connecticut Ave., one of the main arteries of Washington.*

art form (art forms) **1** N-COUNT If you describe an activity as an **art form**, you mean that it is concerned with creating objects, works, or performances that are beautiful or have a certain meaning. ❏ ...*Indian dance and related art forms.* **2** → See feature box at **fine art**

art|ful /ɑːtfəl/ **1** ADJ [usu ADJ n] If you describe someone as **artful**, you mean that they are clever and skillful at achieving what they want, especially by deceiving people. ❏ *Some politicians have realized that there are more artful ways of subduing people than shooting or jailing them.* **2** ADJ [usu ADJ n] If you use **artful** to describe the way someone has done or arranged something, you approve of it because it is clever or elegant. [FORMAL, APPROVAL] ❏ *There is also an artful contrast of shapes.*

art-house also **arthouse** ADJ [ADJ n] An **art-house** film is a film that is intended to be a serious artistic work rather than a piece of popular entertainment.

ar|thrit|ic /ɑːθrɪtɪk/ **1** ADJ [ADJ n] **Arthritic** is used to describe the condition, the pain, or the symptoms of arthritis. ❏ *I developed serious arthritic symptoms and chronic sinusitis.* **2** ADJ An **arthritic** person has arthritis, and cannot move very easily. **Arthritic** joints or hands are affected by arthritis. ❏ ...*an elderly lady who suffered with arthritic hands.*

ar|thri|tis /ɑːθraɪtɪs/ N-UNCOUNT **Arthritis** is a medical condition in which the joints in someone's body are swollen and painful. ❏ *I have a touch of arthritis in the wrist.*

ar|ti|choke /ɑːtɪtʃoʊk/ (artichokes) N-VAR **Artichokes** or **globe artichokes** are round green vegetables that have fleshy leaves arranged like the petals of a flower.

ar|ti|cle ◆◇◇ /ɑːtɪkəl/ (articles) **1** N-COUNT An **article** is a piece of writing that is published in a newspaper or magazine. ❏ ...*a newspaper article.* ❏ *According to an article in Newsweek the drug could have side effects.* **2** N-COUNT You can refer to objects as **articles** of some kind. ❏ ...*articles of clothing.* ❏ *He had stripped the house of all articles of value.* **3** N-COUNT An **article** of a formal agreement or document is a section of it that deals with a particular point. ❏ *The country appears to be violating several articles of the convention.* **4** N-COUNT In grammar, an **article** is a kind of determiner. In English, 'a' and 'an' are called the **indefinite article**, and 'the' is called the **definite article**. **5** PHRASE If you describe something as **the genuine article**, you are emphasizing that it is genuine, and often that it is very good. [EMPHASIS] ❏ *The vodka was the genuine article.*

COLLOCATIONS

article
NOUN **1**
noun + **article**: journal, magazine, newspaper
verb + **article**: read; write; publish
adjective + **article**: in-depth, informative

SYNONYMS

article
NOUN **1**
feature: ...*a special feature on the fund-raising project.*
paper: *He just published a paper in the journal Nature analyzing the fires.*
piece: *I disagree with Andrew Russell over his piece on British Rail.*
item: *There was an item in the paper about him.*

ar|ti|cle of faith (articles of faith) N-COUNT If something is an **article of faith** for a person or group, they believe in it totally. ❏ *For Republicans it is almost an article of faith that this tax should be cut.*

ar|ticu|late (articulates, articulating, articulated)

The adjective is pronounced /ɑːtɪkjələt/. The verb is pronounced /ɑːtɪkjəleɪt/.

1 ADJ If you describe someone as **articulate**, you mean that they are able to express their thoughts and ideas easily and well. [APPROVAL] ❏ *She is an articulate young woman.* **2** V-T When you **articulate** your ideas or feelings, you express them clearly in words. [FORMAL] ❏ *The president has been accused of failing to articulate an overall vision in foreign affairs.* **3** V-T If you **articulate** something, you say it very clearly, so that each word or syllable can be heard. ❏ *He articulated each syllable.* **4** → See feature box at **debate**

ar|ticu|lat|ed /ɑːtɪkjəleɪtɪd/ ADJ An **articulated** vehicle, especially a bus, is made in two or more sections that are joined together by metal bars, so that the vehicle can turn more easily.

ar|ticu|la|tion /ɑːtɪkjələɪʃən/ **1** N-UNCOUNT **Articulation** is the action of producing a sound or word clearly, in speech or music. [FORMAL] **2** N-UNCOUNT [usu N of n] The **articulation** of an idea or feeling is the expression of it, especially in words. [FORMAL] ❏ *This was seen as a way of restricting women's articulation of grievances.*

ar|ti|fact /ɑːtɪfækt/ (artifacts)

in BRIT, usually use **artefact**

N-COUNT An **artifact** is an ornament, tool, or other object that is made by a human being, especially one that is historically or culturally interesting. ❏ *They also repair broken religious artifacts.*

ar|ti|fice /ɑːtɪfɪs/ (artifices) N-VAR **Artifice** is the clever use of tricks and devices. [FORMAL] ❏ *Weegee's photographs are full of artfulness, and artifice.*

ar|ti|fi|cial /ɑːtɪfɪʃəl/ **1** ADJ **Artificial** objects, materials, or processes do not occur naturally and are created by human beings, often using science or technology. ❏ *The city is dotted with small lakes, natural and artificial.* ❏ ...*a wholefood diet free from artificial additives, colors and flavors.* ● **ar|ti|fi|cial|ly** ADV ❏ ...*artificially sweetened lemonade.* **2** ADJ An **artificial** state or situation exists only because someone has created it, and therefore often seems unnatural or unnecessary. ❏ *Even in the artificial environment of an office, our body rhythms continue to affect us.* ● **ar|ti|fi|cial|ly** ADV ❏ ...*state subsidies that have kept retail prices artificially low.*

ar|ti|fi|cial in|semi|na|tion N-UNCOUNT **Artificial insemination** is a medical technique for making a woman pregnant by injecting previously stored sperm into her womb. Female animals can also be made pregnant by artificial insemination. The abbreviation **AI** is also used.

ar|ti|fi|cial in|tel|li|gence N-UNCOUNT **Artificial intelligence** is a type of computer technology concerned with making machines work in an intelligent way, similar to the way that the human mind works.

ar|ti|fi|cial res|pi|ra|tion N-UNCOUNT **Artificial respiration** is the forcing of air into the lungs of someone who has stopped breathing, usually by blowing through their mouth

ar|til|lery /ɑrtɪləri/ **1** N-UNCOUNT **Artillery** consists of large, powerful guns that are transported on wheels and used by an army. ❑ *Using tanks and heavy artillery, they seized the town.* **2** N-SING-COLL **The artillery** is the section of an army that is trained to use large, powerful guns. ❑ *From 1935 to 1937 he was in the artillery.*

ar|ti|san /ɑrtɪzən/ (artisans) N-COUNT An **artisan** is someone whose job requires skill with their hands.

art|ist ♦♦◊ /ɑrtɪst/ (artists) **1** N-COUNT An **artist** is someone who draws or paints pictures or creates sculptures as a job or a hobby. ❑ *...the studio of a great artist.* ❑ *Each poster is signed by the artist.* **2** N-COUNT An **artist** is a person who creates novels, poems, films, or other things which can be considered as works of art. ❑ *His books are enormously easy to read, yet he is a serious artist.* **3** N-COUNT An **artist** is a performer such as a musician, actor, or dancer. ❑ *...a popular artist who has sold millions of records.*

SYNONYMS

artist
NOUN **1**
artisan: *It's great to work with local artisans.*
craftsman: *The table in the kitchen was made by a local craftsman.*
master: *...a portrait by the Dutch master, Vincent van Gogh.*

---

ar|tiste /ɑrtist/ (artistes) N-COUNT [oft supp N] An **artiste** is a professional entertainer, for example, a singer or a dancer. ❑ *...a cabaret artiste.*

ar|tis|tic /ɑrtɪstɪk/ **1** ADJ Someone who is **artistic** is good at drawing or painting, or arranging things in a beautiful way. ❑ *They encourage boys to be sensitive and artistic.* **2** ADJ **Artistic** means relating to art or artists. ❑ *...the campaign for artistic freedom.* • **ar|tis|ti|cal|ly** /ɑrtɪstɪkli/ ADV ❑ *...artistically gifted children.* **3** ADJ An **artistic** design or arrangement is beautiful. ❑ *...an artistic arrangement of stone paving.* • **ar|tis|ti|cal|ly** ADV ❑ *...artistically carved vessels.* **4** → See feature box at **fine art**

art|ist|ry /ɑrtɪstri/ N-UNCOUNT **Artistry** is the creative skill of an artist, writer, actor, or musician. ❑ *...his artistry as a cellist.*

art|less /ɑrtlɪs/ ADJ Someone who is **artless** is simple and honest, and does not think of deceiving other people. ❑ *She was curiously artless.* ❑ *...Hemingway's artless air and charming smile.*

Art Nou|veau /ɑrt nuvoʊ/ also **art nouveau** N-UNCOUNT [oft N n] **Art Nouveau** is a style of decoration and architecture that was common in the 1890s. It is characterized by flowing lines and patterns of flowers and leaves. ❑ *We lunched at the stunning art nouveau Café American.*

artsy /ɑrtsi/ ADJ **Artsy** means the same as **arty**. [INFORMAL]

artsy-fartsy also **arty-farty** ADJ If you describe someone as **artsy-fartsy**, you are criticizing them for being interested in artistic ideas or activities that most people do not think are interesting or worthwhile. [AM, INFORMAL, DISAPPROVAL] ❑ *...an artsy-fartsy pretentious film.*

art|work /ɑrtwɜrk/ (artworks) **1** N-UNCOUNT **Artwork** is drawings and photographs that are prepared in order to be included in something such as a book or advertisement. ❑ *The artwork for the poster was done by my sister.* **2** N-VAR **Artworks** are paintings or sculptures of high quality. ❑ *The museum contains 6,000 contemporary and modern artworks.* ❑ *...a magnificent collection of priceless artwork.*

arty /ɑrti/ ADJ Someone who is **arty** seems very interested in drama, film, music, poetry, or painting. People often describe someone as arty when they want to suggest that the person is pretentious. [INFORMAL] ❑ *Didn't you find her a little bit too arty?* ❑ *...an arty French film*

arty-farty [BRIT] → see **artsy-fartsy**

a|ru|gu|la /ərugələ/ N-UNCOUNT **Arugula** is a vegetable with green leaves that are used in salads. [mainly AM] ❑ *...a small salad of arugula and chopped tomato.*

in BRIT, usually use **rocket**

AS
① CONJUNCTION AND PREPOSITION USES
② USED WITH OTHER PREPOSITIONS AND CONJUNCTIONS

---

① **as** ♦♦♦ /əz, STRONG æz/

→ Please look at meanings **12** – **22** to see if the expression you are looking for is shown under another headword.

1 CONJ If something happens **as** something else happens, it happens at the same time. ❑ *Another police officer has been injured as fighting continued this morning.* ❑ *All the jury's eyes were on him as he continued.* **2** CONJ You use **as** to say how something happens or is done, or to indicate that something happens or is done in the same way as something else. ❑ *I'll behave toward them as I would like to be treated.* ❑ *Today, as usual, he was wearing a three-piece suit.* **3** CONJ You use **as** to introduce short clauses that comment on the truth of what you are saying. ❑ *As you can see, we're still working.* **4** CONJ You can use **as** to mean 'because' when you are explaining the reason for something. ❑ *Enjoy the first hour of the day. This is important as it sets the mood for the rest of the day.* **5** PHRASE You use the structure **as...as** when you are comparing things. ❑ *I never went through a final exam that was as difficult as that one.* • PHRASE **As** is also a conjunction. ❑ *Being a mother isn't as bad as I thought at first!* **6** PHRASE You use **as...as** to emphasize amounts of something. [EMPHASIS] ❑ *She gets as many as eight thousand letters a month.* **7** PHRASE You say **as it were** in order to make what you are saying sound less definite. [VAGUENESS] ❑ *I'd understood the words, but I didn't, as it were, understand the question.* **8** PHRASE You use expressions such as **as it is**, **as it turns out**, and **as things stand** when you are making a contrast between a possible situation and what actually happened or is the case. ❑ *I want to work at home on a Tuesday but as it turns out sometimes it's a Wednesday or a Thursday.* **9** PREP You use **as** when you are indicating what someone or something is or is thought to be, or what function they have. ❑ *He has worked as a diplomat in the U.S., Sudan and Saudi Arabia.* ❑ *The news apparently came as a complete surprise.* **10** PREP If you do something **as** a child or **as** a teenager, for example, you do it when you are a child or a teenager. ❑ *She loved singing as a child and started vocal training at 12.* **11** PREP You use **as** in expressions like **as a result** and **as a consequence** to indicate how two situations or events are related to each other. ❑ *As a result of the growing fears about home security, more people are arranging for someone to stay in their home when they're away.* **12 as ever** → see **ever 13 as a matter of fact** → see **fact 14 as follows** → see **follow** ① **15 as long as** → see **long** ③ **16 as opposed to** → see **opposed 17 as regards** → see **regard 18 as soon as** → see **soon 19 as such** → see **such 20 as well** → see **well** ③ **21 as well as** → see **well** ③ **22 as yet** → see **yet**

② **as** ♦♦♦ /əz, STRONG æz/ **1** PHRASE You use **as for** and **as to** at the beginning of a sentence in order to introduce a slightly different subject that is still connected to the previous one. ❑ *I don't know why the guy yelled at me. And as for going back there, certainly I would never go back, for fear of receiving further abuse.* **2** PHRASE You use **as to** to indicate what something refers to. ❑ *They should make decisions as to whether the student needs more help.* **3** PHRASE If you say that something will happen **as of** a particular date or time, you mean that it will happen from that time on. ❑ *Voting polls have opened as of 8:00am this morning.* **4** PHRASE You use **as if** and **as though** when you are giving a possible explanation for something or saying that something appears to be the case when it is not. ❑ *Anne shrugged, as if she didn't know.*

asap /eɪ ɛs eɪ pi/ ADV [ADV after v] **asap** is an abbreviation for 'as soon as possible.' ❑ *The colonel ordered, "I want two good engines down here asap."*

as|bes|tos /æsbɛstəs, æz-/ N-UNCOUNT **Asbestos** is a gray material that does not burn and that was used in the past as a protection against fire or heat. Clothing and mats are sometimes made from it. ❑ *...asbestos gloves.*

as|cend /əsɛnd/ (ascends, ascending, ascended) **1** V-T If you **ascend** a hill or staircase, you go up it. [WRITTEN] ❑ *Mrs. Clayton had to hold Lizzie's hand as they ascended the steps.* **2** V-I If a staircase or path **ascends**, it leads up to a higher position. [WRITTEN] ❑ *A number of staircases ascend from the cobbled streets*

as|cend|ancy /əsɛndənsi/ also **ascendency** N-UNCOUNT If one group has **ascendancy** over another group, it has more power or influence than the other group. [FORMAL] ☐ *Although geographically linked, the two provinces have long fought for political ascendancy.*

as|cend|ant /əsɛndənt/ PHRASE [v-link PHR] If someone or something is **in the ascendant**, they have or are getting more power, influence, or popularity than other people or things. [FORMAL] ☐ *Radical reformers are once more in the ascendant.*

as|cend|ency /əsɛndənsi/ → see **ascendancy**

as|cend|ing /əsɛndɪŋ/ **1** ADJ [ADJ n] If a group of things is arranged in **ascending** order, each thing is bigger, greater, or more important than the thing before it. ☐ *Now draw or trace ten dinosaurs in ascending order of size.* **2** → see also **ascend**

as|cen|sion /əsɛnʃən/ **1** N-SING [with poss] In some religions, when someone goes to heaven, you can refer to their **ascension** to heaven. ☐ *...the two-day holiday marking the Prophet's ascension to heaven.* **2** N-SING [with poss, usu N to n] The **ascension** of a person to a high rank or important position is the act of reaching this position. [WRITTEN] ☐ *...50 years after his ascension to the Cambodian throne.*

as|cent /əsɛnt/ (**ascents**) **1** N-COUNT An **ascent** is an upward journey, especially when you are walking or climbing. ☐ *In 1955 he led the first ascent of Kangchenjunga, the world's third highest mountain.* **2** N-COUNT An **ascent** is an upward slope or path, especially when you are walking or climbing. ☐ *It was a tough course over a gradual ascent before the big climb of Bluebell Hill.* **3** N-COUNT An **ascent** is an upward, vertical movement. ☐ *Burke pushed the button and the elevator began its slow ascent.*

as|cer|tain /æsərteɪn/ (**ascertains, ascertaining, ascertained**) V-T If you **ascertain** the truth about something, you find out what it is, especially by making a deliberate effort to do so. [FORMAL] ☐ *Through doing this, the teacher will be able to ascertain the extent to which the child understands what he is reading.* ☐ *Once they had ascertained that he was not a spy, they agreed to release him.*

as|cet|ic /əsɛtɪk/ (**ascetics**) ADJ [usu ADJ n] An **ascetic** person has a way of life that is simple and strict, usually because of their religious beliefs. • N-COUNT An **ascetic** is someone who is ascetic.

as|ceti|cism /əsɛtɪsɪzəm/ N-UNCOUNT **Asceticism** is a simple, strict way of life with no luxuries or physical pleasures.

ascor|bic acid /æskɔrbɪk æsɪd/ N-UNCOUNT **Ascorbic acid** is another name for vitamin C. [TECHNICAL]

as|cribe /əskraɪb/ (**ascribes, ascribing, ascribed**) **1** V-T If you **ascribe** an event or condition to a particular cause, you say or consider that it was caused by that thing. [FORMAL] ☐ *An autopsy eventually ascribed the baby's death to sudden infant death syndrome.* **2** V-T If you **ascribe** a quality to someone, you consider that they possess it. [FORMAL] ☐ *We do not ascribe a superior wisdom to government or the state.*

asexu|al /eɪsɛkʃuəl/ **1** ADJ Something that is **asexual** involves no sexual activity. ☐ *Their relationship was totally asexual.* ☐ *...asexual reproduction.* • **asexu|al|ly** ADV ☐ *Many fungi can reproduce asexually.* **2** ADJ **Asexual** creatures and plants have no sexual organs. ☐ *...asexual parasites.* **3** ADJ Someone who is **asexual** is not sexually attracted to other people. ☐ *It is another unfortunate myth of our culture that older people are asexual.*

ash /æʃ/ (**ashes**) **1** N-UNCOUNT [also N in pl] **Ash** is the gray or black powdery substance that is left after something is burned. You can also refer to this substance as **ashes**. ☐ *A cloud of volcanic ash is spreading across wide areas of the Philippines.* ☐ *He brushed the cigarette ash from his sleeve.* **2** N-PLURAL A dead person's **ashes** are their remains after their body has been cremated. ☐ *And she asks him to go back there after her death and scatter her ashes on the lake.* **3** N-VAR An **ash** is a tree that has smooth gray bark and loses its leaves in winter. • N-UNCOUNT **Ash** is the wood from this tree. ☐ *The rafters are made from ash.* **4** → See also color supplement

ashamed /əʃeɪmd/ **1** ADJ [v-link ADJ] If someone is **ashamed**, they feel embarrassed or guilty because of something they do or they have done, or because of their appearance. ☐ *I felt incredibly ashamed of myself for getting so angry.* **2** ADJ [v-link ADJ of n] If you are **ashamed of** someone, you feel embarrassed to be connected with them, often because of their appearance or because you disapprove of something they have done. ☐ *I've never told this to anyone, but it's true, I was terribly ashamed of my mom.*

ash|en /æʃən/ ADJ Someone who is **ashen** looks very pale, especially because they are ill, shocked, or frightened.

ashen-faced ADJ Someone who is **ashen-faced** looks very pale, especially because they are ill, shocked, or frightened. ☐ *The survivors were ashen-faced and visibly shaken.*

ashore /əʃɔr/ ADV Someone or something that comes **ashore** comes from the sea onto the shore. ☐ *Oil has come ashore on a ten mile stretch to the east of Anchorage.*

ash|tan|ga yoga /æʃtɑŋɡə yoʊɡə/ N-UNCOUNT **Ashtanga yoga** is a type of yoga in which you move quickly from one position to another, while controlling your breathing.

ash|tray /æʃtreɪ/ (**ashtrays**) N-COUNT An **ashtray** is a small dish in which smokers can put the ash from their cigarettes and cigars.

Ash Wednes|day N-UNCOUNT **Ash Wednesday** is the first day of Lent.

Asian /eɪʒən/ (**Asians**) ADJ Someone or something that is **Asian** comes from or is associated with Asia. Americans use this term especially to refer to China, Korea, Thailand, Japan, or Vietnam. British people use this term especially to refer to India, Pakistan, and Bangladesh. ☐ *...Asian music.* • N-COUNT An **Asian** is a person who comes from or is associated with a country or region in Asia. ☐ *Many of the shops were run by Asians.*

Asi|at|ic /eɪʒiætɪk/ ADJ [ADJ n] **Asiatic** means belonging or relating to Asia or its people. [OLD-FASHIONED]

aside /əsaɪd/

In addition to the uses shown below, **aside** is used in phrasal verbs such as 'cast aside,' 'stand aside,' and 'step aside.'

1 ADV [ADV after v] If you move something **aside**, you move it to one side of you. ☐ *Sarah closed the book and laid it aside.* **2** ADV [ADV after v] If you take or draw someone **aside**, you take them a little way away from a group of people in order to talk to them in private. ☐ *Latoya grabbed him by the elbow and took him aside.* **3** ADV [ADV after v] If you move **aside**, you get out of someone's way. ☐ *She had been standing in the doorway, but now she stepped aside to let them pass.* **4** ADV [ADV after v] If you set something such as time, money, or space **aside** for a particular purpose, you save it and do not use it for anything else. ☐ *While many parents are putting money aside for college tuition, some are taking on another big expense: buying cars for their teenagers.* **5** ADV [ADV after v] If you brush or sweep **aside** a feeling or suggestion, you reject it. ☐ *Talk to a friend who will really listen and not brush aside your feelings.* **6** ADV You use **aside** to indicate that you have finished talking about something, or that you are leaving it out of your discussion, and that you are about to talk about something else. ☐ *Leaving aside the nutritional argument, these loaves are better value.* **7** PHRASE You use **aside from** when you are making an exception to a general statement. ☐ *The room was empty aside from one man seated beside the fire.* **8** PHRASE You use **aside from** to indicate that you are aware of one aspect of a situation, but that you are going to focus on another aspect. ☐ *Quite aside from her tiredness, Amanda seemed unnaturally abstracted.*

A-side (**A-sides**) N-COUNT The **A-side** of a record that has been released as a single is the main song on it. You can also refer to the side of the record that contains this song as **the A-side**. Compare **B-side**.

asi|nine /æsɪnaɪn/ ADJ If you describe something or someone as **asinine**, you mean that they are very foolish. [FORMAL, DISAPPROVAL] ☐ *...an asinine discussion.*

ask /æsk, æsk/ (**asks, asking, asked**) **1** V-T/V-I If you **ask** someone something, you say something to them in the form of a question because you want to know the answer. ☐ *"How is Frank?" he asked.* ☐ *I asked him his name.* ☐ *She asked me if I'd enjoyed my dinner.* ☐ *Maybe we should adopt the policy of "don't ask, don't tell."* **2** V-T If you **ask** someone to do something, you tell them that you want them to do it. ❑ *We had to ask him to leave.* ❸ V-T If you **ask** to do something, you tell someone that you want to do it. ❑ *I asked to see the Director.* ❹ V-I If you **ask for** something, you say that you would like it. ❑ *I decided to go to the next house and ask for food.* ❺ V-I If you **ask for** someone, you say that you would like to speak to them. ❑ *There's a man at the gate asking for you.* ❻ V-T If you **ask** someone's permission, opinion, or forgiveness, you try to obtain it by making a request. ❑ *Please ask permission from whoever pays the phone bill before making your call.* ❼ V-T If you **ask** someone to an event or place, you invite them to go there. ❑ *Couldn't you ask Juan to the party?* ❽ V-T If someone **is asking** a particular price for something, they are selling it for that price. ❑ *Mr. Pantelaras was asking $6,000 for his collection.* ❾ CONVENTION You reply '**don't ask me**' when you do not know the answer to a question, usually when you are annoyed or surprised that you have been asked. [FEELINGS] ❑ *"She's got other things on her mind, wouldn't you think?" "Don't ask me," murmured Chris. "I've never met her."* ❿ PHRASE You can say '**if you ask me**' to emphasize that you are stating your personal opinion. [EMPHASIS] ❑ *He was nuts, if you ask me.* ⓫ PHRASE If you say that someone **is asking for trouble** or **is asking for it**, you mean that they are behaving in a way that makes it very likely that they will get into trouble. ❑ *To go ahead with the match after such clear advice had been asking for trouble.*

SYNONYMS

ask
VERB
❶
inquire: *I called to inquire about train times.*
question: *This led the therapist to question Jim about his parents and their marriage.*
query: *One of the journalists queried whether sabotage could have been involved.*
❷
request: *Mr Dennis said he had requested access to a telephone.*
demand: *The hijackers are demanding to speak to representatives of both governments.*
plead: *He was kneeling on the floor, pleading for mercy.*
beg: *I begged to be allowed to leave.*

askance /əskæns/ ❶ PHRASE [usu PHR at n] If you **look askance at** someone or something, you have a doubtful or suspicious attitude toward them. ❑ *They have always looked askance at the western notion of democracy.* ❷ PHRASE [usu PHR at n] If you **look askance at** someone, you look at them in a doubtful or suspicious way.

askew /əskyu/ ADJ [v-link ADJ] Something that is **askew** is not straight or not level with what it should be level with. ❑ *There were no shutters at the windows, and some of the doors hung askew.*

ask|ing price (**asking prices**) N-COUNT The **asking price** of something is the price that the person selling it says that they want for it, although they may accept less. ❑ *Offers 15% below the asking price are unlikely to be accepted.*

asleep /əslip/ ❶ ADJ [v-link ADJ] Someone who is **asleep** is sleeping. ❑ *My four-year-old daughter was asleep on the sofa.* ❷ ADJ [be ADJ] If you say that your arm or leg is **asleep**, you mean that it is numb, for example because you have been sitting in an awkward position. [mainly AM] ❑ *Her left leg was asleep from sitting on the floor.* ❸ PHRASE When you **fall asleep**, you start sleeping. ❑ *Sam snuggled down in his pillow and fell asleep.* ❹ PHRASE Someone who is **fast asleep** or **sound asleep** is sleeping deeply. ❑ *They were both fast asleep in their beds.*

USAGE

asleep
Don't use **asleep** in front of a noun. Don't, for example, talk about an '~~asleep child~~.' Instead, you can say a '**sleeping child**.' You also don't say that someone is '~~very asleep~~.' You can say that they are **sound asleep** or **fast asleep**. *Chris is still sound asleep in the other bed.*

as|para|gus /əspærəgəs/ N-UNCOUNT **Asparagus** is a vegetable that is long and green and has small shoots at one end. It is cooked and usually served whole.

as|pect ✦✧ /æspɛkt/ (**aspects**) ❶ N-COUNT An **aspect** of something is one of the parts of its character or nature. ❑ *Climate and weather affect every aspect of our lives.* ❑ *He was interested in all aspects of the work here.* ❷ N-COUNT The **aspect** of a building or window is the direction in which it faces. [FORMAL] ❑ *The house had a southwest aspect.*

SYNONYMS

aspect
NOUN ❶
feature: *The spacious gardens are a special feature of this property.*
point: *The most interesting point about the village was its religion.*
side: *Anxiety has a mental and a physical side.*
factor: *Physical activity is an important factor in maintaining fitness.*
facet: *The caste system shapes nearly every facet of Indian life.*

as|pen /æspən/ (**aspens**) N-VAR An **aspen** is a tall tree with leaves that move a lot in the wind.

as|per|ity /æspɛrɪti/ N-UNCOUNT [oft with N] If you say something with **asperity**, you say it impatiently and severely. [FORMAL] ❑ *"I told you Preskel had no idea," remarked Kemp with some asperity.*

as|per|sions /əspɜrʒ³nz/ PHRASE [usu PHR on n] If you **cast aspersions on** someone or something, you suggest that they are not very good in some way. [FORMAL]

as|phalt /æsfɔlt/ N-UNCOUNT [oft N n] **Asphalt** is a black substance used to make the surfaces of things such as roads and playgrounds.

as|phyxia /æsfɪksiə/ N-UNCOUNT **Asphyxia** is death or loss of consciousness caused by being unable to breathe properly. [MEDICAL] ❑ *Death was due to asphyxia through smoke inhalation.*

as|phyxi|ate /æsfɪksieɪt/ (**asphyxiates, asphyxiating, asphyxiated**) V-T [usu passive] If someone **is asphyxiated**, they die or lose consciousness because they are unable to breathe properly. ❑ *Three people were asphyxiated in the crush for last week's train.* • **as|phyxia|tion** /æsfɪksieɪʃ³n/ N-UNCOUNT ❑ *A postmortem examination found that she died from asphyxiation.*

as|pic /æspɪk/ N-UNCOUNT **Aspic** is a clear shiny jelly made from meat juices. It is used in making cold meat dishes. ❑ *...cold chicken in aspic.*

as|pir|ant /əspaɪrənt, æspərənt/ (**aspirants**) ❶ N-COUNT Someone who is an **aspirant** to political power or to an important job has a strong desire to achieve it. [FORMAL] ❑ *...the young aspirant to power.* ❷ ADJ [ADJ n] **Aspirant** means the same as **aspiring**. [FORMAL] ❑ *...aspirant politicians.*

as|pi|ra|tion /æspɪreɪʃ³n/ (**aspirations**) N-VAR Someone's **aspirations** are their desire to achieve things. ❑ *...the needs and aspirations of our pupils.* ❑ *He is unlikely to send in the army to quell nationalist aspirations.*

as|pi|ra|tion|al /æspɪreɪʃən³l/ ❶ ADJ If you describe someone as **aspirational**, you mean that they have strong hopes of moving to a higher social status. [JOURNALISM] ❑ *...the typical tensions of an aspirational household.* ❷ ADJ If you describe a product as **aspirational**, you mean that it is bought or enjoyed by people who have strong hopes of moving to a higher social class. [JOURNALISM] ❑ *Fine music, particularly opera, has become aspirational, like fine wine or foreign travel.*

as|pire /əspaɪər/ (**aspires, aspiring, aspired**) ❶ V-I If you **aspire to** something such as an important job, you have a strong desire to achieve it. ❑ *...people who aspire to public office.* ❑ *Rice aspired to go to college.* ❷ → see also **aspiring**

as|pi|rin /æspərɪn, -prɪn/ (**aspirins**)

The form **aspirin** can also be used for the plural.

N-VAR **Aspirin** is a mild drug that reduces pain and fever.

as|pir|ing /əspaɪərɪŋ/ ❶ ADJ [ADJ n] If you use **aspiring** to describe someone who is starting a particular career, you mean that they are trying to become successful in it. ❑ *Many aspiring young artists are advised to learn by copying the masters.* ❷ → see also **aspire**

ass /æs/ (**asses**) ❶ N-COUNT Your **ass** is your buttocks. [AM, INFORMAL, VULGAR] ❑ *I jumped back and fell on my ass.*

in BRIT, use **arse**

❷ N-COUNT If you describe someone as an **ass**, you think that they are silly or do silly things. [INFORMAL, DISAPPROVAL] ❑ *He was generally disliked and regarded as a pompous ass.*

assail

3 N-COUNT An **ass** is an animal related to a horse but that is smaller and has long ears. **4 cover your ass** → see **cover** ① **5 a pain in the ass** → see **pain**

as|sail /əseɪl/ (assails, assailing, assailed) **1** V-T If someone **assails** you, they criticize you strongly. [WRITTEN] ❑ *Protesters assailed the proposed fare increase.* **2** V-T If someone **assails** you, they attack you violently. [WRITTEN] ❑ *Her husband was assailed by a young man with a knife in a nearby park.* **3** V-T [usu passive] If you **are assailed** by something unpleasant such as fears or problems, you are greatly troubled by a large number of them. [WRITTEN] ❑ *She is assailed by self-doubt and emotional insecurity.*

as|sail|ant /əseɪlənt/ (assailants) N-COUNT Someone's **assailant** is a person who has physically attacked them. [FORMAL] ❑ *Other partygoers rescued the injured man from his assailant.*

as|sas|sin /əsæsɪn/ (assassins) N-COUNT An **assassin** is a person who assassinates someone. ❑ *He saw the shooting and memorized the license plate of the assassin's car.*

as|sas|si|nate /əsæsɪneɪt/ (assassinates, assassinating, assassinated) **1** V-T When someone important **is assassinated**, they are murdered as a political act. ❑ *Would the U.S. be radically different today if Kennedy had not been assassinated?* • **as|sas|si|na|tion** /əsæsɪneɪʃ⁰n/ (assassinations) N-VAR ❑ *She would like an investigation into the assassination of her husband.* ❑ *He lives in constant fear of assassination.* **2** → See feature box at **history**

as|sault /əsɔlt/ (assaults, assaulting, assaulted) **1** N-COUNT An **assault** by an army is a strong attack made on an area held by the enemy. ❑ *The rebels are poised for a new assault on the government garrisons.* **2** ADJ [ADJ n] **Assault** weapons such as rifles are intended for soldiers to use in battle rather than for purposes such as hunting. **3** N-VAR [oft N on/upon n] An **assault** on a person is a physical attack on them. ❑ *The attack is one of a series of savage sexual assaults on women in the university area.* **4** V-T To **assault** someone means to physically attack them. ❑ *The gang assaulted him with iron bars.* **5** → See feature box at **crime**

COLLOCATIONS

assault
NOUN
1
noun + **assault**: air, ground
adjective + **assault**: aerial, frontal; full-scale, sustained
verb + **assault**: launch, mount, plan
3
adjective + **assault**: domestic, physical, sexual; indecent, serious, vicious, violent; alleged, common, unlawful
verb + **assault**: commit; investigate, report; admit, deny

---

as|sault and bat|tery N-UNCOUNT **Assault and battery** is the crime of attacking someone and causing them physical harm. [LEGAL]

as|sault course (assault courses) N-COUNT An **assault course** is an area of land covered with obstacles such as walls which people, especially soldiers, use to improve their skills and strength. [BRIT]

in AM, use **obstacle course**

as|say /æseɪ/ (assays) N-COUNT An **assay** is a test of a substance to find out what chemicals it contains. It is usually carried out to find out how pure a substance is. [TECHNICAL]

as|sem|blage /əsɛmblɪdʒ/ (assemblages) N-COUNT [oft N of n] An **assemblage** of people or things is a collection of them. [FORMAL] ❑ *He had an assemblage of old junk cars filling the backyard.*

as|sem|ble /əsɛmb⁰l/ (assembles, assembling, assembled) **1** V-T/V-I When people **assemble** or when someone **assembles** them, they come together in a group, usually for a particular purpose such as a meeting. ❑ *There wasn't even a convenient place for students to assemble between classes.* **2** V-T To **assemble** something means to collect it together or to fit the different parts of it together. ❑ *Greenpeace managed to assemble a small flotilla of inflatable boats to waylay the ship at sea.*

as|sem|bler /əsɛmblər/ (assemblers) **1** N-COUNT An **assembler** is a person, a machine, or a company that assembles the individual parts of a vehicle or a piece of equipment such as a computer. **2** N-COUNT An **assembler** is a type of computer program that converts a program written in assembly language into machine language.

as|sem|bly /əsɛmbli/ (assemblies) **1** N-COUNT An **assembly** is a large group of people who meet regularly to make decisions or laws for a particular region or country. ❑ *...the campaign for the first free election to the National Assembly.* **2** N-COUNT An **assembly** is a group of people gathered together for a particular purpose. ❑ *He waited until complete quiet settled on the assembly.* **3** N-UNCOUNT When you refer to rights of **assembly** or restrictions on **assembly**, you are referring to the legal right that people have to gather together. [FORMAL] ❑ *The U.S. Constitution guarantees free speech, freedom of assembly and equal protection.* **4** N-UNCOUNT The **assembly** of a machine, device, or object is the process of fitting its different parts together. ❑ *For the rest of the day, he worked on the assembly of an explosive device.* **5** N-VAR In a school, an **assembly** is a gathering of all the teachers and students for a particular purpose. ❑ *Recently named the nation's top girls' basketball player, she will be honored this morning at a school assembly.*

SYNONYMS

assembly
NOUN **2**
gathering: *...the twenty-second annual gathering of the South Pacific Forum.*
conference: *The President summoned the State Governors to a conference on education.*
rally: *Supporters of the policy are gathering in Delhi for a rally.*
convention: *...the annual convention of the Society of Professional Journalists.*
crowd: *A huge crowd gathered in a square outside the Kremlin walls.*

---

as|sem|bly line (assembly lines) N-COUNT An **assembly line** is an arrangement of workers and machines in a factory, where each worker deals with only one part of a product. The product passes from one worker to another until it is finished.

as|sem|bly|man /əsɛmblimən/ (assemblymen) N-COUNT; N-TITLE An **assemblyman** is a male elected member of a state legislative body in some areas of the U.S.

as|sem|bly plant (assembly plants) N-COUNT An **assembly plant** is a factory where large items such as cars are put together, usually using parts which have been made in other factories.

as|sem|bly|woman /əsɛmbliwʊmən/ (assemblywomen) N-COUNT; N-TITLE An **assemblywoman** is a female elected member of a state legislative body in some areas of the U.S.

as|sent /əsɛnt/ (assents, assenting, assented) **1** N-UNCOUNT If someone gives their **assent** to something that has been suggested, they formally agree to it. ❑ *He gave his assent to the proposed legislation.* **2** V-I If you **assent** to something, you agree to it or agree with it. ❑ *I assented to the request of the American publishers to write this book.*

as|sert /əsɜrt/ (asserts, asserting, asserted) **1** V-T If someone **asserts** a fact or belief, they state it firmly. [FORMAL] ❑ *Mr. Helm plans to assert that the bill violates the First Amendment.* ❑ *The defendants, who continue to assert their innocence, are expected to appeal.* • **as|ser|tion** /əsɜrʃ⁰n/ (assertions) N-VAR ❑ *There is no concrete evidence to support assertions that the recession is truly over.* **2** V-T If you **assert** your authority, you make it clear by your behavior that you have authority. ❑ *After the war, the army made an attempt to assert its authority in the south of the country.* • **as|ser|tion** N-UNCOUNT ❑ *The decision is seen as an assertion of his authority within the company.* **3** V-T If you **assert** your right or claim to something, you insist that you have the right to it. ❑ *The republics began asserting their right to govern themselves.* • **as|ser|tion** N-UNCOUNT ❑ *These institutions have made the assertion of ethnic identity possible.* **4** V-T If you **assert** yourself, you speak and act in a forceful way, so that people take notice of you. ❑ *He's speaking up and asserting himself and doing things he enjoys.*

as|ser|tive /əsɜrtɪv/ **1** ADJ Someone who is **assertive** states their needs and opinions clearly, so that people take notice. ❑ *Debating encourages children to be more assertive.*

• as|ser|tive|ness N-UNCOUNT ☐ Chantelle's assertiveness stirred up his deep-seated sense of inadequacy. ◨ → See feature box at personality

as|sess ✦◇◇ /əsɛs/ (assesses, assessing, assessed) ◧ V-T When you assess a person, thing, or situation, you consider them in order to make a judgment about them. ☐ The test was to assess aptitude rather than academic achievement. ☐ It would be a matter of assessing whether she was well enough to travel. ◨ V-T When you assess the amount of money that something is worth or should be paid, you calculate or estimate it. ☐ Ask them to send you information on how to assess the value of your belongings.

as|sess|ment ✦◇◇ /əsɛsmənt/ (assessments) ◧ N-VAR An assessment is a consideration of someone or something and a judgment about them. ☐ There is little assessment of the damage to the natural environment. ◨ N-VAR An assessment of the amount of money that something is worth or that should be paid is a calculation or estimate of the amount. ☐ Tax assessment is all about comparing values of similar properties.

▸ COLLOCATIONS ◂

assessment
NOUN ◧
noun + **assessment**: impact, risk
adjective + **assessment**: accurate, detailed, honest, objective; damning, downbeat, upbeat, withering; medical, psychiatric
verb + **assessment**: complete, conduct, make, undertake; undergo

▸ SYNONYMS ◂

assessment
NOUN ◧
analysis: We did an analysis of the way that government money was spent.
evaluation: They announced that an inspection team was conducting an evaluation of the building site.
appraisal: What is needed in such cases is a calm appraisal of the situation.
study: ...the first study of English children's attitudes.

as|ses|sor /əsɛsər/ (assessors) N-COUNT An assessor is a person who is employed to calculate the value of something, or the amount of money that should be paid, for example, in tax. [BUSINESS]

as|set ✦✦◇ /æsɛt/ (assets) ◧ N-COUNT Something or someone that is an asset is considered useful or helps a person or organization to be successful. ☐ Our creativity in the field of technology is our greatest asset. ◨ N-PLURAL The assets of a company or a person are all the things that they own. [BUSINESS] ☐ Further probing revealed that the company had assets of $1.5 million.

▸ COLLOCATIONS ◂

asset
NOUN
◧
adjective + **asset**: important, key, prize, valuable; natural
◨
noun + **assets**: liquid, property, state
adjective + **assets**: financial, fixed, net, total; risky
verb + **assets**: acquire, buy, sell, transfer; freeze, seize; manage, protect

▸ SYNONYMS ◂

asset
NOUN ◧
benefit: I'm a great believer in the benefits of this form of therapy.
advantage: A good crowd will be a definite advantage for the team.
blessing: Rivers are a blessing for an agricultural country.

asset-stripping N-UNCOUNT If a person or company is involved in **asset-stripping**, they buy companies cheaply, sell off their assets to make a profit, and then close the companies down. [BUSINESS, DISAPPROVAL]

ass|hole /æshoʊl/ (assholes) N-COUNT If one person calls another person an asshole, they think that person is extremely stupid or has behaved in a stupid way. [AM, VULGAR, DISAPPROVAL]

in BRIT, use **arsehole**

as|sidu|ous /əsɪdʒuəs/ ADJ Someone who is assiduous works hard or does things very thoroughly. ☐ Podulski had been assiduous in learning his adopted language.

as|sign /əsaɪn/ (assigns, assigning, assigned) ◧ V-T If you assign a piece of work to someone, you give them the work to do. ☐ When I taught, I would assign a topic to children that they would write about. ☐ Later in the year, she'll assign them research papers. ◨ V-T If you assign something to someone, you say that it is for their use. ☐ The selling broker is then required to assign a portion of the commission to the buyer broker. ◨ V-T [usu passive] If someone is assigned to a particular place, group, or person, they are sent there, usually in order to work at that place or for that person. ☐ I was assigned to Troop A of the 10th Cavalry. ☐ Did you choose Russia or were you simply assigned there? ◨ V-T If you assign a particular function or value to someone or something, you say they have it. ☐ Under the system, each business must assign a value to each job.

as|sig|na|tion /æsɪɡneɪʃ°n/ (assignations) N-COUNT [oft N with n] An assignation is a secret meeting with someone, especially with a lover. [FORMAL] ☐ She had an assignation with her boyfriend.

as|sign|ment /əsaɪnmənt/ (assignments) N-COUNT An assignment is a task or piece of work that you are given to do, especially as part of your job or studies. ☐ The assessment for the course involves written assignments and practical tests.

as|simi|late /əsɪmɪleɪt/ (assimilates, assimilating, assimilated) ◧ V-T/V-I When people such as immigrants assimilate into a community or when that community assimilates them, they become an accepted part of it. ☐ There is every sign that new Asian-Americans are just as willing to assimilate. ☐ His family tried to assimilate into the White and Hispanic communities. • as|simi|la|tion /əsɪmɪleɪʃ°n/ N-UNCOUNT ☐ They promote social integration and assimilation of minority ethnic groups into the culture. ◨ V-T If you assimilate new ideas, customs, or techniques, you learn them or adopt them. ☐ My mind could only assimilate one impossibility at a time. • as|simi|la|tion N-UNCOUNT ☐ This technique brings life to instruction and eases assimilation of knowledge.

as|sist ✦◇◇ /əsɪst/ (assists, assisting, assisted) ◧ V-T If you assist someone, you help them to do a job or task by doing part of the work for them. ☐ The family decided to assist me with my chores. ◨ V-T/V-I If you assist someone, you give them information, advice, or money. ☐ The public is urgently requested to assist police in tracing this man. ☐ International organizations intensified their activities to locate victims and assist with relief efforts. ◨ V-T/V-I If something assists in doing a task, it makes the task easier to do. ☐ ...a chemical that assists in the manufacture of proteins. ☐ Our sales representatives can assist you in selecting suitable investments.

▸ SYNONYMS ◂

assist
VERB ◧
back: The Prime Minister is backed by the civic movement, Public Against Violence.
support: The Vice President insisted that he supported the hard-working people of New York.
aid: ...a software system to aid managers in advanced decision-making.

as|sis|tance ✦◇◇ /əsɪstəns/ ◧ N-UNCOUNT [oft with poss] If you give someone assistance, you help them do a job or task by doing part of the work for them. ☐ Since 1976 he has been operating the shop with the assistance of volunteers. ◨ N-UNCOUNT If you give someone assistance, you give them information or advice. ☐ Any assistance you could give the police will be greatly appreciated. ◨ N-UNCOUNT [oft supp N] If someone gives a person or country assistance, they help them by giving them money. ☐ ...a viable program of economic assistance. ◨ N-UNCOUNT If something is done with the assistance of a particular thing, that thing is helpful or necessary for doing it. ☐ The translations were carried out with the assistance of a medical dictionary. ◨ PHRASE Someone or something that is of assistance

assistant / assume

to you is helpful or useful to you. ❑ *Can I be of any assistance?* ▣ PHRASE If you **come to** someone's **assistance**, you take action to help them. ❑ *They are appealing to the world community to come to Jordan's assistance.*

SYNONYMS
assistance
NOUN ▣
backing: *The president had the full backing of his government to negotiate a deal.*
aid: *He was forced to turn for aid to his former enemy.*
support: *The prime minister gave his full support to the government's reforms.*

as|sis|tant ◆◇◇ /əsɪstənt/ (assistants) ▣ ADJ [ADJ n] **Assistant** is used in front of titles or jobs to indicate a slightly lower rank. For example, an assistant director is one rank lower than a director in an organization. ❑ *...the assistant secretary of defense.* ▣ N-COUNT Someone's **assistant** is a person who helps them in their work. ❑ *Kalan called his assistant, Hashim, to take over while he went out.* ▣ N-COUNT An **assistant** is a person who works in a store selling things to customers. ❑ *The assistant took the book and checked the price on the back cover.*

SYNONYMS
assistant
NOUN ▣
helper: *One table of six children had nearly as many helpers.*
ally: *He is a close ally of the Prime Minister.*
aide: *...a close aide to the Prime Minister.*

as|sis|tant pro|fes|sor (assistant professors) N-COUNT; N-TITLE An **assistant professor** is a college teacher who ranks above an instructor but below an associate professor. [AM] ❑ *...an assistant professor of mathematics.* ❑ *...Assistant Professor Rob Nideffer.*

as|sis|tant ref|er|ee (assistant referees) N-COUNT An **assistant referee** is the same as a **linesman**.

as|sis|ted liv|ing N-UNCOUNT [oft N n] **Assisted living** is a type of housing specially designed for people who need help in their everyday lives, but who do not need specialist nursing care. In **assisted living** facilities, residents live in independent rooms or apartments, but receive help with day-to-day activities, for example bathing, dressing, preparing meals, and taking their medicines. ❑ *...the one million elderly Americans who live in assisted living facilities.* ❑ *Now she's in assisted living, and her niece and nephew are helping with her affairs.*

Assoc. Assoc. is a written abbreviation for **association**, **associated**, or **associate**.

as|so|ci|ate ◆◇◇ (associates, associating, associated)

The verb is pronounced /əsoʊʃieɪt, -sieɪt/. The noun and adjective are pronounced /əsoʊʃɪt, -siɪt/.

▣ V-T If you **associate** someone or something with another thing, the two are connected in your mind. ❑ *Through science we've got the idea of associating progress with the future.* ▣ V-T If you **are associated with** a particular organization, cause, or point of view, or if you **associate** yourself with it, you support it publicly. ❑ *I haven't been associated with the project over the last year.* ▣ V-I If you say that someone **is associating with** another person or group of people, you mean they are spending a lot of time in the company of people you do not approve of. ❑ *What would they think if they knew that they were associating with a murderer?* ▣ N-COUNT Your **associates** are the people you are closely connected with, especially at work. ❑ *...the restaurant owner's business associates.* ▣ N-COUNT An **associate** is a retail worker who does not have previous experience or qualifications. ❑ *Be sure to get help from the sales associates before buying.* ▣ ADJ [ADJ n] **Associate** is used before a rank or title to indicate a slightly different or lower rank or title. ❑ *Mr. Lin is associate director of the Institute.*

as|so|ci|at|ed ◆◇◇ /əsoʊʃieɪtɪd, -sieɪt-/ ▣ ADJ If one thing is **associated** with another, the two things are connected with each other. ❑ *These symptoms are particularly associated with migraine headaches.* ▣ ADJ [ADJ n] **Associated** is used in the name of a company that is made up of a number of smaller companies that have joined together. ❑ *...the Associated Press.*

SYNONYMS
associated
ADJ ▣
connected: *The dispute is not directly connected to the negotiations.*
related: *...equipment and accessories for diving and related activities.*
allied: *...lectures on subjects allied to health, beauty, and fitness.*

as|so|ci|ate de|gree (associate degrees) N-COUNT An **associate degree** is a college degree that is awarded to a student who has completed a two-year course of study. [AM] ❑ *Such programs lead to an associate degree.*

as|so|ci|ate pro|fes|sor (associate professors) N-COUNT; N-TITLE An **associate professor** is a college teacher who ranks above an assistant professor but below a professor. [AM] ❑ *...an associate professor of psychiatry.* ❑ *...Associate Professor Saifi Karibash.*

as|so|cia|tion ◆◆◇ /əsoʊsieɪʃən, -sieɪ-/ (associations) ▣ N-COUNT An **association** is an official group of people who have the same job, aim, or interest. ❑ *...the National Basketball Association.* ▣ N-COUNT Your **association** with a person or a thing such as an organization is the connection that you have with them. ❑ *...the company's six-year association with retailer J.C. Penney Co.* ▣ N-COUNT If something has particular **associations** for you, it is connected in your mind with a particular memory, idea, or feeling. ❑ *He has a shelf full of things, each of which has associations for him.* ▣ PHRASE If you do something **in association with** someone else, you do it together. ❑ *The changes I instigated in association with the board 18 months ago were because I love this company.*

SYNONYMS
association
NOUN
▣
club: *...a youth club.*
union: *...the question of which countries should join the currency union.*
society: *...the North of England Horticultural Society.*
league: *...the League of Nations.*
coalition: *He was opposed by a coalition of civil rights and women's organizations.*
▣
friendship: *She struck up a close friendship with Desiree during rehearsals.*
relationship: *...the friendly relationship between France and Britain.*
link: *Kiev hopes to cement close links with Bonn.*
tie: *Quebec has always had particularly close ties to France.*

as|so|cia|tive /əsoʊsieɪtɪv, -sieɪ-, -ʃə-/ ADJ [usu ADJ n] **Associative** thoughts are things that you think of because you see, hear, or think of something that reminds you of those things or which you associate with those things. ❑ *The associative guilt was ingrained in his soul.*

as|sort|ed /əsɔrtɪd/ ADJ A group of **assorted** things is a group of similar things that are of different sizes or colors or have different qualities. ❑ *It should be a great week, with overnight stops in assorted hotels in the Adirondacks.*

as|sort|ment /əsɔrtmənt/ (assortments) N-COUNT An **assortment** is a group of similar things that are of different sizes or colors or have different qualities. ❑ *...an assortment of cheese.*

asst. Asst. is an abbreviation for **assistant**.

as|suage /əsweɪdʒ/ (assuages, assuaging, assuaged) ▣ V-T If you **assuage** an unpleasant feeling that someone has, you make them feel it less strongly. [LITERARY] ❑ *To assuage his wife's grief, he took her on a tour of Europe.* ▣ V-T If you **assuage** a need or desire for something, you satisfy it. [LITERARY] ❑ *The meat they'd managed to procure assuaged their hunger.*

as|sume ◆◆◇ /əsum/ (assumes, assuming, assumed) ▣ V-T If you **assume** that something is true, you imagine that it is true, sometimes wrongly. ❑ *It is a misconception to assume that the two continents are similar.* ❑ *If mistakes occurred, they were assumed to be the fault of the commander on the spot.* ▣ V-T If someone **assumes** power or responsibility, they take power or responsibility. ◻ *Mr. Cross will assume the role of CEO with a team of four directors.* **3** V-T If you **assume** a particular expression or way of behaving, you start to look or behave in this way. ◻ *He managed to assume an air of calm.*

as|sumed name (**assumed names**) N-COUNT [usu *under* N] If you do something under an **assumed name**, you do it using a name that is not your real name.

as|sum|ing /əsuːmɪŋ/ CONJ You use **assuming** or **assuming that** when you are considering a possible situation or event, so that you can think about the consequences. ◻ *"Assuming you're right," he said, "there's not much I can do about it, is there?"*

as|sump|tion ♦◇◇ /əsʌmpʃən/ (**assumptions**) N-COUNT If you make an **assumption** that something is true or will happen, you accept that it is true or will happen, often without any real proof. ◻ *You would be making an assumption that's not based on any fact that you could report.*

SYNONYMS

assumption
NOUN
presumption: *...the presumption that a defendant is innocent until proven guilty.*
guess: *Well, we can hazard a guess at the answer.*
inference: *There were two inferences to be drawn from her letter.*
conjecture: *That was a conjecture, not a fact.*
supposition: *There's a popular supposition that we're publicly funded.*

---

as|sur|ance /əʃʊərəns/ (**assurances**) **1** N-VAR If you give someone an **assurance** that something is true or will happen, you say that it is definitely true or will definitely happen, in order to make them feel less worried. ◻ *He would like an assurance that other forces will not move into the territory that his forces vacate.* **2** N-UNCOUNT If you do something with **assurance**, you do it with a feeling of confidence and certainty. ◻ *Masur led the orchestra with assurance.*

as|sure /əʃʊər/ (**assures, assuring, assured**) **1** V-T If you **assure** someone that something is true or will happen, you tell them that it is definitely true or will definitely happen, often in order to make them less worried. ◻ *He hastened to assure me that there was nothing traumatic to report.* ◻ *"Are you sure the raft is safe?" she asked anxiously. "Couldn't be safer," Max assured her confidently.* **2** → see also **assured** **3** V-T To **assure** someone of something means to make certain that they will get it. ◻ *His performance yesterday morning assured him of a record eighth medal.* **4** PHRASE You use phrases such as **I can assure you** or **let me assure you** to emphasize the truth of what you are saying. [EMPHASIS] ◻ *I can assure you that the animals are well cared for.*

as|sured ♦◇◇ /əʃʊərd/ **1** ADJ Someone who is **assured** is very confident and relaxed. ◻ *He was infinitely more assured than in his more recent concert appearances.* **2** ADJ [v-link ADJ] If something is **assured**, it is certain to happen. ◻ *Our victory is assured; nothing can stop us.* **3** ADJ [v-link ADJ *of* n] If you are **assured of** something, you are certain to get it or achieve it. ◻ *Laura Davies is assured of a place in the team.* **4** PHRASE If you say that someone **can rest assured** that something is the case, you mean that it is definitely the case, so they do not need to worry about it. [EMPHASIS] ◻ *Their parents can rest assured that their children's safety will be of paramount importance.*

as|sur|ed|ly /əʃʊərɪdli/ ADV If something is **assuredly** true, it is definitely true. ◻ *He is, assuredly, not alone in believing they will win.* ◻ *"I did not say that."—"You most assuredly did."*

as|ter|isk /æstərɪsk/ (**asterisks**) N-COUNT An **asterisk** is the sign *. It is used especially to indicate that there is further information about something in another part of the text.

astern /əstɜːrn/ ADV [be ADV] Something that is **astern** is at the back of a ship or behind the back part. [TECHNICAL]

as|ter|oid /æstərɔɪd/ (**asteroids**) **1** N-COUNT An **asteroid** is one of the very small planets that move around the sun, especially between Mars and Jupiter. **2** → See feature box at **space**

asth|ma /æzmə/ N-UNCOUNT **Asthma** is a lung condition that causes difficulty in breathing.

asth|mat|ic /æzmætɪk/ (**asthmatics**) **1** N-COUNT People who have asthma are sometimes referred to as **asthmatics**. ◻ *I have been an asthmatic from childhood and was never able to play any sports.* • ADJ **Asthmatic** is also an adjective. ◻ *One child in ten is asthmatic.* **2** ADJ [ADJ n] **Asthmatic** means relating to asthma. ◻ *...asthmatic breathing.*

astig|ma|tism /əstɪgmətɪzəm/ N-UNCOUNT If someone has **astigmatism**, the front of their eye has a slightly irregular shape, so they cannot see properly.

aston|ish /əstɒnɪʃ/ (**astonishes, astonishing, astonished**) V-T If something or someone **astonishes** you, they surprise you very much. ◻ *My news will astonish you.*

aston|ished /əstɒnɪʃt/ ADJ If you are **astonished** by something, you are very surprised about it. ◻ *They were astonished to find the driver was a six-year-old boy.*

aston|ish|ing /əstɒnɪʃɪŋ/ ADJ Something that is **astonishing** is very surprising. ◻ *...an astonishing display of physical strength.* • **aston|ish|ing|ly** ADV ◻ *Andrea was an astonishingly beautiful young woman.*

aston|ish|ment /əstɒnɪʃmənt/ N-UNCOUNT **Astonishment** is a feeling of great surprise. ◻ *I spotted a shooting star which, to my astonishment, was bright green in color.*

astound /əstaʊnd/ (**astounds, astounding, astounded**) V-T If something **astounds** you, you are very surprised by it. ◻ *He used to astound his friends with feats of physical endurance.*

astound|ed /əstaʊndɪd/ ADJ If you are **astounded** by something, you are very shocked or surprised that it could exist or happen. ◻ *I was astounded by its beauty.* ◻ *I am astounded at the comments made by the Senator.*

astound|ing /əstaʊndɪŋ/ ADJ If something is **astounding**, you are shocked or amazed that it could exist or happen. ◻ *The results are quite astounding.*

as|tra|khan /æstrəkæn/ N-UNCOUNT [usu N n] **Astrakhan** is black or gray curly fur from the skins of lambs. It is used for making coats and hats. ◻ *...a coat with an astrakhan collar.*

as|tral /æstrəl/ ADJ **Astral** means relating to the stars. [FORMAL]

astray /əstreɪ/ **1** PHRASE If you **are led astray** by someone or something, you behave badly or foolishly because of them. ◻ *The judge thought he'd been led astray by older children.* **2** PHRASE If someone or something **leads** you **astray**, they make you believe something that is not true, causing you to make a wrong decision. ◻ *The testimony would inflame the jurors, and lead them astray from the facts of the case.* **3** PHRASE If something **goes astray**, it gets lost while it is being taken or sent somewhere. ◻ *Many items of mail being sent to her have gone astray.*

astride /əstraɪd/ PREP If you sit or stand **astride** something, you sit or stand with one leg on each side of it. ◻ *...three youths who stood astride their bicycles and stared.*

as|trin|gent /əstrɪndʒənt/ (**astringents**) N-COUNT An **astringent** is a liquid that you put on your skin to make it less oily or to make cuts stop bleeding. • ADJ [ADJ n] **Astringent** is also an adjective. ◻ *...an astringent lotion.*

PREFIX

astro-
is used to form words which refer to things relating to the stars or to outer space. For example, **astronomy** is the scientific study of the stars, the planets and other objects in space.

---

as|trolo|ger /əstrɒlədʒər/ (**astrologers**) N-COUNT An **astrologer** is a person who uses astrology to try to tell you things about your character and your future.

as|trol|ogy /əstrɒlədʒi/ N-UNCOUNT **Astrology** is the study of the movements of the planets, sun, moon, and stars in the belief that these movements can have an influence on people's lives.

as|tro|naut /æstrənɔːt/ (**astronauts**) N-COUNT An **astronaut** is a person who is trained for traveling in a spacecraft.

as|trono|mer /əstrɒnəmər/ (**astronomers**) **1** N-COUNT An **astronomer** is a scientist who studies the stars, planets, and other natural objects in space. **2** → See feature box at **space**

as|tro|nomi|cal /æstrənɒmɪkəl/ **1** ADJ If you describe an amount, especially the cost of something as **astronomical**, you are emphasizing that it is very large. [EMPHASIS]

astronomy | 74 | **athletics**

❏ *Houses in the subdivision are going for astronomical prices.* ◻ ADJ **Astronomical** means relating to astronomy. ❏ *...the American Astronomical Society.*

as|trono|my /əstrɒnəmi/ N-UNCOUNT **Astronomy** is the scientific study of the stars, planets, and other natural objects in space.

as|tro|physi|cist /æstroʊfɪzɪsɪst/ (astrophysicists) N-COUNT An **astrophysicist** is someone who studies astrophysics.

as|tro|phys|ics /æstroʊfɪzɪks/ N-UNCOUNT **Astrophysics** is the study of the physical and chemical structure of the stars, planets, and other natural objects in space.

As|tro|turf /æstroʊtɜrf/ N-UNCOUNT **Astroturf** is a type of artificial fiber that is used instead of grass on some sports fields. [TRADEMARK] ❏ *Last year our home field was Astroturf and everyone hated it.*

A-student (A-students) also **A student** N-COUNT An **A-student** is a student who regularly receives the highest grades for his or her work. [mainly AM] ❏ *...good, hard-working A students.*

as|tute /əstut/ ADJ If you describe someone as **astute**, you think they show an understanding of behavior and situations, and are skillful at using this knowledge to their own advantage. ❏ *She was politically astute.*

asun|der /əsʌndər/ ADV [ADV after v] If something tears or is torn **asunder**, it is violently separated into two or more parts or pieces. [LITERARY]

asy|lum /əsaɪləm/ (asylums) ◼ N-UNCOUNT If a government gives a person from another country **asylum**, they allow them to stay, usually because they are unable to return home safely for political reasons. ❏ *A significant number of people have applied for asylum in the UK.* ◼ N-COUNT An **asylum** is a psychiatric hospital. [OLD-FASHIONED]

asy|lum seek|er (asylum seekers) N-COUNT An **asylum seeker** is a person who is trying to get asylum in a foreign country. ❏ *Fewer than 7% of asylum seekers are accepted as political refugees.*

asym|met|ric /eɪsɪmɛtrɪk/ ADJ **Asymmetric** means the same as **asymmetrical**.

asym|met|ri|cal /eɪsɪmɛtrɪkᵊl/ ADJ Something that is **asymmetrical** has two sides or halves that are different in shape, size, or style. ❏ *...asymmetrical shapes.*

asym|me|try /eɪsɪmɪtri/ (asymmetries) N-VAR **Asymmetry** is the appearance that something has when its two sides or halves are different in shape, size, or style. ❏ *...the asymmetry of Van de Velde's designs of this period.*

asymp|to|mat|ic /eɪsɪmptəmætɪk/ ADJ If someone with a disease is **asymptomatic**, they do not show any symptoms of the disease. [MEDICAL] ❏ *I had patients who had Covid and were asymptomatic.*

at ♦♦♦ /ət, STRONG æt/

In addition to the uses shown below, **at** is used after some verbs, nouns, and adjectives to introduce extra information. **At** is also used in phrasal verbs such as 'have at' and 'play at.'

◼ PREP You use **at** to indicate the place or event where something happens or is situated. ❏ *He will be at the airport to meet her.* ❏ *I didn't like being alone at home.* ❏ *They agreed to meet at a restaurant in Soho.* ◼ PREP If you are **at** something such as a table, a door, or someone's side, you are next to it or them. ❏ *An assistant sat typing away at a table beside him.* ❏ *At his side was a beautiful young woman.* ◼ PREP When you are describing where someone or something is, you can say that they are **at** a certain distance. You can also say that one thing is **at** an angle in relation to another thing. ❏ *The two journalists followed at a discreet distance.* ◼ PREP If something happens **at** a particular time, that is the time when it happens or begins to happen. ❏ *The funeral will be carried out this afternoon at 3:00.* ◼ PREP If you do something **at** a particular age, you do it when you are that age. ❏ *Zachary started playing violin at age 4.* ◼ PREP If someone is **at** a particular school or college, they go there regularly to study. ❏ *Their daughter is a sophomore at Yale.* ◼ PREP You use **at** to express a rate, frequency, level, or price. ❏ *I drove back down the highway at normal speed.* ❏ *Check the oil at regular intervals, and* have the car serviced regularly. ◼ PREP [PREP amount] You use **at** before a number or amount to indicate a measurement. ❏ *...as unemployment stays pegged at three million.* ◼ PREP If you look at someone or something, you look toward them. If you direct an object or a comment **at** someone, you direct it toward them. ❏ *He looked at Michael and laughed.* ◼ PREP [V PREP n] You can use **at** after verbs such as 'smile' or 'wave' and before nouns referring to people to indicate that you have put on an expression or made a gesture that someone is meant to see or understand. ❏ *She opened the door and stood there, frowning at me.* ◼ PREP [V PREP n] If you point or gesture **at** something, you move your arm or head in its direction so that it will be noticed by someone you are with. ❏ *He pointed at the empty jug and the waiter quickly replaced it.* ◼ PREP If you are working **at** something, you are dealing with it. If you are aiming **at** something, you are trying to achieve it. ❏ *She has worked hard at her marriage.* ◼ PREP [PREP n with poss] If something is done **at** someone's invitation or request, it is done as a result of it. ❏ *She left the light on in the bathroom at his request.* ◼ PREP [v-link PREP n] You use **at** to say that someone or something is in a particular state or condition. ❏ *I am afraid we are not at liberty to disclose that information.* ◼ PREP You use **at** before a possessive pronoun and a superlative adjective to say that someone or something has more of a particular quality than at any other time. ❏ *When I'm on the soccer field, I'm at my happiest.* ◼ PREP You use **at** to say how something is being done. ❏ *Three people were killed by shots fired at random from a minibus.* ◼ PREP [V PREP n] You use **at** to show that someone is doing something repeatedly. ❏ *She lowered the handkerchief which she had kept dabbing at her eyes.* ◼ PREP You use **at** to indicate an activity or task when saying how well someone does it. ❏ *I'm good at my work.* ◼ PREP You use **at** to indicate what someone is reacting to. ❏ *Elena was annoyed at having had to wait so long for him.* ◼ **at all** → see **all** ②

ata|vis|tic /ætəvɪstɪk/ ADJ [usu ADJ n] **Atavistic** feelings or behavior seem to be very primitive, like the feelings or behavior of our earliest ancestors. [FORMAL] ❏ *...an atavistic fear of snakes.*

at bat (at bats) also **at-bat** N-COUNT In baseball, an **at bat** is a turn at hitting the ball. [AM] ❏ *Alfonzo finally hit a homer in his 150th at bat of the season.*

ate /eɪt/ **Ate** is the past tense of **eat**.

at|el|ier /ætəlyeɪ/ (ateliers) N-COUNT An **atelier** is an artist's studio or workshop.

athe|ism /eɪθiɪzəm/ N-UNCOUNT **Atheism** is the belief that there is no God. Compare **agnosticism**. ❏ *Many young people were rejecting the atheism of their Communist rulers.*

athe|ist /eɪθiɪst/ (atheists) N-COUNT An **atheist** is a person who believes that there is no God. Compare **agnostic**.

athe|is|tic /eɪθiɪstɪk/ ADJ **Atheistic** means connected with or holding the belief that there is no God. ❏ *...atheistic philosophers.*

ath|lete ♦◇◇ /æθlit/ (athletes) ◼ N-COUNT An **athlete** is a person who does any kind of physical sports, exercise, or games, especially in competitions. ❏ *Mark Spitz was a great athlete.* ◼ N-COUNT You can refer to someone who is fit and athletic as an **athlete**. ❏ *I was no athlete.* ◼ → See feature box at **Olympic Games**

ath|lete's foot N-UNCOUNT **Athlete's foot** is a fungal infection in which the skin between the toes becomes cracked or peels off.

ath|let|ic /æθlɛtɪk/ ◼ ADJ [ADJ n] **Athletic** means relating to athletes and athletics. ❏ *They have been given college scholarships purely on athletic ability.* ◼ ADJ An **athletic** person is fit, and able to perform energetic movements easily. ❏ *Xandra is an athletic 36-year-old with a 21-year-old's body.*

ath|leti|cism /æθlɛtɪsɪzəm/ N-UNCOUNT **Athleticism** is someone's fitness and ability to perform well at sports or other physical activities.

ath|let|ics /æθlɛtɪks/ ◼ N-UNCOUNT **Athletics** refers to any kind of physical sports, exercise, or games. [AM] ❏ *...students who play intercollegiate athletics.* ◼ N-UNCOUNT **Athletics** refers to track and field sports such as running, the high jump, and the javelin. [mainly BRIT]

in AM, use **track and field**

> **SUFFIX**
>
> **-ation**
> forms nouns that refer to a state or process, or to an instance of that process. *For example,* **formation** *is the process of forming something.*

at|las /ǽtləs/ (atlases) N-COUNT An **atlas** is a book of maps.

ATM /eɪ ti ɛm/ (ATMs) N-COUNT An **ATM** is a machine that allows people to take out money from their bank account by using a special card. **ATM** is an abbreviation for 'automated teller machine.' [mainly AM] ❑ *Keep your ATM card in a safe place.*

in BRIT, usually use **cash dispenser, cashpoint**

at|mos|phere ◆◇◇ /ǽtməsfɪər/ (atmospheres) ■ N-COUNT A planet's **atmosphere** is the layer of air or other gases around it. ❑ *The shuttle Columbia will re-enter Earth's atmosphere tomorrow morning.* ◙ N-COUNT The **atmosphere** of a place is the air that you breathe there. ❑ *These gases pollute the atmosphere of towns and cities.* ◘ N-SING The **atmosphere** of a place is the general impression that you get of it. ❑ *There's still an atmosphere of great hostility and tension in the city.* ◚ N-UNCOUNT If a place or an event has **atmosphere**, it is interesting. ❑ *The old harbor is still full of atmosphere and well worth visiting.* ◛ → See feature box at **global warming**; See also color supplement

> **SYNONYMS**
>
> **atmosphere**
> NOUN ◘
> **feel:** *The room has a warm, cozy feel.*
> **mood:** *First, set the mood with music.*
> **ambience:** *The overall ambience of the room is cozy.*

> **COLLOCATIONS**
>
> **atmosphere**
> NOUN ◘
> noun + **atmosphere:** carnival, festival, party; village
> adjective + **atmosphere:** convivial, friendly, intimate, relaxed; electric, incredible; febrile, hostile, tense
> verb + **atmosphere:** create

at|mos|pher|ic /ǽtməsfɛrɪk/ ■ ADJ **Atmospheric** is used to describe something that relates to the Earth's atmosphere. ❑ *...atmospheric gases.* ◙ ADJ If you describe a place or a piece of music as **atmospheric**, you like it because it has a particular quality that is interesting or exciting and makes you feel a particular emotion. [APPROVAL] ❑ *One of the most atmospheric corners of Prague is the old Jewish ghetto.*

at|mo|spher|ic pres|sure N-UNCOUNT **Atmospheric pressure** is the pressure of the atmosphere on the Earth's surface.

at|mos|pher|ics /ǽtməsfɛrɪks/ N-PLURAL **Atmospherics** are elements in something such as a piece of music or a book which create a certain atmosphere. ❑ *...Dickensian atmospherics.*

at|oll /ǽtɒl/ (atolls) N-COUNT An **atoll** is a ring of coral rock, or a group of coral islands surrounding a lagoon.

at|om /ǽtəm/ (atoms) ■ N-COUNT An **atom** is the smallest amount of a substance that can take part in a chemical reaction. ❑ *...the news that Einstein's former colleagues Otto Hahn and Fritz Strassmann had split the atom.* ◙ → See feature box at **electricity**

atom|ic /ətɒmɪk/ ■ ADJ **Atomic** means relating to power that is produced from the energy released by splitting atoms. ❑ *...atomic energy.* ◙ ADJ [ADJ n] **Atomic** means relating to the atoms of substances. ❑ *...the atomic number of an element.*

atom|ic bomb (atomic bombs) also **atom bomb** N-COUNT An **atomic bomb** or an **atom bomb** is a bomb that causes an explosion by a sudden release of energy that results from splitting atoms.

aton|al /eɪtoʊnəl/ ADJ [usu ADJ n] **Atonal** music is music that is not written or played in any key or system of scales.

atone /ətoʊn/ (atones, atoning, atoned) V-I If you **atone for** something that you have done, you do something to show that you are sorry you did it. [FORMAL] ❑ *He felt he had atoned for what he had done to his son.*

atone|ment /ətoʊnmənt/ N-UNCOUNT [oft N for n] If you do something as an **atonement** for doing something wrong, you do it to show that you are sorry. [FORMAL] ❑ *He's living in a monastery in a gesture of atonement for human rights abuses committed under his leadership.*

atop /ətɒp/ PREP If something is **atop** something else, it is on top of it. [AM] ❑ *Under the newspaper, atop a sheet of paper, lay an envelope.*

A to Z /eɪ tə zi/ (A to Zs) N-SING [usu N of n] An **A to Z** of a particular subject is a book or program that gives information on all aspects of it, arranging it in alphabetical order. ❑ *An A to Z of careers gives helpful information about courses.*

atrium /eɪtriəm/ (atriums) ■ N-COUNT An **atrium** is a part of a building such as a hotel or shopping center that extends up through several floors of the building and often has a glass roof. ◙ N-COUNT The **atrium** is the upper part of each half of the heart. [MEDICAL] ◘ → See also color supplement

atro|cious /ətroʊʃəs/ ■ ADJ If you describe something as **atrocious**, you are emphasizing that its quality is very bad. [EMPHASIS] ❑ *I remain to this day fluent in Hebrew, while my Arabic is atrocious.* ◙ ADJ If you describe someone's behavior or their actions as **atrocious**, you mean that it is unacceptable because it is extremely violent or cruel. ❑ *The judge said he had committed atrocious crimes against women.*

atroc|ity /ətrɒsɪti/ (atrocities) N-VAR An **atrocity** is a very cruel, shocking action. ❑ *The killing was cold-blooded, and those who committed this atrocity should be tried and punished.*

at|ro|phy /ǽtrəfi/ (atrophies, atrophying, atrophied) V-T/V-I If a muscle or other part of the body **atrophies**, it decreases in size or strength, often as a result of an illness. [FORMAL]

at|tach ◆◇◇ /ətǽtʃ/ (attaches, attaching, attached) ■ V-T If you **attach** something to an object, you join it or fasten it to the object. ❑ *We attach labels to things before we file them away.* ❑ *For further information, please contact us on the attached form.* ◙ V-T In computing, if you **attach** a file to a message that you send to someone, you send it with the message but separate from it. ❑ *It is possible to attach executable program files to email.* ◘ → see also **attached** ◚ **no strings attached** → see **string**

> **SYNONYMS**
>
> **attach**
> VERB ■
> **stick:** *Clip the token and stick it on your card.*
> **bind:** *Bind the ends of the cord together with thread.*
> **join:** *The link is used to join the two ends of the chain.*
> **fix:** *It is fixed on the wall.*
> **fasten:** *Mamma fastened the picture on the wall.*

at|ta|ché /ǽtæʃeɪ/ (attachés) N-COUNT [usu supp N] An **attaché** is an employee in an embassy, usually with a special responsibility for something.

at|ta|ché case (attaché cases) N-COUNT An **attaché case** is a flat case for carrying documents.

at|tached /ətǽtʃt/ ■ ADJ [v-link ADJ to n] If you are **attached to** someone or something, you like them very much. ❑ *She is very attached to her family and friends.* ◙ ADJ [v-link ADJ to n] If someone is **attached to** an organization or group of people, they are working with them, often only for a short time. ❑ *Ford was attached to the 101st Airborne Division.*

at|tach|ment /ətǽtʃmənt/ (attachments) ■ N-VAR If you have an **attachment to** someone or something, you are fond of them or loyal to them. ❑ *As a teenager she formed a strong attachment to one of her teachers.* ◙ N-COUNT An **attachment** is a device that can be fixed onto a machine in order to enable it to do different jobs. ❑ *Some models come with attachments for dusting.* ◘ N-COUNT In computing, an **attachment** is a file which is attached separately to a message that you send to someone. ❑ *When you send an email you can also send a file as an attachment and that file can be a graphic, a program, a sound or whatever.* ◚ → See feature box at **email**

at|tack ◆◆◇ /ətǽk/ (attacks, attacking, attacked) ■ V-T/V-I To **attack** a person or place means to try to hurt or damage them using physical violence. ❑ *Fifty civilians in Masawa were killed when government planes attacked the town.* ❑ *The robbers brutally attacked the security guard.* ❑ *They found the least defended area and attacked.* • N-VAR **Attack** is also a noun. ❑ *...a campaign of air attacks on strategic targets.* ◙ V-T If you **attack** a person, belief, idea, or act, you criticize them strongly. ❑ *He publicly* attacked the people who've been calling for secret ballot nominations. • N-VAR [usu with supp] **Attack** is also a noun. ❏ *The role of the state as a prime mover in planning social change has been under attack.* ❸ V-T If something such as a disease, a chemical, or an insect **attacks** something, it harms or spoils it. ❏ *The virus seems to have attacked his throat.* • N-UNCOUNT [also N in pl] **Attack** is also a noun. ❏ *The virus can actually destroy those white blood cells, leaving the body wide open to attack from other infections.* ❹ V-T If you **attack** a job or a problem, you start to deal with it in an energetic way. ❏ *Any attempt to attack the budget problem is going to have to in some way deal with those issues.* ❺ V-T/V-I In games such as soccer, when one team **attacks** the opponent's goal, they try to score a goal. ❏ *Now the U.S. is controlling the ball and attacking the opponent's goal.* ❏ *The goal was just reward for their decision to attack constantly in the second half.* • N-COUNT **Attack** is also a noun. ❏ *Lee was at the hub of some more incisive attacks in the second half.* ❻ N-COUNT An **attack** of an illness is a short period in which you suffer badly from it. ❏ *It had brought on an attack of asthma.* ❼ → see also **counterattack, heart attack** ❽ → See feature box at **debate**

at|tack|er /ətǽkər/ (**attackers**) N-COUNT You can refer to a person who attacks someone as their **attacker**. ❏ *There were signs that she struggled with her attacker before she was stabbed.*

at|tain /ətéɪn/ (**attains, attaining, attained**) V-T If you **attain** something, you gain it or achieve it, often after a lot of effort. [FORMAL] ❏ *Jim is halfway to attaining his pilot's license.*

at|tain|able /ətéɪnəb³l/ ADJ Something that is **attainable** can be achieved. ❏ *...an attainable goal.*

at|tain|ment /ətéɪnmənt/ (**attainments**) ❶ N-UNCOUNT The **attainment** of an aim is the achieving of it. [FORMAL] ❏ *...the attainment of independence.* ❷ N-COUNT An **attainment** is a skill you have learned or something you have achieved. [FORMAL] ❏ *...their educational attainments.*

at|tempt ✦✧✧ /ətémpt/ (**attempts, attempting, attempted**) ❶ V-T If you **attempt** to do something, especially something difficult, you try to do it. ❏ *The only time that we attempted to do something like that was in the city of Philadelphia.* ❷ N-COUNT If you make an **attempt** to do something, you try to do it, often without success. ❏ *...a deliberate attempt to destabilize the defense.* ❸ N-COUNT An **attempt on** someone's life is an attempt to kill them. ❏ *...an attempt on the life of the former Iranian prime minister.*

COLLOCATIONS
attempt
NOUN ❷
noun + **attempt**: assassination, coup; escape, rescue; takeover
adjective + **attempt**: abortive, botched, failed, futile, unsuccessful, vain; desperate; brave, valiant
verb + **attempt**: block, defeat, foil, frustrate, prevent; make

SYNONYMS
attempt
VERB ❶
seek: *He also denied that he would seek to annex the country.*
try: *I tried calling him when I got here, but he wasn't at home.*
aim: *...an appeal which aims to raise funds for cancer research.*
strive: *He strives hard to keep himself very fit.*
endeavor: *They are endeavoring to protect trade union rights*
NOUN ❷
try: *After a few tries, Patrick gave up any attempt to reform her.*
bid: *...Sydney's successful bid for the 2000 Olympic Games®.*
shot: *The heavyweight champion will get a shot at the world title.*
go: *I always wanted to have a go at soccer.*
effort: *...his efforts to reform Italian research.*

at|tempt|ed /ətémptɪd/ ADJ [ADJ n] An **attempted** crime or unlawful action is an unsuccessful effort to commit the crime or carry out the action. ❏ *...a case of attempted murder.*

at|tend ✦✦✧ /əténd/ (**attends, attending, attended**) ❶ V-T/V-I If you **attend** a meeting or other event, you are present at it. ❏ *Thousands of people attended the funeral.* ❏ *The meeting will be attended by finance ministers from many countries.* ❏ *The senator was invited but was unable to attend.* ❷ V-T If you **attend** an institution such as a school, college, or church, you go there regularly. ❏ *They attended college together at the University of Pennsylvania.* ❸ V-I If you **attend** to something, you deal with it. If you **attend** to someone who is hurt or injured, you care for them. ❏ *He took a short leave of absence to attend to personal business.*

COLLOCATIONS
attend
VERB
❶
attend + noun: ceremony, event, function, party, reception, service; conference, hearing, meeting, session; class, course, seminar, workshop; funeral, wedding
❷
attend + noun: college, school, university; church

at|tend|ance /əténdəns/ (**attendances**) ❶ N-UNCOUNT Someone's **attendance** at an event or an institution is the fact that they are present at the event or go regularly to the institution. ❏ *Her attendance in school was sporadic.* ❷ N-VAR The **attendance** at an event is the number of people who are present at it. ❏ *Rain played a big part in the air show's drop in attendance.*

at|tend|ant /əténdənt/ (**attendants**) ❶ N-COUNT An **attendant** is someone whose job is to serve or help people in a place such as a gas station or a parking lot. ❏ *Tony Williams was working as a parking lot attendant in Los Angeles.* ❷ → see also **flight attendant** ❸ N-COUNT The **attendants** at a wedding are people such as the bridesmaids and the ushers, who accompany or help the bride and groom. ❏ *If the bride pays, she has the right to decide on the style of dress worn by her attendants.*

at|tend|ee /əténdí/ (**attendees**) N-COUNT The **attendees** at something such as a meeting or a conference are the people who are attending it. [mainly AM]

at|tend|er /əténdər/ (**attenders**) N-COUNT The **attenders** at a particular place or event are the people who go there. ❏ *He was a regular attender at the opera.*

at|tend|ing /əténdɪŋ/ (**attendings**) N-COUNT An **attending** is a senior doctor in a hospital.

at|ten|tion ✦✦✧ /əténʃ³n/ ❶ N-UNCOUNT If you give someone or something your **attention**, you look at it, listen to it, or think about it carefully. ❏ *You have my undivided attention.* ❏ *Later he turned his attention to the desperate state of housing in the city.* ❷ N-UNCOUNT **Attention** is great interest that is shown in someone or something, particularly by the general public. ❏ *Volume Two, subtitled "The Lawyers," will also attract considerable attention.* ❸ N-UNCOUNT If someone or something is getting **attention**, they are being dealt with or cared for. ❏ *Each year more than two million household injuries need medical attention.* ❹ N-UNCOUNT If you **bring** something to someone's **attention** or **draw** their **attention** to it, you tell them about it or make them notice it. ❏ *If we don't keep bringing this to the attention of the people, nothing will be done.* ❺ PHRASE If someone or something **attracts** your **attention** or **catches** your **attention**, you suddenly notice them. ❏ *A faint aroma of coffee attracted his attention.* ❻ PHRASE If you **pay attention** to someone, you watch them, listen to them, or take notice of them. If you **pay no attention** to someone, you behave as if you are not aware of them or as if they are not important. ❏ *More than ever before, the food industry is paying attention to young consumers.* ❼ PHRASE When people **stand at attention**, they stand straight with their feet together and their arms at their sides. ❏ *Soldiers in full combat gear stood at attention.* ❽ → See feature box at **drive**

COLLOCATIONS
attention
NOUN
❶
adjective + **attention**: careful, close, full, undivided; particular, special
verb + **attention**: give; have
❷
noun + **attention**: media, press
adjective + **attention**: unwanted, unwelcome, international, national, public
verb + **attention**: attract, catch, command, grab; deflect, distract, divert; focus
❸
adjective + **attention**: medical; immediate, urgent
verb + **attention**: receive, require

SYNONYMS

attention
NOUN

1
thought: *Usually at this time, our thoughts are on Christmas.*
mind: *I put what happened during that game in the back of my mind.*
scrutiny: *His private life came under media scrutiny.*
observation: *She has good powers of observation.*

3
care: *Most of the staff specialize in the care of children.*
support: *We hope to continue to have her close support and friendship.*
treatment: *...a veterinary surgeon who specializes in the treatment of wild birds.*

at|ten|tion defi|cit dis|or|der N-UNCOUNT **Attention deficit disorder** is a condition where people, especially children, are unable to concentrate on anything for very long and so find it difficult to learn and often behave in inappropriate ways. The abbreviation **ADD** is often used.

at|ten|tion defi|cit hyper|ac|tiv|ity dis|or|der N-UNCOUNT **Attention deficit hyperactivity disorder** is a condition where people, especially children, are extremely active and unable to concentrate on anything for very long, with the result that they find it difficult to learn and often behave in inappropriate ways. The abbreviation **ADHD** is often used.

attention-grabbing ADJ [usu ADJ n] An **attention-grabbing** remark or activity is one that is intended to make people notice it. ☐ *...an attention-grabbing marketing campaign.*

at|ten|tive /ətɛntɪv/ **1** ADJ If you are **attentive**, you are paying close attention to what is being said or done. ☐ *He wishes the government would be more attentive to detail in their response.* • **at|ten|tive|ly** ADV ☐ *He questioned Chrissie, and listened attentively to what she told him.* **2** ADJ Someone who is **attentive** is helpful and polite. ☐ *At society parties he is attentive to his wife.*

at|tenu|ate /ətɛnyueɪt/ (**attenuates, attenuating, attenuated**) V-T To **attenuate** something means to reduce it or weaken it. [FORMAL] ☐ *You could never eliminate risk, but preparation and training could attenuate it.*

at|tenu|at|ed /ətɛnyueɪtɪd/ ADJ An **attenuated** object is unusually long and thin. [FORMAL] ☐ *...round arches and attenuated columns.*

at|test /ətɛst/ (**attests, attesting, attested**) V-T/V-I To **attest** something or **attest to** something means to say, show, or prove that it is true. [FORMAL] ☐ *Police records attest to his long history of violence.*

at|tic /ætɪk/ (**attics**) N-COUNT An **attic** is a room at the top of a house just below the roof.

at|tire /ətaɪər/ N-UNCOUNT Your **attire** is the clothes you are wearing. [FORMAL] ☐ *...seven women dressed in their finest attire.*

at|tired /ətaɪərd/ ADJ [v-link ADJ] If you describe how someone is **attired**, you are describing how they are dressed. [FORMAL] ☐ *He was faultlessly attired in black coat and striped pants.*

at|ti|tude ✦✧ /ætɪtud/ (**attitudes**) N-VAR Your **attitude** to something is the way that you think and feel about it, especially when this shows in the way you behave. ☐ *...the general change in attitude toward people with disabilities.* ☐ *The foundation encourages positive attitudes to physical exercise amongst young people.*

COLLOCATIONS

attitude
NOUN

adjective + **attitude**: negative, positive; can-do, cavalier, laissez-faire, relaxed; aggressive, caring, hostile, responsible
verb + **attitude**: adopt, develop, reflect; affect, change, influence

SYNONYMS

attitude
NOUN

opinion: *Most who expressed an opinion spoke favorably of Thomas.*
view: *In my view, she should be stopped as soon as possible.*
point of view: *Try to look at this from my point of view.*
perspective: *The death of his father gave him a new perspective on life.*
stance: *They have maintained a consistently neutral stance.*

at|ti|tu|di|nal /ætɪtudᵊnᵊl/ [usu ADJ n] **Attitudinal** means related to people's attitudes and the way they look at their life. [FORMAL] ☐ *Does such an attitudinal change reflect real experiences in daily life?*

at|tor|ney ✦✧ /ətɜrni/ (**attorneys**) **1** N-COUNT In the United States, an **attorney** or **attorney-at-law** is a lawyer. ☐ *...a prosecuting attorney.* ☐ *At the hearing, her attorney did not enter a plea.* **2** → see also **state's attorney**

SYNONYMS

attorney
NOUN

lawyer: *Prosecution and defense lawyers are expected to deliver closing arguments next week.*
solicitor: *You will need advice from the solicitor of the town.*
counsel: *The defense counsel warned that the judge should stop the trial.*
advocate: *She was a skilled advocate, winning many of her cases.*

At|tor|ney Gen|er|al (**Attorneys General**) N-COUNT A country's **Attorney General** is its chief law officer, who advises its government or ruler.

at|tract ✦✧ /ətrækt/ (**attracts, attracting, attracted**) **1** V-T If something **attracts** people or animals, it has features that cause them to come to it. ☐ *The Cardiff Bay project is attracting many visitors.* **2** V-T If someone or something **attracts** you, they have particular qualities which cause you to like or admire them. If a particular quality **attracts** you to a person or thing, it is the reason why you like them. ☐ *He wasn't sure he'd got it right, although the theory attracted him by its logic.* **3** V-T If you **are attracted** to someone, you are interested in them sexually. ☐ *In spite of her hostility, she was attracted to him.* • **at|tract|ed** ADJ [v-link ADJ] ☐ *He was nice looking, but I wasn't deeply attracted to him.* **4** V-T If something **attracts** support, publicity, or money, it receives support, publicity, or money. ☐ *President Mwinyi said his country would also like to attract investment from private companies.* **5 to attract someone's attention** → see **attention**

SYNONYMS

attract
VERB **1**

draw: *The game is currently drawing huge crowds.*
appeal: *On the other hand, the idea appealed to him.*
lure: *They did not realize that they were being lured into a trap.*
entice: *They'll entice doctors to move from the cities by paying them better salaries.*

at|trac|tion /ətrækʃᵊn/ (**attractions**) **1** N-UNCOUNT **Attraction** is a feeling of liking someone, and often of being sexually interested in them. ☐ *Our level of attraction to the opposite sex has more to do with our inner confidence than how we look.* **2** N-COUNT An **attraction** is a feature that makes something interesting or desirable. ☐ *...the attractions of living on the waterfront.* **3** N-COUNT An **attraction** is something that people can go to for interest or enjoyment, for example, a famous building. ☐ *The walled city is an important tourist attraction.*

at|trac|tive ✦✧ /ətræktɪv/ **1** ADJ A person who is **attractive** is pleasant to look at. ☐ *She's a very attractive woman.* ☐ *I thought he was very attractive and obviously very intelligent.* • **at|trac|tive|ness** N-UNCOUNT ☐ *Most of us would maintain that physical attractiveness does not play a major part in how we react to the people we meet.* **2** ADJ Something that is **attractive** has a pleasant appearance or sound. ☐ *The apartment was small but attractive, if rather shabby.* **3** ADJ You can describe something as **attractive** when it seems worth having or doing. ☐ *Smoking is no longer attractive to many young people.* **4** → See feature box at **appearance**

attributable

at|trib|ut|able /ətrɪbyətəbəl/ ADJ [v-link ADJ to n] If something **is attributable to** an event, situation, or person, it is likely that it was caused by that event, situation, or person. ❑ *10,000 deaths a year from chronic lung disease are attributable to smoking.*

at|trib|ute (attributes, attributing, attributed)

The verb is pronounced /ətrɪbyut/. The noun is pronounced /ǽtrɪbyut/.

1 V-T If you **attribute** something to an event or situation, you think that it was caused by that event or situation. ❑ *The quarterback attributes the team's success to the arrival of the new coach.* **2** V-T If you **attribute** a particular quality or feature to someone or something, you think that they have it. ❑ *People were beginning to attribute superhuman qualities to him.* **3** V-T [usu passive] If a piece of writing, a work of art, or a remark **is attributed** to someone, people say that they wrote it, created it, or said it. ❑ *This, and the remaining frescoes, are not attributed to Giotto.* **4** N-COUNT An **attribute** is a quality or feature that someone or something has. ❑ *Cruelty is a normal attribute of human behavior.*

at|tri|tion /ətrɪʃən/ **1** N-UNCOUNT **Attrition** is a process in which you steadily reduce the strength of an enemy by continually attacking them. [FORMAL] ❑ *The rebels have declared a cease-fire in their war of attrition against the government.* **2** N-UNCOUNT At a university or place of work, **attrition** is the decrease in the number of students or employees caused by people leaving and not being replaced. [mainly AM] ❑ *The company cut its workforce through natural attrition and fewer hirings.*

at|tuned /ətund/ **1** ADJ [v-link ADJ to n] If you are **attuned** to something, you can understand and appreciate it. ❑ *He seemed unusually attuned to people's feelings.* **2** ADJ [v-link ADJ to n] If your ears **are attuned** to a sound, you can hear it and recognize it quickly. ❑ *Their ears were still attuned to the sounds of the farm machinery.*

ATV /eɪ ti vi/ (**ATVs**) N-COUNT An **ATV** is a kind of motorbike with four large wheels that people ride for fun or in races. ATV is an abbreviation for **all-terrain vehicle**.

atypi|cal /eɪtɪpɪkəl/ ADJ Someone or something that is **atypical** is not typical of its kind. ❑ *The economy of the province was atypical because it was particularly small.*

auber|gine /oʊbərʒin/ N-VAR [BRIT] → see **eggplant**

auburn /ɔbərn/ COLOR **Auburn** hair is reddish brown. ❑ *...a tall woman with long auburn hair.*

auc|tion ✦◇◇ /ɔkʃən/ (**auctions, auctioning, auctioned**) **1** N-VAR An **auction** is a public sale where items are sold to the person who offers the highest price. ❑ *The painting is expected to fetch up to $400,000 at auction.* **2** V-T If something **is auctioned**, it is sold in an auction. ❑ *Eight drawings by French artist Jean Cocteau will be auctioned next week.*

▶ **auction off** PHRASAL VERB If you **auction off** something, you sell it to the person who offers most for it, often at an auction. ❑ *Any fool could auction off a factory full of engineering machinery.*

auc|tion|eer /ɔkʃənɪər/ (**auctioneers**) N-COUNT An **auctioneer** is a person in charge of an auction.

auda|cious /ɔdeɪʃəs/ ADJ Someone who is **audacious** takes risks in order to achieve something. ❑ *...an audacious plan to win the presidency.* ❑ *He was known for risky tactics that ranged from audacious to outrageous.*

audac|ity /ɔdæsɪti/ N-UNCOUNT **Audacity** is audacious behavior. ❑ *I was shocked at the audacity of the gangsters.*

aud|ible /ɔdɪbəl/ ADJ A sound that is **audible** is loud enough to be heard. ❑ *The Colonel's voice was barely audible.* • **audibly** /ɔdɪbli/ ADV ❑ *Frank sighed audibly.*

audi|ence ✦◇◇ /ɔdiəns/ (**audiences**) **1** N-COUNT-COLL The **audience** at a play, concert, film, or public meeting is the group of people watching or listening to it. ❑ *The entire audience broke into loud applause.* **2** N-COUNT-COLL The **audience** for a television or radio program consists of all the people who watch or listen to it. ❑ *The concert will be broadcast to a worldwide television audience estimated at one billion.* **3** N-COUNT-COLL The **audience** of a writer or artist is the people who read their books or look at their work. ❑ *Say's writings reached a wide audience during his lifetime.*

augur

COLLOCATIONS

audience
NOUN
1
noun + **audience**: movie theater
adjective + **audience**: entire; large, packed, vast
verb + **audience**: attract, delight, entertain, wow; address, face
2
noun + **audience**: radio, studio, TV
adjective + **audience**: live, peak; captive, worldwide
3
adjective + **audience**: potential, receptive, wide
verb + **audience**: reach

SYNONYMS

audience
NOUN **1**
house: *They played in front of a packed house.*
crowd: *The crowd was enormously enthusiastic.*

---

audio ✦◇◇ /ɔdioʊ/ ADJ [ADJ n] **Audio** equipment is used for recording and reproducing sound. ❑ *The software was the first to offer access to audio and video files.*

audio|book /ɔdioʊbʊk/ (**audiobooks**) N-COUNT An **audiobook** is a recorded reading of a book that you can listen to. ❑ *I like to listen to audiobooks while I'm driving.*

audio|tape /ɔdioʊteɪp/ also **audio tape** N-UNCOUNT **Audiotape** is magnetic tape used to record sound. ❑ *Unfortunately, fewer than 5 percent of books are now available in Braille or audiotape.*

audio|visual /ɔdioʊvɪʒuəl/ also **audio-visual** ADJ [ADJ n] **Audio-visual** equipment and materials involve both recorded sound and pictures.

audit /ɔdɪt/ (**audits, auditing, audited**) V-T When an accountant **audits** an organization's accounts, he or she examines the accounts officially in order to make sure that they have been done correctly. ❑ *Each year they audit our accounts and certify them as being true and fair.* • N-COUNT **Audit** is also a noun. ❑ *The bank first learned of the problem when it carried out an internal audit.*

audi|tion /ɔdɪʃən/ (**auditions, auditioning, auditioned**) **1** N-COUNT An **audition** is a short performance given by an actor, dancer, or musician so that a director or conductor can decide if they are good enough to be in a play, film, or orchestra. ❑ *...an audition for a Broadway musical.* **2** V-T/V-I If you **audition** or if someone **auditions** you, you do an audition. ❑ *I was auditioning for the part of a jealous girlfriend.* ❑ *They're auditioning new members for the cast of "Miss Saigon" today.* **3** → See feature box at **theater**

audi|tor /ɔdɪtər/ (**auditors**) N-COUNT An **auditor** is an accountant who officially examines the accounts of organizations.

audi|to|rium /ɔdɪtɔriəm/ (**auditoriums** or **auditoria** /ɔdɪtɔriə/) **1** N-COUNT An **auditorium** is the part of a theater or concert hall where the audience sits. ❑ *Anderson was to sing at the Constitution Hall auditorium.* **2** N-COUNT An **auditorium** is a large room, hall, or building that is used for events such as meetings and concerts. [AM] ❑ *...a high school auditorium.*

audi|tory /ɔdɪtɔri/ ADJ [usu ADJ n] **Auditory** means related to hearing. [TECHNICAL] ❑ *...the limits of the human auditory range.*

au fait /oʊ feɪ/ ADJ GRADED; ADJ [v-link ADJ with n] If you are **au fait** with something, you are familiar with it and know about it. ❑ *...children who are so much more au fait with today's technology.*

Aug. Aug. is a written abbreviation for **August**.

aug|ment /ɔgmɛnt/ (**augments, augmenting, augmented**) V-T To **augment** something means to make it larger, stronger, or more effective by adding something to it. [FORMAL] ❑ *While searching for a way to augment the family income, she began making dolls.*

augur /ɔgər/ (**augurs, auguring, augured**) V-I If something **augurs** well or badly for a person or a future situation, it is a

augury /ˈɔːɡjəri/ (**auguries**) N-COUNT An **augury** is a sign of what will happen in the future. [LITERARY] ❑ *The auguries of death are fast gathering around his head.*

august /ɔːˈɡʌst/ ADJ [usu ADJ n] Someone or something that is **august** is dignified and impressive. [FORMAL] ❑ *...that august body, the United States Senate.*

August ♦♦♦ /ˈɔːɡəst/ (**Augusts**) N-VAR **August** is the eighth month of the year in the Western calendar. ❑ *The world premiere took place in August 1956.* ❑ *The trial will resume on August the twenty-second.*

auk /ɔːk/ (**auks**) N-COUNT An **auk** is a seabird with a heavy body and short tail.

Auld Lang Syne /ˌoʊld læŋ ˈzaɪn/ N-PROPER **Auld Lang Syne** is a Scottish song about friendship that is traditionally sung as clocks strike midnight on New Year's Eve.

aunt ♦♦◊ /ænt, ɑːnt/ (**aunts**) N-FAMILY; N-TITLE Someone's **aunt** is the sister of their mother or father, or the wife of their uncle. ❑ *She wrote to her aunt in Alabama.*

auntie /ˈænti, ˈɑːnti/ (**aunties**) also **aunty** N-FAMILY; N-TITLE Someone's **auntie** is their aunt. [INFORMAL] ❑ *His uncle is dead, but his auntie still lives here.*

au pair /ˌoʊ ˈpɛər/ (**au pairs**) N-COUNT An **au pair** is a young person from a foreign country who lives with a family in order to learn the language and who helps to take care of the children.

aura /ˈɔːrə/ (**auras**) N-COUNT An **aura** is a quality or feeling that seems to surround a person or place or to come from them. ❑ *She had an aura of authority.*

aural /ˈɔːrəl/ ADJ [usu ADJ n] **Aural** means related to the sense of hearing. Compare **oral**. ❑ *He became famous as an inventor of astonishing visual and aural effects.*

aus|pices /ˈɔːspɪsɪz/ PHRASE If something is done **under the auspices of** a particular person or organization, or **under** someone's **auspices**, it is done with their support and approval. [FORMAL] ❑ *.... to meet and discuss peace under the auspices of the United Nations.*

aus|pi|cious /ɔːˈspɪʃəs/ ADJ Something that is **auspicious** indicates that success is likely. [FORMAL] ❑ *His career as a playwright had an auspicious start.*

Aussie /ˈɔːzi/ (**Aussies**) ADJ [ADJ n] **Aussie** means Australian. [INFORMAL] ❑ *...Aussie comedy actor Paul Hogan.* • N-COUNT An **Aussie** is a person from Australia. [INFORMAL]

aus|tere /ɔːˈstɪər/ **1** ADJ If you describe something as **austere**, you approve of its plain and simple appearance. [APPROVAL] ❑ *...a cream linen suit and austere black blouse.* **2** ADJ If you describe someone as **austere**, you disapprove of them because they are strict and serious. [DISAPPROVAL] ❑ *I found her a rather austere, distant, somewhat cold person.* **3** ADJ An **austere** way of life is one that is simple and without luxuries. ❑ *The life of the troops was still comparatively austere.* **4** ADJ An **austere** economic policy is one that reduces people's living standards sharply. ❑ *...a set of very austere economic measures to control inflation.*

aus|ter|ity /ɔːˈstɛrɪti/ N-UNCOUNT **Austerity** is a situation in which people's living standards are reduced because of economic difficulties. ❑ *...the years of austerity which followed the war.*

Aus|tral|asian /ˌɔːstrəˈleɪʒ°n/ ADJ [ADJ n] **Australasian** means belonging or relating to Australasia or to its people.

Aus|tral|ian /ɔːˈstreɪliən/ (**Australians**) **1** ADJ Something that is **Australian** belongs or relates to Australia, or to its people or culture. ❑ *She went solo backpacking for eight months in the Australian outback.* **2** N-COUNT An **Australian** is someone who comes from Australia.

Aus|trian /ˈɔːstriən/ (**Austrians**) **1** ADJ Something that is **Austrian** belongs or relates to Austria, or to its people or culture. ❑ *...the Austrian government.* **2** N-COUNT An **Austrian** is someone who comes from Austria.

Austro- /ˈɔːstroʊ/ COMB IN ADJ **Austro-** combines with adjectives indicating nationality to form adjectives which describe something connected with Austria and another country. ❑ *...the Austro-Hungarian Empire.*

auteur /oʊˈtɜːr/ (**auteurs**) N-COUNT You can refer to a film director as an **auteur** when they have a very strong artistic influence on the films they make.

authen|tic /ɔːˈθɛntɪk/ **1** ADJ An **authentic** person, object, or emotion is genuine. ❑ *...authentic Italian food.* ❑ *She has authentic charm whereas most people simply have nice manners.* • **au|then|tic|ity** /ˌɔːθɛnˈtɪsɪti/ N-UNCOUNT ❑ *There are factors, however, that have cast doubt on the statue's authenticity.* **2** ADJ If you describe something as **authentic**, you mean that it is such a good imitation that it is almost the same as or as good as the original. [APPROVAL] ❑ *...patterns for making authentic frontier-style clothing.* **3** ADJ An **authentic** piece of information or account of something is reliable and accurate. ❑ *I had obtained the authentic details about the birth of the organization.*

authen|ti|cate /ɔːˈθɛntɪkeɪt/ (**authenticates, authenticating, authenticated**) V-T If you **authenticate** something, you state officially that it is genuine after examining it. ❑ *He says he'll have no problem authenticating the stamp.*

author ♦♦◊ /ˈɔːθər/ (**authors**) **1** N-COUNT [oft N of n] The **author** of a piece of writing is the person who wrote it. ❑ *...Jill Phillips, author of the book "Give Your Child Music."* **2** N-COUNT An **author** is a person whose job is writing books. ❑ *Haruki Murakami is Japan's best-selling author.*

SYNONYMS

author
NOUN **1**
novelist: *...a romantic novelist.*
writer: *...detective stories by American writers.*
hack: *...a hack writer of cheap romances.*
columnist: *...the gossip columnists' favorite target.*
journalist: *I am majoring in media studies and hope to become a journalist.*

---

author|ess /ˈɔːθərɪs/ (**authoresses**) N-COUNT An **authoress** is a female author. Most people object to this word, and prefer to be called authors. [OLD-FASHIONED]

autho|rial /ɔːˈθɔːriəl/ ADJ [ADJ n] **Authorial** means relating to the author of something such as a book or play. ❑ *There are times when the book suffers from excessive authorial control.*

author|ing /ˈɔːθərɪŋ/ N-UNCOUNT [oft N n] **Authoring** is the creation of documents, especially for the internet. [COMPUTING] ❑ *...software authoring tools.*

authori|tar|ian /əˌθɔːrɪˈtɛəriən/ ADJ If you describe a person or an organization as **authoritarian**, you are critical of them controlling everything rather than letting people decide things for themselves. [DISAPPROVAL] ❑ *Senior officers could be considering a coup to restore authoritarian rule.*

authori|tari|an|ism /əˌθɔːrɪˈtɛəriənɪzəm/ N-UNCOUNT **Authoritarianism** is the state of being authoritarian or the belief that people with power, especially the State, have the right to control other people's actions. [FORMAL]

authori|ta|tive /əˈθɔːrɪteɪtɪv/ **1** ADJ Someone or something that is **authoritative** gives an impression of power and importance and is likely to be obeyed. ❑ *He has a commanding presence and deep, authoritative voice.* **2** ADJ Someone or something that is **authoritative** has a lot of knowledge of a particular subject. ❑ *The first authoritative study of polio was published in 1840.*

author|ity ♦♦♦ /əˈθɔːrɪti/ (**authorities**) **1** N-PLURAL The **authorities** are the people who have the power to make decisions and to make sure that laws are obeyed. ❑ *This provided a pretext for the authorities to cancel the elections.* **2** N-COUNT An **authority** is an official organization or government department that has the power to make decisions. ❑ *...the Philadelphia Parking Authority.* **3** → see also **local authority 4** N-COUNT Someone who is an **authority on** a particular subject knows a lot about it. ❑ *He's universally recognized as an authority on Russian affairs.* **5** N-UNCOUNT **Authority** is the right to command and control other people. ❑ *A family member in a family business has a position of authority and power.* **6** N-UNCOUNT If someone has **authority**, they have a quality which makes other people take notice of what they say. ❑ *He had no natural authority and no capacity for imposing his will on others.* **7** N-UNCOUNT **Authority** is official permission to do something. ❑ *The prison governor has refused to let him go, saying he must first be given authority from his own superiors.*

authority
NOUN

1
noun + **authorities**: health, immigration, prison, tax
authorities + be + adjective: powerless
verb + **authorities**: alert

2
noun + **authorities**: education, planning
adjective + **authority**: regulatory, relevant, statutory

4
adjective + **authority**: leading

5
adjective + **authority**: moral
verb + **authority**: abuse, assert, exercise

SYNONYMS

authority
NOUN

1
the state: *The state does not collect enough revenue to cover its expenditure.*
the system: *He wants to be the tough rebel who bucks the system.*
the establishment: *What do you expect? This is the establishment we're taking on.*
government: *...fighting between government forces and left-wing rebels.*

5
power: *The police have the power to arrest.*
jurisdiction: *The British police have no jurisdiction over foreign bank accounts.*
supremacy: *The conservative old guard had re-established its political supremacy.*

author|ize /ɔ́θəraɪz/ (**authorizes, authorizing, authorized**)

in BRIT, also use **authorise**

V-T If someone in a position of authority **authorizes** something, they give their official permission for it to happen. ☐ *It would certainly be within his power to authorize a police raid like that.* • **authori|za|tion** /ɔ̀θərɪzeɪʃən/ (**authorizations**) N-VAR ☐ *The United Nations will approve his request for authorization to use military force to deliver aid.*

author|ship /ɔ́θərʃɪp/ N-UNCOUNT The **authorship** of a piece of writing is the identity of the person who wrote it.

autism /ɔ́tɪzəm/ N-UNCOUNT **Autism** is a developmental disorder that can cause someone to have difficulty in communicating with and responding to other people.

autis|tic /ɔtɪ́stɪk/ ADJ If someone is **autistic**, they have a developmental disorder that can cause them to have difficulty in communicating with and responding to other people.

auto ✦✧✧ /ɔ́toʊ/ (**autos**) N-COUNT An **auto** is a car. [AM] ☐ *...the auto industry.*

PREFIX

auto-
forms words that refer to someone doing something to, for, or about themselves. For example, your ***autobiography*** *is an account of your life, which you write yourself.*

auto|bahn /ɔ́toʊbɑn/ (**autobahns**) N-COUNT An **autobahn** is a German highway.

auto|bio|graphi|cal /ɔ̀təbaɪəgrǽfɪkəl/ ADJ An **autobiographical** piece of writing relates to events in the life of the person who has written it. ☐ *...a highly autobiographical novel of a woman's search for identity.*

auto|bi|og|ra|phy /ɔ̀təbaɪɒ́grəfi/ (**autobiographies**) N-COUNT Your **autobiography** is an account of your life, which you write yourself. ☐ *He published his autobiography last fall.*

autoc|ra|cy /ɔtɒ́krəsi/ (**autocracies**) **1** N-UNCOUNT **Autocracy** is government or control by one person who has complete power. ☐ *Many poor countries are abandoning autocracy.* **2** N-COUNT An **autocracy** is a country or organization that is ruled by one person who has complete power. ☐ *She ceded all power to her son-in-law who now runs the country as an autocracy.*

auto|crat /ɔ́təkræt/ (**autocrats**) N-COUNT An **autocrat** is a person in authority who has complete power.

auto|crat|ic /ɔ̀təkrǽtɪk/ ADJ [usu ADJ n] An **autocratic** person or organization has complete power and makes decisions without asking anyone else's advice. ☐ *The people have grown intolerant in recent weeks of the king's autocratic ways.*

Auto|cue /ɔ́toʊkyu/ (**Autocues**) N-COUNT An **Autocue** is the same as a **Teleprompter**. [BRIT, TRADEMARK]

auto|graph /ɔ́təgræf/ (**autographs, autographing, autographed**) **1** N-COUNT An **autograph** is the signature of someone famous that is specially written for a fan to keep. ☐ *He went backstage and asked for her autograph.* **2** V-T If someone famous **autographs** something, they put their signature on it. ☐ *I autographed a copy of one of my books.*

auto|im|mune /ɔ̀toʊɪmyún/ ADJ [usu ADJ n] **Autoimmune** describes medical conditions in which normal cells are attacked by the body's immune system. ☐ *...autoimmune diseases such as rheumatoid arthritis.*

auto|maker /ɔ́toʊmeɪkər/ (**automakers**) N-COUNT An **automaker** is a company that manufactures cars. [AM] ☐ *...General Motors Corp., the world's largest automaker.*

in BRIT, use **car manufacturer**

auto|mate /ɔ́təmeɪt/ (**automates, automating, automated**) V-T To **automate** a factory, office, or process means to put in machines that can do the work instead of people. ☐ *He wanted to use computers to automate the process.* • **auto|ma|tion** /ɔ̀təmeɪ́ʃən/ N-UNCOUNT ☐ *In the last ten years automation has reduced the work force here by half.*

auto|mat|ed /ɔ́təmeɪtɪd/ **1** ADJ An **automated** factory, office, or process uses machines to do the work instead of people. ☐ *The equipment was made on highly automated production lines.* **2** → See feature box at **learning**

auto|mat|ic ✦✧✧ /ɔ̀təmǽtɪk/ (**automatics**) **1** ADJ An **automatic** machine or device is one that has controls that enable it to perform a task without needing to be constantly operated by a person. **Automatic** methods and processes involve the use of such machines. ☐ *Modern trains have automatic doors.* **2** ADJ [ADJ n] An **automatic** weapon is one that keeps firing shots until you stop pulling the trigger. ☐ *Three gunmen with automatic rifles opened fire.* • N-COUNT **Automatic** is also a noun. ☐ *He drew his automatic and began running in the direction of the sounds.* **3** ADJ An **automatic** action is one that you do without thinking about it. ☐ *All of the automatic body functions, even breathing, are affected.* • **auto|mati|cal|ly** /ɔ̀təmǽtɪkli/ ADV ☐ *You will automatically wake up after this length of time.* **4** N-COUNT An **automatic** is a car in which the gears change automatically as the car's speed increases or decreases.

SYNONYMS

automatic
ADJ **1**
mechanized: *...highly-mechanized production methods.*
mechanical: *Most mechanical devices require oil as a lubricant.*
automated: *The equipment was made on highly-automated production lines.*

auto|mat|ic pi|lot also autopilot **1** PHRASE If you are **on automatic pilot** or **on autopilot**, you are acting without thinking about what you are doing, usually because you have done it many times before. **2** N-SING An **automatic pilot** or an **autopilot** is a device in an aircraft that automatically keeps it on a particular course.

auto|mat|ic trans|mis|sion N-UNCOUNT A car that is equipped with **automatic transmission** has a gear system in which the gears change automatically.

automa|ton /ɔtɒ́mətɒn, -tən/ (**automatons** or **automata** /ɔtɒ́mətə/) **1** N-COUNT If you say that someone is an **automaton**, you are critical of them because they behave as if they are so tired or bored that they do things without thinking. [DISAPPROVAL] **2** N-COUNT An **automaton** is a small, mechanical figure that can move automatically.

auto|mo|bile /ɔ́təməbil/ (**automobiles**) N-COUNT An **automobile** is a car. [mainly AM] ☐ *...the automobile industry.*

auto|mo|tive /ɔ̀təmoʊ́tɪv/ ADJ [ADJ n] **Automotive** is used to refer to things relating to cars. ☐ *...a chain of stores selling automotive parts.*

autono|mous /ɔtɒnəməs/ **1** ADJ An **autonomous** country, organization, or group governs or controls itself rather than being controlled by anyone else. ▢ *They proudly declared themselves part of a new autonomous province.* **2** ADJ An **autonomous** person makes their own decisions rather than being influenced by someone else. ▢ *He treated us as autonomous individuals who had to learn to make up our own minds about issues.* **3** ADJ An **autonomous** vehicle is one that can control itself, without needing a person to drive it. ▢ *They are trying to develop autonomous vehicles that could be used in combat.* **4** → See feature box at **learning**

autono|my /ɔtɒnəmi/ **1** N-UNCOUNT **Autonomy** is the control or government of a country, organization, or group by itself rather than by others. ▢ *Activists stepped up their demands for local autonomy last month.* **2** N-UNCOUNT **Autonomy** is the ability to make your own decisions about what to do rather than being influenced by someone else or told what to do. [FORMAL] ▢ *Each of the area managers enjoys considerable autonomy in the running of his or her own area.*

auto|pi|lot /ɔtoupaɪlət/ → see **automatic pilot**

autop|sy /ɔtɒpsi/ (**autopsies**) N-COUNT An **autopsy** is an examination of a dead body by a doctor who cuts it open in order to try to discover the cause of death. ▢ *Macklin had the grim task of carrying out an autopsy on his friend.*

auto|worker /ɔtouwɜrkər/ (**autoworkers**) N-COUNT An **autoworker** is a person who works in the automobile manufacturing industry. [AM] ▢ *...a former autoworker from Cleveland.*

autumn ♦♦◇ /ɔtəm/ (**autumns**) N-VAR **Autumn** is the season between summer and winter when the weather becomes cooler and the leaves fall off the trees. [mainly BRIT]

in AM, usually use **fall**

autum|nal /ɔtʌmnəl/ **1** ADJ **Autumnal** means having features that are characteristic of autumn. [LITERARY] ▢ *...the autumnal colors of the trees.* **2** ADJ **Autumnal** means happening in autumn. ▢ *...the autumnal equinox.*

aux|ilia|ry /ɔgzɪlyəri, -zɪləri/ (**auxiliaries**) **1** ADJ [ADJ n] **Auxiliary** equipment is extra equipment that is available for use when necessary. ▢ *...an auxiliary motor.* **2** ADJ [ADJ n] **Auxiliary** staff and troops assist other staff and troops. ▢ *The government's first concern was to augment the army and auxiliary forces.* **3** N-COUNT An **auxiliary** is a person who is employed to assist other people in their work. Auxiliaries are often medical workers or members of the armed forces. ▢ *Nursing auxiliaries provide basic care, but are not qualified nurses.* **4** N-COUNT In grammar, an **auxiliary** or **auxiliary verb** is a verb that is used with a main verb, for example, to form different tenses or to make the verb passive. In English, the basic auxiliary verbs are 'be,' 'have,' and 'do.' Modal verbs such as 'can' and 'will' are also sometimes called auxiliaries.

avail /əveɪl/ (**avails, availing, availed**) **1** PHRASE If you do something **to no avail** or **to little avail**, what you do fails to achieve what you want. [WRITTEN] ▢ *His efforts were to no avail.* **2** V-T If you **avail** yourself of an offer or an opportunity, you accept the offer or make use of the opportunity. [FORMAL] ▢ *Guests should feel at liberty to avail themselves of your facilities.*

avail|able ♦♦♦ /əveɪləbəl/ **1** ADJ If something you want or need is **available**, you can find it or obtain it. ▢ *Since 1978, the amount of money available to buy books has fallen by 17%.* ▢ *The store has about 500 autographed copies of the book available for purchase.* • **avail|abil|ity** /əveɪləbɪlɪti/ N-UNCOUNT ▢ *...the easy availability of guns.* **2** ADJ [v-link ADJ] Someone who is **available** is not busy and is therefore free to talk to you or to do a particular task. ▢ *Mr. Leach is on holiday and was not available for comment.*

ava|lanche /ævəlæntʃ/ (**avalanches**) N-COUNT An **avalanche** is a large mass of snow that falls down the side of a mountain.

avant-garde /ævɒŋ gɑrd/ ADJ **Avant-garde** art, music, theater, and literature is very modern and experimental. ▢ *...avant-garde concert music.*

ava|rice /ævərɪs/ N-UNCOUNT **Avarice** is extremely strong desire for money and possessions. [LITERARY] ▢ *He paid a month's rent in advance, just enough to satisfy the landlord's avarice.*

ava|ri|cious /ævərɪʃəs/ ADJ [usu ADJ n] An **avaricious** person is very greedy for money or possessions. [DISAPPROVAL] ▢ *He sacrificed his own career so that his avaricious brother could succeed.*

ava|tar /ævətɑr/ (**avatars**) N-COUNT An **avatar** is an image that represents you on the screen in an online game or chatroom. ▢ *My avatar has long hair.*

Ave. N-IN-NAMES **Ave.** is a written abbreviation for **avenue**. ▢ *...90 Dayton Ave.*

avenge /əvɛndʒ/ (**avenges, avenging, avenged**) V-T If you **avenge** a wrong or harmful act, you hurt or punish the person who is responsible for it. ▢ *He has devoted the past five years to avenging his daughter's death.*

av|enue ♦♦◇ /ævɪnyu, -nu/ (**avenues**) **1** N-IN-NAMES **Avenue** is sometimes used in the names of streets. The written abbreviation **Ave.** is also used. ▢ *...the most expensive apartments on Park Avenue.* **2** N-COUNT An **avenue** is a wide, straight road, especially one with trees on either side.

aver /əvɜr/ (**avers, averring, averred**) V-T If you **aver** that something is the case, you say very firmly that it is true. [FORMAL] ▢ *He avers that chaos will erupt if he loses.* ▢ *"Entertaining is something that everyone in the country can enjoy," she averred.*

av|er|age ♦♦◇ /ævərɪdʒ, ævrɪdʒ/ (**averages, averaging, averaged**) **1** N-COUNT An **average** is the result that you get when you add two or more numbers together and divide the total by the number of numbers you added together. ▢ *Take the average of those ratios and multiply by a hundred.* • ADJ [ADJ n] **Average** is also an adjective. ▢ *The average price of goods rose by just 2.2%.* **2** N-SING You use **average** to refer to a number or size that varies but is always approximately the same. ▢ *It takes an average of ten weeks for a house sale to be completed.* **3** N-SING An amount or quality that is **the average** is the normal amount or quality for a particular group of things or people. ▢ *35% of staff time was being spent on repeating work, about the average for a service industry.* • ADJ **Average** is also an adjective. ▢ *$2.20 for a beer is average.* **4** ADJ [ADJ n] An **average** person or thing is typical or normal. ▢ *The average adult man burns 1,500 to 2,000 calories per day.* **5** ADJ Something that is **average** is neither very good nor very bad, usually when you had hoped it would be better. ▢ *I was only average academically.* **6** V-T To **average** a particular amount means to do, get, or produce that amount as an average over a period of time. ▢ *We averaged 42 miles per hour.* **7** PHRASE You say **on average** or **on the average** to indicate that a number is the average of several numbers. ▢ *Shares rose, on average, by 38%.*

av|er|age Joe /ævərɪdʒ dʒoʊ, ævrɪdʒ/ (**average Joes**) N-COUNT An **average Joe** is an average or ordinary man. [mainly AM, INFORMAL] ▢ *I'm just an average Joe.*

averse /əvɜrs/ ADJ [usu with neg, v-link ADJ to n] If you say that you are not **averse** to something, you mean that you like it or want to do it. [FORMAL] ▢ *He's not averse to publicity, of the right kind.*

aver|sion /əvɜrʒən/ (**aversions**) N-VAR If you have an **aversion** to someone or something, you dislike them very much. ▢ *Many people have a natural and emotional aversion to insects.*

avert /əvɜrt/ (**averts, averting, averted**) **1** V-T If you **avert** something unpleasant, you prevent it from happening. ▢ *Talks with the teachers' union over the weekend have averted a strike.* **2** V-T If you **avert** your eyes or gaze from someone or something, you look away from them. ▢ *He avoids any eye contact, quickly averting his gaze when anyone approaches.*

aviary /eɪvieri/ (**aviaries**) N-COUNT An **aviary** is a large cage or covered area in which birds are kept.

avia|tion /eɪvieɪʃən/ N-UNCOUNT **Aviation** is the operation and production of aircraft. ▢ *...the aviation industry.*

avia|tor /eɪvieɪtər/ (**aviators**) N-COUNT An **aviator** is a pilot of a plane, especially in the early days of flying. [OLD-FASHIONED]

avid /ævɪd/ ADJ You use **avid** to describe someone who is very enthusiastic about something that they do. ▢ *He misses not having enough books because he's an avid reader.* • **av|id|ly** ADV [ADV with v] ▢ *Thank you for a most entertaining magazine, which I read avidly each month.*

avi|on|ics /eɪviɒnɪks/ N-UNCOUNT **Avionics** is the science of electronics used in aviation. [TECHNICAL]

avo|ca|do /ævəkɑːdoʊ/ (**avocados**) N-VAR **Avocados** are pear-shaped vegetables, with hard skins and large seeds, which are usually eaten raw.

avo|ca|tion /ævoʊkeɪʃᵊn/ (**avocations**) N-VAR Your **avocation** is a job or activity that you do because you are interested in it, rather than to earn your living. [FORMAL] ▫ He was a printer by trade and naturalist by avocation.

avoid ♦♦♢ /əvɔɪd/ (**avoids, avoiding, avoided**) **1** V-T If you **avoid** something unpleasant that might happen, you take action in order to prevent it from happening. ▫ The pilots had to take emergency action to avoid a disaster. **2** V-T If you **avoid** doing something, you choose not to do it, or you put yourself in a situation where you do not have to do it. ▫ By borrowing from dozens of banks, he managed to avoid giving any of them an overall picture of what he was up to. **3** V-T If you **avoid** a person or thing, you keep away from them. When talking to someone, if you **avoid** the subject, you keep the conversation away from a particular topic. ▫ She eventually had to lock herself in the women's restroom to avoid him. **4** V-T If a person or vehicle **avoids** someone or something, they change the direction they are moving in, so that they do not hit them. ▫ The driver had ample time to brake or swerve and avoid the woman.

avoid|able /əvɔɪdəbᵊl/ ADJ Something that is **avoidable** can be prevented from happening. ▫ The tragedy was entirely avoidable.

avoid|ance /əvɔɪdᵊns/ N-UNCOUNT [usu N of n] **Avoidance** of someone or something is the act of avoiding them. ▫ ...the avoidance of stress.

avow /əvaʊ/ (**avows, avowing, avowed**) V-T If you **avow** something, you admit it or declare it. [FORMAL] ▫ ...a public statement avowing neutrality.

avowed /əvaʊd/ **1** ADJ [ADJ n] If you are an **avowed** supporter or opponent of something, you have declared that you support it or oppose it. [FORMAL] ▫ She is an avowed vegetarian. **2** ADJ [ADJ n] An **avowed** belief or aim is one that you have declared formally or publicly. [FORMAL] ▫ His avowed intention was to bring about reform and spiritual renewal for the church.

avun|cu|lar /əvʌŋkyələr/ ADJ [usu ADJ n] An **avuncular** man or a man with **avuncular** behavior is friendly and helpful toward someone younger. [FORMAL] ▫ He began to talk in his most gentle and avuncular manner.

aw /ɔː/ **1** EXCLAM People sometimes use **aw** to express disapproval, disappointment, or sympathy. [mainly AM, INFORMAL, FEELINGS] ▫ "Aw, leave her alone," Paul said. ▫ Aw, come on, don't be so hard on yourself. **2** EXCLAM People sometimes use **aw** to express encouragement or approval. [mainly AM, INFORMAL, FEELINGS] ▫ Aw, she's got her mother's nose!

await ♦♢♢ /əweɪt/ (**awaits, awaiting, awaited**) **1** V-T If you **await** someone or something, you wait for them. [FORMAL] ▫ Very little was said as we awaited the arrival of the chairman. **2** V-T Something that **awaits** you is going to happen or come to you in the future. [FORMAL] ▫ A surprise awaited them in Wal-Mart.

awake /əweɪk/ **1** ADJ [v-link ADJ, ADJ after v] Someone who is **awake** is not sleeping. ▫ I don't stay awake at night worrying about that. **2** PHRASE Someone who is **wide awake** is fully awake and unable to sleep. ▫ I could not relax and still felt wide awake.

awak|en /əweɪkən/ (**awakens, awakening, awakened**) **1** V-T To **awaken** a feeling in a person means to cause them to start having this feeling. [LITERARY] ▫ The aim of the cruise was to awaken an interest in and an understanding of foreign cultures. **2** V-T/V-I When you **awaken**, or when something or someone **awakens** you, you wake up. [LITERARY] ▫ Unfortunately, Grandma always seems to awaken at awkward moments. ▫ He was snoring when José awakened him.

awak|en|ing /əweɪkənɪŋ/ (**awakenings**) **1** N-COUNT The **awakening** of a feeling or realization is the start of it. ▫ ...the awakening of national consciousness in people. **2** PHRASE If you have a **rude awakening**, you are suddenly made aware of an unpleasant fact. ▫ It was a rude awakening to learn after I left home that I wasn't so special anymore.

award ♦♦♢ /əwɔːrd/ (**awards, awarding, awarded**) **1** N-COUNT An **award** is a prize or certificate that a person is given for doing something well. ▫ The Institute's annual award is presented to organizations that are dedicated to democracy and human rights. **2** N-COUNT In law, an **award** is a sum of money that a court decides should be given to someone. ▫ ...worker's compensation awards. **3** V-T If someone **is awarded** something such as a prize or an examination mark, it is given to them. ▫ She was awarded the prize for both films. **4** V-T To **award** something to someone means to decide that it will be given to that person. ▫ We have awarded the contract to a New York-based company.

award-winning **1** ADJ [ADJ n] An **award-winning** person or thing has won an award, especially an important or valuable one. ▫ ...an award-winning photojournalist. ▫ ...his award-winning film. **2** → See feature box at **book**

aware ♦♦♢ /əwɛər/ **1** ADJ [v-link ADJ] If you are **aware** of something, you know about it. ▫ Smokers are well aware of the dangers to their own health. ▫ He should have been aware of what his junior officers were doing. • **aware|ness** N-UNCOUNT ▫ The 1980s brought an awareness of green issues. **2** ADJ [v-link ADJ] If you are **aware** of something, you realize that it is present or is happening because you hear it, see it, smell it, or feel it. ▫ She was acutely aware of the noise of the city.

awash /əwɒʃ/ **1** ADJ [v-link ADJ] If a place is **awash** with something, it contains a large amount of it. ▫ This is a company that is awash with cash. **2** ADJ [v-link ADJ] If the ground or a floor is **awash**, it is covered in water, often because of heavy rain or as the result of an accident. ▫ The bathroom floor was awash.

away ♦♦♦ /əweɪ/

> **Away** is often used with verbs of movement, such as 'go' and 'drive,' and also in phrasal verbs such as 'do away with' and 'fade away.'

1 ADV If someone or something moves or is moved **away** from a place, they move or are moved so that they are no longer there. If you are **away** from a place, you are not in the place where people expect you to be. ▫ An injured policeman was led away by colleagues. ▫ He walked away from his car. ▫ Jason was away on a business trip. **2** ADV If you look or turn **away** from something, you move your head so that you are no longer looking at it. ▫ She quickly looked away and stared down at her hands. **3** ADV [ADV after v] If you put something **away**, you put it where it should be. If you hide someone or something **away**, you put them in a place where nobody can see them or find them. ▫ I put my journal away and prepared for bed. ▫ All her letters were carefully filed away in folders. **4** ADV [be amount ADV] You use **away** to talk about future events. For example, if an event is a week **away**, it will happen after a week. ▫ ...the Washington summit, now only just over two weeks away. **5** ADV [ADV after v] When a sports team plays **away**, it plays on its opponents' playing court or field. ▫ ...a sensational 4-3 victory for the team playing away. • ADJ [ADJ n] **Away** is also an adjective. ▫ Pittsburgh is about to play an important away game. **6** ADV [ADV after v] You can use **away** to say that something slowly disappears, becomes less significant, or changes so that it is no longer the same. ▫ So much snow has already melted away. ▫ His voice died away in a whisper. **7** ADV You use **away** to show that there has been a change or development from one state or situation to another. ▫ British courts are increasingly moving away from sending young offenders to prison. **8** ADV [ADV after v] You can use **away** to emphasize a continuous or repeated action. [EMPHASIS] ▫ He would often be working away on his word processor late into the night. **9** ADV [ADV after v] You use **away** to show that something is removed. ▫ If you take my work away I can't be happy anymore. **10** PHRASE If something is **away from** a person or place, it is at a distance from that person or place. ▫ The two women were sitting as far away from each other as possible. **11 right away** → see **right** ⑤

awe /ɔː/ (**awes, awed**) **1** N-UNCOUNT **Awe** is the feeling of respect and amazement that you have when you are faced with something wonderful and often rather frightening. ▫ She gazed in awe at the great stones. **2** V-T [usu passive, no cont] If you **are awed** by someone or something, they make you feel respectful and amazed, though often rather frightened. ▫ I am still awed by David's courage.

awe-inspiring ADJ If you describe someone or something as **awe-inspiring**, you are emphasizing that you think that they are remarkable and amazing, although sometimes a little

awe|some /ɔ́səm/ **1** ADJ An **awesome** person or thing is very impressive and often frightening. ❑ *...the awesome responsibility of sending men into combat.* **2** ADJ If you describe someone or something as **awesome**, you are emphasizing that you think that they are very impressive or extraordinary. [INFORMAL, EMPHASIS] ❑ *Melvill called the flight "mind-blowing" and "awesome."*

awe|struck /ɔ́strʌk/ also **awe-struck** ADJ If someone is **awestruck**, they are very impressed and amazed by something. [WRITTEN] ❑ *I stood and gazed at him, awestruck that anyone could be so beautiful.*

aw|ful ◆◇◇ /ɔ́fəl/ **1** ADJ If you say that someone or something is **awful**, you dislike that person or thing or you think that they are not very good. ❑ *We met and I thought he was awful.* ❑ *...an awful smell of paint.* **2** ADJ If you say that something is **awful**, you mean that it is extremely unpleasant, shocking, or bad. ❑ *Her injuries were massive. It was awful.* **3** ADJ [v-link ADJ] If you look or feel **awful**, you look or feel ill. ❑ *I hardly slept at all and felt pretty awful.* **4** ADJ [ADJ n] You can use **awful** with noun groups that refer to an amount in order to emphasize how large that amount is. [EMPHASIS] ❑ *I've got an awful lot of work to do.* ● **aw|ful|ly** ADV ❑ *The caramel looks awfully good.*

awhile /əwaɪl/ ADV **Awhile** means for a short time. ❑ *He worked awhile as a pharmacist in Cincinnati.*

awk|ward /ɔ́kwərd/ **1** ADJ An **awkward** situation is embarrassing and difficult to deal with. ❑ *I was the first to ask him awkward questions but there'll be harder ones to come.* ● **awk|ward|ly** ADV [ADV adj; -ed] ❑ *There was an awkwardly long silence.* **2** ADJ Something that is **awkward** to use or carry is difficult to use or carry because of its design. A job that is **awkward** is difficult to do. ❑ *It was small but heavy enough to make it awkward to carry.* ● **awk|ward|ly** ADV [ADV -ed] ❑ *The front window switches are awkwardly placed on the dashboard.* **3** ADJ An **awkward** movement or position is uncomfortable or clumsy. ❑ *Amy made an awkward gesture with her hands.* ● **awk|ward|ly** ADV [ADV with v] ❑ *He fell awkwardly and went down in agony clutching his right knee.* **4** ADJ Someone who feels **awkward** behaves in a shy or embarrassed way. ❑ *A third of the candidates admitted they felt awkward speaking in meetings.* ● **awk|ward|ly** ADV [ADV with v] ❑ *"This is Malcolm," the girl said awkwardly, to fill the silence.* **5** → See feature box at **personality**

awn|ing /ɔ́nɪŋ/ (awnings) N-COUNT An **awning** is a roof of material placed over a doorway, window, or deck to provide shelter from the rain or sun.

awoke /əwoʊk/ **Awoke** is the past tense of **awake**.

awok|en /əwoʊkən/ **Awoken** is the past participle of **awake**.

AWOL /eɪwɔl/ **1** ADJ [usu v-link ADJ] If someone in the armed forces goes **AWOL**, they leave their post without the permission of a superior officer. **AWOL** is an abbreviation for 'absent without leave.' **2** ADJ [usu v-link ADJ] If you say that someone has gone **AWOL**, you mean that they have disappeared without telling anyone where they were going. [INFORMAL]

awry /əraɪ/ ADJ [v-link ADJ] If something goes **awry**, it does not happen in the way it was planned. ❑ *She was in a fury over a plan that had gone awry.*

ax /ǽks/ (axes, axing, axed)

in BRIT, sometimes in AM, use **axe**

1 N-COUNT An **ax** is a tool used for cutting wood. It consists of a heavy metal blade that is sharp at one edge and attached by its other edge to the end of a long handle. **2** V-T [usu passive] If someone's job or something such as a public service or a television program **is axed**, it is ended suddenly and without discussion. ❑ *Community projects are being axed by hard-pressed social services departments.*

axe /ǽks/ [BRIT] → see **ax**

axes

Pronounced /ǽksɪz/ for meaning 1, and /ǽksiz/ for meaning 2.

1 Axes is the plural of **ax**. **2 Axes** is the plural of **axis**.

axi|om /ǽksiəm/ (axioms) N-COUNT [oft N that] An **axiom** is a statement or idea that people accept as being true. [FORMAL] ❑ *...the long-held axiom that education leads to higher income.*

axio|mat|ic /ǽksiəmǽtɪk/ ADJ If something is **axiomatic**, it seems to be obviously true. [FORMAL]

axis /ǽksɪs/ (axes) **1** N-COUNT An **axis** is an imaginary line through the middle of something. ❑ *...the tilt of the Earth's axis.* **2** N-COUNT An **axis** of a graph is one of the two lines on which the scales of measurement are marked. ❑ *The level of spiritual achievement is plotted along the Y axis, and the degree of physical health is plotted along the X axis.*

axle /ǽksəl/ (axles) N-COUNT An **axle** is a rod connecting a pair of wheels on a car or other vehicle.

aya|tol|lah /aɪətoʊlə/ (ayatollahs) N-COUNT; N-TITLE An **ayatollah** is a type of Muslim religious leader.

aye /aɪ/ (ayes) also **ay** **1** ADV If you vote **aye**, you vote in favor of something. **2** N-PLURAL [the N] **The ayes** are the people who vote in favor of something.

Ay|ur|ved|ic /aɪʊrveɪdɪk/ ADJ [ADJ n] **Ayurvedic** medicine is a type of complementary medicine, originally from India, that uses herbs and other natural treatments. ❑ *...an Ayurvedic practitioner.*

aza|lea /əzeɪlyə/ (azaleas) N-COUNT An **azalea** is a woody plant with shiny, dark-green leaves that produces many brightly-colored flowers in the spring.

az|ure /ǽʒuər/ **1** COLOR [usu COLOR n] **Azure** is used to describe things that are bright blue. [LITERARY] ❑ *...an azure sky.* **2** → See feature box at **hot**

Bb

B also **b** /biː/ (B's, b's) N-VAR **B** is the second letter of the English alphabet.

B2B /biː tə biː/ N-UNCOUNT **B2B** is the selling of goods and services by one company to another using the internet. **B2B** is an abbreviation for 'business to business.' [BUSINESS] ☐ *American analysts have been somewhat cautious in estimating the size of the B2B market.*

B2C /biː tə siː/ N-UNCOUNT **B2C** is the selling of goods and services by businesses to consumers using the internet. **B2C** is an abbreviation for 'business to consumer.' [BUSINESS] ☐ *B2C companies look particularly vulnerable with 19 per cent of them now worth little more than the cash on their balance sheets.*

B4 **B4** is the written abbreviation for 'before,' mainly used in text messages and e-mails.

BA /biː eɪ/ (BAs) also **B.A.** **1** N-COUNT A **BA** is a degree from a college or university in an arts or social science subject. **BA** is an abbreviation for **Bachelor of Arts**. ☐ *I did a BA in film making.* **2** **BA** is written after someone's name to indicate that they have a **BA**. [BRIT] ☐ *...Helen Rich, BA (Hons).*

bab|ble /bæbəl/ (babbles, babbling, babbled) **1** V-I If someone **babbles**, they talk in a confused or excited way. ☐ *Momma babbled on and on about how he was ruining me.* ☐ *They all babbled simultaneously.* **2** V-I If a stream **babbles**, it makes a low murmuring or bubbling sound. ☐ *...a stream babbling in the distance.* **3** N-SING You can refer to people's voices as a **babble** of sound when they are excited and confused, preventing you from understanding what they are saying. ☐ *Kemp knocked loudly so as to be heard above the high babble of voices.* **4** → See feature box at **onomatopoeia**

babe /beɪb/ (babes) **1** N-VOC Some people use **babe** as an affectionate way of addressing someone they love. [INFORMAL, FEELINGS] ☐ *I'm sorry, babe. I didn't mean it.* **2** N-COUNT Some men refer to an attractive young woman as a **babe**. This use could cause offense. [INFORMAL] **3** N-COUNT A **babe** is the same as a baby. [OLD-FASHIONED] ☐ *...newborn babes.*

ba|bel /beɪbəl, bæb-/ N-SING If there is a **babel** of voices, you hear a lot of people talking at the same time, so that you cannot understand what they are saying. ☐ *...a confused babel of sound.*

ba|boon /bæbuːn/ (baboons) N-COUNT A **baboon** is a large monkey that lives in Africa.

baby ♦♦◇ /beɪbi/ (babies) **1** N-COUNT A **baby** is a very young child, especially one that cannot yet walk or talk. ☐ *She used to take care of me when I was a baby.* ☐ *My wife has just had a baby.* **2** N-COUNT [usu N n] A **baby** animal is a very young animal. ☐ *...a baby elephant.* **3** N-COUNT If you refer to someone as a **baby**, you mean that they are behaving in a cowardly way or they are being too sensitive about something. [DISAPPROVAL] ☐ *I know he's an ex-champion boxer, but he can be a big baby sometimes! He hates spiders.* **4** ADJ [ADJ n] **Baby** vegetables are vegetables picked when they are very small. ☐ *Cook the baby potatoes in their skins.* **5** N-VOC; N-COUNT Some people use **baby** as an affectionate way of addressing someone, especially a young woman, or referring to them. [INFORMAL] ☐ *You have to wake up now, baby.*

COLLOCATIONS

baby
NOUN **1**
adjective + **baby**: healthy, newborn, premature; stillborn, unborn
verb + **baby**: adopt, conceive, deliver, expect; breastfeed; lose

---

baby boom (baby booms) N-COUNT [usu sing] A **baby boom** is a period of time when a lot of babies are born in a particular place. [INFORMAL] ☐ *I'm a product of the postwar baby boom.*

baby boom|er (baby boomers) also **baby-boomer** N-COUNT [oft N n] A **baby boomer** is someone who was born during a baby boom, especially during the years after the end of the Second World War. [INFORMAL, mainly JOURNALISM]

baby bug|gy (baby buggies) **1** N-COUNT A **baby buggy** is another word for a **baby carriage**. [AM, OLD-FASHIONED] **2** N-COUNT A **baby buggy** is the same as a **stroller**. [BRIT]

baby car|riage (baby carriages) N-COUNT A **baby carriage** is a small vehicle in which a baby can lie as it is pushed along. [AM]

in BRIT, use **pram**

baby fat N-UNCOUNT **Baby fat** is fat that some children have on their bodies when they are young but that disappears when they grow older and taller. ☐ *Her face had already lost its baby fat.*

ba|by|hood /beɪbihʊd/ N-UNCOUNT Your **babyhood** is the period of your life when you were a baby.

ba|by|ish /beɪbiɪʃ/ ADJ [usu adj n] **Babyish** actions, feelings, or looks are like a baby's, or are immature. ☐ *...a fat, babyish face.* ☐ *I'm ashamed of the babyish nonsense I write.*

baby|sit /beɪbisɪt/ (babysits, babysitting, babysat) V-T/V-I If you **babysit** for someone or **babysit** their children, you look after their children while they are out. ☐ *I promised to babysit for Mrs. Plunkett.* ☐ *She had been babysitting him and his four-year-old sister.* • **baby|sit|ter** N-COUNT ☐ *It can be difficult to find a good babysitter.*

baby talk also **baby-talk** N-UNCOUNT **Baby talk** is the language used by babies when they are just learning to speak, or the way in which some adults speak when they are talking to babies. ☐ *The baby squealed and made cooing noises, while Abigail talked her baby talk.*

baby tooth (baby teeth) N-COUNT [usu pl] Your **baby teeth** are the first teeth that grow in your mouth, which later fall out and are replaced by a second set.

bac|ca|lau|re|ate /bækəlɔːriːət/ (baccalaureates) **1** N-SING A **baccalaureate** is the same as a **bachelor's degree**. [FORMAL] **2** N-COUNT [usu N n] In the United States, a **baccalaureate** is a sermon given to a graduating class, or the religious service in which that sermon is given. **3** N-SING The **baccalaureate** is an examination taken by students at the age of eighteen in France and some other countries.

bach|elor /bætʃələr/ (bachelors) N-COUNT A **bachelor** is a man who has never married. ☐ *...America's most eligible bachelor.*

bach|elor|ette /bætʃələrɛt/ (bachelorettes) N-COUNT A **bachelorette** is a woman who has never married. [mainly AM]

bach|elor|ette par|ty (bachelorette parties) N-COUNT A **bachelorette party** is a party for a woman who is getting married very soon, to which only women are invited. [AM]

in BRIT, use **hen party**, **hen night**

Bach|elor of Arts (Bachelors of Arts) N-COUNT A **Bachelor of Arts** is a first degree from a college or university in an arts or social science subject. The abbreviation **BA** is also used.

Bach|elor of Sci|ence (Bachelors of Science) N-COUNT A **Bachelor of Science** is a first degree from a college or university in a science subject. The abbreviation **BS** is also used.

bach|elor par|ty (bachelor parties) N-COUNT A bachelor party is a party for a man who is getting married very soon, to which only men are invited. [AM]

in BRIT, use **stag party, stag night**

bach|elor's de|gree (bachelor's degrees) **1** N-COUNT A bachelor's degree is a first degree awarded by colleges or universities. **2** → see also BA, BS, BSc

ba|cil|lus /bəsɪləs/ (bacilli /bəsɪlaɪ/) N-COUNT A bacillus is any bacterium that has a long, thin shape.

BACK
① ADVERB USES
② OPPOSITE OF FRONT; NOUN AND ADJECTIVE USES
③ VERB USES

① **back** ♦♦♦ /bæk/

In addition to the uses shown below, **back** is also used in phrasal verbs such as 'date back' and 'fall back on.'

→ Please look at meaning **17** to see if the expression you are looking for is shown under another headword.

1 ADV If you move **back**, you move in the opposite direction to the one in which you are facing or in which you were moving before. ❑ *She stepped back from the door expectantly.* ❑ *He pushed her away and she fell back on the wooden bench.* **2** ADV If you go **back** somewhere, you return to where you were before. ❑ *I went back to bed.* ❑ *I'll be back as soon as I can.* **3** ADV If someone or something is **back** in a particular state, they were in that state before and are now in it again. ❑ *The rail company said it expected services to get slowly back to normal.* **4** ADV If you give or put something **back**, you return it to the person who had it or to the place where it was before you took it. If you get or take something **back**, you then have it again after not having it for a while. ❑ *She handed the knife back.* ❑ *Put it in the freezer.* **5** ADV [ADV after v] If you put a clock or watch **back**, you change the time shown on it so that it shows an earlier time, for example, when the time changes to standard time. ❑ *The clocks go back at 2 o'clock tomorrow morning.* **6** ADV If you write or call **back**, you write to or telephone someone after they have written to or telephoned you. If you look **back** at someone, you look at them after they have started looking at you. ❑ *They wrote back to me and told me I didn't have to do it.* ❑ *If the phone rings, say you'll call back after dinner.* **7** ADV You can say that you go or come **back** to a particular point in a conversation to show that you are mentioning or discussing it again. ❑ *Can I come back to the question of policing once again?* **8** ADV If something is or comes **back**, it is fashionable again after it has been unfashionable for some time. ❑ *Short skirts are back.* **9** ADV If someone or something is kept or situated **back** from a place, they are at a distance away from it. ❑ *Keep back from the edge of the platform.* ❑ *I'm a few miles back from the border.* **10** ADV [ADV after v] If something is held or tied **back**, it is held or tied so that it does not hang loosely over something. ❑ *The curtains were held back by tassels.* **11** ADV [ADV after v] If you lie or sit **back**, you move your body backward into a relaxed sloping or flat position, with your head and body resting on something. ❑ *She lay back and stared at the ceiling.* **12** ADV If you look or shout **back** at someone or something, you turn to look or shout at them when they are behind you. ❑ *Nick looked back over his shoulder and then stopped, frowning.* **13** ADV You use **back** in expressions like **back in Chicago** or **back at the house** when you are giving an account, to show that you are going to start talking about what happened or was happening in the place you mention. ❑ *Meanwhile, back in Everett, Marc Fulmer is busy raising money to help get the project off the ground.* **14** ADV If you talk about something that happened **back** in the past or several years **back**, you are emphasizing that it happened quite a long time ago. [EMPHASIS] ❑ *The story starts back in 1950, when I was five.* **15** ADV If you think **back** to something that happened in the past, you remember it or try to remember it. ❑ *I thought back to the time in 1975 when my son was desperately ill.* **16** PHRASE If someone moves **back and forth**, they repeatedly move in one direction and then in the opposite direction. ❑ *He paced back and forth.* **17 to cast your mind back** → see **mind** ① **18** → See feature box at **drive**

USAGE
back
You never use 'back' with the verb **return**. You do not say, for example, 'He returned back to his office.' You say 'He returned to his office.' *I returned from the Middle East in 1996.*

② **back** ♦♦♦ /bæk/ (backs)

→ Please look at meaning **12** to see if the expression you are looking for is shown under another headword.

1 N-COUNT A person's or animal's **back** is the part of their body between their head and their legs that is on the opposite side to their chest and stomach. ❑ *Her son was lying peacefully on his back.* ❑ *She turned her back to the audience.* **2** N-COUNT The **back** of something is the side or part of it that is toward the rear or farthest from the front. The back of something is normally not used or seen as much as the front. ❑ *...a room at the back of the shop.* ❑ *She raised her hands to the back of her neck.* **3** ADJ [ADJ n] **Back** is used to refer to the side or part of something that is toward the rear or farthest from the front. ❑ *He opened the back door.* ❑ *Ann could remember sitting in the back seat of their car.* **4** N-COUNT The **back** of a chair or sofa is the part that you lean against when you sit on it. ❑ *There was a pink sweater on the back of the chair.* **5** N-COUNT The **back** of something such as a piece of paper or an envelope is the side that is less important. ❑ *Send your answers on the back of a postcard or sealed, empty envelope.* **6** N-COUNT The **back** of a book is the part nearest the end, where you can find the index or the notes, for example. ❑ *The index at the back of the book lists both brand and generic names.* **7** N-UNCOUNT You use **out back** to refer to the area behind a house or other building. You also use **in back** to refer to the rear part of something, especially a car or building. [AM] ❑ *Dan informed her that he would be out back on the patio cleaning his shoes.* ❑ *...the trees in back of the building.* **8** PHRASE If you say that something was done **behind** someone's **back**, you disapprove of it because it was done without them knowing about it, in an unfair or dishonest way. [DISAPPROVAL] ❑ *You eat her food, enjoy her hospitality and then criticize her behind her back.* **9** PHRASE If two or more things are done **back to back**, one follows immediately after the other without any interruption. ❑ *...two half-hour shows, which will be screened back to back.* **10** → see also **back-to-back** **11** PHRASE If you are wearing something **back to front**, you are wearing it with the back of it at the front of your body. If you do something **back to front**, you do it the wrong way around, starting with the part that should come last. [mainly BRIT]

in AM, usually use **backward**

12 to take a back seat → see **seat**

③ **back** ♦♦♦ /bæk/ (backs, backing, backed) **1** V-I If a building **backs** onto something, the back of it faces in the direction of that thing or touches the edge of that thing. ❑ *He lives in a loft that backs onto Friedman's Bar.* **2** V-T/V-I When you **back** a car or other vehicle somewhere or when it **backs** somewhere, it moves backward. ❑ *He backed his car out of the drive.* **3** V-T If you **back** a person or a course of action, you support them, for example, by voting for them or giving them money. ❑ *His defense says it has found a new witness to back his claim that he is a victim of mistaken identity.* **4** V-T If you **back** a particular person, team, or horse in a competition, you predict that they will win, and usually you bet money that they will win. ❑ *She backed the Detroit Lions to beat the Chicago Bears by at least 20-10.* **5** V-T [usu passive] If a singer **is backed** by a band or by other singers, they provide the musical backing for the singer. ❑ *She chose to be backed by a classy trio of acoustic guitar, bass and congas.*

▶ **back away** **1** PHRASAL VERB If you **back away** from a commitment that you made or something that you were involved with in the past, you try to show that you are no longer committed to it or involved with it. ❑ *The company backed away from plans to cut their pay by 15%.* **2** PHRASAL VERB If you **back away**, you walk backward away from someone or something, often because you are frightened of them. ❑ *James got to his feet and started to come over, but the girls hastily backed away.*

▶ **back down** PHRASAL VERB If you **back down**, you withdraw a claim, demand, or commitment that you made earlier, because other people are strongly opposed to it. ❑ *It's too late to back down now.*

▶ **back off** **1** PHRASAL VERB If you **back off**, you move away in order to avoid problems or a fight. ❑ *They backed off in horror.* **2** PHRASAL VERB If you **back off** from a claim, demand, or commitment that you made earlier, or if you **back off** it, you withdraw it. ❑ *A spokesman says the president has backed off from his threat to boycott the conference.*

▶ **back out** PHRASAL VERB If you **back out**, or if you **back out** of something, you decide not to do something that you previously agreed to do. ❑ *The Hungarians backed out of the project in 1989 on environmental grounds.*

▶ **back up** **1** PHRASAL VERB If someone or something **backs up** a statement, they supply evidence to suggest that it is true. ❑ *Radio signals received from the galaxy's center back up the black hole theory.* **2** PHRASAL VERB If you **back up** a computer file, you make a copy of it that you can use if the original file is damaged or lost. [COMPUTING] ❑ *Make a point of backing up your files at regular intervals.* **3** PHRASAL VERB If an idea or intention **is backed up** by action, action is taken to support or confirm it. ❑ *The secretary general says the declaration must now be backed up by concrete and effective actions.* **4** PHRASAL VERB If you **back** someone **up**, you show your support for them. ❑ *His employers backed him up.* **5** PHRASAL VERB If you **back** someone **up**, you help them by confirming that what they are saying is true. ❑ *The girl denied being there, and the man backed her up.* **6** PHRASAL VERB If you **back up**, the car or other vehicle that you are driving moves back a short distance. ❑ *Back up, Hans.* **7** PHRASAL VERB If you **back up**, you move backward a short distance. ❑ *I backed up carefully until I felt the wall against my back.* **8** PHRASAL VERB When a car **backs up** or when you **back** it **up**, the car is driven backward. [AM]

in BRIT, usually use **reverse**

9 → see also **backup**

back|ache /bǽkeɪk/ (backaches) N-VAR **Backache** is a dull pain in your back.

back-alley ADJ [ADJ n] **Back-alley** activities are carried out unofficially, secretly, and often illegally. [AM] ❑ *...a land in which women would be forced into back-alley abortions.*

back|bit|ing /bǽkbaɪtɪŋ/ N-UNCOUNT If you accuse someone of **backbiting**, you mean that they say unpleasant or unkind things about someone who is not present, especially in order to stop them from doing well at work. [DISAPPROVAL]

back|board /bǽkbɔrd/ (backboards) N-COUNT In basketball, the **backboard** is the flat board above each of the baskets.

back|bone /bǽkboʊn/ (backbones) **1** N-COUNT Your **backbone** is the column of small linked bones down the middle of your back. **2** N-UNCOUNT [oft with brd-neg] If you say that someone has no **backbone**, you think that they do not have the courage to do things which need to be done. ❑ *You might be taking drastic measures and you've got to have the backbone to do that.*

back-breaking also **backbreaking** ADJ [usu ADJ n] **Back-breaking** work involves a lot of hard physical effort.

back burn|er also **backburner** N-SING [usu the N] If you put an issue on the **back burner**, you leave it in order to deal with it later because you now consider it to have become less urgent or important. Compare **front burner**. ❑ *Many speculated that the U.S. would put the peace process on the back burner.*

back cata|log (back catalogs) N-COUNT [oft poss N] A musical performer's **back catalog** is the music that they recorded and released in the past rather than their latest recordings.

in BRIT, use **back catalogue**

back|cloth /bǽkklɒθ/ [BRIT] → see **backdrop 1**

back copy (back copies) N-COUNT A **back copy** of a magazine or newspaper is one that was published some time ago and is not the most recent.

back coun|try also **backcountry** N-SING [the N] The **back country** is an area that is a long way from any city and has very few people living in it. [AM] ❑ *They have moved deep into the back country.*

back|coun|try camp|ing /bǽkʌntri kǽmpɪŋ/ N-UNCOUNT **Backcountry camping** is camping in remote places with no facilities, rather than on campsites. ❑ *Exploration and escape are the fundamental attractions of backcountry camping.*

back|court /bǽkkɔrt/ (backcourts) N-COUNT [usu the N] In sports such tennis and badminton, the **backcourt** is the section of each side of the court that is furthest from the net. In basketball, the **backcourt** is the rear part of the court, where the defense plays. You can also use **backcourt** to refer to the members of a team who play mainly in this part of the court.

back|date /bǽkdeɪt/ (backdates, backdating, backdated) also **back-date** V-T If a document or an arrangement **is backdated**, it is valid from a date before the date when it is completed or signed. ❑ *The contract that was signed on Thursday morning was backdated to March 11.*

back|door /bǽkdɔr/ also **back door** **1** ADJ [ADJ n] You can use **backdoor** to describe an action or process if you disapprove of it because you think it has been done in a secret, indirect, or dishonest way. [DISAPPROVAL] ❑ *Firms are using the program as a backdoor way to replace domestic employees with cheaper labor.* ❑ *Critics say this amounts to a backdoor amnesty for illegal aliens.* **2** N-SING [the N, usu prep N] If you say that someone is doing something through or by **the backdoor**, you disapprove of them because they are doing it in a secret, indirect, or dishonest way. [DISAPPROVAL] ❑ *The government must not use this initiative as a means of resolving the pension problem through the back door.*

back|drop /bǽkdrɒp/ (backdrops) **1** N-COUNT A **backdrop** is a large piece of cloth, often with scenery painted on it, that is hung at the back of a stage while a play is being performed. **2** N-COUNT [usu N prep] The **backdrop** to an object or a scene is what you see behind it. ❑ *...the rugged cliffs that formed a backdrop to the village.* **3** N-COUNT [usu N prep] The **backdrop** to an event is the general situation in which it happens. ❑ *The election will take place against a backdrop of increasing instability.*

back|er /bǽkər/ (backers) N-COUNT A **backer** is someone who helps or supports a project, organization, or person, often by giving or lending money. ❑ *I was looking for a backer to assist me in the attempted buyout.*

back|fire /bǽkfaɪər/ (backfires, backfiring, backfired) **1** V-I If a plan or project **backfires**, it has the opposite result to the one that was intended. ❑ *The president's tactics could backfire.* **2** V-I When a motor vehicle or its engine **backfires**, it produces an explosion in the exhaust pipe. ❑ *The car backfired.*

back|gam|mon /bǽkgæmən/ N-UNCOUNT **Backgammon** is a game for two people, played on a board marked with long triangles. Each player has 15 wooden or plastic disks. The players throw dice and move the disks around the board.

back|ground ✦✧ /bǽkgraʊnd/ (backgrounds) **1** N-COUNT Your **background** is the kind of family you come from and the kind of education you have had. It can also refer to such things as your social and racial origins, your financial status, or the type of work experience that you have. ❑ *The Warners were from a Jewish working-class background.* **2** N-COUNT The **background** to an event or situation consists of the facts that explain what caused it. ❑ *The background to the current troubles is provided by the dire state of the country's economy.* ❑ *The meeting takes place against a background of continuing political violence.* **3** N-SING The **background** is sounds, such as music, that you can hear but that you are not listening to with your full attention. ❑ *I kept hearing the sound of applause in the background.* **4** N-COUNT You can use **background** to refer to the things in a picture or scene that are less noticeable or important than the main things or people in it. ❑ *...roses patterned on a blue background.*

SYNONYMS

background
NOUN

1
upbringing: *Martin's upbringing shaped his whole life.*
childhood: *She had a happy childhood.*
nurture: *The human organism learns partly by nature, partly by nurture.*

2
environment: *The twins were brought up in entirely different environments.*
circumstances: *The strategy was too dangerous in the explosive circumstances of the times.*
history: *He couldn't get a new job because of his medical history.*
conditions: *The conditions are ripe for the spread of disease.*

back|ground|er /bækgraʊndər/ (backgrounders) **1** N-COUNT A **backgrounder** is a short article in a newspaper or magazine that provides background information about a particular subject. [AM] □ ...a backgrounder on business prospects for the Asia-Pacific region. **2** N-COUNT A **backgrounder** is a meeting in which government officials give reporters background information about an issue or policy. [mainly AM] □ ...a State Department backgrounder.

back|hand /bækhænd/ (backhands) N-VAR A **backhand** is a shot in tennis or other racket sports, which you make with your arm across your body. □ She practiced her backhand.

back|hand|ed /bækhændɪd/ also **back-handed** **1** ADJ [ADJ n] A **backhanded** compliment is a remark which seems to be an insult but could also be understood as a compliment. A **backhanded** compliment is also a remark which seems to be a compliment but could also be understood as an insult. □ Saying she's improved comes over as a backhanded compliment. **2** ADJ [ADJ n] If you say that someone is doing something in a **backhanded** way, they are doing it indirectly. [DISAPPROVAL] □ In a backhanded way, I think a lot of my energy and strength comes from my campaigning.

back|hoe /bækhoʊ/ (backhoes) N-COUNT A **backhoe** is a large vehicle which is used for moving large amounts of earth. [AM]

back|ing ✦✧ /bækɪŋ/ (backings) **1** N-UNCOUNT If someone has the **backing** of an organization or an important person, they receive support or money from that organization or person in order to do something. □ He said the president had the full backing of his government to negotiate a deal. **2** N-VAR A **backing** is a layer of something such as cloth that is put onto the back of something in order to strengthen or protect it. □ The table mats and coasters have a non-slip, soft green backing.

SYNONYMS

backing
NOUN **1**
support: The prime minister gave his full support to the government's reforms.
approval: The chairman has also given his approval for an investigation into the case.
endorsement: It's important that we get the endorsement of the local colleges.

back is|sue (back issues) N-COUNT A **back issue** of a magazine or newspaper is the same as a **back copy**.

back|lash /bæklæʃ/ N-SING A **backlash** against a tendency or recent development in society or politics is a sudden, strong reaction against it. □ ...the male backlash against feminism.

back|less /bækləs/ ADJ [usu ADJ n] A **backless** dress or top leaves most of a woman's back uncovered down to her waist.

back|log /bæklɒg/ (backlogs) N-COUNT A **backlog** is a number of things which have not yet been done but which need to be done. □ There is a backlog of repairs and maintenance in schools.

back|pack /bækpæk/ (backpacks) **1** N-COUNT A **backpack** is a bag with straps that go over your shoulders, so that you can carry things on your back when you are walking or climbing. **2** → See also color supplement

back|pack|er /bækpækər/ (backpackers) **1** N-COUNT A **backpacker** is a person who goes traveling with a backpack. **2** → See feature box at **tourism**

back|pack|ing /bækpækɪŋ/ N-UNCOUNT If you go **backpacking**, you go traveling with a backpack.

back pay N-UNCOUNT **Back pay** is money which an employer owes an employee for work that he or she did in the past. [BUSINESS] □ He will receive $6,000 in back pay.

back ped|al (back-pedals, back-pedalling or back-pedalling, back-pedaled or back-pedalled) also **backpedal** **1** V-I If you **back-pedal**, you express a different or less forceful opinion about something from the one you have previously expressed. □ Allen back-pedaled, saying that he had had no intention of offending them. □ He appeared to back-pedal on that statement. **2** V-I If you say that someone **back-pedals**, you disapprove of their behavior because they are not doing what they promised. [DISAPPROVAL] □ She's backpedaled twice already. □ The cabinet may backpedal on these commitments. ● **back-pedaling** N-UNCOUNT □ The paper put the controversy on the front page. And the next day, the back-pedaling began.

back|rest /bækrest/ (backrests) N-COUNT The **backrest** of a seat or chair is the part that you rest your back on.

back road (back roads) N-COUNT A **back road** is a small country road with very little traffic.

back|room /bækrum/ (backrooms) also **back-room, back room** **1** N-COUNT A **backroom** is a room that is situated at the back of a building, especially a private room. □ ...the backroom of the officers' club. **2** N-COUNT [oft N n] You can use **backroom** to refer to people in an organization who do important work but are not seen or known about by the public. You can also use **backroom** to refer to a place where such people work. □ Public scrutiny had brought civil servants out from the backroom and into the spotlight. □ ...Mr. Smith's backroom staff. **3** ADJ [ADJ n] If you refer to a deal made by someone such as a politician as a **backroom** deal, you disapprove of it because it has been made in a secret, dishonest way. [DISAPPROVAL] □ They have been calling the presidency decision a backroom deal.

back|seat driv|er (backseat drivers) also **back-seat driver** **1** N-COUNT If you refer to a passenger in a car as a **backseat driver**, they annoy you because they constantly give you advice about how to drive. [DISAPPROVAL] **2** N-COUNT If you refer to someone, especially a politician, as a **backseat driver**, you disapprove of them because they try to influence a situation that does not concern them. [DISAPPROVAL] □ They accused the former president of being a backseat driver.

back|side /bæksaɪd/ (backsides) N-COUNT Your **backside** is the part of your body that you sit on. [INFORMAL] □ The lad fell backwards, landing on his backside.

back|slapping /bækslæpɪŋ/ also **back slapping** N-UNCOUNT **Backslapping** is noisy, cheerful behavior which people use in order to show affection or appreciation to each other. ● ADJ [ADJ n] **Backslapping** is also an adjective. □ Scott breaks away from his back-slapping admirers.

back|slid|ing /bækslaɪdɪŋ/ N-UNCOUNT If you accuse someone of **backsliding**, you disapprove of them because they have failed to do something they promised or agreed to do, or have started again doing something undesirable that they had previously stopped doing. [DISAPPROVAL] □ ...the government's backsliding on free market reforms. □ This may help to maintain the gains you've made and to prevent backsliding.

back|stabbing /bækstæbɪŋ/ **1** N-UNCOUNT **Backstabbing** consists of unkind and disloyal actions or remarks that are likely to harm someone such as a friend or colleague. □ She accused her friends of bullying and backstabbing. **2** ADJ A **backstabbing** person behaves in this way. □ He was not prepared to deal with his backstabbing boss.

back|stage /bæksteɪdʒ/ ADV [ADV after v] In a theater, **backstage** refers to the areas behind the stage. □ He went backstage and asked for her autograph. ● ADJ [ADJ n] **Backstage** is also an adjective. □ ...a backstage pass.

back street (back streets) also **back-street, backstreet** **1** N-COUNT A **back street** in a town or city is a small, narrow street with very little traffic. □ The small church of San Michel is tucked away in a narrow back street of Port-au-Prince. □ ...backstreet garages. **2** N-PLURAL The **back streets** of a town or city are the areas of small, old, poor streets rather than the richer or newer areas. □ ...a kid from the back streets of Billings, Montana.

back|stroke /bækstroʊk/ N-UNCOUNT [also the N] **Backstroke** is a swimming stroke that you do lying on your back. □ "I see you know how to swim very well," she said, watching him do the backstroke.

back talk also **backtalk** N-UNCOUNT If you refer to something that someone says as **backtalk**, you mean that it is rude or shows a lack of respect. You use **backtalk** especially to refer to things said by a child or by someone who is below you in rank or status. [AM, DISAPPROVAL]

back-to-back **1** ADJ [usu ADJ n] **Back-to-back** wins or victories are victories that are gained one after another without any defeats between them. □ ...their first back-to-back victories of the season. **2** → see also **back** ② **9**

back|track /bæktræk/ (backtracks, backtracking, backtracked) also **back-track** **1** V-I If you **backtrack** on a statement or decision you have made, you do or say something that shows that you no longer agree with it or support it. □ The committee backtracked by scrapping the

backup

controversial bonus system. ❑ *His arrest sparked fears that the country was backtracking on market reforms.* • **back|track|ing** N-UNCOUNT ❑ *He promised there would be no backtracking on policies.* **2** V-I If you **backtrack**, you go back along a path or route you have just used. ❑ *Leonard jumped in his car and started backtracking.* ❑ *We had to backtrack to the corner and cross the street.* **3** V-I If you **backtrack** in an account or explanation, you talk about things which happened before the ones you were previously talking about. ❑ *Can we just backtrack a little bit and look at your primary and secondary education?*

back|up /bǽkʌp/ (**backups**) also **back-up** **1** N-VAR **Backup** consists of extra equipment, resources, or people that you can get help or support from if necessary. ❑ *There is no emergency back-up immediately available.* **2** N-VAR If you have something such as a second piece of equipment or set of plans as **backup**, you have arranged for them to be available for use in case the first one does not work. ❑ *Every part of the system has a backup.* **3** N-COUNT The **backup** of a song is the music that is sung or played to accompany the main tune. ❑ *Sharon also sang backup for Barry Manilow.* **4** N-COUNT A **backup** is a long line of traffic stretching back along a road, which moves very slowly or not at all, for example, because of roadwork or an accident. [AM] ❑ *There was a seven-mile backup on the freeway*

in BRIT, use **tailback**

back|up light (**backup lights**) N-COUNT [oft pl] **Backup lights** are the white lights on the back of a vehicle that shine when the vehicle moves backward. [AM] ❑ *The car had a single backup light above the rear license plate.*

in BRIT, use **reversing light**

back|ward /bǽkwərd/

In British English, **backwards** is much more common than **backward** when used as an adverb.

1 ADJ [ADJ n] A **backward** movement or look is in the direction that your back is facing. ❑ *He unlocked the door of apartment two and disappeared inside after a backward glance at Larry.* **2** ADJ If someone takes a **backward** step or a step **backward**, they do something that does not change or improve their situation, but causes them to go back a stage. ❑ *The current U.S. farm bill, however, is a big step backward.* **3** ADJ A **backward** country or society does not have modern industries and machines. ❑ *We need to accelerate the pace of change in our backward country.* **4** ADJ A **backward** child has difficulty in learning. [OFFENSIVE] ❑ *...research into teaching techniques to help backward children.* **5** ADV [ADV after v] If you move or look **backward**, you move or look in the direction that your back is facing. ❑ *The diver flipped over backward into the water.* ❑ *He took two steps backward.* **6** ADV [ADV after v] If you do something **backward**, you do it in the opposite way to the usual way. ❑ *He works backward, building a house from the top downward.* **7** ADV You use **backward** to indicate that something changes or develops in a way that is not an improvement, but is a return to old ideas or methods. ❑ *This country is going backward.* **8** PHRASE If someone or something moves **backward and forward**, they move repeatedly first in one direction and then in the opposite direction. ❑ *Using a gentle, sawing motion, draw the floss backward and forward between the teeth.*

backward-looking also **backward looking** ADJ If you describe someone or something as **backward-looking**, you disapprove of their attitudes, ideas, or actions because they are based on old-fashioned opinions or methods. [DISAPPROVAL] ❑ *...a stagnant, backward-looking culture.*

back|wards /bǽkwərdz/ → see **backward**

back|wash /bǽkwɒʃ/ **1** N-SING The **backwash** of an event or situation is an unpleasant situation that exists after it and as a result of it. ❑ *...the backwash of the events of 1989.* **2** N-UNCOUNT **Backwash** is the backward movement of water caused by something moving through it. ❑ *The skipper pushed the boat hard, creating a broad white backwash at our stern.* **3** N-UNCOUNT **Backwash** is liquid, sometimes mixed with small pieces of food, that goes from your mouth back into a bottle or cup that you drink from. ❑ *I'm not drinking that – it has backwash in it!*

back|water /bǽkwɔtər/ (**backwaters**) **1** N-COUNT A **backwater** is a place that is isolated. ❑ *...a quiet rural backwater.* **2** N-COUNT If you refer to a place or institution as a **backwater**,

88

bad

you think it is not developing properly because it is isolated from ideas and events in other places and institutions. [DISAPPROVAL] ❑ *The state's high schools remain an educational backwater where dropout rates are rising.* ❑ *This agency will be relegated to the backwaters of Washington.*

back|woods /bǽkwʊdz/ N-PLURAL If you refer to an area as the **backwoods**, you mean that it is a long way from large towns or cities and is isolated from modern life. ❑ *...the backwoods of Louisiana.*

back|yard /bǽkyɑrd/ (**backyards**) also **back yard** **1** N-COUNT A **backyard** is an area of land at the back of a house. **2** N-COUNT If you refer to a country's own **backyard**, you are referring to its own territory or to somewhere that is very close and where that country wants to influence events. ❑ *They seem to think that if it isn't happening in their own backyard, it isn't worth worrying about.*

ba|con /béɪkən/ N-UNCOUNT **Bacon** is salted or smoked meat which comes from the back or sides of a pig. ❑ *...bacon and eggs.*

bac|te|ria /bæktɪ́əriə/ N-PLURAL **Bacteria** are very small organisms. Some bacteria can cause disease. ❑ *Chlorine is added to kill bacteria.*

bac|te|rial /bæktɪ́əriəl/ **1** ADJ [ADJ n] **Bacterial** is used to describe things that relate to or are caused by bacteria. ❑ *Cholera is a bacterial infection.* **2** → See feature box at **illness**

bac|te|ri|ol|ogy /bæktɪəriɒ́lədʒi/ N-UNCOUNT **Bacteriology** is the science and the study of bacteria. • **bac|te|rio|logi|cal** /bæktɪəriəlɒ́dʒɪkᵊl/ ADJ [ADJ n] ❑ *...the national bacteriological laboratory.*

bac|te|rium /bæktɪ́əriʊm/ **Bacterium** is the singular of **bacteria**.

bad ♦♦♦ /bǽd/ (**worse, worst**)

In meaning **9**, the comparative form is **badder** and the superlative form is **baddest**.

1 ADJ Something that is **bad** is unpleasant, harmful, or undesirable. ❑ *The bad weather conditions prevented the plane from landing.* ❑ *Experts agree that too much TV is bad for children.* **2** ADJ You use **bad** to indicate that something unpleasant or undesirable is severe or great in degree. ❑ *Glick had a bad accident two years ago and had to give up farming.* ❑ *The floods are described as the worst in nearly fifty years.* **3** ADJ A **bad** idea, decision, or method is not sensible or not correct. ❑ *Giving your address to a man you don't know is a bad idea.* ❑ *The worst thing you can do is underestimate an opponent.* **4** ADJ If you describe a piece of news, an action, or a sign as **bad**, you mean that it is unlikely to result in benefit or success. ❑ *The closure of the project is bad news for her staff.* ❑ *It was a bad start in my relationship with Warr.* **5** ADJ Something that is **bad** is of an unacceptably low standard, quality, or amount. ❑ *Many old people in the United States are living in bad housing.* ❑ *The schools' main problem is that teachers' pay is so bad.* **6** ADJ Someone who is **bad** at doing something is not skillful or successful at it. ❑ *Howard was so bad at basketball.* ❑ *He was a bad driver.* **7** ADJ If you say that it is **bad** that something happens, you mean it is unacceptable, unfortunate, or wrong. ❑ *Not being able to hear doesn't seem as bad to the rest of us as not being able to see.* **8** ADJ [with neg] You can say that something is **not bad** to mean that it is quite good or acceptable, especially when you are rather surprised about this. ❑ *"How much is he paying you?"—"Oh, five thousand."—"Not bad."* ❑ *That's not a bad idea.* **9** ADJ [usu ADJ n] If you describe someone or something as **bad**, you mean that they are very good. [INFORMAL] ❑ *...the baddest bass music from Miami, featuring Dr. Boom & The Dominator.* **10** ADJ If you feel **bad** about something, you feel sorry or guilty about it. ❑ *You don't have to feel bad about relaxing.* ❑ *I feel bad that he's doing most of the work.* **11** ADJ A **bad** child disobeys rules and instructions or does not behave in a polite and correct way. ❑ *You are a bad boy for repeating what I told you.* **12** ADJ If you are in a **bad** mood, you are angry and behave unpleasantly to people. ❑ *She is in a bit of a bad mood because she's just given up smoking.* **13** ADJ If you feel **bad about** something, you feel sorry or guilty about it. ❑ *You don't have to feel bad about relaxing.* ❑ *I feel bad that he's doing most of the work.* **14** ADJ If you have a **bad** back, heart, leg, or eye, it is injured, diseased, or weak. ❑ *Joe has a bad back so we have a hard bed.* **15** ADJ Food that has gone **bad** is not suitable to eat because it has started to decay. ❑ *They bought so* much beef that some went bad. ◨ ADJ **Bad** language is language that contains offensive words such as swear words. ❑ *I don't like to hear bad language in the street.* ◨ → see also **worse, worst** ◨ **bad blood** → see **blood** ◨ **bad luck** → see **luck** ◨ **to get bad press** → see **press**

bad|ass /bǽdæs/ (**badasses**) also **bad-ass** ◨ N-COUNT If you describe someone as a **badass**, you mean that they are very tough or violent. [mainly AM, INFORMAL, VULGAR] ❑ *...the legendary Memphis badass George Tiller.* • **badass** is also an adjective. ❑ *They want to be somebody, want to be able to go home a big, badass Marine.* ◨ ADJ [ADJ n] Some people use **badass** to describe something they think is very good or impressive. [mainly AM, INFORMAL, APPROVAL] ❑ *Recent Emmy-winner Joey Pants is one bust-out, badass dude who deserves a hit.*

bad check (**bad checks**)

in BRIT, use **bad cheque**

N-COUNT A **bad check** is a check that will not be paid because there is a mistake on it, or because there is not enough money in the account of the person who wrote the check.

bad debt (**bad debts**) N-COUNT A **bad debt** is a sum of money that has been lent but is not likely to be repaid. ❑ *The bank set aside 1.1 billion dollars to cover bad debts from business failures.*

bad|dy /bǽdi/ (**baddies**) also **baddie** N-COUNT [usu pl] A **baddy** is a person in a story or film who is considered to be evil or wicked, or who is fighting on the wrong side. You can also refer to the **baddies** in a situation in real life. [mainly BRIT, INFORMAL]

in AM, usually use **bad guy**

bade /bæd, beɪd/ **Bade** is a past tense of **bid**.
badge /bædʒ/ (**badges**) ◨ N-COUNT A **badge** is a piece of metal, cloth or plastic which you wear or carry to show that you work for a particular organization, or that you have achieved something. ❑ *...a police officer's badge.* ◨ N-COUNT A **badge** is a small piece of metal or plastic which you wear in order to show that you support a particular movement, organization, or person. You fasten a badge to your clothes with a pin. [BRIT]

in AM, use **button**

badg|er /bǽdʒər/ (**badgers, badgering, badgered**) ◨ N-COUNT A **badger** is a wild animal which has a white head with two wide black stripes on it. Badgers live underground and usually come up to feed at night. ◨ V-T If you **badger** someone, you repeatedly tell them to do something or repeatedly ask them questions. ❑ *She badgered her doctor time and again, pleading with him to do something.* ❑ *They kept phoning and writing, badgering me to go back.*

bad guy (**bad guys**) N-COUNT [usu pl] A **bad guy** is a person in a story or film who is considered to be evil or wicked, or who is fighting on the wrong side. You can also refer to the **bad guys** in a situation in real life. [INFORMAL] ❑ *In the end the "bad guys" are caught and sent to jail.*

bad hair day (**bad hair days**) N-COUNT [usu sing] People sometimes say they are having a **bad hair day** when they do not feel very happy or relaxed, especially because their hair does not look good. [INFORMAL] ❑ *All this fuss is because Carol is having a bad hair day.*

badi|nage /bǽdɪnɑːʒ, -nɑːʒ/ N-UNCOUNT **Badinage** is humorous or light-hearted conversation that often involves teasing someone. [LITERARY] ❑ *...light-hearted badinage.*

bad|ly /bǽdli/ (**worse, worst**) ◨ ADV [ADV with v] If something is done **badly** or goes **badly**, it is not very successful or effective. ❑ *I was angry because I played so badly.* ❑ *The whole project was badly managed.* ◨ ADV If someone or something is **badly** hurt or **badly** affected, they are severely hurt or affected. ❑ *The bomb destroyed a police station and badly damaged a church.* ❑ *One man was killed and another badly injured.* ◨ ADV [ADV with v] If you want or need something **badly**, you want or need it very much. ❑ *Why do you want to go so badly?* ◨ ADV [ADV with v] If someone behaves **badly** or treats other people **badly**, they act in an unkind, unpleasant, or unacceptable way. ❑ *They have both behaved very badly and I am very hurt.* ◨ ADV [ADV after v] If something reflects **badly** on someone or makes others think **badly** of them, it harms their reputation. ❑ *Teachers know that low exam results will reflect badly on them.* ◨ ADV If a person or their job is **badly** paid, they are not paid very much for what they do. ❑ *You may have to work part-time, in a badly paid job.* ◨ → see also **worse, worst**

USAGE

badly
Don't use 'bad' as an adverb. Don't say, for example, '<s>I did bad on my exam.</s>' Say '*I did badly on my exam.*' *The project was badly managed.*

bad|ly off [BRIT] → see **bad off**
bad|min|ton /bǽdmɪntən/ ◨ N-UNCOUNT **Badminton** is a game played by two or four players on a rectangular court with a high net across the middle. The players try to score points by hitting a small object called a shuttlecock across the net using a racket. ◨ → See also color supplement
bad-mouth (**bad-mouths, bad-mouthing, bad-mouthed**) V-T If someone **bad-mouths** you, they say unpleasant things about you, especially when you are not there to defend yourself. ❑ *Both men continually bad-mouthed each other.*

bad off (**worse off, worst off**)

in BRIT, usually use **badly off**

◨ ADJ [usu v-link ADJ] If you are **bad off**, you are in a bad situation. ❑ *But there were other people worse off than me at the hospital, linked up to respirators and unable to walk.* ◨ ADJ [usu v-link ADJ] If you are **bad off**, you do not have much money. ❑ *An independent study found that the owners are not as bad off as they say, and most are making money.*

bad-tempered ADJ Someone who is **bad-tempered** is not very cheerful and gets angry easily. ❑ *When his headaches developed, Nick became bad-tempered and even violent.*
bae /beɪ/ (**baes**) N-COUNT [usu sing] Your **bae** is someone you are romantically involved with or in love with. [INFORMAL] ❑ *You might give that photo a caption like, "Just another Tuesday with my bae."* ❑ *Hey, bae, thinking about you.*
baf|fle /bǽfᵊl/ (**baffles, baffling, baffled**) V-T If something **baffles** you, you cannot understand it or explain it. ❑ *An apple tree producing square fruit is baffling experts.* • **baf|fling** ADJ ❑ *I was constantly ill, with a baffling array of symptoms.*
baf|fle|ment /bǽfᵊlmənt/ N-UNCOUNT **Bafflement** is the state of being baffled. ❑ *The general response was one of understandable bafflement.*
bag ✦✧ /bæg/ (**bags**) ◨ N-COUNT A **bag** is a container made of thin paper or plastic, for example, one that is used in stores to put things in that a customer has bought. ◨ N-COUNT You can use **bag** to refer to a bag and its contents, or to the contents only. ❑ *...a bag of candy.* ◨ N-COUNT A **bag** is a strong container with one or two handles, used to carry things in. ❑ *She left the hotel carrying a shopping bag.* ◨ N-COUNT A **bag** is the same as a **handbag**. ◨ N-PLURAL If you have **bags** under your eyes, you have folds of skin there, usually because you have not had enough sleep. ❑ *The bags under his eyes have grown darker.* ◨ → see also **sleeping bag** ◨ → See also color supplement
ba|gel /beɪgᵊl/ (**bagels**) N-COUNT A **bagel** is a ring-shaped bread roll.
bag|gage /bǽgɪdʒ/ ◨ N-UNCOUNT Your **baggage** consists of the bags that you take with you when you travel. ❑ *The passengers went through immigration control and collected their baggage.* ◨ N-UNCOUNT You can use **baggage** to refer to someone's emotional problems, fixed ideas, or prejudices. ❑ *How much emotional baggage is he bringing with him into the relationship?*
bag|gage car (**baggage cars**) N-COUNT A **baggage car** is a railroad car, often without windows, which is used to carry luggage, goods, or mail. [AM] ❑ *The coffin was loaded into the baggage car of the train.*

in BRIT, use **van**

bag|gage claim N-SING [usu the N] At an airport, the **baggage claim** is the area where you collect your baggage at the end of your trip. ❑ *Luke and Vlad followed the signs to the baggage claim.*

in BRIT, also use **baggage reclaim**

bag|gage re|claim [BRIT] → see **baggage claim**

bag|ger /bæɡər/ (baggers) N-COUNT A **bagger** is a person whose job is to put customers' purchases into bags at a supermarket or other store. [AM] ❑ *In addition to being a bagger, he's worked at a fast-food restaurant.*

bag|gy /bæɡi/ (baggier, baggiest) ADJ If a piece of clothing is **baggy**, it hangs loosely on your body. ❑ *...a baggy sweater.*

bag lady (bag ladies) N-COUNT A **bag lady** is a homeless woman who carries her possessions in shopping bags. [INFORMAL]

bag|pipes /bæɡpaɪps/

> The form **bagpipe** is used as a modifier.

N-PLURAL [oft *the* N] **Bagpipes** are a musical instrument that is traditionally played in Scotland. You play the bagpipes by blowing air through a pipe into a bag, and then squeezing the bag to force the air out through other pipes.

ba|guette /bæɡɛt/ (baguettes) N-COUNT A **baguette** is a type of long, thin loaf of white bread which is traditionally made in France.

bah /bɑː/ EXCLAM 'Bah' is used in writing to represent a noise that people make in order to express contempt, disappointment, or annoyance. [OLD-FASHIONED] ❑ *Christmas? Bah! Humbug!*

Ba|ha|mian /bəheɪmiən, -hɑː-/ (Bahamians) **1** ADJ **Bahamian** means belonging or relating to the Bahamas or to its people or culture. **2** N-COUNT **Bahamians** are people who come from the Bahamas.

bail /beɪl/ (bails, bailing, bailed)

> The spelling **bale** is also used for meaning **4**, and for meanings **1** and **5** of the phrasal verb.

1 N-UNCOUNT **Bail** is a sum of money that an arrested person or someone else puts forward as a guarantee that the arrested person will attend their trial in a law court. If the arrested person does not attend it, the money will be lost. ❑ *He was freed on bail pending an appeal.* **2** N-UNCOUNT **Bail** is permission for an arrested person to be released after bail has been paid. ❑ *Bilal was held without bail after a court appearance in Detroit.* **3** V-T [usu passive] If someone **is bailed**, they are released while they are waiting for their trial, after paying an amount of money to the court. ❑ *He was bailed to appear on 26 August.* **4** V-I If you **bail**, you use a container to remove water from a boat or from a place which is flooded. ❑ *We kept he afloat for a couple of hours by bailing frantically.* • PHRASAL VERB **Bail out** means the same as **bail**. ❑ *A crew was sent down the shaft to close it off and bail out all the water.* **5** PHRASE If someone who has been arrested **makes bail**, or if another person **makes bail** for them, the arrested person is released on bail. ❑ *Guerrero was ultimately arrested, but he made bail and fled to Colombia.* **6** PHRASE If a prisoner **jumps bail**, he or she does not come back for his or her trial after being released on bail. ❑ *He had jumped bail last year while being tried on drug charges.* **7** → See feature box at **legal**
▶ **bail out** **1** PHRASAL VERB If you **bail** someone **out**, you help them out of a difficult situation, often by giving them money. ❑ *They will discuss how to bail the economy out of its slump.* **2** → see also **bailout** **3** PHRASAL VERB If you **bail** someone **out**, you pay bail on their behalf. ❑ *He has been jailed eight times. Each time, friends bailed him out.* **4** PHRASAL VERB If a pilot **bails out** of an aircraft that is crashing, he or she jumps from it, using a parachute to land safely. ❑ *Reid was forced to bail out of the crippled aircraft.* **5** → see **bail 4**

bail|iff /beɪlɪf/ (bailiffs) N-COUNT A **bailiff** is an official in a court of law who deals with tasks such as keeping control in court. [AM] ❑ *The court bailiff said jurors did not wish to speak to news media until the sentencing.*

bail|out /beɪlaʊt/ (bailouts) **1** N-COUNT [oft N of n] A **bailout** of an organization or individual that has financial problems is the act of helping them by giving them money. [mainly AM] ❑ *...one of the biggest government bailouts of a private company in years.* **2** → See feature box at **banking**

bait /beɪt/ (baits, baiting, baited) **1** N-VAR **Bait** is food which you put on a hook or in a trap in order to catch fish or animals. ❑ *Vivien refuses to put down bait to tempt wildlife to the waterhole.* **2** V-T If you **bait** a hook or trap, you put bait on it or in it. ❑ *He baited his hook with pie.* ❑ *The boys dug pits and baited them.* **3** N-UNCOUNT [also *a* N] To use something as **bait** means to use it to trick or persuade someone to do something. ❑ *Television programs are essentially bait to attract an audience for commercials.* **4** V-T If you **bait** someone, you deliberately try to make them angry by teasing them. ❑ *He delighted in baiting his mother.* **5** PHRASE **Bait and switch** is used to refer to a sales technique in which goods are advertised at low prices in order to attract customers, although only a small number of the low-priced goods are available. ❑ *The classy piano bar next to Maddalena's really sells 11 dishes for the advertised price at lunch. There's no bait and switch here.*

-baiting /-beɪtɪŋ/ **1** COMB IN N-UNCOUNT You use **-baiting** after nouns to refer to the activity of attacking a particular group of people or laughing at their beliefs. **2** COMB IN N-UNCOUNT Badger**-baiting**, bear**-baiting**, and bull**-baiting** involve making these animals fight dogs, while making sure that the animals are unable to defend themselves properly.

baize /beɪz/ N-UNCOUNT **Baize** is a thick woolen material that is used for covering tables on which games such as cards and pool are played.

bake ♦◇◇ /beɪk/ (bakes, baking, baked) **1** V-T/V-I [no passive] If you **bake**, you spend some time preparing and mixing together ingredients to make bread, cakes, pies, or other food which is cooked in the oven. ❑ *How did you learn to bake cakes?* ❑ *I love to bake.* • **bak|ing** N-UNCOUNT [also *the* N] ❑ *On a Thursday she used to do all the baking.* **2** V-T/V-I When a cake or bread **bakes** or when you **bake** it, it cooks in the oven without any extra liquid or fat. ❑ *Bake the cake for 35 to 50 minutes.* ❑ *The batter rises as it bakes.* **3** → see also **baking**

baked beans N-PLURAL **Baked beans** are dried beans cooked with molasses or brown sugar and salt pork in North America or in tomato sauce in Britain. Baked beans are usually sold in cans.

Ba|ke|lite /beɪkəlaɪt/ N-UNCOUNT **Bakelite** is a type of hard plastic that was used in the past for making things such as telephones and radios. [TRADEMARK]

bake-off (bake-offs) N-COUNT A **bake-off** is a cooking competition. ❑ *If you win the bake-off, I'm certain that you get to make a speech.*

bak|er /beɪkər/ (bakers) **1** N-COUNT A **baker** is a person whose job is to bake and sell bread, pastries, and cakes. **2** N-COUNT A **baker** or a **baker's** is a store where bread and cakes are sold. [mainly BRIT]

> in AM, usually use **bakery**

bak|ery /beɪkəri, beɪkri/ (bakeries) N-COUNT A **bakery** is a building where bread, pastries, and cakes are baked, or the store where they are sold. ❑ *A smell of bread drifted from some distant bakery.*

bake|ware /beɪkwɛər/ N-UNCOUNT Pans, trays, and dishes that are used for baking can be referred to as **bakeware**.

bak|ing /beɪkɪŋ/ **1** ADJ You can use **baking** to describe weather or a place that is very hot indeed. ❑ *...a baking July day.* ❑ *The coffins stood in the baking heat surrounded by mourners.* **2** → see also **bake**

bak|ing pow|der (baking powders) N-MASS **Baking powder** is an ingredient used in cake making. It causes cakes to rise when they are in the oven.

bak|ing sheet (baking sheets) N-COUNT A **baking sheet** is a flat piece of metal on which you bake foods such as cookies or pies in an oven.

bak|ing soda N-UNCOUNT **Baking soda** is the same as **bicarbonate of soda**.

bala|cla|va /bæləklɑːvə/ (balaclavas) N-COUNT A **balaclava** is a tight woolen hood that covers every part of your head except your face.

bal|ance ♦♦◇ /bæləns/ (balances, balancing, balanced) **1** V-T/V-I If you **balance** something somewhere, or if it **balances** there, it remains steady and does not fall. ❑ *I balanced on the ledge.* **2** N-UNCOUNT **Balance** is the ability to remain steady when you are standing up. ❑ *The medicines you are currently taking could be affecting your balance.* **3** V-RECIP If you **balance** one thing with something different, each of the things has the same strength or importance. ❑ *Balance spicy dishes with* mild ones. ❑ *The government has to find some way to balance these two needs.* ❑ *Supply and demand on the currency market will generally balance.* ● **bal|anced** ADJ ❑ *This book is a well balanced biography.* **4** N-SING A **balance** is a situation in which all the different parts are equal in strength or importance. ❑ *...the ecological balance of the forest.* **5** N-SING If you say that the **balance** tips in your favor, you start winning or succeeding, especially in a conflict or contest. ❑ *...a powerful new gun which could tip the balance of the war in their favor.* **6** V-T If you **balance** one thing against another, you consider its importance in relation to the other one. ❑ *She carefully tried to balance religious sensitivities against democratic freedom.* **7** V-T If someone **balances** their budget or if a government **balances** the economy of a country, they make sure that the amount of money that is spent is not greater than the amount that is received. ❑ *He balanced his budgets by rigid control over public expenditure.* **8** V-T/V-I If you **balance** your books or make them **balance**, you prove by calculation that the amount of money you have received is equal to the amount that you have spent. ❑ *...teaching them to balance the books.* **9** N-COUNT The **balance** in your bank account is the amount of money you have in it. ❑ *I'd like to check the balance in my account please.* **10** N-SING The **balance** of an amount of money is what remains to be paid for something or what remains when part of the amount has been spent. ❑ *They were due to pay the balance on delivery.* **11** → see also **bank balance** **12** PHRASE If you **keep** your **balance**, for example, when standing in a moving vehicle, you remain standing and do not fall over. If you **lose** your **balance**, you become unsteady and fall over. ❑ *She was holding onto the rail to keep her balance.* **13** PHRASE If you are **off balance**, you are in an unsteady position and about to fall. ❑ *A gust of wind knocked him off balance and he fell face down in the mud.* **14** PHRASE You can say **on balance** to indicate that you are stating an opinion after considering all the relevant facts or arguments. ❑ *On balance he agreed with Christine.* **15** → See feature box at **business**

━━━━━━━━━━━ COLLOCATIONS ━━━━━━━━━━━

balance
NOUN **4**
adjective + **balance**: correct, fair, proper, reasonable, right; perfect; delicate
verb + **balance**: shift, tilt, tip, upset; maintain, strike; redress, restore

━━━━━━━━━━━━ SYNONYMS ━━━━━━━━━━━━

balance
VERB **3**
offset: *The increase in costs was more than offset by higher productivity.*
compensate for: *MPs say it is crucial that a system is found to compensate for inflation.*
redress: *...to redress the economic imbalance between the countries.*
counteract: *This event will counteract such trends.*

bal|anced /bǽlənst/ **1** ADJ A **balanced** report, book, or other document takes into account all the different opinions on something and presents information in a fair and reasonable way. [APPROVAL] ❑ *...a fair, balanced, comprehensive report.* **2** ADJ Something that is **balanced** is pleasing or useful because its different parts or elements are in the correct proportions. [APPROVAL] ❑ *...a balanced diet.* **3** ADJ Someone who is **balanced** remains calm and thinks clearly, even in a difficult situation. [APPROVAL] ❑ *I have to prove myself as a respectable, balanced person.* **4** → see also **balance** **5** → See feature box at **nutrition**

bal|ance of pay|ments (balances of payments) N-COUNT A country's **balance of payments** is the difference, over a period of time, between the payments it makes to other countries for imports and the payments it receives from other countries for exports. [BUSINESS] ❑ *...the chronic American balance-of-payments deficit of the 1960s.*

bal|ance of pow|er N-SING The **balance of power** is the way in which power is distributed between rival groups or countries. ❑ *...changes in the balance of power between the United States and Europe.*

bal|ance of trade (balances of trade) N-COUNT [usu sing] A country's **balance of trade** is the difference in value, over a period of time, between the goods it imports and the goods it exports. [BUSINESS] ❑ *As other nations grow and spend more money on American products, the balance of trade should even out.*

bal|ance sheet (balance sheets) N-COUNT A **balance sheet** is a written statement of the amount of money and property that a company or person has, including amounts of money that are owed or are owing. **Balance sheet** is also used to refer to the general financial state of a company. [BUSINESS] ❑ *Rolls-Royce needed a strong balance sheet.*

bal|anc|ing act (balancing acts) N-COUNT [usu sing] If you perform a **balancing act**, you try to deal successfully with two or more people, groups, or situations that are in opposition to each other. ❑ *...a delicate balancing act between a career, a home, and motherhood.*

bal|co|ny /bǽlkəni/ (balconies) **1** N-COUNT A **balcony** is a platform on the outside of a building, above ground level, with a wall or railing around it. **2** N-SING The **balcony** in a theater or cinema is an area of seats above the main seating area. **3** → See also color supplement

bald /bɔ́ld/ (balder, baldest) **1** ADJ Someone who is **bald** has little or no hair on the top of their head. ❑ *The man's bald head was beaded with sweat.* ● **bald|ness** N-UNCOUNT ❑ *He wears a cap to cover a spot of baldness.* **2** ADJ If a tire is **bald**, its surface has worn down and it is no longer safe to use. **3** ADJ [ADJ n] A **bald** statement is in plain language and contains no extra explanation or information. ❑ *The bald truth is he's just not happy.* ● **bald|ly** ADV [ADV with v] ❑ *"The leaders are outdated," he stated baldly. "They don't relate to young people."*

bald eagle (bald eagles) N-COUNT A **bald eagle** is a large eagle with a white head that lives in North America. It is the national bird of the United States.

bal|der|dash /bɔ́ldərdæʃ/ N-UNCOUNT If you say that something that has been said or written is **balderdash**, you think it is completely untrue or very stupid. [OLD-FASHIONED, DISAPPROVAL]

bald|ing /bɔ́ldɪŋ/ ADJ Someone who is **balding** is beginning to lose the hair on the top of their head. ❑ *He wore a straw hat to keep his balding head from getting sunburned.*

baldy /bɔ́ldi/ (baldies) N-COUNT; N-VOC People sometimes refer to a bald person as a **baldy**, especially if they are talking about them or to them in a friendly or humorous way. Some people might find this offensive. [INFORMAL] ❑ *The actor Patrick Stewart is a long-time baldy and proud of it.* ❑ *Get lost, baldy.*

bale /beɪl/ (bales, baling, baled) **1** N-COUNT A **bale** is a large quantity of something such as hay, cloth, or paper, tied together tightly. ❑ *...bales of hay.* **2** V-T If something such as hay, cloth, or paper **is baled**, it is tied together tightly. ❑ *Once hay has been cut and baled, it has to go through some chemical processes.* **3** → see also **ball**

bale|ful /beɪlfəl/ ADJ [usu ADJ n] **Baleful** means harmful, or expressing harmful intentions. [LITERARY] ❑ *...a baleful look.* ● **bale|ful|ly** ADV [ADV with v] ❑ *He watched her balefully.*

balk /bɔ́k/ (balks, balking, balked) also **baulk** V-I If you **balk** at something, you definitely do not want to do it or to let it happen. ❑ *Even biology undergraduates may balk at animal experiments.* ❑ *Last October the bank balked, alarmed that a $24m profit had turned into a $20m deficit.*

Bal|kani|za|tion /bɔlkənɪzeɪʃən/ also **balkanization**

in BRIT, also use **Balkanisation** and **balkanization**

N-UNCOUNT If you disapprove of the division of a country into separate independent states, you can refer to the **Balkanization** of the country. [DISAPPROVAL] ❑ *We can't accept the fragmentation or balkanization of the country.*

balky /bɔ́ki/ ADJ [usu ADJ n] Someone or something that is **balky** does not behave or work the way you want them to. [mainly AM] ❑ *Surgery to a balky ankle was required.* ❑ *...balky kids.*

ball ✦✧◇ /bɔ́l/ (balls, balling, balled) **1** N-COUNT A **ball** is a round or oval object that is used in games such as tennis, baseball, football, basketball, and soccer. ❑ *...a golf ball.* **2** N-COUNT A **ball** is something or an amount of something that has a round shape. ❑ *Thomas screwed the letter up into a ball.* **3** V-T/V-I When you **ball** something or when it **balls**, it becomes round. ❑ *He picked up the sheets of paper, and balled them tightly in his fists.* **4** N-COUNT The **ball** of your foot or the **ball** of your

ballad

thumb is the rounded part where your toes join your foot or where your thumb joins your hand. **5** N-COUNT A **ball** is a large formal social event at which people dance. ❑ *My Mama and Daddy used to have a grand Christmas ball every year.* **6** PHRASE If you **are having a ball**, you are having a very enjoyable time. [INFORMAL] ❑ *Outside the boys were sitting on the ground and, judging by the gales of laughter, they were having a ball.*
▶ **ball up** PHRASAL VERB If you **ball up** a task or activity, you do it very badly, making a lot of mistakes. [AM, INFORMAL, VULGAR] ❑ *The government has totally balled up the whole assessment process by going to the system they did.*

bal|lad /bæləd/ (**ballads**) **1** N-COUNT A **ballad** is a long song or poem which tells a story in simple language. ❑ *...an eighteenth century ballad about some lost children called the Babes in the Wood.* **2** N-COUNT A **ballad** is a slow, romantic, popular song. ❑ *"You Don't Know Paris" is one of the most beautiful ballads that he ever wrote.* **3** → See feature box at **music**

bal|last /bæləst/ N-UNCOUNT **Ballast** is any substance that is used in ships or hot-air balloons to make them heavier and more stable. Ballast usually consists of water, sand, or iron.

ball bear|ing (**ball bearings**) also **ball-bearing** N-COUNT **Ball bearings** are small metal balls placed between the moving parts of a machine to make the parts move smoothly.

ball boy (**ball boys**) also **ballboy** N-COUNT In a tennis match, the **ball boys** pick up any balls that go into the net or off the court and throw them back to the players. In a baseball game, the **ball boys** are in charge of collecting the balls that are hit out of the field.

bal|le|ri|na /bælərinə/ (**ballerinas**) N-COUNT A **ballerina** is a woman ballet dancer.

bal|let /bæleɪ/ (**ballets**) **1** N-UNCOUNT [also *the* N, oft N n] **Ballet** is a type of very skilled and artistic dancing with carefully planned movements. ❑ *I trained as a ballet dancer.* **2** N-COUNT A **ballet** is an artistic work that is performed by ballet dancers. ❑ *The performance will include the premiere of three new ballets.*

bal|let|ic /bæletɪk/ ADJ [usu ADJ n] If you describe someone's movements as **balletic**, you mean that they have some of the graceful qualities of ballet. ❑ *She dances with balletic grace.*

ball game (**ball games**) also **ballgame** **1** N-COUNT [usu pl] **Ball games** are games that are played with a ball such as tennis, baseball, and football. **2** N-COUNT A **ball game** is a baseball game. [AM] ❑ *I'd still like to go to a ball game.* **3** N-SING You can use **ball game** to describe any situation or activity, especially one that involves competition. [SPOKEN, JOURNALISM] ❑ *Two of his biggest competitors are out of the ball game.* **4** If you say that a situation is **a whole new ball game**, you mean that it is completely different from, or much more difficult than, the previous situation or any situation that you have experienced before. ❑ *He finds himself faced with a whole new ball game.*

ball girl (**ball girls**) also **ballgirl** N-COUNT In a tennis match, the **ball girls** pick up any balls that go into the net or off the court and throw them back to the players. In a baseball game, the **ball girls** are in charge of collecting the balls that are hit out of the field.

ball|gown /bɔːlɡaʊn/ (**ballgowns**) N-COUNT A **ballgown** is a long dress that women wear to formal dances.

bal|lis|tic /bəlɪstɪk/ **1** ADJ [ADJ n] **Ballistic** means relating to ballistics. ❑ *...ballistic missiles.* ❑ *Ballistic tests have matched the weapons with bullets taken from the bodies of victims.* **2** PHRASE If someone **goes ballistic**, they suddenly become very angry. [INFORMAL] ❑ *The singer went ballistic after one member of his band failed to show for a sound check.* **3** PHRASE If something **goes ballistic**, it suddenly becomes very much greater or more powerful, often in a surprising or unwanted way. [INFORMAL] ❑ *August registrations have gone ballistic, accounting now for a quarter of the annual total.*

bal|lis|tics /bəlɪstɪks/ N-UNCOUNT **Ballistics** is the study of the movement of objects that are shot or thrown through the air, such as bullets fired from a gun.

bal|loon /bəluːn/ (**balloons, ballooning, ballooned**) **1** N-COUNT A **balloon** is a small, thin, rubber bag that you blow air into so that it becomes larger and rounder and longer. Balloons are used as toys or decorations. ❑ *She popped a balloon with her fork.* **2** N-COUNT A **balloon** is a large, strong bag filled with gas or hot air, which can carry passengers in a container that hangs underneath it. ❑ *They are to attempt to be the first to circle the Earth non-stop by balloon.* **3** V-I When something **balloons**, it increases rapidly in amount. ❑ *The jail's female and minority populations have both ballooned in recent years.*

bal|loon|ing /bəluːnɪŋ/ N-UNCOUNT **Ballooning** is the sport or activity of flying a hot-air balloon.

bal|loon|ist /bəluːnɪst/ (**balloonists**) N-COUNT A **balloonist** is a person who flies a hot-air balloon.

bal|loon mort|gage (**balloon mortgages**) N-COUNT A **balloon mortgage** is a mortgage on which the repayments are relatively small until the large final payment. [AM]

bal|lot /bælət/ (**ballots, balloting, balloted**) **1** N-COUNT A **ballot** is a secret vote in which people select a candidate in an election, or express their opinion about something. ❑ *The result of the ballot will not be known for two weeks.* **2** N-COUNT A **ballot** is a piece of paper on which you indicate your choice or opinion in a secret vote. ❑ *Election boards will count the ballots by hand.* **3** V-T If you **ballot** a group of people, you find out what they think about a subject by organizing a secret vote. ❑ *The union said they will ballot members on whether to strike.*

SYNONYMS

ballot
NOUN **1**
vote: *Why do you think we should have a vote on that?*
election: *The final election results will be announced on Friday.*
poll: *In 1945, Winston Churchill was defeated at the polls.*
referendum: *Estonia said it too planned to hold a referendum on independence.*

WORD HISTORY

ballot
Ballot comes from Italian *ballotta* meaning 'little ball.' In medieval Venice, people voted by dropping black or white stones or balls into a box.

bal|lot box (**ballot boxes**) **1** N-COUNT A **ballot box** is the box into which ballot papers are put after people have voted. **2** N-SING [*the* N] You can refer to the system of democratic elections as the **ballot box**. ❑ *Martinez expressed confidence of victory at the ballot box.*

bal|lot pa|per (**ballot papers**) N-COUNT A **ballot paper** is a piece of paper on which you indicate your choice or opinion in an election or ballot.

bal|lot rig|ging also **ballot-rigging** N-UNCOUNT **Ballot rigging** is the act of illegally changing the result of an election by producing a false record of the number of votes. ❑ *The poll was widely discredited after allegations of ballot rigging.*

ball|park /bɔːlpɑːrk/ (**ballparks**) also **ball park** **1** N-COUNT A **ballpark** is a park or stadium where baseball is played. ❑ *...one of the oldest and most beautiful ballparks in baseball.* **2** ADJ [ADJ n] A **ballpark** figure or **ballpark** estimate is an approximate figure or estimate. ❑ *I can't give you anything more than just sort of a ballpark figure.*

ball|player /bɔːlpleɪər/ (**ballplayers**) also **ball player** N-COUNT A **ballplayer** is a baseball player. [AM]

ball|point /bɔːlpɔɪnt/ (**ballpoints**) N-COUNT A **ballpoint** or a **ballpoint pen** is a pen with a very small metal ball at the end which transfers the ink from the pen onto a surface.

ball|room /bɔːlrʊm/ (**ballrooms**) N-COUNT A **ballroom** is a very large room that is used for dancing.

ball|room danc|ing N-UNCOUNT **Ballroom dancing** is a type of dancing in which two people dance together using fixed sequences of steps and movements.

balls /bɔːlz/ N-UNCOUNT [oft *the* N to-inf] If you say that someone has **balls**, you mean that they have courage. [INFORMAL, VULGAR, APPROVAL] ❑ *I never had the balls to do anything like this.*
▶ **balls up** [BRIT] → see **ball up**

ball|sy /bɔːlzi/ (**ballsier, ballsiest**) ADJ [oft ADJ n] You can describe a person or their behavior as **ballsy** if you admire them because you think they are energetic and brave. [INFORMAL, VULGAR, APPROVAL] ❑ *...the ballsiest woman I know.* ❑ *...ballsy, gutsy live rap music.*

ball-up (ball-ups) N-COUNT If you make a **ball-up** of something, you do it very badly and make a lot of mistakes. [AM, INFORMAL, VULGAR] ❏ He's made a real ball-up of this.

in BRIT, use **balls-up**

bal|ly|hoo /bǽlihu/ (ballyhoos, ballyhooing, ballyhooed) **1** N-UNCOUNT [also a N] You can use **ballyhoo** to refer to great excitement or anger about something, especially when you disapprove of it because you think it is unnecessary or exaggerated. [DISAPPROVAL] ❏ They announced, amid much ballyhoo, that they had made a breakthrough. **2** V-T [usu passive] If you say that something **is ballyhooed**, you mean that there is a lot of excitement about it and people are claiming that it is very good. You use this word especially when you think the thing is not as exciting or good as people say. [DISAPPROVAL] ❏ The power of red wine to counteract high cholesterol has been ballyhooed in the press. ❏ ...the much-ballyhooed new Star Wars movie.

balm /bɑm/ (balms) **1** N-MASS **Balm** is a sweet-smelling oil that is obtained from some tropical trees and used to make creams that heal wounds or reduce pain. ❏ ...a jar of lip balm. **2** N-UNCOUNT [also a N] If you refer to something as **balm**, you mean that it makes you feel better. [APPROVAL] ❏ The place is balm to the soul.

balmy /bɑmi/ (balmier, balmiest) ADJ [usu ADJ n] **Balmy** weather is fairly warm and pleasant. ❏ ...a balmy summer's evening.

ba|lo|ney /bəlóuni/ (baloneys) **1** N-VAR **Baloney** is the same as **bologna**. [AM] **2** N-UNCOUNT If you say that an idea or statement is **baloney**, you disapprove of it and think it is foolish or wrong. [mainly AM, INFORMAL, DISAPPROVAL] ❏ That's a load of baloney.

bal|sa /bɔ́lsə/ N-UNCOUNT **Balsa** or **balsa wood** is a very light wood from a South American tree.

bal|sam /bɔ́lsəm/ N-UNCOUNT **Balsam** is a sweet-smelling oil that is obtained from certain trees or bushes and used to make medicines and perfumes.

bal|sam|ic vin|egar /bɔlsǽmɪk vɪ́nɪgər/ N-UNCOUNT **Balsamic vinegar** is a type of vinegar that tastes sweet and is made from grape juice.

bal|us|trade /bǽləstreɪd/ (balustrades) N-COUNT A **balustrade** is a railing or wall on a balcony or staircase.

bam|boo /bæmbú/ (bamboos) N-VAR **Bamboo** is a tall tropical plant with hard, hollow stems. The young shoots of the plant can be eaten and the stems are used to make furniture. ❏ ...huts with walls of bamboo.

bam|boo|zle /bæmbúzəl/ (bamboozles, bamboozling, bamboozled) V-T To **bamboozle** someone means to confuse them and often trick them. ❏ He bamboozled Mercer into defeat. ❏ He was bamboozled by con men.

ban ♦♦◊ /bǽn/ (bans, banning, banned) **1** V-T To **ban** something means to state officially that it must not be done, shown, or used. ❏ Canada will ban smoking in all offices later this year. ❏ Last year arms sales were banned. **2** N-COUNT A **ban** is an official ruling that something must not be done, shown, or used. ❏ The general lifted the ban on political parties. **3** V-T If you **are banned** from doing something, you are officially prevented from doing it. ❏ He was banned from driving for three years.

ba|nal /bənǽl, -nǽl, beɪnəl/ ADJ If you describe something as **banal**, you do not like it because you think it is so ordinary that it is not at all effective or interesting. [DISAPPROVAL] ❏ The text is banal.

WORD HISTORY

banal
In Old French, the word **banal** referred to the mill or bakery that was owned by the local lord and that all his tenants had to use. The word came to mean 'common to everyone' and from that, 'commonplace' or 'ordinary.'

ba|na|na /bənǽnə/ (bananas) N-VAR **Bananas** are long curved fruit with yellow skins. ❏ ...a bunch of bananas.

ba|na|na peel (banana peels) N-VAR The thick yellow or green covering of a banana is called a **banana peel**. [AM]

in BRIT, use **banana skin**

ba|na|na re|pub|lic (banana republics) N-COUNT Small, poor countries that are politically unstable are sometimes referred to as **banana republics**. [OFFENSIVE]

ba|na|na split (banana splits) N-COUNT A **banana split** is a kind of dessert. It consists of a banana cut in half along its length, with ice cream, nuts, and sauce on top.

band ♦♦◊ /bǽnd/ (bands, banding, banded) **1** N-COUNT-COLL A **band** is a small group of musicians who play popular music such as jazz, rock, or pop. ❏ He was a drummer in a rock band. **2** N-COUNT-COLL A **band** is a group of musicians who play brass and percussion instruments. ❏ Bands played German marches. **3** N-COUNT-COLL A **band** of people is a group of people who have joined together because they share an interest or belief. ❏ Bands of government soldiers, rebels and just plain criminals have been roaming some neighborhoods. **4** N-COUNT A **band** is a flat, narrow strip of cloth which you wear around your head or wrists, or which forms part of a piece of clothing. ❏ Almost all hospitals use a wrist-band of some kind with your name and details on it. **5** N-COUNT A **band** is a strip of something such as color, light, land, or cloth that contrasts with the areas on either side of it. ❏ ...bands of natural vegetation between strips of crops. **6** N-COUNT A **band** is a strip or loop of metal or other strong material which strengthens something, or which holds several things together. ❏ Surgeon Geoffrey Horne placed a metal band around the knee cap to help it knit back together. **7** → see also **elastic band**, **rubber band** **8** N-COUNT A **band** is a range of numbers or values within a system of measurement. ❏ For an initial service, a 10 megahertz-wide band of frequencies will be needed.
▶ **band together** PHRASAL VERB If people **band together**, they meet and act as a group in order to try and achieve something. ❏ Women banded together to protect each other.

COLLOCATIONS

band
NOUN **1**
noun + **band**: heavy metal, indie, jazz, pop, punk, rock; backing, boy, girl, tribute
verb + **band**: form, join, play in
adjective + **band**: live

band|age /bǽndɪdʒ/ (bandages, bandaging, bandaged) **1** N-COUNT A **bandage** is a long strip of cloth that is wrapped around a wounded part of someone's body to protect or support it. ❏ We put some ointment and a bandage on his knee. **2** V-T If you **bandage** a wound or part of someone's body, you tie a bandage around it. ❏ Apply a dressing to the wound and bandage it.
• PHRASAL VERB **Bandage up** means the same as **bandage**. ❏ I bandaged the leg up and gave her aspirin for the pain.

Band-Aid (Band-Aids) **1** N-VAR A **Band-Aid** is a small piece of sticky tape that you use to cover small cuts or wounds on your body. [mainly AM, TRADEMARK]

in BRIT, use **plaster**

2 ADJ [ADJ n] If you refer to a **Band-Aid** solution to a problem, you mean that you disapprove of it because you think that it will only be effective for a short period. [mainly AM, DISAPPROVAL] ❏ We need long-term solutions, not short-term Band-Aid ones.

ban|dan|na /bændǽnə/ (bandannas) also **bandana** N-COUNT A **bandanna** is a brightly-colored piece of cloth which is worn around a person's neck or head.

B & B /bi ən bi/ (B&Bs) → see **bed and breakfast**

band|ed /bǽndɪd/ ADJ [oft ADJ in/with n] If something is **banded**, it has one or more bands on it, often of a different color which contrasts with the main color. ❏ ...a stark tower, banded in dark and light stone.

-banded /-bǽndɪd/ COMB IN ADJ **-banded** combines with colors to indicate that something has bands of a particular color. ❏ Tables are set with white china and gold-banded silver cutlery.

ban|dit /bǽndɪt/ (bandits) N-COUNT Robbers are sometimes called **bandits**, especially if they are found in areas where the law has broken down. ❏ This is real bandit country.

ban|dit|ry /bǽndɪtri/ N-UNCOUNT **Banditry** is used to refer to acts of robbery and violence in areas where the rule of law has broken down.

band|leader /bǽndlidər/ (bandleaders) N-COUNT A **bandleader** is the person who conducts a band, especially a jazz band.

band|saw /bændsɔː/ (bandsaws) N-COUNT A **bandsaw** is an electric saw that consists of a metal band that turns around and is used for cutting wood, metal, and other materials.

bands|man /bændzmən/ (bandsmen) N-COUNT [usu pl] **Bandsmen** are musicians in a band, especially a military or brass band.

band|stand /bændstænd/ (bandstands) **1** N-COUNT A **bandstand** is a platform with a roof where a military band or a brass band can play in the open air. **2** N-COUNT A **bandstand** is a platform inside a hall or large room where the band that is playing at a dance or other occasion stands. [mainly AM]

band|wagon /bændwægən/ (bandwagons) **1** N-COUNT You can refer to an activity or movement that has suddenly become fashionable or popular as a **bandwagon**. ◻ ...the environmental bandwagon. **2** N-COUNT If someone, especially a politician, jumps or climbs on the **bandwagon**, they become involved in an activity or movement because it is fashionable or likely to succeed and not because they are really interested in it. [DISAPPROVAL] ◻ In recent months many conservative politicians have jumped on the anti-immigrant bandwagon.

band|width /bændwɪdθ/ (bandwidths) N-VAR A **bandwidth** is the range of frequencies used for a particular telecommunications signal, radio transmission, or computer network. ◻ To cope with this amount of data, the system will need a bandwidth of around 100MHz.

ban|dy /bændi/ (bandies, bandying, bandied) V-T If you **bandy** words with someone, you argue with them. ◻ John shook his head. He was tired of bandying words with the man. ◻ The prosecution and defense were bandying accusations back and forth.
▶ **bandy about** also **bandy around** PHRASAL VERB [usu passive] If someone's name or something such as an idea **is bandied about** or **is bandied around**, that person or that thing is discussed by many people in a casual way. [DISAPPROVAL] ◻ Young players now hear various sums bandied around about how much older players are getting.

bane /beɪn/ N-SING [usu the N of n] The **bane** of someone or the **bane** of someone's life is something that frequently makes them feel unhappy or annoyed. ◻ This craving is, of course, the bane of many ex-alcoholics' existence.

bang /bæŋ/ (bangs, banging, banged) **1** N-COUNT; SOUND A **bang** is a sudden loud noise such as the noise of an explosion. ◻ I heard four or five loud bangs. ◻ She slammed the door with a bang. **2** V-I If something **bangs**, it makes a sudden loud noise, once or several times. ◻ The engine spat and banged. **3** V-T/V-I If you **bang** a door or if it **bangs**, it closes suddenly with a loud noise. ◻ ...the sound of doors banging. ◻ All up and down the street the windows bang shut. **4** V-T/V-I If you **bang** on something or if you **bang** it, you hit it hard, making a loud noise. ◻ We could bang on the desks and shout till they let us out. **5** V-T If you **bang** something on something or if you **bang** it down, you quickly and violently put it on a surface, because you are angry. ◻ She banged his dinner on the table. **6** V-T If you **bang** a part of your body, you accidentally knock it against something and hurt yourself. ◻ She'd fainted and banged her head. • N-COUNT **Bang** is also a noun. ◻ ...a nasty bang on the head. **7** V-I If you **bang** into something or someone, you bump or knock them hard, usually because you are not looking where you are going. ◻ I didn't mean to bang into you. **8** ADV [ADV prep] You can use **bang** to emphasize expressions that indicate an exact position or an exact time. [EMPHASIS] ◻ ...bang in the middle of the track. **9** PHRASE [PHR after v] If something begins or ends **with a bang**, it begins or ends with a lot of energy, enthusiasm, or success. ◻ Her career began with a bang in 1986.

Bang|la|deshi /bæŋglədɛʃi/ (Bangladeshis) **1** ADJ [usu ADJ n] **Bangladeshi** means belonging to or relating to Bangladesh, or to its people or culture. **2** N-COUNT The **Bangladeshis** are the people who come from Bangladesh.

ban|gle /bæŋɡəl/ (bangles) N-COUNT A **bangle** is a decorated metal or wooden ring that you can wear around your wrist or ankle.

bangs /bæŋz/ N-PLURAL **Bangs** are hair that is cut so that it hangs over your forehead. [AM] ◻ My bangs were cut short, but the rest of my hair was long.

in BRIT, use **fringe**

bang-up also **bang up** ADJ [ADJ n] Some people use **bang-up** to describe something they think is very good or enjoyable. [mainly AM, INFORMAL] ◻ NET has done a bang-up job of designing its products with service in mind.

ban|ish /bænɪʃ/ (banishes, banishing, banished) **1** V-T If someone or something **is banished** from a place or area of activity, they are sent away from it and prevented from entering it. ◻ John was banished from England. ◻ I was banished to the small bedroom upstairs. **2** V-T If you **banish** something unpleasant, you get rid of it. ◻ ...a public investment program intended to banish the recession.

ban|ish|ment /bænɪʃmənt/ N-UNCOUNT [usu N prep] **Banishment** is the act of banishing someone or the state of being banished. ◻ ...banishment to Devil's Island.

ban|is|ter /bænɪstər/ (banisters) also **bannister** N-COUNT A **banister** is a rail supported by posts and fixed along the side of a staircase. The plural **banisters** can be used to refer to one of these rails. ◻ I still remember sliding down the banisters.

ban|jo /bændʒoʊ/ (banjos) N-VAR [oft the N] A **banjo** is a musical instrument that looks like a guitar with a circular body, a long neck, and four or more strings.

BANK
① FINANCE AND STORAGE
② AREAS AND MASSES
③ OTHER VERB USES
---

① **bank** ✦✦✦ /bæŋk/ (banks, banking, banked) **1** N-COUNT A **bank** is an institution where people or businesses can keep their money. ◻ Students should look to see which bank offers them the service that best suits their financial needs. **2** N-COUNT A **bank** is a building where a bank offers its services. **3** V-I If you **bank with** a particular bank, you have an account with that bank. ◻ I have banked with Coutts & Co. for years. **4** N-COUNT You use **bank** to refer to a store of something. For example, a blood **bank** is a store of blood that is kept ready for use. ◻ ...a national data bank of information on hospital employees.

COLLOCATIONS
bank
NOUN ① **1**
noun + **bank**: investment, merchant, savings
adjective + **bank**: central, commercial, nationalized, retail
---

② **bank** /bæŋk/ (banks) **1** N-COUNT The **banks** of a river, canal, or lake are the raised areas of ground along its edge. ◻ We pedaled north along the east bank of the river. **2** N-COUNT A **bank** of ground is a raised area of it with a flat top and one or two sloping sides. ◻ ...lounging on the grassy bank. **3** N-COUNT A **bank** of something is a long high mass of it. ◻ A bank of clouds had built up along the western horizon. **4** N-COUNT A **bank** of things, especially machines, switches, or dials, is a row of them, or a series of rows. ◻ The typical laborer now sits in front of a bank of dials.

③ **bank** /bæŋk/ (banks, banking, banked) V-I When an aircraft **banks**, one of its wings rises higher than the other, usually when it is changing direction. ◻ A single-engine plane took off and banked above the highway in front of him.
▶ **bank on** PHRASAL VERB If you **bank on** something happening, you expect it to happen and rely on it happening. ◻ Everyone is banking on an economic rebound to help ease the state's fiscal problems.

bank|able /bæŋkəb°l/ ADJ [usu ADJ n] In the entertainment industry, someone or something that is described as **bankable** is very popular and therefore likely to be very profitable. ◻ This movie made him the most bankable star in Hollywood.

bank ac|count (bank accounts) N-COUNT A **bank account** is an arrangement with a bank which allows you to keep your money in the bank and to take some out when you need it. ◻ Paul had at least 17 different bank accounts.

bank bal|ance (bank balances) N-COUNT Your **bank balance** is the amount of money that you have in your bank account at a particular time. ◻ Do you wish to use the Internet simply to check your bank balance?

bank card (bank cards) also **bankcard** **1** N-COUNT A **bank card** is a plastic card that your bank gives you so you can get money from your bank account using a cash machine. It is also called an **ATM** card. **2** N-COUNT A **bank card** is a credit card that is supplied by a bank. [AM]

bank check (bank checks) N-COUNT A **bank check** is a check that you can buy from a bank in order to pay someone who is not willing to accept a personal check. ❏ *Payments should be made by credit card or bank check in U.S. dollars.*

bank draft (bank drafts) N-COUNT A **bank draft** is a check which you can buy from a bank in order to pay someone who is not willing to accept a personal check. ❏ *Payments should be made by credit card or bank draft in U.S. dollars.*

banked /bæŋkt/ **1** ADJ [usu ADJ n] A **banked** stretch of road is higher on one side than the other. ❏ *He struggled to hold the bike down on the banked corners.* **2** ADJ [v-link ADJ] If a place is **banked** with something, it is piled high with that thing. If something is **banked up**, it is piled high. ❏ *Flowerbeds and tubs are banked with summer bedding plants.* ❏ *The snow was banked up along the roadside.*

bank|er ✦✧✧ /bæŋkər/ (bankers) N-COUNT A **banker** is someone who works in banking at a senior level. ❏ *...an investment banker.*

bank holi|day (bank holidays) **1** N-COUNT A **bank holiday** is a public holiday. [mainly BRIT]

in AM, usually use **national holiday**

2 → See feature box at **leisure**

bank|ing ✦✧✧ /bæŋkɪŋ/ N-UNCOUNT **Banking** is the business activity of banks and similar institutions. ❏ *...the online banking revolution.*

VOCABULARY IN CONTEXT

Finance and banking

The most famous **stock market collapse** was probably the one in the United States that led to the Great Depression in 1929. However, there have been other **recessions** caused by **crashes**, both before and after 1929. In 1857, **speculation** on the new railroad industry and risky **investments** in it caused panic. **Shares** fell in value, **investors** lost a lot of money, and the economy crashed, taking two years to recover. More recently, we've seen the **housing bubble** burst, due to the American **subprime mortgage** collapse in 2007. This led to a global **financial crisis** and government **bailouts** of banks worldwide. Whether we are in a **bear** or a **bull market** is hard to determine without hindsight, but even periods of **economic growth** can be suddenly undermined by the risky actions of governments, companies, and even individuals.

bank man|ag|er (bank managers) N-COUNT A **bank manager** is someone who is in charge of a bank, or a particular branch of a bank, and who is involved in making decisions about whether or not to lend money to businesses and individuals. [BUSINESS] ❏ *This may have influenced your bank manager's decision not to give you a loan.*

bank|note /bæŋknoʊt/ (banknotes) also **bank note** N-COUNT **Banknotes** are pieces of paper money. ❏ *...a shopping bag full of banknotes.*

bank rate (bank rates) N-COUNT The **bank rate** is the rate of interest at which a bank lends money, especially the minimum rate of interest that banks are allowed to charge, which is decided from time to time by the country's central bank. ❏ *The United States reduced its main bank rate ten days ago.*

bank|roll /bæŋkroʊl/ (bankrolls, bankrolling, bankrolled) V-T To **bankroll** a person, organization, or project means to provide the financial resources that they need. [mainly AM, INFORMAL] ❏ *The company has bankrolled a couple of local movies.*

bank|rupt /bæŋkrʌpt/ (bankrupts, bankrupting, bankrupted) **1** ADJ People or organizations that go **bankrupt** do not have enough money to pay their debts. [BUSINESS] ❏ *If the firm cannot sell its products, it will go bankrupt.* **2** V-T To **bankrupt** a person or organization means to make them go bankrupt. [BUSINESS] ❏ *The move to the market nearly bankrupted the firm and its director.* **3** N-COUNT A **bankrupt** is a person who has been declared bankrupt by a court of law. ❏ *In total, 80% of bankrupts are men.* **4** ADJ If you say that something is **bankrupt**, you are emphasizing that it lacks any value or worth. [EMPHASIS] ❏ *He really thinks that European civilization is morally bankrupt.* **5** → See feature box at **finance**

bank|rupt|cy /bæŋkrʌptsi/ (bankruptcies) **1** N-UNCOUNT **Bankruptcy** is the state of being bankrupt. [BUSINESS] ❏ *Pan Am is the second airline in two months to file for bankruptcy.* **2** N-COUNT A **bankruptcy** is an instance of an organization or person going bankrupt. [BUSINESS] ❏ *The number of corporate bankruptcies climbed in August.*

bank state|ment (bank statements) N-COUNT A **bank statement** is a printed document showing all the money paid into and taken out of a bank account. Bank statements are usually sent by a bank to a customer at regular intervals.

banned sub|stance (banned substances) N-COUNT In sports, **banned substances** are drugs that competitors are not allowed to take because they could artificially improve their performance.

ban|ner /bænər/ (banners) **1** N-COUNT A **banner** is a long strip of cloth with something written on it. Banners are usually attached to two poles and carried during a protest or rally. ❏ *A large crowd of students followed the coffin, carrying banners and shouting slogans denouncing the government.* **2** PHRASE If someone does something **under the banner of** a particular cause, idea, or belief, they do it saying that they support that cause, idea, or belief. ❏ *Russia was the first country to forge a new economic system under the banner of Marxism.*

ban|ner ad (banner ads) N-COUNT A **banner ad** is a rectangular advertisement on a web page that contains a link to the advertiser's website. ❏ *See our banner ad at this site!*

ban|ner head|line (banner headlines) N-COUNT A **banner headline** is a large headline in a newspaper that stretches across the front page. ❏ *Both newspapers carried the same banner headline, "Where are you, Mr. President?"*

ban|nis|ter /bænɪstər/ → see banister

banns /bænz/ N-PLURAL [the N] When a minister or priest reads or publishes the **banns**, he or she makes a public announcement in church that two people are going to be married. [OLD-FASHIONED]

ban|quet /bæŋkwɪt/ (banquets) N-COUNT A **banquet** is a grand formal dinner. ❏ *...this week's Greater Cleveland Sports Commission awards banquet.* ❏ *...a wedding banquet.*

ban|quet|ing /bæŋkwɪtɪŋ/ ADJ [ADJ n] A **banqueting** hall or room is a large room where banquets are held.

ban|quette /bæŋkɛt/ (banquettes) N-COUNT A **banquette** is a long, low, cushioned seat. Banquettes are usually long enough for more than one person to sit on at a time.

ban|shee /bænʃi/ (banshees) N-COUNT In Irish folk stories, a **banshee** is a female spirit who warns you by her long, sad cry that someone in your family is going to die.

ban|tam /bæntəm/ (bantams) N-COUNT A **bantam** is a breed of small chicken.

bantam|weight /bæntəmweɪt/ (bantamweights) N-COUNT [usu sing, oft N n] A **bantamweight** is a boxer who weighs between 112 and 118 pounds, or a wrestler who weighs between 115 and 126 pounds. A bantamweight is heavier than a flyweight but lighter than a featherweight.

ban|ter /bæntər/ **1** N-UNCOUNT **Banter** is teasing or joking talk that is amusing and friendly. ◻ *As she closed the door, she heard Tom exchanging good-natured banter with Jane.* **2** → See feature box at **socialize**

Ban|tu /bæntu, -tu/ **1** ADJ [ADJ n] **Bantu** means belonging or relating to a group of peoples in central and southern Africa. This use could cause offense. **2** ADJ [ADJ n] **Bantu** languages belong to a group of languages spoken in central and southern Africa. This use could cause offense.

bap|tism /bæptɪzəm/ (**baptisms**) N-VAR A **baptism** is a Christian ceremony in which a person is baptized. Compare **christening**. ◻ *Infants prepared for baptism should be dressed in pure white.*

bap|tis|mal /bæptɪzməl/ ADJ [ADJ n] **Baptismal** means relating to or connected with baptism. [FORMAL] ◻ *...the baptismal ceremony.*

bap|tism of fire (**baptisms of fire**) N-COUNT [usu sing] If someone who has just begun a new job has a **baptism of fire**, they immediately have to cope with very many severe difficulties and obstacles. ◻ *It was Mark's first introduction to emergency duties and he came through his baptism of fire unscathed.*

Bap|tist /bæptɪst/ (**Baptists**) **1** N-COUNT A **Baptist** is a Christian who believes that people should not be baptized until they are old enough to understand the meaning of baptism. **2** ADJ [usu ADJ n] **Baptist** means belonging or relating to Baptists. ◻ *...a Baptist church.*

bap|tize /bæptaɪz/ (**baptizes, baptizing, baptized**)

in BRIT, also use **baptise**

V-T [usu passive] When someone **is baptized**, water is put on their heads or they are covered with water as a sign that their sins have been forgiven and that they have become a member of the Christian church. Compare **christen**. ◻ *At this time she decided to become a Christian and was baptized.*

bar ♦♦◇ /bɑr/ (**bars, barring, barred**) **1** N-COUNT A **bar** is a place where you can buy and drink alcoholic drinks. [mainly AM] ◻ *...Devil's Herd, the city's most popular country and western bar.* **2** → see **snack bar, wine bar** **3** N-COUNT A **bar** is a room in a hotel or other establishment where alcoholic drinks are served. ◻ *Last night in the hotel there was some talk in the bar about drugs.* **4** N-COUNT A **bar** is a counter on which alcoholic drinks are served. ◻ *Michael was standing alone by the bar when Brian rejoined him.* **5** N-COUNT A **bar** is a long, straight, stiff piece of metal. ◻ *...a brick building with bars across the ground floor windows.* **6** PHRASE If you say that someone is **behind bars**, you mean that they are in prison. ◻ *Fisher was behind bars last night, charged with attempted murder.* **7** N-COUNT A **bar** of something is a piece of it which is roughly rectangular. ◻ *What is your favorite chocolate bar?* **8** V-T If you **bar** a door, you place something in front of it or a piece of wood or metal across it in order to prevent it from being opened. ◻ *For added safety, bar the door to the kitchen.* **9** V-T If you **bar** someone's way, you prevent them from going somewhere or entering a place, by blocking their path. ◻ *Harry moved to bar his way.* **10** V-T [usu passive] If someone **is barred** from a place or from doing something, they are officially forbidden to go there or to do it. ◻ *Foreign journalists have been barred from the country since 1982.* **11** N-COUNT If something is a **bar** to doing a particular thing, it prevents someone from doing it. ◻ *One of the fundamental bars to communication is the lack of a universally spoken, common language.* **12** PREP You can use **bar** when you mean 'except.' For example, all the work **bar** the laundry means all the work except the laundry. [mainly BRIT] ◻ *Bar a plateau in 1989, there has been a rise in inflation ever since the mid-1980s.* **13** → see also **barring** **14** N-SING [oft N n] The **bar** is used to refer to the profession of any kind of lawyer in the United States, or of a barrister in England. ◻ *Less than a quarter of graduates from the law school pass the bar exam on the first try.*

in BRIT, use **Bar**

15 N-COUNT In music, a **bar** is one of the several short parts of the same length into which a piece of music is divided. ◻ *She sat down at the piano and played a few bars of a Chopin Polonaise.*

barb /bɑrb/ (**barbs**) **1** N-COUNT A **barb** is a sharp curved point near the end of an arrow or a fish hook that makes it difficult to pull out. **2** N-COUNT A **barb** is an unkind remark meant as a criticism of someone or something. ◻ *The barb stung her exactly the way he hoped it would.*

Bar|ba|dian /bɑrbeɪdiən/ (**Barbadians**) **1** ADJ **Barbadian** means belonging or relating to Barbados or its people. **2** N-COUNT A **Barbadian** is someone who comes from Barbados.

bar|bar|ian /bɑrbɛəriən/ (**barbarians**) **1** N-COUNT In former times, **barbarians** were people from other countries who were thought to be uncivilized and violent. ◻ *The Roman Empire was overrun by Nordic barbarians.* **2** N-COUNT If you describe someone as a **barbarian**, you disapprove of them because they behave in a way that is cruel or uncivilized. [DISAPPROVAL] ◻ *Our math teacher was a bully and a complete barbarian.* • ADJ [usu ADJ n] **Barbarian** is also an adjective. ◻ *We need to fight this barbarian attitude to science.*

bar|bar|ic /bɑrbærɪk/ ADJ If you describe someone's behavior as **barbaric**, you strongly disapprove of it because you think that it is extremely cruel or uncivilized. [DISAPPROVAL] ◻ *This barbaric treatment of animals has no place in any decent society.*

bar|ba|rism /bɑrbərɪzəm/ N-UNCOUNT If you refer to someone's behavior as **barbarism**, you strongly disapprove of it because you think that it is extremely cruel or uncivilized. [DISAPPROVAL] ◻ *We do not ask for the death penalty: barbarism must not be met with barbarism.*

bar|bar|ity /bɑrbærɪti/ (**barbarities**) N-VAR If you refer to someone's behavior as **barbarity**, you strongly disapprove of it because you think that it is extremely cruel. [DISAPPROVAL] ◻ *...the barbarity of war.*

bar|ba|rous /bɑrbərəs/ **1** ADJ If you describe something as **barbarous**, you strongly disapprove of it because you think it is rough and uncivilized. [DISAPPROVAL] ◻ *He thought the poetry of Whitman barbarous.* **2** ADJ If you describe something as **barbarous**, you strongly disapprove of it because you think it is extremely cruel. [DISAPPROVAL] ◻ *...a barbarous attack.*

bar|becue /bɑrbɪkyu/ (**barbecues, barbecuing, barbecued**) also **barbeque, Bar-B-Q** **1** N-COUNT A **barbecue** is a piece of equipment which you use for cooking on in the open air. **2** N-COUNT If someone has a **barbecue**, they cook food on a barbecue in the open air. ◻ *On New Year's Eve we had a barbecue on the beach.* **3** V-T If you **barbecue** food, especially meat, you cook it on a barbecue. ◻ *Tuna can be grilled, fried or barbecued.* ◻ *Here's a way of barbecuing corn-on-the-cob that I learned from my uncle.*

barbed /bɑrbd/ ADJ [usu ADJ n] A **barbed** remark or joke seems polite or humorous, but contains a cleverly hidden criticism. ◻ *...barbed comments.*

barbed wire N-UNCOUNT **Barbed wire** is strong wire with sharp points sticking out of it, and is used to make fences. ◻ *The factory was surrounded by barbed wire.*

bar|bell /bɑrbɛl/ (**barbells**) N-COUNT A **barbell** is a long bar with adjustable weights on either side that people lift to strengthen their arm and shoulder muscles. ◻ *She lifted the barbell in her left hand.*

bar|ber /bɑrbər/ (**barbers**) **1** N-COUNT A **barber** is someone whose job is cutting men's hair. ◻ *My father marched me over to Otto, the local barber, to have my hair cut short.* **2** N-SING A **barber's** is a store where a barber works. [mainly BRIT]

in AM, usually use **barber shop**

barber|shop /bɑrbərʃɒp/ (**barbershops**)

The form **barber shop** is also used for meaning **2**.

1 N-UNCOUNT [oft N n] **Barbershop** is a style of singing where a small group of people, usually men, sing in close harmony and without any musical instruments accompanying them. ◻ *...a barbershop quartet.* **2** N-COUNT A **barbershop** is a place where a barber works.

bar|bi|tu|rate /bɑrbɪtʃərɪt/ (**barbiturates**) N-COUNT A **barbiturate** is a drug which people take to make them calm or to help them to sleep. ◻ *She was addicted to barbiturates.*

Bar-B-Q /bɑrbɪkyu/ → see **barbecue**

bar chart (**bar charts**) N-COUNT A **bar chart** is the same as a **bar graph**.

bar code (**bar codes**) also **barcode** N-COUNT A **bar code** is an arrangement of numbers and parallel lines that is printed on products to be sold in stores. The bar code can be read by computers.

bard /bɑrd/ (bards) N-COUNT A **bard** is a poet. [LITERARY or OLD-FASHIONED]

Bard N-PROPER [the N] People sometimes refer to William Shakespeare as **the Bard**. ❑ ...a new production of the Bard's early tragedy, Richard III.

bare ♦◇◇ /bɛər/ (barer, barest, bares, baring, bared) **1** ADJ If a part of your body is **bare**, it is not covered by any clothing. ❑ She was wearing only a thin robe over a flimsy nightgown, and her feet were bare. **2** ADJ A **bare** surface is not covered or decorated with anything. ❑ They would have liked bare wooden floors throughout the house. **3** ADJ If a tree or a branch is **bare**, it has no leaves on it. ❑ ...an old, twisted tree, many of its limbs brittle and bare. **4** ADJ If a room, cupboard, or shelf is **bare**, it is empty. ❑ His fridge was bare apart from three very withered tomatoes. **5** ADJ An area of ground that is **bare** has no plants growing on it. ❑ That's probably the most bare, bleak, barren and inhospitable island I've ever seen. **6** ADJ [det ADJ n] If someone gives you the **bare** facts or the **barest** details of something, they tell you only the most basic and important things. ❑ Newspaper reporters were given nothing but the bare facts by the superintendent in charge of the investigation. **7** ADJ [det ADJ n] If you talk about the **bare** minimum or the **bare** essentials, you mean the very least that is necessary. ❑ The army would try to hold the western desert with a bare minimum of forces. **8** ADJ [a ADJ amount] **Bare** is used in front of an amount to emphasize how small it is. [EMPHASIS] ❑ Sales are growing for premium wines, but at a bare 2 percent a year. **9** V-T If you **bare** something, you uncover it and show it. [WRITTEN] ❑ Walsh bared his teeth in a grin. **10** PHRASE If someone does something with their **bare hands**, they do it without using any weapons or tools. ❑ He can chop a house brick in half with his bare hands. **11 bare bones** → see **bone**

bare|back /bɛərbæk/ ADV [ADV after v] If you ride **bareback**, you ride a horse without a saddle. ❑ I rode bareback to the paddock. • ADJ [ADJ n] **Bareback** is also an adjective. ❑ She dreamed of being a bareback rider in a circus.

bare-bones 1 ADJ [usu ADJ n] If you describe something as **bare-bones**, you mean that it is reduced to the smallest size, amount, or number that you need. ❑ The mayor will have to slash the city's already bare-bones budget. **2** → see also **bone 4**

bare|faced /bɛərfeɪst/ also **bare-faced** ADJ [ADJ n] You use **barefaced** to describe someone's behavior when you want to emphasize that they do not care that they are behaving wrongly. [EMPHASIS] ❑ ...a barefaced confidence trick. ❑ ...crooked politicians who tell bare-faced lies.

bare|foot /bɛərfʊt/ ADJ Someone who is **barefoot** is not wearing anything on their feet. ❑ I wore a white dress and was barefoot.

bare|headed /bɛərhɛdɪd/ ADJ Someone who is **bareheaded** is not wearing a hat or any other covering on their head. ❑ He was bareheaded in the rain. ❑ I rode bareheaded.

bare|ly ♦◇◇ /bɛərli/ **1** ADV You use **barely** to say that something is only just true or only just the case. ❑ Anastasia could barely remember the ride to the hospital. ❑ It was 90 degrees and the air conditioning barely cooled the room. **2** ADV [ADV before v] If you say that one thing had **barely** happened when something else happened, you mean that the first event was followed immediately by the second. ❑ The water had barely come to a simmer when she cracked four eggs into it.

━━━━ SYNONYMS ━━━━
barely
ADV **1**
only just: The signs of an economic revival are only just beginning.
scarcely: He could scarcely breathe.
━━━━━━━━━━━━━━━━

barf /bɑrf/ (barfs, barfing, barfed) V-I If someone **barfs**, they vomit. [mainly AM, INFORMAL]

bar|fly /bɑrflaɪ/ (barflies) N-COUNT A **barfly** is a person who spends a lot of time drinking in bars. [AM, INFORMAL]

bar|gain ♦◇◇ /bɑrgɪn/ (bargains, bargaining, bargained) **1** N-COUNT Something that is a **bargain** is good value, usually because it has been sold at a lower price than normal. ❑ At this price the wine is a bargain. **2** N-COUNT A **bargain** is an agreement, especially a formal business agreement, in which two people or groups agree what each of them will do, pay, or receive. ❑ I'll make a bargain with you. I'll play hostess if you'll include Matthew in your guest list. **3** V-I When people **bargain** with each other, they discuss what each of them will do, pay, or receive. ❑ They prefer to bargain with individual clients, for cash. • **bar|gain|ing** N-UNCOUNT ❑ The government has called for sensible pay bargaining. **4** PHRASE You use **into the bargain** or **in the bargain** when mentioning an additional quantity, feature, fact, or action, to emphasize the fact that it is also involved. [EMPHASIS] ❑ This machine is designed to save you effort, and keep your work surfaces tidy into the bargain.
▶ **bargain for** also **bargain on** PHRASAL VERB If you have not **bargained for** or **bargained on** something that happens, you did not expect it to happen and so feel surprised or worried by it. ❑ The effects of this policy were more than the government had bargained for.

━━━━ SYNONYMS ━━━━
bargain
VERB **3**
haggle: Ella taught her how to haggle with used furniture dealers.
barter: They have been bartering wheat for cotton and timber.
negotiate: It is not clear whether the President is willing to negotiate with the Democrats.
━━━━━━━━━━━━━━━━

bar|gain base|ment also **bargain-basement** ADJ [ADJ n] If you refer to something as a **bargain basement** thing, you mean that it is cheap and not very good quality. ❑ ...a bargain basement rock musical.

bar|gain hunt|er (bargain hunters) also **bargain-hunter** N-COUNT A **bargain hunter** is someone who is looking for goods that are value for money, usually because they are on sale at a lower price than normal.

bar|gain|ing chip (bargaining chips) N-COUNT In negotiations with other people, a **bargaining chip** is something that you are prepared to give up in order to obtain what you want. ❑ Rubio suggests that oil be used as a bargaining chip in any trade talks.

bar|gain|ing coun|ter [BRIT] → see **bargaining chip**

barge /bɑrdʒ/ (barges, barging, barged) **1** N-COUNT [also by N] A **barge** is a long, narrow boat with a flat bottom. Barges are used for carrying heavy loads, especially on rivers and canals. ❑ Carrying goods by train costs nearly three times more than carrying them by barge. **2** V-I If you **barge into** a place or **barge through** it, you rush or push into it in a rough and rude way. [INFORMAL] ❑ Students tried to barge into the secretariat buildings. **3** V-I If you **barge into** someone or **barge past** them, you bump against them roughly and rudely. [INFORMAL] ❑ He would barge into them and kick them in the shins. **4** → See also color supplement
▶ **barge in** PHRASAL VERB If you **barge in** or **barge in on** someone, you rudely interrupt what they are doing or saying. [INFORMAL] ❑ I'm sorry to barge in like this, but I have a problem I hope you can solve.

bar graph (bar graphs) N-COUNT A **bar graph** is a graph that uses parallel rectangular shapes to represent changes in the size, value, or rate of something or to compare the amount of something relating to a number of different countries or groups. ❑ They made a bar graph to display the results.

bar-hop (bar-hops, bar-hopping, bar-hopped) V-I If a person **bar-hops**, they go from one bar to another having drinks in each one. [AM, INFORMAL] ❑ ...a yearly rite-of-passage in which graduating seniors bar-hop from morning until late afternoon.

bari|tone /bærɪtoʊn/ (baritones) N-COUNT In music, a **baritone** is a man with a fairly deep singing voice that is lower than that of a tenor but higher than that of a bass. ❑ ...the young American baritone Monte Pederson.

bar|ium /bɛəriəm/ N-UNCOUNT **Barium** is a soft, silvery-white metal.

bark /bɑrk/ (barks, barking, barked) **1** V-I When a dog **barks**, it makes a short, loud noise, once or several times. ❑ Don't let the dogs bark. • N-COUNT **Bark** is also a noun. ❑ The Doberman let out a string of roaring barks. **2** V-I If you **bark** at someone, you shout at them aggressively in a loud, rough voice. ❑ I didn't mean to bark at you. **3** N-UNCOUNT **Bark** is the tough material that covers the outside of a tree.

bar|keep|er /bɑrkipər/ (barkeepers) N-COUNT A **barkeeper** is someone who serves drinks behind a bar. [AM]

bar|ley /bɑrli/ N-UNCOUNT **Barley** is a grain that is used to make food, beer, and whiskey. ❑ ...fields of ripening wheat and barley.

bar|ley sug|ar N-UNCOUNT **Barley sugar** is a candy made from boiled sugar.

bar|ley wa|ter N-UNCOUNT **Barley water** is a drink made from barley. It is sometimes flavored with orange or lemon.

bar|maid /bɑ͟ːrmeɪd/ (**barmaids**) N-COUNT A **barmaid** is a woman who serves drinks behind a bar. [mainly BRIT]

> in AM, use **bartender**

bar|man /bɑ͟ːrmən/ (**barmen**) N-COUNT A **barman** is a man who serves drinks behind a bar. [mainly BRIT]

> in AM, use **bartender**

bar mitz|vah /bɑːr mɪ̱tsvə/ (**bar mitzvahs**) N-COUNT A **bar mitzvah** is a religious ceremony that takes place on the thirteenth birthday of a Jewish boy, after which he is regarded as an adult.

barn /bɑːrn/ (**barns**) N-COUNT A **barn** is a building on a farm in which animals, animal food, or crops can be kept.

bar|na|cle /bɑ͟ːrnɪkəl/ (**barnacles**) N-COUNT **Barnacles** are small shellfish that fix themselves tightly to rocks and the bottoms of boats.

barn dance (**barn dances**) N-COUNT A **barn dance** is a social event that people go to for country dancing.

barn|storm /bɑ͟ːrnstɔːrm/ (**barnstorms, barnstorming, barnstormed**) V-T/V-I When people such as politicians or performers **barnstorm**, they travel around the country making speeches or giving shows. [AM] ❑ *He barnstormed across the nation, rallying the people to the cause.* ❑ *The president travels thousands of miles as he barnstorms the country.* ❑ *...his barnstorming campaign for the governorship of Louisiana.*

barn|yard /bɑ͟ːrnjɑːrd/ (**barnyards**) N-COUNT [usu sing, oft the N, oft N n] On a farm, the **barnyard** is the area in front of or next to a barn.

ba|rom|eter /bərɒ̱mɪtər/ (**barometers**) **1** N-COUNT A **barometer** is an instrument that measures air pressure and shows when the weather is changing. ❑ *A man in camp took a barometer reading at half-hour intervals.* **2** N-COUNT If something is a **barometer** of a particular situation, it indicates how things are changing or how things are likely to develop. ❑ *In past presidential elections, Missouri has been a barometer of the rest of the country.*

baro|met|ric /bærəmɛ̱trɪk/ ADJ **Barometric** pressure is the atmospheric pressure that is shown by a barometer.

bar|on /bæ̱rən/ (**barons**) **1** N-COUNT; N-TITLE A **baron** is a man who is a member of the lowest rank of the nobility. [BRIT] ❑ *...their stepfather, Baron Michael Distemple.* **2** N-COUNT You can use **baron** to refer to someone who controls a large part of a particular industry or activity and who is therefore extremely powerful. ❑ *...the battle against the drug barons.* **3** → See feature box at **history**

ba|ro|nial /bərou̱niəl/ **1** ADJ [usu ADJ n] If you describe a house or room as **baronial**, you mean that it is large, impressive, and old-fashioned in appearance, and looks as if it belongs to someone from the upper classes. ❑ *...baronial manor houses.* **2** ADJ [ADJ n] **Baronial** means relating to a baron or barons. ❑ *...the baronial feuding of the Middle Ages.*

baro|ny /bæ̱rəni/ (**baronies**) N-COUNT A **barony** is the rank or position of a baron.

ba|roque /bərou̱k/ **1** ADJ [ADJ n] **Baroque** architecture and art is an elaborate style of architecture and art that was popular in Europe in the seventeenth and early eighteenth centuries. ❑ *The baroque church of San Leonardo is worth a quick look.* ❑ *...a collection from the Middle Ages to the Baroque period.* • N-SING [the N] The baroque style and period in art and architecture are sometimes referred to as **the baroque**. ❑ *...the seventeenth-century taste for the baroque.* **2** ADJ [ADJ n] **Baroque** music is a style of European music that was written in the 18th century.

bar|racks /bæ̱rəks/ (**barracks**)

> **Barracks** is both the singular and plural form.

N-COUNT [oft in names] A **barracks** is a building or group of buildings where soldiers or other members of the armed forces live and work. ❑ *...an army barracks in the north of the city.*

bar|ra|cu|da /bæ̱rəkuːdə/ (**barracudas** or **barracuda**) N-COUNT A **barracuda** is a large tropical sea fish that eats other fish.

bar|rage /bərɑːʒ/ (**barrages, barraging, barraged**)

> Pronounced /bɑ͟ːrɪdʒ/ for meaning **4**.

1 N-COUNT A **barrage** is continuous firing on an area with large guns and tanks. ❑ *The artillery barrage on the city was the heaviest since the ceasefire.* **2** N-COUNT A **barrage** of something such as criticism or complaints is a large number of them directed at someone, often in an aggressive way. ❑ *He was faced with a barrage of angry questions from the floor.* **3** V-T [usu passive] If you **are barraged** by people or things, you have to deal with a great number of people or things you would rather avoid. ❑ *Doctors are complaining about being barraged by drug-company salesmen.* **4** N-COUNT A **barrage** is a structure that is built across a river to control the level of the water. ❑ *...a hydro-electric tidal barrage.*

bar|rel ♦◇◇ /bæ̱rəl/ (**barrels, barreling** or **barrelling, barreled** or **barrelled**) **1** N-COUNT A **barrel** is a large, round container for liquids or food. ❑ *The wine is aged for almost a year in oak barrels.* **2** N-COUNT In the oil industry, a **barrel** is a unit of measurement equal to 42 gallons (159 liters). ❑ *The U.S. consumes more than 19 million barrels of oil each day.* **3** N-COUNT The **barrel** of a gun is the tube through which the bullet moves when the gun is fired. ❑ *The light caught the barrel of the gun.* **4** V-I If a vehicle or person **is barreling** in a particular direction, they are moving very quickly in that direction. [mainly AM] ❑ *The car was barreling down the street at a crazy speed.* **5** PHRASE If you say, for example, that someone moves or buys something **lock, stock, and barrel**, you are emphasizing that they move or buy every part or item of it. [EMPHASIS] ❑ *They received a verbal offer to buy the company lock, stock and barrel.*

barrel-chested ADJ A **barrel-chested** man has a large, rounded chest. ❑ *A barrel-chested young man entered the bedroom.*

-barreled /-bæ̱rəld/ also **-barrelled 1** COMB IN ADJ **-barreled** combines with adjectives to form adjectives that describe a gun which has a barrel or barrels of the specified type. ❑ *...a short-barreled rifle.* ❑ *...a double-barrelled shotgun.* **2** → see also **double-barreled**

bar|rel or|gan (**barrel organs**) N-COUNT A **barrel organ** is a large machine that plays music when you turn the handle on the side. Barrel organs used to be played in the street to entertain people.

bar|ren /bæ̱rən/ **1** ADJ A **barren** landscape is dry and bare, and has very few plants and no trees. ❑ *...the landscape of high barren mountains.* **2** ADJ **Barren** land consists of soil that is so poor that plants cannot grow in it. ❑ *He wants to use the water to irrigate barren desert land.* **3** ADJ [oft ADJ of n] If you describe something such as an activity or a period of your life as **barren**, you mean that you achieve no success during it or that it has no useful results. [WRITTEN] ❑ *...an empty exercise barren of utility.* **4** ADJ [oft ADJ of n] If you describe a room or a place as **barren**, you do not like it because it has almost no furniture or other objects in it. [WRITTEN, DISAPPROVAL] ❑ *The room was austere, nearly barren of furniture or decoration.*

bar|rette /bərɛ̱t/ (**barrettes**) N-COUNT A **barrette** is a small metal or plastic device that a woman uses to hold her hair in position. [AM] ❑ *Sarah's hair was out of her face and held back by a barrette.*

> in BRIT, use **hair slide**

bar|ri|cade /bæ̱rɪkeɪd/ (**barricades, barricading, barricaded**) **1** N-COUNT A **barricade** is a line of vehicles or other objects placed across a road or open space to stop people from getting past, for example, during street fighting or as a protest. ❑ *Large areas of the city have been closed off by barricades set up by the demonstrators.* **2** V-T If you **barricade** something such as a road or an entrance, you place a barricade or barrier across it, usually to stop someone from getting in. ❑ *The rioters barricaded streets with piles of blazing tires.* **3** V-T If you **barricade** yourself inside a room or building, you place barriers across the door or entrance so that other people cannot get in. ❑ *The students have barricaded themselves into their dormitory building.*

bar|ri|er ♦◇◇ /bæ̱riər/ (**barriers**) **1** N-COUNT A **barrier** is something such as a rule, law, or policy that makes it difficult or impossible for something to happen or be achieved. ❑ *Duties and taxes are the most obvious barrier to free trade.* **2** N-COUNT A **barrier** is a problem that prevents two people or groups from agreeing, communicating, or working with each other. ❑ *There is no reason why love shouldn't cross the age barrier.* ❑ *She had been waiting for Simon to break down the barrier between them.* **3** N-COUNT A **barrier** is something such as a fence or wall that is in place to prevent people from moving easily from one area to another. ❑ *The demonstrators broke through heavy police barriers.* **4** N-COUNT A **barrier** is an object or layer that physically prevents something from moving from one place to another. ❑ *A severe storm destroyed a natural barrier between the house and the lake.* **5** N-SING You can refer to a particular number or amount as a **barrier** when you think it is significant, because it is difficult or unusual to go above it. ❑ *They are fearful that unemployment will soon break the barrier of three million.* **6** → See feature box at **global warming, speak**

bar|ri|er meth|od (barrier methods) N-COUNT **Barrier methods** of contraception involve the use of condoms, diaphragms, or other devices that physically prevent the sperm from reaching the egg.

bar|ring /bɑrɪŋ/ PREP You use **barring** to indicate that the person, thing, or event that you are mentioning is an exception to your statement. ❑ *Barring accidents, I believe they will succeed.*

bar|rio /bɑriou/ (barrios) **1** N-COUNT A **barrio** is a mainly Spanish-speaking area in an American city. [AM] ❑ *...the barrios of Santa Cruz.* **2** N-COUNT A **barrio** is an urban district in a Spanish-speaking country. [mainly AM] ❑ *...the barrios of Mexico City.*

bar|ris|ter /bærɪstər/ (barristers) N-COUNT In England and Wales, a **barrister** is a lawyer who represents clients in the higher courts of law.

bar|room /bɑrrum/ (barrooms) also **bar-room** N-COUNT A **barroom** is a room or building in which alcoholic drinks are served over a counter. [mainly AM] ❑ *...a barroom brawl.*

in BRIT, usually use **bar**

bar|row /bæroʊ/ (barrows) **1** N-COUNT A **barrow** is the same as a **wheelbarrow**. **2** N-COUNT A **barrow** is a cart from which fruit or other goods are sold in the street. [BRIT]

in AM, use **pushcart**

3 N-COUNT A **barrow** is a large structure made of earth that people used to build over graves in ancient times.

bar|tender /bɑrtɛndər/ (bartenders) N-COUNT A **bartender** is a person who serves drinks behind a bar. [AM]

in BRIT, use **barmaid, barman**

bar|ter /bɑrtər/ (barters, bartering, bartered) V-T/V-I If you **barter** goods, you exchange them for other goods, rather than selling them for money. ❑ *They have been bartering wheat for cotton and timber.* ❑ *The market-place and street were crowded with those who'd come to barter.* ● N-UNCOUNT **Barter** is also a noun. ❑ *Overall, barter is a very inefficient means of organizing transactions.*

ba|sal /beɪsəl/ ADJ [ADJ n] **Basal** means relating to or forming the base of something. [TECHNICAL] ❑ *...the basal layer of the skin.*

bas|alt /bəsɔlt/ (basalts) **1** N-MASS **Basalt** is a type of black rock that is produced by volcanoes. **2** → See also color supplement

base ♦♦♦ /beɪs/ (bases, basing, based, baser, basest) **1** N-COUNT The **base** of something is its lowest edge or part. ❑ *There was a bike path running along this side of the wall, right at its base.* **2** N-COUNT The **base** of something is the lowest part of it, where it is attached to something else. ❑ *The surgeon placed catheters through the veins and arteries near the base of the head.* **3** N-COUNT The **base** of an object such as a box or vase is the lower surface of it that touches the surface it rests on. ❑ *Remove from the heat and plunge the base of the pan into a bowl of very cold water.* **4** N-COUNT The **base** of an object that has several sections and that rests on a surface is the lower section of it. ❑ *The mattress is best on a solid bed base.* **5** N-COUNT A **base** is a layer of something which will have another layer added to it. ❑ *Mix together the cream cheese, yogurt and honey, and spread over the meringue base.* **6** N-COUNT A position or thing that is a **base** for something is one from which that thing can be developed or achieved. ❑ *The post will give him a powerful political base from which to challenge the Kremlin.* **7** V-T If you **base** one thing on another thing, the first thing develops from the second thing. ❑ *He based his conclusions on the evidence given by the captured prisoners.* ● **based** ADJ [v-link ADJ on/upon n] ❑ *Three of the new products are based on traditional herbal medicines.* **8** N-COUNT A company's client **base** or customer **base** is the group of regular clients or customers that the company gets most of its income from. [BUSINESS] ❑ *The company has been expanding its customer base using trade magazine advertising.* **9** N-COUNT A military **base** is a place that part of the armed forces works from. ❑ *Gunfire was heard at an army base close to the airport.* **10** N-COUNT Your **base** is the main place where you work, stay, or live. ❑ *For most of the spring and early summer her base was her home in Connecticut.* **11** N-COUNT If a place is a **base** for a certain activity, the activity can be carried out at that place or from that place. ❑ *The two hotels are attractive bases from which to explore southeast Tuscany.* **12** N-COUNT The **base** of a substance such as paint or food is the main ingredient of it, to which other substances can be added. ❑ *Just before cooking, drain off any excess marinade and use it as a base for a sauce.* **13** N-COUNT [also N num] A **base** is a system of counting and expressing numbers. The decimal system uses base 10, and the binary system uses base 2. **14** N-COUNT A **base** in baseball or softball is one of the places at each corner of the diamond on the field. A player who is at **first base**, **second base**, or **third base**, is standing at the first, second, or third base in a clockwise direction from home plate. ❑ *The first runner to reach second base in the game was John Flaherty.* **15** ADJ [ADJ n] **Base** is used to describe a price or someone's income when this does not include any additional amounts. ❑ *...an increase of more than twenty percent on the base pay of a typical worker.*

base|ball ♦♦ /beɪsbɔl/ (baseballs) **1** N-UNCOUNT **Baseball** is a game played by two teams of nine players. Each player from one team hits a ball with a bat and then tries to run around three bases and get to home plate before the other team can get the ball back. Compare **softball**. **2** N-COUNT A **baseball** is a small hard ball which is used in the game of baseball. **3** → See also color supplement

base|ball cap (baseball caps) N-COUNT A **baseball cap** is a close-fitting cap with a curved part at the front that sticks out above your eyes. ❑ *He often wore a baseball cap.*

base|board /beɪsbɔrd/ (baseboards) **1** N-COUNT A **baseboard** is a narrow length of wood that goes along the bottom of a wall in a room and makes a border between the walls and the floor. [AM]

in BRIT, use **skirting board**

2 → See feature box at **DIY**

based ♦♦♦ /beɪst/ **1** ADJ [v-link ADJ] If you are **based in** a particular place, that is the place where you live or do most of your work. ❑ *Both firms are based in Kent.* **2** → see also **base**

-based /-beɪst/ **1** COMB IN ADJ **-based** combines with nouns referring to places to mean something positioned or existing mainly in the place mentioned, or operating or organized from that place. ❑ *...a Washington-based organization.* ❑ *...land-based missiles.* **2** COMB IN ADJ **-based** combines with nouns to mean that the thing mentioned is a central part or feature. ❑ *...computer-based jobs.* ❑ *...oil-based sauces.* **3** COMB IN ADJ **-based** combines with adverbs to mean having a particular kind of basis. ❑ *There are growing signs of more broadly-based popular unrest.*

base|less /beɪslɪs/ ADJ If you describe an accusation, rumor, or report as **baseless**, you mean that it is not true and is not based on facts. ❑ *The charges against her are baseless.* ❑ *...baseless allegations of drug taking.*

base|line /beɪslaɪn/ (baselines) also **base-line** **1** N-COUNT [usu sing] The **baseline** of a tennis, badminton, or basketball court is one of the lines at each end of the court that mark the limits of play. ❑ *Martinez, when she served, usually stayed on the baseline.* **2** N-COUNT [usu sing] In baseball, the **baseline** is the line that a player must not cross when running between bases. **3** N-COUNT [usu sing, oft N for n/-ing] A **baseline** is a value or starting point on a scale with which other values can be compared. ❑ *You'll need such information to use as a baseline for measuring progress.*

base|ment /beɪsmənt/ (basements) N-COUNT The **basement** of a building is a floor built partly or completely below ground level. ❑ *They bought an old schoolhouse to live in and built a workshop in the basement.*

base met|al (base metals) N-VAR A **base metal** is a metal such as copper, zinc, tin, or lead that is not a precious metal.

bases

Pronounced /beɪsɪz/ for meaning 1. Pronounced /beɪsiːz/ and hyphenated ba|ses for meaning 2.

■ **Bases** is the plural of **base**. ■ **Bases** is the plural of **basis**.

bash /bæʃ/ (bashes, bashing, bashed) ■ N-COUNT A **bash** is a party or celebration, especially a large one held by an official organization or attended by famous people. [INFORMAL] ❑ *He threw one of the biggest showbiz bashes of the year as a 36th birthday party for his wife.* ■ V-T If someone **bashes** you, they attack you by hitting or punching you hard. [INFORMAL] ❑ *If someone tried to bash my best friend they would have to bash me as well.* ❑ *I bashed him on the head and dumped him in the water.* ■ V-T If you **bash** something, you hit it hard in a rough or careless way. [INFORMAL] ❑ *Too many golfers try to bash the ball out of sand. That spells disaster.*

-basher /-bæʃər/ (-bashers) COMB IN N-COUNT **-basher** combines with nouns to form nouns referring to someone who is physically violent toward a particular type of person, or who is unfairly critical of a particular type of person or group. [DISAPPROVAL] ❑ *Big concessions have been made but it will never be enough to please the union-bashers.*

bash|ful /bæʃfəl/ ADJ Someone who is **bashful** is shy and easily embarrassed. ❑ *He seemed bashful and awkward.* ❑ *...a bashful young lady.* ● **bash|ful|ly** ADV [ADV with v] ❑ *"No," Wang Fu said bashfully.* ● **bash|ful|ness** N-UNCOUNT ❑ *I was overcome with bashfulness when I met her.*

-bashing /-bæʃɪŋ/ ■ COMB IN N-UNCOUNT; ADJ **-bashing** combines with nouns to form nouns or adjectives that refer to strong, public, and often unfair criticism of the people or group mentioned. [JOURNALISM, DISAPPROVAL] ❑ *This is the beginning of Congress-bashing presidential campaign rhetoric.* ■ COMB IN N-UNCOUNT; ADJ **-bashing** combines with nouns to form nouns or adjectives that refer to the activity of violently attacking the people mentioned just because they belong to a particular group or community. [DISAPPROVAL] ■ → see also **bash**

ba|sic ♦♢♢ /beɪsɪk/ ■ ADJ You use **basic** to describe things, activities, and principles that are very important or necessary, and on which others depend. ❑ *...the basic skills of reading, writing and communicating.* ❑ *Access to justice is a basic right.* ■ ADJ **Basic** goods and services are very simple ones which every human being needs. You can also refer to people's **basic** needs for such goods and services. ❑ *...shortages of even the most basic foodstuffs.* ❑ *Hospitals lack even basic drugs for surgical operations.* ■ ADJ [v-link ADJ to n] If one thing is **basic** to another, it is absolutely necessary to it, and the second thing cannot exist, succeed, or be imagined without it. ❑ *...an oily liquid, basic to the manufacture of a host of other chemical substances.* ■ ADJ [ADJ n] You can use **basic** to emphasize that you are referring to what you consider to be the most important aspect of a situation, and that you are not concerned with less important details. [EMPHASIS] ❑ *There are three basic types of tea.* ❑ *The basic design changed little from that patented by Edison more than 100 years ago.* ■ ADJ You can use **basic** to describe something that is very simple in style and has only the most necessary features, without any luxuries. ❑ *We provide 2-person tents and basic cooking and camping equipment.* ■ ADJ [ADJ n] The **basic** rate of income tax is the lowest or most common rate, which applies to people who earn average incomes. ❑ *All this is to be done without big increases in the basic level of taxation.*

BASIC /beɪsɪk/ also **Basic** N-UNCOUNT **BASIC** is a computer language that uses common English words. **BASIC** is an abbreviation for 'Beginner's All-Purpose Symbolic Instruction Code.' [COMPUTING]

ba|si|cal|ly ♦♢♢ /beɪsɪkli/ ■ ADV [ADV with cl/group] You use **basically** for emphasis when you are stating an opinion, or when you are making an important statement about something. [EMPHASIS] ❑ *This gun is designed for one purpose – it's basically to kill people.* ■ ADV You use **basically** to show that you are describing a situation in a simple, general way, and that you are not concerned with less important details. ❑ *Basically you've got two choices.*

SYNONYMS

basically
ADV ■
fundamentally: *He can be very charming, but he is fundamentally a bully.*
essentially: *Essentially, vines and grapes need water, heat, and light.*
primarily: *He believes that violent crime is primarily an urban problem.*

---

ba|sics /beɪsɪks/ ■ N-PLURAL The **basics** of something are its simplest, most important elements, ideas, or principles, in contrast to more complicated or detailed ones. ❑ *They will concentrate on teaching the basics of reading, writing and arithmetic.* ❑ *A strong community cannot be built until the basics are in place.* ■ N-PLURAL **Basics** are things such as simple food, clothes, or equipment that people need in order to live or to deal with a particular situation. ❑ *...supplies of basics such as bread and milk.*

ba|sic train|ing N-UNCOUNT **Basic training** is the training that someone receives when they first join the armed forces. [AM]

bas|il /bæzəl/ N-UNCOUNT **Basil** is a strong-smelling and strong-tasting herb that is used in cooking, especially with tomatoes.

ba|sili|ca /bəzɪlɪkə/ (basilicas) N-COUNT A **basilica** is a church that is rectangular in shape and has a rounded end.

ba|sin /beɪsən/ (basins) ■ N-COUNT A **basin** is a large or deep bowl that you use for holding liquids. ❑ *Water dripped into a basin at the back of the room.* ■ N-COUNT A **basin** of something such as water is an amount of it that is contained in a basin. ❑ *We were given a basin of water to wash our hands in.* ■ N-COUNT A **basin** is a sink. ❑ *...a cast-iron bathtub with a matching basin.* ■ N-COUNT The **basin** of a large river is the area of land around it from which streams run down into it. ❑ *...the Amazon basin.* ■ N-COUNT In geography, a **basin** is a particular region of the world where the Earth's surface is lower than in other places. [TECHNICAL] ❑ *...countries around the Pacific Basin.*

ba|sis ♦♦♢ /beɪsɪs/ (bases /beɪsiːz/) ■ N-SING If something is done on a particular **basis**, it is done according to that method, system, or principle. ❑ *We're going to be meeting there on a regular basis.* ❑ *They want all groups to be treated on an equal basis.* ■ N-SING If you say that you are acting on the **basis** of something, you are giving that as the reason for your action. ❑ *McGregor must remain confined, on the basis of the medical reports we have received.* ■ N-COUNT The **basis** of something is its starting point or an important part of it from which it can be further developed. ❑ *Both factions have broadly agreed that the U.N. plan is a possible basis for negotiation.* ■ N-COUNT The **basis** for something is a fact or argument that you can use to prove or justify it. ❑ *...Japan's attempt to secure the legal basis to send troops overseas.*

COLLOCATIONS

basis
NOUN
■
adjective + **basis**: annual, daily, hourly, monthly, weekly; interim, ongoing, permanent, temporary; full-time, part-time; case-by-case, first-come first-served; consistent, day-to-day, regular; voluntary
■
verb + **basis**: form, lay, provide

---

ba|sis point (basis points) N-COUNT In finance, a **basis point** is one hundredth of a percent (.01%). [BUSINESS] ❑ *The dollar climbed about 30 basis points during the morning session.*

bask /bɑːsk, bæsk/ (basks, basking, basked) ■ V-I If you **bask** in the sunshine, you lie somewhere sunny and enjoy the heat. ❑ *All through the hot, still days of their vacation Amy basked in the sun.* ■ V-I If you **bask** in someone's approval, favor, or admiration, you greatly enjoy their positive reaction toward you. ❑ *He has spent a month basking in the adulation of the fans back in Jamaica.*

bas|ket /bɑ:skɪt, bæs-/ (baskets) **1** N-COUNT A **basket** is a stiff container that is used for carrying or storing objects. Baskets are made from thin strips of materials such as straw, plastic, or wire woven together. ◻ ...big wicker picnic baskets filled with sandwiches. **2** N-COUNT You can use **basket** to refer to a basket and its contents, or to the contents only. ◻ ...a small basket of fruit and snacks. **3** N-COUNT In economics, a **basket** of currencies or goods is the average or total value of a number of different currencies or goods. [BUSINESS] ◻ The dollar has fallen 6.5 percent this year against a basket of currencies from its largest trading partners. **4** N-COUNT In basketball, the **basket** is a net hanging from a ring through which players try to throw the ball in order to score points.

basket|ball ◆◇◇ /bɑ:skɪtbɔ:l, bæs-/ (basketballs) **1** N-UNCOUNT **Basketball** is a game in which two teams of five players each try to score goals by throwing a large ball through a circular net fixed to a metal ring at each end of the court. **2** N-COUNT A **basketball** is a large ball which is used in the game of basketball.

bas|ket case (basket cases) **1** N-COUNT If someone describes a country or organization as a **basket case**, they mean that its economy or finances are in a seriously bad state. [INFORMAL] ◻ The country is an economic basket case with chronic unemployment and rampant crime. **2** N-COUNT If you describe someone as a **basket case**, you think that they are very nervous or unable to function. [INFORMAL, DISAPPROVAL] ◻ You're going to think I'm a basket case when I tell you this.

bas|ket|ry /bæskɪtri/ **1** N-UNCOUNT **Basketry** is baskets made by weaving together thin strips of materials such as wood. **2** N-UNCOUNT **Basketry** is the activity of making baskets. ◻ Eva specializes in one of the most difficult techniques of basketry.

bas-relief /bɑ:rɪli:f, bæs-/ (bas-reliefs) **1** N-UNCOUNT [oft N n] **Bas-relief** is a technique of sculpture in which shapes are carved so that they stand out from the background. ◻ ...a classic white bas-relief design. **2** N-COUNT A **bas-relief** is a sculpture carved on a surface so that it stands out from the background. ◻ ...columns decorated with bas-reliefs.

bass ◆◇◇ (basses)

> Pronounced /beɪs/ for meanings 1 to 4, and /bæs/ for meaning 5. The plural of the noun in meaning 5 is **bass**.

1 N-COUNT A **bass** is a man with a very deep singing voice. ◻ ...the great Russian bass Chaliapin. **2** ADJ [ADJ n] A **bass** drum, guitar, or other musical instrument is one that produces a very deep sound. ◻ ...bass guitarist Dee Murray. **3** N-VAR In popular music, a **bass** is a bass guitar or a double bass. ◻ ...Dave Ranson on bass and Kenneth Blevins on drums. **4** N-UNCOUNT On a stereo system or radio, the **bass** is the ability to reproduce the lower musical notes. The **bass** is also the knob that controls this. ◻ Larger models give more bass. **5** N-VAR **Bass** are edible fish that are found in rivers and the sea. There are several types of bass. ◻ They unloaded their catch of cod and bass. • N-UNCOUNT **Bass** is a piece of this fish eaten as food. ◻ ...a large fresh fillet of sea bass.

bas|set hound /bæsɪt haʊnd/ (basset hounds) N-COUNT A **basset hound** is a dog with short strong legs, a long body, and long ears. It is kept as a pet or used for hunting.

bas|si|net /bæsɪnet/ (bassinets) N-COUNT A **bassinet** is a small bed for a baby that is like a basket. ◻ My baby slept safe from harm in her white wicker bassinet.

bass|ist /beɪsɪst/ (bassists) N-COUNT A **bassist** is someone who plays the bass guitar or the double bass.

bas|soon /bəsu:n/ (bassoons) N-VAR [oft the N] A **bassoon** is a large musical instrument that is shaped like a tube and played by blowing into a reed attached to the end of a curved metal pipe.

bas|soon|ist /bəsu:nɪst/ (bassoonists) N-COUNT A **bassoonist** is someone who plays the bassoon.

bas|tard /bæstərd/ (bastards) **1** N-COUNT A **bastard** is an insulting word which some people use about a person who has behaved very badly. [OFFENSIVE, VULGAR, DISAPPROVAL] **2** N-COUNT [oft N n] A **bastard** is a person whose parents were not married to each other at the time that he or she was born. [OFFENSIVE, OLD-FASHIONED]

bas|tard|ized /bæstərdaɪzd, bæs-/

> in BRIT, also use **bastardised**

ADJ [usu ADJ n] If you refer to something as a **bastardized** form of something else, you mean that the first thing is similar to or copied from the second thing, but is of much poorer quality. [FORMAL, DISAPPROVAL]

baste /beɪst/ (bastes, basting, basted) **1** V-T/V-I If you **baste** meat, you pour hot fat and the juices from the meat itself over it while it is cooking. ◻ Pam was in the middle of basting the turkey. ◻ Bake for 15-20 minutes, basting occasionally. **2** V-T If you **baste** pieces of material together, you sew them together with big, loose stitches in order to hold them firmly or check that they fit, before sewing them more permanently. ◻ Pin and baste the motifs in their correct position.

bas|ti|on /bæstʃən/ (bastions) N-COUNT If a system or organization is described as a **bastion** of a particular way of life, it is seen as being important and effective in defending that way of life. **Bastion** can be used both when you think this way of life should be ended and when you think it should be defended. [FORMAL] ◻ ...a town which had been a bastion of White prejudice. ◻ ...a bastion of spiritual freedom.

bat ◆◇◇ /bæt/ (bats, batting, batted) **1** N-COUNT A **bat** is a specially shaped piece of wood that is used for hitting the ball in baseball, softball, or cricket. ◻ ...a baseball bat. **2** V-I When you **bat**, you have a turn at hitting the ball with a bat in baseball, softball, or cricket. ◻ Pettitte hurt an elbow tendon while batting. **3** N-COUNT A **bat** is a small flying animal that looks like a mouse with wings made of skin. Bats are active at night. **4** PHRASE If something happens **right off the bat**, it happens immediately. [AM] ◻ He learned right off the bat that you can't count on anything in this business. **5** → See also color supplement

bat|boy /bætbɔɪ/ (batboys) N-COUNT A **batboy** is a boy whose job is to take care of equipment that belongs to a baseball team. [AM] ◻ If you are a batboy, then you are holding the bat for the baseball players.

batch /bætʃ/ (batches) N-COUNT A **batch** of things or people is a group of things or people of the same kind, especially a group that is dealt with at the same time or is sent to a particular place at the same time. ◻ ...the current batch of trainee priests. ◻ She brought a large batch of newspaper clippings. ◻ I baked a batch of cookies.

bat|ed /beɪtɪd/ PHRASE [usu PHR after v] If you wait for something **with bated breath**, you wait anxiously to find out what will happen. [FORMAL] ◻ We listened with bated breath to Grandma's stories of her travels.

bath ◆◇◇ /bæθ, bɑ:θ/ (baths, bathing, bathed)

> When the form **baths** is the plural of the noun it is pronounced /bæðz/. When it is used in the present tense of the verb, it is pronounced /bɑ:ðz/ or /bæθs/.

1 N-COUNT A **bath** is the process of washing your body in a bathtub. ◻ The midwife gave him a warm bath. **2** N-COUNT When you **take a bath**, you sit or lie in a bathtub filled with water in order to wash your body. ◻ Take a shower instead of a bath.

> in BRIT, also use **have a bath**

3 V-T If you **bath** someone, especially a child, you wash them in a bathtub. [BRIT]

> in AM, use **bathe**

4 N-COUNT A **bath** is a container, usually a long rectangular one, which you fill with water and sit in while you wash your body. [BRIT]

> in AM, use **bathtub**

5 V-I When you **bath**, you take a bath. [BRIT]

> in AM, use **bathe**

6 N-COUNT A **bath** or a **baths** is a public building containing a swimming pool, and sometimes other facilities that people can use to wash or take a bath. ◻ ...a thriving town with houses, government buildings and public baths. **7** N-COUNT A **bath** is a container filled with a particular liquid, such as a dye or an acid, in which particular objects are placed, usually as part of a manufacturing or chemical process. ◻ ...a developing photograph placed in a bath of fixer.

bathe /beɪð/ (bathes, bathing, bathed) **1** V-I When you bathe, you take a bath. [AM] ☐ *At least 60% of us now bathe or shower once a day.* **2** V-T If you bathe someone, especially a child, you wash them in a bathtub. [AM] ☐ *Back home, Shirley plays with, feeds and bathes the baby.* **3** V-I If you bathe in a sea, river, or lake, you swim, play, or wash yourself in it. Birds and animals can also bathe. [mainly BRIT, FORMAL] ☐ *The police have warned the city's inhabitants not to bathe in the polluted river.* • N-SING Bathe is also a noun. ☐ *They took an early morning bathe in the lake.* • **bath|ing** /beɪðɪŋ/ N-UNCOUNT ☐ *Bathing is not allowed.* **4** V-T If you bathe a part of your body or a wound, you wash it gently or soak it in a liquid. ☐ *Bathe the infected area in a salt solution.* **5** V-T If a place is bathed in light, it is covered with light, especially a gentle, pleasant light. ☐ *The arena was bathed in warm sunshine.* ☐ *I was led to a small room bathed in soft red light.* **6** → see also sunbathe

bathed /beɪðd/ **1** ADJ [v-link ADJ in n] If someone is bathed in sweat, they are sweating a great deal. ☐ *Chantal was writhing in pain and bathed in perspiration.* **2** ADJ [v-link ADJ in n] If someone is bathed in a particular emotion such as love, they feel it constantly in a pleasant way. [LITERARY] ☐ *...a sensation of being bathed in love.*

bath|house /bæθhaʊs/ (bathhouses) also **bath house** N-COUNT A bathhouse is a public or private building containing baths and often other facilities such as a sauna.

bath|ing suit /beɪðɪŋ suːt/ (bathing suits) N-COUNT A bathing suit is a piece of clothing that people wear when they go swimming.

bath|ing trunks /beɪðɪŋ trʌŋks/ N-PLURAL Bathing trunks are shorts that a man wears when he goes swimming.

bath|mat /bæθmæt/ (bathmats) also **bath mat** N-COUNT A bathmat is a mat that you stand on while you dry yourself after getting out of the bathtub or shower.

ba|thos /beɪθɒs, -θəs/ N-UNCOUNT In literary criticism, bathos is a sudden change in speech or writing from a serious or important subject to a ridiculous or very ordinary one. [TECHNICAL]

bath|robe /bæθroʊb/ (bathrobes) **1** N-COUNT A bathrobe is a loose piece of clothing usually made of the same material as towels. You wear it before or after you take a bath or a shower. **2** N-COUNT A bathrobe is a dressing gown.

bath|room ◆◇◇ /bæθruːm/ (bathrooms) **1** N-COUNT A bathroom is a room in a house that contains a bathtub or shower, a sink, and sometimes a toilet. **2** N-SING A bathroom is a room in a house or public building that contains a sink and toilet. [mainly AM] ☐ *She had gone in to use the bathroom.*

in BRIT, usually use **toilet**

3 PHRASE People say that they are going to the bathroom when they want to say that they are going to use the toilet. [POLITENESS] ☐ *Although he had been treated with antibiotics, he went to the bathroom repeatedly.* **4** PHRASE You can say that someone goes to the bathroom to mean that they get rid of waste substances from their body, especially when you want to avoid using words that you think may offend people. [mainly AM, POLITENESS] ☐ *I had to go to the bathroom, but I didn't want to use that awful outhouse. So I went off in the woods.*

in BRIT, use **go to the toilet**

bath salts N-PLURAL You dissolve bath salts in bath water to make the water smell pleasant and as a water softener. ☐ *She poured all of the bath salts into the swirling water of the tub.*

bath tow|el (bath towels) N-COUNT A bath towel is a large towel used for drying your body after you have taken a bath or shower.

bath|tub /bæθtʌb/ (bathtubs) N-COUNT A bathtub is a long, usually rectangular container that you fill with water and sit in to wash your body. [AM] ☐ *...a gigantic pink marble bathtub.*

in BRIT, use **bath**

bath wa|ter also **bathwater** N-UNCOUNT Your bath water is the water in which you sit or lie when you take a bath.

ba|tik /bətiːk, bætɪk/ (batiks) **1** N-UNCOUNT [oft N n] Batik is a process for printing designs on cloth. Wax is put on those areas of the cloth that you do not want to be colored by dye. ☐ *...batik bedspreads.* **2** N-VAR A batik is a cloth which has been printed with a batik design. ☐ *...batik from Bali.*

bat mitz|vah /bɒt mɪtsvə/ (bat mitzvahs) N-COUNT A bat mitzvah is a ceremony that takes place when a Jewish girl is 12 or 13, after which she is regarded as an adult.

ba|ton /bətɒn/ (batons) **1** N-COUNT A baton is a light, thin stick used by a conductor to conduct an orchestra or a choir. ☐ *The maestro raises his baton.* **2** N-COUNT In track and field or track events, a baton is a short stick that is passed from one runner to another in a relay race. ☐ *...their biggest relay outing since dropping the baton in Edmonton last August.* **3** N-COUNT A baton is a short heavy stick which is sometimes used as a weapon by the police. [BRIT]

in AM, use **billy**

bats|man /bætsmən/ (batsmen) N-COUNT The batsman in a game of cricket is the man who is batting. ☐ *He was the greatest batsman of his generation.*

bats|woman /bætswʊmən/ (batswomen) N-COUNT The batswoman in a game of cricket is the woman who is batting. ☐ *She crafted a well-earned reputation as a batswoman and wicketkeeper during her heyday.*

bat|tal|ion /bətæljən/ (battalions) **1** N-COUNT A battalion is a large group of soldiers that consists of three or more companies. ☐ *Ten hours later Anthony was ordered to return to his battalion.* **2** N-COUNT A battalion of people is a large group of them, especially a well-organized, efficient group that has a particular task to do. ☐ *There were battalions of highly paid publicists to see that such news didn't make the press.*

bat|ten /bæt³n/ (battens, battening, battened) **1** N-COUNT A batten is a long strip of wood that is attached to something to strengthen it or to hold it firm. ☐ *...a batten to support the base timbers.* **2** V-T [usu passive] If something is battened in place, it is made secure by having battens attached across it or by being closed firmly. ☐ *The roof was never securely battened down.*

bat|ter /bætər/ (batters, battering, battered) **1** V-T To batter someone means to hit them many times, using fists or a heavy object. ☐ *The passengers were battered by flying luggage and cargo as the cabin lost pressure.* ☐ *The gang battered him unconscious.* • **bat|tered** ADJ ☐ *Her battered body was discovered in a field.* **2** V-T If someone is battered, they are regularly hit and badly hurt by a member of their family or by their partner. ☐ *...evidence that the child was being battered.* ☐ *...boys who witness fathers battering their mothers.* • **bat|ter|ing** N-UNCOUNT ☐ *Leaving the relationship does not mean that the battering will stop.* **3** V-T [usu passive] If a place is battered by wind, rain, or storms, it is seriously damaged or affected by very bad weather. ☐ *The country has been battered by winds of between fifty and seventy miles an hour.* **4** V-T If you batter something, you hit it many times, using your fists or a heavy object. ☐ *They were battering the door, they were trying to break in.* **5** N-VAR Batter is a mixture of flour, eggs, and milk that is used in cooking. ☐ *...pancake batter.* **6** N-COUNT In sports such as baseball and softball, a batter is a person who hits the ball with a wooden bat. ☐ *...batters and pitchers.* **7** → see also battered, battering

bat|tered /bætərd/ ADJ Something that is battered is old and in poor condition because it has been used a lot. ☐ *He drove us in a battered old car.*

bat|ter|ing /bætərɪŋ/ (batterings) N-COUNT If something takes a battering, it suffers very badly as a result of a particular event or action. ☐ *The industry's reputation has taken a battering and its image needs to be restored.*

bat|ter|ing ram (battering rams) also **battering-ram** N-COUNT A battering ram is a long heavy piece of wood that is used to knock down the locked doors of buildings. ☐ *They got a battering ram to smash down the door.*

bat|tery /bætəri/ (batteries) **1** N-COUNT Batteries are small devices that provide the power for electrical items such as radios and children's toys. ☐ *The shavers come complete with batteries.* ☐ *...a battery-operated radio.* **2** N-COUNT A car battery is a rectangular box containing acid that is found in a car engine. It provides the electricity needed to start the car. ☐ *...a car with a dead battery.* **3** N-UNCOUNT Battery is the crime of hitting or beating someone. [mainly AM, LEGAL] ☐ *Lawrence punched a man in a Los Angeles nightclub and was charged with battery.*

battle 4 → see also **assault and battery** 5 N-COUNT A **battery** of equipment such as guns, lights, or computers is a large set of it kept together in one place. ☐ *They stopped beside a battery of abandoned guns.* 6 N-COUNT A **battery** of people or things is a very large number of them. ☐ *...a battery of journalists and television cameras.* 7 → See feature box at **computer, farming**

bat|tle ◆◇◇ /bˈæt əl/ (battles, battling, battled) 1 N-VAR A **battle** is a violent fight between groups of people, especially one between military forces during a war. ☐ *...the victory of King William III at the Battle of the Boyne.* ☐ *...a gun battle between police and drug traffickers.* 2 N-COUNT A **battle** is a conflict in which different people or groups compete in order to achieve success or control. ☐ *...an unfolding political battle over jobs and the economy.* ☐ *...the eternal battle between good and evil in the world.* 3 N-COUNT You can use **battle** to refer to someone's efforts to achieve something in spite of very difficult circumstances. ☐ *...the battle against crime.* ☐ *She has fought a constant battle with her weight.* 4 V-RECIP To **battle** with an opposing group means to take part in a fight or contest against them. You can also say that one group or person **is battling** another. ☐ *In one town thousands of people battled with police and several were reportedly wounded.* ☐ *The sides must battle again for a quarter-final place on December 16.* 5 V-T/V-I To **battle** means to try hard to do something in spite of very difficult circumstances. You can also **battle** something, or **battle** against something or with something. ☐ *Doctors battled throughout the night to save her life.* ☐ *Firefighters are still battling the two blazes.* 6 PHRASE If one group or person **battles it out** with another, they take part in a fight or contest against each other until one of them wins or a definite result is reached. You can also say that two groups or two people **battle it out**. ☐ *She will now battle it out with 50 other hopefuls for a place in the last 10.*

SYNONYMS

battle
NOUN
1
conflict: *...talks aimed at ending four decades of conflict.*
clash: *There were a number of clashes between police and demonstrators.*
combat: *Over 16 million men had died in combat.*
attack: *...a campaign of air attacks on strategic targets.*
2
dispute: *They have won previous payment disputes with the government.*
struggle: *He is currently locked in a power struggle with his Prime Minister.*
debate: *An intense debate is going on within the Israeli government.*

---

battle|ax /bˈæt əlæks/ (battleaxes) also **battleaxe** 1 N-COUNT If someone calls an older woman a **battleax**, they mean she is very difficult and unpleasant because of her fierce and determined attitude. This use could cause offence. [INFORMAL, DISAPPROVAL] 2 N-COUNT A **battleax** is a large ax that was used as a weapon.

bat|tle cruis|er (battle cruisers) also **battlecruiser** N-COUNT A **battle cruiser** is a large fast warship that is lighter than a battleship and moves more easily.

bat|tle cry (battle cries) also **battle-cry** 1 N-COUNT A **battle cry** is a phrase that is used to encourage people to support a particular cause or campaign. ☐ *Their battle cry will be: "Sign this petition before they sign away your country."* 2 N-COUNT A **battle cry** is a shout that soldiers give as they go into battle.

bat|tle fa|tigue N-UNCOUNT **Battle fatigue** is a mental condition of anxiety and depression caused by the stress of fighting in a war. ☐ *...a man suffering from battle fatigue.*

battle|field /bˈæt əlfiːld/ (battlefields) 1 N-COUNT A **battlefield** is a place where a battle is fought. ☐ *...the struggle to save America's Civil War battlefields.* 2 N-COUNT You can refer to an issue or field of activity over which people disagree or compete as a **battlefield**. ☐ *...the domestic battlefield of family life.*

battle|ground /bˈæt əlɡraʊnd/ [BRIT] → see **battlefield**

bat|tle|ments /bˈæt əlmənts/ N-PLURAL The **battlements** of a castle or fortress consist of a wall built around the top, with gaps through which guns or arrows can be fired.

battle|ship /bˈæt əlʃɪp/ (battleships) N-COUNT A **battleship** is a very large, heavily armed warship.

bat|ty /bˈæti/ (battier, battiest) ADJ If you say that someone is **batty**, you mean that they are somewhat eccentric or slightly crazy. [INFORMAL, DISAPPROVAL] ☐ *Laura's going a bit batty.* ☐ *...some batty uncle of theirs.*

bau|ble /bˈɔːb əl/ (baubles) N-COUNT A **bauble** is a small, cheap ornament or piece of jewelry. ☐ *...Christmas trees decorated with colored baubles.*

baulk /bˈɔːk/ → see **balk**

baux|ite /bˈɔːksaɪt/ N-UNCOUNT **Bauxite** is a clay-like substance from which aluminum is obtained.

bawdy /bˈɔːdi/ (bawdier, bawdiest) ADJ A **bawdy** story or joke contains humorous references to sex. [OLD-FASHIONED]

bawl /bˈɔːl/ (bawls, bawling, bawled) 1 V-I If you say that a child **is bawling**, you are annoyed because it is crying loudly. ☐ *One of the toddlers was bawling, and the other had a runny nose.* 2 V-T/V-I If you **bawl**, you shout in a very loud voice, for example, because you are angry or you want people to hear you. ☐ *When I came back to the hotel Laura and Peter were shouting and bawling at each other.* ☐ *Then a voice bawled: "Lay off! I'll kill you, you little rascal!"* • PHRASAL VERB **Bawl out** means the same as **bawl**. ☐ *Someone in the audience bawled out "Not him again!"*
▶ **bawl out** PHRASAL VERB If someone **bawls** you **out**, they tell you off angrily. [INFORMAL] ☐ *I was bawled out at school for not doing my homework.*

bay ◆◇◇ /bˈeɪ/ (bays, baying, bayed) 1 N-COUNT A **bay** is a part of a coast where the land curves inward. ☐ *...a short ferry ride across the bay.* ☐ *...the Bay of Bengal.* 2 N-COUNT A **bay** is a partly enclosed area, inside or outside a building, that is used for a particular purpose. ☐ *The animals are herded into a bay, then led into the barn.* 3 N-COUNT A **bay** is an area of a room that extends beyond the main walls of a house, especially an area with a large window at the front of a house. 4 ADJ A **bay** horse is reddish-brown in color. ☐ *...a 10-year-old bay mare.* 5 V-I [usu cont] If a number of people **are baying** for something, they are demanding something angrily, usually that someone should be punished. ☐ *The referee ignored voices baying for a penalty.* ☐ *Opposition politicians have been baying for his blood.* 6 V-I If a dog or wolf **bays**, it makes loud, long cries. ☐ *A dog suddenly howled, baying at the moon.* 7 PHRASE If you **keep** something or someone **at bay**, or **hold** them **at bay**, you prevent them from reaching, attacking, or affecting you. ☐ *Eating oranges keeps colds at bay.*

bay leaf (bay leaves) N-COUNT A **bay leaf** is a leaf of an evergreen tree that can be dried and used as a herb in cooking.

bayo|net /bˈeɪənɪt, bˈeɪənɛt/ (bayonets) N-COUNT A **bayonet** is a long, sharp blade that can be attached to the end of a rifle and used as a weapon.

bayou /bˈaɪuː/ (bayous) N-COUNT A **bayou** is a slow-moving, marshy area of water in the southern United States, especially Louisiana.

bay win|dow (bay windows) 1 N-COUNT A **bay window** is a window that sticks out from the outside wall of a house.
2 → See also color supplement

ba|zaar /bəzˈɑːr/ (bazaars) 1 N-COUNT In areas such as the Middle East and India, a **bazaar** is a place where there are many small stores and stalls. ☐ *Kamal was a vendor in Cairo's open-air bazaar.* 2 N-COUNT A **bazaar** is a sale to raise money for charity. ☐ *...a church bazaar.*

ba|zoo|ka /bəzˈuːkə/ (bazookas) N-COUNT A **bazooka** is a long, tube-shaped gun that is held on the shoulder and fires rockets.

BBC ◆◆◇ /bˌiː bˌiː sˈiː/ N-PROPER [the N] The **BBC** is a British organization which broadcasts programs on radio and television. **BBC** is an abbreviation for 'British Broadcasting Corporation.' ☐ *The concert will be broadcast live by the BBC.*

BB gun /bˌiː bˌiː ɡˈʌn/ (BB guns) N-COUNT A **BB gun** is a type of airgun that fires small round bullets that are called **BBs**. [AM] ☐ *Sims was carrying a BB gun at the time he was shot.*

BBQ **BBQ** is the written abbreviation for **barbecue**.

BC /bˌiː sˈiː/ also **B.C.** You use **BC** in dates to indicate a number of years or centuries before the year in which Jesus Christ is believed to have been born. Compare **AD**, **BCE**. ☐ *The brooch dates back to the fourth century BC.*

BCE /bi si i/ also **B.C.E.** Non-Christians often use **BCE** instead of **BC** in dates. **BCE** indicates a number of years or centuries before the year in which Jesus Christ is believed to have been born. **BCE** is an abbreviation for 'before the Common Era.' Compare **AD**, **BC**. ☐ ...*Lao-tzu, a sixth-century BCE Chinese teacher.* ☐ *The Babylonian Empire was conquered by the Persian Empire in 539 BCE.*

BE
① AUXILIARY VERB USES
② OTHER VERB USES
---

① **be** ♦♦♦ /bi, STRONG bi/ (**am, are, is, being, was, were, been**)

In spoken English, forms of **be** are often shortened, for example 'I am' can be shortened to 'I'm' and 'was not' can be shortened to 'wasn't.'

1 AUX You use **be** with a present participle to form the continuous tenses of verbs. ☐ *This is happening in every school throughout the country.* ☐ *She didn't always think carefully about what she was doing.* **2 be going to** → see **going** **3** AUX You use **be** with a past participle to form the passive voice. ☐ *Her husband was killed in a car crash.* ☐ *Similar action is being taken by the U.S. government.* **4** AUX You use **be** with an infinitive to indicate that something is planned to happen, that it will definitely happen, or that it must happen. ☐ *The talks are to begin tomorrow.* ☐ *It was to be Johnson's first meeting with the board in nearly a month.* **5 be about to** → see **about** **6** AUX You use **be** with an infinitive to say or ask what should happen or be done in a particular situation, how it should happen, or who should do it. ☐ *What am I to do without him?* ☐ *Who is to say which of them had more power?* **7** AUX You use **was** and **were** with an infinitive to talk about something that happened later than the time you are discussing, and was not planned or certain at that time. ☐ *He started something that was to change the face of China.* **8** AUX You can say that something is **to be** seen, heard, or found in a particular place to mean that people can see it, hear it, or find it in that place. ☐ *Little traffic was to be seen on the streets.*

② **be** ♦♦♦ /bi, STRONG bi/ (**am, are, is, being, was, were, been**)

In spoken English, forms of **be** are often shortened, for example 'I am' can be shortened to 'I'm' and 'was not' can be shortened to 'wasn't.'

1 V-LINK You use **be** to introduce more information about the subject, such as its identity, nature, qualities, or position. ☐ *She's my mother.* ☐ *He is a very attractive man.* ☐ *He is fifty and has been through two marriages.* ☐ *The sky was black.* ☐ *His house is next door.* ☐ *He's still alive, isn't he?* **2** V-LINK You use **be**, with 'it' as the subject, in clauses where you are describing something or giving your judgment of a situation. ☐ *It was too chilly for swimming.* ☐ *Sometimes it is necessary to say no.* ☐ *It is likely that investors will face losses.* ☐ *It's nice having friends to chat to.* **3** V-LINK You use **be** with the impersonal pronoun 'there' in expressions like **there is** and **there are** to say that something exists or happens. ☐ *Clearly there is a problem here.* ☐ *There are very few cars on this street.* **4** V-LINK You use **be** as a link between a subject and a clause and in certain other clause structures, as shown below. ☐ *Our greatest problem is convincing them.* ☐ *All she knew was that I'd had a broken marriage.* ☐ *Local residents said it was as if there had been a nuclear explosion.* **5** V-LINK You use **be** in expressions like **the thing is** and **the point is** to introduce a clause in which you make a statement or give your opinion. [SPOKEN] ☐ *The fact is, the players gave everything they had.* **6** V-LINK The form '**be**' is used occasionally instead of the normal forms of the present tense, especially after 'whether.' [FORMAL] ☐ *They should then be able to refer you to the appropriate type of practitioner, whether it be your GP, dentist, or optician.* **7** PHRASE If you talk about what would happen **if it wasn't for** someone or something, you mean that they are the only thing that is preventing it from happening. ☐ *I could happily move back into an apartment if it wasn't for the fact that I'd miss my garden.*

PREFIX
---

be-
can be added to a noun followed by an '-ed' suffix to form an adjective that indicates that someone or something is covered with or wearing the thing named. For example, a piece of jewelry that is **bedecked** with diamonds is covered with diamonds.

beach ♦◊◊ /bitʃ/ (**beaches, beaching, beached**) **1** N-COUNT A **beach** is an area of sand or stones beside the ocean. ☐ ...*a beautiful sandy beach.* **2** V-T/V-I If something such as a boat **beaches**, or if it **is beached**, it is pulled or forced out of the water and onto land. ☐ *We beached the canoe, running it right up the bank.* ☐ *The boat beached on a mud flat.* **3** → See feature box at **ocean**

COLLOCATIONS

beach
NOUN **1**
noun + **beach**: pebble, sand
adjective + **beach**: deserted, pristine, secluded, unspoiled; pebbly, sandy; beautiful, spectacular
---

beach ball (**beach balls**) N-COUNT A **beach ball** is a large, light ball filled with air, which people play with, especially on the beach.

beach bum (**beach bums**) N-COUNT If you refer to someone as a **beach bum**, you mean that they spend a lot of time enjoying themselves on the beach or in the ocean.

beach chair (**beach chairs**) N-COUNT A **beach chair** is a simple chair with a folding frame, and a piece of canvas as the seat and back. **Beach chairs** are usually used on the beach, on a ship, or in the yard. [AM] ☐ *People sprawl in beach chairs or sit under umbrellas.*

in BRIT, use **deckchair**

beach|comber /bitʃkoʊmər/ (**beachcombers**) also **beach-comber** N-COUNT A **beachcomber** is someone who spends their time wandering along beaches looking for things they can use.

beach|front /bitʃfrʌnt/ ADJ [ADJ n] A **beachfront** house, café, shop, or hotel is situated on or by a beach.

beach|head /bitʃhɛd/ (**beachheads**) also **beach-head** N-COUNT A **beachhead** is an area of land next to the sea or a river where an attacking force has taken control and can prepare to advance further inland.

beach|wear /bitʃwɛər/ N-UNCOUNT **Beachwear** is the things people wear for swimming. [mainly AM] ☐ *There is a boutique where beachwear and sportswear are on sale.*

bea|con /bikən/ (**beacons**) **1** N-COUNT A **beacon** is a light or a fire, usually on a hill or tower, that acts as a signal or a warning. ☐ ...*a huge office tower with aircraft warning beacons on the roof.* **2** N-COUNT If someone acts as a **beacon** to other people, they inspire or encourage them. ☐ *She is a beacon of hope for women navigating the darkest passage of their lives.*

bead /bid/ (**beads**) **1** N-COUNT **Beads** are small pieces of colored glass, wood, or plastic with a hole through the middle. **Beads** are often put together on a piece of string or wire to make jewelry. ☐ ...*a string of beads.* **2** N-COUNT A **bead** of liquid or moisture is a small drop of it. ☐ ...*beads of blood.*

bead|ed /bidɪd/ **1** ADJ [usu ADJ n] A **beaded** dress, cushion, or other object is decorated with beads. **2** ADJ [v-link ADJ with n] If something is **beaded** with a liquid, it is covered in small drops of that liquid. ☐ *The man's bald head was beaded with sweat.*

bead|ing /bidɪŋ/ **1** N-UNCOUNT **Beading** is a narrow strip of wood that is used for decorating or edging furniture and doors. **2** N-UNCOUNT **Beading** is an arrangement of beads used for decorating clothes. ☐ ...*a black velvet bodice with jet black beading.*

beady /bidi/ **1** ADJ [usu ADJ n] **Beady** eyes are small, round, and bright. **2** ADJ [ADJ n] If someone keeps a **beady** eye on a person or organization, they watch them carefully and suspiciously. ☐ *The chairman keeps a beady eye on things.*

bea|gle /bigəl/ (**beagles**) N-COUNT A **beagle** is a short-haired black and brown dog with long ears and short legs. It is kept as a pet and sometimes used for hunting.

beak /bik/ (**beaks**) **1** N-COUNT A bird's **beak** is the hard curved or pointed part of its mouth. ☐ ...*a black bird with a yellow beak.* **2** → See also color supplement

beak|er /bikər/ (**beakers**) **1** N-COUNT A **beaker** is a large cup or glass. [AM] **2** N-COUNT A **beaker** is a glass or plastic jar which is used in chemistry. **3** → See feature box at **experiment**

be-all and end-all PHRASE If something is **the be-all and end-all** to you, it is the only important thing in your life, or the only important feature of a particular activity. ❑ *For some people, competing is the be-all and end-all of their running.*

beam /biːm/ (**beams**, **beaming**, **beamed**) ◼ V-T/V-I If you say that someone **is beaming**, you mean that they have a big smile on their face because they are happy, pleased, or proud about something. [WRITTEN] ❑ *Frances beamed at her friend with undisguised admiration.* ❑ *"Welcome back," she beamed.* ◼ N-COUNT A **beam** is a line of energy, radiation, or particles sent in a particular direction. ❑ *...high-energy laser beams.* ◼ V-T/V-I If radio signals or television pictures **are beamed** somewhere, they are sent there by means of electronic equipment. ❑ *The interview was beamed live across America.* ❑ *The Sci-Fi Channel began beaming into 10 million American homes this week.* ◼ N-COUNT A **beam** of light is a line of light that shines from an object such as a lamp. ❑ *A beam of light slices through the darkness.* ◼ N-COUNT A **beam** is a long thick bar of wood, metal, or concrete, especially one used to support the roof of a building. ❑ *The ceilings are supported by oak beams.*

bean ✦◇◇ /biːn/ (**beans**) ◼ N-COUNT **Beans** such as green **beans**, French **beans**, or fava **beans** are the seeds of a climbing plant or the long thin cases which contain those seeds. ◼ N-COUNT **Beans** such as soybeans and kidney **beans** are the dried seeds of other types of bean plants. ◼ N-COUNT **Beans** such as coffee **beans** or cocoa **beans** are the seeds of plants that are used to produce coffee, cocoa, and chocolate.

bean|bag /biːnbæɡ/ (**beanbags**) also **bean bag** ◼ N-COUNT A **beanbag** is a large round cushion filled with tiny pieces of plastic or rubber. It takes the shape of your body when you sit on it. ◼ N-COUNT A **beanbag** is a small cloth bag usually filled with dried beans and thrown in games.

bean coun|ter (**bean counters**) also **bean-counter** N-COUNT You can describe people such as accountants and business managers as **bean counters** if you disapprove of them because you think they are only interested in money. [DISAPPROVAL] ❑ *...bean counters who tend to focus on controlling expenses.*

bean curd N-UNCOUNT **Bean curd** is the same as **tofu**. [mainly BRIT]

bean|ie /biːni/ (**beanies**) N-COUNT A **beanie** is a small, close-fitting cap. ❑ *He bursts into a breakfast diner with his hair under a woolen beanie.*

bean|pole /biːnpoʊl/ (**beanpoles**) N-COUNT If you call someone a **beanpole**, you are criticizing them because you think that they are extremely tall and thin. [INFORMAL, DISAPPROVAL]

bean sprout (**bean sprouts**) also **beansprout** N-COUNT **Bean sprouts** are small, long, thin shoots grown from beans. They are frequently used in Chinese cooking.

BEAR
① VERB USES
② NOUN USES
---

① **bear** ✦◇◇ /beər/ (**bears**, **bearing**, **bore**, **borne**)
→ Please look at meanings ▯ – ▯ to see if the expression you are looking for is shown under another headword.

◼ V-T If you **bear** something somewhere, you carry it there or take it there. [LITERARY] ❑ *They bore the oblong hardwood box into the kitchen and put it on the table.* ◼ V-T If you **bear** something such as a weapon, you hold it or carry it with you. [FORMAL] ❑ *...the constitutional right to bear arms.* ◼ V-T If one thing **bears** the weight of something else, it supports the weight of that thing. ❑ *The ice was not thick enough to bear the weight of marching men.* ◼ V-T If something **bears** a particular mark or characteristic, it has that mark or characteristic. ❑ *The houses bear the marks of bullet holes and the streets are practically deserted.* ❑ *...notepaper bearing the presidential seal.* ◼ V-T If you **bear** an unpleasant experience, you accept it because you are unable to do anything about it. ❑ *They will have to bear the misery of living in constant fear of war.* ◼ V-T [with neg] If you can't **bear** someone or something, you dislike them very much. ❑ *I can't bear people who make judgements and label me.* ◼ V-T When a woman **bears** a child, she gives birth to him or her. [OLD-FASHIONED] ❑ *Emma bore a son called Karl.* ❑ *She bore him a daughter, Susanna.* ◼ V-T If someone **bears** the cost of something, they pay for it. ❑ *Patients should not have to bear the costs of their own treatment.* ◼ V-T If you **bear** the responsibility for something, you accept responsibility for it. ❑ *After all, he bore no responsibility for what had happened the day before.* ◼ V-T [usu with brd-neg] If one thing **bears** no resemblance or no relationship to another thing, they are not at all similar. ❑ *Their daily menus bore no resemblance whatsoever to what they were actually fed.* ◼ V-T When a plant or tree **bears** flowers, fruit, or leaves, it produces them. ❑ *As the plants grow and start to bear fruit they will need a lot of water.* ▯ V-T If something such as a bank account or an investment **bears** interest, interest is paid on it. [BUSINESS] ❑ *The eight-year bond will bear annual interest of 10.5%.* ▯ V-I If you **bear** left or **bear** right when you are driving or walking along, you turn and continue in that direction. ❑ *Traveling north on 309 to Center Valley, bear right at the fork onto Route 378 North.* ▯ → see also **bore**, **borne** ▯ **to bear the brunt of** → see **brunt** ▯ **to bear fruit** → see **fruit** ▯ **to grin and bear it** → see **grin** ▯ **to bear in mind** → see **mind** ①

▶ **bear out** PHRASAL VERB If someone or something **bears** a person **out** or **bears out** what that person is saying, they support what that person is saying. ❑ *Recent studies have borne out claims that certain perfumes can bring about profound psychological changes.*

▶ **bear with** PHRASAL VERB If you ask someone to **bear with** you, you are asking them to be patient. ❑ *If you'll bear with me, Frank, just let me try to explain.*

SYNONYMS

bear
VERB
① ◼
carry: *He carried the plate through to the dining room.*
lift: *She lifted the last of her drink to her lips.*
hold: *He held the pistol in his right hand.*
① ◼
accept: *Urban dwellers often accept noise as part of city life.*
tolerate: *She can no longer tolerate the position that she's in.*
put up with: *They had put up with bad behavior from their son.*
go through: *He was going through a very difficult time.*

COLLOCATIONS

bear
VERB ① ▯
bear + *noun*: relation, relationship, resemblance
---

② **bear** /beər/ (**bears**) ◼ N-COUNT A **bear** is a large, strong wild animal with thick fur and sharp claws. ◼ N-COUNT In the stock market, **bears** are people who sell shares in expectation of a drop in price, in order to make a profit by buying them back again after a short time. Compare **bull**. [BUSINESS]

bear|able /beərəbəl/ ADJ If something is **bearable**, you feel that you can accept it or deal with it. ❑ *A cool breeze made the heat bearable.*

beard /bɪərd/ (**beards**) N-COUNT A man's **beard** is the hair that grows on his chin and cheeks. ❑ *He's decided to grow a beard.*

beard|ed /bɪərdɪd/ ADJ A **bearded** man has a beard. ❑ *...a bearded 40-year-old sociology professor.*

bear|er /beərər/ (**bearers**) ◼ N-COUNT The **bearer** of something such as a message is the person who brings it to you. ❑ *I hate to be the bearer of bad news.* ◼ N-COUNT A **bearer** of a particular thing is a person who carries it, especially in a ceremony. [FORMAL] ❑ *He was the U.S. flag bearer at the 1976 Montreal Games.* ◼ N-COUNT The **bearer** of something such as a document, a right, or an official position is the person who possesses it or holds it. [FORMAL] ❑ *...the traditional bourgeois notion of the citizen as a bearer of rights.*

bear hug (**bear hugs**) N-COUNT A **bear hug** is a rough, tight, affectionate hug.

bear|ing ✦◇◇ /beərɪŋ/ (**bearings**) ◼ PHRASE If something **has a bearing on** a situation or event, it is relevant to it. ❑ *Experts generally agree that diet has an important bearing on your general health.* ◼ N-SING Someone's **bearing** is the way in which they move or stand. [LITERARY] ❑ *She later wrote warmly of his bearing and behavior.* ◼ PHRASE If you **get** your **bearings** or **find** your **bearings**, you find out where you are or what you should do next. If you **lose** your **bearings**, you do not know where you are or what you should do next. ❑ *A sightseeing tour of the city is included to help you get your bearings.*

-bearing /-bεərɪŋ/ COMB IN ADJ **-bearing** combines with nouns to form adjectives which describe things that hold the specified substance inside them. ❑ *...oil-bearing rocks.* ❑ *...malaria-bearing mosquitoes.*

bear|ish /bεərɪʃ/ ADJ In the stock market, if there is a **bearish** mood, prices are expected to fall. Compare **bullish**. [BUSINESS] ❑ *Dealers said investors remain bearish.*

bear mar|ket (bear markets) **1** N-COUNT A **bear market** is a situation in the stock market when people are selling a lot of shares because they expect the shares will decrease in value and they will be able to make a profit by buying them again after a short time. Compare **bull market**. [BUSINESS] ❑ *Is the bear market in equities over?* **2** → See feature box at **banking**

bear|skin /bεərskɪn/ (bearskins) **1** N-VAR A **bearskin** is the skin and fur of a bear. **2** N-COUNT A **bearskin** is a tall fur hat that is worn by some British soldiers on ceremonial occasions. **3** → See also color supplement

beast /biːst/ (beasts) N-COUNT You can refer to an animal as a **beast**, especially if it is a large, dangerous, or unusual one. [LITERARY] ❑ *...the threats our ancestors faced from wild beasts.*

beast|ly /biːstli/ (beastlier, beastliest) **1** ADJ If you describe something as **beastly**, you mean that it is very unpleasant. [INFORMAL, OLD-FASHIONED] **2** ADJ If you describe someone as **beastly**, you mean that they are behaving unkindly. [INFORMAL, OLD-FASHIONED]

beast of bur|den (beasts of burden) N-COUNT A **beast of burden** is an animal such as an ox or a donkey that is used for carrying or pulling things.

beat ✦✧✧ /biːt/ (beats, beating, beaten)

The form **beat** is used in the present tense and is the past tense.

1 V-T If you **beat** someone or something, you hit them very hard. ❑ *My wife tried to stop them and they beat her.* **2** V-T To **beat** on, at, or against something means to hit it hard, usually several times or continuously for a period of time. ❑ *There was dead silence but for a fly beating against the glass.* ❑ *Nina managed to free herself and began beating at the flames with a pillow.* • N-SING **Beat** is also a noun. ❑ *...the rhythmic beat of the surf.* • **beat|ing** N-SING ❑ *The silence was broken only by the beating of the rain.* **3** V-I When your heart or pulse **beats**, it continually makes regular rhythmic movements. ❑ *I felt my heart beating faster.* • N-COUNT **Beat** is also a noun. ❑ *He could hear the beat of his heart.* • **beat|ing** N-SING ❑ *I could hear the beating of my heart.* **4** V-T/V-I If you **beat** a drum or similar instrument, you hit it in order to make a sound. You can also say a drum **beats**. ❑ *When you beat the drum, you feel good.* ❑ *...drums beating and pipes playing.* • N-SING **Beat** is also a noun. ❑ *...the rhythmical beat of the drum.* **5** N-COUNT The **beat** of a piece of music is the main rhythm that it has. ❑ *...the thumping beat of rock music.* **6** N-COUNT In music, a **beat** is a unit of measurement. The number of beats in a measure of a piece of music is indicated by two numbers at the beginning of the piece. ❑ *It's got four beats to a measure.* **7** V-T If you **beat** eggs, cream, or butter, you mix them thoroughly using a fork or beater. ❑ *Beat the eggs and sugar until they start to thicken.* **8** V-T/V-I When a bird or insect **beats** its wings or when its wings **beat**, its wings move up and down. ❑ *Beating their wings they flew off.* **9** V-T If you **beat** someone in a competition or election, you defeat them. ❑ *In yesterday's game, Switzerland beat the United States two to one.* **10** V-T If someone **beats** a record or achievement, they do better than it. ❑ *He was as eager as his Captain to beat the record.* **11** V-T If you **beat** something that you are fighting against, for example, an organization, a problem, or a disease, you defeat it. ❑ *It became clear that the Union was not going to beat the government.* **12** V-T [usu passive] If an attack or an attempt **is beaten** off or **is beaten** back, it is stopped, often temporarily. ❑ *The rescuers were beaten back by strong winds and currents.* **13** V-T [no cont] If you say that one thing **beats** another, you mean that it is better than it. [INFORMAL] ❑ *Being boss of a software firm beats selling insurance.* **14** V-T To **beat** a time limit or an event means to achieve something before that time or event. ❑ *They were trying to beat the midnight deadline.* **15** N-COUNT A police officer's or journalist's **beat** is the area for which he or she is responsible. ❑ *A policeman was patrolling his regular beat, when he saw a group of boys milling about the street.* **16** → see also **beating** **17** PHRASE If you intend to do something but someone **beats** you **to it**, they do it before you do. ❑ *Don't be too long about it or you'll find someone has beaten you to it.* **18 to beat someone at their own game** → see **game** **19** → See feature box at **competition**

▶ **beat up** PHRASAL VERB If someone **beats** a person **up**, they hit or kick the person many times. ❑ *Then they actually beat her up as well.*

COLLOCATIONS

beat
NOUN **3**
verb + **beat**: miss, skip
VERB
9
beat + noun: opponent, rival, team
10
beat + noun: record

---

beat|able /biːtəbəl/ ADJ [v-link ADJ] Someone who is **beatable** can be defeated. ❑ *All teams are beatable, but it's going to be very, very difficult.*

beat|en ✦✧✧ /biːtən/ **1** **Beaten** is the past participle of **beat**. **2** PHRASE A place that is **off the beaten track** is in an area where not many people live or go. ❑ *Tiny secluded beaches can be found off the beaten track.* **3** → See feature box at **tourism**

beaten-up ADJ A **beaten-up** car or other object is old and in bad condition. ❑ *Her sandals were old and somewhat beaten-up, but very comfortable.*

beat|er /biːtər/ (beaters) N-COUNT [oft n n] A **beater** is a tool or part of a machine that is used for beating things like eggs and cream. ❑ *Whisk the batter with a wire whisk or hand beater until it is smooth and light.*

bea|tif|ic /biːətɪfɪk/ ADJ [usu ADJ n] A **beatific** expression shows or expresses great happiness and calmness. [LITERARY] ❑ *...a beatific smile.*

be|ati|fy /biːætɪfaɪ/ (beatifies, beatifying, beatified) V-T When the Catholic church **beatifies** someone who is dead, it declares officially that they were a holy person, usually as the first step toward making them a saint. ❑ *In May, Pope John Paul is to beatify Gianna Beretta.* • **be|ati|fi|ca|tion** /biːætɪfɪkeɪʃən/ N-UNCOUNT ❑ *Thousands attended the beatification of Juan Diego.*

beat|ing ✦✧✧ /biːtɪŋ/ (beatings) **1** N-COUNT If someone is given a **beating**, they are hit hard many times, especially with something such as a stick. ❑ *...the investigation into the beating of an alleged car thief.* **2** N-SING If something such as a business, a political party, or a team takes a **beating**, it is defeated by a large amount in a competition or an election. ❑ *Our firm has taken a terrible beating in recent years.*

beat|nik /biːtnɪk/ (beatniks) N-COUNT **Beatniks** were young people in the late 1950s who rejected traditional ways of living, dressing, and behaving. People sometimes use the word beatnik to refer to anyone who lives in an unconventional way. ❑ *...a beatnik art student.*

beat-up ADJ [ADJ n] A **beat-up** car or other object is old and in bad condition. [INFORMAL] ❑ *...a beat-up old Fiat.*

beau /boʊ/ (beaux or beaus) N-COUNT [oft poss n] Someone's **beau** is their boyfriend or lover. [OLD-FASHIONED]

Beau|jo|lais /boʊʒəleɪ/ (Beaujolais) also **beaujolais** N-VAR **Beaujolais** is a type of red wine that comes from the region of eastern France called Beaujolais. ❑ *...a fruity Beaujolais.*

beaut /byuːt/ (beauts) N-COUNT You describe someone or something as a **beaut** when you think they are very good. [mainly AM or AUSTRALIAN, INFORMAL]

beau|te|ous /byuːtiəs/ ADJ **Beauteous** means the same as **beautiful**. [LITERARY]

beau|ti|cian /byuːtɪʃən/ (beauticians) N-COUNT A **beautician** is a person whose job is giving people beauty treatments such as doing their nails, treating their skin, and putting on their makeup.

beau|ti|ful ✦✧✧ /byuːtɪfəl/ **1** ADJ A **beautiful** person is very attractive to look at. ❑ *She was a very beautiful woman.* **2** ADJ If you describe something as **beautiful**, you mean that it is very attractive or pleasing. ❑ *New England is beautiful.* ❑ *It was a beautiful morning.* • **beau|ti|ful|ly** /byuːtɪfli/ ADV ❑ *The children behaved beautifully.* **3** ADJ You can describe something that

beautify

someone does as **beautiful** when they do it very skillfully. ❑ *That's a beautiful shot!* • **beau|ti|ful|ly** ADV ❑ *The Sixers played beautifully.*

beau|ti|fy /byúːtɪfaɪ/ (beautifies, beautifying, beautified) V-T If you **beautify** something, you make it look more beautiful. [FORMAL] ❑ *Claire worked to beautify the garden.*

beau|ty ✦✧✧ /byúːti/ (beauties) **1** N-UNCOUNT **Beauty** is the state or quality of being beautiful. ❑ *...an area of outstanding natural beauty.* **2** N-COUNT A **beauty** is a beautiful woman. [JOURNALISM] ❑ *She is known as a great beauty.* **3** N-COUNT You can say that something is a **beauty** when you think it is very good. [INFORMAL] ❑ *It was the one opportunity in the game – the pass was a real beauty, but the shot was poor.* **4** N-COUNT The **beauties** of something are its attractive qualities or features. [LITERARY] ❑ *He was beginning to enjoy the beauties of nature.* **5** ADJ [ADJ n] **Beauty** is used to describe people, products, and activities that are concerned with making someone look beautiful. ❑ *Additional beauty treatments can be booked in advance.* **6** N-COUNT If you say that a particular feature is the **beauty** of something, you mean that this feature is what makes the thing so good. ❑ *There would be no effect on animals – that's the beauty of such water-based materials.*

beau|ty con|test (beauty contests) N-COUNT A **beauty contest** is a competition in which young women are judged in order to decide which one is the most beautiful.

beau|ty mark (beauty marks) N-COUNT A **beauty mark** is a small, dark spot on the skin that is supposed to add to a woman's beauty. [AM, AUSTRALIAN] ❑ *...the little beauty mark on her lower lip.*

> in BRIT, use **beauty spot**

beau|ty pag|eant (beauty pageants) N-COUNT A **beauty pageant** is the same as a **beauty contest**. [AM]

beau|ty par|lor (beauty parlors)

> in BRIT, use **beauty parlour**

N-COUNT A **beauty parlor** is a place where people can go to have beauty treatments, for example to have their hair, nails, or makeup done.

beau|ty queen (beauty queens) N-COUNT A **beauty queen** is a woman who has won a beauty contest.

beau|ty sa|lon (beauty salons) N-COUNT A **beauty salon** is the same as a **beauty parlor**.

beau|ty shop (beauty shops) N-COUNT A **beauty shop** is the same as a **beauty parlor**. [AM]

bea|ver /bíːvər/ (beavers) **1** N-COUNT A **beaver** is a furry animal with a big flat tail and large teeth. Beavers use their teeth to cut wood and build dams in rivers. **2** N-UNCOUNT [oft N n] **Beaver** is the fur of a beaver. ❑ *...a coat with a huge beaver collar.*

be|bop /bíːbɒp/ N-UNCOUNT **Bebop** is a form of jazz music with complex harmonies and rhythms. The abbreviation **bop** is also used.

be|calmed /bɪkάːmd/ **1** ADJ [usu v-link ADJ] If a sailing ship is **becalmed**, it is unable to move because there is no wind. ❑ *We were becalmed off Cape Raoul for several hours.* **2** ADJ If something such as the economy, a company, or a series of talks is **becalmed**, it is not progressing at all, although it should be. [LITERARY] ❑ *...the becalmed peace talks.*

be|came /bɪkéɪm/ **Became** is the past tense of **become**.

be|cause ✦✦✦ /bɪkɒ́z, bɪkʌ́z/ **1** CONJ You use **because** when stating the reason for something. ❑ *He is called Mitch, because his name is Mitchell.* ❑ *Because it is an area of outstanding natural beauty, the number of boats available for hire on the river is limited.* **2** CONJ You use **because** when stating the explanation for a statement you have just made. ❑ *Maybe they just didn't want to ask too many questions, because they rented us a room without even asking to see our papers.* ❑ *The president has played a shrewd diplomatic game because from the outset he called for direct talks.* **3** PHRASE If an event or situation occurs **because of** something, that thing is the reason or cause. ❑ *Many families break up because of a lack of money.*

beck /bék/ PHRASE [v-link PHR] If one person is at another's **beck and call**, they have to be constantly available and ready to do whatever is asked, and this often seems unfair or undesirable.

bedazzled

beck|on /békən/ (beckons, beckoning, beckoned) **1** V-T/V-I If you **beckon** to someone, you signal to them to come to you. ❑ *He beckoned to the waiter.* ❑ *I beckoned her over.* **2** V-I If something **beckons**, it is so attractive to someone that they feel they must become involved in it. ❑ *All the attractions of the peninsula beckon.* **3** V-I If something **beckons** for someone, it is very likely to happen to them. ❑ *The big time beckons for Billy Dodds.*

be|come ✦✦✦ /bɪkʌ́m/ (becomes, becoming, became)

> The form **become** is used in the present tense and is the past participle.

1 V-LINK If someone or something **becomes** a particular thing, they start to change and develop into that thing, or start to develop the characteristics mentioned. ❑ *I first became interested in yoga while I was doing my nursing training.* **2** V-T [no passive, no cont] If something **becomes** someone, it makes them look attractive or it seems right for them. ❑ *Does khaki become you?* **3** PHRASE If you wonder **what** has **become of** someone or something, you wonder where they are and what has happened to them. ❑ *She thought constantly about her family; she might never know what had become of them.*

be|com|ing /bɪkʌ́mɪŋ/ **1** ADJ [usu v-link ADJ] A piece of clothing, a color, or a hairstyle that is **becoming** makes the person who is wearing it look attractive. [OLD-FASHIONED] ❑ *Softer fabrics are much more becoming than stiffer ones.* • **be|com|ing|ly** ADV ❑ *Her dress was of blue silk, quite light, and becomingly open at the neck.* **2** ADJ [usu v-link ADJ] Behavior that is **becoming** is appropriate and proper in the circumstances. ❑ *This behavior is not any more becoming among our politicians than it is among our voters.*

bed ✦✦✧ /béd/ (beds) **1** N-COUNT [also prep N] A **bed** is a piece of furniture that you lie on when you sleep. ❑ *We finally went to bed at about 4am.* ❑ *By the time we got back from dinner, Nona was already in bed.* **2** N-COUNT If a place such as a hospital or a hotel has a particular number of **beds**, it is able to hold that number of patients or guests. **3** N-COUNT A **bed** in a garden or park is an area of ground that has been specially prepared so that plants can be grown in it. ❑ *...beds of strawberries and rhubarb.* **4** N-COUNT A **bed** of shellfish or plants is an area in the sea or in a lake where a particular type of shellfish or plant is found in large quantities. ❑ *The whole lake was rimmed with thick beds of reeds.* **5** N-COUNT The sea **bed** or a river **bed** is the ground at the bottom of the sea or of a river. ❑ *For three weeks a big operation went on to recover the wreckage from the sea bed.* **6** N-COUNT A **bed** of rock is a layer of rock that is found within a larger area of rock. ❑ *Between the white limestone and the grayish pink limestone is a thin bed of clay.* **7** N-COUNT If a recipe or a menu says that something is served on a **bed** of a food such as rice or vegetables, it means it is served on a layer of that food. ❑ *Heat the curry thoroughly and serve it on a bed of rice.* **8** N-COUNT On a vehicle such a truck or a pickup, the **bed** is the long, flat part at the back where goods are carried. ❑ *They loaded about a ton of canned goods into the covered bed of a pickup truck.* **9** → see also **bedding** **10** PHRASE To **go to bed with** someone means to have sex with them. ❑ *I went to bed with him once, just once.* **11** PHRASE When you **make** the **bed**, you neatly arrange the sheets and covers of a bed so that it is ready to sleep in. ❑ *He had made the bed after breakfast.* **12 bed of roses** → see **rose** **13** → See also color supplement

BEd /bíː éd/ (BEds) also **B.Ed** N-COUNT A **BEd** is a degree that usually takes four years to complete and that qualifies someone to teach in a school. **BEd** is an abbreviation for 'Bachelor of Education.' [BRIT]

bed and break|fast (bed and breakfasts) also **bed-and-breakfast** **1** N-UNCOUNT **Bed and breakfast** is a system of accommodations in a hotel or guest house, in which you pay for a room for the night and for breakfast the following morning. The abbreviation **B&B** is also used. ❑ *Bed and breakfast costs from $50 per person per night.* **2** N-COUNT A **bed and breakfast** is a guest house that provides bed and breakfast accommodations. The abbreviation **B&B** is also used. ❑ *The restored home is now a bed-and-breakfast.*

be|daz|zled /bɪdǽzəld/ ADJ [oft ADJ by n] If you are **bedazzled** by someone or something, you are so amazed and impressed by them that you feel confused. ❑ *Many people are bedazzled by fame.*

bed|bug /bɛdbʌg/ (bedbugs) N-COUNT A **bedbug** is a small insect with a round body and no wings that lives in dirty houses and feeds by biting people and sucking their blood when they are in bed.

bed|chamber /bɛdtʃeɪmbər/ (bedchambers) also **bed-chamber** N-COUNT A **bedchamber** is a bedroom. [FORMAL]

bed|clothes /bɛdkloʊz, -kloʊðz/ N-PLURAL **Bedclothes** are the sheets and covers that you put over yourself when you get into bed. [OLD-FASHIONED] ❑ *Momma was cleaning inside, changing the bedclothes.*

bed|ding /bɛdɪŋ/ N-UNCOUNT **Bedding** is sheets, blankets, and covers that are used on beds. ❑ *...a crib with two full sets of bedding.*

bed|ding plant (bedding plants) N-COUNT A **bedding plant** is a plant that lasts for one year. It is put in a flower bed before it flowers, and is then removed when it has finished flowering.

be|deck /bɪdɛk/ (bedecks, bedecking, bedecked) V-T If flags or other ornaments **bedeck** a place, a lot of them have been hung up to decorate it. [LITERARY] ❑ *...flags bedecking the balcony.*

be|decked /bɪdɛkt/ ADJ If a place is **bedecked** with flags or other ornaments, these things have been hung up to decorate it. [LITERARY] ❑ *The palace was bedecked with flags.* • COMB IN ADJ **Bedecked** is also a combining form. ❑ *...a flower-bedecked stage.*

be|dev|il /bɪdɛvəl/ (bedevils, bedeviling or bedevilling, bedeviled or bedevilled) V-T If you **are bedeviled** by something unpleasant, it causes you a lot of problems over a period of time. [FORMAL] ❑ *His career was bedeviled by injury.* ❑ *...a problem that has bedeviled service industries for decades.*

bed|fellow /bɛdfɛloʊ/ (bedfellows) N-COUNT [usu pl] You refer to two things or people as **bedfellows** when they have become associated or related in some way. ❑ *Sex and death are strange bedfellows.*

bed|head /bɛdhɛd/ (bedheads) also **bed-head** ■ N-COUNT A **bedhead** is a board that is attached to the end of a bed behind your head. [BRIT]

in AM, use **headboard**

■ ADJ [ADJ n] If you say that someone has **bedhead** hair, you mean that their hairstyle is deliberately untidy, as if they have been lying in bed. [INFORMAL] ❑ *His face is framed with long bedhead hair that he keeps sweeping back.*

bed|lam /bɛdləm/ N-UNCOUNT **Bedlam** means a great deal of noise and disorder. People often say 'It was bedlam' to mean 'There was bedlam.' ❑ *The crowd went absolutely mad. It was bedlam.*

bed lin|en N-UNCOUNT **Bed linen** is sheets and pillowcases. ❑ *...crisp white cotton bed linen.*

Bedou|in /bɛduɪn, bɛdwɪn/ (Bedouins or Bedouin) ■ N-COUNT A **Bedouin** is a member of a particular Arab tribe. ■ ADJ **Bedouin** means relating to the Bedouin people. ❑ *...Bedouin carpets.*

bed|pan /bɛdpæn/ (bedpans)

in BRIT, also use **bed-pan**

N-COUNT A **bedpan** is a shallow bowl shaped like a toilet seat, which is used instead of a toilet by people who are too ill to get out of bed.

bed|post /bɛdpoʊst/ (bedposts) N-COUNT A **bedpost** is one of the four vertical supports at the corners of a bed with an old-fashioned wooden or iron frame.

be|drag|gled /bɪdrægəld/ ADJ Someone or something that is **bedraggled** looks messy because they have got wet or dirty. ❑ *He looked weary and bedraggled.* ❑ *...a bedraggled group of journalists.*

bed|rid|den /bɛdrɪdən/ ADJ Someone who is **bedridden** is so ill or has such a severe disability that they cannot get out of bed. ❑ *He had to spend two years bedridden with an injury.* ❑ *...bedridden patients.*

bed|rock /bɛdrɒk/ ■ N-SING The **bedrock** of something is the principles, ideas, or facts on which it is based. ❑ *Mutual trust is the bedrock of a relationship.* ❑ *We believe in religious freedom as a bedrock principle of our democracy.* ■ N-UNCOUNT **Bedrock** is the solid rock in the ground which supports all the soil above it.

bed|roll /bɛdroʊl/ (bedrolls) also **bed-roll** N-COUNT A **bedroll** is a rolled-up sleeping bag or other form of bedding that you can carry with you.

bed|room ✦◇◇ /bɛdrum/ (bedrooms) ■ N-COUNT A **bedroom** is a room used for sleeping in. ❑ *...the spare bedroom.* ■ ADJ [ADJ n] If you refer to a place as a **bedroom** community or suburb, you mean that most of the people who live there travel to work in a city or another, larger town a short distance away. [AM] ❑ *This town is becoming a bedroom community of Columbus, 20 miles to the north.*

in BRIT, use **dormitory**

-bedroomed /-bɛdrumd/ COMB IN ADJ **-bedroomed** combines with numbers to form adjectives that indicate how many bedrooms a particular house or apartment has. ❑ *...a two-bedroomed apartment.*

bed|side /bɛdsaɪd/ ■ N-SING [usu N n] Your **bedside** is the area beside your bed. ❑ *She put a cup of tea down on the bedside table.* ■ N-SING If you talk about being at someone's **bedside**, you are talking about being near them when they are ill in bed. ❑ *She kept vigil at the bedside of her critically ill son.*

bed|side man|ner N-SING A doctor's **bedside manner** is the way in which they talk to their patients.

bed|sores /bɛdsɔrz/ N-PLURAL **Bedsores** are sore places on a person's skin, caused by having to lie in bed for a long time without changing position.

bed|spread /bɛdsprɛd/ (bedspreads) N-COUNT A **bedspread** is a decorative cover that is put over a bed, on top of the sheets and blankets.

bed|stead /bɛdstɛd/ (bedsteads) N-COUNT A **bedstead** is the metal or wooden frame of an old-fashioned bed.

bed|time /bɛdtaɪm/ N-UNCOUNT Your **bedtime** is the time when you usually go to bed. ❑ *It was eight-thirty, Trevor's bedtime.* ❑ *...bedtime stories.*

bed|wet|ting /bɛdwɛtɪŋ/ also **bed-wetting** N-UNCOUNT **Bedwetting** means urinating in bed, usually by small children.

bee /bi/ (bees) N-COUNT A **bee** is an insect with a yellow-and-black striped body that makes a buzzing noise as it flies. Bees make honey, and can sting. ❑ *A bee buzzed in the flowers.*

beech /bitʃ/ (beeches) N-VAR A **beech** or a **beech tree** is a tree with a smooth gray trunk. ❑ *...the branch of a huge beech.* • N-UNCOUNT **Beech** is the wood of this tree. ❑ *The worktop is made of solid beech.*

beef /bif/ (beefs, beefing, beefed) N-UNCOUNT **Beef** is the meat of a cow, bull, or ox. ❑ *...roast beef.* ❑ *...beef stew.*
▶ **beef up** PHRASAL VERB If you **beef up** something, you increase, strengthen, or improve it. ❑ *...a campaign to beef up security.* ❑ *Both sides are still beefing up their military strength.*

beef|steak /bifsteɪk/ (beefsteaks) N-VAR **Beefsteak** is steak.

beefy /bifi/ (beefier, beefiest) ADJ [usu ADJ n] Someone, especially a man, who is **beefy** has a big body and large muscles. ❑ *...a beefy red-faced Englishman.*

bee|hive /bihaɪv/ (beehives) N-COUNT A **beehive** is a structure in which bees are kept, which is designed so that the beekeeper can collect the honey that they produce.

bee|keeper /bikipər/ (beekeepers) N-COUNT A **beekeeper** is a person who owns and takes care of bees.

bee|keeping /bikipɪŋ/ N-UNCOUNT **Beekeeping** is the practice of owning and taking care of bees.

bee|line /bilaɪn/ PHRASE [PHR n] If you **make a beeline for** a place, you go to it as quickly and directly as possible. [INFORMAL] ❑ *She made a beeline for the car.*

Beem|er /bimər/ (Beemers) also **Beamer** N-COUNT Some people refer to a BMW automobile as a **Beemer**. [INFORMAL] ❑ *The Beemer's door swung open and Markus Salkow stepped out.*

been /bɪn/ ■ **Been** is the past participle of **be** ① and **be** ②. ■ V-I If you have **been** to a place, you have gone to it or visited it. ❑ *He's already been to Tunisia, and is to go on to Morocco and Mauritania.*

beep /bip/ (beeps, beeping, beeped) ■ N-COUNT; SOUND A **beep** is a short, loud sound like that made by a car horn or a telephone answering machine. ■ V-T/V-I If something such as a horn **beeps**, or you **beep** it, it makes a short, harsh sound. ❑ *My cell phone beeped.* ❑ *He beeped the horn.*

beep|er /bipər/ (beepers) N-COUNT A **beeper** is a portable device that makes a beeping noise, usually to tell you to phone someone or to remind you to do something. ❏ *His beeper sounded and he picked up the telephone.*

beer ✦◇◇ /bɪər/ (beers) N-MASS **Beer** is an alcoholic drink made from grain. ❏ *He sat in the kitchen drinking beer.* • N-COUNT A glass, can, or bottle of beer can be referred to as a **beer**. ❏ *Would you like a beer?*

beer bel|ly (beer bellies) N-COUNT If a man has a **beer belly**, he has a fat stomach because of drinking too much beer. [INFORMAL] ❏ *He was short and fat, with a large beer belly.*

beer gut (beer guts) also **beer-gut** N-COUNT A **beer gut** is the same as a **beer belly**. [INFORMAL]

beer|mat /bɪərmæt/ [BRIT] → see **coaster** 1

beery /bɪəri/ ADJ [usu ADJ n] A **beery** person has drunk a lot of beer. ❏ *...jolly, beery farmers.* ❏ *...beery roars of applause.*

bees|wax /biːzwæks/ N-UNCOUNT **Beeswax** is wax that is made by bees and used especially for making candles and furniture polish.

beet /biːt/ (beets) ◼ N-UNCOUNT **Beet** is a crop with a thick round root. ❏ *...fields of sweet corn and beet.* ◻ N-VAR **Beets** are dark red roots that are eaten as a vegetable. They are often preserved in vinegar. [AM] ❏ *It comes with a garnish of red beets, white cottage cheese and blueberries.*

in BRIT, use **beetroot**

bee|tle /biːtəl/ (beetles) N-COUNT A **beetle** is an insect with a hard covering to its body.

beet|root /biːtruːt/ [BRIT] → see **beet** 2

be|fall /bɪfɔːl/ (befalls, befalling, befell, befallen) V-T If something bad or unlucky **befalls** you, it happens to you. [LITERARY] ❏ *...the disaster that befell the island of Flores.*

be|fit /bɪfɪt/ (befits, befitting, befitted) V-T If something **befits** a person or thing, it is suitable or appropriate for them. [FORMAL] ❏ *They offered him a post befitting his seniority and experience.*

be|fore ✦✦✦ /bɪfɔːr/

In addition to the uses shown below, **before** is used in the phrasal verbs 'go before' and 'lay before.'

◼ PREP If something happens **before** a particular date, time, or event, it happens earlier than that date, time, or event. ❏ *Annie was born a few weeks before Christmas.* ❏ *Before World War II, women were not recruited as intelligence officers.* • CONJ **Before** is also a conjunction. ❏ *Stock prices have climbed close to the peak they'd registered before the stock market crashed.* ◻ PREP [PREP -ing] If you do one thing **before** doing something else, you do it earlier than the other thing. ❏ *He spent his early life in Sri Lanka before moving to Canada.* • CONJ **Before** is also a conjunction. ❏ *He took a cold shower and then toweled off before he put on fresh clothes.* ◼ ADV [n ADV] You use **before** when you are talking about time. For example, if something happened the day **before** a particular date or event, it happened during the previous day. ❏ *The war had ended only a month or so before.* • PREP [n PREP n] **Before** is also a preposition. ❏ *It's interesting that he sent me the book twenty days before the deadline for my book.* • CONJ **Before** is also a conjunction. ❏ *Kelman had a book published in the U.S. more than a decade before a British publisher would touch him.* ◼ CONJ If you do something **before** someone else can do something, you do it when they have not yet done it. ❏ *Before Gallacher could catch up with the ball, Nadlovu had beaten him to it.* ◼ ADV [ADV after v] If someone has done something **before**, they have done it on a previous occasion. If someone has not done something **before**, they have never done it. ❏ *I've been here before.* ❏ *I had met Professor Lown before.* ◼ CONJ If there is a period of time or if several things are done **before** something happens, it takes that amount of time or effort for this thing to happen. ❏ *It was some time before the door opened in response to his ring.* ◼ CONJ If a particular situation has to happen **before** something else happens, this situation must happen or exist in order for the other thing to happen. ❏ *There was additional work to be done before all the troops would be ready.* ◼ PREP If someone is **before** something, they are in front of it. [FORMAL] ❏ *They drove through a tall iron gate and stopped before a large white villa.* ◼ PREP If you tell someone that one place is a certain distance **before** another, you mean that they will come to the first place first. ❏ *The station is on the right, one mile before downtown Romney.* ◼ PREP If you appear or come **before** an official person or group, you go there and answer questions. ❏ *The governor will appear before the committee next Tuesday.* ◼ PREP If something happens **before** a particular person or group, it is seen by or happens while this person or this group is present. ❏ *The game followed a colorful opening ceremony before a crowd of seventy-four thousand.* ◼ PREP [PREP pron] If you have something such as a trip, a task, or a stage of your life **before** you, you must do it or live through it in the future. ❏ *Everyone in the room knew it was the single hardest task before them.* ◼ PREP [v PREP n] When you want to say that one person or thing is more important than another, you can say that they come **before** the other person or thing. ❏ *Her husband and her children came before her needs.* ◼ **before long** → see **long** ③

before|hand /bɪfɔːrhænd/ ADV If you do something **beforehand**, you do it earlier than a particular event. ❏ *How could she tell beforehand that I was going to go out?*

be|friend /bɪfrɛnd/ (befriends, befriending, befriended) V-T If you **befriend** someone, especially someone who is lonely or far from home, you make friends with them. ❏ *The film's about an elderly woman and a young nurse who befriends her.*

be|fud|dle /bɪfʌdəl/ (befuddles, befuddling, befuddled) V-T If something **befuddles** you, it confuses your mind or thoughts. ❏ *...problems that are befuddling them.* • **be|fud|dled** ADJ ❏ *...his befuddled manner.*

beg /bɛg/ (begs, begging, begged) ◼ V-T/V-I If you **beg** someone to do something, you ask them very anxiously or eagerly to do it. ❏ *I begged him to come back to New York with me.* ❏ *We are not going to beg for help anymore.* ◻ V-I [oft cont] If someone who is poor **is begging**, they are asking people to give them food or money. ❏ *I was surrounded by people begging for food.* ❏ *...homeless people begging on the streets.* ❏ *She was living alone, begging food from neighbors.* ◼ **I beg your pardon** → see **pardon**

be|gan /bɪgæn/ **Began** is the past tense of **begin**.

be|get /bɪgɛt/ (begets, begetting, begot, begotten) ◼ V-T To **beget** something means to cause it to happen or be created. [FORMAL] ❏ *Poverty begets debt.* ◻ V-T When a man **begets** a child, he becomes the father of that child. [OLD-FASHIONED]

be|get|ter /bɪgɛtər/ (begetters) N-COUNT [with poss] The **begetter** of something has caused this thing to come into existence. [FORMAL] ❏ *Elvis Presley was the true begetter of modern youth culture.*

beg|gar /bɛgər/ (beggars) N-COUNT A **beggar** is someone who lives by asking people for money or food. ❏ *There are no beggars on the street in Vienna.*

be|gin ✦✦✦ /bɪgɪn/ (begins, beginning, began, begun) ◼ V-T To **begin** to do something means to start doing it. ❏ *He stood up and began to move around the room.* ❏ *The weight loss began to look more serious.* ◻ V-T/V-I When something **begins** or when you **begin** it, it takes place from a particular time onward. ❏ *The problems began last November.* ❏ *He has just begun his fourth year in hiding.* ◼ V-T/V-I If you **begin** with something, or **begin** by doing something, this is the first thing you do. ❏ *Could I begin with a few formalities?* ❏ *...a businessman who began by selling golf shirts from the trunk of his car.* ❏ *He began his career flipping hamburgers.* ◼ V-T/V-I [no cont] You use **begin** to mention the first thing that someone says. ❏ *"Professor Theron," he began, "I'm very pleased to see you."* ❏ *He didn't know how to begin.* ◼ V-I [no cont] If one thing **began as** another thing, it first existed as the other thing before it changed into its present form. ❏ *What began as a local festival has blossomed into an international event.* ◼ V-I [no cont] If you say that a thing or place **begins** somewhere, you are talking about one of its limits or edges. ❏ *The fate line begins close to the wrist.* ◼ V-I [no cont] If a word **begins with** a particular letter, that is the first letter of that word. ❏ *The first word begins with an F.* ◼ PHRASE You use **to begin with** when you are talking about the first stage of a situation, event, or process. ❏ *It was great to begin with but now it's difficult.* ◼ PHRASE You use **to begin with** to introduce the first of several things that you want to say. ❏ *"What do scientists you've spoken with think about that?"—"Well, to begin with, they doubt it's going to work."*

be|gin|ner /bɪgɪnər/ (beginners) N-COUNT A **beginner** is someone who has just started learning to do something

and cannot do it very well yet. ❑ *The course is suitable for both beginners and advanced students.*
be|gin|ning◆◇◇ /bɪgɪnɪŋ/ (beginnings) **1** N-COUNT The **beginning** of an event or process is the first part of it. ❑ *This was also the beginning of her recording career.* **2** N-PLURAL The **beginnings** of something are the signs or events which form the first part of it. ❑ *The discussions were the beginnings of a dialogue with Moscow.* **3** N-SING The **beginning** of a period of time is the time at which it starts. ❑ *The wedding will be at the beginning of March.* **4** N-COUNT The **beginning** of a piece of written material is the first words or sentences of it. ❑ *...the question that was raised at the beginning of this chapter.* **5** N-PLURAL If you talk about the **beginnings** of a person, company, or group, you are referring to their backgrounds or origins. ❑ *His views come from his own humble beginnings.*

SYNONYMS
beginning
NOUN **1**
start: *...1918, four years after the start of the Great War.*
opening: *The opening of the scene depicts Akhnaten and his family in a moment of intimacy.*
outset: *Decide at the outset what kind of learning program you want to follow.*
onset: *With the onset of war, oil prices climbed above $30 a barrel.*

be|gonia /bɪgoʊnyə, -goʊniə/ (begonias) N-COUNT A **begonia** is a garden plant which has large brightly colored flowers.
be|got /bɪgɒt/ **Begot** is the past tense of **beget**.
be|got|ten /bɪgɒtən/ **Begotten** is the past participle of **beget**.
be|grudge /bɪgrʌdʒ/ (begrudges, begrudging, begrudged) **1** V-T [usu with brd-neg] If you do not **begrudge** someone something, you do not feel angry, upset, or jealous that they have it. ❑ *I certainly don't begrudge him the Nobel Prize.* **2** V-T [usu with brd-neg] If you do not **begrudge** something such as time or money, you do not mind giving it up. ❑ *I do not begrudge the money I have lost.*
be|grudg|ing|ly /bɪgrʌdʒɪŋli/ ADV [ADV with v] If you do something **begrudgingly**, you do it unwillingly. ❑ *He agreed to her suggestion begrudgingly.*
be|guile /bɪgaɪl/ (beguiles, beguiling, beguiled) **1** V-T If something **beguiles** you, you are charmed and attracted by it. ❑ *I was beguiled by the romance and exotic atmosphere of the souks in Marrakech.* **2** V-T If someone **beguiles** you **into** doing something, they trick you into doing it. ❑ *He used his newspapers to beguile the readers into buying shares in his company.*
be|guil|ing /bɪgaɪlɪŋ/ ADJ Something that is **beguiling** is charming and attractive. [WRITTEN] ❑ *Mombasa is a town with a beguiling Arabic flavor.* • **be|guil|ing|ly** ADV [ADV adj, ADV with v] ❑ *He was beguilingly boyish and attractive.*
be|gun /bɪgʌn/ **Begun** is the past participle of **begin**.
be|half◆◇◇ /bɪhæf/ **1** PHRASE If you do something **on** someone's **behalf**, you do it for that person as their representative. ❑ *She made an emotional public appeal on her son's behalf.* **2** PHRASE If you feel, for example, embarrassed or angry **on** someone's **behalf**, you feel embarrassed or angry for them. ❑ *"What do you mean?" I asked, offended on Liddie's behalf.*
be|have◆◇◇ /bɪheɪv/ (behaves, behaving, behaved) **1** V-I The way that you **behave** is the way that you do and say things, and the things that you do and say. ❑ *I couldn't believe these people were behaving in this way.* **2** V-T/V-I If you **behave** or **behave yourself**, you act in the way that people think is correct and proper. ❑ *You have to behave.* **3** V-I In science, the way that something **behaves** is the things that it does. ❑ *Under certain conditions, electrons can behave like waves rather than particles.*

SYNONYMS
behave
VERB **1**
act: *He acted as if he hadn't heard any of it.*
react: *'How did he react?'—'Very calmly.'*
conduct yourself: *The way he conducts himself reflects on the party.*

-behaved /-bɪheɪvd/ COMB IN ADJ **-behaved** combines with adverbs such as 'well' or 'badly' to form adjectives that describe people's or animals' behavior. ❑ *They were a very well-behaved crowd.*
be|hav|ior◆◆◇ /bɪheɪvyər/ (behaviors)

in BRIT, use **behaviour**

1 N-VAR People's or animals' **behavior** is the way that they behave. You can refer to a typical and repeated way of behaving as a **behavior**. ❑ *Make sure that good behavior is rewarded.* ❑ *...human sexual behavior.* **2** N-UNCOUNT In science, the **behavior** of something is the way that it behaves. ❑ *It will be many years before anyone can predict a hurricane's behavior with much accuracy.* **3** PHRASE If someone is **on** their **best behavior**, they are trying very hard to behave well. ❑ *The 1,400 fans were on their best behavior and filed out peacefully at the end.* **4** → See feature box at **urban**

COLLOCATIONS
behavior
NOUN
1
adjective + **behavior**: criminal, human, sexual; aggressive, antisocial, inappropriate, unacceptable
verb + **behavior**: change, control, tackle, tolerate; display, exhibit
2
verb + **behavior**: monitor, observe

SYNONYMS
behavior
NOUN **1**
conduct: *He has trouble understanding that other people judge him by his conduct.*
actions: *Jack was the sort of man who did not like his actions questioned.*
demeanor: *...her calm and cheerful demeanor.*
ways: *He said he was against returning to old authoritarian ways.*

be|hav|ior|al /bɪheɪvyərəl/

in BRIT, use **behavioural**

ADJ [ADJ n] **Behavioral** means relating to the behavior of a person or animal, or to the study of their behavior. ❑ *...emotional and behavioral problems.*
be|hav|ior|ism /bɪheɪvyərɪzəm/

in BRIT, use **behaviourism**

N-UNCOUNT **Behaviorism** is the belief held by some psychologists that the only valid method of studying the psychology of people or animals is to observe how they behave. • **be|hav|ior|ist** (behaviorists) N-COUNT ❑ *Animal behaviorists have been studying these monkeys for decades.*
be|head /bɪhɛd/ (beheads, beheading, beheaded) V-T [usu passive] If someone **is beheaded**, their head is cut off, usually because they have been found guilty of a crime. ❑ *At least one hostage was beheaded in that room.*
be|held /bɪhɛld/ **Beheld** is the past tense of **behold**.
be|he|moth /bɪhiməθ/ (behemoths) N-COUNT If you refer to something as a **behemoth**, you mean that it is extremely large, and often that it is unpleasant, inefficient, or difficult to manage. [LITERARY, JOURNALISM, DISAPPROVAL] ❑ *The city is a sprawling behemoth with no heart.* ❑ *...his behemoth 1,047 page book.*
be|hest /bɪhɛst/ PHRASE [PHR after v] If something is done **at** someone's **behest**, it is done because they have ordered or requested it. [FORMAL] ❑ *In 1970, at his new wife's behest, they moved to Dodge City.*
be|hind◆◆◆ /bɪhaɪnd/ (behinds)

In addition to the uses shown below, **behind** is also used in a few phrasal verbs, such as 'fall behind' and 'lie behind.'

1 PREP If something is **behind** a thing or person, it is on the other side of them from you, or nearer their back rather than their front. ❑ *I put one of the cushions behind his head.* ❑ *They were parked behind the truck.* • ADV **Behind** is also an adverb. ❑ *Rising into the hills behind are 800 acres of parkland.* **2** PREP If you are walking or traveling **behind** someone or something, you are following them. ❑ *Keith wandered along behind him.* • ADV [ADV after v]

Behind is also an adverb. ❑ *The troopers followed behind, every muscle tensed for the next gunfire.* **3** PREP If someone is **behind** a desk, counter, or bar, they are on the other side of it from where you are. ❑ *The colonel was sitting behind a cheap wooden desk.* **4** PREP [PREP pron] When you shut a door or gate **behind** you, you shut it after you have gone through it. ❑ *I walked out and closed the door behind me.* **5** N-COUNT Your **behind** is the part of your body that you sit on. **6** PREP The people, reason, or events **behind** a situation are the causes of it or are responsible for it. ❑ *It is still not clear who was behind the killing.* **7** PREP [PREP pron] If something or someone is **behind** you, they support you and help you. ❑ *He had the state's judicial power behind him.* **8** PREP If you refer to what is **behind** someone's outside appearance, you are referring to a characteristic which you cannot immediately see or is not obvious, but which you think is there. ❑ *What lay behind his anger was really the hurt he felt at Grace's refusal.* **9** PREP If you are **behind** someone, you are less successful than them, or have done less or advanced less. ❑ *She finished second behind the American, Ann Cody, in the 800 meters.* • ADV **Behind** is also an adverb. ❑ *The rapid development of technology means that she is now far behind, and will need retraining.* **10** PREP [PREP pron] If an experience is **behind** you, it happened in your past and will not happen again, or no longer affects you. ❑ *Maureen put the nightmare behind her.* **11** PREP [have/v n PREP pron] If you have a particular achievement **behind** you, you have managed to reach this achievement, and other people consider it to be important or valuable. ❑ *He has 20 years of loyal service to Barclays Bank behind him.* **12** PREP If something is **behind** schedule, it is not as far advanced as people had planned. If someone is **behind** schedule, they are not progressing as quickly at something as they had planned. ❑ *The work is 22 weeks behind schedule.* **13** ADV [ADV after v] If you stay **behind**, you remain in a place after other people have gone. ❑ *About 1,200 personnel will remain behind to take care of the air base.* **14** ADV [ADV after v] If you leave something or someone **behind**, you do not take them with you when you go. ❑ *The rebels fled into the mountains, leaving behind their weapons and supplies.* **15** to do something behind someone's back → see back ② **16** behind bars → see bar **17** behind the scenes → see scene **18** behind the times → see time ①

USAGE

behind
Don't use 'of' after **behind**. Don't say, for example, 'They parked the motorcycle behind of some bushes.' Say 'They parked the motorcycle behind some bushes.'

---

behind-the-scenes → see scene

be|hold /bɪhoʊld/ (beholds, beholding, beheld) **1** V-T If you behold someone or something, you see them. [LITERARY] ❑ *She looked into his eyes and beheld madness.* **2** lo and behold → see lo

be|hold|en /bɪhoʊldən/ ADJ [v-link ADJ to n] If you are **beholden** to someone, you are in debt to them in some way or you feel that you have a duty to them because they have helped you. ❑ *We feel really beholden to them for what they've done.*

be|hold|er /bɪhoʊldər/ (beholders) **1** PHRASE [v-link PHR] If you say that something such as beauty or art is **in the eye of the beholder**, you mean that it is a matter of personal opinion. ❑ *Beauty is in the eye of the beholder.* **2** N-COUNT [usu the N in sing] The **beholder** of something is the person who is looking at it. [OLD-FASHIONED]

be|hoove /bɪhuv/ (behooves, behooved)

in BRIT, use **behove**

V-T If it **behooves** you to do something, it is right, necessary, or useful for you to do it. [FORMAL] ❑ *It behooves us to think of these dangers.*

beige /beɪʒ/ COLOR Something that is **beige** is pale brown in color. ❑ *The walls are beige.*

be|ing ♦♢♢ /biɪŋ/ (beings) **1** **Being** is the present participle of **be**. **2** V-LINK **Being** is used in nonfinite clauses where you are giving the reason for something. ❑ *It being a Sunday, the old men had the day off.* ❑ *Little boys, being what they are, might decide to play on it.* **3** N-COUNT You can refer to any real or imaginary creature as a **being**. ❑ *People expect a horse to perform like a car, with no thought for its feelings as a living being.* **4** → see also **human being** **5** N-UNCOUNT **Being** is existence. Something that is in being or comes into being exists. ❑ *Abraham Maslow described psychology as "the science of being."* **6** → see also **well-being** **7** other things being equal → see equal **8** for the time being → see time ③

be|jew|eled /bɪdʒuːəld/ also bejewelled ADJ [usu ADJ n] A **bejeweled** person or object is wearing a lot of jewelry or is decorated with jewels. ❑ *...bejeweled women.* ❑ *...a bejeweled golden tiara.*

be|la|bor /bɪleɪbər/ (belabors, belaboring, belabored)

in BRIT, use **belabour**

V-T If you say that someone **belabors** the point, you mean that they keep on talking about it, perhaps in an annoying or boring way. ❑ *I won't belabor the point, for this is a familiar story.*

be|lat|ed /bɪleɪtɪd/ ADJ A **belated** action happens later than it should have. [FORMAL] ❑ *...the government's belated attempts to alleviate the plight of the poor.*

belch /bɛltʃ/ (belches, belching, belched) **1** V-I If someone **belches**, they make a sudden noise in their throat because air has risen up from their stomach. ❑ *Garland covered his mouth with his hand and belched discreetly.* • N-COUNT **Belch** is also a noun. ❑ *He drank and stifled a belch.* **2** V-T/V-I If a machine or chimney **belches** smoke or fire, or if smoke or fire **belches** from it, large amounts of smoke or fire come out of it. ❑ *Tired old trucks were struggling up the road below us, belching black smoke.* • PHRASAL VERB **Belch out** means the same as **belch**. ❑ *The power-generation plant belched out five tons of ash an hour.*

be|lea|guered /bɪliːɡərd/ ADJ A **beleaguered** person, organization, or project is experiencing a lot of difficulties, opposition, or criticism. [FORMAL] ❑ *There have been seven coup attempts against the beleaguered government.*

bel|fry /bɛlfri/ (belfries) **1** N-COUNT The **belfry** of a church is the top part of its tower, where the bells are. **2** → See also color supplement

Bel|gian /bɛldʒən/ (Belgians) ADJ **Belgian** means belonging or relating to Belgium or to its people. • N-COUNT A **Belgian** is a person who comes from Belgium.

be|lie /bɪlaɪ/ (belies, belying, belied) **1** V-T If one thing **belies** another, it hides the true situation and so creates a false idea or image of someone or something. ❑ *His youthful face belies his 80 years.* **2** V-T If one thing **belies** another, it proves that the other thing is not true or genuine. ❑ *The facts of the situation belie his testimony.*

be|lief ♦♢♢ /bɪliːf/ (beliefs) **1** N-UNCOUNT **Belief** is a feeling of certainty that something exists, is true, or is good. ❑ *One billion people throughout the world are Muslims, united by belief in one god.* **2** N-PLURAL Your religious or political **beliefs** are your views on religious or political matters. ❑ *He refuses to compete on Sundays because of his religious beliefs.* **3** N-SING If it is your **belief** that something is the case, it is your strong opinion that it is the case. ❑ *It is our belief that improvements in health care will lead to a stronger, more prosperous economy.* **4** PHRASE You use **beyond belief** to emphasize that something is true to a very great degree or that it happened to a very great degree. [EMPHASIS] ❑ *We are devastated, shocked beyond belief.* **5** PHRASE If you do one thing **in the belief that** another thing is true or will happen, you do it because you think, usually wrongly, that it is true or will happen. ❑ *Civilians had broken into the building, apparently in the belief that it contained food.*

be|lief sys|tem (belief systems) N-COUNT [oft with poss] The **belief system** of a person or society is the set of beliefs that they have about what is right and wrong and what is true and false. ❑ *...the belief systems of various ethnic groups.*

be|liev|able /bɪliːvəbəl/ ADJ Something that is **believable** makes you think that it could be true or real. ❑ *...believable evidence.*

be|lieve ♦♦♦ /bɪliːv/ (believes, believing, believed) **1** V-T If you **believe** that something is true, you think it is true, but you are not sure. [FORMAL] ❑ *Experts believe that the coming drought will be extensive.* ❑ *We believe them to be hidden here in this apartment.* **2** V-T If you **believe** someone or if you **believe** what they say or write, you accept that they are telling the truth. ❑ *He did not sound as if he believed her.* ❑ *Never believe anything a married man says about his wife.* **3** V-I If you **believe** in fairies, ghosts, or miracles, you are sure that they exist or happen. If you **believe** in a god, you are sure of the existence of that god. ❑ *I don't believe in ghosts.* ❹ V-I If you **believe in** a way of life or an idea, you are in favor of it because you think it is good or right. ❑ *He believed in marital fidelity.* ❺ V-I If you **believe in** someone or what they are doing, you have confidence in them and think that they will be successful. ❑ *If you believe in yourself you can succeed.*

USAGE

believe
Believe is not used in the progressive. Don't say, for example, '*I am believing you.*' Say '*I believe you.*' *I believe that these findings should be presented to your readers.*

SYNONYMS

believe
VERB ❶
suppose: *The problem was more complex than he supposed.*
consider: *I had always considered myself a strong, competent woman.*
assume: *It is a mistake to assume that the two continents are similar.*
gather: *I gather his report is highly critical of the trial judge.*
presume: *'Had he been home all week?'—'I presume so.'*

---

be|liev|er /bɪlivər/ (believers) ❶ N-COUNT If you are a great **believer** in something, you think that it is good, right, or useful. ❑ *Mom was a great believer in herbal medicines.* ❷ N-COUNT A **believer** is someone who is sure that God exists or that their religion is true. ❑ *I made no secret of the fact that I was not a believer.*

be|lit|tle /bɪlɪt³l/ (belittles, belittling, belittled) V-T If you **belittle** someone or something, you say or imply that they are unimportant or not very good. ❑ *We mustn't belittle her outstanding achievement.*

bell ♦◇◇ /bɛl/ (bells) ❶ N-COUNT A **bell** is a device that makes a ringing sound and is used to give a signal or to attract people's attention. ❑ *I had just enough time to finish eating before the bell rang and I was off to my first class.* ❷ N-COUNT A **bell** is a hollow metal object shaped like a cup which has a piece hanging inside it that hits the sides and makes a sound. ❑ *My brother, Nick, was born on a Sunday, when all the church bells were ringing.* ❸ PHRASE If you say that something **rings a bell**, you mean that it reminds you of something, but you cannot remember exactly what it is. [INFORMAL] ❑ *The name doesn't ring a bell.*

bell-bottoms

The form **bell-bottom** is used as a modifier.

N-PLURAL [oft N n] **Bell-bottoms** are trousers that are very wide at the bottom of the leg, near your feet. ❑ *...a Seattle teen in bell-bottoms.* ❑ *...bell-bottom jeans.*

bell|boy /bɛlbɔɪ/ (bellboys) N-COUNT A **bellboy** is the same as a **bellhop**.

belle /bɛl/ (belles) N-COUNT A **belle** is a beautiful woman, especially the most beautiful woman at a party or in a group. [OLD-FASHIONED]

bell|hop /bɛlhɒp/ (bellhops) N-COUNT A **bellhop** is someone who works in a hotel, carrying bags or bringing things to the guests' rooms. [AM]

bel|li|cose /bɛlɪkoʊs/ ADJ You use **bellicose** to refer to aggressive actions or behavior that are likely to start an argument or a fight. [LITERARY] ❑ *He expressed alarm about the government's increasingly bellicose statements.*

-bellied /-bɛlid/ ❶ COMB IN ADJ **-bellied** can be added to an adjective to describe someone or something that has a stomach of a particular kind. ❑ *The fat-bellied officer stood near the door.* ❑ *...the yellow-bellied sea-snake.* ❷ → see also **potbellied**

bel|lig|er|ent /bɪlɪdʒərənt/ ADJ A **belligerent** person is hostile and aggressive. ❑ *...the belligerent statements from both sides which have led to fears of war.* • **bel|lig|er|ence** N-UNCOUNT ❑ *He could be accused of passion, but never belligerence.*

bel|low /bɛloʊ/ (bellows, bellowing, bellowed) ❶ V-T/V-I If someone **bellows**, they shout angrily in a loud, deep voice. ❑ *"I didn't ask to be born!" she bellowed.* ❑ *She prayed she wouldn't come in and find them there, bellowing at each other.* • N-COUNT **Bellow** is also a noun. ❑ *I was distraught and let out a bellow of tearful rage.* ❷ V-I When a large animal such as a bull or an

elephant **bellows**, it makes a loud and deep noise. ❑ *A heifer bellowed in her stall.* ❸ N-COUNT [also a pair of N] A **bellows** is or **bellows** are a device used for blowing air into a fire in order to make it burn more fiercely.

bell pep|per (bell peppers) N-COUNT A **bell pepper** is a hollow green, red, or yellow vegetable with seeds. [mainly AM]

bell ring|er (bell ringers) N-COUNT A **bell ringer** is someone who rings church bells or hand bells, especially as a hobby.

bell|wether /bɛlwɛðər/ (bellwethers) N-COUNT [usu sing, oft N n] If you describe something as a **bellwether**, you mean that it is an indication of the way a situation is changing. [mainly AM, JOURNALISM] ❑ *The Methodist church is viewed as a bellwether of U.S. attitudes in large part.* ❑ *IBM is considered the bellwether stock on Wall Street.*

bel|ly /bɛli/ (bellies) ❶ N-COUNT The **belly** of a person or animal is their stomach or abdomen. ❑ *She laid her hands on her swollen belly.* ❑ *The puppy was rolling over so we could rub his belly.* ❷ PHRASE If a company **goes belly up**, it does not have enough money to pay its debts. [INFORMAL] ❑ *I really can't afford to see this company go belly up.* ❸ → See feature box at **business**; See also color supplement

bel|ly|ache /bɛliek/ (bellyaches, bellyaching, bellyached) also **belly-ache** ❶ N-VAR **Bellyache** is a pain inside your abdomen, especially in your stomach. [INFORMAL] ❷ V-I [usu cont] If you say that someone is **bellyaching**, you mean they complain loudly and frequently about something and you think this is unreasonable or unjustified. [INFORMAL] ❑ *...belly-aching about recession.*

bel|ly but|ton (belly buttons) N-COUNT Your **belly button** is the small hollow just below your waist at the front of your body. [INFORMAL]

bel|ly danc|er (belly dancers) N-COUNT A **belly dancer** is someone who performs a Middle Eastern dance in which they move their hips and abdomen around.

bel|ly laugh (belly laughs) N-COUNT A **belly laugh** is a very loud, deep laugh. ❑ *Each gag was rewarded with a generous belly-laugh.*

be|long ♦◇◇ /bɪlɔŋ/ (belongs, belonging, belonged) ❶ V-I [no cont] If something **belongs to** you, you own it. ❑ *The house had belonged to her family for three of four generations.* ❷ V-I [no cont] You say that something **belongs to** a particular person when you are guessing, discovering, or explaining that it was produced by or is part of that person. ❑ *The handwriting belongs to a male.* ❸ V-I [no cont] If someone **belongs to** a particular group, they are a member of that group. ❑ *I used to belong to a youth club.* ❹ V-I [no cont] If something or someone **belongs in** or **to** a particular category, type, or group, they are of that category, type, or group. ❑ *The judges could not decide which category it belonged in.* ❺ V-I [no cont] If something **belongs to** a particular time, it comes from that time. ❑ *The pictures belong to an era when there was a preoccupation with high society.* ❻ V-I [no cont] If you say that something **belongs to** someone, you mean that person has the right to it. ❑ *...but the last word belonged to Rosanne.* ❼ V-I [no cont] If you say that a time **belongs to** a particular system or way of doing something, you mean that that time is or will be characterized by it. ❑ *The future belongs to democracy.* ❽ V-I [no cont] If a baby or child **belongs to** a particular adult, that adult is his or her parent or the person who is looking after him or her. ❑ *He deduced that the two children belonged to the couple.* ❾ V-I [no cont] If a person or thing **belongs** in a particular place or situation, that is where they should be. ❑ *You don't belong here.* ❑ *They need to feel they belong.*

USAGE

belong
When **belong** is used with meaning ❶, it must be followed by **to**. Don't say, for example, '*This bag belongs me.*' Say '*This bag belongs to me.*' *Everything you see here belongs to me.*

---

be|long|ings /bɪlɔŋɪŋz/ N-PLURAL Your **belongings** are the things that you own, especially things that are small enough to be carried. ❑ *I collected my belongings and left.*

Be|lo|rus|sian /bɛloʊrʌʃ³n/ (Belorussians) ❶ ADJ **Belorussian** means belonging or relating to Belarus or to its people or

beloved 113 **benediction**

culture. **2** N-COUNT A **Belorussian** is a Belorussian citizen, or a person of Belorussian origin.

be|lov|ed /bɪlʌvɪd/ ADJ [ADJ n] A **beloved** person, thing, or place is one that you feel great affection for. ❑ *He lost his beloved wife last year.*

be|low ✦✧✧ /bɪloʊ/ **1** PREP If something is **below** something else, it is in a lower position. ❑ *He appeared from the apartment directly below Leonard's.* ❑ *The sun had already sunk below the horizon.* • ADV **Below** is also an adverb. ❑ *We climbed rather perilously down a rope-ladder to the boat below.* ❑ *...a view to the street below.* **2** PHRASE If something is **below ground** or **below the ground**, it is in the ground. ❑ *They have designed a system which pumps up water from nearly 1,000 feet below ground.* **3** ADV You use **below** in a piece of writing to refer to something that is mentioned later. ❑ *Please write to me at the address below.* **4** PREP If something is **below** a particular amount, rate, or level, it is less than that amount, rate, or level. ❑ *Night temperatures can drop below 15 degrees Celsius.* • ADV **Below** is also an adverb. ❑ *...temperatures at zero or below.* **5** PREP If someone is **below** you in an organization, they are lower in rank. ❑ *Such people often experience less stress than those in the ranks immediately below them.* **6 below par** → see **par**

below the belt → see **belt**

belt ✦✧✧ /bɛlt/ (**belts, belting, belted**) **1** N-COUNT A **belt** is a strip of leather or cloth that you fasten around your waist. ❑ *He wore a belt with a large brass buckle.* **2** → see also **safety belt, seat belt** **3** N-COUNT A **belt** in a machine is a circular strip of rubber that is used to drive moving parts or to move objects along. ❑ *The turning disk is connected by a drive belt to an electric motor.* **4** → see also **conveyor belt** **5** N-COUNT A **belt** of land or sea is a long, narrow area of it that has some special feature. ❑ *Miners in Zambia's northern copper belt have gone on strike.* **6** → see also **commuter belt, green belt** **7** V-T If someone **belts** you, they hit you very hard. If someone **belts** something, they hit it very hard. [INFORMAL] ❑ *"Is it right she belted old George in the gut?" she asked.* ❑ *Torrealba belted the ball into the left-field bleachers.* • N-COUNT **Belt** is also a noun. ❑ *Father would give you a belt over the head with the scrubbing brush.* **8** V-I If you **belt** somewhere, you move or travel there very fast. [INFORMAL] ❑ *Darren and I belted down the stairs and ran out of the house.* **9** PHRASE Something that is **below the belt** is cruel and unfair. ❑ *Do you think it's a bit below the belt what they're doing?* **10** PHRASE If you have to **tighten** your **belt**, you have to spend less money and manage without things because you have less money than you used to have. ❑ *Clearly, if you are spending more than your income, you'll need to tighten your belt.* **11** PHRASE If you have something **under** your **belt**, you have already achieved it or done it. ❑ *Clare is now a full-time author with six books, including four novels, under her belt.* **12** → See feature box at **finance**

▶ **belt out** PHRASAL VERB If you **belt out** a song, you sing or play it very loudly. [INFORMAL] ❑ *He belted out Sinatra and Beatles hits.*

belt|ed /bɛltɪd/ ADJ If someone's jacket or coat, for example, is **belted**, it has a belt fastened round it. ❑ *She wore a brown suede jacket, belted at the waist.*

belt-tightening N-UNCOUNT If you need to do some **belt-tightening**, you must spend less money and manage without things because you have less money than you used to have. ❑ *This will cause further belt-tightening in the public services.*

belt|way /bɛltweɪ/ (**beltways**) N-COUNT A **beltway** is a road that goes around a city or town, to keep traffic away from the center. [AM] ❑ *Interstate 295 is a 20-mile beltway that bypasses Jacksonville's busy downtown area.*

in BRIT, use **ring road**

be|moan /bɪmoʊn/ (**bemoans, bemoaning, bemoaned**) V-T If you **bemoan** something, you express sorrow or dissatisfaction about it. [FORMAL] ❑ *Universities and other research establishments bemoan their lack of funds.*

be|muse /bɪmyuz/ (**bemuses, bemusing, bemused**) V-T If something **bemuses** you, it puzzles or confuses you. ❑ *The sheer quantity of detail would bemuse even the most clear-headed author.*

be|mused /bɪmyuzd/ ADJ If you are **bemused**, you are puzzled or confused. ❑ *He was rather bemused by children.*

be|muse|ment /bɪmyuzmənt/ N-UNCOUNT **Bemusement** is the feeling that you have when you are puzzled or confused by something. ❑ *A look of bemusement spread across their faces.*

bench /bɛntʃ/ (**benches**) **1** N-COUNT A **bench** is a long seat of wood or metal that two or more people can sit on. ❑ *He sat down on a park bench.* **2** N-COUNT A **bench** is a long, narrow table in a factory or laboratory. ❑ *...the laboratory bench.* **3** N-SING-COLL In a court of law, **the bench** is the judge or magistrates. ❑ *The chairman of the bench adjourned the case until October 27.* **4** → See also color supplement

bench|mark /bɛntʃmɑrk/ (**benchmarks**) also **bench mark** N-COUNT A **benchmark** is something whose quality or quantity is known and which can therefore be used as a standard with which other things can be compared. ❑ *The truck industry is a benchmark for the economy.*

bench|mark|ing /bɛntʃmɑrkɪŋ/ N-UNCOUNT In business, **benchmarking** is a process in which a company compares its products and methods with those of the most successful companies in its field, in order to try to improve its own performance. [BUSINESS]

bend ✦✧✧ /bɛnd/ (**bends, bending, bent**) **1** V-I When you **bend**, you move the top part of your body downward and forward. Plants and trees also **bend**. ❑ *I bent over and kissed her cheek.* ❑ *She bent and picked up a plastic bucket.* **2** V-T When you **bend** your head, you move your head forward and downward. ❑ *Rick appeared, bending his head a little to clear the top of the door.* **3** V-T/V-I When you **bend** a part of your body such as your arm or leg, or when it **bends**, you change its position so that it is no longer straight. ❑ *The seat is too far forward and I can't bend my legs.* • **bent** ADJ ❑ *Keep your knees slightly bent.* **4** V-T If you **bend** something that is flat or straight, you use force to make it curved or to put an angle in it. ❑ *Bend the bar into a horseshoe.* • **bent** ADJ ❑ *...a length of bent wire.* **5** V-T/V-I When a road, beam of light, or other long thin thing **bends**, or when something **bends** it, it changes direction to form a curve or angle. ❑ *The road bent slightly to the right.* **6** N-COUNT A **bend** in a road, pipe, or other long thin object is a curve or angle in it. ❑ *The crash occurred on a sharp bend.* **7** V-T If you **bend** rules or laws, you interpret them in a way that allows you to do something they would not normally allow you to do. ❑ *A minority of officers were prepared to bend the rules.* **8** N-PLURAL If deep-sea divers suffer from the **bends**, they experience severe pain and difficulty in breathing as a result of coming to the surface of the ocean too quickly. ❑ *New evidence suggests that exercise could protect divers from the bends.* **9** → see also **bent**

bend|ed /bɛndɪd/ PHRASE [usu PHR after v] If you ask someone for something **on bended knee** or **on bended knees**, you ask them very seriously for it. [FORMAL] ❑ *We beg the government on bended knees not to cut this budget.*

bend|er /bɛndər/ (**benders**) N-COUNT [usu sing, usu *on* n] If someone goes on a **bender**, they drink a very large amount of alcohol. [INFORMAL]

bendy /bɛndi/ (**bendier, bendiest**) ADJ [usu ADJ n] A **bendy** object bends easily into a curved or angled shape. ❑ *...a bendy toy whose limbs bend in every direction.*

be|neath ✦✧✧ /bɪniθ/ **1** PREP Something that is **beneath** another thing is under the other thing. ❑ *She could see the muscles of his shoulders beneath his T-shirt.* ❑ *Four levels of parking beneath the theater was not enough.* • ADV **Beneath** is also an adverb. ❑ *On a shelf beneath he spotted a photo album.* **2** PREP If you talk about what is **beneath** the surface of something, you are talking about the aspects of it which are hidden or not obvious. ❑ *...emotional strains beneath the surface.* ❑ *Somewhere deep beneath the surface lay a caring character.* **3** PREP If you say that someone or something is **beneath** you, you feel that they are not good enough for you or not suitable for you. ❑ *They decided she was marrying beneath her.*

Ben|edic|tine /bɛnɪdɪktɪn, tin/ (**Benedictines**) N-COUNT [oft N n] A **Benedictine** is a monk or nun who is a member of a Christian religious community that follows the rule of St. Benedict. ❑ *...the famous Benedictine abbey of St. Mary.*

ben|edic|tion /bɛnɪdɪkʃən/ (**benedictions**) **1** N-VAR A **benediction** is a kind of Christian prayer. [FORMAL] ❑ *The minister pronounced the benediction.* ❑ *The Pope's hands were raised in benediction.* **2** N-VAR You can refer to something that makes people feel protected and at peace as a **benediction**. ❑ *She could only raise her hand in a gesture of benediction.*

ben|efac|tor /bɛnɪfæktər/ (benefactors) N-COUNT A **benefactor** is someone who helps a person or organization by giving them money. ▫ *In his old age he became a benefactor of the arts.*

be|nefi|cent /bɪnɛfɪsᵊnt/ ADJ [usu ADJ n] A **beneficent** person or thing helps people or results in something good. [FORMAL] ▫ *...optimism about the beneficent effects of new technology.*

ben|efi|cial /bɛnɪfɪʃᵊl/ ADJ Something that is **beneficial** helps people or improves their lives. ▫ *...vitamins that are beneficial to our health.*

bene|fi|ciary /bɛnɪfɪʃieri/ (beneficiaries) **1** N-COUNT Someone who is a **beneficiary** of something is helped by it. ▫ *One of the main beneficiaries of the early election is thought to be the former president.* **2** N-COUNT The **beneficiaries** of a will are legally entitled to receive money or property from someone when that person dies. ▫ *...one of the beneficiaries of the will made by the late Mr. Steil.*

ben|efit ♦♦◇ /bɛnɪfɪt/ (benefits, benefiting or benefitting, benefited or benefitted) **1** N-VAR The **benefit** of something is the help that you get from it or the advantage that results from it. ▫ *Each family farms individually and reaps the benefit of its labor.* ▫ *I'm a great believer in the benefits of this form of therapy.* **2** N-UNCOUNT If something is to your **benefit** or is of **benefit** to you, it helps you or improves your life. ▫ *This could now work to Albania's benefit.* **3** V-T/V-I If you **benefit** from something or if it **benefits** you, it helps you or improves your life. ▫ *Both sides have benefited from the talks.* **4** N-UNCOUNT If you have the **benefit of** some information, knowledge, or equipment, you are able to use it so that you can achieve something. ▫ *Steve didn't have the benefit of a formal college education.* **5** N-VAR **Benefits** are money or other advantages which come from your job, the government, or an insurance company. ▫ *McCary will receive about $921,000 in retirement benefits.* ▫ *...the skyrocketing cost of health care and medical benefits.* **6** N-COUNT [oft N n] A **benefit**, or a **benefit** concert or dinner, is an event that is held in order to raise money for a particular charity or person. ▫ *...a memorial benefit concert for the Bonhoeffer endowment.* **7** → see also **fringe benefit** **8** PHRASE If you **give** someone **the benefit of the doubt**, you treat them as if they are telling the truth or as if they have behaved properly, even though you are not sure that this is the case. ▫ *At first I gave him the benefit of the doubt.* **9** PHRASE If you say that someone is doing something **for the benefit of** a particular person, you mean that they are doing it for that person. ▫ *You need people working for the benefit of the community.* **10** → See feature box at **recycle**

COLLOCATIONS

benefit
NOUN
1
verb + **benefit**: gain, obtain, reap; enjoy
5
noun + **benefit**: disability, employee, housing, unemployment, welfare
adjective + **benefit**: means-tested, unearned
verb + **benefit**: claim, receive
VERB **3**
benefit + adverb: enormously, greatly, hugely; financially; disproportionately

---

Bene|lux /bɛnɪlʌks/ ADJ [ADJ n] The **Benelux** countries are Belgium, the Netherlands, and Luxembourg.

be|nevo|lent /bɪnɛvələnt/ ADJ If you describe a person in authority as **benevolent**, you mean that they are kind and fair. ▫ *The company has proved to be a most benevolent employer.* • **be|nevo|lence** N-UNCOUNT ▫ *A bit of benevolence from people in power is not what we need.*

Ben|ga|li /bɛŋgɔli/ (Bengalis) **1** ADJ **Bengali** means belonging or relating to Bengal, or to its people or language. ▫ *She married a Bengali doctor.* • N-COUNT A **Bengali** is a person who comes from Bangladesh or West Bengal. **2** N-UNCOUNT **Dengali** is the language that is spoken by people who live in Bangladesh and by many people in West Bengal.

be|night|ed /bɪnaɪtɪd/ ADJ [ADJ n] If you describe people or the place where they live as **benighted**, you think they are unfortunate or do not know anything. [LITERARY, DISAPPROVAL] ▫ *Famine hit that benighted country once more.*

be|nign /bɪnaɪn/ **1** ADJ You use **benign** to describe someone who is kind, gentle, and harmless. ▫ *They are normally a more benign audience.* • **be|nign|ly** ADV ▫ *I just smiled benignly and stood back.* **2** ADJ A **benign** substance or process does not have any harmful effects. ▫ *We're taking relatively benign medicines and we're turning them into poisons.* **3** ADJ A **benign** tumor will not cause death or serious harm. [MEDICAL] ▫ *It wasn't cancer, only a benign tumor.* **4** ADJ **Benign** conditions are pleasant or make it easy for something to happen. ▫ *They enjoyed an especially benign climate.*

bent /bɛnt/ **1 Bent** is the past tense and past participle of **bend**. **2** ADJ If an object is **bent**, it is damaged and no longer has its correct shape. ▫ *The trees were all bent and twisted from the wind.* **3** ADJ If a person is **bent**, their body has become curved because of old age or disease. [WRITTEN] ▫ *...a bent, frail, old man.* **4** ADJ [v-link ADJ on/upon n/-ing] If someone is **bent on** doing something, especially something harmful, they are determined to do it. [DISAPPROVAL] ▫ *He's bent on suicide.* **5** N-SING If you have a **bent** for something, you have a natural ability to do it or a natural interest in it. ▫ *His bent for natural history directed him towards his first job.* **6** N-SING If someone is of a particular **bent**, they hold a particular set of beliefs. ▫ *...economists of a socialist bent.*

ben|zene /bɛnzin/ N-UNCOUNT **Benzene** is a clear, colorless liquid which is used to make plastics.

be|queath /bɪkwið/ (bequeaths, bequeathing, bequeathed) V-T If you **bequeath** your money or property to someone, you legally state that they should have it when you die. [FORMAL] ▫ *He bequeathed all his silver to his children.*

be|quest /bɪkwɛst/ (bequests) N-COUNT A **bequest** is money or property which you legally leave to someone when you die. ▫ *The church here was left a bequest to hire doctors who would work with the poor.*

be|rate /bɪreɪt/ (berates, berating, berated) V-T If you **berate** someone, you speak to them angrily about something they have done wrong. [FORMAL] ▫ *Marion berated Joe for the noise he made.*

Ber|ber /bɜrbər/ (Berbers) ADJ **Berber** means belonging or relating to a particular Muslim people in North Africa, or to their language or customs. • N-COUNT A **Berber** is a person from the Berber community.

be|reaved /bɪrivd/ ADJ A **bereaved** person is one who has a relative or close friend who has recently died. ▫ *Mr. Dinkins visited the bereaved family to offer comfort.*

be|reave|ment /bɪrivmənt/ (bereavements) N-VAR **Bereavement** is the sorrow you feel or the state you are in when a relative or close friend dies. ▫ *When Mary died Anne did not share her brother's sense of bereavement.*

be|reft /bɪrɛft/ ADJ If a person or thing is **bereft** of something, they no longer have it. [FORMAL] ▫ *The place seemed to be utterly bereft of human life.*

be|ret /bəreɪ/ (berets) **1** N-COUNT A **beret** is a circular, flat hat that is made of soft material and has no brim. **2** → See also color supplement

ber|ry /bɛri/ (berries) N-COUNT **Berries** are small, round fruit that grow on a bush or a tree. Some berries are edible, for example, blackberries and raspberries.

ber|serk /bərsɜrk, -zɜrk/ **1** ADJ **Berserk** means crazy and out of control. ▫ *He tossed back his head in a howl of berserk laughter.* **2** PHRASE If someone or something **goes berserk**, they lose control of themselves and become very angry or violent. ▫ *When I saw him I went berserk.*

berth /bɜrθ/ (berths, berthing, berthed) **1** PHRASE If you **give** someone or something **a wide berth**, you avoid them because you think they are unpleasant or dangerous, or simply because you do not like them. ▫ *She gives showbiz parties a wide berth.* **2** N-COUNT A **berth** is a bed on a ship or train. ▫ *Goldring booked a berth on the first boat he could.* **3** N-COUNT A **berth** is a space in a harbor where a ship stays for a period of time. ▫ *...the slow passage through the docks to the ship's berth.* **4** V-I When a ship **berths**, it sails into harbor and stops at the quay. ▫ *As the ship berthed in New York, McClintock was with the first immigration officers aboard.*

be|seech /bɪsitʃ/ (beseeches, beseeching, beseeched) V-T If you **beseech** someone to do something, you ask them very

beseeching /bɪsiːtʃɪŋ/ ADJ A **beseeching** expression, gesture, or tone of voice suggests that the person who has or makes it very much wants someone to do something. [LITERARY] ❏ *She looked up at him with beseeching eyes.*
• **be|seech|ing|ly** ADV [ADV after v] ❏ *Hugh looked at his father beseechingly.*

be|set /bɪsɛt/ (besets, besetting)

> The form **beset** is used in the present tense and is the past tense and past participle.

V-T If someone or something **is beset** by problems or fears, they have many problems or fears which affect them severely. ❏ *The country is beset by severe economic problems.* ❏ *The discussions were beset with difficulties.*

be|side ♦◇◇ /bɪsaɪd/ ■ PREP Something that is **beside** something else is at the side of it or next to it. ❏ *On the table beside an empty plate was a pile of books.* ■ → see also **besides** ■ PHRASE If you are **beside yourself** with anger or excitement, you are extremely angry or excited. ❏ *He had shouted down the phone at her, beside himself with anxiety.* ■ **beside the point** → see **point** ③

be|sides ♦◇◇ /bɪsaɪdz/ ■ PREP **Besides** something or **beside** something means in addition to it. ❏ *I think she has many good qualities besides being very beautiful.* • ADV [cl ADV] **Besides** is also an adverb. ❏ *You get to sample lots of baked things and take home masses of cookies besides.* ■ ADV **Besides** is used to emphasize an additional point that you are making, especially one that you consider to be important. ❏ *The house was out of our price range and too big anyway. Besides, I'd grown fond of our little rented house.*

be|siege /bɪsiːdʒ/ (besieges, besieging, besieged) ■ V-T [usu passive] If you **are besieged** by people, many people want something from you and continually bother you. ❏ *She was besieged by the press and the public.* ■ V-T If soldiers **besiege** a place, they surround it and wait for the people in it to stop fighting or resisting. ❏ *The main part of the army moved to Sevastopol to besiege the town.*

be|smirch /bɪsmɜːrtʃ/ (besmirches, besmirching, besmirched) V-T If you **besmirch** someone or their reputation, you say that they are a bad person or that they have done something wrong, usually when this is not true. [LITERARY] ❏ *He has accused local people of trying to besmirch his reputation.*

be|sot|ted /bɪsɒtɪd/ ADJ If you are **besotted** with someone or something, you like them so much that you seem foolish or silly. ❏ *He became so besotted with her that even his children were forgotten.*

be|speak /bɪspiːk/ (bespeaks, bespeaking, bespoke, bespoken) V-T If someone's action or behavior **bespeaks** a particular quality, feeling, or experience, it shows that quality, feeling, or experience. [LITERARY]

be|spec|ta|cled /bɪspɛktəkᵊld/ ADJ [usu ADJ n] Someone who is **bespectacled** is wearing glasses. [WRITTEN] ❏ *Mr. Merrick was a slim, quiet, bespectacled man.*

best ♦♦♦ /bɛst/ ■ **Best** is the superlative of **good**. ❏ *If you want further information the best thing to do is have a word with the driver as you get on the bus.* ■ **Best** is the superlative of **well**. ❏ *James Fox is best known as the author of "White Mischief," and he is currently working on a new book.* ■ N-SING **The best** is used to refer to things of the highest quality or standard. ❏ *We offer only the best to our clients.* ■ N-SING Someone's **best** is the greatest effort or highest achievement or standard that they are capable of. ❏ *Miss Blockey was at her best when she played the piano.* ■ N-SING If you say that something is **the best** that can be done or hoped for, you think it is the most pleasant, successful, or useful thing that can be done or hoped for. ❏ *A draw seems the best they can hope for.* ■ ADV If you like something **best** or like it **the best**, you prefer it. ❏ *The thing I liked best about the show was the music.* ❏ *Mother liked it best when Daniel got money.* ■ **Best** is used to form the superlative of compound adjectives beginning with 'good' and 'well.' For example, the superlative of 'well-known' is 'best-known.' ■ → see also **second best** ■ PHRASE You use **best of all** to indicate that what you are about to mention is the thing that you prefer or that has most advantages out of all the things you have mentioned. ❏ *It was comfortable and cheap: best of all, most of the rent was being paid by two American friends.* ■ PHRASE If someone does something **as best** they **can**, they do it as well as they can, although it is very difficult. ❏ *Let's leave people to get on with their jobs and do them as best they can.* ■ PHRASE You use **at best** to indicate that even if you describe something as favorably as possible or if it performs as well as it possibly can, it is still not very good. ❏ *This policy, they say, is at best confused and at worst non-existent.* ■ PHRASE If you **do** your **best** or **try** your **best** to do something, you try as hard as you can to do it, or do it as well as you can. ❏ *I'll do my best to find out.* ■ PHRASE If you say that something is **for the best**, you mean it is the most desirable or helpful thing that could have happened or could be done, considering all the circumstances. ❏ *Whatever the circumstances, parents are supposed to know what to do for the best.* ■ PHRASE If you say that a particular person **knows best**, you mean that they have a lot of experience and should therefore be trusted to make decisions for other people. ❏ *He was convinced that doctors and dentists knew best.* ■ **to the best of your ability** → see **ability** ■ **to hope for the best** → see **hope** ■ **to the best of sb's knowledge** → see **knowledge** ■ **best of luck** → see **luck** ■ **the best of both worlds** → see **world**

bes|tial /bɛstiəl, bis-/ ADJ If you describe behavior or a situation as **bestial**, you mean that it is very unpleasant or disgusting. ❏ *...the bestial conditions into which the city has sunk.*

bes|ti|al|ity /bɛstiælɪti, bis-/ ■ N-UNCOUNT **Bestiality** is disgusting behavior. [FORMAL] ❏ *It is shocking that humans can behave with such bestiality towards others.* ■ N-UNCOUNT **Bestiality** is sexual activity in which a person has sex with an animal.

best|ie /bɛsti/ (besties) N-COUNT Your **bestie** is your best friend. [INFORMAL] ❏ *She spent the day hanging out with her bestie.*

best man N-SING The **best man** at a wedding is the man who assists the bridegroom.

be|stow /bɪstoʊ/ (bestows, bestowing, bestowed) V-T To **bestow** something **on** someone means to give or present it to them. [FORMAL] ❏ *The United States bestowed honorary citizenship upon England's World War II prime minister, Sir Winston Churchill.*

best prac|tice N-UNCOUNT **Best practice** is the way of running a business or providing a service that is recognized as correct or most effective. ❏ *Schools will work together to share best practice.*

be|stride /bɪstraɪd/ (bestrides, bestriding, bestrode, bestridden) V-T To **bestride** something means to be the most powerful and important person or thing in it. [LITERARY] ❏ *America's media companies bestride the globe.*

best|sell|er /bɛstsɛlər/ (bestsellers) ■ N-COUNT A **bestseller** is a book of which a great number of copies has been sold. ❏ *By mid-August the book was a bestseller.* ■ → See feature box at **book**

best-selling also **bestselling** ■ ADJ [ADJ n] A **best-selling** product such as a book is very popular and a large quantity of it has been sold. ■ ADJ [ADJ n] A **best-selling** author is an author who has sold a very large number of copies of his or her book.

bet ♦◇◇ /bɛt/ (bets, betting)

> The form **bet** is used in the present tense and is the past tense and past participle.

■ V-T/V-I If you **bet** on the result of a horse race, football game, or other event, you give someone a sum of money which they give you back with extra money if the result is what you predicted, or which they keep if it is not. ❏ *Jockeys are forbidden to bet on the outcome of races.* ❏ *I bet $20 on a horse called Premonition.* • **Bet** is also a noun. ❏ *Do you always have a bet on the Kentucky Derby?* • **bet|ting** N-UNCOUNT ❏ *...his thousand-dollar fine for illegal betting.* ■ N-COUNT A **bet** is a sum of money which you give to someone when you bet. ❏ *You can put a bet on almost anything these days.* ■ V-T/V-I [only cont] If someone **is betting** that something will happen, they are hoping or expecting that it will happen. [JOURNALISM] ❏ *The party is betting that the presidential race will turn into a battle for younger voters.* ❏ *People were betting on a further easing of credit conditions.* ■ PHRASE You use expressions such as '**I bet**,' '**I'll bet**,' and '**you can bet**' to indicate that you are sure something is true. [INFORMAL] ❏ *I bet you were good at games when you were at school.* ❏ *I'll bet they'll taste out of this world.* ■ PHRASE If you tell someone that something is a

good bet, you are suggesting that it is the thing or course of action that they should choose. [INFORMAL] ❑ *Your best bet is to choose a guest house.* **6** PHRASE If you say that it is **a good bet** or **a safe bet** that something is true or will happen, you are saying that it is extremely likely to be true or to happen. [INFORMAL] ❑ *It is a safe bet that the current owners will not sell.* **7** PHRASE You use **I bet** or **I'll bet** in reply to a statement to show that you agree with it or that you expected it to be true, usually when you are annoyed or amused by it. [INFORMAL, SPOKEN, FEELINGS] ❑ *"I'd like to ask you something," I said. "I bet you would," she grinned.* **8** PHRASE You say **I bet** or **I'll bet** in reply to a statement to show that you do not believe it or that you doubt that it is true. ❑ *"I only kiss girls," said John. Then he blushed. "I'll bet," said Lisa.* **9** PHRASE You can use **my bet is** or **it's my bet** to give your personal opinion about something, when you are fairly sure that you are right. [INFORMAL] ❑ *My bet is that next year will be different.*

SYNONYMS
---

bet
VERB **1**
gamble: *John gambled heavily on the horses.*
stake: *He has staked his reputation on the outcome.*
NOUN **1**
gamble: *...the French President's risky gamble in calling a referendum.*
stake: *The game was usually played for high stakes between two large groups.*

beta block|er /beɪtə blɒkər/ (**beta blockers**) N-COUNT A **beta blocker** is a drug which is used to treat people who have high blood pressure or heart problems.

bete noire /bet nwɑːr/ also **bête noire** N-SING [oft with poss] If you refer to someone or something as your **bete noire**, you mean that you have a particular dislike for them or that they annoy you a great deal. ❑ *Apple's bete noire in recent years has been timing inventory to meet demand.*

be|tide /bɪtaɪd/ PHRASE [PHR n] If you say **woe betide** anyone who does a particular thing, you mean that something unpleasant will happen to them if they do it. [FORMAL] ❑ *Woe betide anyone who got in his way.*

be|to|ken /bɪtoʊkən/ (**betokens, betokening, betokened**) V-T If something **betokens** something else, it is a sign of this thing. [FORMAL] ❑ *The president alone betokened the national identity.*

be|tray /bɪtreɪ/ (**betrays, betraying, betrayed**) **1** V-T If you **betray** someone who loves or trusts you, your actions hurt and disappoint them. ❑ *When I tell someone I will not betray his confidence I keep my word.* **2** V-T If someone **betrays** their country or their friends, they give information to an enemy, putting their country's security or their friends' safety at risk. ❑ *They offered me money if I would betray my associates.* **3** V-T If you **betray** an ideal or your principles, you say or do something which goes against those beliefs. ❑ *We betray the ideals of our country when we support capital punishment.* **4** V-T If you **betray** a feeling or quality, you show it without intending to. ❑ *She studied his face, but it betrayed nothing.*

be|tray|al /bɪtreɪəl/ (**betrayals**) N-VAR A **betrayal** is an action which betrays someone or something, or the fact of being betrayed. ❑ *She felt that what she had done was a betrayal of Patrick.*

be|troth|al /bɪtroʊðəl/ (**betrothals**) N-VAR A **betrothal** is an agreement to be married. [OLD-FASHIONED]

be|trothed /bɪtroʊðd/ ADJ If you are **betrothed** to someone, you have agreed to marry them. [OLD-FASHIONED] • N-SING [usu poss N] Your **betrothed** is the person you are betrothed to.

BETTER
---
① COMPARING STATES AND QUALITIES
② GIVING ADVICE
③ VERB USES

① **bet|ter** ♦♦♦ /betər/
→ Please look at meaning **15** to see if the expression you are looking for is shown under another headword.
1 **Better** is the comparative of **good**. **2** **Better** is the comparative of **well**. **3** ADV [ADV after v] If you like one thing **better** than another, you like it more. ❑ *I like your interpretation better than the one I was taught.* ❑ *They liked it better when it rained.* **4** ADJ [v-link ADJ] If you are **better** after an illness or injury, you have recovered from it. If you feel **better**, you no longer feel so ill. ❑ *He is much better now, he's fine.* **5** PRON If you say that you expect or deserve **better**, you mean that you expect or deserve a higher standard of achievement, behavior, or treatment from people than they have shown you. ❑ *We expect better of you in the future.* **6** **Better** is used to form the comparative of compound adjectives beginning with 'good' and 'well.' For example, the comparative of 'well-off' is 'better-off.' **7** PHRASE If something changes **for the better**, it improves. ❑ *He dreams of changing the world for the better.* **8** PHRASE If a feeling such as jealousy, curiosity, or anger **gets the better of** you, it becomes too strong for you to hide or control. ❑ *She didn't allow her emotions to get the better of her.* **9** PHRASE If you **get the better of** someone, you defeat them in a contest, fight, or argument. ❑ *He is used to tough defenders, and he usually gets the better of them.* **10** PHRASE If someone **knows better** than to do something, they are old enough or experienced enough to know it is the wrong thing to do. ❑ *She knew better than to argue with Adeline.* **11** PHRASE If you **know better** than someone, you have more information, knowledge, or experience than them. ❑ *He thought he knew better than I did, though he was much less experienced.* **12** CONVENTION You say '**That's better**' in order to express your approval of what someone has said or done, or to praise or encourage them. ❑ *"I came to ask your advice – no, to ask for your help."—"That's better. And how can I help you?"* **13** PHRASE You can say '**so much the better**' or '**all the better**' to indicate that it is desirable that a particular thing is used, done, or available. ❑ *The fog had come in; so much the better when it came to sneaking away.* **14** PHRASE If you intend to do something and then **think better of it**, you decide not to do it because you realize it would not be sensible. ❑ *Alberg opened his mouth, as if to protest. But he thought better of it.* **15** **to be better than nothing** → see **nothing**

② **bet|ter** ♦♦♦ /betər/ **1** PHRASE You use **had better** or **'d better** when you are advising, warning, or threatening someone, or expressing an opinion about what should happen. ❑ *It's half past two. I think we had better go home.* ❑ *You'd better run if you're going to get your ticket.* • ADV In spoken English, people sometimes use **better** without 'had' or 'be' before it. It has the same meaning. ❑ *Better not say too much aloud.* **2** PHRASE You can say that someone **is better** doing one thing than another, or **it is better** doing one thing than another, to advise someone about what they should do. ❑ *Wouldn't it be better putting a time-limit on the task?* **3** PHRASE If you say that someone would **be better off** doing something, you are advising them to do it or expressing the opinion that it would benefit them to do it. ❑ *If you've got bags you're better off taking a taxi.*

③ **bet|ter** ♦♦♦ /betər/ (**betters, bettering, bettered**) **1** V-T If someone **betters** a high achievement or standard, they achieve something higher. ❑ *His throw bettered the American junior record set in 2003.* **2** V-T If you **better** your situation, you improve your social status or the quality of your life. If you **better** yourself, you improve your social status. ❑ *He had dedicated his life to bettering the lot of the oppressed people of South Africa.*

bet|ter|ment /betərmənt/ N-UNCOUNT [oft N of n] The **betterment** of something is the act or process of improving its standard or status. [FORMAL] ❑ *His research is for the betterment of mankind.*

bet|ting /betɪŋ/ PHRASE [PHR that] If you say **the betting is** that something will happen or is true, you are suggesting that it is very likely to happen or to be true. ❑ *The betting is that the experience will make Japan more competitive still.*

be|tween ♦♦♦ /bɪtwiːn/

In addition to the uses shown below, **between** is used in a few phrasal verbs, such as 'come between.'

1 PREP If something is **between** two things or is **in between** them, it has one of the things on one side of it and the other thing on the other side. ❑ *She left the table to stand between the two men.* **2** PREP [PREP pl-n] If people or things travel **between** two places, they travel regularly from one place to the other and back again. ❑ *I spent a lot of time in the early Eighties traveling between Waco and El Paso.* **3** PREP [PREP pl-n] A relationship, discussion, or difference **between** two or more people, groups,

beveled /bɛvəld/ also **bevelled** ADJ [usu ADJ n] If a piece of wood, metal, or glass has **beveled** edges, its edges are cut sloping. ❑ ...a huge mirror with deep beveled edges.

beverage /bɛvərɪdʒ/ (beverages) N-COUNT **Beverages** are drinks. [WRITTEN] ❑ Alcoholic beverages are served in the hotel lounge. ❑ ...artificially sweetened beverages.

bevy /bɛvi/ (bevies) N-COUNT [usu sing, N of n] A **bevy of** people is a group of people all together in one place. ❑ ...a bevy of bright young officers.

bewail /bɪweɪl/ (bewails, bewailing, bewailed) VERB If you **bewail** something, you express great sorrow about it. [JOURNALISM, LITERARY] ❑ ...songs that bewail his dissatisfaction in love.

beware /bɪwɛər/ V-I [only imper and inf] If you tell someone to **beware** of a person or thing, you are warning them that the person or thing may harm them or be dangerous. ❑ Beware of being too impatient with others. ❑ Motorists were warned to beware of slippery conditions.

bewilder /bɪwɪldər/ (bewilders, bewildering, bewildered) V-T If something **bewilders** you, it is so confusing or difficult that you cannot understand it. ❑ The silence from Alex had hurt and bewildered her.

bewildered /bɪwɪldərd/ ADJ If you are **bewildered**, you are very confused and cannot understand something or decide what you should do. ❑ Some shoppers looked bewildered by the sheer variety of goods for sale.

bewildering /bɪwɪldərɪŋ/ ADJ A **bewildering** thing or situation is very confusing and difficult to understand or to make a decision about. ❑ A glance along his bookshelves reveals a bewildering array of interests.

bewilderment /bɪwɪldərmənt/ N-UNCOUNT **Bewilderment** is the feeling of being bewildered. ❑ He shook his head in bewilderment.

bewitch /bɪwɪtʃ/ (bewitches, bewitching, bewitched) V-T If someone or something **bewitches** you, you are so attracted to them that you cannot think about anything else. ❑ She was not moving, as if someone had bewitched her. • **bewitching** ADJ ❑ Frank was a quiet young man with bewitching brown eyes.

beyond ♦♦◊ /bɪyɒnd/ ◼ PREP If something is **beyond** a place or barrier, it is on the other side of it. ❑ On his right was a thriving vegetable garden and beyond it a small orchard of apple trees. • ADV **Beyond** is also an adverb. ❑ The house had a fabulous view out to the Strait of Georgia and the Rockies beyond. ◻ PREP If something happens **beyond** a particular time or date, it continues after that time or date has passed. ❑ Few jockeys continue race-riding beyond the age of 40. • ADV [cl and ADV] **Beyond** is also an adverb. ❑ The financing of home ownership will continue through the 1990s and beyond. ◼ PREP If something extends **beyond** a particular thing, it affects or includes other things. ❑ His interests extended beyond the fine arts to international politics and philosophy. ◼ PREP You use **beyond** to introduce an exception to what you are saying. ❑ He appears to have almost no personal staff, beyond a secretary who can't make coffee. ◼ PREP If something goes **beyond** a particular point or stage, it progresses or increases so that it passes that point or stage. ❑ Their five-year relationship was strained beyond breaking point. ◼ PREP If something is, for example, **beyond** understanding or **beyond** belief, it is so extreme in some way that it cannot be understood or believed. ❑ What Jock had done was beyond my comprehension. ◼ PREP If you say that something is **beyond** someone, or **beyond** their control, you mean that they cannot deal with it. ❑ The situation was beyond her control. ◼ **beyond your wildest dreams** → see **dream**

B-grade /bi greɪd/ ADJ [ADJ n] A **B-grade** person or thing is one that you consider to be inferior or of poor quality. [DISAPPROVAL] ❑ ...a B-grade action movie star.

bhangra /bæŋgrə/ also **Bhangra** N-UNCOUNT **Bhangra** is a form of dance music that comes from India and uses traditional Indian instruments.

bi /baɪ/ ADJ **Bi** means the same as **bisexual**. [INFORMAL]

PREFIX

bi-
forms nouns and adjectives that have two as part of their meaning. For example, if someone is bilingual, they speak two languages.

---

biannual /baɪænyuəl/ ADJ A **biannual** event happens twice a year. ❑ You will need to have a routine biannual examination. • **biannually** ADV [ADV after v] ❑ Only since 1962 has the show been held biannually.

bias /baɪəs/ (biases, biasing, biased) ◼ N-VAR **Bias** is a tendency to prefer one person or thing to another, and to favor that person or thing. ❑ ...his desire to avoid the appearance of bias in favor of one candidate or another. ◻ V-T To **bias** someone means to influence them in favor of a particular choice. ❑ We mustn't allow it to bias our teaching.

biased /baɪəst/ ◼ ADJ If someone is **biased**, they prefer one group of people to another, and behave unfairly as a result. You can also say that a process or system is **biased**. ❑ He seemed a bit biased against women in my opinion. ◻ ADJ [v-link ADJ toward n] If something is **biased toward** one thing, it is more concerned with it than with other things. ❑ University funding was tremendously biased toward scientists.

bib /bɪb/ (bibs) N-COUNT A **bib** is a piece of cloth or plastic which is worn by very young children to protect their clothes while they are eating.

Bible /baɪbəl/ (Bibles) ◼ N-PROPER The **Bible** is the holy book on which the Jewish and Christian religions are based. ◻ N-COUNT A **bible** is a copy of the Bible. ❑ ...a publisher of bibles and hymn books.

Bible Belt N-PROPER [the N] Parts of the southern United States are referred to as **the Bible Belt** because fundamentalist Christians with strong beliefs have a lot of influence there.

biblical /bɪblɪkəl/ ADJ **Biblical** means contained in or relating to the Bible. ❑ The community, whose links with Syria date back to biblical times, is mainly elderly.

bibliography /bɪbliɒgrəfi/ (bibliographies) ◼ N-COUNT A **bibliography** is a list of books on a particular subject. ❑ At the end of this chapter there is a select bibliography of useful books. ◻ N-COUNT A **bibliography** is a list of the books and articles that are referred to in a particular book. ❑ ...the full bibliography printed at the end of the second volume.

bicarb /baɪkɑrb/ N-UNCOUNT **Bicarb** is an abbreviation for bicarbonate of soda. [INFORMAL]

bicarbonate of soda /baɪkɑrbənɪt əv soʊdə/ [mainly BRIT] → see **sodium bicarbonate**

bicentenary /baɪsɛntɛnəri/ [mainly BRIT] → see **bicentennial**

bicentennial /baɪsɛntɛniəl/ (bicentennials) [mainly AM] ◼ N-COUNT A **bicentennial** is a year in which you celebrate something important that happened exactly two hundred years earlier. ◻ ADJ [ADJ n] **Bicentennial** celebrations are held to celebrate a bicentennial.

biceps /baɪsɛps/ N-PLURAL Your **biceps** are the large muscles at the front of the upper part of your arms.

bick|er /bɪkər/ (bickers, bickering, bickered) V-RECIP When people **bicker**, they argue or quarrel about unimportant things. ❑ *I went into medicine to care for patients, not to waste time bickering over budgets.* ❑ *...as states bicker over territory.* • **bick|er|ing** N-UNCOUNT ❑ *The election will end months of political bickering.*

bi|coas|tal /baɪkoʊstəl/ ADJ Someone or something that is **bicoastal** lives or occurs on both the east coast and the west coast of the U.S. [AM]

bi|cy|cle /baɪsɪkəl/ (bicycles) ◼ N-COUNT A **bicycle** is a vehicle with two wheels which you ride by sitting on it and pushing two pedals with your feet. You steer it by turning a bar that is connected to the front wheel. ◪ → See also color supplement

bi|cy|clist /baɪsɪklɪst/ (bicyclists) N-COUNT A **bicyclist** is someone who enjoys cycling. [OLD-FASHIONED]

bid ✦✦◇ /bɪd/ (bids, bidding)

> The form **bid** is used in the present tense and is the past tense and past participle.

◼ N-COUNT A **bid** for something or a **bid** to do something is an attempt to obtain it or do it. [JOURNALISM] ❑ *...Sydney's successful bid for the 2000 Olympic Games.* ◪ N-COUNT A **bid** is an offer to pay a particular amount of money for something that is being sold. ❑ *Hanson made an agreed takeover bid of $351 million.* ◾ V-T/V-I If you **bid** for something or **bid** to do something, you try to obtain it or do it. ❑ *Singapore Airlines is rumored to be bidding for a management contract to run both airports.* ◿ V-I If you **bid** for something that is being sold, you offer to pay a particular amount of money for it. ❑ *She wanted to bid for it.* ❑ *The bank announced its intention to bid.*

SYNONYMS

bid
NOUN ◼
attempt: *...a deliberate attempt to destabilize the defense.*
try: *After a few tries, Patrick had given up any attempt to reform his brother.*
effort: *He made no effort to hide his disappointment.*

---

bid|den /bɪdən/ **Bidden** is a past participle of **bid**. [OLD-FASHIONED]

bid|der /bɪdər/ (bidders) ◼ N-COUNT A **bidder** is someone who offers to pay a certain amount of money for something that is being sold. If you sell something to the highest **bidder**, you sell it to the person who offers the most money for it. ❑ *The sale will be made to the highest bidder subject to a reserve price being attained.* ◪ N-COUNT A **bidder** for something is someone who is trying to obtain it or do it. ❑ *Vodafone is among successful bidders for two licenses to develop cellphone systems in Greece.*

bid|ding /bɪdɪŋ/ ◼ PHRASE If you do something at someone's **bidding**, you do it because they have asked you to do it. [FORMAL] ❑ *At his bidding, the delegates rose and sang the national anthem.* ◪ PHRASE If you say that someone **does** another person's **bidding**, you disapprove of the fact that they do exactly what the other person asks them to do, even when they do not want to. [FORMAL, DISAPPROVAL] ❑ *She is very clever at getting people to do her bidding!* ◾ → see also **bid**

bid|dy /bɪdi/ (biddies) N-COUNT If someone describes an old woman as an old **biddy**, they are saying in an unkind and impolite way that they think she is silly or unpleasant. [INFORMAL, DISAPPROVAL] ❑ *They were gossiping like two old biddies in a tearoom.*

bide /baɪd/ (bides, biding, bided) PHRASE If you **bide** your **time**, you wait for a good opportunity before doing something. ❑ *He was content to bide his time patiently, waiting for the opportunity to approach her.*

bi|det /bɪdeɪ/ (bidets) N-COUNT A **bidet** is a large low bowl in a bathroom, usually with faucets to supply water, for washing your bottom.

bid price (bid prices) N-COUNT The **bid price** of a particular stock or share is the price that investors are willing to pay for it. [BUSINESS] ❑ *Investors feel that the bid price undervalues the company.*

bi|en|nial /baɪɛniəl/ ADJ [ADJ n] A **biennial** event happens or is done once every two years. ❑ *...the biennial Commonwealth conference.*

biff /bɪf/ (biffs, biffing, biffed) V-T If you **biff** someone, you hit them with your fist. [INFORMAL, OLD-FASHIONED]

bi|fo|cals /baɪfoʊkəlz/

> The form **bifocal** is used as a modifier.

N-PLURAL **Bifocals** are glasses with lenses made in two halves. The top part is for looking at things some distance away, and the bottom part is for reading and looking at things that are close. ❑ *Mrs. Bierce wears thick bifocal lenses.*

bi|fur|cate /baɪfərkeɪt/ (bifurcates, bifurcating, bifurcated) V-T/V-I If something such as a line or path **bifurcates** or **is bifurcated**, it divides into two parts which go in different directions. ❑ *The blood supply bifurcates between eight and thirty times before reaching each particular location in the body.* • **bi|fur|ca|tion** /baɪfərkeɪʃən/ (bifurcations) N-VAR ❑ *...the bifurcation between high art and popular culture.*

big ✦✦✦ /bɪg/ (bigger, biggest) ◼ ADJ A **big** person or thing is large in physical size. ❑ *Australia's a big country.* ❑ *Her husband was a big man.* ◪ ADJ Something that is **big** consists of many people or things. ❑ *The crowd included a big contingent from Cleveland.* ◾ ADJ If you describe something such as a problem, increase, or change as a **big** one, you mean it is great in degree, extent, or importance. ❑ *Her problem was just too big for her to tackle on her own.* ◿ ADJ A **big** organization employs many people and has many customers. ❑ *...one of the biggest companies in Italy.* ❺ ADJ [ADJ n, v-link ADJ in n] If you say that someone is **big** in a particular organization, activity, or place, you mean that they have a lot of influence or authority in it. [INFORMAL] ❑ *Their father was very big in the army.* ❻ ADJ [ADJ n] If you call someone a **big** bully or a **big** coward, you are emphasizing your disapproval of them. [INFORMAL, EMPHASIS] ❑ *His personality changed. He turned into a big bully.* ❼ ADJ [ADJ n] Children often refer to their older brother or sister as their **big** brother or sister. ❑ *She always introduces me as her big sister.* ❽ ADJ **Big** words are long or rare words which have meanings that are difficult to understand. [INFORMAL] ❑ *They use a lot of big words.* ❾ PHRASE If you **make it big**, you become successful or famous. [INFORMAL] ❑ *Capone was an underdog hero, a poor boy who made it big.* ❿ PHRASE If you **think big**, you make plans on a large scale, often using a lot of time, effort, or money. ❑ *Maybe we're not thinking big enough.*

biga|mist /bɪgəmɪst/ (bigamists) N-COUNT A **bigamist** is a person who commits the crime of marrying someone when they are already legally married to someone else.

biga|mous /bɪgəməs/ ADJ A **bigamous** marriage is one in which one of the partners is already legally married to someone else.

biga|my /bɪgəmi/ N-UNCOUNT **Bigamy** is the crime of marrying a person when you are already legally married to someone else.

Big Ap|ple N-PROPER [the N] People sometimes refer to the city of New York as the **Big Apple**. [INFORMAL] ❑ *The main attractions of the Big Apple are well documented.*

big band (big bands) N-COUNT A **big band** is a large group of musicians who play jazz or dance music. Big bands were especially popular from the 1930s to the 1950s.

big bang theo|ry N-SING [the N] In astronomy **the big bang theory** is a theory that suggests that the universe was created as a result of an extremely large explosion.

big-box ADJ [ADJ n] A **big-box** store or retailer is a very large store where a great variety of merchandise is sold. [AM] ❑ *Malls and big-box stores have proliferated, while many older urban shopping districts have declined.*

Big Broth|er N-UNCOUNT People sometimes use **Big Brother** to refer to a person, government, or organization when they think it has complete control over people and is always checking what they do. [DISAPPROVAL] ❑ *It's an attempt to control what reaches the public. Big Brother is watching.*

big bucks N-PLURAL If someone earns or spends **big bucks**, they earn or spend a lot of money. [AM, INFORMAL] ❑ *Plastic pipe is easy to install, and doing it yourself saves big bucks.*

big busi|ness ◼ N-UNCOUNT **Big business** is business which involves very large companies and very large sums of money. ❑ *Big business will never let petty nationalism get in the way of a good deal.* ◪ N-UNCOUNT Something that is **big business** is something which people spend a lot of money on, and which has become an important commercial activity. ▫ *Online dating is big business in the United States.*

big cat (big cats) N-COUNT **Big cats** are lions, tigers, and other large wild animals in the cat family.

big city N-SING [the N] **The big city** is used to refer to a large city which seems attractive to someone because they think there are many exciting things to do there, and many opportunities to earn a lot of money. ▫ *...a country girl who dreams of the big city and bright lights.*

big da|ta N-PLURAL; N-UNCOUNT **Big data** is extremely large amounts of information that can only be used with special computers. ▫ *...valuable analysis of big data.*

big deal ◼ N-SING If you say that something is a **big deal**, you mean that it is important or significant in some way. [INFORMAL] ▫ *I felt the pressure on me, winning was such a big deal for the whole family.* ◼ PHRASE If someone **makes a big deal** out of something, they make a fuss about it or treat it as if it were very important. [INFORMAL] ▫ *The Joneses make a big deal out of being "different."* ◼ CONVENTION You can say '**big deal**' to someone to show that you are not impressed by something that they consider important or impressive. [INFORMAL, FEELINGS] ▫ *"You'll miss The Brady Bunch."—"Big deal."*

big fish (big fish) ◼ N-COUNT If you describe someone as a **big fish**, you believe that they are powerful or important in some way. [INFORMAL] ▫ *The four men arrested were described as really big fish by the U.S. Drug Enforcement Agency.* ◼ PHRASE [v-link PHR] If you say that someone is a **big fish in a small pond**, you mean that they are powerful or important but only within a small group of people. [INFORMAL] ▫ *In South Africa, Jani was a big fish in a small pond.*

big game N-UNCOUNT Large wild animals such as lions and elephants that are hunted for sport are often referred to as **big game**.

big|gie /bɪgi/ (biggies) N-COUNT People sometimes refer to something or someone successful, well-known, or big as a **biggie**. [INFORMAL] ▫ *...Hollywood box-office biggies.*

big|gish /bɪgɪʃ/ ADJ Something that is **biggish** is fairly big. [INFORMAL] ▫ *...a biggish room.*

big gun (big guns) N-COUNT If you refer to someone as a **big gun**, you mean that they have a lot of power or influence. [INFORMAL] ▫ *...the legal big guns who will prepare his defense.*

big head (big heads) N-COUNT If you describe someone as a **big head**, you disapprove of them because they think they are very clever and know everything. [INFORMAL, DISAPPROVAL]

big-headed ADJ If you describe someone as **big-headed**, you disapprove of them because they think they are very clever and know everything. [DISAPPROVAL] ▫ *...an arrogant, big-headed man.*

big-hearted ADJ [usu ADJ n] If you describe someone as **big-hearted**, you think they are kind and generous to other people, and always willing to help them. [WRITTEN] ▫ *...a big-hearted Irishman.*

big hit|ter (big hitters) ◼ N-COUNT A **big hitter** is an athlete such as a golfer or tennis player who hits the ball with a lot of force. ▫ *The Uruguayan-born big hitter smashed 28 aces.* ◼ N-COUNT A **big hitter** is a powerful or influential person, especially in business or politics. [INFORMAL] ▫ *He brings a reputation as a big hitter and hard worker.*

big mon|ey N-UNCOUNT **Big money** is an amount of money that seems very large to you, especially money which you get easily. ▫ *They began to make big money during the war.*

big mouth (big mouths) N-COUNT If you say that someone has a **big mouth**, you mean that they tell other people things that should have been kept secret. [INFORMAL, DISAPPROVAL] ▫ *Why don't you shut your big mouth?*

big name (big names) N-COUNT A **big name** is a person who is successful and famous because of their work. ▫ *...all the big names in rock and pop.*

big|ot /bɪgət/ (bigots) N-COUNT If you describe someone as a **bigot**, you mean that they are bigoted. [DISAPPROVAL] ▫ *Anyone who opposes them is branded a racist, a bigot, or a homophobe.*

big|ot|ed /bɪgətɪd/ ADJ Someone who is **bigoted** has strong, unreasonable prejudices or opinions and will not change them, even when they are proved to be wrong. [DISAPPROVAL] ▫ *He was bigoted and racist.*

big|ot|ry /bɪgətri/ N-UNCOUNT **Bigotry** is the possession or expression of strong, unreasonable prejudices or opinions. ▫ *He deplored religious bigotry.*

big screen N-SING [the N] When people talk about **the big screen**, they are referring to movies that are made for movie theaters rather than for television. ▫ *She returns to the big screen to play Candy's overbearing mother, Rose.*

big shot (big shots) N-COUNT A **big shot** is an important and powerful person in a group or organization. [INFORMAL] ▫ *He's a big shot in Chilean politics.*

Big Tech also **big tech** N-UNCOUNT **Big Tech** is used to refer to the biggest technology companies. ▫ *Last week, he and his bandmates turned up the volume in their battle with Big Tech.* ▫ *Many big tech company campuses are like mini resorts.*

big-ticket ADJ [ADJ n] If you describe something as a **big-ticket** item, you mean that it costs a lot of money. [mainly AM] ▫ *Supercomputers are big-ticket items.*

big time also **big-time** ◼ ADJ You can use **big time** to refer to the highest level of an activity or sport where you can achieve the greatest amount of success or importance. If you describe a person as **big time**, you mean they are successful and important. [INFORMAL] ▫ *He took a long time to settle in to big-time football.* ◼ N-SING If someone hits **the big time**, they become famous or successful in a particular area of activity. [INFORMAL] ▫ *He hit the big time with films such as Ghost and Dirty Dancing.* ◼ ADV [ADV after v] You can use **big time** if you want to emphasize the importance or extent of something that has happened. [INFORMAL, EMPHASIS] ▫ *Mike Edwards has tasted success big time.*

big toe (big toes) N-COUNT Your **big toe** is the largest toe on your foot.

big top N-SING The large round tent that a circus uses for its performances is called the **big top**.

big wheel [BRIT] → see **Ferris wheel**

big|wig /bɪgwɪg/ (bigwigs) N-COUNT If you refer to an important person as a **bigwig**, you are being somewhat disrespectful. [INFORMAL, DISAPPROVAL]

bike ✦◊◊ /baɪk/ (bikes, biking, biked) ◼ N-COUNT A **bike** is a bicycle. [INFORMAL] ▫ *When you ride a bike, you exercise all of the leg muscles.* ◼ N-COUNT A **bike** is a motorcycle. [INFORMAL] ▫ *She parked her bike in the alley.* ◼ V-I To **bike** somewhere means to go there on a bicycle. [INFORMAL] ▫ *I biked home from the beach.* ◼ → See also color supplement

bike lane (bike lanes) ◼ N-COUNT A **bike lane** is a part of the road which is intended to be used only by people riding bicycles. ◼ → See feature box at **town**

bike path (bike paths) N-COUNT A **bike path** is a special path on which people can travel by bicycle separately from motor vehicles.

bik|er /baɪkər/ (bikers) ◼ N-COUNT **Bikers** are people who ride around on motorcycles, usually in groups. ▫ *There are always fights going on between rival bikers.* ◼ N-COUNT People who ride bicycles are called **bikers**. [AM] ▫ *And as the morning begins moving toward noon, look out for more bikers and pedestrians.*

in BRIT, use **cyclist**

bike|way /baɪkweɪ/ (bikeways) N-COUNT A **bikeway** is a road, route, or path for the use of bicycles. [AM, AUSTRALIAN]

bi|ki|ni /bɪkiːni/ (bikinis) N-COUNT A **bikini** is a two-piece swimsuit worn by women.

WORD HISTORY

bikini

The **bikini** takes its name from the *Bikini Atoll* in the Marshall Islands in the Pacific Ocean, where an atom bomb was exploded in 1946.

---

bi|ki|ni line N-SING A woman's **bikini line** is the edges of the area where her pubic hair grows.

bi|lat|er|al /baɪlætərəl/ ADJ [ADJ n] **Bilateral** negotiations, meetings, or agreements involve only the two groups or countries that are directly concerned. [FORMAL]

☐ ...bilateral talks between Britain and America. • bi|lat|er|al|ly ADV ☐ The agreement provided for disputes and differences between the two neighbors to be solved bilaterally.

bil|berry /bɪlbəri/ (bilberries) N-COUNT A **bilberry** is a small, round, dark-blue fruit that grows on bushes, especially in northern parts of the world.

bile /baɪl/ **1** N-UNCOUNT **Bile** is a liquid produced by your liver which helps you to digest fat. **2** N-UNCOUNT **Bile** is the bad-smelling liquid that comes out of your mouth when you vomit with no food in your stomach. **3** N-UNCOUNT **Bile** is anger or bitterness toward someone or something. [LITERARY] ☐ He aims his bile at religion, drugs, and politics.

bilge /bɪldʒ/ (bilges) N-COUNT The **bilge** or the **bilges** are the flat bottom part of a ship or boat.

bi|lin|gual /baɪlɪŋgwəl/ **1** ADJ [ADJ n] **Bilingual** means involving or using two languages. ☐ ...bilingual education. **2** ADJ Someone who is **bilingual** can speak two languages equally well, usually because they learned both languages as a child. ☐ He is bilingual in an Asian language and English.

bi|lin|gual|ism /baɪlɪŋgwəlɪzəm/ N-UNCOUNT **Bilingualism** is the ability to speak two languages equally well.

bili|ous /bɪliəs/ **1** ADJ [usu ADJ n] If someone describes the appearance of something as **bilious**, they mean that they think it looks unpleasant and rather disgusting. [WRITTEN, DISAPPROVAL] ☐ ...a bilious shade of green. **2** ADJ [usu ADJ n] **Bilious** is sometimes used to describe the feelings or behavior of someone who is extremely angry or bad-tempered. [WRITTEN] ☐ His speech was a bilious, rancorous attack on young people.

bilk /bɪlk/ (bilks, bilking, bilked) V-T To **bilk** someone out of something, especially money, means to cheat them out of it. [AM, INFORMAL] ☐ They are charged with bilking investors out of millions of dollars.

bill ✦✧ /bɪl/ (bills, billing, billed) **1** N-COUNT A **bill** is a written statement of money that you owe for goods or services. ☐ They couldn't afford to pay the bills. ☐ He paid his bill for the newspapers promptly. **2** V-T [no cont] If you **bill** someone for goods or services you have provided them with, you give or send them a bill stating how much money they owe you for these goods or services. ☐ Are you going to bill me for this? **3** N-COUNT A **bill** is a piece of paper money. [AM] ☐ The case contained a large quantity of U.S. dollar bills.

in BRIT, use **note**

4 N-COUNT In government, a **bill** is a formal statement of a proposed new law that is discussed and then voted on. ☐ This is the toughest crime bill that Congress has passed in a decade. **5** N-SING The **bill** of a show or concert is a list of the entertainers who will take part in it. ☐ Bob Dylan topped the bill. **6** N-SING The **bill** in a restaurant is a piece of paper on which the price of the meal you have just eaten is written and which you are given before you pay. [mainly BRIT]

in AM, usually use **check**

7 V-T [usu passive] If someone **is billed** to appear in a particular show, they have been advertised that they are going to be in it. ☐ She was billed to play the Wicked Queen in "Snow White." • **bill|ing** N-UNCOUNT ☐ ...their quarrels over star billing. **8** V-T If you **bill** a person or event as a particular thing, you advertise them in a way that makes people think they have particular qualities or abilities. ☐ They bill it as California's most exciting museum. **9** N-COUNT A bird's **bill** is its beak. **10** PHRASE If you say that someone or something **fits the bill** or **fills the bill**, you mean that they are suitable for a particular job or purpose. ☐ If you fit the bill, send a CV to Rebecca Rees.

bill|board /bɪlbɔrd/ (billboards) N-COUNT A **billboard** is a very large board on which advertising is displayed.

-billed /-bɪld/ COMB IN ADJ **-billed** combines with adjectives to indicate that a bird has a beak of a particular kind or appearance. ☐ ...yellow-billed ducks.

bil|let /bɪlɪt/ (billets, billeting, billeted) **1** V-T [usu passive] If members of the armed forces **are billeted** in a particular place, that place is provided for them to stay in for a period of time. ☐ The soldiers were billeted in private homes. **2** N-COUNT A **billet** is a house where a member of the armed forces has been billeted.

bill|fold /bɪlfoʊld/ (billfolds) N-COUNT A **billfold** is a small wallet, usually made of leather or plastic, where you can keep paper money and credit cards. [AM] ☐ ...a billfold containing fifteen dollars.

bil|liards /bɪliərdz/

The form **billiard** is used as a modifier.

1 N-UNCOUNT **Billiards** is a game played on a large table, in which you use a long stick called a cue to hit balls against each other or against the walls around the sides of the table. [AM] **2** N-UNCOUNT **Billiards** is a game played on a large table, in which you use a long stick called a cue to hit balls against each other or into pockets around the sides of the table. [BRIT]

in AM, use **pool**

bil|lion ✦✦✦ /bɪlyən/ (billions)

The plural form is **billion** after a number, or after a word or expression referring to a number, such as 'several' or 'a few.'

1 NUM A **billion** is a thousand million. ☐ The Ethiopian foreign debt stands at 3 billion dollars. **2** QUANT-PLURAL [QUANT of pl-n] If you talk about **billions of** people or things, you mean that there is a very large number of them but you do not know or do not want to say exactly how many. ☐ Biological systems have been doing this for billions of years. • PRON You can also use **billions** as a pronoun. ☐ He thought that it must be worth billions.

bil|lion|aire /bɪlyənɛər/ (billionaires) N-COUNT A **billionaire** is an extremely rich person who has money or property worth at least a thousand million dollars.

bil|lionth /bɪlyənθ/ (billionths) **1** ORD The **billionth** item in a series is the one you count as number one billion. ☐ I have to go after Steve Mercer, she thought for probably the billionth time. **2** FRACTION A **billionth** is one of a billion equal parts of something. ☐ ...a billionth of a second.

bill of fare (bills of fare) N-COUNT The **bill of fare** at a restaurant is a list of the food for a meal from which you may choose what you want to eat. [OLD-FASHIONED]

Bill of Rights N-SING A **Bill of Rights** is a written list of citizens' rights which is usually part of the constitution of a country. ☐ And what are your rights according to the Bill of Rights?

bil|low /bɪloʊ/ (billows, billowing, billowed) **1** V-I When something made of cloth **billows**, it swells out and moves slowly in the wind. ☐ The curtains billowed in the breeze. ☐ Her pink dress billowed out around her. **2** V-I When smoke or cloud **billows**, it moves slowly upward or across the sky. ☐ ...thick plumes of smoke billowing from factory chimneys. ☐ Steam billowed out from under the hood. **3** N-COUNT A **billow** of smoke or dust is a large mass of it rising slowly into the air. ☐ ...smokestacks belching billows of almost solid black smoke.

bil|ly /bɪli/ (billies) N-COUNT A **billy** or **billy club** is a short heavy stick which is sometimes used as a weapon by the police. [AM]

in BRIT, use **baton**

bil|ly goat /bɪli goʊt/ (billy goats) N-COUNT A **billy goat** is a male goat.

bim|bo /bɪmboʊ/ (bimbos) N-COUNT If someone calls a young woman a **bimbo**, they think that she is pretty but not very intelligent. This use could cause offense. [INFORMAL, DISAPPROVAL]

bi|month|ly /baɪmʌnθli/ **1** ADJ [usu ADJ n] A **bimonthly** event or publication happens or appears every two months. ☐ ...bimonthly assemblies.

in BRIT, also use **bi-monthly**

• ADV **Bimonthly** is also an adverb. ☐ Under the new plan, customers would pay $45 bimonthly, instead of $18 a month – a substantial increase.

in BRIT, also use **bi-monthly**

2 ADJ A **bimonthly** event or publication happens or appears twice every month. [AM] ☐ In November, it will start bimonthly publication, and in January it goes weekly.

in BRIT, use **fortnightly**

• ADV **Bimonthly** is also an adverb. [AM] ❑ ...*people who get paid weekly, bimonthly and monthly.*

in BRIT, use **fortnightly**

bin /bɪn/ (**bins**) **1** N-COUNT A **bin** is a container that you keep or store things in. ❑ ...*big steel storage bins.* **2** N-COUNT A **bin** is a container that you put garbage or trash in. [mainly BRIT]

in AM, usually use **garbage can**

bi|na|ry /ˈbaɪnəri/ **1** ADJ [usu ADJ n] The **binary** system expresses numbers using only the two digits 0 and 1. It is used especially in computing. ❑ *The message contains Unicode characters and has been sent as a binary attachment.* **2** N-UNCOUNT **Binary** is the binary system of expressing numbers. ❑ *The machine does the calculations in binary.*

bi|na|ry code (**binary codes**) N-VAR **Binary code** is a computer code that uses the binary number system. [COMPUTING] ❑ *The instructions are translated into binary code, a form that computers can easily handle.*

bind /baɪnd/ (**binds, binding, bound**) **1** V-T If something **binds** people together, it makes them feel as if they are all part of the same group or have something in common. ❑ *It is the memory and threat of persecution that binds them together.* ❑ ...*the social and political ties that bind the U.S. to Britain.* **2** V-T If you **are bound** by something such as a rule, agreement, or restriction, you are forced or required to act in a certain way. ❑ *All pharmacists are bound by the society's rules of confidentiality.* ❑ *The authorities will be legally bound to arrest any suspects.* • **bound** ADJ [v link ADJ by n] ❑ *The world of advertising is obviously less bound by convention than the world of banking.* **3** V-T If you **bind** something or someone, you tie rope, string, tape, or other material around them so that they are held firmly. ❑ *Bind the ends of the cord together with thread.* ❑ ...*the red tape which was used to bind the files.* **4** V-T When a book is **bound**, the pages are joined together and the cover is put on. ❑ *Each volume is bound in bright-colored cloth.* ❑ *Their business came from a few big publishers, all of whose books they bound.*

bind|er /ˈbaɪndər/ (**binders**) N-COUNT A **binder** is a hard cover with metal rings inside, which is used to hold loose pieces of paper.

bind|ing /ˈbaɪndɪŋ/ (**bindings**) **1** ADJ A **binding** promise, agreement, or decision must be obeyed or carried out. ❑ ...*proposals for a legally binding commitment on nations to stabilize emissions of carbon dioxide.* **2** N-VAR The **binding** of a book is its cover. ❑ *Its books are noted for the quality of their paper and bindings.* **3** N-VAR **Binding** is a strip of material that you put around the edge of a piece of cloth or other object in order to protect or decorate it. ❑ ...*the Regency mahogany dining table with satinwood binding.* **4** → see also **bind**

bind|weed /ˈbaɪndwiːd/ N-UNCOUNT **Bindweed** is a wild plant that winds itself around other plants and makes it difficult for them to grow.

binge /bɪndʒ/ (**binges, bingeing, binged**) **1** N-COUNT If you go on a **binge**, you do too much of something, such as drinking alcohol, eating, or spending money. [INFORMAL] ❑ *She went on occasional drinking binges.* **2** V-I If you **binge**, you do too much of something, such as drinking alcohol, eating, or spending money. [INFORMAL] ❑ *I haven't binged since 2012.*

binge drink|ing N-UNCOUNT **Binge drinking** is the consumption of large amounts of alcohol within a short period of time. ❑ ...*a disturbing rise in binge drinking among young people.* • **binge drink|er** (**binge drinkers**) N-COUNT ❑ ...*the increasing number of young binge drinkers who have four or more drinks on a night out.*

binge-watch (**binge-watches, binge-watching, binge-watched**) VERB If you **binge-watch** a television series, you watch several episodes one after another in a short time. [INFORMAL] ❑ *It's not uncommon for viewers to binge-watch a whole season of programs in just a couple of evenings.*

bin|go /ˈbɪŋɡoʊ/ **1** N-UNCOUNT **Bingo** is a game in which each player has a card with numbers on it. Someone calls out numbers and if you are the first person to have all your numbers called out, you win the game. ❑ ...*a bingo hall.* **2** EXCLAM You can say '**bingo!**' when something pleasant happens, especially in a surprising, unexpected, or sudden way, or to show that you have just achieved or discovered something. ❑ *She grinned. "Wow, bingo! Got it in one."*

bin lin|er (**bin liners**) N-COUNT A **bin liner** is a plastic bag that you put inside a garbage can or trash can. [BRIT]

in AM, use **garbage bag**

bin|ocu|lars /bɪˈnɒkjələrz/ **1** N-PLURAL [also a pair of N] **Binoculars** consist of two small telescopes joined together side by side, which you look through in order to look at things that are a long distance away. **2** → See also color supplement

PREFIX

bio-
is used at the beginning of nouns and adjectives that refer to life or to the study of living things. *For example,* **bioengineering** *is the study of engineering for medical purposes, such as the design and manufacture of artificial body parts.*

bio|chemi|cal /ˌbaɪoʊˈkɛmɪkəl/ ADJ [ADJ n] **Biochemical** changes, reactions, and mechanisms relate to the chemical processes that happen in living things. ❑ *Starvation brings biochemical changes in the body.*

bio|chem|ist /ˌbaɪoʊˈkɛmɪst/ (**biochemists**) N-COUNT A **biochemist** is a scientist or student who studies biochemistry.

bio|chem|is|try /ˌbaɪoʊˈkɛmɪstri/ **1** N-UNCOUNT **Biochemistry** is the study of the chemical processes that occur in living things. **2** N-UNCOUNT The **biochemistry** of a living thing is the chemical processes that occur in it or are involved in it. ❑ ...*the effects of air pollutants on the biochemistry of plants or animals.*

bio|degrad|able /ˌbaɪoʊdɪˈɡreɪdəbəl/ **1** ADJ Something that is **biodegradable** breaks down or decays naturally without any special scientific treatment, and can therefore be thrown away without causing pollution. ❑ ...*a natural and totally biodegradable plastic.* **2** → See feature box at **recycle**

bio|die|sel /ˈbaɪoʊdiːzəl/ N-UNCOUNT **Biodiesel** is fuel made from natural sources such as plant oils, that can be used in diesel engines.

bio|di|ver|sity /ˌbaɪoʊdaɪˈvɜːrsɪti/ **1** N-UNCOUNT **Biodiversity** is the existence of a wide variety of plant and animal species living in their natural environment. **2** → See feature box at **deforest, ocean**

bio|en|gi|neer|ing /ˌbaɪoʊɛndʒɪˈnɪərɪŋ/ **1** N-UNCOUNT People sometimes use **bioengineering** to talk about genetic engineering. **2** N-UNCOUNT **Bioengineering** is the use of engineering techniques to solve medical problems, for example, to design and make artificial arms and legs.

bio|fu|el /ˈbaɪoʊfjuːəl/ (**biofuels**) N-VAR A **biofuel** is a gas, liquid, or solid from natural sources such as plants that is used as a fuel. ❑ *Biofuels can be mixed with conventional fuels.*

bi|og|ra|pher /baɪˈɒɡrəfər/ (**biographers**) N-COUNT Someone's **biographer** is a person who writes an account of their life. ❑ ...*Picasso's biographer.*

bio|graphi|cal /ˌbaɪəˈɡræfɪkəl/ ADJ **Biographical** facts, notes, or details are concerned with the events in someone's life. ❑ *The book contains few biographical details.*

bi|og|ra|phy /baɪˈɒɡrəfi/ (**biographies**) **1** N-COUNT A **biography** of someone is an account of their life, written by someone else. ❑ ...*recent biographies of Stalin.* **2** N-UNCOUNT **Biography** is the branch of literature which deals with accounts of people's lives. ❑ ...*a volume of biography and criticism.*

biol. Biol. is a written abbreviation for **biology** or **biological**.

bio|logi|cal /ˌbaɪəˈlɒdʒɪkəl/ **1** ADJ **Biological** is used to describe processes and states that occur in the bodies and cells of living things. ❑ *The living organisms somehow concentrated the minerals by biological processes.* • **bio|logi|cal|ly** /ˌbaɪəˈlɒdʒɪkli/ ADV ❑ *Much of our behavior is biologically determined.* **2** ADJ [ADJ n] **Biological** is used to describe activities concerned with the study of living things. ❑ ...*all aspects of biological research associated with leprosy.* **3** ADJ **Biological** weapons and **biological** warfare involve the use of bacteria or other living organisms in order to attack human beings, animals, or plants. ❑ *Such a war could result in the use of chemical and biological weapons.* **4** ADJ [ADJ n] **Biological** pest control is the use of bacteria or other living organisms in order to destroy other organisms which are harmful to plants or crops. ❑ ...*a consultant on biological control of agricultural pests.* **5** ADJ [ADJ n] A child's **biological** parents are the man and woman who caused him or her to be born, rather than other adults who raise him or her. ❑ ...*foster parents for young teenagers whose biological parents have rejected them.* **6** → See feature box at **genetics**

bio|logi|cal clock (biological clocks) N-COUNT [oft poss N] Your **biological clock** is your body's way of registering time. It does not rely on events such as day or night, but on factors such as your habits, your age, and chemical changes taking place in your body. ❑ *For women, the biological clock governs the time for having children.*

bio|logi|cal di|ver|sity N-UNCOUNT **Biological diversity** is the same as **biodiversity**.

bi|ol|ogy /baɪɒlədʒi/ **1** N-UNCOUNT **Biology** is the science which is concerned with the study of living things. • **bi|olo|gist** /baɪɒlədʒɪst/ (biologists) N-COUNT ❑ ...*biologists studying the fruit fly.* **2** N-UNCOUNT The **biology** of a living thing is the way in which its body or cells behave. ❑ *The biology of these diseases is terribly complicated.*

bio|medi|cal /baɪoʊmɛdɪkəl/ ADJ [ADJ n] **Biomedical** research examines the effects of drugs and medical techniques on the biological systems of living creatures. ❑ *Biomedical research will enable many individuals infected with HIV to live longer, more comfortable lives.*

bio|met|ric /baɪoʊmɛtrɪk/ ADJ [ADJ n] **Biometric** tests and devices use biological information about a person to create a detailed record of their personal characteristics. ❑ ...*the use of biometric information such as fingerprints.*

bi|on|ic /baɪɒnɪk/ ADJ [usu ADJ n] In science fiction books or films, a **bionic** person is someone who has special powers, such as being exceptionally strong or having exceptionally good sight, because parts of their body have been replaced by electronic machinery. ❑ ...*the Bionic Woman.*

bio|pic /baɪoʊpɪk/ (biopics) N-COUNT A **biopic** is a film that tells the story of someone's life. [INFORMAL]

bio|pi|ra|cy /baɪoʊpaɪrəsi/ N-UNCOUNT **Biopiracy** is the use of wild plants by international companies to develop medicines, without paying any money to the countries from which they are taken. ❑ *We need laws to protect countries against commercial biopiracy of their natural resources.*

bi|op|sy /baɪɒpsi/ (biopsies) N-VAR A **biopsy** is the removal and examination of fluids or tissue from a patient's body in order to discover why they are ill. ❑ *James had a biopsy of the tumor on his right ear.*

bio|se|cu|rity /baɪoʊsɪkjʊərɪti/ N-UNCOUNT **Biosecurity** is the actions that are taken to prevent dangerous diseases, bacteria or other harmful organisms from spreading. ❑ *The government has issued advice to farmers on animal biosecurity.*

bio|sphere /baɪəsfɪər/ N-SING [usu the N] The **biosphere** is the part of the Earth's surface and atmosphere where there are living things. [TECHNICAL]

bio|tech /baɪoʊtɛk/ N-UNCOUNT [usu N n] **Biotech** means the same as **biotechnology**. ❑ ...*the biotech industry.*

bio|tech|no|logi|cal /baɪoʊtɛknəlɒdʒɪkəl/ ADJ [ADJ n] **Biotechnological** means relating to biotechnology. [TECHNICAL] ❑ ...*modern biotechnological methods of genetic manipulation.*

bio|tech|nol|ogy /baɪoʊtɛknɒlədʒi/ N-UNCOUNT **Biotechnology** is the use of living parts such as cells or bacteria in industry and technology. [TECHNICAL] ❑ ...*the Scottish biotechnology company that developed Dolly the cloned sheep.*

bio|ter|ror|ism /baɪoʊtɛrərɪzəm/ also **bio-terrorism** N-UNCOUNT **Bioterrorism** is terrorism that involves the use of biological weapons. ❑ ...*the threat of bioterrorism.* • **bio|ter|ror|ist** /baɪoʊtɛrərɪst/ (bioterrorists) N-COUNT [oft N n] ❑ ...*the war against bioterrorists.* ❑ ...*a bioterrorist attack.*

bio|weap|on /baɪoʊwɛpən/ (bioweapons) N-COUNT Bioweapons are biological weapons.

bi|par|ti|san /baɪpɑrtɪzən/ ADJ [usu ADJ n] **Bipartisan** means concerning or involving two different political parties or groups. ❑ ...*a bipartisan approach to educational reform.*

bi|ped /baɪpɛd/ (bipeds) N-COUNT A **biped** is a creature with two legs. [TECHNICAL]

bi|plane /baɪpleɪn/ (biplanes) N-COUNT A **biplane** is an old-fashioned type of airplane with two pairs of wings, one above the other.

bi|po|lar /baɪpoʊlər/ **1** ADJ [usu ADJ n] **Bipolar** systems or situations are dominated by two strong and opposing opinions or elements. [FORMAL] ❑ ...*the bipolar world of the Cold War years.* **2** ADJ **Bipolar** means relating to bipolar disorder. ❑ *She is receiving treatment for a bipolar condition.*

bi|po|lar dis|or|der (bipolar disorders) N-VAR **Bipolar disorder** is a mental illness in which a person's state of mind changes between extreme happiness and extreme depression.

birch /bɜrtʃ/ (birches) N-VAR A **birch** is a type of tall tree with thin branches.

bird ✦✦◇ /bɜrd/ (birds) **1** N-COUNT A **bird** is a creature with feathers and wings. Female birds lay eggs. Most birds can fly. **2** → see also **early bird** **3** PHRASE If you refer to two people as **birds of a feather**, you mean that they have the same interests or are very similar. ❑ *We're birds of a feather, you and me, Mr. Plimpton.* **4** PHRASE **A bird in the hand** is something that you already have and do not want to risk losing by trying to get something else. ❑ *Another temporary discount may not be what you want, but at least it is a bird in the hand.* **5** PHRASE If you say that a **little bird** told you about something, you mean that someone has told you about it, but you do not want to say who it was. ❑ *Incidentally, a little bird tells me that your birthday's coming up.* **6** PHRASE If you say that doing something will **kill two birds with one stone**, you mean that it will enable you to achieve two things that you want to achieve, rather than just one. ❑ *We can talk about Union Hill while I get this business over with. Kill two birds with one stone, so to speak.* **7** → See also color supplement

bird|cage /bɜrdkeɪdʒ/ (birdcages) also **bird cage** N-COUNT A **birdcage** is a cage in which birds are kept.

bird feed|er (bird feeders) also **birdfeeder** N-COUNT A **bird feeder** is an object that you fill with seeds or nuts and hang up outside in order attract birds.

bird flu N-UNCOUNT **Bird flu** is a virus that can be transmitted from chickens, ducks, and other birds to people.

birdie /bɜrdi/ (birdies, birdying, birdied) **1** N-COUNT In golf, if you get a **birdie**, you get the golf ball into a hole in one stroke fewer than the number of strokes which has been set as the standard for a good player. **2** V-T If a golfer **birdies** a hole, he or she gets a birdie at that hole. ❑ *He birdied five of the first seven holes.*

bird|life /bɜrdlaɪf/ also **bird life** N-UNCOUNT The **birdlife** in a place is all the birds that live there.

bird|like /bɜrdlaɪk/ also **bird-like** ADJ If someone has a **birdlike** manner, they move or look like a bird. ❑ ...*the birdlike way she darted about.*

bird of para|dise (birds of paradise) N-COUNT A **bird of paradise** is a songbird that is found mainly in New Guinea. The male birds have very brightly colored feathers.

bird of pas|sage (birds of passage) N-COUNT If you refer to someone as a **bird of passage**, you mean that they are staying in a place for a short time before going to another place. ❑ *Most of these emigrants were birds of passage who returned to Spain after a relatively short stay.*

bird of prey (birds of prey) N-COUNT A **bird of prey** is a bird such as an eagle or a hawk that kills and eats other birds and animals.

bird|seed /bɜrdsid/ N-UNCOUNT **Birdseed** is seeds that you give to birds as food. ❑ *She bought a good supply of birdseed for the winter.*

bird's eye view (bird's eye views) N-COUNT [usu sing] You say that you have a **bird's eye view** of a place when you are looking down at it from a great height, so that you can see a long way but everything looks very small.

bird|song /bɜrdsɒŋ/ also **bird song** N-UNCOUNT [also N in pl] **Birdsong** is the sound of a bird or birds calling in a way which sounds musical. ❑ *The air is filled with birdsong.*

bird ta|ble (bird tables) N-COUNT A **bird table** is a small wooden platform on a pole which some people put in their garden in order to put food for the birds on it. [BRIT]

bird-watcher (bird-watchers) also **birdwatcher** N-COUNT A **bird-watcher** is a person whose hobby is watching and studying wild birds in their natural surroundings.

bird-watching also **birdwatching** N-UNCOUNT **Bird-watching** is the activity of watching and studying wild birds in their natural surroundings.

Biro /baɪroʊ/ (Biros) N-COUNT A **Biro** is the same as a **ballpoint**. [BRIT, TRADEMARK]

birth /bɜrθ/ (births) **1** N-VAR When a baby is born, you refer to this event as his or her **birth**. ❑ *It was the birth of his grandchildren that gave him greatest pleasure.* ❑ *She weighed 5lb 7oz at birth.* **2** N-UNCOUNT You can refer to the beginning or origin of something as its **birth**. ❑ *...the birth of popular democracy.* **3** N-UNCOUNT Some people talk about a person's **birth** when they are referring to the social position of the person's family. ❑ *...men of low birth.* **4** → see also **date of birth** **5** PHRASE If, for example, you are French **by birth**, you are French because your parents are French, or because you were born in France. ❑ *Sadrudin was an Iranian by birth.* **6** PHRASE When a woman **gives birth**, she produces a baby from her body. ❑ *She's just given birth to a baby girl.* **7** PHRASE To **give birth to** something such as an idea means to cause it to start to exist. ❑ *In 1980, strikes at the Lenin shipyards gave birth to the Solidarity trade union.* **8** PHRASE The country, town, or village **of** your **birth** is the place where you were born. ❑ *He left the town of his birth five years later for Australia.*

VOCABULARY IN CONTEXT

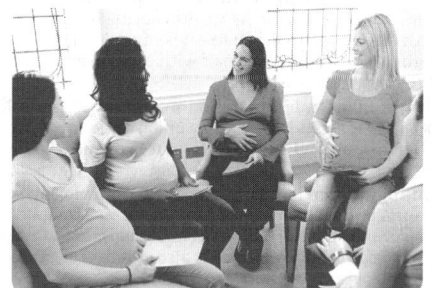

Birth

Most women don't realize they're **pregnant** until a few weeks into their first trimester. Some women will experience **morning sickness**, but around 30% of lucky women don't. Sadly, up to one third of pregnancies end in **miscarriage** at this early stage. In some cases, no **embryo** develops at all, and some women may never even realize they were pregnant. As the **pregnancy** progresses, the **fetus** will have developed limbs, eyes, and organs by the time the **expectant mother** goes for her first **ultrasound** at around 8–12 weeks. This scan is when she will learn her **due date**, |but babies have a habit of being born off-schedule, and they can be either **premature** or **overdue**. Usually, if a woman is two weeks overdue, she will be **induced** by her **midwife** or **obstetrician**. If delivery is planned via **Cesarean**, the mother will not experience **labor** – unless the baby decides to make an early appearance!

birth cer|tifi|cate (birth certificates) N-COUNT Your **birth certificate** is an official document that gives details of your birth, such as the date and place of your birth, and the names of your parents.

birth con|trol N-UNCOUNT **Birth control** means planning whether to have children, and using contraception to prevent having them when they are not wanted. ❑ *Today's methods of birth control make it possible for a couple to choose whether or not to have a child.*

birth|date /bɜrθdeɪt/ (birthdates) N-COUNT Your **birthdate** is the same as your **date of birth**.

birth|day /bɜrθdeɪ, -di/ (birthdays) N-COUNT Your **birthday** is the anniversary of the date on which you were born. ❑ *On his birthday she sent him presents.*

birth|day suit (birthday suits) N-COUNT [poss N] If you are in your **birthday suit**, you are not wearing any clothes. [INFORMAL, HUMOROUS or OLD-FASHIONED]

birth|ing /bɜrθɪŋ/ ADJ [ADJ n] **Birthing** means relating to or used during the process of giving birth. ❑ *The hospital has pioneered the use of birthing pools.*

birth|mark /bɜrθmɑrk/ (birthmarks) N-COUNT A **birthmark** is a mark on someone's skin that has been there since they were born.

birth|place /bɜrθpleɪs/ (birthplaces) **1** N-COUNT Your **birthplace** is the place where you were born. [WRITTEN] ❑ *...Bob Marley's birthplace in the village of Nine Mile.* **2** N-COUNT The **birthplace** of something is the place where it began. ❑ *...Athens, the birthplace of the ancient Olympics.*

birth rate (birth rates) also **birth-rate** N-COUNT The **birth rate** in a place is the number of babies born there for every 1000 people during a particular period of time. ❑ *America's birth rate fell to a record low last year.*

birth|right /bɜrθraɪt/ (birthrights) N-COUNT [usu sing] Something that is your **birthright** is something that you feel you have a basic right to have, simply because you are a human being. ❑ *Freedom is the natural birthright of every human.*

bis|cuit /bɪskɪt/ (biscuits) **1** N-COUNT A **biscuit** is a small round dry cake that is made with baking powder, baking soda, or yeast. [AM] **2** N-COUNT A **biscuit** is a small flat cake that is crisp and usually sweet. [BRIT]

> in AM, use **cookie**

3 PHRASE **Take the biscuit** means the same as **take the cake**. [BRIT]

bi|sect /baɪsɛkt/ (bisects, bisecting, bisected) V-T If something long and thin **bisects** an area or line, it divides the area or line in half. ❑ *The main street bisects the town from end to end.*

bi|sex|ual /baɪsɛkʃuəl/ (bisexuals) ADJ Someone who is **bisexual** is sexually attracted to both men and women. • N-COUNT **Bisexual** is also a noun. ❑ *He was an active bisexual.*

bish|op /bɪʃəp/ (bishops) **1** N-COUNT; N-TITLE; N-VOC A **bishop** is a clergyman of high rank in the Roman Catholic, Anglican, and Orthodox churches. **2** N-COUNT In chess a **bishop** is a piece that can be moved diagonally across the board on squares that are the same color.

bish|op|ric /bɪʃəprɪk/ (bishoprics) **1** N-COUNT A **bishopric** is the area for which a bishop is responsible. **2** N-COUNT A **bishopric** is the rank or office of being a bishop.

bi|son /baɪsən/ (bison)

> Bison is both the singular and plural form.

N-COUNT A **bison** is a large hairy animal with a large head that is a member of the cattle family. Bison used to be very common in North America and Europe. [mainly BRIT]

> in AM, usually use **buffalo**

bis|tro /bistroʊ/ (bistros) N-COUNT A **bistro** is a small, informal restaurant or a bar where food is served.

bit /bɪt/ (bits) **1** QUANT [QUANT of n-uncount] A **bit** of something is a small amount of it. ❑ *All it required was a bit of work.* **2** PHRASE A **bit** means to a small extent or degree. It is sometimes used to make a statement less extreme. [VAGUENESS] ❑ *This girl was a bit strange.* ❑ *I think people feel a bit more confident.* **3** PHRASE You can use **a bit of** to make a statement less forceful. For example, the statement 'It's a bit of a nuisance' is less forceful than 'It's a nuisance.' [VAGUENESS] ❑ *It's all a bit of a mess.* ❑ *Students have always been portrayed as a bit of a joke.* **4** PHRASE **Quite a bit** means quite a lot. ❑ *They're worth quite a bit of money.* ❑ *Things have changed quite a bit.* **5** PHRASE You use **a bit** before 'more' or 'less' to mean a small amount more or a small amount less. ❑ *I still think I have a bit more to offer.* ❑ *Maybe we'll hear a little bit less noise.* **6** PHRASE If you do something **a bit** or do something **for a bit**, you do it for a short time. ❑ *Let's wait a bit.* ❑ *I hope there will be time to talk a bit—or at least ask you about one or two things this evening.* **7** N-COUNT A **bit** of something is a small part or section of it. ❑ *Only a bit of the barley remained.* ❑ *Now comes the really important bit.* **8** N-COUNT A **bit** of something is a small piece of it. ❑ *Only a bit of string looped round a nail in the doorpost held it shut.*

9 N-COUNT You can use **bit** to refer to a particular item or to one of a group or set of things. For example, a **bit** of information is an item of information. ❑ *There was one bit of vital evidence which helped win the case.* **10** N-COUNT In computing, a **bit** is the smallest unit of information that is held in a computer's memory. It is either 1 or 0. Several bits form a byte. **11** N-COUNT A **bit** is 12½ cents; mainly used in expressions such as two **bits**, which means 25 cents, or **four bits**, which means 50 cents. [AM, INFORMAL or OLD-FASHIONED] ❑ *They weren't worth four bits.* **12** **Bit** is the past tense of **bite**. **13** PHRASE If something happens **bit by bit**, it happens in stages. ❑ *Bit by bit I began to understand what they were trying to do.* **14** PHRASE If you **do your bit**, you do something that, to a small or limited extent, helps to achieve something. [BRIT]

in AM, use **do your part**

15 PHRASE You say that one thing is **every bit as** good, interesting, or important as another to emphasize that the first thing is just as good, interesting, or important as the second. [EMPHASIS] ❑ *My dinner jacket is every bit as good as his.* **16** PHRASE If you say that something is **a bit much**, you are annoyed because you think someone has behaved in an unreasonable way. [INFORMAL, FEELINGS] ❑ *Her stage outfit of hot pants, over-the-knee boots and a tube top was a bit much.* **17** PHRASE You use **not a bit** when you want to make a strong negative statement. [EMPHASIS] ❑ *I'm really not a bit surprised.* **18** PHRASE You can use **bits and pieces** to refer to a collection of different things. [INFORMAL] ❑ *The drawers are full of bits and pieces of armor.*

bitch /bɪtʃ/ (**bitches, bitching, bitched**) **1** N-COUNT If someone calls a woman a **bitch**, they are saying in a very rude way that they think her behavior is unpleasant. [OFFENSIVE, VULGAR, DISAPPROVAL] **2** → see also **son of a bitch 3** V-I [oft cont] If you say that someone **is bitching** about something, you mean that you disapprove of the fact that they are complaining about it in an unpleasant way. [INFORMAL, DISAPPROVAL] ❑ *They're forever bitching about everybody else.* **4** N-COUNT A **bitch** is a female dog.

bitchy /bɪtʃi/ (**bitchier, bitchiest**) ADJ If someone is being **bitchy** or is making **bitchy** remarks, they are saying unkind things about someone. [INFORMAL, DISAPPROVAL] ❑ *I'm sorry. I know I was bitchy on the phone.* ● **bitchi|ness** N-UNCOUNT ❑ *There's a lot of bitchiness.*

bit|coin /bɪtkɔɪn/ (**bitcoins**) also **Bitcoin** N-UNCOUNT **Bitcoin** is a digital currency used as a means of payment on the internet. ❑ *Is bitcoin the gold standard of online currency?* ● N-COUNT A **bitcoin** is a unit of this currency. ❑ *Stores in some parts of Berlin now take payments in bitcoins as well as euros.*

bite ◆◆◇ /baɪt/ (**bites, biting, bit, bitten**) **1** V-T/V-I If you **bite** something, you use your teeth to cut into it, for example, in order to eat it or break it. If an animal or person **bites** you, they use their teeth to hurt or injure you. ❑ *Both sisters bit their nails as children.* ❑ *He bit into his sandwich.* ❑ *Every year in this country more than 50,000 children are bitten by dogs.* **2** N-COUNT A **bite** of something, especially food, is the action of biting it. ❑ *He took another bite of apple.* **3** N-COUNT A **bite** of food is the amount of food you take into your mouth when you bite it. ❑ *Look forward to eating the food and enjoy every bite.* **4** N-SING If you have **a bite** to eat, you have a small meal or a snack. [INFORMAL] ❑ *It was time to go home for a little rest and a bite to eat.* **5** V-T/V-I If a snake or a small insect **bites** you, or if it **bites**, it makes a mark or hole in your skin, and often causes the surrounding area of your skin to become painful or itchy. ❑ *When an infected mosquito bites a human, spores are injected into the blood.* **6** N-COUNT A **bite** is an injury or a mark on your body where an animal, snake, or small insect has bitten you. ❑ *Any dog bite, no matter how small, needs immediate medical attention.* **7** V-I When an action or policy begins to **bite**, it begins to have a serious or harmful effect. ❑ *As the sanctions begin to bite there will be more political difficulties ahead.* **8** V-I If an object **bites** into a surface, it presses hard against it or cuts into it. ❑ *There may even be some wire or nylon biting into the flesh.* **9** N-UNCOUNT If you say that a food or drink has **bite**, you like it because it has a strong or sharp taste. ❑ *The olive salad has to have bite and tang.* **10** V-I If a fish **bites** when you are fishing, it takes the hook or bait at the end of your fishing line in its mouth. ❑ *After half an hour, the fish stopped biting and we moved on.* ● N-COUNT **Bite** is also a noun. ❑ *If I don't get a bite in a few minutes I lift the rod and twitch the bait.* **11** PHRASE If someone **bites the hand that feeds** them, they behave badly or in an ungrateful way toward someone who they depend on. ❑ *She may be cynical about the film industry, but ultimately she has no intention of biting the hand that feeds her.* **12** PHRASE If you **bite** your **lip** or your **tongue**, you stop yourself from saying something that you want to say, because it would be the wrong thing to say in the circumstances. ❑ *I must learn to bite my lip.* **13** **to bite the bullet** → see **bullet** **14** **to bite the dust** → see **dust**

> **SYNONYMS**
>
> **bite**
> VERB **1**
> **nibble:** *He started to nibble his biscuit.*
> **gnaw:** *Woodlice attack living plants and gnaw at the stems.*
> **chew:** *Be certain to eat slowly and chew your food extremely well.*
> **crunch:** *Richard crunched into the apple.*

> **COLLOCATIONS**
>
> **bite**
> NOUN **6**
> noun + **bite**: flea, insect, mosquito, spider, tick; dog, shark, snake
> adjective + **bite**: fatal

bite-sized also **bite-size** **1** ADJ [usu ADJ n] **Bite-sized** pieces of food are small enough to fit easily in your mouth. ❑ *...bite-sized pieces of cheese.* **2** ADJ [usu ADJ n] If you describe something as **bite-sized**, you like it because it is small enough to be considered or dealt with easily. [APPROVAL] ❑ *...bite-size newspaper items.*

bit|ing /baɪtɪŋ/ **1** ADJ **Biting** wind or cold is extremely cold. ❑ *...a raw, biting northerly wind.* **2** ADJ **Biting** criticism or wit is very harsh or unkind, and is often caused by such feelings as anger or dislike. ❑ *...the author's biting satire on the church.*

bit|map /bɪtmæp/ (**bitmaps, bitmapping, bitmapped**) N-COUNT A **bitmap** is a type of graphics file on a computer. [COMPUTING] ❑ *...bitmap graphics for representing complex images such as photographs.* ● V-T **Bitmap** is also a verb. ❑ *Bitmapped maps require huge storage space.*

bit part (**bit parts**) also **bit-part** N-COUNT A **bit part** is a small and unimportant role for an actor in a film or play.

bit|ten /bɪt³n/ **Bitten** is the past participle of **bite**.

bit|ter ◆◇◇ /bɪtər/ (**bitterest**) **1** ADJ In a **bitter** argument or conflict, people argue very angrily or fight very fiercely. ❑ *...the scene of bitter fighting during the Second World War.* ❑ *...a bitter attack on the government's failure to support manufacturing.* ● **bit|ter|ly** ADV ❑ *Any such thing would be bitterly opposed by most of the world's democracies.* ● **bit|ter|ness** N-UNCOUNT ❑ *The rift within the organization reflects the growing bitterness of the dispute.* **2** ADJ If someone is **bitter** after a disappointing experience or after being treated unfairly, they continue to feel angry about it. ❑ *She is said to be very bitter about the way she was fired.* ● **bit|ter|ly** ADV ❑ *"And he sure didn't help us," Grant said bitterly.* ● **bit|ter|ness** N-UNCOUNT ❑ *I still feel bitterness and anger towards the person who knocked me down.* **3** ADJ A **bitter** taste is sharp, not sweet, and often slightly unpleasant. ❑ *The leaves taste rather bitter.* **4** ADJ A **bitter** experience makes you feel very disappointed. You can also use **bitter** to emphasize feelings of disappointment. ❑ *The decision was a bitter blow from which he never quite recovered.* ❑ *A great deal of bitter experience had taught him how to lose gracefully.* ● **bit|ter|ly** ADV ❑ *I was bitterly disappointed to have lost yet another race so near the finish.* **5** ADJ **Bitter** weather, or a **bitter** wind, is extremely cold. ❑ *Outside, a bitter east wind was accompanied by flurries of snow.* ● **bit|ter|ly** ADV ❑ *It's been bitterly cold here in Moscow.* **6** **a bitter pill** → see **pill**

bit|ter|ly /bɪtərli/ **1** ADV [ADV adj] You use **bitterly** when you are describing an attitude which involves strong, unpleasant emotions such as anger or dislike. ❑ *We are bitterly upset at what has happened.* **2** → see also **bitter**

bitter|sweet /bɪtərswiːt/ also **bitter-sweet** **1** ADJ If you describe an experience as **bittersweet**, you mean that it has some happy aspects and some sad ones. ❑ *...bittersweet memories of his first appearance for the team.* **2** ADJ A **bittersweet** taste seems bitter and sweet at the same time. ❑ *...a wine with a bitter-sweet flavor.*

bit|ty /bɪti/ (bittier, bittiest) ADJ [ADJ n] If you describe someone or something as a little **bitty** person or thing, you are emphasizing that they are very small. [AM, INFORMAL, EMPHASIS] ❑ *She's just a little bitty wisp of a girl.*

bi|tu|men /bɪtjʊmən/ N-UNCOUNT **Bitumen** is a black sticky substance which is obtained from tar or oil and is used in making roads.

bivou|ac /bɪvuæk/ (bivouacs, bivouacking, bivouacked) **1** N-COUNT A **bivouac** is a temporary camp made by soldiers or mountain climbers. **2** V-I If you **bivouac** in a particular place, you stop and stay in a bivouac there. ❑ *We bivouacked on the outskirts of the city.*

bi|week|ly /baɪwiːkli/ ADJ [ADJ n] A **biweekly** event or publication happens or appears once every two weeks. ❑ *He used to see them at the biweekly meetings.* ❑ *...Beverage Digest, the industry's biweekly newsletter.* • ADV [ADV with v] **Biweekly** is also an adverb. [AM] ❑ *The group meets on a regular basis, usually weekly or biweekly.*

in BRIT, use **fortnightly**

biz /bɪz/ **1** N-SING [oft n N] **Biz** is sometimes used to refer to the entertainment business, especially pop music or films. [INFORMAL, JOURNALISM] ❑ *...a girl in the music biz.* **2** → see also **showbiz**

bi|zarre /bɪzɑːr/ ADJ Something that is **bizarre** is very odd and strange. ❑ *The game was also notable for the bizarre behavior of the team's manager.* • **bi|zarre|ly** ADV ❑ *She dressed bizarrely.*

blab /blæb/ (blabs, blabbing, blabbed) V-T/V-I If someone **blabs** about something secret, they tell people about it. [INFORMAL] ❑ *Her mistake was to blab about their affair.* ❑ *Will you promise not to blab to Mom and Dad?* ❑ *She'll blab it all over the school.*

black ◆◆◆ /blæk/ (blacker, blackest, blacks, blacking, blacked) **1** COLOR Something that is **black** is of the darkest color that there is, the color of the sky at night when there is no light at all. ❑ *She was wearing a black coat with a white collar.* ❑ *He had thick black hair.* **2** ADJ A **Black** person belongs to a race of people with dark skins, especially a race originally from Africa. ❑ *He worked for the rights of Black people.* ❑ *Sherry is Black, tall, slender and soft-spoken.* **3** N-COUNT Black people are sometimes referred to as **Blacks**. This use could cause offense, and it is better to use 'a Black person' or 'Black people.' ❑ *There are about thirty-one million Blacks in the U.S.* **4** ADJ [ADJ n, v n ADJ] **Black** coffee or tea has no milk or cream added to it. ❑ *A cup of black tea or black coffee contains no calories.* **5** ADJ If you describe a situation as **black**, you are emphasizing that it is very bad indeed. [EMPHASIS] ❑ *It was, he said later, one of the blackest days of his political career.* **6** ADJ If someone is in a **black** mood, they feel very miserable and depressed. ❑ *In late 1975, she fell into a black depression.* **7** PHRASE If a person or an organization is **in the black**, they do not owe anyone any money. ❑ *Remington's operations in Japan are now in the black.*

▶ **black out 1** PHRASAL VERB If you **black out**, you lose consciousness for a short time. ❑ *I could feel blood draining from my face. I wondered whether I was about to black out.* **2** PHRASAL VERB If a place **is blacked out**, it is in darkness, usually because it has no electricity supply. ❑ *Large parts of Lima were blacked out after electricity pylons were blown up.* **3** PHRASAL VERB If a film or a piece of writing **is blacked out**, it is prevented from being broadcast or published, usually because it contains information which is secret or offensive. ❑ *TV pictures of the demonstration were blacked out.* **4** PHRASAL VERB If you **black out** a piece of writing, you color over it in black so that it cannot be seen. ❑ *U.S. government specialists went through each page, blacking out any information a foreign intelligence expert could use.* **5** PHRASAL VERB If you **black out** the memory of something, you try not to remember it because it upsets you. ❑ *I tried not to think about it. I blocked it out. It was the easiest way of coping.* **6** → see also **blackout**

black and white also **black-and-white 1** COLOR In a **black and white** photograph or film, everything is shown in black, white, and gray. ❑ *...old black and white film footage.* ❑ *...a black-and-white photo of the two of us together.* **2** ADJ A **black and white** television set shows only black and white pictures. **3** ADJ A **black and white** issue or situation is one that involves issues that seem simple and therefore easy to make decisions about. ❑ *But this isn't a simple black and white affair, Marianne.* **4** PHRASE You say that something is **in black and white** when it has been written or printed, and not just said. ❑ *He'd seen the proof in black and white.*

black|ball /blækbɔːl/ (blackballs, blackballing, blackballed) V-T If the members of a club **blackball** someone, they vote against that person being allowed to join their club. ❑ *Members can blackball candidates in secret ballots.*

black belt (black belts) **1** N-COUNT A **black belt** is worn by someone who has reached a very high standard in a sport such as judo or karate. ❑ *He holds a black belt in karate.* **2** N-COUNT You can refer to someone who has a black belt in a sport such as judo or karate as a **black belt**. ❑ *Murray is a judo black belt.*

black|berry /blækbɛri/ (blackberries) **1** N-COUNT A **blackberry** is a small, soft black or dark purple fruit. **2** N-COUNT A **Blackberry** is a portable, wireless computing device that allows you to send and receive email. [COMPUTING, TRADEMARK]

black|bird /blækbɜːrd/ (blackbirds) **1** N-COUNT A **blackbird** is a common European bird. The male has black feathers and a yellow beak, and the female has brown feathers. **2** N-COUNT A **blackbird** is a common North American bird. The male has black feathers and often a red patch on its wings.

black|board /blækbɔːrd/ (blackboards) N-COUNT A **blackboard** is a dark-colored board that you can write on with chalk. Blackboards are often used by teachers in the classroom.

in AM, also use **chalkboard**

black box (black boxes) **1** N-COUNT A **black box** is an electronic device in an aircraft that records information about its flights. Black boxes are often used to provide evidence about accidents. **2** N-COUNT [usu sing] You can refer to a system or device as a **black box** when you know that it produces a particular result but you have no understanding of how it works. ❑ *They were part of the black box associated with high-flyer management development.*

black|en /blækən/ (blackens, blackening, blackened) **1** V-T/V-I To **blacken** something means to make it black or very dark in color. Something that **blackens** becomes black or very dark in color. ❑ *They spent hours blackening the grate and polishing the fire-irons.* **2** V-T If someone **blackens** your character, they make other people believe that you are a bad person. ❑ *They're trying to blacken our name.*

black eye (black eyes) N-COUNT If someone has a **black eye**, they have a dark-colored bruise around their eye. ❑ *He punched her in the face, giving her a black eye.*

black-eyed pea (black-eyed peas) N-COUNT [usu pl] **Black-eyed peas** are beige seeds with black marks that are eaten as a vegetable. They are from a plant called the cowpea. [AM]

black|head /blækhɛd/ (blackheads) N-COUNT [usu pl] **Blackheads** are small, dark spots on someone's skin caused by blocked pores.

black hole (black holes) **1** N-COUNT **Black holes** are areas in space where gravity is so strong that nothing, not even light, can escape from them. Black holes are thought to be formed by collapsed stars. **2** → See feature box at **space**

black ice N-UNCOUNT **Black ice** is a thin, transparent layer of ice on a road or path that is very difficult to see.

black|ish /blækɪʃ/ COLOR Something that is **blackish** is very dark in color. ❑ *The water was blackish.* ❑ *Katy has long blackish hair.*

black|jack /blækdʒæk/ (blackjacks) **1** N-UNCOUNT **Blackjack** is a card game in which players try to obtain a combination of cards worth 21 points. ❑ *Vicky has lost five hundred dollars playing blackjack.* **2** N-COUNT A **blackjack** is a short, thick stick that is used as a weapon. [AM, INFORMAL] ❑ *Police confiscated guns, knives and blackjacks.*

in BRIT, use **truncheon**

black|list /blæklɪst/ (blacklists, blacklisting, blacklisted) **1** N-COUNT If someone is on a **blacklist**, they are seen by a government or other organization as being one of a number of people who cannot be trusted or who have done something wrong. ❑ *A government official disclosed that they were on a secret blacklist.* **2** V-T [usu passive] If someone is **blacklisted** by a

blackmail

government or organization, they are put on a blacklist. ❏ *He has been blacklisted since being convicted of possessing marijuana in 1969.*

black|mail /blækmeɪl/ (blackmails, blackmailing, blackmailed) **1** N-UNCOUNT **Blackmail** is the action of threatening to reveal a secret about someone, unless they do something you tell them to do, such as giving you money. ❏ *It looks like the pictures were being used for blackmail.* **2** N-UNCOUNT If you describe an action as emotional or moral **blackmail**, you disapprove of it because someone is using a person's emotions or moral values to persuade them to do something against their will. [DISAPPROVAL] ❏ *The tactics employed can range from overt bullying to subtle emotional blackmail.* **3** V-T If one person **blackmails** another person, they use blackmail against them. ❏ *He told her their affair would have to stop, because Jack Smith was blackmailing him.* ❏ *The government insisted that it would not be blackmailed by violence.* • **black|mail|er** (blackmailers) N-COUNT ❏ *The nasty thing about a blackmailer is that his starting point is usually the truth.*

black mark (black marks) N-COUNT A **black mark** against someone is something bad that they have done or a bad quality that they have that affects the way people think about them. ❏ *There was one black mark against him.*

black mar|ket (black markets) N-COUNT If something is bought or sold on the **black market**, it is bought or sold illegally. ❏ *There is a plentiful supply of arms on the black market.*

black mar|ket|eer (black marketeers) N-COUNT A **black marketeer** is someone who sells goods on the black market.

black|ness /blæknɪs/ N-UNCOUNT **Blackness** is the state of being very dark. [LITERARY] ❏ *The twilight had turned to a deep blackness.*

black|out /blækaʊt/ (blackouts) also **black-out 1** N-COUNT A **blackout** is a period of time during a war in which towns and buildings are made dark so that they cannot be seen by enemy planes. ❏ *She had driven ambulances during the blackouts of the Second World War.* ❏ *...blackout curtains.* **2** N-COUNT If a **blackout** is imposed on a particular piece of news, journalists are prevented from broadcasting or publishing it. ❏ *...a media blackout imposed by the Imperial Palace.* **3** N-COUNT If there is a power **blackout**, the electricity supply to a place is temporarily cut off. ❏ *There was an electricity black-out in a large area in the north of the country.* **4** N-COUNT If you have a **blackout**, you temporarily lose consciousness. ❏ *I suffered a black-out which lasted for several minutes.* **5** → See feature box at **electricity**

black pep|per N-UNCOUNT **Black pepper** is pepper which is dark in color and has been made from the dried berries of the pepper plant, including their black outer cases.

black pud|ding [mainly BRIT] → see **blood pudding**

black sheep (black sheep) N-COUNT [usu sing, oft the N of n] If you describe someone as the **black sheep** of their family or of a group that they are a member of, you mean that they are considered bad or worthless by other people in that family or group. [DISAPPROVAL]

black|smith /blæksmɪθ/ (blacksmiths) N-COUNT A **blacksmith** is a person whose job is making things by hand out of metal that has been heated to a high temperature.

black tie also **black-tie 1** ADJ [usu ADJ n] A **black tie** event is a formal social event such as a party at which people wear formal clothes called evening dress. ❏ *...a black-tie dinner for former students.* **2** N-UNCOUNT If someone is dressed in **black tie**, they are wearing formal evening dress, which includes a dinner jacket or tuxedo and a bow tie. ❏ *Most of the guests will be wearing black tie.*

black|top /blæktɒp/ N-UNCOUNT **Blacktop** is a hard black substance which is used as a surface for roads. [AM] ❏ *...waves of heat rising from the blacktop.*

in BRIT, use **tarmac**

blad|der /blædər/ (bladders) **1** N-COUNT Your **bladder** is the part of your body where urine is stored until it leaves your body. ❏ *...an opportunity to empty a full bladder.* **2** → see also **gall bladder**

blade /bleɪd/ (blades) **1** N-COUNT The **blade** of a knife, ax, or saw is the flat sharp part, which is used for cutting. ❏ *Many of them will have sharp blades.* **2** N-COUNT The **blades** of a propeller are the

blank

long, flat parts that turn around. **3** N-COUNT The **blade** of an oar is the thin flat part that you put into the water. **4** N-COUNT A **blade** of grass is a single piece of grass. ❏ *Brian began to tear blades of grass from between the bricks.* **5** → See also color supplement

blah /blɑː/ CONVENTION You use **blah, blah, blah** to refer to something that is said or written without giving the actual words, because you think that they are boring or unimportant. [INFORMAL] ❏ *...the different challenges of their career, their need to change, to evolve, blah blah blah.*

blame ✦✧ /bleɪm/ (blames, blaming, blamed) **1** V-T If you **blame** a person or thing for something bad, or if you **blame** something bad on somebody, you believe or say that they are responsible for it or that they caused it. ❏ *The commission is expected to blame the army for many of the atrocities.* ❏ *Ms. Carey appeared to blame her breakdown on EMI's punishing work schedule.* • N-UNCOUNT **Blame** is also a noun. ❏ *Nothing could relieve my terrible sense of blame.* **2** N-UNCOUNT The **blame** for something bad that has happened is the responsibility for causing it or letting it happen. ❏ *I'm not going to sit around and take the blame for a mistake he made.* **3** V-T [usu with brd-neg] If you say that you do not **blame** someone for doing something, you mean that you consider it was a reasonable thing to do in the circumstances. ❏ *I do not blame them for trying to make some money.* **4** PHRASE If someone is **to blame** for something bad that has happened, they are responsible for causing it. ❏ *If their forces were not involved, then who is to blame?* **5** PHRASE If you say that someone **has only** themselves **to blame** or **has no one but** themselves **to blame**, you mean that they are responsible for something bad that has happened to them and that you have no sympathy for them. ❏ *My life is ruined and I suppose I only have myself to blame.*

blame|less /bleɪmlɪs/ ADJ Someone who is **blameless** has not done anything wrong. ❏ *He feels he is blameless.* ❏ *The U.S. itself, of course, is not entirely blameless in trading matters.*

blanch /blæntʃ/ (blanches, blanching, blanched) **1** V-I If you **blanch**, you suddenly become very pale. ❏ *Simon's face blanched as he looked at Sharpe's blood-drenched uniform.* **2** V-I If you say that someone **blanches** at something, you mean that they find it unpleasant and do not want to be involved with it. ❏ *Everything he had said had been a mistake. He blanched at his miscalculations.*

blanc|mange /bləmɒndʒ/ (blancmanges) N-VAR **Blancmange** is a cold custard that is made from milk, sugar, cornstarch, and flavoring.

bland /blænd/ (blander, blandest) **1** ADJ If you describe someone or something as **bland**, you mean that they are rather dull and unexciting. ❏ *Serle has a blander personality than Howard.* ❏ *It sounds like a commercial: easy on the ear but bland and forgettable.* **2** ADJ Food which is **bland** has very little flavor. ❏ *It tasted bland and insipid, like warmed cardboard.*

blan|dish|ments /blændɪʃmənts/ N-PLURAL [oft with poss] **Blandishments** are pleasant things that someone says to another person in order to persuade them to do something. [FORMAL] ❏ *At first Lewis resisted their blandishments.*

bland|ly /blændli/ ADV [ADV with v] If you do something **blandly**, you do it in a calm and quiet way. ❏ *"It's not important," he said blandly.* ❏ *The nurse smiled blandly.*

blank /blæŋk/ (blanks) **1** ADJ Something that is **blank** has nothing on it. ❏ *We could put some of the pictures over on that blank wall over there.* ❏ *He tore a blank page from his notebook.* **2** N-COUNT A **blank** is a space which is left in a piece of writing or on a printed form for you to fill in particular information. ❏ *Put a word in each blank to complete the sentence.* **3** ADJ If you look **blank**, your face shows no feeling, understanding, or interest. ❏ *Abbot looked blank. "I don't quite follow, sir."* • **blank|ly** ADV [ADV with v] ❏ *She stared at him blankly.* **4** N-SING If your mind or memory is **a blank**, you cannot think of anything or remember anything. ❏ *I'm sorry, but my mind is a blank.* **5** N-COUNT **Blanks** are gun cartridges which contain explosive but do not contain a bullet, so that they cause no harm when the gun is fired. ❏ *...a starter pistol which only fires blanks.* **6** → see also **point-blank** **7** PHRASE If your mind **goes blank**, you are suddenly unable to think of anything appropriate to say, for example in reply to a question.

blank check (blank checks)

[in BRIT, use **blank cheque**]

1 N-COUNT If someone is given a **blank check**, they are given the authority to spend as much money as they need or want. ▫ *We are not prepared to write a blank check for companies that have run into trouble.* **2** N-COUNT If someone is given a **blank check**, they are given the authority to do what they think is best in a particular situation. ▫ *He has, in a sense, been given a blank check to negotiate the new South Africa.*

blan|ket /blˈæŋkɪt/ (blankets, blanketing, blanketed) **1** N-COUNT A **blanket** is a large rectangular piece of thick cloth, especially one that you put on a bed to keep you warm. **2** N-COUNT A **blanket** of something such as snow is a continuous layer of it which hides what is below or beyond it. ▫ *The mud disappeared under a blanket of snow.* **3** V-T If something such as snow **blankets** an area, it covers it. ▫ *More than a foot of snow blanketed parts of Michigan.* **4** ADJ [ADJ n] You use **blanket** to describe something when you want to emphasize that it affects or refers to every person or thing in a group, without any exceptions. [EMPHASIS] ▫ *There's already a blanket ban on foreign unskilled labor in Japan.*

blank verse N-UNCOUNT **Blank verse** is poetry that does not rhyme. In English literature it usually consists of lines with five stressed syllables.

blare /blˈɛər/ (blares, blaring, blared) V-I If something such as a siren or radio **blares**, it makes a loud, unpleasant noise. ▫ *The fire engines were just pulling up, sirens blaring.* ▫ *Music blared from the apartment behind me.* • N-SING **Blare** is also a noun. ▫ *...the blare of a radio through a thin wall.* ► PHRASAL VERB **Blare out** means the same as **blare**. ▫ *Music blares out from every cafe.*

blar|ney /blˈɑːrni/ N-UNCOUNT **Blarney** is things someone says that are flattering and amusing but probably untrue, and which you think they are only saying in order to please you or to persuade you to do something. [DISAPPROVAL]

bla|sé /blɑːzˈeɪ/ also **blase** ADJ [oft ADJ about n] If you describe someone as **blasé**, you mean that they are not easily impressed, excited, or worried by things, usually because they have seen or experienced them before. [DISAPPROVAL] ▫ *They are blasé about their driving skills.* ▫ *...his seemingly blasé attitude.*

blas|pheme /blæsfˈiːm/ (blasphemes, blaspheming, blasphemed) V-I If someone **blasphemes**, they say rude or disrespectful things about God or religion, or they use God's name as a swear word. ▫ *"Don't blaspheme," my mother said.* ▫ *The spiritual leader charged that the book blasphemed against Islam.* • **blas|phem|er** (blasphemers) N-COUNT ▫ *Such a figure is liable to be attacked as a blasphemer.*

blas|phe|mous /blˈæsfəməs/ ADJ You can describe someone who shows disrespect for God or a religion as **blasphemous**. You can also describe what they are saying or doing as **blasphemous**. ▫ *She was accused of being blasphemous.* ▫ *Critics attacked the film as blasphemous.*

blas|phe|my /blˈæsfəmi/ (blasphemies) N-VAR You can describe something that shows disrespect for God or a religion as **blasphemy**. ▫ *He has acted out every kind of blasphemy, including dressing up as the pope in Rome.*

blast ♦◇◇ /blˈæst/ (blasts, blasting, blasted) **1** N-COUNT A **blast** is a big explosion, especially one caused by a bomb. ▫ *250 people were killed in the blast.* **2** V-T If something **is blasted** into a particular place or state, an explosion causes it to be in that place or state. If a hole **is blasted** in something, it is created by an explosion. ▫ *There is a risk that toxic chemicals might be blasted into the atmosphere.* ▫ *The explosion which followed blasted out the wall of her apartment.* **3** V-T If workers **are blasting** rock, they are using explosives to make holes in it or destroy it, for example, so that a road or tunnel can be built. ▫ *Local workmen were blasting the rock face beside the track in order to make it wider.* **4** V-T To **blast** someone means to shoot them with a gun. [JOURNALISM] ▫ *A son blasted his father to death after a lifetime of bullying, a court was told yesterday.* • N-COUNT **Blast** is also a noun. ▫ *Anthony died from a shotgun blast to the face.* **5** V-T If someone **blasts** their way somewhere, they get there by shooting at people or causing an explosion. ▫ *The police were reported to have blasted their way into the house using explosives.* **6** V-T If something **blasts** water or air somewhere, it sends out a sudden, powerful stream of it. ▫ *Blasting cold air over it makes the water evaporate.*

• N-COUNT **Blast** is also a noun. ▫ *Blasts of cold air swept down from the mountains.* **7** V-T/V-I If you **blast** something such as a car horn, or if it **blasts**, it makes a sudden, loud sound. If something **blasts** music, or music **blasts**, the music is very loud. ▫ *...drivers who do not blast their horns.* • N-COUNT **Blast** is also a noun. ▫ *The buzzer suddenly responded in a long blast of sound.* **8** N-SING If you say that something was a **blast**, you mean that you enjoyed it very much. [INFORMAL] ▫ *He went sledding with his daughter. "It was a blast," he said later.* **9** PHRASE If something such as a radio or a heater is on **full blast**, or on **at full blast**, it is producing as much sound or power as it is able to. ▫ *In many of those homes the television is on full blast 24 hours a day.*
▶ **blast off** PHRASAL VERB When a space rocket **blasts off**, it leaves the ground at the start of its journey. ▫ *Columbia is set to blast off at 1:20 a.m. Eastern Time tomorrow.*

blast|ed /blˈæstɪd/ **1** ADJ [ADJ n] Some people use **blasted** to express anger or annoyance at something or someone. [INFORMAL, FEELINGS] **2** ADJ [usu ADJ n] A **blasted** landscape has very few plants or trees, and makes you feel sad or depressed when you look at it. [LITERARY]

blast fur|nace (blast furnaces) N-COUNT A **blast furnace** is a large structure in which iron ore is heated under pressure so that it melts and the pure iron metal separates out and can be collected.

blast|off /blˈæstɒf/ N-UNCOUNT **Blastoff** is the moment when a rocket leaves the ground and rises into the air to begin a journey into space. ▫ *The original planned launch was called off four minutes before blastoff.*

bla|tant /blˈeɪtənt/ ADJ You use **blatant** to describe something bad that is done in an open or very obvious way. [EMPHASIS] ▫ *Outsiders will continue to suffer the most blatant discrimination.* ▫ *...a blatant attempt to spread the blame for the fiasco.*

bla|tant|ly /blˈeɪtəntli/ ADV **Blatantly** is used to add emphasis when you are describing states or situations that you think are bad. [EMPHASIS] ▫ *It became blatantly obvious to me that the band wasn't going to last.* ▫ *For years, blatantly false assertions have gone unchallenged.*

blath|er /blˈæðər/ (blathers, blathering, blathered) V-I If someone **is blathering** on about something, they are talking for a long time about something that you consider boring or unimportant. [INFORMAL] ▫ *The old men blather on and on.* ▫ *Stop blathering.* ▫ *He kept on blathering about police incompetence.* • N-UNCOUNT **Blather** is also a noun. ▫ *Anyone knows that all this is blather.*

blaze /blˈeɪz/ (blazes, blazing, blazed) **1** V-I When a fire **blazes**, it burns strongly and brightly. ▫ *Three people died as wreckage blazed, and rescuers fought to release trapped drivers.* ▫ *The log fire was blazing merrily.* **2** N-COUNT A **blaze** is a large fire which is difficult to control and which destroys a lot of things. [JOURNALISM] ▫ *Some 4,000 firefighters are battling the blaze.* **3** V-I If something **blazes** with light or color, it is extremely bright. [LITERARY] ▫ *The gardens blazed with color.* • N-COUNT **Blaze** is also a noun. ▫ *I wanted the front garden to be a blaze of color.* **4** N-SING A **blaze of** publicity or attention is a great amount of it. ▫ *He was arrested in a blaze of publicity.* **5** V-I If guns **blaze**, or **blaze away**, they fire continuously, making a lot of noise. ▫ *Guns were blazing, flares going up and the sky was lit up all around.* **6 with all guns blazing** → see **gun** **7** → See feature box at **hot**

blaz|er /blˈeɪzər/ (blazers) N-COUNT A **blazer** is a kind of light jacket for men or women that is also often worn by members of a particular group.

blaz|ing /blˈeɪzɪŋ/ **1** ADJ [ADJ n] The **blazing** sun or **blazing hot** weather is very hot. ▫ *Quite a few people were eating outside in the blazing sun.* **2** → See feature box at **hot**

bldg. (bldgs.) Bldg. is a written abbreviation for **building**, and is used especially in the names of buildings. ▫ *...Old National Bank Bldg.*

[in BRIT, also use **bldg**]

bleach /blˈiːtʃ/ (bleaches, bleaching, bleached) **1** V-T If you **bleach** something, you use a chemical to make it white or pale in color. ▫ *These products don't bleach the hair.* ▫ *...bleached pine tables.* **2** V-T/V-I If the sun **bleaches** something, or something **bleaches**, its color gets paler until it is almost white. ❑ *The tree's roots are stripped and hung to season and bleach.* ❑ *He has hair which is naturally black but which has been bleached by the sun.* **3** N-MASS **Bleach** is a chemical that is used to make cloth white, or to clean things thoroughly and kill germs.

bleach|ers /blitʃərz/ N-PLURAL [usu the N] The **bleachers** are a part of an outdoor sports stadium, or the seats in that area, which are usually uncovered and are the least expensive place where people can sit. [AM]

bleak /blik/ (**bleaker, bleakest**) **1** ADJ If a situation is **bleak**, it is bad, and seems unlikely to improve. ❑ *The immediate outlook remains bleak.* • **bleak|ness** N-UNCOUNT ❑ *The continued bleakness of the American job market was blamed.* **2** ADJ If you describe a place as **bleak**, you mean that it looks cold, empty, and unattractive. ❑ *The island's pretty bleak.* **3** ADJ When the weather is **bleak**, it is cold, dull, and unpleasant. ❑ *The weather can be quite bleak on the coast.* **4** ADJ If someone looks or sounds **bleak**, they look or sound depressed, as if they have no hope or energy. ❑ *His face was bleak.* • **bleak|ly** ADV ❑ *"There is nothing left," she says bleakly.*

bleary /blɪəri/ ADJ If your eyes are **bleary**, they look dull or tired, as if you have not had enough sleep or have drunk too much alcohol. ❑ *I arrived bleary-eyed and rumpled.* ❑ *He stared at Leo with great bleary eyes.*

bleat /blit/ (**bleats, bleating, bleated**) **1** V-I When a sheep or goat **bleats**, it makes the sound that sheep and goats typically make. ❑ *From the slope below, the wild goats bleated faintly.* ❑ *...a small flock of bleating ewes and lambs.* • N-COUNT **Bleat** is also a noun. ❑ *...the faint bleat of a distressed animal.* **2** V-I If you say that someone **bleats** about something, you mean that they complain about it in a way which makes them sound weak and irritating. [DISAPPROVAL] ❑ *They are always bleating about "unfair" foreign competition.* ❑ *Don't come bleating to me every time something goes wrong.*

bled /blɛd/ **Bled** is the past tense and past participle of **bleed**.

bleed /blid/ (**bleeds, bleeding, bled**) **1** V-I When you **bleed**, you lose blood from your body as a result of injury or illness. ❑ *His head had struck the sink and was bleeding.* ❑ *He was bleeding profusely.* • **bleed|ing** N-UNCOUNT ❑ *This results in internal bleeding.* **2** V-I If the color of one substance **bleeds** into the color of another substance that it is touching, it goes into the other thing so that its color changes in an undesirable way. ❑ *The coloring pigments from the skins are not allowed to bleed into the grape juice.* **3** V-T If someone is being **bled**, money or other resources are gradually being taken away from them. [DISAPPROVAL] ❑ *We have been gradually bled for twelve years.*

bleed|ing edge

The spelling **bleeding-edge** is used for meaning **2**.

1 N-SING If you are at the **bleeding edge** of a particular field of activity, you are involved in its most advanced or most exciting developments. ❑ *McNally has spent 17 years at the bleeding edge of computing.* **2** ADJ **Bleeding-edge** equipment or technology is the most advanced that there is in a particular field. ❑ *...an aviation facility with bleeding-edge electronics and communications systems.*

bleed|ing heart (**bleeding hearts**) also **bleeding-heart** N-COUNT [oft N n] If you describe someone as a **bleeding heart**, you are criticizing them for being sympathetic toward people who are poor and suffering, without doing anything practical to help. [DISAPPROVAL] ❑ *I'm not a bleeding heart liberal.*

bleep /blip/ (**bleeps, bleeping, bleeped**) **1** N-COUNT A **bleep** is a short, high-pitched sound, usually one of a series, that is made by an electrical device. [mainly BRIT] **2** V-I If something electronic **bleeps**, it makes a short, high-pitched sound. [mainly BRIT] ❑ *When we turned the boat about, the signal began to bleep again constantly.*

▶ **bleep out** PHRASAL VERB In a television or radio program, when someone **bleeps out** an offensive word, they use an electronic device to make the sound of a bleep so that people cannot hear the word. ❑ *Quick-thinking TV bosses bleeped out the abuse.* ❑ *I hope Channel 4 doesn't bleep it out.*

blem|ish /blɛmɪʃ/ (**blemishes, blemishing, blemished**) **1** N-COUNT A **blemish** is a small mark on something that spoils its appearance. ❑ *Every piece is closely scrutinized, and if there is the slightest blemish on it, it is rejected.* **2** N-COUNT A **blemish** on something is a small fault in it. ❑ *This is the one blemish on an otherwise resounding success.* **3** V-T If something

blemishes someone's character or reputation, it spoils it or makes it seem less good than it was in the past. ❑ *He wasn't about to blemish that pristine record.*

blem|ished /blɛmɪʃt/ ADJ [usu ADJ n] You use **blemished** to describe something such as someone's skin or a piece of fruit when its appearance is spoiled by small marks. ❑ *...a skin tonic for oily, blemished complexions.*

blend /blɛnd/ (**blends, blending, blended**) **1** V-RECIP If you **blend** substances together or if they **blend**, you mix them together so that they become one substance. ❑ *Blend the butter with the sugar and beat until light and creamy.* ❑ *Blend the ingredients until you have a smooth cream.* **2** N-COUNT A **blend** of things is a mixture or combination of them that is useful or pleasant. ❑ *The public areas offer a subtle blend of traditional charm with modern amenities.* ❑ *...a blend of wine and sparkling water.* **3** V-RECIP When colors, sounds, or styles **blend**, they come together or are combined in a pleasing way. ❑ *You could paint the walls and ceilings the same color so they blend together.* **4** V-T If you **blend** ideas, policies, or styles, you use them together in order to achieve something. ❑ *His vision is to blend Christianity with "the wisdom of all world religions."* **5** → See feature box at **cooking**

blend|ed learn|ing N-UNCOUNT **Blended learning** includes both classroom and online lessons. ❑ *...a blended learning MBA.*

blend|er /blɛndər/ (**blenders**) N-COUNT A **blender** is an electrical kitchen appliance used for mixing liquids and soft foods together or turning fruit or vegetables into liquid.

bless /blɛs/ (**blesses, blessing, blessed**) **1** V-T When someone such as a priest **blesses** people or things, he or she asks for God's favor and protection for them. ❑ *...asking for all present to bless this couple and their loving commitment to one another.* **2** CONVENTION **Bless** is used in expressions such as 'God bless' or 'bless you' to express affection, thanks, or good wishes. [INFORMAL, SPOKEN, FEELINGS] ❑ *"Bless you, Eva," he whispered.* **3** CONVENTION You can say '**bless you**' to someone who has just sneezed. [SPOKEN, FORMULAE] **4** → see also **blessed, blessing**

bless|ed

Pronounced /blɛst/ for meaning 1, and /blɛsɪd/ for meaning 2.

1 ADJ [v-link ADJ with n] If someone is **blessed with** a particular good quality or skill, they have that good quality or skill. ❑ *Both are blessed with an uncommon ability to fix things.* **2** ADJ [ADJ n] You use **blessed** to describe something that you think is wonderful, and that you are grateful for or relieved about. [APPROVAL] ❑ *The birth of a live healthy baby is a truly blessed event.* • **bless|ed|ly** ADV ❑ *...a wall still blessedly warm from the day's sun.* **3** → see also **bless**

bless|ing /blɛsɪŋ/ (**blessings**) **1** N-COUNT A **blessing** is something good that you are grateful for. ❑ *Rivers are a blessing for an agricultural country.* **2** N-COUNT [with poss] If something is done with someone's **blessing**, it is done with their approval and support. ❑ *With the blessing of the White House, a group of Democrats in Congress is meeting to find additional budget cuts.* **3** N-COUNT A **blessing** is a prayer asking God to look kindly upon the people who are present or the event that is taking place. ❑ *The Reverend Chris Long led the prayers and pronounced the blessing.* **4** → see also **bless**

blew /blu/ **Blew** is the past tense of **blow**.

blight /blaɪt/ (**blights, blighting, blighted**) **1** N-VAR You can refer to something as a **blight** when it causes great difficulties, and damages or spoils other things. ❑ *This discriminatory policy has really been a blight on America.* **2** V-T If something **blights** your life or your hopes, it damages and spoils them. If something **blights** an area, it spoils it and makes it unattractive. ❑ *An embarrassing blunder nearly blighted his career before it got off the ground.* ❑ *...thousands of families whose lives were blighted by unemployment.* **3** N-UNCOUNT **Blight** is a disease which makes plants dry up and die. ❑ *All you can do to prevent potato blight is keep an eye on your crops.*

blimp /blɪmp/ (**blimps**) N-COUNT A **blimp** is the same as an airship.

blind ♦◇◇ /blaɪnd/ (**blinds, blinding, blinded**) **1** ADJ Someone who is **blind** is unable to see because their eyes are damaged. ❑ *I started helping him run the business when he went blind.* • N-PLURAL **The blind** are people who are blind. This use could cause offense. ❑ *He was a teacher of the blind.* • **blind|ness** N-UNCOUNT

❏ *Early diagnosis and treatment can usually prevent blindness.* **2** V-T If something **blinds** you, it makes you unable to see, either for a short time or permanently. ❏ *The sun hit the windshield, momentarily blinding him.* **3** ADJ [v-link ADJ, usu ADJ with n] If you are **blind** with something such as tears or a bright light, you are unable to see for a short time because of the tears or light. ❏ *Her mother groped for the back of the chair, her eyes blind with tears.* • **blind|ly** ADV ❏ *Lettie groped blindly for the glass.* **4** ADJ [v-link ADJ to n] If you say that someone is **blind to** a fact or a situation, you mean that they ignore it or are unaware of it, although you think that they should take notice of it or be aware of it. [DISAPPROVAL] ❏ *David's good looks and impeccable manners had always made him blind to his faults.* • **blind|ness** N-UNCOUNT ❏ *...blindness in government policy to the very existence of the unemployed.* **5** V-T If something **blinds** you to the real situation, it prevents you from realizing that it exists or from understanding it properly. ❏ *He never allowed his love of Australia to blind him to his countrymen's faults.* **6** ADJ You can describe someone's beliefs or actions as **blind** when you think that they seem to take no notice of important facts or behave in an unreasonable way. [DISAPPROVAL] ❏ *...her blind faith in the wisdom of the church.* **7** N-COUNT A **blind** is a roll of cloth or paper which you can pull down over a window as a covering. ❏ *Pulling the blinds up, she let some of the bright sunlight in.* **8** → see also **blinding**, **blindly** **9** PHRASE If you say that someone **is turning a blind eye** to something bad or illegal that is happening, you mean that you think they are pretending not to notice that it is happening so that they will not have to do anything about it. [DISAPPROVAL] ❏ *Teachers are turning a blind eye to pupils smoking at school, a report reveals today.*

blind al|ley (blind alleys) N-COUNT If you describe a situation as a **blind alley**, you mean that progress is not possible or that the situation can have no useful results. ❏ *The Internet has proved a blind alley for many firms.*

blind date (blind dates) N-COUNT A **blind date** is an arrangement made for you to spend a romantic day or evening with someone you have never met before.

blind|ers /bla͟ɪndərz/ N-PLURAL **Blinders** are two pieces of leather that are placed at the side of a horse's eyes so that it can only see straight ahead. [AM]

blind|fold /bla͟ɪndfoʊld/ (blindfolds, blindfolding, blindfolded) **1** N-COUNT A **blindfold** is a strip of cloth that is tied over someone's eyes so that they cannot see. **2** V-T If you **blindfold** someone, you tie a blindfold over their eyes. ❏ *His abductors blindfolded him and drove him to an apartment in southern Beirut.*

blind|ing /bla͟ɪndɪŋ/ **1** ADJ A **blinding** light is extremely bright. ❏ *The doctor worked busily beneath the blinding lights of the delivery room.* **2** ADJ [ADJ n] You use **blinding** to emphasize that something is very obvious. [EMPHASIS] ❏ *The miseries I went through made me suddenly realize with a blinding flash what life was all about.* **3** ADJ **Blinding** pain is very strong pain. ❏ *There was a pain then, a quick, blinding agony that jumped along Danlo's spine.*

blind|ly /bla͟ɪndli/ **1** ADV If you say that someone does something **blindly**, you mean that they do it without having enough information, or without thinking about it. [DISAPPROVAL] ❏ *Don't just blindly follow what the banker says.* ❏ *Without adequate information, many students choose a college almost blindly.* **2** → see also **blind**

blind|side /bla͟ɪndsaɪd/ (blindsides, blindsiding, blindsided) V-T [usu passive] If you say that you **were blindsided** by something, you mean that it surprised you in a negative way. [mainly AM, DISAPPROVAL] ❏ *He complained about being blindsided by the decision.*

blind spot (blind spots) **1** N-COUNT If you say that someone has a **blind spot** about something, you mean that they seem to be unable to understand it or to see how important it is. ❏ *The president has a blind spot on ethical issues.* ❏ *When I was single I never worried about money – it was a bit of a blind spot.* **2** N-COUNT A **blind spot** is an area in your range of vision that you cannot see properly but which you really should be able to see. For example, when you are driving a car, the area just behind your shoulders is often a blind spot.

blind trust (blind trusts) N-COUNT A **blind trust** is a financial arrangement in which someone's investments are managed without the person knowing where the money is invested. **Blind trusts** are used especially by people in public office, so that they cannot be accused of using their position to make money unfairly. [BUSINESS] ❏ *Yang transferred the shares into a blind trust earlier this week.*

bling /blɪŋ/ also **bling-bling** N-UNCOUNT Some people refer to expensive or fancy jewelry or clothes as **bling** or **bling-bling**. [INFORMAL] ❏ *Big-name jewelers are battling it out to get celebrities to wear their bling.* ❏ *...gangsta rap's love of bling-bling.*

blink /blɪŋk/ (blinks, blinking, blinked) **1** V-T/V-I When you **blink** or when you **blink** your eyes, you shut your eyes and very quickly open them again. ❏ *Kathryn blinked and forced a smile.* ❏ *She was blinking her eyes rapidly.* • N-COUNT **Blink** is also a noun. ❏ *He kept giving quick blinks.* **2** V-I When a light **blinks**, it flashes on and off. ❏ *Green and yellow lights blinked on the surface of the harbor.* ❏ *The plane was flying normally for about 15 minutes before a warning light blinked on.* **3** → See feature box at **look**

blink|ers /blɪ͟ŋkərz/ **1** N-PLURAL A car's **blinkers** are the flashing lights that tell you it is going to turn left or right. [AM] **2** N-PLURAL **Blinkers** are the same as **blinders**. [mainly BRIT]

blip /blɪp/ (blips) **1** N-COUNT A **blip** is a small spot of light, sometimes occurring with a short, high-pitched sound, which flashes on and off regularly on a piece of equipment such as a radar screen. **2** N-COUNT A **blip** in a straight line, such as the line on a graph, is a point at which the line suddenly makes a sharp change of direction before returning to its original direction. **3** N-COUNT A **blip** in a situation is a sudden but temporary change or interruption in it. ❏ *Interest rates generally have been declining since last spring, despite a few upward blips in recent weeks.*

bliss /blɪs/ N-UNCOUNT **Bliss** is a state of complete happiness. ❏ *It was a scene of such domestic bliss.*

bliss|ful /blɪ͟sfəl/ **1** ADJ A **blissful** situation or period of time is one in which you are extremely happy. ❏ *We spent a blissful week together.* • **bliss|ful|ly** /blɪ͟sfəli/ ADV ❏ *We're blissfully happy.* **2** ADJ [ADJ n] If someone is in **blissful** ignorance of something unpleasant or serious, they are totally unaware of it. ❏ *Many country towns were still living in blissful ignorance of the post-war crime wave.* • **bliss|ful|ly** ADV ❏ *At first, he was blissfully unaware of the conspiracy against him.*

blis|ter /blɪ͟stər/ (blisters, blistering, blistered) **1** N-COUNT A **blister** is a painful swelling on the surface of your skin. Blisters contain a clear liquid and are usually caused by heat or by something repeatedly rubbing your skin. **2** V-T/V-I When your skin **blisters** or when something **blisters** it, blisters appear on it. ❏ *The affected skin turns red and may blister.* ❏ *The sap of this plant blisters the skin.*

blis|ter|ing /blɪ͟stərɪŋ/ **1** ADJ **Blistering** heat is very great heat. ❏ *...a blistering summer day.* **2** ADJ A **blistering** remark expresses great anger or dislike. ❏ *The president responded to this with a blistering attack on his critics.* **3** ADJ [ADJ n] **Blistering** is used to describe actions in sports to emphasize that they are done with great speed or force. [JOURNALISM, EMPHASIS] ❏ *Sharon Wild set a blistering pace to take the lead.*

blithe /bla͟ɪð/ ADJ You use **blithe** to indicate that something is done casually, without serious or careful thought. [DISAPPROVAL] ❏ *Acts of trespass and petty theft often grew out of the blithe disregard that boys had for private property.* • **blithe|ly** ADV ❏ *Your editorial blithely ignores the hard facts.*

blitz /blɪts/ (blitzes, blitzing, blitzed) **1** N-COUNT If you have a **blitz** on something, you make a big effort to deal with it or to improve it. [INFORMAL] ❏ *Regional accents are still acceptable but there is to be a blitz on incorrect grammar.* **2** N-PROPER The heavy bombing of British cities by German aircraft in 1940 and 1941 is referred to as **the Blitz**. **3** V-T If a city or building is **blitzed** during a war, it is attacked, for example by bombs dropped from enemy aircraft. ❏ *In the autumn of 1940 London was blitzed by an average of two hundred aircraft a night.*

blitz|krieg /blɪ͟tskriːg/ (blitzkriegs) **1** N-COUNT A **blitzkrieg** is a fast and intense military attack that takes the enemy by surprise and is intended to achieve a very quick victory. **2** N-COUNT Journalists sometimes refer to a rapid and powerful attack or campaign in, for example, sports, politics, or advertising as a **blitzkrieg**. [INFORMAL] ❏ *...a blitzkrieg of media hype.*

bliz|zard /blɪzərd/ (blizzards) **1** N-COUNT A **blizzard** is a very bad snowstorm with strong winds. **2** → See feature box at **hot**

bloat|ed /bloʊtɪd/ **1** ADJ If someone's body or a part of their body is **bloated**, it is much larger than normal, usually because it has a lot of liquid or gas inside it. ❑ *...the bloated body of a dead bullock.* **2** ADJ [v-link ADJ] If you feel **bloated** after eating a large meal, you feel very full and uncomfortable. ❑ *Diners do not want to leave the table feeling bloated.*

bloat|ing /bloʊtɪŋ/ N-UNCOUNT **Bloating** is the swelling of a body or part of a body, usually because it has a lot of gas or liquid in it. ❑ *...abdominal bloating and pain.*

blob /blɒb/ (blobs) **1** N-COUNT A **blob** of thick or sticky liquid is a small, often round, amount of it. [INFORMAL] ❑ *...a blob of chocolate mousse.* **2** N-COUNT You can use **blob** to refer to something that you cannot see very clearly, for example because it is in the distance. [INFORMAL] ❑ *You could just see vague blobs of faces.*

bloc /blɒk/ (blocs) N-COUNT A **bloc** is a group of countries that have similar political aims and interests and that act together over some issues. ❑ *...the former Soviet bloc.*

block ✦✦◇ /blɒk/ (blocks, blocking, blocked) **1** N-COUNT A **block** of a substance is a large rectangular piece of it. ❑ *...a block of ice.* **2** N-COUNT A **block** of apartments or offices is a large building containing them. ❑ *...a white-painted apartment block.* **3** N-COUNT A **block** in a town or city is an area of land with streets on all its sides, or the area or distance between such streets. ❑ *He walked around the block three times.* ❑ *She walked four blocks down High Street.* **4** N-COUNT **Blocks** are wooden or plastic cubes, such as those used as toys by children. **5** V-T To **block** a road, channel, or pipe means to put an object across it or in it so that nothing can pass through it or along it. ❑ *Some students today blocked a highway that cuts through the center of the city.* **6** V-T If something **blocks** your view, it prevents you from seeing something because it is between you and that thing. ❑ *...a row of spruce trees that blocked his view of the long north slope of the mountain.* **7** V-T If you **block** someone's way, you prevent them from going somewhere or entering a place by standing in front of them. ❑ *I started to move around him, but he blocked my way.* **8** V-T If you **block** something that is being arranged, you prevent it from being done. ❑ *For years the country has tried to block imports of various cheap foreign products.* **9** N-COUNT [usu N of n] A **block** of something such as tickets or shares is a large quantity of them, especially when they are all sold at the same time and are in a particular sequence or order. ❑ *Those booking a block of seats get them at reduced rates.* **10** N-COUNT If you have a **mental block** or a **block**, you are temporarily unable to do something that you can normally do which involves using, thinking about, or remembering something. ❑ *I cannot do math. I've got a mental block about it.* **11** → see also **stumbling block**
▶ **block out 1** PHRASAL VERB If someone **blocks out** a thought, they try not to think about it. ❑ *She accuses me of having blocked out the past.* **2** PHRASAL VERB Something that **blocks out** light prevents it from reaching a place. ❑ *He pulled down the shades, blocking out the bright sunlight.*

block|ade /blɒkeɪd/ (blockades, blockading, blockaded) **1** N-COUNT A **blockade** of a place is an action that is taken to prevent goods or people from entering or leaving it. ❑ *It's not yet clear who will actually enforce the blockade.* **2** V-T If a group of people **blockade** a place, they stop goods or people from reaching that place. If they **blockade** a road or a port, they stop people from using that road or port. ❑ *About 50,000 people are trapped in the town, which has been blockaded for more than 40 days.*

block|age /blɒkɪdʒ/ (blockages) N-COUNT A **blockage** in a pipe, tube, or tunnel is an object which blocks it, or the state of being blocked. ❑ *The logical treatment is to remove this blockage.*

block|bust|er /blɒkbʌstər/ (blockbusters) N-COUNT A **blockbuster** is a movie or book that is very popular and successful, usually because it is very exciting. [INFORMAL] ❑ *...the latest Hollywood blockbuster.*

block|bust|ing /blɒkbʌstɪŋ/ ADJ [ADJ n] A **blockbusting** film or book is one that is very successful, usually because it is very exciting. [INFORMAL, JOURNALISM] ❑ *...the blockbusting sci-fi movie "Suburban Commando."*

block capi|tals N-PLURAL [usu *in* N] **Block capitals** are simple capital letters that are not decorated in any way.

block|chain /blɒktʃeɪn/ N-UNCOUNT **Blockchain** is a system for storing records of transactions using digital currencies, that can be accessed by linked computers. ❑ *The investment banking industry is keen to utilize blockchain to change the way securities are traded.*

blocked /blɒkt/ also **blocked up** ADJ If something is **blocked** or **blocked up**, it is completely closed so that nothing can get through it. ❑ *The main drain was blocked.* ❑ *His arteries were blocked up again, requiring him to undergo repeat surgery.*

block let|ters N-PLURAL [usu *in* N] **Block letters** are the same as **block capitals**.

block par|ty (block parties) N-COUNT A **block party** is an outdoor party for all the residents of a block or neighborhood. [AM] ❑ *...the Fourth of July parade and block party.*

> in BRIT, use **street party**

block vote (block votes) N-COUNT A **block vote** is a large number of votes that are all cast in the same way by one person on behalf of a group of people.

blog /blɒg/ (blogs, blogging, blogged) **1** N-COUNT A **blog** is a website containing a diary or journal on a particular subject. [COMPUTING] ❑ *When Barbieux started his blog, his aspirations were small; he simply hoped to communicate with a few people.* ● **blog|ger** (bloggers) N-COUNT ❑ *While most bloggers comment on news reported elsewhere, some do their own reporting.* ● **blog|ging** N-UNCOUNT ❑ *...the explosion in the popularity of blogging.* **2** V-I Someone who **blogs** writes a blog. [COMPUTING] ❑ *She blogs about US politics.* ❑ *He'll be blogging from China.*

blogo|sphere /blɒgəsfɪər/ also **blogsphere** /blɒgsfɪər/ N-SING [the N] In computer technology, the **blogosphere** or the **blogsphere** is all the blogs on the internet, considered collectively. [COMPUTING] ❑ *Consequently, even as the blogosphere continues to expand, only a few blogs are likely to emerge as focal points.* ❑ *The blogsphere has changed a lot in the past few years.*

blog|post /blɒgpoʊst/ (blogposts) N-COUNT A **blogpost** is a piece of writing that forms part of a regular blog. [COMPUTING] ❑ *His latest blogpost describes the journey.*

blonde /blɒnd/ (blondes, blonder, blondest)

> The form **blonde** is usually used to refer to women, and **blond** to refer to men.

1 COLOR **Blond** or **blonde** hair can be very light brown or light yellow. ❑ *...a little girl with blonde hair.* **2** ADJ Someone who is **blonde** has blonde hair. ❑ *He was blonder than his brother.* **3** N-COUNT A **blonde** is a woman who has blonde hair. ❑ *...a stunning blonde in her early thirties.*

blonde bomb|shell (blonde bombshells) N-COUNT Journalists sometimes use **blonde bombshell** to refer to a woman with blonde hair who is very attractive. [INFORMAL, JOURNALISM]

blood ✦✦◇ /blʌd/ **1** N-UNCOUNT **Blood** is the red liquid that flows inside your body, which you can see if you cut yourself. ❑ *His shirt was covered in blood.* **2** N-UNCOUNT You can use **blood** to refer to the race or social class of someone's parents or ancestors. ❑ *There was Greek blood in his veins: his ancestors originally bore the name Karajannis.* **3** PHRASE If you say that there is **bad blood** between people, you mean that they have argued about something and dislike each other. ❑ *There is, it seems, some bad blood between Mills and the Baldwins.* **4** PHRASE If something violent and cruel is done **in cold blood**, it is done deliberately and in an unemotional way. [DISAPPROVAL] ❑ *The crime had been committed in cold blood.* **5** → see also **cold-blooded 6** PHRASE If you say that someone has a person's **blood on** their **hands**, you mean that they are responsible for that person's death. ❑ *He has my son's blood on his hands. I hope it haunts him for the rest of his days.* **7** PHRASE If a quality or talent is **in** your **blood**, it is part of your nature, and other members of your family have it too. ❑ *Diplomacy was in his blood: his ancestors had been feudal lords.* **8** PHRASE You can use the expressions **new blood**, **fresh blood**, or **young blood** to refer to people who are brought into an organization to improve it by thinking of new ideas or new ways of doing things. ❑ *There's been a major reshuffle of the cabinet to bring in new blood.* **9 flesh and blood** → see **flesh 10 own flesh and blood** → see **flesh**

blood and thunder ... **bloody**

> **COLLOCATIONS**
> **blood**
> NOUN ■
> verb + **blood**: shed, spill; lose

bl<u>oo</u>d and thun|der also **blood-and-thunder** ADJ [ADJ n] A **blood and thunder** performer or performance is very loud and emotional. ◻ *He was a blood-and-thunder preacher.*

bl<u>oo</u>d bank (**blood banks**) N-COUNT A **blood bank** is a place where blood that has been taken from blood donors is stored until it is needed for people in a hospital.

bl<u>oo</u>d|bath /bl<u>ʌ</u>dbæθ/ (**bloodbaths**) also **blood bath** N-COUNT If you describe an event as a **bloodbath**, you are emphasizing that a lot of people were killed very violently. [EMPHASIS] ◻ *The war degenerated into a bloodbath of tribal killings.*

bl<u>oo</u>d broth|er (**blood brothers**) also **blood-brother** N-COUNT A man's **blood brother** is a man he has sworn to treat as a brother, often in a ceremony which involves mixing a small amount of their blood.

bl<u>oo</u>d count (**blood counts**) N-COUNT Your **blood count** is the number of red and white cells in your blood. A **blood count** can also refer to a medical examination that determines the number of red and white cells in your blood. ◻ *Her blood count was normal.* ◻ *We do a blood count to ensure that all is well.*

bl<u>oo</u>d-curdling also **bloodcurdling** ADJ [usu ADJ n] A **blood-curdling** sound or story is very frightening and horrible. ◻ *...blood-curdling tales.*

bl<u>oo</u>d do|nor (**blood donors**) N-COUNT A **blood donor** is someone who gives some of their blood so that it can be used in operations.

bl<u>oo</u>d feud (**blood feuds**) N-COUNT A **blood feud** is a long-lasting, bitter disagreement between two or more groups of people, particularly family groups. Blood feuds often involve members of each group murdering or fighting with members of the other.

bl<u>oo</u>d group (**blood groups**) N-COUNT [oft poss N] Someone's **blood group** is the type of blood that they have in their body. There are four main types: A, B, AB, and O.

bl<u>oo</u>d|hound /bl<u>ʌ</u>dhaʊnd/ (**bloodhounds**) N-COUNT A **bloodhound** is a large dog with a very good sense of smell. Bloodhounds are often used to find people or other animals by following their scent.

bl<u>oo</u>d|less /bl<u>ʌ</u>dlɪs/ ■ ADJ A **bloodless** coup or victory is one in which nobody is killed. ◻ *Reports from the area indicate that it was a bloodless coup.* ◻ *The campaign would be short and relatively bloodless.* • **blood|less|ly** ADV [ADV with v] ◻ *This war had to be fought fast and relatively bloodlessly.* ❷ ADJ If you describe someone's face or skin as **bloodless**, you mean that it is very pale. ◻ *Her face was gray and bloodless.*

bl<u>oo</u>d|letting /bl<u>ʌ</u>dletɪŋ/ ■ N-UNCOUNT **Bloodletting** is violence or killing between groups of people, especially between rival armies. ◻ *Once again there's been ferocious bloodletting in the township.* ❷ N-UNCOUNT Journalists sometimes refer to a bitter quarrel between two groups of people from within the same organization as **bloodletting**. ◻ *Hopefully a satisfactory solution can be reached without much bloodletting.*

bl<u>oo</u>d|line /bl<u>ʌ</u>dlaɪn/ (**bloodlines**) N-COUNT A person's **bloodline** is their ancestors over many generations, and the characteristics they are believed to have inherited from these ancestors. You can also use **bloodline** to refer to the ancestors of animals such as racehorses.

bl<u>oo</u>d|lust /bl<u>ʌ</u>dlʌst/ N-UNCOUNT [also a N] If you say that someone is driven by a **bloodlust**, you mean that they are acting in an extremely violent way because their emotions have been aroused by the events around them. ◻ *The mobs became driven by a crazed bloodlust to take the city.*

bl<u>oo</u>d mon|ey ■ N-UNCOUNT If someone makes a payment of **blood money** to the family of someone who has been killed, they pay that person's family a sum of money as compensation. ◻ *Defense lawyers have still not agreed to terms for payment of blood money to the victims' families.* ❷ N-UNCOUNT **Blood money** is money that is paid to someone for murdering someone.

bl<u>oo</u>d poi|son|ing N-UNCOUNT **Blood poisoning** is a serious illness resulting from an infection in your blood.

bl<u>oo</u>d pres|sure N-UNCOUNT Your **blood pressure** is the amount of force with which your blood flows around your body. ◻ *Your doctor will monitor your blood pressure.*

bl<u>oo</u>d pres|sure cuff (**blood pressure cuffs**) N-COUNT A **blood pressure cuff** is a medical device consisting of a piece of rubber or similar material that is wrapped around a patient's arm and then inflated in order to measure their blood pressure. [MEDICAL] ◻ *She cried at the application of the blood pressure cuff.*

bl<u>oo</u>d pud|ding (**blood puddings**) N-VAR **Blood pudding** is a thick sausage which has a black skin and is made from pork fat and pig's blood.

bl<u>oo</u>d-red also **blood red** COLOR Something that is **blood-red** is bright red in color. ◻ *...blood-red cherries.*

bl<u>oo</u>d re|la|tion (**blood relations**) also **blood relative** N-COUNT A **blood relation** or **blood relative** is someone who is related to you by birth rather than by marriage.

bl<u>oo</u>d|shed /bl<u>ʌ</u>dʃed/ N-UNCOUNT **Bloodshed** is violence in which people are killed or wounded. ◻ *The government must increase the pace of reforms to avoid further bloodshed.*

bl<u>oo</u>d|shot /bl<u>ʌ</u>dʃɒt/ ADJ If your eyes are **bloodshot**, the parts that are usually white are red or pink. Your eyes can be bloodshot for a variety of reasons, for example, because you are tired or you have drunk too much alcohol. ◻ *John's eyes were bloodshot and puffy.*

bl<u>oo</u>d sis|ter (**blood sisters**) also **blood-sister** N-COUNT A woman's **blood sister** is a woman she has sworn to treat as a sister, often in a ceremony which involves mixing a small amount of their blood.

bl<u>oo</u>d sport (**blood sports**) also **bloodsport** N-COUNT **Blood sports** are sports such as hunting in which animals are killed.

bl<u>oo</u>d|stain /bl<u>ʌ</u>dsteɪn/ (**bloodstains**) N-COUNT A **bloodstain** is a mark on a surface caused by blood.

bl<u>oo</u>d|stained /bl<u>ʌ</u>dsteɪnd/ ADJ Someone or something that is **bloodstained** is covered with blood. ◻ *The killer must have been heavily bloodstained.* ◻ *...bloodstained clothing.*

bl<u>oo</u>d|stock /bl<u>ʌ</u>dstɒk/ N-UNCOUNT [usu N n] Horses that are bred for racing are referred to as **bloodstock**.

bl<u>oo</u>d|stream /bl<u>ʌ</u>dstrim/ (**bloodstreams**) N-COUNT Your **bloodstream** is the blood that flows around your body. ◻ *The disease releases toxins into the bloodstream.*

bl<u>oo</u>d|sucker /bl<u>ʌ</u>dsʌkər/ (**bloodsuckers**) ■ N-COUNT A **bloodsucker** is any creature that sucks blood from a wound that it has made in an animal or person. ❷ N-COUNT If you call someone a **bloodsucker**, you disapprove of them because you think they do not do anything worthwhile but live off the efforts of other people. [DISAPPROVAL] ◻ *At last he was free from the financial bloodsuckers.*

bl<u>oo</u>d test (**blood tests**) N-COUNT A **blood test** is a medical examination of a small amount of your blood.

bl<u>oo</u>d|thirsty /bl<u>ʌ</u>dθɜrsti/ (**bloodthirstier, bloodthirstiest**) ADJ **Bloodthirsty** people are eager to use violence or display a strong interest in violent things. You can also use **bloodthirsty** to refer to very violent situations. ◻ *They were savage and bloodthirsty.* ◻ *...some of the most tragic scenes witnessed even in this bloodthirsty war.*

bl<u>oo</u>d trans|fu|sion (**blood transfusions**) N-VAR A **blood transfusion** is a process in which blood is injected into the body of a person who is badly injured or ill.

bl<u>oo</u>d type (**blood types**) N-COUNT Someone's **blood type** is the same as their **blood group**.

bl<u>oo</u>d ves|sel (**blood vessels**) N-COUNT **Blood vessels** are the narrow tubes through which your blood flows.

bloody ♦◇◇ /bl<u>ʌ</u>di/ (**bloodier, bloodiest, bloodies, bloodying, bloodied**) ■ ADJ If you describe a situation or event as **bloody**, you mean that it is very violent and a lot of people are killed. ◻ *Forty-three demonstrators were killed in bloody clashes.* ❷ ADJ You can describe someone or something as **bloody** if they are covered in a lot of blood. ◻ *He was arrested last October still carrying a bloody knife.* ❸ V-T If you have **bloodied** part of your body, there is blood on it, usually because you have had an accident or you have been attacked. ☐ *One of our children fell and bloodied his knee.*

Bloody Mary /blʌdi mɛəri/ (Bloody Marys) also **bloody mary** N-COUNT A **Bloody Mary** is a drink made from vodka and tomato juice.

bloom /blum/ (blooms, blooming, bloomed) **1** N-COUNT A **bloom** is the flower on a plant. [LITERARY] ☐ *The sweet fragrance of the white blooms makes this climber a favorite.* **2** PHRASE A plant or tree that is **in bloom** has flowers on it. ☐ *...a pink climbing rose in full bloom.* **3** V-I When a plant or tree **blooms**, it produces flowers. When a flower **blooms**, it opens. ☐ *This plant blooms between May and June.* **4** V-I If someone or something **blooms**, they become more good, attractive, popular or successful. ☐ *My passion for photography has bloomed since I moved to the country.* **5** N-UNCOUNT [also a N] If something such as someone's skin has a **bloom**, it has a fresh and healthy appearance. ☐ *The skin loses its youthful bloom.*

bloom|ers /blumərz/ N-PLURAL [also *a pair of* N] **Bloomers** are an old-fashioned kind of women's underwear consisting of wide, loose pants gathered at the knees.

bloom|ing /blumɪŋ/ ADJ Someone who is **blooming** looks attractively healthy and full of energy. ☐ *If they were blooming with confidence they wouldn't need me.* ☐ *She's in blooming health.*

bloop|er /blupər/ (bloopers) N-COUNT A **blooper** is a silly mistake. [mainly AM, INFORMAL] ☐ *...the overwhelming appeal of television bloopers.*

blos|som /blɒsəm/ (blossoms, blossoming, blossomed) **1** N-VAR **Blossom** is the flowers that appear on a tree before the fruit. ☐ *The cherry blossom came out early in Washington this year.* **2** V-I If someone or something **blossoms**, they develop good, attractive, or successful qualities. ☐ *Why do some people take longer than others to blossom?* ☐ *What began as a local festival has blossomed into an international event.* **3** V-I When a tree **blossoms**, it produces blossom. ☐ *Rain begins to fall and peach trees blossom.*

blot /blɒt/ (blots, blotting, blotted) **1** N-COUNT If something is a **blot on** a person's or thing's reputation, it spoils their reputation. ☐ *...a blot on the reputation of the architectural profession.* **2** N-COUNT A **blot** is a drop of liquid that has fallen on to a surface and has dried. ☐ *...an ink blot.* **3** V-T If you **blot** a surface, you remove liquid from it by pressing a piece of soft paper or cloth onto it. ☐ *Before applying makeup, blot the face with a tissue to remove any excess oils.*

▶ **blot out 1** PHRASAL VERB If one thing **blots out** another thing, it is in front of the other thing and prevents it from being seen. ☐ *About the time the three climbers were halfway down, clouds blotted out the sun.* ☐ *The victim's face was blotted out by a camera blur.* **2** PHRASAL VERB If you try to **blot out** a memory, you try to forget it. If one thought or memory **blots out** other thoughts or memories, it becomes the only one that you can think about. ☐ *Are you saying that she's trying to blot out all memory of the incident?* ☐ *The boy has gaps in his mind about it. He is blotting certain things out.*

blotch /blɒtʃ/ (blotches) N-COUNT A **blotch** is a small unpleasant-looking area of color, for example, on someone's skin. ☐ *His face was covered in red blotches, seemingly a nasty case of acne.*

blotched /blɒtʃt/ ADJ [oft ADJ *with* n] Something that is **blotched** has blotches on it. ☐ *Her face is blotched and swollen.* ☐ *...a dozen cargo planes blotched with camouflage colors.*

blotchy /blɒtʃi/ (blotchier, blotchiest) ADJ Something that is **blotchy** has blotches on it. ☐ *My skin goes red and blotchy.* ☐ *...blotchy marks on the leaves.*

blot|ter /blɒtər/ (blotters) N-COUNT A **blotter** is a large sheet of blotting paper kept in a special holder on a desk.

blot|ting pa|per N-UNCOUNT **Blotting paper** is thick soft paper that you use for soaking up and drying ink.

blouse /blaʊs/ (blouses) N-COUNT A **blouse** is a kind of shirt worn by a girl or woman.

BLOW
① VERB USES
② NOUN USES
---

① **blow** ⬥⬥⬦ /bloʊ/ (blows, blowing, blew, blown)
→ Please look at meanings **13** – **15** to see if the expression you are looking for is shown under another headword.

1 V-I When a wind or breeze **blows**, the air moves. ☐ *A chill wind blew at the top of the hill.* **2** V-T/V-I If the wind **blows** something somewhere or if it **blows** there, the wind moves it there. ☐ *The wind blew her hair back from her forehead.* ☐ *Sand blew in our eyes.* **3** V-I If you **blow**, you send out a stream of air from your mouth. ☐ *Danny rubbed his arms and blew on his fingers to warm them.* **4** V-T If you **blow** something somewhere, you move it by sending out a stream of air from your mouth. ☐ *He picked up his mug and blew off the steam.* **5** V-T If you **blow** bubbles or smoke rings, you make them by blowing air out of your mouth through liquid or smoke. ☐ *He blew a ring of blue smoke.* **6** V-T/V-I When a whistle or horn **blows** or someone **blows** it, they make a sound by blowing into it. ☐ *The whistle blew and the train slid forward.* **7** V-T When you **blow** your nose, you force air out of it through your nostrils in order to clear it. ☐ *He took out a handkerchief and blew his nose.* **8** V-T To **blow** something out, off, or away means to remove or destroy it violently with an explosion. ☐ *The can exploded, wrecking the kitchen and bathroom and blowing out windows.* **9** V-T If you **blow** a chance or attempt to do something, you make a mistake which wastes the chance or causes the attempt to fail. [INFORMAL] ☐ *One careless word could blow the whole deal.* ☐ *Oh you fool! You've blown it!* **10** V-T If you say that something **blows** an event, situation, or argument into a particular extreme state, especially an uncertain or unpleasant state, you mean that it causes it to be in that state. ☐ *Someone took an inappropriate use of words on my part and tried to blow it into a major controversy.* **11** V-T If you **blow** a large amount of money, you spend it quickly on luxuries. [INFORMAL] ☐ *My brother lent me some money and I went and blew it all.* **12** → see also **full-blown 13 to blow hot and cold** → see **hot 14 to blow someone a kiss** → see **kiss 15 to blow the whistle** → see **whistle 16** → See feature box at **storm**

▶ **blow away** PHRASAL VERB If you say that you **are blown away** by something, or that it **blows** you **away**, you mean that you are very impressed by it. [INFORMAL] ☐ *I was blown away by the tone and the quality of the story.* ☐ *Everyone I met overwhelmed me and kind of blew me away.*

▶ **blow off** PHRASAL VERB If you **blow** something **off**, you ignore it or choose not to deal with it. [AM, INFORMAL] ☐ *I don't think we can afford just to blow this off.*

▶ **blow out** PHRASAL VERB If you **blow out** a flame or a candle, you blow at it so that it stops burning. ☐ *I blew out the candle.*

▶ **blow over** PHRASAL VERB If something such as trouble or an argument **blows over**, it ends without any serious consequences. ☐ *Wait, and it'll all blow over.*

▶ **blow up 1** PHRASAL VERB If someone **blows** something **up** or if it **blows up**, it is destroyed by an explosion. ☐ *He was jailed for 45 years for trying to blow up a plane.* **2** PHRASAL VERB If you **blow up** something such as a balloon or a tire, you fill it with air. ☐ *Other than blowing up a tire I hadn't done any car maintenance.* **3** PHRASAL VERB If a wind or a storm **blows up**, the weather becomes very windy or stormy. ☐ *A storm blew up over the mountains.* **4** PHRASAL VERB If you **blow up** at someone, you lose your temper and shout at them. [INFORMAL] ☐ *I'm sorry I blew up at you.* **5** PHRASAL VERB If someone **blows** an incident **up** or if it **blows up**, it is made to seem more serious or important than it really is. ☐ *Newspapers blew up the story.* ☐ *The media may be blowing it up out of proportion.* **6** PHRASAL VERB If a photographic image **is blown up**, a large copy is made of it. ☐ *The image is blown up on a large screen.*

USAGE

explode or **blow up**?
If someone destroys a building with a bomb, you say that they **blow** it **up**. Don't say 'He wanted to explode the place.' Say 'He wanted to blow the place up.'
---

② **blow** ⬥⬦ /bloʊ/ (blows) **1** N-COUNT If someone receives a **blow**, they are hit with a fist or weapon. ☐ *He went to the hospital after a blow to the face.* **2** N-COUNT If something that happens is a **blow** to someone or something, it is very upsetting, disappointing, or damaging to them. ☐ *That ruling comes as a blow to environmentalists.*

blow-by-blow ADJ [usu ADJ n] A **blow-by-blow** account of an event describes every stage of it in great detail. [INFORMAL] ☐ *She wanted a blow-by-blow account of what happened.*

blow-dry

blow-dry (blow-dries, blow-drying, blow-dried) V-T If you blow-dry your hair, you dry it with a hairdryer, often to give it a particular style. ❑ *I find it hard to blow-dry my hair.* ❑ *He has blow-dried blond hair.* • N-SING **Blow-dry** is also a noun. ❑ *The price of a cut and blow-dry varies widely.*

blow|hard /bl<u>ou</u>hɑrd/ (blowhards) N-COUNT If you describe someone as a **blowhard**, you mean that they express their opinions very forcefully, and usually in a boastful way. [AM, INFORMAL, DISAPPROVAL] ❑ *He doesn't like to be a blowhard about what he's developed.*

blown /bl<u>ou</u>n/ **Blown** is the past participle of **blow**.

blow|out /bl<u>ou</u>aut/ (blowouts) **1** N-COUNT A **blowout** is a large meal, often a celebration with family or friends, at which people may eat too much. [INFORMAL] ❑ *Once in a while we had a major blowout.* **2** N-COUNT If you have a **blowout** while you are driving a car, one of the tires suddenly bursts. ❑ *A truck traveling south had a blowout and crashed.*

blow|torch /bl<u>ou</u>tɔrtʃ/ (blowtorches) N-COUNT A **blowtorch** is a device that produces a hot flame, and is used to heat metal or remove old paint.

blow-up (blow-ups) also **blowup** **1** N-COUNT A **blow-up** is a photograph or picture that has been made bigger. [INFORMAL] ❑ *...yellowing blow-ups of James Dean.* **2** N-COUNT [oft N with] A **blow-up** is a sudden fierce argument. [INFORMAL] ❑ *He and Cohen appeared to be heading for a major blowup.*

blub|ber /bl<u>ʌ</u>bər/ (blubbers, blubbering, blubbered) **1** N-UNCOUNT **Blubber** is the fat of whales, seals, and similar sea animals. ❑ *The baby whale develops a thick layer of blubber to protect it from the cold sea.* **2** V-I If someone **blubbers**, they cry noisily and in an unattractive way. [INFORMAL] ❑ *She started to blubber like a child.*

bludg|eon /bl<u>ʌ</u>dʒən/ (bludgeons, bludgeoning, bludgeoned) V-T To **bludgeon** someone means to hit them several times with a heavy object. ❑ *He broke into the old man's house and bludgeoned him with a hammer.*

blue ✦✦✧ /bl<u>u</u>/ (bluer, bluest, blues) **1** COLOR Something that is **blue** is the color of the sky on a sunny day. ❑ *There were swallows in the cloudless blue sky.* ❑ *She fixed her pale blue eyes on her father's.* **2** N-PLURAL **The blues** is a type of music which was developed by African American musicians in the southern United States. It is characterized by a slow tempo and a strong rhythm. ❑ *Can White girls sing the blues?* **3** ADJ [v-link ADJ] If you are feeling **blue**, you are feeling sad or depressed, often when there is no particular reason. [INFORMAL] ❑ *There's no earthly reason for me to feel so blue.* **4** ADJ If a U.S. state is described as **blue**, it means that the majority of its residents vote for the Democratic Party in elections, especially in the presidential elections. ❑ *This issue could drive an even bigger wedge between the red and blue states.* **5** → See feature box at **weather**

blue baby (blue babies) N-COUNT A **blue baby** is a baby whose skin is slightly blue because it has been born with something wrong with its heart.

blue|bell /bl<u>u</u>bɛl/ (bluebells) N-COUNT **Bluebells** are plants that have blue bell-shaped flowers on thin upright stems. Bluebells flower in the spring.

blue|berry /bl<u>u</u>bɛri/ (blueberries) N-COUNT A **blueberry** is a small dark blue fruit that is found in North America.

blue-black COLOR Something that is **blue-black** is bluish black in color. ❑ *...blue-black feathers.*

blue-blooded ADJ A **blue-blooded** person is from a royal or noble family. ❑ *...blue-blooded aristocrats.*

blue|bottle /bl<u>u</u>bɒtəl/ (bluebottles) N-COUNT A **bluebottle** is a large fly with a shiny dark-blue body.

blue chip (blue chips) N-COUNT **Blue chip** stocks and shares are an investment which are considered fairly safe to invest in while also being profitable. [BUSINESS] ❑ *Blue chip issues were sharply higher, but the rest of the market actually declined slightly by the end of the day.*

blue-collar ADJ [ADJ n] **Blue-collar** workers work in industry, doing physical work, rather than in offices. ❑ *It wasn't just the blue-collar workers who lost their jobs, it was everyone.*

blue-eyed boy [BRIT] → see **fair-haired boy**

blue|grass /bl<u>u</u>græs/ N-UNCOUNT **Bluegrass** is a style of fast folk music that began in the southern United States.

blur

blue|ish /bl<u>u</u>ɪʃ/ → see **bluish**

blue jeans N-PLURAL [also a pair of N] **Blue jeans** are the same as **jeans**. ❑ *...faded blue jeans.*

blue|print /bl<u>u</u>prɪnt/ (blueprints) **1** N-COUNT A **blueprint** for something is a plan or set of proposals that shows how it is expected to work. ❑ *The president will offer delegates his blueprint for the country's future.* **2** N-COUNT A **blueprint** of an architect's building plans or a designer's pattern is a photographic print consisting of white lines on a blue background. Blueprints contain all of the information that is needed to build or make something. ❑ *...a blueprint of the whole place, complete with heating ducts and wiring.* **3** N-COUNT A genetic **blueprint** is a pattern that is contained within all living cells. This pattern decides how the organism develops and what it looks like. ❑ *The offspring contain a mixture of the genetic blueprint of each parent.*

blue rib|and /bl<u>u</u> rɪbənd/ also **blue ribband** [BRIT] → see **blue ribbon**

blue rib|bon (blue ribbons) N-COUNT If someone or something wins the **blue ribbon** in a competition, they win first prize. The prize is sometimes in the shape of a blue ribbon. [AM] ❑ *We're talking about how Donna won that blue ribbon at the horse show.*

in BRIT, use **blue riband**

blue|stocking /bl<u>u</u>stɒkɪŋ/ (bluestockings) also **bluestocking** N-COUNT A **bluestocking** is an intellectual woman. [OLD-FASHIONED, DISAPPROVAL]

bluesy /bl<u>u</u>zi/ ADJ [usu ADJ n] If you describe a song or the way it is performed as **bluesy**, you mean that it is performed in a way that is characteristic of the blues. ❑ *...bluesy sax-and-strings theme music.*

blue tit (blue tits) N-COUNT A **blue tit** is a small European bird with a blue head, wings, and tail, and a yellow front.

Blue|tooth /bl<u>u</u>tuθ/ N-UNCOUNT [oft N n] **Bluetooth** is a type of short-range wireless technology that allows portable devices such as cell phones, laptops, and PDAs to communicate with each other. [TRADEMARK] ❑ *...the latest Bluetooth technology.*

bluff /bl<u>ʌ</u>f/ (bluffs, bluffing, bluffed) **1** N-VAR A **bluff** is an attempt to make someone believe that you will do something when you do not really intend to do it. ❑ *The letter was a bluff.* ❑ *It is essential to build up the military option and show that this is not a bluff.* **2** PHRASE If you **call** someone's **bluff**, you tell them to do what they have been threatening to do, because you are sure that they will not really do it. ❑ *The socialists have decided to call the opposition's bluff.* **3** V-T/V-I If you **bluff**, you make someone believe that you will do something when you do not really intend to do it, or that you know something when you do not really know it. ❑ *Either side, or both, could be bluffing.* ❑ *In each case the hijackers bluffed the crew using fake grenades.*

blu|ish /bl<u>u</u>ɪʃ/ also **blueish** COLOR Something that is **bluish** is slightly blue in color. ❑ *...bluish-gray eyes.*

blun|der /bl<u>ʌ</u>ndər/ (blunders, blundering, blundered) **1** N-COUNT A **blunder** is a stupid or careless mistake. ❑ *I think he made a tactical blunder by announcing it so far ahead of time.* **2** V-I If you **blunder**, you make a stupid or careless mistake. ❑ *No doubt I had blundered again.* **3** V-I If you **blunder** into a dangerous or difficult situation, you get involved in it by mistake. ❑ *People wanted to know how they had blundered into war, and how to avoid it in the future.* **4** V-I If you **blunder** somewhere, you move there in a clumsy and careless way. ❑ *He had blundered into the table, upsetting the flowers.*

blunt /bl<u>ʌ</u>nt/ (blunter, bluntest, blunts, blunting, blunted) **1** ADJ If you are **blunt**, you say exactly what you think without trying to be polite. ❑ *She is blunt about her personal life.* • **blunt|ly** ADV [ADV with v] ❑ *"I don't believe you!" Jeanne said bluntly.* • **blunt|ness** N-UNCOUNT ❑ *His bluntness got him into trouble.* **2** ADJ [ADJ n] A **blunt** object has a rounded or flat end rather than a sharp one. ❑ *One of them had been struck 13 times over the head with a blunt object.* **3** ADJ A **blunt** knife or blade is no longer sharp and does not cut well. ❑ *The edge is as blunt as an old butter knife.* **4** V-T If something **blunts** an emotion, a feeling, or a need, it weakens it. ❑ *The constant repetition of violence has blunted the human response to it.*

blur /bl<u>ɜ</u>r/ (blurs, blurring, blurred) **1** N-COUNT A **blur** is a shape or area which you cannot see clearly because it has no distinct outline or because it is moving very fast.

❏ Out of the corner of my eye I saw a blur of movement on the other side of the glass. ❷ V-T/V-I When a thing **blurs** or when something **blurs** it, you cannot see it clearly because its edges are no longer distinct. ❏ This creates a spectrum of colors at the edges of objects which blurs the image. • **blurred** ADJ ❏ ...blurred black and white photographs. ❸ V-T If something **blurs** an idea or a distinction between things, that idea or distinction no longer seems clear. ❏ ...her belief that scientists are trying to blur the distinction between "how" and "why" questions. • **blurred** ADJ ❏ The line between fact and fiction is becoming blurred. ❹ V-T/V-I If your vision **blurs**, or if something **blurs** it, you cannot see things clearly. ❏ Her eyes, behind her glasses, began to blur. • **blurred** ADJ ❏ ...visual disturbances like eye-strain and blurred vision. ❺ → See feature box at **eyesight**

Blu-Ray /blʊreɪ/ (**Blu-Rays**) N-VAR **Blu-Ray** is a type of video disk that is used for storing large amounts of high-quality digital information. [TRADEMARK] ❏ Blu-Ray disks store data using a blue laser rather than a regular red one.

blurb /blɜrb/ (**blurbs**) N-COUNT [usu sing, oft the N] The **blurb** about a new book, movie, or exhibition is information about it that is written in order to attract people's interest. [INFORMAL]

blur|ry /blɜri/ (**blurrier, blurriest**) ADJ A **blurry** shape is one that has an unclear outline. ❏ ...a blurry picture of a man.

blurt /blɜrt/ (**blurts, blurting, blurted**) V-T If someone **blurts** something, they say it suddenly, after trying hard to keep quiet or to keep it secret. ❏ "I was looking for Sally," he blurted, and his eyes filled with tears.
▶ **blurt out** PHRASAL VERB If someone **blurts** something **out**, they blurt it. [INFORMAL] ❏ "You're mad," the driver blurted out.

blush /blʌʃ/ (**blushes, blushing, blushed**) V-I When you **blush**, your face becomes redder than usual because you are ashamed or embarrassed. ❏ "Hello, Maria," he said, and she blushed again. • N-COUNT **Blush** is also a noun. ❏ "The most important thing is to be honest," she says, without the trace of a blush.

blush|er /blʌʃər/ (**blushers**) N-MASS **Blusher** is a colored substance that some people put on their cheeks.

blus|ter /blʌstər/ (**blusters, blustering, blustered**) V-T/V-I If you say that someone **is blustering**, you mean that they are speaking aggressively but without authority, often because they are angry or offended. ❏ "That's lunacy," he blustered. ❏ He was still blustering, but there was panic in his eyes. • N-UNCOUNT **Bluster** is also a noun. ❏ ...the bluster of the presidential campaign.

blus|tery /blʌstəri/ ❶ ADJ **Blustery** weather is rough, windy, and often rainy, with the wind often changing in strength or direction. ❏ It's a cold night here, with intermittent rain showers and a blustery wind. ❏ ...a cool, blustery day. ❷ → See feature box at **storm**

Blvd. **Blvd.** is a written abbreviation for **boulevard**. It is used especially in addresses and on maps or signs. ❏ ...1515 Wilson Blvd., Arlington, VA 22209.

in BRIT, also use **Blvd**

BMI /bi ɛm aɪ/ N-COUNT **BMI** is an abbreviation for **body mass index**. [MEDICAL] ❏ A BMI greater than 30 is considered obese.

B-movie (**B-movies**) N-COUNT A **B-movie** is a movie which is produced quickly and cheaply and is often considered to have little artistic value. ❏ ...some old Hollywood B-movie.

bn. also **bn** **bn.** is a written abbreviation for **billion**. ❏ ...total value, dollars $15.6bn.

boa /boʊə/ (**boas**) ❶ N-COUNT A **boa** or a **feather boa** is a long soft scarf made of feathers or of short pieces of very light fabric. ❏ She wore a large pink boa around her neck. ❷ N-COUNT A **boa** is the same as a **boa constrictor**.

boa con|stric|tor /boʊə kənstrɪktər/ (**boa constrictors**) N-COUNT A **boa constrictor** is a large snake that kills animals by wrapping itself round their bodies and squeezing them to death. Boa constrictors are found mainly in South and Central America and the West Indies.

boar /bɔr/ (**boars**)

The plural **boar** can also be used for meaning ❶.

❶ N-COUNT A **boar** or a **wild boar** is a wild pig. ❏ Wild boar are numerous in the valleys. ❷ N-COUNT A **boar** is a male pig.

board ✦✧✧ /bɔrd/ (**boards, boarding, boarded**) ❶ N-COUNT A **board** is a flat, thin, rectangular piece of wood or plastic which is used for a particular purpose. ❏ ...a cutting board. ❷ N-COUNT A **board** is a square piece of wood or stiff cardboard that you use for playing games such as chess. ❏ ...a checkers board. ❸ N-COUNT You can refer to a blackboard or a bulletin board as a **board**. ❏ He wrote a few more notes on the board. ❹ N-COUNT **Boards** are long flat pieces of wood which are used, for example, to make floors or walls. ❏ The floor was drafty bare boards. ❺ N-COUNT The **board** of a company or organization is the group of people who control and direct it. [BUSINESS] ❏ Arthur has made a recommendation, which he wants her to put before the board at a special meeting scheduled for tomorrow afternoon. ❻ → see also **board of directors** ❼ N-COUNT **Board** is used in the names of various organizations which are involved in dealing with a particular kind of activity. ❏ The Scottish tourist board said 33,000 Japanese visited Scotland last year. ❽ V-T When you **board** a train, ship, or aircraft, you get on it in order to travel somewhere. [FORMAL] ❏ I boarded the plane bound for Boston. ❾ N-UNCOUNT **Board** is the food which is provided when you stay somewhere, for example in a hotel. ❏ Free room and board are provided for all hotel staff. ❿ PHRASE If a policy or a situation applies **across the board**, it affects everything or everyone in a particular group. ❏ There are hefty charges across the board for one-way rental. ⓫ PHRASE If something **goes by the board**, it is rejected or ignored, or is no longer possible. ❏ It's a case of not what you know but who you know in this world today and qualifications quite go by the board. ⓬ PHRASE When you are **on board** a train, ship, or aircraft, you are on it or in it. ❏ All 269 people on board the plane were killed. ⓭ PHRASE If someone **sweeps the board** in a competition or election, they win nearly everything that it is possible to win. ❏ Spain swept the board in boys' team competitions. ⓮ PHRASE If you **take on board** an idea or a problem, you begin to accept it or understand it. ❏ You may have to accept their point of view, but hope that they will take on board some of what you have said. ⓯ → See feature box at **theater**
▶ **board up** PHRASAL VERB If you **board up** a door or window, you fix pieces of wood over it so that it is covered up. ❏ Shopkeepers have boarded up their windows.

board and lodg|ing N-UNCOUNT If you are provided with **board and lodging**, you are provided with food and a place to sleep, especially as part of the conditions of a job. [mainly BRIT]

board-certified also **board certified** ADJ A doctor who is **board-certified** has passed tests and meets the standards of a board of specialists in their area of medicine. [AM] ❏ ...a board-certified neurologist.

board game (**board games**) N-COUNT A **board game** is a game such as chess or backgammon that people play by moving small objects around on a board. ❏ ...a new board game played with dice.

board|ing /bɔrdɪŋ/ N-UNCOUNT **Boarding** is an arrangement by which children live at school during the school term. ❏ ...the master in charge of boarding. ❏ Annual boarding fees are $10,350.

board|ing card [BRIT] → see **boarding pass**

board|ing house (**boarding houses**) also **boardinghouse** N-COUNT A **boarding house** is a house that people pay to stay in for a short time.

board|ing pass (**boarding passes**) N-COUNT A **boarding pass** is a card that a passenger must have when boarding a plane or a boat.

board|ing school (**boarding schools**) also **boarding-school** N-VAR A **boarding school** is a school that some or all of the students live in during the school term. Compare **day school**.

board of di|rec|tors (**boards of directors**) N-COUNT A company's **board of directors** is the group of people elected by its shareholders to manage the company. [BUSINESS] ❏ The board of directors has approved the decision unanimously.

board|room /bɔrdrum/ (**boardrooms**) also **board room** N-COUNT The **boardroom** is a room where the board of a company meets. [BUSINESS] ❏ Everyone had already assembled in the boardroom for the 9:00 a.m. session.

board|walk /bɔrdwɔk/ (**boardwalks**) N-COUNT A **boardwalk** is a path made of wooden boards, especially one along a beach. [AM]

boast /boʊst/ (**boasts, boasting, boasted**) ❶ V-T/V-I If someone **boasts** about something that they have done or that they

boastful

own, they talk about it very proudly, in a way that other people may find irritating or offensive. [DISAPPROVAL] ▫ *Witnesses said Furci boasted that he took part in killing them.* ▫ *Carol boasted about her costume.* • N-COUNT **Boast** is also a noun. ▫ *It is the charity's proud boast that it has never yet turned anyone away.* **2** V-T If someone or something can **boast** a particular achievement or possession, they have achieved or possess that thing. ▫ *The houses will boast the latest energy-saving technology.*

boast|ful /bo͞ustfəl/ ADJ If someone is **boastful**, they talk too proudly about something that they have done or that they own. [DISAPPROVAL] ▫ *I'm not being boastful.* ▫ *...boastful predictions.*

boat ♦♦◊ /bo͞ut/ (boats) **1** N-COUNT [also by N] A **boat** is something in which people can travel across water. ▫ *One of the best ways to see the area is in a small boat.* **2** N-COUNT You can refer to a passenger ship as a **boat**. ▫ *When the boat reached Cape Town, we said goodbye.* **3** PHRASE If you say that someone has **missed the boat**, you mean that they have missed an opportunity and may not get another. ▫ *If you don't want to miss the boat, the auction is scheduled for 2:30 p.m. on June 26.* **4** → See also color supplement

---
COLLOCATIONS

boat
NOUN **1**
noun + **boat**: canal, patrol, pleasure, rescue; fishing, sailing
adjective + **boat**: inflatable, wooden
verb + **boat**: moor; sail, steer; capsize

VOCABULARY IN CONTEXT

Boats

A life on the open seas might seem like the dream, but there's one obstacle for many people contemplating sailing the seven seas: **seasickness**. However glamorous the **yacht**, there's nothing glamorous about being sick on one. Once you **set sail**, just thinking about seasickness can bring it on, but it's more likely to start in **choppy seas**. The bigger the boat, the more stable it will be, so **ferries** and **cruise ships** are a safer bet than **dinghies** or fishing **trawlers**. The one boat on which you can be sure to avoid seasickness is a river **barge** since there's no ocean **swell** to cause motion sickness. The good news is that there are plenty of cures for seasickness, and once you find your sealegs, you'll be able to handle most **nautical** adventures.

---

boat|builder /bo͞utbɪldər/ (boatbuilders) also **boat builder** N-COUNT A **boatbuilder** is a person or company that makes boats.

boat|building /bo͞utbɪldɪŋ/ also **boat-building** N-UNCOUNT **Boatbuilding** is the craft or industry of making boats. ▫ *Sunbeam Yachts started boatbuilding in 1870.*

boat|er /bo͞utər/ (boaters) N-COUNT A **boater** or a **straw boater** is a hard straw hat with a flat top and brim that is often worn for certain social occasions in the summer.

boat|house /bo͞uthaʊs/ (boathouses) N-COUNT A **boathouse** is a building at the edge of a lake, in which boats are kept.

boat|ing /bo͞utɪŋ/ N-UNCOUNT **Boating** is traveling on a lake or river in a small boat for pleasure. ▫ *You can go boating or play tennis.*

boat|load /bo͞utloʊd/ (boatloads) also **boat load** N-COUNT [oft N of N] A **boatload** of people or things is a lot of people or things that are, or were, in a boat. ▫ *...a boatload of rice.*

boat|man /bo͞utmən/ (boatmen) N-COUNT A **boatman** is a man who is paid by people to take them across an area of water in a small boat, or a man who hires boats out to them for a short time.

boat peo|ple N-PLURAL **Boat people** are people who escape from their country in small boats to travel to another country in the hope that they will be able to live there. ▫ *...50,000 Vietnamese boat people.*

boat|yard /bo͞utyɑrd/ (boatyards) N-COUNT A **boatyard** is a place where boats are built and repaired or kept.

bob /bɒb/ (bobs, bobbing, bobbed) **1** V-I If something **bobs**, it moves up and down, like something does when it is floating on water. ▫ *Huge balloons bobbed about in the sky above.* **2** V-I If you **bob** somewhere, you move there quickly so that you disappear from view or come into view. ▫ *She handed over a form, then bobbed down again behind a computer screen.*

bobbed /bɒbd/ ADJ If someone's hair is **bobbed**, it is cut in a fairly short hair style with the hair the same length all the way round, except for the front.

bob|bin /bɒbɪn/ (bobbins) N-COUNT A **bobbin** is a small round object on which thread or wool is wound to hold it, for example, on a sewing machine.

bob|ble /bɒbəl/ (bobbles, bobbling, bobbled) **1** V-T If a player **bobbles** a ball, they drop it or fail to control it. [AM] ▫ *The ball was bobbled momentarily, allowing Holloway to race home.* **2** N-COUNT A **bobble** is a small ball of material, usually made of wool, that is used for decorating clothes. [BRIT]

in AM, usually use **tassel**

bob|by pin /bɒbi pɪn/ (bobby pins) N-COUNT A **bobby pin** is a small piece of metal or plastic bent back on itself that someone uses to hold their hair in position. [AM]

in BRIT, use **hairgrip**

bob|by socks /bɒbi sɒks/ also **bobbysox** N-PLURAL **Bobby socks** or **bobbysox** are short socks worn by girls or women. [AM, OLD-FASHIONED]

bob|cat /bɒbkæt/ (bobcats) N-COUNT A **bobcat** is an animal in the cat family that has reddish-brown fur with dark spots or stripes and a short tail. Bobcats live in North America. ▫ *Bobcats roam wild in the mountains.*

bob|sled /bɒbslɛd/ (bobsleds) N-COUNT A **bobsled** is a vehicle with long thin strips of metal fixed to the bottom that is used for racing downhill on ice. [mainly AM]

in BRIT, usually use **bobsleigh**

bob|sleigh /bɒbsleɪ/ (bobsleighs) N-COUNT A **bobsleigh** is the same as a **bobsled**. [BRIT]

bo|da|cious /boʊdeɪʃəs/ [APPROVAL] **1** ADJ If you say that someone or something is **bodacious**, you mean that they are very good or impressive. [mainly AM, INFORMAL] ▫ *...the tasteful and bodacious TT sports coupe.* **2** ADJ If you say that someone is **bodacious**, you mean that they are appealing or sexually attractive. [mainly AM, INFORMAL] ▫ *...such bodacious models as Elle Macpherson and Rachel Williams.* ▫ *...a bodacious physique.*

bode /boʊd/ (bodes, boding, boded) V-I If something **bodes** ill, it makes you think that something bad will happen in the future. If something **bodes** well, it makes you think that something good will happen. [FORMAL] ▫ *She says the way the bill was passed bodes ill for democracy.*

bod|ice /bɒdɪs/ (bodices) N-COUNT The **bodice** of a dress is the part above the waist. ▫ *...a dress with a fitted bodice and circle skirt.*

bod|ice rip|per (bodice rippers) N-COUNT You can refer to a movie or novel that is set in the past and which includes a lot of sex scenes as a **bodice ripper**, especially if you do not think it is very good and is just intended to entertain people. [DISAPPROVAL]

bodice-ripping ADJ [ADJ n] A **bodice-ripping** movie or novel is one that is set in the past and that includes a lot of sex scenes. You use this word especially if you do not think it is very good and is just intended to entertain people. [DISAPPROVAL] ☐ ...bodice-ripping yarns on TV.

bodi|ly /bɒdɪli/ **1** ADJ [ADJ n] Your **bodily** needs and functions are the needs and functions of your body. ☐ ...12-hour shifts without a break in which to eat or attend to bodily needs. **2** ADV [ADV with v] You use **bodily** to indicate that an action involves the whole of someone's body. ☐ I was hurled bodily to the deck.

bodi|ly func|tion (bodily functions) N-COUNT A person's **bodily functions** are the normal physical processes that regularly occur in their body, particularly the ability to urinate and defecate. ☐ The child was not able to speak, walk properly or control bodily functions.

body ◆◆◆ /bɒdi/ (bodies) **1** N-COUNT Your **body** is all your physical parts, including your head, arms, and legs. ☐ The largest organ in the body is the liver. **2** N-COUNT You can also refer to the main part of your body, except for your arms, head, and legs, as your **body**. ☐ Lying flat on the floor, twist your body on to one hip and cross your upper leg over your body. **3** N-COUNT You can refer to a person's dead body as a **body**. ☐ Officials said they had found no traces of violence on the body of the politician. **4** N-COUNT A **body** is an organized group of people who deal with something officially. ☐ She was elected student body president at the University of North Carolina. **5** N-COUNT A **body of** people is a group of people who are together or who are connected in some way. ☐ ...that large body of people which teaches other people how to teach. **6** N-SING The **body** of something such as a building or a document is the main part of it or the largest part of it. ☐ The main body of the church had been turned into a massive television studio. **7** N-COUNT The **body** of a car or airplane is the main part of it, not including its engine, wheels, or wings. ☐ The only shade was under the body of the plane. **8** N-COUNT A **body of** water is a large area of water, such as a lake or an ocean. ☐ It is probably the most polluted body of water in the world. **9** N-COUNT A **body of** information is a large amount of it. ☐ An increasing body of evidence suggests that all of us have cancer cells in our bodies at times during our lives. **10** N-UNCOUNT If you say that an alcoholic drink has **body**, you mean that it has a full and strong flavor. ☐ ...a dry wine with good body. **11** → See feature box at **body language**

COLLOCATIONS

body
NOUN **4**
noun + **body**: government, industry, tourism, trade; review
adjective + **body**: independent, professional, public, representative; advisory, governing, regulatory, ruling, statutory
verb + **body**: create, establish, set up

body ar|mor
in BRIT, use **body armour**
N-UNCOUNT **Body armor** is special protective clothing that people such as soldiers and police officers sometimes wear when they are in danger of being attacked with guns or other weapons.

body bag (body bags) N-COUNT A **body bag** is a specially designed large plastic bag which is used to carry a dead body away, for example when someone has been killed in a battle or an accident. ☐ ...the prospect of young soldiers coming home in body bags.

body blow (body blows) also **body-blow** N-COUNT A **body blow** is something that causes great disappointment and difficulty to someone who is trying to achieve something. ☐ His resignation was a body blow to the team.

body|builder /bɒdibɪldər/ (bodybuilders) also **body builder** N-COUNT A **bodybuilder** is a person who does special exercises regularly in order to make his or her muscles grow bigger.

body|building /bɒdibɪldɪŋ/ also **body building** N-UNCOUNT **Bodybuilding** is the activity of doing special exercises regularly in order to make your muscles grow bigger.

body clock (body clocks) N-COUNT [usu sing] Your **body clock** is the internal biological mechanism that causes your body to automatically behave in particular ways at particular times of the day. ☐ Jet lag is caused because the body clock does not readjust immediately to the time change.

body|guard /bɒdigɑrd/ (bodyguards) N-COUNT A **bodyguard** is a person or a group of people employed to protect someone. ☐ Three of his bodyguards were injured in the attack.

VOCABULARY IN CONTEXT

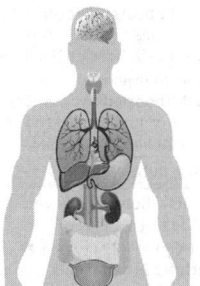

Body parts

Even if you've studied basic anatomy, there's still a lot to know about your amazing body. You might think the hardest bone in your body is the **skull**, but it's actually the **jawbone**. Your **ribs**, on the other hand, can break with a mere sneeze, even though they are there to protect your **heart** and **lungs**. You could survive without a number of your so-called 'vital' organs. For example, if your **stomach**, **spleen**, one **kidney** and one lung, 80% of your **intestines**, 75% of your **liver**, and pretty much all your **reproductive organs** were removed, you'd still live – albeit not very comfortably. The largest organ, of course, is the skin, and it's thickest on the **heels** and **soles** of your feet (more than 15 times thicker than anywhere else on your body). It's thinnest on the **eyelids**.

VOCABULARY IN CONTEXT

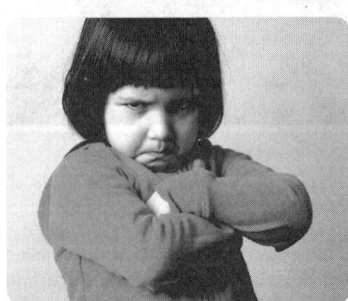

Body language and gestures

The **body language** and **gestures** we use every day are so deeply ingrained that, often, we're not even conscious of doing them. For one day, try noticing how much people express themselves without using words.

For example, a local café: **raising her eyebrows**, the barista holds up some cocoa powder, and the customer **shakes his head**. At the next table, a teenager being scolded **rolls her eyes** and **folds her arms** angrily. A man in a business suit stares at his phone and **fidgets**. He adjusts his tie and **taps his foot** surreptitiously. A guy **flirts** with a girl. He makes direct **eye contact** with her, and she **goes red**. A mother offers her toddler a cupcake. He **nods his head** and claps emphatically.

Why not challenge yourself to pay more attention to this powerful form of **non-verbal communication**?

body lan|guage N-UNCOUNT Your **body language** is the way in which you show your feelings or thoughts to other people by means of the position or movements of your body, rather than with words. ❏ *I can tell by your body language that you're happy with the decision.*

body mass in|dex N-SING A person's **body mass index** is a measurement that represents the relationship between their weight and their height. [MEDICAL] ❏ *...those with a body mass index of 30 and over.*

body odor

in BRIT, use **body odour**

N-UNCOUNT **Body odor** is an unpleasant smell caused by sweat on a person's body.

body poli|tic N-SING [usu the N] The **body politic** is all the people of a nation when they are considered as a complete political group. [FORMAL] ❏ *...the king was the head of the body politic.*

body posi|tiv|ity N-UNCOUNT **Body positivity** is the idea that people should feel happy with and proud of their body, whatever shape or size it is. ❏ *I want to encourage body positivity and self-acceptance in girls like me.*

body-search (body-searches, body-searching, body-searched) also **body search** V-T If a person is **body-searched**, someone such as a police officer searches them while they remain clothed. Compare **strip-search**. ❏ *Foreign journalists were body-searched by airport police.* • N-COUNT **Body search** is also a noun. ❏ *Fans may undergo body searches by security guards.*

body stock|ing (body stockings) N-COUNT A **body stocking** is a piece of clothing that covers the whole of someone's body and fits tightly. Body stockings are often worn by dancers.

body|suit /bɒdisuːt/ (bodysuits) N-COUNT A **bodysuit** is a piece of clothing that fits tightly over the top part of the body and fastens between the legs.

body|work /bɒdiwɜːrk/ N-UNCOUNT The **bodywork** of a motor vehicle is the outside part of it. ❏ *A second hand car dealer will always look at the bodywork rather than the engine.*

Boer /bour, bɔːr/ (Boers) N-COUNT The **Boers** are the descendants of the Dutch people who went to live in South Africa.

bog /bɒg/ (bogs) N-COUNT A **bog** is an area of land that is very wet and muddy.

bo|gey /boʊgi/ (bogeys)

The spelling **bogy** and the plural form **bogies** are also used.

■ N-COUNT A **bogey** is something or someone that people are worried about, perhaps without much cause or reason. ❏ *Age is another bogey for those in the acting business.* ■ N-COUNT In golf, when a player scores a **bogey** at a hole, they take one more shot than the standard that has been fixed for that hole.

bogey|man /bʊgimæn, boʊgi-/ (bogeymen) also **bogey man, boogeyman** ■ N-COUNT [oft the N] A **bogeyman** is an imaginary evil spirit. Some parents tell their children that the bogeyman will catch them if they behave badly. ■ N-COUNT [usu with supp] A **bogeyman** is someone whose ideas or actions are disapproved of by some people, and who is described by them as evil or unpleasant in order to make other people afraid. [DISAPPROVAL] ❏ *The media depict him as a left-wing bogeyman.*

bogged down ADJ If you get **bogged down** in something, it prevents you from making progress or getting something done. ❏ *But why get bogged down in legal details?*

bog|gle /bɒgəl/ (boggles, boggling, boggled) V-T/V-I If you say that the mind **boggles** at something, or that something **boggles** the mind, you mean that it is so strange or amazing that it is difficult to imagine or understand. ❏ *The mind boggles at the possibilities that could be in store for us.*

bog|gy /bɒgi/ (boggier, boggiest) ADJ **Boggy** land is very wet and muddy land.

bo|gus /boʊgəs/ ADJ If you describe something as **bogus**, you mean that it is not genuine. ❏ *...their bogus insurance claim.*

bogy /boʊgi/ (bogies) → see bogey

bo|he|mian /boʊhiːmiən/ (bohemians) ■ ADJ [usu ADJ n] You can use **bohemian** to describe artistic people who live in an unconventional way. ❏ *...a bohemian writer.* ❏ *...the bohemian lifestyle of the French capital.* • N-COUNT A **bohemian** is someone who lives in a bohemian way. ❏ *...this community of writers, artists, and assorted bohemians.* ■ → See feature box at **town**

Bo|he|mian ADJ **Bohemian** means belonging or relating to Bohemia or its people.

boil ✦✧ /bɔɪl/ (boils, boiling, boiled) ■ V-T/V-I When a hot liquid **boils** or when you **boil** it, bubbles appear in it and it starts to change into steam or vapor. ❏ *I stood in the kitchen, waiting for the water to boil.* ❏ *Boil the water in the saucepan and add the sage.* ■ V-T/V-I When you **boil** a pot or a kettle, or put it on to **boil**, you heat the water inside it until it boils. ❏ *He had nothing to do but boil the kettle and make the tea.* ■ V-I [only cont] When a pot **is boiling**, the water inside it has reached boiling point. ❏ *The pot was boiling.* ■ V-T/V-I When you **boil** food, or when it **boils**, it is cooked in boiling water. ❏ *Boil the chick peas, add garlic and lemon juice.* ❏ *I'd peel potatoes and put them on to boil.* ■ V-I [usu cont] If you **are boiling** with anger, you are very angry. ❏ *I used to be all sweetness and light on the outside, but inside I would be boiling with rage.* ■ N-COUNT A **boil** is a red, painful swelling on your skin that contains a thick yellow liquid called pus. ■ → see also **boiling** ■ PHRASE When you **bring a liquid to a boil**, you heat it until it boils. When it **comes to a boil**, it begins to boil. ❏ *Put water, butter and lard into a saucepan and bring slowly to the boil.*

▶ **boil down to** PHRASAL VERB If you say that a situation or problem **boils down to** a particular thing or can **be boiled down to** a particular thing, you mean that this is the most important or the most basic aspect of it. ❏ *What they want boils down to just one thing. It is land.*

▶ **boil over** ■ PHRASAL VERB When a liquid that is being heated **boils over**, it rises and flows over the edge of the container. ❏ *Heat the liquid in a large, wide container rather than a high narrow one, or it can boil over.* ■ PHRASAL VERB When someone's feelings **boil over**, they lose their temper or become violent. ❏ *Sometimes frustration and anger can boil over into direct and violent action.*

boil|er /bɔɪlər/ (boilers) N-COUNT A **boiler** is a device that burns gas, oil, electricity, or coal in order to provide hot water, especially for the central heating in a building.

boil|er|plate /bɔɪlərpleɪt/ (boilerplates) N-VAR A **boilerplate** is a basic written contract that can be used to make many different kinds of contracts. ❏ *...a predictable boilerplate of tax-relief proposals.*

boil|er suit (boiler suits) N-COUNT A **boiler suit** consists of a single piece of clothing that combines pants and a jacket. You wear it over your clothes in order to protect them from dirt while you are working. [BRIT]

in AM, use **overalls**

boil|ing /bɔɪlɪŋ/ ■ ADJ Something that is **boiling** or **boiling hot** is very hot. ❏ *"It's boiling in here," complained Miriam.* ■ ADJ [v-link ADJ] If you say that you are **boiling** or **boiling hot**, you mean that you feel very hot, usually unpleasantly hot. ❏ *When everybody else is boiling hot, I'm freezing!*

boil|ing point ■ N-UNCOUNT The **boiling point** of a liquid is the temperature at which it starts to change into steam or vapor. For example, the boiling point of water is 212° Fahrenheit. ❏ *Heat the cream to boiling point and pour it over the chocolate.* ■ N-UNCOUNT If a situation reaches **boiling point** or **the boiling point**, the people involved have become so angry that they can no longer remain calm and in control of themselves. ❏ *The situation is rapidly reaching boiling point, and the army has been put on stand by.* ❏ *Meanwhile, anger has reached the boiling point among Haitian-Americans in south Florida.*

bois|ter|ous /bɔɪstərəs, -strəs/ ADJ Someone who is **boisterous** is noisy, lively, and full of energy. ❏ *...a boisterous but good-natured crowd.*

bold /boʊld/ (bolder, boldest) ■ ADJ Someone who is **bold** is not afraid to do things that involve risk or danger. ❏ *Amrita becomes a bold, daring rebel.* ❏ *In 1960 this was a bold move.* • **bold|ly** ADV [ADV with v] ❏ *You must act boldly and confidently.* • **bold|ness** N-UNCOUNT ❏ *Don't forget the boldness of his economic program.*

2 ADJ Someone who is **bold** is not shy or embarrassed in the company of other people. ☐ *I don't feel I'm being bold, because it's always been natural for me to just speak out about whatever disturbs me.* • **bold|ly** ADV ☐ *"You should do it," the girl said, boldly.* **3** ADJ A **bold** color or pattern is very bright and noticeable. ☐ *...bold flowers in various shades of red, blue or white.* **4** ADJ **Bold** lines or designs are drawn in a clear, strong way. ☐ *Each picture is shown in color on one page and as a bold outline on the opposite page.* **5** N-UNCOUNT **Bold** is print which is thicker and looks blacker than ordinary printed letters. [TECHNICAL] ☐ *When a candidate is elected his or her name will be highlighted in bold.*

bo|lero (boleros)

Pronounced /bəlɛroʊ/ for meaning 1, and /bəlɛəroʊ/ for meaning 2.

1 N-COUNT A **bolero** is a very short jacket, sometimes without sleeves. **2** N-COUNT The **bolero** is a traditional Spanish dance. ☐ *They danced a romantic bolero together.*

Bo|liv|ian /bəlɪviən/ (Bolivians) ADJ **Bolivian** means belonging or relating to Bolivia or its people. • N-COUNT A **Bolivian** is a person who comes from Bolivia.

bol|lard /bɒlərd/ (bollards) N-COUNT **Bollards** are strong wooden or metal posts on the side of a river or harbor. Boats are tied to them.

bo|lo|gna /bəloʊni/ (bolognas) N-VAR **Bologna** is a type of large smoked sausage, usually made of beef, veal, or pork. [AM] ☐ *...a bologna sandwich.*

Bol|she|vik /boʊlʃɪvɪk, bɒl-/ (Bolsheviks) **1** ADJ **Bolshevik** is used to describe the political system and ideas that Lenin and his supporters introduced in Russia after the Russian Revolution of 1917. ☐ *Seventy-four years after the Bolshevik Revolution, the Soviet era ended.* ☐ *...anti-Bolshevik forces.* **2** N-COUNT A **Bolshevik** was a person who supported Lenin and his political ideas.

Bol|she|vism /boʊlʃɪvɪzəm, bɒl-/ N-UNCOUNT **Bolshevism** is the political system and ideas that Lenin and his supporters introduced in Russia after the Russian Revolution of 1917.

bol|ster /boʊlstər/ (bolsters, bolstering, bolstered) **1** V-T If you **bolster** something such as someone's confidence or courage, you increase it. ☐ *Hopes of an early cut in interest rates bolstered confidence.* **2** V-T If someone tries to **bolster** their position in a situation, they try to strengthen it. ☐ *The country is free to adopt policies to bolster its economy.* **3** N-COUNT A **bolster** is a firm pillow shaped like a long tube which is sometimes put across a bed instead of pillows, or under the ordinary pillows.

bolt /boʊlt/ (bolts, bolting, bolted) **1** N-COUNT A **bolt** is a long metal object that screws into a nut and is used to fasten things together. **2** V-T When you **bolt** one thing to another, you fasten them firmly together, using a bolt. ☐ *The safety belt is easy to fit as there's no need to bolt it to seat belt anchorage points.* ☐ *Bolt the components together.* **3** N-COUNT A **bolt** on a door or window is a metal bar that you can slide across in order to fasten the door or window. ☐ *I heard the sound of a bolt being slowly and reluctantly slid open.* **4** V-T When you **bolt** a door or window, you slide the bolt across to fasten it. ☐ *He reminded her that he would have to lock and bolt the kitchen door after her.* **5** V-I If a person or animal **bolts**, they suddenly start to run very fast, often because something has frightened them. ☐ *The pig rose squealing and bolted.* **6** V-T If you **bolt** your food, you eat it so quickly that you hardly chew it or taste it. ☐ *Being under stress can cause you to miss meals, eat on the move, or bolt your food.* • PHRASAL VERB **Bolt down** means the same as **bolt**. ☐ *I like to think back to high school, when I could bolt down three or four burgers and a pile of French fries.* **7** N-COUNT A **bolt of** lightning is a flash of lightning that is seen as a white line in the sky. ☐ *Suddenly a bolt of lightning crackled through the sky.* **8** PHRASE If someone is sitting or standing **bolt upright**, they are sitting or standing very straight. ☐ *When I pushed his door open, Trevor was sitting bolt upright in bed.* **9** → See also color supplement

bomb ♦♦◊ /bɒm/ (bombs, bombing, bombed) **1** N-COUNT A **bomb** is a device that explodes and damages or destroys a large area. ☐ *Bombs went off at two London train stations.* ☐ *It's not known who planted the bomb.* **2** N-SING Nuclear weapons are sometimes referred to as **the bomb**. ☐ *They are generally thought to have the bomb.* **3** V-T When people **bomb** a place, they attack it with bombs. ☐ *Air force jets bombed the airport.* • **bomb|ing** (bombings) N-VAR ☐ *Aerial bombing of rebel positions is continuing.*

SYNONYMS

bomb
NOUN **1**
explosive: *There were traces of explosives in the bedroom.*
mine: *He stepped on an unexploded mine.*
missile: *...nuclear missiles.*
grenade: *A hand grenade was thrown at an army patrol.*

---

bom|bard /bɒmbɑrd/ (bombards, bombarding, bombarded) **1** V-T If you **bombard** someone with something, you make them face a great deal of it. For example, if you **bombard** them with questions or criticism, you keep asking them a lot of questions or you keep criticizing them. ☐ *He bombarded Catherine with questions to which he should have known the answers.* **2** V-T When soldiers **bombard** a place, they attack it with continuous heavy gunfire or bombs. ☐ *Rebel artillery units have regularly bombarded the airport.*

bom|bard|ment /bɒmbɑrdmənt/ (bombardments) **1** N-VAR A **bombardment** is a strong and continuous attack of gunfire or bombing. ☐ *The city has been flattened by heavy artillery bombardments.* **2** N-VAR A **bombardment** of ideas, demands, questions, or criticisms is an aggressive and exhausting stream of them. ☐ *...the constant bombardment of images urging that work was important.*

bom|bast /bɒmbæst/ N-UNCOUNT **Bombast** is trying to impress people by saying things that sound impressive but have little meaning. [DISAPPROVAL] ☐ *There was no bombast or conceit in his speech.*

bom|bas|tic /bɒmbæstɪk/ ADJ If you describe someone as **bombastic**, you are criticizing them for trying to impress other people by saying things that sound impressive but have little meaning. [DISAPPROVAL] ☐ *He was vain and bombastic.* ☐ *...the bombastic style adopted by his predecessor.*

bomb dis|pos|al N-UNCOUNT [usu N n] **Bomb disposal** is the job of dealing with bombs that have not exploded, by taking out the fuse or by blowing them up in a controlled explosion. ☐ *...an Army bomb disposal squad.*

bombed-out ADJ [ADJ n] A **bombed-out** building has been damaged or destroyed by a bomb. ☐ *...a bombed-out hospital.*

bomb|er /bɒmər/ (bombers) **1** N-COUNT **Bombers** are people who cause bombs to explode in public places. ☐ *Detectives hunting the bombers will be eager to interview him.* **2** N-COUNT A **bomber** is a military aircraft which drops bombs. ☐ *...a high-speed bomber with twin engines.*

bomb|er jack|et (bomber jackets) N-COUNT A **bomber jacket** is a short jacket that is gathered into a band at the waist or hips. ☐ *...a black leather bomber jacket.*

bomb|shell /bɒmʃɛl/ (bombshells) N-COUNT A **bombshell** is a sudden piece of bad or unexpected news. ☐ *His resignation is a political bombshell.* • PHRASE If someone **drops a bombshell**, they give you a sudden piece of bad or unexpected news.

bomb site (bomb sites) also **bombsite** N-COUNT A **bomb site** is an empty area where a bomb has destroyed all the buildings. ☐ *New housing was erected on the old bomb sites.*

bona fide /boʊnə faɪdi/ ADJ [usu ADJ n] If something or someone is **bona fide**, they are genuine or real. [FORMAL] ☐ *We are happy to donate to bona fide charitable causes.*

bona fi|des /boʊnə faɪdiz/ N-PLURAL [usu with poss] Someone's **bona fides** are their good or sincere intentions. [FORMAL] ☐ *Mr. Perks questioned them at length to establish their bona fides.*

bo|nan|za /bənænzə/ (bonanzas) N-COUNT You can refer to a sudden great increase in wealth, success, or luck as a **bonanza**. ☐ *The expected sales bonanza hadn't materialized.*

bond ♦♦◊ /bɒnd/ (bonds, bonding, bonded) **1** N-COUNT A **bond** between people is a strong feeling of friendship, love, or shared beliefs and experiences that unites them. ☐ *The experience created a very special bond between us.* **2** V-RECIP When people **bond** with each other, they form a relationship based on love or shared beliefs and experiences. You can also say that people **bond** or that something **bonds** them. ☐ *Belinda was having difficulty bonding with the baby.* ☐ *They all bonded while writing graffiti* together. **3** N-COUNT A **bond** between people or groups is a close connection that they have with each other, for example because they have a special agreement. ☐ ...*the strong bond between church and nation.* **4** N-COUNT A **bond** between two things is the way in which they stick to one another or are joined in some way. ☐ *If you experience difficulty with the superglue not creating a bond with dry wood, moisten the surfaces with water.* **5** V-RECIP When one thing **bonds** with another, it sticks to it or becomes joined to it in some way. You can also say that two things **bond** together, or that something **bonds** them together. ☐ *In graphite sheets, carbon atoms bond together in rings.* **6** N-COUNT When a government or company issues a **bond**, it borrows money from investors. The certificate that is issued to investors who lend money is also called a **bond**. [BUSINESS] ☐ *Most of it will be financed by government bonds.* **7** → see also **junk bond**

COLLOCATIONS

bond
NOUN **1**
adjective + **bond**: close, special, strong, unbreakable; common
verb + **bond**: create, forge, form; cement, strengthen

---

bond|age /bɒndɪdʒ/ **1** N-UNCOUNT **Bondage** is the condition of being someone's property and having to work for them. ☐ *Masters sometimes allowed their slaves to buy their way out of bondage.* **2** N-UNCOUNT **Bondage** is the condition of not being free because you are strongly influenced by something or someone. [FORMAL] ☐ *All people, she said, lived their lives in bondage to hunger, pain and lust.*

bond|ed /bɒndɪd/ ADJ A **bonded** company has entered into a legal agreement that offers its customers some protection if the company does not fulfill its contract with them. [BUSINESS] ☐ *They are a fully bonded and licensed company.*

bond|hold|er /bɒndhoʊldər/ (bondholders) also **bond holder** N-COUNT A **bondholder** is a person who owns one or more investment bonds. [BUSINESS]

bone ♦◇◇ /boʊn/ (bones, boning, boned) **1** N-VAR Your **bones** are the hard parts inside your body that together form your skeleton. ☐ *Many passengers suffered broken bones.* ☐ *The body is made up primarily of bone, muscle, and fat.* **2** V-T If you **bone** a piece of meat or fish, you remove the bones from it before cooking it. ☐ *Make sure that you do not pierce the skin when boning the chicken thighs.* **3** ADJ [ADJ n] A **bone** tool or ornament is made of bone. ☐ *...a small, expensive pocketknife with a bone handle.* **4** PHRASE The **bare bones** of something are its most basic parts or details. ☐ *There are not even the bare bones of a garden here – I've got nothing.* **5** → see also **bare-bones** **6** PHRASE If something such as costs are cut **to the bone**, they are reduced to the minimum possible. ☐ *It has survived by cutting its costs to the bone.*

▶ **bone up on** PHRASAL VERB If you **bone up** on a subject, you try to find out about it or remind yourself what you have already learned about it. [INFORMAL] ☐ *I had spent the last few months boning up on neurology.*

bone chi|na N-UNCOUNT **Bone china** is a kind of thin china that contains powdered bone.

-boned /-boʊnd/ COMB IN ADJ **-boned** combines with adjectives such as 'big' and 'fine' to form adjectives which describe a person as having a particular type of bone structure or build. ☐ *He was seven years old, small and fine-boned like his mother.*

bone dry also **bone-dry** ADJ If you say that something is **bone dry**, you are emphasizing that it is very dry indeed. [EMPHASIS] ☐ *Now the river bed is bone dry.*

bone mar|row N-UNCOUNT **Bone marrow** is the soft fatty substance inside human or animal bones. ☐ *There are 2,000 children worldwide who need a bone marrow transplant.*

bone meal also **bonemeal** N-UNCOUNT **Bone meal** is a substance made from animal bones that is used as a fertilizer.

bone of con|ten|tion (bones of contention) N-COUNT If a particular matter or issue is a **bone of contention**, it is the subject of a disagreement or argument. ☐ *The main bone of contention is the temperature level of the air-conditioners.*

bon|fire /bɒnfaɪər/ (bonfires) N-COUNT A **bonfire** is a fire that is made outdoors, usually to burn waste. Bonfires are also sometimes lit as part of a celebration. ☐ *With bonfires outlawed in urban areas, gardeners must cart their refuse to a dump.*

WORD HISTORY

bonfire
A **bonfire** is literally a 'bonefire.' Bones were used as fuel in the Middle Ages.

---

bong /bɒŋ/ (bongs) N-COUNT; SOUND A **bong** is a long, deep sound such as the sound made by a big bell.

bon|go /bɒŋgoʊ/ (bongos) N-COUNT A **bongo** is a small drum that you play with your hands.

bon|ho|mie /bɒnəmi/ N-UNCOUNT **Bonhomie** is happy, good-natured friendliness. [FORMAL] ☐ *He was full of bonhomie.*

bon mot /bɒn moʊ/ (bons mots or bon mots) N-COUNT A **bon mot** is a clever, witty remark. [WRITTEN] ☐ *...a cheeky bon mot.*

bon|net /bɒnɪt/ (bonnets) **1** N-COUNT A **bonnet** is a hat with ribbons that are tied under the chin. Bonnets are now worn by babies. In the past, they were also worn by women. **2** N-COUNT The **bonnet** of a car is the metal cover over the engine at the front. [BRIT]

in AM, use **hood**

3 → See also color supplement

bon|sai /bɒnsaɪ/ (bonsai) **1** N-COUNT [oft N n] A **bonsai** is a tree or shrub that has been kept very small by growing it in a little pot and cutting it in a special way. ☐ *...a beautiful Japanese bonsai tree.* **2** N-UNCOUNT **Bonsai** is the art of growing very small shrubs and trees.

bo|nus /boʊnəs/ (bonuses) **1** N-COUNT A **bonus** is an extra amount of money that is added to someone's pay, usually because they have worked very hard. ☐ *Workers in big firms receive a substantial part of their pay in the form of bonuses and overtime.* ☐ *...a $60 bonus.* **2** N-COUNT A **bonus** is something good that you get in addition to something else, and which you would not usually expect. ☐ *We felt we might finish third. Any better would be a bonus.*

bon voy|age /bɒn vɔɪɑːʒ/ CONVENTION You say '**bon voyage**' to someone who is going on a journey, as a way of saying goodbye and wishing them a good trip. [FORMULAE] ☐ *Goodbye! Bon voyage!*

bony /boʊni/ (bonier, boniest) **1** ADJ Someone who has a **bony** face or **bony** hands, for example, has a very thin face or very thin hands, with very little flesh covering their bones. ☐ *...an old man with a bony face and white hair.* **2** ADJ The **bony** parts of a person's or animal's body are the parts made of bone. ☐ *...the bony ridge of the eye socket.*

boo /buː/ (boos, booing, booed) **1** V-T/V-I If you **boo** a speaker or performer, you shout 'boo' or make other loud sounds to indicate that you do not like them, their opinions, or their performance. ☐ *People were booing and throwing things at them.* ☐ *Demonstrators booed and jeered him.* • N-COUNT **Boo** is also a noun. ☐ *She was greeted with boos and hisses.* • **boo|ing** N-UNCOUNT ☐ *The fans are entitled to their opinion but booing doesn't help anyone.* **2** EXCLAM You say '**Boo!**' loudly and suddenly when you want to surprise someone who does not know that you are there.

boob /buːb/ (boobs) N-COUNT [usu pl] A woman's **boobs** are her breasts. [INFORMAL, VULGAR]

boo-boo (boo-boos) **1** N-COUNT A **boo-boo** is a silly mistake or blunder. [AM, INFORMAL] ☐ *O.K. I made a boo-boo. I apologize.* **2** N-COUNT **Boo-boo** is a child's word for a cut or other minor injury. [AM, INFORMAL]

boob tube (boob tubes) **1** N-SING [the N] The **boob tube** is the television. [AM, INFORMAL] ☐ *...hours spent in front of the boob tube.*

in BRIT, use **idiot box**

2 N-COUNT A **boob tube** is a piece of women's clothing made of stretchy material that covers only her chest. [BRIT, INFORMAL]

in AM, use **tube top**

boo|by prize /buːbi praɪz/ (booby prizes) N-COUNT The **booby prize** is a prize given as a joke to the person who comes last in a competition.

booby-trap /buːbi træp/ (booby-traps, booby-trapping, booby-trapped) also **booby trap** **1** N-COUNT [oft N n] A **booby-trap** is something such as a bomb which is hidden

booger

or disguised and which causes death or injury when it is touched. ❑ *Police were checking the area for booby traps.* **2** V-T [usu passive] If something **is booby-trapped**, a booby-trap is placed in it or on it. ❑ *...fears that the area may have been booby-trapped.* ❑ *His booby-trapped car exploded.*

boog|er /bʊgər/ (boogers) N-COUNT A **booger** is a piece of dried mucus that comes from inside your nose. [AM, INFORMAL]

in BRIT, use **bogey**

boogey|man /bʊgimæn/ (boogeymen) → see **bogeyman**

boo|gie /bʊgi/ (boogies, boogying or boogieing, boogied) V-I When you **boogie**, you dance to fast pop music. [INFORMAL, OLD-FASHIONED] ❑ *At night, a good place to boogie through till sunrise is the Pink Panther Bar.*

book ♦♦♦ /bʊk/ (books, booking, booked) **1** N-COUNT A **book** is a number of pieces of paper, usually with words printed on them, which are fastened together and fixed inside a cover of stronger paper or cardboard. Books contain information, stories, or poetry, for example. ❑ *His eighth book came out earlier this year and was an instant bestseller.* ❑ *...the author of a book on politics.* ❑ *...a new book by Rosella Brown.* **2** N-COUNT A **book** of something such as stamps, matches, or tickets is a small number of them fastened together between thin cardboard covers. ❑ *Can I have a book of first class stamps please?* **3** V-T When you **book** something such as a hotel room or a ticket, you arrange to have it or use it at a particular time. ❑ *American officials have booked hotel rooms for the women and children.* ❑ *Laurie booked herself a flight home.* **4** N-PLURAL A company's or organization's **books** are its records of money that has been spent and earned or of the names of people who belong to it. [BUSINESS] ❑ *For the most part he left the books to his managers and accountants.* **5** V-T When a police officer **books** someone, he or she officially records their name and the offense that they may be charged with. ❑ *They took him to the station and booked him for assault with a deadly weapon.* **6** N-COUNT In a very long written work such as the Bible, a **book** is one of the sections into which it is divided. ❑ *...the last book of the Bible.* **7** → see also **booking, checkbook, phone book** **8** PHRASE If you say that someone or something is a **closed book**, you mean that you do not know anything about them. ❑ *Frank Spriggs was a very able man but something of a closed book.* **9** PHRASE If transportation or a hotel, restaurant, or theater is **booked up, fully booked**, or **booked solid**, it has no tickets, rooms, or tables left for a particular time or date. ❑ *The car ferries from the mainland are often fully booked by February.* **10** → See feature box at **business, research**

book|binder /bʊkbaɪndər/ (bookbinders) also **book-binder** N-COUNT A **bookbinder** is a person whose job is fastening books together and putting covers on them.

book|bind|ing /bʊkbaɪndɪŋ/ also **book-binding** N-UNCOUNT **Bookbinding** is the work of fastening books together and putting covers on them.

book|case /bʊkkeɪs/ (bookcases) N-COUNT A **bookcase** is a piece of furniture with shelves that you keep books on.

book club (book clubs) **1** N-COUNT A **book club** is an organization that offers books at reduced prices to its members. **2** N-COUNT A **book club** is the same as a **book group**.

book|end /bʊkɛnd/ (bookends) also **book-end** N-COUNT [usu pl] **Bookends** are a pair of supports used to hold a row of books in an upright position by placing one at each end of the row.

book group (book groups) N-COUNT A **book group** is a group of people who meet regularly to discuss books that they have read.

book|ie /bʊki/ (bookies) N-COUNT A **bookie** is a person whose job is to take your money when you bet and to pay you money if you win. [INFORMAL]

book|ing /bʊkɪŋ/ (bookings) N-COUNT A **booking** is the arrangement that you make when you book something such as a hotel room, a table at a restaurant, or a theater seat. ❑ *There was a mistake over his booking.*

book|ing of|fice (booking offices) N-COUNT A **booking office** is a room where tickets are sold and booked, especially in a theater or station. [BRIT]

in AM, use **ticket office**

book|ish /bʊkɪʃ/ ADJ Someone who is **bookish** spends a lot of time reading serious books. [DISAPPROVAL]

book|keep|er /bʊkkipər/ (bookkeepers) also **book-keeper** N-COUNT A **bookkeeper** is a person whose job is to keep an accurate record of the money that is spent and received by a business or other organization. [BUSINESS]

book|keep|ing /bʊkkipɪŋ/ also **book-keeping** N-UNCOUNT **Bookkeeping** is the job or activity of keeping an accurate record of the money that is spent and received by a business or other organization. [BUSINESS]

book|let /bʊklɪt/ (booklets) N-COUNT A **booklet** is a very thin book that has a paper cover and that gives you information about something. ❑ *...a 48-page booklet of notes for the completion of the form.*

book|mak|er /bʊkmeɪkər/ (bookmakers) N-COUNT A **bookmaker** is the same as a **bookie**.

book|mak|ing /bʊkmeɪkɪŋ/ N-UNCOUNT [oft N n] **Bookmaking** is the activity of taking people's money when they bet and paying them money if they win. ❑ *...an Internet bookmaking business.*

book|mark /bʊkmɑrk/ (bookmarks, bookmarking, bookmarked) **1** N-COUNT A **bookmark** is a narrow piece of card or leather that you put between the pages of a book so that you can find a particular page easily. **2** N-COUNT In computing, a **bookmark** is the address of an internet site that you put into a list on your computer so that you can return to it easily. [COMPUTING] ❑ *This makes it extremely simple to save what you find with an electronic bookmark so you can return to it later.* • V-T **Bookmark** is also a verb. [COMPUTING] ❑ *This site is definitely worth bookmarking.*

book|plate /bʊkpleɪt/ (bookplates) N-COUNT A **bookplate** is a piece of decorated paper that is stuck in the front of a book and on which the owner's name is printed or written.

book|sell|er /bʊksɛlər/ (booksellers) N-COUNT A **bookseller** is a person who sells books.

VOCABULARY IN CONTEXT

Books

As summer approaches, millions of us dream of relaxing on a sunny beach with a **bestseller**. So, which **award-winning novels** will people pack along with their sandals and sunscreen? Some like to lose themselves in the pages of crime fiction, whose **gripping plots** make for **compulsive** reading. Short story **anthologies** are an excellent choice for vacation reading, too, being easy to **dip into** and finish quickly. For those who look forward to the challenge of a complex **narrative** and heavy-going prose it's the ideal time to tackle a great **literary** work, a **tome**. But, let's face it, most of us don't want to struggle through the dense text of an **epic**; we want paperback page-turners and **trilogies**! We want to escape into the **character**-driven tales of **popular fiction** for pure entertainment without taxing our intellect. Happy reading!

book|shelf /bʊkʃɛlf/ (bookshelves) N-COUNT A **bookshelf** is a shelf on which you keep books.

book|shop /bʊkʃɒp/ (bookshops) N-COUNT A **bookshop** is a store where books are sold. [mainly BRIT]

in AM, usually use **bookstore**

book|stall /bʊkstɔl/ (bookstalls) **1** N-COUNT A **bookstall** is a long table from which books and magazines are sold, for example at a conference or in a street market. **2** N-COUNT A **bookstall** is the same as a **newsstand**. [BRIT]

book|store /bʊkstɔr/ (bookstores) N-COUNT A **bookstore** is a store where books are sold. [mainly AM]

in BRIT, usually use **bookshop**

book value (book values) N-COUNT In business, the **book value** of an asset is the value it is given in the account books of the company that owns it. [BUSINESS] ❏ *The insured value of the airplane was greater than its book value.*

book|worm /bʊkwɜrm/ (bookworms) N-COUNT If you describe someone as a **bookworm**, you mean they are very fond of reading. [INFORMAL]

boom ✦✧ /bum/ (booms, booming, boomed) **1** N-COUNT If there is a **boom** in the economy, there is an increase in economic activity, for example, in the number of things that are being bought and sold. ❏ *An economic boom followed, especially in housing and construction.* ❏ *The 1980s were indeed boom years.* **2** N-COUNT A **boom** in something is an increase in its amount, frequency, or success. ❏ *The boom in the sport's popularity has meant more calls for stricter safety regulations.* **3** V-I If the economy or a business **is booming**, the number of things being bought or sold is increasing. ❏ *By 1988 the economy was booming.* ❏ *Sales are booming.* **4** V-T/V-I When something such as someone's voice, a cannon, or a big drum **booms**, it makes a loud, deep sound that lasts for several seconds. ❏ *"Ladies," boomed Helena, without a microphone, "we all know why we're here tonight."* ❏ *Thunder boomed over Crooked Mountain.* • PHRASAL VERB **Boom out** means the same as **boom**. ❏ *Music boomed out from loudspeakers.* ❏ *A megaphone boomed out, "This is the police."* • N-COUNT; SOUND **Boom** is also a noun. ❏ *The stillness of the night was broken by the boom of a cannon.* **5** → See feature box at **population**

─── COLLOCATIONS ───

boom
NOUN
1
noun + **boom**: building, construction, housing; commodities, dotcom, tech
adjective + **boom**: economic; speculative, unprecedented, unsustainable; postwar
verb + **boom**: fuel, stoke
2
noun + **boom**: baby, population, tourism

boom box (boom boxes) N-COUNT A **boom box** is a large portable machine for playing music, especially one that is played loudly in public by young people. [mainly AM, INFORMAL]

boom-bust cy|cle (boom-bust cycles) N-COUNT A **boom-bust cycle** is a series of events in which a rapid increase in business activity in the economy is followed by a rapid decrease in business activity, and this process is repeated again and again. [BUSINESS] ❏ *We must avoid the damaging boom-bust cycles which characterized the 1980s.*

boom|er|ang /buməræŋ/ (boomerangs, boomeranging, boomeranged) **1** N-COUNT A **boomerang** is a curved piece of wood that comes back to you if you throw it in the correct way. Boomerangs were first used by the people who were living in Australia when Europeans arrived there. **2** V-I If a plan **boomerangs**, its result is not the one that was intended and is harmful to the person who made the plan. ❏ *The trick boomeranged, though.* ❏ *He risks defeat in the referendum that he called, but which threatens to boomerang against him.*

boom town (boom towns) N-COUNT A **boom town** is a town that has rapidly become very rich and full of people, usually because industry or business has developed there. ❏ *Brisbane has become the boom town for Australian film and television.*

boon /bun/ (boons) N-COUNT You can describe something as a **boon** when it makes life better or easier for someone. ❏ *It is for this reason that television proves such a boon to so many people.*

boon|docks /bundɒks/ N-PLURAL [the N] If you say that someone lives in the **boondocks**, you mean that they live a long way from any large cities. [AM, INFORMAL, DISAPPROVAL] ❏ *Rural residents are likely to find their lives in the boondocks too restrictive.*

in BRIT, use **sticks**

boon|dog|gle /bundɒgəl/ (boondoggles) N-COUNT People sometimes refer to an official organization or activity as a **boondoggle** when they think it wastes a lot of time and money and does not achieve much. [AM, INFORMAL, DISAPPROVAL] ❏ *The new runway is a billion-dollar boondoggle.*

boon|ies /buniz/ N-PLURAL [the N] The **boonies** are the same as the **boondocks**. [AM, INFORMAL, DISAPPROVAL] ❏ *Why do you live out here in the boonies?*

in BRIT, use **sticks**

boor /bʊər/ (boors) N-COUNT If you refer to someone as a **boor**, you think their behavior and attitudes are rough, uneducated, and rude. [DISAPPROVAL]

boor|ish /bʊərɪʃ/ ADJ **Boorish** behavior is rough, uneducated, and rude. ❏ *...their boorish rejection of the aging movie star.*

boost ✦✧ /bust/ (boosts, boosting, boosted) **1** V-T If one thing **boosts** another, it causes it to increase, improve, or be more successful. ❏ *Lower interest rates can boost the economy by reducing borrowing costs for consumers and businesses.* • N-COUNT **Boost** is also a noun. ❏ *It would get the economy going and give us the boost that we need.* **2** V-T If something **boosts** your confidence or morale, it improves it. ❏ *We need a big win to boost our confidence.* • N-COUNT **Boost** is also a noun. ❏ *It did give me a boost to win such a big event.* **3** N-COUNT [usu sing] If you give someone a **boost**, you push or lift them from behind so that they can reach something. ❏ *He cupped his hands and gave her a boost up to the ledge.*

─── SYNONYMS ───

boost
VERB **1**
increase: *The increased investment will help stabilize the economy.*
build: *The encouragement that young boys receive builds a greater self-confidence.*
develop: *...weekly workshops that are designed to develop acting and theater skills.*
bolster: *Hopes of an early cut in interest rates bolstered confidence.*

─── COLLOCATIONS ───

boost
NOUN
1
noun + **boost**: cash
adjective + **boost**: huge, major, timely, welcome
verb + **boost**: provide; receive
2
noun + **boost**: confidence, ego, morale
VERB
1
boost + noun: economy, growth, profit, sales
2
boost + noun: confidence, morale

boost|er /bustər/ (boosters) **1** N-COUNT [usu n N] A **booster** is something that increases a positive or desirable quality. ❏ *It was amazing what a morale booster her visits proved.* ❏ *Praise is a great confidence booster.* **2** N-COUNT A **booster** is an extra engine in a machine such as a space rocket, which provides an extra amount of power at certain times. ❏ *Ground controllers will then fire the booster, sending the satellite into its proper orbit.* **3** N-COUNT A **booster** is a small injection of a drug that you have some time after a larger injection, in order to make sure that the first injection will remain effective. **4** N-COUNT [oft supp N, N N] A **booster** is someone who supports a sports team, organization, person, or place very enthusiastically. [AM] ❏ *A former associate of Mr. Pierce's was among the project's boosters.*

boost|er seat (booster seats) also **booster cushion** N-COUNT A **booster seat** or a **booster cushion** is a special seat

boot /but/ (boots, booting, booted) **1** N-COUNT Boots are shoes that cover your whole foot and the lower part of your leg. ☐ *He sat in a kitchen chair, reached down and pulled off his boots.* **2** N-COUNT Boots are strong, heavy shoes that cover your ankle and that have thick soles. You wear them to protect your feet, for example, when you are walking or taking part in sports. ☐ *The soldiers' boots resounded in the street.* **3** V-T To boot an illegally parked car means to fit a device to one of its wheels so that it cannot be driven away. [AM] ☐ *Though the city will no longer boot cars, illegally parked vehicles will be towed.*

in BRIT, use **clamp**

4 V-T/V-I If a computer boots or you boot it, it is made ready to use by putting in the instructions it needs in order to start working. [COMPUTING] ☐ *The computer won't boot.* ☐ *Put the CD into the drive and boot the machine.* • PHRASAL VERB **Boot up** means the same as **boot**. ☐ *Go over to your PC and boot it up.* **5** N-COUNT The boot of a car is the same as the **trunk**. [BRIT] **6** PHRASE If you **get the boot** or **are given the boot**, you are told that you are not wanted anymore, either in your job or by someone you are having a relationship with. [INFORMAL] ☐ *She was a disruptive influence, and after a year or two she got the boot.*

boot camp (boot camps) N-VAR In the United States, a boot camp is a camp where people who have just joined the army, navy, or marines are trained. [AM]

bootee /buti/ (bootees or booties) **1** N-COUNT [usu pl] Bootees are short woolen socks that babies wear instead of shoes. **2** N-COUNT Bootees are short boots which come to just above the ankle. [OLD-FASHIONED]

booth /buθ/ (booths) **1** N-COUNT A booth is a small area separated from a larger public area by screens or thin walls where, for example, people can make a telephone call or vote in private. ☐ *I called her from a public phone booth near the entrance to the bar.* **2** N-COUNT A booth in a restaurant or café consists of a table with long fixed seats on two or sometimes three sides of it. ☐ *They sat in a corner booth, away from other diners.*

boot|lace /butleɪs/ (bootlaces) N-COUNT [usu pl] A bootlace is a long thin cord which is used to fasten a boot.

boot|leg /butleg/ (bootlegs, bootlegging, bootlegged) **1** ADJ [ADJ n] Bootleg is used to describe something that is made secretly and sold illegally. ☐ *...a bootleg recording of the band's 1977 tour of Scandinavia.* ☐ *...bootleg liquor.* **2** V-T To bootleg something such as a recording means to make and sell it illegally. ☐ *He has sued a fan for bootlegging his concerts.* ☐ *Avid Bob Dylan fans treasure bootlegged recordings.* • N-COUNT Bootleg is also a noun. ☐ *The record was a bootleg.* • **boot|leg|ger** (bootleggers) N-COUNT ☐ *Bootleggers sold 75 million dollars' worth of copies.*

boot|strap /butstræp/ (bootstraps, bootstrapping, bootstrapped) **1** VERB If you bootstrap an organization or an activity, you set it up or achieve it alone, using very few resources. ☐ *Peterson bootstrapped the company himself and hopes to continue without outside funding.* **2** PHRASE [v inflects] If you have **pulled yourself up by** your **bootstraps**, you have achieved success by your own efforts, starting from very difficult circumstances and without help from anyone.

boo|ty /buti/ N-UNCOUNT Booty is a collection of valuable things stolen from a place, especially by soldiers after a battle. ☐ *Troops destroyed the capital and confiscated many works of art as war booty.*

booze /buz/ (boozes, boozing, boozed) **1** N-UNCOUNT [also the N] Booze is alcoholic drink. [INFORMAL] ☐ *...booze and cigarettes.* **2** V-I If people booze, they drink alcohol. [INFORMAL] ☐ *...a load of drunken businessmen who had been boozing all afternoon.*

boozed /buzd/ ADJ [usu v-link ADJ] If someone is boozed or boozed up, they are drunk. [INFORMAL] ☐ *He's half asleep and a bit boozed.*

booz|er /buzər/ (boozers) N-COUNT A boozer is a person who drinks a lot of alcohol. [INFORMAL] ☐ *I thought he was a bit of a boozer.*

boozy /buzi/ ADJ [usu ADJ n] A boozy person is someone who drinks a lot of alcohol. [INFORMAL] ☐ *...a cheerful, boozy chain-smoker.*

bop /bɒp/ (bops, bopping, bopped) **1** V-I If you bop, you dance to pop music. [INFORMAL] ☐ *He was bopping around, snapping his fingers.* ☐ *Guests bopped and jigged the night away to the disco beat.* **2** → see also **bebop**

bop|per /bɒpər/ → see **teenybopper**

bo|rax /bɔræks/ N-UNCOUNT Borax is a white powder used, for example, in the making of glass and as a cleaning chemical.

bor|del|lo /bɔrdɛloʊ/ (bordellos) N-COUNT A bordello is a brothel. [LITERARY]

bor|der /bɔrdər/ (borders, bordering, bordered) **1** N-COUNT The border between two countries or regions is the dividing line between them. Sometimes **the border** also refers to the land close to this line. ☐ *They fled across the border.* ☐ *Soldiers had temporarily closed the border between the two countries.* **2** V-T A country that borders another country, a sea, or a river is next to it. ☐ *...the European and Arab countries bordering the Mediterranean.* • PHRASAL VERB **Border on** means the same as **border**. ☐ *Both republics border on the Black Sea.* **3** N-COUNT A border is a strip or band around the edge of something. ☐ *...pillowcases trimmed with a hand-crocheted border.* **4** N-COUNT In a garden, a border is a long strip of ground planted with flowers, along the edge of a path or lawn. ☐ *...a lawn flanked by wide herbaceous borders.* **5** V-T If something **is bordered** by another thing, the other thing forms a line along the edge of it. ☐ *...the mile of white sand beach bordered by palm trees and tropical flowers.*

COLLOCATIONS

border
NOUN
1
noun + **border**: desert, land, sea
adjective + **border**: disputed, external, secure; eastern, northern, southern, western
verb + **border**: cross, open, reopen, straddle; close, patrol, seal
3
noun + **border**: flower, garden, shrub
adjective + **border**: herbaceous

SYNONYMS

border
NOUN **1**
frontier: *It wasn't difficult then to cross the frontier.*
boundary: *Drug traffickers operate across national boundaries.*

---

bor|der|land /bɔrdərlænd/ (borderlands) **1** N-SING The borderland between two things is an area which contains features from both of these things so that it is not possible to say that it belongs to one or the other. ☐ *...on the borderland between sleep and waking.* **2** N-COUNT [usu pl] The area of land close to the border between two countries or major areas can be called the **borderlands**. ☐ *...Lebanon's southern borderlands.*

bor|der|line /bɔrdərlaɪn/ (borderlines) **1** N-COUNT The borderline between two different or opposite things is the division between them. ☐ *...a task which involves exploring the borderline between painting and photography.* **2** ADJ Something that is borderline is only just acceptable as a member of a class or group. ☐ *Some were obviously unsuitable and could be ruled out at once. Others were borderline cases.*

bore /bɔr/ (bores, boring, bored) **1** V-T If someone or something bores you, you find them dull and uninteresting. ☐ *Dickie bored him all through the meal with stories of the navy.* **2** PHRASE If someone or something **bores** you **to tears**, **bores** you **to death**, or **bores** you **stiff**, they bore you very much. [INFORMAL, EMPHASIS] ☐ *Monuments and museums bore him to tears.* **3** N-COUNT You describe someone as a **bore** when you think that they talk in a very uninteresting way. ☐ *There is every reason why I shouldn't enjoy his company – he's a bore and a fool.* **4** N-SING You can describe a situation as **a bore** when you find it annoying. ☐ *It's a bore to be sick, and the novelty of lying in bed all day wears off quickly.* **5** V-T If you **bore** a hole in something, you make a deep round hole in it using a special tool. ☐ *Get the special drill bit to bore the correct size hole for the job.* **6** **Bore** is the past tense of **bear**. **7** → see also **bored**, **boring**

bored /bɔrd/ ADJ If you are bored, you feel tired and impatient because you have lost interest in something or because you have nothing to do. ☐ *I am getting very bored with this entire business.*

bore|dom /bɔrdəm/ N-UNCOUNT **Boredom** is the state of being bored. ❑ *He had given up attending lectures out of sheer boredom.*

bore|hole /bɔrhoʊl/ (**boreholes**) N-COUNT A **borehole** is a deep round hole made by a special tool or machine, especially one that is made in the ground when searching for oil or water.

bor|ing /bɔrɪŋ/ ADJ Someone or something **boring** is so dull and uninteresting that they make people tired and impatient. ❑ *Not only are mothers not paid but also most of their boring or difficult work is unnoticed.*

born ♦♦◊ /bɔrn/ ◼ V-T PASSIVE When a baby **is born**, it comes out of its mother's body at the beginning of its life. In formal English, if you say that someone **is born** of someone or to someone, you mean that person is their parent. ❑ *She was born in Milan on April 29, 1923.* ❑ *He was born of German parents and lived most of his life abroad.* ◼ V-T PASSIVE [no cont] If someone **is born** with a particular disease, problem, or characteristic, they have it from the time they are born. ❑ *He was born with only one lung.* ❑ *Some people are born brainy.* ◼ V-T PASSIVE [no cont] You can use **be born** in front of a particular name to show that a person was given this name at birth, although they may be better known by another name. [FORMAL] ❑ *She was born Jenny Harvey on June 11, 1946.* ◼ ADJ [ADJ n] You use **born** to describe someone who has a natural ability to do a particular activity or job. For example, if you are a **born** cook, you have a natural ability to cook well. ❑ *Jack was a born teacher.* ◼ V-T PASSIVE When an idea or organization **is born**, it comes into existence. If something **is born** of a particular emotion or activity, it exists as a result of that emotion or activity. [FORMAL] ❑ *The idea for the show was born in his hospital room.* ❑ *Congress passed the National Security Act, and the CIA was born.* ◼ → see also **newborn**

-born /-bɔrn/ COMB IN ADJ [usu ADJ n] **-born** combines with adjectives that relate to countries or with the names of cities and areas to form adjectives that indicate where someone was born. ❑ *The German-born photographer was admired by writers such as Oscar Wilde.*

born-again ◼ ADJ A **born-again** Christian is a person who has become an evangelical Christian as a result of a religious experience. ◼ ADJ You can use **born-again** to describe someone who has adopted a new set of beliefs or a new way of life and is very enthusiastic about it. ❑ *As a "born-again" cyclist I had decided that this season I would ride in a few races.*

borne /bɔrn/ **Borne** is the past participle of **bear**.

-borne /-bɔrn/ COMB IN ADJ [usu ADJ n] **-borne** combines with nouns to form adjectives that describe the method or means by which something is carried or moved. ❑ *...water-borne diseases.* ❑ *...a mosquito-borne infection.* ❑ *...rocket-borne weapons.*

bor|ough /bɜroʊ/ (**boroughs**) N-COUNT A **borough** is a town, or a district within a large city, which has its own council, government, or local services. ❑ *...the New York City borough of Brooklyn.*

bor|row ♦◊◊ /bɒroʊ/ (**borrows, borrowing, borrowed**) ◼ V-T If you **borrow** something that belongs to someone else, you take it or use it for a period of time, usually with their permission. ❑ *Can I borrow a pen please?* ◼ V-T/V-I If you **borrow** money from someone or from a bank, they give it to you and you agree to pay it back at some time in the future. ❑ *Morgan borrowed $5,000 from his father to form the company 20 years ago.* ❑ *It's so expensive to borrow from finance companies.* ◼ V-T If you **borrow** a book from a library, you take it away for a fixed period of time. ❑ *I couldn't afford to buy any, so I borrowed them from the library.* ◼ V-T If you **borrow** something such as a word or an idea from another language or from another person's work, you use it in your own language or work. ❑ *I borrowed his words for my book's title.*

USAGE

borrow

You don't normally talk about borrowing or lending things that can't be moved. Don't say, for example, 'Can I borrow your garage next week?' Say 'Can I **use** your garage next week?' *You can use our washing machine.*

---

bor|row|er /bɒroʊər/ (**borrowers**) N-COUNT A **borrower** is a person or organization that borrows money. ❑ *Borrowers with a big mortgage should pay for a fixed rate.*

bor|row|ing /bɒroʊɪŋ/ (**borrowings**) N-UNCOUNT [also N in pl] **Borrowing** is the activity of borrowing money. ❑ *We have allowed spending and borrowing to rise in this recession.*

bos|om /bʊzəm/ (**bosoms**) ◼ N-COUNT A woman's breasts are sometimes referred to as her **bosom** or her **bosoms**. [OLD-FASHIONED] ❑ *...a young mother with a baby resting against her ample bosom.* ◼ ADJ [ADJ n] A **bosom** buddy is a friend who you know very well and like very much. ❑ *They were bosom buddies.*

boss ♦♦◊ /bɔs/ (**bosses, bossing, bossed**) ◼ N-COUNT Your **boss** is the person in charge of the organization or department where you work. ❑ *He cannot stand his boss.* ◼ N-COUNT If you are the **boss** in a group or relationship, you are the person who makes all the decisions. [INFORMAL] ❑ *He thinks he's the boss.* ◼ V-T If you say that someone **bosses** you, you mean that they keep telling you what to do in a way that is irritating. ❑ *We cannot boss them into doing more.* • PHRASAL VERB **Boss around** means the same as **boss**. ❑ *He started bossing people around.*

COLLOCATIONS

boss
NOUN ◼
noun + **boss**: company, party, union
adjective + **boss**: former, new

SYNONYMS

boss
NOUN ◼
manager: *The chef, staff, and managers are all Chinese.*
head: *...the head waiter.*
chief: *...a commission appointed by the police chief.*
master: *My master ordered me not to deliver the message except in private.*
supervisor: *...a full-time job as a supervisor at a factory.*

---

bossy /bɒsi/ (**bossier, bossiest**) ADJ If you describe someone as **bossy**, you mean that they enjoy telling people what to do. [DISAPPROVAL] ❑ *She remembers being a rather bossy little girl.*

bot /bɒt/ (**bots**) N-COUNT A **bot** is a computer program that carries out tasks for other programs or users, especially on the internet. [COMPUTING]

bo|tan|ic /bətænɪk/ ADJ [ADJ n] **Botanic** means the same as **botanical**.

bo|tani|cal /bətænɪkəl/ ADJ [ADJ n] **Botanical** books, research, and activities relate to the scientific study of plants. ❑ *The area is of great botanical interest.*

bota|nist /bɒtənɪst/ (**botanists**) N-COUNT A **botanist** is a scientist who studies plants.

bota|ny /bɒtəni/ N-UNCOUNT **Botany** is the scientific study of plants.

botch /bɒtʃ/ (**botches, botching, botched**) ◼ V-T If you **botch** something that you are doing, you do it badly or clumsily. [INFORMAL] ❑ *...a botched job.* • PHRASAL VERB **Botch up** means the same as **botch**. ❑ *I hate having builders botch up repairs on my house.* ◼ N-COUNT If you **make a botch of** something that you are doing, you botch it. [INFORMAL]

botch-up (**botch-ups**) N-COUNT [usu sing] A **botch-up** is the same as a **botch**. [INFORMAL] ❑ *They were victims of a computer botch-up.*

both ♦♦♦ /boʊθ/ ◼ DET You use **both** when you are referring to two people or things and saying that something is true about each of them. ❑ *She cried out in fear and flung both arms up to protect her face.* • QUANT [QUANT of pl-n] **Both** is also a quantifier. ❑ *Both of these women have strong memories of the Vietnam War.* • PRON **Both** is also a pronoun. ❑ *Miss Brown and her friend, both from Brooklyn, were arrested on the 8th of June.* • PRON-EMPH [It PRON] **Both** is also an emphasizing pronoun. ❑ *He visited the Institute of Neurology in Havana where they both worked.* • PREDET [PREDET det pl-n] **Both** is also a predeterminer. [EMPHASIS] ❑ *Both the horses were out, tacked up and ready to ride.* ◼ CONJ You use the structure **both...and** when you are giving two facts or alternatives and emphasizing that each of them is true or possible. ❑ *Now women work both before and after having their children.*

both|er ♦◊◊ /bɒðər/ (**bothers, bothering, bothered**) ◼ V-T/V-I [with brd-neg] If you do not **bother** to do something or if you do not **bother** with it, you do not do it, consider it, or use it because you think it is unnecessary or because you are too lazy. ❑ *Lots of people don't bother to go through a marriage ceremony these days.* ❑ *Nothing I do makes any difference anyway, so why bother?* **2** N-UNCOUNT [also *a* N] **Bother** means trouble or difficulty. You can also use **bother** to refer to an activity which causes this, especially when you would prefer not to do it or get involved with it. ❑ *I usually buy sliced bread – it's less bother.* ❑ *The courts take too long and going to the police is a bother.* **3** V-T/V-I If something **bothers** you, or if you **bother** about it, it worries, annoys, or upsets you. ❑ *Is something bothering you?* ❑ *It bothered me that boys weren't interested in me.* ● **both|ered** ADJ [v-link ADJ] ❑ *I was bothered about the blister on my hand.* **4** V-T If someone **bothers** you, they talk to you when you want to be left alone or interrupt you when you are busy. ❑ *We are playing a trick on a man who keeps bothering me.* **5** PHRASE If you say that you **can't be bothered** to do something, you mean that you are not going to do it because you think it is unnecessary or because you are too lazy. ❑ *I just can't be bothered to look after the house.* **6 hot and bothered** → see **hot**

---SYNONYMS---

bother
NOUN **2**
trouble: *You've caused us a lot of trouble.*
problem: *...the economic problems of the inner city.*
difficulty: *...the difficulty of getting accurate information.*
nuisance: *Sorry to be a nuisance.*
VERB **3**
worry: *I'm still in the early days of my recovery and that worries me.*
trouble: *Is anything troubling you?*
concern: *It concerned her that Bess was developing a crush on Max.*
upset: *She warned me not to say anything to upset him.*

---

both|er|some /bɒðərsəm/ ADJ Someone or something that is **bothersome** is annoying or irritating. [OLD-FASHIONED]

Bo|tox /boʊtɒks/ N-UNCOUNT [oft N n] **Botox** is a substance that is injected into the face in order to make the skin look smoother. [TRADEMARK] ❑ *...Botox injections.*

bot|tle ♦♦◇ /bɒtᵊl/ (**bottles**, **bottling**, **bottled**) **1** N-COUNT A **bottle** is a glass or plastic container in which drinks and other liquids are kept. Bottles are usually round with straight sides and a narrow top. ❑ *There were two empty beer bottles on the table.* ❑ *He was pulling the cork from a bottle of wine.* **2** N-COUNT You can use **bottle** to refer to a bottle and its contents, or to the contents only. ❑ *She had drunk half a bottle of whiskey.* **3** V-T To **bottle** a drink or other liquid means to put it into bottles after it has been made. ❑ *This is a large truck which has equipment to automatically bottle the wine.* **4** N-COUNT A **bottle** is a drinking container used by babies. It has a special rubber part at the top through which they can suck their drink. ❑ *Gary was holding a bottle to the baby's lips.* **5** → see also **bottled**

bot|tled /bɒtᵊld/ ADJ **Bottled** gas is kept under pressure in special metal cylinders which can be moved from one place to another.

bottle-feed (**bottle-feeds**, **bottle-feeding**, **bottle-fed**) V-T If you **bottle-feed** a baby, you give it milk or a liquid like milk in a bottle rather than the baby sucking milk from its mother's breasts. ❑ *New fathers love bottle-feeding their babies.* ❑ *...a bottle-fed baby.*

bottle-green also **bottle green** COLOR Something that is **bottle-green** is dark green in color.

bot|tle|neck /bɒtᵊlnek/ (**bottlenecks**) **1** N-COUNT A **bottleneck** is a place where a road becomes narrow or where it meets another road so that the traffic slows down or stops, often causing traffic jams. **2** N-COUNT A **bottleneck** is a situation that stops a process or activity from progressing. ❑ *He pushed everyone full speed ahead until production hit a bottleneck.*

bottle-opener (**bottle-openers**) N-COUNT A **bottle-opener** is a metal device for removing caps or tops from bottles.

bot|tler /bɒtᵊlər/ (**bottlers**) N-COUNT A **bottler** is a person or company that puts drinks into bottles.

bot|tom ♦♦◇ /bɒtəm/ (**bottoms**) **1** N-COUNT The **bottom** of something is the lowest or deepest part of it. ❑ *He sat at the bottom of the stairs.* ❑ *Answers can be found at the bottom of page 8.* **2** ADJ [ADJ n] The **bottom** thing or layer in a series of things or layers is the lowest one. ❑ *There's an extra pillow in the bottom drawer.* **3** N-COUNT The **bottom** of an object is the flat surface at its lowest point. You can also refer to the inside or outside of this surface as the **bottom**. ❑ *Spread the onion slices on the bottom of the dish.* ❑ *...the bottom of their shoes.* **4** N-SING If you say that **the bottom** has dropped or fallen out of a market or industry, you mean that people have stopped buying the products it sells. [BUSINESS, JOURNALISM] ❑ *The bottom had fallen out of the city's property market.* **5** N-SING [the N, oft N of n] The **bottom** of an organization or career structure is the lowest level in it, where new employees often start. ❑ *He had worked in the theater for many years, starting at the bottom.* **6** N-SING [the N, also no det] If someone is **bottom** or at **the bottom** in a survey, test, or league, their performance is worse than that of all the other people involved. ❑ *He was always bottom of the class.* **7** N-COUNT The lower part of a swimsuit, tracksuit, or pair of pajamas can be referred to as the **bottoms** or the **bottom**. ❑ *She wore blue tracksuit bottoms.* **8** N-SING The **bottom** of a street or yard is the end farthest away from you or from your house. [mainly BRIT]

in AM, usually use **end**

9 N-SING The **bottom** of a table is the end farthest away from where you are sitting. The **bottom** of a bed is the end where you usually rest your feet. [mainly BRIT]

in AM, usually use **end**

10 N-COUNT Your **bottom** is the part of your body that you sit on. [mainly BRIT]

in AM, usually use **behind**

11 → see also **rock bottom** **12** PHRASE You use **at bottom** to emphasize that you are stating what you think is the real nature of something or the real truth about a situation. [EMPHASIS] ❑ *The two systems are, at bottom, conceptual models.* **13** PHRASE If something is **at the bottom of** a problem or an unpleasant situation, it is the real cause of it. ❑ *Often I find that anger and resentment are at the bottom of the problem.* **14** PHRASE If you want to **get to the bottom of** a problem, you want to solve it by finding out its real cause. ❑ *I have to get to the bottom of this.*

---COLLOCATIONS---

bottom
NOUN
1
verb + **bottom**: near, reach
7
noun + **bottom**: bikini, jogging, pajama, sweatsuit

-bottomed /-bɒtəmd/ COMB IN ADJ **-bottomed** can be added to adjectives or nouns to form adjectives that indicate what kind of bottom an object or person has. ❑ *...a glass-bottomed boat.*

bot|tom|less /bɒtəmlɪs/ **1** ADJ If you describe a supply of something as **bottomless**, you mean that it seems so large that it will never run out. ❑ *...big supermarkets and multinationals with apparently bottomless pockets.* **2** ADJ If you describe something as **bottomless**, you mean that it is so deep that it seems to have no bottom. ❑ *His eyes were like bottomless brown pools.* **3** PHRASE If you describe something as a **bottomless pit**, you mean that it seems as if you can take things from it and it will never be empty or put things in it and it will never be full. ❑ *A gold mine is not a bottomless pit, the gold runs out.* ❑ *The problem is we don't have a bottomless pit of resources.*

bot|tom line (**bottom lines**) **1** N-COUNT The **bottom line** in a decision or situation is the most important factor that you have to consider. ❑ *The bottom line is that it's not profitable.* **2** N-COUNT The **bottom line** in a business deal is the least a person is willing to accept. ❑ *She says $95,000 is her bottom line.* **3** N-COUNT The **bottom line** is the total amount of money that a company has made or lost over a particular period of time. [BUSINESS] ❑ *...to force chief executives to look beyond the next quarter's bottom line.*

botu|lism /bɒtʃəlɪzəm/ N-UNCOUNT **Botulism** is a serious form of food poisoning. [MEDICAL]

bou|doir /bˈudwɑr/ (boudoirs) N-COUNT A **boudoir** is a bedroom or private sitting room. [OLD-FASHIONED]

bouf|fant /bufˈɑnt/ ADJ [usu ADJ n] A **bouffant** hairstyle is one in which your hair is high and full. ❑ ...blonde bouffant hairdos.

bou|gain|vil|lea /bˌuɡənvˈɪliə/ (bougainvilleas)

in BRIT, also use **bougainvillaea**

N-VAR **Bougainvillea** is a climbing plant that has red or purple flowers and grows mainly in hot countries.

bough /baʊ/ (boughs) N-COUNT A **bough** is a large branch of a tree. [LITERARY] ❑ I rested my fishing rod against a pine bough.

bought /bɔt/ **Bought** is the past tense and past participle of **buy**.

bouil|la|baisse /bˌulyəbˈeɪs, buyəbˈɛs/ N-UNCOUNT [also a N] **Bouillabaisse** is a rich stew or soup of fish and vegetables.

bouil|lon /bˈulyɒn/ (bouillons) N-VAR **Bouillon** is a liquid made by boiling meat and bones or vegetables in water and used to make soups and sauces.

bouil|lon cube (bouillon cubes) N-COUNT A **bouillon cube** is a solid cube made from dried meat or vegetable juices and other flavorings. Bouillon cubes are used to add flavor to dishes such as stews and soups. [AM]

in BRIT, use **stock cube**

boul|der /bˈoʊldər/ (boulders) N-COUNT A **boulder** is a large rounded rock. ❑ It is thought that the train hit a boulder that had fallen down a cliff on to the track.

boules /bul/ N-UNCOUNT **Boules** is a game in which a small ball is thrown and then the players try to throw other balls as close to the first ball as possible.

boule|vard /bˈuləvɑrd/ (boulevards) N-COUNT A **boulevard** is a wide street in a city, usually with trees along each side. ❑ ...Lenton Boulevard.

bounce /baʊns/ (bounces, bouncing, bounced) ◼ V-T/V-I When an object such as a ball **bounces** or when you **bounce** it, it moves upward from a surface or away from it immediately after hitting it. ❑ My father would burst into the kitchen bouncing a tennis ball. ❑ ...a falling pebble, bouncing down the eroded cliff. • N-COUNT **Bounce** is also a noun. ❑ The wheelchair tennis player is allowed two bounces of the ball. ◼ V-T/V-I If sound or light **bounces off** a surface or **is bounced off** it, it reaches the surface and is reflected back. ❑ Your arms and legs need protection from light bouncing off glass. ◼ V-T/V-I If something **bounces** or if something **bounces** it, it swings or moves up and down. ❑ Her long black hair bounced as she walked. ❑ The car was bouncing up and down as if someone were jumping on it. ◼ V-I If you **bounce** on a soft surface, you jump up and down on it repeatedly. ❑ She lets us do anything, even bounce on our beds. ◼ V-I If someone **bounces** somewhere, they move there in an energetic way, because they are feeling happy. ❑ Moira bounced into the office. ◼ V-T If you **bounce** your ideas off someone, you tell them to that person, in order to find out what they think about them. ❑ It was good to bounce ideas off another mind. ◼ V-T/V-I If a check **bounces** or if someone **bounces** it, the bank refuses to accept it and pay out the money, because the person who wrote it does not have enough money in their account. ❑ Our only complaint would be if the check bounced. ◼ V-I If an email or other electronic message **bounces**, it is returned to the person who sent it because the address was wrong or because of a problem with one of the computers involved in sending it. [COMPUTING] ❑ ...a message saying that your mail has bounced or was unable to be delivered. ◼ → See feature box at **email**

▸ **bounce back** PHRASAL VERB If you **bounce back** after a bad experience, you return very quickly to your previous level of success, enthusiasm, or activity. ❑ We lost two or three early games but we bounced back. ❑ He is young enough to bounce back from this disappointment.

bounc|er /bˈaʊnsər/ (bouncers) N-COUNT A **bouncer** is someone who stands at the door of a club, prevents unwanted people from coming in, and makes people leave if they cause trouble.

bounc|ing /bˈaʊnsɪŋ/ ◼ ADJ [v-link ADJ with n, ADJ n] If you say that someone is **bouncing** with health, you mean that they are very healthy. You can also refer to a **bouncing** baby. ❑ They are bouncing with health in the good weather. ❑ Derek is now the proud father of a bouncing baby girl. ◼ → see also **bounce**

bouncy /bˈaʊnsi/ (bouncier, bounciest) ◼ ADJ Someone or something that is **bouncy** is very lively. ❑ She was bouncy and full of energy. ◼ ADJ A **bouncy** thing can bounce very well or makes other things bounce well. ❑ ...a children's paradise filled with bouncy toys.

bouncy house (bouncy houses) N-COUNT A **bouncy house** is a large object filled with air, often in the shape of a house or castle, which children play on at a fairground or other outdoor event.

━━━━━━━━━━ BOUND ━━━━━━━━━━
① BE BOUND
② OTHER USES

① **bound** ✦◇◇ /baʊnd/ ◼ **Bound** is the past tense and past participle of **bind**. ◼ PHRASE If you say that something **is bound to** happen, you mean that you are sure it will happen, because it is a natural consequence of something that is already known or exists. ❑ There are bound to be price increases next year. ◼ PHRASE If you say that something **is bound to** happen or be true, you feel confident and certain of it, although you have no definite knowledge or evidence. [SPOKEN] ❑ I'll show it to Benjamin. He's bound to know. ◼ ADJ [v-link ADJ to n] If one person, thing, or situation is **bound to** another, they are closely associated with each other, and it is difficult for them to be separated or to escape from each other. ❑ We are as tightly bound to the people we dislike as to the people we love. ◼ ADJ [v link ADJ for n] If a vehicle or person is **bound for** a particular place, they are traveling toward it. ❑ The ship was bound for Italy. • COMB IN ADJ **Bound** is also a combining form. ❑ ...a Texas-bound oil freighter.

② **bound** ✦◇◇ /baʊnd/ (bounds, bounding, bounded) ◼ N-PLURAL **Bounds** are limits which normally restrict what can happen or what people can do. ❑ Changes in temperature occur slowly and are constrained within relatively tight bounds. ❑ ...a forceful personality willing to go beyond the bounds of convention. ◼ V-T If an area of land **is bounded by** something, that thing is situated around its edge. ❑ Kirgizia is bounded by Uzbekistan, Kazakhstan and Tajikistan. ❑ ...the trees that bounded the parking lot. ◼ V-T PASSIVE If someone's life or situation **is bounded** by certain things, those are its most important aspects and it is limited or restricted by them. ❑ Our lives are bounded by work, family and television. ◼ V-I If a person or animal **bounds** in a particular direction, they move quickly with large steps or jumps. ❑ He bounded up the steps and pushed the bell of the door. ◼ N-COUNT A **bound** is a long or high jump. [LITERARY] ❑ With one bound Jack was free. ◼ V-I If the quantity or performance of something **bounds** ahead, it increases or improves quickly and suddenly. ❑ Shares in the company bounded ahead by almost 3 percent. ◼ PHRASE If a place is **out of bounds**, people are not allowed to go there. ❑ For the last few days the area has been out of bounds to foreign journalists. ◼ PHRASE If something is **out of bounds**, people are not allowed to do it, use it, see it, or know about it. ❑ American parents may soon be able to rule violent TV programs out of bounds.

-bound /-baʊnd/ ◼ COMB IN ADJ **-bound** combines with nouns to form adjectives that describe a person who finds it impossible or very difficult to leave the specified place. ❑ Andrew has been left wheelchair-bound after the accident. ❑ I'm pretty desk-bound, which is very frustrating. ◼ COMB IN ADJ **-bound** combines with nouns to form adjectives that describe a place that is greatly affected by the specified type of weather. ❑ ...those calm Pacific regions, which are so unlike the stormy and fog-bound northern seas. ◼ COMB IN ADJ **-bound** combines with nouns to form adjectives that describe something or someone that is prevented from working properly or is badly affected by the specified situation. [WRITTEN] ❑ ...a tradition-bound society. ◼ → see also **duty-bound**, **musclebound**

bounda|ry /bˈaʊndəri/ (boundaries) ◼ N-COUNT The **boundary** of an area of land is an imaginary line that separates it from other areas. ❑ The Bow Brook forms the western boundary of the wood. ◼ N-COUNT The **boundaries** of something such as a subject or activity are the limits that people think that it has. ❑ The boundaries between history and storytelling are always being blurred and muddled.

bound|less /baʊndlɪs/ ADJ If you describe something as **boundless**, you mean that there seems to be no end or limit to it. ❑ *His reforming zeal was boundless.*

boun|ti|ful /baʊntɪfʊl/ **1** ADJ A **bountiful** supply or amount of something pleasant is a large one. ❑ *State aid is less bountiful than it was before.* ❑ *...a bountiful harvest of fruits and vegetables.* **2** ADJ A **bountiful** area or period of time produces or provides large amounts of something, especially food. ❑ *The land is bountiful and no one starves.*

boun|ty /baʊnti/ (bounties) **1** N-VAR You can refer to something that is provided in large amounts as **bounty**. [LITERARY] ❑ *...autumn's bounty of fruits, seeds and berries.* **2** N-COUNT A **bounty** is money that is offered as a reward for doing something, especially for finding or killing a particular person. ❑ *A bounty of $50,000 was put on Dr. Alvarez's head.*

boun|ty hunt|er (bounty hunters) N-COUNT A **bounty hunter** is someone who tries to find or kill someone in order to get the reward that has been offered.

bou|quet /boʊkeɪ, buː-/ (bouquets) **1** N-COUNT A **bouquet** is a bunch of flowers which is attractively arranged. ❑ *The woman carried a bouquet of dried violets.* **2** N-VAR The **bouquet** of something, especially wine, is the pleasant smell that it has. ❑ *...a Sicilian wine with a light red color and a bouquet of cloves.*

bou|quet gar|ni /boʊkeɪ ɡɑːni, buː-/ N-SING [also no det] A **bouquet garni** is a bunch of herbs that are tied together and used in cooking to add flavor to the food.

bour|bon /bɜːrbən/ (bourbons) N-MASS **Bourbon** is a type of whiskey that is made mainly in the United States. ❑ *I poured a little more bourbon into my glass.* • N-COUNT A **bourbon** is a small glass of bourbon.

bour|geois /bʊərʒwɑː/ ADJ If you describe people, their way of life, or their attitudes as **bourgeois**, you disapprove of them because you consider them typical of conventional middle-class people. [DISAPPROVAL] ❑ *He's accusing them of having a bourgeois and limited vision.*

bour|geoi|sie /bʊərʒwɑːziː/ **1** N-SING-COLL [the n] In Marxist theory, the **bourgeoisie** are the middle-class people who own most of the wealth in a capitalist system. [TECHNICAL] ❑ *...the suppression of the proletariat by the bourgeoisie.* **2** → see also petit bourgeoisie

bourse /bʊərs/ (bourses) N-COUNT [also in names] The **bourse** of a European city or region is its stock exchange.

bout /baʊt/ (bouts) **1** N-COUNT If you have a **bout** of an illness or of an unpleasant feeling, you have it for a short period. ❑ *He was recovering from a severe bout of flu.* **2** N-COUNT A **bout** of something that is unpleasant is a short time during which it occurs a great deal. ❑ *The latest bout of violence has claimed twenty-four lives.* **3** N-COUNT A **bout** is a boxing or wrestling match. ❑ *This will be his eighth title bout in 19 months.*

bou|tique /buːtiːk/ (boutiques) N-COUNT A **boutique** is a small store that sells fashionable clothes, shoes, or jewelry.

bou|tique ho|tel (boutique hotels) **1** N-COUNT A **boutique hotel** is a small, high-quality and usually attractive hotel. ❑ *They opened a boutique hotel in Istanbul.* **2** → See feature box at town

bo|vine /boʊvaɪn/ **1** ADJ [usu ADJ n] **Bovine** means relating to cattle. [TECHNICAL] **2** ADJ [usu ADJ n] If you describe someone's behavior or appearance as **bovine**, you think that they are stupid or slow. [DISAPPROVAL] ❑ *I'm depressed by the bovine enthusiasm of the crowd's response.*

BOW
① BENDING OR SUBMITTING
② PART OF A SHIP
③ OBJECTS
---

① **bow** /baʊ/ (bows, bowing, bowed) **1** V-I When you **bow to** someone, you briefly bend your body toward them as a formal way of greeting them or showing respect. ❑ *They bowed low to Louis and hastened out of his way.* • N-COUNT **Bow** is also a noun. ❑ *I gave a theatrical bow and waved.* **2** V-T If you **bow** your head, you bend it downward so that you are looking toward the ground, for example, because you want to show respect or because you are thinking deeply about something. ❑ *The Colonel bowed his head and whispered a prayer of thanksgiving.* **3** V-I If you **bow to** pressure or to someone's wishes, you agree to do what they want you to do. ❑ *Some stores are bowing to consumer pressure and stocking organically grown vegetables.*

▶ **bow out** PHRASAL VERB If you **bow out of** something, you stop taking part in it. [WRITTEN] ❑ *He had bowed out gracefully when his successor had been appointed.*

② **bow** /baʊ/ (bows) **1** N-COUNT The front part of a ship is called the **bow** or the **bows**. The plural **bows** can be used to refer either to one or to more than one of these parts. ❑ *The waves were about five feet high now, and the bow of the boat was leaping up and down.* **2** → See also color supplement

③ **bow** /boʊ/ (bows) **1** N-COUNT A **bow** is a knot with two loops and two loose ends that is used in tying shoelaces and ribbons. ❑ *Add a length of ribbon tied in a bow.* **2** N-COUNT A **bow** is a weapon for shooting arrows that consists of a long piece of curved wood with a string attached to both its ends. ❑ *Some of the raiders were armed with bows and arrows.* **3** N-COUNT The **bow** of a violin or other stringed instrument is a long thin piece of wood with fibers stretched along it that you move across the strings of the instrument in order to play it.

bowd|ler|ize /boʊdləraɪz/ (bowdlerizes, bowdlerizing, bowdlerized)

in BRIT, also use **bowdlerise**

V-T To **bowdlerize** a book or movie means to take parts of it out before publishing it or showing it. [DISAPPROVAL] ❑ *I'm bowdlerizing it – just slightly changing one or two words so listeners won't be upset.* ❑ *...a bowdlerized version of the song.*

bowed

Pronounced /boʊd/ for meaning 1, and /baʊd/ for meaning 2.

1 ADJ Something that is **bowed** is curved. ❑ *...a woman with bowed legs.* **2** ADJ If a person's body is **bowed**, it is bent forward. ❑ *He walked aimlessly along the street, head down and shoulders bowed.*

bow|el /baʊəl/ (bowels) N-COUNT Your **bowels** are the tubes in your body through which digested food passes from your stomach to your anus. ❑ *Symptoms such as stomach pains and irritable bowels can be signs of bowel cancer.*

bow|er /baʊər/ (bowers) N-COUNT A **bower** is a shady, leafy shelter in a garden or wood. [LITERARY]

bowl ♦◇◇ /boʊl/ (bowls, bowling, bowled) **1** N-COUNT A **bowl** is a round container with a wide uncovered top. Some kinds of bowl are used, for example, for serving or eating food from, or in cooking, while other larger kinds are used for washing or cleaning. ❑ *Put all the ingredients into a large bowl.* **2** N-COUNT The contents of a bowl can be referred to as a **bowl** of something. ❑ *...a bowl of soup.* **3** N-COUNT You can refer to the hollow rounded part of an object as its **bowl**. ❑ *He smacked the bowl of his pipe into his hand.* **4** V-T In a sport such as bowling or lawn bowling, when a bowler **bowls** a ball, he or she rolls it down a narrow track or field of grass. ❑ *Neither finalist bowled a particularly strong game.* **5** V-T/V-I In a sport such as cricket, when a bowler **bowls** a ball, he or she throws it down the field toward a batsman. ❑ *I can't see the point of bowling a ball like that.* **6** V-I If you **bowl** along in a car or on a boat, you move along very quickly, especially when you are enjoying yourself. ❑ *Veronica looked at him, smiling, as they bowled along.* **7** → see also bowling

bowl|er /boʊlər/ (bowlers) **1** N-COUNT A **bowler** is someone who plays bowls or goes bowling. **2** N-COUNT The **bowler** in a sport such as cricket is the player who is bowling the ball.

bowl|er hat (bowler hats) N-COUNT A **bowler hat** is a round, hard, black hat with a narrow brim, worn in the past especially by British businessmen. [mainly BRIT]

in AM, use **derby**

bowl|ful /boʊlfʊl/ (bowlfuls) N-COUNT [usu N of n] The contents of a bowl can be referred to as a **bowlful** of something. ❑ *He ate a large bowlful of cereal.* ❑ *I had a mixed salad – a huge bowlful for $3.20.*

bowl|ing /boʊlɪŋ/ **1** N-UNCOUNT **Bowling** is a game in which you roll a heavy ball down a narrow track toward a group of wooden objects and try to knock down as many of them as possible. ❑ *I go bowling for relaxation.* **2** N-UNCOUNT In a sport such as cricket, **bowling** is the action or activity of bowling the ball toward the batsman. ❑ *Much of the bowling was done by Phil Tufnell.*

bowl|ing al|ley (bowling alleys) N-COUNT A **bowling alley** is a building which contains several tracks for bowling.

bowl|ing green (bowling greens) N-COUNT A **bowling green** is an area of very smooth, short grass on which the game of lawn bowling is played.

bow tie /boʊ taɪ/ (bow ties) also **bow-tie** N-COUNT A **bow tie** is a tie in the form of a bow. Bow ties are worn by men, especially for formal occasions.

box ♦♦◇ /bɒks/ (boxes, boxing, boxed) **1** N-COUNT A **box** is a square or rectangular container with hard or stiff sides. Boxes often have lids. ❑ *He reached into the cardboard box beside him.* ❑ *They sat on wooden boxes.* **2** N-COUNT You can use **box** to refer to a box and its contents, or to the contents only. ❑ *She ate two boxes of chocolates.* **3** N-COUNT A **box** is a square or rectangle that is printed or drawn on a piece of paper, a road, or on some other surface. ❑ *For more information, just check the box and send us the form.* **4** N-COUNT A **box** is a small separate area in a theater or at a sports arena or stadium, where a small number of people can sit to watch the performance or game. ❑ *Jim watched the game from a private box.* **5** N-COUNT **Box** is used before a number as a mailing address by people or organizations that rent a post office box. ❑ *...Country Crafts, Box 111, Landisville.* **6** N-UNCOUNT [oft N n] **Box** is a small evergreen tree with dark leaves that is often used to form hedges. ❑ *...box hedges.* **7** V-I To **box** means to fight someone according to the rules of boxing. ❑ *At school I boxed and played rugby.* **8** → see also **boxing**, **post office box**

▸ **box in** **1** PHRASAL VERB If you **are boxed in**, you are unable to move from a particular place because you are surrounded by other people or cars. ❑ *The cabs cut in front of them, trying to box them in.* **2** PHRASAL VERB If something **boxes** you **in**, it puts you in a situation where you have very little choice about what you can do. ❑ *We are not trying to box anybody in, we are trying to find a satisfactory way forward.*

box|car /bɒkskɑr/ (boxcars) N-COUNT A **boxcar** is a railroad car, often without windows, that is used to carry luggage, goods, or mail. [AM]

in BRIT, use **van**

boxed /bɒkst/ **1** ADJ [usu ADJ n] A **boxed** set or collection of things is sold in a box. ❑ *...a boxed set of six cups and saucers.* ❑ *This boxed collection captures 64 of the greatest modern love songs.* **2** → see also **box**

box|er /bɒksər/ (boxers) N-COUNT A **boxer** is someone who takes part in the sport of boxing.

box|er shorts N-PLURAL [also *a pair of* N] **Boxer shorts** are loose-fitting men's underpants that are shaped like the shorts worn by boxers.

box|ing /bɒksɪŋ/ N-UNCOUNT **Boxing** is a sport in which two people wearing large padded gloves fight according to special rules.

box|ing glove (boxing gloves) N-COUNT **Boxing gloves** are big padded gloves worn for boxing.

box|ing ring (boxing rings) N-COUNT A **boxing ring** is a raised square platform with ropes around it in which boxers fight.

box lunch (box lunches) N-COUNT A **box lunch** is food packed in a box, for example a sandwich, that you buy and eat as your lunch. [AM] ❑ *Box lunches can be arranged to take with you on day trips into the valley.*

in BRIT, use **packed lunch**

box num|ber (box numbers) N-COUNT A **box number** is a number used as an address, for example one given by a newspaper for replies to a private advertisement, or one used by an organization for the letters sent to it. ❑ *He produced 1000 leaflets tagged with his phone number and a post office box number.*

box of|fice (box offices) also **box-office** **1** N-COUNT The **box office** in a theater or concert hall is the place where the tickets are sold. ❑ *...the long line of people outside the box-office.* **2** N-SING When people talk about the **box office**, they are referring to the degree of success of a film or play in terms of the number of people who go to watch it or the amount of money it makes. ❑ *The film has taken $180 million at the box office.*

box score (box scores) N-COUNT In baseball and basketball, a **box score** is a printed table of statistics showing how each player performed in a game. [AM]

box|set /bɒksɛt/ (boxsets) also **box set** N-COUNT A **boxset** is a collection of items of the same type, packaged together for sale in a presentation box. ❑ *...a boxset of Rolling Stones classics.* ❑ *...a Harry Potter box set.*

box spring (box springs) N-COUNT A **box spring** is a frame containing rows of coiled springs that is used to provide support for a mattress. You can also use **box springs** to refer to the springs themselves.

box|wood /bɒkswʊd/ N-UNCOUNT **Boxwood** is a type of wood that is obtained from a box tree.

boxy /bɒksi/ (boxier, boxiest) ADJ [usu ADJ n] Something that is **boxy** is similar to a square in shape and usually plain. ❑ *...short boxy jackets.*

boy ♦♦♦ /bɔɪ/ (boys) **1** N-COUNT A **boy** is a child who will grow up to be a man. ❑ *He was still just a boy.* **2** N-COUNT You can refer to a young man as a **boy**, especially when talking about relationships between boys and girls. ❑ *...the age when girls get interested in boys.* **3** N-COUNT Someone's **boy** is their son. [INFORMAL] ❑ *Eric was my cousin Edward's boy.* **4** N-COUNT You can refer to a man as a **boy**, especially when you are talking about him in an affectionate way. [INFORMAL, FEELINGS] ❑ *...the local boy who made president.* **5** EXCLAM Some people say 'boy' or 'oh boy' in order to express feelings of excitement or admiration. [mainly AM, INFORMAL, FEELINGS] ❑ *Oh boy! what resourceful children I have.*

▬▬▬▬▬ COLLOCATIONS ▬▬▬▬▬

boy
NOUN
1
noun + **boy**: baby; country, farm
adjective + **boy**: little, small, young; adolescent, teenage; bad, clever, good, naughty
4
noun + **boy**: pin-up, poster, wonder; birthday
adjective + **boy**: golden

boy band (boy bands) N-COUNT A **boy band** is a band consisting of young men who sing pop music and dance. Boy bands are especially popular with teenagers.

boy|cott /bɔɪkɒt/ (boycotts, boycotting, boycotted) V-T If a country, group, or person **boycotts** a country, organization, or activity, they refuse to be involved with it in any way because they disapprove of it. ❑ *The main opposition parties are boycotting the elections.* • N-COUNT **Boycott** is also a noun. ❑ *Opposition leaders had called for a boycott of the vote.*

boy|friend /bɔɪfrɛnd/ (boyfriends) N-COUNT Someone's **boyfriend** is a man or boy with whom they are having a romantic or sexual relationship. ❑ *...Brenda and her boyfriend Anthony.* ❑ *They don't know if I've got a boyfriend or not.*

boy|hood /bɔɪhʊd/ N-UNCOUNT **Boyhood** is the period of a male person's life during which he is a boy. ❑ *They are rivals who have known each other since boyhood.*

boy|ish /bɔɪɪʃ/ ADJ If you describe a man as **boyish**, you mean that he is like a boy in his appearance or behavior, and you find this characteristic quite attractive. [APPROVAL] ❑ *She was relieved to see his face light up with a boyish grin.* • **boy|ish|ly** ADV ❑ *John grinned boyishly.*

Boy Scout (Boy Scouts) also **boy scout** **1** N-PROPER-COLL [the N] **The Boy Scouts** is an organization for boys which teaches them discipline and practical skills. ❑ *He's in the Boy Scouts.* **2** N-COUNT A **Boy Scout** is a boy who is a member of the Boy Scouts.

bozo /boʊzoʊ/ (bozos) N-COUNT If you say that someone is a **bozo**, you mean that you think they are stupid. [INFORMAL, DISAPPROVAL] ❑ *He makes 'em look like bozos.*

bpm /bi pi ɛm/ **bpm** is written after a number to indicate someone's heart rate. **bpm** is an abbreviation of 'beats per minute.' ❑ *My heart rate shot up from 84 bpm to nearly 100.*

bps /bi pi ɛs/ **bps** is a measurement of the speed at which computer data is transferred, for example, by a modem. **bps** is

Br. an abbreviation for 'bits per second.' [COMPUTING] ▫ *A minimum 28,800 bps modem is probably the slowest you'll want to put up with.*

Br. Br. is a written abbreviation for **British**.

bra /brɑ/ (bras) N-COUNT A bra is a piece of underwear that women wear to support their breasts.

brace /breɪs/ (braces, bracing, braced) **1** V-T If you **brace** yourself for something unpleasant or difficult, you prepare yourself for it. ▫ *He braced himself for the icy plunge into the black water.* **2** V-T If you **brace** yourself **against** something or **brace** part of your body **against** it, you press against something in order to steady your body or to avoid falling. ▫ *Elaine braced herself against the dresser and looked in the mirror.* **3** V-T If you **brace** your shoulders or knees, you keep them stiffly in a particular position. ▫ *He braced his shoulders defiantly as another squall of wet snow slashed across his face.* **4** V-T To **brace** something means to strengthen or support it with something else. ▫ *Overhead, the lights showed the old timbers, used to brace the roof.* **5** N-COUNT A **brace** is a device attached to a part of a person's body, for example, to a weak leg, in order to strengthen or support it. ▫ *He wore leg braces after he had polio in childhood.* **6** N-PLURAL **Braces** are a metal device that can be fastened to a person's teeth in order to help them grow straight. ▫ *I used to have to wear braces.* **7** N-COUNT **Braces** are a pair of written marks {} that you place around words, numbers, or parts of a computer code, for example, to indicate that they are connected in some way or are separate from other parts of the writing or code. [AM]

in BRIT, usually use **curly brackets**

8 N-PLURAL **Braces** are a pair of straps that pass over your shoulders and fasten to your pants at the front and back in order to stop them from falling down. [BRIT]

in AM, use **suspenders**

brace|let /breɪslɪt/ (bracelets) N-COUNT A **bracelet** is a chain or band, usually made of metal, that you wear around your wrist as jewelry.

brac|ing /breɪsɪŋ/ ADJ If you describe something, especially a place, climate, or activity as **bracing**, you mean that it makes you feel fresh and full of energy. ▫ *...a bracing walk.*

brack|en /brækən/ N-UNCOUNT **Bracken** is a large plant with leaves that are divided into many thin sections. It grows on hills and in woods.

brack|et /brækɪt/ (brackets, bracketing, bracketed) **1** N-COUNT If you say that someone or something is in a particular **bracket**, you mean that they come within a particular range, for example, a range of incomes, ages, or prices. ▫ *...a 33% top tax rate on everyone in these high-income brackets.* **2** N-COUNT **Brackets** are pieces of metal, wood, or plastic that are fastened to a wall in order to support something such as a shelf. ▫ *Fix the beam with the brackets and screws.* **3** V-T If two or more people or things **are bracketed** together, they are considered to be similar or related in some way. ▫ *The Magi, Brahmins, and Druids were bracketed together as men of wisdom.* **4** N-COUNT **Brackets** are a pair of marks ( ) that are placed around a series of symbols in a mathematical expression to indicate that those symbols function as one item within the expression. **5** N-COUNT **Brackets** are a pair of written marks ( ) that you place around a word, expression, or sentence in order to indicate that you are giving extra information. [BRIT]

in AM, use **parentheses**

brack|ish /brækɪʃ/ ADJ [usu ADJ n] **Brackish** water is slightly salty and unpleasant. ▫ *...shallow pools of brackish water.*

brag /bræg/ (brags, bragging, bragged) V-T/V-I If you **brag**, you say in a very proud way that you have something or have done something. [DISAPPROVAL] ▫ *He's always bragging that he's a great martial artist.* ▫ *He'll probably go around bragging to his friends.* ▫ *Winn bragged that he had spies in the department.*

Brah|min /brɑmɪn/ (Brahmins) also **Drahman** N-COUNT A **Brahmin** is a Hindu of the highest social rank.

braid /breɪd/ (braids, braiding, braided) **1** N-UNCOUNT **Braid** is a narrow piece of decorated cloth or twisted threads, which is used to decorate clothes or curtains. ▫ *...a plum-colored uniform with lots of gold braid.* **2** V-T If you **braid** hair or a group of threads, you twist three or more lengths of the hair or threads over and under each other to make one thick length. [AM] ▫ *She had almost finished braiding Louisa's hair.*

in BRIT, use **plait**

3 N-COUNT A **braid** is a length of hair that has been divided into three or more lengths and then braided. [AM] ▫ *...a short, energetic woman with her hair in braids.*

in BRIT, use **plait**

braid|ed /breɪdɪd/ ADJ A piece of clothing that is **braided** is decorated with braid.

Braille /breɪl/ N-UNCOUNT **Braille** is a system of printing for blind people. The letters are printed as groups of raised dots that you can feel with your fingers.

brain ♦♦◇ /breɪn/ (brains) **1** N-COUNT Your **brain** is the organ inside your head that controls your body's activities and enables you to think and to feel things such as heat and pain. ▫ *Her father died of a brain tumor.* **2** N-COUNT Your **brain** is your mind and the way that you think. ▫ *Once you stop using your brain you soon go stale.* **3** N-COUNT If someone has **brains** or a good **brain**, they have the ability to learn and understand things quickly, to solve problems, and to make good decisions. ▫ *They were not the only ones to have brains and ambition.* **4** N-COUNT [usu pl] If someone is the **brains** behind an idea or an organization, he or she had that idea or makes the important decisions about how that organization is managed. [INFORMAL] ▫ *Mr. White was the brains behind the scheme.* **5 to rack your brains** → see **rack**

COLLOCATIONS

brain
NOUN
1
adjective + **brain**: human; left, right
verb + **brain**: scan; affect, damage
2
adjective + **brain**: human, teenage; mathematical, sharp, shrewd
verb + **brain**: engage, stimulate, use

VOCABULARY IN CONTEXT

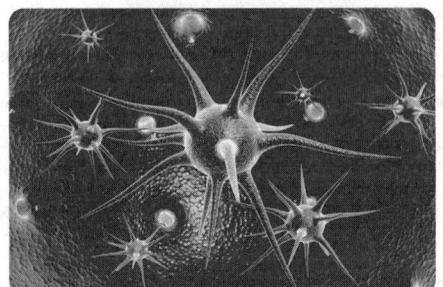

The brain

The brain is the most complex **organ** in the body; it is also the least understood. We know how the brain **functions** in basic terms, but much of its activity is still being investigated. The brain consists of **neurons**: **microscopic** star-shaped **cells** that **emit electrical** and **chemical impulses**. Each neuron is separated from nearby neurons by a small gap called a **synapse**. To transmit information, a neuron creates a chemical signal that travels across the synapse to the next neuron. The chemical signal is **detected** and converted into an electrical signal, called a **nerve impulse**, which travels across the neuron to the next synapse. Here the signal is converted back into a chemical signal and passed across the synapse, and so on. Of course, all of this happens in a **split second**, enabling us to process information and react to it almost instantly.

brain|child /breɪntʃaɪld/ N-SING Someone's **brainchild** is an idea or invention that they have thought up or created. ❑ *The record was the brainchild of rock star Bob Geldof.*

brain dam|age N-UNCOUNT If someone suffers **brain damage**, their brain is damaged by an illness or injury so that they cannot function normally. ❑ *He suffered severe brain damage after a motorbike accident.*

brain-damaged ADJ Someone who is **brain-damaged** has suffered brain damage. ❑ *The accident left the boy severely brain-damaged and almost totally reliant on others.*

brain-dead also **brain dead, braindead** ▪ ADJ If someone is declared **brain-dead**, they have suffered brain death. ▫ ADJ If you say that someone is **brain-dead**, you are saying in a cruel way that you think they are very stupid. [DISAPPROVAL]

brain death N-UNCOUNT **Brain death** occurs when someone's brain stops functioning, even though their heart may be kept beating using a machine.

brain drain N-SING When people talk about a **brain drain**, they are referring to the movement of a large number of scientists or academics away from their own country to other countries where the conditions and salaries are better.

-brained /-breɪnd/ ▪ COMB IN ADJ You can combine **-brained** with nouns to form adjectives that describe the quality of someone's mind when you consider that person to be rather stupid. [DISAPPROVAL] ❑ *...a scatter-brained professor.* ▫ → see also **harebrained**

brain|less /breɪnlɪs/ ADJ If you describe someone or something as **brainless**, you mean that you think that they are stupid. [DISAPPROVAL] ❑ *I got treated as if I was a bit brainless.*

brain|power /breɪnpaʊər/ ▪ N-UNCOUNT **Brainpower** is intelligence or the ability to think. ❑ *She admired Robert's brainpower.* ▫ N-UNCOUNT You can refer to the intelligent people in an organization or country as its **brainpower**. ❑ *A country's principal resource is its brainpower.*

brain|storm /breɪnstɔːrm/ (brainstorms, brainstorming, brainstormed) ▪ N-COUNT If you have a **brainstorm**, you suddenly have a clever idea. [AM] ❑ *"Look," she said, getting a brainstorm, "why don't you invite them here?"*

in BRIT, use **brainwave**

▫ V-T/V-I If a group of people **brainstorm**, they have a meeting in which they all put forward any ideas and suggestions as they can think of. ❑ *The women meet twice a month to brainstorm and set business goals for each other.* ❑ *She brainstormed the possible approaches she might take.* • **brain|storming** N-UNCOUNT ❑ *Hundreds of other ideas had been tried and discarded during two years of brainstorming.*

brain teas|er (brain teasers) also **brain-teaser** N-COUNT A **brain teaser** is a question, problem, or puzzle that is difficult to answer or solve, but is not serious or important.

brain trust (brain trusts) N-COUNT A **brain trust** is a group of experts who advise important people in a government or organization. [AM] ❑ *The president faces conflicting advice from his brain trust.*

brain|wash /breɪnwɒʃ/ (brainwashes, brainwashing, brainwashed) V-T If you **brainwash** someone, you force them to believe something by continually telling them that it is true, and preventing them from thinking about it properly. ❑ *They brainwash people into giving up all their money.*

brain|wave /breɪnweɪv/ (brainwaves) N-COUNT If you have a **brainwave**, you suddenly have a clever idea. [BRIT]

in AM, use **brainstorm**

brainy /breɪni/ (brainier, brainiest) ADJ Someone who is **brainy** is clever and good at learning. [INFORMAL] ❑ *I don't class myself as being very intelligent or brainy.*

braise /breɪz/ (braises, braising, braised) V-T When you **braise** meat or a vegetable, you fry it quickly and then cook it slowly in a covered dish with a small amount of liquid. ❑ *I braised some beans to accompany a shoulder of lamb.* ❑ *...braised cabbage.*

brake /breɪk/ (brakes, braking, braked) ▪ N-COUNT **Brakes** are devices in a vehicle that make it go slower or stop. ❑ *A seagull swooped down in front of her car, causing her to slam on the brakes.* ▫ V-T/V-I When a vehicle or its driver **brakes**, or when a driver brakes a vehicle, the driver makes it slow down or stop by using the brakes. ❑ *He heard tires squeal as the car braked to avoid a collision.* ❑ *He braked the car slightly.* ▪ N-COUNT You can use **brake** in a number of expressions to indicate that something has slowed down or stopped. ❑ *Illness had put a brake on his progress.* ▫ → See also color supplement

bram|ble /bræmbəl/ (brambles) N-COUNT [usu pl] **Brambles** are wild prickly bushes that produce blackberries. ❑ *I became caught in the brambles.*

bran /bræn/ N-UNCOUNT **Bran** is the outer skin of grain that is left when the grain has been used to make flour. ❑ *...oat bran.*

branch ◆◇◇ /brɑːntʃ/ (branches, branching, branched) ▪ N-COUNT The **branches** of a tree are the parts that grow out from its trunk and have leaves, flowers, or fruit growing on them. ❑ *...the upper branches of a row of pines.* ▫ N-COUNT A **branch** of a business or other organization is one of the offices, stores, or groups which belong to it and which are located in different places. ❑ *The local branch of Bank of America is handling the accounts.* ▪ N-COUNT A **branch** of an organization such as the government or the police force is a department that has a particular function. ❑ *Senate employees could take their employment grievances to another branch of government.* ❑ *He had a fascination for submarines and joined this branch of the service.* ▫ N-COUNT A **branch of** a subject is a part or type of it. ❑ *Whole branches of science may not receive any grants.* ▪ N-COUNT A **branch** of your family is a group of its members who are descended from one particular person. ❑ *This is one of the branches of the Roosevelt family.*
▶ **branch off** PHRASAL VERB A road or path that **branches off** from another one starts from it and goes in a slightly different direction. If you **branch off** somewhere, you change the direction in which you are going. ❑ *After a few miles, a small road branched off to the right.*
▶ **branch out** PHRASAL VERB If a person or an organization **branches out**, they do something that is different from their normal activities or work. ❑ *I continued studying moths, and branched out to other insects.*

branch line (branch lines) N-COUNT A **branch line** is a railroad line that goes to small towns rather than one that goes between large cities.

brand ◆◇◇ /brænd/ (brands, branding, branded) ▪ N-COUNT A **brand** of a product is the version of it that is made by one particular manufacturer. ❑ *I don't really like this brand of shampoo.* ❑ *I bought one of the leading brands.* ▫ N-COUNT A **brand of** something such as a way of thinking or behaving is a particular kind of it. ❑ *Joel Hatch brings his own unique brand of humor to the role.* ▪ V-T If someone **is branded** as something bad, people think they are that thing. ❑ *I was instantly branded as a rebel.* ❑ *The company has been branded racist by some of its own staff.* ▫ V-T When you **brand** an animal, you put a permanent mark on its skin in order to show who it belongs to, usually by burning a mark onto its skin. ❑ *The owner couldn't be bothered to brand the cattle.* • N-COUNT **Brand** is also a noun. ❑ *A brand was a mark of ownership burned into the hide of an animal with a hot iron.* ▪ → See feature box at **fashion**

USAGE

brand

Don't talk about the 'mark' of a product. For example, don't say 'What mark of coffee do you drink?' Say 'What **brand** of coffee do you drink?' Don't say 'What mark of car do you drive?' Say 'What **make** of car do you drive?' *This is a very popular **make** of bike.*

SYNONYMS

brand
NOUN ▪
trademark: *Intellectual property law deals with trademarks, copyright, and patents.*
logo: *The product was relaunched with a new website and logo in April.*

---

brand|ed /brændɪd/ ADJ [ADJ n] A **branded** product is one that is made by a well-known manufacturer and has the manufacturer's label on it. [BUSINESS] ❑ *Supermarket lines are often cheaper than branded goods.*

brand im|age (brand images) N-COUNT The **brand image** of a particular brand of a product is the image or impression that people have of it, usually created by advertising. [BUSINESS] ☐ *They can be influenced by brand images that they see for only a fraction of a second.*

brand|ing /brændɪŋ/ N-UNCOUNT The **branding** of a product is the presentation of it to the public in a way that makes it easy for people to recognize or identify. [BUSINESS] ☐ *Local companies find the sites and build the theme parks, while we will look after the branding.*

bran|dish /brændɪʃ/ (brandishes, brandishing, brandished) V-T If you **brandish** something, especially a weapon, you hold it in a threatening way. ☐ *He appeared in the lounge brandishing a knife.*

brand lead|er (brand leaders) N-COUNT The **brand leader** of a particular product is the brand of it that most people choose to buy, or the manufacturer that makes that brand. [BUSINESS] ☐ *In office supplies, we're the brand leader.*

brand name (brand names) N-COUNT The **brand name** of a product is the name the manufacturer gives it and under which it is sold. [BUSINESS] ☐ *The drug is marketed under the brand name Viramune.*

brand-name prod|uct (brand-name products) N-COUNT A **brand-name product** is one which is made by a well-known manufacturer and has the manufacturer's label on it. [BUSINESS] ☐ *In buying footwear, 66% prefer brand-name products.*

brand-new ADJ A **brand-new** object is completely new. ☐ *Yesterday he went off to buy himself a brand-new car.*

bran|dy /brændi/ (brandies) **1** N-MASS **Brandy** is a strong alcoholic drink. It is often drunk after a meal. **2** N-COUNT A **brandy** is a glass of brandy. ☐ *After a couple of brandies Michael started telling me his life story.*

bran|dy snap (brandy snaps) N-COUNT **Brandy snaps** are very thin crisp cookies in the shape of hollow cylinders. They are flavored with ginger and are often filled with cream.

brash /bræʃ/ (brasher, brashest) ADJ If you describe someone or their behavior as **brash**, you disapprove of them because you think that they are too confident and aggressive. [DISAPPROVAL] ☐ *On stage she seems hard, brash and uncompromising.* • **brash|ly** ADV ☐ *I brashly announced to the group that NATO needed to be turned around.*

brass /bræs/ **1** N-UNCOUNT **Brass** is a yellow-colored metal made from copper and zinc. It is used especially for making ornaments and musical instruments. ☐ *The instrument is beautifully made in brass.* **2** N-SING The **brass** is the section of an orchestra which consists of brass wind instruments such as trumpets and horns. ☐ *Consequently even this vast chorus was occasionally overwhelmed by the brass.*

brass band (brass bands) N-COUNT A **brass band** is a band that is made up of brass and percussion instruments.

bras|se|rie /bræsəri/ (brasseries) N-COUNT A **brasserie** is a small and usually cheap restaurant or bar.

bras|si|ca /bræsɪkə/ (brassicas) N-COUNT [oft N n] **Brassicas** are vegetables such as cabbages, broccoli, and turnips.

bras|siere /brəzɪər/ (brassieres) N-COUNT A **brassiere** is the same as a **bra**. [OLD-FASHIONED]

brass rub|bing (brass rubbings) N-COUNT A **brass rubbing** is a picture made by placing a piece of paper over a brass plate that has writing or a picture on it, and rubbing it with a crayon or charcoal.

brassy /bræsi, bræsi/ (brassier, brassiest) **1** ADJ **Brassy** music is bold, harsh, and loud. ☐ *Musicians blast their brassy jazz from street corners.* **2** ADJ If you describe someone's appearance or behavior as **brassy**, you think that they do not have good taste, and that they dress or behave in a way that is too loud or vulgar. [DISAPPROVAL] ☐ *...his brassy new girlfriend.* **3** ADJ Something that is **brassy** has a yellow metallic color and sometimes looks cheap. ☐ *...a woman with big brassy earrings.*

brat /bræt/ (brats) N-COUNT If you call someone, especially a child, a **brat**, you mean that he or she behaves badly or annoys you. [INFORMAL, DISAPPROVAL] ☐ *He's a spoiled brat.*

brat pack (brat packs) N-COUNT A **brat pack** is a group of young people, especially actors or writers, who are popular or successful at the moment. [JOURNALISM] ☐ *...the Hollywood brat pack.*

bra|va|do /brəvɑːdoʊ/ N-UNCOUNT **Bravado** is an appearance of courage or confidence that someone shows in order to impress other people. ☐ *"You won't get away with this," he said with unexpected bravado.*

brave ♦♢ /breɪv/ (braver, bravest, braves, braving, braved) **1** ADJ Someone who is **brave** is willing to do things that are dangerous, and does not show fear in difficult or dangerous situations. ☐ *He was not brave enough to report the loss of the documents.* • **brave|ly** ADV ☐ *Our men wiped them out, but the enemy fought bravely and well.* **2** V-T If you **brave** unpleasant or dangerous conditions, you deliberately expose yourself to them, usually in order to achieve something. [WRITTEN] ☐ *Thousands have braved icy rain to demonstrate their support.*

brave new world N-SING [usu N of n] If someone refers to a **brave new world**, they are talking about a situation or system that has recently been created and that people think will be successful and fair. ☐ *...the brave new world of high-tech, global translation.*

brav|ery /breɪvəri/ N-UNCOUNT **Bravery** is brave behavior or the quality of being brave. ☐ *He deserves the highest praise for his bravery.*

bra|vo /brɑːvoʊ/ EXCLAM Some people say '**bravo**' to express appreciation when someone has done something well. [OLD-FASHIONED] ☐ *"Bravo, Rena! You're right," the students said.*

bra|vu|ra /brəvʊərə/ **1** N-UNCOUNT If you say that someone is doing something with **bravura**, you mean that they are using unnecessary extra actions that emphasize their skill or importance. [LITERARY] ☐ *The film is directed with a technical bravura and visual splendor.* **2** ADJ [ADJ n] A **bravura** performance or piece of work is done with bravura. [LITERARY] ☐ *It was a bravura performance by Denzel Washington.*

brawl /brɔːl/ (brawls, brawling, brawled) **1** N-COUNT A **brawl** is a rough or violent fight. ☐ *He had been in a drunken street brawl.* **2** V-RECIP If someone **brawls**, they fight in a very rough or violent way. ☐ *He was suspended for a year from the university after brawling with police over a speeding ticket.*

brawn /brɔːn/ N-UNCOUNT **Brawn** is physical strength. ☐ *He's got plenty of brains as well as brawn.*

brawny /brɔːni/ ADJ Someone who is **brawny** is strong and has big muscles. ☐ *...a brawny young man.*

bray /breɪ/ (brays, braying, brayed) V-I When a donkey **brays**, it makes a loud harsh sound. ☐ *The donkey brayed and tried to bolt.*

bra|zen /breɪzən/ ADJ If you describe a person or their behavior as **brazen**, you mean that they are very bold and do not care what other people think about them or their behavior. ☐ *They're quite brazen about their bisexuality, it doesn't worry them.* • **bra|zen|ly** ADV ☐ *He was brazenly running a $400,000-a-month drug operation from the prison.*

bra|zier /breɪʒər/ (braziers) **1** N-COUNT A **brazier** is a large metal container in which coal or charcoal is burned to keep people warm when they are outside in cold weather, for example, because of their work. **2** N-COUNT A **brazier** is a grill that you use for cooking, usually with charcoal. [AM]

Bra|zil|ian /brəzɪliən/ (Brazilians) ADJ **Brazilian** means belonging or relating to Brazil, or to its people or culture. • N-COUNT A **Brazilian** is a person who comes from Brazil.

bra|zil nut (brazil nuts) N-COUNT **Brazil nuts** are large nuts with a woody shell that grow on trees in South America and that you can eat. **2** → See also color supplement

breach /briːtʃ/ (breaches, breaching, breached) **1** V-T If you **breach** an agreement, a law, or a promise, you break it. ☐ *The newspaper breached the code of conduct on privacy.* **2** N-VAR A **breach** of an agreement, a law, or a promise is an act of breaking it. ☐ *The congressman was accused of a breach of secrecy rules.* **3** N-COUNT A **breach** in a relationship is a serious disagreement which often results in the relationship ending. [FORMAL] ☐ *Their actions threatened a serious breach in relations between the two countries.* **4** V-T If someone or something **breaches** a barrier, they make an opening in it, usually leaving it weakened or destroyed. [FORMAL] ☐ *The limestone is sufficiently fissured for tree roots to have breached the roof of the cave.* **5** V-T If you **breach** someone's security or their defenses, you manage to get through and attack an area that is heavily guarded and protected. ☐ *The bomber had breached security by* hurling his dynamite from a roof overlooking the building. • N-COUNT **Breach** is also a noun. ❏ ...serious breaches of security at Camp Delta.

breach of the peace (breaches of the peace) N-VAR A **breach of the peace** is noisy or violent behavior in a public place that is illegal because it disturbs other people. [LEGAL] ❏ He admitted causing a breach of the peace. ❏ Four men were found guilty of breach of the peace.

bread ✦✧ /brɛd/ (breads) N-MASS **Bread** is a very common food made from flour, water, and usually yeast. ❏ ...a loaf of bread. ❏ ...bread and butter.

bread and but|ter also bread-and-butter **1** N-UNCOUNT [usu with poss] Something that is the **bread and butter** of a person or organization is the activity or work that provides the main part of their income. ❏ Out-of-state visitors are our bread and butter. **2** ADJ [ADJ n] **Bread-and-butter** issues or matters are ones which are important to most people, because they affect them personally. ❏ The opposition gained support by concentrating on bread-and-butter matters.

bread bas|ket (bread baskets) also **breadbasket** N-COUNT [usu with poss] If an area or region is described as the **bread basket** of a country, it provides a lot of the food for that country because crops grow very easily there. It therefore produces wealth for the country. ❏ The northwest became the country's breadbasket.

bread bin (bread bins) N-COUNT A **bread bin** is the same as a breadbox. [BRIT]

bread|board /brɛdbɔːrd/ (breadboards) also **bread board** N-COUNT A **breadboard** is a flat piece of wood used for cutting bread on.

bread|box /brɛdbɒks/ (breadboxes) also **bread box** N-COUNT A **breadbox** is a wooden, metal, or plastic container for storing bread. [AM]

in BRIT, use **bread bin**

bread|crumb /brɛdkrʌm/ (breadcrumbs) **1** N-COUNT [usu pl] **Breadcrumbs** are tiny pieces of dry bread. They are used in cooking. **2** → See feature box at cooking

bread|fruit /brɛdfruːt/ (breadfruit)

Breadfruit is both the singular and plural form.

N-VAR **Breadfruit** are large round fruit that grow on trees in the Pacific Islands and in tropical parts of America and that, when baked, look and feel like bread.

bread|line /brɛdlaɪn/ N-SING [usu on the N] Someone who is on the **breadline** is very poor indeed. ❏ We lived on the breadline to get our son through college. ❏ They're not exactly on the breadline.

breadth /brɛtθ/ **1** N-UNCOUNT The **breadth** of something is the distance between its two sides. ❏ The breadth of the whole camp was 400 paces. **2** N-UNCOUNT The **breadth** of something is its quality of consisting of or including many different things. ❏ Older people have a tremendous breadth of experience.

bread|winner /brɛdwɪnər/ (breadwinners) also **bread-winner** N-COUNT The **breadwinner** in a family is the person in it who earns the money that the family needs for essential things. ❏ I've always paid the bills and been the breadwinner.

BREAK
① DAMAGE OR DESTROY
② STOP OR CHANGE SOMETHING
③ OTHER USES
④ PHRASAL VERBS

---

① **break** ✦✦✦ /breɪk/ (breaks, breaking, broke, broken) **1** V-T/V-I When an object **breaks** or when you **break** it, it suddenly separates into two or more pieces, often because it has been hit or dropped. ❏ He fell through the window, breaking the glass. ❏ The plate broke. ❏ The plane broke into three pieces. **2** V-T/V-I If you **break** a part of your body such as your leg, your arm, or your nose, or if a bone **breaks**, you are injured because a bone cracks or splits. ❏ She broke a leg in a skiing accident. ❏ Old bones break easily. • N-COUNT **Break** is also a noun. ❏ It has caused a bad break to Gabriella's leg. **3** V-T/V-I If a surface, cover, or seal **breaks** or if something **breaks** it, a hole or tear is made in it, so that a substance can pass through. ❏ Once you've broken the seal of a bottle there's no way you can put it back together again. ❏ The bandage must be put on when the blister breaks. **4** V-T/V-I When a tool or piece of machinery **breaks** or when you **break** it, it is damaged and no longer works. ❏ When the clutch broke, the car was locked into second gear. **5** → see feature box at **global warming**

② **break** ✦✦✦ /breɪk/ (breaks, breaking, broke, broken) **1** V-T If someone **breaks** something, especially a difficult or unpleasant situation that has existed for some time, they end it or change it. ❏ We need to break the vicious cycle of violence and counterviolence. ❏ New proposals have been put forward to break the deadlock among rival factions. • N-COUNT **Break** is also a noun. ❏ Nothing that might lead to a break in the deadlock has been discussed yet. **2** V-T If someone or something **breaks** a silence, they say something or make a noise after a long period of silence. ❏ Hugh broke the silence. "Is she always late?" he asked. **3** V-T/V-I If you **break** with a group of people or a traditional way of doing things, or you **break** your connection with them, you stop being involved with that group or stop doing things in that way. ❏ In 1959, Akihito broke with imperial tradition by marrying a commoner. ❏ They were determined to break from precedent. • N-COUNT **Break** is also a noun. ❏ Making a completely clean break with the past, the couple got rid of all their old furniture. **4** V-T If you **break** a habit or if someone **breaks** you of it, you no longer have that habit. ❏ If you continue to smoke, keep trying to break the habit. **5** V-I If someone **breaks** for a short period of time, they rest or change from what they are doing for a short period. ❏ They broke for lunch. **6** N-COUNT A **break** is a short period of time when you have a rest or a change from what you are doing, especially if you are working or if you are in a boring or unpleasant situation. ❏ They may be able to help with childcare so that you can have a break. ❏ I thought a 15 minute break from his work would do him good. **7** N-COUNT A **break** is a short vacation. ❏ They are currently taking a short break in Spain. **8** V-T If you **break** your journey somewhere, you stop there for a short time so that you can have a rest. ❏ We broke our journey at a small country hotel.

③ **break** ✦✦✦ /breɪk/ (breaks, breaking, broke, broken)
→ Please look at meanings **13** – **21** to see if the expression you are looking for is shown under another headword.

1 V-T If you **break** a rule, promise, or agreement, you do something that you should not do according to that rule, promise, or agreement. ❏ We didn't know we were breaking the law. ❏ The company has consistently denied it had knowingly broken arms embargoes. **2** V-I If you **break** free or loose, you free yourself from something or escape from it. ❏ She broke free by thrusting her elbow into his chest. **3** V-T To **break** the force of something such as a blow or fall means to weaken its effect, for example, by getting in the way of it. ❏ He sustained serious neck injuries after he broke someone's fall. **4** V-I When a piece of news **breaks**, people hear about it from the newspapers, television, or radio. ❏ The news broke that Montgomery was under investigation. **5** V-T When you **break** a piece of bad news to someone, you tell it to them, usually in a kind way. ❏ Then Louise broke the news that she was leaving me. **6** N-COUNT A **break** is a lucky opportunity that someone gets to achieve something. [INFORMAL] ❏ Her first break came when she was chosen out of 100 guitarists auditioning for a spot on Michael Jackson's tour. **7** V-T If you **break** a record, you beat the previous record for a particular achievement. ❏ He has broken the world record in the 100 meters. **8** V-I When day or dawn **breaks**, it starts to grow light after the night has ended. ❏ They continued the search as dawn broke. **9** V-I When a wave **breaks**, it passes its highest point and turns downward, for example, when it reaches the shore. ❏ Danny listened to the waves breaking against the shore. **10** V-T If you **break** a secret code, you work out how to understand it. ❏ It was feared they could break the Allies' codes. **11** V-I If someone's voice **breaks** when they are speaking, it changes its sound, for example, because they are sad or afraid. ❏ Godfrey's voice broke, and halted. **12** V-I When a boy's voice **breaks**, it becomes deeper and sounds more like a man's voice. ❏ He sings with the strained discomfort of someone whose voice hasn't quite broken. **13** V-I If the weather **breaks** or a storm **breaks**, it suddenly becomes rainy or stormy after a period of sunshine. ❏ I've been waiting for the weather to break. **14** → see also **broke**, **broken**, **heartbreak**, **heartbreaking**, **heartbroken**, **outbreak** **15** to break even → see **even** ② **16** to break new ground → see **ground** ③ **17** to break someone's heart → see **heart** ② **18** all hell breaks loose → see **hell** ② **19** to break the ice → see **ice** **20** to break ranks → see **rank** **21** to break wind → see **wind** ①

④ **break** ♦♦♦ /breɪk/ (breaks, breaking, broke, broken)
▶ **break down** ① PHRASAL VERB If a machine or a vehicle **breaks down**, it stops working. ❑ *Their car broke down.* ② PHRASAL VERB If a discussion, relationship, or system **breaks down**, it fails because of a problem or disagreement. ❑ *Talks with business leaders broke down last night.* ③ PHRASAL VERB To **break down** something such as an idea or statement means to separate it into smaller parts in order to make it easier to understand or deal with. ❑ *The report breaks down the results region by region.* ④ PHRASAL VERB When a substance **breaks down** or when something **breaks** it **down**, a biological or chemical process causes it to separate into the substances which make it up. ❑ *Over time, the protein in the eggshell breaks down into its constituent amino acids.* ⑤ PHRASAL VERB If someone **breaks down**, they lose control of themselves and start crying. ❑ *Because he was being so kind and concerned, I broke down and cried.* ⑥ PHRASAL VERB If you **break down** a door or barrier, you hit it so hard that it falls to the ground. ❑ *An unruly mob broke down police barricades and stormed the courtroom.* ⑦ PHRASAL VERB To **break down** barriers or prejudices that separate people or restrict their freedom means to change people's attitudes so that the barriers or prejudices no longer exist. [APPROVAL] ❑ *Women's sports are breaking down the barriers in previously male-dominated domains.* ⑧ → see also **breakdown** ⑨ → See feature box at **global warming**
▶ **break in** ① PHRASAL VERB If someone, usually a thief, **breaks in**, they get into a building by force. ❑ *Masked robbers broke in and made off with $8,000.* ② → see also **break-in** ③ PHRASAL VERB If you **break in** on someone's conversation or activity, you interrupt them. ❑ *O'Leary broke in on his thoughts.* ❑ *Mrs. Southern listened keenly, occasionally breaking in with pertinent questions.* ④ PHRASAL VERB If you **break** someone **in**, you get them used to a new job or situation. ❑ *The band is breaking in a new backing vocalist, who sounds great.* ⑤ PHRASAL VERB If you **break in** something new, you gradually use or wear it for longer and longer periods until it is ready to be used or worn all the time. ❑ *When breaking in an engine, you should refrain from high speeds for the first thousand miles.*
▶ **break into** ① PHRASAL VERB If someone **breaks into** a building, they get into it by force. ❑ *There was no one nearby who might see him trying to break into the house.* ② PHRASAL VERB If someone **breaks into** something they suddenly start doing it. For example, if someone **breaks into** a run they suddenly start running, and if they **break into** song they suddenly start singing. ❑ *The moment she was out of sight she broke into a run.* ③ PHRASAL VERB If you **break into** a profession or area of business, especially one that is difficult to succeed in, you manage to have some success in it. ❑ *She finally broke into films after an acclaimed stage career.*
▶ **break off** ① PHRASAL VERB If part of something **breaks off** or if you **break** it **off**, it comes off or is removed by force. ❑ *The two wings of the aircraft broke off on impact.* ❑ *Grace broke off a large piece of the clay.* ② PHRASAL VERB If you **break off** when you are doing or saying something, you suddenly stop doing it or saying it. ❑ *Barry broke off in mid-sentence.* ③ PHRASAL VERB If someone **breaks off** a relationship, they end it. ❑ *The two West African states had broken off relations two years ago.*
▶ **break out** ① PHRASAL VERB If something such as war, fighting, or disease **breaks out**, it begins suddenly. ❑ *He was 29 when war broke out.* ② PHRASAL VERB If a prisoner **breaks out** of a prison, they escape from it. ❑ *The two men broke out of their cells and cut through a perimeter fence.* ③ → see also **breakout** ④ PHRASAL VERB If you **break out** of a dull situation or routine, you manage to change it or escape from it. ❑ *It's taken a long time to break out of my own conventional training.* ⑤ PHRASAL VERB If you **break out** in a rash or a sweat, a rash or sweat appears on your skin. ❑ *A person who is allergic to cashews may break out in a rash when he consumes these nuts.*
▶ **break through** ① PHRASAL VERB If you **break through** a barrier, you succeed in forcing your way through it. ❑ *Protesters tried to break through a police cordon.* ② PHRASAL VERB If you **break through**, you achieve success even though there are difficulties and obstacles. ❑ *There is still scope for new writers to break through.*
③ → see also **breakthrough**
▶ **break up** ① PHRASAL VERB When something **breaks up** or when you **break** it **up**, it separates or is divided into several smaller parts. ❑ *Civil war could come if the country breaks up.* ❑ *Break up the chocolate and melt it.* ② PHRASAL VERB If you **break up** with your boyfriend, girlfriend, husband, or wife, your relationship with that person ends. ❑ *My girlfriend has broken up with me.* ❑ *He felt appalled by the idea of marriage so we broke up.* ③ PHRASAL VERB If a marriage or romantic relationship **breaks up** or if someone **breaks** it **up**, it ends and the partners separate. ❑ *His first marriage broke up.* ④ PHRASAL VERB When a meeting or gathering **breaks up** or when someone **breaks** it **up**, it is brought to an end and the people involved in it leave. ❑ *A neighbor asked for the music to be turned down and the party broke up.* ❑ *Police used tear gas to break up a demonstration.*

break|able /breɪkəbᵊl/ (breakables) ADJ [usu ADJ n] **Breakable** objects are easy to break by accident. ❑ *Put away any valuable or breakable objects.* • N-PLURAL **Breakables** are breakable objects. ❑ *Keep breakables out of reach of very young children.*

break|age /breɪkɪdʒ/ (breakages) ① N-VAR **Breakage** is the act of breaking something. ❑ *Brushing wet hair can cause stretching and breakage.* ❑ *Check that your insurance policy covers breakages and damage when moving.* ② N-COUNT [usu pl] A **breakage** is something that has been broken. ❑ *We arrived to find the staff cleaning up some breakages, and they asked us where we had been when the earthquake hit.*

break|away /breɪkəweɪ/ ADJ [ADJ n] A **breakaway** group is a group of people who have separated from a larger group, for example, because of a disagreement. ❑ *A breakaway faction of the rebel group has claimed responsibility for the killing.*

break|down /breɪkdaʊn/ (breakdowns) ① N-COUNT The **breakdown** of something such as a relationship, plan, or discussion is its failure or ending. ❑ *...the breakdown of talks between the U.S. and E.U. officials.* ❑ *...the irretrievable breakdown of a marriage.* ② N-COUNT If you have a **breakdown**, you become very depressed, so that you are unable to cope with your life. ❑ *My personal life was terrible. My mother had died, and a couple of years later I had a breakdown.* ③ → see also **nervous breakdown** ④ N-COUNT If a car or a piece of machinery has a **breakdown**, it stops working. ❑ *Her old car was unreliable, so the trip was plagued by breakdowns.* ⑤ N-COUNT A **breakdown** of something is a list of its separate parts. ❑ *The organizers were given a breakdown of the costs.* ⑥ → See feature box at **speak**

break|er /breɪkər/ (breakers) ① N-COUNT **Breakers** are big sea waves, especially at the point when they just reach the shore. ② → see also **icebreaker**, **law-breaker**, **record breaker**, **strikebreaker**

break-even point N-SING When a company reaches **break-even point**, the money it makes from the sale of goods or services is just enough to cover the cost of supplying those goods or services, but not enough to make a profit. [BUSINESS] ❑ *"Terminator 2" finally made $200 million, which was considered to be the break-even point for the picture.*

break|fast ♦◊◊ /brɛkfəst/ (breakfasts, breakfasting, breakfasted) ① N-VAR **Breakfast** is the first meal of the day. It is usually eaten in the early part of the morning. ❑ *What's for breakfast?* ② → see also **bed and breakfast** ③ V-I When you **breakfast**, you have breakfast. [FORMAL] ❑ *We breakfasted on the balcony.*

USAGE

breakfast
You don't usually use 'a' with **breakfast**. Don't say, for example, 'She made a breakfast for everyone.' Say 'She made **breakfast** for everyone.' They had eggs and toast for *breakfast*.

break|fast ta|ble (breakfast tables) N-COUNT [usu sing, the N] You refer to a table as **the breakfast table** when it is being used for breakfast. ❑ *...reading the morning papers at the breakfast table.*

break|fast time also **breakfast-time** N-UNCOUNT [oft prep N] **Breakfast time** is the period of the morning when most people have breakfast. ❑ *By breakfast-time he was already at his desk.*

break-in (break-ins) N-COUNT If there has been a **break-in**, someone has got into a building by force. ❑ *The break-in had occurred just before midnight.*

break|ing point N-UNCOUNT [also *the/a* N] If something or someone has reached **breaking point**, they have so many problems or difficulties that they can no longer cope with them, and may soon collapse or be unable to continue. ❑ *The report on the riot exposed a prison system stretched to breaking point.*

break|neck /breɪknɛk/ ADJ [ADJ n] If you say that something happens or travels at **breakneck** speed, you mean that it happens or travels very fast. ❑ *Jack drove to the hospital at breakneck speed.*

break|out /breɪkaʊt/ (**breakouts**) N-COUNT If there has been a **breakout**, someone has escaped from prison. ❑ *He is thought to have planned a prison breakout of militants suspected of the July bombing.*

break|through /breɪkθruː/ (**breakthroughs**) **1** N-COUNT A **breakthrough** is an important development or achievement. ❑ *The company looks poised to make a significant breakthrough in China.* **2** → See feature box at **success**

break|up /breɪkʌp/ (**breakups**) **1** N-COUNT The **breakup** of a marriage, relationship, or association is the act of it finishing or coming to an end because the people involved decide that it is not working successfully. ❑ *...the acrimonious breakup of the meeting's first session.* **2** N-COUNT The **breakup** of an organization or a country is the act of it separating or dividing into several parts. ❑ *The Justice Department advocated a breakup of the computing multinational.*

break|water /breɪkwɔːtər/ (**breakwaters**) N-COUNT A **breakwater** is a wooden or stone wall that extends from the shore into the sea and is built in order to protect a harbor or beach from the force of the waves.

breast ♦◊◊ /brɛst/ (**breasts**) **1** N-COUNT A woman's **breasts** are the two soft, round parts on her chest that can produce milk to feed a baby. ❑ *She wears a low-cut dress which reveals her breasts.* **2** N-COUNT A person's **breast** is the upper part of his or her chest. [LITERARY] ❑ *He struck his breast in a dramatic gesture.* **3** N-COUNT A bird's **breast** is the front part of its body. ❑ *The cock's breast is tinged with chestnut.* **4** N-SING The **breast** of a shirt, jacket, or coat is the part which covers the top part of the chest. **5** N-VAR You can refer to a piece of meat that is cut from the front of a bird or lamb as **breast**. ❑ *...a chicken breast with vegetables.* **6** → See also color supplement

breast|bone /brɛstboʊn/ (**breastbones**) also **breast bone** N-COUNT Your **breastbone** is the long, flat bone that goes from your throat to the bottom of your ribs and to which your ribs are attached.

breast-feed (**breast-feeds**, **breast-feeding**, **breast-fed**) also **breastfeed, breast feed** V-T/V-I When a woman **breast-feeds**, or **breast-feeds** her baby, she feeds her baby with milk from her breasts, rather than from a bottle. ❑ *Not all women have the choice whether or not to breast feed their babies.* ❑ *Leading scientists claim breast-fed babies are intellectually brighter.* • **breast-feeding** N-UNCOUNT ❑ *There are many advantages to breast feeding.*

breast milk also **breast-milk** N-UNCOUNT **Breast milk** is the white liquid produced by women to breast-feed their babies.

breast|plate /brɛstpleɪt/ (**breastplates**) N-COUNT A **breastplate** is a piece of armor that covers and protects the chest.

breast pock|et (**breast pockets**) N-COUNT [with poss] The **breast pocket** of a coat or jacket is a pocket, usually on the inside, next to the wearer's chest. ❑ *I kept the list in my breast pocket.*

breast|stroke /brɛststroʊk, brɛsstroʊk/ N-UNCOUNT [also *the* N] **Breaststroke** is a swimming stroke that you do lying on your front, moving your arms and legs horizontally in a circular motion. ❑ *I do not yet know how to swim breaststroke effectively.*

breath ♦◊◊ /brɛθ/ (**breaths**) **1** N-VAR Your **breath** is the air that you let out through your mouth when you breathe. If someone has **bad breath**, their breath smells unpleasant. ❑ *I could smell the whiskey on his breath.* **2** N-VAR When you take a **breath**, you breathe in once. ❑ *He took a deep breath, and began to climb the stairs.* ❑ *Gasping for breath, she leaned against the door.* **3** PHRASE If you go outside **for a breath of fresh air** or **for a breath of air**, you go outside because it is unpleasantly warm indoors. ❑ *I had to step outside for a breath of fresh air.* **4** PHRASE If you describe something new or different as **a breath of fresh air**, you mean that it makes a situation or subject more interesting or exciting. [APPROVAL] ❑ *Her brisk treatment of an almost taboo subject was a breath of fresh air.* **5** PHRASE When you **get** your **breath back** after doing something energetic, you start breathing normally again. ❑ *I reached out a hand to steady myself against the house while I got my breath back.* **6** PHRASE If you are **out of breath**, you are breathing very quickly and with difficulty because you have been doing something energetic. ❑ *She was slightly out of breath from running.* **7** PHRASE You can use **in the same breath** or **in the next breath** to indicate that someone says two very different or contradictory things, especially when you are criticizing them. [DISAPPROVAL] ❑ *He hailed this week's arms agreement but in the same breath expressed suspicion about the motivations of the United States.* **8** PHRASE If you are **short of breath**, you find it difficult to breathe properly, for example, because you are ill. You can also say that someone suffers from **shortness of breath**. ❑ *She felt short of breath and flushed.* **9** PHRASE If you say something **under** your **breath**, you say it in a very quiet voice, often because you do not want other people to hear what you are saying. ❑ *Walsh muttered something under his breath.*

breath|able /briːðəbəl/ ADJ A **breathable** fabric allows air to pass through it easily, so that clothing made from it does not become too warm or uncomfortable.

breatha|lyze /brɛθəlaɪz/ (**breathalyzes, breathalyzing, breathalyzed**)

in BRIT, also use **breathalyse**

V-T [usu passive] If the driver of a car **is breathalyzed** by the police, they ask him or her to breathe into a special bag or device in order to test whether he or she has drunk too much alcohol. ❑ *She was breathalyzed and found to be over the limit.*

Breatha|lyz|er /brɛθəlaɪzər/ (**Breathalyzers**)

in BRIT, also use **Breathalyser**

N-COUNT A **Breathalyzer** is a special bag or device that the police use to test whether a driver has drunk too much alcohol. [TRADEMARK] ❑ *Luckily I was never stopped for a Breathalyzer.*

breathe ♦◊◊ /briːð/ (**breathes, breathing, breathed**) **1** V-T/V-I When people or animals **breathe**, they take air into their lungs and let it out again. When they **breathe** smoke or a particular kind of air, they take it into their lungs and let it out again as they breathe. ❑ *He stood there breathing deeply and evenly.* ❑ *No American should have to drive out of town to breathe clean air.* • **breath|ing** N-UNCOUNT ❑ *Her breathing became slow and heavy.* **2 to be breathing down someone's neck** → see **neck** **3 to breathe a sigh of relief** → see **sigh**
▶ **breathe in** PHRASAL VERB When you **breathe in**, you take some air into your lungs. ❑ *She breathed in deeply.*
▶ **breathe out** PHRASAL VERB When you **breathe out**, you send air out of your lungs through your nose or mouth. ❑ *Breathe out and ease your knees in toward your chest.*

SYNONYMS

breathe
VERB **1**
inhale: *He took a long slow breath, inhaling deeply.*
exhale: *Hold your breath for a moment and exhale.*
pant: *She climbed rapidly, until she was panting with the effort.*
gasp: *She gasped for air and drew in a lungful of water.*

---

breath|er /briːðər/ (**breathers**) N-COUNT If you take a **breather**, you stop what you are doing for a short time in order to rest. [INFORMAL] ❑ *Relax and take a breather whenever you feel that you need one.*

breath|ing space (**breathing spaces**) N-VAR A **breathing space** is a short period of time between two activities in which you can recover from the first activity and prepare for the second one. ❑ *Firms need a breathing space if they are to recover.* ❑ *We hope that it will give us some breathing space.*

breath|less /brɛθlɪs/ ADJ If you are **breathless**, you have difficulty in breathing properly, for example, because you have been running or because you are afraid or excited. ❑ *I was a little breathless and my heartbeat was bumpy and fast.* • **breath|less|ly** ADV ❑ *"I'll go in," he said breathlessly.* • **breath|less|ness** N-UNCOUNT ❑ *Asthma causes wheezing and breathlessness.*

breath|taking /brɛθteɪkɪŋ/ also **breath-taking** ADJ If you say that something is **breathtaking**, you are emphasizing that it is extremely beautiful or amazing. [EMPHASIS] ❑ *The house has breathtaking views from every room.* ❑ *Some of their football was breathtaking, a delight to watch.*

breath test (breath tests) N-COUNT A **breath test** is a test carried out by police in which a driver blows into a piece of equipment to show how much alcohol he or she has drunk. ❑ *Police will conduct random breath tests.*

breathy /brɛθi/ ADJ If someone has a **breathy** voice, you can hear their breath when they speak or sing. ❑ *Her voice was suddenly breathy.*

bred /brɛd/ **1 Bred** is the past tense and past participle of **breed**. **2** → see also **ill-bred, purebred, well-bred**

breech /briːtʃ/ (breeches) N-COUNT The **breech** of a gun is the part of the barrel at the back into which you load the bullets.

breeches /brɪtʃɪz/ N-PLURAL [also *a pair of* N] **Breeches** are pants that reach as far as your knees. [OLD-FASHIONED] ❑ *...riding breeches.*

breed ✦✧ /briːd/ (breeds, breeding, bred) **1** N-COUNT A **breed** of a pet animal or farm animal is a particular type of it. For example, terriers are a breed of dog. ❑ *...rare breeds of cattle.* **2** V-T If you **breed** animals or plants, you keep them for the purpose of producing more animals or plants with particular qualities, in a controlled way. ❑ *He lived alone, breeding horses and dogs.* ❑ *He used to breed dogs for the police.* • **breed|ing** N-UNCOUNT ❑ *There is potential for selective breeding for better yields.* **3** V-I When animals **breed**, they have babies. ❑ *Frogs will usually breed in any convenient pond.* • **breed|ing** N-UNCOUNT ❑ *During the breeding season the birds come ashore.* **4** V-T If you say that something **breeds** bad feeling or bad behavior, you mean that it causes bad feeling or bad behavior to develop. ❑ *If they are unemployed it's bound to breed resentment.* **5** → see also **breeding**

---COLLOCATIONS---

breed
NOUN **1**
noun + **breed**: cattle, dog, sheep
adjective + **breed**: exotic, pedigree, rare; dangerous, hardy
VERB **2**
breed + noun: cattle, horses, pigs

breed|er /briːdər/ (breeders) N-COUNT **Breeders** are people who breed animals or plants. ❑ *Her father was a well-known racehorse breeder.*

breed|ing /briːdɪŋ/ **1** N-UNCOUNT If someone says that a person has **breeding**, they mean that they think the person is from a good social background and has good manners. ❑ *It's a sign of good breeding to know the names of all your staff.* **2** → see also **breed**

breed|ing ground (breeding grounds) **1** N-COUNT [usu sing, with supp, usu N *for* n] If you refer to a situation or place as a **breeding ground** for something bad such as crime, you mean that this thing can easily develop in that situation or place. ❑ *Flaws in the system have created a breeding ground for financial scandals.* **2** N-COUNT [with supp] The **breeding ground** for a particular type of creature is the place where this creature breeds easily. ❑ *Warm milk is the ideal breeding ground for bacteria.*

breeze /briːz/ (breezes, breezing, breezed) **1** N-COUNT A **breeze** is a gentle wind. ❑ *...a cool summer breeze.* **2** V-I If you **breeze** into a place or a position, you enter it in a very casual or relaxed manner. ❑ *Lopez breezed into the quarter-finals of the tournament.* **3** V-I If you **breeze through** something such as a game or test, you cope with it easily. ❑ *John seems to breeze effortlessly through his many commitments at work.* **4** → See feature box at **storm**

breeze-block (breeze-blocks) also **breeze block** N-VAR A **breeze-block** is the same as a **cinder block**. [BRIT]

breezy /briːzi/ (breezier, breeziest) ADJ If you describe someone as **breezy**, you mean that they behave in a casual, cheerful, and confident manner. ❑ *...his bright and breezy personality.*

breth|ren /brɛðrɪn/ N-PLURAL You can refer to the members of a particular organization or group, especially a religious group, as **brethren**. [OLD-FASHIONED] ❑ *We must help our brethren, it is our duty.*

brev|ity /brɛvɪti/ N-UNCOUNT [oft N *of* n] The **brevity** of something is the fact that it is short or lasts for only a short time. [FORMAL] ❑ *...the hardship and brevity of human existence.*

brew /bruː/ (brews, brewing, brewed) **1** V-T If you **brew** tea or coffee, you make it by pouring hot water over tea leaves or ground coffee. ❑ *He brewed a pot of coffee.* **2** N-COUNT A **brew** is a particular kind of tea or coffee. It can also be a particular pot of tea or coffee. ❑ *She swallowed a mouthful of the hot strong brew, and wiped her eyes.* **3** V-T If a person or company **brews** beer, they make it. ❑ *I brew my own beer.* **4** V-I [usu cont] If a storm **is brewing**, large clouds are beginning to form and the sky is becoming dark because there is going to be a storm. ❑ *We'd seen the storm brewing when we were out in the boat.* **5** V-I [usu cont] If an unpleasant or difficult situation **is brewing**, it is starting to develop. ❑ *At home a crisis was brewing.*

brew|er /bruːər/ (brewers) N-COUNT **Brewers** are people or companies who make beer.

brew|ery /bruːəri/ (breweries) N-COUNT A **brewery** is a place where beer is made.

bri|ar /braɪər/ (briars) N-COUNT A **briar** is a wild rose with long, prickly stems.

bribe /braɪb/ (bribes, bribing, bribed) **1** N-COUNT A **bribe** is a sum of money or something valuable that one person offers or gives to another in order to persuade him or her to do something. ❑ *He was being investigated for receiving bribes.* **2** V-T If one person **bribes** another, they give them a bribe. ❑ *He was accused of bribing a senior bank official.*

brib|ery /braɪbəri/ N-UNCOUNT **Bribery** is the act of offering someone money or something valuable in order to persuade them to do something for you. ❑ *He was jailed on charges of bribery.*

bric-a-brac /brɪkəbræk/ N-UNCOUNT **Bric-a-brac** is a number of small ornamental objects of no great value.

brick /brɪk/ (bricks) **1** N-VAR **Bricks** are rectangular blocks of baked clay used for building walls, which are usually red or brown. **Brick** is the material made up of these blocks. ❑ *She built bookshelves out of bricks and planks.* **2** PHRASE If you **hit a brick wall** or **come up against a brick wall**, you are unable to continue or make progress because something stops you. [INFORMAL] ❑ *After that my career just seemed to hit a brick wall.*

brick|bat /brɪkbæt/ (brickbats) N-COUNT [usu pl] **Brickbats** are very critical or insulting remarks which are made in public about someone or something.

brick|layer /brɪkleɪər/ (bricklayers) N-COUNT A **bricklayer** is a person whose job is to build walls using bricks.

brick|work /brɪkwɜːrk/ N-UNCOUNT You can refer to the bricks in the walls of a building as the **brickwork**. ❑ *There were cracks in the brickwork.*

brid|al /braɪdəl/ ADJ [ADJ n] **Bridal** is used to describe something that belongs or relates to a bride, or to both a bride and her bridegroom. ❑ *She wore a floor length bridal gown.*

bride /braɪd/ (brides) N-COUNT A **bride** is a woman who is getting married or who has just gotten married. ❑ *Guests toasted the bride and groom with champagne.*

bride|groom /braɪdgruːm/ (bridegrooms) N-COUNT A **bridegroom** is a man who is getting married.

brides|maid /braɪdzmeɪd/ (bridesmaids) N-COUNT A **bridesmaid** is a woman or a girl who helps and accompanies a bride on her wedding day.

bride-to-be (brides-to-be) N-COUNT A **bride-to-be** is a woman who is soon going to be married.

bridge ✦✦✧ /brɪdʒ/ (bridges, bridging, bridged) **1** N-COUNT A **bridge** is a structure that is built over a railroad, river, or road so that people or vehicles can cross from one side to the other. ❑ *He walked back over the railroad bridge.* **2** N-COUNT A **bridge** between two places is a piece of land that joins or connects them. ❑ *...a land bridge linking Serbian territories.* **3** V-T To **bridge** the gap between two people or things means to reduce it or get rid of it. ❑ *It is unlikely that the two sides will be able to bridge their differences.* **4** V-T Something that **bridges** the gap between two very different things has some of the qualities of each of these things. ❑ *...the singer who bridged the gap between pop music and opera.* **5** N-COUNT If something or someone acts as a **bridge** between two people, groups, or things, they connect them.

bridgehead

❏ *We hope this book will act as a bridge between doctor and patient.* **6** N-COUNT The **bridge** is the place on a ship from which it is steered. ❏ *Captain Ronald Warwick was on the bridge when the wave hit.* **7** N-COUNT The **bridge** of your nose is the thin top part of it, between your eyes. ❏ *On the bridge of his hooked nose was a pair of gold rimless spectacles.* **8** N-COUNT The **bridge** of a pair of glasses is the part that rests on your nose. **9** N-COUNT The **bridge** of a violin, guitar, or other stringed instrument is the small piece of wood under the strings that holds them up. **10** N-UNCOUNT **Bridge** is a card game for four players in which the players begin by declaring how many tricks they expect to win.

COLLOCATIONS

bridge
NOUN **1**
noun + **bridge**: pedestrian, railroad
adjective + **bridge**: concrete, wooden; historic; low, narrow, rickety
verb + **bridge**: build, repair; close, open; cross, span
VERB **3**
bridge + noun: divide, gap, gulf

---

bridge|head /brɪdʒhɛd/ (**bridgeheads**) N-COUNT A **bridgehead** is a good position which an army has taken in the enemy's territory and from which it can advance or attack. ❏ *A bridgehead was established.*

bridge loan (**bridge loans**) N-COUNT A **bridge loan** is money that a bank lends you for a short time, for example, so that you can buy a new house before you have sold the one you already own. [AM]

in BRIT, use **bridging loan**

bri|dle /braɪdᵊl/ (**bridles**) N-COUNT A **bridle** is a set of straps that is put around a horse's head and mouth so that the person riding or driving the horse can control it.

bri|dle path (**bridle paths**) also **bridlepath** N-COUNT A **bridle path** is a path intended for people riding horses.

Brie /bri/ also **brie** N-UNCOUNT **Brie** is a type of cheese that comes from France. It is soft and creamy with a white skin.

brief ✦✧✧ /brif/ (**briefer, briefest, briefs, briefing, briefed**) **1** ADJ Something that is **brief** lasts for only a short time. ❏ *She once made a brief appearance on television.* **2** ADJ A **brief** speech or piece of writing does not contain too many words or details. ❏ *In a brief statement, he concentrated entirely on international affairs.* **3** ADJ [v-link ADJ] If you are **brief**, you say what you want to say in as few words as possible. ❏ *Now please be brief – my time is valuable.* **4** ADJ You can describe a period of time as **brief** if you want to emphasize that it is very short. [EMPHASIS] ❏ *For a few brief minutes we forgot the anxiety and anguish.* **5** N-PLURAL [also *a pair of* N] Men's or women's underpants can be referred to as **briefs**. ❏ *A bra and a pair of briefs lay on the floor.* **6** V-T If someone **briefs** you, especially about a piece of work or a serious matter, they give you information that you need before you do it or consider it. ❏ *A department spokesperson briefed reporters.* **7** N-COUNT A **brief** is a document containing all the information relating to a particular legal case, which is used by a lawyer to defend his or her client in court. ❏ *Griffith's expertise is in writing legal briefs.* **8** N-COUNT If someone gives you a **brief**, they officially give you responsibility and instructions for dealing with a particular thing. [mainly BRIT, FORMAL] ❏ *...customs officials with a brief to stop foreign porn coming into the country.* **9** → see also **briefing 10** PHRASE You can say **in brief** to indicate that you are about to say something in as few words as possible or to give a summary of what you have just said. ❏ *In brief, take no risks.*

brief|case /brifkeɪs/ (**briefcases**) **1** N-COUNT A **briefcase** is a case used for carrying documents in. **2** → See also color supplement

brief|er /brifər/ (**briefers**) N-COUNT [usu supp N] A **briefer** is an official who has the job of giving information about something, for example, a war. ❏ *Military briefers say no planes were shot down today.*

brief|ing /brifɪŋ/ (**briefings**) **1** N-VAR A **briefing** is a meeting at which information or instructions are given to people, especially before they do something. ❏ *They're holding a press briefing tomorrow.* **2** → see also **brief**

brilliant

brief|ly /brifli/ **1** ADV [ADV with v] Something that happens or is done **briefly** happens or is done for a very short period of time. ❏ *He smiled briefly.* **2** ADV [ADV with v] If you say or write something **briefly**, you use very few words or give very few details. ❏ *There are four basic alternatives; they are described briefly below.* **3** ADV [ADV with cl] You can say **briefly** to indicate that you are about to say something in as few words as possible. ❏ *Briefly, no less than nine of our agents have passed information to us.*

brig /brɪg/ (**brigs**) **1** N-COUNT A **brig** is a type of ship with two masts and square sails. **2** N-COUNT A **brig** is a prison on a ship, especially a U.S. Navy ship.

Brig. **Brig.** is a written abbreviation for **brigadier**. [BRIT] ❏ *...Brig. Douglas Erskin Crum.*

bri|gade /brɪgeɪd/ (**brigades**) N-COUNT-COLL A **brigade** is one of the groups which an army is divided into. ❏ *...the soldiers of the 173rd Airborne Brigade.*

briga|dier gen|er|al (**brigadier generals**) also **brigadier-general** N-COUNT; N-TITLE In the United States, a **brigadier general** is a senior officer in the armed forces who is often in charge of a brigade and has a rank above colonel and below major general. ❏ *...Brigadier General Gary Whipple of the Louisiana National Guard.*

brig|and /brɪgənd/ (**brigands**) N-COUNT A **brigand** is someone who attacks people and robs them, especially in mountains or forests. [LITERARY] ❏ *...a notorious brigand who hijacked trains.*

bright ✦✦✧ /braɪt/ (**brights, brighter, brightest**) **1** ADJ A **bright** color is strong and noticeable, and not dark. ❏ *...a bright red dress.* ● **bright|ly** ADV ❏ *...a display of brightly colored flowers.* ● **bright|ness** N-UNCOUNT ❏ *You'll be impressed with the brightness and the beauty of the colors.* **2** ADJ A **bright** light, object, or place is shining strongly or is full of light. ❏ *...a bright October day.* ● **bright|ly** ADV [ADV with v] ❏ *...a warm, brightly lit room.* ● **bright|ness** N-UNCOUNT ❏ *An astronomer can determine the brightness of each star.* **3** ADJ If you describe someone as **bright**, you mean that they are quick at learning things. ❏ *I was convinced that he was brighter than average.* **4** ADJ A **bright** idea is clever and original. ❏ *There are lots of books crammed with bright ideas.* **5** ADJ If someone looks or sounds **bright**, they look or sound cheerful and lively. ❏ *The boy was so bright and animated.* ● **bright|ly** ADV [ADV with v] ❏ *He smiled brightly as Ben approached.* **6** ADJ If the future is **bright**, it is likely to be pleasant or successful. ❏ *Both had successful careers and the future looked bright.* **7** N-PLURAL The **brights** on a vehicle are its headlights when they are set to shine their brightest. [AM] ❏ *...a Bronco with its brights on, parked in the middle of the street.*

bright|en /braɪtᵊn/ (**brightens, brightening, brightened**) **1** V-I If someone **brightens** or their face **brightens**, they suddenly look happier. ❏ *Seeing him, she seemed to brighten a little.* ● PHRASAL VERB **Brighten up** means the same as **brighten**. ❏ *He brightened up a bit.* **2** V-I If your eyes **brighten**, you suddenly look interested or excited. ❏ *His eyes brightened and he laughed.* **3** V-T If someone or something **brightens** a place, they make it more colorful and attractive. ❏ *Tubs planted with flowers brightened the area outside the door.* ● PHRASAL VERB **Brighten up** means the same as **brighten**. ❏ *David spotted the pink silk lampshade in a shop and thought it would brighten up the room.* **4** V-T/V-I If someone or something **brightens** a situation or the situation **brightens**, it becomes more pleasant, enjoyable, or favorable. ❏ *That does not do much to brighten the prospects of kids in the city.* **5** V-T/V-I When a light **brightens** a place or when a place **brightens**, it becomes brighter or lighter. ❏ *The sky above the ridge of mountains brightened.* **6** V-I If the weather **brightens**, it becomes less cloudy or rainy, and the sun starts to shine. ❏ *By early afternoon the weather had brightened.*

bright lights N-PLURAL [the N] If someone talks about the **bright lights**, they are referring to life in a big city where you can do a lot of enjoyable and exciting things and be successful. ❏ *The bright lights of Hollywood beckon many.*

bril|liant ✦✧✧ /brɪliənt/ **1** ADJ A **brilliant** person, idea, or performance is extremely clever or skillful. ❏ *She had a brilliant mind.* ● **bril|liant|ly** ADV ❏ *It is a very high quality production, brilliantly written and acted.* ● **bril|liance** N-UNCOUNT ❏ *He was a deeply serious musician who had shown his brilliance very early.* **2** ADJ A **brilliant** career or success is very successful. ❏ *He served four years in prison, emerging to find his brilliant career in ruins.*

brim / brisk

● **bril|liant|ly** ADV ❑ *The strategy worked brilliantly.* **3** ADJ [ADJ n] A **brilliant** color is extremely bright. ❑ *The woman had brilliant green eyes.* ● **bril|liant|ly** ADV [ADV adj/-ed] ❑ *Many of the patterns show brilliantly colored flowers.* ● **bril|liance** N-UNCOUNT ❑ *...an iridescent blue butterfly in all its brilliance.* **4** ADJ You describe light, or something that reflects light, as **brilliant** when it shines very brightly. ❑ *The event was held in brilliant sunshine.* ● **bril|liant|ly** ADV ❑ *It's a brilliantly sunny morning.* ● **bril|liance** N-UNCOUNT ❑ *His eyes became accustomed to the dark after the brilliance of the sun outside.* **5** ADJ You can say that something is **brilliant** when you are very pleased about it or think that it is very good. [mainly BRIT, INFORMAL, SPOKEN] ❑ *If you get a chance to see the show, do go – it's brilliant.*

SYNONYMS

brilliant
ADJ
1
intelligent: *...lively and intelligent conversation.*
sharp: *He is very sharp, a quick thinker, and swift with repartee.*
intellectual: *They were very intellectual and witty.*
clever: *He's a very clever man.*
2
excellent: *The recording quality is excellent.*
wonderful: *It's wonderful to see you.*
marvelous: *He certainly is a marvelous actor.*
superb: *There is a superb 18-hole golf course 6 miles away.*

brim /brɪm/ (brims, brimming, brimmed) **1** N-COUNT The **brim** of a hat is the wide part that sticks outward at the bottom. ❑ *Rain dripped from the brim of his baseball cap.* **2** V-I [usu cont] If someone or something **is brimming with** a particular quality, they are full of that quality. ❑ *The team is brimming with confidence after two straight wins in the tournament.* **3** V-I When your eyes **are brimming with** tears, they are full of fluid because you are upset, although you are not actually crying. ❑ *Michael looked at him imploringly, eyes brimming with tears.* **4** PHRASE If something, especially a container, **is filled to the brim** or **full to the brim** with something, it is filled right up to the top. ❑ *Her glass was filled right up to the brim.*

brim|ful /brɪmfʊl/ ADJ [v-link ADJ of/with n] Someone who is **brimful** of an emotion or quality feels or seems full of it. An object or place that is **brimful** of something is full of it. ❑ *She was brimful of energy and enthusiasm.* ❑ *The United States is brimful with highly paid doctors.*

brim|stone /brɪmstoʊn/ **1** N-UNCOUNT **Brimstone** is the same as **sulfur**. [OLD-FASHIONED] **2** PHRASE When people talk about **fire and brimstone**, they are referring to hell and how they think people are punished there after death. [LITERARY]

brine /braɪn/ (brines) N-MASS **Brine** is salty water, especially salty water that is used for preserving food. ❑ *Soak the walnuts in brine for four or five days.*

bring ◆◆◆ /brɪŋ/ (brings, bringing, brought) **1** V-T If you **bring** someone or something with you when you come to a place, they come with you or you have them with you. ❑ *Remember to bring an apron or an old shirt to protect your clothes.* ❑ *Someone went upstairs and brought down a huge kettle.* **2** V-T If you **bring** something somewhere, you move it there. ❑ *Reaching into her pocket, she brought out a cigarette.* **3** V-T If you **bring** something that someone wants or needs, you get it for them or carry it to them. ❑ *He went and poured a brandy for Dena and brought it to her.* **4** V-T To **bring** something or someone to a place or position means to cause them to come to the place or move into that position. ❑ *I told you about what brought me here.* ❑ *The shock of her husband's arrival brought her to her feet.* **5** V-T If you **bring** something new to a place or group of people, you introduce it to that place or cause those people to hear or know about it. ❑ *...the drive to bring art to the public.* **6** V-T To **bring** someone or something into a particular state or condition means to cause them to be in that state or condition. ❑ *He brought the car to a stop in front of the square.* ❑ *They have brought down income taxes.* **7** V-T If something **brings** a particular feeling, situation, or quality, it makes people experience it or have it. ❑ *He called on the United States to play a more effective role in bringing peace to the region.* ❑ *Her three children brought her joy.* **8** V-T If a period of time **brings** a particular thing, it happens during that time. ❑ *For Sandro, the new year brought disaster.* **9** V-T When you are talking, you can say that something **brings** you to a particular point in order to indicate that you have now reached that point and are going to talk about a new subject. ❑ *And that brings us to the end of this special report from Germany.* **10** V-T [with brd-neg] If you cannot **bring** yourself to do something, you cannot do it because you find it too upsetting, embarrassing, or disgusting. ❑ *It is all very tragic and I am afraid I just cannot bring myself to talk about it at the moment.* **11 to bring something alive** → see **alive** **12 to bring the house down** → see **house** **13 to bring up the rear** → see **rear**

▶ **bring about** PHRASAL VERB To **bring** something **about** means to cause it to happen. ❑ *The only way they can bring about political change is by putting pressure on the country.*

▶ **bring along** PHRASAL VERB If you **bring** someone or something **along**, you bring them with you when you come to a place. ❑ *They brought baby Michael along in a carrier.*

▶ **bring back** **1** PHRASAL VERB Something that **brings back** a memory makes you think about it. ❑ *Your article brought back sad memories for me.* **2** PHRASAL VERB When people **bring back** a practice or fashion that existed at an earlier time, they introduce it again. ❑ *A petition to bring back the hit TV show has been signed by 430,000 fans.*

▶ **bring down** **1** PHRASAL VERB When people or events **bring down** a government or ruler, they cause the government or ruler to lose power. ❑ *They were threatening to bring down the government by withdrawing from the ruling coalition.* **2** PHRASAL VERB If someone or something **brings down** a person or airplane, they cause them to fall, usually by shooting them. ❑ *Military historians may never know what brought down the jet.*

▶ **bring forward** PHRASAL VERB If you **bring forward** a meeting or event, you arrange for it to take place at an earlier date or time than had been planned. ❑ *He had to bring forward an 11 o'clock meeting so that he could get to the funeral on time.*

▶ **bring in** **1** PHRASAL VERB When a government or organization **brings in** a new law or system, they introduce it. ❑ *The government brought in a controversial law under which it could take any land it wanted.* **2** PHRASAL VERB Someone or something that **brings in** money makes it or earns it. ❑ *I have three part-time jobs, which bring in about $24,000 a year.* **3** PHRASAL VERB If you **bring in** someone from outside a team or organization, you invite them to do a job or join in an activity or discussion. ❑ *The firm decided to bring in a new management team.*

▶ **bring out** **1** PHRASAL VERB When a person or company **brings out** a new product, especially a new book or CD, they produce it and put it on sale. ❑ *A journalist all his life, he's now brought out a book.* **2** PHRASAL VERB Something that **brings out** a particular kind of behavior or feeling in you causes you to show it, especially when it is something that you do not normally show. ❑ *He is totally dedicated and brings out the best in his pupils.*

▶ **bring up** **1** PHRASAL VERB When someone **brings up** a child, they look after it until it is an adult. If someone has **been brought up** in a certain place or with certain attitudes, they grew up in that place or were taught those attitudes when they were growing up. ❑ *She brought up four children.* ❑ *He was brought up in Nebraska.* **2** PHRASAL VERB If you **bring up** a particular subject, you introduce it into a discussion or conversation. ❑ *He brought up a subject rarely raised during the course of this campaign.*

bring|er /brɪŋər/ (bringers) N-COUNT [with supp, usu N of n] A **bringer** of something is someone who brings or provides it. [LITERARY] ❑ *He was the bringer of good news.*

brink /brɪŋk/ N-SING If you are on the **brink** of something, usually something important, terrible, or exciting, you are just about to do it or experience it. ❑ *Their economy is teetering on the brink of collapse.*

brink|man|ship /brɪŋkmənʃɪp/ also **brinksmanship** N-UNCOUNT **Brinkmanship** is a method of behavior, especially in politics, in which you deliberately get into dangerous situations which could result in disaster but which could also bring success. [JOURNALISM] ❑ *There is a lot of political brinkmanship involved in this latest development.*

bri|oche /briˈoʊʃ/ (brioches) N-VAR **Brioche** is a kind of sweet bread. ❑ *I'll have coffee and a brioche.*

brisk /brɪsk/ (brisker, briskest) **1** ADJ A **brisk** activity or action is done quickly and in an energetic way. ❑ *Taking a brisk walk can often induce a feeling of well-being.* ● **brisk|ly** ADV [ADV with v]

brisket 157 **broad-minded**

□ *Eve walked briskly down the corridor to her son's room.* ◨ ADJ If trade or business is **brisk**, things are being sold very quickly and a lot of money is being made. □ *Vendors were doing a brisk trade in souvenirs.* • **brisk|ly** ADV [ADV after v] □ *A trader said gold sold briskly on the local market.* ◨ ADJ If the weather is **brisk**, it is cold and fresh. □ *...a typically brisk winter's day on the south coast.* ◨ ADJ Someone who is **brisk** behaves in a busy, confident way which shows that they want to get things done quickly. □ *The Chief summoned me downstairs. He was brisk and businesslike.* • **brisk|ly** ADV [ADV with v] □ *"Anyhow," she added briskly, "it's none of my business."*

bris|ket /brɪskɪt/ N-UNCOUNT **Brisket** is a cut of beef that comes from the breast of the cow.

bris|tle /brɪsᵊl/ (bristles) ◨ N-COUNT **Bristles** are the short hairs that grow on someone's body, especially after they have shaved. The hairs on the top of the head can also be called bristles when they are cut very short. □ *...two days' growth of bristles.* ◨ N-COUNT The **bristles** of a brush are the thick hairs or hairlike pieces of plastic which are attached to it. □ *As soon as the bristles on your toothbrush begin to wear, throw it out.* ◨ N-COUNT **Bristles** are thick, strong animal hairs that feel hard and rough. □ *It has a short stumpy tail covered with bristles.*

bris|tling /brɪslɪŋ/ ◨ ADJ [ADJ n] **Bristling** means thick, hairy, and rough. It is used to describe things such as mustaches, beards, or eyebrows. □ *...a bristling white mustache.* ◨ ADJ [ADJ n] If you describe someone's attitude as **bristling**, you are emphasizing that it is full of energy and enthusiasm. [EMPHASIS] □ *...bristling, exuberant rock'n'roll.*

bris|tly /brɪsli/ ◨ ADJ [usu ADJ n] **Bristly** hair is thick and rough. □ *His bristly red hair was standing on end.* ◨ ADJ If a part of someone's body is **bristly**, it is covered with bristles because it has not been shaved recently. □ *...his bristly cheeks.*

Brit /brɪt/ (Brits) N-COUNT British people are sometimes referred to as **Brits**. [INFORMAL] □ *More than half a million Brits now own homes in Spain.*

Brit|ish /brɪtɪʃ/ ◨ ADJ **British** means belonging or relating to the United Kingdom, or to its people or culture. ◨ N-PLURAL The **British** are the people of Great Britain.

Brit|ish Sum|mer Time N-UNCOUNT **British Summer Time** is a period in the spring and summer during which the clocks are put forward, so that people can have an extra hour of daylight in the evening. [BRIT]

in AM, use **daylight saving time**

Brit|on /brɪtᵊn/ (Britons) N-COUNT A **Briton** is a British citizen, or a person of British origin. [FORMAL] □ *The role is played by seventeen-year-old Briton Jane March.*

brit|tle /brɪtᵊl/ ADJ An object or substance that is **brittle** is hard but easily broken. □ *Pine is brittle and breaks.*

bro /broʊ/ (bros) ◨ N-VOC Some men use **bro** as a friendly way of addressing other men when they are talking to them. [AM, INFORMAL] □ *What do you mean, bro?* ◨ N-COUNT **Bro** is the same as **brother**. [AM, INFORMAL] □ *Bryant said his bro did a great job.*

broach /broʊtʃ/ (broaches, broaching, broached) V-T When you **broach** a subject, especially a sensitive one, you mention it in order to start a discussion on it. □ *Eventually I broached the subject of her early life.*

broad ♦♦♢ /brɔːd/ (broader, broadest) ◨ ADJ Something that is **broad** is wide. □ *His shoulders were broad and his waist narrow.* □ *The hills rise green and sheer above the broad river.* ◨ ADJ A **broad** smile is one in which your mouth is stretched very wide because you are very pleased or amused. □ *He greeted them with a wave and a broad smile.* • **broad|ly** ADV □ *Charles grinned broadly.* ◨ ADJ You use **broad** to describe something that includes a large number of different things or people. □ *A broad range of issues was discussed.* • **broad|ly** ADV [ADV with v] □ *Such policies will do little to resolve long-standing problems more broadly affecting America's global competitiveness.* ◨ ADJ You use **broad** to describe a word or meaning which covers or refers to a wide range of different things. □ *...restructuring in the broad sense of the term.* • **broad|ly** ADV [ADV with v] □ *We define education very broadly and students can study any aspect of its consequences for society.* ◨ ADJ [ADJ n] You use **broad** to describe a feeling or opinion that is shared by many people, or by people of many different kinds. □ *The agreement won broad support in the U.S. Congress.* • **broad|ly** ADV [ADV with v] □ *The new law has been broadly welcomed by road safety organizations.* ◨ in broad daylight → see **daylight**

═══════ SYNONYMS ═══════

broad
ADJ ◨
wide: *...a wide-brimmed sunhat.*
large: *The Pike lives mainly in large rivers and lakes.*
spacious: *The house has a spacious kitchen and dining area.*
expansive: *...an expansive, grassy play area.*

broad|band /brɔːdbænd/ N-UNCOUNT [oft N n] **Broadband** is a method of sending many electronic messages at the same time by using a wide range of frequencies. [COMPUTING] □ *A recent study shows many broadband services lack basic security features.*

broad bean (broad beans) N-COUNT [usu pl] **Broad beans** are the same as **fava beans**. [mainly BRIT]

broad-brush also **broad brush** ADJ [usu ADJ n] A **broad-brush** approach, strategy, or solution deals with a problem in a general way rather than concentrating on details. □ *He's giving a broad-brush approach to the subject.*

broad|cast ♦♢♢ /brɔːdkæst/ (broadcasts, broadcasting)

The form **broadcast** is used in the present tense and is the past tense and past participle of the verb.

◨ N-COUNT A **broadcast** is a program, performance, or speech on the radio or on television. □ *In a broadcast on state radio the government announced that it was willing to resume peace negotiations.* ◨ V-T/V-I To **broadcast** a program means to send it out by radio waves, wires, or satellites so that it can be heard on the radio or seen on television. □ *The concert will be broadcast live on television and radio.* □ *CNN also broadcasts in Europe.*

═══════ COLLOCATIONS ═══════

broadcast
NOUN ◨
noun + **broadcast**: radio, satellite, television; election, news
adjective + **broadcast**: commercial, live, outside; political
verb + **broadcast**: watch
VERB ◨
broadcast + adverb: live, nationally, nightly

═══════ SYNONYMS ═══════

broadcast
VERB ◨
transmit: *The game was transmitted live in Spain and Italy.*
show: *The drama will be shown on American TV next year.*
air: *Tonight, PBS will air a documentary called 'Democracy In Action.'*
televise: *The Grand Prix will be televised by the BBC.*

broad|cast|er /brɔːdkæstər/ (broadcasters) N-COUNT A **broadcaster** is someone who gives talks or takes part in interviews and discussions on radio or television programs. □ *...the prominent naturalist and broadcaster, Sir David Attenborough.*

broad|cast|ing ♦♢♢ /brɔːdkæstɪŋ/ N-UNCOUNT **Broadcasting** is the making and sending out of television and radio programs. □ *If this happens it will change the face of religious broadcasting.*

broad|en /brɔːdᵊn/ (broadens, broadening, broadened) ◨ V-I When something **broadens**, it becomes wider. □ *The trails broadened into roads.* ◨ V-T/V-I When you **broaden** something such as your experience or popularity, or when it **broadens**, the number of things or people that it includes becomes greater. □ *We must broaden our appeal.* □ *I thought you wanted to broaden your horizons.*

broad|ly /brɔːdli/ ◨ ADV [ADV with cl] You can use **broadly** to indicate that something is generally true. □ *The president broadly got what he wanted out of his meeting.* ◨ → see also **broad**

broad|ly based also **broadly-based** ADJ [usu ADJ n] Something that is **broadly based** involves many different kinds of things or people. □ *...a broadly-based political movement for democracy.* □ *This gives children a more broadly based education.*

broad-minded also **broadminded** ADJ If you describe someone as **broad-minded**, you approve of them because they are willing to accept types of behavior that is different from their own. [APPROVAL] ❑ ...*a fair and broad-minded man.*

broad|sheet /brɔdʃit/ (broadsheets) **1** N-COUNT A **broadsheet** is a newspaper that is printed on large sheets of paper. Broadsheets are generally considered to be more serious than other newspapers. Compare **tabloid**. [mainly BRIT] ❑ *Even the broadsheets made it their lead story.* **2** → See feature box at **press**

broad|side /brɔdsaɪd/ (broadsides, broadsiding, broadsided) **1** N-COUNT [oft N *against* n] A **broadside** is a strong written or spoken attack on a person or institution. ❑ *The president continued the broadside against his opponent.* **2** ADV If a ship is **broadside** to something, it has its longest side facing in the direction of that thing. [TECHNICAL] ❑ *The ship was moored broadside to the pier.* **3** ADV [ADV after v] If one vehicle hits another **broadside**, it hits it on the side. ❑ *The Cadillac slammed broadside into a Ford Escort.* **4** V-T If one vehicle **broadsides** another vehicle, it hits the side of the other vehicle. ❑ *The empty coal train broadsided the car and pushed it about 86 feet.*

bro|cade /broʊkeɪd/ (brocades) N-MASS **Brocade** is a thick, expensive material, often made of silk, with a raised pattern on it. ❑ *...a black cloak with gold brocade.*

broc|co|li /brɒkəli/ N-UNCOUNT **Broccoli** is a vegetable with green stalks and green or purple tops.

bro|chure /broʊʃʊr/ (brochures) N-COUNT A **brochure** is a thin magazine with pictures that gives you information about a product or service. ❑ *...travel brochures.*

brogue /broʊg/ (brogues) **1** N-SING If someone has a **brogue**, they speak English with a strong accent, especially Irish or Scots. ❑ *Gill speaks in a quiet Irish brogue.* **2** N-COUNT [usu pl] **Brogues** are thick leather shoes which have an elaborate pattern punched into the leather.

broil /brɔɪl/ (broils, broiling, broiled) V-T When you **broil** food, you cook it using very strong heat directly above it. [AM] ❑ *I'll broil the lobster.*

in BRIT, use **grille**

broil|er /brɔɪlər/ (broilers) **1** N-COUNT A **broiler** is a part of an oven that produces strong heat and cooks food placed underneath it. [AM] ❑ *Remove from heat and finish off under the broiler until cheese melts.*

in BRIT, use **grill**

2 N-COUNT A **broiler** or a **broiler chicken** is a young chicken that is suitable for broiling, roasting, or frying. [AM]

broil|ing /brɔɪlɪŋ/ ADJ If the weather is **broiling**, it is very hot. [AM, INFORMAL] ❑ *...the broiling midday sun.*

broke /broʊk/ **1 Broke** is the past tense of **break**. **2** ADJ [v-link ADJ] If you are **broke**, you have no money. [INFORMAL] ❑ *What do you mean, I've got enough money? I'm as broke as you are.* **3** PHRASE If a company or person **goes broke**, they lose money and are unable to continue in business or to pay their debts. [INFORMAL] ❑ *Balton went broke twice in his career.*

bro|ken /broʊkən/ **1 Broken** is the past participle of **break**. **2** ADJ [ADJ n] A **broken** line is not continuous but has gaps or spaces in it. ❑ *A broken blue line means the course of a waterless valley.* **3** ADJ [ADJ n] You can use **broken** to describe a marriage that has ended in divorce, or a home in which the parents of the family are divorced, when you think this is a sad or bad thing. [DISAPPROVAL] ❑ *She spoke for the first time about the traumas of a broken marriage.* **4** ADJ [ADJ n] If someone talks in **broken** English, for example, or in **broken** French, they speak slowly and make a lot of mistakes because they do not know the language very well. ❑ *Eric could only respond in broken English.*

broken-down ADJ [usu ADJ n] A **broken-down** vehicle or machine no longer works because it has something wrong with it. ❑ *...a broken-down car.*

broken|hearted /broʊkənhɑrtɪd/ ADJ Someone who is **brokenhearted** is very sad and upset because they have had a serious disappointment.

bro|ker ✦◇◇ /broʊkər/ (brokers, brokering, brokered) **1** N-COUNT A **broker** is a person whose job is to buy and sell securities, foreign money, real estate, or goods for other people. [BUSINESS] **2** V-T If a country or government **brokers** an agreement, a ceasefire, or a round of talks, they try to negotiate or arrange it. ❑ *The United Nations brokered a peace in Mogadishu at the end of March.*

bro|ker|age /broʊkərɪdʒ/ (brokerages) N-COUNT A **brokerage** or a **brokerage** firm is a company of brokers. [BUSINESS] ❑ *...Japan's four biggest brokerages.* ❑ *...the nation's largest brokerage firms.*

bro|mance /broʊmæns/ (bromances) N-COUNT A **bromance** is a close but not sexual relationship between two men. [INFORMAL] ❑ *The two men continued their bromance with a trip to the theater.*

bro|mide /broʊmaɪd/ (bromides) **1** N-MASS **Bromide** is a drug that used to be given to people to calm their nerves when they were worried or upset. ❑ *...a dose of bromide.* **2** N-COUNT A **bromide** is a comment that is intended to calm someone down when they are angry, but that has been expressed so often that it has become boring and meaningless. [FORMAL] ❑ *The meeting produced the usual bromides about macroeconomic policy, third-world debt and the environment.*

bron|chial /brɒŋkiəl/ ADJ [ADJ n] **Bronchial** means affecting or concerned with the bronchial tubes. [MEDICAL] ❑ *She suffers from bronchial asthma.*

bron|chial tube (bronchial tubes) **1** N-COUNT [usu pl] Your **bronchial tubes** are the two tubes which connect your windpipe to your lungs. [MEDICAL] **2** → See also color supplement

bron|chi|tis /brɒŋkaɪtɪs/ N-UNCOUNT **Bronchitis** is an illness like a very bad cough, in which your bronchial tubes become sore and infected. ❑ *He was in bed with bronchitis.*

bron|co /brɒŋkoʊ/ (broncos) N-COUNT In the western United States, especially in the 19th century, a wild horse was sometimes referred to as a **bronco**. ❑ *...two cowboys riding bucking broncos.*

Bronx cheer /brɒŋks tʃɪər/ (Bronx cheers) N-COUNT A **Bronx cheer** is a sound that people make by vibrating their lips in order to express disapproval or contempt. [AM, INFORMAL]

in BRIT, use **raspberry**

bronze /brɒnz/ **1** N-UNCOUNT **Bronze** is a yellowish-brown metal which is a mixture of copper and tin. ❑ *...a bronze statue of Giorgi Dimitrov.* **2** COLOR Something that is **bronze** is yellowish-brown in color. ❑ *Her hair shone bronze and gold.*

Bronze Age N-PROPER [the N] The **Bronze Age** was a period of time that began when people started making things from bronze about 4,000–6,000 years ago.

bronzed /brɒnzd/ ADJ Someone who is **bronzed** is attractively brown because they have been in the sun. ❑ *He's bronzed from a short vacation in California.*

bronze med|al (bronze medals) N-COUNT A **bronze medal** is a medal made of bronze or bronze-colored metal that is given as a prize to the person who comes third in a competition, especially a sports contest.

brooch /broʊtʃ/ (brooches) N-COUNT A **brooch** is a piece of jewelry that has a pin at the back so it can be fastened on a dress, blouse, or coat.

brood /brud/ (broods, brooding, brooded) **1** N-COUNT A **brood** is a group of baby birds that were born at the same time to the same mother. ❑ *...a hungry brood of fledglings.* **2** N-COUNT You can refer to someone's young children as their **brood** when you want to emphasize that there are a lot of them. [EMPHASIS] ❑ *...a large brood of children.* **3** V-I If someone **broods** over something, they think about it a lot, seriously and often unhappily. ❑ *She constantly broods about her family.*

brood|ing /brudɪŋ/ ADJ **Brooding** is used to describe an atmosphere or feeling that makes you feel anxious or slightly afraid. [LITERARY] ❑ *The same heavy, brooding silence descended on them.*

broody /brudi/ (broodier, broodiest) **1** ADJ You say that someone is **broody** when they are thinking a lot about something in an unhappy way. ❑ *He became very withdrawn and broody.* **2** ADJ A **broody** hen is ready to lay or sit on eggs.

brook /brʊk/ (brooks, brooking, brooked) **1** N-COUNT A **brook** is a small stream. **2** V-T If someone in a position of authority will **brook** no interference or opposition, they will not accept

broom — bruising

any interference or opposition from others. ❑ *From childhood on, she'd had a plan of action, one that would brook no interference.*

broom /br<u>u</u>m/ (brooms) **1** N-COUNT A **broom** is a kind of brush with a long handle. You use a broom for sweeping the floor. **2** N-UNCOUNT **Broom** is a wild bush with a lot of tiny yellow flowers. **3** → See feature box at **household**

broom|stick /br<u>u</u>mstɪk/ (broomsticks) **1** N-COUNT A **broomstick** is an old-fashioned broom that has a bunch of small sticks at the end. **2** N-COUNT A **broomstick** is the handle of a broom.

Bros. Bros. is a written abbreviation for **brothers**. It is usually used as part of the name of a company. [BUSINESS]

broth /br<u>ɔ</u>θ/ (broths) N-VAR **Broth** is a kind of soup made by boiling meat or vegetables.

broth|el /br<u>ɒ</u>θ°l/ (brothels) N-COUNT A **brothel** is a building where men can go to pay to have sex with prostitutes.

broth|er ♦♦♦ /br<u>ʌ</u>ðər/ (brothers)

> The old-fashioned form **brethren** is still sometimes used as the plural for meanings **3** and **4**.

1 N-COUNT Your **brother** is a boy or a man who has the same parents as you. ❑ *Oh, so you're Peter's younger brother.* **2** → see also **half brother, stepbrother 3** N-COUNT You can describe a man as your **brother** if he belongs to the same race, religion, country, or profession as you, or if he has similar ideas to you. ❑ *He told reporters he'd come to be with his Latvian brothers.* **4** N-TITLE; N-COUNT; N-VOC **Brother** is a title given to a man who belongs to a religious community such as a monastery. ❑ *...Brother Otto.* **5** N-IN-NAMES **Brothers** is used in the names of some companies and stores. ❑ *...the movie company Warner Brothers.*

brother|hood /br<u>ʌ</u>ðərhʊd/ (brotherhoods) **1** N-UNCOUNT **Brotherhood** is the affection and loyalty that you feel for people who you have something in common with. ❑ *People threw flowers into the river between the two countries as a symbolic act of brotherhood.* **2** N-COUNT A **brotherhood** is an organization whose members all have the same political aims and beliefs or the same job or profession. ❑ *...the Brotherhood of Locomotive Engineers.*

brother-in-law (brothers-in-law) N-COUNT Someone's **brother-in-law** is the brother of their husband or wife, or the man who is married to their sister.

broth|er|ly /br<u>ʌ</u>ðərli/ ADJ [usu ADJ n] A man's **brotherly** feelings are feelings of love and loyalty which you expect a brother to show. ❑ *...family loyalty and brotherly love.* ❑ *He gave her a brief, brotherly kiss.*

brought /br<u>ɔ</u>t/ **Brought** is the past tense and past participle of **bring**.

brou|ha|ha /br<u>u</u>hɑhɑ/ N-SING [also no det] A **brouhaha** is an excited and critical fuss or reaction to something. [mainly JOURNALISM, DISAPPROVAL] ❑ *...the recent brouhaha over a congressional pay raise.*

brow /br<u>aʊ</u>/ (brows) **1** N-COUNT Your **brow** is your forehead. ❑ *He wiped his brow with the back of his hand.* **2** N-COUNT [usu pl] Your **brows** are your eyebrows. ❑ *He had thick brown hair and shaggy brows.* **3** N-COUNT The **brow** of a hill is the top part of it. ❑ *He was on the lookout just below the brow of the hill.*

brow|beat /br<u>aʊ</u>bit/ (browbeats, browbeating, browbeaten)

> The form **browbeat** is used in the present tense and is also the past tense.

V-T If someone tries to **browbeat** you, they try to force you to do what they want. ❑ *...attempts to deceive, con, or browbeat the voters.* ❑ *When I backed out of the 100 meters, an older kid tried to browbeat me into it.* • **brow|beat|en** ADJ ❑ *...the browbeaten employees.*

brown ♦♦♦ /br<u>aʊ</u>n/ (browner, brownest, browns, browning, browned) **1** COLOR Something that is **brown** is the color of earth or of wood. ❑ *...her deep brown eyes.* **2** ADJ You can describe a white-skinned person as **brown** when they have been sitting in the sun until their skin has become darker than usual. **3** ADJ **Brown** is used to describe grains that have not had their outer layers removed, and foods made from these grains. ❑ *...brown bread.* ❑ *...spicy tomato sauce served over a bed of brown rice.* **4** V-T/V-I When food **browns** or when you brown food, you cook it, usually for a short time on a high flame. ❑ *Cook for ten minutes until the sugar browns.*

brown-bag (brown-bags, brown-bagging, brown-bagged) **1** V-T If you **brown-bag** your lunch or you **brown-bag** it, you bring your lunch in a bag to work or school. [AM] ❑ *The majority of the time, I brown-bagged my lunch.* **2** ADJ [ADJ n] A **brown-bag** lunch is a meal that you bring in a bag to work or school. [AM] ❑ *Members are advised to bring a brown-bag lunch.*

brown|field /br<u>aʊ</u>nfild/ ADJ [ADJ n] **Brownfield** land is land in a town or city where houses or factories have been built in the past, but which is not being used at the present time.

brownie /br<u>aʊ</u>ni/ (brownies)

> The spelling **Brownie** is used for meaning **2**.

1 N-COUNT [oft n n] **Brownies** are small flat cookies or cakes. They are usually chocolate flavored and have nuts in them. ❑ *...chocolate brownies.* ❑ *...a tray of brownies.* **2** N-PROPER-COLL [the N] **The Brownies** is a junior version of the Girl Scouts for girls between the ages of six and eight. • N-COUNT A **Brownie** is a girl who is a member of the Brownies.

brownie point (brownie points) N-COUNT [usu pl] If someone does something to score **brownie points**, they do it because they think they will be praised for it. [DISAPPROVAL] ❑ *They're just trying to score brownie points with politicians.*

brown|ish /br<u>aʊ</u>nɪʃ/ COLOR Something that is **brownish** is slightly brown in color.

brown|nosing /br<u>aʊ</u>nnoʊzɪŋ/ N-UNCOUNT If you accuse someone of **brownnosing**, you are saying in a rather offensive way that they are agreeing with someone important in order to get their support. [DISAPPROVAL] ❑ *Brownnosing the power brokers won't save you.*

brown|stone /br<u>aʊ</u>nstoʊn/ (brownstones) N-COUNT A **brownstone** is a type of house that was built during the 19th century. Brownstones have a front that is made from a reddish-brown stone. [AM]

brown sugar N-UNCOUNT **Brown sugar** is sugar that has not been refined, or is only partly refined. It is golden brown in color.

browse /br<u>aʊ</u>z/ (browses, browsing, browsed) **1** V-I If you **browse** in a store, you look at things in a fairly casual way, in the hope that you might find something you like. ❑ *I stopped in several bookstores to browse.* ❑ *She browsed in an upscale antiques shop.* • N-COUNT **Browse** is also a noun. ❑ *...a browse around the shops.* **2** V-I If you **browse** through a book or magazine, you look through it in a fairly casual way. ❑ *...sitting on the sofa browsing through the TV pages of the paper.* **3** V-I If you **browse** on a computer, you search for information in computer files or on the internet. [COMPUTING] ❑ *Try browsing around in the network bulletin boards.* **4** V-T/V-I When animals **browse**, they feed on plants. ❑ *...three red deer stags browsing on the fringes of the forest.* **5** → See feature box at **leisure**

brows|er /br<u>aʊ</u>zər/ (browsers) N-COUNT A **browser** is a piece of computer software that you use to search for information on the internet. [COMPUTING] ❑ *You need an up-to-date Web browser.*

bruise /br<u>u</u>z/ (bruises, bruising, bruised) **1** N-COUNT A **bruise** is an injury that appears as a purple mark on your body, although the skin is not broken. ❑ *How did you get that bruise on your cheek?* **2** V-T/V-I If you **bruise** a part of your body, a bruise appears on it, for example, because something hits you. If you **bruise** easily, bruises appear when something hits you only slightly. ❑ *I had only bruised my knee.* • **bruised** ADJ ❑ *I escaped with severely bruised legs.* **3** V-T/V-I If a fruit, vegetable, or plant **bruises** or **is bruised**, it is damaged by being handled roughly, making a mark on the skin. ❑ *Choose a warm, dry day to cut them off the plants, being careful not to bruise them.* ❑ *...bruised tomatoes and cucumbers.* • N-COUNT **Bruise** is also a noun. ❑ *...bruises on the fruit's skin.* **4** V-T [usu passive] If you **are bruised** by an unpleasant experience, it makes you feel unhappy or upset. ❑ *The government will be severely bruised by yesterday's events.*

bruis|er /br<u>u</u>zər/ (bruisers) N-COUNT A **bruiser** is someone who is tough, strong, and aggressive, and enjoys a fight or argument. [INFORMAL, DISAPPROVAL] ❑ *He has a reputation as a political bruiser.*

bruis|ing /br<u>u</u>zɪŋ/ **1** N-UNCOUNT If someone has **bruising** on their body, they have bruises on it. [FORMAL] ❑ *She had quite* severe bruising and a cut lip. **2** ADJ [usu ADJ n] In a **bruising** battle or encounter, people fight or compete with each other in a very aggressive or determined way. [JOURNALISM] ❑ *The administration hopes to avoid another bruising battle over civil rights.*

brunch /brʌntʃ/ (**brunches**) N-VAR **Brunch** is a meal that is eaten in the late morning. It is a combination of breakfast and lunch.

bru|nette /bruːnet/ (**brunettes**) also **brunet** N-COUNT A **brunette** is a woman or girl with dark brown hair.

brunt /brʌnt/ PHRASE To **bear the brunt** or **take the brunt** of something unpleasant means to suffer the main part or force of it. ❑ *Young people are bearing the brunt of unemployment.*

bru|schet|ta /bruʃetə/ (**bruschettas**) N-VAR **Bruschetta** is a slice of toasted bread that is brushed with olive oil and usually covered with chopped tomatoes.

brush ✦✧ /brʌʃ/ (**brushes, brushing, brushed**) **1** N-COUNT A **brush** is an object that has a large number of bristles or hairs fixed to it. You use brushes for painting, for cleaning things, and for making your hair neat. ❑ *We gave him paint and brushes.* ❑ *Stains are removed with buckets of soapy water and scrubbing brushes.* **2** V-T If you **brush** something or **brush** something such as dirt off it, you clean it or make it neat using a brush. ❑ *Have you brushed your teeth?* ❑ *She brushed the powder out of her hair.* • N-SING **Brush** is also a noun. ❑ *I gave it a quick brush with my hairbrush.* **3** V-T If you **brush** something with a liquid, you apply a layer of that liquid using a brush. ❑ *Brush the dough with beaten egg yolk.* **4** V-T If you **brush** something somewhere, you remove it with quick light movements of your hands. ❑ *He brushed his hair back with both hands.* ❑ *She brushed away tears as she spoke of him.* **5** V-T/V-I If one thing **brushes** against another or if you **brush** one thing against another, the first thing touches the second thing lightly while passing it. ❑ *Something brushed against her leg.* ❑ *I felt her dark brown hair brushing the back of my shoulder.* **6** N-COUNT If you have a **brush** with a particular situation, usually an unpleasant one, you almost experience it. ❑ *...the trauma of a brush with death.* **7** N-UNCOUNT **Brush** is an area of rough open land covered with small bushes and trees. You also use **brush** to refer to the bushes and trees on this land. ❑ *...the brush fire that destroyed nearly 500 acres.*

▶ **brush aside** also **brush away** PHRASAL VERB If you **brush aside** or **brush away** an idea, remark, or feeling, you refuse to consider it because you think it is not important or useful, even though it may be. ❑ *Perhaps you shouldn't brush the idea aside too hastily.*

▶ **brush off** **1** PHRASAL VERB If someone **brushes** you **off** when you speak to them, they refuse to talk to you or be nice to you. ❑ *When I tried to talk to her about it she just brushed me off.* **2** → see also **brush-off**

▶ **brush up** also **brush up on** PHRASAL VERB If you **brush up** something or **brush up on** it, you practice it or improve your knowledge of it. ❑ *I had hoped to brush up my Spanish.*

brushed /brʌʃt/ ADJ [ADJ n] **Brushed** cotton, nylon, or other fabric feels soft and furry.

brush-off N-SING If someone gives you the **brush-off** when you speak to them, they refuse to talk to you or be nice to you. [INFORMAL] ❑ *I wanted to keep in touch, but when I called him he gave me the brush-off.*

brush|stroke /brʌʃstroʊk/ (**brushstrokes**) **1** N-COUNT **Brushstrokes** are the marks made on a surface by a painter's brush. ❑ *He paints with harsh, slashing brushstrokes.* **2** → See feature box at **fine art**

brush|wood /brʌʃwʊd/ N-UNCOUNT **Brushwood** consists of small pieces of wood that have broken off trees and bushes.

brush|work /brʌʃwɜːrk/ N-UNCOUNT An artist's **brushwork** is their way of using their brush to put paint on a canvas and the effect that this has in the picture. ❑ *...the texture of the artist's brushwork.*

brusque /brʌsk/ **1** ADJ If you describe a person or their behavior as **brusque**, you mean that they deal with things, or say things, quickly and shortly so that they seem to be rude. ❑ *The doctors are brusque and busy.* **2** → See feature box at **review**

brus|sels sprout /brʌsəlz spraʊt/ (**brussels sprouts**) also **Brussels sprout** N-COUNT **Brussels sprouts** are vegetables that look like tiny cabbages.

bru|tal /bruːt°l/ **1** ADJ A **brutal** act or person is cruel and violent. ❑ *He was the victim of a very brutal murder.* ❑ *...the brutal suppression of anti-government protests.* • **bru|tal|ly** ADV ❑ *Her real parents had been brutally murdered.* **2** ADJ If someone expresses something unpleasant with **brutal** honesty or frankness, they express it in a clear and accurate way, without attempting to disguise its unpleasantness. ❑ *It was refreshing to talk about themselves and their feelings with brutal honesty.* • **bru|tal|ly** ADV ❑ *The talks had been brutally frank.*

bru|tal|ity /bruːtælɪti/ (**brutalities**) N-VAR **Brutality** is cruel and violent treatment or behavior. A **brutality** is an instance of cruel and violent treatment or behavior. ❑ *Her experience of men was of domination and brutality.* ❑ *...police brutality.*

bru|tal|ize /bruːt°laɪz/ (**brutalizes, brutalizing, brutalized**)

in BRIT, also use **brutalise**

1 V-T If an unpleasant experience **brutalizes** someone, it makes them cruel or violent. ❑ *He was brutalized by the experience of being in prison.* **2** V-T If one person **brutalizes** another, they treat them in a cruel or violent way. ❑ *...a 15th century explorer who brutalized people and enslaved them.*

brute /bruːt/ (**brutes**) N-COUNT If you call someone a **brute**, you mean that they are rough, violent, and insensitive. [DISAPPROVAL] ❑ *Custer was an idiot and a brute.*

brut|ish /bruːtɪʃ/ ADJ If you describe a person or their behavior as **brutish**, you think that they are brutal and uncivilized. [DISAPPROVAL] ❑ *The man was brutish and coarse.* ❑ *...brutish bullying.*

BS /biː es/ (**BSs**) also **B.S.** **1** N-COUNT A **BS** or **B.S.** is a first degree from a college or university in a science subject. **BS** is an abbreviation for **Bachelor of Science**. [AM] ❑ *I received a BS in chemistry at Dartmouth.* **2** N-COUNT **BS** or **B.S.** is written after someone's name to indicate that they have a BS. **3** N-UNCOUNT If you describe something as **BS** or **B.S.**, you are saying that it is nonsense or completely untrue. **BS** is an abbreviation for **bullshit**. [mainly AM, INFORMAL, VULGAR, DISAPPROVAL] ❑ *A lot of what he's been hearing from the federal government is BS.*

BSc /biː es siː/ (**BScs**) also **B.Sc.** N-COUNT A **Bachelor of Science** is a first degree from a college or university in a science subject. [mainly BRIT]

in AM, use **BS**

BSE /biː es iː/ N-UNCOUNT **BSE** is a disease that affects the nervous system of cattle and kills them. **BSE** is an abbreviation for 'bovine spongiform encephalopathy.' ❑ *...meat from cattle infected with BSE, or mad cow disease.*

B-side (**B-sides**) N-COUNT The **B-side** of a pop record had the less important or less popular song on it. Compare **A-side**. ❑ *...a compilation of the band's A- and B-sides.*

BTW **BTW** is the written abbreviation for 'by the way,' often used in email. ❑ *BTW, the machine is simply amazing.*

bub|ble /bʌb°l/ (**bubbles, bubbling, bubbled**) **1** N-COUNT **Bubbles** are small balls of air or gas in a liquid. ❑ *Ink particles attach themselves to air bubbles and rise to the surface.* **2** N-COUNT A **bubble** is a hollow ball of soapy liquid that is floating in the air or standing on a surface. ❑ *With soap and water, bubbles and boats, children love bathtime.* **3** N-COUNT In a cartoon, a speech **bubble** is the shape which surrounds the words which a character is thinking or saying. ❑ *All that was missing were speech bubbles saying, "Golly!" and "Wow!"* **4** V-I When a liquid **bubbles**, bubbles move in it, for example, because it is boiling or moving quickly. ❑ *Heat the seasoned stock until it is bubbling.* ❑ *The fermenting wine has bubbled up and over the top.* **5** V-I [usu cont] A feeling, influence, or activity that is **bubbling** away continues to occur. ❑ *...political tensions that have been bubbling away for years.* **6** → See feature box at **banking**

bub|ble bath (**bubble baths**) **1** N-UNCOUNT **Bubble bath** is a liquid that smells nice and makes a lot of bubbles when you add it to your bath water. **2** N-COUNT When you take a **bubble bath**, you lie in a bath of water with bubble bath in it. ❑ *...a long, relaxing bubble bath.*

bub|ble gum also **bubblegum** N-UNCOUNT **Bubble gum** is a type of chewing gum. You can blow it out of your mouth so it makes the shape of a bubble. ❑ *I got bubblegum on the seat of Nanna's car.*

bub|ble tea (bubble teas) N-VAR **Bubble tea** is a sweet drink based on tea mixed with milk or fruit flavorings, with chewy balls made of tapioca floating in it.

bub|bly /bʌbli/ (bubblier, bubbliest) **1** ADJ Someone who is **bubbly** is very lively and cheerful and talks a lot. [APPROVAL] ❑ ...a bubbly girl who loves to laugh. **2** ADJ If something is **bubbly**, it has a lot of bubbles in it. ❑ Melt the butter over a medium-low heat. When it is melted and bubbly, put in the flour.

bu|bon|ic plague /byubɒnɪk pleɪg/ N-UNCOUNT **Bubonic plague** is a serious infectious disease spread by rats. It killed many people during the Middle Ages.

buc|ca|neer /bʌkənɪər/ (buccaneers) N-COUNT A **buccaneer** was a pirate, especially one who attacked and stole from Spanish ships in the 17th and 18th centuries.

buck /bʌk/ (bucks, bucking, bucked) **1** N-COUNT A **buck** is a U.S. or Australian dollar. [INFORMAL] ❑ That would probably cost you about fifty bucks. ❑ Why can't you spend a few bucks on a coat? **2** N-COUNT A **buck** is the male of various animals, including the deer, antelope, rabbit, and kangaroo. **3** ADJ [ADJ n] If someone has **buck** teeth, their upper front teeth stick forward out of their mouth. **4** V-I If a horse **bucks**, it kicks both of its back legs wildly into the air, or jumps into the air wildly with all four feet off the ground. ❑ The stallion bucked as he fought against the reins holding him tightly in. **5** V-T If you **buck** the trend, you obtain different results from others in the same area. If you **buck** the system, you get what you want by breaking or ignoring the rules. ❑ While other newspapers are losing circulation, we are bucking the trend. ❑ To be the tough rebel who bucks the system. **6** PHRASE If you **pass the buck**, you refuse to accept responsibility for something, and say that someone else is responsible. [INFORMAL] ❑ David says the responsibility is Mr. Smith's and it's no good trying to pass the buck.

buck|et /bʌkɪt/ (buckets) **1** N-COUNT A **bucket** is a round metal or plastic container with a handle attached to its sides. Buckets are often used for holding and carrying water. ❑ We drew water in a bucket from the well outside the door. **2** N-COUNT A **bucket** of something such as water is the amount of it that is contained in a bucket. ❑ She threw a bucket of water over them.

buck|et|ful /bʌkɪtfʊl/ (bucketfuls) **1** N-COUNT [usu N of n] A **bucketful** of something is the amount contained in a bucket. **2** PHRASE [PHR after v] If someone produces or gets something **by the bucketful**, they produce or get something in large quantities. [INFORMAL] ❑ Over the years they have sold records by the bucketful.

buck|et list (bucket lists) N-COUNT Your **bucket list** consists of all the things you would really like to do or see in your life. [INFORMAL] ❑ He made a quick visit to the Taj Mahal, just to cross it off his bucket list. ❑ The singer said that performing a James Bond theme song was definitely on her bucket list.

buck|et seat (bucket seats) **1** N-COUNT A **bucket seat** is a seat for one person in a car or airplane which has rounded sides that partly enclose and support the body. **2** → See also color supplement

buck|le /bʌkəl/ (buckles, buckling, buckled) **1** N-COUNT A **buckle** is a piece of metal or plastic attached to one end of a belt or strap, which is used to fasten it. ❑ He wore a belt with a large brass buckle. **2** V-T When you **buckle** a belt or strap, you fasten it. ❑ A door slammed in the house and a man came out buckling his belt. **3** V-T/V-I If an object **buckles** or if something **buckles** it, it becomes bent as a result of very great heat or force. ❑ The door was beginning to buckle from the intense heat. **4** V-I If your legs or knees **buckle**, they bend because they have become very weak or tired. ❑ Mcanally's knees buckled and he crumpled down onto the floor.

▶ **buckle up** PHRASAL VERB When you **buckle up** in a car or airplane, you fasten your seat belt. [INFORMAL] ❑ A sign just ahead of me said, "Buckle Up. It's the Law in Illinois."

buck|led /bʌkəld/ ADJ [ADJ n] **Buckled** shoes have buckles on them, either to fasten them or as decoration.

buck|shot /bʌkʃɒt/ N-UNCOUNT **Buckshot** consists of pieces of lead fired from a gun when hunting animals.

buck|skin /bʌkskɪn/ N-UNCOUNT **Buckskin** is soft, strong leather made from the skin of a deer or a goat.

buck|wheat /bʌkwit/ N-UNCOUNT **Buckwheat** is a type of small black grain used for feeding animals and making flour. **Buckwheat** also refers to the flour itself.

bu|col|ic /byukɒlɪk/ ADJ [usu ADJ n] **Bucolic** means relating to the countryside. [LITERARY] ❑ ...the bucolic surroundings of Chantilly.

bud /bʌd/ (buds) **1** N-COUNT A **bud** is a small pointed lump that appears on a tree or plant and develops into a leaf or flower. ❑ Rosanna's favorite time is early summer, just before the buds open. **2** → see also budding **3** PHRASE If you **nip** something such as bad behavior **in the bud**, you stop it before it can develop very far. [INFORMAL] ❑ It is important to recognize jealousy and to nip it in the bud before it gets out of hand.

Buddha /bʊdə, buːdə/ (Buddhas) **1** N-PROPER [oft the N] **Buddha** is the title given to Gautama Siddhartha, the religious teacher and founder of Buddhism. **2** N-COUNT A **Buddha** is a statue or picture of the Buddha.

Bud|dhism /bʊdɪzəm, buːd-/ N-UNCOUNT **Buddhism** is a religion which teaches that the way to end suffering is by overcoming your desires.

Bud|dhist /bʊdɪst, buːd-/ (Buddhists) **1** N-COUNT A **Buddhist** is a person whose religion is Buddhism. **2** ADJ **Buddhist** means relating or referring to Buddhism. ❑ ...Buddhist monks.

bud|ding /bʌdɪŋ/ **1** ADJ [ADJ n] If you describe someone as, for example, a **budding** businessman or a **budding** artist, you mean that they are starting to succeed or become interested in business or art. ❑ The forum is now open to all budding entrepreneurs. **2** ADJ [ADJ n] You use **budding** to describe a situation that is just beginning. ❑ Our budding romance was over.

bud|dy /bʌdi/ (buddies) N-COUNT A **buddy** is a close friend. [mainly AM] ❑ We became great buddies.

budge /bʌdʒ/ (budges, budging, budged) **1** V-I/V-I [with brd-neg] If someone will not **budge** on a matter, or if nothing **budges** them, they refuse to change their mind or to come to an agreement. ❑ The Americans will not budge on this point. **2** V-T/V-I [with brd-neg] If someone or something will not **budge**, they will not move. If you cannot **budge** them, you cannot make them move. ❑ Her mother refused to budge from Omaha. ❑ The window refused to budge.

budg|eri|gar /bʌdʒərɪgɑr/ (budgerigars) N-COUNT **Budgerigars** are small, brightly-colored birds from Australia that people often keep as pets.

budg|et ✦✧ /bʌdʒɪt/ (budgets, budgeting, budgeted) **1** N-COUNT Your **budget** is the amount of money that you have available to spend. The **budget** for something is the amount of money that a person, organization, or country has available to spend on it. [BUSINESS] ❑ She will design a fantastic new kitchen for you – and all within your budget. ❑ Someone had furnished the place on a tight budget. **2** N-COUNT The **budget** of an organization or country is its financial situation, considered as the difference between the money it receives and the money it spends. [BUSINESS] ❑ The hospital obviously needs to balance the budget each year. **3** V-T/V-I If you **budget** certain amounts of money for particular things, you decide that you can afford to spend those amounts on those things. ❑ The company has budgeted $10 million for advertising. ❑ The movie is only budgeted at $10 million. ❑ I'm learning how to budget. ● **budg|et|ing** N-UNCOUNT ❑ We have continued to exercise caution in our budgeting for the current year. **4** ADJ [ADJ n] **Budget** is used in advertising to suggest that something is being sold cheaply. ❑ Cheap flights are available from budget travel agents from $240. **5** → See feature box at finance, tourism

▶ **budget for** PHRASAL VERB If you **budget for** something, you take account of it when you are deciding how much you can afford to spend on different things. ❑ The authorities had budgeted for some non-payment.

COLLOCATIONS

budget
NOUN
1
noun + **budget**: family, household; aid, defense, education, welfare; advertising, marketing
adjective + **budget**: limited, tight
verb + **budget**: draw up, set; cut, slash
2
adjective + **budget**: balanced
verb + **budget**: balance

-budget /-bʌdʒɪt/ COMB IN ADJ **-budget** combines with adjectives such as 'low' and 'big' to form adjectives that indicate how much money is spent on something, especially the making of a movie. ❑ *They were small, low-budget movies, shot on location.* ❑ *...a big-budget adventure movie starring Mel Gibson.*

budg|et|ary /bʌdʒɪtɛri/ ADJ [ADJ n] A **budgetary** matter or policy is concerned with the amount of money that is available to a country or organization, and how it is to be spent. [FORMAL] ❑ *There are huge budgetary pressures on all governments in Europe to reduce their armed forces.*

budgie /bʌdʒi/ (budgies) N-COUNT A **budgie** is the same as a **budgerigar**. [INFORMAL]

buff /bʌf/ (buffs) ◼ COLOR Something that is **buff** is pale brown in color. ❑ *He took a largish buff envelope from his pocket.* ◼ N-COUNT You use **buff** to describe someone who knows a lot about a particular subject. For example, if you describe someone as a movie **buff**, you mean that they know a lot about movies. [INFORMAL] ❑ *Judge Lanier is a real movie buff.*

buf|fa|lo /bʌfəloʊ/ (buffalo or buffaloes) N-COUNT A **buffalo** is a wild animal like a large cow with horns that curve upward. Buffalo are usually found in southern and eastern Africa.

buff|er /bʌfər/ (buffers, buffering, buffered) ◼ N-COUNT A **buffer** is something that prevents something else from being harmed or that prevents two things from harming each other. ❑ *Keep savings as a buffer against unexpected cash needs.* ◼ V-T If something **is buffered**, it is protected from harm. ❑ *The company is buffered by long-term contracts with growers.* ◼ N-COUNT A **buffer** is an area in a computer's memory where information can be stored for a short time. [COMPUTING]

buff|er state (buffer states) N-COUNT A **buffer state** is a peaceful country situated between two or more larger hostile countries. ❑ *Turkey and Greece were buffer states against the former Soviet Union.*

buff|er zone (buffer zones) N-COUNT A **buffer zone** is an area created to separate opposing forces or groups which belongs to neither of them.

buf|fet (buffets, buffeting, buffeted)

> Pronounced /bʊfeɪ/ for meanings 1 and 2, and /bʌfɪt/ for meaning 3.

◼ N-COUNT A **buffet** is a meal of food that is displayed on a long table at a party or public occasion. Guests usually serve themselves. ❑ *...a buffet lunch.* ◼ N-COUNT A **buffet** is a café, usually in a hotel or station. ❑ *We sat in the station buffet sipping tea.* ◼ V-T If something **is buffeted** by strong winds or by stormy seas, it is repeatedly struck or blown around by them. ❑ *Their plane had been severely buffeted by storms.*

buf|foon /bʌfun/ (buffoons) N-COUNT If you call someone a **buffoon**, you mean that they often do foolish things. [OLD-FASHIONED, DISAPPROVAL]

buf|foon|ery /bʌfunəri/ N-UNCOUNT **Buffoonery** is foolish behavior that makes you laugh. [OLD-FASHIONED]

bug /bʌg/ (bugs, bugging, bugged) ◼ N-COUNT A **bug** is an insect or similar small creature. [INFORMAL] ❑ *We noticed tiny bugs that were all over the walls.* ◼ N-COUNT A **bug** is an illness which is caused by small organisms such as bacteria. [INFORMAL] ❑ *I think I've got a bit of a stomach bug.* ◼ N-COUNT If there is a **bug** in a computer program, there is a mistake in it. [COMPUTING] ❑ *There is a bug in the software.* ◼ N-COUNT A **bug** is a tiny hidden microphone that transmits what people are saying. ❑ *There was a bug on the phone.* ◼ V-T If someone **bugs** a place, they hide tiny microphones in it that transmit what people are saying. ❑ *He heard that they were planning to bug his office.* ◼ V-T If someone or something **bugs** you, they worry or annoy you. [INFORMAL] ❑ *I only did it to bug my parents.* ◼ → See feature box at **illness**

bug|a|boo /bʌgəbu/ (bugaboos) N-COUNT Something or someone that is your **bugaboo** worries or upsets you. [AM] ❑ *Red tape is the bugaboo of small business.*

bug|bear /bʌgbɛr/ (bugbears) N-COUNT A **bugbear** is the same as a **bugaboo**. ❑ *Money is my biggest bugbear.*

bug-eyed ADJ A **bug-eyed** person or animal has eyes that stick out. [INFORMAL] ❑ *...bug-eyed monsters.* ❑ *We were bug-eyed in wonderment.*

bug|gery /bʌgəri/ N-UNCOUNT **Buggery** is anal intercourse.

bug|gy /bʌgi/ (buggies) ◼ N-COUNT A **buggy** is a small lightweight carriage pulled by one horse. ◼ N-COUNT A **buggy** is the same as a **baby buggy**.

bu|gle /byug°l/ (bugles) N-COUNT A **bugle** is a simple brass musical instrument that looks like a small trumpet. Bugles are often used in the army to announce when activities such as meals are about to begin.

bu|gler /byuglər/ (buglers) N-COUNT A **bugler** is someone who plays the bugle.

build ♦♦♦ /bɪld/ (builds, building, built) ◼ V-T If you **build** something, you make it by joining things together. ❑ *Developers are now proposing to build a hotel on the site.* ❑ *The house was built in the early 19th century.* • **build|ing** N-UNCOUNT ❑ *In Japan, the building of Kansai airport continues.* • **built** ADJ [ADV ADJ, ADJ for n, ADJ to-inf] ❑ *Even newly built houses can need repairs.* ❑ *It's a product built for safety.* ◼ V-T If you **build** something into a wall or object, you make it in such a way that it is in the wall or object, or is part of it. ❑ *If the TV was built into the ceiling, you could lie there while watching your favorite program.* ◼ V-T If people **build** an organization, a society, or a relationship, they gradually form it. ❑ *He and a partner set up on their own and built a successful fashion company.* ❑ *Their purpose is to build a fair society and a strong economy.* • **build|ing** N-UNCOUNT ❑ *...the building of the great civilizations of the ancient world.* ◼ V-T If you **build** an organization, system, or product on something, you base it on it. ❑ *We will then have a firmer foundation of fact on which to build theories.* ◼ V-T If you **build** something into a policy, system, or product, you make it part of it. ❑ *We have to build computers into the school curriculum.* ◼ V-T To **build** someone's confidence or trust means to increase it gradually. ❑ *Diplomats hope the meetings will build mutual trust.* • PHRASAL VERB **Build up** means the same as **build**. ❑ *The delegations had begun to build up some trust in one another.* ◼ V-I If you **build** on the success of something, you take advantage of this success in order to make further progress. ❑ *The new regime has no successful economic reforms on which to build.* ◼ V-I If pressure, speed, sound, or excitement **builds**, it gradually becomes greater. ❑ *Pressure built yesterday for postponement of the ceremony.* • PHRASAL VERB **Build up** means the same as **build**. ❑ *Take it slowly and do not let the speed build up.* ◼ N-VAR Someone's **build** is the shape that their bones and muscles give to their body. ❑ *He's described as around thirty years old, six feet tall and of medium build.* ◼ → see also **building**, **built** ◼ → See feature box at **appearance**

▶ **build up** ◼ PHRASAL VERB If you **build up** something or if it **builds up**, it gradually becomes bigger, for example, because more is added to it. ❑ *The regime built up the largest army in Africa.* ❑ *The collection has been built up over the last seventeen years.* ◼ PHRASAL VERB If you **build** someone **up**, you help them to feel stronger or more confident, especially when they have had a bad experience or have been ill. ❑ *Build her up with kindness and a sympathetic ear.* ◼ PHRASAL VERB If you **build** someone or something **up**, you make them seem important or exciting, for example, by talking about them a lot. ❑ *The media will report on it and the tabloids will build it up.* ❑ *The soccer community built him up as the savior of the sport.* ◼ → see also **build 6, 8, build-up, built-up**

build|er /bɪldər/ (builders) N-COUNT A **builder** is a person whose job is to build or repair houses and other buildings. ❑ *The builders have finished the roof.*

build|ing ♦♦♦ /bɪldɪŋ/ (buildings) N-COUNT A **building** is a structure that has a roof and walls, for example, a house or a factory. ❑ *They were on the upper floor of the building.*

COLLOCATIONS

building
NOUN
noun + **building**: farm, government, office, school
adjective + **building**: derelict, historic, Victorian; high-rise, public, residential, tall; brick, stone
verb + **building**: construct, erect, renovate; demolish, destroy; evacuate, occupy

build|ing block (building blocks) N-COUNT [usu N *of*] If you describe something as a **building block** of something, you mean it is one of the separate parts that combine to make that thing. ❑ *...molecules that are the building blocks of all life on earth.*

build|ing per|mit (building permits) N-COUNT In many parts of the United States, a **building permit** is the permission granted by a local authority to build something new or to add something to an existing building.

build|ing site (building sites) N-COUNT A **building site** is an area of land on which a building or a group of buildings is in the process of being built or altered.

build-up (build-ups) also buildup, build up ◼ N-COUNT A **build-up** is a gradual increase in something. ❑ *There has been a build-up of troops on both sides of the border.* ◼ N-COUNT The **build-up** to an event is the way that journalists, advertisers, or other people talk about it a lot in the period of time immediately before it, and try to make it seem important and exciting. ❑ *The exams came, almost an anticlimax after the build-up that the students had given them.*

built /bɪlt/ ◼ **Built** is the past tense and past participle of **build**. ◼ ADJ If you say that someone is **built** in a particular way, you are describing the kind of body they have. ❑ *...a strong, powerfully-built man of 60.* ◼ → see also **well-built**

built-in ADJ [ADJ n] **Built-in** devices or features are included in something as a part of it, rather than being separate. ❑ *...a kitchen with built-in appliances.*

built-up ADJ A **built-up** area is an area such as a town or city which has a lot of buildings in it. ❑ *A speed limit of 30 mph was introduced in built-up areas.*

bulb /bʌlb/ (bulbs) ◼ N-COUNT A **bulb** is the glass part of an electric light or lamp, which gives out light when electricity passes through it. ❑ *The stairwell was lit by a single bulb.* ◼ N-COUNT A **bulb** is a root shaped like an onion that grows into a flower or plant. ❑ *...tulip bulbs.*

bulb|ous /bʌlbəs/ ADJ [usu ADJ n] Something that is **bulbous** is round and fat in a rather ugly way. ❑ *...his bulbous purple nose.*

Bul|gar|ian /bʌlgeəriən/ (Bulgarians) ◼ ADJ **Bulgarian** means belonging or relating to Bulgaria, or to its people, language, or culture. ◼ N-COUNT A **Bulgarian** is a Bulgarian citizen, or a person of Bulgarian origin. ◼ N-UNCOUNT **Bulgarian** is the main language spoken by people who live in Bulgaria.

bulge /bʌldʒ/ (bulges, bulging, bulged) ◼ V-I If something such as a person's stomach **bulges**, it sticks out. ❑ *Jiro waddled closer, his belly bulging and distended.* ❑ *He bulges out of his black T-shirt.* ◼ V-I If someone's eyes or veins **are bulging**, they seem to stick out a lot, often because the person is making a strong physical effort or is experiencing a strong emotion. ❑ *He shouted at his brother, his neck veins bulging.* ◼ V-I [oft cont] If you say that something **is bulging** with things, you are emphasizing that it is full of them. [EMPHASIS] ❑ *They returned home with the car bulging with boxes.* ◼ N-COUNT **Bulges** are lumps that stick out from a surface which is otherwise flat or smooth. ❑ *Why won't those bulges on your hips and thighs go?* ◼ N-COUNT If there is a **bulge** in something, there is a sudden large increase in it. ❑ *...a bulge in aircraft sales.*

bu|limia /bulɪmiə, -liːm-/ N-UNCOUNT **Bulimia** or **bulimia nervosa** is an illness in which a person has a very great fear of becoming fat, and so they make themselves vomit after eating.

bu|limic /bulɪmɪk, -liːm-/ (bulimics) ADJ If someone is **bulimic**, they have bulimia. ❑ *...bulimic patients.* • N-COUNT A **bulimic** is someone who is bulimic. ❑ *...a former bulimic.*

bulk /bʌlk/ (bulks, bulking, bulked) ◼ N-SING You can refer to something's **bulk** when you want to emphasize that it is very large. [WRITTEN, EMPHASIS] ❑ *The truck pulled out of the lot, its bulk unnerving against the dawn.* ◼ N-SING You can refer to a large person's body or to their weight or size as their **bulk**. ❑ *Bannol lowered his bulk carefully into the chair.* ◼ QUANT [QUANT of def-n] The **bulk** of something is most of it. ❑ *The bulk of the text is essentially a review of these original documents.* • PRON **Bulk** is also a pronoun. ❑ *They come from all over the world, though the bulk is from the Indian subcontinent.* ◼ PHRASE If you buy or sell something in **bulk**, you buy or sell it in large quantities. ❑ *Buying in bulk is more economical than shopping for small quantities.*
▶ **bulk up** PHRASAL VERB If someone **bulks up** or if they **bulk up** their body, they put on weight in the form of extra muscle. ❑ *They feel I need to bulk up, and to improve my upper body strength.* ❑ *My friend is obsessed with going to the gym and has really bulked up her arms.*

bulk|head /bʌlkhed/ (bulkheads) N-COUNT A **bulkhead** is a wall that divides the inside of a ship or airplane into separate sections. [TECHNICAL]

bulky /bʌlki/ (bulkier, bulkiest) ADJ Something that is **bulky** is large and heavy. Bulky things are often difficult to move or deal with. ❑ *...bulky items like lawn mowers.*

bull /bʊl/ (bulls) ◼ N-COUNT A **bull** is a male animal of the cow family. ◼ N-COUNT Some other male animals, including elephants and whales, are called **bulls**. ❑ *Suddenly a massive bull elephant with huge tusks charged us.* ◼ N-COUNT In the stock market, **bulls** are people who buy shares in expectation of a price rise, in order to make a profit by selling the shares again after a short time. Compare **bear**. [BUSINESS] ❑ *The bulls argue stock prices are low and there are bargains to be had.* ◼ N-COUNT In the Roman Catholic Church, a papal **bull** is an official statement on a particular subject that is issued by the Pope. ◼ N-UNCOUNT If you say that something is **bull** or a load of **bull**, you mean that it is complete nonsense or absolutely untrue. [INFORMAL] ❑ *I think it's a load of bull.*

bull bar (bull bars) N-COUNT [usu pl] On some motor vehicles, **bull bars** are metal bars fixed to the front that are designed to protect it if it crashes.

bull|dog /bʊldɒg/ (bulldogs) N-COUNT A **bulldog** is a small dog with a large square head and short hair.

bull|doze /bʊldoʊz/ (bulldozes, bulldozing, bulldozed) ◼ V-T If people **bulldoze** something such as a building, they knock it down using a bulldozer. ❑ *She defeated developers who wanted to bulldoze her home to build a supermarket.* ◼ V-T If people **bulldoze** earth, stone, or other heavy material, they move it using a bulldozer. ❑ *They have been cutting down the trees and bulldozing the land.* ◼ V-T If someone **bulldozes** a plan through or **bulldozes** another person into doing something, they get what they want in an unpleasantly forceful way. [DISAPPROVAL] ❑ *Dropping all pretense of reason, they began to bulldoze through the democratic reforms.* ❑ *...to sway public opinion and bulldoze them into adopting uneconomic practices.*

bull|doz|er /bʊldoʊzər/ (bulldozers) N-COUNT A **bulldozer** is a large vehicle with a broad metal blade at the front, which is used for knocking down buildings or moving large amounts of earth.

bul|let /bʊlɪt/ (bullets) ◼ N-COUNT A **bullet** is a small piece of metal with a pointed or rounded end, which is fired out of a gun. ❑ *Two of the police fired 16 bullets each.* ◼ PHRASE If someone **bites the bullet**, they accept that they have to do something unpleasant but necessary. [JOURNALISM] ❑ *Tour operators may be forced to bite the bullet and cut prices.*

bul|letin /bʊlɪtɪn/ (bulletins) ◼ N-COUNT A **bulletin** is a short news report on the radio or television. ❑ *...the early morning news bulletin.* ◼ N-COUNT A **bulletin** is a short official announcement made publicly to inform people about an important matter. ❑ *At 3:30 p.m. a bulletin was released announcing that the president was out of immediate danger.* ◼ N-COUNT A **bulletin** is a regular newspaper or leaflet that is produced by an organization or group such as a school or church.

bul|letin board (bulletin boards) ◼ N-COUNT A **bulletin board** is a board that is usually attached to a wall in order to display notices giving information about something. [mainly AM]

in BRIT, use **noticeboard**

◼ N-COUNT In computing, a **bulletin board** is a system that enables users to send and receive messages of general interest. ❑ *The Internet is the largest computer bulletin board in the world, and it's growing.*

bul|let point (bullet points) N-COUNT A **bullet point** is one of a series of important items for discussion or action in a document, usually marked by a square or round symbol. ❑ *Use bold type for headings and bullet points for noteworthy achievements.*

bullet|proof /bʊlɪtpruːf/ also bullet-proof ADJ Something that is **bulletproof** is made of a strong material that bullets cannot pass through. ❑ *...bulletproof glass.*

bull|fight /bʊlfaɪt/ (bullfights) N-COUNT A **bullfight** is a public entertainment in which people fight and kill bulls. Bullfights take place in Spain, Portugal, and Latin America.

bull|fighter /bʊlfaɪtər/ (bullfighters) N-COUNT A **bullfighter** is the person who tries to injure or kill the bull in a bullfight.

bull|fighting /bʊlfaɪtɪŋ/ N-UNCOUNT **Bullfighting** is the public entertainment in which people try to kill bulls in bullfights.

bull|finch /bʊlfɪntʃ/ (bullfinches) N-COUNT A **bullfinch** is a type of small European bird. The male has a black head and a pinkish-red breast.

bull|frog /bʊlfrɒg/ (bullfrogs) N-COUNT A **bullfrog** is a type of large frog which makes a very loud noise.

bull|horn /bʊlhɔːrn/ (bullhorns) N-COUNT A **bullhorn** is a device for making your voice sound louder in the open air. [AM] ❑ *A bullhorn blared warnings of a bomb scare.*

in BRIT, use **loudhailer**

bul|lion /bʊliən/ N-UNCOUNT **Bullion** is gold or silver, usually in the form of bars. ❑ *The ship was loaded with gold bullion.*

bull|ish /bʊlɪʃ/ ADJ In the stock market, if there is a **bullish** mood, prices are expected to rise. Compare **bearish**. [BUSINESS] ❑ *The market opened in a bullish mood.*

bull mar|ket (bull markets) **1** N-COUNT A **bull market** is a situation in the stock market when people are buying a lot of shares because they expect the shares will increase in value and they will be able to make a profit by selling them again after a short time. Compare **bear market**. [BUSINESS] ❑ *...the decline in prices after the bull market peaked in April 2000.* **2** → See feature box at **banking**

bull|ock /bʊlək/ (bullocks) N-COUNT A **bullock** is a young bull that has been castrated.

bull|pen /bʊlpɛn/ (bullpens) N-COUNT In baseball, a **bullpen** is an area alongside the playing field, where pitchers can practice or warm up. [AM] ❑ *Players from both dugouts and bullpens ran onto the field.*

bull|ring /bʊlrɪŋ/ (bullrings) N-COUNT A **bullring** is a circular area of ground surrounded by rows of seats where bullfights take place.

bull ses|sion (bull sessions) N-COUNT A **bull session** is an informal conversation among a small group of people. [AM, INFORMAL] ❑ *The production actually started as an after-work bull session at a Belgian bar.*

bull's-eye (bull's-eyes) **1** N-COUNT [usu the N in sing] The **bull's-eye** is the small circular area at the center of a target. ❑ *Five of his bullets had hit the bull's-eye.* **2** N-COUNT In shooting or the game of darts, a **bull's-eye** is a shot or throw of a dart that hits the bull's-eye. **3** N-COUNT If something that you do or say hits the **bull's eye**, it has exactly the effect that you intended it to have. [INFORMAL]

bull|shit /bʊlʃɪt/ (bullshits, bullshitting, bullshitted) **1** N-UNCOUNT If you say that something is **bullshit**, you are saying that it is nonsense or completely untrue. [INFORMAL, VULGAR, DISAPPROVAL] ❑ *All the rest I said, all that was bullshit.* **2** V-T/V-I If you say that someone is bullshitting you, you mean that what they are telling you is nonsense or completely untrue. [INFORMAL, VULGAR] ❑ *Don't bullshit me, Brian!* ❑ *He's basically bullshitting.*

bull ter|ri|er (bull terriers) **1** N-COUNT A **bull terrier** is a breed of strong dog with a short, whitish coat and a thick neck. **2** → see also **pit bull terrier**

bull|whip /bʊlwɪp/ (bullwhips) N-COUNT A **bullwhip** is a very long, heavy whip.

bul|ly /bʊli/ (bullies, bullying, bullied) **1** N-COUNT A **bully** is someone who often hurts or frightens other people. ❑ *I fell victim to the office bully.* **2** V-T If someone **bullies** you, they often do or say things to hurt or frighten you. ❑ *I wasn't going to let him bully me.* ● **bul|ly|ing** N-UNCOUNT ❑ *...schoolchildren who were victims of bullying.* **3** V-T If someone **bullies** you into something, they make you do it by using force or threats. ❑ *We think an attempt to bully them into submission would be counterproductive.* ❑ *She used to bully me into doing my schoolwork.*

bully pul|pit N-SING If someone in a prominent job or position publicly expresses their opinions about a particular subject, you can say that they are using their job or position as a **bully pulpit**. [AM] ❑ *He used the bully pulpit of the presidency very effectively.*

bul|wark /bʊlwərk/ (bulwarks) N-COUNT [oft N against/of n] A **bulwark** against something protects you against it. A **bulwark** of something protects it. ❑ *The abbeys were founded in the 12th century by King David as a bulwark against the English.*

bum /bʌm/ (bums, bumming, bummed) **1** N-COUNT A **bum** is a person who has no permanent home or job and who gets [AM, INFORMAL] ❑ *...the bums on the corner fighting over beers.* **2** N-COUNT If someone refers to another person as a **bum**, they think that person is worthless or irresponsible. [INFORMAL, DISAPPROVAL] ❑ *You're all a bunch of bums.* **3** ADJ [ADJ n] Some people use **bum** to describe a situation that they find unpleasant or annoying. [INFORMAL] ❑ *He knows you're getting a bum deal.* **4** V-T If you **bum** something off someone, you ask them for it and they give it to you. [INFORMAL] ❑ *Mind if I bum a cigarette?* **5** a bum rap → see **rap**

bum bag (bum bags) N-COUNT A **bum bag** consists of a small bag attached to a belt which you wear around your waist. You use it to carry things such as money and keys. [BRIT]

in AM, use **fanny pack**

bum|ble /bʌmbəl/ (bumbles, bumbling, bumbled)
▶ **bumble around**

in BRIT, also use **bumble about**

PHRASAL VERB When someone **bumbles around** or bumbles about, they behave in a confused, disorganized way, making mistakes and usually not achieving anything. ❑ *Most of us are novices on the computer – just bumbling around on them.*

bumble|bee /bʌmbəlbiː/ (bumblebees) also **bumble bee** N-COUNT A **bumblebee** is a large hairy bee.

bum|bling /bʌmblɪŋ/ ADJ [ADJ n] If you describe a person or their behavior as **bumbling**, you mean that they behave in a confused, disorganized way, making mistakes and usually not achieving anything. ❑ *...a clumsy, bumbling, inarticulate figure.*

bum|mer /bʌmər/ (bummers) N-COUNT [usu sing] If you say that something is a **bummer**, you mean that it is unpleasant or annoying. [INFORMAL] ❑ *I had a bummer of a day.* ❑ *What a bummer!*

bump /bʌmp/ (bumps, bumping, bumped) **1** V-T/V-I If you **bump** into something or someone, you accidentally hit them while you are moving. ❑ *They stopped walking and he almost bumped into them.* ❑ *She bumped her head against a low branch.* ● N-COUNT **Bump** is also a noun. ❑ *Small children often cry after a minor bump.* **2** N-COUNT A **bump** is the action or the dull sound of two heavy objects hitting each other. ❑ *I felt a little bump and I knew instantly what had happened.* **3** N-COUNT A **bump** is a minor injury or swelling that you get if you bump into something or if something hits you. ❑ *She fell against our coffee table and got a large bump on her forehead.* **4** N-COUNT A **bump** on a road is a raised, uneven part. ❑ *The truck hit a bump and bounced.* **5** V-I If a vehicle **bumps** over a surface, it travels in a rough, bouncing way because the surface is very uneven. ❑ *We left the road, and again bumped over the mountainside.*
▶ **bump into** PHRASAL VERB If you **bump into** someone you know, you meet them unexpectedly. [INFORMAL] ❑ *I happened to bump into Mervyn Johns in the hallway.*

bump|er /bʌmpər/ (bumpers) **1** N-COUNT **Bumpers** are bars at the front and back of a vehicle that protect it if it bumps into something. ❑ *What stickers do you have on the bumper or the back windshield?* **2** ADJ [ADJ n] A **bumper** crop or harvest is one that is larger than usual. ❑ *...a bumper crop of rice.* **3** ADJ [ADJ n] If you say that something is **bumper** size, you mean that it is very large. ❑ *...bumper profits.* **4** PHRASE If traffic is **bumper-to-bumper**, the vehicles are so close to one another that they are almost touching and are moving very slowly. ❑ *...bumper-to-bumper rush-hour traffic.*

bump|er car (bumper cars) N-COUNT A **bumper car** is a small electric car with a wide rubber bumper all around. People drive bumper cars around a special enclosure at an amusement park.

bump|er stick|er (bumper stickers) N-COUNT A **bumper sticker** is a small piece of paper or plastic with words or

bumpkin /bʌmpkɪn/ (bumpkins) N-COUNT If you refer to someone as a **bumpkin**, you think they are uneducated and stupid because they come from the countryside. [DISAPPROVAL] ❑ ...unsophisticated country bumpkins.

bumptious /bʌmpʃəs/ ADJ GRADED; ADJ If you say that someone is **bumptious**, you are criticizing them because they are very pleased with themselves and their opinions. [DISAPPROVAL] ❑ ...a bumptious bureaucrat.

bumpy /bʌmpi/ (bumpier, bumpiest) **1** ADJ A **bumpy** road or path has a lot of bumps on it. ❑ ...bumpy cobbled streets. **2** ADJ A **bumpy** ride is uncomfortable and rough, usually because you are traveling over an uneven surface. ❑ ...a hot and bumpy ride across the desert.

bun /bʌn/ (buns) **1** N-COUNT **Buns** are small bread rolls. They are sometimes sweet and may contain dried fruit or spices. ❑ ...a currant bun. **2** N-COUNT If someone has their hair in a **bun**, they have fastened it tightly on top of their head or at the back of their head in the shape of a ball. **3** N-PLURAL Your **buns** are your buttocks. [mainly AM, INFORMAL] ❑ I'd pinch his buns and kiss his neck.

bunch ✦✧ /bʌntʃ/ (bunches, bunching, bunched) **1** N-COUNT A **bunch** of people is a group of people who share one or more characteristics or who are doing something together. [INFORMAL] ❑ My neighbors are a bunch of busybodies. ❑ We were a pretty inexperienced bunch of people really. **2** N-COUNT A **bunch** of flowers is a number of flowers with their stalks held or tied together. ❑ He had left a huge bunch of flowers in her hotel room. **3** N-COUNT A **bunch** of bananas or grapes is a group of them growing on the same stem. ❑ Lili had fallen asleep clutching a fat bunch of grapes. **4** N-COUNT A **bunch** of keys is a set of keys kept together on a metal ring. ❑ George took out a bunch of keys and went to work on the complicated lock.
▶ **bunch up** also **bunch together** PHRASAL VERB If people or things **bunch up** or if you **bunch** them **up**, they move close to each other so that they form a small tight group. **Bunch together** means the same as bunch up. ❑ They were bunching up, almost stepping on each other's heels. ❑ People were bunched up at all the exits.

bundle /bʌndəl/ (bundles, bundling, bundled) **1** N-COUNT A **bundle** of things is a number of them that are tied together or wrapped in a cloth or bag so that they can be carried or stored. ❑ Lance pulled a bundle of papers out of a folder. ❑ He gathered the bundles of clothing into his arms. **2** N-SING If you describe someone as, for example, a **bundle** of fun, you are emphasizing that they are full of fun. If you describe someone as a **bundle** of nerves, you are emphasizing that they are very nervous. [EMPHASIS] ❑ I remember Mickey as a bundle of fun, great to have around. ❑ Life at high school wasn't a bundle of laughs. **3** V-T If someone **is bundled** somewhere, someone pushes them there in a rough and hurried way. ❑ He was bundled into a car and driven 50 miles to a police station. **4** V-T To **bundle** software means to sell it together with a computer, or with other hardware and software, as part of a set. [COMPUTING] ❑ It's cheaper to buy software bundled with a PC than separately.

bung /bʌŋ/ (bungs) N-COUNT A **bung** is a round piece of wood, cork, or rubber which you use to close the hole in a container such as a barrel or flask.

bungalow /bʌŋɡəloʊ/ (bungalows) **1** N-COUNT A **bungalow** is a house that has only one level, and no stairs. **2** → See also color supplement

━━━━ WORD HISTORY ━━━━
bungalow
Bungalow comes from Hindi banglā meaning 'of Bengal.' A bungalow was originally a house of the style generally occupied by Europeans in Bengal, a one-story house with a veranda around it and a thatched roof.

bungee jumping /bʌndʒi dʒʌmpɪŋ/ N-UNCOUNT If someone goes **bungee jumping**, they jump from a high place such as a bridge or cliff with a long piece of strong elastic cord tied around their ankle connecting them to the bridge or cliff.

bungle /bʌŋɡəl/ (bungles, bungling, bungled) V-T If you **bungle** something, you fail to do it properly, because you make mistakes or are clumsy. ❑ Two prisoners bungled an escape bid after running either side of a lamppost while handcuffed. • N-COUNT **Bungle** is also a noun. ❑ ...an appalling administrative bungle. • **bungling** ADJ ❑ ...a bungling burglar.

bungler /bʌŋɡlər/ (bunglers) N-COUNT A **bungler** is a person who often fails to do things properly because they make mistakes or are clumsy.

bunion /bʌnyən/ (bunions) N-COUNT A **bunion** is a large painful lump on the first joint of a person's big toe.

bunk /bʌŋk/ (bunks) N-COUNT A **bunk** is a narrow bed that is usually attached to a wall, especially in a ship. ❑ He left his bunk and went up on deck again.

bunk bed (bunk beds) **1** N-COUNT **Bunk beds** are two beds that are attached to each other, one above the other, in a frame. **2** → See also color supplement

bunker /bʌŋkər/ (bunkers) **1** N-COUNT A **bunker** is a place, usually underground, that has been built with strong walls to protect it against heavy gunfire and bombing. ❑ ...an extensive network of fortified underground bunkers. **2** N-COUNT A **bunker** is a container for coal or other fuel. **3** N-COUNT On a golf course, a **bunker** is a large area filled with sand that is deliberately put there as an obstacle that golfers must try to avoid. ❑ He put his second shot in a bunker to the left of the green.

bunkum /bʌŋkəm/ N-UNCOUNT If you say that something that has been said or written is **bunkum**, you mean that you think it is completely untrue or very stupid. [INFORMAL, OLD-FASHIONED, DISAPPROVAL]

bunny /bʌni/ (bunnies) N-COUNT A **bunny** or a **bunny rabbit** is a child's word for a rabbit. [INFORMAL]

bunt /bʌnt/ (bunts, bunting, bunted) **1** V-T/V-I In baseball, if you **bunt** or if you **bunt** the ball, you deliberately hit the ball softly, in order to gain an advantage. [AM] ❑ Davis estimated he had been called on to bunt once in six years. ❑ Rich Becker bunted a ball on the third-base side of the mound. **2** N-COUNT In baseball, a **bunt** is the act of bunting a ball or a hit made by bunting the ball. [AM] ❑ Then came a bunt from Russ Davis.

bunting /bʌntɪŋ/ N-UNCOUNT **Bunting** consists of rows of small colored flags that are used to decorate streets and buildings on special occasions. ❑ Red, white and blue bunting hung in the city's renovated train station.

buoy /bui/ (buoys, buoying, buoyed) **1** N-COUNT A **buoy** is a floating object that is used to show ships and boats where they can go and to warn them of danger. **2** V-T If someone in a difficult situation **is buoyed** by something, it makes them feel more cheerful and optimistic. ❑ In May they danced in the streets, buoyed by their victory. • PHRASAL VERB **Buoy up** means the same as buoy. ❑ They are buoyed up by a sense of hope.

buoyancy /bɔɪənsi/ **1** N-UNCOUNT **Buoyancy** is the ability that something has to float on a liquid or in the air. ❑ Air can be pumped into the diving suit to increase buoyancy. **2** N-UNCOUNT **Buoyancy** is a feeling of cheerfulness. ❑ ...a mood of buoyancy and optimism. **3** N-UNCOUNT There is economic **buoyancy** when the economy is growing. ❑ The likelihood is that the slump will be followed by a period of buoyancy.

buoyant /bɔɪənt/ **1** ADJ If you are in a **buoyant** mood, you feel cheerful and behave in a lively way. ❑ You will feel more buoyant and optimistic about the future than you have for a long time. **2** ADJ A **buoyant** economy is a successful one in which there is a lot of trade and economic activity. ❑ We have a buoyant economy and unemployment is considerably lower than the regional average. **3** ADJ A **buoyant** object floats on a liquid. ❑ While there is still sufficient trapped air within the container to keep it buoyant, it will float.

bur /bɜr/ (burs) → see burr

burble /bɜrbəl/ (burbles, burbling, burbled) **1** V-I If something **burbles**, it makes a low continuous bubbling sound. ❑ The water burbled over gravel. ❑ The river gurgled and burbled. **2** V-T/V-I If you say that someone **is burbling**, you mean that they are talking in a confused way. ❑ He burbled something incomprehensible. ❑ Key burbled about the wonderful people who contribute to tourism. ❑ He burbles on about freedom.

'burbs /bɜrbz/ also **burbs** N-PLURAL The **'burbs** are the same as the suburbs. [INFORMAL] ❑ ...a quiet kid from the 'burbs.

bur|den ♦◇◇ /bɜrdᵊn/ (burdens, burdening, burdened)
■ N-COUNT If you describe a problem or a responsibility as a **burden**, you mean that it causes someone a lot of difficulty, worry, or hard work. □ *The developing countries bear the burden of an enormous external debt.* □ *Her death will be an impossible burden on Paul.* ■ N-COUNT A **burden** is a heavy load that is difficult to carry. [FORMAL] □ *...African women carrying burdens on their heads.* ■ V-T If someone **burdens** you with something that is likely to worry you, for example, a problem or a difficult decision, they tell you about it. □ *We decided not to burden him with the news.*

COLLOCATIONS

burden
NOUN ■
noun + **burden**: debt, tax
adjective + **burden**: heavy, huge, intolerable, unsustainable; administrative, economic, financial
verb + **burden**: impose, increase, place; bear, carry, share, shoulder; ease, lift, reduce, shift

---

bur|dened /bɜrdᵊnd/ ■ ADJ [v-link ADJ with/by n] If you are **burdened** with something, it causes you a lot of worry or hard work. □ *Nicaragua was burdened with a foreign debt of $11 billion.* ■ ADJ [v-link ADJ with/by n] If you describe someone as **burdened** with a heavy load, you are emphasizing that it is very heavy and that they are holding it or carrying it with difficulty. [EMPHASIS] □ *Anna arrived burdened by bags and food baskets.*

bur|den|some /bɜrdᵊnsəm/ ADJ If you describe something as **burdensome**, you mean it is worrying or hard to deal with. [WRITTEN] □ *...a burdensome debt.* □ *The load was too burdensome.*

bu|reau /byʊəroʊ/ (bureaus) ■ N-COUNT; N-IN-NAMES A **bureau** is an office, organization, or government department that collects and distributes information. □ *...the Federal Bureau of Investigation.* ■ N-COUNT A **bureau** is an office of a company or organization that has its main office in another city or country. [mainly AM, BUSINESS] □ *...the Wall Street Journal's Washington bureau.* ■ N-COUNT A **bureau** is a chest of drawers. [AM] ■ N-COUNT A **bureau** is a writing desk with shelves and drawers and a lid that opens to form the writing surface. [BRIT]

bu|reau|cra|cy /byʊrɒkrəsi/ (bureaucracies) ■ N-COUNT A **bureaucracy** is an administrative system operated by a large number of officials. □ *State bureaucracies can tend to stifle enterprise and initiative.* ■ N-UNCOUNT **Bureaucracy** refers to all the rules and procedures followed by government departments and similar organizations, especially when you think that these are complicated and cause long delays. [DISAPPROVAL] □ *People usually complain about too much bureaucracy.*

bu|reau|crat /byʊərəkræt/ (bureaucrats) N-COUNT **Bureaucrats** are officials who work in a large administrative system. You can refer to officials as bureaucrats especially if you disapprove of them because they seem to follow rules and procedures too strictly. [DISAPPROVAL] □ *The economy is still controlled by bureaucrats.*

bu|reau|crat|ic /byʊərəkrætɪk/ ADJ **Bureaucratic** means involving complicated rules and procedures which can cause long delays. [DISAPPROVAL] □ *Bureaucratic delays are inevitable.*

bur|geon /bɜrdʒᵊn/ (burgeons, burgeoning, burgeoned) V-I If something **burgeons**, it grows or develops rapidly. [LITERARY] □ *Plants burgeon from every available space.* □ *My confidence began to burgeon later in life.*

burg|er /bɜrgər/ (burgers) N-COUNT A **burger** is a flat round mass of ground meat or minced vegetables that is fried and often eaten in a bread roll. □ *...burger and fries.*

burgh|er /bɜrgər/ (burghers) N-COUNT [usu pl] The **burghers** of a town or city are the people who live there, especially the richer or more respectable people. [OLD-FASHIONED]

bur|glar /bɜrglər/ (burglars) N-COUNT A **burglar** is a thief who enters a house or other building by force. □ *Burglars broke into their home.*

bur|glar alarm (burglar alarms) N-COUNT A **burglar alarm** is an electric device that makes a bell ring loudly if someone tries to enter a building by force.

bur|glar|ize /bɜrgləraɪz/ (burglarizes, burglarizing, burglarized) V-T [usu passive] If a building **is burglarized**, a thief enters it by force and steals things. [AM] □ *Her home was burglarized.*

in BRIT, use **burgle**

bur|gla|ry /bɜrgləri/ (burglaries) ■ N-VAR If someone commits a **burglary**, they enter a building by force and steal things. **Burglary** is the act of doing this. □ *An 11-year-old boy committed a burglary.* ■ → See feature box at **crime**

bur|gle /bɜrgᵊl/ (burgles, burgling, burgled) V-T If a building **is burgled**, a thief enters it by force and steals things. [BRIT] □ *I thought we had been burgled.*

in AM, use **burglarize**

bur|gun|dy /bɜrgəndi/ (burgundies) ■ COLOR **Burgundy** is used to describe things that are purplish-red in color. □ *He was wearing a burgundy polyester jacket.* □ *...burgundy-colored armchairs.* ■ N-MASS **Burgundy** is a type of wine. It can be white or red in color and comes from the region of France called Burgundy. □ *...a bottle of white burgundy.*

bur|ial /bɛriəl/ (burials) N-VAR A **burial** is the act or ceremony of putting a dead body into a grave in the ground. □ *The priest prepared the body for burial.*

bur|ial ground (burial grounds) N-COUNT A **burial ground** is a place where bodies are buried, especially an ancient place. □ *...an ancient burial ground.*

burka /bɜrkə/ (burkas) → see burqa

bur|lap /bɜrlæp/ N-UNCOUNT **Burlap** is a thick, rough fabric that is used for making sacks. [AM] □ *...a burlap sack.*

in BRIT, use **hessian**

bur|lesque /bɜrlɛsk/ (burlesques) N-VAR A **burlesque** is a performance or a piece of writing that makes fun of something by copying it in an exaggerated way. You can also use **burlesque** to refer to a situation in real life that is like this. □ *The book read like a black comic burlesque.* □ *...a trio of burlesque Moscow stereotypes.*

bur|ly /bɜrli/ (burlier, burliest) ADJ A **burly** man has a broad body and strong muscles. □ *He was a big, burly man.*

Bur|mese /bɜrmiːz/ (Burmese) ■ ADJ **Burmese** means belonging or relating to Burma, or to its people, language, or culture. Burma is now known as Myanmar. ■ N-COUNT A **Burmese** is a Burmese citizen or a person of Burmese origin. ■ N-UNCOUNT **Burmese** is the main language spoken by the people who live in Burma, now known as Myanmar.

burn ♦♦◇ /bɜrn/ (burns, burning, burned or burnt) ■ V-I If there is a fire or a flame somewhere, you say that there is a fire or flame **burning** there. □ *Fires were burning out of control in the center of the city.* ■ V-I If something **is burning**, it is on fire. □ *When I arrived one of the vehicles was still burning.* □ *The building housed 1,500 refugees and it burned for hours.* • **burn|ing** N-UNCOUNT □ *When we arrived in our village there was a terrible smell of burning.* ■ V-T If you **burn** something, you destroy or damage it with fire. □ *Protesters set cars on fire and burned a building.* □ *Incineration plants should be built to burn household waste.* • **burn|ing** N-UNCOUNT □ *The French government has criticized the burning of a U.S. flag outside the American embassy.* ■ V-T/V-I If you **burn** a fuel or if it **burns**, it is used to produce heat, light, or energy. □ *The power stations burn coal from the Ruhr region.* ■ V-T/V-I If you **burn** something that you are cooking or if it **burns**, you spoil it by using too much heat or cooking it for too long. □ *I burned the toast.* • **burnt** ADJ □ *...the smell of burnt toast.* ■ V-T If you **burn** part of your body, **burn** yourself, or **are burned** or **burnt**, you are injured by fire or by something very hot. □ *Take care not to burn your fingers.* • N-COUNT **Burn** is also a noun. □ *She suffered appalling burns to her back.* ■ V-T [usu passive] If someone **is burned** or **burned** to death, they are killed by fire. □ *Women were burned as witches in the Middle Ages.* ■ V-I If a light is **burning**, it is shining. [LITERARY] □ *The building was darkened except for a single light burning in a third-story window.* ■ V-T/V-I If you **burn** or get **burned** in the sun, the sun makes your skin become red and sore. □ *Build up your tan slowly and don't allow your skin to burn.* ⑩ V-T/V-I If a part of your body **burns** or if something **burns** it, it has a painful hot or stinging feeling. □ *My eyes burn from staring at the needle.* □ *His face was burning with cold.* ⑪ V-T To **burn** a CD means to write or copy data onto it. [COMPUTING] □ *You can use this software to burn custom compilations of your favorite tunes.* ⑫ → see also **burning** ⑬ **to burn something to the ground** → see **ground** ③ ⑭ **to burn the midnight oil** → see **midnight** ⑮ **to have money to burn** → see **money**

▶ **burn down** PHRASAL VERB If a building **burns down** or if someone **burns** it **down**, it is completely destroyed by fire. ◻ *Six months after Bud died, the house burned down.*

COLLOCATIONS

burn
VERB ❷
burn + *adverb*: brightly, fiercely
NOUN ❻
adjective + **burn**: horrific, serious, severe; minor
verb + **burn**: suffer

---

burned-out also **burnt-out** ❶ ADJ **Burned-out** vehicles or buildings have been so badly damaged by fire that they can no longer be used. ◻ *...a burned-out car.* ❷ ADJ If someone is **burned-out**, they exhaust themselves at an early stage in their life or career because they have achieved too much too quickly. [INFORMAL] ◻ *Everyone I know who kept it up at that intensity is burned-out.*

burn|er /bɜrnər/ (burners) N-COUNT A **burner** is a device which produces heat or a flame, especially as part of a stove or heater. ◻ *He put the frying pan on the gas burner.*

burn|ing /bɜrnɪŋ/ ❶ ADJ You use **burning** to describe something that is extremely hot. ◻ *...the burning desert of central Asia.* • ADV [ADV adj] **Burning** is also an adverb. ◻ *He touched the boy's forehead. It was burning hot.* ❷ ADJ [ADJ n] If you have a **burning** interest in something or a **burning** desire to do something, you are extremely interested in it or want to do it very much. ◻ *I had a burning ambition to become a journalist.* ❸ ADJ [ADJ n] A **burning** issue or question is a very important or urgent one that people feel very strongly about. ◻ *The burning question in this year's debate over the federal budget is: whose taxes should be raised?* ❹ → See feature box at **challenge**

bur|nish /bɜrnɪʃ/ (burnishes, burnishing, burnished) V-T To **burnish** the image of someone or something means to improve their image. [WRITTEN] ◻ *The agency hired a New York public-relations firm to burnish Washington's image.*

bur|nished /bɜrnɪʃt/ ADJ [usu ADJ n] You can describe something as **burnished** when it is bright or smooth. [LITERARY] ◻ *The clouds glowed like burnished gold.*

burn|out /bɜrnaʊt/ also **burn-out** N-UNCOUNT If someone suffers **burnout**, they exhaust themselves at an early stage in their life or career because they have achieved too much too quickly. [INFORMAL]

burnt /bɜrnt/ **Burnt** is a past tense and past participle of **burn**.

burnt-out → see **burned-out**

burp /bɜrp/ (burps, burping, burped) V-I When someone **burps**, they make a noise because air from their stomach has been forced up through their throat. ◻ *Charlie burped loudly.* • N-COUNT **Burp** is also a noun. ◻ *There followed a barely audible burp.*

burqa /bɜrkə/ (burqas) also **burka** N-COUNT A **burqa** is a long garment that covers the whole head and body, including the face, and is worn in public by some women in Islamic countries.

burr /bɜr/ (burrs) also **bur** N-COUNT A **burr** is the part of some plants that contains seeds and that has little hooks on the outside so that it sticks to clothes or fur.

bur|ri|to /bərit̮oʊ/ (burritos) N-COUNT A **burrito** is a tortilla containing a filling of ground beef, chicken, cheese, or beans. [mainly AM]

bur|row /bɜroʊ/ (burrows, burrowing, burrowed) ❶ N-COUNT A **burrow** is a tunnel or hole in the ground that is dug by an animal such as a rabbit. ◻ *Normally timid, they rarely stray far from their burrows.* ❷ V-I If an animal **burrows** into the ground or into a surface, it moves through it by making a tunnel or hole. ◻ *The larvae burrow into cracks in the floor.* ❸ V-I If you **burrow** in a container or pile of things, you search there for something using your hands. ◻ *...the enthusiasm with which he burrowed through old records in search of facts.* ❹ V-I If you **burrow** into something, you move underneath it or press against it, usually in order to feel warmer or safer. ◻ *She turned her face away from him, burrowing into her heap of covers.*

bur|sar /bɜrsər/ (bursars) N-COUNT The **bursar** of a school or college is the person who is in charge of its finances or general administration.

burst ♦◇◇ /bɜrst/ (bursts, bursting)

The form **burst** is used in the present tense and is the past tense and past participle.

❶ V-T/V-I If something **bursts** or if you **burst** it, it suddenly breaks open or splits open and the air or other substance inside it comes out. ◻ *The driver lost control when a tire burst.* ◻ *It is not a good idea to burst a blister.* ❷ V-T/V-I If a dam **bursts**, or if something **bursts** it, it breaks apart because the force of the river is too great. ◻ *A dam burst and flooded their villages.* ❸ V-T If a river **bursts** its banks, the water rises and goes on to the land. ◻ *Monsoons caused the river to burst its banks.* ❹ V-I When a door or lid **bursts** open, it opens very suddenly and violently because someone pushes it or there is great pressure behind it. ◻ *The door burst open and an angry young nurse appeared.* ❺ V-I To **burst** into or out of a place means to enter or leave it suddenly with a lot of energy or force. ◻ *Gunmen burst into his home and opened fire.* ❻ V-I If you say that something **bursts** onto the scene, you mean that it suddenly starts or becomes active, usually after developing quietly for some time. [JOURNALISM] ◻ *He burst onto the fashion scene in the early 1980s.* ❼ N-COUNT A **burst** of something is a sudden short period of it. ◻ *...a burst of machine-gun fire.* ❽ → See feature box at **disaster**
▶ **burst into** ❶ PHRASAL VERB If you **burst into** tears, laughter, or song, you suddenly begin to cry, laugh, or sing. ◻ *She burst into tears and ran from the kitchen.* ❷ PHRASAL VERB If you say that something **bursts into** a particular situation or state, you mean that it suddenly changes into that situation or state. ◻ *This weekend's fighting is threatening to burst into full-scale war.*
❸ **to burst into flames** → see **flame**
▶ **burst out** PHRASAL VERB If someone **bursts out** laughing, crying, or making another noise, they suddenly start making that noise. You can also say that a noise **bursts out**. ◻ *The class burst out laughing.* ◻ *Then the applause burst out.*

burst|ing /bɜrstɪŋ/ ❶ ADJ [v-link ADJ] If a place is **bursting** with people or things, it is full of them. ◻ *The place appears to be bursting with women directors.* ❷ ADJ [v-link ADJ with n] If you say that someone is **bursting with** a feeling or quality, you mean that they have a great deal of it. ◻ *I was bursting with curiosity.* ❸ → see also **burst**

bury ♦◇◇ /bɛri/ (buries, burying, buried) ❶ V-T To **bury** something means to put it into a hole in the ground and cover it up with earth. ◻ *They make the charcoal by burying wood in the ground and then slowly burning it.* ◻ *...squirrels who bury nuts and seeds.* ❷ V-T To **bury** a dead person means to put their body into a grave and cover it with earth. ◻ *They buried the dead in a communal grave.* ◻ *I was horrified that people would think I was dead and bury me alive.* ❸ V-T If someone says they **have buried** one of their relatives, they mean that one of their relatives has died. ◻ *He had buried his wife some two years before he retired.* ❹ V-T If you **bury** something under a large quantity of things, you put it there, often in order to hide it. ◻ *She buried it under some leaves.* ❺ V-T If something **buries** a place or person, it falls on top of them so that it completely covers them and often harms them in some way. ◻ *Latest reports say that mud slides buried entire villages.* ◻ *Their house was buried by a landslide.* ❻ V-T If you **bury** your head or face in something, you press your head or face against it, often because you are unhappy. ◻ *She buried her face in the pillows.* ❼ V-T If something **buries** itself somewhere, or if you **bury** it there, it is pushed very deeply in there. ◻ *The missile buried itself deep in the grassy hillside.* ❽ **to bury the hatchet** → see **hatchet**

bus ♦◇◇ /bʌs/ (buses, busing, bused)

The spellings **busses**, **bussing**, **bussed** are also used for the verb.

❶ N-COUNT [also by N] A **bus** is a large motor vehicle that carries passengers from one place to another. Buses drive along particular routes, and you usually have to pay to travel in them. ◻ *He missed his last bus home.* ❷ V-T/V-I When someone is **bused** to a particular place or when they **bus** there, they travel there on a bus. ◻ *On May Day hundreds of thousands used to be bused in to parade through East Berlin.* ◻ *To get our Colombian visas we bused back to Medellín.* ❸ V-T To **bus** tables means to clear away dirty dishes and reset the tables. [AM] ◻ *As a fund-raiser, police officers will don aprons, take orders and bus tables today.*

bus boy (**bus boys**) N-COUNT A **bus boy** is a man or boy whose job is to set or clear tables in a restaurant. [AM]

bush /bʊʃ/ (bushes) **1** N-COUNT A **bush** is a large plant which is smaller than a tree and has a lot of branches. ☐ *Trees and bushes grew down to the water's edge.* **2** N-SING The wild, uncultivated parts of some hot countries are referred to as the **bush**. ☐ *They walked through the dense Mozambican bush for thirty-six hours.*

bushed /bʊʃt/ ADJ [v-link ADJ] If you say that you are **bushed**, you mean that you are extremely tired. [INFORMAL] ☐ *I'm bushed. I'm going to bed.*

bush|el /bʊʃəl/ (bushels) N-COUNT A **bushel** is a unit of volume that is used for measuring agricultural produce such as corn or beans. A bushel is equivalent in volume to eight gallons (35.2 liters).

bush league (bush leagues) N-COUNT [oft N n] In baseball, a **bush league** is the same as a **minor league**. [AM, INFORMAL] ☐ *...a catcher for a bush league baseball team in Tennessee.*

Bush|man /bʊʃmæn/ (Bushmen) N-COUNT A **Bushman** is an aboriginal person from the southwestern part of Africa, especially the Kalahari desert region.

bushy /bʊʃi/ (bushier, bushiest) **1** ADJ **Bushy** hair or fur is very thick. ☐ *...bushy eyebrows.* **2** ADJ A **bushy** plant has a lot of leaves very close together. ☐ *...strong, sturdy, bushy plants.*

busi|ly /bɪzɪli/ ADV [ADV with v] If you do something **busily**, you do it in a very active way. ☐ *The sales clerks were busily trying to keep up with the demand.*

busi|ness ♦♦♦ /bɪznɪs/ (businesses) **1** N-UNCOUNT **Business** is work relating to the production, buying, and selling of goods or services. ☐ *Jennifer has an impressive academic and business background.* ☐ *...Harvard Business School.* **2** N-UNCOUNT **Business** is used when talking about how many products or services a company is able to sell. If **business** is good, a lot of products or services are being sold and if **business** is bad, few of them are being sold. ☐ *They worried that German companies would lose business.* **3** N-COUNT A **business** is an organization that produces and sells goods or that provides a service. ☐ *The company was a family business.* ☐ *The majority of small businesses fail within the first twenty-four months.* **4** N-UNCOUNT **Business** is work or some other activity that you do as part of your job and not for pleasure. ☐ *I'm here on business.* ☐ *You can't mix business with pleasure.* **5** N-SING You can use **business** to refer to a particular area of work or activity in which the aim is to make a profit. ☐ *May I ask you what business you're in?* **6** N-SING You can use **business** to refer to something that you are doing or concerning yourself with. ☐ *...recording Ben as he goes about his business.* **7** N-UNCOUNT You can use **business** to refer to important matters that you have to deal with. ☐ *The most important business was left to the last.* **8** N-UNCOUNT [poss N] If you say that something is your **business**, you mean that it concerns you personally and that other people have no right to ask questions about it or disagree with it. ☐ *My sex life is my business.* ☐ *If she doesn't want the police involved, that's her business.* **9** N-SING You can use **business** to refer in a general way to an event, situation, or activity. For example, you can say something is 'a wretched business' or you can refer to 'this assassination business.' ☐ *We have sorted out this wretched business at last.* **10** → see also **big business**, **show business** **11** PHRASE If two people or companies **do business** with each other, one sells goods or services to the other. ☐ *I was fascinated by the different people who did business with me.* **12** PHRASE If you say that someone **has no business** to be in a place or to do something, you mean that they have no right to be there or to do it. ☐ *Really I had no business to be there at all.* **13** PHRASE A company that is **in business** is operating and trading. ☐ *You can't stay in business without cash.* **14** PHRASE If a store or company goes **out of business** or is put **out of business**, it has to stop trading because it is not making enough money. ☐ *Thousands of firms could go out of business.* **15** PHRASE In a difficult situation, if you say it is **business as usual**, you mean that people will continue doing what they normally do. ☐ *For the time being it's business as usual for consumers.*

USAGE

business
When you use **business** in the sense of making, buying, and selling goods or services, don't say 'a business.' Don't say, for example, 'We've got a business to do.' Say 'We've got **some business** to do.' *Are you in San Francisco for business or pleasure?*

VOCABULARY IN CONTEXT

Running a business

A successful business owes more to the strength of its business plan than its great product – though many potential **entrepreneurs** think spotting a **niche in the market** is enough to ensure limitless **profits**. As 90% of **startups** fail, half of them in the first five years and the remainder mostly **going belly up** within ten years, **balancing the books** often has as much to do with success as does testing the **market** to see if anyone will pay for your product. You might be lucky and secure **funding** early on from **venture capitalists**, but they will want to take **equity** in your company in return for their **investment**. Securing investment is not the same as successfully running the business. Your company **turnover** might be in the millions, but if your **profit margins** are really tight because **overhead** eats up **revenue**, you'll soon be **CEO** of a failed business.

COLLOCATIONS

business
NOUN
2
business + be + adjective: booming, brisk, good; slow
verb + **business**: lose
3
noun + **business**: family; investment
adjective + **business**: local, small; profitable, successful
verb + **business**: expand, run, set up, start; buy, sell; value
5
noun + **business**: entertainment, music
7
adjective + **business**: important, unfinished

---

busi|ness card (business cards) N-COUNT A person's **business card** or their **card** is a small card that they give to other people, and that has their name and details of their job and company printed on it. ☐ *When we met, he gave me his business card.*

busi|ness class ADJ [ADJ n] **Business class** seating on an airplane costs less than first class but more than economy class. ☐ *You can pay to be upgraded to a business class seat.* • ADV [ADV after v] **Business class** is also an adverb. ☐ *They flew business class.* • N-UNCOUNT **Business class** is the business class seating on an airplane. ☐ *The Australian team will be seated in business class.*

busi|ness end N-SING [usu N of n] The **business end** of a tool or weapon is the end of it that does the work or causes damage rather than the end that you hold. [INFORMAL] ☐ *...the business end of a vacuum cleaner.*

busi|ness hours N-PLURAL **Business hours** are the hours of the day in which a store or a company is open for business. ☐ *All showrooms are staffed during business hours.*

business|like /bɪznɪslaɪk/ ADJ If you describe someone as **businesslike**, you mean that they deal with things in an efficient way without wasting time. ▫ *Mr. Penn sounds quite businesslike.*

business|man ✦✧✧ /bɪznɪsmæn/ (**businessmen**) N-COUNT A **businessman** is a man who works in business. ▫ *...a wealthy businessman who owns a printing business in Orlando.*

business|person /bɪznɪspɜrs³n/ (**businesspeople**) also **business person** N-COUNT **Businesspeople** are people who work in business. ▫ *...businesspeople who serve or supply the security forces.*

busi|ness plan (**business plans**) N-COUNT A **business plan** is a detailed plan for setting up or developing a business, especially one that is written in order to borrow money. ▫ *She learned how to write a business plan for the catering business she wanted to launch.*

busi|ness school (**business schools**) N-COUNT A **business school** is a school or college which teaches business subjects such as economics and management.

business|woman /bɪznɪswʊmən/ (**businesswomen**) N-COUNT A **businesswoman** is a woman who works in business. ▫ *...a successful businesswoman who runs her own international cosmetics company.*

bus lane (**bus lanes**) N-COUNT A **bus lane** is a part of the road which is intended to be used only by buses.

bus|load /bʌsloʊd/ (**busloads**) N-COUNT [usu N *of* n] A **busload** of people is a large number of passengers on a bus. ▫ *...a busload of Japanese tourists.*

bus|man's holi|day /bʌsmənz hɒlɪdeɪ/ N-SING If you have a vacation, but spend it doing something similar to your usual work, you can refer to it as a **busman's holiday**.

buss /bʌs/ (**busses, bussing, bussed**) **1** N-COUNT A **buss** is a kiss. [AM] ▫ *Leaning down, he gave her a brotherly buss.* **2** V-T If you **buss** someone, you kiss them. [AM] ▫ *He bussed her on the cheek.*

bus shel|ter (**bus shelters**) N-COUNT A **bus shelter** is a bus stop that has a roof and at least one open side.

bus stop (**bus stops**) N-COUNT A **bus stop** is a place on a road where buses stop to let passengers on and off.

bust /bʌst/ (**busts, busting, busted**)

The form **bust** is used as the present tense of the verb, and can also be used as the past tense and past participle.

1 V-T If you **bust** something, you break it or damage it so badly that it cannot be used. [INFORMAL] ▫ *They will have to bust the door to get him out.* **2** V-T [usu passive] If someone **is busted**, the police arrest them. [INFORMAL] ▫ *They were busted for possession of cannabis.* **3** V-T If police **bust** a place, they go in it in order to arrest people who are doing something illegal. [INFORMAL] ▫ *Police busted an underground network of illegal sports gambling.* • N-COUNT **Bust** is also a noun. ▫ *Six tons of cocaine were seized last week in Panama's biggest drug bust.* **4** ADJ A company or fund that is **bust** has no money left and has been forced to close down. [INFORMAL] ▫ *It is taxpayers who will pay most of the bill for bailing out bust banks.* **5** PHRASE If a company **goes bust**, it loses so much money that it is forced to close down. [INFORMAL] ▫ *...a Swiss company which went bust last May.* **6** N-COUNT A **bust** is a statue of the head and shoulders of a person. ▫ *...a bronze bust of Thomas Jefferson.* **7** N-COUNT You can use **bust** to refer to a woman's breasts, especially when you are describing their size. ▫ *Good posture helps your bust look bigger.*

-buster /-bʌstər/ (**-busters**) **1** COMB IN N-COUNT **-buster** combines with nouns to form new nouns that refer to someone who breaks a particular law. ▫ *The Security Council will consider taking future actions against sanction-busters.* ▫ *...copyright-busters.* **2** COMB IN N-COUNT **-buster** combines with nouns to form new nouns that refer to someone or something that fights or overcomes the specified crime or undesirable activity. ▫ *Hoover was building his reputation as a crime-buster.* ▫ *...fraud-busters.*

bust|ier /bʌstiər/ (**bustiers**) N-COUNT A **bustier** is a type of close-fitting strapless top worn by women.

bus|tle /bʌs³l/ (**bustles, bustling, bustled**) **1** V-I If someone **bustles** somewhere, they move there in a hurried way, often because they are very busy. ▫ *My mother bustled around the kitchen.* **2** V-I A place that **is bustling** or **bustling** with people or activity is full of people who are very busy or lively. ▫ *The sidewalks are bustling with people.* **3** N-UNCOUNT **Bustle** is busy, noisy activity. ▫ *...the hustle and bustle of modern life.*

busty /bʌsti/ (**bustier, bustiest**) ADJ If you describe a woman as **busty**, you mean that she has large breasts. [INFORMAL]

busy ✦✦✧ /bɪzi/ (**busier, busiest, busies, busying, busied**) **1** ADJ When you are **busy**, you are working hard or concentrating on a task, so that you are not free to do anything else. ▫ *What is it? I'm busy.* ▫ *They are busy preparing for a hectic day's activity on Saturday.* **2** ADJ A **busy** time is a period of time during which you have a lot of things to do. ▫ *It'll have to wait. This is our busiest time.* ▫ *Even with her busy schedule she finds time to watch TV.* **3** ADJ [v-link ADJ] If you say that someone is **busy** thinking or worrying about something, you mean that it is taking all their attention, often to such an extent that they are unable to think about anything else. ▫ *Companies are so busy analyzing the financial implications that they overlook the effect on workers.* **4** V-T If you **busy** yourself with something, you occupy yourself by dealing with it. ▫ *He busied himself with the camera.* ▫ *She busied herself getting towels ready.* **5** ADJ A **busy** place is full of people who are doing things or moving around. ▫ *...a busy commercial street.* **6** ADJ When a telephone line is **busy**, you cannot make your call because the line is already being used by someone else. [mainly AM] ▫ *I tried to reach him, but the line was busy.*

in BRIT, usually use **engaged**

7 → see also **busily** **8** → See feature box at **telephone**

busy|body /bɪzibɒdi, -bʌdi/ (**busybodies**) N-COUNT If you refer to someone as a **busybody**, you are criticizing the way they interfere in other people's affairs. [INFORMAL, DISAPPROVAL] ▫ *This government is full of interfering busybodies.*

busy sig|nal (**busy signals**) N-COUNT If you try to make a telephone call and get a **busy signal**, it means that you cannot make the call because the line is already being used by someone else. [AM] ▫ *I tried the number again, got a busy signal.*

in BRIT, use **engaged tone**

busy|work /bɪziwɜrk/ N-UNCOUNT **Busywork** is work that is intended to keep someone occupied and is not completely necessary. [AM] ▫ *...meaningless busywork.*

but ✦✦✦ /bət, STRONG bʌt/ **1** CONJ You use **but** to introduce something that contrasts with what you have just said, or to introduce something that adds to what you have just said. ▫ *"You said you'd stay till tomorrow."—"I know, Bel, but I think I would rather go back."* ▫ *Place the saucepan over moderate heat until the cider is very hot but not boiling.* **2** CONJ You use **but** when you are about to add something further in a discussion or to change the subject. ▫ *After three weeks, they gradually reduced their sleep to about eight hours. But another interesting thing happened.* **3** CONJ You use **but** after you have made an excuse or apologized for what you are just about to say. ▫ *Please excuse me, but there is something I must say.* ▫ *I'm sorry, but it's nothing to do with you.* **4** CONJ You use **but** to introduce a reply to someone when you want to indicate surprise, disbelief, refusal, or protest. [FEELINGS] ▫ *"I don't think I should stay in this house."—"But why?"* **5** PREP [n PREP n] **But** is used to mean 'except.' ▫ *Europe will be represented in all but two of the seven races.* ▫ *He didn't speak anything but Greek.* **6** ADV **But** is used to mean 'only.' [FORMAL] ▫ *Zach insists that he is but one among many who are fighting for equality.* **7** PHRASE You use **but for** to introduce the only factor that causes a particular thing not to happen or not to be completely true. ▫ *...the small square below, empty but for a dirty white van and a clump of palm trees.* **8** PHRASE You use **but then** or **but then again** before a remark which slightly contradicts what you have just said. ▫ *My husband spends hours in the bathroom, but then again so do I.* **9** PHRASE You use **but then** before a remark which suggests that what you have just said should not be regarded as surprising. ▫ *He was a fine young man, but then so had his father been.* **10 all but** → see **all** ①
11 anything but → see **anything**

bu|tane /byuteɪn, byuteɪn/ N-UNCOUNT **Butane** is a gas that is obtained from petroleum and is used as a fuel.

butch /bʊtʃ/ **1** ADJ If you describe a woman as **butch**, you mean that she behaves or dresses in a masculine way. This use could cause offense. [INFORMAL] **2** ADJ If you describe a man as **butch**, you mean that he behaves in an extremely masculine way. [INFORMAL]

butch|er /bʊtʃər/ (butchers, butchering, butchered)
1 N-COUNT A **butcher** is a storekeeper who cuts up and sells meat. Some butchers also kill animals for meat and make foods such as sausages and meat pies. **2** N-COUNT A **butcher** or a **butcher's** is a store where meat is sold. [mainly BRIT] ❑ *He worked in a butcher's.*

in AM, usually use **butcher shop**

3 V-T To **butcher** an animal means to kill it and cut it up for meat. ❑ *Pigs were butchered, hams were hung to dry from the ceiling.* **4** V-T You can say that someone **has butchered** people when they have killed a lot of people in a very cruel way, and you want to express your horror and disgust. [DISAPPROVAL] ❑ *...rebels who butchered a group of soldiers.*

butch|ery /bʊtʃəri/ **1** N-UNCOUNT You can refer to the cruel killing of a lot of people as **butchery** when you want to express your horror and disgust at this. [DISAPPROVAL] ❑ *In her view, war is simply a legalized form of butchery.* **2** N-UNCOUNT **Butchery** is the work of cutting up meat and preparing it for sale. ❑ *...a carcass hung up for butchery.*

but|ler /bʌtlər/ (butlers) N-COUNT A **butler** is the most important male servant in a wealthy house. ❑ *I called for the butler to clear up the broken crockery.*

butt /bʌt/ (butts, butting, butted) **1** N-COUNT Someone's **butt** is their bottom. [AM, INFORMAL] ❑ *Frieda grinned, pinching him on the butt.* **2** N-COUNT The **butt** or the **butt end** of a weapon or tool is the thick end of its handle. ❑ *Troops used tear gas and rifle butts to break up the protests.* **3** N-COUNT The **butt** of a cigarette or cigar is the small part of it that is left when someone has finished smoking it. ❑ *He dropped his cigarette butt into the street below.* **4** N-COUNT A **butt** is a large barrel used for collecting or storing liquid. ❑ *Make sure your water butt has a top to exclude sunlight.* **5** N-SING If someone or something is the **butt** of jokes or criticism, people often make fun of them or criticize them. ❑ *He is still the butt of cruel jokes about his humble origins.* **6** V-T If a person or animal **butts** you, they hit you with the top of their head. ❑ *Lawrence kept on butting me but the referee did not warn him.*
▶ **butt in 1** PHRASAL VERB If you say that someone **is butting in**, you are criticizing the fact that they are joining in a conversation or activity without being asked to. [DISAPPROVAL] ❑ *Sorry, I don't mean to butt in.* **2** → See feature box at **debate**

but|ter ◆◇◇ /bʌtər/ (butters, buttering, buttered) **1** N-MASS **Butter** is a soft yellow substance made from cream. You spread it on bread or use it in cooking. ❑ *...bread and butter.* **2** V-T If you **butter** something such as bread or toast, you spread butter on it. ❑ *She spread pieces of bread on the counter and began buttering them.*

but|ter bean (butter beans) N-COUNT [usu pl] **Butter beans** are the yellowish flat round seeds of a kind of bean plant. They are eaten as a vegetable, and are usually sold dried rather than fresh.

butter|cup /bʌtərkʌp/ (buttercups) N-COUNT A **buttercup** is a small plant with bright yellow flowers.

butter|fly /bʌtərflaɪ/ (butterflies) N-COUNT A **butterfly** is an insect with large colorful wings and a thin body. ❑ *Butterflies and moths are attracted to the wild flowers.*

butter|milk /bʌtərmɪlk/ N-UNCOUNT **Buttermilk** is the liquid that remains when fat has been removed from cream when butter is being made. You can drink buttermilk or use it in cooking.

butter|scotch /bʌtərskɒtʃ/ **1** N-UNCOUNT **Butterscotch** is a type of hard yellowish-brown candy made from butter and sugar boiled together. **2** N-UNCOUNT [usu n n] A **butterscotch** flavored or colored thing has the flavor or color of butterscotch. ❑ *...butterscotch sauce.*

but|tery /bʌtəri/ ADJ [usu ADJ n] **Buttery** food contains butter or is covered with butter. ❑ *...buttery new potatoes.* ❑ *...the buttery taste of the pastry*

but|tock /bʌtək/ (buttocks) N-COUNT Your **buttocks** are the two rounded fleshy parts of your body that you sit on. ❑ *There were marks on his buttocks I hadn't seen before.*

but|ton ◆◇◇ /bʌtən/ (buttons, buttoning, buttoned)
1 N-COUNT **Buttons** are small hard objects sewn onto shirts, coats, or other pieces of clothing. You fasten the clothing by pushing the buttons through holes called buttonholes. ❑ *...a coat with brass buttons.* **2** V-T If you **button** a shirt, coat, or other piece of clothing, you fasten it by pushing its buttons through the buttonholes. ❑ *Ferguson stood up and buttoned his coat.* • PHRASAL VERB **Button up** means the same as **button**. ❑ *I buttoned up my coat; it was chilly.* ❑ *The young man slipped on the shirt and buttoned it up.* **3** N-COUNT A **button** is a small object on a machine or electrical device that you press in order to operate it. ❑ *He reached for the remote control and pressed the "play" button.* **4** N-COUNT A **button** is a small piece of metal or plastic that you wear in order to show that you support a particular movement, organization, or person. You fasten a button to your clothes with a pin. [AM] ❑ *Wear a campaign button to show support for mothers in prison.*

in BRIT, use **badge**

▶ **button up** → see **button 2**
button-down ADJ [ADJ n] A **button-down** shirt or a shirt with a **button-down** collar has a button under each end of the collar that you can fasten.

but|toned up also **buttoned-up** ADJ If you say that someone is **buttoned up**, you mean that they do not usually talk about their thoughts and feelings. [INFORMAL] ❑ *...the buttoned-up wife of an English clergyman.*

button|hole /bʌtənhoʊl/ (buttonholes) N-COUNT A **buttonhole** is a hole that you push a button through in order to fasten a shirt, coat, or other piece of clothing.

but|ton mush|room (button mushrooms) N-COUNT [usu pl] **Button mushrooms** are small mushrooms used in cooking.

but|tress /bʌtrɪs/ (buttresses) **1** N-COUNT **Buttresses** are supports, usually made of stone or brick, that support a wall. ❑ *...the neo-Gothic buttresses of Riverside Church in Manhattan.* **2** → See also color supplement

bux|om /bʌksəm/ ADJ [usu ADJ n] If you describe a woman as **buxom**, you mean that she has a rounded body and big breasts. ❑ *The buxom Frau Bauer was visibly pleased to see her.*

buy ◆◆◆ /baɪ/ (buys, buying, bought) **1** V-T If you **buy** something, you obtain it by paying money for it. ❑ *He could not afford to buy a house.* ❑ *Lizzie bought herself a mountain bike.* **2** V-T If you talk about the quantity or standard of goods an amount of money **buys**, you are referring to the price of the goods or the value of the money. ❑ *About $70,000 buys a habitable house.* **3** V-T If you **buy** something like time, freedom, or victory, you obtain it but only by offering or giving up something in return. ❑ *It was a risky operation, but might buy more time.* **4** V-T [usu passive] If you say that a person can **be bought**, you are criticizing the fact that they will give their help or loyalty to someone in return for money. [DISAPPROVAL] ❑ *Any number of our military and government officials can be bought.* **5** V-T If you **buy** an idea or a theory, you believe and accept it. [INFORMAL] ❑ *I'm not buying any of that nonsense.* • PHRASAL VERB **Buy into** means the same as **buy**. ❑ *I bought into the popular myth that when I got the new car or the next house, I'd finally be happy.* **6** N-COUNT If something is a good **buy**, it is of good quality and not very expensive. ❑ *This was still a good buy even at the higher price.*
▶ **buy into 1** PHRASAL VERB If you **buy into** a company or an organization, you buy part of it, often in order to gain some control of it. [BUSINESS] ❑ *Other companies could buy into the firm.* **2** → see also **buy 5**
▶ **buy out 1** PHRASAL VERB If you **buy** someone **out**, you buy their share of something such as a company or piece of property that you previously owned together. [BUSINESS] ❑ *The bank had to pay to buy out most of the 200 former partners.* **2** → see also **buyout**
▶ **buy up** PHRASAL VERB If you **buy up** land, property, or a commodity, you buy large amounts of it, or all that is available. ❑ *The mention of price increases sent citizens out to buy up as much as they could.*

buy-back (buy-backs) N-COUNT A **buy-back** is a situation in which a company buys shares back from its investors. [BUSINESS] ❑ *...a share buy-back plan.*

buy|er ◆◆◇ /baɪər/ (buyers) **1** N-COUNT A **buyer** is a person who is buying something or who intends to buy it. ❑ *Car buyers are more interested in safety and reliability than speed.* **2** N-COUNT A

buyer is a person who works for a large store deciding what goods will be bought from manufacturers to be sold in the store. ❑ *Diana is a buyer for a chain of furniture stores.*

buy|er's mar|ket N-SING When there is a **buyer's market** for a particular product, there are more of the products for sale than there are people who want to buy them, so buyers have a lot of choice and can make prices come down. [BUSINESS] ❑ *Real estate remains a buyer's market.*

buy|out /baɪaʊt/ (**buyouts**) ■ N-COUNT A **buyout** is the buying of a company, especially by its managers or employees. [BUSINESS] ❑ *It is thought that a management buyout is one option.* ■ → see also **MBO**

buzz /bʌz/ (**buzzes**, **buzzing**, **buzzed**) ■ V-I If something **buzzes** or **buzzes** somewhere, it makes a long continuous sound, like the noise a bee makes when it is flying. ❑ *The intercom buzzed and he pressed down the appropriate switch.* • N-COUNT; SOUND **Buzz** is also a noun. ❑ *...the irritating buzz of an insect.* ■ V-I If people **are buzzing** around, they are moving around quickly and busily. [WRITTEN] ❑ *A few tourists were buzzing around.* ■ V-I If questions or ideas **are buzzing** around your head, or if your head **is buzzing** with questions or ideas, you are thinking about a lot of things, often in a confused way. ❑ *Many more questions were buzzing around in my head.* ■ V-I [usu cont] If a place **is buzzing** with activity or conversation, there is a lot of activity or conversation there, especially because something important or exciting is about to happen. ❑ *The rehearsal studio is buzzing with lunchtime activity.* ■ N-SING You can use **buzz** to refer to a long continuous sound, usually caused by lots of people talking at once. ❑ *A buzz of excitement filled the courtroom as the defendant was led in.* ■ ADJ [ADJ n] You can use **buzz** to refer to a word, idea, or activity which has recently become extremely popular. ❑ *...the latest buzz phrase in garden design circles.* ■ N-SING [a N] If a place or event has **a buzz** around it, it has a lively, interesting, and modern atmosphere. ❑ *There is a real buzz around the place. Everyone is really excited.* ■ V-T If an aircraft **buzzes** a place, it flies low over it, usually in a threatening way. ❑ *American fighter planes buzzed the city.* ■ → See feature box at **sound**

buz|zard /bʌzərd/ (**buzzards**) N-COUNT A **buzzard** is a large bird of prey.

buzz cut (**buzz cuts**) N-COUNT A **buzz cut** is hairstyle in which the hair is cut very close to the head. [mainly AM] ❑ *He seemed even bigger than before, and he has a buzz cut now.*

buzz|er /bʌzər/ (**buzzers**) N-COUNT A **buzzer** is an electrical device that is used to make a buzzing sound, for example, to attract someone's attention. ❑ *She rang a buzzer at the information desk.*

buzz|saw /bʌzsɔː/ (**buzzsaws**) N-COUNT A **buzzsaw** is an electric tool consisting of a round metal disk with a sharp serrated edge. It is powered by an electric motor and is used for cutting wood and other materials. [AM]

in BRIT, use **circular saw**

buzz|word /bʌzwɜːrd/ (**buzzwords**) also **buzz word** N-COUNT A **buzzword** is a word or expression that has become fashionable in a particular field and is being used a lot by the media. ❑ *Biodiversity was the buzzword of the Rio Earth Summit.*

buzzy /bʌzi/ (**buzzier**, **buzziest**) ADJ If a place, event, or atmosphere is **buzzy**, it is lively, interesting, and modern. [INFORMAL] ❑ *The cafe has an intimate but buzzy atmosphere.*

BY
① WHO DOES SOMETHING OR HOW IT IS DONE
② POSITION OR PLACE
③ TIMES AND AMOUNTS

① **by** ✦✦✦

The preposition is pronounced /baɪ/. The adverb is pronounced /baɪ/.

In addition to the uses shown here, **by** is used in phrasal verbs such as 'abide by,' 'put by,' and 'stand by.'

■ PREP If something is done **by** a person or thing, that person or thing did it. ❑ *The feast was served by his mother and sisters.* ❑ *I was amazed by their discourtesy and lack of professionalism.* ■ PREP If you say that something such as a book, a piece of music, or a painting is **by** a particular person, you mean that this person wrote it or created it. ❑ *A painting by Van Gogh has been sold in New York for more than eighty-two million dollars.* ■ PREP If you do something **by** a particular means, you do it using that thing. ❑ *If you're traveling by car, ask whether there are parking facilities nearby.* ■ PREP [PREP -ing] If you achieve one thing **by** doing another thing, your action enables you to achieve the first thing. ❑ *Make the sauce by boiling the cream and stock together in a pan.* ❑ *The all-female yacht crew made history by becoming the first to sail round the world.* ■ PREP You use **by** in phrases such as 'by chance' or 'by accident' to indicate whether or not an event was planned. ❑ *I met him by chance out walking yesterday.* ❑ *He opened Ingrid's letter by mistake.* ■ PREP [adj/n PREP n] If someone is a particular type of person **by** nature, **by** profession, or **by** birth, they are that type of person because of their nature, their profession, or the family they were born into. ❑ *I am certainly lucky to have a kind wife who is loving by nature.* ❑ *She's a nurse by profession and now runs a counseling service for women.* ■ PREP If something must be done **by** law, it happens according to the law. If something is the case **by** particular standards, it is the case according to the standards. ❑ *Pharmacists are required by law to give the medicine prescribed by the doctor.* ■ PREP If you say what someone means **by** a particular word or expression, you are saying what they intend the word or expression to refer to. ❑ *Stella knew what he meant by "start again."* ■ PREP If you hold someone or something **by** a particular part of them, you hold that part. ❑ *He caught her by the shoulder and turned her around.* ❑ *She was led by the arm to a small room at the far end of the corridor.* ■ PHRASE If you are **by yourself**, you are alone. ❑ *...a dark-haired man sitting by himself in a corner.* ■ PHRASE If you do something **by yourself**, you succeed in doing it without anyone helping you. ❑ *I didn't know if I could raise a child by myself.*

② **by** ✦✦✦ ■ PREP Someone or something that is **by** something else is beside it and close to it. ❑ *Judith was sitting in a rocking chair by the window.* ❑ *Felicity Maxwell stood by the bar and ordered a glass of wine.* • ADV [ADV after v] **By** is also an adverb. ❑ *Large numbers of security police stood by.* ■ PREP [v PREP n] If a person or vehicle goes **by** you, they move past you without stopping. ❑ *A few cars passed close by me.* • ADV [ADV after v] **By** is also an adverb. ❑ *The bomb went off as a police patrol went by.* ■ PREP If you stop **by** a place, you visit it for a short time. ❑ *We had made arrangements to stop by her house in Pacific Grove.* • ADV [ADV after v] **By** is also an adverb. ❑ *I'll stop by after dinner and we'll have that talk.*

USAGE

by
Don't use 'by' with the names of towns or cities. Use **near** instead. *Winston Churchill was born near Oxford.*

---

③ **by** ✦✦✦ /baɪ/ ■ PREP If something happens **by** a particular time, it happens at or before that time. ❑ *By eight o'clock he had arrived at my hotel.* ■ PREP If you do something **by** day, you do it during the day. If you do it **by** night, you do it during the night. ❑ *By day a woman could safely walk the streets.* ■ PREP [PREP num] In arithmetic, you use **by** before the second number in a multiplication or division sum. ❑ *...an annual rate of 22.8 percent (1.9 multiplied by 12).* ■ PREP [PREP num] You use **by** to talk about measurements of area. For example, if a room is twenty feet **by** fourteen feet, it measures twenty feet in one direction and fourteen feet in the other direction. ❑ *Three prisoners were sharing one small cell 3 meters by 2½ meters.* ■ PREP [PREP amount] If something increases or decreases **by** a particular amount, that amount is gained or lost. ❑ *Violent crime has increased by 10 percent since last year.* ■ PREP [PREP the n] Things that are made or sold **by** the million or **by** the dozen are made or sold in those quantities. ❑ *Packages arrived by the dozen from America.* ■ PREP [n PREP n] You use **by** in expressions such as 'minute by minute' and 'drop by drop' to talk about things that happen gradually, not all at once. ❑ *His father began to lose his memory bit by bit, becoming increasingly forgetful.*

bye ✦✧ /baɪ/ also **bye-bye** CONVENTION **Bye** and **bye-bye** are informal ways of saying goodbye. ❑ *Bye, Daddy.*

bye-law → see bylaw

by-election (by-elections) N-COUNT A **by-election** is an election that is held to choose a new member of parliament or another legislature when a member has resigned or died. [mainly BRIT]

Bye|lo|rus|sian /bi̯elo͝urʌʃ°n/ (Byelorussians) **1** ADJ **Byelorussian** means belonging or relating to Byelorussia or to its people or culture. **2** N-COUNT A **Byelorussian** is a Byelorussian citizen, or a person of Byelorussian origin.

by|gone /ba͡ɪgɔn/ ADJ [ADJ n] **Bygone** means happening or existing a very long time ago. ❏ *The book recalls other memories of a bygone age.*

by|law /ba͡ɪlɔ/ (bylaws) also **bye-law, by-law** N-COUNT A **bylaw** is a rule that controls the way an organization is run. [AM] ❏ *Under the company's bylaws, he can continue as chairman until the age of 70.*

by|line /ba͡ɪla͡ɪn/ (bylines) also **by-line** N-COUNT A **byline** is a line at the top of an article in a newspaper or magazine giving the author's name. [TECHNICAL]

BYOD /bi wa͡ɪ o͝u di/ N-UNCOUNT **BYOD** is the practice of allowing employees to use their own computers and smart phones to connect to company information. **BYOD** is an abbreviation for 'bring your own device.' ❏ *The firm has a BYOD policy.*

by|pass /ba͡ɪpæs/ (bypasses, bypassing, bypassed) **1** V-T If you **bypass** someone or something that you would normally have to get involved with, you ignore them, often because you want to achieve something more quickly. ❏ *A growing number of employers are trying to bypass the unions altogether.* **2** N-COUNT A **bypass** is a surgical operation performed on or near the heart, in which the flow of blood is redirected so that it does not flow through a part of the heart that is diseased or blocked. ❏ *...heart bypass surgery.* **3** N-COUNT A **bypass** is a main road that takes traffic around the edge of a town or city rather than through its center. ❏ *A new bypass around the city is being built.* **4** V-T If a road **bypasses** a place, it goes around it rather than through it. ❏ *...money for new roads to bypass cities.* **5** V-T If you **bypass** a place when you are traveling, you avoid going through it. ❏ *The rebel forces simply bypassed the town on their way further south.*

by|product /ba͡ɪprɒdʌkt/ (byproducts) also **by-product** N-COUNT A **byproduct** is something that is produced during the manufacture or processing of another product. ❏ *The raw material for the tire is a byproduct of gasoline refining.*

by|stander /ba͡ɪstændər/ (bystanders) N-COUNT A **bystander** is a person who is present when something happens and who sees it but does not take part in it. ❏ *It looks like an innocent bystander was killed instead of you.*

byte /ba͡ɪt/ (bytes) N-COUNT In computing, a **byte** is a unit of storage approximately equivalent to one printed character. ❏ *...two million bytes of data.*

by|way /ba͡ɪweɪ/ (byways) **1** N-COUNT [usu pl] A **byway** is a small road that is not used by many cars or people. ❏ *...the highways and byways of America.* **2** N-COUNT [usu pl, usu N of n] The **byways** of a subject are the less important or less well known areas of it. ❏ *My research focuses on the byways of children's literature.*

by|word /ba͡ɪwɜrd/ (bywords) **1** N-COUNT [N for n] Someone or something that is a **byword** for a particular quality is well known for having that quality. ❏ *...the Rolls-Royce brand name, a byword for quality.* **2** N-COUNT A **byword** is a word or phrase that people often use. ❏ *Loyalty and support became the bywords of the day.*

byz|an|tine /bɪzəntin/ also **Byzantine** **1** ADJ [ADJ n] **Byzantine** means related to or connected with the Byzantine Empire. ❏ *...Byzantine civilization.* ❏ *There are also several well-preserved Byzantine frescoes.* **2** ADJ [usu ADJ n] If you describe a system or process as **byzantine**, you are criticizing it because it seems complicated or secretive. [DISAPPROVAL]

Cc

C also **c** /siː/ (**C's**, **c's**) **1** N-VAR **C** is the third letter of the English alphabet. **2** N-VAR In music, **C** is the first note in the scale of C major. **3** N-VAR If you get a **C** as a mark for a piece of work or in an exam, your work is average. **4** **c.** is written in front of a date or number to indicate that it is approximate. **c.** is an abbreviation for 'circa.' ❑ *...the museum's re-creation of a New York dining room (c. 1825–35).* **5** **C** or **c** is used as an abbreviation for words beginning with c, such as 'copyright' or 'Celsius.' ❑ *Heat the oven to 180°C.* **6** → see also **C-in-C, c/o**

cab /kæb/ (**cabs**) **1** N-COUNT A **cab** is a taxi. ❑ *Could I use your phone to call a cab?* **2** N-COUNT The **cab** of a truck or train is the front part in which the driver sits. ❑ *The van has additional load space over the driver's cab.*

ca|bal /kəbæl/ (**cabals**) N-COUNT [usu with supp] If you refer to a group of politicians or other people as a **cabal**, you are criticizing them because they meet and decide things secretly. [DISAPPROVAL] ❑ *He had been chosen by a cabal of fellow senators.* ❑ *...a secret government cabal.*

caba|ret /kæbəreɪ/ N-UNCOUNT [oft N n] **Cabaret** is live entertainment consisting of dancing, singing, or comedy acts that are performed in the evening in restaurants or nightclubs. ❑ *Helen made a successful career in cabaret.*

cab|bage /kæbɪdʒ/ (**cabbages**) N-VAR A **cabbage** is a round vegetable with white, green, or purple leaves that is usually eaten cooked.

cab|bie /kæbi/ (**cabbies**) also **cabby** N-COUNT A **cabbie** is a person who drives a taxi. [INFORMAL]

ca|ber /keɪbər/ (**cabers**) N-COUNT A **caber** is a long, heavy, wooden pole. It is thrown into the air as a test of strength in the traditional Scottish sport called 'tossing the caber.'

cab|in /kæbɪn/ (**cabins**) **1** N-COUNT A **cabin** is a small wooden house, especially one in an area of forests or mountains. ❑ *...a log cabin.* **2** N-COUNT A **cabin** is a small room in a ship or boat. ❑ *He showed her to a small cabin.* **3** N-COUNT A **cabin** is one of the areas inside a plane. ❑ *He sat quietly in the first class cabin of the flight looking tired.* **4** → See also color supplement

cab|in crew (**cabin crews**) N-COUNT-COLL The **cabin crew** on an aircraft are the people whose job is to take care of the passengers.

cab|in cruis|er (**cabin cruisers**) N-COUNT A **cabin cruiser** is a motorboat which has a cabin for people to live or sleep in.

cabi|net /kæbɪnɪt/ (**cabinets**) **1** N-COUNT A **cabinet** is a cupboard used for storing things such as medicine or alcoholic drinks or for displaying decorative things in. ❑ *She looked in the medicine cabinet and found some aspirin.* **2** N-COUNT The **cabinet** is a group of the most senior advisers or ministers in a government, who meet regularly to discuss policies. ❑ *The announcement came after a three-hour cabinet meeting.*

COLLOCATIONS

cabinet
NOUN
1
noun + **cabinet**: bathroom, kitchen; display, drinks, medicine, trophy
adjective + **cabinet**: glass, metal, wooden
2
adjective + **cabinet**: shadow
verb + **cabinet**: announce, appoint, form, name; reshuffle

cabinet|maker /kæbɪnɪtmeɪkər/ (**cabinetmakers**) also **cabinet maker** N-COUNT A **cabinetmaker** is a person who makes high-quality wooden furniture.

cab|in fev|er N-SING If you describe someone as having **cabin fever**, you mean that they feel restless and irritable because they have been indoors in one place for too long. ❑ *I've got cabin fever. I've got to get out of here.*

ca|ble /keɪbəl/ (**cables**) **1** N-VAR A **cable** is a kind of very strong, thick rope, made of wires twisted together. ❑ *The miners rode a conveyance attached to a cable made of braided steel wire.* **2** N-VAR A **cable** is a thick wire, or a group of wires inside a rubber or plastic covering, which is used to carry electricity or electronic signals. ❑ *...overhead power cables.* **3** N-UNCOUNT **Cable** is used to refer to television systems in which the signals are sent along underground wires rather than by radio waves. ❑ *They ran commercials on cable systems across the country.*

ca|ble car (**cable cars**) N-COUNT A **cable car** is a vehicle for taking people up mountains or steep hills. It is pulled by a moving cable.

ca|ble tele|vi|sion N-UNCOUNT **Cable television** is a television system in which signals are sent along wires rather than by radio waves.

ca|bling /keɪblɪŋ/ **1** N-UNCOUNT **Cabling** is used to refer to electrical or electronic cables, or to the process of putting them in a place. ❑ *...modern offices equipped with computer cabling.* **2** → see also **cable**

ca|boose /kəbuːs/ (**cabooses**) N-COUNT On a freight train, a **caboose** is a small car, usually at the rear, in which the crew travels. [AM]

in BRIT, use **guard's van**

cab|ri|o|let /kæbriəleɪ/ (**cabriolets**) N-COUNT A **cabriolet** is a type of car with two doors and a convertible top. [mainly AM]

cab stand also **cabstand** (**cab stands**) N-COUNT A **cab stand** is a place where taxis wait for passengers, for example, at an airport or outside a station. [AM]

in BRIT, use **taxi rank**

ca|cao /kəkaʊ/ N-UNCOUNT [oft N n] **Cacao** seeds are the seeds of a tropical tree, from which cocoa and chocolate are made. ❑ *...a group of chemicals found in cacao.* ❑ *...cacao beans.*

cache /kæʃ/ (**caches**) **1** N-COUNT A **cache** is a quantity of things such as weapons that have been hidden. ❑ *A huge arms cache was discovered by police.* **2** N-COUNT A **cache** or **cache memory** is an area of computer memory that is used for temporary storage of data and can be accessed more quickly than the main memory. [COMPUTING] ❑ *In your Web browser's cache are the most recent Web files that you have downloaded.*

ca|chet /kæʃeɪ/ N-SING [with supp] If someone or something has a certain **cachet**, they have a quality which makes people admire them or approve of them. [WRITTEN, APPROVAL] ❑ *A Mercedes carries a certain cachet.*

cack|le /kækəl/ (**cackles, cackling, cackled**) V-I If someone **cackles**, they laugh in a loud unpleasant way, often at something bad that happens to someone else. ❑ *She cackled, pleased to have produced so dramatic a reaction.* • N-COUNT **Cackle** is also a noun. ❑ *He let out a brief cackle.*

ca|copho|ny /kəkɒfəni/ (**cacophonies**) N-COUNT [usu sing, usu N *of* n] You can describe a loud, unpleasant mixture of sounds as a **cacophony**. ◻ *All around was a cacophony of voices.* • **ca|copho|nous** /kəkɒfənəs/ ADJ [usu ADJ n] ◻ *...the cacophonous beat of pop music.*

cac|tus /kæktəs/ (**cactuses** or **cacti** /kæktaɪ/) N-COUNT A **cactus** is a thick, fleshy plant that grows in many hot, dry parts of the world. Cacti have no leaves and many of them are covered in prickles.

cad /kæd/ (**cads**) N-COUNT If you say that a man is a **cad**, you mean that he treats other people, especially women, badly or unfairly. [OLD-FASHIONED] ◻ *He's a scoundrel! A cad!*

CAD /kæd/ N-UNCOUNT **CAD** refers to the use of computer software in the design of things such as cars, buildings, and machines. **CAD** is an abbreviation for 'computer aided design.' [COMPUTING] ◻ *...CAD software.*

ca|dav|er /kədævər/ (**cadavers**) N-COUNT A **cadaver** is a dead body. [FORMAL] ◻ *Cadavers are used to teach med students surgical skills and anatomy.*

ca|dav|er|ous /kədævərəs/ ADJ [usu ADJ n] If you describe someone as **cadaverous**, you mean they are extremely thin and pale. [WRITTEN] ◻ *...a tall man with a long, cadaverous face.*

cad|die /kædi/ (**caddies, caddying, caddied**) also **caddy** ▪ N-COUNT In golf, a **caddie** is a person who carries golf clubs and other equipment for a player. ▪ V-I If you **caddie** for a golfer, you act as their caddie. ◻ *Lil caddied for her son.*

ca|dence /keɪdəns/ (**cadences**) ▪ N-COUNT The **cadence** of someone's voice is the way their voice gets higher and lower as they speak. [FORMAL] ◻ *He recognized the Polish cadences in her voice.* ▪ N-COUNT A **cadence** is the phrase that ends a section of music or a complete piece of music.

ca|den|za /kədɛnzə/ (**cadenzas**) N-COUNT In classical music, a **cadenza** is a long and difficult solo passage in a piece for soloist and orchestra.

ca|det /kədɛt/ (**cadets**) N-COUNT A **cadet** is a young man or woman who is being trained in the armed services or the police force. ◻ *...army cadets.*

cadge /kædʒ/ (**cadges, cadging, cadged**) V-T If someone **cadges** food, money, or help from you, they ask you for it and succeed in getting it. [mainly BRIT, INFORMAL] ◻ *Can I cadge a cigarette?* ◻ *He could cadge a ride from somebody.*

cad|mium /kædmiəm/ N-UNCOUNT **Cadmium** is a soft bluish-white metal that is used in the production of nuclear energy.

ca|dre /kɑdreɪ/ (**cadres**) N-COUNT [usu with supp] A **cadre** is a small group of people who have been specially chosen, trained, and organized for a particular purpose. ◻ *...an elite cadre of international managers.*

Cae|sar|ean /sɪzɛəriən/ (**Caesareans**) also **Cesarean** ▪ N-COUNT [also by N] A **Caesarean** or a **Caesarean section** is an operation in which a baby is lifted out of a woman's uterus through an opening cut in her abdomen. ◻ *My youngest daughter was born by Caesarean.* ▪ → See feature box at **birth**

Cae|sar sal|ad /sizər sæləd/ (**Caesar salads**) also **caesar salad** N-VAR **Caesar salad** is a type of salad containing lettuce, grated cheese, and croutons, served with a dressing of oil, vinegar, and sometimes raw egg.

café /kæfeɪ/ (**cafés**) also **cafe** ▪ N-COUNT A **café** is a place where you can buy drinks, simple meals, and snacks. ▪ N-COUNT [N N] A street **café** or a sidewalk **café** is a café which has tables and chairs on the sidewalk outside it where people can eat and drink. ◻ *...an Italian street café.* ◻ *...sidewalk cafés and boutiques.* ▪ → See feature box at **town**

caf|eteria /kæfɪtɪəriə/ (**cafeterias**) N-COUNT A **cafeteria** is a restaurant where you choose your food from a counter and take it to your table after paying for it. Cafeterias are usually found in public buildings such as hospitals, colleges, and offices.

caf|eti|ère /kæfətyɛər/ (**cafetières**) N-COUNT A **cafetière** is a type of coffeepot that has a disk with small holes in it attached to the lid. You push the lid down to separate the liquid from the ground coffee when it is ready to drink.

caf|feine /kæfin/ N-UNCOUNT **Caffeine** is a chemical substance found in coffee, tea, and cocoa, which affects your brain and body and makes you more active.

caf|tan /kæftæn/ (**caftans**) also **kaftan** ▪ N-COUNT A **caftan** is a long, loose garment with long sleeves, worn by men in some Arab countries. ▪ N-COUNT A **caftan** is a long, loose dress with long sleeves.

cage /keɪdʒ/ (**cages**) N-COUNT A **cage** is a structure of wire or metal bars in which birds or animals are kept. ◻ *I hate to see birds in cages.*

caged /keɪdʒd/ ADJ A **caged** bird or animal is inside a cage. ◻ *Mark was still pacing like a caged animal.*

cag|ey /keɪdʒi/ ADJ If you say that someone is being **cagey** about something, you mean that you think they are deliberately not giving you much information or expressing an opinion about it. ◻ *He is cagey about what he was paid for the business.*

ca|hoots /kəhuts/ PHRASE If you say that one person is **in cahoots** with another, you do not trust the first person because you think that they are planning something secretly with the other. [DISAPPROVAL] ◻ *In his view they were all in cahoots with the police.*

cairn /kɛərn/ (**cairns**) N-COUNT A **cairn** is a pile of stones which marks a boundary, a route across rough ground, or the top of a mountain. A cairn is sometimes also built in memory of someone.

ca|jole /kədʒoʊl/ (**cajoles, cajoling, cajoled**) V-T If you **cajole** someone into doing something, you get them to do it after persuading them for some time. ◻ *It was he who had cajoled Garland into doing the film.*

Ca|jun /keɪdʒən/ (**Cajuns**) ▪ ADJ [usu ADJ n] **Cajun** means belonging or relating to a group of people who live mainly in the state of Louisiana in the United States, and are descended from French people. Cajun is also used to refer to the language and culture of these people. ◻ *They played some Cajun music.* ◻ *...Cajun food.* ▪ N-COUNT A **Cajun** is a person of Cajun origin. ▪ N-UNCOUNT **Cajun** is a dialect of French spoken by Cajun people. ◻ *...the first book ever written in Cajun.*

cake ♦◊◊ /keɪk/ (**cakes**) ▪ N-VAR A **cake** is a sweet food made by baking a mixture of flour, eggs, sugar, and fat in an oven. Cakes may be large and cut into slices or small and intended for one person only. ◻ *...a piece of cake.* ◻ *Would you like some chocolate cake?* ◻ *...a birthday cake.* ▪ N-COUNT Food that is formed into flat round shapes before it is cooked can be referred to as **cakes**. ◻ *...fish cakes.* ▪ N-COUNT A **cake** of soap is a small block of it. ◻ *...a small cake of lime-scented soap.* ▪ PHRASE If someone has done something very stupid, rude, or selfish, you can say that they **take the cake** or that what they have done **takes the cake**, to emphasize your surprise at their behavior. [AM, EMPHASIS]

in BRIT, use **take the biscuit**

▪ **the icing on the cake** → see **icing**

caked /keɪkt/ ADJ [usu v-link ADJ with/in n] If something is **caked** with mud, blood, or dirt, or it has mud, blood, or dirt **caked** on it, it is covered with a thick dry layer of it. ◻ *Her shoes were caked with mud.* ◻ *She had makeup caked on her face to hide her acne scars.* • COMB IN ADJ [usu ADJ n] **Caked** is also a combining form. ◻ *...herds of mud-caked cattle and sheep.*

cake mix (**cake mixes**) N-VAR **Cake mix** is a powder that you mix with eggs and water or milk to make a cake. You bake the mixture in the oven.

cake pan (**cake pans**) N-COUNT A **cake pan** is a metal container that you bake a cake in. [AM] ◻ *Lightly grease and flour a 13-by-9-inch cake pan.*

in BRIT, use **cake tin**

cake tin (**cake tins**) N-COUNT [BRIT] → see **cake pan**

cake|walk /keɪkwɔk/ N-SING [a n] If you describe something as a **cakewalk**, you mean that it is very easy to do or achieve. [INFORMAL] ◻ *Tomorrow's game against Italy should be a cakewalk.*

cal /kæl/ (**cals**) N-COUNT [usu pl, num N] **Cals** are units of measurement for the energy value of food. **Cal** is an abbreviation for 'calorie.' ◻ *...325 cals per serving.*

cal|a|mari /kæləmɑri/ N-UNCOUNT **Calamari** is squid that has been prepared for eating, usually by cutting it into rings, dipping it in a mixture of flour, milk, and eggs, and frying it.

cala|mine /kæləmaɪn/ also **calamine lotion** N-UNCOUNT [oft N n] **Calamine** or **calamine lotion** is a liquid that you can put on your skin when it is sore or itchy.

calamitous

ca|lam|i|tous /kəlæmɪtəs/ ADJ If you describe an event or situation as **calamitous**, you mean it is very unfortunate or serious. [FORMAL] ❑ ...*the calamitous state of the country.*

ca|lam|ity /kəlæmɪti/ (**calamities**) N-VAR A **calamity** is an event that causes a great deal of damage, destruction, or personal distress. [FORMAL] ❑ *He described drugs as the greatest calamity of the age.*

cal|ci|fied /kælsɪfaɪd/ ADJ Body tissue that is **calcified** has become hard because of the presence of substances called calcium salts. ❑ ...*calcified tissue.*

cal|cium /kælsiəm/ N-UNCOUNT **Calcium** is a soft white chemical element which is found in bones and teeth, and also in limestone, chalk, and marble.

cal|cu|lable /kælkjələbᵊl/ ADJ **Calculable** amounts or consequences can be calculated.

cal|cu|late /kælkjəleɪt/ (**calculates, calculating, calculated**) ■ V-T If you **calculate** a number or amount, you discover it from information that you already have, by using arithmetic, mathematics, or a special machine. ❑ *From this you can calculate the total mass in the Galaxy.* ❑ *We calculate that the average size farm in Lancaster County is 65 acres.* ■ V-T If you **calculate** the effects of something, especially a possible course of action, you think about them in order to form an opinion or decide what to do. ❑ *I believe I am capable of calculating the political consequences accurately.*

> **WORD HISTORY**
> **calculate**
> **Calculate** comes from the Latin word *calculare* meaning 'count using small stones,' from *calculus*, meaning 'stone.' The Romans used small stones to count with.

cal|cu|lat|ed /kælkjəleɪtɪd/ ■ ADJ [v-link ADJ to-inf] If something is **calculated** to have a particular effect, it is specially done or arranged in order to have that effect. ❑ *Their movements through the region were calculated to terrify landowners into abandoning their holdings.* ■ ADJ [with brd-neg, v-link ADJ to-inf] If you say that something is not **calculated** to have a particular effect, you mean that it is unlikely to have that effect. ❑ *The liberal agenda is not calculated to help minority groups.* ■ ADJ You can describe a clever or dishonest action as **calculated** when it is very carefully planned or arranged. ❑ *Irene's use of the mop had been a calculated attempt to cover up her crime.* ■ ADJ [ADJ n] If you take a **calculated** risk, you do something which you think might be successful, although you have fully considered the possible bad consequences of your action. ❑ *The president took a calculated political risk in throwing his full support behind the rebels.*

cal|cu|lat|ing /kælkjəleɪtɪŋ/ ADJ If you describe someone as **calculating**, you disapprove of the fact that they deliberately plan to get what they want, often by hurting or harming other people. [DISAPPROVAL] ❑ *Northbridge is a cool, calculating, and clever criminal who could strike again.*

cal|cu|la|tion /kælkjəleɪʃᵊn/ (**calculations**) N-VAR A **calculation** is something that you think about and work out mathematically. **Calculation** is the process of working something out mathematically. ❑ *Leonard made a rapid calculation: he'd never make it in time.*

cal|cu|la|tor /kælkjəleɪtər/ (**calculators**) N-COUNT A **calculator** is a small electronic device that you use for making mathematical calculations. ❑ ...*a pocket calculator.*

cal|cu|lus /kælkjələs/ N-UNCOUNT **Calculus** is a branch of advanced mathematics which deals with variable quantities.

cal|en|dar /kælɪndər/ (**calendars**) ■ N-COUNT A **calendar** is a chart or device which displays the date and the day of the week, and often the whole of a particular year divided up into months, weeks, and days. ❑ *There was a calendar on the wall above, with large squares around the dates.* ■ N-COUNT A **calendar** is a particular system for dividing time into periods such as years, months, and weeks, often starting from a particular point in history. ❑ *The Christian calendar was originally based on the Julian calendar of the Romans.* ■ N-COUNT You can use **calendar** to refer to a series or list of events and activities which take place on particular dates, and which are important for a particular organization, community, or person. ❑ *It is one of the hottest tickets on Washington's social calendar.*

call

cal|en|dar month (**calendar months**) ■ N-COUNT A **calendar month** is one of the twelve months of the year. ❑ *Winners will be selected at the end of each calendar month.* ■ N-COUNT A **calendar month** is the period from a particular date in one month to the same date in the next month, for example from April 4th to May 4th.

cal|en|dar year (**calendar years**) N-COUNT A **calendar year** is a period of twelve months from January 1 to December 31. Compare **fiscal year**. ❑ *In the last calendar year the company had a turnover of $426m.*

calf /kæf/ (**calves** /kævz/) ■ N-COUNT A **calf** is a young cow. ■ N-COUNT Some other young animals, including elephants and whales, are called **calves**. ■ N-COUNT Your **calf** is the thick part at the back of your leg, between your ankle and your knee. ❑ ...*a calf injury.*

calf-length ADJ [ADJ n] **Calf-length** skirts, dresses, and coats come to halfway between your knees and ankles. ❑ ...*a black, calf-length coat.*

calf|skin /kæfskɪn/ N-UNCOUNT [oft N n] **Calfskin** shoes and clothing are made from the skin of a calf. ❑ ...*calfskin boots.*

cal|iber /kælɪbər/

> in BRIT, use **calibre**

■ N-UNCOUNT The **caliber** of a person is the quality or standard of their ability or intelligence, especially when this is high. ❑ *I was impressed by the high caliber of the researchers and analysts.* ■ N-UNCOUNT The **caliber** of something is its quality, especially when it is good. ❑ *The caliber of teaching was very high.* ■ N-COUNT The **caliber** of a gun is the width of the inside of its barrel. [TECHNICAL] ❑ ...*a small caliber rifle.* ■ N-COUNT The **caliber** of a bullet is its diameter. [TECHNICAL] ❑ *She was hit in the head by a .22-caliber bullet.*

cali|brate /kælɪbreɪt/ (**calibrates, calibrating, calibrated**) V-T If you **calibrate** an instrument or tool, you mark or adjust it so that you can use it to measure something accurately. [TECHNICAL] ❑ ...*instructions on how to calibrate a thermometer.*

cali|bre /kælɪbər/ [BRIT] → see **caliber**

cali|co /kælɪkoʊ/ (**calicoes**) ■ N-MASS **Calico** is printed cotton fabric. [AM] ■ N-MASS **Calico** is plain white fabric made from cotton. [BRIT]

cali|per /kælɪpər/ (**calipers**) also **calliper** N-COUNT [usu pl, also *a pair of* N] **Calipers** are an instrument consisting of two long, thin pieces of metal joined together at one end, and are used to measure the size of things.

ca|liph /keɪlɪf/ (**caliphs**) also **calif** N-COUNT; N-TITLE A **caliph** was a Muslim ruler. ❑ ...*the caliph of Baghdad.*

cal|is|then|ics /kælɪsθɛnɪks/ N-PLURAL **Calisthenics** are simple exercises that you can do to keep fit and healthy.

> **CALL**
> ① NAMING
> ② DECLARING, ANNOUNCING, AND DEMANDING
> ③ TELEPHONING AND VISITING
> ④ PHRASAL VERBS

① **call** ◆◆◆ /kɔl/ (**calls, calling, called**)
→ Please look at meanings ■ and ■ to see if the expression you are looking for is shown under another headword.
■ V-T If you **call** someone or something by a particular name or title, you give them that name or title. ❑ *I always wanted to call the dog Mufty for some reason.* ❑ *"Doctor..."—"Will you please call me Sarah?"* ■ V-T If you **call** someone or something a particular thing, you suggest they are that thing or describe them as that thing. ❑ *The speech was interrupted by members of the Republican Party, who called him a traitor.* ❑ *She calls me lazy and selfish.* ■ → see also **so-called** ■ **to call something your own** → see **own** ■ **to call it quits** → see **quit** ■ → See feature box at **illness**

> **USAGE**
> **call**
> Don't use 'as' with **call**. Don't say, for example, 'We decided to call our daughter as Hannah' or 'They called him as a traitor.' Say 'We decided to **call** our daughter Hannah' and 'They **called** him a traitor.' *He **called** the report unfair.*

② **call** ♦♦♦ /kɔl/ (calls, calling, called)
→ Please look at meanings ⑫ – ⑮ to see if the expression you are looking for is shown under another headword.

1 V-T If you **call** something, you say it in a loud voice, because you are trying to attract someone's attention. ◻ *He could hear the others downstairs calling his name.* • PHRASAL VERB **Call out** means the same as **call**. ◻ *The butcher's son called out a greeting.* **2** V-T If you **call** someone, you ask them to come to you by shouting to them. ◻ *She called her young son: "Here, Stephen, come and look at this!"* **3** V-T If you **call** someone such as a doctor or the police, you ask them to come to you, usually by telephoning them. ◻ *He screamed for his wife to call an ambulance.* **4** V-T If someone in authority **calls** something such as a meeting, rehearsal, or election, they arrange for it to take place at a particular time. ◻ *We're going to call a meeting and discuss how we can work with other groups.* **5** V-T [usu passive] If someone **is called** before a court or committee, they are ordered to appear there, usually to give evidence. ◻ *The child waited two hours before she was called to give evidence.* **6** V-T To **call** a game or sporting event means to cancel it, for example because of rain or bad light. [AM] ◻ *We called the next game.* **7** N-COUNT If there is a **call** for something, someone demands that it should happen. ◻ *There have been calls for a new kind of security arrangement.* **8** N-COUNT The **call** of a particular bird or animal is the characteristic sound that it makes. ◻ *...a wide range of animal noises and bird calls.* **9** N-UNCOUNT If there is little or no **call for** something, very few people want it to be done or provided. ◻ *"Have you got just plain chocolate?"—"No, I'm afraid there's not much call for that."* **10** N-SING The **call** of something such as a place is the way it attracts or interests you strongly. ◻ *But the call of the wild was simply too strong and so he set off once more.* **11** PHRASE If someone is **on call**, they are ready to go to work at any time if they are needed, especially if there is an emergency. ◻ *In theory I'm on call day and night.* **12 to call someone's bluff** → see **bluff** **13 to call a halt** → see **halt** **14 to call something into question** → see **question** **15 to call the tune** → see **tune** **16** → See feature box at **telephone**

③ **call** ♦♦♦ /kɔl/ (calls, calling, called) **1** V-T If you **call** someone, you telephone them. ◻ *Would you call me as soon as you find out? My number's in the phone book.* **2** V-I If you **call** somewhere, you make a short visit there. ◻ *A market researcher called at the house where my uncle was living.* • N-COUNT **Call** is also a noun. ◻ *He decided to pay a call on Tommy Cummings.* **3** V-I When a train, bus, or ship **calls** somewhere, it stops there for a short time to allow people to get on or off. ◻ *The steamer calls at several palm-fringed ports along the way.* **4** N-COUNT When you make a telephone **call**, you telephone someone. ◻ *I made a phone call to the United States to talk to a friend.* ◻ *I've had hundreds of calls from other victims.*

④ **call** ♦♦♦ /kɔl/ (calls, calling, called)
▶ **call around**

in BRIT, usually use **ring round**

PHRASAL VERB If you **call around**, you phone several people, usually when you are trying to organize something or to find some information. [mainly AM] ◻ *Call around to find the best bargains.*
▶ **call back** PHRASAL VERB If you **call** someone **back**, you telephone them again or in return for a telephone call that they have made to you. ◻ *If we're not around, she'll take a message and we'll call you back.*
▶ **call for** **1** PHRASAL VERB If something **calls for** a particular action or quality, it needs it or makes it necessary. ◻ *It's a situation that calls for a blend of delicacy and force.* **2** PHRASAL VERB If you **call for** someone, you go to the building where they are, so that you can both go somewhere. ◻ *I'll call for you at seven o'clock.* **3** PHRASAL VERB If you **call for** something, you demand that it should happen. ◻ *They angrily called for Robinson's resignation.*
▶ **call in** **1** PHRASAL VERB If you **call** someone **in**, you ask them to come to and help you or do something for you. ◻ *Call in an architect or engineer to oversee the work.* **2** PHRASAL VERB If you **call in**, you phone a place, such as the place where you work, or a radio or TV station. ◻ *She reached for the phone to call in sick.* ◻ *24 million viewers called in to cast their final votes last night.* **3** → see also **call-in** **4** PHRASAL VERB If you **call in** somewhere, you make a short visit there. ◻ *He just calls in occasionally.*
▶ **call off** PHRASAL VERB If you **call off** an event that has been planned, you cancel it. ◻ *He has called off the trip.*
▶ **call on** also **call upon** **1** PHRASAL VERB If you **call on** someone to do something or **call upon** them to do it, you say publicly that you want them to do it. ◻ *One of Kenya's leading churchmen has called on the government to resign.* **2** PHRASAL VERB If you **call on** someone or **call upon** someone, you pay them a short visit. ◻ *Sofia was intending to call on Miss Kitts.*
▶ **call out** **1** PHRASAL VERB If you **call** someone **out**, you order or request that they come to help, especially in an emergency. ◻ *Colombia has called out the army and imposed emergency measures.* **2** → see also **call** ② **1**
▶ **call up** **1** PHRASAL VERB If you **call** someone **up**, you phone them. [mainly AM] ◻ *When I'm in Pittsburgh, I call him up.* ◻ *He called up the museum.* **2** PHRASAL VERB If someone **is called up**, they are ordered to join the army, navy, or air force. ◻ *The United States has called up some 150,000 military reservists.*
▶ **call upon** → see **call on**

call box (call boxes) also **call-box** N-COUNT A **call box** is a telephone in a box or case, often on a pole, that is at the side of a road and that you can use in emergencies. [mainly AM]

call cen|ter (call centers)

in BRIT, use **call centre**

N-COUNT A **call center** is an office where people work answering or making telephone calls for a particular company.

call|er /kɔlər/ (callers) **1** N-COUNT A **caller** is a person who is making a telephone call. ◻ *An anonymous caller told police what had happened.* **2** N-COUNT A **caller** is a person who comes to see you for a short visit. ◻ *She ushered her callers into a cluttered living room.*

call|er ID N-UNCOUNT A telephone that has **caller ID** displays the telephone number and name of the person who is calling you. [AM] ◻ *The cell phone's caller ID readout told her Frank Montoya was on the line.*

call girl (call girls) N-COUNT A **call girl** is a prostitute who makes appointments by telephone. [OLD-FASHIONED]

cal|lig|ra|pher /kəlɪgrəfər/ (calligraphers) N-COUNT A **calligrapher** is a person skilled in the art of calligraphy. ◻ *She is a skilled calligrapher.*

cal|lig|ra|phy /kəlɪgrəfi/ N-UNCOUNT **Calligraphy** is the art of producing beautiful handwriting using a brush or a special pen.

call-in (call-ins) N-COUNT A **call-in** is a program on radio or television in which people telephone with questions or opinions and their calls are broadcast. [AM] ◻ *...a call-in show on Los Angeles radio station KABC.*

in BRIT, use **phone-in**

call|ing /kɔlɪŋ/ (callings) N-COUNT [usu sing] A **calling** is a profession or career which someone is strongly attracted to, especially one which involves helping other people. ◻ *He was a consultant physician, a serious man dedicated to his calling.*

call|ing card (calling cards) **1** N-COUNT A **calling card** is a small card with personal information about you on it, such as your name and address, which you can give to people when you go to visit them. [mainly AM, OLD-FASHIONED] ◻ *Don't forget to give your calling card to those you'd like to see again.* **2** N-COUNT If you say that someone has left a **calling card**, you mean that they have left evidence that shows they have been in a particular place, especially at the scene of a crime. ◻ *John was studying the medallion in the evidence bag – the killer's calling card.*

cal|li|per /kælɪpər/ → see **caliper**

call let|ters N-PLURAL **Call letters** are the letters and numbers which identify a person, vehicle, or organization that is broadcasting on the radio or sending messages by radio.

cal|lous /kæləs/ ADJ A **callous** person or action is very cruel and shows no concern for other people or their feelings. ◻ *...his callous disregard for human life.* • **cal|lous|ness** N-UNCOUNT ◻ *...the callousness of Raymond's murder.* • **cal|lous|ly** ADV [ADV with v] ◻ *He is accused of callously ill-treating his wife.*

cal|loused /kæləst/ also **callused** ADJ A foot or hand that is **calloused** is covered in calluses. ◻ *...blunt, calloused fingers.*

cal|low /kæloʊ/ ADJ [usu ADJ n] A **callow** young person has very little experience or knowledge of the way they should behave as an adult. [WRITTEN] ◻ *...a callow youth.*

call sign (call signs) N-COUNT A **call sign** is the letters and numbers which identify a person, vehicle, or organization that is broadcasting on the radio or sending messages by radio.

call-up (call-ups) **1** N-COUNT A **call-up** is an occasion on which people are ordered to report for service in the armed forces. ❑ *The call-up of National Guard and reserve units began in late August.* **2** ADJ [ADJ n] If a person gets their **call-up** papers, they receive an official order to join the armed forces. **3** N-COUNT If someone receives a **call-up** to a sports team, they are chosen to play for that team. You can also use **call-up** to refer to a person who is chosen to play for a particular team. ❑ *He spent five seasons in the minors before his first call-up.* ❑ *Chin-Hui was a late-season call-up to the majors.*

cal|lus /kæləs/ (calluses) N-COUNT A **callus** is an unwanted area of thick skin, usually on the palms of your hands or the soles of your feet, which has been caused by something rubbing against it.

call wait|ing **1** N-UNCOUNT **Call waiting** is a telephone service that sends you a signal if another call arrives while you are already on the phone. ❑ *The service includes caller ID, voice mail, and call waiting.* **2** → See feature box at **telephone**

calm ✦✧ /kɑm/ (calmer, calmest, calms, calming, calmed) **1** ADJ A **calm** person does not show or feel any worry, anger, or excitement. ❑ *She is usually a calm and diplomatic woman.* ❑ *Try to keep calm and just tell me what happened.* • N-UNCOUNT [also a N] **Calm** is also a noun. ❑ *He felt a sudden sense of calm, of contentment.* • **calm|ly** ADV ❑ *Alan looked at him and said calmly, "I don't believe you."* **2** ADJ If someone says that a place is **calm**, they mean that it is free from fighting or public disorder, when trouble has recently occurred there or had been expected. [JOURNALISM] ❑ *The city of Sarajevo appears relatively calm today.* • N-UNCOUNT [also a N] **Calm** is also a noun. ❑ *Community and church leaders have appealed for calm and no retaliation.* **3** ADJ If the sea or a lake is **calm**, the water is not moving very much and there are no big waves. ❑ *...the safe, calm waters protected by an offshore reef.* **4** ADJ **Calm** weather is pleasant weather with little or no wind. ❑ *Tuesday was a fine, clear and calm day.* **5** N-UNCOUNT **Calm** is used to refer to a quiet, still, or peaceful atmosphere in a place. ❑ *The house projects an atmosphere of calm and order.* **6** V-T If you **calm** someone, you do something to make them feel less angry, worried, or excited. ❑ *The ruling party's veterans know how to calm their critics.* ❑ *She was breathing quickly and tried to calm herself.* • **calm|ing** ADJ ❑ *...a fresh, cool fragrance which produces a very calming effect on the mind.* **7** V-T To **calm** a situation means to reduce the amount of trouble, violence, or panic there is. ❑ *Officials tried to calm the protesters.* **8** V-I When the sea **calms**, it becomes still because the wind stops blowing strongly. When the wind **calms**, it stops blowing strongly. ❑ *Dawn came. the sea calmed but the cold was as bitter as ever.*
▶ **calm down** **1** PHRASAL VERB If you **calm down**, or if someone **calms** you **down**, you become less angry, upset, or excited. ❑ *Calm down for a minute and listen to me.* ❑ *I'll try a herbal remedy to calm him down.* **2** PHRASAL VERB If things **calm down**, or someone or something **calms** things **down**, the amount of activity, trouble, or panic is reduced. ❑ *We will go back to normal when things calm down.*

▬▬▬ COLLOCATIONS ▬▬▬

calm
NOUN **5**
adjective + **calm**: eerie, preternatural, uneasy; relative
verb + **calm**: maintain, restore

calm|ly /kɑmli/ **1** ADV [ADV with v] You can use **calmly** to emphasize that someone is behaving in a very controlled or ordinary way in a frightening or unusual situation. [WRITTEN, EMPHASIS] ❑ *The gunmen calmly walked away and escaped in a waiting car.* **2** → see also **calm**

ca|lor|ic /kəlɒrɪk/ ADJ [ADJ n] **Caloric** means relating to calories. ❑ *...a daily caloric intake of from 400 to 1200 calories.*

calo|rie /kæləri/ (calories) N-COUNT **Calories** are units used to measure the energy value of food. People who are on diets try to eat food that does not contain many calories. ❑ *Sweetened drinks contain a lot of calories.*

-calorie /-kæləri/ COMB IN ADJ [usu ADJ n] **-calorie** is used after adjectives such as low or high to indicate that food contains a small or a large number of calories. ❑ *...low-calorie margarine.* ❑ *...reduced-calorie mayonnaise.*

calo|rif|ic /kæləɹɪfɪk/ **1** ADJ [usu ADJ n] The **calorific** value of something, or its **calorific** content, is the number of calories it contains. [TECHNICAL] ❑ *...food with a high calorific value.* **2** → See feature box at **nutrition**

cal|um|ny /kæləmni/ (calumnies) N-VAR **Calumny** or a **calumny** is an untrue statement made about someone in order to reduce other people's respect and admiration for them. [FORMAL] ❑ *He was the victim of calumny.*

calve /kæv/ (calves, calving, calved) **1** V-I When a cow **calves**, it gives birth to a calf. ❑ *When his cows calve each year he keeps one or two calves for his family.* **2** V-I Some other female animals, including elephants and whales, are said to **calve** when they give birth to their young. ❑ *The whales migrate some 6,000 miles to breed and calve in the warm lagoons.* **3 Calves** is the plural of **calf**.

Cal|vin|ist /kælvɪnɪst/ (Calvinists) **1** ADJ [ADJ n] **Calvinist** means belonging or relating to a strict Protestant church started by John Calvin. ❑ *...the Calvinist work ethic.* **2** N-COUNT A **Calvinist** is a member of the Calvinist church.

ca|lyp|so /kəlɪpsoʊ/ (calypsos) N-COUNT A **calypso** is a song about a current subject, sung in a style which originally comes from the West Indies.

ca|ma|ra|derie /kɑmərɑdəri/ N-UNCOUNT **Camaraderie** is a feeling of trust and friendship among a group of people who have usually known each other for a long time or gone through some kind of experience together. ❑ *...the loyalty and camaraderie of the wartime Army.*

cam|ber /kæmbər/ (cambers) N-COUNT A **camber** is a gradual downward slope from the center of a road to each side of it.

cam|cord|er /kæmkɔrdər/ (camcorders) N-COUNT A **camcorder** is a portable video camera which records both pictures and sound.

came /keɪm/ **Came** is the past tense of **come** ①.

cam|el /kæm³l/ (camels) **1** N-COUNT A **camel** is a large animal that lives in deserts and is used for carrying goods and people. Camels have long necks and one or two lumps on their backs called humps. **2 the straw that broke the camel's back** → see **straw**

cam|el hair also **camel's hair** ADJ [ADJ n] A **camel hair** coat is made of a kind of soft, thick woolen cloth, usually creamy brown in color.

ca|mel|lia /kəmɪlyə, -mɪliə/ (camellias) N-COUNT A **camellia** is a large bush that has shiny leaves and large white, pink, or red flowers similar to a rose.

Cam|em|bert /kæməmbər/ (Camemberts) N-VAR **Camembert** is a type of cheese that comes from Northern France. It is soft and creamy with a white skin.

cameo /kæmioʊ/ (cameos) **1** N-COUNT A **cameo** is a short description or piece of acting which expresses cleverly and neatly the nature of a situation, event, or person's character. ❑ *...a succession of memorable cameos of American history.* **2** N-COUNT A **cameo** is a small role in a play or movie which is played by a well-known actor or celebrity. ❑ *He played a cameo role, that of a young cancer patient in hospital.* **3** N-COUNT A **cameo** is a piece of jewelry, usually oval in shape, consisting of a raised stone figure or design fixed on to a flat stone of another color. ❑ *...a cameo brooch.*

cam|era ✦✦✧ /kæmrə/ (cameras) **1** N-COUNT A **camera** is a piece of equipment that is used for taking photographs, making movies, or producing television pictures. ❑ *Her grandmother lent her a camera for a school trip to Venice and Egypt.* **2** PHRASE If someone or something is **on camera**, they are being filmed. ❑ *Fay was so impressive on camera that a special part was written in for her.* **3** PHRASE If you do something or if something happens **off camera**, you do it or it happens when not being filmed. ❑ *They were anything but friendly off camera, refusing even to take the same elevator.* **4** PHRASE If a trial is held **in camera**, the public and the press are not allowed to attend. [FORMAL] ❑ *This morning's appeal was held in camera.*

camera|man /kæmrəmæn/ (cameramen) N-COUNT A **cameraman** is a man who operates a camera for television or movies.

cam|era phone (camera phones) N-COUNT A **camera phone** is a cellphone that can also take photographs.

camera-shy ADJ Someone who is **camera-shy** is nervous and uncomfortable about being filmed or about having their photograph taken.

camera|woman /kæmrəwʊmən/ (camerawomen) N-COUNT A **camerawoman** is a woman who operates a camera for television or movies.

camera|work /kæmrəwɜrk/ N-UNCOUNT The **camerawork** in a movie is the way it has been filmed, especially if the style is interesting or unusual in some way. ❏ *The director employs sensuous, atmospheric camerawork and deft dramatic touches.*

cami|sole /kæmɪsoʊl/ (camisoles) N-COUNT A **camisole** is a short piece of clothing that women wear on the top half of their bodies underneath a shirt or blouse, for example. ❏ *...silk camisoles.*

camo|mile /kæməmaɪl/ → see chamomile

camou|flage /kæməflɑʒ/ (camouflages, camouflaging, camouflaged) **1** N-UNCOUNT [also a N, oft N n] **Camouflage** consists of things such as leaves, branches, or brown and green paint, which are used to make it difficult for an enemy to see military forces and equipment. ❏ *They were dressed in camouflage and carried automatic rifles.* ❏ *...a camouflage jacket.* **2** N-UNCOUNT [also a N] **Camouflage** is the way in which some animals are colored and shaped so that they cannot easily be seen in their natural surroundings. ❏ *Confident in its camouflage, being the same color as the rocks, the lizard stands still when it feels danger.* **3** V-T [usu passive] If military buildings or vehicles **are camouflaged**, things such as leaves, branches, or brown and green paint are used to make it difficult for an enemy to see them. ❏ *The entrance was camouflaged with bricks and dirt.* **4** V-T If you **camouflage** something such as a feeling or a situation, you hide it or make it appear to be something different. ❏ *He has never camouflaged his desire to better himself.* • N-UNCOUNT [also a N] **Camouflage** is also a noun. ❏ *There was much laughter – a perfect camouflage for the anxiety of waiting for the verdict in the trial.*

camp ♦♦◊ /kæmp/ (camps, camping, camped) **1** N-COUNT A **camp** is a collection of huts and other buildings that is provided for a particular group of people, such as refugees, prisoners, or soldiers, as a place to live or stay. ❏ *...a refugee camp.* **2** N-COUNT You can refer to a group of people who all support a particular person, policy, or idea as a particular **camp**. ❏ *The press release provoked furious protests from the Gore camp and other top Democrats.* **3** N-VAR A **camp** is an outdoor area with cabins, tents, or trailers where people stay on vacation. **4** N-VAR A **camp** is a collection of tents or trailers where people are living or staying, usually temporarily while they are traveling. ❏ *...gypsy camps.* **5** V-I If you **camp** somewhere, you stay or live there for a short time in a tent or trailer, or in the open air. ❏ *We camped near the beach.* • PHRASAL VERB **Camp out** means the same as **camp**. ❏ *For six months they camped out in a meadow at the back of the house.* • **camp|ing** N-UNCOUNT ❏ *They went camping in the woods.* **6** ADJ If you describe someone's behavior, performance, or style of dress as **camp**, you mean that it is exaggerated and amusing, often in a way that is thought to be typical of some male homosexuals. [INFORMAL] ❏ *James turns in a delightfully camp performance.* **7** → see also concentration camp

---- COLLOCATIONS ----

camp
NOUN
1
noun + **camp**: detention, internment, labor, prison, refugee
3
noun + **camp**: summer
4
verb + **camp**: make, pitch, set up

---

cam|paign ♦♦♦ /kæmpeɪn/ (campaigns, campaigning, campaigned) **1** N-COUNT A **campaign** is a planned set of activities that people carry out over a period of time in order to achieve something such as social or political change. ❏ *During his election campaign he promised to put the economy back on its feet.* ❏ *...a campaign to improve the training of staff.* **2** N-COUNT In a war, a **campaign** is a series of planned movements carried out by armed forces. ❏ *The allies are intensifying their air campaign.* **3** V-I If someone **campaigns** for something, they carry out a planned set of activities over a period of time in order to achieve their aim. ❏ *We are campaigning for law reform.* **4** → see also ad campaign

---- COLLOCATIONS ----

campaign
NOUN **1**
noun + **campaign**: ad, awareness, marketing, poster; election, leadership, re-election, referendum; hate, smear
verb + **campaign**: conduct, launch, mount, run; back, support
adjective + **campaign**: effective, successful; presidential
VERB **3**
campaign + adverb: relentlessly, tirelessly, vigorously, vociferously

---- SYNONYMS ----

campaign
NOUN **1**
drive: *The ANC is about to launch a nationwide recruitment drive.*
appeal: *...an appeal to save a library containing priceless manuscripts.*
push: *They urged negotiators to make a final push to arrive at an agreement.*
offensive: *...a diplomatic offensive.*
crusade: *He made it his crusade to teach children to love books.*
VERB **3**
crusade: *...an adopted boy whose cause is taken up by a crusading lawyer.*
press: *Police might now press for changes in the law.*
push: *Germany is pushing for direct flights to be established.*

---

cam|paign|er /kæmpeɪnər/ (campaigners) N-COUNT A **campaigner** is a person who campaigns for social or political change. ❏ *...anti-war campaigners.*

camp bed (camp beds) N-COUNT A **camp bed** is a small bed that you can fold up. [BRIT]

in AM, use **cot**

camped /kæmpt/ ADJ [v-link ADJ] If people are **camped** or **camped out** somewhere in the open air, they are living, staying, or waiting there, often in tents. ❏ *Most of the refugees are camped high in the mountains.*

camp|er /kæmpər/ (campers) **1** N-COUNT A **camper** is someone who is camping somewhere. ❏ *My fellow campers were already packing up their tents.* **2** N-COUNT A **camper** is a motor vehicle which is equipped with beds and cooking equipment so that you can live, cook, and sleep in it. [mainly AM]

in BRIT, usually use **camper van**

camp|fire /kæmpfaɪər/ (campfires) N-COUNT A **campfire** is a fire that you light out of doors when you are camping.

camp fol|low|er (camp followers) **1** N-COUNT **Camp followers** are people who travel with an army or other group, especially members of soldiers' families, or people who supply goods and services to the army. **2** N-COUNT If you describe someone as a **camp follower**, you mean that they do not officially belong to a particular group or movement but support it for their own advantage. [DISAPPROVAL] ❏ *...the Democratic leader's friends and camp followers.*

camp|ground /kæmpgraʊnd/ (campgrounds) N-COUNT A **campground** is the same as a **campsite**. [mainly AM]

cam|phor /kæmfər/ N-UNCOUNT **Camphor** is a strong-smelling white substance used in various medicines, in mothballs, and in making plastics.

camp|ing site (camping sites) N-COUNT A **camping site** is the same as a **campsite**.

camp|site /kæmpsaɪt/ (campsites) N-COUNT A **campsite** is a place where people who are on vacation can stay in tents.

cam|pus /kæmpəs/ (campuses) N-COUNT [also prep N] A **campus** is an area of land that contains the main buildings of a university or college. ❏ *...during a rally at the campus.*

campy /kæmpi/ ADJ **Campy** means the same as **camp**. ❑ ...a campy spy spoof.

cam|shaft /kæmʃæft/ (**camshafts**) N-COUNT A **camshaft** is a rod in an engine and works to change circular motion into motion up and down or from side to side.

CAN
① MODAL USES
② CONTAINER
---

① **can** ♦♦♦ /kən, STRONG kæn/

Can is a modal verb. It is used with the base form of a verb. The form **cannot** is used in negative statements. The usual spoken form of **cannot** is **can't**, pronounced /kænt/.

1 MODAL You use **can** when you are mentioning a quality or fact about something which people may make use of if they want to. ❑ Tickets can be purchased at the Madstone Theater box office. ❑ A central reservation number can direct you to accommodations that best suit your needs. **2** MODAL You use **can** to indicate that someone has the ability or opportunity to do something. ❑ Don't worry yourself about me, I can take care of myself. ❑ I can't give you details because I don't actually have any details. ❑ The United States will do whatever it can to help Greece. **3** MODAL You use **cannot** to indicate that someone is not able to do something because circumstances make it impossible for them to do it. ❑ We cannot buy food and clothes and pay for rent and utilities on $20 a week. **4** MODAL You use **can** to indicate that something is true sometimes or is true in some circumstances. ❑ ...long-term therapy that can last five years or more. ❑ Exercising alone can be boring. **5** MODAL You use **cannot** and **can't** to state that you are certain that something is not the case or will not happen. ❑ From her knowledge of Douglas's habits, she feels sure that that person can't have been Douglas. ❑ Things can't be that bad. **6** MODAL You use **can** to indicate that someone is allowed to do something. You use **cannot** or **can't** to indicate that someone is not allowed to do something. ❑ Can I really have your jeans when you go? ❑ We can't answer any questions, I'm afraid. **7** MODAL You use **cannot** or **can't** when you think it is very important that something should not happen or that someone should not do something. [EMPHASIS] ❑ It is an intolerable situation and it can't be allowed to go on. **8** MODAL You use **can**, usually in questions, in order to make suggestions or to offer to do something. ❑ What can I do around here? ❑ This elderly woman was struggling out of the train and I said, "Can, can I help you?" **9** MODAL You use **can** in questions in order to make polite requests. You use **can't** in questions in order to request strongly that someone does something. [POLITENESS] ❑ Can I have a look at that? ❑ Why can't you leave me alone? **10** MODAL You use **can** as a polite way of interrupting someone or of introducing what you are going to say next. [FORMAL, SPOKEN] ❑ Can I interrupt you just for a minute? ❑ But if I can interrupt, Joe, I don't think anybody here is personally blaming you. **11** MODAL You use **can** with verbs such as 'imagine,' 'think,' and 'believe' in order to emphasize how you feel about a particular situation. [INFORMAL OR SPOKEN, EMPHASIS] ❑ You can imagine he was terribly upset. ❑ You can't think how glad I was to see them all go. **12** MODAL You use **can** in questions with 'how' to indicate that you feel strongly about something. [SPOKEN, EMPHASIS] ❑ How can millions of dollars go astray? ❑ How can you say such a thing?

② **can** ♦♦♦ /kæn/ (**cans, canning, canned**) **1** N-COUNT A **can** is a metal container in which something such as food, drink, or paint is put. The container is usually sealed to keep the contents fresh. ❑ Several young men were kicking a tin can along the middle of the road. ❑ ...empty beer cans. **2** N-COUNT You can use **can** to refer to a can and its contents, or to the contents only. ❑ She grabbed a can of soda out of the refrigerator. **3** V-T [usu passive] When food or drink **is canned**, it is put into a metal container and sealed so that it will remain fresh. ❑ ...fruits and vegetables that will be canned, skinned, diced, or otherwise processed. **4** V-T If you **are canned**, you are dismissed from your job. [AM, INFORMAL] ❑ The extremists prevailed, and the security chief was canned. **5** N-SING **The can** is the toilet. [AM, INFORMAL] **6** → See feature box at **recycle**

Ca|na|da goose /kænədə gus/ (**Canada geese**) N-COUNT A **Canada** goose is a grayish-brown wild goose that comes from North America.

Ca|na|dian /kəneɪdiən/ (**Canadians**) **1** ADJ **Canadian** means belonging or relating to Canada, or to its people or culture. **2** N-COUNT A **Canadian** is a Canadian citizen, or a person of Canadian origin.

ca|nal /kənæl/ (**canals**) **1** N-COUNT A **canal** is a long, narrow stretch of water that has been made for boats to travel along or to bring water to a particular area. ❑ ...the Grand Union Canal. **2** N-COUNT A **canal** is a narrow tube inside your body for carrying food, air, or other substances. ❑ ...delaying its progress through the alimentary canal.

ca|nal boat (**canal boats**) N-COUNT A **canal boat** is a long, narrow boat used for traveling on canals.

cana|pé /kænəpeɪ/ (**canapés**) N-COUNT [usu pl] **Canapés** are crackers or small pieces of toast with food such as meat, cheese, or pâté on top. They are often served with drinks at parties.

ca|nard /kənɑrd/ (**canards**) N-COUNT A **canard** is an idea or a piece of information that is false, especially one that is spread deliberately in order to harm someone or their work. ❑ The charge that Harding was a political stooge may be a canard.

ca|nary /kənɛəri/ (**canaries**) N-COUNT **Canaries** are small, yellow birds which sing beautifully and are often kept as pets.

ca|nary yel|low COLOR Something that is **canary yellow** is a light or vivid yellow in color. ❑ ...a canary yellow dress.

can-can N-SING [oft the N] The **can-can** is a dance in which the dancers kick their legs in the air to fast music. ❑ ...the can-can dancers from the Moulin Rouge.

can|cel ♦♦◊ /kænsəl/ (**cancels, canceling** or **cancelling, canceled** or **cancelled**) **1** V-T/V-I If you **cancel** something that has been arranged, you stop it from happening. If you **cancel** an order for goods or services, you tell the person or organization supplying them that you no longer wish to receive them. ❑ The Russian foreign minister yesterday canceled his visit to Washington. ❑ Many trains have been cancelled and a limited service is operating on other lines. ❑ The customer called to cancel. • **can|cel|la|tion** /kænsəleɪʃən/ (**cancellations**) N-VAR ❑ Outbursts of violence forced the cancellation of Haiti's first free elections in 1987. **2** V-T If someone in authority **cancels** a document, an insurance policy, or a debt, they officially declare that it is no longer valid or no longer legally exists. ❑ He intends to try to leave the country, in spite of a government order canceling his passport. • **can|cel|la|tion** N-UNCOUNT ❑ ...a march by groups calling for cancellation of Third World debt. **3** V-T To **cancel** a stamp or a check means to mark it to show that it has already been used and cannot be used again. ❑ The new device can also cancel the check after the transaction is complete.
▶ **cancel out** PHRASAL VERB If one thing **cancels out** another thing, the two things have opposite effects, so that when they are combined no real effect is produced. ❑ He wonders if the different influences might not cancel each other out.

SYNONYMS

cancel
VERB **1**
call off: He has called off the trip.
scrap: It had been thought that passport controls would be scrapped.
abandon: The authorities have abandoned any attempt to distribute food.
abort: The decision was made to abort the mission.
---

can|cel cul|ture N-UNCOUNT **Cancel culture** is a culture, especially on social media, in which people stop supporting a person because they are encouraged to do so by someone that person has criticized.

can|cer ♦♦◊ /kænsər/ (**cancers**) N-VAR **Cancer** is a serious disease in which cells in a person's body increase rapidly in an uncontrolled way, producing abnormal growths. ❑ Her mother died of breast cancer. ❑ Jane was just 25 when she learned she had cancer.

Can|cer (**Cancers**) **1** N-UNCOUNT **Cancer** is one of the twelve signs of the zodiac. Its symbol is a crab. People who are born approximately between the 21st of June and the 22nd of July come under this sign. **2** N-COUNT A **Cancer** is a person whose sign of the zodiac is Cancer.

can|cer|ous /kænsərəs/ ADJ Cancerous cells or growths are cells or growths that are the result of cancer. ❑ *The production of these cancerous cells suppresses the production of normal white blood cells.*

can|de|la|bra /kændəlɑbrə/ (candelabras) N-COUNT A candelabra is an ornamental holder for two or more candles.

can|de|la|brum /kændəlɑbrəm/ (candelabrum) N-COUNT A candelabrum is the same as a **candelabra**.

can|did /kændɪd/ ◼ ADJ When you are candid about something or with someone, you speak honestly. ❑ *Natalie is candid about the problems she is having with Steve.* ❑ *I haven't been completely candid with him.* ● **can|did|ly** ADV [usu ADV with v, also ADV adj/adv] ❑ *He admits candidly that he will always be a drug addict.* ◼ ADJ [ADJ n] A candid photograph of someone is one that was taken when the person did not know they were being photographed. ❑ *...candid snaps of off-duty movie stars.*

can|di|da|cy /kændɪdəsi/ (candidacies) N-VAR Someone's candidacy is their position of being a candidate in an election. ❑ *Today he is formally announcing his candidacy for president.*

can|di|date ♦◇ /kændɪdeɪt/ (candidates) ◼ N-COUNT A candidate is someone who is being considered for a position, for example someone who is running in an election or applying for a job. ❑ *The Democratic candidate is still leading in the polls.* ❑ *He is a candidate for the office of governor.* ◼ N-COUNT A candidate is someone who is studying for a degree at a college. [AM] ❑ *He is now a candidate for a Master's degree in social work at San Francisco State University.* ◼ N-COUNT A candidate is a person or thing that is regarded as being suitable for a particular purpose or as being likely to do or be a particular thing. ❑ *Those who are overweight or indulge in high-salt diets are candidates for hypertension.*

COLLOCATIONS
candidate
NOUN ◼
noun + **candidate**: leadership
adjective + **candidate**: external, internal; favored, preferred; likely, obvious, potential, prospective, suitable; mayoral, parliamentary, presidential; vice-presidential
verb + **candidate**: field, put up, run, select; interview

SYNONYMS
candidate
NOUN ◼
contender: *She will be a strong contender for a place in Britain's gymnastics squad.*
competitor: *Blocker, one of the oldest competitors, won the individual silver medal.*
contestant: *The five remaining contestants enter the quarter finals.*
rival: *The world champion finished two seconds ahead of his nearest rival.*

---

can|died /kændid/ ADJ [usu ADJ n] Food such as candied fruit has been covered with sugar or has been cooked in sugar syrup. ❑ *...candied orange peel.*

can|dle /kændᵊl/ (candles) N-COUNT A candle is a stick of hard wax with a piece of string called a wick through the middle. You light the wick in order to give a steady flame that provides light. ❑ *The bedroom was lit by a single candle.*

candle|holder /kændᵊlhoʊldər/ → see **candlestick**

candle|light /kændᵊllaɪt/ N-UNCOUNT Candlelight is the light that a candle produces. ❑ *They dined by candlelight.*

candle|lit /kændᵊllɪt/ ADJ [usu ADJ n] A candlelit room or table is lit by the light of candles. ❑ *...a candlelit dinner for two.*

candle|stick /kændᵊlstɪk/ (candlesticks) also **candleholder** N-COUNT A candlestick is a narrow object with a hole at the top which holds a candle. [mainly AM]

can-do ADJ [ADJ n] If you say that someone has a **can-do** attitude, you approve of them because they are confident and willing to deal with problems or new tasks, rather than complaining or giving up. [INFORMAL, APPROVAL] ❑ *He is known for his optimistic can-do attitude.*

can|dor /kændər/

in BRIT, use **candour**

N-UNCOUNT Candor is the quality of speaking honestly and openly about things. ❑ *...a brash, forceful man, noted both for his candor and his quick temper.*

can|dy /kændi/ (candies) N-VAR Candy is sweet foods such as chocolate or taffy. [AM] ❑ *...a piece of candy.*

in BRIT, usually use **sweets**

can|dy apple (candy apples) N-COUNT A candy apple is an apple coated with hard, red sugar syrup and fixed on a stick. [AM]

in BRIT, use **toffee apple**

can|dy bar (candy bars) N-COUNT A candy bar is a long, thin, sweet food, usually covered in chocolate. [AM]

candy cane (candy canes) N-COUNT A candy cane is a stick of red and white candy with a curve at one end. [AM]

candy|floss /kændiflɒs/ N-UNCOUNT Candyfloss is the same as **cotton candy**. [BRIT]

cane /keɪn/ (canes) ◼ N-VAR Cane is used to refer to the long, hollow, hard stems of plants such as bamboo. Strips of cane are often used to make furniture, and some types of cane can be crushed and processed to make sugar. ❑ *...cane furniture.* ❑ *...cane sugar.* ◼ N-COUNT A cane is a long, thin stick with a curved or round top which you can use to support yourself when you are walking, or which in the past was fashionable to carry with you. ❑ *He wore a gray suit and leaned heavily on his cane.*

ca|nine /keɪnaɪn/ (canines) ◼ ADJ [ADJ n] Canine means relating to dogs. ❑ *...research into canine diseases.* ◼ N-COUNT Canine teeth or canines are pointed teeth near the front of the mouth of humans and of some animals. ◼ → See also color supplement

can|is|ter /kænɪstər/ (canisters) ◼ N-COUNT A canister is a strong, metal container. It is used to hold gases or chemical substances. ❑ *Riot police hurled tear gas canisters and smoke bombs into the crowd.* ◼ N-COUNT A canister is a metal, plastic, or china container with a lid. It is used for storing food such as sugar and flour. ❑ *...a canister of tea.*

can|ker /kæŋkər/ (cankers) ◼ N-COUNT A canker or canker sore is a small sore in the mouth or on the lips. [AM] ◼ N-VAR Canker is a disease which affects the wood of shrubs and trees, making the outer layer come away to expose the inside of the stem. ❑ *In gardens, cankers are most prominent on apples and pear trees.* ◼ N-COUNT A canker is something evil that spreads and affects things or people. [FORMAL] ❑ *...the canker of jealousy.*

can|na|bis /kænəbɪs/ N-UNCOUNT Cannabis is the hemp plant when it is used as a drug. ❑ *...cannabis smokers.*

canned /kænd/ ◼ ADJ [usu ADJ n] Canned music, laughter, or applause on a television or radio program has been recorded beforehand and is added to the program to make it sound as if there is a live audience. ❑ *However, the temptation is always there to add canned laughter in the editing.* ◼ → see also **can** ②

can|nel|lo|ni /kænəloʊni/ N-UNCOUNT Cannelloni is large tube-shaped pieces of pasta that contain a filling of meat, cheese, or vegetables.

can|nery /kænəri/ (canneries) N-COUNT A cannery is a factory where food is canned.

can|ni|bal /kænɪbᵊl/ (cannibals) N-COUNT Cannibals are people who eat the flesh of other human beings. ❑ *...a tropical island inhabited by cannibals.*

can|ni|bal|ism /kænɪbəlɪzəm/ N-UNCOUNT If a group of people practice cannibalism, they eat the flesh of other human beings. ❑ *They were forced to practice cannibalism in order to survive.*

can|ni|bal|is|tic /kænɪbəlɪstɪk/ ADJ [usu ADJ n] Cannibalistic people and practices are connected with cannibalism. ❑ *...lurid cannibalistic feasts.*

can|ni|bal|ize /kænɪbəlaɪz/ (cannibalizes, cannibalizing, cannibalized)

in BRIT, also use **cannibalise**

◼ V-T If you cannibalize something, you take it to pieces and use it to make something else. ❑ *They cannibalized damaged planes for the parts.* ◼ V-T If one of a company's products cannibalizes the company's sales, people buy it instead of any of the company's other products. [BUSINESS] ❑ *A website need not cannibalize existing sales.*

can|non /kænən/ (cannons) **1** N-COUNT A **cannon** is a large gun, usually on wheels, which used to be used in battles. ❑ *The cannons boom, the band plays.* **2** N-COUNT A **cannon** is a heavy automatic gun, especially one that is fired from an aircraft. ❑ *Others carried huge cannons plundered from Russian aircraft.* **3** PHRASE If someone is a **loose cannon**, they do whatever they want and nobody can predict what they are going to do. ❑ *Max is a loose cannon politically.*

can|non|ade /kænəneɪd/ (cannonades) N-COUNT A **cannonade** is an intense continuous attack of gunfire. ❑ *...the distant thunder of a cannonade.*

cannon|ball /kænənbɔl/ (cannonballs) also **cannon ball** N-COUNT A **cannonball** is a heavy metal ball that is fired from a cannon.

can|non fod|der N-UNCOUNT If someone in authority regards people they are in charge of as **cannon fodder**, they do not care if these people are harmed or lost in the course of their work. ❑ *The conscripts were treated as cannon fodder.*

can|not /kænɒt, kənɒt/ **Cannot** is the negative form of **can** ①.

can|ny /kæni/ (cannier, canniest) ADJ [usu ADJ n] A **canny** person is clever and able to think quickly. You can also describe a person's behavior as **canny**. ❑ *He was far too canny to risk giving himself away.*

ca|noe /kənu/ (canoes) **1** N-COUNT A **canoe** is a small, narrow boat that you move through the water using a stick with a wide end called a paddle. **2** → See also color supplement

ca|noe|ing /kənuɪŋ/ N-UNCOUNT **Canoeing** is the sport of using and racing a canoe. ❑ *They went canoeing in the wilds of Canada.*

ca|noe|ist /kənuɪst/ (canoeists) N-COUNT A **canoeist** is someone who is skilled at racing and performing tests of skill in a canoe.

ca|no|la /kənoʊlə/ N-UNCOUNT **Canola** or **canola oil** is a type of vegetable oil used in cooking.

can|on /kænən/ (canons) **1** N-COUNT A **canon** is a member of the clergy who is on the staff of a cathedral. **2** N-COUNT [oft N of n] A **canon** of texts is a list of them that is accepted as genuine or important. [FORMAL] ❑ *...a canon of accepted literary texts.* ❑ *...the Irish literary canon.*

ca|noni|cal /kənɒnɪk³l/ ADJ [ADJ n] If something has **canonical** status, it is accepted as having all the qualities that a thing of its kind should have. ❑ *...Ballard's status as a canonical writer.*

can|on|ize /kænənaɪz/ (canonizes, canonizing, canonized)

in BRIT, also use **canonise**

V-T [usu passive] If a dead person **is canonized**, it is officially announced by the Catholic Church that he or she is a saint. ❑ *Joan of Arc was finally canonized by Pope Benedict XV in 1920.*

can|on law N-UNCOUNT **Canon law** is the law of the Christian church. It has authority only for that church and its members.

ca|noo|dle /kənud³l/ (canoodles, canoodling, canoodled) V-RECIP If two people **are canoodling**, they are kissing and holding each other a lot. [mainly OLD-FASHIONED] ❑ *He was seen canoodling with his new girlfriend.*

can open|er (can openers) **1** N-COUNT A **can opener** is a tool that is used for opening cans of food.

in BRIT, use **tin opener**

2 → See feature box at **household**; See also color supplement

cano|pied /kænəpid/ ADJ [usu ADJ n] A **canopied** building or piece of furniture is covered with a roof or a piece of material supported by poles. ❑ *...a canopied Elizabethan bed.*

cano|py /kænəpi/ (canopies) **1** N-COUNT A **canopy** is a decorated cover, often made of cloth, which is placed above something such as a bed or a seat. **2** N-COUNT A **canopy** is a layer of something that spreads out and covers an area, for example the branches and leaves that spread out at the top of trees in a forest. ❑ *The trees formed such a dense canopy that all beneath was a deep carpet of pine needles.*

cant /kænt/ N-UNCOUNT If you refer to moral or religious statements as **cant**, you are criticizing them because you think the person making them does not really believe what they are saying. [DISAPPROVAL] ❑ *...politicians holding forth with their usual hypocritical cant.*

can't /kænt/ **Can't** is the usual spoken form of 'cannot.'

can|ta|loupe /kænt³loʊp/ (cantaloupes) also **cantaloup** N-COUNT A **cantaloupe** is a type of melon.

can|tan|ker|ous /kæntæŋkərəs/ ADJ [usu ADJ n] Someone who is **cantankerous** is always finding things to argue or complain about. [WRITTEN] ❑ *...a cantankerous old man.*

can|ta|ta /kæntɑtə/ (cantatas) N-COUNT A **cantata** is a fairly short musical work for singers and instruments.

can|teen /kæntin/ (canteens) **1** N-COUNT A **canteen** is a place in a factory or military base where meals or snacks are served to the people who work there. ❑ *Rennie had eaten his supper in the canteen.* **2** N-COUNT A **canteen** is a small metal or plastic bottle for carrying water and other drinks. Canteens are used by soldiers. ❑ *...a full canteen of water.*

can|ter /kæntər/ (canters, cantering, cantered) V-I When a horse **canters**, it moves at a speed that is slower than a gallop but faster than a trot. ❑ *The competitors cantered into the arena to conclude the closing ceremony.* • N-COUNT **Canter** is also a noun. ❑ *Carnac set off at a canter.*

can|ti|lever /kæntɪlivər/ (cantilevers) N-COUNT A **cantilever** is a long piece of metal or wood used in a structure such as a bridge. One end is fastened to something and the other end is used to support part of the structure. ❑ *...the old steel cantilever bridge.*

can|ti|levered /kæntɪlivərd/ ADJ [usu ADJ n] A **cantilevered** structure is constructed using cantilevers. ❑ *...a cantilevered balcony.*

can|ton /kæntɒn/ (cantons) N-COUNT A **canton** is a political or administrative region in some countries, for example Switzerland. ❑ *...the Swiss canton of Berne.*

Can|ton|ese /kæntəniz/ (Cantonese) **1** ADJ **Cantonese** means belonging or relating to the Chinese city of Guangzhou and the province of Guangdong. **2** N-COUNT [usu pl] The **Cantonese** are the people who live in or come from the Chinese city of Guangzhou and the province of Guangdong. **3** N-UNCOUNT **Cantonese** is the language spoken in the mainland Chinese province of Guangdong and its surrounding areas, Hong Kong, Macau, as well as in other parts of the world.

can|ton|ment /kæntoʊnmənt/ (cantonments) N-COUNT A **cantonment** is a group of buildings or a camp where soldiers live.

can|vas /kænvəs/ (canvases) **1** N-UNCOUNT **Canvas** is a strong, heavy cloth that is used for making things such as tents, sails, and bags. ❑ *...a canvas bag.* **2** N-VAR A **canvas** is a piece of canvas or similar material on which an oil painting can be done. **3** N-COUNT A **canvas** is a painting that has been done on canvas. ❑ *The show includes canvases by masters like Carpaccio, Canaletto and Guardi.* **4** → See feature box at **fine art**

can|vass /kænvəs/ (canvasses, canvassing, canvassed) **1** V-I If you **canvass** for a particular person or political party, you go around an area trying to persuade people to vote for that person or party. ❑ *I'm canvassing for the Republican Party.* **2** V-T If you **canvass** public opinion, you find out how people feel about a particular subject. ❑ *Members of Congress are spending the weekend canvassing opinion in their constituencies.*

can|yon /kænyən/ (canyons) N-COUNT; N-IN-NAMES A **canyon** is a long, narrow valley with very steep sides. ❑ *...the Grand Canyon.*

cap ✦✧ /kæp/ (caps, capping, capped) **1** N-COUNT A **cap** is a soft, flat hat with a curved part at the front which is called a visor. ❑ *...a dark blue baseball cap.* **2** N-COUNT A **cap** is a special hat which is worn as part of a uniform. ❑ *...a border guard in olive gray uniform and a cap.* **3** N-COUNT The **cap** of a bottle is its lid. ❑ *She unscrewed the cap of her water bottle and gave him a drink.* **4** V-T If someone says that a good or bad event **caps** a series of events, they mean it is the final event in the series, and the other events were also good or bad. [JOURNALISM] ❑ *The medal capped a fine tournament for the athlete.* **5** → See also color supplement

ca|pa|bil|ity /keɪpəbɪlɪti/ (capabilities) **1** N-VAR If you have the **capability** or the **capabilities** to do something, you have the ability or the qualities that are necessary to do it. ❑ *People experience differences in physical and mental capability depending on the time of day.* ◼ N-VAR A country's military **capability** is its ability to fight in a war. ❑ *Their military capability has gone down because their air force has proved not to be an effective force.*

ca|pable ◆◇◇ /ˈkeɪpəbəl/ ◼ ADJ [v-link ADJ of -ing/n] If a person or thing is **capable of** doing something, they have the ability to do it. ❑ *He appeared hardly capable of conducting a coherent conversation.* ❑ *The kitchen is capable of catering for several hundred people.* ◼ ADJ Someone who is **capable** has the skill or qualities necessary to do a particular thing well, or is able to do most things well. ❑ *She's a very capable speaker.* • **ca|pably** /ˈkeɪpəbli/ ADV [ADV with v] ❑ *It was all dealt with very capably by the police and security people.*

SYNONYMS

capable
ADJ ◼
accomplished: *She is an accomplished painter.*
competent: *He was a loyal, distinguished, and very competent civil servant.*
skilful: *He is widely regarded as Hungary's most skillful politician.*
adept: *He is an adept guitar player.*
proficient: *A great number of Egyptians are proficient in foreign languages.*
able: *...one of the brightest and ablest members of the government.*

ca|pa|cious /kəˈpeɪʃəs/ ADJ [usu ADJ n] Something that is **capacious** has a lot of space to put things in. [FORMAL] ❑ *...her capacious handbag.*

ca|paci|tor /kəˈpæsɪtər/ (**capacitors**) N-COUNT A **capacitor** is a device for accumulating electric charge.

ca|pac|ity ◆◇◇ /kəˈpæsɪti/ (**capacities**) ◼ N-VAR Your **capacity** for something is your ability to do it, or the amount of it that you are able to do. ❑ *Our capacity for giving care, love, and attention is limited.* ❑ *Her mental capacity and temperament are as remarkable as his.* ◼ N-VAR The **capacity** of a container is its volume, or the amount of liquid it can hold, measured in units such as quarts or gallons. ❑ *...containers with a maximum capacity of 200 gallons of water.* ◼ N-UNCOUNT The **capacity** of something such as a factory, industry, or region is the quantity of things that it can produce or deliver with the equipment or resources that are available. ❑ *...the amount of spare capacity in the economy.* ❑ *Bread factories are working at full capacity.* ◼ N-COUNT The **capacity** of a piece of equipment is its size or power, often measured in particular units. ❑ *...an aircraft with a bomb-carrying capacity of 1000 pounds.* ◼ N-COUNT If you do something in a particular **capacity**, you do it as part of a particular job or duty, or because you are representing a particular organization or person. [WRITTEN] ❑ *Ms. Halliwell visited the Philippines in her capacity as a Special Representative of UNICEF.* ◼ N-SING [also no det, oft to N] The **capacity** of a building, place, or vehicle is the number of people or things that it can hold. If a place is filled **to capacity**, it is as full as it can possibly be. ❑ *Each stadium had a seating capacity of about 50,000.* ◼ ADJ [ADJ n] A **capacity** crowd or audience completely fills a theater, sports stadium, or other place. ❑ *A capacity crowd of 76,000 people was at the stadium for the event.*

COLLOCATIONS

capacity
NOUN
◼
adjective + **capacity**: creative, earning, intellectual, mental; diminished, limited
verb + **capacity**: boost, develop
◼
noun + **capacity**: lung, storage
◼
adjective + **capacity**: full, maximum, spare; productive
verb + **capacity**: boost, expand, increase; reduce
◼
noun + **capacity**: engine, fuel

SYNONYMS

capacity
NOUN ◼
ability: *He has the ability to bring out the best in others.*
facility: *He and Marcia shared a facility for languages.*
aptitude: *Some students have more aptitude for academic work than others.*
capability: *People experience differences in mental capability depending on the time of day.*

cape /keɪp/ (**capes**) ◼ N-COUNT; N-IN-NAMES A **cape** is a large piece of land that sticks out into the sea from the coast. ❑ *Naomi James became the first woman to sail solo around the world via Cape Horn.* ◼ N-COUNT A **cape** is a short cloak. ❑ *...a woolen cape.*

ca|per /ˈkeɪpər/ (**capers, capering, capered**) ◼ N-COUNT [usu pl] **Capers** are the small green buds of caper plants. They are usually sold preserved in vinegar. ◼ V-I If you **caper** around, you run and jump around because you are happy or excited. [WRITTEN] ❑ *Children capered around in front of the Smithsonian Institution.*

ca|pil|lary /ˈkæpəleri/ (**capillaries**) N-COUNT **Capillaries** are tiny blood vessels in your body.

capi|tal ◆◆◆ /ˈkæpɪtəl/ (**capitals**) ◼ N-UNCOUNT **Capital** is a large sum of money which you use to start a business, or which you invest in order to make more money. [BUSINESS] ❑ *Companies are having difficulty in raising capital.* ◼ N-UNCOUNT You can use **capital** to refer to buildings or machinery which are necessary to produce goods or to make companies more efficient, but which do not make money directly. [BUSINESS] ❑ *...capital equipment that could have served to increase production.* ◼ N-UNCOUNT **Capital** is the part of an amount of money borrowed or invested which does not include interest. [BUSINESS] ❑ *With a conventional mortgage, the payments consist of both capital and interest.* ◼ N-COUNT The **capital** of a country is the city or town where its government or legislature meets. ❑ *...Kathmandu, the capital of Nepal.* ◼ N-COUNT If a place is the **capital** of a particular industry or activity, it is the place that is most famous for it, because it happens in that place more than anywhere else. ❑ *Colmar has long been considered the capital of the wine trade.* ◼ N-COUNT **Capitals** or **capital letters** are written or printed letters in the form which is used at the beginning of sentences or names. 'T,' 'B,' and 'F' are capitals. ❑ *The name and address are written in capitals.* ◼ ADJ [ADJ n] A **capital** offense is one that is so serious that the person who commits it can be punished by death. ❑ *Espionage is a capital offense in this country.* ◼ PHRASE If you say that someone **is making capital out of** a situation, you disapprove of the way they are gaining an advantage for themselves through other people's efforts or bad luck. [FORMAL, DISAPPROVAL] ❑ *He rebuked the president for trying to make political capital out of the hostage situation.* → see also **working capital**

capi|tal ac|count (**capital accounts**) ◼ N-COUNT A country's **capital account** is the part of its balance of payments that is concerned with the movement of capital. ❑ *...restrictions that affect the capital account of a country's balance of payments.* ◼ N-COUNT A **capital account** is a financial statement showing the capital value of a company on a particular date. [BUSINESS] ❑ *No business can survive without a capital account.*

capi|tal gains N-PLURAL **Capital gains** are the profits that you make when you buy something and then sell it again at a higher price. [BUSINESS] ❑ *He called for the reform of capital gains tax.*

capi|tal goods N-PLURAL **Capital goods** are used to make other products. Compare **consumer goods**. [BUSINESS] ❑ *Most imports from Korea are raw materials and capital goods.*

capi|tal in|flow (**capital inflows**) N-VAR In economics, **capital inflow** is the amount of capital coming into a country, for example in the form of foreign investment. [BUSINESS] ❑ *...a large drop in the capital inflow into America.*

capital-intensive ADJ **Capital-intensive** industries and businesses need the investment of large sums of money. Compare **labor-intensive**. [BUSINESS] ❑ *...highly capital-intensive industries like auto manufacturing or petrochemicals.*

capi|tal|ism /ˈkæpɪtəlɪzəm/ N-UNCOUNT **Capitalism** is an economic and political system in which property, business, and industry are owned by private individuals and not by

capi|tal|ist /kæpɪtᵊlɪst/ (capitalists) **1** ADJ A **capitalist** country or system supports or is based on the principles of capitalism. ❑ *I'm a strong believer in the capitalist system.* **2** N-COUNT A **capitalist** is someone who believes in and supports the principles of capitalism. ❑ *He had hoped to even have a working relationship with the capitalists.* **3** N-COUNT A **capitalist** is someone who owns a business which they run in order to make a profit for themselves. ❑ *They argue that only private capitalists can remake Poland's economy.*

capi|tal|ist|ic /kæpɪtᵊlɪstɪk/ ADJ [ADJ n] **Capitalistic** means supporting or based on the principles of capitalism. ❑ *...the forces of capitalistic greed.* ❑ *...capitalistic economic growth.*

capi|tal|ize /kæpɪtᵊlaɪz/ (capitalizes, capitalizing, capitalized)

in BRIT, also use **capitalise**

1 V-I If you **capitalize** on a situation, you use it to gain some advantage for yourself. ❑ *The rebels seem to be trying to capitalize on the public's discontent with the government.* **2** V-T In business, if you **capitalize** something that belongs to you, you sell it in order to make money. [BUSINESS] ❑ *Our intention is to capitalize the company by any means we can.* **3** V-T If you **capitalize** a letter, you write it as a capital letter. If you **capitalize** a word, you spell it in capital letters, or with the first letter as a capital letter. ❑ *Capitalize all proper nouns but not the articles (a, an) that precede them.*

capi|tal let|ter (capital letters) N-COUNT **Capital letters** are the same as **capitals**.

capi|tal pun|ish|ment N-UNCOUNT **Capital punishment** is punishment which involves the legal killing of a person who has committed a serious crime such as murder. ❑ *Most democracies have abolished capital punishment.*

cap|i|tol /kæpɪtᵊl/ also **Capitol** (capitols) **1** N-COUNT A **capitol** is a government building in which a state legislature meets. [AM] ❑ *Thousands of striking teachers in Washington state will protest in front of the state capitol today.* **2** N-PROPER [the N] **The Capitol** is the government building in Washington, D.C., in which the U.S. Congress meets. [AM] ❑ *Thousands of demonstrators rallied in front of the Capitol.*

ca|pitu|late /kəpɪtʃəleɪt/ (capitulates, capitulating, capitulated) V-I If you **capitulate**, you stop resisting and do what someone else wants you to do. ❑ *The club eventually capitulated and now grants equal rights to women.*

cap|let /kæplɪt/ (caplets) N-COUNT A **caplet** is an oval tablet of medicine. [AM] ❑ *Lenny swallowed the caplets and handed the glass back to Mr. Trancas.*

ca|pon /keɪpɒn, -pən/ (capons) N-COUNT A **capon** is a male chicken that has had its sex organs removed and has been specially fattened up to be eaten.

cap|puc|ci|no /kæpətʃinoʊ/ (cappuccinos) N-UNCOUNT **Cappuccino** is coffee which is made using milk and has froth and sometimes powdered chocolate on top. • N-COUNT A **cappuccino** is a cup of cappuccino.

ca|price /kəpriːs/ (caprices) N-VAR A **caprice** is an unexpected action or decision which has no strong reason or purpose. [FORMAL] ❑ *I lived in terror of her sudden caprices and moods.*

ca|pri|cious /kəprɪʃəs/ ADJ Someone who is **capricious** often changes their mind unexpectedly. ❑ *He was accused of being capricious and undemocratic.*

Cap|ri|corn /kæprɪkɔːrn/ (Capricorns) **1** N-UNCOUNT **Capricorn** is one of the twelve signs of the zodiac. Its symbol is a goat. People who are born approximately between the 22nd of December and the 19th of January come under this sign. **2** N-COUNT A **Capricorn** is a person whose sign of the zodiac is Capricorn.

cap|si|cum /kæpsɪkəm/ (capsicums) N-VAR **Capsicums** are peppers.

cap|size /kæpsaɪz/ (capsizes, capsizing, capsized) V-T/V-I If you **capsize** a boat or if it **capsizes**, it turns upside down in the water. ❑ *The sea got very rough and the boat capsized.*

cap|stan /kæpstən/ (capstans) N-COUNT A **capstan** is a machine consisting of a drum that turns around and pulls in a heavy rope or something attached to a rope, for example an anchor.

cap|sule /kæpsᵊl/ (capsules) **1** N-COUNT A **capsule** is a very small tube containing powdered or liquid medicine, which you swallow. ❑ *...cod liver oil capsules.* **2** N-COUNT A **capsule** is a small container with a drug or other substance inside it, which is used for medical or scientific purposes. ❑ *They first inserted capsules into the animals' mouths.* **3** N-COUNT A space **capsule** is the part of a spacecraft in which people travel, and which often separates from the main rocket. ❑ *A Russian space capsule is currently orbiting the Earth.* **4** N-COUNT A time **capsule** is a container into which people put typical everyday objects from their lives. The container is buried so that people in the future can dig it up, and find out about what life was like in the past. ❑ *Twenty-five years ago they filled a time capsule and buried it.*

Capt. N-TITLE **Capt.** is a written abbreviation for **captain**. ❑ *Capt. Hunt asked which engine was on fire.*

cap|tain ✦✧ /kæptɪn/ (captains, captaining, captained) **1** N-TITLE; N-COUNT; N-VOC In the army, navy, and some other armed forces, a **captain** is an officer of middle rank. ❑ *...Captain Mark Phillips.* ❑ *...a captain in the army.* **2** N-COUNT The **captain** of a sports team is the player in charge of it. ❑ *...Mickey Thomas, the captain of the tennis team.* **3** N-COUNT The **captain** of a ship is the sailor in charge of it. ❑ *...the captain of an excursion boat.* **4** N-COUNT; N-TITLE The **captain** of an airplane is the pilot in charge of it. **5** N-COUNT; N-TITLE In the United States and some other countries, a **captain** is a police officer or firefighter of fairly senior rank. ❑ *...a former Honolulu police captain.* **6** V-T If you **captain** a team or a ship, you are the captain of it. ❑ *He captained the winning team in 1991.*

cap|tain|cy /kæptɪnsi/ N-UNCOUNT The **captaincy** of a team is the position of being captain. ❑ *His captaincy of the team was ended by mild eye trouble.*

cap|tain of in|dus|try (captains of industry) N-COUNT You can refer to the owners or senior managers of industrial companies as **captains of industry**.

cap|tcha /kæptʃə/ (captchas) N-VAR **Captcha** is a system for checking that a human and not a machine is using a computer. **Captcha** is an abbreviation for 'completely automated public Turing test to tell computers and humans apart.' ❑ *We use captcha to screen for spam.*

cap|tion ✦✧ /kæpʃᵊn/ (captions) N-COUNT A **caption** is the words printed underneath a picture or cartoon which explain what it is about. ❑ *The local paper featured me standing on a stepladder with a caption, "Wendy climbs the ladder to success."*

cap|ti|vate /kæptɪveɪt/ (captivates, captivating, captivated) V-T [usu passive] If you **are captivated** by someone or something, you find them fascinating and attractive. ❑ *I was captivated by her brilliant mind.*

cap|ti|vat|ing /kæptɪveɪtɪŋ/ ADJ Someone or something that is **captivating** fascinates or attracts you. ❑ *...her captivating smile and alluring looks.*

cap|tive /kæptɪv/ (captives) **1** ADJ A **captive** person or animal is being kept imprisoned or enclosed. [LITERARY] ❑ *Her heart had begun to pound inside her chest like a captive animal.* • N-COUNT A **captive** is someone who is captive. ❑ *He described the difficulties of surviving for four months as a captive.* **2** ADJ [ADJ n] A **captive** audience is a group of people who are not free to leave a certain place and so have to watch or listen. A **captive** market is a group of people who cannot choose whether or where to buy things. ❑ *We all performed action songs, sketches, and dances before a captive audience of parents and patrons.* **3** PHRASE If you take someone **captive** or hold someone **captive**, you take or keep them as a prisoner. ❑ *Richard was finally released on February 4, one year and six weeks after he'd been taken captive.* **4** → See feature box at **conflict**

cap|tive breed|ing N-UNCOUNT **Captive breeding** is the breeding of wild animals in places such as zoos, especially animals which have become rare in the wild.

cap|tiv|ity /kæptɪvɪti/ N-UNCOUNT **Captivity** is the state of being kept imprisoned or enclosed. ❑ *The great majority of barn owls are reared in captivity.*

cap|tor /kæptər/ (captors) N-COUNT [usu poss N] You can refer to the person who has captured a person or animal as their **captor**. ❑ *They did not know what their captors planned for them.*

cap|ture /kæptʃər/ (captures, capturing, captured)
1 V-T If you **capture** someone or something, you catch them, especially in a war. ❑ *The guerrillas shot down one airplane and captured the pilot.* ❑ *It was a failed attempt to capture more territory from the enemy.* • N-UNCOUNT **Capture** is also a noun. ❑ *...the final battles which led to the army's capture of the town.* **2** V-T [no cont] If something or someone **captures** a particular quality, feeling, or atmosphere, they represent or express it successfully. ❑ *Chef Idris Caldora offers an inspired menu that captures the spirit of the Mediterranean.* **3** V-T If something **captures** your attention or imagination, you begin to be interested or excited by it. If someone or something **captures** your heart, you begin to love them or like them very much. ❑ *...the great names of the past who usually capture the historian's attention.* **4** V-T [usu passive] If an event **is captured** in a photograph or on film, it is photographed or filmed. ❑ *The incident was captured on videotape.* ❑ *The images were captured by TV crews filming outside the base.* **5** → See feature box at **history**

---SYNONYMS---
capture
VERB **1**
catch: *Police say they are confident about catching the gunman.*
arrest: *The police say seven people were arrested for minor offenses.*
seize: *Men carrying sub-machine guns seized the five soldiers and drove them away.*
apprehend: *Police have not apprehended her killer.*

car /kɑr/ (cars) **1** N-COUNT [also by N] A **car** is a motor vehicle with room for a small number of passengers. ❑ *He had left his tickets in his car.* **2** N-COUNT A **car** is one of the separate, long sections of a train that carries passengers. [mainly AM] ❑ *The company manufactured elegant railroad cars.*

in BRIT, usually use **carriage**

3 N-COUNT The separate sections of a train are called **cars** when they are used for a particular purpose. ❑ *He made his way into the dining car for breakfast.* **4** → See feature box at **accident**; See also color supplement

ca|rafe /kəræf/ (carafes) N-COUNT [oft N of n] A **carafe** is a glass container in which you serve water or wine. ❑ *He ordered a carafe of wine.*

car alarm (car alarms) N-COUNT A **car alarm** is a device in a car which makes a loud noise if anyone tries to break into the vehicle. ❑ *He returned to the airport to find his car alarm going off.*

cara|mel /kærəmɛl, -məl, kɑrməl/ (caramels) **1** N-VAR A **caramel** is a chewy sweet food made from sugar, butter, and milk. **2** N-UNCOUNT **Caramel** is burnt sugar used for coloring and flavoring food.

cara|mel|ize /kærəməlaɪz, kɑrmə-/ (caramelizes, caramelizing, caramelized)

in BRIT, also use **caramelise**

1 V-I If sugar **caramelizes**, it turns to caramel as a result of being heated. ❑ *Cook until the sugar starts to caramelize.* **2** V-T If you **caramelize** something such as fruit, you cook it with sugar so that it is coated with caramel. ❑ *...caramelized apples and pears.*

cara|pace /kærəpeɪs/ (carapaces) **1** N-COUNT A **carapace** is the protective shell on the back of some animals such as tortoises or crabs. [FORMAL] **2** N-COUNT [usu with supp] You can refer to an attitude that someone has in order to protect themselves as their **carapace**. [LITERARY] ❑ *The arrogance became his protective carapace.*

car|at /kærət/ (carats) N-COUNT A **carat** is a unit for measuring the weight of diamonds and other precious stones. It is equal to 0.2 grams. ❑ *The gemstone is 28.6 millimeters high and weighs 139.43 carats.*

cara|van /kærəvæn/ (caravans) **1** N-COUNT A **caravan** is a group of people and animals or vehicles who travel together. ❑ *...the old caravan routes from Central Asia to China.* **2** N-COUNT A **caravan** is the same as a **trailer**. [BRIT] → see **trailer 2**

cara|van site (caravan sites) N-COUNT A **caravan site** is the same as a **trailer park**. [BRIT]

cara|way /kærəweɪ/ N-UNCOUNT [oft N n] **Caraway** is a plant with strong-tasting seeds that are used in cooking. Caraway seeds are often used to flavor bread and cakes.

carb /kɑrb/ (carbs) N-COUNT [usu pl] **Carbs** are foods such as potatoes, pasta, and bread, that contain a lot of carbohydrate. ❑ *Eat a wide variety of carbs, fruit, and vegetables.*

car|bine /kɑrbin/ (carbines) N-COUNT A **carbine** is a light automatic rifle.

car|bo|hy|drate /kɑrboʊhaɪdreɪt/ (carbohydrates) N-VAR **Carbohydrates** are substances, found in certain kinds of food, that provide you with energy. Foods such as sugar and bread that contain these substances can also be referred to as **carbohydrates**. ❑ *...carbohydrates such as bread, pasta, or potatoes.*

car|bol|ic acid /kɑrbɒlɪk æsɪd/ N-UNCOUNT **Carbolic acid** or **carbolic** is a liquid that is used as a disinfectant and antiseptic. ❑ *Carbolic acid is usually used for cleaning.* ❑ *She smelled strongly of carbolic soap.*

car bomb (car bombs) N-COUNT A **car bomb** is a bomb which is inside a car, van, or truck.

car|bon /kɑrbən/ **1** N-UNCOUNT **Carbon** is a chemical element that diamonds and coal are made up of. **2** N-UNCOUNT **Carbon** is short for **carbon dioxide**. ❑ *Research has noticed a reduction in the ability of the oceans to absorb carbon.* ❑ *...carbon emissions.*

car|bon|ate /kɑrbəneɪt/ (carbonates) N-VAR [oft N n, N of n] **Carbonate** is used in the names of some substances that are formed from carbonic acid, which is a compound of carbon dioxide and water. ❑ *...1,500 milligrams of calcium carbonate.* ❑ *...carbonate of ammonia solution.*

car|bon|at|ed /kɑrbəneɪtɪd/ ADJ [usu ADJ n] **Carbonated** drinks are drinks that contain small bubbles of carbon dioxide. ❑ *...colas and other carbonated soft drinks.*

car|bon copy (carbon copies) **1** N-COUNT [usu N of n] If you say that one person or thing is a **carbon copy** of another, you mean that they look or behave exactly like them. ❑ *She's a carbon copy of her mother.* **2** N-COUNT A **carbon copy** is a copy of a piece of writing that is made using carbon paper.

car|bon cred|it (carbon credits) N-COUNT [usu pl] **Carbon credits** are an allowance that certain companies have, permitting them to burn a certain amount of fossil fuels. ❑ *By investing in efficient plant it could generate lots of valuable carbon credits to sell to wealthier, more wasteful nations.*

car|bon dat|ing N-UNCOUNT **Carbon dating** is a system of calculating the age of a very old object by measuring the amount of radioactive carbon it contains.

car|bon di|ox|ide /kɑrbən daɪɒksaɪd/ N-UNCOUNT **Carbon dioxide** is a gas. It is produced by animals and people breathing out, and by chemical reactions.

car|bon foot|print (carbon footprints) N-COUNT [oft poss N] Your **carbon footprint** is a measure of the amount of carbon dioxide released into the atmosphere by your activities over a particular period. ❑ *We all need to look for ways to reduce our carbon footprint.*

car|bon mon|ox|ide /kɑrbən mənɒksaɪd/ N-UNCOUNT **Carbon monoxide** is a poisonous gas that is produced especially by the engines of vehicles. ❑ *The limit for carbon monoxide is 4.5 per cent of the exhaust gas.*

car|bon neu|tral ADJ A **carbon neutral** lifestyle, company, or activity does not cause an increase in the overall amount of carbon dioxide in the atmosphere. ❑ *You can make your flights carbon neutral by planting trees to make up for the greenhouse gas emissions.* • **car|bon neu|tral|ity** N-UNCOUNT ❑ *This is consistent with our commitment to carbon neutrality.*

car|bon tax (carbon taxes) N-COUNT A **carbon tax** is a tax on the burning of fuels such as coal, gas, and oil. Its aim is to reduce the amount of carbon dioxide released into the atmosphere.

car|bon trad|ing N-UNCOUNT **Carbon trading** is the practice of buying and selling the right to produce carbon dioxide emissions, so that people, countries, or companies who use a lot of fuel and electricity can buy rights from those that do not use so much.

car|bun|cle /kɑrbʌŋkəl/ (carbuncles) N-COUNT A **carbuncle** is a large swelling under the skin.

car|bu|re|tor /kɑrbəreɪtər/ (carburetors)

in BRIT, use **carburettor**

carcass

N-COUNT A **carburetor** is the part of an engine, usually in a car, in which air and gasoline are mixed together to form a vapor which can be burned.

car|cass /kɑrkəs/ (**carcasses**)

> in BRIT, also use **carcase**

N-COUNT A **carcass** is the body of a dead animal. ❏ *A cluster of vultures crouched on the carcass of a dead buffalo.*

car|cino|gen /kɑrsɪnədʒən, kɑrsɪnədʒɛn/ (**carcinogens**) N-COUNT A **carcinogen** is a substance which can cause cancer. [MEDICAL]

car|cino|gen|ic /kɑrsɪnədʒɛnɪk/ ADJ A substance that is **carcinogenic** is likely to cause cancer. [MEDICAL]

car|ci|no|ma /kɑrsɪnoʊmə/ (**carcinomas**) ◼ N-UNCOUNT **Carcinoma** is a type of cancer. [MEDICAL] ◻ N-COUNT **Carcinomas** are malignant tumors. [MEDICAL]

card ✦✧ /kɑrd/ (**cards**) ◼ N-COUNT A **card** is a piece of stiff paper or thin cardboard on which something is written or printed. ❏ *Check the numbers below against the numbers on your card.* ◻ N-COUNT A **card** is a piece of cardboard or plastic, or a small document, which shows information about you and which you carry with you, for example to prove your identity. ❏ *...they check my bag and press card.* ❏ *...her membership card.* ◼ N-COUNT A **card** is a rectangular piece of plastic, issued by a bank, company, or store, which you can use to buy things or obtain money. ❏ *He paid the whole bill with an American Express card.* ◻ N-COUNT A **card** is a folded piece of stiff paper with a picture and sometimes a message printed on it, which you send to someone on a special occasion. ❏ *She sends me a card on my birthday.* ◼ N-COUNT A **card** is the same as a **postcard**. ❏ *Send your details on a card to the following address.* ◻ N-COUNT A **card** is a piece of thin cardboard carried by someone such as a businessperson in order to give it to other people. A card shows the name, address, telephone number, and other details of the person who carries it. [BUSINESS] ❏ *Here's my card. You may need me.* ◼ N-COUNT **Cards** are thin pieces of cardboard with numbers or pictures printed on them which are used to play various games. ❏ *...a deck of cards.* ◻ N-UNCOUNT If you are playing **cards**, you are playing a game using cards. ❏ *They enjoy themselves drinking wine, smoking, and playing cards.* ◼ N-UNCOUNT **Card** is strong, stiff paper or thin cardboard. ❏ *She put the pieces of card in her pocket.* ◻ → see also **bank card, business card, calling card, credit card, debit card, gold card, greeting card, identity card, playing cards, smart card, wild card** ◼ PHRASE If you say that something is **in the cards**, you mean that it is very likely to happen. ❏ *Last summer she began telling friends that a New Year marriage was in the cards.* ◻ PHRASE If you **have** your **cards read**, you have your fortune told by someone who uses playing cards or tarot cards to tell you about yourself and predict your future. ❏ *The shop had a sign in the window: "Have your cards read here, $25."*

car|da|mom /kɑrdəməm/ (**cardamoms**) also **cardamon** N-VAR **Cardamom** is a spice. It comes from the seeds of a plant grown in Asia.

card|board /kɑrdbɔrd/ N-UNCOUNT **Cardboard** is thick, stiff paper that is used, for example, to make boxes and models. ❏ *...a cardboard box.*

card-carrying ◼ ADJ [ADJ n] A **card-carrying** member of a particular group or political party is an official member of that group or party, rather than someone who supports it. ❏ *I've been a card-carrying member of the party for five years.* ◻ ADJ [ADJ n] If you describe someone as, for example, a **card-carrying** feminist, you are emphasizing the fact that they believe strongly in and try to carry out the ideas of feminism. [EMPHASIS] ❏ *...a card-carrying Christian.*

card game (**card games**) N-COUNT A **card game** is a game that is played using a set of playing cards.

card|holder /kɑrdhoʊldər/ (**cardholders**) N-COUNT A **cardholder** is someone who has a credit card or debit card. ❏ *The average cardholder today carries three to four credit cards.*

car|di|ac /kɑrdiæk/ ADJ [ADJ n] **Cardiac** means relating to the heart. [MEDICAL] ❏ *The man was suffering from cardiac weakness.*

car|di|ac ar|rest (**cardiac arrests**) N-VAR A **cardiac arrest** is a failure of the heart to pump blood. [MEDICAL]

care

car|di|gan /kɑrdɪgən/ (**cardigans**) N-COUNT A **cardigan** is a knitted woolen sweater that you can fasten at the front with buttons or a zipper.

car|di|nal /kɑrdənəl/ (**cardinals**) ◼ N-COUNT; N-TITLE A **cardinal** is a high-ranking priest in the Catholic Church. ❏ *In 1448, Nicholas was appointed a cardinal.* ◻ ADJ [ADJ n] A **cardinal** rule or quality is the one that is considered to be the most important. [FORMAL] ❏ *As a salesperson, your cardinal rule is to do everything you can to satisfy a customer.* ◼ N-COUNT A **cardinal** is a common North American bird. The male has bright red feathers.

car|di|nal num|ber (**cardinal numbers**) N-COUNT A **cardinal number** is a number such as 1, 3, or 10 that tells you how many things there are in a group but not what order they are in. Compare **ordinal number**.

car|di|nal point (**cardinal points**) N-COUNT The **cardinal points** are the four main points of the compass, north, south, east, and west.

car|di|nal sin (**cardinal sins**) N-COUNT If you describe an action as a **cardinal sin**, you are indicating that some people strongly disapprove of it. ❏ *I committed the physician's cardinal sin: I got involved with my patients.*

card in|dex (**card indexes**) N-COUNT A **card index** is a number of cards with information written on them which are arranged in a particular order, usually alphabetical, so that you can find the information you want easily. ❏ *Then he turned to the card index and tore out the entry for Matthew Holmwood.*

car|dio /kɑrdioʊ/ N-UNCOUNT **Cardio** is exercise that is designed to benefit the heart and blood vessels, for example running, swimming, and cycling. ❏ *We go to the gym three times a week and do cardio and weights.* ❏ *...a cardio workout.*

car|di|olo|gist /kɑrdiɒlədʒɪst/ (**cardiologists**) N-COUNT A **cardiologist** is a doctor who specializes in the heart and its diseases.

car|di|ol|ogy /kɑrdiɒlədʒi/ N-UNCOUNT **Cardiology** is the study of the heart and its diseases.

car|dio|vas|cu|lar /kɑrdioʊvæskyələr/ ADJ [ADJ n] **Cardiovascular** means relating to the heart and blood vessels. [MEDICAL] ❏ *Smoking places you at serious risk of cardiovascular and respiratory disease.*

card ta|ble (**card tables**) N-COUNT A **card table** is a small, light table which can be folded up and which is sometimes used for playing games of cards on.

care ✦✦✦ /kɛər/ (**cares, caring, cared**) ◼ V-T/V-I [no cont] If you **care** about something, you feel that it is important and are concerned about it. ❏ *...a company that cares about the environment.* ❏ *...young men who did not care whether they lived or died.* ◻ V-I [no cont] If you **care** for someone, you feel a lot of affection for them. [APPROVAL] ❏ *He wanted me to know that he still cared for me.* ● **car|ing** N-UNCOUNT ❏ *He demonstrates traits of caring and compassion.* ◼ V-I If you **care** for someone or something, you look after them and keep them in a good state or condition. ❏ *They hired a nurse to care for her.* ❏ *...these distinctive cars, lovingly cared for by private owners.* ● N-UNCOUNT **Care** is also a noun. ❏ *Most of the staff specialize in the care of children.* ❏ *...sensitive teeth which need special care.* ◻ V-T/V-I [no cont] You can ask someone if they would **care** for something or if they would **care** to do something as a polite way of asking if they would like to have or do something. [POLITENESS] ❏ *Would you care for some orange juice?* ◼ N-UNCOUNT If you do something with **care**, you give careful attention to it because you do not want to make any mistakes or cause any damage. ❏ *Condoms are an effective method of birth control if used with care.* ◻ N-COUNT Your **cares** are your worries, anxieties, or fears. ❏ *Lean back in a hot bath and forget all the cares of the day.* ◼ → see also **caring, day care, intensive care** ◻ PHRASE You can use **for all I care** to emphasize that it does not matter at all to you what someone does. [EMPHASIS] ❏ *You can go right now for all I care.* ◼ PHRASE If you say that you **couldn't care less** about someone or something, you are emphasizing that you are not interested in them or worried about them. You can also say that you **could care less**, with the same meaning. [EMPHASIS] ❏ *I couldn't care less about the woman.* ❏ *I don't care if they respect me. I could care less.* ◻ PHRASE If someone sends you a letter or package **care of** or **in care**

of a particular person or place, they send it to that person or place, and it is then passed on to you. ❏ *Please write to me care of the publishers.* ❏ *He wrote to me in care of my publisher.* **11** PHRASE If you **take care of** someone or something, you look after them and prevent them from being harmed or damaged. ❏ *There was no one else to take care of their children.* **12** PHRASE If you **take care** to do something, you make sure that you do it. ❏ *Foley followed Albert through the gate, taking care to close the latch.* **13** PHRASE To **take care of** a problem, task, or situation means to deal with it. ❏ *They leave it to the system to try and take care of the problem.* **14** PHRASE You can say '**Who cares?**' to emphasize that something does not matter to you at all. [EMPHASIS] ❏ *"But we might ruin the stove."—"Who cares?"* **15** → See feature box at **drive**

ca|reen /kərin/ (**careens, careening, careened**) V-I To **careen** somewhere means to rush forward in an uncontrollable way. [mainly AM] ❏ *He stood to one side as they careened past him.*

ca|reer ✦✦◇ /kərɪər/ (**careers, careering, careered**) **1** N-COUNT A **career** is the job or profession that someone does for a long period of their life. ❏ *She is now concentrating on a career as a fashion designer.* ❏ *...a career in journalism.* **2** N-COUNT Your **career** is the part of your life that you spend working. ❏ *During his career, he wrote more than fifty plays.* **3** ADJ [ADJ n] **Career** advice or guidance consists of information about different jobs and help with deciding what kind of job you want to do. ❏ *She received very little career guidance when young.* **4** V-I [oft cont] If a person or vehicle **careers** somewhere, they move fast and in an uncontrolled way. ❏ *His car careered into a river.* **5** → See feature box at **work**

COLLOCATIONS

career
NOUN **1**
noun + **career**: acting, coaching, modeling
adjective + **career**: distinguished, glittering, illustrious, successful; academic, managerial, musical, political, professional; international
verb + **career**: forge, pursue; begin, embark on, launch, start; abandon, give up

---
SYNONYMS

career
NOUN **1**
occupation: *I was looking for an occupation which would be an adventure.*
employment: *She was unable to find employment.*
vocation: *It could well be that he has a real vocation.*
livelihood: *...fishermen who depend on the seas for their livelihood.*
profession: *Harper was a teacher by profession.*

---

ca|reer break (**career breaks**) N-COUNT If someone takes a **career break**, they stop working in their particular profession for a period of time, with the intention of returning to it later. [BUSINESS] ❏ *Many women still take career breaks to bring up children.*

ca|reer|ist /kərɪərɪst/ ADJ [usu ADJ n] **Careerist** people are ambitious and think that their career is more important than anything else. ❏ *...careerist politicians.*

ca|reer wom|an (**career women**) N-COUNT A **career woman** is a woman who regards her job and progressing in it as very important.

care|free /kɛərfriː/ ADJ A **carefree** person or period of time does not have or involve any problems, worries, or responsibilities. ❏ *Chantal remembered carefree summers at the beach.*

care|ful ✦✦◇ /kɛərfəl/ **1** ADJ If you are **careful**, you give serious attention to what you are doing, in order to avoid harm, damage, or mistakes. If you are **careful** to do something, you make sure that you do it. ❏ *Be very careful with this stuff, it can be dangerous if it isn't handled properly.* ❏ *Careful on those stairs!* • **care|ful|ly** ADV [ADV with v] ❏ *Have a nice time, dear, and drive carefully.* **2** ADJ **Careful** work, thought, or examination is thorough and shows a concern for details. ❏ *He has decided to prosecute her after careful consideration of all the relevant facts.* • **care|ful|ly** ADV [ADV with v] ❏ *...a vast series of deliberate and carefully planned thefts.* **3** ADJ [v-link ADJ about/of -ing] If you tell someone to be **careful about** doing something, you think that what they intend to do is probably wrong, and that they should think seriously before they do it. ❏ *I think you should be careful about talking of the rebels as heroes.* • **care|ful|ly** ADV [ADV after v] ❏ *He should think carefully about actions like this which play into the hands of his opponents.* **4** ADJ If you are **careful** with something such as money or resources, you use or spend only what is necessary. ❏ *Industries should be more careful with natural resources.*

care|giv|er /kɛərɡɪvər/ (**caregivers**) N-COUNT A **caregiver** is someone who is responsible for taking care of another person, for example, a person who has a disability, or is sick or very young. [mainly AM] ❏ *It is often women who are the primary caregivers.*

in BRIT, usually use **carer**

care|less /kɛərlɪs/ **1** ADJ If you are **careless**, you do not pay enough attention to what you are doing, and so you make mistakes, or cause harm or damage. ❏ *I'm sorry. How careless of me.* ❏ *Some parents are accused of being careless with their children's health.* • **care|less|ly** ADV [ADV with v] ❏ *She was fined $200 for driving carelessly.* • **care|less|ness** N-UNCOUNT ❏ *Errors are sometimes made from simple carelessness.* **2** ADJ If you say that someone is **careless** of something such as their health or appearance, you mean that they do not seem to be concerned about it, or do nothing to keep it in a good condition. ❏ *He had shown himself careless of personal safety where the life of his colleagues might be at risk.*

care|less|ly /kɛərlɪsli/ **1** ADV [ADV with v] If someone does something **carelessly**, they do it without much thought or effort. [WRITTEN] ❏ *He carelessly left the door unlocked.* ❏ *"Oh," he said carelessly. "I'm in no hurry to get back."* **2** → see also **careless**

car|er /kɛərər/ (**carers**) N-COUNT A **carer** is the same as a **caregiver**. [BRIT]

ca|ress /kərɛs/ (**caresses, caressing, caressed**) V-T If you **caress** someone or something, you stroke them gently and affectionately. [WRITTEN] ❏ *He was gently caressing her golden hair.* • N-COUNT **Caress** is also a noun. ❏ *Margaret took me to one side, holding my arm in a gentle caress.*

care|taker /kɛərteɪkər/ (**caretakers**) **1** N-COUNT A **caretaker** is a person whose job it is to take care of a house or property when the owner is not there. ❏ *Slater remained at the house, acting as its caretaker when the family was not in residence.* **2** N-COUNT A **caretaker** is someone who is responsible for looking after another person, for example, a person who has a disability, or is sick or very young. [mainly AM] ❏ *...older people serving as primary caretakers of young children.*

in BRIT, use **carer**

3 N-COUNT A **caretaker** is a person whose job it is to take care of a large building such as a school or an apartment house, and deal with small repairs to it. [BRIT]

in AM, use **janitor**

4 ADJ [ADJ n] A **caretaker** government or leader is in charge temporarily until a new government or leader is appointed. ❏ *The military intends to hand over power to a caretaker government and hold elections within six months.*

care work|er (**care workers**) **1** N-COUNT A **care worker** is someone whose job involves helping people who have particular problems or special needs. **2** → see also **health-care worker**

care|worn /kɛərwɔːrn/ ADJ A person who looks **careworn** looks worried, tired, and unhappy. ❏ *Her face was careworn with anxiety.*

car|go /kɑːrɡoʊ/ (**cargoes**) N-VAR The **cargo** of a ship or plane is the goods that it is carrying. ❏ *The boat calls at the main port to load its regular cargo of bananas.*

car|go pants N-PLURAL [also a pair of N] **Cargo pants** are large, loose pants with lots of pockets. ❏ *...a pair of cream cargo pants.*

Car|ib|bean ✦◇◇ /kærəbiːən, kərɪbiən/ (**Caribbeans**) **1** N-PROPER The **Caribbean** is the sea which is between the West Indies, Central America, and the north coast of South America. **2** ADJ **Caribbean** means belonging or relating to the Caribbean Sea and its islands, or to its people.

❏ ...the Caribbean island of St. Thomas. • N-COUNT A **Caribbean** is a person from a Caribbean island.

cari|bou /kærıbu/ (**caribou**) N-COUNT A **caribou** is a large North American deer.

cari|ca|ture /kærıkətʃər, -tʃʊər/ (**caricatures, caricaturing, caricatured**) **1** N-COUNT A **caricature** of someone is a drawing or description of them that exaggerates their appearance or behavior in a humorous or critical way. ❏ *The poster showed a caricature of Hitler with a devil's horns and tail.* **2** N-COUNT If you describe something as a **caricature** of an event or situation, you mean that it is a very exaggerated account of it. [DISAPPROVAL] ❏ *Hall is angry at what he sees as a caricature of the training offered to modern-day social workers.* **3** V-T If you **caricature** someone, you draw or describe them in an exaggerated way in order to be humorous or critical. ❏ *Her political career has been caricatured in the headlines.*

cari|ca|tur|ist /kærıkətʃʊərıst/ (**caricaturists**) N-COUNT A **caricaturist** is a person who shows other people in an exaggerated way in order to be humorous or critical, especially in drawings or cartoons.

car|ies /keəriz/ N-UNCOUNT **Caries** is decay in teeth. [TECHNICAL] ❏ *...dental caries.*

car|ing ✦◇◇ /keərıŋ/ **1** ADJ If someone is **caring**, they are affectionate, helpful, and sympathetic. ❏ *He is a lovely boy, very gentle and caring.* **2** ADJ [ADJ n] The **caring** professions are those such as nursing and social work that are involved with looking after people who are ill or who need help in coping with their lives. ❏ *The course is also suitable for those in the caring professions.*

SYNONYMS

caring
ADJ **1**
compassionate: *My father was a deeply-compassionate man.*
kind: *She is warm-hearted and kind to everyone and everything.*
warm: *She was a warm and loving mother.*
sympathetic: *It may be that he sees you only as a sympathetic friend.*

---

car|jack|er /kɑrdʒækər/ (**carjackers**) N-COUNT A **carjacker** is someone who attacks and steals from people who are driving their own cars.

car|jack|ing /kɑrdʒækıŋ/ (**carjackings**) N-VAR A **carjacking** is an attack on a person who is driving their own car during which the car or other things may be stolen or they may be harmed physically.

car|load /kɑrloʊd/ (**carloads**) N-COUNT [usu N of n] A **carload** of people or things is as many people or things as a car can carry. ❏ *Wherever he goes, a carload of soldiers goes with him.*

car|mine /kɑrmaın, -mıːn/ COLOR **Carmine** is a deep bright red color. [LITERARY] ❏ *...a tulip with carmine petals.*

car|nage /kɑrnıdʒ/ N-UNCOUNT **Carnage** is the violent killing of large numbers of people, especially in a war. [LITERARY] ❏ *...his strategy for stopping the carnage in Kosovo.*

car|nal /kɑrnəl/ ADJ [usu ADJ n] **Carnal** feelings and desires are sexual and physical, without any spiritual element. [FORMAL] ❏ *Their ruling passion is that of carnal love.*

car|na|tion /kɑrneıʃən/ (**carnations**) N-COUNT A **carnation** is a plant with white, pink, or red flowers.

car|ni|val /kɑrnıvəl/ (**carnivals**) **1** N-COUNT A **carnival** is a public festival during which people play music and sometimes dance in the streets. **2** N-COUNT A **carnival** is a traveling show which is held in a park or field and at which there are machines to ride on, entertainments, and games. [AM]

in BRIT, use **funfair**

car|ni|vore /kɑrnıvɔr/ (**carnivores**) **1** N-COUNT A **carnivore** is an animal that eats meat. [TECHNICAL] **2** N-COUNT If you describe someone as a **carnivore**, you are saying, especially in a humorous way, that they eat meat. ❏ *This is a delicious vegetarian dish that even carnivores love.*

car|nivo|rous /kɑrnıvərəs/ **1** ADJ **Carnivorous** animals eat meat. [TECHNICAL] ❏ *Snakes are carnivorous.* **2** ADJ **Carnivorous** can be used, especially humorously, to describe someone who eats meat.

car|ob /kærəb/ (**carobs**) **1** N-COUNT A **carob** or **carob tree** is a Mediterranean tree that stays green all year round. It has dark brown fruit that tastes similar to chocolate. **2** N-UNCOUNT [oft N n] The dark brown fruit of the carob tree can be referred to as **carob**. It is often made into powder and used instead of chocolate. ❏ *If you crave chocolate, try a carob bar instead.*

car|ol /kærəl/ (**carols**) N-COUNT **Carols** are Christian religious songs that are sung at Christmas. ❏ *The singing of Christmas carols is a custom derived from early dance routines of pagan origin.*

ca|rot|id ar|tery /kərɒtıd ɑrtəri/ (**carotid arteries**) N-COUNT A **carotid artery** is one of the two arteries in the neck that supply the head with blood. [MEDICAL]

ca|rouse /kəraʊz/ (**carouses, carousing, caroused**) V-I If you say that people **are carousing**, you mean that they are behaving very noisily and drinking a lot of alcohol as they enjoy themselves. ❏ *They told him to stay home with his wife instead of going out and carousing with friends.*

carou|sel /kærəsɛl/ (**carousels**) **1** N-COUNT At an airport, a **carousel** is a moving surface from which passengers can collect their luggage. **2** N-COUNT A **carousel** is a large, circular machine with seats, often in the shape of animals or cars. People can sit on it and go around and around for fun.

carp /kɑrp/ (**carps, carping, carped**)

Carp can also be used as the plural form for meaning **1**.

1 N-VAR A **carp** is a kind of fish that lives in lakes and rivers. **2** V-I If you say that someone **is carping**, you mean that they keep criticizing or complaining about someone or something, especially in a way you think is unnecessary or annoying. [DISAPPROVAL] ❏ *He cannot understand why she's constantly carping at him.* • **carp|ing** N-UNCOUNT ❏ *She was in no mood to put up with Blanche's carping.*

car park (**car parks**) also **carpark** N-COUNT A **car park** is an area or building where people can leave their cars. [BRIT]

in AM, use **parking lot**

car|pen|ter /kɑrpıntər/ (**carpenters**) N-COUNT A **carpenter** is a person whose job is making and repairing wooden things.

car|pen|try /kɑrpıntri/ N-UNCOUNT **Carpentry** is the activity of making and repairing wooden things.

car|pet /kɑrpıt/ (**carpets, carpeting, carpeted**) **1** N-VAR A **carpet** is a thick covering of soft material which is laid over a floor or a staircase. ❏ *They put down wooden boards, and laid new carpets on top.* **2** V-T [usu passive] If a floor or a room **is carpeted**, a carpet is laid on the floor. ❏ *The room had been carpeted and the windows glazed with colored glass.*

carpet|bag|ger /kɑrpıtbægər/ (**carpetbaggers**) N-COUNT If you call someone a **carpetbagger**, you disapprove of them because they are trying to become a politician in an area which is not their home, simply because they think they are more likely to succeed there. [AM, DISAPPROVAL]

car|pet bomb|ing N-UNCOUNT **Carpet bombing** is heavy bombing from aircraft, with the intention of hitting as many places as possible in a particular area.

car|pet|ing /kɑrpıtıŋ/ **1** N-UNCOUNT You use **carpeting** to refer to a carpet, or to the type of material that is used to make carpets. ❏ *...a bedroom with wall-to-wall carpeting.* ❏ *Carpeting is a reasonably cheap floor covering.* **2** → see also **carpet**

car phone (**car phones**) N-COUNT A **car phone** is a cellular phone which is designed to be used in a car.

car|pool /kɑrpuːl/ (**carpools, carpooling, carpooled**) also **car pool**, **car-pool** **1** N-COUNT A **carpool** is an arrangement where a group of people take turns driving each other to work, or driving each other's children to school. A **carpool** also refers to the people traveling together in a car. ❏ *His wife stays home to drive the children to school in the carpool.* **2** N-COUNT A **carpool** is a number of cars that are owned by a company or organization for the use of its employees or members. [BUSINESS] **3** V-I If a group of people **carpool**, they take turns driving each other to work, or driving each other's children to school. [mainly AM or AUSTRALIAN] ❏ *The government says fewer Americans are carpooling to work.*

car|port /kɑrpɔrt/ (**carports**) also **car port** N-COUNT A **carport** is a shelter for cars which is attached to a house and consists of a flat roof supported on pillars.

car|rel /kærəl/ (carrels) N-COUNT A **carrel** is a desk with low walls on three sides, at which a student can work in private, especially in a library. ◻ *Merced was pondering this problem one day in his student carrel at the Bradbury library.*

car|riage /kærɪdʒ/ (carriages) **1** N-COUNT [also by N] A **carriage** is an old-fashioned vehicle, usually for a small number of passengers, which is pulled by horses. ◻ *The president-elect followed in an open carriage drawn by six beautiful gray horses.* **2** N-COUNT A **carriage** is the same as a **car**. [mainly BRIT] → see car 2 **3** N-UNCOUNT **Carriage** is the same as a **delivery charge**. [BRIT]

car|ri|er ✦◇◇ /kæriər/ (carriers) **1** N-COUNT A **carrier** is a vehicle that is used for carrying people, especially soldiers, or things. ◻ *There were armored personnel carriers and tanks on the streets.* **2** N-COUNT A **carrier** is a company that provides telecommunications services, such as telephone and internet services. ◻ *...Japan's top wireless carrier.* ◻ *Regional carriers get paid for calls that pass through their switches.* **3** N-COUNT A **carrier** is a passenger airline. ◻ *American Airlines is the third-largest carrier at Denver International Airport.* **4** N-COUNT A **carrier** is a company that transports goods from one place to another by truck. ◻ *The Colorado Motor Carriers Association represents 450 trucking companies across the state.* **5** N-COUNT A **carrier** is a person or an animal that is infected with a disease and so can make other people or animals ill. ◻ *...an AIDS carrier.*

car|ri|er bag (carrier bags) N-COUNT A **carrier bag** is the same as a **shopping bag**. [BRIT]

car|ri|on /kæriən/ N-UNCOUNT **Carrion** is the decaying flesh of dead animals.

car|rot /kærət/ (carrots) **1** N-VAR **Carrots** are long, thin, orange-colored vegetables. They grow under the ground, and have green shoots above the ground. **2** N-COUNT Something that is offered to people in order to persuade them to do something can be referred to as a **carrot**. Something that is meant to persuade people not to do something can be referred to in the same sentence as a 'stick'. ◻ *Why the new emphasis on sticks instead of diplomatic carrots?*

carrot-and-stick ADJ [ADJ n] If an organization has a **carrot-and-stick** approach or policy, they offer people things in order to persuade them to do something and punish them if they refuse to do it. ◻ *The government is proclaiming a carrot-and-stick approach to the problem.*

car|ry ✦✦✦ /kæri/ (carries, carrying, carried) **1** V-T If you **carry** something, you take it with you, holding it so that it does not touch the ground. ◻ *He was carrying a briefcase.* ◻ *She carried her son to the car.* **2** V-T If you **carry** something, you have it with you wherever you go. ◻ *You have to carry a pager so that they can call you in at any time.* **3** V-T If something **carries** a person or thing somewhere, it takes them there. ◻ *Flowers are designed to attract insects which then carry the pollen from plant to plant.* ◻ *The delegation was carrying a message of thanks to President Mubarak.* **4** V-T If a person or animal **is carrying** a disease, they are infected with it and can pass it on to other people or animals. ◻ *The test could be used to screen healthy people to see if they are carrying the virus.* **5** V-T [no passive, no cont] If an action or situation has a particular quality or consequence, you can say that it **carries** it. ◻ *Check that any medication you're taking carries no risk for your developing baby.* **6** V-T If a quality or advantage **carries** someone into a particular position or through a difficult situation, it helps them to achieve that position or deal with that situation. ◻ *He had the ruthless streak necessary to carry him into the cabinet.* **7** V-T If you **carry** an idea or a method to a particular extent, you use or develop it to that extent. ◻ *It's not such a new idea, but I carried it to extremes.* **8** V-T If a newspaper or poster **carries** a picture or a piece of writing, it contains it or displays it. ◻ *Several papers carry the photograph of Mr. Anderson.* **9** V-T [usu passive] In a debate, if a proposal or motion **is carried**, a majority of people vote in favor of it. ◻ *A motion backing its economic policy was carried by 322 votes to 296.* **10** V-T [no cont] If a crime **carries** a particular punishment, a person who is found guilty of that crime will receive that punishment. ◻ *It was a crime of espionage and carried the death penalty.* **11** V-I If a sound **carries**, it can be heard a long way away. ◻ *Even in this stillness Leaphorn doubted if the sound would carry far.* **12** V-T If you **carry** yourself in a particular way, you walk and move in that way. ◻ *They carried themselves with great pride and dignity.* **13** PHRASE If you **get carried away** or **are carried away**, you are so eager or excited about something that you do something hasty or foolish. ◻ *I got completely carried away and almost cried.* **14** **to carry weight** → see **weight**

▶ **carry off** PHRASAL VERB If you **carry** something **off**, you do it successfully. ◻ *He's got the experience and the authority to carry it off.*

▶ **carry on 1** PHRASAL VERB If you **carry on** doing something, you continue to do it. ◻ *The assistant carried on talking.* ◻ *Her bravery has given him the will to carry on with his life and his work.* ◻ *His eldest son Joseph carried on his father's traditions.* **2** PHRASAL VERB If you **carry on** an activity, you do it or take part in it for a period of time. ◻ *The consulate will carry on a political dialogue with Indonesia.*

▶ **carry out** PHRASAL VERB If you **carry out** a threat, task, or instruction, you do it or act according to it. ◻ *The Social Democrats could still carry out their threat to leave the government.* ◻ *Police say they believe the attacks were carried out by nationalists.*

▶ **carry through** PHRASAL VERB If you **carry** something **through**, you do it or complete it, often in spite of difficulties. ◻ *We don't have the confidence that the U.N. will carry through a sustained program.*

carry|all /kæriɔl/ (carryalls) N-COUNT A **carryall** is a large bag made of nylon, canvas, or leather, which you use to carry your clothes and other possessions, for example when you are traveling. [mainly AM] ◻ *He shivered, humping his canvas carryall higher onto his shoulder.*

in BRIT, usually use **holdall**

carry-on ADJ [ADJ n] When you travel by air, your **carry-on** baggage or **carry-on** bag is the baggage or bag you have with you in the plane, rather than the baggage that is carried in the hold. ◻ *Passengers must pass through metal detectors, and their carry-on bags are put through X-ray machines.*

carry|over /kæriouvər/ (carryovers) N-COUNT [usu sing] If something is a **carryover** from an earlier time, it began during an earlier time but still exists or happens now. [AM] ◻ *Her love of these sandwiches was a carryover from the Depression, when she sometimes had nothing else to eat.*

in BRIT, use **carry-over**

car sick ADJ [usu v-link ADJ] If someone feels **car sick**, they feel sick as a result of traveling in a car. ◻ *My eleven-year-old son always gets car sick if we have to travel far.*

cart /kɑrt/ (carts, carting, carted) **1** N-COUNT A **cart** is an old-fashioned wooden vehicle that is used for transporting goods or people. Some carts are pulled by animals. ◻ *...a country where horse-drawn carts far outnumber cars.* **2** N-COUNT A **cart** is a small vehicle with a motor. [AM] ◻ *Cars are prohibited, so transportation is by electric cart or by horse and buggy.* **3** N-COUNT A **cart** or a **shopping cart** is a large metal basket on wheels which is provided by stores such as supermarkets for customers to use while they are in the store. [AM]

in BRIT, use **trolley**

4 V-T If you **cart** things or people somewhere, you carry them or transport them there, often with difficulty. [INFORMAL] ◻ *After their parents died, one of their father's relatives carted off the entire contents of the house.* ◻ *...a neat tote bag for carting around your child's books or toys.*

carte blanche /kɑrt blɒnʃ/ N-UNCOUNT If someone gives you **carte blanche**, they give you the authority to do whatever you think is right. ◻ *They gave him carte blanche to make decisions.*

car|tel /kɑrtɛl/ (cartels) N-COUNT A **cartel** is an association of similar companies or businesses that have grouped together in order to prevent competition and to control prices. [BUSINESS] ◻ *...a drug cartel.*

cart horse (cart horses) N-COUNT A **cart horse** is a large, powerful horse that is used to pull carts or farm machinery. ◻ *Where we use tractors, obviously they used cart horses in those days.*

car|ti|lage /kɑrtɪlɪdʒ/ (cartilages) N-VAR **Cartilage** is a strong, flexible substance in your body, especially around your joints and in your nose. ◻ *Andre Agassi has pulled out of next week's Grand Slam Cup after tearing a cartilage in his chest.*

car|tog|ra|pher /kɑrtɒgrəfər/ (cartographers) N-COUNT A **cartographer** is a person whose job is drawing maps.

car|tog|ra|phy /kɑːtɒgrəfi/ N-UNCOUNT **Cartography** is the art or activity of drawing maps and geographical charts.

car|ton /kɑːtᵊn/ (cartons) ◼ N-COUNT A **carton** is a plastic or cardboard container in which food or drink is sold. ◻ *A quart carton of milk is cheaper than two single pints.* ◼ N-COUNT You can use **carton** to refer to the carton and its contents, or to the contents only. ◻ *He went to the store for a carton of milk.* ◼ N-COUNT A **carton** is a large, strong cardboard box in which goods are stored and transported. [AM] ◻ *Those cartons contain the archives of The New Yorker for the years 1925 to 1980.*

car|toon /kɑːtuːn/ (cartoons) ◼ N-COUNT A **cartoon** is a humorous drawing or series of drawings in a newspaper or magazine. ◻ *Mickey Mouse, Donald Duck, and other Disney cartoon characters gave endless delight to millions of children.* ◼ N-COUNT A **cartoon** is a film in which all the characters and scenes are drawn rather than being real people or objects. ◻ *...a TV set blares out a cartoon comedy.*

car|toon|ist /kɑːtuːnɪst/ (cartoonists) N-COUNT A **cartoonist** is a person whose job is to draw cartoons for newspapers and magazines.

car|toon strip (cartoon strips) N-COUNT A **cartoon strip** is the same as a **comic strip**. [mainly BRIT]

car|tridge /kɑːtrɪdʒ/ (cartridges) ◼ N-COUNT A **cartridge** is a metal or cardboard tube containing a bullet and an explosive substance. Cartridges are used in guns. ◻ *Only four of the five spent cartridges were recovered by police.* ◼ N-COUNT A **cartridge** is part of a machine or device that can be easily removed and replaced when it is worn out or empty. ◻ *Change the filter cartridge as often as instructed by the manufacturer.*

cart|wheel /kɑːtwiːl/ (cartwheels) N-COUNT If you do a **cartwheel**, you do a fast, circular movement with your body. You fall sideways, put your hands on the ground, swing your legs over, and return to a standing position.

carve /kɑːv/ (carves, carving, carved) ◼ V-T/V-I If you **carve** an object, you make it by cutting it out of a substance such as wood or stone. If you **carve** something such as wood or stone into an object, you make the object by cutting it out. ◻ *One of the prisoners has carved a beautiful wooden chess set.* ◻ *I picked up a piece of wood and started carving.* ◼ → see also **carving** ◼ V-T If you **carve** writing or a design on an object, you cut it into the surface of the object. ◻ *He carved his name on his desk.* ◼ V-T If you **carve** a piece of cooked meat, you cut slices from it so that you can eat it. ◻ *Andrew began to carve the chicken.* ◼ → See feature box at **fine art**

▶ **carve out** PHRASAL VERB If you **carve out** a niche or a career, you succeed in getting the position or the career that you want by your own efforts. ◻ *Vick carved out his niche as the fastest quarterback in football.*

▶ **carve up** PHRASAL VERB If you say that someone **carves** something **up**, you disapprove of the way they have divided it into small parts. [DISAPPROVAL] ◻ *He has set about carving up the company which Hammer created from almost nothing.*

carv|er /kɑːvər/ (carvers) N-COUNT [oft n N] A **carver** is a person who carves wood or stone, as a job or as a hobby. ◻ *The industry employed about a thousand carvers.*

carv|ing /kɑːvɪŋ/ (carvings) ◼ N-COUNT A **carving** is an object or a design that has been cut out of a material such as stone or wood. ◻ *...a wood carving of a human hand.* ◼ N-UNCOUNT **Carving** is the art of carving objects, or of carving designs or writing on objects. ◻ *I found wood carving satisfying, and painting fun.*

carv|ing knife (carving knives) N-COUNT A **carving knife** is a long, sharp knife that is used to cut cooked meat.

cas|cade /kæskeɪd/ (cascades, cascading, cascaded) ◼ N-COUNT If you refer to a **cascade** of something, you mean that there is a large amount of it. [LITERARY] ◻ *The women have lustrous cascades of black hair.* ◼ V-I If water **cascades** somewhere, it pours or flows downward very fast and in large quantities. ◻ *She hung on as the freezing, rushing water cascaded past her.*

CASE
① INSTANCES AND OTHER ABSTRACT MEANINGS
② CONTAINERS
③ GRAMMAR TERM
---

① **case** ✦✦✦ /keɪs/ (cases) ◼ N-COUNT A particular **case** is a particular situation or incident, especially one that you are using as an individual example or instance of something. ◻ *Surgical training takes at least nine years, or 11 in the case of obstetrics.* ◻ *In extreme cases, insurance companies can prosecute for fraud.* ◼ N-COUNT A **case** is a person or their particular problem that a doctor, social worker, or other professional is dealing with. ◻ *Dr. Thomas Bracken describes the case of a 45-year-old Catholic priest much given to prayer whose left knee became painful.* ◻ *Some cases of arthritis respond to a gluten-free diet.* ◼ N-COUNT If you say that someone is a sad **case** or a hopeless **case**, you mean that they are in a sad situation or a hopeless situation. ◻ *I knew I was going to make it – that I wasn't a hopeless case.* ◼ → see also **basket case** ◼ N-COUNT A **case** is a crime or mystery that the police are investigating. ◻ *The police have several suspects in the case of five murders committed in Gainesville, Florida.* ◼ N-COUNT The **case** for or against a plan or idea consists of the facts and reasons used to support it or oppose it. ◻ *He sat there while I made the case for his dismissal.* ◻ *Both these facts strengthen the case against fracking.* ◼ N-COUNT In law, a **case** is a trial or other legal inquiry. ◻ *It can be difficult for public figures to win a libel case.* ◼ → see also **test case** ◼ PHRASE You say **in any case** when you are adding something which is more important than what you have just said, but which supports or corrects it. [EMPHASIS] ◻ *The concert was sold out, and in any case, most of the people gathered in the square could not afford the price of a ticket.* ◼ PHRASE If you do something **in case** or **just in case** a particular thing happens, you do it because that thing might happen. ◻ *In case anyone was following me, I made an elaborate detour.* ◼ PHRASE If you do something or have something **in case of** a particular thing, you do it or have it because that thing might happen or be true. ◻ *Many stores along the route have been boarded up in case of trouble.* ◼ PHRASE You use **in case** in expressions like 'in case you didn't know' or 'in case you've forgotten' when you are telling someone in a rather irritated way something that you think is either obvious or none of their business. [FEELINGS] ◻ *She's nervous about something, in case you didn't notice.* ◼ PHRASE You say **in that case** or **in which case** to indicate that what you are going to say is true if the possible situation that has just been mentioned actually exists. ◻ *Perhaps you've some doubts about the attack. In that case it may interest you to know that Miss Woods witnessed it.* ◼ PHRASE You can say that you are doing something **just in case** to refer vaguely to the possibility that a thing might happen or be true, without saying exactly what it is. ◻ *I guess we've already talked about this but I'll ask you again just in case.* ◼ PHRASE If you say that a task or situation is **a case of** a particular thing, you mean that it consists of that thing or can be described as that thing. ◻ *It's not a case of whether anyone would notice or not.* ◼ PHRASE If you say that something **is the case**, you mean that it is true or correct. ◻ *You'll probably notice her having difficulty swallowing. If this is the case, give her plenty of liquids.* ◼ → See feature box at **legal**

COLLOCATIONS

case
NOUN ① ◼
noun + **case**: abuse, fraud, libel, murder, rape; court
adjective + **case**: civil, criminal
verb + **case**: bring; adjourn; hear
---

② **case** /keɪs/ (cases) ◼ N-COUNT A **case** is a container that is specially designed to hold or protect something. ◻ *...a black case for his glasses.* ◼ → see also **bookcase**, **briefcase**

③ **case** /keɪs/ (cases) ◼ N-COUNT In the grammar of many languages, the **case** of a group such as a noun group or adjective group is the form it has which shows its relationship to other groups in the sentence. ◼ → see also **lowercase**, **uppercase**

case|book /keɪsbʊk/ (casebooks) N-COUNT A **casebook** is a written record of the cases dealt with by someone such as a doctor, social worker, or police officer.

case his|to|ry (case histories) N-COUNT A person's **case history** is the record of past events or problems that have affected them, especially their medical history. ◻ *I took her to a homoeopath, who started by taking a very long and detailed case history.*

case law N-UNCOUNT **Case law** is law that has been established by following decisions made by judges in earlier cases. [LEGAL]

case|load /keɪsloʊd/ (**caseloads**) N-COUNT [oft with poss] The **caseload** of someone such as a doctor, social worker, or lawyer is the number of cases that they have to deal with. ▫ *Social workers say the average caseload is 32 families per employee.*

case|ment /keɪsmənt/ (**casements**) N-COUNT A **casement** or a **casement window** is a window that opens by means of hinges, usually at the side.

case-sensitive ADJ In computing, if a written word such as a password is **case-sensitive**, it must be written in a particular form, for example using all capital letters or all small letters, in order for the computer to recognize it. [COMPUTING]

case study (**case studies**) N-COUNT A **case study** is a written account that gives detailed information about a person, group, or thing and their development over a period of time. ▫ *...a large case study of malaria in West African children.*

case|work /keɪswɜrk/ N-UNCOUNT **Casework** is social work that involves actually dealing or working with the people who need help.

case|worker /keɪswɜrkər/ (**caseworkers**) N-COUNT A **caseworker** is someone who does casework.

cash ♦♦◊ /kæʃ/ (**cashes, cashing, cashed**) ◼ N-UNCOUNT **Cash** is money in the form of bills and coins rather than checks. ▫ *...two thousand dollars in cash.* ◼ → see also **hard cash, petty cash** ◼ N-UNCOUNT **Cash** means the same as money, especially money which is immediately available. [INFORMAL] ▫ *...a state-owned financial-services group with plenty of cash.* ◼ V-T If you **cash** a check, you exchange it at a bank for the amount of money that it is worth. ▫ *There are similar charges if you want to cash a check or withdraw money at a branch other than your own.* ▶ **cash in** ◼ PHRASAL VERB If you say that someone **cashes in** on a situation, you are criticizing them for using it to gain an advantage, often in an unfair or dishonest way. [DISAPPROVAL] ▫ *Residents said local gang leaders had cashed in on the violence to seize valuable land.* ◼ PHRASAL VERB If you **cash in** something such as an insurance policy, you exchange it for money. ▫ *Avoid cashing in a policy early as you could lose out heavily.*

cash bar (**cash bars**) N-COUNT A **cash bar** is a bar at a party or similar event where guests can buy drinks. ▫ *At 6 p.m. there will be a reception and cash bar.*

cash cow (**cash cows**) N-COUNT In business, a **cash cow** is a product or investment that steadily continues to be profitable. [BUSINESS] ▫ *The retail division is BT's cash cow.*

cash crop (**cash crops**) N-COUNT A **cash crop** is a crop that is grown in order to be sold. ▫ *Cranberries are a major cash crop in New Jersey.*

cash dis|pens|er (**cash dispensers**) N-COUNT A **cash dispenser** is a machine built into the wall of a bank or other building, which allows people to take out money from their bank account using a special card. [BRIT]

in AM, use **ATM**

cash|ew /kæʃu, kæʃu/ (**cashews**) ◼ N-COUNT A **cashew** or a **cashew nut** is a curved nut that you can eat. ◼ → See also color supplement

cash flow also **cash-flow** N-UNCOUNT The **cash flow** of a firm or business is the movement of money into and out of it. [BUSINESS] ▫ *The company ran into cash-flow problems and faced liquidation.*

cash|ier /kæʃɪər/ (**cashiers**) N-COUNT A **cashier** is a person who customers pay money to or get money from in places such as stores or banks.

cash|ier's check (**cashier's checks**) N-COUNT A **cashier's check** is one which a cashier signs and which is drawn on a bank's own funds. [AM]

cash|ier's desk (**cashier's desks**) N-COUNT A **cashier's desk** is a place in a large store where you pay for the things you want to buy. [AM]

cash|less /kæʃlɪs/ ADJ **Cashless** payments are made using cards or electronic methods rather than physical money. ▫ *The school cafeteria uses a cashless system.*

cash|mere /kæʒmɪər/ N-UNCOUNT **Cashmere** is a kind of very fine, soft wool. ▫ *...a big, soft cashmere sweater.*

cash on de|liv|ery PHRASE [PHR after v] If you pay for goods **cash on delivery**, you pay for them in cash when they are delivered. The abbreviation **C.O.D.** is also used. ▫ *People who ordered were given an option of paying cash on delivery or by credit card.*

cash|point /kæʃpɔɪnt/ (**cashpoints**) N-COUNT A **cashpoint** is the same as a **cash dispenser**. [BRIT]

cash reg|is|ter (**cash registers**) N-COUNT A **cash register** is a machine in a store, bar, or restaurant that is used to add up and record how much money people pay, and in which the money is kept.

cash-starved ADJ A **cash-starved** company or organization does not have enough money to operate properly, usually because another organization, such as the government, is not giving them the money that they need. [BUSINESS, JOURNALISM] ▫ *We are heading for a crisis, with cash-starved councils forced to cut back on vital community services.*

cash-strapped ADJ [usu ADJ n] If a person or organization is **cash-strapped**, they do not have enough money to buy or pay for the things they want or need. [JOURNALISM] ▫ *Union leaders say the wage package is the best they believe the cash-strapped government will offer.*

cas|ing /keɪsɪŋ/ (**casings**) N-COUNT [oft supp N] A **casing** is a substance or object that covers something and protects it. ▫ *...the outer casings of missiles.*

ca|si|no /kəsinoʊ/ (**casinos**) N-COUNT A **casino** is a building or room where people play gambling games such as roulette.

cask /kæsk/ (**casks**) N-COUNT A **cask** is a wooden barrel that is used for storing things, especially alcoholic drink. ▫ *...casks of sherry.*

cas|ket /kæskɪt/ (**caskets**) ◼ N-COUNT A **casket** is a **coffin**. [mainly AM] ◼ N-COUNT A **casket** is a small box in which you keep valuable things. [LITERARY]

cas|sa|va /kəsɑvə/ ◼ N-UNCOUNT **Cassava** is a South American plant with thick roots. It is grown for food. ◼ N-UNCOUNT **Cassava** is a substance that comes from the root of the cassava plant and is used to make flour.

cas|se|role /kæsəroʊl/ (**casseroles**) ◼ N-COUNT A **casserole** is a dish made of meat and vegetables that have been cooked slowly in a liquid. ▫ *...a huge beef casserole, full of herbs, vegetables, and wine.* ◼ N-COUNT A **casserole** or a **casserole dish** is a large heavy container with a lid. You cook casseroles and other dishes in it. ▫ *Place all the chopped vegetables into a casserole dish.*

cas|sette /kəsɛt/ (**cassettes**) N-COUNT [also on N] A **cassette** is a small, flat, rectangular plastic case containing magnetic tape which was used in the past for recording and playing back sound or film. ▫ *His two albums released on cassette sold 10 million copies.*

cas|sock /kæsək/ (**cassocks**) N-COUNT A **cassock** is a long piece of clothing, often black, that is worn by members of the clergy in some churches.

cast ♦♦◊ /kæst/ (**casts, casting**)

The form **cast** is used in the present tense and is the past tense and past participle.

◼ N-COUNT-COLL The **cast** of a play or movie is all the people who act in it. ▫ *The show is very amusing and the cast is very good.* ◼ V-T To **cast** an actor in a play or movie means to choose them to act a particular role in it. ▫ *The world premiere of her new play casts the Australian actor in the lead role.* ▫ *He was cast as a college professor.* ◼ V-T If you **cast** your eyes or **cast** a look in a particular direction, you look quickly in that direction. [WRITTEN] ▫ *He cast a stern glance at the two men.* ▫ *I cast my eyes down briefly.* ◼ V-T If something **casts** a light or shadow somewhere, it causes it to appear there. [WRITTEN] ▫ *The moon cast a bright light over the yard.* ◼ V-T To **cast** doubt on something means to cause people to be unsure about it. ▫ *Last night a top criminal psychologist cast doubt on the theory.* ◼ V-T When you **cast** your vote in an election, you vote. ▫ *About ninety-five per cent of those who cast their votes approve the new constitution.* ◼ V-T To **cast** an object means to make it by pouring a liquid such as hot metal into a specially shaped container and leaving it there until it becomes hard. ▫ *Our door knocker is cast in solid brass.* ◼ N-COUNT A **cast** is a model that has been made by pouring a liquid such as plaster or hot metal onto something or into

castanets 191 **catalytic converter**

something, so that when it hardens it has the same shape as that thing. ❏ *An orthodontist took a cast of the inside of Billy's mouth to make a dental plate.* ◼️ N-COUNT A **cast** is the same as a **plaster cast**. ◼️ **to cast your mind back** → see **mind** ① ◼️ → See feature box at **politics, theater**
▶ **cast aside** PHRASAL VERB If you **cast aside** someone or something, you get rid of them because they are no longer necessary or useful to you. ❏ *We need to cast aside outdated policies.*

cas|ta|nets /kǽstənɛts/ N-PLURAL [also *a pair of* N] **Castanets** are a Spanish musical instrument consisting of two small round pieces of wood or plastic held together by a cord. You hold the castanets in your hand and knock the pieces together with your fingers.

cast|away /kǽstəweɪ/ (castaways) N-COUNT A **castaway** is a person who has managed to swim or float to a lonely island or shore after their boat has sunk.

caste /kǽst/ (castes) ◼️ N-COUNT A **caste** is one of the traditional social classes into which people are divided in a Hindu society. ❏ *In the secretariat, there is a mix of those from the lower and upper castes.* ◼️ N-UNCOUNT **Caste** is the system of dividing people in a society into different social classes. ❏ *Caste is defined primarily by social honor attained through personal lifestyle.*

cas|tel|lat|ed /kǽstəleɪtɪd/ ADJ [usu ADJ n] A **castellated** wall or building looks like a castle. [TECHNICAL] ❏ *...a 19th-century castellated mansion.*

cast|er /kǽstər/ (casters) also **castor** N-COUNT **Casters** are small wheels fitted to a piece of furniture so that it can be moved more easily.

cas|ti|gate /kǽstɪgeɪt/ (castigates, castigating, castigated) V-T If you **castigate** someone or something, you speak to them angrily or criticize them severely. [FORMAL] ❏ *Marx never lost an opportunity to castigate colonialism.*

cast|ing /kǽstɪŋ/ (castings) ◼️ N-COUNT A **casting** is an object or piece of machinery which has been made by pouring a liquid such as hot metal into a container, so that when it hardens it has the required shape. ◼️ → see also **cast**

cast|ing vote (casting votes) N-COUNT When a committee has given an equal number of votes for and against a proposal, the chairperson can give a **casting vote**. This vote decides whether or not the proposal will be passed. ❏ *The vote was tied and a union leader used his casting vote in favor of the return to work.*

cast iron also **cast-iron** ◼️ N-UNCOUNT **Cast iron** is iron which contains a small amount of carbon. It is hard and cannot be bent so it has to be made into objects by casting. ❏ *Made from cast iron, it is finished in graphite enamel.* ◼️ ADJ A **cast-iron** guarantee or alibi is one that is absolutely certain to be effective and will not fail you. ❏ *They would have to offer cast-iron guarantees to invest in long-term projects.*

cas|tle ◆◇◇ /kǽsəl/ (castles) ◼️ N-COUNT A **castle** is a large building with thick, high walls. Castles were built by important people, such as kings, in former times, especially for protection during wars and battles. ◼️ → See also **color supplement**

cast-off (cast-offs) also **castoff** ADJ [ADJ n] **Cast-off** things, especially clothes, are ones which someone no longer uses because they are old or unfashionable, and which they give to someone else or throw away. ❏ *Alexandra looked plump and awkward in her cast-off clothing.* • N-COUNT [usu pl] **Cast-off** is also a noun. ❏ *I never had anything new to wear as a child, only a cousin's cast-offs.*

cas|tor /kǽstər/ → see **caster**

cas|tor oil N-UNCOUNT **Castor oil** is a thick, yellow oil that is obtained from the seeds of the castor oil plant. It has a very unpleasant taste and in former times was used as a medicine.

cas|trate /kǽstreɪt/ (castrates, castrating, castrated) V-T To **castrate** a male animal or a man means to remove his testicles. ❏ *In the ancient world, it was probably rare to castrate a dog or cat.* • **cas|tra|tion** /kæstreɪʃən/ (castrations) N-VAR ❏ *...the castration of male farm animals.*

cas|ual /kǽʒuəl/ ◼️ ADJ If you are **casual**, you are, or you pretend to be, relaxed and not very concerned about what is happening or what you are doing. ❏ *It's difficult for me to be*

casual about anything. • **casu|al|ly** ADV [ADV with v] ❏ *"No need to hurry," Ben said casually.* ◼️ ADJ [ADJ n] A **casual** event or situation happens by chance or without planning. ❏ *What you mean as a casual remark could be misinterpreted.* ◼️ ADJ [ADJ n] **Casual** clothes are ones that you normally wear at home or on vacation, and not on formal occasions. ❏ *I also bought some casual clothes for the weekend.* • **casu|al|ly** ADV ❏ *They were casually dressed.* ◼️ ADJ **Casual** work is done for short periods and not on a permanent or regular basis. [mainly BRIT]

in AM, use **temporary**

casu|al Fri|day (casual Fridays) also **Casual Friday** N-COUNT In some companies, employees are allowed to wear clothes that are more informal than usual on a Friday. This day is known as a **casual Friday**. [AM] ❏ *This denim work shirt is as great with a pair of jeans as it is with a tie on casual Fridays.*

casu|al|ty ◆◇◇ /kǽʒuəlti/ (casualties) ◼️ N-COUNT A **casualty** is a person who is injured or killed in a war or in an accident. ❏ *Troops fired on the demonstrators causing many casualties.* ◼️ N-COUNT A **casualty** of a particular event or situation is a person or a thing that has suffered badly as a result of that event or situation. ❏ *The car industry has been one of the greatest casualties of the recession.* ◼️ N-UNCOUNT **Casualty** is the part of a hospital where people who have severe injuries or sudden illnesses are taken for emergency treatment. [BRIT]

in AM, use **emergency room**

casu|ist|ry /kǽʒuɪstri/ N-UNCOUNT **Casuistry** is the use of clever arguments to persuade or trick people. [FORMAL, DISAPPROVAL]

cat ◆◇◇ /kǽt/ (cats) ◼️ N-COUNT A **cat** is a furry animal that has a long tail and sharp claws. Cats are often kept as pets. ◼️ N-COUNT **Cats** are lions, tigers, and other wild animals in the same family. ❏ *The lion is perhaps the most famous member of the cat family.* ◼️ → see also **fat cat**

cata|clysm /kǽtəklɪzəm/ (cataclysms) N-COUNT A **cataclysm** is an event that causes great change or harm. [FORMAL]

cata|clys|mic /kǽtəklɪzmɪk/ ADJ A **cataclysmic** event is one that changes a situation or society very greatly, especially in an unpleasant way. [FORMAL] ❏ *Few had expected that change to be as cataclysmic as it turned out to be.*

cata|comb /kǽtəkoʊm/ (catacombs) N-COUNT [usu pl] **Catacombs** are ancient underground passages and rooms, especially under a city, where people used to be buried.

Cata|lan /kǽtəlæn/ ◼️ ADJ [usu ADJ n] Something that is **Catalan** belongs or relates to Catalonia, its people, or its language. Catalonia is a region of Spain. ◼️ N-UNCOUNT **Catalan** is one of the languages spoken in Catalonia.

cata|log /kǽtəlɒg/ (catalogs) also **catalogue** ◼️ N-COUNT A **catalog** is a list of things such as the goods you can buy from a particular company, the objects in a museum, or the books in a library. ❏ *...the world's biggest seed catalog.* ◼️ N-COUNT A **catalog** of similar things, especially bad things, is a number of them considered or discussed one after another. ❏ *His story is a catalog of misfortune.*

ca|taly|sis /kətǽlɪsɪs/ N-UNCOUNT **Catalysis** is the speeding up of a chemical reaction by adding a catalyst to it. [TECHNICAL]

cata|lyst /kǽtəlɪst/ (catalysts) ◼️ N-COUNT You can describe a person or thing that causes a change or event to happen as a **catalyst**. ❏ *I very much hope that this case will prove to be a catalyst for change.* ◼️ N-COUNT In chemistry, a **catalyst** is a substance that causes a chemical reaction to take place more quickly.

cata|lyt|ic /kǽtəlɪtɪk/ ◼️ ADJ [ADJ n] In chemistry, a **catalytic** substance or a substance with **catalytic** properties is a substance which increases the speed of a chemical reaction. ❏ *...carbon molecules with unusual chemical and catalytic properties.* ◼️ ADJ [usu ADJ n] If you describe a person or thing as having a **catalytic** effect, you mean that they cause things to happen or they increase the speed at which things happen. [FORMAL] ❏ *Governments do, however, have a vital catalytic role in orchestrating rescue operations.*

cata|lyt|ic con|vert|er (catalytic converters) N-COUNT A **catalytic converter** is a device which is fitted to a car's exhaust to reduce the pollution coming from it.

cata|lyze /kǽtəlaɪz/ (catalyzes, catalyzing, catalyzed)

in BRIT, use **catalyse**

1 V-T If something **catalyzes** a thing or a situation, it makes it active. [FORMAL] ☐ *The Macintosh computer helped catalyze a total change in the way computers were used.* **2** V-T In chemistry, if something **catalyzes** a reaction or event, it causes it to happen. [TECHNICAL] ☐ *The wires do not have a large enough surface to catalyze a big explosion.*

cata|ma|ran /kætəməræn/ (catamarans) **1** N-COUNT A **catamaran** is a sailing boat with two parallel hulls that are held in place by a single deck. **2** → See also color supplement

cata|pult /kǽtəpʌlt/ (catapults, catapulting, catapulted) **1** V-T/V-I If someone or something **catapults** or **is catapulted** through the air, they are thrown very suddenly, quickly, and violently through it. ☐ *We've all seen enough dummies catapulting through windshields in TV warnings to know the dangers of not wearing seat belts.* **2** V-T/V-I If something **catapults** you into a particular state or situation, or if you **catapult** there, you are suddenly and unexpectedly caused to be in that state or situation. ☐ *"Basic Instinct" catapulted her to top status Hollywood.*

cata|ract /kǽtərækt/ (cataracts) N-COUNT **Cataracts** are layers over a person's eyes that prevent them from seeing properly. Cataracts usually develop because of old age or illness. ☐ *In one study, light smokers were found to be more than twice as likely to get cataracts as non-smokers.*

ca|tarrh /kətɑːr/ N-UNCOUNT **Catarrh** is a medical condition in which a lot of mucus is produced in your nose and throat. You may get catarrh when you have a cold.

ca|tas|tro|phe /kətǽstrəfi/ (catastrophes) N-COUNT A **catastrophe** is an unexpected event that causes great suffering or damage. ☐ *From all points of view, war would be a catastrophe.*

cata|stroph|ic /kætəstrɒfɪk/ **1** ADJ Something that is **catastrophic** involves or causes a sudden terrible disaster. ☐ *A tidal wave caused by the earthquake hit the coast causing catastrophic damage.* ☐ *The water shortage in this country is potentially catastrophic.* **2** ADJ If you describe something as **catastrophic**, you mean that it is very bad or unsuccessful. ☐ *...another catastrophic attempt to arrest control from a rival Christian militia.*

cata|ton|ic /kætətɒnɪk/ ADJ If you describe someone as being in a **catatonic** state, you mean that they are not moving or responding at all, usually as a result of illness, shock, or drugs. [MEDICAL] ☐ *The traumatized heroine sinks into a catatonic trance.*

cat|bird seat /kǽtbɜːrd sit/ PHRASE [v-link PHR] If you say that someone is **in the catbird seat**, you think that their situation is very good. [AM, INFORMAL] ☐ *If he had not been hurt, his team would be sitting in the catbird seat.*

cat bur|glar (cat burglars) N-COUNT A **cat burglar** is a thief who steals from houses or other buildings by climbing up walls and entering through windows or through the roof.

cat|call /kǽtkɔːl/ (catcalls) N-COUNT [usu pl] **Catcalls** are loud noises that people make to show that they disapprove of something they are watching or listening to. ☐ *The crowd responded with boos and catcalls.*

CATCH
① HOLD OR TOUCH
② MANAGE TO SEE, HEAR, OR TALK TO
③ OTHER USES
④ PHRASAL VERBS
---

① **catch** ♦♦◇ /kætʃ/ (catches, catching, caught)
→ Please look at meaning ⑥ to see if the expression you are looking for is shown under another headword.

1 V-T If you **catch** a person or animal, you capture them after chasing them, or by using a trap, net, or other device. ☐ *Police say they are confident of catching the gunman.* ☐ *Where did you catch the fish?* **2** V-T If you **catch** an object that is moving through the air, you seize it with your hands. ☐ *I jumped up to catch a ball and fell over.* • N-COUNT **Catch** is also a noun. ☐ *He missed the catch and the game was lost.* **3** V-T If you **catch** a part of someone's body, you take or seize it with your hand, often in order to stop them from going somewhere. ☐ *Liz caught his arm.* ☐ *He knelt beside her and caught her hand in both of his.* **4** V-T If one thing **catches** another, it hits it accidentally or manages to hit it. ☐ *The stinging slap almost caught his face.* ☐ *I may have caught him with my elbow but it was just an accident.* **5** V-I If something **catches** on or in an object, it accidentally becomes attached to the object or stuck in it. ☐ *Her ankle caught on a root, and she almost lost her balance.* **6 to catch hold of something** → see **hold** ①

② **catch** ♦♦◇ /kætʃ/ (catches, catching, caught)
→ Please look at meaning ⑨ to see if the expression you are looking for is shown under another headword.

1 V-T When you **catch** a bus, train, or plane, you get on it in order to travel somewhere. ☐ *We were in plenty of time for Anthony to catch the ferry.* **2** V-T If you **catch** someone doing something wrong, you see or find them doing it. ☐ *He caught a youth breaking into a car.* ☐ *I don't want to catch you pushing yourself into the picture to get some personal publicity.* **3** V-T If you **catch** yourself doing something, especially something surprising, you suddenly become aware that you are doing it. ☐ *I caught myself feeling almost sorry for poor Mr. Laurence.* **4** V-T If you **catch** something or **catch** a glimpse of it, you notice it or manage to see it briefly. ☐ *As she turned back she caught the puzzled look on her mother's face.* **5** V-T If you **catch** something that someone has said, you manage to hear it. ☐ *His ears caught a faint cry.* ☐ *I do not believe I caught your name.* **6** V-T If you **catch** a TV or radio program or an event, you manage to see or listen to it. ☐ *Bill turns on the radio to catch the local news.* **7** V-T If you **catch** someone, you manage to contact or meet them to talk to them, especially when they are just about to go somewhere else. ☐ *I dialed Elizabeth's number thinking I might catch her before she left for work.* **8** V-T If something or someone **catches** you by surprise or at a bad time, you were not expecting them or do not feel able to deal with them. ☐ *She looked as if the photographer had caught her by surprise.* ☐ *I'm sorry but I just cannot say anything. You've caught me at a bad time.* **9 to catch sight of something** → see **sight**

③ **catch** ♦♦◇ /kætʃ/ (catches, catching, caught)
→ Please look at meaning ⑧ to see if the expression you are looking for is shown under another headword.

1 V-T If something **catches** your attention or your eye, you notice it or become interested in it. ☐ *My shoes caught his attention.* **2** V-T If you **catch** a cold or a disease, you become ill with it. ☐ *The more stress you are under, the more likely you are to catch a cold.* **3** V-T If something **catches** the light or if the light **catches** it, it reflects the light and looks bright or shiny. ☐ *They saw the ship's guns, catching the light of the moon.* **4** V-T PASSIVE If you **are caught** in a storm or other unpleasant situation, it happens when you cannot avoid its effects. ☐ *When he was fishing off the island he was caught in a storm and almost drowned.* **5** V-T PASSIVE If you **are caught between** two alternatives or two people, you do not know which one to choose or follow. ☐ *The Jordanian leader is caught between both sides in the dispute.* **6** N-COUNT A **catch** on a window, door, or container is a device that fastens it. ☐ *She fiddled with the catch of her bag.* **7** N-COUNT A **catch** is a hidden problem or difficulty in a plan or an offer that seems surprisingly good. ☐ *The catch is that you work for your supper, and the food and accommodations can be very basic.* **8 to catch fire** → see **fire** ①

COLLOCATIONS

catch
VERB
② ⑨
catch + noun: glimpse, sight
③ **1**
catch + noun: attention, eye
③ **2**
catch + noun: chill, cold, flu, pneumonia
---

④ **catch** ♦♦◇ /kætʃ/ (catches, catching, caught)
▸ **catch on** **1** PHRASAL VERB If you **catch on** to something, you understand it, or realize that it is happening. ☐ *He got what he could out of me before I caught on to the kind of person he'd turned into.* **2** PHRASAL VERB If something **catches on**, it becomes popular. ☐ *The idea has been around for ages without catching on.*
▸ **catch up** **1** PHRASAL VERB If you **catch up** with someone who is in front of you, you reach them by walking faster than

they are walking. ❑ *I stopped and waited for her to catch up.* **2** PHRASAL VERB To **catch up** with someone means to reach the same standard, stage, or level that they have reached. ❑ *Most late developers will catch up with their friends.* ❑ *John began the season better than me but I have fought to catch up.* **3** PHRASAL VERB If you **catch up** on an activity that you have not had much time to do recently, you spend time doing it. ❑ *I was catching up on a bit of reading.* **4** PHRASAL VERB If you **catch up** on friends who you have not seen for some time or on their lives, you talk to them and find out what has happened in their lives since you last talked together. ❑ *The women spent some time catching up on each other's work and families.* **5** PHRASAL VERB If you **are caught up** in something, you are involved in it, usually unwillingly. ❑ *The people themselves weren't part of the conflict; they were just caught up in it.*

▶ **catch up with** **1** PHRASAL VERB When people **catch up with** someone who has done something wrong, they succeed in finding them in order to arrest or punish them. ❑ *The law caught up with him yesterday.* **2** PHRASAL VERB If something **catches up with** you, you are forced to deal with something unpleasant that happened or that you did in the past, which you have been able to avoid until now. ❑ *Although he subsequently became a successful businessman, his criminal past caught up with him.*

Catch-22 /kætʃ twɛntitu/ N-SING [oft N n] If you describe a situation as a **Catch-22**, you mean it is an impossible situation because you cannot do one thing until you do another thing, but you cannot do the second thing until you do the first thing. ❑ *It's a Catch-22 situation here. Nobody wants to support you until you're successful, but without the support how can you ever be successful?*

catch|all /kætʃɔl/ (**catchalls**) also **catch-all** N-COUNT A **catchall** is a term or category which includes many different things. ❑ *Globalization is a catchall to describe increased international trade.* ❑ *Indigestion is a catchall term for any kind of stomach distress.*

catch|er /kætʃər/ (**catchers**) N-COUNT In baseball, the **catcher** is the player who stands behind the batter. The catcher has a special glove for catching the ball.

catch|ing /kætʃɪŋ/ **1** ADJ [v-link ADJ] If a feeling or emotion is **catching**, it has a strong influence on other people and spreads quickly, for example through a crowd. ❑ *Enthusiasm is very catching.* **2** ADJ [v-link ADJ] If an illness or a disease is **catching**, it is easily passed on or given to someone else. [INFORMAL] **3** → See feature box at **illness**

catch|ment /kætʃmənt/ N-UNCOUNT In geography, **catchment** is the process of collecting water, in particular the process of water flowing from the ground and collecting in a river. **Catchment** is also the water that is collected in this way. [TECHNICAL]

catch|ment area (**catchment areas**) N-COUNT In geography, the **catchment area** of a river is the area of land from which water flows into the river. [TECHNICAL]

catch|phrase /kætʃfreɪz/ (**catchphrases**) N-COUNT A **catchphrase** is a sentence or phrase which becomes popular or well-known, often because it is frequently used by a famous person.

catch-up PHRASE If someone **is playing catch-up**, they are trying to equal or better someone else's performance. ❑ *We were playing catch up for most of the game.* ❑ *Yesterday London was playing catch-up after Wall Street's tremendous 500-point gain on Wednesday night.*

catch|word /kætʃwɜrd/ (**catchwords**) N-COUNT A **catchword** is a word or phrase that becomes popular or well-known, for example, because it is associated with a political campaign. ❑ *The catchword he and his supporters have been using is "consolidation."*

catchy /kætʃi/ (**catchier, catchiest**) ADJ If you describe a tune, name, or advertisement as **catchy**, you mean that it is attractive and easy to remember. ❑ *The songs were both catchy and cutting.*

cat|echism /kætɪkɪzəm/ (**catechisms**) N-COUNT [usu sing] In a Catholic, Episcopal, or Orthodox church, the **catechism** is a series of questions and answers about religious beliefs, which has to be learned by people before they can become full members of that church.

cat|egori|cal /kætɪgɒrɪkəl/ ADJ If you are **categorical** about something, you state your views very definitely and firmly. ❑ *...his categorical denial of the charges of sexual harassment.*
● **cat|egori|cal|ly** /kætɪgɒrɪkli/ ADV [ADV with v] ❑ *They totally and categorically deny the charges.*

cat|ego|rize /kætɪgəraɪz/ (**categorizes, categorizing, categorized**)

in BRIT, also use **categorise**

V-T If you **categorize** people or things, you divide them into sets or you say which set they belong to. ❑ *Lindsay, like his films, is hard to categorize.* ❑ *Make a list of your child's toys and then categorize them as sociable or antisocial.* ● **cat|ego|ri|za|tion** /kætɪgərɪzeɪʃən/ (**categorizations**) N-VAR ❑ *Her first novel defies easy categorization.*

cat|ego|ry ✦✧✧ /kætɪgɔri/ (**categories**) N-COUNT If people or things are divided into **categories**, they are divided into groups in such a way that the members of each group are similar to each other in some way. ❑ *This book clearly falls into the category of fictionalized autobiography.*

SYNONYMS

category
NOUN
class: *...the division of the stars into six classes of brightness.*
genre: *...his love of movies and novels in the horror genre.*
sort: *What sort of school did you go to?*
type: *In 1990, 25% of households were of this type.*

---

ca|ter /keɪtər/ (**caters, catering, catered**) **1** V-I To **cater to** a group of people means to provide all the things that they need or want. ❑ *We cater to an exclusive clientele.* **2** V-I To **cater to** something means to take it into account. ❑ *Exercise classes cater to all levels of fitness.* ❑ *...shops that cater to the needs of men.* **3** V-T If a person or company **caters** an occasion such as a wedding or a party, they provide food and drink for all the people there. ❑ *...a full-service restaurant equipped to cater large events.* **4** → see also **catering**

ca|ter|er /keɪtərər/ (**caterers**) N-COUNT **Caterers** are people or companies that provide food and drink for a place such as an office or for special occasions such as weddings and parties. ❑ *The caterers were already laying out the tables for lunch.*

ca|ter|ing /keɪtərɪŋ/ N-UNCOUNT [also the N, oft N n] **Catering** is the activity of providing food and drink for a large number of people, for example, at weddings and parties. ❑ *His catering business made him a millionaire at 41.*

cat|er|pil|lar /kætərpɪlər/ (**caterpillars**) N-COUNT A **caterpillar** is a small, worm-like animal that feeds on plants and eventually develops into a butterfly or moth.

cat|er|waul /kætərwɔl/ (**caterwauls, caterwauling, caterwauled**) V-I If a person or animal **caterwauls**, they make a loud, high, unpleasant noise like the noise that cats make when they fight. ❑ *...shrieking and caterwauling in mock distress.* ● N-COUNT **Caterwaul** is also a noun. ❑ *...blood-curdling caterwauls.* ● **cat|er|waul|ing** N-UNCOUNT ❑ *...high-pitched moaning and caterwauling.*

cat|fight /kætfaɪt/ (**catfights**) N-COUNT A **catfight** is an angry fight or quarrel, especially between women. [INFORMAL] ❑ *A catfight has erupted over who will get top billing.*

cat|fish /kætfɪʃ/ (**catfish**) N-VAR **Catfish** are a type of fish that have long, thin spines around their mouths.

ca|thar|sis /kəθɑrsɪs/ N-UNCOUNT **Catharsis** is getting rid of unhappy memories or strong emotions such as anger or sadness by expressing them in some way. ❑ *He wrote out his rage and bewilderment, which gradually became a form of catharsis leading to understanding.*

ca|thar|tic /kəθɑrtɪk/ ADJ Something that is **cathartic** has the effect of catharsis. [FORMAL] ❑ *His laughter was cathartic, an animal yelp that brought tears to his eyes.*

ca|thedral /kəθidrəl/ (**cathedrals**) N-COUNT A **cathedral** is a very large and important church which has a bishop in charge of it. ❑ *...St. Paul's Cathedral.*

cath|eter /kæθɪtər/ (**catheters**) N-COUNT A **catheter** is a tube which is used to introduce liquids into a human body or to withdraw liquids from it. [MEDICAL]

cath|ode /kǽθoʊd/ (cathodes) N-COUNT A **cathode** is the negative electrode in a cell such as a battery. Compare **anode**.

cathode-ray tube (cathode-ray tubes) N-COUNT A **cathode-ray tube** is a device in televisions and computer terminals which sends an image onto the screen. [TECHNICAL]

Catho|lic ♦◇ /kǽθlɪk/ (Catholics) **1** ADJ The **Catholic** Church is the branch of the Christian Church that accepts the Pope and is based in the Vatican in Rome. ◻ ...the Catholic Church. ◻ ...Catholic priests. **2** ADJ If you describe a collection of things or people as **catholic**, you are emphasizing that they are very varied. ◻ He was a man of catholic tastes, a lover of grand opera, history, and the fine arts. **3** N-COUNT A **Catholic** is a member of the Catholic Church. ◻ At least nine out of ten Mexicans are baptized Catholics.

Ca|tholi|cism /kəθɒlɪsɪzəm/ N-UNCOUNT **Catholicism** is the traditions, the behavior, and the set of Christian beliefs that are held by Catholics. ◻ ...her conversion to Catholicism.

cat|kin /kǽtkɪn/ (catkins) N-COUNT A **catkin** is a long, thin, soft flower that hangs on some trees, for example birch trees and hazel trees.

cat|nap /kǽtnæp/ (catnaps) N-COUNT A **catnap** is a short sleep, usually one which you have during the day. [INFORMAL]

cat|nip /kǽtnɪp/ N-UNCOUNT **Catnip** is an herb with scented leaves, which cats are fond of. ◻ Catnip grows wild in much of the United States.

cat|sup /kǽtsəp/ → see ketchup

cat|tle /kǽtəl/ N-PLURAL **Cattle** are cows and bulls. ◻ ...the finest herd of beef cattle for two hundred miles.

cat|tle guard (cattle guards) N-COUNT A **cattle guard** is a set of metal bars in the surface of a road which prevents cattle and sheep from walking along the road, but allows people and vehicles to pass. [AM]

in BRIT, use **cattle grid**

cat|tle|man /kǽtəlmæn/ (cattlemen) N-COUNT A **cattleman** is a man who takes care of or owns cattle, especially in North America or Australia.

cat|tle mar|ket (cattle markets) **1** N-COUNT A **cattle market** is a market where cattle are bought and sold. **2** N-COUNT If you refer to an event such as a **cattle market**, you disapprove of it because people are judged there only in terms of their sexual attractiveness. [DISAPPROVAL]

cat|tle prod (cattle prods) N-COUNT A **cattle prod** is an object shaped like a long stick. Farmers make cattle move in a particular direction by pushing the cattle prod against the bodies of the animals. ◻ ...an electric cattle prod.

cat|ty /kǽti/ (cattier, cattiest) ADJ If you say that someone is being **catty**, you mean that they are being unpleasant and unkind. [INFORMAL] ◻ ...catty remarks.

catty-corner also **kitty-corner** ADV Something that is **catty-corner** or **kitty-corner** from another thing is placed or arranged diagonally from it. [AM] ◻ There was a police car catty-corner across the street. ◻ ...two 50-foot-tall, steel and aluminum towers standing kitty-corner from each other.

cat|walk /kǽtwɔk/ (catwalks) **1** N-COUNT At a fashion show, the **catwalk** is a narrow platform that models walk along to display clothes. ◻ On the catwalk the models stomped around in thigh-high leather boots. **2** N-COUNT A **catwalk** is a narrow bridge high in the air, for example between two parts of a tall building, on the outside of a large structure, or over a stage. ◻ ...a catwalk overlooking a vast room.

Cau|ca|sian /kɔkeɪʒən/ (Caucasians) ADJ A **Caucasian** person is a White person. [FORMAL] ◻ ...a 25-year-old Caucasian male. ● N-COUNT A **Caucasian** is someone who is Caucasian. ◻ Ann Hamilton was a Caucasian from New England.

cau|cus /kɔkəs/ (caucuses) N-COUNT A **caucus** is a group of people within an organization who share similar aims and interests or who have a lot of influence. [FORMAL] ◻ ...the Black Caucus of minority congressmen.

caught /kɔt/ **Caught** is the past tense and past participle of **catch**.

caul|dron /kɔldrən/ (cauldrons) N-COUNT A **cauldron** is a very large, round metal pot used for cooking over a fire. [LITERARY] ◻ ...a witch's cauldron.

cau|li|flow|er /kɔliflaʊər/ (cauliflowers) N-VAR **Cauliflower** is a large, round vegetable that has a hard, white center surrounded by green leaves.

caulk /kɔk/ (caulks, caulking, caulked) **1** V-T If you **caulk** something such as a boat, you fill small cracks in its surface in order to prevent it from leaking. ◻ He'd offered to caulk the windows. ● **caulk|ing** /kɔkɪŋ/ N-UNCOUNT ◻ ...menial jobs like caulking. **2** N-UNCOUNT **Caulk** is a soft substance that is used to caulk something. ◻ ...a caulk product that isn't sticky to the touch and can be used for quick fill-in jobs.

caus|al /kɔzəl/ ADJ [usu ADJ n] If there is a **causal** relationship between two things, one thing is responsible for causing the other thing. [FORMAL] ◻ Rawlins stresses that it is impossible to prove a causal link between the drug and the deaths.

cau|sal|ity /kɔzælɪti/ N-UNCOUNT **Causality** is the relationship of cause and effect. [FORMAL] ◻ ...the chain of causality that produces an earthquake.

cau|sa|tion /kɔzeɪʃən/ **1** N-UNCOUNT The **causation** of something, usually something bad, is the factors that have caused it. [FORMAL] ◻ The gene is only part of the causation of illness. **2** N-UNCOUNT **Causation** is a study of the factors involved in causing something. [FORMAL]

causa|tive /kɔzətɪv/ ADJ [ADJ n] **Causative** factors are ones which are responsible for causing something. [FORMAL] ◻ Both nicotine and carbon monoxide inhaled with cigarette smoking have been incriminated as causative factors.

'cause /kʌz, kəz/ also **cause** CONJ **'Cause** is an informal way of saying **because**. [SPOKEN] ◻ Hopefully everybody's well-rested 'cause it could be a long day.

cause ♦♦♦ /kɔz/ (causes, causing, caused) **1** N-COUNT The **cause** of an event, usually a bad event, is the thing that makes it happen. ◻ Smoking is the biggest preventable cause of death and disease. **2** N-COUNT A **cause** is an aim or principle which a group of people supports or is fighting for. ◻ Refusing to have one leader has not helped the cause. **3** V-T To **cause** something, usually something bad, means to make it happen. ◻ The insecticide used on some weeds can cause health problems. ◻ This was a genuine mistake, but it did cause me some worry. **4** N-UNCOUNT If you have **cause** for a particular feeling or action, you have good reasons for feeling it or doing it. ◻ Only a few people can find any cause for celebration. **5** PHRASE If you say that something is **for a good cause**, you mean that it is worth doing or giving to because it will help other people, for example by raising money for charity. ◻ The Raleigh International Bike Ride is open to anyone who wants to raise money for a good cause. **6** → See feature box at **global warming**

--- COLLOCATIONS ---

cause
NOUN
1
noun + **cause**: root
adjective + **cause**: underlying; common, likely
4
adjective + **cause**: hopeless, lost; noble, worthy
VERB **3**
cause + noun: controversy, offense, outrage; chaos, damage, harm, havoc; delay, disruption; problem, trouble; death, injury, pain

--- SYNONYMS ---

cause
NOUN **1**
origin: Their medical problems are basically physical in origin.
source: Renewable sources of energy must be used where practical.
root: We got to the root of the problem.
VERB **3**
produce: The talks are aimed at producing a new world trade treaty.
create: Criticizing will only destroy a relationship and create feelings of failure.
lead to: This discovery led to studies of the immune system.
generate: ...the excitement generated by the changes in the world of education.
provoke: His election success has provoked a shocked reaction.

cause célèbre /kɔz səlɛbrə, kouz seɪlɛbrə/ (causes célèbres) also **cause celebre** N-COUNT A **cause célèbre** is an issue, person, or criminal trial that has attracted a lot of public attention and discussion. [FORMAL] ❑ *The Kravchenko trial became a cause célèbre in Paris and internationally.*

cause|way /kɔzweɪ/ (causeways) N-COUNT A **causeway** is a raised path or road that crosses water or wet land.

caus|tic /kɔstɪk/ **1** ADJ **Caustic** chemical substances are very powerful and can dissolve other substances. ❑ *...caustic cleaning agents.* ❑ *Remember that this is caustic; use gloves or a spoon.* **2** ADJ A **caustic** remark is extremely critical, cruel, or bitter. [FORMAL] ❑ *His abrasive wit and caustic comments were an interviewer's nightmare.*

caus|tic soda N-UNCOUNT **Caustic soda** is a powerful chemical substance used to make strong soaps and clean drains.

cau|ter|ize /kɔtəraɪz/ (cauterizes, cauterizing, cauterized)

in BRIT, also use **cauterise**

V-T If a doctor **cauterizes** a wound, he or she burns it with heat or with a chemical in order to close it up and prevent it from becoming infected. ❑ *He cauterized the wound with a piece of red-hot iron.*

cau|tion /kɔʃən/ (cautions, cautioning, cautioned) **1** N-UNCOUNT **Caution** is great care which you take in order to avoid possible danger. ❑ *Extreme caution should be exercised when buying used tires.* **2** V-T/V-I If someone **cautions** you, they warn you about problems or danger. ❑ *Tony cautioned against misrepresenting the situation.* ❑ *The statement clearly was intended to caution Seoul against attempting to block the council's action again.* • N-UNCOUNT **Caution** is also a noun. ❑ *There was a note of caution for the treasury in the figures.* **3 to err on the side of caution** → see **err**

cau|tion|ary /kɔʃənɛri/ ADJ A **cautionary** story or a **cautionary** note to a story is one that is intended to give a warning to people. ❑ *Barely fifteen months later, it has become a cautionary tale of the pitfalls of international mergers and acquisitions.*

cau|tious ◆◇◇ /kɔʃəs/ ADJ Someone who is **cautious** acts very carefully in order to avoid possible danger. ❑ *The scientists are cautious about using enzyme therapy on humans.* • **cau|tious|ly** ADV ❑ *David moved cautiously forward and looked over the edge.*

SYNONYMS

cautious
ADJ
careful: *Students will need careful guidance on their choice of options.*
wary: *They were very wary about giving him a contract.*
prudent: *It is always prudent to start any exercise program gradually at first.*
circumspect: *The banks should have been more circumspect in their dealings.*

cav|al|cade /kævəlkeɪd/ (cavalcades) N-COUNT [oft N of n] A **cavalcade** is a procession of people on horses or in cars or carriages. ❑ *...a cavalcade of limousines and police motorcycles.*

cava|lier /kævəlɪər/ ADJ If you describe a person or their behavior as **cavalier**, you are criticizing them because you think that they do not consider other people's feelings or take account of the seriousness of a situation. [DISAPPROVAL] ❑ *The editor takes a cavalier attitude to the concept of fact checking.*

cav|al|ry /kævəlri/ **1** N-SING The **cavalry** is the part of an army that uses armored vehicles for fighting. ❑ *The 3rd Cavalry went on the offensive.* **2** N-SING The **cavalry** is the group of soldiers in an army who ride horses. ❑ *...a young cavalry officer.*

cav|al|ry|man /kævəlrimæn/ (cavalrymen) N-COUNT A **cavalryman** is a soldier who is in the cavalry, especially one who rides a horse.

cave ◆◇◇ /keɪv/ (caves, caving, caved) N-COUNT A **cave** is a large hole in the side of a cliff or hill, or one that is under the ground. ❑ *Outside the cave mouth the blackness of night was like a curtain.*
▸ **cave in 1** PHRASAL VERB If something such as a roof or a ceiling **caves in**, it collapses inward. ❑ *Part of the roof has caved in.* **2** PHRASAL VERB If you **cave in**, you suddenly stop arguing or resisting, especially when people put pressure on you to stop. ❑ *After a ruinous strike, the union caved in.* ❑ *The judge has caved in to political pressure.*

ca|veat /kæviət/ (caveats) N-COUNT [oft N that] A **caveat** is a warning of a specific limitation of something such as information or an agreement. [FORMAL] ❑ *There was one caveat: he was not to enter into a merger or otherwise weaken the Roche family's control of the firm.*

ca|veat emp|tor /kæviæt ɛmptɔr/ CONVENTION **Caveat emptor** means 'let the buyer beware,' and is a warning to someone buying something that it is their responsibility to identify and accept any faults in it. [FORMAL, WRITTEN]

cave-in (cave-ins) N-COUNT A **cave-in** is the sudden collapse of the roof of a cave or mine.

cave|man /keɪvmæn/ (cavemen) N-COUNT **Cavemen** were men in prehistoric times who lived mainly in caves.

cav|er /keɪvər/ (cavers) N-COUNT A **caver** is someone who goes into underground caves as a sport.

cav|ern /kævərn/ (caverns) N-COUNT A **cavern** is a large, deep cave.

cav|ern|ous /kævərnəs/ ADJ A **cavernous** room or building is very large inside, and so it reminds you of a cave. ❑ *Climbing steep stairs to the choir gallery you peer into a cavernous interior.*

cave|woman /keɪvwʊmən/ (cavewomen) N-COUNT **Cavewomen** were women in prehistoric times who lived mainly in caves.

cavi|ar /kæviɑr/ (caviars) also **caviare** N-MASS **Caviar** is the salted eggs of a fish called a sturgeon.

cav|il /kævəl/ (cavils, caviling, caviled)

in BRIT, use **cavilling, cavilled**

V-I [no passive] If you say that someone **cavils** at something, you mean that they make criticisms of it that you think are unimportant or unnecessary. [FORMAL, DISAPPROVAL] ❑ *Let us not cavil too much.* ❑ *I don't think this is the time to cavil at the wording of the report.* • N-COUNT **Cavil** is also a noun. ❑ *These cavils aside, most of the essays are very good indeed.*

cav|ity /kæviti/ (cavities) **1** N-COUNT A **cavity** is a space or hole in something such as a solid object or a person's body. [FORMAL] ❑ *...a cavity in the roof.* **2** N-COUNT In dentistry, a **cavity** is a hole in a tooth, caused by decay. [TECHNICAL]

ca|vort /kəvɔrt/ (cavorts, cavorting, cavorted) **1** V-I When people **cavort**, they leap about in a noisy and excited way. ❑ *You can enjoy a quick snack while your children cavort in the sand.* **2** V-I **Cavort** is sometimes used by journalists to suggest that people were behaving in a playfully sexual way. ❑ *It was claimed she cavorted with a police sergeant in a Jacuzzi, but she denies this.*

caw /kɔ/ (caws, cawing, cawed) V-I When a bird such as a crow or a rook **caws**, it makes a loud, harsh sound. ❑ *Outside, a raven cawed.*

cay|enne pep|per /kaɪɛn pɛpər/ N-UNCOUNT **Cayenne pepper** or **cayenne** is a red powder with a hot taste which is made from dried peppers and is used to flavor food. ❑ *Season with salt, pepper, and a pinch of cayenne.*

CB /si bi/ N-UNCOUNT **CB**, an abbreviation for 'Citizens' Band,' is a range of radio frequencies which the general public is allowed to use to send messages to each other. It is used especially by truck drivers and other drivers who use radio sets in their vehicles.

CBD /si bi di/ N-UNCOUNT **CBD** is a chemical compound which is one of the substances found in the drug marijuana, and which has some medical uses. **CBD** is an abbreviation for 'cannabidiol.'

cc /si si/ **1** You use **cc** when referring to the volume or capacity of something such as the size of a car engine. **cc** is an abbreviation for 'cubic centimeters.' ❑ *...1,500 cc sports cars.* **2** **cc** is used in email headers or at the end of a business letter to indicate that a copy is being sent to another person. [BUSINESS] ❑ *...cc j.jones@harpercollins.co.uk* ❑ *...cc J. Chater, S. Cooper.*

CCTV /si si ti vi/ N-UNCOUNT **CCTV** is an abbreviation for 'closed-circuit television.' ❑ *...a CCTV camera.*

CD /siː diː/ (CDs) N-COUNT CDs are small plastic disks on which sound, especially music, is recorded. CDs can also be used to store information which can be read by a computer. CD is an abbreviation for 'compact disc.' ▫ *The Beatles' Red and Blue compilations are issued on CD for the first time next month.*

CD burn|er (CD burners) N-COUNT A **CD burner** is a piece of computer equipment that you use for copying data from a computer onto a CD. [COMPUTING] ▫ *Users can download MP3 music files and record them directly onto a CD audio disc using a PC CD burner.*

CD play|er (CD players) N-COUNT A **CD player** is a machine on which you can play CDs.

Cdr also **CDR** N-TITLE **Cdr** is the written abbreviation for Commander when it is used as a title. ▫ *...Cdr A.C. Moore.*

CD-R /siː diː ɑːr/ (CD-Rs) N-COUNT A **CD-R** is a CD which is capable of recording sound and images, for example from another CD or from the internet. **CD-R** is an abbreviation for 'compact disc recordable.'

CD-ROM /siː diː rɒm/ (CD-ROMs) N-COUNT A **CD-ROM** is a CD on which a very large amount of information can be stored and then read using a computer. **CD-ROM** is an abbreviation for 'compact disc read-only memory.' [COMPUTING] ▫ *A single CD-ROM can hold more than 500 megabytes of data.*

CD-ROM drive (CD-ROM drives) N-COUNT A **CD-ROM drive** is the device that you use with a computer to play CD-ROMs. [COMPUTING]

CD-RW /siː diː ɑːr dʌbəljuː/ (CD-RWs) N-COUNT A **CD-RW** is a CD which is capable of recording sound and images, for example from another CD or from the internet. **CD-RW** is an abbreviation for 'compact disc rewritable.'

CD writ|er (CD writers) N-COUNT A **CD writer** is the same as a **CD burner**. [COMPUTING]

CE /siː iː/ Many people now use **CE** in dates to indicate a number of years or centuries after AD 1 or after the year in which Jesus is believed to have been born. Compare **BCE**. ▫ *The Gospel of Mark was written around 70 CE.* ▫ *The language was practically extinct by the sixth century CE.*

cease ♦♢♢ /siːs/ (ceases, ceasing, ceased) **1** V-I If something **ceases**, it stops happening or existing. [FORMAL] ▫ *At one o'clock the rain had ceased.* **2** V-T If you **cease** to do something, you stop doing it. [FORMAL] ▫ *He never ceases to amaze me.* ▫ *The secrecy about the president's condition had ceased to matter.* **3** V-T If you **cease** something, you stop it happening or working. [FORMAL] ▫ *The Tundra Times, a weekly newspaper in Alaska, ceased publication this week.*

▶ SYNONYMS ◀

cease
VERB **2**
stop: *Stop throwing those stones!*
discontinue: *Do not discontinue the treatment without consulting your doctor.*
end: *Talks have resumed to try to end the fighting.*
finish: *As soon as he'd finished eating, he excused himself.*

cease|fire ♦♢♢ /siːsfaɪər/ (ceasefires) N-COUNT A **ceasefire** is an arrangement in which countries or groups of people that are fighting each other agree to stop fighting. ▫ *They have agreed to a ceasefire after three years of conflict.*

cease|less /siːsləs/ ADJ If something, often something unpleasant, is **ceaseless**, it continues for a long time without stopping or changing. [FORMAL] ▫ *There is a ceaseless struggle from noon to night.* • **cease|less|ly** ADV [usu ADV with v] ▫ *The characters complain ceaselessly about food lines, prices, and corruption.*

ce|dar /siːdər/ (cedars) N-COUNT A **cedar** is a large evergreen tree with wide branches and small, thin leaves called needles. • N-UNCOUNT **Cedar** is the wood of this tree. ▫ *The yacht is built of cedar strip planking.*

cede /siːd/ (cedes, ceding, ceded) V-T If someone in a position of authority **cedes** land or power to someone else, they let them have the land or power, often as a result of military or political pressure. [FORMAL] ▫ *Only a short campaign took place in Puerto Rico, but after the war Spain ceded its territory to America.*

ce|dil|la /sɪdɪlə/ (cedillas) N-COUNT A **cedilla** is a symbol that is written under the letter 'c' in French, Portuguese, and some other languages to show that you pronounce it like a letter 's' rather than like a letter 'k.' It is written ç.

cei|lidh /keɪli/ (ceilidhs) N-COUNT A **ceilidh** is an informal entertainment, especially in Scotland or Ireland, at which there is folk music, singing, and dancing.

ceil|ing /siːlɪŋ/ (ceilings) **1** N-COUNT A **ceiling** is the horizontal surface that forms the top part or roof inside a room. ▫ *The rooms were spacious, with tall windows and high ceilings.* **2** N-COUNT A **ceiling** on something such as prices or wages is an official upper limit that cannot be broken. ▫ *...an informal agreement to put a ceiling on salaries.* **3** → see also **glass ceiling**

ce|leb /sɪlɛb/ (celebs) N-COUNT A **celeb** is the same as a **celebrity**. [INFORMAL, mainly JOURNALISM]

cel|ebrant /sɛlɪbrənt/ (celebrants) N-COUNT A **celebrant** is a person who performs or takes part in a religious ceremony. [FORMAL]

cel|ebrate ♦♢♢ /sɛlɪbreɪt/ (celebrates, celebrating, celebrated) **1** V-T/V-I If you **celebrate** an occasion or if you **celebrate**, you do something enjoyable because of a special occasion or to mark someone's success. ▫ *I was in a mood to celebrate.* ▫ *Dick celebrated his 60th birthday Monday.* **2** V-T If an organization or country **is celebrating** an anniversary, it has existed for that length of time and is doing something special because of it. ▫ *The society is celebrating its tenth anniversary this year.* **3** V-T When priests **celebrate** Holy Communion or Mass, they officially perform the actions and ceremonies that are involved. ▫ *Pope John Paul celebrated mass today in a city in central Poland.*

cel|ebrat|ed /sɛlɪbreɪtɪd/ ADJ A **celebrated** person or thing is famous and much admired. ▫ *He was soon one of the most celebrated young painters in England.*

cel|ebra|tion ♦♢♢ /sɛlɪbreɪʃən/ (celebrations) **1** N-COUNT A **celebration** is a special enjoyable event that people organize because something pleasant has happened or because it is someone's birthday or anniversary. ▫ *I can tell you, there was a celebration in our house that night.* **2** N-SING The **celebration** of something is praise and appreciation which is given to it. ▫ *This was not a memorial service but a celebration of his life.*

▶ SYNONYMS ◀

celebration
NOUN **1**
party: *The couple met at a party.*
festivity: *There was a general air of festivity and abandon.*
revelry: *...New Year revelries.*
jubilee: *...Queen Victoria's jubilee.*

▶ COLLOCATIONS ◀

celebration
NOUN **1**
noun + **celebration**: anniversary, birthday, centenary, wedding; goal, victory
adjective + **celebration**: joyous, wild; low-key
celebration + be + adjective: short-lived
verb + **celebration**: organize, plan; attend; spark, trigger

cel|ebra|tory /sɛlɪbrətɔːri/ ADJ [usu ADJ n] A **celebratory** meal, drink, or other activity takes place to celebrate something such as a birthday, anniversary, or victory. ▫ *That night she, Nicholson, and the crew had a celebratory dinner.*

ce|leb|rity /sɪlɛbrɪti/ (celebrities) **1** N-COUNT A **celebrity** is someone who is famous, especially in areas of entertainment such as movies, music, writing, or sports. ▫ *In 1944, at the age of 30, Hersey suddenly became a celebrity.* **2** N-UNCOUNT If a person or thing achieves **celebrity**, they become famous, especially in areas of entertainment such as movies, music, writing, or sports. ▫ *He achieved celebrity as a sports commentator.*

cel|ery /sɛləri/ N-UNCOUNT **Celery** is a vegetable with long, pale green stalks. It is eaten raw in salads. ▫ *...a stick of celery.*

ce|les|tial /sɪlɛstʃəl/ **1** ADJ **Celestial** is used to describe things relating to heaven or to the sky. [LITERARY] ▫ *...the clusters of celestial bodies in the ever-expanding universe.* **2** → See feature box at **space**

celi|ba|cy /sɛlɪbəsi/ N-UNCOUNT **Celibacy** is the state of being celibate. ◻ ...*priests who violate their vows of celibacy.*

celi|bate /sɛlɪbɪt/ (**celibates**) **1** ADJ Someone who is **celibate** does not marry or have sex, because of their religious beliefs. ◻ *The Pope bluntly told the world's priests yesterday to stay celibate.* • N-COUNT A **celibate** is someone who is celibate. ◻ ...*the U.S.A.'s biggest group of celibates.* **2** ADJ Someone who is **celibate** does not have sex during a particular period of their life. ◻ *I was celibate for two years.*

cell ♦♦◊ /sɛl/ (**cells**) **1** N-COUNT A **cell** is the smallest part of an animal or plant that is able to function independently. Every animal or plant is made up of millions of cells. ◻ *Those cells divide and give many other different types of cells.* ◻ ...*blood cells.* **2** N-COUNT A **cell** is a small room in which a prisoner is locked. A **cell** is also a small room in which a monk or nun lives. ◻ *Do you recall how many prisoners were placed in each cell?* **3** → See feature box at **brain**

COLLOCATIONS

cell
NOUN
1
noun + **cell**: blood, brain, fat, nerve, skin; cancer
adjective + **cell**: abnormal, cancerous, dead
2
noun + **cell**: jail, prison

---

cel|lar /sɛlər/ (**cellars**) **1** N-COUNT A **cellar** is a room underneath a building, which is often used for storing things in. ◻ *The box of papers had been stored in a cellar at the family home.* **2** N-COUNT A person's or restaurant's **cellar** is the collection of different wines that they have. ◻ *Choose a superb wine to complement your meal from our extensive wine cellar.*

cel|list /tʃɛlɪst/ (**cellists**) N-COUNT A **cellist** is someone who plays the cello.

cell line (**cell lines**) N-COUNT A **cell line** is a set of cells grown in a laboratory from a single plant or animal cell. ◻ *The work involves growing stem cell lines and examining their surface molecules.*

cell|mate /sɛlmeɪt/ (**cellmates**) N-COUNT [usu with poss] In a prison, someone's **cellmate** is the person they share their cell with.

cel|lo /tʃɛloʊ/ (**cellos**) N-VAR A **cello** is a musical instrument with four strings that looks like a large violin. You play the cello with a bow while sitting down and holding it upright between your legs.

cel|lo|phane /sɛləfeɪn/ N-UNCOUNT **Cellophane** is a thin, transparent material that is used to wrap things. [TRADEMARK] ◻ *She tore off the cellophane, pulled out a cigarette, and lit it.* ◻ ...*a cellophane wrapper.*

cell|phone /sɛlfoʊn/ (**cellphones**) N-COUNT A **cellphone** is the same as a **cellular phone**. [mainly AM]

cel|lu|lar /sɛlyələr/ ADJ **Cellular** means relating to the cells of animals or plants. ◻ *Many toxic effects can be studied at the cellular level.*

cel|lu|lar phone (**cellular phones**) N-COUNT A **cellular phone** or **cellular telephone** is a type of telephone which does not need wires to connect it to a telephone system. [mainly AM]

in BRIT, usually use **mobile phone**

cel|lu|lite /sɛlyəlaɪt/ N-UNCOUNT **Cellulite** is lumpy fat which people may get under their skin, especially on their thighs. ◻ ...*an Italian-made product that is said to eradicate cellulite within weeks.*

cel|lu|loid /sɛlyəlɔɪd/ N-UNCOUNT [oft N N] You can use **celluloid** to refer to movies. **Celluloid** is a type of plastic formerly used for making photographic film. ◻ *King's works seem to lack something on celluloid.*

cel|lu|lose /sɛlyəloʊs/ N-UNCOUNT **Cellulose** is a substance that exists in the cell walls of plants and is used to make paper, plastic, and various fabrics and fibers.

Celsius /sɛlsiəs/ ADJ [n/num ADJ] **Celsius** is a scale for measuring temperature, in which water freezes at 0 degrees and boils at 100 degrees. It is represented by the symbol °C. ◻ *Highest temperatures 11° Celsius, that's 52° Fahrenheit.* • N-UNCOUNT **Celsius** is also a noun. ◻ *The thermometer shows the temperature in Celsius and Fahrenheit.*

Celt /kɛlt, sɛlt/ (**Celts**) N-COUNT If you describe someone as a **Celt**, you mean that they are part of the racial group which comes from Scotland, Wales, Ireland, and some other areas such as Brittany.

Celt|ic /kɛltɪk, sɛl-/ ADJ [usu ADJ n] If you describe something as **Celtic**, you mean that it is connected with the people and the culture of Scotland, Wales, Ireland, and some other areas such as Brittany. ◻ ...*important figures in Celtic tradition.*

ce|ment /sɪmɛnt/ (**cements, cementing, cemented**) **1** N-UNCOUNT **Cement** is a gray powder which is mixed with sand and water in order to make concrete. ◻ *Builders have trouble getting the right amount of cement into their concrete.* **2** N-UNCOUNT **Cement** is the same as **concrete**. ◻ ...*the hard, cold cement floor.* **3** N-UNCOUNT Glue that is made for sticking particular substances together is sometimes called **cement**. ◻ *Stick the pieces on with tile cement.* **4** V-T Something that **cements** a relationship or agreement makes it stronger. ◻ *Nothing cements a friendship between countries so much as trade.* **5** V-T [usu passive] If things **are cemented** together, they are stuck or fastened together. ◻ *Most artificial joints are cemented into place.*

ce|ment mix|er (**cement mixers**) N-COUNT A **cement mixer** is a machine with a large, revolving container into which builders put cement, sand, and water in order to make concrete.

cem|etery /sɛmətɛri/ (**cemeteries**) N-COUNT A **cemetery** is a place where dead people's bodies or their ashes are buried.

ceno|taph /sɛnətæf/ (**cenotaphs**) N-COUNT A **cenotaph** is a structure that is built in honor of soldiers who died in a war.

cen|sor /sɛnsər/ (**censors, censoring, censored**) **1** V-T If someone in authority **censors** letters or the media, they officially examine them and cut out any information that is regarded as secret. ◻ *The military-backed government has heavily censored the news.* **2** V-T If someone in authority **censors** a book, play, or movie, they officially examine it and cut out any parts that are considered to be immoral or inappropriate. ◻ *The Late Show censored the band's live version of their latest song.* **3** N-COUNT A **censor** is a person who has been officially appointed to examine letters or the media and to cut out any parts that are regarded as secret. ◻ *The report was cleared by the American military censors.* **4** N-COUNT A **censor** is a person who has been officially appointed to examine plays, movies, and books and to cut out any parts that are considered to be immoral. ◻ *The movie had to be cut before the board of censors accepted it.*

cen|so|ri|ous /sɛnsɔriəs/ ADJ If you describe someone as **censorious**, you do not like the way they strongly disapprove of and criticize someone else's behavior. [FORMAL, DISAPPROVAL] ◻ *Despite strong principles he was never censorious.*

cen|sor|ship /sɛnsərʃɪp/ N-UNCOUNT **Censorship** is the censoring of books, plays, movies, or reports, especially by government officials, because they are considered immoral or secret in some way. ◻ *The government today announced that press censorship was being lifted.*

cen|sure /sɛnʃər/ (**censures, censuring, censured**) V-T If you **censure** someone for something that they have done, you tell them that you strongly disapprove of it. [FORMAL] ◻ *The ethics committee may take a decision to admonish him or to censure him.* • N-UNCOUNT **Censure** is also a noun. ◻ *It is a controversial policy which has attracted international censure.*

cen|sus /sɛnsəs/ (**censuses**) N-COUNT A **census** is an official survey of the population of a country that is carried out in order to find out how many people live there and to obtain details of such things as people's ages and jobs. ◻ *The detailed assessment of the latest census will be ready in three months.*

cent /sɛnt/ (**cents**) N-COUNT A **cent** is a small unit of money worth one hundredth of some currencies, for example the dollar and the euro. ◻ *A cup of rice which cost thirty cents a few weeks ago is now being sold for up to one dollar.*

cen|taur /sɛntɔr/ (**centaurs**) N-COUNT In classical mythology, a **centaur** is a creature with the head, arms, and chest of a man, and the body and legs of a horse.

cen|te|nar|ian /sɛntɪnɛəriən/ (**centenarians**) N-COUNT A **centenarian** is someone who is a hundred years old or older. ◻ *Many centenarians have lived long and eventful lives.*

cen|te|nary /sɛntɡnəri/ (centenaries) N-COUNT A **centenary** is the same as a **centennial**. [mainly BRIT]

cen|ten|nial /sɛntɛniəl/ N-SING [oft N n] The **centennial** of an event such as someone's birth is the 100th anniversary of that event. [mainly AM] ❑ *The centennial Olympics was in Atlanta, Georgia.*

cen|ter ✦✦✦ /sɛntər/ (centers, centering, centered)

in BRIT, use **centre**

1 N-COUNT The **center** of something is the middle of it. ❑ *A large, wooden table dominates the center of the room.* **2** N-COUNT A **center** is a building where people have meetings, take part in a particular activity, or get help of some kind. ❑ *She now also does pottery classes at a community center.* **3** N-COUNT If an area or town is a **center** for an industry or activity, that industry or activity is very important there. ❑ *New York is also a major international financial center.* **4** N-COUNT The **center** of a town or city is the part where there are the most stores and businesses and where a lot of people come from other areas to work or shop. ❑ *...the city center.* **5** N-COUNT If something or someone is at the **center** of a situation, they are the most important thing or person involved. ❑ *...the man at the center of the controversy.* **6** N-SING If someone or something is the **center** of attention or interest, people are giving them a lot of attention. ❑ *The rest of the cast was used to her being the center of attention.* **7** N-SING In politics, the **center** refers to groups and their beliefs, when they are considered to be neither left-wing nor right-wing. ❑ *The Democrats have become a party of the center.* **8** V-T/V-I If something **centers** or **is centered** on a particular thing or person, that thing or person is the main subject of attention. ❑ *...the improvement was the result of a plan which centered on academic achievement and personal motivation.* ❑ *All his concerns were centered around himself rather than Rachel.* • **-centered** COMB IN ADJ ❑ *...a child-centered approach to teaching.* **9** V-T/V-I If an industry or event **is centered** in a place, or if it **centers** there, it takes place to the greatest extent there. ❑ *The fighting has been centered around the town of Vucovar.* ❑ *The disturbances have centered around the two main university areas.* **10** → see also **community center, shopping center**

cen|tered /sɛntərd/

in BRIT, use **centred**

1 ADJ [v-link ADJ prep] If an industry or event is **centered** in a place, it takes place to the greatest extent there. ❑ *The tremor was centered in the Gulf of Sirte.* **2** → see also **-centered**

-centered /-sɛntərd/

in BRIT, use **-centred**

1 COMB IN ADJ **-centered** can be added to adjectives and nouns to indicate what kind of a center something has. ❑ *...lemon-centered white chocolates.* **2** → see also **center, self-centered**

center|fold /sɛntərfoʊld/ (centerfolds)

in BRIT, use **centrefold**

N-COUNT A **centerfold** is a picture that covers the two central pages of a magazine, especially a photograph of a naked or partly naked woman.

cen|ter for|ward (center forwards)

in BRIT, use **centre-forward**

N-COUNT A **center forward** in a team sport such as soccer or hockey is the player or position in the middle of the front row of attacking players.

cen|ter of grav|ity (centers of gravity)

in BRIT, use **centre of gravity**

N-COUNT The **center of gravity** of an object is a point in it. If this point is above the base of the object, it stays stable, rather than falling over.

center|piece /sɛntərpis/ (centerpieces)

in BRIT, use **centrepiece**

1 N-COUNT The **centerpiece** of something is the best or most interesting part of it. ❑ *The centerpiece of the plan is the idea of regular referendums, initiated by voters.* **2** N-COUNT A **centerpiece** is an ornament which you put in the middle of something, especially a dinner table. ❑ *He was arranging floral centerpieces in the banquet hall.*

cen|ter stage

in BRIT, use **centre stage, centre-stage**

N-UNCOUNT [also the N] If something or someone takes **center stage**, they become very important or noticeable. ❑ *Nuclear proliferation has returned to center stage in international affairs.*

cen|ti|grade /sɛntɪɡreɪd/ ADJ **Centigrade** is a scale for measuring temperature, in which water freezes at 0 degrees and boils at 100 degrees. It is represented by the symbol °C. ❑ *...daytime temperatures of up to forty degrees centigrade.* • N-UNCOUNT **Centigrade** is also a noun. ❑ *The number at the bottom is the recommended water temperature in centigrade.*

cen|ti|li|ter /sɛntɪlitər/ (centiliters)

in BRIT, use **centilitre**

N-COUNT A **centiliter** is a unit of volume in the metric system equal to ten milliliters or one-hundredth of a liter.

cen|ti|me|ter /sɛntɪmitər/ (centimeters)

in BRIT, use **centimetre**

N-COUNT A **centimeter** is a unit of length in the metric system equal to ten millimeters or one-hundredth of a meter. ❑ *...a tiny fossil plant, only a few centimeters high.*

cen|ti|pede /sɛntɪpid/ (centipedes) N-COUNT A **centipede** is a long, thin creature with a lot of legs.

cen|tral ✦✦✦ /sɛntrəl/ **1** ADJ Something that is **central** is in the middle of a place or area. ❑ *...Central America's Caribbean coast.* ❑ *The disruption has now spread and is affecting a large part of central Liberia.* • **cen|tral|ly** ADV ❑ *The main cabin has its full-sized double bed centrally placed with plenty of room around it.* **2** ADJ A place that is **central** is easy to reach because it is in the center of a city, town, or particular area. ❑ *...a central location in the capital.* • **cen|tral|ly** ADV ❑ *...this centrally located hotel, situated on the banks of the river.* **3** ADJ [ADJ n] A **central** group or organization makes all the important decisions that are followed throughout a larger organization or a country. ❑ *There is a lack of trust toward the central government in Rome.* • **cen|tral|ly** ADV ❑ *This is a centrally planned economy.* **4** ADJ The **central** person or thing in a particular situation is the most important one. ❑ *Black dance music has been central to mainstream pop since the early '60s.*

SYNONYMS

central
ADJ **4**
main: *My main concern now is to protect the children.*
chief: *Financial stress is well established as a chief reason for divorce.*
key: *He is expected to be the key witness at the trial.*
principal: *...the country's principal source of foreign exchange earnings.*
fundamental: *A fundamental human right is being withheld from these people.*

---

cen|tral heat|ing N-UNCOUNT **Central heating** is a heating system for buildings. Air or water is heated in one place and travels around a building through pipes and radiators. ❑ *I am thinking of installing central heating.*

cen|tral|ism /sɛntrəlɪzəm/ N-UNCOUNT **Centralism** is a way of governing a country, or organizing something such as industry, education, or politics, which involves having one central group of people who give instructions to everyone else.

cen|tral|ist /sɛntrəlɪst/ (centralists) ADJ [usu ADJ n] **Centralist** organizations govern a country or organize things using one central group of people who control and instruct everyone else. ❑ *...a strong centralist state.* • N-COUNT A **centralist** is someone with centralist views.

cen|tral|ize /sɛntrəlaɪz/ (centralizes, centralizing, centralized)

in BRIT, also use **centralise**

V-T To **centralize** a country, state, or organization means to create a system in which one central group of people gives

centrally heated instructions to regional groups. ☐ *In the mass production era, multinational firms tended to centralize their operations.* • **cen|tral|i|za|tion** /sɛntrəlaɪzeɪʃᵊn/ N-UNCOUNT ☐ *...public hostility to central banks and the centralization of power.*

cen|tral|ly heat|ed ADJ [USU ADJ n] A **centrally heated** building or room has central heating. ☐ *Centrally heated offices tend to be stuffy.*

cen|tral nerv|ous sys|tem (central nervous systems) N-COUNT Your **central nervous system** is the part of your nervous system that consists of the brain and spinal cord.

cen|tral res|er|va|tion (central reservations) N-COUNT The **central reservation** is the strip of ground, often covered with grass, that separates the two sides of a major road. [BRIT]

| in AM, use **median** |

cen|tre /sɛntər/ [BRIT] → see **center**
cen|tred /sɛntərd/ [BRIT] → see **centered**
-centred /-sɛntərd/ [BRIT] → see **-centered**
centre|fold /sɛntərfoʊld/ [BRIT] → see **centerfold**
centre-forward [BRIT] → see **center forward**
cen|tre of grav|ity [BRIT] → see **center of gravity**
centre|piece /sɛntərpis/ [BRIT] → see **centerpiece**
cen|tre stage also **centre-stage** [BRIT] → see **center stage**

cen|tri|fu|gal force /sɛntrɪfyəgᵊl fɔrs, -trɪfəgᵊl/ N-UNCOUNT In physics, **centrifugal force** is the force that makes objects move outward when they are spinning around something or traveling in a curve. ☐ *The juice is extracted by centrifugal force.*

cen|tri|fuge /sɛntrɪfyudʒ/ (centrifuges) N-COUNT A **centrifuge** is a machine that spins mixtures of different substances around very quickly so that they separate by centrifugal force.

cen|trist /sɛntrɪst/ (centrists) ADJ [USU ADJ n] **Centrist** policies and parties are moderate rather than extreme. ☐ *He had left the movement because it had abandoned its centrist policies.* • N-COUNT A **centrist** is someone with centrist views.

cen|tu|ri|on /sɛntʊriən/ (centurions) N-COUNT A **centurion** was an officer in the Roman army.

cen|tu|ry /sɛntʃəri/ (centuries) ◆◆◆ ◼ N-COUNT A **century** is a period of a hundred years that is used when stating a date. For example, the 19th century was the period from 1801 to 1900. ☐ *The material position of the Church had been declining since the late eighteenth century.* ◼ N-COUNT A **century** is any period of a hundred years. ☐ *The drought there is the worst in a century.*

CEO /si i oʊ/ (CEOs) ◼ N-COUNT **CEO** is an abbreviation for chief executive officer. ◼ → See feature box at **business**

ce|ram|ic /sɪræmɪk/ (ceramics) ◼ N-MASS **Ceramic** is clay that has been heated to a very high temperature so that it becomes hard. ☐ *...ceramic tiles.* ◼ N-COUNT [usu pl] **Ceramics** are ceramic ornaments or objects. ☐ *...a collection of Chinese ceramics.* ◼ N-UNCOUNT **Ceramics** is the art of making artistic objects out of clay. ☐ *...a degree in ceramics.*

ce|real /sɪəriəl/ (cereals) ◼ N-MASS **Cereal** or **breakfast cereal** is a food made from grain. It is mixed with milk and eaten for breakfast. ☐ *I have a bowl of cereal every morning.* ◼ N-COUNT **Cereals** are plants such as wheat, corn, or rice that produce grain. ☐ *...the cereal-growing districts of the Midwest.*

cer|ebel|lum /sɛrəbɛləm/ (cerebellums or cerebella) N-COUNT [oft the N] The **cerebellum** is a part of the brain in humans and other mammals that controls the body's movements and balance. [MEDICAL] ☐ *Damage to the cerebellum can disrupt motor activity in other ways.*

cere|bral /sərɪbrəl/ ◼ ADJ If you describe someone or something as **cerebral**, you mean that they are intellectual rather than emotional. [FORMAL] ☐ *Washington struck me as a precarious place from which to publish such a cerebral newspaper.* ◼ ADJ [ADJ n] **Cerebral** means relating to the brain. [MEDICAL] ☐ *...a cerebral hemorrhage.*

cere|bral pal|sy N-UNCOUNT **Cerebral palsy** is a condition caused by damage to a baby's brain before or during its birth, which makes its limbs and muscles permanently weak.

cer|emo|nial /sɛrɪmoʊniəl/ ◼ ADJ [ADJ n] Something that is **ceremonial** relates to a ceremony or is used in a ceremony.

certain
☐ *He represented the nation on ceremonial occasions.* ◼ ADJ A position, function, or event that is **ceremonial** is considered to be representative of an institution, but has very little authority or influence. ☐ *Up to now the post of president has been largely ceremonial.*

cer|emo|ni|ous|ly /sɛrɪmoʊniəsli/ ADV [ADV with v] If someone does something **ceremoniously**, they do it in an extremely formal way. [WRITTEN] ☐ *They ceremoniously cut a piece of ribbon, declaring the exhibition open.* ☐ *He thanked her ceremoniously.*

cer|emo|ny ◆◇◇ /sɛrɪmoʊni/ (ceremonies) ◼ N-COUNT A **ceremony** is a formal event such as a wedding. ☐ *...his grandmother's funeral, a private ceremony attended only by the family.* ◼ N-UNCOUNT **Ceremony** consists of the special things that are said and done on very formal occasions. ☐ *The republic was proclaimed with great ceremony.* ◼ → See feature box at **Olympic Games**

COLLOCATIONS

ceremony
NOUN ◼
noun + **ceremony**: closing, opening; awards, medal, presentation; citizenship, civil union, graduation, marriage, wedding; induction, initiation, swearing-in
adjective + **ceremony**: glittering, glitzy, lavish, star-studded; civil, religious; intimate, low-key
verb + **ceremony**: attend; conduct, hold, host, perform

---

ce|rise /sərɪs/ COLOR Something that is **cerise** is a bright pinkish red.

cert. (certs) **Cert.** is a written abbreviation for **certificate**.

CERTAIN
① BEING SURE
② REFERRING TO AND INDICATING AMOUNT

---

① **cer|tain** ◆◇◇ /sɜrtᵊn/ ◼ ADJ [v-link ADJ] If you are **certain** about something, you firmly believe it is true and have no doubt about it. If you are not **certain** about something, you do not have definite knowledge about it. ☐ *She's absolutely certain she's going to make it in the world.* ☐ *We are not certain whether the appendix had already burst or not.* ◼ ADJ If you say that something is **certain** to happen, you mean that it will definitely happen. ☐ *However, the scheme is certain to meet opposition from fishermen's leaders.* ☐ *It's not certain they'll accept that candidate if he wins.* ☐ *The prime minister is heading for certain defeat if he forces a vote.* ◼ ADJ [v-link ADJ] If you say that something is **certain**, you firmly believe that it is true, or have definite knowledge about it. ☐ *One thing is certain, both have the utmost respect for each other.* ◼ PHRASE If you know something **for certain**, you have no doubt at all about it. ☐ *She couldn't know what time he'd go, or even for certain that he'd go at all.* ◼ PHRASE If you **make certain** that something is the way you want or expect it to be, you take action to ensure that it is. ☐ *Parents should make certain that the children spend enough time doing homework.*

SYNONYMS

certain
ADJ ① ◼
sure: *She was no longer sure how she felt about him.*
positive: *'She's never late. You're sure she said eight?'—'Positive.'*
confident: *I am confident that everything will be fine in time.*
satisfied: *People must be satisfied that the treatment is safe.*
convinced: *He was convinced that I was part of the problem.*

---

② **cer|tain** ◆◆◇ /sɜrtᵊn/ ◼ ADJ [det ADJ, ADJ n] You use **certain** to indicate that you are referring to one particular thing, person, or group, although you are not saying exactly which it is. ☐ *There will be certain people who'll say "I told you so!"* ☐ *You owe a certain person a sum of money.* ◼ ADJ You use **a certain** to indicate that something such as a quality or condition exists, and often to suggest that it is not great in amount or degree. ☐ *That was the very reason why he felt a certain bitterness.* ◼ QUANT [QUANT of def-pl-n] When you refer to **certain** of a group of people or things, you are referring to some particular members of that group. [FORMAL] ☐ *They'll have to give up completely on certain of their studies.*

cer|tain|ly /sɜrtᵊnli/ **1** ADV [ADV with cl/group] You use **certainly** to emphasize what you are saying when you are making a statement. [EMPHASIS] ☐ *The public is certainly getting tired of hearing about it.* ☐ *The bombs are almost certainly part of a much bigger conspiracy.* **2** ADV [ADV as reply] You use **certainly** when you are agreeing with what someone has said. ☐ *"In any case you remained friends."—"Certainly."* **3** ADV [ADV as reply] You say **certainly not** to say 'no' in a strong way. [EMPHASIS] ☐ *"Perhaps it would be better if I withdrew altogether."—"Certainly not!"*

---SYNONYMS---

certainly
ADV **1**
definitely: *Something should definitely be done about that.*
without (a) doubt: *The refugees, without a doubt, are the most vulnerable.*
undoubtedly: *Hanley is undoubtedly a great player.*
unquestionably: *He is unquestionably a star.*

---

cer|tain|ty /sɜrtᵊnti/ (certainties) **1** N-UNCOUNT **Certainty** is the state of being definite or of having no doubts at all about something. ☐ *I have told them with absolute certainty there'll be no change of policy.* **2** N-UNCOUNT [also a N] **Certainty** is the fact that something is certain to happen. ☐ *A general election became a certainty last week.* ☐ *...the certainty of more violence and bloodshed.* **3** N-COUNT [usu pl] **Certainties** are things that nobody has any doubts about. ☐ *There are no certainties in modern Europe.*

cer|ti|fi|able /sɜrtɪfaɪəbᵊl/ ADJ If you describe someone as **certifiable**, you think that their behavior is extremely unreasonable or foolish. [mainly BRIT, INFORMAL, DISAPPROVAL] ☐ *...if he can convince the committee that he is not certifiable.*

cer|tifi|cate /sərtɪfɪkɪt/ (certificates) **1** N-COUNT A **certificate** is an official document stating that particular facts are true. ☐ *...birth certificates.* **2** N-COUNT A **certificate** is an official document that you receive when you have completed a course of study or training. The qualification that you receive is sometimes also called a **certificate**. ☐ *To the right of the fireplace are various framed certificates.*

cer|ti|fied check (certified checks) N-COUNT A **certified check** is a check that is guaranteed by a bank, because the bank has set aside sufficient money in the account. [AM] ☐ *Remember that when the carrier arrives, you must be able to pay the charges with cash or a certified check.*

cer|ti|fied mail N-UNCOUNT [usu by N] If you send a letter or package by **certified mail**, you send it using a mail service which gives you an official record of the fact that it has been mailed and delivered. [AM] ☐ *We recommend that you send your certificates by certified mail.*

cer|ti|fied pub|lic ac|count|ant (certified public accountants) N-COUNT A **certified public accountant** is someone who has received a certificate stating that he or she is qualified to work as an accountant within a particular state. The abbreviation **CPA** is also used. [AM]

cer|ti|fy /sɜrtɪfaɪ/ (certifies, certifying, certified) **1** V-T If someone in an official position **certifies** something, they officially state that it is true. ☐ *The president certified that the project would receive at least $650m from overseas sources.* ☐ *The National Election Council is supposed to certify the results of the election.* • **cer|ti|fi|ca|tion** /sɜrtɪfɪkeɪʃᵊn/ (certifications) N-VAR ☐ *An employer can demand written certification that the relative is really ill.* **2** V-T [usu passive] If someone **is certified** as a particular kind of worker, they are given a certificate stating that they have successfully completed a course of training in their profession. ☐ *They wanted to get certified as divers.* ☐ *...a certified public accountant.* • **cer|ti|fi|ca|tion** N-UNCOUNT ☐ *Students would be offered on-the-job training leading to the certification of their skill in a particular field.*

cer|ti|tude /sɜrtɪtud/ (certitudes) N-UNCOUNT [also N in pl] **Certitude** is the same as **certainty**. [FORMAL] ☐ *We have this definite certitude that Clark will be freed.*

cer|vi|cal /sɜrvɪkᵊl/ **1** ADJ [ADJ n] **Cervical** means relating to the cervix. [MEDICAL] ☐ *Doctors aim to cut the number of women dying from cervical cancer by half this decade.* **2** ADJ [ADJ n] **Cervical** means relating to the neck. [MEDICAL] ☐ *...injury to the cervical spine from motor vehicle collisions.*

cer|vix /sɜrvɪks/ (cervixes or cervices /sərvaɪsiz, sɜrvɪsiz/) N-COUNT The **cervix** is the entrance to the womb. [MEDICAL]

Ce|sar|ean /sɪzɛəriən/ → see Caesarean

ces|sa|tion /seseɪʃᵊn/ N-UNCOUNT [also a N] The **cessation** of something is the stopping of it. [FORMAL] ☐ *He would not agree to a cessation of hostilities.*

cess|pit /sɛspɪt/ (cesspits) N-COUNT A **cesspit** is a hole or tank in the ground into which waste water and sewage flow.

cess|pool /sɛspul/ (cesspools) N-COUNT A **cesspool** is the same as a **cesspit**.

ce|ta|cean /sɪteɪʃᵊn/ (cetaceans) N-COUNT [usu pl] **Cetaceans** are animals such as whales, dolphins, and porpoises.

cf. cf. is used in writing to introduce something that should be considered in connection with the subject you are discussing. ☐ *For the more salient remarks on the matter, cf. "Isis Unveiled," Vol. I.*

CFC /si ɛf si/ (CFCs) N-COUNT **CFCs** are gases that are used in things such as aerosols and refrigerators and can cause damage to the ozone layer. **CFC** is an abbreviation for 'chlorofluorocarbon.' ☐ *...the continued drop in CFC emissions.*

CFS /si ɛf ɛs/ N-UNCOUNT **CFS** is an abbreviation for **chronic fatigue syndrome**.

CGI /si dʒi aɪ/ N-UNCOUNT **CGI** is a type of computer technology that is used to make special effects in movies and on television. **CGI** is an abbreviation for 'computer-generated imagery.' ☐ *Recent, more dramatic use of CGI was seen in "Walking With Dinosaurs."*

ch. (chs) N-VAR **Ch.** is a written abbreviation for **chapter**.

cha-cha /tʃɑ tʃɑ/ (cha-chas) N-COUNT [oft the N] A **cha-cha** is a Latin American dance with small, fast steps.

chafe /tʃeɪf/ (chafes, chafing, chafed) **1** V-T/V-I If your skin **chafes** or **is chafed** by something, it becomes sore as a result of something rubbing against it. ☐ *My shorts were chafing my thighs.* ☐ *His wrists began to chafe against the cloth strips binding them.* ☐ *The messenger bent and scratched at his knee where the strapping chafed.* **2** V-I [no passive] If you **chafe** at something such as a restriction, you feel annoyed about it. [FORMAL] ☐ *He had chafed at having to take orders from another.* ☐ *He was chafing under the company's new ownership.*

chaff /tʃæf/ **1** N-UNCOUNT **Chaff** is the outer part of grain such as wheat. It is removed before the grain is used as food. **2** PHRASE If you **separate the wheat from the chaff** or **sort the wheat from the chaff**, you decide which people or things in a group are good or important and which are not. ☐ *It isn't always easy to separate the wheat from the chaff.*

chaf|finch /tʃæfɪntʃ/ (chaffinches) N-COUNT A **chaffinch** is a small European bird. Male chaffinches have reddish-brown fronts and gray heads.

cha|grin /ʃəgrɪn/ N-UNCOUNT [usu with poss] **Chagrin** is a feeling of disappointment, upset, or annoyance, perhaps because of your own failure. [FORMAL, WRITTEN] ☐ *To the chagrin of their parents, neither Phil nor Pam went to church anymore.*

cha|grined /ʃəgrɪnd/ ADJ [usu v-link ADJ] If you are **chagrined** by something, it disappoints, upsets, or annoys you, perhaps because of your own failure. [WRITTEN] ☐ *The chair of the committee did not appear chagrined by the compromises and delays.*

chain /tʃeɪn/ (chains, chaining, chained) **1** N-COUNT A **chain** consists of metal rings connected together in a line. ☐ *His open shirt revealed a fat gold chain.* **2** N-COUNT A **chain of** things is a group of them existing or arranged in a line. ☐ *...a chain of islands known as the Windward Islands.* **3** N-COUNT A **chain** of stores, hotels, or other businesses is a number of them owned by the same person or company. ☐ *...a large supermarket chain.* **4** N-PLURAL If prisoners are **in chains**, they have thick rings of metal around their wrists or ankles to prevent them from escaping. ☐ *He'd spent four and a half years in windowless cells, much of the time in chains.* **5** V-T If a person or thing **is chained** to something, they are fastened to it with a chain. ☐ *The dogs were chained to a fence.* ☐ *We were sitting together in our cell, chained to the wall.* • PHRASAL VERB **Chain up** means the same as **chain**. ☐ *They kept me chained up every night and released me each day.* **6** N-SING A **chain of** events is a series of them happening one after another. ☐ *...the bizarre chain of events that led to his departure in January 1938.* **7** → See also color supplement

COLLOCATIONS

chain
NOUN [3]
noun + **chain**: hotel, movie theater, restaurant, supermarket; clothing, DIY, fashion; discount
adjective + **chain**: retail

chained /tʃeɪnd/ ADJ [v-link ADJ to n] If you say that someone is **chained to** a person or a situation, you are emphasizing that there are reasons why they cannot leave that person or situation, even though you think they might like to. ❏ *At work, he was chained to a system of boring meetings.*

chain gang (chain gangs) N-COUNT In the United States, a **chain gang** is a group of prisoners who are chained together to do work outside their prison. Chain gangs existed especially in former times.

chain let|ter (chain letters) N-COUNT A **chain letter** is a letter, often with a promise of money, that is sent to several people who send copies on to several more people. Chain letters are illegal in some countries.

chain mail N-UNCOUNT **Chain mail** is a kind of armor made from small, metal rings joined together so that they look like cloth.

chain re|ac|tion (chain reactions) **1** N-COUNT A **chain reaction** is a series of chemical changes, each of which causes the next. **2** N-COUNT A **chain reaction** is a series of events, each of which causes the next. ❏ *The powder immediately ignited and set off a chain reaction of explosions.*

chain saw (chain saws) N-COUNT A **chain saw** is a big saw with teeth fixed in a chain that is driven around by a motor.

chain-smoke (chain-smokes, chain-smoking, chain-smoked) V-T/V-I Someone who **chain-smokes** smokes cigarettes or cigars continuously. ❏ *Melissa had chain-smoked all evening while she waited for a phone call from Tom.*

chain-smoker (chain-smokers) also **chain smoker** N-COUNT A **chain-smoker** is a person who chain-smokes.

chain store (chain stores) N-COUNT A **chain store** is one of several similar stores that are owned by the same person or company, especially one that sells a variety of things.

chair ♦♦◊ /tʃɛər/ (chairs, chairing, chaired) **1** N-COUNT A **chair** is a piece of furniture for one person to sit on, with a back and four legs. ❏ *He rose from his chair and walked to the window.* **2** N-COUNT At a university, a **chair** is the position or job of professor. ❏ *He has been appointed to the chair of sociology.* **3** N-COUNT The person who is the **chair** of a committee or meeting is the person in charge of it. ❏ *She is the chair of the Defense Advisory Committee on Women in the Military.* **4** V-T If you **chair** a meeting or a committee, you are the person in charge of it. ❏ *He was about to chair a meeting in Venice of E.U. foreign ministers.* **5** N-SING **The chair** is the same as the **electric chair**. **6** → See also color supplement

chair lift (chair lifts) also **chairlift** N-COUNT A **chair lift** is a line of chairs that hang from a moving cable and carry people up and down a mountain or ski slope.

chair|man ♦♦◊ /tʃɛərmən/ (chairmen) **1** N-COUNT The **chairman** of a committee, organization, or company is the head of it. ❏ *Glyn Ford is chairman of the committee which produced the report.* **2** N-COUNT; N-VOC The **chairman** of a meeting or debate is the person in charge, who decides when each person is allowed to speak. ❏ *The chairman declared the meeting open.*

COLLOCATIONS

chairman
NOUN [1]
noun + **chairman**: club, committee, company, party; deputy
adjective + **chairman**: former, outgoing; executive, honorary, nonexecutive; acting, interim
verb + **chairman**: appoint, elect

chair|man|ship /tʃɛərmənʃɪp/ (chairmanships) N-VAR The **chairmanship** of a committee or organization is the fact of being its chairperson. Someone's **chairmanship** can also mean the period during which they are chairperson. ❏ *The government has set up a committee under the chairmanship of Professor Roy Goode.*

chair|person /tʃɛərpɜrsən/ (chairpersons) N-COUNT The **chairperson** of a meeting, committee, or organization is the person in charge of it. ❏ *She's the chairperson of the safety committee.*

chair|woman /tʃɛərwʊmən/ (chairwomen) N-COUNT The **chairwoman** of a meeting, committee, or organization is the woman in charge of it. ❏ *Primakov was in Japan meeting with the chairwoman of the Socialist Party there.*

chaise longue /ʃeɪz lɒŋ/ (chaises longues)

The singular and the plural are both pronounced in the same way.

1 N-COUNT A **chaise longue** is a kind of sofa with only one arm and usually a back along half its length. **2** → See also color supplement

chaise lounge /ʃeɪz laʊndʒ/ (chaise lounges) N-COUNT A **chaise lounge** is the same as a **chaise longue**. [AM]

cha|let /ʃæleɪ/ (chalets) **1** N-COUNT A **chalet** is a small wooden house, especially in a mountain area. ❏ *...Swiss ski chalets.* **2** → See also color supplement

chal|ice /tʃælɪs/ (chalices) **1** N-COUNT A **chalice** is a large gold or silver cup with a stem. Chalices are used to hold wine in the Christian service of Holy Communion. **2** → See also color supplement

chalk /tʃɔk/ (chalks, chalking, chalked) **1** N-UNCOUNT **Chalk** is a type of soft, white rock. You can use small pieces of it for writing or drawing with. ❏ *...white cliffs made of chalk.* **2** N-VAR [also N in pl] **Chalk** is small sticks of chalk, or a substance similar to chalk, used for writing or drawing with. ❏ *...somebody writing with a piece of chalk.* **3** V-T If you **chalk** something, you draw or write it using a piece of chalk. ❏ *He chalked the message on the blackboard.*
▶ **chalk up** PHRASAL VERB If you **chalk up** a success, a victory, or a number of points in a game, you achieve it. ❏ *For almost 11 months, the Bosnian army chalked up one victory after another.*

chalk|board /tʃɔkbɔrd/ (chalkboards) N-COUNT A **chalkboard** is a dark-colored board that you can write on with chalk. Chalkboards are often used by teachers in the classroom. [mainly AM] ❏ *The menu was on a chalkboard.*

in BRIT, use **blackboard**

chalky /tʃɔki/ (chalkier, chalkiest) **1** ADJ Something that is **chalky** contains chalk or is covered with chalk. ❏ *The chalky soil around Saumur produces the famous Anjou wines.* **2** ADJ Something that is **chalky** is a pale, dull color or has a powdery texture. ❏ *Her face became a chalky white.*

chal|lenge ♦♦◊ /tʃælɪndʒ/ (challenges, challenging, challenged) **1** N-VAR A **challenge** is something new and difficult which requires great effort and determination. ❏ *The new government's first challenge is the economy.* **2** N-VAR A **challenge** to something is a questioning of its truth or value. A **challenge** to someone is a questioning of their authority. ❏ *The demonstrators have now made a direct challenge to the authority of the government.* **3** PHRASE If someone **rises to the challenge**, they act in response to a difficult situation which is new to them and are successful. ❏ *The new Germany must rise to the challenge of its enhanced responsibilities.* **4** V-T If you **challenge** ideas or people, you question their truth, value, or authority. ❏ *Democratic leaders have challenged the president to sign the bill.* ❏ *The move was immediately challenged by two of the republics.* **5** V-T If you **challenge** someone, you invite them to fight or compete with you in some way. ❏ *Marsyas thought he could play the flute better than Apollo and challenged the god to a contest.* ❏ *He left a note at the scene of the crime, challenging detectives to catch him.* • N-COUNT **Challenge** is also a noun. ❏ *A third presidential candidate emerged to mount a serious challenge and throw the campaign wide open.* **6** → see also **challenging**

COLLOCATIONS

challenge
NOUN
[1]
adjective + **challenge**: big, great, major; daunting, serious, tough
verb + **challenge**: enjoy, relish; pose, present; accept, face, meet, overcome
[5]
noun + **challenge**: leadership, promotion, title
verb + **challenge**: mount

VOCABULARY IN CONTEXT

Challenge

If you prefer a gentle splash in the sea to ice-swimming in freezing waters, you're pretty much like most people. Those who would choose the latter probably enjoy a **challenge**, that is, any situation or task which **tests their abilities**. It's the reason some people have a **burning ambition** for self-imposed and usually **arduous** challenges, like climbing Mount Everest or sailing around the world. Those of us who don't actively seek out **adversity** are still capable of **facing challenges**; we just don't create them unnecessarily.

But there is a received wisdom that **daunting** situations make us stronger and better able to **cope** with **crises** and other challenges when they come our way. The fact is that we all experience **struggles** that range from taking an important exam to dealing with **upheavals** like illness and injury. For this reason, we're often encouraged to leave our **comfort zone** and **overcome** our deepest fears.

chal|lenged /tʃælɪndʒd/ ADJ [adv ADJ] If you say that someone is **challenged** in a particular way, you mean that they have a disability in that area. **Challenged** is often combined with inappropriate words for humorous effect. ❑ ...terms like "vertically challenged" – meaning short. ❑ She ran off with an intellectually challenged ski instructor.

chal|leng|er /tʃælɪndʒər/ (challengers) N-COUNT A **challenger** is someone who competes with you for a position or title that you already have, for example being a sports champion or a political leader. ❑ The strongest challenger, Texas Democrat Martin Frost, has withdrawn from the race.

chal|leng|ing /tʃælɪndʒɪŋ/ **1** ADJ A **challenging** task or job requires great effort and determination. ❑ Mike found a challenging job as a computer programmer. **2** ADJ If you do something in a **challenging** way, you seem to be inviting people to argue with you or compete against you in some way. ❑ Mona gave him a challenging look.

cham|ber ✦✦◇ /tʃeɪmbər/ (chambers) **1** N-COUNT A **chamber** is a large room, especially one that is used for formal meetings. ❑ We are going to be in the council chamber every time he speaks. **2** N-COUNT You can refer to a country's legislature or to one section of it as a **chamber**. ❑ More than 80 parties are contesting seats in the two-chamber parliament. **3** N-COUNT A **chamber** is a room designed and equipped for a particular purpose. ❑ For many, the dentist's office remains a torture chamber.

cham|ber|lain /tʃeɪmbərlɪn/ (chamberlains) N-COUNT A **chamberlain** is the person who is in charge of the household affairs of a king, queen, or person of high social rank.

cham|ber|maid /tʃeɪmbərmeɪd/ (chambermaids) N-COUNT A **chambermaid** is a woman who is employed to clean and tidy the bedrooms in a hotel.

cham|ber mu|sic N-UNCOUNT **Chamber music** is classical music written for a small number of instruments.

cham|ber of com|merce (chambers of commerce) N-COUNT A **chamber of commerce** is an organization of businesspeople that promotes local commercial interests. [BUSINESS]

cham|ber or|ches|tra (chamber orchestras) N-COUNT A **chamber orchestra** is a small orchestra which plays classical music.

cham|ber pot (chamber pots) N-COUNT A **chamber pot** is a round container shaped like a very large cup. Chamber pots used to be kept in bedrooms so that people could urinate in them instead of having to leave their room during the night.

cha|me|le|on /kəmiliən, -mɪlyən/ (chameleons) N-COUNT A **chameleon** is a kind of lizard whose skin changes color to match the color of its surroundings.

cham|ois /ʃæmi/ (chamois) **1** N-COUNT **Chamois** are small animals similar to goats that live in the mountains of Europe and South West Asia. **2** N-COUNT A **chamois** or a **chamois leather** is a soft leather cloth used for cleaning and polishing.

chamo|mile /kæməmil, kæməmail/ also **camomile** N-UNCOUNT **Chamomile** is a scented plant with flowers like small daisies. The flowers can be used to make herbal tea.

champ /tʃæmp/ (champs) N-COUNT [oft n N] A **champ** is the same as a **champion**. [INFORMAL] ❑ ...boxing champ Mike Tyson.

cham|pagne /ʃæmpeɪn/ (champagnes) N-MASS **Champagne** is an expensive French white wine with bubbles in. It is often drunk to celebrate something.

cham|pi|on ✦✦◇ /tʃæmpiən/ (champions, championing, championed) **1** N-COUNT A **champion** is someone who has won the first prize in a competition, contest, or fight. ❑ ...a former Olympic champion. ❑ Kasparov became world champion. **2** N-COUNT If you are a **champion** of a person, a cause, or a principle, you support or defend them. ❑ He received acclaim as a champion of the oppressed. **3** V-T If you **champion** a person, a cause, or a principle, you support or defend them. ❑ He passionately championed the poor. **4** → See feature box at **competition**

SYNONYMS

champion
NOUN **1**
winner: The winner was a horse called Last Town.
victor: He was the eventual victor.
conqueror: He easily overcame Garcia, Saturday's conqueror of Ernie Els.

cham|pi|on|ship ✦✦◇ /tʃæmpiənʃɪp/ (championships) **1** N-COUNT A **championship** is a competition to find the best player or team in a particular sport. ❑ ...the world showjumping championship. **2** N-SING The **championship** refers to the title or status of being a sports champion. ❑ He went on to take the championship.

chance ✦✦✦ /tʃæns/ (chances, chancing, chanced) **1** N-VAR If there is a **chance** of something happening, it is possible that it will happen. ❑ Do you think they have a chance of beating Australia? ❑ There was really very little chance that Ben would ever have led a normal life. **2** N-SING If you have a **chance** to do something, you have the opportunity to do it. ❑ The electoral council announced that all eligible people would get a chance to vote. ❑ Most refugee doctors never get the chance to practice medicine in our hospitals. **3** ADJ [ADJ n] A **chance** meeting or event is one that is not planned or expected. ❑ ...a chance meeting. • N-UNCOUNT **Chance** is also a noun. ❑ ...a victim of chance and circumstance. **4** V-T If you **chance** something, you do it even though there is a risk that you may not succeed or that something bad may happen. ❑ Andy knew the risks. I cannot believe he would have chanced it. **5** PHRASE Something that happens **by chance** was not planned by anyone. ❑ He had met Mr. Maude by chance. **6** PHRASE You can use **by any chance** when you are asking questions in order to find out whether something that you think might be true is actually true. ❑ Are they by any chance related? **7** PHRASE If you say that someone **stands a chance** of achieving something, you mean that they are likely to achieve it. If you say that someone doesn't **stand a chance** of achieving something, you mean that they cannot possibly achieve it. ❑ Being very good at science subjects, I stood a good chance of gaining high grades. **8** PHRASE When you **take a chance**, you try to do something although there is a large risk of danger or failure. ❑ You take a chance on the weather if you vacation in Maine. ❑ Retailers are taking no chances on unknown brands.

chancel

> **COLLOCATIONS**
>
> **chance**
> NOUN ❷
> adjective + **chance**: decent, fair, good, realistic, reasonable; little, outside, slight, slim; excellent, golden, strong
> verb + **chance**: get, have, stand; miss, waste; create, offer; grab, seize, take

chan|cel /tʃænsᵊl/ (**chancels**) N-COUNT The **chancel** is the part of a church containing the altar, where the clergy and the choir usually sit.

chan|cel|lery /tʃɑnsələri, tʃæns-/ (**chanceleries**) ❶ N-COUNT A **chancellery** is the building where a chancellor has their offices. ❷ N-SING [usu the N] The **chancellery** is the officials who work in a chancellor's office. ❏ *He is a former head of the chancellery.*

chan|cel|lor ✦✧✧ /tʃænsələr, -slər/ (**chancellors**) also **Chancellor** ❶ N-TITLE; N-COUNT **Chancellor** is the title of the head of government in Germany and Austria. ❏ *...Chancellor Gerhard Schröder of Germany.* ❷ N-COUNT The head of some American universities is called the **chancellor**. ❸ N-COUNT In Britain, the **Chancellor** is the Chancellor of the Exchequer.

chan|cel|lor of the ex|cheq|uer (**chancellors of the exchequer**) N-COUNT The **chancellor of the exchequer** is the minister in the British government who makes decisions about finance and taxes.

chan|cel|lor|ship /tʃænsələrʃɪp, -slərʃɪp/ N-SING [usu the N] The **chancellorship** is the position of chancellor. Someone's **chancellorship** is the period of time when they are chancellor. ❏ *Austria prospered under Kreisky's chancellorship.*

chan|cer /tʃænsər/ (**chancers**) N-COUNT You can refer to someone as a **chancer** if you think they use opportunities for their own advantage and often pretend to have skills they do not have. [INFORMAL] ❏ *...a corrupt, opportunistic chancer.*

chan|cy /tʃænsi/ (**chancier, chanciest**) ADJ Something that is **chancy** involves a lot of risk or uncertainty. [INFORMAL] ❏ *Investment is becoming a chancy business.*

chan|de|lier /ʃændᵊlɪər/ (**chandeliers**) N-COUNT A **chandelier** is a large, decorative frame which holds light bulbs or candles and hangs from the ceiling. ❏ *A crystal chandelier lit the room.*

change ✦✦✦ /tʃeɪndʒ/ (**changes, changing, changed**) ❶ N-VAR If there is a **change** in something, it becomes different. ❏ *The ambassador appealed for a change in U.S. policy.* ❏ *There are going to have to be some drastic changes.* ❷ → see also **sea change** ❸ N-SING If you say that something is a **change** or makes a **change**, you mean that it is enjoyable because it is different from what you are used to. [APPROVAL] ❏ *It is a complex system, but it certainly makes a change.* ❹ V-I If you **change** from one thing to another, you stop using or doing the first one and start using or doing the second. ❏ *His physician modified the dosage but did not change to a different medication.* ❺ V-T/V-I When something **changes** or when you **change** it, it becomes different. ❏ *We are trying to detect and understand how the climates change.* ❏ *In the union office, the mood gradually changed from resignation to rage.* ❏ *She has now changed into a happy, self-confident woman.* ❏ *They should change the law to make it illegal to own replica weapons.* ❻ V-T To **change** something means to replace it with something new or different. ❏ *I paid $80 to have my car radio fixed and I bet all they did was change a fuse.* • N-COUNT **Change** is also a noun. ❏ *A change of leadership alone will not be enough.* ❼ V-T/V-I When you **change** your clothes or **change**, you take some or all of your clothes off and put on different ones. ❏ *Ben had merely changed his shirt.* ❏ *They had allowed her to shower and change.* ❽ V-T When you **change** a bed or **change** the sheets, you take off the dirty sheets and put on clean ones. ❏ *After changing the bed, I would fall asleep quickly.* ❾ V-T When you **change** a baby or **change** its diaper, you take off the dirty one and put on a clean one. ❏ *She criticizes me for the way I feed or change him.* ❿ V-T/V-I When you **change** buses, trains, or planes or **change**, you get off one bus, train, or plane and get on to another in order to continue your journey. ❏ *At Glasgow I changed trains for Greenock.* ⓫ V-T/V-I When you **change** gear or **change** into another gear, you move the gear lever on a car, bicycle, or other vehicle in order to use a different gear. [mainly BRIT]

in AM, usually use **shift**

⓬ V-T When you **change** money, you exchange it for the same amount of money in a different currency, or in smaller bills or coins. ❏ *You can expect to pay the bank a fee of around 1% to 2% every time you change money.* ⓭ N-COUNT [N of n] A **change of** clothes is an extra set of clothes that you take with you when you go to stay somewhere or to take part in an activity. ❏ *He stuffed a bag with a few changes of clothing.* ⓮ N-UNCOUNT Your **change** is the money that you receive when you pay for something with more money than it costs because you do not have exactly the right amount of money. ❏ *"There's your change."—"Thanks very much."* ⓯ N-UNCOUNT **Change** is coins, rather than paper money. ❏ *Thieves ransacked the office, taking a sack of loose change.* ⓰ N-UNCOUNT If you have **change** for larger bills or coins, you have the same value in smaller bills or coins, which you can give to someone in exchange. ❏ *The courier had change for a $10 bill.* • PHRASE If you **make change**, you give someone smaller bills or coins, in exchange for the same value of larger ones. [AM] ⓱ PHRASE If you say that you are doing something or something is happening **for a change**, you mean that you do not usually do it or it does not usually happen, and you are happy to be doing it or that it is happening. ❏ *Now let me ask you a question, for a change.* ⓲ **to change for the better** → see **better** ① ⓳ **to change hands** → see **hand** ① ⓴ **a change of heart** → see **heart** ② ㉑ **to change your mind** → see **mind** ① ㉒ **to change places** → see **place** ③ ㉓ **to change the subject** → see **subject** ㉔ **to change tack** → see **tack** ㉕ **to change your tune** → see **tune** ㉖ **to change for the worse** → see **worse**

▶ **change over** PHRASAL VERB If you **change over** from one thing to another, you stop doing one thing and start doing the other. ❏ *We are gradually changing over to a completely metric system.*

> **SYNONYMS**
>
> **change**
> NOUN ❶
> **alteration**: *Making some simple alterations to your diet will make you feel fitter.*
> **transformation**: *Chemical transformations occur.*
> **modification**: *Relatively minor modifications were required.*
> VERB ❺
> **alter**: *Little had altered in the village.*
> **transform**: *Your metabolic rate is the speed at which your body transforms food into energy.*
> **revise**: *He soon revised his opinion of the profession.*
> **modify**: *The club members did agree to modify their recruitment policy.*

change|able /tʃeɪndʒəbᵊl/ ADJ Someone or something that is **changeable** is likely to change many times. ❏ *The forecast is for changeable weather.*

change|ling /tʃeɪndʒlɪŋ/ (**changelings**) N-COUNT A **changeling** is a child who was put in the place of another child when they were both babies. In stories changelings were often taken or left by fairies. [LITERARY]

change of life N-SING [the N] The **change of life** is menopause.

change|over /tʃeɪndʒoʊvər/ (**changeovers**) N-COUNT A **changeover** is a change from one activity or system to another. ❏ *He again called for a faster changeover to a market economy.* ❏ *Right now we are in the changeover period between autumn and winter.*

change purse (**change purses**) N-COUNT A **change purse** is a very small bag that people keep their coins in. [AM] ❏ *Eve searched her change purse and found thirty cents.*

in BRIT, use **purse**

chang|ing room (**changing rooms**) N-COUNT A **changing room** is a room where you can change your clothes and usually take a shower, for example at a pool.

chan|nel ✦✦✧ /tʃænᵊl/ (**channels, channeling or channelling, channeled or channelled**) ❶ N-COUNT; N-IN-NAMES A **channel** is a television station. ❏ *...the only serious current affairs program on either channel.* ❏ *...the proliferating number of television channels in America.* ❷ N-COUNT A **channel** is a band of radio waves on which radio messages can be sent and received. ❏ *The radio* channels were filled with the excited, jabbering voices of men going to war. **3** N-COUNT If you do something through a particular **channel**, or particular **channels**, that is the system or organization that you use to achieve your aims or to communicate. ❏ *The government will surely use the diplomatic channels available.* ❏ *The Americans recognize that the U.N. can be the channel for greater diplomatic activity.* **4** N-COUNT A **channel** is a passage along which water flows. ❏ *Keep the drainage channel clear.* **5** N-COUNT A **channel** is a route used by boats. ❏ *...the busy shipping channels of the harbor.* **6** V-T If you **channel** money or resources into something, you arrange for them to be used for that thing, rather than for a wider range of things. ❏ *Jacques Delors wants a system set up to channel funds to the poor countries.* **7** V-T If you **channel** your energies or emotions into something, you concentrate on or do that one thing, rather than a range of things. ❏ *Stephen is channeling his energies into a novel called Blue.*

SYNONYMS

channel
VERB **7**
direct: *Direct the learner's attention to the significant features.*
focus: *Today, he was able to focus his message exclusively on the economy.*
concentrate: *This helps you to be aware of time and concentrate on the immediate task.*

---

channel-hopping N-UNCOUNT **Channel-hopping** is the same as **channel-surfing**. [BRIT]

channel-surfing N-UNCOUNT **Channel-surfing** means switching quickly between different television channels because you are looking for something interesting to watch. [mainly AM]
☐ in BRIT, usually use **channel-hopping**

chant /tʃænt/ (**chants, chanting, chanted**) **1** N-COUNT A **chant** is a word or group of words that is repeated over and over again. ❏ *He was greeted by the chant of "Judas! Judas!"* **2** N-COUNT A **chant** is a religious song or prayer that is sung on only a few notes. ❏ *...a Gregorian chant.* **3** V-T/V-I If you **chant** something or if you **chant**, you repeat the same words over and over again. ❏ *Demonstrators chanted slogans.* ❏ *The crowd chanted "We are with you."* • **chanting** N-UNCOUNT ❏ *A lot of the chanting was in support of the deputy prime minister.* **4** V-T/V-I If you **chant** or if you **chant** something, you sing a religious song or prayer. ❏ *Muslims chanted and prayed.* • **chanting** N-UNCOUNT ❏ *The chanting inside the temple stopped.*

Cha|nu|kah /hɑnəkə/ N-UNCOUNT **Chanukah** is the same as **Hanukkah**.

cha|os ✦✧ /keɪɒs/ N-UNCOUNT **Chaos** is a state of complete disorder and confusion. ❏ *The world's first transatlantic balloon race ended in chaos last night.*

SYNONYMS

chaos
NOUN
disorder: *The emergency room was in disorder.*
confusion: *There was confusion when a man fired shots.*
mayhem: *...the economic mayhem that this country's going through now.*
havoc: *Rioters caused havoc in the center of the town.*

---

cha|ot|ic /keɪɒtɪk/ ADJ Something that is **chaotic** is in a state of complete disorder and confusion. ❏ *My own house feels as filthy and chaotic as a bus terminal.*

chap /tʃæp/ (**chaps**) **1** N-COUNT A **chap** is a man or boy. [mainly BRIT, INFORMAL] ❏ *"I am a very lucky chap," he commented.* *"The doctors were surprised that I was not paralysed."* **2** → see also **chapped**

chap. (**chaps**) N-VAR [num] **Chap.** is a written abbreviation for **chapter**. ❏ *Today the tests are performed in the hospital (see chap. 17).*

chap|el /tʃæpəl/ (**chapels**) **1** N-COUNT A **chapel** is a part of a church which has its own altar and which is used for private prayer. ❏ *...the chapel of the Virgin Mary.* **2** N-COUNT A **chapel** is a small church attached to a hospital, school, or prison. ❏ *We married in the college chapel.* **3** N-VAR A **chapel** is a building used for worship by members of some Christian churches. **Chapel** refers to the religious services that take place there. ❏ *...a Methodist chapel.*

chap|er|one /ʃæpəroʊn/ (**chaperones, chaperoning, chaperoned**) also **chaperon** **1** N-COUNT A **chaperone** is someone who accompanies another person somewhere in order to make sure that they do not come to any harm. **2** V-T [usu passive] If you **are chaperoned** by someone, they act as your chaperone. ❏ *We were chaperoned by our aunt.*

chap|lain /tʃæplɪn/ (**chaplains**) N-COUNT A **chaplain** is a member of the Christian clergy who does religious work in a place such as a hospital, school, prison, or in the armed forces. ❏ *He joined the 40th Division as an army chaplain.*

chap|lain|cy /tʃæplɪnsi/ (**chaplaincies**) **1** N-COUNT A **chaplaincy** is the building or office in which a chaplain works. **2** N-COUNT A **chaplaincy** is the position or work of a chaplain.

chapped /tʃæpt/ ADJ If your skin is **chapped**, it is dry, cracked, and sore. ❏ *...chapped hands.*

chaps /tʃæps/ N-PLURAL **Chaps** are leather leggings without a seat that are sometimes worn by cowboys over their pants. [AM] ❏ *Greenough wears a blue checkered shirt, red scarf and brown chaps.*

chap|ter ✦✧ /tʃæptər/ (**chapters**) **1** N-COUNT [also N num] A **chapter** is one of the parts that a book is divided into. Each chapter has a number, and sometimes a title. ❏ *Chromium supplements were used successfully in the treatment of diabetes (see Chapter 4).* **2** N-COUNT A **chapter** in someone's life or in history is a period of time during which a major event or series of related events takes place. [WRITTEN] ❏ *This had been a particularly difficult chapter in Lebanon's recent history.*

chap|ter house (**chapter houses**) **1** N-COUNT A **chapter house** is the building or set of rooms in the grounds of a cathedral where members of the clergy hold meetings. **2** N-COUNT In a university or college, a **chapter house** is the place where a fraternity or sorority lives or meets. [AM]

char /tʃɑr/ (**chars, charring, charred**) **1** V-T/V-I If food **chars** or if you **char** it, it burns slightly and turns black as it is cooking. ❏ *Toast hazelnuts on a baking sheet until the skins char.* ❏ *Halve the peppers and char the skins under a hot grill.* • **charring** N-UNCOUNT ❏ *The chops should be cooked over moderate heat to prevent excessive charring.* **2** → see also **charred**

char|ac|ter ✦✧ /kærɪktər/ (**characters**) **1** N-COUNT The **character** of a person or place consists of all the qualities they have that make them distinct from other people or places. ❏ *Perhaps there is a negative side to his character that you haven't seen yet.* **2** N-COUNT You use **character** to say what kind of person someone is. For example, if you say that someone is a strange **character**, you mean they are strange. ❏ *It's that kind of courage and determination that makes him such a remarkable character.* **3** N-COUNT The **characters** in a movie, book, or play are the people that it is about. ❏ *The film is autobiographical and the central character is played by Collard himself.* **4** N-COUNT A **character** is a letter, number, or other symbol that is written or printed. ❏ *...a shopping list written in Chinese characters.* **5** N-SING [usu supp N, also in N] If something has a particular **character**, it has a particular quality. ❏ *The financial concessions were of a precarious character.* **6** N-SING You can use **character** to refer to the qualities that people from a particular place are believed to have. ❏ *Individuality is a valued and inherent part of the British character.* **7** N-VAR Your **character** is your personality, especially how reliable and honest you are. If someone is of good **character**, they are reliable and honest. If they are of bad **character**, they are unreliable and dishonest. ❏ *He's begun a series of personal attacks on my character.* **8** N-UNCOUNT If you say that someone has **character**, you mean that they have the ability to deal effectively with difficult, unpleasant, or dangerous situations. [APPROVAL] ❏ *She showed real character in her attempts to win over the crowd.* **9** N-UNCOUNT If you say that a place has **character**, you mean that it has an interesting or unusual quality which makes you notice it and like it. [APPROVAL] ❏ *A soulless shopping center stands across from one of the few buildings with character, the town hall.* **10** N-COUNT If you say that someone is a **character**, you mean that they are interesting, unusual, or amusing. ❏ *He's a nut, a real character.* **11** → See feature box at **book**

char|ac|ter ac|tor (character actors) N-COUNT A **character actor** is an actor who specializes in playing unusual or eccentric people.

char|ac|ter as|sas|si|na|tion (character assassinations) N-VAR A **character assassination** is a deliberate attempt to destroy someone's reputation, especially by criticizing them in an unfair and dishonest way when they are not present. ❑ *A full-scale character assassination of the dead woman got underway in the tabloid press.*

char|ac|ter|ful /kǽrɪktərfəl/ ADJ [usu ADJ n] If you describe something as **characterful**, you mean that it is pleasant, interesting, or unusual. [JOURNALISM] ❑ *...small characterful hotels serving local cuisine.*

char|ac|ter|is|tic ◆◇◇ /ˌkærɪktərɪ́stɪk/ (characteristics) **1** N-COUNT The **characteristics** of a person or thing are the qualities or features that belong to them and make them recognizable. ❑ *Genes determine the characteristics of every living thing.* **2** ADJ A quality or feature that is **characteristic** of someone or something is one which is often seen in them and seems typical of them. ❑ *...the absence of strife between the generations that was so characteristic of such societies.* ❑ *Windmills are a characteristic feature of the Mallorcan landscape.* • **char|ac|ter|is|ti|cal|ly** /ˌkærɪktərɪ́stɪkli/ ADV ❑ *He replied in characteristically robust style.*

SYNONYMS

characteristic
NOUN **1**
feature: *The spacious gardens are a special feature of this property.*
quality: *...the pretentious quality of the poetry.*
attribute: *He has every attribute you could want and could play for any team.*
trait: *Creativity is a human trait.*
property: *A radio signal has both electrical and magnetic properties.*

---

char|ac|teri|za|tion /ˌkærɪktərɪzéɪʃ°n/ (characterizations)
in BRIT, also use **characterisation**
N-VAR **Characterization** is the way an author or an actor describes or shows what a character is like. ❑ *As a writer, I am interested in characterization.*

char|ac|ter|ize /kǽrɪktəraɪz/ (characterizes, characterizing, characterized)
in BRIT, also use **characterise**
1 V-T [usu passive] If something **is characterized** by a particular feature or quality, that feature or quality is an obvious part of it. [FORMAL] ❑ *This election campaign has been characterized by violence.* **2** V-T If you **characterize** someone or something **as** a particular thing, you describe them as that thing. [FORMAL] ❑ *Both companies have characterized the relationship as friendly.*

char|ac|ter|less /kǽrɪktərlɪs/ ADJ If you describe something as **characterless**, you mean that it is dull and uninteresting. ❑ *The town is boring and characterless.* ❑ *...a bland and characterless meal.*

char|ac|ter rec|og|ni|tion N-UNCOUNT **Character recognition** is a process which allows computers to recognize written or printed characters such as numbers or letters and to change them into a form that the computer can use. [COMPUTING] ❑ *...optical character recognition software that allows you to convert a scanned document to an electronic file.*

cha|rade /ʃəréɪd/ (charades) **1** N-COUNT If you describe someone's actions as a **charade**, you mean that their actions are so obviously false that they do not convince anyone. [DISAPPROVAL] ❑ *I wondered why he had gone through the elaborate charade.* **2** N-UNCOUNT **Charades** is a game for teams of players in which one team acts a word or phrase, syllable by syllable, until other players guess the whole word or phrase. ❑ *We are all going to play charades in the library.*

char|broiled /tʃɑ́rbrɔɪld/ also **char-grilled** ADJ **Charbroiled** meat or fish has been cooked so that it burns slightly and turns black. [AM]
in BRIT, use **char-grilled**

char|coal /tʃɑ́rkoʊl/ N-UNCOUNT **Charcoal** is a black substance obtained by burning wood without much air. It can be burned as a fuel, and small sticks of it are used for drawing.

chard /tʃɑrd/ N-UNCOUNT **Chard** is a vegetable with large leaves and thick stalks.

charge ◆◆◆ /tʃɑrdʒ/ (charges, charging, charged) **1** V-T/V-I If you **charge** someone an amount of money, you ask them to pay that amount for something that you have sold to them or done for them. ❑ *Even local nurseries charge $150 a week.* ❑ *Some banks charge if you access your account to determine your balance.* ❑ *The architect charged us a fee of seven hundred and fifty dollars.* **2** V-T To **charge** something **to** a person or organization means to tell the people providing it to send the bill to that person or organization. To **charge** something **to** someone's account means to add it to their account so they can pay for it later. ❑ *Go out and buy a pair of glasses, and charge it to us.* **3** V-T When the police **charge** someone, they formally accuse them of having done something illegal. ❑ *They have the evidence to charge him.* **4** V-I If you **charge** toward someone or something, you move quickly and aggressively toward them. ❑ *He charged through the door to my mother's office.* ❑ *He ordered us to charge.* • N-COUNT **Charge** is also a noun. ❑ *...a bayonet charge.* **5** V-T To **charge** a battery means to pass an electrical current through it in order to make it more powerful or to make it last longer. ❑ *Alex had forgotten to charge the battery.* • PHRASAL VERB **Charge up** means the same as **charge**. ❑ *There was nothing in the brochure about having to drive it every day to charge up the battery.* **6** N-COUNT A **charge** is an amount of money that you have to pay for a service. ❑ *We can arrange this for a small charge.* **7** → see also **service charge** **8** N-COUNT A **charge** is a formal accusation that someone has committed a crime. ❑ *He may still face criminal charges.* **9** N-COUNT If you describe someone as your **charge**, they have been given to you to be taken care of and you are responsible for them. ❑ *The coach tried to get his charges motivated.* **10** N-COUNT An electrical **charge** is an amount of electricity that is held in or carried by something. [TECHNICAL] **11** N-UNCOUNT If you take **charge** of someone or something, you make yourself responsible for them and take control over them. If someone or something is in your **charge**, you are responsible for them. ❑ *A few years ago Bacryl took charge of the company.* ❑ *I have been given charge of this class.* **12** PHRASE If you are **in charge** in a particular situation, you are the most senior person and have control over something or someone. ❑ *Who's in charge here?* **13** PHRASE If something is **free of charge**, it does not cost anything. ❑ *The leaflet is available free of charge from post offices.* **14** → See feature box at **legal**

SYNONYMS

charge
NOUN **6**
price: *...a sharp increase in the price of gas.*
rate: *There is one rate for domestic calls, but there are several rates for international calls.*
cost: *Badges are also available at a cost of $2.50.*
payment: *The fund will make payments of just over $1 billion next year.*
toll: *We pay enough in toll charges to use their roads.*
VERB **3**
accuse: *Her assistant was accused of theft and fraud by the police.*
indict: *He was later indicted on corruption charges.*
impeach: *...an opposition move to impeach the President.*

---

charge|able /tʃɑ́rdʒəb°l/ **1** ADJ If something is **chargeable**, you have to pay a sum of money for it. [FORMAL] ❑ *The day of discharge is not chargeable if rooms are vacated by 12:00 noon.* **2** ADJ If something is **chargeable**, you have to pay tax on it. [BRIT, FORMAL] ❑ *...the taxpayer's chargeable gain.*

charge card (charge cards) **1** N-COUNT A **charge card** is a plastic card that you use to buy goods on credit from a particular store or group of stores. **2** N-COUNT A **charge card** is the same as a **credit card**. [AM]

charged /tʃɑrdʒd/ **1** ADJ [usu adv ADJ] If a situation is **charged**, it is filled with emotion and therefore very tense or exciting. ❑ *There was a highly charged atmosphere.* ❑ *A wedding is an emotionally charged situation.* **2** ADJ [oft adv ADJ] **Charged** particles carry an electrical charge. ☐ ...*negatively charged ions.* **3** → See feature box at **electricity**

char|gé d'af|faires /ʃɑrʒeɪ dæfɛər/ (**chargés d'affaires**)

> The singular and the plural are both pronounced in the same way.

1 N-COUNT A **chargé d'affaires** is a person appointed to act as head of a diplomatic mission in a foreign country while the ambassador is away. **2** N-COUNT A **chargé d'affaires** is the head of a minor diplomatic mission in a foreign country.

charg|er /tʃɑrdʒər/ (**chargers**) N-COUNT A **charger** is a device used for charging or recharging batteries. ☐ *He forgot the charger for his cellphone.*

char-grilled also **chargrilled** ADJ [usu ADJ n] **Char-grilled** meat or fish has been cooked so that it burns slightly and turns black. [BRIT]

> in AM, use **charbroiled**

chari|ot /tʃæriət/ (**chariots**) N-COUNT In ancient times, **chariots** were fast-moving vehicles with two wheels that were pulled by horses.

cha|ris|ma /kərɪzmə/ N-UNCOUNT You say that someone has **charisma** when they can attract, influence, and inspire people by their personal qualities. ☐ *He has neither the policies nor the personal charisma to inspire people.*

char|is|mat|ic /kærɪzmætɪk/ ADJ A **charismatic** person attracts, influences, and inspires people by their personal qualities. ☐ *With her striking looks and charismatic personality, she was noticed far and wide.*

chari|table /tʃærɪtəbəl/ **1** ADJ [ADJ n] A **charitable** organization or activity helps and supports people who are sick, very poor, or who have a disability. ☐ *...charitable work for cancer awareness.* **2** ADJ Someone who is **charitable** to people is kind or understanding toward them. ☐ *They were less than charitable toward the referee.*

char|ity ♦◇◇ /tʃærɪti/ (**charities**) **1** N-COUNT A **charity** is an organization which raises money in order to help people who are sick, very poor, or who have a disability. ☐ *...an AIDS charity.* **2** N-UNCOUNT If you give money to **charity**, you give it to one or more charitable organizations. If you do something for **charity**, you do it in order to raise money for one or more charitable organizations. ☐ *He made substantial donations to charity.* ☐ *Gooch will be raising money for charity.* **3** N-UNCOUNT People who live on **charity** live on money or goods which other people give them because they are poor. ☐ *Her husband is unemployed and the family depends on charity.*

char|ity shop (**charity shops**) N-COUNT A **charity shop** is the same as a **thrift shop**. [BRIT]

char|la|tan /ʃɑrlətən/ (**charlatans**) N-COUNT You describe someone as a **charlatan** when they pretend to have skills or knowledge that they do not really possess. [FORMAL, DISAPPROVAL] ☐ *He was exposed as a charlatan.*

Charles|ton /tʃɑrlstən/ N-SING [usu the N] The **Charleston** is a lively dance that was popular in the 1920s.

char|ley horse /tʃɑrli hɔrs/ (**charley horses**) N-VAR [a N] People sometimes refer to a cramp in the muscles of their leg or arm as a **charley horse**. [AM, INFORMAL]

charm /tʃɑrm/ (**charms, charming, charmed**) **1** N-VAR **Charm** is the quality of being pleasant or attractive. ☐ *"Snow White and the Seven Dwarfs," the 1937 Disney classic, has lost none of its original charm.* **2** N-UNCOUNT Someone who has **charm** behaves in a friendly, pleasant way that makes people like them. ☐ *He was a man of great charm and distinction.* **3** V-T If you **charm** someone, you please them, especially by using your charm. ☐ *He even charmed Mrs Prichard, carrying her shopping and flirting with her.* **4** N-COUNT A **charm** is a small ornament that is fixed to a bracelet or necklace. ☐ *Inside was a gold charm bracelet, with a star charm on it.* **5** N-COUNT A **charm** is an act, saying, or object that is believed to have magic powers. ☐ *They cross their fingers and spit over their shoulders as charms against the evil eye.*

charmed /tʃɑrmd/ ADJ [ADJ n] A **charmed** place, time, or situation is one that is very beautiful or pleasant, and seems slightly separate from the real world or real life. [WRITTEN] ☐ *...the charmed atmosphere of Oxford in the late Twenties.*

charmed cir|cle N-SING If you refer to a group of people as a **charmed circle**, you mean that they seem to have special power or influence, and do not allow anyone else to join their group. [LITERARY] ☐ *...the immense role played by this very small charmed circle of critics.*

charm|er /tʃɑrmər/ (**charmers**) **1** N-COUNT If you refer to someone as a **charmer**, you mean that they behave in a charming way, especially in order to get what they want. [DISAPPROVAL] ☐ *He comes across as an intelligent, sophisticated charmer.* **2** → see also **snake charmer**

charm|ing /tʃɑrmɪŋ/ **1** ADJ If you say that something is **charming**, you mean that it is very pleasant or attractive. ☐ *...a charming little fishing village.* ● **charm|ing|ly** ADV ☐ *There's something charmingly old-fashioned about his brand of entertainment.* **2** ADJ If you describe someone as **charming**, you mean they behave in a friendly, pleasant way that makes people like them. ☐ *...a charming young man.* ☐ *He found her as smart and funny as she is charming.* ● **charm|ing|ly** ADV [ADV after v] ☐ *Calder smiled charmingly and put out his hand. "A pleasure, Mrs. Talbot."*

charm|less /tʃɑrmlɪs/ ADJ If you say that something or someone is **charmless**, you mean that they are unattractive or uninteresting. [WRITTEN] ☐ *...flat, charmless countryside.*

charm of|fen|sive N-SING If you say that someone has launched a **charm offensive**, you disapprove of the fact that they are being very friendly to their opponents or people who are causing problems for them. [JOURNALISM, DISAPPROVAL] ☐ *He launched a charm offensive against opponents of the government.*

char|nel house /tʃɑrnəl haʊs/ (**charnel houses**) N-COUNT A **charnel house** is a place where the bodies and bones of dead people are stored.

charred /tʃɑrd/ ADJ **Charred** plants, buildings, or vehicles have been badly burned and have become black because of fire. ☐ *...the charred remains of a tank.*

chart ♦◇◇ /tʃɑrt/ (**charts, charting, charted**) **1** N-COUNT A **chart** is a diagram, picture, or graph which is intended to make information easier to understand. ☐ *Male unemployment was 14.2%, compared with 5.8% for women (see chart on next page).* **2** → see also **bar chart, flow chart, pie chart** **3** N-COUNT A **chart** is a map of the sea or stars. ☐ *...charts of Greek waters.* **4** V-T If you **chart** an area of land, sea, or sky, or a feature in that area, you make a map of the area or show the feature in it. ☐ *Ptolemy charted more than 1,000 stars in 48 constellations.* **5** V-T If you **chart** the development or progress of something, you observe it and record or show it. You can also say that a report or graph **charts** the development or progress of something. ☐ *One doctor has charted a dramatic rise in local childhood asthma since the road was built.*

SYNONYMS

chart
NOUN **1**
table: *Other research supports the figures in Table 3.3.*
diagram: *You can reduce long explanations to simple charts or diagrams.*
graph: *Recorded information can be viewed via charts and graphs.*
visual: *Remember you want your visuals to reinforce your message.*

---

char|ter ♦◇◇ /tʃɑrtər/ (**charters, chartering, chartered**) **1** N-COUNT A **charter** is a formal document describing the rights, aims, or principles of an organization or group of people. ☐ *...Article 50 of the United Nations Charter.* **2** ADJ [ADJ n] A **charter** plane or boat is one which is rented for use by a particular person or group and which is not part of a regular service. ☐ *...the last charter plane carrying out foreign nationals.* **3** V-T If a person or organization **charters** a plane, boat, or other vehicle, they rent it for their own use. ☐ *He chartered a jet to fly her home from California to Switzerland.*

char|tered /tʃɑrtərd/ ADJ **Chartered** is used to indicate that someone, such as an accountant or a surveyor, has formally qualified in their profession. [BRIT]

> in AM, use **certified**

char|ter mem|ber (**charter members**) N-COUNT [usu N of n] A **charter member** of a club, group, or organization is one of the first members, often one who was involved in setting it up. [AM]

> in BRIT, use **founder member**

chary /tʃɛəri/ ADJ [v-link ADJ] If you are **chary** of doing something, you are fairly cautious about doing it. ❑ *I am chary of making too many idiotic mistakes.*

chase ✦✧✧ /tʃeɪs/ (chases, chasing, chased) **1** V-T/V-I If you **chase** someone, or **chase** after them, you run after them or follow them quickly in order to catch or reach them. ❑ *She chased the thief for 100 yards.* • N-COUNT **Chase** is also a noun. ❑ *He was reluctant to give up the chase.* **2** V-T/V-I If you **are chasing** something you want, such as work or money, or are **chasing after** it, you are trying hard to get it. ❑ *In some areas, 14 people are chasing every job.* ❑ *There are too many schools chasing after too few students.* • N-SING [N *for* n] **Chase** is also a noun. ❑ *They took an invincible lead in the chase for the championship.* **3** V-T/V-I If someone **chases** someone that they are attracted to, or **chases** after them, they try hard to persuade them to have a sexual relationship with them. ❑ *I didn't go around flirting or chasing women.* • N-SING **Chase** is also a noun. ❑ *The chase is always much more exciting than the conquest anyway.* **4** V-T If someone **chases** you from a place, they force you to leave by using threats or violence. ❑ *Many farmers will then chase you off their land quite aggressively.* **5** V-T To **chase** someone from a job or a position or from power means to force them to leave it. ❑ *In the '70s he had been chased out of his job.* **6** V-I If you **chase** somewhere, you run or rush there. ❑ *They chased down the stairs into the narrow, dirty street.* **7** PHRASE If someone **cuts to the chase**, they start talking about or dealing with what is important, instead of less important things. ❑ *Hi everyone, we all know why we are here today, so let's cut to the chase.*

━━━ **COLLOCATIONS** ━━━
chase
NOUN **1**
noun + **chase**: car, police
adjective + **chase**: high-speed
verb + **chase**: begin, continue, join; abandon, give up

chas|er /tʃeɪsər/ (chasers) N-COUNT [oft n N] A **chaser** is an alcoholic drink that you have after you have drunk a stronger or weaker alcoholic drink. ❑ *...whiskey with beer chasers.*

chasm /kæzəm/ (chasms) **1** N-COUNT A **chasm** is a very deep crack in rock, earth, or ice. ❑ *...a yawning fourteen-foot-deep chasm which inexplicably had opened up in the riverbed.* **2** N-COUNT If you say that there is a **chasm** between two things or between two groups of people, you mean that there is a very large difference between them. ❑ *...the chasm that divides the worlds of university and industry.*

chas|sis /tʃæsi, ʃæsi/ (chassis)

> Chassis /tʃæsiz, ʃæsiz/ is also the plural form.

N-COUNT A **chassis** is the framework that a vehicle is built on.

chaste /tʃeɪst/ ADJ If you describe a person or their behavior as **chaste**, you mean that they do not have sex with anyone, or they only have sex with their husband or wife. [OLD-FASHIONED] ❑ *He remained chaste.*

chas|ten /tʃeɪsᵊn/ (chastens, chastening, chastened) V-T [usu passive] If you **are chastened** by something, it makes you regret that you have behaved badly or stupidly. [FORMAL] ❑ *He has clearly not been chastened by his thirteen days in detention.* ❑ *A chastened team flew home for a period of deep contemplation.*
• **chas|tened** ADJ ❑ *The president now seems a more chastened and less confident politician than when he set out a week ago.*

chas|ten|ing /tʃeɪsᵊnɪŋ/ ADJ A **chastening** experience makes you regret that you have behaved badly or stupidly. ❑ *From this chastening experience he learned some useful lessons.*

chas|tise /tʃæstaɪz/ (chastises, chastising, chastised) V-T If you **chastise** someone, you speak to them angrily or punish them for something wrong that they have done. [FORMAL] ❑ *Thomas Rane chastised Peters for his cruelty.* ❑ *The Securities Commission chastised the firm but imposed no fine.* ❑ *I just don't want you to chastise yourself.*

chas|tise|ment /tʃæstaɪzmənt/ N-UNCOUNT [also a N] **Chastisement** is the same as punishment. [OLD-FASHIONED]

chas|tity /tʃæstɪti/ N-UNCOUNT **Chastity** is the state of not having sex with anyone, or of only having sex with your husband or wife. [OLD-FASHIONED] ❑ *He took a vow of chastity and celibacy.*

chat ✦✧✧ /tʃæt/ (chats, chatting, chatted) V-RECIP When people **chat**, they talk to each other in an informal and friendly way. ❑ *The women were chatting.* ❑ *I was chatting to him the other day.* • N-COUNT **Chat** is also a noun. ❑ *I had a chat with John.*

━━━ **COLLOCATIONS** ━━━
chat
VERB **1**
chat + *adverb*: animatedly, excitedly, happily, merrily; amiably
NOUN **1**
adjective + **chat**: cozy, friendly, informal; heart-to-heart, one-to-one, private; brief

châ|teau /ʃætoʊ/ (châteaux /ʃætoʊz/) also **chateau** N-COUNT A **château** is a large country house or castle in France.

chat|elaine /ʃætəleɪn/ (chatelaines) N-COUNT A **chatelaine** is the female owner, or the wife of the owner, of a castle or large country house.

chat room (chat rooms) also **chatroom** N-COUNT A **chat room** is a site on the internet where people can exchange messages about a particular subject. [COMPUTING] ❑ *...a woman I met in a chat room.*

chat show (chat shows) N-COUNT A **chat show** is the same as a **talk show**. [BRIT]

chat|tel /tʃætᵊl/ (chattels) N-VAR **Chattels** are things that belong to you. [OLD-FASHIONED] ❑ *They were slaves, to be bought and sold as chattels.*

chat|ter /tʃætər/ (chatters, chattering, chattered) **1** V-I If you **chatter**, you talk quickly and continuously, usually about things which are not important. ❑ *Everyone's chattering away in different languages.* ❑ *Erica was friendly and chattered about Andrew's children.* • N-UNCOUNT **Chatter** is also a noun. ❑ *...idle chatter.* **2** V-I If your teeth **chatter**, they keep knocking together because you are very cold or very nervous. ❑ *She was so cold her teeth chattered.* **3** V-I When birds or animals **chatter**, they make high-pitched noises. [LITERARY] ❑ *Birds were chattering somewhere, and occasionally he could hear a vehicle pass by.* • N-UNCOUNT **Chatter** is also a noun. ❑ *...almond trees vibrating with the chatter of crickets.*

chatter|box /tʃætərbɒks/ (chatterboxes) N-COUNT A **chatterbox** is someone who talks a lot. [INFORMAL]

chat|ty /tʃæti/ (chattier, chattiest) **1** ADJ Someone who is **chatty** talks a lot in a friendly, informal way. ❑ *She's quite a chatty person.* **2** ADJ A **chatty** style of writing or talking is friendly and informal. ❑ *He wrote a chatty letter to his wife.* **3** → See feature box at **personality**

chauf|feur /ʃoʊfər, ʃoʊfɜr/ (chauffeurs, chauffeuring, chauffeured) **1** N-COUNT The **chauffeur** of a rich or important person is the man or woman who is employed to take care of their car and drive them around in it. **2** V-T If you **chauffeur** someone somewhere, you drive them there in a car, usually as part of your job. ❑ *It was certainly useful to have her there to chauffeur him around.*

chau|vin|ism /ʃoʊvɪnɪzəm/ N-UNCOUNT **Chauvinism** is a strong, unreasonable belief that your own country, sex, race, or religion, is better and more important than any other. [DISAPPROVAL] ❑ *...it may also appeal to the latent chauvinism of many ordinary people.* • **chau|vin|ist** (chauvinists) N-COUNT ❑ *He is arrogant and a bit of a chauvinist.*

chau|vin|is|tic /ʃoʊvɪnɪstɪk/ **1** ADJ If you describe a man or his behavior as **chauvinistic**, you disapprove of him for believing that men are naturally better and more important than women. [DISAPPROVAL] ❑ *My ex-boyfriend Anthony was very chauvinistic.* **2** ADJ [usu ADJ n] If you describe someone as **chauvinistic**, you believe that they think their own country is more important and morally better than any other. [DISAPPROVAL] ❑ *...national narrow mindedness and chauvinistic arrogance.*

cheap ✦✦✧ /tʃiːp/ (cheaper, cheapest) **1** ADJ Goods or services that are **cheap** cost less money than usual or than you expected. ❑ *I'm going to live off campus if I can find somewhere cheap enough.* ❑ *Operating costs are coming down because of cheaper fuel.*

• **cheap|ly** ADV [ADV after v] ❏ *It will produce electricity more cheaply than a nuclear plant.* **2** ADJ [ADJ n] If you describe goods as **cheap**, you mean they cost less money than similar products but their quality is poor. ❏ *Don't resort to cheap imitations; save up for the real thing.* **3** ADJ [ADJ n] If you describe someone's remarks or actions as **cheap**, you mean that they are unkindly or insincerely using a situation to benefit themselves or to harm someone else. [DISAPPROVAL] ❏ *These tests will inevitably be used by politicians to make cheap political points.* **4** ADJ If you describe someone as **cheap**, you are criticizing them for being unwilling to spend money. [AM, DISAPPROVAL] ❏ *Oh, please, Dad, just this once don't be cheap.*

cheap|en /tʃiːpən/ (**cheapens**, **cheapening**, **cheapened**) V-T If something **cheapens** a person or thing, it lowers their reputation or position. ❏ *Making music political cheapens the art.* ❏ *Love is a word cheapened by overuse.*

cheapo /tʃiːpoʊ/ ADJ [ADJ n] **Cheapo** things are very inexpensive and probably of poor quality. [INFORMAL] ❏ *...cheapo deals on wobbly airlines.*

cheap shot (**cheap shots**) N-COUNT A **cheap shot** is a comment someone makes which you think is unfair or unkind. [DISAPPROVAL]

cheap|skate /tʃiːpskeɪt/ (**cheapskates**) N-COUNT If you say that someone is a **cheapskate**, you think that they do not like spending money. [DISAPPROVAL] ❏ *Tell your husband not to be a cheapskate.*

cheat /tʃiːt/ (**cheats**, **cheating**, **cheated**) **1** V-I When someone **cheats**, they do not obey a set of rules which they should be obeying, for example in a game or exam. ❏ *Students may be tempted to cheat in order to get into top schools.* • **cheat|ing** N-UNCOUNT ❏ *In an election in 1988, he was accused of cheating by his opponent.* **2** V-T If someone **cheats** you out of something, they get it from you by behaving dishonestly. ❏ *The company engaged in a deliberate effort to cheat them out of their pensions.* **3** N-COUNT Someone who is a **cheat** does not obey a set of rules which they should be obeying. ❏ *Cheats will be disqualified.*
▶ **cheat on** **1** PHRASAL VERB If someone **cheats on** their husband, wife, or partner, they have a sexual relationship with another person. [INFORMAL] ❏ *I'd found Philippe was cheating on me and I was angry and hurt.* **2** PHRASAL VERB If someone **cheats on** something such as an agreement or their taxes, they do not do what they should do under a set of rules. [mainly AM] ❏ *Their job is to check that none of the signatory countries is cheating on the agreement.*

cheat|er /tʃiːtər/ (**cheaters**) N-COUNT A **cheater** is someone who cheats. [mainly AM]

cheat sheet (**cheat sheets**) N-COUNT A **cheat sheet** is a short list of information that you can use to help you do or remember something. ❏ *If this all sounds too hard to remember, print out the cheat sheet and stick it on the side of your computer screen for quick reference.*

check ♦♦◊ /tʃɛk/ (**checks**, **checking**, **checked**) **1** V-T/V-I If you **check** something such as a piece of information or a document, you make sure that it is correct or satisfactory. ❏ *Check the accuracy of everything in your résumé.* ❏ *I think there is an age limit, but I'd have to check.* ❏ *She hadn't checked whether she had a clean, ironed shirt.* • N-COUNT **Check** is also a noun. ❏ *He is being constantly monitored with regular checks on his blood pressure.* **2** V-I If you **check on** someone or something, you make sure they are in a safe or satisfactory condition. ❏ *Stephen checked on her several times during the night.* **3** V-T If you **check** something that is written on a piece of paper, you put a mark, like a V with the right side extended, next to it to show that something is correct or has been selected or dealt with. [mainly AM] ❏ *To request your free gift, please check the appropriate box below.*

in BRIT, usually use **tick**

4 V-T To **check** something, usually something bad, means to stop it from spreading or continuing. ❏ *Sex education is also expected to help check the spread of AIDS.* **5** V-T When you **check** your baggage at an airport, you give it to an official so that it can be taken on to your plane. [AM] ❏ *We arrived at the airport, checked our baggage and wandered around the gift shops.* • PHRASAL VERB To **check in** your baggage means the same as to **check** it. ❏ *They checked in their luggage and found seats in the departure lounge.* **6** N-COUNT The **check** in a restaurant is a piece of paper on which the price of your meal is written and which you are given before you pay. [mainly AM] ❏ *After coffee, Gastler asked for the check.*

in BRIT, usually use **bill**

7 N-COUNT A pattern of squares, usually of two colors, can be referred to as **checks** or a **check**. ❏ *Styles include stripes and checks.* **8** N-COUNT A **check** is a printed form on which you write an amount of money and who it is to be paid to. Your bank then pays the money to that person from your account. ❏ *He handed me an envelope with a check for $1,500.*

in BRIT, use **cheque**

9 → see also **blank check**, **traveler's check** **10** PHRASE If something or someone **is held in check** or **is kept in check**, they are controlled and prevented from becoming too great or powerful. ❏ *Life on Earth will become unsustainable unless population growth is held in check.* **11** → see also **double-check**, **rain check**
▶ **check in** **1** PHRASAL VERB When you **check in** or **check into** a hotel or clinic, or if someone **checks** you **in**, you arrive and go through the necessary procedures before you stay there. ❏ *I'll call the hotel. I'll tell them we'll check in tomorrow.* ❏ *He has checked into an alcohol treatment center.* **2** PHRASAL VERB When you **check in** at an airport, you arrive and show your ticket before going on a flight. ❏ *He had checked in at Amsterdam's Schiphol airport for a flight to Atlanta.* **3** → see also **check-in**, **check 5**
▶ **check off** PHRASAL VERB When you **check** things **off**, you check or count them while referring to a list of them, to make sure you have considered all of them. ❏ *Once you've checked off the items you ordered, put this record in your file.* ❏ *I haven't checked them off but I would say that's about the number.*
▶ **check out** **1** PHRASAL VERB When you **check out** of a hotel or clinic where you have been staying, or if someone **checks** you **out**, you pay the bill and leave. ❏ *They packed and checked out of the hotel.* ❏ *I was disappointed to miss Bryan, who had just checked out.* **2** PHRASAL VERB If you **check out** something or someone, you find out information about them to make sure that everything is correct or satisfactory. ❏ *Maybe we ought to go down to the library and check it out.* ❏ *We ought to check him out on the computer.* **3** PHRASAL VERB If something **checks out**, it is correct or satisfactory. ❏ *She was in San Diego the weekend Jensen got killed. Her alibi checked out.* **4** PHRASAL VERB If you **check out** a library book, you borrow it for a fixed period of time. ❏ *No books can be checked out after 6 p.m. tomorrow.* **5** → see also **checkout**
▶ **check up** **1** PHRASAL VERB If you **check up** on something, you find out information about it. ❏ *It is certainly worth checking up on your benefit entitlements.* **2** → see also **checkup** **3** PHRASAL VERB If you **check up** on someone, you obtain information about them, usually secretly. ❏ *I'm sure he knew I was checking up on him.*

─── COLLOCATIONS ───

check
NOUN **1**
noun + **check**: health, safety, security; border; background
adjective + **check**: rigorous, stringent, thorough; regular, routine
verb + **check**: carry out, do, make, perform, run; undergo
VERB **1**
check + adverb: carefully, rigorously, thoroughly; periodically, regularly, routinely

─── SYNONYMS ───

check
VERB **1**
examine: *He examined her passport and stamped it.*
test: *Test the water with your wrist.*
verify: *I verified the source from which I got that information.*
vet: *All objects are vetted by a distinguished panel of experts.*
inspect: *Elaine went outside to inspect the playing field.*

check|book /tʃɛkbʊk/ (**checkbooks**)

in BRIT, use **chequebook**

checkbook N-COUNT A **checkbook** is a book of checks which your bank gives you so that you can pay for things by check. [AM] ❑ *The woman took out her checkbook and quickly made out four checks.*

check|book jour|nal|ism N-UNCOUNT **Checkbook journalism** is the practice of paying people large sums of money for information about crimes or famous people in order to get material for newspaper articles. [DISAPPROVAL]

check box (**check boxes**) N-COUNT A **check box** is a small square on a form, questionnaire, or test in which you put a tick to show that you agree with a statement.

checked /tʃɛkt/ ADJ Something that is **checked** has a pattern of small squares, usually of two colors. ❑ *He was wearing blue jeans and a checked shirt.*

check|er /tʃɛkər/ (**checkers**) **1** N-UNCOUNT **Checkers** is a game for two people, played with 24 round pieces on a board. [AM] ❑ *...a game of checkers.*

in BRIT, use **draughts**

2 N-COUNT A **checker** is a person or machine that has the job of checking something. ❑ *Run what you've written through a spell checker before sending.*

checker|board /tʃɛkərbɔrd/ (**checkerboards**)

BRIT also **chequerboard**

1 N-COUNT A **checkerboard** is a square board with 64 black and white squares that is used for playing checkers or chess. [AM]

in BRIT, use **draughts board, chessboard**

2 ADJ [ADJ n] A **checkerboard** pattern is made up of equal-sized squares of two different colors, usually black and white.

check|ered /tʃɛkərd/

in BRIT, usually use **chequered**

1 ADJ [usu ADJ n] If a person or organization has had a **checkered** career or history, they have had a varied past with both good and bad periods. ❑ *Zenker, for his part, regarded Raeder's checkered political career as a distinct liability for a future chief of the navy.* **2** ADJ [ADJ n] Something that is **checkered** has a pattern with squares of two or more different colors. ❑ *...red checkered tablecloths.*

check-in (**check-ins**) N-COUNT At an airport, a **check-in** is the counter or desk where you check in. ❑ *The line at the check-in was already dispersing.*

check-in coun|ter (**check-in counters**) N-COUNT The **check-in counter** at an airport or hotel is the counter or desk where you check in. ❑ *But when I arrived at the check-in counter, I couldn't find my ticket.*

check|ing ac|count (**checking accounts**) N-COUNT A **checking account** is a personal bank account which you can take money out of at any time using your checkbook or bank card. [mainly AM] ❑ *...Commonwealth Bank, where he has his checking account.*

in BRIT, usually use **current account**

check|list /tʃɛklɪst/ (**checklists**) N-COUNT A **checklist** is a list of all the things that you need to do, information that you want to find out, or things that you need to take somewhere, which you make in order to ensure that you do not forget anything. ❑ *Make a checklist of the tools and materials you will need.*

check mark (**check marks**) N-COUNT A **check mark** is a written mark like a ✓. It is used to show that something is correct or has been selected or dealt with. [AM] ❑ *Please make the appropriate check marks on the enclosed form.*

check|mate /tʃɛkmeɪt/ N-UNCOUNT In chess, **checkmate** is a situation in which you cannot stop your king from being captured and so you lose the game.

WORD HISTORY

checkmate
The purpose of the game of chess may be to capture your opponent's king, but in terms of word origins, a player's aim is really to kill the king: **checkmate** comes from the Arabic phrase *shāh māt*, meaning 'the king is dead.'

check|out /tʃɛkaʊt/ (**checkouts**) N-COUNT In a supermarket, a **checkout** is a counter where you pay for things you are buying. ❑ *...the supermarket checkout counter.*

check|point /tʃɛkpɔɪnt/ (**checkpoints**) N-COUNT A **checkpoint** is a place where traffic is stopped so that it can be checked. ❑ *...a bomb explosion close to an army checkpoint.*

check|up /tʃɛkʌp/ (**checkups**) N-COUNT A **checkup** is a medical examination by your doctor or dentist to make sure that there is nothing wrong with your health. ❑ *The disease was detected during a routine checkup.*

ched|dar /tʃɛdər/ (**cheddars**) N-MASS **Cheddar** is a type of hard, yellow cheese, originally made in Britain.

cheek /tʃik/ (**cheeks**) **1** N-COUNT Your **cheeks** are the sides of your face below your eyes. ❑ *Tears were running down her cheeks.* **2** N-COUNT [usu pl] Your **cheeks** are your buttocks. ❑ *My butt cheeks are sore from sitting on this bench too long.* **3** N-SING [also no det] You say that someone has **cheek** when you are annoyed or shocked at something unreasonable that they have done. [mainly BRIT, INFORMAL] ❑ *I'm amazed they had the cheek to ask in the first place.*

cheek|bone /tʃikboʊn/ (**cheekbones**) **1** N-COUNT Your **cheekbones** are the two bones in your face just below your eyes. ❑ *She was very beautiful, with high cheekbones.* **2** → See feature box at **appearance**

cheeky /tʃiki/ (**cheekier, cheekiest**) ADJ If you describe a person or their behavior as **cheeky**, you think that they are slightly rude or disrespectful but in a charming or amusing way. [mainly BRIT] ❑ *The boy was cheeky and casual.*

cheer ♦◇◇ /tʃɪər/ (**cheers, cheering, cheered**) **1** V-T/V-I When people **cheer**, they shout loudly to show their approval or to encourage someone who is doing something such as taking part in a game. ❑ *The crowd cheered as she went up the steps to the bandstand.* ❑ *Hundreds of thousands of jubilant Americans cheered him on his return.* • N-COUNT **Cheer** is also a noun. ❑ *The colonel was rewarded with a resounding cheer from the men.* **2** V-T If you **are cheered** by something, it makes you happier or less worried. ❑ *Stephen noticed that the people around him looked cheered by his presence.* • **cheer|ing** ADJ ❑ *...very cheering news.* **3** CONVENTION People sometimes say '**Cheers**' to each other just before they drink an alcoholic drink. [mainly BRIT]

▶ **cheer on** PHRASAL VERB When you **cheer** someone **on**, you shout loudly in order to encourage them, for example when they are taking part in a game. ❑ *A thousand supporters packed into the stadium to cheer them on.*

▶ **cheer up** PHRASAL VERB When you **cheer up** or when something **cheers** you **up**, you stop feeling depressed and become more cheerful. ❑ *I think he misses her terribly. You might cheer him up.* ❑ *I wrote that song just to cheer myself up.*

SYNONYMS

cheer
VERB **2**
hearten: *The news heartened everybody.*
encourage: *Investors were encouraged by the news.*
brighten: *That really brightened my day.*

cheer|ful /tʃɪərfəl/ **1** ADJ Someone who is **cheerful** is happy and shows this in their behavior. ❑ *Paddy was always cheerful and jolly.* • **cheer|ful|ly** ADV [ADV with v] ❑ *"We've come with good news," Pat said cheerfully.* • **cheer|ful|ness** N-UNCOUNT ❑ *I remember this extraordinary man with particular affection for his unfailing cheerfulness.* **2** ADJ Something that is **cheerful** is pleasant and makes you feel happy. ❑ *The nursery is bright and cheerful, with plenty of toys.* **3** ADJ [usu ADJ n] If you describe someone's attitude as **cheerful**, you mean they are not worried about something, and you think that they should be. ❑ *There is little evidence to support his cheerful assumptions.* • **cheer|ful|ly** ADV [ADV before v] ❑ *He cheerfully ignored medical advice which could have prolonged his life.* **4** → See feature box at **emotion**

cheer|leader /tʃɪərlidər/ (**cheerleaders**) N-COUNT A **cheerleader** is one of the people who leads the crowd in cheering at a large public event, especially a sports event.

cheer|less /tʃɪərlɪs/ ADJ **Cheerless** places or weather are dull and depressing. ❑ *The kitchen was dank and cheerless.* ❑ *...a bleak, cheerless day.*

cheery /tʃɪəri/ (cheerier, cheeriest) ADJ If you describe a person or their behavior as **cheery**, you mean that they are cheerful and happy. ◻ *She was cheery and talked to them about their problems.* • **cheeri|ly** ADV ◻ *"Come on in," she said cheerily.*

cheese ✦◇◇ /tʃiːz/ (cheeses) N-MASS **Cheese** is a solid food made from milk. It is usually white or yellow. ◻ *...bread and cheese.* ◻ *...delicious French cheeses.*

cheese board (cheese boards) also **cheeseboard** N-COUNT [usu sing] A **cheese board** is a board from which cheese is served at a meal.

cheese|burg|er /tʃiːzbɜːrɡər/ (cheeseburgers) N-COUNT A **cheeseburger** is a hamburger with a slice of cheese on top, served on a bun.

cheese|cake /tʃiːzkeɪk/ (cheesecakes) N-VAR **Cheesecake** is a dessert that consists of a crust made from cookie or cracker crumbs covered with a soft sweet filling containing cream cheese.

cheese|cloth /tʃiːzklɒθ/ N-UNCOUNT **Cheesecloth** is cotton cloth that is very thin and light. There are tiny holes between the threads of the cloth. ◻ *...cheesecloth shirts.*

cheesy /tʃiːzi/ (cheesier, cheesiest) **1** ADJ If you describe something as **cheesy**, you mean that it is cheap, unpleasant, or insincere. [INFORMAL, DISAPPROVAL] ◻ *...a cheesy hotel.* ◻ *Politicians persist in imagining that "the people" warm to their cheesy slogans.* **2** ADJ [usu ADJ n] **Cheesy** food is food that tastes or smells of cheese. ◻ *...cheesy biscuits.*

chee|tah /tʃiːtə/ (cheetahs) N-COUNT A **cheetah** is a wild animal that looks like a large cat with black spots on its body. Cheetahs can run very fast.

chef /ʃɛf/ (chefs) N-COUNT A **chef** is a cook in a restaurant or hotel. ◻ *...some of Australia's leading chefs.*

chef's sal|ad (chef's salads) N-VAR A **chef's salad** is a green salad with hard-boiled egg and strips of meat and cheese on top. [AM]

chemi|cal ✦◇◇ /kɛmɪkəl/ (chemicals) **1** ADJ [ADJ n] **Chemical** means involving or resulting from a reaction between two or more substances, or relating to the substances that something consists of. ◻ *...chemical reactions that cause ozone destruction.* ◻ *...the chemical composition of the ocean.* • **chemi|cal|ly** /kɛmɪkli/ ADV ◻ *...chemically treated foods.* **2** N-COUNT **Chemicals** are substances that are used in a chemical process or made by a chemical process. ◻ *The whole food chain is affected by the overuse of chemicals in agriculture.* ◻ *...a chemical company.* **3** → See feature box at **brain**

chemi|cal en|gi|neer (chemical engineers) N-COUNT A **chemical engineer** is a person who designs and constructs the machines needed for industrial chemical processes.

chemi|cal en|gi|neer|ing N-UNCOUNT **Chemical engineering** is the designing and constructing of machines that are needed for industrial chemical processes.

che|mise /ʃəmiːz/ (chemises) N-COUNT A **chemise** is a long, loose piece of underwear worn by women in former times.

chem|ist /kɛmɪst/ (chemists) **1** N-COUNT A **chemist** is a person who does research connected with chemistry or who studies chemistry. ◻ *She worked as a research chemist.* **2** N-COUNT A **chemist** or a **chemist's** is the same as a **drugstore** or a **pharmacy**. [BRIT] **3** N-COUNT A **chemist** is the same as a **druggist** or a **pharmacist**. [BRIT]

chem|is|try /kɛmɪstri/ **1** N-UNCOUNT **Chemistry** is the scientific study of the structure of substances and of the way that they react with other substances. **2** N-UNCOUNT The **chemistry** of an organism or a material is the chemical substances that make it up and the chemical reactions that go on inside it. ◻ *We have literally altered the chemistry of our planet's atmosphere.* **3** N-UNCOUNT If you say that there is **chemistry** between two people, you mean that it is obvious they are attracted to each other or like each other very much. ◻ *...the extraordinary chemistry between Ingrid and Bogart.*

chemo /kiːmoʊ/ N-UNCOUNT **Chemo** is the same as **chemotherapy**. [INFORMAL] ◻ *The first time I had chemo I was quite scared.*

chemo|thera|py /kiːmoʊθɛrəpi/ N-UNCOUNT **Chemotherapy** is the treatment of disease using chemicals. It is often used in treating cancer. ◻ *He had been undergoing chemotherapy for lung cancer.*

che|nille /ʃənil/ N-UNCOUNT **Chenille** is cloth or clothing made from a type of thick furry thread.

cheque /tʃɛk/ (cheques) [BRIT] → see **check 8**

chequebook /tʃɛkbʊk/ (chequebooks) [BRIT] → see **checkbook**

cher|ish /tʃɛrɪʃ/ (cherishes, cherishing, cherished) **1** V-T If you **cherish** something such as a hope or a pleasant memory, you keep it in your mind for a long period of time. ◻ *The president will cherish the memory of this visit to Ohio.* • **cher|ished** ADJ [ADJ n] ◻ *...the cherished dream of a world without wars.* **2** V-T If you **cherish** someone or something, you take good care of them because you love them. ◻ *He genuinely loved and cherished her.* • **cher|ished** ADJ [ADJ n] ◻ *He described the picture as his most cherished possession.* **3** V-T If you **cherish** a right, a privilege, or a principle, you regard it as important and try hard to keep it. ◻ *Chinese people cherish their independence and sovereignty.* • **cher|ished** ADJ [ADJ n] ◻ *Freud called into question some deeply cherished beliefs.*

che|root /ʃəruːt/ (cheroots) N-COUNT A **cheroot** is a cigar with both ends cut flat.

cher|ry /tʃɛri/ (cherries) **1** N-COUNT **Cherries** are small, round fruit with red skins. **2** N-COUNT A **cherry** or a **cherry tree** is a tree that cherries grow on.

cherry-pick (cherry-picks, cherry-picking, cherry-picked) V-T If someone **cherry-picks** people or things, they choose the best ones from a group of them, often in a way that other people consider unfair. ◻ *The team is in debt while others are lining up to cherry-pick their best players.*

cher|ub /tʃɛrəb/ (cherubs) N-COUNT A **cherub** is a kind of angel that is represented in art as a naked child with wings.

che|ru|bic /tʃəruːbɪk/ ADJ If someone looks **cherubic**, they look sweet and innocent like a cherub. [LITERARY] ◻ *...her beaming, cherubic face.*

cher|vil /tʃɜːrvɪl/ N-UNCOUNT **Chervil** is a herb that tastes like aniseed.

Chesh|ire cat /tʃɛʃər kæt/ PHRASE If someone is grinning **like a Cheshire cat** or **like the Cheshire cat**, they are smiling very widely. ◻ *He had a grin on his face like a Cheshire Cat.* ◻ *...a Cheshire Cat smile.*

chess /tʃɛs/ N-UNCOUNT **Chess** is a game for two people, played on a chessboard. Each player has 16 pieces, including a king. Your aim is to move your pieces so that your opponent's king cannot escape being taken. ◻ *He was playing chess with his uncle.*

chess|board /tʃɛsbɔːrd/ (chessboards) N-COUNT A **chessboard** is a square board with 64 black and white squares that is used for playing chess.

chest ✦◇◇ /tʃɛst/ (chests) **1** N-COUNT Your **chest** is the top part of the front of your body where your ribs, lungs, and heart are. ◻ *He crossed his arms over his chest.* ◻ *He was shot in the chest.* **2** N-COUNT A **chest** is a large, heavy box used for storing things. ◻ *At the very bottom of the chest were his carving tools.* ◻ *...a treasure chest.*

chest com|pres|sion (chest compressions) N-VAR **Chest compression** is the act of applying pressure to someone's chest in order to help blood flow through the heart in an emergency situation. ◻ *Give one breath of mouth-to-mouth resuscitation, followed by five chest compressions.*

chest|nut /tʃɛsnʌt, -nət/ (chestnuts) **1** N-COUNT A **chestnut** or **chestnut tree** is a tall tree with broad leaves. **2** N-COUNT **Chestnuts** are the reddish brown nuts that grow on chestnut trees. You can eat chestnuts. **3** COLOR Something that is **chestnut** is dark reddish brown in color. ◻ *...chestnut hair.*

chest of drawers (chests of drawers) N-COUNT A **chest of drawers** is a low, flat piece of furniture with drawers in which you keep clothes and other things.

chev|ron /ʃɛvrən/ (chevrons) N-COUNT A **chevron** is a V shape. ◻ *The chevron or arrow road sign indicates a sharp bend to the left or right.*

chew /tʃuː/ (chews, chewing, chewed) **1** V-T/V-I When you **chew** food, you use your teeth to break it up in your mouth so that it becomes easier to swallow. ◻ *Be certain to eat slowly*

chewing gum and chew your food extremely well. ❑ *Daniel leaned back on the sofa, still chewing on his apple.* **2** V-T If you **chew** gum or tobacco, you keep biting it and moving it around your mouth to taste the flavor of it. You do not swallow it. ❑ *One girl was chewing gum.* **3** V-T If you **chew** your lips or your fingernails, you keep biting them because you are nervous. ❑ *He chewed his lower lip nervously.* **4** V-T/V-I If a person or animal **chews** an object or **chews** on it, they bite it with their teeth. ❑ *They pause and chew their pencils.* ❑ *She chewed through the tape that bound her.*

chew|ing gum N-UNCOUNT **Chewing gum** is a kind of sweet substance that you can chew for a long time. You do not swallow it. ❑ *...a stick of chewing gum.*

chewy /tʃui/ (**chewier, chewiest**) ADJ If food is **chewy**, it needs to be chewed a lot before it becomes soft enough to swallow. ❑ *The meat was too chewy.* ❑ *...chewy chocolate cookies.*

chia|ro|scu|ro /kiærəskyuəroʊ/ N-UNCOUNT **Chiaroscuro** is the use of light and shade in a picture, or the effect produced by light and shade in a place. ❑ *...the natural chiaroscuro of the place.*

chic /ʃik/ **1** ADJ Something or someone that is **chic** is fashionable and sophisticated. ❑ *Her gown was very French and very chic.* **2** N-UNCOUNT **Chic** is used to refer to a particular style or to the quality of being chic. ❑ *...French designer chic.*

Chi|ca|na /tʃikɑnə/ (**Chicanas**) N-COUNT A **Chicana** is an American girl or woman whose family originally came from Mexico. [AM] ❑ *...a Chicana from Michigan.*

chi|can|ery /ʃikeɪnəri/ (**chicaneries**) N-UNCOUNT [also N in pl] **Chicanery** is using cleverness to cheat people. [FORMAL]

Chi|ca|no /tʃikɑnoʊ/ (**chicanos**) N-COUNT A **Chicano** is an American citizen, whose family originally came from Mexico. [AM] ❑ *...views expressed by one young Chicano interviewed by Phinney.*

chi|chi /ʃiʃi/ also **chi-chi** ADJ If you say that something is **chichi**, you mean that it is pretty or stylish, especially in a way that you consider affected. [mainly AM, DISAPPROVAL] ❑ *Two years ago glass bricks were all the rage in chichi homes.* ❑ *Some of the shops were just a bit chichi, I must admit.*

chick /tʃik/ (**chicks**) **1** N-COUNT A **chick** is a baby bird. ❑ *...newly-hatched chicks.* **2** N-COUNT Some men refer to women as **chicks**. This use could cause offense. [INFORMAL]

chicka|dee /tʃikədi/ (**chickadees**) N-COUNT A **chickadee** is a small North American bird with gray and black feathers. [AM]

chick|en ♦◇◇ /tʃikɪn/ (**chickens, chickening, chickened**) **1** N-COUNT **Chickens** are birds which are kept on a farm for their eggs and for their meat. ❑ *Lionel built a coop so that they could raise chickens and have a supply of fresh eggs.* • N-UNCOUNT **Chicken** is the flesh of this bird eaten as food. ❑ *...roast chicken with wild mushrooms.* **2** N-COUNT If someone calls you a **chicken**, they mean that you are afraid to do something. [INFORMAL, DISAPPROVAL] ❑ *I'm scared of the dark. I'm a big chicken.* • ADJ [v-link ADJ] **Chicken** is also an adjective. ❑ *Why are you so chicken, Gregory?* **3** PHRASE If you say that someone **is counting their chickens**, you mean that they are assuming that they will be successful or get something, when this is not certain. ❑ *I don't want to count my chickens before they are hatched.* **4 chickens come home to roost** → see **roost**

▶ **chicken out** PHRASAL VERB If someone **chickens out** of something that they were intending to do, they decide not to do it because they are afraid. [INFORMAL] ❑ *He makes excuses to chicken out of family occasions such as weddings.* ❑ *I had never ridden on a motor-cycle before. But it was too late to chicken out.*

chicken|feed /tʃikɪnfid/ also **chicken feed** N-UNCOUNT If you think that an amount of money is so small it is hardly worth having or considering, you can say that it is **chickenfeed**. ❑ *I was making a million a year, but that's chickenfeed in the pop business.*

chicken|pox /tʃikɪnpɒks/ also **chicken pox** N-UNCOUNT **Chickenpox** is a disease which gives you a high temperature and red spots that itch.

chicken|shit /tʃikɪnʃɪt/ **1** ADJ If you say that someone or something is **chickenshit**, you mean that they are worthless. [AM, INFORMAL, VULGAR] ❑ *I don't want a bunch of nerds telling me whether to take a limo or not. That's all chickenshit.* ❑ *You think I'm chickenshit, don't you?* **2** ADJ If you say that someone is **chickenshit**, you mean that they are cowardly. [AM, VULGAR] ❑ *...djs who are too chickenshit to play experimental music.*

chick|en wire N-UNCOUNT **Chicken wire** is a type of thin wire netting.

chick flick (**chick flicks**) N-COUNT A **chick flick** is a romantic movie that is not very serious and is intended to appeal to women. [INFORMAL]

chick lit N-UNCOUNT **Chick lit** is modern fiction about the lives and romantic problems of young women, usually written by women. [INFORMAL]

chick|pea /tʃikpi/ (**chickpeas**) also **chick pea** N-COUNT [usu pl] **Chickpeas** are hard, round seeds that look like pale brown peas. They can be cooked and eaten.

chick|weed /tʃikwid/ N-UNCOUNT **Chickweed** is a plant with small leaves and white flowers which grows close to the ground.

chico|ry /tʃikəri/ N-UNCOUNT **Chicory** is a plant with crunchy, bitter tasting leaves. It is eaten in salads, and its roots are sometimes used instead of coffee.

chide /tʃaɪd/ (**chides, chiding, chided**) V-T If you **chide** someone, you speak to them angrily because they have done something bad or foolish. [OLD-FASHIONED] ❑ *Jack chided himself for worrying.*

chief ♦♦◇ /tʃif/ (**chiefs**) **1** N-COUNT The **chief** of an organization is the person who is in charge of it. ❑ *...a commission appointed by the police chief.* **2** N-COUNT; N-TITLE The **chief** of a tribe is its leader. ❑ *...Sitting Bull, chief of the Sioux tribes of the Great Plains.* **3** ADJ [ADJ n] **Chief** is used in the job titles of the most senior worker or workers of a particular kind in an organization. ❑ *...the chief test pilot.* **4** ADJ [ADJ n] The **chief** cause, part, or member of something is the most important one. ❑ *Financial stress is well established as a chief reason for divorce.*

SYNONYMS

chief
ADJ **4**
primary: *That's the primary reason the company's share price has held up so well.*
leading: *Britain's future as a leading industrial nation depends on investment.*
main: *What are the main differences and similarities between them?*
prime: *Political stability, meanwhile, will be a prime concern.*
principal: *...the country's principal source of foreign exchange earnings.*

---

chief ex|ecu|tive of|fic|er (**chief executive officers**) N-COUNT The **chief executive officer** of a company is the person who has overall responsibility for the management of that company. The abbreviation **CEO** is often used. [BUSINESS]

Chief Jus|tice (**Chief Justices**) N-COUNT; N-TITLE A **Chief Justice** is the most important judge of a court of law, especially the Supreme Court. ❑ *...Chief Justice Marshall.*

chief|ly /tʃifli/ ADV You use **chiefly** to indicate that a particular reason, emotion, method, or feature is the main or most important one. ❑ *He joined the consular service in China, chiefly because this was one of the few job vacancies.*

Chief of Staff (**Chiefs of Staff**) N-COUNT The **Chiefs of Staff** are the most senior officers in each service of the armed forces. ❑ *...General Carl Vano, the chief of staff of the Army.*

chief|tain /tʃiftən/ (**chieftains**) N-COUNT A **chieftain** is the leader of a tribe. ❑ *...the legendary British chieftain, King Arthur.*

chif|fon /ʃɪfɒn/ (**chiffons**) N-MASS **Chiffon** is a kind of very thin silk or nylon cloth that you can see through. ❑ *...floaty chiffon skirts.*

chi|gnon /ʃinyɒn/ (**chignons**) N-COUNT A **chignon** is a hairstyle in which a woman's hair is tied in a loose knot at the back of her head.

Chi|hua|hua /tʃɪwɑwə/ (**Chihuahuas**) also **chihuahua** N-COUNT A **Chihuahua** is a very small dog with short hair.

chil|blain /tʃɪlbleɪn/ (**chilblains**) N-COUNT [usu pl] **Chilblains** are painful, red swellings which people sometimes get on their fingers or toes in cold weather.

child ♦♦♦ /tʃaɪld/ (**children**) **1** N-COUNT A **child** is a human being who is not yet an adult. ❑ *When I was a child I lived in a country village.* ❑ *...a child of six.* **2** N-COUNT Someone's **children** are their sons and daughters of any age. ❑ *How are the children?* ❑ *His children have left home.* **3** → See feature box at **family**

child|bearing /tʃaɪldbɛərɪŋ/ **1** N-UNCOUNT **Childbearing** is the process of giving birth to babies. **2** ADJ [ADJ n] A woman of **childbearing** age is of an age when women are normally able to give birth to children.

child|birth /tʃaɪldbɜrθ/ N-UNCOUNT **Childbirth** is the act of giving birth to a child. ❏ *She died in childbirth.*

child|care /tʃaɪldkɛər/ N-UNCOUNT **Childcare** refers to taking care of children, and to the facilities which help parents to do so. ❏ *Both partners shared childcare.*

child|hood ✦◇◇ /tʃaɪldhʊd/ (**childhoods**) N-VAR A person's **childhood** is the period of their life when they are a child. ❏ *She had a happy childhood.* ❏ *He was remembering a story heard in childhood.*

child|ish /tʃaɪldɪʃ/ **1** ADJ **Childish** means relating to or typical of a child. ❏ *...childish enthusiasm.* **2** ADJ If you describe someone, especially an adult, as **childish**, you disapprove of them because they behave in an immature way. [DISAPPROVAL] ❏ *...Penny's selfish and childish behavior.*

child|less /tʃaɪldlɪs/ **1** ADJ Someone who is **childless** has no children. ❏ *...childless couples.* **2** → See feature box at **family**

child|like /tʃaɪldlaɪk/ ADJ You describe someone as **childlike** when they seem like a child in their character, appearance, or behavior. ❏ *His most enduring quality is his childlike innocence.*

child prodi|gy (**child prodigies**) N-COUNT A **child prodigy** is a child with a very great talent. ❏ *She was a child prodigy, giving concerts before she was a teenager.*

child|proof /tʃaɪldpruf/ also **child proof** ADJ Something that is **childproof** is designed in a way which ensures that children cannot harm it or be harmed by it. ❏ *The rear doors include childproof locks.*

chil|dren /tʃɪldrən/ **Children** is the plural of **child**.

child sup|port N-UNCOUNT If a parent pays **child support**, they legally have to pay money to help provide things such as food and clothing for a child with whom they no longer live. ❏ *He was imprisoned for failure to pay child support.*

chili /tʃɪli/ (**chilies** or **chilis**) **1** N-VAR **Chilies** are small, red or green peppers. They have a very hot taste and are used in cooking. **2** N-UNCOUNT **Chili** is a dish made from meat or beans, or sometimes both, with a thick sauce of tomatoes, and powdered or fresh chilies.

chili con car|ne /tʃɪli kɒn kɑrni/ N-UNCOUNT **Chili con carne** is a dish made from meat, with a thick sauce of tomatoes, and powdered or fresh chilies.

chili pow|der N-UNCOUNT **Chili powder** is a very hot-tasting powder made mainly from dried chilies. It is used in cooking.

chill /tʃɪl/ (**chills, chilling, chilled**) **1** V-T/V-I When you **chill** something or when it **chills**, you lower its temperature so that it becomes colder but does not freeze. ❏ *Chill the fruit salad until serving time.* ❏ *These doughs can be rolled out while you wait for the pastry to chill.* **2** V-T When cold weather or something cold **chills** a person or a place, it makes that person or that place feel very cold. ❏ *The marble floor was beginning to chill her.* ❏ *Wade placed his chilled hands on the radiator and warmed them.* **3** N-COUNT If something sends a **chill** through you, it gives you a sudden feeling of fear or anxiety. ❏ *The violence used against the students sent a chill through Indonesia.* **4** N-COUNT A **chill** is a mild illness which can give you a slight fever and headache. ❏ *He caught a chill while performing at a rain-soaked open-air venue.* **5** ADJ [ADJ n] **Chill** weather is cold and unpleasant. ❏ *...chill winds, rain and choppy seas.* • N-SING **Chill** is also a noun. ❏ *September is here, bringing with it a chill in the mornings.*

▶ **chill out** PHRASAL VERB To **chill out** means to relax after you have done something tiring or stressful. [INFORMAL] ❏ *After school, we used to chill out in each other's bedrooms.*

chil|lax /tʃɪlæks/ (**chillaxes, chillaxing, chillaxed**) V-I If you **chillax**, you relax and take time out from doing work. [INFORMAL] ❏ *He spent the weekend chillaxing at his beach house.*

chill|er /tʃɪlər/ (**chillers**) N-COUNT A **chiller** is a very frightening movie or novel.

chil|li /tʃɪli/ (**chillies** or **chillis**) [mainly BRIT] → see **chili**

chill|ing /tʃɪlɪŋ/ ADJ If you describe something as **chilling**, you mean that it is frightening. ❏ *He described in chilling detail how he attacked her.* • **chill|ing|ly** ADV ❏ *...the murder of a Chicago teenager in chillingly similar circumstances in February.*

chil|ly /tʃɪli/ (**chillier, chilliest**) **1** ADJ Something that is **chilly** is unpleasantly cold. ❏ *It was a chilly afternoon.* **2** ADJ [v-link ADJ] If you feel **chilly**, you feel rather cold. ❏ *I'm a bit chilly.*

chime /tʃaɪm/ (**chimes, chiming, chimed**) **1** V-T/V-I When a bell or a clock **chimes**, it makes ringing sounds. ❏ *He heard the front doorbell chime.* ❏ *...as the town hall clock chimed three o'clock.* **2** N-COUNT A **chime** is a ringing sound made by a bell, especially when it is part of a clock. ❏ *At that moment a chime sounded from the front of the house.* **3** N-PLURAL **Chimes** are a set of small objects which make a ringing sound when they are blown by the wind. ❏ *...the haunting sound of the wind chimes.*

▶ **chime in** PHRASAL VERB If you **chime in**, you say something just after someone else has spoken. ❏ *"Why?" Pete asked impatiently.—"Yes, why?" Bob chimed in. "It seems like a good idea to me."*

chi|mera /kaɪmɪərə/ (**chimeras**) **1** N-COUNT A **chimera** is an unrealistic idea that you have about something or a hope that you have that is unlikely to be fulfilled. [FORMAL] ❏ *Religious unity remained as much a chimera as ever.* **2** N-COUNT In Greek mythology, a **chimera** is a creature with the head of a lion, the body of a goat, and the tail of a snake.

chim|ney /tʃɪmni/ (**chimneys**) N-COUNT A **chimney** is a pipe through which smoke goes up into the air, usually through the roof of a building. ❏ *Thick, yellow smoke pours constantly out of the chimneys at the steel plant in Katowice.*

chim|ney pot (**chimney pots**) also **chimney-pot** N-COUNT A **chimney pot** is a short, clay pipe which is fixed on top of a chimney.

chim|ney sweep (**chimney sweeps**) N-COUNT A **chimney sweep** is a person whose job is to clean the soot out of chimneys.

chimp /tʃɪmp/ (**chimps**) N-COUNT A **chimp** is the same as a **chimpanzee**. [INFORMAL]

chim|pan|zee /tʃɪmpænzi/ (**chimpanzees**) N-COUNT A **chimpanzee** is a kind of small African ape.

chin /tʃɪn/ (**chins**) N-COUNT Your **chin** is the part of your face that is below your mouth and above your neck. ❏ *...a double chin.*

chi|na /tʃaɪnə/ **1** N-UNCOUNT **China** is a hard white substance made from clay. It is used to make things such as cups, bowls, plates, and ornaments. ❏ *...a small bowl made of china.* **2** N-UNCOUNT Cups, bowls, plates, and ornaments made of china are referred to as **china**. ❏ *Judy collects blue and white china.*

China|town /tʃaɪnətaʊn/ N-UNCOUNT **Chinatown** is the name given to the area in a city where there are many Chinese stores and restaurants, and which is a social center for the Chinese community in the city.

chin|chil|la /tʃɪntʃɪlə/ (**chinchillas**) N-COUNT A **chinchilla** is a small furry animal that is bred for its valuable fur.

Chi|nese /tʃaɪniz/ (**Chinese**) **1** ADJ Something that is **Chinese** relates or belongs to China or its languages or people. • N-COUNT [usu pl] The **Chinese** are the people who come from China. **2** N-UNCOUNT The languages that are spoken in China, especially Mandarin, are often referred to as **Chinese**.

chink /tʃɪŋk/ (**chinks**) **1** N-COUNT A **chink** in a surface is a very narrow crack or opening in it. ❏ *...a chink in the wall.* **2** N-COUNT A **chink of** light is a small patch of light that shines through a small opening in something. ❏ *I noticed a chink of light at the end of the corridor.*

chi|nos /tʃiːnoʊz/ N-PLURAL [also *a pair of* N] **Chinos** are casual, loose pants made from cotton.

chintz /tʃɪnts/ (**chintzes**) N-MASS **Chintz** is a cotton fabric decorated with flowery patterns. ❏ *...chintz curtains.*

chintzy /tʃɪntsi/ (**chintzier, chintziest**) **1** ADJ If you describe something as **chintzy**, you mean that it is showy and looks cheap. [mainly AM, DISAPPROVAL] ❏ *...a chintzy table lamp.* **2** ADJ You can describe someone as **chintzy** if they are mean and seem to spend very little money compared with other people. [AM, INFORMAL, DISAPPROVAL] ❏ *I knew I couldn't afford one of their fabled handbags on my chintzy budget.*

chip ✦◇◇ /tʃɪp/ (**chips, chipping, chipped**) **1** N-COUNT **Chips** or **potato chips** are very thin slices of fried potato that are eaten as a snack. [AM] ❏ *...a package of onion-flavored potato chips.*

in BRIT, use **crisps**

2 N-COUNT **Chips** are long, thin pieces of potato fried in oil or fat and eaten hot, usually with a meal. [BRIT]

> in AM, use **French fries**

3 N-COUNT A silicon **chip** is a very small piece of silicon with electronic circuits on it which is part of a computer or other piece of machinery. ❑ ...*an electronic card containing a chip.* **4** N-COUNT A **chip** is a small piece of something or a small piece which has been broken off something. ❑ *It contains real chocolate chips.* **5** N-COUNT A **chip** in something such as a piece of china or furniture is where a small piece has been broken off it. ❑ *The cup had a small chip.* **6** N-COUNT **Chips** are plastic counters used in gambling to represent money. ❑ *He put the pile of chips in the center of the table and drew a card.* **7** V-T/V-I If you **chip** something or if it **chips**, a small piece is broken off it. ❑ *The blow chipped the woman's tooth.* • **chipped** ADJ ❑ *The wagon's paint was badly chipped on the outside.* **8** → see also **bargaining chip**, **blue chip**

▶ **chip in** PHRASAL VERB When a number of people **chip in**, each person gives some money so that they can pay for something together. [INFORMAL] ❑ *They chip in for the gas.*

chip|board /tʃɪpbɔrd/ N-UNCOUNT **Chipboard** is a hard material made out of very small pieces of wood which have been pressed together. It is often used for making doors and furniture.

chip|munk /tʃɪpmʌŋk/ (chipmunks) N-COUNT A **chipmunk** is a small animal with a large, furry tail and a striped back.

Chippendale /tʃɪpəndeɪl/ ADJ [ADJ n] **Chippendale** is a style of furniture from the eighteenth century. ❑ ...*a pair of Chippendale chairs.*

chip|per /tʃɪpər/ ADJ **Chipper** means cheerful and lively. [OLD-FASHIONED]

chip|pings /tʃɪpɪŋz/ N-PLURAL [usu n N] Wood **chippings** or stone **chippings** are small pieces of wood or stone which are used, for example, to cover surfaces such as paths or roads.

chi|ropo|dist /kɪrɒpədɪst/ (chiropodists) N-COUNT A **chiropodist** is a person whose job is to treat and care for people's feet.

chi|ropo|dy /kɪrɒpədi/ N-UNCOUNT **Chiropody** is the same as **podiatry**. [BRIT]

chi|ro|prac|tic /kaɪrəpræktɪk/ N-UNCOUNT **Chiropractic** is the treatment of injuries by pressing and moving people's joints, especially the spine.

chi|ro|prac|tor /kaɪrəpræktər/ (chiropractors) N-COUNT A **chiropractor** is a person who treats injuries by chiropractic.

chirp /tʃɜrp/ (chirps, chirping, chirped) **1** V-I When a bird or an insect such as a cricket or grasshopper **chirps**, it makes short, high-pitched sounds. ❑ *The crickets chirped faster and louder.* • N-COUNT **Chirp** is also a noun. ❑ *The chirps of the garden birds sounded distant.* • **chirp|ing** N-UNCOUNT ❑ ...*the chirping of birds.* **2** → See feature box at **sound**

chirpy /tʃɜrpi/ (chirpier, chirpiest) ADJ If you describe a person or their behavior as **chirpy**, you mean they are very cheerful and lively. [INFORMAL] ❑ ...*the showbiz world of chirpy chorus girls.* ❑ *She sounded quite chirpy, all she needs is rest.*

chir|rup /tʃɪrəp, tʃɜr-/ (chirrups, chirruping, chirruped) V-T/V-I If a person or bird **chirrups**, they make short, high-pitched sounds. ❑ *"My gosh," she chirruped.* ❑ *I woke up to the sound of larks chirruping.*

chis|el /tʃɪzəl/ (chisels, chiseling or chiselling, chiseled or chiselled) **1** N-COUNT A **chisel** is a tool that has a long metal blade with a sharp edge at the end. It is used for cutting and shaping wood and stone. ❑ ...*a hammer and chisel.* **2** V-T If you **chisel** wood or stone, you cut and shape it using a chisel. ❑ *He set out to chisel a dog out of sandstone.* **3** → See also color supplement

chis|eled /tʃɪzəld/ also **chiselled** **1** ADJ [usu ADJ n] If you say that someone, usually a man, has **chiseled** features, you mean that their face has a strong, clear bone structure. ❑ *His chiseled features resembled a stony mask.* ❑ ...*a chiseled jaw.* **2** → See feature box at **appearance**

chit /tʃɪt/ (chits) N-COUNT A **chit** is a short official note, such as a receipt, an order, or a memo, usually signed by someone in authority. [MILITARY] ❑ *Schrader initialed the chit for the barman.*

chit|chat /tʃɪtʃæt/ also **chit-chat** N-UNCOUNT **Chitchat** is informal talk about things that are not very important. ❑ *Not being a mother, I found the chitchat exceedingly dull.*

chiv|al|ric /ʃɪvælrɪk/ ADJ [ADJ n] **Chivalric** means relating to or connected with the system of chivalry that was believed in and followed by medieval knights. ❑ ...*chivalric ideals.*

chiv|al|rous /ʃɪvəlrəs/ ADJ A **chivalrous** man is polite, kind, and unselfish, especially toward women. [APPROVAL] ❑ *He was handsome, upright, and chivalrous.*

chiv|al|ry /ʃɪvəlri/ **1** N-UNCOUNT **Chivalry** is polite, kind, and unselfish behavior, especially by men toward women. ❑ *Marie seemed to revel in his old-fashioned chivalry.* **2** N-UNCOUNT In the Middle Ages, **chivalry** was the set of rules and way of behaving which knights were expected to follow. ❑ ...*the age of chivalry.*

chives /tʃaɪvz/ N-PLURAL **Chives** are the long, thin, hollow green leaves of a herb with purple flowers. Chives are cut into small pieces and added to food to give it a flavor similar to onions.

chla|myd|ia /kləmɪdiə/ N-UNCOUNT **Chlamydia** is a sexually transmitted disease.

chlo|ride /klɔraɪd/ (chlorides) N-MASS [oft n N] **Chloride** is a chemical compound of chlorine and another substance. ❑ *The scientific name for common salt is sodium chloride.*

chlo|rin|ated /klɔrɪneɪtɪd/ ADJ [usu ADJ n] **Chlorinated** water, for example drinking water or water in a swimming pool, has been cleaned by adding chlorine to it. ❑ ...*swimming in chlorinated pools.*

chlo|rine /klɔrin/ N-UNCOUNT **Chlorine** is a strong-smelling gas that is used to clean water and to make cleaning products.

chloro|fluoro|car|bon /klɔroʊfluəroʊkɑrbən/ (chlorofluorocarbons) N-COUNT **Chlorofluorocarbons** are the same as **CFCs**.

chlo|ro|form /klɔrəfɔrm/ N-UNCOUNT **Chloroform** is a colorless liquid with a strong, sweet smell, which makes you unconscious if you breathe its vapor.

chlo|ro|phyll /klɔrəfɪl/ N-UNCOUNT **Chlorophyll** is a green substance in plants which enables them to use the energy from sunlight in order to grow.

chock-a-block /tʃɒk ə blɒk/ ADJ [v-link ADJ] A place that is **chock-a-block** is very full of people, things, or vehicles. [INFORMAL] ❑ *The small roads are chock-a-block with traffic.*

chock-full ADJ [v-link ADJ] Something that is **chock-full** is completely full. [INFORMAL] ❑ *The 32-page catalog is chock-full of things that add fun to festive occasions.*

cho|co|hol|ic /tʃɒkəhɒlɪk/ (chocoholics) N-COUNT A **chocoholic** is someone who eats a great deal of chocolate and finds it hard to stop themselves from eating it. [INFORMAL] ❑ *The Confectionery Warehouse is a chocoholic's dream.*

choco|late ✦◇◇ /tʃɒkəlɪt, tʃɒklɪt/ (chocolates) **1** N-MASS **Chocolate** is a sweet, hard food made from cacao. It is usually brown in color and is eaten as a candy. ❑ ...*a bar of chocolate.* ❑ *Do you want some chocolate?* **2** N-UNCOUNT **Chocolate** or **hot chocolate** is a drink made from a powder containing chocolate. It is usually made with hot milk. ❑ ...*a small cafeteria where the visitors can buy tea, coffee and chocolate.* **3** N-COUNT **Chocolates** are small candies or nuts covered with a layer of chocolate. They are usually sold in a box. ❑ ...*a box of chocolates.* **4** COLOR **Chocolate** is used to describe things that are dark brown in color. ❑ *The curtains and the bedspread were chocolate velvet.*

━━━━━ **WORD HISTORY** ━━━━━

chocolate
Europeans were first introduced to chocolate at the court of the Aztec king Montezuma II in the 16th century. **Chocolate** or *xocolatl* was a bitter Aztec drink made from cocoa beans. The name *xocolatl* means 'bitter water,' from Aztec *xococ*, meaning 'bitter,' and *atl*, meaning 'water.'

choice ✦✦◇ /tʃɔɪs/ (choices, choicer, choicest) **1** N-COUNT If there is a **choice** of things, there are several of them and you can choose the one you want. ❑ *It's available in a choice of colors.* ❑ *At lunchtime, there's a choice between the buffet or the set menu.*

2 N-COUNT Your **choice** is someone or something that you choose from a range of things. ❑ *Although he was only grumbling, his choice of words made Rodney angry.* **3** ADJ [ADJ n] **Choice** means of very high quality. [FORMAL] ❑ *...a box of their choicest chocolates.* **4** PHRASE If you **have no choice** but to do something or **have little choice** but to do it, you cannot avoid doing it. ❑ *They had little choice but to agree to what he suggested.* **5** PHRASE The thing or person **of** your **choice** is the one that you choose. ❑ *...tickets to see the football team of your choice.* **6** PHRASE The item **of choice** is the one that most people prefer. ❑ *The drug is set to become the treatment of choice for asthma worldwide.*

COLLOCATIONS

choice
NOUN
1
adjective + **choice**: wide
verb + **choice**: offer, provide; limit, restrict
2
noun + **choice**: career, lifestyle
adjective + **choice**: informed, obvious, popular, rational
verb + **choice**: affect, determine, govern, influence; make

---

choir /kwaɪər/ (**choirs**) N-COUNT A **choir** is a group of people who sing together, for example in a church or school. ❑ *He has been singing in his church choir since he was six.*

choir|boy /kwaɪərbɔɪ/ (**choirboys**) N-COUNT A **choirboy** is a boy who sings in a church choir.

choir|girl /kwaɪərgɜrl/ (**choirgirls**) N-COUNT A **choirgirl** is a girl who sings in a church choir.

choir|master /kwaɪərmæstər/ (**choirmasters**) N-COUNT A **choirmaster** is a person whose job is to train a choir.

choke /tʃoʊk/ (**chokes, choking, choked**) **1** V-T/V-I When you **choke** or when something **chokes** you, you cannot breathe properly or get enough air into your lungs. ❑ *A small child could choke on the doll's hair.* ❑ *Dense smoke swirled and billowed, its rank fumes choking her.* ❑ *The girl choked to death after breathing in smoke.* **2** V-T To **choke** someone means to squeeze their neck until they are dead. ❑ *The men pushed him into the entrance of a nearby building, where they choked him with his tie.* **3** V-T [usu passive] If a place **is choked** with things or people, it is full of them and they prevent movement in it. ❑ *The village's roads are choked with traffic.* **4** N-COUNT The **choke** in a car, truck, or other vehicle is a device that reduces the amount of air going into the engine and makes it easier to start. ❑ *It is like driving your car with the choke out all the time.*

choked /tʃoʊkt/ ADJ [ADJ n, v-link ADJ with n] If you say something in a **choked** voice or if your voice is **choked with** emotion, your voice does not have its full sound, because you are upset or frightened. ❑ *"Why did Ben do that?" she asked, in a choked voice.* ❑ *One young conscript rose with a message of thanks, his voice choked with emotion.*

chok|er /tʃoʊkər/ (**chokers**) N-COUNT A **choker** is a necklace or band of material that fits very closely around someone's neck. ❑ *...a pearl choker.*

chol|era /kɒlərə/ N-UNCOUNT **Cholera** is a serious disease that often kills people. It is caused by drinking infected water or by eating infected food. ❑ *...a cholera epidemic.*

chol|er|ic /kɒlərɪk/ ADJ A **choleric** person gets angry very easily. You can also use **choleric** to describe a person who is very angry. [FORMAL] ❑ *...his choleric disposition.* ❑ *He was affable at one moment, choleric the next.*

cho|les|ter|ol /kəlɛstərɒl/ **1** N-UNCOUNT **Cholesterol** is a substance that exists in the fat, tissues, and blood of all animals. Too much cholesterol in a person's blood can cause heart disease. ❑ *...a dangerously high cholesterol level.* **2** → See feature box at **nutrition**

chomp /tʃɒmp/ (**chomps, chomping, chomped**) V-T/V-I If a person or an animal **chomps** their way through food or **chomps** on food, they chew it noisily. [INFORMAL] ❑ *On the diet I would chomp my way through breakfast, even though I'm never hungry in the morning.* ❑ *I lost a tooth while chomping on a French baguette!*

choose /tʃuz/ (**chooses, choosing, chose, chosen**) **1** V-T/V-I If you **choose** someone or something from several

people or things that are available, you decide which person or thing you want to have. ❑ *They will be able to choose their own leaders in democratic elections.* ❑ *There are several patchwork cushions to choose from.* **2** V-T/V-I If you **choose** to do something, you do it because you want to or because you feel that it is right. ❑ *They knew that discrimination was going on, but chose to ignore it.* ❑ *You have the right to remain silent if you choose.*

choosy /tʃuzi/ (**choosier, choosiest**) ADJ Someone who is **choosy** is difficult to please because they will only accept something if it is exactly what they want or if it is of very high quality. [mainly INFORMAL] ❑ *Skiers should be particularly choosy about the insurance policy they buy.*

chop ♦◇◇ /tʃɒp/ (**chops, chopping, chopped**) **1** V-T If you **chop** something, you cut it into pieces with strong, downward movements of a knife or an ax. ❑ *Chop the butter into small pieces.* ❑ *Visitors were set to work chopping wood.* **2** N-COUNT A **chop** is a small piece of meat cut from the ribs of a sheep or pig. ❑ *...grilled lamb chops.* **3** → See feature box at **cooking**
▶ **chop down** PHRASAL VERB If you **chop down** a tree, you cut through its trunk with an ax so that it falls to the ground. ❑ *Sometimes they have to chop down a tree for firewood.*
▶ **chop off** PHRASAL VERB To **chop off** something such as a part of someone's body means to cut it off. ❑ *She chopped off her golden, waist-length hair.*
▶ **chop up** PHRASAL VERB If you **chop** something **up**, you chop it into small pieces. ❑ *Chop up three firm tomatoes.*

SYNONYMS

chop
VERB **1**
cut: *Cut the tomatoes in half vertically.*
fell: *Badly-infected trees should be felled and burned.*
slash: *He came within two minutes of bleeding to death after slashing his wrists.*
hack: *We undertook the task of hacking our way through the jungle.*

---

chop|per /tʃɒpər/ (**choppers**) N-COUNT A **chopper** is a helicopter. [INFORMAL] ❑ *Overhead, the chopper roared and the big blades churned the air.*

chop|ping board (**chopping boards**) N-COUNT A **chopping board** is the same as a **cutting board**. [mainly BRIT]

chop|py /tʃɒpi/ (**choppier, choppiest**) **1** ADJ When water is **choppy**, there are a lot of small waves on it because there is a wind blowing. ❑ *A gale was blowing and the sea was choppy.* **2** → See feature box at **boat**

chop|stick /tʃɒpstɪk/ (**chopsticks**) N-COUNT [usu pl] **Chopsticks** are a pair of thin sticks which people in China and the Far East use to eat their food.

chop suey /tʃɒp sui/ N-UNCOUNT **Chop suey** is a Chinese-style dish that consists of meat and vegetables that have been stewed together.

cho|ral /kɔrəl/ **1** ADJ **Choral** music is sung by a choir. ❑ *His collection of choral music from around the world is called "Voices."* **2** → See feature box at **music**

cho|rale /kəræl, -rɑl/ (**chorales**) **1** N-COUNT A **chorale** is a piece of music sung as part of a church service. ❑ *...a Bach chorale.* **2** N-COUNT A **chorale** is a group of people who sing together. [AM]

chord /kɔrd/ (**chords**) **1** N-COUNT A **chord** is a number of musical notes played or sung at the same time with a pleasing effect. ❑ *I could play a few chords on the guitar and sing a song.* **2** PHRASE If something **strikes a chord** with you, it makes you feel sympathy or enthusiasm. ❑ *Mr. Jenkins's arguments for stability struck a chord with Europe's two most powerful politicians.* **3** → See feature box at **music**

chore /tʃɔr/ (**chores**) **1** N-COUNT A **chore** is a task that you must do but that you find unpleasant or boring. ❑ *She sees exercise primarily as an unavoidable chore.* **2** → See feature box at **housework**

cho|reo|graph /kɔriəgræf/ (**choreographs, choreographing, choreographed**) V-T/V-I When someone **choreographs** a ballet or other dance, they invent the steps and movements and tell the dancers how to perform them. ❑ *Achim had choreographed the dance in Act II himself.*

cho|reo|graphed /kɔ̱riəgræft/ ADJ You describe an activity involving several people as **choreographed** when it is arranged but is intended to appear natural. ◻ ...*a carefully choreographed White House meeting between the two presidents.*

cho|reog|ra|pher /kɔ̱riɒ̱grəfər/ (**choreographers**) N-COUNT A **choreographer** is someone who invents the movements for a ballet or other dance and tells the dancers how to perform them.

cho|reo|graph|ic /kɒ̱riəgræ̱fɪk/ ADJ [usu ADJ n] **Choreographic** means relating to or connected with choreography. ◻ ...*his choreographic work for The Royal Ballet.*

cho|reog|ra|phy /kɒ̱riɒ̱grəfi/ N-UNCOUNT **Choreography** is the inventing of steps and movements for ballets and other dances. ◻ *The choreography of Eric Hawkins is considered radical by ballet audiences.*

chor|is|ter /kɒ̱rɪstər/ (**choristers**) N-COUNT A **chorister** is a singer in a church choir.

chor|tle /tʃɔ̱ː(r)təl/ (**chortles, chortling, chortled**) V-I To **chortle** means to laugh in a way that shows you are very pleased. [WRITTEN] ◻ *There was silence for a moment, then Larry began chortling like an idiot.* • N-COUNT **Chortle** is also a noun. ◻ *He gave a chortle.*

cho|rus /kɔ̱ːrəs/ (**choruses, chorusing, chorused**) ◨ N-COUNT A **chorus** is a part of a song which is repeated after each verse. ◻ *Caroline sang two verses and the chorus of her song.* ◨ N-COUNT A **chorus** is a large group of people who sing together. ◻ *The chorus was singing "The Ode to Joy".* ◨ N-COUNT A **chorus** is a piece of music written to be sung by a large group of people. ◻ ...*the Hallelujah Chorus.* ◨ N-COUNT A **chorus** is a group of singers or dancers who perform together in a show, in contrast to the soloists. ◻ *Students played the lesser parts and sang in the chorus.* ◨ N-COUNT-COLL In drama, a **chorus** is an actor or a group of actors who comment on the action of the play. ◻ *He decides to sort out her life for her, while a pushy Greek chorus dispenses advice from the sidelines.* ◻ ...*commanding performances from Joe Savino as the chorus and Stephen Brennan as the ghost.* ◨ N-COUNT When there is a **chorus** of criticism, disapproval, or praise, that attitude is expressed by a lot of people at the same time. ◻ *The government is defending its economic policies against a growing chorus of criticism.* ◨ V-T When people **chorus** something, they say it or sing it together. [WRITTEN] ◻ *"Hi," they chorused.*

cho|rus girl (**chorus girls**) N-COUNT A **chorus girl** is a young woman who sings or dances as part of a group in a show or movie.

chose /tʃoʊz/ **Chose** is the past tense of **choose**.

cho|sen /tʃoʊzən/ **Chosen** is the past participle of **choose**.

chow /tʃaʊ/ (**chows, chowing, chowed**) ◨ N-UNCOUNT Food can be referred to as **chow**. [AM, INFORMAL] ◻ *Help yourself to some chow.* ◨ N-COUNT A **chow** is a kind of dog that has a thick coat and a curled tail. Chows originally came from China.
▶ **chow down** PHRASAL VERB If you **chow down** on something, you eat a large amount of it quickly and with enthusiasm. [mainly AM, INFORMAL] ◻ *Shane was chowing down on a mammoth hamburger.*

chow|der /tʃaʊdər/ (**chowders**) N-MASS [usu n N] **Chowder** is a thick soup containing pieces of fish.

chow mein /tʃaʊ meɪn/ N-UNCOUNT **Chow mein** is a Chinese-style dish that consists of fried noodles, cooked meat, and vegetables. ◻ ...*chicken chow mein.*

Christ /kraɪst/ N-PROPER **Christ** is one of the names of Jesus, whom Christians believe to be the son of God and whose teachings are the basis of Christianity. ◻ ...*the teachings of Christ.*

chris|ten /krɪ̱sən/ (**christens, christening, christened**) V-T [usu passive] When a baby **is christened**, he or she is given a name during the Christian ceremony of baptism. Compare **baptize**. ◻ *She was born in March and christened in June.*

Chris|ten|dom /krɪ̱səndəm/ N-PROPER All the Christian people and countries in the world can be referred to as **Christendom**. [OLD-FASHIONED]

chris|ten|ing /krɪ̱sənɪŋ/ (**christenings**) N-COUNT A **christening** is a Christian ceremony in which a baby is made a member of the Christian Church and is officially given his or her name. Compare **baptism**. ◻ ...*my granddaughter's christening.*

Christian ✦✧ /krɪ̱stʃən/ (**Christians**) ◨ N-COUNT A **Christian** is someone who follows the teachings of Jesus Christ. ◻ *He was a devout Christian.* ◨ ADJ **Christian** means relating to Christianity or Christians. ◻ ...*the Christian Church.* ◻ *Most of my friends are Christian.*

Chris|ti|an|ity /krɪ̱stiæ̱nɪti/ N-UNCOUNT **Christianity** is a religion that is based on the teachings of Jesus Christ and the belief that he was the son of God. ◻ *He converted to Christianity that day.*

Christian name (**Christian names**) N-COUNT Some people refer to their first names as their **Christian names**. ◻ *Despite my attempts to get him to call me by my Christian name, he insisted on addressing me as "Mr. Kennedy."*

Christian Sci|ence N-UNCOUNT [oft N n] **Christian Science** is a type of Christianity which emphasizes the use of prayer to cure illness. ◻ ...*members of the Christian Science Church.*

Christ|mas ✦✧ /krɪ̱sməs/ (**Christmases**) ◨ N-VAR **Christmas** is a Christian festival when the birth of Jesus Christ is celebrated. Christmas is celebrated on the 25th of December. ◻ *The day after Christmas is generally a busy one for retailers.* ◨ N-VAR **Christmas** is the period of several days around and including Christmas Day. ◻ *During the Christmas holidays there's a tremendous amount of traffic between the Northeast and Florida.*

Christ|mas card (**Christmas cards**) N-COUNT **Christmas cards** are cards with greetings, which people send to their friends and family at Christmas.

Christ|mas Day N-UNCOUNT **Christmas Day** is the 25th of December, when Christmas is celebrated.

Christ|mas Eve N-UNCOUNT **Christmas Eve** is the 24th of December, the day before Christmas Day.

Christ|mas stock|ing (**Christmas stockings**) N-COUNT A **Christmas stocking** is a long sock which children hang up on Christmas Eve. During the night, parents fill the stocking with small presents.

Christ|massy /krɪ̱sməsi/ also **Christmasy** ADJ Something that is **Christmassy** is typical of or suitable for Christmas. [INFORMAL] ◻ *Choose Christmassy colors such as red and green.*

Christ|mas tree (**Christmas trees**) N-COUNT A **Christmas tree** is a fir tree, or an artificial tree that looks like a fir tree, which people put in their houses at Christmas and decorate with colored lights and ornaments.

chro|mat|ic /krəmæ̱tɪk/ ◨ ADJ In music, **chromatic** means related to the scale that consists only of semitones. ◻ ...*the notes of the chromatic scale.* ◨ ADJ [usu ADJ n] **Chromatic** means related to colors.

chrome /kroʊm/ N-UNCOUNT **Chrome** is metal plated with chromium. ◻ ...*old-fashioned chrome taps.*

chro|mium /kroʊ̱miəm/ N-UNCOUNT **Chromium** is a hard, shiny, metallic element, used to make steel alloys and to coat other metals. ◻ ...*chromium-plated fire accessories.*

chro|mo|so|mal /kroʊməsoʊ̱məl/ ADJ [ADJ n] **Chromosomal** means relating to or connected with chromosomes. ◻ ...*chromosomal abnormalities.*

chro|mo|some /kroʊ̱məsoʊm/ (**chromosomes**) ◨ N-COUNT A **chromosome** is a part of a cell in an animal or plant. It contains genes which determine what characteristics the animal or plant will have. ◻ *Each cell of our bodies contains 46 chromosomes.* ◨ → See feature box at **genetics**

chron|ic /krɒ̱nɪk/ ◨ ADJ A **chronic** illness or disability lasts for a very long time. Compare **acute**. ◻ ...*chronic back pain.* • **chroni|cal|ly** /krɒ̱nɪkli/ ADV [ADV adj/-ed] ◻ *Most of them were chronically ill.* ◨ ADJ [ADJ n] You can describe someone's bad habits or behavior as **chronic** when they have behaved like that for a long time and do not seem to be able to stop themselves. ◻ ...*a chronic worrier.* ◨ ADJ A **chronic** situation or problem is very severe and unpleasant. ◻ *One cause of the artist's suicide seems to have been chronic poverty.* • **chroni|cal|ly** ADV [ADV adj/-ed] ◻ *Research and technology are said to be chronically underfunded.*

chron|ic fa|tigue syn|drome N-UNCOUNT **Chronic fatigue syndrome** is an illness that is thought to be caused by a virus, and which affects people for a long period of time. Its symptoms include tiredness and aching muscles. The abbreviation **CFS** is often used.

chroni|cle /krɒnɪkəl/ (chronicles, chronicling, chronicled) **1** V-T To **chronicle** a series of events means to write about them or show them in broadcasts in the order in which they happened. ❑ *The series chronicles the everyday adventures of two eternal bachelors.* **2** N-COUNT A **chronicle** is an account or record of a series of events. ❑ *...this vast chronicle of Napoleonic times.* **3** N-IN-NAMES **Chronicle** is sometimes used as part of the name of a newspaper. ❑ *...the San Francisco Chronicle.*

chrono|logi|cal /krɒnəlɒdʒɪkəl/ ADJ If things are described or shown in **chronological** order, they are described or shown in the order in which they happened. ❑ *I have arranged these stories in chronological order.* • **chrono|logi|cal|ly** ADV ❑ *The exhibition is organized chronologically.*

chro|nol|ogy /krənɒlədʒi/ (chronologies) **1** N-UNCOUNT [oft N *of* n] The **chronology** of a series of past events is the times at which they happened in the order in which they happened. ❑ *She gave him a factual account of the chronology of her brief liaison.* **2** N-COUNT [oft N *of* n] A **chronology** is an account or record of the times and the order in which a series of past events took place. ❑ *The second part of Duffy's book is a detailed chronology of the Reformation.*

chro|nom|eter /krənɒmɪtər/ (chronometers) N-COUNT A **chronometer** is an extremely accurate clock that is used especially by sailors at sea.

chrysa|lis /krɪsəlɪs/ (chrysalises) **1** N-COUNT A **chrysalis** is a butterfly or moth in the stage between being a larva and an adult. **2** N-COUNT A **chrysalis** is the hard, protective covering that a chrysalis has. ❑ *...a butterfly emerging from its chrysalis.*

chry|san|themum /krɪsænθəməm/ (chrysanthemums) N-COUNT A **chrysanthemum** is a large garden flower with many long, thin petals.

chub|by /tʃʌbi/ (chubbier, chubbiest) **1** ADJ A **chubby** person is somewhat fat. ❑ *Do you think I'm too chubby?* **2** → See feature box at **appearance**

chuck /tʃʌk/ (chucks, chucking, chucked) **1** V-T When you **chuck** something somewhere, you throw it there in a casual or careless way. [INFORMAL] ❑ *I took a great dislike to the clock, so I chucked it in the trash.* **2** V-T If you **chuck** your job or some other activity, you stop doing it. [INFORMAL] ❑ *Last summer, he chucked his 10-year career as a stockbroker and headed for the mountains.* **3** PHRASE If someone **chucks it all**, they stop doing their job, and usually move somewhere else. ❑ *Sometimes I'd like to chuck it all and go fishing.* **4** N-COUNT A **chuck** is a device for holding a tool in a machine such as a drill. **5** N-UNCOUNT **Chuck** is a cut of beef.

chuck|le /tʃʌkəl/ (chuckles, chuckling, chuckled) V-I When you **chuckle**, you laugh quietly. ❑ *The banker chuckled and said, "Of course not."* • N-COUNT **Chuckle** is also a noun. ❑ *He gave a little chuckle.*

chug /tʃʌɡ/ (chugs, chugging, chugged) **1** V-I When a vehicle **chugs** somewhere, it goes there slowly, noisily, and with difficulty. ❑ *The train chugs down the track.* **2** V-T If you **chug** something, you drink it very quickly without stopping. [AM, INFORMAL] ❑ *Nadine chugs her beer and orders another.*

chum /tʃʌm/ (chums) N-COUNT [usu with poss] Your **chum** is your friend. [INFORMAL, OLD-FASHIONED] ❑ *...his old chum Anthony.*

chum|my /tʃʌmi/ (chummier, chummiest) ADJ If people or social events are **chummy**, they are pleasant and friendly. [INFORMAL, OLD-FASHIONED]

chump /tʃʌmp/ (chumps) N-COUNT If you call someone a **chump**, you are telling them that they have done something rather stupid or foolish, or that they are always doing stupid things. [INFORMAL, DISAPPROVAL] ❑ *The guy's a chump. I could do a better job myself.*

chunk /tʃʌŋk/ (chunks) **1** N-COUNT **Chunks** of something are thick, solid pieces of it. ❑ *They had to be careful of floating chunks of ice.* ❑ *...a chunk of meat.* **2** N-COUNT A **chunk** of something is a large amount or large part of it. [INFORMAL] ❑ *The company owns a chunk of farmland near the airport.*

chunky /tʃʌŋki/ (chunkier, chunkiest) **1** ADJ A **chunky** person is broad and heavy. ❑ *The soprano was a chunky girl from California.* **2** ADJ A **chunky** object is large and thick. ❑ *Her taste in fiction was for chunky historical romances.* ❑ *...a chunky sweater.*

church ♦♦◇ /tʃɜːrtʃ/ (churches) **1** N-VAR A **church** is a building in which Christians worship. You refer to this place as **church** when you are talking about the time that people spend there. ❑ *...one of the country's most historic churches.* ❑ *...St Helen's Church.* ❑ *The family had gone to church.* **2** N-COUNT A **Church** is one of the groups of people within the Christian religion, for example Catholics or Methodists, that have their own beliefs, clergy, and forms of worship. ❑ *...cooperation with the Catholic Church.* ❑ *Church leaders said he was welcome to return.*

church|goer /tʃɜːrtʃɡoʊər/ (churchgoers) N-COUNT A **churchgoer** is a person who goes to church regularly.

church|man /tʃɜːrtʃmən/ (churchmen) N-COUNT A **churchman** is the same as a **clergyman**. [FORMAL]

Church of Eng|land N-PROPER [the N] **The Church of England** is the main church in England. It has the monarch as its head and it does not recognize the authority of the Pope.

church school (church schools) N-COUNT A **church school** is a school which has a special relationship with a particular branch of the Christian Church, and where there is strong emphasis on worship and the teaching of religion.

church|woman /tʃɜːrtʃwʊmən/ (churchwomen) N-COUNT A **churchwoman** is the same as a **clergywoman**. [FORMAL]

church|yard /tʃɜːrtʃjɑːrd/ (churchyards) N-COUNT A **churchyard** is an area of land around a church where dead people are buried.

churl|ish /tʃɜːrlɪʃ/ ADJ Someone who is **churlish** is unfriendly, bad-tempered, or impolite. [DISAPPROVAL] ❑ *She would think him churlish if he refused.* ❑ *The room was so nice it seemed churlish to argue.*

churn /tʃɜːrn/ (churns, churning, churned) **1** N-COUNT A **churn** is a container which is used for making butter. **2** V-T If something **churns** water, mud, or dust, it moves it about violently. ❑ *...dirt roads now churned into mud by the annual rains.* • PHRASAL VERB **Churn up** means the same as **churn**. ❑ *The recent rain had churned up the waterfall into a muddy whirlpool.* ❑ *Occasionally dolphins slap the water with their tails or churn it up in play.* **3** V-T/V-I If you say that your stomach **is churning**, you mean that you feel sick. You can also say that something **churns** your stomach. ❑ *My stomach churned as I stood up.*
▸ **churn out** PHRASAL VERB To **churn out** something means to produce large quantities of it very quickly. [INFORMAL] ❑ *He began to churn out literary compositions in English.*
▸ **churn up** → see **churn** 2

churn|ing /tʃɜːrnɪŋ/ ADJ [ADJ n] **Churning** water is moving about violently. [LITERARY] ❑ *...anything to take our minds off that gap and the brown, churning water below.*

chute /ʃuːt/ (chutes) **1** N-COUNT A **chute** is a steep, narrow slope down which people or things can slide. ❑ *Passengers escaped from the plane's front exits by sliding down emergency chutes.* **2** N-COUNT A **chute** is a parachute. [INFORMAL] ❑ *You can release the chute with either hand, but it is easier to do it with the left.*

chut|ney /tʃʌtni/ (chutneys) N-MASS **Chutney** is a cold sauce made from fruit, vinegar, sugar, and spices. It is sold in jars and you eat it with meat or cheese. ❑ *...mango chutney.*

chutz|pah /hʊtspə/ also **chutzpa** N-UNCOUNT If you say that someone has **chutzpah**, you mean that you admire the fact that they are not afraid or embarrassed to do or say things that shock, surprise, or annoy other people. [APPROVAL] ❑ *Einstein had the chutzpah to discard long-established theory.*

CIA /siː aɪ eɪ/ N-PROPER [the N] **The CIA** is the government organization in the United States that collects secret information about other countries. **CIA** is an abbreviation for 'Central Intelligence Agency.'

cia|bat|ta /tʃəbɑːtə/ N-UNCOUNT **Ciabatta** or **ciabatta bread** is a type of white Italian bread that is made with olive oil.

ciao /tʃaʊ/ CONVENTION Some people say '**Ciao**' as an informal way of saying goodbye to someone who they expect to see again soon.

ci|ca|da /sɪkeɪdə/ (cicadas) N-COUNT A **cicada** is a large insect that makes a loud, high-pitched noise.

ci|der /saɪdər/ (ciders) N-MASS **Cider** is a drink made from apples. **Cider** does not usually contain alcohol, and if it does contain alcohol, it is usually called **hard cider**. In Britain,

cigar | circulate

cider usually contains alcohol. • N-COUNT A glass of cider can be referred to as a **cider**. ◻ *At the bar he ordered a cider.*

ci|gar /sɪgɑr/ (**cigars**) N-COUNT **Cigars** are rolls of dried tobacco leaves which people smoke. ◻ *He was smoking a big cigar.*

ciga|rette ♦◇◇ /sɪgərɛt/ (**cigarettes**) also **cigaret** N-COUNT **Cigarettes** are small tubes of paper containing tobacco which people smoke. ◻ *He went out to buy a packet of cigarettes.*

ciga|rette butt (**cigarette butts**)

> in BRIT, also use **cigarette end**

N-COUNT A **cigarette butt** or a **cigarette end** is the part of a cigarette that you throw away when you have finished smoking it.

ciga|rette hold|er (**cigarette holders**) N-COUNT A **cigarette holder** is a narrow tube that you can put a cigarette into in order to hold it while you smoke it.

ciga|rette light|er (**cigarette lighters**) N-COUNT A **cigarette lighter** is a device which produces a small flame when you press a switch and which you use to light a cigarette or cigar.

ci|lan|tro /sɪlæntroʊ/ N-UNCOUNT **Cilantro** is the leaves of the coriander plant that are used as an herb. [AM] ◻ *Garnish each plate with a sprig of cilantro and serve.*

C-in-C N-SING A **C-in-C** is the same as a **commander-in-chief**.

cinch /sɪntʃ/ N-SING [*a* N] If you say that something is a **cinch**, you mean that you think it is very easy to do. [INFORMAL] ◻ *It sounds difficult, but compared to full-time work it was a cinch.*

cin|der block /sɪndər blɒk/ (**cinder blocks**) also **cinderblock** N-COUNT [oft N n] A **cinder block** is a large, gray brick made from coal cinders and cement which is used for building. [AM]

> in BRIT, use **breeze-block**

Cinderella /sɪndərɛlə/ (**Cinderellas**) N-COUNT [usu sing, oft N n] If you describe a person or organization as a **Cinderella**, you mean that they receive very little attention and that they deserve to receive more. ◻ *It is a Cinderella of charities, and needs more help.*

cin|ders /sɪndərz/ N-PLURAL **Cinders** are the black pieces that are left after something such as wood or coal has burned away. ◻ *The wind sent sparks and cinders flying.*

cin|ema ♦◇◇ /sɪnəmə/ (**cinemas**) **1** N-UNCOUNT **Cinema** is the business and art of making movies. ◻ *Contemporary African cinema has much to offer.* **2** N-COUNT A **cinema** is a place where people go to watch movies for entertainment. [mainly BRIT]

> in AM, usually use **movie theater**

3 N-SING You can talk about **the cinema** when you are talking about seeing a movie. [mainly BRIT]

> in AM, usually use **the movies**

cin|emat|ic /sɪnɪmætɪk/ ADJ **Cinematic** means relating to movies made for movie theaters. ◻ *...a cinematic masterpiece.*

cin|ema|tog|ra|pher /sɪnɪmətɒgrəfər/ (**cinematographers**) N-COUNT A **cinematographer** is a person who decides what filming techniques should be used during the shooting of a movie.

cin|ema|tog|ra|phy /sɪnɪmətɒgrəfi/ N-UNCOUNT **Cinematography** is the technique of making movies. ◻ *...an admirer of Arthur Jafa's breathtaking cinematography.*

cin|na|mon /sɪnəmən/ N-UNCOUNT **Cinnamon** is a sweet spice used for flavoring food.

ci|pher /saɪfər/ (**ciphers**) also **cypher** N-COUNT A **cipher** is a secret system of writing that you use to send messages. ◻ *...converting their messages into ciphers.*

cir|ca /sɜrkə/ PREP **Circa** is used in front of a particular year to say that this is the approximate date when something happened or was made. [FORMAL] ◻ *The Romans built a fortress there circa A.D. 300 to patrol their empire's eastern border.*

cir|cle ♦♦◇ /sɜrkəl/ (**circles, circling, circled**) **1** N-COUNT A **circle** is a shape consisting of a curved line completely surrounding an area. Every point of the line is the same distance from the center of the area. ◻ *The flag was red, with a large white circle in the center.* **2** N-COUNT A **circle** of something is a round, flat piece or area of it. ◻ *Cut out 4 circles of pastry.* **3** N-COUNT A **circle** of objects or people is a group of them arranged in the shape of a circle. ◻ *...a circle of gigantic stones.* **4** N-COUNT You can refer to a group of people as a **circle** when they meet each other regularly because they are friends or because they belong to the same profession or share the same interests. ◻ *He has a small circle of friends.* **5** V-T/V-I If something **circles** an object or a place, or **circles** around it, it forms a circle around it. ◻ *This is the road that circles the city.* **6** V-T/V-I If an aircraft or a bird **circles** or **circles** something, it moves around in a circle in the air. ◻ *The plane circled, awaiting permission to land.* ◻ *There were two helicopters circling around.* **7** V-T If you **circle** something on a piece of paper, you draw a circle around it. ◻ *Circle the words on this list that you recognize.* **8** → see also **inner circle, vicious circle**
9 → See feature box at **relationship**

SYNONYMS

circle
NOUN **1**
ring: *...a ring of blue smoke.*
disc: *Most shredding machines are based on a revolving disc with replaceable blades.*

---

cir|cuit ♦◇◇ /sɜrkɪt/ (**circuits**) **1** N-COUNT An electrical **circuit** is a complete route which an electric current can flow around. ◻ *Any attempts to cut through the cabling will break the electrical circuit.* **2** → see also **closed-circuit** **3** N-COUNT A **circuit** is a series of places that are visited regularly by a person or group, especially as a part of their job. ◻ *It's a common problem, the one I'm asked about most when I'm on the lecture circuit.* **4** → See feature box at **humor**

cir|cuit board (**circuit boards**) N-COUNT A **circuit board** is the same as a **printed circuit board**.

cir|cuit break|er (**circuit breakers**) N-COUNT A **circuit breaker** is a device which can stop the flow of electricity around a circuit by switching itself off if anything goes wrong. ◻ *There is always an internal circuit breaker to protect the instrument from overload.*

cir|cui|tous /sərkjuɪtəs/ ADJ [usu ADJ n] A **circuitous** route is long and complicated rather than simple and direct. [FORMAL] ◻ *The cabdriver took them on a circuitous route to the police station.*

cir|cuit|ry /sɜrkɪtri/ N-UNCOUNT **Circuitry** is a system of electric circuits. ◻ *The computer's entire circuitry was on a single board.*

cir|cuit train|ing N-UNCOUNT **Circuit training** is a type of physical training in which you do a series of different exercises, each for a few minutes.

cir|cu|lar /sɜrkyələr/ (**circulars**) **1** ADJ Something that is **circular** is shaped like a circle. ◻ *...a circular hole twelve feet wide and two feet deep.* **2** ADJ A **circular** journey or route is one in which you go to a place and return by a different route. ◻ *Both sides of the river can be explored on this circular walk.* **3** N-COUNT A **circular** is an official letter or advertisement that is sent to a large number of people at the same time. ◻ *The proposal has been widely publicized in press information circulars sent to 1,800 newspapers.*

cir|cu|lar saw (**circular saws**) **1** N-COUNT A **circular saw** is a round metal disk with a sharp edge which is used for cutting wood and other materials. **2** → See also color supplement

cir|cu|late /sɜrkyəleɪt/ (**circulates, circulating, circulated**)
1 V-T/V-I If a piece of writing **circulates** or is **circulated**, copies of it are passed around among a group of people. ◻ *The document was previously circulated in New York at the United Nations.* ◻ *Public employees, teachers and liberals are circulating a petition for his recall.* • **cir|cu|la|tion** /sɜrkyəleɪʃən/ N-UNCOUNT ◻ *...an inquiry into the circulation of "unacceptable literature."*
2 V-T/V-I If something such as a rumor **circulates** or is **circulated**, the people in a place tell it to each other. ◻ *Rumors were already beginning to circulate that the project might have to be abandoned.* **3** V-I When something **circulates**, it moves easily and freely within a closed place or system. ◻ *...a virus which circulates via the bloodstream and causes ill health in a variety of organs.* • **cir|cu|la|tion** N-UNCOUNT ◻ *The north pole is warmer than the south and the circulation of air around it is less well contained.* **4** V-I If you **circulate** at a party, you move among the guests and talk to different people. ◻ *If you'll excuse me, I really must circulate.*

cir|cu|la|tion /sɜrkyəleɪʃ⁰n/ (circulations) **1** N-COUNT The **circulation** of a newspaper or magazine is the number of copies that are sold each time it is produced. ❑ *The Daily News once had the highest circulation of any daily in the country.* **2** N-UNCOUNT Your **circulation** is the movement of blood through your body. ❑ *Anyone with heart, lung, or circulation problems should seek medical advice before flying.* **3** → see also **circulate** **4** PHRASE If something such as money is **in circulation**, it is being used by the public. If something is **out of circulation** or has been **withdrawn from circulation**, it is no longer available for use by the public. ❑ *The supply of money in circulation was drastically reduced overnight.* ❑ *...a society like America, with perhaps 180 million guns in circulation.* **5** → See feature box at **press**

cir|cu|la|tory /sɜrkyələtɔri/ ADJ [ADJ n] **Circulatory** means relating to the circulation of blood in the body. [MEDICAL] ❑ *...the human circulatory system.*

cir|cum|cise /sɜrkəmsaɪz/ (circumcises, circumcising, circumcised) V-T [usu passive] If a boy or man **is circumcised**, the loose skin at the end of his penis is cut off. ❑ *He had been circumcised within eight days of birth as required by Jewish law.* • **cir|cum|ci|sion** /sɜrkəmsɪʒ⁰n/ N-UNCOUNT [also a N] ❑ *Jews and Moslems practice circumcision for religious reasons.*

cir|cum|fer|ence /sərkʌmfrəns/ **1** N-UNCOUNT The **circumference** of a circle, place, or round object is the distance around its edge. ❑ *...a scientist calculating the Earth's circumference.* **2** N-UNCOUNT The **circumference** of a circle, place, or round object is its edge. ❑ *Cut the salmon into long strips and wrap it round the circumference of the bread.*

cir|cum|flex /sɜrkəmflɛks/ (circumflexes) N-COUNT A **circumflex** or a **circumflex accent** is a symbol written over a vowel in French and other languages, usually to indicate that it should be pronounced longer than usual. It is used for example in the word 'rôle.'

cir|cum|lo|cu|tion /sɜrkəmloʊkyuʃ⁰n/ (circumlocutions) N-VAR A **circumlocution** is a way of saying or writing something using more words than are necessary instead of being clear and direct. [FORMAL]

cir|cum|navi|gate /sɜrkəmnævɪgeɪt/ (circumnavigates, circumnavigating, circumnavigated) V-T If someone **circumnavigates** the world or an island, they sail all the way around it. [FORMAL] ❑ *For this year at least, our race to circumnavigate the globe in less than 80 days is over.*

cir|cum|scribe /sɜrkəmskraɪb/ (circumscribes, circumscribing, circumscribed) V-T If someone's power or freedom **is circumscribed**, it is limited or restricted. [FORMAL] ❑ *The army evidently fears that, under him, its activities would be severely circumscribed.* ❑ *There are laws circumscribing the right of individual citizens to cause bodily harm to others.*

cir|cum|spect /sɜrkəmspɛkt/ ADJ If you are **circumspect**, you are cautious in what you do and say and do not take risks. [FORMAL] ❑ *The banks should have been more circumspect in their dealings.* • **cir|cum|spect|ly** ADV [ADV after v] ❑ *I would suggest that for the time being you behave as circumspectly as possible in political matters.*

cir|cum|spec|tion /sɜrkəmspɛkʃ⁰n/ N-UNCOUNT [oft with N] **Circumspection** is cautious behavior and a refusal to take risks. [FORMAL] ❑ *This is a region to be treated with circumspection.*

cir|cum|stance ♦◇◇ /sɜrkəmstæns/ (circumstances) **1** N-COUNT The **circumstances** of a particular situation are the conditions which affect what happens. ❑ *Recent opinion polls show that 60 percent favor abortion under certain circumstances.* ❑ *The strategy was too dangerous in the explosive circumstances of the times.* **2** N-PLURAL The **circumstances** of an event are the way it happened or the causes of it. ❑ *I'm making inquiries about the circumstances of Mary Dean's murder.* **3** N-PLURAL Your **circumstances** are the conditions of your life, especially the amount of money that you have. ❑ *...help and support for the single mother, whatever her circumstances.* **4** N-UNCOUNT Events and situations which cannot be controlled are sometimes referred to as **circumstance**. ❑ *There are those, you know, who, by circumstance, end up homeless.* **5** PHRASE You can emphasize that something will not or must not happen by saying that it must not or will not happen **under any circumstances**. [EMPHASIS] ❑ *Racism is wholly unacceptable under any circumstances.* **6** PHRASE You can use **in the circumstances** or **under the circumstances** before or after a statement to indicate that you have considered the conditions affecting the situation before making the statement. ❑ *In the circumstances, Paisley's plans looked highly appropriate.*

SYNONYMS

circumstance
NOUN **1**
conditions: *The conditions are ripe for the spread of disease.*
situation: *She's in a hopeless situation.*
scenario: *In the worst-case scenario, you could become a homeless person.*

---

cir|cum|stan|tial /sɜrkəmstænʃ⁰l/ ADJ [usu ADJ n] **Circumstantial** evidence is evidence that makes it seem likely that something happened, but does not prove it. [FORMAL] ❑ *Fast work by the police had started producing circumstantial evidence.*

cir|cum|vent /sɜrkəmvɛnt/ (circumvents, circumventing, circumvented) V-T If someone **circumvents** a rule or restriction, they avoid having to obey the rule or restriction, in a clever and perhaps dishonest way. [FORMAL] ❑ *Military planners tried to circumvent the treaty.*

cir|cus /sɜrkəs/ (circuses) **1** N-COUNT A **circus** is a group that consists of clowns, acrobats, and animals that travels around to different places and performs shows. ❑ *My real ambition was to work in a circus.* • N-SING The **circus** is the show performed by these people. ❑ *My dad took me to the circus.* **2** N-SING If you describe a group of people or an event as a **circus**, you disapprove of them because they attract a lot of attention but do not achieve anything useful. [DISAPPROVAL] ❑ *It could well turn into some kind of a media circus.*

cir|rho|sis /sɪroʊsɪs/ N-UNCOUNT **Cirrhosis** or **cirrhosis of the liver** is a disease which destroys a person's liver and which can kill them. It is often caused by drinking too much alcohol.

cir|rus /sɪrəs/ (cirri /sɪraɪ/) N-VAR **Cirrus** is a type of thin white cloud that forms at high altitudes. [TECHNICAL]

cis /sɪs/ ADJ Someone who is **cis** has a gender identity which fully corresponds to the sex assigned to them at birth. **Cis** is short for 'cisgender.' ❑ *He said the entertainment industry was full of cis, straight, male characters.*

cis|gen|der /sɪsdʒɛndər/ ADJ Someone who is **cisgender** has a gender identity which fully corresponds to the sex assigned to them at birth. ❑ *I am cisgender. I identify as male and my biological sex is male too.*

cis|tern /sɪstərn/ (cisterns) **1** N-COUNT A **cistern** is a container for storing rain water. [mainly AM]

in BRIT, usually use **water butt**

2 N-COUNT A **cistern** is a container which stores the water supply for a building, or that holds the water for flushing a toilet. [mainly BRIT]

in AM, usually use **tank**

cita|del /sɪtəd⁰l, -dɛl/ (citadels) **1** N-COUNT In the past, a **citadel** was a strong building in or near a city, where people could shelter for safety. ❑ *The citadel at Besançon towered above the river.* **2** N-COUNT [usu N of n] If you describe a system or organization as a **citadel** of a particular way of life, usually one you disapprove of, you mean that it is powerful and effective in defending that way of life. [FORMAL, DISAPPROVAL] ❑ *The business is no longer regarded as a citadel of commerce.*

ci|ta|tion /saɪteɪʃ⁰n/ (citations) **1** N-COUNT A **citation** is an official document or speech which praises a person for something brave or special that they have done. ❑ *His citation says he showed outstanding and exemplary courage.* **2** N-COUNT A **citation** from a book or other piece of writing is a passage or phrase from it. [FORMAL] ❑ *...a 50-minute manifesto with citations from the Koran.* **3** N-COUNT A **citation** is the same as a **summons**. [AM] ❑ *The court could issue a citation and fine Ms. Robbins.* **4** N-COUNT A **citation** is an official piece of paper which orders you to pay a fine or to appear in court because you have committed a traffic offense. [AM] ❑ *The Highway Patrol this year issued 1,018 speeding citations.*

cite ♦◇◇ /saɪt/ (cites, citing, cited) **1** V-T If you **cite** something, you quote it or mention it, especially as an example or proof of what you are saying. [FORMAL] ❑ *She cites a favorite poem by George Herbert.* ❑ *Domestic interest rates are often cited as a major factor affecting exchange rates.* **2** V-T To **cite** a person means to officially name them in a legal case. To **cite** a reason or cause means to state it as the official reason for your case. ❑ *They cited Alex's refusal to return to the marital home.* **3** V-T [usu passive] If someone **is cited**, they are officially ordered to appear before a court. [AM, LEGAL] ❑ *He is the owner of a restaurant chain that was cited for violations of child labor laws.*

in BRIT, use **be summonsed**

4 V-T If a judge **cites** someone, he or she officially names them in a critical way in court. [AM, LEGAL] ❑ *The judge ruled a mistrial and cited the prosecutors for outrageous misconduct.*

SYNONYMS

cite
VERB **1**
quote: *He quoted statistics, saying that the standard of living had fallen.*
name: *She was jailed for refusing to name a source.*
mention: *Ferguson was mentioned in the report as being directly responsible.*
specify: *He has not specified what action he would like them to take.*

citi|zen ♦♦◊ /sɪtɪzᵊn/ (**citizens**) **1** N-COUNT Someone who is a **citizen** of a particular country is legally accepted as belonging to that country. ❑ *...American citizens.* **2** N-COUNT The **citizens** of a town or city are the people who live there. ❑ *...the citizens of Buenos Aires.* **3** ADJ [ADJ n] You describe someone as a **citizen** journalist or a **citizen** scientist, for example, when they are an ordinary person with no special training who does something that is usually done by professionals. ❑ *Several reports are coming from citizen journalists in the area.* **4** → see also **senior citizen** **5** → See feature box at **press**

citi|zen|ry /sɪtɪzᵊnri/ N-SING-COLL The people living in a country, state, or city can be referred to as the **citizenry**. [AM] ❑ *He used the medium of radio when he wanted to enlist public support or reassure the citizenry.*

citi|zen's ar|rest (**citizen's arrests**) N-COUNT If someone makes a **citizen's arrest**, they catch someone who they believe has committed a crime and inform the police. ❑ *Police do not advise the average person to make a citizen's arrest.*

citi|zens band N-PROPER [oft N n] **Citizens band** is a range of radio frequencies which the general public is allowed to use to send messages to each other. It is used especially by truck drivers and other drivers who use radio sets in their vehicles. The abbreviation **CB** is often used. ❑ *...citizens band radios.*

citi|zen|ship /sɪtɪzᵊnʃɪp/ **1** N-UNCOUNT If you have **citizenship** of a country, you are legally accepted as belonging to it. ❑ *After 15 years in the U.S., he has finally decided to apply for American citizenship.* **2** N-UNCOUNT **Citizenship** is the fact of belonging to a community because you live in it, and the duties and responsibilities that this brings. ❑ *Their German peers had a more developed sense of citizenship.*

cit|ric acid /sɪtrɪk æsɪd/ N-UNCOUNT **Citric acid** is a weak acid found in many kinds of fruit, especially citrus fruit such as oranges and lemons.

cit|rus /sɪtrəs/ ADJ [ADJ n] A **citrus** fruit is a juicy fruit with a sharp taste such as an orange, lemon, or grapefruit. ❑ *...citrus groves.*

city ♦♦♦ /sɪti/ (**cities**) N-COUNT A **city** is a large town. ❑ *...the city of Bologna.*

city cen|ter (**city centers**) N-COUNT [oft the N] The **city center** is the busiest part of a city, where most of the shops and businesses are. ❑ *Our offices are in the city center.*

city edi|tor (**city editors**) N-COUNT The **city editor** of a newspaper is the editor who is in charge of local news. [AM] ❑ *"The automobile killed our downtown," claims Jim Snyder, city editor of the Parkersburg News.*

city fa|ther (**city fathers**) N-COUNT You can refer to a member of a city council or city's government as a **city father**. ❑ *The city fathers have just given final approval to a new stadium.*

city hall (**city halls**) also **City Hall** **1** N-COUNT; N-PROPER The **city hall** is the building which a city council uses as its main offices. ❑ *They massed in front of the city hall.* ❑ *...at Philadelphia City Hall.* **2** N-COUNT; N-PROPER **City hall** also refers to government regulations or bureaucracy, which is expressed in the idiom 'You can't fight city hall.'

city plan|ning N-UNCOUNT [oft N n] **City planning** is the planning and design of all the new buildings, roads, and parks in a place in order to make them attractive and convenient for the people who live there. [AM] ❑ *The meetings will include residents, merchants, commercial property owners and city planning officials.*

in BRIT, use **town planning**

city slick|er (**city slickers**) N-COUNT If you refer to someone as a **city slicker**, you mean that they live and work in a city and are stylish and sophisticated. [INFORMAL] ❑ *...the city slickers in the capital.*

city|wide /sɪtiwaɪd/ ADJ **Citywide** activities or situations happen or exist in all parts of a city. [mainly AM] ❑ *This is a citywide problem that has to be addressed as an emergency.*

civ|ic /sɪvɪk/ **1** ADJ [ADJ n] You use **civic** to describe people or things that have an official status in a town or city. ❑ *...the local politicians and civic leaders of Manchester.* **2** ADJ [ADJ n] You use **civic** to describe the duties or feelings that people have because they belong to a particular community. ❑ *...a sense of civic pride.*

civic cen|ter (**civic centers**) N-COUNT In a city or town, a **civic center** is a building or buildings that contain local government offices and often recreational or cultural facilities for the public. [AM] ❑ *The city council wants more parks, an expanded recreation program, and a civic center.*

civ|ics /sɪvɪks/ N-UNCOUNT [oft N n] **Civics** is the study of the rights and duties of the citizens of a society. [mainly AM] ❑ *...my high school civics class.*

civ|il ♦♦◊ /sɪvᵊl/ **1** ADJ [ADJ n] You use **civil** to describe events that happen within a country and that involve the different groups of people in it. ❑ *...civil unrest.* **2** ADJ You use **civil** to describe people or things in a country that are not connected with its armed forces. ❑ *...the U.S. civil aviation industry.* **3** ADJ [ADJ n] You use **civil** to describe things that are connected with the state rather than with a religion. ❑ *They were married on August 9 in a civil ceremony in Venice.* **4** ADJ [ADJ n] You use **civil** to describe the rights that people have within a society. ❑ *...a United Nations covenant on civil and political rights.* **5** ADJ Someone who is **civil** is polite in a formal way, but not particularly friendly. [FORMAL] ❑ *As visitors, the least we can do is be civil to the people in their own land.* • **ci|vil|ity** /sɪvɪlɪti/ N-UNCOUNT ❑ *...civility to underlings.*

civ|il de|fense

in BRIT, use **civil defence**

N-UNCOUNT [oft N n] **Civil defense** is the organization and training of the ordinary people in a country so that they can help the armed forces, medical services, or police force, for example if the country is attacked by an enemy. ❑ *...a civil defense exercise.*

civ|il dis|obedi|ence N-UNCOUNT **Civil disobedience** is the refusal by ordinary people in a country to obey laws or pay taxes, usually as a protest. ❑ *The opposition threatened a campaign of civil disobedience.*

civ|il en|gi|neer (**civil engineers**) N-COUNT A **civil engineer** is a person who plans, designs, and constructs roads, bridges, harbors, and public buildings.

civ|il en|gi|neer|ing N-UNCOUNT **Civil engineering** is the planning, design, and building of roads, bridges, harbors, and public buildings. ❑ *It is believed to be the world's biggest civil engineering project.*

ci|vil|ian ♦♦◊ /sɪvɪlyən/ (**civilians**) **1** N-COUNT In a military situation, a **civilian** is anyone who is not a member of the armed forces. ❑ *The safety of civilians caught up in the fighting must be guaranteed.* **2** ADJ In a military situation, **civilian** is used to describe people or things that are not military. ❑ *...the country's civilian population.* ❑ *...civilian casualties.*

ci|vil|ity /sɪvɪlɪti/ → see **civil**

civi|li|za|tion /sɪvɪlɪzeɪʃᵊn/ (**civilizations**)

in BRIT, also use **civilisation**

civilize / clamber

1 N-VAR A **civilization** is a human society with its own social organization and culture. ☐ *The ancient civilizations of Central and Latin America were founded upon corn.* **2** N-UNCOUNT **Civilization** is the state of having an advanced level of social organization and a comfortable way of life. ☐ *...our advanced state of civilization.*

civi|lize /sɪvɪlaɪz/ (**civilizes**, **civilizing**, **civilized**)

in BRIT, also use **civilise**

V-T To **civilize** a person or society means to educate them and improve their way of life. ☐ *...a comedy about a man who tries to civilize a woman – but she ends up civilizing him.*

civi|lized /sɪvɪlaɪzd/

in BRIT, also use **civilised**

1 ADJ If you describe a society as **civilized**, you mean that it is advanced and has established laws and customs. [APPROVAL] ☐ *I believed that in civilized countries, torture had ended long ago.* **2** ADJ If you describe a person or their behavior as **civilized**, you mean that they are polite and reasonable. ☐ *I wrote to my ex-wife last week. She was very civilized about it.*

civ|il law N-UNCOUNT [oft *the* N] **Civil law** is the part of a country's set of laws which is concerned with the private affairs of citizens, for example, marriage and property ownership, rather than with crime.

civ|il lib|er|ties

The form **civil liberty** is used as a modifier.

N-PLURAL A person's **civil liberties** are the rights they have to say, think, and do what they want as long as they respect other people's rights. ☐ *...his commitment to human rights and civil liberties.* ☐ *...civil liberty campaigners.*

civ|il part|ner|ship (**civil partnerships**) N-VAR A **civil partnership** is a legal relationship between two people that is similar to marriage. ☐ *The two men entered into a civil partnership last year.*

civ|il rights N-PLURAL **Civil rights** are the rights that people have in a society to equal treatment and equal opportunities, whatever their race, sex, or religion. ☐ *...the civil rights movement.*

civ|il serv|ant (**civil servants**) N-COUNT A **civil servant** is a person who works for the local, state, or federal government in the United States, or in the civil service in Britain and some other countries. ☐ *...two senior civil servants.*

civ|il ser|vice N-SING The **civil service** of a country consists of its government departments and all the people who work in them. The departments concerned with military and legal affairs are not part of the civil service. ☐ *...a job in the civil service.*

civ|il un|ion (**civil unions**) N-VAR A **civil union** is a legal relationship between two people that is similar to marriage. ☐ *The two men entered into a civil union last year.*

civ|il war ✦✧ (**civil wars**) **1** N-COUNT A **civil war** is a war which is fought between different groups of people who live in the same country. ☐ *...the American Civil War.* **2** → See feature box at **conflict**

civ|vies /sɪviz/ N-PLURAL [oft *in* N] People in the armed forces use **civvies** to refer to ordinary clothes that are not part of a uniform. [INFORMAL] ☐ *They might have been soldiers in civvies.*

CJD /siː dʒeɪ diː/ N-UNCOUNT **CJD** is an incurable brain disease that affects human beings and is believed to be caused by eating beef from cows infected with BSE. **CJD** is an abbreviation for 'Creutzfeldt-Jakob disease.'

cl **cl** is a written abbreviation for **centiliter**. ☐ *...two 75cl bottles of quality wine.*

clack /klæk/ (**clacks**, **clacking**, **clacked**) V-T/V-I If things **clack** or if you **clack** them, they make a short loud noise, especially when they hit each other. ☐ *The windshield wipers clacked back and forth.* ☐ *I clacked one ski against the other and almost tripped.* • N-SING **Clack** is also a noun. ☐ *...the clack of her shoes on the stairs.* ☐ *Her bracelets were going clack-clack-clack, she was shaking so hard.*

clad /klæd/ **1** ADJ If you are **clad** in particular clothes, you are wearing them. [LITERARY] ☐ *...the figure of a woman, clad in black.* ☐ *Johnson was clad casually in slacks and a light blue golf shirt.* • COMB IN ADJ **Clad** is also a combining form. ☐ *...the leather-clad biker.* **2** ADJ [v-link ADJ *in/with* n] A building, part of a building, or mountain that is **clad** with something is covered by that thing. [LITERARY] ☐ *The walls and floors are clad with ceramic tiles.* • COMB IN ADJ **Clad** is also a combining form. ☐ *...the distant shapes of snow-clad mountains.*

clad|ding /klædɪŋ/ **1** N-UNCOUNT [oft n N] **Cladding** is a covering of tiles, wooden boards, or other material that is fixed to the outside of a building to protect it against bad weather or to make it look more attractive. ☐ *...stone cladding.* **2** N-UNCOUNT **Cladding** is a layer of metal which is put around fuel rods in a nuclear reactor.

claim ✦✦✦ /kleɪm/ (**claims**, **claiming**, **claimed**) **1** V-T If you say that someone **claims** that something is true, you mean they say that it is true but you are not sure whether or not they are telling the truth. ☐ *He claimed that it was all a conspiracy against him.* ☐ *A man claiming to be a journalist threatened to reveal details about her private life.* **2** V-T If you say that someone **claims** responsibility or credit for something, you mean they say that they are responsible for it, but you are not sure whether or not they are telling the truth. ☐ *An underground organization has claimed responsibility for the bomb explosion.* **3** V-T If you **claim** something, you try to get it because you think you have a right to it. ☐ *Now they are returning to claim what was theirs.* **4** V-T If someone **claims** a record, title, or prize, they gain or win it. [JOURNALISM] ☐ *Zhuang claimed the record in 54.64 seconds.* **5** V-T If something or someone **claims** your attention, they need you to spend your time and effort on them. ☐ *There is already a long list of people claiming her attention.* **6** V-T/V-I If you **claim** money from the government, an insurance company, or another organization, you officially apply to them for it, because you think you are entitled to it according to their rules. ☐ *Some 25 percent of the people who are entitled to claim benefits do not do so.* ☐ *John had taken out insurance but when he tried to claim, the insurance company refused to pay.* • N-COUNT **Claim** is also a noun. ☐ *Last time we made a claim on our insurance, they paid up really quickly.* **7** V-T If you **claim** money or other benefits from your employers, you demand them because you think you deserve or need them. ☐ *The union claimed a raise worth four times the rate of inflation.* • N-COUNT **Claim** is also a noun. ☐ *They are making substantial claims for improved working conditions.* **8** V-T If you say that a war, disease, or accident **claims** someone's life, you mean that they are killed in it or by it. [FORMAL] ☐ *The civil war claimed the life of a U.N. interpreter yesterday.* **9** N-COUNT A **claim** is something of which someone says which they cannot prove and which may be false. ☐ *He repeated his claim that the people of Trinidad and Tobago backed his action.* **10** N-COUNT A **claim** is a demand for something that you think you have a right to. ☐ *Rival claims to Macedonian territory caused conflict in the Balkans.* **11** N-COUNT If you have a **claim on** someone or their attention, you have the right to demand things from them or to demand their attention. ☐ *She had no claims on him now.* **12 to stake a claim** → see **stake**

claim|ant /kleɪmənt/ (**claimants**) N-COUNT A **claimant** is someone who asks to be given something which they think they are entitled to. ☐ *The claimants allege that manufacturers failed to warn doctors that their drugs should be used only in limited circumstances.*

claims ad|just|er (**claims adjusters**) also **claims adjustor** N-COUNT A **claims adjuster** is someone who is employed by an insurance company to decide how much money a person making a claim should receive. [AM, BUSINESS]

in BRIT, use **loss adjuster**

clair|voy|ant /kleərvɔɪənt/ ADJ Someone who is believed to be **clairvoyant** is believed to know about future events or to be able to communicate with dead people. ☐ *...clairvoyant powers.*

clam /klæm/ (**clams**) N-COUNT **Clams** are a kind of shellfish which can be eaten.

clam|bake /klæmbeɪk/ (**clambakes**) N-COUNT A **clambake** is a picnic at which clams and other food are served. [AM] ☐ *One of the most popular events is a clambake with unlimited portions of clams, lobster, and seafood salad.*

clam|ber /klæmbər/ (**clambers**, **clambering**, **clambered**) V-I If you **clamber** somewhere, you climb there with difficulty, usually using your hands as well as your feet. ☐ *They clambered up the stone walls of a steeply terraced olive grove.*

clam|my /klǽmi/ (**clammier, clammiest**) ADJ Something that is **clammy** is unpleasantly damp or sticky. ❑ *Think of the clammy hands you get when you visit the dentist!* ❑ *My shirt was clammy with sweat.*

clam|or /klǽmər/ (**clamors, clamoring, clamored**)

in BRIT, use **clamour**

V-I If people **are clamoring** for something, they are demanding it in a noisy or angry way. [JOURNALISM] ❑ *...competing parties clamoring for the attention of the voter.*

clam|or|ous /klǽmərəs/ ADJ [usu ADJ n] If you describe people or their voices as **clamorous**, you mean they are talking loudly or shouting. [LITERARY] ❑ *...the crowded, clamorous streets.*

clam|our [BRIT] → see **clamor**

clamp /klǽmp/ (**clamps, clamping, clamped**) **1** N-COUNT A **clamp** is a device that holds two things firmly together. ❑ *Many openers have a magnet or set of clamps to grip the open lid.* **2** N-COUNT A **clamp** is the same as a **Denver boot**. [mainly BRIT] **3** V-T When you **clamp** one thing **to** another, you fasten the two things together with a clamp. ❑ *Somebody forgot to bring along the U-bolts to clamp the microphones to the pole.* **4** V-T To **clamp** something in a particular place means to put it or hold it there firmly and tightly. ❑ *Simon finished dialing and clamped the phone to his ear.* ❑ *He clamped his lips together.* **5** V-T To **clamp** a car means the same as to **boot** a car. [BRIT]
▶ **clamp down** PHRASAL VERB To **clamp down on** people or activities means to take strong official action to stop or control them. [JOURNALISM] ❑ *If the government clamps down on the movement, that will only serve to strengthen it in the long run.*

clamp|down /klǽmpdaʊn/ (**clampdowns**) N-COUNT [oft N on n] A **clampdown** is a sudden restriction on a particular activity by a government or other authority. [JOURNALISM] ❑ *...a clampdown on the employment of illegal immigrants.*

clan /klǽn/ (**clans**) **1** N-COUNT A **clan** is a group which consists of families that are related to each other. ❑ *...rival clans.* **2** N-COUNT You can refer to a group of people with the same interests as a **clan**. [INFORMAL] ❑ *...a powerful clan of industrialists from Monterrey.*

clan|des|tine /klændɛstɪn/ ADJ Something that is **clandestine** is hidden or kept secret, often because it is illegal. [FORMAL] ❑ *...their clandestine meetings.*

clang /klǽŋ/ (**clangs, clanging, clanged**) V-I When a large metal object **clangs**, it makes a loud noise. ❑ *The door clanged shut behind them.* • N-VAR **Clang** is also a noun. ❑ *He pulled the gates to with a clang.*

clang|or /klǽŋər, klǽŋɡər/ N-SING A **clangor** is a loud or harsh noise. [AM] ❑ *Suddenly, the clangor and shouting ceased.*

in BRIT, use **clangour**

clank /klǽŋk/ (**clanks, clanking, clanked**) V-I When large metal objects **clank**, they make a noise because they are hitting together or hitting against something hard. ❑ *A pan rattled and clanked.* ❑ *"Here we are now," Beth said, as the train clanked into a tiny station.* ❑ *...the clanking noise of the ferry.*

clan|nish /klǽnɪʃ/ ADJ If you describe a group of people as **clannish**, you mean that they often spend time together and may seem unfriendly to other people who are not in the group. [INFORMAL] ❑ *They were a clannish lot, not given to welcoming strangers.*

clans|man /klǽnzmən/ (**clansmen**) N-COUNT [usu pl] **Clansmen** are people who are members of the same **clan**.

clans|woman /klǽnzwʊmən/ (**clanswomen**) N-COUNT [usu pl] **Clanswomen** are women who are members of the same **clan**.

clap /klǽp/ (**claps, clapping, clapped**) **1** V-T/V-I When you **clap**, you hit your hands together to express appreciation or attract attention. ❑ *The men danced and the women clapped.* ❑ *Midge clapped her hands, calling them back to order.* **2** V-T If you **clap** your hand or an object onto something, you put it there quickly and firmly. ❑ *I clapped a hand over her mouth.* **3** N-COUNT A **clap of thunder** is a sudden and loud noise of thunder.

clap|board /klǽbərd, klǽpbɔrd/ (**clapboards**) **1** ADJ [ADJ n] A **clapboard** building has walls which are covered with long, narrow pieces of wood, usually painted white. **2** N-COUNT A **clapboard** consists of two pieces of wood that are connected by a hinge and hit together before each scene when making a film, to make it easier to match the sound and pictures of different scenes. [AM]

in BRIT, use **clapperboard**

clap|trap /klǽptræp/ N-UNCOUNT If you describe something that someone says as **claptrap**, you mean that it is stupid or foolish although it may sound important. [INFORMAL, DISAPPROVAL] ❑ *This is the claptrap that politicians have peddled many times before.*

clar|et /klǽrɪt/ (**clarets**) **1** N-MASS **Claret** is a type of French red wine. **2** COLOR Something that is **claret** is purplish red in color. [LITERARY]

clari|fied /klǽrɪfaɪd/ ADJ **Clarified** butter has been made clear by being heated.

clari|fy /klǽrɪfaɪ/ (**clarifies, clarifying, clarified**) V-T To **clarify** something means to make it easier to understand, usually by explaining it in more detail. [FORMAL] ❑ *Thank you for writing and allowing me to clarify the present position.* • **clari|fi|ca|tion** /klǽrɪfɪkeɪʃən/ (**clarifications**) N-VAR ❑ *The union has written to Detroit asking for clarification of the situation.*

clari|net /klǽrɪnɛt/ (**clarinets**) N-VAR A **clarinet** is a musical instrument in the shape of a pipe. You play the clarinet by blowing into it and covering and uncovering the holes with your fingers.

clari|net|ist /klǽrɪnɛtɪst/ (**clarinetists**) N-COUNT A **clarinetist** is someone who plays the clarinet.

in BRIT, use **clarinettist**

clari|on call (**clarion calls**) N-COUNT A **clarion call** is a strong and emotional appeal to people to do something. [LITERARY] ❑ *Paine's words are a clarion call for democracy.*

clar|ity /klǽrɪti/ **1** N-UNCOUNT The **clarity** of something such as a book or argument is its quality of being well explained and easy to understand. ❑ *...the ease and clarity with which the author explains difficult technical and scientific subjects.* **2** N-UNCOUNT **Clarity** is the ability to think clearly. ❑ *In business circles he is noted for his flair and clarity of vision.* **3** N-UNCOUNT **Clarity** is the quality of being clear in outline or sound. ❑ *This remarkable technology provides far greater clarity than conventional x-rays.*

clash ♦◇◇ /klǽʃ/ (**clashes, clashing, clashed**) **1** V-RECIP When people **clash**, they fight, argue, or disagree with each other. [JOURNALISM] ❑ *A group of 400 demonstrators ripped down the front gate and clashed with police.* ❑ *Behind the scenes, Parsons clashed with almost everyone on the show.* • N-COUNT [oft N between/with n] **Clash** is also a noun. ❑ *There have been a number of clashes between police in riot gear and demonstrators.* **2** V-RECIP Beliefs, ideas, or qualities that **clash** with each other are very different from each other and therefore are opposed. ❑ *Don't make any policy decisions which clash with official company thinking.* • N-COUNT **Clash** is also a noun. ❑ *Inside government, there was a clash of views.* **3** V-RECIP If one color or style **clashes** with another, the colors or styles look ugly together. You can also say that two colors or styles **clash**. ❑ *The red door clashed with the soft, natural tones of the stone walls.* **4** V-I If one event **clashes** with another, the two events happen at the same time so that you cannot attend both of them. [BRIT]

in AM, use **conflict**

5 → See feature box at **conflict**

─── SYNONYMS ───

clash
VERB **1**
fight: *As a child, she fought with her younger sister.*
argue: *They were still arguing; I could hear them down the road.*
disagree: *They can communicate, even when they strongly disagree.*
quarrel: *At one point we quarreled, over something silly.*
feud: *He feuded with his ex-wife.*

─── COLLOCATIONS ───

clash
VERB **1**
clash + *adverb*: repeatedly; angrily, violently
NOUN
1
adjective + **clash**: violent
2
noun + **clash**: culture, personality

clasp /klæsp/ (clasps, clasping, clasped) **1** V-T If you **clasp** someone or something, you hold them tightly in your hands or arms. ◻ *She clasped the children to her.* **2** N-COUNT A **clasp** is a small device that fastens something. ◻ *...the clasp of her handbag.*

class ◆◆◆ /klæs/ (classes, classing, classed) **1** N-COUNT A **class** is a group of students who are taught together. ◻ *He had to spend about six months in a class with younger students.* **2** N-COUNT A **class** is a course of teaching in a particular subject. ◻ *He acquired a law degree by taking classes at night.* **3** N-COUNT A **class** of things is a group of them with similar characteristics. ◻ *Harbor staff noticed that measurements given for the same class of boats differ varied.* **4** N-UNCOUNT If you do something **in class**, you do it during a lesson in school. ◻ *There is lots of reading in class.* **5** N-UNCOUNT If you say that someone or something has **class**, you mean that they are elegant and sophisticated. [INFORMAL, APPROVAL] ◻ *The most elegant woman I've ever met – she had class in every sense of the word.* **6** N-SING The students in a school or college who finish their course in a particular year are often referred to as the **class** of that year. ◻ *These two members of Yale's Class of '57 never miss a reunion.* **7** N-VAR **Class** refers to the division of people in a society into groups according to their social status. ◻ *...the relationship between social classes.* ◻ *What it will do is create a whole new ruling class.* **8** → see also **middle class, upper class, working class** **9** V-T If someone or something **is classed as** a particular thing, they are regarded as belonging to that group of things. ◻ *Since they can and do successfully inter-breed, they cannot be classed as different species.* ◻ *I class myself as an ordinary working person.* **10** → see also **business class, first-class, second-class, world-class**

COLLOCATIONS

class
NOUN
2
noun + **class**: cooking, dance, exercise, yoga; evening, night
verb + **class**: run, teach; attend, go to, take
7
adjective + **class**: lower, middle, ruling, upper; privileged, professional, wealthy

class act (class acts) N-COUNT [usu sing] If you describe someone or something as a **class act**, you mean that they are impressive and of high quality. ◻ *This show will run and run because it's a class act.*

class ac|tion (class actions) N-COUNT [usu sing] A **class action** is a legal case brought by a group of people rather than an individual.

class-conscious ADJ Someone who is **class-conscious** is very aware of the differences between the various classes of people in society, and often has a strong feeling of belonging to a particular class. ◻ *Nineteenth-century Britain was a class-conscious society.* • **class con|scious|ness** N-UNCOUNT ◻ *There was very little snobbery or class consciousness in the wartime navy.*

clas|sic ◆◇◇ /klæsɪk/ (classics) **1** ADJ A **classic** example of a thing or situation has all the features which you expect such a thing or situation to have. ◻ *The debate in the press has been a classic example of hypocrisy.* • N-COUNT **Classic** is also a noun. ◻ *It was a classic of interrogation: first the bully, then the kind one who offers sympathy.* **2** ADJ [ADJ n] A **classic** movie, piece of writing, or piece of music is of very high quality and has become a standard against which similar things are judged. ◻ *...the classic children's film Huckleberry Finn.* • N-COUNT **Classic** is also a noun. ◻ *The record won a gold award and remains one of the classics of modern popular music.* **3** ADJ A **classic** is a book which is well-known and considered to be of a high literary standard. You can refer to such books generally as **the classics**. ◻ *As I grow older, I like to reread the classics regularly.* **4** N-UNCOUNT **Classics** is the study of the ancient Greek and Roman civilizations, especially their languages, literature, and philosophy. ◻ *...a Classics degree.*

clas|si|cal ◆◇◇ /klæsɪkᵊl/ **1** ADJ You use **classical** to describe something that is traditional in form, style, or content. ◻ *Fokine did not change the steps of classical ballet; instead he found new ways of using them.* **2** ADJ **Classical** music is music that is considered to be serious and of lasting value. ◻ *...a classical composer like Beethoven.* **3** ADJ **Classical** is used to describe things which relate to the ancient Greek or Roman civilizations. ◻ *...the healers of ancient Egypt and classical Greece.*

clas|si|cal|ly /klæsɪkli/ **1** ADV [ADV -ed] Someone who has been **classically** trained in something such as art, music, or ballet has learned the traditional skills and methods of that subject. ◻ *Peter is a classically trained pianist.* **2** ADV [ADV adj/-ed] **Classically** is used to indicate that something is based on or reminds people of the culture of ancient Greece and Rome. ◻ *...the classically inspired church of S. Francesco.*

clas|si|cism /klæsɪsɪzəm/ N-UNCOUNT **Classicism** is a style of art practiced especially in the 18th century in Europe. It has simple regular forms and the artist does not attempt to express strong emotions.

clas|si|cist /klæsɪsɪst/ (classicists) **1** N-COUNT A **classicist** is someone who studies the ancient Greek and Roman civilizations, especially their languages, literature, and philosophy. **2** N-COUNT In the arts, especially in architecture, a **classicist** is someone who follows the principles of classicism in their work.

clas|si|fi|ca|tion /klæsɪfɪkeɪʃᵊn/ (classifications) **1** N-COUNT A **classification** is a division or category in a system which divides things into groups or types. ◻ *The government uses a classification system that includes both race and ethnicity.* **2** → see also **classify**

clas|si|fied /klæsɪfaɪd/ ADJ **Classified** information or documents are officially secret. ◻ *He has a security clearance that allows him access to classified information.*

clas|si|fied ad (classified ads) N-COUNT **Classified ads** or **classified advertisements** are small advertisements in a newspaper or magazine. They are usually from a person or company.

clas|si|fieds /klæsɪfaɪdz/ N-PLURAL The **classifieds** are the same as **classified ads**. ◻ *It's common for companies to post job openings on their websites and in newspaper classifieds.*

clas|si|fy /klæsɪfaɪ/ (classifies, classifying, classified) V-T To **classify** things means to divide them into groups or types so that things with similar characteristics are in the same group. ◻ *It is necessary initially to classify the headaches into certain types.* • **clas|si|fi|ca|tion** /klæsɪfɪkeɪʃᵊn/ (classifications) N-VAR ◻ *...the arbitrary classification of knowledge into fields of study.*

class|less /klæslɪs/ ADJ When politicians talk about a **classless** society, they mean a society in which people are not affected by social status. [APPROVAL] ◻ *...the new prime minister's vision of a classless society.*

class|mate /klæsmeɪt/ (classmates) N-COUNT Your **classmates** are students who are in the same class as you at school or college.

class|room /klæsrum/ (classrooms) **1** N-COUNT A **classroom** is a room in a school where lessons take place. **2** → See feature box at **learning**

class sched|ule (class schedules) N-COUNT In a school or college, a **class schedule** is a list that shows the times in the week at which particular subjects are taught. You can also refer to the range of subjects that a student learns or the classes that a teacher teaches as their **class schedule**. [AM] ◻ *They had to be back at their colleges this week to enroll and work out class schedules for the new term.*

in BRIT, usually use **timetable**

classy /klæsi/ (classier, classiest) ADJ If you describe someone or something as **classy**, you mean they are stylish and sophisticated. [INFORMAL] ◻ *The German star put in a classy performance.*

clat|ter /klætər/ (clatters, clattering, clattered) V-I If you say that people or things **clatter** somewhere, you mean that they move there noisily. ◻ *He turned and clattered down the stairs.*

clause /klɔz/ (clauses) **1** N-COUNT A **clause** is a section of a legal document. ◻ *He has a clause in his contract which entitles him to a percentage of the profits.* ◻ *...a compromise document sprinkled with escape clauses.* **2** N-COUNT In grammar, a **clause** is a group of words containing a verb. Sentences contain one or more clauses.

claus|tro|pho|bia /klɔstrəfoʊbiə/ N-UNCOUNT Someone who has **claustrophobia** feels very uncomfortable or anxious when they are in small or enclosed places.

claus|tro|pho|bic /klɔstrəfoʊbɪk/ **1** ADJ You describe a place or situation as **claustrophobic** when it makes you feel uncomfortable and unhappy because you are enclosed or restricted. ❏ *They lived in an unhealthily claustrophobic atmosphere.* ❏ *The house felt too claustrophobic.* **2** ADJ [usu v-link ADJ] If you feel **claustrophobic**, you feel very uncomfortable or anxious when you are in a small, crowded, or enclosed place. ❏ *The churning, pressing crowds made her feel claustrophobic.*

clavi|chord /klævɪkɔrd/ (**clavichords**) N-VAR [oft the N] A **clavichord** is a musical instrument similar to a small piano. When you press the keys, small pieces of metal come up and hit the strings. Clavichords were especially popular during the eighteenth century.

clavi|cle /klævɪkəl/ (**clavicles**) N-COUNT Your **clavicles** are your collarbones. [MEDICAL]

claw /klɔ/ (**claws, clawing, clawed**) **1** N-COUNT The **claws** of a bird or animal are the thin, hard, curved nails at the end of its feet. ❏ *The cat tried to cling to the edge by its claws.* **2** N-COUNT The **claws** of a lobster, crab, or scorpion are the two pointed parts at the end of its legs which are used for holding things. **3** V-I If an animal **claws** at something, it scratches or damages it with its claws. ❏ *The wolf clawed at the tree and howled the whole night.* **4** V-I To **claw** at something mean to try very hard to get hold of it. ❏ *His fingers clawed at Blake's wrist.* **5** V-T If you **claw** your **way** somewhere, you move there with great difficulty, trying desperately to find things to hold on to. ❏ *From the flooded depths of the ship, some did manage to claw their way up iron ladders to the safety of the upper deck.*

clay /kleɪ/ **1** N-MASS **Clay** is a kind of earth that is soft when it is wet and hard when it is dry. Clay is shaped and baked to make things such as pots and bricks. ❏ *...the heavy clay soils of Georgia.* ❏ *As the wheel turned, the potter shaped and squeezed the lump of clay into a graceful shape.* **2** N-UNCOUNT In tennis, matches played on **clay** are played on courts whose surface is covered with finely crushed stones or brick. ❏ *Most tennis is played on hard courts, but a substantial amount is played on clay.*

clay pi|geon (**clay pigeons**) N-COUNT [usu N n] **Clay pigeons** are discs of baked clay which are thrown into the air by a machine as targets for gun shooting practice. ❏ *...hunting and clay-pigeon shooting.*

clean ✦✧ /klin/ (**cleaner, cleanest, cleans, cleaning, cleaned**) **1** ADJ Something that is **clean** is free from dirt or unwanted marks. ❏ *The subway is efficient and spotlessly clean.* ❏ *Tiled kitchen floors are easy to keep clean.* **2** ADJ You say that people or animals are **clean** when they keep themselves or their surroundings clean. ❏ *We like pigs, they're very clean.* **3** ADJ A **clean** fuel or chemical process does not create many harmful or polluting substances. ❏ *Fans of electric cars say they are clean, quiet, and economical.* **4** ADJ If you describe something such as a book, joke, or lifestyle as **clean**, you think that they are not sexually immoral or offensive. [APPROVAL] ❏ *They're trying to show clean, wholesome, decent movies.* ❏ *Flirting is good clean fun.* **5** ADJ If someone has a **clean** reputation or record, they have never done anything illegal or wrong. ❏ *Accusations of tax evasion have tarnished his clean image.* **6** ADJ A **clean** game or fight is carried out fairly, according to the rules. ❏ *He called for a clean fight in the election and an end to "negative campaigning."* • **clean|ly** ADV ❏ *The game had been cleanly fought.* **7** ADJ A **clean** sheet of paper has no writing or drawing on it. ❏ *Take a clean sheet of paper and down the left-hand side make a list.* **8** V-T/V-I If you **clean** something or **clean** dirt off it, you make it free from dirt and unwanted marks, for example by washing or wiping it. ❏ *If something cleans easily, they're easy to clean.* ❏ *Her father cleaned his glasses with a paper napkin.* ❏ *It took half an hour to clean the orange powder off the bathtub.* • **clean|ing** N-UNCOUNT ❏ *The windows will have to be given a thorough cleaning.* **9** V-T/V-I If you **clean** a room or house, you make the inside of it and the furniture in it free from dirt and dust. ❏ *Mary cooked and cleaned for them.* • **clean|ing** N-UNCOUNT ❏ *I do the cleaning myself.* **10** ADV **Clean** is used to emphasize that something was done completely. [INFORMAL, EMPHASIS] ❏ *It burned clean through the seat of my overalls.* ❏ *The thief got clean away with the money.* **11 to clean up** your act → see act **12 to keep your nose clean** → see nose **13 a clean slate** → see slate **14 a clean sweep** → see sweep **15 clean as a whistle** → see whistle

▶ **clean out** PHRASAL VERB If you **clean out** something such as a closet, room, or container, you take everything out of it and clean the inside of it thoroughly. ❏ *Mr. Wall asked if I would help him clean out the barrels.*

▶ **clean up** **1** PHRASAL VERB If you **clean up** a mess or **clean up** a place where there is a mess, you make things neat and free of dirt again. ❏ *Police in the city have been cleaning up the debris left by a day of violent confrontation.* **2** PHRASAL VERB To **clean up** something such as the environment or an industrial process means to make it free from substances or processes that cause pollution. ❏ *Under pressure from the public, many regional governments cleaned up their beaches.* **3** PHRASAL VERB If the police or authorities **clean up** a place or area of activity, they make it free from crime, corruption, and other unacceptable forms of behavior. ❏ *After years of neglect and decline, the city was cleaning itself up.* **4** PHRASAL VERB If you go and **clean up**, you make yourself clean and neat, especially after doing something that has made you dirty. ❏ *Johnny, go inside and get cleaned up.*

SYNONYMS

clean
ADJ **1**
spotless: *Each morning, cleaners make sure everything is spotless.*
immaculate: *Her front room was immaculate.*
pristine: *Now, the house is in pristine condition.*

clean-cut ADJ A man or boy who is **clean-cut** has a neat, tidy appearance. ❏ *...his clean-cut good looks.*

clean eat|ing N-UNCOUNT **Clean eating** is the practice of eating only certain foods that are thought to be healthy and natural. ❏ *This craze for clean eating was responsible for a 30% growth in demand for avocados last year.*

clean|er /klinər/ (**cleaners**) **1** N-COUNT A **cleaner** is someone who is employed to clean the rooms and furniture inside a building. ❏ *...the prison hospital where Sid worked as a cleaner.* **2** N-COUNT A **cleaner** is someone whose job is to clean a particular type of thing. ❏ *He was a window cleaner.* **3** N-COUNT A **cleaner** is a device used for cleaning things. ❏ *...an air cleaner.* **4** → see also **vacuum cleaner** **5** N-COUNT A **cleaner** or a **cleaner's** is a store where things such as clothes are dry-cleaned. ❏ *Did you pick up my suit from the cleaner's?* **6** N-MASS A **cleaner** is a substance used for cleaning things. ❏ *...oven cleaner.*

clean|ing lady (**cleaning ladies**) N-COUNT A **cleaning lady** is a woman who is employed to clean the rooms and furniture inside a building.

clean|ing wom|an (**cleaning women**) N-COUNT A **cleaning woman** is the same as a **cleaning lady**.

clean|li|ness /klɛnlɪnɪs/ N-UNCOUNT **Cleanliness** is the degree to which people keep themselves and their surroundings clean. ❏ *Many of the state's beaches fail to meet minimum standards of cleanliness.*

cleanse /klɛnz/ (**cleanses, cleansing, cleansed**) **1** V-T To **cleanse** a place, person, or organization of something dirty, unpleasant, or evil means to make them free from it. ❏ *Right after your last cigarette, your body will begin to cleanse itself of tobacco toxins.* **2** V-T If you **cleanse** your skin or a wound, you clean it. ❏ *Catherine demonstrated the proper way to cleanse the face.* **3** → see also **ethnic cleansing**

cleans|er /klɛnzər/ (**cleansers**) **1** N-MASS A **cleanser** is a liquid or cream that you use for cleaning your skin. ❏ *...an extremely effective cleanser for dry and sensitive skins.* **2** N-MASS A **cleanser** is a liquid or powder that you use in cleaning kitchens and bathrooms. [mainly AM] ❏ *a certain kind of bathroom cleanser*

clean-shaven ADJ If a man is **clean-shaven**, he does not have a beard or a mustache.

clean|up /klinʌp/ (**cleanups**)

in BRIT, use **clean-up**

N-COUNT A **cleanup** is the removing of dirt, pollution, crime, or corruption from somewhere. ❏ *His supporters want a cleanup of civilian corruption.* ❏ *The governor has now called in the National Guard to assist the cleanup operation.*

CLEAR
① FREE FROM CONFUSION
② FREE FROM PHYSICAL OBSTACLES
③ MORALLY OR LEGALLY RIGHT, POSSIBLE, OR PERMITTED
④ PHRASAL VERBS

① **clear** ♦♦♦ /klɪər/ (clearer, clearest, clears, clearing, cleared)
1 ADJ Something that is **clear** is easy to understand, see, or hear. ❑ *The book is clear, readable, and adequately illustrated.* ❑ *The space telescope has taken the clearest pictures ever of Pluto.* • **clear|ly** ADV ❑ *Whales journey up the coast of California, clearly visible from the beach.* **2** ADJ Something that is **clear** is obvious and impossible to be mistaken about. ❑ *It was a clear case of homicide.* ❑ *It became clear that I hadn't been able to convince Mike.* • **clear|ly** ADV [ADV with cl/group] ❑ *Clearly, the police cannot break the law in order to enforce it.* **3** ADJ If you are **clear** about something, you understand it completely. ❑ *It is important to be clear about what Chomsky is doing here.* ❑ *He is not entirely clear on how he will go about it.* **4** ADJ If your mind or your way of thinking is **clear**, you are able to think sensibly and reasonably, and you are not affected by confusion or by a drug such as alcohol. ❑ *She needed a clear head to carry out her instructions.* • **clear|ly** ADV ❑ *The only time I can think clearly is when I'm alone.* **5** V-T To **clear** your mind or your head means to free it from confused thoughts or from the effects of a drug such as alcohol. ❑ *He walked up Fifth Avenue to clear his head.* **6** CONVENTION You can say '**Is that clear?**' or '**Do I make myself clear?**' after you have told someone your wishes or instructions, to make sure that they have understood you, and to emphasize your authority. ❑ *We're only going for half an hour, and you're not going to buy anything. Is that clear?* **7** PHRASE If you **make** something **clear**, you say something in a way that makes it impossible for there to be any doubt about your meaning, wishes, or intentions. ❑ *Mr. O'Friel made it clear that further insults of this kind would not be tolerated.*

② **clear** ♦♦♦ /klɪər/ (clearer, clearest, clears, clearing, cleared)
→ Please look at meanings **9** and **10** to see if the expression you are looking for is shown under another headword.
1 ADJ A **clear** substance is one which you can see through and which has no color, like clean water. ❑ *...a clear glass panel.* ❑ *...a clear gel.* **2** ADJ If a surface, place, or view is **clear**, it is free of unwanted objects or obstacles. ❑ *The runway is clear – go ahead and land.* ❑ *Caroline prefers her countertops to be clear of clutter.* **3** ADJ If it is a **clear** day or if the sky is **clear**, there is no mist, rain, or cloud. ❑ *On a clear day you can see the coast.* **4** ADJ **Clear** eyes look healthy, attractive, and shining. ❑ *...clear blue eyes.* **5** ADJ If your skin is **clear**, it is healthy and free from blemishes. ❑ *No amount of cleansing or mineral water consumption can guarantee a clear skin.* **6** ADJ If something or someone is **clear** of something else, it is not touching it or is a safe distance away from it. ❑ *As soon as he was clear of the terminal building, he looked around.* **7** V-T When you **clear** an area or place or **clear** something from it, you remove things from it that you do not want to be there. ❑ *To clear the land and harvest the bananas they decided they needed to hire specialist machinery.* ❑ *Workers could not clear the tunnels of smoke.* **8** V-I When fog or mist **clears**, it gradually disappears. ❑ *The early morning mist had cleared.* **9** to **clear the air** → see **air** **10** to **clear your throat** → see **throat** **11** → see also **clearing**, **crystal clear**

③ **clear** ♦♦♦ /klɪər/ (clearer, clearest, clears, clearing, cleared)
1 ADJ If you say that your conscience is **clear**, you mean that you do not think you have done anything wrong. ❑ *Mr. Garcia said his conscience was clear over the jail incidents.* **2** V-T/V-I When a bank **clears** a check or when a check **clears**, the bank agrees to pay the sum of money mentioned on it. ❑ *Banks can still take two or three weeks to clear a check.* **3** V-T If something or someone **clears** the way or the path **for** something to happen, they make it possible. ❑ *The prime minister resigned today, clearing the way for the formation of a new government.* **4** V-T [usu passive] If a course of action **is cleared**, people in authority give permission for it to happen. ❑ *Linda Gradstein has this report from Jerusalem, which was cleared by an Israeli censor.* **5** V-T If someone **is cleared**, they are proved to be not guilty of a crime or mistake. ❑ *She was cleared of murder and jailed for just five years for manslaughter.* **6** PHRASE If someone is **in the clear**, they are not in danger, or are not blamed or suspected of anything. ❑ *It would be stupid to do anything until we know we're in the clear.*

④ **clear** ♦♦♦ /klɪər/ (clears, clearing, cleared)
▶ **clear away** PHRASAL VERB When you **clear** things **away** or **clear away**, you put away the things that you have been using, especially for eating or cooking. ❑ *The waitress had cleared away the plates and brought coffee.*
▶ **clear out 1** PHRASAL VERB If you tell someone to **clear out** of a place or to **clear out**, you are telling them rather rudely to leave the place. [INFORMAL, DISAPPROVAL] ❑ *She turned to the others in the room. "The rest of you clear out of here."* **2** PHRASAL VERB If you **clear out** a container, room, or house, you make it neat and throw away the things in it that you no longer want. ❑ *I took the precaution of clearing out my desk before I left.*
▶ **clear up 1** PHRASAL VERB When you **clear up** or **clear** a place **up**, you make things neat and put them away. ❑ *After breakfast they played while I cleared up.* **2** PHRASAL VERB To **clear up** a problem, misunderstanding, or mystery means to settle it or find a satisfactory explanation for it. ❑ *There should be someone to whom you can turn for any advice or to clear up any problems.* **3** PHRASAL VERB To **clear up** a medical problem, infection, or disease means to cure it or get rid of it. If a medical problem **clears up**, it goes away. ❑ *Antibiotics should be used to clear up the infection.* **4** PHRASAL VERB When the weather **clears up**, it stops raining or being cloudy. ❑ *It all depends on the weather clearing up.*

clear|ance /klɪərəns/ (clearances) **1** N-VAR **Clearance** is the removal of old buildings, trees, or other things that are not wanted from an area. ❑ *...a slum clearance operation in Nairobi.* ❑ *The U.N. pledged to help supervise the clearance of mines.* **2** N-VAR If you get **clearance** to do or have something, you get official approval or permission to do or have it. ❑ *Thai Airways said the plane had been given clearance to land.*

clear|ance sale (clearance sales) N-COUNT A **clearance sale** is a sale in which the goods in a store are sold at reduced prices, because the store wants to get rid of them quickly or is closing down.

clear-cut also **clear cut** ADJ Something that is **clear-cut** is easy to recognize and quite distinct. ❑ *This was a clear-cut case of the original land owner being in the right.*

clear-headed ADJ If you describe someone as **clear-headed**, you mean that they are sensible and think clearly, especially in difficult situations. [APPROVAL] ❑ *...his clear-headed grasp of the laws of economics.*

clear|ing /klɪərɪŋ/ (clearings) N-COUNT A **clearing** is a small area in a forest where there are no trees or bushes. ❑ *A helicopter landed in a clearing in the dense jungle.*

clearing|house /klɪərɪŋhaʊs/ (clearinghouses) **1** N-COUNT If an organization acts as a **clearinghouse**, it collects, sorts, and distributes specialized information. ❑ *The center will act as a clearinghouse for research projects for former nuclear scientists.* **2** N-COUNT A **clearinghouse** is a central bank which deals with all business among the banks that use its services. [BUSINESS]

clear-sighted ADJ If you describe someone as **clear-sighted**, you admire them because they are able to understand situations well and to make sensible judgments and decisions about them. [APPROVAL] ❑ *Try to keep a clear-sighted view of your objective.*

cleat /kliːt/ (cleats) **1** N-PLURAL **Cleats** are shoes with metal pieces attached to the soles to prevent you from slipping when you are playing football or other sports. [AM] ❑ *...a pair of stinky football cleats.* **2** N-COUNT A **cleat** is a kind of hook with two ends which is used to hold ropes, especially on sailing boats.

cleav|age /kliːvɪdʒ/ (cleavages) N-COUNT A woman's **cleavage** is the space between her breasts, especially the top part which you see if she is wearing a dress with a low neck.

cleave /kliːv/ (cleaves, cleaving)

> The past tense can be either **cleaved** or **clove**; the past participle can be **cleaved**, **cloven**, or **cleft** for meaning **1**, and is **cleaved** for meaning **2**.

1 V-T To **cleave** something means to split or divide it into two separate parts, often violently. [LITERARY] ❑ *They just cleave the stone along the cracks.* **2** V-I If someone **cleaves to** something or **to** someone else, they begin or continue to have strong feelings of loyalty toward them. [FORMAL] ❑ *She has cleaved to these principles all her life.*

cleav|er /klivər/ (**cleavers**) N-COUNT A **cleaver** is a knife with a large rectangular blade, used for chopping meat or vegetables. ❑ *...a meat cleaver.*

clef /klɛf/ (**clefs**) N-COUNT A **clef** is a symbol at the beginning of a line of music that indicates the pitch of the written notes.

cleft /klɛft/ (**clefts**) **1** N-COUNT A **cleft** in a rock or in the ground is a narrow opening in it. ❑ *...a narrow cleft in the rocks too small for humans to enter.* **2** N-COUNT A **cleft** in someone's chin is a line down the middle of it. **3** ADJ [ADJ n] If someone has a **cleft** chin, they have a cleft in their chin.

cleft pal|ate (**cleft palates**) N-VAR If someone has a **cleft palate**, they were born with a narrow opening along the roof of their mouth which makes it difficult for them to speak properly.

clema|tis /klɛmətɪs/ (**clematises** or **clematis**) N-VAR A **clematis** is a type of flowering shrub which can be grown to climb up walls or fences. There are many different varieties of clematis.

clem|en|cy /klɛmənsi/ N-UNCOUNT If someone is granted **clemency**, they are punished less severely than they could be. [FORMAL] ❑ *Seventeen prisoners held on death row are to be executed after their pleas for clemency were turned down.*

clem|ent /klɛmənt/ ADJ [usu ADJ n] **Clement** weather is pleasantly mild and dry. [FORMAL]

clem|en|tine /klɛməntaɪn/ (**clementines**) N-COUNT A **clementine** is a fruit that looks like a small orange.

clench /klɛntʃ/ (**clenches, clenching, clenched**) **1** V-T/V-I When you **clench** your fist or your fist **clenches**, you curl your fingers up tightly, usually because you are very angry. ❑ *Alex clenched her fists and gritted her teeth.* ❑ *She pulled at his sleeve and he turned on her, fists clenching again before he saw who it was.* **2** V-T/V-I When you **clench** your teeth or they **clench**, you squeeze your teeth together firmly, usually because you are angry or upset. ❑ *Patsy had to clench her jaw to suppress her anger.* **3** V-T If you **clench** something in your hand or in your teeth, you hold it tightly with your hand or your teeth. ❑ *I clenched the arms of my chair.*

cler|gy /klɜrdʒi/ N-PLURAL The **clergy** are the official leaders of the religious activities of a particular group of believers. ❑ *Stalin deported Catholic clergy to Siberia.*

clergy|man /klɜrdʒimən/ (**clergymen**) N-COUNT A **clergyman** is a male member of the clergy.

clergy|woman /klɜrdʒiwʊmən/ (**clergywomen**) N-COUNT A **clergywoman** is a female member of the clergy.

cler|ic /klɛrɪk/ (**clerics**) N-COUNT A **cleric** is a member of the clergy. ❑ *His grandfather was a Muslim cleric.*

cleri|cal /klɛrɪkᵊl/ **1** ADJ [ADJ n] **Clerical** jobs, skills, and workers are concerned with routine work that is done in an office. ❑ *...a strike by clerical staff in all government departments.* **2** ADJ [ADJ n] **Clerical** means relating to the clergy. ❑ *...Iran's clerical leadership.*

clerk /klɜrk/ (**clerks, clerking, clerked**) **1** N-COUNT A **clerk** is a person who works in an office, bank, or law court and whose job is to keep the records or accounts. ❑ *She was offered a job as a clerk with a travel agency.* **2** N-COUNT In a hotel, office, or hospital, a **clerk** is the person whose job is to answer the telephone and deal with people when they arrive. [mainly AM] ❑ *...a hotel clerk.* **3** N-COUNT A **clerk** is someone who sells things to customers in a store. [AM] ❑ *Now Thomas was working as a clerk in a shop that sold leather goods.* **4** V-I To **clerk** means to work as a clerk. [mainly AM] ❑ *Gene clerked at the auction.*

clev|er ✦✧ /klɛvər/ (**cleverer, cleverest**) **1** ADJ Someone who is **clever** is intelligent and able to understand things easily or plan things well. ❑ *He's a very clever man.* • **clev|er|ly** ADV ❑ *She would cleverly pick up on what I said.* • **clev|er|ness** N-UNCOUNT ❑ *Her cleverness seems to get in the way of her emotions.* **2** ADJ A **clever** idea, book, or invention is extremely effective and shows the skill of the people involved. ❑ *It is a clever and gripping novel, yet something is missing from its heart.* • **clev|er|ly** ADV [ADV -ed] ❑ *...a cleverly designed swimsuit.*

cli|ché /kliʃeɪ/ (**clichés**)

in BRIT, also use **cliche**

N-COUNT A **cliché** is an idea or phrase which has been used so much that it is no longer interesting or effective or no longer has much meaning. [DISAPPROVAL] ❑ *I've learned that the cliché about life not being fair is true.*

cli|chéd /kliʃeɪd/

in BRIT, also use **cliched**

ADJ If you describe something as **clichéd**, you mean that it has been said, done, or used many times before, and is boring or untrue. [DISAPPROVAL] ❑ *The dialogue and acting are tired, clichéd and corny.*

click /klɪk/ (**clicks, clicking, clicked**) **1** V-T/V-I If something **clicks** or if you **click** it, it makes a short, sharp sound. ❑ *The applause rose to a crescendo and cameras clicked.* ❑ *He clicked off the radio.* • N-COUNT **Click** is also a noun. ❑ *The telephone rang three times before I heard a click and then her recorded voice.* **2** V-T/V-I [no passive] If you **click** on an area of a computer screen, you point the cursor at that area and press one of the buttons on the mouse in order to make something happen. [COMPUTING] ❑ *I clicked on a link and recent reviews of the production came up.* ❑ *Click the link and see what happens.* • N-COUNT **Click** is also a noun. ❑ *You can check your email with a click of your mouse.* **3** V-I When you suddenly understand something, you can say that it **clicks**. [INFORMAL] ❑ *When I saw the television report, it all clicked.* **4 to click into place** → see **place** ③ **5** → See feature box at **email, sound**

click|able /klɪkəbᵊl/ ADJ A **clickable** image on a computer screen is one that you can point the cursor at and click on, in order to make something happen. [COMPUTING] ❑ *...a website with clickable maps showing hotel locations.*

click bait N-UNCOUNT **Click bait** is something on a website that encourages people to click on a link. [INFORMAL] ❑ *The images of animals serve as click bait.*

cli|ent ✦✧✧ /klaɪənt/ (**clients**) **1** N-COUNT A **client** of a professional person or organization is a person or company that receives a service from them in return for payment. [BUSINESS] ❑ *...a lawyer and his client.* **2** → see also **customer**

▸ SYNONYMS ◂

client
NOUN
customer: *Our customers have very tight budgets.*
consumer: *...improving public services and consumer rights.*
buyer: *Car buyers are more interested in safety and reliability than speed.*
patron: *Like so many of the hotel's patrons, he adored the food.*
shopper: *Better protection is available for shoppers who use a credit card.*

cli|ent base (**client bases**) N-COUNT A business's **client base** is the same as its **customer base**. [BUSINESS] ❑ *Enviros Consulting has a client base of more than 2,000 organizations worldwide.*

cli|en|tele /klaɪəntɛl, kliɒn-/ N-SING-COLL The **clientele** of a place or organization are its customers or clients. ❑ *This pub had a mixed clientele.*

cli|ent state (**client states**) N-COUNT A **client state** is a country which is controlled or influenced by another larger and more powerful state, or which depends on this state for support and protection. ❑ *...France and its African client states.*

cliff /klɪf/ (**cliffs**) N-COUNT A **cliff** is a high area of land with a very steep side, especially one next to the sea. ❑ *The car rolled over the edge of a cliff.*

cliff|hanger /klɪfhæŋər/ (**cliffhangers**) also **cliff-hanger** N-COUNT A **cliffhanger** is a situation or part of a play or movie that is very exciting or frightening because you are left for a long time not knowing what will happen next. ❑ *The election is likely to be a cliff-hanger.* ❑ *...cliffhanger endings to keep you in suspense.*

cliff|top /klɪftɒp/ (**clifftops**) N-COUNT A **clifftop** is the area of land around the top of a cliff. ❑ *...a house on the clifftop.* ❑ *...25 acres of spectacular clifftop scenery.*

cli|mac|tic /klaɪmæktɪk/ ADJ [ADJ n] A **climactic** moment in a story or a series of events is one in which a very exciting or important event occurs. [FORMAL] ❑ *...the film's climactic scene.*

cli|mate /klaɪmɪt/ (climates) **1** N-VAR The **climate** of a place is the general weather conditions that are typical of it. ☐ ...*the hot and humid climate of Florida*. **2** N-COUNT You can use **climate** to refer to the general atmosphere or situation somewhere. ☐ *The economic climate remains uncertain.* ☐ *...the existing climate of violence and intimidation.* **3** → See feature box at **ecosystem**

SYNONYMS

climate
NOUN **1**
weather: *...the weather conditions.*
temperature: *Coping with severe drops in temperature can be very difficult.*
climes: *He left Britain for the sunnier climes of Southern France.*

---

cli|mate change N-UNCOUNT **Climate change** refers to changes in the earth's climate, especially the gradual rise in temperature caused by high levels of carbon dioxide and other gases. ☐ *Human activity has led to deforestation, species becoming extinct, rising sea levels and climate change.*

cli|mate cri|sis (climate crises) N-VAR If there is a **climate crisis**, very serious danger and damage is likely because of climate change, and special action must be taken. ☐ *This climate crisis is far and away the most serious challenge we've ever faced.* ☐ *This is what climate crisis looks like.*

cli|mate emer|gen|cy N-COUNT If there is a **climate emergency**, very serious danger and damage is likely because of climate change, and special action must be taken. ☐ *Young people are calling for more action on what they say is a climate emergency.*

cli|mate sci|ence N-UNCOUNT **Climate science** is the scientific study of weather conditions that exist in an area over a long period, and how and why they might change. ☐ *He is a professor of climate science at University College London.*

cli|mate sci|en|tist (climate scientists) N-COUNT A **climate scientist** is someone who studies weather conditions, and how and why they might change over time.

cli|mate skep|tic (climate skeptics) N-COUNT A **climate skeptic** is someone who does not believe that changes in the earth's climate risk environmental catastrophe. ☐ *The climate skeptics demonize environmentalists as wanting to wreck the economy.*

cli|mat|ic /klaɪmætɪk/ ADJ [ADJ n] **Climatic** conditions, changes, and effects relate to the general weather conditions of a place. ☐ *...the threat of rising sea levels and climatic change from overheating of the atmosphere.*

cli|ma|tolo|gist /klaɪmətɒlədʒɪst/ (climatologists) N-COUNT A **climatologist** is someone who studies climates.

cli|ma|tol|ogy /klaɪmətɒlədʒi/ N-UNCOUNT **Climatology** is the scientific study of climate.

cli|max /klaɪmæks/ (climaxes, climaxing, climaxed) **1** N-COUNT The **climax** of something is the most exciting or important moment in it, usually near the end. ☐ *For Pritchard, reaching the Olympics was the climax of her career.* ☐ *It was the climax to 24 hours of growing anxiety.* **2** V-T/V-I The event that **climaxes** a sequence of events is an exciting or important event that comes at the end. You can also say that a sequence of events **climaxes** with a particular event. [JOURNALISM] ☐ *The demonstration climaxed two weeks of strikes.*

climb /klaɪm/ (climbs, climbing, climbed) **1** V-T/V-I If you **climb** something such as a tree, mountain, or ladder, or **climb** up it, you move toward the top of it. If you **climb** down it, you move toward the bottom of it. ☐ *Climbing the first hill took half an hour.* ☐ *I told her about him climbing up the drainpipe.* • N-COUNT **Climb** is also a noun. ☐ *...an hour's leisurely climb through olive groves and vineyards.* **2** V-I If you **climb** somewhere, you move there carefully, for example because you are moving into a small space or trying to avoid falling. ☐ *The girls hurried outside, climbed into the car, and drove off.* ☐ *He must have climbed out of his bed.* **3** V-I When something such as an airplane **climbs**, it moves upward to a higher position. When the sun **climbs**, it moves higher in the sky. ☐ *The plane took off for L.A., lost an engine as it climbed, and crashed just off the runway.* **4** V-I When something **climbs**, it increases in value or amount. ☐ *The nation's unemployment rate has been climbing steadily since last June.* ☐ *Prices have climbed by 21% since the beginning of the year.* **5** → see also **climbing** **6** **a mountain to climb** → see **mountain**

SYNONYMS

climb
VERB
1
ascend: *Then we ascend steeply through forests of rhododendron.*
scale: *...the first British woman to scale the world's highest mountain.*
mount: *Llewelyn was mounting the stairs up into the keep.*
clamber: *They clambered up the stone walls of a steeply-terraced olive grove.*
4
increase: *The population continues to increase.*
mount: *The decibel level was mounting.*
go up: *Interest rates went up.*
rise: *Pre-tax profits rose from $842,000 to $1.82m.*

COLLOCATIONS

climb
VERB
1
climb + *noun*: ladder, stairs, steps; hill, mountain; fence, wall
4
climb + *adverb*: rapidly, sharply, steeply; gradually, slowly; steadily
NOUN **1**
adjective + **climb**: steep, stiff; arduous, strenuous; slow, steady; uphill, upward

---

climb|er /klaɪmər/ (climbers) **1** N-COUNT A **climber** is someone who climbs rocks or mountains as a sport or a hobby. ☐ *She was an experienced climber, who had climbed several of the world's tallest mountains.* **2** N-COUNT A **climber** is a plant that grows upward by attaching itself to other plants or objects. ☐ *All good garden centers carry a selection of climbers.*

climb|ing /klaɪmɪŋ/ N-UNCOUNT **Climbing** is the activity of climbing rocks or mountains. ☐ *I had done no skiing, no climbing, and no hiking.*

climb|ing frame (climbing frames) N-COUNT A **climbing frame** is a structure that has been made for children to climb and play on. It consists of metal or wooden bars joined together. [BRIT]

in AM, use **jungle gym**

clime /klaɪm/ (climes) N-COUNT [usu pl, usu adj n] You use **clime** in expressions such as **warmer climes** and **foreign climes** to refer to a place that has a particular kind of climate. [LITERARY] ☐ *He left Seattle for the sunnier climes of Mexico.*

clinch /klɪntʃ/ (clinches, clinching, clinched) **1** V-T If you **clinch** something you are trying to achieve, such as a business deal or victory in a contest, you succeed in obtaining it. ☐ *Her second-place finish in the final race was enough to clinch the overall victory.* **2** V-T The thing that **clinches** an uncertain matter settles it or provides a definite answer. ☐ *Evidently this information clinched the matter.*

clinch|er /klɪntʃər/ (clinchers) N-COUNT A **clincher** is a fact or argument that finally proves something, settles a dispute, or helps someone achieve a victory. [INFORMAL] ☐ *DNA fingerprinting has proved the clincher in this investigation.*

cling /klɪŋ/ (clings, clinging, clung) **1** V-I If you **cling** to someone or something, you hold onto them tightly. ☐ *Another man was rescued as he clung to the riverbank.* ☐ *She had to cling onto the door handle until the pain passed.* **2** V-I If someone **clings** to a position or a possession they have, they do everything they can to keep it even though this may be very difficult. ☐ *Instead, he appears determined to cling to power.* ☐ *Another congressman clung on with a majority of only 18.*

cling|film /klɪŋfɪlm/ also **cling film** N-UNCOUNT **Clingfilm** is a thin, clear, stretchy plastic that you use to cover food in order to keep it fresh. [BRIT]

in AM, use **plastic wrap**

clingy /klɪŋi/ **1** ADJ If you describe someone as **clingy**, you mean that they become very attached to people and depend

clinic

on them too much. [DISAPPROVAL] ❏ *A very clingy child can drive a parent to distraction.* ◼ ADJ **Clingy** clothes fit tightly around your body. ❏ *...long clingy skirts.*

clin|ic ◆◇◇ /klɪnɪk/ (**clinics**) N-COUNT A **clinic** is a building where people go to receive medical advice or treatment. ❏ *...a family planning clinic.*

COLLOCATIONS

clinic
NOUN
noun + **clinic**: abortion, family planning, fertility; health, hospital, pain; addiction, rehab
adjective + **clinic**: dental, medical, prenatal, psychiatric; veterinary; private, walk-in; free
verb + **clinic**: attend, visit; hold, open, run

---

clini|cal /klɪnɪkəl/ ◼ ADJ **Clinical** means involving or relating to the direct medical treatment or testing of patients. [MEDICAL] ❏ *The first clinical trials were expected to begin next year.* • **clini|cal|ly** /klɪnɪkli/ ADV ❏ *She was diagnosed as being clinically depressed.* ◼ ADJ You use **clinical** to describe thought or behavior that is very logical and does not involve any emotion. [DISAPPROVAL] ❏ *All this questioning is so clinical – it kills romance.*

clini|cal tri|al (**clinical trials**) ◼ N-COUNT When a new type of drug or medical treatment undergoes **clinical trials**, it is tested directly on patients to see if it is effective. ❏ *Two rival laser surgery systems are undergoing clinical trials in the U.S.* ◼ → See feature box at **medicine**

cli|ni|cian /klɪnɪʃən/ (**clinicians**) N-COUNT A **clinician** is a doctor who specializes in clinical work.

clink /klɪŋk/ (**clinks, clinking, clinked**) V-RECIP If objects made of glass, pottery, or metal **clink** or if you **clink** them, they touch each other and make a short, light sound. ❏ *She clinked her glass against his.* ❏ *They clinked glasses.* ❏ *The empty whisky bottle clinked against the seat.* ❏ *Their glasses clinked, their eyes met.* • N-COUNT **Clink** is also a noun. ❏ *...the clink of a spoon in a cup.*

clip /klɪp/ (**clips, clipping, clipped**) ◼ N-COUNT A **clip** is a small device, usually made of metal or plastic, that is specially shaped for holding things together. ❏ *She took the clip out of her hair.* ◼ N-COUNT A **clip** from a movie or a radio or television program is a short piece of it that is broadcast separately. ❏ *...an historical film clip of Lenin speaking.* ◼ V-T/V-I When you **clip** things together or when things **clip** together, you fasten them together using a clip or clips. ❏ *He clipped his safety belt to a fitting on the deck.* ◼ V-T If you **clip** something, you cut small pieces from it, especially in order to shape it. ❏ *I saw an old man out clipping his hedge.* ◼ V-T If you **clip** something out of a newspaper or magazine, you cut it out. ❏ *Kids in his neighborhood clipped his picture from the newspaper and carried it around.* ◼ V-I If something **clips** something else, it hits it accidentally at an angle before moving off in a different direction. ❏ *The truck clipped the rear of a tanker and then crashed into a second truck.* ◼ → see also **clipped, clipping, paper clip**

clip|board /klɪpbɔrd/ (**clipboards**) ◼ N-COUNT A **clipboard** is a board with a clip at the top. It is used to hold together pieces of paper that you need to carry around, and provides a firm base for writing. ◼ N-COUNT In computing, a **clipboard** is a file where you can temporarily store text or images from one document until you are ready to use them again. [COMPUTING]

clip-on ADJ [ADJ n] A **clip-on** object is designed to be fastened to something by means of a clip. ❏ *...a clip-on tie.* ❏ *...a clip-on light.*

clipped /klɪpt/ ◼ ADJ **Clipped** means neatly cut. ❏ *...a quiet street of clipped hedges and flowering gardens.* ◼ ADJ If you say that someone has a **clipped** way of speaking, you mean they speak with quick, short sounds, and usually that they sound upper-class. ❏ *Her clipped tones crackled over the telephone line.*

clip|per /klɪpər/ (**clippers**) N-PLURAL [also a pair of N] **Clippers** are a tool used for cutting small amounts from something, especially from someone's hair or nails.

clip|ping /klɪpɪŋ/ (**clippings**) ◼ N-COUNT A **clipping** is an article, picture, or advertisement that has been cut from a newspaper or magazine. ❏ *...bulletin boards crowded with newspaper clippings.* ◼ N-PLURAL **Clippings** are small pieces of something that have been cut from something larger. ❏ *Having mown the lawn, there are all those grass clippings to get rid of.*

clock

clique /klik, klɪk/ (**cliques**) N-COUNT If you describe a group of people as a **clique**, you mean that they spend a lot of time together and seem unfriendly toward people who are not in the group. [DISAPPROVAL] ❏ *He was accepted into the most popular clique on campus.*

cli|quish /klikɪʃ, klɪk-/ ADJ If you describe a group of people or their behavior as **cliquish**, you mean they spend their time only with other members of the group and seem unfriendly toward people who are not in the group. [DISAPPROVAL] ❏ *...cliquish gossip.*

clito|ral /klɪtərəl/ ADJ [ADJ n] **Clitoral** means concerned with or relating to the clitoris. ❏ *...clitoral stimulation.*

clito|ris /klɪtərɪs/ (**clitorises**) N-COUNT The **clitoris** is a part at the front of a woman's sexual organs where she can feel sexual pleasure.

cloak /kloʊk/ (**cloaks**) ◼ N-COUNT A **cloak** is a long, loose, sleeveless piece of clothing which people used to wear over their other clothes when they went out. ◼ N-SING A **cloak of** something such as mist or snow completely covers and hides something. ❏ *Today most of New England will be under a cloak of thick mist.* ◼ N-SING If you refer to something as a **cloak**, you mean that it is intended to hide the truth about something. ❏ *Preparations for the wedding were made under a cloak of secrecy.*

cloak-and-dagger also **cloak and dagger** ADJ [usu ADJ n] A **cloak-and-dagger** activity is one which involves mystery and secrecy. ❏ *She was released from prison in a cloak and dagger operation yesterday.*

cloak|room /kloʊkrum/ (**cloakrooms**) N-COUNT A **cloakroom** is the same as a **coat check**. [OLD-FASHIONED] ❏ *...a cloakroom attendant.*

clob|ber /klɒbər/ (**clobbers, clobbering, clobbered**) V-T If you **clobber** someone, you hit them. [INFORMAL] ❏ *Hillary clobbered him with a vase.*

cloche /klɒʃ/ (**cloches**) N-COUNT A **cloche** is a long, low cover made of glass or clear plastic that is put over young plants to protect them from the cold.

clock ◆◇◇ /klɒk/ (**clocks, clocking, clocked**) ◼ N-COUNT A **clock** is an instrument that shows what time of day it is. ❏ *He was conscious of a clock ticking.* ❏ *...a digital clock.* ◼ N-COUNT A time **clock** in a factory or office is a device that is used to record the hours that people work. Each worker puts a special card into the device when they arrive and leave, and the times are recorded on the card. ❏ *Government workers were made to punch time clocks morning, noon and night.* ◼ V-T To **clock** a particular time or speed in a race means to reach that time or speed. ❏ *Elliott clocked the fastest time this year for the 800 meters.* ◼ V-T [usu passive] If something or someone **is clocked** at a particular time or speed, their time or speed is measured at that level. ❏ *He has been clocked at 11 seconds for 100 meters.* ◼ → see also **alarm clock, o'clock** ◼ PHRASE If you are doing something **against the clock**, you are doing it in a great hurry, because there is very little time. ❏ *The emergency services were working against the clock as the tide began to rise.* ◼ PHRASE If something is done **around the clock** or **round the clock**, it is done all day and all night without stopping. ❏ *Rescue services have been working round the clock to free stranded motorists.* ◼ PHRASE If you want to **turn the clock back** or **put the clock back**, you want to return to a situation that used to exist, usually because the present situation is unpleasant. ❏ *In some ways we wish we could turn the clock back.* ❏ *We cannot put back the clock.* ◼ → See feature box at **time**; See also color supplement

▶ **clock in** PHRASAL VERB When you **clock in** at work, you arrive there or put a special card into a device to show what time you arrived. ❏ *I have to clock in by eight.*

▶ **clock off** PHRASAL VERB When you **clock off** at work, you leave work or put a special card into a device to show what time you left. ❏ *The night duty officer was ready to clock off.*

▶ **clock on** PHRASAL VERB When workers **clock on** at a factory or office, they put a special card into a device to show what time they arrived. ❏ *They arrived to clock on and found the factory gates locked.*

▶ **clock out** PHRASAL VERB **Clock out** means the same as **clock off**. ❏ *She had clocked out of her bank at 5:02pm using her plastic card.*

▶ **clock up** PHRASAL VERB If you **clock up** a large number or total of things, you reach that number or total. [BRIT]

in AM, use **chalk up**

clock tow|er (clock towers) N-COUNT A **clock tower** is a tall, narrow building with a clock at the top.

clock|wise /klɒkwaɪz/ ADV [ADV after v] When something is moving **clockwise**, it is moving in a circle in the same direction as the hands on a clock. ☐ *He told the children to start moving clockwise around the room.* • ADJ [ADJ n] **Clockwise** is also an adjective. ☐ *Gently swing your right arm in a clockwise direction.*

clock|work /klɒkwɜːrk/ **1** ADJ [ADJ n] A **clockwork** toy or device has machinery inside it which makes it move or operate when it is wound up with a key. ☐ *...a clockwork train set.* **2** PHRASE If you say that something happens **like clockwork**, you mean that it happens without any problems or delays, or happens regularly. ☐ *The president's trip is arranged to go like clockwork, everything pre-planned to the minute.*

clod /klɒd/ (clods) N-COUNT [oft N of n] A **clod** of earth is a large lump of earth.

clog /klɒg/ (clogs, clogging, clogged) **1** V-T When something **clogs** a hole or place, it blocks it so that nothing can pass through. ☐ *Dirt clogs the pores, causing blemishes.* **2** N-COUNT **Clogs** are heavy leather or wooden shoes with thick, wooden soles.

clois|ter /klɔɪstər/ (cloisters) N-COUNT A **cloister** is a covered area around a square in a monastery or a cathedral.

clois|tered /klɔɪstərd/ ADJ [usu ADJ n] If you have a **cloistered** way of life, you live quietly and are not involved in the normal busy life of the world around you. ☐ *...the cloistered world of royalty.*

clone /kloʊn/ (clones, cloning, cloned) **1** N-COUNT If someone or something is a **clone** of another person or thing, they are so similar to this person or thing that they seem to be exactly the same as them. ☐ *Tom was in some ways a younger clone of his handsome father.* **2** N-COUNT A **clone** is an animal or plant that has been produced artificially, for example in a laboratory, from the cells of another animal or plant. A clone is exactly the same as the original animal or plant. ☐ *...the world's first human clone.* **3** V-T To **clone** an animal or plant means to produce it as a clone. ☐ *The idea of cloning extinct life forms still belongs to science fiction.*

CLOSE
① SHUTTING OR COMPLETING
② NEARNESS; ADJECTIVE USES
③ NEARNESS; VERB USES

---

① **close** ✦✦✦ /kloʊz/ (closes, closing, closed)

→ Please look at meanings 12 and 13 to see if the expression you are looking for is shown under another headword.

1 V-T/V-I When you **close** something such as a door or lid or when it **closes**, it moves so that a hole, gap, or opening is covered. ☐ *If you are cold, close the window.* ☐ *Zacharias heard the door close.* **2** V-T When you **close** something such as an open book or umbrella, you move the different parts of it together. ☐ *Slowly he closed the book.* **3** V-T If you **close** something such as a computer file or window, you give the computer an instruction to remove it from the screen. [COMPUTING] ☐ *To close your document, press CTRL+W on your keyboard.* **4** V-T/V-I When you **close** your eyes or your eyes **close**, your eyelids move downward, so that you can no longer see. ☐ *Bess closed her eyes and fell asleep.* **5** V-T/V-I When a place **closes** or **is closed**, work or activity stops there for a short period. ☐ *Shops close only on Christmas Day and New Year's Day.* ☐ *Government troops closed the airport.* **6** V-T/V-I If a place such as a factory, store, or school **closes**, or if it **is closed**, all work or activity stops there permanently. ☐ *Many enterprises will be forced to close.* • PHRASAL VERB **Close down** means the same as **close**. ☐ *Minford closed down the business and went into politics.* • **clos|ing** N-SING ☐ *...since the closing of the steel mill in 1984.* **7** V-T To **close** a road or border means to block it in order to prevent people from using it. ☐ *They were cut off from the West in 1948 when their government closed that border crossing.* **8** V-T To **close** a conversation, event, or matter means to bring it to an end or to complete it. ☐ *Judge Isabel Oliva said last night: "I have closed the case. There was no foul play."* ☐ *The governor is said to now consider the matter closed.* **9** V-T If you **close** a bank account, you take all your money out of it and inform the bank that you will no longer be using the account. ☐ *He had closed his account with the bank five years earlier.* **10** V-I On the stock market or the currency markets, if a share price or a currency **closes** at a particular value, that is its value at the end of the day's business. [BUSINESS] ☐ *The U.S. dollar closed higher in Tokyo today.* **11** → see also **closing** **12 to close your eyes to something** → see **eye** ① **13 to close ranks** → see **rank**

▶ **close down** → see **close** ① 6

▶ **close up** **1** PHRASAL VERB If someone **closes up** a building, they shut it completely and securely, often because they are going away. ☐ *Just close up the shop.* ☐ *The summer house had been closed up all year.* **2** PHRASAL VERB If an opening, gap, or something hollow **closes up**, or if you **close** it **up**, it becomes closed or covered. ☐ *Don't use cold water as it shocks the blood vessels into closing up.*

② **close** ✦✦✦ /kloʊs/ (closer, closest)

→ Please look at meanings 16 and 17 to see if the expression you are looking for is shown under another headword.

1 ADJ If one thing or person is **close** to another, there is only a very small distance between them. ☐ *Her lips were close to his head and her breath tickled his ear.* ☐ *The man moved closer, lowering his voice.* • **close|ly** ADV ☐ *They crowded more closely around the stretcher.* **2** ADJ You say that people are **close** to each other when they like each other very much and know each other very well. ☐ *She and Linda became very close.* ☐ *I shared a house with a close friend from school.* • **close|ness** N-UNCOUNT ☐ *I asked whether her closeness to her mother ever posed any problems.* **3** ADJ [ADJ n] Your **close** relatives are the members of your family who are most directly related to you, for example your parents and your brothers or sisters. ☐ *...large changes such as the birth of a child or death of a close relative.* **4** ADJ A **close** ally or partner of someone knows them well and is very involved in their work. ☐ *He was once regarded as one of Mr. Brown's closest political advisers.* **5** ADJ [ADJ n] **Close** contact or cooperation involves seeing or communicating with someone often. ☐ *Both nations are seeking closer links with the West.* • **close|ly** ADV [ADV after v] ☐ *Our agencies work closely with local groups in developing countries.* **6** ADJ If there is a **close** connection or resemblance between two things, they are strongly connected or are very similar. ☐ *There is a close connection between pain and tension.* • **close|ly** ADV ☐ *...a pattern closely resembling a cross.* **7** ADJ **Close** inspection or observation of something is careful and thorough. ☐ *He discovered, on closer inspection, that the rocks contained gold.* • **close|ly** ADV [ADV with v] ☐ *If you look closely at many of the problems in society, you'll see evidence of racial discrimination.* **8** ADJ A **close** competition or election is won or seems likely to be won by only a small amount. ☐ *It is still a close contest between two leading opposition parties.* • **close|ly** ADV ☐ *This will be a closely fought race.* **9** ADJ [v-link ADJ, usu ADJ to n/-ing] If you are **close** to something or if it is **close**, it is likely to happen or come soon. If you are **close** to doing something, you are likely to do it soon. ☐ *She sounded close to tears.* ☐ *A senior White House official said the agreement is close.* **10** ADJ [v-link ADJ, usu ADJ to n] If something is **close** or comes **close** to something else, it almost is, does, or experiences that thing. ☐ *An airliner came close to disaster while approaching Kennedy Airport.* **11** ADJ If the atmosphere somewhere is **close**, it is unpleasantly warm with not enough air. **12** PHRASE Something that is **close by** or **close at hand** is near to you. ☐ *Did a new hair salon open close by?* **13** PHRASE **Close to** a particular amount or distance means slightly less than that amount or distance. ☐ *Sisulu spent close to 30 years in prison.* **14** PHRASE If you look at something **close up**, you look at it when you are very near to it. ☐ *They always look smaller close up.* **15** → see also **close-up** **16** **at close quarters** → see **quarter** **17** **at close range** → see **range**

③ **close** ✦◊◊ /kloʊz/ (closes, closing, closed) V-I If you are **closing** on someone or something that you are following, you are getting nearer and nearer to them. ☐ *I was within 15 seconds of the guy in second place and closing on him.*

▶ **close in** PHRASAL VERB If a group of people **close in** on a person or place, they come nearer and nearer to them and gradually surround them. ☐ *Hitler himself committed suicide as Soviet forces were closing in on Berlin.*

close-cropped /kloʊs krɒpt/ ADJ [usu ADJ n] **Close-cropped** hair or grass is cut very short.

closed /kloʊzd/ **1** ADJ [usu ADJ n] A **closed** group of people does not welcome new people or ideas from outside. ☐ *It was to be a closed circle of no more than twelve women.* ☐ *It is a closed society in*

closed-circuit ADJ [ADJ n] A **closed-circuit** television or video system is one that operates within a limited area such as a building. ❑ *There's a closed-circuit television camera in the reception area.*

the sense that they've not been exposed to many things. **2** → see also **close** ① **3 a closed book** → see **book** **4 behind closed doors** → see **door**

closed sea|son N-SING The **closed season** is the period of the year when it is prohibited to kill certain types of animal or fish. ❑ *A closed season on deer hunting was established on Long Island.*

closed shop (closed shops) N-COUNT If a factory, store, or other business is a **closed shop**, the employees must be members of a particular trade union. [BUSINESS] ❑ *...the trade union which they are required to join under the closed shop agreement.*

close-fitting /kloʊs fɪtɪŋ/ ADJ [usu ADJ n] **Close-fitting** clothes fit tightly and show the shape of your body.

close-knit /kloʊs nɪt/ **1** ADJ [usu ADJ n] A **close-knit** group of people are closely linked, do things together, and take an interest in each other. ❑ *Events over the last year have created a close-knit community.* **2** → See feature box at **relationship**

close-mouthed /kloʊs maʊθt/ ADJ Someone who is **close-mouthed** about something does not say much about it. [AM] ❑ *Lionel was close-mouthed about his private life.*

close|out /kloʊzaʊt/ (closeouts) N-COUNT [oft N n] A **closeout** at a store is a sale at which goods are sold at reduced prices. [AM] ❑ *...the leather skirt she'd found at a closeout sale at Neiman Marcus.*

close-run /kloʊs rʌn/ ADJ [ADJ n] If you describe something such as a race or contest as a **close-run** thing, you mean that it was only won by a very small amount. ❑ *In such a close-run race as this election, the campaign becomes all important.*

clos|et /klɒzɪt/ (closets) N-COUNT A **closet** is a very small room for storing things, especially one without windows. [mainly AM]

clos|et|ed /klɒzɪtɪd/ ADJ If you are **closeted** with someone, you are talking privately to them. [FORMAL OR LITERARY] ❑ *Charles and I were closeted in his study for the briefing session.*

close-up /kloʊs ʌp/ (close-ups) N-COUNT A **close-up** is a photograph or a picture in a film that shows a lot of detail because it is taken very near to the subject. ❑ *...a close-up of Harvey's face.* • PHRASE If you see something **in close-up**, you see it in great detail in a photograph or piece of film which has been taken very near to the subject.

clos|ing /kloʊzɪŋ/ (closings) **1** ADJ [ADJ n] The **closing** part of an activity or period of time is the final part of it. ❑ *He entered the army in the closing stages of the war.* **2** N-COUNT A **closing** is the final meeting between the buyer and seller of a property. [AM]

clos|ing ar|gu|ment (closing arguments) N-COUNT In a court case, a lawyer's **closing argument** is their final speech, in which they give a summary of their case. ❑ *Both sides presented closing arguments this week in the securities fraud trial of Charles Keating.*

clos|ing date (closing dates) N-COUNT [oft N *for* n] The **closing date** for a competition or offer is the final date by which entries or applications must be received. ❑ *The closing date for entries is noon, Friday, January 11.*

clos|ing price (closing prices) N-COUNT On the stock exchange, the **closing price** of a share is its price at the end of a day's business. [BUSINESS] ❑ *The price is slightly above yesterday's closing price.*

clos|ing time (closing times) N-VAR **Closing time** is the time when something such as a store, library, or bar closes and people have to leave. ❑ *We were in the bar until closing time.*

clo|sure /kloʊʒər/ (closures) **1** N-VAR The **closure** of a place such as a business or factory is the permanent ending of the work or activity there. ❑ *...the closure of the steel mill.* ❑ *...protests against the proposed pit closures.* **2** N-COUNT The **closure** of a road or border is the blocking of it in order to prevent people from using it. ❑ *Overnight storms left many streets underwater and forced the closure of road tunnels in the city.* **3** N-UNCOUNT If someone achieves **closure**, they succeed in accepting something bad that has happened to them. [mainly AM] ❑ *I asked McKean if the reunion was meant to achieve closure.*

clot /klɒt/ (clots, clotting, clotted) **1** N-COUNT A **clot** is a sticky lump that forms when blood dries up or becomes thick. ❑ *He needed emergency surgery to remove a blood clot from his brain.* **2** V-I When blood **clots**, it becomes thick and forms a lump. ❑ *The patient's blood refused to clot.*

cloth /klɒθ/ (cloths) **1** N-MASS **Cloth** is fabric which is made by weaving or knitting a substance such as cotton, wool, silk, or nylon. Cloth is used especially for making clothes. ❑ *She began cleaning the wound with a piece of cloth.* **2** N-COUNT A **cloth** is a piece of cloth which you use for a particular purpose, such as cleaning something or covering something. ❑ *Clean the surface with a damp cloth.* **3** → See feature box at **DIY**

cloth cap (cloth caps) **1** N-COUNT A **cloth cap** is a soft flat cap with a stiff, curved part at the front called a visor. Cloth caps are usually worn by men. **2** → See also color supplement

clothe /kloʊð/ (clothes, clothing, clothed) **1** V-T To **clothe** someone means to provide them with clothes to wear. ❑ *She was on her own with two kids to feed and clothe.* **2** → see also **clothed, clothes, clothing**

clothed /kloʊðd/ ADJ If you are **clothed** in a certain way, you are dressed in that way. ❑ *He lay down on the bed fully clothed.* ❑ *She was clothed in a flowered dress.*

clothes ✦✦◇ /kloʊz, kloʊðz/ N-PLURAL **Clothes** are the things that people wear, such as shirts, coats, pants, and dresses. ❑ *Moira walked upstairs to change her clothes.*

clothes horse (clothes horses) **1** N-COUNT A **clothes horse** is a folding frame used inside someone's house to hang laundry on while it dries. **2** N-COUNT If you describe someone as a **clothes horse**, you mean that they are fashionable but think too much about their clothes. [DISAPPROVAL]

clothes|line /kloʊzlaɪn, kloʊðz-/ (clotheslines) also **clothes line** N-COUNT A **clothesline** is a thin rope on which you hang laundry so that it can dry.

clothes|pin /kloʊzpɪn, kloʊðz-/ (clothespins) N-COUNT A **clothespin** is a small device which you use to fasten clothes to a clothesline. [AM]

in BRIT, use **clothes peg**

cloth|ing ✦◇◇ /kloʊðɪŋ/ N-UNCOUNT **Clothing** is the things that people wear. ❑ *Some locals offered food and clothing to the refugees.* ❑ *...the clothing industry.*

clot|ted cream N-UNCOUNT **Clotted cream** is very thick cream made by heating milk gently and taking the cream off the top. It is made mainly in the southwest of England.

cloud ✦◇◇ /klaʊd/ (clouds, clouding, clouded) **1** N-VAR A **cloud** is a mass of water vapor that floats in the sky. Clouds are usually white or gray in color. ❑ *...the varied shapes of the clouds.* ❑ *...a black mass of cloud.* **2** N-COUNT A **cloud** of something such as smoke or dust is a mass of it floating in the air. ❑ *The hens darted away on all sides, raising a cloud of dust.* **3** V-T If you say that something **clouds** your view of a situation, you mean that it makes you unable to understand the situation or judge it properly. ❑ *Perhaps anger had clouded his vision, perhaps his judgment had been faulty.* **4** V-T If you say that something **clouds** a situation, you mean that it makes it unpleasant. ❑ *The atmosphere has already been clouded by the party's anger at the media.* **5** V-T/V-I If glass **clouds** or if moisture **clouds** it, tiny drops of water cover the glass, making it difficult to see through. ❑ *The mirror clouded beside her cheek.* **6** → See feature box at **weather**

---COLLOCATIONS---

cloud
NOUN
1
noun + **cloud**: rain, storm
adjective + **cloud**: black, dark, gray, white; billowing, fluffy, thick
2
noun + **cloud**: ash, dust

---

cloud-based ADJ **Cloud-based** technology allows you to use programs and information that are stored on the internet rather than on your own computer. ❑ *We use a cloud-based communication system.*

cloud|burst /klaʊdbɜrst/ (cloudbursts) N-COUNT A **cloudburst** is a sudden, very heavy fall of rain.

cloud com|pu|ting N-UNCOUNT **Cloud computing** is a model of computer use in which services that are available on the internet are provided to users on a temporary basis. [COMPUTING]

cloud|less /klaʊdlɪs/ ADJ If the sky is **cloudless**, there are no clouds in it.

cloudy /klaʊdi/ (cloudier, cloudiest) **1** ADJ If it is **cloudy**, there are a lot of clouds in the sky. ❑ ...a windy, cloudy day. **2** ADJ A **cloudy** liquid is less clear than it should be. ❑ If the water's cloudy like that, it'll be hard to see anyone underwater.

clout /klaʊt/ (clouts, clouting, clouted) **1** V-T If you **clout** someone, you hit them. [INFORMAL] ❑ Rachel clouted him. • N-COUNT **Clout** is also a noun. ❑ I was half tempted to give one of them a clout myself. **2** N-UNCOUNT A person or institution that has **clout** has influence and power. [INFORMAL] ❑ Mr. Sutherland may have the clout needed to push the two trading giants into a deal.

clove /kloʊv/ (cloves) **1** N-VAR **Cloves** are small dried flower buds which are used as a spice. ❑ ...chicken soup with cloves. **2** N-COUNT A **clove** of garlic is one of the sections of a garlic bulb.

clo|ven hoof /kloʊvən hʊf/ (cloven hooves or cloven hoofs) N-COUNT Animals that have **cloven hooves** have feet that are divided into two parts. Cows, sheep, and goats have cloven hooves.

clo|ver /kloʊvər/ (clovers) N-VAR **Clover** is a small plant with pink or white ball-shaped flowers and usually three round leaves. ❑ ...a four leaf clover.

clover|leaf /kloʊvərlif/ (cloverleafs or cloverleaves) N-COUNT A **cloverleaf** is an arrangement of curved roads, resembling a four-leaf clover, that joins two main roads. [AM] ❑ The 405-167 freeway interchange is a classic cloverleaf, built in the 1960s.

clown /klaʊn/ (clowns, clowning, clowned) **1** N-COUNT A **clown** is a performer in a circus who wears funny clothes and bright makeup, and does silly things in order to make people laugh. **2** N-COUNT If you say that someone is a **clown**, you mean that they say funny things or do silly things to amuse people. ❑ Chapman was the family clown, with a knack for making a joke out of any situation. **3** V-I If you **clown**, you do silly things in order to make people laugh. ❑ He clowned with John Belushi and Bill Murray in National Lampoon shows. • PHRASAL VERB **Clown around** means the same as **clown**. ❑ Bev made her laugh, the way she was always clowning around.

clown|fish /klaʊnfɪʃ/ (clownfish) N-COUNT A **clownfish** is a small, brightly-colored sea fish.

clown|ish /klaʊnɪʃ/ ADJ If you describe a person's appearance or behavior as **clownish**, you mean that they look or behave rather like a clown, and often that they appear rather foolish. ❑ He had a clownish sense of humor.

cloy|ing /klɔɪɪŋ/ ADJ You use **cloying** to describe something that you find unpleasant because it is much too sweet, or too sentimental. ❑ ...the sweet, cloying smell of cheap perfume.

cloze /kloʊz/ (clozes) N-COUNT [usu N n] In language teaching, a **cloze** test is a test in which words are removed from a text and replaced with spaces. The task of the learner is to fill each space with the missing word or a suitable word. [TECHNICAL]

club ✦✦✦ /klʌb/ (clubs, clubbing, clubbed) **1** N-COUNT A **club** is an organization of people interested in a particular activity or subject who usually meet on a regular basis. ❑ ...the Young Republicans Club. ❑ ...a youth club. **2** N-COUNT A **club** is a place where the members of a club meet. ❑ I stopped in at the club for a drink. **3** N-COUNT A **club** is a team which competes in sports competitions. ❑ ...the New York Yankees baseball club. **4** N-COUNT A **club** is the same as **nightclub**. ❑ It's a big dance hit in the clubs. **5** N-COUNT A **club** is a long, thin, metal stick with a piece of wood or metal at one end that you use to hit the ball in golf. ❑ ...a six-iron club. **6** N-COUNT A **club** is a thick, heavy stick that can be used as a weapon. ❑ Men armed with knives and clubs attacked his home. **7** V-T To **club** a person or animal means to hit them with a thick heavy stick or a similar weapon. ❑ Two thugs clubbed him with baseball bats. **8** N-UNCOUNT-COLL **Clubs** is one of the four suits in a pack of playing cards. Each card in the suit is marked with one or more black symbols: ♣. ❑ ...the ace of clubs. • N-COUNT A **club** is a playing card of this suit. ❑ The next player discarded a club.

COLLOCATIONS

club
NOUN
1
noun + **club**: golf; youth
verb + **club**: join, leave; form, found
3
noun + **club**: baseball, football, rugby
adjective + **club**: bottom, top; former, old

---

club|bing /klʌbɪŋ/ N-UNCOUNT **Clubbing** is the activity of going to nightclubs.

club|by /klʌbi/ (clubbier, clubbiest) ADJ GRADED; ADJ If you describe an institution or a group of people as **clubby**, you mean that all the people in it are friendly with each other and do not welcome other people in. [INFORMAL] ❑ Politics is clubby, careerist, and cynical.

club|foot /klʌbfʊt/ (clubfeet)

in BRIT, usually use **club foot**

N-COUNT If someone has a **clubfoot**, they are born with a badly twisted foot.

club|house /klʌbhaʊs/ (clubhouses) N-COUNT A **clubhouse** is a place where the members of a club, especially a sports club, meet.

club soda N-UNCOUNT **Club soda** is fizzy water used for mixing with alcoholic drinks and fruit juice. [mainly AM]

cluck /klʌk/ (clucks, clucking, clucked) V-I When a hen **clucks**, it makes short, low noises. ❑ Several chickens clucked in the garden.

clue /klu/ (clues) **1** N-COUNT A **clue** to a problem or mystery is something that helps you to find the answer to it. ❑ Geneticists in Canada have discovered a clue to the puzzle of why our cells get old and die. **2** N-COUNT A **clue** is an object or piece of information that helps someone solve a crime. ❑ The vital clue to the killer's identity was his nickname, Peanuts. **3** N-COUNT A **clue** in a crossword or game is information which is given to help you to find the answer to a question. ❑ Give me a clue. What's it begin with? **4** PHRASE If you **haven't a clue** about something, you do not know anything about it or you have no idea what to do about it. [INFORMAL] ❑ I haven't a clue what I'll give Carl for his birthday next year.

WORD HISTORY

clue
The word **clue** comes from the old word clew, meaning a ball of wool. In Greek mythology, Ariadne gives Theseus a ball of wool to help him find his way out of the Minotaur's labyrinth. As a result, the word clew started to mean something that shows the way.

---

clue|less /klulɪs/ ADJ [oft ADJ about n] If you describe someone as **clueless**, you are showing your disapproval of the fact that they do not know anything about a particular subject or that they are incapable of doing a particular thing properly. [INFORMAL, DISAPPROVAL] ❑ I came into adult life clueless about a lot of things that most people take for granted.

clump /klʌmp/ (clumps) **1** N-COUNT A **clump** of things such as trees or plants is a small group of them growing together. ❑ ...a clump of trees bordering a side road. **2** N-COUNT A **clump** of things such as wires or hair is a group of them collected together in one place. ❑ I was combing my hair and it was just falling out in clumps.

clumpy /klʌmpi/ (clumpier, clumpiest) ADJ **Clumpy** means big and clumsy. ❑ ...clumpy shoes.

clum|sy /klʌmzi/ (clumsier, clumsiest) **1** ADJ A **clumsy** person moves or handles things in a careless, awkward way, often so that things are knocked over or broken. ❑ I'd never seen a clumsier, less coordinated boxer. • **clum|si|ly** /klʌmzɪli/ ADV [ADV with v] ❑ In the sudden pitch darkness, she scrambled clumsily toward the ladder. • **clum|si|ness** N-UNCOUNT ❑ His clumsiness and ineptitude

clung /klʌŋ/ Clung is the past tense and past participle of **cling**.

clunk /klʌŋk/ (clunks) N-COUNT; SOUND [usu sing] A **clunk** is a sound made by a heavy object hitting something hard. ❑ *Something fell to the floor with a clunk.*

clunk|er /klʌŋkər/ (clunkers) N-COUNT If you describe a machine, especially a car, as a **clunker**, you mean that it is very old and almost falling apart. [AM]

clunky /klʌŋki/ (clunkier, clunkiest) ADJ [usu ADJ n] If you describe something as **clunky**, you mean that it is solid, heavy, and rather awkward. ❑ *...a clunky piece of architecture.*

clus|ter /klʌstər/ (clusters, clustering, clustered) **1** N-COUNT A **cluster** of people or things is a small group of them close together. ❑ *...clusters of men in formal clothes.* **2** V-I If people **cluster** together, they gather together in a small group. ❑ *The passengers clustered together in small groups.*

clus|ter bomb (cluster bombs) N-COUNT A **cluster bomb** is a type of bomb which is dropped from an aircraft. It contains a large number of smaller bombs that spread out before they hit the ground.

clus|tered /klʌstərd/ ADJ If people or things are **clustered** somewhere, there is a group of them close together there. ❑ *Officials were clustered at every open office door, talking excitedly.*

clutch /klʌtʃ/ (clutches, clutching, clutched) **1** V-T/V-I If you **clutch** at something or **clutch** something, you hold it tightly, usually because you are afraid or anxious. ❑ *I staggered and had to clutch at a chair for support.* **2** N-PLURAL If someone is in another person's **clutches**, that person has captured them or has power over them. ❑ *Tony fell into the clutches of an attractive American who introduced him to drugs.* **3** N-COUNT In a vehicle, the **clutch** is the pedal that you press before you change gear. ❑ *Laura let out the clutch and pulled slowly away down the drive.*
4 to clutch at straws → see **straw**

clut|ter /klʌtər/ (clutters, cluttering, cluttered) **1** N-UNCOUNT **Clutter** is a lot of things in a messy state, especially things that are not useful or necessary. ❑ *Caroline prefers her countertops to be clear of clutter.* **2** V-T If things or people **clutter** a place, they fill it in a messy way. ❑ *Empty soft-drink cans lie everywhere. They clutter the desks and are strewn across the floor.* • PHRASAL VERB **Clutter up** means the same as **clutter**. ❑ *The vehicles cluttered up the parking lot.*

cm cm is the written abbreviation for **centimeter** or **centimeters**. ❑ *His height had increased by 2.5 cm.*

Cmdr Cmdr is a written abbreviation for **Commander**. ❑ *...Cmdr Richard Mason.*

PREFIX

co-
forms verbs and nouns that refer to people sharing things or doing things together. *For example, if two people co-write a book, they write it together. The co-author of a book is one of the people who have written it.*

c/o You write c/o before an address on an envelope when you are sending it to someone who is staying or working at that address, often for only a short time. **c/o** is an abbreviation for 'care of.'

Co. ♦♦◊ Co. is used as an abbreviation for **company** when it is part of the name of an organization. [BUSINESS] ❑ *...the Blue Star Amusement Co.*

C.O. /siː oʊ/ (C.O.s) N-COUNT A soldier's **C.O.** is his or her commanding officer.

coach ♦♦◊ /koʊtʃ/ (coaches, coaching, coached) **1** N-COUNT A **coach** is someone who trains a person or team of people in a particular sport. ❑ *Tony Woodcock has joined the team as coach.* **2** N-COUNT A **coach** is a person who is in charge of a sports team. [mainly AM] ❑ *...the women's soccer coach at Rowan University.*
in BRIT, usually use **manager**
3 N-COUNT A **coach** is someone who gives people special teaching in a particular subject, especially in order to prepare them for an examination. ❑ *What you need is a drama coach.* **4** N-COUNT A **coach** is an enclosed vehicle with four wheels which is pulled by horses, and in which people used to travel. Coaches are still used for ceremonial events in some countries, such as Britain. ❑ *...a coach pulled by six black horses.* **5** N-COUNT [also by N] A **coach** is a large, comfortable bus that carries passengers on long trips. [BRIT]
in AM, use **bus**
6 N-COUNT A **coach** is one of the separate sections of a train that carries passengers. [BRIT]
in AM, use **car**
7 V-T When someone **coaches** a person or a team, they help them to become better at a particular sport. ❑ *After her pro playing career, she coached a golf team in San Jose.* **8** V-T If you **coach** someone, you give them special teaching in a particular subject, especially in order to prepare them for an examination. ❑ *He gently coached me in French.*

coach|man /koʊtʃmən/ (coachmen) N-COUNT A **coachman** was a man who drove a coach that was pulled by horses. [OLD-FASHIONED]

coach sta|tion (coach stations) N-COUNT A **coach station** is the same as a **bus station**. [BRIT]

co|agu|late /koʊægyəleɪt/ (coagulates, coagulating, coagulated) V-I When a liquid **coagulates**, it becomes very thick. ❑ *The antibodies will bind to the glycophorin and cause the blood cells to coagulate.* • **co|agu|la|tion** /koʊægyəleɪʃən/ N-UNCOUNT ❑ *Blood becomes stickier to help coagulation in case of a cut.*

coal ♦◊◊ /koʊl/ (coals) **1** N-UNCOUNT **Coal** is a hard, black substance that is extracted from the ground and burned as fuel. ❑ *Gas is cheaper than coal.* **2** N-PLURAL **Coals** are burning pieces of coal. ❑ *The iron teakettle was hissing splendidly over live coals.* **3** → See feature box at **global warming**; See also color supplement

coa|lesce /koʊəlɛs/ (coalesces, coalescing, coalesced) V-I If two or more things **coalesce**, they come together and form a larger group or system. [FORMAL] ❑ *As the number of moisture droplets increases, they begin to coalesce into small rivulets of fluid.* ❑ *His sporting and political interests coalesced admirably in his writing about climbing.*

coal|face /koʊlfeɪs/ (coalfaces) N-COUNT In a coal mine, the **coalface** is the part where the coal is being cut out of the rock.

coal|field /koʊlfiːld/ (coalfields) N-COUNT A **coalfield** is a region where there is coal under the ground. ❑ *The park lies on top of a coalfield.*

coa|li|tion ♦◊◊ /koʊəlɪʃən/ (coalitions) **1** N-COUNT A **coalition** is a government consisting of people from two or more political parties. ❑ *Since June the country has had a coalition government.* **2** N-COUNT A **coalition** is a group consisting of people from different political or social groups who are cooperating to achieve a particular aim. ❑ *He had been opposed by a coalition of about 50 civil rights, women's, and Latino organizations.*

coal mine (coal mines) N-COUNT A **coal mine** is a place where coal is dug out of the ground.

coal min|er (coal miners) N-COUNT A **coal miner** is a person whose job is mining coal.

coal tar also **coal-tar** N-UNCOUNT **Coal tar** is a thick, black liquid made from coal which is used for making drugs and chemical products. ❑ *...coal tar dyes.*

coarse /kɔrs/ (coarser, coarsest) **1** ADJ **Coarse** things have a rough texture because they consist of thick threads or large pieces. ❑ *...a jacket made of very coarse cloth.* • **coarse|ly** ADV ❑ *...coarsely ground black pepper.* **2** ADJ If you describe someone as **coarse**, you mean that he or she talks and behaves in a rude and offensive way. [DISAPPROVAL] ❑ *The soldiers did not bother to moderate their coarse humor in her presence.* • **coarse|ly** ADV [ADV with v] ❑ *The women laughed coarsely at some vulgar joke.*

coars|en /kɔrsən/ (coarsens, coarsening, coarsened) **1** V-T/V-I If something **coarsens** or **is coarsened**, it becomes thicker or rougher in texture. ❑ *Skin thickens, dries, and coarsens after sun exposure.* ❑ *...his gnarled, coarsened features.* **2** V-T/V-I If someone's behavior or speech **coarsens** or if they **coarsen** it, they become less polite or they begin to speak in a less pleasant way. ❑ *Her voice has deepened and coarsened with the years.* ❑ *He had coarsened his voice to an approximation of Cockney.*

coast ✦✧ /koʊst/ (**coasts, coasting, coasted**) **1** N-COUNT The **coast** is an area of land that is next to the sea. ❑ *Campsites are usually situated along the coast, close to beaches.* **2** V-I If a vehicle **coasts** somewhere, it continues to move there with the motor switched off, or without being pushed or pedaled. ❑ *He pushed in the clutch and coasted to a halt.*

coast|al /koʊstᵊl/ ADJ [ADJ n] **Coastal** is used to refer to things that are in the sea or on the land near a coast. ❑ *Local radio stations serving coastal areas often broadcast forecasts for yachtsmen.*

coast|er /koʊstər/ (**coasters**) **1** N-COUNT A **coaster** is a small mat that you put underneath a glass or cup to protect the surface of a table. **2** → see also **roller coaster**

coast guard (**coast guards**) also **Coast Guard, coastguard** N-COUNT The **coast guard** is a part of a country's military forces and is responsible for protecting the coast, carrying out rescues, and doing police work along the coast. [AM] ❑ *The U.S. Coast Guard says it rescued more than 100 Haitian refugees.* • N-COUNT A **coast guard** is a member of the coast guard. [AM] ❑ *The boat was intercepted by U.S. Coast Guards.*

coast|line /koʊstlaɪn/ (**coastlines**) **1** N-VAR A country's **coastline** is the outline of its coast. ❑ *This is some of the most exposed coastline in the world.* **2** → See feature box at **ocean**

coast-to-coast ADJ A **coast-to-coast** journey or route is one that goes from one coast of a country or region to the opposite coast. ❑ *The Massachusetts senator is finishing his coast-to-coast tour across the United States.* • ADV **Coast-to-coast** is also an adverb. ❑ *I drove coast-to-coast in just over two hours.*

coat ✦✧✧ /koʊt/ (**coats, coating, coated**) **1** N-COUNT A **coat** is a piece of clothing with long sleeves which you wear over your other clothes when you go outside. ❑ *He turned off the television, put on his coat, and walked out.* **2** N-COUNT An animal's **coat** is the fur or hair on its body. ❑ *Vitamin B6 is great for improving the condition of dogs' and horses' coats.* **3** N-COUNT A **coat** of paint or varnish is a thin layer of it on a surface. ❑ *The front door needs a new coat of paint.* **4** V-T If you **coat** something **with** a substance or **in** a substance, you cover it with a thin layer of the substance. ❑ *Coat the fish with seasoned flour.*

coat check (**coat checks**) also **coat-check** N-COUNT The **coat check** at a public building such as a theater or club is the place where customers can leave their coats, usually for a small fee. [AM] ❑ *Let's get our coats at the coat check and not come back.*

-coated /koʊtɪd/ **1** COMB IN ADJ [ADJ n] **-coated** combines with color adjectives such as 'white' and 'red,' or words for types of coat like 'fur,' to form adjectives that describe someone as wearing a certain sort of coat. ❑ *At the top of the stairs stood the white-coated doctors.* **2** COMB IN ADJ **-coated** combines with names of substances such as 'sugar' and 'plastic' to form adjectives that describe something as being covered with a thin layer of that substance. ❑ *...chocolate-coated strawberries.*

coat hang|er (**coat hangers**) N-COUNT A **coat hanger** is a curved piece of wood, metal, or plastic that you hang a piece of clothing on.

coat|ing /koʊtɪŋ/ (**coatings**) N-COUNT A **coating** of a substance is a thin layer of it spread over a surface. ❑ *Under the coating of dust and cobwebs, he discovered a fine French Louis XVI clock.*

coat of arms (**coats of arms**) N-COUNT [usu with supp] The **coat of arms** of a family, town, or organization is a special design in the form of a shield that they use as a symbol of their identity.

coat|room /koʊtrum/ (**coatrooms**) also **coat room** N-COUNT A **coatroom** is the same as a **coat check**. [AM]

coat|tails /koʊtteɪlz/ **1** N-PLURAL **Coattails** are the two long pieces at the back of a **tailcoat**. **2** PHRASE [usu PHR after v] If you do something **on the coattails of** someone else, you are able to do it because of the other person's success, and not because of your own efforts. ❑ *They accused him of riding on the coat-tails of the president.*

co|author /koʊɔːθər/ (**coauthors, coauthoring, coauthored**) also **co-author** **1** N-COUNT [oft N *of* n] The **coauthors** of a book, play, or report are the people who have written it together. ❑ *He is coauthor, with Andrew Blowers, of "The International Politics of Nuclear Waste."* **2** V-T If two or more people **co-author** a book, play, or report, they write it together. ❑ *He's co-authored a book on Policy for Tourism.* ❑ *Karen Matthews co-authored the study with Lewis Kullers.*

coax /koʊks/ (**coaxes, coaxing, coaxed**) **1** V-T If you **coax** someone into doing something, you gently try to persuade them to do it. ❑ *After lunch, she watched, listened and coaxed Bobby into talking about himself.* **2** V-T If you **coax** something such as information out of someone, you gently persuade them to give it to you. ❑ *The officer spoke yesterday of her role in trying to coax vital information from the young victim.*

cob /kɒb/ (**cobs**) **1** N-COUNT A **cob** is the same as a **corn cob**. **2** N-COUNT A **cob** is a male swan. **3** N-COUNT A **cob** is a type of short strong horse.

co|balt /koʊbɒlt/ **1** N-UNCOUNT **Cobalt** is a hard, silvery-white metal which is used to harden steel and for producing a blue dye. ❑ *...a country rich in copper, cobalt, and diamonds.* **2** COLOR **Cobalt** or **cobalt blue** is a deep blue color. ❑ *...a woman in a soft cobalt blue dress.*

cob|ble /kɒbᵊl/ (**cobbles, cobbling, cobbled**) N-COUNT **Cobbles** are the same as **cobblestones**. [mainly BRIT]
▶ **cobble together** PHRASAL VERB If you say that someone has **cobbled** something **together**, you mean that they have made or produced it roughly or quickly. [DISAPPROVAL] ❑ *The group had cobbled together a few decent songs.*

cob|bled /kɒbᵊld/ ADJ [usu ADJ n] A **cobbled** street has a surface made of cobblestones. ❑ *...a cobbled courtyard.*

cob|bler /kɒblər/ (**cobblers**) N-COUNT A **cobbler** is a person whose job is to make or mend shoes. [OLD-FASHIONED]

cobble|stone /kɒbᵊlstoʊn/ (**cobblestones**) N-COUNT **Cobblestones** are stones with a rounded upper surface which used to be used for making streets. ❑ *...the narrow, cobblestone streets of the Left Bank.*

co|bra /koʊbrə/ (**cobras**) N-COUNT A **cobra** is a kind of poisonous snake that can make the skin on the back of its neck into a hood.

cob|web /kɒbwɛb/ (**cobwebs**) N-COUNT A **cobweb** is the net which a spider makes for catching insects. ❑ *The windows are cracked and covered in cobwebs.*

cob|webbed /kɒbwɛbd/ ADJ [usu ADJ n] A **cobwebbed** surface is covered with cobwebs. ❑ *...cobwebbed racks of wine bottles.*

coca /koʊkə/ N-UNCOUNT **Coca** is a plant which contains cocaine. The dried leaves of the plant are sometimes chewed for their stimulating effect. ❑ *...illegal crops such as coca.*

co|caine /koʊkeɪn/ N-UNCOUNT **Cocaine** is a powerful drug which some people take for pleasure, but which they can become addicted to.

coc|cyx /kɒksɪks/ (**coccyxes** or **coccyges** /kɒksɪdʒiːz/) N-COUNT The **coccyx** is the small triangular bone at the lower end of the spine in human beings and some apes.

cochi|neal /kɒtʃɪnɪl/ N-UNCOUNT **Cochineal** is a red substance that is used for coloring food.

coch|lea /kɒkliə/ (**cochleae**) **1** N-COUNT The **cochlea** is the spiral-shaped part of the inner ear. **2** → See also **color supplement**

cock /kɒk/ (**cocks**) N-COUNT A **cock** is an adult male chicken. [mainly BRIT]

in AM, use **rooster**

cock|a|mie /kɒkəmeɪmi/ ADJ [usu ADJ n] If you describe something as **cockamamie**, you mean that it is ridiculous or silly. [AM, INFORMAL] ❑ *...some cockamamie story about being late.*

cock-and-bull sto|ry (**cock-and-bull stories**) N-COUNT If you describe something that someone tells you as a **cock-and-bull story**, you mean that you do not believe it is true. [INFORMAL]

cocka|poo /kɒkəpuː/ (**cockapoos**) N-COUNT A **cockapoo** is a kind of dog that is a cross between the cocker spaniel breed and the poodle breed.

cocka|tiel /kɒkətiːl/ (cockatiels) N-COUNT A **cockatiel** is a bird similar to a cockatoo that is often kept as a pet.

cocka|too /kɒkətuː/ (cockatoos) N-COUNT A **cockatoo** is a kind of parrot from Australia or New Guinea which has a bunch of feathers called a crest on its head.

cock|er|el /kɒkərəl, kɒkrəl/ (cockerels) N-COUNT A **cockerel** is a young, male chicken. [mainly BRIT]

cock|er span|iel /kɒkər spæniəl/ (cocker spaniels) N-COUNT A **cocker spaniel** is a breed of small dog with silky hair and long ears.

cock|eyed /kɒkaɪd/ **1** ADJ If you say that an idea or scheme is **cockeyed**, you mean that you think it is very unlikely to succeed. ❑ *She has some cockeyed delusions about becoming a pop star.* **2** ADJ If something is **cockeyed**, it looks wrong because it is not in a level or straight position. ❑ *...dusty photographs hanging at cockeyed angles on the walls.*

cock|le /kɒkəl/ (cockles) N-COUNT [usu pl] **Cockles** are small, edible shellfish.

cock|ney /kɒkni/ (cockneys) **1** N-COUNT [oft N n] A **cockney** is a person who was born in the East End of London. ❑ *...a Cockney cab driver.* **2** N-UNCOUNT **Cockney** is the dialect and accent of the East End of London. ❑ *The man spoke with a Cockney accent.*

cock|pit /kɒkpɪt/ (cockpits) **1** N-COUNT In an airplane or racing car, the **cockpit** is the part where the pilot or driver sits. **2** → See also color supplement

cock|roach /kɒkroʊtʃ/ (cockroaches) N-COUNT A **cockroach** is a large brown insect that is sometimes found in warm places or where food is kept.

cock|sure /kɒkʃʊər/ ADJ Someone who is **cocksure** is so confident and sure of their abilities that they annoy other people. [OLD-FASHIONED, DISAPPROVAL]

cock|tail /kɒkteɪl/ (cocktails) **1** N-COUNT A **cocktail** is an alcoholic drink which contains several ingredients. ❑ *On arrival, guests are offered wine or a champagne cocktail.* **2** N-COUNT A **cocktail** is a mixture of a number of different things, especially ones that do not go together well. ❑ *The court was told she had taken a cocktail of drugs and alcohol.*

cock|tail dress (cocktail dresses) N-COUNT A **cocktail dress** is a short dress that is suitable for formal social occasions.

cock|tail lounge (cocktail lounges) N-COUNT A **cocktail lounge** is a room in a hotel, restaurant, or club where you can buy alcoholic drinks. ❑ *Let's meet in the cocktail lounge at the Hilton.*

cock|tail par|ty (cocktail parties) N-COUNT A **cocktail party** is a party, usually held in the early evening, where cocktails or other alcoholic drinks are served. People often dress quite formally for them.

cocky /kɒki/ (cockier, cockiest) ADJ Someone who is **cocky** is so confident and sure of their abilities that they annoy other people. [INFORMAL, DISAPPROVAL] ❑ *He was a little bit cocky when he was about 11 because he was winning everything.*

co|coa /koʊkoʊ/ **1** N-UNCOUNT **Cocoa** is a brown powder made from the seeds of a tropical tree. It is used in making chocolate. ❑ *...the world's leading cocoa producer.* **2** N-UNCOUNT **Cocoa** is a hot drink made from cocoa powder and milk or water. ❑ *...a cup of cocoa.*

coco|nut /koʊkənʌt/ (coconuts) **1** N-COUNT A **coconut** is a very large nut with a hairy shell, which has white flesh and milky juice inside it. ❑ *...the smell of roasted meats mingled with spices, coconut oil, and ripe tropical fruits.* **2** N-UNCOUNT **Coconut** is the white flesh of a coconut. ❑ *Put 2 cups of grated coconut into a blender or food processor.*

coco|nut milk N-UNCOUNT **Coconut milk** is the milky juice inside coconuts.

coco|nut palm (coconut palms) N-COUNT A **coconut palm** is a tall tree on which coconuts grow.

co|coon /kəkuːn/ (cocoons, cocooning, cocooned) **1** N-COUNT A **cocoon** is a covering of silky threads that the larvae of moths and other insects make for themselves before they grow into adults. ❑ *...like a butterfly emerging from a cocoon.* **2** N-COUNT If you are in a **cocoon** of something, you are wrapped up in it or surrounded by it. ❑ *He stood there in a cocoon of golden light.* **3** N-COUNT If you are living in a **cocoon**, you are in an environment in which you feel protected and safe, and sometimes isolated from everyday life. ❑ *...her innocent desire to envelop her beloved in a cocoon of love.* **4** V-T If something **cocoons** you from something, it protects you or isolates you from it. ❑ *There is nowhere to hide when things go wrong, no organization to cocoon you from blame.*

co|cooned /kəkuːnd/ **1** ADJ If someone is **cocooned** in blankets or clothes, they are completely wrapped in them. ❑ *She is comfortably cocooned in pillows.* ❑ *...my snugly cocooned baby sleeping in his stroller.* **2** ADJ [oft ADJ in/from n] If you say that someone is **cocooned**, you mean that they are isolated and protected from everyday life and problems. ❑ *She was cocooned in a private world of privilege.* ❑ *They were cocooned from the experience of poverty.*

cod /kɒd/ (cod)

> The plural can be either **cod** or **cods**.

N-VAR **Cod** are a type of large edible fish. • N-UNCOUNT **Cod** is this fish eaten as food. ❑ *A Catalan speciality is to serve salt cod cold.*

C.O.D. /siː oʊ diː/ N-UNCOUNT **C.O.D.** is an abbreviation for **cash on delivery**. ❑ *Phone orders are accepted for C.O.D. payment.* ❑ *Shipping charges on orders sent to Canada are paid C.O.D.*

coda /koʊdə/ (codas) **1** N-COUNT A **coda** is a separate passage at the end of something such as a book or a speech that finishes it off. **2** N-COUNT In music, a **coda** is the final part of a fairly long piece of music which is added in order to finish it off in a pleasing way.

cod|dle /kɒdəl/ (coddles, coddling, coddled) V-T To **coddle** someone means to treat them too kindly or protect them too much. [DISAPPROVAL] ❑ *She coddled her youngest son madly.*

code ✦✦✧ /koʊd/ (codes, coding, coded) **1** N-COUNT A **code** is a set of rules about how people should behave or about how something must be done. ❑ *...Article 159 of the state's penal code.* **2** N-COUNT [also in N] A **code** is a system of replacing the words in a message with other words or symbols, so that nobody can understand it unless they know the system. ❑ *They used elaborate secret codes, as when the names of trees stood for letters.* **3** N-COUNT A **code** is a group of numbers or letters which is used to identify something, such as a mailing address or part of a telephone system. ❑ *Callers dialing the wrong area code will not get through.* **4** N-COUNT A **code** is any system of signs or symbols that has a meaning. ❑ *It will need other chips to reconvert the digital code back into normal TV signals.* **5** N-COUNT The genetic **code** of a person, animal, or plant is the information contained in DNA which determines the structure and function of cells, and the inherited characteristics of all living things. ❑ *Scientists provided the key to understanding the genetic code that determines every bodily feature.* **6** V-T If you **code** something means to give it a code or to mark it with its code. ❑ *He devised a way of coding every statement uniquely.* **7** N-UNCOUNT Computer **code** is a system or language for expressing information and instructions in a form which can be understood by a computer. [COMPUTING] ❑ *She began writing software code at the age of nine.* **8** → see also **bar code**, **postcode**, **zip code** **9** → See feature box at **genetics**

SYNONYMS

code
NOUN **1**
principle: *...moral principles.*
rule: *Strictly speaking, this was against the rules.*
ethic: *It is common to distinguish between personal and social ethics.*
etiquette: *...the rules of diplomatic etiquette.*
convention: *It's just a social convention that men don't wear skirts.*
maxim: *I believe in the maxim 'if it ain't broke, don't fix it.'*

---

cod|ed /koʊdɪd/ **1** ADJ **Coded** messages have words or symbols which represent other words, so that the message is secret unless you know the system behind the code. ❑ *In a coded telephone warning, the police were told four bombs had been planted in the area.* **2** ADJ If someone is using **coded** language, they are expressing their opinion in an indirect way, usually because that opinion is likely to offend people. ❑ *They have sent barely coded messages to the secretary of education endorsing this criticism.* **3** ADJ [ADJ n] **Coded** electronic signals use a binary system of digits which can be decoded by an appropriate machine. [TECHNICAL] ❏ *The coded signal is received by satellite dishes.*

co|deine /koʊdin/ N-UNCOUNT **Codeine** is a drug which is used to relieve pain, especially headaches, and the symptoms of a cold.

code name (code names, code naming, code named) also **code-name** ▪ N-COUNT [usu N n] A **code name** is a name used for someone or something in order to keep their identity secret. ❏ *One of their informers was working under the code name Czerny.* ▪ V-T [usu passive] If a military or police operation is **code-named** something, it is given a name which only the people involved in it know. ❏ *The operation was code-named Moonlight Sonata.* ❏ *...a military contingent, code-named Sparrowhawk.*

code of con|duct (codes of conduct) N-COUNT The **code of conduct** for a group or organization is an agreement on rules of behavior for the members of that group or organization. ❏ *Doctors say a new code of conduct is urgently needed to protect the doctor-patient relationship.*

code of prac|tice (codes of practice) N-COUNT A **code of practice** is a set of written rules which explains how people working in a particular profession should behave. ❏ *The auctioneers are violating a code of practice by dealing in stolen goods.*

co|de|pend|ent /koʊdɪpɛndənt/ (codependents) also **co-dependent** ADJ A **codependent** person is in an unsatisfactory relationship with someone who is ill or an addict, but does not want the relationship to end. [TECHNICAL] ❏ *Guys can be codependent, too.* • N-COUNT **Codependent** is also a noun. ❏ *The program is geared toward the problems of being a codependent.* • **co|de|pend|en|cy** N-UNCOUNT ❏ *...the dangers of codependency.*

code word (code words) N-COUNT A **code word** is a word or phrase that has a special meaning, different from its normal meaning, for the people who have agreed to use it in this way. ❏ *...magnum, the code word for launching a radar attack.*

co|dex /koʊdɛks/ (codices) N-COUNT A **codex** is an ancient type of book which was written by hand, not printed.

codg|er /kɒdʒər/ (codgers) N-COUNT [usu adj n] Old **codger** is a disrespectful way of referring to an old man. [DISAPPROVAL]

co|di|ces /koʊdɪsiz, kɒd-/ **Codices** is the plural of **codex**.

codi|cil /kɒdɪsɪl/ (codicils) N-COUNT A **codicil** is an instruction that is added to a will after the main part of it has been written. [LEGAL]

codi|fy /kɒdɪfaɪ/ (codifies, codifying, codified) V-T If you **codify** a set of rules, you define them or present them in a clear and ordered way. ❏ *The latest draft of the agreement codifies the panel's decision.* • **codi|fi|ca|tion** /kɒdɪfɪkeɪʃən/ N-UNCOUNT [usu N of n] ❏ *The codification of the laws began in the 1840s.*

cod|ing /koʊdɪŋ/ N-UNCOUNT **Coding** is a method of making something easy to recognize or distinct, for example by coloring it. ❏ *...a color coding that will ensure easy reference for potential users.*

cod-liver oil also **cod liver oil** N-UNCOUNT **Cod liver oil** is a thick, yellow oil which is given as a medicine, especially to children, because it is full of vitamins A and D.

cod|piece /kɒdpis/ (codpieces) N-COUNT A **codpiece** was a piece of material worn by men in the 15th and 16th centuries to cover their genitals.

co|ed /koʊɛd/ (coeds) ▪ ADJ A **coed** school or college is the same as a coeducational school or college. ❏ *He was educated at a coed high school.* ▪ ADJ [ADJ n] A **coed** sports facility or sport is one that both males and females use or take part in at the same time. [mainly AM] ❏ *You have a choice of co-ed or single-sex swimming exercise classes.*

in BRIT, usually use **mixed**

▪ N-COUNT A **coed** is a female student at a coeducational college or university. [AM, INFORMAL] ❏ *...two University of Florida coeds.*

co|edu|ca|tion|al /koʊɛdʒʊkeɪʃənəl/ ADJ A **coeducational** school, college, or university is attended by both boys and girls. ❏ *The college has been coeducational since 1971.*

co|ef|fi|cient /koʊɪfɪʃənt/ (coefficients) N-COUNT [usu with supp] A **coefficient** is a number that expresses a measurement of a particular quality of a substance or object under specified conditions. [TECHNICAL] ❏ *...production coefficients.*

co|erce /koʊɜrs/ (coerces, coercing, coerced) V-T If you **coerce** someone into doing something, you make them do it, although they do not want to. [FORMAL] ❏ *Potter had argued that the government coerced him into pleading guilty.*

co|er|cion /koʊɜrʃən/ N-UNCOUNT **Coercion** is the act or process of persuading someone forcefully to do something that they do not want to do. ❏ *It was vital that the elections should be free of coercion or intimidation.*

co|er|cive /koʊɜrsɪv/ ADJ [usu ADJ n] **Coercive** measures are intended to force people to do something that they do not want to do. ❏ *The eighteenth-century British Admiralty had few coercive powers over its officers.*

co|ex|ist /koʊɪgzɪst/ (coexists, coexisting, coexisted) V-RECIP If one thing **coexists** with another, they exist together at the same time or in the same place. You can also say that two things **coexist**. ❏ *Newspaper websites can coexist with the newspapers and still bring in healthy profit margins.* ❏ *The different cultures had coexisted peacefully for many years.*

co|ex|ist|ence /koʊɪgzɪstəns/

in BRIT, also use **co-existence**

N-UNCOUNT [oft N of/with/between n] The **coexistence** of one thing with another is the fact that they exist together at the same time or in the same place. ❏ *He also believed in coexistence with the West.*

cof|fee ♦◇◇ /kɒfi/ (coffees) ▪ N-UNCOUNT **Coffee** is a hot drink made with water and ground or powdered coffee beans. ❏ *Would you like some coffee?* • N-COUNT A **coffee** is a cup of coffee. ❏ *I made a coffee.* ▪ N-MASS **Coffee** is the roasted beans or powder from which the drink is made. ❏ *The country exports 9 to 10 million bags of coffee every year.*

cof|fee bar (coffee bars) N-COUNT A **coffee bar** is a small café where nonalcoholic drinks and snacks are sold.

cof|fee bean (coffee beans) N-COUNT [usu pl] **Coffee beans** are small, dark brown beans that are roasted and ground to make coffee. They are the seeds of the coffee plant.

cof|fee break (coffee breaks) N-COUNT A **coffee break** is a short period of time, usually in the morning or afternoon, when you stop working and have a cup of coffee. ❏ *It looks like she'll be too busy to stop for a coffee break.*

cof|fee grind|er (coffee grinders) N-COUNT A **coffee grinder** is a machine for grinding coffee beans.

cof|fee house (coffee houses) also **coffeehouse** N-COUNT A **coffee house** is a kind of bar where people sit to drink coffee and talk.

cof|fee klatch /kɒfi klɑtʃ/ (coffee klatches) also **kaffeeklatsch** N-COUNT A **coffee klatch** is a social event at which coffee is served. [AM] ❏ *There's to be a coffee klatch after church tomorrow for the missionary education committee.*

cof|fee name (coffee names) N-COUNT Your **coffee name** is a name that you give in some situations because it is simpler than your real name. [INFORMAL] ❏ *I gave the woman my coffee name.*

coffee|pot /kɒfipɒt/ (coffeepots) also **coffee pot** N-COUNT A **coffeepot** is a tall, narrow pot with a spout and a lid, in which coffee is made or served.

cof|fee shop (coffee shops) N-COUNT A **coffee shop** is an informal restaurant that sells food and drink, but not normally alcoholic drinks.

cof|fee ta|ble (coffee tables) N-COUNT A **coffee table** is a small, low table in a living room.

coffee-table book (coffee-table books) N-COUNT A **coffee-table book** is a large, expensive book with a lot of pictures, which is designed to be looked at rather than to be read properly, and is usually placed where people can see it easily.

cof|fer /kɒfər/ (coffers) ▪ N-COUNT A **coffer** is a large, strong chest used for storing valuable objects such as money or gold and silver. [OLD-FASHIONED] ▪ N-PLURAL The **coffers** of an organization consist of the money that it has to spend, imagined as being collected together in one place. ❏ *The* proceeds from the lottery go towards sports and recreation, as well as swelling the coffers of the government.

cof|fin /kɒfɪn/ (coffins) **1** N-COUNT A **coffin** is a box in which a dead body is buried or cremated. **2** PHRASE If you say that one thing is **a nail in the coffin** of another thing, you mean that it will help bring about its end or failure. ❑ *A fine would be the final nail in the coffin of the airline.*

cog /kɒg/ (cogs) **1** N-COUNT A **cog** is a wheel with square or triangular teeth around the edge, which is used in a machine to turn another wheel or part. **2** PHRASE [v-link PHR] If you describe someone as **a cog in a machine** or **wheel**, you mean that they are a small part of a large organization or group. ❑ *Mr. Lake was an important cog in the republican campaign machine.*

co|gent /koʊdʒ³nt/ ADJ A **cogent** reason, argument, or example is strong and convincing. [FORMAL] ❑ *Every decision has to be backed up with rational and cogent arguments.* • **co|gen|cy** N-UNCOUNT ❑ *The film makes its points with cogency and force.*

cogi|tate /kɒdʒɪteɪt/ (cogitates, cogitating, cogitated) V-I If you **are cogitating**, you are thinking deeply about something. [FORMAL] ❑ *He sat silently cogitating.* ❑ *We cogitated on the meaning of life.* • **cogi|ta|tion** /kɒdʒɪteɪʃ³n/ N-UNCOUNT ❑ *After much cogitation, we decided to move to the Bahamas.*

cog|nac /koʊnyæk/ (cognacs) also **Cognac** N-MASS **Cognac** is a type of brandy made in the south-west of France. ❑ *...a bottle of Cognac.* • N-COUNT A **cognac** is a glass of cognac. ❑ *Phillips ordered a cognac.*

cog|nate /kɒgneɪt/ ADJ [oft ADJ with n] **Cognate** things are related to each other. [FORMAL] ❑ *...cognate words.*

cog|ni|sance /kɒgnɪzᵊns/ [BRIT] → see **cognizance**

cog|ni|sant /kɒgnɪzᵊnt/ [BRIT] → see **cognizant**

cog|ni|tion /kɒgnɪʃᵊn/ N-UNCOUNT **Cognition** is the mental process involved in knowing, learning, and understanding things. [FORMAL] ❑ *...processes of perception and cognition.*

cog|ni|tive /kɒgnɪtɪv/ ADJ [ADJ n] **Cognitive** means relating to the mental process involved in knowing, learning, and understanding things. [FORMAL] ❑ *As children grow older, their cognitive processes become sharper.*

cog|ni|zance /kɒgnɪzᵊns/

in BRIT, also use **cognisance**

1 PHRASE If you **take cognizance of** something, you take notice of it or acknowledge it. [FORMAL] ❑ *The government failed to take cognizance of their protest.* **2** N-UNCOUNT [oft N of n] **Cognizance** is knowledge or understanding. [FORMAL] ❑ *...the teacher's developing cognizance of the child's intellectual activity.*

cog|ni|zant /kɒgnɪzᵊnt/

in BRIT, also use **cognisant**

ADJ If someone is **cognizant** of something, they are aware of it or understand it. [FORMAL] ❑ *We are cognizant of the problem.*

co|gno|scen|ti /kɒnyəʃɛnti/ N-PLURAL [oft n n] The **cognoscenti** are the people who know a lot about a particular subject. [FORMAL] ❑ *She has an international reputation among film cognoscenti.*

co|hab|it /koʊhæbɪt/ (cohabits, cohabiting, cohabited) **1** V-RECIP If two people **are cohabiting**, they are living together and have a sexual relationship, but are not married. [FORMAL] ❑ *About one-third of all people cohabit at some time in their lives.* ❑ *The dentist left his wife of 15 years and openly cohabited with his receptionist.* ❑ *We had been cohabiting for ten years before we got married.* • **co|habi|ta|tion** /koʊhæbɪteɪʃᵊn/ N-UNCOUNT ❑ *The decline in marriage has been offset by a rise in cohabitation.* **2** → See feature box at **relationship**

co|here /koʊhɪər/ (coheres, cohering, cohered) V-RECIP If the different elements of a piece of writing, a piece of music, or a set of ideas **cohere**, they fit together well so that they form a united whole. ❑ *The various elements of the novel fail to cohere.* ❑ *This coheres with Peel's championing of alternative music.* ❑ *The empire could not cohere as a legitimate whole.*

co|her|ence /koʊhɪərᵊns, -hɛrᵊns/ N-UNCOUNT **Coherence** is a state or situation in which all the parts or ideas fit together well so that they form a united whole. ❑ *The anthology has a surprising sense of coherence.*

co|her|ent /koʊhɪərᵊnt, -hɛrᵊnt/ **1** ADJ If something is **coherent**, it is well planned, so that it is clear and sensible and all its parts go well with each other. ❑ *He has failed to work out a coherent strategy for modernizing the service.* • **co|her|ence** N-UNCOUNT ❑ *The campaign was widely criticized for making tactical mistakes and for a lack of coherence.* **2** ADJ [v-link ADJ] If someone is **coherent**, they express their thoughts in a clear and calm way, so that other people can understand what they are saying. ❑ *He's so calm when he answers questions in interviews. I wish I could be that coherent.* • **co|her|ence** N-UNCOUNT ❑ *This was debated eagerly at first, but with diminishing coherence as the champagne took hold.*

co|he|sion /koʊhiːʒᵊn/ N-UNCOUNT If there is **cohesion** within a society, organization, or group, the different members fit together well and form a united whole. ❑ *By 1990, it was clear that the cohesion of the armed forces was rapidly breaking down.*

co|he|sive /koʊhiːsɪv/ ADJ Something that is **cohesive** consists of parts that fit together well and form a united whole. ❑ *"Daring Adventures" from '86 is a far more cohesive and successful album.*

co|hort /koʊhɔːrt/ (cohorts) N-COUNT [usu poss N] A person's **cohorts** are their friends, supporters, or associates. [DISAPPROVAL] ❑ *Drake and his cohorts were not pleased with my appointment.*

coiffed /kwɑːft/ ADJ [usu adv ADJ] If someone has neatly **coiffed** hair, their hair is very carefully arranged. [FORMAL] ❑ *Her hair was perfectly coiffed.*

coif|fure /kwɑːfjʊər/ (coiffures) N-COUNT A person's **coiffure** is their hairstyle. [FORMAL] ❑ *...her immaculate golden coiffure.*

coif|fured /kwɑːfjʊərd/ ADJ [usu adv ADJ] **Coiffured** means the same as **coiffed**. [FORMAL]

coil /kɔɪl/ (coils) **1** N-COUNT A **coil** of rope or wire is a length of it that has been wound into a series of loops. ❑ *Tod shook his head angrily and slung the coil of rope over his shoulder.* **2** N-COUNT A **coil** is one loop in a series of loops. ❑ *Pythons kill by tightening their coils so that their victim cannot breathe.* **3** N-COUNT A **coil** is a thick spiral of wire through which an electrical current passes.

coiled /kɔɪld/ ADJ [ADJ n] **Coiled** means in the form of a series of loops. ❑ *...a heavy coiled spring.*

coin /kɔɪn/ (coins, coining, coined) **1** N-COUNT A **coin** is a small piece of metal which is used as money. ❑ *...a few loose coins.* **2** V-T If you **coin** a word or a phrase, you are the first person to say it. ❑ *Jaron Lanier coined the term "virtual reality" and pioneered its early development.* **3** PHRASE You say '**to coin a phrase**' to show that you realize you are making a pun or using a cliché. ❑ *Fifty local musicians have, to coin a phrase, banded together to form the Jazz Umbrella.* **4** PHRASE You use **the other side of the coin** to mention a different aspect of a situation. ❑ *On the other side of the coin, there'll be tax incentives for small businesses.*

coin|age /kɔɪnɪdʒ/ **1** N-UNCOUNT **Coinage** is the coins which are used in a country. ❑ *The city produced its own coinage from 1325 to 1864.* **2** N-UNCOUNT **Coinage** is the system of money used in a country. ❑ *In 1783 he secured the adoption of the decimal coinage in Congress.*

co|in|cide /koʊɪnsaɪd/ (coincides, coinciding, coincided) **1** V-RECIP If one event **coincides** with another, they happen at the same time. ❑ *The exhibition coincides with the 50th anniversary of his death.* **2** V-RECIP If the ideas or interests of two or more people **coincide**, they are the same. ❑ *The kids' views on life don't always coincide, but they're not afraid of voicing their opinions.*

co|in|ci|dence /koʊɪnsɪdᵊns/ (coincidences) N-VAR A **coincidence** is when two or more similar or related events occur at the same time by chance and without any planning. ❑ *Mr. Berry said the timing was a coincidence and that his decision was unrelated to Mr. Roman's departure.*

co|in|ci|dent /koʊɪnsɪdᵊnt/ **1** ADJ [oft v-link ADJ with n] **Coincident** events happen at the same time. [FORMAL] ❑ *...coincident birth times.* ❑ *Coincident with the talks, the bank was permitted to open a New York branch.* **2** ADJ [oft v-link ADJ with n] **Coincident** opinions, ideas, or policies are the same or are very similar to each other. [FORMAL] ❑ *Their aims are coincident with ours.* ❑ *Coincident interests with the corporate rich and political directorate are pointed out.*

co|in|ci|dent|al /koʊɪnsɪdɛntᵊl/ ADJ Something that is **coincidental** is the result of a coincidence and has not been deliberately arranged. ▫ *Any resemblance to actual persons, places, or events is purely coincidental.*

co|in|ci|dent|al|ly /koʊɪnsɪdɛntli/ ADV You use **coincidentally** when you want to draw attention to a coincidence. ▫ *Coincidentally, I had once found myself in a similar situation.*

coir /kɔɪər/ N-UNCOUNT **Coir** is a rough material made from coconut shells which is used to make ropes and mats.

coi|tal /koʊɪtᵊl/ ADJ [ADJ n] **Coital** means connected with or relating to sexual intercourse. [TECHNICAL] ▫ *...coital techniques.*

coi|tus /koʊɪtəs/ N-UNCOUNT **Coitus** is sexual intercourse. [TECHNICAL]

coke /koʊk/ **1** N-UNCOUNT **Coke** is a solid, black substance that is produced from coal and is burned as a fuel. ▫ *...a coke-burning stove.* **2** N-UNCOUNT **Coke** is the same as **cocaine**. [INFORMAL]

col. (**cols**) **col.** is a written abbreviation for **column** and **color**.

Col. N-TITLE **Col.** is a written abbreviation for **Colonel** when it is being used as a title in front of someone's name. ▫ *...Col. Frank Weldon.*

cola /koʊlə/ (**colas**) N-MASS **Cola** is a sweet, brown, nonalcoholic carbonated drink. ▫ *...a can of cola.*

col|an|der /kɒləndər, kʌl-/ (**colanders**) N-COUNT A **colander** is a container in the shape of a bowl with holes in it which you wash or drain food in.

cold ♦♦◇ /koʊld/ (**colder, coldest, colds**) **1** ADJ Something that is **cold** has a very low temperature or a lower temperature than is normal or acceptable. ▫ *Rinse the vegetables under cold running water.* ▫ *He likes his tea neither too hot nor too cold.* • **cold|ness** N-UNCOUNT ▫ *She complained about the coldness of his hands.* **2** ADJ If it is **cold**, or if a place is **cold**, the temperature of the air is very low. ▫ *It was bitterly cold.* ▫ *The house is cold because I can't afford to turn the heat on.* • **cold|ness** N-UNCOUNT ▫ *Within a quarter of an hour, the coldness of the night had gone.* **3** ADJ If you are **cold**, your body is at an unpleasantly low temperature. ▫ *I was freezing cold.* **4** ADJ **Cold** colors or **cold** light give an impression of coldness. ▫ *Generally, warm colors advance in painting and cold colors recede.* **5** ADJ A **cold** person does not show much emotion, especially affection, and therefore seems unfriendly and unsympathetic. If someone's voice is **cold**, they speak in an unfriendly, unsympathetic way. [DISAPPROVAL] ▫ *What a cold, unfeeling woman she was.* • **cold|ly** ADV ▫ *"I'll see you in the morning," Hugh said coldly.* • **cold|ness** N-UNCOUNT ▫ *His coldness angered her.* **6** N-UNCOUNT [also the N] Cold weather or low temperatures can be referred to as the **cold**. ▫ *He must have come inside to get out of the cold.* **7** in cold blood → see **blood 8** to get cold feet → see **foot** ① **9** to blow hot and cold → see **hot 10** to pour cold water on something → see **water 11** N-COUNT If you have a **cold**, you have a mild, very common illness which makes you sneeze a lot and gives you a sore throat or a cough. ▫ *I had a pretty bad cold.* **12** PHRASE If you **catch cold**, or **catch a cold**, you become ill with a cold. ▫ *Let's dry our hair so we don't catch cold.* **13** PHRASE If someone is **out cold**, they are unconscious or sleeping very heavily. ▫ *She was out cold but still breathing.*

SYNONYMS

cold
ADJ **1**
chilly: *It was a chilly afternoon.*
biting: *...a raw, biting, northerly wind.*
freezing: *The movie theater was freezing.*
icy: *An icy wind blew hard across the open spaces.*
cool: *I felt a current of cool air.*

---

cold-blooded 1 ADJ Someone who is **cold-blooded** does not show any pity or emotion. [DISAPPROVAL] ▫ *...a cold-blooded murderer.* **2** ADJ **Cold-blooded** animals have a body temperature that changes according to the surrounding temperature. Reptiles, for example, are cold-blooded.

cold call (**cold calls** or **cold-calls, cold-calling, cold-called**)

The form **cold-call** is used for the verb.

1 N-COUNT If someone makes a **cold call**, they telephone or visit someone they have never contacted, without making an appointment, in order to try and sell something. ▫ *She had worked as a call center operator making cold calls for time-share vacations.* **2** V-T/V-I To **cold-call** means to make a cold call. ▫ *You should refuse to meet anyone who cold-calls you with an offer of financial advice.* • **cold-calling** N-UNCOUNT ▫ *We will adhere to strict sales ethics, with none of the cold-calling that has given the industry such a bad name.*

cold com|fort N-UNCOUNT [oft N to/for n] If you say that a slightly encouraging fact or event is **cold comfort** to someone, you mean that it gives them little or no comfort because their situation is so difficult or unpleasant. ▫ *These figures may look good on paper but are cold comfort to the islanders themselves.*

cold cuts N-PLURAL **Cold cuts** are thin slices of cooked meat which are served cold. [AM]

cold fish N-SING If you say that someone is a **cold fish**, you think that they are unfriendly and unemotional. [DISAPPROVAL]

cold frame (**cold frames**) N-COUNT A **cold frame** is a wooden frame with a glass top in which you grow small plants to protect them from cold weather.

cold-hearted ADJ [usu ADJ n] A **cold-hearted** person does not feel any affection or sympathy toward other people. [DISAPPROVAL] ▫ *...a cold-hearted killer.*

cold shoul|der (**cold-shoulders, cold-shouldering, cold-shouldered**)

The form **cold-shoulder** is used for the verb.

1 N-SING [usu the N] If one person gives another the **cold shoulder**, they behave toward them in an unfriendly way, to show them that they do not care about them or that they want them to go away. ▫ *But when Gough looked to Haig for support, he was given the cold shoulder.* **2** V-T If one person **cold-shoulders** another, they give them the cold shoulder. ▫ *Even her own party considered her shrewish and nagging, and cold-shouldered her in the corridors.*

cold snap (**cold snaps**) N-COUNT [usu sing] A **cold snap** is a short period of cold and icy weather.

cold sore (**cold sores**) N-COUNT **Cold sores** are small sore spots that sometimes appear on or near someone's lips and nose when they have a cold. [mainly BRIT]

cold stor|age N-UNCOUNT If something such as food is put in **cold storage**, it is kept in an artificially cooled place in order to preserve it. ▫ *The strawberries are kept in cold storage to prevent them from spoiling during transportation.*

cold sweat (**cold sweats**) N-COUNT [usu sing, usu in/into N] If you are in a **cold sweat**, you are sweating and feel cold, usually because you are very afraid or nervous. ▫ *He awoke from his sleep in a cold sweat.*

cold tur|key N-UNCOUNT **Cold turkey** is the unpleasant physical reaction that people experience when they suddenly stop taking a drug that they have become addicted to. [INFORMAL] ▫ *The quickest way to get her off the drug was to let her go cold turkey.*

Cold War also **cold war** N-PROPER [the N] **The Cold War** was the period of hostility and tension between the Soviet bloc and the Western powers that followed the Second World War. ▫ *...the first major crisis of the post-Cold War era.*

cole|slaw /koʊlslɔ/ N-UNCOUNT **Coleslaw** is a salad of chopped raw cabbage, carrots, onions, and sometimes other vegetables, usually with mayonnaise.

col|ic /kɒlɪk/ N-UNCOUNT **Colic** is an illness in which you get severe pains in your stomach and bowels. Babies especially suffer from colic.

col|icky /kɒlɪki/ ADJ If someone, especially a baby, is **colicky**, they are suffering from colic.

co|li|tis /kəlaɪtɪs/ N-UNCOUNT **Colitis** is an illness in which your colon becomes inflamed. [TECHNICAL]

col|labo|rate /kəlæbəreɪt/ (**collaborates, collaborating, collaborated**) **1** V-RECIP When one person or group **collaborates** with another, they work together, especially on a book or on some research. ▫ *Much later he collaborated with his son Michael on the English translation of a text on food production.* ▫ *He turned his country house into a place where professionals and* amateurs collaborated in the making of music. **2** V-I If someone **collaborates** with an enemy that is occupying their country during a war, they help them. [DISAPPROVAL] ☐ *He was accused of having collaborated with the Communist secret police.*

col|labo|ra|tion /kəlæbəreɪʃ°n/ (**collaborations**) **1** N-VAR **Collaboration** is the act of working together to produce a piece of work, especially a book or some research. ☐ *There is substantial collaboration with neighboring departments.* ☐ *...scientific collaborations.* **2** N-COUNT A **collaboration** is a piece of work that has been produced as the result of people or groups working together. ☐ *He was also a writer of beautiful stories, some of which are collaborations with his fiancée.* **3** N-UNCOUNT **Collaboration** is the act of helping an enemy who is occupying your country during a war. [DISAPPROVAL] ☐ *...rumors of his collaboration with the occupying forces during the war.*

col|labo|ra|tive /kəlæbəreɪtɪv, -ərətɪv/ ADJ [ADJ n] A **collaborative** piece of work is done by two or more people or groups working together. [FORMAL] ☐ *...a collaborative research project.*

col|labo|ra|tor /kəlæbəreɪtər/ (**collaborators**) **1** N-COUNT A **collaborator** is someone that you work with to produce a piece of work, especially a book or some research. ☐ *The Irvine group and their collaborators are testing whether lasers do the job better.* **2** N-COUNT A **collaborator** is someone who helps an enemy who is occupying their country during a war. [DISAPPROVAL] ☐ *Two alleged collaborators were shot dead by masked activists.*

col|lage /kəlɑʒ/ (**collages**) **1** N-COUNT A **collage** is a picture that has been made by sticking pieces of colored paper and cloth onto paper. ☐ *...a collage of words and pictures from magazines.* **2** N-UNCOUNT **Collage** is the method of making pictures by sticking pieces of colored paper and cloth onto paper. ☐ *The illustrations make use of collage, watercolor, and other media.*

col|la|gen /kɒlədʒən/ N-UNCOUNT **Collagen** is a protein that is found in the bodies of people and animals. It is often used as an ingredient in cosmetics or is injected into the face in cosmetic surgery, in order to make the skin look younger. ☐ *The collagen that is included in face creams comes from animal skin.* ☐ *...collagen injections.*

col|lapse ✦✧ /kəlæps/ (**collapses, collapsing, collapsed**) **1** V-I If a building or other structure **collapses**, it falls down very suddenly. ☐ *A section of the Bay Bridge had collapsed.* • N-UNCOUNT **Collapse** is also a noun. ☐ *The governor called for an inquiry into the freeway's collapse.* **2** V-I If something, for example a system or institution, **collapses**, it fails or comes to an end completely and suddenly. ☐ *His business empire collapsed under a massive burden of debt.* • N-UNCOUNT **Collapse** is also a noun. ☐ *The coup's collapse has speeded up the drive to independence.* **3** V-I If you **collapse**, you suddenly faint or fall down because you are very ill or weak. ☐ *He collapsed following a vigorous exercise session at his home.* • N-UNCOUNT **Collapse** is also a noun. ☐ *A few days after his collapse he was sitting up in bed.* **4** V-I If you **collapse** onto something, you sit or lie down suddenly because you are very tired. ☐ *She arrived home exhausted and barely capable of showering before collapsing on her bed.* **5** → See feature box at **banking**

─── SYNONYMS ───
collapse
VERB
1
fall down: *Children jumped from upper floors as the building fell down around them.*
give: *My knees gave under me.*
give way: *The hook in the ceiling had given way.*
cave in: *Part of the roof has caved in.*
2
fail: *He was afraid the revolution they had started would fail.*
fold: *2,500 small businesses were folding each week.*
founder: *The talks have foundered.*
break down: *Talks with business leaders broke down last night.*
fall through: *The deal fell through.*
3
faint: *She suddenly fell forward on to the table and fainted.*
crumple: *He immediately crumpled to the floor.*
pass out: *He felt sick and dizzy, and then passed out.*
keel over: *He then keeled over and fell flat on his back.*
black out: *Samadov said that he felt so ill that he blacked out.*

col|laps|ible /kəlæpsɪb°l/ ADJ [usu ADJ n] A **collapsible** object is designed to be folded flat when it is not being used. ☐ *...a collapsible chair.*

col|lar /kɒlər/ (**collars**) **1** N-COUNT The **collar** of a shirt or coat is the part which fits around the neck and is usually folded over. ☐ *His tie was pulled loose and his collar hung open.* **2** → see also **blue-collar, white-collar 3** N-COUNT A **collar** is a band of leather or plastic which is put around the neck of a dog or cat.

col|lar|bone /kɒlərboʊn/ (**collarbones**) N-COUNT Your **collarbones** are the two long bones which run from your throat to your shoulders. ☐ *Harold had a broken collarbone.*

col|lar|less /kɒlərlɪs/ ADJ [ADJ n] A **collarless** shirt or jacket has no collar.

col|late /kəleɪt/ (**collates, collating, collated**) **1** V-T When you **collate** pieces of information, you gather them all together and examine them. ☐ *Roberts has spent much of his working life collating the data on which the study was based.* **2** V-T If someone, or something such as a photocopier, **collates** pieces of paper, they put them together in the correct order. ☐ *They took sheets of paper off piles, collated them and put them into envelopes.*

col|lat|er|al /kəlætərəl/ N-UNCOUNT **Collateral** is money or property which is used as a guarantee that someone will repay a loan. [FORMAL] ☐ *Many people use personal assets as collateral for small business loans.*

col|lat|er|al dam|age N-UNCOUNT **Collateral damage** is accidental injury to nonmilitary people or damage to nonmilitary buildings which occurs during a military operation. ☐ *To minimize collateral damage, maximum precision in bombing was required.*

col|league ✦✦✧ /kɒliːg/ (**colleagues**) N-COUNT Your **colleagues** are the people you work with, especially in a professional job. ☐ *Without consulting his colleagues, he flew from Los Angeles to Chicago.*

─── SYNONYMS ───
colleague
NOUN
partner: *He's a partner in a Chicago law firm.*
associate: *...the restaurant owner's business associates.*
co-worker: *My co-workers didn't want me to leave.*

col|lect ✦✦✧ /kəlɛkt/ (**collects, collecting, collected**) **1** V-T If you **collect** a number of things, you bring them together from several places or from several people. ☐ *Two young girls were collecting firewood.* ☐ *Elizabeth had been collecting snails for a school project.* **2** V-T If you **collect** things, such as stamps or books, as a hobby, you get a large number of them over a period of time because they interest you. ☐ *I used to collect stamps.* • **col|lect|ing** N-UNCOUNT ☐ *...hobbies like stamp collecting and fishing.* **3** V-T/V-I If a substance **collects** somewhere, or if something **collects**, it keeps arriving over a period of time and is held in that place or thing. ☐ *Methane gas does collect in the mines around here.* **4** V-T If something **collects** light, energy, or heat, it attracts it. ☐ *Like a telescope, it has a curved mirror to collect the sunlight.* **5** V-T/V-I If you **collect** for a charity or for a present for someone, you ask people to give you money for it. ☐ *Are you collecting for charity?* ☐ *The organization has collected $2.5 million for the relief effort.* **6** V-T When you **collect** someone or something, you go and get them from the place where they are waiting for you or have been left for you. [mainly BRIT]

in AM, usually use **pick up**

─── SYNONYMS ───
collect
VERB
1
gather: *I suggest we gather enough firewood to last the night.*
compile: *Councils compiled a register of all adults living in their areas.*
assemble: *Greenpeace managed to assemble enough boats to waylay the ship at sea.*
accumulate: *Households accumulate wealth across a broad spectrum of assets.*
round up: *We've rounded up a selection of products.*
6
fetch: *Sylvia fetched a towel from the bathroom.*
pick up: *We drove to the airport the next morning to pick up Susan.*
get: *Go and get your daddy for me.*

col|lect call (collect calls) N-COUNT A **collect call** is a telephone call which is paid for by the person who receives the call, rather than the person who makes the call. [AM] ❑ *"I want to make a collect call," she said as soon as a voice came on the line.* • PHRASE If you **call collect** when you make a telephone call, the person who you are phoning pays the cost of the call and not you. [AM]

col|lect|ed /kəlɛktɪd/ **1** ADJ [ADJ n] An author's **collected** works or letters are all their works or letters published in one book or in a set of books. ❑ *...the collected works of Rudyard Kipling.* **2** ADJ [usu v-link ADJ] If you say that someone is **collected**, you mean that they are very calm and self-controlled, especially when they are in a difficult or serious situation. ❑ *Police say she was cool and collected during her interrogation.* **3** → see also **collect**

col|lect|ible /kəlɛktəbəl/ also **collectable** ADJ A **collectible** object is one which is valued very highly by collectors because it is rare or beautiful. ❑ *Many of these cushions have survived and are very collectible.*

col|lect|ing /kəlɛktɪŋ/ **1** ADJ [ADJ n] A **collecting** tin or box is the same as a **collection box**. [BRIT] **2** → see also **collect**

col|lec|tion ✦✧ /kəlɛkʃən/ (collections) **1** N-COUNT A **collection** of things is a group of similar things that you have deliberately acquired, usually over a period of time. ❑ *Robert's collection of prints and paintings has been bought over the years.* ❑ *The Art Gallery of Ontario has the world's largest collection of sculptures by Henry Moore.* **2** N-COUNT A **collection** of stories, poems, or articles is a number of them published in one book. ❑ *Two years ago he published a collection of short stories called "Facing The Music."* **3** N-COUNT A **collection** of things is a group of things. ❑ *...a collection of modern glass office buildings.* **4** N-COUNT A fashion designer's new **collection** consists of the new clothes they have designed for the next season. ❑ *Her spring/summer collection for this year predictably uses both simple and rich fabrics.* **5** N-COUNT If you organize a **collection** for charity, you collect money from people to give to charity. ❑ *I asked my principal if he could arrange a collection for a refugee charity.* **6** N-COUNT A **collection** is money that is given by people in church during some Christian services. **7** N-UNCOUNT **Collection** is the act of collecting something from a place or from people. ❑ *Money can be sent to any one of 22,000 agents worldwide for collection.* ❑ *...computer systems to speed up collection of information.*

col|lec|tion agen|cy (collection agencies) N-COUNT A **collection agency** is an organization that obtains payments from people who owe money to others. [mainly AM] ❑ *Missed payments are referred to a collection agency.*

col|lec|tion box (collection boxes) N-COUNT A **collection box** is a box or can that is used to collect money for charity. [AM]

col|lec|tive ✦✧ /kəlɛktɪv/ (collectives) **1** ADJ [ADJ n] **Collective** actions, situations, or feelings involve or are shared by every member of a group of people. ❑ *It was a collective decision.* • **col|lec|tive|ly** ADV ❑ *They collectively decided to recognize the changed situation.* **2** ADJ [ADJ n] A **collective** amount of something is the total obtained by adding together the amounts that each person or thing in a group has. ❑ *Their collective volume wasn't very large.* • **col|lec|tive|ly** ADV [ADV with v] ❑ *In 1968 the states collectively spent $2 billion on it.* **3** ADJ [ADJ n] The **collective** term for two or more types of thing is a general word or expression which refers to all of them. ❑ *Social science is a collective name, covering a series of individual sciences.* • **col|lec|tive|ly** ADV [ADV with v] ❑ *...other sorts of cells (known collectively as white corpuscles).* **4** N-COUNT A **collective** is a business or farm which is run, and often owned, by a group of people. [BUSINESS] ❑ *He will see that he is participating in all the decisions of the collective.*

col|lec|tive bar|gain|ing N-UNCOUNT When a labor union engages in **collective bargaining**, it has talks with an employer about its members' pay and working conditions. [BUSINESS] ❑ *...a new collective-bargaining agreement.*

col|lec|tive noun (collective nouns) N-COUNT A **collective noun** is a noun such as 'family' or 'team' that refers to a group of people or things.

col|lec|tive un|con|scious N-SING [usu the N] In psychology, the **collective unconscious** consists of the basic ideas and images that all people are believed to share because they have inherited them.

col|lec|tiv|ism /kəlɛktɪvɪzəm/ N-UNCOUNT **Collectivism** is the political belief that a country's industries and services should be owned and controlled by the state or by all the people in a country. Socialism and communism are both forms of collectivism.

col|lec|tiv|ist /kəlɛktɪvɪst/ ADJ [usu ADJ n] **Collectivist** means relating to collectivism. ❑ *...collectivist ideals.*

col|lec|ti|vize /kəlɛktɪvaɪz/ (collectivizes, collectivizing, collectivized)

in BRIT, also use **collectivise**

V-T [usu passive] If farms or factories **are collectivized**, they are brought under state ownership and control, usually by combining a number of small farms or factories into one large one. ❑ *Most large businesses were collectivized at the start of the war.* ❑ *He forced the country to collectivize agriculture.* ❑ *...large collectivized farms.* • **col|lec|tivi|za|tion** /kəlɛktɪvaɪzeɪʃən/ N-UNCOUNT [oft N of n] ❑ *...the collectivization of agriculture.*

col|lec|tor /kəlɛktər/ (collectors) **1** N-COUNT A **collector** is a person who collects things of a particular type as a hobby. ❑ *...a stamp collector.* ❑ *...a respected collector of Indian art.* **2** N-COUNT You can use **collector** to refer to someone whose job is to take something such as money, tickets, or garbage from people. For example, a rent **collector** collects rent from people. ❑ *He earned his living as a tax collector.*

col|lec|tor's item (collector's items) N-COUNT A **collector's item** is an object which is highly valued by collectors because it is rare or beautiful.

col|lege ✦✧ /kɒlɪdʒ/ (colleges) **1** N-VAR; N-IN-NAMES A **college** is an institution where students study after they have left secondary school. ❑ *Their daughter Joanna is taking business courses at a local college.* ❑ *Stephanie took up making jewelry after leaving art college this morning.* **2** N-COUNT; N-IN-NAMES At some universities in the United States, **colleges** are divisions which offer degrees in particular subjects. ❑ *...a professor at the University of Florida College of Law.* **3** N-COUNT A **college** is one of the institutions which some British universities are divided into. ❑ *He was educated at Balliol College, Oxford.* **4** → See feature box at **university**

COLLOCATIONS

college
NOUN **1**
noun + **college**: community, liberal arts; art
adjective + **college**: agricultural, naval, secretarial, theological; technical
verb + **college**: attend; finish, leave

---

col|legi|ate /kəlɪdʒɪt, -dʒiːɪt/ ADJ [ADJ n] **Collegiate** means belonging or relating to a college or to college students. [mainly AM] ❑ *The 1933 national collegiate football championship was won by Michigan.* ❑ *...collegiate life.*

col|lide /kəlaɪd/ (collides, colliding, collided) **1** V-RECIP If two or more moving people or objects **collide**, they crash into one another. If a moving person or object **collides** with a person or object that is not moving, they crash into them. ❑ *Two trains collided head-on in Ohio early this morning.* ❑ *Racing up the stairs, he almost collided with Daisy.* **2** V-RECIP If the aims, opinions, or interests of one person or group **collide** with those of another person or group, they are very different from each other and are therefore opposed. ❑ *The aims of the negotiators in New York again seem likely to collide with the aims of the warriors in the field.*

col|lie /kɒli/ (collies) N-COUNT A **collie** or a **collie dog** is a dog with long hair and a long, narrow nose.

col|li|sion /kəlɪʒən/ (collisions) **1** N-VAR A **collision** occurs when a moving object crashes into something. ❑ *They were on their way to the airport when their van was involved in a collision with a car.* **2** N-COUNT A **collision** of cultures or ideas occurs when two very different cultures or people meet and conflict. ❑ *The play represents the collision of three generations.* **3** → See feature box at **accident**, **drive**

col|li|sion course ◼ N-SING [usu on a N, oft N with n] If two or more people or things are on a **collision course**, there is likely to be a sudden and violent disagreement between them. ☐ *The two communities are now on a collision course.* ◼ N-SING [usu on a N, oft N with n] If two or more people or things are on a **collision course**, they are likely to meet and crash into each other violently. ☐ *There is an asteroid on a collision course with the Earth.*

col|lo|cate (collocates, collocating, collocated)

The noun is pronounced /ˈkɒləkɪt/. The verb is pronounced /ˈkɒləkeɪt/.

◼ N-COUNT In linguistics, a **collocate** of a particular word is another word which often occurs with that word. [TECHNICAL] ◼ V-RECIP In linguistics, if one word **collocates** with another, they often occur together. [TECHNICAL] ☐ *"Fast" collocates with "food."*

col|lo|ca|tion /ˌkɒləˈkeɪʃən/ (collocations) N-VAR In linguistics, **collocation** is the way that some words occur regularly whenever another word is used. [TECHNICAL] ☐ *...the basic notion of collocation.*

col|lo|quial /kəˈloʊkwiəl/ ADJ **Colloquial** words and phrases are informal and are used mainly in conversation. ☐ *...a colloquial expression.*

col|lo|qui|al|ism /kəˈloʊkwiəlɪzəm/ (colloquialisms) N-COUNT A **colloquialism** is a colloquial word or phrase.

col|lude /kəˈluːd/ (colludes, colluding, colluded) V-RECIP If one person **colludes** with another, they cooperate with them secretly or illegally. [DISAPPROVAL] ☐ *Several local officials are in jail on charges of colluding with the Mafia.* ☐ *We all colluded in the myth of him as the swanky businessman.*

col|lu|sion /kəˈluːʒən/ N-UNCOUNT [usu N between pl-n, N with n, in N] **Collusion** is secret or illegal cooperation, especially between countries or organizations. [FORMAL, DISAPPROVAL] ☐ *He found no evidence of collusion between record companies and retailers.*

col|lu|sive /kəˈluːsɪv/ ADJ [usu ADJ n] **Collusive** behavior involves secret or illegal cooperation, especially between countries or organizations. [FORMAL, DISAPPROVAL] ☐ *...collusive business practices.*

co|logne /kəˈloʊn/ (colognes) N-MASS **Cologne** is a kind of weak perfume.

Col|om|bian /kəˈlʌmbiən/ (Colombians) ◼ ADJ **Colombian** means belonging or relating to Colombia or its people or culture. ◼ N-COUNT A **Colombian** is a Colombian citizen, or a person of Colombian origin.

co|lon /ˈkoʊlən/ (colons) ◼ N-COUNT A **colon** is the punctuation mark : which you can use in several ways. For example, you can put it before a list of things or before reported speech. ◼ N-COUNT Your **colon** is the part of your intestine above your rectum. ☐ *In the U.S., there are 60,000 deaths a year from colon cancer.* ◼ → See also color supplement

colo|nel ◆◇◇ /ˈkɜːrnəl/ (colonels) N-COUNT; N-TITLE; N-VOC A **colonel** is a senior officer in an army, air force, or the marines. ☐ *This particular place was run by an ex-Army colonel.*

co|lo|nial /kəˈloʊniəl/ ◼ ADJ [ADJ n] **Colonial** means relating to countries that are colonies, or to colonialism. ☐ *...the 31st anniversary of Jamaica's independence from British colonial rule.* ◼ ADJ A **colonial** building or piece of furniture was built or made in a style that was popular in America in the 17th and 18th centuries. [mainly AM] ☐ *...the white colonial houses on the north side of the campus.*

co|lo|ni|al|ism /kəˈloʊniəlɪzəm/ N-UNCOUNT **Colonialism** is the practice by which a powerful country directly controls less powerful countries and uses their resources to increase its own power and wealth. ☐ *...the bitter oppression of slavery and colonialism.*

co|lo|ni|al|ist /kəˈloʊniəlɪst/ (colonialists) ◼ ADJ **Colonialist** means relating to colonialism. ☐ *...the European colonialist powers.* ◼ N-COUNT A **colonialist** is a person who believes in colonialism or helps their country to get colonies. ☐ *...rulers who were imposed on the people by the colonialists.*

co|lon|ic ir|ri|ga|tion /koʊˈlɒnɪk ˌɪrɪˈɡeɪʃən/ (colonic irrigations) N-VAR **Colonic irrigation** is a medical procedure in which a person's colon is washed by injecting water or other fluids into it.

colo|nist /ˈkɒlənɪst/ (colonists) N-COUNT **Colonists** are the people who start a colony or the people who are among the first to live in a particular colony. ☐ *The apple was brought over here by the colonists when they came.*

colo|nize /ˈkɒlənaɪz/ (colonizes, colonizing, colonized)

in BRIT, also use **colonise**

◼ V-T If people **colonize** a foreign country, they go to live there and take control of it. ☐ *The first British attempt to colonize Ireland was in the twelfth century.* ☐ *Liberia was never colonized by the European powers.* ◼ V-T When large numbers of animals **colonize** a place, they go to live there and make it their home. ☐ *Toads are colonizing the whole place.* ◼ V-T [usu passive] When an area **is colonized** by a type of plant, the plant grows there in large amounts. ☐ *The area was then colonized by scrub.*

col|on|nade /ˌkɒləˈneɪd/ (colonnades) N-COUNT A **colonnade** is a row of evenly spaced columns. ☐ *...a colonnade with stone pillars.*

colo|ny /ˈkɒləni/ (colonies) ◼ N-COUNT A **colony** is a country which is controlled by a more powerful country. ☐ *He was born in Algeria, a former colony of France.* ◼ N-COUNT You can refer to a place where a particular group of people lives as a particular kind of **colony**. ☐ *In 1932, he established a school and artists' colony in Stone City, Iowa.* ☐ *...a penal colony.* ◼ N-COUNT A **colony** of birds, insects, or animals is a group of them that live together. ☐ *The islands are famed for their colonies of sea birds.*

col|or ◆◆◆ /ˈkʌlər/ (colors, coloring, colored)

in BRIT, use **colour**

◼ N-COUNT The **color** of something is the appearance that it has as a result of the way in which it reflects light. Red, blue, and green are colors. ☐ *"What color is the car?"—"Red."* ☐ *Judi's favourite color is pink.* ◼ N-COUNT Someone's **color** is the color of their skin. People often use **color** in this way to refer to a person's race. [POLITENESS] ☐ *I don't care what color she is.* ◼ N-VAR A **color** is a substance you use to give something a particular color. Dyes and makeup are sometimes referred to as **colors**. ☐ *It is better to avoid all food colors.* ☐ *Her nail color was coordinated with her lipstick.* ◼ V-T If you **color** something, you use something such as dyes or paint to change its color. ☐ *I've never been one for colouring my hair at home.* ☐ *We'd been making cakes and coloring the posters.* ● **col|or|ing** N-UNCOUNT ☐ *They could not afford to spoil those maps by careless coloring.* ◼ V-I If someone **colors**, their face becomes redder than it normally is, usually because they are embarrassed. ☐ *Andrew couldn't help noticing that she colored slightly.* ◼ V-T If something **colors** your opinion, it affects the way that you think about something. ☐ *All too often it is only the negative images of Ireland that are portrayed, coloring opinions and hiding the true nature of the country.* ◼ ADJ A **color** television, photograph, or picture is one that shows things in all their colors, and not just in black, white, and gray. ☐ *In Japan 99 per cent of all households now have a color television set.* ◼ N-UNCOUNT **Color** is a quality that makes something especially interesting or exciting. ☐ *She had resumed the travel necessary to add depth and color to her novels.* ◼ N-PLURAL A country's national **colors** are the colors of its national flag. ☐ *The Opera House is decorated with the Hungarian national colors: green, red, and white.* ◼ N-PLURAL People sometimes refer to the flag of a particular part of an army, navy, or air force, or the flag of a particular country as its **colors**. ☐ *Troops raised the country's colors in a special ceremony.* ◼ N-PLURAL A sports team's **colors** are the colors of the clothes they wear when they play. ☐ *I was wearing the team's colors.* ◼ → see also **colored, coloring** ◼ PHRASE If a movie or television program is **in color**, it has been made so that you see the picture in all its colors, and not just in black, white, or gray. ☐ *Was he going to show the movie? Was it in color?* ◼ PHRASE **People of color** are people who belong to a race with dark skins. [POLITENESS] ☐ *Black communities spoke up to defend the rights of all people of color.*

▶ **color in** PHRASAL VERB If you **color in** a drawing, you give it different colors using crayons or paints. ☐ *Someone had colored in all the black and white pictures.*

> **COLLOCATIONS**
>
> **color**
> NOUN **1**
> noun + **color**: eye, hair, skin
> adjective + **color**: bold, bright, strong, vibrant, vivid; light, muted, neutral, pale, pastel; cool, rich, warm; dark, deep

col|or|ant /k_ʌ_lərənt/ (**colorants**)

in BRIT, use **colourant**

N-COUNT A **colorant** is a substance that is used to give something a particular color. ❏ ...*a new range of hair colorants.*

col|ora|tion /k_ʌ_ləreɪʃ³n/ N-UNCOUNT The **coloration** of an animal or a plant is the colors and patterns on it. ❏ ...*plants with yellow or red coloration.*

colo|ra|tu|ra /k_ʌ_lərətuərə/ (**coloraturas**) **1** N-UNCOUNT **Coloratura** is very complicated and difficult music for a solo singer, especially in opera. [TECHNICAL] **2** N-COUNT [oft N n] A **coloratura** is a singer who is skilled at singing coloratura. [TECHNICAL]

color-blind

in BRIT, use **colour-blind**

1 ADJ [usu v-link ADJ] Someone who is **color-blind** cannot see the difference between colors, especially between red and green. ❏ *Sixteen times as many men are color-blind as women.* • **color-blindness** N-UNCOUNT ❏ *What exactly is color-blindness and how do you find out if you have it?* **2** ADJ A **color-blind** system or organization does not treat people differently according to their race or nationality. ❏ ...*the introduction of more color-blind anti-poverty programs.* ❏ *Theatre companies have really embraced colour-blind casting.*

color-coded

in BRIT, use **colour-coded**

ADJ Things that are **color-coded** use colors to represent different features or functions. ❏ *The contents are emptied into color-coded buckets.*

col|ored ♦◇◇ /k_ʌ_lərd/

in BRIT, use **coloured**

1 ADJ Something that is **colored** a particular color is that color. ❏ *The illustration shows a cluster of five roses colored apricot orange.* **2** ADJ Something that is **colored** is a particular color or combination of colors, rather than being just white, black, or the color that it is naturally. ❏ *You can often choose between plain white or colored and patterned scarves.* **3** ADJ **Colored** was used in the past to refer to people with dark skins. [OFFENSIVE, OLD-FASHIONED]

col|or|fast /k_ʌ_lərfæst/

in BRIT, use **colourfast**

ADJ A fabric that is **colorfast** has a color that will not get paler when the fabric is washed or worn.

col|or|ful /k_ʌ_lərfəl/

in BRIT, use **colourful**

1 ADJ Something that is **colorful** has bright colors or a lot of different colors. ❏ *The flowers were colorful and the scenery magnificent.* **2** ADJ A **colorful** story is full of exciting details. ❏ *The story she told was certainly colorful, and extended over her life in England, Germany, and Spain.* **3** ADJ A **colorful** character is a person who behaves in an interesting and amusing way. ❏ *Casey Stengel was probably the most colorful character in baseball.*

col|or|ing /k_ʌ_lərɪŋ/

in BRIT, use **colouring**

1 N-UNCOUNT The **coloring** of something is the color or colors that it is. ❏ *Other countries vary the coloring of their bank notes as well as their size.* **2** N-UNCOUNT Someone's **coloring** is the color of their hair, skin, and eyes. ❏ *None of them had their father's dark coloring.* **3** N-UNCOUNT **Coloring** is a substance that is used to give color to food. ❏ *A few drops of green food coloring were added.* **4** → see also **color**

col|or|ing book (**coloring books**)

in BRIT, use **colouring book**

N-COUNT A **coloring book** is a book of simple drawings which children can color in.

col|or|ist /k_ʌ_lərɪst/ (**colorists**)

in BRIT, use **colourist**

1 N-COUNT A **colorist** is someone such as an artist or a fashion designer who uses colors in an interesting and original way. **2** N-COUNT A **colorist** is a hairdresser who specializes in coloring people's hair.

col|ori|za|tion /k_ʌ_lərɪzeɪʃ³n/ N-UNCOUNT **Colorization** is a technique used to add color to old black and white movies. ❏ ...*the colorization of old film classics.*

col|or|ized /k_ʌ_lərаɪzd/ ADJ [usu ADJ n] A **colorized** film is an old black and white movie which has had color added to it using a special technique. ❏ *The film is available in a colorized version.*

col|or|less /k_ʌ_lərlɪs/

in BRIT, use **colourless**

1 ADJ Something that is **colorless** has no color at all. ❏ ...*a colorless, almost odorless liquid.* **2** ADJ If someone's face is **colorless**, it is very pale, usually because they are frightened, shocked, or ill. ❏ *Her face was colorless, and she was shaking.* **3** ADJ **Colorless** people or places are dull and uninteresting. ❏ ...*the much more experienced but colorless general.*

col|or line (**color lines**)

in BRIT, use **colour line**

N-COUNT [usu sing] A **color line** is the set of social, economic or political barriers that exist between different racial groups. ❏ ...*one of the first Black players to break the color line in the deep South.* ❏ *She made numerous efforts to break down color lines in public places.*

col|or scheme (**color schemes**)

in BRIT, use **colour scheme**

N-COUNT In a room or house, the **color scheme** is the way in which colors have been used to decorate it. ❏ ...*a stylish color scheme of olive green and mustard.*

co|los|sal /kəlɒs³l/ ADJ If you describe something as **colossal**, you are emphasizing that it is very large. [EMPHASIS] ❏ *There has been a colossal waste of public money.*

co|los|sus /kəlɒsəs/ (**colossi** /kəlɒsaɪ/) N-COUNT [usu sing, oft N of n] **1** If you describe someone or something as a **colossus**, you think that they are extremely important and great in ability or size. [JOURNALISM, EMPHASIS] ❏ ...*saxophone colossus Sonny Rollins.* ❏ *He became a colossus of the labor movement.* **2** N-COUNT A **colossus** is an extremely large statue.

co|los|to|my /kəlɒstəmi/ (**colostomies**) N-COUNT A **colostomy** is a surgical operation in which a permanent opening from the colon is made. [MEDICAL]

col|our /k_ʌ_lər/ [BRIT] → see **color**
col|our|ant /k_ʌ_lərənt/ [BRIT] → see **colorant**
col|our-blind [BRIT] → see **color-blind**
col|our-coded [BRIT] → see **color-coded**
col|oured /k_ʌ_lərd/ [BRIT] → see **colored**
col|our|fast /k_ʌ_lərfæst/ [BRIT] → see **colorfast**
col|our|ful /k_ʌ_lərfəl/ [BRIT] → see **colorful**
col|our|ing /k_ʌ_lərɪŋ/ [BRIT] → see **coloring**
col|our|ing book [BRIT] → see **coloring book**
col|our|ist /k_ʌ_lərɪst/ [BRIT] → see **colorist**
col|our|less /k_ʌ_lərlɪs/ [BRIT] → see **colorless**
col|our scheme [BRIT] → see **color scheme**

colt /koʊlt/ (**colts**) N-COUNT A **colt** is a young male horse.

colt|ish /koʊltɪʃ/ ADJ A young person or animal that is **coltish** is full of energy but clumsy or awkward, because they lack physical skill or control. ❏ ...*coltish teenagers.*

col|umn ♦◇◇ /kɒləm/ (**columns**) **1** N-COUNT A **column** is a tall, often decorated cylinder of stone which is built to honor someone or forms part of a building. ❏ *Seven massive columns rise up from a marble floor.* **2** N-COUNT A **column** is something that has a tall, narrow shape. ❏ *The explosion sent a column of smoke thousands of feet into the air.* **3** N-COUNT A **column** is a group of people or animals which moves in a long line. ❑ *There were reports of columns of military vehicles appearing on the streets.* ◰ N-COUNT On a printed page such as a page of a dictionary, newspaper, or printed chart, a **column** is one of two or more vertical sections which are read downward. ❑ *We had stupidly been looking at the wrong column of figures.* ◱ N-COUNT In a newspaper or magazine, a **column** is a section that is always written by the same person or is always about the same topic. ❑ *His name features frequently in the social columns of the tabloid newspapers.* ◲ → See feature box at **house**; See also **color supplement**

col|umn|ist /kɒləmnɪst, -əmɪst/ (**columnists**) N-COUNT A **columnist** is a journalist who regularly writes a particular kind of article in a newspaper or magazine. ❑ *Clarence Page is a columnist for the Chicago Tribune.*

coma /koʊmə/ (**comas**) N-COUNT Someone who is in a **coma** is in a state of deep unconsciousness. ❑ *She was in a coma for seven weeks.*

co|ma|tose /koʊmətoʊs/ ◰ ADJ A person who is **comatose** is in a coma. [MEDICAL] ❑ *The right side of my brain had been so severely bruised that I was comatose for a month.* ◱ ADJ [oft ADJ after v] A person who is **comatose** is in a deep sleep, usually because they are tired or have drunk too much alcohol. [INFORMAL] ❑ *Grandpa lies comatose on the sofa.*

comb /koʊm/ (**combs, combing, combed**) ◰ N-COUNT A **comb** is a flat piece of plastic or metal with narrow, pointed teeth along one side, which you use to make your hair neat. ◱ V-T When you **comb** your hair, you make it neat using a comb. ❑ *Salvatore combed his hair carefully.* ◲ V-T If you **comb** a place, you search everywhere in it in order to find someone or something. ❑ *Officers combed the woods for the murder weapon.* ◳ V-I If you **comb** through information, you look at it very carefully in order to find something. ❑ *Eight policemen then spent two years combing through the evidence.*

com|bat ✦◊ (**combats, combating** or **combatting, combated** or **combatted**)

> The noun is pronounced /kɒmbæt/. The verb is pronounced /kəmbæt/.

◰ N-UNCOUNT **Combat** is fighting that takes place in a war. ❑ *Over 16 million men had died in combat.* ❑ *Yesterday saw hand-to-hand combat in the city.* ◱ N-COUNT A **combat** is a battle, or a fight between two people. ❑ *It was the end of a long combat.* ◲ V-T If people in authority **combat** something, they try to stop it from happening. ❑ *Congress has criticized new government measures to combat crime.*

> **SYNONYMS**
>
> **combat**
> NOUN ◰
> **fighting:** *More than nine hundred people have died in the fighting.*
> **war:** *He spent part of the war in the National Guard.*
> **battle:** *...after a gun battle between police and drug traffickers.*
> **action:** *13 soldiers were killed and 10 wounded in action.*
> **conflict:** *...talks aimed at ending four decades of conflict.*

> **COLLOCATIONS**
>
> **combat**
> NOUN
> ◰
> adjective + **combat**: hand-to-hand, mortal, unarmed; aerial, frontline
> ◱
> adjective + **combat**: ferocious, long
> VERB ◲
> **combat** + noun: crime, extremism, fraud, terrorism; disease, obesity

com|bat|ant /kəmbætənt/ (**combatants**) N-COUNT A **combatant** is a person, group, or country that takes part in the fighting in a war. ❑ *I have never suggested that U.N. forces could physically separate the combatants in the region.*

com|bat|ive /kəmbætɪv/ ADJ A person who is **combative** is aggressive and eager to fight or argue. ❑ *He conducted the meeting yesterday in his usual combative style, refusing to admit any mistakes.*

com|bat trou|sers N-PLURAL [also a pair of N] **Combat trousers** are the same as **cargo pants**. [mainly BRIT]

com|bi|na|tion ✦◊ /kɒmbɪneɪʃən/ (**combinations**) N-COUNT A **combination** of things is a mixture of them. ❑ *...a fantastic combination of colors.*

> **SYNONYMS**
>
> **combination**
> NOUN
> **mix:** *The story is a magical mix of fantasy and reality.*
> **mixture:** *They looked at him with a mixture of horror, envy, and awe.*
> **blend:** *...a blend of wine and sparkling water.*
> **compound:** *Honey is a compound of water, sugar, vitamins, and enzymes.*
> **fusion:** *His fusions of jazz, pop, and African melodies have proved highly successful.*

com|bi|na|tion lock (**combination locks**) N-COUNT A **combination lock** is a lock which can only be opened by turning a dial or a number of dials according to a particular series of letters or numbers. ❑ *...a briefcase with combination locks.*

com|bine ✦◊ /kəmbaɪn/ (**combines, combining, combined**) ◰ V-RECIP If you **combine** two or more things or if they **combine**, they exist together. ❑ *The Church has something to say on how to combine freedom with responsibility.* ❑ *Relief workers say it's worse than ever as disease and starvation combine to kill thousands.* ◱ V-RECIP If you **combine** two or more things or if they **combine**, they join together to make a single thing. ❑ *David Jacobs was given the job of combining the data from these 19 studies into one giant study.* ❑ *Combine the flour with 3 tablespoons water to make a paste.* ◲ V-RECIP If two or more groups or organizations **combine** or if someone **combines** them, they join to form a single group or organization. ❑ *...an announcement by Steetley and Tarmac of a joint venture that would combine their brick, tile, and concrete operations.* ◳ V-T If someone or something **combines** two qualities or features, they have both those qualities or features at the same time. ❑ *Their system seems to combine the two ideals of strong government and proportional representation.* ❑ *...a clever, far-sighted lawyer who combines legal expertise with social concern.* ◴ V-T If someone **combines** two activities, they do them both at the same time. ❑ *It is possible to combine a career with being a mother.*

> **SYNONYMS**
>
> **combine**
> VERB ◱
> **mix:** *Mix the ingredients together slowly.*
> **blend:** *Blend the butter with the sugar and beat until light and creamy.*
> **amalgamate:** *The chemical companies had amalgamated into a vast conglomerate.*
> **merge:** *The two countries merged into one.*

com|bined /kəmbaɪnd/ ◰ ADJ [ADJ n] A **combined** effort or attack is made by two or more groups of people at the same time. ❑ *These refugees are taken care of by the combined efforts of the host countries and non-governmental organizations.* ◱ ADJ [ADJ n] The **combined** size or quantity of two or more things is the total of their sizes or quantities added together. ❑ *Such a merger would be the largest in U.S. banking history, giving the two banks' combined assets of some $146 billion.*

com|bine har|vest|er (**combine harvesters**) N-COUNT A **combine harvester** is a large machine which is used on farms to cut, sort, and clean grain.

com|bin|ing form (**combining forms**) N-COUNT A **combining form** is a word that is used, or used with a particular meaning, only when joined to another word. For example, '-legged' as in 'four-legged' and '-fold' as in 'fivefold' are combining forms.

com|bo /kɒmboʊ/ (**combos**) N-COUNT A **combo** is a small group of musicians who play jazz, dance, or popular music. [INFORMAL] ❑ *...a new-wave rock combo.*

com|bus|tible /kəmbʌstɪbəl/ ADJ [usu ADJ n] A **combustible** material or gas catches fire and burns easily. [FORMAL] ❑ *The ability of coal to release a combustible gas has long been known.*

com|bus|tion /kəmbʌstʃən/ N-UNCOUNT **Combustion** is the act of burning something or the process of burning. [TECHNICAL] ❏ *The energy is released by combustion on the application of a match.*

COME

① ARRIVE AT A PLACE
② OTHER USES
③ PHRASES AND PHRASAL VERBS

① **come** ♦♦♦ /kʌm/ (comes, coming, came)

The form **come** is used in the present tense and is the past participle.

1 V-I When a person or thing **comes** to a particular place, especially to a place where you are, they move there. ❏ *Two police officers came into the hall.* ❏ *Come here, Tom.* ❏ *We heard the train coming.* ❏ *The impact blew out some of the windows and the sea came rushing in.* **2** V-T When someone **comes** to do something, they move to the place where someone else is in order to do it, and they do it. Someone can also **come** do something and **come and** do something. However, you always say that someone **came and** did something. ❏ *Eleanor had come to see her.* ❏ *I want you to come visit me.* **3** V-I When you **come to** a place, you reach it. ❏ *He came to a door that led into a passageway.* **4** V-I If something **comes up** to a particular point or **down** to it, it is tall enough, deep enough, or long enough to reach that point. ❏ *The water came up to my chest.*

SYNONYMS

come
VERB ① **1**
arrive: *Fresh groups of guests arrived.*
appear: *A woman appeared at the far end of the street.*
reach: *He did not stop until he reached the door.*
turn up: *Richard had turned up on Christmas Eve with Tony.*

② **come** ♦♦♦ /kʌm/ (comes, coming, came)

The form **come** is used in the present tense and is the past participle.

1 V-I If something **comes apart** or **comes to pieces**, it breaks into pieces. If something **comes off** or **comes away**, it becomes detached from something else. ❏ *The lid won't come off.* ❏ *The pistol came to pieces, easily and quickly.* **2** V-T If someone **comes** to do something, they do it at the end of a long process or period of time. ❏ *She said it so many times that she came to believe it.* **3** V-T You can ask how something **came** to happen when you want to know what caused it to happen or made it possible. ❏ *How did you come to meet him?* **4** V-I When a particular event or time **comes**, it arrives or happens. ❏ *The announcement came after a meeting at the White House.* ❏ *There will come a time when they will have to negotiate.* ● **com|ing** N-SING ❏ *Most of my patients welcome the coming of summer.* **5** V-I If a thought, idea, or memory **comes** to you, you suddenly think of it or remember it. ❏ *He was about to shut the door when an idea came to him.* **6** V-I If money or property is going to **come to** you, you are going to inherit or receive it. ❏ *He did have retirement money coming to him when the factory shut down.* **7** V-I If a case **comes before** a court or tribunal or **comes to** court, it is presented there so that the court or tribunal can examine it. ❏ *The membership application came before the committee in September.* **8** V-I If something **comes to** a particular number or amount, it adds up to it. ❏ *Lunch came to $80.* **9** V-I If someone or something **comes from** a particular place or thing, that place or thing is their origin, source, or starting point. ❏ *Nearly half the students come from overseas.* ❏ *Chocolate comes from the cacao tree.* **10** V-I Something that **comes from** something else or **comes of** it is the result of it. ❏ *There is a feeling of power that comes from driving fast.* ❏ *Some good might come of all this gloomy business.* **11** V-T If someone or something **comes** first, next, or last, they are first, next, or last in a series, list, or competition. ❏ *The two countries have been unable to agree which step should come next.* ❏ *The alphabet might be more rational if all the vowels came first.* **12** V-I If a type of thing **comes** in a particular range of colors, forms, styles, or sizes, it can have any of those colors, forms, styles, or sizes. ❏ *Bikes come in all shapes and sizes.* **13** V-T The next subject in a discussion that you **come to** is the one that you talk about next. ❏ *Finally, I come to the subject of genetic engineering.* **14** V-LINK You use **come** in expressions such as **come to an end** or **come into operation** to indicate that someone or something enters or reaches a particular state or situation. ❏ *The summer came to an end.* ❏ *Their worst fears may be coming true.* **15** PREP You can use **come** before a date, time, or event to mean when it arrives. For example, you can say **come spring** to mean 'when the spring arrives.' ❏ *Come the election on the 20th of May, we will have to decide.*

USAGE

come from
Don't use a progressive form in sentences like these. Don't say, for example, 'Where are you coming from?' or 'I am coming from Zambia.' Say 'Where do you **come from**?' or 'I **come from** Zambia.'

③ **come** ♦♦♦ /kʌm/ (comes, coming, came)

The form **come** is used in the present tense and is the past participle.

1 PHRASE You can use the expression **when it comes down to it** or **when you come down to it** for emphasis, when you are giving a general statement or conclusion. [EMPHASIS] ❏ *When you come down to it, however, the basic problems of life have not changed.* **2** PHRASE You use the expression **come to think of it** to indicate that you have suddenly realized something, often something obvious. ❏ *He was his distant relative, as was everyone else on the island, come to think of it.* **3** PHRASE When you refer to a time or an event **to come** or one that is still **to come**, you are referring to a future time or event. ❏ *I hope in years to come he will reflect on his decision.* **4** PHRASE You can use expressions like **I know where you're coming from** or **you can see where she's coming from** to say that you understand someone's attitude or point of view. ❏ *To understand why they are doing it, it is necessary to know where they are coming from.* **5** → see also **coming**

▶ **come about** PHRASAL VERB When you say how or when something **came about**, you say how or when it happened. ❏ *The peace agreement came about through intense pressure by the international community.* ❏ *That came about when we went to New York last year.*

▶ **come across 1** PHRASAL VERB If you **come across** something or someone, you find them or meet them by chance. ❏ *He came across the jawbone of a 4.5 million-year-old marsupial.* **2** PHRASAL VERB If someone or what they are saying **comes across** in a particular way, they make that impression on people who meet them or are listening to them. ❏ *When sober, he can come across as an extremely pleasant and charming young man.*

▶ **come along 1** PHRASAL VERB You tell someone to **come along** to encourage them in a friendly way to do something, especially to attend something. ❏ *There's a barbecue tonight and you're very welcome to come along.* **2** PHRASAL VERB When something or someone **comes along**, they occur or arrive by chance. ❏ *I waited a long time until a script came along that I thought was genuinely funny.* **3** PHRASAL VERB If something **is coming along**, it is developing or making progress. ❏ *The Pentagon spokesperson says talks are coming along quite well.*

▶ **come around**

in BRIT, also use **come round**

1 PHRASAL VERB If someone **comes around** to your house, they come there to see you. ❏ *Beth came around this morning to apologize.* **2** PHRASAL VERB If you **come around** to an idea, you eventually change your mind and accept it or agree with it. ❏ *It looks like they're coming around to our way of thinking.* **3** PHRASAL VERB When something **comes around**, it happens as a regular or predictable event. ❏ *I hope to be fit when the World Championship comes around next year.* **4** PHRASAL VERB When someone who is unconscious **comes around**, they become conscious again. ❏ *When I came around I was on the kitchen floor.*

▶ **come at** PHRASAL VERB If a person or animal **comes at** you, they move toward you in a threatening way and try to attack you. ❏ *He maintained that he was protecting himself from Mr. Cox, who came at him with an ax.*

▶ **come back 1** PHRASAL VERB If someone comes back to a

place, they return to it. ❏ *He wanted to come back to Washington.* ❏ *She just wanted to go home and not come back.* **2** PHRASAL VERB If something that you had forgotten **comes back** to you, you remember it. ❏ *I'll think of his name in a moment when it comes back to me.* **3** PHRASAL VERB When something **comes back**, it becomes fashionable again. ❏ *I'm glad hats are coming back.* **4** → see also **comeback**

▶ **come between** PHRASAL VERB If someone or something **comes between** two people, or **comes between** a person and a thing, they make the relationship or connection between them less close or happy. ❏ *I don't want this misunderstanding to come between us.*

▶ **come by** PHRASAL VERB To **come by** something means to obtain it or find it. ❏ *How did you come by that check?*

▶ **come down** **1** PHRASAL VERB If the cost, level, or amount of something **comes down**, it becomes less than it was before. ❏ *Interest rates should come down.* ❏ *If you buy three bottles, the bottle price comes down to $10.* **2** PHRASAL VERB If something **comes down**, it falls to the ground. ❏ *The cold rain came down for hours.*

▶ **come down on** **1** PHRASAL VERB If you **come down on** one side of an argument, you declare that you support that side. ❏ *He clearly and decisively came down on the side of the president.* **2** PHRASAL VERB If you **come down on** someone, you criticize them severely or treat them strictly. ❏ *If Douglas came down hard enough on him, Dale would rebel.*

▶ **come down to** PHRASAL VERB If a problem, decision, or question **comes down to** a particular thing, that thing is the most important factor involved. ❏ *The problem comes down to money.* ❏ *I think that it comes down to the fact that people do feel very dependent on their automobiles.*

▶ **come down with** PHRASAL VERB If you **come down with** an illness, you get it. ❏ *Thomas came down with the chickenpox.*

▶ **come for** PHRASAL VERB If people such as soldiers or police **come for** you, they come to find you, usually in order to harm you or take you away, for example to prison. ❏ *Tanya was getting ready to fight if they came for her.*

▶ **come forward** PHRASAL VERB If someone **comes forward**, they make themselves known and offer to help. ❏ *A vital witness came forward to say that she saw Tanner wearing the boots.*

▶ **come in** **1** PHRASAL VERB If information, a report, or a telephone call **comes in**, it is received. ❏ *Reports are now coming in of trouble at yet another jail.* **2** PHRASAL VERB If you have some money **coming in**, you receive it regularly as your income. ❏ *She had no money coming in and no funds.* **3** PHRASAL VERB If someone **comes in** on a discussion, arrangement, or task, they join it. ❏ *Can I come in here too, on both points?* **4** PHRASAL VERB When a new idea, fashion, or product **comes in**, it becomes popular or available. ❏ *It was just when attitudes were really beginning to change and lots of new ideas were coming in.* **5** PHRASAL VERB If you ask where something or someone **comes in**, you are asking what their role is in a particular matter. ❏ *Rose asked again, "But where do we come in, Henry?"* **6** PHRASAL VERB [VP] When the tide **comes in**, the water in the sea gradually moves so that it covers more of the land. ❏ *She became trapped as the tide came in.*

▶ **come in for** PHRASAL VERB If someone or something **comes in for** criticism or blame, they receive it. ❏ *The plans have already come in for fierce criticism.*

▶ **come into** **1** PHRASAL VERB [no passive] If someone **comes into** some money, some property, or a title, they inherit it. ❏ *My father has just come into a fortune in diamonds.* **2** PHRASAL VERB [no passive] If someone or something **comes into** a situation, they have a role in it. ❏ *We don't really know where Hortense comes into all this, Inspector.*

▶ **come off** **1** PHRASAL VERB If something **comes off**, it is successful or effective. ❏ *It was a good try but it didn't really come off.* **2** PHRASAL VERB If someone **comes off** worst in a contest or conflict, they are in the worst position after it. If they **come off** best, they are in the best position. ❏ *Some Democrats still have bitter memories of how they came off worst during the investigation.* **3** CONVENTION You say '**Come off it**' to someone to show them that you think what they are saying is untrue or wrong.

▶ **come on** **1** CONVENTION You say '**Come on**' to someone to encourage them to do something they do not want to do. [SPOKEN] ❏ *Come on Doreen, let's dance.* **2** CONVENTION You say '**Come on**' to someone to encourage them to hurry up. [SPOKEN] ❏ *Come on, darling, we'll be late.* **3** PHRASAL VERB If you have an illness or a headache **coming on**, you can feel it starting. ❏ *Tiredness and fever are much more likely to be a sign of the flu coming on.* **4** PHRASAL VERB If something or someone **is coming on** well, they are developing well or making good progress. ❏ *Leah is coming on very well now and it's a matter of deciding how to fit her into the team.* **5** PHRASAL VERB When something such as a machine or system **comes on**, it starts working or functioning. ❏ *The central heating was coming on and the ancient wooden boards creaked.*

▶ **come on to** PHRASAL VERB If someone **comes on to** you, they show that they are interested in starting a sexual relationship with you. [INFORMAL] ❏ *I met a guy at a party and he came on to me real hard.*

▶ **come out** **1** PHRASAL VERB When a new product such as a book or CD **comes out**, it becomes available to the public. ❏ *The book comes out this week.* **2** PHRASAL VERB If a fact **comes out**, it becomes known to people. ❏ *The truth is beginning to come out about what happened.* **3** PHRASAL VERB When a person **comes out**, they reveal their sexuality or gender identity. ❏ *...the few gay men there who dare to come out.* **4** PHRASAL VERB To **come out** in a particular way means to be in the position or state described at the end of a process or event. ❏ *In this grim little episode of recent American history, few people come out well.* ❏ *So what makes a good marriage? Faithfulness comes out top of the list.* **5** PHRASAL VERB If you **come out** for something, you declare that you support it. If you **come out** against something, you declare that you do not support it. ❏ *Its members had come out virtually unanimously against the tests.* **6** PHRASAL VERB When the sun, moon, or stars **come out**, they appear in the sky. ❏ *Oh, look! The sun's coming out!* **7** PHRASAL VERB When a group of workers **comes out** on strike, they go on strike. [BRIT]

in AM, use **go on strike**

▶ **come over** **1** PHRASAL VERB [no passive] If a feeling or desire, especially a strange or surprising one, **comes over** you, it affects you strongly. ❏ *As I entered the hallway which led to my room that eerie feeling came over me.* **2** PHRASAL VERB If someone or what they are saying **comes over** in a particular way, they make that impression on people who meet them or are listening to them. ❏ *You come over as a capable and amusing companion.* **3** PHRASAL VERB If someone **comes over** to your house or another place, they visit you there. ❏ *Maybe I could come over to your house before the party?*

▶ **come round** → see **come around**

▶ **come through** **1** PHRASAL VERB [no passive] To **come through** a dangerous or difficult situation means to survive it and recover from it. ❏ *The city had faced racial crisis and come through it.* **2** PHRASAL VERB If a feeling or message **comes through**, it is clearly shown in what is said or done. ❏ *The message that comes through is that taxes will have to be raised.* **3** PHRASAL VERB If something **comes through**, it arrives, especially after some procedure has been carried out. ❏ *The father of the baby was waiting for his divorce to come through.* **4** PHRASAL VERB If you **come through** with what is expected or needed from you, you succeed in doing or providing it. ❏ *He puts his administration at risk if he doesn't come through on these promises for reform.*

▶ **come to** PHRASAL VERB When someone who is unconscious **comes to**, they become conscious. ❏ *When he came to and raised his head, he saw Barney.*

▶ **come under** **1** PHRASAL VERB [no passive] If you **come under** attack or pressure, for example, people attack you or put pressure on you. ❏ *The police came under attack from angry crowds.* **2** PHRASAL VERB [no passive] If something **comes under** a particular authority, it is managed or controlled by that authority. ❏ *They were neglected before because they did not come under NATO.* **3** PHRASAL VERB [no passive] If something **comes under** a particular heading, it is in the category mentioned. ❏ *Her articles come under the heading of human interest.*

▶ **come up** **1** PHRASAL VERB If someone **comes up** or **comes up** to you, they approach you until they are standing close to you. ❏ *Her cat came up and rubbed itself against their legs.* **2** PHRASAL VERB If something **comes up** in a conversation or meeting, it is mentioned or discussed. ❏ *The subject came up at work.* **3** PHRASAL VERB If something **is coming up**, it is about to happen or take place. ❏ *We do have elections coming up.* **4** PHRASAL VERB If something **comes up**, it happens

unexpectedly. ☐ *I was delayed – something came up at home.* **5** PHRASAL VERB If a job **comes up** or if something **comes up** for sale, it becomes available. ☐ *A research fellowship came up and I applied for it and got it.* **6** PHRASAL VERB When the sun or moon **comes up**, it rises. ☐ *It will be so great watching the sun come up.* **7** PHRASAL VERB In law, when a case **comes up**, it is heard in a court of law. ☐ *He is one of the reservists who will plead not guilty when their cases come up.*
▶ **come up against** PHRASAL VERB If you **come up against** a problem or difficulty, you are faced with it and have to deal with it. ☐ *We came up against a great deal of resistance in dealing with the case.*

> **Come** is used in a large number of expressions which are explained under other words in this dictionary. For example, the expression 'to come to terms with something' is explained at 'term'.

come|back (comebacks) **1** N-COUNT If someone such as an entertainer or sports personality makes a **comeback**, they return to their profession or sport after a period away. ☐ *The band is making a comeback.* **2** N-COUNT If something makes a **comeback**, it becomes fashionable again. ☐ *Tight fitting T-shirts are making a comeback.*

co|median /kəmiːdiən/ (comedians) **1** N-COUNT A **comedian** is an entertainer whose job is to make people laugh, by telling jokes or funny stories. ☐ *...a stand-up comedian.* **2** → See feature box at **humor**

co|medic /kəmiːdɪk/ ADJ [usu ADJ n] **Comedic** means relating to comedy. [FORMAL] ☐ *...a festival of comedic talent from around the world.*

co|medi|enne /kəmiːdiˈɛn/ (comediennes) **1** N-COUNT A **comedienne** is a female entertainer whose job is to make people laugh, by telling jokes or funny stories. Most people object to this word, and prefer to be called comedians. [OLD-FASHIONED] **2** → See feature box at **humor**

come|down /kʌmdaʊn/

> in BRIT, also use **come-down**

N-SING [a N] If you say that something is **a comedown**, you think that it is not as good as something else that you have just done or had. ☐ *He regarded the new job as a distinct comedown.*

com|edy ♦◇◇ /kɒmədi/ (comedies) **1** N-UNCOUNT **Comedy** consists of types of entertainment, such as plays and movies, or particular scenes in them, that are intended to make people laugh. ☐ *The actor talks about his career in comedy.* **2** N-COUNT A **comedy** is a play, movie, or television program that is intended to make people laugh. ☐ *The movie is a romantic comedy.* **3** → See feature box at **humor**

> **COLLOCATIONS**
>
> **comedy**
> NOUN
> **1**
> adjective + **comedy**: alternative, black, light; musical, physical, stand-up
> **2**
> noun + **comedy**: cult, hit
> adjective + **comedy**: gentle, romantic, satirical, witty

come|ly /kʌmli/ (comelier, comeliest) ADJ [usu ADJ n] A **comely** woman is attractive. [OLD-FASHIONED]

come-on (come-ons) N-COUNT A **come-on** is a gesture or remark which someone makes in order to encourage another person to make sexual advances to them. [INFORMAL] ☐ *He ignores come-ons from the many women who seem to find him attractive.*

com|er /kʌmər/ (comers) **1** N-COUNT [usu pl, supp N] You can use **comers** to refer to people who arrive at a particular place. ☐ *I arrived at the church at two-thirty p.m. to find some early comers outside the main door.* **2** → See also **all-comers, latecomer, newcomer**

com|et /kɒmɪt/ (comets) **1** N-COUNT A **comet** is a bright object with a long tail that travels around the sun. ☐ *Halley's Comet is going to come back in 2061.* **2** → See feature box at **space**

come|up|pance /kʌmʌpəns/ also **come-uppance** N-SING [usu poss N] If you say that someone got their **comeuppance**, you approve of the fact that they have been punished or have suffered for something wrong that they have done. [INFORMAL, APPROVAL] ☐ *The central character is a bad man who shoots people and gets his comeuppance.*

com|fort ♦◇◇ /kʌmfərt/ (comforts, comforting, comforted) **1** N-UNCOUNT If you are doing something in **comfort**, you are physically relaxed and contented, and are not feeling any pain or other unpleasant sensations. ☐ *This will enable the audience to sit in comfort while watching the shows.* **2** N-UNCOUNT **Comfort** is a style of life in which you have enough money to have everything you need. ☐ *Surely there is some way of ordering our busy lives so that we can live in comfort and find spiritual harmony too.* **3** N-UNCOUNT **Comfort** is what you feel when worries or unhappiness stop. ☐ *He welcomed the truce, but pointed out it was of little comfort to families spending Christmas without a loved one.* ☐ *They will be able to take some comfort from inflation figures due on Friday.* **4** N-COUNT If you refer to a person, thing, or idea as a **comfort**, you mean that it helps you to stop worrying or makes you feel less unhappy. ☐ *It's a comfort talking to you.* **5** N-COUNT **Comforts** are things which make your life easier and more pleasant, such as electrical devices you have in your home. ☐ *She enjoys the material comforts this jet-set lifestyle has to offer.* **6** V-T If you **comfort** someone, you make them feel less worried, unhappy, or upset, for example by saying kind things to them. ☐ *Ned put his arm around her, trying to comfort her.* **7** PHRASE If you say that something is, for example, **too close for comfort**, you mean you are worried because it is closer than you would like it to be. ☐ *The bombs fell in the sea, many too close for comfort.*

com|fort|able ♦◇◇ /kʌmftəbəl, -fərtəbəl/ **1** ADJ If a piece of furniture or an item of clothing is **comfortable**, it makes you feel physically relaxed when you use it, for example because it is soft. ☐ *...a comfortable fireside chair.* **2** ADJ If a building or room is **comfortable**, it makes you feel physically relaxed when you spend time in it, for example because it is warm and has nice furniture. ☐ *A home should be comfortable and friendly.* ● **com|fort|ably** ADV ☐ *...the comfortably furnished living room.* **3** ADJ If you are **comfortable**, you are physically relaxed because of the place or position you are sitting or lying in. ☐ *Lie down on your bed and make yourself comfortable.* ● **com|fort|ably** ADV [ADV with v] ☐ *Are you sitting comfortably?* **4** ADJ If you say that someone is **comfortable**, you mean that they have enough money to be able to live without financial problems. ☐ *"Is he rich?"—"He's comfortable."* ● **com|fort|ably** ADV ☐ *Cayton describes himself as comfortably well-off.* **5** ADJ [ADJ n] In a race, competition, or election, if you have a **comfortable** lead, you are likely to win it easily. If you gain a **comfortable** victory or majority, you win easily. ☐ *By half distance we held a comfortable two-lap lead.* ● **com|fort|ably** ADV [ADV with v] ☐ *...the Los Angeles Raiders, who comfortably beat the Bears earlier in the season.* **6** ADJ [v-link ADJ] If you feel **comfortable** with a particular situation or person, you feel confident and relaxed with them. ☐ *Nervous politicians might well feel more comfortable with a step-by-step approach.* ☐ *He liked me and I felt comfortable with him.* ● **com|fort|ably** ADV [ADV after v] ☐ *They talked comfortably of their plans.* **7** ADJ When a sick or injured person is said to be **comfortable**, they are without pain. ☐ *He was described as comfortable in the hospital last night.*

com|fort|ably /kʌmftəbli, -fərtəbli/ **1** ADV [ADV with v] If you manage to do something **comfortably**, you do it easily. ☐ *Only take upon yourself those things that you know you can manage comfortably.* **2** → see also **comfortable**

com|fort|ably off ADJ [usu v-link ADJ] If someone is **comfortably off**, they have enough money to be able to live without financial problems. ☐ *She had no plans to retire even though she is now very comfortably off.*

com|fort|er /kʌmfərtər/ (comforters) **1** N-COUNT A **comforter** is a person or thing that comforts you. ☐ *He became Vivien Leigh's devoted friend and comforter.* **2** N-COUNT A **comforter** is a large cover filled with feathers or similar material that you use like a blanket. [AM]

> in BRIT, use **duvet**

com|fort food N-UNCOUNT If you call something **comfort food**, you mean it is enjoyable to eat and makes you feel

comforting /kʌmfərtɪŋ/ ADJ If you say that something is **comforting**, you mean it makes you feel less worried or unhappy. ❑ *My mother had just died and I found the book very comforting.*

comfort zone (comfort zones) **1** N-COUNT If a situation or activity is out of your **comfort zone**, it does not make you feel secure, comfortable, or in control. ❑ *I like to do things that take me out of my comfort zone.* **2** → See feature box at **challenge**

comfrey /kʌmfri/ N-UNCOUNT **Comfrey** is an herb that is used in medicines.

comfy /kʌmfi/ (comfier, comfiest) ADJ A **comfy** item of clothing, piece of furniture, room, or position is a comfortable one. [INFORMAL] ❑ *...a comfy chair.*

comic /kɒmɪk/ (comics) **1** ADJ If you describe something as **comic**, you mean that it makes you laugh, and is often intended to make you laugh. ❑ *The novel is comic and tragic.* **2** ADJ [ADJ n] **Comic** is used to describe funny entertainment, and the actors and entertainers who perform it. ❑ *Grodin is a fine comic actor.* **3** N-COUNT A **comic** is an entertainer who tells jokes in order to make people laugh. ❑ *...the funniest comic in America.* **4** N-SING The **comics** is the part of a newspaper that contains the comic strips. ❑ *She read the comics in the Philadelphia Inquirer.* **5** N-COUNT A **comic** is a magazine that contains stories told in pictures. [mainly BRIT]

in AM, usually use **comic book**

comical /kɒmɪkᵊl/ ADJ If you describe something as **comical**, you mean that it makes you laugh because it is funny or silly. ❑ *Her expression is almost comical.*

USAGE

comical

Don't use 'comical' to describe things that are intended to make you laugh. Don't say, for example, 'He is a great comical actor.' You say 'He is a great **comic** actor.' *The novel is both comic and tragic.*

---

comic book (comic books) N-COUNT A **comic book** is a magazine that contains stories told in pictures. [mainly AM] ❑ *...comic book heroes such as Spider Man.*

in BRIT, usually use **comic**

comic strip (comic strips) N-COUNT A **comic strip** is a series of drawings that tell a story, especially in a newspaper or magazine.

coming ✦✦✦ /kʌmɪŋ/ **1** ADJ [ADJ n] A **coming** event or time is an event or time that will happen soon. ❑ *This obviously depends on the weather in the coming months.* **2** → see also **come** ①

coming of age **1** N-SING [with supp] When something reaches an important stage of development and is accepted by a large number of people, you can refer to this as its **coming of age**. ❑ *...postwar Germany's final coming-of-age as an independent sovereign state.* **2** N-SING [with poss] Someone's **coming of age** is the time when they become recognized as an adult. ❑ *...traditional coming-of-age ceremonies.*

comings and goings N-PLURAL [with poss] **Comings and goings** refers to the way people keep arriving at and leaving a particular place. ❑ *They noted the comings and goings of the journalists.*

comma /kɒmə/ (commas) N-COUNT A **comma** is the punctuation mark , which is used to separate parts of a sentence or items in a list.

command ✦✦✦ /kəmænd/ (commands, commanding, commanded) **1** V-T If someone in authority **commands** you to do something, they tell you that you must do it. [mainly WRITTEN] ❑ *He commanded his troops to attack.* ❑ *"Get in your car and follow me," she commanded.* • N-VAR **Command** is also a noun. ❑ *The tanker failed to respond to a command to stop.* ❑ *I closed my eyes at his command.* **2** V-T [no cont] If you **command** something such as respect or obedience, you obtain it because you are popular, famous, or important. ❑ *...an excellent physician who commanded the respect of all her colleagues.* **3** V-T If an army or country **commands** a place, they have total control over it.

❑ *Yemen commands the strait at the southern end of the Red Sea.* • N-UNCOUNT **Command** is also a noun. ❑ *...the struggle for command of the air.* **4** V-T An officer who **commands** part of an army, navy, or air force is responsible for controlling and organizing it. ❑ *...the French general who commands the U.N. troops in the region.* • N-UNCOUNT **Command** is also a noun. ❑ *...a small garrison under the command of Major James Craig.* **5** N-COUNT-COLL In the armed forces, a **command** is a group of officers who are responsible for organizing and controlling part of an army, navy, or air force. ❑ *He had authorization from the military command to retaliate.* **6** N-COUNT In computing, a **command** is an instruction that you give to a computer. ❑ *I entered the command into my navigational computer.* **7** N-UNCOUNT If someone has **command** of a situation, they have control of it because they have, or seem to have, power or authority. ❑ *Mr. Baker would take command of the campaign.* **8** N-UNCOUNT Your **command** of something, such as a foreign language, is your knowledge of it and your ability to use this knowledge. ❑ *His command of English was excellent.* **9** PHRASE If you have a particular skill or particular resources **at** your **command**, you have them and can use them fully. ❑ *The country should have the right to defend itself with all legal means at its command.*

commandant /kɒməndænt/ (commandants) N-COUNT; N-TITLE A **commandant** is an army officer in charge of a particular place or group of people.

command economy (command economies) N-COUNT In a **command economy**, business activities and the use of resources are decided by the government, and not by market forces. [BUSINESS] ❑ *...the Czech Republic's transition from a command economy to a market system.*

commandeer /kɒməndɪər/ (commandeers, commandeering, commandeered) **1** V-T If the armed forces **commandeer** a vehicle or building owned by someone else, they officially take charge of it so that they can use it. ❑ *The soldiers commandeered vehicles in the capital and occupied the television station.* ❑ *They drove in a convoy around the city in commandeered cars.* **2** V-T To **commandeer** something owned by someone else means to take charge of it so that you can use it. [DISAPPROVAL] ❑ *The hijacker commandeered the plane on a domestic flight.*

commander ✦✦✦ /kəmændər/ (commanders) **1** N-COUNT; N-TITLE; N-VOC A **commander** is an officer in charge of a military operation or organization. ❑ *The commander and some of the men had been released.* **2** N-COUNT; N-TITLE; N-VOC A **commander** is an officer in the U.S. Navy or the Royal Navy.

COLLOCATIONS

commander
NOUN **1**
noun + **commander**: army; battalion, brigade, platoon, section, squadron
adjective + **commander**: military, naval; senior, supreme; rebel

---

commander-in-chief (commanders-in-chief) N-COUNT; N-TITLE A **commander-in-chief** is an officer in charge of all the forces in a particular area. ❑ *The president of the United States is the commander-in-chief of the armed forces.*

commanding /kəmændɪŋ/ **1** ADJ If you are in a **commanding** position or situation, you are in a strong or powerful position or situation. ❑ *Right now you're in a more commanding position than you have been for ages.* **2** ADJ If you describe someone as **commanding**, you mean that they are powerful and confident. [APPROVAL] ❑ *Lovett was a tall, commanding man with a waxed gray mustache.* **3** → see also **command**

commanding officer (commanding officers) N-COUNT A **commanding officer** is an officer who is in charge of a military unit. ❑ *He got permission from his commanding officer to join me.*

commandment /kəmændmənt/ (commandments) N-COUNT The **Ten Commandments** are the ten rules of behavior which, according to the Old Testament of the Bible, people should obey.

commando /kəmændoʊ/ (commandos or commandoes) **1** N-COUNT A **commando** is a group of soldiers who have been specially trained to carry out surprise attacks. ❏ ...a small commando of marines. **2** N-COUNT A **commando** is a soldier who is a member of a commando. ❏ ...small groups of American commandos.

com|mand per|for|mance (command performances) N-COUNT A **command performance** is a special performance of a play or show, especially one which is given for a head of state.

com|mand post (command posts) N-COUNT A **command post** is a place from which a commander in the army controls and organizes their forces.

com|memo|rate /kəmɛməreɪt/ (commemorates, commemorating, commemorated) V-T To **commemorate** an important event or person means to remember them by means of a special action, ceremony, or specially created object. ❏ One room contained a gallery of paintings commemorating great moments in baseball history. • **com|memo|ra|tion** /kəmɛməreɪʃᵊn/ (commemorations) N-VAR ❏ ...a march in commemoration of Malcolm X.

com|memo|ra|tive /kəmɛmərətɪv, -əreɪtɪv/ ADJ [ADJ n] A **commemorative** object or event is intended to make people remember a particular event or person. ❏ A commemorative stamp will be issued October 15.

com|mence /kəmɛns/ (commences, commencing, commenced) V-T/V-I When something **commences** or you **commence** it, it begins. [FORMAL] ❏ The academic year commences at the beginning of October. ❏ They commenced a systematic search.

com|mence|ment /kəmɛnsmənt/ (commencements) **1** N-UNCOUNT The **commencement** of something is its beginning. [FORMAL] ❏ All applicants should be at least 16 years of age at the commencement of this course. **2** N-VAR **Commencement** is a ceremony at a university, college, or high school at which students formally receive their degrees or diplomas. [AM] ❏ The president gave the commencement address today at the University of Notre Dame.

in BRIT, use **graduation**

com|mend /kəmɛnd/ (commends, commending, commended) **1** V-T If you **commend** someone or something, you praise them formally. [FORMAL] ❏ I commended her for that action. ❏ The reports commend her bravery. • **com|men|da|tion** /kɒməndeɪʃᵊn/ (commendations) N-COUNT ❏ He won a commendation for bravery after risking his life at the scene of a gas blast. **2** V-T If someone **commends** a person or thing **to** you, they tell you that you will find them good or useful. [FORMAL] ❏ I can commend it to him as a realistic course of action.

com|mend|able /kəmɛndəbᵊl/ ADJ If you describe someone's behavior as **commendable**, you approve of it or are praising it. [FORMAL, APPROVAL] ❏ He has acted with commendable speed.

com|men|su|rate /kəmɛnsərɪt/ ADJ [v-link ADJ with/to n, ADJ n] If the level of one thing is **commensurate** with another, the first level is in proportion to the second. [FORMAL] ❏ Employees are paid salaries commensurate with those of teachers.

com|ment ✦✦◇ /kɒmɛnt/ (comments, commenting, commented) **1** V-T/V-I If you **comment** on something, you give your opinion about it or you give an explanation for it. ❏ So far, Mr. Cook has not commented on these reports. ❏ You really can't comment until you know the facts. ❏ One student commented that she preferred literature to social science. **2** N-VAR A **comment** is something that you say which expresses your opinion of something or which gives an explanation of it. ❏ He made his comments at a news conference in Amsterdam. ❏ There's been no comment so far from police about the allegations. **3** CONVENTION People say '**no comment**' as a way of refusing to answer a question, usually when it is asked by a journalist. ❏ No comment. I don't know anything.

[COLLOCATIONS]

comment
VERB **1**
comment + adverb: publicly
NOUN **2**
adjective + **comment**: derogatory, inappropriate, negative, offensive, unacceptable; racist, sexist; positive, upbeat; unhelpful

com|men|tary /kɒmənteri/ (commentaries) **1** N-VAR A **commentary** is a description of an event that is broadcast on radio or television while the event is taking place. ❏ He gave the listening crowd a running commentary. **2** N-COUNT A **commentary** is an article or book which explains or discusses something. ❏ Ms. Rich will be writing a twice-weekly commentary on American society and culture. **3** N-UNCOUNT [also a N, with supp] **Commentary** is discussion or criticism of something. ❏ The show mixed comedy with social commentary.

com|men|tate /kɒmənteɪt/ (commentates, commentating, commentated) V-I To **commentate** means to give a radio or television commentary on an event. ❏ They are in New Hampshire to commentate on the ice hockey.

com|men|ta|tor ✦◇◇ /kɒmənteɪtər/ (commentators) **1** N-COUNT A **commentator** is a broadcaster who gives a radio or television commentary on an event. ❏ ...a sports commentator. **2** N-COUNT A **commentator** is also someone who often writes or broadcasts about a particular subject. ❏ ...a political commentator.

com|merce ✦◇◇ /kɒmɜrs/ **1** N-UNCOUNT **Commerce** is the activities and procedures involved in buying and selling things. ❏ They have made their fortunes from industry and commerce. **2** → see also **chamber of commerce**

[SYNONYMS]

commerce
NOUN **1**
trade: The ministry had direct control over every aspect of foreign trade.
business: Jennifer has an impressive academic and business background.
transaction: Those are the business transactions that count.

com|mer|cial ✦✦◇ /kəmɜrʃᵊl/ (commercials) **1** ADJ **Commercial** means involving or relating to the buying and selling of goods. ❏ Baltimore in its heyday was a major center of industrial and commercial activity. **2** ADJ **Commercial** organizations and activities are concerned with making money or profits, rather than, for example, with scientific research or providing a public service. ❏ The company has indeed become more commercial over the past decade. ❏ Conservationists in Chile are concerned over the effect of commercial exploitation of forests. • **com|mer|cial|ly** ADV ❏ The plane will be commercially viable if 400 can be sold. **3** ADJ [ADJ n] A **commercial** product is made to be sold to the public. ❏ They are the leading manufacturer in both defense and commercial products. • **com|mer|cial|ly** ADV ❏ It was the first commercially available machine to employ artificial intelligence. **4** ADJ A **commercial** vehicle is a vehicle used for carrying goods, or passengers who pay. ❏ The route is used every day by many hundreds of commercial vehicles. **5** ADJ **Commercial** television and radio are paid for by the broadcasting of advertisements, rather than by the government. ❏ There were no commercial radio stations until 1920. **6** ADJ **Commercial** is used to describe something such as a movie or a type of music that is intended to be popular with the public, and is not very original or of high quality. ❏ There's a feeling among a lot of people that music has become too commercial. **7** N-COUNT A **commercial** is an advertisement that is broadcast on television or radio. ❏ Turn the channel – there are too many commercials.

[SYNONYMS]

commercial
ADJ **2**
profitable: It was profitable for them to produce large amounts of food.
salable: Something that is salable is easy to sell to people.
marketable: ...telling them how to turn their prize research projects into marketable products.

com|mer|cial bank (commercial banks) N-COUNT A **commercial bank** is a bank whose main customers are businesses. [BUSINESS]

com|mer|cial break (commercial breaks) N-COUNT A **commercial break** is the interval during a commercial television program, or between programs, during which advertisements are shown. ❏ The movie was aired without commercial breaks.

com|mer|cial|ism /kəmɜrʃəlɪzəm/ N-UNCOUNT
Commercialism is the practice of making a lot of money from things without caring about their quality. [DISAPPROVAL] ❑ *Koons has engrossed himself in a world of commercialism that most modern artists disdain.*

com|mer|cial|ize /kəmɜrʃəlaɪz/ (**commercializes, commercializing, commercialized**)

in BRIT, also use **commercialise**

V-T [usu passive] If something **is commercialized**, it is used or changed in such a way that it makes money or profits, often in a way that people disapprove of. [DISAPPROVAL] ❑ *It seems such a pity that a distinguished and honored name should be commercialized in this way.* ● **com|mer|cial|ized** ADJ ❑ *Rock'n'roll has become so commercialized and safe since punk.*
● **com|mer|ciali|za|tion** /kəmɜrʃəlɪzeɪʃən/ N-UNCOUNT ❑ *...the commercialization of Christmas.*

com|mie /kɒmi/ (**commies**) N-COUNT A **commie** is the same as a **communist**. [INFORMAL, OFFENSIVE, DISAPPROVAL]

com|mis|er|ate /kəmɪzəreɪt/ (**commiserates, commiserating, commiserated**) V-I If you **commiserate with** someone, you show them pity or sympathy when something unpleasant has happened to them. ❑ *When I lost, he commiserated with me.*

com|mis|sari|at /kɒmɪsɛəriət/ (**commissariats**) N-COUNT A **commissariat** is a military department that is in charge of food supplies.

com|mis|sary /kɒmɪsɛri/ (**commissaries**) N-COUNT A **commissary** is a store that provides food and equipment in a place such as a military base or a prison. [AM]

com|mis|sion ♦♦◇ /kəmɪʃən/ (**commissions, commissioning, commissioned**) ◼ V-T If you **commission** something or **commission** someone to do something, you formally arrange for someone to do a piece of work for you. ❑ *The Department of Agriculture commissioned a study into organic farming.* ❑ *You can commission them to paint something especially for you.* ● N-VAR **Commission** is also a noun. ❑ *Our china can be bought off the shelf or by commission.* ◼ N-COUNT A **commission** is a piece of work that someone is asked to do and is paid for. ❑ *Just a few days ago, I finished a commission.* ◼ N-VAR **Commission** is a sum of money paid to a salesperson for every sale that he or she makes. If a salesperson is paid on **commission**, the amount they receive depends on the amount they sell. ❑ *The salespeople work on commission only.* ◼ N-UNCOUNT If a bank or other company charges **commission**, they charge a fee for providing a service, for example for exchanging money or issuing an insurance policy. [BUSINESS] ❑ *Travel agents charge 1 per cent commission on tickets.* ◼ N-COUNT-COLL A **commission** is a group of people who have been appointed to find out about something or to control something. ❑ *The government has set up a commission to look into those crimes.* ◼ N-COUNT If a member of the armed forces receives a **commission**, he or she becomes an officer. ❑ *He accepted a commission as a naval officer.*

com|mis|sion|er ♦♦◇ /kəmɪʃənər/ (**commissioners**) also **Commissioner** N-COUNT A **commissioner** is an important official in a government department or other organization. ❑ *...Alaska's commissioner of education.*

com|mit ♦♦◇ /kəmɪt/ (**commits, committing, committed**)
◼ V-T If someone **commits** a crime or a sin, they do something illegal or bad. ❑ *I have never committed any crime.* ❑ *This is a man who has committed murder.* ◼ V-T If someone **commits** suicide, they deliberately kill themselves. ❑ *There are unconfirmed reports he tried to commit suicide.* ◼ V-T If you **commit** money or resources to something, you decide to use them for a particular purpose. ❑ *They called on Western nations to commit more money to the poorest nations.* ❑ *The company had committed thousands of dollars for a plan to reduce mercury emissions.* ◼ V-T/V-I If you **commit** yourself to something, you say that you will definitely do it. If you **commit** yourself to someone, you decide that you want to have a long-term relationship with them. ❑ *I would advise people to think very carefully about committing themselves to working Sundays.* ❑ *I'd like a friendship that might lead to something deeper, but I wouldn't want to commit myself too soon.* ❑ *He won't commit.* ◼ V-T [with brd-neg] If you do not want to **commit** yourself on something, you do not want to say what you really think about it or what you are going to do. ❑ *It isn't their diplomatic style to commit themselves on such a delicate issue.* ◼ V-T [usu passive] If someone **is committed** to a psychiatric hospital, prison, or other institution, they are officially sent there for a period of time. ❑ *The prisoner has to be committed to a maximum security state hospital.* ◼ V-T If you **commit** something **to** paper or **to** writing, you record it by writing it down. If you **commit** something to memory, you learn it so that you will remember it. ❑ *She had not committed anything to paper about it.* ◼ → See feature box at **crime, prison**

com|mit|ment ♦♦◇ /kəmɪtmənt/ (**commitments**)
◼ N-UNCOUNT **Commitment** is a strong belief in an idea or system. ❑ *...commitment to the ideals of democracy.* ◼ N-COUNT A **commitment** is something which regularly takes up some of your time because of an agreement you have made or because of responsibilities that you have. ❑ *I've got a lot of commitments.* ◼ N-COUNT If you make a **commitment** to do something, you promise that you will do it. ❑ *We made a commitment to keep working together.* ◼ N-VAR **Commitment** is the process of officially sending someone to a prison or a hospital. [AM] ❑ *State law allows involuntary commitment for psychiatric evaluation.*

in BRIT, use **committal**

---- SYNONYMS ----

commitment
NOUN
◼
dedication: *We admire her dedication to the cause of humanity.*
loyalty: *I have sworn an oath of loyalty to the monarchy.*
devotion: *...devotion to the cause of the people and to socialism.*
◼
duty: *I carried out my duties conscientiously.*
responsibility: *...programs to help employees balance work and family responsibilities.*
obligation: *When teachers assign homework, students usually feel an obligation to do it.*

com|mit|tal /kəmɪtəl/ (**committals**) N-VAR **Committal** is the process of officially sending someone to a prison or a hospital.

com|mit|tee ♦♦♦ /kəmɪti/ (**committees**) N-COUNT-COLL A **committee** is a group of people who meet to make decisions or plans for a larger group or organization that they represent. ❑ *...the school yearbook committee.*

---- COLLOCATIONS ----

committee
NOUN
noun + **committee**: executive, management; ethics, finance
adjective + **committee**: advisory, consultative, disciplinary; congressional, ministerial, parliamentary; judicial, scientific, technical
verb + **committee**: appoint, establish, form, set up; appear before; chair, serve on, sit on

com|mode /kəmoʊd/ (**commodes**) N-COUNT A **commode** is a toilet. [AM]

com|mo|di|ous /kəmoʊdiəs/ ADJ [usu ADJ n] A **commodious** room or house is large and has a lot of space. [WRITTEN]

com|mod|ity /kəmɒdɪti/ (**commodities**) N-COUNT A **commodity** is something that is sold for money. [BUSINESS] ❑ *Prices went up on several basic commodities like bread and meat.*

com|mo|dore /kɒmədɔr/ (**commodores**) N-COUNT; N-TITLE A **commodore** is an officer of senior rank in the navy, especially the British Royal Navy.

com|mon ♦♦♦ /kɒmən/ (**commons**) ◼ ADJ If something is **common**, it is found in large numbers or it happens often. ❑ *His name was Hansen, a common name in Norway.* ❑ *Oil pollution is the most common cause of death for seabirds.* ● **com|mon|ly** ADV [ADV with v] ❑ *Parsley is one of the most commonly used herbs.* ◼ ADJ If something is **common** to two or more people or groups, it is done, possessed, or used by them all. ❑ *Moldavians and Romanians share a common language.* ◼ ADJ [ADJ n] When there are more animals or plants of a particular species than there are of related species, then the first species is called **common**.

☐ ...the common house fly. **4** ADJ [ADJ n] **Common** is used to indicate that someone or something is of the ordinary kind and not special in any way. ☐ *Democracy might elevate the common man to a position of political superiority.* **5** ADJ **Common** decency or **common** courtesy is the decency or courtesy which most people have. You usually talk about this when someone has not shown these characteristics in their behavior to show your disapproval of them. [DISAPPROVAL] ☐ *It is common decency to give your seat to anyone in greater need.* **6** ADJ [ADJ n] You can use **common** to describe knowledge, an opinion, or a feeling that is shared by people in general. ☐ *It is common knowledge that swimming is one of the best forms of exercise.* • **com|mon|ly** ADV [ADV -ed] ☐ *A little adolescent rebellion is commonly believed to be healthy.* **7** ADJ If you describe someone or their behavior as **common**, you mean that they show a lack of taste, education, and good manners. [mainly BRIT, DISAPPROVAL] ☐ *She might be a little common at times, but she was certainly not boring.* **8** N-COUNT; N-IN-NAMES A **common** is an area of grassy land, usually in or near a village or small town, where the public is allowed to go. ☐ *We are warning women not to go out on to the common alone.* **9** PHRASE If two or more things have something **in common**, they have the same characteristic or feature. ☐ *The oboe and the clarinet have certain features in common.* **10** PHRASE If two or more people have something **in common**, they share the same interests or experiences. ☐ *He had very little in common with his sister.* **11 common ground** → see **ground** ③ **12** → See feature box at **animal**, **polite**

USAGE

common
Don't use a *that*-clause after **common**. Don't say, for example, 'It is quite common that three generations live under one roof.' You say 'It is quite common **for three generations to live under one roof**.' *It is common **for a child to become** temporarily deaf after an ear infection.*

---

com|mon|al|ity /kɒmənælɪti/ (**commonalities**) N-VAR [oft N of n] **Commonality** is used to refer to a feature or purpose that is shared by two or more people or things. [FORMAL] ☐ *We don't have the same commonality of interest.* ☐ *There are an amazing number of commonalities between the systems.*

com|mon cold (**common colds**) N-COUNT [usu sing, the N] The **common cold** is a mild illness. If you have it, your nose is blocked or runny and you may have a sore throat or a cough.

com|mon de|nomi|na|tor (**common denominators**) **1** N-COUNT In mathematics, a **common denominator** is a number which can be divided exactly by all the denominators in a group of fractions. **2** N-COUNT A **common denominator** is a characteristic or attitude that is shared by all members of a group of people. ☐ *I think the only common denominator of success is hard work.* **3** → see also **lowest common denominator**

com|mon|er /kɒmənər/ (**commoners**) N-COUNT In countries such as Britain which have a nobility, **commoners** are the people who are not members of the nobility. ☐ *It's only the second time a potential heir to the throne has married a commoner.*

com|mon land (**common lands**) N-UNCOUNT [also N in pl] **Common land** is land which everyone is allowed to use.

com|mon law **1** N-UNCOUNT **Common law** is the system of law which is based on judges' decisions and on custom rather than on written laws. ☐ *Canadian libel law is based on English common law.* **2** ADJ [ADJ n] A **common law** relationship is regarded as a marriage because it has lasted a long time, although no official marriage contract has been signed. ☐ *...his common law wife.*

com|mon mar|ket (**common markets**) **1** N-COUNT A **common market** is an organization of countries who have agreed to trade freely with each other and make common decisions about industry and agriculture. [BUSINESS] ☐ *...the Central American Common Market.* **2** N-PROPER [the N] **The Common Market** is the former name of the **European Union**.

com|mon noun (**common nouns**) N-COUNT A **common noun** is a noun such as 'tree,' 'water,' or 'beauty' that is not the name of one particular person or thing. Compare **proper noun**.

com|mon|place /kɒmənpleɪs/ ADJ If something is **commonplace**, it happens often or is often found, and is therefore not surprising. ☐ *Inter-racial marriages have become commonplace.*

com|mon room (**common rooms**) also **common-room** N-COUNT A **common room** is a room in a university or school where people can sit, talk, and relax.

com|mon sense also **commonsense** N-UNCOUNT Your **common sense** is your natural ability to make good judgments and to behave in a practical and sensible way. ☐ *Use your common sense.* ☐ *She always had a lot of common sense.*

com|mon stock N-UNCOUNT **Common stock** refers to the shares in a company that are owned by people who have a right to vote at the company's meetings and to receive part of the company's profits after the holders of preferred stock have been paid. Compare **preferred stock**. [AM, BUSINESS] ☐ *The company priced its offering of 2.7 million shares of common stock at 20 cents a share.*

in BRIT, use **ordinary shares**

common|wealth /kɒmənwɛlθ/ **1** N-PROPER The **commonwealth** is an organization consisting of the United Kingdom and most of the countries that were previously under its rule. ☐ *...the Asian, Caribbean and African members of the commonwealth.* **2** N-IN-NAMES **Commonwealth** is used in the official names of some countries, groups of countries, or parts of countries. ☐ *...the Commonwealth of Australia.*

com|mo|tion /kəmoʊʃən/ (**commotions**) N-VAR A **commotion** is a lot of noise, confusion, and excitement. ☐ *He heard a commotion outside.*

comms /kɒmz/ N-PLURAL **Comms** is an abbreviation for **communications**. [INFORMAL] ☐ *All the ship's comms were down.*

com|mu|nal /kəmyuːnəl/ **1** ADJ [ADJ n] **Communal** means relating to particular groups in a country or society. ☐ *Communal violence broke out in different parts of the country.* **2** ADJ You use **communal** to describe something that is shared by a group of people. ☐ *The inmates ate in a communal dining room.*

com|mune /kɒmyuːn/ (**communes**) N-COUNT A **commune** is a group of people who live together and share many of their possessions and responsibilities. ☐ *Mack lived in a commune.*

com|mu|ni|cable /kəmyuːnɪkəbəl/ ADJ [usu ADJ n] A **communicable** disease is one that can be passed on to other people. [MEDICAL]

com|mu|ni|cant /kəmyuːnɪkənt/ (**communicants**) N-COUNT A **communicant** is a person in the Christian Church who receives communion. [FORMAL]

com|mu|ni|cate ✦✧ /kəmyuːnɪkeɪt/ (**communicates, communicating, communicated**) **1** V-RECIP If you **communicate** with someone, you share or exchange information with them, for example by speaking, writing, or using equipment. You can also say that two people **communicate**. ☐ *My birth mother has never communicated with me.* ☐ *Officials of the CIA depend heavily on email to communicate with each other.* • **com|mu|ni|ca|tion** N-UNCOUNT [oft N with/between n] ☐ *Lithuania hasn't had any direct communication with Moscow.* ☐ *...use of the radio telephone for communication between controllers and pilots.* **2** V-RECIP If one person **communicates** with another, they successfully make each other aware of their feelings and ideas. You can also say that two people **communicate**. ☐ *He was never good at communicating with the players.* ☐ *Family therapy showed us how to communicate with each other.* • **com|mu|ni|ca|tion** N-UNCOUNT ☐ *There was a tremendous lack of communication between us.* ☐ *Good communication with people around you could prove difficult.* **3** V-T If you **communicate** information, a feeling, or an idea to someone, you let them know about it. ☐ *They successfully communicate their knowledge to others.*

com|mu|ni|ca|tion ✦✧ /kəmyuːnɪkeɪʃən/ (**communications**) **1** N-PLURAL **Communications** are the systems and processes that are used to communicate or broadcast information, especially by means of electricity or radio waves. ☐ *...a communications satellite.* **2** N-COUNT A **communication** is a message. [FORMAL] ☐ *The ambassador has brought with him a communication from the president.* **3** → see also **communicate** **4** → See feature box at **body language**, **speak**

com|mu|ni|ca|tive /kəmyuːnɪkeɪtɪv, -kətɪv/ **1** ADJ Someone who is **communicative** talks to people, for example about their feelings, and tells people things. ☐ *She has become a lot more tolerant and communicative.* **2** ADJ [usu ADJ n] **Communicative**

means relating to the ability to communicate. ▢ *We have a very communicative approach to teaching languages.*

com|mun|ion /kəmyunyən/ ◼ N-UNCOUNT [also a N, oft N with n] **Communion** with nature or with a person is the feeling that you are sharing thoughts or feelings with them. ▢ *...communion with nature.* ◼ N-UNCOUNT **Communion** is the Christian ceremony in which people eat bread and drink wine in memory of Christ's death. ▢ *Most villagers took communion only at Easter.*

com|mu|ni|qué /kəmyunɪkeɪ/ (**communiqués**) N-COUNT A **communiqué** is an official statement or announcement. [FORMAL] ▢ *The communiqué said military targets had been hit.*

com|mun|ism /kɒmyənɪzəm/ also **Communism** N-UNCOUNT **Communism** is the political belief that all people are equal, that there should be no private ownership and that workers should control the means of producing things. ▢ *...the ultimate triumph of communism in the world.*

com|mun|ist ◆◆◇ /kɒmyənɪst/ (**communists**) also **Communist** ◼ N-COUNT A **communist** is someone who believes in communism. ▢ *Her family fled Czechoslovakia when the communists seized power in 1947.* ◼ ADJ **Communist** means relating to communism. ▢ *...the Communist Party.*

com|mu|nity ◆◆◆ /kəmyunɪti/ (**communities**) ◼ N-SING-COLL The **community** is all the people who live in a particular area or place. ▢ *He's well liked by people in the community.* ◼ N-COUNT-COLL A particular **community** is a group of people who are similar in some way. ▢ *The police haven't really done anything for the Black community in particular.* ◼ N-UNCOUNT **Community** is friendship between different people or groups, and a sense of having something in common. ▢ *Two of our greatest strengths are diversity and community.* ◼ → See feature box at **garden**

COLLOCATIONS

community
NOUN
◼
adjective + **community**: close-knit, thriving, vibrant; broad, entire, international, local, whole
verb + **community**: benefit, help, serve
◼
noun + **community**: faith, immigrant, minority; arts, business, farming, fishing, mining
adjective + **community**: gay; Christian, Jewish, Muslim; Aboriginal, Asian, Black, ethnic, Indian; medical, scientific

---
SYNONYMS

community
NOUN ◼
society: *...the complexities of South African society.*
public: *The poll is a test of the public's confidence in the government.*
population: *...the local population.*

---

com|mu|nity cen|ter (**community centers**) N-COUNT A **community center** is a place that is specially provided for the people, groups, and organizations in a particular area, where they can go in order to meet one another and do things.

com|mu|nity col|lege (**community colleges**) N-COUNT A **community college** is a local college where students from the surrounding area can take courses in practical or academic subjects. [AM]

com|mu|nity po|lic|ing N-UNCOUNT **Community policing** is a system in which police officers work only in one particular area of the community, so that everyone knows them.

com|mu|nity ser|vice ◼ N-UNCOUNT **Community service** is unpaid work that criminals sometimes do as a punishment instead of being sent to prison. ▢ *He was sentenced to 140 hours' community service for drunk driving.* ◼ N-UNCOUNT **Community service** is unpaid voluntary work that a person performs for the benefit of his or her local community. ▢ *I have been doing community service work in Oakland for the past several years.*

com|mun|ity spread N-UNCOUNT If there is **community spread** of a disease, it spreads widely through a population. ▢ *School closures are in effect in areas where community spread of the virus is high.*

com|mute /kəmyut/ (**commutes, commuting, commuted**) ◼ V-I If you **commute**, you travel a long distance every day between your home and your place of work. ▢ *Mike commutes to Miami every day.* ▢ *McLaren began commuting between Philadelphia and New York.* ● **com|mut|er** (**commuters**) N-COUNT ▢ *There are significant numbers of commuters using our streets.* ◼ N-COUNT A **commute** is the journey that you make when you commute. ▢ *The average Los Angeles commute is over 60 miles a day.*

VOCABULARY IN CONTEXT

Commuting

Unless you can walk to your school or place of employment, you'll know the joy or pain of **commuting**. Getting **stuck in traffic** at **rush hour** leaves many of us **stressed out** before we've even arrived at our desks. The **unpredictability** of bumper-to-bumper traffic is very frustrating when you're running late. In fact, the combination of **congested** roads and impatience can affect a person's well-being. And if you have the option to use **public transportation**, are you better off? With access to good **transportation links**, it may be less stressful to commute by bus or train, but that depends on how many fellow **commuters** you have to share the journey with. Putting up with the **crush** inside subway stations or being **crammed** onto **packed** buses with **standing room** only aren't exactly pleasant ways to start and end each day. But it's not all bad news. Those lucky enough to have quieter commutes can use the time between work and home to **relax**.

---

com|mut|er belt (**commuter belts**) N-COUNT A **commuter belt** is the area surrounding a large city, where many people who work in the city live. ▢ *...people who live in the commuter belt around the capital.*

comp /kɒmp/ (**comps, comping, comped**) ◼ N-UNCOUNT **Comp** is short for **compensation**. [INFORMAL] ▢ *Workers' comp pays for work-related medical problems.* ◼ V-T If someone, or if a place such as a hotel or a restaurant **comps** you, or if they **comp** you to something, they give you a room or a meal without charging you for it. [AM, INFORMAL] ▢ *I comped him his lunch and lent him gas money to get home.*

com|pact /kəmpækt/ (**compacts**) ◼ ADJ **Compact** things are small or take up very little space. You use this word when you think this is a good quality. [APPROVAL] ▢ *...my compact office in Washington.* ◼ ADJ A **compact** person is small but looks strong. ▢ *He was compact, probably no taller than me.* ◼ N-COUNT A **compact** or a **compact car** is a car that is smaller than the average car, and that is economical to run.

com|pact disc (**compact discs**) also **compact disk** N-COUNT [also on N] **Compact discs** are small shiny discs that contain music or computer information. The abbreviation **CD** is also used.

com|pan|ion /kəmpænyən/ (**companions**) N-COUNT A **companion** is someone who you spend time with or who you are traveling with. ▢ *Fred had been her constant companion for the last six years of her life.*

WORD HISTORY

companion
A **companion** was originally someone you liked enough to share a meal with. The Latin word *companio* consists of the roots *com-*, meaning 'with' or 'together,' and *panis*, meaning 'bread.'

com|pan|ion|able /kəmpænyənəbəl/ ADJ If you describe a person as **companionable**, you mean they are friendly and pleasant to be with. [WRITTEN] • **com|pan|ion|ably** /kəmpænyənəbli/ ADV [ADV with v] ❑ *They walked companionably back to the house.*

com|pan|ion|ship /kəmpænyənʃɪp/ N-UNCOUNT **Companionship** is having someone you know and like with you, instead of being on your own. ❑ *I depended on his companionship and on his judgment.*

com|pan|ion|way /kəmpænyənweɪ/ (companionways) N-COUNT A **companionway** is a staircase or ladder that leads from one deck to another on a ship.

com|pa|ny ✦✦✦ /kʌmpəni/ (companies) **1** N-COUNT-COLL; N-IN-NAMES A **company** is a business organization that makes money by selling goods or services. ❑ *Sheila found some work as a secretary in an insurance company.* **2** N-COUNT-COLL; N-IN-NAMES A **company** is a group of opera singers, dancers, or actors who work together. ❑ *...the Phoenix Dance Company.* **3** N-COUNT; N-IN-NAMES A **company** is a group of soldiers that is usually part of a battalion or regiment, and that is divided into two or more platoons. ❑ *The division will consist of two tank companies and one infantry company.* **4** N-UNCOUNT **Company** is having another person or other people with you, usually when this is pleasant or stops you feeling lonely. ❑ *"I won't stay long."—"No, please. I need the company."* ❑ *Ross enjoyed the company of his colleagues.* **5** → see also **joint-stock company, public company** **6** PHRASE If you **have company**, you have a visitor or friend with you. ❑ *He didn't say he had company.* **7** PHRASE If you **keep** someone **company**, you spend time with them and stop them from feeling lonely or bored. ❑ *Why don't you stay here and keep Emma company?*

SYNONYMS

company
NOUN **1**
business: *The company was a family business.*
firm: *The firm's employees were expecting large bonuses.*
corporation: *...multi-national corporations.*
multinational: *...multinationals such as Ford and IBM.*

com|pa|ny car (company cars) N-COUNT A **company car** is a car which an employer gives to an employee to use as their own, usually as a benefit of having a particular job, or because their job involves a lot of driving. [BUSINESS] ❑ *...changes to tax laws for company cars.*

com|pa|rable /kɒmpərəbəl/ **1** ADJ Something that is **comparable** to something else is roughly similar, for example in amount or importance. ❑ *...paying the same wages to men and women for work of comparable value.* ❑ *Farmers were supposed to get an income comparable to that of townspeople.* **2** ADJ If two or more things are **comparable**, they are of the same kind or are in the same situation, and so they can reasonably be compared. ❑ *In other comparable countries, real wages increased much more rapidly.* ❑ *By contrast, the comparable figure for Canada is 16 percent.*

com|para|tive /kəmpærətɪv/ (comparatives) **1** ADJ [ADJ n] You use **comparative** to show that you are judging something against a previous or different situation. For example, **comparative** calm is a situation which is calmer than before or calmer than the situation in other places. ❑ *The task was accomplished with comparative ease.* • **com|para|tive|ly** ADV [ADV adj/adv] ❑ *...a comparatively small nation.* **2** ADJ [ADJ n] A **comparative** study is a study that involves the comparison of two or more things of the same kind. ❑ *...a comparative study of the dietary practices of people from various regions of India.* **3** ADJ [ADJ n] In grammar, the **comparative** form of an adjective or adverb shows that something has more of a quality than something else has. For example, 'bigger' is the comparative form of 'big,' and 'more quickly' is the comparative form of 'quickly.' Compare **superlative**. • N-COUNT **Comparative** is also a noun. ❑ *The comparative of "pretty" is "prettier."*

com|pare ✦◇◇ /kəmpɛər/ (compares, comparing, compared) **1** V-T When you **compare** things, you consider them and discover the differences or similarities between them. ❑ *Compare the two illustrations in Figure 60.* ❑ *Managers analyze their company's data and compare it with data on their competitors.* **2** V-T If you **compare** one person or thing to another, you say that they are like the other person or thing. ❑ *Some commentators compared his work to that of James Joyce.* **3** V-I [usu with neg] If you say that something does not **compare with** something else, you mean that it is much worse. ❑ *The flowers here do not compare with those at home.* **4** V-I If one thing **compares** favorably with another, it is better than the other thing. If it **compares** unfavorably, it is worse than the other thing. ❑ *Our road safety record compares favorably with that of other countries.* **5** → see also **compared**

com|pared ✦✦ /kəmpɛərd/ **1** PHRASE If you say, for example, that one thing is large or small **compared with** another or **compared to** another, you mean that it is larger or smaller than the other thing. ❑ *The room was light and lofty compared to the basement.* **2** PHRASE You talk about one situation or thing **compared with** another or **compared to** another when contrasting the two situations or things. ❑ *In 1800 Ireland's population was nine million, compared to Britain's 16 million.*

com|pari|son ✦◇◇ /kəmpærɪsən/ (comparisons) **1** N-VAR When you make a **comparison**, you consider two or more things and discover the differences between them. ❑ *...a comparison of the Mexican and Guatemalan economies.* ❑ *Its recommendations are based on detailed comparisons between the public and private sectors.* **2** N-COUNT When you make a **comparison**, you say that one thing is like another in some way. ❑ *It is demonstrably an unfair comparison.* **3** PHRASE If you say, for example, that something is large or small **in comparison with**, **in comparison to**, or **by comparison** with something else, you mean that it is larger or smaller than the other thing. ❑ *The amount of carbon dioxide released by human activities that is due to burning coal and oil is small in comparison.*

com|part|ment /kəmpɑrtmənt/ (compartments) **1** N-COUNT A **compartment** is one of the separate parts of an object that is used for keeping things in. ❑ *The fire started in the baggage compartment.* **2** → see also **glove compartment** **3** N-COUNT A **compartment** is one of the separate spaces into which a railroad car is divided. ❑ *On the way home we shared our first class compartment with a group of businessmen.*

com|part|men|tal|ize /kɒmpɑrtmɛntəlaɪz/ (compartmentalizes, compartmentalizing, compartmentalized)

in BRIT, also use **compartmentalise**

V-T To **compartmentalize** something means to divide it into separate sections. ❑ *Some people compartmentalize their lives and don't mix their personal and professional pursuits.* • **com|part|men|tal|ized** ADJ ❑ *...the compartmentalized world of Japanese finance.*

com|pass /kʌmpəs/ (compasses) **1** N-COUNT A **compass** is an instrument that you use for finding directions. It has a dial and a magnetic needle that always points to the north. ❑ *We had to rely on a compass and a lot of luck to get here.* **2** → See also color supplement

com|pas|sion /kəmpæʃən/ N-UNCOUNT **Compassion** is a feeling of pity, sympathy, and understanding for someone who is suffering. ❑ *Patients need time and compassion from their physicians.*

com|pas|sion|ate /kəmpæʃənɪt/ ADJ If you describe someone or something as **compassionate**, you mean that they feel or show pity, sympathy, and understanding for people who are suffering. [APPROVAL] ❑ *My father was a deeply compassionate man.* ❑ *She has a wise, compassionate face.*

com|pas|sion|ate leave N-UNCOUNT **Compassionate leave** is time away from your work that your employer allows you for personal reasons, especially when a member of your family dies or is seriously ill. [BRIT, BUSINESS]

in AM, use **leave of absence**

com|pass point (compass points) N-COUNT A **compass point** is one of the 32 marks on the dial of a compass that show direction, for example north, south, east, and west.

com|pat|ible /kəmpætɪbəl/ **1** ADJ If things, for example systems, ideas, and beliefs, are **compatible**, they work well together or can exist together successfully. ❑ *Free enterprise, he argued, was compatible with Russian values and traditions.* • **com|pat|ibil|ity** /kəmpætɪbɪlɪti/ N-UNCOUNT ❑ *The new regulation has already been criticized by the European Commission regarding its compatibility with EU law.* **2** ADJ If you say that you are **compatible** with someone, you mean that you have a good relationship with them because you have similar opinions and interests. ❑ *Mildred and I are very compatible. She's interested in the things that interest me.* • **com|pat|ibil|ity** N-UNCOUNT ❑ *As a result of their compatibility, Haig and Fraser were able to bring about wide-ranging reforms.* **3** ADJ If one brand of computer or computer equipment is **compatible** with another brand, they can be used together and can use the same software. ❑ *Fujitsu took over another American firm, Amdal, to help it to make and sell machines compatible with IBM in the United States.* • **com|pat|ibil|ity** N-UNCOUNT ❑ *What makes this device stand out from others is its compatibility with multiple software applications.*

com|pat|ri|ot /kəmpeɪtriət/ (compatriots) N-COUNT Your **compatriots** are people from your own country. ❑ *Chris Robertson of Australia beat his compatriot Chris Dittmar in the final.*

com|pel /kəmpɛl/ (compels, compelling, compelled) **1** V-T If a situation, a rule, or a person **compels** you to do something, they force you to do it. ❑ *...the introduction of legislation to compel cyclists to wear a helmet.* **2** PHRASE If you **feel compelled** to do something, you feel that you must do it, because it is the right thing to do. ❑ *Dickens felt compelled to return to the stage for a final goodbye.*

com|pel|ling /kəmpɛlɪŋ/ **1** ADJ A **compelling** argument or reason is one that convinces you that something is true or that something should be done. ❑ *Factual and forensic evidence makes a suicide verdict the most compelling answer to the mystery of his death.* **2** ADJ If you describe something such as a movie or book, or someone's appearance, as **compelling**, you mean you want to keep looking at it or reading it because you find it so interesting. ❑ *...a frighteningly violent yet compelling movie.*

com|pen|dium /kəmpɛndiəm/ (compendiums) N-COUNT A **compendium** is a short but detailed collection of information, usually in a book. ❑ *The Roman Catholic Church has issued a compendium of its teachings.*

com|pen|sate /kɒmpənseɪt/ (compensates, compensating, compensated) **1** V-T To **compensate** someone for money or things that they have lost means to pay them money or give them something to replace those things. ❑ *The damages are designed to compensate victims for their direct losses.* **2** V-I If you **compensate** for a lack of something or for something you have done wrong, you do something to make the situation better. ❑ *The company agreed to keep up high levels of output in order to compensate for supplies lost.* **3** V-I Something that **compensates for** something else balances it or reduces its effects. ❑ *Senators say it is crucial that a mechanism is found to compensate for inflation.* **4** V-I If you try to **compensate** for something that is wrong or missing in your life, you try to do something that removes or reduces the harmful effects. ❑ *Their sense of humor and ability to get along with people are two characteristics that compensate for their lack of experience.*

com|pen|sa|tion /kɒmpənseɪʃən/ (compensations) **1** N-UNCOUNT **Compensation** is money that someone who has experienced loss or suffering claims from the person or organization responsible, or from the state. ❑ *He received one year's salary as compensation for loss of office.* ❑ *They want $20,000 in compensation for each of about 500 claimants.* **2** N-VAR If something is some **compensation** for something bad that has happened, it makes you feel better. ❑ *Helen gained some compensation for her earlier defeat by winning the final open class.*

com|pen|sa|tory /kɒmpɛnsətəri/ **1** ADJ [usu ADJ n] **Compensatory** payments involve money paid as compensation. [FORMAL] ❑ *The jury awarded $11.2 million in compensatory damages.* **2** ADJ [usu ADJ n] **Compensatory** measures are designed to help people who have special problems or disabilities. [FORMAL] ❑ *...compensatory education programs for the developmentally disabled.*

com|pere /kɒmpɛər/ (comperes, compering, compered) also **compère** **1** N-COUNT A **compere** is the same as an **emcee**. [BRIT] **2** V-T/V-I To **compere** a show is the same as to **emcee** it. [BRIT]

com|pete /kəmpiːt/ (competes, competing, competed) **1** V-RECIP When one firm or country **competes** with another, it tries to get people to buy its own goods in preference to those of the other firm or country. You can also say that two firms or countries **compete**. ❑ *The banks have long competed with American Express's charge cards and various store cards.* ❑ *Hardware stores are competing fiercely for business.* **2** V-RECIP If you **compete** with someone for something, you try to get it for yourself and stop the other person from getting it. You can also say that two people **compete** for something. ❑ *Kangaroos compete with sheep and cattle for sparse supplies of food and water.* ❑ *Young men compete with each other for membership in these societies and fraternities.* **3** V-I If you **compete** in a contest or a game, you take part in it. ❑ *He will be competing in the 100-meter race.*

--- SYNONYMS ---

compete
VERB **1**
challenge: *We challenged a team who called themselves 'College Athletes.'*
contest: *He quickly won his party's nomination to contest the elections.*
vie: *The two are vying for the support of New York voters.*
rival: *The image quality obviously cannot rival that of more expensive models.*

com|pe|tence /kɒmpɪtəns/ N-UNCOUNT **Competence** is the ability to do something well or effectively. ❑ *Many people have testified to his competence.*

com|pe|ten|cy /kɒmpɪtənsi/ N-UNCOUNT **Competency** means the same as **competence**. ❑ *...managerial competency.* ❑ *...a competency test.*

com|pe|tent /kɒmpɪtənt/ **1** ADJ Someone who is **competent** is efficient and effective. ❑ *He was a loyal, distinguished and very competent civil servant.* • **com|pe|tent|ly** ADV ❑ *The government performed competently in the face of multiple challenges.* **2** ADJ If you are **competent** to do something, you have the skills, abilities, or experience necessary to do it well. ❑ *Most adults do not feel competent to deal with a medical emergency involving a child.*

com|pet|ing /kəmpiːtɪŋ/ **1** ADJ [ADJ n] **Competing** ideas, requirements, or interests cannot all be right or satisfied at the same time. ❑ *They talked about the competing theories of the origin of life.* ❑ *...the competing demands of work and family.* **2** → see also **compete**

com|pe|ti|tion /kɒmpɪtɪʃən/ (competitions) **1** N-UNCOUNT **Competition** is a situation in which two or more people or groups are trying to get something which not everyone can have. ❑ *There's been some fierce competition for the title.* **2** N-UNCOUNT **Competition** is an activity involving two or more companies, in which each company tries to get people to buy its own goods in preference to the other companies' goods. ❑ *The deal would have reduced competition in the commuter-aircraft market.* ❑ *The farmers have been seeking higher prices as better protection from foreign competition.* **3** N-UNCOUNT The **competition** is the goods or services that a rival organization is selling. ❑ *The American aerospace industry has been challenged by some stiff competition.* **4** N-SING The **competition** is the person or people you are competing with. ❑ *I have to change my approach, the competition is too good now.* **5** N-VAR A **competition** is an event in which many people take part in order to find out who is best at a particular activity. ❑ *...a surfing competition.*

--- COLLOCATIONS ---

competition
NOUN
1
adjective + **competition**: fierce, intense, stiff, tough
3
verb + **competition**: increase, introduce, promote
5
verb + **competition**: hold, organize, run; enter

com|peti|tive /kəmpɛtɪtɪv/ **1** ADJ **Competitive** is used to describe situations or activities in which people or companies compete with each other. ❑ *Only by keeping down costs will America maintain its competitive advantage over other countries.* ❑ *Japan is a highly competitive market system.*

VOCABULARY IN CONTEXT

Competition

When it comes to competition, some people **concede defeat** graciously, while others are **bad losers**. We play games from a very young age, but some adults never grow out of the urge to sulk when they're **beaten fair and square**. However bad losing feels, being **a good sport** earns the respect of your **opponents** and is more likely to give you the opportunity to **triumph** in a **rematch**. A simple congratulations and offering your **rival** a handshake is enough to show them their **victory** hasn't upset you – even if it has! Even some **champions** in their field take defeat badly. Tennis player John McEnroe would throw his racket and shout at the umpire 'You cannot be serious!' when the ball was ruled out.

● **com|peti|tive|ly** ADV [ADV after v] ❑ *He's now back up on the slopes again, skiing competitively.* **2** ADJ A **competitive** person is eager to be more successful than other people. ❑ *He has always been ambitious and fiercely competitive.* ● **com|peti|tive|ly** ADV [ADV after v] ❑ *They worked hard together, competitively and under pressure.* ● **com|peti|tive|ness** N-UNCOUNT ❑ *I can't stand the pace, I suppose, and the competitiveness, and the unfriendliness.* **3** ADJ Goods or services that are at a **competitive** price or rate are likely to be bought, because they are less expensive than other goods of the same kind. ❑ *Only those homes offered for sale at competitive prices will secure interest from serious purchasers.* ● **com|peti|tive|ly** ADV ❑ *...a number of early Martin and Gibson guitars, which were competitively priced.* ● **com|peti|tive|ness** N-UNCOUNT ❑ *It is only on the world market that we can prove the competitiveness and quality of our software.*

com|peti|tor ✦✧✧ /kəmpɛtɪtər/ (**competitors**) **1** N-COUNT A company's **competitors** are companies who are trying to sell similar goods or services to the same people. ❑ *The bank isn't performing as well as some of its competitors.* **2** N-COUNT A **competitor** is a person who takes part in a competition or contest. ❑ *One of the oldest competitors won the individual silver medal.*

com|pi|la|tion /kɒmpɪleɪʃən/ (**compilations**) N-COUNT A **compilation** is a book, CD, or program that contains many different items that have been gathered together, usually ones which have already appeared in other places. ❑ *His latest CD is a compilation of his jazz works over the past decade.*

com|pile /kəmpaɪl/ (**compiles, compiling, compiled**) V-T When you **compile** something such as a report, book, or program, you produce it by collecting and putting together many pieces of information. ❑ *The book took 10 years to compile.*

com|pil|er /kəmpaɪlər/ (**compilers**) **1** N-COUNT [oft N *of* n] A **compiler** is someone who compiles books, reports, or lists of information. **2** N-COUNT A **compiler** is a computer program which converts language that people can use into a code that the computer can understand. [COMPUTING]

com|pla|cen|cy /kəmpleɪsənsi/ N-UNCOUNT **Complacency** is being complacent about a situation. [DISAPPROVAL] ❑ *...a worrying level of complacency about the risks of infection from AIDS.*

com|pla|cent /kəmpleɪsənt/ ADJ A **complacent** person is very pleased with themselves or feels that they do not need to do anything about a situation, even though the situation may be uncertain or dangerous. [DISAPPROVAL] ❑ *We cannot afford to be complacent about our health.*

com|plain ✦✦✧ /kəmpleɪn/ (**complains, complaining, complained**) **1** V-T/V-I If you **complain** about a situation, you say that you are not satisfied with it. ❑ *Miners have complained bitterly that the government did not fulfill their promises.* ❑ *The couple complained about the high cost of visiting Europe.* ❑ *I shouldn't complain, I've got a good job to go back to.* ❑ *"I wish someone would do something about it," he complained.* **2** V-I If you **complain of** pain or illness, you say that you are feeling pain or feeling ill. ❑ *He complained of a headache.*

com|plain|ant /kəmpleɪnənt/ (**complainants**) N-COUNT A **complainant** is a person who starts a court case in a court of law. [LEGAL]

com|plain|er /kəmpleɪnər/ (**complainers**) N-COUNT A **complainer** is someone who complains a lot about their problems or about things they do not like. [DISAPPROVAL] ❑ *He was a terrible complainer – always moaning about something.*

com|plaint ✦✧✧ /kəmpleɪnt/ (**complaints**) **1** N-VAR A **complaint** is a statement in which you express your dissatisfaction with a situation. ❑ *There's been a record number of complaints about the standard of service.* ❑ *People have been reluctant to make formal complaints to the police.* **2** N-COUNT A **complaint** is a reason for complaining. ❑ *My main complaint is that we can't go out on the racecourse anymore.* **3** N-COUNT You can refer to an illness as a **complaint**, especially if it is not very serious. ❑ *Eczema is a common skin complaint which often runs in families.*

SYNONYMS

complaint
NOUN **1**
protest: *The unions called a two-hour strike in protest of the railroad company's announcement.*
objection: *I have no objection to banks making money.*
grumble: *My grumble is with the structure and organization of the material.*
criticism: *...unfair criticism of his tactics.*

---

com|ple|ment (**complements, complementing, complemented**)

> The verb is pronounced /kɒmplɪmɛnt/. The noun is pronounced /kɒmplɪmənt/.

1 V-T If one thing **complements** another, it goes well with the other thing and makes its good qualities more noticeable. ❑ *Nutmeg, parsley and cider all complement the flavor of these beans well.* **2** V-T If people or things **complement** each other, they are different or do something different, which makes them a good combination. ❑ *There will be a written examination to complement the practical test.* **3** N-COUNT Something that is a **complement** to something else complements it. ❑ *The green wallpaper is the perfect complement to the old pine of the dresser.*

com|ple|men|tary /kɒmplɪmɛntəri, -mɛntri/ **1** ADJ **Complementary** things are different from each other but make a good combination. [FORMAL] ❑ *To improve the quality of life through work, two complementary strategies are necessary.* ❑ *He has done experiments complementary to those of Eigen.* **2** ADJ [ADJ n] **Complementary** medicine refers to ways of treating patients which are different from the ones used by most Western doctors, for example acupuncture and homeopathy. ❑ *...combining orthodox treatment with a wide range of complementary therapies.*

com|plete ✦✦✦ /kəmpliːt/ (**completes, completing, completed**) **1** ADJ You use **complete** to emphasize that something is as great in extent, degree, or amount as it possibly can be. [EMPHASIS] ❑ *The house is a complete mess.* ❑ *The rebels had taken complete control.* ❑ *The resignation came as a complete surprise.* ● **com|plete|ly** ADV ❑ *Dozens of homes had been completely destroyed.* ❑ *Make sure that you defrost it completely.* **2** ADJ [ADJ n] You can use **complete** to emphasize that you are referring to the whole of something and not just part of it. [EMPHASIS] ❑ *A complete apartment complex was burned to the ground.* **3** ADJ If something is **complete**, it contains all the parts that it should contain. ❑ *The list may not be complete.* ❑ *...a complete dinner service.* **4** ADJ [ADJ n] The **complete** works of a writer are all their books or poems published together in one book or as a set of books. ❑ *...the Complete Works of William Shakespeare.* **5** ADJ [v-link ADJ] If something is **complete**, it has been finished. ❑ *The work of restoring the farmhouse is complete.* **6** V-T [no cont] To **complete** a set or group means to provide the last item that is needed to make it a full set or group. ❑ *Children don't complete their set of 20 baby teeth until they are two to three years old.* **7** V-T If you **complete** something, you finish doing, making, or producing it. ❑ *Peter Mayle has just completed his first novel.* • **com|ple|tion** /kəmpliːʃ°n/ (**completions**) N-VAR ❑ *The project is nearing completion.* **8** V-T [no cont] If you **complete** something, you do all of it. ❑ *She completed her degree in two years.* **9** V-T If you **complete** a form or questionnaire, you write the answers or information asked for in it. ❑ *Simply complete part 1 of the application.* **10** PHRASE If one thing comes **complete with** another, it has that thing as an extra or additional part. ❑ *The diary comes complete with a gold ballpoint pen.*

com|plex ✦✧ (**complexes**)

The adjective is pronounced /kəmplɛks/ or sometimes /kɒmplɛks/. The noun is pronounced /kɒmplɛks/.

1 ADJ Something that is **complex** has many different parts, and is therefore often difficult to understand. ❑ *...in-depth coverage of today's complex issues.* ❑ *...a complex system of voting.* **2** N-COUNT A **complex** is a group of buildings designed for a particular purpose, or one large building divided into several smaller areas. ❑ *...a low-cost apartment complex*

com|plex|ion /kəmplɛkʃ°n/ (**complexions**) **1** N-COUNT When you refer to someone's **complexion**, you are referring to the natural color or condition of the skin on their face. ❑ *She had short brown hair and a pale complexion.* **2** → See feature box at **appearance**

com|plex|ities /kəmplɛksɪtiz/ N-PLURAL The **complexities** of something are the many complicated factors involved in it. ❑ *...those who find it hardest to cope with the complexities of modern life.*

com|plex|ity /kəmplɛksɪti/ N-UNCOUNT **Complexity** is the state of having many different parts connected or related to each other in a complicated way. ❑ *...a diplomatic tangle of great complexity.*

com|pli|ance /kəmplaɪəns/ N-UNCOUNT **Compliance** with something, for example a law, treaty, or agreement, means doing what you are required or expected to do. [FORMAL] ❑ *Inspectors were sent to visit nuclear sites and verify compliance with the treaty.*

com|pli|ant /kəmplaɪənt/ ADJ If you say that someone is **compliant**, you mean they willingly do what they are asked to do. [FORMAL] ❑ *...a docile and compliant workforce.*

com|pli|cate /kɒmplɪkeɪt/ (**complicates, complicating, complicated**) V-T To **complicate** something means to make it more difficult to understand or deal with. ❑ *What complicates the issue is the burden of history.* ❑ *The day's events, he said, would only complicate the task of the peacekeeping forces.*

com|pli|cat|ed ✦✧ /kɒmplɪkeɪtɪd/ ADJ If you say that something is **complicated**, you mean it has so many parts or aspects that it is difficult to understand or deal with. ❑ *The situation in Lebanon is very complicated.*

com|pli|ca|tion /kɒmplɪkeɪʃ°n/ (**complications**) **1** N-COUNT A **complication** is a problem or difficulty that makes a situation harder to deal with. ❑ *The age difference was a complication to the relationship.* ❑ *There are too many complications to explain now.* **2** N-COUNT A **complication** is a medical problem that occurs as a result of another illness or disease. ❑ *Blindness is a common complication of diabetes.*

com|plic|it /kəmplɪsɪt/ ADJ [usu ADJ in n] If someone is **complicit** in a crime or unfair activity, they are involved in it. [JOURNALISM] ❑ *He did not witness her execution, yet he and the others are complicit in her death.*

com|plic|ity /kəmplɪsɪti/ N-UNCOUNT **Complicity** is involvement with other people in an illegal activity or plan. [FORMAL] ❑ *Recently a number of policemen were sentenced to death for their complicity in the murder.*

com|pli|ment (**compliments, complimenting, complimented**)

The verb is pronounced /kɒmplɪmɛnt/. The noun is pronounced /kɒmplɪmənt/.

1 N-COUNT A **compliment** is a polite remark that you make to someone to show that you like their appearance, appreciate their qualities, or approve of what they have done. ❑ *You can do no harm by paying a woman compliments.* **2** V-T If you **compliment** someone, you give them a compliment. ❑ *They complimented me on the way I looked each time they saw me.*

com|pli|men|tary /kɒmplɪmɛntəri, -mɛntri/ **1** ADJ If you are **complimentary** about something, you express admiration for it. ❑ *The staff have been very complimentary, and so have the customers.* **2** ADJ A **complimentary** seat, ticket, or book is given to you free. ❑ *He had complimentary tickets to take his wife to see the movie.*

com|ply /kəmplaɪ/ (**complies, complying, complied**) V-I If someone or something **complies** with an order or set of rules, they do what is required or expected. ❑ *The commander said that the army would comply with the ceasefire.* ❑ *Some beaches had failed to comply with environmental regulations.*

com|po|nent ✦✧ /kəmpoʊnənt/ (**components**) **1** N-COUNT The **components** of something are the parts that it is made of. ❑ *Enriched uranium is a key component of a nuclear weapon.* ❑ *The management plan has four main components.* **2** ADJ [ADJ n] The **component** parts of something are the parts that make it up. ❑ *Gorbachev failed to keep the component parts of the Soviet Union together.*

com|port /kəmpɔːrt/ (**comports, comporting, comported**) V-T If you **comport** yourself in a particular way, you behave in that way. [FORMAL] ❑ *He comports himself with dignity.*

com|pose /kəmpoʊz/ (**composes, composing, composed**) **1** V-T The things that something **is composed** of are its parts or members. The separate things that **compose** something are the parts or members that form it. ❑ *The force would be composed of troops from NATO countries.* ❑ *Protein molecules compose all the complex working parts of living cells.* **2** V-T/V-I When someone **composes** a piece of music or **composes**, they write music. ❑ *Vivaldi composed a large number of very fine concertos.* **3** V-T If you **compose** something such as a letter, poem, or speech, you write it, often using a lot of concentration or skill. [FORMAL] ❑ *He started at once to compose a reply to Anna.*

com|posed /kəmpoʊzd/ ADJ [usu v-link ADJ] If someone is **composed**, they are calm and able to control their feelings. ❑ *Laura was very calm and composed.*

com|pos|er /kəmpoʊzər/ (**composers**) N-COUNT A **composer** is a person who writes music, especially classical music. ❑ *...music by Strauss, Mozart, Beethoven, and other great composers.*

com|po|site /kəmpɒzɪt/ (**composites**) ADJ A **composite** object or item is made up of several different things, parts, or substances. ❑ *Galton devised a method of creating composite pictures in which the features of different faces were superimposed over one another.* • N-COUNT [usu sing, oft N of n] **Composite** is also a noun. ❑ *Cuba is a composite of diverse traditions and people.*

com|po|si|tion /kɒmpəzɪʃ°n/ (**compositions**) **1** N-UNCOUNT When you talk about the **composition** of something, you are referring to the way in which its various parts are put together and arranged. ❑ *Television has transformed the size and social composition of the audience at great sporting occasions.* **2** N-COUNT The **compositions** of a composer, painter, or other artist are the works of art that they have produced. ❑ *Mozart's compositions are undoubtedly among the world's greatest.* **3** N-COUNT A **composition** is a piece of written work that children write at school. ❑ *We had to write a composition on the subject "My Pet."* **4** → See feature box at **music**

com|posi|tor /kəmpɒzɪtər/ (**compositors**) N-COUNT A **compositor** is a person who arranges the text and pictures of a book, magazine, or newspaper before it is printed.

com|post /kɒmpoʊst/ (**composts, composting, composted**) **1** N-UNCOUNT **Compost** is a mixture of decayed plants and vegetable waste which is added to the soil to help plants grow. ❑ *...a small compost heap.* **2** N-MASS **Compost** is specially treated soil that you buy and use to grow seeds and plants in pots. ❑ *...a 75-pound bag of compost.* **3** V-T To **compost** things such as unwanted bits of plants means to make them into compost.

com|po|sure /kəmpoʊʒər/ N-UNCOUNT **Composure** is the appearance or feeling of calm and the ability to control your feelings. [FORMAL] ❑ *She was a little nervous at first but she soon regained her composure.*

com|pote /kɒmpoʊt/ (compotes) N-VAR A **compote** is fruit stewed with sugar or in syrup.

com|pound /kɒmpaʊnd/ (compounds, compounding, compounded)

> The noun is pronounced /kɒmpaʊnd/. The verb is pronounced /kəmpaʊnd/.

1 N-COUNT A **compound** is an enclosed area of land that is used for a particular purpose. ❑ *They took refuge in the embassy compound.* ❑ *...a military compound.* **2** N-COUNT In chemistry, a **compound** is a substance that consists of two or more elements. ❑ *Organic compounds contain carbon in their molecules.* **3** N-COUNT If something is a **compound** of different things, it consists of those things. [FORMAL] ❑ *Honey is basically a compound of water, two types of sugar, vitamins and enzymes.* **4** ADJ [ADJ n] **Compound** is used to indicate that something consists of two or more parts or things. ❑ *...the big compound eyes of dragonflies.* **5** V-T To **compound** a problem, difficulty, or mistake means to make it worse by adding to it. ❑ *Additional loss of life will only compound the tragedy.* ❑ *The problem is compounded by the medical system here.* **6** ADJ [ADJ n] In grammar, a **compound** noun, adjective, or verb is one that is made up of two or more words, for example 'fire engine,' 'bottle-green,' and 'firelight.' **7** → See also color supplement

com|pound|ed /kɒmpaʊndɪd/ ADJ [v-link ADJ of n] If something is **compounded of** different things, it is a mixture of those things. [FORMAL] ❑ *...an emotion oddly compounded of pleasure and bitterness.*

com|pound frac|ture (compound fractures) N-COUNT A **compound fracture** is a fracture in which the broken bone sticks through the skin.

com|pound in|ter|est N-UNCOUNT **Compound interest** is interest that is calculated both on an original sum of money and on interest which has previously been added to the sum. Compare **simple interest**. [BUSINESS]

com|pre|hend /kɒmprɪhɛnd/ (comprehends, comprehending, comprehended) V-T/V-I [with brd-neg] If you cannot **comprehend** something, you cannot understand it. [FORMAL] ❑ *I just cannot comprehend your attitude.*

com|pre|hen|sible /kɒmprɪhɛnsɪbəl/ ADJ Something that is **comprehensible** can be understood. [FORMAL] ❑ *He spoke abruptly, in barely comprehensible Arabic.*

com|pre|hen|sion /kɒmprɪhɛnʃən/ **1** N-UNCOUNT **Comprehension** is the ability to understand something. [FORMAL] ❑ *This was utterly beyond her comprehension.* **2** N-UNCOUNT **Comprehension** is full knowledge and understanding of the meaning of something. [FORMAL] ❑ *They turned to one another with the same expression of dawning comprehension, surprise, and relief.* **3** → See feature box at **learning**

com|pre|hen|sive /kɒmprɪhɛnsɪv/ ADJ Something that is **comprehensive** includes everything that is needed or relevant. ❑ *The Rough Guide to Nepal is a comprehensive guide to the region.*

SYNONYMS

comprehensive
ADJ
thorough: *This very thorough survey goes back to 1784.*
full: *Full details will be sent to you once your application is accepted.*
complete: *The list may not be complete.*
wide: *The brochure offers a wide choice of hotels, apartments, and vacation homes.*
extensive: *The facilities available are very extensive.*

---

com|pre|hen|sive|ly /kɒmprɪhɛnsɪvli/ ADV Something that is done **comprehensively** is done thoroughly. ❑ *She was comprehensively outplayed by Coetzer.*

com|press /kəmprɛs/ (compresses, compressing, compressed) **1** V-T/V-I When you **compress** something or when it **compresses**, it is pressed or squeezed so that it takes up less space. ❑ *Poor posture, sitting or walking slouched over, compresses the body's organs.* ● **com|pres|sion** /kəmprɛʃən/ N-UNCOUNT ❑ *The compression of the wood is easily achieved.* **2** V-T If you **compress** something such as a piece of writing or a description, you make it shorter. ❑ *He never understood how to organize or compress large masses of material.* **3** V-T [usu passive] If an event **is compressed** into a short space of time, it is given less time to happen than normal or previously. ❑ *The four debates will be compressed into an eight-day period.*

com|pressed /kəmprɛst/ ADJ [usu ADJ n] **Compressed** air or gas is squeezed into a small space or container and is therefore at a higher pressure than normal. It is used especially as a source of power for machines.

com|pres|sor /kəmprɛsər/ (compressors) N-COUNT A **compressor** is a machine or part of a machine that squeezes gas or air and makes it take up less space.

com|prise /kəmpraɪz/ (comprises, comprising, comprised) V-T If you say that something **comprises** or **is comprised of** a number of things or people, you mean it has them as its parts or members. [FORMAL] ❑ *The special cabinet committee comprises Mr. Brown, Mr. Mandelson, and Mr. Straw.* ❑ *The task force is comprised of congressional leaders, cabinet heads and administration officials.*

com|pro|mise /kɒmprəmaɪz/ (compromises, compromising, compromised) **1** N-VAR A **compromise** is a situation in which people accept something slightly different from what they really want, because of circumstances or because they are considering the wishes of other people. ❑ *Encourage your child to reach a compromise between what he wants and what you want.* **2** V-RECIP If you **compromise** with someone, you reach an agreement with them in which you both give up something that you originally wanted. You can also say that two people or groups **compromise**. ❑ *The government has compromised with its critics over monetary policies.* ❑ *"Nine," I said. "Nine thirty," he replied. We compromised on nine fifteen.* **3** V-T If someone **compromises** themselves or **compromises** their beliefs, they do something which damages their reputation for honesty, loyalty, or high moral principles. [DISAPPROVAL] ❑ *...members of the government who have compromised themselves by accepting bribes.*

SYNONYMS

compromise
NOUN **1**
give-and-take: *...a happy relationship where there's a lot of give-and-take.*
concession: *The King made major concessions to end the confrontation with his people.*
trade-off: *The newspaper's headline indicates that there was a trade-off at the summit.*
VERB **2**
concede: *The government conceded some of their demands.*
meet halfway: *The Democrats are willing to meet the president halfway.*

---

com|pro|mis|ing /kɒmprəmaɪzɪŋ/ ADJ If you describe information or a situation as **compromising**, you mean that it reveals an embarrassing or guilty secret about someone. ❑ *How had this compromising picture come into the possession of the press?*

comp time N-UNCOUNT **Comp time** is time off that an employer gives to an employee because the employee has worked overtime. **Comp time** is short for **compensation time**. [AM] ❑ *Comp time is often promised to firefighters and police officers.*

comp|trol|ler /kəntroʊlər, kɒmp-/ (comptrollers) N-COUNT A **comptroller** is someone who is in charge of the accounts of a business or a government department; used mainly in official titles. [BUSINESS] ❑ *...Robert Clarke, U.S. Comptroller of the Currency.*

com|pul|sion /kəmpʌlʃən/ (compulsions) **1** N-COUNT A **compulsion** is a strong desire to do something, which you find difficult to control. ❑ *He felt a sudden compulsion to drop the bucket and run.* **2** N-UNCOUNT If someone uses **compulsion** in order to get you to do something, they force you to do it, for example by threatening to punish you if you do not do it. ❑ *Many universities argued that students learned more when they were in classes out of choice rather than compulsion.*

com|pul|sive /kəmpʌlsɪv/ **1** ADJ [ADJ n] You use **compulsive** to describe people or their behavior when they cannot stop doing something wrong, harmful, or unnecessary. ❑ ...*a compulsive liar.* ❑ *He was a compulsive gambler and often heavily in debt.* **2** ADJ If a book or television program is **compulsive**, it is so interesting that you do not want to stop reading or watching it. ❑ *Her new series is compulsive viewing.* **3** → See feature box at **book**

com|pul|so|ry /kəmpʌlsəri/ ADJ If something is **compulsory**, you must do it or accept it, because it is the law or because someone in a position of authority says you must. ❑ *In East Germany learning Russian was compulsory.*

com|punc|tion /kəmpʌŋkʃən/ N-UNCOUNT If you say that someone has no **compunction** about doing something, you mean that they do it without feeling ashamed or guilty. [DISAPPROVAL] ❑ *He has no compunction about relating how he killed his father.*

com|pu|ta|tion /kɒmpyʊteɪʃən/ (**computations**) N-VAR **Computation** is mathematical calculation. ❑ *The discrepancies resulted from different methods of computation.* ❑ *He took a few notes and made computations.*

com|pu|ta|tion|al /kɒmpyʊteɪʃənəl/ ADJ **Computational** means using computers. ❑ *Students may pursue research in any aspect of computational linguistics.*

com|pute /kəmpyu:t/ (**computes, computing, computed**) V-T To **compute** a quantity or number means to calculate it. ❑ *To compute your scores, merely add or subtract your scores for each item.*

com|put|er ♦♦◊ /kəmpyu:tər/ (**computers**) **1** N-COUNT [also by/on N] A **computer** is an electronic machine that can store and deal with large amounts of information. ❑ *The data are then fed into a computer.* ❑ *The company installed a $650,000 computer system.* **2** → see also **personal computer** **3** → See also color supplement

---
COLLOCATIONS

computer
NOUN **1**
noun + **computer**: desktop, home, laptop
adjective + **computer**: handheld, personal, portable; powerful, sophisticated
verb + **computer**: operate, program, run, use; install, reboot, restart, upgrade; hack, infect

---

com|put|er game (**computer games**) N-COUNT A **computer game** is a game that you play on a computer or on a small piece of electronic equipment.

com|put|er|ize /kəmpyu:təraɪz/ (**computerizes, computerizing, computerized**)

in BRIT, also use **computerise**

V-T To **computerize** a system, process, or type of work means to arrange for a lot of the work to be done by computer. ❑ *I'm trying to make a spreadsheet up to computerize everything that's done by hand at the moment.*

com|put|er|ized /kəmpyu:təraɪzd/

in BRIT, also use **computerised**

1 ADJ A **computerized** system, process, or business is one in which the work is done by computer. ❑ *The National Cancer Institute now has a computerized system that can quickly provide information.* **2** ADJ **Computerized** information is stored on a computer. ❑ *Computerized databases are proliferating fast.*

com|put|er-lit|er|ate ADJ If someone is **computer-literate**, they have enough skill and knowledge to be able to use a computer. ❑ *We look for applicants who are good with numbers, computer-literate, and energetic self-starters.*

com|put|ing /kəmpyu:tɪŋ/ **1** N-UNCOUNT **Computing** is the activity of using a computer and writing programs for it. ❑ *Courses range from cooking to computing.* **2** ADJ [ADJ n] **Computing** means relating to computers and their use. ❑ *Many graduates are employed in the electronics and computing industries.*

com|rade /kɒmræd/ (**comrades**) N-COUNT Your **comrades** are your friends, especially friends that you share a difficult or dangerous situation with. [LITERARY] ❑ *Unlike so many of his comrades, he survived the war.*

VOCABULARY IN CONTEXT

Computers

When it's time to buy a new computer, basing the decision on what you want to use it for saves costly mistakes. The first decision is usually between a **laptop** or a **desktop**, depending on how mobile you need to be. Opting for a laptop then means investigating models according to how much **battery life** they offer; then it's a question of your **operating system** preferences. A large **hard-disk** capacity is most people's next requirement, but those who play a lot of games or work with graphics will prioritize **RAM** capacity. There are two main competitors in the **CPU** market, and they vary in price and quality, so it's crucial to do your research. A **video card** might be important to some users, while others might look for ergonomic **keyboards** and other **hardware**, like an **external DVD drive**, which can be bought separately and plugged in via **USB** or connected **wirelessly**.

com|rade-in-arms (**comrades-in-arms**) also **comrade in arms** N-COUNT [oft poss N] A **comrade-in-arms** is someone who has worked for the same cause or purpose as you and has shared the same difficulties and dangers. ❑ ...*Deng Xiaoping, Mao's long-time comrade-in-arms.*

com|rade|ship /kɒmrædʃɪp/ N-UNCOUNT **Comradeship** is friendship between a number of people who are doing the same work or who share the same difficulties or dangers. ❑ ...*the comradeship of his fellow soldiers.*

con /kɒn/ (**cons, conning, conned**) **1** V-T If someone **cons** you, they persuade you to do something or believe something by telling you things that are not true. [INFORMAL] ❑ *He claimed that the business director had conned him of $10,000.* ❑ *White conned his way into a job as a warehouseman with Dutch airline, KLM.* **2** N-COUNT A **con** is a trick in which someone deceives you by telling you something that is not true. [INFORMAL] ❑ *Snacks that offer miraculous weight loss are a con.* **3 pros and cons** → see **pro** **4** → See feature box at **crime**

con art|ist (**con artists**) N-COUNT A **con artist** is someone who tricks other people into giving them their money or property.

con|cat|ena|tion /kɒnkætəneɪʃən, kən-/ N-UNCOUNT [usu N of n] A **concatenation** of things or events is a series of them linked together. [FORMAL] ❑ ...*the internet, the world's biggest concatenation of computing power.*

con|cave /kɒnkeɪv, kɒnkeɪv/ ADJ A surface that is **concave** curves inward in the middle. ❑ *He has a concave stomach.*

con|ceal /kənsi:l/ (**conceals, concealing, concealed**) **1** V-T If you **conceal** something, you cover it or hide it carefully. ❑ *Frances decided to conceal the machine behind a hinged panel.* **2** V-T If you **conceal** a piece of information or a feeling, you do not let other people know about it. ❑ *Robert could not conceal his relief.* **3** V-T If something **conceals** something else, it covers it and prevents it from being seen. ❑ ...*a pair of carved Indian doors which conceal a built-in cupboard.*

con|ceal|ment /kənsi:lmənt/ N-UNCOUNT **Concealment** is the state of being hidden or the act of hiding something. ❑ *The criminals vainly sought concealment from the searchlight.*

con|cede /kənsiːd/ (concedes, conceding, conceded) **1** V-T If you **concede** something, you admit, often unwillingly, that it is true or correct. ☐ *Bess finally conceded that Nancy was right.* ☐ *"Well," he conceded, "I do sometimes mumble a bit."* **2** V-T If you **concede** something to someone, you allow them to have it as a right or privilege. ☐ *Poland's Communist government conceded the right to establish independent trade unions.* **3** V-T If you **concede** something, you give it to the person who has been trying to get it from you. ☐ *The strike by bank employees ended after employers conceded some of their demands.* **4** V-T If you **concede** a game, contest, or argument, you end it by admitting that you can no longer win. ☐ *Reiner, 56, has all but conceded the race to his rival.* **5** V-T If you **concede** defeat, you accept that you have lost a struggle. ☐ *She has conceded defeat in her bid for the Democratic Party's nomination for governor.* **6** → See feature box at **competition**

con|ceit /kənsiːt/ N-UNCOUNT **Conceit** is too much pride in your abilities or achievements. [DISAPPROVAL] ☐ *Reyes emits confidence without conceit.*

con|ceit|ed /kənsiːtɪd/ ADJ If you say that someone is **conceited**, you are showing your disapproval of the fact that they are far too proud of their abilities or achievements. [DISAPPROVAL] ☐ *I thought he was conceited and arrogant.*

con|ceiv|able /kənsiːvəbəl/ ADJ If something is **conceivable**, you can imagine it or believe it. ☐ *Without their support, the project would not have been conceivable.* • **con|ceiv|ably** /kənsiːvəbli/ ADV [usu ADV before v] ☐ *The mission could conceivably be accomplished within a week.*

con|ceive /kənsiːv/ (conceives, conceiving, conceived) **1** V-T/V-I [usu with brd-neg] If you cannot **conceive** of something, you cannot imagine it or believe it. ☐ *I just can't even conceive of that quantity of money.* ☐ *We could not conceive that he might soon be dead.* **2** V-T/V-I If you **conceive** something as a particular thing, you consider it to be that thing. ☐ *The ancients conceived the earth as afloat in water.* ☐ *We conceive of the family as being in a constant state of change.* **3** V-T If you **conceive** a plan or idea, you think of it and work out how it can be done. ☐ *She had conceived the idea of a series of novels, each of which would reveal some aspect of Chinese life.* **4** V-T/V-I When a woman **conceives** a child or **conceives**, she becomes pregnant. ☐ *Women, he says, should give up alcohol before they plan to conceive.*

con|cen|trate /kɒnsəntreɪt/ (concentrates, concentrating, concentrated) **1** V-T/V-I If you **concentrate** on something, or **concentrate** your mind on it, you give all your attention to it. ☐ *It was up to him to concentrate on his studies and make something of himself.* **2** V-T [usu passive] If something **is concentrated** in an area, it is all there rather than being spread around. ☐ *Italy's industrial districts are concentrated in its north-central and northeastern regions.*

SYNONYMS

concentrate
VERB **1**
pay attention: *I didn't pay any attention at first.*

---

con|cen|trat|ed /kɒnsəntreɪtɪd/ **1** ADJ A **concentrated** liquid has been increased in strength by having water removed from it. ☐ *Sweeten dishes sparingly with honey, or concentrated apple or pear juice.* **2** ADJ A **concentrated** activity is directed with great intensity in one place. ☐ *...a more concentrated effort to reach out to troubled kids.*

con|cen|tra|tion /kɒnsəntreɪʃən/ (concentrations) **1** N-UNCOUNT **Concentration** on something involves giving all your attention to it. ☐ *Neal kept interrupting, breaking my concentration.* **2** N-VAR A **concentration** of something is a large amount of it or large numbers of it in a small area. ☐ *The area has one of the world's greatest concentrations of wildlife.* **3** N-VAR The **concentration** of a substance is the proportion of essential ingredients or substances in it. ☐ *pH is a measure of the concentration of free hydrogen atoms in a solution.* **4** → See feature box at **study**

con|cen|tra|tion camp (concentration camps) N-COUNT A **concentration camp** is a prison in which large numbers of ordinary people are kept in very bad conditions, usually during a war. ☐ *...the ruins of the Nazi concentration camp at Buchenwald.*

con|cen|tric /kənsɛntrɪk/ ADJ [ADJ n] **Concentric** circles or rings have the same center. ☐ *On a blackboard, he drew five concentric circles.*

con|cept /kɒnsɛpt/ (concepts) **1** N-COUNT A **concept** is an idea or abstract principle. ☐ *She added that the concept of arranged marriages is misunderstood in the west.* **2** → See feature box at **study**

con|cep|tion /kənsɛpʃən/ (conceptions) **1** N-VAR A **conception** of something is an idea that you have of it in your mind. ☐ *My conception of a garden was based on gardens I had visited in England.* **2** N-VAR **Conception** is the process in which a woman's egg is fertilized and she becomes pregnant. ☐ *Six weeks after conception, your baby is the size of your little fingernail.*

con|cep|tual /kənsɛptʃuəl/ ADJ [ADJ n] **Conceptual** means related to ideas and concepts formed in the mind. ☐ *...replacing old laws with new within the same conceptual framework.* • **con|cep|tu|al|ly** ADV ☐ *The monograph is conceptually confused, unclear in its structure, and weak in its methodology.*

con|cep|tu|al|ize /kənsɛptʃuəlaɪz/ (conceptualizes, conceptualizing, conceptualized)

in BRIT, also use **conceptualise**

V-T If you **conceptualize** something, you form an idea of it in your mind. ☐ *How we conceptualize things has a lot to do with what we feel.* ☐ *Tiffany conceptualized herself as a mother, whose main task was to feed her baby.*

con|cern /kənsɜːrn/ (concerns, concerning, concerned) **1** N-UNCOUNT **Concern** is worry about a situation. ☐ *The group has expressed concern about reports of political violence in Africa.* ☐ *The move follows growing public concern over the spread of the disease.* **2** V-T [no cont] If something **concerns** you, it worries you. ☐ *The growing number of people seeking refuge in Thailand is beginning to concern Western aid agencies.* • **con|cerned** ADJ ☐ *Academics and employers are concerned that students are not sufficiently prepared for college courses.* **3** V-T If you **concern** yourself with something, you give it attention because you think that it is important. ☐ *I didn't concern myself with politics.* • **con|cerned** ADJ [v-link ADJ with n] ☐ *The agency is more concerned with making arty ads than understanding its clients' businesses.* **4** V-T [no cont] If something such as a book or a piece of information **concerns** a particular subject, it is about that subject. ☐ *The bulk of the book concerns Sandy's two middle-aged children.* • **con|cerned** ADJ [v-link ADJ with n] ☐ *Randolph's work was exclusively concerned with the effects of pollution on health.* **5** V-T [no cont] If a situation, event, or activity **concerns** you, it affects or involves you. ☐ *It was just a little unfinished business from my past, and it doesn't concern you at all.* • **con|cerned** ADJ [n ADJ, v-link ADJ in/with n] ☐ *It's a very stressful situation for everyone concerned.* **6** N-COUNT A **concern** is a fact or situation that worries you. ☐ *His concern was that people would know that he was responsible.* **7** N-COUNT You can refer to a company or business as a **concern**, usually when you are describing what type of company or business it is. [FORMAL, BUSINESS] ☐ *If not a large concern, the Potomac Nursery was at least a successful one.* **8** N-VAR **Concern** for someone is a feeling that you want them to be happy, safe, and well. If you do something out of **concern** for someone, you do it because you want them to be happy, safe, and well. ☐ *Without her care and concern, he had no chance at all.* **9** N-SING If a situation or problem is your **concern**, it is something that you have a duty or responsibility to be involved with. ☐ *The technical aspects were the concern of the Army.* **10** PHRASE If a company is a **going concern**, it is actually doing business, rather than having stopped trading or not yet having started trading. [BUSINESS] ☐ *The receivers will always prefer to sell a business as a going concern.*

COLLOCATIONS

concern
NOUN **1**
noun + **concern**: safety, security
adjective + **concern**: grave, growing, serious, severe; main, primary; immediate, pressing; genuine, legitimate
concern + be + adjective: understandable, unfounded
verb + **concern**: express, raise, voice; address

concerned

> **SYNONYMS**
>
> **concerned**
> ADJ **2**
> **anxious:** *The minister admitted he was anxious about the situation in his country.*
> **worried:** *If you're worried about his progress, discuss it with his teacher.*
> **bothered:** *I was bothered about the blister on my hand.*
> **disturbed:** *Doctors were disturbed that so few patients were women.*

con|cerned ✦✧ /kənsɜ́rnd/ **1** → see concern **2** ADJ [v-link ADJ to-inf] If you are **concerned** to do something, you want to do it because you think it is important. ❑ *We are deeply concerned to get out of this problematic situation.*

con|cern|ing /kənsɜ́rnɪŋ/ **1** PREP You use **concerning** to indicate what a question or piece of information is about. [FORMAL] ❑ *For more information concerning the club, contact Mr. Coldwell.* **2** ADJ [usu it v-link ADJ that] If something is **concerning**, it causes you to feel concerned about it. ❑ *It is particularly concerning that he is working for foreign companies while advising on foreign policy.*

con|cert ✦✧ /kɒ́nsərt/ (concerts) **1** N-COUNT A **concert** is a performance of music. ❑ *...a short concert of piano music.* ❑ *I've been to plenty of live rock concerts.* **2** PHRASE If a musician or group of musicians appears **in concert**, they are giving a live performance. ❑ *I want people to remember Elvis in concert.*

con|cert|ed /kənsɜ́rtɪd/ **1** ADJ [ADJ n] A **concerted** action is done by several people or groups working together. ❑ *Martin Parry, author of the report, says it's time for concerted action by world leaders.* **2** ADJ [ADJ n] If you make a **concerted** effort to do something, you try very hard to do it. ❑ *He made a concerted effort to win me away from my steady, sweet but boring boyfriend.*

con|cert|go|er /kɒ́nsərtgoʊər/ (concertgoers) also **concert-goer** N-COUNT A **concertgoer** is someone who goes to concerts regularly.

con|cer|ti|na /kɒ̀nsərtíːnə/ (concertinas) N-VAR [oft the N] A **concertina** is a musical instrument consisting of two end pieces with stiff paper or cloth that folds up between them. You play the concertina by pressing the buttons on the end pieces while moving them together and apart.

concert|master /kɒ́nsərtmæstər/ (concertmasters) N-COUNT The **concertmaster** of an orchestra is the most senior violin player, who acts as a deputy to the conductor. [AM, AUSTRALIAN]

> in BRIT, use **leader**

con|cer|to /kəntʃɛ́rtoʊ/ (concertos) N-COUNT A **concerto** is a piece of music written for one or more solo instruments and an orchestra. ❑ *...Tchaikovsky's First Piano Concerto.*

con|ces|sion ✦✧ /kənsɛ́ʃⁿn/ (concessions) **1** N-COUNT If you make a **concession** to someone, you agree to let them do or have something, especially in order to end an argument or conflict. ❑ *We made too many concessions and we got too little in return.* **2** N-COUNT A **concession** is a special right or privilege that is given to someone. ❑ *Farmers were granted concessions from the government to develop the farms.* **3** N-COUNT A **concession** is an arrangement where someone is given the right to sell a product or to run a business, especially in a building belonging to another business. [mainly AM, BUSINESS] ❑ *...the man who ran the catering concession at the Rob Roy Links in Palominas.*

> in BRIT, usually use **franchise**

con|ces|sion|aire /kənsɛ̀ʃənɛ́ər/ (concessionaires) N-COUNT A **concessionaire** is a person or company that has the right to sell a product or to run a business, especially in a building belonging to another business. [AM, BUSINESS] ❑ *Concessionaires and shop owners report retail sales are up.*

> in BRIT, use **franchisee**

con|ces|sion|ary /kənsɛ́ʃənɛri/ ADJ [ADJ n] A **concessionary** price is a special price which is lower than the normal one and which is often given to old people, people who are unemployed, and students. [BRIT]

> in AM, use **reduced**

con|ces|sion|er /kənsɛ́ʃənər/ (concessioners) N-COUNT A **concessioner** is the same as a **concessionaire**. [AM, BUSINESS]

> in BRIT, use **franchisee**

con|ces|sive clause /kənsɛ́sɪv klɔːz/ (concessive clauses) N-COUNT A **concessive clause** is a subordinate clause which refers to a situation that contrasts with the one described in the main clause. For example, in the sentence 'Although he was tired, he couldn't get to sleep,' the first clause is a concessive clause. [TECHNICAL]

conch /kɒntʃ, kɒŋk/ (conches) N-COUNT A **conch** is a shellfish with a large shell similar to a snail's. A **conch** or a **conch shell** is the shell of this creature.

con|ci|erge /kɒ̀nsiɛə́rʒ/ (concierges) **1** N-COUNT A **concierge** is an employee of a hotel who assists guests. ❑ *When I asked for the key to the room, the concierge handed me several messages.* **2** N-COUNT A **concierge** is a person, especially in France, who takes care of an apartment house and decides who can enter the building.

con|cili|ate /kənsɪ́lieɪt/ (conciliates, conciliating, conciliated) V-T/V-I If you **conciliate** someone, you try to end a disagreement with them. [FORMAL] ❑ *His duty was to conciliate the people, not to provoke them.* ❑ *The president has a strong political urge to conciliate.* ❑ *He spoke in a low, nervous, conciliating voice.*

con|cili|ation /kənsɪ̀lieɪ́ʃⁿn/ N-UNCOUNT **Conciliation** is willingness to end a disagreement or the process of ending a disagreement. ❑ *Resolving the dispute will require a mood of conciliation on both sides.*

con|cilia|tory /kənsɪ́liətɔri/ ADJ When you are **conciliatory** in your actions or behavior, you show that you are willing to end a disagreement with someone. ❑ *The next time he spoke, he used a more conciliatory tone.*

con|cise /kənsáɪs/ **1** ADJ Something that is **concise** says everything that is necessary without using any unnecessary words. ❑ *Burton's text is concise and informative.* ● **con|cise|ly** ADV [ADV with v] ❑ *He'd delivered his report clearly and concisely.* **2** ADJ [ADJ n] A **concise** edition of a book, especially a dictionary, is shorter than the original edition. ❑ *...Sotheby's Concise Encyclopedia of Porcelain.*

con|clave /kɒ́nkleɪv/ (conclaves) N-COUNT A **conclave** is a meeting at which the discussions are kept secret. The meeting which is held to elect a new Pope is called a conclave.

con|clude ✦✧ /kənklúːd/ (concludes, concluding, concluded) **1** V-T If you **conclude** that something is true, you decide that it is true using the facts you know as a basis. ❑ *Larry had concluded that he had no choice but to accept Paul's words as the truth.* ❑ *So what can we conclude from this debate?* **2** V-T/V-I When you **conclude**, you say the last thing that you are going to say. [FORMAL] ❑ *"It's a waste of time," he concluded.* **3** V-T/V-I When something **concludes**, or when you **conclude** it, you end it. [FORMAL] ❑ *The evening concluded with dinner and speeches.* **4** V-T If one person or group **concludes** an agreement, such as a treaty or business deal, with another, they arrange it. You can also say that two people or groups **conclude** an agreement. [FORMAL] ❑ *Mexico and the Philippines have both concluded agreements with their commercial bank creditors.*

> **SYNONYMS**
>
> **conclude**
> VERB **1**
> **reckon:** *He reckoned he was still fond of her.*
> **assume:** *It is a misconception to assume that the two continents are similar.*
> **infer:** *I inferred from what she said that you have not been well.*
> **deduce:** *Alison had cleverly deduced that I was the author of the letter.*

con|clu|sion ✦✧ /kənklúːʒⁿn/ (conclusions) **1** N-COUNT When you come to a **conclusion**, you decide that something is true after you have thought about it carefully and have considered all the relevant facts. ❑ *Over the years I've come to the conclusion that she's a very great musician.* **2** N-SING The **conclusion** of something is its ending. ❑ *At the conclusion of the program, I asked the children if they had any questions they wanted to ask me.* **3** N-SING The **conclusion** of a treaty or a business deal is the act of arranging it or agreeing on it. ❑ *...the expected conclusion* of a free-trade agreement between Mexico and the United States. **4** PHRASE You say **'in conclusion'** to indicate that what you are about to say is the last thing that you want to say. ❏ *In conclusion, walking is a cheap, safe, enjoyable, and readily available form of exercise.* **5** → See feature box at **debate, research**

COLLOCATIONS

conclusion
NOUN

1
adjective + **conclusion**: definitive, firm, inescapable; tentative; logical, obvious, sensible
verb + **conclusion**: draw, reach

2
adjective + **conclusion**: satisfactory, speedy, successful; final, ultimate; fitting, natural

---
SYNONYMS

conclusion
NOUN **1**

assumption: *We question their assumption that all men and women think alike.*
judgment: *How can he form any judgment of the matter without the figures?*
verdict: *The doctor's verdict was that he was entirely healthy.*
inference: *There were two inferences to be drawn from her letter.*
deduction: *It was a pretty astute deduction.*

---

con|clu|sive /kənklusɪv/ ADJ **Conclusive** evidence shows that something is certainly true. ❏ *Her attorneys claim there is no conclusive evidence that any murders took place.*

con|coct /kənkɒkt/ (**concocts, concocting, concocted**) **1** V-T If you **concoct** an excuse or explanation, you invent one that is not true. ❏ *Mr. Ferguson said the prisoner concocted the story to get a lighter sentence.* **2** V-T If you **concoct** something, especially something unusual, you make it by mixing several things together. ❏ *Eugene was concocting Rossini Cocktails from champagne and pureed raspberries.*

con|coc|tion /kənkɒkʃən/ (**concoctions**) N-COUNT A **concoction** is something that has been made out of several things mixed together. ❏ *...a concoction of honey, yogurt, oats, and apples.*

con|comi|tant /kənkɒmɪtənt/ (**concomitants**) **1** ADJ [ADJ n, v-link ADJ with n] **Concomitant** is used to describe something that happens at the same time as another thing and is connected with it. [FORMAL] ❏ *Cultures that were better at trading saw a concomitant increase in their wealth.* ❏ *This approach was concomitant with the move away from relying solely on official records.* **2** N-COUNT [oft N of n] A **concomitant** of something is another thing that happens at the same time and is connected with it. [FORMAL] ❏ *The right to deliberately alter quotations is not a concomitant of a free press.*

con|cord /kɒnkɔrd/ **1** N-UNCOUNT **Concord** is a state of peaceful agreement. [FORMAL] ❏ *They expressed the hope that he would pursue a neutral and balanced policy for the sake of national concord.* **2** N-UNCOUNT In grammar, **concord** refers to the way that a word has a form appropriate to the number or gender of the noun or pronoun it relates to. For example, in 'He hates it,' there is concord between the singular form of the verb and the singular pronoun 'he.'

con|cord|ance /kənkɔrdəns/ (**concordances**) **1** N-VAR If there is **concordance** between two things, they are similar to each other or consistent with each other. [FORMAL] ❏ *...a partial concordance between theoretical expectations and empirical evidence.* **2** N-COUNT A **concordance** is a list of the words in a text or group of texts, with information about where in the text each word occurs and how often it occurs. The sentences each word occurs in are often given.

con|course /kɒnkɔrs/ (**concourses**) N-COUNT A **concourse** is a wide hall in a public building, for example a hotel, airport, or station.

con|crete ♦⬦⬦ /kɒnkrit/ (**concretes, concreting, concreted**) **1** N-UNCOUNT **Concrete** is a substance used for building which is made by mixing together cement, sand, small stones, and water. ❏ *The posts have to be set in concrete.* ❏ *We sat on the concrete floor.* **2** V-T When you **concrete** something such as a path, you cover it with concrete. ❏ *He merely cleared and concreted the floors.* **3** ADJ You use **concrete** to indicate that something is definite and specific. ❏ *I had no concrete evidence.* ❏ *There were no concrete proposals on the table.* **4** ADJ A **concrete** object is a real, physical object. ❏ *...using concrete objects to teach addition and subtraction.* **5** ADJ [ADJ n] A **concrete** noun is a noun that refers to a physical object rather than to a quality or idea.

SYNONYMS

concrete
ADJ **3**

clear-cut: *This was a clear-cut case of the landowner being in the right.*
black and white: *But this isn't a simple black and white affair, Marianne.*
definite: *We didn't have any definite proof.*
clear: *It was a clear case of homicide.*

---

con|crete jun|gle (**concrete jungles**) N-COUNT If you refer to a city or area as a **concrete jungle**, you mean that it has a lot of modern buildings without grass or trees, and you think it is ugly or unpleasant to live in. [DISAPPROVAL]

con|cu|bine /kɒŋkyubaɪn/ (**concubines**) N-COUNT In former times, a **concubine** was a woman who had a sexual relationship with a man of higher social rank without being married to him.

con|cur /kənk3r/ (**concurs, concurring, concurred**) V-RECIP If one person **concurs** with another person, the two people agree. You can also say that two people **concur**. [FORMAL] ❏ *Local feeling does not necessarily concur with the press.* ❏ *Daniels and Franklin concurred in an investigator's suggestion that the police be commended.*

con|cur|rence /kənk3rəns/ (**concurrences**) **1** N-VAR [oft with poss] Someone's **concurrence** is their agreement to something. [FORMAL] ❏ *Any change requires the general concurrence of all concerned.* **2** N-VAR If there is a **concurrence** of two or more things, they happen at the same time. ❏ *The concurrence of their disappearances had to be more than coincidental.*

con|cur|rent /kənk3rənt/ ADJ **Concurrent** events or situations happen at the same time. ❏ *Galerie St. Etienne is holding three concurrent exhibitions.* ❏ *He will actually be serving three concurrent five-year sentences.* • **con|cur|rent|ly** ADV [ADV with v] ❏ *He was jailed for 33 months to run concurrently with a sentence he is already serving for burglary.*

con|cussed /kənkʌst/ ADJ [usu v-link ADJ] If someone is **concussed**, they lose consciousness or feel sick or confused because they have been hit hard on the head. ❏ *My left arm is badly bruised and I was slightly concussed.*

con|cus|sion /kənkʌʃən/ (**concussions**) N-VAR If you suffer a **concussion** after a blow to your head, you lose consciousness or feel sick or confused. ❏ *Nicky was rushed to the hospital with a concussion.*

con|demn ♦⬦⬦ /kəndɛm/ (**condemns, condemning, condemned**) **1** V-T If you **condemn** something, you say that it is very bad and unacceptable. ❏ *Political leaders united yesterday to condemn the latest wave of violence.* ❏ *Graham was right to condemn his players for lack of ability, attitude, and application.* **2** V-T [usu passive] If someone **is condemned** to a punishment, they are given this punishment. ❏ *He was condemned to life imprisonment.* **3** V-T If circumstances **condemn** you to an unpleasant situation, they make it certain that you will suffer in that way. ❏ *Their lack of qualifications condemned them to a lifetime of boring, usually poorly-paid work.* **4** V-T If authorities **condemn** a building, they officially decide that it is not safe and must be pulled down or repaired. ❏ *The court's ruling clears the way to condemn buildings in the area.* **5** → see also **condemned**

con|dem|na|tion /kɒndɛmneɪʃən/ (**condemnations**) N-VAR **Condemnation** is the act of saying that something or someone is very bad and unacceptable. ❏ *There was widespread condemnation of Saturday's killings.*

con|dem|na|tory /kəndɛmnətɔri/ ADJ **Condemnatory** means expressing strong disapproval. [FORMAL] ❏ *He was justified in some of his condemnatory outbursts.*

con|demned /kəndɛmd/ ADJ A **condemned** man or woman is going to be executed. ❏ *...prison officers who had sat with the condemned man during his last days.*

con|den|sa|tion /kɒndɛnseɪʃᵊn/ N-UNCOUNT **Condensation** consists of small drops of water which form when warm water vapor or steam touches a cold surface such as a window. ❏ *He used his sleeve to wipe the condensation off the glass.* ◾ → See also color supplement

con|dense /kəndɛns/ (condenses, condensing, condensed) ◾ V-T If you **condense** something, especially a piece of writing or a speech, you make it shorter, usually by including only the most important parts. ❏ *When you summarize, you condense an extended idea or argument into a sentence or more in your own words.* ◾ V-T/V-I When a gas or vapor **condenses**, or **is condensed**, it changes into a liquid. ❏ *Water vapor condenses to form clouds.* ◾ → See feature box at **weather**

con|densed /kəndɛnst/ ◾ ADJ [usu ADJ n] A **condensed** book, explanation, or piece of information has been made shorter, usually by including only the most important parts. ❏ *The council was merely given a condensed version of what had already been disclosed in Washington.* ◾ ADJ [usu ADJ n] **Condensed** liquids have been made thicker by removing some of the water in them. ❏ *...condensed mushroom soup.*

con|densed milk N-UNCOUNT **Condensed milk** is very thick, usually sweetened milk that is sold in cans.

con|den|ser /kəndɛnsər/ (condensers) ◾ N-COUNT A **condenser** is a device that cools gases into liquids. ◾ N-COUNT A **condenser** is a device for accumulating electric charge.

con|de|scend /kɒndɪsɛnd/ (condescends, condescending, condescended) ◾ V-T If someone **condescends** to do something, they agree to do it, but in a way which shows that they think they are better than other people and should not have to do it. [DISAPPROVAL] ❏ *When he condescended to speak, he contradicted himself three or four times in the space of half an hour.* ◾ V-I If you say that someone **condescends** to other people, you are showing your disapproval of the fact that they behave in a way which shows that they think they are superior to other people. [DISAPPROVAL] ❏ *Don't condescend to me.*

con|de|scend|ing /kɒndɪsɛndɪŋ/ ADJ If you say that someone is **condescending**, you are showing your disapproval of the fact that they talk or behave in a way which shows that they think they are superior to other people. [DISAPPROVAL] ❏ *I'm fed up with your money and your whole condescending attitude.*

con|de|scen|sion /kɒndɪsɛnʃᵊn/ N-UNCOUNT **Condescension** is condescending behavior. [DISAPPROVAL] ❏ *There was a tinge of condescension in her greeting.*

con|di|ment /kɒndɪmənt/ (condiments) N-COUNT A **condiment** is a substance such as salt, pepper, or mustard that you add to food when you eat it in order to improve the flavor.

con|di|tion ✦✦✦ /kəndɪʃᵊn/ (conditions, conditioning, conditioned) ◾ N-SING [also no det] If you talk about the **condition** of a person or thing, you are talking about the state that they are in, especially how good or bad their physical state is. ❏ *He remains in a critical condition in a California hospital.* ❏ *I received several compliments on the condition of my skin.* ❏ *The two-bedroom chalet is in good condition.* ◾ N-PLURAL The **conditions** under which something is done or happens are all the factors or circumstances which directly affect it. ❏ *It's easy to make a wrong turn here even under ideal weather conditions.* ◾ N-PLURAL The **conditions** in which people live or work are the factors which affect their comfort, safety, or health. ❏ *People are living in appalling conditions.* ❏ *I could not work in these conditions any longer.* ◾ N-COUNT A **condition** is something which must happen or be done in order for something else to be possible, especially when this is written into a contract or law. ❏ *Argentina failed to hit the economic targets set as a condition for loan payments.* ❏ *...terms and conditions of employment.* ◾ N-COUNT If someone has a particular **condition**, they have an illness or other medical problem. ❏ *Doctors suspect he may have a heart condition.* ◾ V-T [usu passive] If someone **is conditioned** by their experiences or environment, they are influenced by them over a period of time so that they do certain things or think in a particular way. ❏ *We are all conditioned by early impressions and experiences.* ❏ *People are conditioned into believing that they have no power over their situation.* • **con|di|tion|ing** N-UNCOUNT ❏ *To a degree, we reflect our social conditioning in the way we act as parents.* ◾ PHRASE When you agree to do something **on condition that** something else happens, you mean that you will only do it if this other thing also happens. ❏ *He agreed to speak to reporters on condition that he was not identified.* ◾ → See feature box at **football, working**

con|di|tion|al /kəndɪʃᵊnᵊl/ ◾ ADJ If a situation or agreement is **conditional** on something, it will only happen or continue if this thing happens. ❏ *Their support is conditional on his proposals meeting their approval.* ❏ *...a conditional offer.* ◾ ADJ [ADJ n] In grammar, a **conditional** clause is a subordinate clause which refers to a situation which may exist or happen. Most conditional clauses begin with 'if' or 'unless,' for example 'If that happens, we'll be in big trouble' and 'You don't have to come unless you want to.' ◾ → See feature box at **university**

con|di|tion|er /kəndɪʃᵊnər/ (conditioners) ◾ N-MASS A **conditioner** is a substance that you can put on your hair after you have shampooed it to make it softer. ◾ N-MASS [oft n n] A **conditioner** is a thick liquid which you can use when you wash clothes in order to make them feel softer. ◾ → see also **air conditioner**

con|do /kɒndoʊ/ (condos) N-COUNT **Condo** means the same as **condominium**. [AM, INFORMAL]

con|do|lence /kəndoʊləns/ (condolences) ◾ N-UNCOUNT A message of **condolence** is a message in which you express your sympathy for someone because one of their friends or relatives has died recently. ❏ *Neil sent him a letter of condolence.* ◾ N-PLURAL When you offer or express your **condolences** to someone, you express your sympathy for them because one of their friends or relatives has died recently. ❏ *He expressed his condolences to the families of the people who died in the incident.*

con|dom /kɒndəm/ (condoms) N-COUNT A **condom** is a covering made of thin rubber which a man can wear on his penis as a contraceptive or as protection against disease during sexual intercourse.

con|do|min|ium /kɒndəmɪniəm/ (condominiums) ◾ N-COUNT A **condominium** is an apartment building in which each apartment is owned by the person who lives there. [AM] ◾ N-COUNT A **condominium** is one of the privately owned apartments in a condominium. [AM]

con|done /kəndoʊn/ (condones, condoning, condoned) V-T [oft with brd-neg] If someone **condones** behavior that is morally wrong, they accept it and allow it to happen. ❏ *I have never encouraged nor condoned violence.*

con|dor /kɒndɔr/ (condors) N-COUNT A **condor** is a large South American bird that eats the meat of dead animals.

con|du|cive /kəndusɪv/ ADJ If one thing is **conducive** to another thing, it makes the other thing likely to happen. ❏ *Make your bedroom as conducive to sleep as possible.*

con|duct ✦✦◇ (conducts, conducting, conducted)

> The verb is pronounced /kəndʌkt/. The noun is pronounced /kɒndʌkt/.

◾ V-T When you **conduct** an activity or task, you organize it and do it. ❏ *I decided to conduct an experiment.* ◾ V-T If you **conduct** yourself in a particular way, you behave in that way. ❏ *The way he conducts himself reflects on the family.* ◾ V-T/V-I When someone **conducts** an orchestra or choir, they stand in front of it and direct its performance. ❏ *Dennis had recently begun a successful career conducting opera.* ❏ *The choral director continued to conduct here and abroad.* ◾ V-T [no cont] If something **conducts** heat or electricity, it allows heat or electricity to pass through it or along it. ❏ *Water conducts heat faster than air.* ◾ N-SING The **conduct** of a task or activity is the way in which it is organized and carried out. ❏ *Also up for discussion will be the conduct of free and fair elections.* ◾ N-UNCOUNT Someone's **conduct** is the way they behave in particular situations. ❏ *For Europeans, the law is a statement of basic principles of civilized conduct.*

COLLOCATIONS

conduct
VERB ◾
conduct + *noun*: experiment, research, review, study, test, trial, poll, survey; inquiry, interview, investigation, operation, search
NOUN ◾
adjective + **conduct**: improper, inappropriate, reprehensible, unacceptable, unsporting; disorderly, unlawful, violent

> **SYNONYMS**
>
> **conduct**
> VERB **1**
> **carry out:** *Police say they believe the attacks were carried out by nationalists.*
> **perform:** *These people have performed outstanding acts of bravery and kindness.*
> **run:** *He ran a lot of tests, and it turned out I had an infection.*
> **execute:** *We are going to execute our campaign plan to the letter.*

con|duct|ed tour (conducted tours) N-COUNT A **conducted tour** is a visit to a building, town, or area during which someone goes with you and explains everything to you.

con|duc|tion /kəndʌkʃ°n/ N-UNCOUNT [usu with supp] **Conduction** is the process by which heat or electricity passes through or along something. [TECHNICAL] □ *Temperature becomes uniform by heat conduction until finally a permanent state is reached.*

con|duc|tive /kəndʌktɪv/ ADJ A **conductive** substance is able to conduct things such as heat and electricity. [TECHNICAL] □ *Salt water is much more conductive than fresh water is.*
• **con|duc|tiv|ity** /kɒndʌktɪvɪti/ N-UNCOUNT □ *...a device which monitors electrical conductivity.*

con|duc|tor /kəndʌktər/ (conductors) **1** N-COUNT A **conductor** is a person who stands in front of an orchestra or choir and directs its performance. **2** N-COUNT On a train, a **conductor** is a person whose job is to travel on the train in order to help passengers and check tickets. [AM]

in BRIT, use **guard**

3 N-COUNT On a streetcar or a bus, the **conductor** is the person whose job is to sell tickets to the passengers. **4** N-COUNT A **conductor** is a substance that heat or electricity can pass through or along. □ *Graphite is a highly efficient conductor of electricity.* **5** → see also **semiconductor**

con|duit /kɒndwɪt, -duɪt/ (conduits) **1** N-COUNT A **conduit** is a small tunnel, pipe, or channel through which water or electrical wires go. **2** N-COUNT [oft N for/to n] A **conduit** is a person or country that links two or more other people or countries. □ *The region became a conduit for drugs produced in Afghanistan.*

cone /koʊn/ (cones) **1** N-COUNT A **cone** is a shape with a circular base ending in a point at the top. □ *...orange traffic cones.* □ *...the streetlight's yellow cone of light.* **2** N-COUNT A **cone** is the fruit of a tree such as a pine or fir. □ *...a bowl of fir cones.* **3** N-COUNT A **cone** is a thin, cone-shaped cookie that is used for holding ice cream. You can also refer to ice cream that you eat in this way as a **cone**. □ *She stopped by the ice-cream shop and had a chocolate cone.*

con|fab /kɒnfæb/ (confabs) N-COUNT A **confab** is an informal, private conversation. [INFORMAL] □ *How about coming over for a little confab?*

con|fec|tion /kənfekʃ°n/ (confections) N-COUNT You can refer to a sweet food that someone has made as a **confection**. [WRITTEN] □ *...a confection made with honey and nuts.*

con|fec|tion|er /kənfekʃənər/ (confectioners) N-COUNT A **confectioner** is a person whose job is making or selling candy and other sweet foods.

con|fec|tion|ers' sug|ar N-UNCOUNT **Confectioners' sugar** is very fine white sugar that is used for making frosting and candy. [AM]

in BRIT, use **icing sugar**

con|fec|tion|ery /kənfekʃəneri/ N-UNCOUNT **Confectionery** is candy and other sweet foods such as cakes. [WRITTEN] □ *...hand-made confectionery.*

con|fed|era|cy /kənfedərəsi/ (confederacies) **1** N-COUNT A **confederacy** is a union of states or people who are trying to achieve the same thing. □ *They've entered this new confederacy because the central government's been unable to control the collapsing economy.* **2** N-PROPER [the N] The 11 southern states that fought against the North in the American Civil War are sometimes referred to as the **Confederacy**.

con|fed|er|ate /kənfedərət/ (confederates) N-COUNT Someone's **confederates** are the people they are working with in a secret activity.

con|fed|era|tion /kənfedəreɪʃ°n/ (confederations) N-COUNT; N-IN-NAMES A **confederation** is an organization or group consisting of smaller groups or states, especially one that exists for business or political purposes. □ *...the Confederation of Indian Industry.*

con|fer /kənfɜr/ (confers, conferring, conferred) **1** V-RECIP When you **confer** with someone, you discuss something with them in order to make a decision. You can also say that two people **confer**. □ *He conferred with Hill and the others in his office.* **2** V-T To **confer** something such as power or an honor on someone means to give it to them. [FORMAL] □ *The constitution also confers large powers on Brazil's 25 constituent states.*

con|fer|ence ♦♦♦ /kɒnfərəns, -frəns/ (conferences) **1** N-COUNT A **conference** is a meeting, often lasting a few days, which is organized on a particular subject or to bring together people who have a common interest. □ *The president took the unprecedented step of summoning all the state governors to a conference on education.* □ *...the Alternative Energy conference.* **2** N-COUNT [also in N] A **conference** is a meeting at which formal discussions take place. □ *They sat down at the dinner table for a conference.* **3** → see also **press conference**

> **SYNONYMS**
>
> **conference**
> NOUN **1**
> **meeting:** *...business meetings.*
> **forum:** *The organization provides a forum where problems can be discussed.*
> **convention:** *...the annual convention of the Society of Professional Journalists.*
> **symposium:** *He had been taking part in an international symposium on population.*
> **convocation:** *...a convocation of the American Youth Congress.*

con|fer|ence call (conference calls) N-COUNT A **conference call** is a phone call in which more than two people take part. [BUSINESS] □ *There are daily conference calls with Washington.*

con|fess /kənfes/ (confesses, confessing, confessed) **1** V-T/V-I If someone **confesses** to doing something, usually something wrong, they admit that they did it. □ *He had confessed to seventeen murders.* □ *I had expected her to confess that she only wrote these books for the money.* □ *Ray changed his mind, claiming that he had been forced into confessing.* **2** V-T/V-I If someone **confesses** or **confesses** their sins, they tell God or a priest about their sins so that they can be forgiven. □ *You just go to the church and confess your sins.*

con|fessed /kənfest/ ADJ [ADJ n] You use **confessed** to describe someone who openly admits that they have a particular fault or have done something wrong. □ *She is a confessed chocaholic.*

con|fes|sion /kənfeʃ°n/ (confessions) **1** N-COUNT A **confession** is a signed statement by someone in which they admit that they have committed a particular crime. □ *They forced him to sign a confession.* **2** N-VAR **Confession** is the act of admitting that you have done something that you are ashamed of or embarrassed about. □ *I have a confession to make.* □ *The diaries are a mixture of confession and observation.* **3** N-VAR If you make a **confession** of your beliefs or feelings, you publicly tell people that this is what you believe or feel. □ *...Tatyana's confession of love.* **4** N-VAR In the Catholic Church and in some other churches, if you go to **confession**, you privately tell a priest about your sins and ask for forgiveness. □ *He never went to Father Porter for confession again.*

con|fes|sion|al /kənfeʃ°nəl/ (confessionals) **1** N-COUNT A **confessional** is the small room in a church where Christians, especially Roman Catholics, go to confess their sins. **2** ADJ A **confessional** speech or writing contains confessions. □ *The convictions rest solely on disputed witness and confessional statements.*

con|fes|sor /kənfesər/ (confessors) **1** N-COUNT A **confessor** is a priest who hears a person's confession. **2** N-COUNT If you describe someone as your **confessor**, you mean that they are the person you can talk to about your secrets or problems. □ *He was their adviser, confidant and confessor.*

con|fet|ti /kənfeti/ N-UNCOUNT **Confetti** is small pieces of colored paper that people throw at a festive occasion such as a wedding.

con|fi|dant /kɒnfɪdænt, -dɑnt/ (**confidants**) N-COUNT [usu with poss] Your **confidant** is a person you can discuss your private problems or feelings with. ❑ ...*a close confidant of the president.*

con|fi|dante /kɒnfɪdænt, -dɑnt/ (**confidantes**) N-COUNT [usu with poss] Your **confidante** is a woman you can discuss your private problems with. ❑ *You are her closest friend and confidante.*

con|fide /kənfaɪd/ (**confides, confiding, confided**) V-T/V-I If you **confide** in someone, you tell them a secret. ❑ *I knew she had some fundamental problems in her marriage because she had confided in me a year earlier.* ❑ *He confided to me that he felt like he was being punished.*

con|fi|dence ♦♦◇ /kɒnfɪdəns/ **1** N-UNCOUNT If you have **confidence** in someone, you feel that you can trust them. ❑ *I have every confidence in you.* ❑ *This has contributed to the lack of confidence in the FDA.* **2** N-UNCOUNT If you have **confidence**, you feel sure about your abilities, qualities, or ideas. ❑ *The band is in excellent form and brimming with confidence.* **3** N-UNCOUNT If you can say something with **confidence**, you feel certain it is correct. ❑ *I can say with confidence that such rumors were totally groundless.* **4** N-UNCOUNT If you tell someone something in **confidence**, you tell them a secret. ❑ *We told you all these things in confidence.* ❑ *Even telling Lois seemed a betrayal of confidence.* • PHRASE If you **take** someone **into** your **confidence**, you tell them a secret.

---SYNONYMS---

confidence
NOUN
1
trust: *He destroyed me and my trust in men.*
belief: *It is our belief that improvements in health care will lead to a stronger, more prosperous economy.*
faith: *She had placed a great deal of faith in Mr Penleigh.*
2
self-assurance: *She displayed considerable self-assurance.*
assurance: *Masur led the orchestra with assurance.*
aplomb: *The whole cast executed the production with truly professional aplomb.*
self-possession: *She found her customary self-possession had deserted her.*

---COLLOCATIONS---

confidence
NOUN
1
noun + **confidence**: business, consumer, investor, market
adjective + **confidence**: complete, full, newfound, renewed; public
confidence + be + adjective: high, sky-high; fragile, low
verb + **confidence**: have, increase, inspire, restore; lose, undermine
2
adjective + **confidence**: great, quiet, supreme
verb + **confidence**: boost, build, exude, gain; lack, lose, shake
4
adjective + **confidence**: strict, utmost

con|fi|dence game (**confidence games**) N-COUNT A **confidence game** is a trick in which someone deceives you by telling you something that is not true, often to trick you out of money. [mainly AM]

in BRIT, usually use **confidence trick**

con|fi|dence man (**confidence men**) N-COUNT A **confidence man** is a man who persuades people to give him their money or property to him by lying to them. [mainly AM]

con|fi|dence trick (**confidence tricks**) N-COUNT A **confidence trick** is the same as a **confidence game**. [mainly BRIT]

con|fi|dent ♦◇◇ /kɒnfɪdənt/ **1** ADJ If you are **confident** about something, you are certain that it will happen in the way you want it to. ❑ *I am confident that everything will come out right in time.* ❑ *Mr. Ryan is confident of success.* • **con|fi|dent|ly** ADV [ADV with v] ❑ *I can confidently promise that this year is going to be very different.* **2** ADJ If a person or their manner is **confident**, they feel sure about their own abilities, qualities, or ideas. ❑ *In time he became more confident and relaxed.* • **con|fi|dent|ly** ADV ❑ *She walked confidently across the hall.* **3** ADJ If you are **confident** that something is true, you are sure that it is true. A **confident** statement is one that the speaker is sure is true. ❑ *She is confident that everybody is on her side.* • **con|fi|dent|ly** ADV [ADV with v] ❑ *We can confidently say we've found a new species.*

con|fi|den|tial /kɒnfɪdɛnʃəl/ **1** ADJ Information that is **confidential** is meant to be kept secret or private. ❑ *She accused them of leaking confidential information about her private life.* • **con|fi|den|tial|ly** ADV ❑ *People can phone in, knowing that any information they give will be treated confidentially.* • **con|fi|den|ti|al|ity** /kɒnfɪdɛnʃiælɪti/ N-UNCOUNT ❑ *...the confidentiality of the client-attorney relationship.* **2** ADJ If you talk to someone in a **confidential** way, you talk to them quietly because what you are saying is secret or private. ❑ *"Look," he said in a confidential tone, "I want you to know that me and Joey are cops."* • **con|fi|den|tial|ly** ADV ❑ *Nash hadn't raised his voice, still spoke rather softly, confidentially.*

con|fi|den|tial|ly /kɒnfɪdɛnʃəli/ **1** ADV [ADV with cl] **Confidentially** is used to say that what you are telling someone is a secret and should not be discussed with anyone else. ❑ *Confidentially, I am not sure that it wasn't above their heads.* **2** → see also **confidential**

con|figu|ra|tion /kənfɪgyəreɪʃən/ (**configurations**) **1** N-COUNT A **configuration** is an arrangement of a group of things. [FORMAL] ❑ *...Stonehenge, in southwestern England, an ancient configuration of giant stones.* **2** N-UNCOUNT The **configuration** of a computer system is the way in which all its parts, such as the hardware and software, are connected together in order for the computer to work. [COMPUTING] ❑ *Prices range from $119 to $199, depending on the particular configuration.*

con|fig|ure /kənfɪgyər/ (**configures, configuring, configured**) V-T If you **configure** a piece of computer equipment, you set it up so that it is ready for use. [COMPUTING] ❑ *How easy was it to configure the software?*

con|fine /kənfaɪn/ (**confines, confining, confined**) **1** V-T To **confine** something to a particular place or group means to prevent it from spreading beyond that place or group. ❑ *Health officials have successfully confined the epidemic to the Tabatinga area.* **2** V-T If you **confine** someone or something, you prevent them from leaving or escaping. ❑ *He was confined in an internment camp in Utah.* ❑ *They decided not to let their new dog run loose, confining it to a fenced enclosure during the day.* **3** V-T If you **confine** yourself or your activities **to** something, you do only that thing and are involved with nothing else. ❑ *He did not confine himself to the one language.*

con|fined /kənfaɪnd/ **1** ADJ [v-link ADJ to n] If something is **confined to** a particular place, it exists only in that place. If it is **confined** to a particular group, only members of that group have it. ❑ *The problem is not confined to Georgia.* **2** ADJ A **confined** space or area is small and enclosed by walls. ❑ *His long legs bent up in the confined space.* **3** ADJ [v-link ADJ to n] If someone is **confined to** a wheelchair, bed, or house, they have to stay there, because they have a disability, or are ill. This use could cause offense. ❑ *He had been confined to a wheelchair since childhood.*

con|fine|ment /kənfaɪnmənt/ N-UNCOUNT **Confinement** is the state of being forced to stay in a prison or another place which you cannot leave. ❑ *She had been held in solitary confinement for four months.*

con|firm ♦♦◇ /kənfɜrm/ (**confirms, confirming, confirmed**) **1** V-T [no cont] If something **confirms** what you believe, suspect, or fear, it shows that it is definitely true. ❑ *X-rays have confirmed that he has not broken any bones.* • **con|fir|ma|tion** /kɒnfərmeɪʃən/ N-UNCOUNT ❑ *They handed her resignation as confirmation of their suspicions.* **2** V-T If you **confirm** something that has been stated or suggested, you say that it is true because you know about it. ❑ *The spokesman confirmed that the area was now in rebel hands.* • **con|fir|ma|tion** N-UNCOUNT ❑ *She glanced over at James for confirmation.* **3** V-T If you **confirm** an arrangement or appointment, you say that it is definite, usually in a letter or on the telephone. ❑ *You make the reservation, and I'll confirm it in writing.* • **con|fir|ma|tion** N-UNCOUNT ❑ *Travel arrangements are subject to confirmation by the head office.* **4** V-T [usu passive]

If someone **is confirmed**, they are formally accepted as a member of a Christian church during a ceremony in which they say they believe what the church teaches. ❑ *He was confirmed as a member of the Methodist Church.* ● **con|fir|ma|tion** (**confirmations**) N-VAR ❑ *...when I was being prepared for Confirmation.* **5** V-T [no cont] If something **confirms** you in your decision, belief, or opinion, it makes you think that you are definitely right. ❑ *It has confirmed me in my decision not to become a nun.* **6** V-T If something **confirms** you **as** something, it shows that you definitely deserve a name, role, or position. ❑ *Her new role could confirm her as one of our leading actors.*

con|fir|ma|tion bias (**confirmation biases**) N-VAR If someone is guilty of **confirmation bias**, they present and interpret information in a way that supports their existing beliefs. ❑ *With easy access to lots of information on the internet, there's a risk of confirmation bias.*

con|firmed /kənfɜrmd/ ADJ [ADJ n] You use **confirmed** to describe someone who has a particular habit or belief that they are very unlikely to change. ❑ *I'm a confirmed bachelor.*

con|fis|cate /kɒnfɪskeɪt/ (**confiscates, confiscating, confiscated**) V-T If you **confiscate** something from someone, you take it away from them, usually as a punishment. ❑ *The law has been used to confiscate assets from people who have committed minor offenses.* ● **con|fis|ca|tion** /kɒnfɪskeɪʃən/ (**confiscations**) N-VAR ❑ *The new laws allow the confiscation of assets purchased with proceeds of the drugs trade.*

con|fit /kɒnfi/ (**confits**) N-MASS **Confit** is meat such as goose or duck which has been cooked and preserved in its own fat. ❑ *...confit of duck.*

con|fla|gra|tion /kɒnfləgreɪʃən/ (**conflagrations**) N-COUNT A **conflagration** is a fire that burns over a large area and destroys property. [FORMAL]

con|flate /kənfleɪt/ (**conflates, conflating, conflated**) V-RECIP If you **conflate** two or more descriptions or ideas, or if they **conflate**, you combine them in order to produce a single one. [FORMAL] ❑ *Her letters conflate past and present.* ❑ *Unfortunately the public conflated fiction with reality and made her into a saint.* ❑ *The two meanings conflated.*

VOCABULARY IN CONTEXT

Conflict

Many countries experience **conflict** in the form of a **civil war**. The English Civil War, also called the Great Rebellion, took place from 1642–1651 between the supporters of King Charles I, called Cavaliers, and the so-called Roundheads, who supported the English Parliament. The first major **clash** on English soil was the Battle of Edgehill and, while both sides claimed **victory**, it was not actually clear who had won. Most of the subsequent fights were **sieges** or **skirmishes** rather than battles, and the **opposing** sides were locked in **stalemate** until, in 1644, the Roundheads decisively **triumphed** over the King's men at the Battle of Marston Moor. This proved to be the first in a series of successes, which ultimately led to the King's **surrender** on May 5, 1646. He was taken **captive** and **executed** in 1649, but the war did not end until Charles I's son, Charles II, was defeated in 1651.

con|flict ✦✦◇ (**conflicts, conflicting, conflicted**)

> The noun is pronounced /kɒnflɪkt/. The verb is pronounced /kənflɪkt/.

1 N-UNCOUNT [oft in/into N] **Conflict** is serious disagreement and argument about something important. If two people or groups are in **conflict**, they have had a serious disagreement or argument and have not yet reached agreement. ❑ *Try to keep any conflict between you and your ex-partner to a minimum.* **2** N-UNCOUNT **Conflict** is a state of mind in which you find it impossible to make a decision. ❑ *...the anguish of his own inner conflict.* **3** N-VAR **Conflict** is fighting between countries or groups of people. [WRITTEN] ❑ *...talks aimed at ending four decades of conflict.* **4** N-VAR A **conflict** is a serious difference between two or more beliefs, ideas, or interests. If two beliefs, ideas, or interests are in **conflict**, they are very different. ❑ *There is a conflict between what they are doing and what you want.* **5** V-RECIP If ideas, beliefs, or accounts **conflict**, they are very different from each other and it seems impossible for them to exist together or to each be true. ❑ *Personal ethics and professional ethics sometimes conflict.* ❑ *He held firm opinions which usually conflicted with mine.* **6** → See feature box at **conflict**

COLLOCATIONS

conflict
NOUN
1
adjective + **conflict**: industrial, political; potential
verb + **conflict**: resolve, settle, solve; avoid, end, prevent
2
adjective + **conflict**: inner, internal
3
adjective + **conflict**: armed, bloody, escalating, military; ethnic, sectarian

con|flu|ence /kɒnfluəns/ N-SING [oft N of n] The **confluence** of two rivers is the place where they join and become one larger river. ❑ *The 160-meter falls mark the dramatic confluence of the rivers Nera and Velino.*

con|form /kənfɔrm/ (**conforms, conforming, conformed**) **1** V-I If something **conforms** to something such as a law or someone's wishes, it is of the required type or quality. ❑ *The lamp has been designed to conform to new safety standards.* **2** V-I If you **conform**, you behave in the way that you are expected or supposed to behave. ❑ *Many children who can't or don't conform are bullied.*

con|form|ist /kənfɔrmɪst/ (**conformists**) ADJ Someone who is **conformist** behaves or thinks like everyone else rather than doing things that are original. ❑ *He may have to become more conformist if he is to prosper again.* ● N-COUNT A **conformist** is someone who is conformist.

con|form|ity /kənfɔrmɪti/ **1** N-UNCOUNT If something happens in **conformity** with something such as a law or someone's wishes, it happens as the law says it should, or as the person wants it to. ❑ *The prime minister is, in conformity with their constitution, chosen by the president.* **2** N-UNCOUNT **Conformity** means behaving in the same way as most other people. ❑ *Excessive conformity is usually caused by fear of disapproval.*

con|found /kənfaʊnd/ (**confounds, confounding, confounded**) V-T If someone or something **confounds** you, they make you feel surprised or confused, often by showing you that your opinions or expectations of them were wrong. ❑ *He momentarily confounded his critics by his cool handling of the hostage crisis.*

con|front ✦✦◇ /kənfrʌnt/ (**confronts, confronting, confronted**) **1** V-T If you **are confronted** with a problem, task, or difficulty, you have to deal with it. ❑ *She was confronted with severe money problems.* **2** V-T If you **confront** a difficult situation or issue, you accept the fact that it exists and try to deal with it. ❑ *We are learning how to confront death.* **3** V-T [usu passive] If you **are confronted** by something that you find threatening or difficult to deal with, it is there in front of you. ❑ *I was confronted with an array of knobs, levers, and switches.* **4** V-T If you **confront** someone, you stand or sit in front of them, especially when you are going to fight, argue, or compete with them. ❑ *She pushed her way through the mob and confronted him face to face.* ❑ *They don't hesitate to open fire when confronted by* police. **5** V-T If you **confront** someone with something, you present facts or evidence to them in order to accuse them of something or force them to deal with a situation. ◻ *She had decided to confront Kathryn with the truth.* ◻ *I could not bring myself to confront him about it.*

SYNONYMS

confront
VERB
2
tackle: *The first reason to tackle these problems is to save children's lives.*
deal with: *She saw a psychiatrist who used hypnotism to help her deal with her fear.*
brave: *Thousands have braved icy rain to demonstrate their support.*
cope: *She has had to cope with losing all her previous status and money.*
face up to: *They had to face up to the fact that they had lost everything.*
4
tackle: *I tackled him about how anyone could live amidst so much poverty.*
challenge: *I challenged him on the hypocrisy of his political attitudes.*
oppose: *Mr Taylor was not bitter towards those who had opposed him.*
stand up to: *He shouted at me, so I shouted back—the first time in my life I'd stood up to him.*

con|fron|ta|tion ♦◇◇ /kɒnfrʌnteɪʃ°n/ (**confrontations**) N-VAR A **confrontation** is a dispute, fight, or battle between two groups of people. ◻ *The commission remains so weak that it will continue to avoid confrontation with governments.*

con|fron|ta|tion|al /kɒnfrʌnteɪʃən°l/ ADJ If you describe the way that someone behaves as **confrontational**, you are showing your disapproval of the fact that they are aggressive and likely to cause an argument or dispute. [DISAPPROVAL] ◻ *The committee's confrontational style of campaigning has made it unpopular.*

con|fus|able /kənfyuːzəb°l/ ADJ **Confusable** words are easily confused because they are very similar.

con|fuse /kənfyuːz/ (**confuses, confusing, confused**) **1** V-T If you **confuse** two things, you get them mixed up, so that you think one of them is the other one. ◻ *I always confuse my left with my right.* ● **con|fu|sion** /kənfyuːʒ°n/ N-UNCOUNT ◻ *Use different colors of felt pen on your sketch to avoid confusion.* **2** V-T To **confuse** someone means to make it difficult for them to know exactly what is happening or what to do. ◻ *My words surprised and confused him.* **3** V-T To **confuse** a situation means to make it complicated or difficult to understand. ◻ *To further confuse the issue, there is an enormous variation in the amount of sleep people feel happy with.*

con|fused /kənfyuːzd/ **1** ADJ If you are **confused**, you do not know exactly what is happening or what to do. ◻ *A survey showed people were confused about what they should eat to stay healthy.* **2** ADJ Something that is **confused** does not have any order or pattern and is difficult to understand. ◻ *The situation remains confused as both sides claim success.*

con|fus|ing /kənfyuːzɪŋ/ ADJ Something that is **confusing** makes it difficult for people to know exactly what is happening or what to do. ◻ *The statement is really confusing.*

con|fu|sion /kənfyuːʒ°n/ (**confusions**) **1** N-VAR If there is **confusion** about something, it is not clear what the true situation is, especially because people believe different things. ◻ *There's still confusion about the number of students.* **2** N-UNCOUNT **Confusion** is a situation in which everything is in disorder, especially because there are lots of things happening at the same time. ◻ *There was confusion when a man fired shots.* **3** → see also **confuse**

con|ga /kɒŋɡə/ (**congas**) N-COUNT If a group of people dance a **conga**, they dance in a long winding line, with each person holding on to the back of the person in front.

con|geal /kəndʒiːl/ (**congeals, congealing, congealed**) V-T/V-I When a liquid **congeals**, it becomes very thick and sticky and almost solid. ◻ *The blood had started to congeal.* ◻ *...congealed soup.*

con|gen|ial /kəndʒiːniəl/ ADJ A **congenial** person, place, or environment is pleasant. [FORMAL] ◻ *He is back in more congenial company.*

con|geni|tal /kəndʒɛnɪt°l/ **1** ADJ [usu ADJ n] A **congenital** disease or medical condition is one that a person has had from birth, but is not inherited. [MEDICAL] ◻ *When John was 17, he died of congenital heart disease.* ● **con|geni|tal|ly** ADV [ADV adj/-ed] ◻ *...congenitally deaf patients.* **2** ADJ [usu ADJ n] A **congenital** characteristic or feature in a person is so strong that you cannot imagine it ever changing, although there may seem to be no reason for it. ◻ *He was a congenital liar and usually in debt.* ● **con|geni|tal|ly** ADV ◻ *I admit to being congenitally lazy.*

con|ger /kɒŋɡər/ (**congers**) N-VAR A **conger** or a **conger eel** is a large fish that looks like a snake.

con|gest|ed /kəndʒɛstɪd/ **1** ADJ A **congested** road or area is extremely crowded and blocked with traffic or people. ◻ *He promised to clear the city's congested roads.* **2** → See feature box at **commute**

con|ges|tion /kəndʒɛstʃ°n/ **1** N-UNCOUNT If there is **congestion** in a place, the place is extremely crowded and blocked with traffic or people. ◻ *The problems of traffic congestion will not disappear in a hurry.* **2** N-UNCOUNT **Congestion** in a part of the body is a medical condition in which the part becomes blocked. ◻ *...nasal congestion.*

con|ges|tion pric|ing N-UNCOUNT **Congestion pricing** refers to money motorists must pay in order to drive in some city areas. Congestion pricing intended to reduce traffic within those areas. ◻ *...the decision on whether to introduce congestion pricing on urban roads.*

con|ges|tive /kəndʒɛstɪv/ ADJ [ADJ n] A **congestive** disease is a medical condition where a part of the body becomes blocked. [MEDICAL] ◻ *...congestive heart failure.*

con|glom|er|ate /kənɡlɒmərɪt/ (**conglomerates**) N-COUNT A **conglomerate** is a large business firm consisting of several different companies. [BUSINESS] ◻ *...the world's second-largest media conglomerate.*

con|glom|era|tion /kənɡlɒməreɪʃ°n/ (**conglomerations**) N-COUNT [usu N of n] A **conglomeration** of things is a group of many different things, gathered together. [FORMAL] ◻ *...a conglomeration of peoples speaking different languages.*

con|gratu|late /kənɡrætʃəleɪt/ (**congratulates, congratulating, congratulated**) **1** V-T If you **congratulate** someone, you say something to show you are pleased that something nice has happened to them. ◻ *She congratulated him on the birth of his son.* ● **con|gratu|la|tion** /kənɡrætʃəleɪʃ°n/ N-UNCOUNT ◻ *We have received many letters of congratulation.* **2** V-T If you **congratulate** someone, you praise them for something good that they have done. ◻ *I really must congratulate the organizers for a well run and enjoyable event.*

con|gratu|la|tions /kənɡrætʃəleɪʃ°nz/ **1** CONVENTION You say '**Congratulations**' to someone in order to congratulate them on something nice that has happened to them or something good that they have done. ◻ *Congratulations, you have a healthy baby girl.* ◻ *Congratulations on your interesting article.* **2** N-PLURAL If you offer someone your **congratulations**, you congratulate them on something nice that has happened to them or on something good that they have done. ◻ *The club also offers its congratulations to D. Brown on her appointment as president.*

con|gratu|la|tory /kənɡrætʃələtɔri/ ADJ A **congratulatory** message expresses congratulations. ◻ *He sent Kim a congratulatory letter.*

con|gre|gant /kɒŋɡrɪɡənt/ (**congregants**) N-COUNT **Congregants** are members of a congregation. [mainly AM]

con|gre|gate /kɒŋɡrɪɡeɪt/ (**congregates, congregating, congregated**) V-I When people **congregate**, they gather together and form a group. ◻ *Visitors congregated on Sunday afternoons to view public exhibitions.*

con|gre|ga|tion /kɒŋɡrɪɡeɪʃ°n/ (**congregations**) N-COUNT-COLL The people who are attending a religious service or who regularly attend a religious service are referred to as the **congregation**. ◻ *Most members of the congregation begin arriving a few minutes before services.*

con|gress /kɒŋgrɪs/ (congresses) N-COUNT-COLL A **congress** is a large meeting that is held to discuss ideas and policies. ❑ *A lot has changed after the party congress.*

Con|gress ✦✧✧ N-PROPER-COLL **Congress** is the elected group of politicians that is responsible for making laws in the United States. It consists of two parts: the House of Representatives and the Senate. ❑ *We want to cooperate with both the administration and Congress.*

con|gres|sion|al ✦✧✧ /kəngrɛʃənəl/ also **Congressional** ADJ [ADJ n] A **congressional** policy, action, or person relates to the U.S. Congress. ❑ *The president explained his plans to congressional leaders.*

congress|man /kɒŋgrɪsmən/ (Congressmen) also **Congressman** N-COUNT; N-TITLE A **Congressman** is a male member of the US Congress, especially of the House of Representatives.

congress|person /kɒŋgrɪspɜrsən/ (Congresspeople) also **Congressperson** N-COUNT A **Congressperson** is a member of the US Congress, especially of the House of Representatives.

congress|woman /kɒŋgrɪswʊmən/ (Congresswomen) also **Congresswoman** N-COUNT; N-TITLE A **Congresswoman** is a female member of the US Congress, especially of the House of Representatives. ❑ *The meeting was organized by Congresswoman Maxine Waters.*

con|gru|ence /kɒŋgruəns/ N-UNCOUNT [also a N, usu N between pl-n] **Congruence** is when two things are similar or fit together well. [FORMAL] ❑ *...a necessary congruence between political, cultural and economic forces.*

con|gru|ent /kɒŋgruənt, kəngru-/ ADJ If one thing is **congruent** with another thing, they are similar or fit together well. [FORMAL] ❑ *They want to work in an organization whose values are congruent with their own.*

coni|cal /kɒnɪkəl/ ADJ [usu ADJ n] A **conical** object is shaped like a cone. ❑ *...floor lamps with conical metal shades.*

co|ni|fer /kɒnɪfər/ (conifers) N-COUNT **Conifers** are a type of trees and shrubs such as pine trees and fir trees. They have fruit called cones, and very thin leaves called needles which they do not normally lose in winter.

co|nif|er|ous /koʊnɪfərəs/ ADJ [usu ADJ n] A **coniferous** forest or wood is made up of conifers.

con|jec|tur|al /kəndʒɛktʃərəl/ ADJ A statement that is **conjectural** is based on information that is not certain or complete. [FORMAL] ❑ *There is something undeniably conjectural about such claims.*

con|jec|ture /kəndʒɛktʃər/ (conjectures, conjecturing, conjectured) **1** N-VAR A **conjecture** is a conclusion that is based on information that is not certain or complete. [FORMAL] ❑ *That was a conjecture, not a fact.* ❑ *There are several conjectures.* **2** V-T/V-I When you **conjecture**, you form an opinion or reach a conclusion on the basis of information that is not certain or complete. [FORMAL] ❑ *He conjectured that some individuals may be able to detect major calamities.*

con|join /kəndʒɔɪn/ (conjoins, conjoining, conjoined) V-RECIP If two or more things **conjoin** or if you **conjoin** them, they are united and joined together. [FORMAL] ❑ *The wisdom of the retired generals and anti-war protesters conjoins.* ❑ *America's rise in rates was conjoined with higher rates elsewhere.* ❑ *...if we conjoin the two responses.*

con|joined twin (conjoined twins) N-COUNT **Conjoined twins** are twins who are born with their bodies joined.

con|ju|gal /kɒndʒəgəl/ ADJ [ADJ n] **Conjugal** means relating to marriage or a married couple's relationship, especially their sexual relationship. [FORMAL] ❑ *...a man deprived of his conjugal rights.*

con|ju|gate /kɒndʒəgeɪt/ (conjugates, conjugating, conjugated) V-T When students or teachers **conjugate** a verb, they give its different forms in a particular order. ❑ *...a child who can read at one and is conjugating Latin verbs at four.*

con|junc|tion /kəndʒʌŋkʃən/ (conjunctions) **1** N-COUNT A **conjunction** of two or more things is the occurrence of them at the same time or place. [FORMAL] ❑ *...the conjunction of two events.* **2** N-COUNT In grammar, a **conjunction** is a word or group of words that joins together words, groups, or clauses. In English, there are coordinating conjunctions such as 'and' and 'but,' and subordinating conjunctions such as 'although,' 'because,' and 'when.' **3** PHRASE [usu PHR with n] If one thing is done in **conjunction** with another, the two things are done or used together. ❑ *Textbooks are designed to be used in conjunction with classroom teaching.*

con|junc|ti|vi|tis /kəndʒʌŋktɪvaɪtɪs/ N-UNCOUNT **Conjunctivitis** is an eye infection which causes the thin skin that covers the eye to become red. [MEDICAL]

con|jure /kɒndʒər/ (conjures, conjuring, conjured) V-T If you **conjure** something out of nothing, you make it appear as if by magic. ❑ *Thirteen years ago she found herself having to conjure a career from thin air.* • PHRASAL VERB **Conjure up** means the same as **conjure**. ❑ *Every day a different chef will be conjuring up delicious dishes in the restaurant.*
▶ **conjure up** **1** PHRASAL VERB If you **conjure up** a memory, picture, or idea, you create it in your mind. ❑ *When he closed his eyes, he could conjure up in exact color almost every event of his life.* **2** → see **conjure**

con|jur|er /kɒndʒərər/ (conjurers) also **conjuror** N-COUNT A **conjurer** is a person who entertains people by doing magic tricks.

conk /kɒŋk/ (conks, conking, conked)
▶ **conk out** PHRASAL VERB If something such as a machine or a vehicle **conks out**, it stops working or breaks down. [INFORMAL] ❑ *The dynamo conked out so we've got no electricity.*

con man (con men) also **conman** N-COUNT A **con man** is a man who persuades people to give him their money or property by lying to them. ❑ *A few years ago she was the victim of a con man.*

con|nect /kənɛkt/ (connects, connecting, connected) **1** V-RECIP If something or someone **connects** one thing to another, or if one thing **connects** to another, or if two things **connect**, the two things are joined together. ❑ *You can connect the speakers to your CD player.* ❑ *I connected the wires for the transformer.* **2** V-RECIP If two things or places **connect** or if something **connects** them, they are joined and people or things can pass between them. ❑ *...the long hallway that connects the rooms.* ❑ *A pedestrian bridge now connects the parking garage with the mall.* **3** V-I If one train or plane, for example, **connects** with another, it arrives at a time which allows passengers to change to the other one in order to continue their trip. ❑ *...a train connecting with a ferry to Ireland.* **4** V-T [usu passive] If a piece of equipment or a place **is connected** to a source of power or water, it is joined to that source so that it has power or water. ❑ *These appliances should not be connected to power supplies.* • PHRASAL VERB **Connect up** means the same as **connect**. ❑ *The shower is easy to install – it needs only to be connected up to the hot and cold water supply.* **5** V-T If you **connect** a person or thing with something, you realize that there is a link or relationship between them. ❑ *I hoped he would not connect me with that now-embarrassing review I'd written seven years earlier.* **6** V-T Something that **connects** a person or thing with something else shows or provides a link or relationship between them. ❑ *A search of Brady's house revealed nothing that could connect him with the robberies.*

con|nect|ed /kənɛktɪd/ **1** ADJ If one thing is **connected** with another, there is a link or relationship between them. ❑ *Have you ever had any skin problems connected with exposure to the sun?* ❑ *The dispute is not directly connected to the negotiations.* **2** → see also **connect**, **well-connected**

con|nec|tion ✦✧✧ /kənɛkʃən/ (connections)

> in BRIT, also use **connexion**

1 N-VAR A **connection** is a relationship between two things, people, or groups. ❑ *There was no evidence of a connection between BSE and the brain diseases recently confirmed in cats.* ❑ *I felt a strong connection between us.* **2** N-COUNT A **connection** is a joint where two wires or pipes are joined together. ❑ *Check all radiators for small leaks, especially round pipework connections.* **3** N-COUNT If a place has good road, rail, or air **connections**, many places can be directly reached from there by car, train, or plane. ❑ *Mexico City has excellent air and rail connections to the rest of the country.* **4** N-COUNT If you get a **connection** at a station or airport, you catch a train, bus, or plane, after getting off another train, bus, or plane, in order to continue your trip. ❑ *My flight was late and I missed the connection.*

> **SYNONYMS**
>
> **connection**
> NOUN ❶
> **relation:** It is a question of the relation of ethics to economics.
> **relationship:** There is a relationship between diet and cancer.
> **link:** ...the link between smoking and lung cancer.
> **association:** Black was considered inappropriate because of its associations with death.
> **correlation:** ...the correlation between smoking and disease.

con|nec|tive /kənɛktɪv/ (**connectives**) N-COUNT In grammar, a **connective** is the same as a **conjunction**.

con|nec|tive tis|sue N-UNCOUNT **Connective tissue** is the substance in the bodies of animals and people which fills in the spaces between organs and connects muscles and bones. [TECHNICAL]

con|nec|tiv|ity /kɒnɛktɪvɪti/ N-UNCOUNT **Connectivity** is the ability of a computing device to connect to other computers or to the internet. [COMPUTING] ❑ ...a DVD player with internet connectivity.

con|nect|or /kənɛktər/ (**connectors**) N-COUNT A **connector** is a device that joins two pieces of equipment, wire, or piping together.

con|niv|ance /kənaɪvəns/ N-UNCOUNT **Connivance** is a willingness to allow or assist something to happen even though you know it is wrong. [DISAPPROVAL] ❑ The deficit had grown with the connivance of the banks. ❑ The goods were exported with official connivance.

con|nive /kənaɪv/ (**connives, conniving, connived**) V-RECIP If one person **connives** with another to do something, they secretly try to achieve something which will benefit both of them. [DISAPPROVAL] ❑ He accused them of conniving with foreign companies to weaken employment rights. ❑ Senior politicians connived to ensure that he was not released.

con|niv|ing /kənaɪvɪŋ/ ADJ [usu ADJ n] If you describe someone as **conniving**, you mean you dislike them because they make secret plans in order to get things for themselves or harm other people. [DISAPPROVAL] ❑ Edith was seen as a conniving, greedy woman.

con|nois|seur /kɒnəsɜr, -sʊər/ (**connoisseurs**) N-COUNT A **connoisseur** is someone who knows a lot about the arts, food, drink, or some other subject. ❑ Sarah tells me you're something of an art connoisseur.

con|no|ta|tion /kɒnəteɪʃən/ (**connotations**) ❶ N-COUNT The **connotations** of a particular word or name are the ideas or qualities which it makes you think of. ❑ It's just one of those words that's got so many negative connotations. ❷ → See feature box at **success**

con|note /kənoʊt/ (**connotes, connoting, connoted**) V-T If a word or name **connotes** something, it makes you think of a particular idea or quality. [FORMAL] ❑ The term "organization" often connotes a sense of neatness.

con|quer /kɒŋkər/ (**conquers, conquering, conquered**) ❶ V-T If one country or group of people **conquers** another, they take complete control of their land. ❑ During 1936, Mussolini conquered Abyssinia. ❷ V-T If you **conquer** something such as a problem, you succeed in ending it or dealing with it successfully. ❑ I was certain that love was quite enough to conquer our differences. ❑ He has never conquered his addiction to smoking.

con|quer|or /kɒŋkərər/ (**conquerors**) N-COUNT The **conquerors** of a country or group of people are the people who have taken complete control of that country or group's land. ❑ The people of an oppressed country obey their conquerors because they want to go on living.

con|quest /kɒŋkwɛst/ (**conquests**) ❶ N-UNCOUNT [also N in pl, oft N of n] **Conquest** is the act of conquering a country or group of people. ❑ He had led the conquest of southern Poland in 1939. ❑ ...the Spanish conquest of Mexico. ❷ N-SING The **conquest** of something such as a problem is success in ending it or dealing with it. ❑ The conquest of inflation has been the Government's overriding economic priority for nearly 15 years.

con|quis|ta|dor /kɒnkwɪstədər/ (**conquistadors** or **conquistadores**) N-COUNT The **conquistadors** were the sixteenth century Spanish conquerors of Central and South America.

con|science /kɒnʃəns/ (**consciences**) ❶ N-COUNT Your **conscience** is the part of your mind that tells you whether what you are doing is right or wrong. If you have a **guilty conscience**, you feel guilty about something because you know it was wrong. If you have a **clear conscience**, you do not feel guilty because you know you have done nothing wrong. ❑ I have battled with my conscience over whether I should actually send this letter. ❑ What if he got a guilty conscience and brought it back? ❷ N-UNCOUNT **Conscience** is doing what you believe is right even though it might be unpopular, difficult, or dangerous. ❑ He refused for reasons of conscience to eat meat. ❸ N-UNCOUNT **Conscience** is a feeling of guilt because you know you have done something that is wrong. ❑ I'm so glad he had a pang of conscience. ❹ PHRASE If you have something **on** your **conscience**, you feel guilty because you know you have done something wrong. ❑ The drunk driver has two deaths on his conscience.

con|sci|en|tious /kɒnʃiɛnʃəs/ ADJ Someone who is **conscientious** is very careful to do their work properly. ❑ We are generally very conscientious about our work. • **con|sci|en|tious|ly** ADV ❑ He studied conscientiously and enthusiastically.

con|sci|en|tious ob|ject|or (**conscientious objectors**) N-COUNT A **conscientious objector** is a person who refuses to join the armed forces because they think that war is morally wrong.

con|scious ♦◇◇ /kɒnʃəs/ ❶ ADJ [v-link ADJ] If you are **conscious** of something, you notice it or realize that it is happening. ❑ He was conscious of the faint, musky aroma of aftershave. ❑ She was very conscious of Max studying her. ❷ ADJ [v-link ADJ] If you are **conscious** of something, you think about it a lot, especially because you are unhappy about it or because you think it is important. ❑ I'm very conscious of my weight. ❸ ADJ A **conscious** decision or action is made or done deliberately with you giving your full attention to it. ❑ I don't think we ever made a conscious decision to have a big family. • **con|scious|ly** ADV [ADV with v] ❑ Sophie was not consciously seeking a replacement after her father died. ❹ ADJ Someone who is **conscious** is awake rather than asleep or unconscious. ❑ She was fully conscious throughout the surgery and knew what was going on. ❺ ADJ [ADJ n] **Conscious** memories or thoughts are ones that you are aware of. ❑ He had no conscious memory of his four-week stay in the hospital. • **con|scious|ly** ADV ❑ Most people cannot consciously remember much before the ages of 3 to 5 years.

-conscious /kɒnʃəs/ COMB IN ADJ **-conscious** combines with words such as 'health,' 'fashion,' 'politically,' and 'environmentally' to form adjectives which describe someone who believes that the aspect of life indicated is important. ❑ We're all becoming increasingly health-conscious these days.

con|scious|ness ♦◇◇ /kɒnʃəsnɪs/ (**consciousnesses**) ❶ N-COUNT Your **consciousness** is your mind and your thoughts. ❑ That idea has been creeping into our consciousness for some time. ❷ N-UNCOUNT The **consciousness** of a group of people is their set of ideas, attitudes, and beliefs. ❑ The Green Party is attempting to shift the American consciousness. ❸ N-UNCOUNT You use **consciousness** to refer to an interest in and knowledge of a particular subject or idea. ❑ Her political consciousness sprang from her upbringing when her father's illness left the family short of money. ❹ N-UNCOUNT **Consciousness** is the state of being awake rather than being asleep or unconscious. If someone **loses consciousness**, they become unconscious, and if they **regain consciousness**, they become conscious after being unconscious. ❑ She banged her head and lost consciousness.

con|scious|ness rais|ing N-UNCOUNT [oft N n] **Consciousness raising** is the process of developing awareness of an unfair situation, with the aim of making people want to help in changing it. ❑ ...consciousness-raising groups.

con|script (**conscripts, conscripting, conscripted**)

> The noun is pronounced /kɒnskrɪpt/. The verb is pronounced /kənskrɪpt/.

❶ N-COUNT A **conscript** is a person who has been made to join the armed forces of a country. ❑ Most of the soldiers are reluctant conscripts. ❷ V-T [usu passive] If someone **is conscripted**, they are officially made to join the armed forces of a country. ❑ He was conscripted into the U.S. army.

con|scrip|tion /kənskrɪpʃən/ N-UNCOUNT **Conscription** is officially making people in a particular country join the armed forces. [FORMAL] ❑ *All adult males will be liable for conscription.*

con|se|crate /kɒnsɪkreɪt/ (**consecrates, consecrating, consecrated**) V-T When a building, place, or object **is consecrated**, it is officially declared to be holy. When a person **is consecrated**, they are officially declared to be a bishop. ❑ *The church was consecrated in 1234.*

con|secu|tive /kənsɛkyətɪv/ ADJ **Consecutive** periods of time or events happen one after the other without interruption. ❑ *The Cup was won for the third consecutive year by the Toronto Maple Leafs.*

con|sen|sual /kənsɛnsuəl/ ◘ ADJ [usu ADJ n] A **consensual** approach, view, or decision is one that is based on general agreement among all the members of a group. ❑ *I hope we can work with others in a consensual way.* ◙ ADJ If sexual activity is **consensual**, both partners willingly take part in it. [LEGAL] ❑ *He claimed the sex was consensual.*

con|sen|sus /kənsɛnsəs/ N-SING [also no det] A **consensus** is general agreement among a group of people. ❑ *The consensus among the world's scientists is that the world is likely to warm up over the next few decades.*

con|sent /kənsɛnt/ (**consents, consenting, consented**) ◘ N-UNCOUNT If you give your **consent** to something, you give someone permission to do it. [FORMAL] ❑ *At approximately 11:30 p.m., Pollard finally gave his consent to the search.* ◙ V-T/V-I If you **consent** to something, you agree to do it or to allow it to be done. [FORMAL] ❑ *He finally consented to go.* ❑ *He asked Ginny if she would consent to a small celebration after the christening.* ◚ → see also **age of consent**

con|sent|ing /kənsɛntɪŋ/ ADJ [ADJ n] A **consenting** adult is a person who is considered to be old enough to make their own decisions about who they have sex with. ❑ *What consenting adults do in private is their own business.*

con|se|quence ♦◇◇ /kɒnsɪkwɛns, -kwəns/ (**consequences**) ◘ N-COUNT The **consequences** of something are the results or effects of it. ❑ *Her lawyer said she understood the consequences of her actions and was prepared to go to jail.* ◙ PHRASE If one thing happens and then another thing happens **in consequence** or **as a consequence**, the second thing happens as a result of the first. ❑ *His death was totally unexpected and, in consequence, no plans had been made for his replacement.* ❑ *Maternity services were to be reduced as a consequence of falling birth rates.* ◚ → See feature box at **disaster**

---- COLLOCATIONS ----

consequence
NOUN ◘
adjective + **consequence**: dire, disastrous, negative, tragic; inevitable, long-term, serious, unintended; economic, social
verb + **consequence**: accept, bear, face, suffer; consider, understand; avoid, escape

---- SYNONYMS ----

consequence
NOUN ◘
result: *She developed asthma as a direct result of the work.*
effect: *Even minor head injuries can cause long-lasting psychological effects.*
outcome: *It's too early to know the outcome of her illness.*
repercussions: *It was an effort which was to have painful repercussions.*
upshot: *So the upshot is we're going for lunch on Friday.*

con|se|quent /kɒnsɪkwɛnt, -kwənt/ ADJ **Consequent** means happening as a direct result of an event or situation. [FORMAL] ❑ *The warming of the Earth and the consequent climatic changes affect us all.*

con|se|quen|tial /kɒnsɪkwɛnʃəl/ ◘ ADJ [ADJ n] **Consequential** means the same as **consequent**. [FORMAL] ❑ *The estimate for extra staff and consequential costs such as accommodation was an annual $9.18 million.* ◙ ADJ Something that is **consequential** is important or significant. [FORMAL] ❑ *From a medical standpoint a week is usually not a consequential delay.*

con|se|quent|ly /kɒnsɪkwɛntli, -kwəntli/ ADV [ADV with cl] **Consequently** means as a result. [FORMAL] ❑ *Grandfather had sustained a broken back while working in the mines. Consequently, he spent the rest of his life in a wheelchair.*

con|serv|an|cy /kənsɜrvənsi/ N-UNCOUNT [usu N n] **Conservancy** is used in the names of organizations that work to preserve and protect the environment. ❑ *...Western Pennsylvania Conservancy.*

con|ser|va|tion /kɒnsərveɪʃən/ ◘ N-UNCOUNT **Conservation** is saving and protecting the environment. ❑ *...a four-nation regional meeting on elephant conservation.* ◙ N-UNCOUNT **Conservation** is saving and protecting historical objects or works of art such as paintings, sculptures, or buildings. ❑ *Then he began his most famous work, the conservation and rebinding of the Book of Kells.* ◚ N-UNCOUNT The **conservation** of a supply of something is the careful use of it so that it lasts for a long time. ❑ *...projects aimed at promoting energy conservation.*

con|ser|va|tion area (**conservation areas**) ◘ N-COUNT In Britain, a **conservation area** is an area where birds and animals are protected. ❑ *...wildlife conservation areas.* ◙ N-COUNT In Britain, a **conservation area** is an area where old buildings are protected and new building is controlled. ❑ *You don't need planning permission unless you live in a conservation area.*

con|ser|va|tion|ist /kɒnsərveɪʃənɪst/ (**conservationists**) N-COUNT A **conservationist** is someone who cares very much about the conservation of the environment and who works to protect it. ❑ *Conservationists say the law must be strengthened.*

con|ser|va|tism /kənsɜrvətɪzəm/ ◘ N-UNCOUNT **Conservatism** is a political philosophy which believes that if changes need to be made to society, they should be made gradually. You can also refer to the political beliefs of a conservative party in a particular country as **conservatism**. ❑ *...the philosophy of modern conservatism.* ◙ N-UNCOUNT **Conservatism** is unwillingness to accept changes and new ideas. ❑ *The conservatism of the literary establishment in this country is astounding.*

con|serva|tive ♦♦◇ /kənsɜrvətɪv/ (**conservatives**)

> The spelling **Conservative** is also used for meaning ◾.

◘ ADJ Someone who is **conservative** has views that are toward the political right. In the U.S. the Republicans are more conservative than the Democrats, who are more liberal. ❑ *...counties whose citizens invariably support the most conservative candidate in any election.* • N-COUNT **Conservative** is also a noun. ❑ *The new judge is 50-year-old David Suitor, who's regarded as a conservative.* ◙ ADJ Someone who is **conservative** or has **conservative** ideas is unwilling to accept changes and new ideas. ❑ *People tend to be more liberal when they're young and more conservative as they get older.* ◚ ADJ If someone dresses in a **conservative** way, their clothes are conventional in style. ❑ *The girl was well dressed, as usual, though in a more conservative style.* • **con|ser|va|tive|ly** ADV [ADV with v] ❑ *She was always very conservatively dressed when we went out.* ◛ ADJ A **conservative** estimate or guess is one in which you are cautious and estimate or guess a low amount which is probably less than the real amount. ❑ *The average fan spends $25 – a conservative estimate based on ticket price and souvenirs.* • **con|ser|va|tive|ly** ADV [ADV with v] ❑ *The bequest is conservatively estimated at $30 million.* ◾ ADJ A **Conservative** politician or voter is a member of or votes for the Conservative Party in Britain and in various other countries. ❑ *Most Conservative MPs appear happy with the government's reassurances.* • N-COUNT **Conservative** is also a noun. ❑ *In 1951 the Conservatives were returned to power.*

---- SYNONYMS ----

conservative
ADJ ◙
traditional: *...traditional parents, who believed in laying down the law for their children.*
conventional: *...a respectable, married woman with conventional opinions.*
proper: *It is right and proper to do this.*
correct: *I think English men are very polite and very correct.*
genteel: *...two women with genteel manners and voices.*

con|ser|va|tor /kənsɜrvətər/ (**conservators**) N-COUNT A **conservator** is someone whose job is to clean and repair historical objects or works of art.

con|serva|tory /kənsɜ́rvətɔri/ (**conservatories**) **1** N-COUNT; N-IN-NAMES A **conservatory** is an institution where musicians are trained. ❑ ...*the New England Conservatory of Music.* **2** N-COUNT A **conservatory** is a room with glass walls and a glass roof, which is attached to a house. People often grow plants in a conservatory.

con|serve /kənsɜ́rv/ (**conserves, conserving, conserved**) **1** V-T If you **conserve** a supply of something, you use it carefully so that it lasts for a long time. ❑ *The factories have closed for the weekend to conserve energy.* **2** V-T To **conserve** something means to protect it from harm, loss, or change. ❑ *...a big increase in U.S. aid to help developing countries conserve their forests.*

con|sid|er ✦✦✦ /kənsɪ́dər/ (**considers, considering, considered**) **1** V-T If you **consider** a person or thing to be something, you have the opinion that this is what they are. ❑ *We don't consider our customers to be mere consumers; we consider them to be our friends.* ❑ *I had always considered myself a strong, competent woman.* **2** V-T If you **consider** something, you think about it carefully. ❑ *The administration continues to consider ways to resolve the situation.* ❑ *You do have to consider the feelings of those around you.* **3** V-T If you **are considering** doing something, you intend to do it, but have not yet made a final decision whether to do it. ❑ *I had seriously considered telling the story from the point of view of the wives.* **4** → see also **considering**

con|sid|er|able ✦✦ /kənsɪ́dərəbəl/ ADJ **Considerable** means great in amount or degree. [FORMAL] ❑ *To be without Pearce would be a considerable blow.* ❑ *Doing it properly makes considerable demands on our time.* • **con|sid|er|ably** ADV ❑ *Children vary considerably in the rate at which they learn these lessons.*

SYNONYMS

considerable
ADJ
marked: *There has been a marked increase in crimes against property.*
substantial: *That is a very substantial improvement in the present situation.*
reasonable: *They will need a reasonable amount of desk area and good light.*
appreciable: *This has not had an appreciable effect on production.*
sizeable: *Harry inherited the house and a sizeable chunk of land.*

con|sid|er|ate /kənsɪ́dərɪt/ ADJ Someone who is **considerate** pays attention to the needs, wishes, or feelings of other people. [APPROVAL] ❑ *I think he's the most charming, most considerate man I've ever known.*

con|sid|era|tion ✦✧ /kənsɪ̀dəreɪ́ʃən/ (**considerations**) **1** N-UNCOUNT **Consideration** is careful thought about something. ❑ *There should be careful consideration about the use of such toxic chemicals.* **2** N-UNCOUNT If something is **under consideration**, it is being discussed. ❑ *Several proposals are under consideration by the state assembly.* **3** N-UNCOUNT If you show **consideration**, you pay attention to the needs, wishes, or feelings of other people. ❑ *Show consideration for your neighbors.* **4** N-COUNT A **consideration** is something that should be thought about, especially when you are planning or deciding something. ❑ *Price has become a more important consideration for shoppers in choosing which store to visit than it was before the recession.* **5** PHRASE If you **take** something **into consideration**, you think about it because it is relevant to what you are doing. ❑ *Safe driving is good driving because it takes into consideration the lives of other people.*

con|sid|ered /kənsɪ́dərd/ **1** ADJ [ADJ n] A **considered** opinion or act is the result of careful thought. ❑ *We would hope to be able to give a considered response to the unions' proposals by the end of the year.* **2** → see also **consider**

con|sid|er|ing ✦✧ /kənsɪ́dərɪŋ/ **1** PREP You use **considering** to indicate that you are thinking about a particular fact when making a judgment or giving an opinion. ❑ *He must be hoping, but considering the situation in June he may be hoping for too much too soon.* **2** CONJ You use **considering that** to indicate that you are thinking about a particular fact when making a judgment or giving an opinion. ❑ *Considering that you are no longer involved with this man, your response is a little extreme.* **3** ADV [cl ADV] When you are giving an opinion or making a judgment, you can use **considering** to suggest that you have thought about all the circumstances, and often that something has succeeded in spite of these circumstances. [SPOKEN] ❑ *I think you're pretty safe, considering.*

con|sign /kənsaɪ́n/ (**consigns, consigning, consigned**) V-T To **consign** something or someone to a place where they will be forgotten about, or to an unpleasant situation or place, means to put them there. [FORMAL] ❑ *For decades, many of Malevich's works were consigned to the basements of Soviet museums.*

con|sign|ment /kənsaɪ́nmənt/ (**consignments**) **1** N-COUNT A **consignment** of goods is a load that is being delivered to a place or person. ❑ *The first consignment of food was flown in yesterday.* **2** PHRASE If goods are sold **on consignment**, the owner is given a percentage of the price once they are sold. ❑ *She sold clothes on consignment to benefit homeless people.*

con|sist ✦✧ /kənsɪ́st/ (**consists, consisting, consisted**) **1** V-I Something that **consists of** particular things or people is formed from them. ❑ *My diet consisted almost exclusively of chocolate-covered cookies and glasses of milk.* **2** V-I Something that **consists in** something else has that thing as its main or only part. ❑ *His work as a consultant consisted in advising foreign companies on the siting of new factories.*

SYNONYMS

consist of
VERB **1**
be made (out) of: *The top of the table is made of glass.*
contain: *Greek yogurt contains much less fat than double cream.*
comprise: *The exhibition comprises 50 oils and watercolors.*
be composed of: *The force would be composed of troops from NATO countries.*

con|sist|en|cy /kənsɪ́stənsi/ **1** N-UNCOUNT **Consistency** is the quality or condition of being consistent. ❑ *She scores goals with remarkable consistency.* **2** N-UNCOUNT The **consistency** of a substance is how thick or smooth it is. ❑ *Dilute the paint with water until it is the consistency of milk.*

con|sist|ent ✦✧ /kənsɪ́stənt/ **1** ADJ Someone who is **consistent** always behaves in the same way, has the same attitudes toward people or things, or achieves the same level of success in something. ❑ *He was never the most consistent of players anyway.* • **con|sist|ent|ly** ADV ❑ *It's something I have consistently denied.* **2** ADJ [v-link ADJ, usu ADJ with n] If one fact or idea is **consistent** with another, they do not contradict each other. ❑ *This result is consistent with the findings of Garnett & Tobin.* **3** ADJ An argument or set of ideas that is **consistent** is one in which no part contradicts or conflicts with any other part. ❑ *A theory should be internally consistent.*

SYNONYMS

consistent
ADJ **1**
constant: *He has been her constant companion for the last four months.*
steady: *...a politician who's steady, almost to the point of being boring.*
reliable: *She was efficient and reliable.*
dependable: *He was a good friend, a dependable companion.*

con|so|la|tion prize (**consolation prizes**) **1** N-COUNT A **consolation prize** is a small prize which is given to a person who fails to win a competition. **2** N-COUNT A **consolation prize** is something that is arranged for or is given to a person to make them feel happier when they have failed to achieve something better. ❑ *Her appointment was seen as a consolation prize after she lost the election.*

con|sole (**consoles, consoling, consoled**)

The verb is pronounced /kənsoʊ́l/. The noun is pronounced /kɒ́nsoʊl/.

1 V-T If you **console** someone who is unhappy about something, you try to make them feel more cheerful. ❑ *"Never mind, Ned," he consoled me.* ❑ *I can console myself with the fact that I'm not alone.* • **con|so|la|tion** /kɒ̀nsəleɪ́ʃən/ (**consolations**) N-VAR ❑ *The only consolation for the baseball team is that they look likely to get another chance.* **2** N-COUNT A **console** is a panel with a number of switches or knobs that is used to operate a machine. ❑ *Several nurses sat before a console of flickering lights and bleeping monitors.*

con|soli|date /kənsplɪdeɪt/ (**consolidates, consolidating, consolidated**) ◼ V-T If you **consolidate** something that you have, for example power or success, you strengthen it so that it becomes more effective or secure. ◻ *The question is: will the junta consolidate its power by force?* ◼ V-T To **consolidate** a number of small groups or companies means to make them into one large organization. ◻ *Judge Charles Schwartz is giving the state 60 days to disband and consolidate Louisiana's four higher education boards.*

con|som|mé /kɒnsəmeɪ/ (**consommés**) N-MASS [oft n n] Consommé is a thin, clear soup, usually made from meat juices. ◻ *...chicken consommé.*

con|so|nant /kɒnsənənt/ (**consonants**) N-COUNT A **consonant** is a sound such as 'p,' 'f,' 'n,' or 't' which you pronounce by stopping the air flowing freely through your mouth. Compare **vowel**.

con|sort (**consorts, consorting, consorted**)

> The verb is pronounced /kənsɔrt/. The noun is pronounced /kɒnsɔrt/.

◼ V-I If you say that someone **consorts with** a particular person or group, you mean that they spend a lot of time with them, and usually that you do not think this is a good thing. [FORMAL, DISAPPROVAL] ◻ *He regularly consorted with known drug-dealers.* ◼ N-COUNT; N-TITLE [oft n n] The ruling monarch's wife or husband is called their **consort**.

con|sor|tium /kənsɔrʃiəm, -ti-/ (**consortia** /kənsɔrʃiə, -ti-/ or **consortiums**) N-COUNT-COLL A **consortium** is a group of people or firms who have agreed to cooperate with each other. [FORMAL] ◻ *The consortium includes some of the biggest building contractors in North America.*

con|spicu|ous /kənspɪkyuəs/ ADJ If someone or something is **conspicuous**, people can see or notice them very easily. ◻ *Most people don't want to be too conspicuous.* ● **con|spicu|ous|ly** ADV ◻ *Britain continues to follow U.S. policy in this and other areas where American policies have most conspicuously failed.*

con|spicu|ous con|sump|tion N-UNCOUNT **Conspicuous consumption** means spending your money in such a way that other people can see how wealthy you are. ◻ *It was an age of conspicuous consumption – those who had money liked to display it.*

con|spira|cy /kənspɪrəsi/ (**conspiracies**) ◼ N-VAR **Conspiracy** is secret planning by a group of people to do something illegal. ◻ *Seven men, all from North Carolina, admitted conspiracy to commit arson.* ◼ N-COUNT A **conspiracy** is an agreement between a group of people which other people think is wrong or is likely to be harmful. ◻ *It's all part of a conspiracy to dispense with the town center altogether and move everything out to the suburbs.*

con|spira|cy theo|rist (**conspiracy theorists**) N-COUNT A **conspiracy theorist** is someone who believes in or spreads conspiracy theories. You use this term to suggest that you think these people are wrong or mistaken. ◻ *The absence of any evidence for such a plot does not deter conspiracy theorists.* ◻ *He may be a brilliant film-maker, but he is also something of a conspiracy theorist.*

con|spira|cy theo|ry (**conspiracy theories**) N-COUNT A **conspiracy theory** is a belief that a group of people are secretly trying to harm someone or achieve something. You usually use this term to suggest that you think this is unlikely. ◻ *Did you ever swallow the conspiracy theory about Kennedy?*

con|spira|tor /kənspɪrətər/ (**conspirators**) N-COUNT A **conspirator** is a person who joins a conspiracy. ◻ *Julius Caesar was murdered by a group of conspirators famously headed by Marcus Junius Brutus.*

con|spira|to|rial /kənspɪrətɔriəl/ ADJ [usu ADJ n] If someone does something such as speak or smile in a **conspiratorial** way, they do it in a way that suggests they are sharing a secret with someone. ◻ *His voice had sunk to a conspiratorial whisper.*

con|spire /kənspaɪər/ (**conspires, conspiring, conspired**) ◼ V-RECIP If two or more people or groups **conspire** to do something illegal or harmful, they make a secret agreement to do it. ◻ *They'd conspired to overthrow the government.* ◻ *...a defendant accused of conspiring with his brother to commit robberies.* ◼ V-T/V-I If events **conspire** to produce a particular result, they seem to work together to cause this result. ◻ *History and geography have conspired to bring the country to a moment of decision.*

con|sta|ble /kʌnstəbəl, kɒn-/ (**constables**) ◼ N-COUNT; N-TITLE In the United States, a **constable** is an official who helps keep the peace in a town. They are lower in rank than a sheriff. ◻ *Courts and magistrates may be set up but they cannot function without sheriffs and constables.* ◼ N-COUNT; N-TITLE; N-VOC In Britain and some other countries, a **constable** is a police officer of the lowest rank.

con|stabu|lary /kənstæbyəleri/ (**constabularies**) ◼ N-COUNT In the United States, a **constabulary** is the constables in a particular area, or the area that they are responsible for. ◼ N-COUNT In Britain and some other countries, a **constabulary** is the police force of a particular area.

con|stan|cy /kɒnstənsi/ ◼ N-UNCOUNT **Constancy** is the quality of staying the same even though other things change. ◻ *We live in a world without constancy.* ◼ N-UNCOUNT **Constancy** is the quality of being faithful and loyal to a particular person or belief. [APPROVAL] ◻ *...those who have proved their constancy in love.* ◼ → See feature box at **time**

con|stant ✦✦◇ /kɒnstənt/ ◼ ADJ You use **constant** to describe something that happens all the time or is always there. ◻ *She suggests that women are under constant pressure to be abnormally thin.* ● *Inflation is a constant threat.* ● **con|stant|ly** ADV ◻ *The direction of the wind is constantly changing.* ◼ ADJ If an amount or level is **constant**, it stays the same over a particular period of time. ◻ *The body feels hot and the temperature remains more or less constant at the new elevated level.* ◼ → See feature box at **weather**

con|stel|la|tion /kɒnstəleɪʃən/ (**constellations**) N-COUNT A **constellation** is a group of stars which form a pattern and have a name. ◻ *...a planet orbiting a star in the constellation of Cepheus.*

con|ster|na|tion /kɒnstərneɪʃən/ N-UNCOUNT **Consternation** is a feeling of anxiety or fear. [FORMAL] ◻ *His decision caused consternation in the art photography community.*

con|sti|pat|ed /kɒnstɪpeɪtɪd/ ADJ [usu v-link ADJ] Someone who is **constipated** has difficulty in getting rid of solid waste from their body.

con|sti|pa|tion /kɒnstɪpeɪʃən/ N-UNCOUNT **Constipation** is a medical condition which causes people to have difficulty getting rid of solid waste from their body. ◻ *Do you suffer from constipation?*

con|stitu|en|cy /kənstɪtʃuənsi/ (**constituencies**) ◼ N-COUNT A particular **constituency** is a section of society that may give political support to a particular party or politician. ◻ *In Iowa, farmers are a powerful political constituency.* ◼ N-COUNT A **constituency** is an area for which someone is elected as the representative in a legislature or government. ◻ *Voters in 17 constituencies are going back to the polls today.*

con|stitu|ent /kənstɪtʃuənt/ (**constituents**) ◼ N-COUNT A **constituent** is someone who lives in a particular constituency, especially someone who is able to vote in an election. ◻ *He told his constituents that he would continue to represent them to the best of his ability.* ◼ N-COUNT A **constituent** of a mixture, substance, or system is one of the things from which it is formed. [FORMAL] ◻ *Caffeine is the active constituent of drinks such as tea and coffee.* ◼ ADJ [ADJ n] The **constituent** parts of something are the things from which it is formed. [FORMAL] ◻ *...a plan to split the company into its constituent parts and sell them separately.*

con|stitu|ent as|sem|bly (**constituent assemblies**) N-COUNT A **constituent assembly** is a body of representatives that is elected to create or change their country's constitution.

con|sti|tute /kɒnstɪtut/ (**constitutes, constituting, constituted**) ◼ V-LINK [no cont] If something **constitutes** a particular thing, it can be regarded as being that thing. ◻ *Testing patients without their consent would constitute a professional and legal offense.* ◼ V-LINK [no cont] If a number of things or people **constitute** something, they are the parts or members that form it. ◻ *China's ethnic minorities constitute less than 7 percent of its total population.*

con|sti|tu|tion ✦◇◇ /kɒnstɪtuʃən/ (**constitutions**) ◼ N-COUNT The **constitution** of a country or organization is the system of laws which formally states people's rights and duties. ◻ *The king was forced to adopt a new constitution which reduced his* powers. **2** N-COUNT Your **constitution** is your health. ▫ *He must have an extremely strong constitution.*

SYNONYMS

constitution
NOUN **1**
code: *...Article 159 of the state's penal code.*
charter: *...the Social Charter of workers' rights.*

---

con|sti|tu|tion|al ✦◇◇ /kɒnstɪtuʃənᵊl/ ADJ **Constitutional** means relating to the constitution of a particular country or organization. ▫ *The issue is one of constitutional and civil rights.*

con|sti|tu|tion|al|ity /kɒnstɪtuʃənælɪti/ N-UNCOUNT [usu the N *of* n] In a particular political system, the **constitutionality** of a law or action is the fact that it is allowed by the constitution. [FORMAL] ▫ *They plan to challenge the constitutionality of the law.*

con|strain /kənstreɪn/ (**constrains**, **constraining**, **constrained**) V-T To **constrain** someone or something means to limit their development or force them to behave in a particular way. [FORMAL] ▫ *Many working parents are too often constrained by inflexible working hours.*

con|straint /kənstreɪnt/ (**constraints**) **1** N-COUNT A **constraint** is something that limits or controls what you can do. ▫ *Their decision to abandon the trip was made because of financial constraints.* **2** N-UNCOUNT **Constraint** is control over the way you behave which prevents you from doing what you want to do. ▫ *Journalists were given the freedom to visit, investigate, and report without constraint.*

con|strict /kənstrɪkt/ (**constricts**, **constricting**, **constricted**) **1** V-T/V-I If a part of your body, especially your throat, **is constricted** or if it **constricts**, something causes it to become narrower. ▫ *Severe migraines can be treated with a drug that constricts the blood vessels.* **2** V-T If something **constricts** you, it limits your actions so that you cannot do what you want to do. ▫ *She objects to the constant testing because it constricts her teaching style.*

con|stric|tion /kənstrɪkʃᵊn/ (**constrictions**) **1** N-COUNT [usu pl] **Constrictions** are rules or factors which limit what you can do and prevent you from doing what you want to do. [FORMAL] ▫ *I hated the constrictions of school.* **2** → see also **constrict**

con|struct /kənstrʌkt/ (**constructs**, **constructing**, **constructed**) **1** V-T If you **construct** something such as a building, road, or machine, you build it or make it. ▫ *His company recently constructed an office building in downtown Denver.* ▫ *The boxes should be constructed from rough-sawn timber.* **2** V-T If you **construct** something such as an idea, a piece of writing, or a system, you create it by putting different parts together. ▫ *He eventually constructed a huge business empire.* ▫ *The novel is constructed from a series of on-the-spot reports.*

con|struc|tion ✦◇◇ /kənstrʌkʃᵊn/ (**constructions**) **1** N-UNCOUNT **Construction** is the building of things such as houses, factories, roads, and bridges. ▫ *He'd already started construction on a hunting lodge.* ▫ *...the downturn in the construction industry.* ▫ *Jim now works in construction.* **2** N-UNCOUNT The **construction** of something such as a vehicle or machine is the making of it. ▫ *...companies who have long experience in the construction of those types of equipment.* **3** N-UNCOUNT The **construction** of something such as a system is the creation of it. ▫ *...the construction of a just system of criminal justice.* **4** N-UNCOUNT You use **construction** to refer to the structure of something and the way it has been built or made. ▫ *The Shakers believed that furniture should be plain, simple, useful, practical, and of sound construction.* **5** N-COUNT You can refer to an object that has been built or made as a **construction**. ▫ *...an impressive steel and glass construction.* **6** N-COUNT A grammatical **construction** is a particular arrangement of words in a sentence, clause, or phrase. ▫ *Avoid complex verbal constructions.*

con|struc|tion pa|per N-UNCOUNT **Construction paper** is a type of stiff, colored paper that children use for drawing and for making things. [AM] ▫ *...a raggedy, three-legged animal cut out of brown construction paper.*

con|struc|tive /kənstrʌktɪv/ ADJ A **constructive** discussion, comment, or approach is useful and helpful rather than negative and unhelpful. ▫ *She welcomes constructive criticism.* ▫ *After their meeting, both men described the talks as frank, friendly and constructive.*

con|struc|tive dis|charge N-UNCOUNT If an employee claims **constructive discharge**, they begin a legal action against their employer in which they claim that they were forced to leave their job because of the behavior of their employer. [BUSINESS] ▫ *The woman claims she was the victim of constructive discharge after being demoted.*

con|struc|tor /kənstrʌktər/ (**constructors**) N-COUNT A racing car **constructor** or aircraft **constructor** is a company that builds cars or aircraft.

con|strue /kənstru/ (**construes**, **construing**, **construed**) V-T If something **is construed** in a particular way, its nature or meaning is interpreted in that way. [FORMAL] ▫ *What may seem helpful behavior to you can be construed as interference by others.* ▫ *He may construe the approach as a hostile act.*

con|sul /kɒnsᵊl/ (**consuls**) N-COUNT; N-TITLE A **consul** is an official who is sent by his or her government to live in a foreign city in order to help other citizens from his or her country who are in that foreign city. ▫ *...Stephanie Sweet, the British Consul in Tangier.*

con|su|lar /kɒnsələr/ ADJ [ADJ n] **Consular** means involving or relating to a consul or the work of a consul. ▫ *U.S. consular officials have visited the men, although they have not yet had access to lawyers.*

con|su|late /kɒnsəlɪt/ (**consulates**) N-COUNT A **consulate** is the place where a consul works. ▫ *...the Canadian consulate in Seattle.*

con|sult ✦◇◇ /kənsʌlt/ (**consults**, **consulting**, **consulted**) **1** V-T/V-I If you **consult** an expert or someone senior to you or **consult** with them, you ask them for their opinion, advice, or permission. ▫ *Consult your doctor about how much exercise you should get.* ▫ *He needed to consult with an attorney.* **2** V-T If you **consult** a book or a map, you look in it or look at it in order to find some information. ▫ *Consult the chart on page 44 for the correct cooking times.* **3** V-RECIP If a person or group of people **consults** with other people or **consults** them, or if two people or groups **consult**, they talk and exchange ideas and opinions about what they might decide to do. ▫ *After consulting with her daughter and manager, she decided to take on the part, on her terms.* ▫ *The two countries will have to consult their allies.*

SYNONYMS

consult
VERB **2**
confer: *He conferred with Hill and the others in his office.*
debate: *He likes to debate issues with his friends.*
deliberate: *The jury deliberated about two hours before returning with the verdict.*
discuss: *The cabinet met today to discuss how to respond to the ultimatum.*

---

con|sul|tan|cy /kənsʌltənsi/ (**consultancies**) **1** N-COUNT A **consultancy** is a company that gives expert advice on a particular subject. ▫ *A survey of 57 hospitals by Newchurch, a consultancy, reveals striking improvements.* **2** N-UNCOUNT **Consultancy** is expert advice on a particular subject which a person or group is paid to provide to a company or organization. [mainly BRIT]

con|sult|ant ✦◇◇ /kənsʌltənt/ (**consultants**) **1** N-COUNT A **consultant** is a person who gives expert advice to a person or organization on a particular subject. ▫ *She is a consultant to the government.* **2** N-COUNT A **consultant** is an experienced doctor with a high position, who specializes in one area of medicine. [BRIT]

in AM, usually use **specialist**

SYNONYMS

consultant
NOUN **2**
specialist: *...a specialist in aviation law.*
adviser: *...a career adviser.*
authority: *He's universally recognized as an authority on Russian affairs.*
expert: *...an expert on trade in that area.*

---

con|sul|ta|tion /kɒnsəlteɪʃᵊn/ (**consultations**) **1** N-VAR A **consultation** is a meeting to discuss something. **Consultation**

is discussion about something. ❑ *Next week he'll be in Florida for consultations with President Vicente Fox.* **2** N-VAR A **consultation** with a doctor or other expert is a meeting with them to discuss a particular problem and get their advice. **Consultation** is the process of getting advice from a doctor or other expert. ❑ *A personal diet plan is devised after a consultation with a nutritionist.* **3** N-COUNT A **consultation** is a meeting where several doctors discuss a patient and his or her condition and treatment. [AM]

con|sul|ta|tive /kənsʌltətɪv/ ADJ A **consultative** committee or document gives advice or makes proposals about a particular problem or subject. ❑ *...the consultative committee on local government finance.*

con|sult|ing room (**consulting rooms**) N-COUNT A **consulting room** is the same as a **doctor's office**. [BRIT]

con|sum|able /kənsuːməbəl/ (**consumables**) ADJ **Consumable** goods are items which are intended to be bought, used, and then replaced. ❑ *...demand for consumable articles.* • N-COUNT **Consumable** is also a noun. ❑ *Suppliers add computer consumables, office equipment and furniture to their product range.*

con|sume /kənsuːm/ (**consumes, consuming, consumed**) **1** V-T If you **consume** something, you eat or drink it. [FORMAL] ❑ *Martha would consume nearly a pound of cheese per day.* **2** V-T To **consume** an amount of fuel, energy, or time means to use it up. ❑ *Some of the most efficient refrigerators consume 70 percent less electricity than traditional models.* **3** → see also **consuming**

con|sumed /kənsuːmd/ ADJ [v-link ADJ with/by n] If you are **consumed** with a feeling or idea, it affects you very strongly. [LITERARY] ❑ *They are consumed with jealousy at her success.*

con|sum|er ✦✦◇ /kənsuːmər/ (**consumers**) **1** N-COUNT A **consumer** is a person who buys things or uses services. ❑ *...claims that tobacco companies failed to warn consumers about the dangers of smoking.* **2** → See feature box at **service**

SYNONYMS

consumer
NOUN **1**

buyer: *Car buyers are more interested in safety and reliability than speed.*
customer: *Our customers have very tight budgets.*

---

con|sum|er con|fi|dence N-UNCOUNT If there is **consumer confidence**, people generally are willing to spend money and buy things. ❑ *The Fed is keen to ensure that rising joblessness does not hit consumer confidence in the new year.*

con|sum|er cred|it N-UNCOUNT **Consumer credit** is money that is lent to people by organizations such as banks and stores so that they can buy things. ❑ *New consumer credit fell to $3.7 billion in August.*

con|sum|er du|rable (**consumer durables**) N-COUNT **Consumer durables** are goods which are expected to last a long time, and are bought infrequently. [BRIT, BUSINESS]

in AM, use **durable goods**

con|sum|er goods N-PLURAL **Consumer goods** are goods bought by people for their own use, rather than by businesses. Compare **capital goods**. [BUSINESS] ❑ *The choice of consumer goods available in local shops is small.*

con|sum|er|ism /kənsuːmərɪzəm/ **1** N-UNCOUNT [oft supp N] **Consumerism** is the belief that it is good to buy and use a lot of goods. ❑ *They have clearly embraced Western consumerism.* **2** N-UNCOUNT **Consumerism** is the protection of the rights and interests of consumers.

con|sum|er|ist /kənsuːmərɪst/ ADJ [usu ADJ n] **Consumerist** economies are ones which encourage people to consume a lot of goods. [BUSINESS, DISAPPROVAL] ❑ *...our consumerist society.*

con|sum|er price in|dex N-SING [usu the N] The **consumer price index** is an official measure of the rate of inflation within a country's economy. The abbreviation **CPI** is also used. ❑ *In May the consumer price index fell by 1.1 per cent.*

con|sum|er so|ci|ety (**consumer societies**) N-COUNT You can use **consumer society** to refer to a society where people think that spending money on goods and services is very important. ❑ *We live in a consumer society in which money is a massive preoccupation.*

con|sum|ing /kənsuːmɪŋ/ **1** ADJ A **consuming** passion or interest is more important to you than anything else. ❑ *He has developed a consuming passion for chess.* **2** → see also **consume, time-consuming**

con|sum|mate (**consummates, consummating, consummated**)

The adjective is pronounced /kɒnsəmɪt, kənsʌmɪt/. The verb is pronounced /kɒnsəmeɪt/.

1 ADJ You use **consummate** to describe someone who is extremely skillful. [FORMAL] ❑ *He acted the part with consummate skill.* **2** V-T If two people **consummate** a marriage or relationship, they make it complete by having sex. [FORMAL] ❑ *His wife divorced him for failing to consummate their marriage.*

con|sump|tion /kənsʌmpʃən/ **1** N-UNCOUNT The **consumption** of fuel or natural resources is the act of using them or the amount used. ❑ *The laws have led to a reduction in fuel consumption in the U.S.* **2** N-UNCOUNT The **consumption** of food or drink is the act of eating or drinking something, or the amount eaten or drunk. [FORMAL] ❑ *Most of the wine was unfit for human consumption.* **3** N-UNCOUNT **Consumption** is the act of buying and using things. ❑ *They were prepared to put people out of work and reduce consumption by strangling the whole economy.* **4** → See feature box at **recycle**

con|sump|tive /kənsʌmptɪv/ ADJ [usu ADJ n] A **consumptive** person has **tuberculosis**. [OLD-FASHIONED]

cont. Cont. is an abbreviation for 'continued,' which is used at the bottom of a page to indicate that a letter or text continues on another page.

con|tact ✦✦◇ /kɒntækt/ (**contacts, contacting, contacted**) **1** N-UNCOUNT [also N in pl, oft N with/between n] **Contact** involves meeting or communicating with someone, especially regularly. ❑ *Opposition leaders are denying any contact with the government in Kabul.* **2** N-UNCOUNT If you come **into contact with** someone or something, you meet that person or thing in the course of your work or other activities. ❑ *Doctors I came into contact with voiced their concern.* **3** N-UNCOUNT When people or things are in **contact**, they are touching each other. ❑ *They compared how these organisms behaved when left in contact with different materials.* ❑ *The cry occurs when air is brought into contact with the baby's larynx.* **4** ADJ [ADJ n] Your **contact** details or number are information such as a telephone number where you can be contacted. ❑ *You must leave your full name and contact details when you phone.* **5** PHRASE If you are **in contact** with someone, you regularly meet them or communicate with them. If you **get in contact** with someone, you start to communicate with them. ❑ *He was in direct contact with the kidnappers.* ❑ *Perhaps you can help us to get in contact with her.* **6** PHRASE If you **make contact** with someone, you find out where they are and talk or write to them. ❑ *How did you make contact with the author?* **7** PHRASE If you **lose contact** with someone who you have been friendly with, you no longer see them, speak to them, or write to them. ❑ *Though they all live nearby, I lost contact with them really quickly.* **8** V-T If you **contact** someone, you telephone them, write to them, or go to see them in order to tell or ask them something. ❑ *Contact the Women's Alliance for further details.* **9** N-COUNT A **contact** is someone you know in an organization or profession who helps you or gives you information. ❑ *Their contact at the United States embassy was Phillip Norton.*

con|tact lens (**contact lenses**) **1** N-COUNT **Contact lenses** are small plastic lenses that you put on the surface of your eyes to help you see better, instead of wearing glasses. **2** → See feature box at **eyesight**

con|tact|less /kɒntæktlɪs/ ADJ A **contactless** credit card or payment system uses technology that recognizes electronic data, and does not require the customer's signature or personal identification number. ❑ *The new system is designed to provide contactless transit cards for use on trains and buses.*

con|tact trac|ing N-UNCOUNT **Contact tracing** is an attempt to control the spread of an infectious disease by identifying and isolating people who have come into contact with it. ❑ *Contact tracing is a central pillar of fighting Ebola.*

con|ta|gion /kənteɪdʒən/ N-UNCOUNT **Contagion** is the spreading of a particular disease by someone touching another person who is already affected by the disease. ❑ *They have been reluctant to admit AIDS patients, in part because of unfounded fears of contagion.*

con|ta|gious /kənteɪdʒəs/ **1** ADJ A disease that is **contagious** can be caught by touching people or things that are infected with it. Compare **infectious**. ❏ ...a highly contagious disease of the lungs. **2** ADJ A feeling or attitude that is **contagious** spreads quickly among a group of people. ❏ Laughing is contagious. **3** → See feature box at **illness**

con|tain ✦✧✧ /kənteɪn/ (**contains, containing, contained**) **1** V-T [no cont] If something such as a box, bag, room, or place **contains** things, those things are inside it. ❏ The envelope contained a Christmas card. ❏ The first two floors of the building contain retail space and a restaurant. **2** V-T [no cont] If a substance **contains** something, that thing is a part of it. ❏ Watermelon contains vitamins and also potassium. **3** V-T [no cont] If writing, speech, or film **contains** particular information, ideas, or images, it includes them. ❏ This sheet contained a list of problems a patient might like to raise with the doctor. **4** V-T [no cont] If a group or organization **contains** a certain number of people, those are the people that are in it. ❏ The committee contains 11 Democrats and nine Republicans. **5** V-T If you **contain** something, you control it and prevent it from spreading or increasing. ❏ More than a hundred firemen are still trying to contain the fire at the plant. **6** → see also **self-contained**

SYNONYMS

contain
VERB **1**
hold: The small bottles don't seem to hold much.
include: The list includes many British internationals.
accommodate: The school was not big enough to accommodate all the children.
enclose: Enclose the pot in a clear polyethylene bag.

---

con|tain|er /kənteɪnər/ (**containers**) **1** N-COUNT A **container** is something such as a box or bottle that is used to hold or store things in. ❏ ...the plastic containers in which fish are stored and sold. **2** N-COUNT A **container** is a very large metal or wooden box used for transporting goods so that they can be loaded easily onto ships and trucks. ❏ The train, carrying loaded containers on flatcars, was 1.2 miles long.

con|tain|er ship (**container ships**) N-COUNT A **container ship** is a ship that is designed for carrying goods that are packed in large metal or wooden boxes.

con|tain|ment /kənteɪnmənt/ **1** N-UNCOUNT **Containment** is the action or policy of keeping another country's power or area of control within acceptable limits or boundaries. **2** N-UNCOUNT [usu N of n] The **containment** of something dangerous or unpleasant is the act or process of keeping it under control within a particular area or place. ❏ Fire crews are hoping they can achieve full containment of the fire before the winds pick up.

con|tami|nant /kəntæmɪnənt/ (**contaminants**) N-COUNT [usu pl] A **contaminant** is something that contaminates a substance such as water or food. [FORMAL] ❏ Contaminants found in poultry will also be found in their eggs.

con|tami|nate /kəntæmɪneɪt/ (**contaminates, contaminating, contaminated**) V-T If something **is contaminated** by dirt, chemicals, or radiation, they make it dirty or harmful. ❏ Have any fish been contaminated in the Arctic Ocean? ● **con|tami|na|tion** /kəntæmɪneɪʃən/ N-UNCOUNT ❏ The contamination of the ocean around Puget Sound may be just the beginning.

con|tem|plate /kɒntəmpleɪt/ (**contemplates, contemplating, contemplated**) **1** V-T If you **contemplate** an action, you think about whether to do it or not. ❏ For a time he contemplated a career as an army medical doctor. **2** V-T If you **contemplate** an idea or subject, you think about it carefully for a long time. ❏ As he lay in his hospital bed that night, he cried as he contemplated his future. ● **con|tem|pla|tion** /kɒntəmpleɪʃən/ N-UNCOUNT ❏ It is a place of quiet contemplation. **3** V-T If you **contemplate** something or someone, you look at them for a long time. ❏ He contemplated his hands, still frowning. ● **con|tem|pla|tion** N-UNCOUNT ❏ He was lost in the contemplation of the landscape for a while. **4** → See feature box at **personality**

con|tem|pla|tive /kəntɛmplətɪv/ ADJ Someone who is **contemplative** thinks deeply, or is thinking in a serious and calm way. ❏ Martin is a quiet, contemplative sort of child.

con|tem|po|ra|neous /kəntɛmpəreɪniəs/ ADJ If two events or situations are **contemporaneous**, they happen or exist during the same period of time. [FORMAL] ❏ ...the contemporaneous development of a separate and recognizable American school of art.

con|tem|po|rary ✦✧✧ /kəntɛmpəreri/ (**contemporaries**) **1** ADJ **Contemporary** things are modern and relate to the present time. ❏ She writes a lot of contemporary music for people like Whitney Houston. **2** ADJ **Contemporary** people or things were alive or happened at the same time as something else you are talking about. ❏ ...drawing upon official records and the reports of contemporary witnesses. **3** N-COUNT Someone's **contemporary** is a person who is or was alive at the same time as them. ❏ Like most of my contemporaries, I grew up in a vastly different world.

SYNONYMS

contemporary
ADJ **1**
modern: ...the problem of materialism in modern society.
current: Current thinking suggests that toxins only have a small part to play.
up-to-date: ...Germany's most up-to-date electric power station.
recent: Sales have fallen by more than 75 percent in recent years.
present-day: Even by present-day standards, these were large aircraft.

---

con|tempt /kəntɛmpt/ N-UNCOUNT If you have **contempt** for someone or something, you have no respect for them or think that they are unimportant. ❏ He has contempt for those beyond his immediate family circle.

con|tempt|ible /kəntɛmptɪbəl/ ADJ If you feel that someone or something is **contemptible**, you feel strong dislike and disrespect for them. [FORMAL] ❏ ...this contemptible act of violence.

con|tempt of court N-UNCOUNT **Contempt of court** is the criminal offense of disobeying an instruction from a judge or a court of law. [LEGAL] ❏ He faced imprisonment for contempt of court.

con|temp|tu|ous /kəntɛmptʃuəs/ ADJ If you are **contemptuous** of someone or something, you do not like or respect them at all. ❏ He was contemptuous of the poor. ❏ He's openly contemptuous of all the major political parties.

con|tend /kəntɛnd/ (**contends, contending, contended**) **1** V-I If you have to **contend with** a problem or difficulty, you have to deal with it or overcome it. ❏ It is time, once again, to contend with racism. **2** V-T If you **contend** that something is true, you state or argue that it is true. [FORMAL] ❏ The government contends that he is fundamentalist. **3** V-RECIP If you **contend** with someone for something such as power, you compete with them to try to get it. ❏ ...the two main groups contending for power. ❏ Small-market clubs such as the Kansas City Royals have had trouble contending with richer teams for championships.

con|tend|er /kəntɛndər/ (**contenders**) N-COUNT A **contender** is someone who takes part in a competition. [JOURNALISM] ❏ Her trainer said yesterday that she would be a strong contender for a place on the Olympic team.

CONTENT
① NOUN USES
② ADJECTIVE USES

---

① **con|tent** ✦✧✧ /kɒntɛnt/ (**contents**) **1** N-PLURAL The **contents** of a container such as a bottle, box, or room are the things that are inside it. ❏ Empty the contents of the pan into the sieve. **2** N-PLURAL The **contents** of a book are its different chapters and sections, usually shown in a list at the beginning of the book. ❏ There is no Table of Contents. **3** N-UNCOUNT [also N in pl, usu N of n] If you refer to the **content** or **contents** of something such as a book, television program, or website, you are referring to the subject that it deals with, the story that it tells, or the ideas that it expresses. ❏ She is reluctant to discuss the content of the play. ❏ Stricter controls were placed on the content of videos. **4** N-UNCOUNT The **content** of something such as an educational course or a program of action is the elements that it consists of. ❏ Previous students have had nothing but praise for the course content and staff. **5** N-SING You can use **content** to refer to the amount or proportion of something that a substance contains. ❏ Sunflower margarine has the same fat content as butter.

②**con|tent** /kəntɛnt/
→ Please look at meaning ❸ to see if the expression you are looking for is shown under another headword.

1 ADJ [v-link ADJ] If you are **content** with something, you are willing to accept it, rather than wanting something more or something better. ☐ *I am content to admire the mountains from below.* ☐ *I'm perfectly content with the way the campaign has gone.*
2 ADJ [v-link ADJ] If you are **content**, you are fairly happy or satisfied. ☐ *He says his daughter is quite content.* **3 to your heart's content** → see **heart** ② **4** → See feature box at **emotion**

con|tent|ed /kəntɛntɪd/ ADJ If you are **contented**, you are satisfied with your life or the situation you are in. ☐ *Whenever he returns to this place, he is happy and contented.*

con|ten|tion /kəntɛnʃən/ (**contentions**) **1** N-COUNT Someone's **contention** is the idea or opinion that they are expressing in an argument or discussion. ☐ *It is my contention that death and murder always lurk as potentials in violent relationships.*
2 N-UNCOUNT If something is a cause of **contention**, it is a cause of disagreement or argument. ☐ *His case has become a source of contention between civil liberties activists and the government.*
3 → see also **bone of contention**

con|ten|tious /kəntɛnʃəs/ ADJ A **contentious** issue causes a lot of disagreement or arguments. [FORMAL] ☐ *Sanctions are expected to be among the most contentious issues.*

con|tent|ment /kəntɛntmənt/ N-UNCOUNT **Contentment** is a feeling of quiet happiness and satisfaction. ☐ *I cannot describe the feeling of contentment that was with me at that time.*

con|tent pro|vid|er (**content providers**) N-COUNT A **content provider** is a company that supplies material such as text, music, or images for use on websites. [COMPUTING] ☐ *...content providers such as MSN and Freeserve.*

con|test ✦✧ (**contests, contesting, contested**)
The noun is pronounced /kɒntɛst/. The verb is pronounced /kəntɛst/.

1 N-COUNT A **contest** is a competition or game that people try to win. ☐ *Few contests in the recent history of boxing have been as thrilling.* **2** N-COUNT A **contest** is a struggle to win power or control. ☐ *The state election in November will be the last such ballot before next year's presidential contest.* **3** V-T If you **contest** a statement or decision, you object to it formally because you think it is wrong or unreasonable. ☐ *Your former employer has to reply within 14 days in order to contest the case.* **4** V-T If someone **contests** an election or competition, they take part in it and try to win it. [BRIT] ☐ *He quickly won his party's nomination to contest the elections.*

con|test|ant /kəntɛstənt/ (**contestants**) N-COUNT A **contestant** in a competition or game show is a person who takes part in it. ☐ *Later he applied to be a contestant on the television show.*

con|text ✦✧ /kɒntɛkst/ (**contexts**) **1** N-VAR The **context** of an idea or event is the general situation that relates to it, and which helps it to be understood. ☐ *We are doing this work in the context of reforms in the economic, social and cultural spheres.* ☐ *It helps to understand the historical context in which Chaucer wrote.* **2** N-VAR The **context** of a word, sentence, or text consists of the words, sentences, or text before and after it which help to make its meaning clear. ☐ *Without a context, I would have assumed it was written by a man.* **3** PHRASE If something is seen **in context** or if it is put **into context**, it is considered together with all the factors that relate to it. ☐ *Taxation is not popular in principle, merely acceptable in context.* **4** PHRASE If a statement or remark is quoted **out of context**, the circumstances in which it was said are not correctly reported, so that it seems to mean something different from the meaning that was intended. ☐ *Thomas says that he has been quoted out of context.*

──── SYNONYMS ────
context
NOUN **1**
circumstances: *The strategy was too dangerous in the explosive circumstances of the times.*
times: *We are in one of the most severe recessions in modern times.*
conditions: *The conditions are ripe for the spread of disease.*
situation: *Army officers said the situation was under control.*

con|tex|tual /kəntɛkstʃuəl/ ADJ [usu ADJ n] A **contextual** issue or account relates to the context of something. [FORMAL] ☐ *The writer builds up a convincing contextual picture of life during the Civil War.*

con|tigu|ous /kəntɪɡjuəs/ ADJ [oft ADJ to/with n] Things that are **contiguous** are next to each other or touch each other. [FORMAL] ☐ *Its vineyards are virtually contiguous with those of Ausone.* ☐ *...two years of travel throughout the 48 contiguous states.*

con|ti|nent ✦✧✧ /kɒntɪnənt/ (**continents**) **1** N-COUNT A **continent** is a very large area of land, such as Africa or Asia, that consists of several countries. ☐ *She loved the African continent.*
2 N-PROPER People sometimes use **the Continent** to refer to the continent of Europe except for Britain. [mainly BRIT] ☐ *Its shops are among the most stylish on the Continent.* **3** → See also color supplement

con|ti|nen|tal /kɒntɪnɛntəl/ (**continentals**) **1** ADJ [ADJ n] **Continental** is used to refer to something that belongs to or relates to a continent. ☐ *The most ancient parts of the continental crust are 4000 million years old.* **2** ADJ The **continental** United States consists of all the states which are situated on the continent of North America, as opposed to Hawaii and territories such as the Virgin Islands. [mainly AM] ☐ *Shipping is included on orders sent within the continental U.S.* **3** ADJ [usu ADJ n] **Continental** means existing or happening in the American colonies during the American Revolution. [AM] ☐ *...George Washington, Commander of the Continental Army.* **4** ADJ [ADJ n] **Continental** means situated on or belonging to the continent of Europe except for Britain. [mainly BRIT] ☐ *He sees no signs of improvement in the U.K. and continental economy.* **5** N-COUNT **Continentals** were soldiers who fought in the Continental Army against the British in the American Revolution. [AM]

con|ti|nen|tal break|fast (**continental breakfasts**)
N-COUNT A **continental breakfast** is breakfast that consists of food such as bread, butter, jam, and a hot drink. There is no cooked food.

con|ti|nen|tal drift N-UNCOUNT **Continental drift** is the slow movement of the Earth's continents toward and away from each other.

con|ti|nen|tal shelf N-UNCOUNT The **continental shelf** is the area which forms the edge of a continent, ending in a steep slope to the depths of the ocean. ☐ *...the deep water off the Continental Shelf.*

con|tin|gen|cy /kəntɪndʒənsi/ (**contingencies**) **1** N-VAR A **contingency** is something that might happen in the future. [FORMAL] ☐ *I need to examine all possible contingencies.* **2** ADJ [ADJ n] A **contingency** plan or measure is one that is intended to be used if a possible situation actually occurs. [FORMAL] ☐ *We have contingency plans.*

con|tin|gent /kəntɪndʒənt/ (**contingents**) **1** N-COUNT A **contingent** of police, soldiers, or military vehicles is a group of them. [FORMAL] ☐ *Nigeria provided a large contingent of troops to the West African Peacekeeping Force.* **2** N-COUNT A **contingent** is a group of people representing a country or organization at a meeting or other event. [FORMAL] ☐ *The American contingent will stay overnight in London.*

con|tin|ual /kəntɪnjuəl/ **1** ADJ [ADJ n] A **continual** process or situation happens or exists without stopping. ☐ *The school has been in continual use since 1883.* ☐ *They felt continual pressure to perform well.* • **con|tinu|al|ly** ADV ☐ *She cried almost continually and threw temper tantrums.* **2** ADJ [ADJ n] **Continual** events happen again and again. ☐ *...the government's continual demands for cash to finance its chronic deficit.* • **con|tinu|al|ly** ADV ☐ *Malcolm was continually changing his mind.*

con|tinu|ance /kəntɪnjuəns/ N-UNCOUNT [usu with poss] The **continuance** of something is its continuation. [FORMAL] ☐ *...thus ensuring the continuance of the human species.*

con|tinu|ation /kəntɪnjueɪʃən/ (**continuations**) **1** N-VAR The **continuation** of something is the fact that it continues, instead of stopping. ☐ *It's the coalition forces who are to blame for the continuation of the war.* **2** N-COUNT Something that is a **continuation of** something else is closely connected with it or forms part of it. ☐ *This chapter is a continuation of Chapter 8.*

con|tinue ✦✦✦ /kəntɪnju/ (**continues, continuing, continued**)
1 V-T/V-I If someone or something **continues** to do something, they keep doing it and do not stop. ☐ *I hope they continue to fight*

for equal justice after I'm gone. ❑ Diana and Roy Jarvis are determined to continue working when they reach retirement age. ◼ V-T/V-I If something **continues** or if you **continue** it, it does not stop. ❑ He insisted that the conflict would continue until conditions were met for a ceasefire. ❑ Outside the building people continue their vigil, huddling around bonfires. ◼ V-T/V-I If you **continue** something or **continue** with something, you start doing it again after a break or interruption. ❑ I went up to my room to continue with my packing. ❑ She looked up for a minute and then continued drawing. ◼ V-T/V-I If something **continues** or if you **continue** it, it starts again after a break or interruption. ❑ He denies 18 charges. The trial continues today. ◼ V-T/V-I If you **continue**, you begin speaking again after a pause or interruption. ❑ "You have no right to intimidate this man," Alison continued. ❑ Tony drank some coffee before he continued. ◼ V-I If you **continue** as something or **continue** in a particular state, you remain in a particular job or state. ❑ He had hoped to continue as a full-time career officer. ◼ V-I If you **continue** in a particular direction, you keep walking or traveling in that direction. ❑ He continued rapidly up the path, not pausing until he neared the Chapter House.

con|tinu|ing edu|ca|tion N-UNCOUNT **Continuing education** is education for adults in a variety of subjects.

con|ti|nu|ity /kɒntɪnuːɪti/ (**continuities**) N-VAR **Continuity** is the fact that something continues to happen or exist, with no great changes or interruptions. ❑ ...a tank designed to ensure continuity of fuel supply during aerobatics.

con|tinu|ous /kəntɪnjuəs/ ◼ ADJ A **continuous** process or event continues for a period of time without stopping. ❑ Residents report that they heard continuous gunfire. ● **con|tinu|ous|ly** ADV ❑ The civil war has raged almost continuously since 1976. ◼ ADJ A **continuous** line or surface has no gaps or holes in it. ❑ ...a continuous line of boats. ◼ ADJ In English grammar, **continuous** verb groups are formed using the auxiliary 'be' and the present participle of a verb, as in 'I'm feeling a bit tired' and 'She had been watching them for some time.' Continuous verb groups are used especially when you are focusing on a particular moment. Compare **simple**.

con|tin|uum /kəntɪnjuəm/ (**continua** /kəntɪnjuə/ or **continuums**) N-COUNT [usu sing] A **continuum** is a set of things on a scale, which have a particular characteristic to different degrees. [FORMAL] ❑ These various complaints are part of a continuum of ill-health.

con|tort /kəntɔːrt/ (**contorts, contorting, contorted**) V-T/V-I If someone's face or body **contorts** or **is contorted**, it moves into an unnatural and unattractive shape or position. ❑ His face contorts as he screams out the lyrics. ❑ A mere touch would contort his already tense body.

con|tor|tion /kəntɔːrʃən/ (**contortions**) N-COUNT **Contortions** are movements of your body or face into unusual shapes or positions. ❑ I had to admire the contortions of the gymnasts.

con|tor|tion|ist /kəntɔːrʃənɪst/ (**contortionists**) N-COUNT A **contortionist** is someone who twists their body into strange and unnatural shapes and positions in order to entertain other people, for example in a circus.

con|tour /kɒntʊər/ (**contours, contouring, contoured**) ◼ N-COUNT You can refer to the general shape or outline of an object as its **contours**. [LITERARY] ❑ ...the texture and color of the skin, the contours of the body. ◼ N-COUNT A **contour** on a map is a line joining points of equal height and indicating hills, valleys, and the steepness of slopes. ❑ ...a contour map showing two hills and this large mountain in the middle.

con|toured /kɒntʊərd/ ADJ [ADJ n] A **contoured** surface has curves and slopes on it, rather than being flat. ❑ ...the lush fairways and contoured greens of the golf course. ❑ Sophia settled into her comfortably contoured seat.

contra|band /kɒntrəbænd/ N-UNCOUNT [oft N n] **Contraband** refers to goods that are taken into or out of a country illegally. ❑ The ship was carrying contraband. ❑ The markets were flooded with contraband goods.

contra|cep|tion /kɒntrəsɛpʃən/ N-UNCOUNT **Contraception** refers to methods of preventing pregnancy. ❑ Use a reliable method of contraception.

contra|cep|tive /kɒntrəsɛptɪv/ (**contraceptives**) ◼ ADJ [ADJ n] A **contraceptive** method or device is used to prevent pregnancy. ❑ ...the contraceptive pill. ◼ N-COUNT A **contraceptive** is a device or drug that prevents a woman from becoming pregnant. ❑ ...oral contraceptives.

con|tract ✦✦◇ (**contracts, contracting, contracted**)

> The noun is pronounced /kɒntrækt/. The verb is pronounced /kəntrækt/.

◼ N-COUNT A **contract** is a legal agreement, usually between two companies or between an employer and employee, which involves doing work for a stated sum of money. ❑ The company won a hefty contract for work on Chicago's tallest building. ❑ Have you read the contract? ◼ V-T If you **contract** with someone to do something, you legally agree to do it for them or for them to do it for you. [FORMAL] ❑ You can contract with us to deliver your cargo. ◼ V-T/V-I When something **contracts** or when something **contracts** it, it becomes smaller or shorter. ❑ Blood is only expelled from the heart when it contracts. ● **con|trac|tion** /kəntrækʃən/ (**contractions**) N-VAR ❑ ...the contraction and expansion of blood vessels. ◼ V-I When something such as an economy or market **contracts**, it becomes smaller. ❑ The manufacturing economy contracted in October for the sixth consecutive month. ◼ V-T [no cont] If you **contract** a serious illness, you become ill with it. [FORMAL] ❑ He contracted AIDS from a blood transfusion. ◼ PHRASE If you are **under contract** to someone, you have signed a contract agreeing to work for them, and for no one else, during a fixed period of time. ❑ The director wanted Olivia de Havilland, then under contract to Warner Brothers. ◼ → See feature box at **working**
▶ **contract out** PHRASAL VERB If a company **contracts out** work, they employ other companies to do it. [BUSINESS] ❑ Firms can contract out work to one another. ❑ When the bank contracted out its cleaning, the new company was cheaper.

--- SYNONYMS ---

contract
NOUN ◼
agreement: It looks as though a compromise agreement has now been reached.
deal: The two sides tried and failed to come to a deal.
pact: Last month, the two countries signed a new non-aggression pact.
settlement: They are not optimistic about a settlement of the eleven-year conflict.
VERB ◼
constrict: Severe migraines can be treated with a drug which constricts the blood vessels.
tighten: Sofia's throat had tightened, and she couldn't speak.
shorten: As they shorten, cells become more prone to disease and death.

---

con|trac|tion /kəntrækʃən/ (**contractions**) ◼ N-COUNT When a woman who is about to give birth has **contractions**, she experiences a very strong, painful tightening of the muscles of her womb. ❑ The contractions were getting stronger. ◼ N-COUNT A **contraction** is a shortened form of a word or words. ❑ "It's" (with an apostrophe) can be used as a contraction for "it is." ◼ → see also **contract**

con|trac|tor /kɒntræktər, kəntræk-/ (**contractors**) N-COUNT A **contractor** is a person or company that does work for other people or organizations. [BUSINESS] ❑ We told the building contractor that we wanted a garage big enough for two cars.

con|trac|tual /kəntræktʃuəl/ ADJ A **contractual** arrangement or relationship involves a legal agreement between people. [FORMAL] ❑ The company has not fulfilled certain contractual obligations. ● **con|trac|tu|al|ly** ADV ❑ He is contractually bound to another year in Los Angeles.

contra|dict /kɒntrədɪkt/ (**contradicts, contradicting, contradicted**) ◼ V-T If you **contradict** someone, you tell them that what they have just said is wrong, or suggest that it is wrong by saying something different. ❑ She dared not contradict him. ❑ His comments appeared to contradict remarks made earlier in the day by the chairman. ◼ V-T If one statement or piece of evidence **contradicts** another, the first one makes the second one appear to be wrong. ❑ Her version contradicted her daughter's.

contra|dic|tion /kɒntrədɪkʃən/ (**contradictions**) N-COUNT If you describe an aspect of a situation as a **contradiction**, you mean that it is completely different from other aspects, and so makes the situation confused or difficult to understand. ❑ *The militants see no contradiction in using violence to bring about a religious state.*

contra|dic|tory /kɒntrədɪktəri/ ADJ If two or more facts, ideas, or statements are **contradictory**, they state or imply that opposite things are true. ❑ *Customs officials have made a series of contradictory statements about the equipment.*

contra|in|di|ca|tion /kɒntraɪndɪkeɪʃən/ (**contraindications**) also **contra-indication** N-COUNT [usu pl] **Contraindications** are specific medical reasons for not using a particular treatment for a medical condition in the usual way. [MEDICAL] ❑ *Contraindications for this drug include liver or kidney impairment.*

con|tral|to /kəntræltoʊ/ (**contraltos**) N-COUNT [oft N n] A **contralto** is a woman with a low singing voice. ❑ *The score calls for a contralto.* ❑ *I had a very low contralto voice.*

con|trap|tion /kəntræpʃən/ (**contraptions**) N-COUNT You can refer to a device or machine as a **contraption**, especially when it looks strange or you do not know what it is used for. ❑ *...a strange contraption called the General Gordon Gas Bath.*

con|trar|ian /kəntreəriən/ (**contrarians**) N-COUNT [oft N n] A **contrarian** is a person who deliberately behaves in a way that is different from the people around them. [FORMAL] ❑ *He is by nature a contrarian.* ❑ *...the young contrarian intellectual.*

con|tra|ry /kɒntreri/ **1** ADJ Ideas, attitudes, or reactions that are **contrary** to each other are completely different from each other. ❑ *This view is contrary to the aims of critical social research for a number of reasons.* **2** PHRASE If you say that something is true **contrary to** other people's beliefs or opinions, you are emphasizing that it is true and that they are wrong. [EMPHASIS] ❑ *Contrary to popular belief, moderate exercise actually decreases your appetite.* **3** PHRASE You use **on the contrary** when you have just said or implied that something is not true and are going to say that the opposite is true. ❑ *It is not an idea around which the community can unite. On the contrary, I see it as one that will divide us.* **4** PHRASE You can use **on the contrary** when you are disagreeing strongly with something that has just been said or implied, or are making a strong negative reply. [EMPHASIS] ❑ *"People just don't do things like that."—"On the contrary, they do them all the time."* **5** PHRASE When a particular idea is being considered, evidence or statements **to the contrary** suggest that this idea is not true or that the opposite is true. ❑ *He continued to maintain that he did nothing wrong, despite clear evidence to the contrary.*

---- USAGE ----

contrary
Don't say 'on the contrary' when you are going to mention something that gives a different opinion from something that you have just said. Don't say, for example, 'I don't like living in the center of the town. On the contrary, it's useful when you want to buy something.' Say 'I don't like living in the center of the town. **On the other hand**, it's useful when you want to buy something.' *It's a difficult job. But, **on the other hand**, the salary is good.*

---

con|trast ✦✧✧ (**contrasts, contrasting, contrasted**)

The noun is pronounced /kɒntræst/. The verb is pronounced /kəntræst/.

1 N-VAR A **contrast** is a great difference between two or more things which is clear when you compare them. ❑ *...the contrast between town and country.* ❑ *The two visitors provided a startling contrast in appearance.* **2** PHRASE You say **by contrast** or **in contrast**, or **in contrast to** something, to show that you are mentioning a very different situation from the one you have just mentioned. ❑ *The private sector, by contrast, has plenty of money to spend.* ❑ *In contrast, the lives of girls in well-to-do families were often very sheltered.* **3** PHRASE If one thing is **in contrast to** another, it is very different from it. ❑ *His public statements have always been in marked contrast to those of his son.* **4** V-T If you **contrast** one thing with another, you point out or consider the differences between those things. ❑ *She contrasted the situation then with the present crisis.* ❑ *Contrast that approach with what goes on in most organizations.* **5** V-RECIP If one thing **contrasts** with another, it is very different from it. ❑ *Johnson's easy charm contrasted sharply with the prickliness of his boss.* **6** N-UNCOUNT **Contrast** is the degree of difference between the darker and lighter parts of a photograph, television picture, or painting. ❑ *...a television with brighter colors, better contrast, and digital sound.*

---- COLLOCATIONS ----

contrast
NOUN
1
adjective + **contrast**: marked, sharp, stark, startling; dynamic
verb + **contrast**: offer, provide, show
1
adjective + **contrast**: complete, total; interesting, refreshing
VERB **5**
contrast + adverb: markedly, sharply, starkly, strikingly; unfavorably

---- SYNONYMS ----

contrast
NOUN **1**
difference: *...the vast difference in size.*
disparity: *...the great disparity of wealth between rich and poor countries.*
VERB **5**
differentiate: *A child may not differentiate between his imagination and the real world.*
distinguish: *It is necessary to distinguish the policies of two successive governments.*

---

contra|vene /kɒntrəviːn/ (**contravenes, contravening, contravened**) V-T To **contravene** a law or rule means to do something that is forbidden by the law or rule. [FORMAL] ❑ *The board has banned the film on the grounds that it contravenes criminal libel laws.* • **contra|ven|tion** /kɒntrəvenʃən/ (**contraventions**) N-VAR ❑ *The government has lent millions of dollars to debt-ridden banks in contravention of local banking laws.*

con|trib|ute ✦✧✧ /kəntrɪbjuːt/ (**contributes, contributing, contributed**) **1** V-I If you **contribute** to something, you say or do things to help to make it successful. ❑ *The three sons also contribute to the family business.* ❑ *I believe that each of us can contribute to the future of the world.* **2** V-T/V-I To **contribute** money or resources to something means to give money or resources to help pay for something or to help achieve a particular purpose. ❑ *The U.S. is contributing $4 billion in loans, credits, and grants.* ❑ *Local businesses have agreed to contribute.* • **con|tribu|tor** (**contributors**) N-COUNT ❑ *Candidates for Congress received 53 percent of their funds from individual contributors.* **3** V-I If something **contributes** to an event or situation, it is one of the causes of it. ❑ *The report says design faults in both the vessels contributed to the tragedy.* **4** → See feature box at **debate**

con|tri|bu|tion ✦✧✧ /kɒntrɪbjuːʃən/ (**contributions**)
1 N-COUNT If you make a **contribution** to something, you do something to help make it successful or to produce it. ❑ *American economists have made important contributions to the field of financial and corporate economics.* **2** N-COUNT A **contribution** is a sum of money that you give in order to help pay for something. ❑ *This list ranked companies that make charitable contributions of a half million dollars or more.*

---- COLLOCATIONS ----

contribution
NOUN
1
adjective + **contribution**: important, major, outstanding, significant; positive, solid, valuable
verb + **contribution**: make; acknowledge, recognize, value
2
noun + **contribution**: employer, pension
adjective + **contribution**: charitable, parental, tax-deductible, voluntary
verb + **contribution**: increase, pay

---

con|tribu|tor /kəntrɪbjətər/ (**contributors**) **1** N-COUNT You can use **contributor** to refer to one of the causes of an event or situation, especially if that event or situation is an unpleasant one. ❑ *Old buses are major contributors to pollution in cities.* **2** → see also **contribute**

con|tribu|tory /kəntrɪbyətɔri/ ADJ [usu ADJ n] A **contributory** factor of a problem or accident is one of the things which caused it. [FORMAL] ❑ ...an allegation of contributory negligence.

con|trite /kəntraɪt, kɒntraɪt/ ADJ [usu v-link ADJ] If you are **contrite**, you are very sorry because you have done something wrong. [FORMAL]

con|triv|ance /kəntraɪvəns/ (**contrivances**) ■ N-VAR If you describe something as a **contrivance**, you disapprove of it because it is unnecessary and artificial. [FORMAL, DISAPPROVAL] ❑ They wear simple clothes and shun modern contrivances. ❑ ...music with a tendency towards contrivance and lack of substance. ■ N-COUNT A **contrivance** is an unfair or dishonest scheme or trick to gain an advantage for yourself. ❑ They always come up with some contrivance to raise prices.

con|trive /kəntraɪv/ (**contrives, contriving, contrived**) V-T If you **contrive** an event or situation, you succeed in making it happen, often by tricking someone. [FORMAL] ❑ The oil companies were accused of contriving a shortage of gasoline to justify price increases.

con|trived /kəntraɪvd/ ADJ If you say that something someone says or does is **contrived**, you think it is false and deliberate, rather than natural and not planned. [DISAPPROVAL] ❑ There was nothing contrived about what he said.

con|trol ♦♦♦ /kəntroʊl/ (**controls, controlling, controlled**) ■ N-UNCOUNT **Control** of an organization, place, or system is the power to make all the important decisions about the way that it is run. ❑ The restructuring involves Mr. Ronson giving up control of the company. • PHRASE If you are **in control** of something, you have the power to make all the important decisions about the way it is run. ❑ Nobody knows who is in control of the club. • PHRASE If something is **under your control**, you have the power to make all the important decisions about the way that it is run. ❑ All the newspapers are under government control. ■ N-UNCOUNT [oft N of/over n] If you have **control** of something or someone, you are able to make them do what you want them to do. ❑ He lost control of his car. • **con|trolled** ADJ ❑ ...a controlled experiment. ■ N-UNCOUNT If you show **control**, you prevent yourself behaving in an angry or emotional way. ❑ He had a terrible temper, and sometimes he would completely lose control. ■ V-T The people who **control** an organization or place have the power to make all the important decisions about the way that it is run. ❑ He now controls the largest retail development empire in southern California. ■ V-T To **control** a piece of equipment, process, or system means to make it work in the way that you want it to work. ❑ ...a computerized system to control the gates. ❑ Scientists would soon be able to manipulate human genes to control the aging process. ■ V-T When a government **controls** prices, wages, or the activity of a particular group, it uses its power to restrict them. ❑ The federal government tried to control rising health-care costs. • N-UNCOUNT **Control** is also a noun. ❑ Control of inflation remains the government's absolute priority. ■ V-T If you **control** yourself, or if you **control** your feelings, voice, or expression, you make yourself behave calmly even though you are feeling angry, excited, or upset. ❑ Jo was advised to learn to control herself. • **con|trolled** ADJ ❑ Her manner was quiet and very controlled. ■ V-T To **control** something dangerous means to prevent it from becoming worse or from spreading. ❑ ...the need to control environmental pollution. ■ N-COUNT A **control** is a device such as a switch or lever which you use in order to operate a machine or other piece of equipment. ❑ I practiced operating the controls. ■ N-VAR **Controls** are the methods that a government uses to restrict increases, for example in prices, wages, or weapons. ❑ Critics question whether price controls would do any good. ■ N-VAR **Control** is used to refer to a place where your documents or luggage are officially checked when you enter a foreign country. ❑ He went straight through Passport Control without incident. ■ → see also **birth control, quality control, remote control, stock control** ■ PHRASE If something is **out of control**, no one has any power over it. ❑ The fire is burning out of control. ■ PHRASE If something harmful is **under control**, it is being dealt with successfully and is unlikely to cause any more harm. ❑ The situation is under control.

con|trol freak (**control freaks**) N-COUNT If you say that someone is a **control freak**, you mean that they want to be in control of every situation they find themselves in. [INFORMAL, DISAPPROVAL]

con|trol|lable /kəntroʊləbəl/ ADJ If something is **controllable** you are able to control or influence it. ❑ This makes the surfboards more controllable. ❑ ...controllable aspects of life.

con|trol|ler /kəntroʊlər/ (**controllers**) ■ N-COUNT A **controller** is a person who has responsibility for a particular organization or for a particular part of an organization. [mainly BRIT] ❑ ...the job of controller of BBC1. ■ → see also **air traffic controller** ■ N-COUNT A **controller** is the same as a **comptroller**.

con|trol tow|er (**control towers**) N-COUNT A **control tower** is a building at an airport from which instructions are given to aircraft when they are taking off or landing. You can also refer to the people who work in a control tower as the **control tower**. ❑ The pilot told the control tower that he'd run into technical trouble.

con|tro|ver|sial ♦◊◊ /kɒntrəvɜrʃəl/ ADJ If you describe something or someone as **controversial**, you mean that they are the subject of intense public argument, disagreement, or disapproval. ❑ Immigration is a controversial issue in many countries.

con|tro|ver|sy ♦◊◊ /kɒntrəvɜrsi/ (**controversies**) N-VAR **Controversy** is a lot of discussion and argument about something, often involving strong feelings of anger or disapproval. ❑ The proposed cuts have caused considerable controversy.

---SYNONYMS---

controversy
NOUN
argument: The issue has caused heated political argument.
contention: They generally tried to avoid subjects of contention between them.
debate: There has been a lot of debate among scholars about this.
disagreement: Congress and the President are still locked in disagreement over the proposals.

---

con|tu|sion /kəntuʒən/ (**contusions**) N-COUNT A **contusion** is a bruise. [MEDICAL]

co|nun|drum /kənʌndrəm/ (**conundrums**) N-COUNT A **conundrum** is a problem or puzzle which is difficult or impossible to solve. [FORMAL] ❑ ...this theological conundrum of the existence of evil and suffering in a world created by a good God.

con|va|lesce /kɒnvəlɛs/ (**convalesces, convalescing, convalesced**) V-I If you **are convalescing**, you are resting and getting your health back after an illness or operation. [FORMAL] ❑ After two weeks, I was allowed home, where I convalesced for three months.

con|va|les|cence /kɒnvəlɛsəns/ N-UNCOUNT **Convalescence** is the period or process of becoming healthy and well again after an illness or operation. [FORMAL] ❑ Also thanks to Lucy and Guthrie Scott for inviting me to stay with them during my convalescence.

con|va|les|cent /kɒnvəlɛsənt/ ADJ [usu ADJ n] **Convalescent** means relating to convalescence. [FORMAL] ❑ ...an officers' convalescent home.

con|vec|tion /kənvɛkʃən/ N-UNCOUNT **Convection** is the process by which heat travels through air, water, and other gases and liquids. [TECHNICAL] ❑ ...clouds which lift warm, moist air by convection high into the atmosphere.

con|vec|tion heat|er (**convection heaters**) N-COUNT A **convection heater** is a heater that heats a room by means of hot air.

con|vene /kənvin/ (**convenes, convening, convened**) V-T/V-I If someone **convenes** a meeting or conference, they arrange for it to take place. You can also say that people **convene** or that a meeting **convenes**. [FORMAL] ❑ Last August he convened a meeting of his closest advisers at Camp David.

con|veni|ence /kənvinyəns/ (**conveniences**) ■ N-UNCOUNT If something is done for your **convenience**, it is done in a way that is useful or suitable for you. ❑ He was happy to make a detour for her convenience. ■ N-COUNT If you describe something as a **convenience**, you mean that it is very useful. ❑ Mail order is a convenience for buyers who are too busy to shop. ■ N-COUNT **Conveniences** are pieces of equipment designed to make your life easier. ❑ ...an apartment with all the modern conveniences. ■ → see also **convenient**

con|veni|ence food N-UNCOUNT **Convenience food** is frozen, dried, or canned food that can be heated and prepared very quickly and easily. ☐ *I know that I rely too much on convenience food.*

con|veni|ence store (convenience stores) N-COUNT A **convenience store** is a small store which sells mainly food and which is usually open until late at night.

con|veni|ent /kənvi:niənt/ ■ ADJ If a way of doing something is **convenient**, it is easy, or very useful or suitable for a particular purpose. ☐ *...a flexible and convenient way of paying for business expenses.* ● **con|veni|ence** N-UNCOUNT ☐ *They may use a credit card for convenience.* ● **con|veni|ent|ly** ADV ☐ *The body spray slips conveniently into your sports bag for freshening up after a game.* ■ ADJ If you describe a place as **convenient**, you are pleased because it is near to where you are, or because you can reach another place from there quickly and easily. [APPROVAL] ☐ *The town is well placed for easy access to Washington D.C. and convenient for Dulles Airport.* ● **con|veni|ent|ly** ADV ☐ *It was very conveniently situated just across the road from the City Reference Library.* ■ ADJ A **convenient** time to do something, for example to meet someone, is a time when you are free to do it or would like to do it. ☐ *She will try to arrange a mutually convenient time and place for an interview.*

con|vent /kɒnvent, -vənt/ (convents) N-COUNT A **convent** is a building in which a community of nuns live.

con|ven|tion ✦◇◇ /kənvɛnʃən/ (conventions) ■ N-VAR A **convention** is a way of behaving that is considered to be correct or polite by most people in a society. ☐ *It's just a social convention that men don't wear skirts.* ■ N-COUNT In art, literature, or the theater, a **convention** is a traditional method or style. ☐ *We go offstage and come back for the convention of the encore.* ■ N-COUNT A **convention** is an official agreement between countries or groups of people. ☐ *...the U.N. convention on climate change.* ■ N-COUNT A **convention** is a large meeting of an organization or political group. ☐ *...the annual convention of the Society of Professional Journalists.* ■ → See feature box at **politics**

con|ven|tion|al ✦◇◇ /kənvɛnʃənəl/ ■ ADJ Someone who is **conventional** has behavior or opinions that are ordinary and normal. ☐ *...a respectable married woman with conventional opinions.* ● **con|ven|tion|al|ly** ADV ☐ *Men still wore their hair short and dressed conventionally.* ■ ADJ A **conventional** method or product is one that is usually used or that has been in use for a long time. ☐ *...the risks and drawbacks of conventional family planning methods.* ● **con|ven|tion|al|ly** ADV [ADV with v] ☐ *Organically grown produce does not differ greatly in appearance from conventionally grown crops.* ■ ADJ **Conventional** weapons and wars do not involve nuclear explosives. ☐ *We must reduce the danger of war by controlling nuclear, chemical, and conventional arms.*

---- SYNONYMS ----

conventional
ADJ ■
traditional: *...traditional parents, who believed in laying down the law for their children.*
conservative: *People tend to be more conservative as they get older.*
respectable: *He came from a perfectly respectable, middle-class family.*

----

con|ven|tion|eer /kənvɛnʃəniər/ (conventioneers) N-COUNT [usu pl] **Conventioneers** are people who are attending a convention. [AM]

con|vent school (convent schools) N-COUNT A **convent school** is a school where many of the teachers are nuns.

con|verge /kənvɜ:rdʒ/ (converges, converging, converged) ■ V-I If people or vehicles **converge on** a place, they move toward it from different directions. ☐ *Hundreds of tractors will converge on the capital.* ■ V-I If roads or lines **converge**, they meet or join at a particular place. [FORMAL] ☐ *As they flow south, the five rivers converge.*

con|ver|gence /kənvɜ:rdʒəns/ (convergences) N-VAR The **convergence** of different ideas, groups, or societies is the process by which they stop being different and become more similar. [FORMAL] ☐ *...the need to move towards greater economic convergence.*

con|ver|sant /kənvɜ:rsənt/ ADJ [v-link ADJ] If you are **conversant with** something, you are familiar with it and able to deal with it. [FORMAL] ☐ *Those in business are not, on the whole, conversant with basic scientific principles.*

con|ver|sa|tion ✦◇◇ /kɒnvərseɪʃən/ (conversations) N-COUNT If you have a **conversation** with someone, you talk with them, usually in an informal situation. ☐ *He's a talkative guy, and I struck up a conversation with him.*

con|ver|sa|tion|al /kɒnvərseɪʃənəl/ ADJ **Conversational** means relating to, or similar to, casual and informal talk. ☐ *What is refreshing is the author's easy, conversational style.*

con|ver|sa|tion|al|ist /kɒnvərseɪʃənəlɪst/ (conversationalists) N-COUNT [usu adj n] A good **conversationalist** is someone who talks about interesting things when they have conversations. ☐ *Joan is a brilliant conversationalist.*

con|verse (converses, conversing, conversed)

The verb is pronounced /kənvɜ:rs/. The noun is pronounced /kɒnvɜ:rs/.

■ V-RECIP If you **converse** with someone, you talk to them. You can also say that two people **converse**. [FORMAL] ☐ *Luke sat directly behind the pilot and conversed with him.* ■ N-SING The **converse** of a statement is its opposite or reverse. [FORMAL] ☐ *What you do for a living is critical to where you settle and how you live – and the converse is also true.*

con|verse|ly /kɒnvɜ:rsli, kənvɜ:rs-/ ADV [ADV with cl] You say **conversely** to indicate that the situation you are about to describe is the opposite or reverse of the one you have just described. [FORMAL] ☐ *Malaysia and Indonesia rely on open markets for forest and fishery products. Conversely, some Asian countries are highly protectionist.*

con|ver|sion /kənvɜ:rʒən/ (conversions) ■ N-VAR **Conversion** is the act or process of changing something into a different state or form. ☐ *...the conversion of disused rail lines into cycle routes.* ■ N-VAR If someone changes their religion or beliefs, you can refer to their **conversion** to their new religion or beliefs. ☐ *...his conversion to Christianity.*

con|vert ✦◇◇ (converts, converting, converted)

The verb is pronounced /kənvɜ:rt/. The noun is pronounced /kɒnvɜ:rt/.

■ V-T/V-I If one thing **is converted** or **converts** into another, it is changed into a different form. ☐ *The signal will be converted into digital code.* ☐ *...naturally occurring substances which the body can convert into vitamins.* ■ V-T If someone **converts** a room or building, they alter it in order to use it for a different purpose. ☐ *By converting the attic, they were able to have two extra bedrooms.* ☐ *...the entrepreneur who wants to convert County Hall into a hotel.* ■ V-T If you **convert** a vehicle or piece of equipment, you change it so that it can use a different fuel. ☐ *Save money by converting your car to run on used vegetable oil.* ■ V-T If you **convert** a quantity from one system of measurement to another, you calculate what the quantity is in the second system. ☐ *Converting metric measurements to U.S. equivalents is easy.* ■ V-T/V-I If someone **converts** you, they persuade you to change your religious or political beliefs. You can also say that someone **converts** to a different religion. ☐ *If you try to convert him, you could find he just walks away.* ☐ *He was a major influence in converting Godwin to political radicalism.* ■ N-COUNT [oft N to n] A **convert** is someone who has changed their religious or political beliefs. ☐ *She, too, was a convert to Roman Catholicism.* ■ N-COUNT [usu N to n] If you describe someone as a **convert** to something, you mean that they have recently become very enthusiastic about it. ☐ *As recent converts to vegetarianism and animal rights, they now live with a menagerie of stray animals.* ■ → See feature box at **recycle**

---- SYNONYMS ----

convert
VERB ■
turn into: *A prince turns into a frog in this cartoon fairytale.*
transform: *Your body transforms food into energy.*
adapt: *Shelves were built to adapt the library for use as an office.*
modify: *The club members did agree to modify their recruitment policy.*
alter: *They have never altered their programs by a single day.*

con|vert|er /kənvɜrtər/ (converters) **1** N-COUNT A **converter** is a device that changes something into a different form. **2** → see also **catalytic converter**

con|vert|ible /kənvɜrtɪbəl/ (convertibles) **1** N-COUNT A **convertible** is a car with a soft roof that can be folded down or removed. ❑ *Her own car is a convertible VW.* **2** ADJ In finance, **convertible** investments or money can be easily exchanged for other forms of investments or money. [BUSINESS] ❑ *...the introduction of a convertible currency.* ● **con|vert|ibil|ity** /kənvɜrtɪbɪlɪti/ N-UNCOUNT ❑ *...the convertibility of the peso.*

con|vex /kɒnveks/ ADJ **Convex** is used to describe something that curves outward in the middle. ❑ *...the large convex mirror above the fireplace.*

con|vey /kənveɪ/ (conveys, conveying, conveyed) V-T To **convey** information or feelings means to cause them to be known or understood by someone. ❑ *When I returned home, I tried to convey the wonder of this machine to my husband.* ❑ *In every one of her pictures she conveys a sense of immediacy.*

con|vey|ance /kənveɪəns/ (conveyances) **1** N-COUNT A **conveyance** is a vehicle. [LITERARY] ❑ *Mahoney had never seen such a conveyance before.* **2** N-UNCOUNT [with supp] The **conveyance** of something is the process of carrying or transporting it from one place to another. [FORMAL] ❑ *...the conveyance of bicycles on trains.*

con|vey|or belt /kənveɪər belt/ (conveyor belts) N-COUNT A **conveyor belt** or a **conveyor** is a continuously moving strip of rubber or metal which is used in factories for moving objects along so that they can be dealt with as quickly as possible. ❑ *The damp bricks went along a conveyor belt into another shed to dry.*

con|vict ✦◇◇ (convicts, convicting, convicted)

The verb is pronounced /kənvɪkt/. The noun is pronounced /kɒnvɪkt/.

1 V-T If someone **is convicted** of a crime, they are found guilty of that crime in a court of law. ❑ *In 1977 he was convicted of murder and sentenced to life imprisonment.* ❑ *There was insufficient evidence to convict him.* **2** N-COUNT A **convict** is someone who is in prison. [JOURNALISM] ❑ *...Neil Jordan's tale of two escaped convicts who get mistaken for priests.*

---- COLLOCATIONS ----

convict
VERB **1**
convict + *adverb*: wrongfully, wrongly; unanimously
NOUN **2**
adjective + **convict**: escaped; former

con|vic|tion ✦◇◇ /kənvɪkʃən/ (convictions) **1** N-COUNT [usu N that] A **conviction** is a strong belief or opinion. ❑ *It is our firm conviction that a step forward has been taken.* **2** N-COUNT If someone has a **conviction**, they have been found guilty of a crime in a court of law. ❑ *He will appeal against his conviction.* **3** N-UNCOUNT If you have **conviction**, you have great confidence in your beliefs or opinions. ❑ *"We shall, sir," said Thorne, with conviction.*

---- COLLOCATIONS ----

conviction
NOUN
1
adjective + **conviction**: deep, firm; ideological, moral, religious
2
verb + **conviction**: obtain, secure, uphold; overturn, quash
3
adjective + **conviction**: absolute, utter
verb + **conviction**: express, have; lack

con|vince ✦◇◇ /kənvɪns/ (convinces, convincing, convinced) **1** V-T If someone or something **convinces** you to do something, they persuade you to do it. ❑ *That weekend in Plattsburgh, he convinced her to go ahead and marry Bud.* **2** V-T If someone or something **convinces** you of something, they make you believe that it is true or that it exists. ❑ *Although I soon convinced him of my innocence, I think he still has serious doubts about my sanity.*

con|vinced ✦◇◇ /kənvɪnst/ ADJ If you are **convinced** that something is true, you feel sure that it is true. ❑ *He was convinced that I was part of the problem.* ❑ *He became convinced of the need for cheap editions of good quality writing.*

---- USAGE ----

convinced
You do not use a 'to'-infinitive after **convinced**. You do not say, for example, 'He is convinced to have failed.' You say 'He is **convinced that he** has failed.' *He was convinced that her mother was innocent.*

con|vinc|ing /kənvɪnsɪŋ/ ADJ If you describe someone or something as **convincing**, you mean that they make you believe that a particular thing is true, correct, or genuine. ❑ *Scientists say there is no convincing evidence that power lines have anything to do with cancer.* ● **con|vinc|ing|ly** ADV ❑ *He argued forcefully and convincingly that they were likely to bankrupt the budget.*

con|viv|ial /kənvɪviəl/ ADJ **Convivial** people or occasions are pleasant, friendly, and relaxed. [FORMAL, APPROVAL] ❑ *...looking forward to a convivial evening.* ❑ *The atmosphere was quite convivial.*

con|vo|ca|tion /kɒnvəkeɪʃən/ (convocations) N-COUNT A **convocation** is a meeting or ceremony attended by a large number of people. [FORMAL] ❑ *...a convocation of the American Youth Congress.*

con|vo|lut|ed /kɒnvəlutɪd/ ADJ If you describe a sentence, idea, or system as **convoluted**, you mean that it is complicated and difficult to understand. [FORMAL, DISAPPROVAL] ❑ *Despite its length and convoluted plot, "Asta's Book" is a rich and rewarding read.*

con|vo|lu|tion /kɒnvəluʃən/ (convolutions) **1** N-COUNT [usu pl] **Convolutions** are curves on an object or design that has a lot of curves. [LITERARY] **2** N-VAR [oft N of n] You can use **convolutions** to refer to a situation that is very complicated. [LITERARY] ❑ *...the thorny convolutions of love.*

con|voy /kɒnvɔɪ/ (convoys) N-COUNT [also *in* n] A **convoy** is a group of vehicles or ships traveling together. ❑ *...a U.N. convoy carrying food and medical supplies.* ❑ *...humanitarian relief convoys.*

con|vulse /kənvʌls/ (convulses, convulsing, convulsed) If someone **convulses** or if they **are convulsed** by or with something, their body moves suddenly in an uncontrolled way. ❑ *Olivia's face convulsed in a series of twitches.* ❑ *He let out a cry that convulsed his bulky frame and jerked his arm.* ❑ *The opposing team were so convulsed with laughter that they almost forgot to hit the ball.*

con|vul|sion /kənvʌlʃən/ (convulsions) N-COUNT If someone has **convulsions**, they suffer uncontrollable movements of their muscles. ❑ *Thirteen per cent said they became unconscious at night and 5 per cent suffered convulsions.*

con|vul|sive /kənvʌlsɪv/ ADJ [usu ADJ n] A **convulsive** movement or action is sudden and cannot be controlled. [FORMAL] ❑ *Convulsive sobs racked her body.*

coo /ku/ (coos, cooing, cooed) **1** V-I When a dove or pigeon **coos**, it makes the soft sounds that doves and pigeons typically make. ❑ *Pigeons fluttered in and out, cooing gently.* **2** V-T/V-I When someone **coos**, they speak in a very soft, quiet voice which is intended to sound attractive. ❑ *She paused to coo at the baby.* ❑ *"Isn't this marvelous?" she cooed.*

cook ✦◇◇ /kʊk/ (cooks, cooking, cooked) **1** V-T/V-I When you **cook** a meal, you prepare food for eating by heating it. ❑ *I have to go and cook dinner.* ❑ *Chefs at the restaurant once cooked for President Kennedy.* ● **cook|ing** N-UNCOUNT ❑ *Her hobbies include music, dancing, sport, and cooking.* **2** V-T/V-I When you **cook** food, or when food **cooks**, it is heated until it is ready to be eaten. ❑ *...some basic instructions on how to cook a turkey.* ❑ *Let the vegetables cook gently for about 10 minutes.* **3** N-COUNT A **cook** is a person whose job is to prepare and cook food, especially in someone's home or in an institution. ❑ *They had a butler, a cook, and a maid.* **4** N-COUNT If you say that someone is a good **cook**, you mean they are good at preparing and cooking food. ❑ *I'm a lousy cook.*
▶ **cook up 1** PHRASAL VERB If someone **cooks up** a dishonest scheme, they plan it. [INFORMAL] ❑ *He must have cooked up his scheme on the spur of the moment.* **2** PHRASAL VERB If someone **cooks up** an explanation or a story, they make it up. [INFORMAL] ❑ *She'll cook up a convincing explanation.*

cook|book /kʊkbʊk/ (cookbooks) N-COUNT A **cookbook** is a book that contains recipes for preparing food.

cook|er /kʊkər/ (cookers) N-COUNT A **cooker** is a large metal device for cooking food using gas or electricity. A cooker usually consists of an oven, a broiler, and some gas burners or electric rings. [BRIT]

in AM, use **stove, range**

cook|ery /kʊkəri/ N-UNCOUNT **Cookery** is the activity of preparing and cooking food. ❏ *The school runs cookery classes throughout the year.*

cookie /kʊki/ (cookies) **1** N-COUNT A **cookie** is a small sweet cake. [mainly AM]

in BRIT, use **biscuit**

2 N-COUNT A **cookie** is a piece of computer software which enables a website you have visited to recognize you if you visit it again. [COMPUTING]

cookie cut|ter (cookie cutters) also **cookie-cutter 1** N-COUNT A **cookie cutter** is a tool that is used for cutting cookies into a particular shape before you bake them. [AM] ❏ *Heart-shaped cookie cutters come in many sizes.* **2** ADJ [usu ADJ n] If you describe something as having a **cookie-cutter** approach or style, you mean that the same approach or style is always used and not enough attention is paid to individual differences. [AM, DISAPPROVAL] ❏ *Too many cookie-cutter condos were built with no attention to consumer needs.*

cookie sheet (cookie sheets) N-COUNT A **cookie sheet** is a flat piece of metal on which you bake foods such as cookies in an oven. [AM]

in BRIT, use **baking sheet**

cook|ing ✦✧✧ /kʊkɪŋ/ **1** N-UNCOUNT **Cooking** is food which has been cooked. ❏ *The menu is based on classic French cooking.* **2** N-UNCOUNT **Cooking** is the activity of preparing food. ❏ *He did the cooking, cleaning, laundry, and home repairs.* **3** ADJ [n] **Cooking** ingredients or equipment are used in cookery. ❏ *Finely slice the cooking apples.* **4** → see also **cook**

VOCABULARY IN CONTEXT

Cooking tips: how to make a plum and apple crumble

A crumble is a traditional British fruit dessert, with a **topping** that has the **texture** of **breadcrumbs**. It is often served with **custard**.

To make a plum and apple crumble, **core** and **peel** the apples, and remove the **pits** from the plums. **Chop** the fruit into fairly small pieces. Then, allow to **simmer** on the **stove** with a little sugar until the fruit is **tender**.

Meanwhile, **blend** flour, butter, and sugar to make a **crumbly** mixture. When the fruit is ready, put it into an **ovenproof** dish and put the crumbly mixture on top. Bake in the oven for 25 minutes, until the topping is **crunchy**.

cook-off (cook-offs) N-COUNT A **cook-off** is a cooking competition. [AM] ❏ *They could do a better job of publicizing the chili cook-off.*

cook|out /kʊkaʊt/ (cookouts) N-COUNT A **cookout** is the same as a **barbecue**. [AM]

cook|top /kʊktɒp/ (cooktops) N-COUNT A **cooktop** is a flat surface on top of a stove or set into a work surface, which can be heated in order to cook things on it. [mainly AM]

cook|ware /kʊkweər/ N-UNCOUNT **Cookware** is the range of pans and pots which are used in cooking. ❏ *...several lines of popular cookware and utensils.*

cool ✦✦✧ /kuːl/ (cooler, coolest, cools, cooling, cooled) **1** ADJ Something that is **cool** has a temperature which is low but not very low. ❏ *I felt a current of cool air.* ❏ *The water was slightly cooler than a child's bath.* **2** ADJ If it is **cool**, or if a place is **cool**, the temperature of the air is low but not very low. ❏ *Thank goodness it's cool in here.* ❏ *Store grains and cereals in a cool, dry place.* • **Cool** is also a noun. ❏ *She walked into the cool of the hallway.* **3** ADJ Clothing that is **cool** is made of thin material so that you do not become too hot in hot weather. ❏ *In warm weather, you should wear clothing that is cool and comfortable.* **4** ADJ [ADJ n] **Cool** colors are light colors which give an impression of coolness. ❏ *Choose a cool color such as cream.* **5** ADJ If you say that a person or their behavior is **cool**, you mean that they are calm and unemotional, especially in a difficult situation. [APPROVAL] ❏ *He was marvelously cool again, smiling as if nothing had happened.* • **cool|ly** ADV ❏ *Everyone must think this situation through calmly and coolly.* **6** ADJ If you say that a person or their behavior is **cool**, you mean that they are unfriendly or not enthusiastic. ❏ *I didn't like him at all. I thought he was cool, aloof, and arrogant.* • **cool|ly** ADV ❏ *"It's your choice, Nina," David said coolly.* **7** ADJ If you say that a person or thing is **cool**, you mean that they are fashionable and attractive. [INFORMAL, APPROVAL] ❏ *He was trying to be really cool and trendy.* ❏ *That's a cool hat.* **8** V-T/V-I When something **cools** or when you **cool** it, it becomes lower in temperature. ❏ *Drain the meat and allow it to cool.* ❏ *Huge fans will have to cool the concrete floor to keep it below 150 degrees.* • PHRASAL VERB To **cool down** means the same as to **cool**. ❏ *Avoid putting your car away until the engine has cooled down.* **9** V-T/V-I When a feeling or emotion **cools**, or when you **cool** it, it becomes less powerful. ❏ *Within a few minutes tempers had cooled.* **10** ADJ [v-link ADJ] If you say that someone is **cool** about something, you mean that they accept it and are not angry or upset about it. [INFORMAL, APPROVAL] ❏ *Bev was really cool about it all.* **11** ADJ If you say that something or someone is **cool**, you think they are excellent in some way. [INFORMAL] ❏ *Kathleen gave me a really cool dress.* ❏ *He's such a cool guy.* **12** → See feature box at **hot**

▶ **cool down 1** PHRASAL VERB → see **cool 8** **2** PHRASAL VERB If someone **cools down** or if you **cool** them **down**, they become less angry than they were. ❏ *He has had time to cool down and look at what happened more objectively.*

▶ **cool off 1** PHRASAL VERB If someone or something **cools off**, or if you **cool** them **off**, they become cooler after having been hot. ❏ *Maybe he's trying to cool off out there in the rain.* ❏ *She made a fanning motion, pretending to cool herself off.* **2** PHRASAL VERB If someone **cools off**, they become less angry than they were. ❏ *We've got to give him some time to cool off.*

cool|ant /kuːlənt/ (coolants) N-MASS **Coolant** is a liquid used to keep a machine or engine cool while it is operating.

cool|er /kuːlər/ (coolers) **1** N-COUNT A **cooler** is a container for keeping things cool, especially drinks. **2** → see also **cool**

cool-headed ADJ If you describe someone as **cool-headed**, you mean that they stay calm in difficult situations. [APPROVAL] ❏ *She has a reputation for being calm and cool-headed.* ❏ *...a cool-headed, responsible statesman.*

cooling-off pe|ri|od (cooling-off periods) N-COUNT A **cooling-off period** is an agreed period of time during which two sides with opposing views try to resolve a dispute before taking any serious action. ❏ *There should be a seven-day cooling-off period between a strike ballot and industrial action.*

cool|ing tow|er (cooling towers) N-COUNT A **cooling tower** is a very large, round, high building which is used to cool water from factories or power stations. ❏ *...landscapes dominated by cooling towers and factory chimneys.*

coon /kuːn/ (coons) **1** N-COUNT A **coon** is a raccoon. [AM, INFORMAL] **2** N-COUNT **Coon** is an extremely offensive word for an African-American. [INFORMAL, VERY OFFENSIVE]

coop /kuːp/ (coops) N-COUNT A **coop** is a cage where you keep small animals or birds such as chickens and rabbits. ❏ *...a chicken coop.*

co-op (co-ops) N-COUNT A **co-op** is a cooperative. [INFORMAL] □ *The co-op sells the art work at exhibitions.*

cooped up /kʊpt ʌp/ ADJ [v-link ADJ] If you say that someone is **cooped up**, you mean that they live or are kept in a place which is too small, or which does not allow them much freedom. □ *He is cooped up in a cramped cell with 10 other inmates.*

cooper /kupər/ (coopers) N-COUNT A **cooper** is a person who makes barrels. [OLD-FASHIONED]

cooperate ◆◇◇ /koʊɒpəreɪt/ (cooperates, cooperating, cooperated)

in BRIT, also use **co-operate**

1 V-RECIP If you **cooperate** with someone, you work with them or help them for a particular purpose. You can also say that two people **cooperate**. □ *The U.N. had been cooperating with the State Department on a plan to find countries willing to take the refugees.* • **cooperation** /koʊɒpəreɪʃən/ N-UNCOUNT □ *A deal with Japan could open the door to economic cooperation with East Asia.* **2** V-I If you **cooperate**, you do what someone has asked or told you to do. □ *He agreed to cooperate with the police investigation.* • **cooperation** N-UNCOUNT □ *The police underlined the importance of the public's cooperation in the hunt for the bombers.*

cooperative /koʊɒpərətɪv/ (cooperatives)

in BRIT, also use **co-operative**

1 N-COUNT A **cooperative** is a business or organization run by the people who work for it, or owned by the people who use it. These people share its benefits and profits. [BUSINESS] □ *They decided a housing cooperative was the way to regenerate the area.* **2** ADJ A **cooperative** activity is done by people working together. □ *He was transferred to FBI custody in a smooth cooperative effort between Egyptian and U.S. authorities.* • **cooperatively** ADV [ADV after v] □ *They agreed to work cooperatively to ease tensions wherever possible.* **3** ADJ If you say that someone is **cooperative**, you mean that they do what you ask them to without complaining or arguing. □ *I made every effort to be cooperative.*

co-opt (co-opts, co-opting, co-opted) **1** V-T If you **co-opt** someone, you persuade them to help or support you. □ *Mr. Wallace tries to co-opt rather than defeat his critics.* **2** V-T If someone **is co-opted** into a group, they are asked by that group to become a member, rather than joining or being elected in the normal way. □ *He was co-opted into the Labour Government of 1964.* □ *He's been authorised to co-opt anyone he wants to join him.* **3** V-T If a group or political party **co-opts** a slogan or policy, they take it, often from another group or political party, and use it themselves. □ *He co-opted many nationalist slogans and cultivated a populist image.*

coordinate (coordinates, coordinating, coordinated)

The verb is pronounced /koʊɔrdɪneɪt/. The noun is pronounced /koʊɔrdɪnət/.

in BRIT, also use **co-ordinate**

1 V-T If you **coordinate** an activity, you organize the various people and things involved in it. □ *Government officials visited the earthquake zone on Thursday morning to coordinate the relief effort.* • **coordinated** ADJ □ *Coalition forces were planning a coordinated effort to attack the drug trade.* □ *...a well-coordinated surprise attack.* • **coordinator** (coordinators) N-COUNT □ *...the party's campaign coordinator, Mr. Peter Mandelson.* **2** V-T If you **coordinate** the different parts of your body, you make them work together efficiently to perform particular movements. □ *You need to coordinate legs, arms, and breathing for the front crawl.* **3** V-RECIP If you **coordinate** clothes or furnishings that are used together, or if they **coordinate**, they are similar in some way and look nice together. □ *She'll show you how to coordinate pattern and colors.* □ *Tie it with fabric bows that coordinate with other furnishings.* **4** N-COUNT The **coordinates** of a point on a map or graph are the two sets of numbers or letters that you need in order to find that point. [TECHNICAL] □ *Can you give me your coordinates?*

coordinating conjunction /koʊɔrdɪneɪtɪŋ kəndʒʌŋkʃən/ (coordinating conjunctions) N-COUNT A **coordinating conjunction** is a word such as 'and,' 'or,' or 'but' which joins two or more words, groups, or clauses of equal status, for example two main clauses. Compare **subordinating conjunction**. [TECHNICAL]

coordination /koʊɔrdɪneɪʃən/

in BRIT, also use **co-ordination**

1 N-UNCOUNT **Coordination** means organizing the activities of two or more groups so that they work together efficiently and know what the others are doing. □ *...the lack of coordination between the civilian and military authorities.* □ *...the coordination of economic policy.* • PHRASE If you do something **in coordination with** someone else, you both organize your activities so that you work together efficiently. **2** N-UNCOUNT **Coordination** is the ability to use the different parts of your body together efficiently. □ *...clumsiness and lack of coordination.*

coot /kut/ (coots) N-COUNT A **coot** is a water bird with black feathers and a white patch on its forehead.

cootie /kuti/ (cooties) N-COUNT **Cooties** are the same as **lice**. [AM, INFORMAL] □ *It was probably infested with cooties.*

cop /kɒp/ (cops, copping, copped) N-COUNT A **cop** is a policeman or policewoman. [INFORMAL] □ *Frank didn't like having the cops know where to find him.*
▶ **cop out** PHRASAL VERB If you say that someone **is copping out**, you mean that they are avoiding doing something they should do. [INFORMAL] □ *The soldiers' families accused the government of copping out.*
▶ **cop to** PHRASAL VERB If you **cop to** something bad or wrong that you have done, you admit that you have done it. [AM, INFORMAL] □ *I left, but you told me to. I'd appreciate it if you'd cop to that.*

cope ◆◇◇ /koʊp/ (copes, coping, coped) **1** V-I If you **cope** with a problem or task, you deal with it successfully. □ *It was amazing how my mother coped bringing up three children on less than thirty dollars a week.* **2** V-I If you have to **cope with** an unpleasant situation, you have to accept it or bear it. □ *Never before has the industry had to cope with war and recession at the same time.* **3** V-I If a machine or a system can **cope** with something, it is large enough or complex enough to deal with it satisfactorily. □ *A giant washing machine copes with the mountain of laundry created by their nine boys and five girls.* **4** → See feature box at **challenge, disaster, success**

SYNONYMS

cope
VERB **1**
manage: *She had managed perfectly well without medication for three years.*
get by: *I'm a survivor. I'll get by.*
deal with: *She saw a psychiatrist who used hypnotism to help her deal with her fear.*

COLLOCATIONS

cope
VERB **1**
cope + adverb: admirably, comfortably, easily, magnificently, well; emotionally, financially, psychologically

copier /kɒpiər/ (copiers) **1** N-COUNT A **copier** is a machine which makes exact copies of writing or pictures on paper, usually by a photographic process. **2** N-COUNT A **copier** is someone who copies what someone else has done. □ *...their reputation as a copier of other countries' designs, patents, and inventions.*

co-pilot (co-pilots) N-COUNT The **co-pilot** of an aircraft is a pilot who assists the chief pilot.

copious /koʊpiəs/ ADJ A **copious** amount of something is a large amount of it. □ *I went out for dinner last night and drank copious amounts of red wine.* • **copiously** ADV □ *The victims were bleeding copiously.*

cop-out (cop-outs) N-COUNT [usu sing] If you refer to something as a **cop-out**, you think that it is a way for someone to avoid doing something that they should do. [INFORMAL, DISAPPROVAL] □ *To decline to vote is a cop-out.* □ *The movie's ending is an unsatisfactory cop-out.*

copper /kɒpər/ **1** N-UNCOUNT **Copper** is a reddish brown metal that is used to make things such as coins and electrical wires. □ *Chile is the world's largest producer of copper.* **2** ADJ **Copper** is sometimes used to describe things that are reddish-brown in color. [LITERARY] ❑ *His hair has reverted back to its original copper hue.* ❸ → See also color supplement

cop|pery /kɒpəri/ ADJ [usu ADJ n] A **coppery** color is reddish-brown like copper. ❑ *...pale coppery leaves.*

cop|pice /kɒpɪs/ (**coppices**) N-COUNT A **coppice** is a small group of trees growing very close to each other. ❑ *...coppices of willow.*

cops-and-robbers ADJ [ADJ n] A **cops-and-robbers** movie, television program, or book is one whose story involves the police trying to catch criminals.

copse /kɒps/ (**copses**) N-COUNT A **copse** is a small group of trees growing very close to each other. ❑ *...a little copse of fir trees.*

cop|ter /kɒptər/ (**copters**) N-COUNT A **copter** is a helicopter. [INFORMAL]

Cop|tic /kɒptɪk/ ADJ [ADJ n] **Coptic** means belonging or relating to a part of the Christian Church that started in Egypt. ❑ *The Coptic Church is among the oldest churches of Christianity.*

copu|la /kɒpyələ/ (**copulas**) N-COUNT A **copula** is the same as a linking verb.

copu|late /kɒpyəleɪt/ (**copulates, copulating, copulated**) V-RECIP If one animal or person **copulates** with another, they have sex. You can also say that two animals or people copulate. [TECHNICAL] ❑ *During the time she is paired to a male, the female allows no other males to copulate with her.* ❑ *Whales take twenty-four hours to copulate.* • **copu|la|tion** /kɒpyəleɪʃən/ (**copulations**) N-VAR ❑ *...acts of copulation.*

copy ♦♦◊ /kɒpi/ (**copies, copying, copied**) ❶ N-COUNT If you make a **copy** of something, you produce something that looks like the original thing. ❑ *The reporter apparently obtained a copy of Steve's resignation letter.* ❷ N-COUNT A **copy** of a book, newspaper, or CD is one of many that are exactly the same. ❑ *I bought a copy of "USA Today" from a street-corner machine.* ❸ V-T If you **copy** something, you produce something that looks like the original thing. ❑ *...lawsuits against companies who have unlawfully copied computer programs.* ❑ *He copied the chart from a book.* ❹ V-T/V-I If you **copy**, or **copy** a piece of writing, you write it again exactly. ❑ *He copied the data into a notebook.* ❑ *We're copying from textbooks because we don't have enough to go round.* • PHRASAL VERB **Copy out** means the same as **copy**. ❑ *He wrote the title on the blackboard, then copied out the text, sentence by sentence.* ❺ V-T If you **copy** a letter, document, or email to someone, you send them a copy of a letter or document that you have sent to someone else. ❑ *He fired off a letter and copied it to the president.* ❻ V-T If you **copy** someone's answer, you look at what that person has written and write the same thing yourself, in order to cheat in a test or exam. ❑ *He would allow John slyly to copy his answers to impossibly difficult algebra questions.* ❼ V-T If you **copy** a person or what they do, you try to do what they do or try to be like them, usually because you admire them or what they have done. ❑ *Children can be seen to copy the behavior of others whom they admire or identify with.* ❑ *He can claim to have been defeated by opponents copying his own tactics.* ❽ → see also **hard copy**

▶ **copy in** PHRASAL VERB If you **copy** someone **in** on something, you send them a copy of something you have written to someone else. [BRIT]

COLLOCATIONS

copy
NOUN
❶
adjective + **copy**: duplicate, exact, identical
verb + **copy**: keep, obtain, receive; enclose, send
❷
noun + **copy**: hardback, paperback
adjective + **copy**: advance, autographed, bound, free; dog-eared, well-thumbed
verb + **copy**: buy, distribute, sell, sign
VERB
❸
copy + noun: document, file, software
copy + adverb: illegally; widely
❹
copy + noun: drawing, text
copy + adverb: painstakingly, verbatim
❼
copy + noun: behavior
copy + adverb: slavishly

---

copy|cat /kɒpikæt/ (**copycats**) also **copy-cat** ❶ ADJ [ADJ n] A **copycat** crime is committed by someone who is copying someone else. ❑ *...a series of copycat attacks by hooligan gangs.* ❷ N-COUNT If you call someone a **copycat**, you are accusing them of copying your behavior, dress, or ideas. [INFORMAL, DISAPPROVAL] ❑ *The Beatles have copycats all over the world.*

copy edi|tor (**copy editors**) N-COUNT A **copy editor** is a person whose job it is to check and correct articles in newspapers or magazines before they are printed. [mainly AM]

in BRIT, also use **sub-editor**

copy|ist /kɒpiɪst/ (**copyists**) N-COUNT A **copyist** copies other people's music or paintings or, in the past, made written copies of documents. ❑ *She copies the true artist's signature as part of a painting, as do most copyists.*

copy ma|chine (**copy machines**) N-COUNT A **copy machine** is the same as a **copier**. [AM]

copy|right /kɒpiraɪt/ (**copyrights**) N-VAR If someone has the **copyright** on a piece of writing or music, it is illegal to reproduce or perform it without their permission. ❑ *Who owns the copyright on this movie?*

copy|right|ed /kɒpiraɪtɪd/ ADJ **Copyrighted** material is protected by a copyright. ❑ *They used copyrighted music without permission.*

copy|writer /kɒpiraɪtər/ (**copywriters**) N-COUNT A **copywriter** is a person whose job is to write the words for advertisements.

co|quette /koʊkɛt/ (**coquettes**) N-COUNT A **coquette** is a woman who behaves in a coquettish way. [OLD-FASHIONED]

co|quet|tish /koʊkɛtɪʃ/ ADJ If you describe a woman as **coquettish**, you mean she acts in a playful way that is intended to make her sexually attractive. [OLD-FASHIONED] ❑ *...a coquettish glance.*

cora|cle /kɒrəkəl/ (**coracles**) N-COUNT In former times, a **coracle** was a simple round rowing boat made of woven sticks covered with animal skins.

cor|al /kɒrəl/ (**corals**) ❶ N-VAR **Coral** is a hard substance formed from the bones of very small sea animals. It is often used to make jewelry. ❑ *The women have elaborate necklaces of turquoise and pink coral.* ❷ N-COUNT **Corals** are very small sea animals. ❑ *The seas around Bermuda are full of colorful corals and fantastic fish.* ❸ COLOR Something that is **coral** is dark orangey-pink in color. ❑ *...coral lipstick.*

cor|al reef (**coral reefs**) ❶ N-COUNT A **coral reef** is a long narrow mass of coral and other substances, the top of which is usually just above or just below the surface of the sea. ❑ *An unspoiled coral reef encloses the bay.* ❷ → See feature box at **ocean**

cord /kɔrd/ (**cords**) ❶ N-VAR **Cord** is strong, thick string. ❑ *The door had been tied shut with a length of nylon cord.* ❷ N-VAR **Cord** is wire covered in rubber or plastic which connects electrical equipment to an electricity supply. ❑ *...electrical cord.* ❑ *...an extension cord.*

cor|dial /kɔrdʒəl/ ADJ **Cordial** means friendly. [FORMAL] ❑ *He had never known him to be so chatty and cordial.* • **cor|di|al|ly** ADV [ADV with v] ❑ *They all greeted me very cordially and were eager to talk about the new project.*

cord|ite /kɔrdaɪt/ N-UNCOUNT **Cordite** is an explosive substance used in guns and bombs.

cord|less /kɔrdlɪs/ ADJ [usu ADJ n] A **cordless** telephone or piece of electric equipment is operated by a battery fitted inside it and is not connected to a supply of electricity. ❑ *The waitress approached Picone with a cordless phone.*

cor|don /kɔrdən/ (**cordons, cordoning, cordoned**) N-COUNT A **cordon** is a line or ring of police, soldiers, or vehicles preventing people from entering or leaving an area. ❑ *Police formed a cordon between the two crowds.*

▶ **cordon off** PHRASAL VERB If police or soldiers **cordon off** an area, they prevent people from entering or leaving an area. ❑ *Police cordoned off part of the city center.* ❑ *The police cordoned everything off.*

cor|don bleu /kɔrdɒn blɜ/ ADJ [ADJ n] **Cordon bleu** is used to describe cooking or cooks of the highest standard. ❑ *I took a cordon bleu cookery course.*

cor|du|roy /kɔrdərɔɪ/ (**corduroys**) **1** N-UNCOUNT **Corduroy** is thick, cotton cloth with parallel raised lines on the outside. **2** N-PLURAL **Corduroys** are pants made out of corduroy.

core ✦✧ /kɔr/ (**cores**, **coring**, **cored**) **1** N-COUNT The **core** of a fruit is the central part of it that contains seeds. ❑ *Someone threw an apple core.* **2** N-COUNT [usu with poss] The **core** of an object, building, or city is the central part of it. ❑ *...the Earth's core.* **3** V-T If you **core** a fruit, you remove its core. ❑ *...machines for peeling and coring apples.* **4** N-SING The **core** of something such as a problem or an issue is the part of it that has to be understood or accepted before the whole thing can be understood or dealt with. ❑ *...the ability to get straight to the core of a problem.* **5** ADJ A **core** team or a **core** group is a group of people who do the main part of a job or piece of work. Other people may also help, but only for limited periods of time. ❑ *We already have our core team in place.* **6** ADJ In a school or college, **core** subjects are a group of subjects that have to be studied. ❑ *The core subjects are English, mathematics and science.* ❑ *I'm not opposed to a core curriculum in principle, but I think requiring a foreign language is unrealistic.* **7** N-SING The **core** businesses or the **core** activities of a company or organization are their most important ones. ❑ *The core activities of social workers were reorganized.* **8** → See feature box at **cooking**

> ### SYNONYMS
> **core**
> NOUN **4**
> **essence**: *Others claim that Ireland's very essence is expressed through the language.*
> **nub**: *That, I think, is the nub of the problem.*
> **heart**: *The heart of the problem is supply and demand.*
> **substance**: *The substance of his discussions doesn't really matter.*
> **crux**: *He said the crux of the matter was economic policy.*

co|re|li|gion|ist /koʊrɪlɪdʒənɪst/ (**coreligionists**) N-COUNT [usu pl, oft poss N] A person's **coreligionists** are people who have the same religion. [FORMAL] ❑ *They will turn for help to their coreligionists in the Middle East.*

cor|gi /kɔrgi/ (**corgis**) N-COUNT A **corgi** is a type of small dog with short legs and a pointed nose.

co|ri|an|der /kɔriændər/ N-UNCOUNT **Coriander** is a plant with seeds that are used as a spice and leaves that are used as an herb.

cork /kɔrk/ (**corks**) **1** N-UNCOUNT **Cork** is a soft, light substance which forms the bark of a type of Mediterranean tree. ❑ *...cork floors.* **2** N-COUNT A **cork** is a piece of cork or plastic that is pushed into the opening of a bottle to close it. ❑ *He popped the cork and the champagne fizzed out over the bottle.*

cork|screw /kɔrkskru/ (**corkscrews**) N-COUNT A **corkscrew** is a device for pulling corks out of bottles.

cor|mo|rant /kɔrmərənt/ (**cormorants**) N-COUNT A **cormorant** is a type of dark-colored bird with a long neck. Cormorants usually live near the ocean and eat fish.

corn /kɔrn/ **1** N-UNCOUNT **Corn** is a tall plant which produces long vegetables covered with yellow seeds. It can also be used to refer to the yellow seeds. ❑ *...rows of corn in an Iowa field.* ❑ *We're having corn-on-the-cob for lunch.* **2** N-UNCOUNT **Corn** is used to refer to crops such as wheat and barley. It can also be used to refer to the seeds from these plants. [BRIT]

> in AM, use **grain**

3 → see also **popcorn**, **sweetcorn**

corn|ball /kɔrnbɔl/ ADJ **Cornball** means the same as **corny**. [mainly AM, DISAPPROVAL] ❑ *...cornball humor.*

corn|bread /kɔrnbrɛd/ also **corn bread** N-UNCOUNT **Cornbread** is bread made from ground corn.

corn cob (**corn cobs**) also **corncob** N-COUNT [usu pl] **Corn cobs** are the long rounded parts of the corn plant on which small yellow seeds grow.

cor|nea /kɔrniə/ (**corneas**) **1** N-COUNT The **cornea** is the transparent skin covering the outside of your eye. **2** → See also color supplement

cor|neal /kɔrniəl/ ADJ [ADJ n] **Corneal** means relating to the cornea. ❑ *...corneal scars.*

corned beef /kɔrnd bif/ N-UNCOUNT **Corned beef** is beef cooked and preserved in salt water.

cor|ner ✦✧ /kɔrnər/ (**corners**, **cornering**, **cornered**) **1** N-COUNT A **corner** is a point or an area where two or more edges, sides, or surfaces of something join. ❑ *He saw the corner of a magazine sticking out from under the blanket.* **2** N-COUNT The **corner** of a room, box, or similar space is the area inside it where its edges or walls meet. ❑ *...a card table in the corner of the living room.* ❑ *The ball hurtled into the far corner of the net.* **3** N-COUNT The **corner** of your mouth or eye is the side of it. ❑ *She flicked a crumb off the corner of her mouth.* **4** N-COUNT The **corner** of a street is the place where one of its sides ends as it joins another street. ❑ *She would spend the day hanging around street corners.* ❑ *We can't have police officers on every corner.* **5** N-COUNT A **corner** is a bend in a road. ❑ *...a sharp corner.* **6** N-COUNT In soccer, hockey, and some other sports, a **corner** is a free shot or kick taken from the corner of the field. ❑ *McPherson took the corner and James crashed his header off the crossbar and over the line.* **7** V-T If you **corner** a person or animal, you force them into a place they cannot escape from. ❑ *A police motorcycle chased his car twelve miles, and cornered him near Gainsborough.* **8** V-T If you **corner** someone, you force them to speak to you when they have been trying to avoid you. ❑ *Thomas managed to corner the young producer-director for an interview.* **9** V-T If a company or place **corners** an area of trade, they gain control over it so that no one else can have any success in that area. [BUSINESS] ❑ *In Germany and other countries Merc have cornered the market in taxis.* **10** V-I If a car, or the person driving it, **corners** in a particular way, the car goes around bends in roads in this way. ❑ *Peter drove jerkily, cornering too fast and fumbling the gears.* **11** PHRASE If you say that something is **around the corner**, you mean that it will happen very soon. ❑ *Economic recovery is just around the corner.* **12** PHRASE If you say that something is **around the corner**, you mean that it is very near. ❑ *My new place is just around the corner.* **13** PHRASE If you **cut corners**, you do something quickly by doing it in a less thorough way than you should. [DISAPPROVAL] ❑ *Take your time, don't cut corners, and follow instructions to the letter.*

> ### COLLOCATIONS
> **corner**
> NOUN **2**
> adjective + **corner**: far, remote; dark, quiet, shady, sheltered

corner|stone /kɔrnərstoʊn/ (**cornerstones**) N-COUNT The **cornerstone** of something is the basic part of it on which its existence, success, or truth depends. [FORMAL] ❑ *Research is the cornerstone of the profession.*

cor|ner store (**corner stores**) N-COUNT A **corner store** is a small store, usually on the corner of a street, that sells mainly food and household goods. [AM]

> in BRIT, use **corner shop**

cor|net /kɔrnɛt/ (**cornets**) **1** N-VAR [oft the N] A **cornet** is a musical instrument that looks like a small trumpet. **2** N-COUNT An ice cream **cornet** is a thin cone-shaped cookie with ice cream in it. [BRIT]

> in AM, use **cone**

corn|field /kɔrnfild/ (**cornfields**) N-COUNT A **cornfield** is a field in which corn is being grown.

corn|flake /kɔrnfleɪk/ (**cornflakes**) N-COUNT [usu pl] **Cornflakes** are small flat pieces of corn eaten with milk as a breakfast cereal. They are popular in the United States and Britain.

corn|flour /kɔrnflaʊər/ also **corn flour** N-UNCOUNT **Cornflour** is the same as **cornstarch**. [BRIT]

corn|flower /kɔrnflaʊər/ (**cornflowers**) N-VAR **Cornflowers** are small plants with flowers that are usually blue. ❑ *Her eyes were a bright, cornflower blue.*

cor|nice /kɔrnɪs/ (**cornices**) N-COUNT A **cornice** is a strip of plaster, wood, or stone which goes along the top of a wall or building.

corn|meal /kɔrnmil/ also **corn meal** N-UNCOUNT **Cornmeal** is a yellow powder made from corn used in cooking.

corn on the cob (corn on the cobs) also **corn-on-the-cob** N-VAR **Corn on the cob** is the long rounded part of the corn plant on which small yellow seeds grow. The seeds are eaten as a vegetable.

corn|row /kɔrnroʊ/ (**cornrows**) also **corn row** N-COUNT [usu pl] If someone wears their hair in **cornrows**, they braid their hair in parallel rows that lie flat upon their head. ❑ ...*a tall Black woman in cornrows.*

corn|starch /kɔrnstɑrtʃ/ also **corn starch** N-UNCOUNT **Cornstarch** is a fine white powder made from corn that is used to make sauces thicker. [AM]

in BRIT, use **cornflour**

cor|nu|co|pia /kɔrnəkoʊpiə, kɔrnyə-/ N-SING A **cornucopia** of things is a large number of different things. [LITERARY] ❑ ...*a table festooned with a cornucopia of fruit.*

corny /kɔrni/ (**cornier, corniest**) ADJ If you describe something as **corny**, you mean that it is obvious or sentimental and not at all original. [DISAPPROVAL] ❑ *I know it sounds corny, but I'm really not motivated by money.* ❑ ...*a corny slapstick movie.*

cor|ol|lary /kɔrəlɛri/ (**corollaries**) N-COUNT [oft with poss] A **corollary** of something is an idea, argument, or fact that results directly from it. [FORMAL] ❑ *The number of prisoners increased as a corollary of the government's determination to combat violent crime.*

co|ro|na /kəroʊnə/ N-SING The sun's **corona** is its outer atmosphere. [TECHNICAL]

coro|nary /kɔrənɛri/ (**coronaries**) **1** ADJ [ADJ n] **Coronary** means belonging or relating to the heart. [MEDICAL] ❑ *If all the coronary arteries are free of significant obstructions, all parts of the heart will receive equal amounts of oxygen.* **2** N-COUNT If someone has a **coronary**, they collapse because the flow of blood to their heart is blocked by a large lump of blood called a clot.

coro|nary throm|bo|sis (**coronary thromboses**) N-VAR If someone has a **coronary thrombosis**, they collapse because the flow of blood to their heart is blocked by a large lump of blood called a clot. [MEDICAL]

coro|na|tion /kɔrəneɪʃən/ (**coronations**) N-COUNT A **coronation** is the ceremony at which a king or queen is crowned.

co|ro|na|vi|rus /kəroʊnəvaɪrəs/ (**coronaviruses**) **1** N-COUNT A **coronavirus** is a type of virus that can cause illnesses such as the common cold, or serious diseases such as SARS and COVID-19. ❑ *The disease is spread mainly by droplets containing the coronavirus.* **2** N-VAR **Coronavirus** is a common way of referring to the disease COVID-19. ❑ *This is how you can protect yourself and others from coronavirus.*

coro|ner /kɔrənər/ (**coroners**) N-COUNT A **coroner** is an official who is responsible for investigating the deaths of people who have died in a sudden, violent, or unusual way. ❑ *The coroner recorded a verdict of accidental death.*

coro|net /kɔrənɛt/ (**coronets**) N-COUNT A **coronet** is a small crown.

Corp. ♦◇◇ **Corp.** is a written abbreviation for **corporation**. [BUSINESS] ❑ ...*Sony Corp. of Japan.*

cor|po|ra /kɔrpərə/ **Corpora** is a plural of **corpus**.

cor|po|ral /kɔrpərəl, -prəl/ (**corporals**) N-COUNT; N-TITLE A **corporal** is a noncommissioned officer in the army or United States Marines. ❑ *The corporal shouted an order at the men.*

cor|po|ral pun|ish|ment N-UNCOUNT **Corporal punishment** is the punishment of people by hitting them. ❑ *Corporal punishment in public schools is forbidden.*

cor|po|rate ♦◇◇ /kɔrpərɪt, -prɪt/ ADJ [ADJ n] **Corporate** means relating to business corporations or to a particular business corporation. [BUSINESS] ❑ ...*top U.S. corporate executives.* ❑ ...*a corporate lawyer.*

cor|po|rate hos|pi|tal|ity N-UNCOUNT **Corporate hospitality** is the entertainment that a company offers to its most valued clients, for example by inviting them to sporting events and providing them with food and drink. [BUSINESS] ❑ ...*corporate hospitality at football games.* ❑ ...*executives in a corporate hospitality tent.*

cor|po|rate raid|er (**corporate raiders**) N-COUNT A **corporate raider** is a person or organization that tries to take control of a company by buying a large number of its shares. [BUSINESS] ❑ *Your present company could be taken over by corporate raiders.*

cor|po|ra|tion ♦◇◇ /kɔrpəreɪʃən/ (**corporations**) N-COUNT; N-IN-NAMES A **corporation** is a large business or company with special rights and powers. [BUSINESS] ❑ ...*multinational corporations.* ❑ *Many voters resented the power of big corporations.*

> **SYNONYMS**
>
> **corporation**
> NOUN
> **multinational:** ...*multinationals such as Ford and IBM.*
> **firm:** *The firm's employees were expecting large bonuses.*
> **company:** ...*the Ford Motor Company.*
> **business:** *The company was a family business.*

cor|po|ra|tion tax N-UNCOUNT **Corporation tax** is a tax that companies have to pay on the profits they make. [BUSINESS]

cor|po|rat|ism /kɔrpərətɪzəm, -prətɪz-/ N-UNCOUNT **Corporatism** is the organization and control of a country by groups who share a common interest or profession. [DISAPPROVAL] ❑ *"The age of corporatism must be put firmly behind us,"* he proclaimed.

cor|po|rat|ist /kɔrpərətɪst, -prətɪst/ ADJ [usu ADJ n] You use **corporatist** to describe organizations, ideas, or systems which follow the principles of corporatism. [DISAPPROVAL] ❑ ...*a corporatist political system.*

cor|po|real /kɔrpɔriəl/ ADJ [usu ADJ n] **Corporeal** means involving or relating to the physical world rather than the spiritual world. [FORMAL] ❑ ...*man's corporeal existence.*

corps /kɔr/ (**corps**)

Corps is both the singular and the plural form.

1 N-COUNT; N-IN-NAMES A **corps** is a part of the army which has special duties. ❑ ...*the Army Medical Corps.* **2** N-COUNT The **Corps** is the United States Marine Corps. [AM] ❑ ...*seventy-five men, all combat veterans, all members of The Corps' most exclusive unit.* **3** N-COUNT A **corps** is a small group of people who do a special job. ❑ ...*the diplomatic corps.*

corps de bal|let /kɔr də bæleɪ/ N-SING In ballet, the **corps de ballet** is the group of dancers who dance together, in contrast to the main dancers, who dance by themselves.

corpse /kɔrps/ (**corpses**) N-COUNT A **corpse** is a dead body, especially the body of a human being. ❑ *Detectives placed the corpse in a body bag.*

cor|pu|lent /kɔrpyələnt/ ADJ If you describe someone as **corpulent**, you mean that they are fat. [LITERARY] ❑ ...*a rather corpulent farmer.*

cor|pus /kɔrpəs/ (**corpora** /kɔrpərə/ or **corpuses**) N-COUNT [usu with supp] A **corpus** is a large collection of written or spoken texts that is used for language research. [TECHNICAL]

cor|pus|cle /kɔrpəsəl, -pʌsəl/ (**corpuscles**) N-COUNT [usu pl] **Corpuscles** are red or white blood cells. ❑ *Deficiency of red corpuscles is caused by a lack of iron.*

cor|ral /kəræl/ (**corrals, corralling, corralled**) **1** N-COUNT A **corral** is a space surrounded by a fence where cattle or horses are kept. **2** V-T To **corral** a person or animal means to capture or confine them. [mainly AM] ❑ *Within hours, police corralled the three men Lewis had named.*

cor|rect ♦♦◇ /kərɛkt/ (**corrects, correcting, corrected**) **1** ADJ If something is **correct**, it is right and true. ❑ *The correct answers can be found at the bottom of page 8.* ❑ *The following information was correct at time of going to press.* • **cor|rect|ly** ADV [ADV with v] ❑ *Did I pronounce your name correctly?* • **cor|rect|ness** N-UNCOUNT ❑ *Ask the investor to check the correctness of what he has written.* **2** ADJ [v-link ADJ] If someone is **correct**, what they have said or thought is true. [FORMAL] ❑ *You are absolutely correct. The leaves are from a bay tree.* **3** ADJ [ADJ n] The **correct** thing or method is the thing or method that is required or is most suitable in a particular situation. ❑ *The use of the correct materials was crucial.* ❑ *White was in no doubt the referee made the correct decision.* • **cor|rect|ly** ADV [ADV with v] ❑ *If correctly executed, this shot will give them a better chance of getting the ball close to the hole.* **4** ADJ If you say that someone is **correct** in doing something, you approve of their action. ☐ *You are perfectly correct in trying to steer your mother toward increased independence.* • **cor|rect|ly** ADV [ADV with cl] ☐ *I think the police commission acted correctly.* **5** ADJ If a person or their behavior is **correct**, their behavior is in accordance with social or other rules. ☐ *He was very polite and very correct.* • **cor|rect|ly** ADV [ADV with v] ☐ *She began speaking politely, even correctly.* • **cor|rect|ness** N-UNCOUNT ☐ *...his stiff-legged gait and formal correctness.* **6** V-T If you **correct** a problem, mistake, or fault, you do something which puts it right. ☐ *He may need surgery to correct the problem.* • **cor|rec|tion** /kərɛkʃ°n/ (**corrections**) N-VAR ☐ *...legislation to require the correction of factual errors.* **7** V-T If you **correct** someone, you say something which you think is more accurate or appropriate than what they have just said. ☐ *"Actually, that isn't what happened," George corrects me.* **8** V-T When someone **corrects** a piece of writing, they look at it and mark the mistakes in it. ☐ *It took an extraordinary effort to focus on preparing his classes or correcting his students' work.*

cor|rec|tion /kərɛkʃ°n/ (**corrections**) **1** N-COUNT **Corrections** are marks or comments made on a piece of work, especially school work, which indicate where there are mistakes and what are the right answers. ☐ *In a group, compare your corrections to Exercise 2A.* **2** N-UNCOUNT **Correction** is the punishment of criminals. [mainly AM] ☐ *...jails and other parts of the correction system.* **3** → see also **correct**

cor|rec|tion|al /kərɛkʃən°l/ ADJ [ADJ n] **Correctional** means related to prisons. [mainly AM] ☐ *He is currently being held in a metropolitan correctional center.*

cor|rec|tion|al fa|cil|ity (**correctional facilities**) N-COUNT A **correctional facility** is a prison or similar institution. [AM] ☐ *...the Utah state correctional facility.*

cor|rec|tions of|fic|er (**corrections officers**) N-COUNT A **corrections officer** is someone who works as a guard at a prison. [AM] ☐ *...a corrections officer in the New Jersey prison system.*

cor|rec|tive /kərɛktɪv/ (**correctives**) **1** ADJ **Corrective** measures or techniques are intended to put right something that is wrong. ☐ *Scientific institutions have been reluctant to take corrective action.* **2** N-COUNT If something is a **corrective** to a particular view or account, it gives a more accurate or fairer picture than there would have been without it. [FORMAL] ☐ *...a useful corrective to the mistaken view that all psychologists are behaviorists.*

cor|re|late /kɒrəleɪt/ (**correlates, correlating, correlated**) **1** V-RECIP If one thing **correlates** with another, there is a close similarity or connection between them, often because one thing causes the other. You can also say that two things **correlate**. [FORMAL] ☐ *Obesity correlates with increased risk for hypertension and stroke.* ☐ *The political opinions of spouses correlate more closely than their heights.* **2** V-T If you **correlate** things, you work out the way in which they are connected or the way they influence each other. [FORMAL] ☐ *Attempts to correlate specific language functions with particular parts of the brain have not advanced very far.*

cor|re|la|tion /kɒrəleɪʃ°n/ (**correlations**) N-COUNT A **correlation** between things is a connection or link between them. [FORMAL] ☐ *...the correlation between smoking and disease.*

cor|rela|tive /kərɛlətɪv/ (**correlatives**) N-COUNT [oft N of n] If one thing is a **correlative** of another, the first thing is caused by the second thing, or occurs together with it. [FORMAL] ☐ *Man has rights only in so far as they are a correlative of duty.*

cor|re|spond /kɒrɪspɒnd/ (**corresponds, corresponding, corresponded**) **1** V-RECIP If one thing **corresponds** to another, there is a close similarity or connection between them. You can also say that two things **correspond**. ☐ *Racegoers will be given a number which will correspond to a horse running in a race.* ☐ *The two maps of the Rockies correspond closely.* • **cor|re|spond|ing** ADJ [ADJ n] ☐ *The rise in interest rates was not reflected in a corresponding rise in the dollar.* **2** V-RECIP If you **correspond** with someone, you write letters to them. You can also say that two people **correspond**. ☐ *She still corresponds with friends she met in Majorca nine years ago.*

cor|re|spond|ence /kɒrɪspɒndəns/ (**correspondences**) **1** N-UNCOUNT [also a N, oft N with n] **Correspondence** is the act of writing letters to someone. ☐ *The judges' decision is final and no correspondence will be entered into.* **2** N-UNCOUNT Someone's **correspondence** is the letters that they receive or send. ☐ *He always replied to his correspondence.* **3** N-COUNT If there is a **correspondence** between two things, there is a close similarity or connection between them. ☐ *In African languages there is a close correspondence between sounds and letters.*

cor|re|spond|ence course (**correspondence courses**) N-COUNT A **correspondence course** is a course in which you study at home, receiving your work by mail and sending it back by mail. ☐ *I took a correspondence course in computing.*

cor|re|spond|ent ◆◇ /kɒrɪspɒndənt/ (**correspondents**) N-COUNT A **correspondent** is a newspaper or television journalist, especially one who specializes in a particular type of news. ☐ *As our Diplomatic Correspondent Mark Brayne reports, the president was given a sympathetic hearing.*

cor|re|spond|ing|ly /kɒrɪspɒndɪŋli/ ADV You use **correspondingly** when describing a situation which is closely connected with one you have just mentioned or is similar to it. ☐ *As his political stature has shrunk, he has grown correspondingly more dependent on the army.*

cor|ri|dor /kɒrɪdər, -dɔr/ (**corridors**) **1** N-COUNT A **corridor** is a long passage in a building, with doors and rooms on one or both sides. [mainly BRIT] ☐ *There were doors on both sides of the corridor.* **2** N-COUNT A **corridor** is a strip of land that connects one country to another or gives it a route to the sea through another country. ☐ *East Prussia and the rest of Germany were separated, in 1919, by the Polish Corridor.* **3** N-COUNT A **corridor** is an area of land between two large cities. ☐ *...the Northeast corridor.*

cor|robo|rate /kərɒbəreɪt/ (**corroborates, corroborating, corroborated**) V-T To **corroborate** something that has been said or reported means to provide evidence or information that supports it. [FORMAL] ☐ *I had access to a wide range of documents which corroborated the story.* • **cor|robo|ra|tion** /kərɒbəreɪʃ°n/ N-UNCOUNT ☐ *He could not get a single witness to establish independent corroboration of his version of the accident.*

cor|robo|ra|tive /kərɒbəreɪtɪv, -rɒbərətɪv/ ADJ [ADJ n] **Corroborative** evidence or information supports an idea, account, or argument. [FORMAL] ☐ *...a written statement supported by other corroborative evidence.*

cor|rode /kəroʊd/ (**corrodes, corroding, corroded**) V-T/V-I If metal or stone **corrodes**, or **is corroded**, it is gradually destroyed by a chemical or by rust. ☐ *He has devised a process for making gold wires which neither corrode nor oxidize.* ☐ *Engineers found the structure had been corroded by moisture.* • **cor|rod|ed** ADJ ☐ *The investigators found that the underground pipes were badly corroded.*

cor|ro|sion /kəroʊʒ°n/ N-UNCOUNT **Corrosion** is the damage that is caused when something is corroded. ☐ *Zinc is used to protect other metals from corrosion.*

cor|ro|sive /kəroʊsɪv/ **1** ADJ A **corrosive** substance is able to destroy solid materials by a chemical reaction. ☐ *Sodium and sulfur are highly corrosive.* **2** ADJ If you say that something has a **corrosive** effect, you mean that it gradually causes serious harm. [FORMAL] ☐ *...the corrosive effects of inflation.*

cor|ru|gat|ed /kɒrəgeɪtɪd/ ADJ **Corrugated** metal or cardboard has been folded into a series of small parallel folds to make it stronger. ☐ *...a hut with a corrugated iron roof.*

cor|rupt /kərʌpt/ (**corrupts, corrupting, corrupted**) **1** ADJ Someone who is **corrupt** behaves in a way that is morally wrong, especially by doing dishonest or illegal things in return for money or power. ☐ *...to save the nation from corrupt politicians of both parties.* **2** V-T/V-I If someone **is corrupted** by something, it causes them to become dishonest and unjust and unable to be trusted. ☐ *It is sad to see a man so corrupted by the desire for money and power.* ☐ *Power tends to corrupt.* **3** V-T To **corrupt** someone means to cause them to stop caring about moral standards. ☐ *...warning that television will corrupt us all.*

cor|rup|tion ◆◇ /kərʌpʃ°n/ N-UNCOUNT **Corruption** is dishonesty and illegal behavior by people in positions of authority or power. ☐ *The president faces 54 charges of corruption and tax evasion.*

cor|sage /kɔrsɑʒ/ (**corsages**) N-COUNT A **corsage** is a very small bunch of flowers that a woman wears on a dress or jacket.

cor|set /kɔ́rsɪt/ (corsets) N-COUNT A **corset** is a stiff piece of underwear worn by some women, especially in the past. It fits tightly around the hips and waist and makes the person wearing it look thinner.

cor|set|ed /kɔ́rsɪtɪd/ ADJ Someone who is **corseted** is wearing a corset.

cor|tege /kɔrtɛ́ʒ/ (corteges) also **cortège** N-COUNT-COLL A **cortege** is a procession of people who are walking or riding in cars to a funeral.

cor|tex /kɔ́rtɛks/ (cortices /kɔ́rtɪsiz/) N-COUNT [usu sing, oft the N] The **cortex** of the brain or of another organ is its outer layer. [MEDICAL] ❏ ...the cerebral cortex.

cor|ti|sone /kɔ́rtɪzoʊn/ N-UNCOUNT **Cortisone** is a hormone used in the treatment of arthritis, allergies, and some skin diseases.

co|rus|cat|ing /kɔ́rəskeɪtɪŋ/ ADJ [usu ADJ n] A **coruscating** speech or performance is lively, intelligent, and impressive. [LITERARY, APPROVAL] ❏ ...coruscating humor.

cor|vette /kɔrvɛ́t/ (corvettes) N-COUNT A **corvette** is a small fast warship that is used to protect other ships from attack.

'cos ♦♢ /kəz, STRONG kʌz/ also **cos** CONJ **'Cos** is an informal way of saying **because**. [BRIT, SPOKEN]

in AM, use **cuz**

cos|met|ic /kɒzmɛ́tɪk/ (cosmetics) **1** N-COUNT **Cosmetics** are substances such as lipstick or powder, which people put on their face to make themselves look more attractive. ❏ ...the cosmetics counter of a department store. **2** ADJ If you describe measures or changes as **cosmetic**, you mean they improve the appearance of a situation or thing but do not change its basic nature, and you are usually implying that they are inadequate. [DISAPPROVAL] ❏ It is a cosmetic measure which will do nothing to help the situation long term.

cos|met|ic sur|gery N-UNCOUNT **Cosmetic surgery** is surgery done to make a person look more attractive. ❏ The champion fighter had cosmetic surgery on his ears to stop them sticking out.

cos|mic /kɒ́zmɪk/ **1** ADJ **Cosmic** means occurring in, or coming from, the part of space that lies outside Earth and its atmosphere. ❏ ...cosmic radiation. **2** ADJ **Cosmic** means belonging or relating to the universe. ❏ ...the cosmic laws governing our world.

cos|mic rays N-PLURAL **Cosmic rays** are rays that reach earth from outer space and consist of atomic nuclei.

cos|mol|ogy /kɒzmɒ́lədʒi/ (cosmologies) **1** N-VAR A **cosmology** is a theory about the origin and nature of the universe. ❏ ...the ideas implicit in Big Bang cosmology. **2** N-UNCOUNT **Cosmology** is the study of the origin and nature of the universe. ● **cos|molo|gist** (cosmologists) N-COUNT ❏ ...astronomers and cosmologists. ● **cos|mo|logi|cal** /kɒzməlɒ́dʒɪkəl/ ADJ [ADJ n] ❏ ...cosmological sciences.

cos|mo|naut /kɒ́zmənɔt/ (cosmonauts) N-COUNT A **cosmonaut** is an **astronaut** from the former Soviet Union.

cos|mo|poli|tan /kɒzməpɒ́lɪtən/ **1** ADJ A **cosmopolitan** place or society is full of people from many different countries and cultures. [APPROVAL] ❏ ...a cosmopolitan city. **2** ADJ Someone who is **cosmopolitan** has had a lot of contact with people and things from many different countries and as a result is very open to different ideas and ways of doing things. [APPROVAL] ❏ The family is rich, and extremely sophisticated and cosmopolitan.

cos|mos /kɒ́zməs, -moʊs/ N-SING The **cosmos** is the universe. [LITERARY] ❏ ...the natural laws of the cosmos.

cos|set /kɒ́sɪt/ (cossets, cosseting or cossetting, cosseted or cossetted) V-T [usu passive] If someone **is cosseted**, everything possible is done for them and they are protected from anything unpleasant. ❏ Our kind of travel is definitely not suitable for people who expect to be cosseted.

cost ♦♦♦ /kɔ́st/ (costs, costing)

The form **cost** is used in the present tense, and is also the past tense and participle, except for meaning **3**, where the form **costed** is used.

1 N-COUNT The **cost** of something is the amount of money that is needed in order to buy, do, or make it. ❏ The cost of a loaf of bread has increased five-fold. ❏ In 1989 the price of coffee fell so low that in many countries it did not even cover the cost of production. **2** V-T If something **costs** a particular amount of money, you can buy, do, or make it for that amount. ❏ This course is limited to 12 people and costs $150. ❏ Painted walls look much more interesting and don't cost much. **3** V-T [usu passive] When something that you plan to do or make **is costed**, the amount of money you need is calculated in advance. ❏ The building work has not been fully costed but runs into millions of dollars. **4** V-T If an event or mistake **costs** you something, you lose that thing as the result of it. ❏ ...a six-year-old boy whose life was saved by an operation that cost him his sight. **5** N-PLURAL Your **costs** are the total amount of money that you must spend on running your home or business. ❏ Costs have been cut by 30 to 50 percent. **6** N-PLURAL If someone is ordered by a court of law to pay **costs**, they have to pay a sum of money toward the expenses of a court case they are involved in. ❏ He was jailed for 18 months and ordered to pay $550 costs. **7** N-UNCOUNT If something is sold **at cost**, it is sold for the same price as it cost the seller to buy it. ❏ ...a store that provided cigarettes and candy bars at cost. **8** N-SING The **cost** of something is the loss, damage, or injury that is involved in trying to achieve it. ❏ In March Mr. Salinas shut down the city's oil refinery at a cost of $500 million and 5,000 jobs. **9** PHRASE If you say that something must be avoided **at all costs**, you are emphasizing that it must be not be allowed to happen under any circumstances. [EMPHASIS] ❏ They told Jacques Delors a disastrous world trade war must be avoided at all costs. **10** PHRASE If you say that something must be done **at any cost**, you are emphasizing that it must be done, even if this requires a lot of effort or money. [EMPHASIS] ❏ This book is of such importance that it must be published at any cost.

SYNONYMS

cost
NOUN **1**
price: ...a sharp increase in the price of petrol.
worth: I went and bought about six dollars' worth of potato chips.
expense: He's bought a big TV at a great expense.
charge: We can arrange this for a small charge.
rate: ...reduced rates for travelers using Gatwick Airport.

cost ac|count|ing N-UNCOUNT **Cost accounting** is the recording and analysis of all the various costs of running a business. [BUSINESS] ❏ But full cost accounting will be introduced without delay.

co|star /koʊ́stɑr/ (costars, costarring, costarred)

in BRIT, also use **co-star**

1 N-COUNT An actor's **costars** are the other actors who also have one of the main parts in a particular movie. ❏ During the filming, Curtis fell in love with his costar, Christine Kaufmann. **2** V-T If a movie **costars** particular actors, they have the main parts in it. ❏ Produced by Oliver Stone, "Wild Palms" costars Dana Delaney, Jim Belushi and Angie Dickinson.

cost-effective ADJ Something that is **cost-effective** saves or makes a lot of money in comparison with the costs involved. ❏ The bank must be run in a cost-effective way. ● **cost-effectively** ADV ❏ The management tries to produce the magazine as cost-effectively as possible. ● **cost-effectiveness** N-UNCOUNT ❏ A report has raised doubts about the cost-effectiveness of the proposals.

cost|ly /kɔ́stli/ (costlier, costliest) ADJ If you say that something is **costly**, you mean that it costs a lot of money, often more than you would want to pay. ❏ Having professionally made curtains can be costly, so why not make your own?

cost of liv|ing N-SING The **cost of living** is the average amount of money that people in a particular place need in order to be able to afford basic food, housing, and clothing. ❏ The cost of living has increased dramatically.

cost-plus ADJ [ADJ n] A **cost-plus** basis for a contract for work to be done is one in which the buyer agrees to pay the seller or contractor all the costs plus a profit. ❏ All vessels were to be built on a cost-plus basis.

cos|tume /kɒ́stum/ (costumes) **1** N-VAR An actor's or performer's **costume** is the set of clothes they wear while

costume jewelry   285   **could**

they are performing. ❑ *Even from a distance, the effect of his fox costume was stunning.* ❑ *The performers, in costume and makeup, were walking up and down backstage.* **2** N-UNCOUNT The clothes worn by people at a particular time in history, or in a particular country, are referred to as a particular type of **costume**. ❑ *...men and women in eighteenth-century costume.* **3** ADJ [ADJ n] A **costume** drama is one which is set in the past and in which the actors wear the type of clothes that were worn in that period. ❑ *...a lavish costume drama set in Ireland and the U.S. in the 1890s.* **4** → See feature box at **theater**

cos|tume jew|el|ry

in BRIT, use **costume jewellery**

N-UNCOUNT **Costume jewelry** is jewelry made from cheap materials.

cos|tume par|ty (costume parties) also **costume ball** N-COUNT A **costume party** or **costume ball** is a party at which the guests try to look like famous people or people from history, from stories, or from particular professions. [AM] ❑ *...a pair of angels' wings and a halo that she'd worn to a costume party just a few months before.*

in BRIT, use **fancy-dress party**

cos|tum|er /kɒstumər/ (costumers) N-COUNT A **costumer** is a person or company that makes or supplies costumes. [AM] ❑ *...the costumers who clothed Sly Stallone in "Judge Dredd."*

cosy /koʊzi/ [BRIT] → see **cozy**

cot /kɒt/ (cots) **1** N-COUNT A **cot** is a narrow bed, usually made of canvas fitted over a frame which can be folded up. [AM]

in BRIT, use **camp bed**

2 N-COUNT A **cot** is a bed for a baby. [BRIT]

in AM, use **crib**

3 → See also color supplement

cot death [BRIT] → see **crib death**

co|terie /koʊtəri/ (coteries) N-COUNT-COLL [usu with supp] A **coterie** of a particular kind is a small group of people who are close friends or have a common interest, and who do not want other people to join them. [FORMAL] ❑ *The songs he recorded were written by a small coterie of dedicated writers.*

cot|tage ✦◇◇ /kɒtɪdʒ/ (cottages) **1** N-COUNT; N-IN-NAMES A **cottage** is a small house, usually in the country. ❑ *They used to have a cottage in N.W. Scotland.* **2** → See also color supplement

---
COLLOCATIONS
---

cottage
NOUN **1**
noun + **cottage**: country, vacation; one-bedroom, two-bedroom
adjective + **cottage**: stone, terraced, thatched; charming, cozy, pretty, quaint

cot|tage cheese N-UNCOUNT **Cottage cheese** is a soft, white, lumpy cheese made from the curds of skim milk.

cot|tage in|dus|try (cottage industries) N-COUNT A **cottage industry** is a small business that is run from someone's home, especially one that involves a craft such as knitting or pottery. [BUSINESS] ❑ *Bookbinding is largely a cottage industry.*

cot|ton ✦◇◇ /kɒtən/ (cottons) **1** N-MASS **Cotton** is a type of cloth made from soft fibers from a particular plant. ❑ *...a cotton shirt.* **2** N-UNCOUNT **Cotton** is a plant which is grown in warm countries and which produces soft fibers used in making cotton cloth. ❑ *...a large cotton plantation in Tennessee.* **3** N-UNCOUNT **Cotton** or **absorbent cotton** is a soft mass of cotton, used especially for applying liquids or creams to your skin. [AM] ❑ *...cotton balls.*

in BRIT, use **cotton wool**

4 N-MASS **Cotton** is thread that is used for sewing, especially thread that is made from cotton. [BRIT]

in AM, use **thread**

5 → See feature box at **sewing**

cot|ton bud (cotton buds) N-COUNT A **cotton bud** is the same as a Q-tip. [BRIT]

cot|ton can|dy N-UNCOUNT **Cotton candy** is a large, pink or white mass of sugar threads that is eaten from a stick. It is sold at fairs or other outdoor events. [AM]

in BRIT, use **candyfloss**

cotton-picking ADJ [ADJ n] **Cotton-picking** is used by some people to emphasize what they are saying. [AM, INFORMAL, EMPHASIS] ❑ *"Just hold on a cotton-picking minute," I said.*

cot|ton swab (cotton swabs) N-COUNT A **cotton swab** is the same as a **swab**.

cotton|tail /kɒtənteɪl/ (cottontails) N-COUNT A **cottontail** is a type of rabbit commonly found in North America. [AM]

cotton|wood /kɒtənwʊd/ (cottonwoods) N-COUNT A **cottonwood** or a **cottonwood tree** is a kind of tree that grows in North America and has seeds that are covered with hairs that look like cotton.

cot|ton wool N-UNCOUNT **Cotton wool** is a soft mass of cotton, used especially for applying liquids or creams to your skin. [BRIT]

in AM, use **cotton**

couch /kaʊtʃ/ (couches) **1** N-COUNT A **couch** is a long, comfortable seat for two or three people. **2** N-COUNT A **couch** is a narrow bed which patients lie on while they are being treated by a psychoanalyst. ❑ *Between films he often winds up spending every single morning on his psychiatrist's couch.*

couch po|ta|to (couch potatoes) N-COUNT A **couch potato** is someone who spends most of their time watching television and does not exercise or have any interesting hobbies. [INFORMAL, DISAPPROVAL] ❑ *...couch potatoes flicking through endless satellite TV channels.*

couch surf|ing **1** N-UNCOUNT **Couch surfing** is the practice of sleeping at the houses of several different people for a period of time without paying. ❑ *He spent a few months couch surfing.* **2** → See feature box at **poverty**

cou|gar /kugər/ (cougars) N-COUNT A **cougar** is a wild member of the cat family. Cougars have brownish-gray fur and live in mountain regions of North and South America. [mainly AM]

in BRIT, usually use **puma**

cough ✦◇◇ /kɔf/ (coughs, coughing, coughed) **1** V-I When you **cough**, you force air out of your throat with a sudden, harsh noise. You often cough when you are ill, or when you are nervous or want to attract someone's attention. ❑ *Graham began to cough violently.* • N-COUNT **Cough** is also a noun. ❑ *Coughs and sneezes spread infections much faster in a warm atmosphere.* • **cough|ing** N-UNCOUNT ❑ *He was then overcome by a terrible fit of coughing.* **2** V-T If you **cough** blood or mucus, it comes up out of your throat or mouth when you cough. ❑ *I started coughing blood so they transferred me to a hospital.* • PHRASAL VERB **Cough up** means the same as **cough**. ❑ *On the chilly seas, Keats became feverish, continually coughing up blood.* **3** N-COUNT A **cough** is an illness in which you cough often and your chest or throat hurts. ❑ *I had a persistent cough for over a month.*

▶ **cough up** **1** PHRASAL VERB If you **cough up** an amount of money, you pay or spend that amount, usually when you would prefer not to. [INFORMAL] ❑ *I'll have to cough up $10,000 a year for tuition.* **2** → see also **cough 2**

cough medi|cine (cough medicines) N-MASS **Cough medicine** is liquid medicine that you take when you have a cough.

cough syr|up (cough syrups) N-MASS **Cough syrup** is a liquid medicine that you take when you have a cough. [mainly AM]

in BRIT, use **cough mixture**

could ✦✦✦ /kəd, STRONG kʊd/

Could is a modal verb. It is used with the base form of a verb. **Could** is sometimes considered to be the past form of **can** ①, but in this dictionary the two words are dealt with separately.

1 MODAL You use **could** to indicate that someone had the ability to do something. You use **could not** or **couldn't** to say that someone was unable to do something. ❑ *I could see that something was terribly wrong.* ❑ *When I left school at 16, I couldn't read or write.* **2** MODAL You use **could** to indicate that something sometimes happened. ❑ *Though he had a temper and could be nasty, it never lasted.* **3** MODAL You use **could have** to indicate that something was a possibility in the past, although it did not actually happen. ❑ *He could have made a fortune as a lawyer.* ❑ *You could have been killed!* **4** MODAL You use **could** to indicate that something is possibly true, or that it may possibly happen. ❑ *Doctors told him the disease could have been caused by years of working in smokey clubs.* ❑ *An improvement in living standards could be years away.* **5** MODAL You use **could not** or **couldn't** to indicate that it is not possible that something is true. ❑ *They argued all the time and thought it couldn't be good for the baby.* ❑ *Anne couldn't be expected to understand the situation.* **6** MODAL You use **could** to talk about a possibility, ability, or opportunity that depends on other conditions. ❑ *Their hope was that a new and better East Germany could be born.* **7** MODAL You use **could** when you are saying that one thing or situation resembles another. ❑ *The charming characters she draws look like they could have walked out of the 1920s.* **8** MODAL You use **could**, or **couldn't** in questions, when you are making offers and suggestions. ❑ *I could call the local doctor.* ❑ *You could look for a career abroad where environmental jobs are better paid and more secure.* ❑ *Couldn't we call a special meeting?* **9** MODAL You use **could** in questions when you are making a polite request or asking for permission to do something. Speakers sometimes use **couldn't** instead of **could** to show that they realize that their request may be refused. [POLITENESS] ❑ *Could I stay tonight?* ❑ *He asked if he could have a cup of coffee.* ❑ *Couldn't I watch you do it?* **10** MODAL You use **could** to say emphatically that someone ought to do the thing mentioned, especially when you are annoyed because they have not done it. You use **why couldn't** in questions to express your surprise or annoyance that someone has not done something. [EMPHASIS] ❑ *We've come to see you, so you could at least stand and greet us properly.* ❑ *Why couldn't she have said something?* **11** MODAL You use **could** when you are expressing strong feelings about something by saying that you feel as if you want to do the thing mentioned, although you do not do it. [EMPHASIS] ❑ *I could kill you! I swear I could!* ❑ *"Welcome back" was all they said. I could have kissed them!* **12** MODAL You use **could** after 'if' when talking about something that you do not have the ability or opportunity to do, but which you are imagining in order to consider what the likely consequences might be. ❑ *If I could afford it, I'd have four television sets.* **13** MODAL You use **could not** or **couldn't** with comparatives to emphasize that someone or something has as much as is possible of a particular quality. For example, if you say 'I couldn't be happier,' you mean that you are extremely happy. [EMPHASIS] ❑ *The rest of the players are great and I couldn't be happier.* **14** MODAL In speech, you use **how could** in questions to emphasize that you feel strongly about something bad that has happened. [EMPHASIS] ❑ *How could you allow him to do something like that?* ❑ *How could I have been so stupid?* **15 could do with** → see **do** ②

couldn't /kʊdənt/ **Couldn't** is the usual spoken form of 'could not.'

could've /kʊdəv/ **Could've** is the usual spoken form of 'could have,' when 'have' is an auxiliary verb.

coun|cil ✦✦✦ /kaʊnsəl/ (councils) **1** N-COUNT-COLL; N-IN-NAMES A **council** is a group of people who are elected to govern a local area such as a city. ❑ *The city council has voted almost unanimously in favor.* **2** N-COUNT-COLL **Council** is used in the names of some organizations. ❑ *...the National Council for Civil Liberties.* ❑ *...the Arts Council.* **3** N-COUNT-COLL In some organizations, the **council** is the group of people that controls or governs it. ❑ *The permanent council of the Organization of American States meets today here in Washington.* **4** N-COUNT A **council** is a specially organized, formal meeting that is attended by a particular group of people. ❑ *President Najibullah said he would call a grand council of all Afghans.*

COLLOCATIONS

council
NOUN **1**
noun + **council**: city, county, district, town
adjective + **council**: local, regional
verb + **council**: contact, elect

SYNONYMS

council
NOUN **4**
committee: *...an elected Management Committee who serve the Association on a voluntary basis.*
board: *...the agenda for the September 12 board meeting.*
panel: *The advisory panel disagreed with the decision.*

---

council|man /kaʊnsəlmən/ (councilmen) N-COUNT; N-TITLE A **councilman** is a man who is a member of a local council. [AM] ❑ *...a city councilman.*

in BRIT, use **councillor**

coun|cil of war (councils of war) N-COUNT A **council of war** is a meeting that is held in order to decide how a particular threat or emergency should be dealt with. [FORMAL]

coun|ci|lor /kaʊnsələr/ (councilors) N-COUNT; N-TITLE A **councilor** is a member of a local council. ❑ *...Councilor Michael Poulter.*

in BRIT, use **councillor**

council|woman /kaʊnsəlwʊmən/ (councilwomen) N-COUNT; N-TITLE A **councilwoman** is a woman who is a member of a local council. [AM] ❑ *...Councilwoman Johnson.*

in BRIT, use **councillor**

coun|sel ✦◇◇ /kaʊnsəl/ (counsels, counseling or counselling, counseled or counselled) **1** N-UNCOUNT **Counsel** is advice. [FORMAL] ❑ *He had always been able to count on her wise counsel.* **2** V-T If you **counsel** someone to take a course of action, or if you **counsel** a course of action, you advise that course of action. [FORMAL] ❑ *My advisers counselled me to do nothing.* **3** V-T If you **counsel** people, you give them advice about their problems. ❑ *...a psychologist who counsels people with eating disorders.* **4** N-COUNT Someone's **counsel** is the lawyer who gives them advice on a legal case and speaks on their behalf in court. ❑ *Singleton's counsel said after the trial that he would appeal.*

coun|sel|ing /kaʊnsəlɪŋ/ also **counselling** N-UNCOUNT **Counseling** is advice which a therapist or other expert gives to someone about a particular problem. ❑ *She will need medical help and counseling to overcome the tragedy.*

coun|se|lor /kaʊnsələr/ (counselors) also **counsellor** **1** N-COUNT A **counselor** is a person whose job is to give advice to people who need it, especially advice on their personal problems. ❑ *Children who have suffered like this should see a counselor experienced in bereavement.* **2** N-COUNT A **counselor** is a young person who supervises children at a summer camp. ❑ *Hicks worked with children as a camp counselor.*

count ✦✦◇ /kaʊnt/ (counts, counting, counted) **1** V-I When you **count**, you say all the numbers one after another up to a particular number. ❑ *He was counting slowly under his breath.* **2** V-T If you **count** all the things in a group, you add them up in order to find how many there are. ❑ *I counted the money. It was more than five hundred dollars.* ❑ *I counted 34 wild goats grazing.* • PHRASAL VERB **Count up** means the same as **count**. ❑ *Couldn't we just count up our ballots and bring them to the courthouse?* **3** V-I If something or someone **counts** for something or **counts**, they are important or valuable. ❑ *It doesn't matter what you've said; what counts is how you act.* **4** V-T/V-I If something **counts** or **is counted** as a particular thing, it is regarded as being that thing, especially in particular circumstances or under particular rules. ❑ *No one agrees on what counts as a desert.* **5** V-T If you **count** something when you are making a calculation, you include it in that calculation. ❑ *It's under 7 percent only because statistics don't count the people who aren't qualified to be in the work force.* **6** N-COUNT A **count** is the action of counting a particular set of things, or the number that you get when you have counted them. ❑ *The final count in last month's referendum showed 56.7 per cent in favor.* **7** N-COUNT You use **count** when referring to the level or amount of something that someone owns or has. ❑ *A glass or two of wine will not significantly add to the calorie count.* **8** N-COUNT In law, a **count** is one of a number of charges brought against someone in court. ❑ *He was indicted by a grand jury on two counts of murder.* **9** N-COUNT; N-TITLE; N-VOC A **count** is a European nobleman. ❑ *Her father was a Polish count.* **10** PHRASE If you **keep count** of a number of

things, you note or keep a record of how many have occurred. If you **lose count** of a number of things, you cannot remember how many have occurred. ❑ *He struggles to keep count of the number of flights he takes yearly.*
▶ **count against** PHRASAL VERB If something **counts against** you, it may cause you to be rejected or punished, or cause people to have a lower opinion of you. ❑ *He is highly regarded, but his youth might count against him.*
▶ **count on** also **count upon** ◼ PHRASAL VERB If you **count on** something or **count upon** it, you expect it to happen and include it in your plans. ❑ *What they did not know was how much support they could count on from Democrats.* ◼ PHRASAL VERB If you **count on** someone or **count upon** them, you rely on them to support you or help you. ❑ *Don't count on Lillian.*
▶ **count out** PHRASAL VERB If you **count out** a sum of money, you count the bills or coins as you put them in a pile one by one. ❑ *Mr. Rohmbauer counted out the money and put it in an envelope.*
▶ **count up** → see **count** 2
▶ **count upon** → see **count on**

COLLOCATIONS

---

count
VERB
◼
count + *adverb*: backward, slowly
◼
count + *noun*: calories, cash, minutes, votes; number
◼
noun + count: opinion

Count /kaʊnt/ (**counts**) also **count** N-COUNT; N-TITLE A **Count** is a European nobleman with the same rank as a British earl. ❑ *Her father was a Polish Count.*

count|able noun /kaʊntəbᵊl naʊn/ (**countable nouns**) N-COUNT A **countable noun** is the same as a **count noun**.

count|down /kaʊntdaʊn/ ◼ N-SING [also no det] A **countdown** is the counting aloud of numbers in reverse order before something happens, especially before a spacecraft is launched. ❑ *The countdown has begun for the launch of the space shuttle.* ◼ → See feature box at **travel**

coun|te|nance /kaʊntɪnəns/ (**countenances, countenancing, countenanced**) ◼ V-T [usu with brd-neg] If someone will not **countenance** something, they do not agree with it and will not allow it to happen. [FORMAL] ❑ *Jake would not countenance Janis's marrying while still a student.* ◼ N-COUNT Someone's **countenance** is their face. [FORMAL]

coun|ter ♦⃟ /kaʊntər/ (**counters, countering, countered**)
◼ N-COUNT In a place such as a store or café, a **counter** is a long, narrow table or flat surface at which customers are served. ❑ *...those guys we see working behind the counter at our local store.* ◼ N-COUNT A **counter** is a mechanical or electronic device which keeps a count of something and displays the total. ❑ *The new answering machine has a call counter.* ◼ N-COUNT A **counter** is a small, flat, round object used in board games. ❑ *...a versatile book which provides boards and counters for fifteen different games.* ◼ V-T/V-I If you do something to **counter** a particular action or process, you do something which has an opposite effect to it or makes it less effective. ❑ *The leadership discussed a plan of economic measures to counter the effects of such a blockade.* ❑ *Sears countered by filing an antitrust lawsuit.* ◼ N-SING Something that is **a counter to** something else has an opposite effect to it or makes it less effective. ❑ *...NATO's traditional role as a counter to the military might of the Warsaw Pact.* ◼ PHRASE If a medicine can be bought **over the counter**, you do not need a prescription to buy it. ❑ *Are you taking any other medicines whether on prescription or bought over the counter?* ❑ *...over-the-counter medicines.* ◼ PHRASE **Over-the-counter** shares are bought and sold directly rather than on a stock exchange. [BUSINESS] ❑ *In national over-the-counter trading yesterday, Clarcor shares tumbled $6.125 to close at $35,625.*

COLLOCATIONS

---

counter
VERB ◼
counter + *noun*: attack, extremism, terrorism, threat; effect; accusation, argument, claim, criticism

---
PREFIX

counter-
forms words that refer to actions or activities that oppose another action or activity. *For example, a **counter-measure** is an action you take to weaken the effect of another action or situation.*

---

counter|act /kaʊntərækt/ (**counteracts, counteracting, counteracted**) V-T To **counteract** something means to reduce its effect by doing something that produces an opposite effect. ❑ *My husband has to take several pills to counteract high blood pressure.*

counter|ar|gu|ment /kaʊntərɑrgyəmənt/ (**counterarguments**) N-COUNT A **counterargument** is an argument that makes an opposing point to another argument. ❑ *...an attempt to develop a counterargument to the labor theory.*

counter|at|tack /kaʊntərətæk/ (**counterattacks, counterattacking, counterattacked**) V-I If you **counterattack**, you attack someone who has attacked you. ❑ *The security forces counterattacked the following day and quelled the unrest.* • N-COUNT **Counterattack** is also a noun. ❑ *The army began its counterattack this morning.*

counter|bal|ance /kaʊntərbæləns/ (**counterbalances, counterbalancing, counterbalanced**) ◼ V-T To **counterbalance** something means to balance or correct it with something that has an equal but opposite effect. ❑ *Add honey to counterbalance the acidity.* ◼ N-COUNT [oft N to n] Something that is a **counterbalance** to something else counterbalances that thing. ❑ *...organizations set up as a counterbalance to groups allied to the ANC.*

coun|ter|bid /kaʊntərbɪd/ (**counterbids**) N-COUNT A **counterbid** is a bid that is made in response to a bid from another person or group, offering the seller more advantages. ❑ *Bass is expected to make a surprise counterbid for First Leisure's family entertainment division on Tuesday, sparking a bid war.*

counter|blast /kaʊntərblæst/ (**counterblasts**) N-COUNT [oft N to n] A **counterblast** is a strong, angry reply to something that has been said, written, or done. [JOURNALISM] ❑ *Other experts delivered a strong counterblast to the professor's claims.*

counter|clockwise /kaʊntərklɒkwaɪz/ ADV [ADV after v] If something is moving **counterclockwise**, it is moving in the opposite direction to the direction in which the hands of a clock move. [AM] ❑ *Rotate the head clockwise and counterclockwise.* • ADJ [ADJ n] **Counterclockwise** is also an adjective. ❑ *The dance moves in a counterclockwise direction.*

in BRIT, use **anticlockwise**

counter|culture /kaʊntərkʌltʃər/ (**countercultures**) N-VAR **Counterculture** is a set of values, ideas, and ways of behaving that are completely different from those of the rest of society. ❑ *...a history of the counterculture.*

counter|es|pio|nage /kaʊntərɛspiənɑʒ/

in BRIT, also use **counter-espionage**

N-UNCOUNT **Counterespionage** is the same as **counterintelligence**.

counter|feit /kaʊntərfɪt/ (**counterfeits, counterfeiting, counterfeited**) ◼ ADJ **Counterfeit** money, goods, or documents are not genuine, but have been made to look exactly like genuine ones in order to deceive people. ❑ *He admitted possessing and delivering counterfeit currency.* • N-COUNT **Counterfeit** is also a noun. ❑ *Levi Strauss says counterfeits of the company's jeans are flooding Europe.* ◼ V-T If someone **counterfeits** something, they make a version of it that is not genuine but has been made to look genuine in order to deceive people. ❑ *...the coins Davies is alleged to have counterfeited.*

counter|foil /kaʊntərfɔɪl/ (**counterfoils**) N-COUNT A **counterfoil** is the part of a check, ticket, or other document that you keep when you give the other part to someone else.

counter|in|tel|li|gence /kaʊntərɪntɛlɪdʒəns/ N-UNCOUNT [oft N n] **Counterintelligence** consists of actions that a country takes in order to find out whether another country is spying on it and to prevent it from doing so. ❑ *...the FBI's department of counterintelligence.* ❑ *...a counter-intelligence officer.*

counter|mand /kaʊntərmænd/ (**countermands, countermanding, countermanded**) V-T If you **countermand**

an order, you cancel it, usually by giving a different order. [FORMAL] ❏ *I can't countermand an order Winger's given.*

counter|meas|ure /kaʊntərmɛʒər/ (**countermeasures**) N-COUNT A **countermeasure** is an action that you take in order to weaken the effect of another action or a situation, or to make it harmless. ❏ *Because the threat never developed, we didn't need to take any real countermeasures.*

counter|move /kaʊntərmuv/ (**countermoves**) N-COUNT A **countermove** is an action that someone takes in response to an action by another person or group. [AM] ❏ *If they had made any sort of move that was in our direction we would have made a countermove already.*

counter|of|fer /kaʊntərɔfər/ (**counteroffers**) N-COUNT A **counteroffer** is an offer that someone makes, for example, for a house or business, in response to an offer by another person or group. ❏ *Many would welcome a counteroffer from a foreign bidder.*

counter|pane /kaʊntərpeɪn/ (**counterpanes**) N-COUNT A **counterpane** is a decorative cover on a bed. [OLD-FASHIONED]

counter|part ♦◇◇ /kaʊntərpɑrt/ (**counterparts**) N-COUNT Someone's or something's **counterpart** is another person or thing that has a similar function or position in a different place. ❏ *As soon as he heard what was afoot, he telephoned his German and Italian counterparts to protest.*

counter|point /kaʊntərpɔɪnt/ (**counterpoints**) N-COUNT [usu sing, oft N to n] Something that is a **counterpoint** to something else contrasts with it in a satisfying way. [JOURNALISM] ❏ *Paris is just a short train journey away, providing the perfect counterpoint to the peace and quiet of Reims.*

counter|pro|duc|tive /kaʊntərprədʌktɪv/ ADJ Something that is **counterproductive** achieves the opposite result from the one that you want to achieve. ❏ *In practice, however, such an attitude is counterproductive.*

counter|revo|lu|tion /kaʊntərrɛvəluʃən/ (**counterrevolutions**) ◼ N-COUNT A **counterrevolution** is a revolution that is intended to reverse the effects of a previous revolution. ❏ *The consequences of the counterrevolution have been extremely bloody.* ◼ N-UNCOUNT You can refer to activities that are intended to reverse the effects of a previous revolution as **counterrevolution**. ❏ *Such actions would be regarded as counterrevolution.*

counter|revo|lu|tion|ary /kaʊntərrɛvəluʃənɛri/ (**counterrevolutionaries**) ◼ ADJ **Counterrevolutionary** activities are activities intended to reverse the effects of a previous revolution. ❏ *...counterrevolutionary propaganda.* ◼ N-COUNT A **counterrevolutionary** is a person who is trying to reverse the effects of a previous revolution.

counter|sign /kaʊntərsaɪn/ (**countersigns, countersigning, countersigned**) V-T If you **countersign** a document, you sign it after someone else has signed it. ❏ *The president has so far refused to countersign the prime minister's desperate decree.*

counter|ten|or /kaʊntərtɛnər/ (**countertenors**) N-COUNT A **countertenor** is a man who sings with a high voice that is similar to a low female singing voice.

coun|ter|ter|ror|ism /kaʊntərtɛrərɪzəm/ N-UNCOUNT **Counterterrorism** consists of activities that are intended to prevent terrorist acts or to get rid of terrorist groups. • **coun|ter|ter|ror|ist** ADJ ❏ *There were gaps in their counterterrorist strategy.*

counter|top /kaʊntərtɒp/ (**countertops**) N-COUNT A **countertop** is a flat surface in a kitchen which is easily cleaned, and on which you can prepare food. [AM] ❏ *She reached for a cloth and began scouring the countertop.*

counter|vail|ing /kaʊntərveɪlɪŋ/ ADJ [ADJ n] A **countervailing** force, power, or opinion is one which is of equal strength to another one but is its opposite or opposes it. [FORMAL] ❏ *Their strategy is expansionist and imperialist, and it is greatest in effect, of course, when there is no countervailing power.*

counter|weight /kaʊntərweɪt/ (**counterweights**) N-COUNT [oft N n] A **counterweight** is an action or proposal that is intended to balance or counter other actions or proposals. ❏ *His no-inflation bill serves as a useful counterweight to proposals less acceptable to the committee.*

coun|tess /kaʊntɪs/ (**countesses**) N-COUNT; N-TITLE; N-VOC A **countess** is a woman who has the same rank as a count or earl, or who is married to a count or earl. ❏ *...the Countess of Lichfield.*

count|ing /kaʊntɪŋ/ ◼ PREP **Not counting** a particular thing means not including that thing. **Counting** a particular thing means including that thing. ❏ *...an average operating profit of 15% to 16% of sales, not counting administrative expenses.* ◼ PHRASE [amount PHR] If you say **and counting** after a number or an amount of something, you mean that the number or amount is continuing to increase. ❏ *There is a 1,700-year-old tea tree still living in southern China which is more than 100 feet tall and counting.*

count|less /kaʊntlɪs/ ADJ [ADJ n] **Countless** means very many. ❏ *She brought joy to countless people through her music.*

count noun (**count nouns**) N-COUNT A **count noun** is a noun such as 'bird,' 'chair,' or 'year' which has a singular and a plural form and is always used after a determiner in the singular.

coun|tri|fied /kʌntrɪfaɪd/ ◼ ADJ [usu ADJ n] You use **countrified** to describe something that seems or looks like something in the country, rather than in a town. ❏ *The house was so handsome, with a lovely countrified garden.* ◼ ADJ [usu ADJ n] **Countrified** is used to describe pop music that sounds similar to country music. [JOURNALISM] ❏ *The sound veers between jazz and countrified blues.*

coun|try ♦♦♦ /kʌntri/ (**countries**) ◼ N-COUNT A **country** is one of the political units which the world is divided into, covering a particular area of land. ❏ *Indonesia is one of the most populous countries in the world.* ❏ *...the boundary between the two countries.* ◼ N-SING The people who live in a particular country can be referred to as the **country**. ❏ *Finally the country got some much-needed good news.* ◼ N-SING The **country** consists of places such as farms, open fields, and villages which are away from towns and cities. ❏ *...a healthy life in the country.* ❏ *She was cycling along a country road near Compiègne.* ◼ N-UNCOUNT A particular kind of **country** is an area of land which has particular characteristics or is connected with a particular well-known person. ❏ *Varese Ligure is a small town in mountainous country east of Genoa.* ◼ N-UNCOUNT **Country** music is popular music from the southern United States. ❏ *For a long time I just wanted to play country music.*

USAGE

country
When you use **country** to talk about a place far away from the city, the only determiner you can use with it is **the**. Don't say, for example, 'I like living in Paris, but my parents prefer to live in a country.' You say 'I like living in Paris, but my parents prefer to live in **the country**.' We have a house in **the country**.

COLLOCATIONS

country
NOUN ◼
adjective + **country**: home, native; developing, poor, rich; foreign
verb + **country**: flee, leave

---

coun|try and west|ern also **country-and-western** N-UNCOUNT [oft N n] **Country and western** is the same as country music. ❏ *...a successful country and western singer.*

coun|try club (**country clubs**) N-COUNT A **country club** is a club in the country where you can play sports and attend social events.

coun|try cous|in (**country cousins**) N-COUNT If you refer to someone as a **country cousin**, you think that they are unsophisticated because they come from the country.

coun|try danc|ing N-UNCOUNT **Country dancing** is traditional dancing in which people dance in rows or circles.

country|man /kʌntrɪmən/ (**countrymen**) ◼ N-COUNT Your **countrymen** are people from your own country. ❏ *He beat his fellow countryman, Andre Agassi, 6-4, 6-3, 6-2.* ◼ N-COUNT A **countryman** is a person who lives in the country rather than in a city or a town. ❏ *He had the red face of a countryman.*

country|side ♦◇◇ /kʌntrɪsaɪd/ N-UNCOUNT The **countryside** is land which is away from towns and cities. ❏ *I've always loved the English countryside.*

countryside NOUN
- **country:** *She was cycling along a country road near Compiègne.*
- **outdoors:** *Life in the great outdoors isn't supposed to be luxurious.*
- **green belt:** *The result will be at least 3,000 houses in our green belt.*

country|wide /kʌntriwaɪd/ ADV [ADV after v, n ADV] Something that happens or exists **countrywide** happens or exists throughout the whole of a particular country. ◻ *Armed robbery and abduction have been on the increase countrywide.* ◻ *They sent out questionnaires to one hundred schools countrywide.* • ADJ [ADJ n] **Countrywide** is also an adjective. ◻ *...a countrywide network of volunteers.*

country|woman /kʌntriwʊmən/ (**countrywomen**) **1** N-COUNT A **countrywoman** is a woman who lives in the country rather than in a city or a town. ◻ *She had the slow, soft voice of a countrywoman.* **2** N-COUNT [usu poss N] Your **countrywomen** are women from your own country. ◻ *Testud lost in straight sets to countrywoman Mary Pierce.*

coun|ty ◆◆◇ /kaʊnti/ (**counties**) N-COUNT A **county** is a region of the U.S., Britain, or Ireland, which has its own local government. ◻ *He arrived at the Palm Beach County courthouse with his mother.*

coun|ty coun|cil (**county councils**) N-COUNT; N-IN-NAMES A **county council** is an organization which runs local government in a county in some parts of the U.S. ◻ *...Delaware County Council.*

coun|ty court (**county courts**) N-COUNT A **county court** is a local court which deals with private disputes between people, but does not deal with serious crimes.

coun|ty seat (**county seats**) N-COUNT A **county seat** is the most important town in a county where the local government is. [AM] ◻ *...Glasgow, the county seat of Barren County, Kentucky.*

coup ◆◇◇ /kuː/ (**coups**) **1** N-COUNT When there is a **coup**, a group of people seize power in a country. ◻ *...a military coup.* **2** N-COUNT A **coup** is an achievement which is thought to be especially good because it was very difficult. ◻ *The sale is a big coup for the auction house.*

COLLOCATIONS
coup
NOUN
1
noun + **coup**: boardroom, leadership, palace
adjective + **coup**: attempted, failed, successful; bloodless, military
verb + **coup**: mount, plot, stage
2
noun + **coup**: propaganda, publicity
adjective + **coup**: major
verb + **coup**: score

SYNONYMS
coup
NOUN **2**
- **achievement:** *Reaching this agreement so quickly was a great achievement.*
- **feat:** *A race car is an extraordinary feat of engineering.*
- **masterstroke:** *Graham pulled a masterstroke by playing Merson in the center of midfield.*
- **accomplishment:** *For a novelist, that's quite an accomplishment.*
- **stroke of genius:** *At the time, his appointment seemed to be a stroke of genius.*

coup de grace /kuː də grɑːs/ N-SING A **coup de grace** is an action or event which finally destroys something, for example, an institution, which has been gradually growing weaker. [FORMAL] ◻ *Irving Kristol delivered the coup de grace in a letter dated June 12: they had decided to reject the proposal.*

coup d'état /kuː deɪtɑː/ (**coups d'état**) N-COUNT When there is a **coup d'état**, a group of people seize power in a country.

coupe /kuːp/ (**coupes**) **1** N-COUNT A **coupe** is a car with a fixed roof, a sloping back, two doors, and seats for four people. [AM]

in BRIT, use **coupé**

2 → See also color supplement

cou|pé /kuːpeɪ/ (**coupés**) N-COUNT A **coupé** is the same as a **coupe**. [BRIT]

cou|ple ◆◆◇ /kʌpᵊl/ (**couples, coupling, coupled**) **1** QUANT [QUANT of pl-n] If you refer to **a couple of** people or things, you mean two or approximately two of them, although the exact number is not important or you are not sure of it. ◻ *Across the street from me there are a couple of police officers standing guard.* ◻ *I think the trouble will clear up in a couple of days.* • DET **Couple** is also a determiner in spoken American English, and is often used before 'more' and 'less.' ◻ *...a couple weeks before the election.* • PRON **Couple** is also a pronoun. ◻ *I've got a couple that don't look too bad.* **2** N-COUNT-COLL A **couple** is two people who are married, living together, or having a sexual relationship. ◻ *The couple have no children.* ◻ *Burglars ransacked an elderly couple's home.* **3** N-COUNT-COLL A **couple** is two people that you see together on a particular occasion or that have some association. ◻ *...as the four couples began the opening dance.* **4** V-T [usu passive] If you say that one thing produces a particular effect when it **is coupled with** another, you mean that the two things combine to produce that effect. ◻ *...a problem that is coupled with lower demand for the machines themselves.*

COLLOCATIONS
couple
NOUN **2**
adjective + **couple**: gay, heterosexual, homosexual, lesbian, same-sex; married, unmarried; childless; elderly, middle-aged, young

SYNONYMS
couple
NOUN
2
- **item:** *She and Gino were an item.*
- **pair:** *He and Paula made an unlikely pair.*
3
- **duo:** *...Britain's former golden duo of Linford Christie and Sally Gunnell.*
- **pair:** *They have hit more runs together than any pair in history.*

cou|plet /kʌplɪt/ (**couplets**) N-COUNT A **couplet** is two lines of poetry which come next to each other, especially two lines that rhyme with each other and are the same length. ◻ *...rhyming couplets.*

cou|pling /kʌplɪŋ/ (**couplings**) **1** N-COUNT [oft supp n] A **coupling** is a device which is used to join two vehicles or pieces of equipment together. ◻ *Before driving away, re-check the trailer coupling.* **2** N-VAR An act of sexual intercourse is sometimes referred to as **coupling**. [FORMAL] ◻ *...sexual couplings.* **3** → see also **couple**

cou|pon /kuːpɒn, kjuː-/ (**coupons**) **1** N-COUNT A **coupon** is a piece of printed paper which allows you to pay less money than usual for a product, or to get it free. ◻ *...a money-saving coupon.* **2** N-COUNT A **coupon** is a small form, for example, in a newspaper or magazine, which you send off to ask for information, to order something, or to enter a competition. ◻ *Mail this coupon with your check or money order.*

cour|age ◆◆◇ /kɜːrɪdʒ/ **1** N-UNCOUNT **Courage** is the quality shown by someone who decides to do something difficult or dangerous, even though they may be afraid. ◻ *General Lewis Mackenzie has impressed everyone with his authority and personal courage.* **2 to pluck up the courage** → see **pluck**

SYNONYMS
courage
NOUN **1**
- **bravery:** *He deserves the highest praise for his bravery.*
- **nerve:** *He never got up enough nerve to meet me.*
- **fortitude:** *He suffered a long series of illnesses with tremendous dignity and fortitude.*
- **daring:** *His daring may have cost him his life.*

cou|ra|geous /kəreɪdʒəs/ ADJ Someone who is **courageous** shows courage. ◻ *The children were very courageous.*

cour|gette /kʊərʒɛt/ (**courgettes**) N-VAR **Courgettes** are long thin vegetables with dark green skin. [BRIT]

in AM, use **zucchini**

cou|ri|er /kʊəriər, kɜr-/ (couriers, couriering, couriered) **1** N-COUNT A **courier** is a person who is paid to take letters and packages direct from one place to another. ◻ ...a motorcycle courier. **2** V-T If you **courier** something somewhere, you send it there by courier. ◻ I couriered it to Darren in New York.

course ♦♦♦ /kɔrs/ (courses) **1** Course is often used in the expression 'of course,' or instead of 'of course' in informal spoken English. See **of course**. **2** N-UNCOUNT [also a N] The **course** of a vehicle, especially a ship or aircraft, is the route along which it is traveling. ◻ Aircraft can avoid each other by altering course to left or right. **3** N-COUNT A **course** of action is an action or a series of actions that you can do in a particular situation. ◻ My best course of action was to help Gill by being sympathetic. **4** N-COUNT A **course** is a series of lessons or lectures on a particular subject. ◻ ...a course in business administration. **5** → see also **correspondence course, refresher course 6** N-COUNT A **course** of medical treatment is a series of treatments that a doctor gives someone. ◻ He had a course of antibiotics to kill the bacterium. **7** N-COUNT A **course** is one part of a meal. ◻ The lunch was excellent, especially the first course. **8** N-COUNT In sports, a **course** is an area of land where races are held or golf is played, or the land over which a race takes place. ◻ Only 12 seconds separated the first three riders on the course. **9** N-COUNT The **course** of a river is the channel along which it flows. ◻ Romantic castles overlook the river's twisting course. **10 in due course** → see **due 11** PHRASE If something happens **in the course of** a particular period of time, it happens during that period of time. ◻ In the course of the 1930s steel production approximately doubled. **12** PHRASE If you do something **as a matter of course**, you do it as part of your normal work or way of life. ◻ If police are carrying arms as a matter of course, then doesn't it encourage criminals to carry them? **13** PHRASE If a ship or aircraft is **on course**, it is traveling along the correct route. If it is **off course**, it is no longer traveling along the correct route. ◻ The ship was sent off course into shallow waters. **14** PHRASE If you are **on course for** something, you are likely to achieve it. ◻ The company is on course for profits of $20m. **15** → See feature box at **learning, university, water**

SYNONYMS

course
NOUN **4**
curriculum: ...the history curriculum.
studies: She gave up her studies to have Alexander.
module: These courses are organized into three four-week modules.

---

course book (course books) also **coursebook** N-COUNT A **course book** is a textbook that students and teachers use as the basis of a course.

course work also **coursework 1** N-UNCOUNT **Course work** is work that students do during a course, rather than in exams, especially work that counts toward a student's final grade. ◻ Some 20 percent of grades are awarded for coursework. **2** → See feature box at **university**

---
court
① NOUN USES
② VERB USES
---

① **court** ♦♦♦ /kɔrt/ (courts) **1** N-COUNT [oft n N, N n, also in/at N] A **court** is a place where legal matters are decided by a judge and jury or by a magistrate. ◻ At this rate, we could find ourselves in the divorce courts! ◻ ...a county court judge. **2** N-COUNT You can refer to the people in a court, especially the judge, jury, or magistrates, as a **court**. ◻ A court at Tampa, Florida has convicted five officials on charges of handling millions of dollars earned from illegal drug deals. **3** N-COUNT [usu supp N, also on/off N] A **court** is an area in which you play a game such as tennis, basketball, badminton, or squash. ◻ The hotel has several tennis and squash courts. **4** N-COUNT The **court** of a king or queen is the place where he or she lives and carries out ceremonial or administrative duties. ◻ She came to visit England, where she was presented at the court of James I. **5** PHRASE If you **go to court** or **take** someone **to court**, you take legal action against them. ◻ They have received at least twenty thousand dollars each but went to court to demand more. **6** PHRASE If a legal matter is decided or settled **out of court**, it is decided without legal action being taken in a court of law. ◻ The Government is anxious to keep the whole case out of court. **7** → See feature box at **legal**

SYNONYMS

court
NOUN ① **3**
field: He was the fastest thing I ever saw on a baseball field.
arena: ...the largest indoor sports arena in the world.
pitch: There was a swimming-pool, cricket pitches, playing fields.
park: Professional baseball has been played in one park or another since 1896.

---

② **court** /kɔrt/ (courts, courting, courted) **1** V-T To **court** a particular person, group, or country means to try to please them or improve your relations with them, often so that they will do something that you want them to do. [JOURNALISM] ◻ Both Democratic and Republican parties are courting former supporters of Ross Perot. **2** V-T If you **court** something such as publicity or popularity, you try to attract it. ◻ Having spent a lifetime avidly courting publicity, Paul has suddenly become secretive. **3** V-T If you **court** something unpleasant such as disaster or unpopularity, you act in a way that makes it likely to happen. ◻ If he thinks he can remain in power by force, he is courting disaster. **4** V-RECIP If you **are courting** someone, you spend a lot of time with them, because you are intending to get married. You can also say that two people **are courting**. [OLD-FASHIONED] ◻ I was courting Billy at 19 and married him when I was 21.

cour|teous /kɜrtiəs/ **1** ADJ Someone who is **courteous** is polite and respectful to other people. ◻ He was a kind and courteous man. ● **cour|teous|ly** ADV ◻ Then he nodded courteously to me and walked off to perform his unpleasant duty. **2** → See feature box at **review**

cour|tesan /kɔrtɪzən/ (courtesans) N-COUNT In former times, a **courtesan** was a woman who had sexual relationships with rich and powerful men for money.

cour|tesy /kɜrtɪsi/ **1** N-UNCOUNT **Courtesy** is politeness, respect, and consideration for others. [FORMAL] ◻ ...a gentleman who behaves with the utmost courtesy towards everyone he meets. **2** N-SING If you refer to the **courtesy** of doing something, you are referring to a polite action. [FORMAL] ◻ By extending the courtesy of a phone call to my clients, I was building a personal relationship with them. **3** ADJ [ADJ n] **Courtesy** is used to describe services that are provided free of charge by an organization to its customers, or to the general public. ◻ A courtesy shuttle bus operates between the hotel and the town. **4** ADJ [ADJ n] A **courtesy** call or a **courtesy** visit is a formal visit that you pay someone as a way of showing them politeness or respect. ◻ The president paid a courtesy call on Emperor Akihito. **5** PHRASE If something is provided **courtesy of** someone or **by courtesy of** someone, they provide it. You often use this expression in order to thank them. ◻ The waitress brings over some congratulatory glasses of champagne, courtesy of the restaurant. **6** → See feature box at **polite**

court|house /kɔrthaʊs/ (courthouses) **1** N-COUNT A **courthouse** is a building in which a court of law meets. [AM] ◻ The two were tried in the same courthouse at the same time, on separate floors.

in BRIT, use **court**

2 N-COUNT A **courthouse** is a building used by the government of a county. [AM] ◻ They were married at the Los Angeles County Courthouse.

cour|ti|er /kɔrtiər/ (courtiers) N-COUNT **Courtiers** were noblemen and women who spent a lot of time at the court of a king or queen.

court|ly /kɔrtli/ ADJ You use **courtly** to describe someone whose behavior is very polite, often in a rather old-fashioned way. [LITERARY] ◻ The waiter made a courtly bow and walked out of the room.

court mar|tial (court martials, court martialing or court martialling, court martialed or court martialled) also **court-martial**

Courts martial is also used as a plural form for the noun.

1 N-VAR A **court martial** is a trial in a military court of a

Court of Appeals

member of the armed forces who is charged with breaking a military law. ❑ *He is due to face a court martial on drugs charges.* **2** V-T [usu passive] If a member of the armed forces **is court martialed**, he or she is tried in a military court. ❑ *I was court martialed and sentenced to six months in a military prison.*

Court of Ap|peals (Courts of Appeals)

in BRIT, use **Court of Appeal**

N-COUNT A **Court of Appeals** is a court which deals with appeals against legal judgments. ❑ *The state Court of Appeals threw out a drug conviction today because a juror did not understand English.*

court of law (courts of law) N-COUNT When you refer to a **court of law**, you are referring to a legal court, especially when talking about the evidence that might be given in a trial. ❑ *We have a witness who would swear to it in a court of law.*

court|room /kɔrtrum/ (courtrooms) N-COUNT A **courtroom** is a room in which a legal court meets.

court|ship /kɔrtʃɪp/ (courtships) **1** N-VAR **Courtship** is the activity of courting or the time during which two people are courting. [OLD-FASHIONED] ❑ *After a short courtship, she accepted his proposal.* **2** N-UNCOUNT The **courtship** of male and female animals is their behavior before they have sex. ❑ *Courtship is somewhat vocal with a lot of displaying by the male.*

court shoe (court shoes) **1** N-COUNT [usu pl] **Court shoes** are shoes worn for sports such as tennis or squash. [AM] **2** N-COUNT **Court shoes** are the same as **pumps**. [BRIT]

court|yard /kɔrtyɑrd/ (courtyards) N-COUNT A **courtyard** is an open area of ground which is surrounded by buildings or walls. ❑ *They walked together through the arch and into the cobbled courtyard.*

cous|cous /kuskus/ N-UNCOUNT **Couscous** is a type of food that is made from crushed steamed wheat, or a dish consisting of this food served with a spicy stew. It is traditionally eaten in North Africa.

cous|in ✦✦◇ /kʌzᵊn/ (cousins) N-COUNT Your **cousin** is the child of your uncle or aunt. ❑ *My cousin Mark helped me to bring in the bags.*

couth /kuθ/ **1** N-UNCOUNT If you say that someone has **couth**, you mean that they have good manners and sophistication. [AM] ❑ *Benny, you have no couth.* **2** N-UNCOUNT If you describe a person or their behavior as **couth**, you mean that they are polite and sophisticated. ❑ *That's the message, only put in a far more couth way.*

cou|ture /kutʊər/ N-UNCOUNT [oft N n] **Couture** is the designing and making of expensive fashionable clothes, or the clothes themselves. [FORMAL] ❑ *...Christian Lacroix's first Paris couture collection.*

cou|tu|ri|er /kutʊəriei/ (couturiers) N-COUNT A **couturier** is a person who designs, makes, and sells expensive, fashionable clothes for women.

cove /koʊv/ (coves) N-COUNT; N-IN-NAMES A **cove** is a part of a coast where the land curves inward so that the sea is partly enclosed. ❑ *The house is situated on a hillside overlooking Fairview Cove.*

cov|en /kʌvən/ (covens) N-COUNT-COLL A **coven** is a group of witches.

cov|enant /kʌvənənt/ (covenants) **1** N-COUNT A **covenant** is a formal written agreement between two or more people or groups of people which is recognized in law. ❑ *...the International Covenant on Civil and Political Rights.* **2** N-COUNT [also by N] A **covenant** is a formal written promise to pay a sum of money each year for a fixed period, especially to a charity. [mainly BRIT]

in AM, usually use **pledge**

---
cover

① VERB USES
② NOUN USES

---

① **cov|er** ✦✦✦ /kʌvər/ (covers, covering, covered) **1** V-T If you **cover** something, you place something else over it in order to protect it, hide it, or close it. ❑ *Cover the casserole with a tight-fitting lid.* ❑ *He whimpered and covered his face.* **2** V-T If one thing **covers** another, it has been placed over it in order to

coverage

protect it, hide it, or close it. ❑ *His finger went up to touch the black patch which covered his left eye.* **3** V-T If one thing **covers** another, it forms a layer over its surface. ❑ *The clouds had spread and covered the entire sky.* **4** V-T To **cover** something **with** or **in** something else means to put a layer of the second thing over its surface. ❑ *The desk was covered with papers.* **5** V-T If you **cover** a particular distance, you travel that distance. ❑ *It would not be easy to cover ten miles on that amount of gas.* **6** V-T An insurance policy that **covers** a person or thing guarantees that money will be paid by the insurance company in relation to that person or thing. ❑ *Their insurer paid the $900 bill, even though the policy did not strictly cover it.* **7** V-T If a law **covers** a particular set of people, things, or situations, it applies to them. ❑ *The law covers four categories of experiments.* **8** V-T If you **cover** a particular topic, you discuss it in a lecture, course, or book. ❑ *Introduction to Chemistry aims to cover important topics in organic chemistry.* **9** V-T If a sum of money **covers** something, it is enough to pay for it. ❑ *Send it to the address given with $2.50 to cover postage and administration.* **10** V-I If you **cover for** someone who is doing something secret or illegal, you give false information or do not give all the information you have, in order to protect them. ❑ *Why would she cover for someone who was trying to kill her?* **11** V-I If you **cover for** someone who is ill or away, you do their work for them while they are not there. ❑ *She did not have enough nurses to cover for those who were sick.* **12** PHRASE If you **cover** your **ass** or **cover** your **butt**, you do something in order to protect yourself, for example against criticism or against accusations of doing something wrong. [INFORMAL, VULGAR]

▶ **cover up** **1** PHRASAL VERB If you **cover** something or someone **up**, you put something over them in order to protect or hide them. ❑ *He fell asleep in the front room so I covered him up with a duvet.* **2** PHRASAL VERB If you **cover up** something that you do not want people to know about, you hide the truth about it. ❑ *He suspects there's a conspiracy to cover up the crime.* ❑ *They knew they had done something terribly wrong and lied to cover it up.* **3** → see also **cover-up**

SYNONYMS

cover
VERB ① **2**
conceal: *The hat concealed her hair.*
screen: *Most of the road behind the hotel was screened by an apartment complex.*
hide: *The man's heavy mustache hid his upper lip completely.*
mask: *A thick, gray cloud masked the sun.*

---

② **cov|er** ✦✦✦ /kʌvər/ (covers) **1** N-COUNT A **cover** is something which is put over an object, usually in order to protect it. ❑ *...a sofa with washable covers.* **2** N-COUNT The **cover** of a book or a magazine is the outside part of it. ❑ *...a small book with a green cover.* **3** N-UNCOUNT **Cover** is protection from enemy attack that is provided for troops or ships carrying out a particular operation, for example, by aircraft. ❑ *They could not provide adequate air cover for ground operations.* **4** N-UNCOUNT **Cover** is trees, rocks, or other places where you shelter from the weather or from an attack, or hide from someone. ❑ *Charles lit the fuses and they ran for cover.* **5** N-UNCOUNT Insurance **cover** is a guarantee from an insurance company that money will be paid by them if it is needed. ❑ *Make sure that the firm's insurance cover is adequate.* **6** N-COUNT Something that is a **cover** for secret or illegal activities seems respectable or normal, and is intended to hide the activities. ❑ *He ran a construction company as a cover for drug dealing.* **7** N-PLURAL The **covers** on your bed are the things such as sheets and blankets that you have on top of you. ❑ *She set her glass down and slid under the covers.* **8** → see also **covering** **9** PHRASE If you **take cover**, you shelter from gunfire, bombs, or the weather. ❑ *Shoppers took cover behind cars as the gunman fired.* **10** PHRASE If you do something **under cover of** a particular situation, you are able to do it without being noticed because of that situation. ❑ *They move under cover of darkness.*

cov|er|age ✦◇◇ /kʌvərɪdʒ/ N-UNCOUNT The **coverage** of something in the news is the reporting of it. ❑ *Now a special TV network gives live coverage of most races.*

COLLOCATIONS

coverage
NOUN
noun + **coverage**: media, news, press, television
adjective + **coverage**: blanket, detailed, extensive, wide; live
verb + **coverage**: expand, extend, provide; receive, watch

cover|alls /kʌvərɔlz/ N-PLURAL [also *a pair of* N] **Coveralls** are a single piece of clothing that combines pants and a jacket. You wear coveralls over your clothes in order to protect them while you are working. [AM] ❑ ...*a man in white coveralls.*

in BRIT, use **overalls**

cov|er charge (**cover charges**) N-COUNT [usu sing] A **cover charge** is a sum of money that you must pay in some restaurants and nightclubs in addition to the money that you pay there for your food and drink.

cov|ered /kʌvərd/ ADJ [ADJ n] A **covered** area is an area that has a roof. ❑ *There are 40 shops and restaurants in a covered mall.*

cov|ered wag|on (**covered wagons**) N-COUNT A **covered wagon** is a wagon that has an arched canvas roof and is pulled by horses. Covered wagons were used by the early American settlers as they traveled across the country.

cov|er girl (**cover girls**) N-COUNT A **cover girl** is an attractive woman whose photograph appears on the front of a magazine.

cov|er|ing /kʌvərɪŋ/ (**coverings**) N-COUNT A **covering** is a layer of something that protects or hides something else. ❑ *Leave a thin covering of fat.*

cov|er|ing let|ter [BRIT] → see **cover letter**

cov|er|let /kʌvərlɪt/ (**coverlets**) N-COUNT A **coverlet** is the same as a **bedspread**. [OLD-FASHIONED]

cov|er let|ter (**cover letters**) N-COUNT A **cover letter** is a letter that you send with a package or with another letter in order to provide extra information. [AM] ❑ *Your cover letter creates the employer's first impression of you.*

cover-mounted also **covermounted** ADJ **Cover-mounted** items such as cassettes, CDs and DVDs are attached to the front of a magazine as free gifts. ❑ *The first issue has a cover-mounted CD-ROM.*

cov|ert /koʊvɜrt, kʌvərt/ ADJ **Covert** activities or situations are secret or hidden. [FORMAL] ❑ *They have been supplying covert military aid to the rebels.* • **cov|ert|ly** ADV ❑ *They covertly observed Lauren, who was sitting between Ned and Algie at a nearby table.*

cover-up (**cover-ups**) also **coverup** N-COUNT A **cover-up** is an attempt to hide a crime or mistake. ❑ *The general denied there'd been any cover-up.*

cov|er ver|sion (**cover versions**) N-COUNT [oft N *of* n] A **cover version** of a song is a version of it recorded by a singer or band who did not originally perform the song. ❑ ...*a new album of Cole Porter cover versions.*

cov|et /kʌvɪt/ (**covets, coveting, coveted**) V-T If you **covet** something, you strongly want to have it for yourself. [FORMAL] ❑ *She coveted his job so openly that their conversations were tense.*

cov|et|ed /kʌvɪtɪd/ ADJ You use **coveted** to describe something that very many people would like to have. ❑ *Allan Little from Radio 4 took the coveted title of reporter of the year.* ❑ ...*one of sport's most coveted trophies.*

cov|et|ous /kʌvɪtəs/ ADJ A **covetous** person has a strong desire to possess something, especially something that belongs to another person. [FORMAL, DISAPPROVAL] ❑ *Even here a red Lamborghini Diablo sports car attracts covetous stares.*

cov|ey /kʌvi/ (**coveys**) N-COUNT [oft N *of* n] A **covey** of grouse or partridges is a small group of them.

COVID-19 also **Covid-19** /koʊvɪdnaɪntin/ N-UNCOUNT COVID-19 is a serious disease which affects your ability to breathe. It is caused by a new type of coronavirus that was first identified in 2019. The short form **Covid** is also used.

cow ✦✧✧ /kaʊ/ (**cows, cowing, cowed**) ◼ N-COUNT A **cow** is a large female animal that is kept on farms for its milk. People sometimes refer to male and female animals of this species as **cows**. ❑ *He kept a few dairy cows.* ❑ *Dad went out to milk the cows.* ◼ N-COUNT Some female animals, including elephants and whales, are called **cows**. ❑ ...*a cow elephant.* ◼ V-T [usu passive] If someone **is cowed**, they are made afraid, or made to behave in a particular way because they have been frightened or badly treated. [FORMAL] ❑ *The government, far from being cowed by these threats, has vowed to continue its policy.* • **cowed** ADJ ❑ *By this time she was so cowed by the beatings that she meekly obeyed.*

cow|ard /kaʊərd/ (**cowards**) N-COUNT If you call someone a **coward**, you disapprove of them because they are easily frightened and avoid dangerous or difficult situations. [DISAPPROVAL] ❑ *She accused her husband of being a coward.*

cow|ard|ice /kaʊərdɪs/ N-UNCOUNT **Cowardice** is cowardly behavior. ❑ *He openly accused his opponents of cowardice.*

cow|ard|ly /kaʊərdli/ ADJ If you describe someone as **cowardly**, you disapprove of them because they are easily frightened and avoid doing dangerous and difficult things. [DISAPPROVAL] ❑ *I was too cowardly to complain.*

cow|bell /kaʊbɛl/ (**cowbells**) N-COUNT A **cowbell** is a small bell that is hung around a cow's neck so that the ringing sound makes it possible to find the cow.

cow|boy /kaʊbɔɪ/ (**cowboys**) ◼ N-COUNT A **cowboy** is a male character in a western. ❑ *Boys used to play at cowboys and Indians.* ◼ N-COUNT A **cowboy** is a man employed to look after cattle in North America, especially in former times. ❑ *In his twenties Roosevelt had sought work as a cowboy on a ranch in the Dakota Territory.*

cow|boy boots N-PLURAL [also *a pair of* N] **Cowboy boots** are high, leather boots, similar to those worn by cowboys. ❑ *He shows up in jeans and cowboy boots.*

cow|er /kaʊər/ (**cowers, cowering, cowered**) V-I If you **cower**, you bend forward and downward because you are very frightened. ❑ *The hostages cowered in their seats.*

cow|girl /kaʊgɜrl/ (**cowgirls**) ◼ N-COUNT A **cowgirl** is a woman employed to look after cattle in North America, especially in former times. ◼ N-COUNT A **cowgirl** is a female rodeo performer.

cow|hide /kaʊhaɪd/ N-UNCOUNT [oft N n] **Cowhide** is leather made from the skin of a cow. ❑ ...*cowhide boots.*

cowl /kaʊl/ (**cowls**) N-COUNT A **cowl** is a large loose hood covering a person's head, or their head and shoulders. Cowls are worn especially by monks.

co|worker /koʊwɜrkər/ (**coworkers**) also **co-worker** N-COUNT Your **coworkers** are the people you work with, especially people on the same job or project as you.

cow|patty /kaʊpæti/ (**cowpatties**) N-COUNT A **cowpatty** is a pile of feces from a cow.

cow|pie /kaʊpaɪ/ (**cowpies**) N-COUNT A **cowpie** is a pile of feces from a cow. [AM]

cow|poke /kaʊpoʊk/ (**cowpokes**) N-COUNT A **cowpoke** is the same as a **cowboy**. [AM] ❑ *Clad in leather chaps, a denim shirt and a white rancher's hat, he looks the quintessential cowpoke.*

cow|shed /kaʊʃɛd/ (**cowsheds**) N-COUNT A **cowshed** is a building where cows are kept or milked.

cow|slip /kaʊslɪp/ (**cowslips**) N-COUNT A **cowslip** is a small wild plant with yellow, sweet-smelling flowers.

cow town (**cow towns**) ◼ N-COUNT If someone describes a town as a **cow town**, they mean that it is small, dull, and old-fashioned. [AM, DISAPPROVAL] ❑ *People thought we were a little cow town.* ◼ N-COUNT A **cow town** is a town or city that is near to cattle ranches. [AM] ❑ *At its peak, Dodge City was the biggest cow town in the West.*

cox /kɒks/ (**coxes**) N-COUNT In a rowboat, the **cox** is the person who gives instructions to the rowers.

cox|swain /kɒksən/ (**coxswains**) N-COUNT The **coxswain** of a lifeboat or other small boat is the person who steers the boat.

coy /kɔɪ/ ◼ ADJ A **coy** person is shy, or pretends to be shy, about love and sex. ❑ *I was sickened by the way Carol charmed all the men by turning coy.* • **coy|ly** ADV [ADV with v] ❑ *She smiled coyly at Algie as he took her hand and raised it to his lips.* ◼ ADJ If someone is being **coy**, they are unwilling to talk about something that they feel guilty or embarrassed about. ❑ *Mr. Alexander is not the slightest bit coy about his ambitions.* • **coy|ly** ADV [ADV with v] ❑ *The administration coyly refused to put a firm figure on the war's costs.*

coy|ote /kaɪoʊti/ (**coyotes**) N-COUNT A **coyote** is a small wolf which lives in the plains of North America.

coy|pu /kɔɪpu/ (**coypus**) N-COUNT A **coypu** is a large South American rodent which lives near water.

cozy /koʊzi/ (**cozies, cozier, coziest**)

in BRIT, use **cosy**

1 ADJ A house or room that is **cozy** is comfortable and warm. ◻ Downstairs there's a breakfast room and guests can relax in the cozy bar. **2** ADJ [v-link ADJ] If you are **cozy**, you are comfortable and warm. ◻ They like to make sure their guests are comfortable and cozy. **3** ADJ You use **cozy** to describe activities that are pleasant and friendly, and involve people who know each other well. ◻ ...a cozy chat between friends. **4** N-COUNT A **cozy** or a **tea cozy** is a soft knitted or fabric cover which you put over a teapot in order to keep the tea hot. ◻ ...unusual miniature tea sets, elegant tea accessories, colorful cozies. ◻ ...a whimsical tea cozy printed with a bright scene of the Tower of London.

CPA /si pi eɪ/ (**CPAs**) N-COUNT **CPA** is an abbreviation for **certified public accountant**. [AM] ◻ He is a CPA in both New York and New Jersey.

CPAP /sipæp/ N-UNCOUNT **CPAP** is a system that continually pushes air into a patient's lungs in order to help them breathe more easily or to prevent them from stopping breathing when they are asleep. **CPAP** is an abbreviation for 'continuous positive airway pressure.' ◻ The use of a CPAP mask at night has eliminated the symptoms of sleep apnea.

CPI /si pi aɪ/ N-SING [usu the N] **CPI** is an abbreviation for **consumer price index**. ◻ The CPI was up 6/10ths of a percent in October.

Cpl. N-TITLE **Cpl.** is the written abbreviation for **corporal** when it is used as a title. ◻ ...Cpl. G. Walker.

CPR /si pi ɑr/ N-UNCOUNT **CPR** is a medical technique for reviving someone whose heart has stopped beating by pressing on their chest and breathing into their mouth. **CPR** is an abbreviation for 'cardiopulmonary resuscitation.' [MEDICAL] ◻ McMullen performed CPR while other bystanders called 911.

CPU /si pi yu/ (**CPUs**) **1** N-COUNT In a computer, the **CPU** is the part that processes all the data and makes the computer work. **CPU** is an abbreviation for 'central processing unit.' [COMPUTING] **2** → See feature box at **computer**

crab /kræb/ (**crabs**) N-COUNT A **crab** is a sea creature with a flat round body covered by a shell, and five pairs of legs with large claws on the front pair. Crabs usually move sideways. • N-UNCOUNT **Crab** is the flesh of this creature eaten as food. ◻ I can't remember when I last had crab.

crab ap|ple (**crab apples**) N-COUNT A **crab apple** is a tree like an apple tree that produces small sour fruit.

crab|by /kræbi/ ADJ Someone who is **crabby** is bad-tempered and unpleasant to people. [INFORMAL]

crab|meat /kræbmit/ also **crab meat** N-UNCOUNT **Crabmeat** is the part of a crab that you eat.

CRACK
① VERB USES
② NOUN AND ADJECTIVE USES
---

① **crack** ✦✦✦ /kræk/ (**cracks, cracking, cracked**) **1** V-T/V-I If something hard **cracks**, or if you **crack** it, it becomes slightly damaged, with lines appearing on its surface. ◻ A gas main had cracked under my neighbor's garage and gas had seeped into our homes. **2** V-T/V-I If something **cracks**, or if you **crack** it, it makes a sharp sound like the sound of a piece of wood breaking. ◻ Thunder cracked in the sky. **3** V-T If you **crack** a hard part of your body, such as your knee or your head, you hurt it by accidentally hitting it hard against something. ◻ He cracked his head on the pavement and was knocked cold. **4** V-T When you **crack** something that has a shell, such as an egg or a nut, you break the shell in order to reach the inside part. ◻ Crack the eggs into a bowl. **5** V-T If you **crack** a problem or a code, you solve it, especially after a lot of thought. ◻ He has finally cracked the system after years of painstaking research. **6** V-I If someone **cracks**, they lose control of their emotions or actions because they are under a lot of pressure. [INFORMAL] ◻ She's calm and strong, and she is just not going to crack. **7** V-I If your voice **cracks** when you are speaking or singing, it changes in pitch because you are feeling a strong emotion. ◻ Her voice cracked and she began to cry. **8** V-T If you **crack** a joke, you tell it. ◻ He drove a Volkswagen, cracked jokes, and talked about beer and girls.

▶ **crack down** **1** PHRASAL VERB If people in authority **crack down** on a group of people, they become stricter in making the group obey rules or laws. ◻ The government has cracked down hard on those campaigning for greater democracy. **2** → see also **crackdown**

▶ **crack up** **1** PHRASAL VERB If someone **cracks up**, they are under such a lot of emotional strain that they become mentally ill. [INFORMAL] ◻ She would have cracked up if she hadn't allowed herself some fun. **2** PHRASAL VERB If you **crack up** or if someone or something **cracks** you **up**, you laugh a lot. [INFORMAL] ◻ She told stories that cracked me up and I swore to write them down so you could enjoy them too.

② **crack** /kræk/ (**cracks**) **1** N-COUNT A **crack** is a very narrow gap between two things, or between two parts of a thing. ◻ Kathryn had seen him through a crack in the curtains. **2** N-COUNT A **crack** is a line that appears on the surface of something when it is slightly damaged. ◻ The plate had a crack in it. **3** N-SING If you open something such as a door, window, or curtain **a crack**, you open it only a small amount. ◻ He went to the door, opened it a crack, and listened. **4** N-COUNT; SOUND A **crack** is a sharp sound, like the sound of a piece of wood breaking. ◻ Suddenly there was a loud crack and glass flew into the car. **5** N-UNCOUNT **Crack** is a very pure form of the drug cocaine. **6** ADJ [ADJ n] A **crack** soldier or sportsman is highly trained and very skillful. ◻ ...a crack undercover police officer. **7** N-COUNT A **crack** is a slightly rude or cruel joke. ◻ Tell Tracy you're sorry for that crack about her weight. **8** → See feature box at **DIY**

crack co|caine also **crack-cocaine** N-UNCOUNT **Crack cocaine** is a form of the drug cocaine which has been purified and made into crystals.

crack|down /krækdaʊn/ (**crackdowns**) N-COUNT A **crackdown** is strong official action that is taken to punish people who break laws. ◻ ...anti-government unrest that ended with the violent army crackdown.

cracked /krækt/ **1** ADJ An object that is **cracked** has lines on its surface because it is damaged. ◻ The ceiling was gray and cracked. ◻ ...a cracked mirror. **2** ADJ A **cracked** voice or a **cracked** musical note sounds rough and unsteady. ◻ When he spoke, his voice was hoarse and cracked.

crack|er /krækər/ (**crackers**) N-COUNT A **cracker** is a thin, crisp piece of baked bread which is often eaten with cheese.

cracker|jack /krækərdʒæk/ ADJ [usu ADJ n] Someone or something that is **crackerjack** is excellent or of very high quality. [AM] ◻ ...a crackerjack attorney. ◻ ...two hours of crackerjack sci-fi drama.

crack|ing /krækɪŋ/ PHRASE If you tell someone to **get cracking**, you are telling them to start doing something immediately. [INFORMAL] ◻ Mark, you'd better get cracking, the sooner the better.

crack|le /krækəl/ (**crackles, crackling, crackled**) **1** V-I If something **crackles**, it makes a rapid series of short, harsh noises. ◻ The radio crackled again. • N-COUNT **Crackle** is also a noun. ◻ ...the crackle of flames and gunfire. **2** → See feature box at **onomatopoeia**

crack|ly /krækəli/ ADJ Something that is **crackly**, especially a recording or broadcast, has or makes a lot of short, harsh noises. ◻ ...a crackly phone line.

crack|pot /krækpɒt/ (**crackpots**) ADJ [ADJ n] If you describe someone or their ideas as **crackpot**, you disapprove of them because you think that their ideas are strange and crazy. [INFORMAL, DISAPPROVAL] ◻ ...crackpot schemes. • N-COUNT A **crackpot** is a crackpot person. ◻ She was no more a crackpot than the rest of us.

crack-up (**crack-ups**) **1** N-COUNT A **crack up** is a mental breakdown. [mainly AM, INFORMAL] ◻ You're clearly having some kind of a crack-up, so I suggest you take three weeks off. **2** N-COUNT A **crack-up** is a motor vehicle accident. [AM, INFORMAL] ◻ In one recent crack-up, two drivers survived with only minor injury.

cra|dle /kreɪdəl/ (**cradles, cradling, cradled**) **1** N-COUNT A **cradle** is a baby's bed with high sides. Cradles often have curved bases so that they rock from side to side. **2** V-T If you **cradle** someone or something in your arms or hands, you hold them carefully and gently. ◻ I cradled her in my arms.

3 → See also color supplement

craft ◆◇◇ /krɑːft/ (crafts, crafting, crafted)

> Craft is both the singular and the plural form for meaning **1**.

1 N-COUNT You can refer to a boat, a spacecraft, or an aircraft as a **craft**. ☐ *With great difficulty, the fisherman maneuvered his small craft close to the reef.* **2** N-COUNT A **craft** is an activity such as weaving, carving, or pottery that involves making things skillfully with your hands. ☐ *...the arts and crafts of the North American Indians.* **3** N-COUNT You can use **craft** to refer to any activity or job that involves doing something skillfully. ☐ *...the craft of writing.* **4** V-T [usu passive] If something **is crafted**, it is made skillfully. ☐ *The windows would probably have been crafted in the latter part of the Middle Ages.* ☐ *...original, hand-crafted bags at affordable prices.*

craft beer (**craft beers**) N-VAR **Craft beer** is beer produced in small quantities, usually by a small, independent company. ☐ *They sell a great range of craft beers.*

craft fair (**craft fairs**) N-COUNT A **craft fair** is an event at which people sell goods they have made.

craft|ly /krɑːftli/ → see crafty

crafts|man /krɑːftsmən/ (**craftsmen**) N-COUNT A **craftsman** is a man who makes things skillfully with his hands. ☐ *The table in the kitchen was made by a local craftsman.*

crafts|man|ship /krɑːftsmənʃɪp/ N-UNCOUNT **Craftsmanship** is the skill that someone uses when they make beautiful things with their hands. ☐ *It is easy to appreciate the craftsmanship of Armani.*

crafts|people /krɑːftspiːpəl/ N-PLURAL **Craftspeople** are people who make things skillfully with their hands. ☐ *...highly skilled craftspeople.*

crafts|wom|an /krɑːftswʊmən/ (**craftswomen**) N-COUNT A **craftswoman** is a woman who makes things skillfully with her hands.

crafty /krɑːfti/ (**craftier, craftiest**) ADJ If you describe someone as **crafty**, you mean that they achieve what they want in a clever way, often by deceiving people. ☐ *...a crafty, lying character who enjoys plotting against others.* ☐ *A crafty look came to his eyes.*

crag /kræg/ (**crags**) N-COUNT A **crag** is a steep rocky cliff or part of a mountain.

crag|gy /krægi/ (**craggier, craggiest**) **1** ADJ [usu ADJ n] A **craggy** cliff or mountain is steep and rocky. ☐ *...tiny villages on craggy cliffs.* **2** ADJ [usu ADJ n] A **craggy** face has large features and deep lines. ☐ *He's a very small man with a lined, craggy face.*

cram /kræm/ (**crams, cramming, crammed**) **1** V-T If you **cram** things or people into a container or place, you put them into it, although there is hardly enough room for them. ☐ *Terry crammed the dirty clothes into his bag.* ☐ *She crammed her mouth with caviar.* **2** V-T/V-I If people **cram** into a place or vehicle or **cram** a place or vehicle, so many of them enter it at one time that it is completely full. ☐ *We crammed into my car and set off.* **3** V-I If you **are cramming for** an examination, you are learning as much as possible in a short time just before you take the examination. ☐ *She was cramming for her Economics exam.* • **cram|ming** N-UNCOUNT ☐ *It would take two or three months of cramming to prepare for Vermont's bar exam.* **4** → See feature box at **commute**

crammed /kræmd/ **1** ADJ If a place is **crammed** with things or people, it is full of them, so that there is hardly room for anything or anyone else. ☐ *The house is crammed with priceless furniture and works of art.* **2** ADJ [v-link ADJ n] If people or things are **crammed** into a place or vehicle, it is full of them. ☐ *Between two and three thousand refugees were crammed into the church buildings.* **3** → See feature box at **commute**

cramp /kræmp/ (**cramps, cramping, cramped**) **1** N-VAR [also N in pl] A **cramp** is a sudden, strong pain caused by a muscle suddenly contracting. You sometimes get cramps in a muscle after you have been making a physical effort over a long period of time. ☐ *Hillsden was complaining of a cramp in his calf muscles.* ☐ *...muscle cramps.* **2** PHRASE If someone or something **cramps your style**, their presence or existence restricts your behavior in some way. [INFORMAL] ☐ *Like more and more women, she believes wedlock would cramp her style.*

cramped /kræmpt/ ADJ A **cramped** room or building is not big enough for the people or things in it. ☐ *There are hundreds of families living in cramped conditions on the floor of the airport lounge.*

cram|pon /kræmpɒn/ (**crampons**) N-COUNT [usu pl] **Crampons** are metal plates with spikes underneath which mountain climbers fasten to the bottom of their boots, especially when there is snow or ice, in order to make climbing easier.

cran|berry /krænbəri/ (**cranberries**) N-COUNT [usu pl, oft N n] **Cranberries** are red berries with a sour taste. They are often used to make juice, or a sauce or jelly that you eat with meat.

crane /kreɪn/ (**cranes, craning, craned**) **1** N-COUNT A **crane** is a large machine that moves heavy things by lifting them in the air. ☐ *The little prefabricated hut was lifted away by a huge crane.* **2** N-COUNT A **crane** is a kind of large bird with a long neck and long legs. **3** V-T/V-I If you **crane** your neck or head, you stretch your neck in a particular direction in order to see or hear something better. ☐ *She craned her neck to get a better view.* ☐ *Children craned to get close to him.*

cra|nial /kreɪniəl/ ADJ [ADJ n] **Cranial** means relating to your cranium. [TECHNICAL] ☐ *...cranial bleeding.*

cra|nium /kreɪniəm/ (**craniums** or **crania** /kreɪniə/) N-COUNT Your **cranium** is the round part of your skull that contains your brain. [TECHNICAL]

crank /kræŋk/ (**cranks, cranking, cranked**) **1** N-COUNT If you call someone a **crank**, you think their ideas or behavior are strange. [INFORMAL, DISAPPROVAL] ☐ *The man with a new idea is a crank until the idea succeeds.* **2** N-COUNT A **crank** is a device that you turn in order to make something move. ☐ *He was idly turning a crank on a strange mechanism strapped to his chest.* **3** V-T If you **crank** an engine or machine, you make it move or function, especially by turning a handle. ☐ *The chauffeur got out to crank the motor.*
▶ **crank out** PHRASAL VERB If you say that a company or person **cranks out** a quantity of similar things, you mean they produce them quickly, in the same way, and are usually implying that the things are not original or are of poor quality. ☐ *In 1933 the studio cranked out fifty-five feature films.* ☐ *The writer must have cranked it out in his lunch-hour.*
▶ **crank up** PHRASAL VERB If you **crank up** a machine or device, you turn it on higher. ☐ *May's warm weather caused Americans to crank up their air conditioners.*

crank|shaft /kræŋkʃɑːft/ (**crankshafts**) N-COUNT A **crankshaft** is the main shaft of an internal combustion engine. ☐ *The engine had a broken crankshaft.*

cranky /kræŋki/ **1** ADJ If someone is **cranky**, they are bad-tempered and complain a lot. [AM, INFORMAL] ☐ *It was a long trek, and Jack and I both started to get cranky.* **2** ADJ If you describe ideas or ways of behaving as **cranky**, you disapprove of them because you think they are strange. [INFORMAL, DISAPPROVAL] ☐ *Vegetarianism has shed its cranky image.*

cran|ny /kræni/ (**crannies**) **1** N-COUNT [usu pl] **Crannies** are very narrow openings or spaces in something. ☐ *They fled like lizards into crannies in the rocks.* **2 every nook and cranny** → see **nook**

crap /kræp/ **1** ADJ If you describe something as **crap**, you think that it is wrong or of very poor quality. [INFORMAL, VULGAR, DISAPPROVAL] ☐ *She later said the book was "crap."* • N-UNCOUNT **Crap** is also a noun. ☐ *It is a tedious, humorless load of crap.* **2** N-UNCOUNT **Crap** is sometimes used to refer to feces. [INFORMAL, VULGAR] ☐ *I look down and I'm standing next to a pile of crap!* **3** N-UNCOUNT **Craps** or **crap** is a gambling game, played mainly in North America, in which you throw two dice and bet what the total will be. ☐ *I'll shoot some craps or play some blackjack.*

crap|py /kræpi/ (**crappier, crappiest**) ADJ [usu ADJ n] If you describe something as **crappy**, you think it is of very poor quality. Many people consider this word offensive. [INFORMAL, DISAPPROVAL] ☐ *...reading a crappy detective novel.*

crap|shoot /kræpʃuːt/ N-SING [a N] If you describe something as a **crapshoot**, you mean that what happens depends entirely on luck or chance. [AM] ☐ *Is buying a computer always a crapshoot?*

crash ◆◆◇ /kræʃ/ (**crashes, crashing, crashed**) **1** N-COUNT A **crash** is an accident in which a moving vehicle hits something and is damaged or destroyed. ❑ *His elder son was killed in a car crash a few years ago.* ◪ N-COUNT A **crash** is a sudden, loud noise. ❑ *Two people recalled hearing a loud crash about 1:30 a.m.* ◪ V-T/V-I If a moving vehicle **crashes** or if the driver **crashes** it, it hits something and is damaged or destroyed. ❑ *The plane crashed mysteriously near the island of Ustica.* ❑ *Her car crashed into the rear of a van.* ◪ V-I If something **crashes** somewhere, it moves and hits something else violently, making a loud noise. ❑ *The door swung inwards to crash against a chest of drawers behind it.* ❑ *My words were lost as the walls above us crashed down, filling the cellar with brick dust.* ◪ V-I If a business or financial system **crashes**, it fails suddenly, often with serious effects. [BUSINESS] ❑ *When the market crashed, they assumed the deal would be cancelled.* • N-COUNT **Crash** is also a noun. ❑ *He predicted correctly that there was going to be a stock market crash.* ◪ V-I If a computer or a computer program **crashes**, it fails suddenly. ❑ *The computer crashed for the second time in 10 days.* ◪ → See feature box at **accident**, **banking**, **onomatopoeia**

COLLOCATIONS

crash
NOUN ◪
noun + **crash**: car, helicopter, plane, train, tram
adjective + **crash**: fatal, near-fatal; head-on, high-speed; horrific
VERB ◪
noun + **crash**: airplane, helicopter, jet, plane; bus, car, motorcycle, truck
crash + noun: airplane, helicopter, jet, plane; bus, car, motorcycle, truck
crash + adverb: headlong, head-on

---

crash bar|ri|er (**crash barriers**) N-COUNT A **crash barrier** is the same as a **guardrail**. [BRIT]

crash course (**crash courses**) N-COUNT A **crash course** in a particular subject is a short course in which you are taught basic facts or skills, for example, before you start a new job. ❑ *I did a 15-week crash course in typing.*

crash hel|met (**crash helmets**) N-COUNT A **crash helmet** is a helmet that motorcyclists wear in order to protect their heads if they have an accident.

crash-land (**crash-lands**, **crash-landing**, **crash-landed**) also **crash land** V-T/V-I If a pilot **crash-lands** an aircraft, or if it **crash-lands**, it lands more quickly and less safely than usual, for example, when there is something wrong with the aircraft, and it cannot land normally. ❑ *He arrives in his biplane and crash lands it in a tree.* ❑ *A light aircraft crash-landed on a putting green yesterday.* • **crash-landing** (**crash-landings**) N-COUNT ❑ *His plane made a crash-landing during a sandstorm yesterday*

crass /kræs/ (**crasser**, **crassest**) ADJ **Crass** behavior is stupid and does not show consideration for other people. ❑ *The government has behaved with crass insensitivity.*

crate /kreɪt/ (**crates**, **crating**, **crated**) ◪ N-COUNT A **crate** is a large box used for transporting or storing things. ❑ *...a pile of wooden crates.* ◪ N-COUNT A **crate** is a plastic or wire box divided into sections that is used for carrying bottles. ◪ N-COUNT You can use **crate** to refer to a crate and its contents, or to the contents only. ❑ *...a crate of oranges.* ◪ V-T [usu passive] If something is **crated** or **crated up**, it is packed in a crate so that it can be transported or stored somewhere safely. ❑ *Equipment and office supplies were crated and shipped.*

cra|ter /kreɪtər/ (**craters**) ◪ N-COUNT A **crater** is a very large hole in the ground, which has been caused by something hitting it or by an explosion. ❑ *The explosion, believed to be a car bomb, left a ten-foot crater in the street.* ◪ → See also color supplement

cra|tered /kreɪtərd/ ADJ [usu ADJ n] If the surface of something is **cratered**, it has many craters in it. ❑ *...the Moon's cratered surface.*

cra|vat /krəvæt/ (**cravats**) N-COUNT A **cravat** is a piece of folded cloth which is worn wrapped around the neck.

crave /kreɪv/ (**craves**, **craving**, **craved**) V-T If you **crave** something, you want to have it very much. ❑ *There may be certain times of day when smokers crave their cigarette.* • **crav|ing** (**cravings**) N-COUNT ❑ *...a craving for sugar.*

cra|ven /kreɪvən/ ADJ Someone who is **craven** is very cowardly. [WRITTEN, DISAPPROVAL] ❑ *They condemned the deal as a craven surrender.*

craw|fish /krɔfɪʃ/ (**crawfish**) N-COUNT A **crawfish** is a small shellfish with five pairs of legs which lives in rivers and streams. You can eat some types of crawfish. [AM]

crawl /krɔl/ (**crawls**, **crawling**, **crawled**) ◪ V-I When you **crawl**, you move forward on your hands and knees. ❑ *Don't worry if your baby seems a little reluctant to crawl or walk.* ❑ *I began to crawl on my hands and knees toward the door.* ◪ V-I When an insect **crawls** somewhere, it moves there quite slowly. ❑ *I watched the moth crawl up the outside of the lampshade.* ◪ V-I If someone or something **crawls** somewhere, they move or progress slowly or with great difficulty. ❑ *I crawled out of bed at nine-thirty.* • N-SING [a N] **Crawl** is also a noun. ❑ *The traffic on the off-ramp slowed to a crawl.* ◪ V-I [only cont] If you say that a place **is crawling with** people or animals, you are emphasizing that it is full of them. [INFORMAL, EMPHASIS] ❑ *This place is crawling with police.* ◪ N-SING The **crawl** is a kind of swimming stroke which you do lying on your front, swinging one arm over your head, and then the other arm. ❑ *I expected him to do 50 lengths of the crawl.*

crawl|er /krɔlər/ (**crawlers**) N-COUNT A **crawler** is a computer program that visits websites and collects information when you do an internet search. [COMPUTING]

crawl space (**crawl spaces**) N-COUNT A **crawl space** is a narrow space under the roof or floor of a building that provides access to the wiring or plumbing. [AM] ❑ *They ran a cable from their machine through a crawl space between the basement and the stage.*

cray|fish /kreɪfɪʃ/ (**crayfish**) N-COUNT A **crayfish** is a small shellfish with five pairs of legs which lives in rivers and streams. You can eat some types of crayfish.

cray|on /kreɪɒn/ (**crayons**) N-COUNT A **crayon** is a rod of colored wax used for drawing.

craze /kreɪz/ (**crazes**) N-COUNT If there is a **craze** for something, it is very popular for a short time. ❑ *...the craze for Mutant Ninja Turtles.*

crazed /kreɪzd/ ADJ **Crazed** people are wild and uncontrolled, and perhaps insane. [WRITTEN] ❑ *A crazed gunman slaughtered five people last night.*

-crazed /-kreɪzd/ COMB IN ADJ **-crazed** combines with nouns to form adjectives that describe people whose behavior is wild and uncontrolled because of the thing the noun refers to. ❑ *...a drug-crazed killer.*

cra|zi|ly /kreɪzɪli/ ◪ ADV [ADV after v] If something moves **crazily**, it moves in a way or in a direction that you do not expect. [WRITTEN] ❑ *The ball bounced crazily over his shoulder into the net.* ◪ → see also **crazy**

cra|zy ✦✧ /kreɪzi/ (**crazier**, **craziest**, **crazies**) ◪ ADJ If you describe someone or something as **crazy**, you think they are very foolish or strange. [INFORMAL, DISAPPROVAL] ❑ *People thought they were all crazy to try to make money from manufacturing.* • **cra|zi|ly** ADV ❑ *The teenagers shook their long, black hair and gesticulated crazily.* ◪ ADJ Someone who is **crazy** is insane. [INFORMAL] ❑ *If I sat home and worried about all this stuff, I'd go crazy.* • N-COUNT **Crazy** is also a noun. ❑ *Outside, mumbling, was one of New York's ever-present crazies.* ◪ ADJ [v-link ADJ about n] If you are **crazy about** something, you are very enthusiastic about it. If you are not **crazy** about something, you do not like it. [INFORMAL] ❑ *He's still crazy about both his work and his hobbies.* • COMB IN ADJ **Crazy** is also a combining form. ❑ *Sports-crazy Coloradans will buy tickets to anything.* ◪ ADJ [v-link ADJ about n] If you are **crazy about** someone, you are deeply in love with them. [INFORMAL] ❑ *We're crazy about each other.*

cra|zy quilt N-SING [N of pl-n] If you describe something as a **crazy quilt** of other things, you mean that it is a mixture of those things without any pattern or order. [AM] ❑ *...a crazy quilt of ethnic neighborhoods.*

creak /kriːk/ (**creaks**, **creaking**, **creaked**) V-I If something **creaks**, it makes a short, high-pitched sound when it moves. ❑ *The bed-springs creaked.* ❑ *The door creaked open.* • N-COUNT **Creak** is also a noun. ❑ *The door was pulled open with a creak.*

creaky /kriːki/ (**creakier**, **creakiest**) ◪ ADJ A **creaky** object creaks when it moves. ❑ *She pushed open a creaky door.* ◪ ADJ

If you describe something as **creaky**, you think it is bad in some way because it is old or old-fashioned. ☐ *...a creaky and corrupt political system.*

cream ♦♦◇ /kriːm/ (creams, creaming, creamed) **1** N-UNCOUNT **Cream** is a thick yellowish-white liquid taken from milk. You can use it in cooking or put it on fruit or desserts. ☐ *...strawberries and cream.* **2** N-UNCOUNT [N *of* n] **Cream** is used in the names of soups that contain cream or milk. ☐ *...cream of mushroom soup.* **3** N-VAR A **cream** is a substance that you rub into your skin, for example, to keep it soft or to heal or protect it. ☐ *Gently apply the cream to the affected areas.* **4** COLOR Something that is **cream** is yellowish-white in color. ☐ *...cream silk stockings.* **5** → see also **ice cream**

▶ **cream off** **1** PHRASAL VERB To **cream off** part of a group of people means to take them away and treat them in a special way, because they are better than the others. [DISAPPROVAL] ☐ *The private schools cream off many of the best pupils.* **2** PHRASAL VERB If a person or organization **creams off** a large amount of money, they take it and use it for themselves. [INFORMAL, DISAPPROVAL] ☐ *This means smaller banks can cream off big profits during lending booms.*

cream cheese N-UNCOUNT **Cream cheese** is a very rich, soft white cheese.

cream|er /kriːmər/ (creamers) N-MASS **Creamer** is a white liquid or powder that is used in coffee or tea instead of milk. ☐ *...coffee whitened with a non-dairy creamer.*

cream|ery /kriːməri/ (creameries) N-COUNT A **creamery** is a place where milk and cream are made into butter and cheese.

cream of tar|tar N-UNCOUNT **Cream of tartar** is a white powder used in baking.

creamy /kriːmi/ (creamier, creamiest) **1** ADJ Food or drink that is **creamy** contains a lot of cream or milk. ☐ *...rich, creamy coffee.* **2** ADJ Food that is **creamy** has a soft, smooth texture and appearance. ☐ *...creamy mashed potato.*

crease /kriːs/ (creases, creasing, creased) **1** N-COUNT **Creases** are lines that are made in cloth or paper when it is crushed or folded. ☐ *She stood up, frowning at the creases in her silk dress.* ☐ *...cream-colored pants with sharp creases.* **2** N-COUNT **Creases** in someone's skin are lines which form where their skin folds when they move. ☐ *...the tiny creases at the corners of his eyes.* ● **creased** ADJ ☐ *Sweat poured down her deeply creased face.* **3** V-T/V-I If cloth or paper **creases** or if you **crease** it, lines form in it when it is crushed or folded. ☐ *Most outfits crease a bit when you are traveling.* ● **creased** ADJ ☐ *His clothes were creased, as if he had slept in them.*

cre|ate ♦♦♦ /krieɪt/ (creates, creating, created) **1** V-T To **create** something means to cause it to happen or exist. ☐ *We set business free to create more jobs.* ☐ *She could create a fight out of anything.* ● **crea|tion** /krieɪʃən/ N-UNCOUNT ☐ *These businesses stimulate the creation of local jobs.* **2** V-T When someone **creates** a new product or process, they invent it or design it. ☐ *It is really great for a radio producer to create a show like this.*

SYNONYMS

create
VERB
1
cause: *Attempts to limit parking around the venue are likely to cause problems.*
lead to: *Ethnic tensions among the republics could lead to civil war.*
bring about: *The only way they can bring about political change is by putting pressure on the country.*
2
make: *She made her own bread.*
form: *They formed a circle and sang 'Auld Lang Syne.'*
produce: *The drug is known to produce side-effects in women.*
invent: *He invented the first electric clock.*
devise: *We devised a scheme to help him.*

---

crea|tion /krieɪʃən/ (creations) **1** N-UNCOUNT [also *the* N] In many religions, **creation** is the making of the universe, earth, and creatures by God. ☐ *...the Creation of the universe as told in Genesis Chapter One.* **2** N-UNCOUNT People sometimes refer to the whole universe as **creation**. [LITERARY] ☐ *The whole of creation is made up of energy.* **3** N-COUNT You can refer to something that someone has made as a **creation**, especially if it shows skill, imagination, or artistic ability. ☐ *The bathroom is entirely my own creation.* **4** → see also **create**

crea|tion|ism /krieɪʃənɪzəm/ N-UNCOUNT **Creationism** is the belief that the account of the creation of the universe in the Bible is true, and that the theory of evolution is incorrect.

crea|tion|ist /krieɪʃənɪst/ (creationists) N-COUNT A **creationist** is someone who believes that the story of the creation of the universe in the Bible is true, and who rejects the theory of evolution.

crea|tive ♦◇◇ /krieɪtɪv/ **1** ADJ A **creative** person has the ability to invent and develop original ideas, especially in the arts. ☐ *Like so many creative people, he was never satisfied.* ● **crea|tiv|ity** /krieɪtɪvɪti/ N-UNCOUNT ☐ *American art reached a peak of creativity in the '50s and '60s.* **2** ADJ **Creative** activities involve the inventing and making of new kinds of things. ☐ *...creative writing.* ☐ *...creative arts.* **3** ADJ If you use something in a **creative** way, you use it in a new way that produces interesting and unusual results. ☐ *...his creative use of words.*

crea|tive ac|count|ing N-UNCOUNT **Creative accounting** is when companies present or organize their accounts in such a way that they gain money for themselves or give a false impression of their profits. [DISAPPROVAL] ☐ *Much of the apparent growth in profits in the 1980s was the result of creative accounting.*

crea|tive writ|ing N-UNCOUNT **Creative writing** is writing such as novels, stories, poems, and plays. ☐ *...a creative writing class.*

crea|tor /krieɪtər/ (creators) **1** N-COUNT The **creator** of something is the person who made it or invented it. ☐ *...Ian Fleming, the creator of James Bond.* **2** N-PROPER God is sometimes referred to as the **Creator**. ☐ *This was the first object placed in the heavens by the Creator.*

crea|ture /kriːtʃər/ (creatures) N-COUNT You can refer to any living thing that is not a plant as a **creature**, especially when it is of an unknown or unfamiliar kind. People also refer to imaginary animals and beings as **creatures**. ☐ *Alaskan Eskimos believe that every living creature possesses a spirit.*

crea|ture com|forts N-PLURAL **Creature comforts** are the things that you need to feel comfortable in a place, for example, good food and modern equipment. ☐ *They appreciate all the creature comforts of home.*

crèche /krɛʃ/ (crèches) also **creche** N-COUNT A **crèche** is a place where small children can be left to be cared for while their parents are doing something else. [BRIT]

in AM, use **day care center**

cred /krɛd/ N-UNCOUNT **Cred** is the same as **street cred**.

cre|dence /kriːdəns/ **1** N-UNCOUNT If something lends or gives **credence** to a theory or story, it makes it easier to believe. [FORMAL] ☐ *Good studies are needed to lend credence to the notion that genuine progress can be made in this important field.* **2** N-UNCOUNT If you give **credence** to a theory or story, you believe it. [FORMAL] ☐ *You're surely not giving any credence to this story of Hythe's?*

cre|den|tials /krɪdɛnʃəlz/ **1** N-PLURAL Someone's **credentials** are their previous achievements, training, and general background, which indicate that they are qualified to do something. ☐ *...her credentials as a Bach specialist.* **2** N-PLURAL Someone's **credentials** are a letter or certificate that proves their identity or qualifications. ☐ *The new ambassador to Lebanon has presented his credentials to the president.*

cred|ibil|ity /krɛdɪbɪlɪti/ N-UNCOUNT If someone or something has **credibility**, people believe in them and trust them. ☐ *The police have lost their credibility.*

cred|ibil|ity gap N-SING A **credibility gap** is the difference between what a person says or promises and what they actually think or do. ☐ *There is a credibility gap developing between employers and employees.*

cred|ible /krɛdɪbəl/ **1** ADJ **Credible** means able to be trusted or believed. ☐ *Her claims seem credible to many.* **2** ADJ A **credible** candidate, policy, or system, for example, is one that appears to have a chance of being successful. ☐ *Mr. Robertson would be a credible candidate.*

cred|it /krɛdɪt/ (credits, crediting, credited) **1** N-UNCOUNT If you are given **credit**, you are allowed to pay for goods or services several weeks or months after you have received them. ❏ *The group can't get credit to buy farming machinery.* **2** N-UNCOUNT If you get the **credit** for something good, people praise you because you are responsible for it, or are thought to be responsible for it. ❏ *We don't mind who gets the credit so long as we don't get the blame.* ❏ *It would be wrong for us to take all the credit.* **3** V-T When a sum of money **is credited** to an account, the bank adds that sum of money to the total in the account. ❏ *She noticed that only $80,000 had been credited to her account.* ❏ *Midland decided to change the way it credited payments to accounts.* **4** V-T If people **credit** someone **with** an achievement or if it **is credited to** them, people say or believe that they were responsible for it. ❏ *The staff are crediting him with having saved Hythe's life.* ❏ *The 74-year-old mayor is credited with helping make Los Angeles the financial capital of the West Coast.* **5** N-COUNT A **credit** is a sum of money which is added to an account. ❏ *The statement of total debits and credits is known as a balance.* **6** N-COUNT A **credit** is an amount of money that is given to someone. ❏ *Senator Bill Bradley outlined his own tax cut, giving families $350 in tax credits per child.* **7** N-PLURAL The list of people who helped to make a movie, a CD, or a television program is called the **credits**. ❏ *It was fantastic seeing my name in the credits.* **8** N-COUNT A **credit** is a successfully completed part of a higher education course, representing about one hour of instruction a week. At universities and colleges you need a certain number of credits to be awarded a degree. ❏ *Through the AP program students can earn college credits in high school.* **9** N-SING If you say that someone is **a credit to** someone or something, you mean that their qualities or achievements will make people have a good opinion of the person or thing mentioned. ❏ *He is one of the greatest players of recent times and is a credit to his profession.* **10** PHRASE To **give** someone **credit for** a good quality means to believe that they have it. ❏ *Bratbakk had more ability than the media gave him credit for.* **11** PHRASE If something is **to** someone's **credit**, they deserve praise for it. ❏ *She had managed to pull herself together and, to her credit, continued to look upon life as a positive experience.*

cred|it|able /krɛdɪtəbəl/ **1** ADJ A **creditable** performance or achievement is of a reasonably high standard. ❏ *They turned out a quite creditable performance.* **2** ADJ If you describe someone's actions or aims as **creditable**, you mean that they are morally good. ❏ *Not a very creditable attitude, I'm afraid.*

cred|it card (credit cards) N-COUNT A **credit card** is a plastic card that you use to buy goods on credit. Compare **charge card**.

cred|it crunch N-SING A **credit crunch** is a period during which there is a sudden reduction in the amount of money that banks and other lenders have available to lend. [JOURNALISM] ❏ *The most common argument for cutting interest rates is to prevent a global credit crunch.*

cred|it hour (credit hours) N-COUNT A **credit hour** in a university or college is one credit earned in a course of study. [AM] ❏ *After all his hard work, he now needs only two credit hours to graduate.*

cred|it lim|it (credit limits) N-COUNT [usu with poss] Your **credit limit** is the amount of debt that you are allowed to have, for example, by your credit card company. ❏ *If you exceed your credit limit, we have the right to suspend or cancel your account.*

cred|it line (credit lines) N-COUNT A person or company's **credit line** is the amount of credit that they are allowed, for example, by a credit card company or a bank. [mainly AM] ❏ *It offered a Gold Visa card and a $6,000 credit line.*

in BRIT, use **credit limit**

credi|tor /krɛdɪtər/ (creditors) N-COUNT Your **creditors** are the people who you owe money to. ❏ *The company said it would pay in full all its creditors except Credit Suisse.*

cred|it rat|ing N-SING Your **credit rating** is a judgment of how likely you are to pay money back if you borrow it or buy things on credit. ❏ *But Cahoot's overdraft rate depends on your credit rating.*

cred|it slip (credit slips) **1** N-COUNT A **credit slip** is a piece of paper that a shop gives you when you return goods that you have bought from it. It states that you are entitled to take goods of the same value without paying for them. [AM]

in BRIT, use **credit note**

2 N-COUNT A **credit slip** is a piece of paper which shows that your account has been credited.

cred|it trans|fer (credit transfers) N-COUNT A **credit transfer** is a direct payment of money from one bank account into another. [BRIT]

in AM, use **money transfer**

cred|it un|ion (credit unions) N-COUNT A **credit union** is a financial institution that offers its members low-interest loans. [mainly AM] ❏ *All the money that we have is tied up in a credit union.*

cred|it|worthy /krɛdɪtwɜrði/ also **credit-worthy** ADJ A **creditworthy** person or organization is one who can safely be lent money or allowed to have goods on credit, for example, because in the past they have always paid back what they owe. ❏ *The Fed wants banks to continue to lend to creditworthy borrowers.* ● **credit|worthi|ness** N-UNCOUNT ❏ *They now take extra steps to verify the creditworthiness of customers.*

cre|do /kridoʊ, kreɪ-/ (credos) N-COUNT A **credo** is a set of beliefs, principles, or opinions that strongly influence the way a person lives or works. [FORMAL] ❏ *Harry's personal credo is doing the best he can.*

cre|du|lity /krɪduliti/ N-UNCOUNT **Credulity** is a willingness to believe that something is real or true. [WRITTEN] ❏ *The plot does stretch credulity.*

credu|lous /krɛdʒələs/ ADJ If you describe someone as **credulous**, you have a low opinion of them because they are too ready to believe what people tell them and are easily deceived. [DISAPPROVAL] ❏ *...quack doctors charming money out of the pockets of credulous health-hungry citizens.*

creed /krid/ (creeds) **1** N-COUNT A **creed** is a set of beliefs, principles, or opinions that strongly influence the way people live or work. [FORMAL] ❏ *...their devotion to their creed of self-help.* **2** N-COUNT A **creed** is a religion. [FORMAL] ❏ *The center is open to all, no matter what race or creed.*

creek /krik/ (creeks) N-COUNT A **creek** is a small stream or river. [AM] ❏ *Follow Austin Creek for a few miles.*

creep /krip/ (creeps, creeping, crept) **1** V-I When people or animals **creep** somewhere, they move quietly and slowly. ❏ *Back I go to the hotel and creep up to my room.* **2** V-I If something **creeps** somewhere, it moves very slowly. ❏ *Mist had crept in again from the sea.* **3** V-I If something **creeps** in or **creeps** back, it begins to occur or becomes part of something without people realizing or without them wanting it. ❏ *Insecurity might creep in.* ❏ *An increasing ratio of mistakes, perhaps induced by tiredness, crept into her game.* **4** V-I If a rate or number **creeps** up to a higher level, it gradually reaches that level. ❏ *The inflation rate has been creeping up to 9.5 per cent.* **5 to make someone's flesh creep** → see **flesh**

creep|er /kripər/ (creepers) N-COUNT **Creepers** are plants with long stems that wind themselves around objects.

creepy /kripi/ (creepier, creepiest) ADJ If you say that something or someone is **creepy**, you mean they make you feel very nervous or frightened. [INFORMAL] ❏ *There were certain places that were really creepy at night.*

creepy-crawly /kripi krɔli/ (creepy-crawlies) N-COUNT [usu pl] You can refer to insects as **creepy-crawlies** when they give you a feeling of fear or disgust. This word is mainly used by children. [INFORMAL, DISAPPROVAL]

cre|mains /krɪmeɪnz/ N-PLURAL [usu poss N] A dead person's **cremains** are their remains after their body has been cremated. [AM] ❏ *Cremains of family members often go unclaimed, leaving funeral homes with heaps of cinders.*

cre|mate /krɪmeɪt/ (cremates, cremating, cremated) V-T [usu passive] When someone **is cremated**, their dead body is burned, usually as part of a funeral service. ❏ *She wants Chris to be cremated.* ● **cre|ma|tion** /krɪmeɪʃən/ (cremations) N-VAR ❏ *At Miss Garbo's request, there was a cremation after a private ceremony.*

crema|to|rium /krɪmətɔriəm, krɛmə-/ (crematoria /krɪmətɔriə, krɛmə-/ or **crematoriums**) N-COUNT A **crematorium** is a building in which the bodies of dead people are burned.

crema|tory /krímətɔri, krɛmə-/ (crematories) N-COUNT A **crematory** is the same as a **crematorium**. [AM]

crème de la crème /krɛm də lɑ krɛm/ N-SING [the N] If you refer to someone or something as **the crème de la crème**, you mean they are the very best person or thing of their kind. [JOURNALISM, APPROVAL] ❑ ...the crème de la crème of fashion designers.

crème fraiche /krɛm frɛʃ/ N-UNCOUNT **Crème fraiche** is a type of thick, slightly sour cream.

cren|e|lat|ed /krɛnᵊleɪtɪd/

in BRIT, sometimes in AM, use **crenellated**

ADJ [usu ADJ n] In a castle, a **crenelated** wall has gaps in the top or openings through which to fire at attackers. [TECHNICAL] ❑ ...crenellated turrets.

cre|ole /kríoʊl/ (creoles) also **Creole** ◼ N-VAR A **creole** is a language that has developed from a mixture of different languages and has become the main language in a particular place. ❑ She begins speaking in the creole of Haiti. ❑ ...French Creole. ◼ N-COUNT A **Creole** is a person of mixed African and European race, who lives in the West Indies and speaks a creole language. ◼ N-COUNT A **Creole** is a person descended from the Europeans who first settled in the West Indies or the southern United States. ◼ ADJ [usu ADJ n] **Creole** means belonging to or relating to the Creole community. ❑ Coconut Rice Balls is a creole dish.

creo|sote /kríəsoʊt/ N-UNCOUNT **Creosote** is a thick, dark liquid made from coal tar which is used to prevent wood from rotting.

crepe /kreɪp/ (crepes) ◼ N-UNCOUNT [oft N n] **Crepe** is a thin fabric with an uneven surface and is made of cotton, silk, or wool. ❑ Use a crepe bandage to support the affected area. ◼ N-UNCOUNT [oft N n] **Crepe** is a type of rubber with a rough surface. ❑ ...a pair of crepe-soled ankle-boots. ◼ N-COUNT A **crepe** is a thin pancake. ❑ ...chicken-filled crepes.

crepe pa|per N-UNCOUNT **Crepe paper** is stretchy paper with an uneven surface. Colored crepe paper is often used for making decorations.

crept /krɛpt/ **Crept** is the past tense and past participle of **creep**.

cre|pus|cu|lar /krɪpʌskyələr/ ADJ [ADJ n] **Crepuscular** means relating to **twilight**. [LITERARY] ❑ ...peering through the crepuscular gloom.

cre|scen|do /krɪʃɛndoʊ/ (crescendos) ◼ N-COUNT A **crescendo** is a noise that gets louder and louder. Some people also use **crescendo** to refer to the point when a noise is at its loudest. ❑ She spoke in a crescendo: "You are a bad girl! You are a wicked girl! You are evil!" ◼ N-COUNT People sometimes describe an increase in the intensity of something, or its most intense point, as a **crescendo**. [JOURNALISM] ❑ There was a crescendo of press criticism.

cres|cent /krɛsᵊnt/ (crescents) ◼ N-COUNT A **crescent** is a curved shape that is wider in the middle than at its ends, like the shape of the moon during its first and last quarters. It is the most important symbol of the Islamic faith. ❑ A glittering Islamic crescent tops the mosque. ❑ ...a narrow crescent of sand dunes. ◼ N-IN-NAMES **Crescent** is sometimes used as part of the name of a street or row of houses that is usually built in a curve. ❑ The address is 44 Colville Crescent.

cress /krɛs/ ◼ N-UNCOUNT **Cress** is a plant with small green leaves that are used in salads or to decorate food. ◼ N-UNCOUNT **Watercress** is sometimes referred to as **cress**.

crest /krɛst/ (crests) ◼ N-COUNT The **crest** of a hill or a wave is the top of it. • PHRASE If you say that you are **on the crest of a wave**, you mean that you are feeling very happy and confident because things are going well for you. ❑ The band is riding on the crest of a wave with the worldwide success of their number-one-selling single. ◼ N-COUNT A bird's **crest** is a group of upright feathers on the top of its head. ❑ Both birds had a dark blue crest. ◼ N-COUNT A **crest** is a design that is the symbol of a noble family, a town, or an organization. ❑ On the wall is the family crest.

crest|ed /krɛstɪd/ ◼ ADJ [ADJ n] A **crested** bird is a bird that has a crest on its head. ❑ ...crested hawks. ◼ ADJ [usu ADJ n] **Crested** objects have on them the crest of a noble family, a town, or an organization. ❑ ...crested writing paper.

crest|fallen /krɛstfɔlən/ ADJ [usu v-link ADJ] If you look **crestfallen**, you look sad and disappointed about something.

cret|in /kríᵗn/ (cretins) N-COUNT If you call someone a **cretin**, you think they are very stupid. [OFFENSIVE, DISAPPROVAL]

cret|in|ous /kríᵗnəs/ ADJ If you describe someone as **cretinous**, you think they are very stupid. [OFFENSIVE, DISAPPROVAL]

cre|vasse /krɪvǽs/ (crevasses) N-COUNT A **crevasse** is a large, deep crack in thick ice or rock. ❑ He fell down a crevasse.

crev|ice /krɛvɪs/ (crevices) N-COUNT A **crevice** is a narrow crack or gap, especially in a rock. ❑ ...a huge boulder with rare ferns growing in every crevice.

crew ✦✧✧ /kru/ (crews, crewing, crewed) ◼ N-COUNT-COLL The **crew** of a ship, an aircraft, or a spacecraft is the people who work on and operate it. ❑ The mission for the crew of the space shuttle is essentially over. ❑ Despite their size, these vessels carry small crews, usually of around twenty men. ◼ N-COUNT A **crew** is a group of people with special technical skills who work together on a task or project. ❑ ...a two-man film crew making a documentary. ◼ V-T/V-I If you **crew** a boat, you work on it as part of the crew. ❑ This neighbor crewed on a ferryboat. ❑ There were to be five teams of three crewing the boat.

crew cut (crew cuts) also **crewcut** N-COUNT A **crew cut** is a hairstyle in which the hair is cut very short.

crew|man /krúmæn/ (crewmen) N-COUNT A **crewman** is a man who is a member of a crew.

crew member (crew members) N-COUNT A **crew member** is a person who is part of a crew.

crew|neck /krúnɛk/ (crewnecks)

in BRIT, use **crew neck**

N-COUNT A **crewneck** or a **crewneck** sweater is a sweater with a round neck.

crib /krɪb/ (cribs) ◼ N-COUNT A **crib** is a bed for a baby. [mainly AM]

in BRIT, usually use **cot**

◼ → See also color supplement

crib death (crib deaths) N-VAR **Crib death** is the sudden death of a baby while it is asleep, although the baby had not previously been ill. [AM] ❑ Mothers wanting to minimize the risk of crib death should breastfeed their babies.

in BRIT, use **cot death**

crick /krɪk/ (cricks) N-COUNT If you have a **crick** in your neck or in your back, you have a pain there caused by muscles becoming stiff.

crick|et ✦✧✧ /krɪkɪt/ (crickets) ◼ N-UNCOUNT **Cricket** is an outdoor game played between two teams. Players try to score points, called runs, by hitting a ball with a wooden bat. ❑ During the summer term we would play cricket at the village ground. ◼ N-COUNT A **cricket** is a small jumping insect that produces short, loud sounds by rubbing its wings together. ◼ → See also color supplement

crick|et|er /krɪkɪtər/ (cricketers) N-COUNT A **cricketer** is a person who plays cricket.

cri|er /kraɪər/ → see **town crier**

crime ✦✦✧ /kraɪm/ (crimes) ◼ N-VAR A **crime** is an illegal action or activity for which a person can be punished by law. ❑ He and Lieutenant Cassidy were checking the scene of the crime. ❑ ...the growing problem of organized crime. ◼ N-COUNT If you say that doing something is a **crime**, you think it is very wrong or a serious mistake. [DISAPPROVAL] ❑ It would be a crime to travel all the way to Australia and not stop in Sydney. ◼ → See feature box at **urban**

COLLOCATIONS

crime
NOUN ◼
noun + **crime**: gun, knife; hate, sex, war; gang, youth
adjective + **crime**: heinous, horrific, violent; organized, serious; petty, victimless, white-collar; unsolved; juvenile
verb + **crime**: combat, fight, prevent, reduce, tackle; investigate, solve; commit, perpetrate

VOCABULARY IN CONTEXT

Crime

Since 1995, there has been a noticeable year-after-year fall in the number of certain crimes being **committed**. **Burglary**, **robbery**, **kidnapping**, **mugging**, and other **assaults** have all been going down. While in many ways, this means that the U.S. is a safer place to live, it does not, however, mean that there is actually less crime overall. As **violent** crime has been dropping, **cybercrime** and **identity theft** have been growing. You are now twice as likely to be **conned** online as you are to have your car stolen. It's much easier and safer for a criminal to send out a **phishing** email than to rob a bank, and such **scams** can be very **lucrative**. It has been estimated that the annual cost of **online fraud** could be more than $20 billion worldwide.

crime scene (crime scenes) N-COUNT A **crime scene** is a place that is being investigated by the police because a crime has taken place there. ❑ *Photographs of the crime scene began to arrive within twenty minutes.*

crime wave also **crimewave** N-SING When more crimes than usual are committed in a particular place, you can refer to this as a **crime wave**. ❑ *The country is in the grip of a teenage crime wave.*

crim|i|nal ♦♦◊ /krˈɪmɪnəl/ (criminals) **1** N-COUNT A **criminal** is a person who has committed a crime. ❑ *A group of gunmen attacked a prison and set free nine criminals.* **2** ADJ **Criminal** means connected with crime. ❑ *Her husband faces various criminal charges.* **3** ADJ If you describe an action as **criminal**, you think it is very wrong or a serious mistake. [DISAPPROVAL] ❑ *He said a full-scale dispute involving strikes would be criminal.* **4** → See feature box at **prison**

crimi|nal court (criminal courts) N-COUNT A **criminal court** is a law court that deals with criminal offenses.

crimi|nal|ize /krˈɪmɪnəlaɪz/ (criminalizes, criminalizing, criminalized)

in BRIT, also use **criminalise**

V-T If a government **criminalizes** an action or person, it officially declares that the action or the person's behavior is illegal. ❑ *There is no move to criminalize alcohol.*

crimi|nol|ogy /krˌɪmɪnˈɒlədʒi/ N-UNCOUNT **Criminology** is the scientific study of crime and criminals. • **crimi|nolo|gist** /krˌɪmɪnˈɒlədʒɪst/ (criminologists) N-COUNT ❑ *...a criminologist at the University of Montreal.*

crimp /krˈɪmp/ (crimps, crimping, crimped) **1** V-T If you **crimp** something such as a piece of fabric or pastry, you make small folds in it. ❑ *Crimp the edges to seal them tightly.* **2** V-T To **crimp** something means to restrict or reduce it. [AM] ❑ *The dollar's recent strength is crimping overseas sales and profits.*

crim|son /krˈɪmzən/ (crimsons) COLOR Something that is **crimson** is deep red in color. ❑ *...a mass of crimson flowers.*

cringe /krˈɪndʒ/ (cringes, cringing, cringed) V-I If you **cringe** at something, you feel embarrassed or disgusted, and perhaps show this feeling in your expression or by making a slight movement. ❑ *Molly had cringed when Ann started picking up the guitar.* ❑ *Chris had cringed at the thought of using her own family for publicity.*

crin|kle /krˈɪŋkəl/ (crinkles, crinkling, crinkled) **1** V-T/V-I If something **crinkles** or if you **crinkle** it, it becomes slightly creased or folded. ❑ *He shrugged whimsically, his eyes crinkling behind his glasses.* ❑ *When she laughs, she crinkles her perfectly-formed nose.* **2** N-COUNT **Crinkles** are small creases or folds.

crin|kly /krˈɪŋkli/ (crinklier, crinkliest) ADJ [usu ADJ n] A **crinkly** object has many small creases or folds in it or in its surface. ❑ *...her big crinkly face.* ❑ *...crinkly paper.*

crino|line /krˈɪnəlɪn/ (crinolines) N-COUNT A **crinoline** was a round frame which women wore under their skirts in the 19th century.

crip|ple /krˈɪpəl/ (cripples, crippling, crippled) **1** N-COUNT A person with a physical disability or a serious permanent injury is sometimes referred to as a **cripple**. [OFFENSIVE] ❑ *She has gone from being a healthy, fit, and sporty young woman to being a cripple.* **2** V-T If someone **is crippled** by an injury, it is so serious that they can never move their body properly again. ❑ *Mr. Easton was crippled in an accident and had to leave his job.* ❑ *He had been warned that another bad fall could cripple him for life.*

crip|pling /krˈɪplɪŋ/ **1** ADJ [ADJ n] A **crippling** illness or disability is one that severely damages your health or your body. ❑ *Arthritis and rheumatism are prominent crippling diseases.* **2** ADJ If you say that an action, policy, or situation has a **crippling** effect on something, you mean it has a very serious, harmful effect. ❑ *The high cost of capital has a crippling effect on many small firms.*

cri|sis ♦♦◊ /krˈaɪsɪs/ (crises /krˈaɪsiːz/) **1** N-VAR A **crisis** is a situation in which something or someone is affected by one or more very serious problems. ❑ *Natural disasters have obviously contributed to the continent's economic crisis.* ❑ *...someone to turn to in moments of crisis.* **2** → See feature box at **banking, challenge, endanger, history**

SYNONYMS

crisis
NOUN **1**
emergency: *The hospital is now open only for emergencies.*
catastrophe: *From all points of view, war would be a catastrophe.*
disaster: *Many had lost all in the disaster and were destitute.*

cri|sis man|age|ment N-UNCOUNT People use **crisis management** to refer to a management style that concentrates on solving the immediate problems occurring in a business rather than looking for long-term solutions. [BUSINESS] ❑ *Today's NSC is overcome by day-to-day crisis management.* ❑ *...a crisis-management team.*

crisp /krˈɪsp/ (crisper, crispest, crisps, crisping, crisped) **1** ADJ Food that is **crisp** is pleasantly hard, or has a pleasantly hard surface. [APPROVAL] ❑ *Bake the potatoes for 15 minutes, till they're nice and crisp.* ❑ *...crisp bacon.* **2** ADJ Weather that is pleasantly fresh, cold, and dry can be described as **crisp**. [APPROVAL] ❑ *...a crisp autumn day.* **3** ADJ **Crisp** cloth or paper is clean and has no creases in it. ❑ *He wore a panama hat and a crisp white suit.* ❑ *I slipped between the crisp clean sheets.* **4** V-T/V-I If food **crisps** or if you **crisp** it, it becomes pleasantly hard, for example, because you have heated it at a high temperature. ❑ *Cook the bacon until it begins to crisp.* **5** N-COUNT **Crisps** are very thin slices of fried potato that are eaten cold as a snack. [BRIT]

in AM, use **chips**

crisp|bread /krˈɪspbrɛd/ (crispbreads) N-VAR **Crispbreads** are thin dry crackers made from wheat or rye. They are often eaten instead of bread by people who want to lose weight.

crispy /krˈɪspi/ (crispier, crispiest) ADJ Food that is **crispy** is pleasantly hard, or has a pleasantly hard surface. [APPROVAL] ❑ *...crispy fried onions.* ❑ *...crispy bread rolls.*

criss-cross /krˈɪs krɒs/ (criss-crosses, criss-crossing, criss-crossed) also **crisscross** **1** V-T If a person or thing **criss-crosses** an area, they travel from one side to the other and back again many times, following different routes. If a number of things **criss-cross** an area, they cross it, and cross over each other. ❑ *They criss-crossed the country by bus.*

2 V-RECIP If two sets of lines or things **criss-cross**, they cross over each other. ☐ *Wires criss-cross between the tops of the poles, forming a grid.* **3** ADJ [ADJ n] A **criss-cross** pattern or design consists of lines crossing each other. ☐ *Slash the tops of the loaves with a serrated knife in a criss-cross pattern.*

cri|teri|on /kraɪtɪəriən/ (**criteria** /kraɪtɪəriə/) N-COUNT A **criterion** is a factor on which you judge or decide something. ☐ *The most important criterion for entry is that applicants must design and make their own work.*

crit|ic ✦◇◇ /krɪtɪk/ (**critics**) **1** N-COUNT A **critic** is a person who writes about and expresses opinions about things such as books, movies, music, or art. ☐ *Mather was a film critic for many years.* **2** N-COUNT Someone who is a **critic** of a person or system disapproves of them and criticizes them publicly. ☐ *The newspaper has been one of the most consistent critics ever of the government.* **3** → See feature box at **theater**

> **SYNONYMS**
> **critic**
> NOUN **1**
> **judge:** *A panel of judges is now selecting the finalists.*
> **reviewer:** *...the reviewer for The Times Literary Supplement.*

criti|cal ✦◇◇ /krɪtɪkəl/ **1** ADJ A **critical** time, factor, or situation is extremely important. ☐ *The incident happened at a critical point in the campaign.* ☐ *He says setting priorities is of critical importance.* • **criti|cal|ly** /krɪtɪkli/ ADV ☐ *Economic prosperity depends critically on an open world trading system.* **2** ADJ A **critical** situation is very serious and dangerous. ☐ *The German authorities are considering an airlift if the situation becomes critical.* • **criti|cal|ly** ADV ☐ *Moscow is running critically low on food supplies.* **3** ADJ If a person is **critical** or in a **critical** condition in a hospital, they are seriously ill. ☐ *Ten of the injured are said to be in critical condition.* • **criti|cal|ly** ADV ☐ *She was critically ill.* **4** ADJ To be **critical** of someone or something means to criticize them. ☐ *His report is highly critical of the trial judge.* • **criti|cal|ly** ADV ☐ *She spoke critically of Lara.* **5** ADJ [ADJ n] A **critical** approach to something involves examining and judging it carefully. ☐ *We need to become critical text-readers.* • **criti|cal|ly** ADV ☐ *Wyman watched them critically.* **6** ADJ [ADJ n] If something or someone receives **critical** acclaim, critics say that they are very good. ☐ *The film met with considerable critical and public acclaim.* **7** → See feature box at **endanger**

> **SYNONYMS**
> **critical**
> ADJ
> **1**
> **crucial:** *...the most crucial election campaign in years.*
> **momentous:** *The past three years have been among the most momentous in world history.*
> **decisive:** *The election campaign has now entered its final, decisive phase.*
> **vital:** *After her release, she was able to give vital information about her kidnapper.*
> **4**
> **scathing:** *He then launched a scathing attack on previous leaders.*
> **disparaging:** *He was critical of the people, disparaging of their crude manners.*
> **derogatory:** *He refused to withdraw derogatory remarks made about his boss.*
> **disapproving:** *Janet gave him a disapproving look.*
> **contemptuous:** *He's openly contemptuous of all the major political parties.*

criti|cal mass 1 N-SING [also no det] In physics, the **critical mass** of a substance is the minimum amount of it that is needed for a nuclear chain reaction. [TECHNICAL] ☐ *In order to make a nuclear explosion, the critical mass must come together within a fraction of a millionth of a second.* **2** N-SING [also no det] A **critical mass** of something is an amount of it that makes it possible for something to happen or continue. ☐ *Only in this way can the critical mass of participation be reached.*

criti|cism ✦◇◇ /krɪtɪsɪzəm/ (**criticisms**) **1** N-VAR **Criticism** is the action of expressing disapproval of something or someone. A **criticism** is a statement that expresses disapproval. ☐ *This policy had repeatedly come under strong criticism on Capitol Hill.* **2** N-UNCOUNT **Criticism** is a serious examination and judgment of something such as a book or play. ☐ *She has published more than 20 books including novels, poetry and literary criticism.*

> **COLLOCATIONS**
> **criticism**
> NOUN **1**
> adjective + **criticism:** constructive, legitimate, widespread; fierce, harsh, heavy, strong; unfair, unjustified, unwarranted
> verb + **criticism:** attract, draw, face, spark; direct, level, voice; deflect, dismiss, reject

> **SYNONYMS**
> **criticism**
> NOUN **1**
> **censure:** *It is a controversial policy which has attracted international censure.*
> **disapproval:** *His action had been greeted with almost universal disapproval.*
> **disparagement:** *Reviewers have been almost unanimous in their disparagement of this book.*
> **denigration:** *...the denigration of minorities in this country.*

criti|cize ✦◇◇ /krɪtɪsaɪz/ (**criticizes, criticizing, criticized**)

in BRIT, also use **criticise**

V-T If you **criticize** someone or something, you express your disapproval of them by saying what you think is wrong with them. ☐ *His mother had rarely criticized him or any of her other children.*

cri|tique /krɪtik/ (**critiques**) N-COUNT A **critique** is a written examination and judgment of a situation or of a person's work or ideas. [FORMAL] ☐ *She had brought a book, a feminist critique of Victorian lady novelists.*

crit|ter /krɪtər/ (**critters**) N-COUNT A **critter** is a living creature. [AM, INFORMAL] ☐ *...little furry critters.*

croak /kroʊk/ (**croaks, croaking, croaked**) **1** V-I When a frog or bird **croaks**, it makes a harsh, low sound. ☐ *Thousands of frogs croaked in the reeds by the riverbank.* • N-COUNT **Croak** is also a noun. ☐ *...the guttural croak of the frogs.* **2** V-T If someone **croaks** something, they say it in a low, rough voice. ☐ *Tiller moaned and managed to croak, "Help me."* • N-COUNT **Croak** is also a noun. ☐ *His voice was just a croak.* **3** V-I When someone **croaks**, they die. [INFORMAL] ☐ *I think the doctors were worried that I was going to croak on their watch.*

croaky /kroʊki/ (**croakier, croakiest**) ADJ If someone's voice is **croaky**, it is low and rough.

cro|chet /kroʊʃeɪ/ (**crochets, crocheting, crocheted**) **1** N-UNCOUNT **Crochet** is a way of making cloth out of cotton or wool by using a needle with a small hook at the end. ☐ *...crochet artwork.* **2** V-T/V-I If you **crochet**, you make cloth by using a needle with a small hook at the end. ☐ *She offered to teach me to crochet.* ☐ *Ma and I crocheted new quilts.* ☐ *...crocheted rugs.*

crock /krɒk/ (**crocks**) **1** N-COUNT A **crock** is a clay pot or jar. [OLD-FASHIONED] **2** N-COUNT [usu sing] If you describe what someone has said as **a crock**, you mean that you think it is foolish, wrong, or untrue. [mainly AM, INFORMAL, DISAPPROVAL] **3** a crock of gold → see gold

crock|ery /krɒkəri/ N-UNCOUNT **Crockery** is the plates, cups, saucers, and dishes that you use at meals. [mainly BRIT]

croco|dile /krɒkədaɪl/ (**crocodiles**) N-COUNT A **crocodile** is a large reptile with a long body and strong jaws. Crocodiles live in rivers and eat meat.

croco|dile tears N-PLURAL If someone is crying **crocodile tears**, their tears and sadness are not genuine or sincere. ☐ *The sight of George shedding crocodile tears made me sick.*

cro|cus /kroʊkəs/ (**crocuses**) N-COUNT **Crocuses** are small white, yellow, or purple flowers that are grown in parks and gardens in the early spring.

crois|sant /krwɑsɒn, krəsɒnt/ (**croissants**) N-VAR **Croissants** are bread rolls in the shape of a crescent that are eaten for breakfast. ☐ *...coffee and croissants.*

crone /kroʊn/ (**crones**) N-COUNT A **crone** is an insulting word for an old woman. [LITERARY]

cro|ny /kroʊni/ (cronies) N-COUNT You can refer to friends that someone spends a lot of time with as their **cronies**, especially when you disapprove of them. [INFORMAL, DISAPPROVAL] ❑ *He played a round of golf with his business cronies.*

cro|ny|ism /kroʊniɪzəm/ N-UNCOUNT If you accuse someone in authority of **cronyism**, you mean that they use their power or authority to get jobs for their friends. [JOURNALISM, DISAPPROVAL]

crook /krʊk/ (crooks, crooking, crooked) **1** N-COUNT A **crook** is a dishonest person or a criminal. [INFORMAL] ❑ *The man is a crook and a liar.* **2** N-COUNT The **crook of** your arm or leg is the soft inside part where you bend your elbow or knee. ❑ *She hid her face in the crook of her arm.* **3** N-COUNT A **crook** is a long pole with a large hook at the end. A crook is carried by a bishop in religious ceremonies, or by a shepherd. **4** V-T If you **crook** your arm or finger, you bend it. ❑ *He crooked his finger: "Come forward," he said.*

crook|ed /krʊkɪd/ **1** ADJ If you describe something as **crooked**, especially something that is usually straight, you mean that it is bent or twisted. ❑ *...the crooked line of his broken nose.* **2** ADJ A **crooked** smile is uneven and bigger on one side than the other. ❑ *Polly gave her a crooked grin.* **3** ADJ If you describe a person or an activity as **crooked**, you mean that they are dishonest or criminal. [INFORMAL] ❑ *...a crooked cop.*

croon /kruːn/ (croons, crooning, crooned) **1** V-T/V-I If you **croon**, you sing or hum quietly and gently. ❑ *He would much rather have been crooning in a smoky bar.* **2** V-T/V-I If one person talks to another in a soft gentle voice, you can describe them as **crooning**, especially if you think they are being sentimental or insincere. ❑ *"Dear boy," she crooned, hugging him heartily.*

croon|er /kruːnər/ (crooners) N-COUNT A **crooner** is a male singer who sings sentimental songs, especially the love songs of the 1930s and 1940s.

crop ♦♦◊ /krɒp/ (crops, cropping, cropped) **1** N-COUNT **Crops** are plants such as wheat and potatoes that are grown in large quantities for food. ❑ *Rice farmers here still plant and harvest their crops by hand.* **2** N-COUNT The plants or fruits that are collected at harvest time are referred to as a **crop**. ❑ *Each year it produces a fine crop of fruit.* ❑ *The U.S. government says that this year's corn crop should be about 8 percent more than last year.* **3** N-COUNT A **crop** is a short hairstyle. ❑ *She had her long hair cut into a boyish crop.* **4** N-SING You can refer to a group of people or things that have appeared recently as a **crop of** people or things. [INFORMAL] ❑ *The present crop of books and documentaries about Marilyn Monroe exploit the thirtieth anniversary of her death.* **5** V-I When a plant **crops**, it produces fruits or parts which people want. ❑ *Although these vegetables adapt well to our temperate climate, they tend to crop poorly.* **6** V-T To **crop** someone's hair means to cut it short. ❑ *She cropped her hair and dyed it blonde.* **7** V-T If you **crop** a photograph, you cut part of it off, in order to get rid of part of the picture or to be able to frame it. ❑ *I decided to crop the picture just above the water line.* **8** → See feature box at **farming**

▶ **crop up** PHRASAL VERB If something **crops up**, it appears or happens, usually unexpectedly. ❑ *His name has cropped up at every selection meeting this season.*

COLLOCATIONS

crop
NOUN
1
noun + **crop**: cereal, potato, root, wheat; cash
verb + **crop**: harvest, produce; plant, sow; damage, destroy
2
adjective + **crop**: bumper, fine, agricultural, staple
4
adjective + **crop**: current, present

---

crop dust|ing also **crop-dusting** N-UNCOUNT [oft N n] **Crop dusting** is the spreading of pesticides on crops, usually from an aircraft. ❑ *...a crop-dusting plane.*

cropped /krɒpt/ **1** ADJ [usu ADJ n] **Cropped** items of clothing are shorter than normal. ❑ *She wore a black t-shirt and cropped jeans.* **2** → see also **crop**

crop|per /krɒpər/ PHRASE If you say that someone **has come a cropper**, you mean that they have had an unexpected and embarrassing failure. [INFORMAL]

crop top (crop tops) N-COUNT A **crop top** is a very short, usually tight, top worn by a girl or a woman.

cro|quet /kroʊkeɪ/ N-UNCOUNT **Croquet** is a game played on grass in which the players use long wooden sticks called mallets to hit balls through metal arches.

cro|quette /kroʊkɛt/ (croquettes) N-COUNT **Croquettes** are small amounts of mashed potato or meat rolled in breadcrumbs and fried.

CROSS
① MOVING ACROSS
② ANGRY

---

① **cross** ♦♦◊ /krɒs/ (crosses, crossing, crossed)
→ Please look at meanings **13** – **16** to see if the expression you are looking for is shown under another headword.

1 V-T/V-I If you **cross** something such as a room, a road, or an area of land or water, you move or travel to the other side of it. If you **cross** to a place, you move or travel over a room, road, or area of land or water in order to reach that place. ❑ *She was partly to blame for failing to look as she crossed the road.* ❑ *Egan crossed to the drinks cabinet and poured a Scotch.* **2** V-T A road, railroad, or bridge that **crosses** an area of land or water passes over it. ❑ *The road crosses the river half a mile outside the town.* **3** V-T If someone or something **crosses** a limit or boundary, for example, the limit of acceptable behavior, they go beyond it. ❑ *I normally never write into magazines but Mr. Stubbs has finally crossed the line.* **4** V-I If an expression **crosses** someone's face, it appears briefly on their face. [WRITTEN] ❑ *Berg tilts his head and a mischievous look crosses his face.* **5** V-T If you **cross** your arms, legs, or fingers, you put one of them on top of the other. ❑ *Jill crossed her legs and rested her chin on one fist, as if lost in deep thought.* **6** V-RECIP Lines or roads that **cross** meet and go across each other. ❑ *...the intersection where Main and Center streets cross.* **7** N-COUNT A **cross** is a shape that consists of a vertical line or piece with a shorter horizontal line or piece across it. It is the most important Christian symbol. ❑ *Around her neck was a cross on a silver chain.* **8** N-COUNT A **cross** is a written mark in the shape of an X. You can use it, for example, to indicate that an answer to a question is wrong, to mark the position of something on a map, or to indicate your vote on a ballot. ❑ *Put a cross next to those activities you like.* **9** N-COUNT In some team sports such as soccer and hockey, a **cross** is the passing of the ball from the side of the field to a player in the center, usually in front of the goal. ❑ *Johnson hit an accurate cross to Groves.* **10** N-SING Something that is **a cross between** two things is neither one thing nor the other, but a mixture of both. ❑ *"Ha!" It was a cross between a laugh and a bark.* **11** ADJ [ADJ n] A **cross** street is a road that crosses another more important road. [AM] ❑ *The Army boys had personnel carriers blockading the cross streets.* **12** → see also **crossing** **13** **to cross your fingers** → see **finger** **14** **cross my heart** → see **heart** ② **15** **to cross your mind** → see **mind** ① **16** **to cross swords** → see **sword**

▶ **cross out** PHRASAL VERB If you **cross out** words on a page, you draw a line through them, because they are wrong or because you want to change them. ❑ *He crossed out "fellow subjects," and instead inserted "fellow citizens."*

SYNONYMS

cross
ADJ ② **1**
angry: *Are you angry with me for some reason?*
irritated: *Not surprisingly, her teacher is getting irritated with her.*
annoyed: *She tapped her forehead and looked annoyed with herself.*
grumpy: *Some folk think I'm a grumpy, old man.*
peevish: *Aubrey had slept little, and that always made him peevish.*

---

② **cross** /krɒs/ (crosser, crossest) ADJ Someone who is **cross** is angry or irritated. ❑ *The women are cross and bored.* ❑ *I'm imagining cross with him.* ● **cross|ly** ADV [ADV with v] ❑ *"No, no, no," Morris said crossly.*

cross|bar /krɒsbɑːr/ (crossbars) **1** N-COUNT A **crossbar** is a horizontal piece of wood attached to two upright pieces, for example, a part of the goal in soccer. **2** N-COUNT The **crossbar**

of a bicycle is the horizontal metal bar between the handlebars and the saddle. **3** → See also color supplement

cross|beam /krɒsbiːm/ (**crossbeams**) N-COUNT A **crossbeam** is a long, thick bar of wood, metal, or concrete that is placed between two walls or other structures, especially in order to support the roof of a building. ❑ *He hung the light from a steel crossbeam in the roof.*

cross|bones /krɒsboʊnz/ → see skull and crossbones

cross-border **1** ADJ [ADJ n] **Cross-border** trade occurs between companies in different countries. ❑ *Currency-conversion costs remain one of the biggest obstacles to cross-border trade.* **2** ADJ [ADJ n] **Cross-border** attacks involve people crossing a border and going a short way into another country. ❑ *...a cross-border raid into Zambian territory.*

cross|bow /krɒsboʊ/ (**crossbows**) N-COUNT A **crossbow** is a weapon consisting of a small, powerful bow that is fixed across a piece of wood, and aimed like a gun.

cross-breed (**cross-breeds**, **cross-breeding**, **cross-bred**) also **crossbreed** **1** V-RECIP If one species of animal or plant **cross-breeds** with another, they reproduce, and new or different animals or plants are produced. You can also say that someone **cross-breeds** something such as an animal or plant. ❑ *By cross-breeding with our native red deer, the sika deer have affected the gene pool.* ❑ *Unfortunately attempts to crossbreed it with other potatoes have been unsuccessful.* ❑ *Dr. Russel is creating an elite herd by cross-breeding goats from around the globe.* ❑ *...a cross-bred labrador.* **2** N-COUNT A **cross-breed** is an animal or a plant that is the result of cross-breeding.

cross-check (**cross-checks**, **cross-checking**, **cross-checked**) V-T/V-I If you **cross-check** information, you check that it is correct using a different method or source from the one originally used to obtain it. ❑ *You have to scrupulously check and cross-check everything you hear.* ❑ *His version will later be cross-checked against that of the university.* ❑ *They want to ensure such claims are justified by cross-checking with other records.*

cross-country **1** N-UNCOUNT **Cross-country** is the sport of running, riding, or skiing across open countryside rather than along roads or around a running track. ❑ *She finished third in the world cross-country championships in Antwerp.* **2** ADJ [ADJ n] A **cross-country** trip takes you from one side of a country to the other. ❑ *...cross-country rail services.* • ADV [ADV after v] **Cross-country** is also an adverb. ❑ *I drove cross-country in his van.*

cross-cultural ADJ [ADJ n] **Cross-cultural** means involving two or more different cultures. ❑ *Minority cultures within the United States often raised issues of cross-cultural conflict.*

cross-current (**cross-currents**) also **crosscurrent** **1** N-COUNT [usu pl] A **cross-current** is a current in a river or sea that flows across another current. ❑ *Cross-currents can sweep the strongest swimmer helplessly away.* **2** N-COUNT [usu pl] You can refer to conflicting ideas or traditions as **cross-currents**. ❑ *...the cross-currents within the party.*

cross-dress (**cross-dresses**, **cross-dressing**, **cross-dressed**) V-I If someone **cross-dresses**, they wear the clothes usually worn by the opposite sex. ❑ *If they want to cross-dress that's fine.* • **cross-dresser** (**cross-dressers**) N-COUNT ❑ *The society maintains that the majority of cross-dressers are heterosexual.* • **cross-dressing** N-UNCOUNT ❑ *Cross-dressing is far more common than we realize.*

cross-examine (**cross-examines**, **cross-examining**, **cross-examined**) V-T When a lawyer **cross-examines** someone during a trial or hearing, he or she questions them about the evidence that they have already given. ❑ *The accused's lawyers will get a chance to cross-examine him.* • **cross-examination** (**cross-examinations**) N-VAR ❑ *...the cross-examination of a witness in a murder case.*

cross-eyed ADJ Someone who is **cross-eyed** has eyes that seem to look toward each other.

cross|fire /krɒsfaɪər/ also **cross-fire** **1** N-UNCOUNT **Crossfire** is gunfire, for example, in a battle, that comes from two or more different directions and passes through the same area. **2** PHRASE [v-link PHR] If you are **caught in the crossfire**, you become involved in an unpleasant situation in which people are arguing with each other, although you do not want to be involved or say which person you agree with. ❑ *They say they are caught in the crossfire between the education establishment and the government.*

cross|ing /krɒsɪŋ/ (**crossings**) **1** N-COUNT A **crossing** is a journey by boat or ship to a place on the other side of an ocean, river, or lake. ❑ *He made the crossing from Cape Town to Sydney in just over twenty-six days.* **2** N-COUNT A **crossing** is a place where two roads, paths, or lines cross. ❑ *She sighed and squatted down next to the crossing of the two trails.* **3** N-COUNT A **crossing** is the same as a **grade crossing** or a **level crossing**.

cross-legged ADV [ADV after v] If someone is sitting **cross-legged**, they are sitting on the floor with their legs bent so that their knees point outward. ❑ *He sat cross-legged on the floor.*

cross|over /krɒsoʊvər/ (**crossovers**) **1** N-VAR A **crossover** of one style and another, especially in music or fashion, is a combination of the two different styles. ❑ *...the contemporary crossover of pop, jazz and funk.* **2** N-SING In music or fashion, if someone makes a **crossover** from one style to another, they become successful outside the style they were originally known for. ❑ *I told her the crossover from acting to singing is easier than singing to acting.*

cross-purposes also **cross purposes** PHRASE If people are **at cross-purposes**, they do not understand each other because they are working toward or talking about different things without realizing it. ❑ *The two friends find themselves at cross-purposes with the officials.*

cross-question (**cross-questions**, **cross-questioning**, **cross-questioned**) V-T If you **cross-question** someone, you ask them a lot of questions about something. ❑ *The police came back and cross-questioned Des again.*

cross-reference (**cross-references**) N-COUNT A **cross-reference** is a note in a book which tells you that there is relevant or more detailed information in another part of the book. ❑ *It concludes with a very useful summary of key points, with cross-references to where each key point is dealt with in the book.*

cross|roads /krɒsroʊdz/ (**crossroads**)

> **Crossroads** is both the singular and the plural form.

1 N-COUNT A **crossroads** is a place where two roads meet and cross each other. ❑ *Turn right at the first crossroads.* **2** N-SING If you say that something is at a **crossroads**, you mean that it has reached a very important stage in its development where it could go one way or another. ❑ *The company was clearly at a crossroads.*

cross-section (**cross-sections**) also **cross section** **1** N-COUNT If you refer to a **cross-section** of particular things or people, you mean a group of them that you think is typical or representative of all of them. ❑ *I was surprised at the cross-section of people there.* **2** N-COUNT [also in N] A **cross-section** of an object is what you would see if you could cut straight through the middle of it. ❑ *...a cross-section of an airplane.*

cross-stitch also **cross stitch** N-UNCOUNT **Cross-stitch** is a type of decorative sewing where one stitch crosses another.

cross|town /krɒstaʊn/ also **cross-town** ADJ [ADJ n] A **crosstown** bus or route is one that crosses the main roads or transportation lines of a town or city. [AM] ❑ *...the crosstown bus that takes me to work.* ❑ *...the long-awaited completion of a crosstown subway.* • ADV **Crosstown** is also an adverb. ❑ *I have trouble these days getting crosstown in Manhattan.*

cross|walk /krɒswɔːk/ (**crosswalks**) N-COUNT A **crosswalk** is a place where pedestrians can cross a street and where drivers must stop to let them cross. [AM]

> in BRIT, usually use **pedestrian crossing**

cross|ways /krɒsweɪz/ → see crosswise

cross|wind /krɒswɪnd/ (**crosswinds**) also **cross-wind** N-COUNT A **crosswind** is a strong wind that blows across the direction that vehicles, boats, or aircraft are traveling in, and that makes it difficult for them to keep moving steadily forward.

cross|wise /krɒswaɪz/ also **crossways** ADV [ADV after v] **Crosswise** means diagonally across something. ❑ *Rinse and slice the zucchini crosswise.*

cross|word /krɒswɜːrd/ (**crosswords**) N-COUNT A **crossword** or **crossword puzzle** is a word game in which you work out the answers and write them in the white squares of a pattern of small black and white squares. ❑ *He could do the Times crossword in 15 minutes.*

crotch /krɒtʃ/ (crotches) **1** N-COUNT Your **crotch** is the part of your body between the tops of your legs. ❑ *Glover kicked him hard in the crotch.* **2** N-COUNT The **crotch** of something such as a pair of pants is the part that covers the area between the tops of your legs. ❑ *They were too long in the crotch.*

crotch|et /krɒtʃɪt/ (crotchets) N-COUNT A **crotchet** is the same as a **quarter note**. [BRIT]

crotch|ety /krɒtʃɪti/ ADJ [usu ADJ n] A **crotchety** person is bad-tempered and easily irritated. [INFORMAL] ❑ *...my cross, crotchety neighbours.*

crouch /kraʊtʃ/ (crouches, crouching, crouched) V-I If you **are crouching**, your legs are bent under you so that you are close to the ground and leaning forward slightly. ❑ *We were crouching in the bushes.* ❑ *I crouched on the ground.* • **Crouch** is also a noun. ❑ *They walked in a crouch, each bent over close to the ground.* • PHRASAL VERB **Crouch down** means the same as **crouch**. ❑ *He crouched down and reached under the mattress.*

croup /kruːp/ N-UNCOUNT [also the N] **Croup** is a disease which children sometimes suffer from that makes it difficult for them to breathe and causes them to cough a lot.

crou|pi|er /kruːpiər/ (croupiers) N-COUNT A **croupier** is the person in charge of a gambling table in a casino, who collects the bets and pays money to the people who have won.

crou|ton /kruːtɒn/ (croutons) N-COUNT [usu pl] **Croutons** are small pieces of toasted or fried bread that are added to soup or a salad just before you eat it.

crow /kroʊ/ (crows, crowing, crowed) **1** N-COUNT A **crow** is a large black bird which makes a loud, harsh noise. ❑ *The crows roosted in Fonsa's Tower.* **2** V-I When a cock **crows**, it makes a loud sound, often early in the morning. ❑ *The cock crows and the dawn chorus begins.* **3** PHRASE If someone **eats crow**, they admit that they have been wrong and apologize, especially in situations where this is humiliating or embarrassing for them. [AM] ❑ *He wanted to make his critics eat crow.*

crow|bar /kroʊbɑːr/ (crowbars) N-COUNT A **crowbar** is a heavy iron bar which is used as a lever.

crowd ♦♦◊ /kraʊd/ (crowds, crowding, crowded) **1** N-COUNT-COLL A **crowd** is a large group of people who have gathered together, for example, to watch or listen to something interesting, or to protest about something. ❑ *A huge crowd gathered in a square outside the Kremlin walls.* ❑ *It took some two hours before the crowd was fully dispersed.* **2** N-COUNT A particular **crowd** is a group of friends, or a set of people who share the same interests or job. [INFORMAL] ❑ *All the old crowd have come out for this occasion.* **3** V-I When people **crowd** around someone or something, they gather closely together around them. ❑ *The hungry refugees crowded around the tractors.* **4** V-T/V-I If people **crowd** into a place or **are crowded** into a place, large numbers of them enter it so that it becomes very full. ❑ *Hundreds of thousands of people have crowded into the center of the Lithuanian capital, Vilnius.* ❑ *One group of journalists were crowded into a minibus.* **5** V-T If a group of people **crowd** a place, there are so many of them there that it is full. ❑ *Thousands of demonstrators crowded the streets shouting slogans.*

crowd|ed /kraʊdɪd/ **1** ADJ If a place is **crowded**, it is full of people. ❑ *He peered slowly around the small crowded room.* **2** ADJ If a place is **crowded**, a lot of people live there. ❑ *...a crowded city of 2 million.* **3** ADJ If your schedule, your life, or your mind is **crowded**, it is full of events, activities, or thoughts. ❑ *Never before has a summit had such a crowded agenda.*

crowd|fund /kraʊdfʌnd/ (crowdfunds, crowdfunding, crowdfunded) VERB If you **crowdfund** a project, you get the money to pay for it by asking a large number of people to each give money. ❑ *She crowdfunded her first book.* ❑ *Their crowdfunded legal fund has already collected more than $150,000.*

crowd|fund|ing /kraʊdfʌndɪŋ/ N-UNCOUNT **Crowdfunding** is when a large number of people each give an amount of money to pay for a project, especially by using a website to collect the money. ❑ *The project was financed through crowdfunding.*

crowd-pleaser (crowd-pleasers) also **crowd pleaser** N-COUNT If you describe a performer, politician, or sports player as a **crowd-pleaser**, you mean they always please their audience. You can also describe an action or event as a **crowd-pleaser**. ❑ *He gets spectacular goals and is a real crowd-pleaser.*

crowd-puller (crowd-pullers) also **crowd puller** N-COUNT If you describe a performer or event as a **crowd-puller**, you mean that they attract a large audience. ❑ *The exhibition is hardly a crowd-puller.*

crowd|sourc|ing /kraʊdsɔːrsɪŋ/ N-UNCOUNT **Crowdsourcing** is the practice of getting ideas or help on a project from a large number of people, usually through the internet. ❑ *We used crowdsourcing to develop the software.*

crown ♦◊◊ /kraʊn/ (crowns, crowning, crowned) **1** N-COUNT A **crown** is a circular ornament, usually made of gold and jewels, which a king or queen wears on their head at official ceremonies. You can also use **crown** to refer to anything circular that is worn on someone's head. ❑ *...a crown of flowers.* **2** N-COUNT Your **crown** is the top part of your head, at the back. ❑ *He laid his hand gently on the crown of her head.* **3** N-COUNT A **crown** is an artificial top piece fixed over a broken or decayed tooth. ❑ *How long does it take to have crowns fitted?* **4** N-PROPER The government of a country that has a king or queen is sometimes referred to as **the Crown**. ❑ *She says the sovereignty of the Crown must be preserved.* ❑ *...a minister of the Crown.* **5** V-T [usu passive] When a king or queen **is crowned**, a crown is placed on their head as part of a ceremony in which they are officially made king or queen. ❑ *Two days later, Juan Carlos was crowned king.* **6** → See also color supplement

crown jew|el (crown jewels) N-PLURAL [the N] **The crown jewels** are the crown, scepter, and other precious objects which are used on important official occasions by the king or queen.

Crown Prince (Crown Princes) N-COUNT [N-TITLE] A **Crown Prince** is a prince who will be king of his country when the present king or queen dies. ❑ *...the crown prince's palace.* ❑ *...Sultan Mahmood's son, Crown Prince Ibrahim Mahmood.*

Crown Prin|cess (Crown Princesses) N-COUNT [N-TITLE] A **Crown Princess** is a princess who is the wife of a Crown Prince, or will be queen of her country when the present king or queen dies. ❑ *...his second wife, Crown Princess Catherine.*

crow's feet N-PLURAL **Crow's feet** are lines or wrinkles which some older people have at the outside corners of their eyes.

crow's nest N-SING On a ship, the **crow's nest** is a small platform high up on the mast, where a person can go to look in all directions.

cru|cial ♦◊◊ /kruːʃəl/ ADJ If you describe something as **crucial**, you mean it is extremely important. ❑ *He had administrators under him but made the crucial decisions himself.* • **cru|cial|ly** ADV ❑ *Chewing properly is crucially important.*

cru|ci|ate liga|ment /kruːʃɪət lɪɡəmənt, -ʃieɪt -/ (cruciate ligaments) N-COUNT A **cruciate ligament** is either of a pair of ligaments that cross at the knee. ❑ *He will be out of the team for the rest of the season after damaging his cruciate ligaments.*

cru|ci|ble /kruːsɪbəl/ (crucibles) **1** N-COUNT A **crucible** is a pot in which metals or other substances can be melted or heated up to very high temperatures. **2** N-SING [oft N of n] **Crucible** is used to refer to a situation in which something is tested or a conflict takes place, often one which produces something new. [LITERARY] ❑ *...a system in which ideas are tested in the crucible of party contention.*

cru|ci|fix /kruːsɪfɪks/ (crucifixes) N-COUNT A **crucifix** is a cross with a figure of Christ on it.

cru|ci|fix|ion /kruːsɪfɪkʃən/ (crucifixions) **1** N-VAR **Crucifixion** is a way of killing people which was common in the Roman Empire, in which they were tied or nailed to a cross and left to die. ❑ *...her historical novel about the crucifixion of Christians in Rome.* **2** N-PROPER **The Crucifixion** is the crucifixion of Christ. ❑ *...the central message of the Crucifixion.*

cru|ci|form /kruːsɪfɔːrm/ ADJ [usu ADJ n] A **cruciform** building or object is shaped like a cross. [FORMAL] ❑ *...a cruciform tower.*

cru|ci|fy /kruːsɪfaɪ/ (crucifies, crucifying, crucified) **1** V-T [usu passive] If someone **is crucified**, they are killed by being tied or nailed to a cross and left to die. ❑ *...the day that Christ was crucified.* **2** V-T To **crucify** someone means to criticize or punish them severely. [INFORMAL] ❑ *She'll crucify me if she finds you still here.*

crud /krʌd/ N-UNCOUNT You use **crud** to refer to any disgustingly dirty or sticky substance. [INFORMAL] ❑ *Remember the motel with all the crud in the pool?*

crude /kruːd/ (cruder, crudest, crudes) **1** ADJ A **crude** method or measurement is not exact or detailed, but may be useful or correct in a rough, general way. ◻ *Standard measurements of blood pressure are an important but crude way of assessing the risk of heart disease or strokes.* • **crude|ly** ADV ◻ *The donors can be split – a little crudely – into two groups.* **2** ADJ If you describe an object that someone has made as **crude**, you mean that it has been made in a very simple way or from very simple parts. ◻ *...crude wooden boxes.* • **crude|ly** ADV ◻ *...a crudely carved wooden form.* **3** ADJ If you describe someone as **crude**, you disapprove of them because they speak or behave in a rude, offensive, or unsophisticated way. [DISAPPROVAL] ◻ *Must you be quite so crude?* • **crude|ly** ADV ◻ *He hated it when she spoke so crudely.* **4** ADJ [ADJ n] **Crude** substances are in a natural or unrefined state, and have not yet been used in manufacturing processes. **5** N-MASS **Crude** is the same as **crude oil**.

crude oil N-UNCOUNT **Crude oil** is oil in its natural state before it has been processed or refined. ◻ *A thousand tons of crude oil has spilled into the sea from an oil tanker.*

cru|di|tés /kruːdɪteɪ/ N-PLURAL **Crudités** are pieces of raw vegetable, often served before a meal.

cru|el /kruːəl/ (crueler or crueller, cruelest or cruellest) **1** ADJ Someone who is **cruel** deliberately causes pain or distress to people or animals. ◻ *Children can be so cruel.* • **cru|el|ly** ADV [ADV with v] ◻ *Douglas was often cruelly tormented by jealous siblings.* **2** ADJ A situation or event that is **cruel** is very harsh and causes people distress. ◻ *...struggling to survive in a cruel world with which they cannot cope.* • **cru|el|ly** ADV ◻ *His life has been cruelly shattered by an event not of his own making.*

cru|el|ty /kruːəlti/ (cruelties) N-VAR **Cruelty** is behavior that deliberately causes pain or distress to people or animals. ◻ *Britain had laws against cruelty to animals but none to protect children.*

cru|et /kruːɪt/ (cruets) N-COUNT A **cruet** is a small glass bottle that contains oil or vinegar and is used at the table at meals. [AM] ◻ *Combine the vinegar, mustard, and oil in a salad cruet.*

cruise ♦◊◊ /kruːz/ (cruises, cruising, cruised) **1** N-COUNT A **cruise** is a vacation during which you travel on a ship or boat and visit a number of places. ◻ *He and his wife were planning to go on a world cruise.* **2** V-T/V-I If you **cruise** an ocean, river, or canal, you travel around it or along it on a cruise. ◻ *She wants to cruise the canals of France in a barge.* ◻ *...a vacation cruising around the Caribbean.* **3** V-I If a car, ship, or aircraft **cruises** somewhere, it moves there at a steady comfortable speed. ◻ *A black and white police car cruised past.*

cruise con|trol **1** N-UNCOUNT In a car or other vehicle, **cruise control** is a system that automatically keeps the vehicle's speed at the same level. ◻ *It came with leather upholstery, air conditioning and cruise control as standard.* **2** PHRASE If you say that someone is **on cruise control** in a contest, you mean that they are winning the contest easily and without needing to make a lot of effort. ◻ *The champs were on cruise control as they eased to victory in this one-sided bore.*

cruise mis|sile (cruise missiles) N-COUNT A **cruise missile** is a missile which carries a nuclear warhead and which is guided by a computer.

cruis|er /kruːzər/ (cruisers) **1** N-COUNT A **cruiser** is a motorboat which has an area for people to live or sleep. ◻ *...a three-hour journey in a small cruiser with indoor and outdoor seating.* **2** N-COUNT A **cruiser** is a large fast warship. ◻ *Italy had lost three cruisers and two destroyers.* **3** N-COUNT A **cruiser** is a police car. [AM] ◻ *Police cruisers surrounded the bank throughout the day.*

cruise ship (cruise ships) **1** N-COUNT A **cruise ship** is a large ship which takes people from place to place on a cruise holiday, and on which entertainment, food, and drink are provided. ◻ *He got a job as a singer on a cruise ship.* **2** → See feature box at **boat**; See also color supplement

crumb /krʌm/ (crumbs) N-COUNT **Crumbs** are tiny pieces that fall from bread, cookies, or cake when you cut it or eat it. ◻ *I stood up, brushing crumbs from my pants.*

crum|ble /krʌmbəl/ (crumbles, crumbling, crumbled) **1** V-T/V-I If something **crumbles**, or if you **crumble** it, it breaks into a lot of small pieces. ◻ *Under the pressure, the flint crumbled into fragments.* **2** V-I If an old building or piece of land **is crumbling**, parts of it keep breaking off. ◻ *The high- and low-rise apartment blocks built in the 1960s are crumbling.* • PHRASAL VERB **Crumble away** means the same as **crumble**. ◻ *Much of the coastline is crumbling away.* **3** V-I If something such as a system, relationship, or hope **crumbles**, it comes to an end. ◻ *Their economy crumbled under the weight of United Nations sanctions.* • PHRASAL VERB **Crumble away** means the same as **crumble**. ◻ *Opposition more or less crumbled away.*

crum|bly /krʌmbli/ (crumblier, crumbliest) **1** ADJ Something that is **crumbly** is easily broken into a lot of little pieces. ◻ *...crumbly cheese.* **2** → See feature box at **cooking**

crum|my /krʌmi/ (crummier, crummiest) ADJ [usu ADJ n] Something that is **crummy** is unpleasant, of very poor quality, or not good enough. [INFORMAL, DISAPPROVAL] ◻ *When I first came here, I had a crummy apartment.*

crum|ple /krʌmpəl/ (crumples, crumpling, crumpled) V-T/V-I If you **crumple** something such as paper or cloth, or if it **crumples**, it is squashed and becomes full of untidy creases and folds. ◻ *She crumpled the paper in her hand.* • PHRASAL VERB **Crumple up** means the same as **crumple**. ◻ *She crumpled up her coffee cup.* • **crum|pled** ADJ ◻ *His uniform was crumpled and untidy.*

crunch /krʌntʃ/ (crunches, crunching, crunched) **1** V-T/V-I If you **crunch** something hard, such as a piece of candy, or if it **crunches**, you crush it noisily between your teeth. ◻ *She sucked an ice cube into her mouth, and crunched it loudly.* **2** V-T/V-I If something **crunches** or if you **crunch** it, it makes a breaking or crushing noise, for example, when you step on it. ◻ *A piece of china crunched under my foot.* • N-COUNT **Crunch** is also a noun. ◻ *She heard the crunch of tires on the gravel driveway.* **3** V-I If you **crunch** across a surface made of very small stones, you move across it causing it to make a crunching noise. ◻ *I crunched across the gravel.* **4** V-T To **crunch** numbers means to do a lot of calculations using a calculator or computer. ◻ *I pored over the books with great enthusiasm, often crunching the numbers until 1:00 a.m.* **5** N-SING You can refer to an important time or event, for example, when an important decision has to be made, as the **crunch**. ◻ *He can rely on my support when the crunch comes.* **6** N-COUNT A situation in which a business or economy has very little money can be referred to as a **crunch**. [BUSINESS] ◻ *The U.N. is facing a cash crunch.*

crunchy /krʌntʃi/ (crunchier, crunchiest) **1** ADJ Food that is **crunchy** is pleasantly hard or crisp so that it makes a noise when you eat it. [APPROVAL] ◻ *...fresh, crunchy vegetables.* **2** → See feature box at **cooking**

cru|sade /kruːseɪd/ (crusades, crusading, crusaded) **1** N-COUNT A **crusade** is a long and determined attempt to achieve something for a cause that you feel strongly about. ◻ *He made it his crusade to teach children to love books.* **2** V-I If you **crusade** for a particular cause, you make a long and determined effort to achieve something for it. ◻ *...a newspaper that has crusaded against the country's cocaine traffickers.*

cru|sad|er /kruːseɪdər/ (crusaders) N-COUNT A **crusader** for a cause is someone who does a lot in support of it. ◻ *He has set himself up as a crusader for higher press and broadcasting standards.*

crush /krʌʃ/ (crushes, crushing, crushed) **1** V-T To **crush** something means to press it very hard so that its shape is destroyed or so that it breaks into pieces. ◻ *Andrew crushed his empty can.* ◻ *...crushed ice.* **2** V-T To **crush** a protest or movement, or a group of opponents, means to defeat it completely, usually by force. ◻ *The military operation was the first step in a plan to crush the uprising.* • **crush|ing** N-UNCOUNT ◻ *...the violent crushing of anti-government demonstrations.* **3** V-T [usu passive] If you **are crushed** by something, it upsets you a great deal. ◻ *Listen to criticism but don't be crushed by it.* **4** V-T [usu passive] If you **are crushed** against someone or something, you are pushed or pressed against them. ◻ *We were at the front, crushed against the stage.* **5** N-COUNT A **crush** is a crowd of people close together, in which it is difficult to move. ◻ *His thirteen-year-old son somehow got separated in the crush.* **6** N-COUNT If you have a **crush** on someone, you are in love with them but do not have a relationship with them. [INFORMAL] ◻ *She had a crush on you, you know.* **7** → See feature box at **commute**

crush|er /krʌʃər/ (crushers) **1** N-COUNT [usu n n] A **crusher** is a piece of equipment used for crushing things. ◻ *...a garlic crusher.* **2** → See also color supplement

crush|ing /krˈʌʃɪŋ/ ADJ [ADJ n] A **crushing** defeat, burden, or disappointment is a very great or severe one. [EMPHASIS] ❑ ...since their crushing defeat in the local elections.

crush|ing|ly /krˈʌʃɪŋli/ ADV [ADV adj] You can use **crushingly** to emphasize the degree of a negative quality. [EMPHASIS] ❑ ...a collection of crushingly bad jokes.

crust /krʌst/ (crusts) **1** N-COUNT The **crust** on a loaf of bread is the outside part. ❑ Cut the crusts off the bread and soak the bread in the milk. **2** N-COUNT A pie's **crust** is its cooked pastry. ❑ The Key lime pie was bursting with flavor. Good crust, too. **3** N-COUNT A **crust** is a hard layer of something, especially on top of a softer or wetter substance. ❑ As the water evaporates, a crust of salt is left on the surface of the soil. **4** N-COUNT The Earth's **crust** is its outer layer. ❑ Earthquakes leave scars in the Earth's crust.

crus|ta|cean /krʌsteɪʃ³n/ (crustaceans) N-COUNT A **crustacean** is an animal with a hard shell and several pairs of legs, which usually lives in water. Crabs, lobsters, and shrimps are crustaceans.

crust|ed /krʌstɪd/ ADJ [oft ADJ with n] If something is **crusted** with a substance, it is covered with a hard or thick layer of that substance. [LITERARY] ❑ ...flat gray stones crusted with lichen. • COMB IN ADJ **Crusted** is also a combining form. ❑ He sat down to remove his mud-crusted boots.

crusty /krʌsti/ (crustier, crustiest) ADJ **Crusty** bread has a hard, crisp outside. ❑ ...crusty French loaves.

crutch /krʌtʃ/ (crutches) **1** N-COUNT A **crutch** is a stick whose top fits around or under the user's arm, which someone with an injured foot or leg uses to support their weight when walking. ❑ I can walk without the aid of crutches. **2** N-SING If you refer to someone or something as a **crutch**, you mean that they give you help or support. ❑ He gave up the crutch of alcohol.

crux /krʌks/ N-SING The **crux** of a problem or argument is the most important or difficult part of it which affects everything else. ❑ He said the crux of the matter was economic policy.

cry ♦♦♢ /kraɪ/ (cries, crying, cried) **1** V-I When you **cry**, tears come from your eyes, usually because you are unhappy or hurt. ❑ I hung up the phone and started to cry. ❑ He cried with anger and frustration. • N-SING **Cry** is also a noun. ❑ A nurse patted me on the shoulder and said, "Have a good cry, dear." • **cry|ing** N-UNCOUNT ❑ She had been unable to sleep for three days because of her 13-week-old son's crying. **2** V-T If you **cry** something, you shout it or say it loudly. ❑ "Nancy Drew," she cried, "you're under arrest!" • PHRASAL VERB **Cry out** means the same as **cry**. ❑ "You're wrong, quite wrong!" Henry cried out, suddenly excited. **3** N-COUNT A **cry** is a loud, high sound that you make when you feel a strong emotion such as fear, pain, or pleasure. ❑ A cry of horror broke from me. **4** N-COUNT A **cry** is a shouted word or phrase, usually one that is intended to attract someone's attention. ❑ Thousands of Ukrainians burst into cries of 'bravo.' **5** N-COUNT You can refer to a public protest about something or an appeal for something as a **cry** of some kind. [JOURNALISM] ❑ There have been cries of outrage about this expenditure. **6** N-COUNT A bird's or an animal's **cry** is the loud, high sound that it makes. ❑ ...the cry of a seagull. **7** → see also **crying** **8** **to cry your eyes out** → see **eye** ① **9** **a shoulder to cry on** → see **shoulder**
▶ **cry out** **1** PHRASAL VERB If you **cry out**, you call out loudly because you are frightened, unhappy, or in pain. ❑ He was crying out in pain when the ambulance arrived. **2** → see also **cry 2**
▶ **cry out for** PHRASAL VERB If you say that something **cries out for** a particular thing or action, you mean that it needs that thing or action very much. ❑ This is a disgraceful state of affairs and cries out for a thorough investigation.

---- COLLOCATIONS ----

cry
NOUN **3**
adjective + **cry**: anguished, plaintive, loud, shrill
verb + **cry**: hear; give, utter
VERB **1**
cry + adverb: hysterically, uncontrollably; quietly, silently; openly

cry|baby /kraɪbeɪbi/ (crybabies) also **cry baby, cry-baby** N-COUNT If you call a child a **crybaby**, you mean that the child cries a lot for no good reason. [INFORMAL, DISAPPROVAL]

cry|ing /kraɪɪŋ/ **1** PHRASE If you say that there is **a crying need for** something, you mean that there is a very great need for it. ❑ There is a crying need for more magistrates from minority communities. **2** → see also **cry**

cryo|gen|ics /kraɪoʊdʒɛnɪks/ N-UNCOUNT **Cryogenics** is a branch of physics that studies what happens to things at extremely low temperatures.

crypt /krɪpt/ (crypts) N-COUNT A **crypt** is an underground room underneath a church or cathedral.

cryp|tic /krɪptɪk/ ADJ A **cryptic** remark or message contains a hidden meaning or is difficult to understand. ❑ He has issued a short, cryptic statement denying the spying charges. • **cryp|ti|cal|ly** ADV [ADV with v] ❑ "Not necessarily," she says cryptically.

cryptocurrency /krɪptoʊkɜrənsi/ (cryptocurrencies) N-VAR **Cryptocurrency** is a kind of digital currency that is created and exchanged using cryptography. It is often shortened to **crypto**. ❑ The kidnappers demanded to be paid in cryptocurrency.

cryptography /krɪptɒgrəfi/ N-UNCOUNT **Cryptography** is the science, skill, or activity of creating and analyzing codes. ❑ They could be using advanced cryptography to hide their operations.

crys|tal ♦♢♢ /krɪst³l/ (crystals) **1** N-COUNT A **crystal** is a small piece of a substance that has formed naturally into a regular symmetrical shape. ❑ ...salt crystals. ❑ ...ice crystals. **2** N-VAR **Crystal** is a transparent rock that is used to make jewelry and ornaments. ❑ She was wearing a strand of crystal beads. **3** N-UNCOUNT **Crystal** is a high quality glass, usually with patterns cut into its surface. ❑ Some of the finest drinking glasses are made from lead crystal. **4** → See feature box at **experiment**

crys|tal ball (crystal balls) N-COUNT If you say that someone, especially an expert, looks into a **crystal ball**, you mean that they are trying to predict the future. Crystal balls are traditionally used by fortune-tellers. ❑ Local economists have looked into their crystal balls and seen something rather nasty.

crys|tal clear **1** ADJ Water that is **crystal clear** is absolutely clear and transparent like glass. ❑ The cliffs, lapped by a crystal-clear sea, remind her of Capri. **2** ADJ If you say that a message or statement is **crystal clear**, you are emphasizing that it is very easy to understand. [EMPHASIS] ❑ The message is crystal clear – if you lose weight, you will feel better.

crys|tal|line /krɪst³laɪn/ **1** ADJ [usu ADJ n] A **crystalline** substance is in the form of crystals or contains crystals. ❑ Diamond is the crystalline form of the element carbon. **2** ADJ [usu ADJ n] **Crystalline** means clear or bright. [LITERARY] ❑ ...a huge plain dotted with crystalline lakes.

crys|tal|lize /krɪst³laɪz/ (crystallizes, crystallizing, crystallized)

in BRIT, also use **crystallise**

1 V-T/V-I If you **crystallize** an opinion or idea, or if it **crystallizes**, it becomes fixed and definite in someone's mind. ❑ He has managed to crystallize the feelings of millions of ordinary Russians. **2** V-T/V-I If a substance **crystallizes**, or something **crystallizes** it, it turns into crystals. ❑ Don't stir or the sugar will crystallize.

crys|tal|lized /krɪst³laɪzd/

in BRIT, also use **crystallised**

ADJ [usu ADJ n] **Crystallized** fruits and candy are covered in sugar which has been melted and then allowed to harden.

C-section (C-sections) also **c-section** N-COUNT A **C-section** is the same as a **Caesarean**. [AM] ❑ C-sections are seldom done at that stage of pregnancy.

CST /si ɛs ti/ [AM] **CST** is an abbreviation for 'Central Standard Time.' ❑ Calls are taken between 7 a.m. and 8 p.m., CST.

cub /kʌb/ (cubs) **1** N-COUNT A **cub** is a young wild animal such as a lion, wolf, or bear. ❑ ...three five-week-old lion cubs. **2** N-PROPER-COLL [the N] **The Cubs** is a junior version of the Boy Scouts for young people between the ages of six and eight. • N-COUNT A **cub** or a **cub scout** is a young person who is a member of the Cubs.

Cu|ban /kyuːbən/ (Cubans) **1** ADJ **Cuban** means belonging or relating to Cuba, or to its people or culture. **2** N-COUNT A **Cuban** is a Cuban citizen, or a person of Cuban origin.

cubby|hole /kʌbi hoʊl/ (cubbyholes) also **cubby-hole** N-COUNT A **cubbyhole** is a very small room or space for storing things. ❑ It's in the cubbyhole under the stairs.

cube /kyub/ (cubes, cubing, cubed) **1** N-COUNT A **cube** is a solid object with six square surfaces which are all the same size. □ ...*cold water with ice cubes in it.* □ ...*a box of sugar cubes.* **2** N-COUNT The **cube** of a number is another number that is produced by multiplying the first number by itself twice. For example, the cube of 2 is 8. **3** V-T When you **cube** food, you cut it into cube-shaped pieces. □ *Remove the seeds and stones and cube the flesh.*

cube root (cube roots) N-COUNT [usu sing, the N of n] The **cube root** of a number is another number that makes the first number when it is multiplied by itself twice. For example, the cube root of 8 is 2.

cu|bic /kyubɪk/ ADJ [ADJ n] **Cubic** is used in front of units of length to form units of volume such as 'cubic meter' and 'cubic foot.' □ ...*3 billion cubic meters of soil.*

cu|bi|cle /kyubɪkᵊl/ (cubicles) **1** N-COUNT A **cubicle** is a very small enclosed area, for example, one where you can take a shower or change your clothes. □ ...*a separate shower cubicle.* **2** N-COUNT A **cubicle** is an area in an office that is separated from the rest of the room by thin walls. □ *I'm not the kind of person to sit in a cubicle behind a desk.*

Cub|ism /kyubɪzəm/ N-UNCOUNT **Cubism** is a style of art, begun in the early twentieth century, in which objects are represented as if they could be seen from several different positions at the same time, using many lines and geometric shapes.

Cub|ist /kyubɪst/ (Cubists) **1** N-COUNT A **Cubist** is an artist who painted in the style of Cubism. **2** ADJ [ADJ n] **Cubist** art is art in the style of Cubism. □ ...*Picasso's seminal Cubist painting, "The Poet."*

cu|boid /kyubɔɪd/ (cuboids) N-COUNT A **cuboid** is a solid object with two square surfaces and four rectangular surfaces. Each surface of a cuboid is the same size as the one opposite to it.

cub re|port|er (cub reporters) N-COUNT A **cub reporter** is a young newspaper journalist who is still being trained. □ *He had been a cub reporter for the Kansas City Star.*

cub scout → see cub

cuck|old /kʌkoʊld/ (cuckolds, cuckolding, cuckolded) **1** N-COUNT A **cuckold** is a man whose wife is having an affair with another man. [LITERARY, OLD-FASHIONED] **2** V-T If a married woman is having an affair, she and her lover are **cuckolding** her husband. [LITERARY, OLD-FASHIONED] □ *His wife had cuckolded him.*

cuckoo /kuku, kuku/ (cuckoos) **1** N-COUNT A **cuckoo** is a bird that has a call of two quick notes, and lays its eggs in other birds' nests. **2** → See feature box at **sound**

cuckoo clock (cuckoo clocks) N-COUNT A **cuckoo clock** is a clock with a door from which a toy cuckoo comes out and makes noises like a cuckoo every hour or half hour.

cu|cum|ber /kyukʌmbər/ (cucumbers) N-VAR A **cucumber** is a long, thin vegetable with a hard, green skin and wet, transparent flesh. It is eaten raw in salads. □ ...*a cheese and cucumber sandwich.*

cud /kʌd/ PHRASE When animals such as cows or sheep **chew the cud**, they chew and swallow their partly digested food over and over again before finally swallowing it.

cud|dle /kʌdᵊl/ (cuddles, cuddling, cuddled) V-T If you **cuddle** someone, you put your arms around them and hold them close as a way of showing your affection. □ *He cuddled the newborn girl.* • N-COUNT **Cuddle** is also a noun. □ *It would have been nice to give him a cuddle and a kiss but there wasn't time.*

cud|dly /kʌdli/ (cuddlier, cuddliest) **1** ADJ A **cuddly** person or animal makes you want to cuddle them. [APPROVAL] □ *He is a small, cuddly man with spectacles.* **2** ADJ [ADJ n] **Cuddly** toys are soft toys that look like animals.

cudg|el /kʌdʒᵊl/ (cudgels) **1** N-COUNT A **cudgel** is a thick, short stick that is used as a weapon. **2** PHRASE [oft PHR for/against n] If you **take up the cudgels** for someone or something, you speak or fight in support of them. □ *The president took up the cudgels in his acceptance speech.*

cue ♦♢♢ /kyu/ (cues, cueing, cued) **1** N-COUNT In the theater or in a musical performance, a performer's **cue** is something another performer says or does that is a signal for them to begin speaking, playing, or doing something. □ *The actors not performing sit at the side of the stage in full view, waiting for their cues.* **2** N-COUNT If you say that something that happens is a **cue** for an action, you mean that people start doing that action when it happens. □ *That was the cue for several months of intense bargaining.* **3** N-COUNT A **cue** is a long, thin wooden stick that is used to hit the ball in games such as billiards, pool, and snooker. **4** V-T If one performer **cues** another, they say or do something which is a signal for the second performer to begin speaking, playing, or doing something. □ *He read the scene, with Seaton cueing him.* **5** → See also color supplement

COLLOCATIONS

cue
NOUN **1**
verb + **cue**: take; miss; provide

cuff /kʌf/ (cuffs) **1** N-COUNT The **cuffs** of a shirt or dress are the parts at the ends of the sleeves, which are thicker than the rest of the sleeve. □ ...*a pale blue shirt with white collar and cuffs.* **2** N-COUNT [usu pl] The **cuffs** on a pair of pants are the parts at the ends of the legs, which are folded up. [AM]

in BRIT, use **turn-up**

3 PHRASE An **off-the-cuff** remark is made without being prepared or thought about in advance. □ *I didn't mean any offense. It was a flippant, off-the-cuff remark.*

cuff|link /kʌflɪŋk/ (cufflinks) N-COUNT [usu pl] **Cufflinks** are small decorative objects used for holding together shirt cuffs around the wrist. □ ...*a pair of gold cufflinks.*

cui|sine /kwɪzin/ (cuisines) N-VAR The **cuisine** of a country or district is the style of cooking that is characteristic of that place. □ *The cuisine of Japan is low in fat.*

cul-de-sac /kʌl di sæk/ (cul-de-sacs) N-COUNT [usu sing] A **cul-de-sac** is a short road which is closed off at one end. □ ...*a four-bedroom detached house in a quiet cul-de-sac.*

culi|nary /kyulənɛri, kʌlə-/ ADJ [ADJ n] **Culinary** means concerned with cooking. [FORMAL] □ ...*advanced culinary skills.*

cull /kʌl/ (culls, culling, culled) **1** V-T [usu passive] If items or ideas are **culled** from a particular source or number of sources, they are taken and gathered together. □ *All this, needless to say, had been culled second-hand from radio reports.* **2** V-T To **cull** animals means to kill the weaker animals in a group in order to reduce their numbers. □ *To save remaining herds and habitat, the national parks department is planning to cull 2000 elephants.* • N-COUNT **Cull** is also a noun. □ *In the reserves of Zimbabwe and South Africa, annual culls are already routine.* • **cull|ing** N-UNCOUNT □ *The culling of seal cubs has led to an outcry from environmental groups.*

cul|mi|nate /kʌlmɪneɪt/ (culminates, culminating, culminated) V-I If you say that an activity, process, or series of events **culminates in** or **with** a particular event, you mean that event happens at the end of it. □ *They had an argument, which culminated in Tom getting drunk.*

cul|mi|na|tion /kʌlmɪneɪʃᵊn/ N-SING Something, especially something important, that is the **culmination** of an activity, process, or series of events happens at the end of it. □ *Their arrest was the culmination of an operation in which 120 other people were detained.*

cu|lottes /kulɒts/ N-PLURAL [also a pair of N] **Culottes** are knee-length women's shorts that look like a skirt.

cul|pable /kʌlpəbᵊl/ ADJ If someone or their conduct is **culpable**, they are responsible for something wrong or bad that has happened. [FORMAL] □ *Their decision to do nothing makes them culpable.* □ ...*manslaughter resulting from culpable negligence.* • **cul|pabil|ity** /kʌlpəbɪlɪti/ N-UNCOUNT □ *He added there was clear culpability on the part of the government.*

cul|prit /kʌlprɪt/ (culprits) **1** N-COUNT When you are talking about a crime or something wrong that has been done, you can refer to the person who did it as the **culprit**. □ *All the men were being deported even though the real culprits in the flight have not been identified.* **2** N-COUNT When you are talking about a problem or bad situation, you can refer to its cause as the **culprit**. □ *About 10% of Japanese teenagers are overweight. Nutritionists say the main culprit is increasing reliance on Western fast food.*

cult /kʌlt/ (cults) **1** N-COUNT A **cult** is a fairly small religious group, especially one which is considered strange. ☐ *The teenager may have been abducted by a religious cult.* **2** N-COUNT The **cult** of something is a situation in which people regard that thing as very important or special. [DISAPPROVAL] ☐ *...the cult of youth that recently gripped publishing.* **3** ADJ [ADJ n] **Cult** is used to describe things that are very popular or fashionable among a particular group of people. ☐ *Since her death, she has become a cult figure.* **4** N-SING Someone or something that is a **cult** has become very popular or fashionable among a particular group of people. ☐ *Violence has become a cult among some young men.*

cult clas|sic (cult classics) N-COUNT A **cult classic** is something such as a movie or book that is considered to be one of the best of its kind by a small group of people.

cul|ti|vate /kʌltɪveɪt/ (cultivates, cultivating, cultivated) **1** V-T If you **cultivate** land or crops, you prepare land and grow crops on it. ☐ *She also cultivated a small garden of her own.* • **cul|ti|va|tion** /kʌltɪveɪʃən/ N-UNCOUNT ☐ *...the cultivation of fruits and vegetables.* **2** V-T If you **cultivate** an attitude, image, or skill, you try hard to develop it and make it stronger or better. ☐ *He has written eight books and has cultivated the image of an elder statesman.* • **cul|ti|va|tion** N-UNCOUNT ☐ *...the cultivation of a positive approach to life and health.* **3** V-T If you **cultivate** someone or **cultivate** a friendship with them, you try hard to develop a friendship with them. ☐ *Howe carefully cultivated Daniel C. Roper, the Assistant Postmaster General.* **4** → See feature box at **garden**

cul|ti|vat|ed /kʌltɪveɪtɪd/ **1** ADJ If you describe someone as **cultivated**, you mean they are well educated and have good manners. [FORMAL] ☐ *His mother was an elegant, cultivated woman.* **2** ADJ [ADJ n] **Cultivated** plants have been developed for growing on farms or in gardens. ☐ *...a mixture of wild and cultivated varieties.*

cul|ti|va|tor /kʌltɪveɪtər/ (cultivators) N-COUNT A **cultivator** is a tool or machine which is used to break up the earth or to remove weeds, for example, in a garden or field.

cul|tur|al ♦♢♢ /kʌltʃərəl/ **1** ADJ **Cultural** means relating to a particular society and its ideas, customs, and art. ☐ *...a deep sense of personal honor which was part of his cultural heritage.* • **cul|tur|al|ly** ADV ☐ *...an informed guide to culturally and historically significant sites.* **2** ADJ [ADJ n] **Cultural** means involving or concerning the arts. ☐ *...the sponsorship of sports and cultural events by tobacco companies.* • **cul|tur|al|ly** ADV ☐ *...one of our better-governed, culturally active regional centers.*

cul|tur|al ap|pro|pria|tion N-UNCOUNT If someone is accused of **cultural appropriation**, people say that they have taken elements of another culture as their own.. ☐ *The urban music industry is often criticized for its racist cultural appropriation.*

cul|tur|al aware|ness N-UNCOUNT Someone's **cultural awareness** is their understanding of the differences between themselves and people from other countries or other backgrounds, especially differences in attitudes and values. ☐ *...programs to promote diversity and cultural awareness within the industry.*

cul|ture ♦♦♢ /kʌltʃər/ (cultures) **1** N-UNCOUNT **Culture** consists of activities such as the arts and philosophy, which are considered to be important for the development of civilization and of people's minds. ☐ *There is just not enough fun and frivolity in culture today.* ☐ *...aspects of popular culture.* **2** N-COUNT A **culture** is a particular society or civilization, especially considered in relation to its beliefs, way of life, or art. ☐ *...people from different cultures.* **3** N-COUNT The **culture** of a particular organization or group consists of the habits of the people in it and the way they generally behave. ☐ *But social workers say that this has created a culture of dependency, particularly in urban areas.* **4** N-COUNT In science, a **culture** is a group of bacteria or cells which are grown, usually in a laboratory as part of an experiment. [TECHNICAL] ☐ *...a culture of human cells.*

SYNONYMS
culture
NOUN **3**
lifestyle: *They enjoyed an income and lifestyle that many people would envy.*
way of life: *Mining activities have totally disrupted the traditional way of life of these people.*

cul|tured /kʌltʃərd/ ADJ If you describe someone as **cultured**, you mean that they have good manners, are well educated, and know a lot about the arts. ☐ *He is a cultured man with a wide circle of friends.*

cul|tured pearl (cultured pearls) N-COUNT A **cultured pearl** is a pearl that is created by putting sand or grit into an oyster.

cul|ture shock N-UNCOUNT [also a N] **Culture shock** is a feeling of anxiety, loneliness, and confusion that people sometimes experience when they first arrive in another country. ☐ *Chuck is jobless, homeless, friendless, and suffering from culture shock.*

cul|vert /kʌlvərt/ (culverts) N-COUNT A **culvert** is a water pipe or sewer that crosses under a road or railroad.

-cum- /-kʌm-/ COMB IN N-COUNT **-cum-** is put between two nouns to form a noun referring to something or someone that is partly one thing and partly another. ☐ *...a dining-room-cum-study.*

cum|ber|some /kʌmbərsəm/ **1** ADJ Something that is **cumbersome** is large and heavy and therefore difficult to carry, wear, or handle. ☐ *Although the machine looks cumbersome, it is actually easy to use.* **2** ADJ A **cumbersome** system or process is very complicated and inefficient. ☐ *...an old and cumbersome computer system.*

cum|in /kʌmɪn, kʊmɪn/ N-UNCOUNT **Cumin** is a sweet-smelling spice, and is popular in Indian cooking.

cum laude /kʊm laʊdeɪ/ ADV If a college student graduates **cum laude**, they receive the third highest honor that is possible. The second-highest grade is known as **magna cum laude**, and the highest grade of all is known as **summa cum laude**. [AM] ☐ *In 1963, she graduated cum laude from Harvard.* ☐ *He graduated magna cum laude.* ☐ *Jeremy Heyl graduated summa cum laude with a degree in Astrophysics.*

cum|mer|bund /kʌmərbʌnd/ (cummerbunds) N-COUNT A **cummerbund** is a wide piece of cloth worn around the waist as part of a man's evening dress.

cu|mu|la|tive /kyuːmyələtɪv/ ADJ If a series of events have a **cumulative** effect, each event makes the effect greater. ☐ *It is simple pleasures, such as a walk on a sunny day, which have a cumulative effect on our mood.*

cu|mu|lo|nim|bus /kyuːmyələnɪmbəs/ (cumulonimbi) also **cumulo-nimbus** N-VAR **Cumulonimbus** is a type of cloud, similar to cumulus, that extends to a great height and is associated with thunderstorms. [TECHNICAL]

cu|mu|lus /kyuːmyələs/ (cumuli /kyuːmyələɪ/) N-VAR **Cumulus** is a type of thick white cloud formed when hot air rises very quickly. ☐ *...huge cumulus clouds.*

cun|ni|lin|gus /kʌnɪlɪŋgəs/ N-UNCOUNT **Cunnilingus** is oral sex which involves someone using their mouth to stimulate a woman's genitals.

cun|ning /kʌnɪŋ/ **1** ADJ Someone who is **cunning** has the ability to achieve things in a clever way, often by deceiving other people. ☐ *These disturbed kids can be cunning.* • **cun|ning|ly** ADV ☐ *They were cunningly disguised in golf clothes.* **2** N-UNCOUNT **Cunning** is the ability to achieve things in a clever way, often by deceiving other people. ☐ *...one more example of the cunning of today's art thieves.*

cunt /kʌnt/ (cunts) **1** N-COUNT **Cunt** is an extremely offensive word that some people use to refer to a woman's genitals. [VULGAR, VERY OFFENSIVE] **2** N-COUNT If someone calls another person a **cunt**, they are expressing extreme contempt for that person. [VULGAR, VERY OFFENSIVE]

cup ♦♦♦ /kʌp/ (cups, cupping, cupped) **1** N-COUNT A **cup** is a small, round container that you drink from. Cups usually have handles and are made from china or plastic. ☐ *...cups and saucers.* **2** N-COUNT You can use **cup** to refer to the cup and its contents, or to the contents only. ☐ *...a cup of coffee.* **3** N-COUNT A **cup** is a unit of measurement used in cooking. It is equal to 16 tablespoons or 8 fluid ounces. ☐ *Gradually add 1 cup of milk, stirring until the liquid is absorbed.* ☐ *...half a cup of sugar.* **4** N-COUNT Things, or parts of things, that are small, round, and hollow in shape can be referred to as **cups**. ☐ *...the brass cups of the small chandelier.* **5** N-COUNT A **cup** is a large metal cup with two handles that is given to the winner of a game or competition. ☐ *The Stars won the Stanley Cup in 1999.* **6** N-IN-NAMES **Cup** is used in the names of some sports competitions in which the prize is a cup. ❑ *Sri Lanka's cricket team will play India in the final of the Asia Cup.* ▸ V-T If you **cup** your **hands**, you make them into a curved shape like a cup. ❑ *He cupped his hands around his mouth and called out for Diane.* ❑ *David knelt, cupped his hands and splashed river water on to his face.* ▸ V-T If you **cup** something in your hands, you make your hands into a curved dish-like shape and support it or hold it gently. ❑ *He cupped her chin in the palm of his hand.* ▸ → See also color supplement

cup|board /kʌbərd/ (**cupboards**) N-COUNT A **cupboard** is a piece of furniture that has one or two doors, usually contains shelves, and is used to store things. ❑ *The kitchen cupboard was stocked with cans of soup and food.*

cup|cake /kʌpkeɪk/ (**cupcakes**) N-COUNT **Cupcakes** are small frosted cakes for one person.

cup|ful /kʌpfʊl/ (**cupfuls**) N-COUNT [usu N *of* n] A **cupful** of something is the amount of something a cup can contain. ❑ *...a cupful of warm milk.*

cu|pid /kyupɪd/ also **Cupid** N-PROPER **Cupid** is the Roman god of love. He is usually shown as a young boy with wings and a bow and arrow. • PHRASE If you say that someone **is playing cupid**, you mean that they are trying to bring two people together to start a romantic relationship.

cu|pid|ity /kyupɪdɪti/ N-UNCOUNT **Cupidity** is a greedy desire for money and possessions. [FORMAL] ❑ *His eyes gave him away, shining with cupidity.*

cu|po|la /kyupələ/ (**cupolas**) N-COUNT A **cupola** is a roof or part of a roof that is shaped like a dome. [FORMAL]

cur /kɜr/ (**curs**) N-COUNT A **cur** is an unfriendly dog, especially a mongrel. [OLD-FASHIONED]

cur|able /kyuərəbəl/ ADJ If a disease or illness is **curable**, it can be cured. ❑ *Most skin cancers are completely curable if detected in the early stages.*

cu|rate (**curates, curating, curated**)

The noun is pronounced /kyuərɪt/. The verb is pronounced /kyuəreɪt/.

▸ N-COUNT A **curate** is a clergyman in the Anglican Church who helps the priest. ▸ V-T [usu passive] If an exhibition is **curated** by someone, they organize it. ❑ *The Hayward exhibition has been curated by the artist Bernard Luthi.*

cu|ra|tive /kyuərətɪv/ ADJ Something that has **curative** properties can cure people's illnesses. [FORMAL] ❑ *Ancient civilizations believed in the curative powers of fresh air and sunlight.*

cu|ra|tor /kyuəreɪtər, kyuəreɪtər/ (**curators**) N-COUNT A **curator** is someone who is in charge of the objects or works of art in a museum or art gallery. ❑ *Peter Forey is curator of fossil fishes at the Natural History Museum.*

cu|ra|to|rial /kyuərətɔriəl/ ADJ [ADJ n] **Curatorial** means relating to curators and their work. [FORMAL] ❑ *...the museum's curatorial team.*

curb /kɜrb/ (**curbs, curbing, curbed**) ▸ V-T If you **curb** something, you control it and keep it within limits. ❑ *...advertisements aimed at curbing the spread of AIDS.* • N-COUNT **Curb** is also a noun. ❑ *He called for much stricter curbs on immigration.* ▸ V-T If you **curb** an emotion or your behavior, you keep it under control. ❑ *He curbed his temper.* ▸ N-COUNT The **curb** is the raised edge of a sidewalk which separates it from the road. [AM] ❑ *I pulled over to the curb.*

in BRIT, use **kerb**

▸ → See feature box at **drive**

curb|stone /kɜrbstoʊn/ (**curbstones**) N-COUNT A **curbstone** is one of the stones that form a curb. [AM] ❑ *There are people sitting on the curbstones.*

in BRIT, use **kerbstone**

curd /kɜrd/ (**curds**) N-VAR [usu pl] **Curds** are the thick white substance that is formed when milk turns sour.

cur|dle /kɜrdəl/ (**curdles, curdling, curdled**) V-T/V-I If milk or eggs **curdle** or if you **curdle** them, they separate into different bits. ❑ *The sauce should not boil or the egg yolk will curdle.* ❑ *The herb has been used for centuries to curdle milk.*

cure ◆◇ /kyuər/ (**cures, curing, cured**) ▸ V-T If doctors or medical treatments **cure** an illness or injury, they cause

it to end or disappear. ❑ *An operation finally cured his shin injury.* ▸ V-T If doctors or medical treatments **cure** a person, they make the person well again after an illness or injury. ❑ *It is an effective treatment and could cure all the leprosy sufferers worldwide.* ❑ *Almost overnight I was cured.* ▸ V-T If someone or something **cures** a problem, they bring it to an end. ❑ *Private firms are willing to make large scale investments to help cure Russia's economic troubles.* ▸ V-T [usu passive] When food, tobacco, or animal skin **is cured**, it is dried, smoked, or salted so that it will last for a long time. ❑ *Legs of pork were cured and smoked over the fire.* ▸ N-COUNT A **cure** for an illness is a medicine or other treatment that cures the illness. ❑ *There is still no cure for a cold.* ▸ N-COUNT A **cure** for a problem is something that will bring it to an end. ❑ *The magic cure for inflation does not exist.*

COLLOCATIONS

cure
VERB
▸
cure + noun: ailment, cancer, disease; hangover
▸
cure + noun: patient
cure + adverb: completely, fully, miraculously
NOUN
▸
adjective + **cure**: effective, miraculous
verb + **cure**: develop, discover, find; research, seek
▸
adjective + **cure**: magic, quick

---

cure-all (**cure-alls**) N-COUNT [oft N *for* n] A **cure-all** is something that is believed, usually wrongly, to be able to solve all the problems someone or something has, or to cure a wide range of illnesses. ❑ *He said the introduction of market discipline to the economy was not a magic cure-all for its problems.*

cur|few /kɜrfyu/ (**curfews**) ▸ N-VAR A **curfew** is a law stating that people must stay inside their houses after a particular time at night, for example, during a war. ❑ *The village was placed under curfew.* ▸ N-VAR **Curfew** or a **curfew** is the time after which a child or student will be punished if they are found outside their home or dormitory. ❑ *They raced back to the dormitory before the nine o'clock curfew.*

cu|rio /kyuəriou/ (**curios**) N-COUNT A **curio** is an object such as a small ornament which is unusual and fairly rare. ❑ *...Oriental curios.* ❑ *...antique and curio shops.*

cu|ri|os|ity /kyuərɪɒsɪti/ (**curiosities**) ▸ N-UNCOUNT **Curiosity** is a desire to know about something. ❑ *Ryle accepted more out of curiosity than anything else.* ❑ *...enthusiasm and genuine curiosity about the past.* ▸ N-COUNT A **curiosity** is something that is unusual, interesting, and fairly rare. ❑ *There is much to see in the way of castles, curiosities, and museums.*

cu|ri|ous ◆◇ /kyuəriəs/ ▸ ADJ If you are **curious** about something, you are interested in it and want to know more about it. • ❑ *Steve was intensely curious about the world I came from.* • **cu|ri|ous|ly** ADV [ADV after v] ❑ *The woman in the shop had looked at them curiously.* ▸ ADJ If you describe something as **curious**, you mean that it is unusual or difficult to understand. ❑ *The pageant promises to be a curious mixture of the ancient and modern.* • **cu|ri|ous|ly** ADV ❑ *Harry was curiously silent through all this.*

curl /kɜrl/ (**curls, curling, curled**) ▸ N-COUNT If you have **curls**, your hair is in the form of tight curves and spirals. ❑ *...the little girl with blonde curls.* ▸ N-COUNT A **curl** of something is a piece or quantity of it that is curved or spiral in shape. ❑ *A thin curl of smoke rose from a rusty stove.* ▸ N-UNCOUNT If your hair has **curl**, it is full of curls. ❑ *Dry curly hair naturally for maximum curl and shine.* ▸ V-T/V-I If your hair **curls** or if you **curl** it, it is full of curls. ❑ *She has hair that refuses to curl.* ❑ *Maria had curled her hair for the event.* ▸ V-T/V-I If your toes, fingers, or other parts of your body **curl**, or if you **curl** them, they form a curved or round shape. ❑ *His fingers curled gently around her wrist.* ❑ *Raise one foot, curl the toes and point the foot downwards.* ▸ V-T/V-I If something **curls** somewhere, or if you **curl** it there, it moves there in a spiral or curve. ❑ *Smoke was curling up the chimney.* ▸ V-I If a person or animal **curls into** a ball, they move into a position in which their body makes a rounded shape. ❑ *He wanted to*

curl into a tiny ball. • PHRASAL VERB **Curl up** means the same as **curl**. ❏ *In colder weather, your cat will curl up into a tight, heat-conserving ball.* ❏ *She curled up next to him.* **5** V-I When a leaf, a piece of paper, or another flat object **curls**, its edges bend toward the center. ❏ *The rose leaves have curled because of an attack by grubs.* • PHRASAL VERB **Curl up** means the same as **curl**. ❏ *The corners of the rug were curling up.*
▶ **curl up** → see curl 7, 8

curl|er /kɜrlər/ (curlers) N-COUNT **Curlers** are small plastic or metal tubes that you roll your hair around in order to make it curly. ❏ *...a woman with her hair in curlers.*

cur|lew /kɜrlyu/ (curlews) N-COUNT A **curlew** is a large, brown bird with long legs and a long, curved beak. Curlews live near water and have a very distinctive cry.

cur|li|cue /kɜrlɪkyu/ (curlicues) N-COUNT [usu pl] **Curlicues** are decorative twists and curls, usually carved or made with a pen. [LITERARY] ❏ *...the Gothic curlicues of cottages and churches.*

curl|ing iron (curling irons) N-COUNT A **curling iron** is a metal device, resembling scissors, that you heat and use to form curls in your hair. ❏ *Then he adds a few quick curls with his curling iron.*

curly /kɜrli/ (curlier, curliest) **1** ADJ **Curly** hair is full of curls. ❏ *I've got naturally curly hair.* **2** ADJ **Curly** is sometimes used to describe things that are curved or spiral in shape. ❏ *...cauliflowers with extra-long curly leaves.*

cur|mudg|eon /kɜrmʌdʒən/ (curmudgeons) N-COUNT If you call someone a **curmudgeon**, you do not like them because they are mean or bad-tempered. [OLD-FASHIONED, DISAPPROVAL] ❏ *...such a terrible old curmudgeon.*

cur|mudg|eon|ly /kɜrmʌdʒənli/ ADJ If you describe someone as **curmudgeonly**, you do not like them because they are mean or bad-tempered. [OLD-FASHIONED, DISAPPROVAL]

cur|rant /kɜrənt/ (currants) **1** N-COUNT **Currants** are small dried black grapes, used especially in cakes. **2** N-COUNT **Currants** are bushes which produce edible red, black, or white berries. The berries are also called **currants**.

cur|ren|cy ✦◇◇ /kɜrənsi/ (currencies) N-VAR The money used in a particular country is referred to as its **currency**. ❏ *Tourism is the country's top earner of foreign currency.* ❏ *More people favor a single European currency than oppose it.*

cur|rent ✦✦✦ /kɜrənt/ (currents) **1** N-COUNT A **current** is a steady and continuous flowing movement of some of the water in a river, lake, or ocean. ❏ *Under normal conditions, the ocean currents of the tropical Pacific travel from east to west.* **2** N-COUNT A **current** is a steady flowing movement of air. ❏ *I felt a current of cool air blowing in my face.* **3** N-COUNT An electric **current** is a flow of electricity through a wire or circuit. ❏ *A powerful electric current is passed through a piece of graphite.* **4** N-COUNT A particular **current** is a particular feeling, idea, or quality that exists within a group of people. ❏ *Each party represents a distinct current of thought.* **5** ADJ **Current** means happening, being used, or being done at the present time. ❏ *The current situation is very different to that in 1990.* • **cur|rent|ly** ADV [ADV before v] ❏ *Twelve potential vaccines are currently being tested on human volunteers.* **6** ADJ Ideas and customs that are **current** are generally accepted and used by most people. ❏ *Current thinking suggests that toxins only have a small part to play in the build-up of cellulite.* **7** → See feature box at **electricity, ocean, population**

┌─ SYNONYMS ─┐
current
ADJ **5**
present: *...the government's present economic difficulties.*
ongoing: *There is an ongoing debate on the issue.*
contemporary: *Only the names are ancient, the characters are modern and contemporary.*
present-day: *...present-day champions of the cause.*
modern: *...the problem of materialism in modern society.*

cur|rent ac|count (current accounts) N-COUNT A **current account** is a personal bank account which you can take money out of at any time using your checkbook or ATM card. [BRIT]

in AM, use **checking account**

cur|rent af|fairs also **current events** N-PLURAL If you refer to **current affairs**, you are referring to political events and problems in society which are discussed in newspapers, and on television and radio. ❏ *I am ill-informed on current affairs.*

cur|rent as|sets (current assets) N-COUNT **Current assets** are assets which a company does not use on a continuous basis, such as stocks and debts, but which can be converted into cash within one year. [BUSINESS] ❏ *The company lists its current assets at $56.9 million.*

cur|rent ev|ents N-PLURAL → see **current affairs**

cur|ricu|lum /kərɪkyələm/ (curriculums or curricula /kərɪkyələ/) **1** N-COUNT A **curriculum** is all the different courses of study that are taught in a school, college, or university. ❏ *Teachers incorporated business skills into the regular school curriculum.* **2** N-COUNT A particular **curriculum** is one particular course of study that is taught in a school, college, or university. ❏ *...the history curriculum.*

cur|ricu|lum vitae /kərɪkyələm vaɪtɪ/ N-SING A **curriculum vitae** is the same as a **CV**.

cur|ried /kɜrid/ ADJ [ADJ n] **Curried** meat or vegetables have been flavored with hot spices.

cur|ry /kɜri/ (curries, currying, curried) **1** N-VAR **Curry** is a dish composed of meat and vegetables, or just vegetables, in a sauce containing hot spices. It is usually eaten with rice and is one of the main dishes of India. ❏ *...vegetable curry.* **2** PHRASE If one person tries to **curry favor** with another, they do things in order to try to gain their support or cooperation. ❏ *Politicians are eager to promote their "happy family" image to curry favor with voters.*

cur|ry pow|der (curry powders) N-MASS **Curry powder** is a powder made from a mixture of spices. It is used in cooking, especially when making curry.

curse /kɜrs/ (curses, cursing, cursed) **1** V-I If you **curse**, you use very impolite or offensive language, usually because you are angry about something. [WRITTEN] ❏ *I cursed and hobbled to my feet.* • N-COUNT **Curse** is also a noun. ❏ *He shot her an angry look and a curse.* **2** V-T If you **curse** someone, you say insulting things to them because you are angry with them. ❏ *Grandma protested, but he cursed her and rudely pushed her aside.* **3** V-T If you **curse** something, you complain angrily about it, especially using very impolite language. ❏ *So we set off again, cursing the delay, toward the west.* **4** N-COUNT If you say that there is a **curse** on someone, you mean that there seems to be a supernatural power causing unpleasant things to happen to them. ❏ *Maybe there is a curse on my family.* **5** N-COUNT You can refer to something that causes a great deal of trouble or harm as a **curse**. ❏ *Apathy is the long-standing curse of democracy.*

curs|ed /kɜrst/ **1** ADJ [v-link ADJ with n] If you are **cursed with** something, you are very unlucky in having it. ❏ *Bulman was cursed with a poor memory for names.* **2** ADJ [usu v-link ADJ] Someone or something that is **cursed** is suffering as the result of a curse. ❏ *The whole family seemed cursed.*

cur|sor /kɜrsər/ (cursors) N-COUNT On a computer screen, the **cursor** is a small shape that indicates where anything that is typed by the user will appear. [COMPUTING] ❏ *He moves the cursor, clicks the mouse.*

cur|sory /kɜrsəri/ ADJ [ADJ n] A **cursory** glance or examination is a brief one in which you do not pay much attention to detail. ❏ *Burke cast a cursory glance at the menu, then flapped it shut.*

curt /kɜrt/ ADJ If you describe someone as **curt**, you mean that they speak or reply in a brief and rather rude way. ❏ *Her tone of voice was curt.* • **curt|ly** ADV [ADV with v] ❏ *"I'm leaving," she said curtly.*

cur|tail /kɜrteɪl/ (curtails, curtailing, curtailed) V-T If you **curtail** something, you reduce or limit it. [FORMAL] ❏ *NATO plans to curtail the number of troops being sent to the region.*

cur|tail|ment /kɜrteɪlmənt/ N-SING [usu N of n] The **curtailment** of something is the act of reducing or limiting it. [FORMAL] ❏ *...the curtailment of presidential power.*

cur|tain ✦◇◇ /kɜrtən/ (curtains) **1** N-COUNT **Curtains** are pieces of material which you hang from the top of a window. ❏ *Her bedroom curtains were drawn.* **2** N-SING In a theater, **the curtain** is the large piece of material that hangs in front of the stage until a performance begins. ❏ *The curtain rises toward the end of the Prelude.*

cur|tain call (curtain calls) also **curtain-call** N-COUNT In a theater, when actors or performers take a **curtain call**, they come forward to the front of the stage after a performance in order to receive the applause of the audience. ☐ *They took 23 curtain calls.*

cur|tained /kɜrtᵊnd/ ADJ [usu ADJ n] A **curtained** window, door, or other opening has a curtain hanging across it. ☐ *...heavily curtained windows.*

curtain-raiser (curtain-raisers) N-COUNT [usu sing] A **curtain-raiser** is an event, especially a sports event or a performance, that takes place before a more important one, or starts off a series of events. [JOURNALISM] ☐ *The three-race series will be a curtain-raiser to the Monaco Grand Prix in May.*

cur|tain rod (curtain rods) N-COUNT A **curtain rod** is a long, narrow pole on which you hang curtains. ☐ *Her mother was there, trying to put a curtain rod up over the little window.*

curt|sy /kɜrtsi/ (curtsies, curtsying, curtsied) also **curtsey** V-I If a woman or a girl **curtsies**, she lowers her body briefly, bending her knees and sometimes holding her skirt with both hands, as a way of showing respect for an important person. ☐ *We were taught how to curtsy to the Queen.* ☐ *Ingrid shook the Duchess's hand and curtsied.* • N-COUNT **Curtsy** is also a noun. ☐ *She gave a curtsy.*

cur|va|ceous /kɜrveɪʃəs/ ADJ If someone describes a woman as **curvaceous**, they think she is attractive because of the curves of her body. [APPROVAL] ☐ *...a curvaceous model.*

cur|va|ture /kɜrvətʃər, -tʃʊər/ N-UNCOUNT [oft N of n] The **curvature** of something is its curved shape, especially when this shape is part of the circumference of a circle. [TECHNICAL] ☐ *...the curvature of the earth.*

curve /kɜrv/ (curves, curving, curved) ◼ N-COUNT A **curve** is a smooth, gradually bending line, for example, part of the edge of a circle. ☐ *...the curve of his lips.* ◼ N-COUNT You can refer to a change in something as a particular **curve**, especially when it is represented on a graph. ☐ *Youth crime overall is on a slow but steady downward curve.* ◼ → see also **learning curve** ◼ V-T/V-I If something **curves**, or if someone or something **curves** it, it has the shape of a curve. ☐ *Her spine curved.* ☐ *...a knife with a slightly curving blade.* ◼ V-I If something **curves**, it moves in a curve, for example, through the air. ☐ *The ball curved strangely in the air.* ◼ PHRASE If someone **throws** you **a curve** or **throws** you **a curve ball**, they surprise you by doing something that you do not expect. [mainly AM] ☐ *At the last minute, I threw them a curve ball by saying, "We're going to bring spouses."* ◼ PHRASE People, products, or ideas that are **ahead of the curve** are more advanced or modern than others of their kind. ☐ *Her fashion designs were always ahead of the curve.*

curved /kɜrvd/ ADJ A **curved** object has the shape of a curve or has a smoothly bending surface. ☐ *...the curved lines of the chairs.*

curvy /kɜrvi/ (curvier, curviest) ADJ If someone describes a woman as **curvy**, they think she is attractive because of the curves of her body. [INFORMAL, APPROVAL]

cush|ion /kʊʃᵊn/ (cushions, cushioning, cushioned) ◼ N-COUNT A **cushion** is a fabric case filled with soft material, which you put on a seat to make it more comfortable. ☐ *...a velvet cushion.* ◼ N-COUNT A **cushion** is a soft pad or barrier, especially one that protects something. ☐ *The company provides a styrofoam cushion to protect the tablets during shipping.* ◼ N-COUNT Something that is a **cushion** against something unpleasant reduces its effect. ☐ *Welfare provides a cushion against hardship.* ◼ V-T Something that **cushions** an object when it hits something protects it by reducing the force of the impact. ☐ *There is also a new steering wheel with an energy-absorbing rim to cushion the driver's head in the worst impacts.* ◼ V-T To **cushion** the effect of something unpleasant means to reduce it. ☐ *They said Western aid was needed to cushion the blows of vital reform.*

cush|ion|ing /kʊʃənɪŋ/ N-UNCOUNT **Cushioning** is something soft that protects what something. ☐ *Running shoes have extra cushioning.*

cushy /kʊʃi/ (cushier, cushiest) ADJ [usu ADJ n] A **cushy** job or situation is pleasant because it does not involve much work or effort. [INFORMAL] ☐ *...a cushy job in the civil service.*

cusp /kʌsp/ PHRASE If you say that someone or something is **on the cusp**, you mean they are between two states, or are about to be in a particular state. ☐ *I am sitting on the cusp of middle age.*

cuss /kʌs/ (cusses, cussing, cussed) V-I If someone **cusses**, they swear at someone or use bad language. [INFORMAL, OLD-FASHIONED] ☐ *Tosh was known to be a man who would cuss and shout.* ☐ *He rails and cusses at those pop stars.*

cus|tard /kʌstərd/ (custards) ◼ N-VAR **Custard** is a baked dessert made of milk, eggs, and sugar. ☐ *...a custard with a caramel sauce.* ◼ N-MASS **Custard** is a sweet, yellow sauce made from milk and eggs or from milk and a powder. It is eaten with fruit and puddings. ☐ *...bananas and custard.* ◼ → See feature box at **cooking**

cus|tard pie (custard pies) N-COUNT **Custard pies** are artificial pies which people sometimes throw at each other as a joke. ☐ *...a custard pie fight.*

cus|to|dial /kʌstoʊdiəl/ ◼ ADJ [ADJ n] If a child's parents are divorced or separated, the **custodial** parent is the parent who has custody of the child. [LEGAL] ☐ *...all the general expenses that come with being the custodial parent.* ◼ ADJ [usu ADJ n] **Custodial** care is help with basic personal needs, for example washing, dressing, and eating. ☐ *In the event that you are mentally or physically disabled, who will provide custodial care and who will pay for it?*

cus|to|dian /kʌstoʊdiən/ (custodians) ◼ N-COUNT The **custodian** of an official building, a company's assets, or something else valuable is the person who is officially in charge of it. ☐ *...the custodian of the holy shrines in Mecca and Medina.* ◼ N-COUNT The **custodian** of a large building such as an office or a school is responsible for cleaning and maintaining it. [AM] ☐ *Augustine Hancock served as an elementary-school custodian for 20 years.*

cus|to|dy /kʌstədi/ ◼ N-UNCOUNT **Custody** is the legal right to keep and take care of a child, especially the right given to a child's mother or father when they get divorced. ☐ *I'm going to go to court to get custody of the children.* ☐ *Child custody is normally granted to the mother.* ◼ N-UNCOUNT If someone is being held in a particular type of **custody**, they are being kept in a place that is similar to a prison. ☐ *The youngster got nine months' youth custody.* ◼ PHRASE Someone who is **in custody** or has been taken **into custody** has been arrested and is being kept in prison until they can be tried in a court. ☐ *Three people appeared in court and two of them were remanded in custody.*

cus|tom /kʌstəm/ (customs) ◼ N-VAR A **custom** is an activity, a way of behaving, or an event which is usual or traditional in a particular society or in particular circumstances. ☐ *The custom of lighting the Olympic flame goes back centuries.* ◼ N-SING If it is your **custom** to do something, you usually do it in particular circumstances. ☐ *It was his custom to approach every problem cautiously.* ◼ → see also **customs**

cus|tom|ary /kʌstəmɛri/ ◼ ADJ **Customary** is used to describe things that people usually do in a particular society or in particular circumstances. [FORMAL] ☐ *It is customary to offer a drink or a snack to guests.* ◼ ADJ [ADJ n] **Customary** is used to describe something that a particular person usually does or has. ☐ *Yvonne took her customary seat behind her desk.*

custom-built ADJ If something is **custom-built**, it is built according to someone's special requirements. ☐ *The machine was custom-built by Steve Roberts.* ☐ *We invested in a custom-built kitchen.*

cus|tom|er ✦✦◇ /kʌstəmər/ (customers) N-COUNT A **customer** is someone who buys goods or services, especially from a store. ☐ *...a satisfied customer.* ☐ *The quality of customer service is extremely important.*

COLLOCATIONS

customer
NOUN
adjective + **customer**: happy, loyal, regular, satisfied; potential, valued
verb + **customer**: attract, help, offer, serve; charge; lose

---

cus|tom|er base (customer bases) N-COUNT A business's **customer base** is all its regular customers, considered as a group. [BUSINESS] ☐ *...Halifax's customer base of 21 million people.*

cus|tom|er re|la|tions ◨ N-PLURAL **Customer relations** are the relationships that a business has with its customers and the way in which it treats them. [BUSINESS] ❑ *Good customer relations require courtesy, professionalism and effective response.* ◪ N-UNCOUNT **Customer relations** is the department within a company that deals with complaints from customers. [BUSINESS] ❑ *...Tucson Electric's customer-relations department.* ◫ → See feature box at **service**

cus|tom|er sat|is|fac|tion ◨ N-UNCOUNT When customers are pleased with the goods or services they have bought, you can refer to this as **customer satisfaction**. ❑ *I really believe that it is possible to both improve customer satisfaction and reduce costs.* ❑ *Customer satisfaction with their service runs at more than 90 percent.* ◪ → See feature box at **service**

cus|tom|er ser|vice ◨ N-UNCOUNT **Customer service** refers to the way that companies behave toward their customers, for example, how well they treat them. [BUSINESS] ❑ *...a mail-order business with a strong reputation for customer service.* ❑ *The firm has an excellent customer service department.* ◪ → See feature box at **service**

cus|tom|ize /kʌstəmaɪz/ (**customizes, customizing, customized**)

| in BRIT, also use **customise** |

V-T If you **customize** something, you change its appearance or features to suit your tastes or needs. ❑ *...a control that allows photographers to customize the camera's basic settings.*

custom-made ADJ If something **is custom-made**, it is made according to someone's special requirements. ❑ *Furniture can also be custom-made to suit your own requirements.* ❑ *...a custom-made suit.*

cus|toms /kʌstəmz/ ◨ N-PROPER **Customs** is the official organization responsible for collecting taxes on goods coming into a country and preventing illegal goods from being brought in. ❑ *What right does Customs have to search my car?* ◪ N-UNCOUNT **Customs** is the place where people arriving from a foreign country have to declare goods that they bring with them. ❑ *He walked through customs.* ◫ ADJ [ADJ n] **Customs** duties are taxes that people pay for importing and exporting goods. ❑ *Personal property which is to be re-exported at the end of your visit is not subject to customs duties.* ◰ → see also **custom**

Cus|toms Ser|vice N-PROPER The **Customs Service** is a United States federal organization which is responsible for collecting taxes on imported and exported goods.

| **CUT** |
| ① PHYSICAL ACTION |
| ② SHORTEN OR REDUCE AMOUNT |
| ③ OTHER USES |
| ④ PHRASAL VERBS |

① **cut** ◆◆◆ /kʌt/ (**cuts, cutting**)

| The form **cut** is used in the present tense and is the past tense and past participle. |

◨ V-T/V-I If you **cut** something, you use a knife or a similar tool to divide it into pieces, or to mark it or damage it. If you **cut** a shape or a hole in something, you make the shape or hole by using a knife or similar tool. ❑ *Mrs. Haines stood nearby, holding scissors to cut a ribbon.* ❑ *Cut the tomatoes in half vertically.* ❑ *The thieves cut a hole in the fence.* ❑ *This little knife cuts really well.* • N-COUNT **Cut** is also a noun. ❑ *Carefully make a cut in the shell with a small serrated knife.* ◪ V-T If you **cut** yourself or **cut** a part of your body, you accidentally injure yourself on a sharp object so that you bleed. ❑ *Johnson cut himself shaving.* ❑ *I started to cry because I cut my finger.* • N-COUNT **Cut** is also a noun. ❑ *He had sustained a cut on his left eyebrow.* ◫ V-T If you **cut** something such as grass, your hair, or your fingernails, you shorten them using scissors or another tool. ❑ *The most recent tenants hadn't even cut the grass.* ❑ *You've had your hair cut, it looks great.* • N-SING **Cut** is also a noun. ❑ *Prices vary from salon to salon, starting at $30 for a cut and blow-dry.* ◰ V-T [usu passive] The way that clothes **are cut** is the way they are designed and made. ❑ *...badly cut blue suits.*

| **SYNONYMS** |

cut
VERB
① ◨
carve: *Andrew began to carve the chicken.*
slice: *Helen sliced the cake.*
hack: *Matthew desperately hacked through the leather.*
chop: *Visitors were put to work chopping wood.*
pierce: *Pierce the skin of the potato with a fork.*
① ◫
clip: *I saw an old man out clipping his hedge.*
mow: *He continued to mow the lawn and do other routine chores.*
trim: *My friend trims my hair every eight weeks.*
prune: *You have to prune a bush if you want fruit.*
② ◰
reduce: *Consumption is being reduced by 25 percent.*
lower: *The Central Bank has lowered interest rates by 2 percent.*
decrease: *Gradually decrease the amount of vitamin C you are taking.*
diminish: *Universities are facing grave problems because of diminishing resources.*
slash: *Everyone agrees that subsidies have to be slashed.*

② **cut** ◆◆◆ /kʌt/ (**cuts, cutting**)

| The form **cut** is used in the present tense and is the past tense and past participle. |

→ Please look at meanings ◖ and ◗ to see if the expression you are looking for is shown under another headword.

◨ V-T If you **cut** something, you reduce it. ❑ *The first priority is to cut costs.* ❑ *The U.N. force is to be cut by 90%.* • N-COUNT [with supp, oft N in n] **Cut** is also a noun. ❑ *The economy needs an immediate 2 percent cut in interest rates.* ◪ V-T If you **cut** a text, broadcast, or performance, you shorten it. If you **cut** a part of a text, broadcast, or performance, you do not publish, broadcast, or perform that part. ❑ *Branagh has cut the play judiciously.* • N-COUNT **Cut** is also a noun. ❑ *It has been found necessary to make some cuts in the text.* ◫ V-I If you **cut across** or **through** a place, you go through it because it is the shortest route to another place. ❑ *Jesse cut across the parking lot and strolled through the main entrance.* ◰ → see also **shortcut** ◱ V-I If you **cut** in front of someone, you move in front of them and take their place. ❑ *Somebody tried to cut in line and a fight broke out.* ◲ V-T To **cut** a supply of something means to stop providing it or stop it from being provided. ❑ *Winds have knocked down power lines, cutting electricity to thousands of people.* • N-COUNT [with supp, usu N in n] **Cut** is also a noun. ❑ *The strike had already led to cuts in electricity and water supplies in many areas.* ◳ **to cut something to the bone** → see **bone** ◴ **to cut corners** → see **corner**

③ **cut** ◆◆◆ /kʌt/ (**cuts, cutting**)

| The form **cut** is used in the present tense and is the past tense and past participle. |

→ Please look at meaning ◖ to see if the expression you are looking for is shown under another headword.

◨ V-T If you **cut** a deck of playing cards, you divide it into two. ❑ *Place the cards face down on the table and cut them.* ◪ V-T If you tell someone to **cut** something, you are telling them in an irritated way to stop it [mainly AM, INFORMAL, FEELINGS] ❑ *"Cut the euphemisms, Daniel," Brenda snapped.* ◫ CONVENTION When the director of a movie says '**cut**,' they want the actors and the camera crew to stop filming. ◰ N-COUNT A **cut** of meat is a piece or type of meat which is cut in a particular way from the animal, or from a particular part of it. ❑ *Use a cheap cut such as spare rib chops.* ◱ N-SING Someone's **cut** of the profits or winnings from something, especially ones that have been obtained dishonestly, is their share. [INFORMAL] ❑ *The agency is expected to take a cut of the money awarded to its client.* ◲ N-COUNT A **cut** is a narrow valley which has been cut through a hill so that a road or railroad track can pass through. [AM]

| in BRIT, use **cutting** |

◳ → see also **cutting** ◴ PHRASE If you say that a situation is **cut and dried**, you mean that it is clear and definite. ❑ *Unfortunately, things cannot be as cut and dried as many people would like.* ◖ **to cut the mustard** → see **mustard**

④ **cut** ♦♦♦ /kʌt/ (cuts, cutting)

> The form **cut** is used in the present tense and is the past tense and past participle.

▶ **cut across** PHRASAL VERB If an issue or problem **cuts across** the division between two or more groups of people, it affects or matters to people in all the groups. ❑ *The problem cuts across all socioeconomic lines and affects all age groups.*

▶ **cut back** **1** PHRASAL VERB If you **cut back** something such as expenditure or **cut back** on it, you reduce it. ❑ *Customers have cut back spending because of the economic slowdown.* ❑ *The Government has cut back on defense spending.* **2** → see also **cutback**

▶ **cut down** **1** PHRASAL VERB If you **cut down** on something or **cut down** something, you use or do less of it. ❑ *He cut down on coffee and cigarettes, and ate a balanced diet.* ❑ *Car owners were asked to cut down travel.* **2** PHRASAL VERB If you **cut down** a tree, you cut through its trunk so that it falls to the ground. ❑ *A vandal with a chainsaw cut down a tree.*

▶ **cut in** PHRASAL VERB If you **cut in** on someone, you interrupt them when they are speaking. ❑ *Immediately, Daniel cut in on Joanne's attempts at reassurance.* ❑ *"Not true," the Duchess cut in.*

▶ **cut off** **1** PHRASAL VERB If you **cut** something **off**, you remove it with a knife or a similar tool. ❑ *Mrs. Johnson cut off a generous piece of the meat.* ❑ *He threatened to cut my hair off.* **2** PHRASAL VERB To **cut** someone or something **off** means to separate them from things that they are normally connected with. ❑ *One of the goals of the campaign is to cut off the elite Republican Guard from its supplies.* ● **cut off** ADJ *Without a car we still felt very cut off.* **3** PHRASAL VERB To **cut off** a supply of something means to stop providing it or stop it from being provided. ❑ *The rebels have cut off electricity from the capital.* **4** PHRASAL VERB If you get **cut off** when you are on the telephone, the line is suddenly disconnected and you can no longer speak to the other person. ❑ *When you do get through, you've got to speak quickly before you get cut off.* **5** → see also **cutoff**

▶ **cut out** **1** PHRASAL VERB If you **cut** something **out**, you remove or separate it from what surrounds it using scissors or a knife. ❑ *I cut it out and pinned it to my studio wall.* **2** PHRASAL VERB If you **cut out** a part of a text, you do not print, publish, or broadcast that part, because to include it would make the text too long or unacceptable. ❑ *I listened to the program and found they'd cut out all the interesting stuff.* **3** PHRASAL VERB To **cut out** something unnecessary or unwanted means to remove it completely from a situation. For example, if you **cut out** a particular type of food, you stop eating it, usually because it is bad for you. ❑ *I've simply cut egg yolks out entirely.* **4** PHRASAL VERB If an object **cuts out** the light, it is between you and the light so that you are in the dark. ❑ *The curtains were half drawn to cut out the sunlight.* **5** PHRASAL VERB If an engine **cuts out**, it suddenly stops working. ❑ *The helicopter crash landed when one of its two engines cut out.* **6** → see also **cut out**

▶ **cut up** PHRASAL VERB If you **cut** something **up**, you cut it into several pieces. ❑ *Halve the tomatoes, then cut them up coarsely.*

cut and dried → see cut ③ 8

cut|away /kʌtəweɪ/ (cutaways) also **cut-away** **1** N-COUNT In a film or video, a **cutaway** or a **cutaway shot** is a picture that shows something different from the main thing that is being shown. ❑ *I asked the cameraman to give me some cutaways for the interviews.* **2** N-COUNT A **cutaway** or a **cutaway** coat or jacket is one which is cut diagonally from the front to the back, so that the back is longer. [AM]

> in BRIT, use **tailcoat**

3 ADJ [ADJ n] A **cutaway** picture shows what something such as a machine looks like inside.

cut|back /kʌtbæk/ (cutbacks) N-COUNT A **cutback** is a reduction that is made in something. ❑ *The region has also been hit hard by cutbacks in defense spending, which has left thousands out of work.*

cute /kyuːt/ (cuter, cutest) **1** ADJ Something or someone that is **cute** is very pretty or attractive, or is intended to appear pretty or attractive. [INFORMAL] ❑ *Oh, look at that dog! He's so cute.* **2** ADJ If you describe someone as **cute**, you think they are sexually attractive. [mainly AM, INFORMAL] ❑ *There was this girl, and I thought she was really cute.* **3** ADJ If you describe someone as **cute**, you mean that they deal with things cleverly. [AM]

❑ *That's a cute trick.* ❑ *The President, trying to be cute, said his liberal arts education had not really prepared him for such complicated issues as this.*

cute|sy /kyuːtsi/ (cutesier, cutesiest) ADJ [usu ADJ n] If you describe someone or something as **cutesy**, you dislike them because you think they are unpleasantly pretty and sentimental. [INFORMAL, DISAPPROVAL] ❑ *...cutesy paintings of owls.*

cut glass also **cut-glass** N-UNCOUNT [oft N n] **Cut glass** is glass that has patterns cut into its surface. ❑ *...a cut-glass bowl.*

cu|ti|cle /kyuːtɪkᵊl/ (cuticles) N-COUNT Your **cuticles** are the skin at the base of each of your nails.

cut|lass /kʌtləs/ (cutlasses) N-COUNT A **cutlass** is a short sword that used to be used by sailors.

cut|lery /kʌtləri/ **1** N-UNCOUNT You can refer to knives and tools used for cutting as **cutlery**. [AM] ❑ *The first catalog featured specialty shavers, accessories, and cutlery.* **2** N-UNCOUNT **Cutlery** consists of the knives, forks, and spoons that you eat your food with. [mainly BRIT]

> in AM, usually use **silverware**

cut|let /kʌtlɪt/ (cutlets) N-COUNT A **cutlet** is a small piece of meat which is usually fried or grilled. ❑ *...grilled lamb cutlets.*

cut|off /kʌtɔːf/ (cutoffs) **1** N-COUNT A **cutoff** or a **cutoff** point is the level or limit at which you decide that something should stop happening. ❑ *The cutoff date for registering is yet to be announced.* **2** N-COUNT The **cutoff** of a supply or service is the complete stopping of the supply or service. ❑ *A total cutoff of supplies would cripple the country's economy.*

cut-offs N-PLURAL **Cut-offs** are short pants made by cutting part of the legs off old pants.

cut|out /kʌtaʊt/ (cutouts) also **cut-out** **1** N-COUNT A cardboard **cutout** is a shape that has been cut from cardboard. ❑ *You'd swear he was a cardboard cut-out except that he'd moved his rifle.* **2** N-COUNT [oft N n] A **cutout** is a device that turns off a machine automatically in particular circumstances. ❑ *Use a kettle with an automatic cut-out so it doesn't boil for longer than necessary.*

cut out ADJ If you are not **cut out** for a particular type of work, you do not have the qualities that are needed to be able to do it well. ❑ *I left medicine anyway. I wasn't really cut out for it.*

cut-rate ADJ [ADJ n] **Cut-rate** goods or services are cheaper than usual. ❑ *...cut-rate auto insurance.*

> in BRIT, usually use **cut-price**

cut|ter /kʌtər/ (cutters) **1** N-COUNT A **cutter** is a tool that you use for cutting through something. ❑ *...wire cutters.* **2** N-COUNT A **cutter** is a person who cuts or reduces something. ❑ *...a glass cutter.*

cut-throat ADJ If you describe a situation as **cut-throat**, you mean that the people or companies involved all want success and do not care if they harm each other in getting it. [DISAPPROVAL] ❑ *...the cut-throat competition in personal computers.*

cut|ting ♦◇◇ /kʌtɪŋ/ (cuttings) **1** N-COUNT A **cutting** from a plant is a part of the plant that you have cut off so that you can grow a new plant from it. ❑ *Take cuttings from it in July or August.* ❑ *Take cuttings from suitable garden tomatoes in late summer.* **2** ADJ A **cutting** remark is unkind and likely to hurt someone's feelings. ❑ *People make cutting remarks to help themselves feel superior or powerful.* **3** N-COUNT A **cutting** is a piece of writing which has been cut from a newspaper or magazine. [BRIT]

> in AM, use **clipping**

cut|ting board (cutting boards) N-COUNT A **cutting board** is a wooden or plastic board that you chop meat and vegetables on. [mainly AM]

> in BRIT, usually use **chopping board**

cut|ting edge

> The spelling **cutting-edge** is used for meaning **2**.

1 N-SING If you are at the **cutting edge** of a particular field of activity, you are involved in its most important or most exciting developments. ❑ *This shipyard is at the cutting edge of world shipbuilding technology.* **2** ADJ **Cutting-edge** techniques or

cutting room equipment are the most advanced that there are in a particular field. ❑ *What we are planning is cutting-edge technology never seen in Australia before.*

cut|ting room N-SING [usu the N] The **cutting room** in a movie production company is the place where the movie is edited. ❑ *Her scene ended up on the cutting room floor.*

cuttle|fish /kʌtᵊlfɪʃ/ (**cuttlefish**) N-COUNT A **cuttlefish** is a sea animal that has a soft body and a hard shell inside.

cuz /kʌz/ also **'cuz** CONJ **Cuz** is an informal way of saying **because**. [AM, SPOKEN] ❑ *I think I actually got into the tobacco business 'cuz I wanted to smoke.*

in BRIT, use **'cos.**

CV /siː viː/ (**CVs**) N-COUNT Your **CV** is a written account of your personal details, your education, and the jobs you have had. CV is an abbreviation for 'curriculum vitae.' [mainly BRIT]

in AM, usually use **résumé**

cwt cwt is a written abbreviation for **hundredweight**.

SUFFIX

-cy
forms nouns that refer to a particular state or quality. For example, **accuracy** is the state or quality of being accurate.

CYA CYA is the written abbreviation for 'see you,' mainly used in text messages and e-mails. [COMPUTING]

cya|nide /saɪənaɪd/ N-UNCOUNT **Cyanide** is a highly poisonous substance. ❑ *His death has all the signs of cyanide poisoning.*

cy|ber|at|tack /saɪbərətæk/ (**cyberattacks**) N-COUNT A **cyberattack** is an attempt to damage or disrupt a computer system, or get information stored on it, by getting into the system without permission. ❑ *The company said its website had been hit by a cyberattack that made the site inaccessible for most of the day.*

cy|ber|bul|ly /saɪbərbʊli/ (**cyberbullies, cyberbullying, cyberbullied**) VERB If someone **cyberbullies** another person, they try to hurt, frighten or threaten them, using the internet. ❑ *Some children use social media to cyberbully their classmates.* ❑ *Thirty per cent of 11-16 year olds have been cyberbullied* ● **cy|ber|bul|ly|ing** N-UNCOUNT ❑ *The girl experienced a high level of cyberbullying.*

cy|ber|café /saɪbərkæfeɪ/ (**cybercafés**) N-COUNT A **cybercafé** is a café where people can pay to use the internet.

cy|ber|crime /saɪbərkraɪm/ ◼ N-UNCOUNT **Cybercrime** is crime committed by means of computers or the internet. ❑ *Security experts say cybercrime and junk mail may increase too.* ◻ → See feature box at **crime**

cy|ber|net|ics /saɪbərnɛtɪks/ N-UNCOUNT **Cybernetics** is a branch of science which involves studying the way electronic machines and human brains work, and developing machines that do things or think in a similar way to people.

cy|ber|punk /saɪbərpʌŋk/ N-UNCOUNT **Cyberpunk** is a type of science fiction.

cy|ber|sex /saɪbərsɛks/ N-UNCOUNT **Cybersex** involves using the internet for sexual purposes, especially by exchanging sexual messages with another person. ❑ *It's a place where you can role-play and have cybersex.*

cy|ber|space /saɪbərspeɪs/ N-UNCOUNT In computer technology, **cyberspace** refers to data banks and networks, considered as a place. [COMPUTING] ❑ *...a report circulating in cyberspace.*

cy|ber|squatting /saɪbərskwɒtɪŋ/ N-UNCOUNT **Cybersquatting** involves buying an internet domain name that might be wanted by another person, business, or organization with the intention of selling it to them and making a profit. [COMPUTING] ● **cy|ber|squatter** (**cybersquatters**) N-COUNT ❑ *The old official club website address has been taken over by cybersquatters.*

cy|ber|stalk|ing /saɪbərstɔːkɪŋ/ N-UNCOUNT **Cyberstalking** is the use of the internet to contact someone or find out information about them in a way that is annoying or frightening. ❑ *The man now faces jail for cyberstalking offenses.*

cy|ber|ter|ror|ism /saɪbərtɛrərɪzəm/ N-UNCOUNT **Cyberterrorism** is the use of computers and the internet to attack or frighten large numbers of people, usually in order to achieve political aims or to force a government to do something. ❑ *The government has pledged more money to fight cyberterrorism and other online attacks.*

cy|borg /saɪbɔːrg/ (**cyborgs**) N-COUNT In science fiction, a **cyborg** is a being that is part human and part machine, or a machine that looks like a human being.

cyc|la|men /sɪkləmən/ (**cyclamen**) N-COUNT A **cyclamen** is a plant with white, pink, or red flowers.

cy|cle ♦⬦ /saɪkᵊl/ (**cycles, cycling, cycled**) ◼ N-COUNT A **cycle** is a series of events or processes that is repeated again and again, always in the same order. ❑ *...the life cycle of the plant.* ◼ N-COUNT A **cycle** is a single complete series of movements in an electrical, electronic, or mechanical process. ❑ *...10 cycles per second.* ◼ N-COUNT A **cycle** is a bicycle. ❑ *We supply the travel ticket for you and your cycle.* ◼ V-I If you **cycle**, you ride a bicycle. ❑ *He cycled to Ingwold.* ● **cy|cling** N-UNCOUNT ❑ *The quiet country roads are ideal for cycling.*

COLLOCATIONS

cycle
NOUN ◼
noun + **cycle**: sleep
adjective + **cycle**: business, economic; menstrual, natural
verb + **cycle**: break, complete, repeat

cy|cle path (**cycle paths**) N-COUNT A **cycle path** is a special path on which people can travel by bicycle separately from motor vehicles. [mainly BRIT]

in AM, use **bike path**

cy|cle|way /saɪkᵊlweɪ/ (**cycleways**) N-COUNT A **cycleway** is a special road, route, or path intended for use by people on bicycles. [BRIT]

in AM, use **bikeway**

cy|clic /sɪklɪk, saɪk-/ ADJ **Cyclic** means the same as **cyclical**.

cy|cli|cal /sɪklɪkᵊl, saɪk-/ ADJ A **cyclical** process is one in which a series of events happens again and again in the same order. ❑ *...the cyclical nature of the airline business.*

cy|clist /saɪklɪst/ (**cyclists**) N-COUNT A **cyclist** is someone who rides a bicycle, or is riding a bicycle. ❑ *...better protection for pedestrians and cyclists.*

cy|clone /saɪkloʊn/ (**cyclones**) N-COUNT A **cyclone** is a violent tropical storm in which the air goes around and around. ❑ *The race was called off as a cyclone struck.*

cyg|net /sɪgnɪt/ (**cygnets**) N-COUNT A **cygnet** is a young swan.

cyl|in|der /sɪlɪndər/ (**cylinders**) ◼ N-COUNT A **cylinder** is an object with flat, circular ends and long, straight sides. ❑ *It was recorded on a wax cylinder.* ◼ N-COUNT A gas **cylinder** is a cylinder-shaped container in which gas is kept under pressure. ❑ *...oxygen cylinders.* ◼ N-COUNT In an engine, a **cylinder** is a cylinder-shaped part in which a piston moves backward and forward. ❑ *...a four-cylinder engine.*

cy|lin|dri|cal /sɪlɪndrɪkᵊl/ ADJ Something that is **cylindrical** is in the shape of a cylinder. ❑ *...a cylindrical aluminium container.* ❑ *It is cylindrical in shape.*

cym|bal /sɪmbᵊl/ (**cymbals**) N-COUNT A **cymbal** is a flat, circular, brass object that is used as a musical instrument. You hit it with a stick or hit two cymbals together, making a loud noise.

cyn|ic /sɪnɪk/ (**cynics**) ◼ N-COUNT A **cynic** is someone who believes that people always act selfishly. ❑ *I have come to be very much of a cynic in these matters.* ◼ → See feature box at **quality**

cyni|cal /sɪnɪkᵊl/ ◼ ADJ If you describe someone as **cynical**, you mean they believe that people always act selfishly. ❑ *...his cynical view of the world.* ● **cyni|cal|ly** ADV [ADV with v] ❑ *The fast-food industry cynically continues to target children.* ◼ ADJ If you are **cynical** about something, you do not believe that it can be successful or that the people involved are honest. ❑ *It's hard not to be cynical about reform.*

cyni|cal|ly /sɪnɪkli/ ■ ADV [usu ADV before v] If you say that someone is **cynically** doing something, you mean they are doing it to benefit themselves and they do not care that they are deceiving, harming, or using people. [DISAPPROVAL] ❏ *He accused the mainstream political parties of cynically exploiting this situation.* ■ → see also **cynical**

cyni|cism /sɪnɪsɪzəm/ ■ N-UNCOUNT **Cynicism** is the belief that people always act selfishly. ❏ *I found Ben's cynicism wearing at times.* ■ N-UNCOUNT **Cynicism** about something is the belief that it cannot be successful or that the people involved are not honorable. ❏ *In an era of growing cynicism about politicians, Mr. Mandela is a model of dignity and integrity.* ■ → See feature box at **quality**

cy|pher /saɪfər/ → see **cipher**

cy|press /saɪprɪs/ (**cypresses**) N-COUNT A **cypress** is a type of conifer.

Cyp|ri|ot /sɪpriət/ (**Cypriots**) ■ ADJ **Cypriot** means belonging or relating to Cyprus, or to its people or culture. ■ N-COUNT A **Cypriot** is a Cypriot citizen, or a person of Cypriot origin.

Cy|ril|lic /sɪrɪlɪk/ also **cyrillic** ADJ [ADJ n] The **Cyrillic** alphabet is the alphabet that is used to write some Slavonic languages, such as Russian and Bulgarian.

cyst /sɪst/ (**cysts**) N-COUNT A **cyst** is a growth containing liquid that appears inside your body or under your skin. ❏ *He had a minor operation to remove a cyst.*

cyst|ic fi|bro|sis /sɪstɪk faɪbroʊsɪs/ N-UNCOUNT **Cystic fibrosis** is a serious disease of the glands which usually affects children and can make breathing difficult.

cys|ti|tis /sɪstaɪtɪs/ N-UNCOUNT **Cystitis** is a bladder infection. [MEDICAL] ❏ *...an attack of cystitis.*

czar /zɑr/ (**czars**) ■ N-COUNT; N-TITLE In former times, the **czar** was the king of Russia. ■ N-COUNT [supp N] A particular kind of **czar** is a person who has been appointed by the government to deal with a particular problem that is affecting the country. ❏ *He promised to appoint an AIDS czar to deal with the disease.*

cza|ri|na /zɑrinə/ (**czarinas**) N-COUNT; N-TITLE In former times, a **czarina** was the queen of Russia or the wife of the czar.

czar|ist /zɑrɪst/ ADJ [usu ADJ n] **Czarist** means belonging to or supporting the system of government by a czar, especially in Russia before 1917.

Czech /tʃɛk/ (**Czechs**) ■ ADJ **Czech** means belonging or relating to the Czech Republic, or to its people, language, or culture. ■ N-COUNT A **Czech** is a Czech citizen, or a person of Czech origin. ■ N-UNCOUNT **Czech** is the language spoken in the Czech Republic.

Czecho|slo|vak /tʃɛkəsloʊvæk, -vɑk/ (**Czechoslovaks**) ■ ADJ [usu ADJ n] **Czechoslovak** means belonging or relating to the former state of Czechoslovakia. ■ N-COUNT A **Czechoslovak** was a Czechoslovak citizen, or a person of Czechoslovak origin.'

Czecho|slo|va|kian /tʃɛkəsləvɑkiən, -vækiən/ (**Czechoslovakians**) ■ ADJ **Czechoslovakian** means the same as **Czechoslovak**. ■ N-COUNT A **Czechoslovakian** was a Czechoslovak citizen, or a person of Czechoslovak origin.

Dd

D also **d** /diː/ (**D's, d's**) N-VAR **D** is the fourth letter of the English alphabet.
d' /-d-/ → see **d'you**
-'d

> Pronounced /-d/ after a vowel sound and /-ɪd/ after a consonant sound.

1 **-'d** is a spoken form of 'had,' especially when 'had' is an auxiliary verb. It is added to the end of the pronoun which is the subject of the verb. For example, 'you had' can be shortened to 'you'd.' **2** **-'d** is a spoken form of 'would.' It is added to the end of the pronoun which is the subject of the verb. For example, 'I would' can be shortened to 'I'd.'
DA /diː eɪ/ (**DAs**) N-COUNT A **DA** is a District Attorney. [AM]
dab /dæb/ (**dabs, dabbing, dabbed**) **1** V-T/V-I If you **dab** something, you touch it several times using quick, light movements. If you **dab** a substance onto a surface, you put it there using quick, light movements. ❑ *She arrived weeping, dabbing her eyes with a tissue.* ❑ *She dabbed iodine on the cuts on her forehead.* **2** N-COUNT A **dab of** something is a small amount of it that is put onto a surface. [INFORMAL] ❑ *...a dab of glue.*
DAB /dæb/ **DAB** is the transmission of digital stereo over conventional radio channels. **DAB** is an abbreviation for **digital audio broadcasting**. ❑ *DAB is the radio system of the 21st century.*
dab|ble /dæbəl/ (**dabbles, dabbling, dabbled**) V-I If you **dabble** in something, you take part in it but not very seriously. ❑ *He dabbled in business.*
dace /deɪs/ (**dace**) N-VAR A **dace** is a type of fish that lives in rivers and lakes.
da|cha /dɑtʃə/ (**dachas**) N-COUNT A **dacha** is a country house in Russia.
dachs|hund /dɑksʊnt/ (**dachshunds**) N-COUNT A **dachshund** is a small dog that has very short legs, a long body, and long ears.

> **WORD HISTORY**
> **dachshund**
> **Dachshund** is a German word meaning *badger-dog*, from *Dachs*, meaning 'badger,' and *Hund*, meaning 'dog.' Dachshunds were originally bred to hunt badgers.

dad ♦◇◇ /dæd/ (**dads**) N-FAMILY Your **dad** is your father. [INFORMAL] ❑ *How do you feel, Dad?*
dad|dy /dædi/ (**daddies**) N-FAMILY Children often call their father **daddy**. [INFORMAL] ❑ *Look at me, Daddy!*
dad|dy long|legs /dædi lɒŋlɛgz/ (**daddy longlegs**) N-COUNT A **daddy longlegs** is a spiderlike insect with a round body and very long thin legs.
daf|fo|dil /dæfədɪl/ (**daffodils**) N-COUNT A **daffodil** is a yellow spring flower with a central part shaped like a tube and a long stem.
daffy /dæfi/ (**daffier, daffiest**) ADJ If you describe a person or thing as **daffy**, you mean that they are strange or foolish, but in an attractive way. [INFORMAL, APPROVAL] ❑ *Daisy called her daffy, but good-hearted.* ❑ *...a daffy storyline.*
dag|ger /dægər/ (**daggers**) N-COUNT A **dagger** is a weapon like a knife with two sharp edges.
dahl|ia /dælyə, dɑl-/ (**dahlias**) N-COUNT A **dahlia** is a flower with a lot of brightly colored petals.
dai|ly ♦◇◇ /deɪli/ **1** ADV [ADV after v] If something happens

daily, it happens every day. ❑ *Cathay Pacific flies daily nonstop to Hong Kong.* • ADJ [ADJ n] **Daily** is also an adjective. ❑ *They held daily press briefings.* **2** ADJ [ADJ n] **Daily** quantities or rates relate to a period of one day. ❑ *...a diet containing adequate daily amounts of fresh fruit.* **3** PHRASE Your **daily life** is the things that you do every day as part of your normal life. ❑ *All of us in our daily life react favorably to people who take us and our views seriously.* **4** → See feature box at **press**
dain|ty /deɪnti/ (**daintier, daintiest**) ADJ If you describe a movement, person, or object as **dainty**, you mean that they are small, delicate, and pretty. ❑ *The girls were dainty and feminine.* • **dain|ti|ly** ADV ❑ *She walked daintily down the steps.*
dai|qui|ri /daɪkɪri, dæk-/ (**daiquiris**) N-COUNT A **daiquiri** is a drink made with rum, lime or lemon juice, sugar, and ice.
dairy /dɛəri/ (**dairies**) **1** N-COUNT A **dairy** is a company that sells milk and food made from milk, such as butter, cream, and cheese. ❑ *In my childhood, local dairies bought milk from local farmers.* **2** ADJ [ADJ n] **Dairy** is used to refer to foods such as butter and cheese that are made from milk. ❑ *He avoids all meat and dairy products.* **3** ADJ [ADJ n] **Dairy** is used to refer to the use of cattle to produce milk rather than meat. ❑ *...a small vegetable and dairy farm.* **4** → See feature box at **nutrition**
dais /deɪɪs/ (**daises**) N-COUNT A **dais** is a raised platform in a hall.
dai|sy /deɪzi/ (**daisies**) N-COUNT A **daisy** is a small wildflower with a yellow center and white petals.

> **WORD HISTORY**
> **daisy**
> **Daisy** comes from Old English *dæges ēage*, meaning 'day's eye.' The flower was given this name because it opens in the daytime and closes at night.

dal /dɑl/ (**dals**) also **dhal** N-VAR **Dal** is an Indian dish made from peas, beans, or lentils.
dale /deɪl/ (**dales**) N-COUNT A **dale** is a valley. [OLD-FASHIONED]
dal|li|ance /dæliəns, dælyəns/ (**dalliances**) **1** N-VAR [oft N with n] If two people have a brief romantic relationship, you can say that they have a **dalliance** with each other, especially if they do not take it seriously. [OLD-FASHIONED] **2** N-COUNT [oft poss N, N with n] Someone's **dalliance** with something is a brief involvement with it. [OLD-FASHIONED] ❑ *...my brief dalliance with higher education.*
dal|ly /dæli/ (**dallies, dallying, dallied**) **1** V-I If you **dally**, you act or move very slowly, wasting time. [OLD-FASHIONED] ❑ *The bureaucrats dallied too long.* ❑ *He did not dally over the choice of a partner.* **2** V-I If someone **dallies** with you, they have a romantic, but not serious, relationship with you. [OLD-FASHIONED] ❑ *His character is a disc jockey who dallies with a female fan.*
Dal|ma|tian /dælmeɪʃən/ (**Dalmatians**) N-COUNT A **Dalmatian** is a large dog with short, smooth, white hair and black or dark brown spots.
dam /dæm/ (**dams**) N-COUNT A **dam** is a wall that is built across a river in order to stop the water from flowing and to make a lake. ❑ *Before the dam was built, Campbell River used to flood in the spring.*
dam|age ♦◇◇ /dæmɪdʒ/ (**damages, damaging, damaged**) **1** V-T To **damage** an object means to break it, spoil it physically, or stop it from working properly. ❑ *He maliciously damaged a car with a baseball bat.* **2** V-T To **damage** something means to cause it to become less good, pleasant, or successful.

...the electoral chaos that damaged Florida's reputation. • **dam|ag|ing** ADJ ❑ The weakened currency could have damaging effects for the economy. ❸ N-UNCOUNT **Damage** is physical harm that is caused to an object. ❑ The blast had serious effects with quite extensive damage to the house. ❹ N-UNCOUNT **Damage** consists of the unpleasant effects that something has on a person, situation, or type of activity. ❑ Incidents of this type cause irreparable damage to relations with the community. ❺ N-PLURAL If a court of law awards **damages** to someone, it orders money to be paid to them by a person who has damaged their reputation or property, or who has injured them. ❑ She is seeking more than $75,000 in damages.

SYNONYMS

damage
VERB
❶
smash: Someone smashed a bottle.
harm: ...a warning that the product may harm the environment.
ruin: Roads and bridges have been destroyed and crops ruined.
devastate: A few days before, a fire had devastated large parts of Windsor Castle.
wreck: He wrecked the garden.
❷
spoil: It's important not to let mistakes spoil your life.
ruin: My wife was ruining her health through worry.
mar: That election was marred by massive cheating.
wreck: His life has been wrecked by the tragedy.

dam|age con|trol N-UNCOUNT **Damage control** is action that is taken to make the bad results of something as small as possible, when it is impossible to avoid bad results completely. [AM] ❑ But Broomfield argues that the long-running case is now an exercise in damage control for the Los Angeles police.

in BRIT, use **damage limitation**

dam|ask /dǽməsk/ (damasks) N-MASS **Damask** is a type of heavy cloth with a pattern woven into it.

dame /deɪm/ (dames) ❶ N-COUNT A **dame** is a woman. This use could cause offense. [AM, INFORMAL, OLD-FASHIONED] ❑ Who does that dame think she is? ❷ N-TITLE **Dame** is a title given to a woman as a special honor because of important service or work that she has done. [BRIT] ❑ ...Dame Judi Dench.

dam|mit /dǽmɪt/ → see damn

damn /dæm/ (damns, damning, damned) ❶ EXCLAM **Damn**, **damn it**, and **dammit** are used by some people to express anger or impatience. [INFORMAL, VULGAR, FEELINGS] ❑ Don't be flippant, damn it! This is serious. ❷ ADJ [ADJ n] **Damn** is used by some people to emphasize what they are saying. [INFORMAL, VULGAR, EMPHASIS] ❑ There's not a damn thing you can do about it now. • ADV [ADV adj/adv] **Damn** is also an adverb. ❑ As it turned out, I was damn right. ❸ V-T If you say that a person or a news report **damns** something such as a policy or action, you mean that they are very critical of it. ❑ ...a sensational book in which she damns the ultra-right party. ❹ → see also **damned, damning** ❺ PHRASE If you say that someone **does not give a damn** about something, you are emphasizing that they do not care about it at all. [INFORMAL, VULGAR, EMPHASIS] ❑ I don't give a damn about the money, Nicole.

dam|nable /dǽmnəbəl/ ADJ [ADJ n] You use **damnable** to emphasize that you dislike or disapprove of something a great deal. [OLD-FASHIONED, VULGAR, EMPHASIS] ❑ What a damnable climate we have! • **dam|nably** /dǽmnəbli/ ADV [ADV adj] ❑ It was damnably unfair that he should suffer so much.

dam|na|tion /dæmneɪʃən/ N-UNCOUNT According to some religions, if someone suffers **damnation**, they have to stay in hell forever after they have died because of their sins. ❑ ...a fear of eternal damnation.

damned /dæmd/ ❶ ADJ [ADJ n] **Damned** is used by some people to emphasize what they are saying, especially when they are angry or frustrated. [INFORMAL, VULGAR, EMPHASIS] ❑ They're a damned nuisance most of the time. • ADV [ADV adj/adv] **Damned** is also an adverb. ❑ We are making a damned good profit, I tell you that. ❷ PHRASE If someone says '**I'm damned if I'm going to do it**' or '**I'll be damned if I'll do it**,' they are emphasizing that they do not intend to do something and think it is

unreasonable for anyone to expect them to do it. [INFORMAL, VULGAR, EMPHASIS] ❑ I was damned if I was going to ask for an explanation and beg to keep my job.

damned|est /dǽmdɪst/ PHRASE [usu PHR to-inf] If you say that you will **do** your **damnedest** to achieve something, you mean that you will try as hard as you can to do it, even though you think that it will take a lot of effort. [INFORMAL, VULGAR] ❑ I did my damnedest to persuade her.

damn fool ADJ [ADJ n] **Damn fool** means 'very stupid.' [AM, INFORMAL, OLD-FASHIONED, VULGAR, EMPHASIS] ❑ What a damn fool thing to do!

damn|ing /dǽmɪŋ/ ADJ If you describe evidence or a report as **damning**, you mean that it suggests very strongly that someone is guilty of a crime or has made a serious mistake. ❑ ...a damning report on safety standards at US space agency NASA.

Damocles /dǽməkliːz/ PHRASE If you say that someone has the **Sword of Damocles** hanging over their head, you mean that they are in a situation in which something very bad could happen to them at any time. [LITERARY]

damp /dæmp/ (damper, dampest, damps, damping, damped) ❶ ADJ Something that is **damp** is slightly wet. ❑ Her hair was still damp. ❑ ...the damp, cold air. ❷ N-UNCOUNT **Damp** is moisture on the inside walls of a house or in the air. ❑ There was damp everywhere and the entire building was in need of rewiring.
▶ **damp down** PHRASAL VERB To **damp down** something such as a strong emotion, an argument, or a crisis means to make it calmer or less intense. ❑ His hand moved to his mouth as he tried to damp down the panic.

damp|en /dǽmpən/ (dampens, dampening, dampened) V-T To **dampen** something such as someone's enthusiasm or excitement means to make it less lively or intense. ❑ Nothing seems to dampen his perpetual enthusiasm. • PHRASAL VERB To **dampen** something **down** means the same as to **dampen** it. ❑ The new penalties were aimed at dampening down consumer spending.

damp|en|er /dǽmpənər/ PHRASE To **put a dampener on** something means the same as to **put a damper on** it. ❑ Boy, did this woman know how to put a dampener on your day.

damp|er /dǽmpər/ (dampers) PHRASE To **put a damper on** something means to have an effect on it which stops it being as enjoyable or as successful as it should be. [INFORMAL] ❑ The cold weather put a damper on our plans.

damp|ness /dǽmpnɪs/ N-UNCOUNT **Dampness** is moisture in the air, or on the surface of something. ❑ It was cooler here, and there was dampness in the air.

dam|sel /dǽmzəl/ (damsels) N-COUNT A **damsel** is a young, unmarried woman. [LITERARY, OLD-FASHIONED] ❑ He keeps coming to the aid of this damsel in distress.

dam|son /dǽmzən/ (damsons) N-COUNT A **damson** is a small, sour, purple plum.

dance ♦♦◇ /dæns/ (dances, dancing, danced) ❶ V-I When you **dance**, you move your body and feet in a way which follows a rhythm, usually in time to music. ❑ Polly had never learned to dance. ❷ V-T If you **dance** a particular kind of dance, you do it or perform it. ❑ Then we put the music on, and we all danced the Charleston. ❸ V-I If you **dance** somewhere, you move there lightly and quickly, usually because you are happy or excited. [LITERARY] ❑ He danced off down the road. ❹ V-I If you say that something **dances**, you mean that it moves around, or seems to move around, lightly and quickly. [LITERARY] ❑ Patterns of light, reflected by the river, dance along the base of the cliffs. ❺ N-COUNT A **dance** is a particular series of graceful movements of your body and feet, which you usually do in time to music. ❑ Sometimes the people doing this dance hold brightly colored scarves. ❻ N-COUNT A **dance** is a social event where people dance with each other. ❑ At the school dance he sat and talked to her all evening. ❼ V-RECIP When you **dance** with someone, the two of you take part in a dance together, as partners. You can also say that two people **dance**. ❑ It's a terrible thing when nobody wants to dance with you. ❑ Shall we dance? • N-COUNT **Dance** is also a noun. ❑ Come and have a dance with me. ❽ N-UNCOUNT **Dance** is the activity of performing dances, as a public entertainment or an art form. ❑ Their contribution to international dance, drama and music is inestimable.

dance floor (dance floors) N-COUNT In a restaurant or night club, the **dance floor** is the area where people can dance. ❏ *Everybody is on the dance floor with the men forming a circle around the women.*

dance hall (dance halls) N-COUNT **Dance halls** were large rooms or buildings where people used to pay to go and dance, usually in the evening. [OLD-FASHIONED]

danc|er /dænsər/ (dancers) **1** N-COUNT A **dancer** is a person who earns money by dancing, or a person who is dancing. ❏ *His girlfriend was a dancer with the New York City Ballet.* **2** N-COUNT If you say that someone is a good **dancer** or a bad **dancer**, you are saying how well or badly they can dance. ❏ *He was the best dancer in LA.*

dance stu|dio (dance studios) N-COUNT A **dance studio** is a place where people pay to learn how to dance.

danc|ing ✦✧✧ /dænsɪŋ/ N-UNCOUNT When people dance for enjoyment or to entertain others, you can refer to this activity as **dancing**. ❏ *All the schools have music and dancing as part of the curriculum.* ❏ *Let's go dancing tonight.*

dan|de|lion /dændɪlaɪən/ (dandelions) N-COUNT A **dandelion** is a wild plant which has yellow flowers with lots of thin petals. When the petals of each flower drop off, a fluffy white ball of seeds grows.

dan|druff /dændrəf/ N-UNCOUNT **Dandruff** is small white pieces of dead skin in someone's hair, or fallen from someone's hair. ❏ *He has very bad dandruff.*

dan|dy /dændi/ (dandies) **1** N-COUNT A **dandy** is someone who thinks a great deal about their appearance and always dresses in fashionable clothes. **2** ADJ If you say that something is **dandy**, you mean it is good or just right. [AM, INFORMAL, OLD-FASHIONED]

Dane /deɪn/ (Danes) N-COUNT A **Dane** is a person who comes from Denmark.

dan|ger ✦✦✧ /deɪndʒər/ (dangers) **1** N-UNCOUNT **Danger** is the possibility that someone may be harmed or killed. ❏ *My friends endured tremendous danger in order to help me.* **2** N-COUNT A **danger** is something or someone that can hurt or harm you. ❏ *...the dangers of smoking.* **3** N-SING If there is a **danger** that something unpleasant will happen, it is possible that it will happen. ❏ *There is a real danger that some people will no longer be able to afford insurance.* ❏ *There was no danger that any of these groups would be elected to power.* **4** PHRASE If someone who has been seriously ill is **out of danger**, they are still ill, but they are not expected to die. ❏ *There is some risk of the lung collapsing again, but he is out of danger.*

dan|ger|ous ✦✦✧ /deɪndʒərəs, deɪndʒrəs/ ADJ If something is **dangerous**, it is able or likely to hurt or harm you. ❏ *It's a dangerous stretch of road.* ❏ *...dangerous drugs.* • **dan|ger|ous|ly** ADV ❏ *He is dangerously ill.*

dan|gle /dæŋgəl/ (dangles, dangling, dangled) **1** V-T/V-I If something **dangles** from somewhere or if you **dangle** it somewhere, it hangs or swings loosely. ❏ *A gold bracelet dangled from his left wrist.* **2** V-T If you say that someone **is dangling** something attractive before you, you mean they are offering it to you in order to try to influence you in some way. ❏ *They dangle hope in front of our eyes, then snatch it clear away.*

Dan|ish /deɪnɪʃ/ **1** ADJ **Danish** means belonging or relating to Denmark, its people, its language, or culture. **2** N-UNCOUNT **Danish** is the language spoken in Denmark. **3** N-COUNT A **Danish** or a **danish** is the same as a **Danish pastry**.

Dan|ish pas|try (Danish pastries) N-COUNT **Danish pastries** are cakes made from sweet pastry. They are often filled with things such as apple or almond paste.

dank /dæŋk/ ADJ A **dank** place, especially an underground place such as a cave, is unpleasantly damp and cold. ❏ *The kitchen was dank and cheerless.*

dap|per /dæpər/ ADJ A man who is **dapper** has a very neat and clean appearance, and always looks smart. ❏ *...a dapper little man.*

dap|pled /dæpəld/ ADJ [ADJ n, v-link ADJ with/by/in n] You use **dappled** to describe something that has dark or light patches on it, or that is made up of patches of light and shade. ❏ *...a dappled horse.* ❏ *The path was dappled with sunlight.*

dare ✦✧✧ /dɛər/ (dares, daring, dared)

> **Dare** sometimes behaves like an ordinary verb, for example, 'He dared to speak' and 'He doesn't dare to speak' and sometimes like a modal, for example, 'He dare not speak.'

1 V-T If you do not **dare** to do something, you do not have enough courage to do it, or you do not want to do it because you fear the consequences. If you **dare** to do something, you do something which requires a lot of courage. ❏ *Most people hate David but they don't dare to say so.* • MODAL **Dare** is also a modal. ❏ *Dare she risk staying where she was?* ❏ *The yen is weakening. But Tokyo dare not raise its interest rates again.* **2** V-T If you **dare** someone to do something, you challenge them to prove that they are not frightened of doing it. ❏ *Over coffee, she lit a cigarette, her eyes daring him to comment.* **3** N-COUNT A **dare** is a challenge which one person gives to another to do something dangerous or frightening. ❏ *Jones broke into a military base on a dare.* **4** PHRASE If you say to someone **'don't you dare'** do something, you are telling them not to do it and letting them know that you are angry. [SPOKEN, FEELINGS] ❏ *Allen, don't you dare go anywhere else, you hear?* **5** PHRASE You say **'how dare you'** when you are very shocked and angry about something that someone has done. [SPOKEN, FEELINGS] ❏ *How dare you pick up the phone and listen in on my conversations!* **6** PHRASE You can use **'I daresay'** or **'I dare say'** before or after a statement to indicate that you believe it is probably true. ❏ *I daresay that the computer would provide a clear answer to that.*

dare|devil /dɛərdɛvəl/ (daredevils) **1** ADJ [ADJ n] **Daredevil** people enjoy doing physically dangerous things. ❏ *A new circus is in town, with Siberian white tigers and daredevil bikers.* • N-COUNT **Daredevil** is also a noun. ❏ *He was a daredevil when young.* **2** ADJ [ADJ n] You use **daredevil** to describe actions that are physically dangerous and require courage. ❏ *The show's full of daredevil feats.*

dare|say /dɛərseɪ/ → see dare 6

dar|ing /dɛərɪŋ/ **1** ADJ People who are **daring** are willing to do or say things which are new or which might shock or anger other people. ❏ *Bergit was probably more daring than I was.* **2** ADJ A **daring** person is willing to do things that might be dangerous. ❏ *His daring rescue saved the lives of the youngsters.* **3** N-UNCOUNT **Daring** is the courage to do things which might be dangerous or which might shock or anger other people. ❏ *His daring may have cost him his life.*

dark ✦✦✧ /dɑrk/ (darker, darkest) **1** ADJ When it is **dark**, there is not enough light to see properly, for example, because it is night. ❏ *It was too dark inside to see much.* ❏ *People usually draw the curtains once it gets dark.* • **dark|ness** N-UNCOUNT ❏ *The light went out, and the room was plunged into darkness.* • **dark|ly** ADV [ADV -ed] ❏ *In a darkly lit, seedy dance hall, hundreds of men lounge around small tables.* **2** ADJ If you describe something as **dark**, you mean that it is black in color, or a shade that is close to black. ❏ *He wore a dark suit and carried a black attaché case.* • **dark|ly** ADV ❏ *The freckles on Joanne's face suddenly stood out darkly against her pale skin.* **3** ADJ If someone has **dark** hair, eyes, or skin, they have brown or black hair, eyes, or skin. ❏ *He had dark, curly hair.* **4** ADJ A **dark** period of time is unpleasant or frightening. ❏ *Once again there's talk of very dark days ahead.* **5** ADJ [ADJ n] A **dark** place or area is mysterious and not fully known about. ❏ *The spacecraft will enable scientists to study some dark corners of the solar system.* **6** ADJ **Dark** thoughts are sad, and show that you are expecting something unpleasant to happen. [LITERARY] ❏ *Troy's endless happy chatter kept me from thinking dark thoughts.* • **dark|ly** ADV [ADV with v] ❏ *She hinted darkly that she might have to resign.* **7** ADJ If you describe something as **dark**, you mean that it is related to things that are serious or unpleasant, rather than lighthearted. ❏ *There's plenty of dark humor in the movie.* • **dark|ly** ADV [ADV adj] ❏ *The afternoon after Wednesday's debut was as darkly comic as the movie itself.* **8** N-SING **The dark** is the lack of light in a place. ❏ *I've always been afraid of the dark.* **9** COMB IN COLOR When you use **dark** to describe a color, you are referring to a shade of that color which is close to black, or seems to have some black in it. ❏ *She was wearing a dark blue dress.* **10** PHRASE If you do something **after dark**, you do it when the sun has set and night has begun. ❏ *They avoid going out alone after dark.* **11** PHRASE If you do something **before dark**, you do it before the sun sets and night begins. ❏ *They'll be back well before dark.*

dark age ⓬ PHRASE If you are **in the dark** about something, you do not know anything about it. ◻ *The investigators admit that they are completely in the dark about the killing.*

dark age (dark ages) also **Dark Age** ❶ N-COUNT If you refer to a period in the history of a society as a **dark age**, you think that it is characterized by a lack of knowledge and progress. [WRITTEN, DISAPPROVAL] ◻ *The Education Secretary accuses teachers of wanting to return to a dark age.* ❷ N-PROPER [the N] **The Dark Ages** are the period of European history between about AD 500 and about AD 1000.

dark cho|co|late N-UNCOUNT **Dark chocolate** is dark brown chocolate that has a stronger and less sweet taste than milk chocolate. [mainly AM] ◻ *I don't like dark chocolate.*

> in BRIT, also use **plain chocolate**

dark|en /dɑrkən/ (darkens, darkening, darkened) ❶ V-T/V-I If something **darkens** or if a person or thing **darkens** it, it becomes darker. ◻ *The sky darkened abruptly.* ❷ V-T/V-I If someone's mood **darkens** or if something **darkens** their mood, they suddenly become unhappy. [LITERARY] ◻ *My sunny mood suddenly darkened.*

dark|ened /dɑrkənd/ ADJ [ADJ n] A **darkened** building or room has no lights on inside it. ◻ *He drove past darkened houses.*

dark glasses N-PLURAL [also *a pair of* N] **Dark glasses** are glasses which have dark-colored lenses to protect your eyes in the sun.

dark horse (dark horses) N-COUNT If you describe someone as a **dark horse**, you mean that people know very little about them, although they may have recently had success or may be about to have success.

dark mat|ter ❶ N-UNCOUNT **Dark matter** is material that is believed to form a large part of the universe, but which has never been seen. ❷ → See feature box at **space**

dark|room /dɑrkrum/ (darkrooms) N-COUNT A **darkroom** is a room which can be sealed off from natural light and is lit only by red light. It is used for developing photographs.

dar|ling /dɑrlɪŋ/ (darlings) ❶ N-VOC You call someone **darling** if you love them or like them very much. [FEELINGS] ◻ *Thank you, darling.* ❷ ADJ [ADJ n] Some people use **darling** to describe someone or something that they love or like very much. [INFORMAL] ◻ *To have a darling baby boy was the greatest gift I could imagine.* ❸ N-COUNT If you describe someone as a **darling**, you are fond of them and think that they are nice. [INFORMAL] ◻ *He's such a darling.*

darn /dɑrn/ (darns, darning, darned) ❶ V-T If you **darn** something knitted or made of cloth, you repair a hole in it by sewing stitches across the hole and then weaving stitches in and out of them. ◻ *Aunt Emilie darned old socks.* ❷ ADJ [ADJ n] People sometimes use **darn** or **darned** to emphasize what they are saying, often when they are annoyed. [INFORMAL, EMPHASIS] ◻ *There's not a darn thing he can do about it.* • ADV [ADV adj/adv] **Darn** is also an adverb. ◻ *...the desire to be free to do just as we darn well please.* ❸ PHRASE You can say **I'll be darned** to show that you are very surprised about something. [AM, INFORMAL, FEELINGS] ◻ *"A talking pig!" he exclaimed. "Well, I'll be darned."*

dart /dɑrt/ (darts, darting, darted) ❶ V-I If a person or animal **darts** somewhere, they move there suddenly and quickly. [WRITTEN] ◻ *Ingrid darted across the deserted street.* ❷ V-T/V-I If you **dart** a look at someone or something, or if your eyes **dart** to them, you look at them very quickly. [LITERARY] ◻ *She darted a sly sideways glance at Bramwell.* ❸ N-COUNT A **dart** is a small, narrow object with a sharp point which can be thrown or shot. ◻ *Markov died after being struck by a poison dart.* ❹ N-UNCOUNT **Darts** is a game in which you throw darts at a round board which has numbers on it. ◻ *I started playing darts at 15.*

dart|board /dɑrtbɔrd/ (dartboards) N-COUNT A **dartboard** is a circular board with numbers on it which is used as the target in a game of darts.

dash /dæʃ/ (dashes, dashing, dashed) ❶ V-I If you **dash** somewhere, you run or go there quickly and suddenly. ◻ *Suddenly she dashed down to the cellar.* • N-SING **Dash** is also a noun. ◻ *...a 160-mile dash to the hospital.* ❷ V-I [no cont] If you say that you have to **dash**, you mean that you are in a hurry and have to leave immediately. [INFORMAL] ◻ *Oh, Tim! I'm sorry but I have to dash.* ❸ V-T If you **dash** something against a wall or other surface, you throw or push it violently, often so hard that it breaks. [LITERARY] ◻ *She seized the doll and dashed it against the stone wall with tremendous force.* ❹ V-T If an event or person **dashes** someone's hopes or expectations, it destroys them by making it impossible that the thing that is hoped for or expected will ever happen. [LITERARY, JOURNALISM] ◻ *Renewed fighting has dashed hopes for a United Nations-organized interim government.* ❺ N-COUNT A **dash** of something is a small quantity of it which you add when you are preparing food or mixing a drink. ◻ *Pour over olive oil and a dash of balsamic vinegar to accentuate the sweetness.* ❻ N-COUNT A **dash** of a quality is a small amount of it that is found in something and often makes it more interesting or distinctive. ◻ *...a story with a dash of mystery thrown in.* ❼ N-COUNT A **dash** is a straight, horizontal line used in writing, for example, to separate two main clauses whose meanings are closely connected. ◻ *...the dash between the birth date and death date.* ❽ N-COUNT The **dash** of a car is its dashboard. ❾ PHRASE If you **make a dash for** a place, you run there very quickly, for example, to escape from someone or something. ◻ *I made a dash for the front door but he got there before me.*

▸ **dash off** ❶ PHRASAL VERB If you **dash off** to a place, you go there very quickly. ◻ *He dashed off to lunch at the Hard Rock Cafe.* ❷ PHRASAL VERB If you **dash off** a piece of writing, you write or compose it very quickly, without thinking about it very much. ◻ *He dashed off a couple of novels.*

dash|board /dæʃbɔrd/ (dashboards) N-COUNT The **dashboard** in a car is the panel facing the driver's seat where most of the instruments and switches are. ◻ *The clock on the dashboard said it was five to two.*

dash|cam /dæʃkæm/ (dashcams) N-COUNT A **dashcam** is a small video camera on the dashboard of a vehicle, that is used to record the view through the windshield. ◻ *The action was captured on a dashcam by another driver.*

dash|ing /dæʃɪŋ/ ADJ A **dashing** person or thing is very stylish and attractive. [OLD-FASHIONED] ◻ *He was the very model of the dashing Air Force pilot.*

das|tard|ly /dæstərdli/ ❶ ADJ [ADJ n] If you describe an action as **dastardly**, you mean it is wicked and intended to hurt someone. [OLD-FASHIONED] ❷ ADJ [ADJ n] If you describe a person as **dastardly**, you mean they are wicked. [OLD-FASHIONED]

DAT /dæt/ N-UNCOUNT **DAT** is a type of magnetic tape used to make very high-quality recordings of sound by recording it in digital form. **DAT** is an abbreviation for **digital audio tape**.

da|ta ◆◆◇ /deɪtə, dætə/

> **datum** is sometimes used as the singular form of **data**.

❶ N-PLURAL; N-UNCOUNT You can refer to information as **data**, especially when it is in the form of facts or statistics that you can analyze. ◻ *The study was based on data from 2,100 women.* ❷ N-UNCOUNT **Data** is information that can be stored and used by a computer program. [COMPUTING] ◻ *This system uses powerful microchips to compress huge amounts of data onto a CD-ROM.* ❸ → See feature box at **global warming**

SYNONYMS

data
NOUN ❶
facts: *His opponent swamped him with facts and figures.*
figures: *New government figures predict that one in two marriages will end in divorce.*
statistics: *Official statistics show real wages declining by 24%.*

---

da|ta bank (data banks) also **databank** N-COUNT A **data bank** is the same as a **database**.

data|base /deɪtəbeɪs, dætə-/ (databases) also **data base** ❶ N-COUNT A **database** is a collection of data that is stored in a computer and that can easily be used and added to. ◻ *The state maintains a database of names of people allowed to vote.* ❷ → See feature box at **research**

da|ta en|try N-UNCOUNT [oft N n] **Data entry** is the activity of putting data into a computer, for example, by using a keyboard. ◻ *...the first Palm computer with a built-in keyboard for easy data entry.* ◻ *...data-entry clerks.*

da|ta min|ing N-UNCOUNT **Data mining** involves collecting information from data stored in a database, for example, in order to find out about people's shopping habits. [COMPUTING] ❑ *Data mining is used to analyze individuals' buying habits.*

da|ta pro|cess|ing N-UNCOUNT **Data processing** is the series of operations that are carried out on data, especially by computers, in order to present, interpret, or obtain information. ❑ *Taylor's company makes data-processing systems.*

da|ta sci|ence N-UNCOUNT **Data science** is the scientific analysis of large amounts of information held on computers, done for example in order to learn about people's shopping or voting behavior. ❑ *The social network has its own in-house team working on data science.*

date ◆◆◇ /deɪt/ (**dates, dating, dated**) **1** N-COUNT A **date** is a specific time that can be named, for example, a particular day or a particular year. ❑ *What's the date today?* **2** N-COUNT A **date** is an appointment to meet someone or go out with them, especially someone with whom you are having, or may soon have, a romantic relationship. ❑ *I have a date with Bob.* **3** V-RECIP If you **are dating** someone, you go out with them regularly because you are having, or may soon have, a romantic relationship with them. You can also say that two people **are dating**. ❑ *For a year I dated a woman who was a research assistant.* **4** N-COUNT If you have a date with someone with whom you are having, or may soon have, a romantic relationship, you can refer to that person as your **date**. ❑ *He lied to Essie, saying his date was one of the girls in the show.* **5** N-COUNT A **date** is a small, dark-brown, sticky fruit with a stone inside. Dates grow on palm trees in hot countries. **6** V-T If you **date** something, you give or discover the date when it was made or when it began. ❑ *I think we can date the decline of Western Civilization quite precisely.* **7** V-T When you **date** something such as a letter or a check, you write that day's date on it. ❑ *Once the decision is reached, he can date and sign the sheet.* **8** V-I If something **dates**, it goes out of fashion and becomes unacceptable to modern tastes. ❑ *Blue and white is the classic color combination for bathrooms. It always looks smart and will never date.* **9** → see also **dated, out of date 10** PHRASE **To date** means up until the present time. ❑ *"Dottie" is by far his best novel to date.*
▶ **date back** PHRASAL VERB If something **dates back** to a particular time, it started or was made at that time. ❑ *The issue is not a new one. It dates back to the 1930s at least.*

dat|ed /ˈdeɪtɪd/ **1** ADJ **Dated** things or ideas seem old-fashioned, although they may once have been fashionable or modern. ❑ *Many of his ideas have value, but some are dated and others are plain wrong.* **2** → See feature box at **upcycle**

date of birth (**dates of birth**) N-COUNT Your **date of birth** is the exact date on which you were born, including the year. ❑ *The registration form showed his date of birth as August 2, 1979.*

date palm (**date palms**) N-COUNT A **date palm** is a palm tree on which dates grow.

date rape N-UNCOUNT **Date rape** is a crime in which someone rapes another person they have met socially.

da|ting /ˈdeɪtɪŋ/ ADJ [ADJ n] **Dating** agencies are for people who are trying to find a girlfriend or boyfriend. ❑ *I joined a dating agency.*

da|tive /ˈdeɪtɪv/ N-SING [the N] In the grammar of some languages, for example, Latin, the **dative**, or the **dative** case, is the case used for a noun when it is the indirect object of a verb, or when it comes after some prepositions.

da|tum /ˈdeɪtəm, ˈdætəm/ N-SING **Datum** is the singular form of **data**. → see **data 1**

daub /dɔb/ (**daubs, daubing, daubed**) V-T When you **daub** a substance such as mud or paint on something, you spread it on that thing in a rough or careless way. ❑ *The makeup woman had been daubing mock blood on Jeremy Fox when last he'd seen her.*

daugh|ter ◆◆◆ /ˈdɔtər/ (**daughters**) N-COUNT Someone's **daughter** is their female child. ❑ *Flora and her daughter Catherine.* ❑ *...the daughter of a university professor.*

daughter-in-law (**daughters-in-law**) N-COUNT Someone's **daughter-in-law** is the wife of their son.

daunt /dɔnt/ (**daunts, daunting, daunted**) V-T If something **daunts** you, it makes you feel slightly afraid or worried about dealing with it. ❑ *a grueling trip that would have daunted a woman half her age.* ● **daunt|ed** ADJ [v-link ADJ] ❑ *It is hard to pick up such a book and not to feel a little daunted.*

daunt|ing /ˈdɔntɪŋ/ **1** ADJ Something that is **daunting** makes you feel slightly afraid or worried about dealing with it. ❑ *He and his wife Jane were faced with the daunting task of restoring the gardens to their former splendor.* **2** → See feature box at **challenge**

daunt|less /ˈdɔntlɪs/ ADJ A **dauntless** person is brave and confident and not easily frightened. [LITERARY] ❑ *...their dauntless courage.*

dau|phin /ˈdɔfɪn, doʊˈfæn/ also **Dauphin** N-SING [the N] In former times, the king and queen of France's oldest son was called the **dauphin**.

daw|dle /ˈdɔdəl/ (**dawdles, dawdling, dawdled**) V-I If you **dawdle**, you spend more time than is necessary going somewhere. ❑ *Eleanor will be back any moment, if she doesn't dawdle.*

dawn /dɔn/ (**dawns, dawning, dawned**) **1** N-VAR **Dawn** is the time of day when light first appears in the sky, just before the sun rises. ❑ *Nancy woke at dawn.* **2** N-SING The **dawn** of a period of time or a situation is the beginning of it. [LITERARY] ❑ *...the dawn of the radio age.* **3** V-I If something **is dawning**, it is beginning to develop or come into existence. [WRITTEN] ❑ *A new century was dawning.* ● **dawn|ing** N-SING ❑ *...the dawning of the space age.*
▶ **dawn on** also **dawn upon** PHRASAL VERB If a fact or idea **dawns on** you, you realize it. ❑ *It gradually dawned on me that I still had talent and ought to run again.*

dawn raid (**dawn raids**) N-COUNT If police officers carry out a **dawn raid**, they go to someone's house very early in the morning to search it or arrest them. ❑ *The dawn raids Tuesday were carried out by about 170 police officers.*

day ◆◆◆ /deɪ/ (**days**) **1** N-COUNT A **day** is one of the seven twenty-four hour periods of time in a week. ❑ *And it has snowed almost every day for the past week.* **2** N-COUNT You can refer to a particular period in history as a particular **day** or as particular **days**. ❑ *He began to talk about the Ukraine of his uncle's day.* ❑ *...his early days of struggle and deep poverty.* **3** it is **early days** → see **early 4** at the end of the day → see end ① **5** the good old days → see old **6** N-VAR **Day** is the time when it is light, or the time when you are up and doing things. ❑ *Twenty-seven million working days are lost each year due to work accidents and sickness.* ❑ *She gives herself one day a week off, on Thursdays.* **7** PHRASE If something happens **day after day**, it happens every day without stopping. ❑ *The newspaper job had me doing the same thing day after day.* **8** PHRASE [V PHR] If you say that something happens **day in, day out** or **day in and day out**, you mean that it happens regularly over a long period of time. ❑ *I used to drink coffee day in, day out.* **9** PHRASE **In this day and age** means in modern times. ❑ *Even in this day and age the old attitudes persist.* **10** PHRASE If you say that something **has seen better days**, you mean that it is old and in poor condition. ❑ *The tweed jacket she wore had seen better days.* **11** PHRASE If you **call it a day**, you decide to stop what you are doing because you are tired of it or because it is not successful. ❑ *Faced with mounting debts, the decision to call it a day was inevitable.* **12** PHRASE If something **makes** your **day**, it makes you feel very happy. [INFORMAL] ❑ *Come on, Bill. Send Tom a card and make his day.* **13** PHRASE **One day** or **some day** or **one of these days** means at some time in the future. ❑ *I too dreamed of living in Dallas one day.* ❑ *I hope some day you will find the woman who will make you happy.* **14** PHRASE If you say that something happened **the other day**, you mean that it happened a few days ago. ❑ *I phoned your office the other day.* **15** PHRASE If someone or something **saves the day** in a situation which seems likely to fail, they manage to make it successful. ❑ *...this story about how he saved the day at his daughter's birthday party.* **16** PHRASE If something happens **from day to day** or **day by day**, it happens each day. ❑ *Your needs can differ from day to day.* **17** PHRASE If it is a month or a year **to the day** since a particular thing happened, it is exactly a month or a year since it happened. ❑ *It was January 19, a year to the day since he had arrived in Singapore.* **18** PHRASE **To this day** means up until and including the present time. ❑ *The controversy continues to this day.* **19** PHRASE If you say that a task is **all in a day's work** for someone, you mean that they do not mind doing it although it may be difficult, because it is part of their job or because they often do it. ❑ *For war reporters, dodging snipers' bullets is all in a day's work.* ⓴ **your day in court** → see **court** ①

-day /-deɪ/ COMB IN ADJ You use **-day** with a number to indicate how long something lasts. ❑ *The Sudanese leader has left for a two-day visit to Zambia.*

day|break /deɪbreɪk/ N-UNCOUNT **Daybreak** is the time in the morning when light first appears. ❑ *Pedro got up every morning before daybreak.*

day care also **daycare** N-UNCOUNT **Day care** is care that is provided during the day for people who cannot take care of themselves, such as small children, old people, or people who are ill. Day care is provided by paid workers. ❑ *She had to contend with day care for her 2-year-old twins being canceled.* ❑ *...a daycare center for elderly people.*

day|dream /deɪdriːm/ (daydreams, daydreaming, daydreamed) ❶ V-I If you **daydream**, you think about pleasant things for a period of time, usually about things that you would like to happen. ❑ *Do you work hard for success rather than daydream about it?* ❑ *He daydreams of being a famous journalist.* ❷ N-COUNT A **daydream** is a series of pleasant thoughts, usually about things that you would like to happen. ❑ *He learned to escape into daydreams of handsome men and beautiful women.*

Day-Glo /deɪ gloʊ/ N-UNCOUNT [usu N n] **Day-Glo** colors are shades of orange, pink, green, and yellow which are so bright that they seem to glow. [TRADEMARK]

day job (day jobs) ❶ N-COUNT Your **day job** is the main job that you do when you are also trying make a career in another field, especially as a singer or an actor. ❑ *Because the band made little money, the members had day jobs to get by.* ❷ PHRASE If someone tells you **not to give up the day job**, they are saying that they think you should continue doing what you are good at, rather than trying something new which they think you will fail at. [HUMOROUS]

day|light /deɪlaɪt/ ❶ N-UNCOUNT **Daylight** is the natural light that there is during the day, before it gets dark. ❑ *Lack of daylight can make people feel depressed.* ❷ N-UNCOUNT **Daylight** is the time of day when it begins to get light. ❑ *Quinn returned shortly after daylight yesterday morning.* ❸ PHRASE If you say that a crime is committed **in broad daylight**, you are expressing your surprise that it is done during the day when people can see it, rather than at night. [EMPHASIS] ❑ *A girl was attacked on a train in broad daylight.*

day|lights /deɪlaɪts/ ❶ PHRASE If you **knock the living daylights out of** someone, or **beat the living daylights out of** them, you hit them very hard many times. [INFORMAL] ❷ PHRASE If someone or something **scares the living daylights out of** you, they make you feel extremely scared. [INFORMAL]

day|light sav|ing time also **daylight savings time, daylight savings** N-UNCOUNT **Daylight saving time** is a period of time in the summer when the clocks are set one hour forward, so that people can have extra light in the evening. [AM]

in BRIT, use **British Summer Time**

day|long /deɪlɒŋ/ also **day-long** ADJ [ADJ n] **Daylong** is used to describe an event or activity that lasts for the whole of one day. [mainly AM] ❑ *...a daylong meeting.*

day nurs|ery (day nurseries) N-COUNT A **day nursery** is a place where children who are too young to go to school can be left all day while their parents are at work. [BRIT]

day off (days off) N-COUNT A **day off** is a day when you do not go to work, even though it is usually a working day. ❑ *It was Mrs. Dearden's day off, and Paul was on duty in her place.*

day of reck|on|ing N-SING [usu the N] If someone talks about the **day of reckoning**, they mean a day or time in the future when people will be forced to deal with an unpleasant situation which they have avoided until now. ❑ *To some union members, the new deal simply delayed the day of reckoning.*

day one N-SING If something happens from **day one** of a process, it happens right from the beginning. If it happens on **day one**, it happens right at the beginning. ❑ *"It's been a battle from day one," Burrell said.*

day re|turn (day returns) N-COUNT A **day return** is a train or bus ticket which allows you to go somewhere and come back on the same day for a lower price than an ordinary return ticket. [BRIT]

in AM, use **round-trip ticket**

day|room (dayrooms) also **day room** N-COUNT A **dayroom** is a room in a hospital where patients can sit and relax during the day.

day school (day schools) N-COUNT A **day school** is a school where the students go home every evening and do not live at the school. Compare **boarding school**.

day|time /deɪtaɪm/ ❶ N-SING [the N, also no det] The **daytime** is the part of a day between the time when it gets light and the time when it gets dark. ❑ *In the daytime he stayed up in his room, sleeping, or listening to music.* ❷ ADJ [ADJ n] **Daytime** television and radio is broadcast during the morning and afternoon on weekdays. ❑ *She took on the role as host of a daytime TV show.*

day-to-day ADJ [ADJ n] **Day-to-day** things or activities exist or happen every day as part of ordinary life. ❑ *I am a vegetarian and use a lot of lentils in my day-to-day cooking.*

day trad|er (day traders) N-COUNT In the stock market, **day traders** are traders who buy and sell particular securities on the same day. [BUSINESS] ❑ *Unlike the day traders, they tended to hold on to stocks for days and weeks, sometimes even months.*

day trip (day trips) also **day-trip** N-COUNT A **day trip** is a trip to a place and back again on the same day, usually for pleasure.

daze /deɪz/ N-SING If someone is in a **daze**, they are feeling confused and unable to think clearly, often because they have had a shock or surprise. ❑ *For an hour I was walking around in a daze.*

dazed /deɪzd/ ADJ If someone is **dazed**, they are confused and unable to think clearly, often because of shock or a blow to the head. ❑ *At the end of the interview I was dazed and exhausted.*

daz|zle /dæzəl/ (dazzles, dazzling, dazzled) ❶ V-T If someone or something **dazzles** you, you are extremely impressed by their skill, qualities, or beauty. ❑ *George dazzled her with his knowledge of the world.* ❷ V-T If a bright light **dazzles** you, it makes you unable to see properly for a short time. ❑ *The sun, glinting from the pool, dazzled me.* ❸ N-SING The **dazzle** of something is a quality it has, such as beauty or skill, which is impressive and attractive. ❑ *The dazzle of stardom and status attracts them.*

dazz|ling /dæzlɪŋ/ ❶ ADJ Something that is **dazzling** is very impressive or beautiful. ❑ *He gave Alberg a dazzling smile.* • **dazz|ling|ly** ADV ❑ *The view was dazzlingly beautiful.* ❷ ADJ A **dazzling** light is very bright and makes you unable to see properly for a short time. ❑ *He shielded his eyes against the dazzling declining sun.* • **dazz|ling|ly** ADV [ADV adj] ❑ *The loading bay seemed dazzlingly bright.* ❸ → See feature box at **light**

DC /di si/ N-UNCOUNT **DC** is used to refer to an electric current that always flows in the same direction. **DC** is an abbreviation for **direct current**.

D-day N-UNCOUNT You can use **D-day** to refer to the day of an important occasion or the beginning of an important activity. ❑ *This is D-day, time for the Walt Disney Co. shareholders' meeting.*

DDT /di di ti/ N-UNCOUNT **DDT** is a poisonous substance used for killing insects.

PREFIX

de-
is added to some verbs to make verbs that mean the opposite. For example, if something **degenerates**, it becomes weaker.

---

dea|con /diːkən/ (deacons) ❶ N-COUNT A **deacon** is a member of the clergy, for example, in the Episcopal or Roman Catholic Church, who is lower in rank than a priest. ❷ N-COUNT A **deacon** is a person who is not ordained but who assists the minister in some Protestant churches.

de|ac|ti|vate /diæktɪveɪt/ (deactivates, deactivating, deactivated) V-T If someone **deactivates** an explosive device or an alarm, they make it harmless or impossible to operate. ❑ *They agreed to deactivate some of their deadliest missiles.*

dead /dɛd/ **1** ADJ A person, animal, or plant that is **dead** is no longer living. ❑ *"You're a widow?"—"Yes. My husband's been dead a year now."* ❑ *The group had shot dead another hostage.* • N-PLURAL **The dead** are people who are dead. ❑ *Two American soldiers were among the dead.* **2** ADJ If you describe a place or a period of time as **dead**, you do not like it because there is very little activity taking place in it. [DISAPPROVAL] ❑ *...some dead little town where the liveliest thing is the flies.* **3** ADJ Something that is **dead** is no longer being used or is finished. ❑ *The dead cigarette was still between his fingers.* **4** ADJ If you say that an idea, plan, or subject is **dead**, you mean that people are no longer interested in it or willing to develop it any further. ❑ *It's a dead issue, Baxter.* **5** ADJ A telephone or piece of electrical equipment that is **dead** is no longer functioning, for example, because it no longer has any electrical power. ❑ *On another occasion I answered the phone and the line went dead.* **6** ADJ [ADJ n] **Dead** is used to mean 'complete' or 'absolute,' especially before the words 'center,' 'silence,' and 'stop.' [EMPHASIS] ❑ *They hurried about in dead silence, with anxious faces.* **7** ADV [ADV prep/adv/adj] **Dead** means 'precisely' or 'exactly.' [EMPHASIS] ❑ *Mars was visible, dead in the center of the telescope.* **8** CONVENTION If you reply '**Over my dead body**' when a plan or action has been suggested, you are emphasizing that you dislike it, and will do everything you can to prevent it. [INFORMAL, EMPHASIS] ❑ *"Let's invite her to dinner."—"Over my dead body!"* **9** PHRASE If you say that a person or animal **dropped dead** or **dropped down dead**, you mean that they died very suddenly and unexpectedly. ❑ *He dropped dead of a heart attack.* **10** PHRASE If you say that you **feel dead** or **are half dead**, you mean that you feel very tired or ill and very weak. [INFORMAL, EMPHASIS] ❑ *I thought you looked half dead at dinner, and who could blame you after that trip.* **11** PHRASE If something happens **in the dead of night**, **at dead of night**, or **in the dead of winter**, it happens in the middle part of the night or the winter, when it is darkest or coldest. [LITERARY] ❑ *All three incidents occurred in the dead of night.* **12** PHRASE If you say that you wouldn't **be seen dead** or **be caught dead** in particular clothes, places, or situations, you are expressing strong dislike or disapproval of them. [INFORMAL, EMPHASIS] ❑ *I wouldn't be seen dead in a straw hat.* **13** PHRASE To **stop dead** means to suddenly stop happening or moving. To **stop** someone or something **dead** means to cause them to suddenly stop happening or moving. ❑ *We all stopped dead and looked at it.* **14 to stop dead in your tracks** → see **track**

SYNONYMS

dead
ADJ **1**
deceased: *...his recently-deceased mother.*
late: *...my late husband.*
extinct: *It has been 250 years since the wolf became extinct in Britain.*

---

dead|beat /dɛdbit/ (**deadbeats**) **1** N-COUNT [oft N n] If you refer to someone as a **deadbeat**, you are criticizing them because they try to avoid paying their debts. [AM, INFORMAL, DISAPPROVAL] ❑ *...deadbeat dads who don't pay child support.* **2** N-COUNT If you describe someone as a **deadbeat**, you are criticizing them because you think they are lazy. [AM, INFORMAL, DISAPPROVAL]

dead-beat also **dead beat** ADJ [v-link ADJ] If you are **dead-beat**, you are very tired and have no energy left. [INFORMAL]

dead duck (**dead ducks**) N-COUNT If you describe someone or something as a **dead duck**, you are emphasizing that you think they have absolutely no chance of succeeding. [INFORMAL, EMPHASIS]

dead|en /dɛdᵊn/ (**deadens, deadening, deadened**) V-T If something **deadens** a feeling or a sound, it makes it less strong or loud. ❑ *He needs morphine to deaden the acute pain in his chest.*

dead end (**dead ends**) also **dead-end** **1** N-COUNT If a street is a **dead end**, there is no way out at one end of it. ❑ *There was another alleyway which came to a dead end just behind the house.* **2** N-COUNT A **dead-end** job or course of action is one that you think is bad because it does not lead to further developments or progress. ❑ *Waitressing was a dead-end job.*

dead|en|ing /dɛdᵊnɪŋ/ ADJ [usu ADJ n] A **deadening** situation destroys people's enthusiasm and imagination. ❑ *She was bored with the deadening routine of her life.*

dead|head /dɛdhɛd/ (**deadheads**) also **dead-head** **1** N-COUNT A **deadhead** is someone who uses a free ticket to see a show, or for a plane or train trip. [AM] **2** N-COUNT If you say that someone is a **deadhead**, you mean that they are stupid or slow. [AM, INFORMAL]

dead heat (**dead heats**) N-COUNT If a race or contest is a **dead heat** or is in a **dead heat**, two or more competitors are joint winners, or are both winning at a particular moment in the race or contest. ❑ *The race ended in a dead heat between two horses.* ❑ *A national poll shows the presidential race in a dead heat.*

dead let|ter (**dead letters**) N-COUNT If you say that a law or agreement is a **dead letter**, you mean that it still exists but people ignore it. ❑ *No one does anything about it and the law becomes a dead letter.*

dead|line /dɛdlaɪn/ (**deadlines**) N-COUNT A **deadline** is a time or date before which a particular task must be finished or a particular thing must be done. ❑ *We were not able to meet the deadline because of manufacturing delays.*

dead|lock /dɛdlɒk/ (**deadlocks**) N-VAR If a dispute or series of negotiations reaches **deadlock**, neither side is willing to give in at all and no agreement can be made. ❑ *They called for a compromise on all sides to break the deadlock in the world trade talks.*

dead|locked /dɛdlɒkt/ ADJ If a dispute or series of negotiations is **deadlocked**, no agreement can be reached because neither side will give in at all. You can also say that the people involved are **deadlocked**. ❑ *The peace talks have been deadlocked over the issue of human rights since August.*

dead|ly /dɛdli/ (**deadlier, deadliest**) **1** ADJ If something is **deadly**, it is likely or able to cause someone's death, or has already caused someone's death. ❑ *He was acquitted on charges of assault with a deadly weapon.* ❑ *...a deadly disease currently affecting dolphins.* **2** ADJ If you describe a person or their behavior as **deadly**, you mean that they will do or say anything to get what they want, without caring about other people. [DISAPPROVAL] ❑ *The Duchess leveled a deadly look at Nikko.* **3** ADJ A **deadly** situation has unpleasant or dangerous consequences. ❑ *...the deadly combination of low expectations and low achievement.* **4** ADV [ADV adj] You can use **deadly** to emphasize that something has a particular quality, especially an unpleasant or undesirable quality. [EMPHASIS] ❑ *Broadcast news was accurate and reliable but deadly dull.*

dead meat N-UNCOUNT If you say that someone is **dead meat**, you mean that they are in very serious trouble that may result in them being hurt or injured in some way. [INFORMAL, SPOKEN]

dead|pan /dɛdpæn/ ADJ **Deadpan** humor is when you appear to be serious and are hiding the fact that you are joking or teasing someone. ❑ *...her natural capacity for irony and deadpan humor.*

dead weight (**dead weights**) **1** N-COUNT A **dead weight** is a load which is surprisingly heavy and difficult to lift. **2** N-COUNT [usu sing] You can refer to something that makes change or progress difficult as a **dead weight**. ❑ *...the dead weight of traditional policies.*

dead wood N-UNCOUNT People or things that have been used for a very long time and that are no longer considered to be useful can be referred to as **dead wood**. [DISAPPROVAL] ❑ *Get the dead wood out of your customer list and bring it up to date.*

deaf /dɛf/ (**deafer, deafest**) **1** ADJ Someone who is **deaf** is unable to hear anything or is unable to hear very well. ❑ *She is now profoundly deaf.* • N-PLURAL **The deaf** are people who are deaf. This use could cause offense. ❑ *Many regular TV programs are captioned for the deaf.* • **deaf|ness** N-UNCOUNT ❑ *The problem of deafness will increase.* **2 to fall on deaf ears** → see **ear** **3 to turn a deaf ear** → see **ear**

deaf|en /dɛfᵊn/ (**deafens, deafening, deafened**) **1** V-T If a noise **deafens** you, it is so loud that you cannot hear anything else at the same time. ❑ *The noise of the typewriters deafened her.* **2** V-T [usu passive] If you **are deafened** by something, you are made deaf by it, or are unable to hear for some time. ❑ *He was deafened by the noise from the gun.* **3** → see also **deafening**

deafen|ing /dɛfᵊnɪŋ/ **1** ADJ A **deafening** noise is a very loud noise. ❑ ...the deafening roar of fighter jets taking off. **2** ADJ If you say there was a **deafening** silence, you are emphasizing that there was no reaction or response to something that was said or done. [EMPHASIS] ❑ What was truly despicable was the deafening silence maintained by the candidates concerning the riots.

deaf-mute (deaf-mutes) N-COUNT A **deaf-mute** is someone who cannot hear or speak. [OLD-FASHIONED, OFFENSIVE]

DEAL
① QUANTIFIER USES
② VERB AND NOUN USES

① **deal** ✦◇◇ /diːl/ QUANT If you say that you need or have **a great deal of** or **a good deal of** a particular thing, you are emphasizing that you need or have a lot of it. [EMPHASIS] ❑ ...a great deal of money. • ADV **Deal** is also an adverb. ❑ As a relationship becomes more established, it also becomes a good deal more complex. • PRON **Deal** is also a pronoun. ❑ Although he had never met Geoffrey Hardcastle, he knew a good deal about him.

② **deal** ✦✦◇ /diːl/ (deals, dealing, dealt) **1** N-COUNT If you make a **deal**, do a **deal**, or cut a **deal**, you complete an agreement or an arrangement with someone, especially in business. [BUSINESS] ❑ He made a deal to testify against the others and wasn't charged. ❑ Japan will have to do a deal with the U.S. on rice imports. **2** N-COUNT If someone has had a **bad deal**, they have been unfortunate or have been treated unfairly. ❑ The people of Hartford have had a bad deal for many, many years. **3** V-I If a person, company, or store **deals in** a particular type of goods, their business involves buying or selling those goods. [BUSINESS] ❑ They deal in antiques. **4** V-T If someone **deals** illegal drugs, they sell them. ❑ I certainly don't deal drugs. **5** V-T If you **deal** playing cards, you give them out to the players in a game of cards. ❑ The croupier dealt each player a card, face down. • PHRASAL VERB **Deal out** means the same as **deal** ② **5**. ❑ Dalton dealt out five cards to each player. **6** → see also **dealings** **7** → see also **wheel and deal**

▶ **deal out 1** PHRASAL VERB If someone **deals out** a punishment or harmful action, they punish or harm someone. [WRITTEN] ❑ ...a failure by the governments of established states to deal out effective punishment to aggressors. **2** → see also **deal** ② **5**

▶ **deal with 1** PHRASAL VERB When you **deal with** something or someone that needs attention, you give your attention to them, and often solve a problem or make a decision concerning them. ❑ ...the way that banks deal with complaints. **2** PHRASAL VERB If you **deal with** an unpleasant emotion or an emotionally difficult situation, you recognize it, and remain calm and in control of yourself in spite of it. ❑ She saw a psychiatrist who used hypnotism to help her deal with her fear. **3** PHRASAL VERB If a book, speech, or movie **deals with** a particular thing, it has that thing as its subject or is concerned with it. ❑ ...the parts of his book which deal with contemporary Paris. **4** PHRASAL VERB If you **deal with** a particular person or organization, you have business relations with them. ❑ When I worked in Florida I dealt with tourists all the time.

SYNONYMS
deal
NOUN ② **1**
agreement: It looks as though a compromise agreement has now been reached.
understanding: We had not set a date for marriage, but there was an understanding between us.
contract: The company won a prestigious contract for work on Europe's tallest building.
pact: Last month, he signed a new non-aggression pact with Germany.

deal|break|er /diːlbreɪkər/ (dealbreakers) N-COUNT A **dealbreaker** is an issue that prevents people from reaching an agreement. ❑ Their refusal to change location was a dealbreaker.

deal|er ✦◇◇ /diːlər/ (dealers) **1** N-COUNT A **dealer** is a person whose business involves buying and selling things. [BUSINESS] ❑ ...an antique dealer. **2** N-COUNT A **dealer** is someone who buys and sells illegal drugs. ❑ They will stay on the job for as long as it takes to clear every dealer from the street.

SYNONYMS
dealer
NOUN **1**
trader: Market traders display an exotic selection of the island's produce.
merchant: Any knowledgeable wine merchant would be able to advise you.
supplier: ...Hillsdown Holdings, one of the U.K.'s biggest food suppliers.

deal|er|ship /diːlərʃɪp/ (dealerships) N-COUNT A **dealership** is a company that sells cars, usually for one car company. [BUSINESS] ❑ ...a car dealership.

deal|ings /diːlɪŋz/ N-PLURAL Someone's **dealings** with a person or organization are the relations that they have with them or the business that they do with them. ❑ He has learned little in his dealings with the international community.

deal|mak|er /diːlmeɪkər/ (dealmakers) N-COUNT A **dealmaker** is someone in business or politics who makes deals. • **deal|mak|ing** N-UNCOUNT [oft N n] ❑ ...a chairman with a reputation for dealmaking. ❑ She prides herself on her dealmaking talents.

dealt /dɛlt/ **Dealt** is the past tense and past participle of **deal** ②.

dean /diːn/ (deans) **1** N-COUNT A **dean** is an important official at a university or college. ❑ She was dean of the University of Washington's Graduate School. **2** N-COUNT A **dean** is a priest who is the main administrator of a large church. ❑ ...Bob Gregg, dean of the Chapel, Stanford Memorial Church.

dear ✦◇◇ /dɪər/ (dearer, dearest, dears) **1** ADJ [ADJ n] You use **dear** to describe someone or something that you feel affection for. ❑ Mrs. Cavendish is a dear friend of mine. **2** ADJ [v-link ADJ to n] If something is **dear to** you or **dear to** your heart, you care deeply about it. ❑ This is a subject very dear to the hearts of academics up and down the country. **3** ADJ [ADJ n] **Dear** is written at the beginning of a letter, followed by the name or title of the person you are writing to. ❑ Dear Peter, I have been thinking about you so much during the past few days. **4** CONVENTION You begin formal letters with '**Dear Sir**' or '**Dear Madam**.' You can also begin them with 'Sir' or 'Madam.' [WRITTEN] ❑ "Dear Sir," she began. **5** N-VOC You can call someone **dear** as a sign of affection. [FEELINGS] ❑ You're a lot like me, dear. **6** EXCLAM You can use **dear** in expressions such as '**oh dear**,' '**dear me**,' and '**dear, dear**' when you are sad, disappointed, or surprised about something. [FEELINGS] ❑ "Oh dear, oh dear." McKinnon sighed. "You, too."

dear|est /dɪərɪst/ ADJ [ADJ n] When you are writing to someone you are very fond of, you can use **dearest** at the beginning of the letter before the person's name or the word you are using to address them. ❑ Dearest Maria, Aren't I terrible, not coming back like I promised?

dear|ly /dɪərli/ **1** ADV [ADV with v] If you love someone **dearly**, you love them very much. [FORMAL, EMPHASIS] ❑ She loved her father dearly. **2** ADV [ADV before v] If you would **dearly** like to do or have something, you would very much like to do it or have it. [FORMAL, EMPHASIS] ❑ I would dearly love to marry. **3** PHRASE If you **pay dearly** for doing something or if it **costs** you **dearly**, you suffer a lot as a result. [FORMAL] ❑ He drank too much and is paying dearly for the pleasure.

dearth /dɜːrθ/ N-SING [usu N of n] If there is a **dearth** of something, there is not enough of it. ❑ Construction had slowed because of a dearth of laborers.

death ✦✦◇ /dɛθ/ (deaths) **1** N-VAR **Death** is the permanent end of the life of a person or animal. ❑ 1.5 million people are in immediate danger of death from starvation. ❑ ...the thirtieth anniversary of Judy Garland's death. **2** N-SING The **death** of something is the permanent end of it. ❑ It meant the death of everything he had ever been or ever hoped to be. **3** PHRASE If you say that someone is **at death's door**, you mean they are very ill and likely to die. [INFORMAL] ❑ He told his boss a tale about his mother being at death's door. **4** PHRASE If you say that you will **fight to the death** for something, you are emphasizing that you will do anything to achieve or protect it, even if you suffer as a consequence. [EMPHASIS] ❑ She'd have fought to the death for that child. **5** PHRASE If you say that something is a **matter of life and death**, you are emphasizing that it is extremely important, often because someone may die or suffer great harm if people do not act immediately. [EMPHASIS] ❏ *Well, never mind, John, it's not a matter of life and death.* ▣ PHRASE If someone **is put to death**, they are executed. [FORMAL] ❏ *Those put to death by firing squad included three generals.* ▣ PHRASE You use **to death** after an adjective or a verb to emphasize the action, state, or feeling mentioned. For example, if you are **frightened to death** or **bored to death**, you are extremely frightened or bored. [EMPHASIS] ❏ *He scares teams to death with his pace and power.*

death|bed /dɛθbɛd/ (**deathbeds**) N-COUNT [usu sing, usu with poss, oft *on* N] If someone is on their **deathbed**, they are in a bed and about to die. ❏ *He promised his mother on her deathbed that he would never marry.*

death blow also **death-blow** N-SING [oft N *to* n] If you say that an event or action deals a **death blow** to something such as a plan or hope, or is a **death blow** to something, you mean that it puts an end to it. [JOURNALISM] ❏ *The deportations would be a death blow to the peace process.*

death camp (**death camps**) N-COUNT A **death camp** is a place where prisoners are kept, especially during a war, and where many of them die or are killed.

death cer|tifi|cate (**death certificates**) N-COUNT A **death certificate** is an official certificate signed by a doctor which states the cause of a person's death.

death knell also **death-knell** N-SING [usu the N *for/of* n] If you say that something sounds the **death knell** for a particular person or thing, you mean it will cause that person or thing to fail, end, or cease to exist. ❏ *The tax increase sounded the death knell for the business.*

death|ly /dɛθli/ ▣ ADV [ADV adj] If you say that someone is **deathly** pale or **deathly** still, you are emphasizing that they are very pale or still, like a dead person. [LITERARY, EMPHASIS] ❏ *Bernadette turned deathly pale.* ▣ ADJ [ADJ n] If you say that there is a **deathly** silence or a **deathly** hush, you are emphasizing that it is very quiet. [LITERARY, EMPHASIS] ❏ *A deathly silence hung over the square.*

death mask (**death masks**) also **death-mask** N-COUNT A **death mask** is a model of someone's face, which is made from a mold that was taken of their face soon after they died.

death pen|al|ty N-SING The **death penalty** is the punishment of death used in some countries for people who have committed very serious crimes. ❏ *If convicted for murder, both men could face the death penalty.*

death rate (**death rates**) N-COUNT The **death rate** is the number of people per thousand who die in a particular area during a particular period of time. ❏ *In Canada the death rate has dropped by a staggering 90 per cent.*

death rat|tle also **death-rattle** N-SING If you say that one thing is the **death rattle** of another, you mean that the first thing is a sign that very soon the second thing will come to an end. [JOURNALISM] ❏ *His rhetoric sounds like the death rattle of a fading leadership.*

death row /dɛθ roʊ/ N-UNCOUNT If someone is on **death row**, they are in the part of a prison which contains the cells for criminals who have been sentenced to death. [AM] ❏ *He has been on death row for 11 years.*

death sen|tence (**death sentences**) N-COUNT A **death sentence** is a punishment of death given by a judge to someone who has been found guilty of a serious crime such as murder. ❏ *His original death sentence was commuted to life in prison.*

death squad (**death squads**) N-COUNT **Death squads** are groups of people who operate illegally and carry out the killing of people such as their political opponents or criminals.

death taxes N-PLURAL **Death taxes** were a tax which had to be paid on the money and property of someone who had died. This tax is now called **estate tax** or **inheritance tax**. [AM]

death throes also **death-throes** ▣ N-PLURAL [usu with poss] The **death throes** of something are its final stages, just before it fails completely or ends. [LITERARY] ▣ N-PLURAL [oft *in* poss N] If a person or animal is in their **death throes**, they are dying and making violent, uncontrolled movements, usually because they are suffering great pain.

death toll (**death tolls**) also **death-toll** N-COUNT The **death toll** of an accident, disaster, or war is the number of people who die in it. ❏ *The death toll continues to rise from yesterday's earthquake.*

death|trap /dɛθtræp/ (**deathtraps**) N-COUNT If you say that a place or vehicle is a **deathtrap**, you mean it is in such bad condition that it might cause someone's death. [INFORMAL] ❏ *Badly built cars can be deathtraps.*

death war|rant (**death warrants**) ▣ N-COUNT A **death warrant** is an official document which orders that someone is to be executed as a punishment for a crime. ▣ PHRASE If you say that someone **is signing their own death warrant**, you mean that they are behaving in a way which will cause their ruin or death. ❏ *By accusing the king of murder, he signed his own death warrant.*

death wish also **death-wish** N-SING A **death wish** is a conscious or unconscious desire to die or be killed.

deb /dɛb/ (**debs**) N-COUNT A **deb** is the same as a **debutante**.

de|ba|cle /dɪbɑːkəl, -bækəl/ (**debacles**)

in BRIT, also use **débâcle**

N-COUNT A **debacle** is an event or attempt that is a complete failure. ❏ *People believed it was a privilege to die for your country, but after the debacle of the war they never felt the same again.*

de|bar /dɪbɑːr, dɪ-/ (**debars, debarring, debarred**) V-T [oft passive] If you **are debarred** from doing something, you are prevented from doing it by a law or regulation. [FORMAL] ❏ *...the decision to debar particular immigrants.*

de|base /dɪbeɪs/ (**debases, debasing, debased**) V-T To **debase** something means to reduce its value or quality. [FORMAL] ❏ *Politicians have debased the meaning of the word "freedom."* ● **de|based** ADJ ❏ *...the debased standards of today's media.*

de|base|ment /dɪbeɪsmənt/ N-UNCOUNT [oft N *of* n] **Debasement** is the action of reducing the value or quality of something. [FORMAL] ❏ *...the debasement of popular culture.*

de|bat|able /dɪbeɪtəbəl/ ADJ If you say that something is **debatable**, you mean that it is not certain. ❏ *It is debatable whether or not the shareholders were ever properly compensated.*

de|bate ♦♦◇ /dɪbeɪt/ (**debates, debating, debated**) ▣ N-VAR A **debate** is a discussion about a subject on which people have different views. ❏ *An intense debate is going on within the Israeli government.* ❏ *There has been a lot of debate among scholars about this.* ▣ N-COUNT A **debate** is a formal discussion, for example, in a parliament or institution, in which people express different opinions about a particular subject and then vote on it. ❏ *He is expected to force a debate in Congress on his immigration reform* ▣ V-RECIP If people **debate** a topic, they discuss it fairly formally, putting forward different views. You can also say that one person **debates** a topic with another person. ❏ *The United Nations Security Council will debate the issue today.* ❏ *Scientists were debating whether an asteroid was about to hit the Earth.* ▣ V-T If you **debate** whether to do something or what to do, you think or talk about possible courses of action before deciding exactly what you are going to do. ❏ *Once outside, he debated whether to walk or drive.*

COLLOCATIONS

debate
NOUN
▣
noun + **debate**: election, independence, referendum; TV
adjective + **debate**: fierce, heated, lively, passionate, robust, vigorous; acrimonious, bitter, divisive, furious; considerable, much; ethical, political; ongoing
verb + **debate**: provoke, spark, trigger; reignite, reopen, revive; fuel, stimulate
▣
adjective + **debate**: congressional, parliamentary; presidential
VERB ▣
debate + noun: issue, matter, question, subject, topic
debate + adverb: fiercely, heatedly, hotly, passionately, vigorously; earnestly, intensely; endlessly; openly, publicly

SYNONYMS

debate
NOUN **1**
discussion: *There was a lot of discussion about the wording of the report.*
argument: *The issue has caused heated political argument.*
dispute: *They have won previous payment disputes with the government.*
controversy: *The proposed cuts have caused considerable controversy.*
VERB **3**
discuss: *I will be discussing the situation with colleagues tomorrow.*
thrash out: *...a sincere effort by two people to thrash out differences.*
argue: *They were still arguing; I could hear them down the road.*
wrangle: *A group of MPs is still wrangling with the government over the timing of elections.*

VOCABULARY IN CONTEXT

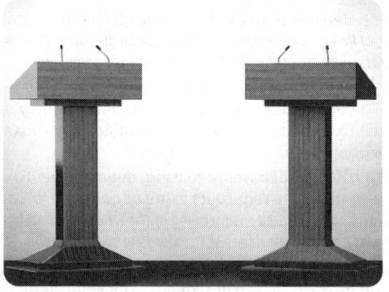

A heated debate

A conversation among climate-change experts turned into a **heated debate** on a prime-time current affairs program last night.

One speaker, who attempted to defend current government policies, was **verbally attacked** and **shouted down** by his opponents. He tried repeatedly to **have his say**, but another guest continued to **butt in** and **talk over him**. Unable to **get a word in edgewise**, he appealed to the host of the program.

The host urged all members of the panel to **hear him out** and not to **jump to conclusions** until his point had been fully **articulated**. Uninterrupted at last, the man **expressed himself** very **eloquently**. His perspective, more than originally anticipated, certainly gave viewers **food for thought**.

The host then **opened the discussion** to members of the studio audience, who **contributed salient points** and offered a range of contrasting opinions.

de|bat|er /dɪbeɪtər/ (**debaters**) N-COUNT [oft adj N] A **debater** is someone who takes part in debates. ❑ *They are skilled debaters.*

de|bauched /dɪbɔːtʃt/ ADJ If you describe someone as **debauched**, you mean they behave in a way that you think is socially unacceptable, for example, because they drink a lot of alcohol or have sex with a lot of people. [OLD-FASHIONED, DISAPPROVAL] ❑ *...a debt-ridden and debauched lifestyle.*

de|bauch|ery /dɪbɔːtʃəri/ N-UNCOUNT You use **debauchery** to refer to the drinking of alcohol or to sexual activity if you disapprove of it or regard it as excessive. [DISAPPROVAL] ❑ *...scenes of drunkenness and debauchery.*

de|ben|ture /dɪbentʃər/ (**debentures**) N-COUNT A **debenture** is a type of savings bond which offers a fixed rate of interest over a long period. Debentures are usually issued by a company or a government agency. [BUSINESS]

de|bili|tate /dɪbɪlɪteɪt/ (**debilitates, debilitating, debilitated**)
1 V-T [usu passive] If you **are debilitated** by something such as an illness, it causes your body or mind to become gradually weaker. [FORMAL] ❑ *Stewart took over yesterday when Russell was debilitated by a stomach virus.* ● **de|bili|tat|ing** ADJ ❑ *...a debilitating illness.* ● **de|bili|tat|ed** ADJ ❑ *Occasionally a patient is so debilitated that he must be fed intravenously.* **2** V-T To **debilitate** an organization, society, or government means to gradually make it weaker. [FORMAL] ❑ *...their efforts to debilitate the political will of the Western alliance.* ● **de|bili|tat|ing** ADJ ❑ *...years of debilitating economic crisis.* ● **de|bili|tat|ed** ADJ ❑ *...the debilitated ruling party.*

de|bil|ity /dɪbɪlɪti/ (**debilities**) N-VAR **Debility** is a weakness of a person's body or mind, especially one caused by an illness. [FORMAL] ❑ *...exhaustion or post-viral debility.*

deb|it /dɛbɪt/ (**debits, debiting, debited**) **1** V-T When your bank **debits** your account, money is taken from it and paid to someone else. ❑ *We will always confirm the revised amount to you in writing before debiting your account.* **2** N-COUNT A **debit** is a record of the money taken from your bank account, for example, when you make a payment. ❑ *The total of debits must balance the total of credits.*

deb|it card (**debit cards**) N-COUNT A **debit card** is a bank card that you can use to pay for things. When you use it the money is taken out of your bank account immediately.

debo|nair /dɛbənɛər/ ADJ A man who is **debonair** is confident, charming, and well dressed. ❑ *Her father walked down the path, debonair in a three-piece suit, hat, and cane.*

de|brief /diːbriːf/ (**debriefs, debriefing, debriefed**) V-T When someone such as a soldier, diplomat, or astronaut **is debriefed**, they are asked to give a report on an operation or task that they have just completed. ❑ *The men have been debriefed by British and Saudi officials.* ❑ *He went to Rio after the CIA had debriefed him.*

de|brief|ing /diːbriːfɪŋ/ (**debriefings**) N-VAR A **debriefing** is a meeting where someone such as a soldier, diplomat, or astronaut is asked to give a report on an operation or task that they have just completed. ❑ *A debriefing would follow this operation, to determine where it went wrong.*

de|bris /dəbriː/ N-UNCOUNT **Debris** is pieces from something that has been destroyed or pieces of trash or unwanted material that are spread around. ❑ *A number of people were killed by flying debris.*

debt ♦♦◊ /dɛt/ (**debts**) **1** N-VAR A **debt** is a sum of money that you owe someone. ❑ *Three years later, he is still paying off his debts.* **2** → see also **bad debt** **3** N-UNCOUNT **Debt** is the state of owing money. ❑ *...a monthly report on the amount of debt owed by consumers.* ● PHRASE If you are **in debt** or **get into debt**, you owe money. If you are **out of debt** or **get out of debt**, you succeed in paying all the money that you owe. ❑ *He was already deeply in debt through gambling losses.* **4** N-COUNT You use **debt** in expressions such as **I owe you a debt** or **I am in your debt** when you are expressing gratitude for something that someone has done for you. [FORMAL, FEELINGS] ❑ *He was so good to me that I can never repay the debt I owe him.* ❑ *I owe a debt of thanks to Joyce Thompson, whose careful and able research was of great help.* **5** → See feature box at **finance, poverty**

COLLOCATIONS

debt
NOUN **1**
noun + **debt**: bank, government, sovereign; credit-card, household, mortgage, student
adjective + **debt**: bad, crippling, toxic; manageable, outstanding, sustainable, unsecured, unsustainable; national
verb + **debt**: clear, pay off, reduce, repay, service; get into, incur, owe

SYNONYMS

debt
NOUN **1**
loan: *The country has no access to foreign loans or financial aid.*
liabilities: *The company had assets of $138 million and liabilities of $120.5 million.*

debt bur|den (debt burdens) N-COUNT A **debt burden** is a large amount of money that one country or organization owes to another and which they find very difficult to repay. ◻ *A lack of competitiveness is likely to ensure the debt burden remains high.*

debt|or /dɛtər/ (debtors) N-COUNT A **debtor** is a country, organization, or person who owes money. ◻ *...important improvements in the situation of debtor countries.*

debt re|lief N-UNCOUNT **Debt relief** is a reduction in the amount of debt that a country has to pay. ◻ *...his crusade to win debt relief for poor countries.*

debt-ridden ADJ [usu ADJ n] **Debt-ridden** countries, companies, or people owe extremely large amounts of money. ◻ *She was a typical debt-ridden American graduate student.*

de|bug /dibʌg/ (debugs, debugging, debugged) V-T When someone **debugs** a computer program, they look for the problems in it and correct them so that it will run properly. [COMPUTING] ◻ *The production lines ground to a halt for hours while technicians tried to debug software.*

de|bunk /dibʌŋk/ (debunks, debunking, debunked) V-T If you **debunk** a widely held belief, you show that it is false. If you **debunk** something that is widely admired, you show that it is not as good as people think it is. ◻ *Historian Michael Beschloss debunks a few myths.*

de|but ✦◇◇ /deɪbyu/ (debuts) N-COUNT The **debut** of a performer or sports player is their first public performance, appearance, or recording. ◻ *She made her debut in a 1937 production of "Hamlet."*

COLLOCATIONS

debut
NOUN
noun + **debut**: big-screen, film, screen, stage; acting
adjective + **debut**: acclaimed, impressive, memorable, sensational; directorial, solo, theatrical; first-class, international; auspicious, promising

---

debu|tante /dɛbyutɑnt/ (debutantes) N-COUNT A **debutante** is a young woman from a wealthy family who has started going to social events with other young people. [OLD-FASHIONED]

Dec. **Dec.** is a written abbreviation for **December**.

dec|ade ✦✦◇ /dɛkeɪd/ (decades) N-COUNT A **decade** is a period of ten years, especially one that begins with a year ending in 0, for example, 1980 to 1989. ◻ *...the last decade of the nineteenth century.*

deca|dent /dɛkədənt/ ADJ If you say that a person or society is **decadent**, you think that they have low moral standards and are interested mainly in pleasure. [DISAPPROVAL] ◻ *...the excesses and stresses of their decadent rock 'n' roll lifestyles.*
• **deca|dence** N-UNCOUNT ◻ *The empire had for years been falling into decadence.*

de|caf /dikæf/ (decafs) N-MASS **Decaf** is decaffeinated coffee. [INFORMAL]

in BRIT, also use **decaff**.

de|caf|fein|at|ed /dikæfɪneɪtɪd/ ADJ **Decaffeinated** coffee or tea has had most of the caffeine removed from it.

de|cal /dikæl/ (decals) N-COUNT **Decals** are pieces of paper with a design on one side. The design can be transferred onto a surface by heating it, soaking it in water, or pressing it hard. [AM]

in BRIT, use **transfer**

de|camp /dikæmp/ (decamps, decamping, decamped) V-I If you **decamp**, you go away from somewhere secretly or suddenly. ◻ *The company is decamping to Asia with 1,700 jobs.*

de|cant /dikænt/ (decants, decanting, decanted) V-T If you **decant** a liquid into another container, you put it into another container. [FORMAL] ◻ *Vintage ports must be decanted to remove natural sediments.*

de|cant|er /dikæntər/ (decanters) N-COUNT A **decanter** is a glass container that you use for serving wine, sherry, or port.

de|capi|tate /dikæpɪteɪt/ (decapitates, decapitating, decapitated) V-T If someone **is decapitated**, their head is cut off. [FORMAL] ◻ *There were nine corpses. Two of them had been decapitated.*

de|car|bon|iza|tion /dikɑrbənaɪzeɪʃ°n/ N-UNCOUNT **Decarbonization** is the process of reducing and removing carbon dioxide output from a country's economy. ◻ *In the face of fierce pressure, the global maritime industry finally set modest goals for decarbonization.*

de|car|bon|ize /dikɑrbənaɪz/ (decarbonizes, decarbonizing, decarbonized) VERB To **decarbonize** a business or an economy is to reduce or remove its carbon dioxide output. ◻ *We need a system that is fair and effective in decarbonizing society.* ◻ *There's no doubt that there are benefits to us in decarbonizing our investment portfolio.*

de|cath|lon /dɪkæθlɒn/ (decathlons) N-COUNT The **decathlon** is a competition in which athletes compete in 10 different sports events.

de|cay /dɪkeɪ/ (decays, decaying, decayed) **1** V-I When something such as a dead body, a dead plant, or a tooth **decays**, it is gradually destroyed by a natural process. ◻ *The bodies buried in the fine ash slowly decayed.* • N-UNCOUNT **Decay** is also a noun. ◻ *When not removed, plaque causes tooth decay and gum disease.* • **de|cayed** ADJ ◻ *Even young children have teeth so decayed they need to be pulled.* **2** V-I If something such as a society, system, or institution **decays**, it gradually becomes weaker or its condition gets worse. ◻ *In practice, the agency system has decayed. Most "agents" now sell only to themselves or their immediate family.* • N-UNCOUNT **Decay** is also a noun. ◻ *There are problems of urban decay and gang violence.*

de|ceased /dɪsist/ (deceased)

Deceased is both the singular and the plural form.

1 N-COUNT The **deceased** is used to refer to a particular person or to particular people who have recently died. [LEGAL] ◻ *The navy is notifying next of kin now that the identities of the deceased have been determined.* **2** ADJ A **deceased** person is one who has recently died. [FORMAL] ◻ *...his recently deceased mother.*

de|ceit /dɪsit/ (deceits) N-VAR **Deceit** is behavior that is deliberately intended to make people believe something which is not true. ◻ *He was living a secret life of deceit and unfaithfulness.*

de|ceit|ful /dɪsitfəl/ ADJ If you say that someone is **deceitful**, you mean that they behave in a dishonest way by making other people believe something that is not true. ◻ *The ambassador called the report deceitful and misleading.*

de|ceive /dɪsiv/ (deceives, deceiving, deceived) **1** V-T If you **deceive** someone, you make them believe something that is not true, usually in order to get some advantage for yourself. ◻ *He has deceived and disillusioned us all.* **2** V-T If something **deceives** you, it gives you a wrong impression and makes you believe something that is not true. ◻ *Do not be deceived by claims on food labels like "light" or "low fat."*

de|cel|er|ate /disɛləreɪt/ (decelerates, decelerating, decelerated) **1** V-I When a vehicle or machine **decelerates** or when someone in a vehicle **decelerates**, the speed of the vehicle or machine is reduced. ◻ *...the sensation of the train decelerating.* • **de|cel|era|tion** /disɛləreɪʃ°n/ N-UNCOUNT ◻ *The harder the brake pedal is pressed, the greater the car's deceleration.* **2** V-I When the rate of something such as inflation or economic growth **decelerates**, it slows down. ◻ *Inflation has decelerated remarkably over the past two years.* • **de|cel|era|tion** N-UNCOUNT ◻ *...a significant deceleration in the annual rate of growth.*

De|cem|ber ✦✦✦ /dɪsɛmbər/ (Decembers) N-VAR **December** is the twelfth and last month of the year in the Western calendar. ◻ *...a bright morning in mid-December.*

de|cen|cy /dis°nsi/ **1** N-UNCOUNT **Decency** is the quality of following accepted moral standards. ◻ *His sense of decency forced him to resign.* **2** PHRASE If you say that someone did not **have the decency** to do something, you are criticizing them because there was a particular action which they did not do but which you believe they ought to have done. [DISAPPROVAL] ◻ *He didn't even have the decency to tell them in person.*

de|cent /dis°nt/ **1** ADJ **Decent** is used to describe something which is considered to be of an acceptable standard or quality. ◻ *He didn't get a decent explanation.* • **de|cent|ly** ADV ◻ *The allies say they will treat their prisoners decently.* **2** ADJ **Decent** is used to describe something which is morally correct or acceptable. ◻ *But, after a decent interval, trade relations began to return to normal.*

● **de|cent|ly** ADV ❑ *And can't you dress more decently – people will think you're a tramp.* ❸ ADJ **Decent** people are honest and behave in a way that most people approve of. ❑ *The majority of people around here are decent people.*

de|cen|tral|ize /disɛntrəlaɪz/ (decentralizes, decentralizing, decentralized)

in BRIT, also use **decentralise**

V-T/V-I To **decentralize** government or a large organization means to move some departments away from the main administrative area, or to give more power to local departments. ❑ *...the need to decentralize and devolve power to regional governments.* ● **de|cen|tral|iza|tion** /disɛntrəlɪzeɪʃ⁰n/ N-UNCOUNT ❑ *He seems set against the idea of increased decentralization and greater powers for regional authorities.*

de|cep|tion /dɪsɛpʃ⁰n/ (deceptions) N-VAR **Deception** is the act of deceiving someone or the state of being deceived by someone. ❑ *He admitted conspiring to obtain property by deception.*

de|cep|tive /dɪsɛptɪv/ ADJ If something is **deceptive**, it encourages you to believe something which is not true. ❑ *Johnston isn't tired of Las Vegas yet, it seems, but appearances can be deceptive.* ● **de|cep|tive|ly** ADV ❑ *The storyline is deceptively simple.*

deci|bel /dɛsɪbɛl/ (decibels) N-COUNT A **decibel** is a unit of measurement which is used to indicate how loud a sound is. ❑ *Continuous exposure to sound above 80 decibels could be harmful.*

de|cide ✦✧✧ /dɪsaɪd/ (decides, deciding, decided) ❶ V-T/V-I If you **decide** to do something, you choose to do it, usually after you have thought carefully about the other possibilities. ❑ *She decided to take a course in philosophy.* ❑ *Think about it very carefully before you decide.* ❷ V-T If a person or group of people **decides** something, they choose what something should be like or how a particular problem should be solved. ❑ *She was still young, he said, and that would be taken into account when deciding her sentence.* ❸ V-T If an event or fact **decides** something, it makes it certain that a particular choice will be made or that there will be a particular result. ❑ *What happens next could decide their destiny.* ❑ *The election will decide if either party controls both houses of Congress.* ❹ V-T If you **decide** that something is true, you form that opinion about it after considering the facts. ❑ *He decided Franklin must be suffering from a bad cold.*
▶ **decide on** PHRASAL VERB If you **decide on** something or **decide upon** something, you choose it from two or more possibilities. ❑ *Denikin held a staff meeting to decide on the next strategic objective.*

de|cid|ed /dɪsaɪdɪd/ ADJ [ADJ n] **Decided** means clear and definite. ❑ *They got involved in a long and exhausting struggle and were at a decided disadvantage in the afternoon.*

de|cid|ed|ly /dɪsaɪdɪdli/ ADV **Decidedly** means to a great extent and in a way that is very obvious. ❑ *He admits there will be moments when he's decidedly uncomfortable at what he sees on the screen.*

de|cidu|ous /dɪsɪdʒuəs/ ❶ ADJ [usu ADJ n] A **deciduous** tree or bush is one that loses its leaves in the fall every year. ❷ → See feature box at **ecosystem**

deci|mal /dɛsɪm⁰l/ (decimals) ❶ ADJ [ADJ n] A **decimal** system involves counting in units of ten. ❑ *The mathematics of ancient Egypt were based on a decimal system.* ❷ N-COUNT A **decimal** is a fraction that is written in the form of a dot followed by one or more numbers which represent tenths, hundredths, and so on: for example, .5, .51, .517. ❑ *...simple math concepts, such as decimals and fractions.*

deci|mal point (decimal points) N-COUNT A **decimal point** is the dot in front of a decimal fraction. ❑ *A waiter omitted the decimal point in the $13.09 bill.*

deci|mate /dɛsɪmeɪt/ (decimates, decimating, decimated) ❶ V-T To **decimate** something such as a group of people or animals means to destroy a very large number of them. ❑ *The pollution could decimate the river's thriving population of kingfishers.* ❷ V-T To **decimate** a system or organization means to reduce its size and effectiveness greatly. ❑ *...a recession which decimated the nation's manufacturing industry.*

de|ci|pher /dɪsaɪfər/ (deciphers, deciphering, deciphered) V-T If you **decipher** a piece of writing or a message, you work out what it says, even though it is very difficult to read or understand. ❑ *I'm still no closer to deciphering the code.*

de|ci|sion ✦✦✦ /dɪsɪʒ⁰n/ (decisions) ❶ N-COUNT When you make a **decision**, you choose what should be done or which is the best of various possible actions. ❑ *I don't want to make the wrong decision and regret it later.* ❷ N-UNCOUNT **Decision** is the act of deciding something or the need to decide something. ❑ *The growing pressures of the crisis may mean that the moment of decision can't be too long delayed.* ❸ N-UNCOUNT **Decision** is the ability to decide quickly and definitely what to do. ❑ *He is very quick-thinking and very much a man of decision.*

> **COLLOCATIONS**
>
> **decision**
> NOUN ❶
> adjective + **decision**: correct, right, wrong; difficult, easy, hard, tough; controversial, unpopular; informed; unanimous; conscious
> verb + **decision**: come to, make, reach; announce; overrule, overturn, reverse

de|ci|sion mak|ing N-UNCOUNT **Decision making** is the process of reaching decisions, especially in a large organization or in government.

de|ci|sive /dɪsaɪsɪv/ ❶ ADJ If a fact, action, or event is **decisive**, it makes certain a particular result. ❑ *...his decisive victory in the presidential elections.* ● **de|ci|sive|ly** ADV ❑ *The plan was decisively rejected by Congress three weeks ago.* ❷ ADJ If someone is **decisive**, they have or show an ability to make quick decisions in a difficult or complicated situation. ❑ *He should give way to a younger, more decisive leader.* ● **de|ci|sive|ly** ADV ❑ *"I'll call for you at ten," she said decisively.* ● **de|ci|sive|ness** N-UNCOUNT ❑ *His supporters admire his decisiveness.*

deck ✦✧✧ /dɛk/ (decks) ❶ N-COUNT A **deck** on a vehicle such as a bus or ship is a lower or upper area of it. ❑ *...a luxury liner with five passenger decks.* ❷ N-COUNT [also on N] The **deck** of a ship is the top part of it that forms a floor in the open air which you can walk on. ❑ *She stood on the deck and waved her hand to them as the steamer moved off.* ❸ N-COUNT A **deck** is a flat wooden area next to a house, where people can sit and relax or eat. ❑ *A natural timber deck leads into the main room of the home.* ❹ N-COUNT A **deck** of cards is a complete set of playing cards. [mainly AM] ❑ *Matt picked up the cards and shuffled the deck.*

in BRIT, usually use **pack**

❺ → See also color supplement

deck chair (deck chairs) ❶ N-COUNT A **deck chair** is a simple chair with a folding frame, and a piece of canvas as the seat and back. Deck chairs are usually used on the beach, on a ship, or in the yard. ❷ → See also color supplement

-decker /-dɛkər/ COMB IN ADJ [ADJ n] **-decker** is used after adjectives like 'double' and 'single' to indicate how many levels or layers something has. ❑ *...a red double-decker bus full of tourists.* ❑ *...a triple-decker peanut butter and jelly sandwich.*

deck|hand /dɛkhænd/ (deckhands) N-COUNT A **deckhand** is a person who does cleaning and other work on the deck of a ship.

deck shoe (deck shoes) ❶ N-COUNT **Deck shoes** are flat casual shoes made of canvas or leather. ❷ → See also color supplement

de|claim /dɪkleɪm/ (declaims, declaiming, declaimed) V-T/V-I If you **declaim**, you speak dramatically, as if you were acting in a theater. [WRITTEN] ❑ *He raised his right fist and declaimed: "Liar and cheat!"* ❑ *He used to declaim French verse to us.*

de|clama|tory /dɪklæmətɔri/ ADJ A **declamatory** phrase, statement, or way of speaking is dramatic and confident. [FORMAL]

dec|la|ra|tion ✦✧✧ /dɛkləreɪʃ⁰n/ (declarations) ❶ N-COUNT A **declaration** is an official announcement or statement. ❑ *The opening speeches sounded more like declarations of war than offerings of peace.* ❷ N-COUNT A **declaration** is a firm, emphatic statement which shows that you have no doubts about what you are saying. ❑ *...declarations of undying love.* ❸ N-COUNT A **declaration** is a written statement about something which you have signed and which can be used as evidence in a court of law. ❑ *On the customs declaration, the sender labeled the freight as agricultural machinery.*

de|clare ✦✦✧ /dɪklɛər/ (declares, declaring, declared) ❶ V-T If you **declare** that something is true, you say that it is true in a

declassify   327   **decoration**

firm, deliberate way. You can also **declare** an attitude or intention. [WRITTEN] ❑ *He declared he would not run for a second term as president.* ❑ *He declared his intention to become the best golfer in the world.* **2** V-T If you **declare** something, you state officially and formally that it exists or is the case. ❑ *The government is ready to declare a permanent ceasefire.* ❑ *His lawyers are confident that the judges will declare Mr. Stevens innocent.* **3** V-T If you **declare** goods that you have bought in another country or money that you have earned, you say how much you have bought or earned so that you can pay tax on it. ❑ *Declaring the wrong income by mistake will no longer lead to an automatic fine.*

de|clas|si|fy /dɪklǽsɪfaɪ/ (**declassifies, declassifying, declassified**) V-T [usu passive] If secret documents or records **are declassified**, it is officially stated that they are no longer secret. ❑ *These reports were only declassified last year.*

de|cline ♦♦◇ /dɪklaɪn/ (**declines, declining, declined**) **1** V-I If something **declines**, it becomes less in quantity, importance, or strength. ❑ *The number of staff has declined from 217,000 to 114,000.* ❑ *Hourly output by workers declined 1.3% in the first quarter.* **2** V-T/V-I If you **decline** something or **decline** to do something, you politely refuse to accept it or do it. [FORMAL] ❑ *He declined their invitation.* ❑ *He offered the boys some coffee. They declined politely.* **3** N-VAR If there is a **decline** in something, it becomes less in quantity, importance, or quality. ❑ *Official figures show a sharp decline in the number of foreign tourists.* **4** PHRASE If something is **in decline** or **on the decline**, it is gradually decreasing in importance, quality, or power. ❑ *Thankfully the smoking of cigarettes is on the decline.* **5** PHRASE If something goes or falls **into decline**, it begins to gradually decrease in importance, quality, or power. ❑ *Libraries are an investment for the future and they should not be allowed to fall into decline.* **6** → See feature box at **population**

---- SYNONYMS ----

decline
VERB
1
fall: *Output will fall by 6%.*
drop: *Temperatures can drop to freezing at night.*
sink: *Salary increases have sunk to around seven percent.*
decrease: *Population growth is decreasing by 1.4% each year.*
lessen: *He is used to a lot of attention from his wife, which will inevitably lessen when the baby is born.*
dwindle: *Exports are dwindling, and the trade deficit is swelling.*
2
refuse: *He offered me a second drink, which I refused.*
reject: *Seventeen publishers rejected the manuscript before Jenks saw its potential.*
turn down: *I thanked him for the offer, but turned it down.*
NOUN **3**
fall: *There was a sharp fall in the value of the pound.*
drop: *The poll indicates a drop in support for the Conservatives.*
decrease: *Interest rates have fallen from 10 percent to 6 percent – a decrease of 40 percent.*
deterioration: *...the slow, steady deterioration of a patient with Alzheimer's disease.*
worsening: *This latest incident is bound to lead to a further worsening of relations between the two countries.*
downturn: *They predicted a severe economic downturn.*

---- COLLOCATIONS ----

decline
NOUN **3**
adjective + **decline**: precipitous, rapid, sharp, steep; gradual, steady; irreversible, terminal
verb + **decline**: halt; reverse; offset
VERB
1
decline + adverb: precipitously, rapidly, sharply, steeply; steadily
2
decline + noun: invitation, offer, request

de|code /diːkoʊd/ (**decodes, decoding, decoded**) **1** V-T If you **decode** a message that has been written or spoken in a code, you change it into ordinary language. ❑ *All he had to do was decode it and pass it over.* **2** V-T A device that **decodes** a broadcast signal changes it into a form that can be displayed on a television screen. ❑ *About 60,000 subscribers have special adapters to receive and decode the signals.*

de|cod|er /diːkoʊdər/ (**decoders**) N-COUNT A **decoder** is a device used to decode messages or signals sent in code, for example, the television signals from a satellite.

de|colo|niza|tion /diːkɒlənaɪzeɪʃən/

in BRIT, also use **decolonisation**

N-UNCOUNT **Decolonization** means giving political independence to a country that was previously a colony.

de|com|mis|sion /diːkəmɪʃən/ (**decommissions, decommissioning, decommissioned**) V-T When something such as a nuclear reactor or a large machine **is decommissioned**, it is taken out of use and taken apart because it is no longer going to be used. ❑ *The ships were to be decommissioned.*

de|com|pose /diːkəmpoʊz/ (**decomposes, decomposing, decomposed**) V-T/V-I When things such as dead plants or animals **decompose**, or when something **decomposes** them, they change chemically and begin to decay. ❑ *...a dead body found decomposing in the woods.* ❑ *The debris slowly decomposes into compost.*

de|com|po|si|tion /diːkɒmpəzɪʃən/ N-UNCOUNT **Decomposition** is the process of decay that takes place when a living thing changes chemically after dying. [FORMAL]

de|com|pres|sion /diːkəmprɛʃən/ **1** N-UNCOUNT **Decompression** is the reduction of the force on something that is caused by the weight of the air. ❑ *Decompression blew out a window in the plane.* **2** N-UNCOUNT [usu N n] **Decompression** is the process of bringing someone back to the normal pressure of the air after they have been deep underwater. ❑ *...a decompression chamber.*

de|con|gest|ant /diːkəndʒɛstənt/ (**decongestants**) N-MASS A **decongestant** is a medicine which helps someone who has a cold to breathe more easily.

de|con|struct /diːkənstrʌkt/ (**deconstructs, deconstructing, deconstructed**) V-T In philosophy and literary criticism, to **deconstruct** an idea or text means to show the contradictions in its meaning, and to show how it does not fully explain what it claims to explain. [TECHNICAL] ❑ *She sets up a framework to deconstruct various categories of film.* • **de|con|struc|tion** /diːkənstrʌkʃən/ N-UNCOUNT ❑ *...the wilful deconstruction of sacred texts.*

de|con|tami|nate /diːkəntæmɪneɪt/ (**decontaminates, decontaminating, decontaminated**) V-T To **decontaminate** something means to remove all germs or dangerous substances from it. ❑ *...procedures for decontaminating pilots hit by chemical weapons.* • **de|con|tami|na|tion** /diːkəntæmɪneɪʃən/ N-UNCOUNT ❑ *The land will require public money for decontamination.*

de|con|trol /diːkəntroʊl/ (**decontrols, decontrolling, decontrolled**) V-T When governments **decontrol** an activity, they remove controls from it so that companies or organizations have more freedom. [mainly AM] ❑ *The Russian government chose not to decontrol oil and gas prices last January.* • N-VAR [oft n n, N of n] **Decontrol** is also a noun. ❑ *...continuing decontrol of banking institutions.*

de|cor /deɪkɔːr/ N-UNCOUNT The **decor** of a house or room is its style of furnishing and decoration. ❑ *The decor is simple – black lacquer panels on white walls.*

deco|rate ♦◇◇ /dɛkəreɪt/ (**decorates, decorating, decorated**) **1** V-T If you **decorate** something, you make it more attractive by adding things to it. ❑ *He decorated his room with pictures of all his favorite sports figures.* **2** V-T/V-I If you **decorate** a room or the inside of a building, you put new paint or wallpaper on the walls and ceiling, and paint the woodwork. ❑ *When they came to decorate the rear bedroom, it was Jemma who had the final say.* ❑ *The boys are planning to decorate when they get the time.*
• **deco|rat|ing** N-UNCOUNT ❑ *I did a lot of the decorating myself.*
• **deco|ra|tion** N-UNCOUNT ❑ *The renovation and decoration took four months.*

deco|ra|tion /dɛkəreɪʃən/ (**decorations**) **1** N-UNCOUNT The **decoration** of a room is its furniture, wallpaper, and ornaments. ❑ *The decoration and furnishings had to be practical* enough for a family home. **2** N-VAR **Decorations** are features that are added to something in order to make it look more attractive. ❑ *The only wall decorations are candles and a single mirror.* **3** N-COUNT **Decorations** are brightly colored objects such as pieces of paper and balloons, which you put up in a room on special occasions to make it look more attractive. ❑ *Colorful streamers and paper decorations had been hung from the ceiling.* **4** → see also **decorate**

deco|ra|tive /dɛkərətɪv, -əreɪtɪv/ ADJ Something that is **decorative** is intended to look pretty or attractive. ❑ *The curtains are for purely decorative purposes and do not open or close.*

deco|ra|tor /dɛkəreɪtər/ (decorators) **1** N-COUNT A **decorator** is a person who is employed to design and decorate the inside of people's houses. [AM] ❑ *...Bloomberg's private palace, with its intricate interior design by decorator Jamie Drake.* **2** → see also **interior decorator**

deco|rous /dɛkərəs/ ADJ **Decorous** behavior is very respectable, calm, and polite. [FORMAL] • **deco|rous|ly** ADV ❑ *He sipped his drink decorously.*

de|co|rum /dɪkɔrəm/ N-UNCOUNT **Decorum** is behavior that people consider to be correct, polite, and respectable. [FORMAL] ❑ *I was treated with decorum and respect throughout the investigation.*

de|cou|ple /dikʌpəl/ (decouples, decoupling, decoupled) V-T If two countries, organizations, or ideas that were connected in some way **are decoupled**, the connection between them is ended. [FORMAL] ❑ *...a conception which decouples culture and politics.* ❑ *The issue threatened to decouple Europe from the United States.*

de|coy /dikɔɪ/ (decoys) N-COUNT If you refer to something or someone as a **decoy**, you mean that they are intended to attract people's attention and deceive them, for example, by leading them into a trap or away from a particular place. ❑ *A plane was waiting at the airport with its engines running but this was just one of the decoys.*

de|crease (decreases, decreasing, decreased)

The verb is pronounced /dɪkris/. The noun is pronounced /dikris/ or /dɪkris/.

1 V-T/V-I When something **decreases** or when you **decrease** it, it becomes less in quantity, size, or intensity. ❑ *Population growth is decreasing by 1.4% each year.* ❑ *The number of independent firms decreased from 198 to 96.* ❑ *Since 1945 air forces have decreased in size.* **2** N-COUNT A **decrease** in the quantity, size, or intensity of something is a reduction in it. ❑ *In Spain and Portugal there has been a decrease in the number of young people out of work.*

de|cree /dɪkri/ (decrees, decreeing, decreed) **1** N-COUNT [also by N] A **decree** is an official order or decision, especially one made by the ruler of a country. ❑ *In July he issued a decree ordering all unofficial armed groups in the country to disband.* **2** N-COUNT A **decree** is a judgment made by a law court. [mainly AM] ❑ *...court decrees.* **3** V-T If someone in authority **decrees** that something must happen, they decide or state this officially. ❑ *The government decreed that all who wanted to live and work in Kenya must hold Kenyan passports.*

de|crep|it /dɪkrɛpɪt/ ADJ Something that is **decrepit** is old and in bad condition. Someone who is **decrepit** is old and weak. ❑ *The film had been shot in a decrepit old police station.*

de|crepi|tude /dɪkrɛpɪtud/ N-UNCOUNT **Decrepitude** is the state of being very old and in poor condition. [FORMAL] ❑ *The building had a general air of decrepitude and neglect.*

de|crimi|nal|ize /dikrɪmɪnəlaɪz/ (decriminalizes, decriminalizing, decriminalized)

in BRIT, also use **decriminalise**

V-T When a criminal offense **is decriminalized**, the law changes so that it is no longer a criminal offense. ❑ *...the question of whether prostitution should be decriminalized.* • **de|crimi|nali|za|tion** /dikrɪmɪnəlɪzeɪʃən/ N-UNCOUNT [oft N of n] ❑ *...a bill calling for the decriminalization of marijuana.*

de|cry /dɪkraɪ/ (decries, decrying, decried) V-T If someone **decries** an idea or action, they criticize it strongly. [FORMAL] ❑ *He is impatient with those who decry the plan.* ❑ *People decried the campaign as a waste of money.*

dedi|cate /dɛdɪkeɪt/ (dedicates, dedicating, dedicated) **1** V-T If you say that someone **has dedicated** themselves to something, you approve of the fact that they have decided to give a lot of time and effort to it because they think that it is important. [APPROVAL] ❑ *For the next few years, she dedicated herself to her work.* • **dedi|cat|ed** ADJ ❑ *He's quite dedicated to his students.* • **dedi|ca|tion** N-UNCOUNT ❑ *We admire her courage, compassion, and dedication to the cause of humanity, justice, and peace.* **2** V-T If someone **dedicates** something such as a book, play, or piece of music to you, they mention your name, for example, in the front of a book or when a piece of music is performed, as a way of showing affection or respect for you. ❑ *She dedicated her first album to Woody Allen, who she says understands her obsession.*

dedi|cat|ed /dɛdɪkeɪtɪd/ **1** ADJ You use **dedicated** to describe someone who enjoys a particular activity very much and spends a lot of time doing it. ❑ *Her great-grandfather had clearly been a dedicated and stoical traveler.* **2** ADJ You use **dedicated** to describe something that is made, built, or designed for one particular purpose or thing. ❑ *Such areas should also be served by dedicated cycle routes.* ❑ *...the world's first museum dedicated to ecology.* **3** → see also **dedicate**

dedi|ca|tion /dɛdɪkeɪʃən/ (dedications) **1** N-COUNT A **dedication** is a message which is written at the beginning of a book, or a short announcement which is sometimes made before a play or piece of music is performed, as a sign of affection or respect for someone. **2** → see also **dedicate**

de|duce /dɪdus/ (deduces, deducing, deduced) V-T If you **deduce** something or **deduce** that something is true, you reach that conclusion because of other things that you know to be true. ❑ *Alison cleverly deduced that I was the author of the letter.* ❑ *The date of the document can be deduced from references to the Civil War.*

de|duct /dɪdʌkt/ (deducts, deducting, deducted) V-T When you **deduct** an amount from a total, you subtract it from the total. ❑ *The company deducted this payment from his compensation.*

de|duct|ible /dɪdʌktɪbəl/ (deductibles) **1** ADJ If a payment or expense is **deductible**, it can be deducted from another sum such as your income, for example, when calculating how much income tax you have to pay. ❑ *Part of the auto-loan interest is deductible as a business expense.* ❑ *...deductible expenses.* **2** N-COUNT A **deductible** is a sum of money which an insured person has to pay toward the cost of an insurance claim. The insurance company pays the rest. [AM] ❑ *Each time they go to a hospital, they have to pay a deductible of $628.*

de|duc|tion /dɪdʌkʃən/ (deductions) **1** N-COUNT A **deduction** is an amount that has been subtracted from a total. ❑ *Most homeowners can get a federal income tax deduction on interest payments to a home equity loan.* **2** N-COUNT A **deduction** is a conclusion that you have reached about something because of other things that you know to be true. ❑ *My mother had made her own shrewd deductions about what was going on.* **3** N-UNCOUNT **Deduction** is the process of reaching a conclusion about something because of other things that you know to be true. ❑ *Miss Allan beamed at him. "You are clever to guess. I'm sure I don't know how you did it."—"Deduction," James said.*

de|duc|tive /dɪdʌktɪv/ ADJ [usu ADJ n] **Deductive** reasoning involves drawing conclusions logically from other things that are already known. [FORMAL]

deed /did/ (deeds) **1** N-COUNT A **deed** is something that is done, especially something that is very good or very bad. [LITERARY] ❑ *The perpetrators of this evil deed must be brought to justice.* **2** N-COUNT A **deed** is a document containing the terms of an agreement, especially an agreement concerning the ownership of land or a building. [LEGAL] ❑ *He asked if I had the deeds to his father's property.*

dee|jay /didʒeɪ/ (deejays, deejaying, deejayed) **1** N-COUNT A **deejay** is the same as a **disc jockey**. [INFORMAL] **2** V-I If someone **deejays**, they introduce and play music on the radio or at a disco. ❑ *Ronson has been deejaying since age 19.*

deem /dim/ (deems, deeming, deemed) V-T If something **is deemed** to have a particular quality or to do a particular thing, it is considered to have that quality or do that thing. [FORMAL] ❑ *French and German were deemed essential.* ❑ *He says he would support the use of force if the UN deemed it necessary.*

deep /diːp/ (**deeper**, **deepest**) **1** ADJ If something is **deep**, it extends a long way down from the ground or from the top surface of something. ❑ *The water is very deep and mysterious looking.* ❑ *Den had dug a deep hole in the center of the garden.* • ADV **Deep** is also an adverb. ❑ *Gingerly, she put her hand in deeper, to the bottom.* • **deep|ly** ADV ❑ *There isn't time to dig deeply and put in manure or compost.* **2** ADJ A **deep** container, such as a closet, extends or measures a long distance from front to back. ❑ *The wardrobe was very deep.* **3** ADJ You use **deep** to emphasize the seriousness, strength, importance, or degree of something. [EMPHASIS] ❑ *I had a deep admiration for Sartre.* ❑ *He wants to express his deep sympathy to the family.* • **deep|ly** ADV ❑ *He loved his brother deeply.* **4** ADJ [ADJ n] If you are in a **deep** sleep, you are sleeping peacefully and it is difficult to wake you. ❑ *Una soon fell into a deep sleep.* • **deep|ly** ADV [ADV after v] ❑ *She slept deeply but woke early.* **5** ADJ [v-link ADJ in n] If you are **deep in** thought or **deep in** conversation, you are concentrating very hard on what you are thinking or saying and are not aware of the things that are happening around you. ❑ *Before long, we were deep in conversation.* **6** ADJ [ADJ n] A **deep** breath or sigh uses or fills the whole of your lungs. ❑ *Cal took a long, deep breath, struggling to control his own emotions.* • **deep|ly** ADV [ADV after v] ❑ *She sighed deeply and covered her face with her hands.* **7** ADJ A **deep** sound is low in pitch. ❑ *His voice was deep and mellow.* **8** ADJ If you describe something such as a problem or a piece of writing as **deep**, you mean that it is important, serious, or complicated. ❑ *They're written as adventure stories. They're not intended to be deep.* **9** ADV **Deep** in an area means a long way inside it. ❑ *Picking up his bag the giant strode off deep into the forest.* **10** ADV If you experience or feel something **deep** inside you or **deep** down, you feel it very strongly even though you do not necessarily show it. ❑ *Deep down, she supported her husband's involvement in the organization.* **11** ADV [ADV in/into n] If you are **deep** in debt, you have a lot of debts. ❑ *He is so deep in debt and desperate for money that he's apparently willing to say anything.* • **deep|ly** ADV [ADV in/into n] ❑ *Because of her medical and her legal bills, she is now penniless and deeply in debt.* **12** COMB IN COLOR You use **deep** to describe colors that are strong and fairly dark. ❑ *The sky was peach colored in the east, deep blue and starry in the west.* ❑ *These Amish cushions in traditional deep colors are available in two sizes.* **13** PHRASE If you say that something **goes deep** or **runs deep**, you mean that it is very serious or strong and is hard to change. ❑ *His anger and anguish clearly went deep.* **14 in deep water** → see **water**

deep dive N-COUNT A **deep dive** into something is a thorough investigation and analysis of it. ❑ *Researchers took a deep dive into the data and made some surprising findings.*

deep|en /diːpən/ (**deepens**, **deepening**, **deepened**) **1** V-T/V-I If a situation or emotion **deepens** or if something **deepens** in it, becomes stronger and more intense. ❑ *If this is not stopped, the financial crisis will deepen.* **2** V-T If you **deepen** your knowledge or understanding of a subject, you learn more about it and become more interested in it. ❑ *The course is an exciting opportunity for anyone wishing to deepen their understanding of themselves and other people.* **3** V-T/V-I When a sound **deepens** or **is deepened**, it becomes lower in tone. ❑ *The music room had been made to reflect and deepen sounds.* **4** V-T If people **deepen** something, they increase its depth by digging out its lower surface. ❑ *The project would deepen the river from 40 to 45 feet, to allow for larger ships.*

deep|fake /diːpfeɪk/ (**deepfakes**) N-UNCOUNT **Deepfake** is a way of adding a digital image or video over another image or video, so that it appears to be part of the original. • N-COUNT A **deepfake** is an image or video that has been changed in this way. ❑ *Deepfakes can be convincing enough to pose a real threat to democracy.*

deep freeze (**deep freezes**) also **deep-freeze**, **deepfreeze** N-COUNT A **deep freeze** is the same as a **freezer**.

deep-fry (**deep-fries**, **deep-frying**, **deep-fried**) V-T If you **deep-fry** food, you fry it in a large amount of fat or oil. ❑ *Heat the oil and deep-fry the fish fillets.*

deep-rooted ADJ [usu ADJ n] **Deep-rooted** means the same as **deep-seated**. ❑ *...long-term solutions to a deep-rooted problem.*

deep-sea **1** ADJ [ADJ n] **Deep-sea** activities take place in the areas of the sea that are a long way from the coast. ❑ *...deep-sea diving.* ❑ *...a deep-sea fisherman.* **2** → See feature box at **ocean**

deep-seated ADJ A **deep-seated** problem, feeling, or belief is difficult to change because its causes have been there for a long time. ❑ *The country is still suffering from deep-seated economic problems.*

deep-set ADJ [usu ADJ n] **Deep-set** eyes seem to be further back in the face than most people's eyes. [WRITTEN] ❑ *He had deep-set brown eyes.*

deep-six (**deep-sixes**, **deep-sixing**, **deep-sixed**) V-T To **deep-six** something means to get rid of it or destroy it. [mainly AM, INFORMAL] ❑ *I'd simply like to deep-six this whole project.*

Deep South N-SING [the N] The **Deep South** consists of the states that are furthest south in the United States.

deep vein throm|bo|sis (**deep vein thromboses**) N-VAR **Deep vein thrombosis** is a serious medical condition in which blood clots form in the legs and can move up to the lungs. The abbreviation **DVT** is also used. [MEDICAL] ❑ *He could have died after developing deep vein thrombosis during a flight to Sydney.*

deer /dɪər/ (**deer**)

Deer is both the singular and the plural form.

N-COUNT A **deer** is a large wild animal that eats grass and leaves. A male deer usually has large, branching horns.

deer|stalker /dɪərstɔːkər/ (**deerstalkers**) N-COUNT A **deerstalker** is an old-fashioned men's hat with parts at the sides which can be folded down to cover the ears.

deets /diːts/ N-PLURAL **Deets** is short for 'details.' [INFORMAL] ❑ *Can I have your credit card deets?*

de|face /dɪfeɪs/ (**defaces**, **defacing**, **defaced**) V-T If someone **defaces** something such as a wall or a notice, they spoil it by writing or drawing things on it. ❑ *It's illegal to deface property.*

de fac|to /di fæktoʊ, deɪ/ ADJ [ADJ n] **De facto** is used to indicate that something is a particular thing, even though it was not planned or intended to be that thing. [FORMAL] ❑ *This might be interpreted as a de facto recognition of the republic's independence.* • ADV [ADV with cl] **De facto** is also an adverb. ❑ *They will be de facto in a state of war.*

defa|ma|tion /defəmeɪʃən/ N-UNCOUNT **Defamation** is the damaging of someone's good reputation by saying something bad and untrue about them. [FORMAL] ❑ *He sued for defamation.*

de|fama|tory /dɪfæmətɔːri/ ADJ Speech or writing that is **defamatory** is likely to damage someone's good reputation by saying something bad and untrue about them. [FORMAL] ❑ *The article was highly defamatory.*

de|fame /dɪfeɪm/ (**defames**, **defaming**, **defamed**) V-T If someone **defames** another person or thing, they say bad and untrue things about them. [FORMAL] ❑ *Sgt. Norwood complained that the article defamed him.*

de|fault /dɪfɔːlt/ (**defaults**, **defaulting**, **defaulted**) **1** V-I If a person, company, or country **defaults on** something that they have legally agreed to do, such as paying some money or doing a piece of work before a particular time, they fail to do it. [LEGAL] ❑ *The credit card business is down, and more borrowers are defaulting on loans.* • N-UNCOUNT **Default** is also a noun. ❑ *The corporation may be charged with default on its contract with the government.* **2** ADJ [ADJ n] A **default** situation is what exists or happens unless someone or something changes it. ❑ *He appeared unimpressed; but then, unimpressed was his default state.* **3** N-UNCOUNT In computing, the **default** is a particular set of instructions which a computer always uses unless the person using the computer gives other instructions. [COMPUTING] ❑ *The default setting on Windows Explorer will not show these files.* **4** PHRASE If something happens **by default**, it happens only because something else which might have prevented it or changed it has not happened. [FORMAL] ❑ *I would rather pay the individuals than let the money go to the State by default.* **5** → See feature box at **finance**

de|fault|er /dɪfɔːltər/ (**defaulters**) N-COUNT A **defaulter** is someone who does not do something that they are legally supposed to do, such as make a payment at a particular time, or appear in a court of law.

de|feat /dɪfiːt/ (**defeats**, **defeating**, **defeated**) **1** V-T If you **defeat** someone, you win a victory over them in a battle, game, or contest. ❑ *His guerrillas defeated the colonial army in 1954.* **2** V-T [usu passive] If a proposal or motion in a debate **is**

defeated, more people vote against it than for it. ☐ *The bill was defeated with support from only two congressmen.* ■3 V-T If a task or a problem **defeats** you, it is so difficult that you cannot do it or solve it. ☐ *The book he most wanted to write was the one which nearly defeated him.* ■4 V-T To **defeat** an action or plan means to cause it to fail. ☐ *The navy played a limited but significant role in defeating the rebellion.* ■5 N-VAR **Defeat** is the experience of being beaten in a battle, game, or contest, or of failing to achieve what you wanted to. ☐ *The most important thing is not to admit defeat until you really have to.* ☐ *...the Sonics' 31-point defeat at Sacramento on Sunday.* ■6 → See feature box at **competition**

SYNONYMS
defeat
VERB ■1
beat: *In yesterday's games, Switzerland beat the United States, two–one.*
conquer: *Early in the Eleventh Century, the whole of England was again conquered by the Vikings.*

de|feat|ism /dɪfiːtɪzəm/ N-UNCOUNT **Defeatism** is a way of thinking or talking which suggests that you expect to be unsuccessful. ☐ *...the mood of economic defeatism.*

de|feat|ist /dɪfiːtɪst/ (**defeatists**) N-COUNT A **defeatist** is someone who thinks or talks in a way that suggests that they expect to be unsuccessful. • ADJ **Defeatist** is also an adjective. ☐ *There is no point going out there with a defeatist attitude.*

def|ecate /dɛfəkeɪt/ (**defecates, defecating, defecated**) V-I When people and animals **defecate**, they get rid of waste matter from their body through their anus. [FORMAL]
• **def|eca|tion** /dɛfəkeɪʃ°n/ N-UNCOUNT ☐ *The drug's side effects can include involuntary defecation.*

de|fect (**defects, defecting, defected**)

The noun is pronounced /diːfɛkt/. The verb is pronounced /dɪfɛkt/.

■1 N-COUNT A **defect** is a fault or imperfection in a person or thing. ☐ *He was born with a hearing defect.* ☐ *A report has pointed out the defects of the present system.* ■2 V-I If you **defect**, you leave your country, political party, or other group, and join an opposing country, party, or group. ☐ *...a KGB officer who defected in 1963.* • **de|fec|tion** /dɪfɛkʃ°n/ (**defections**) N-VAR ☐ *...the defection of at least sixteen parliamentary deputies.*

de|fec|tive /dɪfɛktɪv/ ADJ If something is **defective**, there is something wrong with it and it does not work properly. ☐ *Retailers can return defective merchandise.*

de|fec|tor /dɪfɛktər/ (**defectors**) N-COUNT [usu with supp] A **defector** is someone who leaves their country, political party, or other group, and joins an opposing country, party, or group.

de|fence /dɪfɛns/ [BRIT] → see **defense**

de|fence|less /dɪfɛnslɪs/ [BRIT] → see **defenseless**

de|fend ♦♦◊ /dɪfɛnd/ (**defends, defending, defended**) ■1 V-T If you **defend** someone or something, you take action in order to protect them. ☐ *His courage in defending religious and civil rights inspired many outside the church.* ■2 V-T If you **defend** someone or something when they have been criticized, you argue in support of them. ☐ *He defended his administration's response to the disaster against critics who charge the federal government is moving too slowly.* ■3 V-T When a lawyer **defends** a person who has been accused of something, the lawyer argues on their behalf in a court of law that the charges are not true. ☐ *...a lawyer who defended political prisoners during the military regime.* ☐ *He has hired a lawyer to defend him against the allegation.* ■4 V-T When a sports player plays in the tournament which they won the previous time it was held, you can say that they **are defending** their title. [JOURNALISM] ☐ *Torrence expects to defend her title successfully in the next Olympics.*

SYNONYMS
defend
VERB ■1
protect: *So, what can women do to protect themselves from heart disease?*
guard: *Gunmen guarded homes near the cemetery with shotguns.*
shield: *He shielded his head from the sun with an old sack.*
safeguard: *The interests of minorities will have to be safeguarded under a new constitution.*

de|fend|ant /dɪfɛndənt/ (**defendants**) ■1 N-COUNT A **defendant** is a person who has been accused of breaking the law and is being tried in court. ☐ *The defendant pleaded guilty and was fined $500.* ■2 → See feature box at **legal**

de|fend|er /dɪfɛndər/ (**defenders**) ■1 N-COUNT If someone is a **defender** of a particular thing or person that has been criticized, they argue or act in support of that thing or person. ☐ *...the most ardent defenders of conventional family values.* ■2 N-COUNT A **defender** in a game such as soccer or hockey is a player whose main task is to try and stop the other side from scoring. ☐ *He was NFL's top defender that season.*

de|fense ♦♦◊ /dɪfɛns/ (**defenses**)

Defense in meaning ■7 is pronounced /diːfɛns/.

in BRIT, use **defence**

■1 N-UNCOUNT **Defense** is action that is taken to protect someone or something against attack. ☐ *The land was flat, giving no scope for defense.* ■2 N-UNCOUNT **Defense** is the organization of a country's armies and weapons, and their use to protect the country or its interests. ☐ *Twenty-eight percent of the federal budget is spent on defense.* ☐ *U.S. Defense Secretary visits China.* ■3 N-PLURAL The **defenses** of a country or region are all its armed forces and weapons. ☐ *He emphasized the need to maintain Britain's defenses at a level sufficient to deal with the unexpected.* ■4 N-COUNT A **defense** is something that people or animals can use or do to protect themselves. ☐ *Despite anything the science of medicine may have achieved, the immune system is our main defense against disease.* ■5 N-COUNT [oft N of n, also in N] A **defense** is something that you say or write which supports ideas or actions that have been criticized or questioned. ☐ *Chomsky's defense of his approach goes further.* ■6 N-SING The **defense** is the case that is presented by a lawyer in a trial for the person who has been accused of a crime. You can also refer to this person's lawyers as the **defense**. ☐ *The defense was that the records of the interviews were fabricated by the police.* ■7 N-SING-COLL [oft poss N, also in N] In games such as soccer or hockey, the **defense** is the group of players in a team who try to stop the opposing players from scoring a goal or a point. ☐ *Their defense, so strong last season, has now conceded 12 goals in six games.* ■8 PHRASE If you come to someone's **defense**, you help them by doing or saying something to protect them. ☐ *He realized none of his schoolmates would come to his defense.*

COLLOCATIONS
defense
NOUN
■5
adjective + **defense**: passionate, spirited, successful, vigorous
verb + **defense**: launch, mount
■6
adjective + **defense**: credible, robust, solid

de|fense|less /dɪfɛnslɪs/

in BRIT, use **defenceless**

ADJ If someone or something is **defenseless**, they are weak and unable to defend themselves properly. ☐ *...a savage attack on a defenseless young girl.*

de|fense mecha|nism (**defense mechanisms**) N-COUNT A **defense mechanism** is a way of behaving or thinking which is not conscious or deliberate and is an automatic reaction to unpleasant experiences or feelings such as anxiety and fear. [AM]

in BRIT, use **defence mechanism**.

de|fen|sible /dɪfɛnsɪb°l/ ADJ An opinion, system, or action that is **defensible** is one that people can argue is right or good. ☐ *Her reasons for acting are morally defensible.*

de|fen|sive /dɪfɛnsɪv/ ■1 ADJ You use **defensive** to describe things that are intended to protect someone or something. ☐ *The Government hastily organized defensive measures, deploying searchlights and antiaircraft guns around the target cities.* ■2 ADJ Someone who is **defensive** is behaving in a way that shows they feel unsure or threatened. ☐ *Like their children, parents are often defensive about their private lives.* • **de|fen|sive|ly** ADV

❑ "Oh, I know, I know," said Kate, defensively. **3** ADJ In sports, **defensive** play is play that is intended to prevent your opponent from scoring points against you. ❑ I'd always played a defensive game, waiting for my opponent to make a mistake. • **de|fen|sive|ly** ADV [ADV after v] ❑ We didn't play well defensively in the first half. **4** PHRASE If someone is **on the defensive**, they are trying to protect themselves or their interests because they feel unsure or threatened. ❑ The administration has been on the defensive about the war.

de|fer /dɪfɜr/ (defers, deferring, deferred) **1** V-T If you **defer** an event or action, you arrange for it to happen at a later date, rather than immediately or at the previously planned time. ❑ Customers often defer payment for as long as possible. **2** V-I If you **defer to** someone, you accept their opinion or do what they want you to do, even when you do not agree with it yourself, because you respect them or their authority. ❑ Doctors are encouraged to defer to experts.

def|er|ence /dɛfərəns/ N-UNCOUNT **Deference** is a polite and respectful attitude toward someone, especially because they have an important position. ❑ ...the older political tradition of deference to great leaders.

def|er|en|tial /dɛfərɛnʃəl/ ADJ [oft ADJ to n] Someone who is **deferential** is polite and respectful toward someone else. ❑ They like five-star hotels and deferential treatment. • **def|er|en|tial|ly** ADV ❑ The old man spoke deferentially.

de|fer|ment /dɪfɜrmənt/ (deferments) N-VAR **Deferment** means arranging for something to happen at a later date. [FORMAL] ❑ ...the deferment of debt repayments.

de|fer|ral /dɪfɜrəl/ (deferrals) N-VAR **Deferral** means the same as deferment.

de|fi|ance /dɪfaɪəns/ N-UNCOUNT [oft N of n] **Defiance** is behavior or an attitude which shows that you are not willing to obey someone. ❑ ...his courageous defiance of the government.

de|fi|ant /dɪfaɪənt/ ADJ If you say that someone is **defiant**, you mean they show aggression or independence by refusing to obey someone. ❑ The players are in a defiant mood as they prepare for tomorrow's game. • **de|fi|ant|ly** ADV ❑ They defiantly rejected any talk of a compromise.

de|fib|ril|la|tor /dɪfɪbrɪleɪtər/ (defibrillators) N-COUNT A **defibrillator** is a machine that starts the heart beating normally again after a heart attack, by giving it an electric shock. [MEDICAL]

de|fi|cien|cy /dɪfɪʃənsi/ (deficiencies) **1** N-VAR **Deficiency** in something, especially something that your body needs, is not having enough of it. ❑ They did blood tests on him for signs of vitamin deficiency. **2** N-VAR A **deficiency** that someone or something has is a weakness or imperfection in them. [FORMAL] ❑ The most serious deficiency in NATO's air defense is the lack of an identification system to distinguish friend from foe.

de|fi|cient /dɪfɪʃənt/ ADJ If someone or something is **deficient** in a particular thing, they do not have the full amount of it that they need in order to function normally or work properly. [FORMAL] ❑ ...a diet deficient in vitamin B.

defi|cit ✦✧✧ /dɛfəsɪt/ (deficits) N-COUNT A **deficit** is the amount by which something is less than what is required or expected, especially the amount by which the total money received is less than the total money spent. ❑ They're ready to cut the federal budget deficit for the next fiscal year. ❑ ...a deficit of five billion dollars. • PHRASE If an account or organization is **in deficit**, more money has been spent than has been received.

COLLOCATIONS

deficit
NOUN
noun + **deficit**: budget, pension, trade
verb + **deficit**: cut, eliminate, halve, reduce; tackle

SYNONYMS

deficit
NOUN
shortfall: The government has refused to make up a $30,000 shortfall in funding.
shortage: A shortage of funds is preventing the U.N. from monitoring relief.

defi|cit fi|nanc|ing **1** N-UNCOUNT **Deficit financing** is the financing of government spending through borrowing rather than revenue. [AM] ❑ The overriding problem is the continuing deficit financing of the federal government. **2** N-UNCOUNT **Deficit financing** is the same as deficit spending. [BRIT]

defi|cit spend|ing N-UNCOUNT **Deficit spending** is an economic policy in which a government spends more money raised by borrowing than it receives in revenue. [AM] ❑ ...detailed plans to end deficit spending by early next year.

de|file /dɪfaɪl/ (defiles, defiling, defiled) **1** V-T To **defile** something that people think is important or holy means to do something to it or say something about it which is offensive. [LITERARY] ❑ He had defiled the sacred name of the prophet. **2** N-COUNT A **defile** is a very narrow valley or passage, usually through mountains. [FORMAL]

de|fin|able /dɪfaɪnəbəl/ ADJ Something that is **definable** can be described or identified. ❑ Many suffered from a definable alcohol, drug, or mental disorder. ❑ ...groups broadly definable as conservative.

de|fine ✦✧✧ /dɪfaɪn/ (defines, defining, defined) V-T If you **define** something, you show, describe, or state clearly what it is and what its limits are, or what it is like. ❑ The Convention Against Torture defines torture as any act that inflicts severe pain or suffering, physical or mental.

SYNONYMS

define
VERB
describe: The myth of Narcissus is described in Ovid's work.
interpret: The whole speech could be interpreted as a coded message to the Americans.
characterize: Both companies have characterized the relationship as friendly.

de|fined /dɪfaɪnd/ ADJ [usu adv ADJ] If something is clearly **defined** or strongly **defined**, its outline is clear or strong. ❑ A clearly defined track now leads down to the valley.

defi|nite /dɛfɪnɪt/ **1** ADJ If something such as a decision or an arrangement is **definite**, it is firm and clear, and unlikely to be changed. ❑ It's too soon to give a definite answer. ❑ She made no definite plans for her future. **2** ADJ **Definite** evidence or information is true, rather than being someone's opinion or guess. ❑ We didn't have any definite proof. **3** ADJ [ADJ n] You use **definite** to emphasize the strength of your opinion or belief. [EMPHASIS] ❑ There has already been a definite improvement. **4** ADJ Someone who is **definite** behaves or talks in a firm, confident way. ❑ Mary is very definite about this.

defi|nite ar|ti|cle (definite articles) N-COUNT The word 'the' is sometimes called the **definite article**.

defi|nite|ly ✦✧✧ /dɛfɪnɪtli/ **1** ADV You use **definitely** to emphasize that something is the case, or to emphasize the strength of your intention or opinion. [EMPHASIS] ❑ I'm definitely going to get in touch with these people. **2** ADV [ADV before v] If something has been **definitely** decided, the decision will not be changed. ❑ She had definitely decided that she wanted to continue working with women in prison.

SYNONYMS

definitely
ADV **1**
certainly: The public is certainly getting tired of hearing about it.
clearly: Clearly, the police cannot break the law in order to enforce it.
unquestionably: He is unquestionably a star.
undeniably: Bringing up a baby is undeniably hard work.

defi|ni|tion ✦✧✧ /dɛfɪnɪʃən/ (definitions) **1** N-COUNT A **definition** is a statement giving the meaning of a word or expression, especially in a dictionary. ❑ There is no general agreement on a standard definition of intelligence. • PHRASE If you say that something has a particular quality **by definition**, you mean that it has this quality simply because of what it is. **2** N-UNCOUNT **Definition** is the quality of being clear and distinct. ❑ The first speakers at the conference criticized Prof. Johnson's new program for lack of definition.

> **SYNONYMS**
> **definition**
> NOUN **2**
> **clarity:** *This remarkable technology provides far greater clarity than conventional x-rays.*
> **sharpness:** *The telescope shows us our Universe with wonderful sharpness and clarity.*

de|fini|tive /dɪfɪnɪtɪv/ **1** ADJ Something that is **definitive** provides a firm conclusion that cannot be questioned. ❑ *No one has come up with a definitive answer as to why this should be so.* • **de|fini|tive|ly** ADV ❑ *Law enforcement officials had definitively identified Blanco as a potential suspect.* **2** ADJ A **definitive** book or performance is thought to be the best of its kind that has ever been done or that will ever be done. ❑ *...Ian Macdonald's definitive book on The Beatles.*

de|flate /dɪfleɪt/ (**deflates, deflating, deflated**) **1** V-T If you **deflate** someone or something, you take away their confidence or make them seem less important. ❑ *I hate to deflate your ego, but you seem to have an exaggerated idea of your importance to me.* • **de|flat|ed** ADJ ❑ *When she refused I felt deflated.* **2** V-T/V-I When something such as a tire or balloon **deflates**, or when you **deflate** it, all the air comes out of it. ❑ *We drove a few miles until the tire deflated and we had to stop the car.*

de|fla|tion /dɪfleɪʃən/ N-UNCOUNT **Deflation** is a reduction in economic activity that leads to lower levels of industrial output, employment, investment, trade, profits, and prices. [BUSINESS] ❑ *Deflation is beginning to take hold in the clothing industry.*

de|fla|tion|ary /dɪfleɪʃəneri/ ADJ A **deflationary** economic policy or measure is one that is intended to or likely to cause deflation. [BUSINESS] ❑ *...the government's refusal to implement deflationary measures.*

de|flect /dɪflɛkt/ (**deflects, deflecting, deflected**) **1** V-T If you **deflect** something such as criticism or attention, you act in a way that prevents it from being directed toward you or affecting you. ❑ *Cage changed his name to deflect accusations of nepotism.* **2** V-T To **deflect** someone from a course of action means to make them decide not to continue with it by putting pressure on them or by offering them something desirable. ❑ *The war did not deflect him from the path he had long ago taken.* **3** V-T If you **deflect** something that is moving, you make it go in a slightly different direction, for example, by hitting or blocking it. ❑ *My forearm deflected the first punch.*

de|flec|tion /dɪflɛkʃən/ (**deflections**) **1** N-VAR The **deflection** of something means making it change direction. [TECHNICAL] ❑ *...the deflection of light as it passes through the slits in the grating.* **2** N-COUNT In sports, the **deflection** of a ball, kick, or shot is when the ball hits an object and then travels in a different direction.

de|flow|er /diflaʊər/ (**deflowers, deflowering, deflowered**) V-T When a woman **is deflowered**, she has sex for the first time. [LITERARY, OLD-FASHIONED] ❑ *She was enraged with Taylor because he had deflowered her daughter.*

de|fog|ger /difɒgər/ (**defoggers**) N-COUNT A **defogger** is a device that removes condensation from the window of a vehicle by blowing warm air onto it. [AM] ❑ *...rear window defoggers.*

in BRIT, use **demister**

de|fo|li|ant /difoʊliənt/ (**defoliants**) N-MASS A **defoliant** is a chemical used on trees and plants to make all their leaves fall off. Defoliants are especially used in war to remove protection from an enemy.

de|fo|li|ate /difoʊlieɪt/ (**defoliates, defoliating, defoliated**) V-T To **defoliate** an area or the plants in it means to cause the leaves on the plants to fall off or be destroyed. This is done especially in war to remove protection from an enemy. ❑ *...Agent Orange, the infamous, dioxin-laced cocktail used to defoliate the Vietnamese jungle.* • **de|fo|lia|tion** /difoʊlieɪʃən/ N-UNCOUNT ❑ *...preventing defoliation of trees by caterpillars.*

de|for|est /difɔrɪst/ (**deforests, deforesting, deforested**) V-T [usu passive] If an area **is deforested**, all the trees there are cut down or destroyed. ❑ *...the 400,000 square kilometers of the Amazon basin that have already been deforested.* • **de|for|esta|tion** /difɔrɪsteɪʃən/ N-UNCOUNT ❑ *One percent of Brazil's total forest cover is being lost every year to deforestation.*

> **VOCABULARY IN CONTEXT**

Deforestation

Deforestation is a huge problem that is seriously **endangering biodiversity** in many **habitats** around the world. Many people think of the **rain forests** when they think of deforestation, but, in fact, it is taking place in numerous other irreplaceable forested areas around the world, from the Arctic Circle to the equator. People also assume that deforestation implies vast areas of land being **encroached** upon to provide wood for the paper and furniture industries, but the consequences of the deforestation of even a small area can have far-reaching effects on the local **flora** and **fauna**. Many animals live in a very **specialized** habitat, feeding off one single species of plant or only a few different types of animals. When their **food sources** become **scarce**, many animals **die out** and some species even become **extinct**. This is having devastating consequences that we are only just beginning to understand.

de|form /dɪfɔrm/ (**deforms, deforming, deformed**) V-T/V-I If something **deforms** a person's body or something else, it causes it to have an unnatural shape. In technical English, you can also say that the second thing **deforms** when it changes to an unnatural shape. ❑ *Bad rheumatoid arthritis deforms limbs.* • **de|formed** ADJ ❑ *He was born with a deformed right leg.*

de|form|ity /dɪfɔrmɪti/ (**deformities**) **1** N-COUNT A **deformity** is a part of someone's body which is not the normal shape because of injury or illness, or because they were born this way. ❑ *...facial deformities in babies.* **2** N-UNCOUNT **Deformity** is the condition of having a deformity. ❑ *The object of these movements is to prevent stiffness or deformity of joints.*

de|fraud /dɪfrɔd/ (**defrauds, defrauding, defrauded**) V-T If someone **defrauds** you, they take something away from you or stop you from getting what belongs to you by means of tricks and lies. ❑ *He pleaded guilty to charges of conspiracy to defraud the government.*

de|fray /dɪfreɪ/ (**defrays, defraying, defrayed**) V-T If you **defray** someone's costs or expenses, you give them money which represents the amount that they have spent, for example, while they have been doing something for you or acting on your behalf. [FORMAL] ❑ *The government has committed billions toward defraying the costs of the war.*

de|frock /dɪfrɒk/ (**defrocked**) V-T PASSIVE If a priest **is defrocked**, he is forced to stop being a priest because of bad behavior. ❑ *Mellors was preaching heresy and had to be immediately defrocked.* ❑ *...a defrocked priest.*

de|frost /dɪfrɔst/ (**defrosts, defrosting, defrosted**) **1** V-T/V-I When you **defrost** frozen food or when it **defrosts**, you allow or cause it to become unfrozen so that you can eat it or cook it. ❑ *She has a microwave, but uses it mainly for defrosting bread.* ❑ *Once the turkey has defrosted, remove the giblets.* **2** V-T/V-I When you **defrost** a refrigerator or freezer, you turn it off or press a special switch so that the ice inside it can melt. You can also say that a refrigerator or freezer **is defrosting**. ❑ *Defrost the freezer regularly so that it works at maximum efficiency.*

deft /dɛft/ (defter, deftest) ADJ A **deft** action is skillful and often quick. [WRITTEN] ◻ *With a deft flick of his wrist, he extinguished the match.* ● **deft|ly** ADV ◻ *One of the waiting servants deftly caught him as he fell.*

de|funct /dɪfʌŋkt/ ADJ If something is **defunct**, it no longer exists or has stopped functioning or operating. ◻ *...the leader of the now defunct Social Democratic Party.*

de|fuse /diːfyuːz/ (defuses, defusing, defused) **1** V-T If you **defuse** a dangerous or tense situation, you calm it. ◻ *Police administrators credited the organization with helping defuse potentially violent situations.* **2** V-T If someone **defuses** a bomb, they remove the fuse so that it cannot explode. ◻ *Police have defused a bomb found in a downtown building.*

defy /dɪfaɪ/ (defies, defying, defied) **1** V-T If you **defy** someone or something that is trying to make you behave in a particular way, you refuse to obey them and behave in that way. ◻ *This was the first (and last) time that I dared to defy my mother.* **2** V-T If you **defy** someone to do something, you challenge them to do it when you think that they will be unable to do it or too frightened to do it. ◻ *I defy you to come up with one major accomplishment of the current president.* **3** V-T [no passive, no cont] If something **defies** description or understanding, it is so strange, extreme, or surprising that it is almost impossible to understand or explain. ◻ *It's a devastating and barbaric act that defies all comprehension.*

de|gen|era|cy /dɪdʒɛnərəsi/ N-UNCOUNT If you refer to the behavior of a group of people as **degeneracy**, you mean that you think it is shocking, immoral, or disgusting. [DISAPPROVAL] ◻ *...the moral degeneracy of society.*

de|gen|er|ate (degenerates, degenerating, degenerated)

The verb is pronounced /dɪdʒɛnəreɪt/. The adjective is pronounced /dɪdʒɛnərɪt/.

1 V-I If you say that someone or something **degenerates**, you mean that they become worse in some way, for example, weaker, lower in quality, or more dangerous. ◻ *Inactivity can make your joints stiff, and the bones may begin to degenerate.* ● **de|gen|era|tion** /dɪdʒɛnəreɪʃən/ N-UNCOUNT ◻ *...various forms of physical and mental degeneration.* **2** ADJ If you describe a person or their behavior as **degenerate**, you disapprove of them because you think they have low standards of behavior or morality. [DISAPPROVAL] ◻ *...a group of degenerate computer hackers.* **3** → See feature box at **urban**

de|gen|era|tive /dɪdʒɛnərətɪv, -əreɪtɪv/ ADJ [usu ADJ n] A **degenerative** disease or condition is one that gets worse as time progresses. ◻ *...degenerative diseases of the brain, like Alzheimer's.*

deg|ra|da|tion /dɛgrədeɪʃən/ (degradations) **1** N-VAR You use **degradation** to refer to a situation, condition, or experience which you consider shameful and disgusting, especially one which involves poverty or immorality. [DISAPPROVAL] ◻ *They were sickened by the scenes of misery and degradation they found.* **2** N-UNCOUNT **Degradation** is the process of something becoming worse or weaker, or being made worse or weaker. ◻ *...air pollution, traffic congestion, and the steady degradation of our quality of life.*

de|grade /dɪgreɪd/ (degrades, degrading, degraded) **1** V-T Something that **degrades** someone causes people to have less respect for them. ◻ *...the notion that pornography degrades women.* ● **de|grad|ing** ADJ ◻ *Mr. Porter was subjected to a degrading strip search.* **2** V-T To **degrade** something means to cause it to get worse. [FORMAL] ◻ *...the ability to meet human needs indefinitely without degrading the environment.*

de|gree ✦✦◇ /dɪgriː/ (degrees) **1** N-COUNT You use **degree** to indicate the extent to which something happens or is the case, or the amount which something is felt. ◻ *These man-made barriers will ensure a very high degree of protection for several hundred years.* ◻ *Recent presidents have used television, as well as radio, with varying degrees of success.* ● PHRASE If something has **a degree of** a particular quality, it has a small but significant amount of that quality. **2** N-COUNT A **degree** is a unit of measurement that is used to measure temperatures. It is often written as °, for example, 23°. ◻ *It's over 80 degrees outside.* **3** N-COUNT A **degree** is a unit of measurement that is used to measure angles, and also longitude and latitude. It is often written as °, for example, 23°. ◻ *It was pointing outward at an angle of 45 degrees.* **4** N-COUNT A **degree** is a title or rank given by a university or college when you have completed a course of study there. It can also be given as an honorary title. ◻ *...an engineering degree.* **5** PHRASE You use expressions such as **to some degree**, **to a large degree**, or **to a certain degree** in order to indicate that something is partly true, but not entirely true. [VAGUENESS] ◻ *These statements are, to some degree, all correct.*

COLLOCATIONS

degree
NOUN
1
adjective + **degree**: great, high, large; certain, considerable, fair, reasonable; various, varying
4
adjective + **degree**: postgraduate, undergraduate; honorary
verb + **degree**: gain, obtain, receive

SYNONYMS

degree
NOUN **1**
extent: *Growing up with him soon made me realize the extent of his determination.*
amount: *I still do a certain amount of work for them.*
level: *The exercises are marked according to their level of difficulty.*
proportion: *A large proportion of the dolphins in that area will die.*

---

de|hu|man|ize /diːhyuːmənaɪz/ (dehumanizes, dehumanizing, dehumanized)

in BRIT, also use **dehumanise**

V-T If you say that something **dehumanizes** people, you mean it takes away from them good human qualities such as kindness, generosity, and independence. ◻ *The years of civil war have dehumanized all of us.*

de|hu|midi|fi|er /diːhyuːmɪdɪfaɪər/ (dehumidifiers) N-COUNT A **dehumidifier** is a machine that is used to reduce the amount of moisture in the air.

de|hy|drate /diːhaɪdreɪt/ (dehydrates, dehydrating, dehydrated) **1** V-T [usu passive] When something such as food **is dehydrated**, all the water is removed from it, often in order to preserve it. ◻ *Normally specimens have to be dehydrated.* **2** V-T/V-I If you **dehydrate** or if something **dehydrates** you, you lose too much water from your body so that you feel weak or ill. ◻ *People can dehydrate in weather like this.* ● **de|hy|dra|tion** /diːhaɪdreɪʃən/ N-UNCOUNT ◻ *...a child who's got diarrhea and is suffering from dehydration.*

dei|fi|ca|tion /diːɪfɪkeɪʃən/ N-UNCOUNT [usu with supp] If you talk about the **deification** of someone or something, you mean that they are regarded with very great respect and are not criticized at all. [FORMAL] ◻ *...the deification of science in the 1940s.*

dei|fy /diːɪfaɪ/ (deifies, deifying, deified) V-T [usu passive] If someone **is deified**, they are considered to be a god or are regarded with very great respect. [FORMAL] ◻ *Valentino was virtually deified by legions of female fans.*

deign /deɪn/ (deigns, deigning, deigned) V-T If you say that someone **deigned** to do something, you are expressing your disapproval of the fact that they did it unwillingly, because they thought they were too important to do it. [FORMAL, DISAPPROVAL] ◻ *At last, Harper deigned to speak.*

de|ism /diːɪzəm/ N-UNCOUNT **Deism** is the belief that there is a God who made the world but does not influence human lives.

de|ity /diːɪti/ (deities) N-COUNT A **deity** is a god or goddess. [FORMAL] ◻ *...a deity revered by thousands of Hindus and Buddhists.*

déjà vu /deɪʒɑ vuː/ N-UNCOUNT **Déjà vu** is the feeling that you have already experienced the things that are happening to you now. ◻ *The sense of déjà vu was overwhelming.*

de|ject|ed /dɪdʒɛktɪd/ ADJ If you are **dejected**, you feel miserable or unhappy, especially because you have just been disappointed by something. ◻ *Everyone has days when they feel dejected or down.* ● **de|ject|ed|ly** ADV [ADV with v] ◻ *Passengers lined up dejectedly for the increasingly dirty toilets.*

de|jec|tion /dɪdʒɛkʃən/ N-UNCOUNT **Dejection** is a feeling of sadness that you get, for example, when you have just been disappointed by something. ◻ *There was a slight air of dejection about her.*

de jure /diː ˈdʒʊəri/ ADJ [ADJ n] **De jure** is used to indicate that something legally exists or is a particular thing. [LEGAL] □ ...politicians and kings, de jure leaders of men. • ADV [ADV with cl] **De jure** is also an adverb. □ The Synod's declarations prevailed de jure but not de facto in the Roman Catholic Church down to the Reformation era.

de|lay ✦✦◇ /dɪˈleɪ/ (delays, delaying, delayed) ■ V-T/V-I If you **delay** doing something, you do not do it immediately or at the planned or expected time, but you leave it until later. □ For sentimental reasons I wanted to delay my departure until June. □ They had delayed having children, for the usual reason, to establish their careers. ◎ V-T To **delay** someone or something means to make them late or to slow them down. □ Can you delay him in some way? □ Various setbacks and problems delayed production. ◎ V-I If you **delay**, you deliberately take longer than necessary to do something. □ If he delayed any longer, the sun would be up. ◎ N-VAR If there is a **delay**, something does not happen until later than planned or expected. □ They claimed that such a delay wouldn't hurt anyone. ◎ N-UNCOUNT **Delay** is a failure to do something immediately or in the required or usual time. □ We'll send you a quote without delay.

de|layed ac|tion ADJ [ADJ n] A **delayed action** mechanism causes a delay on the device it is attached to, so that it does not work as soon as you switch it on or operate it. □ ...a type of delayed action parachute.

de|lay|er|ing /dɪˈleɪərɪŋ/ N-UNCOUNT **Delayering** is the process of simplifying the administrative structure of a large organization in order to make it more efficient. [BUSINESS] □ ...downsizing, delayering, and other cost cutting measures.

de|lay|ing tac|tic (delaying tactics) N-COUNT [usu pl] **Delaying tactics** are things that someone does in order to deliberately delay the start or progress of something. □ The Senate is several days from finishing its work because of the delaying tactics of a few members.

de|lec|table /dɪˈlɛktəbəl/ ADJ If you describe something, especially food or drink, as **delectable**, you mean that it is very pleasant. □ ...delectable wine.

de|lec|ta|tion /diːlɛkˈteɪʃən/ PHRASE [PHR with poss] If you do something **for** someone's **delectation**, you do it to give them enjoyment or pleasure. [FORMAL] □ She makes cakes for the delectation of visitors.

del|egate ✦◇ (delegates, delegating, delegated)

The noun is pronounced /ˈdɛlɪɡɪt/. The verb is pronounced /ˈdɛlɪɡeɪt/.

■ N-COUNT A **delegate** is a person who is chosen to vote or make decisions on behalf of a group of other people, especially at a conference or a meeting. □ The Canadian delegate offered no reply. ◎ V-T/V-I If you **delegate** duties, responsibilities, or power to someone, you give them those duties, those responsibilities, or that power so that they can act on your behalf. □ He talks of traveling less, and delegating more authority to his deputies. • **del|ega|tion** N-UNCOUNT □ A key factor in running a business is the delegation of responsibility. ◎ V-T [usu passive] If you **are delegated** to do something, you are given the duty of acting on someone else's behalf by making decisions, voting, or doing some particular work. □ Officials have now been delegated to start work on a draft settlement.

del|ega|tion ✦◇ /dɛlɪˈɡeɪʃən/ (delegations) ■ N-COUNT A **delegation** is a group of people who have been sent somewhere to have talks with other people on behalf of a larger group of people. □ ...the Chinese delegation to the UN talks in New York. ◎ → see also **delegate**

de|lete /dɪˈliːt/ (deletes, deleting, deleted) V-T If you **delete** something that has been written down or stored in a computer, you cross it out or remove it. □ He also deleted files from the computer system.

del|eteri|ous /dɛlɪˈtɪəriəs/ ADJ Something that has a **deleterious** effect on something has a harmful effect on it. [FORMAL] □ Petty crime is having a deleterious effect on community life.

deli /ˈdɛli/ (delis) N-COUNT A **deli** is a **delicatessen**. [INFORMAL]

de|lib|er|ate ✦◇ (deliberates, deliberating, deliberated)

The adjective is pronounced /dɪˈlɪbərɪt/. The verb is pronounced /dɪˈlɪbəreɪt/.

■ ADJ If you do something that is **deliberate**, you planned or decided to do it beforehand, and so it happens on purpose rather than by chance. □ Witnesses say the firing was deliberate and sustained. • **de|lib|er|ate|ly** ADV □ It looks as if the blaze was started deliberately. ◎ ADJ If a movement or action is **deliberate**, it is done slowly and carefully. □ ...stepping with deliberate slowness up the steep paths. • **de|lib|er|ate|ly** ADV [ADV after v] □ The Japanese have acted calmly and deliberately. ◎ V-T/V-I If you **deliberate**, you think about something carefully, especially before making a very important decision. □ She deliberated over the decision for a good few years before she finally made up her mind.

de|lib|era|tion /dɪˌlɪbəˈreɪʃən/ (deliberations) ■ N-UNCOUNT **Deliberation** is the long and careful consideration of a subject. □ In this house nothing is there by chance: it is always the result of great deliberation. ◎ N-PLURAL **Deliberations** are formal discussions where an issue is considered carefully. □ Their deliberations were rather inconclusive.

de|lib|era|tive /dɪˈlɪbərətɪv, -əreɪtɪv/ ADJ [usu ADJ n] A **deliberative** institution or procedure has the power or the right to make important decisions. [FORMAL] □ ...a deliberative body such as the U.S. Senate.

deli|ca|cy /ˈdɛlɪkəsi/ (delicacies) ■ N-UNCOUNT **Delicacy** is the quality of being easy to break or harm, and refers especially to people or things that are attractive or graceful. □ ...the delicacy of a rose. ◎ N-UNCOUNT If you say that a situation or problem is of some **delicacy**, you mean that it is difficult to handle and needs careful and sensitive treatment. □ There was a matter of some delicacy on which he would be grateful for her advice. ◎ N-UNCOUNT If someone handles a difficult situation with **delicacy**, they handle it very carefully, making sure that nobody is offended. □ Both countries are behaving with rare delicacy. ◎ N-COUNT A **delicacy** is a rare or expensive food that is considered especially nice to eat. □ Smoked salmon was considered an expensive delicacy.

deli|cate /ˈdɛlɪkɪt/ ■ ADJ Something that is **delicate** is small and beautifully shaped. □ He had delicate hands. • **deli|cate|ly** ADV [ADV adj/-ed] □ She was a shy, delicately pretty girl with enormous blue eyes. ◎ ADJ Something that is **delicate** has a color, taste, or smell which is pleasant and not strong or intense. □ Young haricot beans have a tender texture and a delicate, subtle flavor. • **deli|cate|ly** ADV [ADV -ed/adj] □ ...a soup delicately flavored with nutmeg. ◎ ADJ If something is **delicate**, it is easy to harm, damage, or break, and needs to be handled or treated carefully. □ Although the coral looks hard, it is very delicate. ◎ ADJ Someone who is **delicate** is not healthy and strong, and becomes ill easily. □ He was far too physically delicate to look after his own garden and was in constant pain. ◎ ADJ You use **delicate** to describe a situation, problem, matter, or discussion that needs to be dealt with carefully and sensitively in order to avoid upsetting things or offending people. □ Ottawa and Washington have to find a delicate balance between the free flow of commerce and legitimate security concerns. • **deli|cate|ly** ADV [ADV with v] □ Clearly, the situation remains delicately poised. ◎ ADJ A **delicate** task, movement, action, or product needs or shows great skill and attention to detail. □ ...a long and delicate operation carried out at a hospital in Pittsburgh. • **deli|cate|ly** ADV [ADV with v] □ ...the delicately embroidered sheets.

deli|ca|tes|sen /dɛlɪkəˈtɛsən/ (delicatessens) N-COUNT A **delicatessen** is a store that sells cold cuts, cheeses, salads, and often a selection of imported foods.

de|li|cious /dɪˈlɪʃəs/ ADJ Food that is **delicious** has a very pleasant taste. □ There's always a wide selection of delicious meals to choose from. • **de|li|cious|ly** ADV [ADV adj/-ed] □ This yogurt has a deliciously creamy flavor.

de|light ✦◇ /dɪˈlaɪt/ (delights, delighting, delighted) ■ N-UNCOUNT **Delight** is a feeling of very great pleasure. □ Throughout the house, the views are a constant source of surprise and delight. □ Andrew roared with delight when he heard Rachel's nickname for the baby. ◎ PHRASE If someone **takes delight** or **takes a delight** in something, they get a lot of pleasure from it. □ Haig took obvious delight in proving his critics wrong. ◎ N-COUNT You can refer to someone or something that gives you great pleasure or enjoyment as a **delight**. [APPROVAL] □ The aircraft was a delight to fly. ◎ V-T If something **delights** you, it gives you a lot of pleasure. □ She has created a style of music that has delighted audiences all over the world.

> **SYNONYMS**
>
> **delight**
> NOUN **1**
> **joy:** *Salter shouted with joy.*
> **happiness:** *I think mostly she was looking for happiness.*
> **ecstasy:** *...a state of almost religious ecstasy.*
> **bliss:** *It was a scene of such domestic bliss.*
> **rapture:** *His speech was received with rapture by his supporters.*

de|light|ed ♦◇◇ /dɪlaɪtɪd/ **1** ADJ If you are **delighted**, you are extremely pleased and excited about something. ❑ *I know Frank will be delighted to see you.* • **de|light|ed|ly** ADV [ADV with v] ❑ *"There!" Jackson exclaimed delightedly.* **2** ADJ If someone invites or asks you to do something, you can say that you would be **delighted** to do it, as a way of showing that you are very willing to do it. [FEELINGS] ❑ *"You have to come to Todd's graduation party."—"I'd be delighted."*

> **SYNONYMS**
>
> **delighted**
> ADJ **1**
> **thrilled:** *He's thrilled to pieces about the news.*
> **ecstatic:** *They were greeted by the cheers of an ecstatic crowd.*
> **jubilant:** *...the jubilant crowds of Paris.*
> **elated:** *I was elated that my second heart bypass had been successful.*

de|light|ful /dɪlaɪtfəl/ ADJ If you describe something or someone as **delightful**, you mean they are very pleasant. ❑ *It was the most delightful garden I had ever seen.* • **de|light|ful|ly** ADV [ADV adj/-ed] ❑ *This delightfully refreshing cologne can be splashed on liberally.*

de|lim|it /dɪlɪmɪt/ (delimits, delimiting, delimited) V-T If you **delimit** something, you fix or establish its limits. [FORMAL] ❑ *This is not meant to delimit what approaches social researchers can adopt.*

de|lin|eate /dɪlɪnieɪt/ (delineates, delineating, delineated) **1** V-T If you **delineate** something such as an idea or situation, you describe it or define it, often in a lot of detail. [FORMAL] ❑ *Biography must to some extent delineate characters.* **2** V-T If you **delineate** a border, you say exactly where it is going to be. [FORMAL] ❑ *...an agreement to delineate the border.*

de|lin|quen|cy /dɪlɪŋkwənsi/ N-UNCOUNT **Delinquency** is criminal behavior, especially that of young people. ❑ *He had no history of delinquency.*

de|lin|quent /dɪlɪŋkwənt/ (delinquents) **1** ADJ Someone, usually a young person, who is **delinquent** repeatedly commits minor crimes. ❑ *...homes for delinquent children.* • N-COUNT **Delinquent** is also a noun. ❑ *...a nine-year-old delinquent.* **2** ADJ A **delinquent** borrower or taxpayer is someone who has failed to pay their debts or taxes. [AM] ❑ *...a legal shortcut to take homes from delinquent borrowers.*

de|liri|ous /dɪlɪriəs/ **1** ADJ Someone who is **delirious** is unable to think or speak in a sensible and reasonable way, usually because they are very ill and have a fever. ❑ *I was delirious and blacked out several times.* **2** ADJ Someone who is **delirious** is extremely excited and happy. ❑ *A raucous crowd of 25,000 delirious fans greeted the team at Grand Central Station.* • **de|liri|ous|ly** ADV ❑ *Dora returned from her honeymoon deliriously happy.*

de|lir|ium /dɪlɪriəm/ N-UNCOUNT If someone is suffering from **delirium**, they are not able to think or speak in a sensible and reasonable way because they are very ill and have a fever. ❑ *In her delirium, she had fallen to the floor several times.*

de|list /dɪlɪst/ (delists, delisting, delisted) V-T/V-I If a company **delists** or if its shares **are delisted**, its shares are removed from the official list of shares that can be traded on the stock market. [BUSINESS] ❑ *The company's stock was delisted from the Nasdaq market in July 2000.*

de|liv|er ♦♦◇ /dɪlɪvər/ (delivers, delivering, delivered) **1** V-T If you **deliver** something somewhere, you take it there. ❑ *The Canadians plan to deliver more food to southern Somalia.* **2** V-T/V-I If you **deliver** something that you have promised to do, make, or produce, you do, make, or produce it. ❑ *They have yet to show that they can really deliver working technologies.* ❑ *The question is, can he deliver?* **3** V-T If you **deliver** a lecture or speech, you give it in public. [FORMAL] ❑ *The president will deliver a speech about schools.* **4** V-T When someone **delivers** a baby, they help the woman who is giving birth to the baby. When a woman **delivers** a baby, she gives birth. ❑ *Although we'd planned to have our baby at home, we never expected to deliver her ourselves!* **5** V-T If someone **delivers** a blow to someone else, they hit them. [WRITTEN] ❑ *Those blows to the head could have been delivered by a woman.*

de|liv|er|ance /dɪlɪvərəns/ N-UNCOUNT [oft N *from* n] **Deliverance** is rescue from imprisonment, danger, or evil. [LITERARY] ❑ *The opening scene shows them celebrating their sudden deliverance from war.*

de|liv|ery ♦◇◇ /dɪlɪvəri/ (deliveries) **1** N-VAR **Delivery** or a **delivery** is the bringing of letters, packages, or other goods to someone's house or to another place where they want them. ❑ *Please allow 28 days for delivery.* ❑ *The uprising is threatening the delivery of humanitarian supplies of food and medicine.* **2** N-VAR **Delivery** is the process of giving birth to a baby. ❑ *In the end, it was an easy delivery: a fine baby boy.* **3** N-COUNT A **delivery** of something is the goods that are delivered. ❑ *I got a delivery of fresh eggs this morning.* **4** ADJ [ADJ n] A **delivery** person or service delivers things to a place. ❑ *...a pizza delivery man.* **5** N-UNCOUNT You talk about someone's **delivery** when you are referring to the way in which they give a speech or lecture. ❑ *His speeches were magnificently written but his delivery was hopeless.*

de|liv|ery charge (delivery charges) N-COUNT A **delivery charge** is the cost of transporting or delivering goods. [AM, FORMAL] ❑ *Again, buyers need to check if delivery charges are included in the price.*

in BRIT, usually use **carriage**

de|liv|ery room (delivery rooms) N-COUNT In a hospital, the **delivery room** is the room where women give birth to their babies.

dell /dɛl/ (dells) N-COUNT A **dell** is a small valley which has trees growing in it. [LITERARY]

del|phin|ium /dɛlfɪniəm/ (delphiniums) N-COUNT A **delphinium** is a plant which has a tall stem with blue flowers growing up it.

del|ta /dɛltə/ (deltas) N-COUNT A **delta** is an area of low, flat land shaped like a triangle, where a river splits and spreads out into several branches before entering the sea. ❑ *...the Mississippi delta.*

de|lude /dɪlud/ (deludes, deluding, deluded) **1** V-T If you **delude** yourself, you let yourself believe that something is true, even though it is not true. ❑ *The president was deluding himself if he thought he was safe from such action.* ❑ *We delude ourselves that we are in control.* **2** V-T To **delude** someone into thinking something means to make them believe what is not true. ❑ *Television deludes you into thinking you have experienced reality, when you haven't.*

de|lud|ed /dɪludɪd/ ADJ Someone who is **deluded** believes something that is not true. ❑ *...deluded fanatics.*

del|uge /dɛlyudʒ/ (deluges, deluging, deluged) **1** N-COUNT A **deluge** of things is a large number of them which arrive or happen at the same time. ❑ *There was a deluge of requests for interviews and statements.* **2** V-T [usu passive] If a place or person **is deluged** with things, a large number of them arrive or happen at the same time. ❑ *During 1933, Papen's office was deluged with complaints.*

de|lu|sion /dɪluʒ³n/ (delusions) **1** N-COUNT A **delusion** is a false idea. ❑ *I was under the delusion that he intended to marry me.* **2** N-UNCOUNT **Delusion** is the state of believing things that are not true. ❑ *Insinuations about her mental state, about her capacity for delusion, were being made.*

deluxe /dɪlʌks/

in BRIT, also use **de luxe**

ADJ [ADJ n, n ADJ] **Deluxe** goods or services are better in quality and more expensive than ordinary ones. ❑ *...a rare, highly prized deluxe wine.*

delve /dɛlv/ (delves, delving, delved) V-I If you **delve** into something, you try to discover new information about it. ❑ *Tormented by her ignorance, Jenny delves into her mother's past.*

dema|gog|ic /dɛməgɒdʒɪk/ ADJ If you say that someone such as a politician is **demagogic**, you are criticizing them because you think they try to win people's support by appealing to their emotions rather than using reasonable arguments. [FORMAL, DISAPPROVAL]

dema|gogue /dɛməgɒg/ (demagogues) also **demagog** N-COUNT [oft adj N] If you say that someone such as a politician is a **demagogue** you are criticizing them because you think they try to win people's support by appealing to their emotions rather than using reasonable arguments. [DISAPPROVAL]

dema|gogy /dɛməgɒdʒi, -goʊdʒi/ also **demagoguery** /dɛməgɔgəri/ N-UNCOUNT You can refer to a method of political rule as **demagogy** or **demagoguery** if you disapprove of it because you think it involves appealing to people's emotions rather than using reasonable arguments. [DISAPPROVAL]

de|mand ◆◆◇ /dɪmænd/ (demands, demanding, demanded) **1** V-T If you **demand** something such as information or action, you ask for it in a very forceful way. ◻ *Human rights groups are demanding an investigation into the shooting.* ◻ *Russia demanded that UNITA send a delegation to the peace talks.* **2** V-T If one thing **demands** another, the first needs the second in order to happen or be dealt with successfully. ◻ *He said the task of reconstruction would demand much patience, hard work, and sacrifice.* **3** N-COUNT A **demand** is a firm request for something. ◻ *There have been demands for services from tenants up there.* **4** N-UNCOUNT If you refer to **demand**, or to the **demand** for something, you are referring to how many people want to have it, do it, or buy it. ◻ *Another flight would be arranged on Saturday if sufficient demand arose.* **5** N-PLURAL The **demands** of something or its **demands** on you are the things which it needs or the things which you have to do for it. ◻ *...the demands and challenges of a new job.* **6** PHRASE If someone or something is **in demand** or **in great demand**, they are very popular and a lot of people want them. ◻ *He was much in demand as a lecturer in the U.S., as well as at universities all over Europe.* **7** PHRASE If something is available or happens **on demand**, you can have it or it happens whenever you want it or ask for it. ◻ *...a system that offers movies on demand.*

USAGE
demand
When **demand** is a verb, don't use 'for' after it. Don't say, for example, '~~They are demanding for higher wages.~~' Say 'They **are demanding** higher wages.'

SYNONYMS
demand
VERB **1**
request: *Mr Dennis said he had requested access to a telephone.*
ask for: *I decided to go to the next house and ask for food.*
order: *The President has ordered a full investigation.*
insist on: *She insisted on being present at all the interviews.*

COLLOCATIONS
demand
VERB **1**
demand + noun: answer, apology, explanation; compensation, money, payment, ransom; action
NOUN **4**
noun + demand: consumer
adjective + demand: growing, increasing, rising, strong; falling, reduced, slowing, weak; domestic, global
verb + demand: meet, satisfy; boost, increase, stimulate; create; reduce, weaken

de|mand|ing /dɪmændɪŋ/ **1** ADJ A **demanding** job or task requires a lot of your time, energy, or attention. ◻ *He tried to return to work, but found he could no longer cope with his demanding job.* **2** ADJ People who are **demanding** are not easily satisfied or pleased. ◻ *Ricky was a very demanding child.* **3** → See feature box at **football**

de|mar|cate /dɪmɑːrkeɪt, diːmɑːrkeɪt/ (demarcates, demarcating, demarcated) V-T If you **demarcate** something, you establish its boundaries or limits. [FORMAL] ◻ *A special UN commission was formed to demarcate the border.*

de|mar|ca|tion /diːmɑːrkeɪʃən/ N-UNCOUNT [oft N n] **Demarcation** is the establishment of boundaries or limits separating two areas, groups, or things. [FORMAL] ◻ *Talks were continuing about the demarcation of the border between the two countries.*

de|mean /dɪmiːn/ (demeans, demeaning, demeaned) V-T To **demean** someone or something means to make people have less respect for them. ◻ *Some groups say that pornography demeans women and incites rape.*

de|mean|ing /dɪmiːnɪŋ/ ADJ Something that is **demeaning** makes people have less respect for the person who is treated in that way, or who does that thing. ◻ *...making demeaning sexist comments.*

de|mean|or /dɪmiːnər/
in BRIT, use **demeanour**
N-UNCOUNT Your **demeanor** is the way you behave, which gives people an impression of your character and feelings. [FORMAL] ◻ *...her calm and cheerful demeanor.*

de|ment|ed /dɪmɛntɪd/ **1** ADJ Someone who is **demented** has a severe mental illness, especially Alzheimer's disease. [MEDICAL, OLD-FASHIONED] **2** ADJ If you describe someone as **demented**, you think that their actions are strange, foolish, or uncontrolled. [INFORMAL, DISAPPROVAL] ◻ *Sid broke into demented laughter.*

de|men|tia /dɪmɛnʃə/ (dementias) N-VAR **Dementia** is a serious illness of the mind. [MEDICAL] ◻ *...a treatment for mental conditions such as dementia and Alzheimer's disease.*

de|mer|it /dɪmɛrɪt/ (demerits) **1** N-COUNT A **demerit** is a mark against someone, or on someone's record, for having done something bad or wrong. [AM, FORMAL] ◻ *Demerits were given to students for late attendance at prayers.* **2** N-COUNT [usu pl, usu with poss] The **demerits** of something or someone are their faults or disadvantages. [FORMAL] ◻ *...articles debating the merits and demerits of the three candidates.*

PREFIX
demi-
is used at the beginning of some words to refer to something equivalent to half of the object or amount indicated by the rest of the word. For example, a *demi-vegetarian* is a person who eats poultry and fish but no red meat.

demi|god /dɛmigɒd/ (demigods) **1** N-COUNT In mythology, a **demigod** is a less important god, especially one who is half god and half human. **2** N-COUNT If you describe a famous or important person such as a politician, writer, or musician as a **demigod**, you mean that you disapprove of the way in which people admire them and treat them like a god. [DISAPPROVAL]

de|mili|ta|rize /diːmɪlɪtəraɪz/ (demilitarizes, demilitarizing, demilitarized)
in BRIT, also use **demilitarise**
V-T To **demilitarize** an area means to ensure that all military forces are removed from it. ◻ *He said the UN had made remarkable progress in demilitarizing the region.*

de|mise /dɪmaɪz/ N-SING The **demise** of something or someone is their end or death. [FORMAL] ◻ *...the demise of the reform movement.*

de|mist|er /diːmɪstər/ (demisters) N-COUNT A **demister** is the same as a **defogger**. [BRIT]

demo /dɛmoʊ/ (demos) **1** N-COUNT A **demo** is a sample recording of someone's music. [INFORMAL] ◻ *He arranged for Reba to record her first demo.* **2** N-COUNT A **demo** is a demonstration of something. [INFORMAL] ◻ *Download free demos of our newest products and upgrades.*

de|mo|bi|lize /diːmoʊbɪlaɪz/ (demobilizes, demobilizing, demobilized)
in BRIT, also use **demobilise**
V-T/V-I If a country or armed force **demobilizes** its troops, or if its troops **demobilize**, its troops are released from service and allowed to go home. ◻ *Dos Santos has demanded that UNITA sign a cease-fire and demobilize its troops.* ● **de|mo|bi|li|za|tion** /diːmoʊbɪlaɪzeɪʃən/ N-UNCOUNT ◻ *The government had previously been opposed to the demobilization of its 100,000 strong army.*

de|moc|ra|cy /dɪmɒkrəsi/ (**democracies**) ◼ N-UNCOUNT **Democracy** is a system of government in which people choose their rulers by voting for them in elections. ◻ *The spread of democracy in Eastern Europe appears to have had negative as well as positive consequences.* ◼ N-COUNT A **democracy** is a country in which the people choose their government by voting for it. ◻ *The new democracies face tough challenges.*

demo|crat /dɛməkræt/ (**democrats**) ◼ N-COUNT A **Democrat** is a member or supporter of a particular political party which has the word 'democrat' or 'democratic' in its title, for example, the Democratic Party in the United States. ◻ *Murray has joined other Senate Democrats in blocking the legislation.* ◼ N-COUNT A **democrat** is a person who believes in the ideals of democracy, personal freedom, and equality. ◻ *This is the time for democrats and not dictators.*

demo|crat|ic /dɛməkrætɪk/ ◼ ADJ A **democratic** country, government, or political system is governed by representatives who are elected by the people. ◻ *Bolivia returned to democratic rule in 1982, after a series of military governments.* • **demo|crati|cal|ly** /dɛməkrætɪkli/ ADV ◻ *That June, Yeltsin became Russia's first democratically elected president.* ◼ ADJ Something that is **democratic** is based on the idea that everyone should have equal rights and should be involved in making important decisions. ◻ *Education is the basis of a democratic society.* • **demo|crati|cal|ly** ADV ◻ *This committee will enable decisions to be made democratically.*

de|moc|ra|tize /dɪmɒkrətaɪz/ (**democratizes, democratizing, democratized**)

in BRIT, also use **democratise**

V-T If a country or a system **is democratized**, it is made democratic. [JOURNALISM] ◻ *a further need to democratize the life of society as a whole.* • **de|moc|ra|ti|za|tion** /dɪmɒkrətɪzeɪʃən/ N-UNCOUNT [oft the N of n] ◻ *...the democratization of Eastern Europe.*

de|mo|graph|ic /dɛməgræfɪk/ (**demographics**) ◼ N-PLURAL The **demographics** of a place or society are the statistics relating to the people who live there. ◻ *...the changing demographics of the United States.* ◼ N-SING A **demographic** is a group of people in a society, especially people in a particular age group. ◻ *The station has won more listeners in the 25–39 demographic.*

de|mog|ra|phy /dɪmɒgrəfi/ N-UNCOUNT **Demography** is the study of the changes in numbers of births, deaths, marriages, and cases of disease in a community over a period of time. • **de|mog|ra|pher** (**demographers**) N-COUNT ◻ *...a politically astute economist and demographer.*

de|mol|ish /dɪmɒlɪʃ/ (**demolishes, demolishing, demolished**) ◼ V-T To **demolish** something such as a building means to destroy it completely. ◻ *A storm moved directly over the island, demolishing buildings and flooding streets.* ◼ V-T If you **demolish** someone's ideas or arguments, you prove that they are completely wrong or unreasonable. ◻ *Our intention was quite the opposite – to demolish rumors that have surrounded him since he took office.*

demo|li|tion /dɛməlɪʃən/ (**demolitions**) N-VAR The **demolition** of a structure, for example, a building, is the act of deliberately destroying it, often in order to build something else in its place. ◻ *The project required the total demolition of the old bridge.*

de|mon /diːmən/ (**demons**) also **daemon** ◼ N-COUNT A **demon** is an evil spirit. ◻ *...a woman possessed by demons.* ◼ N-COUNT If you approve of someone because they are very skilled at what they do or because they do it energetically, you can say that they do it like a **demon**. [APPROVAL] ◻ *She worked like a demon and expected everybody else to do the same.* ◻ *He is a demon organizer.*

de|mon|ic /dɪmɒnɪk/ ADJ **Demonic** means coming from or belonging to a demon or being like a demon. ◻ *...a demonic grin.*

de|mon|ize /diːmənaɪz/ (**demonizes, demonizing, demonized**)

in BRIT, also use **demonise**

V-T If people **demonize** someone, they convince themselves that that person is evil. ◻ *Each side began to demonize the other.*

de|mon|ol|ogy /diːmənɒlədʒi/ N-UNCOUNT **Demonology** is a set of beliefs which says that a particular situation or group of people is evil or unacceptable. ◻ *Large multinational companies are the chief villains in the demonology of contemporary anticapitalists.*

de|mon|strable /dɪmɒnstrəbəl/ ADJ [usu ADJ n] A **demonstrable** fact or quality can be shown to be true or to exist. [FORMAL] ◻ *Without demonstrable progress, the negotiators will begin to see their influence wane.* • **de|mon|strably** /dɪmɒnstrəbli/ ADV ◻ *...demonstrably false statements.*

dem|on|strate /dɛmənstreɪt/ (**demonstrates, demonstrating, demonstrated**) ◼ V-T To **demonstrate** a fact means to make it clear to people. ◻ *The study also demonstrated a direct link between obesity and mortality.* ◻ *They are anxious to demonstrate to the voters that they have practical policies.* ◼ V-T If you **demonstrate** a particular skill, quality, or feeling, you show by your actions that you have it. ◻ *Have they, for example, demonstrated a commitment to democracy?* ◼ V-I When people **demonstrate**, they march or gather somewhere to show their opposition to something or their support for something. ◻ *Some 30,000 angry farmers arrived in Brussels yesterday to demonstrate against possible cuts in subsidies.* ◻ *In the cities vast crowds have been demonstrating for change.* ◼ V-T If you **demonstrate** something, you show people how it works or how to do it. ◻ *A selection of cosmetic companies will be there to demonstrate their new products.*

▌ SYNONYMS ▐

demonstrate
VERB
◼
prove: *...trying to prove how groups of animals have evolved.*
show: *Research shows that a high-fiber diet may protect you from colon cancer.*
establish: *Medical tests established that she was not their biological child.*
indicate: *This indicates whether remedies are suitable for children.*
◼
march: *The demonstrators marched through the capital, chanting slogans and demanding free elections.*
protest: *The students were protesting about overcrowding in the university dorms.*
picket: *100 union members and supporters picketed outside.*

dem|on|stra|tion /dɛmənstreɪʃən/ (**demonstrations**) ◼ N-COUNT A **demonstration** is a march or gathering which people take part in to show their opposition to something or their support for something. ◻ *Riot police used tear gas to break up the demonstration.* ◼ N-COUNT A **demonstration** of something is a talk by someone who shows you how to do it or how it works. ◻ *...a cooking demonstration.* ◼ N-COUNT A **demonstration** of a fact or situation is a clear proof of it. ◻ *It was an unprecedented demonstration of people power by the citizens of Moscow.* ◼ N-COUNT A **demonstration** of a quality or feeling is an expression of it. ◻ *There's been no public demonstration of opposition to the president.*

▌ SYNONYMS ▐

demonstration
NOUN
◼
march: *Organizers expect up to 300,000 protesters to join the march.*
protest: *...a protest march.*
rally: *Supporters of the policy are reported to be gathering in Delhi for a mass rally.*
◼
display: *Normally, such an outward display of affection is reserved for his mother.*
show: *She said goodbye to Hilda with a convincing show of affection.*

de|mon|stra|tive /dɪmɒnstrətɪv/ (**demonstratives**) ◼ ADJ Someone who is **demonstrative** shows affection freely and openly. ◻ *We came from the English tradition of not being demonstrative.* • **de|mon|stra|tive|ly** ADV ◻ *Some children respond more demonstratively than others.* ◼ N-COUNT In grammar, the words 'this,' 'that,' 'these,' and 'those' are sometimes called **demonstratives**.

de|mon|stra|tor /dɛmənstreɪtər/ (**demonstrators**) ◼ N-COUNT **Demonstrators** are people who are marching or gathering somewhere to show their opposition to something or their support for something. ◻ *I saw the police using tear gas to try and break up a crowd of demonstrators.* ◼ N-COUNT A

demoralize

demonstrator is a person who shows people how something works or how to do something. ❏ ...*a demonstrator in a department store*.

de|mor|al|ize /dɪmɒrəlaɪz/ (demoralizes, demoralizing, demoralized)

in BRIT, also use **demoralise**

V-T If something **demoralizes** someone, it makes them lose so much confidence in what they are doing that they want to give up. ❏ *Clearly, one of the objectives is to demoralize the enemy troops in any way they can*. ● **de|mor|al|ized** ADJ ❏ *The Bismarck could now move only at a crawl and her crew were exhausted, hopeless, and utterly demoralized*.

de|mor|al|iz|ing /dɪmɒrəlaɪzɪŋ/

in BRIT, also use **demoralising**

ADJ If something is **demoralizing**, it makes you lose so much confidence in what you are doing that you want to give up. ❏ *Losing their star player was another demoralizing blow for the team*.

de|mote /dɪmoʊt/ (demotes, demoting, demoted) V-T If someone **demotes** you, they give you a lower rank or a less important position than you already have, often as a punishment. ❏ *It's very difficult to demote somebody who has been filling in during maternity leave*. ● **de|mo|tion** /dɪmoʊʃən/ (demotions) N-VAR ❏ *He is seeking redress for what he alleges was an unfair demotion*.

de|mot|ic /dɪmɒtɪk/ **1** ADJ **Demotic** language is the type of informal language used by ordinary people. [FORMAL] ❏ ...*television's demotic style of language*. **2** ADJ [usu ADJ n] **Demotic** is used to describe something or someone that is typical of ordinary people. [FORMAL] ❏ ...*demotic entertainments such as TV soap operas*.

de|mur /dɪmɜr/ (demurs, demurring, demurred) V-I If you **demur**, you say that you do not agree with something or will not do something that you have been asked to do. [FORMAL] ❏ *The doctor demurred, but Piercey was insistent*.

de|mure /dɪmyʊər/ **1** ADJ If you describe someone, usually a young woman, as **demure**, you mean they are quiet and shy, usually in a way that you like and find appealing, and behave very correctly. [APPROVAL] ❏ *She's very demure and sweet*. ● **de|mure|ly** ADV [usu ADV with v] ❏ *She smiled demurely*. **2** ADJ [usu ADJ n] **Demure** clothes do not reveal your body and they give the impression that you are shy and behave correctly. [WRITTEN] ❏ ...*a demure high-necked white blouse*. ● **de|mure|ly** ADV ❏ *She was demurely dressed in a black woolen suit*.

de|mu|tu|al|ize /dimyutʃuəlaɪz/ (demutualizes, demutualizing, demutualized)

in BRIT, also use **demutualise**

V-I If a savings and loan association or an insurance company **demutualizes**, it abandons its mutual status and becomes a different kind of company. [BUSINESS] ❏ *The group won the support of 97 percent of its members for plans to demutualize*. ● **de|mu|tu|ali|za|tion** /dimyutʃuəlɪzeɪʃən/ N-UNCOUNT ❏ *The 503,000 policyholders who voted for demutualization should be represented*.

de|mys|ti|fy /dimɪstɪfaɪ/ (demystifies, demystifying, demystified) V-T If you **demystify** something, you make it easier to understand by giving a clear explanation of it. ❏ *This book aims to demystify medical treatments*.

den /dɛn/ (dens) **1** N-COUNT A **den** is the home of certain types of wild animals such as lions or foxes. **2** N-COUNT Your **den** is a quiet room in your house where you can go to study, work, or relax without being disturbed. [AM] ❏ *The silver-haired retiree sits in his den surrounded by photos of sailing boats*. **3** N-COUNT A **den** is a secret place where people meet, usually for a dishonest purpose. ❏ *I could provide you with the addresses of at least three illegal drinking dens*. **4** N-COUNT If you describe a place as a **den of** a particular type of bad or illegal behavior, you mean that a lot of that type of behavior goes on there. ❏ ...*this den of iniquity called New York City*.

de|na|tion|al|ize /dinæʃənəlaɪz/ (denationalizes, denationalizing, denationalized)

in BRIT, also use **denationalise**

V-T To **denationalize** an industry or business means to transfer it into private ownership so that it is no longer owned and controlled by the state. [OLD-FASHIONED, BUSINESS] ❏ *The government started to denationalize financial institutions*. ● **de|na|tion|ali|za|tion** /dinæʃənəlɪzeɪʃən/ N-UNCOUNT ❏ ...*the denationalization of industry*.

de|ni|al /dɪnaɪəl/ (denials) **1** N-VAR A **denial** of something is a statement that it is not true, does not exist, or did not happen. ❏ *It seems clear that despite official denials, differences of opinion lay behind the ambassador's decision to quit*. **2** N-UNCOUNT The **denial** of something to someone is the act of refusing to let them have it. [FORMAL] ❏ ...*the denial of visas to international relief workers*. **3** N-UNCOUNT In psychology, **denial** is when a person cannot or will not accept an unpleasant truth. ❏ *With major life traumas, like losing a loved one, for instance, the mind's first reaction is denial*.

den|ier /dənɪər/ N-UNCOUNT [num N] **Denier** is used when indicating the thickness of stockings and pantyhose. ❏ ...*fifteen-denier stockings*.

deni|grate /dɛnɪgreɪt/ (denigrates, denigrating, denigrated) V-T If you **denigrate** someone or something, you criticize them unfairly or insult them. ❏ *The amendment prohibits obscene or indecent materials which denigrate the objects or beliefs of a particular religion*. ● **deni|gra|tion** /dɛnɪgreɪʃən/ N-UNCOUNT [usu N of n] ❏ ...*the denigration of minorities in this country*.

den|im /dɛnɪm/ N-UNCOUNT **Denim** is a thick cotton cloth, usually blue, which is used to make clothes. Jeans are made from denim. ❏ ...*a light blue denim jacket*.

den|ims /dɛnɪmz/ N-PLURAL [also *a pair of* N] **Denims** are the same as **jeans**.

deni|zen /dɛnɪzən/ (denizens) N-COUNT [usu N *of* n] A **denizen** of a particular place is a person, animal, or plant that lives or grows in this place. [FORMAL] ❏ *Gannets are denizens of the open ocean*.

de|nomi|na|tion /dɪnɒmɪneɪʃən/ (denominations) **1** N-COUNT A particular **denomination** is a particular religious group which has slightly different beliefs from other groups within the same faith. ❏ *She hosted the conference call including leaders from several denominations*. **2** N-COUNT The **denomination** of a banknote or coin is its official value. ❏ *She paid in cash, in bills of large denominations*.

de|nomi|na|tion|al /dɪnɒmɪneɪʃənəl/ ADJ [ADJ n] **Denominational** means relating to or organized by a particular religious denomination. ❏ ...*a multidenominational group of religious leaders*.

de|nomi|na|tor /dɪnɒmɪneɪtər/ (denominators) **1** N-COUNT In mathematics, the **denominator** is the number which appears under the line in a fraction. **2** → see also **common denominator**, **lowest common denominator**

de|note /dɪnoʊt/ (denotes, denoting, denoted) **1** V-T If one thing **denotes** another, it is a sign or indication of it. [FORMAL] ❏ *Red eyes denote strain and fatigue*. **2** V-T What a symbol **denotes** is what it represents. [FORMAL] ❏ *X denotes those not voting*.

de|noue|ment /deɪnumɒn/ (denouements) also **dénouement** N-COUNT [usu sing] In a book, play, or series of events, the **denouement** is the sequence of events at the end, when things come to a conclusion. ❏ ...*an unexpected dénouement*.

de|nounce /dɪnaʊns/ (denounces, denouncing, denounced) **1** V-T If you **denounce** a person or an action, you criticize them severely and publicly because you feel strongly that they are wrong or evil. ❏ *German leaders all took the opportunity to denounce the attacks and plead for tolerance*. **2** V-T If you **denounce** someone who has broken a rule or law, you report them to the authorities. ❏ *They were at the mercy of informers who might at any moment denounce them*.

dense /dɛns/ (denser, densest) **1** ADJ Something that is **dense** contains a lot of things or people in a small area. ❏ *Where Bucharest now stands, there once was a large, dense forest*. ● **dense|ly** ADV ❏ *Java is a densely populated island*. **2** ADJ **Dense** fog or smoke is difficult to see through because it is very heavy and dark. ❏ *A dense column of smoke rose several miles into the air*. **3** ADJ In science, a **dense** substance is very heavy in relation to its volume. [TECHNICAL] ❏ ...*a small dense star*. **4** → See feature box at **ecosystem**

density

den|sity /dɛnsɪti/ (densities) **1** N-VAR Density is the extent to which something is filled or covered with people or things. ▫ *The region has a very high population density.* **2** N-VAR In science, the **density** of a substance or object is the relation of its mass or weight to its volume. [TECHNICAL] ▫ *Jupiter's moon Io, whose density is 3.5 grams per cubic centimeter, is all rock.*

dent /dɛnt/ (dents, denting, dented) **1** V-T If you **dent** the surface of something, you make a hollow area in it by hitting or pressing it. ▫ *Its brass feet dented the carpet's thick pile.* **2** V-T If something **dents** your confidence or your pride, it makes you realize that you are not as good or successful as you thought. ▫ *Record oil prices have dented consumer confidence.* **3** N-COUNT A **dent** is a hollow in the surface of something which has been caused by hitting or pressing it. ▫ *I was convinced there was a dent in the hood which hadn't been there before.*

den|tal /dɛnt²l/ ADJ [ADJ n] **Dental** is used to describe things that relate to teeth or to the care and treatment of teeth. ▫ *Good oral hygiene and regular dental care are important, whatever your age.*

den|tal floss **1** N-UNCOUNT **Dental floss** is a type of thread that is used to clean between your teeth. **2** → see also **floss**

den|tist /dɛntɪst/ (dentists) N-COUNT A **dentist** is a medical practitioner who is qualified to examine and treat people's teeth. ▫ *Visit your dentist twice a year for a checkup.* • N-SING **The dentist** or **the dentist's** is used to refer to the office or clinic where a dentist works. ▫ *It's worse than being at the dentist's.*

den|tis|try /dɛntɪstri/ N-UNCOUNT **Dentistry** is the work done by a dentist.

den|tist's of|fice (dentist's offices) N-COUNT A **dentist's office** is the room or house where a dentist works. [AM]

in BRIT, use **dentist's surgery**

den|tures /dɛntʃərz/

The form **denture** is used as a modifier.

N-PLURAL **Dentures** are artificial teeth worn by people who no longer have all their own teeth. ▫ *People who wear dentures may sleep better if they leave them in overnight.*

de|nude /dɪnuːd/ (denudes, denuding, denuded) **1** V-T To **denude** an area means to destroy the plants in it. [FORMAL] ▫ *Mining would pollute the lake and denude the forest.* **2** V-T To **denude** someone or something of a particular thing means to take it away from them. [FORMAL] ▫ *The embassy is now denuded of all foreign and local staff.*

de|nun|cia|tion /dɪnʌnsieɪʃ³n/ (denunciations) **1** N-VAR **Denunciation** of someone or something is severe public criticism of them. ▫ *On September 24, he wrote a stinging denunciation of his critics.* **2** N-VAR **Denunciation** is the act of reporting someone who has broken a rule or law to the authorities. ▫ *…memories of the denunciation of French Jews to the Nazis during the Second World War.*

Den|ver boot /dɛnvər buːt/ (Denver boots) N-COUNT A **Denver boot** is a large metal device which is attached to the wheel of an illegally parked car or other vehicle in order to prevent it from being driven away. The driver has to pay to have the device removed. [AM] ▫ *I watched a couple of cops clap a Denver boot on a green Mercedes.*

in BRIT, use **clamp**

deny /dɪnaɪ/ (denies, denying, denied) **1** V-T When you **deny** something, you state that it is not true. ▫ *She denied both accusations.* ▫ *The government has denied that the authorities have uncovered a plot to assassinate the president.* **2** V-T If you **deny** someone something that they need or want, you refuse to let them have it. ▫ *Two federal courts ruled that the military cannot deny prisoners access to lawyers.*

COLLOCATIONS

deny
VERB **1**
deny + noun: allegation, claim, report, rumor, suggestion; accusation, charge; involvement, knowledge, assault, conspiracy, murder
deny + adverb: categorically, emphatically, firmly, strenuously, strongly, consistently, repeatedly; angrily, hotly, vehemently

---

339

depend

de|odor|ant /dioʊdərənt/ (deodorants) N-MASS **Deodorant** is a substance that you can use on your body to hide or prevent the smell of sweat.

de|odor|ize /dioʊdəraɪz/ (deodorizes, deodorizing, deodorized)

in BRIT, also use **deodorise**

V-T If you **deodorize** something, you remove unpleasant smells from it. [FORMAL] ▫ *The machine uses minute quantities of ozone to sterilize and deodorize refrigerated food vehicles.* ▫ *…a deodorizing foot spray.*

de|part /dɪpɑːrt/ (departs, departing, departed) **1** V-T/V-I When something or someone **departs** from a place, they leave it and start a trip to another place. You can also say that someone **departs** a place. ▫ *Flight 43 will depart from Denver at 11:45 a.m. and arrive in Honolulu at 4:12 p.m.* ▫ *In the morning Mr. McDonald departed for Sydney.* **2** V-I If you **depart** from a traditional, accepted, or agreed way of doing something, you do it in a different or unexpected way. ▫ *Why is it in this country that we have departed from good educational sense?*

de|part|ed /dɪpɑːrtɪd/ ADJ [usu ADJ n] **Departed** friends or relatives are people who have died. [FORMAL] ▫ *…departed friends.* • N-PLURAL [the N] **The departed** are people who have died. ▫ *We held services for the departed.*

de|part|ment ✦✦✦ /dɪpɑːrtmənt/ (departments) N-COUNT A **department** is one of the sections in an organization such as a government, business, or university. A department is also one of the sections in a large store. ▫ *…the U.S. Department of Agriculture.* ▫ *He moved to the sales department.*

SYNONYMS

department
NOUN
office: *…Downing Street's press office.*
division: *…the sales division.*

---

de|part|men|tal /dipɑːrtmɛnt³l/ ADJ [ADJ n] **Departmental** is used to describe the activities, responsibilities, or possessions of a department in a government, company, or other organization. ▫ *The Secretary of Education is right to seek a bigger departmental budget.*

de|part|ment store (department stores) N-COUNT A **department store** is a large store which sells many different kinds of goods. ▫ *…the dazzling window displays of world-famous department stores such as Macy's and Bloomingdale's.*

de|par|ture ✦◇ /dɪpɑːrtʃər/ (departures) **1** N-VAR **Departure** or a **departure** is the act of going away from somewhere. ▫ *…the president's departure for Helsinki.* ▫ *They hoped this would lead to the departure of all foreign forces from the country.* **2** N-COUNT If someone does something different or unusual, you can refer to their action as a **departure**. ▫ *Such a move would have been a startling departure from tradition. This is a major departure for the manufacturer as it tries to rapidly double its annual production numbers.*

COLLOCATIONS

departure
NOUN
1
adjective + **departure**: early; scheduled; abrupt, hasty, sudden, unexpected; imminent, impending; acrimonious
verb + **departure**: announce; delay; hasten
2
adjective + **departure**: major, new, significant; dramatic, radical

---

de|par|ture lounge (departure lounges) N-COUNT In an airport, the **departure lounge** is the place where passengers wait before they get onto their plane. ▫ *Passengers will be able to purchase items in the departure lounge and take them on board.*

de|par|ture tax (departure taxes) N-VAR **Departure tax** is a tax that airline passengers have to pay in order to use an airport. ▫ *Many countries charge departure tax in U.S. dollars rather than local currency.*

de|pend ✦✦◇ /dɪpɛnd/ (depends, depending, depended) **1** V-I If you say that one thing **depends** on another, you mean that

de|pend|able /dɪpɛndəbᵊl/ ADJ If you say that someone or something is **dependable**, you approve of them because you feel that you can be sure that they will always act consistently or sensibly, or do what you need them to do. [APPROVAL] ❑ *He was a good friend, a dependable companion.*

de|pend|ant /dɪpɛndənt/ → see **dependent**

de|pend|ence /dɪpɛndəns/ ❶ N-UNCOUNT Your **dependence** on something or someone is your need for them in order to succeed or be able to survive. ❑ *...the city's traditional dependence on tourism.* ❷ N-UNCOUNT If you talk about drug **dependence** or alcohol **dependence**, you are referring to a situation where someone is addicted to drugs or is an alcoholic. ❑ *French doctors tend to regard drug dependence as a form of deep-rooted psychological disorder.* ❸ N-UNCOUNT You talk about the **dependence** of one thing on another when the first thing will be affected or determined by the second. ❑ *...the dependence of politicians on rich donors to fund their increasingly expensive campaigns.*

de|pend|en|cy /dɪpɛndənsi/ (dependencies) ❶ N-COUNT A **dependency** is a country which is controlled by another country. ❑ *...the tiny British dependency of Montserrat in the eastern Caribbean.* ❷ N-UNCOUNT You talk about someone's **dependency** when they have a deep emotional, physical, or financial need for a particular person or thing, especially one that you consider excessive or undesirable. ❑ *We saw his dependency on his mother and worried that he might not survive long if anything happened to her.* ❸ N-VAR If you talk about alcohol **dependency** or chemical **dependency**, you are referring to a situation where someone is an alcoholic or is addicted to drugs. [mainly AM] ❑ *In 2014, he began to show signs of alcohol and drug dependency.*

de|pend|ent /dɪpɛndənt/ (dependents) also **dependant** ❶ ADJ To be **dependent** on something or someone means to need them in order to succeed or be able to survive. ❑ *The local economy is overwhelmingly dependent on oil and gas extraction.* ❷ ADJ [v-link ADJ on/upon n] If one thing is **dependent** on another, the first thing will be affected or determined by the second. ❑ *...companies whose earnings are largely dependent on the performance of the Chinese economy.* ❸ N-COUNT Your **dependents** are the people you support financially, such as your children. [FORMAL] ❑ *Companies with 200 or more workers must offer health benefits to employees and their dependents.*

de|per|son|al|ize /dipɜrsənᵊlaɪz/ (depersonalizes, depersonalizing, depersonalized)

in BRIT, also use **depersonalise**

❶ V-T To **depersonalize** a system or a situation means to treat it as if it did not really involve people, or to treat it as if the people involved were not really important. ❑ *It is true that modern weaponry depersonalized war.* ❷ V-T To **depersonalize** someone means to treat them as if they do not matter because their individual feelings and thoughts are not important. ❑ *She does not feel that the book depersonalizes women.*

the first thing will be affected or determined by the second. ❑ *The cooking time needed depends on the size of the potato.* ❷ V-I If you **depend** on someone or something, you need them in order to be able to survive physically, financially, or emotionally. ❑ *He depended on his writing for his income.* ❸ V-I If you can **depend** on a person, organization, or law, you know that they will support you or help you when you need them. ❑ *"You can depend on me," Cross assured him.* ❹ V-I You use **depend** in expressions such as **it depends** to indicate that you cannot give a clear answer to a question because the answer will be affected or determined by other factors. ❑ *"But how long can you stay in the house?"—"I don't know. It depends."* ❺ PHRASE You use **depending on** when you are saying that something varies according to the circumstances mentioned. ❑ *I tend to have a different answer, depending on the family.*

USAGE

depend

Depend is never an adjective. Don't say, for example, that someone or something 'is depend on' another person or thing. You say that they are **dependent** on that person or thing. *The local economy **is dependent on** oil and gas extraction.*

---

de|pict /dɪpɪkt/ (depicts, depicting, depicted) V-T To **depict** someone or something means to show or represent them in a work of art such as a drawing or painting. ❑ *...a gallery of pictures depicting Lee's most famous battles.*

de|pic|tion /dɪpɪkʃᵊn/ (depictions) N-VAR A **depiction** of something is a picture or a written description of it.

de|pila|tory /dɪpɪlətɔri/ (depilatories) ❶ ADJ [ADJ n] **Depilatory** substances and processes remove unwanted hair from your body. ❑ *...a depilatory cream.* ❷ N-COUNT A **depilatory** is a depilatory substance.

de|plete /dɪplit/ (depletes, depleting, depleted) V-T To **deplete** a stock or amount of something means to reduce it. [FORMAL] ❑ *...substances that deplete the ozone layer.* ● **de|plet|ed** ADJ ❑ *...Lee's worn and depleted army.* ● **de|ple|tion** /dɪpliʃᵊn/ N-UNCOUNT ❑ *...the depletion of underground water supplies.*

de|plet|ed ura|nium N-UNCOUNT **Depleted uranium** is a type of uranium that is used in some bombs.

de|plor|able /dɪplɔrəbᵊl/ ADJ If you say that something is **deplorable**, you think that it is very bad and unacceptable. [FORMAL] ❑ *Many of them live under deplorable conditions.*

de|plore /dɪplɔr/ (deplores, deploring, deplored) V-T If you say that you **deplore** something, you think it is very wrong or immoral. [FORMAL] ❑ *Muslim and Jewish leaders have issued statements deploring the violence and urging the United Nations to take action.*

de|ploy /dɪplɔɪ/ (deploys, deploying, deployed) V-T To **deploy** troops or military resources means to organize or position them so that they are ready to be used. ❑ *The president said he had no intention of deploying ground troops.*

de|ploy|ment /dɪplɔɪmənt/ (deployments) N-VAR The **deployment** of troops, resources, or equipment is the organization and positioning of them so that they are ready for quick action. ❑ *...the deployment of troops into townships.*

de|popu|late /dipɒpyəleɪt/ (depopulates, depopulating, depopulated) V-T To **depopulate** an area means to greatly reduce the number of people living there. ❑ *The famine threatened to depopulate the continent.* ● **de|popu|lat|ed** ADJ ❑ *...a small, rural, and depopulated part of the south-west.* ● **de|popu|la|tion** /dipɒpyəleɪʃᵊn/ N-UNCOUNT ❑ *...rural depopulation.*

de|port /dɪpɔrt/ (deports, deporting, deported) V-T If a government **deports** someone, usually someone who is not a citizen of that country, it sends them out of the country because they have committed a crime or because it believes they do not have the right to be there. ❑ *...a government decision earlier this month to deport all illegal immigrants.* ● **de|por|ta|tion** /dipɔrteɪʃᵊn/ (deportations) N-VAR ❑ *...thousands of migrants facing deportation.*

de|por|tee /dipɔrti/ (deportees) N-COUNT A **deportee** is someone who is being deported.

de|port|ment /dɪpɔrtmənt/ N-UNCOUNT Your **deportment** is the way you behave, especially the way you walk and move. [FORMAL]

de|pose /dɪpoʊz/ (deposes, deposing, deposed) V-T [usu passive] If a ruler or political leader **is deposed**, they are forced to give up their position. ❑ *Mr. Ben Bella was deposed in a coup in 1965.*

de|pos|it ♦◇◇ /dɪpɒzɪt/ (deposits, depositing, deposited) ❶ N-COUNT A **deposit** is a sum of money which is part of the full price of something, and which you pay when you agree to buy it. ❑ *The initial deposit required to open an account is a minimum 100 dollars.* ❷ N-COUNT A **deposit** is a sum of money which is in a bank account or savings account, especially a sum which will be left there for some time. ❸ N-COUNT A **deposit** is an amount of a substance that has been left somewhere as a result of a chemical or geological process. ❑ *...underground deposits of gold and diamonds.* ❹ N-COUNT [usu sing] A **deposit** is a sum of money which you pay when you start renting something. The money is returned to you if you do not damage what you have rented. ❑ *I put down a $500 security deposit for another apartment.* ❺ N-COUNT A **deposit** is a sum of money which you put into a bank account. ❑ *She told me I should make a deposit every week and they'd stamp my book.* ❻ V-T If you **deposit** a sum of money, you put it into a bank account or savings account. ❑ *The customer has to deposit a minimum of $100 monthly.* ❼ V-T

To **deposit** someone or something somewhere means to put them or leave them there. ❏ *Mr. Crenshaw deposited the boys and their suitcases on Mr. Peck's lawn.* **8** V-T If you **deposit** something somewhere, you put it where it will be safe until it is needed again. ❏ *You are advised to deposit valuables in the hotel safe.*

COLLOCATIONS

deposit
NOUN
1
adjective + **deposit**: hefty, minimum; non-refundable, refundable
verb + **deposit**: pay; forfeit, lose; refund
3
noun + **deposit**: coal, gold, iron, mineral; calcium
adjective + **deposit**: glacial, sedimentary; rich; fatty
VERB **8**
deposit + noun: cash, check, money

SYNONYMS

deposit
VERB **6**
place: *Chairs were hastily placed in rows for the parents.*
put: *Leaphorn put the photograph on the desk.*
lay: *Lay a sheet of newspaper on the floor.*
drop: *Drop the noodles into the water.*

---

de|pos|it ac|count (deposit accounts) N-COUNT A **deposit account** is the same as a **savings account**. [BRIT]

depo|si|tion /dɛpəzɪʃ³n/ (depositions) N-COUNT A **deposition** is a formal written statement, made for example, by a witness to a crime, which can be used in a court of law if the witness cannot be present. ❏ *The material would be checked against the depositions from other witnesses.*

de|posi|tor /dɪpɒzɪtər/ (depositors) N-COUNT A bank's **depositors** are the people who have accounts with that bank.

de|posi|tory /dɪpɒzɪtɔri/ (depositories) N-COUNT A **depository** is a place where objects can be stored safely.

de|pot /diːpoʊ/ (depots) **1** N-COUNT A **depot** is a bus station or train station. [AM] ❏ *She was reunited with her boyfriend in the bus depot of Ozark, Alabama.* **2** N-COUNT A **depot** is a place where large amounts of raw materials, equipment, arms, or other supplies are kept until they are needed. ❏ *...food depots.*

de|prave /dɪpreɪv/ (depraves, depraving, depraved) V-T Something that **depraves** someone makes them morally bad or evil. [FORMAL] ❏ *...material likely to deprave or corrupt those who see it.*

de|praved /dɪpreɪvd/ ADJ **Depraved** actions, things, or people are morally bad or evil. ❏ *...a disturbing and depraved movie.*

de|prav|ity /dɪprævɪti/ N-UNCOUNT **Depravity** is very dishonest or immoral behavior. [FORMAL] ❏ *...the absolute depravity that can exist in war.*

dep|re|cate /dɛprɪkeɪt/ (deprecates, deprecating, deprecated) V-T If you **deprecate** something, you criticize it. [FORMAL] ❏ *He deprecated the low quality of entrants to the profession.*

dep|re|cat|ing /dɛprɪkeɪtɪŋ/ ADJ A **deprecating** attitude, gesture, or remark shows that you think that something is not very good, especially something associated with yourself. [WRITTEN] ❏ *Erica made a little deprecating shrug.* • **dep|re|cat|ing|ly** ADV [ADV after v] ❏ *He speaks deprecatingly of his father as a lonely man.*

de|pre|ci|ate /dɪpriːʃieɪt/ (depreciates, depreciating, depreciated) V-T/V-I If something such as a currency **depreciates** or if something **depreciates** it, it loses some of its original value. ❏ *Inflation was rising rapidly; the yuan was depreciating.* ❏ *The demand for foreign currency depreciates the real value of local currencies.* • **de|pre|cia|tion** /dɪpriːʃieɪʃ³n/ (depreciations) N-VAR ❏ *...miscellaneous costs, including machinery depreciation and wages.*

dep|re|da|tion /dɛprɪdeɪʃ³n/ (depredations) N-VAR [usu with supp] The **depredations** of a person, animal, or force are their harmful actions, which usually involve taking or damaging something. [FORMAL] ❏ *Much of the region's environmental depredation is a result of poor planning.*

de|press /dɪprɛs/ (depresses, depressing, depressed) **1** V-T If someone or something **depresses** you, they make you feel sad and disappointed. ❏ *I must admit the state of the country depresses me.* **2** V-T If something **depresses** prices, wages, or figures, it causes them to become less. ❏ *The stronger U.S. dollar depressed sales.*

de|pressed /dɪprɛst/ **1** ADJ If you are **depressed**, you are sad and feel that you cannot enjoy anything, because your situation is so difficult and unpleasant. ❏ *She's been very depressed and upset about this whole situation.* **2** ADJ A **depressed** place or industry does not have enough business or employment to be successful. ❏ *Many states already have enterprise zones and legislation that encourage investment in depressed areas.* **3** → See feature box at **emotion**

de|press|ing /dɪprɛsɪŋ/ ADJ Something that is **depressing** makes you feel sad and disappointed. ❏ *Yesterday's unemployment figures were as depressing as those of the previous 22 months.* • **de|press|ing|ly** ADV ❏ *It all sounded depressingly familiar to Janet.*

de|pres|sion ♦◇◇ /dɪprɛʃ³n/ (depressions) **1** N-VAR **Depression** is a mental state in which you are sad and feel that you cannot enjoy anything, because your situation is so difficult and unpleasant. ❏ *Mr. Thomas was suffering from depression.* **2** N-COUNT A **depression** is a time when there is very little economic activity, which causes a lot of unemployment and poverty. ❏ *He never forgot the hardships he witnessed during the Great Depression of the 1930s.* **3** N-COUNT A **depression** in a surface is an area which is lower than the parts surrounding it. ❏ *...an area pockmarked by rain-filled depressions.* **4** N-COUNT A **depression** is a mass of air that has a low pressure and that often causes rain. ❏ *To the northwest lies a depression with clouds and rain.*

SYNONYMS

depression
NOUN
1
sadness: *It is with a mixture of sadness and joy that I say farewell.*
sorrow: *It was a time of great sorrow.*
unhappiness: *There was a lot of unhappiness in my adolescence.*
misery: *All that money brought nothing but misery and tragedy.*
despondency: *There's a mood of gloom and despondency in the country.*
2
recession: *The recession caused sales to drop off.*
slump: *...the slump of the early 1980s.*
stagnation: *...the stagnation of the steel industry.*

---

de|pres|sive /dɪprɛsɪv/ (depressives) **1** ADJ [usu ADJ n] **Depressive** means relating to depression or to being depressed. ❏ *He's no longer a depressive character.* ❏ *...a severe depressive disorder.* **2** N-COUNT A **depressive** is someone who has depression. **3** → see also **manic-depressive**

dep|ri|va|tion /dɛprɪveɪʃ³n/ (deprivations) N-VAR If you suffer **deprivation**, you do not have or are prevented from having something that you want or need. ❏ *Millions more suffer from serious sleep deprivation caused by long work hours.*

de|prive /dɪpraɪv/ (deprives, depriving, deprived) V-T If you **deprive** someone **of** something that they want or need, you take it away from them, or you prevent them from having it. ❏ *They've been deprived of the fuel necessary to heat their homes.*

de|prived /dɪpraɪvd/ ADJ **Deprived** people or people from **deprived** areas do not have the things that people consider to be essential in life, for example, acceptable living conditions or education. ❏ *...probably the most severely deprived children in the country.*

dept. (depts.) **Dept.** is used as a written abbreviation for **department**, usually in the name of a particular department. ❏ *...the Philadelphia Police Dept.*

in BRIT, use **dept**

depth ♦◇◇ /dɛpθ/ (depths) **1** N-VAR The **depth** of something such as a river or hole is the distance downward from its top surface, or between its upper and lower surfaces. ❏ *The depth of the shaft is 520 yards.* ❏ *The smaller lake ranges from five to fourteen feet in depth.* ❏ *The depth of a standard straight valance is usually* about 12 inches. **2** N-VAR The **depth** of something such as a closet or drawer is the distance between its front surface and its back. **3** N-VAR If an emotion is very strongly or intensely felt, you can talk about its **depth**. ❑ *I am well aware of the depth of feeling that exists in Ontario.* **4** N-UNCOUNT The **depth** of a situation is its extent and seriousness. ❑ *The country's leadership had underestimated the depth of the crisis.* **5** N-UNCOUNT The **depth** of someone's knowledge is the great amount that they know. ❑ *We felt at home with her and were impressed with the depth of her knowledge.* **6** N-PLURAL The **depths** are places that are a long way below the surface of the sea or earth. [LITERARY] ❑ *Leaves, brown with long immersion, rose to the surface and vanished back into the depths.* **7** N-PLURAL If you talk about **the depths of** an area, you mean the parts of it which are very far from the edge. ❑ *...the depths of the countryside.* **8** N-PLURAL If you are in **the depths of** an unpleasant emotion, you feel that emotion very strongly. ❑ *I was in the depths of despair when the baby was terribly sick every day, and was losing weight.* **9** PHRASE If you deal with a subject **in depth**, you deal with it very thoroughly and consider all the aspects of it. ❑ *We will discuss these three areas in depth.* **10** → see also **in-depth** **11** PHRASE If you say that someone is **out of** their **depth**, you mean that they are in a situation that is much too difficult for them to be able to cope with it. ❑ *Mr. Gibson is clearly intellectually out of his depth.* **12** PHRASE If you are **out of** your **depth**, you are in water that is deeper than you are tall, with the result that you cannot stand up with your head above water. ❑ *Somehow I got out of my depth in the pool.*

depth charge (depth charges) N-COUNT A **depth charge** is a type of bomb which explodes under water and which is used especially to destroy enemy submarines.

depu|ta|tion /dɛpyəteɪʃ°n/ (deputations) N-COUNT A **deputation** is a small group of people who have been asked to speak to someone on behalf of a larger group of people, especially in order to make a complaint. ❑ *A deputation of elders from the village arrived headed by its chief.*

de|pute /dɪpyut/ (deputes, deputing, deputed) V-T [usu passive] If you **are deputed** to do something, someone tells or allows you to do it on their behalf. [FORMAL] ❑ *A subcommittee was deputed to investigate the claims.*

depu|tize /dɛpyətaɪz/ (deputizes, deputizing, deputized)

in BRIT, also use **deputise**

1 V-T If you **deputize** someone, you ask them to do something on another person's behalf, for example, attend a meeting. [AM] ❑ *The president said he could deputize the Florida National Guard to help with security.* **2** V-I If you **deputize** for someone, you do something on their behalf, for example, attend a meeting. ❑ *I sometimes had to deputize for him in the kitchen.* ❑ *Herr Schulmann cannot be here to welcome you and has asked me to deputize.*

depu|ty ✦✧ /dɛpyəti/ (deputies) **1** N-COUNT A **deputy** is the second most important person in an organization such as a business or government department. Someone's deputy often acts on their behalf when they are not there. ❑ *...Jack Lang, France's minister for culture, and his deputy, Catherine Tasca.* **2** N-COUNT In some legislatures, the elected members are called **deputies**. ❑ *The president appealed to deputies to approve the plan quickly.* **3** N-COUNT A **deputy** is a police officer. [AM] ❑ *Robyn asked the deputy on duty if she could speak with Sheriff Adkins.* **4** N-COUNT A **deputy** is a person appointed to act on another person's behalf. ❑ *His brother was acting as his deputy in America.*

de|rail /dɪreɪl/ (derails, derailing, derailed) **1** V-T To **derail** something such as a plan or a series of negotiations means to prevent it from continuing as planned. [JOURNALISM] ❑ *The present wave of political killings is the work of people trying to derail peace talks.* **2** V-T/V-I If a train **is derailed** or if it **derails**, it comes off the track on which it is running. ❑ *At least six people were killed and about twenty injured when a train was derailed in an isolated mountain region.*

de|rail|ment /dɪreɪlmənt/ (derailments) N-VAR A **derailment** is an accident in which a train comes off the track on which it is running.

de|ranged /dɪreɪndʒd/ ADJ Someone who is **deranged** behaves in a wild and uncontrolled way, often as a result of mental illness. ❑ *Three years ago today a deranged man shot and killed 14 people in the main square.*

de|range|ment /dɪreɪndʒmənt/ N-UNCOUNT **Derangement** is the state of being mentally ill and unable to think or act in a controlled way. [OLD-FASHIONED]

der|by /dɜrbi/ (derbies) **1** N-PROPER [*the* N] **The Derby** is the name of a race for three-year-old horses that takes place each year. In the United States, it refers particularly to the Kentucky Derby. **2** N-COUNT [oft n N] A **derby** is a sports competition or race where there are no restrictions or limits on who can enter. [AM] ❑ *He caught a 6 pound salmon in the annual fishing derby at Lake Winnipesaukee.* **3** N-COUNT A **derby** is a round, hard hat with a narrow brim which is worn by men. Derbies are no longer very common. [AM]

in BRIT, usually use **bowler hat**

de|regu|late /diregyəleɪt/ (deregulates, deregulating, deregulated) V-T To **deregulate** something means to remove controls and regulations from it. ❑ *...the need to deregulate the U.S. airline industry.*

de|regu|la|tion /diregyəleɪʃ°n/ N-UNCOUNT **Deregulation** is the removal of controls and restrictions in a particular area of business or trade. [BUSINESS] ❑ *Since deregulation, banks are permitted to set their own interest rates.*

der|elict /dɛrɪlɪkt/ (derelicts) **1** ADJ A place or building that is **derelict** is empty and in a bad state of repair because it has not been used or lived in for a long time. ❑ *Her body was found dumped in a derelict warehouse less than a mile from her home.* **2** N-COUNT A **derelict** is a person who has no home or job and who has to live on the streets. [FORMAL] ❑ *I had never seen so many derelicts in one place.*

der|elic|tion /dɛrɪlɪkʃ°n/ N-UNCOUNT If a building or a piece of land is in a state of **dereliction**, it is deserted or abandoned. ❑ *The previous owners had rescued the building from dereliction.*

der|elic|tion of duty N-UNCOUNT **Dereliction of duty** is deliberate or accidental failure to do what you should do as part of your job. [FORMAL] ❑ *He pleaded guilty to willful dereliction of duty.*

de|ride /dɪraɪd/ (derides, deriding, derided) V-T If you **deride** someone or something, you say that they are stupid or have no value. [FORMAL] ❑ *Critics derided the move as too little, too late.*

de ri|gueur /də rɪgɜr/ ADJ [v-link ADJ] If you say that a possession or habit is **de rigueur**, you mean that it is fashionable and therefore necessary for anyone who wants to avoid being considered unfashionable. ❑ *Having the season's hot Prada pumps or Gucci slingbacks is de rigueur.*

de|ri|sion /dɪrɪʒ°n/ N-UNCOUNT If you treat someone or something with **derision**, you express contempt for them. ❑ *He tried to calm them, but was greeted with shouts of derision.*

de|ri|sive /dɪraɪsɪv/ ADJ A **derisive** noise, expression, or remark expresses contempt. ❑ *There was a short, derisive laugh.*

de|ri|sory /dɪraɪsəri, -zə-/ **1** ADJ If you describe something such as an amount of money as **derisory**, you are emphasizing that it is so small or inadequate that it seems silly or not worth considering. [BRIT, DISAPPROVAL] ❑ *She was being paid what I considered a derisory amount of money.* **2** ADJ [usu ADJ n] **Derisory** means the same as **derisive**. ❑ *...derisory remarks about the police.*

deri|va|tion /dɛrɪveɪʃ°n/ (derivations) N-VAR [oft N of n, of adj n] The **derivation** of something, especially a word, is its origin or source. ❑ *The derivation of its name is obscure.*

de|riva|tive /dɪrɪvətɪv/ (derivatives) N-COUNT A **derivative** is something which has been developed or obtained from something else. ❑ *...a poppy-seed derivative similar to heroin.*

de|rive /dɪraɪv/ (derives, deriving, derived) **1** V-T If you **derive** something such as pleasure or benefit **from** a person or from something, you get it from them. [FORMAL] ❑ *Mr. Ying is one of those happy people who derive pleasure from helping others.* **2** V-T/V-I If you say that something such as a word or feeling **derives** or **is derived from** something else, you mean that it comes from that thing. ❑ *The name Anastasia is derived from a Greek word meaning "of the resurrection."* **3** → See feature box at **animal**

der|ma|ti|tis /dɜrmətaɪtɪs/ N-UNCOUNT **Dermatitis** is a medical condition which makes your skin red and painful.

der|ma|tolo|gist /dɜrmətɒlədʒɪst/ (dermatologists) N-COUNT A **dermatologist** is a doctor who specializes in the study of skin and the treatment of skin conditions and diseases. • **der|ma|tol|ogy** N-UNCOUNT ◻ ...drugs used in dermatology.

de|roga|tory /dɪrɒɡətɔri/ ADJ If you make a **derogatory** remark or comment about someone or something, you express your low opinion of them. ◻ He refused to withdraw derogatory remarks made about his boss.

der|rick /dɛrɪk/ (derricks) **1** N-COUNT A **derrick** is a machine that is used to move cargo on a ship by lifting it in the air. **2** N-COUNT A **derrick** is a tower built over an oil well which is used to raise and lower the drill.

derring-do /dɛrɪŋ du/ N-UNCOUNT **Derring-do** is the quality of being bold, often in a showy or foolish way. [OLD-FASHIONED]

der|vish /dɜrvɪʃ/ (dervishes) **1** N-COUNT A **dervish** is a member of a Muslim religious group which has a very active and lively dance as part of its worship. **2** PHRASE [v-link PHR] If you say that someone is **like a dervish**, you mean that they are turning around and around, waving their arms about, or working very quickly. ◻ Brian was whirling like a dervish, slapping at the mosquitoes and moaning.

de|sali|na|tion /disælɪneɪʃ°n/ N-UNCOUNT **Desalination** is the process of removing salt from sea water so that it can be used for drinking, or for watering crops.

des|cant /dɛskænt/ (descants) N-COUNT A **descant** is a tune which is played or sung above the main tune in a piece of music.

de|scend /dɪsɛnd/ (descends, descending, descended) **1** V-T/V-I If you **descend** or if you **descend** a staircase, you move downward from a higher to a lower level. [FORMAL] ◻ Things are cooler and more damp as we descend to the cellar. **2** V-I If a large group of people arrive to see you, especially if their visit is unexpected or causes you a lot of work, you can say that they **have descended** on you. ◻ Some 3,000 city officials will descend on Capitol Hill on Tuesday to lobby for more money. **3** V-I When you want to emphasize that the situation that someone is entering is very bad, you can say that they **are descending into** that situation. [EMPHASIS] ◻ He was ultimately overthrown and the country descended into chaos. **4** V-I If you say that someone **descends to** behavior which you consider unacceptable, you are expressing your disapproval of the fact that they do it. [DISAPPROVAL] ◻ We're not going to descend to such methods.

de|scend|ant /dɪsɛndənt/ (descendants) also **descendent** **1** N-COUNT Someone's **descendants** are the people in later generations who are related to them. ◻ They are descendants of the original English and Scottish settlers. **2** N-COUNT Something modern which developed from an older thing can be called a **descendant** of it. ◻ His design was a descendant of a 1956 device.

de|scend|ed /dɪsɛndɪd/ ADJ [v-link ADJ from n] A person who is **descended from** someone who lived a long time ago is directly related to them. ◻ Anna is descended from pioneers who settled in Colorado in 1898.

de|scend|ent /dɪsɛndənt/ → see **descendant**

de|scend|ing /dɪsɛndɪŋ/ ADJ [ADJ n] When a group of things is listed or arranged in **descending** order, each thing is smaller or less important than the thing before it. ◻ All the other ingredients, including water, have to be listed in descending order by weight.

de|scent /dɪsɛnt/ (descents) **1** N-VAR A **descent** is a movement from a higher to a lower level or position. ◻ Sixteen of the youngsters set off for help, but during the descent three collapsed in the cold and rain. **2** N-COUNT A **descent** is a surface that slopes downward, for example, the side of a steep hill. ◻ On the descents, cyclists spin past cars, freewheeling downhill at tremendous speed. **3** N-SING When you want to emphasize that a situation becomes very bad, you can talk about someone's or something's **descent** into that situation. [EMPHASIS] ◻ his swift descent from respected academic to homeless alcoholic. **4** N-UNCOUNT You use **descent** to talk about a person's family background, for example, their nationality or social status. [FORMAL] ◻ All the contributors were of African descent.

de|scribe ◆◆◆ /dɪskraɪb/ (describes, describing, described) **1** V-T If you **describe** a person, object, event, or situation, you say what they are like or what happened. ◻ We asked her to describe what kind of things she did in her spare time. ◻ She read a poem by Carver which describes their life together. **2** V-T If a person **describes** someone or something **as** a particular thing, he or she believes that they are that thing and says so. ◻ He described it as an extraordinarily tangled and complicated tale. ◻ Even his closest allies describe him as forceful, aggressive, and determined.

▬▬▬ SYNONYMS ▬▬▬
describe
VERB **1**
relate: She related her tale of living on the streets.
report: I reported the theft to the police.
explain: I explained that each person has different ideas of what freedom is.
define: He was asked to define his concept of cool.
detail: The report detailed the human rights abuses committed during the war.

de|scrip|tion ◆◇◇ /dɪskrɪpʃ°n/ (descriptions) **1** N-VAR A **description** of someone or something is an account which explains what they are or what they look like. ◻ Police have issued a description of the man who was aged between fifty and sixty. ◻ The paper provides a detailed description of how to create human embryos by cloning. **2** N-SING If something is **of** a particular **description**, it belongs to the general class of items that are mentioned. ◻ Events of this description occurred daily. **3** N-UNCOUNT You can say that something is **beyond description**, or that it **defies description**, to emphasize that it is very unusual, impressive, terrible, or extreme. [EMPHASIS] ◻ His face is weary beyond description.

▬▬▬ SYNONYMS ▬▬▬
description
NOUN **1**
account: He gave a detailed account of what happened on the fateful night.
report: She came back to give us a progress report on how the project is going.
explanation: There was a hint of shyness in his explanation.
profile: A newspaper published profiles of the candidates' wives.
sketch: I had a basic sketch of a plan.

de|scrip|tive /dɪskrɪptɪv/ ADJ **Descriptive** language or writing indicates what someone or something is like. ◻ The group adopted the simpler, more descriptive title of Angina Support Group.

des|ecrate /dɛsɪkreɪt/ (desecrates, desecrating, desecrated) V-T If someone **desecrates** something which is considered to be holy or very special, they deliberately damage or insult it. ◻ She shouldn't have desecrated the picture of a religious leader. • **des|ecra|tion** /dɛsɪkreɪʃ°n/ N-UNCOUNT ◻ The whole area has been shocked by the desecration of the cemetery.

de|seg|re|gate /disɛɡrɪɡeɪt/ (desegregates, desegregating, desegregated) V-T To **desegregate** something such as a place, institution, or service means to officially stop keeping the people who use it in separate groups, especially groups that are defined by race. ◻ The United States was working to desegregate the military, schools, and all public facilities. ◻ The school system itself is not totally desegregated. • **de|seg|re|ga|tion** /disɛɡrɪɡeɪʃ°n/ N-UNCOUNT ◻ Desegregation may be harder to enforce in rural areas.

de|sen|si|tize /disɛnsɪtaɪz/ (desensitizes, desensitizing, desensitized)

in BRIT, also use **desensitise**

V-T To **desensitize** someone to things such as pain, anxiety, or other people's suffering, means to cause them to react less strongly to them. ◻ ...the language that is used to desensitize us to the terrible reality of war.

des|ert ◆◇◇ (deserts, deserting, deserted)

The noun is usually pronounced /dɛzərt/. The verb and the noun in meaning **6** are pronounced /dɪzɜrt/ and are hyphenated de|sert.

1 N-VAR A **desert** is a large area of land, usually in a hot region, where there is almost no water, rain, trees, or plants. ❏ ...the Sahara Desert. ◪ V-T If people or animals **desert** a place, they leave it and it becomes empty. ❏ Poor farmers are deserting their parched farm fields and coming here looking for jobs. • **de|sert|ed** ADJ ❏ She led them into a deserted side street. ◪ V-T If someone **deserts** you, they go away and leave you, and no longer help or support you. ❏ Mrs. Roding's husband deserted her years ago. • **de|ser|tion** /dɪzɜrʃən/ (**desertions**) N-VAR ❏ It was a long time since she'd referred to her father's desertion. ◪ V-T/V-I If you **desert** something that you support, use, or are involved with, you stop supporting it, using it, or being involved with it. ❏ The sport is being written off as boring and predictable and the fans are deserting in droves. ❏ He was pained to see many youngsters deserting kibbutz life. • **de|ser|tion** N-VAR ❏ They blamed his proposal for much of the mass desertion by the Republican electorate. ◪ V-T/V-I If someone **deserts**, or **deserts** a job, especially a job in the armed forces, they leave that job without permission. ❏ He was a second lieutenant in the army until he deserted. ❏ He deserted from army intelligence last month. ◪ PHRASE If you say that someone got their **just deserts**, you mean that they deserved the unpleasant things that happened to them, because they did something bad. [FEELINGS] ❏ At the end of the book the child's true identity is discovered, and the bad guys get their just deserts. ◪ → See feature box at **ecosystem**

de|sert|er /dɪzɜrtər/ (**deserters**) N-COUNT A **deserter** is someone who leaves their job in the armed forces without permission. ❏ Peters had two deserters followed and shot.

de|ser|ti|fi|ca|tion /dɪzɜrtɪfɪkeɪʃən/ N-UNCOUNT **Desertification** is the process by which a piece of land becomes dry, empty, and unsuitable for growing trees or crops on. ❏ A third of Africa is under threat of desertification.

des|ert is|land /dɛzərt aɪlənd/ (**desert islands**) N-COUNT A **desert island** is a small tropical island, where nobody lives.

de|serve ♦◇◇ /dɪzɜrv/ (**deserves, deserving, deserved**) V-T If you say that a person or thing **deserves** something, you mean that they should have it or receive it because of their actions or qualities. ❏ Government officials clearly deserve some of the blame as well. ❏ These people deserve to make more than the minimum wage.

de|serv|ed|ly /dɪzɜrvɪdli/ ADV You use **deservedly** to indicate that someone deserved what happened to them, especially when it was something good. ❏ He deservedly won the player of the year award.

de|serv|ing /dɪzɜrvɪŋ/ ADJ If you describe a person, organization, or cause as **deserving**, you mean that you think they should be helped. ❏ The money saved could be used for more deserving causes.

des|ic|cat|ed /dɛsɪkeɪtɪd/ ◪ ADJ [usu ADJ n] **Desiccated** things have lost all the moisture that was in them. [FORMAL] ❏ ...desiccated flowers and leaves. ◪ ADJ [ADJ n] **Desiccated** food has been dried in order to preserve it. ❏ ...desiccated coconut.

des|ic|ca|tion /dɛsɪkeɪʃən/ N-UNCOUNT **Desiccation** is the process of becoming completely dried out. [FORMAL] ❏ ...the disastrous consequences of the desiccation of the wetland.

de|sign ♦♦♦ /dɪzaɪn/ (**designs, designing, designed**) ◪ V-T When someone **designs** a garment, building, machine, or other object, they plan it and make a detailed drawing of it from which it can be built or made. ❏ They wanted to design a machine that was both attractive and practical. ◪ V-T When someone **designs** a survey, policy, or system, they plan and prepare it, and decide on all the details of it. ❏ We may be able to design a course to suit your particular needs. ◪ N-UNCOUNT **Design** is the process and art of planning and making detailed drawings of something. ❏ He was a born mechanic with a flair for design. ◪ N-UNCOUNT The **design** of something is the way in which it has been planned and made. ❏ ...a new design of clock. ◪ N-COUNT A **design** is a drawing which someone produces to show how they would like something to be built or made. ❏ When Bernardello asked them to build him a home, they drew up the design in a week. ◪ N-COUNT A **design** is a pattern of lines, flowers, or shapes which is used to decorate something. ❏ Many pictures have been based on simple geometric designs. ◪ V-T PASSIVE If something **is designed** for a particular purpose, it is intended for that purpose. ❏ This project is designed to help homeless people. ◪ → See feature box at **fashion, theater**

COLLOCATIONS

design
VERB ◪
design + noun: building, garden, house, product
NOUN ◪
noun + **design**: costume, fashion, product; garden, set, web
adjective + **design**: industrial, urban
◪
adjective + **design**: contemporary, elegant, good; innovative, intelligent, modern, original
verb + **design**: adapt, improve, modify
◪
verb + **design**: create, draw up
◪
adjective + **design**: floral, geometric, simple, stylish

SYNONYMS

design
VERB ◪
plan: We are planning a new kitchen.
create: It is really great for a radio producer to create a show like this.
produce: The company produces parts for the car industry.
invent: He invented the first electric clock.
NOUN ◪
pattern: ...a golden robe embroidered with purple thread stitched into a pattern of flames.
motif: ...a rose motif.
shape: ...sofas and chairs of contrasting shapes and colors.

---

des|ig|nate (**designates, designating, designated**)

The verb is pronounced /dɛzɪgneɪt/. The adjective is pronounced /dɛzɪgnɪt/.

◪ V-T When you **designate** someone or something as a particular thing, you formally give them that description or name. ❏ ...a man interviewed in one of our studies whom we shall designate as E. ❏ There are efforts under way to designate the bridge a historic landmark. ◪ V-T [usu passive] If something **is designated** for a particular purpose, it is set aside for that purpose. ❏ Some of the rooms were designated as offices. ◪ V-T When you **designate** someone as something, you formally choose them to do that particular job. ❏ Designate someone as the spokesperson. ◪ ADJ [n ADJ] **Designate** is used to describe someone who has been formally chosen to do a particular job, but has not yet started doing it. ❏ Japan's prime minister-designate is completing his cabinet today.

des|ig|nat|ed driv|er (**designated drivers**) N-COUNT [usu sing] The **designated driver** in a group of people traveling together is the one who has agreed to drive, or who is insured to drive.

des|ig|nat|ed hit|ter (**designated hitters**) N-COUNT In baseball, a **designated hitter** is a player who bats in place of the pitcher. ❏ Baker said he will use Shawon Dunston as his designated hitter tonight.

des|ig|na|tion /dɛzɪgneɪʃən/ (**designations**) N-VAR A **designation** is a description, name, or title that is given to someone or something. **Designation** is the fact of giving that description, name, or title. [FORMAL] ❏ Wilderness designation prohibits road building, the use of mechanized equipment and most other developments.

de|sign|er ♦◇◇ /dɪzaɪnər/ (**designers**) ◪ N-COUNT A **designer** is a person whose job is to design things by making drawings of them. ❏ Carolyne is a fashion designer. ◪ ADJ [ADJ n] **Designer** clothes or **designer** labels are expensive, fashionable clothes made by a famous designer, rather than being made in large quantities in a factory. ❏ He wears designer clothes and drives an antique car. ◪ ADJ [ADJ n] You can use **designer** to describe things that are worn or bought because they are fashionable. [INFORMAL] ❏ She sat up and removed her designer sunglasses. ◪ → See feature box at **fashion**

de|sign|er baby (**designer babies**) also **designer child** N-COUNT People sometimes refer to a baby that has developed

de|sir|able /dɪzaɪərəbəl/ **1** ADJ Something that is **desirable** is worth having or doing because it is useful, necessary, or popular. ◻ *Prolonged negotiation was not desirable.* ● **de|sir|abil|ity** /dɪzaɪərəbɪlɪti/ N-UNCOUNT ◻ *...the desirability of democratic reform.* **2** ADJ Someone who is **desirable** is considered to be sexually attractive. ◻ *...the young women of his own age whom his classmates thought most desirable.* ● **de|sir|abil|ity** N-UNCOUNT ◻ *He had not at all overrated Veronica's desirability.*

de|sire ✦✧✧ /dɪzaɪər/ (desires, desiring, desired) **1** N-COUNT A **desire** is a strong wish to do or have something. ◻ *I had a strong desire to help and care for people.* **2** V-T [no cont] If you **desire** something, you want it. [FORMAL] ◻ *She had remarried and desired a child with her new husband.* ● **de|sired** ADJ [ADJ n] ◻ *You may find that just threatening this course of action will produce the desired effect.* **3** N-UNCOUNT **Desire** for someone is a strong feeling of wanting to have sex with them. ◻ *It's common to lose your sexual desire when you have your first child.* **4** → See feature box at **review**

de|sir|ous /dɪzaɪərəs/ ADJ [v-link ADJ of -ing/n] If you are **desirous of** doing something or **desirous of** something, you want to do it very much or want it very much. [FORMAL] ◻ *The enemy is so desirous of peace that he will agree to any terms.*

de|sist /dɪzɪst, -sɪst/ (desists, desisting, desisted) V-I If you **desist** from doing something, you stop doing it. [FORMAL] ◻ *Ford never desisted from trying to persuade him to return to America.*

desk ✦✧ /dɛsk/ (desks) **1** N-COUNT A **desk** is a table, often with drawers, which you sit at to write or work. **2** N-SING The place in a hotel, hospital, airport, or other building where you check in or obtain information is referred to as a particular **desk**. ◻ *I told the girl at the reception desk that I was terribly sorry, but I was half an hour late.* **3** N-SING A particular department of a broadcasting company, or of a newspaper or magazine company, can be referred to as a particular **desk**. ◻ *Let our news desk know as quickly as possible.*

desk clerk (desk clerks) N-COUNT A **desk clerk** is someone who works at the main desk in a hotel. [AM]

in BRIT, use **receptionist**

de|skill /diskɪl/ (deskills, deskilling, deskilled) V-T [oft passive] If workers **are deskilled**, they no longer need special skills to do their work, especially because of modern methods of production. ◻ *Administrative staff may be deskilled through increased automation and efficiency.*

desk|top /dɛsktɒp/ (desktops) also **desk-top** **1** ADJ [ADJ n] **Desktop** computers are a convenient size for using on a desk or table, but are not designed to be portable. ◻ *When launched, the Macintosh was the smallest desktop computer ever produced.* **2** N-COUNT A **desktop** is a desktop computer. ◻ *We have stopped making desktops because no one is making money from them.* **3** N-COUNT The **desktop** of a computer is the display of icons that you see on the screen when the computer is ready to use. ◻ *A dramatic full-sized lightning bolt will then fill your screen's desktop.* **4** → See feature box at **computer**

desk|top pub|lish|ing N-UNCOUNT **Desktop publishing** is the production of printed materials such as newspapers and magazines using a desktop computer and a laser printer, rather than using conventional printing methods. The abbreviation **DTP** is also used.

deso|late /dɛsəlɪt/ **1** ADJ A **desolate** place is empty of people and lacking in comfort. ◻ *...a desolate landscape of flat green fields.* **2** ADJ If someone is **desolate**, they feel very sad, alone, and without hope. [LITERARY] ◻ *He was desolate without her.*

deso|la|tion /dɛsəleɪʃən/ **1** N-UNCOUNT **Desolation** is a feeling of great unhappiness and hopelessness. ◻ *Kozelek expresses his sense of desolation absolutely without self-pity.* **2** N-UNCOUNT If you refer to **desolation** in a place, you mean that it is empty and frightening, for example, because it has been destroyed by a violent force or army. [DISAPPROVAL] ◻ *We looked out upon a scene of desolation and ruin.*

des|pair /dɪspɛər/ (despairs, despairing, despaired) **1** N-UNCOUNT **Despair** is the feeling that everything is wrong and that nothing will improve. ◻ *I looked at my wife in despair.* **2** V-I If you **despair**, you feel that everything is wrong and that nothing will improve. ◻ *"Oh, I despair sometimes," he says in mock sorrow.* **3** V-I If you **despair of** something, you feel that there is no hope that it will happen or improve. If you **despair of** someone, you feel that there is no hope that they will improve. ◻ *He wished to earn a living through writing but despaired of doing so.*

des|patch /dɪspætʃ/ [BRIT] → see **dispatch**

des|pe|ra|do /dɛspərɑːdoʊ/ (desperadoes or desperados) N-COUNT A **desperado** is someone who does illegal, violent things without worrying about the danger. [OLD-FASHIONED]

des|per|ate ✦✧✧ /dɛspərɪt/ **1** ADJ If you are **desperate**, you are in such a bad situation that you are willing to try anything to change it. ◻ *Troops are needed to help get food into Kosovo where people are in desperate need.* ● **des|per|ate|ly** ADV [ADV with v] ◻ *Thousands are desperately trying to leave their battered homes and villages.* **2** ADJ [v-link ADJ] If you are **desperate** for something or **desperate** to do something, you want or need it very much indeed. ◻ *They'd been married nearly four years and June was desperate to start a family.* ● **des|per|ate|ly** ADV [ADV with v] ◻ *He was a boy who desperately needed affection.* **3** ADJ A **desperate** situation is very difficult, serious, or dangerous. ◻ *India's United Nations ambassador said the situation is desperate.*

des|pera|tion /dɛspəreɪʃən/ N-UNCOUNT **Desperation** is the feeling that you have when you are in such a bad situation that you will try anything to change it. ◻ *This feeling of desperation and helplessness was common to most of the refugees.*

des|pic|able /dɛspɪkəbəl/ ADJ If you say that a person or action is **despicable**, you are emphasizing that they are extremely nasty, cruel, or evil. [EMPHASIS] ◻ *The minister, who visited the scene a few hours after the explosion, said it was a despicable crime.*

des|pise /dɪspaɪz/ (despises, despising, despised) V-T If you **despise** something or someone, you dislike them and have a very low opinion of them. ◻ *I can never, ever forgive him. I despise him.*

de|spite ✦✦✧ /dɪspaɪt/ **1** PREP [PREP n/-ing] You use **despite** to introduce a fact which makes the other part of the sentence surprising. ◻ *She has been under house arrest for most of the past decade, despite efforts by the United Nations to have her released.* **2** PREP You use **despite** to introduce an idea that appears to contradict your main statement, without suggesting that this idea is true or that you believe it. ◻ *She told friends she will stand by her husband, despite reports that he sent another woman love notes.*

de|spoil /dɪspɔɪl/ (despoils, despoiling, despoiled) V-T To **despoil** a place means to make it less attractive, valuable, or important by taking things away from it or by destroying it. [FORMAL] ◻ *...people who despoil the countryside.*

de|spond|en|cy /dɪspɒndənsi/ N-UNCOUNT **Despondency** is a strong feeling of unhappiness caused by difficulties which you feel you cannot overcome. ◻ *There's a mood of gloom and despondency in the country.*

de|spond|ent /dɪspɒndənt/ **1** ADJ If you are **despondent**, you are very unhappy because you have been experiencing difficulties that you think you will not be able to overcome. ◻ *He was despondent over the breakup of his marriage.* **2** → See feature box at **emotion**

des|pot /dɛspɒt/ (despots) N-COUNT A **despot** is a ruler or other person who has a lot of power and who uses it unfairly or cruelly.

des|pot|ic /dɪspɒtɪk/ ADJ If you say that someone is **despotic**, you are emphasizing that they use their power over other people in a very unfair or cruel way. [EMPHASIS] ◻ *The country was ruled by a despotic tyrant.*

des|pot|ism /dɛspətɪzəm/ N-UNCOUNT **Despotism** is cruel and unfair government by a ruler or rulers who have a lot of power.

des|sert /dɪzɜːrt/ (desserts) N-MASS **Dessert** is something sweet, such as fruit, pastry, or ice cream, that you eat at the end of a meal. ◻ *She had homemade ice cream for dessert.*

dessert|spoon /dɪzɜːrtspuːn/ (dessertspoons) also **dessert spoon** N-COUNT A **dessertspoon** is a spoon which is midway between the size of a teaspoon and a tablespoon. You use it to eat desserts.

des|sert wine (dessert wines) N-MASS A **dessert wine** is a sweet wine, usually a white wine, that is served with dessert.

de|sta|bi|lize /diːstˈeɪbɪlaɪz/ (destabilizes, destabilizing, destabilized)

in BRIT, also use **destabilise**

V-T To **destabilize** something such as a country or government means to create a situation which reduces its power or influence. ❑ *Their sole aim is to destabilize the Indian government.*

des|ti|na|tion /dɛstɪneɪʃən/ (destinations) N-COUNT The **destination** of someone or something is the place to which they are going or being sent. ❑ *Ellis Island has become one of America's most popular tourist destinations.*

des|tined /dɛstɪnd/ **1** ADJ If something is **destined** to happen or if someone is **destined** to behave in a particular way, that thing seems certain to happen or be done. ❑ *Any economic strategy based on a weak dollar is destined to fail.* **2** ADJ [v-link ADJ for n] If someone is **destined for** a particular place, or if goods are **destined for** a particular place, they are traveling toward that place or will be sent to that place. ❑ *...products destined for Saudi Arabia.*

des|ti|ny /dɛstɪni/ (destinies) **1** N-COUNT A person's **destiny** is everything that happens to them during their life, including what will happen in the future, especially when it is considered to be controlled by someone or something else. ❑ *We are masters of our own destiny.* **2** N-UNCOUNT **Destiny** is the force which some people believe controls the things that happen to you in your life. ❑ *Is it destiny that brings people together, or is it accident?*

des|ti|tute /dɛstɪtut/ ADJ Someone who is **destitute** has no money or possessions. [FORMAL] ❑ *...destitute children who live on the streets.*

des|ti|tu|tion /dɛstɪtuʃən/ N-UNCOUNT **Destitution** is the state of having no money or possessions. [FORMAL]

de-stress (de-stresses, de-stressing, de-stressed) also **destress** V-T/V-I If you **de-stress** or if something **de-stresses** you, you do something that helps you to relax. ❑ *I make sure I make time for fishing because it's how I de-stress.* ❑ *All of these help relax and de-stress you from the rigors of daily life.*

de|stroy ♦♦♢ /dɪstrɔɪ/ (destroys, destroying, destroyed) **1** V-T To **destroy** something means to cause so much damage to it that it is completely ruined or does not exist any more. ❑ *That's a sure recipe for destroying the economy and creating chaos.* **2** V-T To **destroy** someone means to ruin their life or to make their situation impossible to bear. ❑ *If I was younger or more naive, the criticism would have destroyed me.* **3** V-T [usu passive] If an animal **is destroyed**, it is killed, either because it is ill or because it is dangerous. ❑ *Lindsay was unhurt but the horse had to be destroyed.*

de|stroy|er /dɪstrɔɪər/ (destroyers) N-COUNT A **destroyer** is a small, heavily armed warship.

de|struc|tion ♦♦♢ /dɪstrʌkʃən/ **1** N-UNCOUNT **Destruction** is the act of destroying something, or the state of being destroyed. ❑ *...an international agreement aimed at halting the destruction of the ozone layer.* **2** → See feature box at **disaster**

de|struc|tive /dɪstrʌktɪv/ ADJ Something that is **destructive** causes or is capable of causing great damage, harm, or injury. ❑ *...the awesome destructive power of nuclear weapons.*

des|ul|tory /dɛsəltɔri/ ADJ Something that is **desultory** is done in an unplanned and disorganized way, and without enthusiasm. [FORMAL] ❑ *Lynne made desultory conversation with Irene and Alex.*

de|tach /dɪtætʃ/ (detaches, detaching, detached) **1** V-T/V-I If you **detach** one thing from another that it is attached to, you remove it. If one thing **detaches** from another, it becomes separated from it. [FORMAL] ❑ *Detach the white part of the application form and keep it for reference only.* ❑ *They clambered back under the falls to detach the raft from a jagged rock.* **2** V-T If you **detach** yourself from something, you become less involved in it or less concerned about it than you used to be. ❑ *It helps them detach themselves from their problems and become more objective.*

de|tach|able /dɪtætʃəbəl/ ADJ If a part of an object is **detachable**, it has been made so that it can be removed from the object. ❑ *The dresses had detachable collars, cuffs, and sleeves.*

de|tached /dɪtætʃt/ **1** ADJ Someone who is **detached** is not personally involved in something or has no emotional interest in it. ❑ *He tries to remain emotionally detached from the prisoners, but fails.* **2** ADJ A **detached** building is one that is not joined to any other building. ❑ *...a house on the corner with a detached garage.*

de|tach|ment /dɪtætʃmənt/ N-UNCOUNT **Detachment** is the feeling that you have of not being personally involved in something or of having no emotional interest in it. ❑ *She did not care for the idea of socializing with her clients. It would detract from her professional detachment.*

de|tail ♦♦♢ /dɪteɪl/ (details, detailing, detailed)

The pronunciation /dɪteɪl/ is also used for the noun.

1 N-COUNT The **details** of something are its individual features or elements. ❑ *The details of the plan are still being worked out.* ❑ *No details of the discussions have been given.* **2** N-COUNT A **detail** is a minor point or aspect of something, as opposed to the central ones. ❑ *Only minor details now remain to be settled.* **3** N-PLURAL **Details** about someone or something are facts or pieces of information about them. ❑ *See the bottom of this page for details of how to apply for this exciting offer.* **4** N-UNCOUNT You can refer to the small features of something which are often not noticed as **detail**. ❑ *We like his attention to detail and his enthusiasm.* **5** V-T If you **detail** things, you list them or give information about them. ❑ *The report detailed the human rights abuses committed during the war.* **6** N-COUNT [oft N of n] A **detail** of people such as soldiers or prisoners is a small group of them who have been given a special task to carry out. ❑ *...a sergeant with a detail of four men.* **7** PHRASE If someone does not **go into detail** about a subject, or does not **go into the details**, they mention it without explaining it fully or properly. ❑ *He doesn't wish to go into detail about all the events of those days.* **8** PHRASE If you examine or discuss something **in detail**, you do it thoroughly and carefully. ❑ *We examine the wording in detail before deciding on the final text.*

―― COLLOCATIONS ――

detail
NOUN
2
adjective + **detail**: exact, full, further
detail + be + adjective: available
verb + **detail**: announce, give, provide, publish; disclose, leak, release, reveal
3
noun + **details**: account, bank, credit card; contact
adjective + **detail**: intimate, personal; financial, technical

―― SYNONYMS ――

detail
NOUN **1**
feature: *The most unusual feature in the room is an extraordinary pair of candles.*
point: *Many of the points in the report are correct.*
particular: *You will find all the particulars in Chapter 9.*
aspect: *He was interested in all aspects of the work here.*

de|tailed ♦♦♢ /dɪteɪld/ ADJ A **detailed** report or plan contains a lot of details. ❑ *Yesterday's letter contains a detailed account of the decisions.*

de|tain /dɪteɪn/ (detains, detaining, detained) **1** V-T When people such as the police **detain** someone, they keep them in a place under their control. [FORMAL] ❑ *Police have detained two suspects in connection with the attack.* **2** V-T To **detain** someone means to delay them, for example, by talking to them. [FORMAL] ❑ *Millson stood up. "Thank you. We won't detain you any further, Mrs. Stebbing."*

de|tain|ee /diteɪni/ (detainees) N-COUNT A **detainee** is someone who is held prisoner by a government because of his or her political views or activities. ❑ *Earlier this year, Amnesty International called for the release of more than 100 political detainees.*

de|tect /dɪtɛkt/ (detects, detecting, detected) **1** V-T To **detect** something means to find or to discover that it is present somewhere by using equipment or making an investigation.

detectable ☐ ...a sensitive piece of equipment used to detect radiation. ② V-T If you **detect** something, you notice it or sense it, even though it is not very obvious. ☐ Arnold could detect a certain sadness in the old man's face. ③ → See feature box at **brain**

de|tect|able /dɪtɛktəb³l/ ADJ Something that is **detectable** can be noticed or discovered. ☐ Doctors say the disease is probably inherited but not detectable at birth.

de|tec|tion /dɪtɛkʃ³n/ N-UNCOUNT **Detection** is the act of noticing or sensing something. ☐ ...the early detection of breast cancer.

de|tec|tive ♦◇◇ /dɪtɛktɪv/ (**detectives**) ① N-COUNT A **detective** is someone whose job is to discover what has happened in a crime or other situation and to find the people involved. Some detectives work in the police force and others work privately. ☐ Now detectives are appealing for witnesses who may have seen anything suspicious last night. ② ADJ [ADJ n] A **detective** novel or story is one in which a detective tries to solve a crime. ☐ ...Arthur Conan Doyle's classic detective novel.

de|tec|tor /dɪtɛktər/ (**detectors**) N-COUNT A **detector** is an instrument which is used to discover that something is present somewhere, or to measure how much of something there is. ☐ ...a metal detector.

de|tente /deɪtɒnt/ also **détente** N-UNCOUNT [also a N] **Detente** is a state of friendly relations between two countries when previously there had been problems between them. [FORMAL] ☐ ...their desire to pursue a policy of detente.

de|ten|tion /dɪtɛnʃ³n/ (**detentions**) ① N-UNCOUNT [also N in pl] **Detention** is when someone is arrested or put into prison. ☐ ...the detention without trial of government critics. ② N-VAR **Detention** is a punishment for students who misbehave, who are made to stay at school after the other students have gone home. ☐ The teacher kept the boys in detention after school.

de|ten|tion cen|ter (**detention centers**)

in BRIT, use **detention centre**

N-COUNT A **detention center** is a sort of prison, for example, a place where people who have entered a country illegally are kept while a decision is made about what to do with them.

de|ter /dɪtɜr/ (**deters, deterring, deterred**) V-T To **deter** someone from doing something means to make them not want to do it or continue doing it. ☐ Supporters of the death penalty argue that it would deter criminals from carrying guns.

de|ter|gent /dɪtɜrdʒ³nt/ (**detergents**) N-MASS **Detergent** is a chemical substance, usually in the form of a powder or liquid, which is used for washing things such as clothes or dishes. ☐ ...a brand of detergent.

de|terio|rate /dɪtɪəriəreɪt/ (**deteriorates, deteriorating, deteriorated**) V-I If something **deteriorates**, it becomes worse in some way. ☐ There are fears that the situation might deteriorate into full-scale war. • **de|terio|ra|tion** /dɪtɪəriəreɪʃ³n/ N-UNCOUNT ☐ ...concern about the rapid deterioration in relations between the two countries.

de|ter|mi|nant /dɪtɜrmɪnənt/ (**determinants**) N-COUNT [usu with supp] A **determinant** of something causes it to be of a particular kind or to happen in a particular way. [FORMAL]

de|ter|mi|nate /dɪtɜrmɪnɪt/ ADJ [usu ADJ n] **Determinate** means fixed and definite. [FORMAL] ☐ ...a contract for the exclusive possession of land for some determinate period.

de|ter|mi|na|tion /dɪtɜrmɪneɪʃ³n/ ① N-UNCOUNT **Determination** is the quality that you show when you have decided to do something and you will not let anything stop you. ☐ Everyone concerned acted with great courage and determination. ② → see also **determine**

de|ter|mine ♦◇◇ /dɪtɜrmɪn/ (**determines, determining, determined**) ① V-T If a particular factor **determines** the nature of a thing or event, it causes it to be of a particular kind. [FORMAL] ☐ The size of the chicken pieces will determine the cooking time. • **de|ter|mi|na|tion** N-UNCOUNT ☐ ...the gene which is responsible for male sex determination. ② V-T To **determine** a fact means to discover it as a result of investigation. [FORMAL] ☐ The investigation will determine what really happened. ☐ Experts say testing needs to be done on each contaminant to determine the long-term effects on humans. ③ V-T If you **determine** something, you decide about it or settle it. ☐ The Baltic people have a right to determine their own future. • **de|ter|mi|na|tion** (**determinations**) N-COUNT ☐ We must take into our own hands the determination of our future. ④ V-T If you **determine** to do something, you make a firm decision to do it. [FORMAL] ☐ He determined to rescue his two countrymen.

de|ter|mined ♦◇◇ /dɪtɜrmɪnd/ ① ADJ If you are **determined** to do something, you have made a firm decision to do it and will not let anything stop you. ☐ His enemies are determined to ruin him. • **de|ter|mined|ly** ADV ☐ She shook her head, determinedly. ② → See feature box at **quality**

de|ter|min|er /dɪtɜrmɪnər/ (**determiners**) N-COUNT In grammar, a **determiner** is a word which is used at the beginning of a noun group to indicate, for example, which thing you are referring to or whether you are referring to one thing or several. Common English determiners are 'a,' 'the,' 'some,' 'this,' and 'each.'

de|ter|min|ism /dɪtɜrmɪnɪzəm/ N-UNCOUNT [oft adj N] **Determinism** is the belief that all actions and events result from other actions, events, or situations, so people cannot in fact choose what to do. [FORMAL] ☐ I don't believe in historical determinism.

de|ter|min|ist /dɪtɜrmɪnɪst/ (**determinists**) ① N-COUNT A **determinist** is someone who believes in determinism. [FORMAL] ② ADJ **Determinist** ideas are based on determinism. [FORMAL] ☐ The determinist doctrines in question maintained that certain people were born to be slaves.

de|ter|min|is|tic /dɪtɜrmɪnɪstɪk/ ① ADJ **Deterministic** ideas or explanations are based on determinism. [FORMAL] ☐ ...a deterministic view of human progress. ② ADJ **Deterministic** forces and factors cause things to happen in a way that cannot be changed. [FORMAL] ☐ The rise or decline of the United States is not a function of deterministic forces.

de|ter|rence /dɪtɜrəns/ N-UNCOUNT **Deterrence** is the prevention of something, especially war or crime, by having something such as weapons or punishment to use as a threat. ☐ ...policies of nuclear deterrence.

de|ter|rent /dɪtɜrənt/ (**deterrents**) ① N-COUNT A **deterrent** is something that prevents people from doing something by making them afraid of what will happen to them if they do it. ☐ They seriously believe that capital punishment is a deterrent. ② N-COUNT A **deterrent** is a weapon or set of weapons designed to prevent enemies from attacking by making them afraid to do so. ☐ The idea of building a nuclear deterrent is completely off the political agenda. ③ → See feature box at **prison**

de|test /dɪtɛst/ (**detests, detesting, detested**) V-T If you **detest** someone or something, you dislike them very much. ☐ My mother detested him.

de|test|able /dɪtɛstəb³l/ ADJ If you say that someone or something is **detestable**, you mean you dislike them very much. [FORMAL] ☐ I find their views detestable.

de|throne /diθroʊn/ (**dethrones, dethroning, dethroned**) V-T [usu passive] If a king, queen, or other powerful person is **dethroned**, they are removed from their position of power. ☐ He was dethroned and went into exile.

deto|nate /dɛt³neɪt/ (**detonates, detonating, detonated**) V-T/V-I If someone **detonates** a device such as a bomb, or if it **detonates**, it explodes. ☐ Their underground vehicle hit a trip wire that detonated a bomb.

deto|na|tion /dɛt³neɪʃ³n/ (**detonations**) ① N-COUNT A **detonation** is a large or powerful explosion. [FORMAL] ② N-UNCOUNT **Detonation** is the action of causing a device such as a bomb to explode. [FORMAL] ☐ ...accidental detonation of nuclear weapons.

deto|na|tor /dɛt³neɪtər/ (**detonators**) N-COUNT A **detonator** is a small amount of explosive or a piece of electrical or electronic equipment which is used to explode a bomb or other explosive device.

de|tour /ditʊər/ (**detours**) ① N-COUNT If you make a **detour** on a trip, you go by a route which is not the shortest way, because you want to avoid something such as a traffic jam, or because there is something you want to do on the way. ☐ He did not take the direct route to his home, but made a detour around the outskirts of the city. ② N-COUNT A **detour** is a special route for traffic to follow when the normal route is blocked, for

de|tox (detoxes, detoxing, detoxed)

The noun is pronounced /ditɒks/. The verb is pronounced /ditɒks/.

1 N-UNCOUNT [oft N n] **Detox** is treatment given to people who are addicted to drugs or alcohol in order to stop them from being addicted. ❑ *A patient going through acute detox will have an assigned nurse nearby.* ❑ *...a detox therapist.* **2** N-COUNT [oft N n] A **detox** is a treatment that is intended to remove poisonous or harmful substances from your body. ❑ *Overhaul your body with a cleansing detox.* ❑ *Give yourself a healthy glow on our detox diet.* **3** V-T/V-I If someone who is addicted to drugs or alcohol **detoxes**, or if another person **detoxes** them, they undergo treatment which stops them from being addicted. ❑ *He had tried to detox twice by himself, but couldn't.* **4** V-T/V-I If you **detox**, or if something **detoxes** your body, you do something to remove poisonous or harmful substances from your body. ❑ *It might be an idea to detox after the indulgences of Christmas.* ❑ *Honey can help to detox the body.*

de|toxi|fi|ca|tion /ditɒksɪfɪkeɪʃ°n/ **1** N-UNCOUNT **Detoxification** is treatment given to people who are addicted to drugs or alcohol in order to stop them from being addicted. **2** N-UNCOUNT **Detoxification** is treatment that is intended to remove poisonous or harmful substances from your body. ❑ *Detoxification will help keep your bodily systems running smoothly.*

de|toxi|fy /ditɒksɪfaɪ/ (**detoxifies, detoxifying, detoxified**) **1** V-T/V-I If someone who is addicted to drugs or alcohol **detoxifies**, or if they **are detoxified**, they undergo treatment which stops them from being addicted. ❑ *...drugs which block the effects of heroin use and rapidly detoxify addicts.* ❑ *The first thing I did was to get completely detoxified.* **2** V-T/V-I If you **detoxify**, or if something **detoxifies** your body, you do something to remove poisonous or harmful substances from your body. ❑ *Many people have made it a rule to detoxify once a year.* ❑ *Seaweed baths can help to detoxify the body.* **3** V-T To **detoxify** a poisonous substance means to change it chemically so that it is no longer poisonous. ❑ *Vitamin C helps to detoxify pollutants in the body.*

de|tract /dɪtrækt/ (**detracts, detracting, detracted**) V-T/V-I If one thing **detracts** from another, it makes it seem less good or impressive. ❑ *They feared that the publicity surrounding him would detract from their own election campaigns.*

de|trac|tor /dɪtræktər/ (**detractors**) N-COUNT [usu pl, usu with poss] The **detractors** of a person or thing are people who criticize that person or thing. [JOURNALISM] ❑ *This performance will silence many of his detractors.*

det|ri|ment /detrɪmənt/ **1** PHRASE If something happens **to the detriment of** something or **to** a person's **detriment**, it causes harm or damage to them. [FORMAL] ❑ *These tests will give too much importance to written exams to the detriment of other skills.* **2** PHRASE If something happens **without detriment to** a person or thing, it does not harm or damage them. [FORMAL] ❑ *These difficulties have been overcome without detriment to performance.*

det|ri|men|tal /detrɪment°l/ ADJ Something that is **detrimental** to something else has a harmful or damaging effect on it. ❑ *Many foods are suspected of being detrimental to health because of the chemicals and additives they contain.*

de|tri|tus /dɪtraɪtəs/ N-UNCOUNT [with supp] **Detritus** is the small pieces of trash or waste material that remain after an event has finished or when something has been used. [FORMAL] ❑ *...the detritus of war.*

deuce /dus/ (**deuces**) **1** N-VAR [also N in pl] **Deuce** is the score in a game of tennis when both players have forty points. One player has to win two points one after the other to win the game. **2** N-COUNT In card games such as poker, a **deuce** is a playing card with two symbols on it, for example the two of hearts or the two of spades. ❑ *...a pair of deuces.*

de|value /divælyu/ (**devalues, devaluing, devalued**) **1** V-T To **devalue** something means to cause it to be thought less impressive or less deserving of respect. ❑ *They spread tales about her in an attempt to devalue her work.* **2** V-T To **devalue** the currency of a country means to reduce its value in relation to other currencies. ❑ *India has devalued the rupee by about eleven percent.* ● **de|valua|tion** /divælyueɪʃ°n/ (**devaluations**) N-VAR ❑ *It will lead to devaluation of a number of currencies.*

dev|as|tate /devəsteɪt/ (**devastates, devastating, devastated**) V-T If something **devastates** an area or a place, it damages it very badly or destroys it totally. ❑ *The tsunami devastated parts of Indonesia and other countries in the region.*

dev|as|tat|ed /devəsteɪtɪd/ ADJ [v-link ADJ] If you are **devastated** by something, you are very shocked and upset by it. ❑ *Teresa was devastated, her dreams shattered.*

dev|as|tat|ing /devəsteɪtɪŋ/ **1** ADJ If you describe something as **devastating**, you are emphasizing that it is very harmful or damaging. [EMPHASIS] ❑ *Affairs do have a devastating effect on marriages.* **2** ADJ You can use **devastating** to emphasize that something is very shocking, upsetting, or terrible. [EMPHASIS] ❑ *The diagnosis was devastating. She had cancer.* **3** ADJ You can use **devastating** to emphasize that something or someone is very impressive. [EMPHASIS] ❑ *He returned to his best with a devastating display of galloping and jumping.* **4** → See feature box at **endanger**

dev|as|ta|tion /devəsteɪʃ°n/ N-UNCOUNT **Devastation** is severe and widespread destruction or damage. ❑ *The war brought massive devastation and loss of life to the region.*

de|vel|op ♦♦♦ /dɪveləp/ (**develops, developing, developed**) **1** V-I When something **develops**, it grows or changes over a period of time and usually becomes more advanced, complete, or severe. ❑ *It's hard to say at this stage how the market will develop.* ❑ *These clashes could develop into open warfare.* ● **de|vel|oped** ADJ ❑ *Their bodies were well developed and super fit.* **2** V-I If a problem or difficulty **develops**, it begins to occur. ❑ *The space agency says a problem has developed with an experiment aboard the space shuttle.* **3** V-I If you say that a country **develops**, you mean that it changes from being a poor agricultural country to being a rich industrial country. ❑ *All countries, it was predicted, would develop and develop fast.* **4** → see also **developed, developing** **5** V-T/V-I If you **develop** a business or industry, or if it **develops**, it becomes bigger and more successful. [BUSINESS] ❑ *An amateur hatmaker has won a scholarship to pursue her dreams of developing her own business.* ● **de|vel|oped** ADJ ❑ *...the countries that have suffered the most from the absence of more developed financial systems.* **6** V-T To **develop** land or property means to make it more profitable, by building houses or factories or by improving the existing buildings. ❑ *Local entrepreneurs developed fashionable restaurants, bars and discotheques in the area.* ● **de|vel|oped** ADJ ❑ *Developed land was to grow from 5.3% to 6.9%.* **7** V-T If you **develop** a habit, reputation, or belief, you start to have it and it then becomes stronger or more noticeable. ❑ *Mr. Robinson has developed the reputation of a ruthless cost-cutter.* **8** V-T/V-I If you **develop** a skill, quality, or relationship, or if it **develops**, it becomes better or stronger. ❑ *Now you have a good opportunity to develop a greater understanding of each other.* ● **de|vel|oped** ADJ ❑ *...a highly developed instinct for self-preservation.* **9** V-T If a piece of equipment **develops** a fault, it starts to have the fault. ❑ *The aircraft made an unscheduled landing at Logan after developing an electrical fault.* **10** V-T If someone **develops** a new product, they design it and produce it. ❑ *He claims that several countries have developed nuclear weapons secretly.* **11** V-T/V-I If you **develop** an idea, theory, story, or theme, or if it **develops**, it gradually becomes more detailed, advanced, or complex. ❑ *I would like to thank them for allowing me to develop my original idea.* **12** V-T To **develop** photographs means to make negatives or prints from a photographic film. ❑ *...after developing one roll of film.*

SYNONYMS

develop
VERB
1
grow: *The economy continues to grow.*
progress: *Were you surprised that his disease progressed so quickly?*
evolve: *As medical knowledge evolves, beliefs change.*
advance: *Medical technology has advanced considerably.*
flourish: *Business flourished, and within six months they were earning 18,000 rubles a day.*
2
result: *Ignore the early warnings and illness could result.*
arise: *...if a problem arises later in the pregnancy.*
ensue: *A brief but embarrassing silence ensued.*
come about: *That came about when we went to Glastonbury last year.*

developed /dɪvɛləpt/ ADJ If you talk about **developed** countries or the **developed** world, you mean the countries or the parts of the world that are wealthy and have many industries. ❑ *This scarcity is inevitable in less developed countries.*

de|vel|op|er /dɪvɛləpər/ (developers) **1** N-COUNT A **developer** is a person or a company that buys land and builds houses, offices, stores, or factories on it, or buys existing buildings and makes them more modern. [BUSINESS] ❑ *...common land which would have a high commercial value if sold to developers.* **2** N-COUNT A **developer** is someone who develops something such as an idea, a design, or a product. ❑ *John Bardeen was also co-developer of the theory of superconductivity.*

de|vel|op|ing /dɪvɛləpɪŋ/ **1** ADJ [ADJ n] If you talk about **developing** countries or the **developing** world, you mean the countries or the parts of the world that are poor and have few industries. ❑ *Much solar energy is already being used in the developing world.* **2** → See feature box at **disaster**

de|vel|op|ment ♦♦♦ /dɪvɛləpmənt/ (developments) **1** N-UNCOUNT **Development** is the gradual growth or formation of something. ❑ *...an ideal system for studying the development of the embryo.* **2** N-UNCOUNT **Development** is the growth of something such as a business or an industry. [BUSINESS] ❑ *He firmly believes that education and a country's economic development are key factors to progress.* **3** N-UNCOUNT **Development** is the process of making an area of land or water more useful or profitable. ❑ *The talks will focus on economic development of the region.* **4** N-VAR **Development** is the process or result of making a basic design gradually better and more advanced. ❑ *It is spending $850M on research and development to get to the market place as soon as possible with faster microprocessors.* **5** N-COUNT A **development** is an event or incident which has recently happened and is likely to have an effect on the present situation. ❑ *The police spokesman said: "We believe there has been a significant development in the case."* **6** N-COUNT A **development** is an area of houses or buildings which have been built by property developers. ❑ *...a 16-house development planned by Everlast Enterprises.*

COLLOCATIONS

development
NOUN

1
noun + **development**: career, character; language
adjective + **development**: personal, professional

2
noun + **development**: business, property
adjective + **development**: commercial, economic, sustainable
verb + **development**: encourage, promote, support

4
noun + **development**: product, software
adjective + **development**: industrial, technological; exciting

5
adjective + **development**: interesting, major, recent, significant

6
noun + **development**: housing
adjective + **development**: residential; economic, rural, urban

---
SYNONYMS

development
NOUN

1
growth: *The area has seen a rapid population growth.*
increase: *...a sharp increase in productivity.*
expansion: *The company has abandoned plans for further expansion.*

5
event: *...in the wake of recent events in Europe.*
incident: *These incidents were the latest in a series of disputes.*
occurrence: *The lines for food have become a daily occurrence across the country.*

---

de|vel|op|men|tal /dɪvɛləpmɛntəl/ ADJ [usu ADJ n] **Developmental** means relating to the development of someone or something. ❑ *...the emotional, educational, and developmental needs of the child.*

de|vel|op|ment bank (development banks) N-COUNT A **development bank** is a bank that provides money for projects in poor countries or areas. [BUSINESS] ❑ *...the Asian development bank.*

de|vi|ant /diviənt/ ADJ **Deviant** behavior or thinking is different from what people normally consider to be acceptable. ❑ *...the social reactions to deviant and criminal behavior.* ● **de|vi|ance** /diviəns/ N-UNCOUNT ❑ *...sexual deviance, including the abuse of children.*

de|vi|ate /diviert/ (deviates, deviating, deviated) V-I To **deviate** from something means to start doing something different or not planned, especially in a way that causes problems for others. ❑ *They stopped you as soon as you deviated from the script.*

de|via|tion /diviert ʃən/ (deviations) N-VAR **Deviation** means doing something that is different from what people consider to be normal or acceptable. ❑ *Deviation from the norm is not tolerated.*

de|vice ♦♢♢ /dɪvaɪs/ (devices) **1** N-COUNT A **device** is an object that has been invented for a particular purpose, for example, for recording or measuring something. ❑ *...the electronic device that tells the starter when an athlete has moved from his blocks prematurely.* **2** → See feature box at **household**, **study**, **technology**; See also color supplement

---
COLLOCATIONS

device
NOUN **1**
noun + **device**: safety, storage; listening, navigation, recording, tracking
adjective + **device**: electronic, explosive, incendiary, mechanical, medical, nuclear; handheld, mobile, portable; high-tech, simple, sophisticated
verb + **device**: design, develop, test; detonate, install, plant

---
SYNONYMS

device
NOUN **1**
gadget: *...kitchen gadgets, including toasters, kettles, and percolators.*
tool: *I find the best tool for the purpose is a pair of shears.*
instrument: *...instruments for cleaning and polishing teeth.*
appliance: *He learned to use the vacuum cleaner, washing machine, and other household appliances.*
implement: *...knives and other useful implements.*

---

dev|il /dɛvəl/ (devils) **1** N-PROPER In Judaism, Christianity, and Islam, **the Devil** is the most powerful evil spirit. **2** N-COUNT A **devil** is an evil spirit. ❑ *...the idea of angels with wings and devils with horns and hoofs.*

dev|il|ish /dɛvəlɪʃ, dɛvlɪʃ/ **1** ADJ [usu ADJ n] A **devilish** idea or action is cruel or unpleasant. ❑ *...the devilish destructiveness of modern weapons.* **2** ADJ [usu ADJ n] You can use **devilish** to emphasize how extreme or difficult something is. [EMPHASIS] ❑ *...a devilish puzzle.* ● **dev|il|ish|ly** ADV ❑ *It is devilishly painful.*

devil-may-care ADJ [usu ADJ n] If you say that someone has a **devil-may-care** attitude, you mean that they seem relaxed and do not seem worried about the consequences of their actions. [APPROVAL]

dev|il's ad|vo|cate N-UNCOUNT [also with det] If you play **devil's advocate** in a discussion or debate, you express an opinion which you may not agree with but which is very different from what other people have been saying, in order to make the argument more interesting.

de|vi|ous /diviəs/ ADJ If you describe someone as **devious**, you do not like them because you think they are dishonest and like to keep things secret, often in a complicated way. [DISAPPROVAL] ❑ *Newman was certainly devious, prepared to say one thing in print and something quite different in private.*

de|vise /dɪvaɪz/ (devises, devising, devised) V-T If you **devise** a plan, system, or machine, you have the idea for it and design it. ❑ *We devised a scheme to help him.*

de|void /dɪvɔɪd/ ADJ [v-link ADJ of n] If you say that someone or something is **devoid of** a quality or thing, you are emphasizing that they have none of it. [FORMAL, EMPHASIS] ☐ *I have never looked on a face that was so devoid of feeling.*

de|vo|lu|tion /diːvəluːʃən, dɛv-/ N-UNCOUNT **Devolution** is the transfer of some authority or power from a central organization or government to smaller organizations or government departments. ☐ *...the devolution of power to the regions.*

de|volve /dɪvɒlv/ (devolves, devolving, devolved) V-T/V-I If you **devolve** power, authority, or responsibility to a less powerful person or group, or if it **devolves** upon them, it is transferred to them. ☐ *...the need to decentralize and devolve power to regional governments.* ☐ *The best companies are those that devolve responsibility as far as they can.*

de|vote /dɪvoʊt/ (devotes, devoting, devoted) **1** V-T If you **devote** yourself, your time, or your energy to something, you spend all or most of your time or energy on it. ☐ *He decided to devote the rest of his life to scientific investigation.* ☐ *Considerable resources have been devoted to proving him a liar.* **2** V-T If you **devote** a particular proportion of a piece of writing or a speech to a particular subject, you deal with the subject in that amount of space or time. ☐ *He devoted a major section of his massive report to an analysis of U.S. aircraft design.*

de|vot|ed /dɪvoʊtɪd/ **1** ADJ [ADJ n, v-link ADJ to n] Someone who is **devoted** to a person loves that person very much. ☐ *...a loving and devoted husband.* **2** ADJ [v-link ADJ to n, ADJ n] If you are **devoted** to something, you care about it a lot and are very enthusiastic about it. ☐ *I have personally been devoted to this cause for many years.* **3** ADJ [v-link ADJ to n] Something that is **devoted to** a particular thing deals only with that thing or contains only that thing. ☐ *A large part of the Internet is now devoted to blogs.*

devo|tee /dɛvətiː/ (devotees) N-COUNT [with supp, oft N of n] Someone who is a **devotee** of a subject or activity is very enthusiastic about it. ☐ *Mr. Carpenter is obviously a devotee of Britten's music.*

de|vo|tion /dɪvoʊʃən/ **1** N-UNCOUNT **Devotion** is great love, affection, or admiration for someone. ☐ *At first she was flattered by his devotion.* **2** N-UNCOUNT **Devotion** is commitment to a particular activity. ☐ *...devotion to the cause of the people and to socialism.*

de|vo|tion|al /dɪvoʊʃənəl/ ADJ [ADJ n] **Devotional** activities, writings, or objects relate to religious worship. ☐ *...devotional pictures.*

de|vo|tions /dɪvoʊʃənz/ N-PLURAL [oft poss N] Someone's **devotions** are the prayers that they say. ☐ *Normally he performs his devotions twice a day.*

de|vour /dɪvaʊər/ (devours, devouring, devoured) **1** V-T If a person or animal **devours** something, they eat it quickly and eagerly. ☐ *A medium-sized dog will devour at least one can of food plus biscuits per day.* **2** V-T If you **devour** a book or magazine, for example, you read it quickly and with great enthusiasm. ☐ *She began buying and devouring newspapers when she was only 12.*

de|vout /dɪvaʊt/ **1** ADJ A **devout** person has deep religious beliefs. ☐ *She was a devout Christian.* • N-PLURAL **The devout** are people who are devout. ☐ *...priests instructing the devout.* **2** ADJ [ADJ n] If you describe someone as a **devout** supporter or a **devout** opponent of something, you mean that they support it enthusiastically or oppose it strongly. ☐ *Devout Marxists believed fascism was the "last stand of the bourgeoisie."*

de|vout|ly /dɪvaʊtli/ **1** ADV [ADV with v] **Devoutly** is used to emphasize how sincerely or deeply you hope for something or believe in something. [FORMAL, EMPHASIS] ☐ *He devoutly hoped it was true.* **2** ADV [ADV adj, ADV with v] **Devoutly** is used to emphasize how deep someone's religious beliefs are, or to indicate that something is done in a devout way. [EMPHASIS] ☐ *...a devoutly Buddhist country.*

dew /duː/ N-UNCOUNT **Dew** is small drops of water that form on the ground and other surfaces outdoors during the night. ☐ *The dew gathered on the leaves.*

dewy /duːi/ (dewier, dewiest) **1** ADJ Something that is **dewy** is wet with dew. [LITERARY] **2** ADJ If your skin looks **dewy**, it looks soft and glows healthily.

dewy-eyed ADJ If you say that someone is **dewy-eyed**, you are criticizing them because you think that they are unrealistic and think events and situations are better than they really are. [DISAPPROVAL]

dex|ter|ity /dɛkstɛrɪti/ N-UNCOUNT **Dexterity** is skill in using your hands, or sometimes your mind. ☐ *...Reid's dexterity on the guitar.*

dex|ter|ous /dɛkstrəs/ also **dextrous** ADJ Someone who is **dexterous** is very skillful and clever with their hands. ☐ *The robots are not designed to be particularly dexterous or smart.*

dex|trose /dɛkstroʊs/ N-UNCOUNT **Dextrose** is a natural form of sugar that is found in fruits, honey, and in the blood of animals.

dia|be|tes /daɪəbiːtɪs, -tiːz/ N-UNCOUNT **Diabetes** is a medical condition in which someone has too much sugar in their blood.

dia|bet|ic /daɪəbɛtɪk/ (diabetics) **1** N-COUNT A **diabetic** is a person who has diabetes. ☐ *...an insulin-dependent diabetic.* • ADJ **Diabetic** is also an adjective. ☐ *...diabetic patients.* **2** ADJ [ADJ n] **Diabetic** means relating to diabetes. ☐ *He found her in a diabetic coma.*

dia|bol|ic /daɪəbɒlɪk/ **1** ADJ [ADJ n] **Diabolic** is used to describe things that people think are caused by or belong to the Devil. [FORMAL] ☐ *...the diabolic forces which lurk in all violence.* **2** ADJ If you describe something as **diabolic**, you are emphasizing that it is very bad, extreme, or unpleasant. [mainly AM, EMPHASIS] ☐ *Pitt's smile returned, and it was hideously diabolic.*

dia|boli|cal /daɪəbɒlɪkəl/ ADJ If you describe something as **diabolical**, you are emphasizing that it is very bad, extreme, or unpleasant. [INFORMAL, EMPHASIS] ☐ *It was a diabolical error, a schoolboy error.* • **dia|boli|cal|ly** /daɪəbɒlɪkli/ ADV ☐ *...diabolically difficult clues.*

dia|dem /daɪədɛm/ (diadems) N-COUNT A **diadem** is a small crown with precious stones in it.

di|ag|nose /daɪəgnoʊs/ (diagnoses, diagnosing, diagnosed) **1** V-T If someone or something **is diagnosed** as having a particular illness or problem, their illness or problem is identified. If an illness or problem **is diagnosed**, it is identified. ☐ *The soldiers were diagnosed as having flu.* ☐ *Susan had a mental breakdown and was diagnosed with schizophrenia.* **2** → See feature box at **illness**, **medicine**

di|ag|no|sis /daɪəgnoʊsɪs/ (diagnoses) N-VAR **Diagnosis** is the discovery and naming of what is wrong with someone who is ill or with something that is not working properly. ☐ *I need to have a second test to confirm the diagnosis.*

di|ag|nos|tic /daɪəgnɒstɪk/ ADJ [ADJ n] **Diagnostic** equipment, methods, or systems are used for discovering what is wrong with people who are ill or with things that do not work properly. ☐ *...X-rays and other diagnostic tools.*

di|ago|nal /daɪægənəl, -ægn³l/ ADJ A **diagonal** line or movement goes in a sloping direction, for example, from one corner of a square across to the opposite corner. ☐ *...a pattern of diagonal lines.* • **di|ago|nal|ly** ADV ☐ *Vaulting the stile, he headed diagonally across the paddock.*

dia|gram /daɪəgræm/ (diagrams) N-COUNT A **diagram** is a simple drawing which consists mainly of lines and is used, for example, to explain how a machine works. ☐ *...a circuit diagram.*

dia|gram|mat|ic /daɪəgrəmætɪk/ ADJ [usu ADJ n] Something that is in **diagrammatic** form is arranged or drawn as a diagram. ☐ *This is the virus in very crude simple diagrammatic form.*

dial /daɪəl/ (dials, dialing or dialling, dialed or dialled) **1** N-COUNT A **dial** is the part of a machine or instrument such as a clock or watch which shows you the time or a measurement that has been recorded. ☐ *The luminous dial on the clock showed five minutes to seven.* **2** N-COUNT A **dial** is a control on a device or piece of equipment which you can move in order to adjust the setting, for example, to select or change the frequency on a radio or the temperature of a heater. ☐ *He turned the dial on the radio.* **3** V-T/V-I If you **dial** or if you **dial** a number, you turn the dial or press the buttons on a telephone in order to phone someone. ☐ *He lifted the phone and dialed her number.* **4** → See feature box at **telephone**

dia|lect /daɪəlɛkt/ (dialects) N-COUNT [also in N] A **dialect** is a form of a language that is spoken in a particular area. ☐ *It is often appropriate to use the local dialect to communicate your message.*

dia|lec|tic /daɪəlɛktɪk/ (**dialectics**) **1** N-COUNT [with supp, oft the N of/between n] People refer to the **dialectic** or **dialectics** of a situation when they are referring to the way in which two very different forces or factors work together, and the way in which their differences are resolved. [TECHNICAL] ❑ ...the dialectics of class struggle and of socioeconomic change. **2** N-UNCOUNT In philosophy, **dialectics** is a method of reasoning and reaching conclusions by considering theories and ideas together with ones that contradict them. [TECHNICAL]

dia|lec|ti|cal /daɪəlɛktɪkəl/ ADJ [usu ADJ n] In philosophy, **dialectical** is used to describe situations, theories, and methods which depend on resolving opposing factors. ❑ The essence of dialectical thought is division.

dial|ling code (**dialling codes**) N-COUNT A **dialling code** for a particular city or region is the series of numbers that you have to dial before a particular telephone number if you are making a call to that place from a different area. [mainly BRIT]

in AM, use **area code**

dial|ling tone (**dialling tones**) N-COUNT The **dialling tone** is the same as the **dial tone**. [BRIT]

dia|log box (**dialog boxes**) N-COUNT A **dialog box** is a small area containing information or questions that appears on a computer screen when you are performing particular operations. [COMPUTING] ❑ You should now see a dialog box listing all of the print queues on your network.

dia|logue ✦✧ /daɪəlɒg/ (**dialogues**) also **dialog** **1** N-VAR **Dialogue** is communication or discussion between people or groups of people such as governments or political parties. ❑ People of all social standings should be given equal opportunities for dialogue. **2** N-VAR A **dialogue** is a conversation between two people in a book, movie, or play. ❑ Although the dialogue is sharp, the actors move too awkwardly around the stage.

COLLOCATIONS

dialogue
NOUN
1
adjective + **dialogue**: constructive; interfaith, political
verb + **dialogue**: begin, establish, open, start; encourage, promote
2
adjective + **dialogue**: amusing, sharp, snappy, witty; contrived, stilted; spoken
verb + **dialogue**: improvise

---

dial tone (**dial tones**) **1** N-COUNT The **dial tone** is the noise which you hear when you pick up a telephone receiver and which means that you can dial the number you want. ❑ It was only as she tried for the second time that she realized that there was no dial tone.

in BRIT, also use **dialling tone**

2 → See feature box at **telephone**

dial-up ADJ A **dial-up** connection used a modem and a conventional telephone line to connect to the internet. ❑ Fewer and fewer families have to rely on dial-up connections in order to get online.

di|aly|sis /daɪælɪsɪs/ N-UNCOUNT **Dialysis** or **kidney dialysis** is a method of treating kidney failure by using a machine to remove waste material from the kidneys. ❑ I was on dialysis for seven years before my first transplant.

dia|man|te /diəmɒnteɪ/ also **diamanté** N-UNCOUNT [oft N n] **Diamante** jewelry is made from small pieces of cut glass which look like diamonds. ❑ ...diamante earrings.

di|am|eter /daɪæmɪtər/ (**diameters**) N-COUNT [also in n] The **diameter** of a round object is the length of a straight line that can be drawn across it, passing through the middle of it. ❑ ...a tube less than a fifth of the diameter of a human hair.

dia|met|ri|cal|ly /daɪəmɛtrɪkli/ ADV [ADV adj] If you say that two things are **diametrically** opposed, you are emphasizing that they are completely different from each other. [EMPHASIS]

dia|mond /daɪmənd, daɪə-/ (**diamonds**) **1** N-VAR A **diamond** is a hard, bright, precious stone which is clear and colorless. Diamonds are used in jewelry and for cutting very hard substances. ❑ ...a pair of diamond earrings. **2** N-COUNT A **diamond** is a shape with four straight sides of equal length where the opposite angles are the same, but none of the angles is equal to 90°: ♦. ❑ ...forming his hands into the shape of a diamond. **3** N-UNCOUNT-COLL **Diamonds** is one of the four suits of cards in a pack of playing cards. Each card in the suit is marked with one or more red symbols in the shape of a diamond. ❑ He drew the seven of diamonds. • N-COUNT A **diamond** is a playing card of this suit. ❑ ...win the ace of clubs and play a diamond. **4** N-COUNT [usu the N] In baseball, the **diamond** is the square formed by the four bases, or the whole of the playing area. ❑ He would be the best ever to walk out onto the diamond. ❑ Just drive around the city and see all the empty baseball diamonds there are. **5** → See also color supplement

dia|mond ju|bi|lee (**diamond jubilees**) N-COUNT A **diamond jubilee** is the sixtieth anniversary of an important event.

dia|per /daɪpər, daɪə-/ (**diapers**) N-COUNT A **diaper** is a piece of soft towel or paper, which you fasten around a baby's bottom in order to contain its urine and feces. [AM] ❑ He never changed her diapers, never bathed her.

in BRIT, use **nappy**

di|apha|nous /daɪæfənəs/ ADJ [usu ADJ n] **Diaphanous** cloth is very thin and almost transparent. [LITERARY] ❑ ...a diaphanous dress of pale gold.

dia|phragm /daɪəfræm/ (**diaphragms**) **1** N-COUNT Your **diaphragm** is a muscle between your lungs and your stomach. It is used when you breathe. ❑ ...the skill of breathing from the diaphragm. **2** N-COUNT A **diaphragm** is a circular rubber contraceptive device that a woman places inside her vagina. **3** → See also color supplement

dia|rist /daɪərɪst/ (**diarists**) N-COUNT A **diarist** is a person who records things in a diary which is later published.

di|ar|rhea /daɪəriə/

in BRIT, use **diarrhoea**

1 N-UNCOUNT If someone has **diarrhea**, a lot of liquid feces comes out of their body because they are ill. ❑ But the food itself was barely digestible, and many team members suffered from diarrhea or constipation. **2** → See feature box at **illness**

dia|ry ✦✧ /daɪəri/ (**diaries**) N-COUNT A **diary** is a book which has a separate space for each day of the year. You use a diary to write down things you plan to do, or to record what happens in your life day by day. ❑ I had earlier read the entry from Harold Nicholson's diary for July 10, 1940.

di|as|po|ra /daɪæspərə/ N-SING [usu the N] People who come from a particular nation, or whose ancestors came from it, but who now live in many different parts of the world are sometimes referred to as the **diaspora**. [FORMAL] ❑ ...the history of peoples from the African diaspora.

dia|tribe /daɪətraɪb/ (**diatribes**) N-COUNT [usu with supp] A **diatribe** is an angry speech or article which is extremely critical of someone's ideas or activities. ❑ The book is a diatribe against the academic left.

dibs /dɪbz/ N-PLURAL If someone has **dibs** on something, or if they have **first dibs** on it, they have the right to have it before anyone else. [mainly AM, INFORMAL] ❑ Barnett wanted the job, but employees with more years on the job had dibs on the position. ❑ ...a deal that would give her first dibs on anything the non-profit institution produces.

dice /daɪs/ (**dices**, **dicing**, **diced**) **1** N-COUNT A **dice** is a small cube which has between one and six spots or numbers on its sides, and which is used in games to provide random numbers. In old-fashioned English, 'dice' was used only as a plural form, and the singular was **die**, but now 'dice' is used as both the singular and the plural form. ❑ I throw both dice and get double 6. **2** V-T If you **dice** food, you cut it into small cubes. ❑ Dice the onion and boil in the water for about fifteen minutes. **3** PHRASE If you are trying to achieve something and you say that it's **no dice**, you mean that you are having no success or luck with it. If someone asks you for something and you reply **no dice**, you are refusing to do what they ask. ❑ If there'd been a halfway decent house for rent on this island, I would have taken it. But it was no dice. ❑ If the Republicans were to say "no dice," the Democrats would think they have a campaign issue.

dicey /daɪsi/ (dicier, diciest) ADJ Something that is **dicey** is slightly dangerous or uncertain. [INFORMAL] ❑ *There was a dicey moment as one of our party made a risky climb up the cliff wall.*

di|choto|my /daɪkɒtəmi/ (dichotomies) N-COUNT [usu sing, oft N between pl-n] If there is a **dichotomy** between two things, there is a very great difference or opposition between them. [FORMAL] ❑ *There is a dichotomy between the academic world and the industrial world.*

dick /dɪk/ (dicks) **1** N-COUNT A man's **dick** is his penis. [INFORMAL, VULGAR] **2** N-COUNT A **dick** is a private detective. [INFORMAL] ❑ *Most private dicks charge by the hour.*

dick|er /dɪkər/ (dickers, dickering, dickered) V-RECIP If you say that people **are dickering** about something, you mean that they are arguing or disagreeing about it, often in a way that you think is foolish or unnecessary. [mainly AM, OLD-FASHIONED, DISAPPROVAL] ❑ *Management and labor are dickering over pay, benefits, and working conditions.*

dick|head /dɪkhɛd/ (dickheads) N-COUNT If someone calls a man a **dickhead**, they are saying that they think he is very stupid. [INFORMAL, VULGAR, DISAPPROVAL]

dic|tate (dictates, dictating, dictated)

The verb is pronounced /dɪkteɪt, dɪkteɪt/. The noun is pronounced /dɪkteɪt/.

1 V-T If you **dictate** something, you say or read it aloud for someone else to write down. ❑ *Sheldon writes every day of the week, dictating his novels in the morning.* **2** V-T If someone **dictates** something, or **dictates** to someone else, they tell them what they should do or can do. ❑ *What right has one country to dictate the environmental standards of another?* ❑ *What gives them the right to dictate to us what we should eat?* **3** V-T If one thing **dictates** another, the first thing causes or influences the second thing. ❑ *The movie's budget dictated a tough schedule.* ❑ *Of course, a number of factors will dictate how long an apple tree can survive.* **4** V-T You say that logic or common sense **dictates** that a particular thing is the case when you believe strongly that it is the case and that logic or common sense will cause other people to agree. ❑ *Logic dictates that our ancestors could not have held a yearly festival until they figured what a year was.* **5** N-COUNT **Dictates** are principles or rules which you consider to be extremely important. ❑ *We have followed the dictates of our consciences and have done our duty.*

dic|ta|tion /dɪkteɪʃən/ N-UNCOUNT **Dictation** is the speaking or reading aloud of words for someone else to write down. ❑ *...taking dictation from the dean of the graduate school.*

dic|ta|tor /dɪkteɪtər/ (dictators) N-COUNT A **dictator** is a ruler who has complete power in a country, especially power which was obtained by force and is used unfairly or cruelly. ❑ *...foreign dictators who contravene humanitarian conventions.*

dic|ta|tor|ial /dɪktətɔriəl/ ADJ If you describe someone's behavior as **dictatorial**, you do not like the fact that they tell people what to do in a forceful and unfair way. [DISAPPROVAL] ❑ *...his dictatorial management style.*

dic|ta|tor|ship /dɪkteɪtərʃɪp/ (dictatorships) **1** N-VAR **Dictatorship** is government by a dictator. ❑ *...a new era of democracy after a long period of military dictatorship in the country.* **2** N-COUNT A **dictatorship** is a country which is ruled by a dictator or by a very strict and harsh government. ❑ *Every country in the region was a military dictatorship.*

dic|tion /dɪkʃən/ **1** N-UNCOUNT Someone's **diction** is how clearly they speak or sing. ❑ *His diction wasn't very good.* **2** → See feature box at **speak**

dic|tion|ary /dɪkʃənɛri/ (dictionaries) N-COUNT A **dictionary** is a book in which the words and phrases of a language are listed alphabetically, together with their meanings or their translations in another language. ❑ *...a Spanish-English dictionary.*

dic|tum /dɪktəm/ (dictums or dicta) **1** N-COUNT [oft N that] A **dictum** is a saying that describes one aspect of life in an interesting or wise way. ❑ *...the dictum that it is preferable to be roughly right than precisely wrong.* **2** N-COUNT [oft N that] A **dictum** is a formal statement made by someone who has authority. ❑ *...Disraeli's dictum that the first priority of the government must be the health of the people.*

did /dɪd/ **Did** is the past tense of **do** ①.

di|dac|tic /daɪdæktɪk/ **1** ADJ Something that is **didactic** is intended to teach people something, especially a moral lesson. [FORMAL] ❑ *In totalitarian societies, art exists for didactic purposes.* **2** ADJ Someone who is **didactic** tells people things rather than letting them find things out or discussing things. [FORMAL] ❑ *He is more didactic in his approach to the learning process.*

did|dle /dɪdəl/ (diddles, diddling, diddled) **1** V-I [oft v adv] If someone **diddles**, they waste time and do not achieve anything. [AM, INFORMAL] ❑ *...if Congress were to just diddle around and not take any action at all.* **2** V-T If someone **diddles** you, they take money from you dishonestly or unfairly. [mainly BRIT, INFORMAL] ❑ *They diddled their insurance company by making a false claim.*

did|geri|doo /dɪdʒəridu/ (didgeridoos) N-COUNT A **didgeridoo** is an Australian musical instrument that consists of a long pipe which makes a low sound when you blow into it.

didn't ♦♦♦ /dɪdənt/ **Didn't** is the usual spoken form of 'did not.'

die ♦♦♦ /daɪ/ (dies, dying, died) **1** V-T/V-I [no passive] When people, animals, and plants **die**, they stop living. ❑ *A year later my dog died.* ❑ *Sadly, both he and my mother died of cancer.* ❑ *I would die a very happy person if I could stay in music my whole life.* **2** V-I If a machine or device **dies**, it stops completely, especially after a period of working more and more slowly or inefficiently. [WRITTEN] ❑ *Then suddenly, the engine coughed, spluttered, and died.* **3** V-I [only cont] You can say that you **are dying of** thirst, hunger, boredom, or curiosity to emphasize that you are very thirsty, hungry, bored, or curious. [INFORMAL, EMPHASIS] ❑ *Order me a soda, I'm dying of thirst.* **4** V-T/V-I [only cont] You can say that you **are dying for** something or **are dying** to do something to emphasize that you very much want to have it or do it. [INFORMAL, EMPHASIS] ❑ *I'm dying for a breath of fresh air.* **5** V-T/V-I You can use **die** in expressions such as '**I almost died**' or '**I'd die if anything happened**' where you are emphasizing your feelings about a situation, for example, to say that it is very shocking, upsetting, embarrassing, or amusing. [INFORMAL, mainly SPOKEN, EMPHASIS] ❑ *I nearly died when I read what she'd written about me.* ❑ *I nearly died of shame.* ❑ *I thought I'd die laughing.* **6** → see also **dying** **7** PHRASE If you say that something is **to die for**, you mean that you want it or like it very much. [INFORMAL] ❑ *It may be that your property has a stunning view, or perhaps it has a kitchen or bathroom to die for.* **8** PHRASE If you say that habits or attitudes **die hard**, you mean that they take a very long time to disappear or change, so that it may not be possible to get rid of them completely. ❑ *Old habits die hard.* **9** → See feature box at **deforest**, **storm**

▶ **die out** **1** PHRASAL VERB If something **dies out**, it becomes less and less common and eventually disappears completely. ❑ *We used to believe that capitalism would soon die out.* **2** PHRASAL VERB If something such as a fire or wind **dies out**, it gradually stops burning or blowing. [AM] ❑ *Once the fire has died out, the salvage team will move in.*

die|hard /daɪhɑrd/ (diehards) also **die-hard** N-COUNT [oft N n] A **diehard** is someone who is very strongly opposed to change and new ideas, or who is a very strong supporter of a person or idea.

die|sel /dizəl/ (diesels) **1** N-MASS **Diesel** or **diesel oil** is the heavy fuel used in a diesel engine. **2** N-COUNT A **diesel** is a vehicle which has a diesel engine. ❑ *With both models there is a wide choice of engines, including three diesels.*

die|sel en|gine (diesel engines) N-COUNT A **diesel engine** is an internal combustion engine in which oil is burned by very hot air. Diesel engines are used in buses and trucks, and in some trains and cars.

diet ♦♦◊ /daɪət/ (diets, dieting, dieted) **1** N-VAR Your **diet** is the type and variety of food that you regularly eat. ❑ *It's never too late to improve your diet.* **2** N-VAR If you are on a **diet**, you eat special kinds of food or you eat less food than usual because you are trying to lose weight. ❑ *Have you been on a diet? You've lost a lot of weight.* **3** N-COUNT If a doctor puts someone on a **diet**, he or she makes them eat a special type or variety of foods in order to improve their health. ❑ *Certain chronic conditions, such as diabetes, require special diets that should be monitored by your*

dietary

physician. **4** N-COUNT If you are fed on a **diet** of something, especially something unpleasant or of poor quality, you receive or experience a very large amount of it. ▢ *The radio had fed him a diet of pop songs.* **5** V-I If you **are dieting**, you eat special kinds of food or you eat less food than usual because you are trying to lose weight. ▢ *I've been dieting ever since the birth of my fourth child.* **6** ADJ [ADJ n] **Diet** drinks or foods have been specially produced so that they do not contain many calories. ▢ *...sugar-free diet drinks.* **7** → See feature box at **nutrition**

di|etary /daɪətɛri/ ADJ You can use **dietary** to describe anything that concerns a person's diet. ▢ *Dr. Susan Hankinson has studied the dietary habits of more than 50,000 women.*

di|et|er /daɪətər/ (**dieters**) N-COUNT A **dieter** is someone who is on a diet or who regularly goes on diets.

di|etet|ic /daɪətɛtɪk/ ADJ [ADJ n] **Dietetic** food or drink is food or drink that has been specially produced so that it does not contain many calories. [AM, FORMAL] ▢ *All dietetic meals are low in sugar.*

di|eti|cian /daɪətɪʃən/ (**dieticians**) also **dietitian** **1** N-COUNT A **dietician** is a person whose job is to give people advice about the kind of food they should eat. **2** → See feature box at **nutrition**

dif|fer /dɪfər/ (**differs, differing, differed**) **1** V-RECIP If two or more things **differ**, they are unlike each other in some way. ▢ *The story he told police differed from the one he told his mother.* **2** V-RECIP If people **differ** about something, they do not agree with each other about it. ▢ *The two leaders had differed on the issue of sanctions.* ▢ *That is where we differ.* **3** **to agree to differ** → see **agree**

dif|fer|ence ♦♦♢ /dɪfərəns, dɪfrəns/ (**differences**) **1** N-COUNT The **difference** between two things is the way in which they are unlike each other. ▢ *That is the fundamental difference between the two societies.* ▢ *...the vast difference in size.* **2** N-COUNT If people have their **differences** about something, they disagree about it. ▢ *The two communities are learning how to resolve their differences.* **3** N-SING A **difference** between two quantities is the amount by which one quantity is less than the other. ▢ *The difference is 8532.* **4** PHRASE If something **makes** a **difference** or **makes** a lot of **difference**, it affects you and helps you in what you are doing. If something **makes** no **difference**, it does not have any effect on what you are doing. ▢ *Where you live can make such a difference to the way you feel.* **5** PHRASE If there is a **difference of opinion** between two or more people or groups, they disagree about something. ▢ *Was there a difference of opinion over what to do with the Nobel Prize money?*

COLLOCATIONS

difference
NOUN
1
noun + **difference**: age, gender
adjective + **difference**: crucial, fundamental, marked, significant; slight, subtle; cultural, genetic
verb + **difference**: notice, know, tell, understand; explain, show
2
adjective + **difference**: irreconcilable; ideological
verb + **difference**: resolve
3
noun + **difference**: goal; height; price, temperature, time
verb + **difference**: measure; pay, pocket

---

dif|fer|ent ♦♦♦ /dɪfərənt, dɪfrənt/ **1** ADJ If two people or things are **different**, they are not like each other in one or more ways. ▢ *London was different from most European capitals.* ▢ *If he'd attended music school, how might things have been different?* **2** ADJ [v-link ADJ than n/cl] People sometimes say that one thing is **different than** another. This use is acceptable in American English, but is often considered incorrect in British English. ▢ *We're not really any different than they are.* • **dif|fer|ent|ly** ADV ▢ *Every individual learns differently.* **3** ADJ [ADJ n] You use **different** to indicate that you are talking about two or more separate and distinct things of the same kind. ▢ *Different countries specialized in different products.* **4** ADJ [v-link ADJ] You can describe something as **different** when it is unusual and not like others of the same kind. ▢ *The result is interesting and different, but do not attempt the recipe if time is short.*

diffuse

dif|fer|en|tial /dɪfərɛnʃəl/ (**differentials**) N-COUNT In mathematics and economics, a **differential** is a difference between two values in a scale. ▢ *...the wage differential between blue-collar and white-collar workers.*

dif|fer|en|ti|ate /dɪfərɛnʃieɪt/ (**differentiates, differentiating, differentiated**) **1** V-T/V-I If you **differentiate** between things or if you **differentiate** one thing from another, you recognize or show the difference between them. ▢ *A child may not differentiate between his imagination and the real world.* **2** V-T A quality or feature that **differentiates** one thing from another makes the two things different. ▢ *...distinctive policies that differentiate them from the other parties.* • **dif|fer|en|tia|tion** /dɪfərɛnʃieɪʃən/ N-UNCOUNT ▢ *For about six or seven weeks after conception, there is no differentiation between male and female.*

dif|fi|cult ♦♦♦ /dɪfɪkʌlt, -kəlt/ **1** ADJ Something that is **difficult** is not easy to do, understand, or deal with. ▢ *The lack of childcare provisions made it difficult for single mothers to get jobs.* ▢ *It was a very difficult decision to make.* **2** ADJ Someone who is **difficult** behaves in an unreasonable and unhelpful way. ▢ *I had a feeling you were going to be difficult about this.*

dif|fi|cul|ty ♦♦♢ /dɪfɪkʌlti, -kəlti/ (**difficulties**) **1** N-COUNT A **difficulty** is a problem. ▢ *...the difficulty of getting accurate information.* **2** N-UNCOUNT If you have **difficulty** doing something, you are not able to do it easily. ▢ *Do you have difficulty getting up?* **3** PHRASE If someone or something is **in difficulty**, they are having a lot of problems. ▢ *The city's film industry is in difficulty.*

COLLOCATIONS

difficulty
NOUN
1
noun + **difficulty**: breathing, learning
adjective + **difficulty**: economic, financial, practical, technical; serious
verb + **difficulty**: encounter, face; overcome
2
adjective + **difficulty**: considerable, extreme
verb + **difficulty**: experience, find; cause

SYNONYMS

difficulty
NOUN **1**
complication: *An added complication is the growing concern for the environment.*
obstacle: *To succeed, you must learn to overcome obstacles.*
hitch: *After some technical hitches, the show finally got under way.*
snag: *There is a snag though, it costs $9,600 a year.*
hurdle: *The weather will be the biggest hurdle, so I have to be ready.*

---

dif|fi|dent /dɪfɪdənt/ ADJ Someone who is **diffident** is rather shy and does not enjoy talking about themselves or being noticed by other people. ▢ *John was as bouncy and ebullient as Helen was diffident and reserved.* • **dif|fi|dence** /dɪfɪdəns/ N-UNCOUNT ▢ *He tapped on the door, opened it, and entered with a certain diffidence.*

dif|frac|tion /dɪfrækʃən/ N-UNCOUNT In physics, **diffraction** is a change in the direction of a sound wave or a light wave caused by the presence of an obstacle in its path. ▢ *...the diffraction of light that occurs in natural phenomena such as rainbows.*

dif|fuse /dɪfyuz/ (**diffuses, diffusing, diffused**) **1** V-T/V-I If something such as knowledge or information **is diffused**, or if it **diffuses** somewhere, it is made known over a wide area or to a lot of people. [WRITTEN] ▢ *Over time, however, the technology is diffused and adopted by other countries.* ▢ *...to diffuse new ideas obtained from elsewhere.* • **dif|fu|sion** /dɪfyuʒən/ N-UNCOUNT ▢ *...the development and diffusion of ideas.* **2** V-T To **diffuse** a feeling, especially an undesirable one, means to cause it to weaken and lose its power to affect people. ▢ *The presidents will meet to try and diffuse the tensions that threaten to reignite the conflict.* **3** V-T If something **diffuses** light, it causes the light to spread weakly in different directions. ▢ *Diffusing a light also reduces its power.* **4** V-I To **diffuse** or **be diffused** through something means to move and spread through it. ▢ *It allows nicotine to diffuse slowly and steadily into the bloodstream.* • **dif|fu|sion** N-UNCOUNT ▢ *There are data on the rates of diffusion of molecules.*

dig ✦✦✧ /dɪg/ (digs, digging, dug) **1** V-T/V-I If people or animals **dig**, they make a hole in the ground or in a pile of earth, stones, or trash. ❏ *I grabbed the spade and started digging.* ❏ *Dig a large hole and drive the stake in first.* **2** V-I If you **dig** into something such as a deep container, you put your hand in it to search for something. ❏ *He dug into his coat pocket for his keys.* **3** V-T/V-I If you **dig** one thing into another or if one thing **digs** into another, the first thing is pushed hard into the second, or presses hard into it. ❏ *She digs the serving spoon into the moussaka.* **4** V-I If you **dig into** a subject or a store of information, you study it very carefully in order to discover or check facts. ❏ *...as a special congressional enquiry digs deeper into the alleged financial misdeeds of his government.* ❏ *He has been digging into the local archives.* **5** V-T If you **dig** yourself out of a difficult or unpleasant situation, especially one which you caused yourself, you manage to get out of it. ❏ *He's taken these measures to try and dig himself out of a hole.* **6** N-COUNT If you have a **dig** at someone, you say something which is intended to make fun of them or upset them. ❏ *She couldn't resist a dig at Dave after his unfortunate performance.* **7** N-COUNT If you give someone a **dig** in a part of their body, you push them with your finger or your elbow, usually as a warning or as a joke. ❏ *Cassandra silenced him with a sharp dig in the small of the back.* **8 to dig one's heels in** → see **heel** **9** → See feature box at **garden**
▶ **dig out 1** PHRASAL VERB If you **dig** someone or something **out** of a place, you get them out by digging or by forcing them from the things surrounding them. ❏ *...digging minerals out of the Earth.* **2** PHRASAL VERB If you **dig** something **out**, you find it after it has been stored, hidden, or forgotten for a long time. [INFORMAL] ❏ *Recently, I dug out Barstow's novel and read it again.*

COLLOCATIONS

dig
NOUN **8**
adjective + **dig**: good-natured, lighthearted, playful, tongue-in-cheek; sly, subtle; thinly veiled

---

di|gest (digests, digesting, digested)

The verb is pronounced /daɪˈdʒɛst/. The noun is pronounced /ˈdaɪdʒɛst/.

1 V-T/V-I When food **digests** or when you **digest** it, it passes through your body to your stomach. Your stomach removes the substances that your body needs and gets rid of the rest. ❏ *Do not undertake strenuous exercise for a few hours after a meal to allow food to digest.* ❏ *She couldn't digest food properly.* **2** V-T If you **digest** information, you think about it carefully so that you understand it. ❏ *They learn well but seem to need time to digest information.* **3** V-T If you **digest** some unpleasant news, you think about it until you are able to accept it and know how to deal with it. ❏ *All this has upset me. I need time to digest it all.* **4** N-COUNT A **digest** is a collection of pieces of writing. They are published together in a shorter form than they were originally published. ❏ *...the Middle East Economic Digest.*

di|gest|ible /daɪˈdʒɛstɪbəl/ **1** ADJ [oft adv ADJ] **Digestible** food is food that is easy to digest. ❏ *Bananas are easily digestible.* **2** ADJ If a theory or idea is **digestible**, it is easy to understand. ❏ *The book's aim was to make economic theory more digestible.*

di|ges|tion /daɪˈdʒɛstʃən/ (digestions) **1** N-UNCOUNT **Digestion** is the process of digesting food. ❏ *No liquids are served with meals because they interfere with digestion.* **2** N-COUNT Your **digestion** is the system in your body which digests your food. ❏ *Keep your digestion working well by eating plenty of fiber.*

di|ges|tive /daɪˈdʒɛstɪv/ ADJ [ADJ n] You can describe things that are related to the digestion of food as **digestive**. ❏ *...digestive juices that normally work on breaking down our food.*

di|ges|tive sys|tem (digestive systems) **1** N-COUNT [usu poss N] Your **digestive system** is the set of organs in your body that digest the food you eat. **2** → See also color supplement

dig|ger /ˈdɪgər/ (diggers) N-COUNT A **digger** is a machine that is used for digging. ❏ *...a mechanical digger.*

digi|cam /ˈdɪdʒɪkæm/ (digicams) N-COUNT A **digicam** is the same as a **digital camera**. ❏ *Filmmaking was transformed by digital editing, digital f/x, and digicams.*

dig|it /ˈdɪdʒɪt/ (digits) N-COUNT A **digit** is a written symbol for any of the ten numbers from 0 to 9. ❏ *Her telephone number differs from mine by one digit.*

digi|tal ✦✦✧ /ˈdɪdʒɪtəl/ **1** ADJ **Digital** systems record or transmit information in the form of thousands of very small signals. ❏ *The new digital technology would allow a rapid expansion in the number of TV channels.* **2** ADJ [ADJ n] **Digital** devices such as watches or clocks give information by displaying numbers rather than by having a pointer which moves around a dial. Compare **analog**. ❏ *...a digital display.* **3** PHRASE [the/a PHR] People sometimes refer to poorer people's lack of access to the latest computer technology as the **digital divide**. [mainly JOURNALISM] ❏ *Another key factor in the digital divide is connection speed.* **4** → See also color supplement

digi|tal au|dio tape N-UNCOUNT **Digital audio tape** is a type of magnetic tape used to make very high quality recordings of sound by recording it in digital form. The abbreviation **DAT** is often used.

digi|tal cam|era (digital cameras) N-COUNT A **digital camera** is a camera that produces digital images that can be stored on a computer, displayed on a screen, and printed. ❏ *The speed with which digital cameras can take, process, and transmit an image is phenomenal.*

digi|tal im|mi|grant (digital immigrants) N-COUNT A **digital immigrant** is someone who was born before it was common to use things such as personal computers and smart phones. ❏ *At sixty, I'm definitely a digital immigrant.*

digi|tal na|tive (digital natives) N-COUNT A **digital native** is someone who has used the internet, cellphones, or smart phones since they were a child. ❏ *Digital natives like these kids understand the games instinctively.*

digi|tal ra|dio (digital radios) **1** N-UNCOUNT **Digital radio** is radio in which the signals are transmitted in digital form and decoded by the radio receiver. ❏ *...those with access to digital radio, satellite TV, or the Internet.* **2** N-COUNT A **digital radio** is a radio that can receive digital signals. ❏ *Manufacturers are working on a new generation of cheaper digital radios.*

digi|tal re|cord|ing (digital recordings) **1** N-UNCOUNT **Digital recording** is the process of converting sound or images into numbers. **2** N-COUNT A **digital recording** is a recording made by converting sound or images into numbers.

digi|tal tele|vi|sion (digital televisions) **1** N-UNCOUNT **Digital television** is television in which the signals are transmitted in digital form and decoded by the television receiver. ❏ *...the transition to digital television.* **2** N-COUNT A **digital television** is a television that can receive digital signals. ❏ *Other products are also doing well, such as digital cameras and wide screen digital televisions.*

digi|tal TV (digital TVs) **1** N-UNCOUNT **Digital TV** is the same as **digital television**. **2** N-COUNT A **digital TV** is the same as a **digital television**.

dig|it|ize /ˈdɪdʒɪtaɪz/ (digitizes, digitizing, digitized)

in BRIT, also use **digitise**

V-T To **digitize** information means to turn it into a form that can be read easily by a computer. ❏ *The picture is digitized by a scanner.*

dig|ni|fied /ˈdɪgnɪfaɪd/ ADJ If you say that someone or something is **dignified**, you mean they are calm, impressive, and deserve respect. ❏ *He seemed a very dignified and charming man.*

dig|ni|fy /ˈdɪgnɪfaɪ/ (dignifies, dignifying, dignified) **1** V-T To **dignify** something means to make it impressive. [LITERARY] ❏ *Tragic literature dignifies sorrow and disaster.* **2** V-T If you say that a particular reaction or description **dignifies** something you have a low opinion of, you mean that it makes it appear acceptable. [DISAPPROVAL] ❏ *We won't dignify this kind of speculation with a comment.*

dig|ni|tary /ˈdɪgnɪtɛri/ (dignitaries) N-COUNT **Dignitaries** are people who are considered to be important because they have a high rank in government or in a church. ❏ *...an office fund used to entertain visiting dignitaries.*

dig|nity /ˈdɪgnɪti/ **1** N-UNCOUNT If someone behaves or moves with **dignity**, they are calm, controlled, and admirable.

digress ...her extraordinary dignity and composure. **2** N-UNCOUNT If you talk about the **dignity** of people or their lives or activities, you mean that they are valuable and worthy of respect. □ ...the sense of human dignity. **3** N-UNCOUNT Your **dignity** is the sense that you have of your own importance and value, and other people's respect for you. □ She still has her dignity.

di|gress /daɪgrɛs/ (digresses, digressing, digressed) V-I If you **digress**, you move away from the subject you are talking or writing about and talk or write about something different for a while. □ I've digressed a little to explain the situation so far, so let me now recap. □ She digressed from her prepared speech to pay tribute to the president. • **di|gres|sion** /daɪgrɛʃən/ (digressions) N-VAR □ The text is dotted with digressions.

dike /daɪk/ (dikes) **1** N-COUNT A **dike** is a thick wall that is built to stop water flooding onto very low-lying land from a river or from the ocean. **2** → see **dyke 1**

dik|tat /dɪktɑt/ (diktats) N-VAR You use **diktat** to refer to something such as a law or government which people have to obey even if they do not agree with it, especially one which seems unfair. [DISAPPROVAL]

di|lapi|dat|ed /dɪlæpɪdeɪtɪd/ **1** ADJ A building that is **dilapidated** is old and in a generally bad condition. □ ...an old dilapidated barn. **2** → See feature box at **upcycle**

di|late /daɪleɪt/ (dilates, dilating, dilated) V-T/V-I When things such as blood vessels or the pupils of your eyes **dilate** or when something **dilates** them, they become wider or bigger. □ At night, the pupils dilate to allow in more light. • **di|lat|ed** ADJ □ His eyes seemed slightly dilated.

di|la|tory /dɪlətəri/ ADJ Someone or something that is **dilatory** is slow and causes delay. [FORMAL] □ You might expect politicians to smooth things out when civil servants are being dilatory.

dil|do /dɪldoʊ/ (dildos) N-COUNT A **dildo** is an object shaped like a penis, which can be used to get sexual pleasure. [INFORMAL]

di|lem|ma /dɪlɛmə/ (dilemmas) N-COUNT A **dilemma** is a difficult situation in which you have to choose between two or more alternatives. □ He was faced with the dilemma of whether or not to return to his country.

dil|et|tan|te /dɪlətɑnt/ (dilettantes or dilettanti) N-COUNT You can use **dilettante** to talk about someone who seems interested in a subject, especially in art, but who does not really know very much about it. [FORMAL, DISAPPROVAL]

dili|gent /dɪlɪdʒənt/ ADJ Someone who is **diligent** works hard in a careful and thorough way. □ Meyers is a diligent and prolific worker. • **dili|gence** /dɪlɪdʒəns/ N-UNCOUNT □ The police are pursuing their inquiries with great diligence. • **dili|gent|ly** ADV [ADV with v] □ The two sides are now working diligently to resolve their differences.

dill /dɪl/ N-UNCOUNT **Dill** is a herb with yellow flowers and a strong smell.

di|lute /daɪlut/ (dilutes, diluting, diluted) **1** V-T/V-I If a liquid is **diluted** or **dilutes**, it is added to or mixes with water or another liquid, and becomes weaker. □ If you give your baby juice, dilute it well with cooled, boiled water. □ The liquid is then diluted. **2** V-T If someone or something **dilutes** a belief, quality, or value, they make it weaker and less effective. □ There was a clear intention to dilute Black voting power. **3** ADJ A **dilute** liquid is very thin and weak, usually because it has had water added to it. □ ...a dilute solution of bleach.

di|lu|tion /daɪluʃən/ (dilutions) N-COUNT A **dilution** is a liquid that has been diluted with water or another liquid, so that it becomes weaker. □ "Aromatherapy oils" are not pure essential oils but dilutions.

dim /dɪm/ (dimmer, dimmest, dims, dimming, dimmed) **1** ADJ **Dim** light is not bright. □ She stood waiting in the dim light. • **dim|ly** ADV □ Two lamps burned dimly. **2** ADJ A **dim** place is rather dark because there is not much light in it. □ The room was dim and cool and quiet. **3** ADJ A **dim** figure or object is not very easy to see, either because it is in shadow or darkness, or because it is far away. □ Pete's flashlight picked out the dim figures of Bob and Chang. • **dim|ly** ADV □ The shoreline could be dimly seen. **4** ADJ If you have a **dim** memory or understanding of something, it is difficult to remember or is unclear in your mind. □ It seems that the '60s era of social activism is all but a dim memory. • **dim|ly** ADV □ Christina dimly recalled the procedure. **5** ADJ If the future of something is **dim**, you have no reason to feel hopeful or positive about it. □ The prospects for a peaceful solution are dim. **6** ADJ If you describe someone as **dim**, you think that they are stupid. [INFORMAL] □ Sometimes he thought George was a bit dim. **7** V-T/V-I If you **dim** a light or if it **dims**, it becomes less bright. □ Dim the lighting – it is unpleasant to lie with a bright light shining in your eyes. **8** V-T/V-I If your future, hopes, or emotions **dim** or if something **dims** them, they become less good or less strong. □ Their economic prospects have dimmed. **9** V-T/V-I If your memories **dim** or if something **dims** them, they become less clear in your mind. □ Their memory of what happened has dimmed.

dime /daɪm/ (dimes) N-COUNT A **dime** is a U.S. coin worth ten cents. □ The penny meters are slowly being replaced by electronic ones that take nickels, dimes, and quarters.

di|men|sion /dɪmɛnʃən, daɪ-/ (dimensions) **1** N-COUNT A particular **dimension** of something is a particular aspect of it. □ There is a political dimension to the accusations. **2** N-COUNT A **dimension** is a measurement such as length, width, or height. If you talk about the **dimensions** of an object or place, you are referring to its size and proportions. □ Drilling will continue on the site to assess the dimensions of the new oilfield. **3** N-PLURAL If you talk about the **dimensions** of a situation or problem, you are talking about its extent and size. □ The dimensions of the market collapse, in terms of turnover and price, were certainly not anticipated.

di|men|sion|al /dɪmɛnʃənəl, daɪ-/ → see **two-dimensional**, **three-dimensional**

di|min|ish /dɪmɪnɪʃ/ (diminishes, diminishing, diminished) **1** V-T/V-I When something **diminishes**, or when something **diminishes** it, it becomes reduced in size, importance, or intensity. □ The threat of nuclear war has diminished. □ Federalism is intended to diminish the power of the central state. **2** V-T If you **diminish** someone or something, you talk about them or treat them in a way that makes them appear less important than they really are. □ He never put her down or diminished her.

di|min|ished re|spon|sibil|ity N-UNCOUNT In law, **diminished responsibility** is a defense which states that someone is not mentally well enough to be totally responsible for their crime. [mainly BRIT]

di|min|ish|ing re|turns N-UNCOUNT In economics, **diminishing returns** is a situation in which the increase in production, profits, or benefits resulting from something is less than the money or energy that is invested.

dimi|nu|tion /dɪmɪnuʃən/ N-UNCOUNT [usu N of/in n] A **diminution** of something is its reduction in size, importance, or intensity. [FORMAL] □ ...despite a slight diminution in asset value.

di|minu|tive /dɪmɪnyətɪv/ ADJ A **diminutive** person or object is very small. □ Her eyes scanned the room until they came to rest on a diminutive figure standing at the entrance.

dim|mer /dɪmər/ (dimmers) N-COUNT A **dimmer** or a **dimmer switch** is a switch that allows you to gradually change the brightness of an electric light.

dim|ple /dɪmpəl/ (dimples) N-COUNT A **dimple** is a small hollow in someone's cheek or chin, often one that you can see when they smile. □ Bess spoke up, smiling so that her dimples showed.

dim|pled /dɪmpəld/ ADJ Something that is **dimpled** has small hollows in it. □ ...a man with a dimpled chin.

dim sum /dɪm sʌm, sɑm/ N-UNCOUNT **Dim sum** is a Chinese dish of dumplings filled with meat or other ingredients. □ ...huge portions of dim sum.

dim|wit /dɪmwɪt/ (dimwits) N-COUNT If you say that someone is a **dimwit**, you mean that they are ignorant and stupid. [INFORMAL]

dim-witted also **dimwitted** ADJ If you describe someone as **dim-witted**, you are saying in quite an unkind way that you do not think they are very clever. [INFORMAL]

din /dɪn/ N-SING A **din** is a very loud and unpleasant noise that lasts for some time. □ They tried to make themselves heard over the din of the crowd.

di|nar /dinɑr/ (dinars) N-COUNT [num N] The **dinar** is the unit of money that is used in some North African and Middle Eastern countries, and also in the republics which were part of Yugoslavia. • N-SING [the N] The **dinar** is also used to refer to the currency system of these countries.

dine /daɪn/ (dines, dining, dined) **1** V-I [no passive] When you **dine**, you have dinner. [FORMAL] ◻ *He dines alone most nights.* **2** → See feature box at **socialize**

din|er /daɪnər/ (diners) **1** N-COUNT A **diner** is a small cheap restaurant that is often open all day. [AM] **2** N-COUNT The people who are having dinner in a restaurant can be referred to as **diners**. ◻ *They sat in a corner, away from other diners.*

di|nette /daɪnɛt/ (dinettes) N-COUNT A **dinette** is a part of a room, usually in or near the kitchen, that is used in place of a dining room. [mainly AM] ◻ *The elegant study in this 4-bedroom home provides quiet privacy from the big family room and adjoining dinette and kitchen.*

ding|bat /dɪŋbæt/ (dingbats) N-COUNT People sometimes refer to a person who they think is crazy or stupid as a **dingbat**. [AM, INFORMAL, DISAPPROVAL] ◻ *I hope people realize I'm not a dingbat.*

ding-dong /dɪŋ dɒŋ/ SOUND **Ding-dong** is used in writing to represent the sound made by a bell.

din|ghy /dɪŋgi/ (dinghies) **1** N-COUNT A **dinghy** is a small open boat that you sail or row. ◻ *...a rubber dinghy.* **2** → See also color supplement

din|go /dɪŋgoʊ/ (dingoes) N-COUNT A **dingo** is an Australian wild dog.

din|gy /dɪndʒi/ (dingier, dingiest) **1** ADJ A **dingy** building or place is dark and depressing, and perhaps dirty. ◻ *Shaw took me to his dingy office.* **2** ADJ **Dingy** clothes, curtains, or furnishings look dirty or dull. ◻ *...wallpaper with stripes of dingy yellow.*

din|ing car (dining cars) N-COUNT A **dining car** is a car on a train where passengers can have a meal.

din|ing room (dining rooms) N-COUNT The **dining room** is the room in a house where people have their meals, or a room in a hotel where meals are served.

din|ing ta|ble (dining tables) also **dining-table** N-COUNT A **dining table** is a table that is used for having meals on.

dinky /dɪŋki/ ADJ If you describe something as **dinky**, you mean that it is small and unimportant. [AM, INFORMAL, DISAPPROVAL] ◻ *The hotels are full, and the guests have had to go to this dinky little motel way out on Stewart Avenue.*

din|ner ◆◇ /dɪnər/ (dinners) **1** N-VAR **Dinner** is the main meal of the day, usually served in the early part of the evening. ◻ *She invited us to her house for dinner.* ◻ *Would you like to stay and have dinner?* **2** N-VAR Any meal you eat in the middle of the day can be referred to as **dinner**. **3** N-COUNT A **dinner** is a formal social event at which a meal is served. It is held in the evening. ◻ *...a series of official lunches and dinners.*

COLLOCATIONS

dinner
NOUN
1
adjective + **dinner**: candlelight, intimate, romantic
verb + **dinner**: cook, make, prepare
3
noun + **dinner**: awards, charity, fundraising, gala, reunion
adjective + **dinner**: black-tie, fancy, formal; lavish, sumptuous
verb + **dinner**: hold, host; attend

---

din|ner dance (dinner dances) N-COUNT A **dinner dance** is a formal social event where a large number of people come to have dinner and to dance. Dinner dances are held in the evening at hotels, restaurants, and social clubs.

din|ner jack|et (dinner jackets) also **dinner-jacket** N-COUNT A **dinner jacket** is a jacket, usually black, worn at formal social events.

din|ner par|ty (dinner parties) N-COUNT A **dinner party** is a social event where a small group of people are invited to have dinner and spend the evening at someone's house.

din|ner ser|vice (dinner services) N-COUNT A **dinner service** is a set of plates and dishes from which meals are eaten and served. It may also include cups and saucers.

din|ner|time /dɪnərtaɪm/ also **dinner time** N-UNCOUNT [oft prep N] **Dinnertime** is the period of the day when most people have their dinner. ◻ *The telephone call came shortly before dinnertime.*

din|ner|ware /dɪnərwɛər/ N-UNCOUNT You can refer to the plates and dishes you use during a meal as **dinnerware**. [mainly AM]

di|no|saur /daɪnəsɔr/ (dinosaurs) **1** N-COUNT **Dinosaurs** were large reptiles which lived in prehistoric times. **2** N-COUNT If you refer to an organization as a **dinosaur**, you mean that it is large, inefficient, and out of date. [DISAPPROVAL] ◻ *...industrial dinosaurs.*

dint /dɪnt/ PREP-PHRASE If you achieve a result **by dint of** something, you achieve it by means of that thing. [WRITTEN] ◻ *He succeeds by dint of sheer hard work.*

di|oc|esan /daɪɒsɪsən/ ADJ [ADJ n] **Diocesan** means belonging or relating to a diocese. ◻ *...the diocesan synod.*

dio|cese /daɪəsɪs, -siz/ (dioceses) N-COUNT A **diocese** is the area over which a bishop has control.

dio|ra|ma /daɪərɑːmə, -rɑmə/ (dioramas) N-COUNT [oft N of n] A **diorama** is a miniature three-dimensional scene, for example, in a museum, in which models of figures are arranged against a background. ◻ *...a superb diorama of Quebec City as it appeared in 1806.*

di|ox|ide /daɪɒksaɪd/ → see **carbon dioxide**

di|ox|in /daɪɒksɪn/ (dioxins) N-VAR **Dioxins** are poisonous chemicals which occur as a by-product of the manufacture of certain weedkillers and disinfectants.

dip /dɪp/ (dips, dipping, dipped) **1** V-T If you **dip** something in a liquid, you put it into the liquid for a short time, so that only part of it is covered, and take it out again. ◻ *Dip each apple in the syrup until thickly coated.* • N-COUNT **Dip** is also a noun. ◻ *...a quick dip of his toe into the water.* **2** V-T/V-I If you **dip** your hand into a container or **dip** into the container, you put your hand into it in order to take something out of it. ◻ *She dipped a hand into the jar of candies and pulled one out.* ◻ *Nancy dipped into the bowl of popcorn that Hannah had made for them.* **3** V-I If something **dips**, it makes a downward movement, usually quickly. ◻ *Blake jumped in expertly; the boat dipped slightly under his weight.* • N-COUNT **Dip** is also a noun. ◻ *I noticed little things, a dip of the head, a twitch in the shoulder.* **4** V-I If an area of land, a road, or a path **dips**, it goes down quite suddenly to a lower level. ◻ *The road dipped and rose again as it neared the top of Parker Mountain.* • N-COUNT **Dip** is also a noun. ◻ *Where the road makes a dip, soon after a small vineyard on the right, turn right.* **5** V-I If the amount or level of something **dips**, it becomes smaller or lower, usually only for a short period of time. ◻ *Unemployment dipped to 6.9 percent last month.* • N-COUNT **Dip** is also a noun. ◻ *...the current dip in farm spending.* **6** V-I If you **dip into** a book, you take a brief look at it without reading or studying it seriously. ◻ *...a chance to dip into a wide selection of books on Tibetan Buddhism.* **7** V-I If you **dip into** a sum of money that you had intended to save, you use some of it to buy something or pay for something. ◻ *Just when she was ready to dip into her savings, Greg hastened to her rescue.* **8** N-COUNT If you have or take a **dip**, you go for a quick swim in the ocean, a lake, a river, or a swimming pool. ◻ *She flicked through a romantic paperback between occasional dips in the pool.* **9** → See feature box at **book**

Dip. **Dip.** is a written abbreviation for **diploma**.

diph|theria /dɪfθɪəriə, dɪp-/ N-UNCOUNT **Diphtheria** is a dangerous infectious disease which causes fever and difficulty in breathing and swallowing.

diph|thong /dɪfθɒŋ, dɪp-/ (diphthongs) N-COUNT A **diphthong** is a vowel in which the speaker's tongue changes position while it is being pronounced, so that the vowel sounds like a combination of two other vowels. The vowel sound in 'tail' is a diphthong.

di|plo|ma /dɪploʊmə/ (diplomas) N-COUNT A **diploma** is a document which may be awarded to a student who has completed a course of study by a university or college, or by a high school in the United States. ◻ *...a new two-year course leading to a diploma in social work.*

di|plo|ma|cy /dɪploʊməsi/ **1** N-UNCOUNT **Diplomacy** is the activity or profession of managing relations between the governments of different countries. ◻ *Today's Security Council resolution will be a significant success for American diplomacy.*

diplomat | 357 | **directionless**

2 N-UNCOUNT **Diplomacy** is the skill of being careful to say or do things which will not offend people. ❑ *He stormed off in a fury, and it took all Minnelli's powers of diplomacy to get him to return.*

dip|lo|mat ♦♢♢ /dɪpləmæt/ (**diplomats**) N-COUNT A **diplomat** is a senior official who discusses affairs with another country on behalf of his or her own country, usually working as a member of an embassy. ❑ *...a Western diplomat with long experience in Asia.*

dip|lo|mat|ic ♦♢♢ /dɪpləmætɪk/ **1** ADJ **Diplomatic** means relating to diplomacy and diplomats. ❑ *...before the two countries resume full diplomatic relations.* • **dip|lo|mati|cal|ly** /dɪpləmætɪkli/ ADV ❑ *...a growing sense of doubt that the conflict can be resolved diplomatically.* **2** ADJ Someone who is **diplomatic** is careful to say or do things without offending people. ❑ *She is very direct. I tend to be more diplomatic, I suppose.* • **dip|lo|mati|cal|ly** ADV [ADV with v] ❑ *"I really like their sound, although I'm not crazy about their lyrics," he says, diplomatically.*

dip|lo|mat|ic bag (**diplomatic bags**) N-COUNT A **diplomatic bag** is the same as a **diplomatic pouch**. [BRIT]

dip|lo|mat|ic corps (**diplomatic corps**)

Diplomatic corps is both the singular and the plural form.

N-COUNT-COLL The **diplomatic corps** is the group of all the diplomats who work in one city or country.

dip|lo|mat|ic im|mun|ity N-UNCOUNT **Diplomatic immunity** is the freedom from legal action and from paying taxes that a diplomat has in the country in which he or she is working. ❑ *The embassy official claimed diplomatic immunity and was later released.*

dip|lo|mat|ic pouch (**diplomatic pouches**) N-COUNT A **diplomatic pouch** is a bag or container in which mail is sent to and from foreign embassies. Diplomatic pouches are protected by law, so that they are not opened by anyone except the official or embassy they are addressed to. [mainly AM]

in BRIT, usually use **diplomatic bag**

dip|lo|mat|ic ser|vice also **Diplomatic Service** N-PROPER [the N] The **diplomatic service** is the government department that employs diplomats to work in foreign countries. [mainly BRIT]

in AM, usually use **foreign service**

dip|py /dɪpi/ ADJ If you describe someone as **dippy**, you mean that they are slightly odd or unusual, but in a way that you find charming and attractive. [INFORMAL]

dip|stick /dɪpstɪk/ (**dipsticks**) **1** N-COUNT A **dipstick** is a metal rod with marks along one end. It is used to measure the amount of liquid in a container, especially the amount of oil in a car engine. **2** N-COUNT If you call someone a **dipstick**, you are showing that you think they are very stupid or have done something very stupid. [DISAPPROVAL] ❑ *Don't be a total dipstick, Dad.*

dire /daɪər/ **1** ADJ **Dire** is used to emphasize how serious or terrible a situation or event is. [EMPHASIS] ❑ *The government looked as if it would split apart, with dire consequences for domestic peace.* **2** ADJ If you describe something as **dire**, you are emphasizing that it is of very low quality. [INFORMAL, EMPHASIS] ❑ *...a book of children's verse, which ranged from the barely tolerable to the utterly dire.*

di|rect ♦♦♦ /dɪrɛkt, daɪ-/ (**directs, directing, directed**) **1** ADJ **Direct** means moving toward a place or object, without changing direction and without stopping, for example, in a trip. ❑ *They'd come on a direct flight from Athens.* • ADV [ADV after v] **Direct** is also an adverb. ❑ *You can fly direct from Seattle to Europe.* • **di|rect|ly** ADV [ADV after v] ❑ *On arriving in New York, Dylan went directly to Greenwich Village.* **2** ADJ [n] If something is in **direct** heat or light, it is strongly affected by the heat or light, because there is nothing between it and the source of heat or light to protect it. ❑ *All medicines should be stored away from moisture, direct sunlight, and heat.* **3** ADJ You use **direct** to describe an experience, activity, or system which only involves the people, actions, or things that are necessary to make it happen. ❑ *He has direct experience of the process of privatization.* • ADV [ADV after v] **Direct** is also an adverb. ❑ *More farms are selling direct to consumers.* • **di|rect|ly** ADV [ADV with v] ❑ *We cannot measure pain directly. It can only be estimated.* **4** ADJ You use **direct** to emphasize the closeness of a connection between two things. [EMPHASIS] ❑ *They were unable to prove that the unfortunate lady had died as a direct result of his injection.* **5** ADJ If you describe a person or their behavior as **direct**, you mean that they are honest and open, and say exactly what they mean. ❑ *He avoided giving a direct answer.* • **di|rect|ly** ADV [ADV after v] ❑ *At your first meeting, explain simply and directly what you hope to achieve.* • **di|rect|ness** N-UNCOUNT ❑ *Using "I" ensures clarity and directness, and it adds warmth to a piece of writing.* **6** → see also **direction, directly** **7** V-T If you **direct** something at a particular thing, you aim or point it at that thing. ❑ *I reached the cockpit and directed the extinguisher at the fire without effect.* **8** V-T If your attention, emotions, or actions **are directed** at a particular person or thing, you are focusing them on that person or thing. ❑ *The learner's attention needs to be directed to the significant features.* **9** V-T If a remark or look **is directed** at you, someone says something to you or looks at you. ❑ *She could hardly believe the question was directed toward her.* ❑ *The abuse was directed at the TV crews.* **10** V-T If you **direct** someone somewhere, you tell them how to get there. ❑ *Could you direct them to Dr. Lamont's office, please?* **11** V-T When someone **directs** a project or a group of people, they are responsible for organizing the people and activities that are involved. ❑ *Christopher will direct day-to-day operations.* • **di|rec|tion** /dɪrɛkʃən, daɪ-/ N-UNCOUNT ❑ *Organizations need clear direction, set priorities and performance standards, and clear controls.* **12** V-T/V-I When someone **directs** a movie, play, or television program, they are responsible for the way in which it is performed and for telling the actors and assistants what to do. ❑ *He directed various TV shows.*

di|rect ac|tion N-UNCOUNT **Direct action** involves doing something such as going on strike or demonstrating in order to put pressure on an employer or government to do what you want, instead of trying to talk to them.

di|rect cur|rent (**direct currents**) N-VAR A **direct current** is an electric current that always flows in the same direction. The abbreviation **DC** is also used. ❑ *Some kinds of batteries can be recharged by connecting them to a source of direct current.*

di|rect dis|course N-UNCOUNT In grammar, **direct discourse** is speech which is reported by using the exact words that the speaker used. [mainly AM]

in BRIT, usually use **direct speech**

di|rect hit (**direct hits**) N-COUNT If a place suffers a **direct hit**, a bomb, bullet, or other missile that has been aimed at it lands exactly in that place, rather than some distance away. ❑ *The dug-outs were secure from everything but a direct hit.*

di|rec|tion ♦♦♢ /dɪrɛkʃən, daɪ-/ (**directions**) **1** N-VAR A **direction** is the general line that someone or something is moving or pointing in. ❑ *St. Andrews was ten miles in the opposite direction.* ❑ *He got into Margie's car and swung out onto the road in the direction of Larry's shop.* **2** N-VAR A **direction** is the general way in which something develops or progresses. ❑ *They threatened to lead a mass walk-out if the party did not sharply change direction.* **3** N-PLURAL **Directions** are instructions that tell you what to do, how to do something, or how to get somewhere. ❑ *I should know by now not to throw away the directions until we've finished cooking.* **4** → see also **direct**

──── SYNONYMS ────
direction
NOUN **1**
way: *Does anybody know the way to the bathroom?*
course: *Aircraft can avoid each other by altering course to left or right.*
route: *...the most direct route to downtown.*

di|rec|tion|al /dɪrɛkʃənəl, daɪ-/ **1** ADJ If something such as a radio antenna, microphone, or loudspeaker is **directional**, it works most effectively in one direction, rather than equally in all directions at once. [TECHNICAL] ❑ *Unless he was equipped with a directional microphone, he was out of earshot.* **2** ADJ [usu ADJ n] **Directional** means relating to the direction in which something is pointing or going. [TECHNICAL] ❑ *Jets of compressed air gave the aircraft lateral and directional stability.*

di|rec|tion|less /dɪrɛkʃənlɪs, daɪ-/ ADJ If you describe an activity or an organization as **directionless**, you mean that it does not seem to have any point or purpose. If you describe a person as **directionless**, you mean that they do not seem to have any plans or ideas. ❑ ...*his seemingly disorganized and directionless campaign.*

di|rec|tive /dɪrɛktɪv, daɪ-/ (**directives**) N-COUNT A **directive** is an official instruction that is given by someone in authority. ❑ *Thanks to a new directive, food labeling will be more specific.*

di|rect|ly /dɪrɛktli, daɪ-/ **1** ADV [ADV prep/adv] If something is **directly** above, below, or in front of something, it is in exactly that position. ❑ *The second rainbow will be bigger than the first, and directly above it.* **2** ADV [ADV prep/adv] If you do one action **directly** after another, you do the second action as soon as the first one is finished. ❑ *Most guests left directly after the wake.* **3** → see also **direct**

di|rect mail N-UNCOUNT **Direct mail** is a method of marketing which involves companies sending advertising material directly to people who they think may be interested in their products. [BUSINESS] ❑ ...*efforts to solicit new customers by direct mail and television advertising.*

di|rect mar|ket|ing N-UNCOUNT **Direct marketing** is the same as **direct mail**. [BUSINESS] ❑ *The direct marketing industry has become adept at packaging special offers.*

di|rect ob|ject (**direct objects**) N-COUNT In grammar, the **direct object** of a transitive verb is the noun group which refers to someone or something directly affected by or involved in the action performed by the subject. For example, in 'I saw them yesterday,' 'them' is the direct object. Compare **indirect object**.

di|rec|tor ✦✦✦ /dɪrɛktər, daɪ-/ (**directors**) **1** N-COUNT The **director** of a play, movie, or television program is the person who decides how it will appear on stage or screen, and who tells the actors and technical staff what to do. ❑ *"Cut!" the director yelled. "That was perfect."* **2** N-COUNT In some organizations and public authorities, the person in charge is referred to as the **director**. ❑ ...*the director of the intensive care unit at Buffalo General Hospital.* **3** N-COUNT The **directors** of a company are its most senior managers, who meet regularly to make important decisions about how it will be run. [BUSINESS] ❑ *He served on the board of directors of a local bank.* **4** N-COUNT The **director** of a choir is the person who is conducting it. [AM]

in BRIT, use **conductor**

5 → See feature box at **theater**

SYNONYMS

director
NOUN **2**
head: *Heads of government from more than 100 countries gather in Geneva tomorrow.*
manager: ...*She is a marketing manager for Wall's sausages.*
chief: ...*a commission appointed by the police chief.*
boss: *Occasionally, I have to go and ask the boss for a rise.*

di|rec|to|rate /dɪrɛktərɪt, daɪ-/ (**directorates**) **1** N-COUNT A **directorate** is a board of directors in a company or organization. [BUSINESS] ❑ *The bank will be managed by a directorate of around five professional bankers.* **2** N-COUNT A **directorate** is a part of a government department which is responsible for one particular thing. ❑ ...*the CIA's intelligence directorate.*

di|rec|tor gen|er|al (**directors general**) N-COUNT The **director general** of a large organization is the person who is in charge of it. [BUSINESS]

di|rec|to|rial /dɪrɛktɔriəl, daɪrɛk-/ ADJ [ADJ n] **Directorial** means relating to the job of being a movie or theater director. ❑ ...*Sam Mendes' directorial debut.*

di|rec|tor's cut (**director's cuts**) N-COUNT [oft N of n] A **director's cut** is a version of a movie chosen by the movie's director, which expresses the director's artistic aims more fully than the original version. ❑ *Will you be going to see the director's cut of Amadeus?*

di|rec|tor|ship /dɪrɛktərʃɪp, daɪ-/ (**directorships**) N-COUNT A **directorship** is the job or position of a company director. [BUSINESS] ❑ *Barry resigned his directorship in December 1973.*

di|rec|tory /dɪrɛktəri, daɪ-/ (**directories**) **1** N-COUNT A **directory** is a book which gives lists of facts, for example, people's names, addresses, and telephone numbers, or the names and addresses of business companies, usually arranged in alphabetical order. ❑ ...*a telephone directory.* **2** N-COUNT A **directory** is an area of a computer disk which contains one or more files or other directories. [COMPUTING] ❑ *This option lets you search your current directory for files by date, contents, and document summary.* **3** N-COUNT On the World Wide Web, a **directory** is a list of the subjects that you can find information on. [COMPUTING] ❑ *Yahoo is the oldest and best-known Web directory service.*

di|rec|tory as|sis|tance N-UNCOUNT **Directory assistance** is a service which you can telephone to find out someone's telephone number. [AM] ❑ *He dialed directory assistance.*

in BRIT, use **directory enquiries**

di|rect rule N-UNCOUNT **Direct rule** is a system in which a central government rules an area which has had its own parliament or law-making organization in the past.

di|rect speech N-UNCOUNT In grammar, **direct speech** is speech which is reported by using the exact words that the speaker used. [mainly BRIT]

in AM, also use **direct discourse**

di|rect tax (**direct taxes**) N-COUNT A **direct tax** is a tax which a person or organization pays directly to the government, for example, income tax. Compare **indirect tax**. [BUSINESS] ❑ *What people had to pay in direct and indirect taxes had not gone up since 1979.*

di|rect taxa|tion N-UNCOUNT **Direct taxation** is a system in which a government raises money by means of direct taxes.

dirge /dɜrdʒ/ (**dirges**) N-COUNT [usu sing] A **dirge** is a slow, sad song or piece of music. Dirges are sometimes performed at funerals.

dirt /dɜrt/ **1** N-UNCOUNT If there is **dirt** on something, there is dust, mud, or a stain on it. ❑ *I started to scrub off the dirt.* **2** N-UNCOUNT You can refer to the earth on the ground as **dirt**, especially when it is dusty. ❑ *They all sit on the dirt in the dappled shade of a tree.* **3** ADJ [ADJ n] A **dirt** road or track is made from hard earth. A **dirt** floor is made from earth without any cement, stone, or wood laid on it. ❑ *I drove along the dirt road.* **4** N-SING If you say that you have the **dirt** on someone, you mean that you have information that could harm their reputation or career. [INFORMAL] ❑ ...*a sleazy reporter assigned to dig up dirt on Jack.* **5** PHRASE If you say that someone **treats** you **like dirt**, you are angry with them because you think that they treat you unfairly and with no respect. [DISAPPROVAL] ❑ *People think they can treat me like dirt!*

dirt bike (**dirt bikes**) N-COUNT A **dirt bike** is a type of motorbike that is designed to be used on rough ground.

dirt cheap ADJ If you say that something is **dirt cheap**, you are emphasizing that it is very cheap indeed. [INFORMAL, EMPHASIS] ❑ *They're always selling off stuff like that dirt cheap.*

dirt-poor also **dirt poor** ADJ A **dirt-poor** person or place is extremely poor.

dirty ✦◇◇ /dɜrti/ (**dirtier, dirtiest, dirties, dirtying, dirtied**) **1** ADJ If something is **dirty**, it is marked or covered with stains, spots, or mud, and needs to be cleaned. ❑ *She still did not like the woman who had dirty fingernails.* **2** ADJ If you describe an action as **dirty**, you disapprove of it and consider it unfair, immoral, or dishonest. [DISAPPROVAL] ❑ *The gunman had been hired by a rival Mafia family to do the dirty deed.* • ADV [ADV after v] **Dirty** is also an adverb. ❑ *Jim Browne is the kind of fellow who can fight dirty, but make you like it.* **3** ADJ If you describe something such as a joke, a book, or someone's language as **dirty**, you mean that it refers to sex in a way that some people find offensive. ❑ *He laughed at their dirty jokes and sang their raucous ballads.* • ADV [ADV after v] **Dirty** is also an adverb. ❑ *I'm often asked whether they talk dirty to me. The answer is no.* **4** V-T To **dirty** something means to cause it to become dirty. ❑ *He was afraid the dog's hairs might dirty the seats.* **5** PHRASE If someone gives you a **dirty look**, they look at you in a way which shows that they are angry with you. [INFORMAL] ❑ *Jack was being a real pain. Michael gave him a dirty look and walked out.* **6** PHRASE To do someone's **dirty work** means to do a task for them that is dishonest or unpleasant and which they do not want to do themselves. ❑ *As a member of an elite army hit squad, the army*

dirty bomb

would send us out to do their dirty work for them. ◼ PHRASE If you say that an expression is **a dirty word** in a particular group of people, you mean it refers to an idea that they strongly dislike or disagree with. ❑ *Marketing became a dirty word at the company.* ◼ PHRASE If you say that someone **airs** their **dirty laundry in public**, you disapprove of their discussing or arguing about unpleasant or private things in front of other people. There are several other forms of this expression, for example **wash** your **dirty linen in public**, or **wash** your **dirty laundry in public**. [DISAPPROVAL] ❑ *The captain refuses to air the team's dirty laundry in public.*

dirty bomb (dirty bombs) N-COUNT A **dirty bomb** is a nuclear bomb that uses explosives to release radioactive material over a wide area.

dirty trick (dirty tricks) N-COUNT [usu pl] You describe the actions of an organization or political group as **dirty tricks** when you think they are using illegal methods to harm the reputation or effectiveness of their rivals. ❑ *He claimed he was the victim of a dirty tricks campaign.*

dis /dɪs/ (disses, dissing, dissed) also **diss**

in BRIT, sometimes in AM, use **diss**

V-T If someone **disses** you, they criticize you unfairly or speak to you in a way that does not show respect. [INFORMAL] ❑ *He believes that his records speak for themselves and completely ignores those who dis him.*

PREFIX

dis-
can be added to some words to form words that have the opposite meaning. *For example, if someone is dishonest, they are not honest.*

dis|abil|ity /dɪsəbɪlɪti/ (disabilities) ◼ N-COUNT A **disability** is a permanent injury, illness, or physical or mental condition that tends to restrict the way that someone can live their life. ❑ *Facilities for people with disabilities are still insufficient.* ◼ N-UNCOUNT **Disability** is the state of being disabled. ❑ *Disability can make extra demands on financial resources because disabled people need extra care.*

dis|able /dɪseɪbəl/ (disables, disabling, disabled) ◼ V-T If an injury or illness **disables** someone, it affects them so badly that it restricts the way that they can live their life. ❑ *She did all this tendon damage and it really disabled her.* ◼ V-T If someone or something **disables** a system or mechanism, they stop it from working, usually temporarily. ❑ *...if you need to disable a car alarm.*

dis|abled /dɪseɪbəld/ ADJ Someone who is **disabled** has an illness, injury, or condition that tends to restrict the way that they can live their life, especially by making it difficult for them to move about. ❑ *...an insight into the practical problems encountered by disabled people in the workplace.* • N-PLURAL People who are disabled are sometimes referred to as **the disabled**. This use could cause offense. ❑ *There are toilet facilities for the disabled.*

dis|able|ment /dɪseɪbəlmənt/ N-UNCOUNT **Disablement** is the state of being disabled or the experience of becoming disabled. [FORMAL] ❑ *...permanent total disablement resulting in inability to work.*

dis|abuse /dɪsəbjuz/ (disabuses, disabusing, disabused) V-T If you **disabuse** someone of something, you tell them or persuade them that what they believe is in fact untrue. [FORMAL] ❑ *Their view of country people was that they like to please strangers. I did not disabuse them of this notion.*

dis|ad|vant|age /dɪsədvæntɪdʒ/ (disadvantages) ◼ N-COUNT A **disadvantage** is a factor which makes someone or something less useful, acceptable, or successful than other people or things. ❑ *His two main rivals suffer the disadvantage of having been long-term political exiles.* ◼ PHRASE If you are **at a disadvantage**, you have a problem or difficulty that many other people do not have, which makes it harder for you to be successful. ❑ *The children from poor families were at a distinct disadvantage.* ◼ PHRASE If something is **to** your **disadvantage** or works **to** your **disadvantage**, it creates difficulties for you. ❑ *We need a rethink of the present law which works so greatly to the disadvantage of women.*

dis|ad|van|taged /dɪsədvæntɪdʒd/ ADJ People who are **disadvantaged** or live in **disadvantaged** areas live in bad

359

disappoint

conditions and tend not to get a good education or have a reasonable standard of living. ❑ *...the educational problems of disadvantaged children.*

dis|ad|van|ta|geous /dɪsædvəntɛɪdʒəs/ ADJ [oft ADJ to/for n] Something that is **disadvantageous** to you puts you in a worse position than other people. ❑ *The sale of part of the company could be disadvantageous to investors.*

dis|af|fect|ed /dɪsəfɛktɪd/ ADJ **Disaffected** people no longer fully support something such as an organization or political ideal which they previously supported. ❑ *He attracts disaffected voters.*

dis|af|fec|tion /dɪsəfɛkʃən/ N-UNCOUNT [oft N with n] **Disaffection** is the attitude that people have when they stop supporting something such as an organization or political ideal. ❑ *...people's disaffection with their country and its leaders.*

dis|agree /dɪsəgri/ (disagrees, disagreeing, disagreed) ◼ V-RECIP If you **disagree** with someone or **disagree** with what they say, you do not accept that what they say is true or correct. You can also say that two people **disagree**. ❑ *You must continue to see them no matter how much you may disagree with them.* ❑ *They can communicate even when they strongly disagree.* ◼ V-I If you **disagree** with a particular action or proposal, you disapprove of it and believe that it is wrong. ❑ *I respect the president but I disagree with his decision.*

dis|agree|able /dɪsəgriəbəl/ ◼ ADJ Something that is **disagreeable** is unpleasant. ❑ *...a disagreeable odor.* • **dis|agree|ably** /dɪsəgriəbli/ ADV ❑ *The taste is bitter and disagreeably pungent.* ◼ ADJ [usu ADJ n] Someone who is **disagreeable** is unfriendly or unhelpful. ❑ *He's a shallow, disagreeable man.*

dis|agree|ment /dɪsəgrimənt/ (disagreements) ◼ N-UNCOUNT **Disagreement** means objecting to something such as a proposal. ❑ *Britain and France have expressed some disagreement with the proposal.* ◼ N-VAR When there is **disagreement** about something, people disagree or argue about what should be done. ❑ *The United States Congress and the president are still locked in disagreement over proposals to reduce the massive budget deficit.*

dis|al|low /dɪsəlaʊ/ (disallows, disallowing, disallowed) V-T If something **is disallowed**, it is not allowed or accepted officially, because it has not been done correctly. ❑ *The goal was disallowed.*

dis|ap|pear /dɪsəpɪər/ (disappears, disappearing, disappeared) ◼ V-I If you say that someone or something **disappears**, you mean that you can no longer see them, usually because you or they have changed position. ❑ *The black car drove away from them and disappeared.* ◼ V-I If someone or something **disappears**, they go away or are taken away somewhere where nobody can find them. ❑ *...a Japanese woman who disappeared thirteen years ago.* ◼ V-I If something **disappears**, it stops existing or happening. ❑ *The immediate threat of the past has disappeared and the security situation in Europe has significantly improved.*

USAGE

disappear
Don't use **disappeared** as an adjective. If you can't find something because it is not in its usual place, don't say that it 'is disappeared.' You say that it **has disappeared**. *He discovered that a pint of milk had disappeared from the refrigerator.*

dis|ap|pear|ance /dɪsəpɪərəns/ (disappearances) ◼ N-VAR If you refer to someone's **disappearance**, you are referring to the fact that nobody knows where they have gone. ❑ *Her disappearance has baffled police.* ◼ N-COUNT If you refer to the **disappearance** of an object, you are referring to the fact that it has been lost or stolen. ❑ *Police are investigating the disappearance of key files on the killers.* ◼ N-UNCOUNT The **disappearance** of a type of thing, person, or animal is a process in which it becomes less common and finally no longer exists. ❑ *...the virtual disappearance of common dolphins from the western Mediterranean in recent years.*

dis|ap|point /dɪsəpɔɪnt/ (disappoints, disappointing, disappointed) V-T If things or people **disappoint** you, they are

disappointed

not as good as you had hoped, or do not do what you hoped they would do. ❏ *I am afraid I am going to disappoint my parents if I don't go away to college.*

dis|ap|point|ed ♦◇◇ /dɪsəpɔ́ɪntɪd/ **1** ADJ If you are **disappointed**, you are sad because something has not happened or because something is not as good as you had hoped. ❏ *Adamski says he was very disappointed with the mayor's decision.* ❏ *I was disappointed that John was not there.* **2** ADJ [v-link ADJ in n] If you are **disappointed in** someone, you are sad because they have not behaved as well as you expected them to. ❏ *You should have accepted that. I'm disappointed in you.*

SYNONYMS
disappointed
ADJ **1**
disheartened: *He was disheartened by their hostile reaction.*
dissatisfied: *Dissatisfied customers can return the product for a full refund.*
downhearted: *Max sighed, sounding even more downhearted.*

dis|ap|point|ing /dɪsəpɔ́ɪntɪŋ/ ADJ Something that is **disappointing** is not as good or as large as you hoped it would be. ❏ *The wine was excellent, but the meat was overdone and the vegetables disappointing.* • **dis|ap|point|ing|ly** ADV ❏ *Progress is disappointingly slow.*

dis|ap|point|ment /dɪsəpɔ́ɪntmənt/ (**disappointments**) **1** N-UNCOUNT **Disappointment** is the state of feeling disappointed. ❏ *Despite winning the title, their last campaign ended in great disappointment.* **2** N-COUNT Something or someone that is a **disappointment** is not as good as you had hoped. ❏ *For many, their long-awaited homecoming was a bitter disappointment.*

dis|ap|prov|al /dɪsəpruːvᵊl/ N-UNCOUNT If you feel or show **disapproval** of something or someone, you feel or show that you do not approve of them. ❏ *His action had been greeted with almost universal disapproval.*

dis|ap|prove /dɪsəpruːv/ (**disapproves, disapproving, disapproved**) V-I If you **disapprove** of something or someone, you feel or show that you do not like them or do not approve of them. ❏ *Most people disapprove of such violent tactics.*

dis|ap|prov|ing /dɪsəpruːvɪŋ/ ADJ A **disapproving** action or expression shows that you do not approve of something or someone. ❏ *Janet gave him a disapproving look.* • **dis|ap|prov|ing|ly** ADV [ADV after v] ❏ *Antonio looked at him disapprovingly.*

dis|arm /dɪsɑ́rm/ (**disarms, disarming, disarmed**) **1** V-T To **disarm** a person or group means to take away all their weapons. ❏ *We will agree to disarming troops and leaving their weapons at military positions.* **2** V-I If a country or group **disarms**, it gives up the use of weapons, especially nuclear weapons. ❏ *There was still a chance that international pressure would force the country to disarm.* **3** V-T If a person or their behavior **disarms** you, they cause you to feel less angry, hostile, or critical toward them. ❏ *His unease disarmed her.*

dis|arma|ment /dɪsɑ́rməmənt/ N-UNCOUNT **Disarmament** is the act of reducing the number of weapons, especially nuclear weapons, that a country has. ❏ *The goal would be to increase political stability in the region and accelerate the pace of nuclear disarmament.*

dis|arm|ing /dɪsɑ́rmɪŋ/ ADJ If someone or something is **disarming**, they make you feel less angry or hostile. ❏ *Leonard approached with a disarming smile.* • **dis|arm|ing|ly** ADV ❏ *He is, as ever, business-like, and disarmingly honest.*

dis|ar|ray /dɪsəreɪ/ **1** N-UNCOUNT If people or things are in **disarray**, they are disorganized and confused. ❏ *The nation is in disarray following rioting led by the military.* **2** N-UNCOUNT If things or places are in **disarray**, they are in a very disorganized state. ❏ *She was left lying on her side and her clothes were in disarray.*

dis|as|sem|ble /dɪsəsɛmbᵊl/ (**disassembles, disassembling, disassembled**) V-T To **disassemble** something means to take it apart. [FORMAL] ❏ *You'll have to disassemble the drill.*

dis|as|so|ci|ate /dɪsəsoʊʃieɪt, -sieɪt/ (**disassociates, disassociating, disassociated**) **1** V-T If you **disassociate** yourself from something or someone, you say or show that you are not connected with them, usually in order to avoid trouble or blame. ❏ *I wish to disassociate myself from this very sad decision.* **2** V-T If you **disassociate** one group or thing from another, you separate them. ❏ *...an attempt by the president to disassociate the military from politics.*

dis|as|ter ♦◇◇ /dɪzǽstər/ (**disasters**) **1** N-COUNT A **disaster** is a very bad accident such as an earthquake or a plane crash, especially one in which a lot of people are killed. ❏ *It was the second air disaster in the region in less than two months.* **2** N-COUNT If you refer to something as a **disaster**, you are emphasizing that you think it is extremely bad or unacceptable. [EMPHASIS] ❏ *The whole production was just a disaster!* **3** N-UNCOUNT **Disaster** is something which has very bad consequences for you. ❏ *The government brought itself to the brink of fiscal disaster.* **4** PHRASE If you say that something is **a recipe for disaster**, you mean that it is very likely to have unpleasant consequences. ❏ *You give them a gun, and it's a recipe for disaster.*

VOCABULARY IN CONTEXT

Disasters

Natural disasters can kill **vast** numbers of people, but do you know which types of natural disasters are deadliest? If you cast your mind back, you can probably name a few natural disasters which had **tragic consequences**. The **earthquake** in Haiti in 2010, or that which hit Nepal in 2015, for example. Both affected **developing regions** where many buildings were **flimsily** constructed and where the local residents had no **resources** at hand **to cope with** the destruction. Or maybe you are thinking of the **tsunami** which **razed** Fukushima, Japan in 2011? Not only were tens of thousands killed, but the **environmental impact** was made worse by the damage the tsunami caused to the nuclear power station in Fukushima. But the worst natural disaster on record in terms of **loss of** human life wasn't an earthquake or a tsunami; it was a **flood**. In 1931, the Yangtze River **burst its banks** in central China, causing the deaths of around 3.7 million people.

dis|as|ter area (**disaster areas**) **1** N-COUNT A **disaster area** is a part of a country or the world which has been very seriously affected by a disaster such as an earthquake or a flood. ❏ *The region has been declared a disaster area.* **2** N-COUNT [usu sing] If you describe a place, person, or situation as a **disaster area**, you mean that they are in a state of great disorder or failure. [INFORMAL] ❏ *He's a nice man but a disaster area as a politician.*

dis|as|trous /dɪzǽstrəs/ **1** ADJ A **disastrous** event has extremely bad consequences and effects. ❏ *...the recent, disastrous earthquake.* • **dis|as|trous|ly** ADV ❏ *The vegetable harvest is disastrously behind schedule.* **2** ADJ If you describe something as **disastrous**, you mean that it was very unsuccessful. ❏ *...after their disastrous performance in the election.* • **dis|as|trous|ly** ADV ❏ *...debts resulting from the company's disastrously timed venture into property development.*

dis|avow /dɪsəvaʊ/ (**disavows, disavowing, disavowed**) V-T If you **disavow** something, you say that you are not

disavowal 361 **disclose**

connected with it or responsible for it. [FORMAL] ❑ *Dr. Samuels immediately disavowed the newspaper story.*

dis|avow|al /dɪsəvaʊəl/ (disavowals) N-COUNT [oft N of n] A **disavowal** of something is a statement that you are not connected with it or responsible for it, or that you no longer agree with or believe in it. [FORMAL] ❑ *...a public disavowal of his beliefs.*

dis|band /dɪsbænd/ (disbands, disbanding, disbanded) V-T/V-I If someone **disbands** a group of people, or if the group **disbands**, it stops operating as a single unit. ❑ *All the armed groups will be disbanded.*

dis|be|lief /dɪsbɪliːf/ N-UNCOUNT **Disbelief** is not believing that something is true or real. ❑ *She looked at him in disbelief.*

dis|be|lieve /dɪsbɪliːv/ (disbelieves, disbelieving, disbelieved) V-T If you **disbelieve** someone or **disbelieve** something that they say, you do not believe that what they say is true. ❑ *There is no reason to disbelieve him.*

dis|burse /dɪsbɜːrs/ (disburses, disbursing, disbursed) V-T To **disburse** an amount of money means to pay it out, usually from a fund which has been collected for a particular purpose. [FORMAL] ❑ *The aid will not be disbursed until next year.* ❑ *The bank has disbursed over $350m for the project.*

dis|burse|ment /dɪsbɜːrsmənt/ (disbursements) **1** N-UNCOUNT **Disbursement** is the paying out of a sum of money, especially from a fund. [FORMAL] **2** N-COUNT A **disbursement** is a sum of money that is paid out. [FORMAL]

disc /dɪsk/ → see disk

dis|card /dɪskɑːrd/ (discards, discarding, discarded) V-T If you **discard** something, you get rid of it because you no longer want it or need it. ❑ *Read the manufacturer's guidelines before discarding the box.*

dis|cern /dɪsɜːrn/ (discerns, discerning, discerned) **1** V-T If you can **discern** something, you are aware of it and know what it is. [FORMAL] ❑ *You need a long series of data to be able to discern such a trend.* **2** V-T If you can **discern** something, you can just see it, but not clearly. [FORMAL] ❑ *Below the bridge we could just discern a narrow, weedy ditch.*

dis|cern|ible /dɪsɜːrnəbəl/ ADJ If something is **discernible**, you can see it or recognize that it exists. [FORMAL] ❑ *Far away the outline of the island is just discernible.*

dis|cern|ing /dɪsɜːrnɪŋ/ ADJ If you describe someone as **discerning**, you mean that they are able to judge which things of a particular kind are good and which are bad. [APPROVAL] ❑ *Even the most accomplished writers show their work-in-progress to discerning readers.*

dis|cern|ment /dɪsɜːrnmənt/ N-UNCOUNT **Discernment** is the ability to judge which things of a particular kind are good and which are bad.

dis|charge (discharges, discharging, discharged)

The verb is pronounced /dɪstʃɑːrdʒ/. The noun is pronounced /dɪstʃɑːrdʒ/.

1 V-T When someone **is discharged** from a hospital, prison, or one of the armed services, they are officially allowed to leave, or told that they must leave. ❑ *He has a broken nose but may be discharged today.* • N-VAR **Discharge** is also a noun. ❑ *He was given a conditional discharge and ordered to pay Miss Smith $500 compensation.* **2** V-T If someone **discharges** their duties or responsibilities, they do everything that needs to be done in order to complete them. [FORMAL] ❑ *...the quiet competence with which he discharged his many duties.* **3** V-T If something **is discharged** from inside a place, it comes out. [FORMAL] ❑ *The resulting salty water will be discharged at sea.* **4** N-VAR When there is a **discharge** of a substance, the substance comes out from inside somewhere. [FORMAL] ❑ *They develop a fever and a watery discharge from their eyes.* **5** VERB If someone **discharges** a gun, they fire it. [OLD-FASHIONED] ❑ *Lewis was tried for unlawfully and dangerously discharging a weapon.*

dis|ci|ple /dɪsaɪpəl/ (disciples) N-COUNT If you are someone's **disciple**, you are influenced by their teachings and try to follow their example. ❑ *...a major intellectual figure with disciples throughout Europe.*

dis|ci|pli|nar|ian /dɪsɪplɪnɛəriən/ (disciplinarians) N-COUNT If you describe someone as a **disciplinarian**, you mean that they believe in making people obey strict rules of behavior and in punishing severely anyone who disobeys. ❑ *He has a reputation for being a strict disciplinarian.*

dis|ci|pli|nary /dɪsɪplɪnɛri/ ADJ [ADJ n] **Disciplinary** bodies or actions are concerned with making sure that people obey rules or regulations and that they are punished if they do not. ❑ *He will now face a disciplinary hearing for having an affair.*

dis|ci|pline ♦⬦ /dɪsɪplɪn/ (disciplines, disciplining, disciplined) **1** N-UNCOUNT **Discipline** is the practice of making people obey rules or standards of behavior, and punishing them when they do not. ❑ *Order and discipline have been placed in the hands of governing bodies.* **2** N-UNCOUNT **Discipline** is the quality of being able to behave and work in a controlled way which involves obeying particular rules or standards. ❑ *It was that image of calm, control, and discipline that appealed to millions of voters.* **3** N-VAR If you refer to an activity or situation as a **discipline**, you mean that, in order to be successful in it, you need to behave in a strictly controlled way and obey particular rules or standards. ❑ *The discipline of studying music can help children develop good work habits and improve self-esteem.* **4** V-T If someone **is disciplined** for something that they have done wrong, they are punished for it. ❑ *The workman was disciplined by his company but not dismissed.* **5** V-T If you **discipline** yourself to do something, you train yourself to behave and work in a strictly controlled and regular way. ❑ *Discipline yourself to check your messages once a day or every couple of days.* **6** N-COUNT A **discipline** is a particular area of study, especially a subject of study in a college or university. [FORMAL] ❑ *We're looking for people from a wide range of disciplines.* **7** → See feature box at **study**

───── COLLOCATIONS ─────
discipline
NOUN
1
noun + **discipline**: classroom, party
adjective + **discipline**: fiscal, military; strict
verb + **discipline**: enforce, impose, instill; lack; maintain, tighten
2
adjective + **discipline**: physical
verb + **discipline**: lack; require
6
adjective + **discipline**: academic, scientific

───── SYNONYMS ─────
discipline
NOUN
1
punishment: *I have no doubt that the man is guilty and that he deserves punishment.*
penalty: *The maximum penalty is up to 7 years' imprisonment or a $500,000 fine.*
correction: *...jails and other parts of the correction system.*
2
self-control: *I began to wish I'd shown more self-control.*
willpower: *I know I have the willpower to do it.*
restraint: *They behaved with more restraint than I'd expected.*

dis|ci|plined /dɪsɪplɪnd/ ADJ Someone who is **disciplined** behaves or works in a controlled way. ❑ *For me it meant being very disciplined about how I run my life.*

disc jock|ey (disc jockeys) also **disk jockey** N-COUNT A **disc jockey** is someone who plays and introduces music on the radio or at a nightclub.

dis|claim /dɪskleɪm/ (disclaims, disclaiming, disclaimed) V-T If you **disclaim** knowledge of something or **disclaim** responsibility for something, you say that you did not know about it or are not responsible for it. [FORMAL] ❑ *She disclaims any knowledge of her husband's business.*

dis|claim|er /dɪskleɪmər/ (disclaimers) N-COUNT A **disclaimer** is a statement in which a person says that they did not know about something or that they are not responsible for something. [FORMAL] ❑ *The company asserts in a disclaimer that it won't be held responsible for the accuracy of information.*

dis|close /dɪskloʊz/ (discloses, disclosing, disclosed) V-T If you **disclose** new or secret information, you tell people about it. ❑ *Neither side would disclose details of the transaction.*

dis|clo|sure /dɪsklˈoʊʒər/ (disclosures) N-VAR Disclosure is the act of giving people new or secret information. ❑ ...insufficient disclosure of negative information about the company.

dis|co /dˈɪskoʊ/ (discos) N-COUNT A disco is a place or event at which people dance to pop music. ❑ Fridays and Saturdays are regular disco nights.

dis|cog|ra|phy /dɪskˈɒɡrəfi/ (discographies) N-COUNT A discography is a list of all the recordings made by a particular artist or band. [mainly JOURNALISM]

dis|col|or /dɪskˈʌlər/ (discolors, discoloring, discolored)
in BRIT, use **discolour**
V-T/V-I If something discolors or if it is discolored by something else, its original color changes, so that it looks unattractive. ❑ Peas will discolor in contact with the acids in vinaigrette. ● **dis|col|ored** ADJ ❑ Some of the prints were badly discolored. ● **dis|col|ora|tion** /dɪskʌləreɪʃən/ N-UNCOUNT ❑ ...the discoloration of the soil from acid spills.

dis|com|fit /dɪskˈʌmfɪt/ (discomfits, discomfiting, discomfited) V-T If you are discomfited by something, it causes you to feel slightly embarrassed or confused. [WRITTEN] ❑ He will be particularly discomfited by the governor's dismissal of his plan. ❑ The solemn intensity of Jade's gaze discomfited him. ● **dis|com|fit|ed** ADJ [usu v-link ADJ] ❑ Will wanted to do likewise, but felt too discomfited.

dis|com|fi|ture /dɪskˈʌmfɪtʃər/ N-UNCOUNT Discomfiture is a feeling of slight embarrassment or confusion. [WRITTEN]

dis|com|fort /dɪskˈʌmfərt/ (discomforts) **1** N-UNCOUNT Discomfort is a painful feeling in part of your body when you have been hurt slightly or when you have been uncomfortable for a long time. ❑ Steve had some discomfort, but no real pain. **2** N-UNCOUNT Discomfort is a feeling of worry caused by shame or embarrassment. ❑ She hears the discomfort in his voice. **3** N-COUNT Discomforts are conditions which cause you to feel physically uncomfortable. ❑ ...the discomforts of camping.

dis|con|cert /dɪskənsˈɜrt/ (disconcerts, disconcerting, disconcerted) V-T If something disconcerts you, it makes you feel anxious, confused, or embarrassed. ❑ His compliments disconcerted her a little. ● **dis|con|cert|ed** ADJ ❑ He was disconcerted to find his fellow diners already seated.

dis|con|cert|ing /dɪskənsˈɜrtɪŋ/ ADJ If you say that something is disconcerting, you mean that it makes you feel anxious, confused, or embarrassed. ❑ The reception desk is not at street level, which is a little disconcerting. ● **dis|con|cert|ing|ly** ADV ❑ She looks disconcertingly like a familiar aunt or grandmother.

dis|con|nect /dɪskənˈɛkt/ (disconnects, disconnecting, disconnected) **1** V-T To disconnect a piece of equipment means to separate it from its source of power or to break a connection that it needs in order to work. ❑ The device automatically disconnects the ignition when the engine is switched off. **2** V-T [usu passive] If you are disconnected by a gas, electricity, water, or telephone company, they turn off the connection to your house, usually because you have not paid the bill. ❑ You are likely to be given almost three months – until the time of your next bill – before you are disconnected. **3** V-T If you disconnect something from something else, you separate the two things. ❑ He disconnected the IV bottle from the overhead hook and carried it beside the moving cart.

dis|con|nect|ed /dɪskənˈɛktɪd/ ADJ Disconnected things are not linked in any way. ❑ ...sequences of utterly disconnected events.

dis|con|nec|tion /dɪskənˈɛkʃən/ (disconnections) N-VAR [oft the N of n] The disconnection of a gas, water, or electricity supply, or of a telephone, is the act of disconnecting it so that it cannot be used.

dis|con|so|late /dɪskˈɒnsəlɪt/ ADJ Someone who is disconsolate is very unhappy and depressed. [WRITTEN] ❑ He did not have much success, but tried not to get too disconsolate. ● **dis|con|so|late|ly** ADV [ADV with v] ❑ Disconsolately, he walked back down the course.

dis|con|tent /dɪskəntˈɛnt/ (discontents) N-UNCOUNT [also N in pl] Discontent is the feeling that you have when you are not satisfied with your situation. ❑ There are reports of widespread discontent in the capital.

dis|con|tent|ed /dɪskəntˈɛntɪd/ ADJ [oft ADJ with n] If you are discontented, you are not satisfied with your situation. ❑ The Black freedom struggle should be the model for all discontented Americans.

dis|con|tinue /dɪskəntˈɪnyu/ (discontinues, discontinuing, discontinued) **1** V-T If you discontinue something that you have been doing regularly, you stop doing it. [FORMAL] ❑ Do not discontinue the treatment without consulting your doctor. **2** V-T [usu passive] If a product is discontinued, the manufacturer stops making it. ❑ The Leica M2 was discontinued in 1967.

dis|con|ti|nu|ity /dɪskɒntɪnˈuɪti/ (discontinuities) N-VAR Discontinuity in a process is a lack of smooth or continuous development. [FORMAL] ❑ There may appear to be discontinuities between broadcasts.

dis|con|tinu|ous /dɪskəntˈɪnyuəs/ ADJ A process that is discontinuous happens in stages with intervals between them, rather than continuously.

dis|cord /dˈɪskɔrd/ N-UNCOUNT Discord is disagreement and argument between people. [LITERARY]

dis|cord|ant /dɪskˈɔrdənt/ **1** ADJ Something that is discordant is strange or unpleasant because it does not fit in with other things. ❑ His agenda is discordant with ours. **2** ADJ A discordant sound or musical effect is unpleasant to hear.

dis|co|theque /dˈɪskətɛk/ (discotheques) N-COUNT A discotheque is the same as a **disco**. [OLD-FASHIONED]

dis|count✦✧ (discounts, discounting, discounted)

Pronounced /dˈɪskaʊnt/ for meanings 1 and 2, and /dɪskaʊnt/ for meaning 3.

1 N-COUNT A discount is a reduction in the usual price of something. ❑ They are often available at a discount. ❑ All full-time staff get a 20 percent discount. **2** V-T If a store or company discounts an amount or percentage from something that they are selling, they take the amount or percentage off the usual price. ❑ This has forced airlines to discount fares heavily in order to spur demand. **3** V-T If you discount an idea, fact, or theory, you consider that it is not true, not important, or not relevant. ❑ However, traders tended to discount the rumor.

dis|count|er /dˈɪskaʊntər/ (discounters) N-COUNT A discounter is a store or organization which specializes in selling things very cheaply. Discounters usually sell things in large quantities, or offer only a very limited range of goods.

dis|count rate (discount rates) **1** N-COUNT [usu sing] The discount rate is the rate of interest that the central bank of a country charges on the loans that it makes to other banks. [mainly AM] ❑ The Federal Reserve has cut the discount rate five times in 12 months. **2** N-COUNT A discount rate is an amount of interest deducted in advance in the purchase, sale, or loan of negotiable assets. ❑ There are plenty of good deals in fixed and discount rates that homebuyers should consider.

dis|count store (discount stores) N-COUNT A discount store is a store that sells goods at lower prices than usual. [mainly AM] ❑ ...a growing number of shoppers who buy both food and fuel at discount stores.

dis|cour|age /dɪskˈɜrɪdʒ/ (discourages, discouraging, discouraged) **1** V-T If someone or something discourages you, they cause you to lose your enthusiasm about your actions. ❑ It may be difficult to do at first. Don't let this discourage you. ● **dis|cour|aged** ADJ ❑ She was determined not to be too discouraged. ● **dis|cour|ag|ing** ADJ ❑ Today's report is extremely discouraging for the economy. **2** V-T To discourage an action or to discourage someone from doing it means to make them not want to do it. ❑ ...typhoons that discouraged shopping and leisure activities.

dis|cour|age|ment /dɪskˈɜrɪdʒmənt/ N-UNCOUNT Discouragement is the act of trying to make someone not want to do something. ❑ He persevered in the face of active discouragement from those around him.

dis|course /dˈɪskɔrs/ **1** N-UNCOUNT Discourse is spoken or written communication between people, especially serious discussion of a particular subject. ❑ ...a tradition of political discourse. **2** → see also **direct discourse, indirect discourse**

dis|cour|teous /dɪskˈɜrtiəs/ **1** ADJ If you say that someone is discourteous, you mean that they are rude and have no consideration for the feelings of other people. [FORMAL] **2** → See feature box at **polite**

dis|cour|tesy /dɪskˈɜrtɪsi/ (discourtesies) N-VAR Discourtesy is rude and bad-mannered behavior. [FORMAL]

dis|cov|er /dɪskʌvər/ (**discovers, discovering, discovered**) ◼ V-T If you **discover** something that you did not know about before, you become aware of it or learn of it. ❏ *She discovered that they'd escaped.* ❏ *It was difficult for the inspectors to discover which documents were important and which were not.* ◼ V-T If a person or thing **is discovered**, someone finds them, either by accident or because they have been looking for them. ❏ *A few days later his badly beaten body was discovered on a roadside outside the city.* ◼ V-T When someone **discovers** a new place, substance, scientific fact, or scientific technique, they are the first person to find it or become aware of it. ❏ *...the first European to discover America.* ◼ V-T [usu passive] When an actor, musician, or other performer who is not well known **is discovered**, someone recognizes that they have talent and helps them in their career. ❏ *The Beatles were discovered in the early 1960s.*

dis|cov|ery /dɪskʌvəri/ (**discoveries**) ◼ N-VAR If someone makes a **discovery**, they become aware of something that they did not know about before. ❏ *I felt I'd made an incredible discovery.* ◼ N-VAR If someone makes a **discovery**, they are the first to find or become aware of a place, substance, or scientific fact that no one knew about before. ❏ *In that year, two momentous discoveries were made.* ◼ N-VAR When the **discovery** of people or objects happens, someone finds them, either by accident or as a result of looking for them. ❏ *...the discovery and destruction by soldiers of millions of marijuana plants.*

dis|cred|it /dɪskrɛdɪt/ (**discredits, discrediting, discredited**) V-T To **discredit** someone or something means to cause them to lose people's respect or trust. ❏ *...a secret unit within the company that had been set up to discredit its major rival.* • **dis|cred|it|ed** ADJ ❏ *The previous government is, by now, thoroughly discredited.*

dis|cred|it|able /dɪskrɛdɪtəbəl/ ADJ **Discreditable** behavior is not acceptable because people consider it to be shameful and wrong. [FORMAL] ❏ *She had been suspended from her job for discreditable behavior.*

dis|creet /dɪskrit/ ◼ ADJ If you are **discreet**, you are polite and careful in what you do or say, because you want to avoid embarrassing or offending someone. ❏ *They were gossipy and not always discreet.* • **dis|creet|ly** ADV ❏ *I took the phone, and she went discreetly into the living room.* ◼ ADJ If you are **discreet** about something you are doing, you do not tell other people about it, in order to avoid being embarrassed or to gain an advantage. ❏ *We were very discreet about the romance.* • **dis|creet|ly** ADV ❏ *Everyone worked to make him welcome, and, more discreetly, to find out about him.* ◼ ADJ If you describe something as **discreet**, you approve of it because it is small in size or degree, or not easily noticed. [APPROVAL] ❏ *She is wearing a noticeably stylish, feminine dress, plus discreet jewellery.* • **dis|creet|ly** ADV [ADV -ed/adj] ❏ *...stately houses, discreetly hidden behind great avenues of sturdy trees.*

dis|crep|an|cy /dɪskrɛpənsi/ (**discrepancies**) N-VAR If there is a **discrepancy** between two things that ought to be the same, there is a noticeable difference between them. ❏ *...the discrepancy between press and radio reports.*

dis|crete /dɪskrit/ ADJ [usu ADJ n] **Discrete** ideas or things are separate and distinct from each other. [FORMAL] ❏ *...instruction manuals that break down jobs into scores of discrete steps.*

dis|cre|tion /dɪskrɛʃən/ ◼ N-UNCOUNT **Discretion** is the quality of behaving in a quiet and controlled way without drawing attention to yourself or giving away personal or private information. [FORMAL] ❏ *Larsson sometimes joined in the fun, but with more discretion.* ◼ N-UNCOUNT If someone in a position of authority uses their **discretion** or has the **discretion** to do something in a particular situation, they have the freedom and authority to decide what to do. [FORMAL] ❏ *This committee may want to exercise its discretion to look into those charges.* ◼ PHRASE If something happens **at** someone's **discretion**, it can happen only if they decide to do it or give their permission. [FORMAL] ❏ *We may vary the limit at our discretion and will notify you of any change.*

dis|cre|tion|ary /dɪskrɛʃəneri/ ADJ **Discretionary** things are not fixed by rules but are decided on by people in authority, who consider each individual case. ❏ *Magistrates were given wider discretionary powers.*

dis|crimi|nate /dɪskrɪmɪneɪt/ (**discriminates, discriminating, discriminated**) ◼ V-I If you can **discriminate** between two things, you can recognize that they are different. ❏ *He is incapable of discriminating between a good idea and a terrible one.* ◼ V-I To **discriminate** against a group of people or in favor of a group of people means to unfairly treat them worse or better than other groups. ❏ *They believe the law discriminates against women.* ❏ *...legislation which would discriminate in favor of racial minorities.*

dis|crimi|nat|ing /dɪskrɪmɪneɪtɪŋ/ ADJ Someone who is **discriminating** has the ability to recognize things that are of good quality. [APPROVAL] ❏ *More discriminating visitors now tend to shun the area.*

dis|crimi|na|tion /dɪskrɪmɪneɪʃən/ ◼ N-UNCOUNT **Discrimination** is the practice of treating one person or group of people less fairly or less well than other people or groups. ❏ *She is exempt from sex discrimination laws.* ◼ N-UNCOUNT **Discrimination** is knowing what is good or of high quality. ❏ *They cooked without skill and ate without discrimination.* ◼ N-UNCOUNT **Discrimination** is the ability to recognize and understand the differences between two things. ❏ *We will then have an objective measure of how color discrimination and visual acuity develop at the level of the brain.*

dis|crimi|na|tory /dɪskrɪmɪnətɔri/ ADJ **Discriminatory** laws or practices are unfair because they treat one group of people worse than other groups. ❏ *These reforms will abolish racially discriminatory laws.*

dis|cur|sive /dɪskɜrsɪv/ ADJ If a style of writing is **discursive**, it includes a lot of facts or opinions that are not necessarily relevant. [FORMAL] ❏ *...a livelier, more candid and more discursive treatment of the subject.*

dis|cus /dɪskəs/ (**discuses**) ◼ N-COUNT A **discus** is a heavy circular object which athletes try to throw as far as they can as a sport. ◼ N-SING [the N] **The discus** is the sport of throwing a discus. ❏ *He won the discus at the Montreal Olympics.*

dis|cuss /dɪskʌs/ (**discusses, discussing, discussed**) ◼ V-T If you **discuss** something, you talk about it, often in order to reach a decision. ❏ *I will be discussing the situation with colleagues tomorrow.* ◼ V-T If you **discuss** something, you write or talk about it in detail. ❏ *I will discuss the role of diet in cancer prevention in Chapter 7.*

SYNONYMS

discuss
VERB ◼
debate: *He likes to debate issues with his friends.*
thrash out: *...a sincere effort by two people to thrash out their differences.*
argue: *They were still arguing; I could hear them down the road.*

---

dis|cus|sion /dɪskʌʃən/ (**discussions**) ◼ N-VAR If there is **discussion** about something, people talk about it, often in order to reach a decision. ❏ *There was a lot of discussion about the wording of the report.* ❏ *Board members are due to have informal discussions later on today.* • PHRASE If something is **under discussion**, it is still being talked about and a final decision has not yet been reached. ◼ N-COUNT A **discussion** of a subject is a piece of writing or a lecture in which someone talks about it in detail. ❏ *For a discussion of biology and sexual politics, see chapter 4.* ◼ ADJ [ADJ n] A **discussion** document or paper is one that contains information and usually proposals for people to discuss. ❏ *...a NASA discussion paper on long-duration ballooning.* ◼ → See feature box at **debate**

COLLOCATIONS

discussion
NOUN
◼
noun + **discussion**: classroom, group, panel
adjective + **discussion**: earnest, frank, heated, lively; confidential, informal, lengthy; further, ongoing, preliminary
verb + **discussion**: begin, continue, hold, initiate; dominate, join
◼
adjective + **discussion**: detailed, full

---

dis|cus|sion group (**discussion groups**) N-COUNT A **discussion group** is a group of people who meet regularly to discuss a particular subject.

disdain

dis|dain /dɪsdeɪn/ (disdains, disdaining, disdained)
1 N-UNCOUNT If you feel **disdain** for someone or something, you dislike them because you think that they are inferior or unimportant. ❏ *Janet looked at him with disdain.* **2** V-T If you **disdain** someone or something, you regard them with disdain. ❏ *Jackie disdained the servants that her millions could buy.*

dis|dain|ful /dɪsdeɪnfəl/ ADJ [oft ADJ of n] To be **disdainful** means to dislike something or someone because you think they are unimportant or not worth your attention. ❏ *He is highly disdainful of anything to do with the literary establishment.* • **dis|dain|ful|ly** ADV ❏ *"We know all about you," she said disdainfully.*

dis|ease ✦✧ /dɪziːz/ (diseases) **1** N-VAR A **disease** is an illness which affects people, animals, or plants, for example, one which is caused by bacteria or infection. ❏ *...the rapid spread of disease in the area.* **2** → See feature box at **farming**

SYNONYMS

disease
NOUN **1**
illness: *If your child shows any signs of illness, take her to the doctor.*
condition: *Doctors suspect he may have a heart condition.*
complaint: *Eczema is a common skin complaint which often runs in families.*
infection: *Ear infections are common in pre-school children.*
ailment: *The pharmacist can assist you with the treatment of common ailments.*

---

dis|eased /dɪziːzd/ ADJ Something that is **diseased** is affected by a disease. ❏ *The arteries are diseased and a transplant is the only hope.*

dis|em|bark /dɪsɪmbɑːrk/ (disembarks, disembarking, disembarked) V-I When passengers **disembark** from a ship, airplane, or bus, they leave it at the end of their trip. [FORMAL] ❏ *I looked toward the plane. Six passengers had already disembarked.* • **dis|em|bar|ka|tion** /dɪsɛmbɑːrkeɪʃən/ N-UNCOUNT ❏ *Disembarkation is at 7:30 a.m.*

dis|em|bod|ied /dɪsɪmbɒdid/ **1** ADJ [usu ADJ n] **Disembodied** means seeming not to be attached to or to come from anyone. ❏ *A disembodied voice sounded from the back of the cabin.* **2** ADJ [usu ADJ n] **Disembodied** means separated from or existing without a body. ❏ *...a disembodied head.*

dis|em|bow|el /dɪsɪmbaʊəl/ (disembowels, disemboweling, disemboweled)

in BRIT, sometimes in AM, use **disembowelling, disembowelled**

V-T To **disembowel** a person or animal means to remove their internal organs, especially their stomach, intestines, and bowels. ❏ *...sharp claws that can disembowel a human.*

dis|em|pow|er /dɪsɪmpaʊər/ (disempowers, disempowering, disempowered) V-T [oft passive] If someone or something **disempowers** you, they take away your power or influence. ❏ *She feels that women have been disempowered throughout history.*

dis|en|chant|ed /dɪsɪntʃæntɪd/ ADJ If you are **disenchanted** with something, you are disappointed with it and no longer believe that it is good or worthwhile. ❏ *The electorate had grown disenchanted with politics.*

dis|en|chant|ment /dɪsɪntʃæntmənt/ N-UNCOUNT **Disenchantment** is the feeling of being disappointed with something, and no longer believing that it is good or worthwhile. ❏ *There is growing public disenchantment with the educational system.*

dis|en|fran|chise /dɪsɪnfræntʃaɪz/ (disenfranchises, disenfranchising, disenfranchised) V-T To **disenfranchise** a group of people means to take away their right to vote or other rights that most other people have. ❏ *He had been accused of deliberately disenfranchising hundreds of thousands of urban voters.*

dis|en|gage /dɪsɪngeɪdʒ/ (disengages, disengaging, disengaged) V-T/V-I If you **disengage** something, or if it **disengages**, it becomes separate from something which it has been attached to. ❏ *She disengaged the film advance mechanism on the camera.* ❏ *John gently disengaged himself from his sister's tearful embrace.*

disgraceful

dis|en|gaged /dɪsɪngeɪdʒd/ ADJ [oft ADJ from n] If someone is **disengaged** from something, they are not as involved with it as you would expect.

dis|en|gage|ment /dɪsɪngeɪdʒmənt/ N-UNCOUNT [oft N from n] **Disengagement** is a process by which people gradually stop being involved in a conflict, activity, or organization. ❏ *This policy of disengagement from the European war had its critics.*

dis|en|tan|gle /dɪsɪntæŋgəl/ (disentangles, disentangling, disentangled) **1** V-T If you **disentangle** a complicated or confused situation, you make it easier to understand or manage to understand it, by clearly recognizing each separate element. ❏ *In this new book, Harrison brilliantly disentangles complex debates.* ❏ *It's impossible to disentangle the myth from reality.* **2** V-T If you **disentangle** something or someone from an undesirable thing or situation, you separate it from that thing or remove it from that situation. ❏ *They are looking at ways to disentangle him from this major policy decision.* **3** V-T If you **disentangle** something, you separate it from things that are twisted around it, or things that it is twisted or knotted around. ❏ *She clawed at the bushes to disentangle herself.*

dis|equi|lib|rium /dɪsiːkwɪlɪbriəm/ N-UNCOUNT [also a N] **Disequilibrium** is a state in which things are not stable or certain, but are likely to change suddenly. [FORMAL] ❏ *There may be a period of disequilibrium as family members adjust to the new baby.*

dis|es|tab|lish /dɪsɪstæblɪʃ/ (disestablishes, disestablishing, disestablished) V-T To **disestablish** a church or religion means to take away its official status, so that it is no longer recognized as a national institution. [FORMAL] ❏ *It would be right to disestablish the church.* • **dis|es|tab|lish|ment** /dɪsɪstæblɪʃmənt/ N-UNCOUNT ❏ *He advocated the disestablishment of the Anglican church.*

dis|fa|vor /dɪsfeɪvər/

in BRIT, use **disfavour**

N-UNCOUNT [usu in/into N] If someone or something is in **disfavor**, people dislike or disapprove of them. If someone or something falls into **disfavor**, people start to dislike or disapprove of them. [FORMAL] ❏ *Empires are in disfavor these days with good reason.*

dis|fig|ure /dɪsfɪgyər/ (disfigures, disfiguring, disfigured) V-T [usu passive] If someone is **disfigured**, their appearance is spoiled. ❏ *Many of the wounded had been badly disfigured.* • **dis|fig|ured** ADJ ❏ *She tried not to look at the scarred, disfigured face.*

dis|fig|ure|ment /dɪsfɪgyərmənt/ (disfigurements) N-VAR [oft supp N] A **disfigurement** is something, for example, a scar, that spoils a person's appearance. ❏ *He had surgery to correct a facial disfigurement.*

dis|gorge /dɪsgɔːrdʒ/ (disgorges, disgorging, disgorged) V-T If something **disgorges** its contents, it empties them out. [WRITTEN] ❏ *The ground had opened to disgorge a boiling stream of molten lava.*

dis|grace /dɪsgreɪs/ (disgraces, disgracing, disgraced)
1 N-UNCOUNT If you say that someone is in **disgrace**, you are emphasizing that other people disapprove of them and do not respect them because of something that they have done. [EMPHASIS] ❏ *His vice president also had to resign in disgrace.* **2** N-SING If you say that something is **a disgrace**, you are emphasizing that it is very bad or wrong, and that you find it completely unacceptable. [EMPHASIS] ❏ *The way the sales were handled was a complete disgrace.* **3** N-SING You say that someone is **a disgrace** to someone else when you want to emphasize that their behavior causes the other person to feel ashamed. [EMPHASIS] ❏ *Republican leaders called him a disgrace to the party.* **4** V-T If you say that someone **disgraces** someone else, you are emphasizing that their behavior causes the other person to feel ashamed. [EMPHASIS] ❏ *I have disgraced my family's name.*

dis|graced /dɪsgreɪst/ ADJ You use **disgraced** to describe someone whose bad behavior has caused them to lose the approval and respect of the public or of people in authority. ❏ *...the disgraced leader of the coup.*

dis|grace|ful /dɪsgreɪsfəl/ ADJ If you say that something such as behavior or a situation is **disgraceful**, you disapprove of it strongly, and feel that the person or people responsible should be ashamed of it. [DISAPPROVAL] ❏ *It's disgraceful that they have detained him for so long.* • **dis|grace|ful|ly** ADV ❏ *He felt that his brother had behaved disgracefully.*

disgruntled /dɪsgrˈʌntəld/ ADJ If you are **disgruntled**, you are angry and dissatisfied because things have not happened the way that you wanted them to happen. ▫ *Disgruntled employees recently called for his resignation.*

disguise /dɪsgaɪz/ (disguises, disguising, disguised) **1** N-VAR If you are in **disguise**, you are not wearing your usual clothes or you have altered your appearance in other ways, so that people will not recognize you. ▫ *You'll have to travel in disguise.* **2** V-T If you **disguise** yourself, you put on clothes which make you look like someone else or alter your appearance in other ways, so that people will not recognize you. ▫ *She disguised herself as a man so she could fight on the battlefield.* • **disguised** ADJ ▫ *The extremists entered the building disguised as medical workers.* **3** V-T To **disguise** something means to hide it or make it appear different so that people will not know about it or will not recognize it. ▫ *He made no attempt to disguise his agitation.* • **disguised** ADJ ▫ *The proposal is a thinly disguised effort to revive the price controls of the 1970s.*

disgust /dɪsgˈʌst/ (disgusts, disgusting, disgusted) **1** N-UNCOUNT **Disgust** is a feeling of very strong dislike or disapproval. ▫ *He spoke of his disgust at the incident.* **2** V-T To **disgust** someone means to make them feel a strong sense of dislike and disapproval. ▫ *He disgusted many with his boorish behavior.*

disgusted /dɪsgˈʌstɪd/ ADJ If you are **disgusted**, you feel a strong sense of dislike and disapproval at something. ▫ *I'm disgusted with the way that he was treated.* • **disgustedly** ADV [ADV with v] ▫ *"It's a little late for that,"* Ritter said disgustedly.

disgusting /dɪsgˈʌstɪŋ/ **1** ADJ If you say that something is **disgusting**, you are criticizing it because it is extremely unpleasant. ▫ *It tasted disgusting.* **2** ADJ If you say that something is **disgusting**, you mean that you find it completely unacceptable. ▫ *It's disgusting that all this damage has been caused by mindless vandalism.*

dish ♦◇◇ /dɪʃ/ (dishes, dishing, dished) **1** N-COUNT A **dish** is a shallow container with a wide uncovered top. You eat and serve food from dishes and cook food in them. ▫ *...plastic bowls and dishes.* **2** N-COUNT Food that is prepared in a particular style or combination can be referred to as a **dish**. ▫ *There are plenty of vegetarian dishes to choose from.* **3** N-COUNT You can use **dish** to refer to anything that is round and hollow in shape with a wide uncovered top. ▫ *...a dish used to receive satellite broadcasts.* **4** N-PLURAL All the objects that have been used to cook, serve, and eat a meal can be referred to as the **dishes**. ▫ *He'd cooked dinner and washed the dishes.* **5** → see also **satellite dish** **6** PHRASE If you **do the dishes**, you wash the dishes. ▫ *I hate doing the dishes.*
▶ **dish out** **1** PHRASAL VERB If you **dish** something **out**, you distribute it among a number of people. [INFORMAL] ▫ *Doctors, not pharmacists, are responsible for dishing out drugs.* **2** PHRASAL VERB If someone **dishes out** criticism or punishment, they give it to someone. [INFORMAL] ▫ *Do you usually dish out criticism to someone who's doing you a favor?* **3** PHRASAL VERB If you **dish out** food, you serve it to people at the beginning of each course of a meal. [INFORMAL] ▫ *Here the cooks dish out sweet and sour pork.*
▶ **dish up** PHRASAL VERB If you **dish up** food, you serve it. [INFORMAL] ▫ *They dished up a superb meal.*

---- COLLOCATIONS ----

dish
NOUN **2**
noun + **dish**: fish, meat, pasta, vegetable
adjective + **dish**: savory, vegetarian
verb + **dish**: cook, prepare

disharmony /dɪshɑːrməni/ N-UNCOUNT When there is **disharmony**, people disagree about important things and this causes an unpleasant atmosphere. [FORMAL] ▫ *...racial disharmony.*

dishcloth /dɪʃklɒθ/ (dishcloths) **1** N-COUNT A **dishcloth** is a cloth used to dry dishes after they have been washed. **2** N-COUNT A **dishcloth** is a cloth used for washing dishes, pans, and flatware.

disheartened /dɪshɑːrtənd/ ADJ If you are **disheartened**, you feel disappointed about something and have less confidence or less hope about it than you did before. ▫ *He was disheartened by their hostile reaction.*

disheartening /dɪshɑːrtənɪŋ/ ADJ If something is **disheartening**, it makes you feel disappointed and less confident or less hopeful. ▫ *The news was disheartening for investors.*

disheveled /dɪʃɛvəld/
in BRIT, sometimes in AM, use **dishevelled**
ADJ If you describe someone's hair, clothes, or appearance as **disheveled**, you mean that it is very untidy. ▫ *She arrived flushed and disheveled.*

dishevelled /dɪʃɛvəld/ [BRIT] → see **disheveled**

dishonest /dɪsɒnɪst/ ADJ If you say that a person or their behavior is **dishonest**, you mean that they are not truthful or honest and that you cannot trust them. ▫ *It would be dishonest to mislead people and not to present the data as fairly as possible.* • **dishonestly** ADV ▫ *The key issue was whether the four defendants acted dishonestly.*

dishonesty /dɪsɒnɪsti/ N-UNCOUNT **Dishonesty** is dishonest behavior. ▫ *She accused the government of dishonesty and incompetence.*

dishonor /dɪsɒnər/ (dishonors, dishonoring, dishonored)
in BRIT, use **dishonour**
1 V-T If you **dishonor** someone, you behave in a way that damages their good reputation. [FORMAL] ▫ *All of these factors made the family feel that she was dishonoring them.* **2** V-T If someone **dishonors** an agreement, they refuse to act according to its conditions. ▫ *...if your check or money order is insufficient to cover the order total or is dishonored by the bank.* **3** N-UNCOUNT **Dishonor** is a state in which people disapprove of you and lose their respect for you. [FORMAL] ▫ *I have brought shame and dishonor on my family.*

dishonorable /dɪsɒnərəbəl/
in BRIT, use **dishonourable**
ADJ Someone who is **dishonorable** is not honest and does things which you consider to be morally unacceptable. ▫ *Such entertainers were considered lower class and even slightly dishonorable.* • **dishonorably** /dɪsɒnərəbli/ ADV ▫ *He could not bear to be seen to act dishonorably.*

dishrag /dɪʃræg/ (dishrags) N-COUNT A **dishrag** is a cloth used for washing dishes, pans, and flatware. [AM]

dishtowel /dɪʃtaʊəl/ (dishtowels) N-COUNT A **dishtowel** is a cloth used to dry dishes after they have been washed. [AM]
in BRIT, use **tea towel**

dishware /dɪʃwɛər/ N-UNCOUNT **Dishware** is the same as dinnerware. [AM]

dishwasher /dɪʃwɒʃər/ (dishwashers) **1** N-COUNT A **dishwasher** is an electrically operated machine that washes and dries dishes, pans and flatware. **2** N-COUNT A **dishwasher** is a person who is employed to wash dishes, for example at a restaurant, or who usually washes the dishes at home. ▫ *I was a short-order cook and a dishwasher.* **3** → See feature box at **housework**

dishwashing liquid /dɪʃwɒʃɪŋ lɪkwɪd/ (dishwashing liquids) N-MASS **Dishwashing liquid** is a thick soapy liquid which you add to hot water to clean dirty dishes. [AM]

dishwater /dɪʃwɔːtər/ N-UNCOUNT **Dishwater** is water that dishes, pans, and flatware have been washed in.

disillusion /dɪsɪluːʒən/ (disillusions, disillusioning, disillusioned) **1** V-T If a person or thing **disillusions** you, they make you realize that something is not as good as you thought. ▫ *I'd hate to be the one to disillusion him.* **2** N-UNCOUNT **Disillusion** is the same as **disillusionment**. ▫ *There is disillusion with established political parties.*

disillusioned /dɪsɪluːʒənd/ ADJ If you are **disillusioned** with something, you are disappointed, because it is not as good as you had expected or thought. ▫ *I've become very disillusioned with politics.*

disillusionment /dɪsɪluːʒənmənt/ N-UNCOUNT **Disillusionment** is the disappointment that you feel when you discover that something is not as good as you had expected or thought. ▢ *Polls have charted growing disillusionment with the campaign.*

dis|in|cen|tive /dɪsɪnsɛntɪv/ (**disincentives**) N-VAR A **disincentive** is something which discourages people from behaving or acting in a particular way. [FORMAL] ▢ *High marginal tax rates may act as a disincentive to working longer hours.*

dis|in|cli|na|tion /dɪsɪnklɪneɪʃən/ N-SING [usu N to-inf] A **disinclination** to do something is a feeling that you do not want to do it. [FORMAL] ▢ *They are showing a marked disinclination to pursue these opportunities.*

dis|in|clined /dɪsɪnklaɪnd/ ADJ If you are **disinclined** to do something, you do not want to do it. [FORMAL] ▢ *He was disinclined to talk about himself, especially to his students.*

dis|in|fect /dɪsɪnfɛkt/ (**disinfects, disinfecting, disinfected**) V-T If you **disinfect** something, you clean it using a substance that kills germs. ▢ *Chlorine is used to disinfect water.*

dis|in|fect|ant /dɪsɪnfɛktənt/ (**disinfectants**) N-MASS **Disinfectant** is a substance that kills germs. It is used, for example, for cleaning kitchens and bathrooms. ▢ *Effluent from the sedimentation tank is dosed with disinfectant to kill any harmful organisms.*

dis|in|fla|tion /dɪsɪnfleɪʃən/ N-UNCOUNT **Disinflation** is a reduction in the rate of inflation, especially as a result of government policies. ▢ *The 1990s was a period of disinflation, when companies lost much of their power to raise prices.*

dis|in|for|ma|tion /dɪsɪnfərmeɪʃən/ N-UNCOUNT If you accuse someone of spreading **disinformation**, you are accusing them of spreading false information in order to deceive people. ▢ *They spread disinformation in order to discredit politicians.*

dis|in|genu|ous /dɪsɪndʒɛnyuəs/ ADJ Someone who is **disingenuous** is slightly dishonest and insincere in what they say. [FORMAL] ▢ *It would be disingenuous to claim that this is great art.* • **dis|in|genu|ous|ly** ADV ▢ *He disingenuously remarked that he knew nothing about strategy.*

dis|in|her|it /dɪsɪnhɛrɪt/ (**disinherits, disinheriting, disinherited**) V-T If you **disinherit** someone such as your son or daughter, you arrange that they will not become the owner of your money and property after your death, usually because they have done something that you do not approve of. ▢ *He threatened to disinherit her if she refused to obey.*

dis|in|te|grate /dɪsɪntɪgreɪt/ (**disintegrates, disintegrating, disintegrated**) ◼ V-I If something **disintegrates**, it becomes seriously weakened, and is divided or destroyed. ▢ *During October 1918 the Austro-Hungarian Empire began to disintegrate.* • **dis|in|te|gra|tion** /dɪsɪntɪgreɪʃən/ N-UNCOUNT ▢ *...the violent disintegration of Yugoslavia.* ◼ V-I If an object or substance **disintegrates**, it breaks into many small pieces or parts and is destroyed. ▢ *At 420 mph the windshield disintegrated.* • **dis|in|te|gra|tion** N-UNCOUNT ▢ *The report describes the catastrophic disintegration of the aircraft after the explosion.*

dis|in|ter /dɪsɪntɜr/ (**disinters, disinterring, disinterred**) ◼ V-T [usu passive] When a dead body is **disinterred**, it is dug up from out of the ground. ▢ *The bones were disinterred and moved to a burial site.* ◼ V-T If you **disinter** something, you start using it again after it has not been used for a long time. [HUMOROUS] ▢ *...the trend for disinterring sixties soul classics for TV commercials.*

dis|in|ter|est /dɪsɪntərɪst, -ɪntrɪst/ N-UNCOUNT If there is **disinterest** in something, people are not interested in it. ▢ *The fact that Liberia has no oil seems to explain foreign disinterest in its internal affairs.*

dis|in|ter|est|ed /dɪsɪntərɛstɪd, -ɪntrɪstɪd/ ◼ ADJ Someone who is **disinterested** is not involved in a particular situation or not likely to benefit from it and is therefore able to act in a fair and unselfish way. ▢ *The current sole superpower is far from being a disinterested observer.* ◼ ADJ If you are **disinterested** in something, you are not interested in it. Some users of English believe that it is not correct to use **disinterested** with this meaning. ▢ *Lili had clearly regained her appetite but Doran was disinterested in food.*

dis|joint|ed /dɪsdʒɔɪntɪd/ ADJ **Disjointed** words, thoughts, or ideas are not presented in a smooth or logical way and are therefore difficult to understand. ▢ *Sally was used to hearing his complaints, usually in the form of disjointed, drunken ramblings.*

disk /dɪsk/ (**disks**) also **disc** ◼ N-COUNT A **disk** is a flat, circular shape or object. ▢ *The food processor has thin, medium, and thick slicing disks.* ◼ N-COUNT A **disk** is one of the thin, circular pieces of cartilage which separates the bones in your back. ▢ *I had slipped a disk and was frozen in a spasm of pain.* ◼ N-COUNT In a computer, the **disk** is the part where information is stored. ▢ *The program takes up 2.5 megabytes of disk space and can be run on a standard personal computer.* ◼ N-COUNT A **disk** is the same as a **compact disc.** ◼ → see also **disk drive, floppy disk, hard disk**

disk drive (**disk drives**)

in BRIT, also use **disc drive**

N-COUNT The **disk drive** on a computer is the part that contains the disk or into which a disk can be inserted. The disk drive allows you to read information from the disk and store information on the disk.

disk|ette /dɪskɛt/ (**diskettes**) N-COUNT A **diskette** is the same as a **floppy disk.**

disk jock|ey → see **disc jockey**

dis|like /dɪslaɪk/ (**dislikes, disliking, disliked**) ◼ V-T If you **dislike** someone or something, you consider them to be unpleasant and do not like them. ▢ *Liver is a great favorite of his and we don't serve it often because so many people dislike it.* ◼ N-UNCOUNT **Dislike** is the feeling that you do not like someone or something. ▢ *My dislike of thunder and even small earthquakes was due to Mother.* ◼ N-COUNT Your **dislikes** are the things that you do not like. ▢ *Consider what your likes and dislikes are about your job.* ◼ PHRASE If you **take a dislike** to someone or something, you decide that you do not like them. ▢ *He may suddenly take a dislike to foods that he's previously enjoyed.*

dis|lo|cate /dɪsloʊkeɪt, dɪsloʊkeɪt/ (**dislocates, dislocating, dislocated**) ◼ V-T If you **dislocate** a bone or joint in your body, or in someone else's body, it moves out of its proper position in relation to other bones, usually in an accident. ▢ *Harrison dislocated a finger.* ◼ V-T To **dislocate** something such as a system, process, or way of life means to disturb it greatly or prevent it from continuing as normal. ▢ *It would help to end illiteracy and disease, but it would also dislocate a traditional way of life.*

dis|lo|ca|tion /dɪsloʊkeɪʃən/ (**dislocations**) N-VAR [oft N of n] **Dislocation** is a situation in which something such as a system, process, or way of life is greatly disturbed or prevented from continuing as normal. ▢ *Millions of refugees have suffered a total dislocation of their lives.*

dis|lodge /dɪslɒdʒ/ (**dislodges, dislodging, dislodged**) ◼ V-T To **dislodge** something means to remove it from where it was fixed or held. ▢ *Rainfall from a tropical storm dislodged the debris from the slopes of the volcano.* ◼ V-T To **dislodge** a person from a position or job means to remove them from it. ▢ *Congress had sought to dislodge him from the post.*

dis|loy|al /dɪslɔɪəl/ ADJ Someone who is **disloyal** to their friends, family, or country does not support them or does things that could harm them. ▢ *She was so disloyal to her deputy she made his position untenable.*

dis|loy|al|ty /dɪslɔɪəlti/ N-UNCOUNT **Disloyalty** is disloyal behavior. ▢ *Charges had already been made against certain officials suspected of disloyalty.*

dis|mal /dɪzməl/ ◼ ADJ Something that is **dismal** is bad in a sad or depressing way. ▢ *...their dismal record in the Olympics.* ◼ ADJ Something that is **dismal** is sad and depressing, especially in appearance. ▢ *The main part of the hospital is pretty dismal but the children's ward is really lively.*

WORD HISTORY

dismal
In medieval times, **dismal** (from Latin *dies mali*, meaning 'evil days') was the name given to the 24 days of the year (two in each month) that were believed to be unlucky.

dis|man|tle /dɪsmæntəl/ (**dismantles, dismantling, dismantled**) ◼ V-T If you **dismantle** a machine or structure, you carefully separate it into its different parts. ▢ *He asked for immediate help from the United States to dismantle the warheads.*

dismay

2 V-T To **dismantle** an organization or system means to cause it to stop functioning by gradually reducing its power or purpose. ❏ *Public services of all kinds are being dismantled.*

dis|may /dɪsmeɪ/ (dismays, dismaying, dismayed)
1 N-UNCOUNT **Dismay** is a strong feeling of fear, worry, or sadness that is caused by something unpleasant and unexpected. [FORMAL] ❏ *Local politicians have reacted with dismay and indignation.* **2** V-T If you **are dismayed** by something, it makes you feel afraid, worried, or sad. [FORMAL] ❏ *The committee was dismayed by what it had been told.* ● **dis|mayed** ADJ ❏ *He was dismayed at the cynicism of the youngsters.*

dis|mem|ber /dɪsmɛmbər/ (dismembers, dismembering, dismembered) **1** V-T To **dismember** the body of a dead person or animal means to cut or pull it into pieces. ❏ *She then dismembered him, hiding parts of his body in the cellar.* **2** V-T To **dismember** a country or organization means to break it up into smaller parts. ❏ *...Hitler's plans to occupy and dismember Czechoslovakia.*

dis|mem|ber|ment /dɪsmɛmbərmənt/ N-UNCOUNT **Dismemberment** is the cutting or pulling into pieces of a body. **2** N-UNCOUNT [oft N *of* n] **Dismemberment** is the breaking up into smaller parts of a country or organization. ❏ *...the dismemberment of the Warsaw Pact.*

dis|miss ✦✧ /dɪsmɪs/ (dismisses, dismissing, dismissed)
1 V-T If you **dismiss** something, you decide or say that it is not important enough for you to think about or consider. ❏ *Mr. Wakeham dismissed the reports as speculation.* **2** V-T If you **dismiss** something from your mind, you stop thinking about it. ❏ *I dismissed the problem from my mind.* **3** V-T When an employer **dismisses** an employee, the employer tells the employee that they are no longer needed to do the job that they have been doing. ❏ *...the power to dismiss civil servants who refuse to work.* **4** V-T If you **are dismissed** by someone in authority, they tell you that you can go away from them. ❏ *Two more witnesses were called, heard, and dismissed.* **5** V-T When a judge **dismisses** a case against someone, he or she formally states that there is no need for a trial, usually because there is not enough evidence for the case to continue. ❏ *A federal judge dismissed the charges against the doctor yesterday.*

dis|mis|sal /dɪsmɪsəl/ (dismissals) **1** N-VAR When an employee is dismissed from their job, you can refer to their **dismissal**. ❏ *...Mr. Low's dismissal from his post at the head of the commission.* **2** N-UNCOUNT **Dismissal** of something means deciding or saying that it is not important. ❏ *...bureaucratic indifference to people's rights and needs, and high-handed dismissal of public opinion.*

dis|miss|ive /dɪsmɪsɪv/ ADJ If you are **dismissive** of someone or something, you say or show that you think they are not important or have no value. ❏ *Mr. Jones was dismissive of the report, saying it was riddled with inaccuracies.* ● **dis|miss|ive|ly** ADV ❏ *"Critical acclaim from people who don't know what they're talking about is meaningless," he claims dismissively.*

dis|mount /dɪsmaʊnt/ (dismounts, dismounting, dismounted) V-I If you **dismount** from a horse or a bicycle, you get down from it. [FORMAL] ❏ *Emma dismounted and took her horse's bridle.*

dis|obedi|ence /dɪsəbidiəns/ N-UNCOUNT **Disobedience** is deliberately not doing what someone in authority tells you to do, or what a rule or law says that you should do. ❏ *A single act of rebellion or disobedience was often enough to seal a woman's fate.*

dis|obedi|ent /dɪsəbidiənt/ ADJ If you are **disobedient**, you deliberately do not do what someone in authority tells you to do, or what a rule or law says that you should do. ❏ *Her tone was that of a parent to a disobedient child.*

dis|obey /dɪsəbeɪ/ (disobeys, disobeying, disobeyed) V-T/V-I When someone **disobeys** a person or an order, they deliberately do not do what they have been told to do. ❏ *...a naughty boy who often disobeyed his mother and father.*

dis|or|der /dɪsɔrdər/ (disorders) **1** N-VAR A **disorder** is a problem or illness which affects someone's mind or body. ❏ *...a rare nerve disorder that can cause paralysis of the arms.* **2** N-VAR **Disorder** is violence or rioting in public. ❏ *Six months ago America's worst civil disorder in more than 100 years erupted in the city of Los Angeles.* **3** N-UNCOUNT **Disorder** is a state of being untidy, badly prepared, or badly organized. ❏ *The emergency room was in disorder.*

dis|or|dered /dɪsɔrdərd/ ADJ If you describe something as **disordered**, you mean it is untidy and is not neatly arranged. ❏ *...a disordered heap of mossy branches.*

dis|or|der|ly /dɪsɔrdərli/ **1** ADJ If you describe something as **disorderly**, you mean that it is messy, irregular, or disorganized. [FORMAL] ❏ *There were young men and women working away at tables all over the large and disorderly room.* **2** ADJ If you describe someone as **disorderly**, you mean that they are behaving in a noisy, rude, or violent way in public. You can also describe a place or event as **disorderly** if the people there behave in this way. [FORMAL] ❏ *She was jailed for being drunk and disorderly.*

dis|or|der|ly con|duct N-UNCOUNT In law, **disorderly conduct** is the offense of behaving in a dangerous or disturbing way in public. ❏ *The marchers were charged with disorderly conduct and later released.*

dis|or|gani|za|tion /dɪsɔrgənɪzeɪʃən/

in BRIT, also use **disorganisation**

N-UNCOUNT If something is in a state of **disorganization**, it is disorganized. ❏ *The military, he says, is now in a state of disorganization.*

dis|or|gan|ized /dɪsɔrgənaɪzd/

in BRIT, also use **disorganised**

1 ADJ Something that is **disorganized** is in a confused state or is badly planned or managed. ❏ *A report by the state prosecutor described the police action as confused and disorganized.* **2** ADJ Someone who is **disorganized** is very bad at organizing things in their life. ❏ *My boss is completely disorganized and leaves the most important items until very late.*

dis|ori|ent /dɪsɔriənt/ (disorients, disorienting, disoriented)

in BRIT, also use **disorientate**

V-T If something **disorients** you, you lose your sense of direction, or you generally feel lost and uncertain, for example, because you are in an unfamiliar environment. ❏ *An overnight stay at a friend's house disorients me.* ● **dis|ori|ent|ed** ADJ ❏ *I feel dizzy and disoriented.* ● **dis|ori|en|ta|tion** /dɪsɔriənteɪʃən/ N-UNCOUNT ❏ *Morris was so stunned by this that he experienced a moment of total disorientation.*

dis|ori|en|tate /dɪsɔriənteɪt/ (disorientates, disorientating, disorientated) [mainly BRIT] → see **disorient**

dis|own /dɪsoʊn/ (disowns, disowning, disowned) V-T If you **disown** someone or something, you say or show that you no longer want to have any connection with them or any responsibility for them. ❏ *The man who murdered the girl is no son of mine. I disown him.*

dis|par|age /dɪspærɪdʒ/ (disparages, disparaging, disparaged) V-T If you **disparage** someone or something, you speak about them in a way which shows that you do not have a good opinion of them. [FORMAL] ❏ *...Larkin's tendency to disparage literature.*

dis|par|age|ment /dɪspærɪdʒmənt/ N-UNCOUNT [oft N *of* n] **Disparagement** is the act of speaking about someone or something in a way which shows that you do not have a good opinion of them. [FORMAL] ❏ *Reviewers have been almost unanimous in their disparagement of this book.*

dis|par|ag|ing /dɪspærɪdʒɪŋ/ ADJ If you are **disparaging** about someone or something, or make **disparaging** comments about them, you say things which show that you do not have a good opinion of them. ❏ *He was critical of the people, disparaging of their crude manners.*

dis|par|ate /dɪspərɪt/ **1** ADJ **Disparate** things are clearly different from each other in quality or type. [FORMAL] ❏ *Scientists are trying to pull together disparate ideas in astronomy.* **2** ADJ A **disparate** thing is made up of very different elements. [FORMAL] ❏ *...a very disparate nation, with enormous regional differences.*

dis|par|ity /dɪspærɪti/ (disparities) N-VAR If there is a **disparity** between two or more things, there is a noticeable difference between them. [FORMAL] ❏ *...the health disparities between ethnic and socio-economic groups in the U.S.*

dis|pas|sion|ate /dɪspǽʃənɪt/ ADJ Someone who is **dispassionate** is calm and reasonable, and not affected by emotions. ▫ *We, as prosecutors, try to be dispassionate about the cases we bring.* • **dis|pas|sion|ate|ly** ADV [ADV with v] ▫ *He sets out the facts coolly and dispassionately.*

dis|patch /dɪspǽtʃ/ (**dispatches, dispatching, dispatched**)

in BRIT, also use **despatch**

■ V-T If you **dispatch** someone to a place, you send them there for a particular reason. [FORMAL] ▫ *He had been continually dispatching scouts ahead.* • N-UNCOUNT **Dispatch** is also a noun. ▫ *The dispatch of the task force is purely a contingency measure.* ■ V-T If you **dispatch** a message, letter, or parcel, you send it to a particular person or destination. [FORMAL] ▫ *The victory inspired him to dispatch a gleeful telegram to Roosevelt.* • N-UNCOUNT **Dispatch** is also a noun. ▫ *We have 125 cases ready for dispatch.*

dis|patch|er /dɪspǽtʃər/ (**dispatchers**) N-COUNT A **dispatcher** is someone who works for an organization such as the police or the fire department and whose job is to send members of the organization to the places where they are needed. [AM] ▫ *The police dispatcher received the call at around 10:30 a.m.*

dis|pel /dɪspél/ (**dispels, dispelling, dispelled**) V-T To **dispel** an idea or feeling that people have means to stop them having it. ▫ *The president is attempting to dispel the notion that he has neglected the economy.*

dis|pen|sable /dɪspénsəbəl/ ADJ If someone or something is **dispensable**, they are not really needed. ▫ *All those people in the middle are dispensable.*

dis|pen|sa|ry /dɪspénsəri/ (**dispensaries**) N-COUNT A **dispensary** is a place, for example, in a hospital, where medicines are prepared and given out.

dis|pen|sa|tion /dɪspənseɪʃən/ (**dispensations**) ■ N-VAR A **dispensation** is special permission to do something that is normally not allowed. ▫ *They were promised dispensation from military service.* ■ N-UNCOUNT [N of n] **Dispensation of** something is the issuing of it, especially from a position of authority. [FORMAL] ▫ *...our application of consistent standards in the dispensation of justice.*

dis|pense /dɪspéns/ (**dispenses, dispensing, dispensed**) ■ V-T If someone **dispenses** something that they own or control, they give or provide it to a number of people. [FORMAL] ▫ *The union had already dispensed $60000 in grants.* ■ V-T If you obtain a product by getting it out of a machine, you can say that the machine **dispenses** the product. ▫ *For two weeks, the cash machine spewed out receipts apologizing for its inability to dispense money.* ■ V-T When a pharmacist **dispenses** medicine, he or she prepares it, and gives or sells it to the patient or customer. ▫ *Health officials hope to begin dispensing anti-retroviral drugs on a wide scale at the beginning of next year.*

▸ **dispense with** PHRASAL VERB If you **dispense with** something, you stop using it or get rid of it completely, especially because you no longer need it. ▫ *More modern heating systems dispense with the need for a tank.*

dis|pens|er /dɪspénsər/ (**dispensers**) N-COUNT A **dispenser** is a machine or container designed so that you can get an item or quantity of something from it in an easy and convenient way. ▫ *...cash dispensers.*

dis|per|sal /dɪspɜrsəl/ ■ N-UNCOUNT **Dispersal** is the spreading of things over a wide area. ▫ *Plants have different mechanisms of dispersal for their spores.* ■ N-UNCOUNT [oft N of n] The **dispersal** of a crowd involves splitting it up and making the people leave in different directions. ▫ *The police ordered the dispersal of the crowds gathered around the building.*

dis|perse /dɪspɜrs/ (**disperses, dispersing, dispersed**) ■ V-T/V-I When something **disperses** or when you **disperse** it, it spreads over a wide area. ▫ *The oil appeared to be dispersing.* ■ V-T/V-I When a group of people **disperses** or when someone **disperses** them, the group splits up and the people leave in different directions. ▫ *Police fired shots and used tear gas to disperse the demonstrators.*

dis|persed /dɪspɜrst/ ADJ Things that are **dispersed** are situated in many different places, a long way apart from each other. ▫ *...his widely dispersed businesses.*

dis|per|sion /dɪspɜrʃən/ N-UNCOUNT [oft N of n] **Dispersion** is the spreading of people or things over a wide area. [FORMAL] ▫ *The threat will force greater dispersion of their forces.*

dis|pir|it|ed /dɪspɪrɪtɪd/ ADJ If you are **dispirited**, you have lost your enthusiasm and excitement. ▫ *I left eventually at six o'clock feeling utterly dispirited and depressed.*

dis|pir|it|ing /dɪspɪrɪtɪŋ/ ADJ Something that is **dispiriting** causes you to lose your enthusiasm and excitement. ▫ *It's very dispiriting for anyone to be out of a job.*

dis|place /dɪspleɪs/ (**displaces, displacing, displaced**) ■ V-T If one thing **displaces** another, it forces the other thing out of its place, position, or role, and then occupies that place, position, or role itself. ▫ *These factories have displaced tourism as the country's largest source of foreign exchange.* ■ V-T [usu passive] If a person or group of people **is displaced**, they are forced to move away from the area where they live. ▫ *More than 600,000 people were displaced by the tsunami.* ■ → See feature box at **town**

dis|placed per|son (**displaced people** or **displaced persons**) N-COUNT A **displaced person** is someone who has been forced to leave the place where they live, especially because of a war. ▫ *There is an urgent need for food and shelter for these displaced people.*

dis|place|ment /dɪspleɪsmənt/ ■ N-UNCOUNT **Displacement** is the removal of something from its usual place or position by something which then occupies that place or position. [FORMAL] ▫ *...the displacement of traditional agriculture by industrial crops.* ■ N-UNCOUNT **Displacement** is the forcing of people away from the area or country where they live. ▫ *...the gradual displacement of the American Indian.*

dis|play ✦✧ /dɪspleɪ/ (**displays, displaying, displayed**) ■ V-T If you **display** something that you want people to see, you put it in a particular place, so that people can see it easily. ▫ *Among the protesters and war veterans proudly displaying their medals was Aubrey Rose.* • N-UNCOUNT **Display** is also a noun. ▫ *Most of the other artists whose work is on display were his pupils or colleagues.* ■ V-T If you **display** something, you show it to people. ▫ *He displayed his scars to the twelve members of the jury.* ■ V-T If you **display** a characteristic, quality, or emotion, you behave in a way which shows that you have it. ▫ *It was unlike Gordon to display his feelings.* • N-VAR **Display** is also a noun. ▫ *Normally, such an outward display of affection is reserved for his mother.* ■ V-T When a computer **displays** information, it shows it on a screen. ▫ *They started out by looking at the computer screens which display the images.* ■ N-COUNT A **display** is an arrangement of things that have been put in a particular place, so that people can see them easily. ▫ *...a display of your work.* ■ N-COUNT A **display** is a public performance or other event which is intended to entertain people. ▫ *...the fireworks display.* ■ N-COUNT The **display** on a computer screen is the information that is shown there. The screen itself can also be referred to as the **display**. ▫ *A hard copy of the screen display can also be obtained from a printer.*

SYNONYMS

display
VERB ■
show: *The cushions, shown left, measure 20 x 12 inches and cost $39.95.*
present: *We presented the information in a variety of charts.*
exhibit: *His work was exhibited in the best galleries in America, Europe, and Asia.*
NOUN ■
demonstration: *...demonstrations of new products.*
exhibition: *...an exhibition on the natural history of the area.*
presentation: *We gave a slide and video presentation.*

---

dis|please /dɪsplíz/ (**displeases, displeasing, displeased**) V-T If something or someone **displeases** you, they make you annoyed or rather angry. ▫ *Not wishing to displease her, he avoided answering the question.*

dis|pleased /dɪsplízd/ ADJ [v-link ADJ] If you are **displeased** with something, you are annoyed or angry about it. ▫ *Businessmen are displeased with erratic economic policy making.*

dis|pleas|ure /dɪsplɛʒər/ N-UNCOUNT Someone's **displeasure** is a feeling of annoyance that they have about something that has happened. ▫ *The population has already begun to show its displeasure at the slow pace of change.*

dis|port /dɪspɔrt/ (disports, disporting, disported) V-T If you disport yourself somewhere, you amuse yourself there in a happy and energetic way. [HUMOROUS OR OLD-FASHIONED] ❏ ...the rich and famous disporting themselves in glamorous places.

dis|pos|able /dɪspoʊzəbəl/ (disposables) **1** ADJ A disposable product is designed to be thrown away after it has been used. ❏ ...disposable diapers suitable for babies up to 8lbs. • N-COUNT Disposable products can be referred to as **disposables**. ❏ Currently, disposables account for about 80% to 85% of the $3 billion-plus annual diaper market. **2** ADJ [ADJ n] Your **disposable** income is the amount of income you have left after you have paid bills and taxes. ❏ Gerald had little disposable income.

dis|pos|al /dɪspoʊzəl/ **1** PHRASE If you have something **at your disposal**, you are able to use it whenever you want, and for whatever purpose you want. If you say that you are **at someone's disposal**, you mean that you are willing to help them in any way you can. ❏ Do you have this information at your disposal? **2** N-UNCOUNT **Disposal** is the act of getting rid of something that is no longer wanted or needed. ❏ ...methods for the permanent disposal of radioactive waste.

dis|pose /dɪspoʊz/ (disposes, disposing, disposed)
▶ **dispose of** PHRASAL VERB If you **dispose of** something that you no longer want or need, you throw it away. ❏ ...the safest means of disposing of nuclear waste.

dis|posed /dɪspoʊzd/ **1** ADJ [v-link ADJ to-inf] If you are **disposed** to do something, you are willing or eager to do it. [FORMAL] ❏ We passed one or two dwellings, but were not disposed to stop. **2** ADJ You can use **disposed** when you are talking about someone's general attitude or opinion. For example, if you are well or favorably **disposed** to or toward someone or something, you like them or approve of them. [FORMAL] ❏ I saw that the publishers were well disposed toward my book.

dis|po|si|tion /dɪspəzɪʃən/ (dispositions) N-COUNT Someone's **disposition** is the way that they tend to behave or feel. ❏ The rides are unsuitable for people of a nervous disposition.

dis|pos|sess /dɪspəzɛs/ (dispossesses, dispossessing, dispossessed) V-T If you **are dispossessed** of something that you own, especially land or buildings, it is taken away from you. ❏ ...people who were dispossessed of their land under apartheid. ❏ They settled the land, dispossessing many of its original inhabitants. ❏ Droves of dispossessed people emigrated to Canada.

dis|pro|por|tion /dɪsprəpɔrʃən/ (disproportions) N-VAR A **disproportion** is a state in which two things are unequal. [FORMAL] ❏ ...a disproportion in the legal resources available to the two sides.

dis|pro|por|tion|ate /dɪsprəpɔrʃənɪt/ ADJ Something that is **disproportionate** is surprising or unreasonable in amount or size, compared with something else. ❏ A disproportionate amount of time was devoted to one topic. • **dis|pro|por|tion|ate|ly** ADV ❏ There is a disproportionately high suicide rate among prisoners facing very long sentences.

dis|prove /dɪspruv/ (disproves, disproving, disproved, disproven) V-T To **disprove** an idea, belief, or theory means to show that it is not true. ❏ The statistics to prove or disprove his hypothesis will take years to collect.

dis|pu|ta|tion /dɪspyuteɪʃən/ (disputations) N-VAR **Disputation** is discussion on a subject which people cannot agree about. [FORMAL] ❏ After much legal disputation our right to resign was established.

dis|pute /dɪspyut/ (disputes, disputing, disputed) **1** N-VAR A **dispute** is an argument or disagreement between people or groups. ❏ They have won previous pay disputes with the government. **2** V-T If you **dispute** a fact, statement, or theory, you say that it is incorrect or untrue. ❏ He disputed the allegations. ❏ Nobody disputed that Davey was clever. **3** V-RECIP When people **dispute** something, they fight for control or ownership of it. You can also say that one group of people **dispute** something with another group. ❏ The two countries have been disputing the ownership of the fleet. **4** PHRASE If two or more people or groups are **in dispute**, they are arguing or disagreeing about something. ❏ The two countries are in dispute over the boundaries of their coastal waters. **5** PHRASE If something is **in dispute**, people are questioning it or arguing about it. ❏ The schedule for the talks has been agreed, but the location is still in dispute.

COLLOCATIONS

dispute
NOUN **1**
noun + **dispute**: border, contract, pay, trade
adjective + **dispute**: contractual, industrial, legal, territorial; bitter, long-running, ongoing
verb + **dispute**: end, resolve, settle

SYNONYMS

dispute
NOUN **1**
disagreement: My instructor and I had a brief disagreement.
conflict: The two companies came into conflict.
argument: Anny got into an argument with one of the marchers.
strife: Money is a major cause of strife in many marriages.
VERB **2**
question: It never occurs to them to question the doctor's decisions.
challenge: I challenged him on the hypocrisy of his political attitudes.
deny: They all denied ever having seen her.
contest: Her former employer contested the case.

---

dis|quali|fy /dɪskwɒlɪfaɪ/ (disqualifies, disqualifying, disqualified) V-T When someone **is disqualified**, they are officially stopped from taking part in a particular event, activity, or competition, usually because they have done something wrong. ❏ Thomson was disqualified from the 400 meter freestyle. • **dis|quali|fi|ca|tion** /dɪskwɒlɪfɪkeɪʃən/ (disqualifications) N-VAR ❏ Livingston faces a four-year disqualification from athletics.

dis|qui|et /dɪskwaɪɪt/ N-UNCOUNT **Disquiet** is a feeling of worry or anxiety. [FORMAL] ❏ There is growing public disquiet about the cost of such policing.

dis|qui|si|tion /dɪskwɪzɪʃən/ (disquisitions) N-VAR A **disquisition** is a detailed explanation of a particular subject. [FORMAL] ❏ Amanda launched into an authoritative disquisition about contracts.

dis|re|gard /dɪsrɪgɑrd/ (disregards, disregarding, disregarded) V-T If you **disregard** something, you ignore it or do not take account of it. ❏ He disregarded the advice of his executives. • N-UNCOUNT **Disregard** is also a noun. ❏ Whoever planted the bomb showed a total disregard for the safety of the public.

dis|re|pair /dɪsrɪpɛər/ PHRASE [usu v-link PHR] If something is **in disrepair** or is **in a state of disrepair**, it is broken or in bad condition. ❏ The house was unoccupied and in a bad state of disrepair.

dis|repu|table /dɪsrɛpyətəbəl/ ADJ If you say that someone or something is **disreputable**, you are critical of them because they are not respectable or cannot be trusted. [DISAPPROVAL] ❏ ...the noisiest and most disreputable bars.

dis|re|pute /dɪsrɪpyut/ PHRASE If something is brought **into disrepute** or falls **into disrepute**, it loses its good reputation, because it is connected with activities that people do not approve of. ❏ It is a disgrace that such people should bring our profession into disrepute.

dis|re|spect /dɪsrɪspɛkt/ **1** N-UNCOUNT If someone shows **disrespect**, they speak or behave in a way that shows lack of respect for a person, law, or custom. ❏ ...young people with attitudes and complete disrespect for authority. **2** → See feature box at **polite**

dis|re|spect|ful /dɪsrɪspɛktfəl/ ADJ [oft ADJ to/of n] If you are **disrespectful**, you show no respect in the way that you speak or behave to someone. ❏ ...accusations that he had been disrespectful to a police officer. • **dis|re|spect|ful|ly** ADV ❏ They get angry if they think they are being treated disrespectfully.

dis|robe /dɪsroʊb/ (disrobes, disrobing, disrobed) V-I When someone **disrobes**, they remove their clothes. [FORMAL] ❏ She stood up and began to disrobe, folding each garment neatly

dis|rupt /dɪsrʌpt/ (disrupts, disrupting, disrupted) **1** V-T If someone or something **disrupts** an event, system, or process, they cause difficulties that prevent it from continuing or operating in a normal way. ❏ Anti-war protesters disrupted the debate. **2** V-T To **disrupt** a market or a technology is to change the way it works by introducing new methods that are completely different from those that have been used in the past. ❏ If it succeeds, the technology has the potential to seriously disrupt the current market for medical devices.

dis|rup|tion /dɪsrʌpʃᵊn/ (disruptions) N-VAR When there is disruption of an event, system, or process, it is prevented from continuing or operating in a normal way. ❑ *The plan was designed to ensure disruption to business was kept to a minimum.*

dis|rup|tive /dɪsrʌptɪv/ **1** ADJ To be disruptive means to prevent something from continuing or operating in a normal way. ❑ *Alcohol can produce violent, disruptive behavior.* **2** ADJ Disruptive technology involves completely new methods that change the way something such as a market or a type of device works. ❑ *One example of disruptive technology is 3-D printing.*

diss /dɪs/ → see dis

dis|sat|is|fac|tion /dɪssætɪsfækʃᵊn/ (dissatisfactions) N-VAR If you feel dissatisfaction with something, you are not contented or pleased with it. ❑ *She has already expressed her dissatisfaction with this aspect of the policy.*

dis|sat|is|fied /dɪssætɪsfaɪd/ ADJ If you are dissatisfied with something, you are not contented or pleased with it. ❑ *Eighty-two percent of voters are dissatisfied with the way their country is being governed.*

dis|sect /dɪsɛkt, daɪ-/ (dissects, dissecting, dissected) **1** V-T If someone dissects the body of a dead person or animal, they carefully cut it up in order to examine it scientifically. ❑ *We dissected a frog in biology class.* • **dis|sec|tion** /dɪsɛkʃᵊn, daɪ-/ (dissections) N-VAR ❑ *Researchers need a growing supply of corpses for dissection.* **2** V-T If someone dissects something such as a theory, a situation, or a piece of writing, they consider and talk about each detail of it. ❑ *People want to dissect his work and question his motives.* • **dis|sec|tion** (dissections) N-VAR ❑ *...her calm, condescending dissection of my proposals.*

dis|sem|ble /dɪsɛmbᵊl/ (dissembles, dissembling, dissembled) V-T/V-I When people dissemble, they hide their real intentions or emotions. [LITERARY] ❑ *Henry was not slow to dissemble when it served his purposes.*

dis|semi|nate /dɪsɛmɪneɪt/ (disseminates, disseminating, disseminated) V-T To disseminate information or knowledge means to distribute it so that it reaches many people or organizations. [FORMAL] ❑ *They disseminated anti-French propaganda.* • **dis|semi|na|tion** /dɪsɛmɪneɪʃᵊn/ N-UNCOUNT ❑ *He actively promoted the dissemination of scientific ideas about matters such as morality.*

dis|sen|sion /dɪsɛnʃᵊn/ (dissensions) N-UNCOUNT [also N in pl] Dissension is disagreement and argument. [FORMAL] ❑ *The tax cut issue has caused dissension among administration officials.*

dis|sent /dɪsɛnt/ (dissents, dissenting, dissented) **1** N-UNCOUNT Dissent is strong disagreement or dissatisfaction with a decision or opinion, especially one that is supported by most people or by people in authority. ❑ *He is the toughest military ruler yet and has responded harshly to any dissent.* **2** V-I If you dissent, you express disagreement with a decision or opinion, especially one that is supported by most people or by people in authority. [FORMAL] ❑ *Just one of the 10 members dissented.* ❑ *No one dissents from the decision to unify.*

dis|sent|er /dɪsɛntər/ (dissenters) N-COUNT Dissenters are people who say that they do not agree with something that other people agree with or that is official policy. ❑ *The party does not tolerate dissenters in its ranks.*

dis|ser|ta|tion /dɪsərteɪʃᵊn/ (dissertations) N-COUNT A dissertation is a long formal piece of writing on a particular subject, especially for an advanced university degree. ❑ *He is currently writing a dissertation on the Somali civil war.*

dis|ser|vice /dɪssɜrvɪs/ N-SING [oft N to n] If you do someone or something a disservice, you harm them in some way. [FORMAL] ❑ *He said the protesters were doing a disservice to the nation.*

dis|si|dent /dɪsɪdənt/ (dissidents) **1** N-COUNT Dissidents are people who disagree with and criticize their government, especially when it is undemocratic. ❑ *...political dissidents.* **2** ADJ [ADJ n] Dissident people disagree with or criticize their government or a powerful organization they belong to. ❑ *...a dissident Russian novelist.*

dis|simi|lar /dɪsɪmɪlər/ ADJ If one thing is dissimilar to another, or if two things are dissimilar, they are very different from each other. ❑ *His methods were not dissimilar to those used by Freud.* ❑ *It would be difficult to find two men who were more dissimilar.*

dis|simu|late /dɪsɪmyəleɪt/ (dissimulates, dissimulating, dissimulated) V-T/V-I When people dissimulate, they hide their true feelings, intentions, or nature. [FORMAL] ❑ *This man was too injured to dissimulate well.* ❑ *He didn't attempt to dissimulate or conceal his true feelings.*

dis|si|pate /dɪsɪpeɪt/ (dissipates, dissipating, dissipated) **1** V-T/V-I When something dissipates or when you dissipate it, it becomes less or becomes less strong until it disappears or goes away completely. [FORMAL] ❑ *The tension in the room had dissipated.* **2** V-T When someone dissipates money, time, or effort, they waste it in a foolish way. [FORMAL] ❑ *He needs someone who can keep him from dissipating his time and energy on too many different things.*

dis|si|pat|ed /dɪsɪpeɪtɪd/ ADJ If you describe someone as dissipated, you disapprove of them because they spend a lot of time drinking alcohol and enjoying other physical pleasures, and are probably unhealthy because of this. [DISAPPROVAL] ❑ *Flynn was still handsome, though dissipated.*

dis|si|pa|tion /dɪsɪpeɪʃᵊn/ N-UNCOUNT If someone leads a dissipated life, you can also say that they lead a life of dissipation. [LITERARY]

dis|so|ci|ate /dɪsoʊʃieɪt, -sieɪt/ (dissociates, dissociating, dissociated) **1** V-T If you dissociate yourself from something or someone, you say or show that you are not connected with them, usually in order to avoid trouble or blame. ❑ *It seems harder and harder for the president to dissociate himself from these scandals.* **2** V-T If you dissociate one thing from another, you consider the two things as separate from each other, or you separate them. [FORMAL] ❑ *Almost the first lesson they learn is how to dissociate emotion from reason.*

dis|so|lute /dɪsəlut/ ADJ Someone who is dissolute does not care at all about morals and lives in a way that is considered to be wicked and immoral. [DISAPPROVAL]

dis|so|lu|tion /dɪsəluʃᵊn/ **1** N-UNCOUNT [also a N, oft N of n] Dissolution is the act of breaking up officially an organization or institution, or of formally ending a parliament. [FORMAL] ❑ *He stayed on until the dissolution of the firm in 1948.* **2** N-UNCOUNT Dissolution is the act of officially ending a formal agreement, for example, a marriage or a business arrangement. [FORMAL] ❑ *...the statutory requirement for granting dissolution of a marriage.*

dis|solve /dɪzɒlv/ (dissolves, dissolving, dissolved) **1** V-T/V-I If a substance dissolves in liquid or if you dissolve it, it becomes mixed with the liquid and disappears. ❑ *Heat gently until the sugar dissolves.* **2** V-T When an organization or institution is dissolved, it is officially ended or broken up. ❑ *The committee has been dissolved.* **3** V-T When a parliament is dissolved, it is formally ended, so that elections for a new parliament can be held. ❑ *The present assembly will be dissolved on April 30th.* **4** V-T [usu passive] When a marriage or business arrangement is dissolved, it is officially ended. ❑ *The marriage was dissolved in 1976.* **5** V-T/V-I If something such as a problem or feeling dissolves or is dissolved, it becomes weaker and disappears. ❑ *His new-found optimism dissolved.* **6** → See feature box at experiment

dis|so|nance /dɪsənəns/ N-UNCOUNT Dissonance is a lack of agreement or harmony between things. [FORMAL]

dis|suade /dɪsweɪd/ (dissuades, dissuading, dissuaded) V-T If you dissuade someone from doing or believing something, you persuade them not to do or believe it. [FORMAL] ❑ *Doctors had tried to dissuade patients from smoking.* ❑ *She steadfastly maintained that her grandsons were innocent, and nothing could dissuade her from that belief.*

dis|tance ♦♦◇ /dɪstəns/ (distances, distancing, distanced) **1** N-VAR The distance between two points or places is the amount of space between them. ❑ *...the distance between the island and the nearby shore.* **2** N-UNCOUNT When two things are very far apart, you talk about the distance between them. ❑ *The distance wouldn't be a problem.* **3** N-UNCOUNT When you want to emphasize that two people or things do not have a close relationship or are not the same, you can refer to the distance between them. [EMPHASIS] ❑ *There was a vast distance between psychological clues and concrete proof.* **4** N-UNCOUNT Distance is coolness or unfriendliness in the way that someone behaves toward you. [FORMAL] ❑ *There were periods of sulking, of*

pronounced distance, of coldness. ◼️5 ADJ [ADJ n] **Distance** learning or **distance** education involves studying at home and sending your work to a college or university, rather than attending the college or university in person. ❏ *The Internet is often used as a resource and as a tool for distance learning.* ◼️6 N-SING [in/into the N] If you can see something **in the distance**, you can see it, far away from you. ❏ *We suddenly saw her in the distance.* ◼️7 V-T If you **distance** yourself from a person or thing, or if something **distances** you from them, you feel less friendly or positive toward them, or become less involved with them. ❏ *The author distanced himself from some of the comments in his book.*
• **dis|tanced** ADJ [v-link ADJ] ❏ *The party has become too distanced from Black voters.* ◼️8 PHRASE If you are **at a distance** from something, or if you see it or remember it **from a distance**, you are a long way away from it in space or time. ❏ *The only way I can cope with my mother is at a distance.* ◼️9 PHRASE If you **keep** your **distance** from someone or something or **keep** them **at a distance**, you do not become involved with them. ❏ *Jay had always tended to keep his girlfriends at a distance.* ◼️10 → See feature box at **drive**

SYNONYMS

distance
NOUN ◼️1
length: *It is about a meter in length.*
extent: *Their commitment was to maintain the extent of forests, not their biodiversity.*
space: *The space underneath could be used as a storage area.*
span: *It is a very pretty butterfly, with a 2 inch wing span.*

---

dis|tant /dɪstənt/ ◼️1 ADJ **Distant** means very far away. ❏ *The mountains rolled away to a distant horizon.* ◼️2 ADJ You use **distant** to describe a time or event that is very far away in the future or in the past. ❏ *There is little doubt, however, that things will improve in the not too distant future.* ◼️3 ADJ A **distant** relative is one who you are not closely related to. ❏ *He's a distant relative of the mayor.* • **dis|tant|ly** ADV ❏ *The O'Shea girls are distantly related to our family.* ◼️4 ADJ [v-link ADJ] If you describe someone as **distant**, you mean that you find them cold and unfriendly. ❏ *He found her cold, icelike, and distant.* ◼️5 ADJ If you describe someone as **distant**, you mean that they are not concentrating on what they are doing because they are thinking about other things. ❏ *There was a distant look in her eyes from time to time, her thoughts elsewhere.*

dis|tant|ly /dɪstəntli/ ◼️1 ADV **Distantly** means very far away. [LITERARY] ❏ *Distantly, to her right, she could make out the town of Chiffa.* ◼️2 ADV If you are **distantly** aware of something or if you **distantly** remember it, you are aware of it or remember it, but not very strongly. ❏ *She became distantly aware that the light had grown strangely brighter and was flickering gently.* ◼️3 → see also **distant**

dis|taste /dɪsteɪst/ N-UNCOUNT If you feel **distaste** for someone or something, you dislike them and consider them to be unpleasant, disgusting, or immoral. ❏ *He professed a violent distaste for everything related to commerce, production, and money.*

dis|taste|ful /dɪsteɪstfʊl/ ADJ If something is **distasteful** to you, you think it is unpleasant, disgusting, or immoral. ❏ *He found it distasteful to be offered a cold buffet and drinks before witnessing the execution.*

dis|tem|per /dɪstempər/ ◼️1 N-UNCOUNT **Distemper** is a dangerous and infectious disease that can be caught by animals, especially dogs. ◼️2 N-UNCOUNT **Distemper** is a kind of paint sometimes used for painting walls.

dis|tend /dɪstend/ (distends, distending, distended) V-T/V-I If a part of your body **is distended**, or if it **distends**, it becomes swollen and unnaturally large. [FORMAL, MEDICAL] ❏ *Through this incision, the abdominal cavity is distended with carbon dioxide gas.* ❏ *The colon, or large intestine, distends and fills with gas.*
• **dis|tend|ed** ADJ ❏ *...an infant with a distended belly.*

dis|ten|sion /dɪstenʃən/ also **distention** N-UNCOUNT **Distension** is abnormal swelling in a person's or animal's body. [MEDICAL]

dis|till /dɪstɪl/ (distills, distilling, distilled)
in BRIT, use **distil**

◼️1 V-T If a liquid such as whiskey or water **is distilled**, it is heated until it changes into steam or vapor and then cooled until it becomes liquid again. This is usually done in order to make it pure. ❏ *The whiskey had been distilled in 1926 and sat quietly maturing until 1987.* • **dis|til|la|tion** /dɪstɪleɪʃən/ N-UNCOUNT ❏ *Any faults in the original cider stood out sharply after distillation.* ◼️2 V-T If an oil or liquid **is distilled** from a plant, it is produced by a process which extracts the most essential part of the plant. To **distill** a plant means to produce an oil or liquid from it by this process. ❏ *The oil is distilled from the berries of this small tree.* • **dis|til|la|tion** N-UNCOUNT ❏ *The distillation of rose petals to produce rosewater almost certainly originated in Ancient Persia.* ◼️3 V-T If a thought or idea **is distilled** from previous thoughts, ideas, or experiences, it comes from them. If it **is distilled** into something, it becomes part of that thing. ❏ *Reviews are distilled from articles previously published in the main column.* ❏ *Eventually passion was distilled into the natural beauty of a balmy night.* • **dis|til|la|tion** N-SING ❏ *The material below is a distillation of his work.*

dis|till|er /dɪstɪlər/ (distillers) N-COUNT A **distiller** is a person or a company that makes whiskey or a similar strong alcoholic drink by a process of distilling.

dis|till|ery /dɪstɪləri/ (distilleries) N-COUNT A **distillery** is a place where whiskey or a similar strong alcoholic drink is made by a process of distilling.

dis|tinct /dɪstɪŋkt/ ◼️1 ADJ If something is **distinct** from something else of the same type, it is different or separate from it. ❏ *Engineering and technology are disciplines distinct from one another and from science.* • **dis|tinct|ly** ADV [ADV adj] ❏ *...a banking industry with two distinctly different sectors.* ◼️2 ADJ If something is **distinct**, you can hear, see, or taste it clearly. ❏ *...to impart a distinct flavor with a minimum of cooking fat.*
• **dis|tinct|ly** ADV [ADV with v] ❏ *I distinctly heard the loudspeaker calling passengers for the Washington-Miami flight.* ◼️3 ADJ If an idea, thought, or intention is **distinct**, it is clear and definite. ❏ *Now that Tony was no longer present, there was a distinct change in her attitude.* • **dis|tinct|ly** ADV [ADV with v] ❏ *I distinctly remember wishing I had not gotten involved.* ◼️4 ADJ [ADJ n] You can use **distinct** to emphasize that something is great enough in amount or degree to be noticeable or important. [EMPHASIS] ❏ *Being 6ft 3in tall has some distinct disadvantages!* • **dis|tinct|ly** ADV [ADV adj/-ed] ❏ *His government is looking distinctly shaky.* ◼️5 PHRASE If you say that you are talking about one thing **as distinct from** another, you are indicating exactly which thing you mean. ❏ *There's a lot of evidence that oily fish, as distinct from fatty meat, have a beneficial effect.*

dis|tinc|tion /dɪstɪŋkʃən/ (distinctions) ◼️1 N-COUNT A **distinction** between similar things is a difference. ❏ *There are obvious distinctions between the two wine-making areas.* ❏ *The distinction between craft and fine art is more controversial.*
• PHRASE If you **draw a distinction** or **make a distinction**, you say that two things are different. ◼️2 N-COUNT A **distinction** is a special award or honor that is given to someone because of their very high level of achievement. ❏ *The award was established in 1902 as a special distinction for eminent men and women.* ◼️3 N-UNCOUNT **Distinction** is the quality of being very good or better than other things of the same type. [FORMAL] ❏ *Lewis emerges as a composer of distinction and sensitivity.* ◼️4 N-SING If you say that someone or something has the **distinction** of being something, you are drawing attention to the fact that they have the special quality of being that thing. **Distinction** is normally used to refer to good qualities, but can sometimes also be used to refer to bad qualities. ❏ *He has the distinction of being regarded as the Federal Republic's greatest living writer.*

dis|tinc|tive /dɪstɪŋktɪv/ ADJ Something that is **distinctive** has a special quality or feature which makes it easily recognizable and different from other things of the same type. ❏ *...the distinctive odor of chlorine.* • **dis|tinc|tive|ly** ADV [ADV adj/-ed] ❏ *...the distinctively fragrant taste of elderflowers.*

dis|tin|guish /dɪstɪŋgwɪʃ/ (distinguishes, distinguishing, distinguished) ◼️1 V-T/V-I If you can **distinguish** one thing from another or **distinguish** between two things, you can see or understand how they are different. ❏ *Could he distinguish right from wrong?* ❏ *Research suggests that babies learn to see by distinguishing between areas of light and dark.* ◼️2 V-T A feature or quality that **distinguishes** one thing from another causes the two things to be regarded as different, because only the first thing has the feature or quality. ❏ *There is something about music

distinguishable 372 **distrustful**

that distinguishes it from all other art forms. **3** V-T If you can **distinguish** something, you can see, hear, or taste it although it is very difficult to detect. [FORMAL] ❑ There were cries, calls. He could distinguish voices. **4** V-T If you **distinguish** yourself, you do something that makes you famous or important. ❑ Over the next few years he distinguished himself as a leading constitutional scholar. **5** → See feature box at **appearance**

dis|tin|guish|able /dɪstɪŋgwɪʃəbəl/ **1** ADJ If something is **distinguishable** from other things, it has a quality or feature which makes it possible for you to recognize it and see that it is different. ❑ ...features that make their products distinguishable from those of their rivals. **2** ADJ [v-link ADJ] If something is **distinguishable**, you can see or hear it in conditions when it is difficult to see or hear anything. ❑ It was getting light and shapes were more distinguishable.

dis|tin|guished /dɪstɪŋgwɪʃt/ **1** ADJ If you describe a person or their work as **distinguished**, you mean that they have been very successful in their career and have a good reputation. ❑ ...a distinguished academic family. **2** ADJ If you describe someone as **distinguished**, you mean that they look very noble and respectable. ❑ His suit was immaculately cut and he looked very distinguished.

dis|tort /dɪstɔrt/ (distorts, distorting, distorted) **1** V-T If you **distort** a statement, fact, or idea, you report or represent it in an untrue way. ❑ The media distorts reality; it categorizes people as all good or all bad. ● **dis|tort|ed** ADJ ❑ These figures give a distorted view of the significance for the local economy. **2** V-T/V-I If something you can see or hear **is distorted** or **distorts**, its appearance or sound is changed so that it seems unclear. ❑ A painter may exaggerate or distort shapes and forms. ● **dis|tort|ed** ADJ ❑ Sound was becoming more and more distorted through the use of hearing aids.

dis|tor|tion /dɪstɔrʃən/ (distortions) **1** N-VAR **Distortion** is the changing of something into something that is not true or not acceptable. [DISAPPROVAL] ❑ I think it would be a gross distortion of reality to say that they were motivated by self-interest. **2** N-VAR **Distortion** is the changing of the appearance or sound of something in a way that makes it seem strange or unclear. ❑ He demonstrated how audio signals could be transmitted along cables without distortion.

dis|tract /dɪstrækt/ (distracts, distracting, distracted) V-T If something **distracts** you or your attention from something, it takes your attention away from it. ❑ Tom admits that playing video games sometimes distracts him from his homework. ❑ Don't let yourself be distracted by fashionable theories.

dis|tract|ed /dɪstræktɪd/ ADJ If you are **distracted**, you are not concentrating on something because you are worried or are thinking about something else. ❑ She had seemed curiously distracted. ● **dis|tract|ed|ly** ADV [ADV with v] ❑ He looked up distractedly. "Be with you in a second."

dis|tract|ing /dɪstræktɪŋ/ ADJ If you say that something is **distracting**, you mean that it makes it difficult for you to concentrate properly on what you are doing. ❑ I find it slightly distracting to have someone watching me while I work.

dis|trac|tion /dɪstrækʃən/ (distractions) N-VAR A **distraction** is something that turns your attention away from something you want to concentrate on. ❑ Total concentration is required with no distractions.

dis|traught /dɪstrɔt/ ADJ If someone is **distraught**, they are so upset and worried that they cannot think clearly. ❑ Mr. Barker's distraught parents were last night being comforted by relatives.

dis|tress /dɪstrɛs/ (distresses, distressing, distressed) **1** N-UNCOUNT **Distress** is a state of extreme sorrow, suffering, or pain. ❑ Jealousy causes distress and painful emotions. **2** N-UNCOUNT **Distress** is the state of being in extreme danger and needing urgent help. ❑ He expressed concern that the ship might be in distress. **3** V-T If someone or something **distresses** you, they cause you to be upset or worried. ❑ The idea of Toni being in danger distresses him enormously.

dis|tressed /dɪstrɛst/ ADJ If someone is **distressed**, they are upset or worried. ❑ I feel very alone and distressed about my problem.

dis|tress|ing /dɪstrɛsɪŋ/ ADJ If something is **distressing**, it upsets you or worries you. ❑ It is very distressing to see your baby attached to tubes and monitors. ● **dis|tress|ing|ly** ADV ❑ A distressingly large number of firms have been breaking the rules.

dis|trib|ute /dɪstrɪbyut/ (distributes, distributing, distributed) **1** V-T If you **distribute** things, you hand them or deliver them to a number of people. ❑ Students shouted slogans and distributed leaflets. **2** V-T When a company **distributes** goods, it supplies them to the stores or businesses that sell them. [BUSINESS] ❑ We didn't understand how difficult it was to distribute a national paper. **3** V-T To **distribute** a substance **over** something means to scatter it over it. [FORMAL] ❑ Distribute the topping evenly over the fruit.

dis|trib|ut|ed /dɪstrɪbyutɪd/ ADJ If things are **distributed** throughout an area, object, or group, they exist throughout it. ❑ These cells are widely distributed throughout the body.

dis|tri|bu|tion /dɪstrɪbyuʃən/ (distributions) **1** N-UNCOUNT The **distribution** of things involves giving or delivering them to a number of people or places. ❑ ...the council which controls the distribution of foreign aid. **2** N-VAR The **distribution** of something is how much of it there is in each place or at each time, or how much of it each person has. ❑ Mr. Roh's economic planners sought to achieve a more equitable distribution of wealth. **3** → See feature box at **press**

SYNONYMS

distribution
NOUN
1
delivery: ...the delivery of goods and resources.
shipping: ...the international shipping industry.
transport: Local production virtually eliminates transport costs.
2
rationing: The municipal authorities here are preparing for food rationing.
division: The current division of labor between workers and management will alter.
allocation: His sons quarreled bitterly over the allocation of family resources.

---

dis|tri|bu|tion|al /dɪstrɪbyuʃənəl/ **1** ADJ [ADJ n] **Distributional** means relating to the distribution of goods. ❑ What they're doing is setting up distributional networks. **2** ADJ [ADJ n] **Distributional** effects and policies relate to the share of a country's wealth that different groups of people have. [FORMAL] ❑ ...the distributional effects of free markets, which lead to inequalities in income.

dis|tribu|tive /dɪstrɪbyutɪv/ ADJ [ADJ n] **Distributive** means relating to the distribution of goods. ❑ Reorganization is necessary on the distributive side of this industry.

dis|tribu|tor /dɪstrɪbyətər/ (distributors) N-COUNT A **distributor** is a company that supplies goods to stores or other businesses. [BUSINESS] ❑ ...Spain's largest distributor of petroleum products.

dis|tribu|tor|ship /dɪstrɪbyətərʃɪp/ (distributorships) N-COUNT A **distributorship** is a company that supplies goods to stores or other businesses, or the right to supply goods to stores and businesses. [BUSINESS] ❑ ...the general manager of an automobile distributorship.

dis|trict /dɪstrɪkt/ (districts) N-COUNT A **district** is a particular area of a town or country. ❑ I drove around the business district.

Dis|trict At|tor|ney (District Attorneys) N-COUNT In the United States, a **District Attorney** is a lawyer who works for a city, state, or federal government and puts on trial people who are accused of crimes. The abbreviation **DA** is also used.

dis|trict court (district courts) N-COUNT In the United States, a **district court** is a state or federal court that has jurisdiction in a particular district. ❑ A Miami district court has scheduled a hearing for Friday.

dis|trust /dɪstrʌst/ (distrusts, distrusting, distrusted) **1** V-T If you **distrust** someone or something, you think they are not honest, reliable, or safe. ❑ I don't have any particular reason to distrust them. **2** N-UNCOUNT [also a N, oft N of n] **Distrust** is the feeling of doubt that you have toward someone or something you distrust. ❑ What he saw there left him with a profound distrust of all political authority.

dis|trust|ful /dɪstrʌstfəl/ ADJ If you are **distrustful** of someone or something, you think that they are not honest, reliable, or safe. ❑ Voters are deeply distrustful of all politicians.

disturb /dɪstɜrb/ (disturbs, disturbing, disturbed) **1** V-T If you disturb someone, you interrupt what they are doing and upset them. ❑ *Did you sleep well? I didn't want to disturb you. You looked so peaceful.* **2** V-T If something disturbs you, it makes you feel upset or worried. ❑ *I dream about him, dreams so vivid that they disturb me for days.* **3** V-T If something is disturbed, its position or shape is changed. ❑ *He'd placed his notes in the brown envelope. They hadn't been disturbed.* **4** V-T If something disturbs a situation or atmosphere, it spoils it or causes trouble. ❑ *What could possibly disturb such tranquility?*

dis|turb|ance /dɪstɜrbəns/ (disturbances) **1** N-COUNT A disturbance is an incident in which people behave violently in public. ❑ *During the disturbance which followed, three Englishmen were hurt.* **2** N-UNCOUNT Disturbance means upsetting or disorganizing something which was previously in a calm and well-ordered state. ❑ *Successful breeding requires quiet, peaceful conditions with as little disturbance as possible.* **3** N-VAR You can use disturbance to refer to a medical or psychological problem, when someone's body or mind is not working in the normal way. ❑ *Poor educational performance is related to emotional disturbance.*

dis|turbed /dɪstɜrbd/ **1** ADJ A disturbed person is very upset emotionally, and often needs special care or treatment. ❑ *...working with severely emotionally disturbed children.* **2** ADJ You can say that someone is disturbed when they are very worried or anxious. ❑ *Doctors were disturbed that less than 30 percent of the patients were women.* **3** ADJ If you describe a situation or period of time as disturbed, you mean that it is unhappy and full of problems. ❑ *...youngsters from disturbed backgrounds.*

dis|turb|ing /dɪstɜrbɪŋ/ ADJ Something that is disturbing makes you feel worried or upset. ❑ *There was something about him she found disturbing.* • **dis|turb|ing|ly** ADV ❑ *The government has itself recognized the disturbingly high frequency of violent attacks.*

dis|unit|ed /dɪsyunaɪtɪd/ ADJ If a group of people are disunited, there is disagreement and division among them. ❑ *...an increasingly disunited party.*

dis|unity /dɪsyunɪti/ N-UNCOUNT Disunity is lack of agreement among people which prevents them from working together effectively. [FORMAL] ❑ *He had been accused of promoting disunity within the armed forces.*

dis|use /dɪsyus/ N-UNCOUNT [oft into N] If something falls into disuse, people stop using it. If something becomes worse as a result of disuse, it becomes worse because no one uses it. ❑ *...a church which has fallen into disuse.*

dis|used /dɪsyuzd/ ADJ A disused place or building is empty and is no longer used. ❑ *...a disused air field near the village of Ive.*

ditch /dɪtʃ/ (ditches, ditching, ditched) **1** N-COUNT A ditch is a long narrow channel cut into the ground at the side of a road or field. ❑ *Both vehicles ended up in a ditch.* **2** V-T If you ditch something that you have or are responsible for, you abandon it or get rid of it, because you no longer want it. [INFORMAL] ❑ *I decided to ditch the sofa bed.* **3** V-T If someone ditches someone, they end a relationship with that person. [INFORMAL] ❑ *I can't bring myself to ditch him and start again.* **4** V-T/V-I If a pilot ditches an aircraft or if it ditches, the pilot makes an emergency landing. ❑ *One American pilot was forced to ditch his jet in the Gulf.* **5** V-T If someone ditches school or work, they decide not to go to school or work, although they are supposed to go there. [AM, INFORMAL] ❑ *What do you say we ditch school and go to the mall?* **6** → see also last-ditch

dith|er /dɪðər/ (dithers, dithering, dithered) V-I When someone dithers, they hesitate because they are unable to make a quick decision about something. ❑ *We have been living together for five years, and he's still dithering over whether to marry.*

dit|to /dɪtoʊ/ In informal English, you can use ditto to represent a word or phrase that you have just used in order to avoid repeating it. In written lists, ditto can be represented by ditto marks (") under the symbol " – underneath the word that you want to repeat. ❑ *Lister's dead. Ditto three Miami drug dealers and a lady.*

dit|ty /dɪti/ (ditties) N-COUNT A ditty is a short or light-hearted song or poem. [HUMOROUS OR WRITTEN]

dit|zy /dɪtsi/ (ditzier, ditziest) also ditsy ADJ A ditzy person is silly and not very organized. [INFORMAL] ❑ *She may come across as ditzy, but she knows what's she's doing!*

di|uret|ic /daɪyʊərɛtɪk/ (diuretics) N-COUNT A diuretic is a substance which makes your body increase its production of waste fluids, with the result that you need to urinate more often than usual. [MEDICAL OR TECHNICAL] ❑ *Alcohol acts as a diuretic, making you even more dehydrated.* • ADJ Diuretic is also an adjective. ❑ *Many remedies effective in joint disease are primarily diuretic.*

di|ur|nal /daɪɜrnəl/ ADJ [usu ADJ n] Diurnal means happening or active during the daytime. [FORMAL] ❑ *Kangaroos are diurnal animals.*

diva /divə/ (divas) N-COUNT You can refer to a successful and famous female opera singer as a diva.

di|van /dɪvæn, daɪ-/ (divans) **1** N-COUNT A divan is a long soft seat that has no back or arms. **2** → See also color supplement

dive /daɪv/ (dives, diving, dived or dove, dived) **1** V-I If you dive into some water, you jump in head first with your arms held straight above your head. ❑ *He tried to escape by diving into a river.* ❑ *She was standing by a pool, about to dive in.* • N-COUNT Dive is also a noun. ❑ *Pat had earlier made a dive of 80 feet from the Chasm Bridge.* **2** V-I If you dive, you go under the surface of the sea or a lake, using special breathing equipment. ❑ *Bezanik is diving to collect marine organisms.* • N-COUNT Dive is also a noun. ❑ *This sighting occurred during my dive to a sunken wreck off Sardinia.* **3** V-I When birds and animals dive, they go quickly downward, head first, through the air or through water. ❑ *...a pelican which had just dived for a fish.* **4** V-I If you dive in a particular direction or into a particular place, you jump or move there quickly. ❑ *They dived into a taxi.* • N-COUNT Dive is also a noun. ❑ *He made a sudden dive for Uncle Jim's legs to try to trip him up.* **5** V-I It shares, profits, or figures dive, their value falls suddenly and by a large amount. [JOURNALISM] ❑ *They feared the stock could dive after its first day of trading.* ❑ *Profits have dived from $7.7m to $7.1m.* • N-COUNT Dive is also a noun. ❑ *Stock prices took a dive.* **6** N-COUNT If you describe a bar or club as a dive, you mean it is dirty and dark, and not very respectable. [INFORMAL, DISAPPROVAL] ❑ *We've played in all the little clubs and dives around Philadelphia.*

dive-bomb (dive-bombs, dive-bombing, dive-bombed) V-T If a plane dive-bombs an area, it suddenly flies down low over it to drop bombs onto it. ❑ *The Russians had to dive-bomb the cities to regain control.*

dive-bomb|er (dive-bombers) also dive bomber N-COUNT You can refer to a plane that flies down low over a place in order to drop bombs on it as a dive-bomber. ❑ *The port had been attacked by German dive bombers for the past five days.*

div|er /daɪvər/ (divers) N-COUNT A diver is a person who swims under water using special breathing equipment. ❑ *Police divers have recovered the body of a sixteen year old boy.*

di|verge /dɪvɜrdʒ/ (diverges, diverging, diverged) **1** V-RECIP If one thing diverges from another similar thing, the first thing becomes different from the second or develops differently from it. You can also say that two things diverge. ❑ *His interests increasingly diverged from those of his colleagues.* **2** V-RECIP [no cont] If one opinion or idea diverges from another, they contradict each other or are different. You can also say that two opinions or ideas diverge. ❑ *The view of the Estonian government does not diverge that far from Lipmaa's thinking.*

di|ver|gence /dɪvɜrdʒəns/ (divergences) N-VAR A divergence is a difference between two or more things, attitudes, or opinions. [FORMAL] ❑ *There's a substantial divergence of opinion within the party.*

di|ver|gent /dɪvɜrdʒənt/ ADJ Divergent things are different from each other. [FORMAL] ❑ *Two people who have divergent views on this question are George Watt and Bob Marr.*

di|verse /dɪvɜrs/ **1** ADJ If a group of things is diverse, it is made up of a wide variety of things. ❑ *The building houses a wide and diverse variety of antiques.* **2** ADJ Diverse people or things are very different from each other. ❑ *Albert Jones' new style will inevitably put him in touch with a much more diverse and perhaps younger audience.* **3** → See feature box at water

di|ver|si|fy /dɪvɜrsɪfaɪ/ (diversifies, diversifying, diversified) V-T/V-I When an organization or person diversifies into other things, or diversifies their product line, they increase the variety of things that they do or make. ❑ *The company's troubles*

diversion

started only when it diversified into new products. ❑ *As demand has increased, so manufacturers have been encouraged to diversify and improve quality.* ● **di|ver|si|fi|ca|tion** /dɪvɜrsɪfɪkeɪʃᵊn/ (**diversifications**) N-VAR ❑ *The seminar was to discuss diversification of agriculture.*

di|ver|sion /dɪvɜrʒᵊn/ (**diversions**) **1** N-COUNT A **diversion** is an action or event that attracts your attention away from what you are doing or concentrating on. ❑ *...armed robbers who escaped after throwing smoke bombs to create a diversion.* **2** N-COUNT A **diversion** is a special route arranged for traffic to follow when the normal route cannot be used. [BRIT]

| in AM, use **detour** |

3 N-UNCOUNT The **diversion of** something involves changing its course or destination. ❑ *...the illegal diversion of profits from secret arms sales.*

di|ver|sion|ary /dɪvɜrʒəneri/ ADJ A **diversionary** activity is one intended to attract people's attention away from something which you do not want them to think about, know about, or deal with. ❑ *It's thought the fires were started by the prisoners as a diversionary tactic.*

di|ver|sity /dɪvɜrsɪti/ (**diversities**) **1** N-VAR The **diversity** of something is the fact that it contains many very different elements. ❑ *...the cultural diversity of Latin America.* **2** N-SING A **diversity** of things is a range of things which are very different from each other. ❑ *Forslan's object is to gather as great a diversity of genetic material as possible.*

di|vert /dɪvɜrt, daɪ-/ (**diverts, diverting, diverted**) **1** V-T/V-I To **divert** vehicles or travelers means to make them follow a different route or go to a different destination than they originally intended. You can also say that someone or something **diverts** from a particular route or to a particular place. ❑ *We diverted a plane to rescue 100 passengers.* ❑ *The hospital has been diverting trauma patients to other hospitals because it does not have enough surgeons.* **2** V-T To **divert** money or resources means to cause them to be used for a different purpose. ❑ *A wave of deadly bombings has forced the United States to divert funds from reconstruction to security.* **3** V-T To **divert** a phone call means to send it to a different number or place from the one that was dialed by the person making the call. ❑ *He instructed the switchboard staff to divert all Laura's calls to him.* **4** V-T If you say that someone **diverts** your attention from something important or serious, you disapprove of them behaving or talking in a way that stops you thinking about it. [DISAPPROVAL] ❑ *They want to divert the attention of the people from the real issues.*

di|vert|ing /dɪvɜrtɪŋ, daɪ-/ ADJ If you describe something as **diverting**, you mean that it is amusing or entertaining. [OLD-FASHIONED]

di|vest /dɪvɛst, daɪ-/ (**divests, divesting, divested**) **1** V-T If you **divest** yourself of something that you own or are responsible for, you get rid of it or stop being responsible for it. [FORMAL] ❑ *The company divested itself of its oil interests.* **2** V-T If something or someone **is divested** of a particular quality, they lose that quality or it is taken away from them. [FORMAL] ❑ *...in the 1960s, when sexual love had been divested of sin.* ❑ *They have divested rituals of their original meaning.*

di|vide /dɪvaɪd/ (**divides, dividing, divided**) **1** V-T/V-I When people or things **are divided** or **divide** into smaller groups or parts, they become separated into smaller parts. ❑ *The physical benefits of exercise can be divided into three factors.* ❑ *Divide the pastry in half and roll out each piece.* **2** V-T If you **divide** something among people or things, you separate it into several parts or quantities which you distribute to the people or things. ❑ *Divide the sauce among 4 bowls.* **3** V-T If you **divide** a larger number by a smaller number or **divide** a smaller number into a larger number, you calculate how many times the smaller number can fit exactly into the larger number. ❑ *Measure the floor area of the greenhouse and divide it by six.* **4** V-T If a border or line **divides** two areas or **divides** an area into two, it keeps the two areas separate from each other. ❑ *...remote border areas dividing Tamil and Muslim settlements.* **5** V-T/V-I If people **divide** over something or if something **divides** them, it causes strong disagreement between them. ❑ *...the major issues that divided the country.* **6** N-COUNT A **divide** is a significant distinction between two groups, often one that causes conflict. ❑ *I began to notice a definite gender divide.*

diving

▶ **divide up 1** PHRASAL VERB If you **divide** something **up**, you separate it into smaller or more useful groups. ❑ *The idea is to divide up the country into four sectors.* **2** PHRASAL VERB If you **divide** something **up**, you share it out among a number of people or groups in approximately equal parts. ❑ *The aim was to divide up the business, give everyone an equal stake in its future.*

COLLOCATIONS

divide
NOUN **6**
noun + **divide**: class, gender
adjective + **divide**: generational, racial, sectarian
verb + **divide**: bridge, straddle

SYNONYMS

divide
VERB **1**
split: *We split the boards down the middle.*
separate: *Police moved in to separate the two groups.*
cut up: *Halve the tomatoes, then cut them up coarsely.*
partition: *Bedrooms have been created by partitioning a single larger room.*
segregate: *Police segregated the two rival camps of protesters.*

di|vid|ed high|way (**divided highways**) N-COUNT A **divided highway** is a road which has two lanes of traffic traveling in each direction with a strip of grass or concrete down the middle to separate the traffic. [AM]

| in BRIT, use **dual carriageway** |

divi|dend /dɪvɪdɛnd/ (**dividends**) **1** N-COUNT A **dividend** is the part of a company's profits which is paid to people who own shares in the company. [BUSINESS] ❑ *The first quarter dividend has been increased by nearly 4 percent.* **2** PHRASE If something **pays dividends**, it brings advantages at a later date. ❑ *Steps taken now to maximize your health will pay dividends later on.*

COLLOCATIONS

dividend
NOUN **1**
noun + **dividend**: cash, share
adjective + **dividend**: annual, final, interim, quarterly; tax-free
dividend + be + adjective: payable
verb + **dividend**: pay, reap, receive; increase, reinvest; declare

di|vid|er /dɪvaɪdər/ (**dividers**) **1** N-COUNT A **divider** is something which forms a barrier between two areas or sets of things. ❑ *A curtain acted as a divider between this class and another.* **2** N-PLURAL [also *a pair of* N] **Dividers** are an instrument used for measuring lines and for marking points along them. Dividers consist of two pointed arms joined with a hinge.

di|vid|ing line (**dividing lines**) **1** N-COUNT [usu sing, oft N *between* pl-n] A **dividing line** is a distinction or set of distinctions which marks the difference between two types of thing or two groups. ❑ *There's a very thin dividing line between joviality and hysteria.* **2** N-SING [oft N *between* pl-n] The **dividing line** between two areas is the boundary between them. ❑ *...people on both sides of the dividing line between Israel and the occupied territories.*

divi|na|tion /dɪvɪneɪʃᵊn/ N-UNCOUNT **Divination** is the art or practice of discovering what will happen in the future using supernatural means. [FORMAL]

di|vine /dɪvaɪn/ **1** ADJ You use **divine** to describe something that is provided by or relates to a god or goddess. ❑ *He suggested that the civil war had been a divine punishment.* ● **di|vine|ly** ADV ❑ *The law was divinely ordained.* **2** ADJ People use **divine** to express their pleasure or enjoyment of something. ❑ *Her carrot cake is divine.*

di|vine right (**divine rights**) N-COUNT [usu sing] If someone thinks they have a **divine right** to something, they think that it is their right to have it, without making any effort. ❑ *A degree does not give you a divine right to wealth.*

div|ing /daɪvɪŋ/ **1** N-UNCOUNT **Diving** is the activity of working or looking around underwater, using special breathing equipment. ❑ *...equipment and accessories for diving.* **2** N-UNCOUNT **Diving** is the sport or activity in which you

diving bell

jump into water head-first with your arms held straight above your head, usually from a diving board. ❑ *Weight is crucial in diving because the aim is to cause the smallest splash possible.*

div|ing bell (diving bells) N-COUNT A **diving bell** is a container shaped like a bell, in which people can breathe air while they work under water.

div|ing board (diving boards) N-COUNT A **diving board** is a board high above a swimming pool from which people can dive into the water.

di|vin|ity /dɪvɪnɪti/ (divinities) **1** N-UNCOUNT **Divinity** is the study of religion. **2** N-UNCOUNT [oft with poss] **Divinity** is the quality of being divine. ❑ *...a lasting faith in the divinity of Christ's word.* **3** N-COUNT A **divinity** is a god or goddess. ❑ *The three statues above are probably Roman divinities.*

di|vi|sible /dɪvɪzɪbəl/ ADJ [v-link ADJ by num] If one number is **divisible** by another number, the second number can be divided into the first exactly, with nothing left over. ❑ *Twenty-eight is divisible by seven.*

di|vi|sion ✦✧ /dɪvɪʒən/ (divisions) **1** N-UNCOUNT The **division** of a large unit into two or more distinct parts is the act of separating it into these parts. ❑ *...the unification of Germany, after its division into two states at the end of World War Two.* **2** N-UNCOUNT The **division** of something among people or things is its separation into parts which are distributed among the people or things. ❑ *The current division of labor between workers and management will alter.* **3** N-UNCOUNT **Division** is the arithmetical process of dividing one number into another number. ❑ *I taught my daughter how to do division at the age of six.* **4** N-VAR A **division** is a significant distinction or argument between two groups, which causes the two groups to be considered as very different and separate. ❑ *The division between the prosperous west and the impoverished east remains.* **5** N-COUNT In a large organization, a **division** is a group of departments whose work is done in the same place or is connected with similar tasks. ❑ *...the bank's Latin American division.* **6** N-COUNT A **division** is a group of military units which fight as a single unit. ❑ *Several armoured divisions are being moved from Germany.* **7** N-COUNT In some sports, such as soccer, baseball, and basketball, a **division** is one of the groups of teams which make up a league. The teams in each division are of the same level, and they all play against each other during the season. ❑ *Chico State reached the NCAA Division II national finals last season.*

SYNONYMS

division
NOUN **4**
rift: *The serious rifts within the country could lead to civil war.*
disagreement: *There was a disagreement over who should be invited to the conference.*
split: *They were accused of trying to provoke a split in the party.*
feud: *a long and bitter feud between the state government and the villagers.*
schism: *The church seems to be on the brink of schism.*

di|vi|sion|al /dɪvɪʒənəl/ ADJ [ADJ n] **Divisional** means relating to a division of a large organization or group. ❑ *She is divisional sales manager for the Philadelphia region.*

di|vi|sion sign (division signs) N-COUNT A **division sign** is the symbol ÷ used between two numbers to show that the first number has to be divided by the second.

di|vi|sive /dɪvaɪsɪv/ ADJ Something that is **divisive** causes unfriendliness and argument between people. ❑ *Abortion has always been a divisive issue.*

di|vorce ✦✧ /dɪvɔrs/ (divorces, divorcing, divorced) **1** N-COUNT A **divorce** is the formal ending of a marriage by law. ❑ *Numerous marriages now end in divorce.* **2** V-RECIP If two people **divorce** or if one of them **divorces** the other, their marriage is legally ended. ❑ *He and Lillian had got divorced.* ❑ *I am absolutely furious that he divorced me to marry her.* **3** N-SING A **divorce** of one thing from another, or a divorce between two things is a separation between them which is permanent or is likely to be permanent. ❑ *...this divorce of Christian culture from the roots of faith.* **4** V-T If you say that one thing cannot **be divorced from** another, you mean that the two things cannot be considered as different and separate things. ❑ *Good management in the police cannot be divorced from accountability.* ❑ *Democracy cannot be divorced from social and economic progress.*

COLLOCATIONS

divorce
NOUN **1**
adjective + **divorce**: acrimonious, bitter, messy, painful; amicable
verb + **divorce**: finalize, obtain, seek, want; grant

di|vor|cé /dɪvɔrseɪ, -vɔrseɪ/ (divorcés) N-COUNT A **divorcé** is a man who is divorced. [mainly AM]

di|vorced /dɪvɔrst/ **1** ADJ Someone who is **divorced** from their former husband or wife has separated from them and is no longer legally married to them. ❑ *He is divorced, with a young son.* **2** ADJ [v-link ADJ from n] If you say that one thing **is divorced from** another, you mean that the two things are very different and separate from each other. ❑ *...speculative theories divorced from political reality.*

di|vor|cee /dɪvɔrseɪ, -si/ (divorcees) N-COUNT A **divorcee** is someone who is divorced. [mainly BRIT] ❑ *About half of all divorcees remarry within five years of their divorce.*

di|vor|cée /dɪvɔrseɪ, -si/ (divorcées) N-COUNT A **divorcée** is a woman who is divorced. [mainly AM]

div|ot /dɪvət/ (divots) N-COUNT A **divot** is a small piece of grass and earth which is dug out accidentally, for example, by a golf club.

di|vulge /dɪvʌldʒ/ (divulges, divulging, divulged) V-T If you **divulge** a piece of secret or private information, you tell it to someone. [FORMAL] ❑ *Officials refuse to divulge details of the negotiations.*

div|vy /dɪvi/ (divvies, divvying, divvied)
▶ **divvy up** PHRASAL VERB If you **divvy up** something such as money or food, you share it out. [INFORMAL] ❑ *Johnson was free to divvy up his share of the money as he chose.*

Di|wa|li /dɪwɑli/ also **Divali** N-UNCOUNT **Diwali** is a Hindu festival held in honor of Lakshmi, the goddess of wealth. It is celebrated in October or November with the lighting of lamps in homes and temples, and with prayers to Lakshmi.

DIY /di aɪ waɪ/ N-UNCOUNT **DIY** is the activity of making or repairing things yourself, especially in your home. **DIY** is an abbreviation for **do-it-yourself**. [mainly BRIT] ❑ *He's useless at DIY. He won't even put up a shelf.*

VOCABULARY IN CONTEXT

DIY

Decorating a room is easy with the right preparation.

Use drop **cloths** to cover the furniture and carpets, and wear old clothes or **overalls**. Remove any **hooks** or nails with **pliers** and fill in any holes or **cracks**. Using a **screwdriver**, loosen or remove any door **handles** or knockers.

Rub down **plaster** or woodwork with **sandpaper**. When painting window frames, make sure you put **masking tape** over the edges of the glass to protect it.

If putting up **wallpaper**, use a **stepladder** so you can easily reach the full length of the wall. Start patterned wallpaper at the window and work around the room. Measure the height of the room carefully and add ten centimeters, which you can then **trim** at the ceiling and **baseboard**.

diz|zy /dɪzi/ (dizzier, dizziest) **1** ADJ If you feel **dizzy**, you feel that you are losing your balance and are about to fall. ▫ *Her head still hurt, and she felt slightly dizzy and disoriented.* • **diz|zi|ness** N-UNCOUNT ▫ *His head injury causes dizziness and nausea.* **2** ADJ You can use **dizzy** to describe someone who is careless and forgets things, but is easy to like. ▫ *She is famed for playing dizzy blondes.* **3** PHRASE If you say that someone has reached the **dizzy heights** of something, you are emphasizing that they have reached a very high level by achieving it. [HUMOROUS, EMPHASIS] ▫ *I escalated to the dizzy heights of director's secretary.*

diz|zy|ing /dɪziɪŋ/ ADJ You can use **dizzying** to emphasize that something impresses you, though it makes you a bit confused or unsteady. [mainly AM, EMPHASIS] ▫ *...a dizzying array of choices.* ▫ *We're descending now at dizzying speed.*

DJ /diː dʒeɪ/ (DJs) also **D.J.**, **dj** N-COUNT A **DJ** is the same as a disc jockey.

DM /diː ɛm/ (DMs) N-COUNT If you send someone a **DM**, you send them a private message via social media. **DM** is short for 'direct message.' [COMPUTING]

DNA /diː ɛn eɪ/ **1** N-UNCOUNT **DNA** is an acid in the chromosomes in the center of the cells of living things. DNA determines the particular structure and functions of every cell and is responsible for characteristics being passed on from parents to their children. **DNA** is an abbreviation for 'deoxyribonucleic acid.' ▫ *A routine DNA sample was taken.* **2** → See feature box at **genetics**

DNA fin|ger|print|ing N-UNCOUNT **DNA fingerprinting** is the same as **genetic fingerprinting**.

DNA test (DNA tests) N-COUNT A **DNA test** is a test in which someone's DNA is analyzed, for example, to see if they have committed a particular crime or are the parent of a particular child. • **DNA test|ing** N-UNCOUNT ▫ *They took samples from his hair for DNA testing.*

DO
① AUXILIARY VERB USES
② OTHER VERB USES
③ NOUN USES

---

① **do** ♦♦♦ /də, STRONG duː/ (does, doing, did, done)

Do is used as an auxiliary with the simple present tense. Did is used as an auxiliary with the simple past tense. In spoken English, negative forms of **do** are often shortened, for example, **do not** is shortened to **don't** and **did not** is shortened to **didn't**.

1 AUX **Do** is used to form the negative of main verbs, by putting 'not' after 'do' and before the main verb in its infinitive form, that is the form without 'to.' ▫ *They don't want to work.* ▫ *I did not know Jamie had a knife.* **2** AUX **Do** is used to form questions, by putting the subject after 'do' and before the main verb in its infinitive form, that is the form without 'to.' ▫ *Do you like music?* ▫ *What did he say?* **3** AUX **Do** is used in question tags. ▫ *You know about Andy, don't you?* **4** AUX You use **do** when you are confirming or contradicting a statement containing 'do,' or giving a negative or positive answer to a question. ▫ *"Did he think there was anything suspicious going on?"—"Yes, he did."* **5** V-T/V-I **Do** can be used to refer back to another verb group when you are comparing or contrasting two things, or saying that they are the same. ▫ *I make more money than he does.* ▫ *I had fantasies, as do all mothers, about how life would be when my girls were grown.* **6** V-T You use **do** after 'so' and 'nor' to say that the same statement is true for two people or groups. ▫ *You know that's true, and so do I.*

② **do** ♦♦♦ /duː/ (does, doing, did, done)

Do is used in a large number of expressions which are explained under other words in the dictionary. For example, the expression 'easier said than done' is explained at 'easy.'

1 V-T When you **do** something, you take some action or perform an activity or task. **Do** is often used instead of a more specific verb, to talk about a common action involving a particular thing. For example you can say 'do your hair' instead of 'brush your hair.' ▫ *I was trying to do some work.* ▫ *After lunch Elizabeth and I did the dishes.* **2** V-T **Do** can be used to stand for any verb group, or to refer back to another verb group, including one that was in a previous sentence. ▫ *What are you doing?* **3** V-T You can use **do** in a clause at the beginning of a sentence after words like 'what' and 'all,' to give special emphasis to the information that comes at the end of the sentence. [EMPHASIS] ▫ *All she does is complain.* **4** V-T If you **do** a particular thing with something, you use it in that particular way. ▫ *I was allowed to do whatever I wanted with my life.* **5** V-T If you **do** something about a problem, you take action to try to solve it. ▫ *They refuse to do anything about the real cause of crime: poverty.* **6** V-T If an action or event **does** a particular thing, such as harm or good, it has that result or effect. ▫ *A few bombs can do a lot of damage.* **7** V-T If you ask someone what they **do**, you want to know what their job or profession is. ▫ *"What does your father do?"—"Well, he's a civil servant."* **8** V-T If you **are doing** something, you are busy or active in some way, or have planned an activity for some time in the future. ▫ *Are you doing anything tomorrow night?* **9** V-I If you say that someone or something **does** well or badly, you are talking about how successful or unsuccessful they are. ▫ *Connie did well at school and graduated with honors.* **10** V-T You can use **do** when referring to the speed or rate that something or someone achieves or is able to achieve. ▫ *They were doing 70 miles an hour.* **11** V-T If someone **does** drugs, they take illegal drugs. ▫ *I don't do drugs.* **12** V-T/V-I If you say that something will **do** or will **do** you, you mean that there is enough of it or that it is of good enough quality to meet your requirements or to satisfy you. ▫ *Anything to create a scene and attract attention will do.* **13** V-T If you **do** a subject, author, or book, you study them at school or college. [mainly BRIT, SPOKEN] ▫ *She planned to do math at night school.* **14** PHRASE If you say that you **could do with** something, you mean that you need it or would benefit from it. ▫ *I could do with a cup of tea.* **15** PHRASE You can ask someone **what** they **did with** something as another way of asking them where they put it. ▫ *What did you do with that notebook?* **16** PHRASE If you ask **what** someone or something **is doing** in a particular place, you are asking why they are there. ▫ *"Dr. Campbell," he said, clearly surprised. "What are you doing here?"* **17** PHRASE If you say that one thing **has** something **to do with** or **is** something **to do with** another thing, you mean that the two things are connected or that the first thing is about the second thing. ▫ *Mr. Butterfield denies having anything to do with the episode.*

▶ **do away with** **1** PHRASAL VERB To **do away with** something means to remove it completely or put an end to it. ▫ *The long-range goal must be to do away with nuclear weapons altogether.* **2** PHRASAL VERB If one person **does away with** another, the first murders the second. If you **do away with** yourself, you kill yourself. [INFORMAL] ▫ *...a woman whose husband had made several attempts to do away with her.*

▶ **do in** PHRASAL VERB To **do** someone **in** means to kill them. [INFORMAL] ▫ *Whoever did him in removed a man who was brave as well as ruthless.*

▶ **do up** **1** PHRASAL VERB If you **do** something **up**, you fasten it. ▫ *Mari did up the buttons.* **2** PHRASAL VERB If you say that a person or room **is done up** in a particular way, you mean they are dressed or decorated in that way, often a way that is rather ridiculous or extreme. ▫ *...a small salon done up in saffron silks and plum velvet cushions.*

▶ **do without** **1** PHRASAL VERB If you **do without** something you need, want, or usually have, you are able to survive, continue, or succeed although you do not have it. ▫ *We can't do without the help of your organization.* **2** PHRASAL VERB If you say that you could **do without** something, you mean that you would prefer not to have it or it is of no benefit to you. [INFORMAL] ▫ *He could do without her rhetorical questions at five o'clock in the morning.*

③ **do** /duː/ (dos) PHRASE If someone tells you the **dos and don'ts** of a particular situation, they advise you what you should and should not do in that situation. ▫ *Please advise me on the most suitable color print film and some dos and don'ts.*

do. do. is an old-fashioned written abbreviation for **ditto**.

do|able /duːəbəl/ If something is **doable**, it is possible to do it. ▫ *Is this project something that you think is doable?*

DOB also **d.o.b.** DOB is a written abbreviation for **date of birth**, used especially on official forms.

do|ber|man /doʊbərmən/ (dobermans) N-COUNT A **doberman** is a type of large dog with short dark fur. ▫ *...my pet doberman.*

doc /dɒk/ (docs) N-VOC; N-COUNT Some people call a doctor doc. [INFORMAL]

doc|ile /dɒsaɪl/ ADJ A person or animal that is **docile** is quiet, not aggressive, and easily controlled. ❏ ...docile, obedient children. • **do|cil|ity** /dɒsɪlɪti/ N-UNCOUNT ❏ ...a breed of cattle known for their docility. • **docile|ly** ADV [ADV with v] ❏ I heard myself consenting docilely to this suggestion.

dock /dɒk/ (docks, docking, docked) **1** N-COUNT [also in/into N] A **dock** is an enclosed area in a harbor where ships go to be loaded, unloaded, and repaired. ❏ She headed for the docks, thinking that Ricardo might be hiding in one of the boats. **2** N-COUNT A **dock** is a platform for loading vehicles or trains. [AM] ❏ The truck left the loading dock with hoses still attached. **3** N-COUNT A **dock** is a small structure at the edge of water where boats can tie up, especially one that is privately owned. [AM] ❏ He had a house there and a dock and a little aluminum boat. **4** V-T/V-I When a ship **docks** or **is docked**, it is brought into a dock. ❏ The crash happened as the ferry attempted to dock on Staten Island. **5** V-T If you **dock** someone's pay or money, you take some of the money away. ❏ He threatens to dock her fee. **6** V-T If you **dock** someone points in a contest, you take away some of the points that they have. **7** V-RECIP When one spacecraft **docks** or **is docked** with another, the two crafts join together in space. ❏ The space shuttle Atlantis is scheduled to dock with Russia's Mir space station. **8** N-SING In a law court, the **dock** is where the person accused of a crime stands or sits. ❏ What about the odd chance that you do put an innocent man in the dock?

dock|er /dɒkər/ (dockers) N-COUNT A **docker** is a person who works on the docks, loading and unloading ships. [BRIT]

in AM, use **longshoreman**

dock|et /dɒkɪt/ (dockets) N-COUNT A **docket** is a list of cases waiting for trial in a law court. [mainly AM]

dock|side /dɒksaɪd/ N-SING [oft N n] The **dockside** is the part of a dock that is next to the water.

dock work|er (dock workers) also **dockworker** N-COUNT A **dock worker** is a person who works on the docks, loading and unloading ships.

dock|yard /dɒkyɑrd/ (dockyards) N-COUNT A **dockyard** is a place where ships are built, maintained, and repaired.

doc|tor /dɒktər/ (doctors, doctoring, doctored) **1** N-COUNT; N-TITLE; N-VOC A **doctor** is someone who has a degree in medicine and treats people who are sick or injured. ❏ Do not discontinue the treatment without consulting your doctor. **2** N-COUNT; N-TITLE; N-VOC A **dentist** or **veterinarian** can also be called **doctor**. [AM] **3** N-COUNT The **doctor's** is used to refer to the office where a doctor works. ❏ I have an appointment at the doctor's. **4** N-COUNT; N-TITLE A **doctor** is someone who has been awarded the highest academic or honorary degree by a university. ❏ He is a doctor of philosophy. **5** V-T If someone **doctors** something, they change it in order to deceive people. ❏ They doctored the prints, deepening the lines to make her look as awful as possible.

doc|tor|al /dɒktərəl/ ADJ [ADJ n] A **doctoral** thesis or piece of research is written or done in order to obtain a doctorate.

doc|tor|ate /dɒktərɪt/ (doctorates) N-COUNT A **doctorate** is the highest degree awarded by a university. ❏ Professor Lanphier obtained his doctorate in social psychology from the University of Michigan.

Doc|tor of Phi|loso|phy (Doctors of Philosophy) N-COUNT A **Doctor of Philosophy** is someone who has a **Ph.D.**

doc|tor's of|fice (doctor's offices) N-COUNT A **doctor's office** is the room or clinic where a doctor works. [AM] ❏ Some people made it as far as a doctor's office, only to pass out and die within minutes.

doc|tor's sur|gery (doctor's surgeries) N-COUNT A **doctor's surgery** is the same as a **doctor's office**. [BRIT]

doc|tri|naire /dɒktrɪnɛər/ ADJ If you say that someone is **doctrinaire** or has a **doctrinaire** attitude, you disapprove of them because they have fixed principles which they try to force on other people. [FORMAL, DISAPPROVAL] ❏ He is firm but not doctrinaire.

doc|tri|nal /dɒktrɪnəl/ ADJ **Doctrinal** means relating to doctrines. [FORMAL] ❏ Doctrinal differences were vigorously debated among religious leaders.

doc|trine /dɒktrɪn/ (doctrines) N-VAR A **doctrine** is a set of principles or beliefs, especially religious ones. ❏ ...the Marxist doctrine of perpetual revolution.

docu|dra|ma /dɒkyʊdrɑmə/ (docudramas) N-VAR A **docudrama** is a movie based on events that really happened. Docudramas are usually shown on television rather than in movie theaters.

docu|ment (documents, documenting, documented)

The noun is pronounced /dɒkyəmənt/. The verb is pronounced /dɒkyəmɛnt/.

1 N-COUNT A **document** is one or more official pieces of paper with writing on them. ❏ She produces legal documents for a downtown Seattle law firm. **2** N-COUNT A **document** is a piece of text or graphics, for example, a letter, that is stored as a file on a computer and that you can access in order to read it or change it. [COMPUTING] ❏ When you are finished typing, remember to save your document. **3** V-T If you **document** something, you make a detailed record of it in writing or on film or tape. ❏ He wrote a book documenting his prison experiences. **4** → See feature box at **research**

COLLOCATIONS

document
NOUN
1
noun + **document**: court, identity, policy, travel
adjective + **document**: historical, legal; classified, confidential, important; fake, false, genuine, original
verb + **document**: file, obtain, release; forge, leak; prepare, sign
2
verb + **document**: edit, open, save, send

docu|men|tary /dɒkyəmɛntəri, -tri/ (documentaries) **1** N-COUNT A **documentary** is a television or radio program, or a movie, which shows real events or provides information about a particular subject. ❏ ...a TV documentary on homelessness. **2** ADJ [ADJ n] **Documentary** evidence consists of things that are written down. ❏ The government says it has documentary evidence that the two countries were planning military action.

docu|men|ta|tion /dɒkyəmɛnteɪʃən/ N-UNCOUNT **Documentation** consists of documents which provide proof or evidence of something, or are a record of something. ❏ Passengers must carry proper documentation.

dod|der|ing /dɒdərɪŋ/ ADJ [usu ADJ n] If you refer to someone as a **doddering** old man or woman, you are saying in a disrespectful way that they are old and not strong. [DISAPPROVAL] ❏ ...a doddering old man making his will before he's too senile.

dod|dery /dɒdəri/ ADJ Someone who is **doddery** walks in an unsteady way, especially because of old age.

dodge /dɒdʒ/ (dodges, dodging, dodged) **1** V-I If you **dodge**, you move suddenly, often to avoid being hit, caught, or seen. ❏ I dodged back into the alley and waited a minute. **2** V-T If you **dodge** something, you avoid it by quickly moving aside or out of reach so that it cannot hit or reach you. ❏ He desperately dodged a speeding car trying to run him down. **3** V-T If you **dodge** something, you deliberately avoid thinking about it or dealing with it, often by being deceitful. ❏ He boasts of dodging military service by feigning illness. • N-COUNT **Dodge** is also a noun. ❏ This was not just a tax dodge

dodg|em /dɒdʒəm/ (dodgems) N-COUNT [usu pl] A **dodgem** or **dodgem car** is the same as a **bumper car**. [mainly BRIT, TRADEMARK]

dodg|er /dɒdʒər/ (dodgers) **1** N-COUNT [usu n n] A **dodger** is someone who avoids doing a duty or paying a charge, for example, paying taxes or for train travel. ❏ ...tax dodgers who hide their interest earnings. **2** → see also **draft dodger**

dodo /doʊdoʊ/ (dodos or dodoes) **1** N-COUNT A **dodo** was a very large bird that was unable to fly. Dodos are now extinct. **2** N-COUNT If you refer to someone as a **dodo**, you think they are foolish or silly. [INFORMAL, DISAPPROVAL]

doe /doʊ/ (does) N-COUNT A **doe** is an adult female deer, rabbit, or hare.

doer /duər/ (doers) N-COUNT If you refer to someone as a **doer**, you mean that they do jobs promptly and efficiently, without spending a lot of time thinking about them. ❑ *Robertson was a doer, not a thinker.*

does /dəz, STRONG dʌz/ **Does** is the third person singular in the present tense of **do** ①.

doesn't ✦✦✦ /dʌzᵊnt/ **Doesn't** is the usual spoken form of 'does not.'

doff /dɒf/ (**doffs, doffing, doffed**) V-T If you **doff** your hat or coat, you take it off. [OLD-FASHIONED] ❑ *The peasants doff their hats.*

dog ✦✦◇ /dɒg/ (**dogs, dogging, dogged**) **1** N-COUNT A **dog** is a very common four-legged animal that is often kept by people as a pet or to guard or hunt. There are many different breeds of dog. ❑ *The British are renowned as a nation of dog lovers.* **2** N-COUNT People use **dog** to refer to something that they consider unsatisfactory or of poor quality. [AM, INFORMAL, DISAPPROVAL] ❑ *It's a real dog.* **3** V-T If problems or injuries **dog** you, they are with you all the time. ❑ *His career has been dogged by bad luck.* **4** → see also **dogged** **5** PHRASE You use **dog eat dog** to express your disapproval of a situation where everyone wants to succeed and is willing to harm other people in order to do so. [DISAPPROVAL] ❑ *It is very much dog eat dog out there.* **6** PHRASE If you say that something **is going to the dogs**, you mean that it is becoming weaker and worse in quality. [INFORMAL, DISAPPROVAL] ❑ *They sit doing nothing while the country goes to the dogs.*

COLLOCATIONS

dog
VERB **3**
noun + **dog**: accusations, allegations, controversy, rumors, scandal; bad luck, ill health, injury, misfortune, problems; criticism, questions

---

dog col|lar (**dog collars**) **1** N-COUNT A **dog collar** is a collar worn by a dog. **2** N-COUNT A **dog collar** is a stiff, round, white collar that fastens at the back and that is worn by Christian priests and ministers. [INFORMAL]

dog days N-PLURAL The hottest part of the summer is sometimes referred to as the **dog days**. [mainly AM] ❑ *We're well into the dog days of summer.*

dog-eared ADJ A book or piece of paper that is **dog-eared** has been used so much that the corners of the pages are turned down or torn. ❑ *...dog-eared copies of ancient history books.*

dog|fight /dɒgfaɪt/ (**dogfights**) **1** N-COUNT A **dogfight** is a fight between fighter planes, in which they fly close to one another and move very fast. **2** N-COUNT If you say that organizations or people are involved in a **dogfight**, you mean they are struggling very hard against each other in order to succeed. ❑ *The three leading contenders were locked in a dogfight.*

dog|fish /dɒgfɪʃ/ (**dogfish**) N-COUNT A **dogfish** is a small shark. There are several kinds of dogfish.

dog|ged /dɒgɪd/ ADJ [ADJ n] If you describe someone's actions as **dogged**, you mean that they are determined to continue with something even if it becomes difficult or dangerous. ❑ *They have, through sheer dogged determination, slowly gained respect for their efforts.* • **dog|ged|ly** ADV ❑ *She would fight doggedly for her rights as the children's mother.* • **dog|ged|ness** N-UNCOUNT ❑ *Most of my accomplishments came as the result of sheer doggedness rather than talent.*

dog|ger|el /dɒgərᵊl/ N-UNCOUNT If you refer to a poem as **doggerel**, you mean that it is very bad poetry, or that it is funny because it is deliberately bad. [DISAPPROVAL] ❑ *...fragments of meaningless doggerel.*

dog|gie /dɒgi/ (**doggies**) also **doggy** N-COUNT **Doggie** is a child's word for a dog.

dog|gie bag (**doggie bags**) also **doggy bag** N-COUNT If you ask for a **doggie bag** in a restaurant, you ask for any food you have not eaten to be put into a bag for you to take home.

dog|gone /dɒgɔn/ ADJ [ADJ n] People sometimes use **doggone** to emphasize what they are saying, especially when they are annoyed. [AM, INFORMAL, EMPHASIS] ❑ *He's just doing his doggone job.* • ADV [ADV before adj] **Doggone** is also an adverb. ❑ *It was so doggone hot.*

dog|gy /dɒgi/ (**doggies**) → see **doggie**

dog|house /dɒghaʊs/ (**doghouses**) **1** N-COUNT A **doghouse** is a small building made especially for a dog to sleep in. [AM]

in BRIT, use **kennel**

2 PHRASE If you are **in the doghouse**, people are annoyed or angry with you. [INFORMAL] ❑ *Her husband was in the doghouse for leaving her to cope on her own.*

dog|leg /dɒglɛg/ (**doglegs**) also **dog-leg** N-COUNT A **dogleg** is a sharp bend in a road or a path.

dog|ma /dɒgmə/ (**dogmas**) N-VAR If you refer to a belief or a system of beliefs as a **dogma**, you disapprove of it because people are expected to accept that it is true, without questioning it. [DISAPPROVAL] ❑ *Their political dogma has blinded them to the real needs of the country.*

dog|mat|ic /dɒgmætɪk/ ADJ If you say that someone is **dogmatic**, you are critical of them because they are convinced that they are right, and refuse to consider that other opinions might also be justified. [DISAPPROVAL] ❑ *Many writers at this time held rigidly dogmatic views.* • **dog|mati|cal|ly** /dɒgmætɪkli/ ADV [ADV with v] ❑ *Bennett had wanted this list of books to be dogmatically imposed on the nation's universities.*

dog|ma|tism /dɒgmətɪzəm/ N-UNCOUNT If you refer to an opinion as **dogmatism**, you are criticizing it for being strongly stated without considering all the relevant facts or other people's opinions. [DISAPPROVAL] ❑ *We cannot allow dogmatism to stand in the way of progress.*

do-gooder (**do-gooders**) N-COUNT If you describe someone as a **do-gooder**, you mean that they do things which they think will help other people, although you think that they are interfering. [DISAPPROVAL]

dog tag (**dog tags**) N-COUNT [usu pl] **Dog tags** are small rectangular pieces of metal that are worn on a chain around the neck by members of the United States armed forces, as a form of identification.

dog-tired ADJ [v-link ADJ] If you say that you are **dog-tired**, you are emphasizing that you are extremely tired. [INFORMAL, EMPHASIS] ❑ *By dusk we were dog-tired and heading for home.*

dog|wood /dɒgwʊd/ (**dogwoods**) N-VAR A **dogwood** is a tree or bush that has groups of small pink or white flowers surrounded by four large leaves.

doh /doʊ/ also **d'oh** EXCLAM People sometimes say **doh** to show that they have made a silly mistake. [mainly AM, INFORMAL, HUMOROUS] ❑ *"It was the most stupid decision of my whole life," said Jack as he let out a Homer Simpson-style "Doh" to illustrate the folly of his actions.*

doi|ly /dɔɪli/ (**doilies**) N-COUNT A **doily** is a small, round piece of paper or cloth that has a pattern of tiny holes in it. Doilies are put on plates under cakes and sandwiches.

do|ings /duɪŋz/ N-PLURAL [usu with poss] Someone's **doings** are their activities at a particular time. ❑ *Max and Brooke displayed a lively interest in the daily doings of the center.*

do-it-yourself N-UNCOUNT **Do-it-yourself** is the same as **DIY**.

Dol|by /doʊlbi/ N-UNCOUNT [oft N n] **Dolby** is a system which reduces the background noise on recorded sound. [TRADEMARK] ❑ *...built-in speakers with Dolby audio processing.*

dol|ce vita /dɒltʃeɪ vitə/ N-SING [la/the N] People sometimes use **la dolce vita** or the **dolce vita** to mean a life that is full of pleasure and luxury. ❑ *This is where money is made and there's little time for la dolce vita.*

dol|drums /doʊldrəmz/ PHRASE If an activity or situation is **in the doldrums**, it is very quiet and nothing new or exciting is happening. ❑ *The economy is in the doldrums.*

dole /doʊl/ **1** N-UNCOUNT The **dole** or **dole** is money that is given regularly by the government to people who are unemployed. [mainly BRIT]

in AM, usually use **welfare**

2 PHRASE Someone who is **on the dole** is registered as unemployed and receives money from the government. [mainly BRIT]

in AM, usually use **on welfare**

dole|ful /doʊlfəl/ ADJ A **doleful** expression, manner, or voice is depressing and miserable. ❑ *He gave me a long, doleful look.* • **dole|ful|ly** ADV [ADV with v] ❑ *"I don't know why they left," he said dolefully.*

doll /dɒl/ (dolls) N-COUNT A **doll** is a child's toy which looks like a small person or baby.

dol|lar ♦♦♦ /dɒlər/ (dollars) N-COUNT The **dollar** is the unit of money used in the U.S., Canada, Australia, and some other countries. It is represented by the symbol $, the dollar sign. A dollar is divided into one hundred smaller units called cents. ❑ *She gets paid seven dollars an hour.* • N-SING The **dollar** is also used to refer to the American currency system. ❑ *In early trading in Tokyo, the dollar fell sharply against the yen.*

doll|house /dɒlhaʊs/ (dollhouses)

in BRIT, use **doll's house**

N-COUNT A **dollhouse** is a toy in the form of a small house, which contains tiny dolls and furniture for children to play with.

dol|lop /dɒləp/ (dollops) N-COUNT [usu N of n] A **dollop** of soft or sticky food is a large spoonful of it. [INFORMAL] ❑ *...a dollop of cream.*

dol|ly /dɒli/ (dollies) **1** N-COUNT A **dolly** is a child's word for a doll. **2** N-COUNT A **dolly** is a low cart with wheels that is used for moving heavy objects, for example, in a factory. [AM] ❑ *...dozens of vendors pushing dollies stacked high with boxes.*

dol|phin /dɒlfɪn/ (dolphins) **1** N-COUNT A **dolphin** is a mammal which lives in the sea and looks like a large fish with a pointed mouth. **2** → See feature box at **animal**

dolt /doʊlt/ (dolts) N-COUNT If you call someone a **dolt**, you think they are stupid, or have done something stupid. [INFORMAL, DISAPPROVAL]

do|main /doʊmeɪn/ (domains) **1** N-COUNT A **domain** is a particular field of thought, activity, or interest, especially one over which someone has control, influence, or rights. [FORMAL] ❑ *...the great experimenters in the domain of art.* **2** N-COUNT On the internet, a **domain** is a set of addresses that shows, for example, the category or geographical area that an Internet address belongs to. [COMPUTING] ❑ *An Internet society spokeswoman said .org domain users will not experience any disruptions during the transition.*

do|main name (domain names) N-COUNT A **domain name** is the name of a person's or an organization's website on the internet, for example, 'collins.co.uk.' [COMPUTING] ❑ *Users need to find out if a domain name is already registered or is still available.*

dome /doʊm/ (domes) **1** N-COUNT A **dome** is a round roof. ❑ *...the dome of the Capitol.* **2** N-COUNT A **dome** is any object that has a similar shape to a dome. ❑ *...the dome of the hill.*

domed /doʊmd/ ADJ Something that is **domed** is in the shape of a dome. ❑ *...the great hall with its domed ceiling.*

do|mes|tic ♦♦◊ /dəmɛstɪk/ **1** ADJ **Domestic** political activities, events, and situations happen or exist within one particular country. ❑ *...over 100 domestic flights a day to 30 leading U.S. destinations.* **2** → see also **gross domestic product** **3** ADJ [ADJ n] **Domestic** duties and activities are concerned with the running of a home and family. ❑ *...a plan for sharing domestic chores.* **4** ADJ [ADJ n] **Domestic** items and services are intended to be used in people's homes rather than in factories or offices. ❑ *...domestic appliances.* **5** ADJ A **domestic** situation or atmosphere is one which involves a family and their home. ❑ *It was a scene of such domestic bliss.* **6** ADJ A **domestic** animal is one that is not wild and is kept either on a farm to produce food or in someone's home as a pet. ❑ *...a domestic cat.*

---SYNONYMS---

domestic
ADJ
1
internal: *The country stepped up internal security.*
national: *...major national and international issues.*
home: *Europe's software companies still have a growing home market.*
3
household: *...household chores.*
home: *...cheap but healthy home cooking.*

---

do|mes|ti|cate /dəmɛstɪkeɪt/ (domesticates, domesticating, domesticated) V-T When people **domesticate** wild animals or plants, they bring them under control and use them to produce food or as pets. ❑ *We domesticated the dog to help us with hunting.*

do|mes|ti|cat|ed /dəmɛstɪkeɪtɪd/ ADJ Someone who is **domesticated** willingly does household tasks such as cleaning. ❑ *It's true that I have never been very domesticated.*

do|mes|ti|city /doʊmɛstɪsɪti/ N-UNCOUNT **Domesticity** is the state of being at home with your family. ❑ *...a small rebellion against routine and cosy domesticity.*

do|mes|tic vio|lence N-UNCOUNT **Domestic violence** is violence that takes place in the home, especially by one person against their partner. ❑ *Women are still the main victims of domestic violence.*

domi|cile /dɒmɪsaɪl/ (domiciles) N-COUNT [oft with poss] Your **domicile** is the place where you live. [FORMAL]

domi|ciled /dɒmɪsaɪld/ ADJ If you are **domiciled** in a particular place, you live there. [FORMAL] ❑ *Frank is currently domiciled in Berlin.*

domi|nance /dɒmɪnəns/ N-UNCOUNT The **dominance** of a particular person or thing is the fact that they are more powerful, successful, or important than other people or things. ❑ *The latest fighting appears to be an attempt by each group to establish dominance over the other.*

domi|nant /dɒmɪnənt/ ADJ Someone or something that is **dominant** is more powerful, successful, influential, or noticeable than other people or things. ❑ *...a change which would maintain his party's dominant position in Scotland.*

domi|nate ♦♦◊ /dɒmɪneɪt/ (dominates, dominating, dominated) **1** V-T/V-I To **dominate** a situation means to be the most powerful or important person or thing in it. ❑ *The book is expected to dominate the best-seller lists.* ❑ *...countries where life is dominated by war.* ❑ *Selling could continue to dominate as investors play it safe.* • **domi|na|tion** /dɒmɪneɪʃ°n/ N-UNCOUNT ❑ *...the domination of the market by a small number of organizations.* **2** V-T If one country or person **dominates** another, they have power over them. ❑ *He denied that his country wants to dominate Europe.* ❑ *Women are no longer dominated by the men in their relationships.* • **domi|na|tion** N-UNCOUNT ❑ *They had five centuries of domination by the Romans.* **3** V-T If a building, mountain, or other object **dominates** an area, it is so large or impressive that you cannot avoid seeing it. ❑ *It's one of the biggest buildings in this area, and it really dominates this whole place.*

---SYNONYMS---

dominate
VERB **2**
rule: *...the long line of feudal lords who had ruled over this land.*
control: *Most of the countries in the region were controlled by dictators.*
govern: *Their citizens are very thankful they are not governed by a dictator.*

---

domi|nat|ing /dɒmɪneɪtɪŋ/ ADJ A **dominating** person has a very strong personality and influences the people around them. ❑ *She certainly was a dominating figure, a leader who gave her name to a political philosophy.*

domi|neer|ing /dɒmɪnɪərɪŋ/ ADJ If you say that someone is **domineering**, you disapprove of them because you feel that they try to control other people without any consideration for their feelings or opinions. [DISAPPROVAL] ❑ *Mick was stubborn and domineering with a very bad temper.*

do|min|ion /dəmɪnyən/ (dominions) N-COUNT A **dominion** is an area of land that is controlled by a ruler. ❑ *The republic is a dominion of the Brazilian people.*

domi|no /dɒmɪnoʊ/ (dominoes) **1** N-COUNT **Dominoes** are small rectangular blocks marked with two groups of spots on one side. They are used for playing various games. **2** N-UNCOUNT **Dominoes** is a game in which players put dominoes onto a table in turn. ❑ *I used to play dominoes there.*

domi|no ef|fect N-SING If one event causes another similar event, which in turn causes another event, and so on, you can refer to this as a **domino effect**. ❑ *The timetable for trains is so tight that if one is a bit late, the domino effect is enormous.*

don /dɒn/ (dons, donning, donned) V-T If you **don** clothing, you put it on. [WRITTEN] ❑ *He donned his cloak and gloves.*

do|nate /doʊneɪt/ (donates, donating, donated) **1** V-T If you **donate** something to a charity or other organization, you give it to them. ❑ *He frequently donates large sums to charity.*

● **do|na|tion** /doʊneɪʃ³n/ N-UNCOUNT ☐ ...*the donation of his collection to the art gallery.* ■ V-T If you **donate** your blood or a part of your body, you allow doctors to use it to help someone who is ill. ☐ ...*people who are willing to donate their organs for use after death.* ● **do|na|tion** N-UNCOUNT ☐ ...*measures aimed at encouraging organ donation.*

do|na|tion /doʊneɪʃ³n/ (donations) ■ N-COUNT A **donation** is something which someone gives to a charity or other organization. ☐ *Employees make regular donations to charity.* ■ → see also **donate**

done ◆◇◇ /dʌn/ ■ **Done** is the past participle of **do** ①. ■ ADJ [v-link ADJ] A task or activity that is **done** has been completed successfully. ☐ *When her deal is done, the client emerges with her purchase.* ■ ADJ [v-link ADJ] When something that you are cooking is **done**, it has been cooked long enough and is ready. ☐ *As soon as the cake is done, remove it from the oven.* ■ CONVENTION You say '**Done**' when you are accepting a deal, arrangement, or bet that someone has offered to make with you. [SPOKEN, FORMULAE] ☐ *"You lead and we'll look for it."—"Done."*

don|gle /dɒŋg³l/ (dongles) N-COUNT A **dongle** is a small electronic device that you can connect to another device, especially one that gives you access to the internet. [COMPUTING] ☐ *The kit includes a speaker and wi-fi dongle.*

Don Juan /dɒn wɒn, dʒuən/ (Don Juans) N-COUNT If you describe a man as a **Don Juan**, you mean he has had sex with many women.

don|key /dɒŋki/ (donkeys) N-COUNT A **donkey** is an animal which is like a horse but which is smaller and has longer ears.

do|nor /doʊnər/ (donors) ■ N-COUNT A **donor** is someone who gives a part of their body or some of their blood to be used by doctors to help a person who is ill. ☐ *Doctors removed the healthy kidney from the donor.* ■ N-COUNT A **donor** is a person or organization who gives something, especially money, to a charity, organization, or country that needs it. ☐ *Donor countries are becoming more choosy about which countries they are prepared to help.* ■ ADJ [ADJ n] **Donor** organs or parts are organs or parts of the body which people allow doctors to use to help people who are ill. ☐ ...*the severe shortage of donor organs.*

do|nor card (donor cards) N-COUNT A **donor card** is a card which people carry in order to make sure that, when they die, their organs are used by doctors to help people who are ill.

do-nothing ADJ [ADJ n] You can use **do-nothing** to describe people such as politicians who you think have failed to do something. [AM, DISAPPROVAL] ☐ ...*a do-nothing president who ignores domestic concerns.*

don't /doʊnt/ **Don't** is the usual spoken form of 'do not.'

do|nut /doʊnʌt, -nət/ (donuts) → see **doughnut**

doo|dad /dudæd/ (doodads) N-COUNT You can refer to something, especially an electronic device, as a **doodad** when you do not know exactly what is called. [AM, INFORMAL] ☐ *Part of the attraction of photography is gadgets and mechanical doodads.*

doo|dle /dud³l/ (doodles, doodling, doodled) ■ N-COUNT A **doodle** is a pattern or picture that you draw when you are bored or thinking about something else. ☐ *Dillworthy was staring into space, with a scrawl of doodles on the pad in front of him.* ■ V-I When someone **doodles**, they draw doodles. ☐ *He looked across at Jackson, doodling on his notebook.*

doom /dum/ (dooms, dooming, doomed) ■ N-UNCOUNT **Doom** is a terrible future state or event which you cannot prevent. ☐ ...*his warnings of impending doom.* ■ N-UNCOUNT If you have a sense or feeling of **doom**, you feel that things are going very badly and are likely to get even worse. ☐ *Why are people so full of gloom and doom?* ■ V-T If a fact or event **dooms** someone or something to a particular fate, it makes certain that they are going to suffer in some way. ☐ *That argument was the turning point for their marriage, and the one which doomed it to failure.*

doomed /dumd/ ■ ADJ [v-link ADJ] If something **is doomed** to happen, or if you **are doomed** to a particular state, something unpleasant is certain to happen, and you can do nothing to prevent it. ☐ *Their plans seemed doomed to failure.* ■ ADJ Someone or something that is **doomed** is certain to fail or be destroyed. ☐ *I used to pour time and energy into projects that were doomed from the start.*

dooms|day /dumzdeɪ/ ■ N-UNCOUNT **Doomsday** is a day or time when you expect something terrible or unpleasant is going to happen. ☐ ...*the doomsday scenario of civil war between the two factions.* ■ N-PROPER In the Christian religion, **Doomsday** is the last day of the world, on which God will judge everyone.

dooms|day cult (doomsday cults) N-COUNT A **doomsday cult** is a religious cult whose members believe that the world is about to end. [mainly JOURNALISM]

door ◆◆◆ /dɔr/ (doors) ■ N-COUNT A **door** is a piece of wood, glass, or metal, which is moved to open and close the entrance to a building, room, closet, or vehicle. ☐ *I was knocking at the front door but there was no answer.* ■ N-COUNT A **door** is the space in a wall when a door is open. ☐ *She looked through the door of the kitchen. Her daughter was at the stove.* ■ N-PLURAL [amount N down/up] **Doors** is used in expressions such as **a few doors down** or **three doors up** to refer to a place that is a particular number of buildings away from where you are. [INFORMAL] ☐ *Mrs. Cade's house was only a few doors down from her daughter's apartment.* ■ → see also **next door** ■ PHRASE When you **answer the door**, you go and open the door because a visitor has knocked on it or rung the bell. ☐ *Carol answered the door as soon as I knocked.* ■ PHRASE If you say that someone gets or does something **by the back door** or **through the back door**, you are criticizing them for doing it secretly and unofficially. [DISAPPROVAL] ☐ *The government would not allow anyone to sneak in by the back door and seize power by force.* ■ PHRASE If people have talks and discussions **behind closed doors**, they have them in private because they want them to be kept secret. ☐ ...*decisions taken in secret behind closed doors.* ■ PHRASE If someone goes **from door to door** or goes **door to door**, they go along a street calling at each house in turn, for example, selling something. ☐ *They are going from door to door collecting money from civilians.* ■ PHRASE If you talk about a distance or trip **from door to door** or **door to door**, you are talking about the distance from the place where the trip starts to the place where it finishes. ☐ ...*tickets covering the whole trip from door to door.* ■ PHRASE If you say that something helps someone to get their **foot in the door**, you mean that it gives them an opportunity to start doing something new, usually in an area that is difficult to succeed in. ☐ *If we can get our foot in the door, that can help us build our market.* ■ PHRASE If someone **shuts the door in** your **face** or **slams the door in** your **face**, they refuse to talk to you or give you any information. ☐ *Did you say anything to him or just shut the door in his face?* ■ PHRASE If you **lay** something **at** someone's **door**, you blame them for an unpleasant event or situation. ☐ *Much of the blame for the long delay could be laid at the door of the manufacturer.* ■ PHRASE When you are **out of doors**, you are not inside a building, but in the open air. ☐ *The weather was fine enough for working out of doors.* ■ PHRASE If you **see** someone **to the door**, you go to the door with a visitor when they leave. ☐ *Politely he saw her to the door and opened it for her.* ■ PHRASE If someone **shows** you **the door**, they ask you to leave because they are angry with you. ☐ *Would they forgive and forget – or show him the door?* ■ **at death's door** → see **death**

door|bell /dɔrbɛl/ (doorbells) N-COUNT A **doorbell** is a bell on the outside of a house which you can ring so that the people inside know that you want to see them.

do-or-die ■ ADJ [ADJ n] A **do-or-die** battle or struggle is one that involves a determined or desperate effort to succeed. ☐ ...*a do-or-die effort to turn Uniq into a lean and dynamic food business.* ■ PHRASE [v-link PHR n] If something is **do-or-die** for someone or something, it will determine whether they succeed or fail. ☐ *Nobody will know the exact position until Monday, when it is do-or-die for the deal.*

door|keeper /dɔrkipər/ (doorkeepers) N-COUNT A **doorkeeper** is the same as a **doorman**. [BRIT]

door|knob /dɔrnɒb/ (doorknobs) N-COUNT A **doorknob** is a round handle on a door.

door|man /dɔrmæn, -mən/ (doormen) ■ N-COUNT A **doorman** is a man who stands at the door of a building such as a hotel or apartment and helps people who are going in or out.

in BRIT, also use **doorkeeper**

■ N-COUNT A **doorman** is the same as a **bouncer**. [BRIT]

door|mat /dɔrmæt/ (doormats) **1** N-COUNT A **doormat** is a mat by a door which people can wipe their shoes on when they enter a house or building. **2** N-COUNT If you say that someone is a **doormat**, you are criticizing them because they let other people treat them badly, and do not complain or defend themselves when they are being treated unfairly. [INFORMAL, DISAPPROVAL] ☐ *If you always give in to others you will end up feeling like a doormat.*

door|step /dɔrstɛp/ (doorsteps) **1** N-COUNT A **doorstep** is a step in front of a door on the outside of a building. ☐ *...a youth who was sitting on a doorstep, drinking.* **2** PHRASE If a place is **on your doorstep**, it is very near to where you live. If something happens **on your doorstep**, it happens very close to where you live. ☐ *It is easy to lose sight of what is happening on our own doorstep.*

door|stop /dɔrstɒp/ (doorstops) **1** N-COUNT A **doorstop** is a wood or rubber wedge that you put under a door to keep it open. **2** N-COUNT A **doorstop** is a piece of rubber on a wall that prevents it being damaged when a door is opened. **3** N-COUNT A **doorstop** is a heavy object that you use to keep a door open.

door-to-door → see door

door|way /dɔrweɪ/ (doorways) **1** N-COUNT A **doorway** is a space in a wall where a door opens and closes. ☐ *Hannah looked up to see David and another man standing in the doorway.* **2** N-COUNT A **doorway** is a covered space just outside the door of a building. ☐ *...homeless people sleeping in doorways.* **3** → See feature box at **house**

door|woman /dɔrwʊmən/ (doorwomen) **1** N-COUNT A **doorwoman** is a woman who stands at the door of a building such as a hotel or apartment and helps people who are going in or out.

in BRIT, also use **doorkeeper**

2 N-COUNT A **doorwoman** is the same as a **bouncer**. [BRIT] ☐ *It's a far cry from her days as a doorwoman at the Volcano club.*

dope /doʊp/ (dopes, doping, doped) **1** N-UNCOUNT **Dope** is a drug, usually an illegal drug such as marijuana or cocaine. [INFORMAL] ☐ *A man asked them if they wanted to buy some dope.* **2** V-T If someone **dopes** a person or animal or **dopes** their food, they put drugs into their food or force them to take drugs. ☐ *Anyone could have got in and doped the wine.* ☐ *I'd been doped with Somnolin.* **3** N-COUNT If someone calls a person a **dope**, they think that the person is stupid. [INFORMAL, DISAPPROVAL] ☐ *I'm more comfortable with them. I don't feel I'm such a dope.*

doped up ADJ [usu v-link ADJ] If someone is **doped up**, they are in a state where they cannot think clearly because they are under the influence of drugs. [INFORMAL] ☐ *I feel a bit doped up, but I'm okay.*

dopey /doʊpi/ (dopier, dopiest) **1** ADJ Someone who is **dopey** is sleepy, as though they have been drugged. ☐ *The medicine always made him feel dopey and unable to concentrate.* **2** ADJ If you describe someone as **dopey**, you mean that they are rather stupid. [INFORMAL, DISAPPROVAL]

dork /dɔrk/ (dorks) N-COUNT If you say that someone is a **dork**, you think they dress badly in old-fashioned clothes and behave very awkwardly in social situations. [mainly AM, INFORMAL, DISAPPROVAL] ☐ *...their unshakeable conviction that family holidays were strictly for dorks.*

dorm /dɔrm/ (dorms) N-COUNT A **dorm** is the same as a **dormitory**. [INFORMAL]

dor|mant /dɔrmənt/ ADJ Something that is **dormant** is not active, growing, or being used at the present time but is capable of becoming active later on. ☐ *...when the long dormant volcano of Mount St. Helens erupted in 1980.*

dor|mer /dɔrmər/ (dormers) N-COUNT A **dormer** or **dormer window** is a window that is built upright in a sloping roof.

dor|mi|tory /dɔrmɪtɔri/ (dormitories) **1** N-COUNT A **dormitory** is a building at a college or university where students live. [AM] ☐ *She lived in a college dormitory.*

in BRIT, use **hall of residence**

2 N-COUNT A **dormitory** is a large bedroom where several people sleep, for example, in a boarding school. ☐ *...the boys' dormitory.*

dor|mouse /dɔrmaʊs/ (dormice /dɔrmaɪs/) N-COUNT A **dormouse** is a small animal found in Europe that looks like a mouse.

dor|sal /dɔrsəl/ ADJ [ADJ n] **Dorsal** means relating to the back of a fish or animal. [TECHNICAL] ☐ *...a dolphin's dorsal fin.*

DOS /dɒs/ N-UNCOUNT **DOS** is the part of a computer operating system that controls and manages files and programs stored on disk. **DOS** is an abbreviation for 'disk operating system.' [COMPUTING, TRADEMARK] ☐ *Boot from a DOS disk which you know to be virus-free.*

dos|age /doʊsɪdʒ/ (dosages) N-COUNT A **dosage** is the amount of a medicine or drug that someone takes or should take. ☐ *He was put on a high dosage of vitamin C.*

dose /doʊs/ (doses, dosing, dosed) **1** N-COUNT A **dose** of medicine or a drug is a measured amount of it which is intended to be taken at one time. ☐ *One dose of penicillin can wipe out the infection.* **2** V-T If you **dose** a person or animal with medicine, you give them an amount of it. ☐ *The doctor fixed the rib, dosed him heavily with drugs, and said he would probably get better.* • PHRASAL VERB **Dose up** means the same as **dose**. ☐ *I dosed him up with Valium.*

dos|si|er /dɒsieɪ/ (dossiers) N-COUNT A **dossier** is a collection of papers containing information on a particular event, or on a person such as a criminal or a spy. ☐ *The company is compiling a dossier of evidence to back its allegations.*

dost /dʌst/ **Dost** is an old-fashioned second person singular form of the verb 'do.'

dot /dɒt/ (dots, dotting, dotted) **1** N-COUNT A **dot** is a very small round mark, for example, one that is used as the top part of the letter 'i,' as a period, or in the names of websites. ☐ *...a system of painting using small dots of color.* **2** V-T When things **dot** a place or an area, they are scattered or spread all over it. ☐ *Small coastal towns dot the landscape.* **3** → see also **dotted** **4** PHRASE If you arrive somewhere or do something **on the dot**, you arrive there or do it at exactly the time that you were supposed to. ☐ *They appeared on the dot of 9:50 p.m. as always.*

dot|age /doʊtɪdʒ/ N-UNCOUNT [usu poss N] If someone is in their **dotage**, they are very old and becoming weak. ☐ *Even in his dotage, the professor still sits on the committee.*

dot-com (dot-coms) also **dotcom** N-COUNT A **dot-com** is a company that does all or most of its business on the internet. ☐ *...the rise and fall of the dot-coms.*

dote /doʊt/ (dotes, doting, doted) V-I If you say that someone **dotes** on a person or a thing, you mean that they love or care about them very much and ignore any faults they may have. ☐ *He dotes on his nine-year-old son.*

doth /dʌθ/ **Doth** is an old-fashioned third person singular form of the verb 'do.'

dot|ing /doʊtɪŋ/ ADJ If you say that someone is, for example, a **doting** mother, husband, or friend, you mean that they show a lot of love for someone. ☐ *His doting parents bought him his first racing bike at 13.*

dot|ted /dɒtɪd/ **1** ADJ A **dotted** line is a line which is made of a row of dots. ☐ *Cut along the dotted line.* • PHRASE If you **sign on the dotted line**, you formally agree to something by signing an official document. **2** ADJ [v-link ADJ with n] If a place or object is **dotted with** things, it has many of those things scattered over its surface. ☐ *The maps were dotted with the names of small towns.* **3** ADJ [v-link ADJ prep] If things are **dotted** around a place, they can be found in many different parts of that place. ☐ *Many pieces of sculpture are dotted around the house.* **4** → see also **dot**

dot|ty /dɒti/ (dottier, dottiest) ADJ If you say that someone is **dotty**, you mean that they are slightly mad or likely to do strange things. [INFORMAL] ☐ *She was obviously going a bit dotty.*

dou|ble ♦♦◊ /dʌbəl/ (doubles, doubling, doubled) **1** ADJ [ADJ n] You use **double** to indicate that something includes or is made of two things of the same kind. ☐ *...a pair of double doors into the room from the new entrance hall.* **2** ADJ [ADJ n] You use **double** before a singular noun to refer to two things of the same type that occur together, or that are connected in some way. ☐ *...an extremely nasty double murder.* **3** ADJ You use **double** to describe something which is twice the normal size or can hold twice the normal quantity of something. ☐ *...a double helping of ice cream.* **4** ADJ A **double** room is a room intended for two people, usually a couple, to stay or live in. ❑ ...bed and breakfast for $180 for two people in a double room. • N-COUNT **Double** is also a noun. ❑ The Great Western Hotel is ideal, costing around 90 dollars a night for a double. **5** ADJ [ADJ n] A **double** bed is a bed that is wide enough for two people to sleep in. ❑ One bedroom had a double bed and the other had single beds for the boys. **6** ADJ [ADJ n] You use **double** to describe a drink that is twice the normal measure. ❑ He was drinking his double whiskey too fast and scowling. • N-COUNT **Double** is also a noun. ❑ "Give me a whiskey," Debilly said to Francis. "Make it a double." **7** PREDET [PREDET the n] If something is **double** the amount or size of another thing, it is twice as large. ❑ The offer was to start a new research laboratory at double the salary he was then getting. • PRON **Double** is also a pronoun. ❑ On average doctors write just over seven prescriptions each year per patient; in Germany it is double. **8** V-T/V-I When something **doubles** or when you **double** it, it becomes twice as great in number, amount, or size. ❑ The number of managers must double to 100 within 3 years. **9** V-I If a person or thing **doubles** as someone or something else, they have a second job or purpose as well as their main one. ❑ Lots of homes in town double as businesses. • PHRASAL VERB **Double up** means the same as **double**. ❑ The lids of the casserole dishes are designed to double up as baking dishes. **10** N-COUNT If you refer to someone as a person's **double**, you mean that they look exactly like them. ❑ Your mother sees you as her double. **11** N-UNCOUNT In tennis or badminton, when people play **doubles**, two teams consisting of two players on each team play against each other on the same court. ❑ In the doubles, the pair beat Hungary's Renata Csay and Kornelia Szanda. **12** PHRASE If you do something **on the double**, you do it very quickly or immediately. [INFORMAL] ❑ I need a copy of the police report on the double. **13** PHRASE If you are **bent double**, the top half of your body is bent downward so that your head is close to your knees. ❑ I was bent double in agony. **14** PHRASE If you **are seeing double**, there is something wrong with your eyes, and you can see two images instead of one. ❑ For 35 minutes I was walking around in a daze. I was dizzy, seeing double. **15** in **double figures** → see **figure** **16** → See feature box at **population**

▶ **double up** PHRASAL VERB If something **doubles** you **up**, or if you **double up**, you bend your body quickly or violently, for example, because you are laughing a lot or because you are feeling a lot of pain. ❑ ...a savage blow which doubled him up. • PHRASAL VERB **Double over** means the same as **double up**. ❑ Everyone was doubled over in laughter.

dou|ble act (double acts) also **double-act** N-COUNT Two comedians or entertainers who perform together are referred to as a **double act**. Their performance can also be called a **double act**. ❑ ...a famous comedy double act.

dou|ble agent (double agents) N-COUNT A **double agent** is someone who works as a spy for a particular country or organization, but who also works for its enemies.

double-barreled

in BRIT, use **double-barrelled**

1 ADJ [ADJ n] A **double-barreled** gun has two barrels. ❑ ...a double-barreled shotgun. **2** ADJ [ADJ n] **Double-barreled** is used to describe something such as a plan which has two main parts. [JOURNALISM]

dou|ble bass /dʌbəl beɪs/ (double basses) also **double-bass** N-VAR A **double bass** is the largest instrument in the violin family.

dou|ble bill (double bills) also **double-bill** N-COUNT [oft N of n] A **double bill** is a theater performance in which there are two shows on the program.

dou|ble bind (double binds) N-COUNT [usu sing] If you are in a **double bind**, you are in a very difficult situation, because whatever decision you make will have bad results. ❑ Women are caught in a double bind, marginalized in the community if they are not wives and mothers, under excessive pressure to be perfect if they are.

double-blind **1** ADJ A **double-blind** study or experiment compares two groups of people, one of which is being tested while the other is not. Neither the people doing the testing nor the members of the two groups know which group is being tested. ❑ In a double-blind trial, there were some improvements. **2** → See feature box at **medicine**

double-book (double-books, double-booking, double-booked) **1** VERB If you **double-book** something, or if you **double-book**, you book two spaces or services when only one is available to use. ❑ Landlords occasionally double-book the apartment with no hint of apology. ❑ He arrives to find his therapy session is double-booked. **2** → See feature box at **tourism**

double-breasted ADJ [usu ADJ n] A **double-breasted** jacket or suit has two very wide sections at the front of the jacket which fit over one another when you button them up.

double-check (double-checks, double-checking, double-checked) V-T/V-I If you **double-check** something, you examine or test it a second time to make sure that it is completely correct or safe. ❑ Check and double-check spelling and punctuation. ❑ Double-check that the ladder is secure.

dou|ble chin (double chins) N-COUNT [usu sing] If someone has a **double chin**, they have a fold of fat under their chin, making them look as if they have two chins.

double-click (double-clicks, double-clicking, double-clicked) V-T/V-I [no passive] If you **double-click on** an area of a computer screen, you point the cursor at that area and press one of the buttons on the mouse twice quickly in order to make something happen. [COMPUTING] ❑ Go to Control Panel and double-click on Sounds for a list of sounds.

dou|ble cream N-UNCOUNT **Double cream** is the same as **heavy cream**. [BRIT]

double-cross (double-crosses, double-crossing, double-crossed) V-T If someone you trust **double-crosses** you, they do something which harms you instead of doing something they had promised to do. [INFORMAL] ❑ Don't try and double-cross me, Taylor, because I'll kill you.

double-dealing N-UNCOUNT **Double-dealing** is behavior which is deliberately deceitful. ❑ Marriages were broken and lives ruined by the revelation of double-dealing.

double-decker (double-deckers) N-COUNT A **double-decker** or a **double-decker bus** is a bus that has two levels, so that passengers can sit upstairs or downstairs.

double-digit ADJ [ADJ n] A **double-digit** number is between 10 and 99. ❑ Australia had 15 years of double-digit inflation.

dou|ble dip also **double-dip** N-SING [oft N n] In economics, a **double dip** is a period when an economy goes into recession, then briefly recovers, but then goes into another recession. ❑ Dismal economic findings have analysts fearing a double dip. ❑ ...a double-dip recession.

double-edged **1** ADJ If you say that a comment is **double-edged**, you mean that it has two meanings, so that you are not sure whether the person who said it is being critical or is giving praise. ❑ Even his praise is double-edged. **2** ADJ If you say that something is **double-edged**, you mean that its positive effects are balanced by its negative effects, or that its negative effects are greater. ❑ But tourism is double-edged, for although it's boosting the country's economy, the Reef could be damaged. **3** a **double-edged sword** → see **sword**

dou|ble en|ten|dre /dubəl ɒntɒndrə/ (double entendres) N-VAR A **double entendre** is a word or phrase that has two meanings, one of which is rude and often sexual. ❑ He is a master of the pun and the double entendre.

dou|ble fault (double faults) N-COUNT In tennis, if a player serves a **double fault**, they make a mistake with both serves and lose the point.

dou|ble|head|er /dʌbəlhɛdər/ (doubleheaders) N-COUNT A **doubleheader** is a sporting contest between two teams that involves two separate games being played, one after the other, often on the same day. [mainly AM]

dou|ble jeop|ardy N-UNCOUNT In law, **double jeopardy** is the act of prosecuting a person twice for the same offense. [AM] ❑ ...the prohibition against double jeopardy.

dou|ble life (double lives) N-COUNT [usu sing] If you say that someone is living a **double life**, you mean that they lead two separate and very different lives, and they appear to be a different person in each. ❑ She threatened to publicly expose his double life if he left her.

double-park (double-parks, double-parking, double-parked) V-T/V-I If someone **double-parks** their car or their car

double-parks, they park in a road by the side of another parked car. ◻ *Murray double-parked his car.* ◻ *The car pulled in and double-parked in front of the town hall.*

dou|ble play (double plays) N-COUNT In baseball, a **double play** is a play in which two runners are put out. ◻ *There were six double plays in the game: three by each team.*

double-quick ADV [ADV after v] If you say that you will do something **double-quick**, you are emphasizing that you will do it very quickly. [INFORMAL, EMPHASIS] ◻ *Don't worry. We'll have you out of here double-quick.* • PHRASE [PHR after v] **In double-quick time** means the same as **double-quick**. ◻ *I was over the fence in double-quick time.*

double-space (double-spaces, double-spacing, double-spaced) also **double space** ◼ V-T If you **double-space** something you are writing or typing, you include a full line of space between each line of writing. ◻ *Double-space the entire list.* • **double-spaced** ADJ ◻ *...forty pages of double-spaced typescript.* • **dou|ble spac|ing** N-UNCOUNT ◻ *Single spacing is used within paragraphs, double spacing between paragraphs.* ◼ N-COUNT A **double space** is a full line of space between each line of a piece of writing. ◻ *Leave a double space between entries.*

double|speak /dʌbᵊlspiːk/ N-UNCOUNT If you refer to what someone says as **doublespeak**, you are criticizing them for presenting things in a way that is intended to hide the truth or give people the wrong idea. [DISAPPROVAL] ◻ *...the doublespeak so fluently used by governments and their press offices.*

dou|ble stand|ard (double standards) N-COUNT If you accuse a person or institution of applying **double standards** in their treatment of different groups of people, you mean that they unfairly allow more freedom of behavior to one group than to another. [DISAPPROVAL] ◻ *Some residents accused city officials of applying a double standard.*

dou|blet /dʌblɪt/ (doublets) N-COUNT A **doublet** was a short, tight jacket that was worn by men in the fifteenth, sixteenth, and early seventeenth centuries.

double take (double takes) N-COUNT If you do a **double take** when you see or hear something strange or surprising, you hesitate for a moment before reacting to it because you wonder if you really saw or heard it. ◻ *She looked up, then did a double take when she saw my dress and makeup.*

double-talk also **double talk** N-UNCOUNT If you refer to something someone says as **double-talk**, you mean that it can deceive people or is difficult to understand because it has two possible meanings.

dou|ble vi|sion N-UNCOUNT If someone is suffering from **double vision**, they see a single object as two objects, for example, because they are ill or have drunk too much alcohol.

dou|bly /dʌbli/ ◼ ADV You use **doubly** to indicate that there are two aspects or features that are having an influence on a particular situation. ◻ *Employees choosing to move with a relocating company benefit doubly from employer-related housing assistance and lower house prices.* ◼ ADV [ADV adj/adv] You use **doubly** to emphasize that something exists or happens to a greater degree than usual. [EMPHASIS] ◻ *In pregnancy a high fiber diet is doubly important.*

doubt ✦✦◇ /daʊt/ (doubts, doubting, doubted) ◼ N-VAR If you have **doubt** or **doubts** about something, you feel uncertain about it and do not know whether it is true or possible. If you say you have no **doubt** about it, you mean that you are certain it is true. ◻ *This raises doubts about the point of advertising.* ◻ *There is little doubt that man has had an impact on the Earth's climate.* ◼ V-T If you **doubt** whether something is true or possible, you believe that it is probably not true or possible. ◻ *Others doubted whether that would happen.* ◻ *He doubted if he would learn anything new from Maria.* ◼ V-T If you **doubt** something, you believe that it might not be true or genuine. ◻ *No one doubted his ability.* ◼ V-T If you **doubt** someone or **doubt** their word, you think that they may not be telling the truth. ◻ *No one directly involved with the case doubted him.* ◼ PHRASE You say that something is **beyond doubt** or **beyond reasonable doubt** when you are certain that it is true and it cannot be contradicted or disproved. [EMPHASIS] ◻ *A referendum showed beyond doubt that voters wanted independence.* ◼ PHRASE If you are **in doubt** about something, you feel unsure about it. ◻ *He is in no doubt as to what is needed.* ◼ PHRASE If you say that something is **in doubt** or **open to doubt**, you consider it to be uncertain or unreliable. ◻ *The outcome was still in doubt.* ◼ PHRASE You use **no doubt** to emphasize that something seems certain or very likely to you. [EMPHASIS] ◻ *The contract for this will no doubt be widely advertised.* ◼ PHRASE You use **no doubt** to indicate that you accept the truth of a particular point, but that you do not think it is important or contradicts the rest of what you are saying. ◻ *No doubt many will regard these as harsh words, but regrettably they are true.* ◼ PHRASE If you say that something is true **without doubt** or **without a doubt**, you are emphasizing that it is definitely true. [EMPHASIS] ◻ *This was without doubt the most interesting situation that Amanda had ever found herself in.* ◼ CONVENTION You say **I doubt it** as a response to a question or statement about something that you think is untrue or unlikely. ◻ *"Somebody would have seen her."—"I doubt it, not on Monday."* ◼ **the benefit of the doubt** → see **benefit** ◼ **a shadow of a doubt** → see **shadow**

──── COLLOCATIONS ────

doubt
NOUN ◼
adjective + **doubt**: grave, serious; little, slightest; lingering, nagging
verb + **doubt**: cast; express, raise

doubt|er /daʊtər/ (doubters) N-COUNT [usu pl] If you refer to people as **doubters**, you mean that they have doubts about something, especially their religious or political system. ◻ *Some doubters fear this news may not be as good as it appears.*

doubt|ful /daʊtfəl/ ◼ ADJ If it is **doubtful** that something will happen, it seems unlikely to happen or you are uncertain whether it will happen. ◻ *For a time it seemed doubtful that he would move at all.* ◼ ADJ If you are **doubtful** about something, you feel unsure or uncertain about it. ◻ *I was still very doubtful about the chances for success.* • **doubt|ful|ly** ADV [ADV after v] ◻ *Keeton shook his head doubtfully.* ◼ ADJ If you say that something is of **doubtful** quality or value, you mean that it is of low quality or value. [DISAPPROVAL] ◻ *...selling something that is overpriced or of doubtful quality.* ◼ ADJ If a sports player is **doubtful** for a match or event, he or she seems unlikely to play, usually because of injury. [JOURNALISM] ◻ *Forsyth is doubtful for tonight's game with a badly bruised leg.*

doubt|ing Thomas /daʊtɪŋ tɒməs/ (doubting Thomases) N-COUNT If you describe someone as a **doubting Thomas**, you mean they refuse to believe something until they see definite proof or evidence of it.

doubt|less /daʊtlɪs/ ADV [ADV with cl/group] If you say that something is **doubtless** the case, you mean that you think it is probably or almost certainly the case. ◻ *He will doubtless try and persuade his colleagues to change their minds.*

douche /duːʃ/ (douches, douching, douched) ◼ N-COUNT A **douche** is a method of washing the vagina using a stream of water. You also refer to the object which you use to wash the vagina in this way as a **douche**. ◼ V-I To **douche** means to wash the vagina using a stream of water. ◻ *Never douche if you are pregnant.*

dough /doʊ/ (doughs) ◼ N-MASS **Dough** is a fairly firm mixture of flour, water, and sometimes also fat and sugar. It can be cooked to make bread or pastry. ◻ *Roll out the dough into one large circle.* ◼ N-UNCOUNT You can refer to money as **dough**. [INFORMAL] ◻ *He worked hard for his dough.*

dough|nut /doʊnʌt, -nət/ (doughnuts) also **donut** N-COUNT A **doughnut** is a breadlike cake, often in the shape of a ring, made from sweet dough that has been cooked in hot fat.

dough|ty /daʊti/ ADJ [ADJ n] If you describe someone as a **doughty** fighter, you mean they are brave, determined, and not easily defeated. [OLD-FASHIONED, APPROVAL]

doughy /doʊi/ (doughier, doughiest) ADJ If you describe something as **doughy**, you mean that it has a fairly soft texture like dough. ◻ *Add water and mix with a knife to a doughy consistency.*

dour /dʊər, daʊər/ ADJ If you describe someone as **dour**, you mean that they are very serious and unfriendly. ◻ *...a dour, taciturn man.*

douse /daʊs/ (douses, dousing, doused) also **dowse** ◼ V-T If you **douse** a fire, you stop it from burning by pouring a lot of water over it. ◻ *The pumps were started and the crew began to douse the fire with water.* ◼ V-T If you **douse** someone or something with a liquid, you throw a lot of that liquid over them. ◻ *They hurled abuse at their victim as they doused him with gasoline.*

dove (doves)

Pronounced /dʌv/ for meanings 1 and 2, and /doʊv/ for meaning 3.

◼ N-COUNT A **dove** is a bird that looks like a pigeon but is smaller and lighter in color. Doves are often used as a symbol of peace. ◼ N-COUNT In politics, you can refer to people who support the use of peaceful methods to solve difficult situations as **doves**. Compare **hawk**. ◻ *A clear split over tactics appears to be emerging between doves and hawks in the party.* ◼ **Dove** is sometimes used as the past tense of **dive**.

dove|cote /dʌvkoʊt, -koʊt/ (dovecotes) also **dovecot** N-COUNT A **dovecote** is a small building or a container for pigeons or doves to live in.

dove|tail /dʌvteɪl/ (dovetails, dovetailing, dovetailed) V-RECIP If two things **dovetail** or if one thing **dovetails** with another, the two things fit together neatly or have some common characteristics. ◻ *I'm following up a few things that might dovetail.* ◻ *...an attempt to look for areas where U.S. interests can dovetail with Japanese concerns.* ◻ *It is important that we dovetail our respective interests.*

dov|ish /dʌvɪʃ/ also **doveish** ADJ Journalists use **dovish** to describe politicians or governments who are in favor of using peaceful and diplomatic methods to achieve something, rather than using force and violence.

dowa|ger /daʊədʒər/ (dowagers) ◼ ADJ [ADJ n, n ADJ] You use **dowager** to refer to the wife of a dead duke, emperor, or other man of high rank. ◻ *...the Dowager Countess Spencer.* • N-COUNT **Dowager** is also a noun. ◻ *Nobody was allowed to eat in the Empress Dowager's presence.* ◼ N-COUNT If you refer to a woman as a **dowager**, you mean that she is old and rich or looks important. [LITERARY] ◻ *...like stately dowagers on a cruise.*

dow|dy /daʊdi/ (dowdier, dowdiest) ADJ If you describe someone or their clothes as **dowdy**, you mean their clothes are dull and unfashionable. [DISAPPROVAL] ◻ *...clothes which were clean but dowdy.*

dow|el /daʊəl/ (dowels) N-COUNT A **dowel** is a short thin piece of wood or metal which is used for joining larger pieces of wood or metal together.

Dow Jones av|er|age /daʊ dʒoʊnz ævərɪdʒ, ævrɪdʒ/ also **Dow Jones, Dow** N-PROPER [the N] The **Dow Jones Average** is a daily measurement of stock-exchange prices, based on the average price of a selected number of securities. [AM] ◻ *The Dow Jones average closed down 7.49, or 0.1%.*

DOWN
① PREPOSITION AND ADVERB USES
② ADJECTIVE USES
③ VERB USES
④ NOUN USES
---

① **down** ♦♦♦ /daʊn/

Down is often used with verbs of movement, such as 'fall' and 'pull,' and also in phrasal verbs such as 'bring down' and 'calm down.'

→ Please look at meaning ⓭ to see if the expression you are looking for is shown under another headword.

◼ PREP To go **down** something such as a slope or a pipe means to go toward the ground or to a lower level. ◻ *We're going down a mountain.* ◻ *A man came down the stairs to meet them.* • ADV [ADV after v] **Down** is also an adverb. ◻ *She went down to the kitchen again.* ◼ PREP [amount PREP n] If you are a particular distance **down** something, you are that distance below the top or surface of it. ◻ *He managed to cling on to a ledge 40 feet down the rock face.* • ADV [amount ADV] **Down** is also an adverb. ◻ *At the bottom of the pit, some 1,300 feet down, are huge heaps of ore.* ◼ PREP If you go or look **down** something such as a road or river, you go or look along it. If you are **down** a road or river, you are somewhere along it. ◻ *They set off at a jog up one street and down another.*

◼ ADV [ADV after v] You use **down** to say that you are looking or facing in a direction that is toward the ground or toward a lower level. ◻ *She was still looking down at her papers.* ◼ ADV [ADV after v] If you put something **down**, you put it onto a surface. ◻ *Danny put down his glass.* ◼ ADV If an amount of something goes **down**, it decreases. If an amount of something is **down**, it has decreased and is at a lower level than it was. ◻ *Interest rates came down today.* ◻ *Inflation will be down to three percent.* ◼ PHRASE **Down to** a particular detail means including everything, even that detail. **Down to** a particular person means including everyone, even that person. ◻ *The bedroom was an exact replica of the original, perfect right down to the patterns on the wallpaper and the hairbrushes on the dressing table.* ◼ PHRASE If you are **down to** a certain amount of something, you have only that amount left. ◻ *The poor man's down to his last $5.* ◼ PHRASE If someone or something is **down for** a particular thing, it has been arranged that they will do that thing, or that thing will happen. ◻ *Mark had told me that he was down for an interview.* ◼ PHRASE If you pay money **down** on something, you pay part of the money you owe for it. [mainly AM] ◻ *He had a simple, conventional deal and paid 20 percent down at settlement.* ◼ → see also **put down** ◼ PHRASE If people shout '**down with**' something or someone, they are saying that they dislike them and want to get rid of them. [SPOKEN, DISAPPROVAL] ◻ *Demonstrators chanted "down with the rebels."* ◼ **up and down** → see **up** ①

② **down** /daʊn/ ◼ ADJ [v-link ADJ] If you are feeling **down**, you are feeling unhappy or depressed. [INFORMAL] ◻ *The old man sounded really down.* ◼ ADJ [v-link ADJ] If something is **down** on paper, it has been written on the paper. ◻ *That date wasn't down on our news sheet.* ◼ ADJ [v-link ADJ] If a piece of equipment, especially a computer system, is **down**, it is temporarily not working. Compare **up**. ◻ *The computer's down again.*

③ **down** /daʊn/ (downs, downing, downed) ◼ V-T If you say that someone **downs** food or a drink, you mean that they eat or drink it. ◻ *We downed bottles of local wine.* ◼ V-T If something or someone is **downed**, they fall to the ground because they have been hurt or damaged in some way. [JOURNALISM] ◻ *A couple of jet fighters were downed during the five-week rebellion.*

④ **down** /daʊn/ ◼ N-UNCOUNT **Down** consists of the small, soft feathers on young birds. **Down** is used to make bed-covers and pillows. ◻ *... goose down.* ◼ N-UNCOUNT **Down** is very fine hair. ◻ *The whole plant is covered with fine down.*

down-and-dirty ◼ ADJ If you describe a person or their behavior as **down-and-dirty**, you mean that they behave in an unfair or dishonest way in order to gain an advantage. [mainly AM] ◻ *It would likely be a down-and-dirty campaign again.* ◼ ADJ Journalists sometimes refer to a performer or their performance as **down-and-dirty** when they like them because they are bold and direct and perhaps vulgar. [mainly AM] ◻ *It portrays the early Beatles at their most down and dirty.*

down-and-out ADJ If you describe someone as **down-and-out**, you mean that they have no job and nowhere to live, and they have no real hope of improving their situation. ◻ *...a short story about a down-and-out advertising copywriter.*

down-at-heel also **down at heel** ADJ [usu ADJ n] Something that is **down-at-heel** is in bad condition because it has been used too much or has not been cared for properly. If you say that someone is **down-at-heel**, you mean that they are wearing old, worn clothes because they have little money. ◻ *...a down-at-heel disco in central East Berlin.* ◻ *...a down-at-heel family in a trailer park on the outskirts of Dallas.*

down|beat /daʊnbɪt/ ◼ ADJ [usu ADJ n] If people or their opinions are **downbeat**, they are deliberately casual and not enthusiastic about a situation. ◻ *...a downbeat assessment of the year's economic prospects.* ◼ ADJ If you are feeling **downbeat**, you are feeling depressed and without hope. ◻ *They found him in a gloomy, downbeat mood.*

down|cast /daʊnkæst/ ◼ ADJ [usu v-link ADJ] If you are **downcast**, you are feeling sad and without hope. ◻ *Barbara looked increasingly downcast as defeat loomed.* ◼ ADJ [usu v-link ADJ] If your eyes are **downcast**, you are looking toward the ground, usually because you are feeling sad or embarrassed. ◻ *She was silent, her eyes downcast.*

down|er /daʊnər/ (downers) ◼ N-COUNT [usu sing, a N] If you describe a situation as a **downer**, you think that it is very depressing. [INFORMAL] ❑ *For divorced people, Christmas can be a downer.* **2** PHRASE If you are **on a downer**, you are feeling depressed and without hope. [INFORMAL] ❑ *When I arrived, the team was bottom of the league and the whole place was on a real downer.*

down|fall /dˈaʊnfɔːl/ (**downfalls**) **1** N-COUNT The **downfall** of a successful or powerful person or institution is their loss of success or power. ❑ *His lack of experience had led to his downfall.* **2** N-COUNT The thing that was a person's **downfall** caused them to fail or lose power. ❑ *Jeremy's honesty had been his downfall.*

down|grade /dˈaʊngreɪd/ (**downgrades, downgrading, downgraded**) **1** V-T [usu passive] If something **is downgraded**, it is given less importance than it used to have or than you think it should have. ❑ *The boy's condition has been downgraded from critical to serious.* **2** V-T If someone **is downgraded**, their job or status is changed so that they become less important or receive less money. ❑ *There was no criticism of her work until after she was downgraded.*

down|hearted /dˌaʊnhˈɑːtɪd/ ADJ [usu v-link ADJ] If you are **downhearted**, you are feeling sad and discouraged. ❑ *Max sighed, sounding even more downhearted.*

down|hill /dˌaʊnhˈɪl/ **1** ADV If something or someone is moving **downhill** or is **downhill**, they are moving down a slope or are located toward the bottom of a hill. ❑ *He headed downhill toward the river.* • ADJ [ADJ n] **Downhill** is also an adjective. ❑ *...downhill ski runs.* **2** ADV If you say that something is going **downhill**, you mean that it is becoming worse or less successful. ❑ *Since I started to work longer hours things have gone steadily downhill.* **3** ADJ [v-link ADJ] If you say that a task or situation is **downhill** after a particular stage or time, you mean that it is easy to deal with after that stage or time. ❑ *Well, I guess it's all downhill from here.*

down-home also **downhome, down home** ADJ Something that is **down-home** is associated with a simple, rural life, especially in the southern United States. [AM] ❑ *Betty had learned a thing or two about down-home cooking from her mother.*

Down|ing Street /dˈaʊnɪŋ striːt/ N-PROPER **Downing Street** is the street in London in which the British prime minister and chancellor of the exchequer live. You can also use **Downing Street** to refer to the prime minister and his or her officials. ❑ *The prime minister arrived back at Downing Street from Paris this morning.*

down|load /dˌaʊnlˈoʊd/ (**downloads, downloading, downloaded**) V-T To **download** data means to transfer it to or from a computer along a line such as a telephone line, a radio link, or a computer network. ❑ *Users can download their material to a desktop PC back in the office.*

down|load|able /dˌaʊnlˈoʊdəbəl/ ADJ [usu ADJ n] If a computer file or program is **downloadable**, it can be downloaded to another computer. [COMPUTING] ❑ *...downloadable computer games.*

down|market /dˌaʊnmˈɑːkɪt/ also **down-market** ADJ **Downmarket** means the same as **downscale**. [BRIT]

down pay|ment (**down payments**) also **downpayment** N-COUNT If you make a **down payment** on something, you pay only a percentage of the total cost when you buy it. You then finish paying for it later, usually by paying a certain amount every month. ❑ *Celeste asked for the money as a down payment on an old farmhouse.*

down|play /dˌaʊnplˈeɪ/ (**downplays, downplaying, downplayed**) V-T If you **downplay** a fact or feature, you try to make people think that it is less important or serious than it really is. ❑ *Police sources yesterday downplayed the significance of the security breach.*

down|pour /dˈaʊnpɔːr/ (**downpours**) **1** N-COUNT A **downpour** is a sudden and unexpected heavy fall of rain. ❑ *...sheltering from a sudden downpour of rain.* **2** → See feature box at **weather**

down|right /dˈaʊnraɪt/ ADV [ADV adj] You use **downright** to emphasize unpleasant or bad qualities or behavior. [EMPHASIS] ❑ *...ideas that would have been downright dangerous if put into practice.* • ADJ [ADJ n] **Downright** is also an adjective. ❑ *...downright bad manners.*

down|river /dˌaʊnrˈɪvər/ also **down-river** ADV Something that is moving **downriver** is moving toward the mouth of a river, from a point further up the river. Something that is

downriver is toward the mouth of a river. ❑ *By 9:30 we had cast off and were heading downriver.* ❑ *...a big tourist hotel a few hundred yards downriver.* ❑ *Cologne is not so very far downriver from Mainz.* • ADJ [ADJ n] **Downriver** is also an adjective. ❑ *...downriver factories dispensing billows of smoke.*

down|scale /dˈaʊnskeɪl/ ADJ [usu ADJ n] If you describe a product or service as **downscale**, you think that it is cheap and not very good in quality. [AM] ❑ *...downscale department stores.*

in BRIT, use **downmarket**

down|side /dˈaʊnsaɪd/ N-SING The **downside** of a situation is the aspect of it which is less positive, pleasant, or useful than its other aspects. ❑ *The downside of this approach is a lack of clear leadership.*

down|size /dˈaʊnsaɪz/ (**downsizes, downsizing, downsized**) V-T/V-I To **downsize** something such as a business or industry means to make it smaller. [BUSINESS] ❑ *American manufacturing organizations have been downsizing their factories.* ❑ *...today's downsized economy.* • **down|siz|ing** N-UNCOUNT ❑ *...a trend toward downsizing in the personal computer market.*

down|spout /dˈaʊnspaʊt/ (**downspouts**) N-COUNT A **downspout** is a pipe attached to the side of a building, through which rainwater flows from the roof into a drain. [AM] ❑ *He installed rain gutters and downspouts.*

in BRIT, use **drainpipe**

down|stage /dˌaʊnstˈeɪdʒ/ ADV [ADV after v, be ADV] When an actor is **downstage** or moves **downstage**, he or she is or moves toward the front part of the stage. [TECHNICAL] ❑ *Krishna stands downstage in the open area.* • ADJ [ADJ n] **Downstage** is also an adjective. ❑ *...downstage members of the cast.*

down|stairs /dˌaʊnstˈɛərz/ **1** ADV [ADV after v] If you go **downstairs** in a building, you go down a staircase toward the ground floor. ❑ *Denise went downstairs and made some tea.* **2** ADV If something or someone is **downstairs** in a building, they are on the ground floor or on a lower floor than you. ❑ *The telephone was downstairs in the entrance hall.* **3** ADJ [ADJ n] **Downstairs** means situated on the ground floor of a building or on a lower floor than you are. ❑ *She repainted the downstairs rooms and closed off the second floor.* **4** N-SING The **downstairs** of a building is its lower floor or floors. ❑ *The downstairs of the two little houses had been entirely refashioned.*

down|state /dˌaʊnstˈeɪt/ ADJ [ADJ n] **Downstate** means belonging or relating to the parts of a state that are furthest to the south. [AM] ❑ *...people in downstate Illinois.* • ADV **Downstate** is also an adverb. ❑ *Exelon Corp. will explore building a new nuclear reactor downstate.*

down|stream /dˌaʊnstrˈiːm/ ADV Something that is moving **downstream** is moving toward the mouth of a river, from a point further up the river. Something that is **downstream** is further toward the mouth of a river than where you are. ❑ *We had drifted downstream.* • ADJ [ADJ n] **Downstream** is also an adjective. ❑ *Breaking the dam could submerge some downstream cities.*

down|swing /dˈaʊnswɪŋ/ (**downswings**) N-COUNT A **downswing** is a sudden downward movement in something such as an economy, that had previously been improving. ❑ *Industry may disappear if the manufacturing economy remains on a downswing.*

Down syn|drome also **Down's syndrome** N-UNCOUNT **Down syndrome** is a condition that some people are born with. People who have Down syndrome have physical differences, such as shorter stature, and learning difficulties.

down|time /dˈaʊntaɪm/ **1** N-UNCOUNT In industry, **downtime** is the time during which machinery or equipment is not operating. ❑ *On the production line, downtime has been reduced from 55% to 26%.* **2** N-UNCOUNT In computing, **downtime** is time when a computer is not working. ❑ *Downtime due to worm removal from networks cost close to $450 million.* **3** N-UNCOUNT **Downtime** is time when people are relaxing or not working. [mainly AM] ❑ *Downtime in Hollywood can cost a lot of money.*

down-to-earth ADJ If you say that someone is **down-to-earth**, you approve of the fact that they concern themselves with practical things and actions, rather than with abstract theories. [APPROVAL] ❑ *Gloria is probably the most down-to-earth person I've ever met.*

down|town /daʊntaʊn/ ADJ [ADJ n] **Downtown** places are in or toward the center of a large town or city, where the stores and places of business are. [mainly AM] ☐ ...an office in downtown Chicago. • ADV **Downtown** is also an adverb. ☐ By day he worked downtown for American Standard. • N-UNCOUNT [oft the N] **Downtown** is also a noun. ☐ ...in a large vacant area of the downtown.

down|trend /daʊntrend/ N-SING A **downtrend** is a general downward movement in something such as a company's profits or the economy. ☐ The increase slowed to 0.4 percent, possibly indicating the start of a downtrend.

down|trod|den /daʊntrɒdᵊn/ ADJ People who are **downtrodden** are treated very badly by people with power, and do not have the ability or the energy to do anything about it. ☐ The owner is making huge profits at the expense of downtrodden peasants.

down|turn /daʊntɜrn/ (**downturns**) N-COUNT If there is a **downturn** in the economy or in a company or industry, it becomes worse or less successful than it had been. ☐ They predicted a severe economic downturn.

down un|der PHRASE People sometimes refer to Australia and New Zealand as **down under**. [INFORMAL] ☐ For summer skiing down under, there is no better place than New Zealand.

down|ward /daʊnwərd/

The form **downwards** is also used for the adverb.

1 ADJ [ADJ n] A **downward** movement or look is directed toward a lower place or a lower level. ☐ ...a firm downward movement of the hands. **2** ADJ [ADJ n] If you refer to a **downward** trend, you mean that something is decreasing or that a situation is getting worse. ☐ The downward trend in home ownership is likely to continue. **3** ADV If you move or look **downward**, you move or look toward the ground or a lower level. ☐ Benedict pointed downward again with his stick. **4** ADV [ADV after v] If an amount or rate moves **downward**, it decreases. ☐ Inflation is moving firmly downward. **5** ADV [from n ADV] If you want to emphasize that a statement applies to everyone in an organization, you can say that it applies from its leader **downward**. [EMPHASIS] ☐ ...from the president downward.

down|wind /daʊnwɪnd/ ADV If something moves **downwind**, it moves in the same direction as the wind. If something is **downwind**, the wind is blowing toward it. ☐ He attempted to return downwind to the airfield.

downy /daʊni/ (**downier, downiest**) **1** ADJ [usu ADJ n] Something that is **downy** is filled or covered with small soft feathers. ☐ ...the warm downy quilt. **2** ADJ Something that is **downy** is covered with very fine hairs. ☐ ...leaves that are often downy underneath.

dow|ry /daʊəri/ (**dowries**) N-COUNT A woman's **dowry** is the money and goods which, in some cultures, her family gives to the man that she marries.

dowse /daʊs/ (**dowses, dowsing, dowsed**) → see **douse**

doy|en /dɔɪən, dɔɪɛn/ (**doyens**) N-COUNT [usu sing, usu the N of n] If you refer to someone as the **doyen** of a group or profession, you mean that they are the oldest and most experienced and respected member of it. [FORMAL, APPROVAL] ☐ ...the doyen of political interviewers.

doy|enne /dɔɪɛn/ (**doyennes**) N-COUNT [usu sing, usu the N of n] If you refer to a woman as the **doyenne** of a group or profession, you mean that she is the oldest and most experienced and respected woman in it. [FORMAL, APPROVAL] ☐ ...the doyenne of American film critics.

doze /doʊz/ (**dozes, dozing, dozed**) V-I When you **doze**, you sleep lightly or for a short period, especially during the daytime. ☐ For a while she dozed fitfully.

▶ **doze off** PHRASAL VERB If you **doze off**, you fall into a light sleep, especially during the daytime. ☐ I closed my eyes for a minute and must have dozed off.

doz|en /dʌzᵊn/ (**dozens**)

The plural form is **dozen** after a number, or after a word or expression referring to a number, such as 'several' or 'a few.'

1 NUM If you have a **dozen** things, you have twelve of them. ☐ You will be able to take ten dozen bottles free of duty through customs. **2** NUM You can refer to a group of approximately twelve things or people as a **dozen**. You can refer to a group of approximately six things or people as **half a dozen**. ☐ In half a dozen words, he had explained the bond that linked them. **3** QUANT [QUANT of pl-n] If you refer to **dozens of** things or people, you are emphasizing that there are very many of them. [EMPHASIS] ☐ ...a storm which destroyed dozens of homes and buildings. • PRON You can also use **dozens** as a pronoun. ☐ Just as revealing are Mr. Johnson's portraits, of which there are dozens.

dozy /doʊzi/ (**dozier, doziest**) **1** ADJ If you are **dozy**, you are feeling sleepy and not very alert. ☐ Maybe I eat too much and that's what makes me dozy. **2** ADJ If you describe someone as **dozy**, you mean they are rather stupid and slow to understand things. [BRIT, INFORMAL, DISAPPROVAL]

D. Phil. /diː fɪl/ (**D. Phils.**) D. Phil. is an abbreviation for Doctor of Philosophy.

Dr. (**Drs.**) Dr. is a written abbreviation for **Doctor**. ☐ ...Dr. John Hardy of St. Mary's Medical School.

in BRIT, use **Dr**

drab /dræb/ (**drabber, drabbest**) ADJ If you describe something as **drab**, you think that it is dull and boring to look at or experience. ☐ ...his drab little office. • **drab|ness** N-UNCOUNT ☐ ...the dusty drabness of nearby villages.

drach|ma /drækmə/ (**drachmas**) N-COUNT [num N] The **drachma** was the unit of money that was used in Greece. In 2002 it was replaced by the euro. • N-SING [the N] The **drachma** was also used to refer to the Greek currency system. ☐ The drachma disappeared, replaced by the euro when Greece joined the single European currency.

dra|co|nian /dreɪkoʊniən, drə-/ ADJ **Draconian** laws or measures are extremely harsh and severe. [FORMAL] ☐ ...indications that there would be no draconian measures to lower U.S. health care costs.

draft /dræft/ (**drafts, drafting, drafted**) **1** N-COUNT A **draft** is an early version of a letter, book, or speech. ☐ I rewrote his rough draft, which was published under my name. ☐ I faxed a first draft of this article to him. **2** N-COUNT A **draft** is a written order for payment of money by a bank, especially from one bank to another. ☐ Payments must be made in U.S. dollars by a bank draft drawn to the order of the United Nations Postal Administration. **3** N-COUNT A **draft** is a current of air that comes into a place in an undesirable way. [AM] ☐ Block drafts around doors and windows.

in BRIT, use **draught**

4 V-T When you **draft** a letter, book, or speech, you write the first version of it. ☐ He drafted a letter to the editors. **5** V-T [usu passive] If you **are drafted**, you are ordered to serve in the armed forces, usually for a limited period of time. [mainly AM] ☐ During the Second World War, he was drafted into the U.S. Army. **6** V-T If people **are drafted** to do something, they are asked to do a particular job. ☐ She hoped that Fox could be drafted to run the organization. **7** N-SING **The draft** is the practice of ordering people to serve in the armed forces, usually for a limited period of time. [mainly AM] ☐ ...his effort to avoid the draft.

───── SYNONYMS ─────

draft
NOUN **1**
outline: Following is an outline of the survey findings.
plan: ...a detailed plan of action for restructuring the group.
sketch: I had a basic sketch of a plan.

draft dodg|er (**draft dodgers**) N-COUNT A **draft dodger** is someone who avoids joining the armed forces when normally they would have to join. [mainly AM, DISAPPROVAL]

draftee /dræftiː/ (**draftees**) N-COUNT A **draftee** is someone ordered to serve in the armed forces. [AM]

drafts|man /dræftsmən/ (**draftsmen**)

in BRIT, use **draughtsman**

N-COUNT A **draftsman** is a man whose job is to prepare very detailed drawings of machinery, equipment, or buildings.

drafts|man|ship /dræftsmənʃɪp/

in BRIT, use **draughtsmanship**

N-UNCOUNT **Draftsmanship** is the ability to draw well or the art of drawing.

drafts|woman /dræftswʊmən/ (**draftswomen**)

in BRIT, use **draughtswoman**

N-COUNT A **draftswoman** is a woman whose job is to prepare very detailed drawings of machinery, equipment, or buildings.

drafty /dræfti/

in BRIT, use **draughty**

ADJ A **drafty** room or building has currents of cold air blowing through it, usually because the windows and doors do not fit very well.

drag ♦◇◇ /dræg/ (**drags, dragging, dragged**) **1** V-T If you **drag** something, you pull it along the ground, often with difficulty. ◻ He got up and dragged his chair toward the table. **2** V-T To **drag** a computer image means to use the mouse to move the position of the image on the screen, or to change its size or shape. [COMPUTING] ◻ Use your mouse to drag the pictures to their new size. **3** V-T If someone **drags** you somewhere, they pull you there, or force you to go there by physically threatening you. ◻ The vigilantes dragged the men out of the vehicles. **4** V-T If someone **drags** you somewhere you do not want to go, they make you go there. ◻ When you can drag him away from his work, he can also be a devoted father. **5** V-T If you say that you **drag** yourself somewhere, you are emphasizing that you have to make a very great effort to go there. [EMPHASIS] ◻ I find it really hard to drag myself out and exercise regularly. **6** V-T If you **drag** your foot or your leg behind you, you walk with great difficulty because your foot or leg is injured in some way. ◻ He was barely able to drag his poisoned leg behind him. **7** V-T If the police **drag** a river or lake, they pull nets or hooks across the bottom of it in order to look for something. ◻ Police are planning to drag the pond later this morning. **8** V-I If a period of time or an event **drags**, it is very boring and seems to last a long time. ◻ The minutes dragged past. **9** N-SING If something is **a drag on** the development or progress of something, it slows it down or makes it more difficult. ◻ The satellite acts as a drag on the shuttle. **10** N-SING If you say that something is **a drag**, you mean that it is unpleasant or very dull. [INFORMAL, DISAPPROVAL] ◻ As far as shopping for clothes goes, it's a drag. **11** N-COUNT If you take a **drag** on a cigarette or pipe that you are smoking, you take in air through it. [INFORMAL] ◻ He took a drag on his cigarette, and exhaled the smoke. **12** N-UNCOUNT **Drag** is the wearing of women's clothes by men or men's clothes by women, usually as part of an entertainment. ◻ The star wore drag and false eyelashes. • PHRASE If someone is **in drag**, they are wearing clothes usually worn by people of the opposite sex, usually as part of an entertainment. **13** PHRASE If you **drag** your **feet** or **drag** your **heels**, you delay doing something or do it very slowly because you do not want to do it. ◻ The government was dragging its feet, and this was threatening moves toward peace.
▶ **drag out 1** PHRASAL VERB If you **drag** something **out**, you make it last for longer than is necessary. ◻ ...a company that was willing and able to drag out the proceedings for years. **2** PHRASAL VERB If you **drag** something **out** of a person, you persuade them to tell you something that they do not want to tell you. ◻ The families soon discovered that every piece of information had to be dragged out of the authorities.

drag and drop (**drags and drops, dragging and dropping, dragged and dropped**) also **drag-and-drop 1** V-T If you **drag and drop** computer files or images, you move them from one place to another by clicking on them with the mouse and moving them across the screen. ◻ When installing Office, users simply drag and drop the Office folder to their hard drive. **2** N-UNCOUNT **Drag and drop** is a method of moving computer files or images from one place to another by clicking on them with the mouse and moving them across the screen. ◻ Copying software onto an iPod is as easy as drag and drop. • ADJ [ADJ n] **Drag and drop** is also an adjective. ◻ ...a drag and drop text and graphics.

drag|net /drægnet/ N-SING [oft n n] A **dragnet** is a method used by police to catch suspected criminals. A large number of police officers search a specific area, in the hope that they will eventually find the person they are looking for. ◻ ...a massive police dragnet for two suspected terrorists.

drag|on /drægən/ (**dragons**) N-COUNT In stories and legends, a **dragon** is an animal like a big lizard. It has wings and claws, and breathes out fire.

dragon|fly /drægənflaɪ/ (**dragonflies**) N-COUNT **Dragonflies** are brightly colored insects with long, thin bodies and two sets of wings. Dragonflies are often found near slow-moving water.

dra|goon /drəgun/ (**dragoons, dragooning, dragooned**) V-T If someone **dragoons** you into doing something that you do not want to do, they persuade you to do it even though you try hard not to agree. ◻ ...the history professor who had dragooned me into taking the exam.

drag queen (**drag queens**) N-COUNT A **drag queen** is a male entertainer who tells jokes or sings while dressed as a woman. ◻ This was the New York drag queen's first show on these shores. ◻ The neighborhood is given over to performers, stilt walkers and drag queens.

drain ♦◇◇ /dreɪn/ (**drains, draining, drained**) **1** V-T/V-I If you **drain** a liquid from a place or object, you remove the liquid by causing it to flow somewhere else. If a liquid **drains** somewhere, it flows there. ◻ Miners built the tunnel to drain water out of the mines. ◻ Now the focus is on draining the water. **2** V-T/V-I If you **drain** a place or object, you dry it by causing water to flow out of it. If a place or object **drains**, water flows out of it until it is dry. ◻ The authorities have mobilized vast numbers of people to drain flooded land and build or repair dikes. **3** V-T/V-I If you **drain** food or if food **drains**, you remove the liquid that it has been in, especially after it has been cooked or soaked in water. ◻ Drain the pasta well, arrange on four plates and pour over the sauce. **4** V-T/V-I If the color or the blood **drains** or is **drained** from someone's face, they become very pale. You can also say that someone's face **drains** or **is drained** of color. [LITERARY] ◻ Harry felt the color drain from his face. **5** V-T If something **drains** you, it leaves you feeling physically and emotionally exhausted. ◻ My emotional turmoil had drained me. • **drained** ADJ ◻ I began to suffer from headaches, which left me feeling completely drained. • **drain|ing** ADJ ◻ This work is physically exhausting and emotionally draining. **6** V-T If you say that a country's or a company's resources or finances **are drained**, you mean that they are used or spent completely. ◻ The state's finances have been drained by drought and civil disorder. **7** N-COUNT A **drain** is a pipe that carries water or sewage away from a place, or an opening in a surface that leads to the pipe. ◻ Tony built his own house and laid his own drains. **8** N-SING If you say that something is a **drain** on an organization's finances or resources, you mean that it costs the organization a large amount of money, and you do not think that it is worth it. ◻ ...an ultramodern printing plant, which has been a big drain on resources. **9** PHRASE If you say that something is going **down the drain**, you mean that it is being destroyed or wasted. [INFORMAL] ◻ They were aware that their public image was rapidly going down the drain.

drain|age /dreɪnɪdʒ/ N-UNCOUNT **Drainage** is the system or process by which water or other liquids are drained from a place. ◻ Line the pots with pebbles to ensure good drainage.

drain|board /dreɪnbɔrd/ (**drainboards**) N-COUNT [usu the N in sing] A **drainboard** is the place on a sink unit where things such as cups, plates, and flatware are put to drain after they have been washed. [AM]

in BRIT, use **draining board**

drain|ing board (**draining boards**) N-COUNT [usu the N in sing] The **draining board** is the same as a **drainboard**. [mainly BRIT]

drain|pipe /dreɪnpaɪp/ (**drainpipes**) **1** N-COUNT A **drainpipe** is a pipe attached to the side of a building, through which rainwater flows from the roof into a drain. ◻ He evaded police by climbing through a window and shinning down a drainpipe. **2** N-COUNT A **drainpipe** is a pipe through which liquid waste is removed from a building.

drake /dreɪk/ (**drakes**) N-COUNT A **drake** is a male duck.

dram /dræm/ (**drams**) N-COUNT [oft N of n] A **dram** is a small measure of whiskey. [mainly SCOTTISH] ◻ ...a dram of whiskey ◻ Would you care for a dram?

dra|ma ♦◇◇ /drɑmə, dræmə/ (**dramas**) **1** N-COUNT A **drama** is a serious play for the theater, television, or radio, or a serious movie. ◻ He acted in radio dramas. ◻ The movie is a drama about a woman searching for her children. **2** N-UNCOUNT You use **drama** to

drama queen

refer to plays in general or to work that is connected with plays and the theater, such as acting or producing. ❏ *He knew nothing of Greek drama.* **3** N-VAR You can refer to a real situation which is exciting or distressing as **drama**. ❏ *There was none of the drama and relief of a hostage release.*

COLLOCATIONS

drama
NOUN **1**
noun + **drama**: comedy, costume, courtroom, period, sci-fi; cop, crime, detective; radio, TV
adjective + **drama**: comic, fact-based, historical, romantic; gripping

---
SYNONYMS

drama
NOUN **3**
crisis: *...someone to turn to in moments of crisis.*
turmoil: *Her marriage was in turmoil.*
mayhem: *...the economic mayhem that this country's going through now.*
stir: *Her film has caused a stir in America.*
commotion: *He heard a commotion outside.*

---

dra|ma queen (drama queens) N-COUNT If you call someone a **drama queen**, you mean they react to situations in an unnecessarily dramatic or exaggerated way. [INFORMAL] ❏ *Don't worry, he's just being a drama queen.*

dra|mat|ic ✦✦◇ /drəmætɪk/ **1** ADJ A **dramatic** change or event happens suddenly and is very noticeable and surprising. ❏ *A fifth year of drought is expected to have dramatic effects on the California economy.* • **dra|mati|cal|ly** /drəmætɪkli/ ADV ❏ *At speeds above 50 mph, serious injuries dramatically increase.* **2** ADJ A **dramatic** action, event, or situation is exciting and impressive. ❏ *He witnessed many dramatic escapes as people jumped from as high as the fourth floor.* • **dra|mati|cal|ly** ADV ❏ *He tipped his head to one side and sighed dramatically.* **3** ADJ [ADJ n] You use **dramatic** to describe things connected with or relating to the theater, drama, or plays. ❏ *...a dramatic arts major in college.*

SYNONYMS

dramatic
ADJ
1
drastic: *...a drastic reduction in the number of people dying.*
severe: *I suffered from severe bouts of depression.*
radical: *They want a radical reform of the way soccer is run in England.*
extreme: *The scheme has been condemned as extreme.*
2
thrilling: *Our wildlife trips offer a thrilling encounter with wildlife in its natural state.*
sensational: *The world champions suffered a sensational defeat.*
breathtaking: *Some of their soccer was breathtaking, a delight to watch.*
hair-raising: *Her truck is a very large pickup which she drives at hair-raising speeds.*

---

dra|mat|ics /drəmætɪks/ **1** N-UNCOUNT [usu with supp] You use **dramatics** to refer to activities connected with the theater and drama, such as acting in plays or producing them. ❏ *Angela says she longs to join an amateur dramatics class.* ❏ *...the university dramatics society.* **2** N-PLURAL You talk about **dramatics** to express your disapproval of behavior which seems to show too much emotion, and which you think is done deliberately in order to impress people. [DISAPPROVAL] ❏ *...another wearisome outbreak of Nancy's dramatics.*

dra|ma|tis per|so|nae /dræmətɪs pərsoʊnaɪ/ N-PLURAL [the N] The characters in a play are sometimes referred to as the dramatis personae. [TECHNICAL]

drama|tist /dræmətɪst/ (dramatists) N-COUNT A **dramatist** is someone who writes plays.

drama|tize /dræmətaɪz/ (dramatizes, dramatizing, dramatized)

in BRIT, also use **dramatise**

1 V-T [usu passive] If a book or story **is dramatized**, it is written or presented as a play, movie, or television drama. ❏ *...an incident later dramatized in the movie "The Right Stuff."* • **drama|ti|za|tion** /dræmətɪzeɪʃ*ə*n/ (dramatizations) N-COUNT ❏ *...a dramatization of D. H. Lawrence's novel, "Chatterley's Lover."* **2** V-T If you say that someone **dramatizes** a situation or event, you mean that they try to make it seem more serious, more important, or more exciting than it really is. [DISAPPROVAL] ❏ *They have a tendency to show off, to dramatize almost every situation.*

drank /dræŋk/ **Drank** is the past tense of **drink**.

drape /dreɪp/ (drapes, draping, draped) **1** V-T If you **drape** a piece of cloth somewhere, you place it there so that it hangs down in a casual and graceful way. ❏ *Natasha took the coat and draped it over her shoulders.* **2** V-T If someone or something **is draped** in a piece of cloth, they are loosely covered by it. ❏ *...a casket draped in the Virginia flag.* **3** N-COUNT **Drapes** are long heavy curtains. [AM] ❏ *He pulled the drapes shut, locked the door behind him.*

in BRIT, use **curtains**

dra|pery /dreɪpəri/ (draperies) **1** N-UNCOUNT [also N in pl] You can refer to cloth, curtains, or clothing hanging in folds as **drapery** or **draperies**. ❏ *In the dining-room the draperies create an atmosphere of elegance.* **2** N-UNCOUNT **Drapery** is cloth that you buy in a store. [BRIT]

in AM, use **dry goods**

dras|tic /dræstɪk/ **1** ADJ If you have to take **drastic** action in order to solve a problem, you have to do something extreme to solve it. ❏ *Drastic measures are needed to clean up the profession.* **2** ADJ A **drastic** change is a very great change. ❏ *Foreign food aid has led to a drastic reduction in the numbers of people dying of starvation.* • **dras|ti|cal|ly** ADV [ADV with v] ❏ *As a result, services have been drastically reduced.*

draughts /drɑːfts/ N-UNCOUNT **Draughts** is the same as **checkers**. [BRIT]

draughts board (draughts boards) also **draught board** N-COUNT A **draughts board** is the same as a **checkerboard**. [BRIT]

draughts|man /drɑːftsmən/ [BRIT] → see **draftsman**

draughts|man|ship /drɑːftsmənʃɪp/ [BRIT] → see **draftsmanship**

draughts|woman /drɑːftswʊmən/ [BRIT] → see **draftswoman**

draughty /drɑːfti/ [BRIT] → see **drafty**

DRAW

① MAKE A PICTURE
② MOVE, PULL, OR TAKE
③ OTHER USES AND PHRASAL VERBS

---

① **draw** ✦✦✦ /drɔː/ (draws, drawing, drew, drawn)
→ Please look at meaning **2** to see if the expression you are looking for is shown under another headword.

1 V-T/V-I When you **draw**, or when you **draw** something, you use a pencil or pen to produce a picture, pattern, or diagram. ❏ *She would sit there drawing with the pencil stub.* • **draw|ing** N-UNCOUNT ❏ *I like dancing, singing, and drawing.* **2** to draw the line → see **line** ②

② **draw** ✦✦✦ /drɔː/ (draws, drawing, drew, drawn)
→ Please look at meaning **15** to see if the expression you are looking for is shown under another headword.

1 V-I If you **draw** somewhere, you move there slowly. [WRITTEN] ❏ *She drew away and did not smile.* **2** V-T If you **draw** something or someone in a particular direction, you move them in that direction, usually by pulling them gently. [WRITTEN] ❏ *He drew his chair nearer the fire.* ❏ *He put his arm around Caroline's shoulders and drew her close to him.* **3** V-T When you **draw** a curtain or blind, you pull it across a window, either to cover or to uncover it. ❏ *After drawing the curtains, she lit a candle.* **4** V-T If someone **draws** a gun, knife, or other weapon, they pull it out of its container and threaten you with it. ❏ *He drew his dagger and turned to face his pursuers.* **5** V-I When a vehicle **draws** somewhere, it moves there smoothly and steadily. ❏ *Claire had seen the taxi drawing away.* **6** V-T If you **draw** a deep breath, you breathe in deeply once. ❏ *He paused, drawing a deep breath.* **7** V-I If you **draw** on a cigarette, you breathe the smoke from it into your mouth or lungs. ❏ *He drew on an American cigarette.* ■8 V-T To **draw** something such as water or energy **from** a particular source means to take it from that source. ❏ *Villagers still have to draw their water from wells.* ■9 V-T If something that hits you or presses part of your body **draws** blood, it cuts your skin so that it bleeds. ❏ *Any practice that draws blood could increase the risk of getting the virus.* ■10 V-T If you **draw** money out of a bank account, you get it from the account so that you can use it. ❏ *She was drawing out cash from an ATM.* ■11 V-T To **draw** something means to choose it or to be given it, as part of a competition, game, or lottery. ❏ *He put the pile of chips in the center of the table and drew a card.* • N-COUNT **Draw** is also a noun. ❏ *...the final draw for all prize winners takes place on March 17.* ■12 V-T To **draw** something **from** a particular thing or place means to take or get it from that thing or place. ❏ *I draw strength from the millions of women who have faced this challenge successfully.* ■13 V-T If something such as a movie or an event **draws** a lot of people, it is so interesting or entertaining that a lot of people go to it. ❏ *The game is currently drawing huge crowds.* ■14 V-T If someone or something **draws** you, it attracts you very strongly. ❏ *In no sense did he draw her as Alex had done.* ■15 **to draw lots** → see **lot**

③ **draw** ✦✦✦ /drɔː/ (draws, drawing, drew, drawn) ■1 V-T If you **draw** a particular conclusion, you decide that that conclusion is true. ❏ *He draws two conclusions from this.* ■2 V-T If you **draw** a comparison, parallel, or distinction, you compare or contrast two different ideas, systems, or other things. ❏ *...literary critics drawing comparisons between George Sand and George Eliot.* ■3 V-T If you **draw** someone's attention to something, you make them aware of it or make them think about it. ❏ *He was waving his arms to draw their attention.* ■4 V-T If someone or something **draws** a particular reaction, people react to it in that way. ❏ *Such a policy would inevitably draw fierce resistance from farmers.* ■5 V-RECIP In a game or competition, if one person or team **draws** with another one, or if two people or teams **draw**, they have the same number of points or goals at the end of the game. [mainly BRIT] ❏ *Holland and the Republic of Ireland drew one-one.* ❏ *We drew with Ireland in the first game.* • N-COUNT **Draw** is also a noun.

in AM, usually use **tie**

■6 → see also **drawing** ■7 PHRASE When an event or period of time **draws to a close** or **draws to an end**, it finishes. ❏ *Another celebration had drawn to its close.* ■8 PHRASE If an event or period of time **is drawing closer** or **is drawing nearer**, it is approaching. ❏ *Next spring's elections are drawing nearer.*
▶ **draw in** PHRASAL VERB If you **draw** someone **in** or **draw** them **into** something you are involved with, you cause them to become involved with it. ❏ *It won't be easy for you to draw him in.*
▶ **draw on** PHRASAL VERB If you **draw on** or **draw upon** something such as your skill or experience, you make use of it in order to do something. ❏ *He drew on his experience as a yachtsman to make a documentary program.*
▶ **draw up** PHRASAL VERB If you **draw up** a document, list, or plan, you prepare it and write it out. ❏ *They agreed to establish a working party to draw up a formal agreement.*
▶ **draw upon** → see **draw on**

draw|back /drɔːbæk/ (drawbacks) N-COUNT A **drawback** is an aspect of something or someone that makes them less acceptable than they would otherwise be. ❏ *He felt the apartment's only drawback was that it was too small.*

draw|bridge /drɔːbrɪdʒ/ (drawbridges) N-COUNT A **drawbridge** is a bridge that can be pulled up, for example, to allow ships to pass underneath it or to prevent people from getting into a castle.

draw|er /drɔːr/ (drawers) N-COUNT A **drawer** is part of a desk, chest, or other piece of furniture that is shaped like a box and is designed for putting things in. You pull it toward you to open it. ❏ *She opened her desk drawer and took out the manual.*

draw|ers /drɔːrz/ N-PLURAL [also *a pair of* N] **Drawers** are the same as **underpants**. [mainly AM, OLD-FASHIONED] ❏ *I was in my drawers and my T-shirt.*

draw|ing /drɔːɪŋ/ (drawings) ■1 N-COUNT A **drawing** is a picture made with a pencil or pen. ❏ *She did a drawing of me.* ■2 → see also **draw** ①

draw|ing board (drawing boards) ■1 N-COUNT A **drawing board** is a large flat board, often attached to a metal frame so that it looks like a desk, on which you place your paper when you are drawing or designing something. ■2 PHRASE [PHR after v] If you say that you will have to go **back to the drawing board**, you mean that something which you have done has not been successful and that you will have to start again or try another idea.

draw|ing pin (drawing pins) also **drawing-pin** N-COUNT A **drawing pin** is the same as a **thumbtack**. [BRIT]

draw|ing room (drawing rooms) N-COUNT A **drawing room** is a room, especially a large room in a large house, where people sit and relax, or entertain guests. [mainly BRIT, OLD-FASHIONED]

drawl /drɔːl/ (drawls, drawling, drawled) V-T/V-I If someone **drawls**, they speak slowly and not very clearly, with long vowel sounds. ❏ *"I guess you guys don't mind if I smoke?" he drawled.* • N-COUNT **Drawl** is also a noun. ❏ *Jack's southern drawl had become more pronounced as they'd traveled southward.*

drawn /drɔːn/ ■1 **Drawn** is the past participle of **draw**. ■2 ADJ If someone or their face looks **drawn**, their face is thin and they look very tired, ill, worried, or unhappy. ❏ *She looked drawn and tired when she turned toward me.*

drawn-out ADJ You can describe something as **drawn-out** when it lasts or takes longer than you would like it to. ❏ *The road to peace will be long and drawn-out.*

draw|string /drɔːstrɪŋ/ (drawstrings) N-COUNT [usu sing, oft N N] A **drawstring** is a cord that goes through an opening, for example, at the top of a bag or a pair of pants. When the cord is pulled tighter, the opening gets smaller. ❏ *...a velvet bag with a drawstring.*

dray /dreɪ/ (drays) N-COUNT A **dray** is a large flat cart with four wheels which is pulled by horses.

dread /drɛd/ (dreads, dreading, dreaded) ■1 V-T If you **dread** something which may happen, you feel very anxious and unhappy about it because you think it will be unpleasant or upsetting. ❏ *I'm dreading Christmas this year.* ❏ *I dreaded coming back, to be honest.* ■2 N-UNCOUNT **Dread** is a feeling of great anxiety and fear about something that may happen. ❏ *She thought with dread of the cold winters to come.* ■3 → see also **dreaded** ■4 PHRASE If you say that you **dread to think** what might happen, you mean that you are anxious about it because it is likely to be very unpleasant. ❏ *I dread to think what will happen in the case of a major emergency.*

dread|ed /drɛdɪd/ ■1 ADJ [ADJ n] **Dreaded** means terrible and greatly feared. ❏ *No one knew how to treat this dreaded disease.* ■2 ADJ [ADJ n] You can use **the dreaded** to describe something that you, or a particular group of people, find annoying, inconvenient, or undesirable. [INFORMAL, FEELINGS] ❏ *She's a victim of the dreaded hay fever.*

dread|ful /drɛdfəl/ ■1 ADJ If you say that something is **dreadful**, you mean that it is very bad or unpleasant, or very poor in quality. ❏ *They told us the dreadful news.* • **dread|fully** ADV [ADV with v] ❏ *You behaved dreadfully.* ■2 ADJ [ADJ n] **Dreadful** is used to emphasize the degree or extent of something bad. [EMPHASIS] ❏ *We've made a dreadful mistake.* • **dread|fully** ADV ❏ *He looks dreadfully ill.*

dread|locked /drɛdlɒkt/ ADJ [usu ADJ n] A **dreadlocked** person has their hair in dreadlocks. [WRITTEN] ❏ *...the dreadlocked Rastafarian, Bob Marley.*

dread|locks /drɛdlɒks/ N-PLURAL If someone has **dreadlocks**, their hair is divided into a large number of tight strips, like pieces of rope. Dreadlocks are worn especially by Rastafarians.

dream ✦✦✧ /driːm/ (dreams, dreaming, dreamed or dreamt) ■1 N-COUNT A **dream** is a series of events that you experience only in your mind while you are asleep. ❏ *He had a dream about Claire.* ■2 N-COUNT You can refer to a situation or event as a **dream** if you often think about it because you would like it to happen. ❏ *He had finally accomplished his dream of becoming a pilot.* ■3 N-COUNT You can refer to a situation or event that does not seem real as a **dream**, especially if it is very strange or unpleasant. ❏ *When the right woman comes along, this bad dream will be over.* ■4 V-T/V-I When you **dream**, you experience events in your mind while you are asleep. ❏ *Ivor dreamed that he was on a bus.* ❏ *She dreamed about her baby.* ■5 V-T/V-I If you often think about something that you would very much like to happen or have, you can say that you **dream** of it. ❏ *As a schoolgirl, she had* dreamed of becoming a pilot. ❑ For most of us, a brand new designer kitchen is something we can only dream about. ❑ I dream that my son will attend college. **6** V-I [with neg] If you say that you would not **dream of** doing something, you are emphasizing that you would never do it because you think it is wrong or is not possible or suitable for you. [EMPHASIS] ❑ I wouldn't dream of making fun of you. **7** V-T/V-I [with brd-neg] If you say that you never **dreamed** that something would happen, you are emphasizing that you did not think that it would happen because it seemed very unlikely. [EMPHASIS] ❑ I never dreamed that I would be able to afford a home here. **8** ADJ [ADJ n] You can use **dream** to describe something that you think is ideal or perfect, especially if it is something that you thought you would never be able to have or experience. ❑ ...a dream holiday to Jamaica. **9** N-SING If you describe something as a particular person's **dream**, you think that it would be ideal for that person and that he or she would like it very much. ❑ Greece is said to be a botanist's dream. **10** PHRASE If you say that someone does something **like a dream**, you think that they do it very well. If you say that something happens **like a dream**, you mean that it happens successfully without any problems. ❑ She cooked like a dream. **11** PHRASE If you describe someone or something as the person or thing **of** your **dreams**, you mean that you consider them to be ideal or perfect. ❑ This could be the man of my dreams. **12** PHRASE If you say that you could not imagine a particular thing **in** your **wildest dreams**, you are emphasizing that you think it is extremely strange or unlikely. [EMPHASIS] ❑ "Never in my wildest dreams did I think I'd ever accomplish this," said Toni. **13** PHRASE If you describe something as being **beyond** your **wildest dreams**, you are emphasizing that it is better than you could have imagined or hoped for. [EMPHASIS] ❑ She had already achieved success beyond her wildest dreams.

▶ **dream up** PHRASAL VERB If you **dream up** a plan or idea, you work it out or create it in your mind. ❑ I dreamed up a plan to solve both problems at once.

COLLOCATIONS

dream
NOUN **3**
noun + **dream**: boyhood, childhood
adjective + **dream**: distant, impossible, wildest; lifelong
verb + **dream**: fulfill, chase, pursue; achieve, live, realize; crush, dash, shatter

dream|er /drímər/ (**dreamers**) N-COUNT If you describe someone as a **dreamer**, you mean that they spend a lot of time thinking about and planning for things that they would like to happen but which are improbable or impractical. ❑ Far from being a dreamer, she's a level-headed pragmatist.

dreami|ly /drímɪli/ ADV If you say or do something **dreamily**, you say or do it in a way that shows your mind is occupied with pleasant, relaxing thoughts. ❑ "They were divine," she sighs, dreamily.

dream|land /drímlænd/ **1** N-UNCOUNT If a person is in **dreamland**, they are asleep. ❑ Don't insist on a firm mattress if softer ones can send you to dreamland faster. **2** N-UNCOUNT [also a N] If you refer to a situation as **dreamland**, you mean that it represents what someone would like to happen, but that it is completely unrealistic. ❑ In dreamland we play them in the final.

dream|less /drímlɪs/ ADJ [usu ADJ n] A **dreamless** sleep is very deep and peaceful, and without dreams. ❑ He fell into a deep dreamless sleep.

dream|like /drímlaɪk/ ADJ If you describe something as **dreamlike**, you mean it seems strange and unreal. ❑ Her paintings have a naive, dreamlike quality.

dreamt /drɛmt/ **Dreamt** is a past tense and past participle of **dream**.

dream team (**dream teams**) N-COUNT A **dream team** is the best possible group of people to be on a sports team or to do a particular job. ❑ ...basketball's dream team.

dream tick|et N-SING If journalists talk about a **dream ticket**, they are referring to two candidates for political office, for example, president and vice president, or prime minister and deputy prime minister, who they think will be extremely successful.

dreamy /drími/ (**dreamier, dreamiest**) **1** ADJ If you say that someone has a **dreamy** expression, you mean that they are not paying attention to things around them and look as if they are thinking about something pleasant. ❑ His face assumed a sort of dreamy expression. **2** ADJ If you describe something as **dreamy**, you mean that you like it and that it seems gentle and soft, like something in a dream. [APPROVAL] ❑ ...dreamy shots of beautiful sunsets.

dreary /drɪəri/ (**drearier, dreariest**) ADJ If you describe something as **dreary**, you mean that it is dull and depressing. ❑ ...a dreary little town in the Midwest.

dredge /drɛdʒ/ (**dredges, dredging, dredged**) V-T When people **dredge** a harbor, river, or other area of water, they remove mud and unwanted material from the bottom with a special machine in order to make it deeper or to look for something. ❑ Police have spent weeks dredging the lake but have not found his body.

▶ **dredge up** **1** PHRASAL VERB If someone **dredges up** a piece of information they learned a long time ago, or if they **dredge up** a distant memory, they manage to remember it. ❑ ...an American trying to dredge up some French or German learned in high school. **2** PHRASAL VERB If someone **dredges up** a damaging or upsetting fact about your past, they remind you of it or tell other people about it. ❑ She dredges up a minor misdemeanor: "You didn't give me money for the school trip."

dredg|er /drɛdʒər/ (**dredgers**) N-COUNT A **dredger** is a boat with a special machine attached to it, that is used to increase the size of harbors, rivers, and canals.

dregs /drɛgz/ **1** N-PLURAL [usu the N] The **dregs** of a liquid are the last drops left at the bottom of a container, together with any solid pieces that have sunk to the bottom. ❑ Colum drained the dregs from his cup. **2** N-PLURAL [usu the N of n] If you talk about the **dregs** of society or of a community, you mean the people in it who you consider to be the most worthless and bad. [DISAPPROVAL] ❑ He sees dissidents as the dregs of society.

drench /drɛntʃ/ (**drenches, drenching, drenched**) V-T To **drench** something or someone means to make them completely wet. ❑ They turned fire hoses on the people and drenched them. ❑ ...the idea of spending two whole days hanging on to a raft and getting drenched by icy water.

dress ♦♦◇ /drɛs/ (**dresses, dressing, dressed**) **1** N-COUNT A **dress** is a piece of clothing for a woman or girl that covers the body and part or all of the legs. ❑ She was wearing a black dress. **2** N-UNCOUNT You can refer to clothes worn by men or women as **dress**. ❑ He wore formal evening dress. **3** V-T/V-I When you **dress** or **dress** yourself, you put on clothes. ❑ He told Sarah to wait while he dressed. **4** V-T If you **dress** someone, for example, a child, you put clothes on them. ❑ She bathed her and dressed her in clean clothes. **5** V-I If someone **dresses** in a particular way, they wear clothes of a particular style or color. ❑ He dresses in a way that lets everyone know he's got authority. **6** V-I If you **dress for** something, you put on special clothes for it. ❑ We don't dress for dinner here. **7** V-T When someone **dresses** a wound, they clean it and cover it. ❑ The poor child never cried or protested when I was dressing her wounds. **8** → see also **dressing, dressed**

▶ **dress down** PHRASAL VERB If you **dress down**, you wear clothes that are less formal than usual. ❑ She dresses down in dark glasses and baggy clothes to avoid hordes of admirers.

▶ **dress up** **1** PHRASAL VERB If you **dress up** or **dress** yourself **up**, you put on different clothes, in order to make yourself look more formal than usual or to disguise yourself. ❑ You do not need to dress up for dinner. ❑ I just love the fun of dressing up in another era's clothing. **2** PHRASAL VERB If you **dress** someone **up**, you give them special clothes to wear, in order to make them look more formal or to disguise them. ❑ Mother loved to dress me up. **3** PHRASAL VERB If you **dress** something **up**, you try to make it seem more attractive, acceptable, or interesting than it really is. ❑ Politicians are happier to dress up their ruthless ambition as a necessary pursuit of the public good.

dres|sage /drɛsɑː, drə-/ N-UNCOUNT **Dressage** is a competition in which riders on horses have to make their horse perform controlled movements.

dress cir|cle N-SING The **dress circle** is the lowest of the curved rows of seats upstairs in a theater.

dress code (**dress codes**) N-COUNT The **dress code** of a place is the rules about what kind of clothes people are allowed to wear there. ❑ There was a brutally enforced dress code, which required women to be covered from head to toe.

dressed ♦◇◇ /drɛst/ **1** ADJ If you are **dressed**, you are wearing clothes rather than being naked or wearing your nightclothes. If you get **dressed**, you put on your clothes. ❑ *He was fully dressed, including shoes.* **2** ADJ [v-link ADJ] If you are **dressed** in a particular way, you are wearing clothes of a particular color or kind. ❑ *...a tall thin woman dressed in black.* **3** → see also **well-dressed**

dressed up 1 ADJ [usu v-link ADJ] If someone is **dressed up**, they are wearing special clothes, in order to look more formal than usual or in order to disguise themselves. ❑ *You're all dressed up. Are you going somewhere?* **2** ADJ [v-link ADJ as/in n] If you say that something is **dressed up** as something else, you mean that someone has tried to make it more acceptable or attractive by making it seem like that other thing. [DISAPPROVAL] ❑ *He tried to organize things so that the trip would be dressed up as a UN mission.*

dress|er /drɛsər/ (**dressers**) **1** N-COUNT A **dresser** is a chest of drawers, sometimes with a mirror on the top. [mainly AM] **2** N-COUNT You can use **dresser** to refer to the kind of clothes that a person wears. For example, if you say that someone is a **casual dresser**, you mean that they wear casual clothes. ❑ *Mr. Jorgensen was an immaculate dresser.*

dress|ing /drɛsɪŋ/ (**dressings**) **1** N-MASS A salad **dressing** is a mixture of oil, vinegar, and herbs or flavorings, which you pour over salad. ❑ *Mix the ingredients for the dressing in a bowl.* **2** N-COUNT A **dressing** is a covering that is put on a wound to protect it while it heals. ❑ *Miss Finkelstein will put a dressing on your thumb.* **3** N-MASS **Dressing** is a mixture of food that is cooked and then put inside a bird such as a turkey before it is eaten. [AM] ❑ *...cornbread dressing for the first Thanksgiving she cooked at home.*

dressing-down N-SING If someone gives you a **dressing-down**, they speak angrily to you because you have done something bad or foolish. [INFORMAL]

dress|ing gown (**dressing gowns**) also **dressing-gown** N-COUNT A **dressing gown** is a long, loose garment which you wear over your nightclothes when you are not in bed.

dress|ing room (**dressing rooms**) also **dressing-room** **1** N-COUNT A **dressing room** is a room in a theater where performers can dress and get ready for their performance. **2** N-COUNT A **dressing room** is a room at a sports stadium where players can change and get ready for their game. [BRIT]

in AM, use **locker room**

dress|ing ta|ble (**dressing tables**) also **dressing-table** N-COUNT A **dressing table** is a small table in a bedroom. It has drawers underneath and a mirror on top.

dressing-up also **dressing up** N-UNCOUNT **Dressing-up** is the same as **dress-up**. [BRIT]

dress|maker /drɛsmeɪkər/ (**dressmakers**) **1** N-COUNT A **dressmaker** is a person who makes women's or children's clothes. **2** → See feature box at **sewing**

dress|making /drɛsmeɪkɪŋ/ N-UNCOUNT **Dressmaking** is the activity or job of making clothes for women or children.

dress re|hears|al (**dress rehearsals**) **1** N-COUNT The **dress rehearsal** of a play, opera, or show is the final rehearsal before it is performed, in which the performers wear their costumes and the lights and scenery are all used as they will be in the performance. ❑ *We went to all the dress rehearsals together.* **2** N-COUNT You can describe an event as a **dress rehearsal** for a later, more important event when it indicates how the later event will be. ❑ *Yesterday's NEA event looked like a dress rehearsal for the Democratic convention.*

dress shirt (**dress shirts**) N-COUNT A **dress shirt** is a special shirt which men wear on formal occasions. It is worn with a dinner jacket and bow tie.

dress-up 1 N-UNCOUNT When children play **dress-up**, they put on special or different clothes and pretend to be different people. [AM]

in BRIT, use **dressing-up**

2 ADJ [ADJ n] **Dress-up** clothes are stylish clothes which you wear when you want to look elegant or formal. [AM] ❑ *The inns are informal and dress-up clothes are not required for dinner.*

dressy /drɛsi/ (**dressier, dressiest**) **1** ADJ **Dressy** clothes are clothes which you wear when you want to look elegant or formal. **2** → See feature box at **fashion**

drew /druː/ **Drew** is the past tense of **draw**.

drib|ble /drɪbəl/ (**dribbles, dribbling, dribbled**) **1** V-T/V-I If a liquid **dribbles** somewhere, or if you **dribble** it, it drops down slowly or flows in a thin stream. ❑ *Sweat dribbled down Hart's face.* **2** V-T/V-I When players **dribble** the ball in a game such as basketball or soccer, they keep kicking or tapping it quickly in order to keep it moving. ❑ *He dribbled the ball toward Ferris.* ❑ *He dribbled past four defenders.* **3** V-I If a person **dribbles**, saliva drops slowly from their mouth. ❑ *...to protect sheets when the baby dribbles.*

dribs and drabs /drɪbz ən dræbz/ PHRASE [PHR after v] If people or things arrive **in dribs and drabs**, they arrive in small numbers over a period of time rather than arriving all together. [INFORMAL] ❑ *Clients came in dribs and drabs.*

dried /draɪd/ **1** ADJ [ADJ n] **Dried** food or milk has had all the water removed from it so that it will last for a long time. ❑ *...an infusion which may be prepared from the fresh plant or the dried herb.* **2** → see also **dry**

dried fruit (**dried fruits**) N-VAR **Dried fruit** is fruit that has been preserved by being dried.

dried-up 1 ADJ [usu ADJ n] If you describe someone as **dried-up**, you are saying rudely that they are old and dull, and not worth paying attention to. [INFORMAL, DISAPPROVAL] ❑ *...a dried-up old solicitor.* **2** → see also **dry up**

dri|er /draɪər/ → see **dry, dryer**

drift ♦◇◇ /drɪft/ (**drifts, drifting, drifted**) **1** V-I When something **drifts** somewhere, it is carried there by the movement of wind or water. ❑ *We proceeded to drift on up the river.* **2** V-I If someone or something **drifts** into a situation, they get into that situation in a way that is not planned or controlled. ❑ *We need to offer young people drifting into crime an alternative set of values.* **3** V-I If you say that someone **drifts** around, you mean that they travel from place to place without a plan or settled way of life. [DISAPPROVAL] ❑ *You've been drifting from job to job without any real commitment.* **4** V-I To **drift** somewhere means to move there slowly or gradually. ❑ *As rural factories lay off workers, people drift toward the cities.* **5** V-I If sounds **drift** somewhere, they can be heard but they are not very loud. ❑ *Cool summer dance sounds are drifting from the stereo indoors.* **6** V-I If snow **drifts**, it builds up into piles as a result of the movement of the wind. ❑ *The snow, except where it drifted, was only calf-deep.* **7** N-COUNT A **drift** is a movement away from somewhere or something, or a movement toward somewhere or something different. ❑ *...the drift toward the cities.* **8** N-COUNT A **drift** is a mass of snow that has built up into a pile as a result of the movement of wind. ❑ *A nine-year-old boy was trapped in a snow drift.* **9** N-SING The **drift of** an argument or speech is the general point that is being made in it. ❑ *Grace was beginning to get his drift.* **10** → See feature box at **relationship**

▶ **drift off** PHRASAL VERB If you **drift off** to sleep, you gradually fall asleep. ❑ *It was only when he finally drifted off to sleep that the headaches eased.*

drift|er /drɪftər/ (**drifters**) N-COUNT If you describe someone as a **drifter**, you mean that they do not stay in one place or in one job for very long. [DISAPPROVAL]

drift|wood /drɪftwʊd/ N-UNCOUNT **Driftwood** is wood which has been carried onto the shore by the motion of the sea or a river, or which is still floating on the water.

drill /drɪl/ (**drills, drilling, drilled**) **1** N-COUNT A **drill** is a tool or machine that you use for making holes. ❑ *...a dentist's drill.* **2** N-COUNT A **drill** is a routine exercise or activity, in which people practice what they should do in dangerous situations. ❑ *...a fire drill.* **3** V-T/V-I When you **drill into** something, or **drill** a hole in something, you make a hole in it using a drill. ❑ *He drilled into the wall of Lili's bedroom.* **4** V-I When people **drill** for oil or water, they search for it by drilling deep holes in the ground or in the bottom of the sea. ❑ *There have been proposals to drill for more oil.* **5** N-VAR A **drill** is repeated training for a group of people, especially soldiers, so that they can do something quickly and efficiently. ❑ *The Marines carried out landing exercises in a drill that includes 18 ships and 90 aircraft.* **6** → See also color supplement

dri|ly /draɪli/ → see **dry**

drink ♦♦◇ /drɪŋk/ (drinks, drinking, drank, drunk) **1** V-T/V-I When you **drink** a liquid, you take it into your mouth and swallow it. ❏ *He drank his cup of tea.* ❏ *He drank thirstily.* **2** V-I To **drink** means to drink alcohol. ❏ *By his own admission, he was smoking and drinking too much.* • **drink|ing** N-UNCOUNT ❏ *She had left him because of his drinking.* **3** N-COUNT A **drink** is an amount of a liquid which you drink. ❏ *I'll get you a drink of water.* **4** N-COUNT A **drink** is an alcoholic drink. ❏ *She felt like a drink after a hard day.* **5** N-UNCOUNT **Drink** is alcohol, such as beer, wine, or whiskey. [mainly BRIT] ❏ *Too much drink is bad for your health.*
▶ **drink to** PHRASAL VERB When people **drink to** someone or something, they wish them success, good luck, or good health before having an alcoholic drink. ❏ *Let's drink to his memory, eh?*

drink|able /drɪŋkəbəl/ **1** ADJ Water that is **drinkable** is clean and safe for drinking. ❏ *...the pumping stations that provide the main supply of drinkable water for the region.* **2** ADJ If you say that a particular wine, beer, or other drink is **drinkable**, you mean that it tastes quite pleasant. ❏ *The food was good and the wine drinkable.*

drink-drive also **drink drive** ADJ [ADJ n] **Drink-drive** means relating to drink-driving. [BRIT] ❏ *Drink-drive deaths are on the increase again.*

drink-driving N-UNCOUNT **Drink-driving** is the same as **drunk driving**. [BRIT]

drink|er /drɪŋkər/ (drinkers) **1** N-COUNT If someone is a tea **drinker** or a beer **drinker**, for example, they regularly drink tea or beer. ❏ *Sherry drinkers far outnumber wine drinkers or whiskey drinkers.* **2** N-COUNT If you describe someone as a **drinker**, you mean that they drink alcohol, especially in large quantities. ❏ *I'm not a heavy drinker.*

drink|ing /drɪŋkɪŋ/ **1** ADJ [ADJ n] Someone's **drinking** friends or companions are people they regularly drink alcohol with. **2** → see also **drink**

drink|ing foun|tain (drinking fountains) N-COUNT A **drinking fountain** is a device which supplies water for people to drink in places such as streets, parks, or schools.

drink|ing wa|ter N-UNCOUNT **Drinking water** is water which it is safe to drink.

drip /drɪp/ (drips, dripping, dripped) **1** V-T/V-I When liquid **drips** somewhere, or you **drip** it somewhere, it falls in individual small drops. ❏ *Blood dripped from the corner of his mouth.* ❏ *Amid the trees the sea mist was dripping and moisture formed on Tom's glasses.* **2** V-I When something **drips**, drops of liquid fall from it. ❏ *A faucet in the kitchen was dripping.* ❏ *Lou was dripping with perspiration.* **3** V-I [usu cont] If you say that something **is dripping with** a particular thing, you mean that it contains a lot of that thing. [LITERARY] ❏ *They were dazed by window displays dripping with diamonds and furs.* **4** N-COUNT A **drip** is a small individual drop of a liquid. ❏ *Drips of water rolled down the trousers of his uniform.* **5** N-COUNT A **drip** is a piece of medical equipment by which a liquid is slowly passed through a tube into a patient's blood. ❏ *He was put on intravenous drip to treat his dehydration.* **6** → See feature box at **onomatopoeia**

drip-dry ADJ **Drip-dry** clothes or sheets are made of a fabric that dries free of creases when it is hung up wet. ❏ *...drip-dry shirts.*

drip-feed (drip-feeds, drip-feeding, drip-fed) also **drip feed** V-T If you **drip-feed** money into something, you pay the money a little at a time rather than paying it all at once. ❏ *...investors who adopt the sensible policy of drip feeding money into shares.*

drip|ping /drɪpɪŋ/ **1** PHRASE [usu v-link PHR] If you are **dripping wet**, you are so wet that water is dripping from you. ❏ *We were dripping wet from the spray.* **2** N-PLURAL **Drippings** is the fat which comes out of meat when it is fried or roasted, and which can be used for frying food. [AM]

in BRIT, use **dripping**

3 → see also **drip**

drip|py /drɪpi/ ADJ If you describe someone as **drippy**, you mean that they are stupid and weak. If you describe something such as a book or a type of music as **drippy**, you mean that you think it is stupid, dull, and sentimental. [INFORMAL, DISAPPROVAL] ❏ *These men look a bit drippy.* ❏ *...drippy infantile ideas.*

drive ♦♦♦ /draɪv/ (drives, driving, drove, driven) **1** V-T/V-I When you **drive** somewhere, you operate a car or other vehicle and control its movement and direction. ❏ *I drove into town and went to a restaurant for dinner.* ❏ *She never learned to drive.* ❏ *We drove the car down to Richmond for the weekend.* • **driv|ing** N-UNCOUNT ❏ *...a qualified driving instructor.* **2** V-T If you **drive** someone somewhere, you take them there in a car or other vehicle. ❏ *His daughter Carly drove him to the train station.* **3** V-T If something **drives** a machine, it supplies the power that makes it work. ❏ *The current flows into electric motors that drive the wheels.* **4** V-T If you **drive** something such as a nail into something else, you push it in or hammer it in using a lot of effort. ❏ *I had to use our sledgehammer to drive the pegs into the side of the path.* **5** V-T If the wind, rain, or snow **drives** in a particular direction, it moves with great force in that direction. ❏ *Rain drove against the window.* • **driv|ing** ADJ [ADJ n] ❏ *He crashed into a tree in driving rain.* **6** V-T If you **drive** people or animals somewhere, you make them go to or from that place. ❏ *The last offensive drove thousands of people into Thailand.* **7** V-T To **drive** someone into a particular state or situation means to force them into that state or situation. ❏ *The recession and hospital bills drove them into bankruptcy.* **8** V-T The desire or feeling that **drives** a person to do something, especially something extreme, is the desire or feeling that causes them to do it. ❏ *More than once, depression drove him to attempt suicide.* ❏ *Jealousy drives people to murder.* **9** N-COUNT A **drive** is a trip in a car or other vehicle. ❏ *I thought we might go for a drive on Sunday.* **10** N-COUNT A **drive** is a wide piece of hard ground, or sometimes a private road, that leads from the road to a person's house. ❏ *The boys followed Eleanor up the drive to the house.* **11** N-COUNT You use **drive** to refer to the mechanical part of a computer which reads the data on disks, or writes data onto them. ❏ *The firm specialized in supplying pieces of equipment, such as terminals, CD drives, or printers.* **12** → see also **disk drive** **13** N-COUNT A **drive** is a very strong need or desire in human beings that makes them act in particular ways. ❏ *...compelling, dynamic sex drives.* **14** N-UNCOUNT If you say that someone has **drive**, you mean they have energy and determination. ❏ *John will be best remembered for his drive and enthusiasm.* **15** N-SING A **drive** is a special effort made by a group of people for a particular purpose. ❏ *The ANC is about to launch a nationwide recruitment drive.* **16** N-IN-NAMES **Drive** is used in the names of some streets. ❏ *...3091 North Beverly Hills Drive, Beverly Hills, CA.* **17** → see also **driving** **18** → See feature box at **computer**
▶ **drive away** PHRASAL VERB To **drive** people **away** means to make them want to go away or stay away. ❏ *Patrick's rudeness soon drove Monica's friends away.*

drive-by ADJ [ADJ n] A **drive-by** shooting or a **drive-by** murder involves shooting someone from a moving car. ❏ *He was killed by three shots to the head in a drive-by shooting.*

drive-in (drive-ins) N-COUNT A **drive-in** is a restaurant, movie theater, or other commercial place which is specially designed so that customers can use the services provided while staying in their cars. ❏ *...a small neat town, uncluttered by stores, gas stations, or fast food drive-ins.*

driv|el /drɪvəl/ N-UNCOUNT If you describe something that is written or said as **drivel**, you are critical of it because you think it is very silly. [DISAPPROVAL] ❏ *What absolute drivel!*

driv|en /drɪvən/ **Driven** is the past participle of **drive**.

driv|er ♦♦◇ /draɪvər/ (drivers) **1** N-COUNT The **driver** of a vehicle is the person who is driving it. ❏ *The driver got out of his van.* **2** N-COUNT A **driver** is a computer program that controls a device such as a printer. [COMPUTING] ❏ *Printer driver software includes standard features such as print layout and fit-to-page printing.*

COLLOCATIONS

driver
NOUN **1**
noun + **driver**: bus, car, taxi, train; delivery, race; student
adjective + **driver**: drunk, uninsured, unlicensed; female, male, young; careful, experienced, safe
driver + be + adjective: unhurt, uninjured

driv|er|less /dr<u>aɪ</u>vərlɪs/ ADJ A **driverless** vehicle is able to travel without a driver controlling it. ❏ *The company is currently testing a driverless car.*

driv|er's li|cense (driver's licenses) N-COUNT A **driver's license** is a card showing that you are qualified to drive because you have passed a driving test. [AM]

in BRIT, use **driving licence**

driv|er's seat ■ N-SING [usu the N] In a vehicle such as a car or a bus, the **driver's seat** is the seat where the person who is driving sits. ■ PHRASE If you say that someone **is in the driver's seat**, you mean that they are in control in a situation. ❏ *Now he knows he's in the driver's seat and can wait for a better deal.*

drive shaft (drive shafts) N-COUNT A **drive shaft** is a shaft in a car or other vehicle that transfers power from the gear box to the wheels.

drive-through (drive-throughs) also **drive-thru** ADJ [ADJ n] A **drive-through** store, bank, or restaurant is one where you can be served without leaving your car. ❏ *...a drive-through burger bar.* • N-COUNT **Drive-through** is also a noun. ❏ *I got some dinner at a drive-through and headed home.*

drive-thru (drive-thrus) [INFORMAL] → see **drive-through**

drive|way /dr<u>aɪ</u>veɪ/ (driveways) N-COUNT A **driveway** is a piece of hard ground that leads from the road to the front of a house, garage, or other building. ❏ *I was running down the driveway to the car and I lost my balance.*

driv|ing /dr<u>aɪ</u>vɪŋ/ ■ ADJ [ADJ n] The **driving** force or idea behind something that happens or is done is the main thing that has a strong effect on it and makes it happen or be done in a particular way. ❏ *Consumer spending was the driving force behind the economic growth in the summer.* ■ → see also **drive** ■ → See feature box at **electricity**

VOCABULARY IN CONTEXT

Driving

Every time we leave our homes, we trust that **motorists** know the **rules of the road** and are committed to observing them. Driving the **speed limit**, keeping a **safe distance**, and **signaling** appropriately are all basic tenets of sharing the roads. Driving **with due care and attention** is another requirement: indeed, in most driving tests, candidates lose points if they skim the **curb** or accidentally go on the **sidewalk**. But, truly competent driving only comes with experience. For example, it takes skill to **parallel park** or to **back out of** a parking space. Being a good driver takes practice, but it also requires patience. Impatience and **aggressive** driving are the main cause of **collisions** and other road accidents. A recent survey in the U.K. revealed that 94% of drivers had witnessed risky **passing** maneuvers. Driving is a privilege and a responsibility, and the best way to ensure **road safety** is to exercise proper care with regard for others. And, of course, we should not forget to be courteous.

driv|ing li|cence (driving licences) [BRIT] → see **driver's license**

driv|ing li|cense (driving licenses) N-COUNT A **driving license** is the same as a **driver's license**.

driv|ing range (driving ranges) N-COUNT A **driving range** is an outdoor place where you can practice playing golf.

driv|ing school (driving schools) N-COUNT A **driving school** is a business that employs instructors who teach people how to drive a car.

driz|zle /drɪzᵊl/ (drizzles, drizzling, drizzled) ■ N-UNCOUNT [also a N] **Drizzle** is light rain falling in fine drops. ❏ *The drizzle had now stopped and the sun was breaking through.* ■ V-I If it **is drizzling**, it is raining very lightly. ❏ *Clouds had come down and it was starting to drizzle.* ■ → See feature box at **weather**

driz|zly /drɪzli/ (drizzlier, drizzliest) ADJ [oft it v-link ADJ] When the weather is **drizzly**, the sky is dull and gray and it rains steadily but not very hard. ❏ *...a dull, drizzly afternoon.* ❏ *It was dull and slightly drizzly as we left.*

droll /dr<u>oʊ</u>l/ ADJ Something or someone that is **droll** is amusing or witty, sometimes in an unexpected way. [WRITTEN] ❏ *Evelyn is entertaining company, with droll and sardonic observations on nearly everything.*

drone /dr<u>oʊ</u>n/ (drones, droning, droned) ■ V-I If something **drones**, it makes a low, continuous, dull noise. ❏ *Above him an invisible plane droned through the night sky.* • N-SING **Drone** is also a noun. ❏ *I hear the drone of an airplane as it banks across the bay.* ■ V-I If you say that someone **drones**, you mean that they keep talking about something in a boring way. [DISAPPROVAL] ❏ *Chambers' voice droned, maddening as an insect around his head.* • N-SING **Drone** is also a noun. ❏ *The minister's voice was a relentless drone.* • PHRASAL VERB **Drone on** means the same as **drone**. ❏ *Aunt Maimie's voice droned on.* ■ N-COUNT A **drone** is a type of aircraft that does not have a pilot and is controlled by someone on the ground. ❏ *Drones frequently pass over this region.*

drool /dr<u>u</u>l/ (drools, drooling, drooled) ■ V-I To **drool** over someone or something means to look at them with great pleasure, perhaps in an exaggerated or ridiculous way. [DISAPPROVAL] ❏ *Fashion editors drooled over every item.* ■ V-I If a person or animal **drools**, saliva drops slowly from their mouth. ❏ *My dog Jacques is drooling on my shoulder.*

droop /dr<u>u</u>p/ (droops, drooping, drooped) V-I If something **droops**, it hangs or leans downward with no strength or firmness. ❏ *Crook's eyelids drooped and he yawned.* • N-SING **Droop** is also a noun. ❏ *...the droop of his shoulders.*

droopy /dr<u>u</u>pi/ (droopier, droopiest) ADJ If you describe something as **droopy**, you mean that it hangs down with no strength or firmness. ❏ *...a very tall man with a droopy moustache.*

drop ✦✧ /dr<u>ɒ</u>p/ (drops, dropping, dropped) ■ V-T/V-I If a level or amount **drops** or if someone or something **drops** it, it quickly becomes lower. ❏ *Temperatures can drop to freezing at night.* ❏ *His blood pressure had dropped severely.* • N-COUNT **Drop** is also a noun. ❏ *He was prepared to take a drop in wages.* ■ V-T If you **drop** something, you accidentally let it fall. ❏ *I dropped my glasses and broke them.* ■ V-I If something **drops** onto something else, it falls onto that thing. If something **drops** from somewhere, it falls from that place. ❏ *He felt hot tears dropping onto his fingers.* ■ V-T/V-I If you **drop** something somewhere or if it **drops** there, you deliberately let it fall there. ❏ *Drop the noodles into the water.* ❏ *...television footage of bombs dropping on the city* • **drop|ping** N-UNCOUNT [usu N of n] ❏ *...the dropping of the first atomic bomb.* ■ V-T/V-I If a person or a part of their body **drops** to a lower position, or if they **drop** a part of their body to a lower position, they move to that position, often in a tired and lifeless way. ❏ *Nancy dropped into a nearby chair.* ❏ *She let her head drop.* ■ V-I [no cont] To **drop** is used in expressions such as **to be about to drop** and **to dance until you drop** to emphasize that you are exhausted and can no longer continue doing something. [EMPHASIS] ❏ *She looked about to drop.* ■ V-T/V-I If your voice **drops** or if you **drop** your voice, you speak more quietly. ❏ *Her voice will drop to a dismissive whisper.* ■ V-T If you **drop** someone or something somewhere, you take them somewhere and leave them there, usually in a car or other vehicle. ❏ *He dropped me outside the hotel.* • PHRASAL VERB **Drop off** means the same as **drop**. ❏ *Just drop me off at the airport.* ■ V-T If you **drop** an idea, course of action, or habit, you do not continue with it. ❏ *He was told to drop the idea.*

drop-dead

• **drop|ping** N-UNCOUNT ❑ *No explanation was given for the dropping of the charges against them.* ◨ V-T [usu passive] If someone **is dropped** by a sports team or organization, they are no longer included in that team or employed by that organization. ❑ *Alexander has been dropped from his multimillion-dollar-a-year job as spokesman for the company.* ◨ V-I If you **drop** to a lower position in a sports competition, you move to that position. ❑ *She has dropped to third in the world ranking.* ◨ N-COUNT A **drop** of a liquid is a very small amount of it shaped like a little ball. In informal English, you can also use **drop** when you are referring to a very small amount of something such as a drink. ❑ *...a drop of blue ink.* ◨ N-COUNT You use **drop** to talk about vertical distances. For example, a thirty-foot **drop** is a distance of thirty feet between the top of a cliff or wall and the bottom of it. ❑ *There was a sheer drop just outside my window.* ◨ N-PLURAL **Drops** are a kind of medicine which you put drop by drop into your ears, eyes, or nose. ❑ *And he had to have these drops in his eyes as well.* ◨ PHRASE If you **drop a hint**, you give a hint or say something in a casual way. ❑ *Jerry dropped hints that he and Julie were talking about getting married.* ◨ PHRASE If you want someone to **drop the subject**, **drop it**, or **let it drop**, you want them to stop talking about something, often because you are annoyed that they keep talking about it. ❑ *Mary Ann wished he would just drop it.* ◨ **to drop dead** → see **dead** ◨ **at the drop of a hat** → see **hat** ◨ **a drop in the ocean** → see **ocean**

▶ **drop by** ◨ PHRASAL VERB If you **drop by**, you visit someone informally. ❑ *She and Danny will drop by later.* ◨ → See feature box at **socialize**

▶ **drop in** PHRASAL VERB If you **drop in** on someone, you visit them informally, usually without having arranged it. ❑ *Why not drop in for a chat?*

▶ **drop off** ◨ → see drop 8 ◨ PHRASAL VERB If you **drop off** to sleep, you go to sleep. [INFORMAL] ❑ *I must have dropped off to sleep.* ◨ PHRASAL VERB If the level of something **drops off**, it becomes less. ❑ *Two years later, earnings from the stocks had dropped off by nearly 50%.*

▶ **drop out** ◨ PHRASAL VERB If someone **drops out** of college or a race, for example, they leave it without finishing what they started. ❑ *He'd dropped out of high school at the age of 16.* ◨ → see also **dropout**

COLLOCATIONS

drop
VERB ◨
drop + *adverb*: dramatically, sharply, steeply, suddenly; significantly
NOUN ◨
adjective + **drop**: sharp, steep, sudden

SYNONYMS

drop
VERB
◨
decline: *The number of staff has declined from 217,000 to 114,000.*
decrease: *Population growth is decreasing by 1.4% each year.*
fall: *Her weight fell below 100 pounds.*
plummet: *In Tokyo, share prices have plummeted for the sixth successive day.*
dwindle: *The factory's workforce has dwindled from over 4,000 to a few hundred.*
◨
plunge: *At least 50 people died when a bus plunged into a river.*
fall: *Bombs fell in the town.*
plummet: *The jet burst into flames and plummeted to the ground.*

---

drop-dead ADV [ADV adj] If you describe someone as, for example, **drop-dead** gorgeous, you mean that they are so gorgeous that people cannot fail to notice them. [INFORMAL] ❑ *She's tall, blond, and drop-dead gorgeous.* • ADJ [ADJ n] **Drop-dead** is also an adjective. ❑ *...the drop-dead glamor of the designer decade.*

drop-down also **dropdown** ADJ [ADJ n] A **drop-down** menu, list, or box is a list of options that appears on a computer screen when you select an item with a computer mouse. [COMPUTING] ❑ *Select 'Delete all' from the drop-down list.*

drop-down menu (drop-down menus) N-COUNT On a computer screen, a **drop-down menu** is a list of choices that appears when you give the computer a command. ❑ *In the drop-down menu with all your Favorites, right-click on any individual item.*

drop-in ADJ [ADJ n] **Drop-in** centers or services provide information and help for people with particular problems without the need for an appointment. They usually work on a free and informal basis.. ❑ *...a drop-in center for young mothers.*

drop kick (drop kicks) N-COUNT In sports such as football and rugby, a **drop kick** is a kick in which the ball is dropped to the ground and kicked at the moment that it bounces.

drop|let /drɒplɪt/ (droplets) N-COUNT A **droplet** is a very small drop of liquid. ❑ *Droplets of sweat were welling up on his forehead.*

drop-off (drop-offs) N-COUNT [N in n] A **drop-off** in something such as sales or orders is a decrease in them. [mainly AM] ❑ *...a sharp drop-off in orders from Asia.*

drop|out /drɒpaʊt/ (dropouts) also **drop-out** ◨ N-COUNT If you describe someone as a **dropout**, you disapprove of the fact that they have rejected the accepted ways of society, for example, by not having a regular job. [DISAPPROVAL] ❑ *...long-haired, dope-smoking dropouts.* ◨ N-COUNT A **dropout** is someone who has left school or college before they have finished their studies. ❑ *...high-school dropouts.* ◨ ADJ [ADJ n] If you refer to the **dropout** rate, you are referring to the number of people who leave a school or college early, or leave a course or other activity before they have finished it. ❑ *The dropout rate among students is currently one in three.*

drop|per /drɒpər/ (droppers) N-COUNT A **dropper** is a small glass tube with a hollow rubber part on one end which you use for drawing up and dropping small amounts of liquid.

drop|pings /drɒpɪŋz/ N-PLURAL **Droppings** are the feces of birds and small animals. ❑ *...pigeon droppings.*

dross /drɒs/ N-UNCOUNT If you describe something as **dross**, you mean that it is of very poor quality or has no value. [LITERARY, DISAPPROVAL] ❑ *I go through phases where everything I write is just dross.*

drought /draʊt/ (droughts) ◨ N-VAR A **drought** is a long period of time during which no rain falls. ❑ *...a country where drought and famines have killed up to two million people during the last eighteen years.* ◨ → See feature box at **weather**

drove /droʊv/ **Drove** is the past tense of **drive**.

drov|er /droʊvər/ (drovers) N-COUNT A **drover** is someone whose job is to make sheep or cattle move from one place to another in groups.

droves /droʊvz/ N-PLURAL [usu in N, in poss N, N of N] If you say that people are going somewhere or doing something **in droves**, you are emphasizing that there is a very large number of them. [EMPHASIS] ❑ *Scientists are leaving the country in droves.*

drown /draʊn/ (drowns, drowning, drowned) ◨ V-T/V-I When someone **drowns** or **is drowned**, they die because they have gone or been pushed under water and cannot breathe. ❑ *A child can drown in only a few inches of water.* ❑ *Last night a boy was drowned in the river.* ◨ V-I If you say that a person or thing **is drowning** in something, you are emphasizing that they have a very large amount of it, or are completely covered in it. [EMPHASIS] ❑ *...people who gradually find themselves drowning in debt.* ◨ V-T If something **drowns** a sound, it is so loud that you cannot hear that sound properly. ❑ *Clapping drowned the speaker's words for a moment.* • PHRASAL VERB **Drown out** means the same as **drown**. ❑ *Their cheers drowned out the protests of demonstrators.* ◨ PHRASE If you say that someone **is drowning** their **sorrows**, you mean that they are drinking alcohol in order to forget something sad or upsetting that has happened to them. ❑ *Carly drowned her sorrows in vodka cocktails at a South Beach nightclub.*

drowse /draʊz/ (drowses, drowsing, drowsed) V-I If you **drowse**, you are almost asleep or just asleep. ❑ *Nina drowsed for a while.*

drowsy /draʊzi/ (drowsier, drowsiest) ADJ If you feel **drowsy**, you feel sleepy and cannot think clearly. ❑ *He felt pleasantly drowsy and had to fight off the urge to sleep.* • **drowsi|ness** N-UNCOUNT ❑ *Big meals during the day cause drowsiness.*

drub|bing /drʌbɪŋ/ (drubbings) N-COUNT [usu sing] If someone gets a **drubbing**, they are defeated easily. [INFORMAL]

drudge /drʌdʒ/ (drudges) N-COUNT If you describe someone as a **drudge**, you mean they have to work hard at a job which is not very important or interesting.

drudg|ery /drʌdʒəri/ N-UNCOUNT You use **drudgery** to refer to jobs and tasks which are boring or unpleasant but which must be done. ❏ *People want to get away from the drudgery of their everyday lives.*

drug ◆◆◆ /drʌg/ (drugs, drugging, drugged) **1** N-COUNT A **drug** is a chemical which is given to people in order to treat or prevent an illness or disease. ❏ *The drug will be useful to hundreds of thousands of infected people.* **2** N-COUNT **Drugs** are substances that some people take because of their pleasant effects, but which are usually illegal. ❏ *His mother was on drugs, on cocaine.* ❏ *She was sure Leo was taking drugs.* **3** V-T If you **drug** a person or animal, you give them a chemical substance in order to make them sleepy or unconscious. ❏ *She was drugged and robbed.* **4** V-T If food or drink **is drugged**, a chemical substance is added to it in order to make someone sleepy or unconscious when they eat or drink it. ❏ *I wonder now if that drink had been drugged.*

COLLOCATIONS

drug
NOUN
1
noun + **drug**: cancer, diabetes; prescription
adjective + **drug**: anti-inflammatory, antiviral, experimental, generic; lifesaving
verb + **drug**: prescribe
2
adjective + **drug**: banned, illegal, illicit, prohibited; performance-enhancing, recreational
verb + **drug**: deal, smuggle, supply; take, use; possess

SYNONYMS

drug
NOUN **1**
medication: *Are you on any medication?*
medicine: *People in hospitals are dying because of a shortage of medicine.*
remedy: *...natural remedies to help overcome winter infections.*
treatment: *...an effective treatment for eczema.*

---

drug ad|dict (drug addicts) N-COUNT A **drug addict** is someone who is addicted to illegal drugs.

drug|gie /drʌgi/ (druggies) also **druggy** N-COUNT If you refer to someone as a **druggie** you mean they are involved with or addicted to illegal drugs. [INFORMAL, DISAPPROVAL]

drug|gist /drʌgɪst/ (druggists) **1** N-COUNT A **druggist** is the same as a **pharmacist**. [AM]

in BRIT, usually use **chemist**

2 N-COUNT [oft the N] A **druggist** or a **druggist's** is the same as a **pharmacy**. [AM]

in BRIT, usually use **chemist**

drug|store /drʌgstɔr/ (drugstores) N-COUNT A **drugstore** is a store where drugs and medicines are sold, and where you can buy cosmetics, some household goods, and also drinks and snacks. [AM]

Dru|id /druɪd/ (Druids) also **druid** N-COUNT A **Druid** is a priest of the Celtic religion.

drum ◆◇◇ /drʌm/ (drums, drumming, drummed) **1** N-COUNT A **drum** is a musical instrument consisting of a skin stretched tightly over a round frame. You play a drum by beating it with sticks or with your hands. ❏ *...a worker who died after collapsing while beating a drum during a demonstration.* **2** N-COUNT A **drum** is a large cylindrical container which is used to store fuel or other substances. ❏ *...an oil drum.* **3** V-T/V-I If something **drums** on a surface, or if you **drum** something on a surface, it hits it regularly, making a continuous beating sound. ❏ *He drummed his fingers on the leather top of his desk.*

▶ **drum into** PHRASAL VERB If you **drum** something **into** someone, you keep saying it to them until they understand it or remember it. ❏ *Standard examples were drummed into students' heads.*

▶ **drum up** PHRASAL VERB If you **drum up** support or business, you try to get it. ❏ *It is to be hoped that he is merely drumming up business.*

drum|beat /drʌmbit/ (drumbeats) **1** N-COUNT A **drumbeat** is the sound of a beat on a drum. **2** N-COUNT [oft N *of* n] People sometimes describe a series of warnings or continuous pressure on someone to do something as a **drumbeat**. [mainly AM, JOURNALISM]

drum kit (drum kits) N-COUNT A **drum kit** is a set of drums and cymbals.

drum ma|jor (drum majors) N-COUNT A **drum major** is a boy or man who leads a marching band by walking in front of them. [AM]

drum ma|jor|ette (drum majorettes) **1** N-COUNT A **drum majorette** is a girl or woman who leads a marching band by walking in front of them. **2** N-COUNT A **drum majorette** is a girl or woman who wears a uniform and spins a stick and throws it into the air and catches it, often as part of a parade.

drum|mer /drʌmər/ (drummers) N-COUNT A **drummer** is a person who plays a drum or drums in a band or group. ❏ *He was a drummer in a rock band.*

drum|ming /drʌmɪŋ/ **1** N-UNCOUNT **Drumming** is the action of playing the drums. **2** N-UNCOUNT [also a N, oft N *of* n] **Drumming** is the sound or feeling of continuous beating. ❏ *He pointed up to the roof, through which the steady drumming of rain could be heard.* ❏ *His mouth was dry and he felt a drumming in his temples.*

drumroll (drumrolls) also **drum roll** N-COUNT A **drumroll** is a series of drumbeats that follow each other so quickly that they make a continuous sound. A drumroll is often used to show that someone important is arriving, or to introduce someone. ❏ *A long drumroll introduced the trapeze artists.*

drum|stick /drʌmstɪk/ (drumsticks) **1** N-COUNT [usu pl] A **drumstick** is the lower part of the leg of a bird such as a chicken which is cooked and eaten. **2** N-COUNT **Drumsticks** are sticks used for beating a drum.

drunk /drʌŋk/ (drunks) **1** ADJ Someone who is **drunk** has drunk so much alcohol that they cannot speak clearly or behave sensibly. ❏ *I got drunk and had to be carried home.* **2** N-COUNT A **drunk** is someone who is drunk or frequently gets drunk. ❏ *A drunk lay in the alley.* **3** **Drunk** is the past participle of **drink**.

drunk|ard /drʌŋkərd/ (drunkards) N-COUNT A **drunkard** is someone who frequently gets drunk.

drunk driv|ing N-UNCOUNT **Drunk driving** is the offense of driving a vehicle after you have drunk more than the amount of alcohol that is legally allowed. [mainly AM] ❏ *He was arrested for drunk driving.*

in BRIT, usually use **drink-driving**

● **drunk driv|er** (drunk drivers) N-UNCOUNT ❏ *...a car accident caused by a drunk driver.*

drunk|en /drʌŋkən/ **1** ADJ [ADJ n] **Drunken** is used to describe events and situations that involve people who are drunk. ❏ *The pain roused him from his drunken stupor.* **2** ADJ [ADJ n] A **drunken** person is drunk or is frequently drunk. ❏ *Groups of drunken hooligans smashed windows and threw stones.* ● **drunk|en|ly** ADV [ADV with v] ❏ *Once Bob stormed drunkenly into her house and smashed some chairs.* ● **drunk|en|ness** N-UNCOUNT ❏ *He was arrested for drunkenness.*

druth|ers /drʌðərz/ PHRASE You can say that you would do something **if I had my druthers** or **given my druthers** when you mean that you would do it if you were able to choose. [AM] ❏ *If you could have your druthers, what would you be doing?* ❏ *Given my druthers I'd rather write an essay than draw a picture.*

dry ◆◆◇ /draɪ/ (drier or dryer, driest or dryest, dries, drying, dried) **1** ADJ If something is **dry**, there is no water or moisture on it or in it. ❏ *Clean the metal with a soft dry cloth.* ❏ *Pat it dry with a soft towel.* ● **dry|ness** N-UNCOUNT ❏ *...the parched dryness of the air.* **2** ADJ If you say that your skin or hair is **dry**, you mean that it is less oily than, or not as soft as, normal. ❏ *Nothing looks worse than dry, cracked lips.* ● **dry|ness** N-UNCOUNT ❏ *Dryness of the skin can also be caused by living in centrally heated homes and offices.* **3** ADJ If the weather or a period of time is **dry**, there is no rain or there is much less rain than average. ❏ *Exceptionally dry weather over the past year had cut agricultural production.* **4** ADJ A **dry** place or climate is one that gets very little rainfall.

dry-clean

❑ *It was one of the driest and dustiest places in Africa.* • **dry|ness** N-UNCOUNT ❑ *He was advised to spend time in the warmth and dryness of Italy.* **5** ADJ If a river, lake, or well is **dry**, it is empty of water, usually because of hot weather and lack of rain. ❑ *The aquifer which had once fed the wells was pronounced dry.* **6** ADJ If an oil well is **dry**, it is no longer producing any oil. ❑ *To harvest oil and gas profitably from the North Sea, we must focus on the exploitation of small reserves as the big wells run dry.* **7** ADJ If your mouth or throat is **dry**, it has little or no saliva in it, and so feels very unpleasant, perhaps because you are tense or ill. ❑ *His mouth was still dry, he would certainly be glad of a drink.* • **dry|ness** N-UNCOUNT ❑ *Symptoms included frequent dryness in the mouth.* **8** ADJ If someone has **dry** eyes, there are no tears in their eyes; often used with negatives or in contexts where you are expressing surprise that they are not crying. ❑ *There were few dry eyes in the house when I finished.* **9** ADJ **Dry** humor is very amusing, but in a subtle and clever way. [APPROVAL] ❑ *Though the pressure Fulton is under must be considerable, he has retained his dry humor.* • **dry|ness** N-UNCOUNT ❑ *It has a wry dryness you won't recognize.* **10** ADJ If you describe something such as a book, play, or activity as **dry**, you mean that it is dull and uninteresting. [DISAPPROVAL] ❑ *My eyelids were drooping over the dry, academic phrases.* **11** ADJ **Dry** sherry or wine does not have a sweet taste. ❑ *...a glass of chilled, dry white wine.* **12** V-T/V-I When something **dries** or when you **dry** it, it becomes dry. ❑ *Let your hair dry naturally whenever possible.* **13** V-T When you **dry** the dishes after a meal, you wipe the water off the plates, cups, knives, pans, and other things when they have been washed, using a cloth. ❑ *Mrs. Madrigal picked up a towel and began drying dishes next to her daughter.* **14** **high and dry** → see **high** **15** **home and dry** → see **home** ① **16** → See feature box at **humor**

▶ **dry out** **1** PHRASAL VERB If something **dries out** or is **dried out**, it loses all the moisture that was in it and becomes hard. ❑ *If the soil is allowed to dry out the tree could die.* **2** PHRASAL VERB If someone **dries out** or is **dried out**, they stop drinking alcohol. [INFORMAL] ❑ *He checked into Cedars-Sinai Hospital to dry out.*

▶ **dry up** **1** PHRASAL VERB If something **dries up** or if something **dries** it **up**, it loses all its moisture and becomes completely dry and shriveled or hard. ❑ *As the day goes on, the pollen dries up and becomes hard.* **2** PHRASAL VERB If a river, lake, or well **dries up**, it becomes empty of water, usually because of hot weather and a lack of rain. ❑ *Reservoirs are drying up and farmers have begun to leave their land in search of water.* **3** PHRASAL VERB If a supply of something **dries up**, it stops. ❑ *The main source of income, tourism, is expected to dry up completely this summer.* **4** PHRASAL VERB If you **dry up** when you are speaking, you stop in the middle of what you were saying, because you cannot think what to say next. ❑ *When he turned around and saw her, his conversation dried up.*

dry-clean (dry-cleans, dry-cleaning, dry-cleaned) V-T [usu passive] When things such as clothes **are dry-cleaned**, they are cleaned with a liquid chemical rather than with water. ❑ *Natural-filled duvets must be dry-cleaned by a professional.*

dry clean|er (dry cleaners) N-COUNT A **dry cleaner** or a **dry cleaner's** is a store where things can be dry-cleaned.

dry clean|ing also **dry-cleaning** **1** N-UNCOUNT **Dry cleaning** is the action or work of dry-cleaning things such as clothes. ❑ *He owns a dry cleaning business.* **2** N-UNCOUNT **Dry cleaning** is things that have been dry-cleaned, or that are going to be dry-cleaned.

dry dock (dry docks) N-COUNT A **dry dock** is a dock from which water can be removed so that ships or boats can be built or repaired.

dry|er /draɪər/ (dryers) also **drier** **1** N-COUNT A **dryer** is a machine for drying things. There are different kinds of dryers, for example, ones designed for drying clothes, crops, or people's hair or hands. ❑ *...hot air electric hand dryers.* **2** → see also **dry, tumble dryer**

dry-eyed ADJ If you say that someone is **dry-eyed**, you mean that although they are in a very sad situation they are not actually crying. ❑ *At the funeral she was dry-eyed and composed.*

dry goods N-PLURAL **Dry goods** are cloth, thread, clothing, and other related things. [AM]

in BRIT, use **drapery, haberdashery**

dry ice N-UNCOUNT **Dry ice** is a form of solid carbon dioxide that is used to keep things cold and to create smoke in stage shows.

dry|ing N-UNCOUNT [also the N] When you do the **drying**, you dry things such as plates, pans, knives, and cups after they have been washed. [AM]

in BRIT, use **drying up**

dry land N-UNCOUNT [oft on N] If you talk about **dry land**, you are referring to land, in contrast to the sea or the air. ❑ *We were glad to be on dry land again.*

dry rot N-UNCOUNT **Dry rot** is a serious disease of wood. It is caused by a fungus and causes wood to decay. ❑ *The house was riddled with dry rot.*

dry run (dry runs) N-COUNT If you have a **dry run**, you practice something to make sure that you are ready to do it properly. ❑ *The competition is planned as a dry run for the World Cup finals.*

dry|wall /draɪwɔl/ (drywalls) also **dry wall** N-VAR **Drywall** is material such as plasterboard that can be used to make walls without using wet plaster. [AM] ❑ *Walls and ceilings are covered with drywall.* ❑ *Each building had fireproof drywalls to protect the stairwells.*

DSL /di ɛs ɛl/ N-UNCOUNT **DSL** is a method of transmitting digital information at high speed over telephone lines. **DSL** is an abbreviation for 'digital subscriber line.' [COMPUTING]

DTP /di ti pi/ **DTP** is an abbreviation for **desktop publishing**.

DT's /di tiz/ also **dts** N-PLURAL [the N] When alcoholics have the **DT's**, the alcohol causes their bodies to shake and makes them unable to think clearly.

dual /duəl/ ADJ [ADJ n] **Dual** means having two parts, functions, or aspects. ❑ *...his dual role as head of the party and head of state.*

dual carriage|way (dual carriageways) also **dual-carriageway** N-VAR A **dual carriageway** is the same as a **divided highway**. [BRIT]

dual|ism /duəlɪzəm/ N-UNCOUNT **Dualism** is the state of having two main parts or aspects, or the belief that something has two main parts or aspects. [FORMAL] ❑ *...the Gnostic dualism of good and evil struggling for supremacy.*

dual|ity /duælɪti/ (dualities) N-VAR A **duality** is a situation in which two opposite ideas or feelings exist at the same time. [FORMAL]

dub /dʌb/ (dubs, dubbing, dubbed) **1** V-T If someone or something **is dubbed** a particular thing, they are given that description or name. [JOURNALISM] ❑ *Today's session has been widely dubbed as a "make or break" meeting.* **2** V-T [usu passive] If a movie or soundtrack in a foreign language **is dubbed**, a new soundtrack is added with actors giving a translation. ❑ *It was dubbed into Spanish for Mexican audiences.*

du|bi|ous /dubiəs/ **1** ADJ If you describe something as **dubious**, you mean that you do not consider it to be completely honest, safe, or reliable. ❑ *This claim seems to us to be rather dubious.* • **du|bi|ous|ly** ADV ❑ *Carter was dubiously convicted of shooting three White men in a bar.* **2** ADJ [v-link ADJ] If you are **dubious** about something, you are not completely sure about it and have not yet made up your mind about it. ❑ *My parents were a bit dubious about it all at first but we soon convinced them.* • **du|bi|ous|ly** ADV ❑ *He eyed Coyne dubiously.*

dub|step /dʌbstɛp/ N-UNCOUNT **Dubstep** is a type of electronic dance music with a strong bass line.

du|cal /dukəl/ ADJ [ADJ n] **Ducal** places or things belong to or are connected with a duke. [FORMAL]

duch|ess /dʌtʃɪs/ (duchesses) N-COUNT A **duchess** is a woman who has the same rank as a duke, or who is a duke's wife or widow. ❑ *...the Duchess of Kent.*

duchy /dʌtʃi/ (duchies) N-COUNT [oft the N of n] A **duchy** is an area of land that is owned or ruled by a duke. ❑ *...the Duchy of Cornwall.*

duck /dʌk/ (ducks, ducking, ducked) **1** N-VAR A **duck** is a common water bird with short legs, a short neck, and a large flat beak. ❑ *Chickens and ducks scratch around the outbuildings.* • N-UNCOUNT **Duck** is the flesh of this bird when it is eaten as food. ❑ *...honey roasted duck.* **2** V-I If you **duck**, you move your head or the top half of your body quickly downward to avoid

something that might hit you, to avoid being seen, or to hide the expression on your face. ❑ *He ducked in time to save his head from a blow from the poker.* ❸ V-T If you **duck** something such as a blow, you avoid it by moving your head or body quickly downward. ❑ *Hans deftly ducked their blows.* ❹ V-T If you **duck** your head, you move it quickly downward to hide the expression on your face. ❑ *He ducked his head to hide his admiration.* ❺ V-T You say that someone **ducks** a duty or responsibility when you disapprove of the fact that they avoid it. [INFORMAL, DISAPPROVAL] ❑ *The defense secretary ducked the question of whether the United States was winning the war.* ❻ PHRASE You say that criticism is **like water off a duck's back** or **water off a duck's back** to emphasize that it is not having any effect on the person being criticized. [EMPHASIS] ❑ *All the criticism is water off a duck's back to me.* ❼ PHRASE If you **take to** something **like a duck to water**, you discover that you are naturally good at it or that you find it very easy to do. ❑ *Some mothers take to breastfeeding like a duck to water, while others find they need some help to get started.*
▶ **duck out** PHRASAL VERB If you **duck out** of something that you are supposed to do, you avoid doing it. [INFORMAL] ❑ *George ducked out of his forced marriage to a cousin.*

duck|ling /dˈʌklɪŋ/ (**ducklings**) ❶ N-COUNT A **duckling** is a young duck. ❷ → see also **ugly duckling**

duct /dʌkt/ (**ducts**) N-COUNT A **duct** is a pipe, tube, or channel which carries a liquid or gas. ❑ *...a big air duct in the ceiling.*

duct tape N-UNCOUNT **Duct tape** is a strong, sticky tape that you use to bind things together or to seal cracks in something. ❑ *...a broken lid held on with duct tape.*

dud /dʌd/ (**duds**) ADJ [ADJ n] **Dud** means not working properly or not successful. [INFORMAL] ❑ *He replaced a dud valve.* • N-COUNT **Dud** is also a noun. ❑ *The mine was a dud.*

dude /duːd/ (**dudes**) N-COUNT A **dude** is a man. In very informal situations, **dude** is sometimes used as a general form of address to a man. [AM, INFORMAL] ❑ *My doctor is a real cool dude.*

dude ranch (**dude ranches**) N-COUNT A **dude ranch** is an American ranch where people can take vacations during which they can do activities such as horseback riding or camping.

dudg|eon /dʌdʒən/ PHRASE [v-link PHR] If you say that someone is **in high dudgeon**, you are emphasizing that they are very angry or unhappy about something. [EMPHASIS] ❑ *Washington businesses are in high dudgeon over the plan.*

duds /dʌdz/ N-PLURAL **Duds** are clothes. [AM, OLD-FASHIONED] ❑ *...the Super Saturday, where fabulous duds are sold at bargain prices.*

due ◆◆◇ /djuː/ ❶ PHRASE If an event is **due to** something, it happens or exists as a direct result of that thing. ❑ *The country's economic problems are largely due to the weakness of the recovery.* ❷ PHRASE You can say **due to** to introduce the reason for something happening. Some speakers of English believe that it is not correct to use **due to** in this way. ❑ *Due to the large volume of letters he receives Dave regrets he is unable to answer queries personally.* ❸ PHRASE If you say that something will happen or take place **in due course**, you mean that you cannot make it happen any quicker and it will happen when the time is right for it. ❑ *In due course the baby was born.* ❹ PHRASE You can say '**to give** him his **due**,' or '**giving** him his **due**,' when you are admitting that there are some good things about someone, even though there are things that you do not like about them. ❑ *To give Linda her due, she had tried to encourage John in his school work.* ❺ PHRASE You can say '**with due respect**' when you are about to disagree politely with someone. [POLITENESS] ❑ *With all due respect I submit to you that you're asking the wrong question.* ❻ ADJ If something is **due** at a particular time, it is expected to happen, be done, or arrive at that time. ❑ *The results are due at the end of the month.* ❑ *Mr. Carter is due in Washington on Monday.* ❼ ADJ [ADJ n] **Due** attention or consideration is the proper, reasonable, or deserved amount of it under the circumstances. ❑ *After due consideration it was decided to send him away to live with foster parents.* ❽ ADJ [v-link ADJ] Something that is **due**, or that is **due** to someone, is owed to them, either as a debt or because they have a right to it. ❑ *I was sent a check and advised that no further pension was due.* ❾ ADJ [v-link ADJ for n] If someone is **due for** something, that thing is planned to happen or be given to them now, or very soon, often after they have been waiting for it for a long time. ❑ *Although not due for release until 2025, he was let out of his low-security prison to spend a weekend with his wife.* ❿ → See feature box at **birth, drive**

due date ❶ N-UNCOUNT A woman's **due date** is the date on which, according to medical calculations, she is most likely to give birth. ❑ *The due date for the baby is Aug. 14.* ❷ → See feature box at **birth**

duel /djuːəl/ (**duels**) N-COUNT A **duel** is a formal fight between two people in which they use guns or swords in order to settle a quarrel. ❑ *He killed a man in one duel and was himself wounded in another.*

due pro|cess N-UNCOUNT In law, **due process** refers to the carrying out of the law according to established rules and principles. ❑ *The nub of his case is that the principles of fairness and due process were breached.*

duet /djuːˈɛt/ (**duets**) N-COUNT A **duet** is a piece of music sung or played by two people. ❑ *Tonight she sings a duet with her twin sister.*

duf|fel /dʌfəl/ (**duffels**) ❶ N-COUNT A **duffel** is the same as a **duffel bag**. ❷ N-COUNT A **duffel** is the same as a **duffel coat**.

duf|fel bag (**duffel bags**) also **duffle bag** ❶ N-COUNT A **duffel bag** is a bag shaped like a cylinder and made of strong fabric such as canvas. ❷ → See also color supplement

duf|fel coat (**duffel coats**) also **duffle coat** N-COUNT A **duffel coat** is a heavy coat with a hood and long buttons that fasten with loops.

duf|fle /dʌfəl/ → see **duffel bag, duffel coat**

dug /dʌg/ **Dug** is the past tense and past participle of **dig**.

dug|out /dʌgaʊt/ (**dugouts**) ❶ N-COUNT A **dugout** is a small boat that is made by removing the inside of a log. ❷ N-COUNT A **dugout** is a shelter made by digging a hole in the ground and then covering it or tunneling so that the shelter has a roof over it. ❸ N-COUNT [usu the N] The **dugout** at a sports ground is one of the two covered benches at the side of the field where the teams' coaches sit and where players wait when they are not on the field. ❑ *...the visiting team's dugout.*

DUI /diː juː aɪ/ N-UNCOUNT [oft N n] **DUI** is the offense of driving after drinking more than the amount of alcohol that is legally allowed. **DUI** is an abbreviation for 'driving under the influence.' [AM] ❑ *He was arrested for DUI.* ❑ *...DUI offenders.*

duke /djuːk/ (**dukes**) N-COUNT A **duke** is a man with a very high social rank in the nobility of some countries. ❑ *...the Queen and the Duke of Edinburgh.*

duke|dom /djuːkdəm/ (**dukedoms**) ❶ N-COUNT A **dukedom** is the rank or title of a duke. ❑ *...the present heir to the dukedom.* ❷ N-COUNT A **dukedom** is the land owned or ruled over by a duke.

dul|cet /dʌlsɪt/ PHRASE People often use the expression **dulcet tones** to refer to someone's voice. [HUMOROUS] ❑ *"Why, Alex, I'm just going put the pretty flowers you brought me in a vase," she said in dulcet tones.*

dull /dʌl/ (**duller, dullest, dulls, dulling, dulled**) ❶ ADJ If you describe someone or something as **dull**, you mean they are not interesting or exciting. [DISAPPROVAL] ❑ *I felt she found me boring and dull.* • **dull|ness** N-UNCOUNT ❑ *They enjoy anything that breaks the dullness of their routine life.* ❷ ADJ Someone or something that is **dull** is not very lively or energetic. ❑ *The body's natural rhythms mean we all feel dull and sleepy between 1 and 3 pm.* • **dull|ly** ADV [ADV after v] ❑ *His giant face had a rough growth of stubble, his eyes looked dully ahead.* • **dull|ness** N-UNCOUNT ❑ *Did you notice any unusual depression or dullness of mind?* ❸ ADJ A **dull** color or light is not bright. ❑ *The stamp was a dark, dull blue color with a heavy black postmark.* • **dull|ly** ADV [ADV with v] ❑ *The street lamps gleamed dully through the night's mist.* ❹ ADJ You say the weather is **dull** when it is very cloudy. ❑ *It's always dull and raining.* ❺ ADJ **Dull** sounds are not very clear or loud. ❑ *The coffin closed with a dull thud.* • **dull|ly** ADV [ADV after v] ❑ *He heard his heart thump dully but more quickly.* ❻ ADJ [ADJ n] **Dull** feelings are weak and not intense. ❑ *The pain, usually a dull ache, gets worse with exercise.* • **dull|ly** ADV ❑ *His arm throbbed dully.* ❼ V-T/V-I If something **dulls** or if it **is dulled**, it becomes less intense, bright, or lively. ❑ *Her eyes dulled and she gazed blankly.*

dull|ard /d<u>ʌ</u>lərd/ (**dullards**) N-COUNT If you say that someone is a **dullard**, you mean that they are rather boring, unintelligent, and unimaginative. [OLD-FASHIONED]

duly /d<u>u</u>li/ **1** ADV [ADV before v] If you say that something **duly** happened or was done, you mean that it was expected to happen or was requested, and it did happen or it was done. ◻ *Westcott appealed to Waite for an apology, which he duly received.* **2** ADV [ADV before v] If something is **duly** done, it is done in the correct way. [FORMAL] ◻ *He is a duly elected president of the country and we're going to be giving him all the support we can.*

dumb /d<u>ʌ</u>m/ (**dumber, dumbest, dumbs, dumbing, dumbed**) **1** ADJ Someone who is **dumb** is completely unable to speak. [OFFENSIVE] ◻ *...a young deaf and dumb man.* **2** ADJ [v-link ADJ] If someone is **dumb** on a particular occasion, they cannot speak because they are angry, shocked, or surprised. [LITERARY] ◻ *We were all struck dumb for a minute.* **3** ADJ If you call a person **dumb**, you mean that they are stupid or foolish. [INFORMAL, DISAPPROVAL] ◻ *The questions were set up to make her look dumb.* **4** ADJ If you say that something is **dumb**, you think that it is silly and annoying. [AM, INFORMAL, DISAPPROVAL] ◻ *I came up with this dumb idea.*
▶ **dumb down** PHRASAL VERB If you **dumb down** something, you make it easier for people to understand, especially when this spoils it. ◻ *This sounded like a case for dumbing down the magazine, which no one favored.*

dumb|bell (**dumbbells**) also **dumb-bell** **1** N-COUNT A **dumbbell** is a short bar with weights on either side which people use for physical exercise to strengthen their arm and shoulder muscles. **2** N-COUNT If you call a person a **dumbbell**, you mean that they are stupid or foolish. [INFORMAL, DISAPPROVAL]

dumb|found /dʌmfa<u>u</u>nd/ (**dumbfounds, dumbfounding, dumbfounded**) V-T If someone or something **dumbfounds** you, they surprise you very much. ◻ *This suggestion dumbfounded Joe.*

dumb|found|ed /dʌmfa<u>u</u>ndɪd/ ADJ [usu v-link ADJ] If you are **dumbfounded**, you are extremely surprised by something. ◻ *I stood there dumbfounded.*

dumb|struck /d<u>ʌ</u>mstrʌk/ ADJ [usu v-link ADJ] If you are **dumbstruck**, you are so shocked or surprised that you cannot speak. [EMPHASIS]

dumb|wait|er /d<u>ʌ</u>mweɪtər/ (**dumbwaiters**) also **dumb waiter** N-COUNT A **dumbwaiter** is an elevator used to carry food and dishes from one floor of a building to another.

dum|dum /d<u>ʌ</u>m dʌm/ (**dumdums**) N-COUNT A **dumdum** or a **dumdum bullet** is a bullet that is very soft or hollow at the front. Dumdum bullets cause large and serious wounds because they break into small pieces and spread out when they hit someone.

dum-dum /d<u>ʌ</u>m dʌm/ (**dum-dums**) N-COUNT A **dum-dum** is a **dummy**. [AM, INFORMAL] → see **dummy 3**

dum|my /d<u>ʌ</u>mi/ (**dummies**) **1** N-COUNT A **dummy** is the same as a **mannequin**. **2** N-COUNT You can use **dummy** to refer to things that are not real, but have been made to look or behave as if they are real. ◻ *Dummy patrol cars will be set up beside highways to frighten speeding motorists.* **3** N-COUNT If you call a person a **dummy**, you mean that they are stupid or foolish. [AM, INFORMAL, DISAPPROVAL] **4** N-COUNT A baby's **dummy** is the same as a **pacifier**. [BRIT]

dump ✦✧✧ /d<u>ʌ</u>mp/ (**dumps, dumping, dumped**) **1** V-T If you **dump** something somewhere, you put it or unload it there quickly and carelessly. [INFORMAL] ◻ *We dumped our bags at the nearby Grand Hotel and hurried toward the market.* **2** V-T If something is **dumped** somewhere, it is put or left there because it is no longer wanted or needed. [INFORMAL] ◻ *The getaway car was dumped near the freeway.* ● **dump|ing** N-UNCOUNT ◻ *German law forbids the dumping of hazardous waste on German soil.* **3** V-T To **dump** something such as an idea, policy, or practice means to stop supporting or using it. [INFORMAL] ◻ *The party dumped the policy of nationalization in favor of the free market.* **4** V-T If a firm or company **dumps** goods, it sells large quantities of them at prices far below their real value, usually in another country, in order to gain a bigger market share or to keep prices high in the home market. [BUSINESS] ◻ *It produces more than it needs, then dumps its surplus onto the world market.* **5** V-T If you **dump** someone, you end your relationship with them. [INFORMAL] ◻ *My heart sank because I thought he was going to dump me for another girl.* **6** V-T To **dump** computer data or memory means to copy it from one storage system onto another, such as from disk to magnetic tape. [COMPUTING] ◻ *All the data is then dumped into the main computer.* **7** N-COUNT A **dump** is a place where garbage and waste material are left, for example, on open ground outside a town. ◻ *...companies that bring their trash straight to the dump.* **8** N-COUNT If you say that a place is a **dump**, you think it is ugly and unpleasant to live in or visit. [INFORMAL, DISAPPROVAL] ◻ *"What a dump!" Christabel said, standing in the doorway of the youth hostel.* **9** N-COUNT A **dump** is a list of the data that is stored in a computer's memory at a particular time. Dumps are often used by computer programmers to find out what is causing a problem with a program. [COMPUTING] ◻ *...print it out and it'll do a screen dump of what's there.*

dump|ing ground (**dumping grounds**) N-COUNT [usu N for n, supp N] If you say that a place is a **dumping ground** for something, usually something unwanted, you mean that people leave or send large quantities of that thing there. [DISAPPROVAL] ◻ *...a dumping ground for radioactive residues.*

dump|ling /d<u>ʌ</u>mplɪŋ/ (**dumplings**) N-VAR **Dumplings** are small lumps of dough that are cooked and eaten, either with meat and vegetables or as a fruit-filled dessert.

Dump|ster /d<u>ʌ</u>mpstər/ (**Dumpsters**) N-COUNT A **Dumpster** is a large metal container for holding trash. [AM, TRADEMARK]

in BRIT, usually use **skip**

dump|ster fire (**dumpster fires**) N-COUNT If you describe a situation as a **dumpster fire**, you mean that it is in a very disordered state, especially because it has been dealt with very badly. [AM, INFORMAL] ◻ *It was an uncomfortable train wreck, spilling into an awkward dumpster fire.*

dump truck (**dump trucks**) N-COUNT A **dump truck** is a truck whose carrying part can be tipped backward so that the load falls out.

dumpy /d<u>ʌ</u>mpi/ ADJ If you describe someone as **dumpy**, you mean they are short and fat, and are usually implying they are unattractive. [DISAPPROVAL]

dun /d<u>ʌ</u>n/ COLOR Something that is **dun** is a dull gray-brown color. ◻ *...her dun mare.*

dunce /d<u>ʌ</u>ns/ (**dunces**) N-COUNT If you say that someone is a **dunce**, you think they are stupid because they find it difficult or impossible to learn what someone is trying to teach them. [DISAPPROVAL] ◻ *Michael may have been a dunce at mathematics, but he was gifted at languages.*

dune /d<u>u</u>n/ (**dunes**) N-COUNT A **dune** is a hill of sand near the ocean or in a desert. ◻ *Large dunes make access to the beach difficult in places.*

dung /d<u>ʌ</u>ŋ/ N-UNCOUNT **Dung** is feces from animals, especially from large animals such as cattle and horses. ◻ *Workers at Sydney's harbourside Taronga zoo are refusing to collect animal dung in a protest over wages.*

dun|ga|rees /dʌŋgəri͟z/ **1** N-PLURAL [also *a pair of* N] **Dungarees** are the same as **jeans**. [AM] **2** N-PLURAL [also *a pair of* N] **Dungarees** are a one-piece garment consisting of pants, a piece of cloth which covers your chest, and straps which go over your shoulders. [BRIT]

in AM, use **overalls**

dun|geon /d<u>ʌ</u>ndʒ^ən/ (**dungeons**) N-COUNT A **dungeon** is a dark underground prison in a castle.

dunk /d<u>ʌ</u>ŋk/ (**dunks, dunking, dunked**) V-T If you **dunk** something in a liquid, you put it in the liquid, especially for a particular purpose and for a short time. ◻ *Dunk new plants in a bucket of water for an hour or so before planting.*

dun|no /dən<u>oʊ</u>/ **Dunno** is sometimes used in spoken and written English to represent an informal way of saying 'don't know.' ◻ *"How on earth did she get it?"—"I dunno."*

duo /d<u>u</u>oʊ/ (**duos**) **1** N-COUNT A **duo** is two musicians, singers, or other performers who perform together as a pair. ◻ *...a famous dancing and singing duo.* **2** N-COUNT You can refer to two people together as a **duo**, especially when they have something in common. [mainly JOURNALISM] ◻ *...the tragic duo in William Shakespeare's most famous love story.* **3** → See feature box at **humor**

duo|de|nal /djuoudiːnᵊl, duːdᵊnᵊl/ ADJ [ADJ n] **Duodenal** means relating to or contained in the duodenum. [MEDICAL] ❑ ...duodenal ulcers.

duo|de|num /djuoudɪnəm, duːdᵊnəm/ (**duodenums**) N-COUNT Your **duodenum** is the part of your small intestine that is just below your stomach. [MEDICAL]

duo|po|ly /djuːpəli/ (**duopolies**) **1** N-VAR If two companies or people have a **duopoly** on something such as an industry, they share complete control over it and it is impossible for others to become involved in it. [BUSINESS] ❑ ...they are no longer part of a duopoly on overseas routes. **2** N-COUNT A **duopoly** is a group of two companies which are the only ones which provide a particular product or service, and which therefore have complete control over an industry. [BUSINESS] ❑ The proposed merger will create a powerful duopoly.

dupe /djuːp/ (**dupes, duping, duped**) **1** V-T If a person **dupes** you, they trick you into doing something or into believing something which is not true. ❑ ...a plot to dupe stamp collectors into buying fake rarities. **2** N-COUNT A **dupe** is someone who is tricked by someone else. ❑ He was accused of being a dupe of the communists.

du|plex /djuːplɛks/ (**duplexes**) **1** N-COUNT A **duplex** is a house which has been divided into two separate units for two different families or groups of people. [AM] **2** N-COUNT A **duplex** or a **duplex apartment** is an apartment which has rooms on two floors. [AM]

du|pli|cate (**duplicates, duplicating, duplicated**)

The verb is pronounced /djuːplɪkeɪt/. The noun and adjective are pronounced /djuːplɪkɪt/.

1 V-T If you **duplicate** something that has already been done, you repeat or copy it. ❑ His task will be to duplicate his success overseas here at home. • N-COUNT **Duplicate** is also a noun. ❑ The tight race is almost a duplicate of the elections in Georgia and South Dakota last month that pitted a Republican challenger against a Democratic incumbent. **2** V-T To **duplicate** something which has been written, drawn, or recorded onto tape means to make exact copies of it. ❑ ...a business which duplicates video tapes for the movie makers. • N-COUNT [also in n] **Duplicate** is also a noun. ❑ I'm on my way to Switzerland, but I've lost my card. I've got to get a duplicate. **3** ADJ [ADJ n] **Duplicate** is used to describe things that have been made as an exact copy of other things, usually in order to serve the same purpose. ❑ He let himself in with a duplicate key.

du|pli|ca|tion /djuːplɪkeɪʃᵊn/ N-UNCOUNT If you say that there has been **duplication** of something, you mean that someone has done a task unnecessarily because it has already been done before. ❑ There could be a serious loss of efficiency through unnecessary duplication of resources.

du|plic|it|ous /djuːplɪsɪtəs/ ADJ Someone who is **duplicitous** is deceitful. ❑ He is a possessive, duplicitous, and unreasonable man.

du|plic|ity /djuːplɪsɪti/ N-UNCOUNT If you accuse someone of **duplicity**, you mean that they are deceitful. [FORMAL] ❑ Malcolm believed he was guilty of duplicity in his private dealings.

du|rable /djʊərəbᵊl/ ADJ Something that is **durable** is strong and lasts a long time without breaking or becoming weaker. ❑ Fine bone china is eminently practical, since it is strong and durable. • **du|rabil|ity** /djʊərəbɪlɪti/ N-UNCOUNT ❑ Airlines recommend hard-sided cases for durability.

du|rable goods also **durables** N-PLURAL **Durable goods** or **durables** are goods such as televisions or cars which are expected to last a long time, and are bought infrequently. [mainly AM] ❑ ...a 2.6% rise in orders for durable goods in January.

in BRIT, usually use **consumer durables**

du|ra|tion /djʊəreɪʃᵊn/ **1** N-UNCOUNT The **duration** of an event or state is the time during which it happens or exists. ❑ He was given the task of protecting her for the duration of the trial. **2** PHRASE If you say that something will happen **for the duration**, you mean that it will happen for as long as a particular situation continues. ❑ His wounds knocked him out of combat for the duration.

du|ress /djʊərɛs/ N-UNCOUNT [usu **under** n] To do something **under duress** means to do it because someone forces you to do it or threatens you. [FORMAL] ❑ He thought her confession had been made under duress.

dur|ing ♦♦♦ /djʊərɪŋ/ **1** PREP If something happens **during** a period of time or an event, it happens continuously, or happens several times between the beginning and end of that period or event. ❑ Sandstorms are common during the Saudi Arabian winter. **2** PREP If something develops **during** a period of time, it develops gradually from the beginning to the end of that period. ❑ Wages have fallen by more than twenty percent during the past two months. **3** PREP An event that happens **during** a period of time happens at some point or moment in that period. ❑ During his visit, the Pope will also bless the new hospital.

USAGE

during

Don't use **during** to say how long something lasts. Don't say, for example, 'I went to Wales during two weeks.' Say 'I went to Wales for two weeks.'

---

dusk /dʌsk/ N-UNCOUNT **Dusk** is the time just before night when the daylight has almost gone but when it is not completely dark. ❑ We arrived home at dusk.

dusky /dʌski/ **1** ADJ **Dusky** means rather dark. [LITERARY] ❑ He was walking down the road one dusky Friday evening. **2** COMB IN COLOR A **dusky** color is soft rather than bright. [LITERARY] ❑ ...dusky pink carpet.

dust ♦◊◊ /dʌst/ (**dusts, dusting, dusted**) **1** N-UNCOUNT **Dust** is very small dry particles of earth or sand. ❑ Tanks raise huge trails of dust when they move. **2** N-UNCOUNT **Dust** is the very small pieces of dirt which you find inside buildings, for example, on furniture, floors, or lights. ❑ I could see a thick layer of dust on the stairs. **3** N-UNCOUNT **Dust** is a fine powder which consists of very small particles of a substance such as gold, wood, or coal. ❑ The air is so black with diesel fumes and coal dust, I can barely see. **4** V-T/V-I When you **dust** something such as furniture, you remove dust from it, usually using a cloth. ❑ I vacuumed and dusted and polished the living room. **5** V-T/V-I If you **dust** something with a fine substance such as powder or if you **dust** a fine substance onto something, you cover it lightly with that substance. ❑ Lightly dust the fish with flour. **6** PHRASE If you say that something **has bitten the dust**, you are emphasizing that it no longer exists or that it has failed. [HUMOROUS, INFORMAL, EMPHASIS] ❑ In the last 30 years many cherished values have bitten the dust. **7** PHRASE If you say that something will happen when **the dust settles**, you mean that a situation will be clearer after it has calmed down. If you let **the dust settle** before doing something, you let a situation calm down before you try to do anything else. [INFORMAL] ❑ Once the dust had settled Beck defended his decision. **8** PHRASE If you say that something **is gathering dust**, you mean that it has been left somewhere and nobody is using it or doing anything with it. ❑ Many of the machines are gathering dust in basements. **9** → See feature box at **housework**

dust|bin /dʌstbɪn/ (**dustbins**) N-COUNT A **dustbin** is the same as a **garbage can**. [BRIT]

dust bowl (**dust bowls**) also **dustbowl** N-COUNT A **dust bowl** is an area of land, especially in the southern or central United States, that is dry and arid because the soil has been eroded by the wind. [AM] ❑ ...the same fate that befell the midwestern dust bowl in the thirties.

dust|cart /dʌstkɑːt/ (**dustcarts**) N-COUNT A **dustcart** is the same as a **garbage truck**. [BRIT]

dust|er /dʌstər/ (**dusters**) **1** N-COUNT A **duster** is a cloth which you use for removing dust from furniture, ornaments, or other objects. **2** → see also **feather duster**

dust jack|et (**dust jackets**) also **dust-jacket** N-COUNT A **dust jacket** is a loose paper cover which is put on a book to protect it. It often contains information about the book and its author.

dust|man /dʌstmən/ (**dustmen**) N-COUNT A **dustman** is the same as a **garbage collector**. [BRIT]

dust mite (**dust mites**) N-COUNT **Dust mites** are very small creatures that cause allergies. ❑ It's not easy to remove the dust mites from stuffed animals.

dust|pan /dʌstpæn/ (**dustpans**) N-COUNT A **dustpan** is a small flat container made of metal or plastic. You hold it flat on the floor and put dirt and dust into it using a brush.

dust sheet (**dust sheets**) also **dustsheet** N-COUNT A **dust sheet** is a large cloth which is used to cover objects such as furniture in order to protect them from dust.

dust storm (dust storms) N-COUNT A **dust storm** is a storm in which strong winds carry a lot of dust.

dust|up /dʌstʌp/ (dustups) also **dust-up** N-COUNT A **dustup** is a quarrel that often involves some fighting. [AM, INFORMAL] ❑ *He's now facing suspension after a dustup with the referee.*

dusty /dʌsti/ (dustier, dustiest) ▪ ADJ If places, roads, or other things outside are **dusty**, they are covered with tiny bits of earth or sand, usually because it has not rained for a long time. ❑ *They started strolling down the dusty road in the moonlight.* ▪ ADJ If a room, house, or object is **dusty**, it is covered with very small pieces of dirt. ❑ *...a dusty attic.*

Dutch /dʌtʃ/ ▪ ADJ **Dutch** means belonging or relating to the Netherlands, or to its people, language, or culture. ▪ N-PLURAL [the N] The **Dutch** are the people of the Netherlands. ▪ N-UNCOUNT **Dutch** is the language that is spoken by the people who live in the Netherlands. ▪ PHRASE If two or more people **go Dutch**, each of them pays their own bill, for example, in a restaurant. [INFORMAL] ❑ *We went Dutch on a meal in the new restaurant down the block.*

Dutch auc|tion (Dutch auctions) N-COUNT A **Dutch auction** is an auction in which the prices of items are gradually reduced until someone buys them. [mainly AM] ❑ *The Dutch auction it is setting up could prove somewhat confusing to small shareholders, however.*

Dutch cour|age N-UNCOUNT **Dutch courage** is the courage that you get by drinking alcoholic drinks. [INFORMAL]

Dutch|man /dʌtʃmən/ (Dutchmen) N-COUNT A **Dutchman** is a man who is a native of the Netherlands.

Dutch|woman /dʌtʃwumən/ (Dutchwomen) N-COUNT A **Dutchwoman** is a woman who is a native of the Netherlands.

du|ti|ful /djutifəl/ ADJ If you say that someone is **dutiful**, you mean that they do everything that they are expected to do. ❑ *The days of the dutiful wife, who sacrifices her career for her husband, are over.* • **du|ti|ful|ly** ADV [ADV with v] ❑ *The inspector dutifully recorded the date in a large red book.*

duty ♦♦◇ /djuti/ (duties) ▪ N-UNCOUNT **Duty** is work that you have to do for your job. ❑ *Staff must report for duty at their normal place of work.* ▪ N-PLURAL Your **duties** are tasks which you have to do because they are part of your job. ❑ *I carried out my duties conscientiously.* ▪ N-SING If you say that something is your **duty**, you believe that you ought to do it because it is your responsibility. ❑ *I consider it my duty to write to you and thank you.* ▪ N-VAR **Duties** are taxes which you pay to the government on goods that you buy. ❑ *Import duties still average 30%.* ▪ PHRASE If someone such as a police officer or a nurse is **off duty**, they are not working. If someone is **on duty**, they are working. ❑ *I'm off duty.*

COLLOCATIONS

duty
NOUN
▪
adjective + **duty**: heavy, light, onerous; day-to-day, normal
verb + **duty**: carry out, discharge, perform
▪
noun + **duty**: customs, excise, import
verb + **duty**: owe, pay

---

duty-bound also **duty bound** ADJ [v-link ADJ to-inf] If you say you are **duty-bound** to do something, you are emphasizing that you feel it is your duty to do it. [FORMAL, EMPHASIS] ❑ *I felt duty bound to help.*

duty-free ADJ **Duty-free** goods are sold at airports or on planes or ships at a cheaper price than usual because you do not have to pay import tax on them. ❑ *...duty-free cigarettes.*

duty-free shop (duty-free shops) N-COUNT A **duty-free shop** is a shop, for example, at an airport, where you can buy goods at a cheaper price than usual, because no tax is paid on them.

duty of|fic|er (duty officers) N-COUNT In the police or armed forces, a **duty officer** is an officer who is on duty at a particular time. ❑ *I related to the duty officer what I'd seen and was told to telephone the main station.*

du|vet /duveɪ/ (duvets) N-COUNT A **duvet** is the same as a **comforter**. [mainly BRIT]

DVD /di vi di/ (DVDs) ▪ N-COUNT A **DVD** is a disk on which a movie or music is recorded. DVD disks are similar to compact disks but hold a lot more information. **DVD** is an abbreviation for 'digital video disk' or 'digital versatile disk'. ❑ *...a DVD player.* ▪ → See feature box at **computer**

DVD burn|er (DVD burners) N-COUNT A **DVD burner** is a piece of computer equipment that you use for copying data from a computer onto a DVD. [COMPUTING]

DVD-R /di vi di ɑr/ (DVD-Rs) N-COUNT A **DVD-R** is a DVD which is capable of recording sound and images, for example, from another DVD or from the internet. **DVD-R** is an abbreviation for 'digital video disk recordable' or 'digital versatile disk recordable.'

DVD-RW /di vi di ɑr dʌbᵊlyu/ (DVD-RWs) N-COUNT A **DVD-RW** is a DVD which is capable of recording sound and images, for example, from another DVD or from the internet. **DVD-RW** is an abbreviation for 'digital video disk rewritable' or 'digital versatile disk rewritable.'

DVD writ|er (DVD writers) N-COUNT A **DVD writer** is the same as a **DVD burner**. [COMPUTING]

DVT /di vi ti/ (DVTs) N-VAR **DVT** is a serious medical condition caused by blood clots in the legs moving up to the lungs. **DVT** is an abbreviation for **deep vein thrombosis**. [MEDICAL]

dwarf /dwɔrf/ (dwarves, dwarfs, dwarfing, dwarfed)

> The spellings **dwarves** or **dwarfs** are used for the plural form of the noun.

▪ V-T If one person or thing **is dwarfed** by another, the second is so much bigger than the first that it makes them look very small. ❑ *His figure is dwarfed by the huge red McDonald's sign.* ▪ ADJ [ADJ n] **Dwarf** is used to describe varieties or species of plants and animals which are much smaller than the usual size for their kind. ❑ *...dwarf shrubs.* ▪ N-COUNT In children's stories, a **dwarf** is an imaginary creature that is like a small person. Dwarfs often have magical powers. ▪ N-COUNT In former times, people who were much smaller than normal were called **dwarves**. [OFFENSIVE, OLD-FASHIONED]

dwarf plan|et (dwarf planets) N-COUNT A **dwarf planet** is an object in space that is like a small planet but does not completely fit the technical description of a planet. ❑ *Pluto, Eris and the largest asteroid, Ceres, are all dwarf planets.*

dweeb /dwib/ (dweebs) N-COUNT If you call someone a **dweeb**, you are saying in a rather unkind way that you think they are stupid and weak. [mainly AM, INFORMAL, DISAPPROVAL]

dwell /dwɛl/ (dwells, dwelling, dwelt or dwelled) ▪ V-I If you **dwell** on something, especially something unpleasant, you think, speak, or write about it a lot or for quite a long time. ❑ *"I'd rather not dwell on the past," he told me.* ▪ → see also **dwelling**

dwell|er /dwɛlər/ (dwellers) ▪ N-COUNT A city **dweller** or slum **dweller**, for example, is a person who lives in the kind of place or house indicated. ❑ *The number of city dwellers is growing.* ▪ → See feature box at **house**

dwell|ing /dwɛlɪŋ/ (dwellings) N-COUNT A **dwelling** or a **dwelling place** is a place where someone lives. [FORMAL] ❑ *Some 3,500 new dwellings are planned for the area.*

dwelt /dwɛlt/ **Dwelt** is the past tense and past participle of **dwell**.

DWI /di dʌbəlyu aɪ/ N-UNCOUNT [oft N n] **DWI** is the offense of driving after drinking more than the amount of alcohol that is legally allowed. **DWI** is an abbreviation for 'driving while intoxicated.' [AM] ❑ *He'd arranged for his client to pay a stiff fine for charges of DWI and reckless driving.*

dwin|dle /dwɪndᵊl/ (dwindles, dwindling, dwindled) V-I If something **dwindles**, it becomes smaller, weaker, or less in number. ❑ *The factory's workforce has dwindled from over 4,000 to a few hundred.*

dye /daɪ/ (dyes, dyeing, dyed) ▪ V-T If you **dye** something such as hair or cloth, you change its color by soaking it in a special liquid. ❑ *The women prepared, spun, and dyed the wool.* ▪ N-MASS **Dye** is a substance made from plants or chemicals which is mixed into a liquid and used to change the color of something such as cloth or hair. ❑ *...bottles of hair dye.*

dyed-in-the-wool ADJ [ADJ n] If you use **dyed-in-the-wool** to describe someone or their beliefs, you are saying that they have very strong opinions about something, which they refuse to change. ❑ *...a dyed-in-the-wool conservative.*

dying /daɪɪŋ/ **1** Dying is the present participle of **die**. **2** ADJ [ADJ n] A **dying** person or animal is very ill and likely to die soon. ❑ ...*a dying man*. • N-PLURAL The **dying** are people who are dying. ❑ *By the time our officers arrived, the dead and the dying were everywhere.* **3** ADJ [ADJ n] You use **dying** to describe something which happens at the time when someone dies, or is connected with that time. ❑ *It'll stay in my mind till my dying day.* **4** ADJ [ADJ n] The **dying** days or **dying** minutes of a state of affairs or an activity are its last days or minutes. ❑ ...*a story of love and war in the dying days of the Ottoman Empire*. **5** ADJ [ADJ n] A **dying** tradition or industry is becoming less important and is likely to disappear completely. ❑ *Shipbuilding is a dying business.*

dyke /daɪk/ (**dykes**) **1** N-COUNT **Dyke** is an offensive word for a lesbian. [INFORMAL, OFFENSIVE] **2** → see **dike 1**

dy|nam|ic /daɪnæmɪk/ (**dynamics**) **1** ADJ If you describe someone as **dynamic**, you approve of them because they are full of energy or full of new and exciting ideas. [APPROVAL] ❑ *He seemed a dynamic and energetic leader*. • **dy|nami|cal|ly** /daɪnæmɪkli/ ADV ❑ *He's one of the most dynamically imaginative jazz pianists of our time*. **2** ADJ If you describe something as **dynamic**, you approve of it because it is very active and energetic. [APPROVAL] ❑ *South Asia was known as the most dynamic economic region in the world*. **3** ADJ A **dynamic** process is one that constantly changes and progresses. ❑ ...*a dynamic, evolving worldwide epidemic*. **4** N-COUNT The **dynamic** of a system or process is the force that causes it to change or progress. ❑ *The dynamic of the market demands constant change and adjustment*. **5** N-PLURAL The **dynamics** of a situation or group of people are the opposing forces within it that cause it to change. ❑ *What is needed is insight into the dynamics of the social system*.

dy|na|mism /daɪnəmɪzəm/ **1** N-UNCOUNT If you say that someone or something has **dynamism**, you are expressing approval of the fact that they are full of energy or full of new and exciting ideas. [APPROVAL] ❑ ...*a situation that calls for dynamism and new thinking*. **2** N-UNCOUNT If you refer to the **dynamism** of a situation or action, you are referring to the fact that it is changing in an exciting and dramatic way. [APPROVAL] ❑ *Such changes are also indicators of economic dynamism and demographic expansion*.

dy|na|mite /daɪnəmaɪt/ **1** N-UNCOUNT **Dynamite** is a type of explosive that contains nitroglycerin. ❑ *Fifty yards of track was blown up with dynamite*. **2** N-UNCOUNT If you describe a piece of information as **dynamite**, you think that people will react strongly to it. [INFORMAL] ❑ *The book is dynamite, and if she publishes it, there will be no hiding place for her*. **3** N-UNCOUNT If you describe someone or something as **dynamite**, you think that they are exciting. [INFORMAL, APPROVAL] ❑ *The first kiss is dynamite*.

dy|na|mo /daɪnəmoʊ/ (**dynamos**) **1** N-COUNT A **dynamo** is a device that uses the movement of a machine or vehicle to produce electricity. ❑ ...*a bicycle with a dynamo*. **2** N-COUNT If you describe someone as a **dynamo**, you mean that they are very energetic and are always busy and active. ❑ *Myles is a human dynamo*.

dy|nas|tic /daɪnæstɪk/ ADJ [usu ADJ n] **Dynastic** means typical of or relating to a dynasty. ❑ ...*dynastic rule*.

dyn|as|ty /daɪnəsti/ (**dynasties**) **1** N-COUNT A **dynasty** is a series of rulers of a country who all belong to the same family. ❑ *The Seljuk dynasty of Syria was founded in 1094*. **2** N-COUNT A **dynasty** is a period of time during which a country is ruled by members of the same family. ❑ ...*carvings dating back to the Ming dynasty*. **3** N-COUNT A **dynasty** is a family which has members from two or more generations who are important in a particular field of activity, for example, in business or politics. ❑ *This is a family-owned company – the current president is the fourth in this dynasty*. **4** → See feature box at **history**

d'you /dyu, dʒu/ **D'you** is a shortened form of 'do you' or 'did you,' used in spoken English. ❑ *What d'you say?*

dys|en|tery /dɪsənteri/ N-UNCOUNT **Dysentery** is an infection in a person's intestines that causes them to pass a lot of waste, in which blood and mucus are mixed with the person's feces.

dys|func|tion /dɪsfʌŋkʃən/ (**dysfunctions**) **1** N-COUNT If you refer to a **dysfunction** in something such as a relationship or someone's behavior, you mean that it is different from what is considered to be normal. [FORMAL] ❑ *His severe emotional dysfunction was very clearly apparent*. **2** N-VAR If someone has a physical **dysfunction**, part of their body is not working properly. [MEDICAL] ❑ ...*kidney and liver dysfunction*.

dys|func|tion|al /dɪstʌŋkʃənᵊl/ ADJ [usu ADJ n] **Dysfunctional** is used to describe relationships or behavior which are different from what is considered to be normal. [FORMAL] ❑ ...*the characteristics that typically occur in a dysfunctional family*.

dys|lexia /dɪslɛksiə/ N-UNCOUNT If someone has **dyslexia**, they have difficulty with reading because of a slight disorder of their brain. [TECHNICAL]

dys|lex|ic /dɪslɛksɪk/ ADJ If someone is **dyslexic**, they have difficulty with reading because of a slight disorder of their brain. [TECHNICAL]

dys|pep|sia /dɪspɛpʃə, -siə/ N-UNCOUNT **Dyspepsia** is the same as **indigestion**. [OLD-FASHIONED]

dys|praxia /dɪspræksiə/ N-UNCOUNT If someone has **dyspraxia**, they have a brain condition which means they cannot control their body's coordination and movement as well as most people. [TECHNICAL]

dys|tro|phy /dɪstrəfi/ → see **muscular dystrophy**

Ee

E also **e** /iː/ (**E's**, **e's**) N-VAR **E** is the fifth letter of the English alphabet.

PREFIX

e-
is used to form words that indicate that something happens on or uses the internet. **e-** is an abbreviation for 'electronic'. *For example, an **e-book** is an electronic book that you can read on a mobile device such as a tablet.*

each ♦♦♦ /iːtʃ/ **1** DET If you refer to **each** thing or **each** person in a group, you are referring to every member of the group and considering them as individuals. ❑ *Each book is beautifully illustrated.* ❑ *Each year, hundreds of animals are killed in this way.* • PRON **Each** is also a pronoun. ❑ *...two bedrooms, each with three beds.* • PRON-EMPH **Each** is also an emphasizing pronoun. ❑ *We each have different needs and interests.* • ADV [amount ADV] **Each** is also an adverb. ❑ *The children were given one each, handed to them or placed on their plates.* • QUANT [QUANT def-pl-n] **Each** is also a quantifier. ❑ *He handed each of them a page of photos.* ❑ *Each of these exercises takes one or two minutes to do.* **2** QUANT [QUANT def-pl-n] If you refer to **each one** of the members of a group, you are emphasizing that something applies to every one of them. [EMPHASIS] ❑ *He picked up forty of these publications and read each one of them.* **3** PHRASE You can refer to **each and every** member of a group to emphasize that you mean all the members of that group. [EMPHASIS] ❑ *My goal was that each and every person responsible for Yankel's murder be brought to justice.* **4** PRON-RECIP [v PRON, prep PRON] You use **each other** when you are saying that each member of a group does something to the others or has a particular connection with the others. ❑ *We looked at each other in silence, each equally shocked.* ❑ *Both sides are willing to make allowances for each other's political sensitivities.*

eager ♦♦♦ /ˈiːɡər/ **1** ADJ If you are **eager** to do or have something, you want to do or have it very much. ❑ *Robert was eager to talk about life in the Army.* ❑ *When my own son was five years old, I became eager for another baby.* • **eager|ness** N-UNCOUNT ❑ *...an eagerness to learn.* **2** ADJ If you look or sound **eager**, you look or sound as if you expect something interesting or enjoyable to happen. ❑ *Arty sneered at the crowd of eager faces around him.* • **eager|ly** ADV ❑ *"So what do you think will happen?" he asked eagerly.* • **eager|ness** N-UNCOUNT ❑ *It was the voice of a woman speaking with breathless eagerness.*

SYNONYMS

eager
ADJ **1**
anxious: *He is anxious to meet them.*
keen: *She's still keen to keep in touch.*
impatient: *He was impatient to get home.*
raring: *Sarah's here and raring to meet you.*

eagle /ˈiːɡəl/ (**eagles**) **1** N-COUNT An **eagle** is a large bird that lives by eating small animals. **2** N-COUNT In golf, if you get an **eagle**, you get the golf ball into a hole in two strokes fewer than the number of strokes which has been set as the standard for a good player.

eagle-eyed ADJ If you describe someone as **eagle-eyed**, you mean that they watch things very carefully and seem to notice everything. ❑ *Three marijuana plants were found by eagle-eyed police officers.*

ear ♦⬦⬦ /ɪər/ (**ears**) **1** N-COUNT Your **ears** are the two parts of your body, one on each side of your head, with which you hear sounds. ❑ *He whispered something in her ear.* **2** N-SING If you have an **ear** for music or language, you are able to hear its sounds accurately and to interpret them or reproduce them well. ❑ *Moby certainly has a fine ear for a tune.* **3** N-COUNT **Ear** is often used to refer to people's willingness to listen to what someone is saying. ❑ *What would cause the masses to give him a far more sympathetic ear?* **4** N-COUNT The **ears** of a cereal plant such as corn or barley are the parts at the top of the stem that contain the seeds or grains. ❑ *American farmers use machines to pick the ears of corn from the plants.* **5** PHRASE If a request **falls on deaf ears** or if the person to whom the request is made **turns a deaf ear** to it, they take no notice of it. ❑ *I hope that our appeals will not fall on deaf ears.* **6** PHRASE If you **play by ear** or **play** a piece of music **by ear**, you play music by relying on your memory rather than by reading printed music. ❑ *Neil sat at the piano and began playing, by ear, the music he'd heard his older sister practicing.* **7** PHRASE [usu PHR for n] If you say that someone **has a tin ear** for something, you mean that they do not have any natural ability for it and cannot appreciate or understand it fully. ❑ *Worst of all, for a playwright specializing in characters who use the vernacular, he has a tin ear for dialogue.* **8** **music to your ears** → see **music** **9** → See also color supplement

ear|ache /ˈɪəreɪk/ (**earaches**) N-COUNT An **earache** is a pain in the inside part of your ear. ❑ *He had an earache and a fever.*

ear ca|nal (**ear canals**) **1** N-COUNT Your **ear canal** is the tube that opens in your outer ear and leads inside your ear. ❑ *Your hearing can be affected by ear wax blocking the ear canal.* **2** → See also color supplement

ear|drum /ˈɪərdrʌm/ (**eardrums**) also **ear drum** **1** N-COUNT Your **eardrums** are the thin pieces of tightly stretched skin inside each ear that vibrate when sound waves reach them. ❑ *The blast burst Ollie Williams' eardrum.* **2** → See also color supplement

ear|ful /ˈɪərfəl/ N-SING [a N] If you say that you got **an earful**, you mean that someone spoke angrily to you for a long time. [INFORMAL] ❑ *I bet Sue gave you an earful when you got home.*

earl /ɜːrl/ (**earls**) N-COUNT An **earl** is a British nobleman. ❑ *...the first Earl of Birkenhead.*

earl|dom /ˈɜːrldəm/ (**earldoms**) N-COUNT An **earldom** is the rank or title of an earl.

ear|li|er ♦♦♦ /ˈɜːrliər/ **1** **Earlier** is the comparative of **early**. **2** ADV **Earlier** is used to refer to a point or period in time before the present or before the one you are talking about. ❑ *As mentioned earlier, the university supplements this information with an interview.* ❑ *...political reforms announced by the president earlier this year.* • ADJ [ADJ n] **Earlier** is also an adjective. ❑ *Earlier reports of gunshots have not been substantiated.*

ear|li|est /ˈɜːrliɪst/ **1** **Earliest** is the superlative of **early**. **2** PHRASE **At the earliest** means not before the date or time mentioned. ❑ *The first official results are not expected until Tuesday at the earliest.*

ear|lobe /ˈɪərloʊb/ (**earlobes**) also **ear lobe** N-COUNT Your **earlobes** are the soft parts at the bottom of your ears. ❑ *...the holes in her earlobes.*

ear|ly ♦♦♦ /ˈɜːrli/ (**earlier**, **earliest**) **1** ADV [ADV after v] **Early** means before the usual time that a particular event or activity happens. ❑ *I knew I had to get up early.* • ADJ [ADJ n] **Early** is also an adjective. ❑ *I decided that I was going to take early*

early bird 403 **earth**

retirement. **2** ADJ [ADJ n] **Early** means near the beginning of a day, week, year, or other period of time. ❑ ...*in the 1970s and the early 1980s.* ❑ *She was in her early teens.* • ADV **Early** is also an adverb. ❑ *We'll hope to see you some time early next week.* **3** ADV [ADV after v] **Early** means before the time that was arranged or expected. ❑ *She arrived early to get a place at the front.* • ADJ **Early** is also an adjective. ❑ *I'm always early.* **4** ADJ [ADJ n] **Early** means near the beginning of a period in history, or in the history of something such as the world, a society, or an activity. ❑ ...*the early stages of pregnancy.* ❑ ...*Fassbinder's early films.* **5** ADJ [ADJ n] **Early** means near the beginning of something such as a piece of work or a process. ❑ ...*the book's early chapters.* • ADV **Early** is also an adverb. ❑ ...*an incident that occurred much earlier in the game.* **6** ADJ [ADJ n] **Early** refers to plants that flower or crop before or at the beginning of the main season. ❑ ...*these early cabbages and cauliflowers.* • ADV [ADV with v] **Early** is also an adverb. ❑ *This early flowering gladiolus is not very hardy.* **7** ADJ [ADJ n] **Early** reports or indications of something are the first reports or indications about it. [FORMAL] ❑ *The early indications look encouraging.* **8** PHRASE You can use **as early as** to emphasize that a particular time or period is surprisingly early. [EMPHASIS] ❑ *Inflation could fall back into single figures as early as this month.*

ear|ly bird (early birds) **1** N-COUNT An **early bird** is someone who does something or goes somewhere very early, especially very early in the morning. ❑ *We've always been early birds, getting up at 5:30 or 6 a.m.* **2** ADJ [ADJ n] An **early bird** deal or special is one that is available at a reduced price, but that you must buy earlier than you would normally. ❑ *Early bird discounts are usually available at the beginning of the season.*

ear|ly warn|ing also **early-warning** ADJ [ADJ n] An **early warning** system warns people that something bad is likely to happen, for example that a machine is about to stop working, or that a country is being attacked.

ear|mark /ɪərmɑrk/ (earmarks, earmarking, earmarked) **1** V-T If resources such as money **are earmarked** for a particular purpose, they are reserved for that purpose. ❑ ...*the extra money being earmarked for the new projects.* ❑ *China has earmarked more than $20 billion for oil exploration.* **2** V-T [usu passive] If something **has been earmarked** for closure or disposal, for example, people have decided that it will be closed or got rid of. ❑ *Their support meant that he was not forced to sell the business which was earmarked for disposal last year.* **3** N-COUNT [with poss] The **earmark** of something or someone is their most typical quality or feature. [AM] ❑ *Davis's solo work exhibits all the earmarks of his style: it is hesitant, tentative, spare.*

ear|muffs /ɪərmʌfs/ also **ear muffs** N-PLURAL [also *a pair of* N] **Earmuffs** consist of two thick soft pieces of cloth joined by a band, which you wear over your ears to protect them from the cold.

earn ✦✧ /ɜrn/ (earns, earning, earned) **1** V-T If you **earn** money, you receive money in return for work that you do. ❑ *What a lovely way to earn a living.* **2** V-T If something **earns** money, it produces money as profit or interest. ❑ ...*a bank account that earns little or no interest.* **3** V-T If you **earn** something such as praise, you get it because you deserve it. ❑ *Companies must earn a reputation for honesty.* **4** → See feature box at **work**

COLLOCATIONS

earn
VERB
1
earn + *noun*: income, living, salary, wage
3
earn + *noun*: praise, reputation, respect, right; victory
earn + *adverb*: deservedly, rightly

SYNONYMS

earn
VERB **1**
get: *They get a salary of $21,000 a year.*
make: *How much did we make?*
be paid: *Students were paid substantial sums of money to lie in bed all day.*
bring in: *I have a part-time job, which brings in about $14,000 a year.*

earn|er /ɜrnər/ (earners) N-COUNT An **earner** is someone or something that earns money or produces profit. ❑ ...*a typical wage earner.*

ear|nest /ɜrnɪst/ **1** PHRASE If something is done or happens **in earnest**, it happens to a much greater extent and more seriously than before. ❑ *Campaigning will begin in earnest tomorrow.* **2** ADJ **Earnest** people are very serious and sincere in what they say or do, because they think that their actions and beliefs are important. ❑ *Catherine was a pious, earnest woman.*

ear|nest|ly /ɜrnɪstli/ **1** ADV [ADV with v] If you say something **earnestly**, you say it very seriously, often because you believe that it is important or you are trying to persuade someone else to believe it. ❑ *"Did you?" she asked earnestly.* **2** ADV If you do something **earnestly**, you do it in a thorough and serious way, intending to succeed. ❑ *She always listened earnestly as if this might help her to understand.*

earn|ings ✦✧ /ɜrnɪŋz/ N-PLURAL Your **earnings** are the sums of money that you earn by working. ❑ *Average weekly earnings rose by 1.5% in July.*

SYNONYMS

earnings
NOUN
income: *Over a third of their income comes from comedy shows.*
pay: ...*their complaints about their pay and conditions.*
wages: *His wages have gone up.*
salary: *The lawyer was paid a huge salary.*
takings: *The hotel said that their takings were fifteen to twenty thousand dollars a week.*

ear|phone /ɪərfoʊn/ (earphones) **1** N-COUNT **Earphones** are a small piece of equipment that you wear over or inside your ears so that you can listen to a radio or recorded music without anyone else hearing. **2** → See also color supplement

ear|piece /ɪərpis/ (earpieces) N-COUNT The **earpiece** of a telephone receiver, hearing aid, or other device is the part that you hold up to your ear or put into your ear.

ear|plug /ɪərplʌg/ (earplugs) N-COUNT [usu pl] **Earplugs** are small pieces of a soft material that you put into your ears to keep out noise, water, or cold air.

ear|ring /ɪərɪŋ/ (earrings) N-COUNT **Earrings** are pieces of jewelry that you attach to your ears. ❑ ...*a pair of diamond earrings.*

ear|shot /ɪərʃɒt/ PHRASE If you are **within earshot** of someone or something, you are close enough to be able to hear them. If you are **out of earshot**, you are too far away to hear them. ❑ *It is within earshot of a main road.*

ear-splitting ADJ [usu ADJ n] An **ear-splitting** noise is very loud. ❑ ...*ear-splitting screams.*

earth ✦✧ /ɜrθ/ **1** N-PROPER **Earth** or **the Earth** is the planet on which we live. People usually say **Earth** when they are referring to the planet as part of the universe, and **the Earth** when they are talking about the planet as the place where we live. ❑ *The space shuttle Atlantis returned safely to Earth today.* **2** N-SING The **earth** is the land surface on which we live and move around. ❑ *The earth shook and swayed and the walls of neighboring houses fell around them.* **3** N-UNCOUNT **Earth** is the substance on the land surface of the earth, for example clay or sand, in which plants grow. ❑ *The road winds for miles through parched earth, scrub and cactus.* **4** N-SING The **earth** in an electric plug or piece of electrical equipment is the same as the **ground** ①. [BRIT] **5** → see also **down-to-earth** **6** PHRASE **On earth** is used for emphasis in questions that begin with words such as 'how,' 'why,' 'what,' or 'where.' It is often used to suggest that there is no obvious or easy answer to the question being asked. [EMPHASIS] ❑ *How on earth did that happen?* **7** PHRASE **On earth** is used for emphasis after some negative noun groups, for example 'no reason.' [EMPHASIS] ❑ *There was no reason on earth why she couldn't have moved in with us.* **8** PHRASE If you come **down to earth** or **back to earth**, you have to face the reality of everyday life after a period of great excitement. ❑ *When he came down to earth after his win he admitted: "It was an amazing feeling."* **9** → See also color supplement

SYNONYMS

earth
NOUN
1
globe: *70% of our globe's surface is water.*
world: *It's a beautiful part of the world.*
3
soil: *We have the most fertile soil in Europe.*
mud: *Their truck got stuck in the mud.*
dirt: *They all sit on the dirt in the dappled shade of a tree.*

earth|bound /ɜrθbaʊnd/ ADJ If something is **earthbound**, it is unable to fly, or is on the ground rather than in the air or in space. ❏ *...earthbound telescopes.*

earth|en /ɜrθən/ **1** ADJ [ADJ n] **Earthen** containers and objects are made of clay that is baked so that it becomes hard. **2** ADJ [ADJ n] An **earthen** floor, bank, or mound is made of hard earth.

earthen|ware /ɜrθənwɛər/ **1** ADJ [ADJ n] **Earthenware** bowls, pots, or other objects are made of clay that is baked so that it becomes hard. ❏ *...earthenware pots.* **2** N-UNCOUNT **Earthenware** objects are referred to as **earthenware**. ❏ *...colorful Italian china and earthenware.*

earth|ling /ɜrθlɪŋ/ (**earthlings**) N-COUNT [usu pl] **Earthling** is used in science fiction to refer to a human being who lives on the planet Earth.

earth|ly /ɜrθli/ **1** ADJ [ADJ n] **Earthly** means happening in the material world of our life on earth and not in any spiritual life or life after death. ❏ *...the need to confront evil during the earthly life.* **2** ADJ [ADJ n] **Earthly** is used for emphasis in phrases such as **no earthly reason**. If you say that there is **no earthly reason** why something should happen, you are emphasizing that there is no reason at all why it should happen. [EMPHASIS] ❏ *There is no earthly reason why they should ever change.*

earth-moving also **earthmoving** ADJ [ADJ n] **Earth-moving** equipment is machinery that is used for digging and moving large amounts of soil. ❏ *The earth-moving trucks and cement mixers lay idle.*

earth|quake /ɜrθkweɪk/ (**earthquakes**) **1** N-COUNT An **earthquake** is a shaking of the ground caused by movement of the Earth's crust. ❏ *...the San Francisco earthquake of 1906.* **2** → See feature box at **disaster**

earth sci|ence (**earth sciences**) also **Earth science** N-VAR **Earth sciences** are sciences such as geology and geography that are concerned with the study of the earth. ❏ *Her husband taught Earth sciences.* ❏ *Her specialty is math, earth science, and chemistry.*

earth|shaking /ɜrθʃeɪkɪŋ/ → see **earth-shattering**

earth-shattering also **earthshaking** ADJ Something that is **earth-shattering** is very surprising or shocking. ❏ *...earth-shattering news.*

earth|work /ɜrθwɜrk/ (**earthworks**) N-COUNT [usu pl] **Earthworks** are large structures of earth that have been built for defense, especially ones built a very long time ago.

earth|worm /ɜrθwɜrm/ (**earthworms**) N-COUNT An **earthworm** is a kind of worm that lives in the ground.

earthy /ɜrθi/ (**earthier, earthiest**) **1** ADJ If you describe someone as **earthy**, you mean that they are open and direct, and talk about subjects that other people avoid or feel ashamed about. [APPROVAL] ❏ *...his extremely earthy humor.* **2** ADJ If you describe something as **earthy**, you mean it looks, smells, or feels like earth. ❏ *I'm attracted to warm, earthy colors.*

ear|wig /ɪərwɪg/ (**earwigs**) N-COUNT An **earwig** is a small, thin, brown insect that has a pair of claws at the back end of its body.

WORD HISTORY

earwig
Earwig comes from Old English *earwicga*, meaning 'ear insect.' It was once believed that earwigs would creep into people's ears.

ease ✦✧✧ /iz/ (**eases, easing, eased**) **1** PHRASE If you do something **with ease**, you do it easily, without difficulty or effort. ❏ *Anne was intelligent and capable of passing her exams with ease.* **2** N-UNCOUNT If you talk about the **ease of** a particular activity, you are referring to the way that it has been made easier to do, or to the fact that it is already easy to do. ❏ *For ease of reference, only the relevant extracts of the regulations are included.* **3** N-UNCOUNT **Ease** is the state of being very comfortable and able to live as you want, without any worries or problems. ❏ *She lived a life of ease.* **4** V-T/V-I If something unpleasant **eases** or if you **ease** it, it is reduced in degree, speed, or intensity. ❏ *Tensions had eased.* ❏ *I gave him some brandy to ease the pain.* **5** V-T/V-I If you **ease** your way somewhere or **ease** somewhere, you move there slowly, carefully, and gently. If you **ease** something somewhere, you move it there slowly, carefully, and gently. ❏ *I eased my way toward the door.* ❏ *He eased his foot off the accelerator.* **6** PHRASE If you are **at ease**, you are feeling confident and relaxed, and are able to talk to people without feeling nervous or anxious. If you put someone **at ease**, you make them feel at ease. ❏ *It is essential to feel at ease with your therapist.* **7** PHRASE If you are **ill at ease**, you feel somewhat uncomfortable, anxious, or worried. ❏ *He appeared embarrassed and ill at ease with the sustained applause that greeted him.*
▶ **ease up** **1** PHRASAL VERB If something **eases up**, it is reduced in degree, speed, or intensity. ❏ *The rain had eased up.* **2** PHRASAL VERB If you **ease up**, you start to make less effort. ❏ *He told supporters not to ease up even though he's leading in the presidential race.*

COLLOCATIONS

ease
NOUN **2**
adjective + **ease**: apparent, comparative, consummate, relative
VERB
4
ease + noun: burden, congestion, pain, pressure
noun + **ease**: pain, tension; rain
ease + adverb: gradually, slightly, somewhat
5
ease + adverb: gently, slowly

easel /iz³l/ (**easels**) N-COUNT An **easel** is a frame that supports a picture which an artist is painting or drawing.

easi|ly ✦✧✧ /izɪli/ **1** ADV You use **easily** to emphasize that something is very likely to happen, or is very likely to be true. [EMPHASIS] ❏ *It could easily be another year before the economy starts to show some improvement.* **2** ADV [ADV after v] You use **easily** to say that something happens more quickly or more often than is usual or normal. ❏ *He had always cried very easily.* **3** → see also **easy**

east ✦✦✦ /ist/ also **East** **1** N-UNCOUNT [also the N] The **east** is the direction where the sun rises. ❏ *...the vast swamps that lie to the east of the River Nile.* **2** N-SING The **east** of a place, country, or region is the part which is in the east. ❏ *...a village in the east of the country.* **3** ADV [ADV after v] If you go **east**, you travel toward the east. ❏ *To drive, go east on Route 9.* **4** ADV Something that is **east** of a place is positioned to the east of it. ❏ *...just east of the center of town.* **5** ADJ [ADJ n] The **east** edge, corner, or part of a place or country is the part toward the east. ❏ *...a low line of hills running along the east coast.* **6** ADJ [ADJ n] **East** is used in the names of some countries, states, and regions in the east of a larger area. ❏ *He had been on safari in East Africa with his son.* **7** ADJ An **east** wind is a wind that blows from the east. ❏ *...a bitter east wind.* **8** N-SING **The East** is used to refer to the southern and eastern part of Asia, including India, China, and Japan. ❏ *Every so often, a new martial art arrives from the East.* **9** → see also **Middle East, Far East** **10** → See also color supplement

east|bound /istbaʊnd/ ADJ [ADJ n] **Eastbound** roads or vehicles lead to or are traveling toward the east. [FORMAL] ❏ *All eastbound traffic was stopped until 8 a.m.*

East|er /istər/ (**Easters**) N-VAR [oft N n] **Easter** is a Christian festival when Jesus Christ's return to life is celebrated. It is celebrated on a Sunday in March or April. ❏ *"Happy Easter," he yelled.*

East|er egg (**Easter eggs**) N-COUNT An **Easter egg** is a cooked egg with a decorated shell, or an egg made of chocolate, that is given as a present at Easter. In some countries, Easter eggs are hidden and children then look for them.

east|er|ly /istərli/ **1** ADJ An **easterly** point, area, or direction is to the east or toward the east. ❑ *He progressed slowly along the coast in an easterly direction.* **2** ADJ An **easterly** wind is a wind that blows from the east. ❑ *It was a beautiful September day, with stiff easterly winds.*

east|ern ♦♦◊ /istərn/ **1** ADJ [ADJ n] **Eastern** means in or from the east of a region, state, or country. ❑ *...Eastern Europe.* **2** ADJ [ADJ n] **Eastern** means coming from or associated with the people or countries of the East, such as India, China, or Japan. ❑ *In many Eastern countries massage was and is a part of everyday life.*

east|ern|er /istərnər/ (**easterners**) N-COUNT An **easterner** is a person who was born in or who lives in the eastern part of a place or country, especially an American from the East Coast of the U.S. [mainly AM]

east|ern|most /istərnmoʊst/ ADJ [usu ADJ n] The **easternmost** part of an area or the **easternmost** place is the one that is farthest toward the east. [FORMAL]

East|er Sun|day N-UNCOUNT **Easter Sunday** is the Sunday in March or April when Easter is celebrated.

East Ger|man (**East Germans**) ADJ **East German** is used to describe things that belonged or related to the former German Democratic Republic. • N-COUNT **East Germans** were people from the German Democratic Republic.

east|ward /istwərd/

The form **eastwards** is also used.

ADV [ADV after v] **Eastward** or **eastwards** means toward the east. ❑ *A powerful snow storm is moving eastward.* • ADJ **Eastward** is also an adjective. ❑ *...the eastward expansion of the city.*

easy ♦♦♦ /izi/ (**easier, easiest**) **1** ADJ If a job or action is **easy**, you can do it without difficulty or effort, because it is not complicated and causes no problems. ❑ *The shower is easy to install.* ❑ *This is not an easy task.* • **easi|ly** ADV ❑ *Dress your child in layers of clothes you can remove easily.* **2** ADJ If you describe an action or activity as **easy**, you mean that it is done in a confident, relaxed way. If someone is **easy** about something, they feel relaxed and confident about it. ❑ *He was an easy person to talk to.* • **easi|ly** ADV [ADV with v] ❑ *They talked amiably and easily about a range of topics.* **3** ADJ If you say that someone has an **easy** life, you mean that they live comfortably without any problems or worries. ❑ *She has not had an easy life.* **4** ADJ If you say that something is **easy** or too **easy**, you are criticizing someone because they have done the most obvious or least difficult thing, and have not considered the situation carefully enough. [DISAPPROVAL] ❑ *That's easy for you to say.* **5** PHRASE If you tell someone to **go easy on** something, you are telling them to use only a small amount of it. [INFORMAL] ❑ *Go easy on the alcohol.* **6** PHRASE If you tell someone to **go easy on**, or **be easy on**, a particular person, you are telling them not to punish or treat that person very severely. [INFORMAL] ❑ *"Go easy on him," Sam repeated, opening the door.* **7** PHRASE If someone tells you to **take it easy** or **take things easy**, they mean that you should relax and not do very much at all. [INFORMAL] ❑ *It is best to take things easy for a week or two.* **8** → see also **easily**

> **SYNONYMS**
>
> **easy**
> ADJ **1**
> **simple:** *The job itself had been simple enough.*
> **straightforward:** *Disposable diapers are pretty straightforward to put on.*
> **effortless:** *...effortless and elegant Italian cooking.*

easy chair (**easy chairs**) **1** N-COUNT An **easy chair** is a large, comfortable padded chair. **2** → See also color supplement

easy|going /izigoʊɪŋ/

in BRIT, use **easy-going**

ADJ If you describe someone as **easygoing**, you mean that they are not easily annoyed, worried, or upset, and you think this is a good quality. [APPROVAL] ❑ *He was easygoing and good-natured.*

easy lis|ten|ing N-UNCOUNT **Easy listening** is gentle, relaxing music. Some people do not like this kind of music because they do not think that it is very interesting or exciting. ❑ *...a radio played softly, tuned to an easy-listening station.*

eat ♦♦◊ /it/ (**eats, eating, ate, eaten**) **1** V-T/V-I When you **eat** something, you put it into your mouth, chew it, and swallow it. ❑ *She was eating a sandwich.* ❑ *I ate slowly and without speaking.* **2** V-I If you **eat** sensibly or healthily, you eat food that is good for you. ❑ *...a campaign to persuade people to eat more healthily.* **3** V-T/V-I If you **eat**, you have a meal. ❑ *Let's go out to eat.* ❑ *We ate lunch together every day.* **4** V-T [only cont] If something is **eating** you, it is annoying or worrying you. [INFORMAL] ❑ *"What the hell's eating you?" he demanded.* **5 dog eat dog** → see **dog** **6 to eat crow** → see **crow**

▸ **eat away** PHRASAL VERB If one thing **eats away** another or **eats away** at another, it gradually destroys or uses it up. ❑ *Water pours through the roof, encouraging rot to eat away the interior of the house.*

▸ **eat into** **1** PHRASAL VERB If something **eats into** your time or your resources, it uses them, when they should be used for other things. ❑ *Responsibilities at home and work eat into his time.* **2** PHRASAL VERB If a substance such as acid or rust **eats into** something, it destroys or damages its surface. ❑ *Ulcers occur when the stomach's natural acids eat into the lining of the stomach.*

> **SYNONYMS**
>
> **eat**
> VERB **1**
> **consume:** *...serving chocolate ice-cream for the children to consume in the kitchen.*
> **swallow:** *You are asked to swallow a capsule containing vitamin B.*
> **devour:** *She devoured half an apple pie.*

> **COLLOCATIONS**
>
> **eat**
> VERB **1**
> **eat** + adverb: healthily, properly, sensibly, well

eat|en /it³n/ **Eaten** is the past participle of **eat**.

eat|en up ADJ [v-link ADJ with n] If someone is **eaten up with** jealousy, curiosity, or desire, they feel it very intensely. [INFORMAL] ❑ *Don't waste your time being eaten up with envy.*

eat|er /itər/ (**eaters**) N-COUNT You use **eater** to refer to someone who eats in a particular way or who eats particular kinds of food. ❑ *I've never been a fussy eater.*

eat|ery /itəri/ (**eateries**) N-COUNT An **eatery** is a place where you can buy and eat food. [JOURNALISM] ❑ *...one of the most elegant old eateries in town.*

eat|ing ap|ple (**eating apples**) N-COUNT An **eating apple** is an ordinary apple that is usually eaten raw rather than cooked.

eat|ing dis|or|der (**eating disorders**) N-COUNT An **eating disorder** is a medical condition such as bulimia or anorexia in which a person does not eat in a normal or healthy way. ❑ *Anyone can develop an eating disorder, but young women are most vulnerable.*

eau de co|logne /oʊ də kəloʊn/ also **eau de Cologne** N-UNCOUNT **Eau de cologne** is a fairly weak, sweet-smelling perfume.

eaves /ivz/ N-PLURAL The **eaves** of a house are the lower edges of its roof. ❑ *There were icicles hanging from the eaves.*

eaves|drop /ivzdrɒp/ (**eavesdrops, eavesdropping, eavesdropped**) V-I If you **eavesdrop** on someone, you listen secretly to what they are saying. ❑ *The government illegally eavesdropped on his telephone conversations.*

e-banking N-UNCOUNT **E-banking** is the use of the internet to operate your bank account. ❑ *How do I sign onto e-banking?*

ebb /ɛb/ (**ebbs, ebbing, ebbed**) **1** V-I When the tide or the sea **ebbs**, its level gradually falls. ❑ *When the tide ebbs, you can paddle out for a mile and barely get your ankles wet.* **2** N-COUNT The **ebb** or the **ebb** tide is one of the regular periods, two per day, when the sea gradually falls to a lower level as the tide moves away from the land. ❑ *...the spring ebb tide.* **3** V-I If someone's life, support, or feeling **ebbs**, it becomes weaker and gradually disappears. [FORMAL] ❑ *Were there occasions when enthusiasm ebbed?* • PHRASAL VERB **Ebb away** means the same as **ebb**. ❑ *I his little girl's life ebbed away.* **4** PHRASE If someone or something is **at a low ebb** or **at** their **lowest ebb**, they are not very successful or profitable. ❑ *...a time when everyone is tired and at a low ebb.*

e-bike (e-bikes) N-COUNT An **e-bike** is a bicycle that can be powered by electricity as well as by pedaling. **E-bike** is an abbreviation for 'electronic bike.' ◻ *With my e-bike, I could explore the beautiful hills without working up a sweat.* ② → See also color supplement

Ebola /ɪboʊlə/ also **Ebola virus** N-UNCOUNT [oft N n] **Ebola** or the **Ebola virus** is a virus that causes a fever and internal bleeding, usually resulting in death. ◻ *Ebola is not as easily spread as viruses such as smallpox.*

eb|ony /ɛbəni/ ① N-UNCOUNT [oft N n] **Ebony** is a very hard, heavy, dark-colored wood. ◻ *...a small ebony cabinet.* ② ADJ Something that is **ebony** is a very deep black color. [LITERARY] ◻ *He had rich, soft ebony hair.*

e-book (e-books) N-COUNT An **e-book** is a book which is produced for reading on a computer screen. **E-book** is an abbreviation for **electronic book**. ◻ *In addition to the classics, the new e-books will include a host of Rough Guide titles.*

ebul|lient /ɪbʌliənt, -bʊl-/ ADJ If you describe someone as **ebullient**, you mean that they are lively and full of enthusiasm or excitement about something. [FORMAL] ◻ *...the ebullient president.* • **ebul|lience** /ɪbʌliəns, -bʊl-/ N-UNCOUNT ◻ *His natural ebullience began to return.*

e-business (e-businesses) ① N-COUNT An **e-business** is a business that uses the internet to sell goods or services, especially one that does not also have stores or offices that people can visit or phone. [BUSINESS] ◻ *...JSL Trading, an e-business in Vancouver.* ② N-UNCOUNT **E-business** is the buying, selling, and ordering of goods and services using the internet. [BUSINESS] ◻ *...proven e-business solutions.*

e-card (e-cards) N-COUNT An **e-card** is a digital card that you send over the internet on a special occasion. ◻ *She sent me an e-card for my birthday.*

ec|cen|tric /ɪksɛntrɪk/ (eccentrics) ADJ If you say that someone is **eccentric**, you mean that they behave in a strange way, and have habits or opinions that are different from those of most people. ◻ *He is an eccentric character who likes wearing a beret and dark glasses.* • N-COUNT An **eccentric** is an eccentric person. ◻ *Askew used several names, and had a reputation as an eccentric.*

ec|cen|tri|city /ɛksɛntrɪsɪti/ (eccentricities) ① N-UNCOUNT **Eccentricity** is unusual behavior that other people consider strange. ◻ *She is unusual to the point of eccentricity.* ② N-COUNT **Eccentricities** are ways of behaving that people think are strange, or habits or opinions that are different from those of most people. ◻ *We all have our eccentricities.*

ec|cle|si|as|tic /ɪkliziæstɪk/ (ecclesiastics) N-COUNT An **ecclesiastic** is a priest or member of the clergy in the Christian Church. [FORMAL]

ec|cle|si|as|ti|cal /ɪkliziæstɪkᵊl/ ADJ **Ecclesiastical** means belonging to or connected with the Christian Church. ◻ *My ambition was to travel upward in the ecclesiastical hierarchy.*

ECG /i si dʒi/ (ECGs) N-VAR **ECG** is an abbreviation for **electrocardiogram**. [mainly BRIT]

in AM, use **EKG**

eche|lon /ɛʃəlɒn/ (echelons) N-COUNT An **echelon** in an organization or society is a level or rank in it. [FORMAL] ◻ *...the lower echelons of society.*

echo ✦✧✧ /ɛkoʊ/ (echoes, echoing, echoed) ① N-COUNT An **echo** is a sound caused by a noise being reflected off a surface such as a wall. ◻ *He listened and heard nothing but the echoes of his own voice in the cave.* ② V-I If a sound **echoes**, it is reflected off a surface and can be heard again after the original sound has stopped. ◻ *His feet echoed on the hardwood floor.* ③ V-I In a place that **echoes**, a sound is reflected off a surface, and is repeated after the original sound has stopped. ◻ *The room echoed.* ◻ *The corridor echoed with the barking of a dozen dogs.* ④ V-T If you **echo** someone's words, you repeat them or express agreement with their attitude or opinion. ◻ *Their views often echo each other.* ⑤ N-COUNT A detail or feature that reminds you of something else can be referred to as an **echo**. ◻ *The accident has echoes of past disasters.* ⑥ V-T If one thing **echoes** another, the first is a copy of a particular detail or feature of the other. ◻ *Pinks and beiges were chosen to echo the colors of the ceiling.* ⑦ V-I If something **echoes**, it continues to be discussed and remains important or influential in a particular situation or among a particular group of people. ◻ *The old fable continues to echo down the centuries.*

echo|lo|ca|tion /ɛkoʊloʊkeɪʃᵊn/ also **echo-location** N-UNCOUNT **Echolocation** is a system used by some animals to determine the position of an object by measuring how long it takes for an echo to return from the object. [TECHNICAL] ◻ *Most bats navigate by echolocation.*

e-cigarette (e-cigarettes) N-COUNT An **e-cigarette** is a hand-held object that some people use to simulate the effect of smoking. **E-cigarette** is an abbreviation for 'electronic cigarette.'

éclair /eɪklɛər/ (éclairs) also **eclair** N-COUNT An **éclair** is a long thin cake made of light pastry that is filled with cream and usually has chocolate on top.

ec|lec|tic /ɪklɛktɪk/ ADJ An **eclectic** collection of objects, ideas, or beliefs is wide-ranging and comes from many different sources. [FORMAL] ◻ *...an eclectic collection of paintings, drawings, and prints.*

ec|lec|ti|cism /ɪklɛktɪsɪzəm/ N-UNCOUNT [usu with supp] **Eclecticism** is the principle or practice of choosing or involving objects, ideas, and beliefs from many different sources. [FORMAL] ◻ *...her cultural eclecticism.*

eclipse /ɪklɪps/ (eclipses, eclipsing, eclipsed) ① N-COUNT An **eclipse** of the sun is an occasion when the moon is between the Earth and the sun, so that for a short time you cannot see part or all of the sun. An **eclipse** of the moon is an occasion when the Earth is between the sun and the moon, so that for a short time you cannot see part or all of the moon. ◻ *...an eclipse of the sun.* ◻ *...the solar eclipse on May 21.* ② V-T If one thing **is eclipsed** by a second thing that is bigger, newer, or more important than it, the first thing is no longer noticed because the second thing gets all the attention. ◻ *...the space program has been eclipsed by other pressing needs.*

PREFIX
---

eco-
forms nouns and adjectives that refer to something related to the environment. *For example,* **eco-friendly** *products do not harm the environment.*

eco-friendly ADJ **Eco-friendly** products or services are less harmful to the environment than other similar products or services. ◻ *...eco-friendly laundry detergent.*

eco|logi|cal /ɛkəlɒdʒɪkᵊl, ik-/ [ADJ n] **Ecological** means involved with or concerning ecology. ◻ *Large dams have harmed Siberia's delicate ecological balance.* • **eco|logi|cal|ly** /ɛkəlɒdʒɪkli, ik-/ ADV ◻ *It is economical to run and ecologically sound.*

ecolo|gist /ɪkɒlədʒɪst/ (ecologists) N-COUNT An **ecologist** is a person who studies ecology. ◻ *Ecologists argue that the benefits of treating sewage with disinfectants are doubtful.*

ecol|ogy /ɪkɒlədʒi/ (ecologies) ① N-UNCOUNT **Ecology** is the study of the relationships between plants, animals, people, and their environment, and the balances between these relationships. ◻ *...a professor in ecology.* ② N-VAR When you talk about the **ecology** of a place, you are referring to the pattern and balance of relationships between plants, animals, people, and the environment in that place. ◻ *...the ecology of the rocky Negev desert in Israel.*

e-commerce N-UNCOUNT **E-commerce** is the same as **e-business**. [BUSINESS] ◻ *...the anticipated explosion of e-commerce.*

eco|nom|ic ✦✦✦ /ɛkənɒmɪk, ik-/ ① ADJ **Economic** means concerned with the organization of the money, industry, and trade of a country, region, or society. ◻ *...Poland's radical economic reforms.* • **eco|nomi|cal|ly** /ɛkənɒmɪkli, ik-/ ADV ◻ *...an economically depressed area.* ② ADJ If something is **economic**, it produces a profit. ◻ *Critics say that the new system may be more economic but will lead to a decline in program quality.* ③ → See feature box at **banking**

SYNONYMS
---

economic
ADJ ①
financial: *The company is in financial difficulty.*
fiscal: *...in 1987, when the government tightened fiscal policy.*
monetary: *Some countries tighten monetary policy to avoid inflation.*
budgetary: *There are budgetary pressures on all governments to reduce their armed forces.*

eco|nomi|cal /ˌiːkəˈnɒmɪkəl, ɪk-/ **1** ADJ Something that is **economical** does not require a lot of money to operate. For example, a car that only uses a small amount of gasoline is economical. ❏ ...plans to trade in their car for something smaller and more economical. ● **eco|nomi|cal|ly** ADV [ADV after v] ❏ Services could be operated more efficiently and economically. **2** ADJ Someone who is **economical** spends money sensibly and does not want to waste it on things that are unnecessary. A way of life that is economical does not require a lot of money. ❏ ...ideas for economical housekeeping. **3** ADJ **Economical** means using the minimum amount of time, effort, or language that is necessary. ❏ His gestures were economical, his words generally mild.

eco|nom|ics ♦◇◇ /ˌiːkəˈnɒmɪks, ɪk-/ N-UNCOUNT **Economics** is the study of the way in which money, industry, and commerce are organized in a society. ❏ His younger sister is studying economics.

> **SYNONYMS**
>
> **economics**
> NOUN
> **finance:** ...a major player in the world of high finance.
> **commerce:** They have made their fortunes from industry and commerce.

eco|no|mies of scale N-PLURAL **Economies of scale** are the financial advantages that a company gains when it produces large quantities of products. [BUSINESS] ❏ Some companies are simply trying to get bigger to achieve economies of scale.

eco|no|mist ♦◇◇ /ɪˈkɒnəmɪst/ (**economists**) N-COUNT An **economist** is a person who studies, teaches, or writes about economics.

eco|no|mize /ɪˈkɒnəmaɪz/ (**economizes, economizing, economized**)

> in BRIT, also use **economise**

V-I If you **economize**, you save money by spending it very carefully. ❏ We're going to have to economize from now on.

eco|no|my ♦♦♦ /ɪˈkɒnəmi/ (**economies**) **1** N-COUNT An **economy** is the system according to which the money, industry, and commerce of a country or region are organized. ❏ ...Africa's most industrialized economy. **2** N-COUNT A country's **economy** is the wealth that it gets from business and industry. ❏ The Japanese economy grew at an annual rate of more than 10 percent. **3** N-UNCOUNT **Economy** is the use of the minimum amount of money, time, or other resources needed to achieve something, so that nothing is wasted. ❏ ...improvements in the fuel economy of cars. **4** ADJ [ADJ n] **Economy** services such as travel are cheap and have no luxuries or extras. ❏ ...the limitations that come with economy travel. **5** → see **economy class 6** ADJ [ADJ n] **Economy** is used to describe large packs of products that are cheaper than normal sized packs. ❏ ...an economy pack containing 150 assorted screws. **7** PHRASE If you describe an attempt to save money as **a false economy**, you mean that you have not saved any money as you will have to spend a lot more later. ❏ A cheap bed can be a false economy, so spend as much as you can afford.

> **COLLOCATIONS**
>
> **economy**
> NOUN **1**
> noun + **economy**: market, world
> adjective + **economy**: fragile, weak, dynamic, healthy, strong; advanced, capitalist, emerging; domestic, global, local, regional
> verb + **economy**: boost, revive, stimulate, strengthen

eco|no|my class ADJ [ADJ n] On an airplane, an **economy class** ticket or seat is the cheapest available. ❏ The price includes two economy class airfares from Brisbane to Los Angeles.

economy-class syn|drome N-UNCOUNT **Economy-class syndrome** is a serious medical condition caused by blood clots in the legs moving up to the lungs; used especially in connection with long-haul flights. ❏ Lemon juice can help to prevent economy-class syndrome by improving blood circulation.

eco|sys|tem /ˈiːkoʊsɪstəm, ɪk-/ (**ecosystems**) **1** N-COUNT An **ecosystem** is all the plants and animals that live in a particular area together with the complex relationship that exists between them and their environment. [TECHNICAL] ❏ ...the forest ecosystem. **2** → See feature box at **endanger, water**

VOCABULARY IN CONTEXT

Ecosystems

Have you ever wondered how an **ecosystem** is named? Well, many ecosystems are named after the **vegetation** that can be found there – and the vegetation depends on the **climate**. There are six primary **terrestrial** ecosystems: **tundra**, taiga, **temperate deciduous forest**, **tropical rainforest**, **grassland**, and **desert**. Many of their names refer to the plants – deciduous forest, rainforest, and grassland, for example – while references to climate are also common, as in tropical and temperate. The vegetation varies so greatly from one ecosystem to another that this is often the easiest way to distinguish between them. Compare the **arid** emptiness of a desert ecosystem, where few plants grow, to the **lush** grasslands of the African **Savannah**, or the **dense green woodlands** of Canada. Each is a miniature world in itself, providing a **habitat** for all the **living organisms** that call it home.

eco|tar|ian /ˌiːkoʊˈtɛəriən, ɪk-/ N-COUNT An **ecotarian** is a person who eats only food that has been produced in a way that does not harm the environment. ❏ Strictly speaking, you don't have to be a vegetarian or a vegan to be an ecotarian. ● ADJ **Ecotarian** is also an adjective. ❏ We try to follow an ecotarian diet.

eco|tec|ture /ˈiːkoʊtɛktʃə, ɪk-/ N-UNCOUNT **Ecotecture** is a type of architecture with designs based on ecological principles such as sustainability and environmental impact.

eco|tour|ism /ˈiːkoʊtʊərɪzəm, ɪk-/

> in BRIT, use **eco-tourism**

N-UNCOUNT **Ecotourism** is the business of providing vacations and related services that are not harmful to the environment of the area. [BUSINESS] ● **eco|tour|ist** /ˈiːkoʊtʊərɪst, ɪk-/ (**ecotourists**) N-COUNT ❏ ...an environmentally sensitive project to cater to ecotourists.

ecru /ˈɛkruː, ˈeɪk-/ COLOR Something that is **ecru** is pale, creamy white in color.

ec|sta|sy /ˈɛkstəsi/ (**ecstasies**) **1** N-VAR **Ecstasy** is a feeling of very great happiness. ❏ ...a state of almost religious ecstasy. **2** N-UNCOUNT **Ecstasy** is an illegal drug that makes people feel happy and energetic. ❏ The teenager died after taking ecstasy on her birthday.

ec|stat|ic /ɛkˈstætɪk/ **1** ADJ If you are **ecstatic**, you feel very happy and full of excitement. ❏ His wife gave birth to their first child, and he was ecstatic about it. ● **ec|stati|cal|ly** /ɛkˈstætɪkli/ ADV ❏ We are both ecstatically happy. **2** ADJ [ADJ n] You can use **ecstatic** to describe reactions that are very enthusiastic and excited. For example, if someone receives an **ecstatic** reception or an **ecstatic** welcome, they are greeted with great enthusiasm and excitement. ❏ They gave an ecstatic reception to the speech.

ec|top|ic /ɛkˈtɒpɪk/ ADJ [usu ADJ n] An **ectopic** pregnancy occurs when an embryo develops outside a woman's uterus, for example in one of her fallopian tubes.

ecu|meni|cal /ɛkyumɛnɪkᵊl, ik-/ ADJ [usu ADJ n] **Ecumenical** activities, ideas, and movements try to unite different Christian churches. [FORMAL] ❑ ...ecumenical church services.

ecu|men|ism /ɛkyumənɪzəm, ɪkyu-/ N-UNCOUNT **Ecumenism** is the belief that the different Christian churches should be as united as possible, and can also be used to refer to actions based on this belief. [FORMAL]

ec|ze|ma /ɛksəmə, ɛgzə-, ɪgzi-/ N-UNCOUNT **Eczema** is a skin condition that makes your skin itch and become sore, rough, and broken.

ed. (**eds**) ed. is a written abbreviation for **editor**.

SUFFIX

-ed
is added to verbs to make the past tense and past participle. Past participle forms are often used as adjectives that indicate that something has been affected in some way. For example, **cooked** food is food that has been cooked.

---

eddy /ɛdi/ (**eddies**) N-COUNT An **eddy** is a movement in water or in the air that goes around and around instead of flowing in one continuous direction.

edge ✦✧ /ɛdʒ/ (**edges, edging, edged**) **1** N-COUNT The **edge** of something is the place or line where it stops, or the part of it that is farthest from the middle. ❑ We were on a hill, right on the edge of town. ❑ She was standing at the water's edge. **2** N-COUNT The **edge** of something sharp such as a knife or an ax is its sharp or narrow side. ❑ ...the sharp edge of the sword. **3** V-I If someone or something **edges** somewhere, they move very slowly in that direction. ❑ He edged closer to the telephone, ready to grab it. **4** N-SING The **edge** of something, especially something bad, is the point at which it may start to happen. ❑ They have driven the rhino to the edge of extinction. **5** N-SING If someone or something has an **edge**, they have an advantage that makes them stronger or more likely to be successful than another thing or person. ❑ The three days Uruguay have to prepare could give them the edge over Brazil. **6** N-SING If you say that someone or something has **an edge**, you mean that they have a powerful quality. ❑ Featuring new bands gives the show an edge. **7** N-SING If someone's voice has an **edge** to it, it has a sharp, bitter, or emotional quality. ❑ But underneath the humor is an edge of bitterness. **8** → see also **cutting edge, leading edge** **9** PHRASE If you or your nerves are **on edge**, you are tense, nervous, and unable to relax. ❑ My nerves were constantly on edge. **10** PHRASE If something **takes the edge off** an unpleasant situation, it weakens its effect or intensity. ❑ Poor health took the edge off her performance.

▶ **edge out** PHRASAL VERB If someone **edges out** someone else, they just manage to beat them or get in front of them in a game, race, or contest. ❑ In the second race, the American competitor edged out the Ethiopian runner by less than a second.

COLLOCATIONS

edge
NOUN **1**
adjective + **edge**: inner, inside, outer, outside; jagged, ragged, rough

---

edged /ɛdʒd/ ADJ [v-link ADJ with/in n] If something is **edged** with a particular thing, that thing forms a border around it. ❑ ...a large lawn edged with flowers and shrubs. • COMB IN ADJ **Edged** is also a combining form. ❑ ...clutching a lace-edged handkerchief.

-edged /-ɛdʒd/ **1** COMB IN ADJ **-edged** combines with words such as 'sharp,' 'raw,' and 'dark' to form adjectives that describe art or writing that is very powerful or critical. [JOURNALISM] ❑ ...a sharp-edged satire that puts the Hollywood system under the microscope. ❑ ...the raw-edged vitality and daring of these works. **2** → see also **edge, edged, hard-edged**

edge|wise /ɛdʒwaɪz/ **1** PHRASE If you say that you **cannot get a word in edgewise**, you are complaining that you do not have the opportunity to speak because someone else is talking so much. [INFORMAL, DISAPPROVAL] ❑ Ernest dominated the conversation - Zhou could hardly get a word in edgewise. **2** → See feature box at **debate**

edg|ing /ɛdʒɪŋ/ (**edgings**) N-VAR **Edging** is something that is put along the borders or sides of something else, usually to make it look attractive. ❑ ...the satin edging on the baby's blanket.

edgy /ɛdʒi/ (**edgier, edgiest**) ADJ If someone is **edgy**, they are nervous and anxious, and seem likely to lose control of themselves. [INFORMAL] ❑ She was nervous and edgy, still chain-smoking.

ed|ible /ɛdɪbᵊl/ ADJ If something is **edible**, it is safe to eat and not poisonous. ❑ ...edible fungi.

edict /idɪkt/ (**edicts**) N-COUNT An **edict** is a command or instruction given by someone in authority. [FORMAL] ❑ He issued an edict that none of his writings be destroyed.

edi|fi|ca|tion /ɛdɪfɪkeɪʃᵊn/ N-UNCOUNT [oft with poss] If something is done for your **edification**, it is done to benefit you in some way, for example by teaching you about something. [FORMAL] ❑ Demonstrations, films, and videotapes are shown for your edification.

edi|fice /ɛdɪfɪs/ (**edifices**) N-COUNT An **edifice** is a large and impressive building. [FORMAL] ❑ The taxi driver reeled off a list of historic edifices they must not fail to visit.

edi|fy|ing /ɛdɪfaɪɪŋ/ **1** ADJ If you describe something as **edifying**, you mean that it benefits you in some way, for example by teaching you about something. [FORMAL] ❑ In the 18th century art was seen, along with music and poetry, as something edifying. **2** ADJ [with brd-neg] You say that something is not very **edifying** when you want to express your disapproval or dislike of it, or to suggest that there is something unpleasant or unacceptable about it. [DISAPPROVAL] ❑ It all brought back memories of a not very edifying past.

edit ✦✧ /ɛdɪt/ (**edits, editing, edited**) **1** V-T If you **edit** a text such as an article or a book, you correct and adapt it so that it is suitable for publishing. ❑ The majority of contracts give the publisher the right to edit a book after it's done. **2** V-T If you **edit** a book or a series of books, you collect several pieces of writing by different authors and prepare them for publishing. ❑ This collection of essays is edited by Ellen Knight. ❑ He edits the literary journal, Murmur. **3** V-T If you **edit** a movie or a television or radio program, you choose some of what has been filmed or recorded and arrange it in a particular order. ❑ He taught me to edit and splice film. **4** V-T Someone who **edits** a newspaper, magazine, or journal is in charge of it. ❑ I used to edit the college paper in the old days.

SYNONYMS

edit
VERB **1**
revise: Three editors handled the work of revising the articles for publication.
rewrite: The script was rewritten constantly during filming.
redraft: The speech had already been redrafted 22 times.

---

edi|tion ✦✧ /ɪdɪʃᵊn/ (**editions**) **1** N-COUNT An **edition** is a particular version of a book, magazine, or newspaper that is printed at one time. **2** N-COUNT An **edition** is the total number of copies of a particular book or newspaper that are printed at one time. ❑ The second edition was published only in Canada. **3** N-COUNT An **edition** is a single television or radio program that is one of a series about a particular subject. ❑ ...an interview featured on last week's edition of "60 Minutes." **4** → See feature box at **press**

edi|tor ✦✧ /ɛdɪtər/ (**editors**) **1** N-COUNT An **editor** is the person who is in charge of a newspaper or magazine and who decides what will be published in each edition of it. ❑ Her father was the former editor of the Saturday Review. **2** N-COUNT An **editor** is a journalist who is responsible for a particular section of a newspaper or magazine. ❑ Mike later became the sports editor for The Beacon. **3** N-COUNT An **editor** is a person who checks and corrects texts before they are published. ❑ Your role as editor is important, for you can look at a piece of writing objectively. **4** N-COUNT An **editor** is a radio or television journalist who reports on a particular type of news. ❑ ...our economics editor, Tom Goldberg. **5** N-COUNT An **editor** is a person who prepares a movie, or a radio or television program, by selecting some of what has been filmed or recorded and putting it in a particular order. ❑ A few years earlier, she had worked at 20th Century Fox as a film editor. **6** N-COUNT An **editor** is a person who collects pieces of writing by different authors and prepares them for publication in a book or a series of books. ❑ Michael Rosen is the editor of the anthology. **7** N-COUNT An **editor** is a computer program that enables you

editorial

to change and correct stored data. [COMPUTING] ☐ *To edit it, you need to run the built-in Windows Registry editor.*

COLLOCATIONS

editor NOUN

1
noun + **editor**: magazine, newspaper, tabloid; assistant, deputy, executive
adjective + **editor**: contributing, founding, managing

2
noun + **editor**: fashion, features, news, picture; economics, politics, science, sports

---

edi|to|rial /ɛdɪtɔ:riəl/ (editorials) **1** ADJ [ADJ n] **Editorial** means involved in preparing a newspaper, magazine, or book for publication. ☐ *I went to the editorial board meetings when I had the time.* **2** ADJ [ADJ n] **Editorial** means involving the attitudes, opinions, and contents of something such as a newspaper, magazine, or television program. ☐ *We are not about to change our editorial policy.* **3** N-COUNT An **editorial** is an article in a newspaper that gives the opinion of the editor or owner on a topic or item of news. ☐ *In an editorial, The New York Times suggests the victory could turn nasty.*

edi|to|ri|al|ize /ɛdɪtɔ:riəlaɪz/ (editorializes, editorializing, editorialized)

in BRIT, also use **editorialise**

V-I If someone **editorializes**, they express their opinion about something rather than just stating facts; mainly used in contexts where you are talking about journalists and newspapers. ☐ *Other papers have editorialized, criticizing the government for rushing to judgment on this individual.*

edi|tor|ship /ɛdɪtərʃɪp/ (editorships) N-VAR [oft poss N, N of n] The **editorship** of a newspaper or magazine is the position of its editor, or his or her work as its editor. ☐ *Under his editorship, the newspaper has introduced regular sports coverage.*

edu|cate /ɛdʒʊkeɪt/ (educates, educating, educated) **1** V-T [usu passive] When someone, especially a child, **is educated**, he or she is taught at a school or college. ☐ *He was educated at Yale and Stanford.* **2** V-T To **educate** people means to teach them better ways of doing something or a better way of living. ☐ *...World AIDS Day, an event designed to educate people about AIDS.*

edu|cat|ed /ɛdʒʊkeɪtɪd/ ADJ Someone who is **educated** has a high standard of learning. ☐ *The new CEO is an educated, amiable, and decent man.*

-educated /-ɛdʒʊkeɪtɪd/ **1** COMB IN ADJ **-educated** combines with nouns and adjectives to form adjectives indicating where someone was educated. ☐ *He is a Harvard-educated lawyer from Miami.* **2** COMB IN ADJ **-educated** combines with adverbs to form adjectives indicating how much education someone has had and how good it was. ☐ *Many of the immigrants are well-educated.* ☐ *...impoverished, undernourished, and ill-educated workers.*

edu|cat|ed guess (educated guesses) N-COUNT An **educated guess** is a guess that is based on a certain amount of knowledge and is therefore likely to be correct. ☐ *Estimating the right cooking time will always be an educated guess.*

edu|ca|tion /ɛdʒʊkeɪʃən/ (educations) **1** N-VAR **Education** involves teaching people various subjects, usually at a school or college, or being taught. ☐ *They're cutting funds for education.* **2** N-UNCOUNT **Education** of a particular kind involves teaching the public about a particular issue ☐ *...better health education.* **3** → see also further education, higher education **4** → See feature box at **university**

COLLOCATIONS

education NOUN

1
noun + **education**: school, state, university; adult
adjective + **education**: comprehensive, further, higher, secondary; compulsory, formal, general, private; vocational
verb + **education**: promote, provide; complete, receive

2
noun + **education**: health, sex, science
adjective + **education**: physical, religious

409

effect

SYNONYMS

education NOUN **1**
teaching: *The government funds university teaching.*
schooling: *He had little formal schooling.*
instruction: *Most area colleges offer some instruction in Chinese.*

---

edu|ca|tion|al /ɛdʒʊkeɪʃənəl/ **1** ADJ **Educational** matters or institutions are concerned with or relate to education. ☐ *...the Japanese educational system.* **2** ADJ An **educational** experience teaches you something. ☐ *The staff should make sure the kids have an enjoyable and educational day.*

SYNONYMS

educational ADJ
1
academic: *Their academic standards are high.*
pedagogical: *...the pedagogical methods used in the classroom.*
2
instructive: *...an entertaining and instructive documentary.*
illuminating: *His autobiography provides an illuminating insight into his mind.*
enlightening: *...an enlightening talk on the work done at the animal park.*
didactic: *In totalitarian societies, art exists for didactic purposes.*
instructional: *...instructional material designed to help you with your lifestyle.*

---

edu|ca|tion|al|ist /ɛdʒʊkeɪʃənəlɪst/ (educationalists) N-COUNT An **educationalist** is someone who is specialized in the theories and methods of education. [BRIT]

in AM, use **educator**

edu|ca|tion|al psy|chol|ogy N-UNCOUNT **Educational psychology** is the area of psychology concerned with the study and assessment of teaching methods, and with helping individual students who have educational problems. • **edu|ca|tion|al psy|cholo|gist** (educational psychologists) N-COUNT ☐ *An assessment by an independent educational psychologist was essential.*

edu|ca|tive /ɛdʒʊkeɪtɪv/ ADJ Something that has an **educative** role teaches you something. [FORMAL] ☐ *...the educative value of allowing broadcasters into their courts.*

edu|ca|tor /ɛdʒʊkeɪtər/ (educators) **1** N-COUNT An **educator** is a person who educates people. [AM] ☐ *What more could an educator hope for than a student's desire to learn.* ☐ *...a passionate and dedicated nursing educator.* **2** N-COUNT An **educator** is someone who is specialized in the theories and methods of education. [mainly AM]

in BRIT, use **educationalist**

edu|tain|ment /ɛdʒuteɪnmənt/ N-UNCOUNT People use **edutainment** to refer to things such as computer games that are designed to be entertaining and educational at the same time. ☐ *...the increased demand for edutainment software.*

Ed|ward|ian /ɛdwɔːrdiən/ ADJ [usu ADJ n] **Edwardian** means belonging to, connected with, or typical of Britain in the first decade of the 20th century, when Edward VII was king. ☐ *...the Edwardian era.*

eel /iːl/ (eels) N-VAR An **eel** is a long, thin fish that looks like a snake. • N-UNCOUNT **Eel** is the flesh of this fish eaten as food. ☐ *...smoked eel.*

eerie /ɪəri/ (eerier, eeriest) ADJ If you describe something as **eerie**, you mean that it seems strange and frightening, and makes you feel nervous. ☐ *I walked down the eerie dark path.* • **eeri|ly** /ɪərɪli/ ADV ☐ *Monrovia after the fighting is eerily quiet.*

ef|face /ɪfeɪs/ (effaces, effacing, effaced) **1** V-T To **efface** something means to destroy or remove it so that it cannot be seen anymore. [FORMAL] ☐ *...an event that has helped efface the country's traditional image.* **2** → see also **self-effacing**

ef|fect /ɪfɛkt/ (effects, effecting, effected) **1** N-VAR The **effect** of one thing on another is the change that the first thing causes in the second thing. ☐ *Parents worry about the effect of music on their adolescent's behavior.* **2** N-COUNT An **effect** is an impression that someone creates deliberately, for example in a place or in a piece of writing. ☐ *The whole effect is cool, light, and airy.* **3** N-PLURAL A person's **effects** are the things that they have with them at a particular time, for example when they are arrested or admitted to a hospital, or the things that they owned when they died. [FORMAL] ☐ *His daughters were collecting his effects.* **4** N-PLURAL The **effects** in a movie are the specially created sounds and scenery. ☐ *It's got a gripping story, great acting, superb sets, and stunning effects.* **5** V-T If you **effect** something that you are trying to achieve, you succeed in causing it to happen. [FORMAL] ☐ *Prospects for effecting real political change seemed to have taken a major step backward.* **6** → see also greenhouse effect, side-effect, special effect **7** PHRASE If you say that someone is doing something **for effect**, you mean that they are doing it in order to impress people and to draw attention to themselves. ☐ *The southern accent was put on for effect.* **8** PHRASE You add **in effect** to a statement or opinion that is not precisely accurate, but that you feel is a reasonable description or summary of a particular situation. [VAGUENESS] ☐ *That deal would create, in effect, the world's biggest airline.* **9** PHRASE If you **put**, **bring**, or **carry** a plan or idea **into effect**, you cause it to happen in practice. ☐ *These and other such measures ought to have been put into effect in 1985.* **10** PHRASE If a law or policy **takes effect** or **comes into effect** at a particular time, it officially begins to apply or be valid from that time. If it **remains in effect**, it still applies or is still valid. ☐ *...the ban on new logging permits which will take effect in July.* **11** PHRASE You can say that something **takes effect** when it starts to produce the results that are intended. ☐ *The second injection should only have been given once the first drug had taken effect.* **12** PHRASE You use **effect** in expressions such as **to good effect** and **to no effect** in order to indicate how successful or impressive an action is. ☐ *Mr. Morris feels the museum is using advertising to good effect.* **13** PHRASE You use **to this effect**, **to that effect**, or **to the effect that** to indicate that you have given or are giving a summary of something that was said or written, and not the actual words used. ☐ *I understand that a circular to this effect will be issued in the next few weeks.* **14** → See feature box at endanger

---

SYNONYMS

effect
NOUN **1**
result: *A real pizza oven gives better results than an ordinary home oven.*
consequence: *An economic crisis may have tremendous consequences for our global security.*
outcome: *It's too early to know the outcome of her illness.*
end result: *The end result of this will be unity.*
aftermath: *In the aftermath of the coup, the troops opened fire on the demonstrators.*
influence: *Many other medications have an influence on cholesterol levels.*
impact: *The major impact of this epidemic worldwide is yet to come.*

---

ef|fec|tive ◆◆◇ /ɪfɛktɪv/ **1** ADJ Something that is **effective** works well and produces the results that were intended. ☐ *The project looks at how we could be more effective in encouraging students to enter teacher training.* ☐ *Simple antibiotics are effective against this organism.* ● **ef|fec|tive|ly** ADV ☐ *Services need to be organized more effectively than they are at present.* ● **ef|fec|tive|ness** N-UNCOUNT ☐ *...the effectiveness of computers as an educational tool.* **2** ADJ [ADJ n] **Effective** means having a particular role or result in practice, though not officially or in theory. ☐ *They have had effective control of the area since the security forces left.* **3** ADJ [v-link ADJ] When something such as a law or an agreement becomes **effective**, it begins officially to apply or be valid. ☐ *The new rules will become effective in the next few days.*

SYNONYMS

effective
ADJ **1**
efficient: *This was done in an efficient and competent manner.*
successful: *How successful will this new treatment be?*
useful: *The police gained a great deal of useful information about the organization.*
productive: *Training makes workers highly productive.*
helpful: *A predominantly liquid diet for a day or two may be helpful.*

---

ef|fec|tive|ly /ɪfɛktɪvli/ ADV You use **effectively** with a statement or opinion to indicate that it is not accurate in every detail, but that you feel it is a reasonable description or summary of a particular situation. ☐ *The region was effectively independent.*

ef|fec|tual /ɪfɛktʃuəl/ ADJ If an action or plan is **effectual**, it succeeds in producing the results that were intended. [FORMAL] ☐ *This is the only effectual way to secure our present and future happiness.*

ef|femi|nate /ɪfɛmɪnɪt/ ADJ If you describe a man or boy as **effeminate**, you think he behaves, looks, or sounds like a woman or girl. [DISAPPROVAL] ☐ *...a skinny, effeminate guy in lipstick and earrings.*

ef|fer|ves|cent /ɛfərvɛsᵊnt/ **1** ADJ An **effervescent** liquid is one that contains or releases bubbles of gas. ☐ *...an effervescent mineral water.* **2** ADJ If you describe someone as **effervescent**, you mean that they are lively, entertaining, enthusiastic, and exciting. [APPROVAL] ☐ *...her winning smile and effervescent personality.* ● **ef|fer|ves|cence** N-UNCOUNT ☐ *He wrote about Gillespie's effervescence, magnetism, and commitment.*

ef|fete /ɪfit/ ADJ If you describe someone as **effete**, you are criticizing them for being weak and powerless. [FORMAL, DISAPPROVAL] ☐ *...the charming but effete Russian gentry of the 1840s.*

ef|fi|ca|cious /ɛfɪkeɪʃəs/ ADJ Something that is **efficacious** is effective. [FORMAL] ☐ *The nasal spray was new on the market and highly efficacious.*

ef|fi|ca|cy /ɛfɪkəsi/ N-UNCOUNT If you talk about the **efficacy** of something, you are talking about its effectiveness and its ability to do what it is supposed to. [FORMAL] ☐ *Recent medical studies confirm the efficacy of a healthier lifestyle.*

ef|fi|cien|cy /ɪfɪʃᵊnsi/ N-UNCOUNT **Efficiency** is the quality of being able to do a task successfully, without wasting time or energy. ☐ *There are many ways to increase agricultural efficiency in the poorer areas of the world.*

ef|fi|cient ◆◇◇ /ɪfɪʃᵊnt/ ADJ If something or someone is **efficient**, they are able to do tasks successfully, without wasting time or energy. ☐ *With today's more efficient contraception women can plan their families and careers.* ● **ef|fi|cient|ly** ADV ☐ *I work very efficiently and am decisive, and accurate in my judgement.*

ef|fi|gy /ɛfɪdʒi/ (**effigies**) **1** N-COUNT An **effigy** is a quickly and roughly made figure, often ugly or amusing, that represents someone you hate or feel contempt for. **2** N-COUNT An **effigy** is a statue or carving of a famous person. [FORMAL]

eff|ing /ɛfɪŋ/ ADJ [ADJ n] Some people use **effing** to emphasize a word or phrase, especially when they are feeling angry or annoyed. [INFORMAL, VULGAR, EMPHASIS] ☐ *She told him it was none of his effing business.*

ef|flu|ent /ɛfluənt/ (**effluents**) N-MASS **Effluent** is liquid waste material that comes out of factories or sewage works. [FORMAL] ☐ *The effluent from the factory was dumped into the river.*

ef|fort ◆◆◆ /ɛfərt/ (**efforts**) **1** N-VAR If you make an **effort** to do something, you try very hard to do it. ☐ *He made no effort to hide his disappointment.* ☐ *Finding a cure requires considerable time and effort.* **2** N-UNCOUNT [usu with N, also a N] If you say that someone did something with **effort** or with **an effort**, you mean it was difficult for them to do. [WRITTEN] ☐ *She took a deep breath and sat up slowly and with great effort.* **3** N-COUNT An **effort** is a particular series of activities that is organized by a group of people in order to achieve something. ☐ *...a famine relief effort in Angola.* **4** N-SING If you say that something is **an effort**, you mean that an unusual amount of physical or mental energy is needed to do it. ☐ *Carrying the equipment while hiking in the forest was an effort.* **5** PHRASE If you **make the effort** to do something, you do it, even though you need extra energy to do it or you do not really want to. ☐ *I don't get lonely now because I make the effort to see people.*

COLLOCATIONS

effort
NOUN
1
adjective + **effort**: determined, last-ditch, worthwhile; solo, team
verb + **effort**: make, renew, require; praise, recognize; block, hamper
3
noun + **effort**: conservation, recovery, relief, rescue; peace, war

ef|fort|less /ˈɛfərtlɪs/ **1** ADJ Something that is **effortless** is done easily and well. ❏ *...effortless and elegant Italian cooking.* • **ef|fort|less|ly** ADV ❏ *Her son Peter adapted effortlessly to his new surroundings.* **2** ADJ You use **effortless** to describe a quality that someone has naturally and does not have to learn. ❏ *She liked him above all for his effortless charm.*

ef|fron|tery /ɪfrˈʌntəri/ N-UNCOUNT **Effrontery** is behavior that is bold, rude, or disrespectful. [FORMAL, DISAPPROVAL] ❏ *The man had the effrontery to be sarcastic.*

ef|fu|sion /ɪfyˈuʒᵊn/ (**effusions**) N-VAR If someone expresses their emotions or ideas with **effusion**, they express them with more enthusiasm and for longer than is usual or expected. ❏ *He advised him not to get too excited by her effusions of empathy and respect.*

ef|fu|sive /ɪfyˈusɪv/ ADJ If you describe someone as **effusive**, you mean that they express pleasure, gratitude, or approval in a very enthusiastic way. ❏ *He was effusive in his praise for the general.* • **ef|fu|sive|ly** ADV ❏ *She greeted them effusively.*

EFL /ˌi ɛf ɛl/ N-UNCOUNT [oft N n] **EFL** is the teaching of English to people whose first language is not English. **EFL** is an abbreviation for 'English as a Foreign Language.' ❏ *...an EFL teacher.*

e.g. /ˌi dʒi/ **e.g.** is an abbreviation that means 'for example.' It is used before a noun, or to introduce another sentence. ❏ *We need helpers of all types, e.g., geologists and teachers.*

egali|tar|ian /ɪɡælɪtɛəriən/ ADJ **Egalitarian** means supporting or following the idea that all people are equal and should have the same rights and opportunities. ❏ *I still believe in the notion of an egalitarian society.*

egali|tari|an|ism /ɪɡælɪtɛəriənɪzəm/ N-UNCOUNT **Egalitarianism** is used to refer to the belief that all people are equal and should have the same rights and opportunities, and to actions that are based on this belief.

egg ✦✧ /ˈɛɡ/ (**eggs, egging, egged**) **1** N-COUNT An **egg** is an oval object that is produced by a female bird and contains a baby bird. Other animals such as reptiles and fish also lay eggs. ❏ *...a baby bird hatching from its egg.* **2** N-VAR In many countries, **eggs** often means hen's eggs, eaten as food. ❏ *Break the eggs into a shallow bowl and beat them lightly.* **3** N-COUNT **Egg** is used to refer to an object in the shape of a hen's egg. ❏ *...a chocolate egg.* **4** N-COUNT An **egg** is a cell that is produced in the bodies of female animals and humans. If it is fertilized by a sperm, a baby develops from it. ❏ *It only takes one sperm to fertilize an egg.* **5** PHRASE If someone puts **all** their **eggs in one basket**, they put all their effort or resources into doing one thing so that, if it fails, they have no alternatives left. ❏ *The key word here is diversify; don't put all your eggs in one basket.* **6** PHRASE If someone has **egg on** their **face** or has **egg all over** their **face**, they have been made to look foolish. ❏ *If they take this game lightly they could end up with egg on their faces.*
▶ **egg on** PHRASAL VERB If you **egg** a person **on**, you encourage them to do something, especially something dangerous or foolish. ❏ *He was lifting up handfuls of leaves and throwing them at her. She was laughing and egging him on.*

egg cup (**egg cups**) also **eggcup** N-COUNT An **egg cup** is a small container in which you put a boiled egg while you eat it.

egg|head /ˈɛɡhɛd/ (**eggheads**) N-COUNT If you think someone is more interested in ideas and theories than in practical actions you can say they are an **egghead**. [INFORMAL, DISAPPROVAL] ❏ *The committee was dominated by self-important eggheads.*

egg|nog /ˈɛɡnɒɡ/ also **egg nog** N-UNCOUNT **Eggnog** is a drink made from eggs, milk, sugar, spices, and often alcohol such as rum or brandy.

egg|plant /ˈɛɡplænt/ (**eggplants**) N-VAR An **eggplant** is a vegetable with a smooth, dark purple skin. [AM]

in BRIT, use **aubergine**

egg|shell /ˈɛɡʃɛl/ (**eggshells**) also **egg shell** N-VAR An **eggshell** is the hard covering on the outside of an egg.

egg tim|er (**egg timers**) also **egg-timer** N-COUNT An **egg timer** is a device that measures the time needed to boil an egg.

egg whisk (**egg whisks**) N-COUNT An **egg whisk** is a piece of kitchen equipment used for mixing the different parts of an egg together.

ego /ˈiɡoʊ, ˈɛɡoʊ/ (**egos**) N-VAR Someone's **ego** is their sense of their own worth. For example, if someone has a large **ego**, they think they are very important and valuable. ❏ *He had a massive ego, never would he admit he was wrong.*

ego|cen|tric /ˌiɡoʊsɛntrɪk, ˌɛɡ-/ ADJ Someone who is **egocentric** thinks only of themselves and their own wants, and does not consider other people. [DISAPPROVAL] ❏ *He was egocentric, a man of impulse who expected those around him to serve him.*

ego|ism /ˈiɡoʊɪzəm, ˈɛɡ-/ N-UNCOUNT **Egoism** is the same as **egotism**. [DISAPPROVAL]

ego|ist /ˈiɡoʊɪst, ˈɛɡ-/ (**egoists**) N-COUNT An **egoist** is the same as an **egotist**. [DISAPPROVAL]

ego|is|tic /ˌiɡoʊɪstɪk, ˌɛɡ-/ ADJ **Egoistic** means the same as **egotistic**. [DISAPPROVAL]

ego|ma|ni|ac /ˌiɡoʊmeɪniæk, ˌɛɡ-/ (**egomaniacs**) N-COUNT An **egomaniac** is someone who thinks only of themselves and does not care if they harm other people in order to get what they want. [DISAPPROVAL] ❏ *Arnie is clever enough, but he's also an egomaniac.*

ego|tism /ˈiɡətɪzəm, ˈɛɡ-/ N-UNCOUNT **Egotism** is the quality of being egotistic. [DISAPPROVAL]

ego|tist /ˈiɡətɪst, ˈɛɡ-/ (**egotists**) N-COUNT An **egotist** is someone who is egotistic. [DISAPPROVAL]

ego|tis|tic /ˌiɡətɪstɪk, ˌɛɡ-/

The form **egotistical** is also used.

ADJ Someone who is **egotistic** or **egotistical** behaves selfishly and thinks they are more important than other people. [DISAPPROVAL] ❏ *Susan and Deborah share an intensely selfish, egotistic streak.*

ego trip (**ego trips**) N-COUNT If you say that someone is on an **ego trip**, you are criticizing them for doing something for their own satisfaction and enjoyment, often to show that they think they are more important than other people. [INFORMAL, DISAPPROVAL] ❏ *I was on an ego trip and only cared about earning a fortune.*

egre|gious /ɪɡriˈdʒəs/ ADJ [usu ADJ n] **Egregious** means very bad and offensive. [FORMAL] ❏ *...the most egregious abuses of human rights.*

Egyp|tian /ɪdʒɪpʃᵊn/ (**Egyptians**) **1** ADJ **Egyptian** means belonging or relating to Egypt or to its people, language, or culture. **2** N-COUNT The **Egyptians** are the people who come from Egypt. **3** ADJ **Egyptian** means related to or connected with ancient Egypt. ❏ *...the Egyptian pharaoh.* **4** N-COUNT The **Egyptians** were the people who lived in ancient Egypt.

eh /eɪ/ CONVENTION **Eh** is used in writing to represent a noise that people make as a response in conversation, for example to express agreement or to ask for something to be explained or repeated. ❏ *Let's talk all about it outside, eh?*

Eid /ˈid/ N-UNCOUNT **Eid** is an Islamic religious festival that takes place at the end of Ramadan. ❏ *...the recurrent festivals like Eid, Christmas, or Diwali.*

eider|down /ˈaɪdərdaʊn/ (**eiderdowns**) N-COUNT An **eiderdown** is a bed covering, placed on top of sheets and blankets, that is filled with small soft feathers or warm material. [mainly BRIT]

in AM, usually use **comforter**

eight ✦✦✦ /ˈeɪt/ (**eights**) NUM **Eight** is the number 8. ❏ *So far eight workers have been killed.*

eight|een ✦✦✦ /eɪtˈin/ NUM **Eighteen** is the number 18. ❏ *He was employed by them for eighteen years.*

eight|eenth ✦✦ /eɪtˈinθ/ ORD The **eighteenth** item in a series is the one that you count as number eighteen. ❏ *The siege is now in its eighteenth day.*

eighth ✦✦✧ /ˈeɪtθ/ (**eighths**) **1** ORD The **eighth** item in a series is the one that you count as number eight. ❏ *...the eighth prime minister of India.* **2** FRACTION An **eighth** is one of eight equal parts of something. ❏ *The Kuban produces an eighth of Russia's grain, meat, and milk.*

eighth note (**eighth notes**) N-COUNT An **eighth note** is a musical note that has a time value equal to half a quarter note. [AM]

in BRIT, use **quaver**

eighti|eth /eɪtiəθ/ ORD The **eightieth** item in a series is the one that you count as number eighty. ▫ *Mr. Stevens recently celebrated his eightieth birthday.*

eighty /eɪti/ (**eighties**) **1** NUM **Eighty** is the number 80. ▫ *Eighty horses trotted up.* **2** N-PLURAL When you talk about the **eighties**, you are referring to numbers between 80 and 89. For example, if you are **in your eighties**, you are aged between 80 and 89. If the temperature is **in the eighties**, the temperature is between 80 and 89 degrees. ▫ *He was in his late eighties and had become the country's most respected elder statesman.* **3** N-PLURAL **The eighties** is the decade between 1980 and 1989. ▫ *He ran a property development business in the eighties.*

either /iːðər, aɪðər/ **1** CONJ You use **either** in front of the first of two or more alternatives, when you are stating the only possibilities or choices that there are. The other alternatives are introduced by 'or.' ▫ *Sightseeing is best done either by tour bus or by bicycles.* ▫ *The former president was demanding that he should be either put on trial or set free.* **2** CONJ You use **either** in a negative statement in front of the first of two alternatives to indicate that the negative statement refers to both the alternatives. ▫ *There had been no indication of either breathlessness or any loss of mental faculties right until his death.* **3** PRON You can use **either** to refer to one of two things, people, or situations, when you want to say that they are both possible and it does not matter which one is chosen or considered. ▫ *There were glasses of iced champagne and cigars. Unfortunately not many of either were consumed.* • QUANT [QUANT of def-pl-n] **Either** is also a quantifier. ▫ *Do either of you smoke or drink heavily?* • DET **Either** is also a determiner. ▫ *...a special Indian drug police that would have the authority to pursue suspects into either country.* **4** PRON [with brd-neg] You use **either** in a negative statement to refer to each of two things, people, or situations to indicate that the negative statement includes both of them. ▫ *She warned me that I'd never marry or have children.—"I don't want either."* • QUANT **Either** is also a quantifier. ▫ *There are no simple answers to either of those questions.* • DET **Either** is also a determiner. ▫ *He sometimes couldn't remember either man's name.* **5** ADV [ADV after v, with brd-neg] You use **either** by itself in negative statements to indicate that there is a similarity or connection with a person or thing that you have just mentioned. ▫ *He did not even say anything to her, and she did not speak to him either.* **6** ADV [ADV after v] When one negative statement follows another, you can use **either** at the end of the second one to indicate that you are adding an extra piece of information, and to emphasize that both are equally important. ▫ *Don't agree, but don't argue either.* **7** DET You can use **either** to introduce a noun that refers to each of two things when you are talking about both of them. ▫ *The basketball nets hung down from the ceiling at either end of the gymnasium.*

> **USAGE**
> **either**
> Don't use **either** without **of** in front of a plural noun or pronoun. Don't say, for example 'He was better dressed than either us.' Say 'He was better dressed than **either of us**.' *I don't know either of them very well.*

ejacu|late /ɪdʒækyəleɪt/ (**ejaculates, ejaculating, ejaculated**) V-I When a man **ejaculates**, sperm comes out through his penis. ▫ *...a tendency to ejaculate quickly.* • **ejacu|la|tion** /ɪdʒækyəleɪʃən/ (**ejaculations**) N-VAR ▫ *Each male ejaculation will contain up to 300 million sperm.*

eject /ɪdʒɛkt/ (**ejects, ejecting, ejected**) **1** V-T If you **eject** someone from a place, you force them to leave. ▫ *Officials used guard dogs to eject the protesters.* • **ejec|tion** /ɪdʒɛkʃən/ (**ejections**) N-VAR ▫ *...the ejection and manhandling of hecklers at the meeting.* **2** V-T To **eject** something means to remove it or push it out forcefully. ▫ *He aimed his rifle, fired a single shot, then ejected the spent cartridge.* **3** V-I When a pilot **ejects** from an aircraft, he or she leaves the aircraft quickly using an ejector seat, usually because the plane is about to crash. ▫ *The pilot ejected from the plane and escaped injury.*

ejec|tor seat (**ejector seats**) N-COUNT An **ejector seat** is a special seat that can throw the pilot out of a fast military aircraft in an emergency.

eke /iːk/ (**ekes, eking, eked**) PHRASE If you **eke a living** or **eke out an existence**, you manage to survive with very little money. ▫ *That forced peasant farmers to try to eke a living off steep hillsides.* ▫ *He was eking out an existence on a few dollars a day.*
▸ **eke out** PHRASAL VERB If you **eke out** something, for example, a victory, you obtain it with difficulty. [AM] ▫ *They are a team that always seemed to eke out victory when the going got tough.*

EKG /iː keɪ dʒiː/ (**EKGs**) N-VAR **EKG** is an abbreviation for **electrocardiogram**. [AM] ▫ *An EKG was done before the exercise and immediately after.*

elabo|rate (**elaborates, elaborating, elaborated**)

> The adjective is pronounced /ɪlæbərɪt/. The verb is pronounced /ɪlæbəreɪt/.

1 ADJ You use **elaborate** to describe something that is very complex because it has a lot of different parts. ▫ *...an elaborate research project.* **2** ADJ **Elaborate** plans, systems, and procedures are complicated because they have been planned in very great detail, sometimes too much detail. ▫ *...elaborate efforts at the highest level to conceal the problem.* • **elabo|rate|ly** ADV ▫ *It was clearly an elaborately planned operation.* **3** ADJ **Elaborate** clothing or material is made with a lot of detailed artistic designs. ▫ *He is known for his elaborate costumes.* **4** V-T If you **elaborate** a plan or theory, you develop it by making it more complicated and more effective. ▫ *His task was to elaborate policies that would make a market economy compatible with a clean environment.* • **elabo|ra|tion** /ɪlæbəreɪʃən/ N-UNCOUNT ▫ *...the elaboration of specific policies and mechanisms.* **5** V-I If you **elaborate** on something that has been said, you say more about it, or give more details. ▫ *A spokesman declined to elaborate on a statement released late yesterday.*

élan /eɪlɑːn/ also **elan** N-UNCOUNT If you say that someone does something with **élan**, you mean that they do it in an energetic and confident way. [LITERARY]

elapse /ɪlæps/ (**elapses, elapsing, elapsed**) V-I When time **elapses**, it passes. [FORMAL] ▫ *Forty-eight hours have elapsed since his arrest.*

elas|tic /ɪlæstɪk/ **1** N-UNCOUNT **Elastic** is a rubber material that stretches when you pull it and returns to its original size and shape when you let it go. Elastic is often used in clothes to make them fit tightly, for example, around the waist. ▫ *Make a mask with long ears and attach a piece of elastic to go around the back of the head.* **2** ADJ Something that is **elastic** is able to stretch easily and then return to its original size and shape. ▫ *Beat it until the dough is slightly elastic.*

elas|ti|cat|ed /ɪlæstɪkeɪtɪd/ [BRIT] → see **elasticized**

elas|tic band (**elastic bands**) N-COUNT An **elastic band** is a thin circle of very stretchy rubber that you can put around things in order to hold them together. [mainly BRIT]

> in AM, use **rubber band**

elas|tic|ity /ɪlæstɪsɪti, iːlæst-/ N-UNCOUNT The **elasticity** of a material or substance is its ability to return to its original shape, size, and condition after it has been stretched. ▫ *Daily facial exercises help to retain the skin's elasticity.*

elas|ti|cized /ɪlæstɪsaɪzd/ ADJ If a piece of clothing or part of a piece of clothing is **elasticized**, elastic has been sewn or woven into it to make it fit better and to help it keep its shape. [AM] ▫ *The matching pants have an elasticized waist with drawstrings.*

> in BRIT, use **elasticated**

Elas|to|plast /ɪlæstəplæst/ (**Elastoplasts**) N-VAR **Elastoplast** is the same as **Band-Aid**. [BRIT, TRADEMARK]

elat|ed /ɪleɪtɪd/ ADJ If you are **elated**, you are extremely happy and excited because of something that has happened. ▫ *I was elated that my recent second bypass had been successful.*

ela|tion /ɪleɪʃən/ N-UNCOUNT **Elation** is a feeling of great happiness and excitement about something that has happened. ▫ *His supporters have reacted to the news with elation.*

el|bow /ɛlboʊ/ (**elbows, elbowing, elbowed**) **1** N-COUNT Your **elbow** is the part of your arm where the upper and lower halves are joined. ▫ *He slipped and fell, badly bruising an elbow.* **2** V-T If you **elbow** people aside or **elbow** your way somewhere, you push people with your elbows in order to move somewhere. ❑ *They also claim that the security team elbowed aside a steward.* **3** V-T If someone or something **elbows** their way somewhere, or **elbows** other people or things out of the way, they achieve success by being aggressive and determined. ❑ *Non-state firms gradually elbow aside the inefficient state-owned ones.* **4 to rub elbows with** → see **rub**

el|bow bump (**elbow bumps**) N-COUNT If people greet each other with an **elbow bump**, they briefly touch their elbows together.

el|bow grease N-UNCOUNT People use **elbow grease** to refer to the strength and energy that you use when doing physical work like rubbing or polishing. [INFORMAL] ❑ *It took a considerable amount of polish and elbow grease before the brass shone.*

el|bow room 1 N-UNCOUNT **Elbow room** is the freedom to do what you want to do or need to do in a particular situation. [INFORMAL] ❑ *His speech was designed to give himself more political elbow room.* **2** N-UNCOUNT If there is enough **elbow room** in a place or vehicle, it is not too small or too crowded. [INFORMAL] ❑ *There was not much elbow room in the cockpit of a Snipe.*

el|der /ɛldər/ (**elders**) **1** ADJ [ADJ n, the ADJ, the ADJ of n] The **elder** of two people is the one who was born first. ❑ *...his elder brother.* **2** N-COUNT A person's **elder** is someone who is older than them, especially someone quite a lot older. [FORMAL] ❑ *They have no respect for their elders.* **3** N-COUNT In some societies, an **elder** is one of the respected older people who have influence and authority. ❑ *...a meeting of political figures and tribal elders.*

elder|berry /ɛldərbɛri/ (**elderberries**) **1** N-COUNT [usu pl] **Elderberries** are the edible black berries that grow on an elder bush or tree. **2** N-VAR An **elderberry** is an elder bush or tree.

el|der|ly ✦✧✧ /ɛldərli/ ADJ You use **elderly** as a polite way of saying that someone is old. [POLITENESS] ❑ *There was an elderly couple on the terrace.* • N-PLURAL **The elderly** are people who are old. This use could cause offense. ❑ *The elderly are a formidable force in any election.*

SYNONYMS

elderly
ADJ
old: *He was considered too old for the job.*
aged: *She has an aged parent who's capable of being very difficult.*
ageing: *John lives with his ageing mother.*
geriatric: *The geriatric patients will be moved out.*

el|der states|man (**elder statesmen**) **1** N-COUNT An **elder statesman** is an old and respected politician or former politician who still has influence because of his or her experience. **2** N-COUNT [usu with supp] An experienced and respected member of an organization or profession is sometimes referred to as an **elder statesman**.

el|der states|woman (**elder statesmen**) **1** N-COUNT An **elder statesman** is an old and respected politician or former politician who still has influence because of her experience. **2** N-COUNT [usu with supp] An experienced and respected member of an organization or profession is sometimes referred to as an **elder statesman**.

eld|est /ɛldɪst/ ADJ The **eldest** person in a group is the one who was born before all the others. ❑ *The eldest child was a daughter called Fatiha.* ❑ *David was the eldest of three boys.*

e-learning 1 N-UNCOUNT **E-learning** is learning that takes place by means of computers and the internet. **2** → See feature box at **learning**

SYNONYMS

elect
VERB **1**
vote for: *They would vote for the candidate who was nearest what they wanted.*
choose: *They will be able to choose their own leaders in democratic elections.*
pick: *She had picked ten people to interview for six sales jobs in London.*
select: *Voters are selecting candidates for both U.S. Senate seats and congressional seats.*

elect ✦✦✧ /ɪlɛkt/ (**elects, electing, elected**) **1** V-T When people **elect** someone, they choose that person to represent them, by voting for them. ❑ *The people of the Philippines have voted to elect a new president.* ❑ *The University of Washington elected him dean in 1956.* **2** V-T If you **elect** to do something, you choose to do it. [FORMAL] ❑ *The girls will probably elect to stay with their mother.* **3** ADJ [n ADJ] **Elect** is added after words such as 'president' or 'governor' to indicate that a person has been elected to the post but has not officially started to carry out the duties involved. [FORMAL] ❑ *...the date when the president-elect takes office.*

elec|tion ✦✦✦ /ɪlɛkʃən/ (**elections**) **1** N-VAR An **election** is a process in which people vote to choose a person or group of people to hold an official position. ❑ *...Poland's first fully free elections for more than fifty years.* ❑ *During his election campaign he promised to put the economy back on its feet.* **2** N-UNCOUNT [usu with poss] The **election** of a particular person or group of people is their success in winning an election. ❑ *...the election of the Democrat candidate last year.* ❑ *It was his fifth election.*

COLLOCATIONS

election
NOUN **1**
adjective + **election**: federal, mayoral, municipal, parliamentary, presidential; local, national, primary; forthcoming, upcoming; free and fair
verb + **election**: call, hold; contest, fight; lose, win

SYNONYMS

election
NOUN **1**
vote: *Why do you think we should have a vote on that?*
the polls: *The polls have closed in the Pakistan parliamentary elections.*
ballot: *The result of the ballot will not be known for two weeks.*
referendum: *The party said it too planned to hold a referendum on independence.*

elec|tion|eer|ing /ɪlɛkʃənɪərɪŋ/ N-UNCOUNT **Electioneering** is the activities that politicians and their supporters carry out in order to persuade people to vote for them or their political party in an election, for example making speeches and visiting voters.

elec|tive /ɪlɛktɪv/ (**electives**) **1** ADJ [usu ADJ n] An **elective** post or committee is one to which people are appointed as a result of winning an election. [FORMAL] ❑ *Buchanan has never held elective office.* **2** ADJ [usu ADJ n] **Elective** surgery is surgery that you choose to have before it becomes essential. [FORMAL] **3** N-COUNT An **elective** is a subject that a student can choose to study as part of his or her course. [AM]

in BRIT, use **option**

elec|tor /ɪlɛktər/ (**electors**) N-COUNT An **elector** is a person who has the right to vote in an election. ❑ *There are now 117 cardinals who can be cardinal electors, that is, eligible to enter the secret conclave that will choose the next pope*

elec|tor|al ✦✧✧ /ɪlɛktərəl/ ADJ [ADJ n] **Electoral** is used to describe things that are connected with elections. ❑ *The Mongolian Democratic Party is campaigning for electoral reform.* • **elec|tor|al|ly** ADV ❑ *He believed that the policies were both wrong and electorally disastrous.*

elec|tor|al col|lege N-SING [the N] The **electoral college** is the system that is used in the United States in presidential elections. The electors in the electoral college act as representatives for each state, and they elect the president and vice president. [AM]

elec|tor|ate /ɪlɛktərɪt/ (**electorates**) N-COUNT-COLL The **electorate** of a country or area is all the people in it who have the right to vote in an election. ❑ *He has the backing of almost a quarter of the electorate.*

elec|tric ✦✧✧ /ɪlɛktrɪk/ **1** ADJ An **electric** device or machine works by means of electricity, rather than using some other source of power. ❑ *...her electric guitar.* **2** ADJ [ADJ n] An **electric** current, voltage, or charge is one that is produced by electricity. **3** ADJ [ADJ n] **Electric** plugs, sockets, or power lines are designed to carry electricity. ❑ *More people are deciding that electric power lines could present a health risk.* **4** ADJ [ADJ n] **Electric** is used to refer to the supply of electricity. [INFORMAL] ❑ *An average electric bill might go up $2 or $3 per month.* **5** ADJ If you describe the atmosphere of a place or event as **electric**, you mean that people are in a state of great excitement. ❑ *The mood in the hall was electric.*

elec|tri|cal /ɪlɛktrɪkᵊl/ **1** ADJ **Electrical** goods, equipment, or appliances work by means of electricity. ❏ ...*shipments of electrical equipment.* ● **elec|tri|cal|ly** /ɪlɛktrɪkli/ ADV [ADV -ed] ❏ ...*electrically powered vehicles.* **2** ADJ **Electrical** systems or parts supply or use electricity. ❏ ...*lighting and other electrical systems on the new runway.* **3** ADJ **Electrical** energy is energy in the form of electricity. ❏ ...*brief pulses of electrical energy.* ● **elec|tri|cal|ly** ADV ❏ ...*electrically charged particles.* **4** ADJ [ADJ n] **Electrical** industries, engineers, or workers are involved in the production and supply of electricity or electrical products. ❏ ...*company representatives from the electrical industry.* **5** → See feature box at **brain**, **electricity**

elec|tri|cal en|gi|neer (electrical engineers) N-COUNT An **electrical engineer** is a person who uses scientific knowledge to design, construct, and maintain electrical devices.

elec|tri|cal en|gi|neer|ing N-UNCOUNT **Electrical engineering** is the designing, constructing, and maintenance of electrical devices.

elec|tric blan|ket (electric blankets) N-COUNT An **electric blanket** is a blanket with electrical wires inside it that keep the blanket warm.

elec|tric blue also **electric-blue** COLOR Something that is **electric blue** is very bright blue in color.

elec|tric chair (electric chairs) N-COUNT The **electric chair** is a rarely-used method for killing criminals, in which a person is strapped to a special chair and killed by a powerful electric current. ❏ *Murderer Walter Kemmler was the first man to die in the electric chair.*

elec|tri|cian /ɪlɛktrɪʃᵊn, ilɛk-/ (electricians) N-COUNT An **electrician** is a person whose job is to install and repair electrical equipment.

elec|tric|ity ♦◇◇ /ɪlɛktrɪsɪti, ilɛk-/ N-UNCOUNT **Electricity** is a form of energy that can be carried by wires and is used for heating and lighting, and to provide power for machines. ❏ *We moved into a cabin with electricity but no running water.*

VOCABULARY IN CONTEXT

Electricity

Electricity is a form of **energy** that gets its name from **electrons**. An **atom** is made up of a nucleus and one or more **negatively-charged** electrons that **orbit the nucleus**. Simply put, electricity is created when electrons jump from the orbit of one neutron to that of another. This **flow** of negatively charged particles is called **electrical current**. Of course, electricity exists in the natural world, too; think of **lightning** and **static electricity**. But it took humans a long time, and a lot of dangerous experiments to learn how to **harness** this energy form for our own use. Since the work of Benjamin Franklin (who discovered that electricity could be harnessed), Nikola Tesla (who invented the alternating current electricity supply system we still use today), and Thomas Edison (who invented, amongst other things, the electric light bulb), electricity has become the **driving force** behind our modern lifestyles. We **rely on** it for heat, food, light, and comfort. Just think about how lost we are without it during a **blackout**!

WORD HISTORY

electricity
Electricity comes from the Greek word *ēlektron*, meaning 'amber.' The ancient Greeks had found out that if you rub a piece of amber, it will attract small particles by the force that we now understand to be electricity.

elec|tric shock (electric shocks) N-COUNT If you get an **electric shock**, you get a sudden painful feeling when you touch something connected to a supply of electricity.

elec|tri|fi|ca|tion /ɪlɛktrɪfɪkeɪʃᵊn/ N-UNCOUNT The **electrification** of a house, town, or area is the connecting of that place to a supply of electricity. ❏ ...*rural electrification.*

elec|tri|fied /ɪlɛktrɪfaɪd/ ADJ [ADJ n] An **electrified** fence or other barrier has been connected to a supply of electricity, so that a person or animal that touches it will get an electric shock. ❏ *The house was surrounded by an electrified fence.*

elec|tri|fy /ɪlɛktrɪfaɪ/ (electrifies, electrifying, electrified) **1** V-T [usu passive] If people **are electrified** by an event or experience, it makes them feel very excited and surprised. ❏ *The world was electrified by his courage and resistance.* ● **elec|tri|fy|ing** ADJ ❏ *He gave an electrifying performance.* **2** V-T [usu passive] When a rail system or rail line **is electrified**, electric cables are put over the tracks, or electric rails are put beside them, so that the trains can be powered by electricity. ❏ *The railroad line was electrified as long ago as 1974.*

PREFIX

electro-
is used to form words that refer to electricity or processes involving electricity. *For example, if someone is **electrocuted**, they are killed or injured by electricity.*

elec|tro|car|dio|gram /ɪlɛktroʊkɑrdiəgræm/ (electrocardiograms) N-COUNT If someone has an **electrocardiogram**, doctors use special equipment to measure the electric currents produced by that person's heart in order to see whether it is working normally.

e|lec|tro|chem|i|cal /ɪlɛktroʊkɛmɪkᵊl/ ADJ [ADJ n] An **electrochemical** process or reaction is one in which electricity is produced by a chemical reaction. ❏ *The technology uses an electrochemical process to produce electricity.*

elec|tro|cute /ɪlɛktrəkyut/ (electrocutes, electrocuting, electrocuted) **1** V-T If someone **is electrocuted**, they are accidentally killed or badly injured when they touch something connected to a source of electricity. ❏ *Three people were electrocuted by falling power lines.* **2** V-T [usu passive] If a criminal **is electrocuted**, he or she is executed using electricity. ❏ *He was electrocuted for a murder committed when he was 17.* ● **elec|tro|cu|tion** /ɪlɛktrəkyuʃᵊn/ (electrocutions) N-VAR ❏ *The court pronounced him guilty and sentenced him to death by electrocution.*

elec|trode /ɪlɛktroʊd/ (electrodes) N-COUNT An **electrode** is a small piece of metal or other substance that is used to take an electric current to or from a source of power, a piece of equipment, or a living body. ❏ *Two electrodes that measure changes in the body's surface moisture are attached to the palms of your hands.*

elec|troly|sis /ɪlɛktrɒlɪsɪs, i-/ N-UNCOUNT **Electrolysis** is the process of passing an electric current through a substance in order to produce chemical changes in the substance. [TECHNICAL]

elec|tro|lyte /ɪlɛktrəlaɪt/ (electrolytes) N-COUNT An **electrolyte** is a substance, usually a liquid, that electricity can pass through. [TECHNICAL]

elec|tro|mag|net /ɪlɛktroʊmægnɪt/ (electromagnets) N-COUNT An **electromagnet** is a magnet that consists of a piece of iron or steel surrounded by a coil. The metal becomes magnetic when an electric current is passed through the coil.

elec|tro|mag|net|ic /ɪlɛktroʊmægnɛtɪk/ ADJ [usu ADJ n] **Electromagnetic** is used to describe the electrical and magnetic forces or effects produced by an electric current. ❏ ...*electromagnetic fields.*

elec|tron /ɪlɛktrɒn/ (electrons) **1** N-COUNT An **electron** is a tiny particle of matter that is smaller than an atom and has a negative electrical charge. [TECHNICAL] ☐ *Most things are balanced – with equal numbers of electrons and protons.* **2** → See feature box at **electricity**

elec|tron|ic ✦✧✧ /ɪlɛktrɒnɪk, i-/ **1** ADJ [ADJ n] An **electronic** device has transistors or silicon chips that control and change the electric current passing through the device. ☐ *...expensive electronic equipment.* **2** ADJ An **electronic** process or activity involves the use of electronic devices. ☐ *...electronic music.* • **elec|troni|cal|ly** ADV [ADV with v] ☐ *Data is transmitted electronically.*

elec|tron|ic book (electronic books) N-COUNT An **electronic book** is the same as an **e-book**. [COMPUTING]

elec|tron|ic mail N-SING **Electronic mail** is the same as **email**.

elec|tron|ic pub|lish|ing N-UNCOUNT **Electronic publishing** is the publishing of documents in a form that can be read on a computer, for example, as a CD-ROM.

elec|tron|ics /ɪlɛktrɒnɪks, i-/ N-UNCOUNT **Electronics** is the technology of using transistors and silicon chips, especially in devices such as radios, televisions, and computers. ☐ *...Ohio's three main electronics companies.*

elec|tron micro|scope (electron microscopes) N-COUNT An **electron microscope** is a type of very powerful microscope that uses electrons instead of light to produce a magnified image of something. ☐ *...specimens that can only be observed under a powerful electron microscope.*

el|egant ✦✧✧ /ɛlɪgənt/ **1** ADJ If you describe a person or thing as **elegant**, you mean that they are pleasing and graceful in appearance or style. ☐ *Patricia looked beautiful and elegant as always.* • **el|egance** N-UNCOUNT ☐ *The furniture managed to combine practicality with elegance.* • **el|egant|ly** ADV ☐ *...a tall, elegantly dressed man with a mustache.* **2** ADJ If you describe a piece of writing, an idea, or a plan as **elegant**, you mean that it is simple, clear, and clever. ☐ *The document impressed me with its elegant simplicity.* • **el|egant|ly** ADV ☐ *...an elegantly simple idea.* **3** → See feature box at **fashion**

SYNONYMS

elegant
ADJ **1**
stylish: *...a very attractive and very stylish woman of 27.*
sophisticated: *Claude was a charming, sophisticated companion.*
refined: *...refined and well-dressed ladies.*
chic: *Her gown was very French and very chic.*
graceful: *...graceful ballerinas.*

---

el|egi|ac /ɛlɪdʒaɪək/ ADJ Something that is **elegiac** expresses or shows sadness. [LITERARY] ☐ *The music has a dreamy, elegiac quality.*

el|egy /ɛlɪdʒi/ (elegies) N-COUNT An **elegy** is a sad poem, often about someone who has died. ☐ *...a touching elegy for a lost friend.*

el|ement ✦✦✧ /ɛlɪmənt/ (elements) **1** N-COUNT The different **elements** of something are the different parts it contains. ☐ *The exchange of prisoners of war was one of the key elements of the UN's peace plan.* **2** N-COUNT A particular **element** of a situation, activity, or process is an important quality or feature that it has or needs. ☐ *Physical fitness has now become an important element in our lives.* **3** N-COUNT When you talk about **elements** within a society or organization, you are referring to groups of people who have similar aims, beliefs, or habits. ☐ *The government must weed out criminal elements from within the security forces.* **4** N-COUNT If something has an **element** of a particular quality or emotion, it has a certain amount of this quality or emotion. ☐ *These reports clearly contain elements of propaganda.* **5** N-COUNT An **element** is a substance such as gold, oxygen, or carbon that consists of only one type of atom. **6** N-COUNT The **element** in an electric or water heater is the metal part that changes the electric current into heat. **7** N-PLURAL You can refer to the weather, especially wind and rain, as **the elements**. ☐ *The area where most refugees are waiting is exposed to the elements.* **8** PHRASE If you say that someone is **in their element**, you mean that they are in a situation they enjoy. ☐ *My stepmother was in her element, organizing everything.*

SYNONYMS

element
NOUN **1**
component: *The management plan has four main components.*
part: *Respect is a very important part of any relationship.*
feature: *Patriotic songs have long been a feature of Kuwaiti life.*
factor: *Physical activity is an important factor in maintaining fitness.*
aspect: *Climate and weather affect every aspect of our lives.*
ingredient: *I think that is one of the major ingredients of his success.*

---

el|emen|tal /ɛlɪmɛntəl/ ADJ **Elemental** feelings and types of behavior are simple, basic, and forceful. [LITERARY] ☐ *...the elemental life they would be living in this new colony.*

el|emen|ta|ry /ɛlɪmɛntəri, -tri/ ADJ Something that is **elementary** is very simple and basic. ☐ *Literacy now includes elementary computer skills.*

el|emen|ta|ry school (elementary schools) N-VAR An **elementary school** is a school where children are taught for the first six or sometimes seven years of their education. [mainly AM] ☐ *The move from elementary school to middle school or junior high can be difficult.*

el|ephant /ɛlɪfənt/ (elephants) N-COUNT An **elephant** is a very large animal with a long, flexible nose called a trunk, which it uses to pick up things. Elephants live in India, Africa, and other parts of Asia.

el|ephan|tine /ɛlɪfæntin, -taɪn/ ADJ If you describe something as **elephantine**, you mean that you think it is large and clumsy. [WRITTEN, DISAPPROVAL] ☐ *...elephantine clumsiness.* ☐ *His legs were elephantine.*

el|evate /ɛlɪveɪt/ (elevates, elevating, elevated) **1** V-T [usu passive] When someone or something achieves a more important rank or status, you can say that they **are elevated** to it. [FORMAL] ☐ *He was elevated to the post of president.* • **el|eva|tion** /ɛlɪveɪʃən/ N-UNCOUNT ☐ *The elevation of the assistant coach to the head coaching position within only 9 months was a surprise.* **2** V-T If you **elevate** something to a higher status, you consider it to be better or more important than it really is. ☐ *Don't elevate your superiors to superstar status.* **3** V-T To **elevate** something means to increase it in amount or intensity. [FORMAL] ☐ *Emotional stress can elevate blood pressure.* **4** V-T If you **elevate** something, you raise it higher. ☐ *A few times a day, elevate feet above heart level.* ☐ *I built a platform to elevate the bed.*

el|evat|ed /ɛlɪveɪtɪd/ **1** ADJ [usu ADJ n] A person, job, or role that is **elevated** is very important or of very high rank. ☐ *His career has blossomed and that has given him a certain elevated status.* **2** ADJ [usu ADJ n] If thoughts or ideas are **elevated**, they are on a high moral or intellectual level. ☐ *...the magazine's elevated tone.* **3** ADJ [usu ADJ n] If land or buildings are **elevated**, they are raised up higher than the surrounding area. ☐ *An elevated platform on the stage collapsed during rehearsals.*

el|eva|tion /ɛlɪveɪʃən/ (elevations) **1** N-COUNT The **elevation** of a place is its height above sea level. ☐ *We're probably at an elevation of about 13,000 feet above sea level.* **2** N-COUNT An **elevation** is a piece of ground that is higher than the area around it. ☐ *...the monument was on an elevation, which could be seen from the church.*

el|eva|tor /ɛlɪveɪtər/ (elevators) N-COUNT An **elevator** is a device that carries people or goods up and down inside tall buildings. [AM] ☐ *We took the elevator to the fourteenth floor.*

in BRIT, use **lift**

elev|en ✦✦✧ /ɪlɛvən/ (elevens) NUM **Eleven** is the number 11. ☐ *...the Princess and her eleven friends.*

elev|enth ✦✧✧ /ɪlɛvənθ/ ORD The **eleventh** item in a series is the one that you count as number eleven. ☐ *We were working on the eleventh floor.*

elev|enth hour N-SING [usu at the N, N n] If someone does something at **the eleventh hour**, they do it at the last possible moment. ☐ *He postponed his trip at the eleventh hour.* ☐ *...last night's eleventh-hour agreement.*

elf /ɛlf/ (elves) N-COUNT In fairy tales, **elves** are small magical beings who play tricks on people.

elf|in /ɛlfɪn/ ADJ [usu ADJ n] If you describe someone as **elfin**, you think that they are attractive because they are small and have delicate features. [APPROVAL] ▫ ...a little boy with an elfin face.

elic|it /ɪlɪsɪt/ (elicits, eliciting, elicited) **1** V-T If you **elicit** a response or a reaction, you do or say something that makes other people respond or react. ▫ Mr. Norris said he was hopeful that his request would elicit a positive response. **2** V-T If you **elicit** a piece of information, you get it by asking the right questions. [FORMAL] ▫ My letters to her have elicited no response.

elide /ɪlaɪd/ (elides, eliding, elided) **1** V-T If you **elide** something, especially a distinction, you leave it out or ignore it. [FORMAL] ▫ These habits of thinking elide the difference between what is common and what is normal. **2** V-T In linguistics, if you **elide** a word, you do not pronounce or write it fully. [TECHNICAL] ▫ He complained about announcers eliding their words.

eli|gible /ɛlɪdʒɪbəl/ ADJ Someone who is **eligible** to do something is qualified or able to do it, for example, because they are old enough. ▫ Almost half the population are eligible to vote in today's election. • **eli|gibil|ity** /ɛlɪdʒɪbɪlɪti/ N-UNCOUNT ▫ The rules covering eligibility for benefits changed in the 1980s. **2** ADJ An **eligible** man or woman is not yet married and is thought by many people to be a suitable partner. ▫ He's the most eligible bachelor in Japan.

elimi|nate ✦✧ /ɪlɪmɪneɪt/ (eliminates, eliminating, eliminated) **1** V-T To **eliminate** something, especially something you do not want or need, means to remove it completely. [FORMAL] ▫ Recent measures have not eliminated discrimination in employment. • **elimi|na|tion** N-UNCOUNT ▫ ...the prohibition and elimination of chemical weapons. **2** V-T PASSIVE When a person or team **is eliminated** from a competition, they are defeated and so stop participating in the competition. ▫ I was eliminated from the 400 meters in the semi-finals. **3** V-T If someone says that they **have eliminated** an enemy, they mean that they have killed them. By using the word 'eliminate,' they are trying to make the action sound more positive than if they used the word 'kill.' ▫ He declared war on the government and urged right-wingers to eliminate their opponents.

SYNONYMS

eliminate
VERB **1**
get rid of: There's corruption, and we're going to get rid of it.
remove: Most of her fears had been removed.
abolish: The whole system should be abolished.
eradicate: They are already battling to eradicate illnesses such as malaria.
banish: ...diseases that have been banished for centuries.
do away with: The long-range goal must be to do away with nuclear weapons altogether.

---

elimi|na|tion /ɪlɪmɪneɪʃən/ N-UNCOUNT **Elimination** is the process of getting rid of waste products from your body by going to the bathroom. [FORMAL] ▫ Breast-feeding is as natural as sex or elimination or any other bodily function. **2** → see **eliminate** 1

elimi|na|tion game (elimination games) N-COUNT [usu n n] In sports, an **elimination game** is a game that decides which team or player will take part in the next stage of a particular competition. [AM] ▫ ...a world title elimination game.

| in BRIT, use **eliminator** |

elimi|na|tor /ɪlɪmɪneɪtər/ [BRIT] → see **elimination game**

elite /ɪlit, eɪ-/ (elites) **1** N-COUNT You can refer to the most powerful, rich, or talented people within a particular group, place, or society as the **elite**. ▫ ...a government comprised mainly of the elite. **2** ADJ [ADJ n] **Elite** people or organizations are considered to be the best of their kind. ▫ ...the elite troops of the president's bodyguard.

elit|ism /ɪlitɪzəm, eɪ-/ N-UNCOUNT **Elitism** is the quality or practice of being elitist. ▫ It became difficult to promote conventional ideas of excellence without being instantly accused of elitism.

elit|ist /ɪlitɪst, eɪ-/ (elitists) **1** ADJ **Elitist** systems, practices, or ideas favor the most powerful, rich, or talented people within a group, place, or society. [DISAPPROVAL] ▫ He worries about a time when college athletics become even more elitist than they are now. **2** N-COUNT An **elitist** is someone who has elitist ideas or is part of an elite. [DISAPPROVAL] ▫ He was an elitist who had no time for the masses.

elix|ir /ɪlɪksər/ (elixirs) N-COUNT [oft N of n] An **elixir** is a liquid that is considered to have magical powers. [LITERARY] ▫ ...the elixir of life.

Eliza|bethan /ɪlɪzəbiθən/ ADJ [usu ADJ n] **Elizabethan** means belonging to or connected with England in the second half of the sixteenth century, when Elizabeth I was Queen. ▫ ...Elizabethan England. ▫ ...the Elizabethan theater.

elk /ɛlk/ (elk or elks) N-VAR An **elk** is a type of large deer. Elk have big horns called antlers and are found in Northern Europe, Asia, and North America.

el|lipse /ɪlɪps/ (ellipses) N-COUNT An **ellipse** is an oval shape similar to a circle but longer and flatter. ▫ The Earth orbits in an ellipse.

el|lip|sis /ɪlɪpsɪs/ N-UNCOUNT In linguistics, **ellipsis** means leaving out words rather than repeating them unnecessarily; for example, saying 'I want to go but I can't' instead of 'I want to go but I can't go.' [TECHNICAL]

el|lip|ti|cal /ɪlɪptɪkəl/ **1** ADJ Something that is **elliptical** has the shape of an ellipse. [FORMAL] ▫ ...the moon's elliptical orbit. **2** ADJ **Elliptical** references to something are indirect rather than clear. [FORMAL] ▫ ...elliptical references to problems best not aired in public. • **el|lip|ti|cal|ly** /ɪlɪptɪkli/ ADV [ADV after v] ▫ He spoke only briefly and elliptically about the mission.

elm /ɛlm/ (elms) N-VAR An **elm** is a tree that has broad leaves which it loses in winter. • N-UNCOUNT **Elm** is the wood of this tree. ▫ It was a good table too, sturdily constructed of elm.

elo|cu|tion /ɛləkyuʃən/ N-UNCOUNT **Elocution** is how clearly someone speaks or sings. ▫ When I was 11 my mother sent me to elocution lessons.

elon|gate /ɪlɔŋgeɪt/ (elongates, elongating, elongated) V-T/V-I If you **elongate** something or if it **elongates**, you stretch it so that it becomes longer. [FORMAL] ▫ "Mom," she intoned, elongating the word. ▫ In this exercise, the muscles are elongating rather than contracting.

elon|gat|ed /ɪlɔŋgeɪtɪd/ ADJ If something is **elongated**, it is very long and thin, often in an unnatural way. ▫ The light from my candle threw his elongated shadow on the walls.

elope /ɪloʊp/ (elopes, eloping, eloped) V-RECIP When two people **elope**, they go away secretly together to get married. ▫ My girlfriend Lynn and I eloped. ▫ In 1912 he eloped with Frieda von Richthofen.

elo|quent /ɛləkwənt/ **1** ADJ Speech or writing that is **eloquent** is well expressed and effective in persuading people. ▫ I heard him make a very eloquent speech at that dinner. • **elo|quence** N-UNCOUNT ▫ ...the eloquence of his prose. • **elo|quent|ly** ADV ▫ Juanita speaks eloquently about her art. **2** ADJ A person who is **eloquent** is good at speaking and able to persuade people. [APPROVAL] ▫ He was eloquent about his love of books. • **elo|quence** N-UNCOUNT ▫ She can speak with an eloquence that is almost inspirational. **3** → See feature box at **debate**

else ✦✦✦ /ɛls/ **1** ADJ You use **else** after words such as 'anywhere,' 'someone,' and 'what' to refer in a vague way to another person, place, or thing. ▫ If I can't make a living at painting, at least I can teach someone else to paint. ▫ We had nothing else to do on those long trips. • ADV [adv ADV] **Else** is also an adverb. ▫ I never wanted to live anywhere else. **2** ADJ [pron-indef ADJ] You use **else** after words such as 'everyone,' 'everything,' and 'everywhere' to refer in a vague way to all the other people, things, or places except the one you are talking about. ▫ As I try to be truthful, I expect everyone else to be truthful. • ADV [adv ADV] **Else** is also an adverb. ▫ It was cheaper than everywhere else we had looked. **3** PHRASE You use **or else** after stating a logical conclusion, to indicate that what you are about to say is evidence for that conclusion. ▫ Evidently no lessons have been learned or else the government would not have handled the problem so badly. **4** PHRASE You use **or else** to introduce a statement that indicates the unpleasant results that will occur if someone does or does not do something. ▫ This time we really need to succeed or else people will start giving us funny looks. **5** PHRASE You use **or else** to introduce the second of two possibilities when you do not know which one is true. ▫ You are either a total genius or else you must be totally crazy. **6** PHRASE **Above all else** is used to emphasize that a particular thing is more important than other things. [EMPHASIS] ▫ Above all else I hate the cold. **7** PHRASE You can say '**if nothing else**' to indicate that what you are mentioning is, in your opinion, the only good thing in a particular situation.

elsewhere ◆◇◇ /ɛlswɛər/ ADV **Elsewhere** means in other places or to another place. ❑ *Almost 80 percent of the state's residents were born elsewhere.* ❑ *They were living well, in comparison with people elsewhere in the world.*

elu|ci|date /ɪlu:sɪdeɪt/ (**elucidates**, **elucidating**, **elucidated**) V-T/V-I If you **elucidate** something, you make it clear and easy to understand. [FORMAL] ❑ *Haig went on to elucidate his personal principle of war.* ❑ *There was no need for him to elucidate.* • **elu|ci|da|tion** /ɪlu:sɪdeɪʃᵊn/ N-UNCOUNT ❑ *...Geraldo's attempts at elucidation.*

elude /ɪlu:d/ (**eludes**, **eluding**, **eluded**) ◼ V-T [no passive] If something that you want **eludes** you, you fail to obtain it. ❑ *Sleep eluded her.* ◼ V-T If you **elude** someone or something, you avoid them or escape from them. ❑ *He eluded the police for 13 years.* ◼ V-T [no passive] If a fact or idea **eludes** you, you do not succeed in understanding it, realizing it, or remembering it. ❑ *The appropriate word eluded him.*

elu|sive /ɪlu:sɪv/ ADJ Something or someone that is **elusive** is difficult to find, describe, remember, or achieve. ❑ *Here late-night taxis are elusive and far from cheap.*

elves /ɛlvz/ **Elves** is the plural of **elf**.

'em /əm, STRONG ɛm/ PRON **'em** is an informal way of saying or writing **them**. ❑ *There was also two other men there with 'em too.*

PREFIX
---

em-
is added to words to form verbs that describe the process of putting someone into a particular state, condition, or place, or to form adjectives and nouns that describe that process or those states and conditions. It is used before *b-*, *m-*, and *p-*. For example, if someone **embarrasses** you, they make you feel nervous or stupid in a social situation.

ema|ci|at|ed /ɪmeɪʃieɪtɪd/ ADJ A person or animal that is **emaciated** is extremely thin and weak because of illness or lack of food. ❑ *...horrific television pictures of emaciated prisoners.*

VOCABULARY IN CONTEXT

Email and the internet

One of the biggest problems for almost anyone with an email address isn't **spam** (a decent email provider will send most of it to your **junk mail folder**) but **phishing** emails. Most people know never to open an **attachment** in an email from someone they don't know, but email scammers have other methods. First, the email address may look very similar to a real website you use. Then, they either try to trick you into revealing **passwords** or bank details, or they try to get you to **click** on a link that infects your computer with **viruses**, or with **malware** that downloads **software** to your computer. If your **firewall** doesn't protect you, you could end up with scammers **hacking** into your bank account. Simply **scrolling** through the email won't hurt, but don't reply as it might lead to more contact from them. In many cases, any email you send them will simply **bounce back** anyway.

email /i:meɪl/ (**emails**, **emailing**, **emailed**) also **e-mail** ◼ N-VAR **Email** is a system of sending written messages electronically from one computer to another. **Email** is an abbreviation of 'electronic mail. ❑ *You can contact us by email.* ❑ *Do you want to send an E-mail?* ◼ V-T If you **email** someone, you send them an email. ❑ *Jamie emailed me to say he couldn't come.*

ema|nate /ɛməneɪt/ (**emanates**, **emanating**, **emanated**) ◼ V-T/V-I If a quality **emanates** from you, or if you **emanate** a quality, you give people a strong sense that you have that quality. [FORMAL] ❑ *Intelligence and cunning emanated from him.* ◼ V-I If something **emanates** from somewhere, it comes from there. [FORMAL] ❑ *The heady aroma of wood smoke emanated from the stove.*

ema|na|tion /ɛməneɪʃᵊn/ N-COUNT An **emanation** is a form of energy or a mass of tiny particles that comes from something. [FORMAL]

eman|ci|pate /ɪmænsɪpeɪt/ (**emancipates**, **emancipating**, **emancipated**) V-T If people **are emancipated**, they are freed from unpleasant or unfair social, political, or legal restrictions. [FORMAL] ❑ *Some convicts formed relationships and settled in Australia after they were emancipated.* ❑ *That war preserved the Union and emancipated enslaved people.* • **eman|ci|pa|tion** /ɪmænsɪpeɪʃᵊn/ N-UNCOUNT [oft N *of* n] ❑ *...the emancipation of women.*

eman|ci|pat|ed /ɪmænsɪpeɪtɪd/ ADJ If you describe someone as **emancipated**, you mean that they behave in a less restricted way than is traditional in their society. ❑ *She is an emancipated woman.*

emas|cu|late /ɪmæskjʊleɪt/ (**emasculates**, **emasculating**, **emasculated**) ◼ V-T If someone or something **is emasculated**, they have been made weak and ineffective. [DISAPPROVAL] ❑ *Left-wing dissidents have been emasculated and marginalized.* ❑ *The company tried to emasculate the unions.* • **emas|cu|la|tion** /ɪmæskjʊleɪʃᵊn/ N-UNCOUNT ❑ *...the emasculation of fundamental freedoms.* ◼ V-T [usu passive] If a man **is emasculated**, he loses his male role, identity, or qualities. [DISAPPROVAL] ❑ *Tosh was known to be a man who feared no-one, yet he was clearly emasculated by the situation.*

em|balm /ɪmbɑ:m/ (**embalms**, **embalming**, **embalmed**) V-T [usu passive] If a dead person **is embalmed**, their body is preserved using chemicals. ❑ *His body was embalmed.* ❑ *...the embalmed body of Lenin.*

em|bank|ment /ɪmbæŋkmənt/ (**embankments**) N-COUNT An **embankment** is a thick wall of earth that is built to carry a road or railroad track over an area of low ground, or to prevent water from a river or the sea from flooding the area. ❑ *They climbed a steep embankment.* ❑ *...a railroad embankment.*

em|bar|go /ɪmbɑ:rɡoʊ/ (**embargoes**, **embargoing**, **embargoed**) ◼ N-COUNT If one country or group of countries imposes an **embargo** against another, it forbids trade with that country. ❑ *The United Nations imposed an arms embargo against the country.* ◼ V-T If goods of a particular kind **are embargoed**, people are not allowed to import them from a particular country or export them to a particular country. ❑ *The fruit was embargoed.* ❑ *They embargoed oil shipments to the U.S.*

em|bark /ɪmbɑ:rk/ (**embarks**, **embarking**, **embarked**) ◼ V-I If you **embark** on something new, difficult, or exciting, you start doing it. ❑ *He's embarking on a new career as a writer.* ◼ V-I When someone **embarks** on a ship, they go on board before the start of a journey. ❑ *They embarked on a ship bound for Europe.*

em|bar|rass /ɪmbærəs/ (**embarrasses**, **embarrassing**, **embarrassed**) ◼ V-T If something or someone **embarrasses** you, they make you feel shy or ashamed. ❑ *His clumsiness embarrassed him.* ◼ V-T If something **embarrasses** a public figure such as a politician or an organization such as a political party, it causes problems for them. ❑ *Aides spoke of disposing of records that would embarrass the governor.*

em|bar|rassed /ɪmbærəst/ ADJ A person who is **embarrassed** feels shy, ashamed, or guilty about something. ❑ *He looked a bit embarrassed.*

em|bar|rass|ing /ɪmbærəsɪŋ/ ◼ ADJ Something that is **embarrassing** makes you feel shy or ashamed. ❑ *That was an embarrassing situation for me.* • **em|bar|rass|ing|ly** ADV ❑ *The lyrics of the song are embarrassingly banal.* ◼ ADJ Something that is

embarrassing to a public figure such as a politician or an organization such as a political party causes problems for them. ❑ *He has put the administration in an embarrassing position.*

em|bar|rass|ment /ɪmbærəsmənt/ (**embarrassments**) **1** N-VAR **Embarrassment** is the feeling you have when you are embarrassed. ❑ *I think I would have died of embarrassment.* ❑ *We apologize for any embarrassment this may have caused.* **2** N-COUNT An **embarrassment** is an action, event, or situation that causes problems for a politician, political party, government, or other public group. ❑ *The poverty figures were undoubtedly an embarrassment to the president.* **3** N-SING If you refer to a person as **an embarrassment**, you mean that you disapprove of them but cannot avoid your connection with them. [DISAPPROVAL] ❑ *You have been an embarrassment to us from the day Doug married you.*

em|bas|sy ✦◇◇ /ɛmbəsi/ (**embassies**) N-COUNT An **embassy** is a group of government officials, headed by an ambassador, who represent their government in a foreign country. The building in which they work is also called an **embassy**. ❑ *The American embassy has already complained.*

em|bat|tled /ɪmbætəld/ **1** ADJ [usu ADJ n] If you describe a person, group, or organization as **embattled**, you mean that they are having a lot of problems or difficulties. ❑ *The embattled president also denied recent claims that he was being held hostage by his own soldiers.* **2** ADJ [ADJ n] An **embattled** area is one that is involved in the fighting in a war, especially one that is surrounded by enemy forces. ❑ *Both sides say they want to try to reach a political settlement in the embattled north and east of the island.*

em|bed /ɪmbɛd/ (**embeds, embedding, embedded**) **1** V-T If an object **embeds** itself in a substance or thing, it becomes fixed there firmly and deeply. ❑ *One of the bullets passed through Andrea's chest before embedding itself in a wall.* • **em|bed|ded** ADJ ❑ *The fossils at Dinosaur Cove are embedded in hard sandstone.* **2** V-T [usu passive] If something such as an attitude or feeling **is embedded** in a society or system, or in someone's personality, it becomes a permanent and noticeable feature of it. ❑ *This agreement will be embedded in a state treaty to be signed soon.* • **em|bed|ded** ADJ ❑ *I think that hatred of the other is deeply embedded in our society.*

em|bel|lish /ɪmbɛlɪʃ/ (**embellishes, embellishing, embellished**) **1** V-T If something **is embellished** with decorative features or patterns, it has those features or patterns on it and they make it look more attractive. ❑ *The boat was embellished with carvings in red and blue.* ❑ *Ivy leaves embellish the front of the dresser.* **2** V-T If you **embellish** a story, you make it more interesting by adding details that may be untrue. ❑ *I launched into the parable, embellishing the story with invented dialogue and extra details.*

em|bel|lish|ment /ɪmbɛlɪʃmənt/ (**embellishments**) N-VAR An **embellishment** is a decoration added to something to make it seem more attractive or interesting. ❑ *...Renaissance embellishments.* ❑ *...public buildings with little bits of decoration and embellishment.*

em|ber /ɛmbər/ (**embers**) N-COUNT [usu pl] The **embers** of a fire are small pieces of wood or coal that remain and glow with heat after the fire has finished burning.

em|bez|zle /ɪmbɛzəl/ (**embezzles, embezzling, embezzled**) V-T If someone **embezzles** money that their organization or company has placed in their care, they take it and use it illegally for their own purposes. ❑ *One former director embezzled $34 million in company funds.*

em|bez|zle|ment /ɪmbɛzəlmənt/ N-UNCOUNT **Embezzlement** is the crime of embezzling money. ❑ *He was later charged with embezzlement.*

em|bit|tered /ɪmbɪtərd/ ADJ If someone is **embittered**, they feel angry and unhappy because of harsh, unpleasant, and unfair things that have happened to them. ❑ *He had turned into an embittered, hardened adult.*

em|bla|zoned /ɪmbleɪzənd/ ADJ If something is **emblazoned** with a design, words, or letters, they are clearly drawn, printed, or sewn on it. ❑ *The republic's new flag was emblazoned with the ancient symbol of the Greek Macedonian dynasty.* ❑ *...a T-shirt with "Mustique" emblazoned on it.*

em|blem /ɛmbləm/ (**emblems**) **1** N-COUNT An **emblem** is a design representing a country or organization. ❑ *...the emblem of the Soviet Union.* **2** N-COUNT An **emblem** is something that represents a quality or idea. ❑ *The eagle was an emblem of strength and courage.*

em|blem|at|ic /ɛmbləmætɪk/ **1** ADJ If something, such as an object in a picture, is **emblematic** of a particular quality or an idea, it symbolically represents the quality or idea. ❑ *Dogs are emblematic of faithfulness.* **2** ADJ [usu v-link ADJ of n] If you say that something is **emblematic** of a state of affairs, you mean that it is characteristic of it and represents its most typical features. ❑ *The killing in Pensacola is emblematic of a lot of the violence that is happening around the world.*

em|bodi|ment /ɪmbɒdimənt/ N-SING If you say that someone or something is the **embodiment** of a quality or idea, you mean that that is their most noticeable characteristic or the basis of all they do. [FORMAL] ❑ *A baby is the embodiment of vulnerability.*

em|body /ɪmbɒdi/ (**embodies, embodying, embodied**) **1** V-T To **embody** an idea or quality means to be a symbol or expression of that idea or quality. ❑ *Jack Kennedy embodied all the hopes of the 1960s.* ❑ *For twenty-nine years, Checkpoint Charlie embodied the Cold War.* **2** V-T If something **is embodied** in a particular thing, the second thing contains or consists of the first. ❑ *The proposal has been embodied in a draft resolution.*

em|bold|en /ɪmboʊldən/ (**emboldens, emboldening, emboldened**) V-T If you **are emboldened** by something, it makes you feel confident enough to behave in a particular way. ❑ *The president was steadily emboldened by the discovery that he faced no opposition.* ❑ *Four days of non-stop demonstrations have emboldened the anti-government protesters.*

em|bo|lism /ɛmbəlɪzəm/ (**embolisms**) N-COUNT [oft adj n] An **embolism** is a serious medical condition that occurs when an artery becomes blocked, usually by a blood clot.

em|bossed /ɪmbɒst/ ADJ If a surface such as paper or wood is **embossed** with a design, the design stands up slightly from the surface. ❑ *The paper on the walls was pale gold, embossed with swirling leaf designs.*

em|brace /ɪmbreɪs/ (**embraces, embracing, embraced**) **1** V-RECIP If you **embrace** someone, you put your arms around them and hold them tightly, usually in order to show your love or affection for them. You can also say that two people **embrace**. ❑ *Penelope came forward and embraced her sister.* ❑ *At first people were sort of crying for joy and embracing each other.* • N-COUNT **Embrace** is also a noun. ❑ *...a young couple locked in an embrace.* **2** V-T If you **embrace** a change, political system, or idea, you accept it and start supporting it or believing in it. [FORMAL] ❑ *He embraces the new information age.* • N-SING **Embrace** is also a noun. ❑ *The marriage signaled James's embrace of the Catholic faith.* **3** V-T If something **embraces** a group of people, things, or ideas, it includes them in a larger group or category. [FORMAL] ❑ *...a theory that would embrace the whole field of human endeavor.*

em|broi|der /ɪmbrɔɪdər/ (**embroiders, embroidering, embroidered**) **1** V-T/V-I If something such as clothing or cloth **is embroidered** with a design, the design is stitched into it. ❑ *The collar was embroidered with very small red strawberries.* ❑ *I have a pillow with my name embroidered on it.* **2** V-T/V-I If you **embroider** a story or account of something, or if you **embroider** on it, you try to make it more interesting by adding details that may be untrue. ❑ *He told some lies and sometimes just embroidered the truth.*

em|broi|dery /ɪmbrɔɪdəri/ (**embroideries**) **1** N-VAR **Embroidery** consists of designs stitched into cloth. ❑ *The shorts had blue embroidery over the pockets.* **2** N-UNCOUNT **Embroidery** is the activity of stitching designs onto cloth. ❑ *She learned sewing, knitting, and embroidery.* **3** → See feature box at **sewing**

em|broil /ɪmbrɔɪl/ (**embroils, embroiling, embroiled**) V-T If someone **embroils** you in a fight or an argument, they get you deeply involved in it. ❑ *Any hostilities could result in retaliation and further embroil U.N. troops in fighting.*

em|broiled /ɪmbrɔɪld/ ADJ [v-link ADJ] If you become **embroiled** in a fight or argument, you become deeply involved in it. ❑ *The government insisted that troops should not become embroiled in further battles.*

em|bryo /ɛmbrioʊ/ (**embryos**) **1** N-COUNT An **embryo** is an unborn animal or human being in the very early stages of development. ❑ *There are 24,000 frozen embryos in clinics across the country.* **2** ADJ [ADJ n] An **embryo** idea, system, or organization is in the very early stages of development, but is expected to grow stronger. ❑ *They are an embryo party of government.* **3** → See feature box at **birth**

em|bry|ol|ogy /ˌembriˈɒlədʒi/ N-UNCOUNT **Embryology** is the scientific study of embryos and their development. • **em|bry|olo|gist** /ˌembriˈɒlədʒɪst/ (**embryologists**) N-COUNT ❏ ...*a genetic embryologist at the hospital.*

em|bry|on|ic /ˌembriˈɒnɪk/ ADJ An **embryonic** process, idea, organization, or organism is one that is at a very early stage in its development. [FORMAL] ❏ ...*the country's embryonic democracy.* ❏ *At the time, he was trying to recruit members for his embryonic resistance group.*

em|cee /ˌemˈsiː/ (**emcees, emceeing, emceed**) **1** N-COUNT An **emcee** is the same as a **master of ceremonies**. [AM] **2** V-T/V-I To **emcee** an event or performance of something means to act as master of ceremonies for it. [AM] ❏ *I'm going to be emceeing a costume contest.* ❏ *That first night I emceed I was absolutely terrified.*

em|er|ald /ˈemərəld, ˈemrəld/ (**emeralds**) **1** N-COUNT An **emerald** is a precious stone that is clear and bright green. **2** COLOR Something that is **emerald** is bright green in color. ❏ ...*an emerald valley.* **3** → See also color supplement

emerge ♦♦◊ /ɪˈmɜːrdʒ/ (**emerges, emerging, emerged**) **1** V-I To **emerge** means to come out from an enclosed or dark space such as a room or a vehicle, or from a position where you could not be seen. ❏ *Richard was waiting outside the door as she emerged.* ❏ *She then emerged from the courthouse to thank her supporters.* **2** V-I If you **emerge from** a difficult or bad experience, you come to the end of it. ❏ *There is growing evidence that the economy is at last emerging from recession.* **3** V-T/V-I If a fact or result **emerges** from a period of thought, discussion, or investigation, it becomes known as a result of it. ❏ ...*the growing corruption that has emerged in the past few years.* ❏ *It soon emerged that neither the July nor August mortgage payment had been collected.* **4** V-I If someone or something **emerges** as a particular thing, they become recognized as that thing. [JOURNALISM] ❏ *Vietnam has emerged as the world's third-biggest rice exporter.* **5** V-I When something such as an organization or an industry **emerges**, it comes into existence. [JOURNALISM] ❏ ...*the new republic that emerged in October 1917.*

SYNONYMS

emerge
VERB
1
appear: *A woman appeared at the far end of the street.*
come: *Two police officers came into the hall.*
arrive: *Fresh groups of guests arrived.*
materialize: *Tamsin materialized at her side, notebook at the ready.*
surface: *He surfaced, gasping for air.*
3
come out: *The truth is beginning to come out about what happened.*
transpire: *It transpired that Paolo had left his driver's license at home.*
reveal: *After the fire, it was revealed that officials had never inspected the factory.*

---

emer|gence /ɪˈmɜːrdʒəns/ N-UNCOUNT The **emergence** of something is the process or event of its coming into existence. ❏ ...*the emergence of new global players.*

emer|gen|cy ♦♦◊ /ɪˈmɜːrdʒənsi/ (**emergencies**) **1** N-COUNT An **emergency** is an unexpected and difficult or dangerous situation, especially an accident, that happens suddenly and that requires quick action to deal with it. ❏ *He deals with emergencies promptly.* **2** ADJ [ADJ n] An **emergency** action is one that is done or arranged quickly and not in the normal way, because an emergency has occurred. ❏ *Yesterday, the center's board held an emergency meeting.* **3** ADJ [ADJ n] **Emergency** equipment or supplies are those intended for use in an emergency. ❏ *The plane is carrying emergency supplies for refugees.*

emer|gen|cy brake (**emergency brakes**) N-COUNT In a vehicle, the **emergency brake** is a brake that the driver operates with his or her hand or foot, and uses, for example, in emergencies or when parking. [mainly AM] ❏ *He stopped just as his truck tilted down the steep incline, put on the emergency brake, and stepped out.*

emer|gen|cy room (**emergency rooms**) N-COUNT The **emergency room** is the room or department in a hospital where people who have severe injuries or sudden illnesses are taken for emergency treatment. The abbreviation **ER** is often used. [mainly AM] ❏ *She began hyperventilating and was rushed to the emergency room.*

emer|gen|cy ser|vices N-PLURAL The **emergency services** are the public organizations whose job is to take quick action to deal with emergencies when they occur, especially the fire department, the police, and the ambulance service. ❏ ...*members of the emergency services.*

emer|gent /ɪˈmɜːrdʒənt/ ADJ [ADJ n] An **emergent** country, political movement, or social group is one that is becoming powerful or coming into existence. [WRITTEN] ❏ ...*an emergent state.* ❏ ...*an emergent nationalist movement.*

emeri|tus /ɪˈmerɪtəs/ ADJ [ADJ n, n ADJ] **Emeritus** is used with a professional title to indicate that the person bearing it has retired but keeps the title as an honor. ❏ ...*emeritus professor of physics.* ❏ *He will continue as chairman emeritus.*

em|ery /ˈeməri, ˈemri/ N-UNCOUNT [usu N n] **Emery** is a hard, rough mineral that is put on paper or cloth and used for cleaning or polishing things. ❏ *File across the tip of each nail with an emery board to smooth the edges.*

emet|ic /ɪˈmetɪk/ (**emetics**) **1** N-COUNT An **emetic** is something that is given to someone to swallow, in order to make them vomit. **2** ADJ Something that is **emetic** makes you vomit.

emi|grant /ˈemɪgrənt/ (**emigrants**) N-COUNT An **emigrant** is a person who has left their own country to live in another country. Compare **immigrant**. ❏ ...*Irish emigrants to America.*

emi|grate /ˈemɪgreɪt/ (**emigrates, emigrating, emigrated**) V-I If you **emigrate**, you leave your own country to live in another country. ❏ *He emigrated to Belgium.* • **emi|gra|tion** /ˌemɪˈgreɪʃən/ N-UNCOUNT ❏ ...*the huge emigration of workers to the West.*

émi|gré /ˈemɪgreɪ/ (**émigrés**) also **emigre** N-COUNT An **émigré** is someone who has left their own country and lives in a different country for political reasons. ❏ *Several hundred refugees and émigrés demonstrated outside the main entrance.*

emi|nence /ˈemɪnəns/ N-UNCOUNT **Eminence** is the quality of being very well-known and highly respected. ❏ *Many of the pilots were to achieve eminence in the aeronautical world.*

emi|nent /ˈemɪnənt/ ADJ An **eminent** person is well-known and respected, especially because they are good at their profession. ❏ ...*an eminent scientist.*

emi|nent do|main N-UNCOUNT **Eminent domain** is the legal right that a government has to buy private land within its borders and to compensate the owner of the land. [AM] ❏ *Officials planned to use eminent domain to force 18 residents and businesses off their properties.*

emi|nent|ly /ˈemɪnəntli/ ADV [ADV adj/-ed] You use **eminently** in front of an adjective describing a positive quality in order to emphasize the quality expressed by that adjective. [EMPHASIS] ❏ *His books on diplomatic history were eminently readable.*

emir /eˈmɪər/ (**emirs**) N-COUNT [usu the N] An **emir** is a Muslim ruler. ❏ ...*the Emir of Kuwait.*

emir|ate /ˈemɪərɪt, ˈemərɪt/ (**emirates**) N-COUNT [oft in names] An **emirate** is a country that is ruled by an emir.

em|is|sary /ˈemɪseri/ (**emissaries**) N-COUNT An **emissary** is a representative sent by one government or leader to another. [FORMAL] ❏ ...*the president's special emissary to Hanoi.*

emis|sion /ɪˈmɪʃən/ (**emissions**) **1** N-VAR An **emission** of something such as gas or radiation is the release of it into the atmosphere. [FORMAL] ❏ *The emission of gases such as carbon dioxide should be stabilized at their present level.* **2** N-COUNT [usu pl] **Emissions** refers to the gases that are released into the atmosphere. ❏ *Sulfur emissions from steel mills become acid rain.*

emit /ɪˈmɪt/ (**emits, emitting, emitted**) **1** V-T If something **emits** heat, light, gas, or a smell, it produces it and sends it out by means of a physical or chemical process. [FORMAL] ❏ *The new device emits a powerful circular column of light.* **2** V-T To **emit** a sound or noise means to produce it. [FORMAL] ❏ *Whitney blinked and emitted a long, low whistle.* **3** → See feature box at **brain**

emo|ji /ɪˈmoʊdʒi/ (**emojis**) N-COUNT An **emoji** is a digital image that is used to express an emotion in an electronic communication such as an email or text message. [COMPUTING] ❏ *He added a 'wink' emoji to show that he was joking.*

emol|lient /ɪmpliənt/ (emollients) **1** N-MASS An **emollient** is a liquid or cream that you put on your skin to make it softer or to reduce pain. [FORMAL] **2** ADJ [ADJ n] An **emollient** cream or other substance makes your skin softer or reduces pain. [FORMAL]

emolu|ment /ɪmplyəmənt/ (emoluments) N-COUNT [usu pl] **Emoluments** are money or other forms of payment that a person receives for doing work. [FORMAL] ❑ *He could earn up to a million dollars a year in salary and emoluments from many directorships.*

emo|ti|con /ɪmoutɪkɒn/ (emoticons) N-COUNT An **emoticon** is a symbol used in email to show how someone is feeling. :-) is an emoticon showing happiness. [COMPUTING]

emo|tion ✦◇◇ /ɪmoʊʃ°n/ (emotions) **1** N-VAR An **emotion** is a feeling such as happiness, love, fear, anger, or hatred, which can be caused by the situation that you are in or the people you are with. ❑ *Happiness was an emotion that Jerry was having to relearn.* **2** N-UNCOUNT **Emotion** is the part of a person's character that consists of their feelings, as opposed to their thoughts. ❑ *...the split between reason and emotion.*

VOCABULARY IN CONTEXT

Emotions

Everyone can have a bad day, but if someone is continually feeling **hopeless** or **short-tempered** and not experiencing any **joy** or pleasure in daily life, it might mean they are **depressed**. People who have problems managing their anger can end up depressed because being constantly **furious** takes up so much mental energy. There's simply nothing left to channel into feeling **cheerful** in general, or being **thrilled** by some unexpected good news. It's okay to be **despondent** when life is difficult, or **fuming** when someone steals your parking spot, but if those feelings don't disappear, counseling may be a sensible step. No one can be **over the moon** every time they greet the dawn of a new day, but it's worth remembering that people who are generally **content** with their lives tend to live longer.

SYNONYMS

emotion
NOUN **1**
feeling: *Strong feelings of pride welled up in me.*
sentiment: *I must agree with the sentiments expressed by my colleague.*

emo|tion|al ✦◇◇ /ɪmoʊʃən°l/ **1** ADJ **Emotional** means concerned with emotions and feelings. ❑ *I needed this man's love, and the emotional support he was giving me.* • **emo|tion|al|ly** ADV [ADV adj/-ed] ❑ *Are you saying that you're becoming emotionally involved with me?* **2** ADJ An **emotional** situation or issue is one that causes people to have strong feelings. ❑ *Abortion is a very emotional issue.* • **emo|tion|al|ly** ADV [ADV adj/-ed] ❑ *In an emotionally charged speech, he said he was resigning.* **3** ADJ If someone is or becomes **emotional**, they show their feelings very openly, especially because they are upset. ❑ *He is a very emotional man.*

SYNONYMS

emotional
ADJ **3**
passionate: *...a passionate and combative speech.*
sentimental: *I'm trying not to be sentimental about the past.*
temperamental: *...a man given to temperamental outbursts and paranoia.*
excitable: *Mary sat beside Elaine, who today seemed excitable.*

emo|tion|al in|tel|li|gence N-UNCOUNT **Emotional intelligence** is used to refer to people's interpersonal and communication skills. ❑ *This is an age when we boast of our emotional intelligence and we claim to feel each other's pain.*

emo|tion|less /ɪmoʊʃ°nlɪs/ ADJ If you describe someone as **emotionless**, you mean that they do not show any feelings or emotions.

emo|tive /ɪmoʊtɪv/ ADJ An **emotive** situation or issue is likely to make people feel strong emotions. ❑ *Embryo research is an emotive issue.*

em|pa|thet|ic /ɛmpəθɛtɪk/ **1** ADJ Someone who is **empathetic** has the ability to share another person's feelings or emotions as if they were their own. [FORMAL] ❑ *...Clinton's skills as an empathetic listener.* **2** → See feature box at **quality**

em|pa|thize /ɛmpəθaɪz/ (empathizes, empathizing, empathized)

in BRIT, also use **empathise**

V-I If you **empathize** with someone, you understand their situation, problems, and feelings because you have been in a similar situation. ❑ *I clearly empathize with the people who live in those neighborhoods.* ❑ *Parents must make use of their natural ability to empathize.*

em|pa|thy /ɛmpəθi/ N-UNCOUNT **Empathy** is the ability to share another person's feelings and emotions as if they were your own. ❑ *Having begun my life in a children's home, I have great empathy with the little ones.*

em|per|or /ɛmpərər/ (emperors) N-COUNT; N-TITLE An **emperor** is a man who rules an empire or is the head of state in an empire. ❑ *...the emperor of Japan.*

em|pha|sis ✦◇◇ /ɛmfəsɪs/ (emphases /ɛmfəsiːz/) **1** N-VAR **Emphasis** is special or extra importance that is given to an activity or to a part or aspect of something. ❑ *Too much emphasis is placed on research.* **2** N-VAR **Emphasis** is extra force that you put on a syllable, word, or phrase when you are speaking in order to make it seem more important. ❑ *The emphasis is on the first syllable of the last word.*

SYNONYMS

emphasis
NOUN **1**
importance: *We have always stressed the importance of economic reform.*
weight: *The scientists involved put different weight on the conclusions of different models.*
significance: *Ideas about the social significance of religion have changed over time.*
stress: *Japanese car makers are placing even more stress on European sales.*
attention: *The conference may help to focus attention on the economy.*

em|pha|size ✦◇◇ /ɛmfəsaɪz/ (emphasizes, emphasizing, emphasized)

in BRIT, also use **emphasise**

V-T To **emphasize** something means to indicate that it is particularly important or true, or to draw special attention to it. ❑ *But it's also been emphasized that no major policy changes can be expected to come out of the meeting.*

SYNONYMS

emphasize
VERB
stress: *They also stress the need for better transportation and health care.*
highlight: *Once again, the 'Free Press' prefers not to highlight these facts.*
accentuate: *His shaved head accentuates his large, round face.*
flag: *I think there are more important issues, and I just wanted to flag that.*

em|phat|ic /ɪmfætɪk/ **1** ADJ An **emphatic** response or statement is one made in a forceful way, because the speaker feels very strongly about what they are saying. ❑ *His response was immediate and emphatic.* **2** ADJ [v-link ADJ] If you are **emphatic** about something, you use forceful language that shows you feel very strongly about what you are saying. ❑ *The rebels are emphatic that this is not a surrender.* **3** ADJ An **emphatic** win or victory is one in which the winner has won by a large amount or distance. ❑ *Yesterday's emphatic victory was their fifth in succession.*

em|phati|cal|ly /ɪmfætɪkli/ **1** ADV [ADV with v] If you say something **emphatically**, you say it in a forceful way that shows you feel very strongly about what you are saying. ❑ *"No fast food," she said emphatically.* **2** ADV [ADV with cl/group] You use **emphatically** to emphasize the statement you are making. [EMPHASIS] ❑ *Making people feel foolish is emphatically not my strategy.*

em|phy|sema /ɛmfɪsiːmə/ N-UNCOUNT **Emphysema** is a serious medical condition that occurs when the lungs become larger and do not work properly, causing difficulty in breathing.

em|pire ♦◇◇ /ɛmpaɪər/ (empires) **1** N-COUNT An **empire** is a number of individual nations that are all controlled by the government or ruler of one particular country. ❑ *...the Roman Empire.* **2** N-COUNT You can refer to a group of companies controlled by one person as an **empire**. ❑ *...the global Murdoch media empire.*

em|piri|cal /ɪmpɪrɪkəl/ ADJ **Empirical** evidence or study relies on practical experience rather than theories. ❑ *There is no empirical evidence to support his thesis.* ● **em|piri|cal|ly** ADV ❑ *They approached this part of their task empirically.*

em|piri|cism /ɪmpɪrɪsɪzəm/ N-UNCOUNT **Empiricism** is the belief that people should rely on practical experience and experiments, rather than on theories, as a basis for knowledge. ● **em|piri|cist** (empiricists) N-COUNT [FORMAL] ❑ *He was an unswerving empiricist with little time for theory.*

em|place|ment /ɪmpleɪsmənt/ (emplacements) N-COUNT [usu pl, usu supp N] **Emplacements** are specially prepared positions from which a heavy gun can be fired. [TECHNICAL] ❑ *There are gun emplacements every 500 yards along the road.*

em|ploy ♦◇◇ /ɪmplɔɪ/ (employs, employing, employed) **1** V-T If a person or company **employs** you, they pay you to work for them. ❑ *The company employs 18 workers.* ❑ *More than 3,000 local workers are employed in the tourism industry.* **2** V-T If you **employ** certain methods, materials, or expressions, you use them. ❑ *The group will employ a mix of tactics to achieve its aim.* **3** V-T [usu passive] If your time **is employed** in doing something, you are using the time you have to do that thing. ❑ *Your time could be usefully employed in attending night classes.*

em|ploy|able /ɪmplɔɪəbəl/ ADJ Someone who is **employable** has skills or abilities that are likely to help them get a job. ❑ *People need basic education if they are to become employable.* ❑ *...employable adults.*

em|ployee ♦♦◇ /ɪmplɔɪiː/ (employees) **1** N-COUNT An **employee** is a person who is paid to work for an organization or for another person. ❑ *He is an employee of Fuji Bank.* **2** → See feature box at **working**

SYNONYMS

employee
NOUN
worker: *Wages have been frozen and workers laid off.*
staff: *...members of staff.*
hand: *He now works as a farm hand.*

---

em|ploy|er ♦◇◇ /ɪmplɔɪər/ (employers) **1** N-COUNT Your **employer** is the person or organization that you work for. ❑ *He had been sent to Rome by his employer.* **2** → See feature box at **working**

em|ploy|ment ♦◇◇ /ɪmplɔɪmənt/ **1** N-UNCOUNT **Employment** is the fact of having a job. ❑ *She was unable to find employment.* **2** N-UNCOUNT **Employment** is the fact of employing someone. ❑ *...the employment of children under nine.* **3** N-UNCOUNT **Employment** is the work that is available in a country or area. ❑ *...economic policies designed to secure full employment.* **4** → See feature box at **work**

SYNONYMS

employment
NOUN **1**
work: *Fewer and fewer people are finding work.*
job: *...overseas job vacancies.*
position: *He left a career in teaching to take up a position with the Arts Council.*
post: *She had earlier resigned her post as the president's assistant.*

---

em|ploy|ment agen|cy (employment agencies) N-COUNT An **employment agency** is a company whose business is to help people to find work and help employers to find the workers they need. [BUSINESS]

em|po|rium /ɛmpɔːriəm/ (emporiums or emporia /ɛmpɔːriə/) N-COUNT An **emporium** is a store or large shop. [FORMAL]

em|power /ɪmpaʊər/ (empowers, empowering, empowered) **1** V-T If someone **is empowered** to do something, they have the authority or power to do it. [FORMAL] ❑ *The army is now empowered to operate on a shoot-to-kill basis.* **2** V-T To **empower** someone means to give them the means to achieve something, for example, to become stronger or more successful. ❑ *You must delegate effectively and empower people to carry out their roles with your full support.* **3** → See feature box at **success**

em|pow|er|ment /ɪmpaʊərmənt/ N-UNCOUNT The **empowerment** of a person or group of people is the process of giving them power and status in a particular situation. ❑ *This government believes very strongly in the empowerment of women.*

em|press /ɛmprɪs/ (empresses) N-COUNT; N-TITLE An **empress** is a woman who rules an empire or who is the wife of an emperor. ❑ *...Catherine II, Empress of Russia.*

emp|ti|ness /ɛmptinɪs/ **1** N-UNCOUNT A feeling of **emptiness** is an unhappy or frightening feeling that nothing is worthwhile, especially when you are very tired or have just experienced something upsetting. ❑ *The result later in life may be feelings of emptiness and depression.* **2** N-UNCOUNT The **emptiness** of a place is the fact that there is nothing in it. ❑ *...the emptiness of the desert.*

emp|ty ♦◇◇ /ɛmpti/ (emptier, emptiest, empties, emptying, emptied) **1** ADJ An **empty** place, vehicle, or container is one that has no people or things in it. ❑ *The room was bare and empty.* ❑ *...empty cans of beer.* **2** ADJ An **empty** gesture, threat, or relationship has no real value or meaning. ❑ *His father had threatened disinheritance, but both men had known it was an empty threat.* **3** ADJ If you describe a person's life or a period of time as **empty**, you mean that nothing interesting or valuable happens in it. ❑ *My life was very hectic but empty before I met him.* **4** ADJ If you feel **empty**, you feel unhappy and have no energy, usually because you are very tired or have just experienced something upsetting. ❑ *I feel so empty, my life just doesn't seem worth living any more.* **5** V-T If you **empty** a container, or **empty** something out of it, you remove its contents, especially by tipping it up. ❑ *I emptied the ashtray.* ❑ *Empty the noodles and liquid into a serving bowl.* **6** V-T/V-I If someone **empties** a room or place, or if it **empties**, everyone in it goes away. ❑ *The stadium emptied at the end of the first day of games.* **7** V-I A river or canal that **empties into** a lake, river, or sea flows into it. ❑ *The Milwaukee River empties into Lake Michigan near that pipe.* **8** N-COUNT **Empties** are bottles or containers that no longer have anything in them. ❑ *After breakfast we'll take the empties down in the sack.*

empty-handed ADJ [ADJ after v] If you come away from somewhere **empty-handed**, you have failed to get what you wanted. ❑ *Delegates from the warring sides held a new round of peace talks but went away empty-handed.*

empty-headed ADJ If you describe someone as **empty-headed**, you mean that they are not very intelligent and often do silly things.

emu /iːmjuː/ (emus or emu) N-COUNT An **emu** is a large Australian bird that cannot fly.

emu|late /ɛmjʊleɪt/ (emulates, emulating, emulated) V-T If you **emulate** something or someone, you imitate them because you admire them a great deal. [FORMAL] ❑ *Sons are traditionally expected to emulate their fathers.*

emul|si|fi|er /ɪmʌlsɪfaɪər/ (emulsifiers) N-MASS An **emulsifier** is a substance used in food manufacturing that helps to combine liquids of different thicknesses.

emul|si|fy /ɪmʌlsɪfaɪ/ (emulsifies, emulsifying, emulsified) V-T/V-I When two liquids of different thicknesses **emulsify** or when they **are emulsified**, they combine. [TECHNICAL] ❑ *It is the pressure which releases the coffee oils; these emulsify and give the coffee its rich, velvety texture.* ❑ *Whisk the cream into the mixture to emulsify it.* ❑ *Beeswax acts as an emulsifying agent.* ❑ *...emulsified oil.*

emul|sion /ɪmʌlʃ°n/ (emulsions) **1** N-MASS **Emulsion** or **emulsion paint** is a water-based paint used for painting walls and ceilings. ❑ *...an undercoat of white emulsion paint.* ❑ *...a matt emulsion.* **2** N-MASS An **emulsion** is a liquid or cream which is a mixture of two or more liquids, such as oil and water, that do not naturally mix together.

PREFIX

en-
is added to words to form verbs that describe the process of putting someone into a particular state, condition, or place, or to form adjectives and nouns that describe that process or those states and conditions. *For example, if something* **enriches** *your life, it makes your life better or more enjoyable.*

en|able ✦✧ /ɪneɪb°l/ (enables, enabling, enabled) **1** V-T If someone or something **enables** you to do a particular thing, they give you the opportunity to do it. ❑ *The new test should enable doctors to detect the disease early.* **2** V-T To **enable** something to happen means to make it possible for it to happen. ❑ *The hot sun enables the grapes to reach optimum ripeness.* **3** V-T To **enable** someone to do something means to give them permission or the right to do it. ❑ *...legislation which enables young people to do a form of alternative service.*

SYNONYMS

enable
VERB **1**
allow: *She said this would allow more effective planning.*
permit: *This method of cooking also permits heat to penetrate from both sides.*
facilitate: *The new airport will facilitate the development of tourism.*
let: *I can't let myself be distracted by those things.*

en|act /ɪnækt/ (enacts, enacting, enacted) **1** V-T When a government or authority **enacts** a proposal, they make it into a law. [TECHNICAL] ❑ *The authorities have failed so far to enact a law allowing unrestricted emigration.* **2** V-T If people **enact** a story or play, they perform it by acting. ❑ *She often enacted the stories told to her by her father.* **3** V-T [usu passive] If a particular event or situation **is enacted**, it happens; used especially to talk about something that has happened before. [JOURNALISM] ❑ *It was a scene enacted month after month for eight years.*

en|act|ment /ɪnæktmənt/ (enactments) N-VAR The **enactment** of a law is the process in a legislature by which the law is agreed upon and made official. [TECHNICAL] ❑ *We support the call for the enactment of a Bill of Rights.*

enam|el /ɪnæm°l/ (enamels) **1** N-MASS **Enamel** is a substance like glass that can be heated and put onto metal, glass, or pottery in order to decorate or protect it. ❑ *...a white enamel saucepan.* **2** N-MASS **Enamel** is a hard, shiny paint that is used especially for painting metal and wood. ❑ *...enamel polymer paints.* **3** N-UNCOUNT **Enamel** is the hard white substance that forms the outer part of a tooth.

enam|eled /ɪnæm°ld/
in BRIT, use **enamelled**
ADJ [ADJ n] An **enameled** object is decorated or covered with enamel. ❑ *...enameled plates.*

enam|el|ing /ɪnæməlɪŋ/
in BRIT, use **enamelling**
N-UNCOUNT **Enameling** is the decoration of something such as jewelry with enamel.

en|am|ored /ɪnæmərd/
in BRIT, use **enamoured**
ADJ If you are **enamored** of something, you like or admire it a lot. If you are not **enamored** of something, you dislike or disapprove of it. [LITERARY] ❑ *I became totally enamored of the wildflowers there.*

en bloc /ɒn blɒk/ ADV [ADV after v, n ADV] If a group of people do something **en bloc**, they do it all together and at the same time. If a group of people or things are considered **en bloc**, they are considered as a group, rather than separately. ❑ *The selectors should resign en bloc.*

en|camped /ɪnkæmpt/ ADJ If people, especially soldiers, are **encamped** somewhere, they have set up camp there. ❑ *He made his way back to the farmyard where his regiment was encamped.*

en|camp|ment /ɪnkæmpmənt/ (encampments) N-COUNT [usu with supp] An **encampment** is a group of tents or other shelters in a particular place, especially when they are used by soldiers or refugees. ❑ *...a large military encampment.*

en|cap|su|late /ɪnkæpsəleɪt, -syu-/ (encapsulates, encapsulating, encapsulated) V-T To **encapsulate** particular facts or ideas means to represent all their most important aspects in a very small space or in a single object or event. ❑ *A Wall Street Journal editorial encapsulated the views of many conservatives.*

en|case /ɪnkeɪs/ (encases, encasing, encased) V-T If a person or an object **is encased** in something, they are completely covered or surrounded by it. ❑ *When nuclear fuel is manufactured it is encased in metal cans.* ❑ *These weapons also had a heavy brass guard which encased almost the whole hand.*

SUFFIX

-ence, -ency
form nouns that refer to a particular action, state, or quality. *For example,* **dependence** *is the state of being dependent, and* **efficiency** *is the quality of being efficient.*

en|cepha|li|tis /ɛnsɛfəlaɪtɪs/ N-UNCOUNT **Encephalitis** is a medical condition in which the brain becomes swollen. ❑ *Encephalitis still attacks one child in 1,000 who catches measles.*

en|chant /ɪntʃænt/ (enchants, enchanting, enchanted) **1** V-T If you **are enchanted** by someone or something, they cause you to have feelings of great delight or pleasure. ❑ *Dena was enchanted by the house.* **2** V-T In fairy tales and legends, to **enchant** someone or something means to put a magic spell on them. ❑ *...Celtic stories of cauldrons and enchanted vessels.*

en|chant|ing /ɪntʃæntɪŋ/ ADJ If you describe someone or something as **enchanting**, you mean that they are very attractive or charming. ❑ *She's an absolutely enchanting child.*

en|chant|ment /ɪntʃæntmənt/ (enchantments) **1** N-UNCOUNT If you say that something has **enchantment**, you mean that it makes you feel great delight or pleasure. Your **enchantment** with something is the fact of your feeling great delight and pleasure because of it. ❑ *The wilderness campsite had its own peculiar enchantment.* ❑ *Alonzo's enchantment with orchids dates back to 1951.* **2** N-COUNT In fairy tales and legends, an **enchantment** is a magic spell.

en|chant|ress /ɪntʃæntrɪs/ (enchantresses) N-COUNT In fairy tales and legends, an **enchantress** is a woman who uses magic to put spells on people and things.

en|chi|la|da /ɛntʃɪlɑːdə/ (enchiladas) N-COUNT An **enchilada** is a Mexican dish consisting of a tortilla which is rolled around a filling of meat or cheese and served with a chili sauce.

en|cir|cle /ɪnsɜrk°l/ (encircles, encircling, encircled) V-T To **encircle** something or someone means to surround or enclose them, or to go around them. ❑ *A forty-foot-high concrete wall encircles the jail.*

en|clave /ɛnkleɪv, ɒn-/ (enclaves) N-COUNT An **enclave** is an area within a country or a city where people live who have a different nationality or culture from the people living in the surrounding country or city. ❑ *Nagorno-Karabakh is an Armenian enclave inside Azerbaijan.*

en|close /ɪnkloʊz/ (encloses, enclosing, enclosed) **1** V-T If a place or object **is enclosed** by something, the place or object is inside that thing or completely surrounded by it. ❑ *The rules state that samples must be enclosed in two watertight containers.* ❑ *Enclose the flower in a small muslin bag.* **2** V-T If you **enclose** something with a letter, you put it in the same envelope as the letter. ❑ *I have enclosed a check for $100.*

en|closed /ɪnkloʊzd/ ADJ [usu ADJ n] An **enclosed** community of monks or nuns does not have any contact with the outside world. ❑ ...*monks and nuns from enclosed orders.*

en|clo|sure /ɪnkloʊʒər/ (**enclosures**) N-COUNT An **enclosure** is an area of land that is surrounded by a wall or fence and that is used for a particular purpose. ❑ *This enclosure was so vast that the outermost wall could hardly be seen.*

en|code /ɪnkoʊd/ (**encodes, encoding, encoded**) V-T If you **encode** a message or some information, you put it into a code or express it in a different form or system of language. ❑ *The two parties encode confidential data in a form that is not directly readable by the other party.*

en|com|pass /ɪnkʌmpəs/ (**encompasses, encompassing, encompassed**) ◼ V-T If something **encompasses** particular things, it includes them. ❑ *His repertoire encompassed everything from Bach to Schoenberg.* ◻ V-T To **encompass** a place means to completely surround or cover it. ❑ *The map shows the rest of the western region, encompassing nine states.*

en|core /ɒŋkɔr, -koʊr/ (**encores**) N-COUNT An **encore** is a short extra performance at the end of a longer one, that an entertainer gives because the audience asks for it. ❑ *Lang's final encore last night was "Barefoot."*

en|coun|ter ✦✧ /ɪnkaʊntər/ (**encounters, encountering, encountered**) ◼ V-T If you **encounter** problems or difficulties, you experience them. ❑ *Every day of our lives we encounter major and minor stresses of one kind or another.* ◻ V-T If you **encounter** someone, you meet them, usually unexpectedly. [FORMAL] ❑ *Did you encounter anyone in the building?* ◼ N-COUNT An **encounter** with someone is a meeting with them, particularly one that is unexpected or significant. ❑ *The author tells of a remarkable encounter with a group of South Vietnamese soldiers.* ◼ N-COUNT An **encounter** is a particular type of experience. ❑ ...*a sexual encounter.*

SYNONYMS

encounter
VERB ◼
experience: *Widows seem to experience more distress than do widowers.*
face: *The immense difficulties facing European businessmen were only too evident.*
suffer: *They suffered another setback in their efforts to obtain support for reforms.*
undergo: *He underwent an agonizing 48-hour wait for the test results.*

---

en|cour|age ✦✧ /ɪnkɜrɪdʒ/ (**encourages, encouraging, encouraged**) ◼ V-T If you **encourage** someone, you give them confidence, for example by letting them know that what they are doing is good and telling them that they should continue to do it. ❑ *When things aren't going well, he encourages me, telling me not to give up.* ◻ V-T [usu passive] If someone **is encouraged by** something that happens, it gives them hope or confidence. ❑ *Investors were encouraged by the news.* • **en|cour|aged** ADJ [v-link ADJ] ❑ *We were very encouraged after over 17,000 pictures were submitted.* ◼ V-T If you **encourage** someone to do something, you try to persuade them to do it, for example, by telling them that it would be a pleasant thing to do, or by trying to make it easier for them to do it. You can also **encourage** an activity. ❑ *Herbie Hancock was encouraged by his family to learn music at a young age.* ◼ V-T If something **encourages** a particular activity or state, it causes it to happen or increase. ❑ ...*a natural substance that encourages cell growth.*

en|cour|age|ment /ɪnkɜrɪdʒmənt/ (**encouragements**) N-VAR **Encouragement** is the activity of encouraging someone, or something that is said or done in order to encourage them. ❑ *Friends gave me a great deal of encouragement.*

en|cour|ag|ing /ɪnkɜrɪdʒɪŋ/ ADJ Something that is **encouraging** gives people hope or confidence. ❑ *There are encouraging signs of an artistic revival.* ❑ *The results have been encouraging.* • **en|cour|ag|ing|ly** ADV ❑ *The people at the next table watched me eat and smiled encouragingly.*

en|croach /ɪnkroʊtʃ/ (**encroaches, encroaching, encroached**) ◼ V-I If one thing **encroaches** on another, the first thing spreads or becomes stronger, and slowly begins to restrict the power, range, or effectiveness of the second thing. [FORMAL, DISAPPROVAL] ❑ *The new institutions do not encroach on political power.* ◻ V-I If something **encroaches** on a place, it spreads and takes over more and more of that place. [FORMAL] ❑ *The shrubs encroached ever more on the twisting drive.* ◼ → See feature box at **deforest**

en|croach|ment /ɪnkroʊtʃmənt/ (**encroachments**) N-VAR You can describe the action or process of encroaching on something as **encroachment**. [FORMAL, DISAPPROVAL] ❑ *It's a sign of the encroachment of commercialism in medicine.*

en|crus|ta|tion /ɛnkrʌsteɪʃən/ (**encrustations**) N-VAR An **encrustation** is a hard and thick layer on the surface of something that has built up over a long period of time.

en|crust|ed /ɪnkrʌstɪd/ ADJ [oft ADJ with n] If an object is **encrusted** with something, its surface is covered with a layer of that thing. ❑ ...*a blue coat that was thickly encrusted with gold loops.*

en|crypt /ɪnkrɪpt/ (**encrypts, encrypting, encrypted**) V-T If a document or piece of information **is encrypted**, it is written in a special code, so that only certain people can read it. ❑ *Account details are encrypted to protect privacy.* ❑ ...*a program that will encrypt the information before sending.* ❑ ...*encrypted signals.* • **en|cryp|tion** /ɪnkrɪpʃən/ N-UNCOUNT [oft N n] ❑ *It is currently illegal to export this encryption technology from the U.S.*

en|cum|ber /ɪnkʌmbər/ (**encumbers, encumbering, encumbered**) V-T If you **are encumbered** by something, it prevents you from moving freely or doing what you want. ❑ *Lead weights and air cylinders encumbered the divers as they walked to the shore.* ❑ *It is still laboring under the debt that it was encumbered with in the 1980s.* • **en|cum|bered** ADJ [v-link ADJ, usu ADJ with/by n] ❑ *The rest of the world is less encumbered with legislation.*

en|cum|brance /ɪnkʌmbrəns/ (**encumbrances**) N-COUNT An **encumbrance** is something or someone that encumbers you. [FORMAL] ❑ *Magdalena considered the past an irrelevant encumbrance.*

-ency → see **-ence**

en|cyc|li|cal /ɪnsɪklɪkəl/ (**encyclicals**) N-COUNT An **encyclical** is an official letter written by the pope and sent to all Roman Catholic bishops, usually in order to make a statement about the official teachings of the church.

en|cy|clo|pedia /ɪnsaɪkləpidiə/ (**encyclopedias**) also **encyclopaedia** N-COUNT An **encyclopedia** is a book or set of books in which facts about many different subjects or about one particular subject are arranged for reference, usually in alphabetical order.

en|cy|clo|pedic /ɪnsaɪkləpidɪk/ also **encyclopaedic** ADJ [usu ADJ n] If you describe something as **encyclopedic**, you mean that it is very full, complete, and thorough in the amount of knowledge or information that it has. ❑ *He had an encyclopedic knowledge of plants.* ❑ ...*an almost overwhelmingly encyclopedic volume.*

END

① NOUN USES
② VERB USES
③ PHRASAL VERBS

---

① **end** ✦✦✦ /ɛnd/ (**ends**)
→ Please look at meanings ㉑ – ㉓ to see if the expression you are looking for is shown under another headword.
◼ N-SING The **end** of something such as a period of time, an event, a book, or a movie is the last part of it or the final point in it. ❑ *The report is expected by the end of the year.* ❑ ...*families who settled in the region at the end of the 17th century.* ◻ N-COUNT An **end** to something or the **end** of it is the act or result of stopping it so that it does not continue any longer. ❑ *The government today called for an end to the violence.* ❑ *I was worried she would walk out or bring the interview to an end.* ◼ N-COUNT The two **ends** of something long and narrow are the two points or parts of it that are farthest away from each other. ❑ *The company is planning to place surveillance equipment at both ends of the tunnel.* ◼ N-COUNT The **end** of a long, narrow object such as a finger or a pencil is the tip or smallest edge of it, usually the part that is furthest away from you. ❑ *He tapped the ends of his fingers together.* ◼ N-COUNT **End** is used to refer to either of the two extreme points of a scale, or of something that you are considering as a scale. ❑ ...*two aspiring actors from opposite ends*

of the social scale. ⑥ N-COUNT The other **end** is one of two places that are connected because people are communicating with each other by telephone or writing, or are traveling from one place to the other. ▢ *When he answered the phone, Fred was at the other end.* ⑦ N-COUNT If you refer to a particular **end** of a project or piece of work, you mean a part or aspect of it, such as a part of it that is done by a particular person or in a particular place. [SPOKEN] ▢ *You take care of your end, kid, I'll take care of mine.* ⑧ N-COUNT An **end** is the purpose for which something is done or toward which you are working. ▢ *The police force is being manipulated for political ends.* ⑨ PHRASE If something is **at an end**, it has finished and will not continue. ▢ *The recession is definitely at an end.* ⑩ PHRASE If something **comes to an end**, it stops. ▢ *The cold war came to an end.* ⑪ PHRASE You say **at the end of the day** when you are talking about what happens after a long series of events or what appears to be the case after you have considered the relevant facts. [INFORMAL] ▢ *At the end of the day it's up to them to decide.* ⑫ PHRASE You say **in the end** when you are saying what is the final result of a series of events, or what is your final conclusion after considering all the relevant facts. ▢ *I toyed with the idea of calling the police, but in the end I didn't.* ⑬ PHRASE If you find it difficult to **make ends meet**, you cannot manage very well financially because you hardly have enough money for the things you need. ▢ *With Betty's salary they barely made ends meet.* ⑭ PHRASE **No end** means a lot. [INFORMAL] ▢ *Teachers inform me that Todd's behavior has improved no end.* ⑮ PHRASE When something happens for hours, days, weeks, or years **on end**, it happens continuously and without stopping for the amount of time that is mentioned. ▢ *He is a wonderful companion and we can talk for hours on end.* ⑯ PHRASE Something that is **on end** is upright, instead of in its normal or natural position, for example, lying down, flat, or on its longest side. ▢ *Wet books should be placed on end with their pages kept apart.* ⑰ PHRASE To **put an end to** something means to cause it to stop. ▢ *Only a political solution could put an end to the violence.* ⑱ PHRASE If a process or person has reached **the end of the road**, they are unable to progress any further. ▢ *Given the results of the vote, is this the end of the road for the hardliners in Congress?* ⑲ PHRASE If you say that something bad is **not the end of the world**, you are trying to stop yourself or someone else being so upset by it, by suggesting that it is not the worst thing that could happen. ▢ *Obviously I'd be disappointed if we don't make it, but it wouldn't be the end of the world.* ⑳ **the end of your tether** → see **tether** ㉑ **to make your hair stand on end** → see **hair** ㉒ **to be on the receiving end** → see **receive** ㉓ **to get the wrong end of the stick** → see **stick** ①

② **end** ♦♦♦ /ɛnd/ (ends, ending, ended) ❶ V-T/V-I When a situation, process, or activity **ends**, or when something or someone **ends** it, it reaches its final point and stops. ▢ *The meeting quickly ended and Steve and I left the room.* • **end|ing** N-SING ▢ *The ending of a marriage by death is different in many ways from an ending caused by divorce.* ❷ V-T/V-I If you say that someone or something **ends** a period of time in a particular way, you are indicating what the final situation was like. You can also say that a period of time **ends** in a particular way. ▢ *The markets ended the week on a quiet note.* ❸ V-I If a period of time **ends**, it reaches its final point. ▢ *Reports usually come out about three weeks after each month ends.* ❹ V-T/V-I If something such as a book, speech, or performance **ends** with a particular thing or the writer or performer **ends** it with that thing, its final part consists of the thing mentioned. ▢ *His statement ended with the words: "Pray for me."* ▢ *The book ends on a lengthy description of Hawaii.* ❺ V-I If a situation or event **ends** in a particular way, it has that particular result. ▢ *The incident could have ended in tragedy.* ▢ *Our conversations ended with him saying he would try to be more understanding.* ❻ V-I If an object **ends with** or in a particular thing, it has that thing on its tip or point, or as its last part. ▢ *It has three pairs of legs, each ending in a large claw.* ❼ V-I A journey, road, or river that **ends** at a particular place stops there and goes no further. ▢ *The highway ended at an intersection.* ❽ V-I If you say that something **ends** at a particular point, you mean that it is applied or exists up to that point, and no further. ▢ *Heather is also 25 and from Boston, but the similarity ends there.* ❾ V-I If you **end** by doing something or **end in a particular state**, you do that thing or get into that state even though you did not originally intend to. ▢ *They ended by making themselves miserable.* ❿ PHRASE If someone **ends it all**, they kill themselves. ▢ *He grew suicidal, thinking up ways to end it all.*

③ **end** ♦♦♦ /ɛnd/ (ends, ending, ended)
▶ **end up** ❶ PHRASAL VERB If someone or something **ends up** somewhere, they eventually arrive there, usually by accident. ▢ *She fled with her children, moving from neighbor to neighbor and ending up in a friend's basement.* ❷ PHRASAL VERB If you **end up** doing something or **end up** in a particular state, you do that thing or get into that state even though you did not originally intend to. ▢ *If you don't know what you want, you might end up getting something you don't want.* ▢ *Every time they went dancing they ended up in a bad mood.*

SYNONYMS

end
NOUN ① ❶
close: *As 1999 drew to a close, the story was changing.*
finish: *I intend to continue it and see the job through to the finish.*
ending: *The movie has a Hollywood happy ending.*
stop: *His daughter should have stood up and put a stop to all these rumors.*
VERB ② ❶
finish: *The teaching day finishes around 4pm.*
stop: *The music stopped and the lights were turned up.*
halt: *He criticized the government for failing to halt economic decline.*
cease: *At one o'clock the rain had ceased.*
terminate: *Her next remark abruptly terminated the conversation.*

---

en|dan|ger /ɪndeɪndʒər/ (endangers, endangering, endangered) ❶ V-T To **endanger** something or someone means to put them in a situation where they might be harmed or destroyed completely. ▢ *The debate could endanger the proposed Mideast peace talks.* ❷ → See feature box at **deforest**

VOCABULARY IN CONTEXT

Endangered animals

Animals become **endangered** for a number of different reasons. Some, such as the black rhino or the Sumatran elephant, are **hunted** for the **ivory** that their **horns** or **tusks** provide. Others, such as the Bornean orangutan, and many species of tiger and gorilla, become endangered when their **habitats** are destroyed to provide land for housing or farming, or by pollution from factories or garbage. But by far the most worrying addition to the list of endangered species in recent years is bees. Any animal that becomes extinct or **critically-endangered** creates an irreversible **knock-on effect** to the **ecosystem**. However, bees **pollinate** many plants which humans and animals alike rely on as a source of food. The disappearance of bees could create an international **food crisis** with **devastating effects** in as little as a few years.

---

en|dan|gered spe|cies (endangered species) N-COUNT An **endangered species** is an animal species that is in danger of becoming extinct. ▢ *The beetles are on the list of endangered species.*
en|dear /ɪndɪər/ (endears, endearing, endeared) V-T If something **endears** you to someone or if you **endear** yourself

endearing

to them, you become popular with them and well liked by them. ❏ *Their taste for gambling has endeared them to Las Vegas casino owners.*

en|dear|ing /ɪndɪərɪŋ/ ADJ [v-link ADJ] If you describe someone's behavior as **endearing**, you mean that it causes you to feel very fond of them. ❏ *She has such an endearing personality.*

en|dear|ment /ɪndɪərmənt/ (**endearments**) N-VAR An **endearment** is a loving or affectionate word or phrase that you say to someone you love. ❏ *No term of endearment crossed their lips.* ❏ *...flattering endearments.*

en|deav|or /ɪndɛvər/ (**endeavors, endeavoring, endeavored**)

> in BRIT, use **endeavour**

1 V-T If you **endeavor** to do something, you try very hard to do it. [FORMAL] ❏ *They are endeavoring to protect labor union rights.* **2** N-VAR An **endeavor** is an attempt to do something, especially something new or original. [FORMAL] ❏ *The company's creative endeavors are thriving.* ❏ *Extracting information about the large-scale composition of a planet from a sample weighing a millionth of a gram was a fascinating example of scientific endeavor.*

en|dem|ic /ɛndɛmɪk/ **1** ADJ If a disease or illness is **endemic** in a place, it is frequently found among the people who live there. [TECHNICAL] ❏ *Polio was then endemic among children my age.* **2** ADJ If you say that a condition or problem is **endemic**, you mean that it is very common and strong, and cannot be dealt with easily. [WRITTEN] ❏ *Nepotism and corruption seem to be endemic in the system.*

end|game /ɛndgeɪm/ (**endgames**) **1** N-VAR In chess, **endgame** refers to the final stage of a game, when only a few pieces are left on the board and one of the players must win soon. **2** N-COUNT Journalists sometimes refer to the final stages of something such as a war, dispute, or contest as an **endgame**. [JOURNALISM] ❏ *The political endgame is getting closer.*

end|ing /ɛndɪŋ/ (**endings**) **1** N-COUNT You can refer to the last part of a book, story, play, or movie as the **ending**, especially when you are considering the way that the story ends. ❏ *The movie has a Hollywood happy ending.* **2** N-COUNT The **ending** of a word is the last part of it. ❏ *...common word endings, like "ing" in walking.* **3** → see also **end** ②

en|dive /ɛndaɪv/ (**endives**) **1** N-VAR **Endive** is a type of plant with bitter-tasting leaves that are eaten in salads, and roots that can be cooked and used instead of coffee. [AM]

> in BRIT, use **chicory**

2 N-VAR **Endive** is a type of plant with crisp curly leaves that is eaten in salads.

end|less /ɛndlɪs/ ADJ If you say that something is **endless**, you mean that it is very large or lasts for a very long time, and it seems as if it will never stop. ❏ *...the endless hours I spent on homework.* ● **end|less|ly** ADV ❏ *They talk about it endlessly.*

endo|crine /ɛndəkraɪn/ ADJ [ADJ n] The **endocrine** system is the system of glands that produce hormones for the bloodstream, such as the pituitary or thyroid glands. [MEDICAL]

en|dorse /ɪndɔrs/ (**endorses, endorsing, endorsed**) **1** V-T If you **endorse** someone or something, you say publicly that you support or approve of them. ❏ *I can endorse their opinion wholeheartedly.* **2** V-T If you **endorse** a product or company, you appear in advertisements for it. ❏ *The twins endorsed a line of household cleaning products.*

en|dorse|ment /ɪndɔrsmənt/ (**endorsements**) **1** N-COUNT An **endorsement** is a statement or action that shows you support or approval of something or someone. ❏ *This is a powerful endorsement for his softer style of government.* **2** N-COUNT An **endorsement** for a product or company involves appearing in advertisements for it or showing support for it. ❏ *His commercial endorsements for everything from running shoes to breakfast cereals will take his earnings to more than ten million dollars a year.*

en|dow /ɪndaʊ/ (**endows, endowing, endowed**) **1** V-T [usu passive] You say that someone **is endowed** with a particular desirable ability, characteristic, or possession when they have it by chance or by birth. ❏ *You are endowed with wealth, good health and a lively intellect.* **2** V-T If you **endow** something **with** a

energy

particular feature or quality, you provide it with that feature or quality. ❏ *Herbs have been used for centuries to endow a whole range of foods with subtle flavors.* **3** V-T If someone **endows** an institution, scholarship, or project, they provide a large amount of money that will produce the income needed to pay for it. ❏ *The ambassador has endowed a $1 million public-service fellowships program.*

en|dow|ment /ɪndaʊmənt/ (**endowments**) N-COUNT An **endowment** is a gift of money that is made to an institution or community in order to provide it with an annual income. ❏ *...the National Endowment for the Arts.*

end prod|uct (**end products**) N-COUNT [oft N of n] The **end product** of something is the thing that is produced or achieved by means of it. ❏ *It is the end product of exhaustive research and development.*

end re|sult (**end results**) N-COUNT The **end result** of an activity or a process is the final result that it produces. ❏ *The end result is very good and very successful.*

en|dur|ance /ɪndʊrəns/ N-UNCOUNT **Endurance** is the ability to continue with an unpleasant or difficult situation, experience, or activity over a long period of time. ❏ *The exercise obviously will improve strength and endurance.*

en|dure /ɪndʊər/ (**endures, enduring, endured**) **1** V-T If you **endure** a painful or difficult situation, you experience it and do not avoid it or give up, usually because you cannot. ❏ *The company endured heavy financial losses.* **2** V-I If something **endures**, it continues to exist without any loss in quality or importance. ❏ *Somehow the language endures and continues to survive.* ● **en|dur|ing** ADJ ❏ *This chance meeting was the start of an enduring friendship.*

end user (**end users**) N-COUNT The **end user** of a piece of equipment is the user that it has been designed for, rather than the person who installs or maintains it. [COMPUTING] ❏ *You have to be able to describe things in a form that the end user can understand.*

end zone (**end zones**) N-COUNT In football, an **end zone** is one of the areas at each end of the field that the ball must cross for a touchdown to be scored.

en|ema /ɛnɪmə/ (**enemas**) N-COUNT If someone has an **enema**, a liquid is put into their rectum in order to make them empty their bowels, for example before they have an operation.

en|emy ✦✧ /ɛnəmi/ (**enemies**) **1** N-COUNT If someone is your **enemy**, they hate you or want to harm you. ❏ *Imagine loving your enemy and doing good to those who hated you.* **2** N-COUNT If someone is your **enemy**, they are opposed to you and to what you think or do. ❏ *Her political enemies were quick to pick up on this series of disasters.* **3** N-SING-COLL [the n, N n] The **enemy** is an army or other force that is opposed to you in a war, or a country with which your country is at war. ❏ *The enemy were pursued for two miles.* **4** N-COUNT If one thing is the **enemy of** another thing, the second thing cannot happen or succeed because of the first thing. [FORMAL] ❏ *Reform, as we know, is the enemy of revolution.*

en|er|get|ic /ɛnərdʒɛtɪk/ **1** ADJ If you are **energetic** in what you do, you have a lot of enthusiasm and determination. ❏ *Ibrahim is 59, strong looking, enormously energetic and accomplished.* ● **en|er|geti|cal|ly** /ɛnərdʒɛtɪkli/ ADV [ADV with v] ❏ *He had worked energetically all day on his new book.* **2** ADJ An **energetic** person is very active and does not feel at all tired. An **energetic** activity involves a lot of physical movement and power. ❏ *Ten year-olds are incredibly energetic.* ● **en|er|geti|cal|ly** ADV [ADV with v] ❏ *David chewed energetically on the gristly steak.*

en|er|gize /ɛnərdʒaɪz/ (**energizes, energizing, energized**)

> in BRIT, also use **energise**

V-T To **energize** someone means to give them the enthusiasm and determination to do something. ❏ *He helped energize and mobilize millions of people around the nation.* ❏ *I am completely energized and feeling terrific.* ● **en|er|giz|ing** ADJ ❏ *Acupuncture has a harmonizing and energizing effect on mind and body.*

en|er|gy ✦✦✧ /ɛnərdʒi/ (**energies**) **1** N-UNCOUNT **Energy** is the ability and strength to do active physical things and the feeling that you are full of physical power and life. ❏ *He was saving his* energy for next week's race in Tucson. **2** N-UNCOUNT **Energy** is determination and enthusiasm about doing things. [APPROVAL] ☐ *You have drive and energy for those things you are interested in.* **3** N-COUNT Your **energies** are the efforts and attention that you can direct toward a particular aim. ☐ *She had started to devote her energies to teaching rather than performing.* **4** N-UNCOUNT **Energy** is the power from sources such as electricity and coal that makes machines work or provides heat. ☐ *...those who favor nuclear energy.* **5** → See feature box at **electricity, recycle**

COLLOCATIONS

energy
NOUN
1
verb + **energy**: expend, waste; conserve, save
4
noun + **energy**: wave, wind
adjective + **energy**: alternative, clean, green, low-carbon, renewable; atomic, nuclear, solar
verb + **energy**: generate, produce; conserve, save; waste

---

energy-efficient also **energy efficient** ADJ A device or building that is **energy-efficient** uses relatively little energy to provide the power it needs. ☐ *...energy-efficient light bulbs.* ☐ *...information on how to make your home more energy efficient.*

en|er|vat|ed /ˈɛnərveɪtɪd/ ADJ If you feel **enervated**, you feel tired and weak. [FORMAL]

en|er|vat|ing /ˈɛnərveɪtɪŋ/ ADJ Something that is **enervating** makes you feel tired and weak. [FORMAL]

en|fant ter|ri|ble /ɒnfɒn tɛriblə/ (**enfants terribles**) N-COUNT [usu sing, usu the N of n] If you describe someone as an **enfant terrible**, you mean that they are clever but unconventional, and often cause problems or embarrassment for their friends or families. [LITERARY] ☐ *He became known as the enfant terrible of Chicago theater.*

en|fee|bled /ɪnˈfiːbəld/ ADJ If someone or something is **enfeebled**, they have become very weak. [FORMAL] ☐ *He finds himself politically enfeebled.* ☐ *...the already enfeebled newspaper.*

en|fold /ɪnˈfoʊld/ (**enfolds, enfolding, enfolded**) **1** V-T If something **enfolds** an object or person, it covers, surrounds, or is wrapped around that object or person. [LITERARY] ☐ *Aurora felt the opium haze enfold her.* ☐ *Winona was now comfortably enfolded in a woolly dressing-gown.* **2** V-T If you **enfold** someone or something, you hold them close in a very gentle, loving way. [LITERARY] ☐ *Ted came up behind him, enfolding him in his arms.*

en|force /ɪnˈfɔːrs/ (**enforces, enforcing, enforced**) **1** V-T If people in authority **enforce** a law or a rule, they make sure that it is obeyed, usually by punishing people who do not obey it. ☐ *Boulder was one of the first cities in the nation to enforce a ban on smoking.* **2** V-T To **enforce** something means to force or cause it to be done or to happen. ☐ *They struggled to limit the cost by enforcing a low-tech specification.* **3** → See feature box at **football**

en|force|able /ɪnˈfɔːrsəbəl/ ADJ If something such as a law or agreement is **enforceable**, it can be enforced. ☐ *...the creation of legally enforceable contracts.*

en|force|ment /ɪnˈfɔːrsmənt/ N-UNCOUNT If someone carries out the **enforcement** of an act or rule, they enforce it. ☐ *The doctors want stricter enforcement of existing laws.*

en|fran|chise /ɪnˈfræntʃaɪz/ (**enfranchises, enfranchising, enfranchised**) V-T To **enfranchise** someone means to give them the right to vote in elections. [FORMAL] ☐ *The company voted to enfranchise its 120 women members.*

en|fran|chise|ment /ɪnˈfræntʃaɪzmənt/ N-UNCOUNT [oft N of n] **Enfranchisement** is the condition of someone being enfranchised. [FORMAL] ☐ *...a time of working-class enfranchisement.*

en|gage /ɪnˈgeɪdʒ/ (**engages, engaging, engaged**) **1** V-I If you **engage in** an activity, you do it or are actively involved with it. [FORMAL] ☐ *I have never engaged in drug trafficking.* **2** V-T If something **engages** you or your attention or interest, it keeps you interested in it and thinking about it. ☐ *They never learned skills to engage the attention of the others.* **3** V-T If you **engage** someone **in** conversation, you have a conversation with them. ☐ *They tried to engage him in conversation.* **4** V-I If you **engage with** something or **with** a group of people, you get involved with that thing or group and feel that you are connected with it or have real contact with it. ☐ *She found it hard to engage with office life.* • **en|gage|ment** N-UNCOUNT ☐ *...the candidate's apparent lack of engagement with younger voters.* **5** V-T If you **engage** someone to do a particular job, you appoint them to do it. [FORMAL] ☐ *We engaged the services of a famous engineer.* **6** → see also **engaged, engaging**

en|gaged /ɪnˈgeɪdʒd/ **1** ADJ [v-link ADJ in/on n] Someone who is **engaged in** a particular activity is doing that thing. [FORMAL] ☐ *...the various projects he was engaged in.* **2** ADJ When two people are **engaged**, they have agreed to marry each other. ☐ *We got engaged on my eighteenth birthday.* **3** ADJ If a telephone or a telephone line is **engaged**, it is already being used by someone else so that you are unable to speak to the person you are phoning. [BRIT]

in AM, use **busy**

4 ADJ If a public toilet is **engaged**, it is already being used by someone else. [mainly BRIT]

in AM, usually use **occupied**

en|gaged tone [BRIT] → see **busy signal**

en|gage|ment /ɪnˈgeɪdʒmənt/ (**engagements**) **1** N-COUNT An **engagement** is an arrangement that you have made to do something at a particular time. [FORMAL] ☐ *He had an engagement at a restaurant at eight.* **2** N-COUNT An **engagement** is an agreement that two people have made with each other to get married. ☐ *I've broken off my engagement to Arthur.* **3** N-COUNT You can refer to the period of time during which two people are engaged as their **engagement**. ☐ *We spoke every night during our engagement.* **4** N-VAR A military **engagement** is an armed conflict between two enemies. ☐ *The constitution prohibits them from military engagement on foreign soil.* **5** → see also **engage**

en|gage|ment ring (**engagement rings**) N-COUNT An **engagement ring** is a ring worn by someone who is engaged to be married.

en|gag|ing /ɪnˈgeɪdʒɪŋ/ ADJ An **engaging** person or thing is pleasant, interesting, and entertaining. ☐ *...one of her most engaging and least known novels.*

en|gen|der /ɪnˈdʒɛndər/ (**engenders, engendering, engendered**) V-T If someone or something **engenders** a particular feeling, atmosphere, or situation, they cause it to occur. [FORMAL] ☐ *It helps engender a sense of common humanity.*

en|gine ♦◇◇ /ˈɛndʒɪn/ (**engines**) **1** N-COUNT The **engine** of a car or other vehicle is the part that produces the power which makes the vehicle move. ☐ *He got into the driving seat and started the engine.* **2** N-COUNT An **engine** is also the large vehicle that pulls a train. ☐ *In 1941, the train would have been pulled by a steam engine.* **3** → See also color supplement

-engined /ˈɛndʒɪnd/ COMB IN ADJ **-engined** combines with other words to show the number or type of engines that something has. ☐ *...the world's biggest twin-engined airliner.*

en|gi|neer ♦◇◇ /ˌɛndʒɪˈnɪər/ (**engineers, engineering, engineered**) **1** N-COUNT An **engineer** is a person who uses scientific knowledge to design, construct, and maintain engines and machines or structures such as roads, railroads, and bridges. **2** N-COUNT An **engineer** is a person who repairs mechanical or electrical devices. ☐ *They will send a service engineer to fix it.* **3** N-COUNT An **engineer** is a person who is responsible for maintaining the engine of a ship while it is at sea. **4** V-T [usu passive] When a vehicle, bridge, or building **is engineered**, it is planned and constructed using scientific methods. ☐ *Its spaceship was engineered by Bert Rutan, renowned for designing the Voyager.* **5** V-T If you **engineer** an event or situation, you arrange for it to happen, in a clever or indirect way. ☐ *Some people believe that his murder was engineered by Stalin.*

en|gi|neer|ing ♦◇◇ /ˌɛndʒɪˈnɪərɪŋ/ **1** N-UNCOUNT **Engineering** is the work involved in designing and constructing engines and machinery or structures such as roads and bridges. **Engineering** is also the subject studied by people who want to do this work. ☐ *...graduates with degrees in engineering.* **2** → see also **genetic engineering**

en|gine room (**engine rooms**) N-COUNT On a boat or a ship, the **engine room** is the place where the engines are.

2 N-COUNT [oft the N of n] If you refer to something as the **engine room** of an organization or institution, you mean it is the most important or influential part of that organization or institution. ❑ *These firms are regarded as the engine room of the economy.*

Eng|lish ✦✧ /ɪ́ŋglɪʃ/ **1** N-UNCOUNT **English** is the language spoken by people who live in Great Britain and Ireland, the United States, Canada, Australia, and many other countries. **2** ADJ **English** means belonging or relating to England, or to its people or language. It is also often used to mean belonging or relating to Great Britain, although many people object to this. ❑ *...the English way of life.* • N-PLURAL **The English** are English people. ❑ *It is often said that the English are reserved.*

Eng|lish|man /ɪ́ŋglɪʃmən/ (**Englishmen**) N-COUNT An **Englishman** is a man who comes from England.

Eng|lish muf|fin (**English muffins**) N-COUNT **English muffins** are flat, round bread rolls that you split in half and usually eat hot with butter. [AM] ❑ *You can even get peanut butter and jelly on an English muffin for breakfast.*

Eng|lish|woman /ɪ́ŋglɪʃwʊmən/ (**Englishwomen**) N-COUNT An **Englishwoman** is a woman who comes from England.

en|gorged /ɪngɔ́ːrdʒd/ ADJ [oft ADJ with n] Something that is **engorged** is swollen, usually because it has been filled with a particular fluid. ❑ *The tissues become engorged with blood.*

en|grave /ɪngreɪv/ (**engraves, engraving, engraved**) V-T If you **engrave** something with a design or words, or if you **engrave** a design or words on it, you cut the design or words into its surface. ❑ *Your wedding ring can be engraved with a personal inscription at no extra cost.* ❑ *The store will also engrave your child's name on the side.* ❑ *...a bottle engraved with her name.*

en|graved /ɪngreɪvd/ ADJ [v-link ADJ in/on/upon n] If you say that something is **engraved** on your mind or memory or on your heart, you are emphasizing that you will never forget it, because it has made a very strong impression on you. [EMPHASIS] ❑ *Her image is engraved upon my heart.*

en|grav|er /ɪngreɪvər/ (**engravers**) N-COUNT An **engraver** is someone who cuts designs or words on metal, glass, or wood.

en|grav|ing /ɪngreɪvɪŋ/ (**engravings**) **1** N-COUNT An **engraving** is a picture or design that has been cut into a surface. **2** N-COUNT An **engraving** is a picture that has been printed from a plate on which designs have been cut. ❑ *...a color engraving of oranges and lemons.*

en|grossed /ɪngroʊst/ ADJ If you are **engrossed** in something, it holds your attention completely. ❑ *Tony didn't notice because he was too engrossed in his work.*

en|gross|ing /ɪngroʊsɪŋ/ ADJ Something that is **engrossing** is very interesting and holds your attention completely. [APPROVAL] ❑ *He is an engrossing subject for a book.*

en|gulf /ɪngʌ́lf/ (**engulfs, engulfing, engulfed**) **1** V-T If one thing **engulfs** another, it completely covers or hides it, often in a sudden and unexpected way. ❑ *A seven-year-old boy was found dead after a landslide engulfed an apartment block.* **2** V-T If a feeling or emotion **engulfs** you, you are strongly affected by it. ❑ *...the pain that engulfed him.*

en|hance ✦✧ /ɪnhǽns/ (**enhances, enhancing, enhanced**) V-T To **enhance** something means to improve its value, quality, or attractiveness. ❑ *The White House is eager to protect and enhance that reputation.*

▶ **SYNONYMS** ◀

enhance
VERB
improve: *He said he was going to improve his football skills.*
strengthen: *The dollar strengthened against most other currencies.*
embellish: *Ivy leaves embellish the front of the dresser.*
perfect: *...girls who needed to perfect their English.*
polish: *They just need to polish their technique.*

en|hance|ment /ɪnhǽnsmənt/ (**enhancements**) N-VAR The **enhancement** of something is the improvement of it in relation to its value, quality, or attractiveness. [FORMAL] ❑ *Music is merely an enhancement to the power of her words.*

en|hanc|er /ɪnhǽnsər/ (**enhancers**) N-COUNT [usu n N] An **enhancer** is a substance or a device that makes a particular thing look, taste, or feel better. ❑ *Cinnamon is an excellent flavor enhancer.*

enig|ma /ɪnɪ́gmə/ (**enigmas**) N-COUNT [usu sing] If you describe something or someone as an **enigma**, you mean they are mysterious or difficult to understand. ❑ *The concept of time management remains an enigma for many.*

en|ig|mat|ic /ɛnɪgmǽtɪk/ ADJ Someone or something that is **enigmatic** is mysterious and difficult to understand. ❑ *She starred in one of Welles's most enigmatic films.* • **en|ig|mati|cal|ly** ADV ❑ *"Corbiere didn't deserve this," she said enigmatically.*

en|join /ɪndʒɔ́ɪn/ (**enjoins, enjoining, enjoined**) **1** V-T If you **enjoin** someone to do something, you order them to do it. If you **enjoin** an action or attitude, you order people to do it or have it. [FORMAL] ❑ *She enjoined me strictly not to tell anyone else.* ❑ *Islam enjoins tolerance.* **2** V-T If a judge **enjoins** someone from doing something, they order them not to do it. If a judge **enjoins** an action, they order people not to do it. [AM, FORMAL] ❑ *The judge enjoined Varityper from using the ad in any way.* ❑ *...a preliminary injunction enjoining the practice.*

en|joy ✦✧ /ɪndʒɔ́ɪ/ (**enjoys, enjoying, enjoyed**) **1** V-T If you **enjoy** something, you find pleasure and satisfaction in doing it or experiencing it. ❑ *Ross had always enjoyed the company of women.* ❑ *He was a guy who enjoyed life to the full.* **2** V-T If you **enjoy** yourself, you do something that you like doing or you take pleasure in the situation that you are in. ❑ *I am really enjoying myself at the moment.* **3** V-T If you **enjoy** something such as a right, benefit, or privilege, you have it. [FORMAL] ❑ *The average German will enjoy 40 days' paid holiday this year.*

▶ **SYNONYMS** ◀

enjoy
VERB **1**
like: *What music do you like best?*
relish: *He ate quietly, relishing his meal.*
take delight in: *Generations of adults and children have taken delight in the story.*
revel in: *Reveling in her freedom, she got a hotel room and stayed for several days.*

en|joy|able /ɪndʒɔ́ɪəbəl/ ADJ Something that is **enjoyable** gives you pleasure. ❑ *It was much more enjoyable than I had expected.*

en|joy|ment /ɪndʒɔ́ɪmənt/ N-UNCOUNT **Enjoyment** is the feeling of pleasure and satisfaction that you have when you do or experience something that you like. ❑ *I apologize if your enjoyment of the movie was spoiled.*

en|large /ɪnlɑ́rdʒ/ (**enlarges, enlarging, enlarged**) **1** V-T/V-I When you **enlarge** something or when it **enlarges**, it becomes bigger. ❑ *The college has announced its intention to enlarge its stadium.* **2** V-I If you **enlarge** on something that has been mentioned, you give more details about it. [FORMAL] ❑ *He didn't enlarge on the form that the interim government and assembly would take.*

en|large|ment /ɪnlɑ́rdʒmənt/ (**enlargements**) **1** N-UNCOUNT The **enlargement** of something is the process or result of making it bigger. ❑ *There is insufficient space for enlargement of the buildings.* **2** N-COUNT An **enlargement** is a photograph that has been made bigger. ❑ *Ordering reprints and enlargements is easier than ever.*

en|larg|er /ɪnlɑ́rdʒər/ (**enlargers**) N-COUNT An **enlarger** is a device that makes an image larger.

en|light|en /ɪnlaɪtən/ (**enlightens, enlightening, enlightened**) V-T [no cont] To **enlighten** someone means to give them more knowledge and greater understanding about something. [FORMAL] ❑ *A few dedicated doctors have fought for years to enlighten the profession.* • **en|light|en|ing** ADJ ❑ *...an enlightening talk on the work done at the charity.*

en|light|ened /ɪnlaɪtənd/ ADJ If you describe someone or their attitudes as **enlightened**, you mean that they have sensible, modern attitudes and ways of dealing with things. [APPROVAL] ❑ *...an enlightened policy.*

en|light|en|ment /ɪnlaɪtənmənt/ **1** N-UNCOUNT **Enlightenment** means the act of enlightening or the state of being enlightened. ❑ *Stella had a moment of enlightenment.* **2** N-UNCOUNT In Buddhism, **enlightenment** is a final spiritual state in which everything is understood and there is no more suffering or desire. ❑ *...a sense of deep peace and spiritual enlightenment.*

en|list /ɪnlɪst/ (enlists, enlisting, enlisted) **1** V-T/V-I If someone **enlists** or **is enlisted**, they join the army, navy, marines, or air force. ❑ *He enlisted in the 82nd Airborne 20 years ago.* ❑ *He enlisted as a private in the Mexican War.* **2** V-T If you **enlist** the help of someone, you persuade them to help or support you in doing something. ❑ *I had to cut down a tree and enlist the help of seven neighbors to get it out of the yard!*

en|list|ed /ɪnlɪstɪd/ ADJ [usu ADJ n] An **enlisted** man or woman is a member of the armed forces who is below the rank of officer.

en|list|ment /ɪnlɪstmənt/ (enlistments) **1** N-UNCOUNT **Enlistment** is the act of joining the army, navy, marines, or air force. ❑ *...the enlistment of volunteers in a national service program.* **2** N-VAR **Enlistment** is the period of time for which someone is a member of one of the armed forces. ❑ *At the end of my term of enlistment I decided to return to civilian life.*

en|liv|en /ɪnlaɪvᵊn/ (enlivens, enlivening, enlivened) V-T To **enliven** events, situations, or people means to make them more lively or cheerful. ❑ *Even the most boring meeting was enlivened by Dan's presence.*

en masse /ɒn mæs/ ADV If a group of people do something **en masse**, they do it all together and at the same time. ❑ *The people marched en masse.*

en|meshed /ɪnmɛʃt/ ADJ [v-link ADJ] If you are **enmeshed** in or with something, usually something bad, you are involved in it and cannot easily escape from it. ❑ *All too often they become enmeshed in deadening routines.* ❑ *...as her life gets enmeshed with Andrew's.*

en|mity /ɛnmɪti/ (enmities) N-VAR **Enmity** is a feeling of hatred toward someone that lasts for a long time. ❑ *I think there is an historic enmity between them.*

en|no|ble /ɪnnoʊbᵊl/ (ennobles, ennobling, ennobled) **1** V-T To **ennoble** someone or something means to make them more dignified and morally better. [LITERARY] ❑ *...the enduring fundamental principles of life that ennoble mankind.* • **en|no|bling** ADJ ❑ *...the ennobling and civilizing power of education.* **2** V-T [usu passive] If someone **is ennobled**, they are made a member of a country's nobility. [FORMAL] ❑ *...the son of a financier who had been ennobled.*

en|nui /ɒnwiː/ N-UNCOUNT **Ennui** is a feeling of being tired, bored, and dissatisfied. [LITERARY]

enor|mity /ɪnɔːrmɪti/ **1** N-UNCOUNT If you refer to the **enormity** of something that you consider to be a problem or difficulty, you are referring to its very great size, extent, or seriousness. ❑ *I was numbed by the enormity of the responsibility.* **2** N-UNCOUNT If you refer to the **enormity** of an event, you are emphasizing that it is terrible and frightening. [EMPHASIS] ❑ *...the enormity of the disaster.*

enor|mous ✦✧✧ /ɪnɔːrməs/ **1** ADJ Something that is **enormous** is extremely large in size or amount. ❑ *The main bedroom is enormous.* **2** ADJ You can use **enormous** to emphasize the great degree or extent of something. [EMPHASIS] ❑ *It was an enormous disappointment.* • **enor|mous|ly** ADV ❑ *This book was enormously influential.*

SYNONYMS

enormous
ADJ **1**
huge: *...a tiny, little woman with huge, black glasses.*
vast: *...farmers who own vast stretches of land.*
massive: *...a massive steam boat.*
great: *The room had a great bay window.*
immense: *...an immense cloud of smoke.*
gigantic: *...gigantic rocks.*

---

enough ✦✦✦ /ɪnʌf/ **1** DET **Enough** means as much as you need or as much as is necessary. ❑ *They had enough cash for a one-way ticket.* • ADV **Enough** is also an adverb. ❑ *I was old enough to work and earn money.* ❑ *Do you believe that sentences for criminals are tough enough at present?* • PRON **Enough** is also a pronoun. ❑ *Although the police say efforts are being made, they are not doing enough.* • QUANT [QUANT of def-n] **Enough** is also a quantifier. ❑ *All parents worry about whether their child is getting enough of the right foods.* • ADJ [n ADJ] **Enough** is also an adjective. ❑ *Her disappearance and death would give proof enough of Charles' guilt.* **2** PRON If you say that something is **enough**, you mean that you do not want it to continue any longer or get any worse. ❑ *I met him only the once, and that was enough.* ❑ *I think I have said enough.* • QUANT [QUANT of def-n] **Enough** is also a quantifier. ❑ *Ann had heard enough of this.* • DET **Enough** is also a determiner. ❑ *Would you shut up, please! I'm having enough trouble with these children!* • ADV [adj ADV] **Enough** is also an adverb. ❑ *I'm serious, things are difficult enough as they are.* **3** ADV [adj/adv ADV] You can use **enough** to say that something is the case to a moderate or fairly large degree. ❑ *Winters is a common enough surname.* **4** ADV You use **enough** in expressions such as **strangely enough** and **interestingly enough** to indicate that you think a fact is strange or interesting. ❑ *Strangely enough, the last thing he thought of was his beloved Tanya.* **5** PHRASE If you say that you **have had enough**, you mean that you are unhappy with a situation and you want it to stop. ❑ *I had had enough of other people for one night.* **6 fair enough** → see **fair** **7 sure enough** → see **sure**

en|quire /ɪnkwaɪər/ → see **inquire**

en|quir|er /ɪnkwaɪərər/ → see **inquirer**

en|quiry /ɪnkwaɪəri/ → see **inquiry**

en|rage /ɪnreɪdʒ/ (enrages, enraging, enraged) V-T If you are **enraged** by something, it makes you extremely angry. ❑ *Many were enraged by the discriminatory practice.*

en|rap|ture /ɪnræptʃər/ (enraptures, enrapturing, enraptured) V-T If something or someone **enraptures** you, you think they are wonderful or fascinating. [LITERARY] ❑ *The place at once enraptured me.* ❑ *The 20,000-strong audience listened, enraptured.* ❑ *...an enraptured audience.*

en|rich /ɪnrɪtʃ/ (enriches, enriching, enriched) **1** V-T To **enrich** something means to improve its quality, usually by adding something to it. ❑ *It is important to enrich the soil prior to planting.* **2** V-T To **enrich** someone means to increase the amount of money that they have. ❑ *He will drain, rather than enrich, the country.*

en|rich|ment /ɪnrɪtʃmənt/ N-UNCOUNT **Enrichment** is the act of enriching someone or something or the state of being enriched. ❑ *...the enrichment of society.*

en|roll /ɪnroʊl/ (enrolls, enrolling, enrolled)

in BRIT, use **enrol**

V-T/V-I If you **enroll** or **are enrolled** at an institution or in a class, you officially join it. ❑ *Cherny was enrolled at the University in 1945.* ❑ *Her mother enrolled her in acting classes.*

en|roll|ment /ɪnroʊlmənt/ **1** N-UNCOUNT **Enrollment** is the act of enrolling at an institution or in a class. ❑ *A fee is charged for each year of study and is payable at enrollment.* **2** N-UNCOUNT **Enrollment** is the total number of students enrolled. ❑ *The district's enrollment is expected to stabilize in 2006-07 at 10,200 students.*

en route /ɒn ruːt/ → see **route**

en|sconced /ɪnskɒnst/ ADJ [v-link ADJ] If you are **ensconced** somewhere, you are settled there firmly or comfortably and have no intention of moving or leaving. ❑ *Brian was ensconced behind the bar.*

en|sem|ble /ɒnsɒmbᵊl/ (ensembles) N-COUNT An **ensemble** is a group of musicians, actors, or dancers who regularly perform together. ❑ *...an ensemble of young musicians.*

en|shrine /ɪnʃraɪn/ (enshrines, enshrining, enshrined) V-T If something such as an idea or a right **is enshrined** in something such as a constitution or law, it is protected by it. ❑ *This system is enshrined in our Constitution.* ❑ *The apartheid system which enshrined racism in law still existed.*

en|shroud /ɪnʃraʊd/ (enshrouds, enshrouding, enshrouded) V-T To **enshroud** something means to cover it completely so that it can no longer be seen. [LITERARY] ❑ *...clouds that enshrouded us in twilight.* ❑ *...the culture of secrecy that enshrouds our politics.*

en|sign /ɛnsaɪn, ɛnsᵊn/ (ensigns) **1** N-COUNT An **ensign** is a flag flown on a ship to show what country the ship belongs to. **2** N-COUNT; N-TITLE An **ensign** is a junior officer in the United States Navy or Coast Guard. ❑ *He had been a naval ensign stationed off Cuba.* ❑ *...Ensign Smith.*

en|slave /ɪnsleɪv/ (enslaves, enslaving, enslaved) **1** V-T To **enslave** someone means to make them into a slave. ❑ *They'd been enslaved and had to do what they were told.* ❑ *I'd die myself before*

I'd let anyone enslave your folk ever again. ❏ George was born to an enslaved African mother. **2** V-T To **enslave** a person or society means to trap them in a situation from which they cannot escape. ❏ ...the various cultures, cults and religions that have enslaved human beings for untold years. ❏ It would be a tragedy if both sexes were enslaved to the god of work.

en|slave|ment /ɪnsleɪvmənt/ **1** N-UNCOUNT [oft N of n] **Enslavement** is the act of making someone into a slave or the state of being a slave. ❏ ...the enslavement of African people. **2** N-UNCOUNT **Enslavement** is the state of being trapped in a situation from which it is difficult to escape. ❏ [+ to] He has only ever signed one-year deals to avoid enslavement to the sport.

en|snare /ɪnsneər/ (ensnares, ensnaring, ensnared) **1** V-T If you **ensnare** someone, you gain power over them, especially by using dishonest or deceitful methods. ❏ He was concerned the campaign could ensnare innocent people. ❏ They were ensnared in a legal nightmare. **2** V-T If an animal **is ensnared**, it is caught in a trap. ❏ The spider must wait for prey to be ensnared on its web.

en|sue /ɪnsuː/ (ensues, ensuing, ensued) V-I [no cont] If something **ensues**, it happens immediately after another event, usually as a result of it. ❏ If the Europeans did not reduce subsidies, a trade war would ensue.

en|su|ing /ɪnsuːɪŋ/ **1** ADJ [n] **Ensuing** events happen immediately after other events. ❏ The ensuing argument had been bitter. **2** ADJ [det ADJ] **Ensuing** hours, months, or years follow the time you are talking about. ❏ The two companies grew tenfold in the ensuing ten years.

en suite /ɒn swiːt/ ADJ [ADJ n] An **en suite** bathroom is next to a bedroom and can only be reached by a door in the bedroom. An **en suite** bedroom has an en suite bathroom. [BRIT]

In AM, use **private bathroom**

en|sure ◆◆◇ /ɪnʃʊər/ (ensures, ensuring, ensured) V-T To **ensure** something, or to **ensure** that something happens, means to make certain that it happens. [FORMAL] ❏ We must ensure that all patients have access to high quality care.

SYNONYMS

ensure
VERB
guarantee: Surplus resources alone do not guarantee growth.
secure: Graham's achievements helped secure him the job.
assure: Ways must be found to assure our children a decent start in life.
make certain: To make extra certain, a police helicopter kept watch from the skies.

en|tail /ɪnteɪl/ (entails, entailing, entailed) V-T If one thing **entails** another, it involves it or causes it. [FORMAL] ❏ Such a decision would entail a huge political risk in the midst of the presidential campaign.

en|tan|gle /ɪntæŋgəl/ (entangles, entangling, entangled) **1** V-T If one thing **entangles** itself with another, the two things become caught together very tightly. ❏ The blade of the oar had entangled itself with the strap of her bag. **2** V-T If something **entangles** you in problems or difficulties, it causes you to become involved in problems or difficulties from which it is hard to escape. ❏ Bureaucracy can entangle applications for months.

en|tan|gled /ɪntæŋgəld/ **1** ADJ If something is **entangled** in something such as a rope, wire, or net, it is caught in it very firmly. ❏ Divers battled for hours to try to free a whale entangled in crab nets. **2** ADJ [v-link ADJ] If you become **entangled** in problems or difficulties, you become involved in problems or difficulties from which it is hard to escape. ❏ This case was bound to get entangled in international politics.

en|tan|gle|ment /ɪntæŋgəlmənt/ (entanglements) **1** N-COUNT An **entanglement** is a complicated or difficult relationship or situation. ❏ ...a military and political entanglement the president probably doesn't want. **2** N-VAR If things become entangled, you can refer to this as entanglement. ❏ Many dolphins are accidentally killed through entanglement with fishing equipment.

en|tente /ɒntɒnt/ (ententes) N-VAR An **entente** or an **entente cordiale** is a friendly agreement between two or more countries. ❏ The French entente with Great Britain had already been significantly extended.

en|ter ◆◆◇ /entər/ (enters, entering, entered) **1** V-T/V-I When you **enter** a place such as a room or building, you go into it or come into it. [FORMAL] ❏ He entered the room briskly and stood near the door. ❏ When Spinks entered they all turned to look at him. **2** V-T If you **enter** an organization or institution, you start to work there or become a member of it. ❏ He entered the firm as a junior associate. **3** V-T If something new **enters** your mind, you suddenly think about it. ❏ Dreadful doubts began to enter my mind. **4** V-T [with brd-neg] If it does not **enter** your head to do, think, or say something, you do not think of doing that thing although you should have. ❏ It never enters his mind that anyone is better than him. **5** V-T If someone or something **enters** a particular situation or period of time, they start to be in it or part of it. ❏ The war has entered its second month. ❏ A million young people enter the labor market each year. **6** V-T If you **enter** a competition, race, or examination, you officially state that you will compete or take part in it. ❏ I run so well I'm planning to enter some races. ❏ As a boy soprano he entered many competitions, winning several gold medals. **7** V-T If you **enter** someone for a race or competition, you officially state that they will compete or take part in it. ❏ His wife Marie secretly entered him for the championship. **8** V-T If you **enter** something in a notebook, register, or financial account, you write it down. ❏ Each week she meticulously entered in her notebooks all sums received. **9** V-T To **enter** information into a computer or database means to record it there by typing it on a keyboard. ❏ When a baby is born, they enter that baby's name into the computer.
▶ **enter into** PHRASAL VERB If you **enter into** something such as an agreement, discussion, or relationship, you become involved in it. You can also say that two people **enter into** something. [FORMAL] ❏ I have not entered into any financial agreements with them. ❏ The United States and Canada may enter into an agreement that would allow easier access to jobs across the border.

SYNONYMS

enter
VERB **2**
join: He joined the army five years ago.
enlist: He enlisted as a private in the Mexican War.
enroll: He enrolled in a degree course at London's Royal College of Art.
sign up: He signed up as a steward with P&O Lines.

en|ter|prise ◆◆◇ /entərpraɪz/ (enterprises) **1** N-COUNT An **enterprise** is a company or business. [BUSINESS] ❏ There are plenty of small industrial enterprises. **2** N-COUNT An **enterprise** is something new, difficult, or important that you do or try to do. ❏ Horse breeding is indeed a risky enterprise. **3** N-UNCOUNT **Enterprise** is the activity of managing companies and businesses and starting new ones. [BUSINESS] ❏ He is still involved in voluntary work promoting local enterprise. **4** N-UNCOUNT **Enterprise** is the ability to think of new and effective things to do, together with an eagerness to do them. [APPROVAL] ❏ ...the spirit of enterprise worthy of a free and industrious people.

SYNONYMS

enterprise
NOUN **1**
company: Sheila found some work as a secretary in an insurance company.
firm: ...a firm of chemical engineers.
business: The company was a family business.
operation: Thorn's electronics operation employs around 5,000 people.

en|ter|prise zone (enterprise zones) N-COUNT An **enterprise zone** is an area, usually a depressed or inner-city area, where the government offers advantages in order to attract new businesses. [BUSINESS] ❏ Because it is in an enterprise zone, taxes on non-food items are 3.5% instead of the usual 7%.

en|ter|pris|ing /entərpraɪzɪŋ/ ADJ An **enterprising** person is willing to try out new, unusual ways of doing or achieving something. ❏ Some enterprising members found ways of reducing their expenses or raising their incomes.

en|ter|tain ◆◆◇ /entərteɪn/ (entertains, entertaining, entertained) **1** V-T/V-I If a performer, performance, or activity **entertains** you, it amuses you, interests you, or gives you pleasure. ❏ *They were entertained by top singers, dancers and celebrities.* • **en|ter|tain|ing** ADJ ❏ *To generate new money the sport needs to be more entertaining.* **2** V-T/V-I If you **entertain**, or **entertain** people, you provide food and drink for them, for example, when you have invited them to your house. ❏ *I don't like to entertain guests anymore.* ❏ *He loves to entertain.* • **en|ter|tain|ing** N-UNCOUNT ❏ *...a cozy area for entertaining and relaxing.* **3** V-T If you **entertain** an idea or suggestion, you allow yourself to consider it as possible or as worth thinking about seriously. [FORMAL] ❏ *How foolish I am to entertain doubts.* **4** → See feature box at **socialize**

en|ter|tain|er /ɛntərteɪnər/ (**entertainers**) N-COUNT An **entertainer** is a person whose job is to entertain audiences, for example, by telling jokes, singing, or dancing. ❏ *Some have called him the greatest entertainer of the twentieth century.*

en|ter|tain|ment ✦✧✧ /ɛntərteɪnmənt/ (**entertainments**) N-VAR **Entertainment** consists of performances of plays and movies, and activities such as reading and watching television, that give people pleasure. ❏ *...the world of entertainment and international stardom.*

en|thrall /ɪnθrɔːl/ (**enthralls, enthralling, enthralled**) V-T If you **are enthralled** by something, you enjoy it and give it your complete attention and interest. ❏ *The passengers were enthralled by the scenery.*

en|throne /ɪnθroʊn/ (**enthrones, enthroning, enthroned**) **1** V-T [usu passive] When kings, queens, emperors, or bishops **are enthroned**, they officially take on their role during a special ceremony. [FORMAL] ❏ *Emperor Akihito of Japan has been enthroned in Tokyo.* ❏ *He is expected to be enthroned early next year as the spiritual leader.* **2** V-T If an idea **is enthroned**, it has an important place in people's life or thoughts. [JOURNALISM] ❏ *He was forcing the state to enthrone a particular brand of modernism.*

en|throne|ment /ɪnθroʊnmənt/ (**enthronements**) N-COUNT [usu sing, usu with poss] The **enthronement** of a king, queen, emperor, or bishop is a ceremony in which they officially take on their role. [FORMAL] ❏ *...the enthronement of their new emperor.*

en|thuse /ɪnθuːz/ (**enthuses, enthusing, enthused**) **1** V-I If you **enthuse** about something, you talk about it in a way that shows how excited you are about it. ❏ *Elizabeth David enthuses about the taste, fragrance and character of Provencal cuisine.* **2** V-T If you **are enthused** by something, it makes you feel excited and enthusiastic. ❏ *I was immediately enthused.*

en|thu|si|asm ✦✧✧ /ɪnθuːziæzəm/ (**enthusiasms**) **1** N-VAR **Enthusiasm** is great eagerness to be involved in a particular activity that you like and enjoy or that you think is important. ❏ *Their skill and enthusiasm has gotten them on the team.* **2** N-COUNT An **enthusiasm** is an activity or subject that interests you very much and that you spend a lot of time on. ❏ *Draw him out about his current enthusiasms and future plans.*

COLLOCATIONS

enthusiasm
NOUN **1**
adjective + **enthusiasm**: contagious, infectious; boundless, unbridled; boyish, youthful
verb + **enthusiasm**: express, share, show; dampen, lose; generate, inject, muster

en|thu|si|ast /ɪnθuːziæst/ (**enthusiasts**) N-COUNT An **enthusiast** is a person who is very interested in a particular activity or subject and who spends a lot of time on it. ❏ *He is a great sports enthusiast.*

en|thu|si|as|tic /ɪnθuːziæstɪk/ ADJ If you are **enthusiastic** about something, you show how much you like or enjoy it by the way that you behave and talk. ❏ *Tom was very enthusiastic about the place.* • **en|thu|si|as|ti|cal|ly** /ɪnθuːziæstɪkli/ ADV ❏ *The announcement was greeted enthusiastically.*

en|tice /ɪntaɪs/ (**entices, enticing, enticed**) V-T To **entice** someone to go somewhere or to do something means to try to persuade them to go to that place or to do that thing. ❏ *They'll entice thousands of doctors to move from the cities to the rural areas by paying them better salaries.* ❏ *Retailers have tried almost everything, from cheap credit to free flights, to entice shoppers through their doors.*

en|tice|ment /ɪntaɪsmənt/ (**enticements**) N-VAR An **enticement** is something that makes people want to do a particular thing. ❏ *...a second disk that offers, among other enticements, an interactive tour of Hogwarts.*

en|tic|ing /ɪntaɪsɪŋ/ ADJ Something that is **enticing** is extremely attractive and makes you want to get it or to become involved with it. ❏ *A prospective premium of about 30 percent on their initial investment is enticing.*

en|tire ✦✦✧ /ɪntaɪər/ ADJ [det ADJ] You use **entire** when you want to emphasize that you are referring to the whole of something, for example, the whole of a place, time, or population. [EMPHASIS] ❏ *He had spent his entire life in China as a doctor.* ❏ *There are only 60 swimming pools in the entire country.*

SYNONYMS

entire
ADJ
whole: *We spent the whole summer in Italy that year.*
complete: *A complete city block was burned to the ground.*

en|tire|ly ✦✦✧ /ɪntaɪərli/ **1** ADV **Entirely** means completely and not just partly. ❏ *...an entirely new approach.* ❏ *Their price depended almost entirely on their scarcity.* ❏ *This administration is not entirely free of suspicion.* **2** ADV **Entirely** is also used to emphasize what you are saying. [EMPHASIS] ❏ *I agree entirely.*

SYNONYMS

entirely
ADV **1**
completely: *...something completely different.*
totally: *Young people want something totally different from the old ways.*
wholly: *For urban areas this approach was wholly inadequate.*
utterly: *Everything about the country seemed utterly different from what I remembered.*

en|tirety /ɪntaɪərti, -taɪriti/ PHRASE If something is used or affected **in its entirety**, the whole of it is used or affected. ❏ *The peace plan has not been accepted in its entirety by all parties.*

en|ti|tle ✦✧✧ /ɪntaɪt°l/ (**entitles, entitling, entitled**) **1** V-T If you **are entitled** to something, you have the right to have it or do it. ❏ *If the warranty is limited, the terms may entitle you to a replacement or refund.* ❏ *They are entitled to first class travel.* **2** V-T [usu passive] If the title of something such as a book, movie, or painting is, for example, 'Sunrise,' you can say that it **is entitled** 'Sunrise.' ❏ *...a performance entitled "United States."*

en|ti|tle|ment /ɪntaɪt°lmənt/ (**entitlements**) N-VAR An **entitlement** to something is the right to have it or do it. [FORMAL] ❏ *They lose their entitlement to welfare when they start work.*

en|tity /ɛntɪti/ (**entities**) N-COUNT An **entity** is something that exists separately from other things and has a clear identity of its own. [FORMAL] ❏ *...the earth as a living entity.*

en|tomb /ɪntuːm/ (**entombs, entombing, entombed**) **1** V-T If something **is entombed**, it is buried or permanently trapped by something. [FORMAL] ❏ *The city was entombed in volcanic lava.* ❏ *The Tel, an artificial mountain, entombs Jericho's ancient past.* **2** V-T [usu passive] When a person's dead body **is entombed**, it is buried in a grave or put into a tomb. [FORMAL] ❏ *Neither of them had any idea how long the body had been entombed.*

ento|mol|ogy /ɛntəmɒlədʒi/ N-UNCOUNT **Entomology** is the study of insects. • **ento|molo|gist** /ɛntəmɒlədʒɪst/ (**entomologists**) N-COUNT ❏ *...a research entomologist.*

en|tou|rage /ɒntʊrɑːʒ/ (**entourages**) N-COUNT A famous or important person's **entourage** is the group of assistants, servants, or other people who travel with them. ❏ *Rachel was quickly whisked away by her entourage.*

en|trails /ɛntreɪlz, -trəlz/ N-PLURAL The **entrails** of people or animals are their inside parts, especially their intestines.

ENTRANCE
① NOUN USES
② VERB USE

① **en|trance** ✦✦✧ /ɛntrəns/ (**entrances**) **1** N-COUNT The **entrance** to a place is the way into it, for example, a door or gate. ❏ *Beside the entrance to the church, turn right.* ❏ *He was driven out of a side entrance with his hand covering his face.* **2** N-COUNT You can refer to someone's arrival in a place as their **entrance**, especially when you think that they are trying to be noticed and admired. ☐ *If she had noticed her father's entrance, she gave no indication.* ❸ N-COUNT When a performer makes his or her **entrance** onto the stage, he or she comes onto the stage. ☐ *When he made his entrance on stage there was uproar.* ❹ N-UNCOUNT If you gain **entrance** to a particular place, you manage to get in there. [FORMAL] ☐ *Hewitt had gained entrance to the Hall by pretending to be a heating engineer.* ❺ N-UNCOUNT If you gain **entrance** to a particular profession, society, or institution, you are accepted as a member of it. ☐ *Many students have insufficient science and mathematics background to gain entrance to engineering school.* ❻ N-SING If you make an **entrance** into a particular activity or system, you succeed in becoming involved in it. ☐ *The acquisition helped BCCI make its initial entrance into the U.S. market.*

SYNONYMS

entrance
NOUN ①❷
entry: *He made his triumphant entry into Mexico City.*
arrival: *He was dead on arrival at the nearby hospital.*
appearance: *...last Christmas, when there'd been the welcome appearance of Cousin Fred.*

---

② **en|trance** /ɪntrɑːns/ (**entrances, entrancing, entranced**) V-T If something or someone **entrances** you, they cause you to feel delight and wonder, often so that all your attention is taken up and you cannot think about anything else. ☐ *As soon as I met Dick, he entranced me because he has a lovely voice.* • **en|tranced** ADJ ☐ *He is entranced by the kindness of her smile.*

en|trance fee (**entrance fees**) N-COUNT An **entrance fee** is a sum of money that you pay before you enter a place such as an amusement park or museum, or that you have to pay in order to join an organization or institution.

en|trance hall (**entrance halls**) N-COUNT The **entrance hall** of a large house, hotel, or other large building, is the area just inside the main door.

en|trant /ˈɛntrənt/ (**entrants**) ❶ N-COUNT An **entrant** is a person who is taking part in a competition. ☐ *All items entered for the competition must be the entrant's own work.* ❷ N-COUNT An **entrant** is a person or company who has recently become a member of an institution or market. ☐ *...the company that made a name for itself as an early entrant in the digital video-recorder market.*

en|trap /ɪntræp/ (**entraps, entrapping, entrapped**) V-T If you **entrap** someone, you trick or deceive them and make them believe or do something wrong. [FORMAL] ☐ *The police have been given extra powers to entrap drug traffickers.* ☐ *He claimed the government had entrapped him into doing something that he would not have done otherwise.*

en|trap|ment /ɪntræpmənt/ N-UNCOUNT **Entrapment** is the practice of arresting someone by using unfair or illegal methods. [LEGAL] ☐ *...allegations of police entrapment.*

en|treat /ɪntriːt/ (**entreats, entreating, entreated**) V-T If you **entreat** someone to do something, you ask them very politely and seriously to do it. [FORMAL] ☐ *He entreated them to delay their departure.* ☐ *"Call me Earl!" he entreated.*

en|treaty /ɪntriːti/ (**entreaties**) N-VAR [oft N *to* n] An **entreaty** is a very polite, serious request. [FORMAL] ☐ *She declined the Republican Party's entreaties to run for his seat.*

en|trée /ˈɒntreɪ/ (**entrées**) also **entree** ❶ N-COUNT [oft N *into* n] If you have an **entrée** to a social group, you are accepted and made to feel welcome by them. ☐ *She had an entree into the city's cultivated society.* ❷ N-COUNT At restaurants or formal dinners, the **entrée** is the main course, or sometimes a dish before the main course. ☐ *Dinner features a hot entrée of chicken, veal, or lamb.*

en|trench /ɪntrɛntʃ/ (**entrenches, entrenching, entrenched**) V-T If something such as power, a custom, or an idea is **entrenched**, it is firmly established, so that it would be difficult to change it. ☐ *...a series of measures designed to entrench democracy and the rule of law.* • **en|trenched** ADJ ☐ *The recession remains deeply entrenched.*

en|trench|ment /ɪntrɛntʃmənt/ (**entrenchments**) ❶ N-COUNT [usu pl] **Entrenchments** are a series of long deep holes called trenches that are dug for defense by soldiers in war. ❷ N-UNCOUNT **Entrenchment** means the firm establishment of a system or your own position in a situation. ☐ *...the entrenchment of democratic norms.*

en|tre|pre|neur /ˌɒntrəprəˈnɜːr, -ˈnʊər/ (**entrepreneurs**) ❶ N-COUNT An **entrepreneur** is a person who sets up businesses and business deals. [BUSINESS] ❷ → See feature box at **business**

en|tre|pre|neur|ial /ˌɒntrəprəˈnɜːriəl, -ˈnʊər-/ ADJ **Entrepreneurial** means having the qualities that are needed to succeed as an entrepreneur. [BUSINESS] ☐ *...her prodigious entrepreneurial flair.*

en|tre|pre|neur|ship /ˌɒntrəprəˈnɜːrʃɪp, -ˈnʊər-/ N-UNCOUNT **Entrepreneurship** is the state of being an entrepreneur, or the activities associated with being an entrepreneur.

en|tro|py /ˈɛntrəpi/ N-UNCOUNT **Entropy** is a state of disorder, confusion, and disorganization. [TECHNICAL]

en|trust /ɪntrʌst/ (**entrusts, entrusting, entrusted**) V-T If you **entrust** something important to someone or **entrust** them with it, you make them responsible for looking after it or dealing with it. ☐ *He entrusted his cash to a business partner for investment in a series of projects.* ☐ *They can be entrusted to solve major national problems.*

en|try ♦♦◊ /ˈɛntri/ (**entries**) ❶ N-UNCOUNT If you gain **entry** to a particular place, you are able to go in. ☐ *You can gain entry to the club only through a member.* ☐ *Entry to the museum is free.* • PHRASE **No Entry** is used on signs to indicate that you are not allowed to go into a particular area or go through a particular door or gate. ❷ N-COUNT You can refer to someone's arrival in a place as their **entry**, especially when you think that they are trying to be noticed and admired. ☐ *He made his triumphal entry into Mexico City.* ❸ N-UNCOUNT Someone's **entry** into a particular society or group is their joining of it. ☐ *...China's entry into the World Trade Organization.* ❹ N-COUNT An **entry** in a diary, account book, computer file, or reference book is a short piece of writing in it. ☐ *Violet's diary entry for April 20, 1917 records Brigit admitting to the affair.* ❺ N-COUNT An **entry** for a competition is a piece of work, a story or drawing, or the answers to a set of questions, which you complete in order to take part in the competition. ☐ *The closing date for entries is December 31.* ❻ N-SING Journalists sometimes use **entry** to refer to the total number of people taking part in an event or competition. For example, if a competition has an **entry** of twenty people, twenty people take part in it. ☐ *Our competition has attracted a huge entry.* ❼ N-UNCOUNT **Entry** in a competition is the act of taking part in it. ☐ *Entry to this competition is by invitation only.* ❽ N-COUNT The **entry** to a place is the way into it, for example a door or gate. ☐ *...the towering marble archway that marked the entry to the Pelican Point development.*

COLLOCATIONS

entry
NOUN
❶
noun + **entry**: museum
adjective + **entry**: direct, free; forced, unlawful
verb + **entry**: gain, seek; grant, guarantee, permit; bar, deny, prevent, refuse
❹
noun + **entry**: diary, dictionary, journal
❺
adjective + **entry**: winning
verb + **entry**: send, submit; judge

---

entry-level ❶ ADJ **Entry-level** is used to describe basic low-cost versions of products such as cars or computers that are suitable for people who have no previous experience or knowledge of them. [BUSINESS] ☐ *Several companies are offering new, entry-level models in hopes of attracting more buyers.* ❷ ADJ **Entry-level** jobs are suitable for people who do not have previous experience or qualifications in a particular area of work. [BUSINESS] ☐ *Many entry-level jobs were filled by high school grads.*

entry|way /ˈɛntriweɪ/ (**entryways**) N-COUNT An **entryway** is a passage that is used as an entrance to a building. [mainly AM]

en|twine /ɪntwaɪn/ (entwines, entwining, entwined)
■ V-RECIP If one thing **is entwined** with another thing, or if you **entwine** two things, the two things are twisted around each other. ◻ *His dazed eyes stare at the eels, which still writhe and entwine.* ◻ *Facing each other, the giraffes entwine their necks in the most astonishing manner.* ◻ *He entwined his fingers with hers.* ◻ *...with silk ribbons and flowers entwined in their hair.*
■ V-T/V-I If two things **entwine** or **are entwined**, they closely resemble or are linked to each other, and they are difficult to separate or identify. ◻ *The book entwines the personal and the political to chart the history of four generations of the family.* ◻ *Once, years ago, he told me our lives should entwine.* ● **en|twined** ADJ [oft ADJ with n] ◻ *...before media manipulation became entwined with management.*

enu|mer|ate /ɪnjuːməreɪt/ (enumerates, enumerating, enumerated) V-T When you **enumerate** a list of things, you name each one in turn. ◻ *I enumerate the work that will have to be done.*

enun|ci|ate /ɪnʌnsieɪt/ (enunciates, enunciating, enunciated) ■ V-T/V-I When you **enunciate** a word or part of a word, you pronounce it clearly. [FORMAL] ◻ *His voice was harsh as he enunciated each word carefully.* ◻ *She enunciates very slowly and carefully.* ● **enun|cia|tion** /ɪnʌnsieɪʃən/ N-UNCOUNT ◻ *...his grammar always precise, his enunciation always perfect.*
■ → See feature box at **speak**

en|vel|op /ɪnvɛləp/ (envelops, enveloping, enveloped) V-T If one thing **envelops** another, it covers or surrounds it completely. ◻ *That lovely, rich fragrant smell of the forest enveloped us.*

en|velope /ɛnvəloʊp, ɒn-/ (envelopes) ■ N-COUNT An **envelope** is the rectangular paper cover in which you send a letter to someone through the mail. ■ PHRASE If someone **pushes the envelope**, they do something to a greater degree or in a more extreme way than it has ever been done before. ◻ *There's a valuable place for fashion and design that pushes the envelope a bit.*

en|vi|able /ɛnviəbəl/ ADJ You describe something such as a quality as **enviable** when someone else has it and you wish that you had it too. ◻ *This country, unlike other big economies, is in the enviable position of having a budget surplus.*

en|vi|ous /ɛnviəs/ ADJ If you are **envious** of someone, you want something that they have. ◻ *I don't think I'm envious of your success.* ◻ *Do I sound envious? I pity them, actually.* ● **en|vi|ous|ly** ADV [ADV with v] ◻ *"You haven't changed," I am often enviously told.*

en|vi|ron|ment ◆◆◇ /ɪnvaɪrənmənt, -vaɪərn-/ (environments)
■ N-VAR Someone's **environment** is all the circumstances, people, things, and events around them that influence their life. ◻ *Students in our schools are taught in a safe, secure environment.* ◻ *Our characters are formed not by heredity but by environment.* ■ N-COUNT Your **environment** consists of the particular natural surroundings in which you live or exist, considered in relation to their physical characteristics or weather conditions. ◻ *...a safe environment for marine mammals.* ■ N-SING **The environment** is the natural world of land, sea, air, plants, and animals. ◻ *...persuading people to respect the environment.*

SYNONYMS

environment
NOUN
■
conditions: *The conditions are ripe for the spread of disease.*
circumstances: *The strategy was too dangerous in the explosive circumstances of the times.*
situation: *She's in a hopeless situation.*
background: *The meeting takes place against a background of continuing political violence.*
■
habitat: *Few countries have as rich a diversity of habitat as South Africa.*
territory: *A cat's territory remains fixed for as long as the cat dominates it.*

COLLOCATIONS

environment
NOUN
■
adjective + **environment**: safe, secure, stable, supportive; challenging, competitive, hostile, relaxed; economic, political, social
■
verb + **environment**: help, protect, respect, save; damage, harm, pollute

---

en|vi|ron|men|tal ◆◆◇ /ɪnvaɪrənmɛntəl, -vaɪərn-/ ■ ADJ [ADJ n] **Environmental** means concerned with the protection of the natural world of land, sea, air, plants, and animals. ◻ *Environmental groups plan to stage public protests during the conference.* ● **en|vi|ron|men|tal|ly** ADV [ADV adj] ◻ *...the high price of environmentally friendly goods.* ■ ADJ [ADJ n] **Environmental** means relating to or caused by the surroundings in which someone lives or something exists. ◻ *It protects against environmental hazards such as wind and sun.* ■ → See feature box at **disaster**, **recycle**

en|vi|ron|men|tal|ism /ɪnvaɪrənmɛntəlɪzəm, -vaɪərn-/ N-UNCOUNT **Environmentalism** is used to describe actions and policies that show a concern with protecting and preserving the natural environment, for example, by preventing pollution.

en|vi|ron|men|tal|ist /ɪnvaɪrənmɛntəlɪst, -vaɪərn-/ (environmentalists) N-COUNT An **environmentalist** is a person who is concerned with protecting and preserving the natural environment, for example, by preventing pollution.

en|vi|rons /ɪnvaɪrənz, -vaɪərnz/ N-PLURAL [with poss] The **environs** of a place consist of the area immediately surrounding it. [FORMAL] ◻ *...the environs of Paris.* ◻ *The town and its environs are inviting, with recreational attractions and art museums.*

en|vis|age /ɪnvɪzɪdʒ/ (envisages, envisaging, envisaged) V-T If you **envisage** something, you imagine that it is true, real, or likely to happen. ◻ *He envisages the possibility of establishing direct diplomatic relations in the future.*

en|vi|sion /ɪnvɪʒən/ (envisions, envisioning, envisioned) V-T If you **envision** something, you envisage it. [AM] ◻ *In the future we envision a federation of companies.* ◻ *Alana never envisioned her college career ending like this.*

en|voy /ɛnvɔɪ, ɒn-/ (envoys) ■ N-COUNT An **envoy** is someone who is sent as a representative from one government or political group to another. ◻ *A U.S. envoy is expected in the region this month to collect responses to the proposal.* ■ N-COUNT An **envoy** is a diplomat in an embassy who is immediately below the ambassador in rank.

envy /ɛnvi/ (envies, envying, envied) ■ N-UNCOUNT **Envy** is the feeling you have when you wish you could have the same thing or quality that someone else has. ◻ *Gradually he began to acknowledge his feelings of envy toward his mother.* ■ V-T If you **envy** someone, you wish that you had the same things or qualities that they have. ◻ *I don't envy the young ones who've become TV superstars and know no other world.* ■ N-SING If a thing or quality is **the envy of** someone, they wish very much that they could have or achieve it. ◻ *Their economy is the envy of the developing world.*

en|zyme /ɛnzaɪm/ (enzymes) N-COUNT An **enzyme** is a chemical substance found in living creatures that produces changes in other substances without being changed itself. [TECHNICAL]

eon /iːɒn/ (eons) N-COUNT An **eon** is an extremely long period of time. [AM]

in BRIT, sometimes in AM, use **aeon**

EP /iː piː/ (EPs) N-COUNT An **EP** is a record which lasts for about 8 minutes on each side. **EP** is an abbreviation for 'extended play.'

ep|aulet /ɛpəlɛt/ (epaulets) also **epaulette** N-COUNT [usu pl] **Epaulets** are decorations worn on the shoulders of certain uniforms, especially military ones.

épée /eɪpeɪ, ɛpeɪ/ (épées) also **epee** N-COUNT An **épée** is a thin, light sword that is used in the sport of fencing.

ephem|era /ɪfɛmərə/ ■ N-UNCOUNT You can refer to things which last for only a short time as **ephemera**. [LITERARY]
■ N-PLURAL [oft adj n] **Ephemera** are things people collect such as old postcards, posters, and bus tickets, which were only intended to last a short time when they were produced. ◻ *...tickets and other printed ephemera.*

ephem|er|al /ɪfɛmərəl/ ADJ If you describe something as **ephemeral**, you mean that it lasts only for a short time. [FORMAL] ☐ *He talked about the country's ephemeral unity being shattered by the defeat.*

epic /ɛpɪk/ (epics) **1** N-COUNT An **epic** is a long book, poem, or movie whose story extends over a long period of time or tells of great events. ☐ *...the Middle High German epic, "Nibelungenlied," written about 1200.* • ADJ **Epic** is also an adjective. ☐ *...epic narrative poems.* **2** ADJ Something that is **epic** is very large and impressive. ☐ *...Columbus's epic voyage of discovery.* **3** → See feature box at **book**

epi|cen|ter /ɛpɪsɛntər/ (epicenters)

in BRIT, use **epicentre**

1 N-COUNT [usu with poss] The **epicenter** of an earthquake is the place on the Earth's surface directly above the point where it starts, and is the place where it is felt most strongly. ☐ *The epicenter of the quake was near the town of Potenza.* **2** N-COUNT [oft N of n] The **epicenter** of something bad is the place where is it most common or intense. ☐ *The city became the epicenter of the crisis.*

epi|cure /ɛpɪkyʊər/ (epicures) N-COUNT An **epicure** is someone who enjoys eating food that is of very good quality, especially unusual or rare food. [FORMAL]

epi|cu|rean /ɛpɪkyʊəriən/ ADJ [usu ADJ n] **Epicurean** food is of very good quality, especially unusual or rare food. [FORMAL] ☐ *...an epicurean dish.*

epi|dem|ic /ɛpɪdɛmɪk/ (epidemics) **1** N-COUNT If there is an **epidemic** of a particular disease somewhere, it affects a very large number of people there and spreads quickly to other areas. ☐ *A flu epidemic is sweeping through Moscow.* **2** N-COUNT If an activity that you disapprove of is increasing or spreading rapidly, you can refer to this as an **epidemic** of that activity. [DISAPPROVAL] ☐ *...an epidemic of serial killings.*

epi|dem|i|ol|ogist /ɛpɪdimiɒlədʒɪst/ (epidemiologists) N-COUNT An **epidemiologist** is a doctor who specializes in the occurrence, distribution, and control of epidemic diseases.

epi|demi|ol|ogy /ɛpɪdimiɒlədʒi/ N-UNCOUNT **Epidemiology** is a branch of medicine that is concerned with the occurrence, distribution, and control of disease. ☐ *...major contributions to the understanding of the epidemiology, diagnosis and treatment of liver diseases.*

epi|der|mis /ɛpɪdɜrmɪs/ N-SING Your **epidermis** is the thin, protective, outer layer of your skin. [TECHNICAL]

epi|dur|al /ɛpɪdʊərəl/ (epidurals) N-COUNT An **epidural** is a type of anesthetic injected into a person's spine so that they cannot feel anything from the waist downward. Epidurals are sometimes given to women when they are giving birth.

epi|gram /ɛpɪgræm/ (epigrams) N-COUNT An **epigram** is a short saying or poem that expresses an idea in a very clever and amusing way.

epi|graph /ɛpɪgræf/ (epigraphs) N-COUNT [usu N to n] An **epigraph** is a quotation at the beginning of a book or chapter of a book. ☐ *The epigraph to O'Rourke's book is from de Quincey's Confessions of an English Opium Eater.*

epi|lep|sy /ɛpɪlɛpsi/ N-UNCOUNT **Epilepsy** is a brain condition that causes a person to suddenly lose consciousness and sometimes to have seizures. ☐ *Shawna suffers from epilepsy.*

epi|lep|tic /ɛpɪlɛptɪk/ **1** ADJ Someone who is **epileptic** has epilepsy. ☐ *He was epileptic and refused to take medication for his condition.* **2** ADJ [ADJ n] An **epileptic** seizure is caused by epilepsy. ☐ *He suffered an epileptic seizure.*

epi|logue /ɛpɪlɒg/ (epilogues) also **epilog** N-COUNT [usu the N in sing] An **epilogue** is a passage or speech that is added to the end of a book or play as a conclusion.

epi|pha|ny /ɪpɪfəni/ (epiphanies) N-COUNT An **epiphany** is a moment of sudden insight or understanding. ☐ *...Isaac Newton's epiphany about gravity and a falling apple.*

Epipha|ny /ɪpɪfəni/ N-UNCOUNT **Epiphany** is a Christian festival on the 6th of January that celebrates the arrival of the wise men who came to see Jesus of Nazareth soon after he was born.

epis|co|pal /ɪpɪskəpəl/ **1** ADJ [ADJ n] **Episcopal** means relating to a branch of the Anglican Church in the U.S. and Scotland. ☐ *...the Episcopal bishop of New York.* ☐ *...the Protestant Episcopal church.* **2** ADJ [ADJ n] **Episcopal** means relating to bishops. [FORMAL] ☐ *...episcopal conferences.*

Epis|co|pa|li|an /ɪpɪskəpeɪliən/ (Episcopalians) **1** ADJ [ADJ n] **Episcopalian** means belonging to the Episcopal Church. **2** N-COUNT An **Episcopalian** is a member of the Episcopal Church.

epi|sode /ɛpɪsoʊd/ (episodes) **1** N-COUNT You can refer to an event or a short period of time as an **episode** if you want to suggest that it is important or unusual, or has some particular quality. ☐ *This episode is bound to be a deep embarrassment for Washington.* **2** N-COUNT An **episode** of something such as a series on television or a story in a magazine is one of the separate parts in which it is broadcast or published. ☐ *The final episode will be shown next Sunday.*

epi|sod|ic /ɛpɪsɒdɪk/ ADJ Something that is **episodic** occurs at irregular and infrequent intervals. [FORMAL] ☐ *...episodic attacks of fever.*

epis|tle /ɪpɪsəl/ (epistles) **1** N-COUNT An **epistle** is a letter. [LITERARY] **2** N-COUNT [usu N to n] In the Bible, the **Epistles** are a series of books in the New Testament that were originally written as letters to the early Christians.

epis|to|lary /ɪpɪstəlɛri/ ADJ [ADJ n] An **epistolary** novel or story is one that is written as a series of letters. [FORMAL]

epi|taph /ɛpɪtæf/ (epitaphs) N-COUNT An **epitaph** is a short piece of writing about someone who is dead, often carved on their gravestone.

epi|thet /ɛpɪθɛt/ (epithets) N-COUNT An **epithet** is an adjective or short phrase that is used as a way of criticizing or praising someone. [FORMAL] ☐ *"Tactless" is one of the kinder epithets applied to him.*

epito|me /ɪpɪtəmi/ N-SING If you say that a person or thing is the **epitome** of something, you are emphasizing that they are the best possible example of it. [FORMAL, EMPHASIS] ☐ *Maureen was the epitome of sophistication.*

epito|mize /ɪpɪtəmaɪz/ (epitomizes, epitomizing, epitomized)

in BRIT, also use **epitomise**

V-T If you say that something or someone **epitomizes** a particular thing, you mean that they are a perfect example of it. ☐ *Seafood is a regional specialty epitomized by Captain Anderson's Restaurant.*

EPO /i pi oʊ/ also **epo** N-UNCOUNT **EPO** is a drug that can improve performance in sports and is used illegally by some athletes. **EPO** is short for 'erythropoietin.'

epoch /ɛpək/ (epochs) N-COUNT If you refer to a long period of time as an **epoch**, you mean that important events or great changes took place during it. ☐ *This marked an epoch in the social history of the city.*

epoch-making ADJ [usu ADJ n] An **epoch-making** change or declaration is considered to be the extremely important because it is likely to have a significant effect on a particular period of time. ☐ *It was meant to sound like an epoch-making declaration.* ☐ *...the epoch-making changes now taking place in Eastern Europe.*

epony|mous /ɪpɒnɪməs/ ADJ [ADJ n] An **eponymous** hero or heroine is the character in a play or book whose name is the title of that play or book. [FORMAL]

epoxy /ɪpɒksi/ N-UNCOUNT [oft N n] **Epoxy** resin or adhesive contains an artificial substance used as a very strong glue.

Ep|som salts /ɛpsəm sɔlts/ N-UNCOUNT **Epsom salts** is a kind of white powder that you can mix with water and drink as a medicine to help you empty your bowels, or add to water that you soak your feet in.

EQ /i kyu/ (EQs) N-VAR A person's **EQ** is a measure of their interpersonal and communication skills. **EQ** is an abbreviation for 'emotional quotient.' Compare **IQ**. ☐ *Guy was elected leader and then found to have the highest EQ on a nominal measure.*

eq|uable /ɛkwəbəl/ ADJ If you describe someone as **equable**, you mean that they are calm, cheerful, and fair with

equal other people, even in difficult circumstances. ❑ *He was a man of the most equable temper.* ● **eq|uably** ADV [ADV after v] ❑ *She wasn't prepared to respond equably to Richardson's mood, and she spoke curtly.*

equal ✦◇◇ /ˈiːkwəl/ (**equals**, **equaling**, **equaled**)

in BRIT, sometimes in AM, use **equalling**, **equalled**

1 ADJ If two things are **equal** or if one thing is **equal** to another, they are the same in size, number, standard, or value. ❑ *Investors can borrow an amount equal to the property's purchase price.* ❑ *...in a population having equal numbers of men and women.* **2** ADJ If different groups of people have **equal** rights or are given **equal** treatment, they have the same rights or are treated the same as each other, however different they are. ❑ *We will be demanding equal rights at work.* ❑ *...the commitment to equal opportunities.* **3** ADJ [v-link ADJ] If you say that people are **equal**, you mean that they have or should have the same rights and opportunities as each other. ❑ *We are equal in every way.* **4** N-COUNT Someone who is your **equal** has the same ability, status, or rights as you have. ❑ *She was one of the boys, their equal.* **5** ADJ [v-link ADJ to n] If someone is **equal** to a particular job or situation, they have the necessary ability, strength, or courage to deal successfully with it. ❑ *She was determined that she would be equal to any test the corporation put to them.* **6** V-LINK If something **equals** a particular number or amount, it is the same as that amount or the equivalent of that amount. ❑ *9 percent interest less 7 percent inflation equals 2 percent.* **7** V-T To **equal** something or someone means to be as good or as great as them. ❑ *The victory equaled the team's best in history.* **8** PHRASE If you say '**other things being equal**' or '**all things being equal**' when talking about a possible situation, you mean if nothing unexpected happens or if there are no other factors that affect the situation. ❑ *It appears reasonable to assume that, other things being equal, most hostel tenants would prefer single to shared rooms.*

SYNONYMS

equal
ADJ
1
identical: *The two parties fought the last election on almost identical platforms.*
equivalent: *Calls for equivalent wage increases are bound to be heard.*
the same: *Its gross domestic product will be roughly the same as that of the US.*
uniform: *The price rises will not be uniform across the country.*
2
fair: *I wanted them to get a fair deal.*
evenhanded: *The administration wants to ensure the meetings appear evenhanded.*
equitable: *We believe you can redistribute this money in a way that's equitable.*

equali|ty /ɪˈkwɒlɪti/ N-UNCOUNT **Equality** is the same status, rights, and responsibilities for all the members of a society, group, or family. ❑ *...equality of the sexes.*

equal|ize /ˈiːkwəlaɪz/ (**equalizes**, **equalizing**, **equalized**)

in BRIT, also use **equalise**

V-T To **equalize** a situation means to give everyone the same rights or opportunities, for example, in education, wealth, or social status. ❑ *Such measures are needed to equalize wage rates between countries.* ● **equali|za|tion** /ˌiːkwəlaɪˈzeɪʃ°n/ N-UNCOUNT ❑ *...the equalization of parenting responsibilities between men and women.*

equal|ly ✦◇◇ /ˈiːkwəli/ **1** ADV **Equally** means in sections, amounts, or spaces that are the same size as each other. ❑ *Try to get into the habit of eating at least three small meals a day, at equally spaced intervals.* **2** ADV **Equally** means to the same degree or extent. ❑ *All these techniques are equally effective.* **3** ADV **Equally** is used to introduce another comment on the same topic, that balances or contrasts with the previous comment. ❑ *Subscribers should be allowed call-blocking services, but equally, they should be able to choose whether to accept calls from blocked numbers.*

USAGE

equally
Don't use '**equally**' in front of **as** when you are comparing things. Don't say, for example, 'He is equally as tall as his brother.' Say 'He is **as tall as** his brother.' *He was **just as shocked as** I was. He was an excellent pianist. Irene was **equally brilliant**.*

SYNONYMS

equally
ADV **1**
evenly: *The loss of jobs has been far more evenly spread across the regions.*
uniformly: *Microwaves heat water uniformly.*
fairly: *Water was precious, and it had to be shared fairly between individuals.*

equal op|por|tu|nities N-PLURAL **Equal opportunities** refers to the policy of giving everyone the same opportunities for employment, pay and promotion, without discriminating against particular groups. [BUSINESS] ❑ *The profession's leaders must take action now to promote equal opportunities for all.*

equal op|por|tu|nity N-UNCOUNT **Equal opportunity** refers to the policy of giving everyone the same opportunities for employment, pay, and promotion, without discriminating against particular groups. [BUSINESS] ❑ *The bill is needed to create equal opportunity for women.*

equal op|por|tu|nity em|ploy|er (**equal opportunity employers**) N-COUNT An **equal opportunity employer** is an employer who gives people the same opportunities for employment, pay, and promotion, without discrimination against anyone. [BUSINESS] ❑ *The police force is committed to being an equal opportunity employer.*

equal sign (**equal signs**) N-COUNT An **equal sign** is the sign =, which is used in arithmetic to indicate that two numbers or sets of numbers are equal.

equa|nim|ity /ˌiːkwəˈnɪmɪti, ˌɛk-/ N-UNCOUNT [oft with N] **Equanimity** is a calm state of mind and attitude to life, so that you never lose your temper or become upset. [FORMAL] ❑ *His sense of humor allowed him to face adversaries with equanimity.*

equate /ɪˈkweɪt/ (**equates**, **equating**, **equated**) V-T/V-I If you **equate** one thing with another, or if you say that one thing **equates** with another, you believe that they are strongly connected. ❑ *American culture is not the only one to equate wealth with virtue.* ❑ *The author doesn't equate liberalism and conservatism.* ● **equa|tion** N-UNCOUNT ❑ *The equation of gangsterism with business in general in Coppola's film was intended to be subversive.*

equa|tion /ɪˈkweɪʒ°n/ (**equations**) **1** N-COUNT An **equation** is a mathematical statement saying that two amounts or values are the same, for example 6x4=12x2. **2** N-COUNT An **equation** is a situation in which two or more parts have to be considered together so that the whole situation can be understood or explained. ❑ *The equation is simple: research breeds new products.* ❑ *The party fears the equation between higher spending and higher taxes.*

equa|tor /ɪˈkweɪtər/ N-SING The **equator** is an imaginary line around the middle of the Earth at an equal distance from the North Pole and the South Pole.

equa|to|rial /ˌiːkwəˈtɔːriəl, ˌɛk-/ ADJ [usu ADJ n] Something that is **equatorial** is near or at the equator. ❑ *...the equatorial island with a hundred and twenty thousand people living there.*

eq|uer|ry /ˈɛkwəri/ (**equerries**) N-COUNT [oft N to n] An **equerry** is an officer of a royal household or court who acts as a personal assistant to a member of the royal family.

eques|trian /ɪˈkwɛstriən/ ADJ **Equestrian** means connected with the activity of riding horses. ❑ *...his equestrian skills.*

eques|tri|an|ism /ɪˈkwɛstriənɪzəm/ N-UNCOUNT **Equestrianism** refers to sports in which people demonstrate their skill at riding and controlling a horse.

equi|dis|tant /ˌiːkwɪˈdɪstənt/ ADJ A place that is **equidistant** from two other places is the same distance away from each of these places. ❑ *Altus is equidistant from Ozark and Cotton Town.*

equi|lat|eral /ˌiːkwɪˈlætərəl/ ADJ [usu ADJ n] A shape or figure that is **equilateral** has sides that are all the same length. [TECHNICAL] ❑ *...an equilateral triangle.*

equi|lib|rium /iːkwɪlɪbriəm/ (equilibria) **1** N-VAR **Equilibrium** is a balance between several different influences or aspects of a situation. [FORMAL] ❑ *Stocks seesawed ever lower until prices found some new level of equilibrium.* **2** N-UNCOUNT Someone's **equilibrium** is their normal calm state of mind. ❑ *I paused in the hall to take three deep breaths to restore my equilibrium.*

equine /ˈiːkwaɪn/ ADJ [ADJ n] **Equine** means connected with or relating to horses. ❑ *...an outbreak of equine influenza.*

equi|nox /ˈiːkwɪnɒks, ˈek-/ (equinoxes) N-COUNT [oft supp N] An **equinox** is one of the two days in the year when day and night are of equal length. ❑ *In the Chinese calendar, the Spring Equinox always occurs in the second month.*

equip /ɪˈkwɪp/ (equips, equipping, equipped) **1** V-T If you **equip** a person or thing with something, you give them the tools or equipment that are needed. ❑ *They try to equip their vehicles with gadgets to deal with every possible contingency.* ❑ *Owners of restaurants have to equip them to admit people with disabilities.* **2** V-T If something **equips** you for a particular task or experience, it gives you the skills and attitudes you need for it, especially by educating you in a particular way. ❑ *Relative poverty, however, did not prevent Martin from equipping himself with an excellent education.*

equip|ment ♦♦◇ /ɪˈkwɪpmənt/ N-UNCOUNT **Equipment** consists of the things that are used for a particular purpose, such as a hobby or job. ❑ *...computers, electronic equipment and machine tools.*

USAGE

equipment
Equipment is an uncountable noun. Don't talk about 'equipments' or 'an equipment.' You can talk about a single item as a **piece of equipment**. *This radio is an important piece of equipment. ...kitchen equipment.*

---

equi|table /ˈekwɪtəbəl/ ADJ Something that is **equitable** is fair and reasonable in a way that gives equal treatment to everyone. ❑ *He has urged them to come to an equitable compromise that gives Hughes his proper due.*

equi|ties /ˈekwɪtiz/ **1** N-PLURAL **Equities** are shares in a company that are owned by people who have a right to vote at the company's meetings and to receive part of the company's profits after the holders of preference shares have been paid. [BUSINESS] ❑ *Investors have poured money into U.S. equities.* **2** → see also **preference shares**

equi|ty ♦◇◇ /ˈekwɪti/ **1** N-UNCOUNT In finance, your **equity** is the sum of your assets, for example the value of your house, once your debts have been subtracted from it. [BUSINESS] ❑ *To capture his equity, Murphy must either sell or refinance.* **2** → See feature box at **business**

equiva|lence /ɪˈkwɪvələns/ N-UNCOUNT If there is **equivalence** between two things, they have the same use, function, size, or value. ❑ *...the equivalence of science and rationality*

equiva|lent ♦◇◇ /ɪˈkwɪvələnt/ (equivalents) **1** N-SING If one amount or value is the **equivalent** of another, they are the same. ❑ *Mr. Li's pay is the equivalent of about $80 a month.* ● ADJ **Equivalent** is also an adjective. ❑ *If they want to change an item in the budget, they will have to propose equivalent cuts elsewhere.* **2** N-COUNT The **equivalent** of someone or something is a person or thing that has the same function in a different place, time, or system. ❑ *...the Red Cross emblem, and its equivalent in Muslim countries, the Red Crescent.* ● ADJ **Equivalent** is also an adjective. ❑ *...a decrease of 10% in property investment compared with the equivalent period last year.* **3** N-SING You can use **equivalent** to emphasize the great or severe effect of something. [EMPHASIS] ❑ *His party has just suffered the equivalent of a near-fatal heart attack.*

equivo|cal /ɪˈkwɪvəkəl/ **1** ADJ If you are **equivocal**, you are deliberately vague in what you say, because you want to avoid speaking the truth or making a decision. [FORMAL] ❑ *Many were equivocal about the idea.* ❑ *His equivocal response has done nothing to dampen the speculation.* **2** ADJ If something is **equivocal**, it is difficult to understand, interpret, or explain, often because it has aspects that seem to contradict each other. [FORMAL] ❑ *Research in this area is somewhat equivocal.* ❑ *He was tortured by an awareness of the equivocal nature of his position.*

equivo|cate /ɪˈkwɪvəkeɪt/ (equivocates, equivocating, equivocated) V-I When someone **equivocates**, they deliberately use vague language in order to deceive people or to avoid speaking the truth. ❑ *He is equivocating a lot about what is going to happen if and when there are elections.* ❑ *He had asked her once again about her finances. And again she had equivocated.* ● **equivo|ca|tion** /ɪkwɪvəˈkeɪʃən/ N-UNCOUNT [usu without N] ❑ *Why doesn't the president say so without equivocation?*

er /ɜːr/ **Er** is used in writing to represent the sound that people make when they hesitate, especially while they decide what to say next. ❑ *Sorry about those, er, marks.*

ER /iː ˈɑːr/ (ERs) N-COUNT The **ER** is the part of a hospital where people who have severe injuries or sudden illnesses are taken for emergency treatment. **ER** is an abbreviation for **emergency room**. [AM] ❑ *...people who come to the ER thinking they're having heart attacks.*

SUFFIX

-er
1 forms nouns that refer to a person who performs a particular action, often because it is their job. For example, a **teacher** is someone who teaches.
2 also forms nouns which refer to tools and machines that perform a particular action. For example, a **scanner** is a machine that scans things.

---

era ♦◇◇ /ˈɪərə/ (eras) N-COUNT You can refer to a period of history or a long period of time as an **era** when you want to draw attention to a particular feature or quality that it has. ❑ *...the nuclear era.* ❑ *...the Reagan-Bush era.*

SYNONYMS

era
NOUN
time(s): *We are in one of the most severe recessions in modern times.*
age: *...the age of steam and steel.*
period: *...the most difficult periods of history.*
epoch: *This was the beginning of a major epoch of world history.*
day(s): *He was one of the finest observers of his day.*

---

eradi|cate /ɪˈrædɪkeɪt/ (eradicates, eradicating, eradicated) V-T To **eradicate** something means to get rid of it completely. [FORMAL] ❑ *They are already battling to eradicate illnesses such as malaria and tetanus.* ● **eradi|ca|tion** /ɪrædɪˈkeɪʃən/ N-UNCOUNT ❑ *...a significant contribution toward the eradication of corruption.*

erase /ɪˈreɪs/ (erases, erasing, erased) **1** V-T If you **erase** a thought or feeling, you destroy it completely so that you can no longer remember something or no longer feel a particular emotion. ❑ *They are desperate to erase the memory of that last defeat.* **2** V-T If you **erase** sound that has been recorded on a tape or information which has been stored in a computer, you completely remove or destroy it. ❑ *An intruder broke into the campaign headquarters and managed to erase 17,000 names from computer files.* **3** V-T If you **erase** something such as writing or a mark, you remove it, usually by rubbing it with a cloth. ❑ *It was unfortunate that she had erased the message.*

eras|er /ɪˈreɪsər/ (erasers) N-COUNT An **eraser** is an object, for example, a piece of rubber or a felt pad, that is used for removing something that has been written using a pencil or chalk. [AM]

eras|ure /ɪˈreɪʃər/ N-UNCOUNT [oft N of n] The **erasure** of something is the removal, loss, or destruction of it. [FORMAL] ❑ *Globalization is the erasure of national borders for economic purposes.*

ere /ɛər/ CONJ **Ere** means the same as 'before.' [LITERARY, OLD-FASHIONED] ❑ *Take the water ere the clock strikes twelve.*

e-reader (e-readers) N-COUNT An **e-reader** is a device that you can carry with you and use to download and read texts in electronic form. **E-reader** is an abbreviation for 'e-book reader.' ❑ *The number of people who owned an e-reader nearly doubled over the recent holiday season.*

erect /ɪˈrekt/ (erects, erecting, erected) **1** V-T If people **erect** something such as a building, bridge, or barrier, they build it or create it. [FORMAL] ❑ *Opposition demonstrators have erected barricades in roads leading to the parliament building.* ❑ *The building was erected in 1900–1901.* **2** V-T If you **erect** a system, a theory, or an institution, you create it. ❑ *Officials have stressed the importance of erecting a solid regional infrastructure to facilitate trade.*

erection

3 ADJ People or things that are **erect** are straight and upright. ▫ *Stand reasonably erect, your arms hanging naturally.*

erec|tion /ɪrɛkʃən/ (erections) **1** N-COUNT If a man has an **erection**, his penis is stiff, swollen, and sticking up because he is sexually aroused. **2** N-UNCOUNT The **erection** of something is the act of building it or placing it in an upright position. ▫ *...the erection of temporary fencing to protect hedges.*

er|ga|tive /ɜrgətɪv/ ADJ An **ergative** verb is a verb that can be both transitive and intransitive, where the subject of the intransitive verb is the same as the object of the transitive verb. For example, 'open' is an ergative verb because you can say 'The door opened' or 'She opened the door.'

ergo /ɜrgoʊ/ ADV [ADV with cl] **Ergo** is sometimes used instead of 'therefore' to introduce a clause in which you mention something that is the consequence or logical result of what you have just said. [FORMAL OR LITERARY] ▫ *Neither side would have a real incentive to start a war. Ergo, peace would reign.*

er|go|nom|ics /ɜrgənɒmɪks/ N-UNCOUNT **Ergonomics** is the study of how equipment and furniture can be arranged so that people can do work or other activities more efficiently and comfortably.

er|mine /ɜrmɪn/ N-UNCOUNT [oft N n] **Ermine** is expensive white fur that comes from small animals called stoats.

erode /ɪroʊd/ (erodes, eroding, eroded) **1** V-T/V-I If rock or soil **erodes** or **is eroded** by the weather, sea, or wind, it cracks and breaks so that it is gradually destroyed. ▫ *The storm washed away buildings and roads and eroded beaches.* **2** V-T/V-I If someone's authority, right, or confidence **erodes** or **is eroded**, it is gradually destroyed or removed. [FORMAL] ▫ *His critics say his fumbling on the issue of reform has eroded his authority.* **3** V-T/V-I If the value of something **erodes** or **is eroded** by something such as inflation or age, its value decreases. ▫ *Competition in the financial marketplace has eroded profits.*

erog|enous /ɪrɒdʒɪnəs/ ADJ [usu ADJ n] An **erogenous** part of your body is one where sexual pleasure can be felt or caused. [FORMAL] ▫ *Your body contains many erogenous zones, areas that lead to a feeling of sexual excitement when they are caressed.*

ero|sion /ɪroʊʒən/ **1** N-UNCOUNT **Erosion** is the gradual destruction and removal of rock or soil in a particular area by rivers, the sea, or the weather. ▫ *...erosion of the river valleys.* **2** N-UNCOUNT The **erosion** of a person's authority, rights, or confidence is the gradual destruction or removal of them. ▫ *...the erosion of confidence in world financial markets.* **3** N-UNCOUNT The **erosion** of support, values, or money is a gradual decrease in its level or standard. ▫ *...the erosion of moral standards.*

erot|ic /ɪrɒtɪk/ ADJ If you describe something as **erotic**, you mean that it involves sexual feelings or arouses sexual desire. ▫ *It might sound like a fantasy, but it wasn't an erotic experience at all.*

eroti|ca /ɪrɒtɪkə/ N-UNCOUNT **Erotica** means works of art that show or describe sexual activity, and that are intended to arouse sexual feelings.

eroti|cism /ɪrɒtɪsɪzəm/ N-UNCOUNT **Eroticism** is sexual excitement, or the quality of being able to arouse sexual excitement. [FORMAL] ▫ *Almost all of Massenet's works are pervaded with an aura of eroticism.*

err /ɜr, ɛr/ (errs, erring, erred) **1** V-I If you **err**, you make a mistake. [FORMAL] ▫ *It criticizes the main contractor for seriously erring in its estimates.* **2** PHRASE If you **err on the side of** caution, for example, you decide to act in a cautious way, rather than take risks. ▫ *They may be wise to err on the side of caution.*

er|rand /ɛrənd/ (errands) **1** N-COUNT An **errand** is a short trip that you make in order to do a job, for example, when you go to a store to buy something. ▫ *She went off on some errand.* **2** PHRASE If you **run an errand** for someone, you do or get something for them, usually by making a short trip somewhere. ▫ *Run an errand for me, will you? Go find Roger for me.*

er|rant /ɛrənt/ ADJ [ADJ n] **Errant** is used to describe someone whose actions are considered unacceptable or wrong by other people. For example, an errant husband is unfaithful to his partner. [FORMAL] ▫ *Usually his cases involved errant husbands and wandering wives.*

er|rat|ic /ɪrætɪk/ ADJ Something that is **erratic** does not follow a regular pattern, but happens at unexpected times or moves along in an irregular way. ▫ *Argentina's erratic inflation rate threatens to upset the plans.* ● **er|rati|cal|ly** /ɪrætɪkli/ ADV ▫ *Police stopped him for driving erratically.*

er|ro|neous /ɪroʊniəs/ ADJ Beliefs, opinions, or methods that are **erroneous** are incorrect or only partly correct. ▫ *Some people have the erroneous notion that one can contract AIDS by giving blood.* ● **er|ro|neous|ly** ADV [ADV with v] ▫ *It had been widely and erroneously reported that Armstrong had refused to give evidence.*

er|ror ◆◇◇ /ɛrər/ (errors) **1** N-VAR An **error** is something you have done that is considered to be incorrect or wrong, or that should not have been done. ▫ *NASA discovered a mathematical error in its calculations.* **2** PHRASE If you do something **in error** or if it happens **in error**, you do it or it happens because you have made a mistake, especially in your judgment. ▫ *The plane was shot down in error by a NATO missile.* **3** PHRASE If someone sees **the error of** their **ways**, they realize or admit that they have made a mistake or behaved badly. ▫ *I wanted an opportunity to talk some sense into him and try to make him see the error of his ways.*

COLLOCATIONS

error
NOUN **1**
noun + **error**: driver, pilot
adjective + **error**: unforced; uncharacteristic; administrative, clerical, factual, tactical; costly, glaring, grave; basic, fundamental
verb + **error**: correct, rectify; make; admit

SYNONYMS

error
NOUN **1**
mistake: *Jonathan says it was his mistake.*
slip: *We must be well prepared; there must be no slips.*
blunder: *He made a tactical blunder by announcing it so soon.*
oversight: *William was angered and embarrassed by his oversight.*

---

er|satz /ɛərzɑts, -sɑts/ ADJ [usu ADJ n] If you describe something as **ersatz**, you dislike it because it is not genuine and is a poor imitation of something better. [WRITTEN, DISAPPROVAL] ▫ *...the ersatz Gothic architecture of Yale.*

erst|while /ɜrstwaɪl/ ADJ [ADJ n] You use **erstwhile** to describe someone that used to be the type of person indicated, but no longer is. [FORMAL] ▫ *He fled to Brazil with Gloria Lopez, an erstwhile friend of his wife's.*

eru|dite /ɛryədaɪt/ ADJ If you describe someone as **erudite**, you mean that they have or show great academic knowledge. You can also use **erudite** to describe something such as a book or a style of writing. [FORMAL] ▫ *He was never dull, always erudite and well informed.* ▫ *She wrote in an original and highly erudite style.*

eru|di|tion /ɛryədɪʃən/ N-UNCOUNT **Erudition** is great academic knowledge. [FORMAL] ▫ *His erudition was apparently endless.*

erupt /ɪrʌpt/ (erupts, erupting, erupted) **1** V-I When a volcano **erupts**, it throws out a lot of hot, melted rock called lava, as well as ash and steam. ▫ *The volcano erupted in 1980, devastating a large area of Washington state.* ● **erup|tion** /ɪrʌpʃən/ (eruptions) N-VAR ▫ *...the volcanic eruption of Tambora in 1815.* **2** V-I If violence or fighting **erupts**, it suddenly begins or gets worse in an unexpected, violent way. [JOURNALISM] ▫ *Heavy fighting erupted there today after a two-day cease-fire.* ● **erup|tion** N-COUNT ▫ *...this sudden eruption of violence.* **3** V-I When people in a place suddenly become angry or violent, you can say that they **erupt** or that the place **erupts**. [JOURNALISM] ▫ *In Los Angeles, the neighborhood known as Watts erupted into riots.* **4** V-I You say that someone **erupts** when they suddenly have a change in mood, usually becoming quite noisy. ▫ *Then, without warning, she erupts into laughter.* ● **erup|tion** N-COUNT ▫ *...an eruption of despair.*

es|ca|late /ɛskəleɪt/ (escalates, escalating, escalated) **1** V-T/V-I If a bad situation **escalates** or if someone or something **escalates** it, it becomes greater in size, seriousness, or intensity. [JOURNALISM] ▫ *Both unions and management fear the dispute could escalate.* ▫ *The protests escalated into five days of rioting.* ● **es|ca|la|tion** /ɛskəleɪʃən/ (escalations) N-VAR ▫ *The threat of nuclear escalation remains.* **2** → See feature box at **population**

es|ca|la|tor /ˈɛskəleɪtər/ (escalators) N-COUNT An **escalator** is a moving staircase on which people can go from one level of a building to another. ☐ *Take the escalator to the third floor and it's the last office on the left.*

es|ca|lope /ɪsˈkɒləp, ˈɛskəloʊp/ (escalopes) N-COUNT An **escalope** is a thin slice of meat without a bone. [mainly BRIT]

in AM, use **scallop**

es|ca|pade /ˈɛskəpeɪd/ (escapades) N-COUNT An **escapade** is an exciting and somewhat dangerous adventure. ☐ *...the scene of Robin Hood's escapades.*

es|cape ✦✦◇ /ɪsˈkeɪp/ (escapes, escaping, escaped) **1** V-I [no passive] If you **escape** from a place, you succeed in getting away from it. ☐ *A prisoner has escaped from a jail in northern Texas.* ☐ *They are reported to have escaped to the other side of the border.* **2** N-COUNT Someone's **escape** is the act of escaping from a particular place or situation. ☐ *The man made his escape.* **3** V-T/V-I You can say that you **escape** when you survive something such as an accident. ☐ *The two officers were extremely lucky to escape serious injury.* ☐ *The man's girlfriend managed to escape unhurt.* • N-COUNT **Escape** is also a noun. ☐ *I hear you had a very narrow escape on the bridge.* **4** N-COUNT If something is an **escape**, it is a way of avoiding difficulties or responsibilities. ☐ *But for me television is an escape.* **5** ADJ [ADJ n] You can use **escape** to describe things that allow you to avoid difficulties or problems. For example, an **escape route** is an activity or opportunity that lets you improve your situation. An **escape clause** is part of an agreement that allows you to avoid having to do something that you do not want to do. ☐ *We all need the occasional escape route from the boring, routine aspects of our lives.* **6** V-T If something **escapes** you or **escapes** your attention, you do not know about it, do not remember it, or do not notice it. ☐ *It was an actor whose name escapes me for the moment.* **7** V-I When gas, liquid, or heat **escapes**, it comes out from a pipe, container, or place. ☐ *Leave a vent open to let some moist air escape.* **8** → see also **fire escape**

es|cape art|ist (escape artists) N-COUNT An **escape artist** is someone who entertains audiences by being tied up and placed in a dangerous situation, then escaping from it. [mainly AM]

es|capee /ɪskeɪˈpiː/ (escapees) N-COUNT An **escapee** is a person who has escaped from somewhere, especially from prison.

es|cape room (escape rooms) N-COUNT An **escape room** is a room containing puzzles and games which you must solve in order to win or to get out of the room.

es|cap|ism /ɪsˈkeɪpɪzəm/ N-UNCOUNT If you describe an activity or type of entertainment as **escapism**, you mean that it makes people think about pleasant things instead of the uninteresting or unpleasant aspects of their life. ☐ *Horoscopes are merely harmless escapism.*

es|cap|ist /ɪsˈkeɪpɪst/ ADJ **Escapist** ideas, activities, or types of entertainment make people think about pleasant or unlikely things instead of the uninteresting or unpleasant aspects of their life. ☐ *...a little escapist fantasy.*

es|ca|polo|gist /ɛskəˈpɒlədʒɪst/ (escapologists) N-COUNT An **escapologist** is the same as an **escape artist**. [BRIT]

es|carp|ment /ɪsˈkɑːrpmənt/ (escarpments) N-COUNT An **escarpment** is a wide, steep slope on a hill or mountain.

es|chew /ɪsˈtʃuː/ (eschews, eschewing, eschewed) V-T If you **eschew** something, you deliberately avoid doing it or becoming involved in it. [FORMAL] ☐ *Although he appeared to enjoy a jet-setting life, he eschewed publicity and avoided nightclubs.*

e-scooter (e-scooters) N-COUNT An **e-scooter** is a light, battery-powered scooter, ridden standing up. ☐ *Leave your car at home and instead, whiz around on an e-scooter.*

es|cort (escorts, escorting, escorted)

The noun is pronounced /ˈɛskɔːrt/. The verb is pronounced /ɪsˈkɔːrt/.

1 V-T If you **escort** someone somewhere, you accompany them there, usually in order to make sure that they leave a place or get to their destination. ☐ *I escorted him to the door.* **2** N-COUNT An **escort** is a person who travels with someone in order to protect or guard them. ☐ *He arrived with a police escort shortly before half past nine.* • PHRASE If someone is taken somewhere **under escort**, they are accompanied by guards, either because they have been arrested or because they need to be protected. **3** N-COUNT An **escort** is a person who accompanies another person to a social event. Sometimes people are paid to be escorts. ☐ *My sister needed an escort for a company dinner.*

es|crow /ˈɛskroʊ/ N-UNCOUNT [oft N n] **Escrow** is money or property that is given to someone, but kept by another person until the first person has done a particular thing or met particular requirements. [mainly AM, LEGAL] ☐ *They had $96,000 in their escrow account.* ☐ *His stake has been held in escrow since the start of the year.*

Es|ki|mo /ˈɛskɪmoʊ/ (Eskimos) N-COUNT An **Eskimo** is a member of the group of peoples who live in Alaska, Northern Canada, eastern Siberia, and other parts of the Arctic. These peoples now usually call themselves Inuits or Yupiks, and the term Eskimo could cause offense.

ESL /iː ɛs ɛl/ **ESL** is taught to people whose native language is not English but who live in a society in which English is the main language or one of the main languages. **ESL** is an abbreviation for 'English as a second language.'

esopha|gus /ɪsˈpɒfəɡəs/ (esophaguses) N-COUNT Your **esophagus** is the part of your body that carries the food from the throat to the stomach. ☐ *...cancer of the esophagus.*

eso|ter|ic /ˌɛsəˈtɛrɪk/ ADJ If you describe something as **esoteric**, you mean it is known, understood, or appreciated by only a small number of people. [FORMAL] ☐ *...esoteric knowledge.*

ESP /iː ɛs piː/ N-UNCOUNT **ESP** is an abbreviation for extrasensory perception.

esp. **esp.** is a written abbreviation for **especially**.

es|pe|cial /ɪsˈpɛʃəl/ ADJ [ADJ n] **Especial** means unusual or special in some way. [FORMAL] ☐ *Joyce took especial care to include her.*

es|pe|cial|ly ✦✦◇ /ɪsˈpɛʃəli/ **1** ADV [ADV with cl/group] You use **especially** to emphasize that what you are saying applies more to one person, thing, time, or area than to any others. [EMPHASIS] ☐ *Millions of wild flowers color the valleys, especially in April and May.* **2** ADV [ADV adj/adv] You use **especially** to emphasize a characteristic or quality. [EMPHASIS] ☐ *Babies lose heat much faster than adults, and are especially vulnerable to the cold in their first month.*

───── SYNONYMS ─────

especially
ADV
1
particularly: *Keep your office space looking good, particularly your desk.*
in particular: *Why should he notice her car in particular?*
specifically: *Death frightens me, specifically my own death.*
2
specially: *What was specially enjoyable about that job?*
particularly: *Progress has been particularly disappointing.*
exceptionally: *The conditions under ground were exceptionally hot.*
extremely: *These headaches are extremely common.*

Es|pe|ran|to /ˌɛspəˈræntoʊ/ N-UNCOUNT **Esperanto** is an invented language that consists of parts of several European languages, and that was designed to help people from different countries communicate with each other.

es|pio|nage /ˈɛspiənɑːʒ/ N-UNCOUNT **Espionage** is the activity of finding out the political, military, or industrial secrets of your enemies or rivals by using spies. [FORMAL] ☐ *The authorities have arrested several people suspected of espionage.*

es|pla|nade /ˈɛsplənɑːd/ (esplanades) N-COUNT [usu the N in sing] The **esplanade**, usually in a town by the sea, is a wide, open road where people walk for pleasure.

e-sports also **esports** N-PLURAL **E-sports** are video games played competitively in front of spectators. ☐ *...an e-sports arena.*

es|pous|al /ɪsˈpaʊzəl/ N-SING [usu poss N of n] A government's or person's **espousal** of a particular policy, cause, or belief is their strong support of it. [FORMAL] ❑ *The author's espousal of unpopular causes has certainly alienated large sections of the establishment.*

es|pouse /ɪspaʊz/ (**espouses, espousing, espoused**) V-T If you **espouse** a particular policy, cause, or belief, you become very interested in it and give your support to it. [FORMAL] ❑ *She ran away with him to Mexico and espoused the revolutionary cause.*

es|pres|so /ɛspresoʊ/ (**espressos**) N-UNCOUNT **Espresso** coffee is made by forcing steam or boiling water through ground coffee beans. ❑ *...Italian espresso coffee.* • N-COUNT An **espresso** is a cup of espresso coffee.

es|prit de corps /ɛspriː də kɔːr/ N-UNCOUNT **Esprit de corps** is a feeling of loyalty and pride that is shared by the members of a group who consider themselves to be different from other people in some special way. [FORMAL]

espy /ɪspaɪ/ (**espies, espying, espied**) V-T If you **espy** something, you see or notice it. [OLD-FASHIONED] ❑ *Here, from a window, did Guinevere espy a knight standing in a woodman's cart.*

Esq. Esq. is used sometimes after names as a written abbreviation for **esquire** to indicate that the person is a lawyer. ❑ *...Harold T. Cranford, Esq.*

es|quire /ɛskwaɪər/ N-TITLE **Esquire** is a title that can be used after a lawyer's name. [AM]

es|say /ɛseɪ/ (**essays**) ◼ N-COUNT An **essay** is a short piece of writing on a particular subject written by a student. ❑ *We asked Jason to write an essay about his hometown.* ◻ N-COUNT An **essay** is a short piece of writing on a particular subject that is written by a writer for publication. ❑ *...Thomas Malthus's essay on population.*

es|say|ist /ɛseɪɪst/ (**essayists**) N-COUNT An **essayist** is a writer who writes essays for publication.

es|sence /ɛsəns/ (**essences**) ◼ N-UNCOUNT The **essence** of something is its basic and most important characteristic that gives it its individual identity. ❑ *The essence of consultation is to listen to, and take account of, the views of those consulted.* • PHRASE You use **in essence** to emphasize that you are talking about the most important or central aspect of an idea, situation, or event. [FORMAL, EMPHASIS] ❑ *Though complicated in detail, local taxes are in essence simple.* • PHRASE If you say that something **is of the essence**, you mean that it is absolutely necessary in order for a particular action to be successful. [FORMAL] ❑ *Speed was of the essence in a project of this type.* ◻ N-MASS **Essence** is a very concentrated liquid that is used for flavoring food or for its smell. ❑ *...a few drops of vanilla essence.*

es|sen|tial ✦✧ /ɪsɛnʃəl/ (**essentials**) ◼ ADJ Something that is **essential** is extremely important or absolutely necessary to a particular subject, situation, or activity. ❑ *It was absolutely essential to separate crops from the areas that animals used as pasture.* ❑ *As they must also sprint over short distances, speed is essential.* ◻ N-COUNT The **essentials** are the things that are absolutely necessary for the situation you are in or for the task you are doing. ❑ *The apartment contained the basic essentials for bachelor life.* ◼ ADJ The **essential** aspects of something are its most basic or important aspects. ❑ *Most authorities agree that play is an essential part of a child's development.* ◻ N-PLURAL The **essentials** are the most important principles, ideas, or facts of a particular subject. ❑ *...the essentials of everyday life, such as eating and exercise.*

SYNONYMS

essential
ADJ ◼
vital: *The port is vital to supply relief to millions of drought victims.*
necessary: *We will do whatever is necessary to stop them.*
critical: *He says setting priorities is of critical importance.*
crucial: *...the most crucial election campaign in years.*
indispensable: *...the indispensable guide for any traveler to France.*
key: *Education is likely to be a key issue in the next election.*

es|sen|tial|ly ✦✧ /ɪsɛnʃəli/ ◼ ADV [ADV with cl/group] You use **essentially** to emphasize a quality that someone or something has, and to say that it is their most important or basic quality. [FORMAL, EMPHASIS] ❑ *It's been believed for centuries that great writers, composers, and scientists are essentially quite different from ordinary people.* ◻ ADV You use **essentially** to indicate that what you are saying is mainly true, although some parts of it are wrong or more complicated than has been stated. [FORMAL, VAGUENESS] ❑ *His analysis of urban use of agricultural land has been proved essentially correct.*

es|sen|tial work|er (**essential workers**) N-COUNT An **essential worker** is someone without whose work society cannot function properly, such as a teacher, nurse or bus driver. ❑ *Average house prices in many places are unaffordable for essential workers such as nurses and teachers.*

SUFFIX

-est
You add **-est** to many short adjectives to form superlatives. For example, the superlative of 'nice' is **nicest** and the superlative of 'happy' is **happiest**.

es|tab|lish ✦✧ /ɪstæblɪʃ/ (**establishes, establishing, established**) ◼ V-T If someone **establishes** something such as an organization, a type of activity, or a set of rules, they create it or introduce it in such a way that it is likely to last for a long time. ❑ *The UN has established detailed criteria for who should be allowed to vote.* ◻ V-RECIP If you **establish** contact with someone, you start to have contact with them. You can also say that two people, groups, or countries **establish** contact. [FORMAL] ❑ *We had already established contact with the museum.* ◼ V-T If you **establish** that something is true, you discover facts that show that it is definitely true. [FORMAL] ❑ *Medical tests established that she was not their own child.* ❑ *It will be essential to establish how the money is being spent.* • **es|tab|lished** ADJ ❑ *That link is an established medical fact.* ◻ V-T If you **establish** yourself, your reputation, or a good quality that you have, you succeed in doing something, and achieve respect or a secure position as a result of this. ❑ *This is going to be the show where up-and-coming comedians will establish themselves.* ❑ *He has established himself as a pivotal figure in state politics.*

es|tab|lished /ɪstæblɪʃt/ ADJ If you use **established** to describe something such as an organization, you mean that it is well known because it has existed for a long time. ❑ *These range from established companies to start-ups.*

es|tab|lish|ment ✦✧ /ɪstæblɪʃmənt/ (**establishments**) ◼ N-SING The **establishment** of an organization or system is the act of creating it or beginning it. [FORMAL] ❑ *The establishment of the regional government in 1980 did not end terrorism.* ◻ N-COUNT An **establishment** is a store, business, or organization occupying a particular building or place. [FORMAL] ❑ *...a scientific research establishment.* ◼ N-SING You refer to the people who have power and influence in the running of a country, society, or organization as the **establishment**. ❑ *While scientists were once considered cranks and outsiders to the system, we are now part of the establishment.*

SYNONYMS

establishment
NOUN ◻
organization: *Most of these specialized schools are provided by volunteer organizations.*
institution: *Class size varies from one type of institution to another.*
body: *...the Chairman of the police representative body, the Police Federation.*

es|tate ✦✧ /ɪsteɪt/ (**estates**) ◼ N-COUNT An **estate** is a large area of land in the country which is owned by a person, family, or organization. ❑ *He spent holidays at the 300-acre estate of his aunt and uncle.* ◻ N-COUNT Someone's **estate** is all the money and property that they leave behind when they die. [LEGAL] ❑ *His estate was valued at $150,000.* ◼ → see also **real estate**

es|tate agen|cy (**estate agencies**) N-COUNT An **estate agency** is a company that sells houses and land for people. [BRIT]

in AM, use **real estate agency**

es|tate agent (**estate agents**) N-COUNT An **estate agent** is someone who works for a company that sells houses and land for people. [BRIT]

in AM, use **Realtor**

es|tate car (**estate cars**) N-COUNT An **estate car** is a car with a long body, a door at the rear, and space behind the back seats. [BRIT]

in AM, use **station wagon**

es|teem /ɪstim/ ◼ N-UNCOUNT **Esteem** is the admiration and respect that you feel toward another person. [FORMAL] ❏ *He is held in high esteem by colleagues in the construction industry.* ◼ → see also **self-esteem**

es|teemed /ɪstimd/ ADJ You use **esteemed** to describe someone who you greatly admire and respect. [FORMAL] ❏ *He was esteemed by his neighbors.* ❏ *It is indeed an honor to serve my country in such an esteemed position.*

es|thete /ɛsθit/ → see **aesthete**

es|thet|ic /ɛsθɛtɪk/ → see **aesthetic**

es|ti|mable /ɛstɪməbᵊl/ ADJ [usu ADJ n] If you describe someone or something as **estimable**, you mean that they deserve admiration. [FORMAL] ❏ *...the estimable Miss Cartwright.*

es|ti|mate ◆◆◇ (estimates, estimating, estimated)

> The verb is pronounced /ɛstɪmeɪt/. The noun is pronounced /ɛstɪmɪt/.

◼ V-T If you **estimate** a quantity or value, you make an approximate judgment or calculation of it. ❏ *Try to estimate how many steps it will take to get to a close object.* ❏ *I estimate that total cost for treatment will go from $9,000 to $12,500.* ● **es|ti|mat|ed** ADJ ❏ *There are an estimated 90,000 gangsters in the country.* ◼ N-COUNT An **estimate** is an approximate calculation of a quantity or value. ❏ *...the official estimate of the election result.* ◼ N-COUNT An **estimate** is a judgment about a person or situation that you make based on the available evidence. ❏ *I hadn't been far wrong in my estimate of his grandson's capabilities.* ◼ N-COUNT An **estimate** from someone who you employ to do a job for you, such as a builder or a plumber, is a written statement of how much the job is likely to cost. ❏ *Quotes and estimates can be prepared by computer on the spot.*

SYNONYMS

estimate
VERB ◼
guess: *Paula reached for her camera, guessing distance and exposure.*
calculate: *From this, you can calculate the total mass in the galaxy.*
evaluate: *The market situation is difficult to evaluate.*
gauge: *He gauged the wind at over thirty knots.*
NOUN ◼
guess: *He'd taken her pulse and made a guess at her blood pressure.*
calculation: *Leonard made a rapid calculation: he'd never make it in time.*
reckoning: *By my reckoning we were seven or eight kilometers from Borj Mechaab.*
ballpark estimate/figure: *Ballpark estimates indicate a price tag of $90 million a month.*

---

es|ti|ma|tion /ɛstɪmeɪʃᵊn/ (estimations) ◼ N-SING Your **estimation** of a person or situation is the opinion or impression that you have formed about them. [FORMAL] ❏ *He has gone down considerably in my estimation.* ◼ N-COUNT An **estimation** is an approximate calculation of a quantity or value. ❏ *...estimations of pre-tax profits of 12.25 million.*

es|tranged /ɪstreɪndʒd/ ◼ ADJ An **estranged** wife or husband is no longer living with their husband or wife. ❏ *...his estranged wife.* ◼ ADJ If you are **estranged** from your family or friends, you have quarreled with them and are not communicating with them. [FORMAL] ❏ *Joanna spent most of her twenties virtually estranged from her father.* ◼ ADJ [v-link ADJ] If you describe someone as **estranged** from something such as society or their profession, you mean that they no longer seem involved in it. [FORMAL] ❏ *Arran became increasingly estranged from the mainstream of Hollywood.*

es|trange|ment /ɪstreɪndʒmənt/ (estrangements) N-VAR **Estrangement** is the state of being estranged from someone or the length of time for which you are estranged. [FORMAL] ❏ *The trip will bring to an end years of estrangement between the two countries.*

es|tro|gen /ɛstrədʒᵊn/ N-COUNT **Estrogen** is a hormone produced in the ovaries of female animals. Estrogen controls the reproductive cycle and prepares the body for pregnancy. ❏ *Low estrogen levels are associated with stress.*

es|tu|ary /ɛstʃueri/ (estuaries) ◼ N-COUNT; N-IN-NAMES An **estuary** is the wide part of a river where it joins the sea. ❏ *Sturgeon fishing has been pretty good in the estuary.* ◼ → See feature box at **water**

e-tailer /iteɪlər/ (e-tailers) also **etailer** N-COUNT An **e-tailer** is a person or company that sells products on the internet. [COMPUTING] ❏ *This company is the biggest wine e-tailer in California.*

e-tailing /iteɪlɪŋ/ also **etailing** N-UNCOUNT **E-tailing** is the business of selling products on the internet. [COMPUTING] ❏ *Electronic retailing has predictably become known as e-tailing.*

et al. /ɛt æl, -ɑl/ **et al.** is used after a name or a list of names to indicate that other people are also involved. It is used especially when referring to books or articles that were written by more than two people. ❏ *...Blough et al.*

etc. ◆◇◇ /ɛt sɛtərə, -sɛtrə/ **etc.** is used at the end of a list to indicate that you have mentioned only some of the items involved and have not given a full list. **etc.** is a written abbreviation for 'etcetera.' ❏ *She knew all about my schoolwork, my hospital work, etc.*

et|cet|era /ɛtsɛtərə, -sɛtrə/ also **et cetera** → see **etc.**

etch /ɛtʃ/ (etches, etching, etched) ◼ V-T If a line or pattern is **etched** into a surface, it is cut into the surface by means of acid or a sharp tool. You can also say that a surface **is etched** with a line or pattern. ❏ *Crosses were etched into the walls.* ❏ *Windows are etched with the vehicle identification number.* ◼ V-T PASSIVE If something **is etched** on your memory, you remember it very clearly, usually because it has some special importance for you. [LITERARY] ❏ *The ugly scene in the study was still etched on her mind.*

etch|ing /ɛtʃɪŋ/ (etchings) N-COUNT An **etching** is a picture printed from a metal plate that has had a design cut into it with acid.

eter|nal /ɪtɜrnᵊl/ ◼ ADJ Something that is **eternal** lasts forever. ❏ *...the quest for eternal youth.* ● **eter|nal|ly** ADV ❏ *She is eternally grateful to her family for their support.* ◼ ADJ If you describe something as **eternal**, you mean that it seems to last forever, often because you think it is boring or annoying. ❏ *In the background was that eternal hum.*

eter|nal tri|an|gle (eternal triangles) N-COUNT [usu sing] You use **the eternal triangle** to refer to a relationship involving love and jealousy between three people.

eter|nity /ɪtɜrnɪti/ ◼ N-UNCOUNT **Eternity** is time without an end or a state of existence outside time, especially the state that some people believe they will pass into after they have died. ❏ *I have always found the thought of eternity terrifying.* ◼ N-SING If you say that a situation lasted for **an eternity**, you mean that it seemed to last an extremely long time, usually because it was boring or unpleasant. ❏ *The war continued for an eternity.*

etha|nol /ɛθənɔl, -nɒl/ N-UNCOUNT **Ethanol** is another name for alcohol. [TECHNICAL]

ether /iθər/ N-UNCOUNT **Ether** is a colorless liquid that burns easily. It is used in industry and in medicine as an anesthetic. ❏ *...a sweetish smell of ether and iodine.*

ethe|real /ɪθɪəriəl/ ADJ Someone or something that is **ethereal** has a delicate beauty. [FORMAL] ❏ *She's the prettiest, most ethereal romantic heroine in the movies.*

Ether|net /iθərnɛt/ N-UNCOUNT [oft N n] In computing, **Ethernet** is a type of local area network. [TRADEMARK] ❏ *Thanks to its Ethernet card, you can link straight into your network at the office.*

eth|ic /ɛθɪk/ (ethics) ◼ N-PLURAL **Ethics** are moral beliefs and rules about right and wrong. ❏ *Refugee workers said such action was a violation of medical ethics.* ◼ N-PLURAL Someone's **ethics** are the moral principles about right and wrong behavior that they believe in. ❏ *He told the police that he had thought honestly about the ethics of what he was doing.* ◼ N-UNCOUNT **Ethics** is the study of questions about what is morally right and wrong. ❏ *...the teaching of ethics and moral philosophy.* ◼ N-SING An **ethic** of a particular kind is an idea or moral belief that influences the behavior, attitudes, and philosophy of a group of people. ❏ *...the ethic of public service.*

ethi|cal /ɛθɪkᵊl/ ◼ ADJ **Ethical** means relating to beliefs about right and wrong. ❏ *...the medical, nursing and ethical issues* surrounding terminally-ill people. • **ethi|cal|ly** /ɛθɪkli/ ADV ❑ *Attorneys are ethically and legally bound to absolute confidentiality.* **2** ADJ If you describe something as **ethical**, you mean that it is morally right or morally acceptable. ❑ *The trade association promotes ethical business practices.* • **ethi|cal|ly** ADV [ADV after v] ❑ *Mayors want local companies to behave ethically.*

Ethio|pian /iθioupiən/ (**Ethiopians**) ADJ **Ethiopian** means belonging or relating to Ethiopia, or to its people, language, or culture. • N-COUNT An **Ethiopian** is an Ethiopian citizen, or a person of Ethiopian origin.

eth|nic ✦✧ /ɛθnɪk/ **1** ADJ **Ethnic** means connected with or relating to different racial or cultural groups of people. ❑ *...a survey of Britain's ethnic minorities.* • **eth|ni|cal|ly** /ɛθnɪkli/ ADV ❑ *...a predominantly young, ethnically mixed audience.* **2** ADJ [ADJ n] You can use **ethnic** to describe people who belong to a particular racial or cultural group but who, usually, do not live in the country where most members of that group live. ❑ *There are still several million ethnic Germans in Russia.* • **eth|ni|cal|ly** ADV [ADV adj] ❑ *...a large ethnically Albanian population.* **3** ADJ **Ethnic** clothing, music, or food is characteristic of the traditions of a particular ethnic group, and different from what is usually found in modern Western culture. ❑ *...a magnificent range of ethnic fabrics.*

eth|nic cleans|ing N-UNCOUNT **Ethnic cleansing** is the process of using violent methods to force certain groups of people out of a particular area or country. [DISAPPROVAL] ❑ *In late May, government forces began the "ethnic cleansing" of the area around the town.*

eth|nic|ity /ɛθnɪsɪti/ (**ethnicities**) N-VAR **Ethnicity** is the state or fact of belonging to a particular ethnic group. ❑ *He said his ethnicity had not been important to him.*

eth|no|cen|tric /ɛθnoʊsɛntrɪk/ ADJ If you describe something as **ethnocentric**, you disagree with it because it is based on the belief that one particular race or nationality of people is superior to all others. [DISAPPROVAL] ❑ *Her work is open to the criticism that it is ethnocentric.*

eth|no|graph|ic /ɛθnəgræfɪk/ ADJ **Ethnographic** refers to things that are connected with or relate to ethnography.

eth|nog|ra|phy /ɛθnɒgrəfi/ N-UNCOUNT **Ethnography** is the branch of anthropology in which different cultures are studied and described.

ethos /iθɒs/ N-SING An **ethos** is the set of ideas and attitudes that is associated with a particular group of people or a particular type of activity. [FORMAL] ❑ *The whole ethos of the hotel is effortless service.*

ethyl al|co|hol /ɛθəl ælkəhɒl/ N-UNCOUNT **Ethyl alcohol** is the same as **ethanol**. [TECHNICAL]

e-ticket (**e-tickets**) N-COUNT An **e-ticket** is a ticket in electronic form rather than one printed on paper. **E-ticket** is an abbreviation for 'electronic ticket.' ❑ *Your e-ticket is attached to this email.*

eti|ol|ogy /itɪplədʒi/ (**etiologies**) also **aetiology** N-VAR [oft the N of n] The **etiology** of a disease or a problem is the study of its causes. ❑ *...the etiology of psychiatric disorder.*

eti|quette /ɛtɪkɪt, -kɛt/ **1** N-UNCOUNT **Etiquette** is a set of customs and rules for polite behavior, especially among a particular class of people or in a particular profession. ❑ *This was such a great breach of etiquette, he hardly knew what to do.* **2** → See feature box at **polite**

ety|mo|logi|cal /ɛtɪməlɒdʒɪkəl/ ADJ [usu ADJ n] **Etymological** means concerned with or relating to etymology. [FORMAL] ❑ *"Gratification" and "gratitude" have the same etymological root.*

ety|mol|ogy /ɛtɪmɒlədʒi/ (**etymologies**) **1** N-UNCOUNT **Etymology** is the study of the origins and historical development of words. **2** N-COUNT The **etymology** of a particular word is its history.

EU /i yu/ N-PROPER The **EU** is an organization of European countries that have joint policies on matters such as trade, agriculture, and finance. **EU** is an abbreviation for **European Union**. ❑ *...the ten new EU members.*

euca|lyp|tus /yukəlɪptəs/ (**eucalyptuses** or **eucalyptus**) N-VAR [oft N n] A **eucalyptus** is an evergreen tree, originally from Australia, that is grown to provide wood, gum, and an oil that is used in medicines.

Eucha|rist /yukərɪst/ N-SING [usu the N] The **Eucharist** is the Christian religious ceremony in which Christ's last meal with his disciples is celebrated by eating bread and drinking wine.

eugen|ics /yudʒɛnɪks/ N-UNCOUNT **Eugenics** is the study of methods to improve the human race by carefully selecting parents who will produce the healthiest children. [TECHNICAL, DISAPPROVAL]

eulo|gize /yulədʒaɪz/ (**eulogizes**, **eulogizing**, **eulogized**)

in BRIT, also use **eulogise**

1 V-T If you **eulogize** someone who has died, you make a speech praising them, usually at their funeral. [AM] ❑ *Leaders from around the world eulogized the Egyptian president.* **2** V-T/V-I If you **eulogize** someone or something, you praise them very highly. [FORMAL] ❑ *She eulogized him virtually right up to their sudden break-up.* ❑ *The boss eulogized about Steven's versatility.*

eulogy /yulədʒi/ (**eulogies**) **1** N-COUNT A **eulogy** is a speech or piece of writing that praises someone or something very much. [FORMAL] **2** N-COUNT A **eulogy** is a speech, usually at a funeral, in which a person who has just died is praised. [AM]

eunuch /yunək/ (**eunuchs**) N-COUNT A **eunuch** is a man who has had his testicles removed.

eu|phe|mism /yufəmɪzəm/ (**euphemisms**) N-COUNT A **euphemism** is a polite word or expression that is used to refer to things that people may find upsetting or embarrassing to talk about, for example sex, the human body, or death. ❑ *The term "early retirement" is nearly always a euphemism for layoffs nowadays.*

eu|phe|mis|tic /yufəmɪstɪk/ ADJ **Euphemistic** language uses polite, pleasant, or neutral words and expressions to refer to things that people may find unpleasant, upsetting, or embarrassing to talk about, for example, sex, the human body, or death. ❑ *...a euphemistic way of saying that someone has been lying.* • **eu|phe|mis|ti|cal|ly** /yufəmɪstɪkli/ ADV [ADV with v] ❑ *...political prisons, called euphemistically "reeducation camps."*

eupho|ria /yufɔriə/ N-UNCOUNT **Euphoria** is a feeling of intense happiness and excitement. ❑ *There was euphoria after the election.*

euphor|ic /yufɔrɪk/ ADJ If you are **euphoric**, you feel intense happiness and excitement. ❑ *The war had received euphoric support from the public.*

Eura|sian /yʊəreɪʒən/ (**Eurasians**) **1** ADJ **Eurasian** means concerned with or relating to both Europe and Asia. ❑ *...the whole of the Eurasian continent.* **2** N-COUNT A **Eurasian** is a person who has one European and one Asian parent or whose family comes from both Europe and Asia. • ADJ **Eurasian** is also an adjective. ❑ *She married into a leading Eurasian family in Hong Kong.*

eure|ka /yʊərikə/ EXCLAM Someone might say '**eureka**' when they suddenly find or realize something, or when they solve a problem. [HUMOROUS, OLD-FASHIONED] ❑ *"Eureka! I've got it!"*

euro /yʊəroʊ/ (**euros**) N-COUNT The **euro** is a unit of currency that is used by several member countries of the European Union. ❑ *Millions of words have been written about the introduction of the euro.*

PREFIX

Euro-
is used to form words that describe or refer to something that is connected with Europe or with the European Union. *For example, a **Eurocentric** view focuses on European culture and society, often with the result that people in other parts of the world are not considered.*

Euro|bond /yʊəroʊbɒnd/ (**Eurobonds**) also **eurobond** N-COUNT **Eurobonds** are bonds which are issued in a particular European currency and sold to people from a country with a different currency.

Euro|cen|tric /yʊəroʊsɛntrɪk/ ADJ If you describe something as **Eurocentric**, you disapprove of it because it focuses on Europe and the needs of European people, often with the result that people in other parts of the world suffer in some way. [DISAPPROVAL] ❑ *...the insultingly Eurocentric bias in the education system.*

Eu|ro|pean /jʊərəpiən/ (**Europeans**) **1** ADJ **European** means belonging or relating to, or coming from Europe. ❑ ...in some other European countries. **2** N-COUNT A **European** is a person who comes from Europe. ❑ Three-quarters of working-age Americans work, compared with roughly 60% of Europeans.

Eu|ro|pean Un|ion N-PROPER The **European Union** is an organization of European countries that have joint policies on matters such as commerce, agriculture, and finance.

Eu|ro|scep|tic /jʊəroʊskɛptɪk/ (**Eurosceptics**) also **Euro-sceptic, eurosceptic** N-COUNT A **Eurosceptic** is someone, especially a politician, who is opposed to closer links between Britain and the European Union. [BRIT] • ADJ [usu ADJ n] **Eurosceptic** is also an adjective. ❑ ...Eurosceptic MPs.

eu|ro|zone /jʊəroʊzoʊn/ also **Eurozone** N-SING [the N] The **eurozone** is all those countries that have adopted the euro currency, considered as a group.

eu|tha|na|sia /juːθəneɪʒə/ N-UNCOUNT **Euthanasia** is the practice of killing someone who is very ill and will never get better in order to end their suffering, usually done at their request or with their consent. ❑ ...those in favor of voluntary euthanasia.

evacu|ate /ɪvækjueɪt/ (**evacuates, evacuating, evacuated**) **1** V-T To **evacuate** someone means to send them to a place of safety, away from a dangerous building, town, or area. ❑ They were planning to evacuate the seventy American officials still in the country. • **evacu|ation** /ɪvækjueɪʃ°n/ (**evacuations**) N-VAR ❑ ...the evacuation of the sick and wounded. ❑ An evacuation of the city's four-million inhabitants is planned for later this week. **2** V-T If people **evacuate** a place, they move out of it for a period of time, especially because it is dangerous. ❑ The fire is threatening about sixty homes, and residents have evacuated the area. • **evacu|ation** N-VAR ❑ ...the mass evacuation of the Bosnian town of Srebrenica.

evac|uee /ɪvækjuiː/ (**evacuees**) N-COUNT An **evacuee** is someone who has been sent away from a dangerous place to somewhere safe, especially during a war.

evade /ɪveɪd/ (**evades, evading, evaded**) **1** V-T If you **evade** something, you find a way of not doing something that you really ought to do. ❑ By his own admission, he evaded paying taxes as a Florida real-estate speculator. **2** V-T If you **evade** a question or a topic, you avoid talking about it or dealing with it. ❑ Too many companies, she says, are evading the issue. **3** V-T If you **evade** someone or something, you move so that you can avoid meeting them or avoid being touched or hit. ❑ She turned and gazed at the river, evading his eyes.

evalu|ate /ɪvæljueɪt/ (**evaluates, evaluating, evaluated**) V-T If you **evaluate** something or someone, you consider them in order to make a judgment about them, for example about how good or bad they are. ❑ The market situation is difficult to evaluate. • **evalu|ation** /ɪvæljueɪʃ°n/ (**evaluations**) N-VAR ❑ ...the opinions and evaluations of college supervisors.

evalu|ative /ɪvæljuətɪv/ ADJ Something that is **evaluative** is based on an assessment of the values, qualities, and significance of a particular person or thing. [FORMAL] ❑ ...ten years of evaluative research.

eva|nes|cent /ɛvənɛs°nt/ ADJ Something that is **evanescent** gradually disappears from sight or memory. [FORMAL OR LITERARY] ❑ ...the evanescent scents of summer herbs.

evan|geli|cal /iːvændʒɛlɪk°l, ɛvən-/ **1** ADJ **Evangelical** Christians emphasize the importance of the Bible and the need for a personal belief in Christ. ❑ ...an evangelical Christian. **2** ADJ [usu ADJ n] If you describe someone's behavior as **evangelical**, you mean that it is very enthusiastic. ❑ With almost evangelical fervor, Markman warns against sunbathing.

evan|gelism /ɪvændʒəlɪzəm/ N-UNCOUNT **Evangelism** is the teaching of Christianity, especially to people who are not Christians.

evan|gelist /ɪvændʒəlɪst/ (**evangelists**) N-COUNT An **evangelist** is a person who travels from place to place in order to try to convert people to Christianity. • **evan|gelis|tic** ADJ ❑ ...a youth-oriented evangelistic magazine.

evan|gelize /ɪvændʒəlaɪz/ (**evangelizes, evangelizing, evangelized**)

in BRIT, also use **evangelise**

V-T If someone **evangelizes** a group or area, they try to convert people to their religion, especially Christianity. ❑ ...missionaries who went to evangelize faraway countries.

evapo|rate /ɪvæpəreɪt/ (**evaporates, evaporating, evaporated**) **1** V-T/V-I When a liquid **evaporates**, or **is evaporated**, it changes from a liquid state to a gas, because its temperature has increased. ❑ Moisture is drawn to the surface of the fabric so that it evaporates. ❑ The water is evaporated by the sun. • **evapo|ra|tion** /ɪvæpəreɪʃ°n/ N-UNCOUNT ❑ The soothing, cooling effect is caused by the evaporation of the sweat on the skin. **2** V-I If a feeling, plan, or activity **evaporates**, it gradually becomes weaker and eventually disappears completely. ❑ My anger evaporated and I wanted to cry. **3** → See feature box at **experiment**; See also color supplement

evapo|rat|ed milk N-UNCOUNT **Evaporated milk** is thick, concentrated milk that is sold in cans.

eva|sion /ɪveɪʒ°n/ (**evasions**) **1** N-VAR **Evasion** means deliberately avoiding something that you are supposed to do or deal with. ❑ He was arrested for tax evasion. **2** N-VAR If you accuse someone of **evasion** when they have been asked a question, you mean that they are deliberately avoiding giving a clear direct answer. ❑ We want straight answers. No evasions.

eva|sive /ɪveɪsɪv/ **1** ADJ If you describe someone as **evasive**, you mean that they deliberately avoid giving clear direct answers to questions. ❑ He was evasive about the circumstances of his first meeting with Stanley Dean. • **eva|sive|ly** ADV [ADV with v] ❑ "Until I can speak to your husband I can't come to any conclusion about that," Manuel said evasively. **2** PHRASE If you **take evasive action**, you deliberately move away from someone or something in order to avoid meeting them or being hit by them. ❑ At least four high-flying warplanes had to take evasive action.

eve /iːv/ (**eves**) **1** N-COUNT The **eve** of a particular event or occasion is the day before it, or the period of time just before it. ❑ ...on the eve of his 27th birthday. **2** → see also **Christmas Eve, New Year's Eve**

EVEN

① DISCOURSE USES
② ADJECTIVE USES
③ PHRASAL VERB USE

---

① **even** /iːv°n/ **1** ADV You use **even** to suggest that what comes just after or just before it in the sentence is rather surprising. ❑ He kept calling me for years, even after he got married. ❑ Some of Edward's remarks were so scathing that even Jane was surprised. **2** ADV [ADV compar] You use **even** with comparative adjectives and adverbs to emphasize a quality that someone or something has. [EMPHASIS] ❑ On television he made an even stronger impact as an interviewer. **3** PHRASE You use **even if** or **even though** to indicate that a particular fact does not make the rest of your statement untrue. ❑ Cynthia is not ashamed of what she does, even if she ends up doing something wrong. **4** PHRASE You use **even so** to introduce a surprising fact that relates to what you have just said. [SPOKEN] ❑ The bus was only half full. Even so, a young man asked Nina if the seat next to her was taken. **5** PHRASE You use **even then** to say that something is the case in spite of what has just been stated or whatever the circumstances may be. ❑ Peace could come only gradually, in carefully measured steps. Even then, it sounds almost impossible to achieve.

② **even** /iːv°n/

→ Please look at meaning **8** to see if the expression you are looking for is shown under another headword.

1 ADJ An **even** measurement or rate stays at about the same level. ❑ How important is it to have an even temperature when you're working? • **even|ly** ADV ❑ He looked at Ellen, breathing evenly in her sleep. **2** ADJ An **even** surface is smooth and flat. ❑ The tables are fitted with a glass top to provide an even surface. **3** ADJ If there is an **even** distribution or division of something, each person, group, or area involved has an equal amount. ❑ Divide the dough into 12 even pieces and shape each piece into a ball. • **even|ly** ADV ❑ The meat is divided evenly and boiled in a stew. **4** ADJ An **even** contest or competition is equally balanced between the two sides who are taking part. ❑ It was an even game. • **even|ly** ADV [ADV -ed] ❑ They must choose between two evenly matched candidates for governor. **5** ADJ An **even** number can be divided exactly by the number two. **6** ADJ [ADJ n] If there is an **even** chance that something will happen, the chances that it will or will not happen are equal. ◻ *They have a more than even chance of winning the next election.* **7** PHRASE When a company or a person running a business **breaks even**, they make neither a profit nor a loss. [BUSINESS] ◻ *The airline hopes to break even next year and return to profit the following year.* **8** **to be on an even keel** → see **keel**

③ **even** /iːvᵊn/ (**evens**, **evening**, **evened**)

▶ **even out** PHRASAL VERB If something **evens out**, or if you **even** it **out**, the differences between the different parts of it are reduced. ◻ *The power-balance has evened out in the interim government.*

even|hand|ed /iːvᵊnhændɪd/ ADJ If someone is **evenhanded**, they are completely fair, especially when they are judging other people or dealing with two groups of people. ◻ *...an evenhanded approach to the war on drugs.*

eve|ning ✦✦◇ /iːvnɪŋ/ (**evenings**) N-VAR The **evening** is the part of each day between the end of the afternoon and the time when you go to bed. ◻ *All he did that evening was sit around the house.* ◻ *Supper is from 5:00 to 6:00 in the evening.*

eve|ning class (**evening classes**) N-COUNT An **evening class** is a class for adults that is taught in the evening rather than during the day. ◻ *He's trying to learn English fast with evening classes twice a week.*

eve|ning dress (**evening dresses**) **1** N-UNCOUNT **Evening dress** consists of the formal clothes that people wear to formal occasions in the evening. **2** N-COUNT An **evening dress** is a special dress, usually a long one, that a woman wears to a formal occasion in the evening.

eve|ning prim|rose (**evening primroses**) N-VAR **Evening primrose** is a tall plant with yellow flowers that open in the evening. Its seeds are used to make medicine.

even|song /iːvᵊnsɒŋ/ N-UNCOUNT **Evensong** is the evening service in the Anglican Church.

event ✦✦✦ /ɪvɛnt/ (**events**) **1** N-COUNT An **event** is something that happens, especially when it is unusual or important. You can use **events** to describe all the things that are happening in a particular situation. ◻ *A new inquiry into the events of the day was opened in 2002.* **2** N-COUNT An **event** is a planned and organized occasion, for example a social gathering or a sports tournament. ◻ *...major sporting events.* **3** N-COUNT An **event** is one of the races or competitions that are part of an organized occasion such as a sports tournament. ◻ *The main events start at 1 p.m.* **4** PHRASE You use **in the event of**, **in the event that**, and **in that event** when you are talking about a possible future situation, especially when you are planning what to do if it occurs. ◻ *The bank has agreed to give an immediate refund in the unlikely event of an error being made.* **5** PHRASE You say **in any event** after you have been discussing a situation, in order to indicate that what you are saying is true or possible, in spite of anything that has happened or may happen. ◻ *In any event, the bowling alley restaurant proved quite acceptable.*

COLLOCATIONS

event
NOUN
1
adjective + **event**: major, significant; historical, recent; tragic
2
noun + **event**: charity, fundraising; music, sporting, swimming
adjective + **event**: major, special; social
verb + **event**: hold, host, stage; organize, plan; attend

---

even-tempered ADJ If someone is **even-tempered**, they are usually calm and do not easily get angry.

event|ful /ɪvɛntfəl/ ADJ If you describe an event or a period of time as **eventful**, you mean that a lot of interesting, exciting, or important things have happened during it. ◻ *This has been an eventful year for Tom, both professionally and personally.*

even|tual /ɪvɛntʃuəl/ ADJ [ADJ n] You use **eventual** to indicate that something happens or is the case at the end of a process or period of time. ◻ *There are many who believe that civil war will be the eventual outcome of the racial tension in the country.*

even|tu|al|ity /ɪvɛntʃuælɪti/ (**eventualities**) N-COUNT An **eventuality** is a possible future event or result, especially one that is unpleasant or surprising. [FORMAL] ◻ *Every eventuality is covered, from running out of gas to needing water.*

even|tu|al|ly ✦✦◇ /ɪvɛntʃuəli/ **1** ADV **Eventually** means in the end, especially after a lot of delays, problems, or arguments. ◻ *Eventually, the army caught up with him in Latvia.* **2** ADV **Eventually** means at the end of a situation or process or as the final result of it. ◻ *Eventually your child will leave home to lead her own life as a fully independent adult.*

SYNONYMS

eventually
ADV **1**
finally: *The food finally arrived at the end of last week and distribution began.*
in the end: *I toyed with the idea of calling the police, but in the end I didn't.*
ultimately: *...a tough but ultimately worthwhile struggle.*

---

ever ✦✦✦ /ɛvər/

Ever is an adverb that you use to add emphasis in negative sentences, commands, questions, and conditional structures.

1 ADV **Ever** means at any time. It is used in questions and negative statements. ◻ *I'm not sure I'll ever trust people again.* ◻ *Neither of us had ever skied.* **2** ADV You use **ever** in expressions such as '**did you ever**' and '**have you ever**' to express surprise or shock at something you have just seen, heard, or experienced, especially when you expect people to agree with you. [EMPHASIS] ◻ *Have you ever seen anything like it?* **3** ADV You use **ever** after comparatives and superlatives to emphasize the degree to which something is true or when you are comparing a present situation with the past or the future. [EMPHASIS] ◻ *She's got a great voice and is singing better than ever.* ◻ *We probably take less exercise than ever before.* **4** ADV [ADV adj/adv] You use **ever** to say that something happens more all the time. ◻ *They grew ever further apart.* **5** ADV [ADV before v] You can use **ever** for emphasis after 'never.' [INFORMAL, EMPHASIS] ◻ *I can never, ever, forgive myself.* **6** ADV [quest ADV] You use **ever** in questions beginning with words such as 'why,' 'when,' and 'who' when you want to emphasize your surprise or shock. [EMPHASIS] ◻ *Why ever didn't you tell me?* **7** PHRASE If something has been the case **ever since** a particular time, it has been the case all the time from then until now. ◻ *He's been there ever since you left!* • ADV **Ever** is also an adverb. ◻ *I simply gave in to him, and I've regretted it ever since.* **8** → see also **forever** **9** PHRASE You use the expression **all** someone **ever does** when you want to emphasize that they do the same thing all the time, and this annoys you. [EMPHASIS] ◻ *All she ever does is complain.* **10** PHRASE You say **as ever** in order to indicate that something or someone's behavior is not unusual because it is like that all the time or very often. ◻ *As ever, the meals are primarily fish-based.* **11** **hardly ever** → see **hardly**

ever- /ɛvər-/ COMB IN ADJ You use **ever** in adjectives such as **ever-increasing** and **ever-present**, to show that something exists or continues all the time. ◻ *...the ever-increasing traffic on our roads.*

ever|green /ɛvərgriːn/ (**evergreens**) N-COUNT An **evergreen** is a tree or bush that has green leaves all year long. ◻ *Holly, like ivy and mistletoe, is an evergreen.* • ADJ **Evergreen** is also an adjective. ◻ *Plant evergreen shrubs around the end of the month.*

ever|lasting /ɛvərlæstɪŋ/ ADJ Something that is **everlasting** never comes to an end. ◻ *...a message of peace and everlasting life.*

ever|more /ɛvərmɔːr/ also **ever more** ADV [ADV with v, oft *for* ADV] **Evermore** means for all the time in the future. ◻ *The editor's decision is final and shall evermore remain so.* ◻ *They will bitterly regret what they have done for ever more.*

every ✦✦✦ /ɛvri/ **1** DET You use **every** to indicate that you are referring to all the members of a group or all the parts of something and not only some of them. ◻ *Every room has a window facing the ocean.* ◻ *Record every expenditure you make.* • ADJ [poss ADJ n] **Every** is also an adjective. ◻ *His every utterance will*

everybody 443 **evil**

be scrutinized. **2** DET You use **every** in order to say how often something happens or to indicate that something happens at regular intervals. ❏ *We were made to attend meetings every day.* ❏ *A burglary occurs every three minutes in London.* **3** DET You use **every** in front of a number when you are saying what proportion of people or things something happens to or applies to. ❏ *Two out of every three people have a cell phone.* **4** DET You can use **every** before some nouns, for example 'sign,' 'effort,' 'reason,' and 'intention' in order to emphasize what you are saying. [EMPHASIS] ❏ *The Congressional Budget Office says the federal deficit shows every sign of getting larger.* ❏ *I think that there is every chance that you will succeed.* **5** ADJ [poss ADJ n] If you say that someone's **every** whim, wish, or desire will be satisfied, you are emphasizing that everything they want will happen or be provided. [EMPHASIS] ❏ *Dozens of servants had catered to his every whim.* **6** PHRASE You use **every** in the expressions **every now and then**, **every now and again**, **every once in a while**, and **every so often** in order to indicate that something happens occasionally. ❏ *Stir the batter every now and then to keep it from separating.* **7** PHRASE If something happens **every other day** or **every second day**, for example, it happens one day, then does not happen the next day, then happens the day after that, and so on. You can also say that something happens **every third week**, **every fourth year**, and so on. ❏ *I went home every other week.* **8 every bit as good as** → see **bit**

every|body ♦◇◇ /ɛvribɒdi, -bʌdi/ PRON-INDEF **Everybody** means the same as **everyone**.

every|day /ɛvrideɪ/ ADJ You use **everyday** to describe something that happens or is used every day, or forms a regular and basic part of your life, so it is not especially interesting or unusual. ❏ *In the course of my everyday life, I had very little contact with teenagers.*

every|man /ɛvrimæn/ N-SING **Everyman** is used to refer to people in general. If you say, for example, that a character in a movie or book is an **everyman**, you mean that the character has experiences and emotions that are like those of any ordinary person. ❏ *Douglas plays a frustrated everyman who suddenly loses control under the pressure of daily life.*

every|one ♦◇◇ /ɛvriwʌn/ also **everybody 1** PRON-INDEF You use **everyone** or **everybody** to refer to all the people in a particular group. ❏ *Everyone on the street was shocked when they heard the news.* ❏ *Not everyone thinks that the government is being particularly generous.* **2** PRON-INDEF You use **everyone** or **everybody** to refer to all people. ❏ *Everyone wrestles with self-doubt and feels like a failure at times.* ❏ *Everyone needs some free time for rest and relaxation.*

every|place /ɛvripleɪs/ ADV **Everyplace** means the same as **everywhere**.

every|thing ♦♦◇ /ɛvriθɪŋ/ **1** PRON-INDEF You use **everything** to refer to all the objects, actions, activities, or facts in a particular situation. ❏ *He'd gone to Seattle long after everything else in his life had changed.* **2** PRON-INDEF You use **everything** to refer to all possible or likely actions, activities, or situations. ❏ *"This should have been decided long before now."—"We can't think of everything."* ❏ *Najib and I do everything together.* **3** PRON-INDEF You use **everything** to refer to a whole situation or to life in general. ❏ *She says everything is going smoothly.* ❏ *Is everything all right?* **4** PRON-INDEF If you say that someone or something is **everything**, you mean you consider them to be the most important thing in your life, or the most important thing that there is. ❏ *I love him. He is everything to me.* **5** PRON-INDEF If you say that someone or something has **everything**, you mean they have all the things or qualities that most people consider to be desirable. ❏ *This man had everything. He had the house, the sailboat and a full life with friends and family.*

every|where ♦◇◇ /ɛvriwɛər/ also **everyplace 1** ADV You use **everywhere** to refer to a whole area or to all the places in a particular area. ❏ *Working people everywhere object to paying taxes.* ❏ *We went everywhere together.* **2** ADV You use **everywhere** to refer to all the places that someone goes to. ❏ *Mary Jo is still accustomed to traveling everywhere in style.* **3** ADV You use **everywhere** to emphasize that you are talking about a large number of places, or all possible places. [EMPHASIS] ❏ *I saw her picture everywhere.* **4** ADV If you say that someone or something is **everywhere**, you mean that they are present in a place in very large numbers. ❏ *There were cartons of cigarettes everywhere.*

every|woman /ɛvriwʊmən/ N-SING **Everywoman** is used to refer to women in general. If you say, for example, that a character in a film or book is an **everywoman**, you mean that the character has experiences and emotions that are like those of any ordinary person. ❏ *She became an everywoman, and finally started getting roles on television.*

evict /ɪvɪkt/ (**evicts**, **evicting**, **evicted**) **1** V-T If someone is **evicted** from the place where they are living, they are forced to leave it, usually because they have broken a law or contract. ❏ *They were evicted from their apartment after their mother became addicted to drugs.* ❏ *In the first week, the city police evicted ten families.* **2** → See feature box at **poverty**

evic|tion /ɪvɪkʃən/ (**evictions**) N-VAR **Eviction** is the act or process of officially forcing someone to leave a house or piece of land. ❏ *He was facing eviction, along with his wife and family.*

evi|dence ♦♦◇ /ɛvɪdəns/ **1** N-UNCOUNT **Evidence** is anything that you see, experience, read, or are told that causes you to believe that something is true or has really happened. ❏ *Ganley said he'd seen no evidence of widespread fraud.* **2** N-UNCOUNT **Evidence** is the information that is used in a court of law to try to prove something. Evidence is obtained from documents, objects, or witnesses. [LEGAL] ❏ *The evidence against him was purely circumstantial.* **3** PHRASE If you **give evidence** in a court of law or an official inquiry, you officially say what you know about people or events, or describe an occasion at which you were present. ❏ *The forensic scientists who carried out the original tests will be called to give evidence.* **4** PHRASE If someone or something **is in evidence**, they are present and can be clearly seen. ❏ *Few soldiers were in evidence.*

---SYNONYMS---

evidence
NOUN **1**
proof: *This is not necessarily proof that he is wrong.*
testimony: *This book is testimony to a very individual kind of courage.*
indication: *He gave no indication that he was ready to compromise.*
mark: *The mark of a civilized society is that it looks after its weakest members.*

evi|dent /ɛvɪdənt/ **1** ADJ If something is **evident**, you notice it easily and clearly. ❏ *His footprints were clearly evident in the heavy dust.* ❏ *The threat of inflation is already evident in bond prices.* **2** ADJ You use **evident** to show that you are certain about a situation or fact and your interpretation of it. [EMPHASIS] ❏ *It was evident that Martha was concerned about something.* **3** → see also **self-evident**

evi|dent|ly /ɛvɪdəntli, -dɛnt-/ **1** ADV You use **evidently** to say that something is obviously true, for example, because you have seen evidence of it yourself. ❏ *The man wore a bathrobe and had evidently just come from the bathroom.* **2** ADV You use **evidently** to show that you think something is true or have been told something is true, but that you are not sure, because you do not have enough information or proof. ❏ *From childhood, he was evidently at once rebellious and precocious.* **3** ADV [ADV with cl] You can use **evidently** to introduce a statement or opinion and to emphasize that you feel that it is true or correct. [FORMAL, EMPHASIS] ❏ *Evidently, it has nothing to do with social background.*

evil ♦◇◇ /iːvəl/ (**evils**) **1** N-UNCOUNT **Evil** is a powerful force that some people believe to exist, and that causes wicked and bad things to happen. ❏ *There's always a conflict between good and evil in his plays.* **2** N-UNCOUNT **Evil** is used to refer to all the wicked and bad things that happen in the world. ❏ *He could not, after all, stop all the evil in the world.* **3** N-COUNT If you refer to an **evil**, you mean a very unpleasant or harmful situation or activity. ❏ *Higher taxes may be a necessary evil.* **4** ADJ If you describe someone as **evil**, you mean that they are very wicked by nature and take pleasure in doing things that harm other people. ❏ *...the country's most evil terrorists.* **5** ADJ If you describe something as **evil**, you mean that you think it causes a great deal of harm to people and is morally bad. ❏ *A judge yesterday condemned heroin as evil.* **6** ADJ If you describe something as **evil**, you mean that you think it is influenced by the devil. ❏ *I think this is an evil spirit at work.* **7** PHRASE If you have two choices, but think that they are both bad, you can describe the less bad one as **the lesser of two evils**, or **the lesser evil**. ❏ *People voted for him as the lesser of two evils.*

SYNONYMS

evil
NOUN **3**
wrong: *Johnson didn't seem to be able to tell the difference between right and wrong.*
vice: *...allegations of how she worked in a 'seedy vice den.'*
sin: *Was it the sin of pride to have believed too much in themselves?*
ADJ **5**
wicked: *She described the shooting as a wicked attack.*
immoral: *...those who think that birth control and abortion are immoral.*
heinous: *They are capable of the most heinous acts.*
depraved: *...a disturbing and depraved movie.*

evil|doer /ˈiːvəldʊər/ (**evildoers**) also **evil-doer** N-COUNT If you describe someone as an **evildoer**, you mean that they are wicked, and that they deliberately cause harm or suffering to others. [LITERARY or OLD-FASHIONED]

evil eye **1** N-SING [the N] Some people believe that **the evil eye** is a magical power to cast a spell on someone or something by looking at them, so that bad things happen to them. **2** N-SING [usu the] If someone gives you the **evil eye**, they look at you in an unpleasant way, usually because they dislike you or are jealous of you.

evince /ɪˈvɪns/ (**evinces, evincing, evinced**) V-T If someone or something **evinces** a particular feeling or quality, they show that feeling or quality, often indirectly. [FORMAL] ▫ *The entire production evinces authenticity and a real respect for the subject matter.*

evis|cer|ate /ɪˈvɪsəreɪt/ (**eviscerates, eviscerating, eviscerated**) **1** V-T To **eviscerate** a person or animal means to remove their internal organs, such as their heart, lungs, and stomach. [FORMAL] **2** V-T If you say that something will **eviscerate** an organization or system, you are emphasizing that it will make the organization or system much weaker or much less powerful. [FORMAL, EMPHASIS] ▫ *Democrats say the petition will eviscerate state government.*

evo|ca|tion /ˌevəˈkeɪʃən, ˌiːvoʊ-/ (**evocations**) N-VAR [usu N of n] An **evocation** of something involves creating an image or impression of it. [FORMAL] ▫ *...a perfect evocation of the period.*

evoca|tive /ɪˈvɒkətɪv/ ADJ If you describe something as **evocative**, you mean that it is good or interesting because it produces pleasant memories, ideas, emotions, and responses in people. [FORMAL] ▫ *Her story is sharply evocative of Italian provincial life.*

evoke /ɪˈvoʊk/ (**evokes, evoking, evoked**) V-T To **evoke** a particular memory, idea, emotion, or response means to cause it to occur. [FORMAL] ▫ *...the scene evoking memories of those old movies.*

evo|lu|tion /ˌevəˈluːʃən, ˌiːv-/ (**evolutions**) **1** N-UNCOUNT **Evolution** is a process of gradual change that takes place over many generations, during which species of animals, plants, or insects slowly change some of their physical characteristics. ▫ *...the evolution of plants and animals.* **2** N-VAR **Evolution** is a process of gradual development in a particular situation or thing over a period of time. [FORMAL] ▫ *...a crucial period in the evolution of modern physics.*

evo|lu|tion|ary /ˌevəˈluːʃəneri, ˌiːv-/ ADJ **Evolutionary** means relating to a process of gradual change and development. ▫ *...an evolutionary process.*

evo|lu|tion|ist /ˌevəˈluːʃənɪst, ˌiːv-/ (**evolutionists**) N-COUNT An **evolutionist** is someone who accepts the scientific theory that all living things evolved from a few simple life forms.

evolve /ɪˈvɒlv/ (**evolves, evolving, evolved**) **1** V-I When animals or plants **evolve**, they gradually change and develop into different forms. ▫ *The bright plumage of many male birds was thought to have evolved to attract females.* ▫ *Birds are widely believed to have evolved from dinosaurs.* **2** V-T/V-I If something **evolves** or you **evolve** it, it gradually develops over a period of time into something different and usually more advanced. ▫ *...a tiny airline which eventually evolved into Pakistan International Airlines.* ▫ *Popular music evolved from folk songs.*

ewe /juː/ (**ewes**) N-COUNT A **ewe** is an adult female sheep.

ewer /ˈjuːər/ (**ewers**) N-COUNT A **ewer** is a large jug with a wide opening. [OLD-FASHIONED]

ex /ɛks/ (**exes**) N-COUNT [usu poss N] Someone's **ex** is the person they used to be married to or used to have a romantic or sexual relationship with. [INFORMAL] ▫ *He's different from my ex.* ▫ *...one of her exes.*

PREFIX

ex-
forms words that refer to people who are no longer a particular thing. For example, an **ex-police officer** is someone who is no longer a police officer.

ex|ac|er|bate /ɪɡˈzæsərbeɪt/ (**exacerbates, exacerbating, exacerbated**) V-T If something **exacerbates** a problem or bad situation, it makes it worse. [FORMAL] ▫ *Longstanding poverty has been exacerbated by racial divisions.* • **ex|ac|er|ba|tion** /ɪɡˌzæsərˈbeɪʃən/ N-UNCOUNT ▫ *...the exacerbation of global problems.*

ex|act ♦♦◊ /ɪɡˈzækt/ (**exacts, exacting, exacted**) **1** ADJ **Exact** means correct in every detail. For example, an **exact** copy is the same in every detail as the thing it is copied from. ▫ *I don't remember the exact words.* ▫ *The exact number of protest calls has not been revealed.* • **ex|act|ly** ADV ▫ *Try to locate exactly where the smells are entering the room.* ▫ *Both drugs will be exactly the same.* **2** ADJ [ADJ n] You use **exact** before a noun to emphasize that you are referring to that particular thing and no other, especially something that has a particular significance. [EMPHASIS] ▫ *I hadn't really thought about it until this exact moment.* • **ex|act|ly** ADV [ADV n/wh] ▫ *These are exactly the people who do not vote.* **3** V-T When someone **exacts** something, they demand and obtain it from another person, especially because they are in a superior or more powerful position. [FORMAL] ▫ *Already he has exacted a written apology from the chairman of the commission.* **4** V-T If someone **exacts** revenge on a person, they have their revenge on them. ▫ *She uses the media to help her exact a terrible revenge.* **5** V-T If something **exacts** a high price, it has a bad effect on a person or situation. ▫ *The sheer physical effort had exacted a heavy price.* **6** → see also **exacting** **7** PHRASE You say **to be exact** to indicate that you are slightly correcting or giving more detailed information about what you have been saying. ▫ *A small number – five, to be exact – have been bad.*

SYNONYMS

exact
ADJ **1**
accurate: *This provides an accurate way of monitoring levels of carbon dioxide.*
detailed: *Yesterday's letter contains a detailed account of the decisions.*
precise: *What he has to say is precise and to the point.*
correct: *The following information was correct at the time of going to press.*
specific: *I asked him to be more specific.*

ex|act|ing /ɪɡˈzæktɪŋ/ ADJ You use **exacting** to describe something or someone that demands hard work and a great deal of care. ▫ *She didn't think that he was well enough to carry out such an exacting task.*

ex|acti|tude /ɪɡˈzæktɪtuːd/ N-UNCOUNT **Exactitude** is the quality of being very accurate and careful. [FORMAL] ▫ *...the precision and exactitude of current genetic mapping.*

ex|act|ly ♦♦◊ /ɪɡˈzæktli/ **1** ADV You use **exactly** before an amount, number, or position to emphasize that it is no more, no less, or no different from what you are stating. [EMPHASIS] ▫ *Each corner had a guard tower, each of which was exactly ten meters in height.* **2** ADV [ADV as reply] If you say '**Exactly**,' you are agreeing with someone or emphasizing the truth of what they say. If you say '**Not exactly**,' you are telling them politely that they are wrong in part of what they are saying. ▫ *Eve nodded, almost approvingly. "Exactly."* **3** ADV You use **not exactly** to indicate that a meaning or situation is slightly different from what people think or expect. [VAGUENESS] ▫ *He's not exactly homeless, he just hangs out in this park.* **4** ADV You can use **not exactly** to show that you mean the opposite of what you are saying. [EMPHASIS] ▫ *This was not exactly what I wanted to hear.* **5** ADV [ADV with quest] You use **exactly** with a question to show that you disapprove of what the person you are talking to is doing or saying. [DISAPPROVAL] ▫ *What exactly do you mean?* **6** → see also **exact**

exactness 445 **exasperating**

> **SYNONYMS**
> **exactly**
> ADV **1**
> **accurately:** *The test can accurately predict what a bigger explosion would do.*
> **precisely:** *Nobody knows precisely how many people are still living in the camp.*
> **correctly:** *You have to correctly answer each question.*

ex|act|ness /ɪgzæktnɪs/ N-UNCOUNT [usu with supp] **Exactness** is the quality of being very accurate and precise. ❑ *He recalls his native Bombay with cinematic exactness.*

ex|act sci|ence N-SING [usu with brd-neg] If you say that a particular activity is not an **exact science**, you mean that there are no set rules to follow or it does not produce very accurate results. ❑ *Forecasting floods is not an exact science.*

ex|ag|ger|ate /ɪgzædʒəreɪt/ (**exaggerates, exaggerating, exaggerated**) **1** V-T/V-I If you **exaggerate**, you indicate that something is, for example, worse or more important than it really is. ❑ *He thinks I'm exaggerating.* • **ex|ag|gera|tion** /ɪgzædʒəreɪʃᵊn/ (**exaggerations**) N-VAR ❑ *Like many stories about him, it smacks of exaggeration.* **2** V-T If something **exaggerates** a situation, quality, or feature, it makes the situation, quality, or feature appear greater, more obvious, or more important than it really is. ❑ *These figures exaggerate the loss of competitiveness.*

ex|ag|ger|at|ed /ɪgzædʒəreɪtɪd/ ADJ Something that is **exaggerated** is or seems larger, better, worse, or more important than it actually needs to be. ❑ *Western fears, he insists, are greatly exaggerated.*

ex|alt /ɪgzɔːlt/ (**exalts, exalting, exalted**) V-T To **exalt** someone or something means to praise them very highly. [FORMAL] ❑ *His work exalts all those virtues that we, as Americans, are taught to hold dear.*

ex|al|ta|tion /ɛgzɔːlteɪʃᵊn/ N-UNCOUNT **Exaltation** is an intense feeling of great happiness. [FORMAL] ❑ *The city was swept up in the mood of exaltation.*

ex|alt|ed /ɪgzɔːltɪd/ ADJ Someone or something that is at an **exalted** level is at a very high level, especially with regard to rank or importance. [FORMAL] ❑ *You must decide how to make the best use of your exalted position.*

exam /ɪgzæm/ (**exams**) **1** N-COUNT An **exam** is a formal test that you take to show your knowledge or ability in a particular subject, or to obtain a qualification. ❑ *I don't want to take any more exams.* **2** N-COUNT If you have a medical **exam**, a doctor looks at your body, feels it, or does simple tests in order to check how healthy you are. [mainly AM] ❑ *These medical exams have shown I am in perfect physical condition.*

> **USAGE**
> **exam**
> Don't use 'make.' Don't say, for example, '~~We made another change to exam.~~' You say that people **take**, **sit for**, or **do** an exam or a test. *Many children want to take these exams. Students must sit for an entrance exam.*

ex|ami|na|tion ♦◇◇ /ɪgzæmɪneɪʃᵊn/ (**examinations**) **1** N-COUNT An **examination** is a formal test that you take to show your knowledge or ability in a particular subject, or to obtain a qualification. [FORMAL] ❑ *...college examination results.* **2** → see also **examine** **3** N-COUNT If you have a medical **examination**, a doctor looks at your body, feels it, or does simple tests in order to check how healthy you are. ❑ *You must see your doctor for a thorough examination.*

> **SYNONYMS**
> **examination**
> NOUN
> **exam:** *I don't want to take any more exams.*
> **test:** *Out of a total of 2,602 students only 922 passed the test.*
> **assessment:** *The assessments are supposed to help teachers predict students' exam grades.*

ex|am|ine ♦♦◇ /ɪgzæmɪn/ (**examines, examining, examined**) **1** V-T If you **examine** something, you look at it carefully. ❑ *He examined her passport and stamped it.* • **ex|ami|na|tion** /ɪgzæmɪneɪʃᵊn/ (**examinations**) N-VAR ❑ *The navy is to carry out an examination of the wreck tomorrow.* **2** V-T If a doctor **examines** you, he or she looks at your body, feels it, or does simple tests in order to check how healthy you are. ❑ *Another doctor examined her and could still find nothing wrong.* • **ex|ami|na|tion** N-VAR ❑ *He was later discharged after an examination at the hospital.* **3** V-T If an idea, proposal, or plan **is examined**, it is considered very carefully. ❑ *The plans will be examined by officials.* • **ex|ami|na|tion** N-VAR ❑ *The government said it was studying the implications, which "required very careful examination and consideration."* **4** V-T [usu passive] If you **are examined**, you are given a formal test in order to show your knowledge of a subject. ❑ *...learning to cope with the pressures of being judged and examined by our teachers.*

> **SYNONYMS**
> **examine**
> VERB **1**
> **inspect:** *Elaine went outside to inspect the playing field.*
> **study:** *Debbie studied her friend's face for a moment.*
> **vet:** *She was secretly vetted before she ever undertook any work for me.*
> **check:** *It's worth checking each item for obvious flaws.*
> **survey:** *He pushed himself to his feet and surveyed the room.*
> **scrutinize:** *The results were carefully scrutinized.*

ex|ami|nee /ɪgzæmɪniː/ (**examinees**) N-COUNT An **examinee** is someone who is taking an exam. [FORMAL]

ex|am|in|er /ɪgzæmɪnər/ (**examiners**) **1** N-COUNT An **examiner** is a person who conducts an examination. ❑ *...FBI senior fingerprint examiner Terry Green.* **2** → see also **medical examiner**

ex|am|ple ♦♦♦ /ɪgzæmpᵊl/ (**examples**) **1** N-COUNT An **example** of something is a particular situation, object, or person that shows that what is being claimed is true. ❑ *The doctors gave numerous examples of patients being expelled from the hospital.* **2** N-COUNT An **example** of a particular class of objects or styles is something that has many of the typical features of such a class or style, and that you consider clearly represents it. ❑ *Symphonies 103 and 104 stand as perfect examples of early symphonic construction.* **3** N-COUNT If you refer to a person or their behavior as an **example** to other people, you mean that he or she behaves in a good or correct way that other people should copy. [APPROVAL] ❑ *He is a model professional and an example to the younger boys.* **4** PHRASE You use **for example** to introduce and emphasize something that shows that something is true. ❑ *Take, for example, the simple sentence: "The man climbed up the hill."* **5** PHRASE If you **follow** someone's **example**, you behave in the same way as they did in the past, or in a similar way, especially because you admire them. ❑ *Following the example set by her father, she has fulfilled her role and done her duty.* **6** PHRASE To **make an example of** someone who has done something wrong means to punish them severely as a warning to other people not to do the same thing. ❑ *Let us at least see our courts make an example of these despicable criminals.* **7** PHRASE If you **set an example**, you encourage or inspire people by your behavior to behave or act in a similar way. ❑ *An officer's job was to set an example.*

> **USAGE**
> **example**
> When someone mentions an example, you say that they are **giving** an example. Don't say '~~Could you say me an example?~~' Say 'Could you give me an example?'

ex|as|per|ate /ɪgzæspəreɪt/ (**exasperates, exasperating, exasperated**) V-T If someone or something **exasperates** you, they annoy you and make you feel frustrated or upset. ❑ *The sheer futility of it all exasperates her.* • **ex|as|pera|tion** /ɪgzæspəreɪʃᵊn/ N-UNCOUNT ❑ *Mahoney clenched his fist in exasperation.*

ex|as|per|at|ed /ɪgzæspəreɪtɪd/ ADJ If you describe a person as **exasperated**, you mean that they are frustrated or angry because of something that is happening or something that another person is doing. ❑ *The president was clearly exasperated by the whole saga.*

ex|as|per|at|ing /ɪgzæspəreɪtɪŋ/ ADJ [usu v-link ADJ] If you describe someone or something as **exasperating**, you mean

excavate

that you feel angry or frustrated by them or by what they do. ☐ *Herrera could be exasperating to his colleagues.*

ex|ca|vate /ˈɛkskəveɪt/ (excavates, excavating, excavated) **1** V-T When archeologists or other people **excavate** a piece of land, they remove earth carefully from it and look for things such as pots, bones, or buildings that are buried there, in order to discover information about the past. ☐ *A new Danish expedition is again excavating the site in annual summer digs.* • **ex|ca|va|tion** /ˌɛkskəˈveɪʃən/ (excavations) N-VAR ☐ *She worked on the excavation of a Mayan archeological site.* **2** V-T To **excavate** means to dig a hole in the ground, for example, in order to build there. ☐ *A contractor was hired to drain the reservoir and to excavate soil from one area for replacement with clay.* • **ex|ca|va|tion** N-VAR ☐ *...the excavation of canals.*

ex|ca|va|tor /ˈɛkskəveɪtər/ (excavators) N-COUNT An **excavator** is a large machine that is used for digging, for example, when people are building something.

ex|ceed /ɪkˈsiːd/ (exceeds, exceeding, exceeded) **1** V-T If something **exceeds** a particular amount or number, it is greater or larger than that amount or number. [FORMAL] ☐ *Its research budget exceeds $700 million a year.* **2** V-T If you **exceed** a limit or rule, you go beyond it, even though you are not supposed to or it is against the law. [FORMAL] ☐ *He accepts that he was exceeding the speed limit.*

ex|ceed|ing|ly /ɪkˈsiːdɪŋli/ ADV **Exceedingly** means very or very much. [OLD-FASHIONED] ☐ *We had an exceedingly good lunch.*

ex|cel /ɪkˈsɛl/ (excels, excelling, excelled) V-T/V-I If someone **excels** in something or **excels** at it, they are very good at doing it. ☐ *Mary was a better rider than either of them and she excelled at outdoor sports.* ☐ *Academically he began to excel.*

ex|cel|lence /ˈɛksələns/ N-UNCOUNT If someone or something has the quality of **excellence**, they are extremely good in some way. ☐ *...the top award for excellence in journalism and the arts.*

Ex|cel|len|cy /ˈɛksələnsi/ (Excellencies) N-VOC [POSS N] You use expressions such as **Your Excellency** or **Her Excellency** when you are addressing or referring to officials of very high rank, such as ambassadors or governors. [POLITENESS] ☐ *I am reluctant to trust anyone totally, Your Excellency.*

ex|cel|lent ✦✧✧ /ˈɛksələnt/ **1** ADJ Something that is **excellent** is extremely good. ☐ *The recording quality is excellent.* • **ex|cel|lent|ly** ADV ☐ *They're both playing excellently.* **2** EXCLAM Some people say '**Excellent!**' to show that they approve of something. [FEELINGS] ☐ *"Excellent!" he shouted, yelping happily at the rain. "Now we'll see how this boat really performs!"*

ex|cept ✦✦✧ /ɪkˈsɛpt/ **1** PREP You use **except** to introduce the only thing or person that a statement does not apply to, or a fact that prevents a statement from being completely true. ☐ *I wouldn't have accepted anything except a job in New York.* • CONJ **Except** is also a conjunction. ☐ *Freddie would tell me nothing about what he was writing, except that it was to be a Christmas play.* **2** PHRASE You use **except** or **except for** to introduce the only thing or person that prevents a statement from being completely true. ☐ *He hadn't eaten a thing except for one forkful of salad.*

SYNONYMS

except
PREP **1**
aside from: *The room was empty aside from one man seated beside the fire.*
other than: *She makes no reference to any feminist work other than her own.*
excepting: *This has been the source of meat for much of this region excepting Japan.*
bar: *Bar a plateau in 1989, inflation has gone up ever since.*
excluding: *The total costs, excluding the plane, are in the neighborhood of $140,000.*

---

ex|cept|ed /ɪkˈsɛptɪd/ ADV [N ADV] You use **excepted** after you have mentioned a person or thing to show that you do not include them in the statement you are making. [FORMAL] ☐ *Jeremy excepted, the men seemed personable.*

ex|cept|ing /ɪkˈsɛptɪŋ/ PREP You use **excepting** to introduce the only thing that prevents a statement from being completely true. [FORMAL] ☐ *The source of meat for much of this region (excepting Japan) has traditionally been the pig.*

excess baggage

ex|cep|tion ✦✧✧ /ɪkˈsɛpʃən/ (exceptions) **1** N-COUNT An **exception** is a particular thing, person, or situation that is not included in a general statement, judgment, or rule. ☐ *Few guitarists can sing as well as they can play; Eddie, however, is an exception.* ☐ *The law makes no exceptions.* **2** PHRASE If you make a general statement, and then say that something or someone is **no exception**, you are emphasizing that they are included in that statement. [EMPHASIS] ☐ *Marketing is applied to everything these days, and books are no exception.* **3** PHRASE If you **take exception to** something, you feel offended or annoyed by it, usually with the result that you complain about it. ☐ *He also took exception to having been spied on.* **4** PHRASE You use **with the exception of** to introduce a thing or person that is not included in a general statement that you are making. ☐ *Yesterday was a day off for everybody, with the exception of Lorenzo.* **5** PHRASE You use **without exception** to emphasize that the statement you are making is true in all cases. [EMPHASIS] ☐ *The vehicles are without exception old, rusty and dented.*

ex|cep|tion|al /ɪkˈsɛpʃənəl/ **1** ADJ You use **exceptional** to describe someone or something that has a particular quality, usually a good quality, to an unusually high degree. [APPROVAL] ☐ *...children with exceptional ability.* • **ex|cep|tion|al|ly** ADV [ADV adj/adv] ☐ *He's an exceptionally talented dancer and needs to practice several hours every day.* **2** ADJ **Exceptional** situations and incidents are unusual and only likely to happen infrequently. [FORMAL] ☐ *A review panel concluded that there were no exceptional circumstances that would warrant a lesser penalty for him.* • **ex|cep|tion|al|ly** ADV [ADV with cl] ☐ *Exceptionally, in times of emergency, we may send a team of experts.*

ex|cerpt ✦✧✧ /ˈɛksɜːrpt/ (excerpts) N-COUNT An **excerpt** is a short piece of writing or music taken from a larger piece. ☐ *...an excerpt from Tchaikovsky's Nutcracker.*

SYNONYMS

excerpt
NOUN
extract: *Read this extract from an information booklet.*
passage: *He reads a passage from Milton.*
quotation: *She illustrated her argument with quotations from Pasternak.*
cutting: *Here are the press cuttings and reviews.*
quote: *The article starts with a quote from an unnamed member of the cabinet.*

---

ex|cess ✦✧✧ (excesses)

The noun is pronounced /ɪkˈsɛs/ or /ˈɛksɛs/. The adjective is pronounced /ˈɛksɛs/.

1 N-VAR An **excess** of something is a larger amount than is needed, allowed, or usual. ☐ *An excess of house plants in a small apartment can be oppressive.* **2** ADJ [ADJ n] **Excess** is used to describe amounts that are greater than what is needed, allowed, or usual. ☐ *After cooking the fish, pour off any excess fat.* **3** ADJ [ADJ n] **Excess** is used to refer to additional amounts of money that need to be paid for services and activities that were not originally planned or taken into account. [FORMAL] ☐ *Make sure that you don't have to pay expensive excess charges.* **4** PHRASE **In excess of** means more than a particular amount. [FORMAL] ☐ *The value of the company is well in excess of $2 billion.* **5** PHRASE If you do something **to excess**, you do it too much. [DISAPPROVAL] ☐ *I was reasonably fit, played a lot of tennis, and didn't smoke or drink to excess.*

SYNONYMS

excess
NOUN **1**
surfeit: *Rationing had put an end to a surfeit of biscuits long ago.*
plethora: *A plethora of new operators will be allowed to enter the market.*
glut: *There's a glut of agricultural products in Western Europe.*
surplus: *There would normally be a surplus of properties on the market at this time of year.*

---

ex|cess bag|gage also **excess luggage** **1** N-UNCOUNT On an airplane flight, **excess baggage** is baggage that is larger or weighs more than your ticket allows, so that you have to pay extra to take it on board. **2** N-UNCOUNT You can use **excess**

excessive / **exclusive**

baggage to talk about problems or events from someone's past which you think still worry them, especially when you think these things make it difficult for the person to cope or develop. ❑ *The good thing about these younger players is that they are not carrying any excess baggage from less successful times.* **8** → See feature box at **tourism**

ex|ces|sive /ɪksɛsɪv/ ADJ If you describe the amount or level of something as **excessive**, you disapprove of it because it is more or higher than is necessary or reasonable. [DISAPPROVAL] ❑ *Their spending on research is excessive and is slowing developments of new treatments.* ● **ex|ces|sive|ly** ADV ❑ *Managers are also accused of paying themselves excessively high salaries.*

ex|change ✦✧ /ɪkstʃeɪndʒ/ (**exchanges, exchanging, exchanged**) **1** V-RECIP If two or more people **exchange** things of a particular kind, they give them to each other at the same time. ❑ *We exchanged addresses.* ❑ *The two men exchanged glances.* ● N-COUNT **Exchange** is also a noun. ❑ *He ruled out any exchange of prisoners with the militants.* **2** V-T If you **exchange** something, you replace it with a different thing, especially something that is better or more satisfactory. ❑ *...the chance to sell back or exchange goods.* **3** N-COUNT An **exchange** is a brief conversation, usually an angry one. [FORMAL] ❑ *There've been some bitter exchanges between the two groups.* **4** N-COUNT An **exchange** of fire, for example, is an incident in which people use guns or missiles against each other. ❑ *There was an exchange of fire during which the gunman was wounded.* **5** N-COUNT An **exchange** is an arrangement in which people from two different countries visit each other's country, to strengthen links between them. ❑ *...a series of sporting and cultural exchanges with Seoul.* **6** → see also **foreign exchange, stock exchange** **7** PHRASE If you do or give something **in exchange** for something else, you do it or give it in order to get that thing. ❑ *It is illegal for public officials to solicit gifts or money in exchange for favors.*

SYNONYMS

exchange
VERB **1**
swap: *Some hostages were swapped for convicted prisoners.*
trade: *They traded land for goods and money.*
switch: *In half an hour, they'd switched the tags on every cable.*
barter: *They have been bartering wheat for cotton and timber.*

ex|change rate ✦✧ (**exchange rates**) N-COUNT The **exchange rate** of a country's unit of currency is the amount of another country's currency that you get in exchange for it. ❑ *...a high exchange rate for the Canadian dollar.*

Ex|cheq|uer /ɪkstʃɛkər/ N-PROPER The **Exchequer** is the department in the British government responsible for receiving, issuing, and accounting for money belonging to the state.

ex|cise /ɛksaɪz/ (**excises**) N-VAR **Excise** is a tax that the government of a country puts on particular goods, such as cigarettes and alcoholic drinks, which are produced for sale in its own country. ❑ *...this year's rise in excise duties.* ❑ *...an excise tax on wine and tobacco.*

ex|cit|able /ɪksaɪtəbəl/ ADJ If you describe someone as **excitable**, you mean that they behave in a nervous way and become excited very easily. ❑ *Mary sat beside Elaine, who today seemed excitable.*

ex|cite /ɪksaɪt/ (**excites, exciting, excited**) **1** V-T If something **excites** you, it makes you feel very happy, eager, or enthusiastic. ❑ *I only take on work that excites me, even if it means turning down lots of money.* **2** V-T If something **excites** a particular feeling, emotion, or reaction in someone, it causes them to experience it. ❑ *Daniel's early exposure to motor racing did not excite his interest.*

ex|cit|ed /ɪksaɪtɪd/ **1** ADJ If you are **excited**, you are so happy that you cannot relax, especially because you are thinking about something pleasant that is going to happen to you. ❑ *I was excited about the possibility of playing football again.* ● **ex|cit|ed|ly** ADV [ADV with v] ❑ *"You're coming?" he said excitedly. "That's fantastic! That's incredible!"* **2** ADJ If you are **excited**, you are worried or angry about something, and so you are very alert and cannot relax. ❑ *I don't think there's any reason to get excited about inflation.* ● **ex|cit|ed|ly** ADV [ADV with v] ❑ *Larry rose excitedly to the edge of his seat, shook a fist at us and spat.*

ex|cite|ment /ɪksaɪtmənt/ (**excitements**) N-VAR You use **excitement** to refer to the state of being excited, or to something that excites you. ❑ *Everyone is in a state of great excitement.*

ex|cit|ing ✦✧ /ɪksaɪtɪŋ/ ADJ If something is **exciting**, it makes you feel very happy or enthusiastic. ❑ *The race itself is very exciting.*

SYNONYMS

exciting
ADJ
gripping: *...Craig Thomas's gripping tale of espionage.*
thrilling: *Our wildlife trips offer a thrilling encounter with wildlife in its natural state.*
exhilarating: *It was exhilarating to be on the road again, and his spirits rose.*
electrifying: *He gave an electrifying performance.*

ex|claim /ɪkskleɪm/ (**exclaims, exclaiming, exclaimed**) V-T Writers sometimes use **exclaim** to show that someone is speaking suddenly, loudly, or emphatically, often because they are excited, shocked, or angry. ❑ *"He went back to the lab," Inez exclaimed impatiently.*

ex|cla|ma|tion /ɛkskləmeɪʃən/ (**exclamations**) N-COUNT An **exclamation** is a sound, word, or sentence that is spoken suddenly, loudly, or emphatically and that expresses excitement, admiration, shock, or anger. ❑ *Sue gave an exclamation as we got a clear sight of the house.*

ex|cla|ma|tion point (**exclamation points**) also **exclamation mark** N-COUNT An **exclamation point** is the sign ! which is used in writing to show that a word, phrase, or sentence is an exclamation.

ex|clude /ɪksklud/ (**excludes, excluding, excluded**) **1** V-T If you **exclude** someone from a place or activity, you prevent them from entering it or taking part in it. ❑ *Many of the youngsters feel excluded.* **2** V-T If you **exclude** something that has some connection with what you are doing, you deliberately do not use it or consider it. ❑ *In some schools, Christmas carols are being modified to exclude any reference to Christ.* **3** V-T [usu with brd-neg] To **exclude** a possibility means to decide or prove that it is wrong and not worth considering. ❑ *I cannot entirely exclude the possibility that some form of pressure was applied to the neck.* **4** V-T To **exclude** something such as the sun's rays or harmful germs means to prevent them physically from reaching or entering a particular place. ❑ *This was intended to exclude the direct rays of the sun.*

ex|clud|ing /ɪkskludɪŋ/ PREP You use **excluding** before mentioning a person or thing to show that you are not including them in your statement. ❑ *Excluding water, half of the body's weight is protein.*

ex|clu|sion /ɪksklu³ən/ (**exclusions**) **1** N-VAR The **exclusion** of something is the act of deliberately not using, allowing, or considering it. ❑ *It calls for the exclusion of all commercial lending institutions from the college loan program.* **2** N-UNCOUNT **Exclusion** is the act of preventing someone from entering a place or taking part in an activity. ❑ *His problems went well beyond exclusion from the Christmas celebrations.* **3** PHRASE If you do one thing **to the exclusion of** something else, you only do the first thing and do not do the second thing at all. ❑ *Diane had dedicated her life to caring for him to the exclusion of all else.*

ex|clu|sion|ary /ɪksklu³nɛri/ ADJ Something that is **exclusionary** excludes a particular person or group of people. [FORMAL] ❑ *...exclusionary business practices.*

ex|clu|sion zone (**exclusion zones**) N-COUNT An **exclusion zone** is an area where people are not allowed to go or where they are not allowed to do a particular thing, for example because it would be dangerous.

ex|clu|sive /ɪksklusɪv/ (**exclusives**) **1** ADJ If you describe something as **exclusive**, you mean that it is limited to people who have a lot of money or who are privileged, and is therefore not available to everyone. ❑ *It used to be a private, exclusive club, and now it's open to all New Yorkers.* **2** ADJ Something that is **exclusive** is used or owned by only one person or group, and not shared with anyone else. ❑ *Our group will have exclusive use of a 60-foot boat.* **3** ADJ If a newspaper, magazine, or broadcasting organization describes one of its reports as **exclusive**, they mean it is a special report that does not appear in any other publication or on any other channel. ☐ *He told the magazine in an exclusive interview: "All my problems stem from drinking."* • N-COUNT An **exclusive** is an exclusive article or report. ☐ *Some papers thought they had an exclusive.* ◨ ADJ If a company states that its prices, goods, or services are **exclusive** of something, that thing is not included in the stated price, although it usually still has to be paid for. ☐ *...the average cost of a three-course dinner exclusive of tax, tip and beverage.* ◧ PHRASE If two things are **mutually exclusive**, they are separate and very different from each other, so that it is impossible for them to exist or happen together. ☐ *They both have learned that ambition and successful fatherhood can be mutually exclusive.*

ex|clu|sive|ly /ɪkskluːsɪvli/ ADV **Exclusively** is used to refer to situations or activities that involve only the thing or things mentioned, and nothing else. ☐ *...an exclusively male domain.*

ex|com|muni|cate /ˌɛkskəmjuːnɪkeɪt/ (**excommunicates, excommunicating, excommunicated**) V-T If a Roman Catholic or member of the Orthodox Church **is excommunicated**, it is publicly and officially stated that the person is no longer a member of the church. This is a punishment for some very great wrong that they have done. ☐ *Eventually, he was excommunicated along with his mentor.* ☐ *In 1766 he excommunicated the village for its "depraved diversion."* • **ex|com|mu|ni|ca|tion** /ˌɛkskəmjuːnɪkeɪʃən/ (**excommunications**) N-VAR ☐ *...the threat of excommunication.*

ex|co|ri|ate /ɪkskɔːrieɪt/ (**excoriates, excoriating, excoriated**) V-T To **excoriate** a person or organization means to criticize them severely, usually in public. [FORMAL] ☐ *He proceeded to excoriate me in front of the nurses.*

ex|cre|ment /ˈɛkskrɪmənt/ N-UNCOUNT **Excrement** is the solid waste that is passed out of a person or animal's body through their bowels. [FORMAL] ☐ *The cage smelled of excrement.*

ex|cre|ta /ɪkskriːtə/ N-UNCOUNT **Excreta** is the waste matter, such as urine or feces, which is passed out of a person or animal's body. [FORMAL, TECHNICAL]

ex|crete /ɪkskriːt/ (**excretes, excreting, excreted**) V-T When a person or animal **excretes** waste matter from their body, they get rid of it in feces, urine, or sweat. [FORMAL] ☐ *Your open pores excrete sweat and dirt.*

ex|cru|ci|at|ing /ɪkskruːʃieɪtɪŋ/ ADJ If you describe something as **excruciating**, you are emphasizing that it is extremely painful, either physically or emotionally. [EMPHASIS] ☐ *I was in excruciating pain and one leg wouldn't move.*

ex|cur|sion /ɪkskɜːrʒən/ (**excursions**) ◨ N-COUNT You can refer to a short trip as an **excursion**, especially if it is taken for pleasure or enjoyment. ☐ *In Bermuda, Sam's father took him on an excursion to a coral barrier.* ◨ N-COUNT An **excursion** is a trip or visit to an interesting place, especially one that is arranged or recommended by a travel agency or tourist organization. ☐ *Another pleasant excursion is Matamoros, 18 miles away.* ◨ → See feature box at **leisure**

ex|cus|able /ɪkskjuːzəbəl/ ADJ If you say that someone's wrong words or actions are **excusable**, you mean that they can be understood and forgiven. ☐ *I then realized that he had made a simple but excusable historical mistake.*

ex|cuse ♦◇◇ (**excuses, excusing, excused**)

The noun is pronounced /ɪkskjuːs/. The verb is pronounced /ɪkskjuːz/.

◨ N-COUNT An **excuse** is a reason that you give in order to explain why something has been done or has not been done, or in order to avoid doing something. ☐ *It is easy to find excuses for his indecisiveness.* ☐ *If you stop making excuses and do it you'll wonder what took you so long.* • PHRASE If you say that there is **no excuse** for something, you are emphasizing that it should not happen, or expressing disapproval that it has happened. [DISAPPROVAL] ☐ *There's no excuse for behavior like that.* ◨ V-T To **excuse** someone or **excuse** their behavior means to provide reasons for their actions, especially when other people disapprove of these actions. ☐ *Trying to excuse himself by blaming you was despicable.* ◨ V-T If you **excuse** someone for something wrong that they have done, you forgive them for it. ☐ *Many people might have excused them for shirking some of their responsibilities.* ◨ V-T [usu passive] If someone **is excused** from a duty or responsibility, they are told that they do not have to carry it out. ☐ *She is usually excused from her duties during summer vacation.* ◨ V-T If you **excuse** yourself, you use a phrase such as 'Excuse me' as a polite way of saying that you are about to leave. ☐ *He excused himself and went up to his room.* ◨ CONVENTION You say '**Excuse me**' when you want to politely get someone's attention, especially when you are about to ask them a question. [FORMULAE] ☐ *Excuse me, but are you Mr. Honig?* ◨ CONVENTION You use **excuse me** to apologize to someone when you have disturbed or interrupted them. [FORMULAE] ☐ *Excuse me interrupting, but there's something I need to say.* ◨ CONVENTION You use **excuse me** or a phrase such as **if you'll excuse me** as a polite way of indicating that you are about to leave or that you are about to stop talking to someone. [POLITENESS] ☐ *"Excuse me," she said to José, and left the room.* ◨ CONVENTION You use **excuse me**, but to indicate that you are about to disagree with someone. ☐ *Excuse me, but I want to know what all this has to do with us.* ◨ PHRASE You say **excuse me** to apologize when you have bumped into someone, or when you need to move past someone in a crowd. [FORMULAE] ☐ *Saying excuse me, Seaton pushed his way into the crowded living room.* ◨ CONVENTION You say **excuse me** to apologize when you have done something slightly embarrassing or impolite, such as burping, hiccuping, or sneezing. [FORMULAE] ◨ CONVENTION You say '**Excuse me?**' to show that you want someone to repeat what they have just said. [AM, FORMULAE] ☐ *"Excuse me?" Kate said, not sure she'd heard correctly.*

USAGE

excuse
You say that someone **makes** an excuse. Don't say 'I said an excuse.' *I made an excuse and left the meeting early.*

---

ex-directory ADJ If a person or their telephone number is **ex-directory**, the number is not listed in the telephone directory, and the telephone company will not give it to people who ask for it. [BRIT]

in AM, use **unlisted**

exec /ɪgzɛk/ (**execs**) N-COUNT **Exec** is an abbreviation for **executive**. [INFORMAL]

ex|ecrable /ˈɛksɪkrəbəl/ ADJ If you describe something as **execrable**, you mean that it is very bad or unpleasant. [FORMAL] ☐ *Accusing us of being disloyal to cover his own sorry behavior is truly execrable.* ☐ *...an execrable meal.*

ex|ecu|table /ˌɛksɪkjuːtəbəl/ ADJ [usu ADJ n] An **executable** file or program contains software that runs when it is opened. ☐ *Some emails may contain executable programs that delete your anti-virus software.*

ex|ecute ♦◇◇ /ˈɛksɪkjuːt/ (**executes, executing, executed**) ◨ V-T To **execute** someone means to kill them as a punishment for a serious crime. ☐ *He said nobody had been executed as a direct result of the events.* ☐ *One group claimed to have executed the hostage.* • **ex|ecu|tion** /ˌɛksɪkjuːʃən/ (**executions**) N-VAR ☐ *Execution by lethal injection is scheduled for July 30th.* ◨ V-T If you **execute** a plan, you carry it out. [FORMAL] ☐ *We are going to execute our campaign plan to the letter.* • **ex|ecu|tion** N-UNCOUNT ☐ *U.S. forces are fully prepared for the execution of any action once the order is given by the president.* ◨ V-T If you **execute** a difficult action or movement, you successfully perform it. ☐ *The landing was skillfully executed.* ◨ → See feature box at **conflict**

ex|ecu|tion|er /ˌɛksɪkjuːʃənər/ (**executioners**) N-COUNT An **executioner** is a person who has the job of executing criminals.

ex|ecu|tive ♦♦◇ /ɪgzɛkjətɪv/ (**executives**) ◨ N-COUNT An **executive** is someone who is employed by a business at a senior level. Executives decide what the business should do, and ensure that it is done. ☐ *...an advertising executive.* ◨ ADJ [ADJ n] The **executive** sections and tasks of an organization are concerned with the making of decisions and with ensuring that decisions are carried out. ☐ *A successful job search needs to be as well organised as any other executive task.* ◨ ADJ [ADJ n] **Executive** goods are expensive products designed or intended for executives and other people at a similar social or economic level. ☐ *...an executive briefcase.* ◨ N-SING [the N, N n] The **executive** committee or board of an organization is a committee within that organization that has the authority to make decisions and ensures that these decisions are carried out. ❑ *They opted to put an executive committee in charge of the project rather than a single person.* **5** N-SING [the N, N n] **The executive** is the part of the government of a country that is concerned with carrying out decisions or orders, as opposed to the part that makes laws or the part that deals with criminals. ❑ *The government, the executive and the judiciary are supposed to be separate.*

SYNONYMS

executive
NOUN **1**
manager: *...a retired bank manager.*
director: *She served on the board of directors of a local bank.*
chairperson: *She's the chairperson of the safety committee.*

ex|ecu|tive or|der (executive orders) N-COUNT An **executive order** is a regulation issued by a member of the executive branch of government. It has the same authority as a law. [AM] ❑ *The president issued an executive order banning such activities.*

ex|ecu|tive privi|lege N-UNCOUNT **Executive privilege** is the right that a member of the executive branch of government has to withhold information about matters that they consider to be confidential. [AM] ❑ *So far, no documents are being withheld on grounds of executive privilege.*

ex|ecu|tor /ɪɡzɛkyətər/ (executors) N-COUNT An **executor** is someone whose name you write in your will when you want them to be responsible for dealing with your affairs after your death. [LEGAL]

ex|egesis /ɛksɪdʒisɪs/ (exegeses /ɛksɪdʒisiz/) N-VAR An **exegesis** is an explanation and interpretation of a piece of writing after very careful study. [FORMAL] ❑ *...the kind of academic exegesis at which Isaacs excels.* ❑ *...a substantial exegesis of his work.*

ex|em|plar /ɪɡzɛmplɑr/ (exemplars) **1** N-COUNT [oft N of n] An **exemplar** is someone or something that is considered to be so good that they should be copied or imitated. [FORMAL] ❑ *They viewed their new building as an exemplar of taste.* **2** N-COUNT [oft N of n] An **exemplar** is a typical example of a group or class of things. [FORMAL] ❑ *One of the wittiest exemplars of the technique was M. C. Escher.*

ex|em|pla|ry /ɪɡzɛmpləri/ ADJ If you describe someone or something as **exemplary**, you think they are extremely good. ❑ *Underpinning this success has been an exemplary record of innovation.*

ex|em|pli|fy /ɪɡzɛmplɪfaɪ/ (exemplifies, exemplifying, exemplified) V-T If a person or thing **exemplifies** something such as a situation, quality, or class of things, they are a typical example of it. [FORMAL] ❑ *The room's style exemplifies their ideal of "beauty and practicality."*

ex|empt /ɪɡzɛmpt/ (exempts, exempting, exempted) **1** ADJ If someone or something is **exempt** from a particular rule, duty, or obligation, they do not have to follow it or do it. ❑ *Men in college were exempt from military service.* **2** V-T To **exempt** a person or thing from a particular rule, duty, or obligation means to state officially that they are not bound or affected by it. ❑ *South Carolina claimed the power to exempt its citizens from the obligation to obey federal law.* • **ex|emp|tion** /ɪɡzɛmpʃən/ (exemptions) N-VAR [oft N from n] ❑ *...the exemption of employer-provided health insurance from taxation.*

ex|er|cise ◆◇◇ /ɛksərsaɪz/ (exercises, exercising, exercised) **1** V-T If you **exercise** something such as your authority, your rights, or a good quality, you use it or put it into effect. [FORMAL] ❑ *They are merely exercising their right to free speech.* • N-SING **Exercise** is also a noun. ❑ *Social structures are maintained through the exercise of political and economic power.* **2** V-I When you **exercise**, you move your body energetically in order to get in shape and to remain healthy. ❑ *She exercises two or three times a week.* • N-UNCOUNT **Exercise** is also a noun. ❑ *Lack of exercise can lead to feelings of depression and exhaustion.* **3** V-T If a movement or activity **exercises** a part of your body, it keeps it strong, healthy, or in good condition. ❑ *They call rowing the perfect sport. It exercises every major muscle group.* **4** N-COUNT **Exercises** are a series of movements or actions that you do in order to get in shape, remain healthy, or practice for a particular physical activity. ❑ *I do special neck and shoulder exercises.* **5** N-COUNT [usu pl, also on n] **Exercises** are military activities and operations that are not part of a real war, but that allow the armed forces to practice for a real war. ❑ *General Powell predicted that in the future it might even be possible to stage joint military exercises.* **6** N-COUNT An **exercise** is a short activity or piece of work that you do, in school for example, which is designed to help you learn a particular skill. ❑ *Try working through the opening exercises in this chapter.*

COLLOCATIONS

exercise
VERB **1**
exercise + *noun*: authority, control, influence, jurisdiction, power; caution, discretion, restraint; right
NOUN **2**
noun + **exercise**: breathing, relaxation
adjective + **exercise**: aerobic, vigorous; regular

ex|er|cise bike (exercise bikes) **1** N-COUNT An **exercise bike** is a special bicycle that does not move, so that you can exercise on it at home or at a gym. **2** → See also color supplement

ex|er|cise book (exercise books) N-COUNT An **exercise book** is a book with printed exercises for students to complete.

ex|ert /ɪɡzɜrt/ (exerts, exerting, exerted) **1** V-T If someone or something **exerts** influence, authority, or pressure, they use it in a strong or determined way, especially in order to produce a particular effect. [FORMAL] ❑ *He exerted considerable influence on the thinking of the scientific community on these issues.* **2** V-T If you **exert** yourself, you make a great physical or mental effort, or work hard to do something. ❑ *Do not exert yourself unnecessarily.* • **ex|er|tion** (exertions) N-UNCOUNT [also N in pl] ❑ *He clearly found the physical exertion exhilarating.*

ex|fo|li|ate /ɛksfoʊlieɪt/ (exfoliates, exfoliating, exfoliated) V-T/V-I To **exfoliate**, or **exfoliate** your skin, means to remove the dead cells from its surface using something such as a brush or a special cream. ❑ *Exfoliate your back at least once a week.* • **ex|fo|li|at|ing** ADJ ❑ *...a gentle exfoliating cream.* • **ex|fo|lia|tion** /ɛksfoʊlieɪʃən/ N-UNCOUNT ❑ *There is little doubt that skin does benefit from exfoliation.*

ex gra|tia /ɛks ɡreɪʃiə/ ADJ [usu ADJ n] An **ex gratia** payment is one that is given as a favor or gift and not because it is legally necessary. [FORMAL]

ex|hale /ɛksheɪl/ (exhales, exhaling, exhaled) V-T/V-I When you **exhale**, you breathe out the air that is in your lungs. [FORMAL] ❑ *Hold your breath for a moment and exhale.*

ex|haust ◆◇◇ /ɪɡzɔst/ (exhausts, exhausting, exhausted) **1** V-T If something **exhausts** you, it makes you so tired, either physically or mentally, that you have no energy left. ❑ *Don't exhaust him.* • **ex|haust|ed** ADJ ❑ *She was too exhausted and distressed to talk about the tragedy.* • **ex|haust|ing** ADJ ❑ *It was an exhausting schedule she had set herself.* **2** V-T If you **exhaust** something such as money or food, you use or finish it all. ❑ *We have exhausted all our material resources.* **3** V-T If you **have exhausted** a subject or topic, you have talked about it so much that there is nothing more to say about it. ❑ *She and Chantal must have exhausted the subject of school.* **4** N-UNCOUNT [also N in pl] **Exhaust** is the gas or steam that is produced when the engine of a vehicle is running. ❑ *...the exhaust from a car engine.* ❑ *The city's streets are filthy and choked with exhaust fumes.* **5** N-COUNT The **exhaust** is the same as the **exhaust pipe**. [BRIT]

ex|haus|tion /ɪɡzɔstʃən/ N-UNCOUNT **Exhaustion** is the state of being so tired that you have no energy left. ❑ *He is suffering from exhaustion.*

ex|haus|tive /ɪɡzɔstɪv/ ADJ If you describe a study, search, or list as **exhaustive**, you mean that it is very thorough and complete. ❑ *This is by no means an exhaustive list but it gives an indication of the many projects taking place.* • **ex|haus|tive|ly** ADV ❑ *Martin said these costs were scrutinized exhaustively by independent accountants.*

ex|haust pipe (exhaust pipes) N-COUNT The **exhaust pipe** is the pipe that carries the gas out of the engine of a vehicle.

ex|hib|it /ɪɡzɪbɪt/ (exhibits, exhibiting, exhibited) **1** V-T If someone or something shows a particular quality, feeling, or type of behavior, you can say that they **exhibit** it. [FORMAL] ❑ *He has exhibited symptoms of anxiety and overwhelming worry.* **2** V-T [usu passive] When a painting, sculpture, or object of interest **is exhibited**, it is put in a public place such as a museum or art gallery so that people can come to look at it. You can also say that animals **are exhibited** in a zoo. ☐ *His work was exhibited in the best galleries in America, Europe and Asia.* ● **ex|hi|bi|tion** N-UNCOUNT ☐ *Five large pieces of the wall are currently on exhibition.* **3** V-I When artists **exhibit**, they show their work in public. ☐ *He has also exhibited at galleries and museums in New York and Washington.* **4** N-COUNT An **exhibit** is a painting, sculpture, or object of interest that is displayed to the public in a museum or art gallery. ☐ *Shona showed me around the exhibits.* **5** N-COUNT An **exhibit** is a public display of paintings, sculpture, or objects of interest in a museum or art gallery. [AM] ☐ *...an exhibit at the Metropolitan Museum of Art.* **6** N-COUNT An **exhibit** is an object that a lawyer shows in court as evidence in a legal case. ☐ *The jury has already asked to see more than 40 exhibits from the trial.* **7** → See feature box at **fine art**

ex|hi|bi|tion ◆◇◇ /ɛksɪbɪʃən/ (**exhibitions**) **1** N-COUNT An **exhibition** is a public event at which pictures, sculptures, or other objects of interest are displayed, for example at a museum or art gallery. ☐ *...an exhibition of expressionist art.* **2** N-SING An **exhibition of** a particular skillful activity is a display or example of it that people notice or admire. ☐ *He responded in champion's style by treating the fans to an exhibition of power and speed.* **3** → see also **exhibit 2**

ex|hi|bi|tion game (**exhibition games**) N-COUNT In sports, an **exhibition game** is a game that is not part of a competition, and is played for entertainment or practice, often without any serious effort to win. [AM]

ex|hi|bi|tion|ism /ɛksɪbɪʃənɪzəm/ N-UNCOUNT **Exhibitionism** is behavior that tries to get people's attention all the time, and especially behavior that most people think is silly. [DISAPPROVAL] ☐ *There is an element of exhibitionism in the parents' performance too.*

ex|hi|bi|tion|ist /ɛksɪbɪʃənɪst/ (**exhibitionists**) N-COUNT An **exhibitionist** is someone who tries to get people's attention all the time by behaving in a way that most people think is silly. [DISAPPROVAL]

ex|hibi|tor /ɪgzɪbɪtər/ (**exhibitors**) N-COUNT An **exhibitor** is a person or company whose work or products are being shown in an exhibition. ☐ *Schedules will be sent out to all exhibitors.*

ex|hila|rat|ed /ɪgzɪləreɪtɪd/ ADJ [usu v-link ADJ] If you are **exhilarated** by something, it makes you feel very happy and excited. [FORMAL] ☐ *He felt strangely exhilarated by the brisk, blue morning.*

ex|hil|arat|ing /ɪgzɪləreɪtɪŋ/ ADJ If you describe an experience or feeling as **exhilarating**, you mean that it makes you feel very happy and excited. ☐ *It was exhilarating to be on the road again and his spirits rose.*

ex|hila|ra|tion /ɪgzɪləreɪʃən/ N-UNCOUNT **Exhilaration** is a strong feeling of excitement and happiness. ☐ *The exhilaration of winning such a famous event has stayed with him.*

ex|hort /ɪgzɔrt/ (**exhorts, exhorting, exhorted**) V-T If you **exhort** someone to do something, you try hard to persuade or encourage them to do it. [FORMAL] ☐ *Kennedy exhorted his listeners to turn away from violence.* ☐ *He exhorted his companions, "Try to accomplish your aim with diligence."* ● **ex|hor|ta|tion** /ɛgzɔrteɪʃən/ (**exhortations**) N-VAR ☐ *Foreign funds alone are clearly not enough, nor are exhortations to reform.*

ex|hume /ɪgzum/ (**exhumes, exhuming, exhumed**) V-T [usu passive] If a dead person's body **is exhumed**, it is taken out of the ground where it is buried, especially so that it can be examined in order to find out how the person died. [FORMAL] ☐ *His remains have been exhumed from a cemetery in Queens.* ● **ex|hu|ma|tion** /ɛgzyumeɪʃən/ (**exhumations**) N-VAR ☐ *Detectives ordered the exhumation when his wife said she believed he had been killed.*

exi|gen|cy /ɛksɪdʒənsi/ (**exigencies**) N-COUNT [usu pl, usu N of n] The **exigencies** of a situation or a job are the demands or difficulties that you have to deal with as part of it. [FORMAL] ☐ *...the exigencies of a wartime economy.*

ex|ile ◆◇◇ /ɛksaɪl, ɛgz-/ (**exiles, exiling, exiled**) **1** N-UNCOUNT If someone is living in **exile**, they are living in a foreign country because they cannot live in their own country, usually for political reasons. ☐ *He is now living in exile in Egypt.* ☐ *He returned from exile earlier this year.* **2** V-T If someone **is exiled**, they are living in a foreign country because they cannot live in their own country, usually for political reasons. ☐ *His second wife, Hilary, had been widowed, then exiled from South Africa.* ☐ *They threatened to exile her in southern Spain.* **3** N-COUNT An **exile** is someone who has been exiled. ☐ *He is also an exile, a native of Palestine who has long given up the idea of going home.* **4** V-T [usu passive] If you say that someone **has been exiled** from a particular place or situation, you mean that they have been sent away from it or removed from it against their will. ☐ *He served less than a year of a five-year prison sentence, but was permanently exiled from the sport.* ● N-UNCOUNT **Exile** is also a noun. ☐ *...the Left's long exile from power from 1958 to 1981.*

ex|ist ◆◆◇ /ɪgzɪst/ (**exists, existing, existed**) **1** V-I [no cont] If something **exists**, it is present in the world as a real thing. ☐ *He thought that if he couldn't see something, it didn't exist.* ☐ *Research opportunities exist in a wide range of areas.* **2** V-I To **exist** means to live, especially under difficult conditions or with very little food or money. ☐ *I was barely existing.* ☐ *Some people exist on melons or coconuts for weeks at a time.*

SYNONYMS

exist
VERB **1**
endure: *Somehow the language endures and continues to survive.*
remain: *Many of the differences in everyday life remain.*
stand: *Although exceptions could be made, the rule still stands.*

---

ex|ist|ence ◆◆◇ /ɪgzɪstəns/ (**existences**) **1** N-UNCOUNT The **existence** of something is the fact that it is present in the world as a real thing. ☐ *...the existence of other galaxies.* ☐ *Public worries about accidents are threatening the very existence of the nuclear power industry.* **2** N-COUNT You can refer to someone's way of life as an **existence**, especially when they live under difficult conditions. ☐ *You may be stuck with a miserable existence for the rest of your life.*

SYNONYMS

existence
NOUN **1**
being: *The Kingdom of Italy formally came into being on March 17, 1861.*
actuality: *It exists in dreams rather than actuality.*
continuation: *What we'll see in the future is, in fact, a continuation of that trend.*
maintenance: *...the importance of natural food to the maintenance of health.*

---

ex|ist|ent /ɪgzɪstənt/ **1** ADJ You can describe something as **existent** when it exists. [FORMAL] ☐ *Their remedy lay within the range of existent technology.* **2** → see also **nonexistent**

ex|is|ten|tial /ɛgzɪstɛnʃəl/ **1** ADJ [ADJ n] **Existential** means relating to human existence and experience. [FORMAL] ☐ *Existential questions requiring religious answers still persist.* **2** ADJ [ADJ n] You use **existential** to describe fear, anxiety, and other feelings that are caused by thinking about human existence and death. [FORMAL] ☐ *"What if there's nothing left at all?" he cried, lost in some intense existential angst.*

ex|is|ten|tial|ism /ɛgzɪstɛnʃəlɪzəm/ N-UNCOUNT **Existentialism** is a philosophy that stresses the importance of human experience, and says that everyone is responsible for the results of their own actions. [TECHNICAL]

ex|is|ten|tial|ist /ɛgzɪstɛnʃəlɪst/ (**existentialists**) **1** N-COUNT An **existentialist** is a person who agrees with the philosophy of existentialism. **2** ADJ If you describe a person or their philosophy as **existentialist**, you mean that their beliefs are based on existentialism. ☐ *...existentialist theories.*

ex|ist|ing ◆◆◇ /ɪgzɪstɪŋ/ ADJ [ADJ n] **Existing** is used to describe something that is now present, available, or in operation, especially when you are contrasting it with something that is planned for the future. ☐ *...the need to improve existing products and develop new lines.* ☐ *Existing timbers are replaced or renewed.*

exit /ɛgzɪt, ɛksɪt/ (**exits, exiting, exited**) **1** N-COUNT The **exit** is the door through which you can leave a public building. ☐ *He picked up the case and walked toward the exit.* **2** N-COUNT An **exit** on a highway is a place where traffic can leave it. ☐ *She continued to the next exit, got off the highway and pulled into a*

exit poll | **expect**

parking lot. **3** N-COUNT If you refer to someone's **exit**, you are referring to the way that they left a room or building, or the fact that they left it. [FORMAL] ❏ *I made a hasty exit and managed to open the gate.* **4** N-COUNT If you refer to someone's **exit**, you are referring to the way that they left a situation or activity, or the fact that they left it. [FORMAL] ❏ *It was his earliest exit in the tournament he had dominated for over a decade.* **5** V-T/V-I If you **exit** from a room or building, you leave it. [FORMAL] ❏ *She exits into the tropical storm.* ❏ *As I exited the final display, I entered a hexagonal room.* **6** V-T If you **exit** a computer program or system, you stop running it. [COMPUTING] ❏ *I can open other applications without having to exit Adobe.* • N-SING **Exit** is also a noun. ❏ *Press Exit to return to your document.*

exit poll (exit polls) N-COUNT An **exit poll** is a survey in which people who have just voted in an election are asked which candidate they voted for. ❏ *Exit polls showed Mr Ventura was backed by supporters of all ages.*

exit strat|egy (exit strategies) N-COUNT [usu sing] In politics and business, an **exit strategy** is a way of ending your involvement in a situation such as a military operation or a business arrangement. ❏ *The fear is that we have no exit strategy from this conflict.*

exit visa (exit visas) N-COUNT An **exit visa** is an official stamp in someone's passport, or an official document, which allows them to leave the country that they are visiting or living in.

exo|dus /ɛksədəs/ N-SING If there is an **exodus** of people from a place, a lot of people leave that place at the same time. ❏ *The medical system is facing collapse because of an exodus of doctors.*

ex of|fi|cio /ɛks əfɪʃioʊ/ ADJ [ADJ n] **Ex officio** is used to describe something such as a rank or privilege that someone is entitled to because of the job or position they have. [FORMAL] ❏ *...ex officio members of the Advisory Council.* ❏ *...an ex officio degree.*

ex|on|er|ate /ɪgzɒnəreɪt/ (exonerates, exonerating, exonerated) V-T If a court, report, or person in authority **exonerates** someone, they officially say or show that that person is not responsible for something wrong or unpleasant that has happened. [FORMAL] ❏ *The official report basically exonerated everyone.* ❏ *An investigation exonerated the school from any blame.* • **ex|on|era|tion** /ɪgzɒnəreɪʃᵊn/ N-UNCOUNT ❏ *They expected complete exoneration for their clients.*

ex|or|bi|tant /ɪgzɔrbɪtənt/ ADJ If you describe something such as a price or fee as **exorbitant**, you are emphasizing that it is much higher than it should be. [EMPHASIS] ❏ *Exorbitant housing prices have created an acute shortage of affordable housing for the poor.*

ex|or|cism /ɛksɔrsɪzəm, -sər-/ (exorcisms) N-VAR **Exorcism** is the removing of evil spirits from a person or place by the use of prayer. ❏ *The exorcism was broadcast on television.*

ex|or|cist /ɛksɔrsɪst, -sər-/ (exorcists) N-COUNT An **exorcist** is someone who performs exorcisms.

ex|or|cize /ɛksɔrsaɪz, -sər-/ (exorcizes, exorcizing, exorcized)

in BRIT, also use **exorcise**

1 V-T If you **exorcize** a painful or unhappy memory, you succeed in removing it from your mind. ❏ *He confronted his childhood trauma and tried to exorcize the pain.* **2** V-T To **exorcize** an evil spirit or to **exorcize** a place or person means to force the spirit to leave the place or person by means of prayers and religious ceremonies. ❏ *They came to our house and exorcized me.*

ex|ot|ic /ɪgzɒtɪk/ ADJ Something that is **exotic** is unusual and interesting, usually because it comes from or is related to a distant country. ❏ *...brilliantly colored, exotic flowers.*
• **ex|oti|cal|ly** ADV ❏ *...exotically beautiful scenery.*

ex|oti|ca /ɪgzɒtɪkə/ N-PLURAL You use **exotica** to refer to objects that you think are unusual and interesting, usually because they come from or are related to a distant country.

ex|oti|cism /ɪgzɒtɪsɪzəm/ N-UNCOUNT **Exoticism** is the quality of seeming unusual or interesting, usually because of associations with a distant country.

ex|pand ♦◇◇ /ɪkspænd/ (expands, expanding, expanded) **1** V-T/V-I If something **expands** or **is expanded**, it becomes larger. ❏ *Engineers noticed that the pipes were not expanding as expected.* ❏ *We have to expand the size of the image.* **2** V-T/V-I If something such as a business, organization, or service **expands**, or if you **expand** it, it becomes bigger and includes more people, goods, or activities. [BUSINESS] ❏ *The popular ceramics industry expanded toward the middle of the 19th century.*
3 → See feature box at **population**
▶ **expand on** also **expand upon** PHRASAL VERB If you **expand on** or **expand upon** something, you give more information or details about it when you write or talk about it. ❏ *The president used today's speech to expand on remarks he made last month.*

--- SYNONYMS ---

expand
VERB **1**
increase: *The population continues to increase.*
grow: *The economy continues to grow.*
extend: *This year they have introduced three new products to extend their range.*
develop: *Over the last few years, tourism here has developed considerably.*
enlarge: *...the plan to enlarge Ewood Park into a 30,000 seat stadium.*

ex|panse /ɪkspæns/ (expanses) N-COUNT An **expanse** of something, usually sea, sky, or land, is a very large amount of it. ❏ *...a vast expanse of grassland.*

ex|pan|sion ♦◇◇ /ɪkspænʃᵊn/ (expansions) N-VAR **Expansion** is the process of becoming greater in size, number, or amount. ❏ *...the rapid expansion of private health insurance.*

--- SYNONYMS ---

expansion
NOUN
increase: *...a sharp increase in productivity.*
development: *Education is central to a country's economic development.*
growth: *The area has seen a rapid population growth.*
spread: *The greatest hope for reform is the gradual spread of information.*

ex|pan|sion|ary /ɪkspænʃənɛri/ **1** ADJ [usu ADJ n] **Expansionary** economic policies are intended to expand the economy of a country. **2** ADJ [usu ADJ n] **Expansionary** policies or actions are intended to increase the amount of land that a particular country rules. [DISAPPROVAL] ❏ *The full extent of their expansionary ambitions was not yet evident to many observers in the West.*

ex|pan|sion|ism /ɪkspænʃənɪzəm/ N-UNCOUNT If you refer to a country's **expansionism**, you disapprove of its policy of increasing its land and power. [DISAPPROVAL] ❏ *Soviet expansionism was considered a real threat.*

ex|pan|sion|ist /ɪkspænʃənɪst/ ADJ If you describe a country or organization as **expansionist**, you disapprove of it because it has a policy of increasing its land and power. [DISAPPROVAL] ❏ *...the intended victim of his expansionist foreign policy.*

ex|pan|sive /ɪkspænsɪv/ ADJ If you are **expansive**, you talk a lot, or are friendly or generous, because you are feeling happy and relaxed. ❏ *He was becoming more expansive as he relaxed.*

ex|pat|ri|ate /ɛkspeɪtriət, -pæt-/ (expatriates) N-COUNT An **expatriate** is someone who is living in a country that is not their own. ❏ *...British expatriates in Spain.* • ADJ [ADJ n] **Expatriate** is also an adjective. ❏ *The expatriate vote could help determine who wins in November.*

ex|pect ♦♦♦ /ɪkspɛkt/ (expects, expecting, expected) **1** V-T If you **expect** something to happen, you believe that it will happen. ❏ *...a workman who expects to lose his job in the next few weeks.* ❏ *The talks are expected to continue until tomorrow.* **2** V-T [usu cont] If you **are expecting** something or someone, you believe that they will be delivered to you or come to you soon, often because this has been arranged earlier. ❏ *I wasn't expecting a visitor.* **3** V-T If you **expect** something, or **expect** a person to do something, you believe that it is your right to have that thing, or the person's duty to do it for you. ❏ *He wasn't expecting our hospitality.* ❏ *I do expect to have some time to myself in the evenings.* **4** V-T [with brd-neg] If you tell someone not to **expect** something, you mean that the thing is unlikely to happen as they have planned or imagined, and they should not hope that it will. ❏ *Don't expect an instant cure.* ❏ *You cannot expect to like all the people you will work with.* **5** V-T/V-I [only cont] If you say that a woman **is expecting** a baby, or that she **is expecting**, you mean that

expectancy she is pregnant. ☐ *She was expecting another baby.* ▪ PHRASE You say '**I expect**' to suggest that a statement is probably correct, or a natural consequence of the present situation, although you have no definite knowledge. [SPOKEN] ☐ *I expect you can guess what follows.* ☐ *I expect you're tired.*

ex|pec|tan|cy /ɪkspɛktənsi/ N-UNCOUNT **Expectancy** is the feeling or hope that something exciting, interesting, or good is about to happen. ☐ *The supporters had a tremendous air of expectancy.*

ex|pec|tant /ɪkspɛktənt/ ▪ ADJ If someone is **expectant**, they are excited because they think something interesting is about to happen. ☐ *An expectant crowd gathered.* • **ex|pect|ant|ly** ADV [ADV after v] ☐ *The others waited, looking at him expectantly.* ▪ ADJ [ADJ n] An **expectant** mother or father is someone whose baby is going to be born soon. ☐ *...a magazine for expectant mothers.* ▪ → See feature box at **birth**

ex|pec|ta|tion ✦◇◇ /ɛkspɛkteɪʃən/ (expectations) ▪ N-UNCOUNT [also N in pl] Your **expectations** are your strong hopes or beliefs that something will happen or that you will get something that you want. ☐ *Their hope, and their expectation, was that she was going to be found safe and that she would be returned to her family.* ▪ N-COUNT A person's **expectations** are strong beliefs they have about the proper way someone should behave or something should happen. ☐ *Jamieson had determined to live up to the expectations of the company.*

COLLOCATIONS

expectation
NOUN ▪
noun + **expectation**: analyst, inflation, market
adjective + **expectation**: high, low; realistic, reasonable, unrealistic
verb + **expectation**: beat, defy, surpass; dampen, lower, raise; fulfill, meet

---

ex|pec|to|rant /ɪkspɛktərənt/ (expectorants) N-COUNT An **expectorant** is a cough medicine that helps you to cough up mucus from your lungs. [MEDICAL]

ex|pedi|en|cy /ɪkspiːdiənsi/ N-UNCOUNT **Expediency** means doing what is convenient rather than what is morally right. [FORMAL] ☐ *This was a matter less of morals than of expediency.*

ex|pedi|ent /ɪkspiːdiənt/ (expedients) ▪ N-COUNT An **expedient** is an action that achieves a particular purpose, but may not be morally right. ☐ *The curfew regulation is a temporary expedient made necessary by a sudden emergency.* ▪ ADJ If it is **expedient** to do something, it is useful or convenient to do it, even though it may not be morally right. ☐ *Governments frequently ignore human rights abuses in other countries if it is politically expedient to do so.*

ex|pedite /ɛkspɪdaɪt/ (expedites, expediting, expedited) V-T If you **expedite** something, you cause it to be done more quickly. [FORMAL] ☐ *We tried to help you expedite your plans.*

ex|pedi|tion /ɛkspɪdɪʃən/ (expeditions) ▪ N-COUNT An **expedition** is an organized trip made for a particular purpose such as exploration. ☐ *...Byrd's 1928 expedition to Antarctica.* ▪ N-COUNT You can refer to a group of people who are going on an expedition as an **expedition**. ☐ *Forty-three members of the expedition were killed.* ▪ N-COUNT An **expedition** is a short trip that you make for pleasure. ☐ *...Officer Goss was on a fishing expedition.*

ex|pedi|tion|ary force /ɛkspɪdɪʃənɛri fɔrs/ (expeditionary forces) N-COUNT An **expeditionary force** is a group of soldiers who are sent to fight in a foreign country. [MILITARY]

ex|pedi|tious /ɛkspɪdɪʃəs/ ADJ **Expeditious** means quick and efficient. [FORMAL] ☐ *The judge said that arbitration was a fair and expeditious decision-making process.* • **ex|pedi|tious|ly** ADV [ADV with v] ☐ *The matter has certainly been handled expeditiously by the authorities.*

ex|pel /ɪkspɛl/ (expels, expelling, expelled) ▪ V-T [usu passive] If someone **is expelled** from a school or organization, they are officially told to leave because they have behaved badly. ☐ *More than five-thousand high school students have been expelled for cheating.* ▪ V-T If people **are expelled** from a place, they are made to leave it, often by force. ☐ *An American academic was expelled from the country yesterday.* ☐ *They were told that they should expel the refugees.* ▪ V-T To **expel** something means to force it

experience out from a container or from your body. ☐ *As the lungs exhale this waste, gas is expelled into the atmosphere.*

ex|pend /ɪkspɛnd/ (expends, expending, expended) V-T To **expend** something, especially energy, time, or money, means to use it or spend it. [FORMAL] ☐ *Children expend a lot of energy and may need more high-energy food than adults.*

ex|pend|able /ɪkspɛndəb°l/ ADJ If you regard someone or something as **expendable**, you think it is acceptable to get rid of them, abandon them, or allow them to be destroyed when they are no longer needed. [FORMAL] ☐ *Once our services cease to be useful to them, we're expendable.* ☐ *During the recession, training budgets were seen as an expendable luxury.*

ex|pendi|ture /ɪkspɛndɪtʃər/ (expenditures) ▪ N-VAR **Expenditure** is the spending of money on something, or the money that is spent on something. [FORMAL] ☐ *Policies of tax reduction must lead to reduced public expenditure.* ▪ → See feature box at **finance**

ex|pense ✦◇◇ /ɪkspɛns/ (expenses) ▪ N-VAR **Expense** is the money that something costs you or that you need to spend in order to do something. ☐ *He's bought a big TV at vast expense so that everyone can see properly.* ▪ N-PLURAL **Expenses** are amounts of money that you spend while doing something in the course of your work, which will be paid back to you afterwards. [BUSINESS] ☐ *Her airfare and hotel expenses were paid by the committee.* ▪ PHRASE If you do something **at** someone's **expense**, they provide the money for it. ☐ *Should architects continue to be trained for five years at public expense?* ▪ PHRASE If someone laughs or makes a joke **at** your **expense**, they do it to make you seem foolish. ☐ *I think he's having fun at our expense.* ▪ PHRASE If you achieve something **at the expense of** someone, you do it in a way that might cause them some harm or disadvantage. ☐ *According to this study, women have made notable gains at the expense of men.* ▪ PHRASE If you say that someone does something **at the expense of** another thing, you are expressing concern that they are not doing the second thing, because the first thing uses all their resources. [DISAPPROVAL] ☐ *The orchestra has more discipline now, but at the expense of spirit.* ▪ PHRASE If you **go to** the **expense** of doing something, you do something that costs a lot of money. If you **go to** great **expense** to do something, you spend a lot of money in order to achieve it. ☐ *Why go to the expense of buying an electric saw when you can borrow one?*

COLLOCATIONS

expense
NOUN
▪
noun + **expense**: household, living, office; funeral
adjective + **expense**: additional, considerable, vast; legal, medical, parliamentary; day-to-day, monthly
verb + **expense**: incur; justify; fiddle
▪
noun + **expense**: hotel, travel
verb + **expense**: claim, deduct; cover, pay, reimburse

---

ex|pense ac|count (expense accounts) N-COUNT An **expense account** is an arrangement between an employer and an employee that allows the employee to spend the company's money on things relating to their job, such as traveling or dealing with clients. [BUSINESS] ☐ *He put Elizabeth's motel bill and airfare on his expense account.*

ex|pen|sive ✦✦◇ /ɪkspɛnsɪv/ ADJ If something is **expensive**, it costs a lot of money. ☐ *Renewable energy is still more expensive than fossil fuels.* • **ex|pen|sive|ly** ADV ☐ *She was expensively dressed, with fine furs and jewels.*

SYNONYMS

expensive
ADJ
costly: *Having professionally-made curtains can be costly.*
pricey: *Medical insurance is very pricey.*
overpriced: *I had an overpriced cup of coffee in the hotel cafeteria.*
exorbitant: *Exorbitant housing prices have created an acute shortage of affordable housing for the poor.*

---

ex|peri|ence ✦✦✦ /ɪkspɪəriəns/ (experiences, experiencing, experienced) ▪ N-UNCOUNT **Experience** is knowledge or skill in a particular job or activity that you have gained because you have done that job or activity for a long time. ❏ *He has also had managerial experience on every level.* **2** N-UNCOUNT **Experience** is used to refer to the past events, knowledge, and feelings that make up someone's life or character. ❏ *I should not be in any danger here, but experience has taught me caution.* **3** N-COUNT An **experience** is something that you do or that happens to you, especially something important that affects you. ❏ *His only experience of gardening so far proved immensely satisfying.* **4** V-T If you **experience** a particular situation, you are in that situation or it happens to you. ❏ *We had never experienced this kind of vacation before and had no idea what to expect.* **5** V-T If you **experience** a feeling, you feel it or are affected by it. ❏ *Widows seem to experience more distress than widowers.* • N-SING **Experience** is also a noun. ❏ *...the experience of pain.* **6** → See feature box at **service**

COLLOCATIONS

experience
NOUN
1
noun + **experience**: life, work
adjective + **experience**: first-hand, invaluable, personal, practical; managerial; extensive, previous
verb + **experience**: gain
3
noun + **experience**: dining, learning, shopping
adjective + **experience**: bad, common, memorable, traumatic; positive, valuable
verb + **experience**: enjoy, share
VERB
4
experience + noun: difficulty, hardship, loss, problem; change, symptom; life
5
experience + noun: anxiety, distress, pain

---

ex|pe|ri|enced /ɪkspɪəriənst/ ADJ If you describe someone as **experienced**, you mean that they have been doing a particular job or activity for a long time, and therefore know a lot about it or are very skillful at it. ❏ *...lawyers who are experienced in these matters.* ❏ *It's a team packed with experienced and mature professionals.*

ex|peri|en|tial /ɪkspɪəriɛnʃ°l/ ADJ **Experiential** means relating to or resulting from experience. [FORMAL] ❏ *Learning has got to be active and experiential.*

ex|peri|ment ✦✧ (experiments, experimenting, experimented)

> The noun is pronounced /ɪkspɛrɪmənt/. The verb is pronounced /ɪkspɛrɪmɛnt/.

1 N-VAR An **experiment** is a scientific test done in order to discover what happens to something in particular conditions. ❏ *The astronauts are conducting a series of experiments to learn more about how the body adapts to weightlessness.* **2** V-I If you **experiment with** something or **experiment on** it, you do a scientific test on it in order to discover what happens to it in particular conditions. ❏ *In 1857 Mendel started experimenting with peas in his monastery garden.* ❏ *The scientists have experimented on the tiny neck arteries of rats.* • **ex|peri|men|ta|tion** /ɪkspɛrɪmɛntɛɪʃ°n/ N-UNCOUNT ❏ *...the ethical aspects of animal experimentation.* **3** N-VAR An **experiment** is the trying out of a new idea or method in order to see what it is like and what effects it has. ❏ *As an experiment, we bought Ted a watch.* **4** V-I To **experiment** means to try out a new idea or method to see what it is like and what effects it has. ❏ *...if you like cooking and have the time to experiment.* • **ex|peri|men|ta|tion** N-UNCOUNT ❏ *Decentralization and experimentation must be encouraged.* **5** → See feature box at **research**

USAGE

experiment
You usually say that someone **conducts** or **does** an experiment. Don't say '~~We decided to make an experiment.~~' Say 'We decided to **conduct** an experiment.'

---

ex|peri|men|tal /ɪkspɛrɪmɛnt°l/ **1** ADJ Something that is **experimental** is new or uses new ideas or methods, and might be modified later if it is unsuccessful. ❏ *...an experimental air-conditioning system.* **2** ADJ [ADJ n] **Experimental** means using, used in, or resulting from scientific experiments. ❏ *...the main techniques of experimental science.* • **ex|peri|men|tal|ly** ADV [ADV with v] ❏ *...an ecology laboratory, where communities of species can be studied experimentally under controlled conditions.* **3** ADJ An **experimental** action is done in order to see what it is like, or what effects it has. ❏ *The senator is ready to argue for an experimental lifting of the ban.* • **ex|peri|men|tal|ly** ADV [ADV with v] ❏ *This system is being tried out experimentally at many universities.*

VOCABULARY IN CONTEXT

Experiment

What do you think happens when you heat a **saline solution**? Before beginning your experiment, write your **hypothesis** down. To carry out the experiment, first make a saline solution by mixing 10g of salt into 10ml of water in a **beaker**. Stir the mixture well to ensure all the salt has **dissolved**; then pour the solution into an evaporating dish. Before the next step, make sure you put on your safety **goggles**. Set up a **tripod** over a Bunsen burner and put a **wire mesh** on top of the tripod. Then place the evaporating dish on the wire mesh. Remember not to light the Bunsen burner until you have put your evaporating dish in place! As the solution is heated, the water will **evaporate**, leaving solid **salt crystals** behind in the dish. Was your hypothesis correct?

---

ex|pert ✦✧✧ /ɛkspɜrt/ (experts) **1** N-COUNT An **expert** is a person who is very skilled at doing something or who knows a lot about a particular subject. ❏ *...a yoga expert.* **2** ADJ Someone who is **expert** at doing something is very skilled at it. ❏ *The Japanese are expert at lowering manufacturing costs.* • **ex|pert|ly** ADV [ADV with v] ❏ *Shopkeepers expertly rolled spices up in bay leaves.* **3** ADJ [ADJ n] If you say that someone has **expert** hands or an **expert** eye, you mean that they are very skillful or experienced in using their hands or eyes for a particular purpose. ❏ *Harvey cured the pain with his own expert hands.* **4** ADJ [ADJ n] **Expert** advice or help is given by someone who has studied a subject thoroughly or who is very skilled at a particular job. ❏ *We'll need an expert opinion.*

ex|per|tise /ɛkspɜrtiz/ N-UNCOUNT **Expertise** is special skill or knowledge that is acquired by training, study, or practice. ❏ *She was not an accountant and didn't have the expertise to verify all of the financial details.*

ex|pert wit|ness (expert witnesses) N-COUNT In a court case, an **expert witness** is someone such as a doctor or other professional who testifies about and gives opinions on subjects and issues that have been raised in the particular court case. ❏ *Flynn often testifies as an expert witness in court cases.*

ex|pi|ate /ɛkspieɪt/ (expiates, expiating, expiated) V-T If you **expiate** guilty feelings or bad behavior, you do something to indicate that you are sorry for what you have done. [FORMAL] ❏ *It seemed that Alice was expiating her father's sins with her charity work.* • **ex|pia|tion** /ɛkspieɪʃ°n/ N-UNCOUNT ❏ *...an often painful process of evaluation and expiation.*

expiration

ex|pi|ra|tion /ɛkspɪreɪʃᵊn/ **1** N-UNCOUNT [oft the N of n] The **expiration** of a fixed period of time is its ending. ☐ ...about ten days before the expiration of my leave of absence. **2** N-UNCOUNT [usu the N of n] The **expiration** of something such as a contract, deadline, or visa is the time when it comes to an end or stops being valid. [AM] ☐ This will allow them to stay in the United States beyond the expiration of their visas.

ex|pi|ra|tion date (expiration dates) N-COUNT The **expiration date** on a food container is the date by which the food should be sold or eaten before it starts to decay. [AM] ☐ But soda past its expiration date goes flat and loses much of its taste.

ex|pire /ɪkspaɪər/ (expires, expiring, expired) V-I When something such as a contract, deadline, or visa **expires**, it comes to an end or is no longer valid. ☐ He had lived illegally in the United States for five years after his visitor's visa expired.

ex|pi|ry /ɪkspaɪəri/ N-UNCOUNT The **expiry** of something such as a contract, deadline, or visa is the time that it comes to an end or stops being valid. [BRIT]

in AM, use **expiration**

ex|plain ◆◇◇ /ɪkspleɪn/ (explains, explaining, explained) **1** V-T/V-I If you **explain** something, you give details about it or describe it so that it can be understood. ☐ Not every judge, however, has the ability to explain the law in simple terms. ☐ Don't sign anything until your lawyer has explained the contract to you. ☐ Professor Griffiths explained how the drug appears to work. **2** V-T/V-I If you **explain**, or **explain** something that has happened, you give people reasons for it, especially in an attempt to justify it. ☐ "Let me explain, sir."—"Don't tell me about it. I don't want to know." ☐ Before she ran away, she left a note explaining her actions. ☐ Explain why you didn't telephone.

▶ **explain away** PHRASAL VERB If someone **explains away** a mistake or a bad situation they are responsible for, they try to indicate that it is unimportant or that it is not really their fault. ☐ He evaded her questions about the war and tried to explain away the atrocities.

ex|pla|na|tion ◆◇◇ /ɛkspləneɪʃᵊn/ (explanations) **1** N-COUNT [also of/in n] If you give an **explanation** of something that has happened, you give people reasons for it, especially in an attempt to justify it. ☐ She told the court she would give a full explanation of the prosecution's decision on Monday. **2** N-COUNT If you say there is an **explanation** for something, you mean that there is a reason for it. ☐ The deputy airport manager said there was no apparent explanation for the crash. **3** N-COUNT If you give an **explanation** of something, you give details about it or describe it so that it can be understood. ☐ He has given a very clear explanation of his remarks and the context in which they were made.

SYNONYMS

explanation
NOUN
1
interpretation: The opposition Conservative Party had a different interpretation of the figures.
clarification: The union has written to Zurich asking for clarification of the situation.
2
reason: There is a reason for every important thing that happens.
cause: The causes are a complex blend of local and national tensions.
excuse: It is easy to find excuses for his indecisiveness.
motive: Police have ruled out robbery as a motive for the killing.

ex|pla|na|tory /ɪksplænətəri/ ADJ **Explanatory** statements or theories are intended to make people understand something by describing it or giving the reasons for it. [FORMAL] ☐ These statements are accompanied by a series of explanatory notes.

ex|ple|tive /ɛksplitɪv/ (expletives) N-COUNT An **expletive** is a rude word or expression such as 'Damn!' that people say when they are annoyed, excited, or in pain. [FORMAL]

ex|pli|cable /ɛksplɪkəbᵊl/ ADJ If something is **explicable**, it can be explained and understood because it is logical or sensible. [FORMAL] ☐ The older I grow, the stranger and less explicable the world appears to me.

exploit

ex|pli|cate /ɛksplɪkeɪt/ (explicates, explicating, explicated) V-T To **explicate** something means to explain it and make it clear. [FORMAL] ☐ We shall have to explicate its basic assumptions before we can assess its implications. • **ex|pli|ca|tion** /ɛksplɪkeɪʃᵊn/ (explications) N-VAR ☐ The jury listened to his impassioned explication of article 306. ☐ McKen criticizes the lack of explication of what the term "areas" means.

ex|plic|it /ɪksplɪsɪt/ **1** ADJ Something that is **explicit** is expressed or shown clearly and openly, without any attempt to hide anything. ☐ Sexually explicit scenes in movies and books were taboo under the old regime. • **ex|plic|it|ly** ADV ☐ The play was the first commercially successful work dealing explicitly with homosexuality. **2** ADJ [v-link ADJ, oft ADJ about n] If you are **explicit** about something, you speak about it very openly and clearly. ☐ He was explicit about his intention to overhaul the party's internal voting system. • **ex|plic|it|ly** ADV [ADV with v] ☐ She has been talking very explicitly about AIDS to these groups.

ex|plode ◆◇◇ /ɪksploʊd/ (explodes, exploding, exploded) **1** V-T/V-I If an object such as a bomb **explodes** or if someone or something **explodes** it, it bursts loudly and with great force, often causing damage or injury. ☐ They were clearing up when the second bomb exploded. **2** V-I If someone **explodes**, they express strong feelings suddenly and violently. ☐ Do you fear that you'll burst into tears or explode with anger in front of her? ☐ "What happened!" I exploded. **3** V-I If something **explodes**, it increases suddenly and rapidly in number or intensity. ☐ The population explodes to 40,000 during the tourist season. **4** V-T If someone **explodes** a theory or myth, they prove that it is wrong or impossible. ☐ Electricity privatization has exploded the myth of cheap nuclear power.

USAGE

explode or blow up?
If someone destroys a building with a bomb, you say that they **blow** it **up**. Don't say 'He wanted to explode the place.' Say 'He wanted to **blow** the place **up**.'

ex|ploit ◆◇◇ (exploits, exploiting, exploited)

The verb is pronounced /ɪksplɔɪt/. The noun is pronounced /ɛksplɔɪt/.

1 V-T If you say that someone is **exploiting** you, you think that they are treating you unfairly by using your work or ideas and giving you very little in return. ☐ Critics claim he exploited Black musicians for personal gain. • **ex|ploi|ta|tion** /ɛksplɔɪteɪʃᵊn/ N-UNCOUNT ☐ Extra payments should be made to protect the interests of the staff and prevent exploitation. **2** V-T If you say that someone is **exploiting** a situation, you disapprove of them because they are using it to gain an advantage for themselves, rather than trying to help other people or do what is right. [DISAPPROVAL] ☐ The government and its opponents compete to exploit the troubles to their advantage. • **ex|ploi|ta|tion** N-SING ☐ ...the exploitation of the famine by local politicians. **3** V-T If you **exploit** something, you use it well, and achieve something or gain an advantage from it. ☐ You'll need a good antenna to exploit the radio's performance. **4** V-T To **exploit** resources or raw materials means to develop them and use them for industry or commercial activities. ☐ I think we're being very shortsighted in not exploiting our own coal. • **ex|ploi|ta|tion** N-UNCOUNT ☐ ...the planned exploitation of its potential oil and natural gas reserves. **5** N-COUNT If you refer to someone's **exploits**, you mean the brave, interesting, or amusing things that they have done. ☐ His wartime exploits were later made into a movie and a television series.

SYNONYMS

exploit
VERB **1**
abuse: He showed how the rich and powerful can abuse their position.
take advantage of: She took advantage of him even after they were divorced.
use: Why do I have the feeling I'm being used again?
ill-treat: They said they had not been ill-treated in captivity.
NOUN **5**
feat: This seems to me an impressive feat.
adventure: I set off for a new adventure on the first day of the year.
stunt: In a bold promotional stunt, he smashed his car into a passing truck.
deed: His heroic deeds were celebrated in every corner of India.

ex|ploit|able /ɪksplɔɪtəbəl/ **1** ADJ If something is **exploitable**, it can be used or developed to make a profit. ❑ *Exploitable raw materials were in short supply.* ❑ *Of 27 new wells drilled, 16 have proved exploitable.* **2** ADJ An **exploitable** situation can be used by someone to their own advantage. ❑ *Your hope was I'd make some exploitable mistake.*

ex|ploita|tive /ɪksplɔɪtətɪv/ ADJ If you describe something as **exploitative**, you disapprove of it because it treats people unfairly by using their work or ideas for its own advantage, and giving them very little in return. [FORMAL, DISAPPROVAL] ❑ *...the increasingly exploitative nature of free-market capitalism.*

ex|ploit|er /ɪksplɔɪtər/ (**exploiters**) N-COUNT If you refer to people as **exploiters**, you disapprove of them because they exploit other people in an unfair and cruel way. [FORMAL, DISAPPROVAL]

ex|plora|tory /ɪksplɔrətɔri/ ADJ **Exploratory** actions are done in order to discover something or to learn the truth about something. ❑ *Exploratory surgery revealed her liver cancer.*

ex|plore ◆◇◇ /ɪksplɔr/ (**explores, exploring, explored**) **1** V-T/V-I If you **explore**, or **explore** a place, you travel around it to find out what it is like. ❑ *I just wanted to explore on my own.* ❑ *After exploring the old part of town there is a guided tour of the cathedral.* ● **ex|plo|ra|tion** /ɛkspləreɪʃən/ (**explorations**) N-VAR ❑ *We devote several days to the exploration of the magnificent Maya sites of Copan.* **2** V-T If you **explore** an idea or suggestion, you think over it or comment on it in detail, in order to assess it carefully. ❑ *The movie is eloquent as it explores the relationship between artist and instrument.* ● **ex|plo|ra|tion** N-VAR ❑ *I looked forward to the exploration of their theories.* **3** V-I If people **explore for** a substance such as oil or minerals, they study an area and do tests on the land to see whether they can find it. ❑ *Central to the operation is a mile-deep well, dug originally to explore for oil.* ● **ex|plo|ra|tion** N-UNCOUNT ❑ *...a Dallas-based oil and gas exploration and production concern.* **4** V-T If you **explore** something with your hands or fingers, you touch it to find out what it feels like. ❑ *He explored the wound with his finger, trying to establish its extent.*

---SYNONYMS---

explore
VERB **2**
investigate: *Gas officials are investigating the cause of the explosion.*
consider: *The government is being asked to consider the plan.*
research: *She spent two years in South Florida researching and filming her documentary.*
examine: *The plans will be examined by E.U. ministers.*
analyze: *You need to analyze what is causing the stress in your life.*

---

ex|plor|er /ɪksplɔrər/ (**explorers**) N-COUNT An **explorer** is someone who travels to places about which very little is known, in order to discover what is there. ❑ *...the travels of Columbus, Magellan, and many other explorers.*

ex|plo|sion ◆◇◇ /ɪksploʊʒən/ (**explosions**) **1** N-COUNT An **explosion** is a sudden, violent burst of energy, such as one caused by a bomb. ❑ *After the second explosion, all of London's main train and subway stations were shut down.* **2** N-VAR An **explosion** is the act of deliberately causing a bomb or similar device to explode. ❑ *Bomb disposal experts blew up the bag in a controlled explosion.* **3** N-COUNT An **explosion** is a large rapid increase in the number or amount of something. ❑ *The study also forecast an explosion in the diet soft-drink market.* **4** N-COUNT An **explosion** is a sudden violent expression of someone's feelings, especially anger. ❑ *Every time they met, Myra anticipated an explosion.* **5** N-COUNT An **explosion** is a sudden and serious political protest or violence. ❑ *...the explosion of protest and violence sparked off by the killing of seven workers.*

ex|plo|sive /ɪksploʊsɪv/ (**explosives**) **1** N-VAR An **explosive** is a substance or device that can cause an explosion. ❑ *...one-hundred-and-fifty pounds of Semtex explosive.* **2** ADJ Something that is **explosive** is capable of causing an explosion. ❑ *The explosive device was timed to go off at the rush hour.* **3** ADJ An **explosive** growth is a sudden, rapid increase in the size or quantity of something. ❑ *The explosive growth in casinos is one of the most conspicuous signs of Westernization.* **4** ADJ An **explosive** situation is likely to have difficult, serious, or dangerous effects. ❑ *He appeared to be treating the potentially explosive situation with some sensitivity.* **5** ADJ If you describe someone as **explosive**, you mean that they tend to express sudden violent anger. ❑ *He's inherited his father's explosive temper.*

expo /ɛkspoʊ/ (**expos**) also **Expo** N-COUNT An **expo** is a large event where goods, especially industrial goods, are displayed. ❑ *...Asia's largest computer expo.*

ex|po|nent /ɪkspoʊnənt/ (**exponents**) **1** N-COUNT An **exponent** of an idea, theory, or plan is a person who supports and explains it, and who tries to persuade other people that it is a good idea. [FORMAL] ❑ *...a leading exponent of test-tube baby techniques.* **2** N-COUNT An **exponent** of a particular skill or activity is a person who is good at it. ❑ *The Alvin Ailey American Dance Theater was formed in the 1950s and quickly established itself as a leading exponent of progressive choreography and contemporary dance.*

ex|po|nen|tial /ɛkspənɛnʃəl/ [usu ADJ n] **Exponential** means growing or increasing very rapidly. [FORMAL] ❑ *The policy tried to check the exponential growth of public expenditure.* ● **ex|po|nen|tial|ly** ADV [ADV after v] ❑ *The quantity of chemical pollutants has increased exponentially.*

ex|port ◆◆◇ (**exports, exporting, exported**)

The verb is pronounced /ɪkspɔrt/. The noun is pronounced /ɛkspɔrt/.

1 V-T/V-I To **export** products or raw materials means to sell them to another country. ❑ *The nation also exports beef.* ❑ *They expect the antibiotic products to be exported to Southeast Asia and Africa.* ❑ *The company now exports to Japan.* ● N-UNCOUNT [also N in pl] **Export** is also a noun. ❑ *...the production and export of cheap casual wear.* ❑ *A lot of our land is used to grow crops for export.* **2** N-COUNT **Exports** are goods sold to another country and sent there. ❑ *Ghana's main export is cocoa.* **3** V-T To **export** something means to introduce it into another country or make it happen there. ❑ *It has exported inflation at times.* **4** V-T In computing, if you **export** files or information from one type of software into another type, you change their format so that they can be used in the new software. ❑ *Files can be exported in ASCII or PCX formats.*

ex|port|able /ɪkspɔrtəbəl/ ADJ **Exportable** products are suitable for being exported. ❑ *They are reliant on a very limited number of exportable products.*

ex|port|er /ɛkspɔrtər, ɪkspɔrtər/ (**exporters**) N-COUNT An **exporter** is a country, company, or person that sells and sends goods to another country. ❑ *...the world's second-biggest exporter of agricultural products.*

ex|pose ◆◆◇ /ɪkspoʊz/ (**exposes, exposing, exposed**) **1** V-T To **expose** something that is usually hidden means to uncover it so that it can be seen. ❑ *Lowered sea levels exposed the shallow continental shelf beneath the Bering Sea.* **2** V-T To **expose** a person or situation means to reveal that they are bad or immoral in some way. ❑ *...the story of how the press helped expose the truth about the Nixon administration.* **3** V-T If someone **is exposed to** something dangerous or unpleasant, they are put in a situation in which it might affect them. ❑ *They had not been exposed to most diseases common to urban populations.* ❑ *A wise mother never exposes her children to the slightest possibility of danger.* **4** V-T If someone **is exposed to** an idea or feeling, usually a new one, they are given experience of it, or introduced to it. ❑ *...local people who've not been exposed to glimpses of Western life before.*

---SYNONYMS---

expose
VERB
1
reveal: *A gray carpet was removed to reveal the original pine floor.*
uncover: *Archeologists have uncovered an 11,700-year-old hunting camp in Alaska.*
show: *He showed his teeth in a humorless grin.*
bare: *He bared his muscular, hairy chest for a women's magazine.*
2
reveal: *It was revealed that officials had never inspected the factory.*
disclose: *Neither side would disclose details of the transaction.*
betray: *She studied his face, but it betrayed nothing.*
give away: *They felt like they were giving away company secrets.*
leak: *He revealed who leaked a confidential police report.*

ex|po|sé /ɛkspoʊzeɪ/ (**exposés**) N-COUNT [oft N of n] An **exposé** is a movie or piece of writing that reveals the truth about a situation or person, especially something involving shocking facts. ❑ *The movie is an exposé of prison conditions in the South.*

ex|posed /ɪkspoʊzd/ ADJ If a place is **exposed**, it has no natural protection against bad weather or enemies, for example, because it has no trees or is on very high ground. ❑ *...an exposed hillside in Connecticut.*

ex|po|si|tion /ɛkspəzɪʃ°n/ (**expositions**) ◨ N-COUNT [oft N of n] An **exposition** of an idea or theory is a detailed explanation or account of it. [FORMAL] ❑ *Aristotle was valued because of his clear exposition of rational thought.* ◨ N-COUNT An **exposition** is an exhibition in which something such as goods or works of art are shown to the public. ❑ *...an art exposition.*

ex|pos|tu|late /ɪkspɒstʃəleɪt/ (**expostulates, expostulating, expostulated**) V-T/V-I If you **expostulate**, you express strong disagreement with someone. [FORMAL] ❑ *"For heaven's sake!" Dot expostulated. "They're cheap and they're useful."* ❑ *For a moment I thought she was going to expostulate.* ❑ *His family expostulated with him.*

ex|po|sure ♦◇◇ /ɪkspoʊʒər/ (**exposures**) ◨ N-UNCOUNT **Exposure** to something dangerous means being in a situation where it might affect you. ❑ *Exposure to lead is known to damage the brains of young children.* ◨ N-UNCOUNT **Exposure** is the harmful effect on your body caused by very cold weather. ❑ *He was suffering from exposure and shock but his condition was said to be stable.* ◨ N-UNCOUNT The **exposure** of a well-known person is the revealing of the fact that they are bad or immoral in some way. ❑ *He undertook increasingly dangerous assignments until his exposure as a spy.* ◨ N-UNCOUNT **Exposure** is publicity that a person, company, or product receives. ❑ *All the candidates have been getting an enormous amount of exposure on television and in the press.* ◨ N-COUNT In photography, an **exposure** is a single photograph. [TECHNICAL] ❑ *Larger drawings tend to require two or three exposures to cover them.*

─── **SYNONYMS** ───

exposure
NOUN
◨
hypothermia: *He was unconscious and suffering hypothermia.*
frostbite: *The survivors suffered from frostbite.*
◨
publicity: *The case has generated enormous publicity in Brazil.*
hype: *My products aren't based on advertising hype; they sell by word of mouth.*
promotion: *In 1984, the company spent a lot of money on advertising and promotion.*
attention: *Volume Two, sub-titled 'The Lawyers,' will also attract considerable attention.*

ex|pound /ɪkspaʊnd/ (**expounds, expounding, expounded**) V-T If you **expound** an idea or opinion, you give a clear and detailed explanation of it. [FORMAL] ❑ *Schmidt continued to expound his views on economics and politics.* • PHRASAL VERB **Expound on** means the same as **expound**. ❑ *Lawrence expounded on the military aspects of guerrilla warfare.*

ex|press ♦♦◇ /ɪksprɛs/ (**expresses, expressing, expressed**) ◨ V-T When you **express** an idea or feeling, or **express** yourself, you show what you think or feel. ❑ *He expressed grave concern at American attitudes.* ◨ V-T If an idea or feeling **expresses** itself in some way, it can be clearly seen in someone's actions or in its effects on a situation. ❑ *The anxiety of the separation often expresses itself as anger toward the child for getting lost.* ◨ ADJ [ADJ n] An **express** command or order is one that is clearly and deliberately stated. [FORMAL] ❑ *This mighty electricity-generating power station was built on the express orders of the president.* • **ex|press|ly** ADV [ADV before v] ❑ *He has expressly forbidden her to go out on her own.* ◨ ADJ [ADJ n] If you refer to an **express** intention or purpose, you are emphasizing that it is a deliberate and specific one that you have before you do something. [EMPHASIS] ❑ *The express purpose of the flights was to get Americans out of the danger zone.* • **ex|press|ly** ADV ❑ *...projects expressly designed to support cattle farmers.* ◨ ADJ [ADJ n] **Express** is used to describe special services provided by companies or organizations such as the U.S. Postal Service, in which things are sent or done faster than usual for a higher price. ❑ *A special express service is available by fax.* • ADV **Express** is also an adverb. ❑ *Send it express.* ◨ N-COUNT An **express** or an **express** train is a fast train that stops at very few stations. ❑ *Punctually at 7:45, the express to Kuala Lumpur left Singapore station.* ◨ → See feature box at **debate**

─── **COLLOCATIONS** ───

express
VERB ◨
express + *noun*: concern, disappointment, dismay, frustration, outrage, regret; confidence, optimism; desire, hope, wish; opinion, view; support, sympathy; doubts, reservations
express + *adverb*: freely, openly, privately, publicly; clearly, eloquently, forcefully; frequently, repeatedly

─── **SYNONYMS** ───

express
VERB ◨
communicate: *They successfully communicate their knowledge to others.*
convey: *Please convey my congratulations to the bride and groom.*
articulate: *He was accused of failing to articulate an overall vision in foreign affairs.*
state: *'Our relationship is totally platonic,' she stated.*
verbalize: *...his inability to verbalize his feelings.*

ex|pres|sion ♦◇◇ /ɪksprɛʃ°n/ (**expressions**) ◨ N-VAR The **expression** of ideas or feelings is the showing of them through words, actions, or artistic activities. ❑ *Laughter is one of the most infectious expressions of emotion.* ❑ *...the rights of the individual to freedom of expression.* ◨ N-VAR Your **expression** is the way that your face looks at a particular moment. It shows what you are thinking or feeling. ❑ *Levin sat there, an expression of sadness on his face.* ◨ N-UNCOUNT **Expression** is the showing of feeling when you are acting, singing, or playing a musical instrument. ❑ *I think I put more expression into my lyrics than a lot of other singers do.* ◨ N-COUNT An **expression** is a word or phrase. ❑ *She spoke in a quiet voice but used remarkably coarse expressions.*

─── **SYNONYMS** ───

expression
NOUN
◨
look: *Sally spun around, a feigned look of surprise on her face.*
face: *He was walking around with a sad face.*
air: *Jennifer regarded him with an air of amusement.*
◨
phrase: *He used a phrase I hate: 'You have to be cruel to be kind.'*
saying: *We also realize the truth of that old saying: Charity begins at home.*
term: *Myocardial infarction is the medical term for a heart attack.*
idiom: *Proverbs and idioms may become worn with over-use.*
proverb: *An old proverb says, 'The enemy of my enemy is my friend.'*

ex|pres|sion|ism /ɪksprɛʃ°nɪzəm/ N-UNCOUNT **Expressionism** is a style of art, literature, and music that uses symbols and exaggeration to represent emotions, rather than representing physical reality.

ex|pres|sion|ist /ɪksprɛʃ°nɪst/ (**expressionists**) ◨ N-COUNT An **expressionist** is an artist, writer, or composer who uses the style of expressionism. ◨ ADJ [USU ADJ n] **Expressionist** artists, writers, composers, or works use the style of expressionism. ❑ *...an extraordinary collection of expressionist paintings.*

ex|pres|sion|less /ɪksprɛʃ°nlɪs/ ADJ If you describe someone's face as **expressionless**, you mean that they are not showing their feelings.

ex|pres|sive /ɪksprɛsɪv/ ADJ If you describe a person or their behavior as **expressive**, you mean that their behavior clearly indicates their feelings or intentions. ❑ *You can train people to be more expressive.* ❑ *...the present fashion for intuitive, expressive painting.* • **ex|pres|sive|ly** ADV [ADV with v] ❑ *He moved his hands expressively.*

ex|press|way /ɪksprɛsweɪ/ (**expressways**) N-COUNT An **expressway** is a wide road that is specially designed to carry a lot of traffic moving quickly. It has no stop signs or signals, and traffic traveling in one direction is separated from the traffic traveling in the opposite direction.

ex|pro|pri|ate /ɛksproʊprieɪt/ (**expropriates, expropriating, expropriated**) V-T If a government or other authority **expropriates** someone's property, they take it away from them for public use. [LEGAL] ❑ *The Bolsheviks expropriated the property of the landowners.* • **ex|pro|pria|tion** /ɛksproʊprieɪʃən/ (**expropriations**) N-VAR [oft N of n] ❑ ...*the expropriation of property.* ❑ *Ownership is not clear because of expropriations in the Nazi era.*

ex|pul|sion /ɪkspʌlʃən/ (**expulsions**) **1** N-VAR **Expulsion** is when someone is forced to leave a school, university, or organization. ❑ *Her hatred of authority led to her expulsion from high school.* **2** N-VAR **Expulsion** is when someone is forced to leave a place. [FORMAL] ❑ ...*the expulsion of migrant workers.*

ex|punge /ɪkspʌndʒ/ (**expunges, expunging, expunged**) V-T If you **expunge** something, you get rid of it completely, because it causes problems or bad feelings. [FORMAL] ❑ *The revolutionaries expunged domestic opposition.* ❑ *The experience was something he had tried to expunge from his memory.* ❑ *His name was expunged from the record books.*

ex|pur|gate /ɛkspərgeɪt/ (**expurgates, expurgating, expurgated**) V-T If someone **expurgates** a piece of writing, they remove parts of it before it is published because they think those parts will offend or shock people. [FORMAL] ❑ *He heavily expurgated the work in its second edition.* • **ex|pur|gat|ed** ADJ ❑ *It was first published in 1914 in a highly expurgated version.*

ex|quis|ite /ɪkskwɪzɪt, ɛkskwɪzɪt/ ADJ Something that is **exquisite** is extremely beautiful or pleasant, especially in a delicate way. ❑ *The Indians brought in exquisite beadwork to sell.* • **ex|quis|ite|ly** ADV ❑ ...*exquisitely crafted dollshouses.*

ex-serviceman (**ex-servicemen**) N-COUNT An **ex-serviceman** is a man who used to be in a country's army, navy, or air force. [BRIT]

in AM, use **veteran**

ex-servicewoman (**ex-servicewomen**) N-COUNT An **ex-servicewoman** is a woman who used to be in a country's army, navy, or air force. [BRIT]

in AM, use **veteran**

ext. [N num] Ext. is the written abbreviation for **extension** when it is used to refer to a particular telephone number. ❑ *For a full festival program call 206-555-7115, ext. 239.*

ex|tant /ɛkstənt, ɪkstænt/ ADJ If something is **extant**, it is still in existence, in spite of being very old. [FORMAL] ❑ *Two fourteenth-century manuscripts of this text are still extant.* ❑ *The oldest extant document is dated 1492.*

ex|tem|po|rize /ɪkstɛmpəraɪz/ (**extemporizes, extemporizing, extemporized**)

in BRIT, also use **extemporise**

V-I If you **extemporize**, you speak, act, or perform something immediately, without rehearsing or preparing it beforehand. [FORMAL] ❑ *He completely departed from the text and extemporized in a very energetic fashion.*

ex|tend ♦♦◊ /ɪkstɛnd/ (**extends, extending, extended**) **1** V-I If you say that something, usually something large, **extends** for a particular distance or **extends** from one place to another, you are indicating its size or position. ❑ *The caves extend for some 12 miles.* ❑ *The main stem will extend to around 12 ft, if left to develop naturally.* **2** V-I If an object **extends from** a surface or place, it sticks out from it. ❑ *A table extended from the front of her desk to create a T-shaped seating arrangement.* **3** V-I If an event or activity **extends** over a period of time, it continues for that time. ❑ *The normal cyclone season extends from December to April.* **4** V-I If something **extends** to a group of people, things, or activities, it includes or affects them. ❑ *The service also extends to wrapping and delivering gifts.* ❑ *The talks will extend to the church, human rights groups, and other social organizations.* **5** V-T If you **extend** something, you make it longer or bigger. ❑ *This year they have introduced three new products to extend their range.* ❑ *The building was extended in 1500.* **6** V-I If a piece of equipment or furniture **extends**, its length can be increased. ❑ ...*a table that extends to accommodate extra guests.* **7** V-T If you **extend** something, you make it last longer than before or end at a later date. ❑ *They have extended the deadline by twenty-four hours.* **8** V-T If you **extend** something **to** other people or things, you make it include or affect more people or things. ❑ *It might be possible to extend the technique to other crop plants.* **9** V-T If someone **extends** their hand, they stretch out their arm and hand to shake hands with someone. ❑ *The man extended his hand: "I'm Chuck."*

┌─── SYNONYMS ───┐
extend
VERB **5**
widen: *The search for my brother widened.*
increase: *The population continues to increase.*
develop: *She won a grant to develop her own business.*
enlarge: ...*the plan to enlarge Ewood Park into a 30,000 seat stadium.*
broaden: *We must broaden our appeal.*
└─────────────────┘

ex|tend|able /ɪkstɛndəbəl/ ADJ [usu ADJ n] Something that is **extendable** can be made longer. ❑ *These were hung in place with extendable rods.*

ex|tend|ed /ɪkstɛndɪd/ **1** ADJ [ADJ n] If something happens for an **extended** period of time, it happens for a long period of time. ❑ *Obviously, any child who receives dedicated teaching over an extended period is likely to improve.* **2** → see also **extend**

ex|tend|ed fam|ily (**extended families**) **1** N-COUNT An **extended family** is a family group that includes relatives such as uncles, aunts, and grandparents, as well as parents, children, and brothers and sisters. ❑ *The pregnant woman in such a community has the support of all the womenfolk in her extended family.* **2** → See feature box at **family**

ex|ten|sion /ɪkstɛnʃən/ (**extensions**) **1** N-COUNT An **extension** is a new room or building that is added to an existing building or group of buildings. ❑ *We are thinking of having an extension built, as we now require an extra bedroom.* **2** N-COUNT An **extension** is a new section of a road or railroad that is added to an existing road or railroad. ❑ ...*a proposed extension to the No. 7 subway line.* **3** N-COUNT An **extension** is an extra period of time for which something lasts or is valid, usually as a result of official permission. ❑ *He first entered the country on a six-month visa, and was given a further extension of six months.* **4** N-COUNT Something that is an **extension** of something else is a development of it that includes or affects more people, things, or activities. ❑ *Our web page is an extension of everything we do.* **5** N-COUNT [also N num] An **extension** is a telephone line that is connected to the switchboard of a company or institution, and that has its own number. The written abbreviation **ext.** is also used. ❑ *She can get me on extension 308.* **6** N-COUNT An **extension** is a part connected to a piece of equipment in order to make it reach something further away. ❑ ...*a 30-foot extension cord.*

ex|ten|sive ♦◊◊ /ɪkstɛnsɪv/ **1** ADJ Something that is **extensive** covers or includes a large physical area. ❑ ...*an extensive tour of Latin America.* • **ex|ten|sive|ly** ADV [ADV after v] ❑ *Mark, however, needs to travel extensively with his varied business interests.* **2** ADJ Something that is **extensive** covers a wide range of details, ideas, or items. ❑ *She recently completed an extensive study of elected officials who began their political careers before the age of 35.* • **ex|ten|sive|ly** ADV ❑ *All these issues have been extensively researched in recent years.* **3** ADJ If something is **extensive**, it is very great. ❑ *The security forces have extensive powers of search and arrest.* • **ex|ten|sive|ly** ADV ❑ *Hydrogen is used extensively in industry for the production of ammonia.*

ex|tent ♦◊◊ /ɪkstɛnt/ **1** N-SING If you are talking about how great, important, or serious a difficulty or situation is, you can refer to the **extent** of it. ❑ *The government itself has little information on the extent of industrial pollution.* **2** N-SING The **extent** of something is its length, area, or size. ❑ *Industry representatives made it clear that their motivation was only to maintain the extent of forests, not their biodiversity.* **3** PHRASE You use expressions such as **to a large extent**, **to some extent**, or **to a certain extent** in order to indicate that something is partly true, but not entirely true. [VAGUENESS] ◻ *It was and, to a large extent, still is a good show.* ◻ *To some extent this was the truth.* ◼ PHRASE You use expressions such as **to what extent**, **to that extent**, or **to the extent that** when you are discussing how true a statement is, or in what ways it is true. [VAGUENESS] ◻ *It's still not clear to what extent this criticism is originating from within the ruling party.* ◼ PHRASE You use expressions such as **to the extent of**, **to the extent that**, or **to such an extent that** in order to emphasize that a situation has reached a difficult, dangerous, or surprising stage. [EMPHASIS] ◻ *Ford kept his suspicions to himself, even to the extent of going to jail for a murder he obviously didn't commit.* ◼ → See feature box at **football**

SYNONYMS

extent
NOUN ◼
scale: *However, he underestimates the scale of the problem.*
magnitude: *No one realized the magnitude of the problem.*
degree: *These barriers will ensure a very high degree of protection.*
level: *The exercises are marked according to their level of difficulty.*
amount: *I still do a certain amount of work for them.*

ex|tenu|at|ing /ɪkstɛnyueɪtɪŋ/ ADJ [usu ADJ n] If you say that there are **extenuating** circumstances for a bad situation or wrong action, you mean that there are reasons or factors that partly excuse it. [FORMAL] ◻ *The defendants decide to admit their guilt, but insist that there are extenuating circumstances.*

ex|te|ri|or /ɪkstɪəriər/ (**exteriors**) ◼ N-COUNT The **exterior** of something is its outside surface. ◻ *The exterior of the building was a masterpiece of architecture, elegant and graceful.* ◼ N-COUNT You can refer to someone's usual appearance or behavior as their **exterior**, especially when it is very different from their real character. ◻ *According to Mandy, Pat's tough exterior hides a shy and sensitive soul.* ◼ ADJ [ADJ n] You use **exterior** to refer to the outside parts of something or things that are outside something. ◻ *The exterior walls were made of preformed concrete.*

ex|ter|mi|nate /ɪkstɜrmɪneɪt/ (**exterminates, exterminating, exterminated**) V-T To **exterminate** a group of people or animals means to kill all of them. ◻ *A huge effort was made to exterminate the rats.* • **ex|ter|mi|na|tion** /ɪkstɜrmɪneɪʃən/ N-UNCOUNT ◻ *...the extermination of hundreds of thousands of their brethren.*

ex|ter|mi|na|tor /ɪkstɜrmɪneɪtər/ (**exterminators**) N-COUNT An **exterminator** is a person whose job is to kill animals such as rats or mice, because they are annoying or dangerous.

ex|ter|nal /ɪkstɜrnəl/ ◼ ADJ **External** is used to indicate that something is on the outside of a surface or body, or that it exists, happens, or comes from outside. ◻ *...a much reduced heat loss through external walls.* • **ex|ter|nal|ly** ADV ◻ *Vitamins can be applied externally to the skin.* ◼ ADJ [ADJ n] **External** means involving or intended for foreign countries. ◻ *...the commissioner for external affairs.* ◻ *...Jamaica's external debt.* • **ex|ter|nal|ly** ADV ◻ *...protecting the value of the dollar both internally and externally.* ◼ ADJ [ADJ n] **External** means happening or existing in the world in general and affecting you in some way. ◻ *Such events occur only when the external conditions are favorable.* ◼ → See feature box at **computer**

ex|ter|nal|ize /ɪkstɜrnəlaɪz/ (**externalizes, externalizing, externalized**)

in BRIT, also use **externalise**

V-T If you **externalize** your ideas or feelings, you express them openly, in words or actions. [FORMAL] ◻ *These are some people who tend to externalize blame when anything goes wrong at work.*

ex|ter|nals /ɪkstɜrnəlz/ N-PLURAL When you talk about **externals**, you are referring to the features of a situation that are obvious but not important or central. ◻ *All that the tourists see are the externals of our faith.*

ex|tinct /ɪkstɪŋkt/ ◼ ADJ A species of animal or plant that is **extinct** no longer has any living members, either in the world or in a particular place. ◻ *At the current rate of decline, many of the rain forest animals could become extinct in less than 10 years.* ◼ ADJ If a particular kind of worker, way of life, or type of activity is **extinct**, it no longer exists, because of changes in society.

◻ *Herbalism had become an all but extinct skill in the Western world.* ◼ ADJ An **extinct** volcano is one that does not erupt or is not expected to erupt anymore. ◻ *Its tallest volcano, long extinct, is Olympus Mons.* ◼ → See feature box at **deforest**

ex|tinc|tion /ɪkstɪŋkʃən/ ◼ N-UNCOUNT The **extinction** of a species of animal or plant is the death of all its remaining living members. ◻ *An operation is beginning to try to save a species of crocodile from extinction.* ◼ N-UNCOUNT If someone refers to the **extinction** of a way of life or type of activity, they mean that the way of life or activity stops existing. ◻ *The loggers say their jobs are faced with extinction because of declining timber sales.*

ex|tin|guish /ɪkstɪŋgwɪʃ/ (**extinguishes, extinguishing, extinguished**) ◼ V-T If you **extinguish** a fire or a light, you stop it from burning or shining. [FORMAL] ◻ *It took about 50 minutes to extinguish the fire.* ◼ V-T If something **extinguishes** a feeling or idea, it destroys it. ◻ *The message extinguished her hopes of Richard's return.*

ex|tin|guish|er /ɪkstɪŋgwɪʃər/ (**extinguishers**) N-COUNT An **extinguisher** is the same as a **fire extinguisher**.

ex|tol /ɪkstoʊl/ (**extols, extolling, extolled**) also **extoll** V-T If you **extol** something or someone, you praise them enthusiastically. ◻ *Now experts are extolling the virtues of the humble potato.*

ex|tort /ɪkstɔrt/ (**extorts, extorting, extorted**) V-T If someone **extorts** money from you, they get it from you using force, threats, or other unfair or illegal means. ◻ *Corrupt government officials were extorting money from him.* ◻ *Her kidnapper extorted a $175,000 ransom for her release.*

ex|tor|tion /ɪkstɔrʃən/ N-UNCOUNT **Extortion** is the crime of obtaining something from someone, especially money, by using force or threats. ◻ *He has been charged with extortion and abusing his powers.*

ex|tor|tion|ate /ɪkstɔrʃənɪt/ ADJ If you describe something such as a price as **extortionate**, you are emphasizing that it is much greater than it should be. [EMPHASIS] ◻ *...a specially prepared menu on which basic dishes are charged at extortionate prices.*

ex|tor|tion|ist /ɪkstɔrʃənɪst/ (**extortionists**) N-COUNT An **extortionist** is a person who commits the crime of obtaining something from someone by using force or threats.

ex|tra ✦✧ /ɛkstrə/ (**extras**) ◼ ADJ [ADJ n] You use **extra** to describe an amount, person, or thing that is added to others of the same kind, or that can be added to others of the same kind. ◻ *Police warned motorists to allow extra time to get to work.* ◻ *There's an extra blanket in the bottom drawer of the cupboard.* ◼ ADJ [v-link ADJ] If something is **extra**, you have to pay more money for it in addition to what you are already paying for something. ◻ *For foreign orders postage is extra.* • PRON **Extra** is also a pronoun. ◻ *She won't pay any extra.* • ADV **Extra** is also an adverb. ◻ *You may be charged 10% extra for this service.* ◼ N-COUNT **Extras** are additional amounts of money that are added to the price that you have to pay for something. ◻ *There are no hidden extras.* ◼ N-COUNT **Extras** are things that are not necessary in a situation, activity, or object, but that make it more comfortable, useful, or enjoyable. ◻ *Optional extras include cooking classes at a top restaurant.* ◼ N-COUNT The **extras** in a movie are the people who play unimportant parts, for example, as members of a crowd. ◻ *In 1944, Kendall entered films as an extra.* ◼ ADV [ADV adj/adv] You can use **extra** in front of adjectives and adverbs to emphasize the quality that they are describing. [INFORMAL, EMPHASIS] ◻ *I said you'd have to be extra careful.*

PREFIX

extra-
◼ forms adjectives that refer to something being outside or beyond something else. For example, something that is **extraordinary** is more than ordinary, that is, very special.
◼ also forms adjectives that refer to something having a large amount of a particular quality. For example, if something is **extra-strong**, it is very strong.

ex|tract (**extracts, extracting, extracted**)

The verb is pronounced /ɪkstrækt/. The noun is pronounced /ɛkstrækt/.

extraction   459   **extreme**

1 V-T To **extract** a substance means to obtain it from something else, for example, by using industrial or chemical processes. ❏ *...the traditional method of pick and shovel to extract coal.* ❏ *Citric acid can be extracted from the juice of oranges, lemons, limes or grapefruit.* • **ex|trac|tion** N-UNCOUNT ❏ *Petroleum engineers plan and manage the extraction of oil.* **2** V-T If you **extract** something from a place, you take it out or pull it out. ❏ *He extracted a small notebook from his hip pocket.* **3** V-T When a dentist **extracts** a tooth, they remove it from the patient's mouth. ❏ *A dentist may decide to extract the tooth to prevent recurrent trouble.* • **ex|trac|tion (extractions)** N-VAR ❏ *In those days, dentistry was basic. Extractions were carried out without anesthetic.* **4** V-T If you say that someone **extracts** something, you disapprove of them because they take it for themselves to gain an advantage. [DISAPPROVAL] ❏ *He sought to extract the maximum political advantage from the cut in interest rates.* **5** V-T If you **extract** information or a response **from** someone, you get it from them with difficulty, because they are unwilling to say or do what you want. ❏ *He made the mistake of trying to extract further information from our director.* **6** V-T If you **extract** a particular piece of information, you obtain it from a larger amount or source of information. ❏ *I've simply extracted a few figures.* ❏ *Britain's trade figures can no longer be extracted from export-and-import documentation at ports.* **7** V-T PASSIVE If part of a book or text **is extracted** from a particular book, it is printed or published. [JOURNALISM] ❏ *This material has been extracted from "Collins GoodWood Handbook."* **8** N-COUNT An **extract** from a book or piece of writing is a small part of it that is printed or published separately. ❏ *Read this extract from an information booklet about the work of an airline cabin crew.* **9** N-MASS **Extract** is a very concentrated liquid that is used for flavoring food or for its smell. ❏ *Blend in the vanilla extract, lemon peel, and walnuts.*

ex|trac|tion /ɪkstrækʃən/ **1** N-UNCOUNT [with supp] If you say, for example, that someone is of French **extraction**, you mean that they or their family originally came from France. [FORMAL] ❏ *Her real father was of Italian extraction.* **2** → see also **extract**

ex|trac|tor /ɪkstræktər/ **(extractors)** **1** N-COUNT [with supp] An **extractor** is a device that squeezes liquid out of something. ❏ *...a juice extractor.* **2** N-COUNT An **extractor** or **extractor fan** is a device that is attached to a window or wall to draw smells, steam, or hot air out of a room. [mainly BRIT]

in AM, use **ventilator**

extra|cur|ricu|lar /ˌɛkstrəkəˈrɪkyələr/ ADJ [ADJ n] **Extracurricular** activities are activities for students that are not part of their course. [FORMAL] ❏ *Each child had participated in extracurricular activities at school.* ❏ *...extracurricular sports.* **2** ADJ [ADJ n] **Extracurricular** activities are activities that someone does outside of their normal work. [INFORMAL] ❏ *The money he made from these extracurricular activities enabled him to pursue other ventures.*

extra|dite /ˈɛkstrədaɪt/ **(extradites, extraditing, extradited)** V-T If someone **is extradited**, they are officially sent back to their own or another country or state to be tried for a crime that they have been accused of. [FORMAL] ❏ *A judge agreed to extradite him to Texas.* • **ex|tra|di|tion** /ˌɛkstrəˈdɪʃən/ **(extraditions)** N-VAR ❏ *A New York court turned down the British government's request for his extradition.*

extra|mari|tal /ˌɛkstrəˈmærɪtəl/ ADJ [usu ADJ n] An **extramarital** affair is a sexual relationship between a married person and another person who is not their husband or wife. ❏ *Her husband has admitted having an extramarital affair.*

extra|neous /ɪkstreɪniəs/ ADJ [usu ADJ n] **Extraneous** things are not relevant or essential to the situation you are involved in or the subject you are talking about. [FORMAL] ❏ *To avoid delays, she wanted the disaster relief legislation to be kept free of extraneous matters.*

extraor|di|naire /ˌɛkstrɔːrdɪˈnɛər/ ADJ [n ADJ] If you describe someone as being, for example, a musician **extraordinaire**, you are saying it in a slightly humorous way that you think they are an extremely good musician. ❏ *...George Kuchar, filmmaker extraordinaire.*

extraor|di|nary ✦✧✧ /ɪkstrɔːrdəˌnɛri/ **1** ADJ If you describe something or someone as **extraordinary**, you mean that they have some extremely good or special quality. [APPROVAL] ❏ *We've made extraordinary progress as a society in that regard.* ❏ *The task requires extraordinary patience and endurance.* • **extraor|di|nari|ly** /ɪkstrɔːrdəˈnɛrɪli/ ADV [ADV adj] ❏ *She's extraordinarily disciplined.* **2** ADJ If you describe something as **extraordinary**, you mean that it is very unusual or surprising. [EMPHASIS] ❏ *What an extraordinary thing to happen!* • **extraor|di|nari|ly** ADV ❏ *Apart from the hair, he looked extraordinarily unchanged.* **3** ADJ [ADJ n] An **extraordinary** meeting is arranged to deal with a particular situation or problem, rather than happening regularly. [FORMAL] ❏ *The U.S. has called for an extraordinary emergency meeting of the UN Human Rights Commission to examine the crisis.*

ex|trapo|late /ɪkstræpəleɪt/ **(extrapolates, extrapolating, extrapolated)** V-T If you **extrapolate from** known facts, you use them as a basis for general statements about a situation or about what is likely to happen in the future. [FORMAL] ❏ *Extrapolating from his latest findings, he reckons about 80% of these deaths might be attributed to smoking.* • **ex|trapo|la|tion** /ɪkˌstræpəˈleɪʃən/ **(extrapolations)** N-VAR ❏ *His estimate of half a million HIV-positive cases was based on an extrapolation of the known incidence of the virus.*

extra|sen|so|ry per|cep|tion /ˌɛkstrəˌsɛnsəri pərˈsɛpʃən/ N-UNCOUNT **Extrasensory perception** means knowing without using your ordinary senses such as sight and hearing. Some people believe this is possible. The abbreviation **ESP** is also used.

extra|ter|res|trial /ˌɛkstrətəˈrɛstriəl/ **(extraterrestrials)** **1** ADJ [usu ADJ n] **Extraterrestrial** means happening, existing, or coming from somewhere beyond the planet Earth. [FORMAL] ❏ *NASA has started a 10-year search for extraterrestrial intelligence.* ❏ *...extraterrestrial rocks.* **2** N-COUNT **Extraterrestrials** are living creatures that some people think exist or may exist in another part of the universe.

ex|tra time N-UNCOUNT If a game of soccer, hockey, or basketball goes into **extra time**, the game continues for a set period after it would usually have ended because both teams have the same score. [BRIT]

in AM, use **overtime**

ex|trava|gance /ɪkstrævəgəns/ **(extravagances)** **1** N-UNCOUNT **Extravagance** is the spending of more money than is reasonable or than you can afford. ❏ *When the company went under, tales of his extravagance surged through the industry.* **2** N-COUNT An **extravagance** is something that you spend money on but cannot really afford. ❏ *Why waste money on such extravagances?*

ex|trava|gant /ɪkstrævəgənt/ **1** ADJ Someone who is **extravagant** spends more money than they can afford or uses more of something than is reasonable. ❏ *We are not extravagant; restaurant meals are a luxury and designer clothes are out.* • **ex|trava|gant|ly** ADV [ADV with v] ❏ *The day before they left Jeff had shopped extravagantly for presents for the whole family.* **2** ADJ Something that is **extravagant** costs more money than you can afford or uses more of something than is reasonable. ❏ *Her aunt gave her an uncharacteristically extravagant gift.* ❏ *Baking a whole cheese in pastry may seem extravagant.* • **ex|trava|gant|ly** ADV [ADV adj/-ed] ❏ *By supercar standards, though, it is not extravagantly priced for a beautifully engineered machine.* **3** ADJ **Extravagant** behavior is extreme behavior that is often done for a particular effect. ❏ *He was extravagant in his admiration of Hellas.* • **ex|trava|gant|ly** ADV ❏ *She had on occasion praised him extravagantly.* **4** ADJ **Extravagant** claims or ideas are unrealistic or impractical. [DISAPPROVAL] ❏ *Don't be afraid to consider apparently extravagant ideas.*

ex|trava|gan|za /ɪkˌstrævəˈgænzə/ **(extravaganzas)** N-COUNT An **extravaganza** is a very elaborate and expensive show or performance. ❏ *...a magnificent fireworks extravaganza.*

ex|treme ✦✧✧ /ɪkstriːm/ **(extremes)** **1** ADJ **Extreme** means very great in degree or intensity. ❏ *The girls were afraid of snakes and picked their way along with extreme caution.* ❏ *...people living in extreme poverty.* **2** ADJ You use **extreme** to describe situations and behavior that are much more severe or unusual than you would expect, especially when you disapprove of them because of this. [DISAPPROVAL] ❏ *The extreme case was Poland, where 29 parties won seats.* ❏ *It is hard to imagine Jesse capable of anything so extreme.* **3** ADJ You use **extreme** to describe opinions, beliefs, or political movements that you disapprove of because they are very different from those that most people would accept as reasonable or normal. [DISAPPROVAL] ❑ *This extreme view hasn't captured popular opinion.* **4** N-COUNT You can use **extremes** to refer to situations or types of behavior that have opposite qualities to each other, especially when each situation or type of behavior has such a quality to the greatest degree possible. ❑ *...a "middle way" between the extremes of success and failure, wealth and poverty.* **5** ADJ [ADJ n] The **extreme** end or edge of something is its farthest end or edge. ❑ *...the room at the extreme end of the corridor.* **6** PHRASE If a person **goes to extremes** or **takes** something **to extremes**, they do or say something in a way that people consider to be unacceptable, unreasonable, or foolish. ❑ *The police went to the extremes of installing the most advanced safety devices in the man's house.*

SYNONYMS
extreme
ADJ **1**
great: *Benjamin Britten did not live to a great age.*
high: *High winds have knocked down trees and power lines.*
considerable: *Doing it properly makes considerable demands on our time.*
severe: *I suffered from severe bouts of depression.*
intense: *He was sweating from the intense heat.*
acute: *The report has caused acute embarrassment to the government.*

ex|treme|ly ♦♦◇ /ɪkstriːmli/ ADV [ADV adj/adv] You use **extremely** in front of adjectives and adverbs to emphasize that the specified quality is present to a very great degree. [EMPHASIS] ❑ *My cellphone is extremely useful.* ❑ *Three of them are working extremely well.*

SYNONYMS
extremely
ADV
highly: *Mr Singh was a highly successful salesman.*
particularly: *Progress has been particularly disappointing.*
severely: *...the severely-depressed construction industry.*
exceptionally: *He's an exceptionally-talented dancer.*
intensely: *The fast-food business is intensely competitive.*

ex|treme sport (**extreme sports**) N-COUNT **Extreme sports** are exciting, physically dangerous sports such as bungee jumping or snowboarding.

ex|tre|mis /ɪkstriːmɪs/ → see **in extremis**

ex|trem|ism /ɪkstriːmɪzəm/ N-UNCOUNT **Extremism** is the behavior or beliefs of extremists. ❑ *Greater demands were being placed on the police by growing violence and left and right-wing extremism.*

ex|trem|ist /ɪkstriːmɪst/ (**extremists**) **1** N-COUNT If you describe someone as an **extremist**, you disapprove of them because they try to bring about political change by using violent or extreme methods. [DISAPPROVAL] ❑ *He said the country needed a strong intelligence service to counter espionage, terrorism, and foreign extremists.* ❑ *A previously unknown extremist group has said it carried out Friday's bomb attack.* **2** ADJ If you say that someone has **extremist** views, you disapprove of them because they believe in bringing about change by using violent or extreme methods. [DISAPPROVAL] ❑ *...his determination to purge the party of extremist views.*

ex|trem|ity /ɪkstrɛmɪti/ (**extremities**) **1** N-COUNT [with supp] The **extremity** of something is its farthest end or edge. [FORMAL] ❑ *...a small port on the north-western extremity of the Iberian peninsula.* ❑ *...the extremities of the airplane.* **2** N-PLURAL [oft with poss] Your **extremities** are the end parts of your body, especially your hands and feet. ❑ *He found that his extremities grew cold.* **3** N-UNCOUNT [also N in pl, oft N *of* n] The **extremity** of a situation or of someone's behavior is the degree to which it is severe, unusual, or unacceptable. ❑ *In spite of the extremity of her seclusion she was sane.* ❑ *In the past, the region had been protected by its forbidding geography and the extremities of its climate.*

ex|tri|cate /ɛkstrɪkeɪt/ (**extricates, extricating, extricated**) **1** V-T If you **extricate** yourself or another person **from** a difficult or serious situation, you free yourself or the other person from it. ❑ *It represents a last-ditch attempt by the country to extricate itself from its economic crisis.* ❑ *She tugged on Hart's arm to extricate him from the circle of men with whom he'd been talking.* **2** V-T If you **extricate** someone or something from a place where they are trapped or caught, you succeed in freeing them. [FORMAL] ❑ *He endeavored to extricate the car, digging with his hands in the blazing sunshine.*

ex|trin|sic /ɪkstrɪnsɪk/ ADJ [ADJ n] **Extrinsic** reasons, forces, or factors exist outside the person or situation they affect. [FORMAL] ❑ *Nowadays there are fewer extrinsic pressures to get married.*

extro|vert /ɛkstrəvɜːrt/ (**extroverts**) **1** ADJ Someone who is **extrovert** is very active, lively, and friendly. [mainly BRIT] ❑ *His footballing skills and extrovert personality won the hearts of the public.*

in AM, usually use **extroverted**

● N-COUNT An **extrovert** is someone who is extrovert. **2** → See feature box at **personality**

extro|vert|ed /ɛkstrəvɜːrtɪd/ ADJ Someone who is **extroverted** is very active, lively, and friendly. [mainly AM] ❑ *Some young people who were easy-going and extroverted as children become self-conscious in early adolescence.*

ex|trude /ɪkstruːd/ (**extrudes, extruding, extruded**) V-T [usu passive] If a substance **is extruded**, it is forced or squeezed out through a small opening. [TECHNICAL] ❑ *These crystals are then embedded in a plastic, and the plastic is extruded as a wire.* ❑ *I work in the extruded tube business.*

ex|tru|sion /ɪkstruːʒən/ (**extrusions**) N-VAR **Extrusion** is the act or process of extruding something. [TECHNICAL]

exu|ber|ance /ɪgzuːbərəns/ N-UNCOUNT **Exuberance** is behavior that is energetic, excited, and cheerful. ❑ *Her burst of exuberance and her brightness overwhelmed me.*

exu|ber|ant /ɪgzuːbərənt/ ADJ If you are **exuberant**, you are full of energy, excitement, and cheerfulness. ❑ *So the exuberant young girl with dark hair and blue eyes decided to become a screen actress.* ● **exu|ber|ant|ly** ADV ❑ *They both laughed exuberantly.*

ex|ude /ɪgzuːd, ɪksuːd/ (**exudes, exuding, exuded**) **1** V-T/V-I If someone **exudes** a quality or feeling, or if it **exudes**, they show that they have it to a great extent. [FORMAL] ❑ *The guerrillas exude confidence. Every town, they say, is under their control.* ❑ *She exudes an air of relaxed calm.* **2** V-T/V-I If something **exudes** a liquid or smell or if a liquid or smell **exudes** from it, the liquid or smell comes out of it slowly and steadily. [FORMAL] ❑ *Nearby was a factory which exuded a pungent smell.*

ex|ult /ɪgzʌlt/ (**exults, exulting, exulted**) V-T/V-I If you **exult** in a triumph or success that you have had, you feel and show great happiness and pleasure because of it. [WRITTEN] ❑ *He was exulting in a win at the show earlier that day.* ❑ *Some individual investors exulted at the record.* ❑ *I exulted and wept for joy.* ❑ *"This is what I've longed for during my entire career," Kendall exulted.* ● **ex|ul|ta|tion** /ɛgzʌlteɪʃən/ N-UNCOUNT ❑ *I felt a tremendous sense of relief and exultation.*

ex|ult|ant /ɪgzʌltənt/ ADJ If you are **exultant**, you feel very happy and proud about something you have done. [FORMAL] ❑ *An exultant party leader said: "He will be an excellent MP."* ● **ex|ult|ant|ly** ADV [ADV with v] ❑ *"We cannot lose the war!" he shouted exultantly.*

EYE
① PART OF THE BODY, ABILITY TO SEE
② PART OF AN OBJECT

① **eye** ♦♦♦ /aɪ/ (**eyes, eyeing** or **eying, eyed**)
→ Please look at meanings **25** – **27** to see if the expression you are looking for is shown under another headword.

1 N-COUNT Your **eyes** are the parts of your body with which you see. ❑ *I opened my eyes and looked.* ❑ *...a tall, thin white-haired lady with piercing dark brown eyes.* **2** V-T If you **eye** someone or something in a particular way, you look at them carefully in that way. ❑ *Sally eyed Claire with interest.* ❑ *We eyed each other thoughtfully.* **3** N-COUNT You use **eye** when you are talking about a person's ability to judge things or about the way in which they are considering or dealing with things. ❑ *William was a man of discernment, with an eye for quality.* ❑ *He first learned to fish under the watchful eye of his grandmother.* **4** → see also **black eye** **5** PHRASE If you say that something happens **before**

your **eyes**, **in front of** your **eyes**, or **under** your **eyes**, you are emphasizing that it happens where you can see it clearly and often implying that it is surprising or unpleasant. [EMPHASIS] ❑ *A lot of them died in front of our eyes.* **6** PHRASE If you **cast** your **eye** or **run** your **eye** over something, you look at it or read it quickly. ❑ *I would be grateful if he could cast an expert eye over it and tell me what he thought of it.* **7** PHRASE If something **catches** your **eye**, you suddenly notice it. ❑ *As she turned back, a movement across the lawn caught her eye.* **8** → see also **eye-catching** **9** PHRASE If you **catch** someone's **eye**, you do something to attract their attention, so that you can speak to them. ❑ *He tried to catch Annie's eye as he walked by her seat.* **10** PHRASE If you **make eye contact** with someone, you look at them at the same time as they look at you, so that you are both aware that you are looking at each other. If you **avoid eye contact** with someone, you deliberately do not look straight at them because you feel awkward or embarrassed. ❑ *She was looking at me across the room, and we made eye contact several times.* ❑ *I walked down the high street, avoiding eye contact with passers-by.* **11** PHRASE If you **close** your **eyes to** something bad or if you **shut** your **eyes to** it, you ignore it. ❑ *Most governments must simply be shutting their eyes to the problem.* **12** PHRASE If you **cry** your **eyes out**, you cry very hard. [INFORMAL] ❑ *He didn't mean to be cruel but I cried my eyes out.* **13** PHRASE If there is something **as far as the eye can see**, there is a lot of it and you cannot see anything else beyond it. ❑ *There are pine trees as far as the eye can see.* **14** PHRASE If you say that someone **has an eye for** something, you mean that they are good at noticing it or making judgments about it. ❑ *Susan has a keen eye for detail, so each dress is beautifully finished.* **15** PHRASE You use expressions such as **in his eyes** or **to her eyes** to indicate that you are reporting someone's opinion and that other people might think differently. ❑ *The other serious problem in the eyes of the new government is communalism.* **16** PHRASE If you **keep** your **eyes open** or **keep an eye out** for someone or something, you watch for them carefully. [INFORMAL] ❑ *I ask the mounted patrol to keep their eyes open.* **17** PHRASE If you **keep an eye on** something or someone, you watch them carefully, for example to make sure that they are satisfactory or safe, or not causing trouble. ❑ *I went for a run there, keeping an eye on the children the whole time.* **18** PHRASE If you say that **all eyes are on** something or that the **eyes of the world are on** something, you mean that everyone is paying careful attention to it and what will happen. [JOURNALISM] ❑ *All eyes will be on tomorrow's vote.* **19** PHRASE If someone **has** their **eye on** you, they are watching you carefully to see what you do. ❑ *A spokesman for the store said: "He comes here quite a lot. We've had our eye on him before."* **20** PHRASE If you **have** your **eye on** something, you want to have it. [INFORMAL] ❑ *If you're saving up for a new outfit you've had your eye on, cheap dinners for a month might let you buy it.* **21** PHRASE If you say that you did something **with** your **eyes open** or **with** your **eyes wide open**, you mean that you knew about the problems and difficulties that you were likely to have. ❑ *We want all our members to undertake this trip responsibly, with their eyes open.* **22** PHRASE If something **opens** your **eyes**, it makes you aware that something is different from the way that you thought it was. ❑ *Watching your child explore the world about her can open your eyes to delights long forgotten.* **23** PHRASE If you **see eye to eye** with someone, you agree with them and have the same opinions and views. ❑ *Yuriko saw eye to eye with Yul on almost every aspect of the production.* **24** PHRASE When you **take** your **eyes off** the thing you have been watching or looking at, you stop looking at it. ❑ *She took her eyes off the road to glance at me.* **25 to turn a blind eye** → see **blind 26 to feast your eyes** → see **feast 27 in your mind's eye** → see **mind** ① **28** → See feature box at **body language**, **speak**; See also color supplement

▶ **eye up** **1** PHRASAL VERB If someone **eyes** you **up**, they look at you in a way that shows they consider you attractive. [mainly BRIT, INFORMAL] ❑ *...a slob who eyes up the women and makes lewd comments.* ❑ *The women sit in the corner and men eye them up.* **2** → See feature box at **look**

② **eye** /aɪ/ (**eyes**) **1** N-COUNT An **eye** is a small metal loop that a hook fits into, as a fastening on a piece of clothing. ❑ *There were lots of hooks and eyes in Victorian costumes!* **2** N-COUNT The **eye** of a needle is the small hole at one end that the thread passes through. ❑ *The only difficult part was threading the cotton through the eye of the needle!* **3** N-SING The **eye of** a storm, tornado, or hurricane is the center of it. ❑ *The eye of the hurricane hit Florida just south of Miami.*

eye|ball /aɪbɔl/ (**eyeballs, eyeballing, eyeballed**) **1** N-COUNT Your **eyeballs** are your whole eyes, rather than just the part which can be seen between your eyelids. **2** V-T If you **eyeball** someone or something, you stare at them. [INFORMAL] ❑ *"Can you handle that?" Savage asked, eyeballing Cameron.* **3** PHRASE You use **up to the eyeballs** to emphasize that someone is in an undesirable state to a very great degree. [INFORMAL, EMPHASIS] ❑ *He is out of a job and up to his eyeballs in debt.*

eye|brow /aɪbraʊ/ (**eyebrows**) **1** N-COUNT Your **eyebrows** are the lines of hair that grow above your eyes. **2** PHRASE If something causes you to **raise an eyebrow** or to **raise** your **eyebrows**, it causes you to feel surprised or disapproving. ❑ *An intriguing item on the news pages caused me to raise an eyebrow over my morning coffee.* ❑ *He raised his eyebrows over some of the suggestions.* **3** → See feature box at **body language**

eye can|dy also **eye-candy** N-UNCOUNT **Eye candy** is used to refer to people or things that are attractive to look at but are not interesting in other ways. [INFORMAL] ❑ *Back then, women on TV were mostly seen as eye candy.* ❑ *Animation has stopped being eye-candy for kids and geeks and become mainstream entertainment.*

eye-catching ADJ Something that is **eye-catching** is very noticeable. ❑ *...a series of eye-catching ads.*

-eyed /-aɪd/ COMB IN ADJ **-eyed** combines with adjectives to form adjectives that indicate the color, shape, or size of a person's eyes, or indicate the kind of expression that they have. ❑ *...a blonde-haired, blue-eyed little girl.* ❑ *She watched open-eyed as the plane took off.*

eye drops N-PLURAL **Eye drops** are medicine that you put in your eyes one drop at a time.

eye|ful /aɪfʊl/ (**eyefuls**) N-COUNT [usu sing, oft N of n] If you get an **eyeful** of something, especially of something that you would not normally see, you are able to get a good look at it. [INFORMAL] ❑ *Then she bent over and gave him an eyeful of her tattoos.*

eye|glasses /aɪglæsɪz/ N-PLURAL **Eyeglasses** are two lenses in a frame that some people wear in front of their eyes in order to help them see better. [AM, FORMAL] ❑ *...the 140 million Americans who wear eyeglasses or contact lenses.*

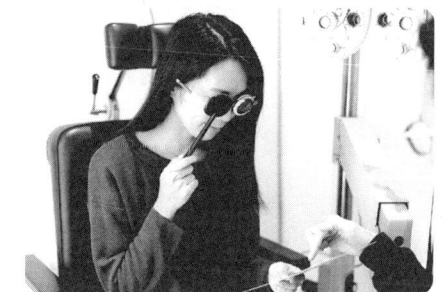

VOCABULARY IN CONTEXT

Eyesight

When was the last time you had your **eyesight** tested? Less than one third of the world has **20/20 vision**, so the chances are that you need glasses or **contact lenses**, even if you didn't last time you went to the **optician**. If you find yourself **squinting** because you have **blurred vision** when trying to read a sign, you're instinctively trying to reduce the amount of light that hits your **retina** in order to **focus** better, just like a photographer does with a camera. It won't harm your eyesight, but getting a pair of glasses to counteract being **farsighted** or **nearsighted** is probably a more effective solution. The other advantage to having an eye test is that the optician can identify health problems like **glaucoma**, diabetes, and high blood pressure.

eye|lash /aɪlæʃ/ (eyelashes) N-COUNT Your **eyelashes** are the hairs that grow on the edges of your eyelids.

eye|let /aɪlɪt/ (eyelets) N-COUNT An **eyelet** is a small hole with a metal or leather ring around it in cloth, for example, on a sail. You can put cord, rope, or string through it.

eye|lid /aɪlɪd/ (eyelids) ◼ N-COUNT Your **eyelids** are the two pieces of skin that cover your eyes when they are closed. ◼ → See feature box at **body**

eye|liner /aɪlaɪnər/ (eyeliners) N-MASS **Eyeliner** is a special kind of pencil that is used on the edges of their eyelids to look more attractive.

eye-opener (eye-openers) N-COUNT If you describe something as an **eye-opener**, you mean that it surprises you and that you learn something new from it. [INFORMAL] ❑ *Writing these scripts has been quite an eye-opener for me. It proves that you can do anything if the need is urgent.*

eye patch (eye patches) N-COUNT An **eye patch** is a piece of material that you wear over your eye when you have damaged or injured it.

eye|piece /aɪpiːs/ (eyepieces) N-COUNT The **eyepiece** of a microscope or telescope is the piece of glass at one end, where you put your eye in order to look through the instrument.

eye-popping ADJ [usu ADJ n] Something that is **eye-popping** is very impressive or striking. ❑ *...a plan to raise property taxes by an eye-popping $2 billion.* ❑ *For sure, there is little shortage of eye-popping scenery around here.*

eye|roll /aɪroʊl/ (eyerolls) N-COUNT If someone does an **eyeroll**, they move their eyes round and upward, sometimes when they are bored or annoyed. ❑ *Apparently, a sign of approaching relationship apocalypse is the spousal eyeroll at dinner parties.*

eye shad|ow (eye shadows) also **eye-shadow**, **eyeshadow** N-MASS **Eye shadow** is a substance that you can brush on your eyelids in order to make them a different color.

eye|sight /aɪsaɪt/ ◼ N-UNCOUNT Your **eyesight** is your ability to see. ❑ *He suffered from poor eyesight and could no longer read properly.* ◼ → See feature box on previous page

eye sock|et (eye sockets) N-COUNT Your **eye sockets** are the two hollow parts on either side of your face, where your eyeballs are.

eye|sore /aɪsɔːr/ (eyesores) N-COUNT [usu sing] You describe a building or place as an **eyesore** when it is extremely ugly and you dislike it or disapprove of it. [DISAPPROVAL] ❑ *Poverty leads to slums, which are an eyesore and a health hazard.*

eye strain N-UNCOUNT If you suffer from **eye strain**, you feel pain around your eyes or at the back of your eyes, because you are very tired or should be wearing glasses.

eye|teeth /aɪtiːθ/ PHRASE If you say that you would **give** your **eyeteeth** for something, you mean that you want it very much and you would do anything to get it. [INFORMAL] ❑ *She has the job most of us would give our eyeteeth for.*

eye|wear /aɪwɛər/ N-UNCOUNT **Eyewear** is sometimes used to talk about eyeglasses and sunglasses.

eye|wit|ness /aɪwɪtnɪs/ (eyewitnesses) N-COUNT An **eyewitness** is a person who was present at an event and can therefore describe it, for example in a law court. ❑ *Eyewitnesses say the police then opened fire on the crowd.*

ey|rie /ɪəri/ [BRIT] → see **aerie**

e-zine /iːzin/ (e-zines) N-COUNT An **e-zine** is a website which contains the kind of articles, pictures, and advertisements that you would find in a magazine.

Ff

F also **f** /ɛf/ (**F's, f's**) N-VAR **F** is the sixth letter of the English alphabet.

fab /fæb/ ADJ If you say that something is **fab**, you are emphasizing that you think it is very good. [INFORMAL, EMPHASIS] ❑ *The dancing is fab.*

fa|ble /feɪbᵊl/ (**fables**) **1** N-VAR A **fable** is a story which teaches a moral lesson. Fables sometimes have animals as the main characters. ❑ *...the fable of the tortoise and the hare.* **2** N-VAR You can describe a statement or explanation that is untrue but that many people believe as **fable**. ❑ *Is reincarnation fact or fable?*

fa|bled /feɪbᵊld/ ADJ [ADJ n] If you describe a person or thing as **fabled**, especially someone or something remarkable, you mean that they are well known because they are often talked about or a lot of stories are told about them. ❑ *...the fabled city of Troy.*

fab|ric ♦◇◇ /fæbrɪk/ (**fabrics**) **1** N-MASS **Fabric** is cloth or other material produced by weaving together cotton, nylon, wool, silk, or other threads. Fabrics are used for making things such as clothes, curtains, and sheets. ❑ *...small squares of red cotton fabric.* **2** N-SING The **fabric** of a society or system is its basic structure, with all the customs and beliefs that make it work successfully. ❑ *The fabric of society has been deeply damaged by the previous regime.* **3** → See feature box at **sewing**

SYNONYMS

fabric
NOUN **1**
cloth: *She began cleaning the wound with a piece of cloth.*
material: *...the thick material of her skirt.*
textile: *...decorative textiles for the home.*

fab|ri|cate /fæbrɪkeɪt/ (**fabricates, fabricating, fabricated**) V-T If someone **fabricates** information, they invent it in order to deceive people. ❑ *All four claim that officers fabricated evidence against them.* • **fab|ri|ca|tion** /fæbrɪkeɪʃᵊn/ (**fabrications**) N-VAR ❑ *She described the interview as a "complete fabrication."*

fabu|lous /fæbjələs/ ADJ If you describe something as **fabulous**, you are emphasizing that you like it a lot or think that it is very good. [INFORMAL, EMPHASIS] ❑ *This is a fabulous album. It's fresh, varied, fun.*

fa|cade /fəsɑd/ (**facades**) also **façade** **1** N-COUNT The **facade** of a building, especially a large one, is its front wall or the wall that faces the street. ❑ *...the repairs to the building's facade.* **2** N-SING A **facade** is an outward appearance which is deliberately false and gives you a wrong impression about someone or something. ❑ *They hid the troubles plaguing their marriage behind a facade of family togetherness.*

FACE
① NOUN USES
② VERB AND PHRASAL VERB USES

①**face** ♦♦♦ /feɪs/ (**faces**)
→ Please look at meanings ⑲ and ⑳ to see if the expression you are looking for is shown under another headword.

1 N-COUNT Your **face** is the front part of your head from your chin to the top of your forehead, where your mouth, eyes, nose, and other features are. ❑ *He rolled down his window and stuck his face out.* ❑ *He was going red in the face and breathing with difficulty.* ❑ *She had a beautiful face.* **2** N-COUNT If your **face** is happy, sad, or serious, for example, the expression on your face shows that you are happy, sad, or serious. ❑ *He was walking around with a sad face.* **3** N-COUNT The **face** of a cliff, mountain, or building is a vertical surface or side of it. ❑ *Harrer was one of the first to climb the north face of the Eiger.* **4** N-COUNT The **face** of a clock or watch is the surface with the numbers or hands on it, which shows the time. ❑ *It was too dark to see the face of my watch.* **5** N-SING If you say that the **face** of an area, institution, or field of activity is changing, you mean its appearance or nature is changing. ❑ *...the changing face of the countryside.* **6** N-SING If you refer to something as the particular **face of** an activity, belief, or system, you mean that it is one particular aspect of it, in contrast to other aspects. ❑ *Brothels, she insists, are the acceptable face of prostitution.* **7** N-UNCOUNT If you lose **face**, you do something which makes you appear weak and makes people respect or admire you less. If you do something in order to save **face**, you do it in order to avoid appearing weak and losing people's respect or admiration. ❑ *They don't want a war, but they don't want to lose face.* ❑ *To cancel the airport would mean a loss of face for the present governor.* **8** → see also **face value** **9** PHRASE If someone or something is **face down**, their face or front points downward. If they are **face up**, their face or front points upward. ❑ *All the time Stephen was lying face down and unconscious in the bathtub.* **10** PHRASE If you come **face to face** with someone, you meet them and can talk to them or look at them directly. ❑ *We were strolling into the town when we came face to face with Jacques Dubois.* **11** PHRASE If you come **face to face with** a difficulty or reality, you cannot avoid it and have to deal with it. ❑ *Eventually, he came face to face with discrimination again.* **12** PHRASE If an action or belief **flies in the face of** accepted ideas or rules, it seems to completely oppose or contradict them. ❑ *...scientific principles that seem to fly in the face of common sense.* **13** PHRASE If you take a particular action or attitude **in the face of** a problem or difficulty, you respond to that problem or difficulty in that way. ❑ *The president has called for national unity in the face of the violent anti-government protests.* **14** PHRASE If you **make a face**, you show a feeling such as dislike or disgust by putting an exaggerated expression on your face, for example, by sticking out your tongue. ❑ *Opening the door, she made a face at the musty smell.* **15** PHRASE You say '**on the face of it**' when you are describing how something seems when it is first considered, in order to suggest that people's opinion may change when they know or think more about the subject. ❑ *On the face of it that seems to make sense. But the figures don't add up.* **16** PHRASE If you **show** your **face** somewhere, you go there and see people, although you are not welcome, are somewhat unwilling to go, or have not been there for some time. ❑ *If she shows her face again back in Massachusetts she'll find a warrant for her arrest waiting.* **17** PHRASE If you manage to keep **a straight face**, you manage to look serious, although you want to laugh. ❑ *What went through Tom's mind I can't imagine, but he did manage to keep a straight face.* **18** PHRASE If you say something **to** someone's **face**, you say it openly in their presence. ❑ *Her opponent called her a liar to her face.* **19** **to shut the door in someone's face** → see **door** **20** **to have egg on your face** → see **egg** **21** → See feature box at **challenge**

②**face** ♦♦♦ /feɪs/ (**faces, facing, faced**)
→ Please look at meaning **8** to see if the expression you are looking for is shown under another headword.

1 V-T/V-I If someone or something **faces** a particular thing, person, or direction, they are positioned opposite them or are looking in that direction. ❑ *They stood facing each other.*

❏ *Our house faces south.* **2** V-T If you **face** someone or something, you turn so that you are looking at them. ❏ *She stood up from the table and faced him.* **3** V-T If you have to **face** a person or group, you have to stand or sit in front of them and talk to them, although it may be difficult and unpleasant. ❏ *Christie looked relaxed and calm as he faced the press.* **4** V-T If you **face** or **are faced** with something difficult or unpleasant, or if it **faces** you, it is going to affect you and you have to deal with it. ❏ *Williams faces life in prison if convicted of attempted murder.* ❏ *The immense difficulties facing European businessmen in Russia were only too evident.* **5** V-T If you **face** the truth or **face** the facts, you accept that something is true. If you **face** someone with the truth or with the facts, you try to make them accept that something is true. ❏ *Although your heart is breaking, you must face the truth that a relationship has ended.* ❏ *He accused the Government of refusing to face facts about the economy.* • PHRASAL VERB **Face up to** means the same as **face**. ❏ *I have grown up now and I have to face up to my responsibilities.* **6** V-T [with neg] If you cannot **face** something, you do not feel able to do it because it seems so difficult or unpleasant. ❏ *I couldn't face the prospect of spending a Saturday night there, so I decided to press on.* ❏ *My children want me with them for Christmas Day, but I can't face it.* **7** PHRASE You use the expression '**let's face it**' when you are stating a fact or making a comment about something which you think the person you are talking to may find unpleasant or be unwilling to admit. ❏ *Let's face it, stardom isn't for everybody.* **8 to face the music** → see **music**

▸ **face up to** → see **face** ② 5

face card (**face cards**) N-COUNT A **face card** is any of the twelve cards in a deck which has a picture of a face. The face cards are kings, queens, and jacks. ❏ *She won millions of dollars at blackjack by keeping track of the aces and face cards played.*

face|cloth /feɪsklɒθ/ (**facecloths**) also **face cloth** N-COUNT A **facecloth** is the same as a **washcloth**.

face cream (**face creams**) N-MASS **Face cream** is a thick substance that you rub into your face in order to keep it soft.

-faced /-feɪst/ **1** COMB IN ADJ **-faced** combines with adjectives to form other adjectives that describe someone's face or expression. ❏ *...a slim, thin-faced man.* ❏ *The committee walked out, grim-faced and shocked.* **2** → see also **ashen-faced, barefaced, poker-faced, red-faced, shamefaced, straight-faced, two-faced**

face flan|nel (**face flannels**) N-COUNT A **face flannel** is a small cloth made of toweling which you use for washing yourself. [BRIT]

in AM, use **washcloth**

face|less /feɪslɪs/ ADJ If you describe someone or something as **faceless**, you dislike them because they are uninteresting and have no character. [DISAPPROVAL] ❏ *Ordinary people are at the mercy of faceless bureaucrats.*

face|lift /feɪslɪft/ (**facelifts**) also **face-lift** **1** N-COUNT If you give a place or thing a **facelift**, you do something to make it look better or more attractive. ❏ *Nothing gives a room a faster facelift than a coat of paint.* **2** N-COUNT A **facelift** is an operation in which a surgeon tightens the skin on someone's face in order to make them look younger. ❏ *I had a facelift last year, which went wrong.*

face mask (**face masks**) **1** N-COUNT A **face mask** is a device that you wear over your face, for example, to prevent yourself from breathing bad air or from spreading germs, or to protect your face when you are in a dangerous situation. **2** N-COUNT A **face mask** is a thick substance which you spread on your face, allow to dry for a short time, and then remove, in order to clean your skin thoroughly. [mainly AM]

face-off (**face-offs**) N-COUNT [oft N between/with n] A **face-off** is an argument or conflict that is intended to settle a dispute. [mainly AM] ❏ *A face-off between Congress and the White House appears to be in the making.*

face pow|der (**face powders**) N-MASS **Face powder** is a very fine soft powder which you put on your face in order to make it look smoother.

face-saver (**face-savers**) N-COUNT A **face-saver** is an action or excuse which prevents damage to your reputation or the loss of people's respect for you. [JOURNALISM]

face-saving ADJ [ADJ n] A **face-saving** action is one which prevents damage to your reputation or the loss of people's respect for you. ❏ *The decision appears to be a face-saving compromise which will allow the governor to remain in office.*

fac|et /fæsɪt/ (**facets**) **1** N-COUNT A **facet** of something is a single part or aspect of it. ❏ *The caste system shapes nearly every facet of Indian life.* **2** N-COUNT The **facets** of a diamond or other precious stone are the flat surfaces that have been cut on its outside.

face-time N-UNCOUNT **Face-time** is time that you spend talking directly to someone, rather than talking by phone or email. ❏ *I need some face-time with the senator.*

fa|cetious /fəsiʃəs/ ADJ If you say that someone is being **facetious**, you are criticizing them because they are making humorous remarks or saying things that they do not mean in a situation where they ought to be serious. [DISAPPROVAL] ❏ *The woman eyed him coldly. "Don't be facetious," she said.*

face to face → see **face** ①

face value **1** N-SING The **face value** of things such as coins, paper money, investment documents, or tickets is the amount of money that they are worth, and that is written on them. ❏ *Tickets were selling at twice their face value.* **2** PHRASE If you take something **at face value**, you accept it and believe it without thinking about it very much, even though it might be untrue. ❏ *Public statements from the various groups involved should not necessarily be taken at face value.*

fa|cial /feɪʃl/ (**facials**) **1** ADJ [ADJ n] **Facial** means appearing on or being part of your face. ❏ *Cross didn't answer; his facial expression didn't change.* **2** N-COUNT A **facial** is a sort of beauty treatment in which someone's face is massaged, and creams and other substances are rubbed into it. ❏ *Where's the best place to get a facial in New York City?*

fa|cie /feɪʃi/ → see **prima facie**

fac|ile /fæsl/ ADJ If you describe someone's arguments or suggestions as **facile**, you are criticizing them because their ideas are too simple and indicate a lack of careful, intelligent thinking. [DISAPPROVAL] ❏ *This subject is admittedly too complex for facile summarization.*

fa|cili|tate /fəsɪlɪteɪt/ (**facilitates, facilitating, facilitated**) V-T To **facilitate** an action or process, especially one that you would like to happen, means to make it easier or more likely to happen. ❏ *The new airport will facilitate the development of tourism.*

fa|cili|ta|tor /fəsɪlɪteɪtər/ (**facilitators**) N-COUNT A **facilitator** is a person or organization that helps another person or organization to do or to achieve a particular thing. [FORMAL] ❏ *The conference is chaired by a highly skilled facilitator who has been fully trained.*

fa|cil|ity ✦◇ /fəsɪlɪti/ (**facilities**) **1** N-COUNT **Facilities** are buildings, pieces of equipment, or services that are provided for a particular purpose. ❏ *What recreational facilities are now available?* **2** N-COUNT A **facility** is something such as an additional service provided by an organization or an extra feature on a machine which is useful but not essential. ❏ *One of the new models has the facility to reproduce speech as well as text.* **3** N-COUNT [usu sing, usu N for n, N to-inf] If you have a **facility** for something, for example learning a language, you find it easy to do. ❏ *He and Marcia shared a facility for languages.*

fac|ing /feɪsɪŋ/ N-UNCOUNT **Facing** is fabric which is stitched inside the edges of a piece of clothing in order to make them look neat and strengthen them.

fac|simi|le /fæksɪmɪli/ (**facsimiles**) **1** N-COUNT [oft N of n, N n] A **facsimile** of something is a copy or an imitation of it. [FORMAL] ❏ *...a facsimile edition of Beethoven's musical manuscripts.* **2** N-COUNT A **facsimile** is the same as a **fax**. [FORMAL]

fact ✦✦✦ /fækt/ (**facts**) **1** N-COUNT **Facts** are pieces of information that can be discovered. ❏ *There is so much information you can almost effortlessly find the facts for yourself.* ❏ *His opponent swamped him with facts and figures.* **2** PHRASE You use the **fact that** after some verbs or prepositions, especially in expressions such as **in view of the fact that, apart from the fact that,** and **despite the fact that,** to link the verb or preposition with a clause. ❏ *His chances do not seem good in view of the fact that the Chief Prosecutor has already voiced his public disapproval.* ❏ *Despite the fact that the disease is so prevalent,*

fact-finding   465   **fade**

treatment is still far from satisfactory. **3** PHRASE You use **the fact that** instead of a simple that-clause either for emphasis or because the clause is the subject of your sentence. ❑ *My family now accepts the fact that I don't eat sugar or bread.* **4** PHRASE You use **in fact, in actual fact,** or **in point of fact** to indicate that you are giving more detailed information about what you have just said. ❑ *We've had a pretty bad time while you were away. In fact, we very nearly split up this time.* ❑ *He apologized as soon as he realized what he had done. In actual fact he wrote a nice little note to me.* **5** PHRASE You use **in fact, in actual fact,** or **in point of fact** to introduce or draw attention to a comment that modifies, contradicts, or contrasts with a previous statement. ❑ *That sounds rather simple, but in fact it's very difficult.* ❑ *They complained that they had been trapped inside the police station, but in fact most were seen escaping over the adjacent roofs to safety in nearby buildings.* **6** PHRASE You use **as a matter of fact** to introduce a statement that gives more details about what has just been said, or an explanation of it, or something that contrasts with it. ❑ *The local people saw the suffering to which these deportees were subjected. And, as a matter of fact, the local people helped the victims.* **7** PHRASE If you say that you know something **for a fact,** you are emphasizing that you are completely certain that it is true. [EMPHASIS] ❑ *I know for a fact that baby corn is very expensive in Europe.* **8** PHRASE You use **the fact is** or **the fact of the matter is** to introduce and draw attention to a summary or statement of the most important point about what you have been saying. ❑ *The fact is blindness hadn't stopped the children from doing many of the things that sighted children enjoy.* **9** N-VAR When you refer to something as a **fact** or as **fact,** you mean that you think it is true or correct. ❑ *...a statement of verifiable historical fact.*

> ### SYNONYMS
> **fact**
> NOUN **1**
> **truth:** *Is it possible to separate truth from fiction?*
> **reality:** *Fiction and reality were increasingly blurred.*
> **certainty:** *There are no certainties in modern Europe.*

fact-finding ADJ [ADJ n] A **fact-finding** mission or visit is one whose purpose is to get information about a particular situation, especially for an official group. ❑ *A UN fact-finding mission is on its way to the region.*

fac|tion ✦✧ /fˈækʃən/ (**factions**) N-COUNT A **faction** is an organized group of people within a larger group, which opposes some of the ideas of the larger group and fights for its own ideas. ❑ *A peace agreement will be signed by the leaders of the country's warring factions.*

> ### COLLOCATIONS
> **faction**
> NOUN
> noun + **faction:** rebel, rival; army, guerrilla
> adjective + **faction:** competing, feuding, opposing, warring; armed, militant; breakaway, dominant, hardline, powerful
> verb + **faction:** head, lead; unite

fac|tion|al /fˈækʃənəl/ ADJ **Factional** arguments or disputes involve two or more small groups from within a larger group. ❑ *...factional disputes between the various groups that make up the leadership.*

fac|tion|al|ism /fˈækʃənəlɪzəm/ N-UNCOUNT **Factionalism** refers to arguments or disputes between two or more small groups from within a larger group. ❑ *There has been a substantial amount of factionalism within the movement.*

fact of life (**facts of life**) **1** N-COUNT You say that something which is not pleasant is a **fact of life** when there is nothing you can do to change it so you must accept it. ❑ *Stress is a fact of life from time to time for all of us.* **2** N-PLURAL [the N] If you tell a child about **the facts of life,** you tell him or her about sexual intercourse and how babies are born. ❑ *There comes a time when children need to know more than the basic facts of life.*

fac|tor ✦✦ /fˈæktər/ (**factors, factoring, factored**) **1** N-COUNT A **factor** is one of the things that affects an event, decision, or situation. ❑ *Physical activity is an important factor in maintaining fitness.* **2** N-COUNT If an amount increases by a **factor** of two, for example, or by a **factor** of eight, then it becomes two times bigger or eight times bigger. ❑ *The cost of butter quadrupled and bread prices increased by a factor of five.* **3** N-SING You can use **factor** to refer to a particular level on a scale of measurement. ❑ *A sunscreen with a protection factor of 30 allows you to stay in the sun without burning.*
▶ **factor in** also **factor into** PHRASAL VERB If you **factor** a particular cost or element **into** a calculation you are making, or if you **factor** it **in,** you include it. ❑ *You'd better consider this and factor this into your decision making.*

> ### COLLOCATIONS
> **factor**
> NOUN **1**
> noun + **factor:** fear, risk
> adjective + **factor:** critical, crucial, deciding, decisive, significant; contributing, contributory; important, key, major, motivating; economic, environmental, psychological, social; aggravating, mitigating

fac|to|ry ✦✧ /fˈæktəri, -tri/ (**factories**) N-COUNT A **factory** is a large building where machines are used to make large quantities of goods. ❑ *He owned furniture factories in New York State.*

> ### SYNONYMS
> **factory**
> NOUN
> **plant:** *The plant provides forty percent of the country's electricity.*
> **works:** *The steel works could be seen for miles.*
> **mill:** *...a textile mill.*
> **workshop:** *...the railroad workshops.*

fac|to|ry floor N-SING [the N] The **factory floor** refers to the workers in a factory, as opposed to the managers. It can also refer to the area where they work. ❑ *He had worked on the factory floor for 16 years.*

fac|to|ry out|let (**factory outlets**) also **factory store** N-COUNT [oft N n] A **factory outlet** is the same as an **outlet** or **outlet store.**

fac|to|ry ship (**factory ships**) N-COUNT A **factory ship** is a large fishing boat which has equipment for processing the fish that are caught, for example, by cleaning or freezing them, before it returns to port.

fac|to|tum /fˈæktoʊtəm/ (**factotums**) N-COUNT A **factotum** is a servant who is employed to do a wide variety of jobs for someone. [FORMAL]

fact sheet (**fact sheets**) N-COUNT A **fact sheet** is a short, printed document with information about a particular subject, especially a summary of information that has been given on a radio or television program. ❑ *...the institute's free fact sheet, Driving Abroad.*

fac|tual /fˈæktʃuəl/ ADJ Something that is **factual** is concerned with facts or contains facts, rather than giving theories or personal interpretations. ❑ *The editorial contained several factual errors.*

fac|ul|ty /fˈækəlti/ (**faculties**) **1** N-COUNT Your **faculties** are your physical and mental abilities. ❑ *He was drunk and not in control of his faculties.* **2** N-VAR A **faculty** is all the teaching staff of a university or college, or of one department. [AM] ❑ *The faculty agreed on a change in the requirements.* ❑ *How can faculty improve their teaching so as to encourage creativity?* **3** → See feature box at **university**

fad /fˈæd/ (**fads**) N-COUNT You use **fad** to refer to an activity or topic of interest that is very popular for a short time, but which people become bored with very quickly. ❑ *Hamnett does not believe environmental concern is a passing fad.*

fad|dish /fˈædɪʃ/ ADJ If you describe something as **faddish,** you mean that it has no real value and that it will not remain popular for very long. ❑ *...faddish footwear.*

fade ✦✧ /fˈeɪd/ (**fades, fading, faded**) **1** V-T/V-I When a colored object **fades** or when the light **fades** it, it gradually becomes paler. ❑ *All color fades – especially under the impact of direct sunlight.* ❑ *No matter how soft the light is, it still fades carpets and curtains in every room.* ● **fad|ed** ADJ ❑ *...a girl in a faded dress.* **2** V-I When light **fades,** it slowly becomes less bright. When a sound **fades,** it slowly becomes less loud. ❑ *Seaton lay on his bed and gazed at the ceiling as the light faded.* **3** V-I If memories, feelings, or possibilities **fade**, they slowly become less intense or less strong. ❑ *Sympathy for the rebels, the government claims, is beginning to fade.* ❑ *Prospects for peace had already started to fade.*

fae|cal /fiːkəl/ [BRIT] → see **fecal**

fae|ces /fiːsiːz/ [BRIT] → see **feces**

fag /fæg/ (**fags**) N-COUNT **Fag** is a very offensive word for someone who is gay. [mainly AM, INFORMAL, OFFENSIVE]

fag end (**fag ends**) also **fag-end** N-COUNT [usu sing, N of n] If you refer to the **fag end** of something, you mean the last part of it, especially when you consider this part boring or unimportant. [INFORMAL] ❑ *He never had much confidence in his judgement at the fag-end of the working day.*

fag|got /fægət/ (**faggots**) N-COUNT A **faggot** is a very offensive word for someone who is gay. [AM, INFORMAL, OFFENSIVE]

Fahr|en|heit /færənhaɪt/ ADJ [n/num ADJ] **Fahrenheit** is a scale for measuring temperature, in which water freezes at 32 degrees and boils at 212 degrees. It is represented by the symbol °F. ❑ *By mid-morning, the temperature was already above 100 degrees Fahrenheit.* • N-UNCOUNT **Fahrenheit** is also a noun. ❑ *He was asked for the boiling point of water in Fahrenheit.*

fail ✦✦✦ /feɪl/ (**fails, failing, failed**) **1** V-T/V-I If you **fail** to do something that you were trying to do, you are unable to do it or do not succeed in doing it. ❑ *The party failed to win the election.* ❑ *He failed in his attempt to take control of the company.* **2** V-I If an activity, attempt, or plan **fails**, it is not successful. ❑ *We tried to develop plans for them to get along, which all failed miserably.* ❑ *He was afraid the revolution they had started would fail.* ❑ *...a failed military coup.* **3** V-T If someone or something **fails** to do a particular thing that they should have done, they do not do it. [FORMAL] ❑ *Some schools fail to require any homework.* ❑ *He failed to file tax returns for last year.* **4** V-I If something **fails**, it stops working properly, or does not do what it is supposed to do. ❑ *The lights mysteriously failed, and we stumbled around in complete darkness.* **5** V-I If a business, organization, or system **fails**, it becomes unable to continue in operation or in existence. [BUSINESS] ❑ *So far this year, 104 banks have failed.* ❑ *...a failed hotel business.* **6** V-I If something such as your health or a physical quality **is failing**, it is becoming gradually weaker or less effective. ❑ *He was 58, and his health was failing rapidly.* ❑ *Here in the hills, the light failed more quickly.* **7** V-T If someone **fails** you, they do not do what you had expected or trusted them to do. ❑ *We waited twenty-one years, don't fail us now.* **8** V-T If someone **fails** a test, examination, or course, they perform badly in it and do not reach the standard that is required. ❑ *I lived in fear of failing my final exams.* • N-COUNT **Fail** is also a noun. ❑ *It's the difference between a pass and a fail.* **9** V-T If someone **fails** you in a test, examination, or course, they judge that you have not reached a high enough standard in it. ❑ *...the two professors who had failed him during his first year of law school.* **10** PHRASE You say **if all else fails** to suggest what could be done in a certain situation if all the other things you have tried are unsuccessful. ❑ *If all else fails, I could always drive a truck.* **11** PHRASE You use **without fail** to emphasize that something always happens. [EMPHASIS] ❑ *He attended every meeting without fail.* **12** PHRASE You use **without fail** to emphasize an order or a promise. [EMPHASIS] ❑ *On the 30th you must without fail hand in some money for Alex.*

fail|ing /feɪlɪŋ/ (**failings**) **1** N-COUNT The **failings** of someone or something are their faults or unsatisfactory features. ❑ *Like many of her compatriots, she blamed the country's failings on futile attempts to catch up with the West.* **2** PHRASE You say **failing that** to introduce an alternative, in case what you have just said is not possible. ❑ *Find someone who will let you talk things through, or failing that, write down your thoughts.*

fail-safe also **failsafe** ADJ [usu ADJ n] Something that is **fail-safe** is designed or made in such a way that nothing dangerous can happen if a part of it goes wrong. ❑ *The camera has a built-in failsafe device which prevents it from working if the right signals aren't received.*

fail|ure ✦✦◊ /feɪljər/ (**failures**) **1** N-UNCOUNT **Failure** is a lack of success in doing or achieving something, especially in relation to a particular activity. ❑ *This policy is doomed to failure.* ❑ *Three attempts on the 200-meter record ended in failure.* **2** N-UNCOUNT Your **failure** to do a particular thing is the fact that you do not do it, even though you were expected to do it. ❑ *They see their failure to produce an heir as a curse from God.* **3** N-COUNT If something is a **failure**, it is not a success. ❑ *The marriage was a failure and they both wanted to be free of it.* **4** N-COUNT If you say that someone is a **failure**, you mean that they have not succeeded in a particular activity, or that they are unsuccessful at everything they do. ❑ *Despite the many honors he received, he often considered himself a failure.* **5** N-VAR If there is a **failure** of something, for example, a machine or part of the body, it goes wrong and stops working or developing properly. ❑ *There were also several accidents mainly caused by engine failures on take-off.* **6** N-VAR If there is a **failure** of a business or bank, it is no longer able to continue operating. [BUSINESS] ❑ *Business failures rose 16% last month.* **7** → See feature box at **success**

COLLOCATIONS

failure
NOUN
2
adjective + **failure**: abject, catastrophic, heroic, systemic; complete, total
3
adjective + **failure**: complete, total
5
noun + **failure**: heart, kidney, liver, organ; engine, system
adjective + **failure**: renal, respiratory; mechanical
verb + **failure**: cause; suffer

faint /feɪnt/ (**fainter, faintest, faints, fainting, fainted**) **1** ADJ A **faint** sound, color, mark, feeling, or quality has very little strength or intensity. ❑ *He became aware of the soft, faint sounds of water dripping.* ❑ *There was still the faint hope deep within him that she might never need to know.* • **faint|ly** ADV ❑ *He was already asleep in the bed, which smelled faintly of mildew.* **2** ADJ [ADJ n] A **faint** attempt at something is one that is made without proper effort and with little enthusiasm. ❑ *Caroline made a faint attempt at a laugh.* ❑ *A faint smile crossed the Monsignor's face and faded quickly.* • **faint|ly** ADV [ADV after v] ❑ *John smiled faintly and shook his head.* **3** ADJ [v-link ADJ] Someone who is **faint** feels weak and unsteady as if they are about to lose consciousness. ❑ *Other signs of angina are nausea, sweating, feeling faint and shortness of breath.* **4** V-I If you **faint**, you lose consciousness for a short time, especially because you are hungry, or because of pain, heat, or shock. ❑ *She suddenly fell forward on to the table and fainted.* • N-COUNT **Faint** is also a noun. ❑ *She slumped to the ground in a faint.*

faint|est /feɪntɪst/ ADJ [ADJ n, with neg] You can use **faintest** for emphasis in negative statements. For example, if you say that someone hasn't the **faintest** idea what to do, you are emphasizing that they do not know what to do. [EMPHASIS] ❑ *I haven't the faintest idea how to care for a snake.*

faint-hearted also **fainthearted** **1** ADJ If you describe someone or their behavior as **faint-hearted**, you mean that they are not very confident and do not take strong action because they are afraid of failing. ❑ *This is no time to be faint-hearted.* **2** PHRASE [usu v-link PHR] If you say that something is **not for the faint-hearted**, you mean that it is an extreme or very unusual example of its kind, and is not suitable for people who like only safe and familiar things. ❑ *It's a movie about a serial killer and not for the faint-hearted.*

fair ✦✦◊ /feər/ (**fairer, fairest, fairs**) **1** ADJ Something or someone that is **fair** is reasonable, right, and just. ❑ *It didn't seem fair to leave out her father.* ❑ *Do you feel they're paying their fair share?* ❑ *I wanted them to get a fair deal.* • **fair|ly** ADV ❑ *...demonstrating concern for employees and solving their problems quickly and fairly.* **2** ADJ [ADJ n] A **fair** amount, degree, size, or distance is quite a large amount, degree, size, or distance. ❑ *My neighbors across the street travel a fair amount.* **3** ADJ [ADJ n] A **fair** guess or idea about something is one that is likely to be correct. ❑ *It's a fair guess to say that the damage will be extensive.* **4** ADJ If you describe someone or something as **fair**, you mean that they are average in standard or quality, neither very good nor very bad. ❑ *Reimar had a fair command of English.* **5** ADJ Someone who is **fair**, or who has **fair** hair, has light-colored hair. ❑ *Both children were very like Robina, but were much fairer than she was.* • COMB IN ADJ **Fair** is also a combining form. ❑ *...a tall,* fair-haired man. **6** ADJ **Fair** skin is very pale and usually burns easily. ❑ *It's important to protect my fair skin from the sun.* • COMB IN ADJ **Fair** is also a combining form. ❑ *Fair-skinned people who spend a great deal of time in the sun have the greatest risk of skin cancer.* **7** ADJ When the weather is **fair**, it is quite sunny and not raining. [FORMAL] ❑ *Weather conditions were fair.* **8** N-COUNT A county, state, or country **fair** is an event where there are, for example, displays of goods and animals, and amusements, games, and competitions. ❑ *Every fall I go to the county fair.* **9** N-COUNT A **fair** is an event at which people display and sell goods, especially goods of a particular type. ❑ *...an antiques fair.* **10** → see also **trade fair** **11** PHRASE You use **fair enough** when you want to say that a statement, decision, or action seems reasonable to a certain extent, but that perhaps there is more to be said or done. [mainly SPOKEN] ❑ *If you don't like it, fair enough, but that's hardly a justification to attack the whole thing.* **12** PHRASE If you say that someone won a competition **fair and square**, you mean that they won honestly and without cheating. ❑ *There are no excuses. We were beaten fair and square.* **13** → See feature box at **competition**

fair game N-UNCOUNT If you say that someone is **fair game**, you mean that it is acceptable to criticize or attack them, usually because of the way that they behave. ❑ *Politicians were always considered fair game by cartoonists.*

fair|ground /fɛərgraʊnd/ (fairgrounds) N-COUNT A **fairground** is an area of land where a fair is held.

fair-haired boy (fair-haired boys) N-COUNT [oft poss N] Someone's **fair-haired boy** is a young man who they like better than anyone else and who therefore receives better treatment than other people. [AM, DISAPPROVAL]

in BRIT, use **blue-eyed boy**

fair|ly ✦✧ /fɛərli/ **1** ADV [ADV adj/adv] **Fairly** means to quite a large degree. For example, if you say that something is **fairly** old, you mean that it is old but not very old. ❑ *We did fairly well but only fairly well.* **2** ADV [ADV adj/adv] You use **fairly** instead of 'very' to add emphasis to an adjective or adverb without making it sound too forceful. [VAGUENESS] ❑ *Were you always fairly bright at school?* ❑ *You've got to be fairly single-minded about it.* **3** → see also **fair**

SYNONYMS

fairly
ADV **1**
moderately: *...a moderately-attractive woman.*
rather: *I grew up in rather unusual circumstances.*
somewhat: *He concluded that Oswald was somewhat abnormal.*
reasonably: *She was reasonably sure that he had tonsillitis.*

fair-minded ADJ [oft ADJ n] A **fair-minded** person always tries to be fair and reasonable, and always listens to other people's opinions. ❑ *She is one of the most fair-minded people I know.*

fair|ness /fɛərnɪs/ N-UNCOUNT **Fairness** is the quality of being reasonable, right, and just. ❑ *...concern about the fairness of the election campaign.*

fair play N-UNCOUNT If you refer to someone's attitude or behavior as **fair play**, you approve of it because it shows respect and sympathy toward everyone, even toward people who are thought to be wrong or to deserve punishment. [APPROVAL] ❑ *...a legal system that is unmatched anywhere in the world for its justice and sense of fair play.*

fair trade N-UNCOUNT **Fair trade** is the practice of buying goods directly from producers in developing countries at a fair price. ❑ *...fair trade coffee.*

fair|way /fɛərweɪ/ (fairways) N-COUNT [usu the N] The **fairway** on a golf course is the long strip of short grass between each tee and green.

fair-weather ADJ [ADJ n] You use **fair-weather** to refer to someone who offers help to someone, or who takes part in a particular activity, only when it is easy or pleasant for them to do so. [DISAPPROVAL] ❑ *...a fair-weather friend.*

fairy /fɛəri/ (fairies) N-COUNT A **fairy** is an imaginary creature with magical powers. Fairies are often represented as small people with wings.

fairy god|mother (fairy godmothers) **1** N-COUNT A **fairy godmother** is a female character in fairy stories who has magical powers and protects one of the main characters.

2 N-SING [poss N] If you call a woman your **fairy godmother**, you are saying in a slightly humorous way that she has been very helpful in your life, often at times when you thought you had problems that could not be solved.

fairy|land /fɛərilænd/ (fairylands) **1** N-UNCOUNT **Fairyland** is the imaginary place where fairies live. **2** N-VAR If you describe a place as a **fairyland**, you mean that it has a delicate beauty. ❑ *If you came with me to one of my toy shops, you'd think you were stepping into a fairyland.*

fairy sto|ry (fairy stories) N-COUNT A **fairy story** is the same as a **fairy tale**.

fairy tale (fairy tales) also **fairytale** N-COUNT A **fairy tale** is a story for children involving magical events and imaginary creatures. ❑ *She was like a princess in a fairy tale.*

fait ac|com|pli /feɪt ækɒmpliː, fɛt/ (faits accomplis) N-COUNT [usu sing] If something is a **fait accompli**, it has already been decided or done and cannot be changed. [FORMAL] ❑ *They became increasingly annoyed that they were being presented with a fait accompli.*

faith ✦✧ /feɪθ/ (faiths) **1** N-UNCOUNT If you have **faith** in someone or something, you feel confident about their ability or goodness. ❑ *People have lost faith in the government.* **2** N-UNCOUNT **Faith** is strong religious belief in a particular God. ❑ *Umberto Eco's loss of his own religious faith is reflected in his novels.* **3** N-COUNT A **faith** is a particular religion, for example, Christianity, Buddhism, or Islam. ❑ *England shifted officially from a Catholic to a Protestant faith in the 16th century.* **4** PHRASE If you do something **in good faith**, you seriously believe that what you are doing is right, honest, or legal, even though this may not be the case. ❑ *This report was published in good faith but we regret any confusion which may have been caused.*

COLLOCATIONS

faith
NOUN
1
adjective + **faith**: blind, complete
verb + **faith**: keep, restore; lose; repay
3
adjective + **faith**: religious; deep, unwavering
verb + **faith**: shake, test

faith|ful /feɪθfəl/ **1** ADJ Someone who is **faithful** to a person, organization, idea, or activity remains firm in their belief in them or support for them. ❑ *She had been faithful to her promise to guard this secret.* • N-PLURAL **The faithful** are people who are faithful to someone or something. ❑ *He spends his time making speeches at factories or gatherings of the Party faithful.* • **faith|ful|ly** ADV [ADV with v] ❑ *He has since 1965 faithfully followed and supported every twist and turn of government policy.* **2** ADJ Someone who is **faithful** to their husband, wife, or lover does not have a sexual relationship with anyone else. ❑ *I'm very faithful when I love someone.* **3** ADJ A **faithful** account, translation, or copy of something represents or reproduces the original accurately ❑ *Colin Welland's screenplay is faithful to the novel.* • **faith|ful|ly** ADV [ADV with v] ❑ *When I adapt something I translate from one meaning to another as faithfully as I can.*

faith|ful|ly /feɪθfəli/ **1** CONVENTION When you start a formal or business letter with 'Dear Sir' or 'Dear Madam,' you write **Yours faithfully** before your signature at the end. **2** → see also **faithful**

faith heal|er (faith healers) N-COUNT A **faith healer** is someone who believes they can treat and heal sick people using prayer or supernatural powers.

faith heal|ing also **faith-healing** N-UNCOUNT **Faith healing** is the treatment of a sick person by someone who believes that they are able to heal people through prayer or a supernatural power.

faith|less /feɪθlɪs/ ADJ If you say that someone is **faithless**, you mean that they are disloyal or dishonest. ❑ *She decided to divorce her increasingly faithless and unreliable husband.*

fa|ji|ta /fəhiːtə/ (fajitas) N-COUNT [usu pl] A **fajita** is a Mexican dish consisting of a tortilla wrapped around strips of meat and vegetables. ❑ *...chicken fajitas.*

fake /feɪk/ (fakes, faking, faked) **1** ADJ A **fake** fur or a **fake** painting, for example, is a fur or painting that has been made to look valuable or genuine, usually in order to deceive people. ❏ *The bank manager is said to have issued fake certificates.* • N-COUNT A **fake** is something that is fake. ❏ *The gallery is filled with famous works of art, and every one of them is a fake.* **2** V-T If someone **fakes** something, they try to make it look valuable or genuine, although in fact it is not. ❏ *It's safer to fake a tan with make-up rather than subject your complexion to the harsh rays of the sun.* ❏ *...faked evidence.* **3** V-T If you **fake** a feeling, emotion, or reaction, you pretend that you are experiencing it when you are not. ❏ *He tried to fake sincerity as he smiled at them.* **4** N-COUNT Someone who is a **fake** is not what they claim to be, for example, because they do not have the qualifications that they claim to have. ❏ *I think Jack is a good man. He isn't a fake.* **5** → See feature box at **truth**

fake news N-UNCOUNT If you describe information as **fake news**, you mean that it is false even though it is being reported as news, for example by the media.

fal|con /fɒlkən, fæl-/ (**falcons**) N-COUNT A **falcon** is a bird of prey that can be trained to hunt other birds and animals.

fal|con|er /fɒlkənər, fæl-/ (**falconers**) N-COUNT A **falconer** is someone who trains and uses falcons for hunting.

fal|con|ry /fɒlkənri, fæl-/ N-UNCOUNT **Falconry** is the skill of training falcons to hunt, and the sport of using them to hunt.

fall ♦♦♦ /fɔːl/ (**falls, falling, fell, fallen**)
→ Please look at meanings **17** – **21** to see if the expression you are looking for is shown under another headword.
1 V-I If someone or something **falls**, they move quickly downward onto or toward the ground, by accident or because of a natural force. ❏ *He has again fallen from his horse.* ❏ *Bombs fell in the town.* • N-COUNT **Fall** is also a noun. ❏ *The helmets are designed to withstand impacts equivalent to a fall from a bicycle.* **2** V-I If a person or structure that is standing somewhere **falls**, they move from their upright position, so that they are then lying on the ground. ❏ *The woman gripped the shoulders of her man to stop herself from falling.* ❏ *He lost his balance and fell backward.* • N-COUNT **Fall** is also a noun. ❏ *She broke her right leg in a bad fall.* • PHRASAL VERB **Fall down** means the same as **fall**. ❏ *I hit him so hard he fell down.* • **fall|en** ADJ [ADJ n] ❏ *A number of roads have been blocked by fallen trees.* **3** V-I When rain or snow **falls**, it comes down from the sky. ❏ *Winds reached up to 100 mph in some places with an inch of rain falling within 15 minutes.* • N-COUNT **Fall** is also a noun. ❏ *One night there was a heavy fall of snow.* **4** → see also **rainfall** **5** V-I If you **fall** somewhere, you allow yourself to drop there in a hurried or disorganized way, often because you are very tired. ❏ *Totally exhausted, he tore his clothes off and fell into bed.* **6** V-I If something **falls**, it decreases in amount, value, or strength. ❏ *Output will fall by 6%.* ❏ *The rate of convictions has fallen.* • N-COUNT **Fall** is also a noun. ❏ *There was a sharp fall in the value of the dollar.* **7** V-I If a powerful or successful person **falls**, they suddenly lose their power or position. ❏ *Regimes fall, revolutions come and go, but places never really change.* • N-SING **Fall** is also a noun. ❏ *Following the fall of the military dictator in March, the country has had a civilian government.* **8** V-I If a place **falls** in a war or election, an enemy army or a different political party takes control of it. ❏ *Croatian army troops retreated from northern Bosnia and the area fell to the Serbs.* • N-SING **Fall** is also a noun. ❏ *...the fall of Rome.* **9** V-I If you say that something or someone **falls into** a particular group or category, you mean that they belong in that group or category. ❏ *The problems generally fall into two categories.* **10** V-I If a celebration or other special event **falls on** a particular day or date, it happens to be on that day or date. ❏ *...the oddly named Quasimodo Sunday which falls on the first Sunday after Easter.* **11** V-I When light or shadow **falls** on something, it covers it. ❏ *Nancy, out of the corner of her eye, saw the shadow that suddenly fell across the doorway.* **12** V-I If you say that someone's eyes **fell** on something, you mean they suddenly noticed it. [WRITTEN] ❏ *As he laid the flowers on the table, his eye fell upon a note in Grace's handwriting.* **13** V-I When night or darkness **falls**, night begins and it becomes dark. ❏ *As darkness fell outside, they sat down to eat at long tables.* **14** V-LINK You can use **fall** to show that someone or something passes into another state. For example, if someone **falls ill**, they become ill, and if something **falls into disrepair**, it is then in a state of disrepair. ❏ *It is almost impossible to visit Florida without falling in love with the state.* ❏ *Almost without exception these women fall victim to exploitation.* **15** N-PLURAL; N-IN-NAMES You can refer to a **waterfall** as the **falls**. ❏ *The falls have always been an insurmountable obstacle for salmon and sea trout.* **16** N-VAR **Fall** is the season between summer and winter when the weather becomes cooler. [AM] ❏ *He was elected judge in the fall of 2011.* **17** → see also **fallen** **18** PHRASE To **fall to pieces** means the same as to **fall apart**. ❏ *At that point the radio handset fell to pieces.* **19** **to fall foul of** → see **foul** **20** **to fall flat** → see **flat** ① **21** **to fall into place** → see **place** ③ **22** → See feature box at **relationship**

▶ **fall apart** **1** PHRASAL VERB If something **falls apart**, it breaks into pieces because it is old or badly made. ❏ *The work was never finished and bit by bit the building fell apart.* **2** PHRASAL VERB If an organization or system **falls apart**, it becomes disorganized or unable to work effectively, or breaks up into its different parts. ❏ *It means that the agreement is in danger of falling apart.* **3** PHRASAL VERB If you say that someone **is falling apart**, you mean that they are becoming emotionally disturbed and are unable to think calmly or to deal with the difficult or unpleasant situation that they are in. [INFORMAL] ❏ *I was falling apart. I wasn't getting any sleep.*

▶ **fall back on** PHRASAL VERB If you **fall back on** something, you do it or use it after other things have failed. ❏ *When necessary, instinct is the most reliable resource you can fall back on.*

▶ **fall behind** **1** PHRASAL VERB If you **fall behind**, you do not make progress or move forward as fast as other people. ❏ *Boris is falling behind all the top players.* **2** PHRASAL VERB If you **fall behind** with something or let it **fall behind**, you do not do it or produce it when you should, according to an agreement or schedule. ❏ *He faces losing his home after falling behind with the payments.* ❏ *Thousands of people could die because the relief effort has fallen so far behind.*

▶ **fall for** **1** PHRASAL VERB If you **fall for** someone, you are strongly attracted to them and start loving them. ❏ *He was fantastically handsome – I just fell for him right away.* **2** PHRASAL VERB If you **fall for** a lie or trick, you believe it or are deceived by it. ❏ *It was just a line to get you out here, and you fell for it!*

▶ **fall off** **1** PHRASAL VERB If something **falls off**, it separates from the thing to which it was attached and moves toward the ground. ❏ *When your exhaust pipe falls off, you have to replace it.* **2** PHRASAL VERB If the degree, amount, or size of something **falls off**, it decreases. ❏ *Unemployment is rising again and retail buying has fallen off.*

▶ **fall out** **1** PHRASAL VERB If something such as a person's hair or a tooth **falls out**, it comes out. ❏ *Her hair started falling out as a result of radiation treatment.* **2** PHRASAL VERB If you **fall out** with someone, you have an argument and stop being friendly with them. You can also say that two people **fall out**. ❏ *She fell out with her husband.* **3** → see also **fallout**

▶ **fall over** PHRASAL VERB If a person or object that is standing **falls over**, they accidentally move from their upright position so that they are then lying on the ground or on the surface supporting them. ❏ *If he drinks more than two glasses of wine he falls over.*

▶ **fall through** PHRASAL VERB If an arrangement, plan, or deal **falls through**, it fails to happen. ❏ *They wanted to turn the estate into a private golf course and offered $20 million, but the deal fell through.*

▶ **fall to** PHRASAL VERB If a responsibility, duty, or opportunity **falls to** someone, it becomes their responsibility, duty, or opportunity. ❏ *He's been very unlucky that no chances have fallen to him.*

USAGE

fall
Fall is an intransitive verb. You can't say that someone 'falls' something. Don't say, for example, 'He yelled and fell the tray.' You say 'He yelled and **dropped** the tray.' *She bumped into a chair and **dropped** her plate.*

SYNONYMS

fall
VERB
1
drop: *He felt hot tears dropping onto his fingers.*
plunge: *At least 50 people died when a bus plunged into a river.*
plummet: *The jet burst into flames and plummeted to the ground.*
collapse: *The roof collapsed in a roar of rock and rubble.*
tumble: *A small boy tumbled off a third floor fire escape.*
6
decrease: *Population growth is decreasing by 1.4% each year.*
decline: *The number of staff has declined from 217,000 to 114,000.*
go down: *Income from sales tax went down.*
slump: *Net profits slumped by 41%.*

fal|la|cious /fəleɪʃəs/ ADJ If an idea, argument, or reason is **fallacious**, it is wrong because it is based on a fallacy. [FORMAL] ☐ *Their main argument is fallacious.*

fal|la|cy /fæləsi/ (fallacies) N-VAR A **fallacy** is an idea which many people believe to be true, but which is in fact false because it is based on incorrect information or reasoning. ☐ *It's a fallacy that the affluent give relatively more to charity than the less prosperous.*

fall|back /fɔlbæk/ ADJ [ADJ n] Someone's **fallback** position is what they will do if their plans do not succeed, or if something unexpected happens. [JOURNALISM] ☐ *Yesterday's vote itself was a retreat from an earlier fallback position.*

fall|en /fɔlən/ **Fallen** is the past participle of **fall**.

fall guy (fall guys) N-COUNT If someone is the **fall guy**, they are blamed for something which they did not do or which is not their fault. [INFORMAL] ☐ *He claims he was made the fall guy for the affair.*

fal|lible /fælɪbəl/ ADJ If you say that someone or something is **fallible**, you mean that they are not perfect and are likely to make mistakes or to fail in what they are doing. [FORMAL] ☐ *They are only human and all too fallible.* • **fal|libil|ity** /fælɪbɪlɪti/ N-UNCOUNT [usu with supp] ☐ *Errors may have been made due to human fallibility.*

falling-off N-SING [N of/in n] If there is a **falling-off** of an activity, there is a decrease in its amount or intensity. ☐ *There has been a falling-off in box office income and other earnings.*

fall-off (fall-offs) also **falloff** N-COUNT [usu sing] A **fall-off** in something such as sales or orders is a decrease in them. ☐ *A surge in domestic sales helped compensate for a fall-off in export sales.*

fal|lo|pian tube /fəloʊpiən tub/ (fallopian tubes) N-COUNT A woman's **fallopian tubes** are the two tubes in her body along which eggs pass from her ovaries to her womb.

fall|out /fɔlaʊt/ **1** N-UNCOUNT **Fallout** is the radiation that affects a particular place or area after a nuclear explosion has taken place. ☐ *They were exposed to radioactive fallout during nuclear weapons tests.* **2** N-UNCOUNT If you refer to the **fallout** from something that has happened, you mean the unpleasant consequences that follow it. ☐ *Grundy lost his job in the fallout from the incident.*

fal|low /fæloʊ/ **1** ADJ **Fallow** land has been dug or plowed but nothing has been planted in it, especially so that its quality or strength has a chance to improve. ☐ *The fields lay fallow.* **2** ADJ [usu ADJ n] A **fallow** period is a time when very little is being achieved. ☐ *There followed something of a fallow period professionally, until a job came up in the summer.*

false ♦◇◇ /fɔls/ **1** ADJ If something is **false**, it is incorrect, untrue, or mistaken. ☐ *It was quite clear the president was being given false information by those around him.* ☐ *You do not know whether what you're told is true or false.* • **false|ly** ADV [ADV with v] ☐ *...a man who is falsely accused of a crime.* **2** ADJ You use **false** to describe objects which are artificial but which are intended to look like the real thing or to be used instead of the real thing. ☐ *...a set of false teeth.* **3** ADJ If you describe a person or their behavior as **false**, you are criticizing them for being insincere or for hiding their real feelings. [DISAPPROVAL] ☐ *"Thank you," she said with false enthusiasm.* • **false|ly** ADV ☐ *They smiled at one another, somewhat falsely.*

false alarm (false alarms) N-COUNT When you think something dangerous is about to happen, but then discover that you were mistaken, you can say that it was a **false alarm**. ☐ *...a bomb threat that turned out to be a false alarm.*

false|hood /fɔlshʊd/ (falsehoods) **1** N-UNCOUNT **Falsehood** is the quality or fact of being untrue or of being a lie. ☐ *She called the verdict a victory of truth over falsehood.* **2** N-COUNT A **falsehood** is a lie. [FORMAL] ☐ *He accused them of knowingly spreading falsehoods about him.*

false move PHRASE You use **one false move** to introduce the very bad or serious consequences which will result if someone makes a mistake, even a very small one. ☐ *One false move and I knew Sarah would be dead.*

false posi|tive (false positives) N-COUNT [oft N n] A **false positive** is a mistaken result of a scientific test. For example, if the result of a pregnancy test is a false positive, it indicates that a woman is pregnant when she is not. ☐ *...a high rate of false positive results.*

false start (false starts) **1** N-COUNT A **false start** is an attempt to start something, such as a speech, project, or plan, which fails because you were not properly prepared or ready to begin. ☐ *Any economic reform, he said, faced false starts and mistakes.* **2** N-COUNT If there is a **false start** at the beginning of a race, one of the competitors moves before the person who starts the race has given the signal. ☐ *He powered away after two false starts to win comfortably.*

fal|set|to /fɔlsɛtoʊ/ (falsettos) N-COUNT [usu sing, oft in N, N n] If a man sings or speaks in a **falsetto**, his voice is high-pitched, and higher than a man's normal voice. ☐ *He sang to himself in a soft falsetto.* ☐ *...a falsetto voice.*

fal|si|fy /fɔlsɪfaɪ/ (falsifies, falsifying, falsified) V-T If someone **falsifies** something, they change it or add untrue details to it in order to deceive people. ☐ *The charges against him include fraud, bribery, and falsifying business records.*

fal|ter /fɔltər/ (falters, faltering, faltered) **1** V-I If something **falters**, it loses power or strength in an uneven way, or no longer makes much progress. ☐ *Normal life is at a standstill, and the economy is faltering.* **2** V-I If you **falter**, you lose your confidence and stop doing something or start making mistakes. ☐ *I have not faltered in my quest for a new future.*

fal|ter|ing /fɔltərɪŋ/ ADJ A **faltering** attempt, effort, or movement is uncertain because the person doing it is nervous or weak, or does not really know what to do. ☐ *Leaning on Jon, Michael took faltering steps to the bathroom.*

fam /fæm/ (fams) N-COUNT **Fam** is short for **family**. [INFORMAL] ☐ *He met her while vacationing with the fam in the Maldives.*

fame /feɪm/ N-UNCOUNT If you achieve **fame**, you become very well-known. ☐ *At the height of his fame, his every word was valued.* ☐ *The movie earned him international fame.*

famed /feɪmd/ ADJ If people, places, or things are **famed** for a particular thing, they are very well known for it. ☐ *The city is famed for its outdoor restaurants.*

fa|mil|ial /fəmɪlyəl, -iəl/ ADJ [usu ADJ n] **Familial** means relating to families in general, or typical of a family. [FORMAL] ☐ *Gerard also took on wider familial responsibilities.*

fa|mil|iar ♦◇◇ /fəmɪlyər/ ADJ **1** If someone or something is **familiar** to you, you recognize them or know them well. ☐ *He talked of other cultures as if they were more familiar to him than his own.* ☐ *They are already familiar faces on our TV screens.* • **fa|mili|ar|ity** /fəmɪliærɪti/ N-UNCOUNT ☐ *Tony was unnerved by the uncanny familiarity of her face.* **2** ADJ [v-link ADJ with n] If you are **familiar with** something, you know or understand it well. ☐ *Most people are familiar with this figure from Wagner's opera.* • **fa|mili|ar|ity** N-UNCOUNT ☐ *The enemy would always have the advantage of familiarity with the rugged terrain.* **3** ADJ If someone you do not know well behaves in a **familiar** way toward you, they treat you very informally in a way that you might find offensive. [DISAPPROVAL] ☐ *It isn't appropriate for an officer to be overly familiar with an enlisted man.* • **fa|mili|ar|ity** N-UNCOUNT ☐ *She needed to control her surprise at the familiarity with which her host greeted the head waiter.* • **fa|mili|ar|ly** ADV ☐ *"Gerald, isn't it?" I began familiarly.*

fa|mili|ar|ity /fəmɪliærɪti/ **1** PHRASE **Familiarity** is used especially in the expression **familiarity breeds contempt** to say that if you know a person or situation very well, you can easily lose respect for that person or become careless in that situation. **2** → see also **familiar**

fa|mil|iar|ize /fəmɪlyəraɪz/ (familiarizes, familiarizing, familiarized)

in BRIT, also use **familiarise**

V-T If you **familiarize** yourself **with** something, or if someone **familiarizes** you **with** it, you learn about it and start to understand it. ☐ *The goal of the experiment was to familiarize the people with the new laws.*

fa|mili|ar|ly /fəmɪlyərli/ PHRASE If you say that something or someone is **familiarly known** as a particular thing or **familiarly called** a particular thing, you are giving the name that people use informally to refer to them. ☐ *...Ann Hamilton's father, familiarly known as "Hank."*

fami|ly /fæmɪli, fæmli/ (**families**) **1** N-COUNT-COLL A **family** is a group of people who are related to each other, especially parents and their children. ❏ *There's room in there for a family of five.* ❏ *Does he have any family?* **2** N-COUNT-COLL When people talk about a **family**, they sometimes mean children. ❏ *They decided to start a family.* **3** N-COUNT-COLL When people talk about their **family**, they sometimes mean their ancestors. ❏ *Her family came to Los Angeles at the turn of the century.* **4** ADJ [ADJ n] You can use **family** to describe things that belong to a particular family. ❏ *He returned to the family home.* **5** ADJ [ADJ n] You can use **family** to describe things that are designed to be used or enjoyed by both parents and children. ❏ *It had been designed as a family house.* **6** N-COUNT A **family** of animals or plants is a group of related species. ❏ *...foods in the cabbage family, such as Brussels sprouts.*

COLLOCATIONS

family
NOUN **1**
adjective + **family**: extended, immediate; nuclear, single-parent; dysfunctional, happy, ordinary

VOCABULARY IN CONTEXT

Families

The concept of the **nuclear family** might seem outdated to many, but it still exists, even though definitions of the term have become so broad as to be almost meaningless. The term is often confused with the idea of 2.4 children per couple, but it has always included families with an **only child** or multiple children. It now encompasses **single-parent** families and a wide variety of other family structures. Not all connections have to be **flesh and blood**, as families with **adopted** children and families with **stepchildren** from previous relationships would also count within this category. Perhaps a nuclear family is best described as married or divorced adults who are either **raising children**, or who may be **childless** but *could do so in theory*. The term does not cover **extended families**, where three generations live under one roof. Also, **siblings** or friends that live together are not considered to be nuclear families.

fami|ly doc|tor (**family doctors**) N-COUNT [oft poss N] A **family doctor** is a doctor who does not specialize in any particular area of medicine, but who has a medical practice in which he or she treats all types of illness. [OLD-FASHIONED]

fami|ly man (**family men**) **1** N-COUNT A **family man** is a man who is very fond of his partner and children and likes to spend a lot of time with them. ❏ *I'm very much a family man and need to be close to those I love.* **2** N-COUNT A **family man** is a man who has a partner and children. ❏ *I am a family man with a mortgage.*

fami|ly name (**family names**) N-COUNT Your **family name** is your surname.

fami|ly plan|ning N-UNCOUNT **Family planning** is the practice of using contraception to control the number of children you have. ❏ *...a family planning clinic.*

fami|ly room (**family rooms**) N-COUNT A **family room** in a house is a room that is intended for the use of a family with children. ❏ *The present owners added a new kitchen, a front porch and a family room.*

fami|ly tree (**family trees**) N-COUNT A **family tree** is a chart that shows all the people in a family over many generations and their relationship to one another.

fami|ly val|ues N-PLURAL People sometimes refer to traditional moral values and standards as **family values**. ❏ *During the Washington meeting, Reverend Jackson called for a return to family values.*

fam|ine /fæmɪn/ (**famines**) N-VAR **Famine** is a situation in which large numbers of people have little or no food, and many of them die. ❏ *Thousands of refugees are trapped by war, drought and famine.*

fam|ished /fæmɪʃt/ ADJ [usu v-link ADJ] If you are **famished**, you are very hungry. [INFORMAL] ❏ *Isn't dinner ready? I'm famished.*

fa|mous /feɪməs/ ADJ Someone or something that is **famous** is very well known. ❏ *...one of Kentucky's most famous landmarks.*

fa|mous|ly /feɪməsli/ ADV You use **famously** to refer to a fact that is well known, usually because it is remarkable or extreme. ❏ *Authors are famously ignorant about the realities of publishing.*

fan /fæn/ (**fans, fanning, fanned**) **1** N-COUNT If you are a **fan** of someone or something, especially a famous person or a sport, you like them very much and are very interested in them. ❏ *If you're a Billy Crystal fan, you'll love this movie.* ❏ *I am a great fan of rave music.* **2** N-COUNT A **fan** is a piece of electrical or mechanical equipment with blades that go around and around. It keeps a room or machine cool or gets rid of unpleasant smells. ❏ *He cools himself in front of an electric fan.* **3** N-COUNT A **fan** is a flat object that you hold in your hand and wave in order to move the air and make yourself feel cooler. ❏ *...hundreds of dancing girls waving peacock fans.* **4** V-T If you **fan** yourself or your face when you are hot, you wave a fan or other flat object in order to make yourself feel cooler. ❏ *She would have to wait in the truck, fanning herself with a piece of cardboard.*
▶ **fan out** PHRASAL VERB If a group of people or things **fan out**, they move forward away from a particular point in different directions. ❏ *The main body of British, American, and French troops had fanned out to the west.*

COLLOCATIONS

fan
NOUN **1**
noun + **fan**: cricket, football, rugby, sports; music
adjective + **fan**: big, great, huge; diehard, loyal

fa|nat|ic /fənætɪk/ (**fanatics**) **1** N-COUNT If you describe someone as a **fanatic**, you disapprove of them because you consider their behavior or opinions to be very extreme, for example, in the way they support particular religious or political ideas. [DISAPPROVAL] ❏ *I am not a religious fanatic but I am a Christian.* **2** N-COUNT If you say that someone is a **fanatic**, you mean that they are very enthusiastic about a particular activity, sport, or way of life. ❏ *Both Rod and Phil are football fanatics.* **3** ADJ **Fanatic** means the same as **fanatical**.

fa|nati|cal /fənætɪkəl/ ADJ If you describe someone as **fanatical**, you disapprove of them because you consider their behavior or opinions to be very extreme. [DISAPPROVAL] ❏ *He is a fanatical fan of Mozart.*

fa|nati|cism /fənætɪsɪzəm/ N-UNCOUNT **Fanaticism** is fanatical behavior or the quality of being fanatical. [DISAPPROVAL] ❏ *...a protest against intolerance and religious fanaticism.*

fan base (**fan bases**) also **fanbase** N-COUNT [usu sing with poss] The **fan base** of someone such as a pop star or a pop group is their fans, considered as a whole. ❏ *His fan base is mostly middle-aged ladies.*

fan belt (**fan belts**) N-COUNT In a car engine, the **fan belt** is the belt that drives the fan which keeps the engine cool.

fan|boy /fænbɔɪ/ (**fanboys**) N-COUNT A **fanboy** is a boy or a young man who is very enthusiastic about and interested in a particular thing such as a movie, entertainer, or type of music. [INFORMAL] ❏ *Comic book fanboys will love this.*

fan|ci|er /fænsiər/ (fanciers) **1** N-COUNT [supp N] A **fancier** is someone who has a very strong liking for something, or a very strong interest in it. ❑ ...*pigeon fanciers.* **2** → see also **fancy** ①

fan|ci|ful /fænsɪfəl/ ADJ If you describe an idea as **fanciful**, you disapprove of it because you think it comes from someone's imagination, and is therefore unrealistic or unlikely to be true. [DISAPPROVAL] ❑ ...*fanciful ideas about Martian life.*

fan club (fan clubs) N-COUNT A **fan club** is an organized group of people who all admire the same person or thing, for example, a singer or a band. Members of the fan club receive information and can take part in activities such as trips to concerts.

FANCY
① ELABORATE OR EXPENSIVE
② WANTING, LIKING, OR THINKING
---

① **fan|cy** /fænsi/ (fancier, fanciest) **1** ADJ If you describe something as **fancy**, you mean that it is special, unusual, or elaborate, for example because it has a lot of decoration. ❑ *The magazine was packaged in a fancy plastic case with attractive graphics.* **2** ADJ If you describe something as **fancy**, you mean that it is very expensive or of very high quality, and you often dislike it because of this. [INFORMAL] ❑ *My parents sent me to a fancy private school.*

② **fan|cy** ◆◇◇ /fænsi/ (fancies, fancying, fancied) **1** V-T If you **fancy** yourself as a particular kind of person or fancy yourself doing a particular thing, you like the idea of being that kind of person or doing that thing. [mainly BRIT] ❑ *So you fancy yourself as the boss someday?* **2** V-T If you say that someone **fancies** themselves as a particular kind of person, you mean that they think, often wrongly, that they have the good qualities which that kind of person has. ❑ *She fancies herself a bohemian.* **3** V-T If you **fancy** something, you want to have it or to do it. [mainly BRIT, INFORMAL] ❑ *I just fancied a drink.* **4** V-T If you **fancy** someone, you feel attracted to them, especially in a sexual way. [BRIT, INFORMAL] **5** EXCLAM You say '**fancy**' or '**fancy that**' when you want to express surprise or disapproval. [FEELINGS] ❑ *'Fancy that!' smiled Conti.* **6** PHRASE If you **take a fancy to** someone or something, you start liking them, usually for no understandable reason. ❑ *Sylvia took quite a fancy to him.* **7** PHRASE If something **takes** your **fancy** or **tickles** your **fancy**, you like it a lot when you see it or think of it. ❑ *She makes most of her own clothes, copying any fashion which takes her fancy.*

fan|cy dress N-UNCOUNT [oft N n] **Fancy dress** is clothing that you wear for a party at which everyone tries to look like a famous person or a person from a story, from history, or from a particular profession. ❑ *Guests were told to come in fancy dress.*

fancy-free footloose and fancy-free → see **footloose**

fan|dan|go /fændæŋgoʊ/ (fandangos) N-COUNT [oft the n] A **fandango** is a Spanish dance in which two people dance very close together.

fan|dom /fændəm/ (fandoms) **1** N-UNCOUNT **Fandom** is the state of being an enthusiastic fan of something or someone. ❑ *Fandom has become increasingly interactive in the internet age.* **2** N-COUNT Someone's or something's **fandom** is their group of enthusiastic fans. ❑ *The fandom reacted with rage to news of the series being canceled.*

fan|fare /fænfeər/ (fanfares) **1** N-COUNT A **fanfare** is a short, loud tune played on trumpets or other similar instruments to announce a special event. ❑ *The ceremony opened with a fanfare of trumpets.* **2** N-VAR [oft N of n] If something happens with a **fanfare**, it happens or is announced with a lot of publicity. If something happens without a **fanfare**, it happens without a lot of fuss or publicity. ❑ *...a fanfare of publicity.*

fang /fæŋ/ (fangs) N-COUNT **Fangs** are the two long, sharp, upper teeth that some animals have. ❑ *The cobra sank its venomous fangs into his hand.*

fan|girl /fæŋgɜrl/ (fangirls) N-COUNT A **fangirl** is a girl or young woman who is very enthusiastic about and interested in a particular thing such as a movie, entertainer, or type of music. [INFORMAL] ❑ *This is a site for fangirls.*

fan|light /fænlaɪt/ (fanlights) N-COUNT A **fanlight** is a small window over a door or above another window.

fan mail N-UNCOUNT **Fan mail** is mail that is sent to a famous person by their fans. ❑ ...*six boxes of fan mail.*

fan|ny /fæni/ (fannies) N-COUNT [usu poss N] Someone's **fanny** is their buttocks. [AM, INFORMAL, OLD-FASHIONED]

fan|ny pack (fanny packs) **1** N-COUNT A **fanny pack** is a small bag attached to a belt which you wear around your waist. You use it to carry things such as money and keys. [AM] ❑ *This lightweight zoom camera will fit comfortably into a fanny pack or coat pocket.* **2** → See also color supplement

fan|ta|sia /fænteɪʒə/ (fantasias) N-COUNT [usu sing] A **fantasia** is a piece of music that is not written in a traditional or fixed form. [TECHNICAL]

fan|ta|sist /fæntəsɪst, -zɪst/ (fantasists) N-COUNT A **fantasist** is someone who tells lies about their life in order to make it sound more exciting.

fan|ta|size /fæntəsaɪz/ (fantasizes, fantasizing, fantasized)

in BRIT, also use **fantasise**

V-T/V-I If you **fantasize** about an event or situation that you would like to happen, you give yourself pleasure by imagining that it is happening, although it is untrue or unlikely to happen. ❑ *I fantasized about writing music.*

fan|tas|tic /fæntæstɪk/ **1** ADJ If you say that something is **fantastic**, you are emphasizing that you think it is very good or that you like it a lot. [INFORMAL, EMPHASIS] ❑ *I have a fantastic social life.* **2** ADJ [ADJ n] A **fantastic** amount or quantity is an extremely large one. ❑ ...*fantastic amounts of money.* ● **fan|tas|ti|cal|ly** /fæntæstɪkli/ ADV [ADV adj/adv] ❑ ...*a fantastically expensive restaurant.*

fan|ta|sy ◆◇◇ /fæntəsi/ (fantasies) **1** N-COUNT A **fantasy** is a pleasant situation or event that you think about and that you want to happen, especially one that is unlikely to happen. ❑ ...*fantasies of romance and true love.* **2** N-VAR You can refer to a story or situation that someone creates from their imagination and that is not based on reality as **fantasy**. ❑ *The movie is more of an ironic fantasy than a horror story.* **3** N-UNCOUNT **Fantasy** is the activity of imagining things. ❑ ...*a world of imagination, passion, fantasy, reflection.* **4** ADJ [ADJ n] **Fantasy** football, baseball, or another sport is a game in which players choose an imaginary team and score points based on the actual performances of the members of their team in real games. ❑ *Haskins said he has been playing fantasy baseball for the past five years.*

fan|zine /fænzin/ (fanzines) N-COUNT A **fanzine** is a magazine written by and for people who are fans of, for example, a particular band or football team.

FAO [BRIT] You use **FAO** when addressing a letter or parcel to a particular person. **FAO** is a written abbreviation for 'for the attention of.'

in AM, use **Attn.**

FAQ /fæk/ (FAQs) N-VAR **FAQ** is used especially on websites to refer to questions about a particular topic. **FAQ** is an abbreviation for 'frequently asked question' or 'frequently asked questions.'

FAR
① DISTANT IN SPACE OR TIME
② THE EXTENT TO WHICH SOMETHING HAPPENS
③ EMPHATIC USES
---

① **far** ◆◆◆ /fɑr/

→ Please look at meaning **6** to see if the expression you are looking for is shown under another headword.

1 ADV If one place, thing, or person is **far** away from another, there is a great distance between them. ❑ *I know a nice little Italian restaurant not far from here.* ❑ *Both of my sisters moved even farther away from home.* **2** ADV If you ask how **far** a place is, you are asking what distance it is from you or from another place. If you ask how **far** someone went, you are asking what distance they reached, or what place they reached. ❑ *How far is Pawtucket from Providence?* ❑ *How far is it to Malcy?* ❑ *She followed the tracks as far as the road.* **3** ADV A time or event that is **far** away in the future or the past is a long time from the present or from a particular point in time. ❑ ...*hidden conflicts whose* roots lie far back in time. ❑ I can't see any farther than the next six months. **4** ADJ [ADJ n] When there are two things of the same kind in a place, the **far** one is the one that is a greater distance from you. ❑ He had wandered to the far end of the room. **5** ADJ [ADJ n] You can use **far** to refer to the part of an area or object that is the greatest distance from the center in a particular direction. For example, the **far** north of a country is the part of it that is the greatest distance to the north. ❑ A storm was brewing off Port Angeles in the far north of Washington State. **6** near and far → see **near**

Far has two comparatives, **farther** and **further**, and two superlatives, **farthest** and **furthest**. Farther and farthest are used mainly in sense **1**, and are dealt with here. Further and furthest are dealt with in separate entries.

② **far** ◆◆◆ /fɑr/ **1** ADV You can use **far** to talk about the extent or degree to which something happens or is true. ❑ How far did the movie tell the truth about his life? **2** ADV You can talk about how **far** someone or something gets to describe the progress that they make. ❑ Discussions never progressed very far. ❑ Think of how far we have come in a little time. **3** ADV [ADV with v] You can talk about how **far** a person or action goes to describe the degree to which someone's behavior or actions are extreme. ❑ It's still not clear how far the regime will go to implement its own plans. ❑ Competition can be healthy, but if it is pushed too far it can result in bullying. **4** ADV [as/so ADV as] You can use **far** in expressions like '**as far as I know**' and '**so far as I remember**' to indicate that you are not absolutely sure of the statement you are about to make or have just made, and you may be wrong. [VAGUENESS] ❑ It only lasted a couple of years, as far as I know. **5** PHRASE If you say that someone **will go far**, you mean that they will be very successful in their career. ❑ I was very impressed with their talent. They will go far. **6** PHRASE Someone or something that is **far gone** is in such a bad state or condition that not much can be done to help or improve them. ❑ In his last few days the pain seemed to have stopped, but by then he was so far gone that it was no longer any comfort. **7** PHRASE You can use the expression '**as far as I can see**' when you are about to state your opinion of a situation, or have just stated it, to indicate that it is your personal opinion. ❑ That's the problem as far as I can see. **8** PHRASE If you say that something only goes **so far** or can only go **so far**, you mean that its extent, effect, or influence is limited. ❑ Their loyalty only went so far. **9** PHRASE If you tell or ask someone what has happened **so far**, you are telling or asking them what has happened up until the present point in a situation or story, and often implying that something different might happen later. ❑ It's been quiet so far. ❑ So far, they have met with no success. **10** PHRASE You can say **so far so good** to express satisfaction with the way that a situation or activity is progressing, developing, or happening. [FEELINGS] ❑ Of course, it's a case of so far, so good, but it's only one step.

③ **far** ◆◆◆ /fɑr/ **1** ADV You can use **far** to mean 'very much' when you are comparing two things and emphasizing the difference between them. For example, you can say that something is **far better** or **far worse** than something else to indicate that it is very much better or worse. You can also say that something is, for example, **far too big** to indicate that it is very much too big. [EMPHASIS] ❑ Women who eat plenty of fresh vegetables are far less likely to suffer anxiety or depression. ❑ The police say the response has been far better than expected. **2** ADJ [ADJ n] You can describe people with extreme left-wing or right-wing political views as the **far** left or the **far** right. ❑ The far right is now a greater threat than the extreme left. **3** PHRASE You use the expression **by far** when you are comparing something or someone with others of the same kind, in order to emphasize how great the difference is between them. For example, you can say that something is **by far the best** or **the best by far** to indicate that it is definitely the best. [EMPHASIS] ❑ By far the most important issue for them is unemployment. **4** PHRASE If you say that something is **far from** a particular thing or **far from** being the case, you are emphasizing that it is not that particular thing or not at all the case, especially when people expect or assume that it is. [EMPHASIS] ❑ It was obvious that much of what they recorded was far from the truth. ❑ Far from being relaxed, we both felt so uncomfortable we hardly spoke. **5** PHRASE You can use the expression '**far from it**' to emphasize a negative statement that you have just made. [EMPHASIS] ❑ Being dyslexic does not mean that one is unintelligent. Far from it.

far|away /fɑrəweɪ/ ADJ [ADJ n] A **faraway** place is a long distance from you or from a particular place. ❑ They have just returned from faraway places with wonderful stories to tell.

farce /fɑrs/ (**farces**) **1** N-COUNT A **farce** is a humorous play in which the characters become involved in complicated and unlikely situations. ❑ ...an off-Broadway farce called "Lucky Stiff." **2** N-UNCOUNT **Farce** is the style of acting and writing that is typical of farces. ❑ The plot often borders on farce. **3** N-SING [also no det] If you describe a situation or event as a **farce**, you mean that it is so disorganized or ridiculous that you cannot take it seriously. [DISAPPROVAL] ❑ The elections have been reduced to a farce.

far|ci|cal /fɑrsɪkəl/ ADJ If you describe a situation or event as **farcical**, you mean that it is so silly or extreme that you are unable to take it seriously. [DISAPPROVAL] ❑ ...a farcical nine months' jail sentence imposed yesterday on a killer. **2** → See feature box at **humor**

fare ◆◇◇ /fɛər/ (**fares, faring, fared**) **1** N-COUNT A **fare** is the money that you pay for a trip that you make, for example, in a bus, train, or taxi. ❑ He could barely afford the fare. **2** V-I If you say that someone or something **fares** well or badly, you are referring to the degree of success they achieve in a particular situation or activity. ❑ It is unlikely that the marine industry will fare any better in September.

Far East N-PROPER The **Far East** is used to refer to all the countries of Eastern Asia, including China, Japan, the Democratic People's Republic of Korea, the Republic of Korea, and Indonesia.

fare|well /fɛərwɛl/ (**farewells**) CONVENTION **Farewell** means the same as **goodbye**. [LITERARY, OLD-FASHIONED] • N-COUNT **Farewell** is also a noun. ❑ They said their farewells there at the cafe.

far-fetched ADJ If you describe a story or idea as **far-fetched**, you are criticizing it because you think it is unlikely to be true or practical. [DISAPPROVAL] ❑ The storyline was too far-fetched and none of the actors was particularly good.

far-flung (**farther-flung, farthest-flung**) ADJ [ADJ n] **Far-flung** places are a very long distance away from where you are or from important places. ❑ American soldiers were dispatched to far-flung regions of the globe. ❑ ...one of the farthest-flung outposts of the old Roman Empire.

farm ◆◆◆ /fɑrm/ (**farms, farming, farmed**) **1** N-COUNT A **farm** is an area of land, together with the buildings on it, that is used for growing crops or raising animals, usually in order to sell them. ❑ Farms in France are much smaller than those in the United States or even Britain. **2** N-COUNT A mink **farm** or a fish **farm**, for example, is a place where a particular kind of animal or fish is bred and kept in large quantities in order to be sold. ❑ ...trout fresh from a local trout farm. **3** V-T/V-I If you **farm** an area of land, you grow crops or keep animals on it. ❑ They farmed some of the best land in the country. ❑ Bease has been farming for 30 years. **4** → See feature box at **farming**
▶ **farm out** PHRASAL VERB If you **farm out** something that is your responsibility, you send it to other people for them to deal with or look after. ❑ Scores of U.S. companies farm out software development. ❑ She may have farmed the child out in order to remarry.

═══ COLLOCATIONS ═══

farm
NOUN **1**
noun + **farm**: dairy, pig, sheep
adjective + **farm**: organic
VERB **3**
farm + adverb: intensively, organically, sustainably

farm|er ◆◆◇ /fɑrmər/ (**farmers**) **1** N-COUNT A **farmer** is a person who owns or manages a farm. **2** → See feature box at **farming**

farm|ers' mar|ket (**farmers' markets**) also **farmers market** N-COUNT A **farmers' market** is a market where food growers sell their produce directly to the public.

farm|hand /fɑrmhænd/ (**farmhands**) also **farm hand** N-COUNT A **farmhand** is a person who is employed to work on a farm.

farm|house /fɑrmhaʊs/ (**farmhouses**) ◼ N-COUNT A **farmhouse** is the main house on a farm, usually where the farmer lives. ◼ → See also color supplement

farm|ing /fɑrmɪŋ/ ◼ N-UNCOUNT **Farming** is the activity of growing crops or keeping animals on a farm. ❑ ...a career in farming. ◼ → See feature box at **global warming**

VOCABULARY IN CONTEXT

Farming

Humans have **farmed the land** since prehistoric times. Since then, **farming techniques** have changed radically. Of course, nowadays, the exploding population of the world and our newly-acquired taste for daily portions of meat and year-round strawberries have led to **intensive farming practices**, such as **battery farming**, over-use of **pesticides**, and **genetically modified crops**. But many people are worried about the long-term effects of these methods on our health. **Organic farming practices** are becoming more widespread and are gaining in popularity. **Organically grown agricultural products** are at risk from **plagues** of insects and **disease**, which can wipe out a crop, and the farmer's profits, overnight. Organic **livestock farmers** need to provide ample space for their animals, and good-quality, natural **feed**. **Parasites** or diseases can affect their **herds**, too. For all of these reasons, organic **produce** is more expensive for the consumer. But for many people, the health benefits far outweigh the increased cost.

farm|land /fɑrmlænd/ (**farmlands**) N-UNCOUNT [also N in pl] **Farmland** is land which is farmed, or which is suitable for farming. ❑ It is surrounded by 62 acres of farmland.

farm|yard /fɑrmyɑrd/ (**farmyards**) N-COUNT On a farm, the **farmyard** is an area of land near the farmhouse which is enclosed by walls or buildings. ❑ ...farmyard animals including chickens, geese and rabbits.

far off (**further off, furthest off**) ◼ ADJ If you describe a moment in time as **far off**, you mean that it is a long time from the present, either in the past or the future. ❑ In those far off days it never entered anyone's mind that a woman could be prime minister. ◼ ADJ If you describe something as **far off**, you mean that it is a long distance from you or from a particular place. ❑ ...stars in far-off galaxies. • ADV [ADV after v] **Far off** is also an adverb. ❑ The band was playing far off in their blue and yellow uniforms.

far out also **far-out** ADJ [usu v-link ADJ] If you describe something as **far out**, you mean that it is very strange or extreme. [INFORMAL] ❑ Fantasies cannot harm you, no matter how bizarre or far out they are.

far|ra|go /fərɑgoʊ/ (**farragoes** or **farragos**) N-COUNT [oft N of n] If you describe something as a **farrago**, you are critical of it because you think it is a confused mixture of different types of things. [FORMAL, DISAPPROVAL]

far-reaching ADJ If you describe actions, events, or changes as **far-reaching**, you mean that they have a very great influence and affect a great number of things. ❑ The economy is in danger of collapse unless far-reaching reforms are implemented.

far|ri|er /færiər/ (**farriers**) N-COUNT A **farrier** is a person who fits horseshoes onto horses.

Farsi /fɑrsi/ N-UNCOUNT **Farsi** is a language that is spoken in Iran.

far|sighted /fɑrsaɪtɪd/ also **far-sighted** ◼ ADJ If you describe someone as **farsighted**, you admire them because they understand what is likely to happen in the future, and therefore make wise decisions and plans. [APPROVAL] ❑ Haven't farsighted economists been telling us that in the future we will work less, not more? ◼ ADJ **Farsighted** people cannot see things clearly that are close to them, and therefore need to wear glasses. ◼ → See feature box at **eyesight**

fart /fɑrt/ (**farts, farting, farted**) V-I If someone **farts**, air is forced out of their body through their anus. [INFORMAL, VULGAR] ❑ He'd been farting all night. • N-COUNT **Fart** is also a noun. ❑ ...a loud fart.

far|ther /fɑrðər/ **Farther** is a comparative form of **far**.

far|thest /fɑrðɪst/ **Farthest** is a superlative form of **far**.

fas|cia /fæʃiə, feɪʃə/ (**fascias**) ◼ N-COUNT The **fascia** of a cellphone is its detachable cover. ◼ N-COUNT In a car, the **fascia** is the part surrounding the instruments and dials. [BRIT, FORMAL]

in AM, use **dashboard**

fas|ci|nate /fæsɪneɪt/ (**fascinates, fascinating, fascinated**) V-T If something **fascinates** you, it interests and delights you so much that your thoughts tend to concentrate on it. ❑ Politics fascinated Franklin's father.

fas|ci|nat|ed /fæsɪneɪtɪd/ ADJ If you are **fascinated** by something, you find it very interesting and attractive, and your thoughts tend to concentrate on it. ❑ I sat on the stairs and watched, fascinated.

fas|ci|nat|ing /fæsɪneɪtɪŋ/ ADJ If you describe something as **fascinating**, you find it very interesting and attractive, and your thoughts tend to concentrate on it. ❑ Madagascar is the most fascinating place I have ever been to.

fas|ci|na|tion /fæsɪneɪʃ°n/ ◼ N-UNCOUNT **Fascination** is the state of being greatly interested in or delighted by something. ❑ I've had a lifelong fascination with the sea and with small boats. ◼ → See feature box at **recycle, time**

fas|cism /fæʃɪzəm/ N-UNCOUNT **Fascism** is a set of right-wing political beliefs that includes strong control of society and the economy by the state, a powerful role for the armed forces, and the stopping of political opposition. ❑ ...the rise of fascism in the 1930s.

fas|cist /fæʃɪst/ (**fascists**) ADJ You use **fascist** to describe organizations, ideas, or systems which follow the principles of fascism. ❑ ...an upsurge of support for extreme rightist, nationalist and fascist organizations. • N-COUNT A **fascist** is someone who has fascist views. ❑ ...a reluctant supporter of Mussolini's Fascists.

fash|ion ♦♦◇ /fæʃ°n/ (**fashions**) ◼ N-UNCOUNT **Fashion** is the area of activity that involves styles of clothing and appearance. ❑ There are 20 full-color pages of fashion for men. ◼ N-COUNT A **fashion** is a style of clothing or a way of behaving that is popular at a particular time. ❑ In the early seventies I wore false eyelashes, as was the fashion. ❑ The demand for perfume resulted in a fashion for fancy scent bottles. ◼ N-SING If you do something in a particular **fashion** or after a particular **fashion**, you do it in that way. ❑ There is another drug called DHE that works in a similar fashion. ◼ → see also **old-fashioned** ◼ PHRASE If something is **in fashion**, it is popular and approved of at a particular time. If it is **out of fashion**, it is not popular or approved of. ❑ That sort of house is back in fashion. ◼ → See feature box on next page

fash|ion|able /fæʃ°nəb°l/ ADJ Something or someone that is **fashionable** is popular or approved of at a particular time. ❑ It became fashionable to eat certain kinds of fish. • **fash|ion|ably** ADV ❑ ...women who are fashionably dressed.

fash|ion vic|tim (**fashion victims**) N-COUNT A **fashion victim** is someone who thinks that being fashionable is more important than looking nice, and as a result often wears very fashionable clothes that do not suit them or that make them look silly. [DISAPPROVAL]

VOCABULARY IN CONTEXT

Fashion

Two **fashion design** students from London have smashed the market with a simple but highly successful idea. They developed their **brand**, Fasho, for people who can't find clothes to **suit** them. Fasho offers two services. One: they sell their own **up-to-the-minute** original **designs**; two: they source the **styles** that customers ask for, and customize them on request. One testimonial is from a woman who dreaded attending **dressy** events because everything she tried on in department stores made her feel **frumpy** or **overdressed**. The Fasho fellows listened and found some **elegant** and **timeless** designs that were simple but **structured**. Fasho says they wanted to bridge the gap between the unaffordable **haute couture** of the **high-end designers** and the mass-produced sameness of **off-the-peg** clothing in the shopping malls. Keep **styling**, guys!

fast ✦✦◊ /fæst/ (faster, fastest, fasts, fasting, fasted) **1** ADJ **Fast** means happening, moving, or doing something at great speed. You also use **fast** in questions or statements about speed. ❑ ...fast cars with flashing lights and sirens. ❑ The only question is how fast the process will be. • ADV [ADV with v] **Fast** is also an adverb. ❑ They work terrifically fast. ❑ It would be nice to go faster and break the world record. ❑ How fast would the disease develop? **2** ADJ [v-link ADJ] If a watch or clock is **fast**, it is showing a time that is later than the real time. ❑ That clock's an hour fast. **3** ADJ If colors or dyes are **fast**, they do not come out of the fabrics they are used on when they get wet. ❑ The fabric was ironed to make the colors fast. **4** ADV [ADV after v] You use **fast** to say that something happens without any delay. ❑ When you've got a crisis like this you need professional help – fast! • ADJ [ADJ n] **Fast** is also an adjective. ❑ That would be an astonishingly fast action on the part of the Congress. **5** ADV [ADV after v] If you hold something **fast**, you hold it tightly and firmly. If something is stuck **fast**, it is stuck very firmly and cannot move. ❑ She climbed the staircase cautiously, holding fast to the rail. **6** ADV [ADV after v] If you hold **fast** to a principle or idea, or if you stand **fast**, you do not change your mind about it, even though people are trying to persuade you to. ❑ We can only try to hold fast to the age-old values of honesty, decency and concern for others. **7** V-I If you **fast**, you eat no food for a period of time, usually for either religious or medical reasons, or as a protest. ❑ I fasted for a day and a half and asked God to help me. • N-COUNT **Fast** is also a noun. ❑ The fast is broken at sunset, traditionally with dates and water. • **fast|ing** N-UNCOUNT ❑ ...the Muslim holy month of fasting and prayer. **8** PHRASE Someone who is **fast asleep** is completely asleep. ❑ When he went upstairs five minutes later, she was fast asleep.

fast|ball /fæstbɔl/ (fastballs) N-COUNT In baseball, a **fastball** is a ball that is pitched very fast. ❑ Soriano hit Peavy's first pitch, a 90-mph fastball, down the left-field line.

fast-breeder re|ac|tor (fast-breeder reactors) N-COUNT A **fast-breeder reactor** or a **fast-breeder** is a kind of nuclear reactor that produces more plutonium than it uses.

fas|ten /fæsᵊn/ (fastens, fastening, fastened) **1** V-T/V-I When you **fasten** something, you close it by means of buttons or a strap, or some other device. If something **fastens** with buttons or straps, you can close it in this way. ❑ She got quickly into her Mini and fastened the seat-belt. ❑ Her long fair hair was fastened at the nape of her neck by an elastic band. **2** V-T If you **fasten** one thing to another, you attach the first thing to the second, for example, with a piece of string or tape. ❑ There were no instructions on how to fasten the carrying strap to the box. **3** → see also **fastening**

fas|ten|er /fæsᵊnər/ (fasteners) N-COUNT A **fastener** is a device such as a button, zipper, or small hook that fastens something, especially clothing.

fas|ten|ing /fæsᵊnɪŋ/ (fastenings) N-COUNT A **fastening** is something such as a clasp or zipper that you use to fasten something and keep it shut. ❑ The sundress has a neat back zipper fastening.

fast food N-UNCOUNT **Fast food** is hot food, such as hamburgers and French fries, that you obtain from particular types of restaurants, and which is served quickly after you order it. ❑ James works at a fast food restaurant.

fast for|ward (fast forwards, fast forwarding, fast forwarded) also **fast-forward** V-T/V-I When you **fast forward** the tape in a video or when you **fast forward**, you make the tape go forward. Compare **rewind**. ❑ Just fast forward the video.

fas|tidi|ous /fæstɪdiəs, fə-/ ADJ If you say that someone is **fastidious**, you mean that they pay great attention to detail because they like everything to be very neat, accurate, and in good order. ❑ ...her fastidious attention to historical detail.

fast lane (fast lanes) **1** N-COUNT On a highway, the **fast lane** is the part of the road where the vehicles that are traveling fastest go. ❑ I cut across the expressway and took the fast lane back to Miami. **2** N-SING If someone is living in the **fast lane**, they have a very busy, exciting life, although they sometimes seem to take a lot of risks. ❑ ...a tale of life in the fast lane.

fast|ness /fæstnɪs/ (fastnesses) N-COUNT [with supp] A **fastness** is a place, such as a castle, which is considered safe because it is difficult to reach or easy to defend against attack. [LITERARY] ❑ They could have withdrawn into the mountain fastness of Eryri.

fast track (fast tracks, fast tracking, fast tracked) also **fast-track** **1** N-SING The **fast track** to a particular goal, especially in politics or in your career, is the quickest route to achieving it. ❑ Football is good at launching young men on the fast track to fame. **2** V-T To **fast track** something means to make it happen or progress faster or earlier than normal. ❑ A Federal Court case had been fast tracked to Wednesday.

fat ✦✦◊ /fæt/ (fatter, fattest, fats) **1** ADJ If you say that a person or animal is **fat**, you mean that they have a lot of flesh on their body and that they weigh too much. You usually use the word **fat** when you think that this is a bad thing. [DISAPPROVAL] ❑ I could eat what I liked without getting fat. **2** N-MASS **Fat** is a substance contained in foods such as meat, cheese, and butter which forms an energy store in your body. ❑ An easy way to cut the amount of fat in your diet is to avoid eating red meats. **3** N-VAR **Fat** is a solid or liquid substance obtained from animals or vegetables, which is used in cooking. ❑ When you use oil or fat for cooking, use as little as possible. **4** ADJ A **fat** object, especially a book, is very thick or wide. ❑ ..."Europe in Figures," a fat book published on September 22nd. **5** ADJ [ADJ n] A **fat** profit or fee is a large one. [INFORMAL] ❑ They are set to make a big fat profit. **6** N-UNCOUNT **Fat** is the extra flesh that animals and humans have under their skin, which is used to store energy and to help keep them warm. ❑ Because you're not burning calories, everything you eat turns to fat. **7** PHRASE If you say that there is **fat chance** of something happening, you mean that you do not believe that it will happen. [INFORMAL, mainly SPOKEN, FEELINGS] ❑ "Would your car be easy to steal?"—"Fat chance. I've got a device that shuts down the gas and ignition."

fa|tal /feɪtᵊl/ **1** ADJ A **fatal** action has very undesirable effects. ❑ It would be fatal for the nation to overlook the urgency of the situation. ❑ He made the fatal mistake of compromising early. • **fa|tal|ly** ADV [ADV with v] ❑ Failure now could fatally damage his chances in the future. **2** ADJ A **fatal** accident or illness causes someone's death. ❑ ...the fatal stabbing of a police sergeant. • **fa|tal|ly** ADV ❑ The dead soldier is reported to have been fatally wounded in the chest.

fa|tal|ism /feɪtᵊlɪzəm/ N-UNCOUNT **Fatalism** is a feeling that you cannot control events or prevent unpleasant things from happening, especially when this feeling stops you from making decisions or making an effort. ❏ *There's a certain mood of fatalism now among the radicals.*

fa|tal|is|tic /feɪtᵊlɪstɪk/ ADJ [oft ADJ about n] If someone is **fatalistic** about something, especially an unpleasant event or situation, they feel that they cannot change or control it, and therefore that there is no purpose in trying. ❏ *People we spoke to today were really rather fatalistic about what's going to happen.*

fa|tal|ity /fətælɪti/ (fatalities) **1** N-COUNT A **fatality** is a death caused by an accident or by violence. [FORMAL] ❏ *Drunk driving fatalities have decreased more than 10 percent over the past 10 years.*
2 → See feature box at **accident**

fat cat (fat cats) N-COUNT If you refer to a businessman or politician as a **fat cat**, you are indicating that you disapprove of the way they use their wealth and power. [INFORMAL, BUSINESS, DISAPPROVAL] ❏ *...the fat cats who run the bank.*

fate ♦◊◊ /feɪt/ (fates) **1** N-UNCOUNT [also N in pl] **Fate** is a power that some people believe controls and decides everything that happens, in a way that cannot be prevented or changed. You can also refer to **the fates**. ❏ *I see no use arguing with fate.* ❏ *...the fickleness of fate.* **2** N-COUNT A person's or thing's **fate** is what happens to them. ❏ *The Russian Parliament will hold a special session later this month to decide his fate.* ❏ *He seems for a moment to be again holding the fate of the country in his hands.*

fat|ed /feɪtɪd/ **1** ADJ [oft ADJ to-inf] If you say that a person is **fated** to do something, or that something is **fated**, you mean that it seems to have been decided by fate before it happens, and nothing can be done to avoid or change it. ❏ *He was fated not to score.* ❏ *...stories of desperation, fated love, treachery and murder.*
2 → see also **ill-fated**

fate|ful /feɪtfəl/ ADJ If an action or a time when something happened is described as **fateful**, it is considered to have an important, and often very bad, effect on future events. ❏ *It was a fateful decision, one which was to break the Government.*

fa|ther ♦♦♦ /fɑðər/ (fathers, fathering, fathered) **1** N-FAMILY Your **father** is your male parent. You can also call someone your **father** if he brings you up as if he were this man. ❏ *His father was a painter.* ❏ *He would be a good father to my children.*
2 V-T When a man **fathers** a child, he makes a woman pregnant and their child is born. ❏ *She claims Mark fathered her child.* **3** N-COUNT The man who invented or started something is sometimes referred to as the **father of** that thing. ❏ *...Max Dupain, regarded as the father of modern photography.*

COLLOCATIONS

father
NOUN **1**
adjective + **father**: absent, biological, estranged, married; beloved, devoted, loving, proud
verb + **father**: become

Father Christ|mas N-PROPER **Father Christmas** is the name given to an imaginary old man with a long white beard and a red coat. Traditionally, young children in many countries are told that he brings their Christmas presents. [BRIT]

in AM, use **Santa Claus**

fa|ther fig|ure (father figures) also **father-figure** N-COUNT If you describe someone as a **father figure**, you mean that you feel able to turn to that person for advice and support in the same way that you might turn to your father. ❏ *She believed her daughter needed a father-figure.* ❏ *He became a father figure to the whole company.*

father|hood /fɑðərhʊd/ N-UNCOUNT **Fatherhood** is the state of being a father. ❏ *...the joys of fatherhood.*

father-in-law (fathers-in-law) N-COUNT Someone's **father-in-law** is the father of their husband or wife.

father|land /fɑðərlænd/ (fatherlands) N-COUNT [usu sing] If someone is very proud of the country where they or their ancestors were born, they sometimes refer to it as the **fatherland**. The word **fatherland** is particularly associated with Germany. ❏ *They were willing to serve the fatherland in its hour of need.*

fa|ther|less /fɑðərlɪs/ ADJ You describe children as **fatherless** when their father has died or does not live with them. ❏ *...widows and fatherless children.* ❏ *They were left fatherless.*

fa|ther|ly /fɑðərli/ ADJ [usu ADJ n] **Fatherly** feelings or actions are like those of a kind father. ❏ *His voice filled with fatherly concern.*

Fa|ther's Day N-UNCOUNT **Father's Day** is the third Sunday in June, when children give cards and presents to their fathers to show that they love them.

fath|om /fæðəm/ (fathoms, fathoming, fathomed)
1 N-COUNT A **fathom** is a measurement of 6 feet or 1.8 meters, used when referring to the depth of water. ❏ *We sailed into the bay and dropped anchor in five fathoms of water.* **2** V-T [no cont, oft with brd-neg] If you cannot **fathom** something, you are unable to understand it, although you think carefully about it. ❏ *I really couldn't fathom what Steiner was talking about.*
• PHRASAL VERB **Fathom out** means the same as **fathom**. ❏ *We're trying to fathom out what's going on.*

fath|om|less /fæðəmlɪs/ ADJ Something that is **fathomless** cannot be measured or understood because it gives the impression of being very deep, mysterious, or complicated. ❏ *...the fathomless space of the universe.* ❏ *The silence was fathomless and overwhelming.*

fa|tigue /fətig/ (fatigues) **1** N-UNCOUNT **Fatigue** is a feeling of extreme physical or mental tiredness. ❏ *She continued to have severe stomach cramps, aches, fatigue, and depression.* **2** N-UNCOUNT You can say that people are suffering from a particular kind of **fatigue** when they have been doing something for a long time and feel they can no longer continue to do it. ❏ *...compassion fatigue caused by endless TV and celebrity appeals.*
3 N-UNCOUNT **Fatigue** in metal or wood is a weakness in it that is caused by repeated stress. Fatigue can cause the metal or wood to break. ❏ *The problem turned out to be metal fatigue in the fuselage.* **4** N-PLURAL **Fatigues** are clothes that soldiers wear when they are fighting or when they are doing routine jobs. ❏ *He never expected to return home wearing combat fatigues.*

fa|tigued /fətigd/ ADJ [usu v-link ADJ] If you are feeling **fatigued**, you are suffering from extreme physical or mental tiredness.

fa|tigu|ing /fətigɪŋ/ ADJ Something that is **fatiguing** makes you feel extremely physically or mentally tired. ❏ *This was the heaviest and most fatiguing work of all.*

fat|so /fætsoʊ/ (fatsos or fatsoes) N-COUNT; N-VOC If someone calls another person a **fatso**, they are saying in an unkind way that the person is fat. [INFORMAL, DISAPPROVAL] ❏ *When I was a little girl, there was this mean boy who called me fatso all the time.*

fat|ten /fætᵊn/ (fattens, fattening, fattened) V-T If you say that someone **is fattening** something such as a business or its profits, you mean that they are increasing the value of the business or its profits, in a way that you disapprove of. [BUSINESS, DISAPPROVAL] ❏ *They have kept the price of sugar artificially high and so fattened the company's profits.* • PHRASAL VERB **Fatten up** means the same as **fatten**. ❏ *The Government is making the taxpayer pay to fatten up a public sector business for private sale.*

fat|ten|ing /fætᵊnɪŋ/ ADJ Food that is **fattening** is considered to make people fat easily. ❏ *Some foods are more fattening than others.*

fat|ty /fæti/ (fattier, fattiest) **1** ADJ **Fatty** food contains a lot of fat. ❏ *Don't eat fatty food or chocolates.* **2** ADJ [ADJ n] **Fatty** acids or **fatty** tissues, for example, contain or consist of fat.
3 → See feature box at **nutrition**

fatu|ous /fætʃuəs/ ADJ If you describe a person, action, or remark as **fatuous**, you think that they are extremely silly, showing a lack of intelligence or thought. [FORMAL, DISAPPROVAL] ❏ *The Chief was left speechless by this fatuous remark.*

fat|wa /fætwɑ/ (fatwas) also **fatwah** N-COUNT A **fatwa** is a religious order issued by a Muslim leader.

fau|cet /fɔsɪt/ (faucets) N-COUNT A **faucet** is a device that controls the flow of a liquid or gas from a pipe or container. Sinks and baths have faucets attached to them. [mainly AM] ❏ *She turned off the faucet and dried her hands.*

in BRIT, use **tap**

fault /fɔlt/ (faults, faulting, faulted) **1** N-SING If a bad or undesirable situation is your **fault**, you caused it or are responsible for it. ❑ *There was no escaping the fact: it was all his fault.* **2** N-COUNT A **fault** is a mistake in what someone is doing or in what they have done. ❑ *It is a big fault to think that you can learn how to manage people in business school.* **3** N-COUNT A **fault** in someone or something is a weakness in them or something that is not perfect. ❑ *His manners had always made her blind to his faults.* **4** N-COUNT A **fault** is a large crack in the surface of the earth. ❑ *...the San Andreas Fault.* **5** N-COUNT A **fault** in tennis is a service that is wrong according to the rules. ❑ *He caught the ball on his first toss and then served a fault.* **6** V-T [with brd-neg] If you cannot **fault** someone, you cannot find any reason for criticizing them or the things that they are doing. ❑ *You can't fault them for lack of invention.* **7** PHRASE If someone or something is **at fault**, they are to blame or are responsible for a particular situation that has gone wrong. ❑ *He could never accept that he had been at fault.* **8** PHRASE If you **find fault** with something or someone, you look for mistakes and complain about them. ❑ *I was disappointed whenever the cook found fault with my work.* **9** → See feature box at **review**

fault|less /fɔltlɪs/ ADJ Something that is **faultless** is perfect and has no mistakes at all. ❑ *...Mary Thomson's faultless and impressive performance on the show.*

fault line (fault lines) **1** N-COUNT A **fault line** is a long crack in the surface of the earth. Earthquakes usually occur along fault lines. **2** N-COUNT A **fault line** in a system or process is an area of it that seems weak and likely to cause problems or failure. ❑ *These issues have created a stark fault line within the Peace Process.*

faulty /fɔlti/ **1** ADJ A **faulty** piece of equipment has something wrong with it and is not working properly. ❑ *The money will be used to repair faulty equipment.* **2** ADJ If you describe someone's argument or reasoning as **faulty**, you mean that it is wrong or contains mistakes, usually because they have not been thinking in a logical way. ❑ *Their interpretation was faulty – they had misinterpreted things.*

faun /fɔn/ (fauns) N-COUNT A **faun** is an imaginary creature which is like a man with goat's legs and horns.

fau|na /fɔnə/ (faunas) **1** N-COUNT-COLL Animals, especially the animals in a particular area, can be referred to as **fauna**. [TECHNICAL] ❑ *...the flora and fauna of the African jungle.* **2** → See feature box at **deforest**

faux pas /foʊ pɑ/ (faux pas) N-COUNT A **faux pas** is a socially embarrassing action or mistake. [FORMAL] ❑ *It was not long before I realized the enormity of my faux pas.*

fava bean /fɑvə bin/ (fava beans) N-COUNT [usu pl] **Fava beans** are flat round beans that are light green in color and are eaten as a vegetable. [AM]

fa|vor /feɪvər/ (favors, favoring, favored)
in BRIT, use **favour**

1 N-UNCOUNT If you regard something or someone with **favor**, you like or support them. ❑ *It remains to be seen if the show will find favor with an audience.* ❑ *No one would look with favor on the continuing military rule.* **2** N-COUNT If you do someone a **favor**, you do something for them even though you do not have to. ❑ *I've come to ask you to do me a favor.* **3** V-T If you **favor** something, you prefer it to the other choices available. ❑ *The French say they favor a transition to democracy.* **4** V-T If you **favor** someone, you treat them better or in a kinder way than you treat other people. ❑ *The company has no rules about favoring U.S. citizens during layoffs.* **5** PHRASE If you are **in favor of** something, you support it and think that it is a good thing. ❑ *I wouldn't be in favor of income tax cuts.* ❑ *Yet this is a Government which proclaims that it is all in favor of openness.* **6** PHRASE If someone makes a judgment **in** your **favor**, they say that you are right about something. ❑ *The Supreme Court ruled in Fitzgerald's favor.* **7** PHRASE If something is **in** your **favor**, it helps you or gives you an advantage. ❑ *The protection that farmers have enjoyed amounts to a bias in favor of the countryside.* **8** PHRASE If one thing is rejected **in favor of** another, the second thing is done or chosen instead of the first. ❑ *The policy was rejected in favor of a more cautious approach.* **9** PHRASE If someone or something is **in favor**, people like or support them. If they are **out of favor**, people no longer like or support them. ❑ *Governments and party leaders can only hope to remain in favor with the public for so long.*

fa|vor|able /feɪvərəbəl, feɪvrəbəl/
in BRIT, use **favourable**

1 ADJ [ADJ n, v-link ADJ to n] If your opinion or your reaction is **favorable** to something, you agree with it and approve of it. ❑ *The president's convention speech received favorable reviews.* **2** ADJ **Favorable** conditions make something more likely to succeed or seem more attractive. ❑ *It's believed the conditions in which the elections are being held are too favorable to the government.* **3** ADJ If you make a **favorable** comparison between two things, you say that the first is better than or as good as the second. ❑ *The movie bears favorable technical comparison with Hollywood productions costing 10 times as much.*

fa|vor|ite /feɪvərɪt, feɪvrɪt/ (favorites)
in BRIT, use **favourite**

1 ADJ [ADJ n] Your **favorite** thing or person of a particular type is the one you like most. ❑ *He celebrated by opening a bottle of his favorite champagne.* • N-COUNT **Favorite** is also a noun. ❑ *The Metropole is my favorite. I love those huge, anonymous hotels.* • PHRASE If you refer to something as an **old favorite**, you mean that it has been in existence for a long time and everyone knows it or likes it. ❑ *This recipe is an adaptation of an old favorite.* **2** N-COUNT The **favorite** in a race or contest is the competitor that is expected to win. In a team game, the team that is expected to win is referred to as the **favorites**. ❑ *The U.S. team is considered one of the favorites in next month's games.*

USAGE

favorite
Your **favorite** thing or person is the one you like more than all the others. Don't use 'most' with **favorite**. Don't say, for example, 'What is is your most favorite movie?' Say 'What is your **favorite** movie?'

COLLOCATIONS

favorite
NOUN **2**
noun + **favorite**: promotion, race, title
adjective + **favorite**: clear, firm, hot, overwhelming; equal, joint, odds-on

---

fa|vor|it|ism /feɪvərɪtɪzəm, feɪvrɪt-/
in BRIT, use **favouritism**

N-UNCOUNT If you accuse someone of **favoritism**, you disapprove of them because they unfairly help or favor one person or group much more than another. [DISAPPROVAL] ❑ *Maria loved both the children. There was never a hint of favoritism.*

fawn /fɔn/ (fawns) **1** N-COUNT A **fawn** is a very young deer. ❑ *The fawn ran to the top of the ridge.* **2** COLOR **Fawn** is a pale yellowish-brown color. ❑ *Tania was standing there in her light fawn coat.*

fax /fæks/ (faxes, faxing, faxed) **1** N-COUNT [also by n] A **fax** or a **fax machine** is a piece of equipment used to copy documents by sending information electronically along a telephone line, and to receive copies that are sent in this way. ❑ *...a reception desk with telephone and fax.* **2** N-COUNT You can refer to a copy of a document that is transmitted by a fax machine as a **fax**. ❑ *I sent him a long fax, saying I didn't need a maid.* **3** V-T If you **fax** a document to someone, you send it from one fax machine to another. ❑ *I faxed a copy of the agreement to each of the investors.* ❑ *Did you fax him a reply?*

faze /feɪz/ (fazes, fazed) V-T [no cont, oft with brd-neg] If something **fazes** you, it surprises, shocks, or frightens you, so that you do not know what to do. [INFORMAL] ❑ *Big concert halls do not faze Melanie.*

FBI /ɛf bi aɪ/ N-PROPER [the N] The **FBI** is a government agency in the United States that investigates crimes in which a national law is broken or in which the country's security is threatened. **FBI** is an abbreviation for 'Federal Bureau of Investigation.'

FDA /ɛf di eɪ/ N-PROPER [the N] **FDA** is an abbreviation for **Food and Drug Administration**. ❑ *The FDA has approved a new treatment for a rare blood disorder.*

fe|al|ty /fiəlti/ N-UNCOUNT In former times, if someone swore **fealty** to their ruler, they promised to be loyal to him or her.

fear ✦✦✦ /fɪər/ (fears, fearing, feared) **1** N-VAR **Fear** is the unpleasant feeling you have when you think that you are in danger. ❏ *I was sitting on the floor shivering with fear because a bullet had been fired through a window.* **2** N-VAR A **fear** is a thought that something unpleasant might happen or might have happened. ❏ *These youngsters are motivated by fear of failure.* ❏ *Then one day his worst fears were confirmed.* **3** N-VAR If you say that there is a **fear** that something unpleasant or undesirable will happen, you mean that you think it is possible or likely. ❏ *There is a fear that the freeze on bank accounts could prove a lasting deterrent to investors.* **4** N-VAR If you have **fears for** someone or something, you are very worried because you think that they might be in danger. ❏ *He also spoke of his fears for the future of his country's culture.* **5** V-T If you **fear** someone or something, you are frightened because you think that they will harm you. ❏ *It seems to me that if people fear you they respect you.* **6** V-T If you **fear** something unpleasant or undesirable, you are worried that it might happen or might have happened. ❏ *She had feared she was coming down with pneumonia or bronchitis.* **7** V-I If you **fear for** someone or something, you are very worried because you think that they might be in danger. ❏ *Carla fears for her son.* **8** PHRASE If you are **in fear of** doing or experiencing something unpleasant or undesirable, you are very worried that you might have to do it or experience it. ❏ *Many older people live in fear of assault and murder.* **9** PHRASE If you take a particular course of action **for fear of** something, you take the action in order to prevent that thing happening. ❏ *She was afraid to say anything to them for fear of hurting their feelings.*

COLLOCATIONS

fear
NOUN **3**
noun + **fear**: safety, security, terrorism; inflation, recession
adjective + **fear**: irrational, unfounded; genuine, grave, intense, well-founded; deep, deep-seated
fear + be + adjective: groundless, unjustified
verb + **fear**: prompt, raise, spark; fuel, stoke; allay, calm, dispel, ease; express, voice

---

fear|ful /fɪərfəl/ **1** ADJ If you are **fearful** of something, you are afraid of it. [FORMAL] ❏ *Bankers were fearful of a world banking crisis.* **2** ADJ [ADJ n] You use **fearful** to emphasize how serious or bad a situation is. [FORMAL, EMPHASIS] ❏ *The region is in a fearful recession.*

fear|less /fɪərlɪs/ ADJ If you say that someone is **fearless**, you mean that they are not afraid at all, and you admire them for this. [APPROVAL] ❏ *...his fearless campaigning for racial justice.*

fear|some /fɪərsəm/ ADJ **Fearsome** is used to describe things that are frightening, for example, because of their large size or extreme nature. ❏ *He had developed a fearsome reputation for intimidating people.*

fea|sible /fizəbəl/ ADJ If something is **feasible**, it can be done, made, or achieved. ❏ *She questioned whether it was feasible to stimulate investment in these regions.* • **fea|sibil|ity** /fizəbɪlɪti/ N-UNCOUNT ❏ *The committee will study the feasibility of setting up a national computer network.*

feast /fist/ (feasts, feasting, feasted) **1** N-COUNT A **feast** is a large and special meal. ❏ *Lunch was a feast of meat and vegetables, cheese, yogurt and fruit, with unlimited wine.* ❏ *The fruit was often served at wedding feasts.* **2** N-COUNT A **feast** is a day or time of the year when a special religious celebration takes place. ❏ *The Jewish feast of Passover began last night.* **3** V-I If you **feast on** a particular food, you eat a large amount of it with great enjoyment. ❏ *They feasted well into the afternoon on mutton and corn stew.* **4** V-I If you **feast**, you take part in a feast. ❏ *Only a few feet away, their captors feasted in the castle's banqueting hall.* • **feast|ing** N-UNCOUNT ❏ *The feasting, drinking, dancing and revelry continued for several days.* **5** PHRASE If you **feast your eyes on** something, you look at it for a long time with great attention because you find it very attractive. ❏ *She stood feasting her eyes on the view.*

feat /fit/ (feats) N-COUNT If you refer to an action, or the result of an action, as a **feat**, you admire it because it is an impressive and difficult achievement. [APPROVAL] ❏ *A racing car is an extraordinary feat of engineering.*

feath|er /fɛðər/ (feathers) **1** N-COUNT A bird's **feathers** are the soft covering on its body. Each **feather** consists of a lot of smooth hairs on each side of a thin stiff center. ❏ *...a hat that she had made herself from black ostrich feathers.* **2** → see also feathered **3** to ruffle someone's feathers → see ruffle

feath|er boa → see boa

feath|er dust|er (feather dusters) N-COUNT A **feather duster** is a stick with a bunch of real or artificial feathers attached to one end. It is used for dusting and cleaning things.

feath|ered /fɛðərd/ ADJ If you describe something as **feathered**, you mean that it has feathers on it. ❏ *Her mother was the proud lady in the feathered hat.*

feather|weight /fɛðərweɪt/ (featherweights) N-COUNT A **featherweight** is a professional boxer who weighs between 118 and 126 pounds or 54 and 57 kilograms, which is one of the lowest weight ranges.

feath|ery /fɛðəri/ **1** ADJ If something is **feathery**, it has an edge divided into a lot of thin parts so that it looks soft. ❏ *The foliage was soft and feathery.* **2** ADJ **Feathery** is used to describe things that are soft and light. ❏ *...flurries of small, feathery flakes of snow.*

fea|ture ✦✦✧ /fitʃər/ (features, featuring, featured) **1** N-COUNT A **feature** of something is an interesting or important part or characteristic of it. ❏ *Patriotic songs have long been a feature of life here.* ❏ *The spacious gardens are a special feature of this property.* **2** N-COUNT A **feature** is a special article in a newspaper or magazine, or a special program on radio or television. ❏ *We are delighted to see the Sunday Times running a long feature on breast cancer.* **3** N-COUNT A **feature** or a **feature movie** is a full-length movie about a fictional situation, as opposed to a short movie or a documentary. ❏ *...the first feature-length cartoon, Snow White and the Seven Dwarfs.* **4** N-COUNT A geographical **feature** is something noticeable in a particular area of country, for example, a hill, river, or valley. ❏ *...one of the area's oddest geographical features - an eight-mile bank of pebbles shelving abruptly into the sea.* **5** N-PLURAL Your **features** are your eyes, nose, mouth, and other parts of your face. ❏ *His features seemed to change.* **6** V-T When something such as a movie or exhibition **features** a particular person or thing, they are an important part of it. ❏ *It's a great movie and it features a Spanish actor who is going to be a world star within a year.* ❏ *The hour-long program will be updated each week and feature highlights from recent games.* **7** V-I If someone or something **features** in something such as a show, exhibition, or magazine, they are an important part of it. ❏ *Jon featured in one of the show's most thrilling episodes.* **8** → See feature box at animal, appearance, press

---

COLLOCATIONS

feature
NOUN **1**
noun + **feature**: design, period; safety
adjective + **feature**: extra, important, key, special; distinctive, distinguishing, original, striking
verb + **feature**: add, offer; include, retain
VERB **6**
feature + adverb: heavily, prominently, regularly, strongly

SYNONYMS

feature
NOUN **1**
aspect: *He was interested in all aspects of the work here.*
characteristic: *...their physical characteristics.*
point: *The most interesting point about the village was its religion.*
side: *He is in charge of the civilian side of the U.N. mission.*

---

fea|ture|less /fitʃərlɪs/ ADJ If you say that something is **featureless**, you mean that it has no interesting features or characteristics. ❏ *Malone looked out at the gray-green featureless landscape.*

Feb. Feb. is a written abbreviation for **February**.

fe|brile /fibrəl, fɛb-/ ADJ **Febrile** behavior is intensely and nervously active. [LITERARY] ❏ *The news plunged the nation into a febrile, agitated state.*

Feb|ru|ary ✦✦✦ /fɛbyuɛri, fɛbru-/ (Februaries) N-VAR **February** is the second month of the year in the Western calendar. ❏ *He joined the Army in February 1943.* ❏ *His exhibition opens on February 5.*

fe|cal /fiːkəl/ ADJ **Fecal** means referring or relating to feces. [FORMAL] ◻ *One of the ways the parasite spreads is through fecal matter.*

fe|ces /fiːsiz/ N-UNCOUNT **Feces** is the solid waste substance that people and animals get rid of from their body by passing it through the anus. [FORMAL] ◻ *...grass contaminated by feces from infected dogs.*

feck|less /fɛklɪs/ ADJ If you describe someone as **feckless**, you mean that they lack determination or strength, and are unable to do anything properly. [FORMAL, DISAPPROVAL] ◻ *He regarded the young man as feckless and irresponsible.*

fe|cund /fiːkənd, fɛk-/ **1** ADJ Land or soil that is **fecund** is able to support the growth of a large number of strong healthy plants. [FORMAL] ◻ *The pampas are still among the most fecund lands in the world.* **2** ADJ If you describe something as **fecund**, you approve of it because it produces a lot of good or useful things. [FORMAL, APPROVAL] ◻ *It has now become clear how extraordinarily fecund a decade was the 1890s.*

fed /fɛd/ **1** **Fed** is the past tense and past participle of **feed**. **2** → see also **fed up** **3** N-SING [*the* N] The **Fed** is the **Federal Reserve**. [INFORMAL] ◻ *The Fed has already eased rates three times since late October.*

fed|er|al ♦♦♢ /fɛdərəl/ **1** ADJ [ADJ n] A **federal** country or system of government is one in which the different states or provinces of the country have important powers to make their own laws and decisions. ◻ *Five of the six provinces are to become autonomous regions in a new federal system of government.* **2** ADJ [ADJ n] **Federal** also means belonging or relating to the national government of a federal country rather than to one of the states within it. ◻ *The federal government controls just 6% of the education budget.* • **fed|er|al|ly** ADV [ADV -ed] ◻ *...residents of public housing and federally subsidized apartments.*

fed|er|al|ism /fɛdərəlɪzəm/ N-UNCOUNT **Federalism** is belief in or support for a federal system of government, or this system itself. ◻ *They argue that the amendment undermines Canadian federalism.*

fed|er|al|ist /fɛdərəlɪst/ (**federalists**) ADJ Someone or something that is **federalist** believes in, supports, or follows a federal system of government. ◻ *The new constitution includes federalist principles.* • N-COUNT **Federalist** is also a noun. ◻ *Many Quebeckers are federalists.*

Fed|er|al Re|serve N-SING [*the* N] In the United States, the **Federal Reserve** is the central banking system, which is responsible for setting policy on monetary matters such as money supply and interest rates. ◻ *...the Federal Reserve's influence on the American economy.*

fed|er|at|ed /fɛdəreɪtɪd/ ADJ [ADJ n, v-link ADJ to n] **Federated** states or societies are ones that have joined together for a common purpose. ◻ *Whether to stay in the federated state or become independent is a decision that has to be made by the people.*

fed|era|tion ♦♢♢ /fɛdəreɪʃən/ (**federations**) **1** N-COUNT A **federation** is a federal country. ◻ *...the Russian Federation.* **2** N-COUNT A **federation** is a group of societies or other organizations which have joined together, usually because they share a common interest. ◻ *...the American Federation of Government Employees.*

> **SYNONYMS**
>
> **federation**
> NOUN **2**
> **union:** *...the question of which countries should join the currency union.*
> **association:** *...the British Medical Association.*
> **alliance:** *The two parties were still too far apart to form an alliance.*
> **coalition:** *It's a coalition of about 50 civil rights, women's, and Latino organizations.*

fe|do|ra /fɪdɔːrə/ (**fedoras**) N-COUNT A **fedora** is a type of hat which has a brim and is made from a soft material such as velvet.

fed up ADJ [v-link ADJ] If you are **fed up**, you are unhappy, bored, or tired of something, especially something that you have been experiencing for a long time. [INFORMAL] ◻ *I'm fed up with visiting temples and never want to see another one again.* ◻ *He had become fed up with city life.*

fee ♦♦♢ /fiː/ (**fees**) **1** N-COUNT A **fee** is a sum of money that you pay to be allowed to do something. ◻ *He paid his license fee, and walked out with a brand-new driver's license.* **2** N-COUNT A **fee** is the amount of money that a person or organization is paid for a particular job or service that they provide. ◻ *Lawyer's fees can be substantial.* **3** → See feature box at **university**

> **COLLOCATIONS**
>
> **fee**
> NOUN **1**
> noun + **fee**: course, school, university; admission, booking, entry, exit, registration
> adjective + **fee**: annual, monthly; hefty, high; fixed, flat
> verb + **fee**: pay; charge

> **SYNONYMS**
>
> **fee**
> NOUN **1**
> **charge:** *We can arrange this for a small charge.*
> **cost:** *Badges are also available at a cost of $2.50.*
> **bill:** *They couldn't afford to pay the bills.*
> **toll:** *We pay enough in toll charges to use their roads.*

fee|ble /fiːbəl/ (**feebler, feeblest**) **1** ADJ If you describe someone or something as **feeble**, you mean that they are weak. ◻ *He told them he was old and feeble and was not able to walk so far.* • **fee|bly** ADV [ADV with v] ◻ *His left hand moved feebly at his side.* **2** ADJ If you describe something that someone says as **feeble**, you mean that it is not very good or convincing. ◻ *This is a particularly feeble argument.* • **fee|bly** ADV [ADV with v] ◻ *I said "Sorry," very feebly, feeling rather embarrassed.*

feed ♦♦♢ /fiːd/ (**feeds, feeding, fed**) **1** V-T If you **feed** a person or animal, you give them food to eat and sometimes actually put it in their mouths. ◻ *We brought along pieces of old bread and fed the birds.* • **feed|ing** N-UNCOUNT ◻ *The feeding of dairy cows has undergone a revolution.* **2** V-T To **feed** a family or a community means to supply food for them. ◻ *Feeding a hungry family can be expensive.* **3** V-I When an animal **feeds**, it eats or drinks something. ◻ *After a few days the caterpillars stopped feeding.* **4** V-T/V-I When a baby **feeds**, or when you **feed** it, it drinks breast milk or milk from a bottle. ◻ *When a baby is thirsty, it feeds more often.* **5** V-T To **feed** something to a place, means to supply it to that place in a steady flow. ◻ *...blood vessels that feed blood to the brain.* **6** V-T If you **feed** something into a container or piece of equipment, you put it into it. ◻ *He took the compact disc from her, then fed it into the player.* **7** V-T If you **feed** a plant, you add substances to it to make it grow well. ◻ *Feed plants to encourage steady growth.* **8** V-I If one thing **feeds** on another, it becomes stronger as a result of the other thing's existence. ◻ *The drinking and the guilt fed on each other.* **9** V-T To **feed** information into a computer means to gradually put it into it. ◻ *An automatic weather station feeds information on wind direction to the computer.* **10** N-MASS [usu n N] Animal **feed** is food given to animals, especially farm animals. ◻ *The grain just rotted and all they could use it for was animal feed.* **11** N-COUNT A **feed** is a system that tells a user when an item is available to read, for example on social media. ◻ *I saw the news on my Twitter feed.* **12** **to bite the hand that feeds you** → see **bite** **13** **mouths to feed** → see **mouth** **14** → See feature box at **farming**

> **COLLOCATIONS**
>
> **feed**
> VERB **1**
> **feed** + adverb: properly, regularly; intravenously
> NOUN **13**
> noun + **feed**: news, satellite
> adjective + **feed**: live

feed|back /fiːdbæk/ **1** N-UNCOUNT If you get **feedback** on your work or progress, someone tells you how well or badly you are doing, and how you could improve. If you get good feedback you have worked or performed well. ◻ *Continue to ask for feedback on your work.* **2** N-UNCOUNT **Feedback** is the unpleasant high-pitched sound produced by a piece of electrical equipment when part of the signal that comes out goes back into it. ◻ *The microphone screeched with feedback.*

feed|er /fiːdər/ (**feeders**) **1** ADJ [ADJ n] A **feeder** road, railroad line, or river is a smaller one that leads to a more important one. **2** N-COUNT [usu N n] **Feeder** airline and rail services connect major routes and local destinations. ❏ *...an American network of feeder airports.* **3** N-COUNT [oft N n] A **feeder** school or team provides students or players for a larger or more important one. **4** N-COUNT [oft n n] A **feeder** is a container that you fill with food for birds or animals.

feed|ing ground (**feeding grounds**) N-COUNT [usu with supp] The **feeding ground** of a group of animals or birds, is the place where they find food and eat. ❏ *The mud is a feeding ground for large numbers of birds.*

feel ♦♦♦ /fiːl/ (**feels, feeling, felt**) **1** V-LINK If you **feel** a particular emotion or physical sensation, you experience it. ❏ *I am feeling very depressed.* ❏ *Suddenly I felt a sharp pain in my shoulder.* ❏ *I felt as if all my strength had gone.* ❏ *I felt like I was being kicked in the teeth every day.* **2** V-LINK [no cont] If you talk about how an experience or event **feels**, you talk about the emotions and sensations connected with it. ❏ *It feels good to have finished a piece of work.* ❏ *The speed at which everything moved felt strange.* ❏ *Within five minutes of arriving back from vacation, it feels as if I've never been away.* **3** V-LINK [no cont] If you talk about how an object **feels**, you talk about the physical quality that you notice when you touch or hold it. For example, if something **feels** soft, you notice that it is soft when you touch it. ❏ *The metal felt smooth and cold.* ❏ *The ten-foot oars felt heavy and awkward.* • N-SING **Feel** is also a noun. ❏ *He remembered the feel of her skin.* **4** V-LINK [no cont] If you talk about how the weather **feels**, you describe the weather, especially the temperature or whether or not you think it is going to rain or snow. ❏ *It felt wintry cold that day.* **5** V-T/V-I If you **feel** an object, you touch it deliberately with your hand, so that you learn what it is like, for example, what shape it is or whether it is rough or smooth. ❏ *The doctor felt his head.* ❏ *Feel how soft the skin is in the small of the back.* **6** V-T [no cont] If you can **feel** something, you are aware of it because it is touching you. ❏ *Through several layers of clothes I could feel his muscles.* **7** V-T If you **feel** something happening, you become aware of it because of the effect it has on your body. ❏ *She felt something being pressed into her hands.* ❏ *He felt something move beside him.* **8** V-T If you **feel** yourself doing something or being in a particular state, you are aware that something is happening to you which you are unable to control. ❏ *I felt myself blush.* ❏ *If at any point you feel yourself becoming tense, make a conscious effort to relax.* **9** V-T [no cont] If you **feel** the presence of someone or something, you become aware of them, even though you cannot see or hear them. ❏ *He felt her eyes on him.* ❏ *I could feel that a man was watching me very intensely.* **10** V-T [no cont] If you **feel** that something is the case, you have a strong idea in your mind that it is the case. ❏ *I feel that not enough is being done to protect the local animal life.* ❏ *I feel certain that it will all turn out well.* **11** V-T [no cont] If you **feel** that you should do something, you think that you should do it. ❏ *I feel I should resign.* ❏ *You need not feel obliged to contribute.* **12** V-T/V-I [no cont] If you talk about how you **feel** about something, you talk about your opinion, attitude, or reaction to it. ❏ *We'd like to know what you feel about abortion.* ❏ *She feels guilty about spending less time lately with her two kids.* **13** V-I If you **feel like** doing something or having something, you want to do it or have it because you are in the right mood for it and think you would enjoy it. ❏ *Neither of them felt like going back to sleep.* **14** → see also **feeling, felt** **15** **feel free** → see **free**

▶ **feel for** **1** PHRASAL VERB If you **feel for** something, for example, in the dark, you try to find it by moving your hand around until you touch it. ❏ *I felt for my wallet and papers in my inside pocket.* **2** PHRASAL VERB If you **feel for** someone, you have sympathy for them. ❏ *She cried on the phone and I really felt for her.*

feel|er /fiːlər/ (**feelers**) **1** N-COUNT [usu pl] An insect's **feelers** are the two thin stalks on its head with which it touches and senses things around it. **2** N-PLURAL If you put out **feelers**, you make careful, quiet contacts with people in order to get information from them, or to find out what their reaction will be to a suggestion. ❏ *When vacancies occur, the office puts out feelers to the universities.*

feel|good /fiːlɡʊd/ also **feel-good** **1** ADJ [ADJ n] A **feelgood** movie is a movie which presents people and life in a way which makes the people who watch it feel happy and optimistic. ❏ *This could be the feelgood movie of the season.* **2** PHRASE When journalists refer to **the feelgood factor**, they mean that people are feeling hopeful and optimistic about the future. [BRIT]

feel|ing ♦♦◇ /fiːlɪŋ/ (**feelings**) **1** N-COUNT A **feeling** is an emotion, such as anger or happiness. ❏ *It gave me a feeling of satisfaction.* ❏ *He was unable to contain his own destructive feelings.* **2** N-COUNT If you have a **feeling** of hunger, tiredness, or other physical sensation, you experience it. ❏ *I also had a strange feeling in my neck.* ❏ *Focus on the feeling of relaxation.* **3** N-COUNT If you have a **feeling** that something is the case or that something is going to happen, you think that is probably the case or that it is probably going to happen. ❏ *I have a feeling that everything will be all right.* **4** N-PLURAL Your **feelings** about something are the things that you think and feel about it, or your attitude toward it. ❏ *Everyone knows what my feelings are on that.* ❏ *I think that sums up the feelings of most discerning and intelligent Indians.* **5** N-PLURAL When you refer to someone's **feelings**, you are talking about the things that might embarrass, offend, or upset them. For example, if you hurt someone's **feelings**, you upset them by something that you say or do. ❏ *He was afraid of hurting my feelings.* **6** N-UNCOUNT **Feeling** is a way of thinking and reacting to things which is emotional and not planned rather than logical and practical. ❏ *He was prompted to a rare outburst of feeling.* **7** N-UNCOUNT **Feeling for** someone is love, affection, sympathy, or concern for them. ❏ *Thomas never lost his feeling for Harriet.* **8** N-UNCOUNT **Feeling** in part of your body is the ability to experience the sense of touch in this part of the body. ❏ *After the accident he had no feeling in his legs.* **9** N-UNCOUNT **Feeling** is used to refer to a general opinion that a group of people has about something. ❏ *There is still some feeling in the art world that the market for such works may be declining.* **10** N-SING If you have a **feeling of being** in a particular situation, you feel that you are in that situation. ❏ *I had the terrible feeling of being left behind to bring up the baby while he had fun.* **11** N-SING If something such as a place or book creates a particular kind of **feeling**, it creates a particular kind of atmosphere. ❏ *That's what we tried to portray in the book, this feeling of opulence and grandeur.* **12** → see also **feel** **13** PHRASE **Bad feeling** or **ill feeling** is bitterness or anger which exists between people, for example, after they have had an argument. ❏ *There's been some bad feeling between the two families.* **14** PHRASE **Hard feelings** are feelings of anger or bitterness toward someone who you have had an argument with or who has upset you. If you say '**no hard feelings**,' you are making an agreement with someone not to be angry or bitter about something. ❏ *I don't want any hard feelings between our companies.*

> **SYNONYMS**
>
> **feeling**
> NOUN **4**
> **opinion:** *I wasn't asking for your opinion, Dick.*
> **view:** *You should also make your views known to your local representative.*
> **attitude:** *His attitude made me angry.*
> **belief:** *It is our belief that improvements in health care will lead to a stronger economy.*

feel|ing|ly /fiːlɪŋli/ ADV [ADV after v] If someone says something **feelingly**, they say it in a way which shows that they have very strong feelings about what they are saying. ❏ *"It's what I want," she said feelingly.*

feet /fiːt/ **Feet** is the plural of **foot**.

feign /feɪn/ (**feigns, feigning, feigned**) V-T If someone **feigns** a particular feeling, attitude, or physical condition, they try to make other people think that they have it or are experiencing it, although this is not true. [FORMAL] ❏ *One morning, I didn't want to go to school, and decided to feign illness.*

feint /feɪnt/ (**feints, feinting, feinted**) V-I In sports or military conflict, if someone **feints**, they make a brief movement in a different direction from the one they intend to follow, as a way of confusing or deceiving their opponent. ❏ *I feinted to the left, then to the right.* ❏ *They feinted and concentrated forces against the most fortified line of the enemy side.*

feisty /faɪsti/ (**feistier, feistiest**) ADJ If you describe someone as **feisty**, you mean that they are tough, independent, and spirited, often when you would not expect them to be, for example, because they are old or ill. ❏ *At 66, she was as feisty as ever.*

fe|lici|tous /fɪlɪsɪtəs/ ADJ If you describe a remark or idea as **felicitous**, you approve of it because it seems particularly suitable in the circumstances. [FORMAL, APPROVAL] ❑ *Her prose style is not always felicitous; she tends to repetition.*

fe|lic|ity /fɪlɪsɪti/ **1** N-UNCOUNT **Felicity** is great happiness and pleasure. [LITERARY] ❑ *...joy and felicity.* **2** N-UNCOUNT **Felicity** is the quality of being good, pleasant, or desirable. [LITERARY] ❑ *...his conversational manner and easy verbal felicity.*

fe|line /fiːlaɪn/ (**felines**) **1** ADJ [ADJ n] **Feline** means belonging or relating to the cat family. **2** ADJ [usu ADJ n] You can use **feline** to describe someone's appearance or movements if they are elegant or graceful in a way that makes you think of a cat. [LITERARY] ❑ *She moves with feline grace.* **3** N-COUNT A **feline** is an animal that belongs to the cat family. ❑ *The 16-pound feline is so fat she can hardly walk.*

fell /fɛl/ (**fells, felling, felled**) **1** **Fell** is the past tense of **fall**. **2** V-T [usu passive] If trees **are felled**, they are cut down. ❑ *Badly infected trees should be felled and burned.* **3** **in one fell swoop** → see **swoop**

fel|la /fɛlə/ (**fellas**) also **feller** N-COUNT [usu with supp] You can refer to a man as a **fella**. [INFORMAL, OLD-FASHIONED] ❑ *He's an intelligent man and a nice fella.*

fel|la|tio /fəleɪʃioʊ, -ʃoʊ/ N-UNCOUNT **Fellatio** is oral sex which involves someone using their mouth to stimulate their partner's penis.

fel|low ✦✧✧ /fɛloʊ/ (**fellows**) **1** ADJ [ADJ n] You use **fellow** to describe people who are in the same situation as you, or people you feel you have something in common with. ❑ *She discovered, to her pleasure, a talent for making her fellow guests laugh.* **2** N-COUNT A **fellow** is a man or boy. [INFORMAL, OLD-FASHIONED] ❑ *By all accounts, Rodger would appear to be a fine fellow.* **3** N-COUNT A **fellow** of an academic or professional association is someone who is a specially elected member of it, usually because of their work or achievements or as a mark of honor. ❑ *...the fellows of the Zoological Society.* **4** N-PLURAL [poss N] Your **fellows** are the people who you work with, do things with, or who are like you in some way. [FORMAL] ❑ *He stood out in terms of competence from all his fellows.*

fel|low feel|ing also **fellow-feeling** N-UNCOUNT **Fellow feeling** is sympathy and friendship that exists between people who have shared similar experiences or difficulties.

fel|low|ship /fɛloʊʃɪp/ (**fellowships**) **1** N-COUNT A **fellowship** is a group of people that join together for a common purpose or interest. ❑ *...the National Schizophrenia Fellowship.* **2** N-COUNT A **fellowship** at a university is a post which involves research work. ❑ *He was offered a research fellowship at Yale.* **3** N-UNCOUNT **Fellowship** is a feeling of friendship that people have when they are talking or doing something together and sharing their experiences. ❑ *...a sense of community and fellowship.*

fel|on /fɛlən/ (**felons**) N-COUNT A **felon** is a person who is guilty of committing a felony. [LEGAL] ❑ *He's a convicted felon.*

felo|ny /fɛləni/ (**felonies**) N-COUNT In countries where the legal system distinguishes between very serious crimes and less serious ones, a **felony** is a very serious crime such as armed robbery. [LEGAL] ❑ *He pleaded guilty to six felonies.*

felt /fɛlt/ **1** **Felt** is the past tense and past participle of **feel**. **2** N-UNCOUNT [oft N n] **Felt** is a thick cloth made from wool or other fibers packed tightly together. ❑ *She had on an old felt hat.*

felt-tip (**felt-tips**) N-COUNT A **felt-tip** or a **felt-tip pen** is a pen which has a piece of fiber at the end that the ink comes through.

fem. **fem.** is a written abbreviation for **female** or **feminine**.

fe|male ✦✧✧ /fiːmeɪl/ (**females**) **1** ADJ Someone who is **female** is a woman or a girl. ❑ *...a sixteen-piece dance band with a female singer.* **2** ADJ [ADJ n] **Female** matters and things relate to, belong to, or affect women rather than men. ❑ *...female infertility.* **3** N-COUNT Women and girls are sometimes referred to as **females** when they are being considered as a type. ❑ *Hay fever affects males more than females.* **4** N-COUNT You can refer to any creature that can lay eggs or produce babies from its body as a **female**. ❑ *Each female will lay just one egg in April or May.* • ADJ **Female** is also an adjective. ❑ *...the scent given off by the female aphid to attract the male.*

femi|nine /fɛmɪnɪn/ **1** ADJ **Feminine** qualities and things relate to or are considered typical of women, in contrast to men. ❑ *...traditional feminine roles.* **2** ADJ Someone or something that is **feminine** has qualities that are considered typical of women, especially being pretty or gentle. [APPROVAL] ❑ *I've always been attracted to very feminine women.* **3** ADJ In some languages, a **feminine** noun, pronoun, or adjective has a different form from a masculine or neuter one, or behaves in a different way.

femi|nin|ity /fɛmɪnɪnɪti/ **1** N-UNCOUNT A woman's **femininity** is the fact that she is a woman. ❑ *...the drudgery behind the ideology of motherhood and femininity.* **2** N-UNCOUNT **Femininity** means the qualities that are considered to be typical of women. ❑ *I wonder if there isn't a streak of femininity in him, a kind of sweetness.*

femi|nism /fɛmɪnɪzəm/ N-UNCOUNT **Feminism** is the belief and aim that women should have the same rights, power, and opportunities as men. ❑ *...Barbara Johnson, that champion of radical feminism.*

femi|nist /fɛmɪnɪst/ (**feminists**) **1** N-COUNT A **feminist** is a person who believes in and supports feminism. ❑ *Only 16 percent of young women in the survey considered themselves feminists.* **2** ADJ [ADJ n] **Feminist** groups, ideas, and activities are involved in feminism.

femi|nize /fɛmɪnaɪz/ (**feminizes, feminizing, feminized**)

in BRIT, also use **feminise**

V-T To **feminize** something means to make it into something that involves mainly women or is thought suitable for or typical of women. [FORMAL] ❑ *...their governments' policies of feminizing low-paid factory work.* ❑ *...a feminized pinstriped suit.*

femme fa|tale /fæm fətɑːl/ (**femmes fatales**) N-COUNT [usu sing] If a woman has a reputation as a **femme fatale**, she is considered to be very attractive sexually, and likely to cause problems for anyone who is attracted to her.

fe|mur /fiːmər/ (**femurs**) **1** N-COUNT Your **femur** is the large bone in the upper part of your leg. **2** → See also color supplement

fen /fɛn/ (**fens**) N-VAR **Fen** is used to refer to an area of low, flat, wet land. ❑ *This is fen country – the mills drive pumps that drain the land.*

fence ✦✧✧ /fɛns/ (**fences, fencing, fenced**) **1** N-COUNT A **fence** is a barrier between two areas of land, made of wood or wire supported by posts. ❑ *Villagers say the fence would restrict public access to the hills.* **2** N-COUNT A **fence** in show jumping or horse racing is an obstacle or barrier that horses have to jump over. ❑ *The horse fell at the last fence.* **3** V-T If you **fence** an area of land, you surround it with a fence. ❑ *The first task was to fence the wood to exclude sheep.* **4** PHRASE If you **sit on the fence**, you avoid supporting a particular side in a discussion or argument. ❑ *They are sitting on the fence and refusing to commit themselves.*

fenc|ing /fɛnsɪŋ/ **1** N-UNCOUNT **Fencing** is a sport in which two competitors fight each other using very thin swords. The ends of the swords are covered and the competitors wear protective clothes, so that they do not hurt each other. ❑ *...the amateur fencing champion.* **2** N-UNCOUNT Materials such as wood or wire that are used to make fences are called **fencing**. ❑ *...old wooden fencing.*

fend /fɛnd/ (**fends, fending, fended**) V-I If you have to **fend for** yourself, you have to look after yourself without relying on help from anyone else. ❑ *The woman and her young baby had been thrown out and left to fend for themselves.*

▶ **fend off** **1** PHRASAL VERB If you **fend off** unwanted questions, problems, or people, you stop them from affecting you or defend yourself from them, but often only for a short time and without dealing with them completely. ❑ *He looked relaxed and determined as he fended off questions from the world's Press.* **2** PHRASAL VERB If you **fend off** someone who is attacking you, you use your arms or something such as a stick to defend yourself from their blows. ❑ *He raised his hand to fend off the blow.*

fend|er /fɛndər/ (**fenders**) **1** N-COUNT The **fenders** of a car are the parts of the body over the wheels. [AM] ❑ *Todd sat on the front fender, his legs dangling toward the ground.* **2** → See also color supplement

feng shui /fʌŋ ʃweɪ/ N-UNCOUNT **Feng shui** is a Chinese art which is based on the belief that the way you arrange things

fen|nel /fɛnᵊl/ N-UNCOUNT **Fennel** is a plant with a crisp rounded base and feathery leaves. It can be eaten as a vegetable or the leaves can be used as a herb.

fe|ral /fɛrəl, fɪər-/ ADJ [usu ADJ n] **Feral** animals are wild animals that are not owned or controlled by anyone, especially ones that belong to species which are normally owned and kept by people. [FORMAL] ❑ ...feral cats.

fer|ment (ferments, fermenting, fermented)

> The noun is pronounced /fɜrmɛnt/. The verb is pronounced /fərmɛnt/.

■ N-UNCOUNT **Ferment** is excitement and trouble caused by change or uncertainty. ❑ The whole country has been in a state of political ferment for some months. ■ V-T/V-I If a food, drink, or other natural substance **ferments**, or if it **is fermented**, a chemical change takes place in it so that alcohol is produced. This process forms part of the production of alcoholic drinks such as wine and beer. ❑ The dried grapes are allowed to ferment until there is no sugar left and the wine is dry. • **fer|men|ta|tion** /fɜrmɛnteɪʃᵊn/ N-UNCOUNT ❑ Yeast is essential for the fermentation that produces alcohol.

fern /fɜrn/ (ferns) N-VAR A **fern** is a plant that has long stems with feathery leaves and no flowers. There are many types of fern.

fe|ro|cious /fərouʃəs/ ■ ADJ A **ferocious** animal, person, or action is very fierce and violent. ❑ By its very nature a lion is ferocious. ■ ADJ A **ferocious** war, argument, or other form of conflict involves a great deal of anger, bitterness, and determination. ❑ Fighting has been ferocious.

fe|roc|ity /fərɒsɪti/ N-UNCOUNT The **ferocity** of something is its fierce or violent nature. ❑ The armed forces seem to have been taken by surprise by the ferocity of the attack.

fer|ret /fɛrɪt/ (ferrets, ferreting, ferreted) N-COUNT A **ferret** is a small, fierce animal which is used for hunting rabbits and rats.

▶ **ferret out** PHRASAL VERB If you **ferret out** some information, you discover it by searching for it very thoroughly. [INFORMAL] ❑ The team is trying to ferret out missing details. ❑ I leave it to the reader to ferret these out.

> **WORD HISTORY**
> **ferret**
> **Ferret** comes from Old French *furet* meaning 'little thief,' from Latin *fūr*, meaning 'thief.'

Fer|ris wheel /fɛrɪs wil/ (Ferris wheels) also **ferris wheel** N-COUNT A **Ferris wheel** is a very large upright wheel with cars around the edge of it which people can ride in. Ferris wheels are often found at amusement parks or carnivals. [AM]

> in BRIT, also use **big wheel**

fer|rous /fɛrəs/ ADJ [ADJ n] **Ferrous** means containing or relating to iron. ❑ ...ferrous metals. ❑ ...ferrous chloride.

fer|rule /fɛrᵊl/ (ferrules) N-COUNT A **ferrule** is a metal or rubber cap that is fixed onto the end of a stick or post in order to prevent it from splitting or wearing down. [FORMAL]

fer|ry /fɛri/ (ferries, ferrying, ferried) ■ N-COUNT [also by N] A **ferry** is a boat that transports passengers and sometimes also vehicles, usually across rivers or short stretches of sea. ❑ They had recrossed the River Gambia by ferry. ■ V-T If a vehicle **ferries** people or goods, it transports them, usually by means of regular trips between the same two places. ❑ Every day, a plane arrives to ferry guests to and from Bird Island Lodge. ■ → See feature box at **boat**; See also color supplement

fer|ry|boat /fɛribout/ (ferryboats) N-COUNT A **ferryboat** is a boat used as a ferry.

fer|tile /fɜrtᵊl/ ■ ADJ Land or soil that is **fertile** is able to support the growth of a large number of strong healthy plants. ❑ ...fertile soil. • **fer|til|ity** /fɜrtɪlɪti/ N-UNCOUNT ❑ He was able to bring large sterile acreages back to fertility. ■ ADJ A **fertile** mind or imagination is able to produce a lot of good, original ideas. ❑ ...a product of Flynn's fertile imagination. ■ ADJ [ADJ n] A situation or environment that is **fertile** in relation to a particular activity or feeling encourages the activity or feeling. ❑ ...a fertile breeding ground for disharmony of one kind or another. ■ ADJ A person or animal that is **fertile** is able to reproduce and have babies or young. ❑ The operation cannot be reversed to make her fertile again. • **fer|til|ity** N-UNCOUNT ❑ Doctors will tell you that pregnancy is the only sure test for fertility.

fer|ti|lize /fɜrtᵊlaɪz/ (fertilizes, fertilizing, fertilized)

> in BRIT, also use **fertilise**

■ V-T When an egg from the ovary of a woman or female animal **is fertilized**, a sperm from the male joins with the egg, causing a baby or young animal to begin forming. A female plant **is fertilized** when its reproductive parts come into contact with pollen from the male plant. ❑ Certain varieties cannot be fertilized with their own pollen. ❑ ...the normal sperm levels needed to fertilize the egg. • **fer|ti|li|za|tion** /fɜrtᵊlɪzeɪʃᵊn/ N-UNCOUNT ❑ From fertilization until birth is about 266 days. ■ V-T To **fertilize** land means to improve its quality in order to make plants grow well on it, by spreading solid animal waste or a chemical mixture on it. ❑ The feces contain nitrogen which fertilizes the soil.

fer|ti|liz|er /fɜrtᵊlaɪzər/ (fertilizers)

> in BRIT, also use **fertiliser**

N-MASS **Fertilizer** is a substance such as solid animal waste or a chemical mixture that you spread on the ground in order to make plants grow more successfully. ❑ ...farming without any purchased chemical, fertilizer or pesticide.

fer|vent /fɜrvᵊnt/ ADJ A **fervent** person has or shows strong feelings about something, and is very sincere and enthusiastic about it. ❑ ...a fervent admirer of Morisot's work. • **fer|vent|ly** ADV ❑ Their claims will be fervently denied.

fer|vor /fɜrvər/

> in BRIT, use **fervour**

N-UNCOUNT **Fervor** for something is a very strong feeling for or belief in it. [FORMAL] ❑ They were concerned only with their own religious fervor.

fes|ter /fɛstər/ (festers, festering, festered) ■ V-I If you say that a situation, problem, or feeling **is festering**, you disapprove of the fact that it is being allowed to grow more unpleasant or full of anger, because it is not being properly recognized or dealt with. [DISAPPROVAL] ❑ Resentments are starting to fester. ■ V-I If a wound **festers**, it becomes infected, making it worse. ❑ The wound is festering, and gangrene has set in.

fes|ti|val ✦✦◇ /fɛstɪvᵊl/ (festivals) ■ N-COUNT A **festival** is an organized series of events such as musical concerts or drama productions. ❑ Many towns hold their own summer festivals of music, theater, and dance. ■ N-COUNT A **festival** is a day or time of the year when people do not go to work or school and celebrate some special event, often a religious event. ❑ Shavuot is a two-day festival for Orthodox Jews. ■ → See feature box at **humor**

fes|tive /fɛstɪv/ ■ ADJ Something that is **festive** is special, colorful, or exciting, especially because of a holiday or celebration. ❑ The town has a festive holiday atmosphere. ■ ADJ [ADJ n] **Festive** means relating to a holiday or celebration, especially Christmas. ❑ With Christmas just around the corner, you should start your festive cooking now.

fes|tive sea|son N-SING [usu the N] People sometimes refer to the Christmas period as the **festive season**.

fes|tiv|ity /fɛstɪvɪti/ (festivities) ■ N-UNCOUNT **Festivity** is the celebration of something in a happy way. ❑ There was a general air of festivity and abandon. ■ N-COUNT **Festivities** are events that are organized in order to celebrate something. ❑ The festivities included a huge display of fireworks.

fes|toon /fɛstun/ (festoons, festooning, festooned) V-T [usu passive] If something **is festooned** with, for example, lights, balloons, or flowers, large numbers of these things are hung from it or wrapped around it, especially in order to decorate it. ❑ The temples are festooned with lights.

feta /fɛtə/ N-UNCOUNT **Feta** is a type of salty white cheese made from goats' or sheep's milk. It is traditionally made in Greece.

fe|tal /fitᵊl/ ADJ [ADJ n] **Fetal** is used to describe something that relates to or is like a fetus. ❑ ...somewhere between the fourth and fifth month of fetal development.

fe|tal po|si|tion (fetal positions) N-COUNT [usu a/the N] If someone is in the **fetal position**, their body is curled up like a fetus in the womb. [AM] ❑ *She lay in a fetal position, turned away from him to the wall.*

fetch /fɛtʃ/ (fetches, fetching, fetched) **1** V-T If you **fetch** something or someone, you go and get them from the place where they are. ❑ *Sylvia fetched a towel from the bathroom.* ❑ *Fetch me a glass of water.* **2** V-T If something **fetches** a particular sum of money, it is sold for that amount. ❑ *The painting is expected to fetch between two and three million dollars.* **3** → see also **far-fetched**

fetch|ing /fɛtʃɪŋ/ ADJ If you describe someone or something as **fetching**, you think that they look very attractive. [OLD-FASHIONED] ❑ *Sue was sitting up in bed, looking very fetching in a flowered bed jacket.*

fete /feɪt, fɛt/ (fetes, feting, feted) also **fête** **1** N-COUNT A **fete** is a fancy party or celebration. [AM] ❑ *The pop star flew 100 friends in from London and Paris for a two-day fete.* **2** V-T [usu passive] If someone **is feted**, they are celebrated, welcomed, or admired by the public. ❑ *Vera Wang was feted in New York this week at a spectacular dinner.*

fet|id /fɛtɪd, fi-/ ADJ [usu ADJ n] **Fetid** water or air has a very strong unpleasant smell. [FORMAL] ❑ *...the fetid river of waste.* ❑ *...the fetid stench of vomit.*

fet|ish /fɛtɪʃ/ (fetishes) **1** N-COUNT [oft n N] If someone has a **fetish**, they have an unusually strong liking or need for a particular object or activity, as a way of getting sexual pleasure. ❑ *...rubber and leather fetishes.* ❑ *...fetish wear for sexual arousal.* **2** N-COUNT [usu with supp] If you say that someone has a **fetish** for doing something, you disapprove of the fact that they do it very often or enjoy it very much. [DISAPPROVAL] ❑ *What began as a postwar fetish for sunbathing is rapidly developing into a world health crisis.* **3** N-COUNT In some cultures, a **fetish** is an object, especially a carved object, which is considered to have religious importance or magical powers.

fet|ish|ism /fɛtɪʃɪzəm/ N-UNCOUNT **Fetishism** involves a person having a strong liking or need for a particular object or activity which gives them sexual pleasure and excitement.

fet|ish|ist /fɛtɪʃɪst/ (fetishists) N-COUNT [usu n N] A **fetishist** is a person who has a strong liking or need for a particular object or activity in order to experience sexual pleasure and excitement. ❑ *...a foot fetishist.*

fet|lock /fɛtlɒk/ (fetlocks) N-COUNT A horse's **fetlock** is the back part of its leg, just above the hoof.

fet|ter /fɛtər/ (fetters, fettering, fettered) **1** V-T If you say that you **are fettered** by something, you dislike it because it prevents you from behaving or moving in a free and natural way. [LITERARY, DISAPPROVAL] ❑ *...a private trust which would not be fettered by bureaucracy.* ❑ *The black mud fettered her movements.* **2** N-PLURAL You can use **fetters** to refer to things such as rules, traditions, or responsibilities that you dislike because they prevent you from behaving in the way you want. [LITERARY, DISAPPROVAL]

fet|tle /fɛt°l/ PHRASE If you say that someone or something is **in fine fettle**, you mean that they are in very good health or condition. [INFORMAL, OLD-FASHIONED] ❑ *You seem in fine fettle.*

fe|tus /fitəs/ (fetuses) **1** N-COUNT A **fetus** is an animal or human being in its later stages of development before it is born. ❑ *Pregnant women who are heavy drinkers risk damaging the unborn fetus.* **2** → See feature box at **birth**

feud /fyud/ (feuds, feuding, feuded) **1** N-COUNT A **feud** is a quarrel in which two people or groups remain angry with each other for a long time, although they are not always fighting or arguing. ❑ *...a long and bitter feud between the state government and the villagers.* **2** V-RECIP If one person or group **feuds** with another, they have a quarrel that lasts a long time. You can also say that two people or groups **feud**. ❑ *He feuded with his ex-wife.*

feu|dal /fyud°l/ **1** ADJ [ADJ n] **Feudal** means relating to the system or the time of feudalism. ❑ *...the emperor and his feudal barons.* **2** → See feature box at **history**

feu|dal|ism /fyud°lɪzəm/ N-UNCOUNT **Feudalism** was a system in which people were given land and protection by people of higher rank, and worked and fought for them in return. ❑ *As feudalism decayed in the West it gave rise to a mercantile class.*

fe|ver /fivər/ (fevers) **1** N-VAR If you have a **fever** when you are ill, your body temperature is higher than usual. ❑ *My Uncle Jim had a high fever.* **2** → see also **hay fever**

fe|ver blis|ter (fever blisters) N-COUNT **Fever blisters** are small sore spots that sometimes appear on or near someone's lips and nose when they have a cold. [AM]

in BRIT, use **cold sore**

fe|vered /fivərd/ **1** ADJ [usu ADJ n] **Fevered** is used to describe feelings of great excitement, and the activities that result from them. [WRITTEN] ❑ *Meg was in a state of fevered anticipation.* ❑ *...fevered speculation over the leadership.* **2** ADJ [usu ADJ n] If a person is **fevered**, or they have a **fevered** brow, they are suffering from a fever. [LITERARY]

fe|ver|ish /fivərɪʃ/ **1** ADJ **Feverish** activity is done extremely quickly, often in a state of nervousness or excitement because you want to finish it as soon as possible. ❑ *Hours of feverish activity lay ahead. The tents had to be erected, the stalls set up.* **2** ADJ If you are **feverish**, you are suffering from a fever. ❑ *A feverish child refuses to eat and asks only for cold drinks.* • **fe|ver|ish|ly** ADV ❑ *He slept feverishly all afternoon and into the night.*

fe|ver pitch N-UNCOUNT [oft at N] If something is at **fever pitch**, it is in an extremely active or excited state. ❑ *Campaigning is reaching fever pitch for elections on November 6.*

few ✦✦✦ /fyu/ (fewer, fewest) **1** DET You use **a few** to indicate that you are talking about a small number of people or things. You can also say **a very few**. ❑ *I gave a dinner party for a few close friends.* ❑ *Here are a few more ideas to consider.* • PRON **Few** is also a pronoun. ❑ *Doctors work an average of 90 hours a week, while a few are on call for up to 120 hours.* • QUANT [QUANT of def-pl-n] **Few** is also a quantifier. ❑ *There are many ways eggs can be prepared; here are a few of them.* **2** DET You use **few** to indicate that you are talking about a small number of people or things. You can use 'so,' 'too,' and 'very' in front of **few**. ❑ *She had few friends, and was generally not functioning up to her potential.* ❑ *Few members planned to vote for him.* • PRON **Few** is also a pronoun. ❑ *Few can survive more than a week without water.* • QUANT [QUANT of def-pl-n] **Few** is also a quantifier. ❑ *Few of the beach houses still had lights on.* • ADJ **Few** is also an adjective. ❑ *...spending her few waking hours in front of the TV.* **3** ADJ [adj/det ADJ n] You use **few** after adjectives and determiners to indicate that you are talking about a small number of things or people. ❑ *The past few weeks of her life had been the most pleasant she could remember.* ❑ *...in the last few chapters.* **4** N-SING **The few** means a small set of people considered as separate from the majority, especially because they share a particular opportunity or quality that the others do not have. ❑ *This should not be an experience for the few.* **5** PHRASE You use **as few as** before a number to suggest that it is surprisingly small. [EMPHASIS] ❑ *One study showed that even as few as ten cigarettes a day can damage fertility.* **6** PHRASE Things that are **few and far between** are very rare or do not happen very often. [EMPHASIS] ❑ *Visitors to the town were few and far between.* **7** PHRASE You use **no fewer than** to emphasize that a number is surprisingly large. [EMPHASIS] ❑ *No fewer than thirteen foreign ministers attended the session.*

fey /feɪ/ ADJ If you describe someone as **fey**, you mean that they behave in a shy, childish, or unpredictable way, and you are often suggesting that this is unnatural or insincere. [LITERARY] ❑ *Her fey charm and eccentric ways were legendary.*

fez /fɛz/ (fezzes) **1** N-COUNT A **fez** is a round, red hat with no brim and a flat top. **2** → See also color supplement

ff. also **ff** **1** In a book or magazine, when **ff.** is written it refers to the page or line mentioned and two or more pages or lines after it. ❑ *...p. 173 ff.* **2** In a piece of music, **ff.** is a written abbreviation for **fortissimo**.

FGM /ɛf dʒi ɛm/ N-UNCOUNT **FGM** is the practice of cutting off some or all of the outer sex organs of a girl or woman. It is illegal in many countries. **FGM** is an abbreviation for 'female genital mutilation.'

fi|an|cé /fiɑnseɪ, fiɑnseɪ/ (fiancés) N-COUNT [usu poss N] Someone's **fiancé** is the man to whom they are engaged to be married.

fi|an|cée /fiɑnseɪ, fiɑnseɪ/ (fiancées) N-COUNT [usu poss N] Someone's **fiancée** is the woman to whom they are engaged to be married.

fi|as|co /fiæskoʊ/ (**fiascos**) N-COUNT If you describe an event or an attempt to do something as a **fiasco**, you are emphasizing that it fails completely. [EMPHASIS] ❑ *The blame for the Charleston fiasco did not lie with him.*

fiat /fiæt, faɪ-/ (**fiats**) N-COUNT [also by N] If something is done by **fiat**, it is done because of an official order given by someone in authority. [FORMAL] ❑ *He has tried to impose solutions to the country's problems by fiat.*

fib /fɪb/ (**fibs, fibbing, fibbed**) ■ N-COUNT A **fib** is a small, unimportant lie. [INFORMAL] ❑ *She told innocent fibs like anyone else.* ■ V-I If someone **is fibbing**, they are telling lies. [INFORMAL] ❑ *He laughs loudly when I accuse him of fibbing.*

fi|ber /faɪbər/ (**fibers**)

in BRIT, use **fibre**

■ N-COUNT A **fiber** is a thin thread of a natural or artificial substance, especially one that is used to make cloth or rope. ❑ *If you look at the paper under a microscope you will see the fibers.* ■ N-COUNT A **fiber** is a thin piece of flesh like a thread which connects nerve cells in your body or which muscles are made of. ❑ *...the nerve fibers.* ■ N-VAR A particular **fiber** is a type of cloth or other material that is made from or consists of threads. ❑ *The ball is made of rattan – a natural fiber.* ■ N-UNCOUNT **Fiber** consists of the parts of plants or seeds that your body cannot digest. Fiber is useful because it makes food pass quickly through your body. ❑ *Most vegetables contain fiber.* ■ → See feature box at **nutrition**

fiber|glass /faɪbərglæs/

in BRIT, use **fibreglass**

■ N-UNCOUNT **Fiberglass** is plastic strengthened with short, thin threads of glass. ■ N-UNCOUNT **Fiberglass** is a material made from short, thin threads of glass which can be used to stop heat from escaping.

fi|ber op|tics

The spelling **fibre optics** is used in British English. The form **fiber optic** is used as a modifier.

■ N-UNCOUNT **Fiber optics** is the use of long thin threads of glass to carry information in the form of light. ■ ADJ [ADJ n] **Fiber optic** means relating to or involved in fiber optics. ❑ *...fiber optic cables.*

fi|broid /faɪbrɔɪd/ (**fibroids**) N-COUNT [usu pl] **Fibroids** are lumps of fibrous tissue that form in a woman's womb, often causing pain. [MEDICAL]

fi|brous /faɪbrəs/ ADJ [usu ADJ n] A **fibrous** object or substance contains a lot of fibers or fiber, or looks as if it does. ❑ *...fibrous tissue.*

fibu|la /fɪbyələ/ (**fibulae**) ■ N-COUNT Your **fibula** is the outer bone of the two bones in the lower part of your leg. [MEDICAL] ■ → See also color supplement

fick|le /fɪkəl/ ■ ADJ If you describe someone as **fickle**, you disapprove of them because they keep changing their mind about what they like or want. [DISAPPROVAL] ❑ *The group has been notoriously fickle in the past.* ■ ADJ If you say that something is **fickle**, you mean that it often changes and is unreliable. ❑ *New England's weather can be fickle.*

fic|tion /fɪkʃən/ (**fictions**) ■ N-UNCOUNT **Fiction** refers to books and stories about imaginary people and events, rather than books about real people or events. ❑ *Immigrant tales have always been popular themes in fiction.* ■ → see also **science fiction** ■ N-UNCOUNT A statement or account that is **fiction** is not true. ❑ *The truth or fiction of this story has never been truly determined.* ■ N-COUNT If something is a **fiction**, it is not true, although people sometimes pretend that it is true. ❑ *Total recycling is a fiction.* ■ → See feature box at **book**

fic|tion|al /fɪkʃənəl/ ADJ **Fictional** characters or events occur only in stories, plays, or movies and never actually existed or happened. ❑ *It is drama featuring fictional characters.*

fic|tion|al|ize /fɪkʃənəlaɪz/ (**fictionalizes, fictionalizing, fictionalized**)

in BRIT, also use **fictionalise**

V-T To **fictionalize** an account of something that really happened means to tell it as a story, with some details changed or added. ❑ *We had to fictionalize names.* ❑ *...a fictionalized account of a true and horrific story.*

fic|ti|tious /fɪktɪʃəs/ ■ ADJ **Fictitious** is used to describe something that is false or does not exist, although some people claim that it is true or exists. ❑ *We're interested in the source of these fictitious rumors.* ■ ADJ A **fictitious** character, thing, or event occurs in a story, play, or movie but never really existed or happened. ❑ *The persons and events portrayed in this production are fictitious.*

fid|dle /fɪdəl/ (**fiddles, fiddling, fiddled**) ■ V-I If you **fiddle with** an object, you keep moving it or touching it with your fingers. ❑ *Harriet fiddled with a pen on the desk.* ■ V-I If you **fiddle with** something, you change it in minor ways. ❑ *She told Whistler that his portrait of her was finished and to stop fiddling with it.* ■ V-I If you **fiddle with** a machine, you adjust it. ❑ *He turned on the radio and fiddled with the knob until he got a talk show.* ■ N-VAR Some people call violins **fiddles**, especially when they are used to play folk music. ❑ *Hardy played the fiddle at local dances.*

fid|dler /fɪdələr/ (**fiddlers**) N-COUNT A **fiddler** is someone who plays the violin, especially one who plays folk music.

fid|dling /fɪdəlɪŋ/ ■ N-UNCOUNT Violin playing, especially in folk music, is sometimes referred to as **fiddling**. ■ ADJ [usu ADJ n] You can describe something as **fiddling** if it is small, unimportant, or difficult to do. ❑ *...the daunting amount of fiddling technical detail.*

fi|del|ity /fɪdɛlɪti/ ■ N-UNCOUNT **Fidelity** is loyalty to a person, organization, or set of beliefs. [FORMAL] ❑ *People have failed to act in fidelity to their vows.* ■ N-UNCOUNT **Fidelity** to a sexual partner is not having a sexual relationship with anyone else. ❑ *Wanting fidelity implies you're thinking about a major relationship.*

fidg|et /fɪdʒɪt/ (**fidgets, fidgeting, fidgeted**) ■ V-I If you **fidget**, you keep moving your hands or feet slightly or changing your position slightly, for example, because you are nervous, bored, or excited. ❑ *Brenda fidgeted in her seat.* • PHRASAL VERB **Fidget around** and **fidget about** mean the same as **fidget**. ❑ *There were two new arrivals, fidgeting around, waiting to ask questions.* ■ V-I If you **fidget with** something, you keep moving it or touching it with your fingers with small movements, for example, because you are nervous or bored. ❑ *He fidgeted with his tie.* ■ → See feature box at **body language**

fidg|ety /fɪdʒɪti/ ADJ Someone who is **fidgety** keeps fidgeting, for example, because they are nervous or bored.

fi|du|ci|ary /fɪduʃiɛri/ ADJ [usu ADJ n] **Fiduciary** is used to talk about things which relate to a trust, or to the people who are in charge of a trust. [LEGAL] ❑ *They have a case against their directors for breach of fiduciary duty.*

fief /fif/ (**fiefs**) N-COUNT In former times, a **fief** was a piece of land given to someone by their lord, to whom they had a duty to provide particular services in return.

field ♦♦◊ /fild/ (**fields, fielding, fielded**) ■ N-COUNT A **field** is an area of grass, for example, in a park or on a farm. A **field** is also an area of land on which a crop is grown. ❑ *...a field of wheat.* ■ N-COUNT A sports **field** is an area of grass where sports are played. ❑ *...a football field.* ❑ *He was the fastest thing I ever saw on a baseball field.* ■ N-COUNT A **field** is an area of land or sea bed under which large amounts of a particular mineral have been found. ❑ *...an extensive natural gas field in Alaska.* ■ N-COUNT A magnetic, gravitational, or electric **field** is the area in which that particular force is strong enough to have an effect. ❑ *Some people are worried that electromagnetic fields from electric power lines could increase the risk of cancer.* ■ N-COUNT A particular **field** is a particular subject of study or type of activity. ❑ *Each of the authors of the tapes is an expert in his field.* ■ N-COUNT A **field** is an area of a computer's memory or a program where data can be entered, edited, or stored. [COMPUTING] ❑ *Go to a site like Yahoo! Finance and enter "AOL" in the Get Quotes field.* ■ N-COUNT Your **field** of vision or your visual **field** is the area that you can see without turning your head. ❑ *Our field of vision is surprisingly wide.* ■ N-COUNT-COLL The **field** is a way of referring to all the competitors taking part in a particular race or sports contest. ❑ *Going into the fourth lap, the two most broadly experienced riders led the field.* ■ ADJ [ADJ n] You use **field** to describe work or study that is done in a real, natural environment rather than in a theoretical way or in

fielder

controlled conditions. ❑ *I also conducted a field study among the boys about their attitude to relationships.* ■❿ V-I [usu cont] In a game of baseball or cricket, the team that **is fielding** is trying to catch the ball, while the other team is trying to hit it. ❑ *When we are fielding, the umpires keep looking at the ball.* ■⓫ V-T If you say that someone **fields** a question, you mean that they answer it or deal with it, usually successfully. [JOURNALISM] ❑ *He was later shown on television, fielding questions.* ■⓬ V-T If a sports team **fields** a particular number or type of players, the players are chosen to play for the team on a particular occasion. ❑ *We're going to field an exciting and younger team.* ■⓭ V-T If a candidate in an election is representing a political party, you can say that the party **is fielding** that candidate. [JOURNALISM] ❑ *There are signs that the new party aims to field candidates in elections scheduled for February next year.* ■⓮ → see also **minefield, playing field**

---SYNONYMS---

field
NOUN ■①
land: *Good agricultural land is in short supply.*
meadow: *Its forests and meadows also make it great for country walks.*
paddock: *The family kept horses in the paddock in front of the house.*
pasture: *The cows are out now, grazing in the pasture.*

---

field|er /fíldər/ (**fielders**) N-COUNT A **fielder** is a player in baseball or cricket who is fielding or one who has a particular skill at fielding. ❑ *He hit 10 home runs in the Coast League and he's also a good fielder.*

field event (**field events**) N-COUNT A **field event** is a track and field contest such as the high jump or throwing the discus or javelin, rather than a race.

field-glasses also **field glasses** N-PLURAL **Field-glasses** are the same as **binoculars**. [FORMAL]

field goal (**field goals**) ■① N-COUNT In football, a **field goal** is a score of three points that is gained by kicking the ball through the opponent's goalposts above the crossbar. ❑ *Stoyanovich kicked a 52-yard field goal, placing it squarely between Miami's goalposts.* ■② N-COUNT In basketball, a **field goal** is a goal that is scored by throwing the ball through the basket during normal play.

field hand (**field hands**) N-COUNT A **field hand** is someone who is employed to work on a farm. [mainly AM]

field hock|ey N-UNCOUNT [oft N n] **Field hockey** is an outdoor game played on a grass field between two teams of 11 players who use long curved sticks to hit a small ball and try to score goals. [AM]

field mar|shal (**field marshals**) also **field-marshal** N-COUNT; N-TITLE A **field marshal** is an officer in the army who has the highest rank.

field mouse (**field mice**) also **fieldmouse** N-COUNT A **field mouse** is a mouse with a long tail that lives in fields and woods.

field sport (**field sports**) N-COUNT [usu pl] Hunting, shooting birds, and fishing with a rod are referred to as **field sports** when they are done mainly for pleasure.

field-test (**field-tests, field-testing, field-tested**) also **field test** V-T If you **field-test** a new piece of equipment, you test it in a real, natural environment. ❑ *We've field-tested them ourselves and are happy that they work.*

field trip (**field trips**) A **field trip** is a trip made by students and a teacher to see or study something, for example a museum, a factory, or a historical site. ❑ *Rachel enjoyed the class field trip to the aquarium in Boston.*

field|work /fíldwɜrk/ also **field work** N-UNCOUNT **Fieldwork** is the gathering of information about something in a real, natural environment, rather than in a place of study such as a laboratory or classroom. ❑ *...anthropological fieldwork.*

fiend /fínd/ (**fiends**) ■① N-COUNT If you describe someone as a **fiend**, you mean that they are extremely wicked or cruel. [WRITTEN] ❑ *We must catch the fiend who did this.* ■② N-COUNT [n N] **Fiend** can be used after a noun to refer to a person who is very interested in the thing mentioned, and enjoys having a lot of it or doing it often. ❑ *...if you're a heavy coffee drinker or a tea fiend.*

fiend|ish /fíndɪʃ/ ■① ADJ [usu ADJ n] A **fiendish** plan, action, or device is very clever or imaginative. [INFORMAL] ❑ *...a fiendish plot.* • **fiend|ish|ly** ADV [usu ADV adj] ❑ *This figure is reached by a fiendishly clever equation.* ■② ADJ [ADJ n] A **fiendish** problem or task is very difficult and challenging. [INFORMAL] ❑ *...the fiendish difficulty of the questions.* • **fiend|ish|ly** ADV [ADV adj] ❑ *Their trade laws are fiendishly complex.* ■③ ADJ [usu ADJ n] A **fiendish** person enjoys being cruel. ❑ *This was a fiendish act of wickedness.*

fierce ✦✧✧ /fɪ́ərs/ (**fiercer, fiercest**) ■① ADJ A **fierce** animal or person is very aggressive or angry. ❑ *They look like the teeth of some fierce animal.* • **fierce|ly** ADV ❑ *"I don't know," she said fiercely.* ■② ADJ **Fierce** feelings or actions are very intense or enthusiastic, or involve great activity. ❑ *Consumers have a wide array of choices and price competition is fierce.* ❑ *The town was captured after a fierce battle with rebels.* • **fierce|ly** ADV ❑ *He has always been ambitious and fiercely competitive.*

fiery /fáɪəri/ (**fierier, fieriest**) ■① ADJ If you describe something as **fiery**, you mean that it is burning strongly or contains fire. [LITERARY] ❑ *A helicopter crashed in a fiery explosion in Vallejo.* ■② ADJ You can use **fiery** for emphasis when you are referring to bright colors such as red or orange. [LITERARY, EMPHASIS] ❑ *The sky turned from fiery orange to lemon yellow.*

fi|es|ta /fiɛ́stə/ (**fiestas**) N-COUNT A **fiesta** is a time of public entertainment and parties, usually on a special religious holiday, especially in Spain or Latin America.

fife /fáɪf/ (**fifes**) N-COUNT A **fife** is a musical instrument like a small flute.

fif|teen ✦✦✧ /fɪftíːn/ (**fifteens**) NUM **Fifteen** is the number 15. ❑ *Fifteen new episodes of the police drama are scheduled for next year.*

fif|teenth ✦✦✧ /fɪftíːnθ/ ORD The **fifteenth** item in a series is the one that you count as number fifteen. ❑ *...the invention of the printing press in the fifteenth century.*

fifth ✦✦✧ /fɪ́fθ/ (**fifths**) ■① ORD The **fifth** item in a series is the one that you count as number five. ❑ *Joe has recently returned from his fifth trip to Australia.* ■② FRACTION A **fifth** is one of five equal parts of something. ❑ *India spends over a fifth of its budget on defense.* ■③ N-SING If you take or plead the **fifth**, you take the **Fifth Amendment**.

Fifth Amend|ment N-SING [the N] In American law, if someone takes the **Fifth Amendment**, they refuse to answer a question because they think it might show that they are guilty of a crime. You can also say that someone invokes, pleads, or claims the Fifth Amendment. ❑ *Enron Chairman and CEO Kenneth Lay took the Fifth Amendment during his congressional testimony.*

fifth col|umn|ist (**fifth columnists**) N-COUNT A **fifth columnist** is someone who secretly supports and helps the enemies of the country or organization they are in.

fif|ti|eth ✦✦✧ /fɪ́ftiəθ/ ORD The **fiftieth** item in a series is the one that you count as number fifty. ❑ *He retired in 1970, on his fiftieth birthday.*

fif|ty ✦✦✧ /fɪ́fti/ (**fifties**) ■① NUM **Fifty** is the number 50. ■② N-PLURAL When you talk about the **fifties**, you are referring to numbers between 50 and 59. For example, if you are in your **fifties**, you are aged between 50 and 59. If the temperature is **in the fifties**, the temperature is between 50 and 59 degrees. ❑ *I probably look as if I'm in my fifties rather than my seventies.* ■③ N-PLURAL The **fifties** is the decade between 1950 and 1959. ❑ *He began performing in the early fifties, singing and playing guitar.*

fifty-fifty ADV [ADV after v] If something such as money or property is divided or shared **fifty-fifty** between two people, each person gets half of it. [INFORMAL] ❑ *The proceeds of the sale are split fifty-fifty.* • ADJ **Fifty-fifty** is also an adjective. ❑ *The new firm was owned on a fifty-fifty basis by the two parent companies.*

fig /fíg/ (**figs**) ■① N-COUNT A **fig** is a soft sweet fruit that grows in hot areas. It is full of tiny seeds and is often eaten dried. ■② N-COUNT A **fig** or a **fig tree** is a tree on which figs grow.

fig. In books and magazines, **fig.** is used as an abbreviation for **figure** in order to tell the reader which picture or diagram is being referred to. ❑ *Draw the basic outlines in black felt-tip pen (see fig. 4).*

fight ✦✦✦ /fáɪt/ (**fights, fighting, fought**) ■① V-T/V-I If you **fight** something unpleasant, you try in a determined way to prevent it or stop it from happening. ❑ *More units to fight forest fires are planned.* ❑ *I've spent a lifetime fighting against racism and prejudice.*

• N-COUNT **Fight** is also a noun. □ ...*the fight against drug addiction.* **2** V-I If you **fight** for something, you try in a determined way to get it or achieve it. □ *Lee had to fight hard for his place on the expedition.* □ *I told him how we had fought to hold on to the company.* • N-COUNT **Fight** is also a noun. □ *I too am committing myself to continue the fight for justice.* **3** V-T/V-I If a person or army **fights** in a battle or a war, they take part in it. □ *He fought in the war and was taken prisoner by the Americans.* □ *If I were a young man I would sooner go to prison than fight for this country.* • **fight|ing** N-UNCOUNT □ *More than nine hundred people have died in the fighting.* **4** V-T If you **fight** your way to a place, you move toward it with great difficulty, for example, because there are a lot of people or obstacles in your way. □ *I fought my way into a carriage just before the doors closed.* **5** V-T/V-I To **fight** means to take part in a boxing match. □ *In a few hours' time one of the world's most famous boxers will be fighting here for the first time.* □ *I'd like to fight him because he's undefeated and I want to be the first man to beat him.* **6** V-T If you **fight** an election, you are a candidate in the election and try to win it. □ *He helped raise almost $40 million to fight the election campaign.* **7** V-T If you **fight** a case or a court action, you make a legal case against someone in a very determined way, or you put forward a defense when a legal case is made against you. □ *Watkins sued the Army and fought his case in various courts for 10 years.* **8** V-T/V-I If you **fight** an emotion or desire, you try very hard not to feel it, show it, or act on it, but do not always succeed. □ *I desperately fought the urge to giggle.* □ *He fought with the urge to smoke one of the cigars he'd given up a while ago.* **9** V-RECIP If an army or group **fights** a battle with another army or group, they oppose each other with weapons. You can also say that two armies or groups **fight** a battle. □ *Police fought a gun battle with a gang which used hand grenades against them.* **10** V-RECIP If one person **fights** with another, or **fights** them, the two people hit or kick each other because they want to hurt each other. You can also say that two people **fight**. □ *As a child she fought with her younger sister.* □ *I did fight him, I punched him but it was like hitting a wall.* • N-COUNT [oft N with n] **Fight** is also a noun. □ *He had a fight with Smith and bloodied his nose.* **11** V-RECIP If one person **fights** with another, or **fights** them, they have an angry disagreement or quarrel. You can also say that two people **fight**. [INFORMAL] □ *She was always arguing with him and fighting with him.* □ *Gwendolen started fighting her teachers.* • N-COUNT **Fight** is also a noun. □ *We think maybe he took off because he had a big fight with his dad the night before.* **12** N-COUNT A **fight** is a boxing match. □ *The referee stopped the fight.* **13** N-COUNT You can use **fight** to refer to a contest such as an election or a sports competition. [JOURNALISM] □ *...the fight for power between the two parties.* **14** N-UNCOUNT **Fight** is the desire or ability to keep fighting. □ *I thought that we had a lot of fight in us.* **15** PHRASE Someone who **is fighting for** their **life** is making a great effort to stay alive, either when they are being physically attacked or when they are very ill. □ *He is still fighting for his life in the hospital.*
▶ **fight back** **1** PHRASAL VERB If you **fight back against** someone or something that is attacking or harming you, you resist them actively or attack them. □ *We should take some comfort from the ability of the judicial system to fight back against corruption.* **2** PHRASAL VERB If you **fight back** an emotion or a desire, you try very hard not to feel it, show it, or act on it. □ *She fought back the tears.*
▶ **fight off** **1** PHRASAL VERB If you **fight off** something, for example, an illness or an unpleasant feeling, you succeed in getting rid of it and in not letting it overcome you. □ *Unfortunately these drugs are quite toxic and hinder the body's ability to fight off infection.* **2** PHRASAL VERB If you **fight off** someone who has attacked you, you fight with them, and succeed in making them go away or stop attacking you. □ *She fought off three armed robbers.*

COLLOCATIONS

fight
VERB
1
fight + *noun*: cancer, crime, terrorism
2
fight + *noun*: battle, war

fight|back /ˈfaɪtbæk/ N-SING A **fightback** is an effort made by a person or group of people to get back into a strong position when they seem likely to lose something such as an election or an important sports competition. [BRIT, JOURNALISM]

in AM, use **comeback**

fight|er ◆◇◇ /ˈfaɪtər/ (**fighters**) **1** N-COUNT A **fighter** or a **fighter plane** is a fast military aircraft that is used for destroying other aircraft. □ *...a fighter pilot.* **2** N-COUNT If you describe someone as a **fighter**, you approve of them because they continue trying to achieve things in spite of great difficulties or opposition. [APPROVAL] □ *From the start it was clear this tiny girl was a real fighter.* **3** N-COUNT A **fighter** is a person who physically fights another person, especially a professional boxer. □ *He was a real street fighter who'd do anything to win.* **4** → see also **firefighter**

fight|ing chance N-SING [a N; oft N of n/-ing] If you say that someone has a **fighting chance** of success, you are emphasizing that they have some chance of success after a hard struggle. □ *The airline has a fighting chance of surviving.*

fig leaf (**fig leaves**) **1** N-COUNT A **fig leaf** is a large leaf which comes from the fig tree. A fig leaf is sometimes used in painting and sculpture to cover the genitals of a naked body. **2** N-COUNT [usu with supp] People sometimes refer disapprovingly to something which is intended to hide or prevent an embarrassing situation as a **fig leaf**. [JOURNALISM, DISAPPROVAL] □ *This deal is little more than a fig leaf for the continued destruction of the landscape.*

fig|ment /ˈfɪɡmənt/ PHRASE If you say that something is a **figment** of someone's **imagination**, you mean that it does not really exist and that they are just imagining it. □ *The attack wasn't just a figment of my imagination.*

fig|ura|tive /ˈfɪɡjərətɪv/ **1** ADJ If you use a word or expression in a **figurative sense**, you use it with a more abstract or imaginative meaning than its ordinary literal one. □ *...an event that will change your route – in both the literal and figurative sense.* • **fig|ura|tive|ly** ADV □ *I saw that she was, both literally and figuratively, up against a wall.* **2** ADJ **Figurative** art is a style of art in which people and things are shown in a realistic way. □ *His career spanned some 50 years and encompassed both abstract and figurative painting.*

fig|ure ◆◆◆ /ˈfɪɡjər/ (**figures, figuring, figured**) **1** N-COUNT A **figure** is a particular amount expressed as a number, especially a statistic. □ *It would be very nice if we had a true figure of how many people in this country haven't got a job.* □ *It will not be long before the inflation figure starts to fall.* **2** N-COUNT A **figure** is any of the ten written symbols from 0 to 9 that are used to represent a number. □ *...the glowing red figures on the radio alarm clock which read 4:22 a.m.* **3** N-COUNT You refer to someone that you can see as a **figure** when you cannot see them clearly or when you are describing them. □ *Ernie saw the dim figure of Rose in the chair.* **4** N-COUNT In art, a **figure** is a person in a drawing or a painting, or a statue of a person. □ *...a life-size bronze figure of a brooding, hooded woman.* **5** N-COUNT Your **figure** is the shape of your body. □ *Take pride in your health and your figure.* **6** N-COUNT Someone who is referred to as a **figure** of a particular kind is a person who is well-known and important in some way. □ *The movement is supported by key figures in the three main political parties.* **7** N-COUNT If you say that someone is, for example, a mother **figure** or a hero **figure**, you mean that other people regard them as the type of person stated or suggested. □ *Daniel Boone, the great hero figure of the frontier.* **8** N-COUNT [also N num] In books and magazines, the diagrams which help to show or explain information are referred to as **figures**. □ *If you look at a world map (see Figure 1) you can identify the major wine-producing regions.* **9** N-COUNT In geometry, a **figure** is a shape, especially a regular shape. [TECHNICAL] □ *Draw a pentagon, a regular five-sided figure.* **10** N-PLURAL An amount or number that is in single **figures** is between zero and nine. An amount or number that is in double **figures** is between ten and ninety-nine. You can also say, for example, that an amount or number is in three **figures** when it is between one hundred and nine hundred and ninety-nine. □ *Inflation, which has usually been in single figures, is running at more than 12%.* **11** V-T If you **figure** that something is the case, you think or guess that it is the case. [INFORMAL] □ *She figured that both she and Ned had learned a lot from the experience.* **12** V-I If you say '**That figures**' or 'It figures,' you mean that the fact referred to is not surprising. [INFORMAL] ❑ *When I finished, he said, "Yeah. That figures."* ⓭ V-I [no passive] If a person or thing **figures** in something, they appear in or are included in it. ❑ *Human rights violations figured prominently in the report.* ⓮ → See feature box at **population**

▶ **figure out** PHRASAL VERB If you **figure out** a solution to a problem or the reason for something, you succeed in solving it or understanding it. [INFORMAL] ❑ *It took them about one month to figure out how to start the equipment.* ❑ *They're trying to figure out the politics of this whole situation.*

SYNONYMS

figure
NOUN
❷
digit: *Her phone number differs from mine by one digit.*
number: *We were only one number away from winning the jackpot.*
numeral: *...a flat, square wristwatch with classic Roman numerals.*
❹
outline: *He could see only the hazy outline of the goalposts.*
form: *...the form of the body.*
silhouette: *...the distinctive silhouette of his ears.*

-figure /fɪɡyər/ COMB IN ADJ [ADJ n] **-figure** combines with a number, usually 'five,' 'six,' or 'seven,' to form adjectives which say how many figures are in a number. These adjectives usually describe a large amount of money. For example, a six-figure sum is between 100,000 and 999,999. ❑ *Columbia Pictures paid him a six-figure sum for the rights.*

fig|ure eight (**figure eights**) N-COUNT A **figure eight** is something that has the shape of the number 8, for example, a knot or a movement done by a skater. [AM]

figure|head /fɪɡyərhɛd/ (**figureheads**) ❶ N-COUNT If someone is the **figurehead** of an organization or movement, they are recognized as being its leader, although they have little real power. ❑ *The president will be little more than a figurehead.* ❷ N-COUNT A **figurehead** is a large wooden model of a person that was put just under the pointed front of a sailing ship in former times.

figure-hugging ADJ **Figure-hugging** clothes fit very close to the body of the person who is wearing them.

fig|ure of speech (**figures of speech**) N-COUNT A **figure of speech** is an expression or word that is used with a metaphorical rather than a literal meaning. ❑ *"The leopard cannot change his spots" is just a figure of speech.*

fig|ure skat|ing N-UNCOUNT **Figure skating** is ice skating in an attractive pattern, usually with spins and jumps included.

figu|rine /fɪɡyərin/ (**figurines**) N-COUNT A **figurine** is a small ornamental model of a person.

fila|ment /fɪləmənt/ (**filaments**) N-COUNT A **filament** is a very thin piece or thread of something, for example, the piece of wire inside a light bulb.

filch /fɪltʃ/ (**filches, filching, filched**) V-T If you say that someone **filches** something, you mean they steal it, especially when you do not consider this to be a very serious crime. [INFORMAL] ❑ *He filched pills from the psychiatrist.*

file ✦✦◇ /faɪl/ (**files, filing, filed**) ❶ N-COUNT A **file** is a box or a folded piece of heavy paper or plastic in which letters or documents are kept. ❑ *...a file of insurance papers.* ❷ N-COUNT A **file** is a collection of information about a particular person or thing. ❑ *We already have files on people's tax details.* ❸ N-COUNT In computing, a **file** is a set of related data that has its own name. ❑ *Be sure to save the revised version of the file under a new filename.* ❹ N-COUNT A **file** is a hand tool which is used for rubbing hard objects to make them smooth, shape them, or cut through them. ❺ V-T If you **file** a document, you put it in the correct file. ❑ *They are all filed alphabetically under author.* ❻ V-T/V-I If you **file** a formal or legal accusation, complaint, or request, you make it officially. ❑ *I filed for divorce on the grounds of adultery a few months later.* ❼ V-T When someone **files** a report or a news story, they send or give it to their employer. ❑ *He had to rush back to the office and file a housing story before the secretaries went home.* ❽ V-T If you **file** an object, you smooth it,

shape it, or cut it with a file. ❑ *Manicurists are skilled at shaping and filing nails.* ❾ → see also **rank and file** ❿ PHRASE A group of people who are walking or standing **in single file** or **single file** are in a line, one behind the other. ❑ *We were walking in single file to the lake.*

file cabi|net (**file cabinets**) N-COUNT A **file cabinet** is a piece of office furniture, usually made of metal, which has drawers in which files are kept.

file|name /faɪlneɪm/ (**filenames**) N-COUNT In computing, a **filename** is a name that you give to a particular document. ❑ *Save your outline with a filename such as homeless.doc.*

file-sharing also **file sharing** N-UNCOUNT [oft N n] **File-sharing** is a method of distributing computer files, for example, files containing music, among a large number of users. [COMPUTING] ❑ *...legal action to close down file-sharing sites offering music for free.*

fi|let /fɪleɪ, fɪlɛɪ/ (**filets**) N-COUNT [oft N of n] A **filet** of meat or fish is the same as a **fillet**. [mainly AM] ❑ *...a choice of filet of beef, grilled marinated chicken or broiled salmon.*

fil|ial /fɪliəl/ ADJ [ADJ n] You can use **filial** to describe the duties, feelings, or relationships which exist between a son or daughter and his or her parents. [FORMAL] ❑ *His father would accuse him of neglecting his filial duties.*

fili|bus|ter /fɪlɪbʌstər/ (**filibusters, filibustering, filibustered**) ❶ N-COUNT A **filibuster** is a long slow speech made to use up time so that a vote cannot be taken and a law cannot be passed. [mainly AM] ❑ *Senator Seymour has threatened a filibuster to block the bill.* ❷ V-T/V-I If a politician **filibusters**, he or she makes a long slow speech in order to use up time so that a vote cannot be taken and a law cannot be passed. [mainly AM] ❑ *They simply threatened to filibuster until the Senate adjourns.* ❑ *A group of senators plans to filibuster a measure that would permit drilling in Alaska.*

fili|gree /fɪlɪgri/ N-UNCOUNT [oft N n] The word **filigree** refers to delicate ornamental designs made with gold or silver wire.

fil|ing cabi|net (**filing cabinets**) N-COUNT A **filing cabinet** is a piece of office furniture, usually made of metal, which has drawers in which files are kept.

fil|ings /faɪlɪŋz/ ❶ N-PLURAL [usu n N] **Filings** are very small pieces of a substance, especially a metal, that are produced when it is filed or cut. ❑ *...iron filings.* ❑ *...metal filings.* ❷ N-PLURAL Court **filings** are cases filed in a court of law. [AM, AUSTRALIAN] ❑ *In court filings, they argued that the settlement was inadequate.*

Fili|pi|no /fɪlɪpinoʊ/ (**Filipinos**) ❶ ADJ **Filipino** means belonging or relating to the Philippines, or to its people or culture. ❷ N-COUNT A **Filipino** is a person who comes from the Philippines.

fill ✦✦◇ /fɪl/ (**fills, filling, filled**) ❶ V-T/V-I If you **fill** a container or area, or if it **fills**, an amount of something enters it that is enough to make it full. ❑ *She went to the bathroom, filled a glass with water, returned to the bed.* ❑ *The boy's eyes filled with tears.* • PHRASAL VERB **Fill up** means the same as **fill**. ❑ *Warehouses at the frontier between the two countries fill up with sacks of rice and flour.* ❷ V-T If something **fills** a space, it is so big, or there are such large quantities of it, that there is very little room left. ❑ *He cast his eyes at the rows of cabinets that filled the enormous work area.* • PHRASAL VERB **Fill up** means the same as **fill**. ❑ *...the complicated machines that fill up today's laboratories.* • **filled** ADJ [v-link ADJ with n] ❑ *...four museum buildings filled with historical objects.* ❸ V-T If you **fill** a crack or hole, you put a substance into it in order to make the surface smooth again. ❑ *Fill small holes with wood filler in a matching color.* • PHRASAL VERB **Fill in** means the same as **fill**. ❑ *Start by filling in any cracks and gaps between window and door frames and the wall.* ❹ V-T If a sound, smell, or light **fills** a space, or the air, it is very strong or noticeable. ❑ *In the parking lot of the school, the siren filled the air.* ❺ V-T If something **fills** you with an emotion, or if an emotion **fills** you, you experience this emotion strongly. ❑ *I admired my father, and his work filled me with awe and curiosity.* ❻ V-T If you **fill** a period of time with a particular activity, you spend the time in this way. ❑ *If she wants a routine to fill her day, let her do community work.* • PHRASAL VERB **Fill up** means the same as **fill**. ❑ *On Thursday night she went to her yoga class, glad to have something to fill up the evening.* ❼ V-T If something **fills** a need or a gap, it puts an end to this need or gap by existing or being active. ❑ *She brought him a sense of fun, of gaiety that filled a gap in his life.* ❽ V-T If something **fills** a role, position, or function, they have that role or position, or perform that function, often successfully. ❑ *Dena was filling the role of diplomat's wife with the skill she had learned over the years.* ❾ V-T If a company or organization **fills** a job vacancy, they choose someone to do the job. If someone **fills** a job vacancy, they accept a job that they have been offered. ❑ *A vacancy has arisen which I intend to fill.* ❿ V-T When a dentist **fills** someone's tooth, he or she puts a filling in it. ❑ *Dentists fill teeth and repair broken ones.* ⓫ V-T If you **fill** an order or a prescription, you provide the things that are asked for. [mainly AM] ❑ *A pharmacist can fill any prescription if, in his or her judgment, the prescription is valid.* ⓬ **to fill the bill** → see **bill**

▸ **fill in** ❶ PHRASAL VERB If you **fill in** a form or other document requesting information, you write information in the spaces on it. ❑ *Fill in the coupon and send it first class to the address shown.* ❷ PHRASAL VERB If you **fill in** a shape, you cover the area inside the lines with color or shapes so that none of the background is showing. ❑ *With a lip pencil, outline lips and fill them in.* ❸ PHRASAL VERB If you **fill** someone **in**, you give them more details about something that you know about. [INFORMAL] ❑ *He filled her in on Wilbur Kantor's visit.* ❹ PHRASAL VERB If you **fill in** for someone, you do the work or task that they normally do because they are unable to do it. ❑ *Vice-presidents' wives would fill in for first ladies.* ❺ → see also **fill 3**

▸ **fill out** ❶ PHRASAL VERB If you **fill out** a form or other document requesting information, you write information in the spaces on it. [mainly AM] ❑ *Fill out the application carefully, and keep copies of it.* ❷ PHRASAL VERB If someone or something **fills out**, they become fuller, thicker, or rounder. ❑ *A girl may fill out before she reaches her full height.*

▸ **fill up** ❶ PHRASAL VERB If you **fill up** or **fill** yourself **up** with food, you eat so much that you do not feel hungry. ❑ *Fill up on potatoes, bread and pasta, which are high in carbohydrate and low in fat.* ❷ PHRASAL VERB A type of food that **fills** you **up** makes you feel that you have eaten a lot, even though you have only eaten a small amount. ❑ *Potatoes fill us up without overloading us with calories.* ❸ → see also **fill 1, 2, 6**

fill|er /fɪlər/ (**fillers**) ❶ N-MASS **Filler** is a substance used for filling cracks or holes, especially in walls, car bodies, or wood. ❷ N-COUNT You can describe something as a **filler** when it is being used or done because there is a need for something and nothing better is available. [INFORMAL] ❸ → see also **stocking filler**

fil|let /fɪleɪ/ (**fillets, filleting, filleted**) ❶ N-VAR **Fillet** is a strip of meat, especially beef, that has no bones in it. ❑ *...fillet of beef with shallots.* ❑ *...chicken breast fillets.* ❷ N-COUNT A **fillet** of fish is the side of a fish with the bones removed. ❑ *...anchovy fillets.* ❸ V-T When you **fillet** fish or meat, you prepare it by taking the bones out. ❑ *Fillet the fish and roll the fillets in flour.*

fill-in (**fill-ins**) N-COUNT [oft N *for* n] If someone is a **fill-in** for another person, they replace them for a period of time. [AM] ❑ *He was a fill-in for Primeau, who was out with a concussion.*

fill|ing /fɪlɪŋ/ (**fillings**) ❶ N-COUNT A **filling** is a small amount of metal or plastic that a dentist puts in a hole in a tooth to prevent further decay. ❑ *The longer your child can go without needing a filling, the better.* ❷ N-MASS The **filling** in something such as a cake, pie, or sandwich is a substance or mixture that is put inside it. ❑ *Spread some of the filling over each cold pancake and then either roll or fold.* ❸ N-MASS The **filling** in a piece of soft furniture or in a cushion is the soft substance inside it. ❑ *...second-hand sofas with old-style foam fillings.* ❹ ADJ Food that is **filling** makes you feel full when you have eaten it. ❑ *Although it is tasty, crab is very filling.*

fill|ing sta|tion (**filling stations**) N-COUNT A **filling station** is a place where you can buy gasoline and oil for your car.

fil|lip /fɪlɪp/ (**fillips**) N-COUNT [usu sing, oft N *to/for* n] If someone or something gives a **fillip** to an activity or person, they suddenly encourage or improve them. [WRITTEN] ❑ *The news gave a fillip to the telecommunications sector.*

fil|ly /fɪli/ (**fillies**) N-COUNT A **filly** is a young female horse.

film ✦✦✦ /fɪlm/ (**films, filming, filmed**) ❶ N-COUNT A **film** consists of moving pictures that have been recorded so that they can be shown in a theater or on television. A film tells a story, or shows a real situation. [mainly BRIT] ❑ *Everything about the film was good. Good acting, good story, good fun.* ❷ N-COUNT A **film** of powder, liquid, or oil is a very thin layer of it. ❑ *The sea is coated with a film of raw sewage.* ❸ V-T If you **film** something, you use a camera to take moving pictures which can be shown on a screen or on television. ❑ *He had filmed her life story.* ❹ N-UNCOUNT **Film** of something is moving pictures of a real event that are shown on television or on a screen. ❑ *He likes to look at film of old-time players.* ❺ N-UNCOUNT [also N in pl] The making of films, considered as a form of art or a business, can be referred to as **film** or **films**. ❑ *...people working in film and television.* ❻ N-UNCOUNT Plastic **film** is a very thin sheet of plastic used to wrap and cover things. [BRIT]

in AM, use **plastic wrap**

❼ N-VAR A **film** is the narrow roll of plastic that is used in a camera to take photographs. ❑ *The photographers had already shot a dozen rolls of film.*

COLLOCATIONS

film
NOUN ❶
noun + **film**: action, documentary, feature, horror, sci-fi, war
adjective + **film**: animated, classic, short
verb + **film**: direct, make, produce, shoot; watch

film|ic /fɪlmɪk/ ADJ [ADJ n] **Filmic** means related to films. [FORMAL] ❑ *...a new filmic style.*

film|ing /fɪlmɪŋ/ N-UNCOUNT **Filming** is the activity of making a film including the acting, directing, and camera shots. ❑ *Filming was due to start next month.*

film|maker /fɪlmmeɪkər/ (**filmmakers**) N-COUNT A **filmmaker** is someone involved in making films, in particular a director or producer.

film noir /fɪlm nwɑr/ (**films noir**) N-VAR **Film noir** refers to a type of movie or a style of filmmaking which shows the world as a dangerous or depressing place where many people suffer, especially because of the greed or cruelty of others. ❑ *...a remake of the 1947 film noir classic, Kiss of Death.*

film star (**film stars**) N-COUNT A **film star** is a famous actor who appears in films. [mainly BRIT]

filmy /fɪlmi/ (**filmier, filmiest**) ADJ [usu ADJ n] A **filmy** fabric or substance is very thin and almost transparent. ❑ *...filmy nightgowns.*

filo /fiːloʊ/ also **filo pastry** N-UNCOUNT **Filo** or **filo pastry** is a type of light pastry made of thin layers. It is traditionally used in Greek cooking.

Filo|fax /faɪləfæks/ (**Filofaxes**) N-COUNT A **Filofax** is a type of personal filing system in the form of a small book with pages that can easily be added or removed. [TRADEMARK]

fil|ter /fɪltər/ (**filters, filtering, filtered**) ❶ V-T To **filter** a substance means to pass it through a device which is designed to remove certain particles contained in it. ❑ *The best prevention for cholera is to boil or filter water, and eat only well-cooked food.* ❷ V-I If light or sound **filters** into a place, it comes in weakly or slowly, either through a partly covered opening, or from a long distance away. ❑ *Light filtered into my kitchen through the soft, green shade of the honey locust tree.* ❸ V-I When news or information **filters** through to people, it gradually reaches them. ❑ *It took months before the findings began to filter through to the politicians.* ❑ *News of the attack quickly filtered through the college.* ❹ N-COUNT A **filter** is a device through which a substance is passed when it is being filtered. ❑ *...a paper coffee filter.* ❺ N-COUNT A **filter** is a device through which sound or light is passed and which blocks or reduces particular sound or light frequencies. ❑ *You might use a yellow filter to improve the clarity of a hazy horizon.*

▸ **filter out** PHRASAL VERB To **filter out** something from a substance or from light means to remove it by passing the substance or light through something acting as a filter. ❑ *Children should have glasses which filter out UV rays.* ❑ *Plants and trees filter carbon dioxide out of the air and produce oxygen.*

fil|ter tip (filter tips) N-COUNT A **filter tip** is a small device at the end of a cigarette that reduces the amount of dangerous substances that pass into the smoker's body. **Filter tips** are cigarettes that are manufactured with these devices.

filth /fɪlθ/ **1** N-UNCOUNT **Filth** is a disgusting amount of dirt. ◻ *Thousands of tons of filth and sewage pour into the Ganges every day.* **2** N-UNCOUNT People refer to words or pictures, usually ones relating to sex, as **filth** when they think they are very disgusting and rude. [DISAPPROVAL] ◻ *The dialogue was all filth and innuendo.*

filthy /fɪlθi/ (filthier, filthiest) **1** ADJ Something that is **filthy** is very dirty. ◻ *He never washed, and always wore a filthy old jacket.* **2** ADJ If you describe something as **filthy**, you mean that you think it is morally very unpleasant and disgusting, sometimes in a sexual way. [DISAPPROVAL] ◻ *Apparently, well known actors were at these filthy parties.*

fil|tra|tion /fɪltreɪʃ°n/ N-UNCOUNT **Filtration** is the process of filtering a substance. ◻ *This enzyme would make the filtration of beer easier.* ◻ *...water filtration systems.*

fin /fɪn/ (fins) **1** N-COUNT A fish's **fins** are the flat parts which stick out of its body and help it to swim and keep its balance. **2** N-COUNT A **fin** on something such as an airplane, rocket, or bomb is a flat part which sticks out and which is intended to help control its movement. **3** → See also color supplement

fi|nal ♦♦◊ /faɪn°l/ (finals) **1** ADJ [det ADJ] In a series of events, things, or people, the **final** one is the last one. ◻ *Astronauts will make a final attempt today to rescue a communications satellite from its useless orbit.* ◻ *This is the fifth and probably final day of testimony before the Senate Judiciary Committee.* **2** ADJ [ADJ n] **Final** means happening at the end of an event or series of events. ◻ *You must have been on stage until the final curtain.* **3** ADJ If a decision or someone's authority is **final**, it cannot be changed or questioned. ◻ *The judges' decision is final.* **4** N-COUNT The **final** is the last game or contest in a series and decides who is the winner. ◻ *...the Gold Cup final.* **5** → see also **quarterfinal**, **semifinal** **6** N-PLURAL The **finals** of a sports tournament consist of a smaller tournament that includes only players or teams that have won earlier games. The finals decide the winner of the whole tournament. ◻ *Poland knows it has a chance of qualifying for the World Cup Finals.*

COLLOCATIONS

final
NOUN **5**
verb + **final**: contest, play; make, qualify for, reach; lose, win

fi|na|le /fɪnɑli, -næli/ (finales) N-COUNT The **finale** of a show, piece of music, or series of shows is the last part of it or the last one of them, especially when this is exciting or impressive. ◻ *...the finale of Shostakovich's Fifth Symphony.*

fi|nal|ist /faɪn°lɪst/ (finalists) N-COUNT A **finalist** is someone who reaches the last stages of a competition or tournament by doing well or winning in its earlier stages. ◻ *The twelve finalists will be listed in the Sunday Times.*

fi|nal|ity /faɪnælɪti/ N-UNCOUNT [oft N of n] **Finality** is the quality of being final and impossible to change. If you say something with **finality**, you say it in a way that shows that you have made up your mind about something and do not want to discuss it further. [FORMAL] ◻ *Young children have difficulty grasping the finality of death.*

fi|nal|ize /faɪn°laɪz/ (finalizes, finalizing, finalized)

in BRIT, also use **finalise**

V-T If you **finalize** something such as a plan or an agreement, you complete the arrangements for it, especially by discussing it with other people. ◻ *Negotiators from the three countries finalized the agreement in August.* ◻ *We are saying nothing until all the details have been finalized.*

fi|nal|ly ♦♦◊ /faɪn°li/ **1** ADV You use **finally** to suggest that something happens after a long period of time, usually later than you wanted or expected it to happen. ◻ *The food finally arrived at the end of last week and distribution began.* **2** ADV [with cl/group] You use **finally** to indicate that something is last in a series of actions or events. ◻ *The action slips from comedy to melodrama and finally to tragedy.*

fi|nance ♦♦◊ /faɪnæns, fɪnæns/ (finances, financing, financed) **1** V-T When someone **finances** something such as a project or a purchase, they provide the money that is needed to pay for them. ◻ *The fund has been used largely to finance the construction of federal prisons.* • N-UNCOUNT **Finance** is also a noun. ◻ *A United States delegation is in Japan seeking finance for a major scientific project.* **2** N-UNCOUNT [also N in pl] **Finance** is the commercial or government activity of managing money, debt, credit, and investment. ◻ *...a major player in the world of high finance.* ◻ *The report recommends an overhaul of public finances.* **3** N-UNCOUNT [also N in pl] You can refer to the amount of money that you have and how well it is organized as your **finances**. ◻ *Be prepared for unexpected news concerning your finances.*

COLLOCATIONS

finance
NOUN
1
noun + **finance**: government
adjective + **finance**: corporate, public; shaky, strained; sound
2
noun + **finance**: consumer, household, mortgage, vehicle
adjective + **finance**: personal, private
verb + **finance**: arrange, provide, raise; secure
VERB **1**
finance + noun: acquisition, deal, project, purchase
finance + adverb: privately, publicly

VOCABULARY IN CONTEXT

Personal finance

Being good with money is about more than just avoiding **going bankrupt** every month. While it's partly about not **living beyond your means**, it's also about keeping track of your **income** and **expenditures**, and understanding different types of **debt** and how to manage them. **Financially literate** people plan a **budget** each month and stick to it. They might **splurge** every once in a while, but they plan for those treats, perhaps by **tightening their belts** in other months. They only take out a **loan** or **mortgage** after calculating the **interest** and the **repayments** to minimize the risk of **defaulting** on payments. They avoid the temptation of **pay day loans**, which offer short-term, **unsecured debt** on small amounts of money at extremely high **interest rates**.

fi|nance charge (finance charges) N-COUNT **Finance charges** are fees or interest that you pay when you borrow money or buy something on credit. [mainly AM] ◻ *...cards with annual fees up to $75 and finance charges of 18% APR or more.*

fi|nance com|pa|ny (finance companies) N-COUNT A **finance company** is a business which lends money to people and charges them interest while they pay it back. [BUSINESS]

fi|nan|cial ♦♦◊ /faɪnænʃ°l, fɪn-/ **1** ADJ **Financial** means relating to or involving money. ◻ *The company is in financial difficulties.* • **fi|nan|cial|ly** ADV ◻ *She would like to be more financially independent.* **2** → See feature box at **banking**, **finance**

SYNONYMS

financial
ADJ
economic: *The pace of economic growth is picking up.*
budgetary: *There are huge budgetary pressures on governments to reduce their armed forces.*
monetary: *Some countries tighten monetary policy to avoid inflation.*
fiscal: *...in 1987, when the government tightened fiscal policy.*

fi|nan|cial ad|vis|er (financial advisers) N-COUNT A **financial adviser** is someone whose job it is to advise people about financial products and services. [BUSINESS]

fi|nan|cial con|sult|ant (financial consultants) N-COUNT A **financial consultant** is the same as a **financial adviser**. [BUSINESS]

fi|nan|cial ser|vices

The form **financial service** is used as a modifier.

N-PLURAL A company or organization that provides **financial services** is able to help you do things such as make investments or get a mortgage. [BUSINESS] ❏ *...using the Internet to shop for financial services and other products nationwide.* ❏ *...financial service companies.*

fi|nan|ci|er /fɪnænsɪər, faɪ-/ (financiers) N-COUNT A **financier** is a person, company, or government that provides money for projects or businesses. [BUSINESS] ❏ *Private banks became the main financiers of developing countries.*

finch /fɪntʃ/ (finches) N-COUNT A **finch** is a small bird with a short strong beak.

find ♦♦♦ /faɪnd/ (finds, finding, found)
→ Please look at meanings **15** and **16** to see if the expression you are looking for is shown under another headword.

1 V-T If you **find** someone or something, you see them or learn where they are. ❏ *The police also found a pistol.* ❏ *They have spent ages looking at the map and can't find a trace of anywhere called Darrowby.* **2** V-T If you **find** something that you need or want, you succeed in achieving or obtaining it. ❏ *Many people here cannot find work.* ❏ *He has to apply for a permit and we have to find him a job.* **3** V-T If you **find** someone or something in a particular situation, they are in that situation when you see them or come into contact with them. ❏ *They found her walking alone and depressed on the beach.* ❏ *She returned to her home to find her back door forced open.* **4** V-T If you **find** yourself doing something, you are doing it without deciding or intending to do it. ❏ *It's not the first time that you've found yourself in this situation.* ❏ *I found myself having more fun than I had had in years.* **5** V-T If you **find** that something is the case, you become aware of it or realize that it is the case. ❏ *The two biologists found, to their surprise, that both groups of birds survived equally well.* ❏ *At my age I would find it hard to get another job.* **6** V-T When a court or jury decides that a person on trial is guilty or innocent, you say that the person **has been found** guilty or not guilty. ❏ *She was found guilty of manslaughter and put on probation for two years.* **7** V-T You can use **find** to express your reaction to someone or something. ❏ *I find most of the young men of my own age so boring.* ❏ *I find it ludicrous that nothing has been done to protect passengers from fire.* **8** V-T If you **find** a feeling such as pleasure or comfort in a particular thing or activity, you experience the feeling mentioned as a result of this thing or activity. ❏ *How could anyone find pleasure in hunting and killing this beautiful creature?* **9** V-T If you **find** the time or money to do something, you succeed in making or obtaining enough time or money to do it. ❏ *I was just finding more time to write music.* **10** V-T PASSIVE If something **is found** in a particular place or thing, it exists in that place. ❏ *Two thousand of France's 4,200 species of flowering plants are found in the park.* **11** N-COUNT If you describe someone or something that has been discovered as a **find**, you mean that they are valuable, interesting, good, or useful. ❏ *Another of his lucky finds was a pair of candleholders.* **12** → see also **finding**, **found** **13** PHRASE If you **find your way** somewhere, you successfully get there by choosing the right way to go. ❏ *He was an expert at finding his way, even in strange surroundings.* **14** PHRASE If something **finds** its **way** somewhere, it comes to that place, especially by chance. ❏ *It is one of the very few Michelangelos that have found their way out of Italy.* **15 to find fault with** → see **fault** **16 to find one's feet** → see **foot** ①
17 → See feature box at **work**

▶ **find out 1** PHRASAL VERB If you **find** something **out**, you learn something that you did not already know, especially by making a deliberate effort to do so. ❏ *It makes you want to watch the next episode to find out what's going to happen.* ❏ *I was relieved to find out that my problems were due to a genuine disorder.* **2** PHRASAL VERB If you **find** someone **out**, you discover that they have been doing something dishonest. ❏ *Her face was so grave, I wondered for a moment if she'd found me out.*

find|er /faɪndər/ (finders) N-COUNT You can refer to someone who finds something as the **finder** of that thing. ❏ *The finder of a wallet who takes it home may be guilty of theft.*

fin de siè|cle /fæn də sjɛklə/ also **fin-de-siècle** ADJ [ADJ n] **Fin de siècle** is used to describe something that is thought to be typical of the end of the nineteenth century, especially when it is considered stylish or exaggerated. [WRITTEN] ❏ *...fin de siècle decadence.*

find|ing /faɪndɪŋ/ (findings) **1** N-COUNT Someone's **findings** are the information they get or the conclusions they come to as the result of an investigation or some research. ❏ *One of the main findings of the survey was the confusion about the facilities already in place.* **2** N-COUNT The **findings** of a court are the decisions that it reaches after a trial or an investigation. ❏ *The government hopes the court will announce its findings before the end of the month.* **3** → See feature box at **research**

FINE
① ADJECTIVE USES
② PUNISHMENT

① **fine** ♦♦◇ /faɪn/ (finer, finest) **1** ADJ You use **fine** to describe something that you admire and think is very good. ❏ *There is a fine view of the countryside.* ❏ *This is a fine book.* • **fine|ly** ADV [ADV -ed] ❏ *They are finely engineered boats.* **2** ADJ [v-link ADJ] If you say that you are **fine**, you mean that you are in good health or reasonably happy. ❏ *Lina is fine and sends you her love and best wishes.* **3** ADJ If you say that something is **fine**, you mean that it is satisfactory or acceptable. ❏ *The skiing is fine.* ❏ *Everything was going to be just fine.* • ADV **Fine** is also an adverb. ❏ *All the instruments are working fine.* **4** ADJ Something that is **fine** is very delicate, narrow, or small. ❏ *The heat scorched the fine hairs on her arms.* • **fine|ly** ADV [ADV with v] ❏ *Chop the ingredients finely and mix them together.* **5** ADJ **Fine** objects or clothing are of good quality, delicate, and expensive. ❏ *We waited in our fine clothes.* **6** ADJ A **fine** detail or distinction is very delicate, small, or exact. ❏ *Johnson likes the broad outline but is reserving judgment on the fine detail.* • **fine|ly** ADV ❏ *They had to take the finely balanced decision to let the visit proceed.* **7** ADJ A **fine** person is someone you consider good, moral, and worth admiring. [APPROVAL] ❏ *He was an excellent journalist and a very fine man.* **8** ADJ When the weather is **fine**, the sun is shining and it is not raining. ❏ *He might be doing some gardening if the weather is fine.* **9** CONVENTION You say **'fine'** or **'that's fine'** to show that you do not object to an arrangement, action, or situation that has been suggested. [FORMULAE] ❏ *If competition is the best way to achieve it, then, fine.*

SYNONYMS

fine
ADJ
① **2**
healthy: *We need to lead more balanced lives to be healthy and happy.*
well: *I'm not very well today; I can't come in.*
fit: *A fit person can usually master easy ski runs within a few days.*
① **3**
satisfactory: *I never got a satisfactory answer.*
all right: *'How was school?'—'It was all right.'*
okay: *I guess for a fashionable restaurant like this, the prices are okay.*

② **fine** ♦◇◇ /faɪn/ (fines, fining, fined) **1** N-COUNT A **fine** is a punishment in which a person is ordered to pay a sum of money because they have done something illegal or broken a rule. **2** V-T If someone **is fined**, they are punished by being ordered to pay a sum of money because they have done something illegal or broken a rule. ❏ *She was fined $300 and banned from driving for one month.*

fine art

COLLOCATIONS

fine
NOUN ② **1**
noun + **fine**: parking, speeding, traffic; library
adjective + **fine**: heavy, hefty, maximum; unpaid
verb + **fine**: impose, issue; face, pay, receive

fine art (**fine arts**) **1** N-UNCOUNT [also N in pl] Painting and sculpture, in which objects are produced that are beautiful rather than useful, can be referred to as **fine art** or as the **fine arts**. ❑ *He deals in antiques and fine art.* **2** PHRASE If you **have something down to a fine art**, you are able to do it in a very skillful or efficient way because you have had a lot of experience of doing it. ❑ *They've got fruit retailing down to a fine art. You can be sure that your pears will ripen in day.*

VOCABULARY IN CONTEXT

Fine art

The scope of **fine art** is broad. There is disagreement among some experts about which **art forms** constitute fine art, but generally it's agreed that fine art refers to **artistic** works created purely for **aesthetic** purposes. In other words, fine art is specifically for looking at and enjoying. This is as opposed to **applied art** – for example, fashion design – which goes beyond being **visually** pleasing to having a practical purpose; a function. Think of your favorite painting. What do you like about it? The **brushstrokes** of oil on **canvas**? Or is it a **watercolor**? Is it a **portrait** of someone? Is it a **landscape** that you love? Is it **abstract**? Either way, it's fine art, as are drawing and **sculpture**. From the **masterpieces** that Michelangelo and Rodin **carved** to the **pencil sketches** of Picasso and Leonardo da Vinci, fine art is **exhibited** in thousands of galleries around the world for our viewing pleasure and appreciation.

fine print N-UNCOUNT In a contract or agreement, the **fine print** is the same as the **small print**.

fin|ery /ˈfaɪnəri/ N-UNCOUNT If someone is dressed in their **finery**, they are wearing the elegant and impressive clothes and jewelry that they wear on special occasions. [LITERARY] ❑ *...the guests in all their finery.*

fi|nesse /fɪˈnɛs/ N-UNCOUNT If you do something with **finesse**, you do it with great skill and style. ❑ *...handling momentous diplomatic challenges with tact and finesse.*

fine-tooth comb also **fine tooth comb** PHRASE If you say that you will **go over** something **with a fine-tooth comb** or **go through** something **with a fine-tooth comb**, you are emphasizing that you will search it thoroughly or examine it very carefully. [EMPHASIS]

fine-tune (**fine-tunes**, **fine-tuning**, **fine-tuned**) V-T If you **fine-tune** something, you make very small and precise changes to it in order to make it as successful or effective as it possibly can be. ❑ *We do not try to fine-tune the economy on the basis of short-term predictions.*

fin|ger ♦♦◊ /ˈfɪŋgər/ (**fingers, fingering, fingered**) **1** N-COUNT Your **fingers** are the long thin parts at the end of each hand, sometimes also including the thumb. ❑ *She suddenly held up a* small, bony finger and pointed across the room. ❑ *She ran her fingers through her hair.* **2** N-COUNT The **fingers** of a glove are the parts that a person's fingers fit into. ❑ *He bit the fingers of his right glove and pulled it off.* **3** N-COUNT A **finger of** something such as smoke or land is an amount of it that is shaped rather like a finger. ❑ *...a thin finger of land that separates Pakistan from the former Soviet Union.* **4** V-T If you **finger** something, you touch or feel it with your fingers. ❑ *He fingered the few coins in his pocket.* **5** PHRASE If you **cross** your **fingers**, you put one finger on top of another and hope for good luck. If you say that someone **is keeping their fingers crossed**, you mean they are hoping for good luck. ❑ *He crossed his fingers, asking for luck for the first time in his life.* **6** PHRASE If you say that someone did not **lay a finger on** a particular person or thing, you are emphasizing that they did not touch or harm them at all. [EMPHASIS] ❑ *I must make it clear I never laid a finger on her.* **7** PHRASE If you say that a person does not **lift a finger** or **raise a finger** to do something, especially to help someone, you are critical of them because they do nothing. [DISAPPROVAL] ❑ *She never lifted a finger around the house.* **8** PHRASE If you **point the finger at** someone or **point an accusing finger at** someone, you blame them or accuse them of doing wrong. ❑ *He said he wasn't pointing an accusing finger at anyone in the government or the army.* **9** PHRASE If you **put** your **finger on** something, for example, a reason or problem, you see and identify exactly what it is. ❑ *Midge couldn't quite put her finger on the reason.*

fin|ger|ing /ˈfɪŋgərɪŋ/ N-UNCOUNT **Fingering** is the method of using the most suitable finger to play each note when you are playing a musical instrument, especially the piano.

finger|mark /ˈfɪŋgərmɑːrk/ (**fingermarks**) N-COUNT A **fingermark** is a mark which is made when someone puts a dirty or oily finger onto a clean surface. [BRIT]

finger|nail /ˈfɪŋgərneɪl/ (**fingernails**) N-COUNT Your **fingernails** are the thin hard areas at the end of each of your fingers.

finger|print /ˈfɪŋgərprɪnt/ (**fingerprints, fingerprinting, fingerprinted**) **1** N-COUNT **Fingerprints** are marks made by a person's fingers which show the lines on the skin. Everyone's fingerprints are different, so they can be used to identify criminals. ❑ *The detective discovered no fewer than 35 fingerprints.* ❑ *...his fingerprint on the murder weapon.* • PHRASE If the police **take** someone's **fingerprints**, they make that person press their fingers onto a pad covered with ink, and then onto paper, so that they know what that person's fingerprints look like. **2** V-T [usu passive] If someone **is fingerprinted**, the police take their fingerprints. ❑ *He took her to jail, where she was fingerprinted and booked.*

finger|tip /ˈfɪŋgərtɪp/ (**fingertips**) also **finger-tip** **1** N-COUNT Your **fingertips** are the ends of your fingers. ❑ *The butter and flour are rubbed together with the fingertips.* **2** PHRASE If you say that something is **at** your **fingertips**, you approve of the fact that you can reach it easily or that it is easily available to you. [APPROVAL] ❑ *I had the information at my fingertips and hadn't used it.*

finger|tip search (**fingertip searches**) N-COUNT [oft N of n] When the police carry out a **fingertip search** of a place, they examine it for evidence in a very detailed way. [BRIT] ❑ *Officers continued a fingertip search of the area yesterday.*

fin|icky /ˈfɪnɪki/ ADJ If you say that someone is **finicky**, you mean that they are worried about small details and are difficult to please. [DISAPPROVAL] ❑ *Even the most finicky eater will find something appetizing here.*

fin|ish ♦♦◊ /ˈfɪnɪʃ/ (**finishes, finishing, finished**) **1** V-T When you **finish** doing or dealing with something, you do or deal with the last part of it, so that there is no more for you to do or deal with. ❑ *As soon as he'd finished eating, he excused himself.* ❑ *Mr. Gould was given a standing ovation and loud cheers when he finished his speech.* • PHRASAL VERB **Finish up** means the same as **finish**. [AM] ❑ *We waited a few minutes outside his office while he finished up his meeting.* **2** V-T When you **finish** something that you are making or producing, you reach the end of making or producing it, so that it is complete. ❑ *The consultants had been working to finish a report this week.* • PHRASAL VERB **Finish off** and **finish up** mean the same as **finish**. ❑ *Now she is busy finishing off a biography of Queen Caroline.* **3** V-T/V-I When something such as a course, show, or sale **finishes**, especially at a planned time, it ends. ❑ *The teaching day finishes at around 4 p.m.* **4** V-T/V-I You

say that someone or something **finishes** a period of time or an event in a particular way to indicate what the final situation was like. You can also say that a period of time or an event **finishes** in a particular way. ▫ *The two of them finished by kissing each other goodbye.* ▫ *The evening finished with the welcoming of three new members.* **5** V-I If someone **finishes** second, for example, in a race or competition, they are in second place at the end of the race or competition. ▫ *He finished second in the championship four years in a row.* **6** V-I To **finish** means to reach the end of saying something. ▫ *Her eyes flashed, but he held up a hand. "Let me finish."* **7** N-SING [the N, with poss] The **finish** of something is the end of it or the last part of it. ▫ *I intend to continue it and see the job through to the finish.* **8** N-COUNT The **finish** of a race is the end of it. ▫ *Win a trip to see the finish of the Tour de France!* **9** N-COUNT If the surface of something that has been made has a particular kind of **finish**, it has the appearance or texture mentioned. ▫ *The finish and workmanship of the woodwork were excellent.* **10** → see also **finished** **11** PHRASE If you add **the finishing touches** to something, you add or do the last things that are necessary to complete it. ▫ *Right up until the last minute, workers were still putting the finishing touches on the pavilions.*
▶ **finish off** **1** PHRASAL VERB If you **finish off** something that you have been eating or drinking, you eat or drink the last part of it with the result that there is none left. ▫ *Kelly finished off his coffee.* **2** PHRASAL VERB If someone **finishes off** a person or thing that is already badly injured or damaged, they kill or destroy them. ▫ *They meant to finish her off, swiftly and without mercy.* **3** → see also **finish 2**
▶ **finish up** **1** PHRASAL VERB If you **finish up** something that you have been eating or drinking, you eat or drink the last part of it. ▫ *Finish up your drinks now, please.* **2** → see also **finish 1, 2**
▶ **finish with** PHRASAL VERB If you **finish with** someone or something, you stop dealing with them or being involved with them. ▫ *My boyfriend was threatening to finish with me.*

fin|ished /fɪnɪʃt/ **1** ADJ [v-link ADJ with n] Someone who is **finished with** something is no longer doing it or dealing with it or is no longer interested in it. ▫ *One suspects he will be finished with boxing.* **2** ADJ [v-link ADJ] Something that is **finished** no longer exists or is no longer happening. ▫ *After each game is finished, a message flashes on the screen.* **3** ADJ [v-link ADJ] Someone or something that is **finished** is no longer important, powerful, or effective. ▫ *Her power over me is finished.*

fin|ish|ing line [BRIT] → see **finish line**

fin|ish|ing school (finishing schools) N-VAR A **finishing school** is a private school where rich or upper-class young women are taught manners and other social skills that are considered to be suitable for them. ▫ *...a Swiss finishing school.*

fin|ish line (finish lines) N-COUNT In a race, the **finish line** is the place on the track or course where the race officially ends.

fi|nite /faɪnaɪt/ ADJ Something that is **finite** has a definite fixed size or extent. [FORMAL] ▫ *...a finite set of elements.* ▫ *Only a finite number of situations can arise.*

Finn /fɪn/ (Finns) N-COUNT The **Finns** are the people of Finland.

Finn|ish /fɪnɪʃ/ **1** ADJ **Finnish** means belonging or relating to Finland or to its people, language, or culture. **2** N-UNCOUNT **Finnish** is the language spoken in Finland.

fir /fɜr/ (firs) N-VAR A **fir** or a **fir tree** is a tall evergreen tree that has thin needle-like leaves.

FIRE
① BURNING, HEAT, OR ENTHUSIASM
② SHOOTING OR ATTACKING
③ DISMISSAL
---

① **fire** ♦♦◇ /faɪər/ (fires, firing, fired)
→ Please look at meanings **11** – **13** to see if the expression you are looking for is shown under another headword.
1 N-UNCOUNT **Fire** is the hot, bright flames produced by things that are burning. ▫ *They saw a big flash and a huge ball of fire reaching hundreds of feet into the sky.* **2** N-COUNT **Fire** or a **fire** is an occurrence of uncontrolled burning which destroys buildings, forests, or other things. ▫ *87 people died in a fire at the club.* ▫ *A forest fire is sweeping across portions of north Maine this evening.* **3** N-COUNT A **fire** is a burning pile of wood, coal, or other fuel that you make, for example, to use for heat, light, or cooking. ▫ *There was a fire in the grate.* **4** N-COUNT A **fire** is a device that uses electricity or gas to give out heat and warm a room. [BRIT]

in AM, use **heater**

5 V-T When a pot or clay object **is fired**, it is heated at a high temperature in a special oven, as part of the process of making it. ▫ *After the pot is dipped in this mixture, it is fired.* **6** V-I When the engine of a motor vehicle **fires**, an electrical spark is produced which causes the fuel to burn and the engine to work. ▫ *The engine fired and we moved off.* **7** V-T If you **fire** someone with enthusiasm, you make them feel very enthusiastic. If you **fire** someone's imagination, you make them feel interested and excited. ▫ *...the potential to fire the imagination of an entire generation.* ▫ *It was Allen who fired this rivalry with real passion.* **8** PHRASE If an object or substance **catches fire**, it starts burning. ▫ *The blast caused several buildings to catch fire.* **9** PHRASE If something is **on fire**, it is burning and being damaged or destroyed by an uncontrolled fire. ▫ *The captain radioed that the ship was on fire.* **10** PHRASE If you **set fire to** something or if you **set** it **on fire**, you start it burning in order to damage or destroy it. ▫ *They set fire to vehicles outside that building.* **11 to have irons in the fire** → see **iron** **12 like a house on fire** → see **house** **13 where there's smoke there's fire** → see **smoke**

▶ **fire up** **1** PHRASAL VERB If you **fire up** a machine, you switch it on. ▫ *Fire up your engine and head out.* **2** PHRASAL VERB If you **fire** someone **up**, you make them feel very enthusiastic or motivated. ▫ *The president knows his task is to fire up the delegates.*

② **fire** ♦♦◇ /faɪər/ (fires, firing, fired) **1** V-T/V-I If someone **fires** a gun or a bullet, or if they **fire**, a bullet is sent from a gun that they are using. ▫ *Seven people were wounded when soldiers fired rubber bullets to disperse crowds.* • **fir|ing** N-UNCOUNT ▫ *The firing continued even while the protestors were fleeing.* **2** V-T If you **fire** an arrow, you send it from a bow. ▫ *He fired an arrow into a clearing in the forest.* **3** V-T If you **fire** questions at someone, you ask them a lot of questions very quickly, one after another. ▫ *They were bombarded by more than 100 representatives firing questions on pollution.* **4** N-UNCOUNT You can use **fire** to refer to the shots fired from a gun or guns. ▫ *His car was raked with fire from automatic weapons.* **5** PHRASE If someone **holds** their **fire** or **holds fire**, they stop shooting or they wait before they start shooting. ▫ *Devereux ordered his men to hold their fire until the ships got closer.* **6** PHRASE If you are in the **line of fire**, you are in a position where someone is aiming their gun at you. If you move into their **line of fire**, you move into a position between them and the thing they were aiming at. ▫ *He cheerfully blows away any bad guy stupid enough to get in his line of fire.* **7** PHRASE If you **open fire** on someone, you start shooting at them. ▫ *Then without warning, the troops opened fire on the crowd.* **8** PHRASE If you **return fire** or you **return** someone's **fire**, you shoot back at someone who has shot at you. ▫ *The soldiers returned fire after being attacked.* **9** PHRASE If you come **under fire** or are **under fire**, someone starts shooting at you. ▫ *The Belgians fell back as the infantry came under fire.* **10** PHRASE If you come **under fire** from someone or are **under** fire, they criticize you strongly. ▫ *The president's plan first came under fire from critics who said he hadn't included enough spending cuts.*

③ **fire** /faɪər/ (fires, firing, fired) V-T If an employer **fires** you, they dismiss you from your job. ▫ *If he hadn't been so good at the rest of his job, I probably would have fired him.* • **fir|ing** (firings) N-COUNT ▫ *There was yet another round of firings.*

fire alarm (fire alarms) N-COUNT A **fire alarm** is a device that makes a noise, for example, with a bell, to warn people when there is a fire. ▫ *The smoke sets off the fire alarm.*

fire|arm /faɪərɑrm/ (firearms) N-COUNT **Firearms** are guns. [FORMAL] ▫ *He was also charged with illegal possession of firearms.*

fire|ball /faɪərbɔl/ (fireballs) N-COUNT A **fireball** is a ball of fire, for example, one at the center of a nuclear explosion.

fire|bomb /faɪərbɒm/ (firebombs, firebombing, firebombed) **1** N-COUNT A **firebomb** is a type of bomb which is designed to cause fires. **2** V-T To **firebomb** a building, vehicle, or place means to set fire to it using a firebomb. ▫ *Protestors firebombed the embassy building yesterday.* • **fire|bombing** (firebombings) N-VAR ▫ *The homes bore evidence of firebombing.*

fire|brand /ˈfaɪərbrænd/ (firebrands) N-COUNT If you describe someone as a **firebrand**, especially someone who is very active in politics, you mean that they are always trying to make people take strong action. ❑ ...his reputation as a young firebrand.

fire|break /ˈfaɪərbreɪk/ (firebreaks) also **fire break** N-COUNT A **firebreak** is an area of open land in a wood or forest that has been created to stop a fire from spreading.

fire|cracker /ˈfaɪərkrækər/ (firecrackers) N-COUNT A **firecracker** is a firework that makes several loud bangs when it is lit.

-fired /-faɪərd/ COMB IN ADJ [usu ADJ n] **-fired** combines with nouns which refer to fuels to form adjectives which describe power stations, machines, or devices that operate by means of that fuel. ❑ ...coal-fired power stations. ❑ Most of the food is cooked on a large wood-fired oven.

fire de|part|ment (fire departments) N-COUNT-COLL [usu the N] The **fire department** is an organization which has the job of putting out fires. [AM]

fire drill (fire drills) N-VAR When there is a **fire drill** in a particular building, the people who spend time there practice what to do if there is a fire.

fire-eater (fire-eaters) N-COUNT **Fire-eaters** are performers who put flaming rods into their mouths in order to entertain people.

fire en|gine (fire engines) N-COUNT A **fire engine** is a large vehicle which carries firefighters and equipment for putting out fires.

fire es|cape (fire escapes) also **fire-escape** N-COUNT A **fire escape** is a metal staircase on the outside of a building, which can be used to escape from the building if there is a fire.

fire ex|tin|guish|er (fire extinguishers) also **fire-extinguisher** N-COUNT A **fire extinguisher** is a metal cylinder which contains water or chemicals at high pressure which can put out fires.

fire|fight /ˈfaɪərfaɪt/ (firefights) N-COUNT A **firefight** is a battle in a war which involves the use of guns rather than bombs or any other sort of weapon. [JOURNALISM] ❑ U.S. Marines had a firefight with local gunmen this morning.

fire|fighter /ˈfaɪərfaɪtər/ (firefighters) N-COUNT [usu pl] **Firefighters** are people whose job is to put out fires.

fire|fighting /ˈfaɪərfaɪtɪŋ/ N-UNCOUNT [oft N n] **Firefighting** is the work of putting out fires. ❑ There was no firefighting equipment.

fire|fly /ˈfaɪərflaɪ/ (fireflies) N-COUNT A **firefly** is a type of beetle that produces light from its body.

fire|guard /ˈfaɪərɡɑːrd/ (fireguards) N-COUNT A **fireguard** is a screen made of strong wire that you put around a fire so that people cannot accidentally burn themselves.

fire|house /ˈfaɪərhaʊs/ (firehouses) also **fire house** N-COUNT A **firehouse** is a building where fire trucks are kept, and where firefighters wait until they are called to put out a fire. [AM] ❑ ...the city's busiest firehouse.

fire hy|drant (fire hydrants) N-COUNT A **fire hydrant** is a pipe in the street from which firefighters can obtain water for putting out a fire.

fire|light /ˈfaɪərlaɪt/ N-UNCOUNT [also the N] **Firelight** is the light that comes from a fire. ❑ In the firelight his head gleamed with sweat.

fire|man /ˈfaɪərmən/ (firemen) N-COUNT A **fireman** is a man whose job is to put out fires.

fire|place /ˈfaɪərpleɪs/ (fireplaces) N-COUNT In a room, the **fireplace** is the place where a fire can be lit and the area on the wall and floor surrounding this place. ❑ In the evenings, we gathered around the fireplace and talked in hushed whispers.

fire|power /ˈfaɪərpaʊər/ N-UNCOUNT The **firepower** of an army, ship, tank, or aircraft is the amount of ammunition it can fire. ❑ The U.S. also had superior firepower.

fire|proof /ˈfaɪərpruːf/ ADJ Something that is **fireproof** cannot be damaged by fire. ❑ ...fireproof clothing.

fire-retardant /ˈfaɪərrɪtɑːrdənt/ ADJ **Fire-retardant** substances make the thing that they are applied to burn more slowly. ❑ ...fire-retardant foam.

fire sale (fire sales) ■ N-COUNT A **fire sale** is an event in which goods are sold cheaply because the store or storeroom they were in has been damaged by fire. ■ N-COUNT [oft N n] If you describe a sale of goods or other assets as a **fire sale**, you mean that everything is being sold very cheaply. ❑ They're likely to hold big fire sales to liquidate their inventory.

fire ser|vice (fire services) N-COUNT-COLL [usu the N] The **fire service** is an organization which has the job of putting out fires. [BRIT]

in AM, use **fire department**

fire|side /ˈfaɪərsaɪd/ (firesides) N-COUNT [usu sing] If you sit by the **fireside** in a room, you sit near the fireplace. ❑ ...winter evenings by the fireside. ❑ ...cozy fireside chats.

fire sta|tion (fire stations) N-COUNT A **fire station** is a building where fire trucks are kept, and where firefighters wait until they are called to put out a fire.

fire|storm /ˈfaɪərstɔːrm/ (firestorms) also **fire storm** ■ N-COUNT A **firestorm** is a fire that is burning uncontrollably, usually in a place that has been bombed. ■ N-COUNT [usu with supp] If you say that there is a **firestorm** of protest or criticism, you are emphasizing that there is a great deal of very fierce protest or criticism. [AM, EMPHASIS] ❑ The speech has resulted in a firestorm of controversy.

fire truck (fire trucks) N-COUNT A **fire truck** is a large vehicle which carries firefighters and equipment for putting out fires. [mainly AM, AUSTRALIAN]

fire|wall /ˈfaɪərwɔːl/ (firewalls) ■ N-COUNT A **firewall** is a computer system or program that automatically prevents an unauthorized person from gaining access to a computer when it is connected to a network such as the internet. [COMPUTING] ❑ New technology should provide a secure firewall against hackers. ■ → See feature box at **email**

fire|wood /ˈfaɪərwʊd/ N-UNCOUNT **Firewood** is wood that has been cut into pieces so that it can be burned on a fire. ❑ Young Geoffrey made money by chopping and selling firewood.

fire|work /ˈfaɪərwɜːrk/ (fireworks) N-COUNT **Fireworks** are small objects that are lit to entertain people on special occasions. They contain chemicals and burn brightly or attractively, often with a loud noise, when you light them. ❑ They drank champagne, set off fireworks and tooted their car horns.

fir|ing line (firing lines) ■ N-COUNT If you are in the **firing line** in a conflict, you are in a position where someone is aiming their gun at you. ❑ Any hostages in the firing line would have been sacrificed. ■ N-SING [the N, usu in/out of N] If you say that someone is in the **firing line**, you mean that they are being criticized, blamed, or attacked for something. ❑ Foreign banks are in the firing line too.

fir|ing squad (firing squads) N-COUNT [also by N] A **firing squad** is a group of soldiers who are ordered to shoot and kill a person who has been found guilty of committing a crime. ❑ He was executed by firing squad.

firm ♦♦♦ /fɜːrm/ (firms, firmer, firmest) ■ N-COUNT A **firm** is an organization which sells or produces something or which provides a service which people pay for. ❑ The firm's employees were expecting large bonuses. ❑ ...a legal assistant at a Chicago law firm. ■ ADJ If something is **firm**, it does not change much in shape when it is pressed but is not completely hard. ❑ Fruit should be firm and in excellent condition. ■ ADJ If someone's grip is **firm** or if they perform a physical action in a **firm** way, they do it with quite a lot of force or pressure but also in a controlled way. ❑ The quick handshake was firm and cool. ● **firm|ly** ADV [ADV after v] ❑ She held me firmly by the elbow and led me to my aisle seat. ■ ADJ If you describe someone as **firm**, you mean they behave in a way that shows that they are not going to change their mind, or that they are the person who is in control. ❑ She had to be firm with him. "I don't want to see you again." ● **firm|ly** ADV [ADV with v] ❑ "A good night's sleep is what you want," he said firmly. ■ ADJ A **firm** decision or opinion is definite and unlikely to change. ❑ He made a firm decision to leave Fort Multry by boat. ● **firm|ly** ADV ❑ Political values and opinions are firmly held, and can be slow to change. ■ ADJ [ADJ n] **Firm** evidence or information is based on facts and so is likely to be true. ❑ This man may have killed others but unfortunately we have no firm evidence. ■ ADJ You use **firm** to describe control or a basis or position when it is strong and unlikely to be ended or removed. ❑ Although the Yakutians are a minority, they have firm control of the territory. ● **firm|ly** ADV ❑ This tradition is also firmly rooted in the past. ■ ADJ

If something is **firm**, it does not shake or move when you put weight or pressure on it, because it is strongly made or securely fastened. ❑ *If you have to climb up, use a firm platform or a sturdy ladder.* ● **firm|ly** ADV ❑ *The front door is locked and all the windows are firmly shut.* **9** PHRASE If someone **stands firm**, they refuse to change their mind about something. ❑ *The council is standing firm against the protest.*

▶ **firm up** **1** PHRASAL VERB If you **firm up** something or if it **firms up**, it becomes firmer and more solid. ❑ *This treatment helps tone the body, firm up muscles and tighten the skin.* **2** PHRASAL VERB If you **firm** something **up** or if it **firms up**, it becomes clearer, stronger, or more definite. ❑ *We can give you more detail as our plans firm up.*

COLLOCATIONS

firm
NOUN **1**
noun + **firm**: accounting, consulting, investment, law; building, energy, engineering
adjective + **firm**: architectural, financial, legal, pharmaceutical; large, medium-sized, small
verb + **firm**: found, set up

SYNONYMS

firm
NOUN **1**
company: *Sheila found some work as a secretary in an insurance company.*
business: *The company was a family business.*
corporation: *...multi-national corporations.*
ADJ **2**
hard: *He shuffled his feet on the hard, wooden floor.*
solid: *The snow had melted, but the lake was still frozen solid.*
stiff: *His waterproof trousers were brand new and stiff.*
rigid: *...rigid plastic containers.*

fir|ma|ment /fɜrməmənt/ **1** N-SING [the N] **The firmament** is the sky or heaven. [LITERARY] ❑ *There are no stars in the firmament.* **2** N-SING [the N, usu with supp] If you talk about **the firmament** in a particular organization or field of activity, you mean the top of it. ❑ *He was rich, and a rising star in the political firmament.*

firm|ware /fɜrmwɛər/ N-UNCOUNT In computer systems, **firmware** is a set of commands which are stored on a chip rather than as part of a program, because the computer uses them very often. [COMPUTING]

first ✦✦✦ /fɜrst/ **1** ORD The **first** thing, person, event, or period of time is the one that happens or comes before all the others of the same kind. ❑ *She lost 16 pounds in the first month of her diet.* ❑ *...the first few flakes of snow.* ● PRON **First** is also a pronoun. ❑ *The second paragraph startled me even more than the first.* **2** ORD When something happens or is done for the **first** time, it has never happened or been done before. ❑ *This is the first time she has experienced disappointment.* ● ADV [ADV with v] **First** is also an adverb. ❑ *Anne and Steve got engaged two years after they had first started going out.* **3** ORD The **first** thing, person, or place in a line is the one that is nearest to you or nearest to the front. ❑ *Before him, in the first row, sat the president.* **4** ORD You use **first** to refer to the best or most important thing or person of a particular kind. ❑ *The first duty of any government must be to protect the interests of the taxpayers.* **5** ADV If you do something **first**, you do it before anyone else does, or before you do anything else. ❑ *I do not remember who spoke first, but we all expressed the same opinion.* ❑ *First, tell me what you think of my products.* **6** ADV [ADV before v] You use **first** when you are talking about what happens in the early part of an event or experience, in contrast to what happens later. ❑ *When he first came home he wouldn't say anything about what he'd been doing.* ● ORD **First** is also an ordinal. ❑ *She told him that her first reaction was disgust.* **7** ADV [ADV after v] In order to emphasize your determination not to do a particular thing, you can say that rather than do it, you would do something else **first**. [EMPHASIS] ❑ *I'll die first, before I let you have all my money!* **8** N-SING An event that is described as **a first** has never happened before and is important or exciting. ❑ *It is a first for New York. An outdoor exhibition of Fernando Botero's sculpture on Park Avenue.* **9** PRON [the PRON that] **The first** you hear of something or the **first** you know about it is the time when you first become aware of it. ❑ *We heard it on the TV last night – that was the first we heard of it.* **10** PHRASE You use **first of all** to introduce the first of a number of things that you want to say. ❑ *The cut in the interest rates has not had very much impact in California for two reasons. First of all, banks are still afraid to loan.* **11** PHRASE You use **at first** when you are talking about what happens in the early stages of an event or experience, or just after something else has happened, in contrast to what happens later. ❑ *At first, he seemed surprised by my questions.* **12** PHRASE If you say that someone or something **comes first** for a particular person, you mean they treat or consider that person or thing as more important than anything else. ❑ *There's no time for boyfriends, my career comes first.* **13** PHRASE You say '**first-come first-served**' to indicate that a group of people or things will be dealt with or given something in the order in which they arrive. ❑ *There will be five buses, first-come first-served.* **14** PHRASE If you learn or experience something **at first hand**, you experience it yourself or learn it directly rather than being told about it by other people. ❑ *He arrived in Natal to see at first hand the effects of the recent heavy fighting.* **15** PHRASE If you say that you **do not know the first thing about** something, you are emphasizing that you know absolutely nothing about it. [EMPHASIS] ❑ *You don't know the first thing about farming.* **16** PHRASE If you **put** someone or something **first**, you treat or consider them as more important than anything else. ❑ *Somebody has to think for the child and put him first.* **17 first and foremost** → see **foremost**

-first /-fɜrst/ COMB IN ADV [ADV after v] **-first** combines with nouns like 'head' and 'feet' to indicate that someone moves with the part that is mentioned pointing in the direction in which they are moving. ❑ *He overbalanced and fell head first.*

first aid N-UNCOUNT **First aid** is simple medical treatment given as soon as possible to a person who is injured or who suddenly becomes ill. ❑ *There are many emergencies which need prompt first aid treatment.*

First Amend|ment N-SING [the N] The **First Amendment** is the part of the U.S. Constitution that guarantees people the right of free speech, as well as freedom of religion, assembly, and petition. ❑ *Thornburgh said such demands wouldn't violate the First Amendment.*

first|born /fɜrstbɔrn/ N-SING [oft N n] Someone's **firstborn** is their first child. ❑ *She was my firstborn.*

first-class also **first class** **1** ADJ If you describe something or someone as **first-class**, you mean that they are extremely good and of the highest quality. ❑ *The food was first-class.* **2** ADJ [ADJ n] You use **first-class** to describe something that is in the group that is considered to be of the highest standard. ❑ *They always stayed in first-class hotels.* **3** ADJ [ADJ n] **First-class** accommodations on a train, airplane, or ship are the best and most expensive type of accommodations. ❑ *He won himself two first-class tickets to fly to Dublin.* ● ADV [ADV after v] **First-class** is also an adverb. ❑ *She had never flown first class before.* ● N-UNCOUNT **First-class** is the first-class accommodations on a train, airplane, or ship. ❑ *He paid for and was assigned a cabin in first class.* **4** ADJ [ADJ n] In the United States, **first-class** postage is the type of postage that is used for sending letters and postcards. ❑ *Two first-class stamps, please.*

first cous|in (**first cousins**) N-COUNT [oft with poss] Someone's **first cousin** is the same as their **cousin**. Compare **second cousin**.

first-degree **1** ADJ [ADJ n] In the United States, **first-degree** is used to describe crimes that are considered to be the most serious of their kind. For example, **first-degree** murder is when a murder is planned before it is carried out. ❑ *She was charged with first-degree murder.* ❑ *He pleaded guilty to a charge of first-degree robbery.* **2** ADJ [ADJ n] A **first-degree** burn is one of the least severe kind, where only the surface layer of the skin has been burned.

first ever also **first-ever** ADJ [usu ADJ n] Something that is the **first ever** one of its kind has never happened before. ❑ *It's the first-ever meeting between leaders of the two countries.*

First Fami|ly N-SING [the N] The **First Family** is the U.S. president and their spouse and children. [AM] ❑ *...the cameras which followed the First Family on their difficult vacation.*

first floor (first floors) **1** N-COUNT The **first floor** of a building is the one at ground level. [AM] **2** N-COUNT The **first floor** of a building is the floor immediately above the one at ground level. [BRIT]

> in AM, use **second floor**

first fruits N-PLURAL [usu N of n] The **first fruits** of a project or activity are the earliest results or profits. ☐ *The deal is one of the first fruits of a liberalization of foreign investment law.*

first hand also **first-hand, firsthand 1** ADJ [ADJ n] **First hand** information or experience is gained or learned directly, rather than from other people or from books. ☐ *School trips give children firsthand experience not available in the classroom.* • ADV [ADV after v] **First-hand** is also an adverb. ☐ *We've been through Germany and seen first-hand what's happening there.* **2 at first hand** → see **first**

first lady (first ladies) also **First Lady 1** N-COUNT [usu the N in sing] The **First Lady** in a country or state is the wife of the president or state governor, or a woman who performs the official duties normally performed by the wife. ☐ *America's First Lady stood on the sweeping staircase of the White House.* **2** N-COUNT [usu sing, N of n] If you refer to a woman as the **first lady of** something, you mean that you consider her to be better at the thing mentioned than any other person. ☐ *...the first lady of song, Ella Fitzgerald.*

first lan|guage (first languages) N-COUNT Someone's **first language** is the language that they learned first and speak best; used especially when someone speaks more than one language.

first|ly /fɜrstli/ ADV [ADV with cl/group] You use **firstly** in speech or writing when you want to give a reason, make a point, or mention an item that will be followed by others connected with it. ☐ *The program is now seven years behind schedule as a result, firstly of increased costs, then of technical problems.*

first name (first names) N-COUNT Your **first name** is the first of the names that were given to you when you were born. ☐ *Her first name was Mary. I don't know what her surname was.*

first night (first nights) N-COUNT [oft N n] The **first night** of a show, play, or performance is the first public performance of it.

first of|fend|er (first offenders) N-COUNT A **first offender** is a person who has been found guilty of a crime for the first time.

first per|son N-SING [the N] A statement in **the first person** is a statement about yourself, or about yourself and someone else. The subject of a statement like this is 'I' or 'we.' ☐ *He tells the story in the first person.*

first-rate also **first rate** ADJ If you say that something or someone is **first-rate**, you mean that they are extremely good and of the highest quality. [APPROVAL] ☐ *People who used his service knew they were dealing with a first-rate professional.*

first-timer (first-timers) N-COUNT A **first-timer** is someone who does something for the first time. ☐ *Gabrielle entered this year's charts faster than any first-timer before her.*

First World N-PROPER [the N, N n] The most prosperous and industrialized parts of the world are sometimes referred to as the **First World**. Compare **Third World**. [OLD-FASHIONED] ☐ *We in the First World cannot continue to isolate ourselves in our wealth and good fortune.* ☐ *...wealthy First World countries.*

First World War N-PROPER [the N] The **First World War** or **World War I** is the war that was fought between 1914 and 1918 in Europe.

fir tree (fir trees) N-COUNT A **fir tree** is the same as a **fir**.

fis|cal ✦◇◇ /fɪskəl/ ADJ [ADJ n] **Fiscal** is used to describe something that relates to government money or public money, especially taxes. ☐ *...in 1987, when the government tightened fiscal policy.*

> **SYNONYMS**
>
> **fiscal**
> ADJ
> **financial:** *The company is in financial difficulties.*
> **economic:** *...Poland's radical, economic reforms.*
> **monetary:** *Some countries tighten monetary policy to avoid inflation.*
> **budgetary:** *There are huge budgetary pressures on all governments in Europe.*

fis|cal cliff (fiscal cliffs) N-COUNT A **fiscal cliff** is a situation in which sudden changes in government spending and tax have a big and sudden effect on a country's economy. ☐ *The country is fast approaching the fiscal cliff.*

fis|cal year (fiscal years) N-COUNT A **fiscal year** is a period of twelve months, used by government, business, and other organizations in order to calculate their budgets, profits, and losses. Compare **calendar year**. [BUSINESS] ☐ *...the budget for the coming fiscal year.*

fish ✦◆◇ /fɪʃ/ (fish or fishes, fishes, fishing, fished)

> The form **fish** is usually used for the plural, but **fishes** can also be used.

1 N-COUNT A **fish** is a creature that lives in water and has a tail and fins. There are many different kinds of fish. ☐ *An expert angler was casting his line and catching a fish every time.* **2** N-UNCOUNT **Fish** is the flesh of a fish eaten as food. ☐ *Does dry white wine go best with fish?* **3** V-I If you **fish**, you try to catch fish, either for food or as a form of sport or recreation. ☐ *Brian remembers learning to fish in the Colorado River.* **4** V-I If you say that someone is **fishing** for information or praise, you disapprove of the fact that they are trying to get it from someone in an indirect way. [DISAPPROVAL] ☐ *He didn't want to create the impression that he was fishing for information.* **5** → see also **fishing 6** → See also color supplement

fish and chips N-PLURAL **Fish and chips** are fish fillets coated with batter and deep-fried, eaten with French fries. ☐ *Bring me back a takeout of fish and chips.*

fish|bowl /fɪʃboʊl/ (fishbowls) also **fish bowl 1** N-COUNT A **fishbowl** is a glass bowl in which you can keep fish as pets. ☐ *...the round fishbowl in which Samson the goldfish spent his days.* **2** N-COUNT [usu sing] You can use **fishbowl** to describe a place or situation that is open to observation. ☐ *The members of the family lived in a fishbowl where their behavior was constantly scrutinized.* ☐ *...in the fishbowl of the White House.*

fish cake (fish cakes) also **fishcake** N-COUNT A **fish cake** is a mixture of fish and potato that is made into a flat round shape, covered in breadcrumbs, and fried.

fisher|man /fɪʃərmən/ (fishermen) N-COUNT A **fisherman** is a person who catches fish as a job or for sport. ☐ *The Algarve is a paradise for fishermen whether river anglers or deep-sea fishermen.*

fish|ery /fɪʃəri/ (fisheries) **1** N-COUNT **Fisheries** are areas of the sea where fish are caught in large quantities for commercial purposes. ☐ *...the fisheries off Newfoundland.* **2** N-COUNT A **fishery** is a place where fish are bred and reared.

fish|ing ✦◇◇ /fɪʃɪŋ/ N-UNCOUNT **Fishing** is the sport, hobby, or business of catching fish. ☐ *Despite the poor weather the fishing has been pretty good.*

fish|ing rod (fishing rods) N-COUNT A **fishing rod** is a long thin pole which has a line and hook attached to it and which is used for catching fish.

fish|ing tack|le N-UNCOUNT **Fishing tackle** consists of all the equipment that is used in the sport of fishing, such as fishing rods, lines, hooks, and bait.

fish knife (fish knives) N-COUNT A **fish knife** is a knife that you use when you eat fish. It has a wide flat blade and does not have a sharp edge.

fish|monger /fɪʃmʌŋɡər, -mɒŋ-/ (fishmongers) **1** N-COUNT A **fishmonger** is a storekeeper who sells fish. [mainly BRIT] **2** N-COUNT [oft the N] The **fishmonger** or the **fishmonger's** is a store where fish is sold. [mainly BRIT]

fish|net /fɪʃnɛt/ N-UNCOUNT [usu N n] **Fishnet** tights or stockings are made from a stretchy fabric which has wide holes between its threads, rather like the holes in a fishing net.

fish slice (fish slices) also **fish-slice** N-COUNT A **fish slice** is a kitchen tool which consists of a flat part with narrow holes in it attached to a handle. It is used for turning or serving fish or other food that is cooked in a frying pan. [BRIT]

> in AM, use **spatula**

fish stick (fish sticks) N-COUNT [usu pl] **Fish sticks** are small long pieces of fish covered in breadcrumbs. They are usually sold in frozen form. [AM]

fish|tail /fɪʃteɪl/ (fishtails, fishtailing, fishtailed) V-I If a vehicle **fishtails**, the rear of the vehicle swings around in an

fishy /fɪʃi/ (fishier, fishiest) **1** ADJ A **fishy** taste or smell reminds you of fish. **2** ADJ If you describe a situation as **fishy**, you feel that someone is not telling the truth or behaving completely honestly. [INFORMAL] ☐ *There seems to be something fishy going on.*

fis|sion /fɪʃ°n/ N-UNCOUNT Nuclear **fission** is the splitting of the nucleus of an atom to produce a large amount of energy or cause a large explosion.

fis|sure /fɪʃər/ (fissures) N-COUNT A **fissure** is a deep crack in something, especially in rock or in the ground.

fist /fɪst/ (fists) N-COUNT Your hand is referred to as your **fist** when you have bent your fingers in toward the palm in order to hit someone, to make an angry gesture, or to hold something. ☐ *Angry protesters with clenched fists shouted their defiance.*

fist bump (fist bumps) N-COUNT If people greet each other with a **fist bump**, they briefly touch their clenched fists together.

fist|fight /fɪstfaɪt/ (fistfights) also **fist fight** N-COUNT A **fistfight** is a fight in which people punch each other. ☐ *Their argument almost ended in a fistfight.*

fist|ful /fɪstfʊl/ (fistfuls) N-COUNT [usu N *of* n] A **fistful** of things is the number of them that you can hold in your fist. ☐ *Mandy handed him a fistful of coins.*

fisti|cuffs /fɪstɪkʌfs/ N-UNCOUNT **Fisticuffs** is fighting in which people try to hit each other with their fists. [HUMOROUS or OLD-FASHIONED]

FIT
① BEING RIGHT OR GOING IN THE RIGHT PLACE
② HEALTHY
③ UNCONTROLLABLE MOVEMENTS OR EMOTIONS
---

① **fit** ◆◆◇ /fɪt/ (fits, fitting, fitted *or* fit)
→ Please look at meanings **14** – **16** to see if the expression you are looking for is shown under another headword.

1 V-T/V-I If something **fits**, it is the right size and shape to go onto a person's body or onto a particular object. ☐ *The sash, kimono, and other garments were made to fit a child.* ☐ *She has to go to the men's department to find trousers that fit at the waist.* **2** V-T [usu passive] If you **are fitted** for a particular piece of clothing, you try it on so that the person who is making it can see where it needs to be altered. ☐ *She was being fitted for her wedding dress.* **3** V-I If something **fits** somewhere, it can be put there or is designed to be put there. ☐ *...a pocket computer which is small enough to fit into your pocket.* ☐ *He folded his long legs to fit under the table.* **4** V-T If you **fit** something into a particular space or place, you put it there. ☐ *...she fitted her key in the lock.* ☐ *Who could cut the millions of stone blocks and fit them together?* **5** V-T If you **fit** something somewhere, you attach it there, or put it there carefully and securely. ☐ *Fit hinge bolts to give extra support to the door lock.* ☐ *Peter had built the overhead ladders, and the next day he fitted them to the wall.* **6** V-T/V-I If something **fits** something else or **fits** into it, it goes together well with that thing or is able to be part of it. ☐ *Her daughter doesn't fit the current feminine ideal.* ☐ *Fostering is a full-time job and you should carefully consider how it will fit into your career.* **7** V-T You can say that something **fits** a particular person or thing when it is appropriate or suitable for them or it. ☐ *The punishment must always fit the crime.* **8** V-T If something **fits** someone for a particular task or role, it makes them good enough or suitable for it. [FORMAL] ☐ *...a man whose past experience fits him for the top job in education.* **9** N-SING If something is a good **fit**, it fits well. ☐ *Eventually he was happy that the sills and doors were a reasonably good fit.* **10** ADJ If something is **fit** for a particular purpose, it is suitable for that purpose. ☐ *Of the seven bicycles we had, only two were fit for the road.* **11** ADJ If someone is **fit** to do something, they have the appropriate qualities or skills that will allow them to do it. ☐ *You're not fit to be a mother!* ☐ *In a word, this government isn't fit to rule.* • **fit|ness** N-UNCOUNT ☐ *There is a debate about his fitness for the highest office.* **12** PHRASE If you say that someone **sees fit** to do something, you mean that they are entitled to do it, but that you disapprove of their decision to do it. [FORMAL, DISAPPROVAL] ☐ *He's not a friend, you say, yet you saw fit to lend him money.* **13** → see also **fitted, fitting 14** to fit the bill → see **bill 15** to fit like a glove → see **glove 16** not in a fit state → see **state**

▶ **fit in 1** PHRASAL VERB If you manage to **fit** a person or task **in**, you manage to find time to deal with them. ☐ *We work long hours both outside and inside the home and we rush around trying to fit everything in.* **2** PHRASAL VERB If you **fit in** as part of a group, you seem to belong there because you are similar to the other people in it. ☐ *She was great with the children and fit in beautifully.* **3** PHRASAL VERB If you say that someone or something **fits in**, you understand how they form part of a particular situation or system. ☐ *He knew where I fitted in and what he had to do to get the best out of me.*

▶ **fit out** PHRASAL VERB If you **fit** someone or something **out**, or you **fit** them **up**, you provide them with equipment and other things that they need. ☐ *We helped to fit him out for a trip to the Baltic.* ☐ *I suggest we fit you up with an office suite.*

▶ **fit up** PHRASAL VERB → see **fit out**

COLLOCATIONS

fit
VERB ① **1**
fit + *adverb*: comfortably, neatly, snugly; nicely, perfectly
ADJ ② **1**
adverb + **fit**: extremely, incredibly, supremely; mentally, physically; fairly, pretty, reasonably
---

② **fit** ◆◇◇ /fɪt/ (fitter, fittest) ADJ Someone who is **fit** is healthy and physically strong. ☐ *An averagely fit person can master easy ski runs within a few days.* • **fit|ness** N-UNCOUNT ☐ *Squash was once thought to offer all-round fitness.*

③ **fit** /fɪt/ (fits) **1** N-COUNT If you have a **fit of** coughing or laughter, you suddenly start coughing or laughing in an uncontrollable way. ☐ *Halfway down the cigarette she had a fit of coughing.* **2** N-COUNT If you do something in a **fit of** anger or panic, you are very angry or afraid when you do it. ☐ *Pattie shot Tom in a fit of jealous rage.* **3** N-COUNT If someone has a **fit** they suddenly lose consciousness and their body makes uncontrollable movements. ☐ *About two in every five epileptic fits occur during sleep.* **4** N-COUNT If someone has a **fit** or throws a **fit**, they suddenly become very agitated because they are angry or worried about something. [INFORMAL] ☐ *When my landlady said she wanted to keep $380 of my deposit to paint the walls, I threw a fit.* ☐ *"Cathy will have a fit when she finds out you bought all that fishing gear," Harrington said.*

fit|ful /fɪtfəl/ ADJ Something that is **fitful** happens for irregular periods of time or occurs at irregular times, rather than being continuous. ☐ *Colin drifted off into a fitful sleep.*

fit|ted /fɪtɪd/ **1** ADJ A **fitted** piece of clothing is designed so that it is the same size and shape as your body rather than being loose. ☐ *...baggy trousers with fitted jackets.* **2** ADJ [ADJ n] A **fitted** sheet has the corners sewn so that they fit over the corners of the mattress and do not have to be folded.

fit|ter /fɪtər/ (fitters) N-COUNT A **fitter** is a person whose job is to put together, adjust, or install machinery or equipment. ☐ *George was a fitter at the shipyard.*

fit|ting /fɪtɪŋ/ (fittings) **1** N-COUNT A **fitting** is one of the smaller parts on the outside of a piece of equipment or furniture, for example, a handle or a faucet. ☐ *...brass light fittings.* ☐ *...industrial fittings for kitchen and bathroom.* **2** N-COUNT If someone has a **fitting**, they try on a piece of clothing that is being made for them to see if it fits. ☐ *She lunched and shopped and went for fittings for clothes she didn't need.* **3** N-PLURAL **Fittings** are things such as ovens or heaters, that are fitted inside a building, but can be removed if necessary. ☐ *...a detailed list of what fixtures and fittings are included in the purchase price.* **4** ADJ Something that is **fitting** is right or suitable. ☐ *A solitary man, it was perhaps fitting that he should have died alone.* • **fit|ting|ly** ADV ☐ *He closed out his career, fittingly, by hitting a home run.*

-fitting /-fɪtɪŋ/ COMB IN ADJ **-fitting** combines with adjectives or adverbs such as 'close,' 'loose,' or 'tightly' to show that something is the size indicated in relation to the thing it is on, in, or next to. ☐ *She was dressed in a white, loose-fitting shirt.* ☐ *...glass bottles with tight-fitting caps.*

five ◆◆◆ /faɪv/ (fives) NUM **Five** is the number 5. ☐ *I spent five years there and had a really good time.*

fiv|er /faɪvər/ (fivers) N-COUNT A **fiver** is a five dollar bill. [INFORMAL]

fix ♦◊◊ /fɪks/ (fixes, fixing, fixed) **1** V-T If you **fix** something which is damaged or which does not work properly, you repair it. ❏ *He cannot fix the electricity.* **2** V-T If you **fix** a problem or a bad situation, you deal with it and make it satisfactory. ❏ *It's not too late to fix the problem, although time is clearly getting short.* **3** V-T If you **fix** some food or a drink for someone, you make it or prepare it for them. ❏ *Sarah fixed some food for us.* ❏ *Let me fix you a drink.* **4** V-T If you **fix** your hair, clothes, or makeup, you arrange or adjust them so you look neat and tidy, showing you have taken care with your appearance. [INFORMAL] ❏ *"I've got to fix my hair," I said and retreated to my bedroom.* **5** V-T If you **fix** something, for example, a date, price, or policy, you decide and say exactly what it will be. ❏ *He's going to fix a time when I can see him.* ❏ *The date of the election was fixed.* **6** V-T If you **fix** something for someone, you arrange for it to happen or you organize it for them. ❏ *I've fixed it for you to see Bonnie Lachlan.* ❏ *It's fixed. He's going to meet us at the airport.* ❏ *He vanished after you fixed him with a job.* **7** V-T If something **is fixed** somewhere, it is attached there firmly or securely. ❏ *It is fixed on the wall.* ❏ *Most blinds can be fixed directly to the top of the window-frame.* **8** V-T/V-I If you **fix** your eyes **on** someone or something or if your eyes **fix on** them, you look at them with complete attention. ❏ *She fixes her steel-blue eyes on an unsuspecting local official.* ❏ *Her soft brown eyes fixed on Kelly.* **9** V-T If someone or something **is fixed in** your mind, you remember them well, for example, because they are very important, interesting, or unusual. ❏ *Leonard was now fixed in his mind.* **10** V-T If someone **fixes** a gun, camera, or radar **on** something, they point it at that thing. ❏ *The U.S. crew fixed its radar on the Turkish ship.* **11** V-T If someone **fixes** a race, election, contest, or other event, they make unfair or illegal arrangements or use deception to affect the result. [DISAPPROVAL] ❏ *They offered opposing players bribes to fix a decisive game.* • N-COUNT **Fix** is also a noun. ❏ *It's all a fix, a deal they've made.* **12** V-T If you accuse someone of **fixing** prices, you accuse them of making unfair arrangements to charge a particular price for something, rather than allowing market forces to decide it. [BUSINESS, DISAPPROVAL] ❏ *...a suspected cartel that had fixed the price of steel for the construction market.* **13** N-COUNT You can refer to a solution to a problem as a **fix**. [INFORMAL] ❏ *Many of those changes could just be a temporary fix.* **14** → see also **quick fix** **15** N-SING If you get **a fix on** someone or something, you have a clear idea or understanding of them. [INFORMAL] ❏ *It's been hard to get a steady fix on what's going on.* **16** → see also **fixed**

▶ **fix up 1** PHRASAL VERB If you **fix** something **up**, you do work that is necessary in order to make it more suitable or attractive. ❏ *I've fixed up Matthew's old room.* **2** PHRASAL VERB If you **fix** someone **up with** something they need, you provide it for them. ❏ *We'll fix him up with a tie.* **3** PHRASAL VERB If you **fix** something **up**, you arrange it. [BRIT]

COLLOCATIONS

fix
NOUN **13**
noun + **fix**: bug, software
adjective + **fix**: easy, instant, short-term, temporary

---

fix|at|ed /fɪkseɪtɪd/ ADJ [v-link ADJ on/with/by n] If you accuse someone of being **fixated** on a particular thing, you mean that they think about it to an extreme and excessive degree. ❏ *But by then the administration wasn't paying attention, for top officials were fixated on Kuwait.*

fixa|tion /fɪkseɪʃ°n/ (fixations) N-COUNT [usu sing, usu with supp] If you accuse a person of having a **fixation** on something or someone, you mean they think about a particular subject or person to an extreme and excessive degree. ❏ *The country's fixation on the war may delay a serious examination of domestic needs.*

fixa|tive /fɪksətɪv/ (fixatives) N-MASS **Fixative** is a liquid used to preserve the surface of things such as a drawings or photographs.

fixed ♦◊◊ /fɪkst/ **1** ADJ You use **fixed** to describe something which stays the same and does not or cannot vary. ❏ *They issue a fixed number of shares that trade publicly.* ❏ *Many restaurants offer fixed-price menus.* **2** ADJ If you say that someone has **fixed** ideas or opinions, you mean that they do not often change their ideas and opinions, although perhaps they should. ❏ *...people who have fixed ideas about things.* **3** ADJ If someone has a **fixed** smile on their face, they are smiling even though they do not feel happy or pleased. ❏ *I had to go through the rest of the evening with a fixed smile on my face.* **4** PHRASE Someone who is of **no fixed address** does not have a permanent place to live. [FORMAL] ❏ *They are not able to get a job interview because they have no fixed address.* **5** → see also **fix**

fixed as|set (fixed assets) N-COUNT **Fixed assets** are assets which a company uses on a continuous basis, such as property and machinery. [BUSINESS] ❏ *Investment in fixed assets is important to ensure that the latest technology is available to business.*

fix|ed|ly /fɪksɪdli/ ADV [ADV after v] If you stare **fixedly** at someone or something, you look at them steadily and continuously for a period of time. [LITERARY] ❏ *I stared fixedly at the statue.*

fix|er /fɪksər/ (fixers) N-COUNT If someone is a **fixer**, he or she is the sort of person who solves problems and gets things done. [mainly BRIT, JOURNALISM]

fix|ings /fɪksɪŋz/ **1** N-PLURAL **Fixings** are extra items that are used to decorate or complete something, especially a meal. [AM] ❏ *He bought a hot dog and had it covered with all the fixings.* **2** N-PLURAL **Fixings** are items such as nails and screws which are used to fix things such as furniture together. [BRIT]

fix|ity /fɪksɪti/ N-UNCOUNT [oft N of n] If you talk about the **fixity** of something, you talk about the fact that it does not change or weaken. [WRITTEN] ❏ *She believed in the fixity of the class system.*

fix|ture /fɪkstʃər/ (fixtures) N-COUNT **Fixtures** are fittings or furniture which belong to a building and are legally part of it, for example, a bathtub or a toilet. ❏ *...a detailed list of what fixtures and fittings are included in the purchase price.*

fizz /fɪz/ (fizzes, fizzing, fizzed) V-I If a drink **fizzes**, it produces a lot of little bubbles of gas and makes a sound like a long 's.' ❏ *After a while their mother was back, holding a tray of glasses that fizzed.* • N-UNCOUNT **Fizz** is also a noun. ❏ *I wonder if there's any fizz left in the lemonade.*

fiz|zle /fɪz°l/ (fizzles, fizzling, fizzled) V-I If something **fizzles**, it ends in a weak or disappointing way after starting off strongly. ❏ *Our relationship fizzled into nothing.* • PHRASAL VERB **Fizzle out** means the same as **fizzle**. ❏ *The railway strike fizzled out on its second day as drivers returned to work.*

fizzy /fɪzi/ (fizzier, fizziest) ADJ **Fizzy** liquids contain small bubbles of carbon dioxide. They make a sound like a long 's' when you pour them. ❏ *...fizzy water.*

fjord /fyɔrd/ (fjords) also **fiord** N-COUNT A **fjord** is a strip of sea that comes into the land between high cliffs, especially in Norway.

flab /flæb/ N-UNCOUNT If you say that someone has **flab**, you mean they have loose flesh on their body because they are rather fat, especially when you are being critical of them. [DISAPPROVAL] ❏ *Don had a hefty roll of flab overhanging his waistband.*

flab|ber|gast|ed /flæbərgæstɪd/ ADJ If you say that you are **flabbergasted**, you are emphasizing that you are extremely surprised. [EMPHASIS] ❏ *Everybody was flabbergasted when I announced I was going to emigrate to Australia.*

flab|by /flæbi/ (flabbier, flabbiest) **1** ADJ **Flabby** people are rather fat, with loose flesh over their bodies. [DISAPPROVAL] ❏ *This exercise is great for getting rid of flabby arms.* **2** ADJ If you describe something as **flabby**, you are criticizing it for being disorganized or wasteful. [DISAPPROVAL] ❏ *You hear talk about American business being flabby.*

flac|cid /flæksɪd, flæsɪd/ ADJ You use **flaccid** to describe a part of someone's body when it is unpleasantly soft and not hard or firm. ❏ *I picked up her wrist. It was limp and flaccid.*

flack /flæk/ N-UNCOUNT **Flack** is another spelling of **flak**. ❏ *I took a lot of flack for not playing up to expectations.*

flag ♦◊◊ /flæg/ (flags, flagging, flagged) **1** N-COUNT A **flag** is a piece of cloth which can be attached to a pole and which is used as a sign, signal, or symbol of something, especially of a particular country. ❑ *The Marines climbed to the roof of the embassy building to raise the American flag.* ❷ N-COUNT Journalists sometimes refer to the **flag** of a particular country or organization as a way of referring to the country or organization itself and its values or power. ❑ *Every person who serves under the American flag will answer to his or her own superiors and to military law.* ❸ V-I If you **flag** or if your spirits **flag**, you begin to lose enthusiasm or energy. ❑ *His enthusiasm was in no way flagging.*

COLLOCATIONS

flag
NOUN ❶
adjective + **flag**: checkered, red, white; national
verb + **flag**: fly, unfurl, wave; hoist, raise

Flag Day N-UNCOUNT In the United States, **Flag Day** is the 14th of June, the anniversary of the day in 1777 when the Stars and Stripes became the official U.S. flag.

flag|el|la|tion /flædʒəleɪʃᵊn/ N-UNCOUNT **Flagellation** is the act of beating yourself or someone else, usually as a religious punishment. [FORMAL]

flagged /flægd/ ADJ A **flagged** path or area of ground is covered with large, flat, square pieces of stone.

flag|on /flægən/ (flagons) ❶ N-COUNT A **flagon** is a wide bottle in which liquids such as wine are sold. [OLD-FASHIONED] ❷ N-COUNT A **flagon** is a jug with a narrow neck in which wine or another drink is served. [OLD-FASHIONED]

flag|pole /flægpoʊl/ (flagpoles) N-COUNT A **flagpole** is a tall pole on which a flag can be displayed. ❑ *The new Namibian flag was hoisted up the flagpole.*

fla|grant /fleɪgrənt/ ADJ [ADJ n] You can use **flagrant** to describe an action, situation, or someone's behavior that you find extremely bad or shocking in a very obvious way. [DISAPPROVAL] ❑ *The judge called the decision "a flagrant violation of international law."*

flag|ship /flægʃɪp/ (flagships) ❶ N-COUNT The **flagship** of a group of things that are owned or produced by a particular organization is the most important one. ❑ *The company plans to open a flagship store in New York this month.* ❷ N-COUNT A **flagship** is the most important ship in a fleet of ships, especially the one on which the commander of the fleet is sailing. [mainly BRIT]

flag|staff /flægstæf/ (flagstaffs) N-COUNT A **flagstaff** is the same as a **flagpole**.

flag|stone /flægstoʊn/ (flagstones) N-COUNT [usu pl] **Flagstones** are large, flat, square pieces of stone which are used for covering a path or area of ground.

flag-waving N-UNCOUNT You can use **flag-waving** to refer to the expression of feelings for a country in a loud or exaggerated way, especially when you disapprove of this. [DISAPPROVAL] ❑ *The real costs of the war have been ignored in the flag-waving of recent months.*

flail /fleɪl/ (flails, flailing, flailed) V-T/V-I If your arms or legs **flail** or if you **flail** them about, they wave about in an energetic but uncontrolled way. ❑ *His arms were flailing in all directions.* • PHRASAL VERB **Flail around** means the same as **flail**. ❑ *He started flailing around and hitting Vincent in the chest.*

flair /fleər/ ❶ N-SING If you have a **flair for** a particular thing, you have a natural ability to do it well. ❑ *...a friend who has a flair for languages.* ❷ N-UNCOUNT If you have **flair**, you do things in an original, interesting, and stylish way. [APPROVAL] ❑ *Their work has all the usual punch, panache and flair you'd expect.*

flak /flæk/ N-UNCOUNT If you get a lot of **flak** from someone, they criticize you severely. If you take **flak**, you get the blame for something. [INFORMAL] ❑ *The president is getting a lot of flak for that.*

flake /fleɪk/ (flakes, flaking, flaked) ❶ N-COUNT A **flake** is a small thin piece of something, especially one that has broken off a larger piece. ❑ *...flakes of paint.* ❑ *Large flakes of snow began swiftly to fall.* ❷ V-I If something such as paint **flakes**, small thin pieces of it come off. ❑ *They can see how its colors have faded and where paint has flaked.* • PHRASAL VERB **Flake off** means the same as **flake**. ❑ *The surface corrosion was worst where the paint had flaked off.* ❸ N-COUNT If you refer to someone as a **flake**, you mean that you think they are very unreliable. [INFORMAL] ❑ *Sophie turned out to be such a flake. She said she'd meet me here and instead I'm just lying around this hotel room and I'm totally bored.*

flak jack|et (flak jackets) N-COUNT A **flak jacket** is a thick sleeveless jacket that soldiers and police officers sometimes wear to protect themselves against bullets.

flaky /fleɪki/ (flakier, flakiest) ❶ ADJ Something that is **flaky** breaks easily into small thin pieces or tends to come off in small thin pieces. ❑ *...a small patch of red, flaky skin.* ❷ ADJ If you describe an idea, argument, or person as **flaky**, you mean that they are rather eccentric and unreliable. [INFORMAL, DISAPPROVAL] ❑ *He wondered if the idea wasn't just a little too flaky, a little too outlandish.*

flam|boy|ant /flæmbɔɪənt/ ADJ If you say that someone or something is **flamboyant**, you mean that they are very noticeable, stylish, and exciting. ❑ *Freddie Mercury was a flamboyant star of the hard rock scene.* • **flam|boy|ance** N-UNCOUNT ❑ *Campese was his usual mixture of flamboyance and flair.*

flame /fleɪm/ (flames, flaming, flamed) ❶ N-VAR A **flame** is a hot bright stream of burning gas that comes from something that is burning. ❑ *The heat from the flames was so intense that roads melted.* ❷ N-COUNT A **flame** is an online message which severely criticizes or attacks someone. [INFORMAL, COMPUTING] ❑ *The best way to respond to a flame is to ignore it.* • V-T **Flame** is also a verb. ❑ *Ever been flamed?* ❸ → see also **flaming** ❹ PHRASE If something **bursts into flames** or **bursts into flame**, it suddenly starts burning strongly. ❑ *She managed to scramble out of the vehicle as it burst into flames.* ❺ PHRASE Something that is **in flames** is on fire. ❑ *I woke to a city in flames.* ❻ → See feature box at **Olympic Games**

fla|men|co /fləmɛŋkoʊ/ (flamencos) N-VAR **Flamenco** is a Spanish dance that is danced to a special type of guitar music.

flame|proof /fleɪmpruːf/ also **flame-proof** ADJ [usu ADJ n] **Flameproof** cooking dishes can withstand direct heat, so they can be used, for example, on top of a stove, or under a broiler.

flame-retardant /fleɪmrɪtɑːrdənt/ ADJ **Flame-retardant** is the same as **fire-retardant**.

flame thrower (flame throwers) N-COUNT A **flame thrower** is a gun that can send out a stream of burning liquid and that is used as a weapon or for clearing plants from an area of ground.

flam|ing /fleɪmɪŋ/ ADJ **Flaming** is used to describe something that is burning and producing a lot of flames. ❑ *The plane, which was full of fuel, scattered flaming fragments over a large area.*

fla|min|go /fləmɪŋgoʊ/ (flamingos or flamingoes) N-COUNT A **flamingo** is a bird with pink feathers, long thin legs, a long neck, and a curved beak. Flamingos live near water in warm areas.

flam|mable /flæməbᵊl/ ADJ **Flammable** chemicals, gases, cloth, or other things catch fire and burn easily. ❑ *...flammable liquids such as gasoline or kerosene.*

flan /flæn, flɑn/ (flans) ❶ N-VAR A **flan** is a custard dessert with a caramel sauce. [AM] ❷ N-VAR A **flan** is a food that has a base and sides of pastry or sponge cake. The base is filled with fruit or savory food.

flange /flændʒ/ (flanges) N-COUNT A **flange** is a projecting edge on an object. Its purpose is to strengthen the object or to connect it to another object. ❑ *...a steel plate with mounting flange.*

flank /flæŋk/ (flanks, flanking, flanked) ❶ N-COUNT An animal's **flank** is its side, between the ribs and the hip. ❑ *He put his hand on the dog's flank.* ❷ N-COUNT A **flank** of an army or navy force is one side of it when it is organized for battle. ❑ *The assault element, led by Captain Ramirez, opened up from their right flank.* ❸ N-COUNT The side of anything large can be referred to as its **flank**. ❑ *They continued along the flank of the mountain.* ❹ V-T If something **is flanked** by things, it has them on both sides of it, or sometimes has them on one side of it. ❑ *The altar was flanked by two Christmas trees.*

flan|nel /flænᵊl/ (flannels) ❶ N-UNCOUNT [oft N n] **Flannel** is a soft cloth, usually made of cotton or wool, that is used for making clothes. ❑ *He wore a faded red flannel shirt.* ❷ N-COUNT

A **flannel** is a small cloth that you use for washing yourself. [BRIT]

in AM, use **washcloth**

flap /flæp/ (flaps, flapping, flapped) **1** V-T/V-I If something such as a piece of cloth or paper **flaps** or if you **flap** it, it moves quickly up and down or from side to side. ◻ *Gray sheets flapped on the clothes line.* **2** V-T/V-I If a bird or insect **flaps** its wings or if its wings **flap**, the wings move quickly up and down. ◻ *The bird flapped its wings furiously.* **3** V-T If you **flap** your arms, you move them quickly up and down as if they were the wings of a bird. ◻ *...a kid running and flapping her arms.* **4** N-COUNT A **flap** of cloth or skin, for example, is a flat piece of it that can move freely up and down or from side to side because it is held or attached by only one edge. ◻ *He drew back the tent flap and strode out into the blizzard.* **5** N-COUNT A **flap** on the wing of an aircraft is an area along the edge of the wing that can be raised or lowered to control the movement of the aircraft. ◻ *...the sudden slowing as the flaps were lowered.* **6** → See also color supplement

flap|jack /flæpdʒæk/ (flapjacks) N-COUNT **Flapjacks** are the same as **pancakes**. [AM]

flap|per /flæpər/ (flappers) N-COUNT A **flapper** was a young woman in the 1920s who dressed or behaved in an unconventional way. ◻ *She'd had to wear her short, auburn hair flat like a twenties flapper for the play.*

flare /flɛər/ (flares, flaring, flared) **1** N-COUNT A **flare** is a small device that produces a bright flame. Flares are used as signals, for example, on ships. ◻ *...a ship which had fired a distress flare.* **2** V-I If a fire **flares**, the flames suddenly become larger. ◻ *Camp fires flared like beacons in the dark.* • PHRASAL VERB **Flare up** means the same as **flare**. ◻ *Don't spill too much fat on the barbecue as it could flare up.* **3** V-I If something such as trouble, violence, or conflict **flares**, it starts or becomes more violent. ◻ *Even as the president appealed for calm, trouble flared in several American cities.* • PHRASAL VERB **Flare up** means the same as **flare**. ◻ *Dozens of people were injured as fighting flared up.* **4** V-I If people's tempers **flare**, they get angry. ◻ *Tempers flared and harsh words were exchanged.*

flared /flɛərd/ ADJ [usu ADJ n] **Flared** skirts or pants are wider at the bottom or at the end of the legs than at the top. ◻ *In the 1970s they all had flared pants.*

flare-up (flare-ups) N-COUNT If there is a **flare-up** of violence or of an illness, it suddenly starts or gets worse. ◻ *There's been a flare-up of violence in South Africa.*

flash ✦◇◇ /flæʃ/ (flashes, flashing, flashed) **1** N-COUNT A **flash** is a sudden burst of light or of something shiny or bright. ◻ *A sudden flash of lightning lit everything up for a second.* ◻ *The wire snapped at the wall plug with a blue flash.* **2** V-T/V-I If a light **flashes** or if you **flash** a light, it shines with a sudden bright light, especially as quick, regular flashes of light. ◻ *Lightning flashed among the distant dark clouds.* ◻ *He lost his temper after a driver flashed her headlights as he overtook.* **3** V-I If something **flashes** past or by, it moves past you so fast that you cannot see it properly. ◻ *It was a busy road, cars flashed by every few minutes.* **4** V-I If something **flashes through** or **into** your mind, you suddenly think about it. ◻ *A ludicrous thought flashed through Harry's mind.* **5** V-T If you **flash** something such as an identification card, you show it to people quickly and then put it away again. [INFORMAL] ◻ *Halim flashed his official card, and managed to get hold of a soldier to guard the Land Rover.* **6** V-T/V-I If a picture or message **flashes** up on a screen, or if you **flash** it onto a screen, it is displayed there briefly or suddenly, and often repeatedly. ◻ *The figures flash up on the scoreboard.* ◻ *The words "Good Luck" were flashing on the screen.* **7** V-T If you **flash** a look or a smile at someone, you suddenly look at them or smile at them. [WRITTEN] ◻ *I flashed a look at Sue.* **8** N-UNCOUNT **Flash** is the use of special bulbs to give more light when taking a photograph. ◻ *He was one of the first people to use high speed flash in bird photography.* **9** N-COUNT A **flash** is the same as a **flashlight**. [AM, INFORMAL] ◻ *Stopping to rest, Pete shut off the flash.* **10** PHRASE If you say that something happens **in a flash**, you mean that it happens suddenly and lasts only a very short time. ◻ *The answer had come to him in a flash.* **11** PHRASE If you say that someone reacts to something **quick as a flash**, you mean that they react to it extremely quickly. ◻ *Quick as a flash, the man said, "I have to, don't I?"*

COLLOCATIONS

flash
NOUN **1**
noun + **flash**: lightning
adjective + **flash**: blinding, bright, vivid; blue, white; sudden

---

flash|back /flæʃbæk/ (flashbacks) **1** N-COUNT In a movie, novel, or play, a **flashback** is a scene that returns to events in the past. ◻ *There is even a flashback to the murder itself.* **2** N-COUNT If you have a **flashback** to a past experience, you have a sudden and very clear memory of it. ◻ *He has recurring flashbacks to the night his friends died.*

flash|bulb /flæʃbʌlb/ (flashbulbs) also **flash bulb** N-COUNT A **flashbulb** is a small bulb that can be attached to a camera. It makes a bright flash of light so that you can take photographs indoors.

flash card (flash cards) also **flashcard** N-COUNT **Flash cards** are cards which are sometimes used in the teaching of reading or a foreign language. Each card has words or a picture on it.

flash drive (flash drives) N-COUNT A **flash drive** is a small, lightweight smart card. It can be plugged into a computer where it functions as a kind of portable hard drive.

flash|er /flæʃər/ (flashers) N-COUNT A **flasher** is someone who deliberately exposes their genitals to people in public places. [INFORMAL]

flash flood (flash floods) N-COUNT A **flash flood** is a sudden rush of water over dry land, usually caused by a great deal of rain.

flash|gun /flæʃgʌn/ (flashguns) N-COUNT A **flashgun** is a device that you can attach to, or that is part of, a camera. It makes bright flashes of light so that you can take photographs indoors.

flash|light /flæʃlaɪt/ (flashlights) N-COUNT [also by n] A **flashlight** is a small electric light which gets its power from batteries and which you can carry in your hand. [mainly AM] ◻ *Len studied it a moment in the beam of his flashlight.*

flash mob (flash mobs) N-COUNT A **flash mob** is a group of people who arrange by phone or online to meet suddenly in a public place to do something for a short time. ◻ *...a flash mob performing a song and dance routine.*

flash|point /flæʃpɔɪnt/ (flashpoints) **1** N-VAR A **flashpoint** is the moment at which a conflict, especially a political conflict, suddenly gets worse and becomes violent. ◻ *The immediate flashpoint was Wednesday's big rally.* **2** N-COUNT A **flashpoint** is a place which people think is dangerous because political trouble may start there and then spread to other areas or countries. ◻ *The more serious flashpoints are outside the capital.*

flashy /flæʃi/ (flashier, flashiest) ADJ If you describe a person or thing as **flashy**, you mean they are fashionable and noticeable, but in a somewhat vulgar way. [INFORMAL, DISAPPROVAL] ◻ *He was much less flashy than his brother.*

flask /flæsk/ (flasks) **1** N-COUNT A **flask** is a bottle which you use for carrying drinks around with you. ◻ *He took out a metal flask from a canvas bag.* • N-COUNT A **flask** of liquid is the flask and the liquid which it contains. ◻ *There are some sandwiches here and a flask of coffee.* **2** N-COUNT A **flask** is a bottle or other container which is used in science laboratories and industry for holding liquids. ◻ *Flasks for the transport of spent fuel are extremely strong containers made of steel or steel and lead.*

FLAT

① SURFACES, SHAPES, AND POSITIONS
② OTHER USES
③ AN APARTMENT

---

① **flat** ✦✦◇ /flæt/ (flats, flatter, flattest) **1** ADJ Something that is **flat** is level, smooth, or even, rather than sloping, curved, or uneven. ◻ *Tiles can be fixed to any surface as long as it's flat, firm and dry.* ◻ *...windows which a thief can reach from a drainpipe or flat roof.* **2** ADJ **Flat** means horizontal and not upright. ◻ *Two men near him threw themselves flat.* **3** PHRASE If you **fall flat** on your face, you fall over. ◻ *A man walked in off the street and fell flat on his face, unconscious.* **4** ADJ A **flat** object is not very tall or deep in

flat relation to its length and width. ❑ *Ellen is walking down the drive with a square flat box balanced on one hand.* **5** ADJ **Flat** land is level, with no high hills or other raised parts. ❑ *To the north lie the flat and fertile farmlands of Nebraska.* **6** ADJ **Flat** shoes have no heels or very low heels. ❑ *People wear slacks, sweaters, flat shoes, and all manner of casual attire for travel.* • N-PLURAL **Flats** are flat shoes. [AM] ❑ *His mother looked ten years younger in jeans and flats.* **7** ADJ A **flat** tire, ball, or balloon does not have enough air in it. ❑ *One vehicle with a flat tire can bring the highway to a standstill.* **8** N-COUNT You can refer to one of the broad flat surfaces of an object as **the flat of** that object. ❑ *He slammed the counter with the flat of his hand.* **9** N-COUNT A **flat** is a tire that does not have enough air in it. ❑ *Then, after I finally got back on the highway, I developed a flat.* **10** N-COUNT A low flat area of uncultivated land, especially an area where the ground is soft and wet, can be referred to as **flats** or a **flat**. ❑ *The salt marshes and mud flats attract large numbers of waterfowl.* **11** ADJ If you have **flat** feet, the arches of your feet are too low. ❑ *The condition of flat feet runs in families.*

② **flat** ✦✧◇ /flæt/ (flatter, flattest) **1** ADJ A drink that is **flat** has lost its fizz. ❑ *Could this really stop the champagne from going flat?* **2** ADJ A **flat** battery has lost some or all of its electrical charge. [BRIT]

| in AM, use **dead** |

3 ADV [num n ADV] If you say that something happened, for example, in ten seconds **flat** or ten minutes **flat**, you are emphasizing that it happened surprisingly quickly and only took ten seconds or ten minutes. [EMPHASIS] ❑ *You're sitting behind an engine that'll move you from 0 to 60mph in six seconds flat.* **4** ADJ [ADJ n] A **flat** rate, price, or percentage is one that is fixed and which applies in every situation. ❑ *Fees are charged at a flat rate, rather than on a percentage basis.* **5** ADJ If trade or business is **flat**, it is slow and inactive, rather than busy and improving or increasing. ❑ *During the first eight months of this year, sales of big pickups were up 14% while car sales stayed flat.* **6** ADJ [n ADJ] **Flat** is used after a letter representing a musical note to show that the note should be played or sung half a tone lower than the note which otherwise matches that letter. **Flat** is often represented by the symbol ♭ after the letter. ❑ *...Schubert's B flat Piano Trio (Opus 99).* **7** ADJ If someone's singing or a musical instrument is **flat**, their singing or the instrument is slightly lower in pitch than it should be. ❑ *He had been fired because his singing was flat.* • ADV [ADV after v] **Flat** is also an adverb. ❑ *Her vocal range was limited, and she had a tendency to sing flat.* **8** ADJ [ADJ n] A **flat** denial or refusal is definite and firm, and is unlikely to be changed. ❑ *The Foreign Ministry has issued a flat denial of any involvement.* • **flat|ly** ADV ❑ *He flatly refused to discuss it.* **9** ADJ If you describe something as **flat**, you mean that it is dull and not exciting or interesting. ❑ *The past few days have seemed comparatively flat and empty.* **10** PHRASE If an event or attempt **falls flat** or **falls flat on** its **face**, it is unsuccessful. ❑ *Liz meant it as a joke but it fell flat.* **11** PHRASE If you do something **flat out**, you do it as fast or as hard as you can. ❑ *Everyone is working flat out to try to trap those responsible.* ❑ *...a flat-out sprint.* **12** PHRASE You use **flat out** to emphasize that something is completely the case. [mainly AM, INFORMAL, EMPHASIS] ❑ *That allegation is a flat-out lie.*

③ **flat** /flæt/ (flats) N-COUNT A **flat** is a set of rooms for living in, usually on one floor and part of a larger building. A flat usually includes a kitchen and bathroom. [BRIT]

| in AM, use **apartment** |

flat|bed /flætbɛd/ (flatbeds) also **flatbed truck** N-COUNT [oft N n] A **flatbed** or a **flatbed truck** is a truck that has a long flat platform with no sides.

flat-chested ADJ If you describe a woman as **flat-chested**, you mean that she has small breasts. [DISAPPROVAL] ❑ *This bra will take flat-chested girls and give them exactly what they want.*

flat|fish /flætfɪʃ/ (flatfish) N-VAR **Flatfish** are sea fish with flat wide bodies, for example, flounder or sole.

flat-footed 1 ADJ If you are **flat-footed**, the arches of your feet are too low. ❑ *He told me I was flat-footed.* **2** ADJ It you describe a person or action as **flat-footed**, you think they are clumsy, awkward, or foolish. [DISAPPROVAL] ❑ *...flat-footed writing.*

flat|lands /flætlændz/ N-PLURAL **Flatlands** are areas where the land is very flat. [mainly AM] ❑ *...the featureless flatlands of the Midwest.*

flat|mate /flætmeɪt/ (flatmates) also **flat-mate** N-COUNT Someone's **flatmate** is a person who shares a flat with them. [BRIT]

| in AM, use **roommate** |

flat racing N-UNCOUNT **Flat racing** is horse racing which does not involve jumping over fences.

flat|screen /flætskrin/ (flatscreens) ADJ A **flatscreen** television or computer monitor has a flat screen. ❑ *They finally replaced their 40-year-old television with a flatscreen TV.* • N-COUNT **Flatscreen** is also a noun. ❑ *...a 42-inch digital flatscreen.*

flat|ten /flætᵊn/ (flattens, flattening, flattened) **1** V-T/V-I If you **flatten** something or if it **flattens**, it becomes flat or flatter. ❑ *He carefully flattened the wrappers and put them between the leaves of his book.* ❑ *The dog's ears flattened slightly as Cook spoke his name.* • PHRASAL VERB **Flatten out** means the same as **flatten**. ❑ *The hills flattened out just south of the mountain.* **2** V-T To **flatten** something such as a building, town, or plant means to destroy it by knocking it down or crushing it. ❑ *...explosives capable of flattening a five-story building.* ❑ *...bombing raids flattened much of the area.* **3** V-T If you **flatten** yourself against something, you press yourself flat against it, for example, to avoid getting in the way or being seen. ❑ *He flattened himself against a brick wall as I passed.* **4** V-T If you **flatten** someone, you make them fall over by hitting them violently. ❑ *"I've never seen a woman flatten someone like that," said a crew member. "She knocked him out cold."*

flat|ter /flætər/ (flatters, flattering, flattered) **1** V-T If someone **flatters** you, they praise you in an exaggerated way that is not sincere, because they want to please you or to persuade you to do something. [DISAPPROVAL] ❑ *I knew she was just flattering me.* **2** V-T If you **flatter** yourself that something good is the case, you believe that it is true, although others may disagree. If someone says to you '**you're flattering yourself**' or '**don't flatter yourself**,' they mean that they disagree with your good opinion of yourself. ❑ *I flatter myself that this campaign will put an end to the war.* **3** → see also **flat** ①, **flat** ②, **flattered, flattering**

flat|tered /flætərd/ ADJ [v-link ADJ] If you are **flattered** by something that has happened, you are pleased about it because it makes you feel important or special. ❑ *She was flattered by Roberto's long letter.*

flat|ter|ing /flætərɪŋ/ **1** ADJ If something is **flattering**, it makes you appear more attractive. ❑ *It wasn't a very flattering photograph.* **2** ADJ If someone's remarks are **flattering**, they praise you and say nice things about you. ❑ *Most of his colleagues had positive, even flattering things to say.*

flat|tery /flætəri/ N-UNCOUNT **Flattery** consists of flattering words or behavior. [DISAPPROVAL] ❑ *He is ambitious and susceptible to flattery.*

flatu|lence /flætʃələns/ N-UNCOUNT **Flatulence** is too much gas in a person's intestines, which causes an uncomfortable feeling.

flat|ware /flætwɛər/ N-UNCOUNT You can refer to the knives, forks, and spoons that you eat your food with as **flatware**. [AM] ❑ *An assortment of pots, pans, plates, cups, and flatware is provided.*

flat white (flat whites) N-COUNT A **flat white** is a cup of strong coffee with hot milk poured on top, similar to a **latte** but smaller and less milky.

flaunt /flɔnt/ (flaunts, flaunting, flaunted) V-T If you say that someone **flaunts** their possessions, abilities, or qualities, you mean that they display them in a very obvious way, especially in order to try to obtain other people's admiration. [DISAPPROVAL] ❑ *They drove around in Rolls-Royces, openly flaunting their wealth.*

flau|tist /flɔtɪst, flaʊ-/ (flautists) N-COUNT A **flautist** is someone who plays the flute.

fla|vor ✦✧◇ /fleɪvər/ (flavors, flavoring, flavored)

| in BRIT, use **flavour** |

1 N-VAR The **flavor** of a food or drink is its taste. ❑ *I always add some paprika for extra flavor.* **2** N-COUNT If something is

flavored

orange **flavor** or beef **flavor**, it is made to taste of orange or beef. ❏ *It has an orange flavor and smooth texture.* **3** V-T If you **flavor** food or drink, you add something to it to give it a particular taste. ❏ *Lime preserved in salt is a North African specialty which is used to flavor chicken dishes.*

fla|vored /fleɪvərd/
[in BRIT, use **flavoured**]
ADJ [oft ADJ with n] If a food is **flavored**, various ingredients have been added to it so that it has a distinctive flavor. ❏ *...meat flavored with herbs.* ❏ *Many of these recipes are highly flavored.*

-flavored /-fleɪvərd/
[in BRIT, use **-flavoured**]
COMB IN ADJ **-flavored** is used after nouns such as 'strawberry' or 'chocolate' to indicate that a food or drink is flavored with strawberry or chocolate. ❏ *...strawberry-flavored candies.*

fla|vor|ful /fleɪvərfəl/
[in BRIT, use **flavourful**]
ADJ **Flavorful** food has a strong, pleasant taste and is good to eat. [APPROVAL] ❏ *This was an incredibly flavorful dish in every way.* ❏ *The steak was flavorful and cooked as ordered.*

fla|vor|ing /fleɪvərɪŋ/ (**flavorings**)
[in BRIT, use **flavouring**]
N-VAR **Flavorings** are substances that are added to food or drink to give it a particular taste. ❏ *...lemon flavoring.*

fla|vor|less /fleɪvərlɪs/
[in BRIT, use **flavourless**]
ADJ **Flavorless** food is uninteresting because it does not taste strongly of anything.

fla|vor|some /fleɪvərsəm/
[in BRIT, use **flavoursome**]
ADJ **Flavorsome** means the same as **flavorful**. [APPROVAL]

flaw /flɔ/ (**flaws**) **1** N-COUNT A **flaw** in something such as a theory or argument is a mistake in it, which causes it to be less effective or valid. ❏ *There were, however, a number of crucial flaws in his monetary theory.* **2** N-COUNT A **flaw** in someone's character is an undesirable quality that they have. ❏ *The only flaw in his character seems to be a short temper.* **3** N-COUNT A **flaw** in something such as a pattern or material is a fault in it that should not be there. ❏ *It's like having a flaw in a piece of material – the longer you leave it, the weaker it gets.*

flawed /flɔd/ ADJ Something that is **flawed** has a mark, fault, or mistake in it. ❏ *These tests were so seriously flawed as to render the results meaningless.*

flaw|less /flɔlɪs/ ADJ If you say that something or someone is **flawless**, you mean that they are extremely good and that there are no faults or problems with them. ❏ *Discovery's takeoff this morning from Cape Canaveral was flawless.* • **flaw|less|ly** ADV ❏ *Each stage of the battle was carried off flawlessly.*

flax /flæks/ N-UNCOUNT **Flax** is a plant with blue flowers. Its stem is used for making thread, rope, and cloth, and its seeds are used for making linseed oil.

flax|en /flæksən/ ADJ [ADJ n] **Flaxen** hair is pale yellow in color. [LITERARY]

flay /fleɪ/ (**flays, flaying, flayed**) V-T When someone **flays** an animal or person, they remove their skin, usually when they are dead.

flea /fli/ (**fleas**) N-COUNT A **flea** is a very small jumping insect that has no wings and feeds on the blood of humans or animals.

flea mar|ket (**flea markets**) N-COUNT A **flea market** is an outdoor market which sells cheap used goods and sometimes also very old furniture.

fleck /flɛk/ (**flecks**) N-COUNT **Flecks** are small marks on a surface, or objects that look like small marks. ❏ *He went to the men's room to wash flecks of blood from his shirt.*

flecked /flɛkt/ ADJ [oft ADJ with n] Something that is **flecked** with something is marked or covered with small bits of it. ❏ *His hair was increasingly flecked with gray.* • COMB IN ADJ **Flecked** is also a combining form. ❏ *He was attired in a plain, mud-flecked uniform.*

fled /flɛd/ **Fled** is the past tense and past participle of **flee**.

fledg|ling /flɛdʒlɪŋ/ (**fledglings**) **1** N-COUNT A **fledgling** is a young bird that has its feathers and is learning to fly. ❏ *...when fledglings are almost ready to leave the nests.* **2** ADJ [ADJ n] You use **fledgling** to describe a person, organization, or system that is new or without experience. ❏ *...the country's fledgling democracy.*

flee ✦◇◇ /fli/ (**flees, fleeing, fled**) V-T/V-I [no passive] If you **flee** from something or someone, or **flee** a person or thing, you escape from them. [WRITTEN] ❏ *He slammed the bedroom door behind him and fled.* ❏ *...refugees fleeing persecution or torture.*

SYNONYMS

flee
VERB
run away: *After his beating, Colin ran away and hasn't been heard from since.*
bolt: *The pig rose, squealing, and bolted.*
escape: *He was fatally wounded as he tried to escape.*
abscond: *He was ordered to appear the following day, but absconded.*

---

fleece /flis/ (**fleeces, fleecing, fleeced**) **1** N-COUNT A sheep's **fleece** is the coat of wool that covers it. ❏ *...a special protein which triggers the animal to shed its fleece.* **2** N-COUNT A **fleece** is the wool that is cut off one sheep in a single piece. ❏ *Wool can be spun from fleeces.* **3** V-T If you **fleece** someone, you get a lot of money from them by tricking them or charging them too much. [INFORMAL] ❏ *She claims he fleeced her out of thousands of dollars.* **4** N-VAR **Fleece** is a soft warm artificial fabric. A **fleece** is also a jacket or other garment made from this fabric. ❏ *...white leather slippers with fleece lining.*

fleecy /flisi/ (**fleecier, fleeciest**) **1** ADJ [usu ADJ n] **Fleecy** clothes, blankets, or other objects are made of a soft light material. ❏ *...fleecy walking jackets.* **2** ADJ Something that is **fleecy** is light and soft in appearance. ❏ *It was a lovely afternoon with a blue sky and a few fleecy white clouds.*

fleet ✦◇◇ /flit/ (**fleets**) **1** N-COUNT A **fleet** is a group of ships organized to do something together, for example, to fight battles or to catch fish. ❏ *A fleet sailed for New South Wales to establish the first European settlement in Australia.* **2** N-COUNT A **fleet** of vehicles is a group of them, especially when they all belong to a particular organization or business, or when they are all going somewhere together. ❏ *With its own fleet of trucks, the company delivers most orders overnight.*

fleet|ing /flitɪŋ/ ADJ **Fleeting** is used to describe something which lasts only for a very short time. ❏ *The girls caught only a fleeting glimpse of the driver.* • **fleet|ing|ly** ADV ❏ *A smile passed fleetingly across his face.*

Flem|ish /flɛmɪʃ/ **1** ADJ **Flemish** means belonging or relating to the region of Flanders in northern Europe, or to its people, language, or culture. **2** N-UNCOUNT **Flemish** is a language spoken in Belgium.

flesh /flɛʃ/ (**fleshes, fleshing, fleshed**) **1** N-UNCOUNT **Flesh** is the soft part of a person's or animal's body between the bones and the skin. ❏ *...the pale pink flesh of trout and salmon.* **2** N-UNCOUNT You can use **flesh** to refer to human skin and the human body, especially when you are considering it in a sexual way. ❏ *...the warmth of her flesh.* **3** N-UNCOUNT The **flesh** of a fruit or vegetable is the soft inside part of it. ❏ *Cut the flesh from the olives and discard the stones.* **4** PHRASE You use **flesh and blood** to emphasize that someone has human feelings or weaknesses, often when contrasting them with machines. [EMPHASIS] ❏ *I'm only flesh and blood, like anyone else.* **5** PHRASE If you say that someone is your **own flesh and blood**, you are emphasizing that they are a member of your family. [EMPHASIS] ❏ *The kid, after all, was his own flesh and blood. He deserved a second chance.* **6** PHRASE If something **makes** your **flesh creep** or **makes** your **flesh crawl**, it makes you feel disgusted, shocked or frightened. ❏ *It makes my flesh creep to think of it.* **7** PHRASE If you meet or see someone **in the flesh**, you actually meet or see them, rather than, for example, seeing them in a movie or on television. ❏ *The first thing viewers usually say when they see*

flesh-colored

me in the flesh is "You're smaller than you look on TV." ☑ → See feature box at **family**

▶ **flesh out** PHRASAL VERB If you **flesh out** something such as a story or plan, you add details and more information to it. ❏ *Permission for a warehouse development has already been granted and the developers are merely fleshing out the details.*

flesh-colored ADJ Something that is **flesh-colored** is the color of any shade of a person's skin.

flesh wound (flesh wounds) N-COUNT A **flesh wound** is a wound that breaks the skin but does not damage the bones or any of the body's important internal organs.

fleshy /flɛʃi/ (fleshier, fleshiest) ☑ ADJ If you describe someone as **fleshy**, you mean that they are a little too fat. ❏ *He was well-built, but too fleshy to be impressive.* ☑ ADJ **Fleshy** parts of the body or **fleshy** plants are thick and soft. ❏ *...fleshy fruits like apples, plums, pears, peaches.*

flew /fluː/ **Flew** is the past tense of **fly**.

flex /flɛks/ (flexes, flexing, flexed) ☑ V-T If you **flex** your muscles or parts of your body, you bend, move, or stretch them for a short time in order to exercise them. ❏ *He slowly flexed his muscles and tried to stand.* ☑ N-VAR A **flex** is an electric cable containing two or more wires that is connected to an electrical appliance. [mainly BRIT]

in AM, use **cord**

☑ to flex your muscles → see **muscle**

flex|ible /flɛksɪbəl/ ☑ ADJ A **flexible** object or material can be bent easily without breaking. ❏ *...brushes with long, flexible bristles.* • **flexi|bil|ity** /flɛksɪbɪlɪti/ N-UNCOUNT ❏ *The flexibility of the lens decreases with age; it is therefore common for our sight to worsen as we get older.* ☑ ADJ Something or someone that is **flexible** is able to change easily and adapt to different conditions and circumstances as they occur. [APPROVAL] ❏ *...flexible working hours.* • **flexi|bil|ity** N-UNCOUNT ❏ *The flexibility of distance learning would be particularly suited to busy managers.*

SYNONYMS

flexible
ADJ ☑
pliable: *As your baby grows bigger, his bones become less pliable.*
elastic: *Beat it until the dough is slightly elastic.*
supple: *The leather is supple and sturdy enough to last for years.*
bendy: *...a bendy toy whose limbs bend in every direction.*

---

flexi|tar|ian /flɛksɪtɛəriən/ (flexitarians) ADJ Someone who is **flexitarian** eats mostly vegetarian food, but eats meat or fish occasionally. • N-COUNT A **flexitarian** is someone who is flexitarian. ❏ *I stopped eating meat as a teenager, but I now call myself a flexitarian.*

flex|time /flɛkstaɪm/ also **flexitime** ☑ N-UNCOUNT **Flextime** is a system that allows employees to vary the time that they start or finish work, provided that an agreed total number of hours are spent at work. [BUSINESS] ❏ *I have recently introduced flextime for all my staff.* ☑ → See feature box at **working**

flick /flɪk/ (flicks, flicking, flicked) ☑ V-T/V-I If something **flicks** in a particular direction, or if someone **flicks** it, it moves with a short, sudden movement. ❏ *His tongue flicked across his lips.* ❏ *He flicked his cigarette out of the window.* • N-COUNT **Flick** is also a noun. ❏ *...a flick of a paintbrush.* ☑ V-T If you **flick** something away, or off something else, you remove it with a quick movement of your hand or finger. ❏ *Shirley flicked a piece of lint from the sleeve of her black suit.* ☑ V-T If you **flick** something such as a whip or a towel, or **flick** something with it, you hold one end of it and move your hand quickly up and then forward, so that the other end moves. ❏ *She sighed and flicked a dishcloth at the counter.* • N-COUNT **Flick** is also a noun. ❏ *...a flick of the whip.* ☑ V-T If you **flick** a switch, or **flick** an electrical appliance on or off, you press the switch sharply so that it moves into a different position and works the equipment. ❏ *Sam was flicking a flashlight on and off.* ☑ V-I If you **flick through** a book or magazine, you turn its pages quickly, for example, to get a general idea of its contents or to look for a particular item. If you **flick through** television channels, you continually change channels very quickly, usually using a remote control. ❏ *She was flicking through some magazines on a table.* • N-SING

Flick is also a noun. ❏ *I thought I'd have a quick flick through some recent issues.*

flick|er /flɪkər/ (flickers, flickering, flickered) ☑ V-I If a light or flame **flickers**, it shines unsteadily. ❏ *Fluorescent lights flickered, and then the room was blindingly bright.* • N-COUNT **Flicker** is also a noun. ❏ *Looking through the window I saw the flicker of flames.* ☑ → See feature box at **light**

flick-knife (flick-knives) also **flick knife** N-COUNT A **flick-knife** is a knife with a blade in the handle that springs out when a button is pressed. [BRIT]

in AM, use **switchblade**

fli|er /flaɪər/ → see **flyer**

flight /flaɪt/ (flights) ☑ N-COUNT A **flight** is a trip made by flying, usually in an airplane. ❏ *The flight will take four hours.* ☑ N-COUNT [also N num] You can refer to an airplane carrying passengers on a particular trip as a particular **flight**. ❏ *BA flight 286 was two hours late.* ☑ N-COUNT A **flight** of steps or stairs is a set of steps or stairs that lead from one level to another without changing direction. ❏ *We walked in silence up a flight of stairs and down a long corridor.* ☑ N-UNCOUNT **Flight** is the action of flying, or the ability to fly. ❏ *Supersonic flight could become a routine form of travel in the 21st century.* ☑ N-UNCOUNT **Flight** is the act of running away from a dangerous or unpleasant situation or place. ❏ *The family was often in flight, hiding out in friends' houses.*

COLLOCATIONS

flight
NOUN
☑
adjective + **flight**: cheap, direct, scheduled; domestic, internal, long-haul, short-haul, transatlantic; connecting, direct, nonstop
verb + **flight**: book; cancel, delay
☑
verb + **flight**: catch, take; board

---

flight at|tend|ant (flight attendants) N-COUNT On an airplane, the **flight attendants** are the people whose job is to take care of the passengers and serve their meals.

flight deck (flight decks) ☑ N-COUNT On an aircraft carrier, the **flight deck** is the flat open surface on the deck where aircraft take off and land. ☑ N-COUNT On a large airplane, the **flight deck** is the area at the front where the pilot works and where all the controls are.

flight|less /flaɪtlɪs/ ADJ [ADJ n] A **flightless** bird or insect is unable to fly because it does not have the necessary type of wings.

flight of capi|tal N-SING When people lose confidence in a particular economy or market and withdraw their investment from it, you can refer to a **flight of capital** from that economy or market. [BUSINESS] ❏ *TI has seen its shares suffer because of a flight of capital to telecom and internet-related businesses.*

flight re|cord|er (flight recorders) N-COUNT On an airplane, the **flight recorder** is the same as the **black box**.

flight risk (flight risks) N-COUNT If someone who has been charged with a crime is a **flight risk**, they are considered likely to attempt to escape to another country before their trial. ❏ *US authorities are opposing his request for bail, saying that he is a flight risk.*

flighty /flaɪti/ (flightier, flightiest) ADJ If you say that someone is **flighty**, you disapprove of them because they are not very serious or reliable and keep changing from one activity, idea, or partner to another. [DISAPPROVAL] ❏ *Isabelle was a frivolous little fool, vain and flighty.*

flim|sy /flɪmzi/ (flimsier, flimsiest) ☑ ADJ A **flimsy** object is weak because it is made of a weak material, or is badly made. ❏ *...a flimsy wooden door.* ☑ ADJ **Flimsy** cloth or clothing is thin and does not give much protection. ❏ *...a very flimsy pink chiffon nightgown.* ☑ ADJ If you describe something such as evidence or an excuse as **flimsy**, you mean that it is not very good or convincing. ❏ *The charges were based on very flimsy evidence.* ☑ → See feature box at **disaster**

flinch /flɪntʃ/ (flinches, flinching, flinched) ☑ V-I [usu neg] If you **flinch**, you make a small sudden movement, especially

fling

when something surprises you or hurts you. ❏ *Leo stared back at him without flinching.* **2** V-I If you **flinch** from something unpleasant, you are unwilling to do it or think about it, or you avoid doing it. ❏ *The world community should not flinch in the face of this challenge.*

fling /flɪŋ/ (**flings, flinging, flung**) **1** V-T If you **fling** something somewhere, you throw it there using a lot of force. ❏ *The woman flung the cup at him.* **2** V-T If you **fling yourself** somewhere, you move or jump there suddenly and with a lot of force. ❏ *He flung himself to the floor.* **3** V-T If you **fling** a part of your body in a particular direction, especially your arms or head, you move it there suddenly. ❏ *She flung her arms around my neck and kissed me.* **4** V-T If you **fling** someone to the ground, you push them very roughly so that they fall over. ❏ *The youth got him by the front of his shirt and flung him to the ground.* **5** V-T If you **fling** something into a particular place or position, you put it there in a quick or angry way. ❏ *Peter flung his shoes into the corner.* **6** V-T If you **fling yourself** into a particular activity, you do it with a lot of enthusiasm and energy. ❏ *She flung herself into her career.* **7 Fling** can be used instead of 'throw' in many expressions that usually contain 'throw.' **8** N-COUNT If two people have a **fling**, they have a brief sexual relationship. [INFORMAL] ❏ *She claims she had a brief fling with him 30 years ago.*

flint /flɪnt/ (**flints**) **1** N-UNCOUNT **Flint** is a very hard grayish-black stone that was used in former times for making tools. ❏ *...a flint arrowhead.* ❏ *...eyes the color of flint.* **2** N-COUNT A **flint** is a small piece of flint which can be struck with a piece of steel to produce sparks. **3** → See also color supplement

flint|lock /flɪntlɒk/ (**flintlocks**) N-COUNT [oft N N] A **flintlock** gun is a type of gun that was used in former times. It is fired by pressing a trigger which causes a spark struck from a flint to light gunpowder.

flinty /flɪnti/ (**flintier, flintiest**) ADJ If you describe a person or someone's character or expression as **flinty**, you mean they are harsh and show no emotion. ❏ *...her flinty stare.* ❏ *...a man of flinty determination.*

flip /flɪp/ (**flips, flipping, flipped**) **1** V-T If you **flip** a device on or off, or if you **flip** a switch, you turn it on or off by pressing the switch quickly. ❏ *He didn't flip on the headlights until he was two blocks away.* ❏ *Then he walked out, flipping the lights off.* **2** V-I If you **flip** through the pages of a book, for example, you quickly turn over the pages in order to find a particular one or to get an idea of the contents. ❏ *He was flipping through a magazine in the living room.* **3** V-T/V-I If something **flips** over, or if you **flip** it over or into a different position, it moves or is moved into a different position. ❏ *The plane then flipped over and burst into flames.* **4** V-T If you **flip** something, especially a coin, you use your thumb to make it turn over and over, as it goes through the air. ❏ *I pulled a coin from my pocket and flipped it.*

flip|chart /flɪptʃɑrt/ (**flipcharts**) N-COUNT A **flipchart** is a stand with large sheets of paper which is used when presenting information at a meeting. ❏ *There are three conference rooms each of which is equipped with a screen, flipchart and audio visual equipment.*

flip-flop (**flip-flops, flip-flopping, flip-flopped**) **1** N-PLURAL **Flip-flops** are open shoes which are held on your feet by a strap that goes between your toes. **2** V-I If you say that someone, especially a politician, **flip-flops** on a decision, you are critical of them because they change their decision, so that they do or think the opposite. [mainly AM, INFORMAL, DISAPPROVAL] ❏ *He has been criticized for flip-flopping on several key issues.* ❏ *He seemed so sure of his decision, how could he flip-flop so dramatically now?* • N-COUNT **Flip-flop** is also a noun. ❏ *The president's flip-flops on taxes made him appear indecisive.* **3** → See also color supplement

flip|pant /flɪpənt/ ADJ If you describe a person or what they say as **flippant**, you are criticizing them because you think they are not taking something as seriously as they should. [DISAPPROVAL] ❏ *Don't be flippant, damn it! This is serious!* ❏ *He now dismisses that as a flippant comment.*

flipped /flɪpt/ ADJ [ADJ n] **Flipped** learning is a way of teaching in which students first learn about subjects for themselves online and then discuss them with their teacher. ❏ *Stanforth said he was planning to take the flipped classroom several stages further.*

flip|per /flɪpər/ (**flippers**) **1** N-COUNT [usu pl] **Flippers** are flat pieces of rubber that you can wear on your feet to help you swim more quickly, especially underwater. **2** N-COUNT [usu pl] The **flippers** of an animal that lives in water, for example, a seal or a penguin, are the two or four flat limbs which it uses for swimming.

flip side also **flipside 1** N-SING [the N] The **flip side** of a record is the side that does not have the main song on it. ❏ *"What's on the flip side?"* **2** N-SING The **flip side** of a situation consists of the less obvious or less pleasant aspects of it. ❏ *The trade deficit is the flip side of a rapidly expanding economy.*

flirt /flɜrt/ (**flirts, flirting, flirted**) **1** V-RECIP If you **flirt** with someone, you behave as if you are sexually attracted to them, in a playful or not very serious way. ❏ *Dad's flirting with all the ladies, or they're all flirting with him, as usual.* • **flir|ta|tion** /flɜrteɪʃən/ (**flirtations**) N-VAR [oft N with n] ❏ *She was aware of his attempts at flirtation.* **2** N-COUNT Someone who is a **flirt** likes to flirt a lot. ❏ *I've always been a real flirt, I had a different boyfriend every week.* **3** V-I If you **flirt** with the idea of something, you consider it but do not do anything about it. ❏ *My mother used to flirt with Anarchism.* • **flir|ta|tion** N-VAR ❏ *...the party's brief flirtation with economic liberalism.* **4** → See feature box at **body language**

flir|ta|tious /flɜrteɪʃəs/ ADJ Someone who is **flirtatious** behaves toward someone else as if they are sexually attracted to them, usually not in a very serious way. ❏ *He was dashing, self-confident and flirtatious.*

flir|ty /flɜrti/ (**flirtier, flirtiest**) **1** ADJ If you describe someone as **flirty**, you mean that they behave toward someone else as if they are sexually attracted to them, usually not in a very serious way. ❏ *She is amazingly flirty and sensual.* ❏ *She had an appealing flirty smile.* **2** ADJ **Flirty** clothes are feminine and sexy.

flit /flɪt/ (**flits, flitting, flitted**) **1** V-I If you **flit** around or **flit** between one place and another, you go to lots of places without staying for very long in any of them. ❏ *Laura flits about New York hailing taxis at every opportunity.* **2** V-I If someone **flits** from one thing or situation to another, they move or turn their attention from one to the other very quickly. ❏ *He's prone to flit between subjects with amazing ease.* **3** V-I If something such as a bird or a bat **flits** about, it flies quickly from one place to another. ❏ *...the parrot that flits from tree to tree.*

float /floʊt/ (**floats, floating, floated**) **1** V-T/V-I If something or someone **is floating** in a liquid, they are on or just below the surface, and are being supported by it. You can also **float** something on a liquid. ❏ *They noticed fifty and twenty dollar bills floating in the water.* ❏ *It's below freezing and small icebergs are floating by.* **2** V-I Something that **floats** lies on or just below the surface of a liquid when it is put in it and does not sink. ❏ *They will also float if you drop them in the water.* **3** V-I Something that **floats** in or through the air hangs in it or moves slowly and gently through it. ❏ *The white cloud of smoke floated away.* **4** V-T If you **float** a project, plan, or idea, you suggest it for others to think about. ❏ *The French had floated the idea of placing the diplomatic work in the hands of the UN.* **5** V-T If a company director **floats** their company, they start to sell shares in it to the public. [BUSINESS] ❏ *He floated his firm on the stock market.* **6** V-T/V-I If a government **floats** its country's currency or allows it to **float**, it allows the currency's value to change freely in relation to other currencies. [BUSINESS] ❏ *On January 15th Brazil was forced to float its currency.* **7** N-COUNT A **float** is a light object that is used to help someone or something float. ❏ *Floats will provide confidence in the water.* **8** N-COUNT A **float** is a small object attached to a fishing line which floats on the water and moves when a fish has been caught. **9** N-COUNT A **float** is a truck on which displays and people in special costumes are carried in a parade. ❏ *...a procession of makeshift floats bearing loudspeakers and banners.*

float|ing vot|er (**floating voters**) N-COUNT A **floating voter** is a person who is not a firm supporter of any political party, and whose vote in an election is difficult to predict. [BRIT]

in AM, use **swing voter**

flock /flɒk/ (**flocks, flocking, flocked**) **1** N-COUNT-COLL A **flock** of birds, sheep, or goats is a group of them. ❏ *They kept a small* flock of sheep. **2** N-COUNT-COLL You can refer to a group of people or things as a **flock of** them to emphasize that there are a lot of them. [EMPHASIS] ❑ *These cases all attracted flocks of famous writers.* **3** V-I If people **flock** to a particular place or event, a very large number of them go there, usually because it is pleasant or interesting. ❑ *The public has flocked to the show.* ❑ *The criticisms will not stop people flocking to see the movie.*

floe /floʊ/ → see **ice floe**

flog /flɒg/ (flogs, flogging, flogged) V-T If someone **is flogged**, they are hit hard with a whip or stick as a punishment. ❑ *In these places people starved, were flogged, were clubbed to death.* • **flog|ging** (floggings) N-VAR ❑ *He gets dragged off to court and sentenced to a flogging and life imprisonment.*

flood ♦♦♢ /flʌd/ (floods, flooding, flooded) **1** N-VAR If there is a **flood**, a large amount of water covers an area which is usually dry, for example, when a river flows over its banks or a pipe bursts. ❑ *More than 70 people were killed in the floods, caused when a dam burst.* ❑ *This is the type of flood dreaded by cavers.* **2** V-T/V-I If something such as a river or a burst pipe **floods** an area that is usually dry or if the area **floods**, it becomes covered with water. ❑ *The kitchen flooded.* **3** V-I If a river **floods**, it overflows, especially after very heavy rain. ❑ *...the relentless rain that caused twenty rivers to flood.* **4** V-I If you say that people or things **flood** into a place, you are emphasizing that they arrive there in large numbers. [EMPHASIS] ❑ *Refugees flooded into the country.* ❑ *Inquiries flooded in from all over the world.* **5** V-T If you **flood** a place with a particular type of thing, or if a particular type of thing **floods** a place, the place becomes full of so many of them that it cannot hold or deal with any more. ❑ *Manufacturers are destroying American jobs by flooding the market with cheap imports.* **6** N-COUNT If you say that **a flood** of people or things arrive somewhere, you are emphasizing that a very large number of them arrive there. [EMPHASIS] ❑ *The system broke down, unable to cope with the flood of refugees.* **7** → See feature box at **disaster**

flood|gates /flʌdgeɪts/ PHRASE [usu PHR to/for n] If events **open the floodgates** to something, they make it possible for that thing to happen much more often or much more seriously than before. ❑ *A decision against the cigarette companies could open the floodgates to many more lawsuits.*

flood|ing /flʌdɪŋ/ N-UNCOUNT If **flooding** occurs, an area of land that is usually dry is covered with water after heavy rain or after a river or lake flows over its banks. ❑ *The flooding, caused by three days of torrential rain, is the worst in sixty-five years.*

flood|light /flʌdlaɪt/ (floodlights, floodlighting, floodlit) **1** N-COUNT **Floodlights** are very powerful lamps that are used outside to light public buildings, sports grounds, and other places at night. ❑ *A group of men were playing soccer under the glare of floodlights.* **2** V-T If a building or place **is floodlit**, it is lit by floodlights. ❑ *In the evening the facade is floodlit.*

flood plain (flood plains) also **floodplain** N-COUNT A **flood plain** is a flat area on the edge of a river, where the ground consists of soil, sand, and rock left by the river when it floods.

floor ♦♦♢ /flɔːr/ (floors, flooring, floored) **1** N-COUNT The **floor** of a room is the part of it that you walk on. ❑ *Jack's sitting on the floor watching TV.* **2** N-COUNT A **floor** of a building is all the rooms that are on a particular level. ❑ *The café was on the top floor of the hospital.* **3** N-COUNT The ocean **floor** is the ground at the bottom of an ocean. The valley **floor** is the ground at the bottom of a valley. ❑ *They spend hours feeding on the ocean floor.* **4** N-COUNT The place where official debates and discussions are held, especially between members of a legislature, is referred to as the **floor**. ❑ *The issues were debated on the floor of the House.* **5** N-SING-COLL In a debate or discussion, **the floor** is the people who are listening to the arguments being put forward but who are not among the main speakers. ❑ *The president is taking questions from the floor.* **6** V-T [usu passive] If you **are floored** by something, you are unable to respond to it because you are so surprised by it. ❑ *He was floored by the announcement.* **7** → see also **floored, flooring, dance floor, first floor, ground floor, shop floor** **8** PHRASE If someone **has the floor**, they are the person who is speaking in a debate or discussion. ❑ *Since I have the floor for the moment, I want to go back to a previous point.* **9** PHRASE If you **take to the floor**, you start dancing at a dance or disco. ❑ *The happy couple and their respective parents took to the floor.* **10** PHRASE If you **wipe the floor with** someone, you defeat them completely in a competition or discussion. [INFORMAL]

❑ *He could wipe the floor with the opposition.* **11** → See feature box at **ocean**

floor|board /flɔːrbɔːrd/ (floorboards) N-COUNT **Floorboards** are the long pieces of wood that a wooden floor is made up of.

floored /flɔːrd/ ADJ A room or part of a room that is **floored** with a particular material has a floor made of that material. ❑ *The aisle was floored with ancient bricks.* • COMB IN ADJ **Floored** is also a combining form. ❑ *They had to cross the large marble-floored hall.*

floor|ing /flɔːrɪŋ/ (floorings) N-MASS **Flooring** is a material that is used to make the floor of a room. ❑ *Quarry tiles are a popular kitchen flooring.*

floor lamp (floor lamps) N-COUNT A **floor lamp** is a tall electric light which stands on the floor in a living room. [mainly AM]

in BRIT, usually use **standard lamp**

floor show (floor shows) also **floorshow** N-COUNT A **floor show** is a series of performances by dancers, singers, or comedians at a nightclub.

floo|zy /fluːzi/ (floozies) N-COUNT If someone refers to a woman as a **floozy**, they disapprove of her because she has many casual sexual relationships. [INFORMAL, OLD-FASHIONED, DISAPPROVAL]

flop /flɒp/ (flops, flopping, flopped) **1** V-I If you **flop** into a chair, for example, you sit down suddenly and heavily because you are so tired. ❑ *Bunbury flopped down upon the bed and rested his tired feet.* **2** V-I If something **flops** onto something else, it falls there heavily or untidily. ❑ *The briefcase flopped onto the desk.* **3** V-I If something **flops**, it is completely unsuccessful. [INFORMAL] ❑ *The movie flopped badly at the box office.* **4** N-COUNT If something is a **flop**, it is completely unsuccessful. [INFORMAL] ❑ *It is the public who decide whether a movie is a hit or a flop.*

flop|house /flɒphaʊs/ (flophouses) N-COUNT A **flophouse** is a kind of cheap hotel in a city for people who have no home and very little money. [AM, INFORMAL]

flop|py /flɒpi/ (floppier, floppiest) ADJ Something that is **floppy** is loose rather than stiff, and tends to hang downward. ❑ *...the girl with the floppy hat and glasses.*

flop|py disk (floppy disks) N-COUNT A **floppy disk** is a small magnetic disk that is used for storing computer data and programs. Floppy disks are used especially with personal computers.

flo|ra /flɔːrə/ **1** N-UNCOUNT-COLL You can refer to plants as **flora**, especially the plants growing in a particular area. [FORMAL] ❑ *...the variety of food crops and flora which now exists in Dominica.* **2** → See feature box at **deforest**

flo|ral /flɔːrəl/ **1** ADJ A **floral** fabric or design has flowers on it. ❑ *...a bright yellow floral fabric.* **2** ADJ [ADJ n] You can use **floral** to describe something that contains flowers or is made of flowers. ❑ *...eye-catching floral arrangements.*

flo|ret /flɒrɪt/ (florets) **1** N-COUNT On a flowering plant, a **floret** is a small flower that is part of a larger flower. **2** N-COUNT On vegetables such as broccoli and cauliflower, a **floret** is one of the small, flower-shaped pieces which make up the part of the vegetable that you eat.

flor|id /flɒrɪd/ **1** ADJ If you describe something as **florid**, you disapprove of the fact that it is complicated and extravagant rather than plain and simple. [DISAPPROVAL] ❑ *...florid language.* **2** ADJ Someone who is **florid** always has a red face. ❑ *Jacobs was a stout, florid man.*

flo|rist /flɒrɪst/ (florists) **1** N-COUNT A **florist** is a storekeeper who arranges and sells flowers and sells houseplants. **2** N-COUNT A **florist** or a **florist's** is a store where flowers and houseplants are sold. ❑ *He bought her some roses at the florist's in the mall.*

floss /flɒs/ (flosses, flossing, flossed) **1** N-UNCOUNT You can use **floss** to refer to fine soft threads of some kind. ❑ *Craft Resources also sells yarn and embroidery floss.* **2** → see also **dental floss** **3** V-T/V-I When you **floss**, you use a special kind of strong string to clean between your teeth and gums. ❑ *Brush your teeth after each meal and floss daily.* ❑ *She was flossing her teeth at the time.*

flo|ta|tion /floʊteɪʃən/ (**flotations**) N-VAR The **flotation** of a company is the selling of shares in it to the public. [BUSINESS] ◻ *Prudential's flotation will be the third largest this year, behind Kraft Foods and Agere Systems.*

flo|til|la /fləˈtɪlə/ (**flotillas**) N-COUNT A **flotilla** is a group of small ships, usually military ships.

flot|sam /ˈflɒtsəm/ **1** N-UNCOUNT **Flotsam** is useless material, for example bits of wood and plastic, that is floating on the ocean or has been left by the ocean on the shore. ◻ *The water was full of flotsam and refuse.* **2** PHRASE You can use **flotsam and jetsam** to refer to small or unimportant items that are found together, especially ones that have no connection with each other. ◻ *...cereal boxes, bottles, and all the flotsam and jetsam of the kitchen.*

flounce /flaʊns/ (**flounces, flouncing, flounced**) **1** V-I If you **flounce** somewhere, you walk there quickly with exaggerated movements, in a way that shows you are annoyed or upset. ◻ *She flounced out of my room in a huff.* ◻ *She will flounce and argue when asked to leave the room.* **2** N-COUNT A **flounce** is a piece of cloth that has been sewn into folds and put around the edge of something, for example, a skirt, dress, tablecloth, or curtain. ◻ *...a gown with a flounced hem.*

floun|der /ˈflaʊndər/ (**flounders, floundering, floundered**) **1** V-I If something **is floundering**, it has many problems and may soon fail completely. ◻ *What a pity that his career was left to flounder.* **2** V-I If you say that someone **is floundering**, you are criticizing them for not making decisions or for not knowing what to say or do. [DISAPPROVAL] ◻ *Right now, you've got a president who's floundering, trying to find some way to get his campaign jump-started.* **3** V-I If you **flounder** in water or mud, you move in an uncontrolled way, trying not to sink. ◻ *Three men were floundering about in the water.*

flour /ˈflaʊər/ (**flours**) N-MASS **Flour** is a white or brown powder that is made by grinding grain. It is used to make bread, cakes, and pastry.

flour|ish /ˈflɜrɪʃ/ (**flourishes, flourishing, flourished**) **1** V-I If something **flourishes**, it is successful, active, or common, and developing quickly and strongly. ◻ *Business flourished and within six months they were earning 18,000 roubles a day.* ● **flour|ish|ing** ADJ ◻ *Boston quickly became a flourishing port.* **2** V-I If a plant or animal **flourishes**, it grows well or is healthy because the conditions are right for it. ◻ *The plant flourishes particularly well in slightly harsher climes.* ● **flour|ish|ing** ADJ ◻ *...a flourishing fox population.* **3** V-T If you **flourish** an object, you wave it about in a way that makes people notice it. ◻ *He flourished the glass to emphasize the point.* ● N-COUNT **Flourish** is also a noun. ◻ *He took his cap from under his arm with a flourish and pulled it low over his eyes.*

floury /ˈflaʊəri/ **1** ADJ Something that is **floury** is covered with flour or tastes of flour. ◻ *She wiped her floury hands on her apron.* ◻ *...floury biscuits.* **2** ADJ [usu ADJ n] **Floury** potatoes get soft around the edges and break up when they are cooked. [BRIT]

flout /flaʊt/ (**flouts, flouting, flouted**) V-T If you **flout** something such as a law, an order, or an accepted way of behaving, you deliberately do not obey it or follow it. ◻ *...illegal campers who persist in flouting the law.*

flow ◆◇ /floʊ/ (**flows, flowing, flowed**) **1** V-I If a liquid, gas, or electrical current **flows** somewhere, it moves there steadily and continuously. ◻ *A stream flowed gently down into the valley.* ◻ *The current flows into electric motors that drive the wheels.* ● N-VAR **Flow** is also a noun. ◻ *It works only in the veins, where the blood flow is slower.* **2** V-I If a number of people or things **flow** from one place to another, they move there steadily in large groups, usually without stopping. ◻ *Large numbers of refugees continue to flow from the troubled region into the no-man's land.* ● N-VAR **Flow** is also a noun. ◻ *She watched the frantic flow of cars and buses along the street.* **3** V-I If information or money **flows** somewhere, it moves freely between people or organizations. ◻ *A lot of this information flowed through other police departments.* ● N-VAR **Flow** is also a noun. ◻ *...the opportunity to control the flow of information.* **4** → see also **cash flow** **5** PHRASE If you say that an activity, or the person who is performing the activity, is **in full flow**, you mean that the activity has started and is being carried out with a great deal of energy and enthusiasm. ◻ *Lunch at Harry's Bar was in full flow when Irene made a splendid entrance.* **6** → See feature box at **electricity**

SYNONYMS

flow
VERB **1**
stream: *Tears streamed down their faces.*
gush: *Piping-hot water gushed out.*
run: *Wash the rice in cold water until the water runs clear.*

---

flow chart (**flow charts**) N-COUNT A **flow chart** or a **flow diagram** is a diagram which represents the sequence of actions in a particular process or activity. ◻ *This flow chart, shown below, summarizes the overall costing process.*

flow|er ◆◇ /ˈflaʊər/ (**flowers, flowering, flowered**) **1** N-COUNT A **flower** is the part of a plant which is often brightly colored, grows at the end of a stem, and only survives for a short time. ◻ *Each individual flower is tiny.* **2** N-COUNT A **flower** is a stem of a plant that has one or more flowers on it and has been picked, usually with others, for example, to give as a present or to put in a vase. ◻ *...a bunch of flowers sent by a new admirer.* **3** N-COUNT **Flowers** are small plants that are grown for their flowers as opposed to trees, shrubs, and vegetables. ◻ *...a lawned area surrounded by screening plants and flowers.* **4** V-I When a plant or tree **flowers**, its flowers appear and open. ◻ *Several of these rhododendrons will flower this year for the first time.* **5** V-I When something **flowers**, for example, a political movement or a relationship, it gets stronger and more successful. ◻ *Their relationship flowered.* **6** → See also color supplement

flow|er ar|rang|ing N-UNCOUNT **Flower arranging** is the art or hobby of arranging cut flowers in a way which makes them look attractive.

flower|bed /ˈflaʊərbɛd/ (**flowerbeds**) N-COUNT A **flowerbed** is an area of ground in a garden or park which has been specially prepared so that flowers can be grown in it.

flow|ered /ˈflaʊərd/ ADJ [ADJ n] **Flowered** paper or cloth has a pattern of flowers on it. ◻ *She was wearing a flowered cotton dress.*

flow|er|ing /ˈflaʊərɪŋ/ **1** N-UNCOUNT The **flowering** of something such as an idea or artistic style is the development of its popularity and success. ◻ *He may be happy with the flowering of new thinking, but he has yet to contribute much to it himself.* **2** ADJ [ADJ n] **Flowering** shrubs, trees, or plants are those which produce noticeable flowers. ◻ *...a late summer flowering plant like an aster.*

flower|pot /ˈflaʊərpɒt/ (**flowerpots**) N-COUNT A **flowerpot** is a container that is used for growing plants.

flow|er pow|er N-UNCOUNT **Flower power** is an old-fashioned way of referring to hippies and the culture associated with hippies in the late 1960s and early 1970s. ◻ *...the era of flower power.*

flow|ery /ˈflaʊəri/ **1** ADJ A **flowery** smell is strong and sweet, like flowers. ◻ *Amy thought she caught the faintest drift of Isabel's flowery perfume.* **2** ADJ [usu ADJ n] **Flowery** cloth, paper, or china has a lot of flowers printed or painted on it. ◻ *The baby, dressed in a flowery jumpsuit, waved her rattle.* **3** ADJ **Flowery** speech or writing contains long or literary words and expressions. ◻ *They were using uncommonly flowery language.*

flown /floʊn/ **Flown** is the past participle of **fly**.

fl. oz. **fl. oz.** is a written abbreviation for **fluid ounce**.

flu /fluː/ N-UNCOUNT [also the N] **Flu** is an illness which is similar to a bad cold but more serious. It often makes you feel very weak and makes your muscles hurt. ◻ *I got the flu.*

flub /flʌb/ (**flubs, flubbing, flubbed**) **1** V-T If you **flub** something that you are trying to do, you are unsuccessful or you do it badly. [AM, INFORMAL] ◻ *If you try a sales technique and flub it, not making a sale, will you try it again?* **2** N-COUNT A **flub** is a mistake or an unsuccessful attempt to do something. [AM, INFORMAL] ◻ *...a flub that made listeners cringe.*

fluc|tu|ate /ˈflʌktʃueɪt/ (**fluctuates, fluctuating, fluctuated**) V-I If something **fluctuates**, it changes a lot in an irregular way. ◻ *Body temperature can fluctuate if you are ill.* ● **fluc|tua|tion** /ˌflʌktʃueɪʃən/ (**fluctuations**) N-VAR ◻ *Don't worry about tiny fluctuations in your weight.*

flue /fluː/ (**flues**) N-COUNT A **flue** is a pipe or long tube that acts as a chimney, taking smoke away from a device such as a heater, fire, or stove.

flu|ent /flu̱ənt/ **1** ADJ Someone who is **fluent** in a particular language can speak the language easily and correctly. You can also say that someone speaks **fluent** French, Chinese, or some other language. ◻ *She studied eight foreign languages but is fluent in only six of them.* • **flu|en|cy** N-UNCOUNT ◻ *To work as a translator, you need fluency in at least one foreign language.* • **flu|ent|ly** ADV ◻ *He spoke three languages fluently.* **2** ADJ If your speech, reading, or writing is **fluent**, you speak, read, or write easily, smoothly, and clearly with no mistakes. ◻ *He had emerged from being a hesitant and unsure candidate into a fluent debater.* • **flu|en|cy** N-UNCOUNT ◻ *His son was praised for speeches of remarkable fluency.* • **flu|ent|ly** ADV [ADV with v] ◻ *Alex didn't read fluently till he was nearly seven.*

fluff /flʌ̱f/ (fluffs, fluffing, fluffed) **1** N-UNCOUNT **Fluff** consists of soft threads or fibers in the form of small, light balls or lumps. For example, you can refer to the fur of a small animal as **fluff**. ◻ *The nest contained two chicks: just small gray balls of fluff.* **2** V-T If you **fluff** something that you are trying to do, you are unsuccessful or you do it badly. [INFORMAL] ◻ *She fluffed her interview at Harvard.*

fluffy /flʌ̱fi/ (fluffier, fluffiest) **1** ADJ If you describe something such as a towel or a toy animal as **fluffy**, you mean that it is very soft. ◻ *...fluffy white towels.* **2** ADJ A cake or other food that is **fluffy** is very light because it has a lot of air in it. ◻ *Cream together the margarine and sugar with a wooden spoon until light and fluffy.*

flu|id /flu̱ɪd/ (fluids) **1** N-MASS A **fluid** is a liquid. [FORMAL] ◻ *The blood vessels may leak fluid, which distorts vision.* ◻ *Make sure that you drink plenty of fluids.* **2** ADJ **Fluid** movements or lines or designs are smooth and graceful. ◻ *His painting became less illustrational and more fluid.*

flu|id ounce (fluid ounces) N-COUNT [num N, oft N *of* n] A **fluid ounce** is a measurement of liquid. There are sixteen fluid ounces in a pint.

fluke /flu̱k/ (flukes) N-COUNT [usu sing, also by N] If you say that something good is a **fluke**, you mean that it happened accidentally rather than by being planned or arranged. [INFORMAL] ◻ *The discovery was something of a fluke.*

flum|mox /flʌ̱məks/ (flummoxes, flummoxing, flummoxed) V-T [usu passive] If someone **is flummoxed** by something, they are confused by it and do not know what to do or say. ◻ *The two leaders were flummoxed by the suggestion.* • **flum|moxed** ADJ ◻ *No wonder Josef was feeling a bit flummoxed.*

flung /flʌ̱ŋ/ **Flung** is the past tense and past participle of **fling**.

flunk /flʌ̱ŋk/ (flunks, flunking, flunked) V-T If you **flunk** an exam or a course, you fail to reach the required standard. [mainly AM, INFORMAL] ◻ *Your son is upset because he flunked a history exam.*
▶ **flunk out** PHRASAL VERB If you **flunk out**, you are dismissed from a school or college because your grades are not satisfactory. [mainly AM, INFORMAL] ◻ *He flunked out, a school official told CNN.* ◻ *If he doesn't find a solution to his problem soon, he'll surely flunk out of college.*

flunky /flʌ̱ŋki/ (flunkies) also **flunkey** N-COUNT If you refer to someone as a **flunky**, you disapprove of the fact that they associate themselves with someone who is powerful and carry out small, unimportant jobs for them in the hope of being rewarded. [DISAPPROVAL]

fluo|res|cent /flʊˌrɛ̱sᵊnt/ **1** ADJ A **fluorescent** surface, substance, or color has a very bright appearance when light is directed onto it, as if it is actually shining itself. ◻ *...a piece of fluorescent tape.* **2** ADJ A **fluorescent** light shines with a very hard, bright light and is usually in the form of a long strip. ◻ *Fluorescent lights flickered, and then the room was brilliantly, blindingly bright.*

fluori|da|tion /flʊərɪdeɪ̱ʃᵊn/ N-UNCOUNT **Fluoridation** is the action or process of adding fluoride to a water supply. ◻ *...fluoridation of the water supply.*

fluo|ride /flʊəraɪd/ N-UNCOUNT **Fluoride** is a mixture of chemicals that is sometimes added to drinking water and toothpaste because it is considered to be good for people's teeth.

fluo|rine /flʊərin/ N-UNCOUNT **Fluorine** is a pale yellow, poisonous gas. It is used in the production of uranium and other chemicals.

flur|ry /flɜ̱ri/ (flurries) **1** N-COUNT A **flurry** of something such as activity or excitement is a short intense period of it. ◻ *...a flurry of diplomatic activity aimed at ending the war.* **2** N-COUNT A **flurry** of something such as snow is a small amount of it that suddenly appears for a short time and moves in a quick, swirling way. ◻ *The Alps expect heavy cloud over the weekend with light snow flurries and strong winds.*

flush /flʌ̱ʃ/ (flushes, flushing, flushed) **1** V-I If you **flush**, your face gets red because you are hot or ill, or because you are feeling a strong emotion such as embarrassment or anger. ◻ *Do you sweat a lot or flush a lot?* • N-COUNT **Flush** is also a noun. ◻ *There was a slight flush on his cheeks.* • **flushed** ADJ ◻ *Her face was flushed with anger.* **2** V-T/V-I When someone **flushes** a toilet after using it, they fill the toilet bowl with water in order to clean it, usually by pressing a handle or pulling a chain. You can also say that a toilet **flushes**. ◻ *She flushed the toilet and went back in the bedroom.* • N-COUNT **Flush** is also a noun. ◻ *He heard the flush of a toilet.* **3** V-T If you **flush** something down the toilet, you get rid of it by putting it into the toilet bowl and flushing the toilet. ◻ *He was found trying to flush the pills down the toilet.* **4** V-T If you **flush** a part of your body, you clean it or make it healthier by using a large amount of liquid to get rid of dirt or harmful substances. ◻ *Flush the eye with clean cold water for at least 15 minutes.* • PHRASAL VERB **Flush out** means the same as **flush**. ◻ *...an "alternative" therapy that gently flushes out the colon to remove toxins.* **5** V-T If you **flush** dirt or a harmful substance out of a place, you get rid of it by using a large amount of liquid. ◻ *That won't flush out all the sewage, but it should unclog some stinking drains.* **6** V-T If you **flush** people or animals out of a place where they are hiding, you find or capture them by forcing them to come out of that place. ◻ *They flushed them out of their hiding places.*

flushed /flʌ̱ʃt/ ADJ [v-link ADJ *with* n] If you say that someone is **flushed with** success or pride you mean that they are very excited by their success or pride. ◻ *Grace was flushed with the success of the venture.*

flus|ter /flʌ̱stər/ (flusters, flustering, flustered) V-T If you **fluster** someone, you make them feel nervous and confused by rushing them and preventing them from concentrating on what they are doing. ◻ *The General refused to be flustered.* • **flus|tered** ADJ ◻ *She was so flustered that she forgot her reply.*

flute /flu̱t/ (flutes) N-VAR A **flute** is a musical instrument of the woodwind family. You play it by blowing over a hole near one end while holding it sideways to your mouth.

flut|ed /flu̱tɪd/ ADJ [usu ADJ n] Something that is **fluted** has shallow curves cut into it. ◻ *...the fluted wooden post of the porch.*

flut|ing /flu̱tɪŋ/ ADJ If you describe someone's voice as **fluting**, you mean that it goes up and down a lot, and usually that it is high pitched. ◻ *Her voice, small and fluting, stopped abruptly.* ◻ *...a fluting and melodic Scottish accent.*

flut|ist /flu̱tɪst/ (flutists) N-COUNT A **flutist** is someone who plays the flute. [AM]

flut|ter /flʌ̱tər/ (flutters, fluttering, fluttered) **1** V-T/V-I If something thin or light **flutters**, or if you **flutter** it, it moves up and down or from side to side with a lot of quick, light movements. ◻ *Her chiffon skirt was fluttering in the night breeze.* ◻ *...a butterfly fluttering its wings.* • N-COUNT **Flutter** is also a noun. ◻ *...a flutter of white cloth.* **2** V-I If something light such as a small bird or a piece of paper **flutters** somewhere, it moves through the air with small quick movements. ◻ *The paper fluttered to the floor.*

flux /flʌ̱ks/ N-UNCOUNT If something is in a state of **flux**, it is constantly changing. ◻ *Education remains in a state of flux which will take some time to settle down.*

fly ♦♦♦ /fla̱ɪ/ (flies, flying, flew, flown)
→ Please look at meanings **15** to **20** to see if the expression you are looking for is shown under another headword.

1 N-COUNT A **fly** is a small insect with two wings. There are many kinds of flies, and the most common are black in color. ◻ *Flies buzzed on the animals' swishing tails.* **2** N-COUNT The front opening on a pair of pants is referred to as the **fly**. It usually consists of a zipper or row of buttons behind a band of cloth. ◻ *I'm the kind of person who checks to see if my fly is undone.* **3** V-I When something such as a bird, insect, or aircraft **flies**, it moves through the air. ◻ *The planes flew through the clouds.*

4 V-I If you **fly** somewhere, you travel there in an aircraft. ❑ *He flew to Los Angeles.* ❑ *He flew back to London.* **5** V-T/V-I When someone **flies** an aircraft, they control its movement in the air. ❑ *Parker had successfully flown both aircraft.* ❑ *He flew a small plane to Cuba.* ❑ *I learned to fly in Vietnam.* • **flying** N-UNCOUNT ❑ *...a flying instructor.* **6** V-T To **fly** someone or something somewhere means to take or send them there in an aircraft. ❑ *It may be possible to fly the women and children out on Thursday.* **7** V-I If something such as your hair **is flying** about, it is moving about freely and loosely in the air. ❑ *His long, uncovered hair flew back in the wind.* **8** V-T/V-I If you **fly** a flag or if it **is flying**, you display it at the top of a pole. ❑ *They flew the flag of the African National Congress.* **9** V-I If you say that someone or something **flies** in a particular direction, you are emphasizing that they move there with a lot of speed or force. [EMPHASIS] ❑ *She flew to their bedsides when they were ill.* **10** → see also **flying** **11** PHRASE If you say that someone wouldn't **hurt a fly** or wouldn't **harm a fly**, you are emphasizing that they are very kind and gentle. [EMPHASIS] ❑ *Ray wouldn't hurt a fly.* **12** PHRASE If you **let fly**, you attack someone, either physically by hitting them, or with words by insulting them. ❑ *A simmering dispute ended with her letting fly with a stream of obscenities.* **13** PHRASE If you **send** someone or something **flying** or if they **go flying**, they move through the air and fall down with a lot of force. ❑ *The blow sent the young man flying.* **14** PHRASE [V PHR] If you do something **on the fly**, you do it quickly or automatically, without planning it in advance. [mainly AM] ❑ *You've got to be able to make decisions on the fly as deadlines loom.* **15 to fly in the face of** → see **face** ① **16 to fly off the handle** → see **handle 17** a **fly in the ointment** → see **ointment 18 when pigs fly** → see **pig 19 sparks fly** → see **spark 20 time flies** → see **time** ⑤
▶ **fly into** PHRASAL VERB If you **fly into** a bad temper or a panic, you suddenly become very angry or anxious and show this in your behavior. ❑ *Losing a game would cause him to fly into a rage.*

fly|away /fl**aɪ**əweɪ/ ADJ [usu ADJ n] **Flyaway** hair is very soft and fine. [WRITTEN]

fly ball (**fly balls**) also **flyball** N-COUNT In baseball, a **fly ball** is a ball that is hit very high. ❑ *Mike Lowell hit a fly ball to center fielder Doug Glanville.*

fly|by /fl**aɪ**baɪ/ (**flybys**) also **fly-by** N-COUNT A **flyby** is a flight made by an aircraft or a spacecraft over a particular place in order to record details about it.

fly-by-night ADJ [ADJ n] A **fly-by-night** businessperson is someone who wants to make money very quickly, without caring about the quality or honesty of the service they offer. [INFORMAL, DISAPPROVAL] ❑ *...fly-by-night operators who fail to complete jobs.*

fly-drive ADJ [ADJ n] On a **fly-drive** vacation, you travel part of the way to your destination by airplane, and collect a rental car at the airport so that you can drive the rest of the way. [BRIT]

fly|er /fl**aɪ**ər/ (**flyers**) also **flier** **1** N-COUNT A **flyer** is a pilot of an aircraft. ❑ *The American flyers sprinted for their planes and got into the cockpit.* **2** N-COUNT You can refer to someone who travels by airplane as a **flyer**. ❑ *...regular business flyers.* **3** N-COUNT A **flyer** is a small printed notice which is used to advertise a particular company, service, or event. ❑ *Thousands of flyers advertising the tour were handed out during the festival.*

fly-fishing also **fly fishing** N-UNCOUNT **Fly-fishing** is a method of fishing in which a silk or nylon model of a small winged insect is used as bait.

fly|ing /fl**aɪ**ɪŋ/ **1** ADJ [ADJ n] A **flying** animal has wings and is able to fly. ❑ *...species of flying insects.* **2** PHRASE If someone or something **gets off to a flying start**, or **makes a flying start**, they start very well, for example, in a race or a new job. ❑ *Advertising revenue in the new financial year has got off to a flying start.*

fly|ing fish (**flying fish** or **flying fishes**) N-VAR **Flying fish** are a type of fish that live in warm seas. They have large fins that enable them to move forward in the air when they jump out of the water.

fly|ing sau|cer (**flying saucers**) N-COUNT A **flying saucer** is a round, flat object which some people say they have seen in the sky and which they believe to be a spacecraft from another planet. [OLD-FASHIONED]

fly|leaf /fl**aɪ**liːf/ (**flyleaves**) N-COUNT The **flyleaf** of a book is a page at the front that has nothing printed on it.

fly|over /fl**aɪ**oʊvər/ (**flyovers**) N-COUNT A **flyover** is a structure which carries one road over the top of another road. [BRIT]

in AM, use **overpass**

fly|weight /fl**aɪ**weɪt/ (**flyweights**) N-COUNT A **flyweight** is a boxer who weighs 112 pounds or less.

fly|wheel /fl**aɪ**wiːl/ (**flywheels**) N-COUNT A **flywheel** is a heavy wheel that is part of some engines. It regulates the engine's rotation, making it operate at a steady speed.

FM /ɛf ɛm/ **FM** is a method of transmitting radio waves that can be used to broadcast high quality sound. **FM** is an abbreviation for 'frequency modulation.'

foal /foʊl/ (**foals, foaling, foaled**) **1** N-COUNT A **foal** is a very young horse. **2** V-I When a female horse **foals**, it gives birth. ❑ *The mare is due to foal today.*

foam /foʊm/ (**foams**) **1** N-UNCOUNT **Foam** consists of a mass of small bubbles that are formed when air and a liquid are mixed together. ❑ *The water curved round the rocks in great bursts of foam.* **2** N-MASS **Foam** is used to refer to various kinds of manufactured products which have a soft, light texture like a thick liquid. ❑ *...shaving foam.* **3** N-MASS **Foam** or **foam rubber** is soft rubber full of small holes which is used, for example, to make mattresses and cushions. ❑ *...modern three-piece suites filled with foam rubber.*

foamy /f**oʊ**mi/ (**foamier, foamiest**) ADJ A **foamy** liquid has a mass of small bubbles on its surface or consists of a mass of bubbles. ❑ *...foamy waves.* ❑ *Whisk the egg whites until they are foamy but not stiff.*

fob /fɒb/ (**fobs, fobbing, fobbed**) N-COUNT A **fob** is a short chain that has a key or a watch attached to the end. The **fob** can also refer to the watch that is attached to the chain.
▶ **fob off** PHRASAL VERB If someone **fobs** you **off**, they tell you something just to stop you from asking questions. [DISAPPROVAL] ❑ *I've asked her about it but she fobs me off.* ❑ *Don't be fobbed off with excuses.*

fo|cal /f**oʊ**kəl/ **1** ADJ [ADJ n] **Focal** is used to describe something that relates to the point where a number of rays or lines meet. ❑ *...the focal plane of the telescope.* **2** ADJ [ADJ n] **Focal** is used to describe something that is very important. ❑ *...the focal center of the city.*

fo|cal point /f**oʊ**kəl pɔɪnt/ (**focal points**) N-COUNT The **focal point** of something is the thing that people concentrate on or pay most attention to. ❑ *The focal point for the town's many visitors is the museum.*

fo'c'sle /f**oʊ**ksəl/ → see **forecastle**

fo|cus ◆◆◇ /f**oʊ**kəs/ (**focuses, focusing** or **focussing, focused** or **focussed**)

The plural of the noun can be either **focuses** or **foci** /f**oʊ**saɪ/.

1 V-T/V-I If you **focus** on a particular topic or if your attention **is focused** on it, you concentrate on it and think about it, discuss it, or deal with it, rather than dealing with other topics. ❑ *The research effort has focused on tracing the effects of growing levels of five compounds.* ❑ *Today he was able to focus his message exclusively on the economy.* **2** V-T/V-I If you **focus** your eyes or if your eyes **focus**, your eyes adjust so that you can clearly see the thing that you want to look at. If you **focus** a camera, telescope, or other instrument, you adjust it so that you can see clearly through it. ❑ *Kelly couldn't focus his eyes well enough to tell if the figure was male or female.* ❑ *His eyes slowly began to focus on what looked like a small dark ball.* **3** V-T If you **focus** rays of light on a particular point, you pass them through a lens or reflect them from a mirror so that they meet at that point. ❑ *Magnetic coils focus the electron beams into fine spots.* **4** N-COUNT The **focus** of something is the main topic or main thing that it is concerned with. ❑ *The UN's role in promoting peace is increasingly the focus of international attention.* ❑ *The new system is the focus of controversy.* **5** N-COUNT Your **focus** on something is the special attention that you pay it. ❑ *He said his sudden focus on foreign policy was not motivated by presidential politics.* **6** N-UNCOUNT If you say that something has a **focus**, you

focused — mean that you can see a purpose in it. ❑ *Somehow, though, their latest CD has a focus that the others have lacked.* **7** N-UNCOUNT You use **focus** to refer to the fact of adjusting your eyes or a camera, telescope, or other instrument, and to the degree to which you can see clearly. ❑ *His focus switched to the little white ball.* **8** PHRASE If an image or a camera, telescope, or other instrument is **in focus**, the edges of what you see are clear and sharp. ❑ *Pictures should be in focus, with realistic colors and well composed groups.* **9** PHRASE If something is **in focus**, it is being discussed or its purpose and nature are clear. ❑ *We want to keep the real issues in focus.* **10** PHRASE If an image or a camera, telescope, or other instrument is **out of focus**, the edges of what you see are unclear. ❑ *In some of the pictures the subjects are out of focus while the background is sharp.* **11** → See feature box at **eyesight**, **look**

COLLOCATIONS

focus
VERB **1**
focus + *noun*: attention, mind; effort, energy, resources; debate, discussion
noun + **focus**: attention, discussion, investigation, research, study
focus + *adverb*: entirely, exclusively, solely, totally; heavily, mainly, primarily
NOUN **5**
adjective + **focus**: clear, intense, narrow, relentless, sharp; main, primary, sole; increased, renewed
verb + **focus**: shift, switch; increase, narrow, sharpen; keep, maintain

---
SYNONYMS

focus
VERB **1**
concentrate: *Water companies should concentrate on reducing waste.*
direct: *The learner's attention needs to be directed to the significant features.*
home in: *The critics immediately homed in on the group's newly-elected members.*

---

fo|cused /foʊkəst/ also **focussed** ADJ [usu v-link ADJ] If you describe someone or something as **focused**, you approve of the fact that they have a clear and definite purpose. [APPROVAL] ❑ *I spent the next year just wandering. I wasn't focused.*

fo|cus group (**focus groups**) N-COUNT A **focus group** is a specially selected group of people who are intended to represent the general public. Focus groups have discussions in which their opinions are recorded as a form of market research. ❑ *The market research company BMRB conducted 12 focus groups for the project.*

fod|der /fɒdər/ **1** N-UNCOUNT **Fodder** is food that is given to cows, horses, and other animals. ❑ *...fodder for horses* **2** N-UNCOUNT If you say that something is **fodder** for a particular purpose, you mean that it is useful for that purpose and perhaps nothing else. [DISAPPROVAL] ❑ *The press conference simply provided more fodder for another attack on his character.*

foe /foʊ/ (**foes**) N-COUNT Someone's **foe** is their enemy. [WRITTEN] ❑ *But he soon discovers that his old foe may be leading him into a trap.*

foe|tal /fiːt°l/ [BRIT] → see **fetal**
foet|id /fɛtɪd/ [BRIT] → see **fetid**
foe|tus /fiːtəs/ [BRIT] → see **fetus**

fog /fɒg/ (**fogs**) **1** N-VAR When there is **fog**, there are tiny drops of water in the air which form a thick cloud and make it difficult to see things. ❑ *The crash happened in thick fog.* **2** N-SING A **fog** is an unpleasant cloud of something such as smoke inside a building or room. ❑ *...a fog of stale cigarette smoke.*

fog bank (**fog banks**) N-COUNT A **fog bank** is an area of thick fog, especially at sea.

fog|bound /fɒgbaʊnd/ ADJ If you are **fogbound** in a place or if the place is **fogbound**, thick fog makes it dangerous or impossible to go anywhere. ❑ *He was fogbound at JFK airport.* ❑ *...a fogbound highway.*

fo|gey /foʊgi/ → see **fogy**

fog|gy /fɒgi/ (**foggier, foggiest**) **1** ADJ When it is **foggy**, there is fog. ❑ *It's quite foggy now.* **2** PHRASE If you say that you **haven't the foggiest** or you **haven't the foggiest idea**, you are emphasizing that you do not know something. [INFORMAL, EMPHASIS] ❑ *I did not have the foggiest idea what he meant.*

fog|horn /fɒghɔːrn/ (**foghorns**) N-COUNT A **foghorn** is a piece of equipment that makes a loud noise and is used to warn ships about the position of land and other ships in fog.

fo|gy /foʊgi/ (**fogies**) also **fogey** N-COUNT If you describe someone as a **fogy** or an **old fogy**, you mean that they are boring and old-fashioned. [INFORMAL, DISAPPROVAL] ❑ *I don't want to sound like I'm some old fogy.*

foi|ble /fɔɪb°l/ (**foibles**) N-COUNT A **foible** is a habit or characteristic that someone has which is considered rather strange, foolish, or bad but which is also considered unimportant. ❑ *...human foibles and weaknesses.*

foie gras /fwɑː grɑː/ N-UNCOUNT **Foie gras** is a food made from the livers of geese that were specially fed so that their livers became very large.

foil /fɔɪl/ (**foils, foiling, foiled**) **1** N-UNCOUNT **Foil** consists of sheets of metal as thin as paper. It is used to wrap food in. ❑ *Pour cider around the meat and cover with foil.* **2** V-T If you **foil** someone's plan or attempt to do something, for example, to commit a crime, you succeed in stopping them from doing what they want. [JOURNALISM] ❑ *A brave police chief foiled an armed robbery by grabbing the raider's shotgun.*

foist /fɔɪst/ (**foists, foisting, foisted**)
▸ **foist on** PHRASAL VERB If you say that someone **foists** something **on** you, or **foists** it **upon** you, you dislike the way that they force you to listen to it or experience it. [DISAPPROVAL] ❑ *I don't see my role as foisting my beliefs on them.* ❑ *A man who murdered his wife tried to foist the responsibility for his crime onto a neighbor.*

fold ♦◇◇ /foʊld/ (**folds, folding, folded**) **1** V-T If you **fold** something such as a piece of paper or cloth, you bend it so that one part covers another part, often pressing the edge so that it stays in place. ❑ *He folded the paper carefully.* ❑ *Fold the omelette in half.* **2** V-T/V-I If a piece of furniture or equipment **folds** or if you can **fold** it, you can make it smaller by bending or closing parts of it. ❑ *The back of the bench folds forward to make a table.* ❑ *This portable seat folds flat for easy storage.* • PHRASAL VERB **Fold up** means the same as **fold**. ❑ *When not in use it folds up out of the way.* **3** V-T If you **fold** your arms or hands, you bring them together and cross or link them, for example, over your chest. ❑ *Meer folded his arms over his chest and turned his head away.* **4** N-COUNT A **fold** in a piece of paper or cloth is a bend that you make in it when you put one part of it over another part and press the edge. ❑ *Make another fold and turn the ends together.* **5** N-COUNT The **folds** in a piece of cloth are the curved shapes which are formed when it is not hanging or lying flat. ❑ *The priest fumbled in the folds of his gown.* **6** → See feature box at **body language**
▸ **fold up** **1** PHRASAL VERB If you **fold** something **up**, you make it into a smaller, neater shape by folding it, usually several times. ❑ *She folded it up, and tucked it into her purse.* **2** → see also **fold 2**

SUFFIX

-fold
combines with numbers to form adverbs which say how much an amount has increased by. For example, if an amount increases **fourfold**, it is four times greater than it was originally.

---

fold|er /foʊldər/ (**folders**) **1** N-COUNT A **folder** is a thin piece of cardboard in which you can keep loose papers. **2** N-COUNT A **folder** is a group of files that are stored together on a computer. **3** → See feature box at **email**

fold-up ADJ [ADJ n] A **fold-up** piece of furniture or equipment is one that is specially designed so that it can be folded into a smaller shape in order to be stored.

fo|li|age /foʊliɪdʒ/ N-UNCOUNT The leaves of a plant are referred to as its **foliage**. ❑ *...shrubs with gray or silver foliage.*

fo|lic acid /foʊlɪk æsɪd, fɒl-/ N-UNCOUNT **Folic acid** is one of the B group of vitamins. It is found in green vegetables and fruit.

fo|lio /fóuliou/ (**folios**) N-COUNT A **folio** is a book made with paper of a large size, used especially in the early centuries of European printing. ☐ *Richard told me of three 16th-century folio volumes on alchemy.*

folk ✦✧✧ /fóuk/ (**folks**)

> Folk can also be used as the plural form for meaning **1**.

1 N-PLURAL You can refer to people as **folk** or **folks**. ☐ *Country folk can tell you that there are certain places which animals avoid.* ☐ *These are the folks from the local TV station.* **2** N-PLURAL You can refer to your close family, especially your mother and father, as your **folks**. [INFORMAL] ☐ *I've been avoiding my folks lately.* **3** N-VOC You can use **folks** as a term of address when you are talking to several people. [INFORMAL] ☐ *"It's a question of money, folks," I said.* **4** ADJ [ADJ n] **Folk** art and customs are traditional or typical of a particular community or nation. ☐ *...South American folk art.* **5** ADJ [ADJ n] **Folk** music is music which is traditional or typical of a particular community or nation. • N-UNCOUNT **Folk** is also a noun. ☐ *...a variety of music including classical and folk.*

folk|lore /fóuklɔr/ N-UNCOUNT **Folklore** is the traditional stories, customs, and habits of a particular community or nation. ☐ *In Chinese folklore the bat is a symbol of good fortune.*

folk song (**folk songs**) also **folksong** N-COUNT A **folk song** is a traditional song that is typical of a particular community or nation.

folk|sy /fóuksi/ (**folksier, folksiest**) **1** ADJ [usu ADJ n] If you describe something as **folksy**, you mean that it is simple and has a style characteristic of folk craft and tradition. You sometimes use **folksy** to show disapproval of something because it seems unsophisticated. ☐ *...folksy country furniture.* **2** ADJ [usu ADJ n] If you describe someone as **folksy**, you mean that they are friendly and informal in their behavior. [AM, APPROVAL] ☐ *...an elderly, folksy postman.*

fol|li|cle /fɒlɪkᵊl/ (**follicles**) N-COUNT A **follicle** is one of the small hollows in the skin which hairs grow from.

FOLLOW

① GO OR COME AFTER
② ACT ACCORDING TO SOMETHING, OBSERVE SOMETHING
③ UNDERSTAND
④ PHRASAL VERBS

---

① **fol|low** ✦✦✦ /fɒlou/ (**follows, following, followed**)
→ Please look at meanings **16** – **18** to see if the expression you are looking for is shown under another headword.

1 V-T/V-I If you **follow** someone who is going somewhere, you move along behind them because you want to go to the same place. ☐ *We followed him up the steps into a large hall.* ☐ *Please follow me, madam.* ☐ *They took him into a small room and I followed.* **2** V-T If you **follow** someone who is going somewhere, you move along behind them without their knowledge, in order to catch them or find out where they are going. ☐ *She realized that the Mercedes was following her.* **3** V-T If you **follow** someone to a place where they have recently gone and where they are now, you go to join them there. ☐ *He followed Janice to New York, where she was preparing an exhibition.* **4** V-T/V-I An event, activity, or period of time that **follows** a particular thing happens or comes after that thing, at a later time. ☐ *...the rioting and looting that followed the verdict.* ☐ *Other problems may follow.* **5** V-T If you **follow** one thing with another, you do or say the second thing after you have done or said the first thing. ☐ *Her first major role was in Martin Scorsese's "Goodfellas" and she followed this with a part in Spike Lee's "Jungle Fever."* • PHRASAL VERB **Follow up** means the same as **follow**. ☐ *The book proved such a success that the authors followed it up with "The Messianic Legacy."* **6** V-T/V-I If it **follows** that a particular thing is the case, that thing is a logical result of something else being true or being the case. ☐ *Just because a bird does not breed one year, it does not follow that it will fail the next.* ☐ *If the explanation is right, two things follow.* **7** V-T/V-I If you refer to the words that **follow** or **followed**, you are referring to the words that come next or came next in a piece of writing or speech. ☐ *What follows is an eye-witness account.* ☐ *There followed a list of places where Hans intended to visit.* **8** V-T If you **follow** a path, route, or set of signs, you go somewhere using the path, route, or signs to direct you. ☐ *If they followed the road, they would be certain to reach a village.* ☐ *All we had to do was follow the map.* **9** V-T If something such as a path or river **follows** a particular route or line, it goes along that route or line. ☐ *Our route follows the Pacific coast through densely populated neighborhoods.* **10** V-T If you **follow** something with your eyes, or if your eyes **follow** it, you watch it as it moves or you look along its route or course. ☐ *Ann's eyes followed a police car as it drove slowly past.* **11** V-T Something that **follows** a particular course of development happens or develops in that way. ☐ *His release turned out to follow the pattern set by that of the other six hostages.* **12** V-T If you **follow** someone in what you do, you do the same thing or job as they did previously. ☐ *He followed his father and became a surgeon.* **13** PHRASE You use **as follows** in writing or speech to introduce something such as a list, description, or an explanation. ☐ *The winners are as follows: E. Walker; R. Foster; R. Gates; A. Mackintosh.* **14** PHRASE You use **followed by** to say what comes after something else in a list or ordered set of things. ☐ *Potatoes are still the most popular food, followed by white bread.* **15** → see also **following** **16** **to follow in someone's footsteps** → see **footstep** **17** **to follow your nose** → see **nose** **18** **to follow suit** → see **suit**

SYNONYMS

follow
VERB ① **2**
pursue: *She pursued the man who had stolen a woman's bag.*
track: *He thought he had better track this wolf and kill it.*
chase: *She chased the thief for 100 yards.*
trail: *Two detectives were trailing him.*

---

② **fol|low** ✦✦✦ /fɒlou/ (**follows, following, followed**) **1** V-T If you **follow** advice, an instruction, or a recipe, you act or do something in the way that it indicates. ☐ *Take care to follow the instructions carefully.* **2** V-T If you **follow** what someone else has done, you do it too because you think it is a good thing or because you want to copy them. ☐ *His admiration for the athlete did not extend to the point where he would follow his example in taking drugs.* **3** V-T If you **follow** something, you take an interest in it and keep informed about what happens. ☐ *...the millions of people who follow football because they genuinely love it.* **4** V-T If you **follow** a particular religion or political belief, you have that religion or belief. ☐ *"Do you follow any particular religion?"—"Yes, we're all Hindus."*

COLLOCATIONS

follow
VERB ② **1**
follow + noun: guidelines, instructions, procedures, rules

---

③ **fol|low** ✦✦✦ /fɒlou/ (**follows, following, followed**) **1** V-T/V-I If you are able to **follow** something such as an explanation or the story of a movie, you understand it as it continues and develops. ☐ *Can you follow the plot so far?* ☐ *I'm sorry, I don't follow.* **2** → see also **following**

④ **fol|low** ✦✦✦ /fɒlou/ (**follows, following, followed**)
▶ **follow through** PHRASAL VERB If you **follow through** an action, plan, or idea or **follow through** with it, you continue doing or thinking about it until you have done everything possible. ☐ *The leadership has been unwilling to follow through the implications of these ideas.* ☐ *I was trained to be an actor but I didn't follow it through.*
▶ **follow up 1** PHRASAL VERB If you **follow up** something that has been said, suggested, or discovered, you try to find out more about it or take action about it. ☐ *State police are following up several leads.* **2** → see also **follow** ① **5**, **follow-up**

fol|low|er /fɒlouər/ (**followers**) N-COUNT A **follower** of a particular person, group, or belief is someone who supports or admires this person, group, or belief. ☐ *...followers of the Zulu Inkatha movement.*

fol|low|ing ✦✦✧ /fɒlouɪŋ/ (**followings**) **1** PREP **Following** a particular event means after that event. ☐ *In the centuries following Christ's death, Christians genuinely believed the world was about to end.* **2** ADJ [det ADJ] The **following** day, week, or year is the day, week, or year after the one you have just mentioned. ☐ *The following day the picture appeared on the front pages of every newspaper in the world.* ☐ *We went to dinner the following Monday* evening. **3** ADJ [det ADJ] You use **following** to refer to something that you are about to mention. ❑ *Write down the following information: name of product, type, date purchased and price.* • PRON [the PRON] **The following** refers to the thing or things that you are about to mention. ❑ *The following is a paraphrase of what was said.* **4** N-COUNT A person or organization that has a **following** has a group of people who support or admire their beliefs or actions. ❑ *Australian rugby league enjoys a huge following in New Zealand.*

SYNONYMS

following
ADJ **2**
next: *I got up early the next morning.*
subsequent: *Those concerns were overshadowed by subsequent events.*
successive: *Jackson was the winner for a second successive year.*
consecutive: *They won the Cup for the third consecutive year.*
ensuing: *The ensuing argument had been bitter.*

follow-on N-SING [also no det, usu N to n] A **follow-on** is something that is done to continue or add to something done previously. ❑ *This course for bridge players with some experience is intended as a follow-on to the Beginners' course.*

follow-through (follow-throughs) **1** N-UNCOUNT [also a N, oft N prep] A **follow-through** is something that completes an action or a planned series of actions. ❑ *...the task of finding a durable solution to the refugee problem as a follow-through to the very temporary measures.* **2** N-VAR A **follow-through** is a movement that completes an action such as hitting a ball. ❑ *Focus on making a short, firm follow-through.*

follow-up (follow-ups) N-VAR A **follow-up** is something that is done to continue or add to something done previously. ❑ *She is working on a follow-up to her last solo album.*

folly /fɒli/ (follies) N-VAR If you say that a particular action or way of behaving is **folly** or a **folly**, you mean that it is foolish. ❑ *It's sheer folly to build nuclear power stations in a country that has dozens of earthquakes every year.*

foment /foʊmɛnt/ (foments, fomenting, fomented) V-T If someone or something **foments** trouble or violent opposition, they cause it to develop. [FORMAL] ❑ *They accused strike leaders of fomenting violence.*

FOMO /foʊmoʊ/ FOMO is the written and sometimes spoken abbreviation for 'fear of missing out,' used to talk about the belief of some people that others are having a good time without them. [INFORMAL]

fond /fɒnd/ (fonder, fondest) **1** ADJ [v-link ADJ of n] If you are **fond of** someone, you feel affection for them. ❑ *I am very fond of Michael.* • **fondness** N-UNCOUNT ❑ *...a great fondness for children.* **2** ADJ [ADJ n] You use **fond** to describe people or their behavior when they show affection. ❑ *a fond father.* • **fondly** ADV [ADV after v] ❑ *Liz saw their eyes meet fondly across the table.* **3** ADJ [v-link ADJ of n/-ing] If you are **fond of** something, you like it or you like doing it very much. ❑ *He was fond of marmalade.* • **fondness** N-UNCOUNT ❑ *I've always had a fondness for chocolate cake.* **4** ADJ [ADJ n] If you have **fond** memories of someone or something, you remember them with pleasure. ❑ *I have very fond memories of living in our village.* • **fondly** ADV [ADV with v] ❑ *My dad took us there when I was about four and I remembered it fondly.* **5** ADJ [ADJ n] You use **fond** to describe hopes, wishes, or beliefs which you think are foolish because they seem unlikely to be fulfilled. ❑ *My fond hope is that we will be ready by Christmastime.* • **fondly** ADV [ADV with v] ❑ *I fondly imagined that surgery meant a few stitches and an overnight stay in the hospital.*

fondant /fɒndənt/ N-UNCOUNT [oft N n] **Fondant** is a sweet paste made from sugar and water. ❑ *...fondant cakes.*

fondle /fɒndəl/ (fondles, fondling, fondled) V-T If you **fondle** someone or something, you touch them gently with a stroking movement, usually in a sexual way. ❑ *He tried to kiss her and fondle her.*

fondue /fɒndu/ (fondues) N-VAR A **fondue** is a melted sauce. It can be melted cheese into which you dip bread, a pot of hot oil into which you dip pieces of meat or vegetables, or melted chocolate into which you dip pieces of fruit.

font /fɒnt/ (fonts) N-COUNT In printing, a **font** is a set of characters of the same style and size. ❑ *...the immense variety of fonts available in Microsoft Word and Publisher.*

food ♦♦♦ /fud/ (foods) **1** N-MASS **Food** is what people and animals eat. ❑ *Enjoy your food.* ❑ *...frozen foods.* **2** → see also **fast food, junk food** **3** PHRASE If you give someone **food for thought**, you make them think carefully about something. ❑ *Her speech offers much food for thought.* **4** → See feature box at **debate, deforest, endanger, recycle**

Food and Administration N-PROPER [the N] In the United States, the **Food and Drug Administration** is a government department that is responsible for making sure that foods and drugs are safe.

food bank (food banks) N-COUNT A **food bank** is a place that collects food that has been donated and gives it to people who are poor or homeless. [AM] ❑ *...charities that provide food for the poor, such as soup kitchens and food banks.*

food chain (food chains) N-COUNT [usu sing] The **food chain** is a series of living things which are linked to each other because each thing feeds on the one next to it in the series. ❑ *The whole food chain is affected by the overuse of chemicals in agriculture.*

food court (food courts) N-COUNT A **food court** is a place, for example, in a shopping mall, that has several small restaurants and a common eating area. ❑ *At O'Hare's food court near the international terminal, it's tough to find a seat.*

food desert (food deserts) N-COUNT If you refer to an area as a **food desert**, you mean that there is little fresh or healthy food there. ❑ *People living in so-called food deserts were at greater risk of poor diet and being overweight or obese.* ❑ *In clear view of the Hollywood sign, there were food deserts, poverty and hunger all around me.*

foodie /fudi/ (foodies) also **foody** N-COUNT **Foodies** are people who enjoy cooking and eating different kinds of food. [INFORMAL] ❑ *Other neighborhoods in the city offer foodies a choice of Chinese, Portuguese or Greek food.*

food mixer (food mixers) also **food-mixer** N-COUNT A **food mixer** is a piece of electrical equipment that is used to mix food such as cake batter.

food poisoning **1** N-UNCOUNT If you get **food poisoning**, you become ill because you have eaten food that has gone bad. **2** → See feature box at **illness**

food processor (food processors) N-COUNT A **food processor** is a piece of electrical equipment that is used to mix, chop, or beat food, or to make it into a liquid.

food stamp (food stamps) N-COUNT [usu pl] In the United States, **food stamps** are official vouchers that are given to people with low incomes to be exchanged for food.

foodstuff /fudstʌf/ (foodstuffs) N-VAR **Foodstuffs** are substances which people eat. ❑ *...basic foodstuffs such as sugar, cooking oil and cheese.*

foody /fudi/ → see **foodie**

fool ♦◇◇ /ful/ (fools, fooling, fooled) **1** N-COUNT If you call someone a **fool**, you are indicating that you think they are not at all sensible and show a lack of good judgment. [DISAPPROVAL] ❑ *"You fool!" she shouted.* **2** ADJ [ADJ n] **Fool** is used to describe an action or person that is not at all sensible and shows a lack of good judgment. [mainly AM, INFORMAL, DISAPPROVAL] ❑ *What a damn fool thing to do!* **3** V-T If someone **fools** you, they deceive or trick you. ❑ *I don't think you can fool people for long.* ❑ *Don't be fooled by his appearance.* **4** V-I If you say that a person **is fooling with** something or someone, you mean that the way they are behaving is likely to cause problems. ❑ *What are you doing fooling with such a staggering sum of money?* **5** PHRASE If you **make a fool of** someone, you make them seem silly by telling people about something stupid that they have done, or by tricking them. ❑ *Your brother is making a fool of you.* **6** PHRASE If you **make a fool of** yourself, you behave in a way that makes other people think that you are silly or lacking in good judgment. ❑ *He was drinking and making a fool of himself.* **7** PHRASE If you **play the fool** or **act the fool**, you behave in a playful, childish, and foolish way, usually in order to make other people laugh. ❑ *They used to play the fool together, calling each other silly names and giggling.*

▶ **fool around** PHRASAL VERB If you **fool around**, you behave in a silly, dangerous, or irresponsible way. ❑ *They were fooling around on an Army firing range.*

foolhardy

SYNONYMS

fool
NOUN **1**
simpleton: 'But Ian's such a simpleton,' she laughed.
idiot: I knew I'd been an idiot to stay there.
dunce: Michael may have been a dunce at mathematics, but he was gifted at languages.
dolt: He's a first-class dolt who insists on doing things his way.
VERB **3**
deceive: He has deceived and disillusioned us all.
trick: Stephen is going to be pretty upset when he finds out how you tricked him.
mislead: Jack was furious with his London doctors for having misled him.
dupe: ...a plot to dupe stamp collectors into buying fake rarities.

fool|hardy /fu̱lhɑːdi/ ADJ If you describe behavior as foolhardy, you disapprove of it because it is extremely risky. [DISAPPROVAL] ◻ When he tested an early vaccine on himself, some described the act as foolhardy.

fool|ish /fu̱lɪʃ/ **1** ADJ If someone's behavior or action is foolish, it is not sensible and shows a lack of good judgment. ◻ It would be foolish to raise hopes unnecessarily. ● **fool|ish|ly** ADV ◻ He admitted that he had acted foolishly. ● **fool|ish|ness** N-UNCOUNT ◻ They don't accept any foolishness when it comes to spending money. **2** ADJ If you look or feel foolish, you look or feel so silly or ridiculous that people are likely to laugh at you. ◻ I just stood there feeling foolish and watching him. ● **fool|ish|ly** ADV [ADV after v] ◻ He saw me standing there, grinning foolishly at him.

fool|proof /fu̱lpruːf/ ADJ Something such as a plan or a machine that is foolproof is so well designed, easy to understand, or easy to use that it cannot go wrong or be used wrongly. ◻ The system is not 100 per cent foolproof.

fool's gold **1** N-UNCOUNT Fool's gold is a substance that is found in rock and that looks very like gold. **2** N-UNCOUNT If you say that a plan for getting money is fool's gold, you mean that it is foolish to carry it out because you are sure that it will fail or cause problems. [DISAPPROVAL] ◻ The establishment seems to be off on another quest for fool's gold.

fool's para|dise N-SING [a N] If you say that someone is living in a fool's paradise, you are criticizing them because they are not aware that their present happy situation is likely to change and get worse. [DISAPPROVAL] ◻ ...living in a fool's paradise of false prosperity.

FOOT
① PART OF BODY
② UNIT OF MEASUREMENT
③ LOWER END OF SOMETHING

① **foot** ✦✦✦ /fu̱t/ (feet)
→ Please look at meanings **21** – **23** to see if the expression you are looking for is shown under another headword.

1 N-COUNT Your feet are the parts of your body that are at the ends of your legs, and that you stand on. ◻ She stamped her foot again. ◻ ...a foot injury. **2** ADJ [ADJ n] A foot brake or foot pump is operated by your foot rather than by your hand. ◻ I tried to reach the foot brakes but I couldn't. **3** ADJ [ADJ n] A foot patrol or foot soldiers walk rather than traveling in vehicles or on horseback. ◻ Paratroopers and foot-soldiers entered the building on the government's behalf. **4** → see also **footing** **5** PHRASE If you get **cold feet** about something, you become nervous or frightened about it because you think it will fail. ◻ The Government is getting cold feet about the reforms. **6** PHRASE If you say that someone **is finding** their **feet** in a new situation, you mean that they are starting to feel confident and to deal with things successfully. ◻ I don't know anyone here but I am sure I will manage when I find my feet. **7** PHRASE If you say that someone has their **feet on the ground**, you approve of the fact that they have a sensible and practical attitude toward life, and do not have unrealistic ideas. [APPROVAL] ◻ In that respect he needs to keep his feet on the ground and not get carried away. **8** PHRASE If you go somewhere **on foot**, you walk, rather than using any form of transport. ◻ We rowed ashore, then explored the island on foot for the rest of the day. **9** PHRASE If you are **on your feet**, you are standing up. ◻ Everyone was on their feet applauding wildly.

510

football field

10 PHRASE If you say that someone or something is **on their feet** again after an illness or difficult period, you mean that they have recovered and are back to normal. ◻ You need someone to take the pressure off and help you get back on your feet. **11** PHRASE If you say that someone always **lands on their feet**, you mean that they are always successful or lucky, although they do not seem to achieve this by their own efforts. ◻ He has good looks and charm, and always lands on his feet. **12** PHRASE If someone **puts** their **foot down**, they use their authority in order to stop something from happening. ◻ He had planned to go skiing on his own in March but his wife had decided to put her foot down. **13** PHRASE If someone **puts** their **foot down** when they are driving, they drive as fast as they can. [BRIT] **14** PHRASE If someone **puts** their **foot in it** or **puts** their **foot in** their **mouth**, they accidentally do or say something which embarrasses or offends people. [INFORMAL] ◻ Our chairman has really put his foot in it, poor man, though he doesn't know it. **15** PHRASE If you **put** your **feet up**, you relax or have a rest, especially by sitting or lying with your feet supported off the ground. ◻ After supper he'd put his feet up and read. **16** PHRASE If you never **put a foot wrong**, you never make any mistakes. [mainly BRIT] ◻ When he's around, we never put a foot wrong. **17** PHRASE If you say that someone **sets foot** in a place, you mean that they enter it or reach it, and you are emphasizing the significance of their action. If you say that someone never **sets foot** in a place, you are emphasizing that they never go there. [EMPHASIS] ◻ ...the day the first man set foot on the moon. **18** PHRASE If someone has to **stand on** their **own two feet**, they have to be independent and manage their life without help from other people. ◻ My father didn't mind whom I married, so long as I could stand on my own two feet and wasn't dependent on my husband. **19** PHRASE If you get or rise **to** your **feet**, you stand up. ◻ Malone got to his feet and followed his superior out of the suite. ◻ The delegates cheered and rose to their feet. **20** PHRASE If someone **gets off on the wrong foot** in a new situation, they make a bad start by doing something in completely the wrong way. ◻ Even though they called the election and had been preparing for it for some time, they got off on the wrong foot. **21** foot in the door → see **door 22** to drag your feet → see **drag 23** to vote with your feet → see **vote**

② **foot** ✦✦✦ /fu̱t/ (feet) N-COUNT A foot is a unit for measuring length, height, or depth, and is equal to 12 inches or 30.48 centimeters. When you are giving measurements, the form 'foot' is often used as the plural instead of the plural form 'feet.' ◻ This beautiful and curiously shaped lake lies at around fifteen thousand feet. ◻ He occupies a cell 10 foot long, 6 foot wide and 10 foot high.

③ **foot** /fu̱t/ (feet) **1** N-SING The **foot** of something is the part that is farthest from its top. ◻ David called to the children from the foot of the stairs. ◻ ...the foot of the hill. **2** N-SING The **foot** of a bed is the end nearest to the feet of the person lying in it. ◻ Friends stood at the foot of the bed, looking at her with serious faces.

foot|age /fu̱tɪdʒ/ N-UNCOUNT **Footage** of a particular event is a film of it or the part of a film which shows this event. ◻ They are planning to show exclusive footage from this summer's festivals.

foot-and-mouth dis|ease N-UNCOUNT **Foot-and-mouth disease** or **foot-and-mouth** is a serious and highly infectious disease that affects cattle, sheep, pigs, and goats.

foot|ball ✦✦ /fu̱tbɔːl/ (footballs) **1** N-UNCOUNT **Football** is a game played by two teams of eleven players using an oval ball. Players carry the ball in their hands or throw it to each other as they try to score goals that are called touchdowns. [AM] ◻ Two blocks beyond our school was a field where boys played football. **2** N-COUNT A **football** is a ball that is used for playing football. ◻ ...a heavy leather football. **3** N-UNCOUNT **Football** is a game played by two teams of eleven players using a round ball. Players kick the ball to each other and try to score goals by kicking the ball into a large net. [BRIT] **4** → See feature box on next page

in AM, use **soccer**

foot|ball|er /fu̱tbɔːlər/ (footballers) N-COUNT A **footballer** is a person who plays football (soccer), especially as a profession. [BRIT]

in AM, use **soccer player**

foot|ball field (football fields) N-COUNT A **football field** is an area of grass where football is played.

in BRIT, also use **football pitch**

VOCABULARY IN CONTEXT

Football

When you say 'football,' what sport are you talking about? That depends on where you are. If you are in the United States, the game of football is a **team** sport that is played on a **rectangular** field with a **goal** at either end. However, this is about the **extent** of the similarities between the game called football in the U.S. and the one that shares its name in the rest of the world. **Soccer**, as football is known in the U.S., is the world's most popular sport. It is played by over 250 million people in more than 200 countries. It's difficult to say which game of football is more **demanding**, as both require athletes to be in **peak condition** to perform well. Furthermore, both games rely on **referees** to **enforce** the rules, and we can't overlook the fact that these officials have a lot of power in determining the outcomes of games.

foot|bridge /fʊtbrɪdʒ/ (**footbridges**) N-COUNT A **footbridge** is a narrow bridge for people traveling on foot.

foot-dragging N-UNCOUNT If you accuse someone of **foot-dragging**, you mean that they are deliberately delaying making a decision about something that is important to you. [DISAPPROVAL] ❑ ...foot-dragging on international environmental policy. ❑ He accused the company of "shameful foot-dragging."

-footed /-fʊtɪd/ ■ COMB IN ADJ **-footed** combines with words such as 'heavy' or 'light' to form adjectives which indicate how someone moves or walks. ❑ ...a slim, light-footed little man. ❑ He was a nimble-footed boy of ten. ■ → see also **foot** ①, **flat-footed**, **sure-footed**

foot|er /fʊtər/ (**footers**) N-COUNT A **footer** is text such as a name or page number that can be automatically displayed at the bottom of each page of a printed document. Compare **header**. [COMPUTING] ❑ Page Mode shows headers, footers, footnotes and page numbers.

foot|fall /fʊtfɔl/ (**footfalls**) N-COUNT A **footfall** is the sound that is made by someone walking each time they take a step. [LITERARY] ❑ She heard the priest's familiar, flat footfall on the staircase.

foot|hills /fʊthɪlz/ N-PLURAL The **foothills** of a mountain or a range of mountains are the lower hills or mountains around its base. ❑ Pasadena lies in the foothills of the San Gabriel mountains.

foot|hold /fʊthoʊld/ (**footholds**) ■ N-COUNT A **foothold** is a strong or favorable position from which further advances or progress may be made. ❑ Businesses are investing millions of dollars to gain a foothold in this new market. ■ N-COUNT A **foothold** is a place such as a small hole or area of rock where you can safely put your foot when climbing. ❑ He lowered his legs until he felt he had a solid foothold on the rockface beneath him.

foot|ing /fʊtɪŋ/ ■ N-UNCOUNT If something is put on a particular **footing**, it is defined, established, or changed in a particular way, often so that it is able to develop or exist successfully. ❑ The new law will put official corruption on the same legal footing as treason. ■ N-UNCOUNT If you are on a particular kind of **footing** with someone, you have that kind of relationship with them. ❑ They decided to put their relationship on a more formal footing. ■ N-UNCOUNT You refer to your **footing** when you are referring to your position and how securely your feet are placed on the ground. For example, if you lose your **footing**, your feet slip and you fall. ❑ He was cautious of his footing, wary of the edge.

foot|lights /fʊtlaɪts/ N-PLURAL In a theater, the **footlights** are the row of lights along the front of the stage.

foot|locker /fʊtlɒkər/ (**footlockers**) also **foot locker** N-COUNT A **footlocker** is a large box for keeping personal possessions in, especially one that is placed at the end of a bed. [AM]

foot|loose /fʊtlus/ ■ ADJ If you describe someone as **footloose**, you mean that they have no responsibilities or commitments, and are therefore free to do what they want and go where they want. ❑ People that are single tend to be more footloose. ■ PHRASE [usu v-link PHR] If you describe someone as **footloose and fancy-free**, you mean that they are not married or in a similar relationship, and you therefore consider them to have very few responsibilities or commitments.

foot|man /fʊtmən/ (**footmen**) N-COUNT A **footman** is a male servant who typically does jobs such as opening doors or serving food, and who often wears a special uniform.

foot|note /fʊtnoʊt/ (**footnotes**) ■ N-COUNT A **footnote** is a note at the bottom of a page in a book which provides more detailed information about something that is mentioned on that page. ■ N-COUNT If you refer to what you are saying as a **footnote**, you mean that you are adding some information that is related to what has just been mentioned. ❑ As a footnote, I should add that there was one point on which his bravado was more than justified. ■ N-COUNT If you describe an event as a **footnote**, you mean that it is fairly unimportant although it will probably be remembered. ❑ I'm afraid that his name will now become a footnote in history.

foot|path /fʊtpæθ/ (**footpaths**) N-COUNT A **footpath** is a path for people to walk on, especially in the countryside.

foot|print /fʊtprɪnt/ (**footprints**) N-COUNT A **footprint** is a mark in the shape of a foot that a person or animal makes in or on a surface. ❑ His footprints were clearly evident in the heavy dust.

foot|sie /fʊtsi/ PHRASE [usu PHR with n] If someone **plays footsie** with you, they touch your feet with their own feet, for example, under a table, often as a playful way of expressing their romantic or sexual feelings toward you. [INFORMAL]

foot sol|dier (**foot soldiers**) N-COUNT The **foot soldiers** of a particular organization are people who seem unimportant and who do not have a high position but who do a large amount of very important and often very boring work.

foot|step /fʊtstɛp/ (**footsteps**) ■ N-COUNT A **footstep** is the sound or mark that is made by someone walking each time their foot touches the ground. ❑ I heard footsteps outside. ■ PHRASE If you **follow in** someone's **footsteps**, you do the same things as they did earlier. ❑ My father is extremely proud that I followed in his footsteps and became a doctor.

foot|stool /fʊtstul/ (**footstools**) N-COUNT A **footstool** is a small low stool that you can rest your feet on when you are sitting in a chair.

foot|wear /fʊtwɛər/ ■ N-UNCOUNT **Footwear** refers to things that people wear on their feet, for example, shoes and boots. ❑ Some football players get paid millions for endorsing footwear. ■ → See also color supplement

foot|work /fʊtwɜrk/ ■ N-UNCOUNT [usu supp N] **Footwork** is the way in which you move your feet, especially in sports such as boxing, soccer, or tennis, or in dancing. ❑ This exercise improves your coordination, balance, timing and footwork. ■ N-UNCOUNT [supp N] If you refer to someone's **footwork** in a difficult situation, you mean the clever way they deal with it. ❑ In the end, his brilliant legal footwork paid off. ❑ It'll take some very fancy footwork by government officials to defuse the situation.

fop|pish /fɒpɪʃ/ ADJ If you describe someone as **foppish**, you disapprove of the fact that they dress in beautiful, expensive clothes and are very proud of their appearance. [mainly BRIT, OLD-FASHIONED, DISAPPROVAL]

for

FOR
① SAYING WHO OR WHAT SOMETHING RELATES TO, OR WHO BENEFITS
② MENTIONING A PURPOSE, REASON, OR DESTINATION
③ BEFORE NUMBERS, AMOUNTS, AND TIMES
④ WANTING OR SUPPORTING

① **for** ♦♦♦ /fər, STRONG fɔːr/
→ Please look at meanings **17** – **19** to see if the expression you are looking for is shown under another headword.

1 PREP If something is **for** someone, they are intended to have it or benefit from it. ❑ *Isn't that enough for you?* ❑ *...a table for two.* ❑ *He wanted all the running of the business for himself.* **2** PREP If you work or do a job **for** someone, you are employed by them. ❑ *I knew he worked for a security firm.* ❑ *Have you had any experience writing for radio?* **3** PREP If you speak or act **for** a particular group or organization, you represent them. ❑ *She appears nightly on the television news, speaking for the State Department.* **4** PREP If someone does something **for** you, they do it so that you do not have to do it. ❑ *If your pharmacy doesn't stock the product you want, have them order it for you.* ❑ *I hold a door open for an old person.* **5** PREP [adj/n PREP] If you feel a particular emotion **for** someone, you feel it on their behalf. ❑ *This is the best thing you've ever done – I am so happy for you!* **6** PREP [adj/n PREP] If you feel a particular emotion **for** someone or something, they are the object of that emotion, and you feel it when you think about them. ❑ *John, I'm sorry for Steve, but I think you've made the right decisions.* **7** PREP You use **for** after words such as 'time,' 'space,' 'money,' or 'energy' when you say how much there is or whether there is enough of it in order to be able to do or use a particular thing. ❑ *Many new trains have space for wheelchair users.* ❑ *...a huge room with plenty of room for books.* **8** PREP You use **for** when you make a statement about something in order to say how it affects or relates to someone, or what their attitude is to it. ❑ *What matters for most scientists is money and facilities.* ❑ *For her, books were as necessary to life as bread.* **9** PREP [PREP n to-inf] After some adjective, noun, and verb phrases, you use **for** to introduce the subject of the action indicated by the following infinitive verb. ❑ *It might be possible for a single woman to be accepted as a foster parent.* ❑ *I had made arrangements for my affairs to be dealt with by one of my children.* **10** PREP [with neg] If you say that something is not **for** you, you mean that you do not enjoy it or that it is not suitable for you. [INFORMAL] ❑ *Wendy decided the sport was not for her.* **11** PREP [PREP n to-inf] If it is **for** you to do something, it is your responsibility or right to do it. ❑ *I wish you would come back to Washington with us, but that's for you to decide.* **12** PREP **For** is the preposition that is used after some nouns, adjectives, or verbs in order to introduce more information or to indicate what a quality, thing, or action relates to. ❑ *Reduced-calorie cheese is a great substitute for cream cheese.* ❑ *Parking lot owners should be legally responsible for protecting vehicles.* **13** PREP If a word or expression has the same meaning as another word or expression, you can say that the first one is another word or expression **for** the second one. ❑ *The technical term for sunburn is erythema.* **14** PREP To be named **for** someone means to be given the same name as them. [AM] ❑ *The Brady Bill is named for former White House Press Secretary James Brady.* **15** PREP You use **for** in a piece of writing when you mention information which will be found somewhere else. ❑ *For further information on the life of William James Sidis, see Amy Wallace, "The Prodigy."* **16** PREP **For** is used in conditional sentences, in expressions such as **'if not for'** and **'were it not for,'** to introduce the only thing which prevents the main part of the sentence from being true. ❑ *If not for John, Brian wouldn't have learned the truth.* ❑ *The earth would be a frozen ball if it were not for the radiant heat of the sun.* **17** **as for** → see as ②
18 **but for** → see but **19** **for all** → see all ③

USAGE

for
Don't use 'for' with an -ing form when saying why someone does something. Don't say, for example, 'He went to the city for finding work.' You say 'He went to the city **to find** work' or 'He went to the city **in order to find** work.' *People would stroll down the path to admire the garden.*

② **for** ♦♦♦ /fər, STRONG fɔːr/ **1** PREP [PREP n/-ing] You use **for** when you state or explain the purpose of an object, action, or activity. ❑ *...drug users who use unsterile equipment for injections of drugs.* ❑ *The knife for cutting sausage was sitting in the sink.* **2** PREP [n PREP n/-ing] You use **for** after nouns expressing reason or cause. ❑ *He's soon to make a speech explaining his reasons for going.* ❑ *The county hospital could find no physical cause for Sumner's problems.* **3** PREP If something is **for** sale, hire, or use, it is available to be sold, hired, or used. ❑ *Freshwater fish for sale.* ❑ *...a room for rent.* **4** PREP If you do something **for** a particular occasion, you do it on that occasion or to celebrate that occasion. ❑ *He asked his daughter what she would like for her birthday.* **5** PREP If you leave **for** a particular place or if you take a bus, train, plane, or boat **for** a place, you are going there. ❑ *They would be leaving for Rio early the next morning.*

③ **for** ♦♦♦ /fər, STRONG fɔːr/ **1** PREP [PREP amount] You use **for** to say how long something lasts or continues. ❑ *The toaster was on for more than an hour.* ❑ *They talked for a bit.* **2** PREP [PREP amount] You use **for** to say how far something extends. ❑ *We drove on for a few miles.* **3** PREP [PREP amount] If something is bought, sold, or done **for** a particular amount of money, that amount of money is its price. ❑ *We got the bus back to Tange for 30 cents.* ❑ *The Martins sold their house for about 1.4 million dollars.* **4** PREP If something is planned **for** a particular time, it is planned to happen then. ❑ *...the Baltimore Boat Show, planned for January 21 – 29.* ❑ *The designer will be unveiling her latest fashions for fall and winter.* **5** PHRASE You use expressions such as **for the first time** and **for the last time** when you are talking about how often something has happened before. ❑ *He was married for the second time.* **6** PREP You use **for** when you say that an aspect of something or someone is surprising in relation to other aspects of them. ❑ *He was tall for an eight-year-old.* **7** PREP You use **for** with 'every' when you are stating a ratio, to introduce one of the things in the ratio. ❑ *For every farm job that is lost, two or three other jobs in the area are put at risk.* **8** PREP [n PREP n] You can use **for** in expressions such as **dollar for dollar** or **mile for mile** when you are making comparisons between the values or qualities of different things. ❑ *...the Antarctic, mile for mile one of the planet's most lifeless areas.*

④ **for** ♦♦♦ /fər, STRONG fɔːr/ **1** PREP If you say that you are **for** a particular activity, you mean that this is what you want or intend to do. ❑ *Right, who's for a toasted sandwich then?* **2** PREP If you are **for** something, you agree with it or support it. ❑ *Are you for or against public transportation?* **3** PREP [n/v PREP n] You use **for** after words such as 'argue,' 'case,' 'evidence,' or 'vote' in order to introduce the thing that is being supported or proved. ❑ *Another union has voted for industrial action in support of a pay claim.* ❑ *The case for nuclear power is impressive.* • ADV [ADV after v] **For** is also an adverb. ❑ *833 delegates voted for, and only 432 against.* **4** PHRASE If you say that you are **all for** doing something, you agree or strongly believe that it should be done, but you are also often suggesting that other people disagree with you or that there are practical difficulties. ❑ *He is all for players earning what they can while they are in the game.*

In addition to the uses shown below, **for** is used after some verbs, nouns, and adjectives in order to introduce extra information, and in phrasal verbs such as 'account for' and 'make up for.' It is also used with some verbs that have two objects in order to introduce the second object.

for|age /fɒrɪdʒ/ (**forages**, **foraging**, **foraged**) **1** V-I If someone **forages for** something, they search for it in a busy way. ❑ *They were forced to forage for clothing and fuel.* **2** V-I When animals **forage**, they search for food. ❑ *We disturbed a wild boar that had been foraging by the roadside.*

for|ay /fɒreɪ/ (**forays**) **1** N-COUNT If you make a **foray** into a new or unfamiliar type of activity, you start to become involved in it. ❑ *Emporio Armani, the Italian fashion house, has made a discreet foray into furnishings.* **2** N-COUNT You can refer to a short trip that you make as a **foray** if it seems to involve excitement or risk, for example, because it is to an unfamiliar place or because you are looking for a particular thing. ❑ *Most guests make at least one foray into the town.* **3** N-COUNT If a group of soldiers make a **foray** into enemy territory, they make a quick attack there, and then return to their own territory. ❑ *These base camps were used by the PKK guerrillas to make forays into Turkey.*

for|bade /fərbæd, -beɪd/ Forbade is the past tense of **forbid**.

for|bear /fɔrbɛər/ (forbears, forbearing, forbore, forborne) V-T/V-I If you **forbear** to do something, you do not do it although you have the opportunity or the right to do it. [FORMAL] ❏ *I forbore to comment on this.* ❏ *Protesters largely forbore from stone-throwing and vandalism.*

for|bear|ance /fɔrbɛərəns/ N-UNCOUNT If you say that someone has shown **forbearance**, you admire them for behaving in a calm and sensible way about something that they have a right to be very upset or angry about. [FORMAL, APPROVAL] ❏ *All the Greenpeace people behaved with impressive forbearance and dignity.*

for|bear|ing /fɔrbɛərɪŋ/ ADJ Someone who is **forbearing** behaves in a calm and sensible way at a time when they would have a right to be very upset or angry. [FORMAL, APPROVAL]

for|bid /fərbɪd, fɔr-/ (forbids, forbidding, forbade, forbidden) **1** V-T If you **forbid** someone to do something, or if you **forbid** an activity, you order that it must not be done. ❏ *They'll forbid you to marry.* ❏ *She was shut away and forbidden to read.* **2** V-T If something **forbids** a particular course of action or state of affairs, it makes it impossible for the course of action or state of affairs to happen. ❏ *His own pride forbids him to ask Arthur's help.*

for|bid|den /fərbɪdᵊn, fɔr-/ **1** ADJ If something is **forbidden**, you are not allowed to do it or have it. ❏ *Smoking was forbidden everywhere.* **2** ADJ A **forbidden** place is one that you are not allowed to visit or enter. ❏ *This was a forbidden area for foreigners.* **3** ADJ **Forbidden** is used to describe things that people strongly disapprove of or feel guilty about, and that are not often mentioned or talked about. ❏ *The war was a forbidden subject.* ❏ *People sometimes fantasize as a substitute for acting out forbidden desires.*

for|bid|den fruit (forbidden fruits) N-VAR **Forbidden fruit** is a source of pleasure that involves breaking a rule or doing something that you are not supposed to do. ❏ *...the forbidden fruit of an illicit romance.*

for|bid|ding /fərbɪdɪŋ, fɔr-/ ADJ If you describe a person, place, or thing as **forbidding**, you mean they have a severe, unfriendly, or threatening appearance. ❏ *There was something a little severe and forbidding about her face.* ❏ *...a huge, forbidding building.*

FORCE
① VERB USES
② NOUN USES: POWER OR STRENGTH
③ THE ARMY, POLICE, ETC.
---

① **force** ✦✦✦ /fɔrs/ (forces, forcing, forced) **1** V-T If someone **forces** you to do something, they make you do it even though you do not want to, for example, by threatening you. ❏ *He took two women hostage and forced them to drive away from the area.* ❏ *They were grabbed by three men who appeared to force them into a car.* **2** V-T If a situation or event **forces** you to do something, it makes it necessary for you to do something that you would not otherwise have done. ❏ *A back injury forced her to withdraw from Wimbledon.* ❏ *He turned right, down a dirt road that forced him into four-wheel drive.* **3** V-T If someone **forces** something **on** or **upon** you, they make you accept or use it when you would prefer not to. ❏ *To force this agreement on the nation is wrong.* **4** V-T If you **force** something into a particular position, you use a lot of strength to make it move there. ❏ *They were forcing her head under the icy waters, drowning her.* **5** V-T If someone **forces** a lock, a door, or a window, they break the lock or fastening in order to get into a building without using a key. ❏ *That evening police forced the door of the apartment and arrested Mr. Roberts.* **6** PHRASE If you **force** your **way** through or into somewhere, you have to push or break things that are in your way in order to get there. ❏ *The miners forced their way through a police cordon.*

② **force** ✦✦✦ /fɔrs/ (forces) **1** N-UNCOUNT If someone uses **force** to do something, or if it is done by **force**, strong and violent physical action is taken in order to achieve it. ❏ *The government decided against using force to break up the demonstrations.* **2** N-UNCOUNT **Force** is the power or strength which something has. ❏ *The force of the explosion shattered the windows of several buildings.* **3** N-UNCOUNT The **force** of something is the powerful effect or quality that it has. ❏ *He changed our world through the force of his ideas.* **4** N-UNCOUNT **Force** is used before a number to indicate a wind of a particular speed or strength, especially a very strong wind. ❏ *The airlift was conducted in force ten winds.* **5** N-COUNT If you refer to someone or something as a **force** in a particular type of activity, you mean that they have a strong influence on it. ❏ *For years the army was the most powerful political force in the country.* ❏ *The band is still an innovative force in music.* **6** N-COUNT You can use **forces** to refer to processes and events that do not appear to be caused by human beings, and are therefore difficult to understand or control. ❏ *...the protection of mankind against the forces of nature: epidemics, predators, floods, hurricanes.* ❏ *The principle of market forces was applied to some of the country's most revered institutions.* **7** N-VAR In physics, a **force** is the pulling or pushing effect that something has on something else. ❏ *...the Earth's gravitational force.* **8** PHRASE If you do something from **force of habit**, you do it because you have always done it in the past, rather than because you have thought carefully about it. ❏ *He looked around from force of habit, but nobody paid any attention to him.* **9** PHRASE A law, rule, or system that is **in force** exists or is being used. ❏ *Although the new tax is already in force, you have until November to lodge an appeal.* **10** PHRASE When people do something **in force**, they do it in large numbers. ❏ *Voters turned out in force for their first taste of multiparty elections.* **11** PHRASE If you **join forces** with someone, you work together in order to achieve a common aim or purpose. ❏ *Both groups joined forces to persuade voters to approve a tax break for the industry.*

③ **force** ✦✦✦ /fɔrs/ (forces) **1** N-COUNT **Forces** are groups of soldiers or military vehicles that are organized for a particular purpose. ❏ *...the deployment of American forces in the region.* **2** N-PLURAL The **forces** means the army, the navy, or the air force, or all three. ❏ *The more senior you become in the forces, the more likely you are to end up in a desk job.* **3** N-SING The **force** is sometimes used to mean the police force. ❏ *It was hard for a police officer to make friends outside the force.* **4** → see also **air force, armed forces, labor force, workforce**

forced /fɔrst/ **1** ADJ [ADJ n] A **forced** action is something that you do because someone else makes you do it. ❏ *A system of forced labor was used on the cocoa plantations.* **2** ADJ [ADJ n] A **forced** action is something that you do because circumstances make it necessary. ❏ *He made a forced landing on a highway.* **3** ADJ If you describe something as **forced**, you mean it does not happen naturally and easily. ❏ *...a forced smile.*

force-feed (force-feeds, force-feeding, force-fed) V-T If you **force-feed** a person or animal, you make them eat or drink by pushing food or drink down their throat. ❏ *Production of the foie gras pt involves force-feeding geese and ducks so that their livers swell.*

force field (force fields) N-COUNT A **force field** is an area of energy, such as magnetic energy, that surrounds an object or place. ❏ *...a giant force field that protects the planet from solar winds.*

force|ful /fɔrsfəl/ **1** ADJ If you describe someone as **forceful**, you approve of them because they express their opinions and wishes in a strong, emphatic, and confident way. [APPROVAL] ❏ *He was a man of forceful character, with considerable insight and diplomatic skills.* • **force|ful|ly** ADV [ADV with v] ❏ *Mrs. Dambar was talking very rapidly and somewhat forcefully.* **2** ADJ Something that is **forceful** has a very powerful effect and causes you to think or feel something very strongly. ❏ *It made a very forceful impression on me.* • **force|ful|ly** ADV [ADV with v] ❏ *Daytime television tended to remind her too forcefully of her own situation.* **3** ADJ A **forceful** point or argument in a discussion is one that is good, valid, and convincing. ❏ *You may need to be armed with some forceful arguments to persuade a partner into seeing things your way.*

for|ceps /fɔrsɛps/ N-PLURAL [also *a pair of* N] **Forceps** are an instrument consisting of two long narrow arms. Forceps are used by a doctor to hold things.

for|cible /fɔrsɪbᵊl/ ADJ **Forcible** action involves physical force or violence. ❏ *Reports are coming in of the forcible resettlement of villagers from the countryside into towns.*

ford /fɔrd/ (fords, fording, forded) **1** N-COUNT A **ford** is a shallow place in a river or stream where it is possible to cross safely without using a boat. **2** V-T If you **ford** a river or stream, you cross it without using a boat, usually at a shallow point. ❑ *They were guarding the bridge, so we forded the river.*

fore /fɔr/ **1** PHRASE If someone or something comes **to the fore** in a particular situation or group, they become important or popular. ❑ *A number of low-budget independent films brought new directors and actors to the fore.* **2** ADJ [ADJ n] **Fore** is used to refer to parts at the front of an animal, ship, or aircraft. ❑ *There had been no direct damage in the fore part of the ship.*

fore|arm /fɔrɑrm/ (**forearms**) N-COUNT Your **forearm** is the part of your arm between your elbow and your wrist. ❑ *...the tattoo on his forearm.*

fore|armed /fɔrɑrmd/ PHRASE If you say '**Forewarned is forearmed**,' you are saying that if you know about a problem or situation in advance, you will be able to deal with it when you need to.

fore|bear /fɔrbɛər/ (**forebears**) N-COUNT [usu with poss] Your **forebears** are your ancestors. [LITERARY] ❑ *I'll come back to the land of my forebears.*

fore|bod|ing /fɔrboʊdɪŋ/ (**forebodings**) N-VAR **Foreboding** is a strong feeling that something terrible is going to happen. ❑ *His triumph was overshadowed by an uneasy sense of foreboding.*

fore|cast ♦◇◇ /fɔrkæst/ (**forecasts, forecasting, forecasted**)

The forms **forecast** and **forecasted** can both be used for the past tense and past participle.

1 N-COUNT A **forecast** is a statement of what is expected to happen in the future, especially in relation to a particular event or situation. ❑ *...a forecast of a 2.25 percent growth in the economy.* ❑ *He delivered his election forecast.* **2** V-T If you **forecast** future events, you say what you think is going to happen in the future. ❑ *They forecast a humiliating defeat for the president.* **3** → see also **weather forecast**

---SYNONYMS---

forecast
NOUN **1**
prediction: *Weather prediction has never been a perfect science.*
projection: *...the company's projection of 11 million visitors for the first year.*
prognosis: *...a gloomy prognosis for the team's championship prospects.*
prophecy: *The youth, too, fulfilled the prophecy.*

---

fore|cast|er /fɔrkæstər/ (**forecasters**) N-COUNT A **forecaster** is someone who uses detailed knowledge about a particular activity in order to work out what they think will happen in that activity in the future. ❑ *Some of the nation's top economic forecasters say the economic recovery is picking up speed.*

fore|cas|tle /foʊksəl/ (**forecastles**) also **fo'c'sle** N-COUNT [usu the N in sing] The **forecastle** is the part at the front of a ship where the sailors live.

fore|close /fɔrkloʊz/ (**forecloses, foreclosing, foreclosed**) V-I If the person or organization that lent someone money **forecloses**, they take possession of a property that was bought with the borrowed money, for example, because regular repayments have not been made. [BUSINESS] ❑ *The bank foreclosed on the mortgage for his previous home.*

fore|clo|sure /fɔrkloʊʒər/ (**foreclosures**) N-VAR **Foreclosure** is when someone who has lent money to a person or organization does something so that they can buy property takes possession of the property because the money has not been repaid. [BUSINESS] ❑ *If homeowners can't keep up the payments, they face foreclosure.*

fore|court /fɔrkɔrt/ (**forecourts**) **1** N-COUNT [usu the] In sports such as tennis and badminton, the **forecourt** is the section of each side of the court that is nearest to the net. **2** N-COUNT The **forecourt** of a large building or gas station is the open area at the front of it.

fore|deck /fɔrdɛk/ (**foredecks**) N-COUNT [usu N SING, the N] The **foredeck** is the part of the deck at the front of a ship.

fore|father /fɔrfɑðər/ (**forefathers**) N-COUNT [usu pl, usu poss N] Your **forefathers** are your ancestors, especially your male ancestors. [LITERARY] ❑ *They were determined to go back to the land of their forefathers.*

fore|finger /fɔrfɪŋɡər/ (**forefingers**) N-COUNT Your **forefinger** is the finger that is next to your thumb. ❑ *He took the pen between his thumb and forefinger.*

fore|foot /fɔrfʊt/ (**forefeet**) N-COUNT [usu pl] A four-legged animal's **forefeet** are its two front feet.

fore|front /fɔrfrʌnt/ **1** N-SING If you are at **the forefront** of a campaign or other activity, you have a leading and influential position in it. ❑ *They have been at the forefront of the campaign for political change.* **2** N-SING If something is at **the forefront** of people's minds or attention, they think about it a lot because it is particularly important to them. ❑ *Senior citizen issues were always at the forefront of his mind.*

fore|go /fɔrɡoʊ/ (**foregoes, foregoing, forewent, foregone**) also **forgo** V-T If you **forgo** something, you decide to do without it, although you would like it. [FORMAL] ❑ *Many skiers are happy to forego a summer vacation to go skiing.*

fore|going /fɔrɡoʊɪŋ, fɔrɡoʊ-/ PRON [the PRON] You can refer to what has just been stated or mentioned as **the foregoing**. [FORMAL] ❑ *You might think from the foregoing that the French want to phase accents out. Not at all.* • ADJ [ADJ n] **Foregoing** is also an adjective. ❑ *The foregoing paragraphs were written in 1985.*

fore|gone /fɔrɡɒn/ **1 Foregone** is the past participle of **forego**. **2** PHRASE If you say that a particular result is **a foregone conclusion**, you mean you are certain that it will happen. ❑ *Most voters believe the result is a foregone conclusion.*

fore|ground /fɔrɡraʊnd/ (**foregrounds**) **1** N-VAR The **foreground** of a picture or scene you are looking at is the part or area of it that appears nearest to you. ❑ *He is the bowler-hatted figure in the foreground of Orpen's famous painting.* **2** N-SING If something or someone is in the **foreground**, or comes to the **foreground**, they receive a lot of attention. ❑ *This is another worry that has come to the foreground in recent years.*

fore|hand /fɔrhænd/ (**forehands**) N-COUNT A **forehand** is a shot in tennis or squash in which the palm of your hand faces the direction in which you are hitting the ball. ❑ *Agassi saw his chance and, with another lightning forehand, reached match point.*

fore|head /fɔrhɛd, fɒrɪd/ (**foreheads**) N-COUNT Your **forehead** is the area at the front of your head between your eyebrows and your hair. ❑ *...the lines on her forehead.*

for|eign ♦♦♦ /fɔrɪn/ **1** ADJ Something or someone that is **foreign** comes from or relates to a country that is not your own. ❑ *She was on her first foreign vacation without her parents.* ❑ *...a foreign language.* **2** ADJ [ADJ n] In politics and journalism, **foreign** is used to describe people, jobs, and activities relating to countries that are not the country of the person or government concerned. ❑ *...the German foreign minister.* ❑ *I am the foreign correspondent in Washington of La Tribuna newspaper of Honduras.* **3** ADJ A **foreign** object is something that has got into something else, usually by accident, and should not be there. [FORMAL] ❑ *The patient's immune system would reject the transplanted organ as a foreign object.*

for|eign body (**foreign bodies**) N-COUNT A **foreign body** is an object that has come into something else, usually by accident, and should not be in it. [FORMAL] ❑ *...a foreign body in the eye.*

for|eign|er ♦◇◇ /fɔrɪnər/ (**foreigners**) N-COUNT A **foreigner** is someone who belongs to a country that is not your own. ❑ *They are discouraged from becoming close friends with foreigners.*

for|eign ex|change (**foreign exchanges**) **1** N-PLURAL **Foreign exchanges** are the institutions or systems involved with changing one currency into another. ❑ *On the foreign exchanges, the U.S. dollar is up point forty-five.* **2** N-UNCOUNT **Foreign exchange** is used to refer to foreign currency that is obtained through the foreign exchange system. ❑ *...an important source of foreign exchange.* **3** N-COUNT [oft N n] A **foreign exchange** is an arrangement in which people from two different countries visit each other's country, to strengthen links between them. ❑ *He recently hosted a foreign exchange student from Argentina.*

for|eign ser|vice N-SING [the N] The **foreign service** is the government department that employs diplomats to work in foreign countries. [AM]

fore|knowl|edge /fɔrnɒlɪdʒ/ N-UNCOUNT [oft N of n] If you have **foreknowledge** of an event or situation, you have some knowledge of it before it actually happens. ❑ *She has maintained that the General had foreknowledge of the plot.*

fore|leg /fɔ:rlɛg/ (forelegs) N-COUNT [usu pl] A four-legged animal's **forelegs** are its two front legs.

fore|lock /fɔ:rlɒk/ (forelocks) N-COUNT A **forelock** is a piece of hair that falls over your forehead. [OLD-FASHIONED]

fore|man /fɔ:rmən/ (foremen) **1** N-COUNT A **foreman** is a man in charge of a group of workers. ◻ *He still visited the dairy daily, but left most of the business details to his manager and foreman.* **2** N-COUNT The **foreman** of a jury is the man who is chosen as their leader. ◻ *There was applause as the foreman of the jury announced the verdict.*

fore|most /fɔ:rmoʊst/ **1** ADJ The **foremost** thing or person in a group is the most important or best. ◻ *He was one of the world's foremost scholars of ancient Indian culture.* **2** PHRASE You use **first and foremost** to emphasize the most important quality of something or someone. [EMPHASIS] ◻ *It is first and foremost a trade agreement.*

fore|name /fɔ:rneɪm/ (forenames) N-COUNT Your **forename** is your first name. Your **forenames** are your names other than your surname. [FORMAL] ◻ *...the unusual spelling of his forename.*

fore|noon /fɔ:rnu:n/ N-SING The **forenoon** is the morning. [OLD-FASHIONED]

fo|ren|sic /fərɛnsɪk/ (forensics) **1** ADJ [ADJ n] **Forensic** is used to describe the work of scientists who examine evidence in order to help the police solve crimes. ◻ *They were convicted on forensic evidence alone.* ◻ *Forensic experts searched the area for clues.* **2** N-UNCOUNT **Forensics** is the use of scientific techniques to solve crimes. ◻ *...the newest advances in forensics.*

fore|play /fɔ:rpleɪ/ N-UNCOUNT **Foreplay** is activity such as kissing and stroking when it takes place before sexual intercourse.

fore|run|ner /fɔ:rrʌnər/ (forerunners) N-COUNT If you describe a person or thing as the **forerunner** of someone or something similar, you mean they existed before them and either influenced their development or were a sign of what was going to happen. ◻ *...a machine which, in some respects, was the forerunner of the modern helicopter.*

fore|see /fɔ:rsi:/ (foresees, foreseeing, foresaw, foreseen) V-T If you **foresee** something, you expect and believe that it will happen. ◻ *He did not foresee any problems.*

fore|see|able /fɔ:rsi:əbəl/ **1** ADJ If a future event is **foreseeable**, you know that it will happen or that it can happen, because it is a natural or obvious consequence of something else that you know. ◻ *It seems to me that this crime was foreseeable and this death preventable.* **2** PHRASE If you say that something will happen **for the foreseeable future**, you think that it will continue to happen for a long time. ◻ *Profit and dividend growth looks above average for the foreseeable future.*

fore|shad|ow /fɔ:rʃædoʊ/ (foreshadows, foreshadowing, foreshadowed) V-T If something **foreshadows** an event or situation, it suggests that it will happen. ◻ *What are the signs that foreshadow a suicide?*

fore|shore /fɔ:rʃɔ:r/ (foreshores) N-COUNT [usu sing] Beside the sea, a lake, or a wide river, the **foreshore** is the part of the shore which is between the highest and lowest points reached by the water.

fore|short|en /fɔ:rʃɔ:rtən/ (foreshortens, foreshortening, foreshortened) V-T To **foreshorten** someone or something means to draw them, photograph them, or see them from an unusual angle so that the parts of them that are furthest away seem smaller than they really are. ◻ *She could see herself in the reflecting lenses, which had grotesquely foreshortened her.*

fore|sight /fɔ:rsaɪt/ N-UNCOUNT Someone's **foresight** is their ability to see what is likely to happen in the future and to take appropriate action. [APPROVAL] ◻ *They had the foresight to invest in new technology.*

fore|skin /fɔ:rskɪn/ (foreskins) N-VAR A man's **foreskin** is the skin that covers the end of his penis.

for|est ✦◇◇ /fɔ:rɪst/ (forests) **1** N-VAR A **forest** is a large area where trees grow close together. ◻ *Parts of the forest are still dense and inaccessible.* **2** → See feature box at **ecosystem**

fore|stall /fɔ:rstɔ:l/ (forestalls, forestalling, forestalled) V-T If you **forestall** someone, you realize what they are likely to do and prevent them from doing it. ◻ *Large numbers of police were in the square to forestall any demonstrations.*

for|est|ed /fɔ:rɪstɪd/ ADJ A **forested** area is an area covered in trees growing closely together. ◻ *...a thickly forested valley.* ◻ *Only 8 percent of the area is forested.*

for|est|er /fɔ:rɪstər/ (foresters) N-COUNT A **forester** is a person whose job is to look after the trees in a forest and to plant new ones.

for|est land (forest lands) also **forestland** N-VAR **Forest land** is land that is mainly covered by forest. [AM] ◻ *More than 24,000 acres of forest land have burned in California.*

for|est|ry /fɔ:rɪstri/ N-UNCOUNT **Forestry** is the science or skill of growing and taking care of trees in forests, especially in order to obtain wood. ◻ *...his great interest in forestry.*

fore|taste /fɔ:rteɪst/ (foretastes) N-COUNT [usu a N of n] If you describe an event as a **foretaste** of a future situation, you mean that it suggests to you what that future situation will be like. ◻ *It was a foretaste of things to come.*

fore|tell /fɔ:rtɛl/ (foretells, foretelling, foretold) V-T If you **foretell** a future event, you predict that it will happen. [LITERARY] ◻ *...prophets who have foretold the end of the world.*

fore|thought /fɔ:rθɔ:t/ N-UNCOUNT If you act with **forethought**, you think carefully before you act about what will be needed, or about what the consequences will be. ◻ *With a little forethought many accidents could be avoided.*

fore|told /fɔ:rtoʊld/ **Foretold** is the past tense and past participle of **foretell**.

for|ever /fərɛvər, fɔ:r-/ **1** ADV [ADV with v] If you say that something will happen or continue **forever**, you mean that it will always happen or continue. ◻ *I think that we will live together forever.* **2** ADV [ADV after v] If something has gone or changed **forever**, it has gone or changed completely and permanently. ◻ *The old social order was gone forever.* **3** ADV [ADV after v] If you say that something **takes forever** or **lasts forever**, you are emphasizing that it takes or lasts a very long time, or that it seems to. [INFORMAL, EMPHASIS] ◻ *The drive seemed to take forever.*

fore|warn /fɔ:rwɔ:rn/ (forewarns, forewarning, forewarned) **1** V-T If you **forewarn** someone about something, you warn them in advance that it is going to happen. ◻ *The travel guide had forewarned me of what to expect.* **2 forewarned is forearmed** → see **forearmed**

fore|went /fɔ:rwɛnt/ **Forewent** is the past tense of **forego**.

fore|woman /fɔ:rwʊmən/ (forewomen) **1** N-COUNT A **forewoman** is a woman in charge of a group of workers. ◻ *By 17, she was a forewoman at a city stationer.* **2** N-COUNT The **forewoman** of a jury is the woman who is chosen as their leader. ◻ *He did not react as the jury forewoman announced the verdict.*

fore|word /fɔ:rwɜ:rd/ (forewords) N-COUNT The **foreword** to a book is an introduction by the author or by someone else. ◻ *She has written the foreword to a book of recipes.*

forex /fɔ:rɛks/ N-UNCOUNT **Forex** is an abbreviation for **foreign exchange**. ◻ *...the forex market.*

for|feit /fɔ:rfɪt/ (forfeits, forfeiting, forfeited) **1** V-T If you **forfeit** something, you lose it or are forced to give it up because you have broken a rule or done something wrong. ◻ *He was ordered to forfeit more than $1.5m.* **2** V-T If you **forfeit** something, you give it up willingly, especially so that you can achieve something else. ◻ *Do you think that they would forfeit profit in the name of safety?* **3** N-COUNT A **forfeit** is something that you have to give up because you have done something wrong. ◻ *That is the forfeit he must pay.*

for|fei|ture /fɔ:rfɪtʃər/ (forfeitures) N-VAR [oft N of n] **Forfeiture** is the action of forfeiting something. [LEGAL] ◻ *...the forfeiture of illegally obtained profits.* ◻ *Both face maximum forfeitures of about $1.2 million.*

for|gave /fərgeɪv/ **Forgave** is the past tense of **forgive**.

forge /fɔ:rdʒ/ (forges, forging, forged) **1** V-RECIP If one person or institution **forges** an agreement or relationship with another, they create it with a lot of hard work, hoping that it will be strong or lasting. ◻ *The prime minister is determined to forge a good relationship with the country's new leader.* ◻ *They agreed to forge closer economic ties.* **2** V-T If someone **forges** something such as paper money, a document, or a painting, they copy it or make it so that it looks genuine, in order to deceive people.

❑ He admitted seven charges including forging passports. ❑ They used forged documents to leave the country. • **forg|er** (forgers) N-COUNT ❑ ...the most prolific art forger in the country.

▶ **forge ahead** PHRASAL VERB If you **forge ahead** with something, you continue with it and make a lot of progress with it. ❑ He again pledged to forge ahead with his plans for reform.

for|gery /fɔrdʒəri/ (forgeries) **1** N-UNCOUNT **Forgery** is the crime of forging money, documents, or paintings. ❑ He was found guilty of forgery. **2** N-COUNT You can refer to a forged document, bill, or painting as a **forgery**. ❑ The letter was a forgery.

for|get ♦♦◊ /fərgɛt/ (forgets, forgetting, forgot, forgotten) **1** V-T If you **forget** something or **forget** how to do something, you cannot think of it or think how to do it, although you knew it or knew how to do it in the past. ❑ She forgot where she left the car and it took us two days to find it. **2** V-T/V-I If you **forget** something or **forget** to do it, you fail to think about it or fail to remember to do it, for example, because you are thinking about other things. ❑ She never forgets her daddy's birthday. ❑ She forgot to lock her door one day and two men got in. ❑ When I close my eyes, I forget about everything. **3** V-T If you **forget** something that you had intended to bring with you, you do not bring it because you did not think about it at the right time. ❑ Once when we were going to Paris, I forgot my passport. **4** V-T/V-I If you **forget** something or someone, you deliberately put them out of your mind and do not think about them any more. ❑ I hope you will forget the bad experience you had today. ❑ I found it very easy to forget about Sumner. **5** CONVENTION You say '**Forget it**' in reply to someone as a way of telling them not to worry or bother about something, or as an emphatic way of saying no to a suggestion. [SPOKEN, FORMULAE] ❑ "Sorry, Liz. I think I was a bit rude to you."—"Forget it, but don't do it again!" **6** PHRASE You say **not forgetting** a particular thing or person when you want to include them in something that you have already talked about. ❑ Leave a message, not forgetting your name and address.

for|get|ful /fərgɛtfəl/ ADJ Someone who is **forgetful** often forgets things. ❑ My mother has become very forgetful and confused.

forget-me-not (forget-me-nots) N-COUNT A **forget-me-not** is a small plant with tiny blue flowers.

for|get|table /fərgɛtəbəl/ ADJ If you describe something or someone as **forgettable**, you mean that they do not have any qualities that make them special, unusual, or interesting. ❑ He has acted in three forgettable action movies.

for|giv|able /fərgɪvəbəl/ ADJ If you say that something bad is **forgivable**, you mean that you can understand it and can forgive it in the circumstances. ❑ Is infidelity ever forgivable?

for|give /fərgɪv/ (forgives, forgiving, forgave, forgiven) **1** V-T If you **forgive** someone who has done something bad or wrong, you stop being angry with them and no longer want to punish them. ❑ Hopefully Jane will understand and forgive you, if she really loves you. ❑ Irene forgave Terry for stealing her money. ❑ He could forgive Petal anything if the children were safe. **2** V-T **Forgive** is used in polite expressions and apologies like '**forgive me**' and '**forgive my ignorance**' when you are saying or doing something that might seem rude, silly, or complicated. [POLITENESS] ❑ Forgive me, I don't mean to insult you. ❑ I do hope you'll forgive me but I've got to leave. **3** V-T PASSIVE If you say that someone could **be forgiven for** doing something, you mean that they were wrong or mistaken, but not seriously, because many people would have done the same thing in those circumstances. ❑ Looking at the figures, you could be forgiven for thinking the recession is already over.

for|give|ness /fərgɪvnɪs/ N-UNCOUNT If you ask for **forgiveness**, you ask to be forgiven for something wrong that you have done. ❑ ...a spirit of forgiveness and national reconciliation.

for|giv|ing /fərgɪvɪŋ/ ADJ Someone who is **forgiving** is willing to forgive. ❑ Voters can be remarkably forgiving of presidents who fail to keep their campaign promises.

for|go /fɔrgoʊ/ → see forego

for|got /fərgɒt/ **Forgot** is the past tense of **forget**.

for|got|ten /fərgɒtən/ **Forgotten** is the past participle of **forget**.

fork /fɔrk/ (forks, forking, forked) **1** N-COUNT A **fork** is a tool used for eating food which has a row of three or four long metal points at the end. ❑ ...knives and forks. **2** N-COUNT A **fork** in a road, path, or river is a point at which it divides into two parts and forms a 'Y' shape. ❑ We arrived at a fork in the road. ❑ The road divides; you should take the right fork. **3** V-T If you **fork** food **into** your mouth or **onto** a plate, you put it there using a fork. ❑ He forked an egg onto a piece of bread and folded it into a sandwich. **4** V-I [no cont] If a road, path, or river **forks**, it forms a fork. ❑ Beyond the village the road forked. **5** N-COUNT A garden **fork** is a tool used for breaking up soil which has a row of three or four long metal points at the end. [mainly BRIT]

in AM, usually use **pitchfork**

6 → See also color supplement

▶ **fork out** PHRASAL VERB If you **fork out** for something, you spend a lot of money on it. [INFORMAL] ❑ Visitors to the castle had to fork out for a guidebook.

▶ **fork over** PHRASAL VERB If you **fork** something **over** to someone, for example money, you give it to them. [INFORMAL] ❑ Nonresidents who work in Philadelphia fork over 3.88 percent of their pay to the city.

forked /fɔrkt/ ADJ [usu ADJ n] Something that divides into two parts and forms a 'Y' shape can be described as **forked**. ❑ Jaegers are swift black birds with long forked tails.

forked light|ning N-UNCOUNT **Forked lightning** is lightning that divides into two or more parts near the ground.

fork|ful /fɔrkfʊl/ (forkfuls) N-COUNT [usu N of n] You can refer to an amount of food on a fork as a **forkful** of food. ❑ I put a forkful of fillet steak in my mouth.

fork|lift truck /fɔrklɪft trʌk/ (forklift trucks) N-COUNT A **forklift truck** or a **forklift** is a small vehicle with two movable parts on the front that are used to lift heavy loads.

for|lorn /fɔrlɔrn/ **1** ADJ If someone is **forlorn**, they feel alone and unhappy. [LITERARY] ❑ One of the demonstrators, a young woman, sat forlorn on the sidewalk. **2** ADJ A **forlorn** hope or attempt is one that you think has no chance of success. ❑ Peasants have left the land in the forlorn hope of finding a better life in cities.

form ♦♦♦ /fɔrm/ (forms, forming, formed) **1** N-COUNT A **form** of something is a type or kind of it. ❑ He contracted a rare form of cancer. ❑ I am against hunting in any form. **2** N-COUNT When something can exist or happen in several possible ways, you can use **form** to refer to one particular way in which it exists or happens. ❑ They received a benefit in the form of a tax reduction. **3** N-COUNT The **form** of something is its shape. ❑ ...the form of the body. **4** N-COUNT You can refer to something that you can see as a **form** if you cannot see it clearly, or if its outline is the clearest or most striking aspect of it. ❑ His form lay still under the blankets. **5** N-COUNT A **form** is a paper with questions on it and spaces marked where you should write the answers. Forms usually ask you to give details about yourself, for example, when you are applying for a job or joining an organization. ❑ You will be asked to fill in a form with details of your birth and occupation. **6** V-T/V-I When a particular shape **forms** or **is formed**, people or things move or are arranged so that this shape is made. ❑ A line formed to use the bathroom. ❑ They formed a circle and sang "Auld Lang Syne." **7** V-T If something is arranged or changed so that it becomes similar to a thing with a particular structure or function, you can say that it **forms** that thing. ❑ These panels folded up to form a screen some five feet tall. **8** V-T If something consists of particular things, people, or features, you can say that they **form** that thing. ❑ ...the articles that formed the basis of Randolph's book. **9** V-T If you **form** an organization, group, or company, you start it. ❑ They tried to form a study group on human rights. **10** V-T/V-I When something natural **forms** or **is formed**, it begins to exist and develop. ❑ The stars must have formed 10 to 15 billion years ago. **11** V-T/V-I If you **form** a relationship, a habit, or an idea, or if it **forms**, it begins to exist and develop. ❑ You know what foods you should eat, but haven't formed the habit of eating them. ❑ An idea formed in his mind. **12** V-T If you say that something **forms** a person's character or personality, you mean that it has a strong influence on them and causes them to develop in a particular way. ❑ Anger at injustice formed his character. **13** N-UNCOUNT In sports, **form** refers to the ability or success of a person or animal over a period of time. ❑ His form this season has been brilliant.

SYNONYMS

form
NOUN [1]
type: ...several types of lettuce.
kind: The party needs a different kind of leadership.
sort: What sort of school did you go to?
variety: She has 12 varieties of old-fashioned roses.

for|mal ♦♦◊ /fɔ́rməl/ (formals) [1] ADJ **Formal** speech or behavior is very correct and serious rather than relaxed and friendly, and is used especially in official situations. ❏ *He wrote a very formal letter of apology to Douglas.* • **for|mal|ly** ADV [ADV with v] ❏ *He took her back to Vincent Square in a taxi, saying goodnight formally on the doorstep.* • **for|mal|ity** /fɔrmǽlɪti/ N-UNCOUNT ❏ *Lillith's formality and seriousness amused him.* [2] ADJ [ADJ n] A **formal** action, statement, or request is an official one. ❏ *UN officials said a formal request was passed to American authorities.* ❏ *No formal announcement had been made.* • **for|mal|ly** ADV [ADV with v] ❏ *Diplomats haven't formally agreed to Anderson's plan.* [3] ADJ **Formal** occasions are special occasions at which people wear elegant clothes and behave according to a set of accepted rules. ❏ *One evening the company arranged a formal dinner after the play.* • N-COUNT **Formal** is also a noun. ❏ *...a wide array of events, including school formals and speech nights, weddings, and balls.* [4] ADJ [ADJ n] **Formal** clothes are very elegant clothes that are suitable for formal occasions. ❏ *They wore ordinary ties instead of the more formal high collar and cravat.* • **for|mal|ly** ADV ❏ *It was really too warm for her to dress so formally.* [5] ADJ [ADJ n] **Formal** education or training is given officially, usually in a school, college, or university. ❏ *Wendy didn't have any formal dance training.* • **for|mal|ly** ADV [ADV -ed] ❏ *Usually only formally-trained artists from established schools are chosen.* [6] → see also **formality**

SYNONYMS

formal
ADJ [2]
official: *An official announcement is expected in the next few days.*
proper: *The Supreme Court will ensure that the proper procedures have been followed.*
correct: *We were surprised by their sporting and correct behavior.*

for|mal|de|hyde /fɔrmǽldɪhaɪd/ N-UNCOUNT **Formaldehyde** is a strong-smelling gas, used especially to preserve parts of animals or plants for biological study.

for|mal|ism /fɔ́rməlɪzəm/ N-UNCOUNT **Formalism** is a style, especially in art, in which great attention is paid to the outward form or appearance rather than to the inner reality or significance of things. • **for|mal|ist** ADJ [ADJ n] ❏ *...art based on formalist principles.*

for|mal|ity /fɔrmǽlɪti/ (formalities) [1] N-COUNT If you say that an action or procedure is just a **formality**, you mean that it is done only because it is normally done, and that it will not have any real effect on the situation. ❏ *Some contracts are a mere formality.* [2] N-COUNT **Formalities** are formal actions or procedures that are carried out as part of a particular activity or event. ❏ *They are whisked through the immigration and customs formalities in a matter of minutes.* [3] → see also **formal**

for|mal|ize /fɔ́rməlaɪz/ (formalizes, formalizing, formalized)

in BRIT, also use **formalise**

V-T If you **formalize** a plan, idea, arrangement, or system, you make it formal and official. ❏ *A recent treaty signed by Russia, Canada and Japan formalized an agreement to work together to stop the pirates.*

for|mat /fɔ́rmæt/ (formats, formatting, formatted) [1] N-COUNT The **format** of something is the way or order in which it is arranged and presented. ❏ *I had met with him to explain the format of the program and what we had in mind.* [2] N-COUNT The **format** of a piece of computer software, a movie or a musical recording is the type of equipment on which it is designed to be used or played. For example, possible formats for a movie are DVD and video cassette. ❏ *His latest album is available on all formats.* [3] V-T To **format** a computer disk means to run a program so that the disk can be written on. [COMPUTING] ❏ *...a menu that includes the choice to format a disk.* [4] V-T To **format** a piece of computer text or graphics means to arrange the way in which it appears when it is printed or is displayed on a screen. [COMPUTING] ❏ *When text is saved from a Web page, it is often very badly formatted with many short lines.*

for|ma|tion /fɔrmeɪʃən/ (formations) [1] N-UNCOUNT The **formation** of something is the starting or creation of it. ❏ *Time is running out for the formation of a new government.* [2] N-UNCOUNT The **formation** of an idea, habit, relationship, or character is the process of developing and establishing it. ❏ *My profession had an important influence in the formation of my character and temperament.* [3] N-COUNT If people or things are in **formation**, they are arranged in a particular pattern as they move. ❏ *He was flying in formation with seven other jets.* [4] N-COUNT A rock or cloud **formation** is rock or cloud of a particular shape or structure. ❏ *...a vast rock formation shaped like a pillar.*

for|ma|tive /fɔ́rmətɪv/ ADJ A **formative** period of time or experience is one that has an important and lasting influence on a person's character and attitudes. ❏ *She was born in Barbados but spent her formative years growing up in Miami.*

for|mer ♦♦◊ /fɔ́rmər/ [1] ADJ [ADJ n] **Former** is used to describe someone who used to have a particular job, position, or role, but no longer has it. ❏ *The unemployed executives include former sales managers, directors and accountants.* ❏ *...former president Richard Nixon.* [2] ADJ [ADJ n] **Former** is used to refer to countries which no longer exist or whose boundaries have changed. ❏ *...the former Soviet Union.* [3] ADJ [ADJ n] **Former** is used to describe something which used to belong to someone or which used to be a particular thing. ❏ *...the former home of Robert E. Lee.* [4] PRON [the PRON] When two people, things, or groups have just been mentioned, you can refer to the first of them as **the former**. ❏ *They grappled with the problem of connecting the electricity and water supplies. The former proved simple compared with the latter.*

COLLOCATIONS

former
ADJ [1]
former + noun: boss, captain, chairman, director, head; leader, manager, president

SYNONYMS

former
ADJ [1]
previous: *She has a teenage daughter from a previous marriage.*
one-time: *She's 87 years old and a one-time member of the Ziegfeld Follies.*
ex-: *...an ex-soldier.*
earlier: *Earlier reports of gunshots have not been substantiated.*
erstwhile: *Erstwhile workers may have become managers.*

for|mer|ly /fɔ́rmərli/ ADV If something happened or was true **formerly**, it happened or was true in the past. ❏ *He had formerly been in the navy.*

form-fitting ADJ [usu ADJ n] **Form-fitting** clothes fit very closely to the body of the person who is wearing them. **Form-fitting** is usually used to describe clothes worn by women. [AM] ❏ *...a black, form-fitting designer frock.*

For|mi|ca /fɔrmaɪkə/ N-UNCOUNT **Formica** is a hard plastic that is used for covering surfaces such as kitchen tables or counters. [TRADEMARK]

for|mi|dable /fɔ́rmɪdəbəl, fɔrmɪ́d-/ ADJ If you describe something or someone as **formidable**, you mean that you feel slightly frightened by them because they are very great or impressive. ❏ *We have a formidable task ahead of us.*

form|less /fɔ́rmlɪs/ ADJ Something that is **formless** does not have a clear or definite structure or shape. ❏ *A series of largely formless images rushed across the screen.*

form let|ter (form letters) N-COUNT A **form letter** is a single copy of a letter that has been reproduced in large numbers and sent to many people. [mainly AM] ❏ *Remember: personal letters carry much more weight than form letters.*

for|mu|la ♦◊◊ /fɔ́rmyələ/ (formulae /fɔ́rmyəli/ or formulas) [1] N-COUNT A **formula** is a plan that is invented in order to deal with a particular problem. ❏ *...a peace formula.* [2] N-COUNT A **formula** is a group of letters, numbers, or other symbols which represents a scientific or mathematical rule.

formulaic

☐ *He developed a mathematical formula describing the distances of the planets from the Sun.* **3** N-COUNT In science, the **formula** for a substance is a list of the amounts of various substances which make up that substance, or an indication of the atoms that it is composed of. ☐ *Glucose and fructose have the same chemical formula but have very different properties.* **4** N-SING A **formula for** a particular situation, usually a good one, is a course of action or a combination of actions that is certain or likely to result in that situation. ☐ *After he was officially pronounced the world's oldest man, he offered this simple formula for a long and happy life.*

for|mu|laic /fɔrmyəleɪɪk/ ADJ If you describe a way of saying or doing something as **formulaic**, you are criticizing it because it is not original and has been used many times before in similar situations. [DISAPPROVAL] ☐ *His paintings are contrived and formulaic.*

for|mu|late /fɔrmyəleɪt/ (formulates, formulating, formulated) **1** V-T If you **formulate** something such as a plan or proposal, you invent it, thinking about the details carefully. ☐ *Little by little, he formulated his plan for escape.* **2** V-T If you **formulate** a thought, opinion, or idea, you express it or describe it using particular words. ☐ *I was impressed by the way he could formulate his ideas.*

for|mu|la|tion /fɔrmyəleɪʃᵊn/ (formulations) **1** N-VAR A **formulation** is the way in which you express your thoughts and ideas. ☐ *This is a far weaker formulation than is in the draft resolution which is being proposed.* **2** N-UNCOUNT The **formulation** of something such as a policy or plan is the process of creating or inventing it. ☐ *...the process of policy formulation and implementation.* **3** N-VAR The **formulation** of something such as a medicine or a beauty product is the way in which different ingredients are combined to make it. You can also say that the finished product is a **formulation**. [mainly BRIT]

for|ni|cate /fɔrnɪkeɪt/ (fornicates, fornicating, fornicated) V-RECIP To **fornicate** means to have sex with someone you are not married to. [FORMAL, DISAPPROVAL] • **for|ni|ca|tion** /fɔrnɪkeɪʃᵊn/ N-UNCOUNT ☐ *Fornication is a crime in some countries.*

for-profit ADJ [ADJ n] A **for-profit** organization is one that is run with the aim of making a profit. [BUSINESS] ☐ *Gerber has been running her own for-profit school in southern Florida for 17 years.*

for|sake /fərseɪk/ (forsakes, forsaking, forsook /fərsʊk/, forsaken) **1** V-T If you **forsake** someone, you leave them when you should have stayed, or you stop helping them or looking after them. [LITERARY, DISAPPROVAL] ☐ *I still love him and I would never forsake him.* **2** V-T If you **forsake** something, you stop doing it, using it, or having it. [LITERARY] ☐ *He doubted their claim to have forsaken military solutions to the civil war.*

for|sak|en /fərseɪkᵊn/ **1** ADJ [ADJ n] A **forsaken** place is not lived in, used, or looked after. [LITERARY] ☐ *The delta region of the Rio Grande river was a forsaken land of thickets and swamps.* **2** → see also **godforsaken**

for|swear /fɔrswɛər/ (forswears, forswearing, forswore, forsworn) V-T If you **forswear** something, you promise that you will stop doing it, having it, or using it. [FORMAL or LITERARY] ☐ *The party was offered a share of government if it forswore violence.*

for|sythia /fərsɪθiə/ (forsythias) N-VAR Forsythia is a bush whose yellow flowers appear in the spring before the leaves have grown.

fort /fɔrt/ (forts) **1** N-COUNT; N-IN-NAMES A **fort** is a building or a place with a wall or fence around it where soldiers can stay and be safe from the enemy. **2** PHRASE If you **hold the fort** for someone or if you **hold down the fort**, you take care of things for them while they are somewhere else or are busy doing something else. ☐ *His business partner is holding the fort while he is away.* ☐ *"I'll hold down the fort until he's back," Clark said.*

forte /fɔrteɪ/ (fortes)

Also pronounced /fɔrt/ for meaning 1.

1 N-COUNT [usu sing, poss N] You can say that a particular activity is your **forte** if you are very good at it. ☐ *Shipley's forte is being able to do a lot of things at the same time with ease.* **2** ADV [ADV after v] A piece of music that is played **forte** is played loudly. [TECHNICAL]

forth /fɔrθ/

In addition to the uses shown below, **forth** is also used in the phrasal verbs 'put forth' and 'set forth.'

1 ADV [ADV after v] When someone goes **forth** from a place, they leave it. [LITERARY] ☐ *Go forth into the desert.* **2** ADV [ADV after v] If one thing brings **forth** another, the first thing produces the second. [LITERARY] ☐ *My reflections brought forth no conclusion.* **3** ADV [ADV after v] When someone or something is brought **forth**, they are brought to a place or moved into a position where people can see them. [LITERARY] ☐ *Pilate ordered Jesus to be brought forth.* **4 back and forth** → see **back** ① **5 to hold forth** → see **hold** ④

forth|com|ing /fɔrθkʌmɪŋ/ **1** ADJ [ADJ n] A **forthcoming** event is planned to happen soon. ☐ *...his opponents in the forthcoming elections.* **2** ADJ [v-link ADJ] If something that you want, need, or expect is **forthcoming**, it is given to you or it happens. [FORMAL] ☐ *They promised that the money would be forthcoming.* ☐ *One source predicts no major shift in policy will be forthcoming at the committee hearings.* **3** ADJ If you say that someone is **forthcoming**, you mean that they willingly give information when you ask them. ☐ *William, sadly, was not very forthcoming about any other names he might have, where he lived or what his phone number was.*

forth|right /fɔrθraɪt/ ADJ If you describe someone as **forthright**, you admire them because they show clearly and strongly what they think and feel. [APPROVAL] ☐ *...a deeply religious man with forthright opinions.*

forth|with /fɔrθwɪθ/ ADV [ADV with v] **Forthwith** means immediately. [FORMAL] ☐ *I could have you arrested forthwith!*

for|ti|eth /fɔrtiəθ/ ORD The **fortieth** item in a series is the one that you count as number forty. ☐ *It was the fortieth anniversary of the death of the composer.*

for|ti|fi|ca|tion /fɔrtɪfɪkeɪʃᵊn/ (fortifications) **1** N-COUNT [usu pl] **Fortifications** are buildings, walls, or ditches that are built to protect a place and make it more difficult to attack. ☐ *The government has started building fortifications along its eastern border.* **2** → see also **fortify**

for|ti|fied wine (fortified wines) N-MASS **Fortified wine** is an alcoholic drink such as sherry or port that is made by mixing wine with a small amount of brandy or strong alcohol.

for|ti|fy /fɔrtɪfaɪ/ (fortifies, fortifying, fortified) **1** V-T To **fortify** a place means to make it stronger and more difficult to attack, often by building a wall or ditch round it. ☐ *...soldiers working to fortify an airbase in Bahrain.* **2** V-T [usu passive] If food or drink **is fortified**, another substance is added to it to make it healthier or stronger. ☐ *Choose margarine or butter fortified with vitamin D.* ☐ *All sherry is made from wine fortified with brandy.*

for|tis|si|mo /fɔrtɪsɪmoʊ/ ADV [ADV after v] A piece of music that is played **fortissimo** is played very loudly. [TECHNICAL]

for|ti|tude /fɔrtɪtud/ N-UNCOUNT If you say that someone has shown **fortitude**, you admire them for being brave, calm, and uncomplaining when they have experienced something unpleasant or painful. [FORMAL, APPROVAL] ☐ *He suffered a long series of illnesses with tremendous dignity and fortitude.*

fort|night /fɔrtnaɪt/ (fortnights) N-COUNT A **fortnight** is a period of two weeks. [mainly BRIT] ☐ *I hope to be back in a fortnight.*

fort|night|ly /fɔrtnaɪtli/ ADJ A **fortnightly** event or publication happens or appears once every two weeks. [BRIT]

in AM, use **biweekly**

• ADV **Fortnightly** is also an adverb.

for|tress /fɔrtrɪs/ (fortresses) N-COUNT A **fortress** is a castle or other large strong building, or a well-protected place, which is intended to be difficult for enemies to enter. ☐ *...a 13th-century fortress.*

for|tui|tous /fɔrtuɪtəs/ ADJ You can describe something as **fortuitous** if it happens, by chance, to be very successful or pleasant. ☐ *Their success is the result of a fortuitous combination of circumstances.*

for|tu|nate /fɔrtʃənɪt/ ADJ If you say that someone or something is **fortunate**, you mean that they are lucky. ☐ *He was extremely fortunate to survive.* ☐ *She is in the fortunate position of having plenty of choice.*

for|tu|nate|ly /fɔrtʃənɪtli/ ADV **Fortunately** is used to introduce or indicate a statement about an event or situation that is good. ❑ *Fortunately, the weather that winter was reasonably mild.*

for|tune ✦◇◇ /fɔrtʃən/ (**fortunes**) **1** N-COUNT You can refer to a large sum of money as a **fortune** or a small **fortune** to emphasize how large it is. [EMPHASIS] ❑ *He made a small fortune in the property boom.* **2** N-COUNT Someone who has a **fortune** has a very large amount of money. ❑ *He made his fortune in car sales.* **3** N-UNCOUNT **Fortune** or good **fortune** is good luck. Ill **fortune** is bad luck. ❑ *Investors are starting to wonder how long their good fortune can last.* **4** N-PLURAL If you talk about someone's **fortunes** or the **fortunes** of something, you are talking about the extent to which they are doing well or being successful. ❑ *The company had to do something to reverse its sliding fortunes.* **5** PHRASE When someone **tells** your **fortune**, they tell you what they think will happen to you in the future, which they say is shown, for example, by the lines on your hand. ❑ *I was just going to have my fortune told by a gypsy.*

for|tune cookie (**fortune cookies**) N-COUNT A **fortune cookie** is a sweet, crisp cookie which contains a piece of paper which is supposed to say what will happen to you in the future. Fortune cookies are often served in Chinese restaurants.

fortune-teller (**fortune-tellers**) N-COUNT A **fortune-teller** is a person who tells you what they think will happen to you in the future, after looking at something such as the lines on your hand.

for|ty ✦✦✦ /fɔrti/ (**forties**) **1** NUM **Forty** is the number 40. **2** N-PLURAL When you talk about the **forties**, you are referring to numbers between 40 and 49. For example, if you are in your **forties**, you are aged between 40 and 49. If the temperature is in the **forties**, the temperature is between 40 and 49 degrees. ❑ *He was a big man in his forties, smartly dressed in a suit and tie.* **3** N-PLURAL **The forties** is the decade between 1940 and 1949. ❑ *Steel cans were introduced sometime during the forties.*

fo|rum /fɔrəm/ (**forums**) **1** N-COUNT A **forum** is a place, situation, or group in which people exchange ideas and discuss issues, especially important public issues. ❑ *Members of the council agreed that was an important forum for discussion.* **2** → See feature box at **learning**

for|ward ✦✦✦ /fɔrwərd/ (**forwards, forwarding, forwarded**) **1** ADV [ADV after v] If you move or look **forward**, you move or look in a direction that is in front of you. ❑ *He came forward with his hand out. "Mr. and Mrs. Selby?" he said.* ❑ *She fell forward on to her face.* **2** ADV **Forward** means in a position near the front of something such as a building or a vehicle. ❑ *The best seats are in the aisle and as far forward as possible.* • ADJ [ADJ n] **Forward** is also an adjective. ❑ *Reinforcements were needed to allow more troops to move to forward positions.* **3** ADV If you say that someone looks **forward**, you approve of them because they think about what will happen in the future and plan for it. [APPROVAL] ❑ *Now the leadership wants to look forward, and to outline a strategy for the rest of the century.* ❑ *People should forget and look forward.* • ADJ [ADJ n] **Forward** is also an adjective. ❑ *The university system requires more forward planning.* **4** ADV [ADV after v] If you move a clock or watch **forward**, you change the time shown on it so that it shows a later time, for example, when the time changes to daylight saving time. ❑ *When we put the clocks forward in March we go into daylight saving time.* **5** ADV [from n ADV] When you are referring to a particular time, if you say that something was true **from** that time **forward**, you mean that it became true at that time, and continued to be true afterward. ❑ *Velazquez's work from that time forward was confined largely to portraits of the royal family.* **6** ADV You use **forward** to indicate that something progresses or improves. ❑ *And by boosting economic prosperity in Mexico, Canada and the United States, it will help us move forward on issues that concern all of us.* ❑ *They just couldn't see any way forward.* **7** ADV [ADV after v] If something or someone is put **forward**, or comes **forward**, they are suggested or offered as suitable for a particular purpose. ❑ *Over the years several similar theories have been put forward.* ❑ *Investigations have ground to a standstill because no witnesses have come forward.* **8** V-T If a letter or message **is forwarded** to someone, it is sent to the place where they are, after having been sent to a different place earlier. ❑ *When he's out on the road, office calls are forwarded to the cellular phone in his truck.* **9** N-COUNT In basketball, soccer, or hockey, a **forward** is a player whose usual position is in the opponents' half of the field, and whose usual job is to attack or score goals. ❑ *Junior forward Sam McCracken added 14 points for the home team.* **10 backward and forward** → see **backward**

for|ward|ing ad|dress (**forwarding addresses**) N-COUNT A **forwarding address** is an address that you give to someone when you go and live somewhere else so that they can send your mail on to you. ❑ *The former owner had not left any forwarding address.*

forward-looking ADJ If you describe a person or organization as **forward-looking**, you approve of the fact that they think about the future or have modern ideas. [APPROVAL]

for|wards /fɔrwərdz/ → see **forward**

for|ward slash (**forward slashes**) N-COUNT A **forward slash** is the sloping line / that separates letters, words, or numbers.

for|went /fɔrwɛnt/ **Forwent** is the past tense of **forgo**.

fos|sil /fɒsəl/ (**fossils**) N-COUNT A **fossil** is the hard remains of a prehistoric animal or plant that are found inside a rock.

fos|sil fuel (**fossil fuels**) also **fossil-fuel** N-MASS **Fossil fuel** is fuel such as coal or oil that is formed from the decayed remains of plants or animals. ❑ *Burning fossil fuels uses oxygen and produces carbon dioxide.*

fos|sil|ize /fɒsɪlaɪz/ (**fossilizes, fossilizing, fossilized**)

in BRIT, also use **fossilise**

1 V-T/V-I If the remains of an animal or plant **fossilize** or **are fossilized**, they become hard and form fossils, instead of decaying completely. ❑ *The tissue and cartilage of a nose are too soft to fossilize.* ❑ *The survival of the proteins depends on the way in which bones are fossilized.* ❑ *...fossilized dinosaur bones.* **2** V-T/V-I If you say that ideas, attitudes, or ways of behaving **have fossilized** or **have been fossilized**, you are criticizing the fact that they are fixed and unlikely to change, in spite of changing situations or circumstances. [DISAPPROVAL] ❑ *They seem to want to fossilize the environment in which people live and work.* ❑ *Needs change while policies fossilize.* • **fos|sil|ized** ADJ ❑ *...these fossilized organizations.*

fos|ter /fɒstər/ (**fosters, fostering, fostered**) **1** ADJ [ADJ n] **Foster** parents are people who officially take a child into their family for a period of time, without becoming the child's legal parents. The child is referred to as their **foster** child. ❑ *Little Jack was placed with foster parents.* **2** V-T If you **foster** a child, you take it into your family for a period of time, without becoming its legal parent. ❑ *She has since gone on to find happiness by fostering more than 100 children.* **3** V-T To **foster** something such as an activity or idea means to help it to develop. ❑ *The point of this is to foster global communication.*

fought /fɔt/ **Fought** is the past tense and past participle of **fight**.

foul /faʊl/ (**fouler, foulest, fouls, fouling, fouled**) **1** ADJ If you describe something as **foul**, you mean it is dirty and smells or tastes unpleasant. ❑ *...foul polluted water.* **2** ADJ **Foul** language is offensive and contains swear words or rude words. ❑ *The teachers had to deal with her foul language, disruptive behavior, and low academic performance.* **3** ADJ If someone has a **foul** temper or is in a **foul** mood, they become angry or violent very suddenly and easily. ❑ *Collins was in a foul mood even before the interviews began.* **4** ADJ **Foul** weather is unpleasant, windy, and stormy. ❑ *No amount of foul weather, whether hail, wind, rain or snow, seems to deter them.* **5** V-T If an animal **fouls** a place, it drops feces onto the ground. ❑ *It is an offense to let your dog foul a footpath.* **6** V-T In a game or sport, if a player **fouls** another player, they touch them or block them in a way which is not allowed according to the rules. ❑ *Nowitzki fouled Mitchell early in the third quarter.* **7** N-COUNT A **foul** is an act in a game or sport that is not allowed according to the rules. ❑ *Harridge was charged with a flagrant foul and ejected from the game.* • ADJ [ADJ n] **Foul** is also an adjective. ❑ *...a foul tackle.* **8** PHRASE If you **run foul of** someone or **fall foul of** them, you do something which gets you into trouble with them. ❑ *He had fallen foul of the FBI.*

▶ **foul up** PHRASAL VERB If someone or something **fouls up**, or if they **foul** something **up**, they make a serious mistake that causes things to go badly wrong. ❑ *A computer software glitch fouled up their presentation.*

foul line (foul lines) **1** N-COUNT In basketball, the **foul line** is the line from which a player tries to throw the ball through the basket after they have been fouled. **2** N-COUNT In other sports, the **foul lines** are the lines that form the boundaries of the playing area. ◻ ...a machine that determines whether a tennis ball has fallen outside the foul line.

foul-mouthed ADJ If you describe someone as **foul-mouthed**, you disapprove of them because they use offensive words or say very rude things. [DISAPPROVAL]

foul play 1 N-UNCOUNT **Foul play** is criminal violence or activity that results in a person's death. ◻ The report says it suspects foul play was involved in the deaths of two journalists. **2** N-UNCOUNT **Foul play** is unfair or dishonest behavior, especially during a sports game. ◻ Players were warned twice for foul play.

foul-up (foul-ups) N-COUNT A **foul-up** is something that has gone seriously wrong as a result of someone's mistakes or carelessness. [INFORMAL] ◻ A series of technical foul-ups delayed the launch of the new product.

found ♦◊◊ /faʊnd/ (founds, founding, founded) **1 Found** is the past tense and past participle of **find**. **2** V-T When an institution, company, or organization **is founded** by someone or by a group of people, they get it started, often by providing the necessary money. ◻ The New York Free-Loan Society was founded in 1892. ◻ His father founded the American Socialist Party. • **foun|da|tion** /faʊndeɪʃ³n/ N-SING [with poss] ◻ ...the foundation of the National Association of Evangelicals in 1942. • **found|ing** N-SING ◻ The firm has never had an unprofitable year since its founding 65 years ago. **3** V-T [usu passive] When a town, important building, or other place **is founded** by someone or by a group of people, they cause it to be built. ◻ The town was founded in 1610. **4** → see also **founded, founding**

SYNONYMS

found
VERB **2**
establish: The School was established in 1989 by an Italian professor.
set up: The two sides agreed to set up a commission to investigate claims.
institute: We will institute a number of measures to better safeguard the public.
inaugurate: Pan Am inaugurated the first scheduled international flight.

foun|da|tion ♦◊◊ /faʊndeɪʃ³n/ (foundations) **1** N-COUNT The **foundation** of something such as a belief or way of life is the things on which it is based. ◻ Best friends are the foundation of my life. ◻ The issue strikes at the very foundation of our community. **2** N-COUNT A **foundation** is an organization which provides money for a special purpose such as research or charity. ◻ ...the National Foundation for Educational Research. **3** N-PLURAL The **foundations** of a building or other structure are the layer of bricks or concrete below the ground that it is built on. **4** N-UNCOUNT If a story, idea, or argument has no **foundation**, there are no facts to prove that it is true. ◻ The allegations were without foundation. **5** N-MASS **Foundation** is a skin-colored cream that you put on your face before putting on the rest of your makeup. ◻ Use foundation and/or face powder afterward for an even skin tone. **6** → see also **found**

SYNONYMS

foundation
NOUN **1**
basis: Both have agreed that the U.N. plan is a possible basis for negotiation.
mainstay: Fish and rice were the mainstays of the country's diet.
pillar: The pillar of her economic policy was keeping tight control over money supply.

foun|da|tion stone (foundation stones) **1** N-COUNT [oft with poss] A **foundation stone** is a large block of stone built into a large public building near the bottom. It is often involved in a ceremony for the opening of the building, and has writing on it recording this. ◻ The official foundation stone for the dam was laid in 1961. **2** N-COUNT [usu N of n] The **foundation stone** of something is the basic, important thing which its existence or success depends on. ◻ ...these foundation stones of the future: education, training, research, development.

found|ed /faʊndɪd/ **1** ADJ [v-link ADJ on n] If something is **founded on** a particular thing, it is based on it. ◻ The criticisms are founded on facts as well as on convictions. **2** → see also **found**

found|er ♦◊◊ /faʊndər/ (founders, foundering, foundered) **1** N-COUNT The **founder** of an institution, organization, or building is the person who got it started or caused it to be built, often by providing the necessary money. ◻ He was one of the founders of the university's medical faculty. **2** V-I If something such as a plan or project **founders**, it fails because of a particular point, difficulty, or problem. ◻ The talks have foundered, largely because of the reluctance of some members of the government to do a deal with criminals.

SYNONYMS

founder
NOUN **1**
initiator: ...one of the major initiators of the tumultuous changes in Eastern Europe.
architect: ...Russia's chief architect of economic reform.
creator: I have always believed that a garden dies with its creator.
originator: ...the originator of the theory of relativity.

found|ing /faʊndɪŋ/ **1** ADJ [ADJ n] **Founding** means relating to the starting of a particular institution or organization. ◻ The committee held its founding congress in the capital, Riga. **2** → see also **found**

found|ing fa|ther (founding fathers) **1** N-COUNT [oft N of n] The **founding father** of an institution, organization, or idea is the person who sets it up or who first develops it. [LITERARY] **2** N-PROPER-PLURAL The **Founding Fathers** of the United States were the members of the American Constitutional Convention of 1787.

found|ing mem|ber (founding members) N-COUNT [usu N of n] A **founding member** of a club, group, or organization is one of the first members, often one who was involved in setting it up.

in AM, use **charter member**

found|ling /faʊndlɪŋ/ (foundlings) N-COUNT A **foundling** is a baby that has been abandoned by its parents, often in a public place, and that has then been found by someone. [OLD-FASHIONED]

found|ry /faʊndri/ (foundries) N-COUNT A **foundry** is a place where metal or glass is melted and formed into particular shapes.

fount /faʊnt/ (founts) N-COUNT [usu sing, N of n] If you describe a person or thing as the **fount of** something, you are saying that they are an important source or supply of it. [LITERARY] ◻ To the young boy his father was the fount of all knowledge.

foun|tain /faʊntɪn/ (fountains) **1** N-COUNT A **fountain** is an ornamental feature in a pool or lake which consists of a long narrow stream of water that is forced up into the air by a pump. ◻ ...the fountains on the 16th Street Mall. **2** N-COUNT A **fountain** of a liquid is an amount of it which is sent up into the air and falls back. [LITERARY] ◻ The volcano spewed a fountain of molten rock 650 feet in the air.

foun|tain pen (fountain pens) N-COUNT A **fountain pen** is a pen which uses ink that you have drawn up inside it from a bottle.

four ♦♦♦ /fɔr/ (fours) **1** NUM **Four** is the number 4. ◻ Judith is married with four children. **2** PHRASE If you are **on all fours**, your knees, feet, and hands are on the ground. ◻ She crawled on all fours over to the window.

four-letter word (four-letter words) N-COUNT A **four-letter word** is a short word that people consider to be rude or offensive, usually because it refers to sex or other private bodily functions.

four-poster bed (four-poster beds) **1** N-COUNT A **four-poster bed** or a **four-poster** is a large old-fashioned bed that has a tall post at each corner and sometimes has curtains that can be drawn around it. **2** → See also color supplement

four|some /fɔrsəm/ (foursomes) N-COUNT-COLL A **foursome** is a group of four people or things. ◻ The foursome released their second CD this month.

four-square also **foursquare** ADJ [v-link ADJ prep] To stand four-square behind someone or something means to be firm in your support of that person or thing. ☐ *They stood four-square behind their chief, and they would not accept pressure on him to resign.*

four|teen ✦✦✦ /fɔrtin/ (**fourteens**) NUM **Fourteen** is the number 14. ☐ *I'm fourteen years old.*

four|teenth ✦✦ /fɔrtinθ/ ORD The **fourteenth** item in a series is the one that you count as number fourteen. ☐ *The Festival, now in its fourteenth year, has become a major international jazz event.*

fourth ✦✦ /fɔrθ/ (**fourths**) **1** ORD The **fourth** item in a series is the one that you count as number four. ☐ *Last year's winner was in fourth place.* **2** FRACTION A **fourth** is one of four equal parts of something. [AM] ☐ *Three-fourths of the public say they favor a national referendum on the issue.*

fourth di|men|sion N-SING [the N] In physics, **the fourth dimension** is time. The other three dimensions, which exist in space, are length, width, and height. [TECHNICAL]

fourth es|tate N-SING [the N] Journalists are sometimes referred to collectively as the **fourth estate**. ☐ *How does the fourth estate simultaneously serve an audience that is both consumer and citizen?*

fourth|ly /fɔrθli/ ADV [ADV with cl] You say **fourthly** when you want to make a fourth point or give a fourth reason for something. ☐ *Fourthly, the natural enthusiasm of the student teachers should be maintained.*

Fourth of July N-SING [usu the N] In the United States, the **Fourth of July** is a national holiday when people celebrate the Declaration of Independence in 1776. The **Fourth of July** is also known as **Independence Day**. ☐ *...a Fourth of July picnic.*

four-wheel drive (**four-wheel drives**) N-COUNT A **four-wheel drive** is a vehicle in which all four wheels receive power from the engine to help with steering. This makes the vehicle easier to drive on rough roads or surfaces such as sand or snow.

fowl /faʊl/ (**fowls**)

> Fowl can also be used as the plural form.

N-COUNT A **fowl** is a bird, especially one that can be eaten as food, such as a duck or a chicken. ☐ *Carve the fowl into 8 pieces.*

fox /fɒks/ (**foxes**) N-COUNT A **fox** is a wild animal which looks like a dog and has reddish-brown fur, a pointed face and ears, and a thick tail. Foxes eat smaller animals.

fox|glove /fɒksɡlʌv/ (**foxgloves**) N-VAR A **foxglove** is a tall plant that has pink or white flowers shaped like bells growing up its stem.

fox|hole /fɒkshoʊl/ (**foxholes**) N-COUNT A **foxhole** is a small hole which soldiers dig as a shelter from the enemy and from which they can shoot.

fox|hound /fɒkshaʊnd/ (**foxhounds**) N-COUNT A **foxhound** is a type of dog that is trained to hunt foxes.

fox-hunting also **foxhunting** N-UNCOUNT **Fox-hunting** is a sport in which people riding horses chase a fox across the countryside. Dogs called hounds are used to find the fox.

fox|trot /fɒkstrɒt/ (**foxtrots**) N-COUNT [usu sing] The **foxtrot** is a type of dance which involves a combination of long slow steps and short fast steps.

foxy /fɒksi/ (**foxier, foxiest**) **1** ADJ If you describe someone as **foxy**, you mean that they are deceitful in a clever, secretive way. ☐ *He had wary, foxy eyes.* **2** ADJ If someone calls a woman **foxy**, they mean that she is physically and sexually attractive. [mainly AM, INFORMAL]

foy|er /fɔɪər, fɔɪeɪ, fwaɪeɪ/ (**foyers**) N-COUNT The **foyer** is the large area where people meet or wait just inside the main doors of a building such as a theater or hotel. ☐ *I went and waited in the foyer.*

Fr. **1** Fr. is a written abbreviation for **French** or **franc**. **2** Fr. is a written abbreviation for **Father** when it is used in titles before the name of a Catholic priest.

fra|cas /freɪkəs, fræk-/ N-SING A **fracas** is a rough, noisy quarrel or fight.

frack /fræk/ (**fracks, fracking, fracked**) VERB To **frack** is to get oil or gas from rock by forcing liquid or sand into the rock. ☐ *The company could apply for a licence to frack.* ☐ *They used the technique of pumping water from long range to frack the rock.*

frack|ing /frækɪŋ/ N-UNCOUNT **Fracking** is a method of getting oil or gas from rock by forcing liquid and sand into the rock. ☐ *Local people are opposed to fracking in the area.*

frac|tal /fræktəl/ (**fractals**) N-COUNT [oft N n] In geometry, a **fractal** is a shape made up of parts that are the same shape as itself and are of smaller and smaller sizes.

frac|tion /frækʃən/ (**fractions**) **1** N-COUNT A **fraction** of something is a tiny amount or proportion of it. ☐ *She hesitated for a fraction of a second before responding.* ☐ *Here's how to eat like the stars, at a fraction of the cost.* **2** N-COUNT A **fraction** is a number that can be expressed as a proportion of two whole numbers. For example, 1/2 and 1/3 are both fractions. ☐ *The students had a grasp of decimals, percentages and fractions.*

frac|tion|al /frækʃənəl/ ADJ [usu ADJ n] If something is **fractional**, it is very small in size or degree. ☐ *...a fractional hesitation.* • **frac|tion|al|ly** /frækʃənəli/ ADV [ADV group] ☐ *Murphy, Sinclair's young teammate, was fractionally behind him.*

frac|tious /frækʃəs/ ADJ If you describe someone as **fractious**, you disapprove of them because they become upset or angry very quickly about small unimportant things. [DISAPPROVAL] ☐ *Nancy was in a fractious mood.* ☐ *The children were predictably fractious.*

frac|ture /fræktʃər/ (**fractures, fracturing, fractured**) **1** N-COUNT A **fracture** is a crack or break in something, especially a bone. ☐ *At least one-third of all women over ninety have sustained a hip fracture.* **2** V-T/V-I If something such as a bone **is fractured** or **fractures**, it gets a crack or break in it. ☐ *You've fractured a rib, maybe more than one.* ☐ *One strut had fractured and been crudely repaired in several places.* **3** V-T/V-I If something such as an organization or society **is fractured** or **fractures**, it splits into several parts or stops existing. [FORMAL] ☐ *His policy risks fracturing the coalition.*

frag|ile /frædʒəl/ **1** ADJ If you describe a situation as **fragile**, you mean that it is weak or uncertain, and unlikely to be able to resist strong pressure or attack. [JOURNALISM] ☐ *The fragile economies of several southern African nations could be irreparably damaged.* • **fra|gil|ity** /frədʒɪlɪti/ N-UNCOUNT ☐ *By mid-1988 there were clear indications of the extreme fragility of the Right-wing coalition.* **2** ADJ Something that is **fragile** is easily broken or damaged. ☐ *He leaned back in his fragile chair.* • **fra|gil|ity** N-UNCOUNT ☐ *Older drivers are more likely to be seriously injured because of the fragility of their bones.*

frag|ment (**fragments, fragmenting, fragmented**)

> The noun is pronounced /frægmənt/. The verb is pronounced /frægmɛnt/.

1 N-COUNT A **fragment** of something is a small piece or part of it. ☐ *The only reminder of the shooting is a few fragments of metal in my shoulder.* ☐ *She read everything, digesting every fragment of news.* **2** V-T/V-I If something **fragments** or **is fragmented**, it breaks or separates into small pieces or parts. ☐ *The clouds fragmented and out came the sun.* • **frag|men|ta|tion** /frægmɛnteɪʃən/ N-UNCOUNT ☐ *...the extraordinary fragmentation of styles on the music scene.*

frag|men|tary /frægməntɛri/ ADJ Something that is **fragmentary** is made up of small or unconnected pieces. ☐ *Any action on the basis of such fragmentary evidence would be foolish.*

fra|grance /freɪɡrəns/ (**fragrances**) **1** N-VAR A **fragrance** is a pleasant or sweet smell. ☐ *...a shrubby plant with a strong characteristic fragrance.* **2** N-MASS **Fragrance** is a pleasant-smelling liquid which people put on their bodies to make themselves smell nice. ☐ *The advertisement is for a men's fragrance.*

fra|grant /freɪɡrənt/ ADJ Something that is **fragrant** has a pleasant, sweet smell. ☐ *...fragrant oils and perfumes.*

frail /freɪl/ (**frailer, frailest**) **1** ADJ Someone who is **frail** is not very strong or healthy. ☐ *She lay in bed looking frail.* **2** ADJ Something that is **frail** is easily broken or damaged. ☐ *The frail boat rocked as he clambered in.*

frail|ty /freɪlti, freɪəl-/ (**frailties**) **1** N-VAR If you refer to the **frailties** or **frailty** of people, you are referring to their weaknesses. ☐ *...the frailties of human nature.* **2** N-UNCOUNT **Frailty** is the condition of having poor health. ☐ *She died after a long period of increasing frailty.*

frame ✦✦✦ /freɪm/ (**frames, framing, framed**) **1** N-COUNT The **frame** of a picture or mirror is the wood, metal, or plastic that

frame of mind is fitted around it, especially when it is displayed or hung on a wall. ▫ *Estelle kept a photograph of her mother in a silver frame on the kitchen mantelpiece.* **2** N-COUNT The **frame** of an object such as a building, bicycle, chair, or window is the arrangement of wooden, metal, or plastic bars between which other material is fitted, and which give the object its strength and shape. ▫ *He supplied housebuilders with modern timber frames.* ▫ *With difficulty he released the mattress from the metal frame, and groped beneath it.* **3** N-COUNT The **frames** of a pair of glasses are all the metal or plastic parts of it, but not the lenses. ▫ *He was wearing new glasses with gold wire frames.* **4** N-COUNT A **frame** of movie film is one of the many separate photographs that it consists of. ▫ *Standard 8mm projects at 16 frames per second.* **5** V-T [usu passive] When a picture or photograph **is framed**, it is put in a frame. ▫ *The picture is now ready to be mounted and framed.* **6** V-T [usu passive] If an object **is framed** by a particular thing, it is surrounded by that thing in a way that makes the object more striking or attractive to look at. ▫ *The swimming pool is framed by tropical gardens.* **7** V-T If someone **frames** an innocent person, they make other people think that that person is guilty of a crime, by lying or inventing evidence. [INFORMAL] ▫ *I need to find out who tried to frame me.* **8** N-COUNT You can refer to someone's body as their **frame**, especially when you are describing the general shape of their body. ▫ *Their belts are pulled tight against their bony frames.* **9** → See also color supplement

COLLOCATIONS

frame
NOUN
1
noun + **frame**: picture
adjective + **frame**: carved, gilded, gilt, silver, wooden
2
noun + **frame**: bed, door, window; metal, steel, timber
adjective + **frame**: lightweight, rigid
3
adjective + **frame**: lanky, slender, slight, wiry; bulky, muscular, stocky

frame of mind (**frames of mind**) N-COUNT Your **frame of mind** is the mood that you are in, which causes you to have a particular attitude to something. ▫ *Lewis was not in the right frame of mind to continue.*

frame of ref|er|ence (**frames of reference**) N-COUNT [usu with supp] A **frame of reference** is a particular set of beliefs or ideas on which you base your judgment of things. ▫ *We know we're dealing with someone with a different frame of reference.*

frame-up (**frame-ups**) N-COUNT A **frame-up** is a situation where someone pretends that an innocent person has committed a crime by deliberately lying or inventing evidence. [INFORMAL] ▫ *He was innocent and the victim of a frame-up.*

frame|work /freɪmwɜrk/ (**frameworks**) **1** N-COUNT A **framework** is a particular set of rules, ideas, or beliefs which you use in order to deal with problems or to decide what to do. ▫ *...within the framework of federal regulations.* **2** N-COUNT A **framework** is a structure that forms a support or frame for something. ▫ *...wooden shelves on a steel framework.*

franc /fræŋk/ (**francs**) N-COUNT [num N] The **franc** was the unit of currency that was used in France and Belgium, before it was replaced by the euro. It is also the unit of currency in some other countries where French is spoken. ▫ *The price of grapes had shot up to 32 francs a kilo.* ● N-SING [the N] **The franc** was used to refer to the currency systems of France and Belgium, before it was replaced by the euro. It is also used to refer to the currency systems of some other countries where French is spoken. ▫ *The Swiss franc has remained surprisingly strong.*

fran|chise /fræntʃaɪz/ (**franchises, franchising, franchised**) **1** N-COUNT A **franchise** is an authority that is given by an organization to someone, allowing them to sell its goods or services or to take part in an activity which the organization controls. [BUSINESS] ▫ *...fast-food franchises.* ▫ *...the franchise to build and operate the tunnel.* **2** V-T If a company **franchises** its business, it sells franchises to other companies, allowing them to sell its goods or services. [BUSINESS] ▫ *She has recently franchised her business.* **3** N-UNCOUNT [also the N] **Franchise** is the right to vote in an election. ▫ *...the introduction of universal franchise.*

fratricidal

fran|chi|see /fræntʃaɪziː/ (**franchisees**) N-COUNT A **franchisee** is a person or group of people who buy a particular franchise. [BUSINESS] ▫ *...National Restaurants, a New York franchisee for Pizza Hut.*

fran|chi|ser /fræntʃaɪzər/ (**franchisers**) N-COUNT A **franchiser** is an organization which sells franchises. [BUSINESS] ▫ *Coca-Cola, Pepsi and Cadbury use franchisers to manufacture, bottle and distribute their products within geographical areas.*

PREFIX

Franco-
occurs in words connected with France and the French language. *For example, the Franco-German border is the border between France and Germany.*

Fran|co|phone /fræŋkəfoʊn/ (**Francophones**) N-COUNT [oft N n] A **Francophone** is someone who speaks French, especially someone who speaks it as their first language. [FORMAL]

frank /fræŋk/ (**franker, frankest**) ADJ If someone is **frank**, they state or express things in an open and honest way. ▫ *"It is clear that my client has been less than frank with me," said his lawyer.* ● **frank|ly** ADV [ADV with v] ▫ *You can talk frankly to me.* ● **frank|ness** N-UNCOUNT ▫ *The reaction to his frankness was hostile.*

frank|fur|ter /fræŋkfɜrtər/ (**frankfurters**) N-COUNT A **frankfurter** is a type of smoked sausage.

frank|in|cense /fræŋkɪnsɛns/ N-UNCOUNT **Frankincense** is a substance which is obtained from a tree and which smells pleasant when it is burned. It is used especially in religious ceremonies.

frank|ly /fræŋkli/ **1** ADV You use **frankly** when you are expressing an opinion or feeling to emphasize that you mean what you are saying, especially when the person you are speaking to may not like it. [EMPHASIS] ▫ *"You don't give a damn about my feelings, do you."—"Quite frankly, I don't."* ▫ *Frankly, Thomas, this question of your loan is beginning to worry me.* **2** → see also **frank**

fran|tic /fræntɪk/ **1** ADJ If you are **frantic**, you are behaving in a wild and uncontrolled way because you are frightened or worried. ▫ *A bird had been locked in and was by now quite frantic.* ● **fran|ti|cal|ly** /fræntɪkli/ ADV [ADV with v] ▫ *She clutched frantically at Emily's arm.* **2** ADJ If an activity is **frantic**, things are done quickly and in an energetic but disorganized way, because there is very little time. ▫ *A busy night in the restaurant can be frantic in the kitchen.* ● **fran|ti|cal|ly** ADV [ADV with v] ▫ *We have been frantically trying to save her life.*

frape /freɪp/ (**frapes, fraping, fraped**) V-T If someone **frapes** you, they add comments or pictures that appear to come from you to a social networking website without your permission. [INFORMAL] ▫ *I didn't post the comment – my friend Max fraped me!*

fra|ter|nal /frətɜrnəl/ **1** ADJ [usu ADJ n] **Fraternal** actions show strong links of friendship between two people or groups of people. [FORMAL] ▫ *...the fraternal assistance of our colleagues and comrades.* **2** ADJ [usu ADJ n] **Fraternal** twins are twins born from two eggs, so they are not exactly the same. They look different from each other and may be different sexes.

fra|ter|nity /frətɜrnɪti/ (**fraternities**) **1** N-COUNT You can refer to people who have the same profession or the same interests as a particular **fraternity**. ▫ *...the spread of stolen guns among the criminal fraternity.* **2** N-UNCOUNT **Fraternity** refers to friendship and support between people who feel they are closely linked to each other. [FORMAL] ▫ *Bob needs the fraternity of others who share his mission.* **3** N-COUNT In the United States, a **fraternity** is a society of male university or college students. ▫ *He must have been the most popular guy at the most popular fraternity in college.*

frat|er|nize /frætərnaɪz/ (**fraternizes, fraternizing, fraternized**)

in BRIT, also use **fraternise**

V-RECIP If you **fraternize** with someone, you associate with them in a friendly way. ▫ *At these conventions, executives fraternized with the key personnel of other banks.* ▫ *Mrs. Zuckerman does not fraternize widely.*

frat|ri|cid|al /frætrɪsaɪdəl/ ADJ [ADJ n] A **fratricidal** war or conflict is one in which people kill members of their own society or social group. [FORMAL]

frat|ri|cide /frǽtrɪsaɪd/ N-UNCOUNT If someone commits fratricide, they kill their brother. [FORMAL]

fraud ◆◇◇ /frɔːd/ (frauds) **1** N-VAR Fraud is the crime of gaining money or financial benefits by a trick or by lying. ❑ *He was jailed for two years for fraud and deception.* **2** N-COUNT A fraud is something or someone that deceives people in a way that is illegal or dishonest. ❑ *He's a fraud and a cheat.* **3** → See feature box at **crime**

SYNONYMS

fraud
NOUN **1**
deception: *He admitted conspiring to obtain property by deception.*
deceit: *They have been involved in a campaign of deceit.*
treachery: *He was deeply wounded by the treachery of close aides and old friends.*
trickery: *They are notorious for resorting to trickery in order to impress their clients.*

---

fraud squad (fraud squads) N-COUNT [oft N n] The fraud squad is a part of a police force whose job is to investigate crimes involving fraud.

fraudu|lent /frɔ́ːdʒələnt/ **1** ADJ A fraudulent activity is deliberately deceitful, dishonest, or untrue. ❑ *...fraudulent claims about being a nurse.* • **fraudu|lent|ly** ADV [ADV with v] ❑ *All 5,000 of the homes were fraudulently obtained.* **2** → See feature box at **truth**

fraught /frɔːt/ **1** ADJ [v-link ADJ with n] If a situation or action is fraught with problems or risks, it is filled with them. ❑ *The earliest operations employing this technique were fraught with dangers.* **2** ADJ If you say that a situation or action is fraught, you mean that it is worrisome or difficult. ❑ *It has been a somewhat fraught day.*

fray /freɪ/ (frays, fraying, frayed) **1** V-T/V-I If something such as cloth or rope frays, or if something frays it, its threads or fibers start to come apart from each other and spoil its appearance. ❑ *The fabric is very fine or frays easily.* ❑ *The stitching had begun to fray at the edges.* **2** V-T/V-I If your nerves or your temper fray, or if something frays them, you become nervous or easily annoyed because of mental strain and anxiety. ❑ *Tempers began to fray as the two teams failed to score.*

fraz|zle /frǽzəl/ PHRASE If you **wear yourself to a frazzle**, or if you **are worn to a frazzle**, you feel mentally and physically exhausted because you have been working too hard or because you have been constantly worrying about something. ❑ *She's worn to a frazzle with her silly speech competition.*

fraz|zled /frǽzəld/ ADJ If you are frazzled, or if your nerves are frazzled, you feel mentally and physically exhausted. ❑ *...a place to calm the most frazzled tourist.* ❑ *I need to rest my frazzled nerves.*

freak /friːk/ (freaks) **1** ADJ [ADJ n] A freak event or action is one that is a very unusual or extreme example of its type. ❑ *Weir broke his leg in a freak accident playing golf.* **2** N-COUNT If you describe someone as a particular kind of freak, you are emphasizing that they are very enthusiastic about a thing or activity, and often seem to think about nothing else. [INFORMAL] ❑ *Diaz is a fitness freak who's trained in martial arts.* **3** N-COUNT People are sometimes referred to as freaks when their behavior or attitude is very different from that of the majority of people. [DISAPPROVAL]

freak|ish /fríːkɪʃ/ ADJ [usu ADJ n] Something that is freakish is remarkable because it is not normal or natural. ❑ *...his freakish voice varying from bass to soprano.*

freaky /fríːki/ (freakier, freakiest) ADJ If someone or something is freaky, they are very unusual in some way. [INFORMAL] ❑ *This guy bore a really freaky resemblance to Jones.*

freck|le /frékəl/ (freckles) N-COUNT Freckles are small light brown spots on someone's skin, especially on their face. ❑ *He had short ginger-colored hair and freckles.*

freck|led /frékəld/ ADJ If a part of your body is freckled, it has freckles on it. ❑ *...a slight man with auburn hair and a freckled face.*

free ◆◆◆ /friː/ (freer, freest, frees, freeing, freed)
→ Please look at meanings **18** and **19** to see if the expression you are looking for is shown under another headword.

1 ADJ If something is **free**, you can have it or use it without paying for it. ❑ *The seminars are free, with lunch provided.* **2 free of charge** → see **charge** **3** ADJ Someone or something that is **free** is not restricted, controlled, or limited, for example, by rules, customs, or other people. ❑ *The government will be free to pursue its economic policies.* ❑ *The elections were free and fair.* • **free|ly** ADV [ADV with v] ❑ *They cast their votes freely and without coercion on election day.* **4** ADJ Someone who is **free** is no longer a prisoner or a slave. ❑ *He walked from the court house a free man.* **5** ADJ [v-link ADJ of/from n] If someone or something is **free of** or **free from** an unpleasant thing, they do not have it or they are not affected by it. ❑ *...a future far more free of fear.* ❑ *She retains her slim figure and is free of wrinkles.* **6** ADJ [v-link ADJ of n] A sum of money or type of goods that is **free of** tax or duty is one that you do not have to pay tax on. ❑ *This benefit is free of tax under current legislation.* **7** → see also **duty-free, interest-free, tax-free** **8** ADJ If you have a **free** period of time or are **free** at a particular time, you are not working or occupied then. ❑ *She spent her free time shopping.* ❑ *I used to write during my free periods at school.* **9** ADJ If something such as a table or seat is **free**, it is not being used or occupied by anyone, or is not reserved for anyone to use. ❑ *There was only one seat free on the train.* **10** ADJ If you get something **free** or if it gets **free**, it is no longer trapped by anything or attached to anything. ❑ *He pulled his arm free, and strode for the door.* **11** ADJ [ADJ n] When someone is using one hand or arm to hold or move something, their other hand or arm is referred to as their **free** one. ❑ *He snatched up the receiver and his free hand groped for the switch on the bedside lamp.* **12** V-T If you **free** someone of something that is unpleasant or restricting, you remove it from them. ❑ *It will free us of a whole lot of debt.* **13** V-T To **free** a prisoner or a slave means to let them go or release them from prison. ❑ *Israel is set to free more Lebanese prisoners.* **14** V-T To **free** someone or something means to make them available for a task or function that they were previously not available for. ❑ *Toolbelts free both hands and lessen the risk of dropping hammers.* ❑ *His deal with Disney will run out shortly, freeing him to pursue his own project.* • PHRASAL VERB **Free up** means the same as **free**. ❑ *It can handle even the most complex graphic jobs, freeing up your computer for other tasks.* **15** V-T If you **free** someone or something, you remove them from the place in which they have been trapped or become fixed. ❑ *Rescue workers tried to free him by cutting away part of the car.* **16** PHRASE You say '**feel free**' when you want to give someone permission to do something, in a very willing way. [INFORMAL, FORMULAE] ❑ *If you have any questions at all, please feel free to ask me.* **17** PHRASE If you do something or get something **for free**, you do it without being paid or get it without having to pay for it. [INFORMAL] ❑ *I wasn't expecting you to do it for free.* **18 to give someone a free hand** → see **hand** ① **19 to give someone free rein** → see **rein** **20** → See feature box at **legal**

▶ **free up** **1** PHRASAL VERB To **free up** a market, economy, or system means to make it operate with fewer restrictions and controls. [BUSINESS] ❑ *...policies for freeing up markets and extending competition.* **2** → see **free 12**

-free /-friː/ COMB IN ADJ **-free** combines with nouns to form adjectives that indicate that something does not have the thing mentioned, or has only a little of it. For example, sugar-free drinks do not contain any sugar, and lead-free gasoline is made using only a small amount of lead. ❑ *...a salt-free diet.*

free agent (free agents) **1** N-COUNT If you say that someone is a **free agent**, you are emphasizing that they can do whatever they want to do, because they are not responsible to anyone or for anyone. ❑ *We are not free agents; we abide by the decisions of our president.* **2** N-COUNT If an athlete is a **free agent**, he or she is free to sign a contract with any team. [AM]

free and easy also **free-and-easy** ADJ Someone or something that is **free and easy** is casual and informal. ❑ *...the free and easy atmosphere of these cafés.*

free as|so|cia|tion N-UNCOUNT Free association is a psychological technique in which words or images are used to suggest other words or images in a nonlogical way. ❑ *The volume consists of short poems interspersed by eight "Meditations," longish poems of free association.*

free|bie /frˈiːbi/ (**freebies**) N-COUNT A **freebie** is something that you are given, usually by a company, without having to pay for it. [INFORMAL]

free|dom ♦♦◊ /frˈiːdəm/ (**freedoms**) **1** N-UNCOUNT [also N in pl] **Freedom** is the state of being allowed to do what you want to do. **Freedoms** are instances of this. ◻ ...*freedom of speech*. ◻ *The United Nations Secretary-General has spoken of the need for individual freedoms and human rights*. **2** N-UNCOUNT When prisoners or slaves are set free or escape, they gain their **freedom**. ◻ ...*the agreement worked out by the UN, under which all hostages and detainees would gain their freedom*. **3** N-UNCOUNT **Freedom from** something you do not want means not being affected by it. ◻ ...*all the freedom from pain that medicine could provide*.

free|dom fight|er (**freedom fighters**) N-COUNT If you refer to someone as a **freedom fighter**, you mean that they belong to a group that is trying to change the government of their country using violent methods, and you agree with or approve of this. [APPROVAL]

free|dom of speech N-UNCOUNT **Freedom of speech** is the same as **free speech**. ◻ ...*a country where freedom of speech may not be allowed*.

free en|ter|prise N-UNCOUNT **Free enterprise** is an economic system in which businesses compete for profit without much government control. [BUSINESS] ◻ ...*a believer in democracy and free enterprise*.

free fall (**free falls**) also **free-fall** **1** N-VAR [oft *into/in* N] If the value or price of something goes into **free fall**, it starts to fall uncontrollably. [JOURNALISM] ◻ *Sterling went into free fall*. ◻ *The price did a free fall*. **2** N-UNCOUNT In parachuting, **free fall** is the part of the jump before the parachute opens.

free-floating ADJ [ADJ n] **Free-floating** things or people are able to move freely and are not controlled or directed by anything. ◻ ...*a system of free-floating exchange rates*.

Free|fone /frˈiːfoʊn/ also **freefone**, **freephone** N-UNCOUNT [usu N num, N n] A **Freefone** telephone number is one which you can dial without having to pay for the call. [BRIT, TRADEMARK]

in AM, use **toll-free**

free-for-all (**free-for-alls**) **1** N-SING A **free-for-all** is a situation in which several people or groups are trying to get something for themselves and there are no controls on how they do it. **2** N-COUNT A **free-for-all** is a disorganized fight or argument which lots of people join in.

free form also **free-form** ADJ [ADJ n] A **free form** work of art or piece of music has not been created according to a standard style or convention. ◻ ...*free-form jazz*.

free|hand /frˈiːhænd/ ADJ [ADJ n] A **freehand** drawing is drawn without using instruments such as a ruler or a compass. ◻ ...*freehand sketches*. • ADV [ADV after v] **Freehand** is also an adverb. ◻ *Use a template or stencil or simply do it freehand*.

free|hold /frˈiːhoʊld/ (**freeholds**) **1** N-VAR If you have the **freehold** of a building or piece of land, it is yours for life and there are no conditions regarding your ownership. ◻ *People owning leasehold homes will be given a new right to buy the freehold of their property*. **2** ADJ If a building or piece of land is **freehold**, you can own it for life. ◻ *The property register will also say whether the property is freehold or leasehold*.

free|holder /frˈiːhoʊldər/ (**freeholders**) N-COUNT A **freeholder** is someone who owns the freehold to a particular piece of land.

free kick (**free kicks**) N-COUNT In a game of soccer or rugby, when there is a **free kick**, the ball is given to a member of one side to kick because a member of the other side has broken a rule.

free|lance /frˈiːlæns/ ADJ Someone who does **freelance** work or who is, for example, a **freelance** journalist or photographer is not employed by one organization, but is paid for each piece of work they do by the organization they do it for. [BUSINESS] ◻ *Michael Cross is a freelance journalist*. • ADV [ADV after v] **Freelance** is also an adverb. ◻ *He is now working freelance from his home in New Hampshire*.

free|lancer /frˈiːlænsər/ (**freelancers**) N-COUNT A **freelancer** is someone who does freelance work.

free|loader /frˈiːloʊdər/ (**freeloaders**) N-COUNT If you refer to someone as a **freeloader**, you disapprove of them because they take advantage of other people's kindness, for example, by accepting food or accommodations from them, without giving anything in return. [INFORMAL, DISAPPROVAL]

free love N-UNCOUNT A belief in **free love** is the belief that it is acceptable and good to have sexual relationships without marrying, often several relationships at the same time. [OLD-FASHIONED]

free|ly /frˈiːli/ **1** ADV **Freely** means many times or in large quantities. ◻ *We have referred freely to his ideas*. ◻ *George was spending very freely*. **2** ADV [ADV after v] If you can talk **freely**, you can talk without needing to be careful about what you say. ◻ *She wondered whether he had someone to whom he could talk freely*. **3** ADV [ADV with v] If someone gives or does something **freely**, they give or do it willingly, without being ordered or forced to do it. ◻ *Danny shared his knowledge freely with anyone interested*. **4** ADV [ADV after v] If something or someone moves **freely**, they move easily and smoothly, without any obstacles or resistance. ◻ *The clay court was slippery and he was unable to move freely*. **5** → see also **free**

free mar|ket (**free markets**) N-COUNT A **free market** is an economic system in which business organizations decide things such as prices and wages, and are not controlled by the government. [BUSINESS] ◻ ...*the creation of a free market*.

free-marketeer (**free-marketeers**) N-COUNT A **free-marketeer** is someone, especially a politician, who is in favor of letting market forces control the economy. [BUSINESS] ◻ *Free-marketeers would argue that governments do not need to intervene in the currency and interest rate process unduly*.

Free|mason /frˈiːmeɪsən/ (**Freemasons**) N-COUNT A **Freemason** is a member of a large secret society. Freemasons promise to help each other, and use a system of secret signs in order to recognize each other.

free|masonry /frˈiːmeɪsənri/ **1** N-UNCOUNT **Freemasonry** is the organization of the Freemasons and their beliefs and practices. ◻ *He was very active in Freemasonry*. **2** N-UNCOUNT **Freemasonry** is the friendly feeling that exists between people who are of the same kind or who have the same interests. ◻ ...*the freemasonry of sailors*.

free pass (**free passes**) N-COUNT A **free pass** is an official document that allows a person to travel or to enter a particular building without having to pay.

free port (**free ports**) N-COUNT A **free port** is a port or airport where goods can be brought in from foreign countries without payment of duty if they are going to be exported again. [BUSINESS]

freer /frˈiːər/ **Freer** is the comparative of **free**.

free radi|cal (**free radicals**) N-COUNT [usu pl] **Free radicals** are atoms that contain one or more unpaired electrons. Free radicals are believed to be a cause of aging, heart disease, and some cancers. [TECHNICAL]

free-range ADJ **Free-range** means relating to a system of keeping animals in which they can move and feed freely on an area of open ground. ◻ ...*free-range eggs*.

free ride (**free rides**) N-COUNT [usu sing: *a* N] If you say that someone is getting a **free ride** in a particular situation, you mean that they are getting some benefit from it without putting any effort into achieving it themselves. [DISAPPROVAL] ◻ ...*the parents who'd rather live on welfare and get a free ride*.

free|sia /frˈiːʒə/ (**freesias**) N-VAR **Freesias** are small plants with yellow, pink, white, or purple flowers that are shaped like tubes.

free speech N-UNCOUNT **Free speech** is the right to express your opinions in public. ◻ *Many experts in constitutional law have warned that the rule violates the right to free speech*.

free spir|it (**free spirits**) N-COUNT If you describe someone as a **free spirit**, you admire them because they are independent and live as they want to live rather than in a conventional way. [APPROVAL]

fre|est /frˈiːɪst/ **Freest** is the superlative of **free**.

free|stand|ing /frístǽndɪŋ/ also **free-standing** ADJ A **freestanding** piece of furniture or other object is not attached to anything, or stands on its own away from other things. ❑ *...a small freestanding cast-iron stove.*

free|style /fríːstaɪl/ ADJ [ADJ n] **Freestyle** is used to describe sports competitions, especially in swimming, wrestling, and skiing, in which competitors can use any style or method that they like when they take part. ❑ *...the 100m freestyle swimming event.* • N-SING **Freestyle** is also a noun. ❑ *She won the 400-meter freestyle.*

free|think|er /friːθɪŋkər/ (**freethinkers**) also **free-thinker** N-COUNT If you refer to someone as a **freethinker**, you admire them because they work out their own ideas rather than accepting generally accepted views. [APPROVAL]

free-to-air ADJ [usu ADJ n] **Free-to-air** television programs and channels are broadcast to all televisions and do not require a subscription or payment. • ADV **Free to air** is also an adverb. ❑ *The fight will be televised free to air on the Fox Network.*

free trade N-UNCOUNT [oft N n] **Free trade** is trade between different countries that is carried on without particular government regulations such as subsidies or taxes. ❑ *...the idea of a free trade pact between the US and Mexico.*

free|ware /fríːwɛər/ N-UNCOUNT **Freeware** is computer software that you can use without payment. [COMPUTING] ❑ *Is there a freeware program that I can use to produce my own clip art?*

free|way /fríːweɪ/ (**freeways**) N-COUNT A **freeway** is a major road that has been specially built for fast travel over long distances. Freeways have several lanes and special places where traffic gets on and leaves. [AM] ❑ *The speed limit on the freeway is 55mph.*

free|wheel /fríːwiːl/ (**freewheels, freewheeling, freewheeled**) also **free-wheel** V-I If you **freewheel**, you travel, usually downhill, on a bicycle without using the pedals, or in a vehicle without using the engine. ❑ *He freewheeled back down the course.*

free|wheel|ing /fríːwiːlɪŋ/ ADJ [usu ADJ n] If you refer to someone's **freewheeling** lifestyle or attitudes, you mean that they behave in a casual, relaxed way without feeling restricted by rules or accepted ways of doing things. ❑ *He has given up his freewheeling lifestyle to settle down with his baby daughter.*

free will ◼ N-UNCOUNT If you believe in **free will**, you believe that people have a choice in what they do and that their actions have not been decided in advance by God or by any other power. ❑ *...the free will of the individual.* ◼ PHRASE If you do something **of your own free will**, you do it by choice and not because you are forced to do it. ❑ *Would Bethany return of her own free will, as she had promised?*

freeze ♦◇◇ /fríːz/ (**freezes, freezing, froze, frozen**) ◼ V-T/V-I If a liquid or a substance containing a liquid **freezes**, or if something **freezes** it, it becomes solid because of low temperatures. ❑ *If the temperature drops below 0°C, water freezes.* ❑ *The ground froze solid.* ◼ V-T/V-I If you **freeze** something such as food, you preserve it by storing it at a temperature below freezing point. You can also talk about how well food **freezes**. ❑ *You can freeze the soup at this stage.* ◼ V-I When **it freezes** outside, the temperature falls below freezing point. ❑ *What if it rained and then froze all through those months?* • N-COUNT **Freeze** is also a noun. ❑ *The trees were damaged by a freeze in December.* ◼ V-I If you **freeze**, you feel extremely cold. ❑ *The windows didn't fit at the bottom so for a while we froze even in the middle of summer.* ◼ V-I If someone who is moving **freezes**, they suddenly stop and become completely still and quiet. [WRITTEN] ❑ *She froze when the beam of the flashlight struck her.* ◼ V-T If the government or a company **freeze** things such as prices or wages, they state officially that they will not allow them to increase for a fixed period of time. [BUSINESS] ❑ *They want the government to freeze prices.* • N-COUNT **Freeze** is also a noun. ❑ *A wage freeze was imposed on all staff earlier this month.* ◼ V-T If someone in authority **freezes** something such as a bank account, fund, or property, they obtain a legal order which states that it cannot be used or sold for a particular period of time. [BUSINESS] ❑ *The governor's action freezes 300,000 accounts.* • N-COUNT [with supp] **Freeze** is also a noun. ❑ *...a freeze on private savings.* ◼ → see also **freezing, frozen**

COLLOCATIONS

freeze
VERB
◼
freeze + *noun*: food; eggs, embryo
◼
freeze + *noun*: pay, price, wage
NOUN ◼
noun + **freeze**: pay, price, wage
verb + **freeze**: announce, impose, put

---

freeze-dried ADJ **Freeze-dried** food has been preserved by a process of rapid freezing and drying. ❑ *...freeze-dried instant mashed potatoes.* ❑ *...freeze-dried coffee granules.*

freeze-frame (**freeze-frames**) N-COUNT A **freeze-frame** from a movie is an individual picture from it, produced by stopping the movie or video at that point.

freez|er /fríːzər/ (**freezers**) N-COUNT A **freezer** is a large container like a refrigerator in which the temperature is kept below freezing point so that you can store food inside it for long periods.

freez|ing /fríːzɪŋ/ ◼ ADJ If you say that something is **freezing** or **freezing cold**, you are emphasizing that it is very cold. [EMPHASIS] ❑ *The movie theater was freezing.* ◼ ADJ [v-link ADJ] If you say that you are **freezing** or **freezing cold**, you are emphasizing that you feel very cold. [EMPHASIS] ❑ *"You must be freezing," she said.* ◼ N-UNCOUNT **Freezing** means the same as **freezing point**. ❑ *It's 15 degrees below freezing.* ◼ → see also **freeze**

freez|ing point (**freezing points**) also **freezing-point** ◼ N-UNCOUNT **Freezing point** is 32° Fahrenheit or 0° Celsius, the temperature at which water freezes. Freezing point is often used when talking about the weather. ❑ *The temperature remained below freezing point throughout the day.* ◼ N-COUNT The **freezing point** of a particular substance is the temperature at which it freezes. ❑ *It was the seventeenth century before Newton determined the freezing point of water.*

freight /fréɪt/ ◼ N-UNCOUNT **Freight** is the movement of goods by trucks, trains, ships, or airplanes. ❑ *France derives 16% of revenue from air freight.* ◼ N-UNCOUNT **Freight** is goods that are transported by trucks, trains, ships, or airplanes. ❑ *...26 tons of freight.*

freight car (**freight cars**) N-COUNT On a train, a **freight car** is a large container in which goods are transported. [mainly AM]

freight|er /fréɪtər/ (**freighters**) N-COUNT A **freighter** is a large ship or airplane that is designed for carrying freight.

freight train (**freight trains**) N-COUNT A **freight train** is a train on which goods are transported.

French /fréntʃ/ ◼ ADJ **French** means belonging or relating to France, or its people, language, or culture. ◼ N-PLURAL The **French** are the people who come from France. ◼ N-UNCOUNT **French** is the language spoken by people who live in France and in parts of some other countries, including Belgium, Canada, and Switzerland. ❑ *The villagers spoke French.*

French bean (**French beans**) N-COUNT [usu pl] A **French bean** is the same as a **green bean**. [BRIT]

French bread N-UNCOUNT **French bread** is white bread which is baked in long, thin loaves.

French Ca|na|dian (**French Canadians**) also **French-Canadian** ◼ ADJ **French Canadian** means belonging or relating to people who come from the part of Canada where French is spoken. ◼ N-COUNT **French Canadians** are Canadians whose native language is French.

French door (**French doors**) N-COUNT [usu pl] **French doors** are a pair of glass doors which you go through into a garden or onto a balcony.

French dress|ing ◼ N-UNCOUNT **French dressing** is a thin sauce made of oil, vinegar, salt, and spices which you put on salad. ◼ N-UNCOUNT **French dressing** is a creamy pinkish-orange sauce which you put on salad. [AM]

French fries N-PLURAL **French fries** are long, thin pieces of potato fried in oil or fat.

French horn (**French horns**) N VAR [oft the N] A **French horn** is a musical instrument of the brass family. It is shaped like a long metal tube with one wide end, wound around in a circle.

You play the French horn by blowing into it and moving valves in order to obtain different notes.

French kiss (French kisses, French kissing, French kissed) V-RECIP If one person **French kisses** another, they kiss each other using their tongues. You can also say that two people **are French kissing.** ❑ *This boy David tried to French kiss me.* ❑ *At the age of 13, I was taught to French kiss.* • N-COUNT **French kiss** is also a noun ❑ *...her first real French kiss.*

French|man /frɛntʃmən/ (**Frenchmen**) N-COUNT A **Frenchman** is a man who comes from France.

French pol|ish N-UNCOUNT **French polish** is a type of varnish which is painted onto wood so that the wood has a hard shiny surface.

French toast N-UNCOUNT **French toast** is toast made by dipping a slice of bread into beaten egg and milk and then frying it.

French win|dow (**French windows**) ◼ N-COUNT [usu pl] **French windows** are the same as **French doors**. [BRIT] ◼ → See also color supplement

French|woman /frɛntʃwʊmən/ (**Frenchwomen**) N-COUNT A **Frenchwoman** is a woman who comes from France.

fre|net|ic /frɪnɛtɪk/ ADJ If you describe an activity as **frenetic**, you mean that it is fast and energetic, but rather uncontrolled. ❑ *...the frenetic pace of life in New York.*

fren|zied /frɛnzid/ ADJ **Frenzied** activities or actions are wild, excited, and uncontrolled. ❑ *...the frenzied activity of the election.*

fren|zy /frɛnzi/ (**frenzies**) N-VAR **Frenzy** or a **frenzy** is great excitement or wild behavior that often results from losing control of your feelings. ❑ *"Get out!" she ordered in a frenzy.*

fre|quen|cy /frikwənsi/ (**frequencies**) ◼ N-UNCOUNT The **frequency** of an event is the number of times it happens during a particular period. ❑ *The frequency of Kara's phone calls increased rapidly.* ◼ N-VAR In physics, the **frequency** of a sound wave or a radio wave is the number of times it vibrates within a specified period of time. ❑ *You can't hear waves of such a high frequency.* ❑ *...a frequency of 24 kilohertz.*

fre|quent ✦✦◇ /frikwənt/ ADJ If something is **frequent**, it happens often. ❑ *Bordeaux is on the main Paris-Madrid line so there are frequent trains.* • **fre|quent|ly** ADV ❑ *Iron and folic acid supplements are frequently given to pregnant women.*

SYNONYMS

frequent
ADJ
common: *Earthquakes are not common in this part of the world.*
usual: *She's smiling her usual friendly smile.*
repeated: *He did not return the money, despite repeated reminders.*
everyday: *...the everyday problems of living in the city.*
regular: *This condition usually clears up with regular shampooing.*
recurrent: *...buildings in which staff suffer recurrent illness.*
persistent: *His cough grew more persistent, until it never stopped.*

---

fres|co /frɛskoʊ/ (**frescoes** or **frescos**) ◼ N-COUNT A **fresco** is a picture that is painted on a plastered wall when the plaster is still wet. ◼ → see also **alfresco**

fresh ✦✦◇ /frɛʃ/ (**fresher, freshest**) ◼ ADJ [ADJ n] A **fresh** thing or amount replaces or is added to a previous thing or amount. ❑ *He asked the police, who carried out the original investigation, to make fresh inquiries.* ◼ ADJ Something that is **fresh** has been done, made, or experienced recently. ❑ *There were no fresh car tracks or footprints in the snow.* ❑ *A puppy stepped in the fresh cement.* ◼ ADJ **Fresh** food has been picked or produced recently, and has not been preserved, for example, by being frozen or put in a can. ❑ *...locally caught fresh fish.* ◼ ADJ If you describe something as **fresh**, you like it because it is new and exciting. ❑ *These designers are full of fresh ideas.* ◼ ADJ If you describe something as **fresh**, you mean that it is pleasant, bright, and clean in appearance. ❑ *Gingham fabrics always look fresh and pretty.* ◼ ADJ If something smells, tastes, or feels **fresh**, it is clean or cool. ❑ *The air was fresh and for a moment she felt revived.* ◼ ADJ If you feel **fresh**, you feel full of energy and enthusiasm. ❑ *It's vital we are as fresh as possible for those games.* ◼ ADJ **Fresh** paint is not yet dry. [AM] ❑ *There was fresh paint on the walls.* ◼ ADJ [v-link ADJ from/out of n] If you are **fresh from** a particular place or experience, you have just come from that place or you have just had that experience. You can also say that someone is **fresh out of** a place. ❑ *I returned to the office, fresh from the airport.*

fresh- /frɛʃ-/ COMB IN ADJ [ADJ n] **Fresh-** is added to past participles in order to form adjectives which describe something as having been recently made or done. ❑ *...a vase of fresh-cut flowers.* ❑ *...a meadow of fresh-mown hay.*

fresh air N-UNCOUNT [also the N] You can describe the air outside as **fresh air**, especially when you mean that it is good for you because it does not contain dirt or dangerous substances. ❑ *"Let's take the baby outside," I suggested. "We all need some fresh air."*

fresh|en /frɛʃən/ (**freshens, freshening, freshened**) ◼ V-I If the wind **freshens**, it becomes stronger and colder. ❑ *The wind had freshened.*
▸ **freshen up** ◼ PHRASAL VERB If you **freshen** something **up**, you make it clean and pleasant in appearance or smell. ❑ *A thorough brushing helps to freshen up your mouth.* ❑ *My room needed a coat of paint to freshen it up.* ◼ PHRASAL VERB If you **freshen up**, you wash your hands and face and make yourself look neat and tidy. ❑ *After Martine had freshened up, they went for a long walk.*

fresh|er /frɛʃər/ (**freshers**) ◼ N-COUNT **Fresher** is the comparative form of **fresh**. ◼ N-COUNT [usu pl] **Freshers** are students who have just started their first year at a university or college. [BRIT, INFORMAL]

in AM, use **freshman**

fresh|ly /frɛʃli/ ADV [ADV -ed] If something is **freshly** made or done, it has been recently made or done. ❑ *...freshly baked bread.*

fresh|man /frɛʃmən/ (**freshmen**) N-COUNT In the United States, a **freshman** is a student who is in his or her first year at a high school or college.

fresh|water /frɛʃwɔːtər/ ◼ ADJ [ADJ n] A **freshwater** lake contains water that is not salty, usually in contrast to the sea. **Freshwater** creatures live in water that is not salty. ❑ *...Lake Balaton, the largest freshwater lake in Europe.* ◼ → See feature box at **water**

fret /frɛt/ (**frets, fretting, fretted**) ◼ V-T/V-I If you **fret** about something, you worry about it. ❑ *I was working all hours and constantly fretting about everyone else's problems.* ❑ *But congressional staffers fret that the project will eventually cost billions more.* ◼ N-COUNT The **frets** on a musical instrument such as a guitar are the raised lines across its neck.

fret|ful /frɛtfəl/ ADJ If someone is **fretful**, they behave in a way that shows that they are worried or unhappy about something. ❑ *Don't assume your baby automatically needs feeding if she's fretful.*

fret|work /frɛtwɜːrk/ N-UNCOUNT [oft N n] **Fretwork** is wood or metal that has been decorated by cutting pieces of it out to make a pattern.

Freud|ian /frɔɪdiən/ ADJ [usu ADJ n] **Freudian** means relating to the ideas and methods of the psychiatrist Freud, especially to his ideas about people's subconscious sexual feelings. ❑ *...the Freudian theory about daughters falling in love with their father.*

Freud|ian slip (**Freudian slips**) N-COUNT If someone accidentally says something that reveals their subconscious feelings, especially their sexual feelings, this is referred to as a **Freudian slip**.

Fri. Fri. is a written abbreviation for **Friday**.

fri|ar /fraɪər/ (**friars**) N-COUNT A **friar** is a member of one of several Catholic religious orders.

fric|tion /frɪkʃən/ (**frictions**) ◼ N-UNCOUNT [also N in pl] If there is **friction** between people, there is disagreement and argument between them. ❑ *Sara sensed that there had been friction between her parents.* ◼ N-UNCOUNT **Friction** is the force that makes it difficult for things to move freely when they are touching each other. ❑ *The pistons are graphite-coated to reduce friction.*

Fri|day ✦✦✦ /fraɪdeɪ, -di/ (**Fridays**) N-VAR **Friday** is the day after Thursday and before Saturday. ❑ *Mr. Cook is intending to go to the Middle East on Friday.* ❑ *...Friday November 6.*

fridge /frɪdʒ/ (**fridges**) N-COUNT A **fridge** is the same as a **refrigerator**. [INFORMAL]

friend /frɛnd/ (friends) **1** N-COUNT A **friend** is someone who you know well and like, but who is not related to you. ❑ *I had a long talk about this with my best friend.* ❑ *She never was a close friend of mine.* **2** N-COUNT If one country refers to another as a **friend**, they mean that the other country is not an enemy of theirs. ❑ *The president said that Japan is now a friend and international partner.* **3** N-PLURAL If you are **friends** with someone, you are their friend and they are yours. ❑ *I still wanted to be friends with Alison.* ❑ *We remained good friends.* **4** N-PLURAL; N-IN-NAMES The **friends** of a country, cause, organization, or a famous politician are the people and organizations who help and support them. ❑ *...the friends of Israel.* **5** PHRASE If you **make friends** with someone, you begin a friendship with them. You can also say that two people **make friends**. ❑ *He has made friends with the kids on the street.* ❑ *Dennis made friends easily.*

▬▬▬▬▬ COLLOCATIONS ▬▬▬▬▬
friend
NOUN
1
noun + **friend**: childhood, college, family, school, university
adjective + **friend**: best, close, dear, good, great; lifelong, long-time, old; loyal, true; female, male; mutual
5
verb + **friend**: become, make, remain, stay

friend|less /frɛndlɪs/ ADJ Someone who is **friendless** has no friends. ❑ *The boy was unhappy because he thought he was friendless.*

friend|ly ✦✧✧ /frɛndli/ (friendlier, friendliest, friendlies) **1** ADJ If someone is **friendly**, they behave in a pleasant, kind way, and like to be with other people. ❑ *Godfrey had been friendly to me.* ❑ *...a man with a pleasant, friendly face.* • **friend|li|ness** N-UNCOUNT ❑ *She also loves the friendliness of the people.* **2** ADJ [v-link ADJ] If you are **friendly** with someone, you like each other and enjoy spending time together. ❑ *I'm friendly with his mother.* **3** ADJ You can describe another country or their government as **friendly** when they have good relations with your own country rather than being an enemy. ❑ *...a worsening in relations between the two previously friendly countries.* **4** N-COUNT In sports, a **friendly** is a game which is not part of a competition, and is played for entertainment or practice, often without any serious effort to win. [BRIT]

in AM, use **exhibition game**

• ADJ [ADJ n] **Friendly** is also an adjective.

▬▬▬▬▬ USAGE ▬▬▬▬▬
friendly
Friendly is never an adverb. Don't say, for example, 'He behaved friendly.' Say 'He behaved **in a friendly way**.' *She smiled at him in a friendly way.*

-friendly /-frɛndli/ **1** COMB IN ADJ **-friendly** combines with nouns to form adjectives which describe things that are not harmful to the specified part of the natural world. ❑ *...environment-friendly technologies.* **2** COMB IN ADJ **-friendly** combines with nouns to form adjectives which describe things which are intended for or suitable for the specified person, especially things that are easy for them to understand, appreciate, or use. ❑ *...customer-friendly banking facilities.* **3** → see also **user-friendly**

friend|ly fire N-UNCOUNT If you come under **friendly fire** during a battle, you are accidentally shot at by people on your own side, rather than by your enemy. ❑ *An extraordinarily high percentage of allied casualties were caused by friendly fire.*

friend|ship ✦✧✧ /frɛndʃɪp/ (friendships) **1** N-VAR A **friendship** is a relationship between two or more friends. ❑ *Giving advice when it's not called for is the quickest way to end a good friendship.* ❑ *She struck up a close friendship with Desiree during the week of rehearsals.* **2** N-VAR **Friendship** is a relationship between two countries in which they help and support each other. ❑ *The president set the targets for the future to promote friendship with East Europe.* **3** N-UNCOUNT You use **friendship** to refer in a general way to the state of being friends, or the feelings that friends have for each other. ❑ *...a hobby which led to a whole new world of friendship and adventure.*

friend zone (friend zones) N-COUNT If you are in someone's **friend zone**, you are considered only as a friend by them, and not as a romantic partner. [INFORMAL] ❑ *I get along well with women, but I always end up in the friend zone.*

fries /fraɪz/ N-PLURAL **Fries** are long, thin pieces of potato fried in oil or fat.

frieze /friːz/ (friezes) **1** N-COUNT A **frieze** is a decoration high up on the walls of a room or just under the roof of a building. It consists of a long panel of carving or a long strip of paper with a picture or pattern on it. **2** → See also color supplement

frig|ate /frɪɡət/ (frigates) **1** N-COUNT A **frigate** is a fairly small ship owned by the navy that can move at fast speeds. Frigates are often used to protect other ships. **2** → See also color supplement

frig|ging /frɪɡɪŋ/ ADJ [ADJ n] **Frigging** is used by some people to emphasize what they are saying, especially when they are angry or annoyed about something. [INFORMAL, VULGAR, EMPHASIS]

fright /fraɪt/ (frights) **1** N-UNCOUNT **Fright** is a sudden feeling of fear, especially the fear that you feel when something unpleasant surprises you. ❑ *The steam pipes rattled suddenly, and Franklin jumped with fright.* ❑ *The birds smashed into the top of their cages in fright.* **2** N-COUNT A **fright** is an experience which makes you suddenly afraid. ❑ *The snake picked up its head and stuck out its tongue which gave everyone a fright.*

fright|en /fraɪtᵊn/ (frightens, frightening, frightened) **1** V-T If something or someone **frightens** you, they cause you to suddenly feel afraid, anxious, or nervous. ❑ *He knew that Soli was trying to frighten him, so he smiled to hide his fear.* **2** PHRASE If something **frightens the life out of** you, **frightens the wits out of** you, or **frightens** you **out of your wits**, it causes you to feel suddenly afraid or gives you a very unpleasant shock. [EMPHASIS] ❑ *Fairground rides are intended to frighten the life out of you.*

▶ **frighten away** also **frighten off** **1** PHRASAL VERB If you **frighten away** a person or animal or **frighten** them **off**, you make them afraid so that they run away or stay some distance away from you. ❑ *The fishermen said the company's seismic survey was frightening away fish.* **2** PHRASAL VERB To **frighten** someone **away** or **frighten** them **off** means to make them nervous so that they decide not to become involved with a particular person or activity. ❑ *Repossessions have frightened buyers off.*
▶ **frighten off** → see **frighten away**

fright|ened /fraɪtᵊnd/ ADJ If you are **frightened**, you are anxious or afraid, often because of something that has just happened or that you think may happen. ❑ *She was frightened of making a mistake.*

fright|en|ing /fraɪtᵊnɪŋ/ ADJ If something is **frightening**, it makes you feel afraid, anxious, or nervous. ❑ *It was a very frightening experience and they were very courageous.* • **fright|en|ing|ly** ADV ❑ *The country is frighteningly close to possessing nuclear weapons.*

fright|ful /fraɪtfᵊl/ **1** ADJ **Frightful** means very bad or unpleasant. [OLD-FASHIONED] ❑ *My father was unable to talk about the war, it was so frightful.* **2** ADJ [ADJ n] **Frightful** is used to emphasize the extent or degree of something, usually something bad. [INFORMAL, OLD-FASHIONED, EMPHASIS] ❑ *He got himself into a frightful muddle.*

frig|id /frɪdʒɪd/ **1** ADJ **Frigid** means extremely cold. [FORMAL] ❑ *A snowstorm hit the West today, bringing with it frigid temperatures.* **2** ADJ [usu v-link ADJ] If someone, especially a woman, is described as **frigid**, they find it difficult to become sexually aroused. Frigid is often used to show disapproval.

frill /frɪl/ (frills) **1** N-COUNT A **frill** is a long narrow strip of cloth or paper with many folds in it, which is attached to something as a decoration. ❑ *...curtains with frills.* **2** N-COUNT If you describe something as having no **frills**, you mean that it has no extra features, but is acceptable or good if you want something simple. [APPROVAL]

frilled /frɪld/ ADJ [ADJ n] A **frilled** item of clothing is decorated with a frill or frills.

frilly /frɪli/ (frillier, frilliest) ADJ [usu ADJ n] **Frilly** items of clothing or fabric have a lot of frills on them. ❑ *...maids in frilly aprons.*

fringe /frɪndʒ/ (**fringes**) **1** N-COUNT A **fringe** is a decoration attached to clothes, or other objects such as curtains, consisting of a row of hanging strips or threads. ❑ *The jacket had leather fringes.* **2** N-COUNT To be on the **fringe** or the **fringes** of a place means to be on the outside edge of it, or to be in one of the parts that are farthest from its center. ❑ *...Black townships located on the fringes of the city.* **3** N-COUNT The **fringe** or the **fringes** of an activity or organization are its less important, least typical, or most extreme parts, rather than its main and central part. ❑ *The party remained on the fringe of the political scene until last year.* **4** N-COUNT A **fringe** is hair which is cut so that it hangs over your forehead. [BRIT]

| in AM, use **bangs** |

5 ADJ [ADJ n] **Fringe** groups or events are less important or popular than other related groups or events. ❑ *The monarchists are a small fringe group who quarrel fiercely among themselves.*

fringe ben|efit (**fringe benefits**) N-COUNT **Fringe benefits** are extra things that some people get from their job in addition to their salary, for example, a car. [BUSINESS] ❑ *...insecure, badly paid jobs without any of the fringe benefits such as healthcare.*

fringed /frɪndʒd/ **1** ADJ [ADJ n] **Fringed** clothes, curtains, or lampshades are decorated with fringes. ❑ *Emma wore a fringed scarf round her neck.* **2** ADJ [v-link ADJ with n] If a place or object is **fringed with** something, that thing forms a border around it or is situated along its edges. ❑ *Her eyes were large and brown and fringed with incredibly long lashes.*

Fris|bee /frɪzbi/ (**Frisbees**) N-COUNT A **Frisbee** is a light plastic disk that one person throws to another as a game. [TRADEMARK]

frisk /frɪsk/ (**frisks, frisking, frisked**) V-T If someone **frisks** you, they search you, usually with their hands in order to see if you are hiding a weapon or something else such as drugs in your clothes. ❑ *Drago pushed him up against the wall and frisked him.*

frisky /frɪski/ (**friskier, friskiest**) ADJ A **frisky** animal or person is energetic and playful, and may be difficult to control. ❑ *His horse was feeling frisky, and he had to hold the reins tightly.*

fris|son /frisɒn/ (**frissons**) N-COUNT A **frisson** is a short, sudden feeling of excitement or fear. [LITERARY] ❑ *A frisson of apprehension rippled around the theater.*

frit|ter /frɪtər/ (**fritters, frittering, frittered**) N-COUNT [usu n N] **Fritters** are round pieces of fruit, vegetables, or meat that are dipped in batter and fried. ❑ *...apple fritters.*

▶ **fritter away** PHRASAL VERB If someone **fritters away** time or money, they waste it on unimportant or unnecessary things. ❑ *The firm soon started frittering away the cash it was generating.* ❑ *I seem to fritter my time away.*

fri|vol|ity /frɪvɒlɪti/ (**frivolities**) N-VAR If you refer to an activity as **frivolity**, you think that it is amusing and rather silly, rather than serious and sensible. ❑ *There is a serious message at the core of all this frivolity.* ❑ *He was one of my most able pupils, but far too easily distracted by frivolities.*

frivo|lous /frɪvələs/ **1** ADJ If you describe someone as **frivolous**, you mean they behave in a silly or light-hearted way, rather than being serious and sensible. ❑ *I just decided I was a bit too frivolous to be a doctor.* **2** ADJ If you describe an activity as **frivolous**, you disapprove of it because it is not useful and wastes time or money. [DISAPPROVAL] ❑ *The group says it wants politicians to stop wasting public money on what it believes are frivolous projects.*

frizz /frɪz/ N-UNCOUNT **Frizz** is frizzy hair. ❑ *Manic brushing will only cause frizz.*

friz|zy /frɪzi/ (**frizzier, frizziest**) ADJ **Frizzy** hair is very tightly curled. ❑ *Carol's hair had a slightly frizzy perm.*

fro /froʊ/ **to and fro** → see **to** ①

frock /frɒk/ (**frocks**) N-COUNT A **frock** is a dress. [OLD-FASHIONED]

frock coat (**frock coats**) also **frock-coat** N-COUNT A **frock coat** was a long coat that was worn by men in the 19th century.

frog /frɒg/ (**frogs**) N-COUNT A **frog** is a small creature with smooth skin, big eyes, and long back legs which it uses for jumping. Frogs usually live near water.

frog|man /frɒgmən/ (**frogmen**) N-COUNT A **frogman** is someone whose job involves diving and working underwater, especially in order to mend or search for something. Frogmen wear special rubber suits and shoes, and carry equipment to help them to breathe underwater.

frog-march (**frog-marches, frog-marching, frog-marched**) also **frogmarch** V-T If you **are frog-marched** somewhere, someone takes you there by force, holding you by the arms or another part of your body so that you have to walk along with them. ❑ *He was frog-marched through the kitchen and out into the yard.* ❑ *They arrested the men and frog-marched them to the local police station.*

fro-ing → see **to-ing and fro-ing**

frol|ic /frɒlɪk/ (**frolics, frolicking, frolicked**) V-I When people or animals **frolic**, they play or move in a lively, happy way. ❑ *Tourists sunbathe and frolic in the ocean.*

FROM

① MENTIONING THE SOURCE, ORIGIN, OR STARTING POINT
② MENTIONING A RANGE OF TIMES, AMOUNTS, OR THINGS
③ MENTIONING SOMETHING YOU WANT TO PREVENT OR AVOID

---

① **from** ♦♦♦ /frəm, STRONG frʌm/ **1** PREP If something comes **from** a particular person or thing, or if you get something **from** them, they give it to you or they are the source of it. ❑ *He appealed for information from anyone who saw the attackers.* ❑ *...an anniversary present from his wife.* **2** PREP Someone who comes **from** a particular place lives in that place or originally lived there. Something that comes **from** a particular place was made in that place. ❑ *...an art dealer from Zurich.* ❑ *Katy Jones is nineteen and comes from Biloxi.* **3** PREP A person **from** a particular organization works for that organization. ❑ *...a representative from the Israeli embassy.* **4** PREP If someone or something moves or is moved **from** a place, they leave it or are removed, so that they are no longer there. ❑ *The guests watched as she fled from the room.* **5** PREP If you take one thing or person **from** another, you move that thing or person so that they are no longer with the other or attached to the other. ❑ *In many bone transplants, bone can be taken from other parts of the patient's body.* **6** PREP If you take something **from** an amount, you reduce the amount by that much. ❑ *The $103 is deducted from Mrs. Adams' salary.* **7** PREP **From** is used in expressions such as **away from** or **absent from** to say that someone or something is not present in a place where they are usually found. ❑ *Her husband worked away from home a lot.* **8** PREP If you return **from** a place or an activity, you return after being in that place or doing that activity. ❑ *My son has just returned from Amsterdam.* **9** PREP If you are back **from** a place or activity, you have left it and have returned to your former place. ❑ *Elaine was just back from work when he called.* **10** PREP If you see or hear something **from** a particular place, you are in that place when you see it or hear it. ❑ *Visitors see the painting from behind a plate glass window.* **11** PREP [V PREP n] If something hangs or sticks out **from** an object, it is attached to it or held by it. ❑ *Hanging from his right wrist is a heavy gold bracelet.* ❑ *...large fans hanging from ceilings.* **12** PREP [amount PREP n] You can use **from** when giving distances. For example, if a place is fifty miles **from** another place, the distance between the two places is fifty miles. ❑ *...a small park only a few hundred yards from Zurich's main shopping center.* ❑ *How far is it from here?* **13** PREP If a road or railroad line goes **from** one place to another, you can travel along it between the two places. ❑ *...the road from St. Petersburg to Tallinn.* **14** PREP [v PREP n] **From** is used, especially in the expression **made from**, to say what substance has been used to make something. ❑ *...bread made from white flour.* **15** PREP If something changes **from** one thing to another, it stops being the first thing and becomes the second thing. ❑ *The expression on his face changed from sympathy to surprise.* ❑ *Unemployment has fallen from 7.5 to 7.2%.* **16** PREP [PREP n/-ing] You use **from** after some verbs and nouns when mentioning the cause of something. ❑ *The problem simply resulted from a difference of opinion.* ❑ *They really do get pleasure from spending money on other people.* **17** PREP You use **from** when you are giving the reason for an opinion. ❑ *She knew from experience that Dave was about to tell her the truth.* ❑ *He sensed from the expression on her face that she had something to say.*

from

USAGE

from

① Don't use 'from' to say that something started to happen at a particular time in the past and is still happening now. Don't say, for example, 'I have lived here from 1984.' Say 'I have lived here **since** 1984.' *He has been a teacher since 1998.*

② Don't use 'from' to say who wrote a book, play, or piece of music. Don't say, for example, 'Have you seen any plays from Ibsen?' You say 'Have you seen any plays **by** Ibsen?' *We listened to some pieces by Mozart.*

② **from** ♦♦♦ /frəm, STRONG frʌm/ ◼ PREP You can use **from** when you are talking about the beginning of a period of time. ❏ *She studied painting from 1926 and also worked as a commercial artist.* ❏ *Breakfast is available to travelers from 6 a.m.* ◻ PREP [PREP n/-ing] You say **from** one thing **to** another when you are stating the range of things that are possible, or when saying that the range of things includes everything in a certain category. ❏ *There are 94 countries represented in Barcelona, from Algeria to Zimbabwe.*

③ **from** ♦♦♦ /frəm, STRONG frʌm/ PREP **From** is used after verbs with meanings such as 'protect,' 'free,' 'keep,' and 'prevent' to introduce the action that does not happen, or that someone does not want to happen. ❏ *Such laws could protect the consumer from harmful or dangerous remedies.*

In addition to the uses shown here, **from** is used in phrasal verbs such as 'date from' and 'grow away from.'

fro|mage frais /froʊmɑʒ freɪ/ (**fromage frais**) N-VAR **Fromage frais** is a thick, creamy dessert that is made from milk and often flavored with fruit. A **fromage frais** is a small pot of fromage frais.

frond /frɒnd/ (**fronds**) N-COUNT [usu with supp] A **frond** is a long leaf which has an edge divided into lots of thin parts. ❏ *...palm fronds.*

front ♦♦♦ /frʌnt/ (**fronts**) ◼ N-COUNT The **front** of something is the part of it that faces you, or that faces forward, or that you normally see or use. ❏ *One man sat in an armchair, and the other sat on the front of the desk.* ❏ *Stand at the front of the line.* ◻ N-COUNT The **front** of a building is the side or part of it that faces the street. ❏ *Attached to the front of the house, there was a large veranda.* ◼ N-COUNT In a war, the **front** is a line where two opposing armies are facing each other. ❏ *Sonja's husband is fighting at the front.* ◻ → see also **front line** ◼ N-COUNT If you say that something is happening on a particular **front**, you mean that it is happening with regard to a particular situation or field of activity. ❏ *...research across a wide academic front.* ◼ N-COUNT If someone puts on a particular kind of **front**, they pretend to have a particular quality. ❏ *Michael kept up a brave front both to the world and in his home.* ◼ N-COUNT An organization or activity that is a **front** for one that is illegal or secret is used to hide it. ❏ *...a firm later identified by the police as a front for crime syndicates.* ◼ N-COUNT In relation to the weather, a **front** is a line where a mass of cold air meets a mass of warm air. ❏ *The snow signaled the arrival of a front, and a high-pressure area seemed to be settling in.* ◼ N-SING A person's or animal's **front** is the part of their body between their head and their legs that is on the opposite side to their back. ❏ *When baby is lying on his front, hold something so that he has to raise his head to see it.* ◼ ADJ [ADJ n] **Front** is used to refer to the side or part of something that is toward the front or nearest to the front. ❏ *I went out there on the front porch.* ❏ *She was only six and still missing her front teeth.* ◼ ADJ [ADJ n] The **front page** of a newspaper is the outside of the first page, where the main news stories are printed. ❏ *The front page carries a photograph of the two foreign ministers.* ◼ → see also **front-page** ◼ PHRASE If a person or thing is **in front**, they are ahead of others in a moving group, or further forward than someone or something else. ❏ *Officers will crack down on lunatic motorists who speed or drive too close to the car in front.* ◼ PHRASE Someone who is **in front in a** competition or contest at a particular point is winning at that point. ❏ *For once, he was in front in the jockeys' title race.* ◼ PHRASE If someone or something is **in front of** a particular thing, they are facing it, ahead of it, or close to the front part of it. ❏ *She sat down in front of her dressing-table mirror to look at herself.* ❏ *Something darted out in front of my car, and my car hit it.* ◼ PHRASE

front woman

If you do or say something **in front of** someone else, you do or say it when they are present. ❏ *They never argued in front of their children.*

front|age /frʌntɪdʒ/ (**frontages**) N-COUNT [also no det] A **frontage** of a building is a wall which faces a public place such as a street or a river. ❏ *The restaurant has a river frontage.*

front|al /frʌntəl/ ADJ **Frontal** means relating to or involving the front of something, for example, the front of an army, a vehicle, or the brain. [FORMAL] ❏ *Military leaders are not expecting a frontal assault by the rebels.*

front and cen|ter ADJ If a topic or question is **front and center**, a lot of attention is being paid to it or a lot of people are talking about it. [AM] ❏ *I think the media has done an extraordinary job of keeping the story front and center.*

front burn|er N-SING [usu on the N] If an issue is on the **front burner**, it receives a lot of attention because it is considered to be more urgent or important than other issues. Compare **back burner**. ❏ *It helps to put an important issue back on the front burner.*

front desk N-SING The **front desk** in a hotel is the desk or office that books rooms for people and answers their questions. [mainly AM] ❏ *Call the hotel's front desk and cancel your early morning wake-up call.*

front door (**front doors**) N-COUNT The **front door** of a house or other building is the main door, which is usually in the wall that faces a street.

fron|tier /frʌntɪər, frɒn-/ (**frontiers**) ◼ N-COUNT When you are talking about the western part of America before the twentieth century, you use **frontier** to refer to the area beyond the part settled by Europeans. ❏ *...a far-flung outpost on the frontier.* ◻ N-COUNT The **frontiers** of something, especially knowledge, are the limits to which it extends. ❏ *...pushing back the frontiers of science.* ◼ N-COUNT A **frontier** is a border between two countries. ❏ *It wasn't difficult then to cross the frontier.*

fron|tiers|man /frʌntɪərzmən/ (**frontiersmen**) N-COUNT A **frontiersman** is a man who lives near a frontier, used especially of men who used to live on the U.S. frontier. [mainly AM] ❏ *...a manuscript about the dying breed of frontiersman and their harsh life in Canada's northern wilderness.*

fron|tis|piece /frʌntɪspis/ (**frontispieces**) N-COUNT [usu sing] The **frontispiece** of a book is a picture at the beginning, opposite the page with the title on.

front line (**front lines**) also **front-line** ◼ N-COUNT The **front line** is the place where two opposing armies are facing each other and where fighting is going on. ❏ *...a massive concentration of soldiers on the front line.* ◻ PHRASE Someone who is **in the front line** has to play a very important part in defending or achieving something. ❏ *Information officers are in the front line of putting across government policies.*

front man (**front men**) N-COUNT [oft N for n] If you say that someone is a **front man** for a group or organization, you mean that their role is to represent and give a good impression of it to the public, especially when it is not very respectable or popular. [DISAPPROVAL] ❏ *He is the company's front man in L.A.*

front of|fice (**front offices**) N-COUNT [usu sing] The **front office** of a company or other organization is the room or rooms where staff deal with the public. The executives of a company or other organization are sometimes referred to collectively as the **front office**. [AM] ❏ *All requests must be made in writing on a Change of Program form, which is available at the front office of the Cultural Center.* ❏ *Several of his front-office executives view Piniella as the best candidate.*

front-page ADJ [ADJ n] A **front-page** article or picture appears on the front page of a newspaper because it is very important or interesting. ❏ *...a front-page article in last week's paper.*

front-runner (**front-runners**) N-COUNT In a competition or contest, the **front-runner** is the person who seems most likely to win it. ❏ *Neither of the front-runners in the presidential election is a mainstream politician.*

front woman (**front women**) N-COUNT [oft N for n] If you say that someone is a **front woman** for a group or organization, you mean that their role is to represent and give a good impression of it to the public, especially when it is not very respectable or popular. [DISAPPROVAL] ❏ *She is the front woman*

frost /frɔst/ (frosts, frosting, frosted) **1** N-VAR When there is frost or a frost, the temperature outside falls below freezing point and the ground becomes covered in ice crystals. ☐ *There is frost on the ground and snow is forecast.* **2** V-T If you frost a cake, you cover and decorate it with frosting. [AM] ☐ *She was frosting the cupcakes while we talked.*

frost|bite /frɔstbaɪt/ N-UNCOUNT Frostbite is a condition in which parts of your body, such as your fingers or toes, become seriously damaged as a result of being very cold. ☐ *The survivors suffered from frostbite.*

frost|bitten /frɔstbɪtᵊn/ ADJ If a person or a part of their body is frostbitten, they are suffering from frostbite.

frost|ed /frɔstɪd/ **1** ADJ Frosted glass is glass that you cannot see through clearly. ☐ *The top half of the door to his office was of frosted glass.* **2** ADJ Frosted means covered with frost. ☐ *...the frosted trees.* **3** ADJ Frosted means covered with something that looks like frost. ☐ *...frosted blue eye shadow.* **4** ADJ Frosted means covered with frosting. [AM] ☐ *...a plate of frosted cupcakes.*

frost|ing /frɔstɪŋ/ N-UNCOUNT Frosting is a sweet substance made from powdered sugar that is used to cover and decorate cakes. [AM] ☐ *...a huge pastry with green frosting on it.*

frosty /frɔsti/ (frostier, frostiest) **1** ADJ If the weather is frosty, the temperature is below freezing. ☐ *...sharp, frosty nights.* **2** ADJ You describe the ground or an object as frosty when it is covered with frost. ☐ *The street was deserted except for a cat lifting its paws off the frosty stones.*

froth /frɔθ/ (froths, frothing, frothed) **1** N-UNCOUNT Froth is a mass of small bubbles on the surface of a liquid. ☐ *...the froth of bubbles on the top of a glass of beer.* **2** V-I If a liquid froths, small bubbles appear on its surface. ☐ *The sea froths over my feet.*

frothy /frɔθi/ (frothier, frothiest) ADJ [usu ADJ n] A frothy liquid has lots of bubbles on its surface. ☐ *...frothy milk shakes.*

frown /fraʊn/ (frowns, frowning, frowned) **1** V-I When someone frowns, their eyebrows become drawn together, because they are annoyed, worried, or puzzled, or because they are concentrating. ☐ *Nancy shook her head, frowning.* ☐ *He frowned at her anxiously.* • N-COUNT Frown is also a noun. ☐ *There was a deep frown on the boy's face.* **2** → See feature box at polite

▶ **frown upon** also **frown on** PHRASAL VERB If something is frowned upon or is frowned on, people disapprove of it. ☐ *This practice is frowned upon as being wasteful.*

froze /froʊz/ Froze is the past tense of freeze.

fro|zen /froʊzᵊn/ **1** Frozen is the past participle of freeze. **2** ADJ If the ground is frozen, it has become very hard because the weather is very cold. ☐ *It was bitterly cold now and the ground was frozen hard.* **3** ADJ Frozen food has been preserved by being kept at a very low temperature. ☐ *Frozen fish is a very healthy convenience food.* **4** ADJ If you say that you are frozen, or a part of your body is frozen, you are emphasizing that you feel very cold. [EMPHASIS] ☐ *He put one hand up to his frozen face.* ☐ *I'm frozen out here.* • PHRASE Frozen stiff means the same as frozen.

fruc|tose /frʌktoʊs, -koʊz/ N-UNCOUNT Fructose is a sweet substance which occurs naturally in fruit and vegetables. It is sometimes used to make food sweeter.

fru|gal /fruːgᵊl/ **1** ADJ People who are frugal or who live frugal lives do not spend much money on themselves. ☐ *She lives a frugal life.* • **fru|gal|ity** /fruːgæliti/ N-UNCOUNT ☐ *We must practice the strictest frugality and economy.* **2** ADJ A frugal meal is small and not expensive. ☐ *The diet was frugal: cheese and water, rice and beans.*

fruit ♦♦♢ /fruːt/ (fruit, fruits, fruiting, fruited)

The plural form is usually **fruit**, but can also be **fruits**.

1 N-VAR Fruit or a fruit is something which grows on a tree or bush and which contains seeds or a pit covered by a substance that you can eat. ☐ *Fresh fruit and vegetables provide fiber and vitamins.* ☐ *...bananas and other tropical fruits.* **2** V-I If a plant fruits, it produces fruit. ☐ *The scientists will study the variety of trees and observe which are fruiting.* **3** N-COUNT The fruits or the fruit of someone's work or activity are the good things that result from it. ☐ *The team has really worked hard and we're all enjoying the fruits of that labor.* **4** → see also kiwi fruit **5** PHRASE If the effort that you put into something or a particular way of doing something bears fruit, it is successful and produces good results. ☐ *Eleanor's work among the women will, I trust, bear fruit.*

USAGE

fruit
Don't use 'fruits' to talk about several oranges, bananas, etc. Use **some fruit**. For example, don't say 'I'm going to the market to buy some fruits.' Say 'I'm going to the market to buy **some fruit**.' *...a table with some fruit on it.*

fruit bowl (fruit bowls) N-COUNT A fruit bowl is a large bowl in which fruit is kept and displayed.

fruit|cake /fruːtkeɪk/ (fruitcakes) also **fruit cake** **1** N-VAR A fruitcake is a cake that contains raisins, currants, and other dried fruit. **2** N-COUNT If you refer to someone as a fruitcake, you mean that they are crazy or that their behavior is very strange. [INFORMAL, DISAPPROVAL]

fruit cock|tail (fruit cocktails) N-VAR Fruit cocktail is a mixture of pieces of different kinds of fruit eaten as part of a meal.

fruit fly (fruit flies) N-COUNT Fruit flies are very small flies which eat fruit and rotting plants.

fruit|ful /fruːtfəl/ ADJ Something that is fruitful produces good and useful results. ☐ *We had a long, happy, fruitful relationship.*

frui|tion /fruːɪʃᵊn/ N-UNCOUNT If something comes to fruition, it starts to succeed and produce the results that were intended or hoped for. [FORMAL] ☐ *These plans take time to come to fruition.*

fruit|less /fruːtlɪs/ ADJ Fruitless actions, events, or efforts do not achieve anything at all. ☐ *It was a fruitless search.*

fruit ma|chine (fruit machines) N-COUNT A fruit machine is a machine used for gambling. You put money into it and if a particular combination of symbols, especially fruit, appears, you win money. [BRIT]

in AM, use **slot machine**

fruit sal|ad (fruit salads) N-VAR Fruit salad is a mixture of pieces of different kinds of fruit. It is usually eaten as a dessert.

fruity /fruːti/ (fruitier, fruitiest) **1** ADJ Something that is fruity smells or tastes of fruit. ☐ *This shampoo smells fruity and leaves the hair beautifully silky.* **2** ADJ A fruity voice or laugh is pleasantly rich and deep. ☐ *Jerrold laughed again, a solid, fruity laugh.*

frumpy /frʌmpi/ (frumpier, frumpiest) **1** ADJ If you describe someone or someone's clothes as frumpy, you mean that their clothes are dull and not fashionable. [DISAPPROVAL] ☐ *...bulky, frumpy clothes.* **2** → See feature box at fashion

frus|trate ♦♢♢ /frʌstreɪt/ (frustrates, frustrating, frustrated) **1** V-T If something frustrates you, it upsets or angers you because you are unable to do anything about the problems it creates. ☐ *These questions frustrated me.* • **frus|trat|ed** ADJ ☐ *Roberta felt frustrated and angry.* • **frus|tra|tion** /frʌstreɪʃᵊn/ (frustrations) N-VAR ☐ *The results show the level of frustration among hospital doctors.* **2** V-T If someone or something frustrates a plan or attempt to do something, they prevent it from succeeding. ☐ *The government has deliberately frustrated his efforts to gain work permits for his foreign staff.*

frus|trat|ing /frʌstreɪtɪŋ/ ADJ Something that is frustrating annoys you or makes you angry because you cannot do anything about the problems it causes. ☐ *The current situation is very frustrating for us.*

fry ♦♦♢ /fraɪ/ (fries, frying, fried) **1** V-T When you fry food, you cook it in a pan that contains hot fat or oil. ☐ *Fry the breadcrumbs until golden brown.* **2** N-PLURAL Fries are the same as French fries.

fry|er /fraɪər/ (fryers) N-COUNT [oft n n] A fryer is a type of deep pan which you can use to fry food in hot oil.

fry|ing pan (frying pans) N-COUNT A frying pan is a flat metal pan with a long handle, in which you fry food.

ft. ft. is a written abbreviation for feet or foot. ☐ *Flying at 1,000 ft., he heard a peculiar noise from the rotors.*

fuch|sia /fyuʃə/ (fuchsias) N-VAR A **fuchsia** is a plant or a small bush which has pink, purple, or white flowers. The flowers hang downward, with their outer petals curved backward.

fuck /fʌk/ (fucks, fucking, fucked)

> Fuck is a vulgar and offensive word.

1 EXCLAM **Fuck** is used to express anger or annoyance. [OFFENSIVE, VULGAR, FEELINGS] **2** V-RECIP To **fuck** someone means to have sex with them. [OFFENSIVE, VULGAR]
▶ **fuck off** PHRASAL VERB [usu imper] Telling someone to **fuck off** is an insulting way of telling them to go away. [OFFENSIVE, VULGAR]

fuck|er /fʌkər/ (fuckers) N-COUNT If someone calls a person a **fucker**, they are insulting them. [OFFENSIVE, VULGAR, DISAPPROVAL]

fuck|ing /fʌkɪŋ/ ADJ [ADJ n] **Fucking** is used by some people to emphasize a word or phrase, especially when they are feeling angry or annoyed. [OFFENSIVE, VULGAR, EMPHASIS] • ADV [ADV adj] **Fucking** is also an adverb.

fud|dled /fʌdəld/ ADJ Someone who is **fuddled** cannot think clearly, for example, because they are very tired or slightly drunk. ❑ *Fuddled by brandy, her brain fumbled over the events of the night.*

fuddy-duddy /fʌdi dʌdi, dʌdi/ (fuddy-duddies) N-COUNT If you describe someone as a **fuddy-duddy**, you are criticizing or making fun of them because they are old-fashioned in their appearance or attitudes. [OLD-FASHIONED, DISAPPROVAL] ❑ *He didn't want all those old fuddy-duddies around.*

fudge /fʌdʒ/ (fudges, fudging, fudged) **1** N-UNCOUNT **Fudge** is a soft brown candy that is made from butter, cream, and sugar. **2** V-T If you **fudge** something, you avoid making a clear and definite decision, distinction, or statement about it. ❑ *Both have fudged their calculations and avoided specifics.*

fuel ♦♦◊ /fyuəl/ (fuels, fueling or fuelling, fueled or fuelled) **1** N-MASS **Fuel** is a substance such as coal, oil, or gasoline that is burned to provide heat or power. ❑ *They ran out of fuel.* **2** V-T To **fuel** a situation means to make it become worse or more intense. ❑ *The result will inevitably fuel speculation about the prime minister's future.*

fuel cell (fuel cells) N-COUNT [oft N n] A **fuel cell** is a device, similar to a battery, that converts chemicals into electricity. ❑ *Instead of exhaust fumes, the fuel-cell car produces soap and water.*

fueled /fyuəld/ also **fuelled** ADJ [v-link ADJ by n] A machine or vehicle that **is fueled by** a particular substance works by burning that substance. ❑ *She's cooking on a stove fueled by dried animal dung.*

fuel in|jec|tion N-UNCOUNT **Fuel injection** is a system in the engines of some vehicles which forces fuel directly into the part of the engine where it is burned.

fuel rod (fuel rods) N-COUNT **Fuel rods** are metal tubes containing nuclear fuel. They are used in some nuclear reactors.

fu|gi|tive /fyudʒɪtɪv/ (fugitives) N-COUNT A **fugitive** is someone who is running away or hiding, usually in order to avoid being caught by the police. ❑ *The rebel leader was a fugitive from justice.*

fugue /fyug/ (fugues) N-COUNT A **fugue** is a piece of music that begins with a simple tune which is then repeated by other voices or instrumental parts with small variations. [TECHNICAL]

SUFFIX

-ful
forms nouns that refer to the amount of a substance that something contains or can contain. *For example, a handful of sand is the amount of sand that you can hold in your hand.*

---

ful|crum /fʊlkrəm/ N-SING [oft N of n] If you say that someone or something **is the fulcrum** of an activity or situation, you mean that they have a very important effect on what happens. [FORMAL] ❑ *The decision is the strategic fulcrum of the Budget.*

ful|fill ♦◊◊ /fʊlfɪl/ (fulfills, fulfilling, fulfilled)

> in BRIT, also use **fulfil**

1 V-T If you **fulfill** something such as a promise, dream, or hope, you do what you said or hoped you would do. ❑ *The president fulfilled his promise of announcing a date for the referendum.* **2** V-T To **fulfill** a task, role, or requirement means to do or be what is required, necessary, or expected. ❑ *Without them you will not be able to fulfill the tasks you have before you.* **3** V-T If something **fulfills** you, or if you **fulfill** yourself, you feel happy and satisfied with what you are doing or with what you have achieved. ❑ *The war was the biggest thing in her life and nothing after that quite fulfilled her.* • **ful|filled** ADJ ❑ *She has courageously continued to lead a fulfilled life.* • **ful|fil|ling** ADJ ❑ *...a fulfilling career.*

SYNONYMS

fulfill
VERB
1
carry out: *Commitments have been made with very little intention of carrying them out.*
perform: *We're looking for people who have performed outstanding acts of bravery.*
execute: *We are going to execute our campaign plan to the letter.*
2
comply with: *The commander said that the army would comply with the ceasefire.*
meet: *Only a third of the candidates met the entry requirements.*
satisfy: *The procedures should satisfy certain basic requirements.*

---

ful|fill|ment /fʊlfɪlmənt/ **1** N-UNCOUNT **Fulfillment** is a feeling of satisfaction that you get from doing or achieving something, especially something useful. ❑ *...professional fulfillment.* **2** N-UNCOUNT The **fulfillment** of a promise, threat, request, hope, or duty is the event or act of it happening or being made to happen. ❑ *Visiting Angkor was the fulfillment of a childhood dream.*

FULL

① CONTAINING AS MANY PEOPLE/THINGS AS POSSIBLE
② COMPLETE, INCLUDING THE MAXIMUM POSSIBLE
③ OTHER USES

---

① **full** ♦♦♦ /fʊl/ (fuller, fullest) **1** ADJ If something is **full**, it contains as much of a substance or as many objects as it can. ❑ *Once the container is full, it stays shut until you turn it clockwise.* **2** ADJ [v-link ADJ of n] If a place or thing **is full of** things or people, it contains a large number of them. ❑ *The case was full of clothes.* ❑ *The streets are still full of debris from two nights of rioting.* **3** ADJ You say that a place or vehicle is **full** when there is no space left in it for any more people or things. ❑ *The parking lot was full when I left about 10:45.* ❑ *They stay here a few hours before being sent to refugee camps, which are now almost full.* **4** ADJ [v-link ADJ] If your hands or arms are **full**, you are carrying or holding as much as you can carry. ❑ *Sylvia entered, her arms full of packages.* **5** ADJ [v-link ADJ] If you feel **full**, you have eaten or drunk so much that you do not want anything else. ❑ *It's healthy to eat when I'm hungry and to stop when I'm full.* • **full|ness** N-UNCOUNT ❑ *High fiber diets give the feeling of fullness.*

② **full** ♦♦♦ /fʊl/ (fuller, fullest)
→ Please look at meanings **12** – **14** to see if the expression you are looking for is shown under another headword.

1 ADJ [v-link ADJ of n] If someone or something **is full of** a particular feeling or quality, they have a lot of it. ❑ *I feel full of confidence and so open to possibilities.* ❑ *Mom's face was full of pain.* **2** ADJ [ADJ n] You use **full** before a noun to indicate that you are referring to all the details, things, or people that it can possibly include. ❑ *Full details will be sent to you once your application has been accepted.* ❑ *May I have your full name?* **3** ADJ [ADJ n] **Full** is used to describe a sound, light, or physical force which is being produced with the greatest possible power or intensity. ❑ *From his study came the sound of Mahler, playing at full volume.* ❑ *Officials say the operation will be carried out in full daylight.* **4** ADJ [ADJ n] You use **full** to emphasize the completeness, intensity, or extent of something. [EMPHASIS] ❑ *We should conserve oil and gas by making full use of other energy sources.* ❑ *The lane leading to the farm was in full view of the house windows.* **5** ADJ A **full** statement or report contains a lot of information and detail. ❑ *They gave a full account of their meeting with the president.* **6** ADJ If you say that someone has or leads a **full** life, you approve of the fact that they are always busy and do a lot of different things. [APPROVAL] ❑ *You will be successful in whatever you do and you will have a very full and interesting life.* **7** ADJ [ADJ n] You use **full** to refer to something which gives you all the rights, status, or importance for a particular position or activity, rather than just some of them. ❑ *How did the meeting go, did you get your full membership?* **8** ADV [ADV prep] You use **full** to emphasize the force or directness with which someone or something is hit or looked at. [EMPHASIS] ❑ *She kissed him full on the mouth.* **9** PHRASE You say that something has been done or described **in full** when everything that was necessary has been done or described. ❑ *The medical experts have yet to report in full.* **10** PHRASE If you say that a person **knows full well** that something is true, especially something unpleasant, you are emphasizing that they are definitely aware of it, although they may behave as if they are not. [EMPHASIS] ❑ *He knew full well he'd be ashamed of himself later.* **11** PHRASE Something that is done or experienced **to the full** is done to as great an extent as is possible. ❑ *She probably has a good mind, which should be used to the full.* **12 full blast** → see **blast** **13 to have your hands full** → see **hand** ① **14 in full swing** → see **swing**

③ **full** ✦✦✦ /fʊl/ (**fuller**, **fullest**) **1** ADJ [ADJ n] A **full** flavor is strong and rich. ❑ *Italian plum tomatoes have a full flavor, and are best for cooking.* **2** ADJ If you describe a part of someone's body as **full**, you mean that it is rounded and quite large. ❑ *The Juno Collection specializes in large sizes for ladies with a fuller figure.* **3** ADJ A **full** skirt or sleeve is wide and has been made from a lot of fabric. ❑ *My wedding dress has a very full skirt so I need to wear a good quality slip.* • **full|ness** N-UNCOUNT ❑ *The coat has raglan sleeves, and is cut to give fullness at the back.* **4** ADJ When there is a **full** moon, the moon appears as a bright, complete circle. ❑ *...those nights when the moon is full.*

full|back /fʊlbæk/ (**fullbacks**) **1** N-COUNT In football, a **fullback** is a player on the attacking team whose position is behind the quarterback. [AM] **2** N-COUNT In soccer or rugby, a **fullback** is a defending player whose position is toward the goal which their team is defending.

full-blooded ADJ [ADJ n] **Full-blooded** behavior and actions are carried out with great commitment and enthusiasm. ❑ *Experts are agreed that full-blooded market reform is the only way to save the economy.*

full-blown ADJ [ADJ n] **Full-blown** means having all the characteristics of a particular type of thing or person. ❑ *Before becoming a full-blown director, he worked as the film editor on Citizen Kane.*

full-bodied ADJ A **full-bodied** wine has a full, rich flavor. ❑ *...a soft but full-bodied wine with concentrated blackcurrant flavor.*

full dress N-UNCOUNT Someone who is in **full dress** is wearing all the clothes needed for a ceremony or formal occasion.

full-flavored

in BRIT, use **full-flavoured**

ADJ **Full-flavored** food or wine has a pleasant fairly strong taste.

full-fledged ADJ **Full-fledged** means complete or fully developed. ❑ *Hungary is to have a full-fledged Stock Exchange from today.*

full-frontal also **full frontal** **1** ADJ [usu ADJ n] If there is **full-frontal** nudity in a photograph or movie, you can see the whole of the front part of someone's naked body, including the genitals. ❑ *Will this set a precedent for full-frontal nudity in movies?* **2** ADJ [usu ADJ n] If you use **full-frontal** to describe someone's criticism or way of dealing with something, you are emphasizing that it is very strong and direct. [EMPHASIS] ❑ *...a full-frontal attack on the opposition leader.*

full-grown ADJ An animal or plant that is **full-grown** has reached its full adult size and stopped growing. ❑ *...a full-grown male orang-utan.*

full house (**full houses**) N-COUNT If a theater has a **full house** for a particular performance, it has as large an audience as it can hold. ❑ *...playing to a full house.*

full-length **1** ADJ [ADJ n] A **full-length** book, record, or movie is the normal length, rather than being shorter than normal. ❑ *...his first full-length recording in well over a decade.* **2** ADJ [ADJ n] A **full-length** coat or skirt is long enough to reach the lower part of a person's leg, almost to the ankles. A full-length sleeve reaches a person's wrist. **3** ADJ [ADJ n] **Full-length** curtains or other furnishings reach to the floor. **4** ADJ [ADJ n] A **full-length** mirror or painting shows the whole of a person. **5** ADV [ADV after v] Someone who is lying **full-length**, is lying down flat and stretched out. ❑ *She stretched herself out full-length.*

full marks N-PLURAL If you get **full marks** in a test or exam, you get everything right and gain the maximum number of points. [BRIT]

in AM, use **a perfect score**

full|ness /fʊlnɪs/ **1** → see **full** ① **2** PHRASE If you say that something will happen **in the fullness of time**, you mean that it will eventually happen after a long time or after a long series of events. [WRITTEN] ❑ *...a mystery that will be revealed in the fullness of time.*

full-on ADJ **Full-on** is used to describe things or activities that have all the characteristics of their type, or are done in the strongest or most extreme way possible. [INFORMAL] ❑ *What they were really good at was full-on rock'n'roll.*

full-page ADJ [ADJ n] A **full-page** advertisement, picture, or article in a newspaper or magazine uses a whole page.

full-scale **1** ADJ [ADJ n] **Full-scale** means as complete, intense, or great in extent as possible. ❑ *...the possibility of a full-scale nuclear war.* **2** ADJ [ADJ n] A **full-scale** drawing or model is the same size as the thing that it represents. ❑ *...working, full-scale prototypes.*

full-size also **full-sized** ADJ [ADJ n] A **full-size** or **full-sized** model or picture is the same size as the thing or person that it represents. ❑ *I made a full-size cardboard model.*

full stop (**full stops**) N-COUNT A **full stop** is the punctuation mark . which you use at the end of a sentence when it is not a question or exclamation. [BRIT]

in AM, use **period**

full-strength → see **strength**

full-throated ADJ [ADJ n] A **full-throated** sound coming from someone's mouth, such as a shout or a laugh, is very loud. ❑ *...full-throated singing.*

full-time also **full time** **1** ADJ **Full-time** work or study involves working or studying for the whole of each normal working week rather than for part of it. ❑ *...a full-time job.* • ADV [ADV after v] **Full-time** is also an adverb. ❑ *Deirdre works full-time.* **2** → See feature box at **working**

full-timer (**full-timers**) N-COUNT A **full-timer** is someone who works full-time. ❑ *The company employs six full-timers and one part-time worker.*

full up also **full-up** **1** ADJ [v-link ADJ] Something that is **full up** has no space left for any more people or things. ❑ *The prisons are all full up.* **2** ADJ [v-link ADJ] If you are **full up** you have eaten or drunk so much that you do not want to eat or drink anything else. [INFORMAL] ❑ *He found that he was so full-up from all the liquid in his diet that he hardly had room for his evening meal.*

ful|ly ✦✦◇ /fʊli/ **1** ADV **Fully** means to the greatest degree or extent possible. ❑ *She was fully aware of my thoughts.* **2** ADV [ADV with v] You use **fully** to say that a process is completely finished. ❑ *He had still not fully recovered.* **3** ADV [ADV with v] If you describe, answer, or deal with something **fully**, you leave out nothing that should be mentioned or dealt with. ❑ *Fiers promised to testify fully and truthfully.*

---- SYNONYMS ----

fully
ADV **1**
completely: *Make sure that you defrost it completely.*
entirely: *Their price depended almost entirely on their scarcity.*
wholly: *A second referendum would be wholly undemocratic.*
utterly: *Such an allegation is utterly without foundation.*
totally: *The fire totally destroyed the top floor.*

fully-fledged ADJ **Fully-fledged** means the same as **full-fledged**. [BRIT]

ful|mi|nate /fʊlmɪneɪt, fʌl-/ (**fulminates**, **fulminating**, **fulminated**) V-I If you **fulminate** against someone or something, you criticize them angrily. [FORMAL] ❑ *They all fulminated against the new curriculum.*

ful|some /fʊlsəm/ ADJ If you describe expressions of praise, apology, or gratitude as **fulsome**, you disapprove of them

fumble /fʌmbᵊl/ (fumbles, fumbling, fumbled) **1** V-I If you **fumble** for something or **fumble** with something, you try to reach for it or hold it in a clumsy way. ❑ *She crept from the bed and fumbled for her dressing gown.* **2** V-I When you are trying to say something, if you **fumble** for the right words, you speak in a clumsy and unclear way. ❑ *I fumbled for something to say.*

fume /fyum/ (fumes, fuming, fumed) **1** N-PLURAL **Fumes** are the unpleasant and often unhealthy smoke and gases that are produced by fires or by things such as chemicals, fuel, or cooking. ❑ *...car exhaust fumes.* **2** V-T/V-I If you **fume** over something, you express annoyance and anger about it. ❑ *"It's monstrous!" Jackie fumed.* **3** → See feature box at **emotion**

fu|mi|gate /fyumɪgeɪt/ (fumigates, fumigating, fumigated) V-T If you **fumigate** something, you get rid of germs or insects from it using special chemicals. ❑ *...fruit which has been treated with insecticide and fumigated.* • **fu|mi|ga|tion** /fyumɪgeɪʃᵊn/ N-UNCOUNT ❑ *Methods of control involved poisoning and fumigation.*

fun ♦♦◇ /fʌn/ **1** N-UNCOUNT You refer to an activity or situation as **fun** if you think it is pleasant and enjoyable and it causes you to feel happy. ❑ *It's been a learning adventure and it's also been great fun.* ❑ *It could be fun to watch them.* **2** N-UNCOUNT If you say that someone is **fun**, you mean that you enjoy being with them because they say and do interesting or amusing things. [APPROVAL] ❑ *Liz was fun to be with.* **3** ADJ [ADJ n] If you describe something as a **fun** thing, you mean that you think it is enjoyable. If you describe someone as a **fun** person, you mean that you enjoy being with them. [INFORMAL] ❑ *It was a fun evening.* **4** PHRASE If you do something **for fun** or **for the fun of it**, you do it in order to enjoy yourself rather than because it is important or necessary. ❑ *We used to drive too fast, just for fun.* **5** PHRASE If you do something **in fun**, you do it as a joke or for amusement, without intending to cause any harm. ❑ *Don't say such things, even in fun.* **6** PHRASE If you **make fun of** someone or something or **poke fun at** them, you laugh at them, tease them, or make jokes about them in a way that causes them to seem ridiculous. ❑ *Don't make fun of me.*

┌─ SYNONYMS ─┐
fun
NOUN **1**
amusement: *Steamships tooted at us as sailors on deck waved in amusement.*
pleasure: *He gets huge pleasure from ballet and contemporary dance.*
enjoyment: *...her enjoyment of the beauty of the countryside.*

func|tion ♦♦◇ /fʌŋkʃᵊn/ (functions, functioning, functioned) **1** N-COUNT The **function** of something or someone is the useful thing that they do or are intended to do. ❑ *The main function of the investment banks is to raise capital for industry.* **2** N-COUNT A **function** is a large formal dinner or party. ❑ *...a private function hosted by one of his students.* **3** V-I If a machine or system **is functioning**, it is working or operating. ❑ *The authorities say the prison is now functioning normally.* **4** V-I If someone or something **functions** as a particular thing, they do the work or fulfill the purpose of that thing. ❑ *On weekdays, one third of the room functions as workspace.* **5** → See feature box at **brain**

┌─ COLLOCATIONS ─┐
function
NOUN
1
noun + **function**: brain, kidney, liver, lung; memory
adjective + **function**: bodily, cognitive; basic, important, primary; administrative
verb + **function**: exercise, fulfill, perform, serve; affect, impair
2
noun + **function**: charity, gala
adjective + **function**: official, social
verb + **function**: attend; host, organize
VERB **3**
function + adverb: efficiently, normally, properly, smoothly

┌─ SYNONYMS ─┐
function
NOUN **1**
purpose: *The purpose of the occasion was to raise money for medical supplies.*
job: *Their main job is to preserve health rather than treat illness.*
role: *...the drug's role in preventing more serious effects of infection.*
VERB **3**
work: *The pump doesn't work, and we have no running water.*
run: *We told him to wait out front with the engine running.*
operate: *The number of these machines operating around the world has increased dramatically.*

func|tion|al /fʌŋkʃᵊnᵊl/ **1** ADJ **Functional** things are useful rather than decorative. ❑ *...modern, functional furniture.* **2** ADJ **Functional** equipment works or operates in the way that it is supposed to. ❑ *We have fully functional smoke alarms on all staircases.*

func|tion|al|ism /fʌŋkʃᵊnᵊlɪzəm/ N-UNCOUNT **Functionalism** is the idea that the most important aspect of something, especially the design of a building or piece of furniture, is how it is going to be used or its usefulness. [TECHNICAL]

func|tion|al|ity /fʌŋkʃᵊnælɪti/ N-UNCOUNT The **functionality** of a computer or other machine is how useful it is or how many functions it can perform. ❑ *It is significantly more compact than any comparable laptop, with no loss in functionality.*

func|tion|ary /fʌŋkʃᵊnɛri/ (functionaries) N-COUNT A **functionary** is a person whose job is to do administrative work, especially for a government or a political party. [FORMAL]

func|tion key (function keys) N-COUNT **Function keys** are the keys along the top of a computer keyboard, usually numbered from F1 to F12. Each key is designed to make a particular thing happen when you press it. [COMPUTING] ❑ *Just hit the F5 function key to send and receive your e-mails.*

fund ♦♦◇ /fʌnd/ (funds, funding, funded) **1** N-PLURAL **Funds** are amounts of money that are available to be spent, especially money that is given to an organization or person for a particular purpose. ❑ *The concert will raise funds for research into AIDS.* **2** → see also **fund-raising** **3** N-COUNT A **fund** is an amount of money that is collected or saved for a particular purpose. ❑ *...a scholarship fund for undergraduate engineering students.* **4** → see also **trust fund** **5** V-T When a person or organization **funds** something, they provide money for it. ❑ *The Bush Foundation has funded a variety of faculty development programs.* ❑ *The airport is being privately funded by a construction group.*

fun|da|men|tal ♦◇◇ /fʌndəmɛntᵊl/ **1** ADJ You use **fundamental** to describe things, activities, and principles that are very important or essential. They affect the basic nature of other things or are the most important element upon which other things depend. ❑ *Our constitution embodies all the fundamental principles of democracy.* ❑ *A fundamental human right is being withheld from these people.* **2** ADJ You use **fundamental** to describe something which exists at a deep and basic level, and is therefore likely to continue. ❑ *But on this question, the two leaders have very fundamental differences.* **3** ADJ [v-link ADJ to n] If one thing **is fundamental to** another, it is absolutely necessary to it, and the second thing cannot exist, succeed, or be imagined without it. ❑ *He believes better relations with China are fundamental to the well-being of the area.* **4** ADJ [ADJ n] You can use **fundamental** to show that you are referring to what you consider to be the most important aspect of a situation, and that you are not concerned with less important details. ❑ *The fundamental problem lies in their inability to distinguish between reality and invention.*

┌─ SYNONYMS ─┐
fundamental
ADJ **1**
central: *...a central part of their culture.*
key: *Education is likely to be a key issue in the next election.*
basic: *Access to justice is a basic right.*
essential: *Jordan promised to trim the city budget without cutting essential services.*

fun|da|men|tal|ism /fʌndəmɛntəlɪzəm/ N-UNCOUNT
Fundamentalism is the belief in the original form of a religion or theory, without accepting any later ideas. ▫ *Religious fundamentalism was spreading in the region.* • **fun|da|men|tal|ist** (**fundamentalists**) N-COUNT ▫ *...fundamentalist Christians.*

fun|da|men|tal|ly /fʌndəmɛntəli/ **1** ADV [ADV with cl/group] You use **fundamentally** for emphasis when you are stating an opinion, or when you are making an important or general statement about something. [EMPHASIS] ▫ *Fundamentally, women like him for his sensitivity and charming vulnerability.* **2** ADV [ADV with v] You use **fundamentally** to indicate that something affects or relates to the deep, basic nature of something. ▫ *He disagreed fundamentally with the president's judgment.* ▫ *Environmentalists say the treaty is fundamentally flawed.*

fun|da|men|tals /fʌndəmɛntəlz/ N-PLURAL The **fundamentals** of something are its simplest, most important elements, ideas, or principles, in contrast to more complicated or detailed ones. ▫ *They agree on fundamentals, like the need for further political reform.*

fund|ing ✦◇◇ /fʌndɪŋ/ **1** N-UNCOUNT **Funding** is money which a government or organization provides for a particular purpose. ▫ *They hope for government funding for the program.* **2** → See feature box at **business**

fund man|ag|er (**fund managers**) N-COUNT A **fund manager** is someone whose job involves investing the money contained in a fund, for example, a mutual fund, on behalf of another person or organization. ▫ *...Doug Johnson, a fund manager for Seattle-based Safeco Asset Management.*

fund|rais|er /fʌndreɪzər/ (**fundraisers**) also **fund-raiser** **1** N-COUNT A **fundraiser** is an event which is intended to raise money for a particular purpose, for example, for a charity. ▫ *Organize a fundraiser for your church.* **2** N-COUNT A **fundraiser** is someone who works to raise money for a particular purpose, for example, for a charity. ▫ *...a fundraiser for the Democrats.*

fund-raising also **fundraising** N-UNCOUNT **Fund-raising** is the activity of collecting money to support a charity or political campaign or organization. ▫ *Encourage her to get involved in fund-raising for charity.*

fu|ner|al /fyunərəl/ (**funerals**) N-COUNT A **funeral** is the ceremony that is held when the body of someone who has died is buried or cremated. ▫ *The funeral will be held in Joplin, Missouri.*

fu|ner|al di|rec|tor (**funeral directors**) N-COUNT A **funeral director** is a person whose job is to arrange funerals.

fu|ner|al home (**funeral homes**) N-COUNT A **funeral home** is a place where a funeral director works and where dead people are prepared for burial or cremation.

fu|ner|al par|lor (**funeral parlors**) N-COUNT A **funeral parlor** is the same as a **funeral home**.

fu|ner|ary /fyunərɛri/ ADJ [ADJ n] **Funerary** means relating to funerals, burials, or cremations. [FORMAL] ▫ *...funerary monuments.*

fu|nereal /fyunɪəriəl/ ADJ [usu ADJ n] A **funereal** tone, atmosphere, or color is very sad and serious and would be suitable for a funeral. ▫ *He addressed the group in funereal tones.*

fun|fair /fʌnfɛər/ (**funfairs**) N-COUNT A **funfair** is an event held in a park or field at which people pay to ride on various machines for amusement or try to win prizes in games. The people who organize and operate it usually take it from one place to another. [BRIT]

in AM, use **carnival, fair**

fun|gal /fʌŋgəl/ ADJ [usu ADJ n] **Fungal** means caused by, consisting of, or relating to fungus. ▫ *Athlete's foot is a fungal infection.*

fun|gi /fʌndʒaɪ, fʌŋgaɪ/ **Fungi** is the plural of **fungus**.

fun|gi|cide /fʌndʒɪsaɪd, fʌŋgɪ-/ (**fungicides**) N-MASS A **fungicide** is a chemical that can be used to kill fungus or to prevent it from growing.

fun|gus /fʌŋgəs/ (**fungi**) N-MASS A **fungus** is a plant that has no flowers, leaves, or green coloring, such as a mushroom or a toadstool. Other types of fungus such as mold are extremely small and look like a fine powder.

fun|house /fʌnhaʊs/ (**funhouses**) also **fun house** N-COUNT [oft N n] A **funhouse** is a building in an amusement park that contains amusing or frightening objects or rooms. [mainly AM] ▫ *When she looks in the mirror, though, her face warps out of focus as if the reflection is from a funhouse mirror.*

fu|nicu|lar /fyunɪkyələr/ N-SING A **funicular** or a **funicular railway** is a type of railroad which goes up a very steep hill or mountain. A machine at the top of the slope pulls the cars up the rails by a steel rope.

funk /fʌŋk/ (**funks**) **1** N-UNCOUNT **Funk** is a style of dance music based on jazz and blues, with a strong, repeated bass part. ▫ *...a mixture of experimental jazz, soul and funk.* **2** N-COUNT [usu sing] A **funk** is a state of mind in which you feel sad or depressed. ▫ *I was at loose ends and in a funk.* ▫ *She's really helped me out of the funk I was in.*

funky /fʌŋki/ (**funkier, funkiest**) **1** ADJ **Funky** jazz, blues, or pop music has a very strong, repeated bass part. ▫ *It's a funky sort of rhythm.* **2** ADJ If you describe something or someone as **funky**, you mean that they are stylish and modern in an unconventional way. [APPROVAL] ▫ *She would love to buy her daughter funky little leopard-print skirts.* ▫ *The place is quirky, funky and dazzlingly imaginative in design.* **3** ADJ Something that is **funky** has a strong, offensive odor. ▫ *There were dirty clothes everywhere, and they all had that funky overripe smell.*

fun|nel /fʌnəl/ (**funnels, funneling** or **funnelling, funneled** or **funnelled**) **1** N-COUNT A **funnel** is an object with a wide, circular top and a narrow short tube at the bottom. Funnels are used to pour liquids into containers which have a small opening, for example, bottles. ▫ *Rain falls through the funnel into the jar below.* **2** N-COUNT A **funnel** is a metal chimney on a ship or railroad engine powered by steam. ▫ *...a ship with three masts and two funnels.* **3** N-COUNT You can describe as a **funnel** something that is narrow, or narrow at one end, through which a substance flows and is directed. ▫ *Along the road, funnels of dark gray smoke rose from bombed villages.* **4** V-T/V-I If something **funnels** somewhere or is **funneled** there, it is directed through a narrow space. ▫ *The winds came from the north, across the plains, funneling down the valley.* **5** V-T If you **funnel** money, goods, or information from one place or group to another, you cause it to be sent there as it becomes available. ▫ *He secretly funneled credit-card information to counterfeiters.* **6** → See also color supplement

fun|ni|ly /fʌnɪli/ PHRASE You use **funnily enough** to indicate that, although something is surprising, it is true or really happened. ▫ *Funnily enough I can remember what I had for lunch on July 5th, 1956, but I've forgotten what I had for breakfast today.*

fun|ny ✦◇◇ /fʌni/ (**funnier, funniest**) **1** ADJ Someone or something that is **funny** is amusing and likely to make you smile or laugh. ▫ *I'll tell you a funny story.* **2** ADJ If you describe something as **funny**, you think it is strange, surprising, or puzzling. ▫ *Children get some very funny ideas sometimes!* ▫ *There's something funny about him.* **3** ADJ If you feel **funny**, you feel slightly ill. [INFORMAL] ▫ *My head had begun to ache and my stomach felt funny.* **4** → See feature box at **humor**

fun|ny bone (**funny bones**) N-COUNT [usu sing] Your **funny bone** is the soft part of your elbow which gives you an uncomfortable feeling on your skin if it is hit. [INFORMAL]

funny|man /fʌnimæn/ (**funnymen**) N-COUNT [usu sing] A **funnyman** is a male comedian. [JOURNALISM] ▫ *...Hollywood funnyman Billy Crystal.*

fur /fɜr/ (**furs**) **1** N-MASS **Fur** is the thick and usually soft hair that grows on the bodies of many mammals. ▫ *This creature's fur is short, dense and silky.* **2** N-MASS **Fur** is an artificial fabric that looks like fur and is used, for example, to make clothing, soft toys, and seat covers. **3** N-VAR **Fur** is the fur-covered skin of an animal that is used to make clothing or small carpets. ▫ *She had on a black coat with a fur collar.* ▫ *...the trading of furs from Canada.* **4** N-COUNT A **fur** is a coat made from real or artificial fur, or a piece of fur worn around your neck. ▫ *There were women in furs and men in comfortable overcoats.*

fu|ri|ous /fyʊəriəs/ **1** ADJ Someone who is **furious** is extremely angry. ▫ *He is furious at the way his wife has been treated.* • **fu|ri|ous|ly** ADV ▫ *He stormed out of the apartment, slamming the door furiously behind him.* **2** ADJ **Furious** is also used to describe something that is done with great energy, effort, speed, or

furl violence. ❏ *A furious gunbattle ensued.* • **fu|ri|ous|ly** ADV ❏ *Officials worked furiously to repair the center court.* ❸ → See feature box at **emotion**

furl /fɜrl/ (**furls, furling, furled**) V-T When you **furl** something made of fabric such as an umbrella, sail, or flag, you roll or fold it up because it is not going to be used. ❏ *An attempt was made to furl the headsail.* ❏ *...a furled umbrella.*

fur|long /fɜrlɔŋ/ (**furlongs**) N-COUNT A **furlong** is a unit of length that is equal to 220 yards or 201.2 meters. ❏ *"Although he was beaten in his first race at seven furlongs, I was thrilled with his performance," the trainer said.*

fur|lough /fɜrloʊ/ (**furloughs, furloughing, furloughed**) ❶ N-VAR If workers are given **furlough**, they are told to stay away from work for a certain period because there is not enough for them to do. ❏ *This could mean a massive furlough of government workers.* ❷ V-T If people who work for a particular organization **are furloughed**, they are given a furlough. ❏ *We regret to inform you that you are being furloughed indefinitely.*

fur|nace /fɜrnɪs/ (**furnaces**) N-COUNT A **furnace** is a container or enclosed space in which a very hot fire is made, for example, to melt metal, burn trash, or produce heat for a building or house.

fur|nish /fɜrnɪʃ/ (**furnishes, furnishing, furnished**) ❶ V-T If you **furnish** a room or building, you put furniture and furnishings into it. ❏ *Many proprietors try to furnish their hotels with antiques.* ❷ V-T If you **furnish** someone with something, you provide or supply it. [FORMAL] ❏ *They'll be able to furnish you with the rest of the details.*

fur|nished /fɜrnɪʃt/ ❶ ADJ A **furnished** room or house is available to be rented together with the furniture in it. ❷ ADJ [adv ADJ] When you say that a room or house is **furnished** in a particular way, you are describing the kind or amount of furniture that it has in it. ❏ *We drank tea by lamplight in his sparsely furnished house.*

fur|nish|ings /fɜrnɪʃɪŋz/ N-PLURAL The **furnishings** of a room or house are the furniture, curtains, carpets, and decorations such as pictures. ❏ *To enable rental increases, you have to have luxurious furnishings.*

fur|ni|ture ♦⬦ /fɜrnɪtʃər/ N-UNCOUNT **Furniture** consists of large objects such as tables, chairs, or beds that are used in a room for sitting or lying on or for putting things on or in. ❏ *Each piece of furniture in their home suited the style of the house.*

fu|ror /fyʊərɔr, -ər/ N-SING A **furor** is a very angry or excited reaction by people to something. ❏ *...an international furor over the plan.*

fur|ri|er /fɜriər/ (**furriers**) N-COUNT A **furrier** is a person who makes or sells clothes made from fur.

fur|row /fɜroʊ/ (**furrows**) ❶ N-COUNT A **furrow** is a long, thin line in the earth which a farmer makes in order to plant seeds or to allow water to flow along. ❏ *...furrows of roses and corn.* ❷ N-COUNT A **furrow** is a deep, fairly wide line in the surface of something. ❏ *I saw a dark brown fertile field in which a plow was cutting large furrows.* ❸ N-COUNT A **furrow** is a deep fold or line in the skin of someone's face. ❏ *He was his old self again, except for the deep furrows that marked the corners of his mouth.*

fur|ry /fɜri/ (**furrier, furriest**) ❶ ADJ A **furry** animal is covered with thick, soft hair. ❏ *People like having small furry animals to stroke, but pets can be expensive to feed.* ❷ ADJ If you describe something as **furry**, you mean that it has a soft rough texture like fur. ❏ *The leaves are soft, round and rather furry.*

fur|ther ♦♦⬦ /fɜrðər/ (**furthers, furthering, furthered**)

Further is a comparative form of far. It is also a verb.

❶ ADV [ADV with v] **Further** means to a greater extent or degree. ❏ *Inflation is below 5% and set to fall further.* ❏ *The rebellion is expected to further damage the country's image.* ❷ ADV [ADV with v] If you go or get **further** with something, or take something **further**, you make some progress. ❏ *They lacked the scientific personnel to develop the technical apparatus much further.* ❸ ADV [ADV after v] If someone goes **further** in a discussion, they make a more extreme statement or deal with a point more thoroughly. ❏ *To have a better comparison, we need to go further and address such issues as repairs and insurance.* ❹ ADV [ADV adv/prep] **Further** means a greater distance than before or than something else. ❏ *People are living further away from their jobs.* ❏ *He came to a halt at a crossroads fifty yards further on.* ❺ ADV [ADV adv/prep] **Further** is used in expressions such as **'further back'** and **'further ahead'** to refer to a point in time that is earlier or later than the one you are talking about. ❏ *Looking still further ahead, by the end of the next century world population is expected to be about ten billion.* ❻ ADJ [ADJ n, pron-indef ADJ] A **further** thing, number of things, or amount of something is an additional thing, number of things, or amount. ❏ *Further evidence of slowing economic growth is likely to emerge this week.* ❼ V-T If you **further** something, you help it to progress, to be successful, or to be achieved. ❏ *Education needn't only be about furthering your career.*

fur|ther|ance /fɜrðərəns/ N-UNCOUNT [N of n] The **furtherance of** something is the activity of helping it to be successful or be achieved. [FORMAL] ❏ *The thing that matters is the furtherance of research in this country.*

fur|ther edu|ca|tion N-UNCOUNT **Further education** is the education of people who have left school but who are not at a university or a college of education. [BRIT]

in AM, use **continuing education, adult education**

further|more /fɜrðərmɔr/ ADV [ADV with cl] **Furthermore** is used to introduce a piece of information or opinion that adds to or supports the previous one. [FORMAL] ❏ *Furthermore, they claim that any such interference is completely ineffective.*

further|most /fɜrðərmoʊst/ ADJ [ADJ n] The **furthermost** one of a number of similar things is the one that is the greatest distance away from a place. ❏ *We walked to the furthermost point and then sat on the sand dunes.*

fur|thest /fɜrðɪst/

Furthest is a superlative form of far.

❶ ADV [ADV with v] **Furthest** means to a greater extent or degree than ever before or than anything or anyone else. ❏ *The south, where prices have fallen furthest, will remain the weakest market.* ❷ ADV **Furthest** means at a greater distance from a particular point than anyone or anything else, or for a greater distance than anyone or anything else. ❏ *The risk of thunder is greatest in those areas furthest from the coast.* • ADJ [ADJ n] **Furthest** is also an adjective. ❏ *...the furthest point from earth that any controlled spacecraft has ever been.*

fur|tive /fɜrtɪv/ ADJ If you describe someone's behavior as **furtive**, you disapprove of them behaving as if they want to keep something secret or hidden. [DISAPPROVAL] ❏ *With a furtive glance over her shoulder, she unlocked the door and entered the house.*

fury /fyʊəri/ N-UNCOUNT **Fury** is violent or very strong anger. ❏ *She screamed, her face distorted with fury and pain.*

fuse /fyuz/ (**fuses, fusing, fused**)

The spelling **fuze** is also used for meaning ❷.

❶ N-COUNT A **fuse** is a safety device in an electric plug or circuit. It contains a piece of wire which melts when there is a fault so that the flow of electricity stops. ❏ *The fuse blew as he pressed the button to start the motor.* ❷ N-COUNT A **fuse** is a device on a bomb or firework which delays the explosion so that people can move a safe distance away. ❏ *A bomb was deactivated at the last moment, after the fuse had been lit.* ❸ V-RECIP When things **fuse** or **are fused**, they join together physically or chemically, usually to become one thing. You can also say that one thing **fuses** with another. ❏ *The skull bones fuse between the ages of fifteen and twenty-five.* ❏ *Manufactured glass is made by fusing various types of sand.*

fuse box (**fuse boxes**) N-COUNT [oft the N in sing] The **fuse box** is the box that contains the fuses for all the electric circuits in a building. It is usually attached to a wall.

fused /fyuzd/ ADJ If an electric plug or circuit is **fused**, it has a fuse in it.

fu|se|lage /fyusɪlɑʒ, -lɪdʒ, -zɪ-/ (**fuselages**) ❶ N-COUNT The **fuselage** is the main body of an airplane, missile, or rocket. It is usually cylindrical in shape. ❏ *The force of the impact ripped apart the plane's fuselage.* ❷ → See also color supplement

fu|sil|lade /fyusɪlɑd, -leɪd, -zɪ-/ N-SING [usu N of n] A **fusillade** of shots or objects is a large number of them fired or thrown at the same time. [FORMAL] ❏ *Both were killed in a fusillade of bullets fired at close range.*

fu|sion /fyuʒᵊn/ (fusions) **1** N-COUNT A **fusion** of different qualities, ideas, or things is something new that is created by joining them together. ❑ *His previous fusions of jazz, pop and African melodies have proved highly successful.* **2** N-VAR The **fusion** of two or more things involves joining them together to form one thing. ❑ *His final reform was the fusion of regular and reserve forces.* **3** N-UNCOUNT In physics, **fusion** is the process in which atomic particles combine and produce a large amount of nuclear energy. ❑ *...research into nuclear fusion.*

fuss /fʌs/ (fusses, fussing, fussed) **1** N-SING [also no det] **Fuss** is anxious or excited behavior which serves no useful purpose. ❑ *I don't know what all the fuss is about.* **2** V-I If you **fuss**, you worry or behave in a nervous, anxious way about unimportant matters or rush around doing unnecessary things. ❑ *Carol fussed about getting me a drink.* ❑ *My wife was fussing over the food and clothing we were going to take.* ❑ *"Stop fussing," he snapped.* **3** V-I If you **fuss over** someone, you pay them a lot of attention and do things to make them happy or comfortable. ❑ *Auntie Hilda and Uncle Jack couldn't fuss over them enough.* **4** PHRASE If you **make a fuss** or **kick up a fuss** about something, you become angry or excited about it and complain. [INFORMAL] ❑ *I don't know why everybody makes such a fuss about a few mosquitoes.* **5** → See feature box at **review**

fussy /fʌsi/ (fussier, fussiest) ADJ Someone who is **fussy** is very concerned with unimportant details and is difficult to please. [DISAPPROVAL] ❑ *She is not fussy about her food.*

fus|ty /fʌsti/ (fustier, fustiest) **1** ADJ If you describe something or someone as **fusty**, you disapprove of them because they are old-fashioned in attitudes or ideas. [DISAPPROVAL] ❑ *The fusty old establishment refused to recognize the demand for popular music.* **2** ADJ [usu n] A **fusty** place or thing has a smell that is not fresh or pleasant. ❑ *...fusty old carpets.*

fu|tile /fyutᵊl/ ADJ If you say that something is **futile**, you mean there is no point in doing it, usually because it has no chance of succeeding. ❑ *He brought his arm up in a futile attempt to ward off the blow.*

fu|til|ity /fyutɪlɪti/ N-UNCOUNT **Futility** is a total lack of purpose or usefulness. ❑ *Brown's article tells of the tragedy and futility of war.*

fu|ton /futɒn/ (futons) **1** N-COUNT A **futon** is a piece of furniture which consists of a thin mattress on a low wooden frame which can be used as a bed or folded up to make a chair. **2** → See also color supplement

fu|ture ♦♦♦ /fyutʃər/ (futures) **1** N-SING The **future** is the period of time that will come after the present, or the things that will happen then. ❑ *The spokesman said no decision on the proposal was likely in the immediate future.* ❑ *He was making plans for the future.* **2** ADJ [ADJ n] **Future** things will happen or exist after the present time. ❑ *She said if the world did not act conclusively now, it would only bequeath the problem to future generations.* ❑ *...the future king and queen.* **3** N-COUNT Someone's **future**, or the **future** of something, is what will happen to them or what they will do after the present time. ❑ *His future depends on the outcome of the elections.* ❑ *...a proposed national conference on the country's political future.* **4** N-PLURAL When people trade in **futures**, they buy stocks and shares, commodities such as coffee or oil, or foreign currency at a price that is agreed at the time of purchase for items which are delivered some time in the future. [BUSINESS] ❑ *This report could spur some buying in corn futures when the market opens today.* **5** PHRASE You use **in the future** when saying what will happen from now on, which will be different from what has previously happened. ❑ *I asked her to be more careful in the future.*

---- COLLOCATIONS ----

future
NOUN **1**
adjective + **future**: bright, rosy, secure; uncertain, unclear; distant, foreseeable, immediate, long-term, near; bleak
verb + **future**: predict; secure; shape

---

fu|tur|ism /fyutʃərɪzəm/ N-UNCOUNT **Futurism** was a modern artistic and literary movement in the early twentieth century.

fu|tur|ist /fyutʃərɪst/ (futurists) **1** N-COUNT **Futurists** were artists and writers who were followers of futurism. **2** N-COUNT A **futurist** is someone who makes predictions about what is going to happen, on the basis of facts about what is happening now. [mainly AM]

fu|tur|is|tic /fyutʃərɪstɪk/ **1** ADJ Something that is **futuristic** looks or seems very modern and unusual, like something from the future. ❑ *The theater is a futuristic steel and glass structure.* **2** ADJ [ADJ n] A **futuristic** movie or book tells a story that is set in the future, when things are different. ❑ *...the futuristic hit movie, "Terminator 2."*

fu|tur|ol|ogy /fyutʃərɒlədʒi/ N-UNCOUNT **Futurology** is the activity of trying to predict what is going to happen, on the basis of facts about what is happening now. ❑ *The way a good investor does really well is by engaging in successful futurology.*
● **fu|tur|olo|gist** /fyutʃərɒlədʒɪst/ (futurologists) N-COUNT ❑ *In his March 1984 report Wanger analyzed some predictions made by futurologists in 1972.*

fuze /fyuz/ → see **fuse 2**

fuzz /fʌz/ **1** N-UNCOUNT [also a N] **Fuzz** is a mass of short, curly hairs. **2** N-PLURAL [usu the N] The **fuzz** are the police. [INFORMAL, OLD-FASHIONED]

fuzzy /fʌzi/ (fuzzier, fuzziest) **1** ADJ **Fuzzy** hair sticks up in a soft, curly mass. ❑ *He had fuzzy black hair and bright black eyes.* **2** ADJ If something is **fuzzy**, it has a covering that feels soft and like fur. ❑ *...fuzzy material.* **3** ADJ A **fuzzy** picture, image, or sound is unclear and hard to see or hear. ❑ *A couple of fuzzy pictures have been published.* **4** ADJ If you or your thoughts are **fuzzy**, you are confused and cannot think clearly. ❑ *He had little patience for fuzzy ideas.*

FYI **FYI** is a written abbreviation for 'for your information,' often used in notes and documents when giving someone additional information about something. ❑ *FYI: Walton appeared in a grand total of 49 career tournament games.*

Gg

G also **g** /dʒiː/ (**G's, g's**) N-VAR G is the seventh letter of the English alphabet.

gab /gæb/ PHRASE If someone has **the gift of gab**, they are able to speak easily and confidently, and to persuade people. [APPROVAL] ❏ *I have the gift of gab, so I'd make a good salesperson.*

gab|ar|dine /ˈgæbərdin/ (**gabardines**)

in BRIT, also use **gaberdine**

1 N-UNCOUNT [also N in pl, oft N n] Gabardine is a fairly thick cloth which is used for making coats, suits, and other clothes. **2** N-COUNT A **gabardine** is a coat made from gabardine.

gab|ble /ˈgæbəl/ (**gabbles, gabbling, gabbled**) V-T/V-I If you **gabble**, you say things so quickly that it is difficult for people to understand you. [INFORMAL] ❏ *Marcello sat on the floor and gabbled excitedly.* ❏ *She gabbles on about drug dealers and journalists.* ❏ *One of the soldiers gabbled something and pointed at the front door.*

ga|ble /ˈgeɪbəl/ (**gables**) N-COUNT A **gable** is the triangular part at the top of the end wall of a building, between the two sloping sides of the roof.

ga|bled /ˈgeɪbəld/ ADJ [usu ADJ n] A **gabled** building or roof has a gable.

gad /gæd/ (**gads, gadding, gadded**) V-I If you **gad** about, you go to a lot of different places looking for amusement or entertainment. [INFORMAL] ❏ *Don't think you'll keep me here while you gad about.*

gad|fly /ˈgædflaɪ/ (**gadflies**) N-COUNT If you refer to someone as a **gadfly**, you believe that they deliberately annoy or challenge other people, especially people in authority.

gadg|et /ˈgædʒɪt/ (**gadgets**) N-COUNT A **gadget** is a small machine or device which does something useful. You sometimes refer to something as a **gadget** when you are suggesting that it is complicated and unnecessary. ❏ *...sales of kitchen gadgets including toasters, kettles, and percolators.*

gadg|et|ry /ˈgædʒɪtri/ N-UNCOUNT [oft adj n] **Gadgetry** is small machines or devices which do something useful. ❏ *...a passion for the latest electronic gadgetry.*

Gael|ic /ˈgeɪlɪk, ˈgælɪk/ **1** N-UNCOUNT **Gaelic** is a language spoken by people in parts of Scotland and Ireland. ❏ *We weren't allowed to speak Gaelic at school.* • ADJ **Gaelic** is also an adjective. ❏ *...the Gaelic language.* **2** ADJ **Gaelic** means coming from or relating to Scotland and Ireland, especially the parts where Gaelic is spoken. ❏ *...an evening of Gaelic music and drama.*

gaff /gæf/ (**gaffs**) **1** N-COUNT [oft N n] On a boat, a **gaff** is a pole which is attached to a mast in order to support a particular kind of sail. **2** N-COUNT A **gaff** is a pole with a point or hook at one end, which is used for catching large fish. **3** → see also **gaffe**

gaffe /gæf/ (**gaffes**) also **gaff** N-COUNT A **gaffe** is a stupid or careless mistake, for example when you say or do something that offends or upsets people. ❏ *He made an embarrassing gaffe at the convention last weekend.* ❏ *...social gaffes committed by high-ranking individuals.*

gag /gæg/ (**gags, gagging, gagged**) **1** N-COUNT A **gag** is something such as a piece of cloth that is tied around or put inside someone's mouth in order to stop them from speaking or shouting. ❏ *His captors had put a gag of thick leather in his mouth.* **2** V-T If someone **gags** you, they tie a piece of cloth around your mouth or put a cloth inside it in order to stop you from speaking or shouting. ❏ *I gagged him with a towel.* **3** V-T If a person **is gagged** by someone in authority, they are prevented from expressing their opinion or from publishing certain information. [DISAPPROVAL] ❏ *Judges must not be gagged.* **4** V-I If you **gag**, you cannot swallow and nearly vomit. ❏ *I knelt by the toilet and gagged.* **5** N-COUNT A **gag** is a joke. [INFORMAL] ❏ *The running gag is that the band never gets to play.* **6** N-COUNT A **gag** is a humorous trick that you play on someone. [AM, INFORMAL] ❏ *Richard must have thought colleagues were playing a gag on him.*

gaga /ˈgɑːgɑː/ ADJ [v-link ADJ] If someone goes **gaga** over a person or thing, they like them very much. [INFORMAL] ❏ *...the man everyone is going gaga over.*

gag|gle /ˈgægəl/ (**gaggles**) N-COUNT-COLL [usu N of n] You can use **gaggle** to refer to a group of people, especially if they are noisy or disorganized. [DISAPPROVAL] ❏ *A gaggle of journalists sit in a hotel foyer waiting impatiently.*

gag or|der (**gag orders**) N-COUNT If a judge puts a **gag order** on information relating to a legal case, people involved in the case are banned from discussing it in public or writing about it. [AM] ❏ *Reporters published information that a judge had put a gag order on.*

in BRIT, use **gagging order**

gag rule (**gag rules**) N-COUNT A **gag rule** is an official restriction that forbids people from discussing something in a particular place. [AM] ❏ *...voters who see the gag rule as a restriction on free speech.*

gai|ety /ˈgeɪɪti/ N-UNCOUNT **Gaiety** is a feeling, attitude, or atmosphere of liveliness and fun. ❏ *Music rang out, adding to the gaiety and life of the market.*

gai|ly /ˈgeɪli/ **1** ADV [ADV with v] If you do something **gaily**, you do it in a lively, happy way. ❏ *Magda laughed gaily.* **2** ADV [ADV -ed] Something that is **gaily** colored or **gaily** decorated is colored or decorated in a bright, pretty way. ❏ *He put on a gaily colored shirt.* ❏ *...gaily painted front doors.*

gain ♦♦◊ /geɪn/ (**gains, gaining, gained**) **1** V-T/V-I If a person or place **gains** something such as an ability or quality, they gradually get more of it. ❏ *Students can gain valuable experience by working on the campus radio or magazine.* ❏ *His reputation abroad has gained in stature.* **2** V-T/V-I If you **gain** from something such as an event or situation, you get some advantage or benefit from it. ❏ *The company didn't disclose how much it expects to gain from the two deals.* ❏ *There is absolutely nothing to be gained by feeling bitter.* **3** V-T To **gain** something such as weight or speed means to have an increase in that particular thing. ❏ *Some people do gain weight after they stop smoking.* ❏ *The BMW started coming forward, passing the other cars and gaining speed as it approached.* • N-VAR [usu with supp] **Gain** is also a noun. ❏ *News on new home sales is brighter, showing a gain of nearly 8% in June.* **4** V-T If you **gain** something, you obtain it, especially after a lot of hard work or effort. ❏ *To gain a promotion, you might have to work overtime.* **5** PHRASE If something such as an idea or an ideal **gains ground**, it gradually becomes more widely known or more popular. ❏ *There are strong signs that his views are gaining ground.*

SYNONYMS

gain
VERB
1
acquire: *I recently acquired some wood from a holly tree.*
receive: *They will receive their awards at a ceremony in Stockholm.*
obtain: *Evans was trying to obtain a false passport and other documents.*
2
benefit: *Both sides have benefitted from the talks.*
profit: *Jennifer felt she might profit from a more relaxed lifestyle.*

gain|er /ɡeɪnər/ (gainers) N-COUNT [oft adj N] A **gainer** is a person or organization that gains something from a particular situation. ❏ *Overall, there were more losers than gainers.*

gain|ful /ɡeɪnfʊl/ ADJ [ADJ n] If you are in **gainful** employment, you have a job for which you are paid. [FORMAL] ❏ *...opportunities for gainful employment.* ● **gain|ful|ly** ADV [ADV -ed] ❏ *Both parents were gainfully employed.*

gain|say /ɡeɪnseɪ/ (gainsays, gainsaying, gainsaid) V-T [with brd-neg] If there is no **gainsaying** something, it is true or obvious and everyone would agree with it. [FORMAL] ❏ *There is no gainsaying the fact that they have been responsible for a great building.*

gait /ɡeɪt/ (gaits) N-COUNT A particular kind of **gait** is a particular way of walking. [WRITTEN] ❏ *...a tubby little man in his fifties, with sparse hair and a rolling gait.*

gal /ɡæl/ (gals) N-COUNT; N-VOC **Gal** is used in written English to represent the word 'girl' as it is pronounced in a particular accent. ❏ *...a Southern gal who wants to make it in the movies.*

gal. also **gal**. **gal.** is a written abbreviation for **gallon** or **gallons**. ❏ *...gas prices averaging nearly $2 per gal.*

gala /ɡeɪlə/ (galas) N-COUNT A **gala** is a special public celebration, entertainment, performance, or festival. ❏ *...a gala evening at the Metropolitan Opera House.*

ga|lac|tic /ɡəlæktɪk/ ADJ [ADJ n] **Galactic** means relating to galaxies.

gal|axy /ɡæləksi/ (galaxies) also **Galaxy** ◼ N-COUNT A **galaxy** is an extremely large group of stars and planets that extends over many billions of light years. ❏ *Astronomers have discovered a distant galaxy.* ◼ N-PROPER **The Galaxy** is the extremely large group of stars and planets to which the Earth and the solar system belong. ❏ *The Galaxy consists of over 100 billion stars.* ◼ → See feature box at **space**

gale /ɡeɪl/ (gales) ◼ N-COUNT A **gale** is a very strong wind. ❏ *...forecasts of fierce gales over the next few days.* ◼ N-COUNT You can refer to the loud noise made by a lot of people all laughing at the same time as a **gale** of laughter or **gales** of laughter. [WRITTEN] ❏ *This was greeted with gales of laughter from the audience.* ◼ → See feature box at **hot**, **storm**

gale-force ADJ [ADJ n] A **gale-force** wind is a very strong wind.

gall /ɡɔːl/ (galls, galling, galled) ◼ N-UNCOUNT If you say that someone has the **gall** to do something, you are criticizing them for behaving in a rude or disrespectful way. [DISAPPROVAL] ❏ *He has the gall to accuse reporters of exploiting a tragedy for their own ends.* ◼ V-T If someone's action **galls** you, it makes you feel very angry or annoyed, often because it is unfair to you and you cannot do anything about it. ❏ *It must have galled him that Nick thwarted each of these measures.*

gal|lant /ɡælənt/

Pronounced /ɡələnt/ or /ɡælənt/ for meaning 2.

◼ ADJ If someone is **gallant**, they behave bravely and honorably in a dangerous or difficult situation. [OLD-FASHIONED] ❏ *The gallant soldiers lost their lives so that peace might reign again.* ● **gal|lant|ly** ADV [ADV with v] ❏ *The town responded gallantly to the war.* ◼ ADJ If a man is **gallant**, he is kind, polite, and considerate toward women. [OLD-FASHIONED] ❏ *Douglas was a complex man, thoughtful, gallant, and generous.* ● **gal|lant|ly** ADV [ADV with v] ❏ *He gallantly kissed Marie's hand as we prepared to leave.*

gal|lant|ry /ɡæləntri/ ◼ N-UNCOUNT **Gallantry** is bravery shown by someone who is in danger, for example when they are fighting in a war. [FORMAL] ❏ *He was awarded the Silver Star for gallantry.* ◼ N-UNCOUNT **Gallantry** is considerate, kind, and polite behavior toward other people, especially women. [FORMAL] ❏ *It's that time of year, when thoughts turn to romance and gallantry.*

gall blad|der (gall bladders) ◼ N-COUNT Your **gall bladder** is the organ in your body which contains bile and is next to your liver. ◼ → See also color supplement

gal|leon /ɡæliən/ (galleons) ◼ N-COUNT A **galleon** is a sailing ship with three masts. Galleons were used mainly in the fifteenth to seventeenth centuries. ◼ → See also color supplement

gal|lery ◆◇◇ /ɡæləri/ (galleries) ◼ N-COUNT; N-IN-NAMES A **gallery** is a place that has permanent exhibitions of works of art in it. ❏ *...an art gallery.* ◼ N-COUNT A **gallery** is a privately owned building or room where people can look at and buy works of art. ❏ *The painting is in the gallery upstairs.* ◼ N-COUNT A **gallery** is an area high above the ground at the back or at the sides of a large room or hall. ❏ *A crowd already filled the gallery.* ◼ N-COUNT **The gallery** in a theater or concert hall is an area high above the ground that usually contains the cheapest seats. ❏ *They had been forced to find cheap tickets in the gallery.* ● PHRASE If you **play to the gallery**, you do something in public in a way which you hope will impress people. ❏ *I must tell you that in my opinion you're both now playing to the gallery.*

gal|ley /ɡæli/ (galleys) ◼ N-COUNT On a ship or aircraft, the **galley** is the kitchen. ❏ *I awake to the smell of sizzling bacon in the galley.* ◼ N-COUNT In former times, a **galley** was a ship with sails and a lot of oars, which was often rowed by slaves or prisoners. ❏ *...his months pulling the oar on the galleys.*

Gal|lic /ɡælɪk/ ADJ [usu ADJ n] **Gallic** means the same as **French**. You sometimes use **Gallic** to describe ideas, feelings, or actions that you think are very typical of France and French people. ❏ *The proposal has provoked howls of Gallic indignation.*

gal|li|vant /ɡælɪvænt/ (gallivants, gallivanting, gallivanted) V-I Someone who **is gallivanting** around goes to a lot of different places looking for amusement and entertainment. [OLD-FASHIONED] ❏ *He is still gallivanting around Europe.*

gal|lon /ɡælən/ (gallons) N-COUNT A **gallon** is a unit of measurement for liquids that is equal to eight pints or 3.785 liters. ❏ *...80 million gallons of water a day.*

gal|lop /ɡæləp/ (gallops, galloping, galloped) ◼ V-T/V-I When a horse **gallops**, it runs very fast so that all four legs are off the ground at the same time. If you **gallop** a horse, you make it gallop. ❏ *The horses galloped away.* ◼ V-I If you **gallop**, you ride a horse that is galloping. ❏ *Major Winston galloped into the distance.* ◼ N-SING A **gallop** is a ride on a horse that is galloping. ❏ *I was forced to attempt a gallop.* ◼ V-I If something such as a process **gallops**, it develops very quickly and is often difficult to control. ❏ *China's economy galloped ahead.* ◼ PHRASE If you do something **at a gallop**, you do it very quickly. ❏ *I read the book at a gallop.*

gal|lows /ɡæloʊz/ (gallows) N-COUNT A **gallows** is a wooden frame used to execute criminals by hanging.

gall|stone /ɡɔːlstoʊn/ (gallstones) N-COUNT A **gallstone** is a small, painful lump which can develop in your gall bladder.

Gallup poll /ɡæləp poʊl/ (Gallup polls) N-COUNT A **Gallup poll** is an opinion poll carried out by an official organization and used especially in forecasting the results of elections. [TRADEMARK] ❏ *A recent Gallup poll suggests that no political group is likely to win an outright majority in the next Salvadoran parliament.*

ga|lore /ɡəlɔːr/ ADJ [n ADJ] You use **galore** to emphasize that something you like exists in very large quantities. [INFORMAL, WRITTEN, EMPHASIS] ❏ *You'll be able to win prizes galore.*

ga|loshes /ɡəlɒʃɪz/ N-PLURAL **Galoshes** are waterproof shoes, usually made of rubber, which you wear over your ordinary shoes to prevent them from getting wet.

gal|va|nize /ɡælvənaɪz/ (galvanizes, galvanizing, galvanized)

in BRIT, also use **galvanise**

V-T To **galvanize** someone means to cause them to take action, for example by making them feel very excited, afraid, or angry. ❏ *The aid appeal has galvanized the country's business community.*

gal|va|nized /ɡælvənaɪzd/

in BRIT, also use **galvanised**

ADJ [usu ADJ n] **Galvanized** metal, especially iron and steel, has been covered with zinc in order to protect it from rust and other damage. ❏ *...corrosion-resistant galvanized steel.* ❏ *...galvanized nails.*

gam|bit /ɡæmbɪt/ (gambits) ◼ N-COUNT [usu with supp] A **gambit** is an action or set of actions which you carry out in order to try to gain an advantage in a situation or game.

❑ He sees the proposal as more of a diplomatic gambit than a serious defense proposal. ❑ Campaign strategists are calling the plan a clever political gambit. **2** N-COUNT [usu with supp] A **gambit** is a remark which you make to someone in order to start or continue a conversation with them. ❑ His favorite opening gambit is: "You are so beautiful, will you be my next wife?" ❑ Bernard made no response to Tom's conversational gambits.

gam|ble /gæmbəl/ (gambles, gambling, gambled) **1** N-COUNT A **gamble** is a risky action or decision that you take in the hope of gaining money, success, or an advantage over other people. ❑ Yesterday, he named his cabinet and took a big gamble in the process. **2** V-T/V-I If you **gamble** on something, you take a risky action or decision in the hope of gaining money, success, or an advantage over other people. ❑ Few firms will be willing to gamble on new products. ❑ They are not prepared to gamble their careers on this matter. **3** V-T/V-I If you **gamble** an amount of money, you bet it in a game such as cards or on the result of a race or competition. People who **gamble** usually do it frequently. ❑ Most people visit Las Vegas to gamble their hard-earned money. ❑ John gambled heavily on the horses.

gam|bler /gæmblər/ (gamblers) **1** N-COUNT A **gambler** is someone who gambles regularly, for example in card games or on horse racing. ❑ There was a fellow in that casino tonight who's a very heavy gambler. **2** N-COUNT If you describe someone as a **gambler**, you mean that they are ready to take risks in order to gain advantages or success. ❑ He had never been afraid of failure: he was a gambler, ready to go off somewhere else and start all over again.

gam|bling /gæmblɪŋ/ N-UNCOUNT **Gambling** is the act or activity of betting money, for example in card games or on horse racing. ❑ Gambling is a form of entertainment.

gam|bol /gæmbəl/ (gambols, gamboling, gamboled)

in BRIT, use **gambolling, gambolled**

V-I If animals or people **gambol**, they run or jump about in a playful way. ❑ ...the sight of newborn lambs gamboling in the fields.

game ♦♦♦ /geɪm/ (games) **1** N-COUNT A **game** is an activity or sport usually involving skill, knowledge, or chance, in which you follow fixed rules and try to win against an opponent or to solve a puzzle. ❑ ...the wonderful game of football. ❑ ...a playful game of hide-and-seek. **2** N-COUNT A **game** is one particular occasion on which a game is played. ❑ It was the first game of the season. ❑ He regularly watched our games from the stands. **3** N-COUNT A **game** is a part of a match, for example in tennis or bridge, consisting of a fixed number of points. ❑ She won six games to love in the second set. **4** N-PLURAL **Games** are an organized event in which competitions in several sports take place. ❑ ...the 1996 Olympic Games at Atlanta. **5** N-COUNT You can use **game** to describe a way of behaving in which a person uses a particular plan, usually in order to gain an advantage for himself or herself. ❑ Until now, the Americans have been playing a very delicate political game. **6** N-UNCOUNT Wild animals or birds that are hunted for sport and sometimes cooked and eaten are referred to as **game**. ❑ As men who shot game for food, they were natural marksmen. **7** ADJ [v-link ADJ] If you are **game** for something, you are willing to do something new, unusual, or risky. ❑ He said he's game for a similar challenge next year. **8** PHRASE If someone or something **gives the game away**, they reveal a secret or reveal their feelings, and this puts them at a disadvantage. ❑ The faces of the two conspirators gave the game away! **9** PHRASE If you **are new to** a particular **game**, you have not done a particular activity or been in a particular situation before. ❑ Don't forget that she's new to this game and will take a while to complete the task. **10** PHRASE If you **beat** someone **at** their **own game**, you use the same methods that they have used, but more successfully, so that you gain an advantage over them. ❑ He must anticipate the maneuvers of the other lawyers and beat them at their own game. **11** PHRASE If you say that someone is **playing games** or **playing silly games**, you mean that they are not treating a situation seriously and you are annoyed with them. [DISAPPROVAL] ❑ This seemed to annoy Professor Steiner. "Don't play games with me!" he thundered. **12** → See feature box at **Olympic Games**

game bird (game birds) N-COUNT [usu pl] **Game birds** are birds which are shot for food or for sport.

game chan|ger /geɪm tʃeɪndʒər/ (game changers) N-COUNT If something is a **game changer**, it has a big and important effect on something, usually making the difference between one thing happening and another. ❑ The experience was a game changer in their relationship.

game chan|ging /geɪm tʃeɪndʒɪŋ/ ADJ If something is **game changing**, it has a big and important effect on something, usually making the difference between one thing happening and another. ❑ It was a good idea, but I didn't think it was game changing.

game|keeper /geɪmkiːpər/ (gamekeepers) N-COUNT A **gamekeeper** is a person who takes care of the wild animals or birds that are kept on someone's land for hunting.

game|ly /geɪmli/ ADV [ADV with v] If you do something **gamely**, you do it bravely or with a lot of effort. ❑ He gamely defended his organization's decision.

game park (game parks) N-COUNT A **game park** is a large area of land, especially in Africa, where wild animals can live safely.

game plan (game plans) **1** N-COUNT [usu poss N] In sport, a team's **game plan** is their plan for winning a match. ❑ The home team kept quiet, stuck to their game plan, and quietly racked up the points. **2** N-COUNT [oft poss N] Someone's **game plan** is the actions they intend to take and the policies they intend to adopt in order to achieve a particular thing. ❑ If he has a game plan for winning the deal, only he understands it. ❑ He is unlikely to alter his game plan.

game|play /geɪmpleɪ/ N-UNCOUNT The **gameplay** of a computer game is the way that it is designed and the skills that you need in order to play it. ❑ On PC, the game had it all – imaginative story line and characters, challenging gameplay, superb graphics.

gamer /geɪmər/ (gamers) N-COUNT A **gamer** is someone who plays computer games.

game re|serve (game reserves) N-COUNT A **game reserve** is a large area of land, especially in Africa, where wild animals can live safely.

games con|sole (games consoles) N-COUNT A **games console** is an electronic device used for playing computer games on a television screen. [BRIT] ❑ This Christmas sees the launch of a new games console.

game show (game shows) N-COUNT **Game shows** are television programs on which people play games in order to win prizes. ❑ Being a good game show host means getting to know your contestants.

games|man|ship /geɪmzmənʃɪp/ N-UNCOUNT **Gamesmanship** is the art or practice of winning a game by clever methods which are not against the rules but are very close to cheating. ❑ ...a remarkably successful piece of diplomatic gamesmanship.

gam|ete /gæmiːt/ (gametes) N-COUNT **Gamete** is the name for the two types of male and female cells that join together to make a new creature. [TECHNICAL]

gam|ine /gæmiːn/ ADJ [usu ADJ N] If you describe a girl or a woman as **gamine**, you mean that she is attractive in a boyish way. ❑ She had a gamine charm which men found irresistibly attractive. • N-SING **Gamine** is also a noun. ❑ ...a snub-nosed gamine.

gam|ing /geɪmɪŋ/ N-UNCOUNT **Gaming** means the same as **gambling**. ❑ ...offenses connected with vice, gaming, and drugs.

gam|ma /gæmə/ (gammas) N-VAR **Gamma** is the third letter of the Greek alphabet.

gam|ma rays N-PLURAL **Gamma rays** are a type of electromagnetic radiation that has a shorter wavelength and higher energy than X-rays.

gam|ut /gæmət/ **1** N-SING [usu the N of n] The **gamut of** something is the complete range of things of that kind, or a wide variety of things of that kind. ❑ As the story unfolded throughout the past week, I experienced the gamut of emotions: shock, anger, sadness, disgust, confusion. **2** PHRASE To **run the gamut of** something means to include, express, or experience all the different things of that kind, or a wide variety of them. ❑ The show runs the gamut of 20th century design.

gan|der /gændər/ (ganders) N-COUNT A **gander** is a male goose.

gang /gæŋ/ (gangs, ganging, ganged) **1** N-COUNT A **gang** is a group of people, especially young people, who go around together and often deliberately cause trouble. ❏ *During the fight with a rival gang he lashed out with his flick knife.* ❏ *Gang members were behind a lot of the violence.* **2** N-COUNT A **gang** is a group of criminals who work together to commit crimes. ❏ *Police were hunting for a gang that had allegedly stolen fifty-five cars.* ❏ *...an underworld gang.* **3** N-SING The **gang** is a group of friends who frequently meet. [INFORMAL] ❏ *Come on over, we've got lots of the old gang here.* **4** N-COUNT A **gang** is a group of workers who do physical work together. ❏ *...a gang of laborers.*
▶ **gang up** PHRASAL VERB If people **gang up** on someone, they unite against them for a particular reason, for example in a fight or argument. [INFORMAL] ❏ *Harrison complained that his colleagues ganged up on him.* ❏ *All the other parties ganged up to keep them out of power.*

gang|buster /gæŋbʌstər/ (gangbusters) PHRASE If something is **going gangbusters**, it is going strongly and doing very well. If someone **comes on like gangbusters**, they behave very energetically and sometimes aggressively. [AM] ❏ *The economy was still going gangbusters.* ❏ *The team, who struggled early, came on like gangbusters at precisely the right time.*

gang|land /gæŋlænd/ ADJ [ADJ n] **Gangland** is used to describe activities or people that are involved in organized crime. ❏ *It's been suggested they were gangland killings.* ❏ *...one of Italy's top gangland bosses.*

gan|gling /gæŋglɪn/ ADJ [ADJ n] **Gangling** is used to describe a young person who is tall, thin, and clumsy in their movements. ❏ *His gangling, awkward gait has earned him the name Spiderman.* ❏ *...his gangling, bony frame.*

gan|gly /gæŋgli/ (ganglier, gangliest) ADJ [usu ADJ n] If you describe someone as **gangly**, you mean that they are tall and thin and have a slightly awkward or clumsy manner.

gang|plank /gæŋplæŋk/ (gangplanks) N-COUNT [usu the N in sing] The **gangplank** is a short bridge or platform that can be placed between the side of a ship or boat and the shore, so that people can get on or off.

gang-rape (gang-rapes, gang-raping, gang-raped) V-T [usu passive] If someone **is gang-raped**, they are raped by a group of people. ❏ *The woman was gang-raped by three men.* ● N-VAR **Gang rape** is also a noun.

gan|grene /gæŋgrin/ N-UNCOUNT **Gangrene** is the decay that can occur in a part of a person's body if the blood stops flowing to it, for example as a result of illness or injury. ❏ *Once gangrene has developed, the tissue is dead, and the only hope is to contain the damage.*

gan|gre|nous /gæŋgrɪnəs/ ADJ **Gangrenous** is used to describe a part of a person's body that has been affected by gangrene. ❏ *...patients with gangrenous limbs.*

gang|sta /gæŋstə/ also **gangsta rap** N-UNCOUNT **Gangsta** or **gangsta rap** is a form of rap music in which the words often refer to crime and violence.

gang|ster /gæŋstər/ (gangsters) N-COUNT A **gangster** is a member of an organized group of violent criminals. ❏ *...a gangster movie.*

gan|net /gænɪt/ (gannets) N-COUNT **Gannets** are large, white sea birds that live on cliffs.

gan|try /gæntri/ (gantries) N-COUNT A **gantry** is a high, metal structure that supports a set of road signs, railway signals, or other equipment. ❏ *On top of the gantry the American flag flew.* ❏ *...the lighting gantries.*

gap /gæp/ (gaps) **1** N-COUNT A **gap** is a space between two things or a hole in the middle of something solid. ❏ *He pulled the thick curtains together, leaving just a narrow gap.* **2** N-COUNT A **gap** is a period of time when you are not busy or when you stop doing something that you normally do. ❏ *There followed a gap of four years, during which William joined the Army.* **3** N-COUNT If there is something missing from a situation that prevents it from being complete or satisfactory, you can say that there is a **gap**. ❏ *The manifesto calls for a greater effort to recruit young scientists to fill the gap left by a wave of retirements expected over the next decade.* **4** N-COUNT A **gap** between two groups of people, things, or sets of ideas is a big difference between them. ❏ *...the gap between rich and poor.* ❏ *America's trade gap widened.*

COLLOCATIONS

gap
NOUN
3
verb + **gap**: fill; create, identify, leave
4
noun + **gap**: age, gender, pay, wealth
adjective + **gap**: widening, yawning
verb + **gap**: bridge, close, narrow, reduce; widen

---

gape /geɪp/ (gapes, gaping, gaped) **1** V-I If you **gape**, you look at someone or something in surprise, usually with an open mouth. ❏ *His secretary stopped taking notes to gape at me.* ❏ *He was not the type to wander around gaping at everything like a tourist.* **2** V-I If you say that something such as a hole or a wound **gapes**, you are emphasizing that it is big or wide. [EMPHASIS] ❏ *The front door was missing. A hole gaped in the roof.* ● **gap|ing** ADJ ❏ *The aircraft took off with a gaping hole in its fuselage.*

gap-fill (gap-fills) N-COUNT In language teaching, a **gap-fill** test is an exercise in which words are removed from a text and replaced with spaces. The learner has to fill each space with the missing word or a suitable word. [BRIT]

in AM, use **cloze exercise**

gap-toothed ADJ [usu ADJ n] If you describe a person or their smile as **gap-toothed**, you mean that some of that person's teeth are missing, or that there are wide spaces between their teeth. ❏ *...a broad, gap-toothed grin.*

gar|age /gərɑʒ/ (garages) **1** N-COUNT A **garage** is a building in which you keep a car. A garage is often built next to or as part of a house. ❏ *They have turned the garage into a study.* **2** N-COUNT; N-IN-NAMES A **garage** is a place where you can get your car repaired. ❏ *Nancy took her car to a local garage for a check-up.*

gar|age sale (garage sales) N-COUNT If you have a **garage sale**, you sell things such as clothes, toys, and household items that you do not want, usually in your garage. [mainly AM]

garb /gɑrb/ N-UNCOUNT Someone's **garb** is the clothes they are wearing, especially when these are unusual. [WRITTEN] ❏ *...a familiar figure in civilian garb.* ❏ *He wore the garb of a scout.*

gar|bage /gɑrbɪdʒ/ **1** N-UNCOUNT **Garbage** is waste material, especially waste from a kitchen. [mainly AM] ❏ *This morning a bomb in a garbage bag exploded and injured 15 people.* **2** N-UNCOUNT If someone says that an idea or opinion is **garbage**, they are emphasizing that they believe it is untrue or unimportant. [INFORMAL, DISAPPROVAL] ❏ *I personally think this is complete garbage.*

gar|bage can (garbage cans) N-COUNT A **garbage can** is a container that you put waste material into. [AM] ❏ *A bomb planted in a garbage can exploded early today.*

in BRIT, use **dustbin**

gar|bage col|lec|tor (garbage collectors) N-COUNT A **garbage collector** is a person whose job is to take people's garbage away. [AM]

in BRIT, use **refuse collector**

gar|bage dis|pos|al (garbage disposals) N-COUNT A **garbage disposal** or a **garbage disposal unit** is a small machine in the kitchen sink that breaks down waste matter so that it does not block the sink. [AM]

in BRIT, use **waste disposal**

gar|bage dump (garbage dumps) N-COUNT A **garbage dump** is a place where waste material is left. [AM]

in BRIT, use **rubbish tip**

gar|bage man (garbage men) N-COUNT A **garbage man** is the same as a **garbage collector**. [AM]

gar|bage truck (garbage trucks) N-COUNT A **garbage truck** is a large truck which collects the garbage from outside people's houses. [AM]

in BRIT, use **dustcart**

garbed /gɑrbd/ ADJ [v-link ADJ in n] If someone is **garbed** in particular clothes, they are wearing those clothes. [LITERARY]

❑ *He was garbed in sweater, tweed jacket, and leather boots.* • COMB IN ADJ [usu ADJ n] **Garbed** is also a combining form. ❑ *...the small, blue-garbed woman with a brown, wrinkled face.*

gar|bled /gɑ́rbᵊld/ ADJ A **garbled** message or report contains confused or wrong details, often because it is spoken by someone who is nervous or in a hurry. ❑ *The Coast Guard needs to decipher garbled messages in a few minutes.*

gar|den ♦♦◊ /gɑ́rdᵊn/ (gardens, gardening, gardened) **1** N-COUNT A **garden** is the part of a yard which is used for growing flowers and vegetables. ❑ *...the most beautiful garden on Earth.* **2** V-I If you **garden**, you do work in your garden such as weeding or planting. ❑ *Jim gardened at the homes of friends on weekends.* • **gar|den|ing** N-UNCOUNT ❑ *I have taken up gardening again.* **3** N-PLURAL **Gardens** are places like a park that have areas of plants, trees, and grass, and that people can visit and walk around. ❑ *The Gardens are open from 10:30 a.m. until 5:00 p.m.* **4** N-IN-NAMES **Gardens** is sometimes used as part of the name of a street. ❑ *He lives at 9 Acacia Gardens.*

VOCABULARY IN CONTEXT

Gardening

Gardening is more than a genteel hobby for the middle-class and middle-aged. More and more people are discovering the joy, and other benefits, it brings. This is not about vast **landscaped** spaces and **manicured lawns**, it's about the value of **planting** and **growing** things together. With more than half of the world's population living in cities, **community gardening** has been growing significantly in popularity. It's something special when people come together to clear an **overgrown** area and lovingly **cultivate** a garden that everyone can enjoy. It's hard work physically; it takes a lot of energy to **dig** and **weed**, but the rewards are worth it. And the numbers who want to feel the **soil** under their fingernails continue to increase. In the U.S., many residents in **urban** neighborhoods also rely on community gardens to provide fresh fruit and vegetables.

gar|den apart|ment (garden apartments) N-COUNT A **garden apartment** is an apartment that has direct access to a garden, yard, or lawn. [AM] ❑ *Alice Cummings lived in a cheap garden apartment behind a car wash.*

in BRIT, use **garden flat**

gar|den|er /gɑ́rdənər/ (gardeners) **1** N-COUNT A **gardener** is a person who is paid to work in someone else's garden. ❑ *She employed a gardener.* **2** N-COUNT A **gardener** is someone who enjoys working in their own garden growing flowers or vegetables. ❑ *The majority of sweet peas are still bred by enthusiastic amateur gardeners.*

gar|denia /gɑrdíniə/ (gardenias) N-COUNT A **gardenia** is a type of large, white or yellow flower with a very pleasant smell. A **gardenia** is also the bush on which these flowers grow.

gar|den par|ty (garden parties) N-COUNT [usu sing] A **garden party** is a formal party that is held out-of-doors, especially in a large private garden, during the afternoon.

gar|den-variety ADJ [usu ADJ n] You can use **garden-variety** to describe something you think is ordinary and not special in any way. [mainly AM] ❑ *The experiment itself is garden-variety science.*

in BRIT, usually use **common-or-garden**

gar|gan|tuan /gɑrgǽntʃuən/ ADJ [usu ADJ n] If you say that something is **gargantuan**, you are emphasizing that it is very large. [WRITTEN, EMPHASIS] ❑ *...a marketing event of gargantuan proportions.* ❑ *...a gargantuan corruption scandal.*

gar|gle /gɑ́rgᵊl/ (gargles, gargling, gargled) V-I If you **gargle**, you wash your mouth and throat by filling your mouth with a liquid, tipping your head back and using your throat to blow bubbles through the liquid, and finally spitting it out. ❑ *Try gargling with salt water as soon as a cough begins.*

gar|goyle /gɑ́rgɔɪl/ (gargoyles) N-COUNT A **gargoyle** is a decorative stone carving on old buildings. It is usually shaped like the head of a strange and ugly creature, and water drains through it from the roof of the building.

gar|ish /gέərɪʃ/ ADJ You describe something as **garish** when you dislike it because it is very bright in an unattractive, showy way. [DISAPPROVAL] ❑ *They climbed the garish, purple-carpeted stairs.*

gar|land /gɑ́rlənd/ (garlands) N-COUNT A **garland** is a circular decoration made from flowers and leaves. People sometimes wear garlands of flowers on their heads or around their necks. ❑ *They wore blue silk dresses with cream sashes and garlands of summer flowers in their hair.*

gar|lic /gɑ́rlɪk/ N-UNCOUNT **Garlic** is the small, white, round bulb of a plant that is related to the onion plant. Garlic has a very strong smell and taste and is used in cooking. ❑ *...a clove of garlic.*

gar|licky /gɑ́rlɪki/ ADJ [usu ADJ n] Something that is **garlicky** tastes or smells of garlic. ❑ *...a garlicky salad.* ❑ *...garlicky breath.*

gar|ment /gɑ́rmənt/ (garments) **1** N-COUNT A **garment** is a piece of clothing; used especially in contexts where you are talking about the manufacture or sale of clothes. ❑ *Many of the garments have the customers' name tags sewn into the linings.* **2** → See feature box at **sewing**

gar|ner /gɑ́rnər/ (garners, garnering, garnered) V-T If someone **has garnered** something useful or valuable, they have gained it or collected it. [FORMAL] ❑ *Durham had garnered three times as many votes as Carey.* ❑ *He has garnered extensive support for his proposals.*

gar|net /gɑ́rnɪt/ (garnets) N-COUNT A **garnet** is a hard, shiny stone that is used in making jewelry. Garnets can be red, yellow, or green in color.

gar|nish /gɑ́rnɪʃ/ (garnishes, garnishing, garnished) **1** N-VAR A **garnish** is a small amount of salad, herbs, or other food that is used to decorate cooked or prepared food. ❑ *...a garnish of chopped raw onion, tomato, and fresh coriander.* **2** V-T If you **garnish** cooked or prepared food, you decorate it with a garnish. ❑ *She had finished the vegetables and was garnishing the roast.*

gar|ret /gǽrɪt/ (garrets) N-COUNT A **garret** is a small room at the top of a house.

gar|ri|son /gǽrɪsᵊn/ (garrisons, garrisoning, garrisoned) **1** N-COUNT-COLL A **garrison** is a group of soldiers whose task is to guard the town or building where they live. ❑ *...a five-hundred-man French army garrison.* **2** N-COUNT A **garrison** is the buildings which the soldiers live in. ❑ *The approaches to the garrison have been heavily mined.* **3** V-T To **garrison** a place means to put soldiers there in order to protect it. You can also say that soldiers **are garrisoned** in a place. ❑ *American troops still garrisoned the country.* ❑ *No other soldiers were garrisoned there.*

gar|rote /gərɒ́t/ (garrotes, garroting, garroted) also **garrotte** **1** V-T If someone **is garroted**, they are killed by having something such as a piece of wire or cord pulled tightly around their neck. ❑ *The two guards had been garroted.* **2** N-COUNT A **garrote** is a piece of wire or cord used to garrote someone.

gar|ru|lous /gǽrələs/ ADJ If you describe someone as **garrulous**, you mean that they talk a great deal, especially about unimportant things. ❑ *...a garrulous old woman.*

gar|ter /gɑ́rtər/ (garters) **1** N-COUNT [usu pl] **Garters** are the fastenings which hold up a woman's stockings. [AM]

in BRIT, use **suspenders**

garter belt

2 N-COUNT A **garter** is a piece of elastic worn around the top of a stocking or sock in order to prevent it from slipping down.

gar|ter belt (garter belts) N-COUNT A **garter belt** is a piece of underwear that is used for holding up stockings. [AM]

in BRIT, use **suspender belt**

gas ♦♦◊ /gæs/ (gases, gasses, gassing, gassed)

The form **gases** is the plural of the noun. The form **gasses** is the third person singular of the verb.

1 N-UNCOUNT **Gas** is a substance like air that is neither liquid nor solid, and burns easily. It is used as a fuel for cooking and heating. ❏ *Coal is actually cheaper than gas.* **2** N-VAR A **gas** is any substance that is neither liquid nor solid, for example oxygen or hydrogen. ❏ *Helium is a very light gas.* **3** N-MASS **Gas** is a poisonous gas that can be used as a weapon. ❏ *The problem was that the exhaust gases contain many toxins.* **4** N-UNCOUNT **Gas** is the fuel which is used to drive motor vehicles. [AM] ❏ *...a tank of gas.*

in BRIT, use **petrol**

5 V-T To **gas** a person or animal means to kill them by making them breathe poisonous gas. ❏ *Hundreds of thousands of rabbits are to be gassed because they are destroying the environment.*
6 → see also **gas mask, greenhouse gas, tear gas**

gas cham|ber (gas chambers) N-COUNT A **gas chamber** is a room that has been specially built so that it can be filled with poisonous gas in order to kill people or animals.

gas|eous /gæsiəs, gæʃəs/ ADJ [usu ADJ n] You use **gaseous** to describe something which is in the form of a gas, rather than a solid or liquid. ❏ *Freon exists both in liquid and gaseous states.*

gas fire (gas fires) N-COUNT A **gas fire** is a fire that produces heat by burning gas.

gas guz|zler (gas guzzlers) also **gas-guzzler** N-COUNT If you say that a car is a **gas guzzler** you mean that it uses a lot of fuel and is not cheap to run. [AM, INFORMAL]

gash /gæʃ/ (gashes, gashing, gashed) **1** N-COUNT A **gash** is a long, deep cut in your skin or in the surface of something. ❏ *There was an inch-long gash just above his right eye.* **2** V-T If you **gash** something, you accidentally make a long and deep cut in it. ❏ *He gashed his leg while felling trees.*

gas|ket /gæskɪt/ (gaskets) N-COUNT A **gasket** is a flat piece of soft material that you put between two joined surfaces in a pipe or engine in order to make sure that gas and oil cannot escape.

gas|light /gæslaɪt/ (gaslights) also **gas light** N-COUNT A **gaslight** is a lamp that produces light by burning gas.
• N-UNCOUNT **Gaslight** is also the light that the lamp produces. ❏ *He would show his collection by gaslight.*

gas|man /gæsmæn/ (gasmen) N-COUNT [usu the N in sing] The **gasman** is a man who works for a gas company, repairing gas appliances in people's houses, or checking how much gas they have used. [INFORMAL]

gas mask (gas masks) N-COUNT A **gas mask** is a device that you wear over your face in order to protect yourself from poisonous gases.

gaso|line /gæsəlin/ N-UNCOUNT **Gasoline** is the fuel which is used to drive motor vehicles. [AM]

in BRIT, use **petrol**

gasp /gæsp/ (gasps, gasping, gasped) **1** N-COUNT A **gasp** is a short, quick breath of air that you take in through your mouth, especially when you are surprised, shocked, or in pain. ❏ *An audible gasp went around the court as the jury announced the verdict.* **2** V-I When you **gasp**, you take a short, quick breath through your mouth, especially when you are surprised, shocked, or in pain. ❏ *She gasped for air and drew in a lungful of water.* **3** PHRASE You describe something as **the last gasp** to emphasize that it is the final part of something or happens at the last possible moment. [EMPHASIS] ❏ *...the last gasp of a dying system of censorship.*

gas pe|dal (gas pedals) N-COUNT [usu the N] The **gas pedal** is another name for the **accelerator**. [mainly AM]

gas ring (gas rings) N-COUNT A **gas ring** is a metal device on top of a cooker or stove, where you can burn gas in order to cook food on it. [BRIT]

in AM, use **burner**

gas sta|tion (gas stations) N-COUNT A **gas station** is a place where you can buy fuel for your car. [AM]

in BRIT, use **petrol station**

gas|sy /gæsi/ (gassier, gassiest) ADJ Something that is **gassy** contains a lot of bubbles or gas. ❏ *The champagne was sweet and too gassy.*

gas tank (gas tanks) N-COUNT The **gas tank** in a motor vehicle is the container for gas. [AM] ❏ *I pulled into a Getty station and asked the attendant to check my oil and fill the gas tank.*

in BRIT, use **petrol tank**

gas|tric /gæstrɪk/ ADJ [ADJ n] You use **gastric** to describe processes, pain, or illnesses that occur in someone's stomach. [MEDICAL] ❏ *He suffered from diabetes and gastric ulcers.*

gas|tric band (gastric bands) N-COUNT A **gastric band** is a device that is fitted inside the body around someone's stomach to make it smaller in order to help them lose weight. [MEDICAL] ❏ *The surgeon fits an adjustable gastric band to restrict the amount that someone can eat.*

gas|tro|en|teri|tis /gæstroʊɛntəraɪtɪs/

in BRIT, also use **gastro-enteritis**

N-UNCOUNT **Gastroenteritis** is an illness in which the lining of your stomach and intestines becomes swollen and painful. [MEDICAL]

gas|tro|in|tes|ti|nal /gæstroʊɪntɛstɪnəl/ ADJ [ADJ n] **Gastrointestinal** means relating to the stomach and intestines. [MEDICAL]

gas|tro|nome /gæstrənoʊm/ (gastronomes) N-COUNT A **gastronome** is someone who enjoys preparing and eating good food, especially unusual or expensive food. [FORMAL]

gas|tro|nom|ic /gæstrənɒmɪk/ ADJ [ADJ n] **Gastronomic** is used to describe things that are concerned with good food. [FORMAL] ❏ *Paris is the gastronomic capital of the world.* ❏ *She is sampling gastronomic delights along the Riviera.*

gas|trono|my /gæstrɒnəmi/ N-UNCOUNT **Gastronomy** is the activity and knowledge involved in preparing and appreciating good food. [FORMAL] ❏ *Burgundy has always been considered a major center of gastronomy.*

gas|works /gæswɜrks/ (gasworks) also **gas works** N-COUNT A **gasworks** is a factory where gas is made, usually from coal, so that it can be used as a fuel.

gate ♦◊◊ /geɪt/ (gates) **1** N-COUNT A **gate** is a structure like a door which is used at the entrance to a field, a garden, or the grounds of a building. ❏ *He opened the gate and started walking up to the house.* **2** N-COUNT In an airport, a **gate** is a place where passengers leave the airport and get on their airplane. ❏ *Passengers with hand luggage can go straight to the departure gate to check in there.* **3** N-UNCOUNT The **gate** is the total amount of money that is paid by the people who go to a sports match or other event.

gate|crash /geɪtkræʃ/ (gatecrashes, gatecrashing, gatecrashed) V-T/V-I If someone **gatecrashes** a party or other social event, they go to it, even though they have not been invited. ❏ *Scores of people tried desperately to gatecrash the party.* • **gate|crash|er** (gatecrashers) N-COUNT ❏ *Panic set in as gatecrashers tried to force their way through the narrow doors and corridors.*

gat|ed com|mu|nity (gated communities) N-COUNT A **gated community** is an area of houses and sometimes shops that is surrounded by a wall or fence and has an entrance that is guarded. [mainly AM]

gate|house /geɪthaʊs/ (gatehouses) N-COUNT A **gatehouse** is a small house next to a gate on the edge of a park or country estate.

gate|keeper /geɪtkipər/ (gatekeepers) N-COUNT A **gatekeeper** is a person who is in charge of a gate and who allows people through it.

gate|post /geɪtpoʊst/ (**gateposts**) N-COUNT A **gatepost** is a post in the ground which a gate is hung from, or which it is fastened to when it is closed.

gate|way /geɪtweɪ/ (**gateways**) **1** N-COUNT A **gateway** is an entrance where there is a gate. ❑ *He walked across the park and through a gateway.* **2** N-COUNT A **gateway to** somewhere is a place which you go through because it leads you to a much larger place. ❑ *Denver is the gateway to some of the best skiing in the world.* **3** N-COUNT If something is a **gateway to** a job, career, or other activity, it gives you the opportunity to make progress or get further success in that activity. ❑ *The prestigious title offered a gateway to success in the highly competitive world of modeling.* **4** N-COUNT In computing, a **gateway** connects different computer networks so that information can be passed between them. [COMPUTING] ❑ *The network has a gateway into the hospital mainframe.*

gate|way drug (**gateway drugs**) N-COUNT A **gateway drug** is a drug such as marijuana that is believed by some people to lead to the use of more harmful drugs such as heroin or cocaine.

gath|er ✦✧ /gæðər/ (**gathers, gathering, gathered**) **1** V-T/V-I If people **gather** somewhere, or if someone **gathers** people somewhere, they come together in a group. ❑ *In the evenings, we gathered around the fireplace and talked.* **2** V-T If you **gather** things, you collect them together so that you can use them. ❑ *I suggest we gather enough firewood to last the night.* • PHRASAL VERB **Gather up** means the same as **gather**. ❑ *When Steinberg had gathered up his papers, he went out.* **3** V-T If you **gather** information or evidence, you collect it, especially over a period of time and after a lot of hard work. ❑ *...a private detective using a hidden tape recorder to gather information.* **4** V-T If something **gathers** speed, momentum, or force, it gradually becomes faster or more powerful. ❑ *Demands for his dismissal have gathered momentum in recent weeks.* **5** V-T When you **gather** something such as your strength, courage, or thoughts, you make an effort to prepare yourself to do something. ❑ *You must gather your strength for the journey.* • PHRASAL VERB **Gather up** means the same as **gather**. ❑ *She was gathering up her courage to approach him when he called to her.* **6** V-T You use **gather** in expressions such as '**I gather**' and '**as far as I can gather**' to introduce information that you have found out, especially when you have found it out in an indirect way. ❑ *I gather his report is highly critical of the trial judge.* ❑ *"He speaks English," she said to Graham. "I gathered that."* **7** **to gather dust** → see **dust**
▶ **gather up** → see **gather 2, 5**

gath|er|er /gæðərər/ (**gatherers**) N-COUNT [usu n n] A **gatherer** is someone who collects or gathers a particular thing. ❑ *...professional intelligence gatherers.*

gath|er|ing /gæðərɪŋ/ (**gatherings**) **1** N-COUNT A **gathering** is a group of people meeting together for a particular purpose. ❑ *...the twenty-second annual gathering of the South Pacific Forum.* **2** ADJ [ADJ n] If there is **gathering** darkness, the light is gradually decreasing, usually because it is nearly night. ❑ *The lighthouse beam was quite distinct in the gathering dusk.* **3** → see also **gather** **4** → See feature box at **socialize**

gator /geɪtər/ (**gators**) also **'gator** N-COUNT A **gator** is the same as an **alligator**. [AM, INFORMAL]

gauche /goʊʃ/ ADJ If you describe someone as **gauche**, you mean that they are awkward and uncomfortable in the company of other people. ❑ *We're all a bit gauche when we're young.*

gau|cho /gaʊtʃoʊ/ (**gauchos**) N-COUNT A **gaucho** is a South American cowboy.

gaudy /gɔːdi/ (**gaudier, gaudiest**) ADJ If something is **gaudy**, it is very brightly colored and showy. [DISAPPROVAL] ❑ *...her gaudy orange-and-purple floral hat.*

gauge /geɪdʒ/ (**gauges, gauging, gauged**) **1** V-T If you **gauge** the speed or strength of something, or if you gauge an amount, you measure or calculate it, often by using a device of some kind. ❑ *He gauged the wind at over thirty knots.* **2** N-COUNT [oft n n] A **gauge** is a device that measures the amount or quantity of something and shows the amount measured. ❑ *...temperature gauges.* **3** V-T If you **gauge** people's actions, feelings, or intentions in a particular situation, you carefully consider and judge them. ❑ *His mood can be gauged by his reaction to the most trivial of incidents.* **4** N-SING A **gauge** of someone's feelings or a situation is a fact or event that can be used to judge them. ❑ *The index is the government's chief gauge of future economic activity.*

gaunt /gɔːnt/ **1** ADJ If someone looks **gaunt**, they look very thin, usually because they have been very ill or worried. ❑ *Looking gaunt and tired, he denied there was anything to worry about.* **2** ADJ [ADJ n] If you describe a building as **gaunt**, you mean it is very plain and unattractive. [LITERARY] ❑ *Above on the hillside was a large, gaunt, gray house.*

gaunt|let /gɔːntlɪt/ (**gauntlets**) **1** N-COUNT **Gauntlets** are long, thick, protective gloves. ❑ *The smart biker also wears boots, gauntlets, and protective clothing.* **2** PHRASE If you **pick up the gauntlet** or **take up the gauntlet**, you accept the challenge that someone has made. ❑ *She picked up the gauntlet in her incisive keynote address to the conference.* **3** PHRASE If you **run the gauntlet**, you go through an unpleasant experience in which a lot of people criticize or attack you. ❑ *The trucks tried to drive to the American base, running the gauntlet of marauding bands of gunmen.* **4** PHRASE If you **throw down the gauntlet** to someone, you say or do something that challenges them to argue or compete with you. ❑ *The company has thrown down the gauntlet to competitors by giving the best guarantee on the market.*

gauze /gɔːz/ N-UNCOUNT **Gauze** is a type of light, soft cloth with tiny holes in it. ❑ *Strain the juice through a piece of gauze or a sieve.*

gauzy /gɔːzi/ ADJ [ADJ n] **Gauzy** material is light, soft, and thin, so that you can see through it. ❑ *...thin, gauzy curtains.*

gave /geɪv/ **Gave** is the past tense of **give**.

gav|el /gæv^əl/ (**gavels**) N-COUNT A **gavel** is a small wooden hammer that the person in charge of a law court, an auction, or a meeting bangs on a table to get people's attention.

gawd /gɔːd/ EXCLAM **Gawd** is used to represent the word 'God' pronounced in a particular accent or tone of voice, especially to show that someone is bored, irritated, or shocked. [INFORMAL, WRITTEN] ❑ *I thought, oh my gawd!*

gawk /gɔːk/ (**gawks, gawking, gawked**) V-I To **gawk** at someone or something means to stare at them in a rude, stupid, or unthinking way. [INFORMAL] ❑ *The youth continued to gawk at her and did not answer.* ❑ *Tens of thousands came to gawk.*

gawky /gɔːki/ (**gawkier, gawkiest**) ADJ If you describe someone, especially a young person, as **gawky**, you mean they are awkward and clumsy. ❑ *...a gawky lad with pimples.*

gay ✦✦ /geɪ/ ADJ A **gay** person is homosexual. ❑ *...a gay male couple.*

gay mar|riage (**gay marriages**) N-COUNT A **gay marriage** is marriage between two people of the same sex.

gaze /geɪz/ (**gazes, gazing, gazed**) **1** V-I If you **gaze** at someone or something, you look steadily at them for a long time, for example because you find them attractive or interesting, or because you are thinking about something else. ❑ *...gazing at herself in the mirror.* ❑ *Sitting in his wicker chair, he gazed reflectively at the fire.* **2** N-COUNT You can talk about someone's **gaze** as a way of describing how they are looking at something, especially when they are looking steadily at it. [WRITTEN] ❑ *The Monsignor turned his gaze from the flames to meet the Colonel's.* ❑ *She felt increasingly uncomfortable under the woman's steady gaze.* **3** PHRASE If someone or something is **in the public gaze**, they are receiving a lot of attention from the general public. ❑ *You won't find a couple more in the public gaze than Michael and Lizzie.* **4** → See feature box at **look, space**

ga|zebo /gəzeɪboʊ, gəziːboʊ/ (**gazebos**) N-COUNT A **gazebo** is a small building with open sides. Gazebos are often put up in gardens so that people can sit in them to enjoy the view.

ga|zelle /gəzel/ (**gazelles**) N-COUNT A **gazelle** is a type of small African or Asian animal similar to a deer. Gazelles move very quickly and gracefully.

ga|zette /gəzet/ (**gazettes**) N-IN-NAMES [n N] **Gazette** is often used in the names of newspapers. ❑ *...the Arkansas Gazette.*

gaz|et|teer /gæzɪtɪər/ (**gazetteers**) N-COUNT A **gazetteer** is a book or a part of a book which lists and describes places.

G.B. /dʒiː biː/ N-PROPER **G.B.** is an abbreviation for **Great Britain**.

GDP /dʒi di pi/ (GDPs) N-VAR In economics, a country's **GDP** is the total value of goods and services produced within a country in a year, not including its income from investments in other countries. **GDP** is an abbreviation for **gross domestic product**. Compare **GNP**.

gear ✦✧ /gɪər/ (gears, gearing, geared) **1** N-COUNT The **gears** on a machine or vehicle are a device for changing the rate at which energy is changed into motion. ▫ *On hills, he must use low gears.* ▫ *The car was in fourth gear.* **2** N-UNCOUNT The **gear** involved in a particular activity is the equipment or special clothing that you use. ▫ *About 100 officers in riot gear were needed to break up the fight.* ▫ *...fishing gear.* **3** N-UNCOUNT **Gear** means clothing. [INFORMAL] ▫ *I used to wear trendy gear but it just looked ridiculous.* **4** V-T PASSIVE If someone or something **is geared to** or **toward** a particular purpose, they are organized or designed in order to achieve that purpose. ▫ *Colleges are not always geared to the needs of mature students.* ▫ *My training was geared toward winning gold.* **5** → See also color supplement
▶ **gear up** PHRASAL VERB If someone **is gearing up for** a particular activity, they are preparing to do it. If they **are geared up to** do a particular activity, they are prepared to do it. ▫ *...another indication that the country is gearing up for an election.*

COLLOCATIONS

gear
NOUN **2**
noun + **gear**: camping, diving, fishing, riding; combat, lifting, riot
adjective + **gear**: high-tech, outdoor, protective

---

gear|box /gɪərbɒks/ (gearboxes) N-COUNT A **gearbox** is the system of gears in an engine or vehicle.

gear|head /gɪərhed/ (gearheads) N-COUNT A **gearhead** is someone who likes and is very interested in cars. [AM, INFORMAL]

gear lev|er [BRIT] → see gearshift

gear|shift /gɪərʃɪft/ (gearshifts) N-COUNT In a vehicle, the **gearshift** is the lever that you use to change gear in a car or other vehicle.

gear stick [BRIT] → see gearshift

GED /dʒi i di/ (GEDs) N-COUNT A **GED** is an American educational qualification which is equivalent to a high school diploma. **GED** is an abbreviation for 'General Equivalency Diploma.' [AM] ▫ *She attended Crane High School and got her GED from Jones Commercial High School.*

gee /dʒi/ EXCLAM People sometimes say **gee** to emphasize a reaction or remark. [AM, INFORMAL, EMPHASIS] ▫ *Gee, it's hot.*

geek /gik/ (geeks) **1** N-COUNT You can refer to someone who is very skilled in a specific subject as a **geek**. [INFORMAL] ▫ *She happily admits she is known as a math geek.* **2** N-COUNT If you call someone a **geek**, you are saying in an unkind way that they are unfashionable and behave awkwardly in social situations. [INFORMAL, DISAPPROVAL]

geeky /giki/ (geekier, geekiest) ADJ If you describe someone as **geeky**, you think they look or behave like a geek. [INFORMAL]

geese /gis/ **Geese** is the plural of **goose**.

gee whiz also **gee whizz 1** EXCLAM People sometimes say **gee whiz** in order to express a strong reaction to something or to introduce a remark or response. [AM, INFORMAL, FEELINGS] ▫ *Gee whiz, they carried on and on, they loved the evening.* **2** ADJ [ADJ n] You use **gee whiz** to describe something that is new, exciting, and impressive, but that is perhaps more complicated or showy than it needs to be. [mainly AM, INFORMAL] ▫ *The trend now is toward "lifestyle" electronics – black, shiny gee-whiz things that people like to own.*

gee|zer /gizər/ (geezers) N-COUNT Some people use **geezer** to refer to an old or eccentric man. [INFORMAL, OLD-FASHIONED] ▫ *...an old geezer with thinning gray hair.*

Geiger coun|ter /gaɪgər kaʊntər/ (Geiger counters) N-COUNT A **Geiger counter** is a device which finds and measures radioactivity.

gei|sha /geɪʃə, gi-/ (geishas) N-COUNT A **geisha** is a Japanese woman who is specially trained in music, dancing, and the art of conversation. Her job is to entertain men.

gel /dʒɛl/ (gels, gelling, gelled)

The spelling **jell** is usually used for meanings **1** and **2**.

1 V-RECIP If people **gel** with each other, or if two groups of people **gel**, they work well together because their skills and personalities fit together well. ▫ *They have gelled very well with the rest of the side.* ▫ *Their partnership gelled, and scriptwriting for television followed.* **2** V-I If a vague shape, thought, or creation **gels**, it becomes clearer or more definite. ▫ *Even if her interpretation has not yet gelled into a satisfying whole, she displays real musicianship.* **3** N-MASS **Gel** is a thick, jelly-like substance, especially one used to keep your hair in a particular style.

gela|tin /dʒɛlətən/ (gelatins) also **gelatine** N-MASS **Gelatin** is a clear tasteless powder that is used to make liquids become firm, for example when you are making desserts.

ge|lati|nous /dʒɪlætənəs/ ADJ **Gelatinous** substances or mixtures are wet and sticky. ▫ *Pour a cup of the gelatinous mixture into the blender.*

geld|ing /gɛldɪŋ/ (geldings) N-COUNT A **gelding** is a male horse that has been castrated.

gel|ig|nite /dʒɛlɪgnaɪt/ N-UNCOUNT **Gelignite** is a type of explosive.

gem /dʒɛm/ (gems) **1** N-COUNT A **gem** is a jewel or stone that is used in jewelry. ▫ *The mask is formed of a gold-platinum alloy inset with emeralds and other gems.* **2** N-COUNT If you describe something or someone as a **gem**, you mean that they are especially pleasing, good, or helpful. [INFORMAL] ▫ *...a gem of a hotel, Castel Clara.*

Gemi|ni /dʒɛmɪni/ (Geminis) **1** N-UNCOUNT **Gemini** is one of the twelve signs of the zodiac. Its symbol is a pair of twins. People who are born approximately between May 21st and June 20th come under this sign. **2** N-COUNT A **Gemini** is a person whose sign of the zodiac is Gemini.

gem|stone /dʒɛmstoʊn/ (gemstones) **1** N-COUNT A **gemstone** is a jewel or stone used in jewelry. **2** → See also color supplement

Gen. Gen. is a written abbreviation for **General**. ▫ *Gen. de Gaulle sensed that nuclear weapons would fundamentally change the nature of international relations.*

gen|darme /ʒɒndɑrm/ (gendarmes) N-COUNT A **gendarme** is a member of the French police force.

gen|der /dʒɛndər/ (genders) **1** N-UNCOUNT **Gender** is the state of being male or female in relation to the social and cultural roles that are considered appropriate for men and women. ▫ *It is illegal to discriminate on the grounds of race, gender or sexual orientation.* ▫ *Gender stereotyping can be as damaging for men as it can for women.* ▫ *Some people experience a mismatch between their gender identity and their biological sex.* **2** N-COUNT You can use **gender** to refer to one of a range of identities that includes female, male, a combination of both, and neither. ▫ *Membership is open to people of all genders.* ▫ *The new law would allow people to change gender by filling in a form.* ▫ *Each of them identifies with a different gender from the one they were born with.* **3** N-VAR Some people refer to the fact that a person is male or female as his or her **gender**. ▫ *Women are sometimes denied opportunities solely because of their gender.* **4** N-COUNT Some people refer to all male people or all female people as a particular **gender**. ▫ *While her observations may be true about some men, they could hardly apply to the entire gender.* **5** N-VAR In grammar, the **gender** of a noun, pronoun, or adjective is whether it is masculine, feminine, or neuter. A word's gender can affect its form and behavior. In English, only personal pronouns such as 'she,' reflexive pronouns such as 'itself,' and possessive determiners such as 'his' have gender. ▫ *In both Welsh and Irish the word for "moon" is of feminine gender.*

gender- /dʒɛndər/ COMB IN ADJ **Gender-** combines with adjectives to refer to things that relate to people's gender or to people who have a particular gender identity. ▫ *Each electoral list must be as gender-balanced as possible.*

gen|der bend|er (gender benders) N-COUNT People sometimes use **gender bender** to refer to a man who dresses or behaves like a woman, or a woman who dresses or behaves like a man. This use could cause offense. [INFORMAL]
• **gender-bending** ADJ [ADJ n] ▫ *Hilary Swank lived for a month as a man to prepare for her Oscar-winning, gender-bending breakthrough role.*

gendered /dʒɛndərd/ ▮ ADJ If something is **gendered**, it is related to or involves one particular gender. ❑ *'Anyone' is inconsistently treated as plural to avoid a gendered pronoun.* ▮ ADJ If something is **gendered**, it is determined or limited by gender. ❑ *Hysteria has persisted as one of the most gendered of diseases.*

gender-fluid ADJ Someone who is **gender-fluid** does not identify exclusively with any gender. ❑ *I told them I consider myself gender-fluid.*

gen|der iden|tity (gender identities) N-VAR A person's **gender identity** is their understanding of whether they are female, male, a combination of both, or neither. ❑ *At that time, she was changing her gender identity from male to female.* ❑ *...people whose sense of gender identity is seen as different from typical norms.*

gender-neutral ▮ ADJ Something that is **gender-neutral** is suitable for people of any gender. ❑ *...gender-neutral clothing.* ▮ ADJ **Gender-neutral** language does not refer to one particular gender. For example, 'police officer' is a gender-neutral form of 'policeman' or 'policewoman.'

gen|der re|as|sign|ment /dʒɛndər riəsaɪnmənt/ N-UNCOUNT **Gender reassignment** is the process of changing a person's physical sexual characteristics from male to female or from female to male with an operation and other medical procedures.

gender-variant ADJ A **gender-variant** person expresses themselves in a way that is different from that which is traditionally considered as normal for a man or woman. ❑ *...a support and advice service for gender-variant children, teenagers and their families.* • **gen|der vari|ance** N-UNCOUNT ❑ *There is mounting scientific evidence that gender variance is an innate condition.*

gene ♦◇◇ /dʒiːn/ (genes) ▮ N-COUNT A **gene** is the part of a cell in a living thing which controls its physical characteristics, growth, and development. ❑ *The gene for asthma has been identified.* ▮ → See feature box at **genetics**

ge|neal|ogy /dʒiːniælədʒi/ N-UNCOUNT **Genealogy** is the study of the history of families, especially through studying historical documents to discover the relationships between particular people and their families. • **ge|nea|logi|cal** /dʒiːniəlɒdʒɪkəl/ ADJ [ADJ n] ❑ *He had engaged in genealogical research on his family shortly before the War.*

gene edit|ing N-UNCOUNT **Gene editing** involves adding or removing DNA from a gene by a scientific process. ❑ *With gene editing, you remove certain segments and replace them.*

gen|era /dʒɛnərə/ **Genera** is the plural of **genus**.

gen|er|al ♦♦♦ /dʒɛnrəl/ (generals) ▮ N-COUNT; N-TITLE; N-VOC A **general** is a high-ranking officer in the armed forces, usually in the army. ❑ *The General's visit to Sarajevo is part of preparations for the deployment of extra troops.* ▮ ADJ [ADJ n] If you talk about the **general** situation somewhere or about something in **general** terms, you are describing the situation as a whole rather than considering its details or exceptions. ❑ *The figures represent a general decline in employment.* ❑ *...a general deterioration in the quality of life.* • PHRASE If you describe something **in general terms**, you describe it without giving details. ▮ ADJ [ADJ n] You use **general** to describe several items or activities when there are too many of them or when they are not important enough to mention separately. ❑ *$2,500 for software is soon swallowed up in general costs.* ▮ ADJ [ADJ n] You use **general** to describe something that involves or affects most people, or most people in a particular group. ❑ *The project should raise general awareness about bullying.* ▮ ADJ [ADJ n] If you describe something as **general**, you mean that it is not restricted to any one thing or area. ❑ *...a general ache radiating from the back of the neck.* ❑ *...a general sense of well-being.* ▮ ADJ [ADJ n] **General** is used to describe a person's job, usually as part of their title, to indicate that they have complete responsibility for the administration of an organization or business. [BUSINESS] ❑ *He joined Sanders Roe, moving on later to become general manager.* ▮ → see also **generally** ▮ PHRASE You use **in general** to indicate that you are talking about something as a whole, rather than about part of it. ❑ *I think we need to improve our educational system in general.* ▮ PHRASE You say **in general** to indicate that you are referring to most people or things in a particular group. ❑ *People in general will support us.*

gen|er|al elec|tion ♦◇◇ (general elections) N-COUNT In the United States, a **general election** is a local, state, or national election where the candidates have been selected by a primary election. Compare **primary**. ❑ *Street raised $10 million during his primary and general election.*

gen|er|al hos|pi|tal (general hospitals) N-COUNT; N-IN-NAMES A **general hospital** is a hospital that does not specialize in the treatment of particular illnesses or patients. ❑ *...one of the city's general hospitals.* ❑ *...the Massachusetts General Hospital in Boston.*

gen|er|al|ity /dʒɛnəræliti/ (generalities) ▮ N-COUNT A **generality** is a general statement that covers a range of things, rather than being concerned with specific instances. [FORMAL] ❑ *I'll start with some generalities and then examine a few specific examples.* ❑ *He avoided this tricky question and talked in generalities.* ▮ N-UNCOUNT The **generality** of a statement or description is the fact that it is a general one, rather than a specific, detailed one. ❑ *That there are problems with this kind of definition is hardly surprising, given its level of generality.*

gen|er|ali|za|tion /dʒɛnrəlaɪzeɪʃən/ (generalizations)

in BRIT, also use **generalisation**

N-VAR A **generalization** is a statement that seems to be true in most situations or for most people, but that may not be completely true in all cases. ❑ *He is making sweeping generalizations to get his point across.*

gen|er|al|ize /dʒɛnrəlaɪz/ (generalizes, generalizing, generalized)

in BRIT, also use **generalise**

▮ V-I If you **generalize**, you say something that seems to be true in most situations or for most people, but that may not be completely true in all cases. ❑ *Critics love to generalize, to formulate trends into which all new work must be fitted, however contradictory.* ▮ V-T If you **generalize** something such as an idea, you apply it more widely than its original context, as if it was true in many other situations. ❑ *A child first labels the household pet cat as a "cat" and then generalizes this label to other animals that look like it.*

gen|er|al|ized /dʒɛnrəlaɪzd/

in BRIT, also use **generalised**

▮ ADJ **Generalized** means involving many different things, rather than one or two specific things. ❑ *...a generalized discussion about admirable singers.* ▮ ADJ You use **generalized** to describe medical conditions or problems which affect the whole of someone's body, or the whole of a part of their body. [MEDICAL] ❑ *She experienced an increase in generalized aches and pains.*

gen|er|al knowl|edge N-UNCOUNT **General knowledge** is knowledge about many different things, as opposed to detailed knowledge about one particular subject. ❑ *...a general-knowledge quiz show.*

gen|er|al|ly ♦♦◇ /dʒɛnrəli/ ▮ ADV You use **generally** to give a summary of a situation, activity, or idea without referring to the particular details of it. ❑ *University teachers generally have admitted a lack of enthusiasm about their subjects.* ▮ ADV You use **generally** to say that something happens or is used on most occasions but not on every occasion. ❑ *As women we generally say and feel too much about these things.* ❑ *In the diet, it is generally true that the darker the fruit the higher its iron content.*

SYNONYMS

generally
ADV ▮
usually: *Usually, the work is boring.*
typically: *It typically takes a day or two, depending on size.*
normally: *Normally, the transportation system in Paris carries 950,000 passengers a day.*
on the whole: *On the whole, people miss the opportunity to enjoy leisure.*
mostly: *...men and women, mostly in their 30s.*

---

gen|er|al prac|tice (general practices) ▮ N-VAR When a doctor is in **general practice**, he or she treats sick people at an office, and does not specialize in a particular type of medicine. ❑ *In recent years, doctors have been trained specifically for general practice.* ❑ *The sample was selected from the medical records of two general practices.* ▮ N-UNCOUNT When lawyers deal with all kinds of legal matters, rather than specializing in one kind of law, you can say they have a **general practice** or are **in general practice**. [mainly AM]

gen|er|al prac|ti|tion|er (general practitioners) N-COUNT A **general practitioner** is the same as a GP. [FORMAL]

gen|er|al pub|lic N-SING-COLL You can refer to the people in a society as **the general public**, especially when you are contrasting people in general with a small group. ❑ *These charities depend on the compassionate feelings and generosity of the general public.*

gen|er|al store (general stores) N-COUNT A **general store** is a store, especially in a small town, where many different sorts of goods are sold. [mainly AM] ❑ *...the old-fashioned general store where Rockwell purchased everything from pipe tobacco to paints and supplies.*

gen|er|al strike (general strikes) N-COUNT A **general strike** is a situation where most or all of the workers in a country are on strike and are refusing to work.

gen|er|ate ✦◇◇ /dʒɛnəreɪt/ (generates, generating, generated) **1** V-T To **generate** something means to cause it to begin and develop. ❑ *The labor secretary said the reforms would generate new jobs.* **2** V-T To **generate** a form of energy or power means to produce it. ❑ *The company, New England Electric, burns coal to generate power.*

──────────── SYNONYMS ────────────

generate
VERB **1**
create: *We set business free to create more jobs in Britain.*
produce: *The drug is known to produce side-effects in women.*
cause: *Any attempts are likely to cause problems.*
bring about: *So how do we bring about political change?*
give rise to: *This can give rise to high blood-pressure.*

gen|era|tion ✦✦◇ /dʒɛnəreɪʃ³n/ (generations) **1** N-COUNT A **generation** is all the people in a group or country who are of a similar age, especially when they are considered as having the same experiences or attitudes. ❑ *...the younger generation of party members.* **2** N-COUNT A **generation** is the period of time, usually considered to be about thirty years, that it takes for children to grow up and become adults and have children of their own. ❑ *Within a generation, flight has become the method used by many travelers.* **3** N-COUNT [N of n] You can use **generation** to refer to a stage of development in the design and manufacture of machines or equipment. ❑ *...a new generation of Apple computers.* **4** ADJ [ord ADJ n] **Generation** is used to indicate how long members of your family have had a particular nationality. For example, second generation means that you were born in the country you live in, but your parents were not. ❑ *...second-generation Jamaicans in New York.*

──────────── COLLOCATIONS ────────────

generation
NOUN **1**
adjective + **generation**: current, future, next, previous; older, younger, unborn; whole
verb + **generation**: educate, influence, inspire

──────────── SYNONYMS ────────────

generation
NOUN **1**
age group: *...a style that would appeal to all age groups.*
peer group: *...peer group pressure.*

gen|era|tion|al /dʒɛnəreɪʃənəl/ ADJ [usu ADJ n] **Generational** means relating to a particular generation, or to the relationship between particular generations. ❑ *People's lifestyles are usually fixed by generational habits and fashions.*

gen|era|tion gap (generation gaps) N-COUNT If you refer to the **generation gap**, you are referring to a difference in attitude and behavior between older people and younger people, which may cause them to argue or may prevent them from understanding each other fully.

gen|era|tive /dʒɛnərətɪv/ **1** ADJ If something is **generative**, it is capable of producing something or causing it to develop. [FORMAL] ❑ *...the generative power of the sun.* **2** ADJ [ADJ n] In linguistics, **generative** is used to describe linguistic theories or models which are based on the idea that a single set of rules can explain how all the possible sentences of a language are formed. [TECHNICAL]

gen|era|tor /dʒɛnəreɪtər/ (generators) **1** N-COUNT A **generator** is a machine which produces electricity. ❑ *The house is far from water mains and electricity and relies on its own generators.* **2** N-COUNT A **generator** of something is a person, organization, product, or situation which produces it or causes it to happen. ❑ *The company has been a very good cash generator.*

ge|ner|ic /dʒɪnɛrɪk/ (generics) **1** ADJ You use **generic** to describe something that refers or relates to a whole class of similar things. ❑ *Parmesan is a generic term used to describe a family of hard Italian cheeses.* **2** ADJ A **generic** drug or other product is one that does not have a trademark and that is known by a general name, rather than the manufacturer's name. ❑ *Doctors sometimes prescribe cheaper generic drugs instead of more expensive brand names.* • N-COUNT **Generic** is also a noun. ❑ *The program saved $11 million by substituting generics for brand-name drugs.*

gen|er|os|ity /dʒɛnərɒsɪti/ N-UNCOUNT If you refer to someone's **generosity**, you mean that they are generous, especially in doing or giving more than is usual or expected. ❑ *There are stories about his generosity, the massive amounts of money he gave to charities.*

gen|er|ous ✦◇◇ /dʒɛnərəs/ **1** ADJ A **generous** person gives more of something, especially money, than is usual or expected. ❑ *Dietler is generous with his time and money.* • **gen|er|ous|ly** ADV [ADV with v] ❑ *We would like to thank all the judges who gave so generously of their time.* **2** ADJ A **generous** person is friendly, helpful, and willing to see the good qualities in someone or something. ❑ *He was always generous in sharing his enormous knowledge.* • **gen|er|ous|ly** ADV [ADV with v] ❑ *The students generously gave them instruction in social responsibility.* **3** ADJ A **generous** amount of something is much larger than is usual or necessary. ❑ *He should be able to keep his room tidy with the generous amount of storage space.* • **gen|er|ous|ly** ADV ❑ *Season the steaks generously with salt and pepper.*

gen|esis /dʒɛnɪsɪs/ N-SING [usu with poss] The **genesis** of something is its beginning, birth, or creation. [FORMAL] ❑ *The project had its genesis two years earlier.*

gene splic|ing N-UNCOUNT **Gene splicing** is a technique that combines genetic material from different places. ❑ *In the movie, the scientists use gene splicing to create a bigger dinosaur.*

gene thera|py N-UNCOUNT **Gene therapy** is the use of genetic material to treat disease.

ge|net|ic /dʒɪnɛtɪk/ **1** ADJ You use **genetic** to describe something that is concerned with genetics or with genes. ❑ *Cystic fibrosis is the most common fatal genetic disease in the United States.* • **ge|neti|cal|ly** /dʒɪnɛtɪkli/ ADV ❑ *Some people are genetically predisposed to diabetes.* **2** → See feature box at **genetics, medicine**

ge|neti|cal|ly modi|fied 1 ADJ **Genetically modified** plants and animals have had one or more genes changed, for example so that they resist pests and diseases better. **Genetically modified** food contains ingredients made from genetically modified plants or animals. The abbreviation **GM** is often used. ❑ *Top supermarkets are to ban many genetically modified foods.* **2** → See feature box at **farming**

ge|net|ic en|gi|neer|ing N-UNCOUNT **Genetic engineering** is the science or activity of changing the genetic structure of an animal, plant, or other organism in order to make it stronger or more suitable for a particular purpose. ❑ *Scientists have used genetic engineering to protect tomatoes against the effects of freezing.*

ge|net|ic fin|ger|print|ing N-SING **Genetic fingerprinting** is a method of identifying people using the genetic material in their bodies.

ge|neti|cist /dʒɪnɛtɪsɪst/ (geneticists) N-COUNT A **geneticist** is a person who studies or specializes in genetics.

ge|net|ics /dʒɪnɛtɪks/ N-UNCOUNT **Genetics** is the study of heredity and how qualities and characteristics are passed on from one generation to another by means of genes. ❑ *Genetics is also bringing about dramatic changes in our understanding of cancer.*

VOCABULARY IN CONTEXT

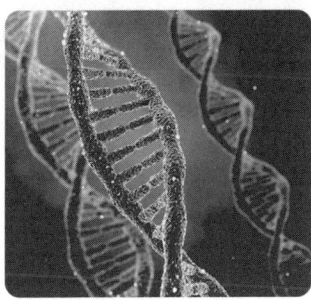

Genetics

Genetics is the study of the **biological** history of humans, or in fact any living **organism**. Our **genes** are made up of **DNA** (short for 'deoxyribonucleic acid') – **molecules** containing a **genetic code** that enables us to grow and develop into adult humans with specific physical and personality **traits**. These DNA molecules are arranged in pairs in a spiral, ladder-like shape known as a 'double helix'. A complete set of human DNA is called a **human genome**. Each genome contains 23 pairs of **chromosomes**, and each pair contains one gene from the father and one from the mother. You may think that as we are all so different from each other in so many ways, the **variation** between the genes of one person and another must be huge. In fact, 99.9% of our DNA is shared with all humans. This means that these differences are contained in only 0.1% of our genes.

gen|ial /dʒiːnyəl/ ADJ Someone who is **genial** is kind and friendly. [APPROVAL] ❑ *Bob was always genial and welcoming.* • **gen|ial|ly** ADV ❑ *"If you don't mind," Mrs. Dambar said genially.* • **ge|ni|al|ity** /dʒiːniæliti/ N-UNCOUNT ❑ *He soon recovered his habitual geniality.*

ge|nie /dʒiːni/ (genies) **1** N-COUNT In stories from Arabia and Persia, a **genie** is a spirit which appears and disappears by magic and obeys the person who controls it. **2** PHRASE If you say that **the genie is out of the bottle** or that someone **has let the genie out of the bottle**, you mean that something has happened which has made a great and permanent change in people's lives, especially a bad change.

geni|tal /dʒɛnɪtəl/ N-PLURAL Someone's **genitals** are their external sexual organs. ❑ *Without thinking, Neil cupped his hands over his genitals.* **2** ADJ [ADJ n] **Genital** means relating to a person's external sexual organs. ❑ *Wear loose clothing in the genital area.*

geni|ta|lia /dʒɛnɪteɪliə/ N-PLURAL A person's or animal's **genitalia** are their external sexual organs. [FORMAL]

geni|tive /dʒɛnɪtɪv/ N-SING [the N] In the grammar of some languages, **the genitive**, or **the genitive case**, is a noun case which is used mainly to show possession. In English grammar, a noun or name with 's added to it, for example 'dog's' or 'Anne's', is sometimes called **the genitive form**.

ge|ni|us /dʒiːnyəs/ (geniuses) **1** N-UNCOUNT **Genius** is very great ability or skill in a particular subject or activity. ❑ *This is the mark of her real genius as a designer.* ❑ *The man had genius and had made his mark in the aviation world.* **2** N-COUNT A **genius** is a highly talented, creative, or intelligent person. ❑ *Chaplin was not just a genius, he was among the most influential figures in film history.*

geno|cid|al /dʒɛnəsaɪdəl/ ADJ [USU ADJ n] **Genocidal** means relating to genocide or carrying out genocide. ❑ *They have been accused of genocidal crimes.*

geno|cide /dʒɛnəsaɪd/ N-UNCOUNT **Genocide** is the deliberate murder of a whole community or race. ❑ *They have alleged that acts of genocide and torture were carried out.*

ge|nome /dʒiːnoʊm/ (genomes) **1** N-COUNT In biology, a **genome** is the particular number and arrangement of chromosomes within the cells of an organism such as an animal or plant that distinguishes it from other types of organism. [TECHNICAL] ❑ *...the mapping of the human genome.* **2** → See feature box at **genetics**

ge|nom|ic /dʒiːnɒmɪk/ ADJ [ADJ n] **Genomic** means relating to genomes. [TECHNICAL] ❑ *...genomic research.*

ge|nom|ics /dʒiːnɒmɪks/ N-SING **Genomics** is the study of genomes. [TECHNICAL] ❑ *...the genomics revolution.*

gen|re /ʒɒnrə/ (genres) N-COUNT A **genre** is a particular type of literature, painting, music, film, or other art form which people consider as a class because it has special characteristics. [FORMAL] ❑ *...his love of films and novels in the horror genre.*

gent /dʒɛnt/ (gents) **1** N-COUNT **Gent** is an informal and old-fashioned word for **gentleman**. ❑ *Mr. Blake was a gent. He knew how to behave.* **2** N-VOC **Gents** is used when addressing men in an informal, humorous way, especially in the expression 'ladies and gents.' [HUMOROUS, INFORMAL] ❑ *Don't be left standing, ladies and gents, while a bargain slips past your eyes.*

gen|teel /dʒɛntiːl/ **1** ADJ A **genteel** person is respectable and well-mannered, and comes or seems to come from a high social class. ❑ *It was a place to which genteel families came in search of health and quiet.* **2** ADJ A **genteel** place or area is quiet and traditional, but may also be old-fashioned and dull. ❑ *...the genteel towns of Winchester and Chichester.*

gen|tian /dʒɛnʃən/ (gentians) N-COUNT A **gentian** is a small plant with a blue or purple flower shaped like a bell which grows in mountain regions.

Gen|tile /dʒɛntaɪl/ (Gentiles) also **gentile** N-COUNT A **Gentile** is a person who is not Jewish. • ADJ [USU ADJ n] **Gentile** is also an adjective. ❑ *...a flood of Jewish and Gentile German refugees.*

gen|til|ity /dʒɛntɪlɪti/ N-UNCOUNT **Gentility** is the fact or appearance of belonging to a high social class. ❑ *The hotel has an air of faded gentility.*

gen|tle ✦✧ /dʒɛntəl/ (gentler, gentlest) **1** ADJ Someone who is **gentle** is kind, mild, and calm. ❑ *My son was a quiet and gentle man who liked sports and enjoyed life.* • **gen|tly** ADV [ADV with v] ❑ *She smiled gently at him.* • **gen|tle|ness** N-UNCOUNT ❑ *...the gentleness with which she treated her pregnant mother.* **2** ADJ **Gentle** actions or movements are performed in a calm and controlled manner, with little force. ❑ *...a gentle game of tennis.* • **gen|tly** ADV ❑ *Patrick took her gently by the arm and led her to a chair.* **3** ADJ A **gentle** slope or curve is not steep or severe. ❑ *...gentle, rolling meadows.* • **gen|tly** ADV ❑ *With its gently rolling hills it looks like Tuscany.* **4** ADJ A **gentle** heat is a fairly low heat. ❑ *Cook for 30 minutes over a gentle heat.* • **gen|tly** ADV [ADV with v] ❑ *Add the onion and cook gently for about 5 minutes.*

gentle|man ✦✧ /dʒɛntəlmən/ (gentlemen) **1** N-COUNT If you say that a man is a **gentleman**, you mean he is polite and educated, and can be trusted. ❑ *He was always such a gentleman.* **2** N-COUNT A **gentleman** is a man who comes from a family of high social standing. ❑ *...this wonderful portrait of English gentleman Joseph Greenway.* **3** N-COUNT; N-VOC You can address men as **gentlemen**, or refer politely to them as **gentlemen**. [POLITENESS] ❑ *This way, please, ladies and gentlemen.* ❑ *It seems this gentleman was waiting for the doctor.*

gentle|man|ly /dʒɛntəlmənli/ ADJ [USU ADJ n] If you describe a man's behavior as **gentlemanly**, you approve of him because he has good manners. [APPROVAL] ❑ *He was respected by all who knew him for his kind and gentlemanly consideration.*

gentle|man's agree|ment (gentleman's agreements) also **gentlemen's agreement** A **gentleman's agreement** or a **gentlemen's agreement** is an informal agreement in which people trust one another to do what they have promised. The agreement is not written down and does not have any legal force. ❑ *She made a gentleman's agreement with her buyer.*

gentle|woman /dʒɛntəlwʊmən/ (gentlewomen) N-COUNT A **gentlewoman** is a woman of high social standing, or a woman who is cultured, educated, and well-mannered. [OLD-FASHIONED]

gen|tri|fy /dʒɛntrɪfaɪ/ (gentrifies, gentrifying, gentrified) **1** V-T [USU PASSIVE] When a street or area **is gentrified**, it becomes a more expensive place to live because wealthy people move into the area and buy the houses where people

with less money used to live. ❑ *The local neighborhood, like so many areas of Manhattan, is gradually being gentrified.* • **gen|tri|fi|ca|tion** /dʒɛntrɪfɪkeɪʃ°n/ N-UNCOUNT ❑ *...the gentrification of the area.*
2 → See feature box at **town**

genu|flect /dʒɛnyʊflɛkt/ (**genuflects**, **genuflecting**, **genuflected**) **1** V-I If you **genuflect**, you bend one or both knees and bow, especially in church, as a sign of respect. [FORMAL] ❑ *He genuflected in front of the altar.* **2** V-I You can say that someone **is genuflecting** to something when they are giving it a great deal of attention and respect, especially if you think it does not deserve this. [mainly JOURNALISM, DISAPPROVAL] ❑ *They refrained from genuflecting to the laws of political economy.*

genu|ine ◆◇◇ /dʒɛnyuɪn/ **1** ADJ **Genuine** is used to describe people and things that are exactly what they appear to be, and are not false or an imitation. ❑ *There was a risk of genuine refugees being returned to Vietnam.* ❑ *...genuine leather.* **2** ADJ **Genuine** refers to things such as emotions that are real and not pretended. ❑ *If this offer is genuine, I will gladly accept it.* • **genu|ine|ly** ADV ❑ *He was genuinely surprised.* **3** ADJ If you describe a person as **genuine**, you approve of them because they are honest, truthful, and sincere in the way they live and in their relationships with other people. [APPROVAL] ❑ *She is very caring and very genuine.*

SYNONYMS

genuine
ADJ
1
authentic: *...authentic Italian food.*
real: *...the smell of real leather.*
actual: *The segments are filmed using either local actors or the actual people involved.*
legitimate: *The New York Times has a legitimate claim to be a national newspaper.*
2
heartfelt: *My heartfelt sympathy goes out to all the relatives.*
sincere: *He accepted her apologies as sincere.*
honest: *What do you think of the school, in your honest opinion?*

WORD HISTORY

genuine
The word **genuine** comes from the Latin word *genu*, meaning 'knee.' This can be explained by a Roman custom in which a father used to put a newborn baby on his knee as a way of formally recognizing that the child was his.

---

ge|nus /dʒinəs/ (**genera** /dʒɛnərə/) N-COUNT A **genus** is a class of similar things, especially a group of animals or plants that includes several closely related species. [TECHNICAL] ❑ *...a genus of plants called Sinningia.* **2** → See feature box at **animal**

PREFIX

geo-
is used at the beginning of words that refer to the whole of the world or to the Earth's surface. *For example, geology is the study of the Earth's structure, surface, and origins.*

---

geo|en|gi|neer|ing /dʒioʊɛndʒɪnɪərɪŋ/ N-UNCOUNT **Geoengineering** is the use of scientific processes to improve the environment, especially to stop the Earth becoming any hotter. ❑ *The company is involved in several geoengineering projects.*

ge|og|ra|pher /dʒiɒgrəfər/ (**geographers**) N-COUNT A **geographer** is a person who studies geography or is an expert in it.

geo|graphi|cal /dʒiəgræfɪk°l/

The form **geographic** /dʒiəgræfɪk/ is also used.

ADJ **Geographical** or **geographic** means concerned with or relating to geography. ❑ *Its geographical location stimulated overseas mercantile enterprise.* • **geo|graphi|cal|ly** /dʒiəgræfɪkli/ ADV ❑ *It is geographically more diverse than any other continent.*

ge|og|ra|phy /dʒiɒgrəfi/ **1** N-UNCOUNT **Geography** is the study of the countries of the world and of such things as the land, seas, climate, towns, and population. **2** N-UNCOUNT The **geography** of a place is the way that features such as rivers, mountains, towns, or streets are arranged within it. ❑ *...policemen who knew the local geography.*

geo|lo|ca|tion /dʒioʊloʊkeɪʃ°n/ N-UNCOUNT **Geolocation** is the use of technology to find the location of an internet or cellphone user. ❑ *The company uses geolocation to spot whether criminals may be trying to transfer money from a new location.*

geo|logi|cal /dʒiəlɒdʒɪk°l/ ADJ **Geological** means relating to geology. ❑ *With geological maps, books, and atlases you can find out all the proven sites of precious minerals.*

ge|ol|ogy /dʒiɒlədʒi/ **1** N-UNCOUNT **Geology** is the study of the Earth's structure, surface, and origins. ❑ *He was visiting professor of geology at the University of Georgia.* • **ge|olo|gist** (**geologists**) ❑ *Geologists have studied the way that heat flows from the earth.* **2** N-UNCOUNT The **geology** of an area is the structure of its land, together with the types of rocks and minerals that exist within it. ❑ *...the geology of Asia.*

geo|met|ric /dʒiəmɛtrɪk/

The form **geometrical** /dʒiəmɛtrɪk°l/ is also used.

1 ADJ **Geometric** or **geometrical** patterns or shapes consist of regular shapes or lines. ❑ *Geometric designs were popular wall decorations in the 14th century.* **2** ADJ **Geometric** or **geometrical** means relating to or involving the principles of geometry. ❑ *Euclid was trying to convey his idea of a geometrical point.*

ge|om|etry /dʒiɒmɪtri/ **1** N-UNCOUNT **Geometry** is the branch of mathematics concerned with the properties and relationships of lines, angles, curves, and shapes. ❑ *...the very ordered way in which mathematics and geometry describe nature.* **2** N-UNCOUNT The **geometry** of an object is its shape or the relationship of its parts to each other. ❑ *...the geometry of the curved roof.*

geo|physi|cal /dʒioʊfɪzɪk°l/ ADJ [usu ADJ n] **Geophysical** means relating to geophysics.

geo|physi|cist /dʒioʊfɪzɪsɪst/ (**geophysicists**) N-COUNT A **geophysicist** is someone who studies or specializes in geophysics.

geo|phys|ics /dʒioʊfɪzɪks/ N-UNCOUNT **Geophysics** is the branch of geology that uses physics to examine the Earth's structure, climate, and oceans.

geo|po|liti|cal /dʒioʊpəlɪtɪk°l/ ADJ [usu ADJ n] **Geopolitical** means relating to or concerned with geopolitics. ❑ *Early resolution of geopolitical issues would be beneficial.*

geo|poli|tics /dʒioʊpɒlɪtɪks/ N-UNCOUNT **Geopolitics** is concerned with politics and the way that geography affects politics or relations between countries.

Geor|gian /dʒɔrdʒ°n/ ADJ **Georgian** means belonging to or connected with Britain in the eighteenth and early nineteenth centuries, during the reigns of King George I to King George IV. ❑ *...the restoration of his Georgian house.*

geo|ther|mal /dzioʊθɜrm°l/ ADJ [ADJ n] **Geothermal** energy is heat that is produced inside the earth. ❑ *One house is heated and cooled with geothermal energy.* ❑ *...the geothermal activity on the surface of Iceland.*

ge|ra|nium /dʒɪreɪniəm/ (**geraniums**) N-COUNT A **geranium** is a plant with red, pink, or white flowers.

ger|bil /dʒɜrbɪl/ (**gerbils**) N-COUNT A **gerbil** is a small, furry animal that is often kept as a pet.

geri|at|ric /dʒɛriætrɪk/ (**geriatrics**) **1** ADJ [ADJ n] **Geriatric** is used to describe things relating to the illnesses and medical care of old people. [MEDICAL] ❑ *There is a question mark over the future of geriatric care.* **2** N-COUNT If you describe someone as a **geriatric**, you are implying that they are old and that their mental or physical condition is poor. This use could cause offense. [DISAPPROVAL] ❑ *He will complain about having to spend time with such a boring bunch of geriatrics.*

germ /dʒɜrm/ (**germs**) **1** N-COUNT A **germ** is a very small organism that causes disease. ❑ *Chlorine is widely used to kill germs.* **2** N-SING The **germ** of something such as an idea is something which developed or might develop into that thing. ❑ *This was the germ of a book.* **3** → See feature box at **illness**

Ger|man /dʒɜrmən/ (**Germans**) **1** ADJ **German** means belonging or relating to Germany. • N-COUNT A **German** is a

germane /dʒɜrmeɪn/ ADJ [oft ADJ to n] Something that is germane to a situation or idea is connected with it in an important way. [FORMAL] ❑ ...the suppression of a number of documents which were very germane to the case. ❑ Fenton was a good listener, and his questions were germane.

Ger|man|ic /dʒɜrmænɪk/ **1** ADJ If you describe someone or something as Germanic, you think that their appearance or behavior is typical of German people or things. ❑ He asked in his Germanic English if I was enjoying France. **2** ADJ Germanic is used to describe the ancient culture and language of the peoples of northern Europe. ❑ ...the Germanic tribes of pre-Christian Europe.

Ger|man mea|sles N-UNCOUNT German measles is a disease which causes you to have a cough, a sore throat, and red spots on your skin.

Ger|man shep|herd (German shepherds) N-COUNT A German shepherd is a large, usually fierce dog that is used to guard buildings or by the police to help them find criminals. [mainly AM] ❑ ...his eighty-five-pound German shepherd Spike.

in BRIT, also use **Alsatian**

ger|mi|nate /dʒɜrmɪneɪt/ (germinates, germinating, germinated) **1** V-T/V-I If a seed germinates or if it is germinated, it starts to grow. ❑ Some seed varieties germinate fast, so check every day or so. • **ger|mi|na|tion** /dʒɜrmɪneɪʃ°n/ N-UNCOUNT [usu with supp] ❑ The poor germination of your seed could be because the soil was too cold. **2** V-I If an idea, plan, or feeling germinates, it comes into existence and begins to develop. ❑ ...a big book that was germinating in his mind.

germ war|fare N-UNCOUNT Germ warfare is the use of germs in a war in order to cause disease in enemy troops, or to destroy crops that they might use as food. ❑ ...an international treaty banning germ warfare.

ger|on|tol|ogy /dʒɛrəntɒlədʒi/ N-UNCOUNT Gerontology is the study of the process by which we get old, how our bodies change, and the problems that old people have.

ger|ry|man|der|ing /dʒɛrimændərɪŋ/ N-UNCOUNT Gerrymandering is the act of altering political boundaries in order to give an unfair advantage to one political party or group of people. [DISAPPROVAL]

ger|und /dʒɛrənd/ (gerunds) N-COUNT A gerund is a noun formed from a verb which refers to an action, process, or state. In English, gerunds end in '-ing,' for example 'running' and 'thinking.'

ge|stalt /ɡəʃtælt/ N-SING In psychology, a gestalt is something that has particular qualities when you consider it as a whole which are not obvious when you consider only the separate parts of it. [TECHNICAL]

ges|ta|tion /dʒɛsteɪʃ°n/ N-UNCOUNT **1** Gestation is the process in which babies grow inside their mother's body before they are born. [TECHNICAL] ❑ ...the seventeenth week of gestation. ❑ The gestation period can be anything between 95 and 150 days. **2** N-UNCOUNT Gestation is the process in which an idea or plan develops. [FORMAL] ❑ ...the period of gestation of this design.

ges|ticu|late /dʒɛstɪkjʊleɪt/ (gesticulates, gesticulating, gesticulated) V-I If you gesticulate, you make movements with your arms or hands, often while you are describing something that is difficult to express in words. [mainly WRITTEN] ❑ A man with a paper hat upon his head was gesticulating wildly. ❑ The architect was gesticulating at a hole in the ground. • **ges|ticu|la|tion** /dʒɛstɪkjʊleɪʃ°n/ (gesticulations) N-COUNT [also N in pl] ❑ We communicated mainly by signs, gesticulation, and mime.

ges|ture ♦◇◇ /dʒɛstʃər/ (gestures, gesturing, gestured) **1** N-COUNT A gesture is a movement that you make with a part of your body, especially your hands, to express emotion or information. ❑ Sarah made a menacing gesture with her fist. **2** N-COUNT A gesture is something that you say or do in order to express your attitude or intentions, often something that you know will not have much effect. ❑ He questioned the government's commitment to peace and called on it to make a gesture of good will. **3** V-I If you gesture, you use movements of your hands or head in order to tell someone something or draw their attention to something. ❑ I gestured toward the boathouse, and he looked inside. **4** → See feature box at **body language**

COLLOCATIONS

gesture
NOUN
1
noun + **gesture**: hand
adjective + **gesture**: obscene, offensive, rude, threatening
verb + **gesture**: make
2
noun + **gesture**: goodwill
adjective + **gesture**: dramatic, generous, grand; romantic, spontaneous, symbolic, token; empty
verb + **gesture**: appreciate, welcome; reciprocate, return
VERB **3**
gesture + adverb: angrily, rudely, vaguely, wildly

SYNONYMS

gesture
NOUN
1
sign: They gave Lavalle the thumbs-up sign.
signal: As soon as it was dark, Mrs Evans gave the signal.
motion: He made a neat, chopping motion with his hand.
2
token: As a token of goodwill, I'm going to write another letter.
demonstration: ...physical demonstrations of affection.
expression: Laughter is one of the most infectious expressions of emotion.
display: Normally, such an outward display of affection is reserved for his mother.

GET

① CHANGING, CAUSING, MOVING, OR REACHING
② OBTAINING, RECEIVING, OR CATCHING
③ PHRASES AND PHRASAL VERBS

① **get** ♦♦♦ /ɡɛt/ (gets, getting, got, gotten or got)

In most of its uses **get** is a fairly informal word.

1 V-LINK You use get with adjectives to mean 'become.' For example, if someone gets cold, they become cold, and if they get angry, they become angry. ❑ The boys were getting bored. ❑ From here on, it can only get better. **2** V-LINK Get is used with expressions referring to states or situations. For example, to get into trouble means to start being in trouble. ❑ Half the pleasure of an evening out is getting ready. ❑ Perhaps I shouldn't say that – I might get into trouble. **3** V-T To get someone or something into a particular state or situation means to cause them to be in it. ❑ I don't know if I can get it clean. ❑ Brian will get them out of trouble. **4** V-T If you get someone to do something, you cause them to do it by asking, persuading, or telling them to do it. ❑ ...a long campaign to get U.S. politicians to take the AIDS epidemic more seriously. **5** V-T If you get something done, you cause it to be done. ❑ I might benefit from getting my teeth fixed. **6** V-I To get somewhere means to move there. ❑ I got off the bed and opened the door. ❑ How can I get past her without her seeing me? **7** V-I When you get to a place, you arrive there. ❑ Generally I get to work at 9:30 a.m. **8** V-T To get something or someone into a place or position means to cause them to move there. ❑ Mack got his wallet out. ❑ Go and get your coat on. **9** AUX Get is often used in place of 'be' as an auxiliary verb to form passives. ❑ A pane of glass got broken. **10** V-T If you get to do something, you eventually or gradually reach a stage at which you do it. ❑ No one could figure out how he got to be so wealthy. **11** V-T If you get to do something, you manage to do it or have the opportunity to do it. ❑ How do these people get to be the bosses of major companies? ❑ Do you get to see him often? **12** V-T You can use get in expressions like get moving, get going, and get working when you want to tell people to begin moving, going, or working quickly. ❑ I aim to be at the lake before dawn, so let's get moving. **13** V-I If you get to a particular stage in your life or in something you are

get

doing, you reach that stage. ❑ *We haven't gotten to the stage of a full-scale military conflict.* ❑ *It got to the point where I was so ill I was waiting to die.* **14** V-T/V-I You can use **get** to talk about the progress that you are making. For example, if you say that you are **getting somewhere**, you mean that you are making progress, and if you say that something **won't get** you **anywhere**, you mean it will not help you to progress at all. ❑ *Radical factions say the talks are getting nowhere and they want to withdraw.* ❑ *This bout of self-pity was getting me nowhere.* **15** V-LINK When it **gets** to be a particular time, it is that time. If it **is getting** toward a particular time, it is approaching that time. ❑ *It got to be after 1 a.m. and I was exhausted.* ❑ *It was getting toward evening when we got back.* **16** V-I If something that has continued for some time **gets to** you, it starts causing you to suffer. ❑ *That's the first time I lost my cool in 20 years in this job. This whole thing's getting to me.*

② **get** ♦♦♦ /gɛt/ (**gets, getting, got, gotten** or **got**) **1** V-T If you **get** something that you want or need, you obtain it. ❑ *I got a job at the sawmill.* **2** V-T If you **get** something, you receive it or are given it. ❑ *I'm getting a bike for my birthday.* ❑ *He gets a lot of letters from women.* **3** V-T If you **get** someone or something, you go and bring them to a particular place. ❑ *I came down this morning to get the newspaper.* ❑ *Go and get me a large brandy.* **4** V-T If you **get** a particular result, you obtain it from some action that you take, or from a calculation or experiment. ❑ *What do you get if you multiply six by nine?* **5** V-T If you **get** a particular price for something that you sell, you obtain that amount of money by selling it. ❑ *He can't get a good price for his crops.* **6** V-T If you **get** the time or opportunity to do something, you have the time or opportunity to do it. ❑ *You get time to think in prison.* **7** V-T If you **get** an idea, impression, or feeling, you begin to have that idea, impression, or feeling as you learn or understand more about something. ❑ *I get the feeling that you're an honest man.* **8** V-T If you **get** a feeling or benefit from an activity or experience, the activity or experience gives you that feeling or benefit. ❑ *Charles got a shock when he saw him.* ❑ *She gets enormous pleasure out of working freelance.* **9** V-T If you **get** a look, view, or glimpse of something, you manage to see it. ❑ *Young men climbed on buses and fences to get a better view.* **10** V-T If you **get** a joke or **get** the point of something that is said, you understand it. ❑ *Did you get that joke, Ann? I'll explain later.* **11** V-T If you **get** an illness or disease, you become ill with it. ❑ *When I was five I got measles.* **12** V-T When you **get** a train, bus, plane, or boat, you leave a place on a particular train, bus, plane, or boat. ❑ *It'll be a dollar to get the bus.* **13** → see also **got**

③ **get** ♦♦♦ /gɛt/ (**gets, getting, got, gotten** or **got**) **1** PHRASE You can say that something is, for example, **as good as you can get** to mean that it is as good as it is possible for that thing to be. ❑ *Consort has a population of 714 and is about as rural and isolated as you can get.* ❑ *...the diet that is as near to perfect as you can get it.* **2** PHRASE If you say **you can't get away from** something or **there is no getting away from** something, you are emphasizing that it is true, even though people might prefer it not to be true. [INFORMAL, EMPHASIS] ❑ *There is no getting away from the fact that he is on the left of the party.* **3** PHRASE If you **get away from it all**, you take a vacation in a place that is very different from where you normally live and work. ❑ *...the ravishing island of Ischia, where rich Italians get away from it all.* **4** PHRASE You can use **you get** instead of 'there is' or 'there are' to say that something exists, happens, or can be experienced. [SPOKEN] ❑ *That's where you get some differences of opinion.*

▶ **get across** PHRASAL VERB When an idea **gets across** or when you **get** it **across**, you succeed in making other people understand it. ❑ *Officers felt their point of view was not getting across to the generals.*

▶ **get along** PHRASAL VERB If you **get along with** someone, you have a friendly relationship with them. You can also say that two people **get along**. ❑ *It's impossible to get along with him.*

▶ **get around** **1** PHRASAL VERB To **get around** a problem or difficulty means to overcome it. ❑ *None of these countries has found a way yet to get around the problem of the polarization of wealth.* **2** PHRASAL VERB If you **get around** a rule or law, you find a way of doing something that the rule or law is intended to prevent, without actually breaking it. ❑ *Although tobacco ads are prohibited, companies get around the ban by sponsoring music shows.* **3** PHRASAL VERB If news **gets around**, it becomes well known as a result of being told to lots of people. ❑ *They threw him out because word got around that he was taking drugs.* **4** PHRASAL VERB If you **get around** someone, you persuade them to allow you to do or have something by pleasing them or flattering them. ❑ *Max could always get around her.* **5** PHRASAL VERB If you **get around**, you visit a lot of different places as part of your way of life. ❑ *He claimed to be a journalist, and he got around.* **6** PHRASAL VERB The way that someone **gets around** is the way that they walk or go from one place to another. ❑ *It is difficult for Gail to get around since she broke her leg.*

▶ **get around to** PHRASAL VERB When you **get around to** doing something that you have delayed doing or have been too busy to do, you finally do it. ❑ *I said I would write to you, but as usual I never got around to it.*

▶ **get at** **1** PHRASAL VERB To **get at** something means to succeed in reaching it. ❑ *A goat was standing up against a tree on its hind legs, trying to get at the leaves.* **2** PHRASAL VERB If you **get at** the truth about something, you succeed in discovering it. ❑ *We want to get at the truth. Who killed him? And why?* **3** PHRASE If you ask someone **what they are getting at**, you are asking them to explain what they mean, usually because you think that they are being unpleasant or are suggesting something that is untrue. ❑ *"What are you getting at now?" demanded Rick.*

▶ **get away** **1** PHRASAL VERB If you **get away**, you succeed in leaving a place or a person's company. ❑ *She'd gladly have gone anywhere to get away from the city.* **2** PHRASAL VERB If you **get away**, you go away for a period of time in order to have a vacation. ❑ *He is too busy to get away.* **3** PHRASAL VERB When someone or something **gets away**, or when you **get** them **away**, they escape. ❑ *Dr. Dunn was apparently trying to get away when he was shot.*

▶ **get away with** PHRASAL VERB If you **get away with** doing something wrong or risky, you do not suffer any punishment or other bad consequences because of it. ❑ *The criminals know how to play the system and get away with it.*

▶ **get back** **1** PHRASAL VERB If someone or something **gets back** to a state they were in before, they are then in that state again. ❑ *Then life started to get back to normal.* **2** PHRASAL VERB If you **get back** to a subject that you were talking about before, you start talking about it again. ❑ *It wasn't until we sat down to eat that we got back to the subject of Tom Halliday.* **3** PHRASAL VERB If you **get** something **back** after you have lost it or after it has been taken from you, you then have it again. ❑ *You have 14 days in which you can cancel the contract and get your money back.*

▶ **get back to** **1** PHRASAL VERB If you **get back to** an activity, you start doing it again after you have stopped doing it. ❑ *I think I ought to get back to work.* **2** PHRASAL VERB If you **get back to** someone, you contact them again after a short period of time, often by telephone. ❑ *We'll get back to you as soon as possible.*

▶ **get by** PHRASAL VERB If you can **get by** with what you have, you can manage to live or do things in a satisfactory way. ❑ *I'm a survivor. I'll get by.*

▶ **get down** **1** PHRASAL VERB If something **gets** you **down**, it makes you unhappy. ❑ *At times when my work gets me down, I like to fantasize about being a farmer.* **2** PHRASAL VERB If you **get down**, you lower your body until you are sitting, kneeling, or lying on the ground. ❑ *"Get down!" she yelled. "Somebody's shooting!"*

▶ **get down to** PHRASAL VERB If you **get down to** something, especially something that requires a lot of attention, you begin doing it. ❑ *With the election out of the way, the government can get down to business.*

▶ **get in** **1** PHRASAL VERB If a political party or a politician **gets in**, they are elected. ❑ *If the Republicans got in they might decide to change it.* **2** PHRASAL VERB If you **get** something **in**, you manage to do it at a time when you are very busy doing other things. ❑ *I plan to get a few lessons in.* **3** PHRASAL VERB When a train, bus, or plane **gets in**, it arrives. ❑ *We would have come straight here, except our flight got in too late.*

▶ **get into** **1** PHRASAL VERB If you **get into** a particular kind of work or activity, you manage to become involved in it. ❑ *He was eager to get into politics.* **2** PHRASAL VERB If you **get into** a school, college, or university, you are accepted there as a student. ❑ *I was working hard to get into Yale.*

▶ **get off** **1** PHRASAL VERB If someone who has broken a law or rule **gets off**, they are not punished, or are given only a

getaway

very small punishment. ❏ *He is likely to get off with a small fine.* ▪ PHRASAL VERB If you tell someone to **get off** a piece of land or a property, you are telling them to leave, because they have no right to be there and you do not want them there. ❏ *I told you. Get off the farm.* ▪ PHRASAL VERB You can tell someone to **get off** when they are touching something and you do not want them to. ❏ *I kept telling him to get off.*
▶ **get on** PHRASAL VERB If you **get on** with something, you continue doing it or start doing it. ❏ *Jane got on with her work.*
▶ **get on to** PHRASAL VERB If you **get on to** a topic when you are speaking, you start talking about it. ❏ *We got on to the subject of relationships.*
▶ **get out** ▪ PHRASAL VERB If you **get out**, you leave a place because you want to escape from it, or because you are made to leave it. ❏ *They probably wanted to get out of the country.* ▪ PHRASAL VERB If you **get out**, you go to places and meet people, usually in order to have a more enjoyable life. ❏ *Get out and enjoy yourself, make new friends.* ▪ PHRASAL VERB If you **get out** of an organization or a commitment, you withdraw from it. ❏ *I wanted to get out of the group, but they wouldn't let me.* ▪ PHRASAL VERB If news or information **gets out**, it becomes known. ❏ *If word got out now, a scandal could be disastrous.*
▶ **get out of** PHRASAL VERB If you **get out of** doing something that you do not want to do, you succeed in avoiding doing it. ❏ *It's amazing what people will do to get out of paying taxes.*
▶ **get over** ▪ PHRASAL VERB If you **get over** an unpleasant or unhappy experience or an illness, you recover from it. ❏ *It took me a very long time to get over the shock of her death.* ▪ PHRASAL VERB If you **get over** a problem or difficulty, you overcome it. ❏ *"How would they get over that problem?" he wondered.*
▶ **get round** [BRIT] → see **get around**
▶ **get round to** [BRIT] → see **get around to**
▶ **get through** ▪ PHRASAL VERB If you **get through** a task or an amount of work, especially when it is difficult, you complete it. ❏ *I think you can get through the first two chapters.* ▪ PHRASAL VERB If you **get through** a difficult or unpleasant period of time, you manage to live through it. ❏ *It is hard to see how people will get through the winter.* ▪ PHRASAL VERB If you **get through** to someone, you succeed in making them understand something that you are trying to tell them. ❏ *An old friend might well be able to get through to her and help her.* ▪ PHRASAL VERB If you **get through** to someone, you succeed in contacting them on the telephone. ❏ *Look, I can't get through to this number.* ▪ PHRASAL VERB If a law or proposal **gets through**, it is officially approved by something such as a parliament or committee. ❏ *Such a radical proposal would never get through Congress.* ▪ → See feature box at **telephone**
▶ **get together** ▪ PHRASAL VERB When people **get together**, they meet in order to discuss something or to spend time together. ❏ *A whole range of people from all backgrounds can get together and enjoy themselves.* ▪ → see also **get-together** ▪ PHRASAL VERB If you **get** something **together**, you organize it. ❏ *Paul and I were getting a band together, and we needed a new record deal.* ▪ PHRASAL VERB If you **get** an amount of money **together**, you succeed in getting all the money that you need in order to pay for something. ❏ *Now you've finally got enough money together to put a down payment on your dream home.*
▶ **get up** ▪ PHRASAL VERB When someone who is sitting or lying down **gets up**, they rise to a standing position. ❏ *I got up and walked over to where he was.* ▪ PHRASAL VERB When you **get up**, you get out of bed. ❏ *They have to get up early in the morning.*

get|away /gɛtəweɪ/ (**getaways**) ▪ N-COUNT If someone makes a **getaway**, they leave a place quickly, especially after committing a crime or when trying to avoid someone. ❏ *They made their getaway on a stolen motorcycle.* ▪ N-COUNT A **getaway** is a short vacation somewhere. [INFORMAL] ❏ *Weekend tours are ideal for families who want a short getaway.*

got-go PHRASE If something happens or is true **from the get-go**, it happens or is true from the beginning of a process or activity. [mainly AM, INFORMAL] ❏ *From the get-go, there was no question about his ability.*

get|ting /gɛtɪŋ/ **Getting** is the present participle of **get**.

get-together (**get-togethers**) ▪ N-COUNT A **get-together** is an informal meeting or party, usually arranged for a particular purpose. ❏ *...a get-together I had at my home.* ▪ → See feature box at **socialize**

get-up (**get-ups**) also **getup** N-COUNT If you refer to a set of clothes as a **get-up**, you think that they are unusual or ridiculous. [INFORMAL, DISAPPROVAL] ❏ *Naturally he couldn't work in this get-up.*

gey|ser /gaɪzər/ (**geysers**) N-COUNT A **geyser** is a hole in the Earth's surface from which hot water and steam are forced out, usually at irregular intervals of time.

Gha|na|ian /gɑːneɪən/ (**Ghanaians**) ADJ Something that is **Ghanaian** belongs or relates to Ghana or to its people. • N-COUNT **Ghanaians** are people who are Ghanaian.

ghast|ly /gæstli/ (**ghastlier, ghastliest**) ADJ If you describe someone or something as **ghastly**, you mean that you find them very unpleasant or shocking. [INFORMAL] ❏ *...a mother accompanied by her ghastly, unruly child.* ❏ *It was the worst week of my life. It was ghastly.*

GHB /dʒiː eɪtʃ biː/ N-UNCOUNT **GHB** is a drug with some medical uses, which some people take illegally to make them feel happy and energetic. **GHB** is an abbreviation for 'gamma hydroxybutyrate.'

ghee /giː/ N-UNCOUNT **Ghee** is a hard fat that is obtained by heating butter made from the milk of a cow or a buffalo. **Ghee** is used in Indian cooking.

gher|kin /gɜːrkɪn/ (**gherkins**) N-COUNT **Gherkins** are small green cucumbers that have been preserved in vinegar.

ghet|to /gɛtoʊ/ (**ghettos** or **ghettoes**) N-COUNT A **ghetto** is a part of a city in which many poor people or many people of a particular race, religion, or nationality live separately from everyone else. ❏ *...the Black ghettos of New York and Los Angeles.*

ghet|to blast|er (**ghetto blasters**) N-COUNT A **ghetto blaster** is a large portable radio and cassette or CD player with built-in speakers, especially one that is played loudly in public by young people. [INFORMAL]

ghost /goʊst/ (**ghosts**) ▪ N-COUNT A **ghost** is the spirit of a dead person that someone believes they can see or feel. ❏ *...the ghost of Marie Antoinette.* ▪ N-COUNT The **ghost of** something, especially of something bad that has happened, is the memory of it. ❏ *...the ghost of anti-Americanism.*

ghost|ly /goʊstli/ ▪ ADJ Something that is **ghostly** seems unreal or unnatural and may be frightening because of this. ❏ *...Sonia's ghostly laughter.* ▪ ADJ [ADJ n] A **ghostly** presence is the ghost or spirit of a dead person. ❏ *...the ghostly presences which haunt these islands.*

ghost sto|ry (**ghost stories**) N-COUNT A **ghost story** is a story about ghosts.

ghost town (**ghost towns**) N-COUNT A **ghost town** is a town that used to be busy and wealthy but is now poor and deserted. ❏ *Mogadishu is said to be a virtual ghost town, deserted by two-thirds of its residents.*

ghost|write /goʊstraɪt/ (**ghostwrites, ghostwriting, ghostwrote, ghostwritten**) V-T [usu passive] If a book or other piece of writing **is ghostwritten**, it is written by a writer for another person, for example a politician or athlete, who then publishes it as his or her own work. ❏ *Articles were ghostwritten by company employees.*

ghost|writ|er /goʊstraɪtər/ (**ghostwriters**) N-COUNT A **ghostwriter** is someone who writes a book or other published work instead of the person who is named as the author.

ghoul /guːl/ (**ghouls**) N-COUNT A **ghoul** is an imaginary evil spirit. **Ghouls** are said to steal bodies from graves and eat them.

ghoul|ish /guːlɪʃ/ ▪ ADJ [usu ADJ n] **Ghoulish** people and things show an unnatural interest in things such as human suffering, death, or dead bodies. [DISAPPROVAL] ❏ *They are there only to satisfy their ghoulish curiosity.* ▪ ADJ [usu ADJ n] Something that is **ghoulish** looks or behaves like a ghoul. ❏ *...the ghoulish apparitions at the window.*

GHQ /dʒiː eɪtʃ kjuː/ N-UNCOUNT **GHQ** is used to refer to the place where the people who organize military forces or a military operation work. **GHQ** is an abbreviation for 'General Headquarters.' [MILITARY] ❏ *...the dispatches he was carrying from GHQ to the Eighth Army.*

GI /dʒiː aɪ/ (**GIs**) N-COUNT A **GI** is a soldier in the United States armed forces, especially the army. ❏ *...the GIs who came to Europe to fight the Nazis.*

gi|ant /dʒaɪənt/ (giants) **1** ADJ [ADJ n] Something that is described as **giant** is much larger or more important than most others of its kind. □ ...*America's giant car maker, General Motors.* □ ...*a giant oak table.* **2** N-COUNT **Giant** is often used to refer to any large, successful business organization or country. [JOURNALISM] □ ...*Japanese electronics giant, Sony.* **3** N-COUNT A **giant** is an imaginary person who is very big and strong, especially one mentioned in old stories. □ ...*a Nordic saga of giants.*

SYNONYMS

giant
ADJ **1**
huge: ...*a tiny, little woman with huge, black glasses.*
vast: ...*Afrikaner farmers who own vast stretches of land.*
enormous: *The main bedroom is enormous.*
immense: ...*an immense cloud of smoke.*
gigantic: ...*gigantic rocks.*

---

giant-sized ADJ [usu ADJ n] An object that is **giant-sized** is much bigger than objects of its kind usually are. □ ...*a giant-sized TV.*

gib|ber /dʒɪbər/ (gibbers, gibbering, gibbered) V-I If you say that someone **is gibbering**, you mean that they are talking very fast and in a confused manner. [INFORMAL] □ *Everyone is gibbering insanely, nerves frayed, as showtime approaches.* □ *I was a gibbering wreck by this stage.*

gib|ber|ish /dʒɪbərɪʃ/ N-UNCOUNT If you describe someone's words or ideas as **gibberish**, you mean that they do not make any sense. □ *When he was talking to a girl he could hardly speak, and when he did speak he talked gibberish.*

gib|bet /dʒɪbɪt/ (gibbets) N-COUNT A **gibbet** is a **gallows**. [OLD-FASHIONED]

gib|bon /gɪbən/ (gibbons) N-COUNT A **gibbon** is an ape with very long arms and no tail that lives in southern Asia.

gibe /dʒaɪb/ [BRIT] → see **jibe**

gib|lets /dʒɪblɪts/ N-PLURAL **Giblets** are the parts such as the heart and liver that you remove from inside a chicken or other bird before you cook and eat it. Some people cook the giblets separately to make soup or a gravy.

gid|dy /gɪdi/ (giddier, giddiest) **1** ADJ If you feel **giddy**, you feel unsteady and think that you are about to fall over, usually because you are not well. □ *He felt giddy and light-headed.* **2** ADJ If you feel **giddy** with delight or excitement, you feel so happy or excited that you find it hard to think or act normally. □ *Anthony was giddy with self-satisfaction.*

GIF /gɪf/ (GIFs) N-COUNT A **GIF** is a computer file that is used on the internet for sending images, especially moving images. **GIF** is an abbreviation for 'Graphic Interchange Format.' □ *Please send the data as a GIF.*

gift /gɪft/ (gifts) **1** N-COUNT A **gift** is something that you give someone as a present. □ ...*a gift of $50.00.* □ *They believed the unborn child was a gift from God.* **2** N-COUNT If someone has a **gift** for doing something, they have a natural ability for doing it. □ *As a youth he discovered a gift for teaching.*

gift cer|tifi|cate (gift certificates) N-COUNT A **gift certificate** is a card or piece of paper that you buy at a store and give to someone, which entitles the person to exchange it for goods worth the same amount. [mainly AM] □ *Readers whose submissions are published will receive a $25 gift certificate from Harrowsmith Books.*

in BRIT, also use **gift voucher, gift token**

gift|ed /gɪftɪd/ **1** ADJ Someone who is **gifted** has a natural ability to do something well. □ ...*one of the most gifted players in the world.* **2** ADJ A **gifted** child is much more intelligent or talented than average. □ ...*a state program for gifted children.*

gift-wrapped ADJ [usu ADJ n] A **gift-wrapped** present is wrapped in pretty paper.

gig /gɪg/ (gigs) N-COUNT A **gig** is a live performance by someone such as a musician or a comedian. [INFORMAL] □ *The two bands join forces for a gig at Madison Square Garden on November 28.*

gi|ga|byte /gɪgəbaɪt/ (gigabytes) N-COUNT In computing, **gigabyte** is one thousand and twenty-four megabytes.

gi|gan|tic /dʒaɪgæntɪk/ ADJ If you describe something as **gigantic**, you are emphasizing that it is extremely large in size, amount, or degree. [EMPHASIS] □ *In Red Rock Valley the road is bordered by gigantic rocks.*

gig econo|my N-SING The **gig economy** is a job market which consists of short-term or part-time work done by people who are self-employed or on temporary contracts. [BRIT] □ *There has been a huge increase in the number of people working in the gig economy as independent contractors.*

gig|gle /gɪgᵊl/ (giggles, giggling, giggled) **1** V-T/V-I If someone **giggles**, they laugh in a childlike way, because they are amused, nervous, or embarrassed. □ *Both girls began to giggle.* □ *"I beg your pardon?" she giggled.* • N-COUNT **Giggle** is also a noun. □ *She gave a little giggle.* **2** N-PLURAL If you say that someone has **the giggles**, you mean they cannot stop giggling. □ *I was so nervous I got the giggles.* **3** → See feature box at **humor**

gig|gly /gɪgli/ ADJ Someone who is **giggly** keeps laughing in a childlike way, because they are amused, nervous, or drunk. □ *Ray was very giggly and joking all the time.* □ ...*giggly girls.*

gigo|lo /dʒɪgəloʊ/ (gigolos) N-COUNT [usu sing] A **gigolo** is a man who is paid to be the lover of a rich and usually older woman. [DISAPPROVAL]

gild /gɪld/ (gilds, gilding, gilded) V-T If you **gild** a surface, you cover it in a thin layer of gold or gold paint. □ *Carve the names and gild them.* □ ...*gilded statues.*

gild|ing /gɪldɪŋ/ N-UNCOUNT **Gilding** is a layer of gold or gold paint that is put on something.

gill /gɪl/ (gills) **1** N-COUNT [usu pl] **Gills** are the organs on the sides of fish and other water creatures through which they breathe. **2** → See also color supplement

gilt /gɪlt/ ADJ A **gilt** object is covered with a thin layer of gold or gold paint. □ ...*marble columns and gilt spires.*

gim|let /gɪmlɪt/ ADJ [ADJ n] If you say that someone has **gimlet** eyes, you mean that they look at people or things very carefully, and seem to notice every detail. [WRITTEN] □ *'Have you read the whole book?' she asks, gimlet-eyed.*

gim|me /gɪmi/ **Gimme** is sometimes used in written English to represent the words 'give me' when they are pronounced informally. □ *"Gimme a break, kid! You know how much those things cost?"*

gim|mick /gɪmɪk/ (gimmicks) N-COUNT A **gimmick** is an unusual and unnecessary feature or action whose purpose is to attract attention or publicity. [DISAPPROVAL] □ *It is just a public relations gimmick.*

gim|mick|ry /gɪmɪkri/ N-UNCOUNT If you describe features or actions as **gimmickry**, you mean they are not necessary or useful, and their only purpose is to attract attention or publicity. [DISAPPROVAL] □ *No gimmickry or hoopla is necessary.*

gim|micky /gɪmɪki/ ADJ If you describe something as **gimmicky**, you think it has features which are not necessary or useful, and whose only purpose is to attract attention or publicity. [INFORMAL, DISAPPROVAL] □ *The campaign was gimmicky, but it had a serious side to it.*

gin /dʒɪn/ (gins) N-MASS **Gin** is a strong, colorless, alcoholic drink made from grain and juniper berries. • N-COUNT A **gin** is a glass of gin. □ ...*another gin and tonic.*

gin|ger /dʒɪndʒər/ **1** N-UNCOUNT **Ginger** is the root of a plant that is used to flavor food. It has a sweet, spicy flavor and is often sold in powdered form. **2** COLOR **Ginger** is used to describe things that are orangey brown in color. □ *She was a mature lady with dyed ginger hair.*

gin|ger ale (ginger ales) N-MASS **Ginger ale** is a sweet, carbonated non-alcoholic drink flavored with ginger. □ *I live mostly on coffee and ginger ale.* • N-COUNT A glass of ginger ale can be referred to as a **ginger ale**.

gin|ger beer (ginger beers) N-MASS **Ginger beer** is a carbonated drink that is made from syrup and ginger and has a strong flavor. • N-COUNT A glass of ginger beer can be referred to as a **ginger beer**.

ginger|bread /dʒɪndʒərbrɛd/ N-UNCOUNT **Gingerbread** is a sweet cake or cookie that is flavored with ginger. It is often made in the shape of a person or an animal.

gin|ger|ly /dʒɪndʒərli/ ADV [ADV with v] If you do something **gingerly**, you do it in a careful manner, usually because you expect it to be dangerous, unpleasant, or painful. [WRITTEN] ❑ *She was touching the dressing gingerly with both hands.*

ging|ham /gɪŋəm/ N-UNCOUNT **Gingham** is cotton cloth which has a woven pattern of small squares, usually in white and one other color. ❑ *...a gingham apron.* ❑ *...gingham check shorts.*

gin|seng /dʒɪnsɛŋ/ N-UNCOUNT **Ginseng** is the root of a plant found in countries such as China, Russia, and America which some people believe is good for your health.

gip|sy /dʒɪpsi/ [BRIT] → see **Gypsy**

gi|raffe /dʒɪræf/ (giraffes) N-COUNT A **giraffe** is a large African animal with a very long neck, long legs, and dark patches on its body.

gird /gɜrd/ (girds, girding, girded) V-T If you **gird** yourself **for** a battle or contest, you prepare yourself for it. [LITERARY] ❑ *With audiences in the U.S. falling for the first time in a generation, Hollywood is girding itself for recession.*

gird|er /gɜrdər/ (girders) N-COUNT A **girder** is a long, thick piece of steel or iron that is used in the framework of buildings and bridges.

gir|dle /gɜrdəl/ (girdles) N-COUNT A **girdle** is a piece of underwear that fits tightly around the stomach and hips.

girl ◆◆◆ /gɜrl/ (girls) **1** N-COUNT A **girl** is a female child. ❑ *...an eleven-year-old girl.* **2** N-COUNT You can refer to someone's daughter as a **girl**. ❑ *We had a little girl.* **3** N-COUNT Young women are sometimes referred to as **girls**. This use could cause offense. ❑ *...a pretty twenty-year-old girl.* **4** N-COUNT Some people use **girl** to refer to a person's girlfriend. [INFORMAL] ❑ *I've been with my girl for nine years.*

girl band (girl bands) N-COUNT A **girl band** is a band consisting of young women who sing pop music and dance.

girl|friend /gɜrlfrɛnd/ (girlfriends) **1** N-COUNT Someone's **girlfriend** is a girl or woman with whom they are having a romantic or sexual relationship. ❑ *He had been going out with his girlfriend for seven months.* **2** N-COUNT A **girlfriend** is a female friend. ❑ *I met a girlfriend for lunch.*

Girl Guide (Girl Guides) also **girl guide 1** N-PROPER [the N] In Britain, the Guides used to be called **the Girl Guides**. **2** N-COUNT In Britain, a **Girl Guide** was a girl who was a member of the Girl Guides.

girl|hood /gɜrlhʊd/ N-UNCOUNT [oft poss N] **Girlhood** is the period of a female person's life during which she is a girl. ❑ *She had shared responsibility for her brother since girlhood.* ❑ *Her girlhood dream had been to study painting.*

girlie /gɜrli/ also **girly 1** ADJ [ADJ n] **Girlie** magazines or calendars show photographs of naked or almost naked women. [INFORMAL] **2** ADJ **Girlie** things are suitable for girls or women rather than men or boys. A **girlie** person likes girlie things. [INFORMAL, DISAPPROVAL] ❑ *She swapped her plain suit for a girlie dress.* ❑ *She's a tomboy, not a girlie girl at all.*

girl|ish /gɜrlɪʃ/ ADJ [usu ADJ n] If you describe a woman as **girlish**, you mean she behaves, looks, or sounds like a young girl, for example because she is shy, excited, or lively. ❑ *She gave a little girlish giggle.*

Girl Scout (Girl Scouts) **1** N-PROPER-COLL [the N] **The Girl Scouts** is an organization for girls which teaches them to become practical and independent. **2** N-COUNT In the United States, a **Girl Scout** is a girl who is a member of the Girl Scouts.

girth /gɜrθ/ (girths) N-VAR The **girth** of an object, for example a person's or an animal's body, is its width or thickness, considered as the measurement around its circumference. [FORMAL] ❑ *A girl he knew had upset him by commenting on his increasing girth.*

gist /dʒɪst/ N-SING The **gist of** a speech, conversation, or piece of writing is its general meaning. ❑ *He related the gist of his conversation to Sam.*

GIVE

① USED WITH NOUNS DESCRIBING ACTIONS
② TRANSFERRING
③ OTHER USES, PHRASES, AND PHRASAL VERBS

---

① **give** ◆◆◆ /gɪv/ (gives, giving, gave, given) **1** V-T [no cont] You can use **give** with nouns that refer to physical actions. The whole expression refers to the performing of the action. For example, **She gave a smile** means almost the same as 'She smiled.' ❑ *She stretched her arms out and gave a great yawn.* ❑ *He gave her a fond smile.* **2** V-T You use **give** to say that a person does something for another person. For example, if you **give** someone a lift, you take them somewhere in your car. ❑ *I gave her a lift back to her house.* ❑ *He was given mouth-to-mouth resuscitation.* **3** V-T You use **give** with nouns that refer to information, opinions, or greetings to indicate that something is communicated. For example, if you **give** someone some news, you tell it to them. ❑ *He gave no details.* ❑ *Would you like to give me your name?* **4** V-T You use **give** to say how long you think something will last or how much you think something will be. ❑ *A recent poll gave Campbell a 68 percent support rating.* **5** V-T [no cont, no passive, with brd-neg] People use **give** in expressions such as **I don't give a damn** to show that they do not care about something. [INFORMAL, FEELINGS] ❑ *They don't give a damn about the country.* **6** V-T If someone or something **gives** you a particular idea or impression, it causes you to have that idea or impression. ❑ *They gave me the impression that they were doing exactly what they wanted in life.* **7** V-T If someone or something **gives** you a particular physical or emotional feeling, it makes you experience it. ❑ *He gave me a shock.* **8** V-T If you **give** a performance or speech, you perform or speak in public. ❑ *Kotto gives a stupendous performance.* **9** V-T If you **give** something thought or attention, you think about it, concentrate on it, or deal with it. ❑ *I've been giving it some thought.* **10** V-T If you **give** a party or other social event, you organize it. ❑ *That evening, I gave a dinner party for a few close friends.*

② **give** ◆◆◆ /gɪv/ (gives, giving, gave, given) **1** V-T/V-I If you **give** someone something that you own or have bought, you provide them with it, so that they have it or can use it. ❑ *They gave us T-shirts and stickers.* ❑ *He gave money to the World Health Organization to help defeat smallpox.* ❑ *Many people are still giving to charity despite hard times.* **2** V-T If you **give** someone something that you are holding or that is near you, you pass it to them, so that they are then holding it. ❑ *Give me that pencil.* **3** V-T To **give** someone or something a particular power or right means to allow them to have it. ❑ *The new law would give the president the power to appoint the central bank's chairman.*

③ **give** ◆◆◆ /gɪv/ (gives, giving, gave, given)

→ Please look at meanings **8** – **11** to see if the expression you are looking for is shown under another headword.

1 V-I If something **gives**, it collapses or breaks under pressure. ❑ *My knees gave under me.* **2** V-T PASSIVE You say that you **are given** to understand or believe that something is the case when you do not want to say how you found out about it, or who told you. [FORMAL, VAGUENESS] ❑ *We were given to understand that he was ill.* **3** → see also **given** **4** PHRASE You use **give me** to say that you would rather have one thing than another, especially when you have just mentioned the thing that you do not want. ❑ *"I hate Sundays," he said. "They're endless. Give me a Saturday night any day."* **5** PHRASE If you say that something requires **give-and-take**, you mean that people must compromise or cooperate for it to be successful. ❑ *...a happy relationship where there's a lot of give-and-take.* **6** PHRASE **Give or take** is used to indicate that an amount is approximate. For example, if you say that something is fifty years old, **give or take** a few years, you mean that it is approximately fifty years old. ❑ *They grow to a height of 12 in. – give or take a couple of inches.* **7** PHRASE If an audience is asked to **give it up for** a performer, they are being asked to applaud. [INFORMAL] ❑ *Ladies and gentlemen, give it up for Fred Durst.* **8 to give the game away** → see **game** **9 to give notice** → see **notice** **10 to give rise to** → see **rise** **11 to give way** → see **way** ②

▶ **give away** **1** PHRASAL VERB If you **give away** something that you own, you give it to someone, rather than selling it, often because you no longer want it. ❑ *He was giving his collection away for free.* **2** PHRASAL VERB If someone **gives away** an advantage, they accidentally cause their opponent or enemy to have that advantage. ❑ *Military advantages should not be given away.* **3** PHRASAL VERB If you **give away** information that should be kept secret, you reveal it to other people.

give-and-take □ *She would give nothing away.* ◼ PHRASAL VERB To **give** someone or something **away** means to show their true nature or identity, which is not obvious. □ *He tried to sound calm, but the tone of his voice gave him away.*

▶ **give back** PHRASAL VERB If you **give** something **back**, you return it to the person who gave it to you. □ *I gave the textbook back to him.* □ *You gave me back the projector.*

▶ **give in** ◼ PHRASAL VERB If you **give in**, you admit that you are defeated or that you cannot do something. □ *"I wasn't going to give in. I wasn't going to fall. I was going to fight like hell."* ◼ PHRASAL VERB If you **give in**, you agree to do something that you do not want to do. □ *I pressed my parents until they finally gave in and registered me for skating classes.*

▶ **give off** also **give out** PHRASAL VERB If something **gives off** or **gives out** a gas, heat, or a smell, it produces it and sends it out into the air. □ *...natural gas, which gives off less carbon dioxide than coal.*

▶ **give out** ◼ PHRASAL VERB If you **give out** a number of things, you distribute them among a group of people. □ *There were people at the entrance giving out leaflets.* ◼ PHRASAL VERB If you **give out** information, you make it known to people. □ *He wouldn't give out any information.* ◼ → see **give off**

▶ **give over to** also **give up to** PHRASAL VERB If something **is given over** or **given up to** a particular use, it is used entirely for that purpose. □ *Much of the garden was given over to vegetables.*

▶ **give up** ◼ PHRASAL VERB If you **give up** something, you stop doing it or having it. □ *The Coast Guard had given up all hope of finding the two divers alive.* ◼ PHRASAL VERB If you **give up**, you decide that you cannot do something and stop trying to do it. □ *After a fruitless morning sitting at his desk he had given up.* ◼ PHRASAL VERB If you **give up** your job, you resign from it. □ *She gave up her job to join her husband's campaign.* ◼ PHRASAL VERB If you **give up** something that you have or that you are entitled to, you allow someone else to have it. □ *One of the men with him gave up his place on the bench.* ◼ PHRASAL VERB If you **give yourself up**, you let the police or other people know where you are, after you have been hiding from them. □ *A 28-year-old man later gave himself up and will appear in court today.* ◼ → See feature box at **success**

▶ **give up on** PHRASAL VERB If you **give up on** something or someone, you decide that you will never succeed in doing what you want to with them, and you stop trying. □ *He urged them not to give up on peace efforts.*

▶ **give up to** → see **give over to**

give-and-take → see **give** ③ 5

give|away /gɪveɪ/ (giveaways) also **give-away** N-COUNT A **giveaway** is something that a company or organization gives to someone, usually in order to encourage people to buy a particular product. □ *Free book giveaway for all who attend.*

giv|en ♦♢♢ /gɪvən/ ◼ **Given** is the past participle of **give**. ◼ ADJ [det ADJ] If you talk about, for example, any **given** position or a **given** time, you mean the particular position or time that you are discussing. □ *In chess there are typically about 36 legal moves from any given board position.* ◼ PREP **Given** is used when indicating a possible situation in which someone has the opportunity or ability to do something. For example, **given the chance** means 'if I had the chance.' □ *Write down the sort of thing you would like to do, given the opportunity.* ◼ PHRASE If you say **given that** something is the case, you mean taking that fact into account. □ *Usually, I am sensible with money, as I have to be, given that I don't earn that much.* ◼ PREP If you say **given** something, you mean taking that thing into account. □ *Given the uncertainty over Leigh's future I was left with little other choice.*

giv|en name (given names) N-COUNT [oft with poss] A **given name** is a person's first name, which they are given at birth in addition to their surname. [FORMAL]

giv|er /gɪvər/ (givers) N-COUNT You can refer to a person or organization that gives or supplies a particular thing as a **giver** of that thing. □ *That country is the largest giver of aid among the wealthy countries of the West.* • COMB IN N-COUNT **Giver** is also a combining form. □ *...if the money-givers do not have specific projects in view.*

giz|mo /gɪzmoʊ/ (gizmos) N-COUNT [usu with supp] A **gizmo** is a device or small machine that performs a particular task, usually in a new and efficient way. People often use **gizmo** to refer to a device or machine when they do not know what it is really called. [INFORMAL] □ *...a plastic gizmo for holding a coffee cup on the dashboard.*

gla|cé /glæseɪ/ ADJ [ADJ n] **Glacé** fruits are fruits that have been preserved in a thick, sugary syrup and then dried. □ *...pieces of glacé cherry.*

gla|cial /gleɪʃəl/ ◼ ADJ **Glacial** means relating to or produced by glaciers or ice. [TECHNICAL] □ *...a true glacial landscape with U-shaped valleys.* ◼ ADJ [usu ADJ n] If you say that something moves or changes at a **glacial** pace, you are emphasizing that it moves or changes very slowly. [EMPHASIS] □ *Change occurs at a glacial pace.*

gla|cia|tion /gleɪsieɪʃən/ (glaciations) N-VAR In geology, **glaciation** is the process by which the land is covered by glaciers. **Glaciations** are periods when this happens. [TECHNICAL]

gla|cier /gleɪʃər/ (glaciers) N-COUNT A **glacier** is an extremely large mass of ice which moves very slowly, often down a mountain valley.

glad ♦♢♢ /glæd/ ◼ ADJ [v-link ADJ] If you are **glad** about something, you are happy and pleased about it. □ *The people seem genuinely glad to see you.* □ *I'd be glad if the boys slept a little longer so I could do some ironing.* • **glad|ly** ADV [ADV with v] □ *Malcolm gladly accepted the invitation.* ◼ ADJ [v-link ADJ to-inf] If you say that you will be **glad** to do something, usually for someone else, you mean that you are willing and eager to do it. [FEELINGS] □ *I'll be glad to show you everything.* • **glad|ly** ADV [ADV with v] □ *The counselors will gladly babysit during their free time.*

glad|den /glædən/ (gladdens, gladdening, gladdened) ◼ PHRASE [V and N inflect] If you say that something **gladdens** someone's **heart**, you mean that it makes them feel pleased and hopeful. [WRITTEN] □ *...a conclusion that should gladden the hearts of all animal-rights activists.* ◼ V-T If something **gladdens** you, it makes you feel happy and pleased. [LITERARY] □ *Charles's visit surprised and gladdened him.*

glade /gleɪd/ (glades) N-COUNT A **glade** is a grassy space without trees in a wood or forest. [LITERARY]

gladia|tor /glædieɪtər/ (gladiators) ◼ N-COUNT In the time of the Roman Empire, a **gladiator** was a man who had to fight against other men or wild animals in order to entertain an audience. ◼ N-COUNT You can refer to an athlete or a performer as a **gladiator** in order to emphasize how brave or dangerous their actions are. [JOURNALISM, EMPHASIS] □ *This is an arena for gladiators only, for the Titans of the track.*

gladio|lus /glædioʊləs/ (gladioli /glædioʊlaɪ/) N-COUNT A **gladiolus** is a type of plant with long, thin leaves and several large, brightly colored flowers.

glad rags N-PLURAL You can refer to clothes that you wear to parties and other special occasions as your **glad rags**. [INFORMAL, OLD-FASHIONED]

glam /glæm/ ◼ ADJ **Glam** is short for glamorous. [INFORMAL] □ *She was always glam. She looked like a star.* ◼ N-UNCOUNT **Glam** is short for glamour. [INFORMAL] □ *...the gleam and glam of New York's Carnegie Hall.*

glam|or /glæmər/ N-UNCOUNT → see **glamour**

glam|or|ize /glæməraɪz/ (glamorizes, glamorizing, glamorized)

in BRIT, also use **glamorise**

V-T If someone **glamorizes** something, they make it look or seem more attractive than it really is, especially in a movie, book, or program. [DISAPPROVAL] □ *Filmmakers have often been accused of glamorizing organized crime.* □ *...a glamorized view of the past.*

glam|or|ous /glæmərəs/ ADJ If you describe someone or something as **glamorous**, you mean that they are more attractive, exciting, or interesting than ordinary people or things. □ *...some of the world's most beautiful and glamorous women.*

glam|our /glæmər/ also **glamor** N-UNCOUNT **Glamour** is the quality of being more attractive, exciting, or interesting than ordinary people or things. □ *...the glamour of show biz.*

glance ♦♢♢ /glæns/ (glances, glancing, glanced) ◼ V-I If you **glance** at something or someone, you look at them very quickly and then look away again immediately. ❑ *He glanced at his watch.* **2** V-I If you **glance through** or **at** a newspaper, report, or book, you spend a short time looking at it without reading it very carefully. ❑ *I picked up the phone book and glanced through it.* **3** N-COUNT A **glance** is a quick look at someone or something. ❑ *Trevor and I exchanged a glance.* **4** PHRASE If you see something **at a glance**, you see or recognize it immediately, and without having to think or look carefully. ❑ *One could tell at a glance that she was a compassionate person.* **5** PHRASE If you say that something is true or seems to be true **at first glance**, you mean that it seems to be true when you first see it or think about it, but that your first impression may be wrong. ❑ *At first glance, organic farming looks much more expensive for the farmer.* **6** → See feature box at **look**

SYNONYMS

glance
VERB **1**
peep: *Now and then, she peeped to see if he was noticing her.*
peek: *On two occasions, she had peeked at him through a crack in the wall.*
glimpse: *She glimpsed a group of people standing on the bank of a river.*
NOUN **3**
peep: *'Fourteen minutes,' Chris said, taking a peep at his watch.*
peek: *American firms have been paying outrageous fees for a peek at the technical data.*
glimpse: *Some of the fans had waited 24 hours to catch a glimpse of their heroine.*

glanc|ing /glɑːnsɪŋ/ ADJ [ADJ n] A **glancing** blow is one that hits something at an angle rather than from directly in front. ❑ *The car struck him a glancing blow on the hip.*

gland /glænd/ (**glands**) N-COUNT [usu supp n] A **gland** is an organ in the body which produces chemical substances for the body to use or get rid of. ❑ *...the hormones secreted by our endocrine glands.*

glan|du|lar /glændʒʊlər/ ADJ [usu ADJ n] **Glandular** means relating to or affecting your glands. [TECHNICAL] ❑ *...the amount of fat and glandular tissue in the breasts.*

glan|du|lar fe|ver N-UNCOUNT **Glandular fever** is the same as **mononucleosis**. [BRIT]

glare /gleər/ (**glares, glaring, glared**) **1** V-I If you **glare** at someone, you look at them with an angry expression on your face. ❑ *The old woman glared at him.* ❑ *Jacob glared and muttered something.* **2** N-COUNT A **glare** is an angry, hard, and unfriendly look. ❑ *His glasses magnified his irritable glare.* **3** V-I If the sun or a light **glares**, it shines with a very bright light which is difficult to look at. ❑ *The sunlight glared.* **4** N-UNCOUNT **Glare** is very bright light that is difficult to look at. ❑ *...the glare of a car's headlights.* **5** N-SING If someone is in **the glare of** publicity or public attention, they are constantly being watched and talked about by a lot of people. ❑ *Norma is said to dislike the glare of publicity.*

glar|ing /gleərɪŋ/ **1** ADJ If you describe something bad as **glaring**, you are emphasizing that it is very obvious and easily seen or noticed. [EMPHASIS] ❑ *I never saw such a glaring example of misrepresentation.* ● **glar|ing|ly** ADV ❑ *It was glaringly obvious.* **2** → see also **glare**

glas|nost /glæznɒst/ N-UNCOUNT **Glasnost** is a policy of making a government more open and democratic. The word **glasnost** was originally used to describe the policies of President Gorbachev in the former Soviet Union in the 1980s.

glass ✦✧ /glɑːs, glæs/ (**glasses**) **1** N-UNCOUNT **Glass** is a hard, transparent substance that is used to make things such as windows and bottles. ❑ *...a pane of glass.* **2** N-COUNT A **glass** is a container made from glass, which you can drink from and which does not have a handle. ❑ *Grossman raised the glass to his lips.* ● N-COUNT The contents of a glass can be referred to as a **glass** of something. ❑ *...a glass of milk.* **3** N-UNCOUNT **Glass** is used to mean objects made of glass, for example drinking containers and bowls. ❑ *There's a glittering array of glass to choose from at markets.* **4** N-PLURAL **Glasses** are two lenses in a frame that some people wear in front of their eyes in order to help them see better. ❑ *He took off his glasses.* **5** → See feature box at **recycle**; See also color supplement

COLLOCATIONS

glass
NOUN
1
adjective + **glass**: bulletproof
verb + **glass**: break, shatter, smash
2
verb + **glass**: drain, empty; raise

glass ceil|ing (**glass ceilings**) N-COUNT When people refer to a **glass ceiling**, they are talking about the attitudes and traditions in a society that prevent women from rising to the top jobs. [JOURNALISM] ❑ *In her current role she broke through the glass ceiling as the first woman to reach senior management level in the company.*

glassed-in ADJ [usu ADJ n] A **glassed-in** room or building has large windows instead of walls.

glass fi|ber

in BRIT, use **glass fibre**

N-UNCOUNT **Glass fiber** is another name for **fiberglass**.

glass|ware /glɑːsweər/ N-UNCOUNT **Glassware** consists of objects made of glass, such as bowls, drinking containers, and ornaments.

glassy /glɑːsi/ (**glassier, glassiest**) ADJ If you describe something as **glassy**, you mean that it is very smooth and shiny, like glass. [WRITTEN] ❑ *The water was glassy.* ❑ *...glassy green pebbles.*

glau|co|ma /glaʊkoʊmə/ **1** N-UNCOUNT **Glaucoma** is an eye disease which can cause people to gradually go blind. **2** → See feature box at **eyesight**

glaze /gleɪz/ (**glazes, glazing, glazed**) **1** N-COUNT A **glaze** is a thin layer of liquid which is put on a piece of pottery and becomes hard and shiny when the pottery is heated in a very hot oven. ❑ *...hand-painted French tiles with decorative glazes.* **2** N-COUNT A **glaze** is a thin layer of beaten egg, milk, or other liquid that you spread onto food in order to make the surface shine and look attractive. ❑ *Brush the glaze over the top and sides of the hot cake.* **3** V-T When you **glaze** food such as bread or pastry, you spread a layer of beaten egg, milk, or other liquid onto it before you cook it in order to make its surface shine and look attractive. ❑ *Glaze the pie with beaten egg.*
▶ **glaze over** PHRASAL VERB If your eyes **glaze over**, they become dull and lose all expression, usually because you are bored or are thinking about something else. ❑ *...movie actors whose eyes glaze over as soon as the subject wavers from themselves.*

glazed /gleɪzd/ **1** ADJ If you describe someone's eyes as **glazed**, you mean that their expression is dull or dreamy, usually because they are tired or are having difficulty concentrating on something. ❑ *Doctors with glazed eyes sat chain-smoking in front of a television set.* **2** ADJ **Glazed** pottery is covered with a thin layer of a hard, shiny substance. ❑ *...a large glazed pot.* **3** ADJ A **glazed** window or door has glass in it. ❑ *...the new office, with glazed windows to the corridor.*

gla|zier /gleɪziər/ (**glaziers**) N-COUNT A **glazier** is someone whose job is fitting glass into windows and doors.

gleam /gliːm/ (**gleams, gleaming, gleamed**) **1** V-I If an object or a surface **gleams**, it reflects light because it is shiny and clean. ❑ *His black hair gleamed in the sun.* **2** N-COUNT A **gleam of** something is a faint sign of it. ❑ *There was a gleam of hope for a peaceful settlement.* **3** → See feature box at **light**

glean /gliːn/ (**gleans, gleaning, gleaned**) V-T If you **glean** something such as information or knowledge, you learn or collect it slowly and patiently, and perhaps indirectly. ❑ *At present we're gleaning information from all sources.*

glee /gliː/ N-UNCOUNT **Glee** is a feeling of happiness and excitement, often caused by someone else's misfortune. ❑ *His victory was greeted with glee by his fellow American golfers.*

glee|ful /gliːfʊl/ ADJ Someone who is **gleeful** is happy and excited, often because of someone else's bad luck. [WRITTEN] ❑ *He took an almost gleeful delight in showing how wrong they can be.*
● **glee|ful|ly** ADV [ADV with v] ❑ *I spent the rest of their visit gleefully boring them with tedious details.*

glen /glen/ (**glens**) N-COUNT [oft in names] A **glen** is a deep, narrow valley, especially in the mountains of Scotland or Ireland.

glib /glɪb/ ADJ If you describe what someone says as **glib**, you disapprove of it because it implies that something is simple or easy, or that there are no problems involved, when this is not the case. [DISAPPROVAL] ☐ ...the glib talk of "past misery." • **glib|ly** ADV [ADV with v] ☐ We talk glibly of equality of opportunity.

glide /glaɪd/ (glides, gliding, glided) **1** V-I If you **glide** somewhere, you move silently and in a smooth and effortless way. ☐ Waiters glide between tightly packed tables bearing trays of pasta. **2** V-I When birds or airplanes **glide**, they float on air currents. ☐ Our only companion is the wandering albatross, which glides effortlessly and gracefully behind the yacht.

glid|er /glaɪdər/ (gliders) N-COUNT A **glider** is an aircraft without an engine, which flies by floating on air currents.

glid|ing /glaɪdɪŋ/ N-UNCOUNT **Gliding** is the sport or activity of flying in a glider.

glim|mer /glɪmər/ (glimmers, glimmering, glimmered) **1** V-I If something **glimmers**, it produces or reflects a faint, gentle, often unsteady light. ☐ The moon glimmered faintly through the mists. **2** N-COUNT A **glimmer** is a faint, gentle, often unsteady light. ☐ In the east there is the slightest glimmer of light. **3** N-COUNT A **glimmer of** something is a faint sign of it. ☐ Despite an occasional glimmer of hope, this campaign has not produced any results. **4** → See feature box at **light**

glim|mer|ing /glɪmərɪŋ/ (glimmerings) N-COUNT [N of n] A **glimmering of** something is a faint sign of it. ☐ ...a glimmering of understanding. ☐ ...the first glimmerings of civilization.

glimpse /glɪmps/ (glimpses, glimpsing, glimpsed) **1** N-COUNT If you get a **glimpse** of someone or something, you see them very briefly and not very well. ☐ Some of the fans had waited 24 hours outside the hotel to catch a glimpse of their heroine. **2** V-T If you **glimpse** someone or something, you see them very briefly and not very well. ☐ She glimpsed a group of people standing on the bank of a river. **3** N-COUNT A **glimpse** of something is a brief experience of it or an idea about it that helps you understand or appreciate it better. ☐ Is this a glimpse into the future of advertising? **4** → See feature box at **look**

glint /glɪnt/ (glints, glinting, glinted) **1** V-I If something **glints**, it produces or reflects a quick flash of light. [WRITTEN] ☐ The sea glinted in the sun. ☐ Sunlight glinted on his glasses. **2** N-COUNT [usu N of n] A **glint** is a quick flash of light. [WRITTEN] ☐ ...glints of sunlight.

glis|ten /glɪsᵊn/ (glistens, glistening, glistened) V-I If something **glistens**, it shines, usually because it is wet or oily. ☐ The calm sea glistened in the sunlight. ☐ Deborah's face was white and glistening with sweat.

glitch /glɪtʃ/ (glitches) N-COUNT A **glitch** is a problem that stops something from working properly or being successful. [INFORMAL] ☐ Manufacturing glitches have limited the factory's output.

glit|ter /glɪtər/ (glitters, glittering, glittered) **1** V-I If something **glitters**, light comes from or is reflected off different parts of it. ☐ The bay glittered in the sunshine. **2** N-UNCOUNT **Glitter** consists of tiny, shining pieces of metal. It is glued to things for decoration. ☐ Cut out a piece of sandpaper and sprinkle it with glitter. **3** N-UNCOUNT You can use **glitter** to refer to superficial attractiveness or to the excitement connected with something. ☐ She was blinded by the glitter and the glamour of her own life.

glit|te|ra|ti /glɪtərɑːti/ N-PLURAL The **glitterati** are rich and famous people such as actors and rock stars. [JOURNALISM] ☐ He just happens to astound everyone he meets from international footballers to the Hollywood glitterati.

glit|ter|ing /glɪtərɪŋ/ ADJ [ADJ n] You use **glittering** to indicate that something is very impressive or successful. ☐ ...a brilliant school pupil destined for a glittering academic career. ☐ ...a glittering array of celebrities.

glit|tery /glɪtəri/ ADJ Something that is **glittery** shines with a lot of very small points of light. ☐ ...a gold suit and a glittery bow tie.

glitz /glɪts/ N-UNCOUNT You use **glitz** to refer to something that is exciting and attractive in a showy way. ☐ ...the glitz of Beverly Hills.

glitzy /glɪtsi/ (glitzier, glitziest) ADJ Something that is **glitzy** is exciting and attractive in a showy way. ☐ ...Aspen, Colorado, one of the glitziest ski resorts in the world.

gloat /gloʊt/ (gloats, gloating, gloated) V-I If someone is **gloating**, they are showing pleasure at their own success or at other people's failure in an arrogant and unpleasant way. [DISAPPROVAL] ☐ He had never been a malicious man, certainly not one to gloat over the tragedies of others.

glob /glɒb/ (globs) N-COUNT [usu N of n] A **glob** of something soft or liquid is a small, round amount of it. [INFORMAL] ☐ ...oily globs of soup.

glob|al ♦◇◇ /gloʊbᵊl/ **1** ADJ You can use **global** to describe something that happens in all parts of the world or affects all parts of the world. ☐ ...a global ban on nuclear testing. • **glob|al|ly** ADV ☐ ...a globally familiar trade name. **2** ADJ A **global** view or vision of a situation is one in which all the different aspects of it are considered. ☐ ...a global vision of contemporary societies. **3** → See feature box at **population**, **weather**

> **SYNONYMS**
>
> **global**
> ADJ **1**
> **worldwide:** Today, doctors are fearing a worldwide epidemic.
> **international:** ...emergency aid from the international community.
> **world:** ...his personal contribution to world history.

glob|al|ize /gloʊbəlaɪz/ (globalizes, globalizing, globalized)

in BRIT, also use **globalise**

V-T/V-I When industry **globalizes** or **is globalized**, companies from one country link with companies from another country in order to do business with them. [BUSINESS] ☐ One way to lower costs will be to forge alliances with foreign companies or to expand internationally through appropriate takeovers – in short, to "globalize." • **glob|ali|za|tion** /gloʊbəlaɪzeɪʃᵊn/ N-UNCOUNT ☐ Trends toward the globalization of industry have dramatically affected food production in California.

glob|al north also **Global North** N-SING The **global north** consists of the richest and most industrialized countries, which are mainly in the northern part of the world.

glob|al po|si|tion|ing sys|tem (global positioning systems) N-COUNT A **global positioning system** is a system that uses signals from satellites to find out the position of an object. The abbreviation **GPS** is also used.

glob|al reach N-SING When people talk about the **global reach** of a company or industry, they mean its ability to have customers in many different parts of the world. [BUSINESS] ☐ The company does not yet have the global reach of its bigger competitors. ☐ It would have to grow by acquisitions or joint ventures to achieve global reach.

glob|al south also **Global South** N-SING The **global south** consists of the poorest and least industrialized countries, which are mainly in the southern part of the world.

glob|al vil|lage N-SING People sometimes refer to the world as a **global village** when they want to emphasize that all the different parts of the world form one community linked together by electronic communications, especially the internet. ☐ Now that we are all part of the global village, everyone becomes a neighbor.

glob|al warm|ing N-UNCOUNT **1 Global warming** is the gradual rise in the Earth's temperature caused by high levels of carbon dioxide and other gases in the atmosphere. ☐ The threat of global warming will eventually force the U.S. to slow down its energy consumption. **2** → See feature box on next page

globe /gloʊb/ (globes) **1** N-SING You can refer to the world as the **globe** when you are emphasizing how big it is or that something happens in many different parts of it. ☐ ...bottles of beer from every corner of the globe. ☐ 70% of our globe's surface is water. **2** N-COUNT A **globe** is a ball-shaped object with a map of the world on it. It is usually fixed on a stand. ☐ Three large globes stand on the floor. **3** N-COUNT Any ball-shaped object can be referred to as a **globe**. ☐ The overhead light was covered now with a white globe.

globe ar|ti|choke (globe artichokes) → see **artichoke**

globe-trot (globe-trots, globe-trotting, globe-trotted) also **globetrot** V-I [usu cont] If someone spends their time **globe-trotting**, they spend a lot of time traveling to different parts of the world. [INFORMAL] ☐ The son of a diplomat, he

VOCABULARY IN CONTEXT

Global warming

Evidence of **global warming** is everywhere. Since the year 2000, **data** collected by NASA has confirmed scientists' worst suspicions. And perhaps the most worrying fact is that the rise in temperatures is actually **accelerating**. So why is the Earth heating up at such an **alarming rate**, and why now? Well, global warming is **caused by** an **accumulation** of carbon dioxide and other **pollutants** in the **atmosphere**. Normally, any excess heat would escape out into space, but these pollutants, which take many years to **break down**, have formed a **barrier** in the **upper regions** of the atmosphere, **trapping heat** and causing temperatures to rise. Where do these pollutants come from? Fossil fuels, such as **coal** or **petroleum**, are a **major source** of carbon dioxide. There are many other sources of pollutants, however, such as **intensive livestock farming**, which has increased drastically in recent years in order to **supply** the human race's ever-increasing demand for meat.

---

has spent much of his life globe-trotting. • **globe-trotting** ADJ ❑ ...globe-trotting academic superstars. • **globe-trotter** (**globe-trotters**) N-COUNT ❑ Does this mean that India is on the shortlist of must-see countries for globe-trotters?

globu|lar /glɒbyʊlər/ ADJ [usu ADJ n] A **globular** object is shaped like a ball. [FORMAL] ❑ The globular seed capsule contains numerous small seeds.

glob|ule /glɒbyul/ (**globules**) N-COUNT [usu pl, oft N of n] **Globules** of a liquid or of a soft substance are tiny, round particles of it. ❑ ...globules of saliva. ❑ Our bone marrow contains fat in the form of small globules.

glock|en|spiel /glɒkənʃpil/ (**glockenspiels**) N-COUNT [oft the N] A **glockenspiel** is a musical instrument which consists of metal bars of different lengths arranged like the keyboard of a piano. You play the glockenspiel by hitting the bars with wooden hammers.

gloom /glum/ ❶ N-SING The **gloom** is a state of near darkness. ❑ ...the gloom of a foggy November morning. ❷ N-UNCOUNT **Gloom** is a feeling of sadness and lack of hope. ❑ ...the deepening gloom over the economy.

gloomy /glumi/ (**gloomier, gloomiest**) ❶ ADJ If a place is **gloomy**, it is almost dark so that you cannot see very well ❑ Inside it's gloomy after all that sunshine. ❷ ADJ If people are **gloomy**, they are unhappy and have no hope. ❑ Miller is gloomy about the fate of the serious playwright in America. • **gloomi|ly** ADV [ADV with v] ❑ He tells me gloomily that he has been called up for army service. ❸ ADJ If a situation is **gloomy**, it does not give you much hope of success or happiness. ❑ ...a gloomy picture of an economy sliding into recession. ❑ Officials say the outlook for next year is gloomy.

glo|ri|fied /glɔrɪfaɪd/ ADJ [ADJ n] You use **glorified** to indicate that something is less important or impressive than its name suggests. ❑ So really I'd just be a glorified secretary?

glo|ri|fy /glɔrɪfaɪ/ (**glorifies, glorifying, glorified**) V-T To **glorify** something means to praise it or make it seem good or special, usually when it is not. ❑ This magazine in no way glorifies gangs.

• **glo|ri|fi|ca|tion** /glɔrɪfɪkeɪʃən/ N-UNCOUNT ❑ ...the glorification of violence.

glo|ri|ous /glɔriəs/ ❶ ADJ Something that is **glorious** is very beautiful and impressive. ❑ ...a glorious rainbow in the air. ❑ She had missed the glorious blooms of the desert spring. • **glo|ri|ous|ly** ADV ❑ A tree, gloriously lit by autumn, pressed against the windowpane. ❷ ADJ If you describe something as **glorious**, you are emphasizing that it is wonderful and it makes you feel very happy. [EMPHASIS] ❑ The win revived glorious memories of his championship-winning days. • **glo|ri|ous|ly** ADV ❑ ...her gloriously happy love life. ❸ ADJ A **glorious** career, victory, or occasion involves great fame or success. ❑ Harrison had a glorious career spanning more than six decades. • **glo|ri|ous|ly** ADV ❑ But the mission was successful, gloriously successful.

glo|ry /glɔri/ (**glories**) ❶ N-UNCOUNT **Glory** is the fame and admiration that you gain by doing something impressive. ❑ Walsham had his moment of glory when he won a 20km race. ❷ N-PLURAL A person's **glories** are the occasions when they have done something people greatly admire which makes them famous. ❑ The album sees them re-living past glories but not really breaking any new ground.

gloss /glɒs/ (**glosses, glossing, glossed**) ❶ N-SING A **gloss** is a bright shine on the surface of something. ❑ Sheets of rain were falling and produced a black gloss on the asphalt. ❷ N-UNCOUNT **Gloss** is an appearance of attractiveness or good quality which sometimes hides less attractive features or poor quality. ❑ Television commercials might seem more professional, but beware of mistaking the gloss for the content. ❸ N-SING If you put **a gloss** on a bad situation, you try to make it seem more attractive or acceptable by giving people a false explanation or interpretation of it. ❑ He used his diary to put a fine gloss on the horrors the regime perpetrated. ❹ N-MASS **Gloss** is the same as **gloss paint**. ❺ V-T If you **gloss** a difficult word or idea, you provide an explanation of it. ❑ "Aventure" is often glossed as simply good or bad "fortune" or "chance."

▶ **gloss over** PHRASAL VERB If you **gloss over** a problem, a mistake, or an embarrassing moment, you try to make it seem unimportant by ignoring it or by dealing with it very quickly. ❑ Some foreign governments gloss over human rights abuses.

glos|sa|ry /glɒsəri/ (**glossaries**) N-COUNT A **glossary** of special, unusual, or technical words or expressions is an alphabetical list of them giving their meanings, for example at the end of a book on a particular subject. ❑ A glossary of terms is included for the reader's convenience.

gloss paint N-UNCOUNT **Gloss paint** is paint that forms a shiny surface when it dries. ❑ ...a fresh coat of white gloss paint.

glossy /glɒsi/ (**glossier, glossiest**) ❶ ADJ **Glossy** means smooth and shiny. ❑ ...glossy black hair. ❷ ADJ You can describe something as **glossy** if you think that it has been designed to look attractive but has little practical value or may have hidden faults. ❑ ...a glossy new office. ❸ ADJ [ADJ n] **Glossy** magazines, leaflets, books, and photographs are produced on expensive, shiny paper. ❑ ...a glossy magazine.

glove /glʌv/ (**gloves**) ❶ N-COUNT **Gloves** are pieces of clothing which cover your hands and wrists and have individual sections for each finger. You wear gloves to keep your hands warm or dry or to protect them. ❑ He stuck his gloves in his pocket. ❷ PHRASE If you say that something **fits like a glove**, you are emphasizing that it fits exactly. [EMPHASIS] ❑ I gave one of the bikinis to my sister Sara and it fit like a glove.

glove com|part|ment (**glove compartments**) also **glove box** N-COUNT The **glove compartment** in a car is a small enclosed space or shelf below the front windshield.

gloved /glʌvd/ ADJ [usu ADJ n] A **gloved** hand has a glove on it. [mainly WRITTEN]

glow /gloʊ/ (**glows, glowing, glowed**) ❶ N-COUNT A **glow** is a dull, steady light, for example the light produced by a fire when there are no flames. ❑ The cigarette's red glow danced about in the darkness. ❷ N-SING A **glow** is a pink color on a person's face, usually because they are healthy or have been exercising. ❑ The moisturizer gave my face a healthy glow that lasted all day. ❸ N-SING If you feel a **glow** of satisfaction or achievement, you have a strong feeling of pleasure because of something that you have done or that has happened. ❑ Exercise will give you a glow of satisfaction at having achieved something. ❹ V-I If

glower

something **glows**, it produces a dull, steady light. ❑ *The night lantern glowed softly in the darkness.* **5** V-I If someone's skin **glows**, it looks pink because they are healthy or excited, or have been doing physical exercise. ❑ *Her freckled skin glowed with health again.* **6** V-I If someone **glows** with an emotion such as pride or pleasure, the expression on their face shows how they feel. ❑ *The expectant mothers that Amy had encountered positively glowed with pride.* **7** → see also **glowing** **8** → See feature box at **light**

glow|er /gl<u>au</u>ər/ (**glowers, glowering, glowered**) V-I If you **glower** at someone or something, you look at them angrily. ❑ *He glowered at me but said nothing.*

glow|er|ing /gl<u>au</u>ərɪŋ/ **1** ADJ [usu ADJ n] If you describe a person as **glowering**, you mean they look angry and bad-tempered. [WRITTEN] ❑ *...his glowering good looks.* **2** ADJ [usu ADJ n] If you describe a place as **glowering**, you mean that it looks dark and threatening. [WRITTEN] ❑ *...glowering castle walls.*

glow|ing /gl<u>ou</u>ɪŋ/ **1** ADJ A **glowing** description or opinion about someone or something praises them highly or supports them strongly. ❑ *The media has been speaking in glowing terms of the relationship between the two countries.* **2** → see also **glow**

glow|worm /gl<u>ou</u>wɜrm/ (**glowworms**) N-COUNT A **glowworm** is a type of beetle that produces light from its body.

glu|cose /gl<u>u</u>kous/ N-UNCOUNT **Glucose** is a type of sugar that gives you energy.

glue /gl<u>u</u>/ (**glues, glueing** or **gluing, glued**) **1** N-MASS **Glue** is a sticky substance used for joining things together, often for repairing broken things. ❑ *...a tube of glue.* **2** V-T If you **glue** one object to another, you stick them together using glue. ❑ *Glue the fabric around the window.* ❑ *The material is cut and glued in place.* **3** V-T PASSIVE If you say that someone **is glued to** something, you mean that they are giving it all their attention. ❑ *They are all glued to the Olympic Games.*

glue sniff|ing N-UNCOUNT **Glue sniffing** is the practice of breathing the vapor from glue in order to become intoxicated.

glum /gl<u>ʌ</u>m/ (**glummer, glummest**) ADJ Someone who is **glum** is sad and quiet because they are disappointed or unhappy about something. ❑ *She was very glum and was obviously missing her children.* ● **glum|ly** ADV [ADV with v] ❑ *When Eleanor returned, I was still sitting glumly on the couch.*

glut /gl<u>ʌ</u>t/ (**gluts, glutting, glutted**) **1** N-COUNT [usu sing, usu with supp] If there is a **glut** of something, there is so much of it that it cannot all be sold or used. ❑ *Exports have become increasingly important to wineries as they battle a global wine glut.* **2** V-T If a market **is glutted** with something, there is a glut of that thing. [BUSINESS] ❑ *The region is glutted with hospitals.*

glu|ta|mate /gl<u>u</u>təmeɪt/ → see **monosodium glutamate**

glute /gl<u>u</u>t/ (**glutes**) N-COUNT Your **glutes** are the large muscles in your buttocks. [INFORMAL] ❑ *Every time you do this exercise you can feel your glutes getting stronger.*

glu|ten /gl<u>u</u>tᵊn/ N-UNCOUNT **Gluten** is a substance found in cereal grains such as wheat.

glu|ti|nous /gl<u>u</u>tɪnəs/ ADJ Something that is **glutinous** is very sticky. ❑ *The sauce was glutinous and tasted artificial.* ❑ *...soft and glutinous mud.*

glut|ton /gl<u>ʌ</u>tᵊn/ (**gluttons**) **1** N-COUNT If you think that someone eats too much and is greedy, you can say they are a **glutton**. [DISAPPROVAL] ❑ *I can't control my eating. It's hard when people don't understand and call you a glutton.* **2** N-COUNT [N for n] If you say that someone is a **glutton for** something, you mean that they enjoy or need it very much. ❑ *He was a glutton for hard work.* ❑ *Ivy must be a glutton for punishment.*

glut|ton|ous /gl<u>ʌ</u>tənəs/ ADJ If you think that someone eats too much or is greedy, you can say they are **gluttonous**. ❑ *...a selfish, gluttonous and lazy person.*

glut|tony /gl<u>ʌ</u>təni/ N-UNCOUNT **Gluttony** is the act or habit of eating too much or being greedy.

glyc|er|in /gl<u>ɪ</u>sərɪn/

in BRIT, usually use **glycerine**

N-UNCOUNT **Glycerin** is a thick, sweet, colorless liquid that is used especially in making medicine, explosives, and antifreeze for cars.

GM /dʒ<u>i</u> ɛm/ ADJ **GM** crops have had one or more genes changed, for example in order to make them resist pests better. **GM** food contains ingredients made from GM crops. **GM** is an abbreviation for **genetically modified**. ❑ *Many of us may be eating food containing GM ingredients without realizing it.*

gm.

The plural can be **gm.** or **gms**.

gm. is a written abbreviation for **gram**. ❑ *...450 gm. mixed soft summer fruits.*

GM-free ADJ **GM-free** products or crops are products or crops that do not contain any genetically modified material. ❑ *...GM-free soya.* ❑ *...food that is meant to be GM-free.*

GMO /dʒ<u>i</u> ɛm o<u>u</u>/ (**GMOs**) N-COUNT A **GMO** is an animal, plant, or other organism whose genetic structure has been changed by genetic engineering. **GMO** is an abbreviation for 'genetically modified organism.' ❑ *...the presence of GMOs in many processed foods.*

GMT /dʒ<u>i</u> ɛm t<u>i</u>/ **GMT** is the standard time in Great Britain which is used to calculate the time in the rest of the world. **GMT** is an abbreviation for **Greenwich Mean Time**. ❑ *New Mexico is seven hours behind GMT.*

gnarled /n<u>ɑ</u>rld/ **1** ADJ A **gnarled** tree is twisted and strangely shaped because it is old. ❑ *...a large and beautiful garden full of ancient gnarled trees.* **2** ADJ A person who is **gnarled** looks very old because their skin has lines on it or their body is bent. If someone has **gnarled** hands, their hands are twisted as a result of old age or illness. ❑ *...gnarled old men.* ❑ *His hands were gnarled with arthritis.*

gnash /n<u>æ</u>ʃ/ (**gnashes, gnashing, gnashed**) PHRASE If you say that someone **is gnashing** their **teeth**, you mean they are angry or frustrated about something. ❑ *If you couldn't attend either of the concerts and are currently gnashing your teeth at having missed out, don't despair.*

gnat /n<u>æ</u>t/ (**gnats**) N-COUNT A **gnat** is a very small flying insect that bites people and usually lives near water.

gnaw /n<u>ɔ</u>/ (**gnaws, gnawing, gnawed**) **1** V-T/V-I If people or animals **gnaw** something or **gnaw** at it, they bite it repeatedly. ❑ *Woodlice attack living plants and gnaw at the stems.* **2** V-I If a feeling or thought **gnaws at** you, it causes you to keep worrying. [WRITTEN] ❑ *...the nagging disquiet that had gnawed at him for days.*

gnoc|chi /n<u>ɒ</u>ki, ny<u>ɒ</u>ki/ N-PLURAL **Gnocchi** are a type of pasta consisting of small round balls made from flour and sometimes potato.

gnome /n<u>ou</u>m/ (**gnomes**) N-COUNT In children's stories, a **gnome** is an imaginary creature that is like a tiny old man with a beard and pointed hat.

gno|mic /n<u>ou</u>mɪk/ ADJ [usu ADJ n] A **gnomic** remark is brief and seems wise but is difficult to understand. [WRITTEN] ❑ *...the somewhat gnomic utterances of John Maynard Keynes in his General Theory.*

GNP /dʒ<u>i</u> ɛn p<u>i</u>/ (**GNPs**) N-VAR In economics, a country's **GNP** is the total value of all the goods produced and services provided by that country in one year. **GNP** is an abbreviation for **gross national product**. Compare **GDP**.

gnu /n<u>u</u>, ny<u>u</u>/ (**gnus**) N-COUNT A **gnu** is a large African animal similar to an ox.

GO
① MOVING OR LEAVING
② LINK VERB USES
③ OTHER VERB USES, NOUN USES, AND PHRASES
④ PHRASAL VERBS

① **go** ✦✦✦ /g<u>ou</u>/ (**goes, going, went, gone**)

In most cases the past participle of **go** is **gone**, but occasionally you use 'been': see **been**.

1 V-T/V-I When you **go** somewhere, you move or travel there. ❑ *We went to Rome.* ❑ *I went home for the weekend.* ❑ *It took us an* hour to go three miles. **2** V-I When you **go**, you leave the place where you are. ❏ *Let's go.* **3** V-T/V-I You use **go** to say that someone leaves the place where they are and does an activity, often a leisure activity. ❏ *We went swimming very early.* ❏ *Maybe they've just gone shopping.* ❏ *He went for a walk.* **4** V-T/V-I When you **go** do something, you move to a place in order to do it and you do it. You can also use **go and** do something, but you always say that someone **went and** did something. ❏ *I have to go see the doctor.* ❏ *I finished my beer, then went and got another.* **5** V-I If you **go to** school, work, or church, you attend it regularly as part of your normal life. ❏ *She will have to go to school.* **6** V-I When you say where a road or path **goes**, you are saying where it begins or ends, or what places it is to. ❏ *There's a mountain road that goes from Blairstown to Millbrook Village.* **7** V-I You can use **go** with words like 'further' and 'beyond' to show the degree or extent of something. ❏ *The governor went further by agreeing that all policy announcements should be made first in the House.* **8** V-I If you say that a period of time **goes** quickly or slowly, you mean that it seems to pass quickly or slowly. ❏ *The weeks go so quickly!* **9** V-I If you say where money **goes**, you are saying what it is spent on. ❏ *Most of my money goes toward bills.* **10** V-I If you say that something **goes to** someone, you mean that it is given to them. ❏ *A lot of credit must go to the chairman and his father.* **11** V-I If someone **goes on** television or radio, they take part in a television or radio program. ❏ *The president has gone on television to defend stringent new security measures.* **12** V-I If something **goes**, someone gets rid of it. ❏ *Exactly how many jobs will go remains unclear.* **13** V-I If someone **goes**, they leave their job, usually because they are forced to. ❏ *He had made a humiliating tactical error and he had to go.* **14** V-I If something **goes into** something else, it is put in it as one of the parts or elements that form it. ❏ *...the really interesting ingredients that go into the dishes that we all love to eat.* **15** V-I If something **goes** in a particular place, it belongs there or should be put there, because that is where you normally keep it. ❏ *The shoes go on the shoe shelf.* **16** V-I If you say that one number **goes into** another number a particular number of times, you are dividing the second number by the first. ❏ *Six goes into thirty five times.* **17** V-I If one of a person's senses, such as their sight or hearing, **is going**, it is getting weak and they may soon lose it completely. [INFORMAL] ❏ *His eyes are going; he says he has glaucoma.* **18** V-I If something such as a light bulb or a part of an engine **is going**, it is no longer working properly and will soon need to be replaced. ❏ *I thought it looked as though the battery was going.*

② **go** ♦♦♦ /goʊ/ (goes, going, went, gone) V-LINK You can use **go** to say that a person or thing changes to another state or condition. For example, if someone **goes crazy**, they become crazy, and if something **goes bad**, it deteriorates. ❏ *I'm going bald.* ❏ *Sometimes food goes bad, but people don't know it, so they eat it anyway and then they get sick.*

③ **go** ♦♦♦ /goʊ/ (goes, going, went, gone) **1** V-I You use **go** to talk about the way something happens. For example, if an event or situation **goes well**, it is successful. ❏ *She says everything is going smoothly.* **2** V-I If a machine or device **is going**, it is working. ❏ *What about my copier? Can you get it going again?* **3** V-RECIP If something **goes with** something else, or if two things **go together**, they look or taste good together. ❏ *I was searching for a pair of gray gloves to go with my new gown.* ❏ *I can see that some colors go together and some don't.* **4** V-T/V-I You use **go** to introduce something you are quoting. For example, you say **the story goes** or **the argument goes** just before you quote all or part of it. ❏ *The story goes that she went home with him that night.* ❏ *The story goes like this.* **5** V-T You use **go** when indicating that something makes or produces a sound. For example, if you say that something **goes** 'bang,' you mean it produces the sound 'bang.' ❏ *She stopped in front of a painting of a dog and she started going "woof woof."* **6** V-T You can use **go** instead of 'say' when you are quoting what someone has said or what you think they will say. [INFORMAL] ❏ *He goes to me: "Oh, what do you want?"* **7** N-COUNT A **go** is an attempt at doing something. ❏ *I always wanted to have a go at football.* ❏ *She won on her first go.* **8** N-COUNT [poss N] If it is your **go** in a game, it is your turn to do something, for example to play a card or move a piece. ❏ *Now whose go is it?* **9** → see also **going**, **gone** **10** PHRASE If you do something **as** you **go along**, you do it while you are doing another thing, without preparing it beforehand. ❏ *Learning how to become a parent takes time. It's a skill you learn as you go along.* **11** CONVENTION If someone says '**Where do we go from here?**' they are asking what should be done next, usually because a problem has not been solved in a satisfactory way. **12** PHRASE If you say that someone is **making a go of** something such as a business or relationship, you mean that they are having some success with it. ❏ *I knew we could make a go of it and be happy.* **13** PHRASE If you say that someone is always **on the go**, you mean that they are always busy and active. [INFORMAL] ❏ *I got a new job this year where I am on the go all the time.* **14** PHRASE If you say that there are a particular number of things **to go**, you mean that they still remain to be dealt with. ❏ *I still had another five operations to go.* **15** PHRASE If you say that there is a certain amount of time **to go**, you mean that there is that amount of time left before something happens or ends. ❏ *There is a week to go until the elections.* **16** PHRASE If you are in a café or restaurant and ask for an item of food **to go**, you mean that you want to take it with you and not eat it there. [mainly AM] ❏ *... large fries to go.*

in BRIT, use **to take away**

④ **go** ♦♦♦ /goʊ/ (goes, going, went, gone)
▶ **go about** **1** PHRASAL VERB The way you **go about** a task or problem is the way you approach it and deal with it. ❏ *I want him back, but I just don't know how to go about it.* **2** PHRASAL VERB When you **are going about** your normal activities, you are doing them. ❏ *We were simply going about our business when we were pounced upon by these police officers.*
▶ **go after** PHRASAL VERB If you **go after** something, you try to get it, catch it, or hit it. ❏ *We're not going after civilian targets.*
▶ **go against** **1** PHRASAL VERB If a person or their behavior goes against your wishes, beliefs, or expectations, their behavior is the opposite of what you want, believe in, or expect. ❏ *Changes are being made here which go against my principles and I cannot agree with them.* **2** PHRASAL VERB If a decision, vote, or result **goes against** you, you do not get the decision, vote, or result that you wanted. ❏ *The mayor will resign if the vote goes against him.*
▶ **go ahead** **1** PHRASAL VERB If someone **goes ahead** with something, they begin to do it or make it, especially after planning, promising, or asking permission to do it. ❏ *The district board will vote today on whether to go ahead with the plan.* **2** PHRASAL VERB If a process or an organized event **goes ahead**, it takes place or is carried out. ❏ *The event will go ahead as planned in Chicago next summer.*
▶ **go along with** **1** PHRASAL VERB If you **go along with** a rule, decision, or policy, you accept it and obey it. ❏ *Whatever the majority decided I was prepared to go along with.* **2** PHRASAL VERB If you **go along with** a person or an idea, you agree with them. ❏ *"I don't think a government has properly done it for about the past twenty-five years."—"I'd go along with that."*
▶ **go around** **1** PHRASAL VERB If you **go around** to someone's house, you go to visit them at their house. ❏ *I asked them to go around to the house to see if they were there.* **2** PHRASAL VERB If you **go around** in a particular way, you behave or dress in that way, often as part of your normal life. ❏ *I got in the habit of going around with bare feet.* **3** PHRASAL VERB If a piece of news or a joke **is going around**, it is being told by many people in the same period of time. ❏ *There's a nasty sort of rumor going around about it.* **4** PHRASAL VERB If there is enough of something to **go around**, there is enough of it to be shared among a group of people, or to do all the things for which it is needed. ❏ *Eventually we will not have enough water to go around.*
▶ **go away** **1** PHRASAL VERB If you **go away**, you leave a place or a person's company. ❏ *I think we need to go away and think about this.* **2** PHRASAL VERB If you **go away**, you leave a place and spend a period of time somewhere else, especially as a vacation. ❏ *Why don't you and I go away this weekend?*
▶ **go back on** PHRASAL VERB If you **go back on** a promise or agreement, you do not do what you promised or agreed to do. ❏ *The budget crisis has forced the president to go back on his word.*
▶ **go back to** **1** PHRASAL VERB If you **go back to** a task or activity, you start doing it again after you have stopped doing it for a period of time. ❏ *I now look forward to going back to work as soon as possible.* **2** PHRASAL VERB If you **go back to** a particular

▶ **go before** ◼ PHRASAL VERB Something that has **gone before** has happened or been discussed at an earlier time. ❑ *This is a rejection of most of what has gone before.* ◼ PHRASAL VERB To **go before** a judge, tribunal, or court of law means to be present there as part of an official or legal process. ❑ *The case went before Justice Henry on December 23 and was adjourned.*

▶ **go by** ◼ PHRASAL VERB If you say that time **goes by**, you mean that it passes. ❑ *My grandmother was becoming more and more sad and frail as the years went by.* ◼ PHRASAL VERB If you **go by** something, you use it as a basis for a judgment or action. ❑ *If they prove that I was wrong, then I'll go by what they say.*

▶ **go down** ◼ PHRASAL VERB If a price, level, or amount **goes down**, it becomes lower or less than it was. ❑ *Income from sales tax went down.* ◼ PHRASAL VERB Crime has gone down 70 percent. ◼ PHRASAL VERB If you **go down** on your knees or on all fours, you lower your body until it is supported by your knees, or by your hands and knees. ❑ *I went down on my knees and prayed for guidance.* ◼ PHRASAL VERB If you say that a remark, idea, or type of behavior **goes down** in a particular way, you mean that it gets a particular kind of reaction from a person or group of people. ❑ *Lawyers advised their clients that a neat appearance went down well with the judges.* ◼ PHRASAL VERB When the sun **goes down**, it goes below the horizon. ❑ *...the glow left in the sky after the sun has gone down.* ◼ PHRASAL VERB If a ship **goes down**, it sinks. If a plane **goes down**, it crashes out of the sky. ❑ *Their aircraft went down during a training exercise.* ◼ PHRASAL VERB If a computer **goes down**, it stops functioning temporarily. ❑ *The main computers went down for 30 minutes.* ◼ PHRASAL VERB [usu cont] Something that **is going down** is happening. [INFORMAL] ❑ *The patrol can detect if something is going down or is about to go down.*

▶ **go for** ◼ PHRASAL VERB If you **go for** a particular thing or way of doing something, you choose it. ❑ *People tried to persuade him to go for a more gradual reform program.* ◼ PHRASAL VERB If you **go for** someone, you attack them. ❑ *Pantieri went for him, gripping him by the throat.* ◼ PHRASAL VERB If you say that a statement you have made about one person or thing also **goes for** another person or thing, you mean that the statement is also true of this other person or thing. ❑ *It is illegal to dishonor reservations; that goes for restaurants as well as customers.* ◼ PHRASAL VERB If something **goes for** a particular price, it is sold for that amount. ❑ *Some old machines go for as much as 35,000 dollars.*

▶ **go in** PHRASAL VERB If the sun **goes in**, a cloud comes in front of it and it can no longer be seen. ❑ *The sun went in, and the breeze became cold.*

▶ **go in for** PHRASAL VERB If you **go in for** a particular activity, you decide to do it as a hobby or interest. ❑ *They go in for tennis and bowling.*

▶ **go into** ◼ PHRASAL VERB If you **go into** something, you describe or examine it fully or in detail. ❑ *It was a private conversation and I don't want to go into details about what was said.* ◼ PHRASAL VERB If you **go into** something, you decide to do it as your job or career. ❑ *Mr. Pok has now gone into the tourism business.* ◼ PHRASAL VERB If an amount of time, effort, or money **goes into** something, it is spent or used to do it, get it, or make it. ❑ *Is there a lot of effort and money going into this sort of research?*

▶ **go off** ◼ PHRASAL VERB If an explosive device or a gun **goes off**, it explodes or fires. ❑ *A few minutes later the bomb went off, destroying the vehicle.* ◼ PHRASAL VERB If an alarm bell **goes off**, it makes a sudden loud noise. ❑ *Then the fire alarm went off. I just grabbed my clothes and ran out.* ◼ PHRASAL VERB If an electrical device **goes off**, it stops operating. ❑ *As the water came in the windows, all the lights went off.*

▶ **go off with** ◼ PHRASAL VERB If someone **goes off with** another person, they leave their husband, wife, or lover and have a relationship with that person. ❑ *I suppose Carolyn went off with some man she'd fallen in love with.* ◼ PHRASAL VERB If someone **goes off with** something that belongs to another person, they leave and take it with them. ❑ *He's gone off with my passport.*

▶ **go on** ◼ PHRASAL VERB If you **go on** doing something, or **go on with** an activity, you continue to do it. ❑ *Unemployment is likely to go on rising this year.* ❑ *I'm all right here. Go on with your work.* ◼ PHRASAL VERB If something **is going on**, it is happening. ❑ *While this conversation was going on, I was listening with earnest attention.* ◼ PHRASAL VERB If a process or institution **goes on**, it continues to happen or exist. ❑ *The population failed to understand the necessity for the war to go on.* ◼ PHRASAL VERB If you say that a period of time **goes on**, you mean that it passes. ❑ *Renewable energy will become progressively more important as time goes on.* ◼ PHRASAL VERB If you **go on** to do something, you do it after you have done something else. ❑ *Alliss retired from golf in 1969 and went on to become a successful broadcaster.* ◼ PHRASAL VERB If you **go on** to a place, you go to it from the place that you have reached. ❑ *He goes on to New Orleans tomorrow.* ◼ PHRASAL VERB If you **go on**, you continue saying something or talking about something. ❑ *Meer cleared his throat several times before he went on.* ◼ PHRASAL VERB If you **go on about** something, you continue talking about the same thing, often in an annoying way. [INFORMAL] ❑ *He's always going on about his son and daughter.* ◼ PHRASAL VERB [only imper] You say '**Go on**' to someone to persuade or encourage them to do something. [INFORMAL] ❑ *Go on, it's fun.* ◼ PHRASAL VERB If you talk about the information you have to **go on**, you mean the information you have available to base an opinion or judgment on. ❑ *But you have to go on the facts.* ◼ PHRASAL VERB If an electrical device **goes on**, it begins operating. ❑ *A light went on at seven every evening.*

▶ **go out** ◼ PHRASAL VERB If you **go out**, you leave your home in order to do something enjoyable, for example to go to a party, a bar, or the movies. ❑ *I'm going out tonight.* ◼ PHRASAL VERB If you **go out** with someone, the two of you spend time together socially, and have a romantic or sexual relationship. ❑ *I once went out with a French man.* ◼ PHRASAL VERB If you **go out** to do something, you make a deliberate effort to do it. ❑ *You do not go out to injure opponents.* ◼ PHRASAL VERB If a light **goes out**, it stops shining. ❑ *The bedroom light went out after a moment.* ◼ PHRASAL VERB If something that is burning **goes out**, it stops burning. ❑ *The fire seemed to be going out.* ◼ PHRASAL VERB If a message **goes out**, it is announced, published, or sent out to people. ❑ *Word went out that a column of tanks was on its way.* ◼ PHRASAL VERB When the tide **goes out**, the water in the sea gradually moves back to a lower level. ❑ *The tide was going out.* ◼ PHRASE You can say '**My heart goes out to him**' or '**My sympathy goes out to her**' to express the strong sympathy you have for someone in a difficult or unpleasant situation. [FEELINGS] ❑ *My heart goes out to Mrs. Adams and her fatherless children.*

▶ **go over** PHRASAL VERB If you **go over** a document, incident, or problem, you examine, discuss, or think about it very carefully. ❑ *I won't know how successful it is until an accountant has gone over the books.*

▶ **go round** → see **go around**

▶ **go through** ◼ PHRASAL VERB If you **go through** an experience or a period of time, especially an unpleasant or difficult one, you experience it. ❑ *He was going through a very difficult time.* ◼ PHRASAL VERB If you **go through** a lot of things such as papers or clothes, you look at them, usually in order to sort them into groups or to search for a particular item. ❑ *It was evident that someone had gone through my possessions.* ◼ PHRASAL VERB If you **go through** a list, story, or plan, you read or check it from beginning to end. ❑ *Going through his list of customers is a massive job.* ◼ PHRASAL VERB If a law, agreement, or official decision **goes through**, it is approved by a legislature or committee. ❑ *The bill might have gone through if the economy was growing.*

▶ **go through with** PHRASAL VERB If you **go through with** an action you have decided on, you do it, even though it may be very unpleasant or difficult for you. ❑ *Richard pleaded for Belinda to reconsider and not to go through with the divorce.*

▶ **go under** PHRASAL VERB If a business or project **goes under**, it becomes unable to continue in operation or in existence. [BUSINESS] ❑ *If one firm goes under it could provoke a cascade of bankruptcies.*

▶ **go up** ◼ PHRASAL VERB If a price, amount, or level **goes up**, it becomes higher or greater than it was. ❑ *Interest rates went up.* ❑ *The cost has gone up to $1.95 a minute.* ◼ PHRASAL VERB When a building, wall, or other structure **goes up**, it is built or fixed in place. ❑ *He noticed a new building going up near Whitaker Park.* ◼ PHRASAL VERB If something **goes up**, it explodes or starts to burn, usually suddenly and with great intensity. ❑ *The hotel*

went up in flames. **4** PHRASAL VERB If a shout or cheer **goes up**, it is made by a lot of people together. ❑ *A cheer went up from the other passengers.*
▶ **go with 1** PHRASAL VERB If one thing **goes with** another thing, the two things officially belong together, so that if you get one, you also get the other. ❑ *...the lucrative $250,000 salary that goes with the job.* **2** PHRASAL VERB If one thing **goes with** another thing, it is usually found or experienced together with the other thing. ❑ *For many women, the status which goes with being a wife is important.*
▶ **go without** PHRASAL VERB If you **go without** something that you need or usually have or do, you do not get it or do it. ❑ *I have known what it is like to go without food for days.*

goad /goʊd/ (**goads, goading, goaded**) V-T If you **goad** someone, you deliberately make them feel angry or irritated, often causing them to react by doing something. ❑ *Charles was always goading me.* • N-COUNT **Goad** is also a noun. ❑ *Her presence was just one more goad to Joanna's unraveling nerves.*

go-ahead 1 N-SING If you give someone or something the **go-ahead**, you give them permission to start doing something. ❑ *Chuck gave Pellman the go-ahead to speak publicly about the injury he sustained.* **2** ADJ [ADJ n] A **go-ahead** person or organization tries hard to succeed, often by using new methods. ❑ *Fairview Estate is one of the oldest and the most go-ahead wine producers in South Africa.*

goal ♦♦◊ /goʊl/ (**goals**) **1** N-COUNT In games such as soccer or hockey, the **goal** is the space into which the players try to get the ball in order to score a point for their team. ❑ *The Dragons had only one shot on goal.* **2** N-COUNT In games such as soccer or hockey, a **goal** is when a player gets the ball into the goal, or the point that is scored by doing this. ❑ *They scored five goals in the first half of the match.* **3** N-COUNT Something that is your **goal** is something that you hope to achieve, especially when much time and effort will be needed. ❑ *It's a matter of setting your own goals and following them.* **4** → See feature box at **football**

SYNONYMS

goal
NOUN **3**
aim: *The aim of the festival is to increase awareness of such traditions.*
target: *...course repeaters who failed to reach their target grades.*
objective: *Our main objective was the recovery of the child safe and well.*
end: *The police force is being manipulated for political ends.*
purpose: *The purpose of the occasion was to raise money for medical supplies.*

---

goalie /ˈgoʊli/ (**goalies**) N-COUNT A **goalie** is the same as a **goalkeeper**. [INFORMAL]

goal|keeper /ˈgoʊlkiːpər/ (**goalkeepers**) N-COUNT A **goalkeeper** is the player on a sports team whose job is to guard the goal.

goal|keeping /ˈgoʊlkiːpɪŋ/ N-UNCOUNT In games such as soccer and hockey, **goalkeeping** refers to the activity of guarding the goal. ❑ *They were thankful for the excellent goalkeeping of John Lukic.*

goal|less /ˈgoʊlləs/ ADJ In games such as soccer, a **goalless** draw is a game which ends without any goals having been scored. ❑ *The fixture ended in a goalless draw.*

goal line (**goal lines**) N-COUNT In games such as football and soccer, a **goal line** is one of the lines at each end of the field over which the ball must pass in order to score a goal.

goal|mouth /ˈgoʊlmaʊθ/ (**goalmouths**) N-COUNT In games such as soccer, the **goalmouth** is the area just in front of the goal.

goal|post /ˈgoʊlpoʊst/ (**goalposts**) also **goal post** N-COUNT A **goalpost** is one of the two upright wooden posts that are connected by a crossbar and form the goal in games such as soccer and hockey.

goal|tender /ˈgoʊltɛndər/ (**goaltenders**) N-COUNT A **goaltender** is the same as a **goalkeeper**. [AM] ❑ *...the league's two best goaltenders.*

goal|tending /ˈgoʊltɛndɪŋ/ N-UNCOUNT **Goaltending** is the same as **goalkeeping**. [AM] ❑ *The goaltending and defense are among the weakest in the league.*

goat /goʊt/ (**goats**) N-COUNT A **goat** is a farm animal or a wild animal that is about the size of a sheep. Goats have horns, and hairs on their chin which resemble a beard.

goat cheese (**goat cheeses**) also **goat's cheese** N-MASS **Goat cheese** is cheese made from goat's milk.

goatee /goʊˈtiː/ (**goatees**) N-COUNT A **goatee** is a very short, pointed beard that covers a man's chin but not his cheeks.

gob /gɒb/ (**gobs**) N-COUNT [N of n] A **gob** of a thick, unpleasant liquid is a small amount of it. [INFORMAL] ❑ *...a gob of spit.*

gob|bet /ˈgɒbɪt/ (**gobbets**) **1** N-COUNT A **gobbet** of something soft, especially food, is a small lump or piece of it. ❑ *...gobbets of meat.* **2** N-COUNT A **gobbet** of information is a small piece of it.

gob|ble /ˈgɒbəl/ (**gobbles, gobbling, gobbled**) V-T If you **gobble** food, you eat it quickly and greedily. ❑ *Pete gobbled all the lentil stew.* • PHRASAL VERB **Gobble down** and **gobble up** mean the same as **gobble**. ❑ *There were dangerous beasts in the river that might gobble you up.*

gob|ble|dy|gook /ˈgɒbəldiɡuːk/ also **gobbledegook** N-UNCOUNT If you describe a speech or piece of writing as **gobbledygook**, you are criticizing it for seeming like nonsense and being very technical or complicated. [INFORMAL, DISAPPROVAL] ❑ *When he asked questions, the answers came back in Wall Street gobbledygook.*

go-between (**go-betweens**) N-COUNT A **go-between** is a person who takes messages between people who are unable or unwilling to meet each other. ❑ *He will act as a go-between to try and work out an agenda.*

gob|let /ˈgɒblɪt/ (**goblets**) **1** N-COUNT A **goblet** is a type of cup without handles and usually with a long stem. **2** → See also color supplement

gob|lin /ˈgɒblɪn/ (**goblins**) N-COUNT In fairy stories, a **goblin** is a small, ugly creature which usually enjoys causing trouble.

go-cart (**go-carts**) also **go-kart** N-COUNT A **go-cart** is a very small motor vehicle with four wheels, used for racing.

go-carting also **go-karting** N-UNCOUNT **Go-carting** is the sport of racing or riding on go-carts.

god ♦♦◊ /gɒd/ (**gods**) **1** N-PROPER The name **God** is given to the spirit or being who is worshipped as the creator and ruler of the world, especially by Jews, Christians, and Muslims. ❑ *He believes in God.* **2** CONVENTION People sometimes use **God** in exclamations to emphasize something that they are saying, or to express surprise, fear, or excitement. This use could cause offense. [EMPHASIS] ❑ *Oh my God, he's shot somebody.* ❑ *Good God, it's Mr. Harper!* **3** N-COUNT In many religions, a **god** is one of the spirits or beings that are believed to have power over a particular part of the world or nature. ❑ *...Zeus, king of the gods.* **4** N-COUNT Someone who is admired very much by a person or group of people, and who influences them a lot, can be referred to as a **god**. ❑ *To his followers he was a god.* **5** PHRASE You can say **God knows**, **God only knows**, or **God alone knows** to emphasize that you do not know something. [EMPHASIS] ❑ *God alone knows what she thinks.* **6** PHRASE If someone says **God knows** in reply to a question, they mean that they do not know the answer. [EMPHASIS] ❑ *"Where is he now?"—"God knows."* **7** PHRASE If someone uses expressions such as **what in God's name**, **why in God's name**, or **how in God's name**, they are emphasizing how angry, annoyed, or surprised they are. [INFORMAL, EMPHASIS] ❑ *What in God's name do you expect me to do?* **8** PHRASE If a person thinks they are **God's gift** to someone or something, they think they are perfect or extremely good. [INFORMAL] ❑ *Are men God's gift to women? Some of them think they are.* **9** PHRASE If someone **plays God**, they act as if they have unlimited power and can do anything they want. [DISAPPROVAL] ❑ *You have no right to play God in my life!* **10** PHRASE You can use **God** in expressions such as **I hope to God**, or **I wish to God**, or **I swear to God**, in order to emphasize what you are saying. [EMPHASIS] ❑ *I hope to God they are paying you well.* **11** PHRASE If you say **God willing**, you are saying that something will happen if all goes well. ❑ *God willing, there will be a breakthrough.* **12 honest to God** → see **honest** **13 for God's sake** → see **sake** **14 thank God** → see **thank**

god-awful ADJ [usu ADJ n] If someone says that something is **god-awful**, they think it is very unpleasant. This word could cause offense. [INFORMAL, EMPHASIS]

god|child /gɒdtʃaɪld/ (**godchildren**) N-COUNT [usu with poss] In the Christian religion, your **godchild** is a person that you promise to help bring up in the Christian faith.

god|dammit /gɒdæmɪt/ also **goddamnit, goddamn it** EXCLAM Some people say **goddammit** when they are angry or irritated. This use could cause offense. [INFORMAL, FEELINGS]

god|damn /gɒdæm/ also **goddam, goddamned** ADJ [ADJ n] Some people use **goddamn** when they are angry, surprised, or excited. This use could cause offense. [INFORMAL, FEELINGS] • ADV [ADV adj] *Goddamn is also an adverb.*

god|damned /gɒdæmd/ ADJ [ADJ n] **Goddamned** means the same as **goddamn**. This use could cause offense. [INFORMAL, FEELINGS]

god|daughter /gɒddɔːtər/ (**goddaughters**) also **god-daughter** N-COUNT A **goddaughter** is a female godchild.

god|dess /gɒdɪs/ (**goddesses**) N-COUNT In many religions, a **goddess** is a female spirit or being that is believed to have power over a particular part of the world or nature. ❑ *...Diana, the goddess of the hunt.*

god|father /gɒdfɑːðər/ (**godfathers**) ◼ N-COUNT A **godfather** is a male godparent. ◻ N-COUNT A powerful man who is at the head of a criminal organization is sometimes referred to as a **godfather**. ❑ *...the feared godfather of the Mafia.* ◼ N-COUNT [N *of* n] You can refer to a man who started or developed something such as a style of music as the **godfather of** that thing. [JOURNALISM] ❑ *...the godfather of soul, James Brown.*

God-fearing ADJ [usu ADJ n] A **God-fearing** person is religious and behaves according to the moral rules of their religion. ❑ *They brought up their children to be God-fearing Christians.*

god|forsaken /gɒdfɔːseɪkən/ also **God-forsaken** ADJ [ADJ n] If you say that somewhere is a **godforsaken** place, you dislike it a lot because you find it very boring and depressing. [DISAPPROVAL] ❑ *I don't want to stay here, in this job and in this God-forsaken country.*

God|head /gɒdhed/ N-SING [usu the N] The **Godhead** is the essential nature of God.

god|less /gɒdlɪs/ ADJ [usu ADJ n] If you say that a person or group of people is **godless**, you disapprove of them because they do not believe in God. [DISAPPROVAL] ❑ *...a godless and alienated society.* • **god|less|ness** N-UNCOUNT ❑ *...his assaults on the godlessness of America.*

god|like /gɒdlaɪk/ ADJ [usu ADJ n] A **godlike** person or a person with **godlike** qualities is admired or respected very much as if he or she were perfect. ❑ *His energy and talent elevate him to godlike status.* ❑ *They were godlike in their wisdom and compassion.*

god|li|ness /gɒdlɪnɪs/ ◼ N-UNCOUNT **Godliness** is the quality of being godly. ◻ PHRASE If someone says that **cleanliness is next to godliness**, they are referring to the idea that people have a moral duty to keep themselves and their homes clean.

god|ly /gɒdli/ (**godlier, godliest**) ADJ [usu ADJ n] A **godly** person is someone who is deeply religious and shows obedience to the rules of their religion. ❑ *...a learned and godly preacher.*

god|mother /gɒdmʌðər/ (**godmothers**) ◼ N-COUNT A **godmother** is a female godparent. ◻ N-COUNT You can refer to a woman who started or developed something such as a style of music as the **godmother of** that thing. [JOURNALISM] ❑ *...the godmother of British show business.*

god|parent /gɒdpeərənt, -pær-/ (**godparents**) N-COUNT In the Christian religion, if you are the **godparent** of a younger person, you promise to help bring them up in the Christian faith.

god|send /gɒdsend/ N-SING [*a* N] If you describe something as **a godsend**, you are emphasizing that it helps you very much. [EMPHASIS] ❑ *Pharmacists are a godsend when you don't feel sick enough to call the doctor.*

god|son /gɒdsʌn/ (**godsons**) N-COUNT A **godson** is a male godchild.

God|speed /gɒdspiːd/ also **godspeed** CONVENTION The term **Godspeed** is sometimes used in order to wish someone success and safety, especially if they are about to go on a long and dangerous journey. [FORMAL] ❑ *I know you will join me in wishing them Godspeed.*

-goer /-gouər/ (**-goers**) COMB IN N-COUNT **-goer** is added to words such as 'theater,' 'church,' and 'movie' to form nouns which describe people who regularly go to that type of place or event. ❑ *They are regular churchgoers.* ❑ *...excited partygoers.*

go|fer /goufər/ (**gofers**) N-COUNT A **gofer** is a person whose job is to do simple and rather boring tasks for someone. [INFORMAL]

go-getter (**go-getters**) N-COUNT If someone is a **go-getter**, they are very energetic and eager to succeed. [APPROVAL]

gog|gle /gɒgəl/ (**goggles, goggling, goggled**) ◼ V-I If you **goggle** at something, you stare at it with your eyes wide open, usually because you are surprised by it. ❑ *She goggled at me.* ❑ *He goggled in bewilderment.* ◻ N-PLURAL [also *a pair of* N] **Goggles** are large glasses that fit closely to your face around your eyes to protect them from such things as water, wind, or dust. ◼ → See feature box at **experiment**

go-go ◼ ADJ [ADJ n] A **go-go** dancer is someone whose job involves dancing to pop music in nightclubs while wearing very few clothes. [OLD-FASHIONED] ◻ ADJ [ADJ n] A **go-go** period of time is a time when people make a lot of money and businesses are growing. A **go-go** company is very energetic and is growing fast. [mainly AM, BUSINESS] ❑ *Current economic activity is markedly slower than during the go-go years of the mid to late 1980s.* ❑ *It will be a go-go business with pre-tax profits forecast to climb from $152 million last year to $200 million.*

going ✦✦✦ /goʊɪŋ/ ◼ PHRASE If you say that something **is going to** happen, you mean that it will happen in the future, usually quite soon. ❑ *I think it's going to be successful.* ❑ *You're going to enjoy this.* ◻ PHRASE You say that you **are going to** do something to express your intention or determination to do it. ❑ *I'm going to go to bed.* ❑ *He announced that he's going to resign.* ◼ N-UNCOUNT You use **the going** to talk about how easy or difficult it is to do something. You can also say that something is, for example, **hard going** or **tough going**. ❑ *He has her support to fall back on when the going gets tough.* ◻ ADJ [ADJ n] The **going** rate or the **going** salary is the usual amount of money that you expect to pay or receive for something. ❑ *That's about half the going price on world markets.* ◼ → see also **go** ① ◻ PHRASE If someone or something **has** a lot **going for** them, they have a lot of advantages. ❑ *This area has a lot going for it.* ◼ PHRASE When you **get going**, you start doing something or start a journey, especially after a delay. ❑ *Now what about that shopping list? I've got to get going.* ◻ PHRASE If you say that someone should do something **while the going is good**, you are advising them to do it while things are going well and they still have the opportunity, because you think it will become much more difficult to do. ❑ *People are leaving in the thousands while the going is good.* ◼ PHRASE If you **keep going**, you continue doing things or doing a particular thing. ❑ *I like to keep going. I hate to sit still.* ◼ **going concern** → see **concern**

-going /-goʊɪŋ/ ◼ COMB IN N-UNCOUNT [oft N n] **-going** is added to nouns such as 'theater,' 'church,' and 'movie' to form nouns which describe the activity of going to that type of place or event. ❑ *...his partygoing days as a student.* ◻ COMB IN ADJ [usu ADJ n] **-going** is added to nouns such as 'ocean' and 'sea' to form adjectives which describe vehicles that are designed for that type of place. ❑ *...one of the largest oceangoing liners in the world.* ◼ COMB IN ADJ [usu ADJ n] **-going** is added to nouns that refer to directions to form adjectives which describe things that are moving in that direction. ❑ *The material can absorb outward-going radiation from the earth.* ◼ → see also **easygoing, ongoing, outgoing, thoroughgoing**

going-over N-SING If you give someone or something a **going-over**, you examine them thoroughly. [INFORMAL] ❑ *Michael was given a complete going-over and then treated for mononucleosis.*

goings-on N-PLURAL If you describe events or activities as **goings-on**, you mean that they are strange, interesting, amusing, or dishonest. ❑ *The Mexican girl had found out about the goings-on in the factory.*

goi|ter /gɔɪtər/ (**goiters**) N-VAR **Goiter** is a disease of the thyroid gland that makes a person's neck very swollen.

go-kart (**go-karts**) N-COUNT A **go-kart** is a very small motor vehicle with four wheels, used for racing.

go-karting N-UNCOUNT **Go-karting** is the sport of racing or riding on go-karts.

gold /goʊld/ (golds) **1** N-UNCOUNT Gold is a valuable, yellow-colored metal that is used for making jewelry and ornaments, and as an international currency. ☐ ...a sapphire set in gold. ☐ The price of gold was going up. **2** N-UNCOUNT Gold is jewelry and other things that are made of gold. ☐ We handed over all our gold and money. **3** COLOR Something that is gold is a bright yellow color, and is often shiny. ☐ I'd been wearing Michel's black and gold shirt. **4** N-VAR A gold is the same as a gold medal. [INFORMAL] ☐ His ambition was to win gold at the Olympic Games. **5** PHRASE If you say that a child is being as good as gold, you are emphasizing that they are behaving very well and are not causing you any problems. [EMPHASIS] ☐ The boys were as good as gold on our walk. **6** PHRASE If you say that someone has a heart of gold, you are emphasizing that they are very good and kind to other people. [EMPHASIS] ☐ They are all good boys with hearts of gold. They would never steal. **7** → See also color supplement

gold card (gold cards) N-COUNT A gold card is a special type of credit card that gives you extra benefits such as a higher spending limit.

gold digger (gold diggers) N-COUNT A gold digger is a person who has a relationship with someone who is rich in order to get money or expensive things from them. [DISAPPROVAL]

gold dust N-UNCOUNT Gold dust is gold in the form of a fine powder.

gold|en /ˈɡoʊldən/ **1** ADJ Something that is golden is bright yellow in color. ☐ She combed and arranged her golden hair. **2** ADJ Golden things are made of gold. ☐ ...a golden chain with a golden locket. **3** ADJ [ADJ n] If you describe something as golden, you mean it is wonderful because it is likely to be successful and rewarding, or because it is the best of its kind. ☐ He says there's a golden opportunity for peace which must be seized. **4** PHRASE If you refer to a man as a golden boy or a woman as a golden girl, you mean that they are especially popular and successful. ☐ When the movie came out the critics went wild, hailing Tarantino as the golden boy of the 1990s.

gold|en age (golden ages) N-COUNT [oft N of n] A golden age is a period of time during which a very high level of achievement is reached in a particular field of activity, especially in art or literature. ☐ You grew up in the golden age of American children's books.

gold|en hand|shake (golden handshakes) N-COUNT A golden handshake is a large sum of money that a company gives to an employee when he or she leaves, as a reward for long service or good work. [BUSINESS] ☐ And if Mr. Pell, 49, is axed following a takeover, he would be in line to collect a golden handshake of $1 million.

gold|en hel|lo (golden hellos) N-COUNT A golden hello is a sum of money that a company offers to a person in order to persuade them to join the company. [BUSINESS] ☐ Most people recognize the need to pay a golden hello to attract the best.

gold|en ju|bi|lee (golden jubilees) N-COUNT A golden jubilee is the 50th anniversary of an important or special event. ☐ The company is celebrating its golden jubilee.

gold|en oldie (golden oldies) N-COUNT People sometimes refer to something such as a song that is still popular even though it is old as a golden oldie. [INFORMAL]

gold|en para|chute (golden parachutes) N-COUNT A golden parachute is an agreement to pay a large amount of money to a senior executive of a company if they are forced to leave. [BUSINESS] ☐ Golden parachutes entitle them to a full year's salary if they get booted out of the company.

gold|en rule (golden rules) N-COUNT A golden rule is a principle you should remember because it will help you to be successful. ☐ Hanson's golden rule is to add value to whatever business he buys.

gold|en wed|ding (golden weddings) N-COUNT A golden wedding or a golden wedding anniversary is the 50th anniversary of a wedding.

gold|field /ˈɡoʊldfiːld/ (goldfields) N-COUNT A goldfield is an area of land where gold is found.

gold|fish /ˈɡoʊldfɪʃ/ (goldfish)

Goldfish is both the singular and the plural form.

N-COUNT Goldfish are small gold or orange fish which are often kept as pets.

gold leaf N-UNCOUNT Gold leaf is gold that has been beaten flat into very thin sheets and is used for decoration, for example to form the letters on the cover of a book.

gold med|al (gold medals) N-COUNT A gold medal is a medal made of gold which is awarded as first prize in a contest or competition. ☐ ...her ambition to win a gold medal at the Winter Olympics.

gold|mine /ˈɡoʊldmaɪn/ N-SING If you describe something such as a business or idea as a goldmine, you mean that it produces large profits. ☐ The book is a goldmine.

gold-plated ADJ Something that is gold-plated is covered with a very thin layer of gold. ☐ ...marble bathrooms with gold-plated faucets.

gold-rimmed ADJ [usu ADJ n] Gold-rimmed glasses have gold-colored frames.

gold rush (gold rushes) N-COUNT A gold rush is a situation when a lot of people suddenly go to a place where gold has been discovered.

gold|smith /ˈɡoʊldsmɪθ/ (goldsmiths) N-COUNT A goldsmith is a person whose job is making jewelry and other objects using gold.

golf /ɡɒlf/ N-UNCOUNT Golf is a game in which you use long sticks called clubs to hit a small, hard ball into holes that are spread out over a large area of grassy land. ☐ "Do you play golf?" he asked me suddenly.

golf ball (golf balls) N-COUNT A golf ball is a small, hard, white ball which people use when they are playing golf.

golf club (golf clubs) **1** N-COUNT A golf club is a long, thin, metal stick with a piece of wood or metal at one end that you use to hit the ball in golf. **2** N-COUNT A golf club is a social organization which provides a golf course and a building to meet in for its members. **3** → See also color supplement

golf course (golf courses) N-COUNT A golf course is a large area of grass which is specially designed for people to play golf on.

golf|er /ˈɡɒlfər/ (golfers) N-COUNT A golfer is a person who plays golf for pleasure or as a profession. ☐ ...one of the world's top golfers.

golf|ing /ˈɡɒlfɪŋ/ **1** ADJ [ADJ n] Golfing is used to describe things that involve the playing of golf or that are used while playing golf. ☐ He was wearing a cream silk shirt and a tartan golfing cap. **2** N-UNCOUNT Golfing is the activity of playing golf. ☐ You can play tennis or go golfing.

gol|ly /ˈɡɒli/ **1** EXCLAM Some people say golly to indicate that they are very surprised by something. [INFORMAL, OLD-FASHIONED, FEELINGS] ☐ "Golly," he says, "Isn't it exciting!" **2** EXCLAM Some people say by golly to emphasize that something did happen or should happen. [INFORMAL, OLD-FASHIONED, EMPHASIS] ☐ By golly we can do something about it this time.

gon|do|la /ˈɡɒndələ/ (gondolas) **1** N-COUNT A gondola is a long, narrow boat that is used especially in Venice. It has a flat bottom and curves upward at both ends. A person stands at one end of the boat and uses a long pole to move and steer it. **2** → See also color supplement

gone /ɡɔːn/ **1** Gone is the past participle of go. **2** ADJ [v-link ADJ] When someone is gone, they have left the place where you are and are no longer there. When something is gone, it is no longer present or no longer exists. ☐ He knows how hard it was for her while he was gone. ☐ He's already been gone four hours!

gon|er /ˈɡɔːnər/ (goners) N-COUNT If you say that someone is a goner, you mean that they are about to die, or are in such danger that nobody can save them. [INFORMAL] ☐ She fell so heavily I thought she was a goner.

gong /ɡɒŋ/ (gongs) N-COUNT A gong is a large, flat, circular piece of metal that you hit with a hammer to make a sound like a loud bell. Gongs are sometimes used as musical instruments, or to give a signal that it is time to do something. ☐ On the stroke of seven, a gong summons guests into the dining room.

gon|na /ˈɡɒnə/ Gonna is used in written English to represent the words 'going to' when they are pronounced informally. ☐ Then what am I gonna do?

gon|or|rhea /gɒnəriə/

in BRIT, use **gonorrhoea**

N-UNCOUNT **Gonorrhea** is a sexually transmitted disease.

goo /guː/ N-UNCOUNT You can use **goo** to refer to any thick, sticky substance, for example, mud or paste. [INFORMAL] ❑ *...a sticky goo of pineapple and coconut.*

GOOD
① DESCRIBING QUALITY, EXPRESSING APPROVAL
② BENEFICIAL
③ MORALLY RIGHT
④ OTHER USES
---

① **good** ♦♦♦ /gʊd/ (better, best)

→ Please look at meanings 18 – 24 to see if the expression you are looking for is shown under another headword.

1 ADJ **Good** means pleasant or enjoyable. ❑ *We had a really good time together.* ❑ *I know they would have a better life here.* **2** ADJ **Good** means of a high quality, standard, or level. ❑ *Exercise is just as important to health as good food.* ❑ *His parents wanted Raymond to have the best possible education.* **3** ADJ If you are **good at** something, you are skillful and successful at doing it. ❑ *He was very good at his work.* ❑ *I'm not very good at singing.* **4** ADJ If you describe a piece of news, an action, or an effect as **good**, you mean that it is likely to result in benefit or success. ❑ *On balance, biotechnology should be good news for developing countries.* ❑ *I think the response was good.* **5** ADJ A **good** idea, reason, method, or decision is a sensible or valid one. ❑ *They thought it was a good idea to make some offenders do community service.* ❑ *There is good reason to doubt this.* **6** ADJ If you say that **it is good** that something should happen or **good** to do something, you mean it is desirable, acceptable, or right. ❑ *I think it's good that some people are going.* **7** N-UNCOUNT [with brd-neg] If someone or something is **no good** or is **not any good**, they are not satisfactory or are of a low standard. ❑ *If the weather's no good then I won't take any pictures.* **8** ADJ A **good** estimate or indication of something is an accurate one. ❑ *We have a fairly good idea of what's going on.* ❑ *This is a much better indication of what a school is really like.* **9** ADJ If you get a **good** deal or a **good** price when you buy or sell something, you receive a lot in exchange for what you give. ❑ *Whether such properties are a good deal will depend on individual situations.* **10** ADJ Someone who is in a **good** mood is cheerful and pleasant to be with. ❑ *People were in a pretty good mood.* ❑ *He exudes natural charm and good humor.* **11** [ADJ n] If people are **good** friends, they get along well together and are very close. ❑ *She and Gavin are good friends.* **12** ADJ [a ADJ n] You use **good** to emphasize the great extent or degree of something. [EMPHASIS] ❑ *We waited a good fifteen minutes.* **13** CONVENTION You say '**Good**' or '**Very good**' to express pleasure, satisfaction, or agreement with something that has been said or done, especially when you are in a position of authority. ❑ *"Are you all right?"—"I'm fine."—"Good. So am I."* ❑ *Oh good, Tom's just come in.* **14** PHRASE If you say **it's a good thing** that something is the case, you mean that it is fortunate. ❑ *It's a good thing you aren't married.* **15** PHRASE If you say that something or someone is **as good as new**, you mean that they are in a very good condition or state, especially after they have been damaged or ill. ❑ *I only use that on special occasions, so it's as good as new.* **16** PHRASE You use **good old** before the name of a person, place, or thing when you are referring to them in an affectionate way. [FEELINGS] ❑ *Good old Harry. Reliable to the end.* **17** → see also **best, better** ① **18 in good faith** → see **faith 19 so far so good** → see **far** ② **20 the good old days** → see **old 21 in good shape** → see **shape 22 to stand someone in good stead** → see **stead 23 in good time** → see **time** ④ **24 too good to be true** → see **true**

SYNONYMS

good
ADJ
① **2**
excellent: *The recording quality is excellent.*
first-class: *The food was first-class.*
splendid: *The book includes a wealth of splendid photographs.*
superb: *There is a superb 18-hole golf course 6 miles away.*
---

① **3**
proficient: *A great number of Egyptians are proficient in foreign languages.*
skilled: *...a network of highly-skilled observers of wildlife.*
able: *They are bright, intelligent, able, and confident.*
capable: *She's a very capable speaker.*
adept: *He is an adept guitar player.*

① **4**
positive: *The separation from his sister had a positive effect on John.*
beneficial: *Using computers has a beneficial effect on children's learning.*
favorable: *His ability to talk tough while eating fast made a favorable impression on his dining companions.*

② **good** ♦♦♦ /gʊd/ (better, best) **1** ADJ [v-link ADJ for n] If something is **good for** a person or organization, it benefits them. ❑ *Rain water was once considered to be good for the complexion.* **2** N-SING [with poss] If something is done for the **good** of a person or organization, it is done in order to benefit them. ❑ *The president urged him to resign for the good of the country.* ❑ *Victims want to see justice done not just for themselves, but for the greater good of society.* **3** N-UNCOUNT If you say that doing something is **no good** or does **not** do **any good**, you mean that doing it is not of any use or will not bring any success. ❑ *It's no good worrying about it now.* ❑ *We gave them water and kept them warm, but it didn't do any good.* **4** PHRASE If you say that something will **do** someone **good**, you mean that it will benefit them or improve them. ❑ *The outing will do me good.* ❑ *It's probably done you good to get away for a few hours.* **5** → see also **best, better** ①

③ **good** ♦♦♦ /gʊd/ (better, best)

→ Please look at meaning 6 to see if the expression you are looking for is shown under another headword.

1 N-UNCOUNT **Good** is what is considered to be right according to moral standards or religious beliefs. ❑ *Good and evil may co-exist within one family.* **2** ADJ Someone who is **good** is morally correct in their attitudes and behavior. ❑ *The president is a good man.* **3** ADJ Someone, especially a child, who is **good** obeys rules and instructions and behaves in a socially correct way. ❑ *The children were very good.* ❑ *I'm going to be a good boy now.* **4** ADJ Someone who is **good** is kind and thoughtful. ❑ *You are good to me.* ❑ *Her good intentions were thwarted almost immediately.* **5** → see also **best, better** ① **6 good as gold** → see **gold**

④ **good** ♦♦♦ /gʊd/

→ Please look at meanings 5 – 8 to see if the expression you are looking for is shown under another headword.

1 PHRASE **As good as** can be used to mean 'almost.' ❑ *His career is as good as over.* **2** PHRASE If something changes or disappears **for good**, it never changes back or comes back as it was before. ❑ *Some of the nation's manufacturing jobs may be gone for good.* **3** PHRASE If someone **makes good** a threat or promise or **makes good on** it, they do what they have threatened or promised to do. [mainly AM] ❑ *He was confident the allies would make good on their pledges.* **4** → see also **goods 5 good gracious** → see **gracious 6 good grief** → see **grief 7 good heavens** → see **heaven 8 good lord** → see **lord**

good after|noon CONVENTION You say '**Good afternoon**' when you are greeting someone in the afternoon. [FORMAL, FORMULAE]

good|bye /gʊdbaɪ/ (goodbyes) also **good-bye, good-by 1** CONVENTION You say '**Goodbye**' to someone when you or they are leaving, or at the end of a telephone conversation. [FORMULAE] **2** N-COUNT When you say your **goodbyes**, you say something such as 'Goodbye' when you leave. ❑ *He said his goodbyes knowing that a long time would pass before he would see his child again.* ❑ *Perry and I exchanged goodbyes.* **3** PHRASE If you **say goodbye** or **wave goodbye** to something that you want or usually have, you accept that you are not going to have it. ❑ *He has probably said goodbye to his last chance of Olympic gold.* **4 to kiss something goodbye** → see **kiss**

good day CONVENTION People sometimes say '**Good day**' instead of 'Hello' or 'Goodbye.' [OLD-FASHIONED, FORMULAE] ❑ *Well, I'd better be off. Good day to you.*

good eve|ning CONVENTION You say '**Good evening**' when you are greeting someone in the evening. [FORMAL, FORMULAE]

good-for-nothing (good-for-nothings) ADJ [ADJ n] If you describe someone as **good-for-nothing**, you think that they are lazy or irresponsible. ❏ ...a good-for-nothing fourteen-year-old son who barely knows how to read and count. • N-COUNT **Good-for-nothing** is also a noun. ❏ ...lazy good-for-nothings.

Good Friday N-UNCOUNT **Good Friday** is the day on which Christians remember the crucifixion of Jesus Christ. It is the Friday before Easter Sunday.

good guy (good guys) N-COUNT [usu pl] You can refer to the good characters in a movie or story as the **good guys**. You can also refer to the **good guys** in a situation in real life. [INFORMAL] ❏ There was a fine line between the good guys and the bad guys.

good-humored

in BRIT, use **good-humoured**

ADJ A **good-humored** person or atmosphere is pleasant and cheerful. ❏ Charles was brave and remarkably good-humored. ❏ It was a good-humored conference.

goodie /gʊdi/ (goodies) → see goody

good-looking (better-looking, best-looking) **1** ADJ Someone who is **good-looking** has an attractive face. ❏ Cassandra noticed him because he was good-looking. **2** → See feature box at appearance

good|ly /gʊdli/ ADJ [ADJ n] A **goodly** amount or part of something is a fairly large amount or part of it, often more than was expected. [FORMAL] ❏ Laski spent a goodly part of his lecturing life in American universities.

good morn|ing CONVENTION You say '**Good morning**' when you are greeting someone in the morning. [FORMAL, FORMULAE]

good-natured ADJ A **good-natured** person or animal is naturally friendly and does not get angry easily. ❏ Bates looks like a good-natured fellow.

good|ness /gʊdnɪs/ **1** EXCLAM People sometimes say '**goodness**' or '**my goodness**' to express surprise. [FEELINGS] ❏ Goodness, I wonder if he knows. **2 for goodness' sake** → see **sake** **3 thank goodness** → see **thank** **4** N-UNCOUNT **Goodness** is the quality of being kind, helpful, and honest. ❏ He retains a faith in human goodness.

good night also **goodnight 1** CONVENTION You say '**Good night**' to someone late in the evening before one of you goes home or goes to sleep. [FORMULAE] **2** PHRASE If you **say good night** to someone or **kiss** them **good night**, you say something such as 'Good night' to them or kiss them before one of you goes home or goes to sleep. ❏ Eleanor went upstairs to say good night to the children. ❏ Both men rose to their feet and kissed her goodnight.

goods ◆◇ /gʊdz/ **1** N-PLURAL **Goods** are things that are made to be sold. ❏ Money can be exchanged for goods or services. **2** N-PLURAL Your **goods** are the things that you own and that can be moved. ❏ You can give your unwanted goods to charity.

COLLOCATIONS

goods
NOUN
1
noun + **goods**: consumer, household
adjective + **goods**: counterfeit, damaged, faulty, stolen; durable, electrical, electronic, manufactured
verb + **goods**: export, import; return
2
adjective + **goods**: worldly

SYNONYMS

goods
NOUN **1**
merchandise: No one will buy merchandise hearing this logo.
stock: We took the decision to withdraw a quantity of stock from sale.
product: Try to get the best product at the lowest price.
wares: Vendors displayed their wares in baskets or on the ground.

---

goods train (goods trains) N-COUNT A **goods train** is a train that transports goods and not people. [BRIT]

in AM, use **freight train**

good-tempered ADJ A **good-tempered** person or animal is naturally friendly and pleasant and does not easily get angry or upset. ❏ He was a happy, good-tempered child. ❏ ...a horse that is quiet and good-tempered.

good|will /gʊdwɪl/ **1** N-UNCOUNT **Goodwill** is a friendly or helpful attitude toward other people, countries, or organizations. ❏ I invited them to dinner, a gesture of goodwill. **2** N-UNCOUNT The **goodwill** of a business is something such as its good reputation, which increases the value of the business. [BUSINESS] ❏ We do not want to lose the goodwill built up over 175 years.

goody /gʊdi/ (goodies) also **goodie 1** N-COUNT [usu pl] You can refer to pleasant, exciting, or attractive things as **goodies**. [INFORMAL] ❏ ...a little bag of goodies. **2** N-COUNT [usu pl] You can refer to the heroes or the morally good characters in a movie or story as the **goodies**. You can also refer to the **goodies** in a situation in real life. [BRIT, INFORMAL]

in AM, usually use **good guy**

goody bag (goody bags) **1** N-COUNT A **goody bag** is a bag of little gifts, often given away by manufacturers in order to encourage people to try their products. [INFORMAL] **2** N-COUNT A **goody bag** is a bag of little gifts or candy that children are sometimes given at a children's party. [mainly AM]

goody-goody (goody-goodies) N-COUNT If you call someone a **goody-goody**, you mean they behave extremely well in order to please people in authority. [INFORMAL, DISAPPROVAL]

goo|ey /gui/ (gooier, gooiest) ADJ If you describe a food or other substance as **gooey**, you mean that it is very soft and sticky. [INFORMAL] ❏ ...a lovely, gooey, sticky mess.

goof /guf/ (goofs, goofing, goofed) **1** V-I If you **goof** or **goof up**, you make a silly mistake. [INFORMAL] ❏ We goofed last week at the end of our interview with the band. • N-COUNT **Goof** is also a noun. ❏ But was it, in fact, a hideous goof? **2** N-COUNT If you call someone a **goof**, you think they are silly. [INFORMAL, DISAPPROVAL] ❏ I could write for TV as well as any of those goofs.
▶ **goof off** PHRASAL VERB If someone **goofs off**, they spend their time doing nothing, often when they should be working. [mainly AM, INFORMAL] ❏ I saw a few films and generally kind of goofed off all day.

goofy /gufi/ (goofier, goofiest) ADJ If you describe someone or something as **goofy**, you think they are rather silly or ridiculous. [INFORMAL] ❏ ...a goofy smile.

Google /guːgəl/ N-PROPER **Google** is a popular internet search engine. It scans the Web to find Web pages that are relevant to the words you have typed in the search box. [TRADEMARK] ❏ A search on Google for "free ring tones" yields more than a million sites.

goon /gun/ (goons) **1** N-COUNT A **goon** is a person who is paid to hurt or threaten people. [AM, INFORMAL] ❏ He and the other goon began to beat me up. **2** N-COUNT If you call someone a **goon**, you think they behave in a silly way. [OLD-FASHIONED, DISAPPROVAL]

goose /gus/ (geese) **1** N-COUNT A **goose** is a large bird that has a long neck and webbed feet. Geese are often farmed for their meat. **2** N-UNCOUNT **Goose** is the meat from a goose that has been cooked. ❏ ...roast goose.

goose|berry /gʊsberi/ (gooseberries) N-COUNT A **gooseberry** is a small green fruit that has a sharp taste and is covered with tiny hairs.

goose bumps N-PLURAL If you get **goose bumps**, the hairs on your skin stand up so that it is covered with tiny bumps. You get goose bumps when you are cold, frightened, or excited.

goose pim|ples N-PLURAL **Goose pimples** are the same as **goose bumps**.

goose-step (goose-steps, goose-stepping, goose-stepped) V-I When soldiers **goose-step**, they lift their legs high and do not bend their knees as they march. ❏ ...photos of soldiers goose-stepping beside fearsome missiles.

go|pher /goʊfər/ (gophers) **1** N-COUNT A **gopher** is a small animal that looks somewhat like a rat and lives in holes in the ground. Gophers are found in Canada and the U.S. **2** N-PROPER In computing, **Gopher** is a program that collects information for you from many databases across the internet.

gore /gɔr/ (gores, goring, gored) **1** V-T [usu passive] If someone **is gored** by an animal, they are badly wounded by its horns or tusks. ❑ *Carruthers had been gored by a rhinoceros.* **2** N-UNCOUNT **Gore** is blood from a wound that has become thick. ❑ *There were pools of blood and gore on the pavement.*

gorge /gɔrdʒ/ (gorges, gorging, gorged) **1** N-COUNT A **gorge** is a deep, narrow valley with very steep sides, usually where a river passes through mountains or an area of hard rock. ❑ *...the deep gorge between these hills.* **2** V-T/V-I If you **gorge on** something or **gorge** yourself on it, you eat lots of it in a very greedy way. ❑ *I could spend each day gorging on chocolate.*

gor|geous /gɔrdʒəs/ **1** ADJ If you say that something is **gorgeous**, you mean that it gives you a lot of pleasure or is very attractive. [INFORMAL] ❑ *...gorgeous mountain scenery.* ❑ *It's a gorgeous day.* **2** ADJ If you describe someone as **gorgeous**, you think that they are very attractive. [INFORMAL] ❑ *The cosmetics industry uses gorgeous women to sell its skincare products.*

go|ril|la /gərɪlə/ (gorillas) N-COUNT A **gorilla** is a very large ape. It has long arms, black fur, and a black face.

gorse /gɔrs/ N-UNCOUNT **Gorse** is a dark green bush that grows in Europe. It has small yellow flowers and sharp prickles.

gory /gɔri/ (gorier, goriest) ADJ **Gory** situations involve people being injured or dying in a horrible way. ❑ *...the gory details of Mayan human sacrifices.*

gosh /gɒʃ/ EXCLAM Some people say '**Gosh**' when they are surprised. [OLD-FASHIONED] ❑ *Gosh, there's a lot of noise.*

gos|ling /gɒzlɪŋ/ (goslings) N-COUNT A **gosling** is a baby goose.

go-slow (go-slows) N-COUNT A **go-slow** is a protest by workers in which they deliberately work slowly in order to cause problems for their employers. [BRIT]

in AM, use **slowdown**

gos|pel /gɒspəl/ (gospels) **1** N-COUNT; N-IN-NAMES In the New Testament of the Bible, the **Gospels** are the four books which describe the life and teachings of Jesus Christ. ❑ *...the parable in St. Matthew's Gospel.* **2** N-SING In the Christian religion, the **gospel** refers to the message and teachings of Jesus Christ, as explained in the New Testament. ❑ *I didn't shirk my duties. I visited the sick and I preached the gospel.* **3** N-UNCOUNT **Gospel** or **gospel music** is a style of religious music that uses strong rhythms and vocal harmony. It is especially popular among Black Christians in the southern United States. ❑ *I had to go to church, so I grew up singing gospel.* **4** N-UNCOUNT If you take something as **gospel**, or it is the **gospel truth**, you believe that it is completely true. ❑ *He wouldn't say this if it weren't the gospel truth.*

gos|sa|mer /gɒsəmər/ ADJ You use **gossamer** to indicate that something is very light, thin, or delicate. [LITERARY] ❑ *...the daring gossamer dresses of sheer black lace.*

gos|sip /gɒsɪp/ (gossips, gossiping, gossiped) **1** N-UNCOUNT [also a N] **Gossip** is informal conversation, often about other people's private affairs. ❑ *He spent the first hour talking gossip.* ❑ *There has been much gossip about the possible reasons for his absence.* **2** V-RECIP If you **gossip with** someone, you talk informally, especially about other people or local events. You can also say that two people **gossip**. ❑ *We spoke, debated, gossiped into the night.* ❑ *Eva gossiped with Sarah.* **3** N-COUNT If you describe someone as a **gossip**, you mean that they enjoy talking informally to people about the private affairs of others. [DISAPPROVAL] ❑ *He was a vicious gossip.* **4** → See feature box at **truth**

gos|sip col|umn (gossip columns) N-COUNT A **gossip column** is a part of a newspaper or magazine where the activities and private lives of famous people are discussed. ❑ *The jet-setting couple made frequent appearances in the gossip columns.* • **gos|sip col|umn|ist** (gossip columnists) N-COUNT ❑ *...a Hollywood gossip columnist.*

gos|sipy /gɒsɪpi/ **1** ADJ [usu ADJ n] If you describe a book or account as **gossipy**, you mean it is informal and full of interesting but often unimportant news or information about people. ❑ *...a chatty, gossipy account of Forster's life.* **2** ADJ [usu ADJ n] If you describe someone as **gossipy**, you are critical of them because they talk about other people's private lives a great deal. [DISAPPROVAL] ❑ *...gossipy old women.*

got ✦✦✦ /gɒt/ **1** **Got** is the past tense and sometimes the past participle of **get**. **2** PHRASE You use **have got** to say that someone has a particular thing, or to mention a quality or characteristic that someone or something has. In informal American English, people sometimes just use 'got'. [SPOKEN] ❑ *I've got a coat just like this.* ❑ *After a pause he asked, "You got any identification?"* **3** PHRASE You use **have got to** when you are saying that something is necessary or must happen in the way stated. In informal American English, the 'have' is sometimes omitted. [SPOKEN] ❑ *I'm not happy with the situation, but I've just got to accept it.* ❑ *You got to come clean about things.* **4** PHRASE People sometimes use **have got to** in order to emphasize that they are certain that something is true, because of the facts or circumstances involved. In informal American English, the 'have' is sometimes omitted. [SPOKEN, EMPHASIS] ❑ *"You've got to be joking!" he wisely replied.*

got|cha /gɒtʃə/ EXCLAM **Gotcha** is used in written English to represent the words 'got you' when they are pronounced informally. ❑ *Gotcha, didn't I?*

Goth|ic /gɒθɪk/ **1** ADJ **Gothic** architecture and religious art was produced in the Middle Ages. Its features include tall pillars, high curved ceilings, and pointed arches. ❑ *...a vast, lofty Gothic cathedral.* ❑ *...Gothic stained glass windows.* **2** ADJ In **Gothic** stories, strange, mysterious adventures happen in dark and lonely places such as graveyards and old castles. ❑ *This novel is not science fiction, nor is it Gothic horror.*

got|ta /gɒtə/ **Gotta** is used in written English to represent the words 'got to' when they are pronounced informally, with the meaning 'have to' or 'must.' ❑ *Prices are high and our kids gotta eat.*

got|ten /gɒtən/ **Gotten** is the past participle of **get** in American English.

gouge /gaʊdʒ/ (gouges, gouging, gouged) V-T If you **gouge** something, you make a hole or a long cut in it, usually with a pointed object. ❑ *I punched him and gouged his face with the diamond ring he had given me.*
▶ **gouge out** PHRASAL VERB To **gouge out** a piece or part of something means to cut, dig, or force it from the surrounding surface. You can also **gouge out** a hole in the ground. ❑ *He has accused her of threatening to gouge his eyes out.*

gourd /gʊrd, gɔrd/ (gourds) **1** N-COUNT A **gourd** is a large, round fruit with a hard skin. You can also use **gourd** to refer to the plant on which this fruit grows. **2** N-COUNT A **gourd** is a container made from the hard, dry skin of a gourd fruit. Gourds are often used to carry water or for decoration.

gour|mand /gʊrmɒnd/ (gourmands) N-COUNT A **gourmand** is a person who enjoys eating and drinking in large amounts. [FORMAL, DISAPPROVAL] ❑ *The food here satisfies gourmands rather than gourmets.*

gour|met /gʊrmeɪ/ (gourmets) **1** ADJ [ADJ n] **Gourmet** food is nicer or more unusual or sophisticated than ordinary food, and is often more expensive. ❑ *Flavored coffee is sold at gourmet food stores and coffee shops.* ❑ *The couple share a love of gourmet cooking.* **2** N-COUNT A **gourmet** is someone who enjoys good food, and who knows a lot about food and wine. ❑ *The seafood here is a gourmet's delight.*

gout /gaʊt/ N-UNCOUNT **Gout** is a disease which causes people's joints to swell painfully, especially in their toes.

Gov. N-TITLE **Gov.** is a written abbreviation for **Governor**. ❑ *...Gov. Thomas Kean of New Jersey.*

gov|ern ✦✧✧ /gʌvərn/ (governs, governing, governed) **1** V-T To **govern** a place such as a country, or its people, means to be officially in charge of the place, and to have responsibility for making laws, managing the economy, and controlling public services. ❑ *They go to the polls on Friday to choose the people they want to govern their country.* **2** V-T If a situation or activity **is governed** by a particular factor, rule, or force, it is controlled by that factor, rule, or force. ❑ *Marine insurance is governed by a strict series of rules and regulations.*

gov|ern|ance /gʌvərnəns/ **1** N-UNCOUNT The **governance** of a country is the way in which it is governed. [FORMAL] ❑ *...he will meet with officials from several countries to discuss ways to promote good governance.* **2** N-UNCOUNT The **governance** of a company or organization is the way in which it is managed.

[FORMAL] ❑ ...a dramatic move away from the traditional view of governance in education.

gov|er|ness /gʌvərnɪs/ (**governesses**) N-COUNT In the past, a **governess** was a woman who was employed by a family to live with them and educate their children.

gov|ern|ing /gʌvərnɪŋ/ ADJ [ADJ n] A **governing** body or organization is one which controls a particular activity. ❑ The league became the governing body for amateur fencing in the U.S.

gov|ern|ment ♦♦♦ /gʌvərnmənt/ (**governments**) **1** N-COUNT-COLL The **government** of a country is the group of people who are responsible for governing it. ❑ The Government has insisted that confidence is needed before the economy can improve. ❑ ...democratic governments in countries like Britain and the U.S. **2** N-UNCOUNT **Government** consists of the activities, methods, and principles involved in governing a country or other political unit. ❑ The first four years of government were completely disastrous.

gov|ern|men|tal /gʌvərnmɛntəl/ ADJ [ADJ n] **Governmental** means relating to a particular government, or to the practice of governing a country. ❑ ...a governmental agency for providing financial aid to developing countries.

gov|er|nor ♦♦◊ /gʌvərnər/ (**governors**) **1** N-COUNT; N-TITLE In some systems of government, a **governor** is a person who is in charge of the political administration of a state, colony, or region. ❑ He was governor of Iowa in the late 1970s. **2** N-COUNT A **governor** is a member of a committee which controls an organization such as a university or a hospital. ❑ Wayne Hansen was added to the board of governors at City University, Bellevue.

gov|er|nor|ship /gʌvərnərʃɪp/ (**governorships**) N-COUNT The **governorship** of a particular state, colony, or region is the position of being its governor. **Governorship** is also used to refer to the period of time a particular person spends being the governor of a state, colony, or region. ❑ The governorship went to a Democrat, Mrs. Anne Richards.

govt. Govt. is a written abbreviation for **government**.

gown /gaʊn/ (**gowns**) **1** N-COUNT A **gown** is a dress, usually a long dress, which women wear on formal occasions. ❑ The new ball gown was a great success. **2** N-COUNT A **gown** is a loose black garment worn on formal occasions by people such as lawyers and academics. ❑ ...an old headmaster in a flowing black gown.

GP /dʒi pi/ (**GPs**) also **G.P.** N-COUNT A **GP** is a doctor who does not specialize in any particular area of medicine, but who has a medical practice in which he or she treats all types of illness. **GP** is an abbreviation for 'general practitioner.' ❑ Her husband called their local GP.

GPA /dʒi pi eɪ/ (**GPAs**) N-COUNT **GPA** is an abbreviation for **grade point average**. [AM] ❑ You've got to have a good GPA to get into graduate school. ❑ People who achieve high scores on the SAT tend to earn high college GPAs in the future.

GPS /dʒi pi ɛs/ (**GPSs**) N-COUNT **GPS** is an abbreviation for **global positioning system**. ❑ GPS operates best near the equator. ❑ ...a GPS receiver.

grab ♦◊◊ /græb/ (**grabs, grabbing, grabbed**) **1** V-T If you **grab** something, you take it or pick it up suddenly and roughly. ❑ I managed to grab her hand. **2** V-I If you **grab at** something, you try to grab it. ❑ He was clumsily trying to grab at Alfred's arms. • N-COUNT [usu sing, N for/at n] **Grab** is also a noun. ❑ I made a grab for the knife. **3** V-T If you **grab** someone who is walking past, you succeed in getting their attention. [INFORMAL] ❑ Grab that waiter, Mary Ann. **4** V-T If you **grab** someone's attention, you do something in order to make them notice you. ❑ I jumped on the wall to grab the attention of the crowd. **5** V-T If you **grab** something such as food, drink, or sleep, you manage to get some quickly. [INFORMAL] ❑ Grab a beer. **6** to **grab hold of** → see **hold** ① **7** PHRASE If something is **up for grabs**, it is available to anyone who is interested. [INFORMAL] ❑ The famous Ritz hotel is up for grabs for $100 million.

grab bag (**grab bags**) **1** N-COUNT A **grab bag** is a game in which you take a prize out of a container full of hidden prizes. [AM]

in BRIT, use **lucky dip**

2 N-COUNT [usu N of n] A **grab bag** of things, ideas, or people is a varied group of them. ❑ ...a fascinating grab-bag of documents about the life of Liszt.

grace /greɪs/ (**graces, gracing, graced**) **1** N-UNCOUNT If someone moves with **grace**, they move in a smooth, controlled, and attractive way. ❑ He moved with the grace of a trained boxer. **2** N-PLURAL The **graces** are the ways of behaving and doing things which are considered polite and well-mannered. ❑ She didn't fit in and she had few social graces. **3** V-T If you say that something **graces** a place or a person, you mean that it makes them more attractive. [FORMAL] ❑ He went to the beautiful old Shaker dresser that graced this homely room. **4** N-UNCOUNT In Christianity and some other religions, **grace** is the kindness that God shows to people because He loves them. ❑ It was only by the grace of God that no one died. **5** N-VAR When someone says **grace** before or after a meal, they say a prayer in which they thank God for the food and ask Him to bless it. ❑ Leo, will you say grace?

grace|ful /greɪsfəl/ **1** ADJ Someone or something that is **graceful** moves in a smooth and controlled way that is attractive to watch. ❑ His movements were so graceful they seemed effortless. • **grace|ful|ly** ADV [ADV with v] ❑ She stepped gracefully onto the stage. **2** ADJ Something that is **graceful** is attractive because it has a pleasing shape or style. ❑ His handwriting, from earliest young manhood, was flowing and graceful. • **grace|ful|ly** ADV [ADV adj/-ed] ❑ She loved the gracefully high ceiling, with its white-painted cornice.

grace|less /greɪslɪs/ **1** ADJ Something that is **graceless** is unattractive and not at all interesting or charming. ❑ It was a massive, graceless house. **2** ADJ A **graceless** movement is clumsy and uncontrolled. ❑ ...a graceless pirouette. • **grace|less|ly** ADV [ADV with v] ❑ He dropped gracelessly into a chair opposite her. **3** ADJ If you describe someone as **graceless**, you mean that their behavior is impolite. ❑ She couldn't stand his blunt, graceless manner. • **grace|less|ly** ADV [ADV with v] ❑ The task fell to Mr. Harris to deliver this bad news. It was gracelessly done.

gra|cious /greɪʃəs/ **1** ADJ If you describe someone as **gracious**, you mean that they are very well-mannered and pleasant. [FORMAL] ❑ She is a lovely and gracious woman. **2** ADJ If you describe the behavior of someone in a position of authority or high social standing as **gracious**, you mean that they behave in a polite and considerate way. [FORMAL] ❑ She closed with a gracious speech of thanks. • **gra|cious|ly** ADV [ADV with v] ❑ Hospitality at the presidential guest house was graciously declined. **3** ADJ You use **gracious** to describe the comfortable way of life of wealthy people. ❑ He drove through the gracious suburbs with the swimming pools and tennis courts. **4** EXCLAM Some people say **good gracious** or **goodness gracious** in order to express surprise or annoyance. [FEELINGS] ❑ Good gracious, look at that specimen, will you?

grad /græd/ (**grads**) N-COUNT [oft N n] A **grad** is a **graduate**. [mainly AM, INFORMAL]

gra|da|tion /greɪdeɪʃən/ (**gradations**) N-COUNT [usu pl, with supp] **Gradations** are small differences or changes in things. [FORMAL] ❑ But TV images require subtle gradations of light and shade.

grade ♦◊◊ /greɪd/ (**grades, grading, graded**) **1** V-T If something **is graded**, its quality is judged, and it is often given a number or a name that indicates how good or bad it is. ❑ Dust masks are graded according to the protection they offer. ❑ Hampshire College does not grade the students' work. **2** N-COUNT The **grade** of a product is its quality, especially when this has been officially judged. ❑ ...a good grade of plywood. • COMB IN ADJ **Grade** is also a combining form. ❑ ...weapons-grade plutonium. **3** N-COUNT Your **grade** in an examination or piece of written work is the mark you get, usually in the form of a letter or number, that indicates your level of achievement. ❑ What grade are you hoping to get? **4** N-COUNT Your **grade** in a company or organization is your level of importance or your rank. ❑ Staff turnover is particularly high among junior grades. **5** N-COUNT In the United States, a **grade** is a group of classes in which all the children are of a similar age. When you are six years old you go into the first grade and you leave school after the twelfth grade. ❑ Mr. White teaches first grade in south Georgia. **6** N-COUNT A **grade** is a slope. [AM] ❑ She drove up a steep grade and then began the long descent into the desert.

in BRIT, use **gradient**

7 N-COUNT Someone's **grade** is their military rank. [AM] ❑ I was a naval officer, lieutenant junior grade. **8** PHRASE If someone

makes the grade, they succeed, especially by reaching a particular standard. ❑ *She had a strong desire to be a dancer but failed to make the grade.* **9** → See feature box at **learning**

COLLOCATIONS

grade
NOUN **2**
adjective + **grade**: fine, high, premium, top; low, standard
3
noun + **grade**: exam
adjective + **grade**: good, high; low, poor
verb + **grade**: achieve, obtain

SYNONYMS

grade
VERB **1**
classify: *Rocks can be classified according to their mode of origin.*
rate: *He is generally rated Italy's No. 3 industrialist.*
group: *The fact sheets are grouped into seven sections.*
rank: *Mr Short does not even rank in the world's top ten.*

---

grade cross|ing (grade crossings) N-COUNT A **grade crossing** is a place where a railroad track crosses a road at the same level. [AM]

> in BRIT, use **level crossing**

grad|ed read|er (graded readers) N-COUNT A **graded reader** is a story that has been adapted for people learning to read or learning a foreign language. Graded readers avoid using difficult grammar and vocabulary.

grade point av|er|age (grade point averages) also **grade-point average** N-COUNT A student's **grade point average** is a measure of their academic achievement, based on an average of all the grades they receive. [AM] ❑ *At her old high school in Hamilton, Ohio, she earned a 4.0 grade point average.*

-grader /-greɪdər/ (-graders) COMB IN N-COUNT **-grader** combines with words such as 'first' and 'second' to form nouns which refer to a child or young person who is in a particular grade in the American education system. ❑ *...a sixth-grader at the Latta School.*

grade school (grade schools) N-VAR In the United States, a **grade school** is the same as an **elementary school**. ❑ *I was just in grade school at the time, but I remember it perfectly.*

gra|di|ent /ˈgreɪdiənt/ (gradients) N-COUNT A **gradient** is a slope, or the degree to which the ground slopes. [mainly BRIT]

> in AM, usually use **grade**

grad|ual /ˈgrædʒuəl/ ADJ A **gradual** change or process occurs in small stages over a long period of time, rather than suddenly. ❑ *Losing weight is a slow, gradual process.*

gradu|al|ly ♦◇◇ /ˈgrædʒuəli/ ADV [ADV with v] If something changes or is done **gradually**, it changes or is done in small stages over a long period of time, rather than suddenly. ❑ *Electricity lines to 30,000 homes were gradually being restored yesterday.*

SYNONYMS

gradually
ADV
steadily: *The company has steadily been losing market share.*
slowly: *My resentment of her slowly began to fade.*
bit by bit: *Bit by bit, I began to understand what they were trying to do.*
step-by-step: *I am not rushing things, and I'm taking it step-by-step.*

---

gradu|ate ♦◇◇ (graduates, graduating, graduated)

The noun is pronounced /ˈgrædʒuɪt/. The verb is pronounced /ˈgrædʒueɪt/.

1 N-COUNT A **graduate** is a student who has successfully completed a course at a high school, college, or university. ❑ *The top one-third of all high school graduates are entitled to an education at California State University.* **2** V-I When a student **graduates**, they complete their studies successfully and leave their school or university. ❑ *When the boys graduated from high school, Ann moved to a small town in Vermont.* **3** V-I If you **graduate** from one thing to another, you go from a less important job or position to a more important one. ❑ *Bruce graduated to chef at the Bear Hotel.*

COLLOCATIONS

graduate
NOUN **1**
noun + **graduate**: college, university; arts, economics, law, science
adjective + **graduate**: unemployed; new, recent; bright, skilled
verb + **graduate**: employ, recruit; attract, produce

---

gradu|at|ed /ˈgrædʒueɪtɪd/ **1** ADJ [ADJ n] **Graduated** means increasing by regular amounts or grades. ❑ *The U.S. military wants to avoid the graduated escalation that marked the Vietnam War.* **2** ADJ [ADJ n] **Graduated** jars are marked with lines and numbers which show particular measurements. ❑ *...a graduated tube marked in millimeters.*

gradu|ate school (graduate schools) N-VAR In the United States, a **graduate school** is a division of a university or college where graduate students are taught. ❑ *She was in graduate school, studying for a master's degree in social work.*

gradu|ate stu|dent (graduate students) N-COUNT In the United States, a **graduate student** is a student with a bachelor's degree from a university who is studying or doing research at a more advanced level. [AM]

> in BRIT, use **postgraduate**

gradua|tion /ˌgrædʒuˈeɪʃən/ (graduations) **1** N-UNCOUNT **Graduation** is the successful completion of a course of study at a university, college, or school, for which you receive a degree or diploma. ❑ *They asked what his plans were after graduation.* **2** N-COUNT A **graduation** is a special ceremony at a university, college, or school, at which degrees and diplomas are given to students who have successfully completed their studies. ❑ *...the graduation ceremony at Yale.*

graf|fi|ti /grəˈfiːti/ **1** N-UNCOUNT-COLL **Graffiti** is words or pictures that are written or drawn in public places, for example on walls or posters. ❑ *Buildings old and new are thickly covered with graffiti.* **2** → See feature box at **urban**

graft /græft/ (grafts, grafting, grafted) **1** N-COUNT A **graft** is a piece of healthy skin or bone, or a healthy organ, which is attached to a damaged part of your body by a medical operation in order to replace it. ❑ *I am having a skin graft on my arm soon.* **2** V-T [usu passive] If a piece of healthy skin or bone or a healthy organ **is grafted** onto a damaged part of your body, it is attached to that part of your body by a medical operation. ❑ *The top layer of skin has to be grafted onto the burns.* **3** V-T If a part of one plant or tree **is grafted** onto another plant or tree, they are joined together so that they will become one plant or tree, often in order to produce a new variety. ❑ *Pear trees are grafted on quince rootstocks.*

gra|ham crack|er /ˈgreɪəm ˌkrækər/ (graham crackers) N-COUNT A **graham cracker** is a thin, crisp cookie made from wholewheat flour. [AM] ❑ *She gave each of us graham crackers.*

Grail /greɪl/ also **grail** **1** N-PROPER The **Grail** or the **Holy Grail** is the cup that was believed to have been used by Jesus Christ at the Last Supper. In medieval times, many people tried to find the Grail without success. **2** N-SING [oft the N of n] If you describe something as a **grail** or a **holy grail**, you mean that someone is trying very hard to obtain or achieve it. ❑ *The discovery is being hailed as the Holy Grail of astronomy.*

grain ♦◇◇ /greɪn/ (grains) **1** N-COUNT A **grain** of wheat, rice, or other cereal crop is a seed from it. ❑ *...a grain of wheat.* **2** N-MASS **Grain** is a cereal crop, especially wheat or corn, that has been harvested and is used for food or in trade. ❑ *...a bag of grain.* **3** N-COUNT A **grain** of something such as sand or salt is a tiny, hard piece of it. ❑ *...a grain of sand.* **4** to **take something with a grain of salt** → see **salt** **5** N-SING [N of n] A **grain of** a quality is a very small amount of it. ❑ *There's more than a grain of truth in that.* **6** N-SING The **grain** of a piece of wood is the direction of its fibers. You can also refer to the pattern of lines on the surface of the wood as **the grain**. ❑ *Brush the paint generously over the wood in the direction of the grain.* **7** PHRASE If you say that an idea or action **goes against the grain**, you mean that it is very difficult for you to accept it or do it, because it conflicts with your previous ideas, beliefs, or principles. ❏ *Privatization goes against the grain of their principle of opposition to private ownership of industry.*

grain elevator (grain elevators) N-COUNT A **grain elevator** is a building in which grain such as corn is stored and which contains machinery for moving the grain. [AM]

grainy /ɡreɪni/ (grainier, grainiest) **1** ADJ A **grainy** photograph looks as if it is made up of lots of spots, which make the lines or shapes in it difficult to see. ❏ *...grainy black and white photos.* **2** ADJ [usu ADJ n] **Grainy** means having a rough surface or texture, or containing small bits of something. ❏ *...the grainy tree trunk.* ❏ *Do not use a grainy mustard.*

gram /ɡræm/ (grams)

in BRIT, also use **gramme**

N-COUNT A **gram** is a unit of weight. One thousand grams are equal to one kilogram. ❏ *A soccer ball weighs about 400 grams.*

-gram /-ɡræm/ (-grams) COMB IN N-COUNT **-gram** combines with nouns to form other nouns which refer to someone who dresses up in order to a bring a message to someone else, as a practical joke. ❏ *They sent him a kissogram.*

grammar /ɡræmər/ **1** N-UNCOUNT **Grammar** is the ways that words can be put together in order to make sentences. ❏ *He doesn't have mastery of the basic rules of grammar.* **2** N-UNCOUNT Someone's **grammar** is the way in which they obey or do not obey the rules of grammar when they write or speak. ❏ *His vocabulary was sound and his grammar excellent.*

grammarian /ɡrəmɛəriən/ (grammarians) N-COUNT A **grammarian** is someone who studies the grammar of a language and writes books about it or teaches it.

grammar school (grammar schools) N-VAR; N-IN-NAMES A **grammar school** is the same as an **elementary school**. [AM] ❏ *Jennifer hadn't been home to watch television in the afternoon since grammar school.*

grammatical /ɡrəmætɪkəl/ **1** ADJ [ADJ n] **Grammatical** is used to indicate that something relates to grammar. ❏ *Should the teacher present grammatical rules to students?* **2** ADJ If someone's language is **grammatical**, it is considered correct because it obeys the rules of grammar. ❏ *...a new test to determine whether students can write grammatical English.*

gramme /ɡræm/ (grammes) [BRIT] → see gram

gramophone /ɡræməfoʊn/ (gramophones) N-COUNT A **gramophone** is an old-fashioned type of record player. ❏ *...a wind-up gramophone with a big horn.* ❏ *...gramophone records.*

granary /ɡrænəri/ (granaries) N-COUNT A **granary** is a building that is used for storing grain.

grand ✦✧ /ɡrænd/ (grander, grandest, grand)

The form **grand** is used as the plural for meaning **6**.

1 ADJ If you describe a building or a piece of scenery as **grand**, you mean that its size or appearance is very impressive. ❏ *This grand building in the center of town used to be the hub of the capital's social life.* **2** ADJ **Grand** plans or actions are intended to achieve important results. ❏ *Hamilton revealed his grand design for the economic future of the United States.* **3** ADJ People who are **grand** think they are important or socially superior. [DISAPPROVAL] ❏ *He is grander and even richer than the Prince of Wales.* **4** ADJ [ADJ n] A **grand** total is one that is the final amount or the final result of a calculation. ❏ *It came to a grand total of $220,329.* **5** ADJ [ADJ n] **Grand** is often used in the names of buildings such as hotels, especially when they are very large. ❏ *They stayed at The Grand Hotel, Budapest.* **6** N-COUNT A **grand** is a thousand dollars or a thousand pounds. [INFORMAL] ❏ *They're paying you ten grand now for those adaptations of old plays.*

grandad /ɡrændæd/ (grandads) → see granddad

grandaddy /ɡrændædi/ (grandaddies) → see granddaddy

grandchild /ɡræntʃaɪld/ (grandchildren) N-FAMILY Someone's **grandchild** is the child of their son or daughter. ❏ *Mary loves her grandchildren.*

granddad /ɡrændæd/ (granddads) also **grandad** N-FAMILY Your **granddad** is your grandfather. [INFORMAL] ❏ *My granddad is 85.*

granddaddy /ɡrændædi/ (granddaddies) also **grandaddies** N-FAMILY Some people refer to or address their grandfather as **granddaddy**. [AM, INFORMAL]

granddaughter /ɡrændɔtər/ (granddaughters) N-FAMILY Someone's **granddaughter** is the daughter of their son or daughter. ❏ *...a drawing of my granddaughter Amelia.*

grandee /ɡrændi/ (grandees) N-COUNT In the past, a **grandee** was a Spanish prince of the highest rank.

grandeur /ɡrændʒər/ **1** N-UNCOUNT If something such as a building or a piece of scenery has **grandeur**, it is impressive because of its size, its beauty, or its power. ❏ *Venezuela is the ideal starting point to explore the grandeur and natural beauty of South America.* **2** N-UNCOUNT Someone's **grandeur** is the great importance and social status that they have, or think they have. ❏ *He is wholly concerned with his own grandeur.*

grandfather /ɡrænfɑðər/ (grandfathers) N-FAMILY Your **grandfather** is the father of your father or mother. ❏ *His grandfather was a professor.*

grandfather clock (grandfather clocks) **1** N-COUNT A **grandfather clock** is an old-fashioned type of clock in a tall wooden case which stands upright on the floor. **2** → See also color supplement

grandiloquent /ɡrændɪləkwənt/ ADJ **Grandiloquent** language or behavior is very formal, literary, or exaggerated, and is used by people when they want to seem important. [FORMAL, DISAPPROVAL]

grandiose /ɡrændioʊs/ ADJ If you describe something as **grandiose**, you mean it is bigger or more elaborate than necessary. [DISAPPROVAL] ❏ *The sad truth is that not one of Tim's grandiose plans has even begun.*

grand jury (grand juries) N-COUNT A **grand jury** is a jury, usually in the United States, which considers a criminal case in order to decide if someone should be tried in a court of law. ❏ *They have already given evidence before a grand jury in Washington.*

grandly /ɡrændli/ **1** ADV You say that someone speaks or behaves **grandly** when they are trying to impress other people. [DISAPPROVAL] ❏ *He grandly declared that "international politics is a struggle for power."* **2** ADV You use **grandly** in expressions such as 'grandly named' or 'grandly called' to say that the name of a place or thing makes it sound much more impressive than it really is. ❏ *Lucille's home was very grandly called a chateau, though in truth it was nothing more than a large farm.*

grandma /ɡrænmɑ/ (grandmas) N-FAMILY Your **grandma** is your grandmother. [INFORMAL] ❏ *Grandma was from Scotland.*

grandmaster /ɡrændmæstər/ (grandmasters) also **grand master** N-COUNT; N-TITLE In chess, a **grandmaster** is a player who has achieved a very high standard in tournaments.

grandmother /ɡrænmʌðər/ (grandmothers) N-FAMILY Your **grandmother** is the mother of your father or mother. ❏ *My grandmothers are both widows.*

grandpa /ɡrænpɑ/ (grandpas) N-FAMILY Your **grandpa** is your grandfather. [INFORMAL] ❏ *Grandpa was not yet back from the war.*

grandparent /ɡrænpɛərənt, -pær-/ (grandparents) N-FAMILY Your **grandparents** are the parents of your father or mother. ❏ *Tammy was raised by her grandparents.*

grand piano (grand pianos) N-COUNT A **grand piano** is a large piano whose strings are set horizontally to the ground. Grand pianos are used especially for giving concerts and making recordings.

Grand Prix /ɡrɑ̃ pri/ N-COUNT [usu with supp] A **Grand Prix** is one of a series of races for very powerful racing cars; also used sometimes in the names of competitions in other sports. ❏ *He never won the British Grand Prix.*

grand slam (grand slams) **1** ADJ [ADJ n] In some sports, a **grand slam** tournament is a major one. ❏ *...her 39 grand slam titles.* • N-COUNT **grand slam** is also a noun. ❏ *It's my first grand slam and I am hoping to make a good impression.* **2** N-COUNT If someone wins a **grand slam**, they win all the major tournaments in a season in a particular sport, for example in golf or tennis. ❏ *Welsh dreams came true when they won the grand slam.* **3** N-COUNT In baseball, a **grand slam** is a home run that is hit when there are players standing at all of the bases. ❏ *Pujols' grand slam was the third by a Cardinals player this season.*

grand|son /grænsʌn/ (grandsons) N-FAMILY Someone's **grandson** is the son of their son or daughter. ☐ *My grandson's birthday was on Tuesday.*

grand|stand /grændstænd/ (grandstands) N-COUNT A **grandstand** is a covered stand with rows of seats for people to sit on at sporting events.

grand|stand|ing /grændstændɪŋ/ N-UNCOUNT **Grandstanding** means behaving in a way that makes people pay attention to you instead of thinking about more important matters. [mainly AM] ☐ *Opponents of the measure say it's political grandstanding that could prove devastating to the economy.*

grand tour (grand tours) also **Grand Tour** N-COUNT The **grand tour** was a journey around the main cities of Europe that young men from rich families used to make as part of their education.

gran|ite /grænɪt/ (granites) **1** N-MASS **Granite** is a very hard rock used in building. **2** → See also color supplement

gran|ny /græni/ (grannies) also **grannie** N-FAMILY Some people refer to their grandmother as **granny**. [INFORMAL] ☐ *...my old granny.*

gra|no|la /grənoʊlə/ N-UNCOUNT **Granola** is a breakfast cereal usually consisting of oats, wheatgerm, sesame seeds, and dried fruit or nuts. [AM] ☐ *I'll bring you some coffee and a bag of granola for breakfast.*

grant ✦✦◇ /grænt/ (grants, granting, granted) **1** N-COUNT A **grant** is an amount of money that a government or other institution gives to an individual or to an organization for a particular purpose such as education or home improvements. ☐ *They'd got a special grant to encourage research.* **2** V-T If someone in authority **grants** you something, or if something **is granted** to you, you are allowed to have it. [FORMAL] ☐ *France has agreed to grant him political asylum.* ☐ *Some parents tend to grant more independence to their children than other parents do.* **3** V-T If you **grant** that something is true, you accept that it is true, even though your opinion about it does not change. ☐ *The magistrates granted that the charity was justified in bringing the action.* **4** PHRASE If you say that someone **takes** you **for granted**, you are complaining that they benefit from your help, efforts, or presence without showing that they are grateful. ☐ *What right has the family to take me for granted, Martin?* **5** PHRASE If you **take** something **for granted**, you believe that it is true or accept it as normal without thinking about it. ☐ *I was amazed that virtually all the things I took for granted up north just didn't happen here.* **6** PHRASE If you **take it for granted** that something is the case, you believe that it is true or you accept it as normal without thinking about it. ☐ *He seemed to take it for granted that he should speak as a representative.* **7** → See feature box at **university**

COLLOCATIONS

grant
NOUN **1**
verb + **grant**: award, give, make; obtain, receive; apply for
VERB **2**
grant + noun: access, approval, exemption, leave, permission, wish; asylum, citizenship, immunity; bail, injunction, pardon, parole; request

---
SYNONYMS

grant
NOUN **1**
allowance: *She gets an allowance for looking after Lillian.*
award: *...workers' compensation awards.*
donation: *Employees make regular donations to charity.*
handout: *Soldiers oversee the food handouts.*

---

grant|ed /græntɪd/ CONJ You use **granted** or **granted that** at the beginning of a clause to say that something is true, before you make a comment on it. ☐ *Granted that the firm has not broken the law, is the law what it should be?* • ADV [ADV with cl] **Granted** is also an adverb. ☐ *Granted, he doesn't look too bad for his age, but I don't care for him.*

granu|lar /grænyʊlər/ ADJ [usu ADJ n] **Granular** substances are composed of a lot of granules, or feel or look as if they are composed of a lot of granules. ☐ *...a granular fertilizer.*

granu|lat|ed sug|ar /grænyʊleɪtɪd ʃʊgər/ N-UNCOUNT **Granulated sugar** is sugar that is in the form of grains, and is usually white.

gran|ule /grænyul/ (granules) N-COUNT [usu pl, oft supp N] **Granules** are small, round pieces of something. ☐ *She was spooning coffee granules into cups.*

grape /greɪp/ (grapes) **1** N-COUNT **Grapes** are small green or purple fruit which grow in bunches. Grapes can be eaten raw, used for making wine, or dried. ☐ *...a bunch of grapes.* **2** PHRASE If you describe someone's attitude as **sour grapes**, you mean that they say something is worthless or undesirable because they want it themselves but cannot have it. ☐ *These accusations have been going on for some time now, but it is just sour grapes.*

grape|fruit /greɪpfrut/ (grapefruit)

> The plural can also be **grapefruits**.

N-VAR A **grapefruit** is a large, round, yellow fruit, similar to an orange, that has a sharp, slightly bitter taste.

grape|vine /greɪpvaɪn/ N-SING If you hear or learn something on or through **the grapevine**, you hear it or learn it in casual conversation with other people. ☐ *I had heard through the grapevine that he was quite critical of what we were doing.*

graph /græf/ (graphs) N-COUNT A **graph** is a mathematical diagram which shows the relationship between two or more sets of numbers or measurements. ☐ *...a graph showing that breast cancer deaths rose about 20 percent from 1960 to 1985.*

gra|phene /græfin/ N-UNCOUNT **Graphene** is a very thin, strong material which consists of a single layer of carbon atoms, arranged in a pattern of six-sided shapes. ☐ *Graphene is used for energy generation.*

graph|ic /græfɪk/ (graphics) **1** ADJ If you say that a description or account of something unpleasant is **graphic**, you are emphasizing that it is clear and detailed. [EMPHASIS] ☐ *The descriptions of sexual abuse are graphic.* • **graphi|cal|ly** /græfɪkli/ ADV [ADV with v] ☐ *Here, graphically displayed, was confirmation of the entire story.* **2** ADJ [ADJ n] **Graphic** means concerned with drawing or pictures, especially in publishing, industry, or computing. ☐ *...fine and graphic arts.* **3** N-UNCOUNT **Graphics** is the activity of drawing or making pictures, especially in publishing, industry, or computing. ☐ *...a computer manufacturer that specializes in graphics.* **4** N-COUNT **Graphics** are drawings and pictures that are composed using simple lines and sometimes strong colors. ☐ *The Agriculture Department today released a new graphic to replace the old symbol.*

graphi|cal /græfɪkəl/ ADJ [ADJ n] A **graphical** representation of something uses graphs or similar images to represent statistics or figures. ☐ *A graphical representation of results is shown in figure 1.*

graph|ic de|sign N-UNCOUNT **Graphic design** is the art of designing advertisements, magazines, and books by combining pictures and words. ☐ *...the graphic design department.*

graph|ic de|sign|er (graphic designers) N-COUNT A **graphic designer** is a person who designs advertisements, magazines, and books by combining pictures and words.

graph|ite /græfaɪt/ N-UNCOUNT **Graphite** is a soft black substance that is a form of carbon. It is used in pencils and electrical equipment.

graph|ol|ogy /græfɒlədʒi/ N-UNCOUNT **Graphology** is the study of people's handwriting in order to discover what sort of personality they have.

graph pa|per N-UNCOUNT **Graph paper** is paper that has small squares printed on it so that you can use it for drawing graphs.

grap|ple /græpəl/ (grapples, grappling, grappled) **1** V-I If you **grapple** with a problem or difficulty, you try hard to solve it. ☐ *The economy is just one of several critical problems the country is grappling with.* **2** V-RECIP If you **grapple** with someone, you take hold of them and struggle with them, as part of a fight. You can also say that two people **grapple**. ☐ *He was grappling with an alligator in a lagoon.*

grasp /græsp/ (grasps, grasping, grasped) **1** V-T If you **grasp** something, you take it in your hand and hold it very firmly. ☐ *He grasped both my hands.* **2** N-SING A **grasp** is a very firm hold or grip. ☐ *His hand was taken in a warm, firm grasp.* **3** N-SING If you say that something is in someone's **grasp**, you disapprove of the fact that they possess or control it. If something slips from your **grasp**, you lose it or lose control of it. ❏ *The people in your grasp are not guests, they are hostages.* ❏ *She allowed victory to slip from her grasp.* ◨ V-T If you **grasp** something that is complicated or difficult to understand, you understand it. ❏ *The government has not yet grasped the seriousness of the crisis.* ◨ N-SING A **grasp** of something is an understanding of it. ❏ *They have a good grasp of foreign languages.* ◨ PHRASE If you say that something is **within** someone's **grasp**, you mean that it is very likely that they will achieve it. ❏ *Peace is now within our grasp.*

grasp|ing /ɡrǽspɪŋ/ ADJ If you describe someone as **grasping**, you are criticizing them for wanting to get and keep as much money as possible, and for being unwilling to spend it. [DISAPPROVAL] ❏ *...a greedy, grasping, drug-ridden individual.*

grass ◆◇◇ /ɡrǽs/ (**grasses**) ◨ N-MASS **Grass** is a very common plant consisting of large numbers of thin, spiky, green leaves that cover the surface of the ground. ❏ *Small things stirred in the grass around the tent.* ◨ PHRASE If you say **the grass is greener** somewhere else, you mean that other people's situations always seem better or more attractive than your own, but may not really be so. ❏ *He was very happy with us but wanted to see if the grass was greener elsewhere.*

grass|hopper /ɡrǽshɒpər/ (**grasshoppers**) N-COUNT A **grasshopper** is an insect with long back legs that jumps high into the air and makes a high, vibrating sound.

grass|land /ɡrǽslænd/ (**grasslands**) ◨ N-UNCOUNT [also N in pl] **Grassland** is land covered with wild grass. ❏ *...areas of open grassland.* ◨ → See feature box at **ecosystem**

grass|roots /ɡrǽsruːts/ N-PLURAL The **grassroots** of an organization or movement are the ordinary people who form the main part of it, rather than its leaders. ❏ *You have to join the party at grassroots level from what I understand.*

grassy /ɡrǽsi/ (**grassier**, **grassiest**) ADJ A **grassy** area of land is covered in grass. ❏ *The buildings are hidden behind grassy banks.*

grate /ɡreɪt/ (**grates**, **grating**, **grated**) ◨ N-COUNT A **grate** is a framework of metal bars in a fireplace, which holds the wood or coal. ❏ *A wood fire burned in the grate.* ◨ V-T If you **grate** food such as cheese or carrots, you rub it over a metal tool called a grater so that the food is cut into very small pieces. ❏ *Grate the cheese into a mixing bowl.* ◨ V-I When something **grates**, it rubs against something else, making a harsh, unpleasant sound. ❏ *His chair grated as he got to his feet.* ◨ V-I If something such as someone's behavior **grates on** you or **grates**, it makes you feel annoyed. ❏ *His manner always grated on me.*

grate|ful /ɡreɪtfʊl/ ADJ If you are **grateful** for something that someone has given you or done for you, you have warm, friendly feelings toward them and wish to thank them. ❏ *She was grateful to him for being so good to her.* ● **grate|ful|ly** ADV [ADV with v] ❏ *"That's kind of you, Sally," Claire said gratefully.*

grat|er /ɡreɪtər/ (**graters**) ◨ N-COUNT A **grater** is a kitchen tool which has a rough surface that you use for cutting food into very small pieces. ◨ → See feature box at **household**; See also color supplement

grati|fy /ɡrǽtɪfaɪ/ (**gratifies**, **gratifying**, **gratified**) ◨ V-T If you **are gratified** by something, it gives you pleasure or satisfaction. [FORMAL] ❏ *Mr. Dambar was gratified by his response.* ● **grati|fy|ing** ADJ ❏ *We took a chance and we've won. It's very gratifying.* ● **grati|fi|ca|tion** /ɡrǽtɪfɪkeɪʃən/ N-UNCOUNT ❏ *He is waiting for them to recognize him and eventually they do, much to his gratification.* ◨ V-T If you **gratify** your own or another person's desire, you do what is necessary to please yourself or them. [FORMAL] ❏ *We gratified our friend's curiosity.* ● **grati|fi|ca|tion** N-UNCOUNT ❏ *...sexual gratification.*

grat|in /ɡrǽtæn/ (**gratins**) N-VAR A **gratin** is a dish containing vegetables or sometimes meat or fish. It is covered with cheese or cheese sauce and baked in the oven. ❏ *fresh salmon with potato and cheese gratin.*

grat|ing /ɡreɪtɪŋ/ (**gratings**) ◨ N-COUNT A **grating** is a flat, metal frame with rows of bars across it, which is fastened over a window or over a hole in a wall or the ground. ❏ *...an open grating in the sidewalk.* ◨ ADJ [usu ADJ n] A **grating** sound is harsh and unpleasant. ❏ *She recognized the grating voice of Dr. Sarnoff.*

gra|tis /ɡrǽtɪs, ɡrɑː-/ ADV [ADV after v] If something is done or provided **gratis**, it does not have to be paid for. ❏ *David gives the first consultation gratis.* ● ADJ **Gratis** is also an adjective. ❏ *What I did for you was free, gratis, you understand?*

grati|tude /ɡrǽtɪtuːd/ N-UNCOUNT **Gratitude** is the state of feeling grateful. ❏ *I wish to express my gratitude to Kathy Davis for her immense practical help.*

gra|tui|tous /ɡrətuːɪtəs/ ADJ If you describe something as **gratuitous**, you mean that it is unnecessary, and often harmful or upsetting. ❏ *There's too much crime and gratuitous violence on TV.* ● **gra|tui|tous|ly** ADV ❏ *They wanted me to change the title to something less gratuitously offensive.*

gra|tu|ity /ɡrətuːɪti/ (**gratuities**) N-COUNT A **gratuity** is a gift of money to someone who has done something for you. [FORMAL] ❏ *The porter expects a gratuity.*

grave ◆◇◇ (**graves**, **graver**, **gravest**)

Pronounced /ɡreɪv/, except for meaning **4**, when it is pronounced /ɡrɑːv/.

◨ N-COUNT A **grave** is a place where a dead person is buried. ❏ *They used to visit her grave twice a year.* ◨ ADJ A **grave** event or situation is very serious, important, and worrying. ❏ *He said that the situation in his country is very grave.* ● **grave|ly** ADV ❏ *They had gravely impaired the credibility of the government.* ◨ ADJ A **grave** person is quiet and serious in their appearance or behavior. ❏ *Anxiously, she examined his unusually grave face.* ● **grave|ly** ADV ❏ *"I think I've covered that business more than adequately," he said gravely.* ◨ ADJ [ADJ n] In some languages, such as French, a **grave** accent is a symbol that is placed over a vowel in a word to show how the vowel is pronounced. For example, the word 'mère' has a grave accent over the first 'e.' ◨ PHRASE If you say that someone who is dead would **turn** or **turn over in their grave** at something that is happening now, you mean that they would be very shocked or upset by it, if they were alive. ❏ *Darwin must be turning in his grave at the thought of what is being perpetrated in his name.*

SYNONYMS

grave
NOUN ◨
tomb: *The tomb was overgrown with ivy.*
vault: *He ordered that Matilda's body be buried in the family vault.*
sepulcher: *His body is in the sepulcher.*
ADJ ◨
serious: *The government still faces very serious difficulties.*
critical: *Its day-to-day finances are in a critical state.*
severe: *I suffered from severe bouts of depression.*

grave|digger /ɡreɪvdɪɡər/ (**gravediggers**) N-COUNT A **gravedigger** is a person whose job is to dig the graves in which dead people can be buried.

grav|el /ɡrǽvəl/ N-UNCOUNT **Gravel** consists of very small stones. It is often used to make paths. ❏ *...a gravel path leading to the front door.*

grav|eled /ɡrǽvəld/

in BRIT, use **gravelled**

ADJ [ADJ n] A **graveled** path, road, or area has a surface made of gravel.

grav|el|ly /ɡrǽvəli/ (**gravellier**, **gravelliest**) ◨ ADJ [usu ADJ n] A **gravelly** voice is low and rather rough and harsh. ❏ *There's a triumphant note in his gravelly voice.* ◨ ADJ A **gravelly** area of land is covered in or full of small stones. ❏ *Water runs through the gravelly soil very quickly.*

grave|side /ɡreɪvsaɪd/ (**gravesides**) N-COUNT [usu sing, oft at N] You can refer to the area around a grave as the **graveside**, usually when you are talking about the time when someone is buried. ❏ *Both women wept at his graveside.*

grave|stone /ɡreɪvstoʊn/ (**gravestones**) N-COUNT A **gravestone** is a large stone with words carved into it, which is placed on a grave.

grave|yard /ɡreɪvjɑːrd/ (**graveyards**) N-COUNT A **graveyard** is an area of land, sometimes near a church, where dead people are buried. ❏ *They made their way to a graveyard to pay their traditional respects to the dead.*

grave|yard shift (graveyard shifts) N-COUNT [usu the N] If someone works the **graveyard shift**, they work during the night. [mainly AM]

gravi|tas /ɡrævɪtæs/ N-UNCOUNT If you say that someone has **gravitas**, you mean that you respect them because they seem serious and intelligent. [FORMAL] ❑ *He is pale, dark, and authoritative, with the gravitas you might expect of a Nobel prize winner.*

gravi|tate /ɡrævɪteɪt/ (gravitates, gravitating, gravitated) V-I If you **gravitate** toward a particular place, thing, person, or activity, you are attracted by it and go to it or get involved in it. ❑ *You naturally gravitate toward people with shared values.*

gravi|ta|tion /ɡrævɪteɪʃən/ N-UNCOUNT In physics, **gravitation** is the force which causes objects to be attracted toward each other because they have mass. [TECHNICAL]

gravi|ta|tion|al /ɡrævɪteɪʃənəl/ ADJ [ADJ n] **Gravitational** means relating to or resulting from the force of gravity. [TECHNICAL] ❑ *If a spacecraft travels faster than 11 km a second, it escapes the Earth's gravitational pull.*

grav|ity /ɡrævɪti/ **1** N-UNCOUNT **Gravity** is the force that causes things to drop to the ground. ❑ *Arrows would continue to fly forward forever in a straight line were it not for gravity, which brings them down to earth.* **2** N-UNCOUNT The **gravity** of a situation or event is its extreme importance or seriousness. ❑ *The president said those who grab power through violence deserve punishment which matches the gravity of their crime.* **3** N-UNCOUNT The **gravity** of someone's behavior or speech is the extremely serious way in which they behave or speak. ❑ *There was an appealing gravity to everything she said.*

gra|vy /ɡreɪvi/ (gravies) N-MASS **Gravy** is a sauce made from the juices that come from meat when it cooks.

gra|vy boat (gravy boats) N-COUNT A **gravy boat** is a long, narrow jug that is used to serve gravy.

gra|vy train (gravy trains) N-COUNT [oft on the N] If an organization or person earns a lot of money without doing much work, you can say that they are on the **gravy train**. [JOURNALISM, DISAPPROVAL] ❑ *The business community wants, of course, to stay on the gravy train.*

gray ✦✦◇ /ɡreɪ/ (grayer, grayest)

in BRIT, use **grey**

1 COLOR **Gray** is the color of ashes or of clouds on a rainy day. ❑ *...a gray suit.* **2** ADJ If the weather is **gray**, there are many clouds in the sky and the light is dull. ❑ *It was a gray, wet, April Sunday.* **3** ADJ If you describe a situation as **gray**, you mean that it is dull, unpleasant, or difficult. ❑ *Brazilians look gloomily forward to a New Year that even the president admits will be gray and cheerless.* **4** ADJ If you describe someone or something as **gray**, you think that they are boring and unattractive, and very similar to other things or other people. [DISAPPROVAL] ❑ *Miles is one of those little gray men you find in every company.* **5** → See feature box at **appearance**

gray area (gray areas) N-COUNT If you refer to something as a **gray area**, you mean that it is unclear, for example because nobody is sure how to deal with it or who is responsible for it, or it falls between two separate categories of things. ❑ *At the moment, the law on compensation is very much a gray area.*

gray|ing /ɡreɪɪŋ/ ADJ [usu ADJ n] If someone has **graying** hair, there is a lot of gray hair mixed with the person's natural color. ❑ *...a small, wiry man with graying hair.*

gray|ish /ɡreɪɪʃ/ ADJ **Grayish** means slightly gray in color. ❑ *The building was of grayish plaster and looked old.* • COMB IN COLOR **Grayish** is also a combining form. ❑ *...grayish green leaves.*

gray mar|ket **1** N-SING **Gray market** goods are bought unofficially and then sold to customers at lower prices than usual. [BUSINESS] ❑ *Gray market perfumes and toiletries are now commonly sold by mail.* **2** N-SING **Gray market** shares are sold to investors before they have been officially issued. [BUSINESS] ❑ *An unofficial gray market in the shares has been operating for about two weeks.*

gray mat|ter N-UNCOUNT You can refer to your intelligence or your brains as **gray matter**. [INFORMAL] ❑ *...an unsolved equation which has caused his gray matter to work overtime.*

graze /ɡreɪz/ (grazes, grazing, grazed) **1** V-T/V-I When animals **graze** or **are grazed**, they eat the grass or other plants that are growing in a particular place. You can also say that a field **is grazed** by animals. ❑ *Five cows graze serenely around a massive oak.* ❑ *Several horses grazed the meadowland.* **2** V-T If you **graze** a part of your body, you injure your skin by scraping against something. ❑ *I had grazed my knees a little.* **3** N-COUNT A **graze** is a small wound caused by scraping against something. ❑ *Although cuts and grazes are not usually very serious, they can be quite painful.* **4** V-T If something **grazes** another thing, it touches that thing lightly as it passes by. ❑ *A bullet had grazed his arm.*

graz|ing /ɡreɪzɪŋ/ N-UNCOUNT **Grazing** or **grazing land** is land on which animals graze. ❑ *He had nearly a thousand acres of grazing and arable land.*

GRE /dʒi ɑr i/ N-PROPER The **GRE** is the examination which you have to take to be admitted to graduate schools. **GRE** is an abbreviation for 'Graduate Record Examination.'

grease /ɡris/ (greases, greasing, greased) **1** N-UNCOUNT **Grease** is a thick, oily substance which is put on the moving parts of cars and other machines in order to make them work smoothly. ❑ *...grease-stained hands.* **2** V-T If you **grease** a part of a car, machine, or device, you put grease on it in order to make it work smoothly. ❑ *I greased front and rear hubs and adjusted the brakes.* **3** N-UNCOUNT **Grease** is an oily substance that is produced by your skin. ❑ *His hair is thick with grease.* **4** N-UNCOUNT **Grease** is animal fat that is produced by cooking meat. You can use **grease** for cooking. ❑ *He could smell the bacon grease.* **5** V-T If you **grease** a dish, you put a small amount of fat or oil around the inside of it in order to prevent food from sticking to it during cooking. ❑ *Grease two sturdy baking sheets and heat the oven to 400 degrees.*

grease|paint /ɡrispeɪnt/ N-UNCOUNT **Greasepaint** is an oily substance used by actors as makeup.

grease|proof pa|per /ɡrispruf peɪpər/ N-UNCOUNT **Greaseproof paper** is a special kind of paper which does not allow fat or oil to pass through it. It is mainly used in cooking or to wrap food. [BRIT]

in AM, use **wax paper**

greasy /ɡrisi, -zi/ (greasier, greasiest) ADJ Something that is **greasy** has grease on it or in it. ❑ *He propped his elbows upon a greasy counter.*

greasy spoon (greasy spoons) N-COUNT A **greasy spoon** is a small, cheap, unattractive café that serves mostly fried food. [INFORMAL]

great ✦✦✦ /ɡreɪt/ (greater, greatest, greats) **1** ADJ [ADJ n] You use **great** to describe something that is very large. **Great** is more formal than **big**. ❑ *The room had a great bay window.* **2** ADJ **Great** means large in amount or degree. ❑ *Benjamin Britten did not live to a great age.* **3** ADJ You use **great** to describe something that is important, famous, or exciting. ❑ *...the great cultural achievements of the past.* • **great|ness** N-UNCOUNT ❑ *A nation must take certain risks to achieve greatness.* **4** ADJ You can describe someone who is successful and famous for their actions, knowledge, or skill as **great**. ❑ *He has the potential to be a great player.* • **great|ness** N-UNCOUNT ❑ *Abraham Lincoln achieved greatness.* **5** N-PLURAL The **greats** in a particular subject or field of activity are the people who have been most successful or famous in it. [JOURNALISM] ❑ *...all the greats of Hollywood.* **6** ADJ If you describe someone or something as **great**, you approve of them or admire them. [INFORMAL, APPROVAL] ❑ *Arturo has this great place in Cozumel.* ❑ *They're a great bunch of guys.* **7** ADJ [feel ADJ] If you **feel great**, you feel very healthy, energetic, and enthusiastic. ❑ *I feel just great.* **8** ADJ You use **great** in order to emphasize the size or degree of a characteristic or quality. [EMPHASIS] ❑ *...a great big Italian wedding.* **9** EXCLAM You say **great** in order to emphasize that you are pleased or enthusiastic about something. [FEELINGS] ❑ *Oh great! That'll be good for Fred.*

PREFIX

great-
is used before some nouns that refer to relatives. Nouns formed in this way refer to a relative who is a further generation away from you. *For example, your **great-aunt** is the aunt of one of your parents.*

Great Brit|ain /ɡreɪt brɪtᵊn/ N-PROPER **Great Britain** is the island consisting of England, Scotland, and Wales, which together with Northern Ireland makes up the United Kingdom.

great|coat /ɡreɪtkoʊt/ (**greatcoats**) also **great coat** N-COUNT A **greatcoat** is a long, thick coat that is worn especially as part of a uniform. ❑ ...*an army greatcoat.*

great|er /ɡreɪtər/ ◼ ADJ **Greater** is the comparative of **great**. ◼ ADJ [ADJ n] **Greater** is used with the name of a large city to refer to the city together with the surrounding urban and suburban area. ❑ ...*Greater Los Angeles.* ◼ ADJ [ADJ n] **Greater** is used with the name of a country to refer to a larger area which includes that country and other land which used to belong to it, or which some people believe should belong to it. ❑ ...*Greater Syria.*

great|ly /ɡreɪtli/ ADV You use **greatly** to emphasize the degree or extent of something. [FORMAL, EMPHASIS] ❑ *People would benefit greatly from a pollution-free vehicle.*

grebe /ɡriːb/ (**grebes**) N-COUNT A **grebe** is a type of water bird.

Gre|cian /ɡriːʃᵊn/ ADJ [usu ADJ n] **Grecian** is used to describe something which is in the style of things from ancient Greece. ❑ ...*elegant Grecian columns.*

greed /ɡriːd/ N-UNCOUNT **Greed** is the desire to have more of something, such as food or money, than is necessary or fair. ❑ ...*an insatiable greed for personal power.*

greedy /ɡriːdi/ (**greedier, greediest**) ADJ If you describe someone as **greedy**, you mean that they want to have more of something such as food or money than is necessary or fair. ❑ *He attacked greedy bosses for awarding themselves big raises.* ● **greedi|ly** ADV [ADV with v] ❑ *Laurie ate the pastries greedily and with huge enjoyment.*

Greek /ɡriːk/ (**Greeks**) ◼ ADJ **Greek** means belonging or relating to Greece. ◼ N-COUNT A **Greek** is a person who comes from Greece. ◼ N-UNCOUNT **Greek** is the language used in Greece. ❑ *I had to learn Greek.* ◼ N-UNCOUNT **Greek** or **Ancient Greek** was the language used in Greece in ancient times.

green ♦♦♦ /ɡriːn/ (**greener, greenest, greens**) ◼ COLOR **Green** is the color of grass or leaves. ❑ *Yellow and green together make a pale green.* ◼ ADJ A place that is **green** is covered with grass, plants, and trees and not with houses or factories. ❑ *Every street ends at a park or bit of green space.* ● **green|ness** N-UNCOUNT ❑ ...*the lush greenness of the river valleys.* ◼ ADJ [ADJ n] **Green** issues and political movements relate to or are concerned with the protection of the environment. ❑ *The power of the Green movement in Germany has made that country a leader in the drive to recycle more waste materials.* ◼ ADJ If you say that someone or something is **green**, you mean that they harm the environment as little as possible. ❑ ...*trying to persuade governments to adopt greener policies.* ● **green|ness** N-UNCOUNT ❑ *If you'd like to recognize the greenness of an individual or organization, why not nominate them for an Environmental Achievement Award.* ◼ N-COUNT **Greens** are members of green political movements. ❑ *The Greens see themselves as a radical alternative to the two major political parties.* ◼ N-COUNT A **green** is a smooth, flat area of grass around a hole on a golf course. ❑ ...*the 18th green.* ◼ N-COUNT A **green** is an area of land covered with grass, especially in a town or in the middle of a village. ❑ ...*the village green.* ◼ ADJ If you say that someone is **green**, you mean that they have had very little experience of life or a particular job. ❑ *He was a young fellow, very green, very immature.* ◼ PHRASE If someone has **a green thumb**, they are very good at gardening and their plants grow well. [AM] ❑ *She has an unbelievably green thumb, she can grow anything.*

□ in BRIT, use **green fingers**

◼ **to give someone the green light** → see **light** ① ◼ → See feature box at **ecosystem**

green|back /ɡriːnbæk/ (**greenbacks**) N-COUNT A **greenback** is a United States banknote such as a dollar bill. [AM, INFORMAL]

green bean (**green beans**) N-COUNT [usu pl] **Green beans** are long, narrow beans that are eaten as a vegetable.

green belt (**green belts**) also **greenbelt** ◼ N-VAR A **green belt** is an area of land with fields or parks around a town or city, where people are not allowed to build houses or factories by law. ❑ *The room features a 20 feet wall of glass that overlooks a greenbelt.* ◼ → See feature box at **town**

Green Be|ret (**Green Berets**) N-COUNT A **Green Beret** is an American or British **commando**. [INFORMAL]

green card (**green cards**) N-COUNT A **green card** is a document showing that someone who is not a citizen of the United States has permission to live and work there. ❑ *Nicollette married Harry so she could get a green card.*

green en|er|gy N-UNCOUNT **Green energy** is power that comes from sources that do not harm the environment and are always available, such as wind and sunlight.

green|ery /ɡriːnəri/ N-UNCOUNT Plants that make a place look attractive are referred to as **greenery**. ❑ *Adriana misses the trees and greenery of her native mountains.*

green|gage /ɡriːnɡeɪdʒ/ (**greengages**) N-COUNT A **greengage** is a greenish yellow plum with a sweet taste.

green|grocer /ɡriːnɡroʊsər/ (**greengrocers**) ◼ N-COUNT A **greengrocer** is a storekeeper who sells fruit and vegetables. [mainly BRIT] ◼ N-COUNT A **greengrocer** or a **greengrocer's** is a store where fruit and vegetables are sold. [mainly BRIT]

green|house /ɡriːnhaʊs/ (**greenhouses**) ◼ N-COUNT A **greenhouse** is a glass building in which you grow plants that need to be protected from bad weather. ◼ ADJ [ADJ n] **Greenhouse** means relating to or causing the greenhouse effect. ❑ ...*controls on greenhouse emissions.*

green|house ef|fect ◼ N-SING The **greenhouse effect** is the problem caused by increased quantities of gases such as carbon dioxide in the air. These gases trap the heat from the sun, and cause a gradual rise in the temperature of the Earth's atmosphere. ❑ ...*gases that contribute to the greenhouse effect.* ◼ → See also color supplement

green|house gas (**greenhouse gases**) N-VAR **Greenhouse gases** are the gases which are responsible for causing the greenhouse effect. The main greenhouse gas is carbon dioxide.

green|ing /ɡriːnɪŋ/ N-SING [also no det, oft N of n] The **greening** of a person or organization means that the person or organization is becoming more aware of environmental issues. [JOURNALISM] ❑ *They can take the credit for the greening of local politics.*

green|ish /ɡriːnɪʃ/ COLOR Something that is **greenish** is slightly green in color. ❑ ...*his cold greenish eyes.* ● COMB IN COLOR **Greenish** is also a combining form. ❑ ...*greenish yellow flowers.*

green|mail /ɡriːnmeɪl/ N-UNCOUNT **Greenmail** is when a company buys enough shares in another company to threaten a takeover and makes a profit if the other company buys back its shares at a higher price. [mainly AM, BUSINESS] ❑ *Family control would prevent any hostile takeover or greenmail attempt.*

green on|ion (**green onions**) N-COUNT **Green onions** are small onions with long green leaves. [mainly AM]

□ in BRIT, usually use **spring onion**

Green Par|ty N-PROPER The **Green Party** is a political party that is particularly concerned about protecting the environment.

green pep|per (**green peppers**) N-COUNT A **green pepper** is an unripe pepper that is used in cooking or eaten raw in salads.

green revo|lu|tion also **Green Revolution** N-SING The **green revolution** is the increase in agricultural production that has been made possible by the use of new types of crops and new farming methods, especially in developing countries.

green|room /ɡriːnrʊm/ (**greenrooms**) also **green room** N-COUNT A **greenroom** is a room in a theater or television studio where performers can rest.

green sal|ad (**green salads**) N-VAR A **green salad** is a salad made mainly with lettuce and other green vegetables.

green screen (**green screens**) N-COUNT A **green screen** is a blank green background that can be used to create special effects in a movie, by adding in images created by a computer. ❑ *The scene was first shot with actors on a green screen then the backdrop was created.*

green tea (green teas) N-MASS **Green tea** is tea made from tea leaves that have been steamed and dried quickly. ◻ ...*a cup of green tea.* ◻ *Many Japanese and Chinese teas are green teas.*

green wall (green walls) N-COUNT A **green wall** is a wall with plants growing in a layer of soil on its surface.

Green|wich Mean Time /grɛnɪtʃ miːn taɪm/ → see GMT

greeny /griːni/ ADJ **Greeny** means slightly green in color. ◻ ...*greeny sea water.* • COMB IN COLOR **Greeny** is also a combining form. ◻ ...*a lightweight, greeny gray wool suit.*

greet /griːt/ (greets, greeting, greeted) **1** V-T When you **greet** someone, you say 'Hello' or shake hands with them. ◻ *She liked to be home to greet Steve when he came in from school.* **2** V-T [usu passive] If something **is greeted** in a particular way, people react to it in that way. ◻ *His research was greeted with skepticism by advocates for children, who thought it was based on faulty data.*

greet|ing /griːtɪŋ/ (greetings) N-VAR A **greeting** is something friendly that you say or do when you meet someone. ◻ *His greeting was familiar and friendly.* ◻ *They exchanged greetings.*

greet|ing card (greeting cards)

in BRIT, use **greetings card**

N-COUNT A **greeting card** is a folded card with a picture on the front and greetings inside that you give or send to someone, for example on their birthday.

gre|gari|ous /grɪgɛəriəs/ **1** ADJ Someone who is **gregarious** enjoys being with other people. ◻ *She is such a gregarious and outgoing person.* **2** ADJ **Gregarious** animals or birds normally live in large groups. ◻ *Snow geese are very gregarious birds.*

grem|lin /grɛmlɪn/ (gremlins) N-COUNT A **gremlin** is a tiny imaginary evil spirit that people say is the cause of a problem, especially in a machine, which they cannot explain properly or locate. ◻ *The microphones went dead as if the technical gremlins had struck again.*

gre|nade /grɪneɪd/ (grenades) N-COUNT A **grenade** or a **hand grenade** is a small bomb that can be thrown by hand. ◻ *A hand grenade was thrown at an army patrol.*

grew /gruː/ **Grew** is the past tense of **grow**.

grey /greɪ/ [BRIT] → see **gray**

grey area [BRIT] → see **gray area**

grey|hound /greɪhaʊnd/ (greyhounds) **1** N-COUNT A **greyhound** is a dog with a thin body and long thin legs, which can run very fast. Greyhounds sometimes run in races and people bet on them. ◻ ...*his love of greyhound racing.* **2** N-COUNT In the United States, a **Greyhound** or a **Greyhound bus** is a bus that travels between towns or cities rather than within a particular town or city. [AM, TRADEMARK] ◻ *I didn't fly. I took the Greyhound.*

grey|ing /greɪɪŋ/ [BRIT] → see **graying**

grey|ish /greɪɪʃ/ [BRIT] → see **grayish**

grey mar|ket [BRIT] → see **gray market**

grey mat|ter [BRIT] → see **gray matter**

grid /grɪd/ (grids) **1** N-COUNT A **grid** is something which is in a pattern of straight lines that cross over each other, forming squares. On maps, the grid is used to help you find a particular thing or place. ◻ ...*a grid of ironwork.* ◻ ...*a grid of narrow streets.* **2** N-COUNT A **grid** is a network of wires and cables by which sources of power, such as electricity, are distributed throughout a country or area. ◻ ...*breakdowns in communications and electric-power grids.* **3** N-COUNT The **grid** or the **starting grid** is the starting line on a car-racing track. ◻ *The Ferrari driver was starting second on the grid.*

grid|dle /grɪdᵊl/ (griddles) N-COUNT A **griddle** is a round, flat, heavy piece of metal which is placed on a stove or over a fire and used for cooking.

grid|iron /grɪdaɪərn/ **1** N-SING Football is sometimes referred to as **gridiron**. [AM] ◻ ...*the greatest quarterback in gridiron history.* **2** N-UNCOUNT The field of play in football is sometimes referred to as the **gridiron**. [AM] ◻ *Joe Gibbs has returned to the Washington Redskins after 11 years away from the gridiron.*

grid|lock /grɪdlɒk/ **1** N-UNCOUNT **Gridlock** is the situation that exists when all the roads in a particular place are so full of vehicles that none of them can move. ◻ *The streets are wedged solid with the chaos of poorly regulated parking and near-constant traffic gridlock.* **2** N-UNCOUNT You can use **gridlock** to refer to a situation in an argument or dispute when neither side is prepared to give in, so no agreement can be reached. ◻ *He agreed that these policies would lead to gridlock in the future.*

grief /griːf/ (griefs) **1** N-VAR **Grief** is a feeling of extreme sadness. ◻ ...*a huge outpouring of national grief for the victims of the shootings.* **2** PHRASE If something **comes to grief**, it fails. If someone **comes to grief**, they fail in something they are doing, and may be hurt. ◻ *So many marriages have come to grief over lack of money.* **3** EXCLAM Some people say '**Good grief**' when they are surprised or shocked. [FEELINGS] ◻ *"He's been arrested for theft and burglary."—"Good grief!"*

grief-stricken ADJ If someone is **grief-stricken**, they are extremely sad about something that has happened. [FORMAL] ◻ ...*the grief-stricken family.* ◻ *The queen was grief-stricken over his death.*

griev|ance /griːvəns/ (grievances) N-VAR If you have a **grievance** about something that has happened or been done, you believe that it was unfair. ◻ *They had a legitimate grievance.* ◻ *The main grievance of the drivers is the imposition of higher fees for driver's licenses.*

grieve /griːv/ (grieves, grieving, grieved) V-I If you **grieve** over something, especially someone's death, you feel very sad about it. ◻ *He's grieving over his dead wife and son.* ◻ *I didn't have any time to grieve.*

griev|ous /griːvəs/ **1** ADJ If you describe something such as a loss as **grievous**, you mean that it is extremely serious or worrying in its effects. ◻ *Mr. Morris said the victims had suffered from a very grievous mistake.* • **griev|ous|ly** ADV [ADV with v] ◻ *Birds, sea life and the coastline all suffered grievously.* **2** ADJ A **grievous** injury to your body is one that causes you great pain and suffering. ◻ *He survived in spite of suffering grievous injuries.* • **griev|ous|ly** ADV ◻ *A first aider was trying to comfort the grievously injured women.*

grif|fin /grɪfɪn/ (griffins) also **griffon** N-COUNT In mythology, a **griffin** is a winged creature with the body of a lion and the head of an eagle.

grill /grɪl/ (grills, grilling, grilled) **1** N-COUNT A **grill** is a flat frame of metal bars on which food can be cooked over a fire. ◻ *Jerry forced scrap wood through the vents in the grill to stoke the fire.* **2** N-COUNT A **grill** is a part of a stove which produces strong direct heat to cook food that has been placed underneath it. [BRIT]

in AM, use **broiler**

3 V-T/V-I When you **grill** food, or when it **grills**, you cook it on metal bars above a fire or barbecue. ◻ *Grill the steaks over a wood or charcoal fire that is quite hot.* **4** V-T/V-I When you **grill** food, or when it **grills**, you cook it in a stove using very strong heat directly above it. [BRIT] ◻ *Grill the meat for 20 minutes on each side.* ◻ *Apart from peppers and eggplant, many other vegetables grill well.*

in AM, use **broil**

• **grill|ing** N-UNCOUNT ◻ *The breast can be cut into portions for grilling.* **5** V-T If you **grill** someone about something, you ask them a lot of questions for a long period of time. [INFORMAL] ◻ *Grill your travel agent about the facilities for families with children.* • **grill|ing** (grillings) N-COUNT ◻ *He faced a hostile grilling from the committee's Republicans.* **6** N-COUNT A **grill** is a restaurant that serves grilled food. ◻ ...*patrons of the Savoy Grill.*

grille /grɪl/ (grilles) also **grill** N-COUNT A **grille** is a framework of metal bars or wire which is placed in front of a window or a piece of machinery, in order to protect it or to protect people. ◻ *The single window was protected by a rusted iron grille.*

grim /grɪm/ (grimmer, grimmest) **1** ADJ A situation or piece of information that is **grim** is unpleasant, depressing, and difficult to accept. ◻ *They painted a grim picture of growing crime.* ◻ *There was further grim economic news yesterday.* **2** ADJ A place that is **grim** is unattractive and depressing in appearance. ◻ *The city might be grim at first, but there is a vibrancy and excitement.*

gri|mace /grɪməs, grɪmeɪs/ (grimaces, grimacing, grimaced) V-I If you **grimace**, you twist your face in an ugly way because you are annoyed, disgusted, or in pain. [WRITTEN] ◻ *She started to sit up, grimaced, and sank back weakly against the pillow.* • N-COUNT

Grimace is also a noun. ❑ *He took another drink of his coffee. "Awful," he said with a grimace.*

grime /graɪm/ N-UNCOUNT **Grime** is dirt that has collected on the surface of something. ❑ *Kelly got the grime off his hands before rejoining her in the kitchen.*

Grim Reap|er N-SING [the N] **The Grim Reaper** is an imaginary character who represents death. He looks like a skeleton, wears a long, black cloak with a hood, and carries a scythe.

grimy /ˈgraɪmi/ (**grimier**, **grimiest**) ADJ Something that is **grimy** is very dirty. ❑ *...a grimy industrial city.*

grin /grɪn/ (**grins**, **grinning**, **grinned**) **1** V-I When you **grin**, you smile broadly. ❑ *He grins, delighted at the memory.* ❑ *Sarah tried several times to catch Philip's eye, but he just grinned at her.* **2** N-COUNT A **grin** is a broad smile. ❑ *...a big grin on her face.* **3** PHRASE If you **grin and bear it**, you accept a difficult or unpleasant situation without complaining because you know there is nothing you can do to make things better. ❑ *They cannot stand the sight of each other, but they will just have to grin and bear it.*

grind /graɪnd/ (**grinds**, **grinding**, **ground**) **1** V-T If you **grind** a substance such as corn, you crush it between two hard surfaces or with a machine until it becomes a fine powder. ❑ *Store the peppercorns in an airtight container and grind the pepper as you need it.* • PHRASAL VERB **Grind up** means the same as **grind**. ❑ *He makes his own paint, grinding up the pigment with a little oil.* **2** V-T If you **grind** something into a surface, you press and rub it hard into the surface using small circular or sideways movements. ❑ *"Well," I said, grinding my cigarette nervously into the granite step.* • PHRASE If you **grind** your **teeth**, you rub your upper and lower teeth together as though you are chewing something. **3** V-T If you **grind** something, you make it smooth or sharp by rubbing it against a hard surface. ❑ *It was beyond my ability to grind a blade this broad.* **4** V-I If a vehicle **grinds** somewhere, it moves there very slowly and noisily. ❑ *Tanks had crossed the border at five fifteen and were grinding south.* **5** N-SING The **grind** of a machine is the harsh, scraping noise that it makes, usually because it is old or is working too hard. ❑ *The grind of heavy machines could get on their nerves.* **6** N-SING If you refer to routine tasks or activities as the **grind**, you mean they are boring and take up a lot of time and effort. [INFORMAL, DISAPPROVAL] ❑ *Life continues to be a terrible grind for the ordinary person.* **7** PHRASE If a country's economy or something such as a process **grinds to a halt**, it gradually becomes slower or less active until it stops. ❑ *Higher unemployment figures might suggest that the economy has ground to a halt.* **8** PHRASE If a vehicle **grinds to a halt**, it stops slowly and noisily. ❑ *The tanks ground to a halt after a hundred yards because the fuel had been siphoned out.*
▶ **grind down** PHRASAL VERB If you say that someone **grinds** you **down**, you mean that they treat you very harshly and cruelly, reducing your confidence or your will to resist them. ❑ *"You see," said Hughes, "there's people who want to humiliate you and grind you down."*
▶ **grind up** → see grind 1

grind|er /ˈgraɪndər/ (**grinders**) **1** N-COUNT In a kitchen, a **grinder** is a device for crushing food such as coffee or meat into small pieces or into a powder. ❑ *...an electric coffee grinder.* **2** N-COUNT A **grinder** is a machine or tool for sharpening, smoothing, or polishing the surface of something. ❑ *The grinder is used for making precision tooling.*

grind|ing /ˈgraɪndɪŋ/ **1** ADJ [ADJ n] If you describe a bad situation as **grinding**, you mean it never gets better, changes, or ends. ❑ *Their grandfather had left his village in order to escape the grinding poverty.* • **grind|ing|ly** ADV [ADV adj] ❑ *Nursing was ill-paid and grindingly hard work.* **2** PHRASE [PHR after v] If you say that something comes to a **grinding halt**, you are emphasizing that it stops very suddenly, especially before it was meant to. [EMPHASIS] ❑ *A car will come to a grinding halt if you put water in the gas tank.* **3** → see also grind

grind|stone /ˈgraɪndstoʊn/ (**grindstones**) N-COUNT A **grindstone** is a large, round stone that turns like a wheel and is used for sharpening knives and tools.

grin|go /ˈgrɪŋgoʊ/ (**gringos**) N-COUNT **Gringo** is sometimes used by people from Latin America to refer to people from other countries, especially the United States and Britain. [OFFENSIVE]

grip ♦◇◇ /grɪp/ (**grips**, **gripping**, **gripped**) **1** V-T If you **grip** something, you take hold of it with your hand and continue to hold it firmly. ❑ *She gripped the rope.* **2** N-COUNT A **grip** is a firm, strong hold on something. ❑ *His strong hand eased the bag from her grip.* **3** N-SING Someone's **grip** on something is the power and control they have over it. ❑ *The president maintains an iron grip on his country.* **4** V-T If something **grips** you, it affects you very strongly. ❑ *The entire community has been gripped by fear.* **5** V-T [usu passive] If you **are gripped** by something such as a story or a series of events, your attention is concentrated on it and held by it. ❑ *The nation is gripped by the dramatic story.* • **grip|ping** ADJ ❑ *The film turned out to be a gripping thriller.* **6** N-UNCOUNT If things such as shoes or car tires have **grip**, they do not slip. ❑ *...a new way of reinforcing rubber which gives car tires a better grip.* **7** PHRASE If you **come to grips with** a problem, you consider it seriously, and start taking action to deal with it. ❑ *The administration's first task is to come to grips with the economy.* **8** PHRASE If you **get a grip** on yourself, you make an effort to control or improve your behavior or work. ❑ *Part of me was very frightened and I consciously had to get a grip on myself.* **9** PHRASE If a person, group, or place is **in the grip of** something, they are being severely affected by it. **10** PHRASE If you **lose** your **grip**, you become less efficient, less confident, and less able to deal with things. ❑ *He wondered if perhaps he was getting old and losing his grip.* **11** PHRASE If you say that someone has a **grip on reality**, you mean they recognize the true situation and do not have mistaken ideas about it. ❑ *Shakur loses his fragile grip on reality and starts blasting away at friends and foes alike.* **12** → See feature box at **book**

COLLOCATIONS

grip
NOUN
2
adjective + **grip**: firm, strong, tight; loose
3
adjective + **grip**: firm, iron, tight, vice-like; tenuous
verb + **grip**: keep, maintain; lose
VERB
1
grip + adverb: firmly, tightly
4
noun + **grip**: fear, fever, mania, panic; crisis

---

gripe /graɪp/ (**gripes**, **griping**, **griped**) **1** V-I If you say that someone **is griping**, you mean they are annoying you because they keep on complaining about something. [INFORMAL, DISAPPROVAL] ❑ *Why are football players griping when the average salary is half a million dollars?* • **grip|ing** N-UNCOUNT ❑ *Still, the griping went on.* **2** N-COUNT A **gripe** is a complaint about something. [INFORMAL] ❑ *My only gripe is that one main course and one dessert were unavailable.*

grip|ing /ˈgraɪpɪŋ/ ADJ [ADJ n] A **griping** pain is a sudden, sharp pain in your stomach or bowels.

gris|ly /ˈgrɪzli/ (**grislier**, **grisliest**) ADJ Something that is **grisly** is extremely unpleasant, and usually involves death and violence. ❑ *He was insane when he carried out the grisly murders.*

grist /grɪst/ PHRASE If you say that something is **grist for the mill**, you mean that it is useful for a particular purpose or helps support someone's point of view. ❑ *The press desperately needs new information, and everything we do is grist for the mill.*

gris|tle /ˈgrɪsəl/ N-UNCOUNT **Gristle** is a tough, rubbery substance found in meat, especially in meat of poor quality, which is unpleasant to eat.

grit /grɪt/ (**grits**, **gritting**, **gritted**) **1** N-UNCOUNT **Grit** is very small pieces of stone. ❑ *He felt tiny pieces of grit and sand peppering his knees.* **2** N-UNCOUNT If someone has **grit**, they have the determination and courage to continue doing something even though it is very difficult. ❑ *If they gave gold medals for grit, Karen would be right up there on the winners' podium.* **3** N-PLURAL **Grits** are coarsely ground grains of corn which are cooked and eaten for breakfast or as part of a meal in the southern United States. [AM] ❑ *I want grits with my eggs instead of hash browns.* **4** V-T If you **grit** your **teeth**, you press your upper and lower teeth tightly together, usually because you are angry about something. ❑ *Gritting my teeth, I did my best to stifle one or two remarks.* **5** PHRASE If you **grit** your **teeth**, you make up your

gritty /ɡrɪti/ (grittier, grittiest) **1** ADJ Something that is **gritty** contains grit, is covered with grit, or has a texture like that of grit. ◻ *The sheets fell on the gritty floor, and she just let them lie.* **2** ADJ Someone who is **gritty** is brave and determined. ◻ *We have to prove how gritty we are.* **3** ADJ A **gritty** description of a tough or unpleasant situation shows it in a very realistic way. ◻ *...gritty social comment.*

grizzled /ɡrɪzəld/ ADJ [usu ADJ n] A **grizzled** person or a person with **grizzled** hair has hair that is gray or partly gray.

grizzly /ɡrɪzli/ (grizzlies) **1** N-COUNT A **grizzly** or a **grizzly bear** is a large, fierce, grayish brown bear. ◻ *...two grizzly bear cubs.* **2** → see also **grisly**

groan /ɡroʊn/ (groans, groaning, groaned) **1** V-I If you **groan**, you make a long, low sound because you are in pain, or because you are upset or unhappy about something. ◻ *Slowly, he opened his eyes. As he did so, he began to groan with pain.* ◻ *They glanced at the man on the floor, who began to groan.* • N-COUNT **Groan** is also a noun. ◻ *She heard him let out a pitiful, muffled groan.* **2** V-T If you **groan** something, you say it in a low, unhappy voice. ◻ *"My leg – I think it's broken," Eric groaned.* **3** V-I If you **groan** about something, you complain about it. ◻ *His parents were beginning to groan about the price of college tuition.* • N-COUNT **Groan** is also a noun. ◻ *Listen sympathetically to your child's moans and groans about what she can't do.* **4** V-I If wood or something made of wood **groans**, it makes a loud sound when it moves. ◻ *The timbers groan and creak and the floorboards shift.* **5** V-I If you say that something such as a table **groans** under the weight of food, you are emphasizing that there is a lot of food on it. [EMPHASIS] ◻ *The bar counter groans under the weight of huge plates of the freshest fish.* **6** V-I [usu cont] If you say that someone or something **is groaning under** the weight of something, you think there is too much of that thing. [DISAPPROVAL] ◻ *Consumers were groaning under the weight of high interest rates.*

grocer /ɡroʊsər/ (grocers) **1** N-COUNT A **grocer** is a storekeeper who sells foods such as flour, sugar, and canned foods. **2** N-COUNT A **grocer** or a **grocer's** is the same as a **grocery**. [mainly BRIT]

grocery /ɡroʊsəri, ɡroʊsri/ (groceries) **1** N-COUNT A **grocery** or a **grocery store** is a small store that sells foods such as flour, sugar, and canned goods. [mainly AM] ◻ *They run a small grocery store.* **2** → see also **supermarket 3** N-PLURAL **Groceries** are foods you buy at a grocery or at a supermarket. ◻ *...a small bag of groceries.*

grog /ɡrɒɡ/ N-UNCOUNT **Grog** is a drink made by mixing a strong spirit, such as rum or whiskey, with water.

groggy /ɡrɒɡi/ (groggier, groggiest) ADJ [usu v-link ADJ] If you feel **groggy**, you feel weak and rather ill. [INFORMAL] ◻ *She was feeling a little groggy when I saw her.*

groin /ɡrɔɪn/ (groins) N-COUNT Your **groin** is the front part of your body between your legs. ◻ *I underwent an operation on my groin once.*

groom /ɡruːm/ (grooms, grooming, groomed) **1** N-COUNT A **groom** is the same as a **bridegroom**. ◻ *...the bride and groom.* **2** N-COUNT A **groom** is someone whose job is to look after the horses in a stable and to keep them clean. **3** V-T If you **groom** an animal, you clean its fur, usually by brushing it. ◻ *The horses were exercised and groomed with special care.* **4** V-T [usu passive] If you **are groomed** for a special job, someone prepares you for it by teaching you the skills you will need. ◻ *George was already being groomed for the top job.*

groomed /ɡruːmd/ ADJ You use **groomed** in expressions such as **well groomed** and **badly groomed** to say how neat and clean a person is. ◻ *...a very well groomed man.*

grooming /ɡruːmɪŋ/ N-UNCOUNT **Grooming** refers to the things that people do to keep themselves clean and make their face, hair, and skin look nice. ◻ *...a growing concern for personal grooming.*

groove /ɡruːv/ (grooves) N-COUNT A **groove** is a deep line cut into a surface. ◻ *Prior to assembly, grooves were made in the shelf, base, and sides to accommodate the back panel.*

grooved /ɡruːvd/ ADJ Something that is **grooved** has grooves on its surface. ◻ *The inscriptions are fresh and deep grooved.*

groovy /ɡruːvi/ (groovier, grooviest) ADJ If you describe something as **groovy**, you mean that it is attractive, fashionable, or exciting. [INFORMAL, OLD-FASHIONED] ◻ *...the grooviest club in San Francisco.*

grope /ɡroʊp/ (gropes, groping, groped) **1** V-I If you **grope** for something that you cannot see, you try to find it by moving your hands around in order to feel it. ◻ *With his left hand he groped for the knob, turned it, and pulled the door open.* **2** V-T If you **grope** your way to a place, you move there, holding your hands in front of you and feeling the way because you cannot see anything. ◻ *I didn't turn on the light, but groped my way across the room.* **3** V-I If you **grope** for something, for example the solution to a problem, you try to think of it, when you have no real idea what it could be. ◻ *He groped for solutions to his problems.*

gross ♦♦♢ /ɡroʊs/ (grosser, grossest, grosses, grossing, grossed)

> The plural of the number is **gross**.

1 ADJ [ADJ n] You use **gross** to describe something unacceptable or unpleasant to a very great amount, degree, or intensity. ◻ *The company was guilty of gross negligence.* • **grossly** ADV [ADV -ed/adj] ◻ *Funding of education had been grossly inadequate for years.* **2** ADJ If you say that someone's speech or behavior is **gross**, you think it is very coarse, vulgar, or unacceptable. [DISAPPROVAL] ◻ *He abused the Admiral in the grossest terms.* **3** ADJ If you describe something as **gross**, you think it is very unpleasant. [INFORMAL, DISAPPROVAL] ◻ *They had a commercial on the other night for Drug Free America that was so gross I thought Dad was going to faint.* **4** ADJ [v-link ADJ] If you describe someone as **gross**, you mean that they are extremely fat and unattractive. [DISAPPROVAL] ◻ *I only resist things like chocolate if I feel really gross.* **5** ADJ [ADJ n] **Gross** means the total amount of something, especially money, before any has been taken away. ◻ *...a fixed rate account guaranteeing 10.4% gross interest or 7.8% net until October.* • ADV [ADV after v] **Gross** is also an adverb. ◻ *Interest is paid gross, rather than having tax deducted.* **6** ADJ [ADJ n] **Gross** means the total amount of something, after all the relevant amounts have been added together. ◻ *Gross sales reached nearly $2 million a year.* **7** V-T If a person or a business **grosses** a particular amount of money, they earn that amount of money before tax has been taken away. [BUSINESS] ◻ *The company grossed $16.8 million last year.* **8** NUM A **gross** is a group of 144 things. ◻ *In all honesty he could not have justified ordering more than twelve gross of the disks.*

SYNONYMS

gross
ADJ **1**
flagrant: *The judge called the decision 'a flagrant violation of international law.'*
glaring: *I never saw such a glaring example of misrepresentation.*
blatant: *...a blatant attempt to spread the blame for the fiasco.*
barefaced: *...crooked politicians who tell barefaced lies.*
obvious: *...the need to rectify what is an obvious injustice.*

---

gross domestic product (gross domestic products) N-VAR A country's **gross domestic product** is the total value of all the goods it has produced and the services it has provided in a particular year, not including its income from investments in other countries. [BUSINESS]

gross national product (gross national products) N-VAR A country's **gross national product** is the total value of all the goods it has produced and the services it has provided in a particular year, including its income from investments in other countries. [BUSINESS]

grotesque /ɡroʊtɛsk/ (grotesques) **1** ADJ You say that something is **grotesque** when it is so unnatural, unpleasant, and exaggerated that it upsets or shocks you. ◻ *...the grotesque disparities between the wealthy few and nearly everyone else.* • **grotesquely** ADV ◻ *He called it the most grotesquely tragic experience he's ever had.* **2** ADJ If someone or something is **grotesque**, they are very ugly. ◻ *They tried to avoid looking at his grotesque face and his crippled body.* • **grotesquely** ADV [ADV adj/-ed] ◻ *Their arms and legs were grotesquely swollen.* **3** N-COUNT A **grotesque** is a person who is very ugly in a strange or

grotto 577 **groundhog**

unnatural way, especially one in a novel or painting. ❏ *Grass's novels are peopled with outlandish characters: grotesques, clowns, scarecrows, dwarfs.*

grot|to /grɒtoʊ/ (**grottoes** or **grottos**) N-COUNT A **grotto** is a small cave with interesting or attractively shaped rocks. ❏ *Water trickles through an underground grotto.*

grouch /graʊtʃ/ (**grouches**) **1** N-COUNT A **grouch** is someone who is always complaining in a bad-tempered way. [INFORMAL, DISAPPROVAL] ❏ *He's an old grouch but she puts up with him.* **2** N-COUNT A **grouch** is a bad-tempered complaint. [INFORMAL] ❏ *One of his grouches is the system of payment.*

grouchy /graʊtʃi/ (**grouchier, grouchiest**) ADJ If someone is **grouchy**, they are very bad-tempered and complain a lot. [INFORMAL, DISAPPROVAL] ❏ *Your grandmother has nothing to stop her from being bored, grouchy, and lonely.*

GROUND
① NOUN USES
② VERB AND ADJECTIVE USES
③ PHRASES
---

① **ground** ♦♦♦ /graʊnd/ (**grounds**) **1** N-SING [the N] The **ground** is the surface of the earth. ❏ *Forty or fifty women were sitting cross-legged on the ground.* ❏ *We slid down the roof and dropped to the ground.* • PHRASE Something that is **below ground** is under the Earth's surface or under a building. Something that is **above ground** is on top of the earth's surface. **2** N-SING If you say that something takes place on the **ground**, you mean it takes place on the surface of the earth and not in the air. ❏ *Coordinating airline traffic on the ground is as complicated as managing the traffic in the air.* **3** N-SING The **ground** is the soil and rock on the earth's surface. ❏ *The ground had eroded.* **4** N-UNCOUNT You can refer to land as **ground**, especially when it has very few buildings or when it is considered to be special in some way. ❏ *...a stretch of waste ground.* **5** N-COUNT You can use **ground** to refer to an area of land, sea, or air which is used for a particular activity. ❏ *The best fishing grounds are around the islands.* **6** N-PLURAL The **grounds** of a large or important building are the garden or area of land which surrounds it. ❏ *...the palace grounds.* **7** N-VAR You can use **ground** to refer to a place or situation in which particular methods or ideas can develop and be successful. ❏ *The company has maintained its reputation as the developing ground for new techniques.* **8** N-UNCOUNT You can use **ground** in expressions such as **on shaky ground** and **the same ground** to refer to a particular subject, area of experience, or basis for an argument. ❏ *Sensing she was on shaky ground, Marie changed the subject.* ❏ *This is the most solid ground for optimism.* **9** N-UNCOUNT **Ground** is used in expressions such as **gain ground, lose ground**, and **give ground** in order to indicate that someone gets or loses an advantage. [JOURNALISM] ❏ *There are signs that the party is gaining ground in the latest polls.* **10** N-VAR If something is **grounds for** a feeling or action, it is a reason for it. If you do something **on the grounds** of a particular thing, that thing is the reason for your action. ❏ *In the interview he gave some grounds for optimism.* ❏ *The court overturned that decision on the grounds that the prosecution had withheld crucial evidence.* **11** N-COUNT [usu sing] The **ground** in an electric plug or piece of electrical equipment is the wire through which electricity passes into the ground and which makes the equipment safe. [AM] ❏ *...an insulated ground.*

in BRIT, use **earth**

② **ground** ♦♦♦ /graʊnd/ (**grounds, grounding, grounded**) **1** V-T If an argument, belief, or opinion **is grounded** in something, that thing is used to justify it. ❏ *Her argument was grounded in fact.* **2** V-T If an aircraft or its passengers **are grounded**, they are made to stay on the ground and are not allowed to take off. ❏ *The civil aviation minister ordered all the planes to be grounded.* **3** V-T When parents **ground** a child, they forbid them to go out and enjoy themselves for a period of time, as a punishment. ❏ *They grounded him for a month, and banned television.* **4** V-T/V-I If a ship or boat **is grounded** or if it **grounds**, it touches the bottom of the sea, lake, or river it is on, and is unable to move off. ❏ *Residents have been told to stay away from the region where the ship was grounded.* ❏ *The boat finally grounded on a soft, underwater bank.* **5** V-T If something **grounds** you, it causes you to have a sensible and practical attitude toward life and not to have unrealistic ideas. ❏ *These things have grounded me and made me who I am.* • **ground|ed** ADJ ❏ *She seems very grounded and down-to-earth.* **6** ADJ **Ground** meat has been cut into very small pieces in a machine. [mainly AM] ❏ *...The sausages are made of coarsely ground pork.*

in BRIT, usually use **minced**

7 Ground is the past tense and past participle of **grind**. **8** → see also **grounding**

③ **ground** ♦♦♦ /graʊnd/ **1** PHRASE If you **break new ground**, you do something completely different or you do something in a completely different way. [APPROVAL] ❏ *Gellhorn may have broken new ground when she filed her first report on the Spanish Civil War.* **2** PHRASE If you say that a town or building **is burned to the ground** or **is razed to the ground**, you are emphasizing that it has been completely destroyed by fire. [EMPHASIS] ❏ *The town was razed to the ground after the French Revolution.* **3** PHRASE If two people or groups find **common ground**, they agree about something, especially when they do not agree about other things. ❏ *The participants seem unable to find common ground on the issue of agriculture.* **4** PHRASE If you **hit the ground running**, you start a new activity with a lot of enthusiasm and energy and do not waste any time. ❏ *We want our students to hit the ground running after they graduate.* **5** PHRASE The **middle ground** between two groups, ideas, or plans involves things which do not belong to either of these groups, ideas, or plans but have elements of each, often in a less extreme form. ❏ *The sooner we find a middle ground between freedom of speech and protection of the young, the better for everyone.* **6** PHRASE If something such as a project gets **off the ground**, it begins or starts functioning. ❏ *We help small companies to get off the ground.* **7** PHRASE If you **prepare the ground** for a future event, course of action, or development, you make it easier for it to happen. ❏ *...a political initiative which would prepare the ground for war.* **8** PHRASE If you **shift** your **ground** or **change** your **ground**, you change the basis on which you are arguing. ❏ *Robert considered this, then shifted his ground slightly in line with a new thought.* **9** PHRASE If you **stand** your **ground** or **hold** your **ground**, you do not run away from a situation, but face it bravely. ❏ *She had to force herself to stand her ground when she heard someone approaching.*

ground ball (**ground balls**) also **groundball** N-COUNT In baseball, a **ground ball** is a ball that is hit along the ground rather than in the air. ❏ *Albert Belle hit a ground ball that appeared destined for right field.*

ground|break|ing /graʊndbreɪkɪŋ/ ADJ [usu ADJ n] You use **groundbreaking** to describe things which you think are significant because they provide new and positive ideas, and influence the way people think about things. ❏ *...his groundbreaking novel on women's rights.* ❏ *...groundbreaking research.*

ground cloth (**ground cloths**) N-COUNT A **ground cloth** is a piece of waterproof material that you put on the ground to sleep on when you are camping. [AM]

in BRIT, use **groundsheet**

ground crew (**ground crews**) N-COUNT-COLL At an airport, the people who take care of the planes when they are on the ground are called the **ground crew**. ❏ *The airport ground crew tried to dissuade the pilot from taking off.*

ground|er /graʊndər/ (**grounders**) N-COUNT A **grounder** is the same as a **ground ball**. ❏ *Travis Lee then hit a grounder to second baseman Mark Bellhorn.*

ground floor (**ground floors**) **1** N-COUNT The **ground floor** of a building is the floor that is level or almost level with the ground outside. ❏ *She showed him around the ground floor of the empty house.*

in AM, also use **first floor**

2 PHRASE If you **get in on the ground floor**, you become involved in a business or plan in the early stages, in order to gain an advantage. ❏ *A supplier wants to get in on the ground floor and grow with the business.*

ground|hog /graʊndhɒg/ (**groundhogs**) N-COUNT A **groundhog** is a type of small animal with reddish brown fur that is found in North America.

ground|ing /ɡraʊndɪŋ/ N-SING If you have a **grounding** in a subject, you know the basic facts or principles of that subject, especially as a result of a particular course of training or instruction. ☐ *The degree provides a thorough grounding in both mathematics and statistics.*

ground|less /ɡraʊndlɪs/ ADJ If you say that a fear, accusation, or story is **groundless**, you mean that it is not based on evidence and is unlikely to be true or valid. ☐ *Fears that the world was about to run out of fuel proved groundless.*

ground lev|el N-UNCOUNT [oft prep N] If something is at **ground level**, it is at the same level as the ground, as opposed to being higher up or below the surface. ☐ *The hotel is set on three floors. There's a bar and cafe at ground level.* ☐ *The remaining section of woodland is cut down to ground level.*

ground plan (ground plans) ◼ N-COUNT A **ground plan** is a plan of any floor of a building. ◼ N-COUNT A **ground plan** is a basic plan for future action.

ground rule (ground rules) N-COUNT The **ground rules** for something are the basic principles on which future action will be based. ☐ *The panel says the ground rules for the current talks should be maintained.*

ground|sheet /ɡraʊndʃiːt/ (groundsheets) also **ground sheet** N-COUNT A **groundsheet** is a piece of waterproof material which you put on the ground to sleep on when you are camping. [mainly BRIT]

in AM, also use **ground cloth**

grounds|keeper /ɡraʊndzkiːpər/ (groundskeepers) N-COUNT A **groundskeeper** is a person whose job is to look after a park or sports ground.

grounds|man /ɡraʊndzmən/ [BRIT] → see **groundskeeper**

ground squir|rel (ground squirrels) N-COUNT A **ground squirrel** is a rodent such as a chipmunk or a gopher. [AM] ☐ *Ground squirrels are normally active by day and sleep at night.*

ground staff ◼ N-COUNT-COLL The people who are paid to maintain a sports ground are called the **ground staff**. ☐ *The ground staff do all they can to prepare the field.* ◼ N-COUNT-COLL At an airport, the **ground staff** are the employees of airlines who do not fly with the planes, but who work in the airport helping passengers and providing information. ☐ *He planned to subcontract everything from the airplanes to the ground staff.*

ground|swell /ɡraʊndswɛl/ N-SING [with supp, usu N of n] A sudden growth of public feeling or support for something is often called a **groundswell**. [JOURNALISM] ☐ *There is undoubtedly a groundswell of support for the idea of a strong central authority.* ☐ *The groundswell of opinion is in favor of a referendum.*

ground|water /ɡraʊndwɔːtər/ N-UNCOUNT **Groundwater** is water that is found under the ground. Groundwater has usually passed down through the soil and become trapped by rocks.

ground|work /ɡraʊndwɜːrk/ N-SING The **groundwork** for something is the early work on it which forms the basis for further work. ☐ *Yesterday's meeting was to lay the groundwork for the task ahead.*

ground zero N-UNCOUNT People sometimes use **ground zero** to refer to the site of a disaster such as a nuclear explosion. However, it is used especially in relation to the destruction of the World Trade Center in New York on September 11, 2001. [mainly AM] ☐ *Within a half-mile from ground zero, death from radiation poisoning will occur within twelve hours.* ☐ *...Liberty Travel, located just blocks from ground zero in Manhattan.*

group ♦♦♦ /ɡruːp/ (groups, grouping, grouped) ◼ N-COUNT-COLL A **group** of people or things is a number of people or things that are together in one place at one time. ☐ *The trouble involved a small group of football fans.* ◼ N-COUNT A **group** is a set of people who have the same interests or aims, and who organize themselves to work or act together. ☐ *Members of an environmental group are staging a protest inside a chemical plant.* ◼ N-COUNT A **group** is a set of people, organizations, or things which are considered together because they have something in common. ☐ *She is among the most promising players in her age group.* ◼ N-COUNT A **group** is a number of separate commercial or industrial firms that all have the same owner. [BUSINESS] ☐ *The group made a pretax profit of $1.05 million.* ◼ N-COUNT A **group** is a number of musicians who perform together, especially ones who play popular music. ☐ *At school he played bass in a pop group called The Urge.* ◼ V-T/V-I If a number of things or people are **grouped together** or **group together**, they are together in one place or within one organization or system. ☐ *Plants are grouped into botanical "families" that have certain characteristics in common.* ☐ *The Species Survival Network groups together 80 international environmental organizations.* ◼ → see also **grouping, pressure group**

COLLOCATIONS

group
NOUN ◼
adjective + **group**: ethnic, religious, social; large, small; advisory
noun + **group**: campaign, lobby, pressure
verb + **group**: form, join, lead

groupie /ɡruːpi/ (groupies) N-COUNT A **groupie** is someone who is a fan of a particular band, singer, or other famous person, and follows them around.

group|ing /ɡruːpɪŋ/ (groupings) N-COUNT A **grouping** is a set of people or things that have something in common. ☐ *There were two main political groupings pressing for independence.*

group thera|py N-UNCOUNT **Group therapy** is a form of psychiatric treatment in which a group of people discuss their problems with each other.

grouse /ɡraʊs/ (grouses, grousing, groused)

The form **grouse** is used as the plural for meaning ◼.

◼ N-COUNT [oft N n] A **grouse** is a wild bird with a round body. Grouse are often shot for sport and can be eaten. ☐ *Her yell sent nearby grouse running for cover.* ☐ *The party had been to the grouse moors that morning.* • N-UNCOUNT **Grouse** is the flesh of this bird eaten as food. ☐ *The menu included roast grouse.* ◼ V-T/V-I If you **grouse**, you complain. ☐ *"How come we never know what's going on?" he groused.* ☐ *When they groused about the parking regulations, they did it with good humor.* ◼ N-COUNT A **grouse** is a complaint. ☐ *There have been grouses about interest rates and housing prices.*

grout /ɡraʊt/ (grouts, grouting, grouted) ◼ N-UNCOUNT **Grout** is a thin mixture of sand, water, and cement or lime, which is used to fill in the spaces between tiles that are attached to a wall. ◼ V-T If you **grout** the tiles on a wall, you use grout to fill in the spaces between the tiles. ☐ *Make sure that your tiles are thoroughly grouted and sealed.*

grove /ɡroʊv/ (groves) N-COUNT [usu with supp] A **grove** is a group of trees that are close together. ☐ *...an olive grove.*

grov|el /ɡrɒvəl/ (grovels, groveling, groveled)

in BRIT, use **grovelling, grovelled**

◼ V-I If you say that someone **grovels**, you think they are behaving too respectfully toward another person, for example because they are frightened or because they want something. [DISAPPROVAL] ☐ *I don't grovel to anybody.* ☐ *Speakers have been shouted down, classes disrupted, teachers made to grovel.* ◼ V-I If you **grovel**, you crawl on the ground, for example in order to find something. ☐ *We groveled around the room on our knees.*

grow ♦♦♦ /ɡroʊ/ (grows, growing, grew, grown) ◼ V-I When people, animals, and plants **grow**, they increase in size and change physically over a period of time. ☐ *We stop growing at maturity.* ◼ V-I If a plant or tree **grows** in a particular place, it is alive there. ☐ *The station had roses growing at each end of the platform.* ◼ V-T If you **grow** a particular type of plant, you put seeds or young plants in the ground and take care of them as they develop. ☐ *Lettuce was grown by the ancient Romans.* ◼ V-I When someone's hair **grows**, it gradually becomes longer. Your nails also **grow**. ☐ *Then the hair began to grow again and I felt terrific.* ◼ V-T If someone **grows** their hair, or **grows** a beard or mustache, they stop cutting their hair or shaving so that their hair becomes longer. You can also **grow** your nails. ☐ *I'd better start growing my hair.* ◼ V-I If someone **grows** mentally, they change and develop in character or attitude. ☐ *They began to grow as individuals.* ◼ V-LINK You use **grow** to say that someone or something gradually changes until they have a new quality, feeling, or attitude. ☐ *I grew a little afraid of the guy next door.*

He's growing old. ■ V-I If an amount, feeling, or problem **grows**, it becomes greater or more intense. □ *From 2000 to 2002, the number of uninsured grew by almost 4 million.* □ *Opposition grew and the government agreed to negotiate.* ■ V-I If one thing **grows into** another, it develops or changes until it becomes that thing. □ *The boys grew into men.* ■ V-I If something such as an idea or a plan **grows out of** something else, it develops from it. □ *The idea for this book grew out of conversations with Philippa Brewster.* ■ V-I If the economy or a business **grows**, it increases in wealth, size, or importance. [BUSINESS] □ *The economy continues to grow.* ■ V-T If someone **grows** a business, they take actions that will cause it to increase in wealth, size, or importance. [BUSINESS] □ *To grow the business, he needs to develop management expertise and innovation across his team.* ■ → see also **grown** ■ → See feature box at **farming, garden**

▶ **grow apart** PHRASAL VERB If people who have a close relationship **grow apart**, they gradually start to have different interests and opinions from each other, and their relationship starts to fail. □ *He and his wife grew apart.*

▶ **grow into** PHRASAL VERB When a child **grows into** an item of clothing, they become taller or bigger so that it fits them properly. □ *It's a little big, but she'll soon grow into it.*

▶ **grow on** PHRASAL VERB If someone or something **grows on** you, you start to like them more and more. □ *Slowly and strangely, the place began to grow on me.*

▶ **grow out of** ■ PHRASAL VERB If you **grow out of** a type of behavior or an interest, you stop behaving in that way or having that interest, as you develop or change. □ *Most children who stammer grow out of it.* ■ PHRASAL VERB When a child **grows out of** an item of clothing, they become so tall or big that it no longer fits them properly. □ *You've grown out of your shoes again.*

▶ **grow up** ■ PHRASAL VERB When someone **grows up**, they gradually change from being a child into being an adult. □ *She grew up in Tokyo.* ■ → see also **grown-up** ■ PHRASAL VERB If you tell someone to **grow up**, you are telling them to stop behaving in a silly or childish way. [INFORMAL, DISAPPROVAL] □ *It's time you grew up.* ■ PHRASAL VERB If something **grows up**, it starts to exist and then becomes larger or more important. □ *A variety of heavy industries grew up alongside the port.*

COLLOCATIONS

grow
VERB ■
noun + **grow**: business, demand, economy, industry, market; profit, revenue, sales
grow + adverb: fast, quickly, rapidly; significantly, steadily, strongly; slowly

grow|er /ˈɡroʊər/ (growers) N-COUNT A **grower** is a person who grows large quantities of a particular plant or crop in order to sell them. □ *The state's apple growers are fighting an uphill battle against foreign competition.*

grow|ing pains ■ N-PLURAL [usu with poss] If a person or organization has **growing pains**, they experience temporary difficulties and problems at the beginning of a particular stage of development. □ *There's some sympathy for this new country's growing pains.* ■ N-PLURAL If children suffer from **growing pains**, they have pain in their muscles or joints that is caused by unusually fast growth.

grow|ing sea|son (growing seasons) N-COUNT [usu sing] The **growing season** in a particular country or area is the period in each year when the weather and temperature is right for plants and crops to grow.

growl /ɡraʊl/ (growls, growling, growled) ■ V-I When a dog or other animal **growls**, it makes a low noise in its throat, usually because it is angry. □ *The dog was biting, growling, and wagging its tail.* • N-COUNT **Growl** is also a noun. □ *Their noise modulated to a concerted menacing growl punctuated by sharp yaps.* ■ V-T If someone **growls** something, they say something in a low, rough, and angry voice. [WRITTEN] □ *His fury was so great he could hardly speak. He growled some unintelligible words at Pete.* • N-COUNT **Growl** is also a noun. □ *...with an angry growl of contempt for her own weakness.*

grown /ɡroʊn/ ADJ [ADJ n] A **grown** man or woman is one who is fully developed and mature, both physically and mentally. □ *I've never seen a group of grown men laugh so much.*

grown-up (grown-ups)

The spelling **grownup** is also used. The syllable **up** is not stressed when it is a noun.

■ N-COUNT A **grown-up** is an adult. □ *Jan was almost a grown-up.* ■ ADJ Someone who is **grown-up** is physically and mentally mature and no longer depends on their parents or another adult. □ *I seem to have everything anyone could want – a good husband, a lovely home, grown-up children who're doing well.* ■ ADJ If you say that someone is **grown-up**, you mean that they behave in an adult way, often when they are in fact still a child. □ *She's very grown-up.* ■ ADJ **Grown-up** things seem suitable for or typical of adults. [INFORMAL] □ *Her songs tackle grown-up subjects.*

growth ◆◆◇ /ɡroʊθ/ (growths) ■ N-UNCOUNT The **growth** of something such as an industry, organization, or idea is its development in size, wealth, or importance. □ *...the growth of nationalism.* □ *...Japan's enormous economic growth.* ■ N-UNCOUNT [also a N] The **growth** in something is the increase in it. □ *A steady growth in the popularity of two smaller parties may upset the polls.* □ *The area has seen a rapid population growth.* ■ ADJ [ADJ n] A **growth** industry, area, or market is one that is increasing in size or activity. [BUSINESS] □ *Computers and electronics are growth industries and need skilled technicians.* ■ N-UNCOUNT Someone's **growth** is the development and progress of their character. □ *...the child's emotional and intellectual growth.* ■ N-UNCOUNT **Growth** in a person, animal, or plant is the process of increasing in physical size and development. □ *...hormones which control fertility and body growth.* ■ N-VAR You can use **growth** to refer to plants that have recently developed or that developed at the same time. □ *This helps to ripen new growth and makes it flower profusely.* ■ N-COUNT A **growth** is a lump that grows inside or on a person, animal, or plant, and that is caused by a disease. □ *This type of surgery could even be used to extract cancerous growths.* ■ → See feature box at **banking**

grub /ɡrʌb/ (grubs, grubbing, grubbed) ■ N-COUNT A **grub** is a young insect which has just come out of an egg and looks like a short, fat worm. ■ N-UNCOUNT **Grub** is food. [INFORMAL] □ *Get yourself some grub and come and sit down.* ■ V-I If you **grub** around, you search for something. □ *I simply cannot face grubbing through all this paper.*

grub|by /ˈɡrʌbi/ (grubbier, grubbiest) ■ ADJ A **grubby** person or object is rather dirty. □ *His white coat was grubby and stained.* ■ ADJ If you call an activity or someone's behavior **grubby**, you mean that it is not completely honest or respectable. [DISAPPROVAL] □ *...the grubby business of politics.*

grudge /ɡrʌdʒ/ (grudges) N-COUNT If you have or bear a **grudge** against someone, you have unfriendly feelings toward them because of something they did in the past. □ *He appears to have a grudge against certain players.*

grudge match (grudge matches) N-COUNT You can call a contest between two people or groups a **grudge match** when they dislike each other. □ *This is something of a grudge match against a long-term enemy.*

grudg|ing /ˈɡrʌdʒɪŋ/ ADJ A **grudging** feeling or action is felt or done very unwillingly. □ *He even earned his opponents' grudging respect.* • **grudg|ing|ly** ADV [ADV with v] □ *The film studio grudgingly agreed to allow him to continue working.*

gru|el /ˈɡruəl/ N-UNCOUNT **Gruel** is a food made by boiling oats with water or milk.

gru|el|ing /ˈɡruəlɪŋ/

in BRIT, use **gruelling**

ADJ A **grueling** activity is extremely difficult and tiring to do. □ *He had complained of exhaustion after his grueling schedule over the past week.*

grue|some /ˈɡruːsəm/ ADJ Something that is **gruesome** is extremely unpleasant and shocking. □ *There has been a series of gruesome murders in the capital.*

gruff /ɡrʌf/ ■ ADJ A **gruff** voice sounds low and rough. □ *He picked up the phone expecting to hear the president's gruff voice.* • **gruff|ly** ADV □ *"Well, never mind now," he said gruffly.* ■ ADJ If you describe someone as **gruff**, you mean that they seem rather unfriendly or bad tempered. □ *His gruff exterior concealed one of the kindest hearts.*

grum|ble /grˈʌmbəl/ (grumbles, grumbling, grumbled)
1 V-T/V-I If someone **grumbles**, they complain about something in a bad-tempered way. ❑ *They grumble about how hard they have to work.* ❑ *Taft grumbled that the law so favored the criminal that trials seemed like a game of chance.* • N-COUNT **Grumble** is also a noun. ❑ *My only grumble is that I don't see enough of them.* **2** V-I If something **grumbles**, it makes a low continuous sound. [LITERARY] ❑ *It was quiet now, the thunder had grumbled away to the west.* • N-SING [usu N *of* n] **Grumble** is also a noun. ❑ *One could often hear, far to the east, the grumble of guns.* **3** → See feature box at **review**

grum|py /grˈʌmpi/ (grumpier, grumpiest) ADJ If you say that someone is **grumpy**, you mean that they are bad tempered and miserable. ❑ *Some folks think I'm a grumpy old man.* • **grumpi|ly** ADV [ADV with v] ❑ *"I know, I know," said Ken, grumpily, without looking up.*

grunge /grʌndʒ/ N-UNCOUNT [oft N n] **Grunge** is the name of a fashion and of a type of music. **Grunge** fashion involves wearing clothes which look old and messy. **Grunge** music is played on guitars and is very loud. ❑ *...uncount Grunge is dirt.* • **grun|gy** ADJ [AM, INFORMAL] ❑ *...grungy motel rooms.*

grunt /grʌnt/ (grunts, grunting, grunted) **1** V-T/V-I If you **grunt**, you make a low sound, especially because you are annoyed or not interested in something. ❑ *The driver grunted, convinced that Michael was crazy.* ❑ *Harvey grunted disgustedly as he tossed in his cards.* • N-COUNT [oft N *of* n] **Grunt** is also a noun. ❑ *Their replies were no more than grunts of acknowledgement.* **2** V-I When an animal **grunts**, it makes a low, rough noise. ❑ *...the sound of a pig grunting.* **3** N-COUNT A **grunt** is a soldier of low rank in the infantry or the marines. [AM, INFORMAL] ❑ *I'm just a grunt. I have to follow everybody's orders.*

grunt work N-UNCOUNT [usu the N] If you do the **grunt work**, you do the hard work or the less interesting part of the work that needs to be done. [AM, INFORMAL] ❑ *Too many people had too little patience for the grunt work necessary for long-term success.*

in BRIT, use **donkey work**

GSM /dʒiː ɛs ɛm/ N-UNCOUNT **GSM** is a digital mobile telephone system. **GSM** is an abbreviation for 'global system for mobile communication.' ❑ *Their latest financial performance was a direct result of consistent growth in GSM cell phone subscribers.*

G-spot /dʒiː spɒt/ (G-spots) N-COUNT A woman's **G-spot** is an area inside her vagina that is supposed to produce a very intense orgasm when stimulated. ❑ *...orgasm resulting from G-spot stimulation.*

G-string /dʒiː strɪŋ/ (G-strings) N-COUNT A **G-string** is a narrow band of cloth that is worn between a person's legs to cover their sexual organs, and that is held up by a narrow string around the waist.

gua|ca|mo|le /gwɑːkəmoʊli/ N-UNCOUNT **Guacamole** is a cold food from Mexico made of crushed avocados and other ingredients such as tomatoes and chilies.

gua|no /gwɑːnoʊ/ N-UNCOUNT **Guano** is the feces of sea birds and bats. It is used as a fertilizer.

guar|an|tee ♦♦◇ /gærəntiː/ (guarantees, guaranteeing, guaranteed) **1** V-T If one thing **guarantees** another, the first is certain to cause the second thing to happen. ❑ *Surplus resources alone do not guarantee growth.* **2** N-COUNT Something that is a **guarantee** of something else makes it certain that it will happen or that it is true. ❑ *A famous old name on a firm is not necessarily a guarantee of quality.* **3** V-T If you **guarantee** something, you promise that it will definitely happen, or that you will do or provide it for someone. ❑ *Most states guarantee the right to free and adequate education.* ❑ *We guarantee that you will find a community with which to socialize.* • N-COUNT **Guarantee** is also a noun. ❑ *The editors can give no guarantee that they will fulfil their obligations.* **4** N-COUNT [also *under* N] A **guarantee** is a written promise by a company to replace or repair a product free of charge if it has any faults within a particular time. ❑ *Whatever a guarantee says, when something goes wrong, you can still claim your rights from the store.* **5** V-T If a company **guarantees** its product or work, they provide a guarantee for it. ❑ *Some builders guarantee their work.* ❑ *All our electric blankets are guaranteed for three years.* **6** N-COUNT A **guarantee** is money or something valuable that you give to someone to show that you will do what you have promised. ❑ *Males between 18 and 20 had to leave a deposit as a guarantee of returning to do their military service.*

guar|an|teed /gærəntiːd/ **1** ADJ [v-link ADJ] If you say that something is **guaranteed** to happen, you mean that you are certain that it will happen. ❑ *Reports of this kind are guaranteed to cause anxiety.* ❑ *It's guaranteed that my colleagues think I'm deranged.* ❑ *Success is not guaranteed.* **2** → see also **guarantee**

guar|an|tor /gærəntɔːr/ (guarantors) N-COUNT A **guarantor** is a person who gives a guarantee or who is bound by one. [LEGAL] ❑ *Someone thinking about acting as a guarantor should be clear what their obligations will be.*

guard ♦♦◇ /gɑːrd/ (guards, guarding, guarded) **1** V-T If you **guard** a place, person, or object, you stand near them in order to watch and protect them. ❑ *Gunmen guarded homes near the cemetery with shotguns.* **2** V-T If you **guard** someone, you watch them and keep them in a particular place to stop them from escaping. ❑ *Marines with rifles guarded them.* **3** N-COUNT A **guard** is someone such as a soldier, police officer, or prison officer who is guarding a particular place or person. ❑ *The prisoners overpowered their guards and locked them in a cell.* **4** N-SING-COLL A **guard** is a specially organized group of people, such as soldiers or police officers, who protect or watch someone or something. ❑ *We have a security guard around the whole area.* **5** V-T If you **guard** some information or advantage that you have, you try to protect it or keep it for yourself. ❑ *He closely guarded her identity.* **6** N-COUNT [usu with supp] A **guard** is a protective device which covers a part of someone's body or a dangerous part of a piece of equipment. ❑ *...the chin guard of my helmet.* **7** N-COUNT On a train, a **guard** is a person whose job is to travel on the train in order to help passengers, check tickets, and make sure that the train travels safely and on time. [BRIT]

in AM, use **conductor**

8 → see also **guarded**, **bodyguard**, **coast guard**, **lifeguard** **9** PHRASE If someone **catches** you **off guard**, they surprise you by doing something you do not expect. If something **catches** you **off guard**, it surprises you by happening when you are not expecting it. ❑ *Charm the audience and catch them off guard.* **10** PHRASE If you **lower** your **guard**, let your **guard** down, or **drop** your **guard**, you relax when you should be careful and alert, often with unpleasant consequences. ❑ *The ANC could not afford to lower its guard until everything had been carried out.* ❑ *You can't let your guard down.* **11** PHRASE If you are **on** your **guard** or **on guard**, you are being very careful because you think a situation might become difficult or dangerous. ❑ *The police have questioned him thoroughly, and he'll be on his guard.* **12** PHRASE If someone is **on guard**, they are on duty and responsible for guarding a particular place or person. ❑ *Police were on guard at Barnet town hall.* **13** PHRASE If you **stand guard**, you stand near a particular person or place because you are responsible for watching or protecting them. ❑ *One young policeman stood guard outside the locked embassy gates.* **14** PHRASE If someone is **under guard**, they are being guarded. ❑ *Three men were arrested and one was under guard in a hospital.*
▶ **guard against** PHRASAL VERB If you **guard against** something, you are careful to prevent it from happening, or to avoid being affected by it. ❑ *The armed forces were on high alert to guard against any retaliation.*

COLLOCATIONS

guard
NOUN
3
noun + **guard**: border, palace, prison; security
verb + **guard**: overpower; hire, post, station
adjective + **guard**: armed, uniformed
4
adjective + **guard**: armed; presidential
VERB
1
guard + noun: building, compound, embassy, entrance; border
noun + **guard**: officers, soldiers, troops
guard + adverb: carefully, heavily
2
guard + noun: prisoner
5
guard + noun: privacy, secret
guard + adverb: closely, heavily, jealously

guard dog (guard dogs) N-COUNT A **guard dog** is a fierce dog that has been specially trained to protect a particular place.

guard|ed /gɑrdɪd/ ADJ If you describe someone as **guarded**, you mean that they are careful not to show their feelings or give away information. ☐ *The boy gave him a guarded look.*

guard|ian /gɑrdiən/ (guardians) **1** N-COUNT A **guardian** is someone who has been legally appointed to take charge of the affairs of another person, for example a child or someone who is mentally ill. ☐ *Destiny's legal guardian was her grandmother.* **2** N-COUNT The **guardian** of something is someone who defends and protects it. ☐ *...an institution acting as the guardian of democracy in Europe.*

guard|ian an|gel (guardian angels) N-COUNT A **guardian angel** is a spirit who is believed to protect and guide a particular person.

guard|ian|ship /gɑrdiənʃɪp/ N-UNCOUNT [usu with poss] **Guardianship** is the position of being a guardian. ☐ *...depriving mothers of the guardianship of their children.*

guard of hon|our (guards of honour) N-COUNT A **guard of honour** is an official parade of troops, usually to celebrate or honor a special occasion, such as the visit of a head of state. [BRIT]

in AM, use **honor guard**

guard|rail /gɑrdreɪl/ (guardrails) also **guard rail** N-COUNT A **guardrail** is a railing that is placed along the edge of something such as a staircase, path, or boat, so that people can hold onto it or so that they do not fall over the edge.

guards|man /gɑrdzmən/ (guardsmen) also **Guardsman** N-COUNT A **guardsman** is a male soldier who is a member of the National Guard.

guards|woman /gɑrdzwʊmən/ (guardswomen) also **Guardswoman** N-COUNT A **guardswoman** is a female soldier who is a member of the National Guard.

gua|va /gwɑvə/ (guavas) N-VAR A **guava** is a round, yellow, tropical fruit with pink or white flesh and hard seeds.

gu|ber|na|to|rial /guːbərnətɔriəl/ ADJ [ADJ n] **Gubernatorial** means relating to or connected with the post of governor. ☐ *...a well-known Dallas lawyer and former Texas gubernatorial candidate.*

guer|ril|la ♦◊◊ /gərɪlə/ (guerrillas) also **guerilla** N-COUNT A **guerrilla** is someone who fights as part of an unofficial army, usually against an official army or police force. ☐ *The guerrillas threatened to kill their hostages.*

guer|ril|la mar|ket|ing N-UNCOUNT [oft N n] **Guerrilla marketing** is trying to sell or publicize a product using unusual and low-cost methods, usually in public places, for example by organizing events or placing objects that get people's attention. [BUSINESS] ☐ *The graffiti is actually a clever piece of guerrilla marketing.*

guess ♦♦◊ /gɛs/ (guesses, guessing, guessed) **1** V-T/V-I If you **guess** something, you give an answer or provide an opinion which may not be true because you do not have definite knowledge about the matter concerned. ☐ *Yvonne guessed that he was a very successful publisher or a banker.* ☐ *You can only guess at what mental suffering they endure.* ☐ *Guess what I did for the whole of the first week.* **2** V-T If you **guess** that something is the case, you correctly form the opinion that it is the case, although you do not have definite knowledge about it. ☐ *By now you will have guessed that I'm back in Ohio.* ☐ *He should have guessed what would happen.* **3** N-COUNT A **guess** is an attempt to give an answer or provide an opinion which may not be true because you do not have definite knowledge about the matter concerned. ☐ *My guess is that the chance that these vaccines will work is zero.* ☐ *He'd taken her pulse and made a guess at her blood pressure.* **4** PHRASE If you say that something is **anyone's guess** or **anybody's guess**, you mean that no one can be certain about what is really true. [INFORMAL] ☐ *Just when this will happen is anyone's guess.* **5** PHRASE You say **at a guess** to indicate that what you are saying is only an estimate or what you believe to be true, rather than being a definite fact. [mainly BRIT, VAGUENESS] ☐ *At a guess he's been dead for two days.* **6** PHRASE You say **I guess** to show that you are slightly uncertain or reluctant about what you are saying. [mainly AM, INFORMAL, VAGUENESS] ☐ *I guess he's right.* ☐ *"I think you're being paranoid."—"Yeah. I guess so."* **7** PHRASE If someone **keeps** you **guessing**, they do not tell you what you want to know. ☐ *The author's intention is to keep everyone guessing until the bitter end.* **8** CONVENTION You say **guess what** to draw attention to something exciting, surprising, or interesting that you are about to say. [INFORMAL] ☐ *Guess what, I just got my first part in a movie.*

guess|ti|mate /gɛstɪmət/ (guesstimates) N-COUNT A **guesstimate** is an approximate calculation which is based mainly or entirely on guessing. [INFORMAL] ☐ *The 30 percent figure may be no more than a guesstimate.*

guess|work /gɛswɜrk/ N-UNCOUNT **Guesswork** is the process of trying to guess or estimate something without knowing all the facts or information. ☐ *The question of who planted the bomb remains a matter of guesswork.*

guest ♦♦◊ /gɛst/ (guests) **1** N-COUNT A **guest** is someone who is visiting you or is at an event because you have invited them. ☐ *She was a guest at the wedding.* **2** N-COUNT A **guest** is someone who visits a place or organization or appears on a radio or television show because they have been invited to do so. ☐ *...a frequent talk show guest.* ☐ *Dr. Gerald Jeffers is the guest speaker.* **3** N-COUNT A **guest** is someone who is staying in a hotel. ☐ *I was the only hotel guest.* **4** CONVENTION If you say **be my guest** to someone, you are giving them permission to do something. ☐ *If anybody wants to work on this, be my guest.*

COLLOCATIONS

guest
NOUN
1
noun + **guest**: dinner, house, party, wedding
adjective + **guest**: honored, overnight, royal; unexpected, uninvited
verb + **guest**: entertain, greet, invite, offer
2
noun + **guest**: celebrity, star, surprise
adjective + **guest**: regular, special
verb + **guest**: welcome

---

guest book (guest books) N-COUNT A **guest book** is a book in which guests write their names and addresses when they have been staying in someone's house or in a hotel.

guest house (guest houses) also **guesthouse** **1** N-COUNT A **guest house** is a small hotel. **2** N-COUNT A **guest house** is a small house in the grounds of a large house, where visitors can stay. [AM]

guest of hon|or (guests of honor)

in BRIT, use **guest of honour**

N-COUNT If you say that someone is the **guest of honor** at a dinner or other social occasion, you mean that they are the most important guest.

guest room (guest rooms) N-COUNT A **guest room** is a bedroom in a house or hotel for visitors or guests to sleep in.

guest work|er (guest workers) N-COUNT A **guest worker** is a person, especially one from a poor country, who lives and works in a different country for a period of time.

guff /gʌf/ N-UNCOUNT If you say that what someone has said or written is **guff**, you think that it is nonsense. [INFORMAL, DISAPPROVAL]

guf|faw /gʌfɔ/ (guffaws, guffawing, guffawed) **1** N-COUNT A **guffaw** is a very loud laugh. ☐ *He bursts into a loud guffaw.* **2** V-T/V-I To **guffaw** means to laugh loudly. ☐ *As they guffawed loudly, the ticket collector arrived.* ☐ *"Ha, ha," everyone guffawed.* *"It's one of Viv's shock tactics."* **3** → See feature box at **humor**

GUI /gui/ (GUIs) N-COUNT [oft N n] In computing, a **GUI** is a type of screen interface that is found on most computers, consisting of menus and icons that can be controlled by a mouse. **GUI** is an abbreviation for 'graphical user interface.' ☐ *The goal of a GUI is to present the user with as few decision points as possible.*

guid|ance /gaɪdəns/ N-UNCOUNT **Guidance** is help and advice. ☐ *...an opportunity for young people to improve their performance under the guidance of professional coaches.*

guid|ance coun|se|lor (guidance counselors)

in BRIT, use **guidance counsellor**

N-COUNT A **guidance counselor** is a person who works in a

guid|ance sys|tem (guidance systems) N-COUNT The **guidance system** of a missile or rocket is the device that controls its course. ❑ *The guidance systems didn't work and the missile couldn't hit its target.*

guide ✦✧ /gaɪd/ (guides, guiding, guided) **1** N-COUNT; N-IN-NAMES A **guide** is a book that gives you information or instructions to help you do or understand something. ❑ *Our 10-page guide will help you to change your life for the better.* **2** N-COUNT; N-IN-NAMES A **guide** is a book that gives tourists information about a town, area, or country. ❑ *The Rough Guide to Paris lists accommodations for as little as $35 a night.* **3** N-COUNT A **guide** is someone who shows tourists around places such as museums or cities. ❑ *We've arranged a walking tour of the city with your guide.* **4** V-T If you **guide** someone around a city, museum, or building, you show it to them and explain points of interest. ❑ *...a young Egyptologist who guided us through tombs and temples with enthusiasm.* **5** N-COUNT A **guide** is someone who shows people the way to a place in a difficult or dangerous region. ❑ *The mountain people say that, with guides, the journey can be done in fourteen days.* **6** N-COUNT A **guide** is something that can be used to help you plan your actions or to form an opinion about something. ❑ *As a rough guide, a horse needs 2.5 percent of its body weight in food every day.* **7** V-T If you **guide** someone somewhere, you go there with them in order to show them the way. ❑ *He took the bewildered Elliott by the arm and guided him out.* **8** V-T If you **guide** a vehicle somewhere, you control it carefully to make sure that it goes in the right direction. ❑ *Captain Shelton guided his plane down the runway and took off.* **9** V-T If something **guides** you somewhere, it gives you the information you need in order to go in the right direction. ❑ *They sailed across the Caribbean with only a compass to guide them.* **10** V-T If something or someone **guides** you, they influence your actions or decisions. ❑ *He should have let his instinct guide him.* ❑ *Development has been guided by a concern for the ecology of the area.* **11** V-T If you **guide** someone through something that is difficult to understand or to achieve, you help them to understand it or to achieve success in it. ❑ *Gym owner David Barton will guide them through a workout.*

---- COLLOCATIONS ----

guide
NOUN **1**
adjective + **guide**: handy, helpful, interactive, step-by-step; authoritative, informative, reliable

----

guide|book /gaɪdbʊk/ (guidebooks) also **guide book** N-COUNT A **guidebook** is a book that gives tourists information about a town, area, or country.

guid|ed mis|sile (guided missiles) N-COUNT A **guided missile** is a missile whose direction can be controlled while it is in the air.

guide dog (guide dogs) N-COUNT A **guide dog** is a dog that has been trained to lead a blind person. [mainly BRIT]

in AM, usually use **seeing-eye dog**

guid|ed tour (guided tours) N-COUNT [oft N *of* n] If someone takes you on a **guided tour** of a place, they show you the place and tell you about it.

guid|ed writ|ing N-UNCOUNT [oft N n] In language teaching, when students do **guided writing** activities, they are given an outline in words or pictures to help them write. ❑ *...some guided writing tasks.*

guide|line /gaɪdlaɪn/ (guidelines) **1** N-COUNT If an organization issues **guidelines** on something, it issues official advice about how to do it. ❑ *The government should issue clear guidelines on the content of religious education.* **2** N-COUNT A **guideline** is something that can be used to help you plan your actions or to form an opinion about something. ❑ *A written IQ test is merely a guideline.*

guild /gɪld/ (guilds) N-COUNT A **guild** is an organization of people who do the same job. ❑ *...the Writers' Guild of America.*

guil|der /gɪldər/ (guilders) N-COUNT [num N] A **guilder** was a unit of money that was used in the Netherlands. In 2002 it was replaced by the euro. • N-SING [*the* N] **The guilder** was also used to refer to the Dutch currency system. ❑ *During the turmoil in the foreign-exchange markets the guilder remained strong.*

guile /gaɪl/ N-UNCOUNT **Guile** is the quality of being good at deceiving people in a clever way. ❑ *I love children's innocence and lack of guile.*

guile|less /gaɪlləs/ ADJ If you describe someone as **guileless**, you mean that they behave openly and truthfully and do not try to deceive people. [WRITTEN, APPROVAL] ❑ *Joanne was so guileless that Claire had no option but to believe her.*

guil|lo|tine /gɪlətin/ (guillotines, guillotining, guillotined) **1** N-COUNT [also *by* N] A **guillotine** is a device used to execute people, especially in France in the past. A sharp blade was raised up on a frame and dropped onto the person's neck. ❑ *One after the other Danton, Robespierre and the rest went to the guillotine.* **2** V-T [usu passive] If someone **is guillotined**, they are killed with a guillotine. **3** N-COUNT A **guillotine** is a device used for cutting paper.

guilt /gɪlt/ **1** N-UNCOUNT **Guilt** is an unhappy feeling that you have because you have done something wrong or think that you have done something wrong. ❑ *Her emotions had ranged from anger to guilt in the space of a few seconds.* **2** N-UNCOUNT **Guilt** is the fact that you have done something wrong or illegal. ❑ *The trial is concerned only with the determination of guilt according to criminal law.*

guilt com|plex (guilt complexes) N-COUNT If you say that someone has a **guilt complex** about something, you mean that they feel very guilty about it, in a way that you consider is exaggerated, unreasonable, or unnecessary. [DISAPPROVAL]

guilt-ridden ADJ If a person is **guilt-ridden**, they feel very guilty about something. ❑ *In the first week of January, thousands of guilt-ridden people signed up for fitness courses or embarked on diets.*

guilty ✦✧ /gɪlti/ (guiltier, guiltiest) **1** ADJ If you feel **guilty**, you feel unhappy because you think that you have done something wrong or have failed to do something which you should have done. ❑ *I feel so guilty, leaving all this to you.* • **guilti|ly** ADV [ADV with v] ❑ *He glanced guiltily over his shoulder.* **2** ADJ [ADJ n] **Guilty** is used of an action or fact that you feel guilty about. ❑ *Many may be keeping it a guilty secret.* **3 guilty conscience** → see **conscience** **4** ADJ If someone is **guilty** of a crime or offense, they have committed that crime or offense. ❑ *They were found guilty of murder.* **5** ADJ If someone is **guilty** of doing something wrong, they have done that thing. ❑ *He claimed Mr. Brooke had been guilty of a "gross error of judgment."* **6** → See feature box at **legal**

---- SYNONYMS ----

guilty
ADJ
1
ashamed: *I felt incredibly ashamed of myself for getting so angry.*
sorry: *She was very sorry about all the trouble she'd caused.*
rueful: *He shook his head and gave me a rueful smile.*
contrite: *She was instantly contrite. 'Oh, I am sorry! You must forgive me.'*
remorseful: *He was genuinely remorseful.*
5
culpable: *Their decision to do nothing makes them culpable.*
responsible: *He still felt responsible for her death.*
to blame: *If their forces were not involved, then who is to blame?*

----

guinea /gɪni/ (guineas) N-COUNT A **guinea** is an old British unit of money that was worth £1.05. Guineas are still sometimes used, for example in auctions.

guinea fowl (guinea fowl) N-COUNT A **guinea fowl** is a large, gray, African bird that is often eaten as food.

guinea pig (guinea pigs) **1** N-COUNT If someone is used as a **guinea pig** in an experiment, something is tested on them that has not been tested on people before. ❑ *Dr. Roger Altounyan used himself as a human guinea pig.* **2** N-COUNT A **guinea pig** is a small, furry animal without a tail. Guinea pigs are often kept as pets.

guise /gaɪz/ (guises) N-COUNT You use **guise** to refer to the outward appearance or form of someone or something, which is often temporary or different from their real nature. ❑ *He turned up at an Easter party in the guise of a white rabbit.*

gui|tar /gɪtɑr/ (guitars) N-VAR A **guitar** is a musical instrument with six strings and a long neck. You play the guitar by plucking or strumming the strings.

gui|tar|ist /gɪtɑrɪst/ (guitarists) N-COUNT A **guitarist** is someone who plays the guitar.

gu|lag /gulæg/ (gulags) N-COUNT A **gulag** is a prison camp where conditions are extremely bad and the prisoners are forced to work very hard. The name **gulag** comes from the prison camps in the former Soviet Union.

gulch /gʌltʃ/ (gulches) N-COUNT [oft in names] A **gulch** is a long, narrow valley with steep sides which has been made by a stream flowing through it. [mainly AM] ❏ ...California Gulch.

gulf /gʌlf/ (gulfs) ◼ N-COUNT A **gulf** is an important or significant difference between two people, things, or groups. ❏ Within society, there is a growing gulf between rich and poor. ◼ N-COUNT A **gulf** is a large area of sea which extends a long way into the surrounding land. ❏ Hurricane Andrew was last night heading into the Gulf of Mexico.

Gulf N-PROPER [the N, oft N n] **The Gulf** is used to refer to the Gulf of Mexico or the Persian Gulf and the surrounding countries. ❏ ...the Gulf crisis. ❏ ...the Gulf War. ❏ ...the oil wells of the Gulf.

gull /gʌl/ (gulls) N-COUNT A **gull** is a common sea bird.

gul|let /gʌlɪt/ (gullets) N-COUNT Your **gullet** is the tube that goes from your mouth to your stomach.

gul|ley /gʌli/ (gulleys) → see gully

gul|lible /gʌlɪbəl/ ADJ If you describe someone as **gullible**, you mean they are easily tricked because they are too trusting. ❏ What point is there in admitting that the stories fed to the gullible public were false? ● **gul|li|bil|ity** /gʌlɪbɪlɪti/ N-UNCOUNT ❏ Was she taking part of the blame for her own gullibility?

gul|ly /gʌli/ (gullies) also **gulley** N-COUNT A **gully** is a long, narrow valley with steep sides. ❏ The bodies of the three climbers were located at the bottom of a steep gully.

gulp /gʌlp/ (gulps, gulping, gulped) ◼ V-T If you **gulp** something, you eat or drink it very quickly by swallowing large quantities of it at once. ❏ She quickly gulped her soda. ● PHRASAL VERB **Gulp down** means the same as **gulp**. ❏ Paige gulped down more coffee and a candy bar from the machine. ◼ V-T/V-I If you **gulp**, you swallow air, often making a noise in your throat as you do so, because you are nervous or excited. [WRITTEN] ❏ I gulped, and then proceeded to tell her the whole story. ◼ V-T If you **gulp** air, you breathe in a large amount of air quickly through your mouth. ❏ She gulped air into her lungs. ◼ N-COUNT A **gulp** of air, food, or drink, is a large amount of it that you swallow at once. ❏ I took in a large gulp of air.

gum /gʌm/ (gums) ◼ N-MASS **Gum** is a substance, usually tasting of mint, which you chew for a long time but do not swallow. ❏ I do not permit chewing gum in public. ◼ N-COUNT Your **gums** are the areas of firm, pink flesh inside your mouth, which your teeth grow out of. ❏ The toothbrush gently removes plaque without damaging the gums or causing bleeding.

gum|ball /gʌmbɔl/ (gumballs) N-COUNT **Gumballs** are round, brightly colored balls of chewing gum. [mainly AM]

gum|bo /gʌmboʊ/ (gumbos) ◼ N-VAR **Gumbo** is a type of soup or stew from the southern United States. It can be made with chicken or fish, and usually contains okra. ◼ N-UNCOUNT In parts of the United States, **gumbo** is another name for **okra**.

gum|drop /gʌmdrɒp/ (gumdrops) N-COUNT A **gumdrop** is a chewy candy which feels like firm rubber and usually tastes of fruit.

gum|my /gʌmi/ ADJ Something that is **gummy** is sticky. ❏ My eyes are gummy.

gump|tion /gʌmpʃən/ ◼ N-UNCOUNT [oft the N to-inf] If someone has the **gumption** to do something, they are brave enough to do it. ❏ He suspected that deep down, she admired him for having the gumption to disagree with her. ◼ N-UNCOUNT If someone has **gumption**, they are able to think what it would be sensible to do in a particular situation, and they do it. [INFORMAL] ❏ Surely anyone with marketing gumption should be able to sell good books at any time of year.

gum|shoe /gʌmʃu/ (gumshoes) N-COUNT A **gumshoe** is a detective. [AM, INFORMAL, OLD-FASHIONED] ❏ ...an FBI gumshoe.

gum tree (gum trees) N-COUNT A **gum tree** is a tree such as a eucalyptus that produces gum.

gun ♦♢ /gʌn/ (guns, gunning, gunned) ◼ N-COUNT A **gun** is a weapon from which bullets or other things are fired. ❏ He fled, pointing the gun at officers as they chased him. ❏ He just seemed like a normal military guy who liked guns. ◼ N-COUNT A **gun** or a **starting gun** is an object like a gun that is used to make a noise to signal the start of a race. ❏ The starting gun blasted and they were off. ◼ V-T To **gun** an engine or a vehicle means to make it start or go faster by pressing on the accelerator pedal. [mainly AM] ❏ He gunned his engine and drove off. ◼ → see also **shotgun** ◼ PHRASE If you come out **with guns blazing** or **with all guns blazing**, you put all your effort and energy into trying to achieve something. ❏ The company came out with guns blazing. ◼ PHRASE If you **jump the gun**, you do something before everyone else or before the proper or right time. [INFORMAL] ❏ It wasn't due to be released until September 10, but some booksellers have jumped the gun and decided to sell it early. ◼ PHRASE If you **stick to** your **guns**, you continue to have your own opinion about something even though other people are trying to tell you that you are wrong. [INFORMAL] ❏ He should have stuck to his guns and refused to meet her.

▶ **gun down** PHRASAL VERB If someone **is gunned down**, they are shot and severely injured or killed. [JOURNALISM] ❏ He had been gunned down and killed at point-blank range.

COLLOCATIONS

gun
NOUN ◼
noun + **gun**: anti-aircraft, hand, laser; imitation, replica, toy
adjective + **gun**: heavy; loaded
verb + **gun**: brandish, carry, draw, hold; fire, load, point

---

gun|boat /gʌnboʊt/ (gunboats) N-COUNT A **gunboat** is a small ship which has several large guns fixed on it.

gun con|trol N-UNCOUNT [oft N n] **Gun control** refers to the laws that restrict the possession and use of guns. ❏ France has tight gun-control laws for handguns, but not for hunting rifles.

gun dog (gun dogs) also **gundog** N-COUNT A **gun dog** is a dog that has been trained to work with a hunter or gamekeeper, especially to find and carry back birds or animals that have been shot.

gun|fight /gʌnfaɪt/ (gunfights) N-COUNT A **gunfight** is a fight between people using guns. ● **gun|fighter** (gunfighters) N-COUNT ❏ Eastwood plays retired gunfighter Will Munny.

gun|fire /gʌnfaɪər/ N-UNCOUNT **Gunfire** is the repeated shooting of guns. ❏ The sound of gunfire and explosions grew closer.

gung ho /gʌŋ hoʊ/ also **gung-ho** ADJ If you say that someone is **gung ho**, you mean that they are very enthusiastic or eager to do something, for example to fight in a battle. [INFORMAL] ❏ He has warned some of his more gung ho generals about the consequences of an invasion. ❏ Senate Republicans are less gung-ho about tax cuts.

gunk /gʌŋk/ N-UNCOUNT You use **gunk** to refer to any soft, sticky substance, especially if it is unpleasant. [INFORMAL]

gun|man /gʌnmən/ (gunmen) N-COUNT A **gunman** is a man who uses a gun to commit a crime such as murder or robbery. [JOURNALISM] ❏ Two policemen were killed when gunmen opened fire on their patrol vehicle.

gun|ner /gʌnər/ (gunners) N-COUNT A **gunner** is an ordinary soldier in an artillery regiment.

gun|nery /gʌnəri/ N-UNCOUNT [usu N n] **Gunnery** is the activity of firing large guns. [MILITARY] ❏ During the Second World War the area was used for gunnery practice.

gun|point /gʌnpɔɪnt/ PHRASE If you are held **at gunpoint**, someone is threatening to shoot and kill you if you do not obey them. ❏ She and her two daughters were held at gunpoint by a gang who burst into their home.

gun|powder /gʌnpaʊdər/ N-UNCOUNT **Gunpowder** is an explosive substance that is used to make fireworks or cause explosions.

gun|runner /gʌnrʌnər/ (gunrunners)

in BRIT, use **gun-runner**

N-COUNT A **gunrunner** is someone who takes or sends guns into a country secretly and illegally.

gun|running /gʌnrʌnɪŋ/ N-UNCOUNT **Gunrunning** is the activity of taking or sending guns into a country secretly and illegally.

in BRIT, use **gun-running**

gun|ship /gʌnʃɪp/ (gunships) → see helicopter gunship

gun|shot /gʌnʃɒt/ (gunshots) **1** N-UNCOUNT **Gunshot** is used to refer to bullets that are fired from a gun. ❏ *They had died of gunshot wounds.* **2** N-COUNT A **gunshot** is the firing of a gun or the sound of a gun being fired. ❏ *They heard thousands of gunshots.*

gun-shy ADJ [usu v-link ADJ] If someone is **gun-shy**, they are nervous or afraid. ❏ *The electric-power industry is gun-shy about building more large plants.*

gun|slinger /gʌnslɪŋər/ (gunslingers) N-COUNT A **gunslinger** is someone, especially a criminal, who uses guns in fighting.

gun|smith /gʌnsmɪθ/ (gunsmiths) N-COUNT A **gunsmith** is someone who makes and repairs guns.

gup|py /gʌpi/ (guppies) N-COUNT A **guppy** is a small, brightly colored tropical fish.

gur|gle /gɜrgəl/ (gurgles, gurgling, gurgled) **1** V-I If water is **gurgling**, it is making the sound that it makes when it flows quickly and unevenly through a narrow space. ❏ *...a narrow stone-edged channel along which water gurgles unseen.* • N-COUNT **Gurgle** is also a noun. ❏ *We could hear the swish and gurgle of water against the hull.* **2** V-I If someone, especially a baby, **is gurgling**, they are making a sound in their throat similar to the gurgling of water. ❏ *Henry gurgles happily in his baby chair.* • N-COUNT **Gurgle** is also a noun. ❏ *There was a gurgle of laughter on the other end of the line.*

gur|ney /gɜni/ (gurneys) N-COUNT A **gurney** is a bed on wheels that is used in hospitals for moving sick or injured people. [AM] ❏ *A man on a gurney was being handled by an orderly.*

in BRIT, use **trolley**

guru /guru/ (gurus) **1** N-COUNT A **guru** is a person who some people regard as an expert or leader. ❏ *Fashion gurus dictate crazy ideas such as squeezing oversized bodies into tight trousers.* **2** N-COUNT; N-TITLE A **guru** is a religious and spiritual leader and teacher, especially in Hinduism.

gush /gʌʃ/ (gushes, gushing, gushed) **1** V-T/V-I When liquid **gushes** out of something, or when something **gushes** a liquid, the liquid flows out very quickly and in large quantities. ❏ *Piping-hot water gushed out.* **2** N-SING [usu N of n] A **gush** of liquid is a sudden, rapid flow of liquid, or a quantity of it that suddenly flows out. ❏ *I heard a gush of water.* **3** V-T/V-I If someone **gushes**, they express their admiration or pleasure in an exaggerated way. ❏ *"Oh, it was brilliant," he gushes.* • **gush|ing** ADJ ❏ *He delivered a gushing speech.*

gussy /gʌsi/ (gussies, gussying, gussied)
▶ **gussy up** PHRASAL VERB If someone **is gussied up**, they are dressed in a fancy or very fashionable way. If something **is gussied up**, it is made more interesting or attractive. [mainly AM, INFORMAL, OLD-FASHIONED] ❏ *They all got gussied up.* ❏ *...plans to gussy up the venues, offering better food and game arcades.*

gust /gʌst/ (gusts, gusting, gusted) **1** N-COUNT A **gust** is a short, strong, sudden rush of wind. ❏ *A gust of wind drove down the valley.* **2** V-I When the wind **gusts**, it blows with short, strong, sudden rushes. ❏ *The wind gusted again.* **3** N-COUNT [N of n] If you feel a **gust** of emotion, you feel the emotion suddenly and intensely. ❏ *...a small gust of pleasure.* **4** → See feature box at **storm**

gus|to /gʌstoʊ/ N-UNCOUNT [usu with N] If you do something with **gusto**, you do it with energetic and enthusiastic enjoyment. [APPROVAL] ❏ *Hers was a minor part, but she played it with gusto.*

gusty /gʌsti/ (gustier, gustiest) ADJ [usu ADJ n] **Gusty** winds are very strong and irregular. ❏ *Weather forecasts predict more high weather, gusty winds, and lightning strikes.*

gut /gʌt/ (guts, gutting, gutted) **1** N-PLURAL A person's or animal's **guts** are all the organs inside them. ❏ *By the time they finish, the crew are standing ankle-deep in fish guts.* **2** V-T When someone **guts** a dead animal or fish, they prepare it for cooking by removing all the organs from inside it. ❏ *It is not always necessary to gut the fish prior to freezing.* **3** N-SING [the/poss N] The **gut** is the tube inside the body of a person or animal through which food passes while it is being digested. ❏ *Toxins can leak from the gut into the bloodstream.* **4** N-UNCOUNT **Guts** is the will and courage to do something that is difficult or unpleasant, or which might have unpleasant results. [INFORMAL] ❏ *The new governor has the guts to push through unpopular tax increases.* **5** ADJ A **gut** feeling is based on instinct or emotion rather than reason. ❏ *Let's have your gut reaction to the facts as we know them.* **6** N-COUNT You can refer to someone's stomach as their **gut**, especially when it is very large and sticks out. [INFORMAL] ❏ *His gut sagged out over his belt.* **7** V-T To **gut** a building means to destroy the inside of it so that only its outside walls remain. ❏ *Over the weekend, a firebomb gutted a building where 60 people lived.* **8** N-UNCOUNT **Gut** is string made from part of the stomach of an animal. Traditionally, it is used to make the strings of sports rackets or musical instruments such as violins. ❏ *Gerald's violin strings are made of gut rather than steel.* **9** PHRASE If you **hate someone's guts**, you dislike them very much. [INFORMAL, EMPHASIS] ❏ *We hate each other's guts.* **10** PHRASE If you say that you **are working** your **guts out**, you are emphasizing that you are working as hard as you can. [INFORMAL, EMPHASIS] ❏ *Most have worked their guts out and made sacrifices.*

gut|less /gʌtlɪs/ ADJ If you describe someone as **gutless**, you think they have a weak character and lack courage or determination. [DISAPPROVAL] ❏ *By attacking me, by attacking my wife, he has proved himself to be a gutless coward.*

gutsy /gʌtsi/ (gutsier, gutsiest) ADJ If you describe someone as **gutsy**, you mean they show courage or determination. [INFORMAL, APPROVAL] ❏ *I've always been drawn to tough, gutsy women.* ❏ *They admired his gutsy and emotional speech.*

gut|ter /gʌtər/ (gutters) **1** N-COUNT The **gutter** is the edge of a road next to the pavement, where rainwater collects and flows away. ❏ *It is supposed to be washed down the gutter and into the city's vast sewerage system.* **2** N-COUNT A **gutter** is a plastic or metal channel attached to the lower edge of the roof of a building, which rainwater drains into. ❏ *Did you fix the gutter?* **3** N-SING If someone is in **the gutter**, they are very poor and live in a very bad way. ❏ *Instead of ending up in jail or in the gutter he was remarkably successful.*

gut|ter|ing /gʌtərɪŋ/ N-UNCOUNT **Guttering** consists of the plastic or metal channels attached to the lower edge of the roof of a building, which rainwater drains into.

gut|ter press N-SING You can refer to newspapers and magazines which print mainly stories about sex and crime as **the gutter press**. [BRIT, DISAPPROVAL]

in AM, use **scandal sheets**

gut|tur|al /gʌtərəl/ ADJ **Guttural** sounds are harsh sounds that are produced at the back of a person's throat. ❏ *Joe had a low, guttural voice with a Midwestern accent.*

gut-wrenching ADJ **Gut-wrenching** events or experiences make you feel extremely shocked or upset. [mainly JOURNALISM] ❏ *Going to court can be an expensive, time-consuming, and gut-wrenching experience that is best avoided.*

guy ◆◇◇ /gaɪ/ (guys) **1** N-COUNT A **guy** is a man. [INFORMAL] ❏ *I was working with a guy from Milwaukee.* **2** N-VOC; N-PLURAL [you N] Americans sometimes address a group of people, whether they are male or female, as **guys** or **you guys**. [INFORMAL] ❏ *Hi, guys. How are you doing?*

guy rope (guy ropes) N-COUNT A **guy rope** is a rope or wire that has one end fastened to a tent or pole and the other end fixed to the ground, so that it keeps the tent or pole in position.

guz|zle /gʌzəl/ (guzzles, guzzling, guzzled) **1** V-T/V-I If you **guzzle** something, you drink it or eat it quickly and greedily. [INFORMAL] ❏ *Melissa had guzzled gin and tonics like they were lemonade.* **2** V-T If you say that a vehicle **guzzles** fuel, you mean that it uses a lot of it in a way that is wasteful and unnecessary. ❏ *The plane was deafeningly noisy, guzzled fuel, and left a trail of smoke.* • **-guzzling** COMB IN ADJ [ADJ n] ❏ *The boom of the 1980s led to a taste for gas-guzzling cars.* ❏ *...big, energy-guzzling houses.* **3** → see also **gas guzzler**

gym /dʒɪm/ (gyms) **1** N-COUNT A **gym** is a club, building, or large room, usually containing special equipment, where people go to do physical exercise and get fit. ❏ *While the boys are golfing, I work out in the gym.* **2** N-UNCOUNT **Gym** is the

gymkhana activity of doing physical exercises in a gym, especially at school. □ ...*gym classes*.

gym|kha|na /dʒɪmkɑnə/ (gymkhanas) N-COUNT A **gymkhana** is an event in which people ride horses in competition.

gym|na|sium /dʒɪmneɪziəm/ (gymnasiums or gymnasia /dʒɪmneɪziə/) N-COUNT A **gymnasium** is the same as a **gym**. [FORMAL]

gym|nast /dʒɪmnæst/ (gymnasts) N-COUNT A **gymnast** is someone who is trained in gymnastics.

gym|nas|tics /dʒɪmnæstɪks/

The form **gymnastic** is used as a modifier.

N-UNCOUNT **Gymnastics** consists of physical exercises that develop your strength, coordination, and ease of movement. □ *She competes in gymnastics, with hopes of making it to the Olympics.*

gy|ne|col|ogy /gaɪnɪkɒlədʒi/

in BRIT, use **gynaecology**

N-UNCOUNT **Gynecology** is the branch of medical science that deals with women's diseases and medical conditions. • **gy|ne|colo|gist** (gynecologists) N-COUNT □ *Gynecologists at the hospital have successfully used the drug on 60 women.* • **gy|ne|co|logi|cal** /gaɪnɪkəlɒdʒɪkᵊl/ ADJ [ADJ n] □ *Breast examination is a part of a routine gynecological examination.*

gyp /dʒɪp/ (gyps, gypping, gypped) V-T To **gyp** someone means to cheat or swindle them. [mainly AM, INFORMAL, OFFENSIVE] □ *Bill came to believe he had been gypped.* □ *So you were gypped out of one quarter – twenty-five thousand dollars – of the promised amount?*

gyp|sum /dʒɪpsəm/ N-UNCOUNT **Gypsum** is a soft white substance that looks like chalk and which is used to make plaster of Paris.

Gyp|sy /dʒɪpsi/ (Gypsies) also **Gipsy** N-COUNT A **Gypsy** is a member of a race of people who travel from place to place, usually in caravans, rather than living in one place. Some Gypsies object to this name, and prefer to be called Romany. □ *I'm proud of being brought up by Gypsies.* • ADJ **Gypsy** is also an adjective. □ *...the largest Gypsy community of any country.*

gy|rate /dʒaɪreɪt/ (gyrates, gyrating, gyrated) **1** V-I If you **gyrate**, you dance or move your body quickly with circular movements. □ *The woman began to gyrate to the music.* □ *...a room stuffed full of gasping, gyrating bodies.* • **gy|ra|tion** /dʒaɪreɪʃᵊn/ (gyrations) N-COUNT [usu pl] □ *Prince continued his enthusiastic gyrations on stage.* **2** V-I To **gyrate** means to turn around and around in a circle, usually very fast. □ *The Sun, Moon, and the planets formed from a huge spinning gas cloud that collapsed into a gyrating disk.* **3** V-I If things such as prices or currencies **gyrate**, they move up and down in a rapid and uncontrolled way. [JOURNALISM] □ *Interest rates began to gyrate up toward 20 percent in 1980 and then down and up again.* • **gy|ra|tion** N-COUNT [usu pl, with supp] □ *...the gyrations of the currency markets.*

gyro /dʒaɪroʊ/ (gyros) N-COUNT A **gyro** is the same as a **gyroscope**. [AM, INFORMAL] □ *We have six gyros on board.*

gy|ro|scope /dʒaɪrəskoʊp/ (gyroscopes) N-COUNT A **gyroscope** is a device that contains a disc turning on an axis that can turn freely in any direction, so that the disc maintains the same position whatever the position or movement of the surrounding structure.

Hh

H also **h** /eɪtʃ/ (**H's, h's** /ˈeɪtʃɪz/) H is the eighth letter of the English alphabet.

ha

> The pronunciation /hɑ/ is used and the spelling **hah** is sometimes used in meaning **1**.

1 EXCLAM **Ha** is used in writing to represent a noise that people make to show they are surprised, annoyed, or pleased about something. ▫ *"Ha!" said James. "Think I'd trust you?"* **2** → see also **ha ha** **3 ha** is a written abbreviation for **hectare**.

ha|beas cor|pus /ˌheɪbiəs ˈkɔrpəs/ N-UNCOUNT **Habeas corpus** is a writ that states that a person cannot be kept in prison unless they have first been brought before a court of law, which decides whether it is legal for them to be kept in prison.

hab|er|dash|er /ˈhæbərdæʃər/ (**haberdashers**) **1** N-COUNT A **haberdasher** is a storekeeper who makes and sells men's clothes. [AM] **2** N-COUNT A **haberdasher** or a **haberdasher's** is a store where men's clothes are sold. [AM]

hab|er|dash|ery /ˈhæbərdæʃəri/ (**haberdasheries**) **1** N-UNCOUNT **Haberdashery** is men's clothing sold in a store. [AM] **2** N-UNCOUNT **Haberdashery** is small articles for sewing, such as buttons, zippers, and thread, which are sold in a haberdasher's store. [BRIT]

> in AM, use **notions**

3 N-COUNT A **haberdashery** is a store selling haberdashery.

hab|it ♦◇◇ /ˈhæbɪt/ (**habits**) **1** N-VAR A **habit** is something that you do often or regularly. ▫ *He has an endearing habit of licking his lips when he's nervous.* ▫ *Many people add salt to their food out of habit, without even tasting it first.* **2** N-COUNT A **habit** is an action considered bad that someone does repeatedly and finds it difficult to stop doing. ▫ *A good way to break the habit of eating too quickly is to put your knife and fork down after each mouthful.* **3** N-COUNT A drug **habit** is an addiction to a drug such as heroin or cocaine. ▫ *She became a prostitute in order to pay for her cocaine habit.* **4** PHRASE If you say that someone is **a creature of habit**, you mean that they usually do the same thing at the same time each day, rather than doing new and different things. ▫ *Jesse is a creature of habit and always eats breakfast.* **5** PHRASE If you are **in the habit of** doing something, you do it regularly or often. If you **get into the habit of** doing something, you begin to do it regularly or often. ▫ *They were in the habit of giving two or three dinner parties a month.* **6** PHRASE If you **make a habit of** doing something, you do it regularly or often. ▫ *You can phone me at work as long as you don't make a habit of it.*

SYNONYMS

habit
NOUN **1**
mannerism: *His mannerisms are more those of a preoccupied math professor.*
way: *He denounces people who urge him to alter his ways.*
quirk: *Brown was fascinated by people's quirks and foibles.*
foible: *...human foibles and weaknesses.*
idiosyncrasy: *Everyone has a few little idiosyncrasies.*

---

hab|it|able /ˈhæbɪtəbəl/ ADJ If a place is **habitable**, it is good enough for people to live in. ▫ *Making the house habitable was a major undertaking.*

habi|tat /ˈhæbɪtæt/ (**habitats**) **1** N-VAR The **habitat** of an animal or plant is the natural environment in which it normally lives or grows. ▫ *In its natural habitat, the hibiscus will grow up to 25 ft.* **2** → See feature box at **deforest, ecosystem, endanger**

habi|ta|tion /ˌhæbɪˈteɪʃən/ N-UNCOUNT **Habitation** is the activity of living somewhere. [FORMAL] ▫ *The recent survey found that 20 percent of rented dwellings are unfit for human habitation.*

ha|bitu|al /həˈbɪtʃuəl/ **1** ADJ A **habitual** action, state, or way of behaving is one that someone usually does or has, especially one that is considered to be typical or characteristic of them. ▫ *If bad posture becomes habitual, you risk long-term effects.* • **ha|bitu|al|ly** ADV ▫ *His mother had a patient who habitually flew into rages.* **2** ADJ [ADJ n] You use **habitual** to describe someone who usually or often does a particular thing. ▫ *Three out of four of them would become habitual criminals if actually sent to jail.*

ha|bitu|at|ed /həˈbɪtʃueɪtɪd/ ADJ If you are **habituated** to something, you have become used to it. [FORMAL] ▫ *People in the area are habituated to the idea of learning from the person above how to do the work.*

ha|bitué /həˈbɪtʃueɪ/ (**habitués**) N-COUNT [usu with supp, oft N *of* n] Someone who is a **habitué** of a particular place often visits that place. [FORMAL] ▫ *Kiki and Man Ray, who lived just down the street, were habitués of this bar.*

haci|en|da /ˌhæsiˈendə/ (**haciendas**) N-COUNT A **hacienda** is a large ranch or plantation, especially in a Spanish-speaking country. ▫ *...an old colonial coffee hacienda in the Andes.*

hack /hæk/ (**hacks, hacking, hacked**) **1** V-T/V-I If you **hack** something or **hack** at it, you cut it with strong, rough strokes using a sharp tool such as an ax or a knife. ▫ *An armed gang barged onto the train and began hacking and shooting anyone in sight.* ▫ *Matthew desperately hacked through the leather.* **2** V-I If someone **hacks into** a computer system, they break into the system, especially in order to get secret information. ▫ *The saboteurs had demanded money in return for revealing how they hacked into the systems.* • **hack|ing** N-UNCOUNT ▫ *...the common and often illegal art of computer hacking.* **3** N-COUNT If you refer to a politician as a **hack**, you disapprove of them because they are too loyal to their party and perhaps do not deserve the position they have. [DISAPPROVAL] ▫ *Far too many party hacks from the old days still hold influential jobs.* **4** N-COUNT If you refer to a professional writer, such as a journalist, as a **hack**, you disapprove of them because they write for money without worrying very much about the quality of their writing. [DISAPPROVAL] ▫ *...tabloid hacks, always eager to find victims in order to sell newspapers.* **5** N-COUNT A **hack** is the same as a **taxi**. [AM] ▫ *I will pay for a hack. There is no need for you to return home on foot.* **6** PHRASE If you say that someone **can't hack it** or **couldn't hack it**, you mean that they do not or did not have the qualities needed to do a task or cope with a situation. [INFORMAL] ▫ *You have to be strong and confident, and never give the slightest impression that you can't hack it.* **7** → See feature box at **email**

hack|er /ˈhækər/ (**hackers**) N-COUNT A computer **hacker** is someone who tries to break into computer systems, especially in order to get secret information. ▫ *...a hacker who steals credit card numbers.*

hack|ing /ˈhækɪŋ/ **1** ADJ [ADJ n] A **hacking** cough is a dry, painful cough with a harsh, unpleasant sound. **2** → see also **hack**

hack|les /ˈhækəlz/ PHRASE If something **raises** your **hackles** or makes your **hackles rise**, it makes you feel angry and hostile.

hack|neyed /ˈhæknid/ ADJ If you describe something such as a saying or an image as **hackneyed**, you think it is no longer likely to interest, amuse, or affect people because it has been used, seen, or heard many times before. ❑ *Power corrupts and absolute power corrupts absolutely. That's the old hackneyed phrase, but it's true.*

hack|saw /hæksɔː/ (**hacksaws**) **1** N-COUNT A **hacksaw** is a small saw used for cutting metal. **2** → See also color supplement

had

> The auxiliary verb is pronounced /həd, STRONG hæd/. For the main verb, and for meanings **2** to **5**, the pronunciation is /hæd/.

1 Had is the past tense and past participle of **have**. **2** AUX **Had** is sometimes used instead of 'if' to begin a clause which refers to a situation that might have happened but did not. For example, the clause 'had she been elected' means the same as 'if she had been elected.' ❑ *Had he succeeded, he would have acquired a monopoly.* **3** PHRASE If you **have been had**, someone has tricked you, for example by selling you something at too high a price. [INFORMAL] ❑ *If your customer thinks he's been had, you have to make him happy.* **4** PHRASE If you say that someone **has had it**, you mean they are in very serious trouble or have no hope of succeeding. [INFORMAL] ❑ *But if the teacher is unsympathetic, you've had it.* **5** PHRASE If you say that you **have had it**, you mean that you are very tired of something or very annoyed about it, and do not want to continue doing it or it to continue happening. [INFORMAL] ❑ *I've had it. Let's call it a day.*

had|dock /hædək/ (**haddock**) N-VAR **Haddock** is a type of edible saltwater fish found in the North Atlantic. ❑ *...fishing boats which normally catch a mix of cod, haddock, and whiting.* • N-UNCOUNT **Haddock** is this fish eaten as food.

Ha|des /heɪdiːz/ N-PROPER In Greek mythology, **Hades** was a place under the earth where people went after they died.

hadn't /hædənt/ **Hadn't** is the usual spoken form of 'had not.'

haema|tol|ogy /hiːmətɒlədʒi/ → see **hematology**

haemo|glo|bin /hiːməgloʊbɪn/ → see **hemoglobin**

haemo|philia /hiːməfɪliə/ → see **hemophilia**

haemo|phili|ac /hiːməfɪliæk/ → see **hemophiliac**

haem|or|rhage /hɛmərɪdʒ/ → see **hemorrhage**

haem|or|rhoid /hɛmərɔɪd/ → see **hemorrhoid**

hag /hæg/ (**hags**) N-COUNT If someone refers to a woman as a **hag**, they mean that she is ugly, old, and unpleasant. [OFFENSIVE, DISAPPROVAL]

hag|gard /hægərd/ ADJ Someone who looks **haggard** has a tired expression and shadows under their eyes, especially because they are ill or have not had enough sleep. ❑ *He was pale and a bit haggard.*

hag|gis /hægɪs/ (**haggises**) N-VAR A **haggis** is a large sausage, usually shaped like a ball, which is made from minced sheep's meat contained inside the skin from a sheep's stomach. **Haggis** is traditionally made and eaten in Scotland.

hag|gle /hægəl/ (**haggles, haggling, haggled**) V-RECIP If you **haggle**, you argue about something before reaching an agreement, especially about the cost of something that you are buying. ❑ *Ella showed her the best places to go for a good buy, and taught her how to haggle with used furniture dealers.* ❑ *Of course he'll still haggle over the price.* • **hag|gling** N-UNCOUNT ❑ *After months of haggling, they recovered only three-quarters of what they had lent.*

hah /hɑː/ → see **ha**

ha ha also **ha ha ha 1** EXCLAM **Ha ha** is used in writing to represent the sound that people make when they laugh. ❑ *I dropped my bag at the officer's feet. The bank notes fell out. "Ha ha ha!" he laughed. "Got no money, uh?"* **2** EXCLAM People sometimes say '**ha ha**' to show that they are not amused by what you have said, or do not believe it. [SPOKEN] ❑ *He said "vegetarians unite," and I looked at him and said "yeah, ha ha."*

hai|ku /haɪkuː/ (**haikus** or **haiku**) N-VAR A **haiku** is a short poem consisting of words with a total of seventeen syllables, arranged on three lines.

hail /heɪl/ (**hails, hailing, hailed**) **1** V-T [usu passive] If a person, event, or achievement **is hailed** as important or successful, they are praised publicly. ❑ *Faulkner has been hailed as the greatest American novelist of his generation.* **2** N-UNCOUNT **Hail** consists of small balls of ice that fall like rain from the sky. ❑ *...a sharp short-lived storm with heavy hail.* **3** V-I When it **hails**, hail falls like rain from the sky. ❑ *It started to hail, huge great stones.* **4** N-SING A **hail of** things, usually small objects, is a large number of them that hit you at the same time and with great force. ❑ *The victim was hit by a hail of bullets.* **5** V-I Someone who **hails from** a particular place was born there or lives there. [FORMAL] ❑ *He hails from Memphis.* **6** V-T If you **hail** a taxi, you wave at it in order to stop it because you want the driver to take you somewhere. ❑ *I hurried away to hail a taxi.*

Hail Mary /heɪl mɛəri/ (**Hail Marys**) N-COUNT A **Hail Mary** is a prayer to the Virgin Mary that is said by Roman Catholics.

hail|stone /heɪlstoʊn/ (**hailstones**) N-COUNT [usu pl] **Hailstones** are small balls of ice that fall like rain from the sky.

hail|storm /heɪlstɔːrm/ (**hailstorms**) also **hail storm** N-COUNT A **hailstorm** is a storm during which it hails.

hair ♦♦◇ /hɛər/ (**hairs**) **1** N-VAR Your **hair** is the fine threads that grow in a mass on your head. ❑ *I wash my hair every night.* ❑ *I get some gray hairs but I pull them out.* **2** N-VAR **Hair** is the short, fine threads that grow on different parts of your body. ❑ *The majority of men have hair on their chest.* **3** N-VAR **Hair** is the threads that cover the body of an animal such as a dog, or make up a horse's mane and tail. ❑ *I am allergic to cat hair.* **4** PHRASE If you **let** your **hair down**, you relax completely and enjoy yourself. ❑ *...the world-famous Oktoberfest, a time when everyone in Munich really lets their hair down.* **5** PHRASE Something that **makes** your **hair stand on end** shocks or frightens you very much. ❑ *This was the kind of smile that made your hair stand on end.* **6** PHRASE If you say that someone has **not a hair out of place**, you are emphasizing that they are extremely neat and well dressed. [EMPHASIS] ❑ *She had a lot of makeup on and not a hair out of place.* **7** PHRASE If you say that someone **is splitting hairs**, you mean that they are making unnecessary distinctions between things when the differences between them are so small they are not important. ❑ *Don't split hairs. You know what I'm getting at.*

hair|brush /hɛərbrʌʃ/ (**hairbrushes**) N-COUNT A **hairbrush** is a brush that you use to brush your hair.

hair care also **haircare** N-UNCOUNT **Hair care** is all the things people do to keep their hair clean, healthy looking, and attractive. ❑ *...an American maker of haircare products.*

hair|cut /hɛərkʌt/ (**haircuts**) **1** N-COUNT If you get a **haircut**, someone cuts your hair for you. ❑ *Your hair is all right; it's just that you need a haircut.* **2** N-COUNT A **haircut** is the style in which your hair has been cut. ❑ *Who's that guy with the funny haircut?*

hair|do /hɛərduː/ (**hairdos**) N-COUNT A **hairdo** is the style in which your hair has been cut and arranged. [INFORMAL]

hair|dresser /hɛərdrɛsər/ (**hairdressers**) **1** N-COUNT A **hairdresser** is a person who cuts, colors, and arranges people's hair. **2** N-COUNT A **hairdresser** or a **hairdresser's** is a place where a hairdresser works. ❑ *I work in this new hairdresser's.*

hair|dressing /hɛərdrɛsɪŋ/ N-UNCOUNT **Hairdressing** is the job or activity of cutting, coloring, and arranging people's hair. ❑ *...personal services such as hairdressing and dry cleaning.*

hair|dry|er /hɛərdraɪər/ (**hairdryers**) also **hairdrier** N-COUNT A **hairdryer** is a machine that you use to dry your hair.

-haired /-hɛərd/ COMB IN ADJ **-haired** combines with adjectives to describe the length, color, or type of hair that someone has. ❑ *He was a small, dark-haired man.*

hair|grip /hɛərgrɪp/ (**hairgrips**) also **hair-grip** N-COUNT A **hairgrip** is a small piece of metal or plastic bent back on itself, which you use to hold your hair in position. [BRIT]

> in AM, use **bobby pin**

hair|less /hɛərlɪs/ ADJ A part of your body that is **hairless** has no hair on it.

hair|line /hɛərlaɪn/ (**hairlines**) **1** N-COUNT [usu sing, oft poss N] Your **hairline** is the edge of the area where your hair grows on your head. ❑ *Joanne had a small dark birthmark near her hairline.* **2** ADJ [ADJ n] A **hairline** crack or gap is very narrow or fine. ❑ *He suffered a hairline fracture of the right index finger.* **3** → See feature box at **appearance**

hair|net /hɛərnɛt/ (**hairnets**) N-COUNT A **hairnet** is a small net that can be worn over the hair in order to keep it in place.

hair|piece /hɛərpiːs/ (**hairpieces**) N-COUNT A **hairpiece** is a piece of false hair that some people wear on their head if they are bald or if they want to make their own hair seem longer or thicker.

hair|pin /hɛərpɪn/ (hairpins) **1** N-COUNT A **hairpin** is a thin piece of metal wire bent back on itself which someone uses to hold their hair in position. **2** N-COUNT A **hairpin** is the same as a **hairpin turn**.

hair|pin turn (hairpin turns) N-COUNT A **hairpin turn** or a **hairpin** is a very sharp bend in a road, where the road turns back in the opposite direction. [AM]

hair-raising ADJ A **hair-raising** experience, event, or story is very frightening but can also be exciting. ❑ ...stories of spying, abductions, hair-raising chases and narrow escapes.

hair's breadth N-SING [a N] A **hair's breadth** is a very small degree or amount. ❑ The dollar fell to within a hair's breadth of its all-time low.

hair shirt (hair shirts) **1** N-COUNT A **hair shirt** is a shirt made of rough uncomfortable cloth which some religious people used to wear to punish themselves. **2** N-COUNT If you say that someone is wearing a **hair shirt**, you mean that they are trying to punish themselves to show they are sorry for something they have done. ❑ No one is asking you to put on a hair shirt and give up all your luxuries.

hair|spray /hɛərspreɪ/ (hairsprays) N-MASS **Hairspray** is a sticky substance that you spray out of a can onto your hair in order to hold it in place.

hair|style /hɛərstaɪl/ (hairstyles) N-COUNT Your **hairstyle** is the style in which your hair has been cut or arranged. ❑ I think her new short hairstyle looks simply great.

hair|stylist /hɛərstaɪlɪst/ (hairstylists) also **hair stylist** N-COUNT A **hairstylist** is someone who cuts and arranges people's hair, especially in order to get them ready for a photograph or movie.

hair-trigger ADJ [ADJ n] If you describe something as **hair-trigger**, you mean that it is likely to change very violently and suddenly. ❑ His boozing, arrogance, and hair-trigger temper have often led him into ugly nightclub brawls. ❑ A hair-trigger situation has been created which could lead to an outbreak of war at any time.

hairy /hɛəri/ (hairier, hairiest) **1** ADJ Someone or something that is **hairy** is covered with hairs. ❑ He was wearing shorts which showed his long, muscular, hairy legs. **2** ADJ If you describe a situation as **hairy**, you mean that it is exciting, worrying, and somewhat frightening. [INFORMAL] ❑ His driving was a bit hairy.

hajj /hædʒ/ also **haj, Hajj** N-SING [usu the N] In the Islamic religion, the **hajj** is the pilgrimage to Mecca that Muslims are required to make. ❑ Some 50,000 Nigerian Muslims annually go on the Hajj to Mecca in Saudi Arabia.

hake /heɪk/ (hake) N-VAR A **hake** is a type of large edible saltwater fish. • N-UNCOUNT Hake is this fish eaten as food.

halal /həlɑːl/ N-UNCOUNT [usu N n] **Halal** is meat from animals that have been killed according to Muslim law. ❑ ...a halal butcher's shop.

hal|cy|on /hælsiən/ ADJ [ADJ n] A **halcyon** time is a time in the past that was peaceful or happy. [LITERARY] ❑ It was all a far cry from those halcyon days in 1990, when he won three tournaments around the European tour.

hale /heɪl/ ADJ [usu v-link ADJ] If you describe people, especially people who are old, as **hale**, you mean that they are healthy. [OLD-FASHIONED] ❑ She is remarkable and I'd like to see her remain hale and hearty for years yet.

half ✦✦✦ /hæf/ (halves /hævz/) **1** FRACTION **Half** of a number, an amount, or an object is one of two equal parts that together make up the whole number, amount, or object. ❑ She wore a diamond ring worth half a million dollars. ❑ More than half of all U.S. households are heated with natural gas. • PREDET **Half** is also a predeterminer. ❑ We just sat and talked for half an hour or so. ❑ They had only received half the money promised. • ADJ [ADJ n] **Half** is also an adjective. ❑ ...a half measure of fresh lemon juice. **2** ADV You use **half** to say that something is only partly the case or happens to only a limited extent. ❑ His eyes were half closed. ❑ His refrigerator frequently looked half empty. **3** N-COUNT In games such as football, soccer, rugby, and basketball, games are divided into two equal periods of time which are called **halves**. ❑ The only goal was scored by Jakobsen early in the second half. **4** ADV [ADV adj] You use **half** to say that someone has parents of different nationalities. For example, if you are **half** German, one of your parents is German but the other is not. ❑ She was half Italian and half English. **5** PHRASE You use **half past** to refer to a time that is thirty minutes after a particular hour. ❑ "What time were you planning lunch?"—"Half past twelve, if that's convenient." **6** ADV [ADV adj] You can use **half** before an adjective describing an extreme quality, as a way of emphasizing and exaggerating something. [INFORMAL, EMPHASIS] ❑ He felt half dead with tiredness. • PREDET **Half** can also be used in this way with a noun referring to a long period of time or a large quantity. ❑ I thought about you half the night. **7** ADV You use **not half** to emphasize a negative quality that someone has. [EMPHASIS] ❑ You're not half the man you think you are. **8** PHRASE If two people **go halves**, they divide the cost of something equally between them. ❑ She went halves on gas.

COLLOCATIONS

half
NOUN
1
adjective + **half**: first, latter, second; bottom, left, right, upper; eastern, northern, southern, western
3
adjective + **half**: first, opening, second
verb + **half**: dominate; start

---

half-assed ADJ [usu ADJ n] **Half-assed** remarks, ideas, or actions are poorly planned or poorly performed. [mainly AM, VULGAR, DISAPPROVAL] ❑ ...a half-assed comment I'd made on television. ❑ The organization does a pretty half-assed job of running many of the national parks.

half|back /hæfbæk/ (halfbacks) also **half back, half-back** N-COUNT In football, a **halfback** is an attacking player who stands behind the front line and runs with the ball. ❑ Berwanger was a halfback for the University of Chicago Maroons.

half-baked ADJ [usu ADJ n] If you describe an idea or plan as **half-baked**, you mean that it has not been properly thought out, and so is stupid or impractical. [DISAPPROVAL] ❑ This is another half-baked scheme that isn't going to work.

half brother (half brothers) N-COUNT Someone's **half brother** is a boy or man who has either the same mother or the same father as they have.

half-day (half-days) also **half day** N-COUNT A **half-day** is a day when you work only in the morning or in the afternoon, but not all day. ❑ "If I could have just what I wanted," Sharon mused, "I'd work half days."

half|heart|ed /hæfhɑːrtɪd/ ADJ If someone does something in a **halfhearted** way, they do it without any real effort, interest, or enthusiasm. ❑ ...a halfhearted apology. • **half|heart|ed|ly** ADV [ADV with v] ❑ I can't do anything halfheartedly. I have to do everything 100 percent.

half-hour (half-hours) N-COUNT [oft N n] A **half-hour** is a period of thirty minutes. ❑ ...a lecture which led to a half-hour of stimulating dialogue afterwards. ❑ ...the half-hour wait before he was rescued.

half-life (half-lives) also **half life** N-COUNT The **half-life** of a radioactive substance is the amount of time that it takes to lose half its radioactivity.

half-mast PHRASE [usu PHR after v] If a flag is flying **at half-mast**, it is flying from the middle of the pole, not the top, to show respect and sorrow for someone who has just died.

half meas|ure (half measures) also **half-measure** N-COUNT [usu pl] If someone refers to policies or actions as **half measures**, they are critical of them because they think that they are not forceful enough and are therefore of little value. [DISAPPROVAL] ❑ They have already declared their intention to fight on rather than settle for half-measures.

half note (half notes) N-COUNT A **half note** is a musical note that has a time value equal to two quarter notes. [AM]

half-price **1** ADJ If something is **half-price**, it costs only half what it usually costs. ❑ Main courses are half price from 12:30 p.m. to 2 p.m. ❑ A half-price suit still cost $400. **2** N-UNCOUNT If something is sold at or for **half-price**, it is sold for only half of what it usually costs. ❑ By yesterday she was selling off stock at half-price.

half sister (half sisters) N-COUNT Someone's **half sister** is a girl or woman who has either the same mother or the same father as they have.

half-timbered ADJ Half-timbered is used to describe old buildings that have wooden beams showing in the brick and plaster walls, both on the inside and the outside of the building.

half|time /hæftaɪm/ N-UNCOUNT Halftime is the short period of time between the two parts of a sports event such as a football, rugby, or basketball game, when the players take a short rest. ☐ *The game started in brilliant sunshine but during halftime fog closed in.*

half-truth (half-truths) also half truth N-COUNT If you describe statements as **half-truths**, you mean that they are only partly based on fact and are intended or likely to deceive people. ☐ *The article had been full of errors and half truths.*

half|way /hæfweɪ/ **1** ADV Halfway means in the middle of a place or between two points, at an equal distance from each of them. ☐ *He was halfway up the ladder.* **2** ADV [ADV prep/adv] Halfway means in the middle of a period of time or of an event. ☐ *By then, it was October and we were more than halfway through our tour.* • ADJ [ADJ n] Halfway is also an adjective. ☐ *Cleveland held a 12-point advantage at the halfway point.* **3** PHRASE If you **meet** someone **halfway**, you accept some of the points they are making so that you can come to an agreement with them. ☐ *The Democrats are willing to meet the president halfway.* **4** ADV [ADV adj] Halfway means fairly or reasonably. [INFORMAL] ☐ *You need hard currency to get anything halfway decent.*

half|way house (halfway houses) **1** N-COUNT A **halfway house** is a home for people such as former prisoners, psychiatric patients, or drug addicts who can stay there for a limited period of time to get used to life outside prison or a hospital. **2** N-SING A **halfway house** is an arrangement or thing that has some of the qualities of two different things. ☐ *...a halfway house between traditional and third-generation cellular networks.*

half-wit (half-wits) also halfwit **1** N-COUNT If you describe someone as a **half-wit**, you think they have behaved in a stupid, silly, or irresponsible way. [INFORMAL, DISAPPROVAL] **2** N-COUNT A **half-wit** is a person who has little intelligence. [OLD-FASHIONED]

half-witted ADJ If you describe someone as **half-witted**, you think they are very stupid, silly, or irresponsible. [INFORMAL, DISAPPROVAL]

half-yearly **1** ADJ [ADJ n] Half-yearly means happening in the middle of a calendar year or a financial year. [BRIT]

in AM, use **semiannual**

2 ADJ [ADJ n] A company's **half-yearly** profits are the profits that it makes in six months. [BRIT]

in AM, use **semiannual**

hali|but /hælɪbət/ (halibut) N-VAR A **halibut** is a large flat fish. • N-UNCOUNT Halibut is this fish eaten as food.

hali|to|sis /hælɪtoʊsɪs/ N-UNCOUNT If someone has **halitosis**, their breath smells unpleasant. [FORMAL]

hall ♦♢♢ /hɔːl/ (halls) **1** N-COUNT The **hall** in a house or an apartment is the area just inside the front door, into which some of the other rooms open. ☐ *The lights were on in the hall and in the bedroom.* **2** N-COUNT A **hall** in a building is a long passage with doors into rooms on both sides of it. [mainly AM] ☐ *There are 10 rooms along each hall.* **3** N-COUNT A **hall** is a large room or building which is used for public events such as concerts, exhibitions, and meetings. ☐ *We picked up our conference materials and filed into the lecture hall.* **4** → see also **town hall**

hal|le|lu|jah /hælɪluːjə/ also alleluia **1** EXCLAM Hallelujah is used in religious songs and worship as an exclamation of praise and thanks to God. **2** EXCLAM People sometimes say 'Hallelujah!' when they are pleased that something they have been waiting a long time for has finally happened. ☐ *Hallelujah! College days are over!*

hall|mark /hɔːlmɑːrk/ (hallmarks) **1** N-COUNT The **hallmark** of something or someone is their most typical quality or feature. ☐ *It's a technique that has become the hallmark of his movies.* **2** N-COUNT A **hallmark** is an official mark put on things made of gold, silver, or platinum that indicates the quality of the metal, where the object was made, and who made it. ☐ *Early pieces of Scottish silver carry the hallmarks of individual silversmiths.*

hal|lo /hæloʊ/ → see **hello**

hall of fame (halls of fame) **1** N-SING [with supp] If you say that someone is a member of a particular **hall of fame**, you mean that they are one of the most famous people in that area of activity. ☐ *She certainly scaled the heights of fashion's hall of fame.* **2** N-COUNT A **hall of fame** is a type of museum where people can see things relating to famous people who are connected with a particular area of activity.

hall of resi|dence (halls of residence) **1** N-COUNT Halls of residence are buildings with rooms or apartments, usually built by universities or colleges, in which students live during the term. [mainly BRIT]

in AM, use **dormitory**

2 → See feature box at **university**

hal|lowed /hæloʊd/ **1** ADJ [ADJ n] Hallowed is used to describe something that is respected and admired, usually because it is old, important, or has a good reputation. ☐ *They protested that there was no place for a school of commerce in their hallowed halls of learning.* **2** ADJ [ADJ n] Hallowed is used to describe something that is considered to be holy. ☐ *...hallowed ground.*

Hal|low|een /hæloʊiːn/ also Hallowe'en N-UNCOUNT Halloween is the night of the 31st of October and is traditionally said to be the time when ghosts and witches can be seen. On Halloween, children often dress up in costumes and go from door to door asking their neighbors for candy.

hal|lu|ci|nate /həluːsɪneɪt/ (hallucinates, hallucinating, hallucinated) V-I If you **hallucinate**, you see things that are not really there, either because you are ill or because you have taken a drug. ☐ *Hunger made him hallucinate.*

hal|lu|ci|na|tion /həluːsɪneɪʃən/ (hallucinations) N-VAR A **hallucination** is the experience of seeing something that is not really there because you are ill or have taken a drug. ☐ *The drug induces hallucinations at high doses.*

hal|lu|ci|na|tory /həluːsɪnətɔːri/ ADJ [usu ADJ n] Hallucinatory is used to describe something that is like a hallucination or is the cause of a hallucination. ☐ *It was an unsettling show. There was a hallucinatory feel from the start.*

hal|lu|cino|gen /həluːsɪnədʒən/ (hallucinogens) N-COUNT A **hallucinogen** is a substance such as a drug which makes you hallucinate.

hal|lu|ci|no|gen|ic /həluːsɪnədʒɛnɪk/ ADJ [usu ADJ n] A **hallucinogenic** drug is one that makes you hallucinate.

hall|way /hɔːlweɪ/ (hallways) **1** N-COUNT A **hallway** in a building is a long passage with doors into rooms on both sides of it. ☐ *They took the elevator up to the third floor and walked along the quiet hallway.* **2** N-COUNT A **hallway** in a house or an apartment is the area just inside the front door, into which some of the other rooms open. ☐ *...the coats hanging in the hallway.*

halo /heɪloʊ/ (haloes or halos) N-COUNT A **halo** is a circle of light that is shown in pictures around the head of a holy figure such as a saint or angel.

halo|gen /hælədʒən/ (halogens) N-VAR [oft N n] A **halogen** is one of a group of chemical elements that includes chlorine, fluorine, and iodine. Halogens are often used in lighting and heating devices. ☐ *...a halogen lamp.*

halt ♦♢♢ /hɔːlt/ (halts, halting, halted) **1** V-T/V-I When a person or a vehicle **halts** or when something **halts** them, they stop moving in the direction they were going and stand still. ☐ *They halted at a short distance from the house.* **2** V-T/V-I When something such as growth, development, or activity **halts** or when you **halt** it, it stops completely. ☐ *Striking workers halted production at the auto plant yesterday.* **3** PHRASE If someone **calls a halt to** something such as an activity, they decide not to continue with it or to end it immediately. ☐ *The Russian government had called a halt to the construction of a new project in the Rostov region.* **4** PHRASE If someone or something comes **to a halt**, they stop moving. ☐ *The elevator creaked to a halt at the ground floor.* **5** PHRASE If something such as growth, development, or activity comes or grinds **to a halt** or is brought **to a halt**, it stops completely. ☐ *Her political career came to a halt in December 2008.*

COLLOCATIONS

halt
VERB ②
halt + *noun*: construction, growth, production; decline, slide, spread
halt + *adverb*: abruptly, briefly, suddenly, temporarily

---

hal|ter /hɔltər/ (**halters**) ① N-COUNT A piece of clothing with a **halter** has a strap that goes around the back of the neck, rather than a strap over each shoulder. • ADJ [ADJ n] **Halter** is also an adjective. ☐ *She wore shorts and a halter top.* ② N-COUNT A **halter** is a piece of leather or rope that is fastened around the head of a horse so that it can be led easily.

hal|ter|neck /hɔltərnɛk/ → see **halter** 1

halt|ing /hɔltɪŋ/ ADJ If you speak or do something in a **halting** way, you speak or do it slowly and with a lot of hesitation, usually because you are uncertain about what to say or do next. ☐ *In a halting voice she said that she wished to make a statement.* • **halt|ing|ly** ADV [ADV with v] ☐ *She spoke haltingly of her deep upset and hurt.*

halve /hæv/ (**halves, halving, halved**) ① V-T/V-I When you **halve** something or when it **halves**, it is reduced to half its previous size or amount. ☐ *Dr. Lee believes that men who exercise can halve their risk of colon cancer.* ② V-T If you **halve** something, you divide it into two equal parts. ☐ *Halve the pineapple and scoop out the inside.* ③ **Halves** is the plural of **half**.

ham /hæm/ (**hams**) N-VAR **Ham** is meat from the top of the back leg of a pig, specially treated so that it can be kept for a long period of time. ☐ *...ham sandwiches.*

ham|burg|er /hæmbɜrgər/ (**hamburgers**) N-COUNT A **hamburger** is ground meat which has been shaped into a flat circle. Hamburgers are fried or grilled and then eaten, often on a bun.

WORD HISTORY

hamburger
Hamburgers are named after their city of origin, Hamburg in Germany. The word 'hamburger' has nothing to do with ham, but the 'burger' part has now been taken as a noun in its own right, on the basis of which we now have veggieburgers, cheeseburgers, and so on.

---

ham-fisted ADJ If you describe someone as **ham-fisted**, you mean that they are clumsy, especially in the way that they use their hands. ☐ *They can all be made in minutes by even the most ham-fisted of cooks.*

ham|let /hæmlɪt/ (**hamlets**) N-COUNT A **hamlet** is a very small village.

ham|mer /hæmər/ (**hammers, hammering, hammered**) ① N-COUNT A **hammer** is a tool that consists of a heavy piece of metal at the end of a handle. It is used, for example, to hit nails into a piece of wood or a wall, or to break things into pieces. ☐ *He used a hammer and chisel to chip away at the wall.* ② V-T If you **hammer** an object such as a nail, you hit it with a hammer. ☐ *To avoid damaging the tree, hammer a wooden peg into the hole.* ③ V-T If you **hammer** on a surface, you hit it several times in order to make a noise, or to emphasize something you are saying when you are angry. ☐ *We had to hammer and shout before they would open up.* ☐ *A crowd of reporters was hammering on the door.* ④ V-T/V-I If you **hammer** something such as an idea into people or you **hammer** at it, you keep repeating it forcefully so that it will have an effect on people. ☐ *He hammered it into me that I had not suddenly become a rotten goalkeeper.* ⑤ V-T If you say that someone **hammers** another person, you mean that they attack, criticize, or punish the other person severely. ☐ *Democrats insisted they will continue to hammer the President on his tax plan.* ⑥ V-T In sports, if you say that one player or team **hammered** another, you mean that the first player or team defeated the second completely and easily. ☐ *He hammered the young left-hander in three straight sets.* ⑦ N-COUNT In track and field, a **hammer** is a heavy weight on a piece of wire, which the athlete throws as far as possible. • N-SING The **hammer** also refers to the sport of throwing the hammer. ☐ *Events like the hammer and the discus are not traditional crowd-pleasers in the West.* ⑧ N-COUNT The **hammer** is the largest bone of the three small bones in the ear of mammals. ⑨ PHRASE If you say that someone was going at something **hammer and tongs**, you mean that they were doing it with great energy. ☐ *He loved gardening. He went at it hammer and tongs as soon as he got back from work.* ☐ *They yell, shout and argue. For six hours a night they go at it, hammer and tongs.* ⑩ → See also color supplement

▶ **hammer out** PHRASAL VERB If people **hammer out** an agreement or treaty, they succeed in producing it after a long or difficult discussion. ☐ *I think we can hammer out a solution.*

ham|mock /hæmək/ (**hammocks**) ① N-COUNT A **hammock** is a piece of strong cloth or netting which is hung between two supports and used as a bed. ② → See also color supplement

ham|per /hæmpər/ (**hampers, hampering, hampered**) ① V-T If someone or something **hampers** you, they make it difficult for you to do what you are trying to do. ☐ *The bad weather hampered rescue operations.* ② N-COUNT A **hamper** is a basket containing food of various kinds that is given to people as a present. ☐ *...a luxury food hamper.* ③ N-COUNT A **hamper** is a large basket with a lid, used especially for carrying food. ☐ *...a picnic hamper.* ④ N-COUNT A **hamper** is a storage container for soiled clothing. ☐ *He tossed his damp towel into the laundry hamper.*

ham|ster /hæmstər/ (**hamsters**) N-COUNT A **hamster** is a small furry animal which is similar to a mouse, and which is often kept as a pet.

ham|string /hæmstrɪŋ/ (**hamstrings, hamstringing, hamstrung**) ① N-COUNT A **hamstring** is a length of tissue or tendon behind your knee which joins the muscles of your thigh to the bones of your lower leg. ☐ *Webster has not played since suffering a hamstring injury in the opening game.* ② V-T [usu v-link ADJ by n] If you are **hamstrung** by a person, problem, or difficulty, they make it very difficult for you to take any action. ☐ *Rural schools were hamstrung by their inability to attract and keep experienced staff.*

HAND

① NOUN USES AND PHRASES
② VERB USES

---

① **hand** ♦♦♦ /hænd/ (**hands**)
→ Please look at meanings ㊳ – ㊵ to see if the expression you are looking for is shown under another headword.

① N-COUNT Your **hands** are the parts of your body at the end of your arms. Each hand has four fingers and a thumb. ☐ *I put my hand into my pocket and pulled out the letter.* ② N-SING The **hand** of someone or something is their influence in an event or situation. ☐ *The hand of the military authorities can be seen in the entire electoral process.* ③ N-PLURAL If you say that something is in a particular person's **hands**, you mean that they are taking care of it, own it, or are responsible for it. ☐ *I feel that possibly the majority of these dogs are in the wrong hands.* ☐ *We're in safe hands.* ④ N-SING If you ask someone for **a hand** with something, you are asking them to help you in what you are doing. ☐ *Come and give me a hand in the garden.* ⑤ N-SING If someone asks an audience to give someone **a hand**, they are asking the audience to clap loudly, usually before or after that person performs. ☐ *Let's give 'em a big hand.* ⑥ N-COUNT In a game of cards, your **hand** is the set of cards that you are holding in your hand at a particular time or the cards that are dealt to you at the beginning of the game. ☐ *He carefully inspected his hand.* ⑦ N-COUNT The **hands** of a clock or watch are the thin pieces of metal or plastic that indicate what time it is. ☐ *The hands of the clock on the wall moved with a slight click. Half past ten.* ⑧ PHRASE If something is **at hand, near at hand**, or **close at hand**, it is very near in place or time. ☐ *Having the right equipment at hand will be enormously helpful.* ⑨ PHRASE If someone experiences a particular kind of treatment, especially unpleasant treatment, **at the hands of** a person or organization, they receive it from them. ☐ *The civilian population was suffering greatly at the hands of the security forces.* ⑩ PHRASE If you do something **by hand**, you do it using your hands rather than a machine. ☐ *Each pleat was stitched in place by hand.* ⑪ PHRASE When something **changes hands**, its ownership changes, usually because it is sold to someone else. ▫ *The firm has changed hands many times over the years.* **12** PHRASE If you **have** your **hands full** with something, you are very busy because of it. ▫ *She had her hands full with new arrivals.* **13** PHRASE If someone gives you **a free hand**, they give you the freedom to use your own judgment and to do exactly as you wish. ▫ *He gave Stephanie a free hand in the decoration.* **14** PHRASE If you **get** your **hands on** something or **lay** your **hands on** something, you manage to find it or obtain it, usually after some difficulty. [INFORMAL] ▫ *Patty began reading everything she could get her hands on.* **15** PHRASE If two people are **hand in hand**, they are holding each other's nearest hand, usually while they are walking or sitting together. People often do this to show their affection for each other. ▫ *I saw them making their way, hand in hand, down the path.* **16** PHRASE If two things go **hand in hand**, they are closely connected and cannot be considered separately from each other. ▫ *For us, research and teaching go hand in hand.* **17** PHRASE If you **have a hand in** something such as an event or activity, you are involved in it. ▫ *He thanked all who had a hand in his release.* **18** PHRASE If two people **are holding hands**, they are holding each other's nearest hand, usually while they are walking or sitting together. People often do this to show their affection for each other. ▫ *She approached a young couple holding hands on a bench.* **19** PHRASE The job or problem **in hand** is the job or problem that you are dealing with at the moment. ▫ *The business in hand was approaching some kind of climax.* **20** PHRASE If a situation is **in hand**, it is under control. ▫ *The organizers say that matters are well in hand.* **21** PHRASE If you **lend** someone **a hand**, you help them. ▫ *I'd be glad to lend a hand.* **22** PHRASE If someone **lives hand to mouth** or **lives from hand to mouth**, they have hardly enough food or money to live on. ▫ *I have a wife and two children and we live from hand to mouth on what I earn.* **23** → see also **hand-to-mouth 24** PHRASE If you tell someone to **keep** their **hands off** something or to **take** their **hands off** it, you are telling them in a slightly aggressive way not to touch it or interfere with it. ▫ *Keep your hands off my milk.* **25** PHRASE If you do not know something **off hand**, you do not know it without having to ask someone else or look it up in a book. [SPOKEN] ▫ *I can't think of any off hand.* **26** PHRASE If you have a problem or responsibility **on your hands**, you have to deal with it. If it is **off** your **hands**, you no longer have to deal with it. ▫ *They now have yet another drug problem on their hands.* **27** PHRASE If someone or something is **on hand**, they are near and able to be used if they are needed. ▫ *There are experts on hand to give you all the help and advice you need.* **28** PHRASE You use **on the one hand** to introduce the first of two contrasting points, facts, or ways of looking at something. It is always followed later by 'on the other hand' or 'on the other.' ▫ *On the one hand, if the body doesn't have enough cholesterol, we would not be able to survive. On the other hand, if the body has too much cholesterol, the excess begins to line the arteries.* **29** PHRASE You use **on the other hand** to introduce the second of two contrasting points, facts, or ways of looking at something. ▫ *The movie lost money; reviews, on the other hand, were by and large favorable.* **30** PHRASE If a person or a situation **gets out of hand**, you are no longer able to control them. ▫ *His drinking got out of hand.* **31** PHRASE If you dismiss or reject something **out of hand**, you do so immediately and do not consider believing or accepting it. ▫ *I initially dismissed the idea out of hand.* **32** PHRASE If you **take** something or someone **in hand**, you take control or responsibility over them, especially in order to improve them. ▫ *She took the twins in hand, encouraging them to turn their thoughts to the future.* **33** PHRASE If you say that your **hands are tied**, you mean that something is preventing you from acting in the way that you want to. ▫ *Politicians are always saying that they want to help us but their hands are tied.* **34** PHRASE If you **try** your **hand** at an activity, you attempt to do it, usually for the first time. ▫ *He tried his hand at fishing, but he wasn't really very good at it.* **35** PHRASE If you **turn** your **hand to** something such as a practical activity, you learn about it and do it for the first time. ▫ *...a person who can turn his hand to anything.* **36** PHRASE If you **wash** your **hands of** someone or something, you refuse to be involved with them any more or to take responsibility for them. ▫ *He seems to have washed his hands of the job.* **37** PHRASE If you **win hands down**, you win very easily. ▫ *We have been beaten in some games which we should have won hands down.* **38 with one's bare hands** → see **bare 39 to shake someone's hand** → see **shake 40 to shake hands** → see **shake 41** → See feature box at **work**

② hand ✦✦◇ /hænd/ (**hands, handing, handed**) V-T If you **hand** something to someone, you pass it to them. ▫ *He handed me a little rectangle of white paper.*
▶ **hand back** PHRASAL VERB If you **hand back** something that you have borrowed or taken from someone, you return it to them. ▫ *He handed the book back.*
▶ **hand down** PHRASAL VERB If you **hand down** something such as knowledge, a possession, or a skill, you give or leave it to people who belong to a younger generation. ▫ *The idea of handing down his knowledge from generation to generation is important to McLean.*
▶ **hand in** **1** PHRASAL VERB If you **hand in** something such as homework or something that you have found, you give it to a teacher, police officer, or other person in authority. ▫ *I'm supposed to have handed in a first draft of my dissertation.* **2** PHRASAL VERB If you **hand in** your notice or resignation, you tell your employer, in speech or in writing, that you no longer wish to work there. ▫ *I handed my notice in on Saturday.*
▶ **hand on** PHRASAL VERB If you **hand** something **on**, you give it or transfer it to another person, often someone who replaces you. ▫ *Natural resources should be handed on to the next generation intact.*
▶ **hand out** **1** PHRASAL VERB If you **hand** things **out** to people, you give one or more to each person in a group. ▫ *One of my jobs was to hand out the prizes.* **2** PHRASAL VERB When people in authority **hand out** something such as advice or permission to do something, they give it to people. ▫ *I listened to a lot of people handing out a lot of advice.* **3** → see also **handout**
▶ **hand over** **1** PHRASAL VERB If you **hand** something **over** to someone, you give them the responsibility for dealing with a particular situation or problem. ▫ *I wouldn't dare hand this project over to anyone else.* **2** PHRASAL VERB If you **hand over** to someone or **hand** something **over** to them, you give them the responsibility for dealing with a particular situation or problem. ▫ *The present leaders have to decide whether to hand over to a younger generation.*

hand- /hænd-/ COMB IN ADJ [COMB -ed] **Hand-** combines with past participles to indicate that something has been made by someone using their hands or using tools rather than by machines. ▫ *...handcrafted jewelry.* ▫ *...handbuilt cars.*

hand|bag /hændbæg/ (**handbags**) **1** N-COUNT A **handbag** is a small bag which a woman uses to carry things such as her money and keys in when she goes out. **2** → See also color supplement

hand|ball /hændbɔl/ also **hand-ball** N-UNCOUNT **Handball** is a sport in which players try to score points by hitting a small ball against a wall with their hand.

hand|bill /hændbɪl/ (**handbills**) N-COUNT A **handbill** is a small printed notice which is used to advertise a particular company, service, or event.

hand|book /hændbʊk/ (**handbooks**) N-COUNT A **handbook** is a book that gives you advice and instructions about a particular subject, tool, or machine. ▫ *a handbook on pool maintenance.*

hand|brake /hændbreɪk/ (**handbrakes**) also **hand brake** N-COUNT In a vehicle, the **handbrake** is a brake which the driver operates with his or her hand, for example, when parking. [mainly BRIT]

in AM, usually use **emergency brake**

hand|cart /hændkɑrt/ (**handcarts**) also **hand-cart** N-COUNT A **handcart** is a small cart with two wheels which is pushed or pulled along and is used for transporting goods.

hand|clap /hændklæp/ (**handclaps**) N-COUNT If a group of people give a **handclap**, they clap their hands. [BRIT]

hand|cuff /hændkʌf/ (**handcuffs, handcuffing, handcuffed**) **1** N-PLURAL [also *a pair of* N] **Handcuffs** are two metal rings which are joined together and can be locked around someone's wrists, usually by the police during an arrest. ▫ *He was led away to jail in handcuffs.* **2** V-T If you **handcuff** someone, you put handcuffs around their wrists. ▫ *They tried to handcuff him but, despite his injuries, he fought his way free.*

hand|ful /hændfʊl/ (**handfuls**) **1** N-SING A **handful** of people or things is a small number of them. ▫ *He surveyed the handful of customers at the bar.* **2** N-COUNT A **handful** of something is the amount of it that you can hold in your hand. ▫ *She scooped up* a handful of sand and let it trickle through her fingers. **3** N-SING If you say that someone, especially a child, is a **handful**, you mean that they are difficult to control. [INFORMAL] ❑ *Zara can be a handful sometimes.*

hand gre|nade (hand grenades) N-COUNT A **hand grenade** is the same as a **grenade**.

hand|gun /hændgʌn/ (handguns) also **hand gun** N-COUNT A **handgun** is a gun that you can hold, carry, and fire with one hand.

hand|held /hændheld/ (handhelds) ADJ A **handheld** device such as a camera or a computer is small and light enough to be used while you are holding it. ❑ *...a handheld electric mixer.* • N-COUNT **Handheld** is also a noun. ❑ *Users will be able to use their handhelds to look up timetables on the net, search for a local hotel, and check their bank accounts.*

hand|hold /hændhoʊld/ (handholds) N-COUNT A **handhold** is a small hole or hollow in something such as rock or a wall that you can put your hand in if you are trying to climb it. ❑ *I found handholds and hoisted myself along.*

handi|cap /hændikæp/ (handicaps, handicapping, handicapped) **1** N-COUNT A **handicap** is a physical or mental disability. ❑ *He lost his leg when he was ten, but learned to overcome his handicap.* **2** N-COUNT A **handicap** is an event or situation that places you at a disadvantage and makes it harder for you to do something. ❑ *Being a foreigner was not a handicap.* **3** V-T If an event or a situation **handicaps** someone or something, it places them at a disadvantage. ❑ *Greater levels of stress may seriously handicap some students.* **4** N-COUNT In golf, a **handicap** is an advantage given to someone who is not a good player, in order to make the players more equal. As you improve, your handicap gets lower. ❑ *I see your handicap is down from 16 to 12.* **5** N-COUNT In horse racing, a **handicap** is a race in which some competitors are given a disadvantage of extra weight in an attempt to give everyone an equal chance of winning. ❑ *...the Melbourne Cup, a two-mile handicap.*

handi|capped /hændikæpt/ ADJ Someone who is **handicapped** has a physical or mental disability that prevents them from living a totally normal life. Many people who have a disability find this word offensive. [OFFENSIVE] ❑ *I'm going to work two days a week teaching handicapped kids to fish.* • N-PLURAL You can refer to people who are handicapped as **the handicapped**. [OFFENSIVE] ❑ *...measures to prevent discrimination against the handicapped.*

handi|craft /hændikræft/ (handicrafts) **1** N-COUNT [usu pl] **Handicrafts** are activities such as embroidery and pottery which involve making things with your hands in a skillful way. **2** N-COUNT [usu pl] **Handicrafts** are the objects that are produced by people doing handicrafts. ❑ *She sells handicrafts to the tourists.*

handi|work /hændiwɜrk/ N-UNCOUNT [usu with poss] You can refer to something that you have done or made yourself as your **handiwork**. ❑ *The architect stepped back to admire his handiwork.*

hand|ker|chief /hæŋkərtʃɪf/ (handkerchiefs) N-COUNT A **handkerchief** is a small square piece of fabric which you use for blowing your nose.

han|dle ♦♦◇ /hænd²l/ (handles, handling, handled) **1** N-COUNT A **handle** is a small round object or a lever that is attached to a door and is used for opening and closing it. ❑ *I turned the handle and found the door was open.* **2** N-COUNT A **handle** is the part of an object such as a tool, bag, or cup that you hold in order to be able to pick up and use the object. ❑ *...a broom handle.* **3** V-T If you say that someone can **handle** a problem or situation, you mean that they have the ability to deal with it successfully. ❑ *To tell the truth, I don't know if I can handle the job.* **4** V-T If you talk about the way that someone **handles** a problem or situation, you mention whether or not they are successful in achieving the result they want. ❑ *I think I would handle a meeting with Mr. Siegel very badly.* • **han|dling** N-UNCOUNT ❑ *The family has criticized the military's handling of Robert's death.* **5** V-T If you **handle** a particular area of work, you have responsibility for it. ❑ *She handled travel arrangements for the press corps during the presidential campaign.* **6** V-T When you **handle** something, you hold it or move it with your hands. ❑ *Wear rubber gloves when handling cat litter.* **7** PHRASE If you **fly off the handle**, you suddenly and completely lose your temper. [INFORMAL] ❑ *He flew off the handle at the slightest thing.* **8** → See feature box at **DIY**

SYNONYMS

handle
VERB **3**
manage: *How did your mother manage when your father left?*
deal with: *The agreement would allow other vital problems to be dealt with.*
cope: *The problems were an annoyance, but we managed to cope.*
tackle: *The first reason to tackle these problems is to save children's lives.*

handle|bar /hænd²lbɑr/ (handlebars) **1** N-COUNT The **handlebar** or **handlebars** of a bicycle consist of a curved metal bar with handles at each end which are used for steering. **2** → See also color supplement

handle|bar mus|tache (handlebar mustaches) also **handlebar moustache** N-COUNT A **handlebar mustache** is a long thick mustache with curled ends.

han|dler /hændlər/ (handlers) **1** N-COUNT A **handler** is someone whose job is to be in charge of and control an animal. ❑ *Fifty officers, including dog handlers, are searching for her.* **2** N-COUNT A **handler** is someone whose job is to deal with a particular type of object. ❑ *...baggage handlers at the airport.*

han|dling /hændlɪŋ/ N-UNCOUNT [usu with supp] A vehicle's **handling** is how easy it is to control safely in difficult driving conditions or when going round bends.

hand lug|gage N-UNCOUNT When you travel by air, your **hand luggage** is the luggage you have with you in the plane, rather than the luggage that is carried in the hold. ❑ *...a ban on all knives in hand luggage.*

hand|made /hændmeɪd/ also **hand-made** ADJ **Handmade** objects have been made by someone using their hands or using tools rather than by machines. ❑ *Because they're handmade, each one varies slightly.*

hand|maiden /hændmeɪdᵊn/ (handmaidens) **1** N-COUNT A **handmaiden** is a female servant. [LITERARY, OLD-FASHIONED] **2** N-COUNT [N of/to n] If one thing is the **handmaiden** of another, the first thing helps the second or makes it possible. [FORMAL] ❑ *The fear is that science could become the handmaiden of industry.*

hand-me-down (hand-me-downs) **1** N-COUNT [usu pl] **Hand-me-downs** are things, especially clothes, which have been used by someone else before you and which have been given to you for your use. ❑ *Edward wore Andrew's hand-me-downs.* **2** ADJ [ADJ n] **Hand-me-down** is used to describe things, especially clothes, which have been used by someone else before you and which have been given to you for your use. ❑ *Most of the boys wore hand-me-down military shirts from their fathers.*

hand|out /hændaʊt/ (handouts) **1** N-COUNT A **handout** is a gift of money, clothing, or food, which is given free to poor people. ❑ *Each family is being given a cash handout of six thousand rupees.* **2** N-COUNT If you call money that is given to someone a **handout**, you disapprove of it because you believe that the person who receives it has done nothing to earn or deserve it. [DISAPPROVAL] ❑ *Using government money to keep honest, hardworking workers in their jobs is easier for politicians to justify than handouts for greedy bankers.* **3** N-COUNT A **handout** is a document which contains news or information about something and which is given, for example, to journalists or members of the public. ❑ *Booklets and written handouts are useful.* **4** N-COUNT A **handout** is a paper given out to students by a teacher, that contains a summary of the information or topics that will be dealt with in a lesson. ❑ *Many teachers are opting for group discussions instead of handouts.*

hand|over /hændoʊvər/ (handovers) N-COUNT [usu sing, oft N of n] The **handover** of something is when possession or control of it is given by one person or group of people to another. ❑ *The handover is expected to be completed in the next ten years.*

hand|pick /hændpɪk/ (handpicks, handpicking, handpicked) also **hand-pick** V-T If someone **is handpicked**, they are very carefully chosen by someone in authority for a particular purpose or a particular job. ❑ *He was handpicked for this job by the Admiral.* ❑ *He was able to handpick his successor.*

hand|rail /hǽndreɪl/ (handrails) N-COUNT A **handrail** is a long piece of metal or wood which is attached near stairs or places where people could slip and fall, and which people can hold on to for support.

hand sani|tizer (hand sanitizers) N-MASS **Hand sanitizer** is a liquid or gel that you use to clean your hands. ❑ *Supplies of hand sanitizer ran out in some areas.*

hand|set /hǽndset/ (handsets) **1** N-COUNT The **handset** of a telephone is the part that you hold next to your face in order to speak and listen. ❑ *...the cord that connects the telephone handset to the phone itself.* **2** N-COUNT You can refer to a device such as the remote control of a television or stereo as a **handset**. ❑ *The timer is operated by four buttons on the remote control handset.*

hands-free **1** ADJ [ADJ n] A **hands-free** telephone or other device can be used without being held in your hand. ❑ *...legislation to ban both handheld and hands-free cellphones in moving vehicles.* **2** → See feature box at **technology**

hand|shake /hǽndʃeɪk/ (handshakes) **1** N-COUNT If you give someone a **handshake**, you take their right hand with your own right hand and hold it firmly or move it up and down, as a sign of greeting or to show that you have agreed about something such as a business deal. ❑ *He has a strong handshake.* **2** → see also **golden handshake**

hands-off ADJ A **hands-off** policy or approach to something consists of not being personally or directly involved in it. ❑ *...the state's traditional hands-off attitude toward big business.*

hand|some /hǽnsəm/ **1** ADJ A **handsome** man has an attractive face with regular features. ❑ *...a tall, dark, handsome sheep farmer.* **2** ADJ [ADJ n] A **handsome** sum of money is a large or generous amount. [FORMAL] ❑ *They will make a handsome profit on the property.* • **hand|some|ly** ADV [ADV with v] ❑ *He was rewarded handsomely for his efforts.*

hands-on ADJ **Hands-on** experience or work involves actually doing a particular thing, rather than just talking about it or getting someone else to do it. ❑ *This hands-on management approach often stretches his workday from 6 a.m. to 11 p.m.*

hand|stand /hǽndstænd/ (handstands) N-COUNT If you do a **handstand**, you balance yourself upside down on your hands with your body and legs straight up in the air.

hand-to-hand also **hand to hand** ADJ [ADJ n] **Hand-to-hand** fighting is fighting where the people are very close together, using either their hands or weapons such as knives. ❑ *There was, reportedly, hand-to-hand combat in the streets.*

hand-to-mouth also **hand to mouth** ADJ A **hand-to-mouth** existence is a way of life in which you have hardly enough food or money to live on. ❑ *Unloved and uncared-for, they live a meaningless hand to mouth existence.* • ADV [ADV after v] **Hand to mouth** is also an adverb. ❑ *I just can't live hand to mouth, it's too frightening.*

hand tool (hand tools) N-COUNT **Hand tools** are fairly simple tools which you use with your hands, and which are usually not powered.

hand|wash /hǽndwɒʃ/ (handwashes, handwashing, handwashed) V-T [V n] If you **handwash** something, you wash it by hand rather than in a washing machine.

hand-wringing also **handwringing** N-UNCOUNT If you accuse someone of **hand-wringing**, you mean that they are expressing sorrow about a bad situation but are saying that they are unable to change it. [DISAPPROVAL] ❑ *...despite all the public hand-wringing about the importance of voting.*

hand|writing /hǽndraɪtɪŋ/ N-UNCOUNT Your **handwriting** is your style of writing with a pen or pencil. ❑ *The address was in Anna's handwriting.*

hand|written /hǽndrɪtən/ ADJ A piece of writing that is **handwritten** is one that someone has written using a pen or pencil rather than by typing it. ❑ *...a handwritten note.*

handy /hǽndi/ (handier, handiest) **1** ADJ Something that is **handy** is useful. ❑ *The book gives handy hints on looking after indoor plants.* **2** PHRASE If something **comes in handy**, it is useful in a particular situation. ❑ *The $20 check came in very handy.* **3** ADJ A thing or place that is **handy** is nearby and therefore easy to get or reach. ❑ *It would be good to have a pencil and paper handy.*

handy|man /hǽndimæn/ (handymen) N-COUNT A **handyman** is a man who earns money by doing small jobs for people such as making and repairing things in their houses. You can also describe a man who is good at making or repairing things in his home as a **handyman**.

handy|woman /hǽndiwʊmən/ (handywomen) N-COUNT A **handywoman** is a woman who earns money by doing small jobs for people such as making and repairing things in their houses. You can also describe a woman who is good at making or repairing things in her home as a **handywoman**.

hang ✦✦◇ /hǽŋ/ (hangs, hanging, hung or hanged)

> The form **hanged** is used as the past tense and past participle for meaning **5**.

1 V-T/V-I If something **hangs** in a high place or position, or if you **hang** it there, it is attached there so it does not touch the ground. ❑ *Notices painted on sheets hang at every entrance.* ❑ *...small hanging lanterns.* • PHRASAL VERB **Hang up** means the same as **hang**. ❑ *I found his jacket, which was hanging up in the hallway.* **2** V-I If a piece of clothing or fabric **hangs** in a particular way or position, that is how it is worn or arranged. ❑ *...a ragged fur coat that hung down to her calves.* **3** V-I If something **hangs** loose or **hangs** open, it is partly fixed in position, but is not firmly held, supported, or controlled, often in such a way that it moves freely. ❑ *...her long golden hair which hung loose about her shoulders.* **4** V-T [usu passive] If something such as a wall **is hung with** pictures or other objects, they are attached to it. ❑ *The walls were hung with huge modern paintings.* **5** V-T/V-I If someone **is hanged** or if they **hang**, they are killed, usually as a punishment, by having a rope tied around their neck and the support taken away from under their feet. ❑ *He was convicted and sentenced to be hanged.* ❑ *He hanged himself two hours after arriving.* **6** V-I If something such as someone's breath or smoke **hangs** in the air, it remains there without appearing to move or change position. ❑ *His breath was hanging in the air before him.* **7** V-I If a possibility **hangs over** you, it worries you and makes your life unpleasant or difficult because you think it might happen. ❑ *A constant threat of unemployment hangs over thousands of university researchers.* **8** → see also **hung** **9** PHRASE If you **get the hang of** something such as a skill or activity, you begin to understand or realize how to do it. [INFORMAL] ❑ *It's a bit tricky at first till you get the hang of it.* **10** PHRASE If you tell someone to **hang in there** or to **hang on in there**, you are encouraging them to keep trying to do something and not to give up even though it might be difficult. [INFORMAL] ❑ *Hang in there and you never know what is achievable.* **11** → See feature box at **personality**

▶ **hang back** **1** PHRASAL VERB If you **hang back**, you move or stay slightly behind a person or group, usually because you are shy or nervous about something. ❑ *I saw him step forward momentarily but then hang back, nervously massaging his hands.* **2** PHRASAL VERB If a person or organization **hangs back**, they do not do something immediately. ❑ *They will then hang back on closing the deal.*

▶ **hang on** **1** PHRASAL VERB If you ask someone to **hang on**, you ask them to wait or stop what they are doing or saying for a moment. [INFORMAL] ❑ *Can you hang on for a minute?* **2** PHRASAL VERB If you **hang on**, you manage to survive, achieve success, or avoid failure in spite of great difficulties or opposition. ❑ *He hung on to finish second.* **3** PHRASAL VERB If you **hang on to** or **hang onto** something that gives you an advantage, you succeed in keeping it for yourself, and prevent it from being taken away or given to someone else. ❑ *The driver was unable to hang on to his lead.* **4** PHRASAL VERB If you **hang on to** or **hang onto** something, you hold it very tightly, for example to stop it from falling or to support yourself. ❑ *She was conscious of a second man hanging on to the rail.* ❑ *...a flight attendant who helped save the life of a pilot by hanging onto his legs.* **5** PHRASAL VERB If you **hang on to** or **hang onto** something, you keep it for a longer time than you would normally expect. [INFORMAL] ❑ *You could, alternatively, hang onto it in the hope that it will be worth millions in 10 years time.* **6** PHRASAL VERB If one thing **hangs on** another, it depends on it in order to be successful. ❑ *Much hangs on the success of the election.*

▶ **hang out** **1** PHRASAL VERB If you **hang out** clothes that you have washed, you hang them on a clothes line to dry. ❑ *I was worried I wouldn't be able to hang my laundry out.* **2** PHRASAL VERB If you **hang out** in a particular place or area, you go and stay there for no particular reason, or spend a lot of time

there. [INFORMAL] ❑ *I often used to hang out in supermarkets.*
▶ **hang up** ❶ → see **hang** 1 ❷ PHRASAL VERB If you **hang up** or you **hang up** the phone, you end a phone call. If you **hang up** on someone you are speaking to on the phone, you end the phone call suddenly and unexpectedly, usually because you are angry or upset with the person you are speaking to. ❑ *Mom hung up the phone.* ❑ *Don't hang up!*

hang|ar /hæŋər/ (hangars) N-COUNT A **hangar** is a large building in which aircraft are kept.

hang|dog /hæŋdɒg/ also **hang-dog** ADJ [usu adj n] If you say that someone has a **hangdog** expression on their face, you mean that they look sad, and often guilty or ashamed.

hang|er /hæŋər/ (hangers) N-COUNT A **hanger** is the same as a **coat hanger**.

hanger-on (hangers-on) N-COUNT If you describe someone as a **hanger-on**, you are critical of them because they are trying to be friendly with a richer or more important person, especially in order to gain an advantage for themselves. [DISAPPROVAL] ❑ *For every one or two talented people in any group of artists, there are hordes of talentless hangers-on.*

hang glid|er (hang gliders) also **hang-glider** N-COUNT A **hang glider** is a type of glider, made from a large piece of cloth attached to a frame. It is used to fly from high places, with the pilot hanging underneath.

hang glid|ing N-UNCOUNT **Hang gliding** is the activity of flying in a hang glider.

hang|ing /hæŋɪŋ/ (hangings) N-COUNT A **hanging** is a large piece of cloth that you put as a decoration on a wall.

hang|ing bas|ket (hanging baskets) N-COUNT A **hanging basket** is a basket with small ropes or chains attached so that it can be hung from a hook. Hanging baskets are usually used for displaying plants or storing fruit and vegetables.

hang|man /hæŋmæn/ (hangmen) N-COUNT A **hangman** is a man whose job is to execute people by hanging them.

hang|out /hæŋaʊt/ (hangouts) N-COUNT [with supp] If a place is a **hangout** for a particular group of people, they spend a lot of time there because they can relax and meet other people there. [INFORMAL] ❑ *By the time he was sixteen, Malcolm already knew most of the city's teenage hangouts.*

hang|over /hæŋoʊvər/ (hangovers) ❶ N-COUNT If someone wakes up with a **hangover**, they feel sick and have a headache because they drank a lot of alcohol the night before. ❑ *It was a great night and I had a massive hangover.* ❷ N-COUNT Something that is a **hangover** from the past is an idea or way of behaving which people used to have in the past but which people no longer generally have. ❑ *As a hangover from rationing, they mixed butter and margarine.*

hang-up (hang-ups) N-COUNT If you have a **hang-up** about something, you have a feeling of fear, anxiety, or embarrassment about it. [INFORMAL] ❑ *I don't have any hang-ups about my body.*

hank /hæŋk/ (hanks) N-COUNT [oft N *of* n] A **hank** of wool, rope, or string is a length of it which has been loosely wound.

hank|er /hæŋkər/ (hankers, hankering, hankered) V-I If you **hanker** after something, you want it very much. ❑ *I hankered after a floor-length brown suede coat.*

hank|er|ing /hæŋkərɪŋ/ (hankerings) N-COUNT [usu N *for/after* n, N to-inf] A **hankering** for something is a desire or longing for it. ❑ *From time to time we all get a hankering for something a little different.*

hanky /hæŋki/ (hankies) also **hankie** N-COUNT A **hanky** is the same as a handkerchief. [INFORMAL]

hanky-panky /hæŋki pæŋki/ ❶ N-UNCOUNT If you describe behavior as **hanky-panky**, you disapprove of it because it is dishonest or breaks rules. [DISAPPROVAL] ❑ *The government has been offering tax credits, accelerated depreciation, and other economic hanky-panky.* ❷ N-UNCOUNT **Hanky-panky** is sexual activity between two people, especially when this is regarded as improper or not serious. [HUMOROUS, INFORMAL] ❑ *Does this mean no hanky-panky after lights out?*

han|som /hænsəm/ (hansoms) N-COUNT In former times, a **hansom** or a **hansom cab** was a horse-drawn carriage with two wheels and a fixed hood.

Ha|nuk|kah /hɑnəkə/ also **Hanukah**, **Chanukah** N-UNCOUNT **Hanukkah** is a Jewish festival that celebrates the rededication of the Temple in Jerusalem in 165 B.C. It begins in November or December and lasts for eight days.

hap|haz|ard /hæphæzərd/ ADJ If you describe something as **haphazard**, you are critical of it because it is not at all organized or is not arranged according to a plan. [DISAPPROVAL] ❑ *The investigation does seem haphazard.* • **hap|haz|ard|ly** ADV ❑ *She looked at the books jammed haphazardly in the shelves.*

hap|less /hæplɪs/ ADJ [ADJ n] A **hapless** person is unlucky. [FORMAL] ❑ *...his hapless victim.*

hap|pen ✦✦✦ /hæpən/ (happens, happening, happened) ❶ V-I Something that **happens** occurs or is done without being planned. ❑ *We cannot say for sure what will happen.* ❷ V-I If something **happens**, it occurs as a result of a situation or course of action. ❑ *She wondered what would happen if her parents found her.* ❸ V-I When something, especially something unpleasant, **happens to** you, it takes place and affects you. ❑ *If we had been spotted at that point, I don't know what would have happened to us.* ❹ V-T If you **happen** to do something, you do it by chance. If it **happens** that something is the case, it occurs by chance. ❑ *We happened to discover we had a friend in common.* ❺ PHRASE You use **as it happens** in order to introduce a statement, especially one that is rather surprising. ❑ *He called Amy to see if she knew where his son was. As it happened, Amy did know.*

hap|pen|ing /hæpənɪŋ/ (happenings) N-COUNT **Happenings** are things that happen, often in a way that is unexpected or hard to explain. ❑ *The Budapest office plans to hire freelance reporters to cover the latest happenings.*

hap|pen|stance /hæpənstæns/ N-UNCOUNT [also *a* N, oft by N] If you say that something happened by **happenstance**, you mean that it happened because of certain circumstances, although it was not planned by anyone. [WRITTEN] ❑ *I came to live at the farm by happenstance.*

hap|pi|ly /hæpɪli/ ❶ ADV [ADV with cl] You can add **happily** to a statement to indicate that you are glad that something happened. ❑ *Happily, his neck injuries were not serious.* ❷ → see also **happy**

hap|py ✦✦◇ /hæpi/ (happier, happiest) ❶ ADJ Someone who is **happy** has feelings of pleasure, usually because something nice has happened or because they feel satisfied with their life. ❑ *Marina was a confident, happy child.* • **hap|pi|ly** ADV ❑ *Margery and he had been happily picnicking with the children.* • **hap|pi|ness** N-UNCOUNT ❑ *I think mostly she was looking for happiness.* ❷ ADJ A **happy** time, place, or relationship is full of happy feelings and pleasant experiences, or has an atmosphere in which people feel happy. ❑ *Except for her illnesses, she had a particularly happy childhood.* ❑ *It had always been a happy place.* ❸ ADJ [v-link ADJ] If you are **happy** about a situation or arrangement, you are satisfied with it, for example, because you think that something is being done in the right way. ❑ *If you are not happy about a repair, go back and complain.* ❑ *He's happy that I deal with it myself.* ❹ ADJ [v-link ADJ] If you say you are **happy** to do something, you mean that you are very willing to do it. ❑ *I'll be happy to answer questions if there are any.* • **hap|pi|ly** ADV [ADV with v] ❑ *If I've caused any offense over something I have written, I will happily apologize.* ❺ ADJ [ADJ n] **Happy** is used in greetings and other conventional expressions to say that you hope someone will enjoy a special occasion. ❑ *Happy Birthday!*

happy-go-lucky ADJ Someone who is **happy-go-lucky** enjoys life and does not worry about the future.

hap|py hour (happy hours) N-VAR In a bar, **happy hour** is a period when drinks are sold more cheaply than usual to encourage people to come to the bar.

hara-kiri /hærə kɪri/ N-UNCOUNT In former times, if a Japanese person committed **hara-kiri**, they killed themselves by cutting their own stomach open, in order to avoid dishonor.

ha|rangue /həræŋ/ (harangues, haranguing, harangued) V-T If someone **harangues** you, they try to persuade you to accept their opinions or ideas in a forceful way. ❑ *An argument ensued, with various band members joining in and haranguing him and his girlfriend for over two hours.*

har|ass /həræs, hærəs/ (harasses, harassing, harassed) V-T If someone **harasses** you, they trouble or annoy you, for example by attacking you repeatedly or by causing you as many problems as they can. ❑ *A woman reporter complained one of them sexually harassed her in the locker room.*

har|assed /hərǽst, hǽrəst/ ADJ If you are **harassed**, you are anxious and tense because you have too much to do or too many problems to cope with. ❑ *This morning, looking harassed and drawn, Lewis tendered his resignation.*

har|ass|ment /hərǽsmənt, hǽrəs-/ N-UNCOUNT **Harassment** is behavior which is intended to trouble or annoy someone, for example repeated attacks on them or attempts to cause them problems. ❑ *Another survey found that 51 percent of women had experienced some form of sexual harassment in their working lives.*

har|bin|ger /hɑ́rbɪndʒər/ (**harbingers**) N-COUNT [usu N *of* n] Something that is a **harbinger** of something else, especially something bad, is a sign that it is going to happen. [LITERARY] ❑ *The November air stung my cheeks, a harbinger of winter.*

har|bor ✦✧✧ /hɑ́rbər/ (**harbors, harboring, harbored**)

> in BRIT, use **harbour**

1 N-COUNT; N-IN-NAMES A **harbor** is an area of the sea at the coast which is partly enclosed by land or strong walls, so that boats can be left there safely. ❑ *She led us to a room with a balcony overlooking the harbor.* **2** V-T If you **harbor** an emotion, thought, or secret, you have it in your mind over a long period of time. ❑ *He might have been murdered by a former client or someone harboring a grudge.* **3** V-T If a person or country **harbors** someone who is wanted by the police, they let them stay in their house or country and offer them protection. ❑ *A police spokesperson said the community they was harboring criminals.*

har|bor|master /hɑ́rbərmæstər/ (**harbormasters**) also **harbor master**

> in BRIT, use **harbourmaster** or **harbour master**

N-COUNT A **harbormaster** is the official in charge of a harbor.

hard ✦✦✦ /hɑ́rd/ (**harder, hardest**) **1** ADJ Something that is **hard** is very firm and stiff to touch and is not easily bent, cut, or broken. ❑ *He shuffled his feet on the hard wooden floor.* • **hard|ness** N-UNCOUNT ❑ *He felt the hardness of the iron railing press against his spine.* **2** ADJ Something that is **hard** is very difficult to do or deal with. ❑ *It's hard to tell what effect this latest move will have.* ❑ *That's a very hard question.* **3** ADV [ADV after v] If you work **hard** doing something, you are very active or work intensely, with a lot of effort. ❑ *I'll work hard. I don't want to let him down.* • ADJ [ADJ n] **Hard** is also an adjective. ❑ *I admired him as a true scientist and hard worker.* **4** ADJ **Hard** work involves a lot of activity and effort. ❑ *Coping with three babies is very hard work.* ❑ *...a hard day's work.* **5** ADV [ADV after v] If you look, listen, or think **hard**, you do it carefully and with a great deal of attention. ❑ *He looked at me hard.* • ADJ **Hard** is also an adjective. ❑ *It might be worth taking a long hard look at your frustrations and resentments.* **6** ADV [ADV after v] If you strike or take hold of something **hard**, you strike or take hold of it with a lot of force. ❑ *I kicked a trash can very hard and broke my toe.* • ADJ [ADJ n] **Hard** is also an adjective. ❑ *Anthony gave the door a hard push.* **7** ADV [ADV after v] You can use **hard** to indicate that something happens intensely and for a long time. ❑ *I've never seen Terry laugh so hard.* **8** ADJ If a person or their expression is **hard**, they show no kindness or sympathy. ❑ *His father was a hard man.* **9** ADJ [v-link ADJ *on* n] If you are **hard on** someone, you treat them severely or unkindly. ❑ *Don't be so hard on him.* • ADV [ADV after v] **Hard** is also an adverb. ❑ *He said the security forces would continue to crack down hard on the protestors.* **10** ADJ [v-link ADJ *on* n] If you say that something is **hard on** a person or thing, you mean it affects them in a way that is likely to cause them damage or suffering. ❑ *The gray light was hard on the eyes.* **11** ADJ If you have a **hard** life or a **hard** period of time, your life or that period is difficult and unpleasant for you. ❑ *It had been a hard life for her.* • **hard|ness** N-UNCOUNT ❑ *In America, people don't normally admit to the hardness of life.* **12** ADJ [ADJ n] **Hard** evidence or facts are definitely true and do not need to be questioned. ❑ *He wanted more hard evidence.* **13** ADJ [ADJ n] **Hard** drugs are very strong illegal drugs such as heroin or cocaine. ❑ *He then graduated from soft drugs to hard ones.* **14** PHRASE If you say that something is **hard going**, you mean it is difficult and requires a lot of effort. ❑ *The talks had been hard going at the start.* **15** PHRASE To be **hard hit** by something means to be affected very severely by it. ❑ *This area has been particularly hard hit by the recession.* **16** PHRASE If someone **plays hard to get**, they pretend not to be interested in another person or in what someone is trying to persuade them to do. ❑ *Remember what I told you: play hard to get. He'll lap it up.*

hard and fast ADJ [usu with brd-neg, usu ADJ n] If you say that there are no **hard and fast** rules, or that there is no **hard and fast** information about something, you are indicating that there are no fixed or definite rules or facts. ❑ *There are no hard and fast rules, but rather traditional guidelines as to who pays for what.*

hard|back /hɑ́rdbæk/ (**hardbacks**) N-COUNT [also in n] A **hardback** is a book which has a stiff hard cover. Compare **paperback**. ❑ *The book was published in hardback last October.*

hard|ball /hɑ́rdbɔl/ PHRASE If someone **plays hardball**, they will do anything that is necessary to achieve or get what they want, even if this involves being harsh or unfair. [mainly AM] ❑ *She is playing hardball in a world dominated by men 20 years her senior.*

hard-bitten ADJ [usu ADJ n] If you describe someone as **hard-bitten**, you are critical of them because they do not show much emotion or have much sympathy for other people, usually because they have experienced many unpleasant things. [DISAPPROVAL] ❑ *...a cynical hard-bitten journalist.*

hard|board /hɑ́rdbɔrd/ N-UNCOUNT **Hardboard** is a material which is made by pressing very small pieces of wood very closely together to form a thin, slightly flexible sheet.

hard-boiled also **hard boiled 1** ADJ A **hard-boiled** egg has been boiled in its shell until the whole of the inside is solid. **2** ADJ You use **hard-boiled** to describe someone who is tough and does not show much emotion. ❑ *She's hard-boiled, tough, and funny.*

hard cash N-UNCOUNT **Hard cash** is money in the form of bills and coins as opposed to a check or a credit card. ❑ *There is no confusion about what the real dividend is since the payment comes in hard cash.*

hard ci|der N-UNCOUNT **Hard cider** is an alcoholic drink that is made from apples. [AM]

hard copy (**hard copies**) N-VAR A **hard copy** of a document is a printed version of it, rather than a version that is stored on a computer. ❑ *...eight pages of hard copy.*

hard core also **hard-core 1** N-SING [oft N *of* n, N n] You can refer to the members of a group who are the most committed to its activities or who are the most involved in them as a **hard core** of members or as the **hard-core** members. ❑ *We've got a hard core of customers that have stood by us.* ❑ *A hard-core group of right-wing senators had hoped to sway their colleagues.* **2** ADJ [ADJ n] **Hard-core** pornography shows sex in a detailed way, often violent or extreme sex. Compare **soft-core**.

hard-core porn N-UNCOUNT **Hard-core porn** is pornography that shows sex in a detailed way, often violent or extreme sex.

hard|cover /hɑ́rdkʌvər/ (**hardcovers**) N-COUNT [also in n] A **hardcover** is a book which has a stiff hard cover. Compare **softcover**. [AM]

hard cur|ren|cy (**hard currencies**) N-VAR A **hard currency** is one which is unlikely to lose its value and so is considered to be a good one to have or to invest in. ❑ *The country is running short of hard currency to pay for imports.*

hard disk (**hard disks**) **1** N-COUNT A computer's **hard disk** is a stiff magnetic disk on which data and programs can be stored. **2** → See feature box at **computer**

hard-drinking ADJ [ADJ n] If you describe someone as a **hard-drinking** person, you mean that they frequently drink large quantities of alcohol.

hard drive (**hard drives**) also **hard-drive** N-COUNT A computer's **hard drive** is its hard disk, or the part that contains and operates the hard disk, which is used for storing and retrieving data. ❑ *You can store your entire CD collection on the computer's hard drive.*

hard-earned ADJ A **hard-earned** victory or **hard-earned** cash is a victory or money that someone deserves because they have worked hard for it. ❑ *Whoever lifts the trophy will know that theirs has been a hard-earned victory.* ❑ *Before you part with your hard-earned cash, make sure that you are happy that you are getting value for money.*

hard-edged ADJ If you describe something such as a style, play, or article as **hard-edged**, you mean you admire it because it is powerful, critical, or unsentimental. [APPROVAL] ❑ *...hard-edged drama.*

hard|en /hɑrdªn/ (hardens, hardening, hardened) **1** V-T/V-I When something **hardens** or when you **harden** it, it becomes stiff or firm. ☐ *Mold the mixture into shape while hot, before it hardens.* **2** V-T/V-I When an attitude or opinion **hardens** or is **hardened**, it becomes harsher, stronger, or fixed. ☐ *Their action can only serve to harden the attitude of landowners.* • **hard|en|ing** N-SING ☐ *...a hardening of the government's attitude toward rebellious parts of the army.* **3** V-T/V-I When events **harden** people or when people **harden**, they become less easily affected emotionally and less sympathetic and gentle than they were before. ☐ *Her years of drunken bickering hardened my heart.* **4** V-I If you say that someone's face or eyes **harden**, you mean that they suddenly look serious or angry. ☐ *His smile died and the look in his face hardened.*

hard|ened /hɑrdªnd/ ADJ [usu ADJ n] If you describe someone as **hardened**, you mean that they have had so much experience of something bad or unpleasant that they are no longer affected by it in the way that other people would be. ☐ *...hardened criminals.* ☐ *...hardened politicians.*

hard hat (hard hats) **1** N-COUNT A **hard hat** is a hat made from a hard material, which people wear to protect their heads on construction sites or in factories, or when riding a horse. **2** → See also color supplement

hard|headed /hɑrdhɛdɪd/ also **hard-headed** ADJ You use **hardheaded** to describe someone who is practical and determined to get what they want or need, and who does not allow emotions to affect their actions. ☐ *...a hardheaded and shrewd businesswoman.*

hard-hearted ADJ If you describe someone as **hard-hearted**, you disapprove of the fact that they have no sympathy for other people and do not care if people are hurt or made unhappy. [DISAPPROVAL] ☐ *You would have to be pretty hard-hearted not to feel something for him.*

hard-hitting ADJ [usu ADJ n] If you describe a report or speech as **hard-hitting**, you like the way it talks about difficult or serious matters in a bold and direct way. [JOURNALISM, APPROVAL] ☐ *In a hard-hitting speech to the IMF, he urged Third World countries to undertake sweeping reforms.*

hard la|bor

in BRIT, use **hard labour**

N-UNCOUNT **Hard labor** is hard physical work which people have to do as punishment for a crime. ☐ *The sentence of the court was twelve years' hard labor.*

hard-line also **hardline** ADJ If you describe someone's policy or attitude as **hard-line**, you mean that it is strict or extreme, and that they refuse to change it. ☐ *The United States has taken a lot of criticism for its hard-line stance.*

hard-liner ♦◇◇ (hard-liners) also **hardliner** N-COUNT [usu pl] The **hard-liners** in a group such as a political party are the people who support a strict, fixed set of ideas that are often extreme, and who refuse to accept any change in them. ☐ *Hardliners warned the president he would not be welcome.*

hard luck also **hard-luck 1** N-UNCOUNT If you say that someone had some **hard luck**, or that a situation was **hard luck** on them, you mean that something bad happened to them and you are implying that it was not their fault. [INFORMAL] ☐ *We had a bit of hard luck this season.* **2** N-UNCOUNT [poss N] If someone says that a bad situation affecting you is just your **hard luck**, they do not care about it or think you should be helped, often because they think it is your fault. [INFORMAL] ☐ *If the forces of law had not uncovered Stein in the seven-year interval that was their hard luck.* **3** CONVENTION You can say '**hard luck**' to someone to show that you are sorry they have not got or done something that they had wanted to get or do. [INFORMAL, FEELINGS] ☐ *Hard luck, but don't despair too much.* **4** ADJ [ADJ n] A **hard-luck** story is an account of something bad that happened to someone, which was not their fault. ☐ *...a hard-luck story in which he or she is the victim.*

hard|ly ♦♦◇ /hɑrdli/ **1** ADV You use **hardly** to modify a statement when you want to emphasize that it is only a small amount or detail which makes it true, and that therefore it is best to consider the opposite statement as being true. [EMPHASIS] ☐ *I hardly know you.* ☐ *I've hardly slept in three days.* **2** ADV [ADV ever/any] You use **hardly** in expressions such as **hardly ever**, **hardly any**, and **hardly anyone** to mean almost never, almost none, or almost no one. ☐ *We hardly ever eat fish.* ☐ *Most of the others were so young they had hardly any experience.* **3** ADV [ADV n] You use **hardly** before a negative statement in order to emphasize that something is usually true or usually happens. [EMPHASIS] ☐ *Hardly a day goes by without a visit from someone.* **4** ADV [can/could ADV inf] When you say you can **hardly** do something, you are emphasizing that it is very difficult for you to do it. [EMPHASIS] ☐ *My garden was covered with so many butterflies that I could hardly see the flowers.* **5** ADV You use **hardly** to mean 'not' when you want to suggest that you are expecting your listener or reader to agree with your comment. ☐ *We have not seen the letter, so we can hardly comment on it.* **6** CONVENTION You use '**hardly**' to mean 'no,' especially when you want to express surprise or annoyance at a statement that you disagree with. [SPOKEN] ☐ *"They all thought you were marvelous!"—"Well, hardly."*

SYNONYMS

hardly
ADV **1**
barely: *Anastasia could barely remember the ride to the hospital.*
scarcely: *He could scarcely breathe.*

---

hard-nosed ADJ [usu ADJ n] You use **hard-nosed** to describe someone who is tough and realistic, and who makes decisions on practical grounds rather than emotional ones. [INFORMAL] ☐ *If nothing else, Doug is a hard-nosed businessman.*

hard of hear|ing ADJ [usu v-link ADJ] Someone who is **hard of hearing** is not able to hear properly.

hard-on (hard-ons) N-COUNT If a man has a **hard-on**, he has an erection. [VULGAR] ☐ *The thought of this had stirred him up; he actually had a hard-on.*

hard-pressed also **hard pressed 1** ADJ If someone is **hard-pressed**, they are under a great deal of strain and worry, usually because they do not have enough money. [JOURNALISM] ☐ *The region's hard-pressed consumers are spending less on luxuries.* **2** ADJ [v-link ADJ to-inf] If you will be **hard-pressed** to do something, you will have great difficulty doing it. ☐ *This year the airline will be hard-pressed to make a profit.*

hard rock N-UNCOUNT [oft N n] **Hard rock** is a type of very loud rock music with a fast beat. ☐ *...a hard rock band.*

hard sell N-SING A **hard sell** is a method of selling in which the salesperson puts a lot of pressure on someone to make them buy something. ☐ *...a company whose hard sell techniques were exposed by a consumer program.*

hard|ship /hɑrdʃɪp/ (hardships) N-VAR **Hardship** is a situation in which your life is difficult or unpleasant, often because you do not have enough money. ☐ *Many people are suffering economic hardship.*

hard shoul|der (hard shoulders) N-COUNT [usu the N in sing] The **hard shoulder** is the area at the side of a highway or other road where you are allowed to stop if your car breaks down. [mainly BRIT]

in AM, use **shoulder**

hard up also **hard-up** ADJ If you are **hard up**, you have very little money. [INFORMAL] ☐ *Her parents were very hard up.*

hard|ware /hɑrdwɛər/ **1** N-UNCOUNT In computer systems, **hardware** refers to the machines themselves as opposed to the programs which tell the machines what to do. Compare **software**. ☐ *To be totally secure, you need a piece of hardware that costs about $200.* **2** N-UNCOUNT Military **hardware** is the machinery and equipment that is used by the armed forces, such as tanks, aircraft, and missiles. ☐ *...the billions which are spent on military hardware.* **3** N-UNCOUNT **Hardware** refers to tools and equipment that are used in the home and garden, for example nuts and bolts, screwdrivers, and hinges. ☐ *...a shop from which an uncle had sold hardware and timber.* **4** → See feature box at **computer**

hard|ware store (hardware stores) N-COUNT A **hardware store** is a store where articles for the house and garden such as tools, nails, and building supplies are sold.

hard-wearing also **hard wearing** ADJ Something that is **hard-wearing** is strong and well made so that it lasts for a

hard|wired /hɑrdwaɪərd/ also **hard-wired** **1** ADJ A **hardwired** part of a computer forms part of its hardware. **2** ADJ If an ability, approach, or type of activity is **hardwired** into the brain, it is a basic one and cannot be changed. ❑ *Others think that the rules for what is "musical" are hardwired in our brains to some degree.*

hard-won ADJ [usu ADJ n] If you describe something that someone has gained or achieved as **hard-won**, you mean that they worked hard to gain or achieve it. ❑ *The dispute could destroy Australia's hard-won reputation for industrial stability.*

hard|wood /hɑrdwʊd/ (**hardwoods**) N-MASS [oft N n] **Hardwood** is wood such as oak, teak, and mahogany, which is very strong and hard. ❑ *...hardwood floors.*

hard|working /hɑrdwɜrkɪŋ/ also **hard-working** ADJ If you describe someone as **hardworking**, you mean that they work very hard. ❑ *He was hardworking and energetic.*

har|dy /hɑrdi/ (**hardier, hardiest**) ADJ Plants that are **hardy** are able to survive cold weather. ❑ *The silver-leaved varieties of cyclamen are not quite as hardy.*

hare /hɛər/ (**hares**) N-VAR A **hare** is an animal like a rabbit but larger with long ears, long legs, and a small tail.

hare|brained /hɛərbreɪnd/ also **hare-brained** ADJ [usu ADJ n] You use **harebrained** to describe a scheme or theory which you consider to be very foolish and which you think is unlikely to be successful or true. [DISAPPROVAL] ❑ *This isn't the first harebrained scheme he's had.*

har|em /hɛərəm, hær-/ (**harems**) N-COUNT In the past, if a man, especially a Muslim, had several wives or sexual partners living in his house, they were often referred to as his **harem**.

hark /hɑrk/ (**harks, harking, harked**)
▶ **hark back to** PHRASAL VERB If you say that one thing **harks back to** another thing in the past, you mean it is similar to it or takes it as a model. ❑ *...pitched roofs, which hark back to the Victorian era.*

har|lequin /hɑrlɪkwɪn/ (**harlequins**) **1** ADJ [ADJ n] You use **harlequin** to describe something that has a lot of different colors, often in a diamond pattern. [WRITTEN] ❑ *...the striking harlequin floor.* **2** N-COUNT In some forms of theater, a **harlequin** is a comic character who wears a mask and brightly-colored tights.

har|lot /hɑrlət/ (**harlots**) N-COUNT **Harlot** is an offensive and old-fashioned word for a prostitute. [OFFENSIVE, OLD-FASHIONED, DISAPPROVAL]

harm ♦◇◇ /hɑrm/ (**harms, harming, harmed**) **1** V-T To **harm** a person or animal means to cause them physical injury, usually on purpose. ❑ *The hijackers seemed anxious not to harm anyone.* **2** N-UNCOUNT **Harm** is physical injury to a person or an animal which is usually caused on purpose. ❑ *All dogs are capable of doing harm to human beings.* **3** V-T To **harm** a thing, or sometimes a person, means to damage them or make them less effective or successful than they were. ❑ *...a warning that the product may harm the environment.* **4** N-UNCOUNT **Harm** is the damage to something which is caused by a particular course of action. ❑ *The abuse of your powers does harm to all other officers who do their job properly.* **5** PHRASE If you say **it does no harm** to do something or **there is no harm** in doing something, you mean that it might be worth doing, and you will not be blamed for doing it. ❑ *They are not always willing to take on untrained workers, but there's no harm in asking.* **6** PHRASE If someone or something is **out of harm's way**, they are in a safe place away from danger or from the possibility of being damaged. ❑ *For parents, it is an easy way of keeping their children entertained, or simply out of harm's way.* **7** PHRASE If you say that there is **no harm done**, you are telling someone not to worry about something that has happened because it has not caused any serious injury or damage. ❑ *There, now, you're all right. No harm done.* **8** PHRASE If you say that someone or something **will come to no harm** or that **no harm will come** to them, you mean that they will not be hurt or damaged in any way. ❑ *There is always a lifeguard to ensure that no one comes to any harm.*

harm|ful /hɑrmfəl/ ADJ Something that is **harmful** has a bad effect on something else, especially on a person's health. ❑ *...the harmful effects of smoking.*

harm|less /hɑrmlɪs/ **1** ADJ Something that is **harmless** does not have any bad effects, especially on people's health. ❑ *This experiment was harmless to the animals.* **2** ADJ If you describe someone or something as **harmless**, you mean that they are not important and therefore unlikely to annoy other people or cause trouble. ❑ *He seemed harmless enough.*

har|mon|ic /hɑrmɒnɪk/ ADJ **Harmonic** means composed, played, or sung using two or more notes which sound right and pleasing together. ❑ *I had been looking for ways to combine harmonic and rhythmic structures.*

har|moni|ca /hɑrmɒnɪkə/ (**harmonicas**) N-COUNT [oft the N] A **harmonica** is a small musical instrument. You play the harmonica by moving it across your lips and blowing and sucking air through it.

har|mo|ni|ous /hɑrmoʊniəs/ ADJ A **harmonious** relationship, agreement, or discussion is friendly and peaceful. ❑ *Their harmonious relationship resulted in part from their similar goals.* ● **har|mo|ni|ous|ly** ADV [ADV after v] ❑ *To live together harmoniously as men and women is an achievement.*

har|mo|nize /hɑrmənaɪz/ (**harmonizes, harmonizing, harmonized**)

in BRIT, also use **harmonise**

1 V-RECIP If two or more things **harmonize** with each other, they fit in well with each other. ❑ *How well all her garments harmonized with each other.* **2** V-T When governments or organizations **harmonize** laws, systems, or regulations, they agree in a friendly way to make them the same or similar. ❑ *The leaders have agreed to harmonize their national policies on immigration and asylum.* **3** V-I When people **harmonize**, they sing or play notes which are different from the main tune but which sound nice with it. ❑ *...a perfectly pitched gospel group that harmonized perfectly.*

har|mo|ny /hɑrməni/ (**harmonies**) **1** N-UNCOUNT If people are living in **harmony** with each other, they are living together peacefully rather than fighting or arguing. ❑ *...the notion that mankind should dominate nature rather than live in harmony with it.* **2** N-VAR **Harmony** is the pleasant combination of different notes of music played at the same time. ❑ *...singing in harmony.* **3** N-UNCOUNT The **harmony** of something is the way in which its parts are combined into a pleasant arrangement. ❑ *...the ordered harmony of the universe.* **4** → See feature box at **music**

har|ness /hɑrnɪs/ (**harnesses, harnessing, harnessed**) **1** V-T If you **harness** something such as an emotion or natural source of energy, you bring it under your control and use it. ❑ *...a monumental project to harness the power of the river for electricity.* **2** N-COUNT A **harness** is a set of straps which fit under a person's arms and fasten around their body in order to keep a piece of equipment in place or to prevent the person moving from a place. **3** N-COUNT A **harness** is a set of leather straps and metal links fastened around a horse's head or body so that the horse can have a carriage, cart, or plow fastened to it. **4** V-T [usu passive] If a horse or other animal **is harnessed**, a harness is put on it, especially so that it can pull a carriage, cart, or plow. ❑ *On Sunday the horses were harnessed to a heavy wagon for a day-long ride over the border.* **5** → See feature box at **electricity**

harp /hɑrp/ (**harps, harping, harped**) N-VAR A **harp** is a large musical instrument consisting of a row of strings stretched from the top to the bottom of a frame. You play the harp by plucking the strings with your fingers.
▶ **harp on** PHRASAL VERB If you say that someone **harps on** a subject, or **harps on** about it, you mean that they keep on talking about it in a way that other people find annoying. ❑ *Jones harps on this theme more than on any other.*

harp|ist /hɑrpɪst/ (**harpists**) N-COUNT A **harpist** is someone who plays the harp.

har|poon /hɑrpun/ (**harpoons, harpooning, harpooned**) **1** N-COUNT A **harpoon** is a long pointed weapon with a long rope attached to it, which is fired or thrown by people hunting whales or large sea fish. **2** V-T To **harpoon** a whale or large fish means to hit it with a harpoon. ❑ *Norwegian whalers said yesterday they had harpooned a female minke whale.*

harp|si|chord /hɑrpsɪkɔrd/ (harpsichords) N-VAR [oft the N] A **harpsichord** is an old-fashioned musical instrument similar to a small piano. When you press the keys, the strings are pulled, rather than being hit by hammers as in a piano.

har|py /hɑrpi/ (harpies) **1** N-COUNT [usu pl, oft the N] In classical mythology, the **harpies** were creatures with the bodies of birds and the faces of women. They flew quickly and were cruel and greedy. **2** N-COUNT If you refer to a woman as a **harpy**, you mean that she is very cruel or nasty. [LITERARY, DISAPPROVAL] ❏ ...a snobby, scheming harpy who sells off the family silverware.

har|ri|dan /hærɪdən/ (harridans) N-COUNT If you call a woman a **harridan**, you mean that she is unpleasant and aggressive. [FORMAL, DISAPPROVAL] ❏ She was a mean old harridan.

har|row /hæroʊ/ (harrows) N-COUNT A **harrow** is a piece of farm equipment consisting of a row of blades attached to a heavy frame. When it is pulled over plowed land, the blades break up large lumps of soil.

har|row|ing /hæroʊɪŋ/ ADJ A **harrowing** experience is extremely upsetting or disturbing. ❏ You've had a harrowing time this past month.

har|ry /hæri/ (harries, harrying, harried) V-T If someone **harries** you, they keep bothering you or trying to get something from you. ❏ He is increasingly active in harrying the government in late-night debates. ● **har|ried** ADJ ❏ ...harried shoppers scurrying from one crowded store to another.

harsh /hɑrʃ/ (harsher, harshest) **1** ADJ **Harsh** climates or conditions are very difficult for people, animals, and plants to live in. ❏ ...the harsh desert environment. ● **harsh|ness** N-UNCOUNT ❏ ...the harshness of their living conditions. **2** ADJ **Harsh** actions or speech are unkind and show no understanding or sympathy. ❏ He said many harsh and unkind things about his opponents. ● **harsh|ly** ADV [ADV with v] ❏ She's been told that her husband is being harshly treated in prison. ● **harsh|ness** N-UNCOUNT ❏ ...treating him with great harshness. **3** ADJ Something that is **harsh** is so hard, bright, or rough that it seems unpleasant or harmful. ❏ Tropical colors may look rather harsh in our dull northern light. ● **harsh|ness** N-UNCOUNT ❏ As the wine ages, it loses its bitter harshness. **4** ADJ **Harsh** voices and sounds are ones that are rough and unpleasant to listen to. ❏ It's a pity she has such a loud harsh voice. ● **harsh|ly** ADV [ADV with v] ❏ Chris laughed harshly. ● **harsh|ness** N-UNCOUNT ❏ Then in a tone of abrupt harshness, he added, "Open these trunks!" **5** ADJ If you talk about **harsh** realities or facts, or the **harsh** truth, you are emphasizing that they are true or real, although they are unpleasant and people try to avoid thinking about them. [EMPHASIS] ❏ The harsh truth is that luck plays a big part in who will live or die.

har|vest /hɑrvɪst/ (harvests, harvesting, harvested) **1** N-SING The **harvest** is the gathering of a crop. ❏ There was about 300 million tons of grain in the fields at the start of the harvest. **2** N-COUNT A **harvest** is the crop that is gathered in. ❏ Millions of people are threatened with starvation as a result of drought and poor harvests. **3** V-T When you **harvest** a crop, you gather it in. ❏ Rice farmers here still plant and harvest their crops by hand. **4** V-T If someone **harvests** data, they collect it from different sources, for example on the internet. ❏ Millions of social media users have unknowingly had their personal data harvested.

har|vest|er /hɑrvɪstər/ (harvesters) **1** N-COUNT A **harvester** is a machine which cuts and often collects crops such as wheat, corn, or vegetables. **2** → see also **combine harvester** **3** N-COUNT You can refer to a person who cuts, picks, or gathers crops as a **harvester**.

has

The auxiliary verb is pronounced /həz/, STRONG hæz/. The main verb is usually pronounced /hæz/.

Has is the third person singular of the present tense of **have**.

has-been (has-beens) N-COUNT If you describe someone as a **has-been**, you are indicating in an unkind way that they were important or respected in the past, but they are not now. [DISAPPROVAL] ❏ ...the so-called experts and various has-beens who foist opinions on us.

hash /hæʃ/ (hashes, hashing, hashed) **1** N-UNCOUNT **Hash** is a dish made from meat cut into small lumps and fried with other ingredients such as onions or potato. ❏ ...corned beef hash. **2** N-COUNT [usu sing] A **hash** is the sign #, found on telephone keypads and computer keyboards. [mainly BRIT, SPOKEN]

in AM, usually use **pound sign**

3 PHRASE If you **make a hash of** a job or task, you do it very badly. [INFORMAL] ❏ The government made a total hash of things and squandered a small fortune.
▶ **hash out** **1** PHRASAL VERB [also V n P] If people **hash out** something such as a plan or an agreement, they decide on it after a lot of discussion. [AM] ❏ The House and Senate are to begin soon hashing out an agreement for sanctions legislation. **2** PHRASAL VERB If people **hash out** a problem or a dispute, they discuss it thoroughly until they reach an agreement. [AM] ❏ ...while the parties try to hash out their differences in court.

hash browns also **hashed browns** N-PLURAL **Hash browns** or **hashed browns** are potatoes that have been chopped into small pieces, formed into small cakes, and cooked on a grill or in a frying pan.

hash|ish /hæʃiʃ/ N-UNCOUNT **Hashish** is an illegal drug made from the hemp plant which some people smoke like a cigarette to make them feel relaxed. [OLD-FASHIONED]

hash|tag /hæʃtæg/ (hashtags) N-COUNT A **hashtag** is a word or phrase that has the hash symbol (#) in front of it, to show that it is the topic of a message on social media. [COMPUTING] ❏ Over the course of the day, dozens of memories were collected under the hashtag #Remembering_Challenger.

hasn't /hæzənt/ **Hasn't** is the usual spoken form of 'has not.'

hasp /hɑsp hæsp/ (hasps) N-COUNT A **hasp** is a flat piece of metal with a long hole in it, fastened to the edge of a door or lid. To close the door or lid, you push the hasp over a metal loop fastened to the other part and put a lock through the loop.

has|sle /hæsəl/ (hassles, hassling, hassled) **1** N-VAR A **hassle** is a situation that is difficult and involves problems, effort, or arguments with people. [INFORMAL] ❏ I don't think it's worth the money or the hassle. **2** V-T If someone **hassles** you, they cause problems for you, often by repeatedly telling you or asking you to do something, in an annoying way. [INFORMAL] ❏ Then my husband started hassling me.

has|sock /hæsək/ (hassocks) **1** N-COUNT A **hassock** is a thick cushion or padded stool that you sit on or rest your feet on. **2** N-COUNT A **hassock** is a cushion for kneeling on in a church. [mainly BRIT]

hast /hæst/ **Hast** is an old-fashioned second person singular form of the verb 'have.' It is used with 'thou' which is an old-fashioned form of 'you.'

haste /heɪst/ **1** N-UNCOUNT **Haste** is the quality of doing something quickly, sometimes too quickly so that you are careless and make mistakes. ❏ In their haste to escape the rising water, they dropped some expensive equipment. **2** PHRASE If you do something **in haste**, you do it quickly and hurriedly, and sometimes carelessly. ❏ Don't act in haste or be hot-headed.

has|ten /heɪsən/ (hastens, hastening, hastened) **1** V-T If you **hasten** an event or process, often an unpleasant one, you make it happen faster or sooner. ❏ But if he does this, he may hasten the collapse of his own country. **2** V-T If you **hasten** to do something, you are quick to do it. ❏ She more than anyone had hastened to sign the contract.

has|ty /heɪsti/ (hastier, hastiest) **1** ADJ A **hasty** movement, action, or statement is sudden, and often done in reaction to something that has just happened. ❏ Donald had overturned a chair in his hasty departure. ● **hasti|ly** /heɪstɪli/ ADV [ADV with v] ❏ The council was hastily convened after his father said he was resigning. **2** ADJ If you describe a person or their behavior as **hasty**, you mean that they are acting too quickly, without thinking carefully, for example because they are angry. [DISAPPROVAL] ❏ A number of the United States' allies had urged him not to make a hasty decision. ● **hasti|ly** ADV [ADV with v] ❏ I decided that nothing should be done hastily, that things had to be sorted out carefully.

hat ✦✧✧ /hæt/ (hats) **1** N-COUNT A **hat** is a head covering, often with a brim around it, which is usually worn outdoors to give protection from the weather. ❏ ...a plump woman in a red hat. **2** N-COUNT If you say that someone is wearing a particular **hat**, you mean that they are performing a particular role at that time. If you say that they wear several **hats**, you mean that they have several roles or jobs. ◻ *Now I'll take off my "friend hat" and put on my "therapist hat."* ■ PHRASE If you say that you are ready to do something **at the drop of a hat**, you mean that you are willing to do it immediately, without hesitating. ◻ *India is one part of the world I would go to at the drop of a hat.* ■ PHRASE If you tell someone to **keep** a piece of information **under** their **hat**, you are asking them not to tell anyone else about it. ◻ *Look, if I tell you something, will you promise to keep it under your hat?* ■ PHRASE If you say that you take your **hat off to** someone, you mean that you admire them for something that they have done. [APPROVAL] ◻ *I take my hat off to Mr. Clarke for taking this action.* ■ PHRASE To **pull** something **out of the hat** means to do something unexpected which helps you to succeed, often when you are failing. ◻ *There are expectations that he'll pull a cease-fire out of a hat.* ■ PHRASE In competitions, if you say that the winners will be drawn or picked **out of the hat**, you mean that they will be chosen randomly, so everyone has an equal chance of winning. ◻ *The first 10 correct entries drawn out of the hat will win a pair of tickets, worth $30 each.* ■ → See also color supplement

hat|box /hǽtbɒks/ (**hatboxes**) N-COUNT A **hatbox** is a cylindrical box in which a hat can be carried and stored.

hatch /hætʃ/ (**hatches, hatching, hatched**) ■ V-T/V-I When a baby bird, insect, or other animal **hatches**, or when it **is hatched**, it comes out of its egg by breaking the shell. ◻ *The young disappeared soon after they were hatched.* ■ V-T/V-I When an egg **hatches** or when a bird, insect, or other animal **hatches** an egg, the egg breaks open and a baby comes out. ◻ *The eggs hatch after a week or ten days.* ■ V-T If you **hatch** a plot or a scheme, you think of it and work it out. ◻ *He has accused opposition parties of hatching a plot to assassinate the pope.* ■ N-COUNT A **hatch** is an opening in the deck of a ship, through which people or cargo can go. You can also refer to the door of this opening as a **hatch**. ◻ *He stuck his head up through the hatch*

hatch|back /hǽtʃbæk/ (**hatchbacks**) ■ N-COUNT A **hatchback** is a car with an extra door at the back which opens upward. ■ → See also color supplement

hatch|ery /hǽtʃəri/ (**hatcheries**) N-COUNT A **hatchery** is a place where people control the hatching of eggs, especially fish eggs.

hatch|et /hǽtʃɪt/ (**hatchets**) ■ N-COUNT A **hatchet** is a small ax that you can hold in one hand. ■ PHRASE If two people **bury the hatchet**, they become friendly again after a quarrel or disagreement. ◻ *It is time to bury the hatchet and forget about what has happened in the past.*

hatch|et job (**hatchet jobs**) N-COUNT [usu sing, oft N *on* n] To do a **hatchet job** on someone or something means to say or write something mentioning many bad things about them, which harms their reputation. [INFORMAL] ◻ *Unfortunately, his idea of bold journalism was a hatchet job, portraying the staff in a negative light.*

hatch|et man (**hatchet men**) N-COUNT You can refer to someone who makes changes in an organization by getting rid of lots of people as a **hatchet man**, especially if you think they do so in an unnecessarily harsh way. [INFORMAL, DISAPPROVAL]

hatch|way /hǽtʃweɪ/ (**hatchways**) N-COUNT A **hatchway** is the same as a **hatch**.

hate ♦◇◇ /heɪt/ (**hates, hating, hated**) ■ V-T If you **hate** someone or something, you have an extremely strong feeling of dislike for them. ◻ *Most people hate him, but they don't dare to say so, because he still rules the country.* • N-UNCOUNT **Hate** is also a noun. ◻ *I was 17 and filled with a lot of hate.* ■ V-T [no cont] If you say that you **hate** something such as a particular activity, you mean that you find it very unpleasant. ◻ *Ted hated parties, even gatherings of people he liked individually.* ◻ *He hates to be interrupted during training.* ◻ *He hated coming home to the empty house.* ■ V-T [no cont] You can use **hate** in expressions such as '**I hate to trouble you**' or '**I hate to bother you**' when you are apologizing to someone for interrupting them or asking them to do something. [POLITENESS] ◻ *I hate to rush you but I have another appointment later on.* ■ V-T [no cont] You can use **hate** in expressions such as '**I hate to say it**' or '**I hate to tell you**' when you want to express regret about what you are about to say, because you think it is unpleasant or should not be the case. [FEELINGS] ◻ *I hate to tell you this, but tomorrow's your last day.* ■ **to hate someone's guts** → see **gut** ■ V-T [no cont] You can use **hate** in expressions such as '**I hate to see**' or '**I hate to think**' when you are emphasizing that you find a situation or an idea unpleasant. [EMPHASIS] ◻ *I just hate to see you doing this to yourself.* ■ V-T [no cont] You can use **hate** in expressions such as '**I'd hate to think**' when you hope that something is not true or that something will not happen. ◻ *I'd hate to think my job would not be secure if I left it temporarily.*

hate cam|paign (**hate campaigns**) N-COUNT [usu sing] A **hate campaign** is a series of actions which are intended to harm or upset someone, or to make other people have a low opinion of them. ◻ *The media has waged a virulent hate campaign against her.*

hate crime (**hate crimes**) N-COUNT A **hate crime** is a crime against a person that is motivated by feelings of hatred for his or her race, religion, sexuality, or gender.

hate|ful /heɪtfʊl/ ■ ADJ Someone or something that is **hateful** is extremely bad or unpleasant. [OLD-FASHIONED] ◻ *I'm sorry. That was a hateful thing to say.* ■ ADJ Someone who is **hateful** hates someone else. ◻ *These are not necessarily hateful, malicious people.*

hate mail also **hate-mail** N-UNCOUNT If someone receives **hate mail**, they receive unpleasant or threatening letters or emails.

hat|er /heɪtər/ (**haters**) N-COUNT [N *of* n] If you call someone a **hater of** something, you mean that they strongly dislike that thing. ◻ *Braccio was a hater of idleness.* • COMB IN N-COUNT **Hater** is also a combining form. ◻ *He was reputed to be a woman-hater.*

hath /hæθ/ **Hath** is an old-fashioned third person singular form of the verb 'have.'

hat|pin /hǽtpɪn/ (**hatpins**) N-COUNT A **hatpin** is a metal pin which can be pushed through a woman's hat and through her hair to keep the hat in position.

ha|tred /heɪtrɪd/ N-UNCOUNT **Hatred** is an extremely strong feeling of dislike for someone or something. ◻ *Her hatred of them would never lead her to murder.*

hat trick (**hat tricks**) also **hat-trick** N-COUNT A **hat trick** is a series of three achievements, especially in a sports event, for example three goals scored by the same person in a soccer game. ◻ *I scored a hat-trick in my first game.*

haugh|ty /hɔti/ ADJ [usu ADJ n] You use **haughty** to describe someone's behavior or appearance when you disapprove of the fact that they seem to be very proud and to think that they are better than other people. [DISAPPROVAL] ◻ *He spoke in a haughty tone.* • **haugh|ti|ly** /hɔtɪli/ ADV ◻ *Toni looked at him rather haughtily.*

haul /hɔl/ (**hauls, hauling, hauled**) ■ V-T If you **haul** something which is heavy or difficult to move, you move it using a lot of effort. ◻ *A crane had to be used to haul the car out of the stream.* ■ V-T [usu passive] If someone **is hauled** before a court or someone in authority, they are made to appear before them because they are accused of having done something wrong. ◻ *He was hauled before the managing director and fired.* • PHRASAL VERB **Haul up** means the same as **haul**. ◻ *He was hauled up before the board of trustees.* ■ N-COUNT A **haul** is a quantity of things that are stolen, or a quantity of stolen or illegal goods found by police or customs. ◻ *The size of the drug haul shows that the international trade in heroin is still flourishing.* ■ PHRASE If you say that a task or a journey is a **long haul**, you mean that it takes a long time and a lot of effort. ◻ *Revitalizing the economy will be a long haul.* ■ → see also **long-haul**

haul|er /hɔlər/ (**haulers**) N-COUNT A **hauler** is a company or a person that transports goods by road. [AM]

haunch /hɔntʃ/ (**haunches**) ■ PHRASE [V PHR] If you get down **on** your **haunches**, you lower yourself toward the ground so that your legs are bent under you and you are balancing on your feet. ◻ *Edgar squatted on his haunches.* ■ N-COUNT [usu pl] The **haunches** of an animal or person are the area of the body which includes the bottom, the hips, and the tops of the legs.

haunt /hɔnt/ (**haunts, haunting, haunted**) ■ V-T If something unpleasant **haunts** you, you keep thinking or worrying about it over a long period of time. ◻ *He would always be haunted by that scene in Well Park.* ■ V-T Something that **haunts** a person or organization regularly causes them problems over a long

haunted

period of time. ☐ *The stigma of being a bankrupt is likely to haunt him for the rest of his life.* **3** N-COUNT A place that is the **haunt** of a particular person is one which they often visit because they enjoy going there. ☐ *The islands are a favorite summer haunt for yacht owners.* **4** V-T A ghost or spirit that **haunts** a place or a person regularly appears in the place, or is seen by the person and frightens them. ☐ *His ghost is said to haunt some of the rooms, banging a toy drum.*

haunt|ed /hɔ́ntɪd/ **1** ADJ A **haunted** building or other place is one where a ghost regularly appears. ☐ *Tracy said the cabin was haunted.* **2** ADJ Someone who has a **haunted** expression looks very worried or troubled. ☐ *She looked so haunted, I almost didn't recognize her.*

haunt|ing /hɔ́ntɪŋ/ ADJ **Haunting** sounds, images, or words remain in your thoughts because they are very beautiful or sad. ☐ *...the haunting calls of wild birds in the mahogany trees.*
● **haunt|ing|ly** ADV ☐ *Each one of these ancient towns is hauntingly beautiful.*

haute cou|ture /óʊt kutyʊə́r/ **1** N-UNCOUNT **Haute couture** refers to the designing and making of high-quality fashion clothes, or to the clothes themselves. [FORMAL] **2** → See feature box at **fashion**

hau|teur /hoʊtɜ́r/ N-UNCOUNT You can use **hauteur** to describe behavior which you think is proud and arrogant. [FORMAL, DISAPPROVAL] ☐ *Once, she had been put off by his hauteur.*

HAVE

① AUXILIARY VERB USES
② USED WITH NOUNS DESCRIBING ACTIONS
③ OTHER VERB USES AND PHRASES
④ MODAL PHRASES

---

① **have** ♦♦♦ /həv, STRONG hæv/ (has, having, had)

In spoken English, forms of **have** are often shortened, for example **I have** is shortened to **I've** and **has not** is shortened to **hasn't**.

1 AUX You use the forms **have** and **has** with a past participle to form the present perfect tense of verbs. ☐ *Alex has already gone.* ☐ *What have you found so far?* ☐ *Frankie hasn't been feeling well for a long time.* **2** AUX You use the form **had** with a past participle to form the past perfect tense of verbs. ☐ *When I met her, she had just returned from a job interview.* **3** AUX **Have** is used in question tags. ☐ *You haven't sent her away, have you?* **4** AUX You use **have** when you are confirming or contradicting a statement containing 'have,' 'has,' or 'had,' or answering a question. ☐ *"You'd never seen the Marilyn Monroe film?"—"No I hadn't."* **5** AUX The form **having** with a past participle can be used to introduce a clause in which you mention an action which had already happened before another action began. ☐ *He arrived in San Francisco, having left New Jersey on January 19th.*

USAGE

have

You use a progressive form to say that an activity is taking place. For example, don't say '~~He has a bath at the moment.~~' Say '*He **is having** a bath at the moment.*' *The children **are having** a party.*

---

② **have** ♦♦♦ /hæv/ (has, having, had)

Have is used in combination with a wide range of nouns, where the meaning of the combination is mostly given by the noun.

1 V-T [no passive] You can use **have** followed by a noun to talk about an action or event, when it would be possible to use the same word as a verb. For example, you can say '**I had a look at the photos**' instead of 'I looked at the photos.' ☐ *I went out and had a walk around.* ☐ *We had a laugh over that one.* **2** V-T [no passive] In normal spoken or written English, people use **have** with a wide range of nouns to talk about actions and events, often instead of a more specific verb. For example people are more likely to say '**we had ice cream**' or '**she's had a shock**' than 'we ate ice cream,' or 'she's suffered a shock.' ☐ *Come and have a meal with us tonight.* ☐ *We will be having a meeting to decide what to do.*

---

③ **have** ♦♦♦ /hæv/ (has, having, had)

For meanings **1** – **4**, people often use **have gotten** in spoken American English or **have got** in spoken British English, instead of **have**. In this case, **have** is pronounced as an auxiliary verb. For more information and examples of the use of 'have got' and 'have gotten,' see **got**.

→ Please look at meanings **17** and **18** to see if the expression you are looking for is shown under another headword.

1 V-T [no passive] You use **have** to say that someone or something owns a particular thing, or when you are mentioning one of their qualities or characteristics. ☐ *Oscar had a new bicycle.* ☐ *I want to have my own business.* ☐ *She had no job and no money.* ☐ *You have beautiful eyes.* ☐ *Do you have any brothers and sisters?* **2** V-T [no passive] If you **have** something to do, you are responsible for doing it or must do it. ☐ *He had plenty of work to do.* **3** V-T [no passive] You can use **have** instead of 'there is' to say that something exists or happens. For example, you can say '**you have no alternative**' instead of 'there is no alternative,' or '**she had a good view from her window**' instead of 'there was a good view from her window.' ☐ *He had two tenants living with him.* **4** V-T [no passive] If you **have** something such as a part of your body in a particular position or state, it is in that position or state. ☐ *Mary had her eyes closed.* ☐ *They had the curtains open.* **5** V-T [no passive] If you **have** something done, someone does it for you or you arrange for it to be done. ☐ *I had your rooms cleaned and aired.* ☐ *They had him killed.* **6** V-T [no passive] If someone **has** something unpleasant happen to them, it happens to them. ☐ *We had our money stolen.* **7** V-T [no passive] If you **have** someone do something, you persuade, cause, or order them to do it. ☐ *The bridge is not as impressive as some guides would have you believe.* **8** V-T [no passive] If someone **has** you by a part of your body, they are holding you there and they are trying to hurt you or force you to go somewhere. ☐ *He had her by the arm and he was screaming at her.* **9** V-T [no passive] If you **have** something from someone, they give it to you. ☐ *You can have my ticket.* ☐ *Can I have your name please?* **10** V-T [no passive] If you **have** an illness or disability, you suffer from it. ☐ *I had a headache.* **11** V-T [no passive] If a woman **has** a baby, she gives birth to it. If she **is having** a baby, she is pregnant. ☐ *My wife has just had a baby boy.* **12** V-T [with neg] You can use **have** in expressions such as '**I won't have it**' or '**I'm not having that,**' to mean that you will not allow or put up with something. ☐ *I'm not having any of that nonsense.* **13** PHRASE You can use **has it** in expressions such as '**rumor has it that**' or '**as legend has it**' when you are quoting something that you have heard, but you do not necessarily think it is true. [VAGUENESS] ☐ *Rumor has it that tickets were being sold for $300.* **14** PHRASE If someone **has it in for** you, they do not like you and they want to make life difficult for you. [INFORMAL] ☐ *He's always had it in for the Dawkins family.* **15** PHRASE If you **have it in** you, you have abilities and skills which you do not usually use and which only show themselves in a difficult situation. ☐ *"You were brilliant!" he said. "I didn't know you had it in you."* **16** PHRASE If you **have it out** or **have things out** with someone, you discuss a problem or disagreement very openly with them, even if it means having an argument, because you think this is the best way to solve the problem. ☐ *Why not have it out with your critic, discuss the whole thing face to face?* **17 to be had** → see **had** **18 to have had it** → see **had**

④ **have** ♦♦♦ /hæv, hæf/ (has, having, had) **1** PHRASE You use **have to** when you are saying that something is necessary or required, or must happen. If you do not **have to** do something, it is not necessary or required. ☐ *He had to go to Germany.* ☐ *You have to be careful what you say on TV.* **2** PHRASE You can use **have to** in order to say that you feel certain that something is true or will happen. ☐ *There has to be some kind of way out.*

ha|ven /héɪvən/ (havens) **1** N-COUNT A **haven** is a place where people or animals feel safe, secure, and happy. ☐ *...Lake Baringo, a freshwater haven for a mixed variety of birds.* **2** → see also **safe haven**

have-nots PHRASE If you refer to two groups of people as **haves and have-nots**, you mean that the first group are very wealthy and the second group are very poor. You can also refer generally to poor people as **have-nots**.

haven't /hˈævənt/ Haven't is the usual spoken form of 'have not.'

haves /hˈævz/ haves and have-nots → see have-nots

hav|oc /hˈævək/ **1** N-UNCOUNT **Havoc** is great disorder and confusion. ❑ *Rioters caused havoc in the center of the town.* **2** PHRASE If one thing **plays havoc with** another or **wreaks havoc on** it, it prevents it from continuing or functioning as normal, or damages it. ❑ *The weather played havoc with airline schedules.*

haw /hˈɔː/ (haws, hawing, hawed) **1** N-COUNT **Haws** are the red berries produced by hawthorn trees in the fall. **2** EXCLAM Writers sometimes use '**haw haw**' to show that one of their characters is laughing, especially in a rather unpleasant or superior way. ❑ *Look at the plebs! Getting all muddy! Haw haw haw!* **3** PHRASE If you **hem and haw**, you take a long time to say something because you cannot think of the right words, or because you are not sure what to say. ❑ *Tim hemmed and hawed, but finally told his boss the truth.*

hawk /hˈɔːk/ (hawks) **1** N-COUNT A **hawk** is a large bird with a short, hooked beak, sharp claws, and very good eyesight. Hawks catch and eat small birds and animals. **2** N-COUNT In politics, if you refer to someone as a **hawk**, you mean that they believe in using force and violence to achieve something, rather than using more peaceful or diplomatic methods. Compare **dove**. ❑ *Both hawks and doves have expanded their conditions for ending the war.* **3** PHRASE If you **watch** someone **like a hawk**, you observe them very carefully, usually to make sure that they do not make a mistake or do something you do not want them to do. ❑ *If we hadn't watched him like a hawk, he would have escaped.*

hawk|er /hˈɔːkər/ (hawkers) N-COUNT You can use **hawker** to refer to a person who tries to sell things by calling at people's homes or standing in the street, especially when you do not approve of this activity. [DISAPPROVAL]

hawk|ish /hˈɔːkɪʃ/ ADJ Journalists use **hawkish** to describe politicians or governments who are in favor of using force to achieve something, rather than using peaceful and diplomatic methods. ❑ *He is one of the most hawkish members of the new cabinet.*

haws|er /hˈɔːzər/ (hawsers) N-COUNT A **hawser** is a large heavy rope, especially one used on a ship.

haw|thorn /hˈɔːθɔːrn/ (hawthorns) N-VAR A **hawthorn** is a small tree which has sharp thorns and produces white or pink flowers.

hay /hˈeɪ/ **1** N-UNCOUNT **Hay** is grass which has been cut and dried so that it can be used to feed animals. ❑ *...bales of hay.* **2** PHRASE If you say that someone **is making hay** or **is making hay while the sun shines**, you mean that they are taking advantage of a situation that is favorable to them while they have the chance to. ❑ *We knew war was coming, and were determined to make hay while we could.*

hay fe|ver N-UNCOUNT If someone has **hay fever**, they sneeze and their eyes itch, because they are allergic to grass or flowers.

hay|stack /hˈeɪstæk/ (haystacks) **1** N-COUNT A **haystack** is a large, solid pile of hay, often covered with a straw roof to protect it, which is left in the field until it is needed. **2** PHRASE If you are trying to find something and say that it is like looking for **a needle in a haystack**, you mean that you are extremely unlikely to find it.

hay|wire /hˈeɪwaɪər/ ADJ [v-link ADJ] If something goes **haywire**, it goes out of control or starts doing the wrong thing. [INFORMAL] ❑ *Many people think the legal system has gone haywire.*

haz|ard /hˈæzərd/ (hazards, hazarding, hazarded) **1** N-COUNT A **hazard** is something which could be dangerous to you, your health or safety, or your plans or reputation. ❑ *A new report suggests that chewing gum may be a health hazard.* **2** V-T If you **hazard** or if you **hazard a guess**, you make a suggestion about something which is only a guess and which you know might be wrong. ❑ *I would hazard a guess that they'll do fairly well in the next election.*

WORD HISTORY

hazard
This word comes from the Arabic *al zahr*, meaning 'the dice.' Traditionally, games using dice have involved risk, and this has led to the word **hazard** being used to refer to risk and danger.

haz|ard|ous /hˈæzərdəs/ ADJ Something that is **hazardous** is dangerous, especially to people's health or safety. ❑ *They have no way to dispose of the hazardous waste they produce.*

haze /hˈeɪz/ (hazes) **1** N-VAR **Haze** is light mist, caused by particles of water or dust in the air, which prevents you from seeing distant objects clearly. Haze often forms in hot weather. ❑ *They vanished into the haze near the horizon.* **2** N-SING If there is a **haze** of something such as smoke or steam, you cannot see clearly through it. [LITERARY] ❑ *Dan smiled at him through a haze of smoke and steaming coffee.*

ha|zel /hˈeɪzəl/ (hazels) **1** N-VAR A **hazel** is a small tree which produces nuts that you can eat. **2** COLOR **Hazel** eyes are greenish brown in color.

hazel|nut /hˈeɪzəlnʌt/ (hazelnuts) **1** N-COUNT **Hazelnuts** are nuts from a hazel tree, which can be eaten. **2** → See also color supplement

haz|ing /hˈeɪzɪŋ/ (hazings) N-VAR [oft N n] **Hazing** is a ritual practiced in some universities and other institutions, in which a new member of a club or society is humiliated or abused. [AM] ❑ *Her son had been the victim of fraternity hazing.* ❑ *...a hazing featuring broken glass.* ❑ *...a vicious hazing ritual.*

hazy /hˈeɪzi/ (hazier, haziest) **1** ADJ **Hazy** weather conditions are those in which things are difficult to see, because of light mist, hot air, or dust. ❑ *The air was thin and crisp, filled with hazy sunshine and frost.* **2** ADJ If you are **hazy** about ideas or details, or if they are **hazy**, you are uncertain or confused about them. ❑ *I'm a bit hazy about that.* **3** ADJ If things seem **hazy**, you cannot see things clearly, for example because you are feeling ill. ❑ *My vision has grown so hazy.*

H-bomb (H-bombs) N-COUNT An **H-bomb** is a bomb in which energy is released from hydrogen atoms.

HDTV /ˌeɪtʃ diː tiː viː/ N-UNCOUNT [oft N n] **HDTV** is a television system that provides a clearer image than conventional television systems. **HDTV** is an abbreviation for 'high-definition television.' ❑ *She said the quality of digital TV is noticeably better, especially HDTV.* ❑ *Connect directly to your PC, laptop, and HDTV.*

he ♦♦♦ /hi, STRONG hiː/

He is a third person singular pronoun. He is used as the subject of a verb.

1 PRON-SING You use **he** to refer to a man, boy, or male animal. ❑ *He could never quite remember all our names.* **2** PRON-SING In written English, **he** is sometimes used to refer to a person without saying whether that person is a man or a woman. Many people prefer to use 'he or she' or 'they' as an alternative to 'he.' ❑ *The teacher should encourage the child to proceed as far as he can.*

H.E. N-TITLE **H.E.** is a written abbreviation for **His Excellency** or **Her Excellency** and is used in the title of an important official such as an ambassador. ❑ *...H.E. the Italian Ambassador.*

HEAD
① NOUN AND ADVERB USES
② VERB USES
③ PHRASES

① **head** ♦♦♦ /hˈɛd/ (heads) **1** N-COUNT Your **head** is the top part of your body, which has your eyes, mouth, and brain in it. ❑ *She turned her head away from him.* **2** N-COUNT You can use **head** to refer to your mind and your mental abilities. ❑ *...an exceptional analyst who could do complex math in his head.* **3** N-SING The **head** of a line of people or vehicles is the front of it, or the first person or vehicle in the line. ❑ *He made his way to the head of the line.* **4** N-COUNT The **head** of a company or organization is the person in charge of it and in charge of the people in it. ❑ *Heads of government from more than 100 countries gather in Geneva tomorrow.* **5** N-COUNT The **head** of something long and thin is the end which is wider than or a different shape from the rest, and which is often considered to be the most important part. ❑ *There should be no exposed screw heads.* **6** ADV If you flip a coin and it comes down **heads**, you can see the side of the coin which has a picture of a head on it. ❑ *"We might flip a coin for it," suggested Ted. "If it's heads, then we'll talk."* **7** → See also color supplement

② **head** ♦♦♦ /hˈɛd/ (heads, heading, headed) **1** V-T If someone or something **heads** a line or procession, they are at the front

headache · 602 · **headline**

of it. ▫ *The parson, heading the procession, had just turned right toward the churchyard.* **2** V-T If something **heads** a list or group, it is at the top of it. ▫ *Running a business heads the list of ambitions among the 1,000 people interviewed by Good Housekeeping magazine.* **3** V-T If you **head** a department, company, or organization, you are the person in charge of it. ▫ *...the youngest, most ambitious professor ever to head the department.* **4** V-T/V-I If you **are heading** or **are headed** for a particular place, you are going toward that place. ▫ *He was headed for the bus stop.* ▫ *It is not clear how many of them will be heading back to Saudi Arabia tomorrow.* **5** V-T/V-I If something or someone **is heading for** or **is headed for** a particular result, the situation they are in is developing in a way that makes that result very likely. ▫ *The latest talks aimed at ending the civil war appear to be heading for deadlock.* **6** V-T [usu passive] If a piece of writing **is headed** a particular title, it has that title written at the beginning of it. ▫ *One chapter is headed, "Beating the Test."* **7** V-T If you **head** a ball in soccer, you hit it with your head in order to make it go in a particular direction. ▫ *He headed the ball across the face of the goal.* **8** → see also **heading**

③ **head** ♦♦♦ /hɛd/ **1** PHRASE You use **a head** or **per head** after stating a cost or amount in order to indicate that that cost or amount is for each person in a particular group. ▫ *This simple chicken dish costs less than $3 a head.* **2** PHRASE If you have **a head for** something, you can deal with it easily. For example, if you have a **head for figures**, you can do arithmetic easily, and if you have a **head for heights**, you can climb to a great height without feeling afraid. ▫ *I don't have a head for business.* **3** PHRASE If you **get** a fact or idea **into your head**, you suddenly realize or think that it is true and you usually do not change your opinion about it. ▫ *Once they get an idea into their heads, they never give up.* **4** PHRASE If you say that someone has **got** or **gotten** something **into their head**, you mean that they have finally understood or accepted it, and you are usually criticizing them because it has taken them a long time to do this. ▫ *Managers have at last got it into their heads that they can no longer rest content with inefficient operations.* **5** PHRASE If alcoholic drink **goes to** your **head**, it makes you feel drunk. ▫ *That wine was strong, it went to your head.* **6** PHRASE If you say that something such as praise or success **goes to** someone's **head**, you are criticizing them because you think that it makes them too proud or confident. [DISAPPROVAL] ▫ *Ford is definitely not a man to let a little success go to his head.* **7** PHRASE If you are **head over heels** or **head over heels in love**, you are very much in love. ▫ *I was very attracted to men and fell head over heels many times.* **8** PHRASE If you **keep** your **head**, you remain calm in a difficult situation. If you **lose** your **head**, you panic or do not remain calm in a difficult situation. ▫ *She was able to keep her head and not panic.* **9** PHRASE Phrases such as **laugh** your **head off** and **scream** your **head off** can be used to emphasize that someone is laughing or screaming a lot or very loudly. [EMPHASIS] ▫ *He carried on telling a joke, laughing his head off.* **10** PHRASE If something such as an idea, joke, or comment goes **over** someone's **head**, it is too difficult for them to understand. ▫ *I admit that a lot of the ideas went way over my head.* **11** PHRASE If someone does something **over** another person's **head**, they do it without asking them or discussing it with them, especially when they should do so because the other person is in a position of authority. ▫ *He was reprimanded for trying to go over the heads of senior officers.* **12** PHRASE If you say that something unpleasant or embarrassing **rears its ugly head** or **raises its ugly head**, you mean that it occurs, often after not occurring for some time. ▫ *There was a problem which reared its ugly head about a week after she moved back in.* **13** PHRASE If you **stand on** your **head**, you balance upside down with the top of your head and your hands on the ground. ▫ *He was photographed standing on his head doing yoga.* **14** PHRASE If you say that you cannot **make head nor tail of** something or you cannot **make heads or tails of** it, you are emphasizing that you cannot understand it at all. [INFORMAL] ▫ *I couldn't make head nor tail of the damn film.* **15** PHRASE If somebody **takes it into** their **head** to do something, especially something strange or foolish, they suddenly decide to do it. ▫ *He suddenly took it into his head to go out to Australia to stay with his son.* **16** PHRASE If a problem or disagreement **comes to a head** or **is brought to a head**, it becomes so bad that something must be done about it. ▫ *These problems came to a head in September when five of the staff were fired.* **17** PHRASE If two or more people **put** their **heads**

together, they talk about a problem they have and try to solve it. ▫ *So everyone put their heads together and eventually an amicable arrangement was reached.* **18** PHRASE If you **keep** your **head above water**, you just avoid getting into difficulties; used especially to talk about business. ▫ *We are keeping our head above water, but our cash flow position is not too good.* **19** PHRASE If you say that **heads will roll** as a result of something bad that has happened, you mean that people will be punished for it, especially by losing their jobs. ▫ *The group's problems have led to speculation that heads will roll.*

> **Head** is used in a large number of expressions which are explained under other words in the dictionary. For example, the expression 'off the top of your head' is explained at 'top.'

head|ache /hɛdeɪk/ (**headaches**) **1** N-COUNT If you have a **headache**, you have a pain in your head. ▫ *I have had a terrible headache for the last two days.* **2** N-COUNT If you say that something is a **headache**, you mean that it causes you difficulty or worry. ▫ *The airline's biggest headache is the increase in the price of aviation fuel.*

head|band /hɛdbænd/ (**headbands**) N-COUNT A **headband** is a narrow strip of material which you can wear around your head across your forehead, for example to keep hair or sweat out of your eyes.

head|board /hɛdbɔrd/ (**headboards**) N-COUNT A **headboard** is an upright board at the end of a bed where you lay your head.

head-butt (**head-butts, head-butting, head-butted**) also **headbutt** V-T If someone **head-butts** you, they hit you with the top of their head. ▫ *He was said to have head-butted one policeman and stamped on another's hand.* • N-COUNT **Head-butt** is also a noun. ▫ *The cuts could only have been made by head-butts.*

head count (**head counts**) N-COUNT If you do a **head count**, you count the number of people present. You can also use **head count** to talk about the number of people that are present at an event, or that an organization employs. ▫ *The troops rushed back onto the chopper and took off – but a head count showed one man was missing.*

head|dress /hɛddrɛs/ (**headdresses**) N-COUNT A **headdress** is something that is worn on a person's head for decoration.

head|er /hɛdər/ (**headers**) N-COUNT A **header** is text such as a name or a page number that can be automatically displayed at the top of each page of a printed document. Compare **footer**. [COMPUTING] ▫ *...page formatting like headers, footers, and page numbers.*

head|first /hɛdfɜrst/ also **head-first** ADV [ADV after v] If you move **headfirst** in a particular direction, your head is the part of your body that is furthest forward as you are moving. ▫ *He had apparently fallen headfirst down the stairwell.*

head|gear /hɛdgɪər/ also **head gear** N-UNCOUNT You use **headgear** to refer to hats or other things worn on the head.

head|hunt /hɛdhʌnt/ (**headhunts, headhunting, headhunted**) V-T If someone who works for a particular company **is headhunted**, they leave that company because another company has approached them and offered them another job with better pay and higher status. ▫ *She was soon headhunted by an investment bank.*

head|hunter /hɛdhʌntər/ (**headhunters**) N-COUNT A **headhunter** is a person who tries to persuade someone to leave their job and take another job which has better pay and more status. ▫ *...a headhunter for a bank.*

head|ing /hɛdɪŋ/ (**headings**) **1** N-COUNT A **heading** is the title of a piece of writing, which is written or printed at the top of the page. ▫ *...helpful chapter headings.* **2** → see also **head** ②

head|land /hɛdlənd/ (**headlands**) N-COUNT A **headland** is a narrow piece of land which sticks out from the coast into the ocean.

head|less /hɛdlɪs/ ADJ If the body of a person or animal is **headless**, the head has been cut off.

head|light /hɛdlaɪt/ (**headlights**) **1** N-COUNT A vehicle's **headlights** are the large powerful lights at the front. ▫ *Motorists were forced to turn on their headlights at midday.* **2** → See also color supplement

head|line ♦♢♢ /hɛdlaɪn/ (**headlines, headlining, headlined**) **1** N-COUNT A **headline** is the title of a newspaper story, printed in large letters at the top of the story, especially on the front page. ▫ *The front cover of your July 28 issue has the headline: "Time for*

headline-grabbing 603 **health**

action." **2** N-PLURAL The **headlines** are the main points of the news which are read on radio or television. ❏ *I'm Claudia Polley with the news headlines.* **3** V-T [usu passive] If a newspaper or magazine article **is headlined** a particular thing, that is the headline that introduces it. ❏ *The article was headlined "Tell us the truth."* **4** PHRASE Someone or something that **hits the headlines** or **grabs the headlines** gets a lot of publicity from the media. ❏ *El Salvador first hit the world headlines at the beginning of the 1980s.*

COLLOCATIONS

headline
NOUN **1**
noun + **headline**: banner, newspaper, tabloid
adjective + **headline**: back-page, front-page; national; lurid, negative, sensational
verb + **headline**: dominate, grab, hit, hog; run

---

headline-grabbing ADJ [usu ADJ n] A **headline-grabbing** statement or activity is one that is intended to attract a lot of attention, especially from the media. ❏ *...a series of headline-grabbing announcements.*

head|lin|er /hɛdlaɪnər/ (**headliners**) N-COUNT A **headliner** is the main performer or group of performers in a show. ❏ *Headliners at the event will include David Sanborn, Roberta Flack and Bob James.*

head|lock /hɛdlɒk/ (**headlocks**) N-COUNT A **headlock** is a hold in wrestling in which a wrestler grips his opponent's head between his elbow and the side of his body. ❏ *The guard put a youth in a headlock and dragged him away.*

head|long /hɛdlɔŋ/ **1** ADV [ADV after v] If you move **headlong** in a particular direction, you move there very quickly. ❏ *He ran headlong for the open door.* **2** ADV [ADV after v] If you fall or move **headlong**, you fall or move with your head furthest forward. ❏ *She missed her footing and fell headlong down the stairs.* **3** ADV [ADV after v] If you rush **headlong** into something, you do it quickly without thinking carefully about it. ❏ *Do not leap headlong into decisions.* • ADJ [ADJ n] **Headlong** is also an adjective. ❏ *...the headlong rush to independence.*

head|man /hɛdmən/ (**headmen**) N-COUNT A **headman** is the chief or leader of a tribe in a village.

head|master /hɛdmæstər/ (**headmasters**) N-COUNT A **headmaster** is the head teacher of a private school.

head of state (**heads of state**) N-COUNT A **head of state** is the leader of a country, for example a president, king, or queen. ❏ *The authorities have still not named a new head of state.*

head-on 1 ADV [ADV after v] If two vehicles hit each other **head-on**, they hit each other with their fronts pointing toward each other. ❏ *The car collided head-on with a van.* • ADJ [ADJ n] **Head-on** is also an adjective. ❏ *Their car was in a head-on collision with a truck.* **2** ADJ [ADJ n] A **head-on** conflict or approach is direct, without any attempt to compromise or avoid the issue. ❏ *The only victors in a head-on clash between the president and the assembly would be the hardliners on both sides.* • ADV [ADV after v] **Head-on** is also an adverb. ❏ *Once again, I chose to confront the issue head-on.* **3** → See feature box at **accident**

head|phones /hɛdfoʊnz/ **1** N-PLURAL [also *a pair of* N] **Headphones** are a pair of padded speakers which you wear over your ears in order to listen to a radio, recorded music, or for using a phone without other people hearing it. ❏ *...while out cycling one evening and listening to your program on headphones.* **2** → See also color supplement

head|quartered /hɛdkwɔrtərd/ V-T PASSIVE If an organization **is headquartered** in a particular place, that is where its main offices are. ❏ *The company is headquartered in Chicago.*

head|quarters /hɛdkwɔrtərz/ N-SING-COLL The **headquarters** of an organization are its main offices. ❏ *...fraud squad officers from Chicago's police headquarters.*

head|rest /hɛdrɛst/ (**headrests**) N-COUNT A **headrest** is the part of the back of a seat on which you can lean your head, especially one on the front seat of a car.

head|room /hɛdrum/ N-UNCOUNT **Headroom** is the amount of space below a roof or bridge. ❏ *The forecabin, with 6ft headroom, also has plenty of room to stand and get dressed.*

head|scarf /hɛdskɑrf/ (**headscarves**) also **head scarf** N-COUNT A **headscarf** is a scarf that is worn on the head.

head|set /hɛdsɛt/ (**headsets**) **1** N-COUNT A **headset** is a small pair of headphones that you can use for listening to a radio or recorded music, or for using a telephone. ❏ *During the race Mr. Taylor talks to the driver using a headset.* **2** N-COUNT A **headset** is a piece of equipment that you wear on your head so you can see computer images or images from a camera in front of your eyes. ❏ *Soon the wearer of a virtual reality headset will be able to be "present" at sporting or theatrical events staged thousands of miles away.*

head|space /hɛdspeɪs/ N-UNCOUNT You can use **headspace** to refer to someone's mental condition. [INFORMAL] ❏ *Most of what they do is to get players in the right headspace.*

head start (**head starts**) N-COUNT If you have a **head start** on other people, you have an advantage over them in something such as a competition or race. ❏ *A good education gives your child a head start in life.*

head|stone /hɛdstoʊn/ (**headstones**) N-COUNT A **headstone** is a large stone which stands at one end of a grave, usually with the name of the dead person carved on it.

head|strong /hɛdstrɔŋ/ ADJ If you refer to someone as **headstrong**, you are slightly critical of the fact that they are determined to do what they want. ❏ *He's young, very headstrong, but he's a good man underneath.*

heads-up N-SING If you give someone a **heads-up** about something that is going to happen, you tell them about it before it happens. [AM] ❏ *When the airlines decided to enforce these rules without giving anyone a heads-up, it created a lot of problems for travelers.*

head-to-head (**head-to-heads**) **1** ADJ [usu ADJ n] A **head-to-head** contest or competition is one in which two people or groups compete directly against each other. ❏ *Missouri then won a head to head tiebreaker with Colorado.* • ADV [V ADV] **Head-to-head** is also an adverb. ❏ *Canadian business cannot compete head-to-head with American business.* **2** N-COUNT [usu sing] A **head-to-head** is a head-to-head contest or competition. ❏ *...a head-to-head between the champion and the aspiring champion.*

head|waters /hɛdwɔtərz/ also **head-waters**, **head waters** N-PLURAL [oft N *of* n] The **headwaters** of a river are the smaller streams near its source, which combine to form the river. ❏ *...the headwaters of the Amazon river.*

head|way /hɛdweɪ/ PHRASE If you **make headway**, you progress toward achieving something. ❏ *There was concern in the city that police were making little headway in the investigation.*

head|wind /hɛdwɪnd/ (**headwinds**) N-COUNT A **headwind** is a wind which blows in the direction opposite the one in which you are moving.

head|woman /hɛdwʊmən/ (**headwomen**) N-COUNT A **headwoman** is the female chief or leader of a tribe in a village.

head|word /hɛdwɜrd/ (**headwords**) N-COUNT In a dictionary, a **headword** is a word which is followed by an explanation of its meaning.

heady /hɛdi/ (**headier**, **headiest**) ADJ A **heady** drink, atmosphere, or experience strongly affects your senses, for example, by making you feel drunk or excited. ❏ *...in the heady days just after their marriage.*

heal ♦♢♢ /hil/ (**heals**, **healing**, **healed**) **1** V-T/V-I When a broken bone or other injury **heals**, or if someone or something **heals** it, it becomes healthy and normal again. ❏ *Within six weeks the bruising had gone, but it was six months before it all healed.* **2** V-T/V-I If you **heal** something such as a rift or a wound, or if it **heals**, the situation is put right so that people are friendly or happy again. ❏ *We have begun to heal the wounds of war in our society.*

heal|er /hilər/ (**healers**) N-COUNT A **healer** is a person who heals people, especially a person who heals through prayer and religious faith.

health ♦♦♦ /hɛlθ/ **1** N-UNCOUNT A person's **health** is the condition of their body and the extent to which it is free from illness or is able to resist illness. ❏ *If you don't look after your health, no one else will.* **2** N-UNCOUNT **Health** is a state in which a person is not suffering from any illness and is feeling well. ❏ *In the hospital they nursed me back to health.* **3** N-UNCOUNT The

health of something such as an organization or a system is its success and the fact that it is working well. ❏ *There's no way to predict the future health of the banking industry.* **4** → See feature box at **medicine**

health care ✦◇ also **healthcare** **1** N-UNCOUNT [oft N n] **Health care** is the various services for the prevention or treatment of illness and injuries. ❏ *Nobody wants to pay more for health care.* ❏ *...the nation's health care system.* **2** → See feature box at **medicine**

health-care work|er (health-care workers) N-COUNT A **health-care worker** is someone who works in a hospital or health center.

health cen|ter (health centers)
in BRIT, use **health centre**
N-COUNT A **health center** is a building in which a group of doctors have offices where their patients can visit them.

health club (health clubs) N-COUNT A **health club** is a private club that people go to in order to do exercise and have beauty treatments.

health farm (health farms) N-COUNT A **health farm** is a hotel where people go to build muscles or lose weight by exercising and eating special food. [mainly BRIT]
in AM, use **spa**

health food (health foods) N-MASS [oft N n] **Health foods** are natural foods without artificial ingredients that people believe are good for health.

health|ful /hɛlθfəl/ ADJ Something that is **healthful** is good for your health. ❏ *Does the college cafeteria provide a healthful diet?*

health main|te|nance or|gani|za|tion (health maintenance organizations) N-COUNT A **health maintenance organization** is an organization to which you pay a fee and that allows you to use only doctors and hospitals which belong to the organization. The abbreviation **HMO** is often used. [AM] ❏ *...a health maintenance organization for retired workers in northern California.*

healthy ✦◆◇ /hɛlθi/ (healthier, healthiest) **1** ADJ Someone who is **healthy** is well and is not suffering from any illness. ❏ *Most of us need to lead more balanced lives to be healthy and happy.* ● **healthi|ly** /hɛlθɪli/ ADV ❏ *What I really want is to live healthily for as long as possible.* **2** ADJ Something that is **healthy** is good for your health. ❏ *...a healthy diet.* **3** ADJ A **healthy** organization or system is successful. ❏ *...an economically healthy socialist state.* **4** ADJ A **healthy** amount of something is a large amount that shows success. ❏ *He predicts a continuation of healthy profits in the current financial year.* **5** ADJ If you have a **healthy** attitude about something, you show good sense. ❏ *She has a refreshingly healthy attitude to work.*

heap /hip/ (heaps, heaping, heaped) **1** N-COUNT A **heap** of things is a pile of them, especially a pile arranged in a rather messy way. ❏ *...a heap of bricks.* **2** V-T If you **heap** things in a pile, you arrange them in a large pile. ❏ *Mrs. Madrigal heaped more carrots onto Michael's plate.* ● PHRASAL VERB **Heap up** means the same as **heap**. ❏ *Off to one side, the militia was heaping up wood for a bonfire.* **3** V-T If you **heap** praise or criticism **on** someone or something, you give them a lot of praise or criticism. ❏ *The head of the navy heaped scorn on both the methods and motives of the conspirators.* **4** QUANT **Heaps of** something or a **heap of** something is a large quantity of it. [INFORMAL] ❏ *You have heaps of time.*

heaped /hipt/ ADJ [v-link ADJ with n] A container or a surface that is **heaped with** things has a lot of them in it or on it in a pile, often so many that it cannot hold any more. ❏ *The large desk was heaped with papers.*

heap|ing /hipɪŋ/ ADJ [ADJ n] A **heaping** spoonful has the contents of the spoon piled up above the edge. [AM] ❏ *Add one heaping tablespoonful of salt.*

hear ✦✦✦ /hɪər/ (hears, hearing, heard /hɜrd/) **1** V-T/V-I When you **hear** a sound, you become aware of it through your ears. ❏ *She heard no further sounds.* ❏ *They heard the protesters shout: "No more fascism!"* ❏ *He doesn't hear very well.* **2** V-T If you **hear** something such as a lecture or a piece of music, you listen to it. ❏ *You can hear commentary on the game at halftime.* ❏ *I don't think you've ever heard Doris talking about her emotional life before.* **3** V-T When a judge or a court of law **hears** a case, or evidence in a case, they listen to it officially in order to make a decision about it. [FORMAL] ❏ *The jury has heard evidence from defense witnesses.* **4** V-I If you **hear** from someone, you receive a letter or telephone call from them. ❏ *Drop us a line, it's always great to hear from you.* **5** V-T/V-I If you **hear** some news or information about something, you find out about it by someone telling you, or from the radio or television. ❏ *My mother heard of this school through Leslie.* ❏ *He had heard that the trophy had been sold.* **6** V-I [no cont] If you **have heard of** something or someone, you know about them, but not in great detail. ❏ *Many people haven't heard of reflexology.* **7** PHRASE If you say that you **have heard** something **before**, you mean that you are not interested in it, or do not believe it, or are not surprised about it, because you already know about it or have experienced it. ❏ *Frank shrugs wearily. He has heard it all before.* **8** PHRASE If you say that you **can't hear** yourself **think**, you are complaining and emphasizing that there is a lot of noise, and that it is disturbing you or preventing you from doing something. [INFORMAL, EMPHASIS] ❏ *...those noisy late-night clubs where you can't even hear yourself think.* **9** PHRASE If you say that you **won't hear of** someone doing something, you mean that you refuse to let them do it. ❏ *I've always wanted to be an actor but Dad wouldn't hear of it.* **10** → See feature box at **debate**

hear|er /hɪərər/ (hearers) N-COUNT Your **hearers** are the people who are listening to you speak. [FORMAL]

hear|ing ✦◇◇ /hɪərɪŋ/ (hearings) **1** N-UNCOUNT A person's or animal's **hearing** is the sense which makes it possible for them to be aware of sounds. ❏ *His mind still seemed clear and his hearing was excellent.* **2** N-COUNT A **hearing** is an official meeting which is held in order to collect facts about an incident or problem. ❏ *After more than two hours of pandemonium, the judge adjourned the hearing until next Tuesday.* **3** PHRASE If someone gives you **a fair hearing** or **a hearing**, they listen to you when you give your opinion about something. ❏ *Weber gave a fair hearing to anyone who held a different opinion.* **4** PHRASE If someone says something **in** your **hearing** or **within** your **hearing**, you can hear what they say because they are with you or near you. ❏ *No one spoke disparagingly of her father in her hearing.*

COLLOCATIONS

hearing
NOUN **2**
noun + **hearing**: court, tribunal; appeal, bail, extradition, parole
adjective + **hearing**: disciplinary; preliminary; fair
verb + **hearing**: adjourn; attend; schedule

hear|ing aid (hearing aids) N-COUNT A **hearing aid** is a device which people with hearing difficulties wear in their ear to enable them to hear better.

hear|ing dog (hearing dogs) N-COUNT **Hearing dogs** are dogs that have been specially trained to help people with hearing difficulties.

hearing-impaired ADJ A **hearing-impaired** person cannot hear as well as most people. ❏ *Some hearing-impaired children may work harder to overcome their disability.* ● N-PLURAL **The hearing-impaired** are people who are hearing-impaired. This use could cause offense. ❏ *The hearing-impaired say digital phones interfere with hearing aids.*

hear|say /hɪərseɪ/ N-UNCOUNT **Hearsay** is information which you have been told but do not know to be true. ❏ *Much of what was reported to them was hearsay.*

hearse /hɜrs/ (hearses) N-COUNT A **hearse** is a large car that carries the coffin at a funeral.

HEART
① NOUN USES
② PHRASES

① **heart** ✦✦✦ /hɑrt/ (hearts) **1** N-COUNT Your **heart** is the organ in your chest that pumps the blood around your body. People also use **heart** to refer to the area of their chest that is closest to their heart. ❏ *The bullet had passed less than an inch from Andrea's heart.* **2** N-COUNT You can refer to someone's **heart** when you are talking about their deep feelings and beliefs.

[LITERARY] ◻ *Alik's words filled her heart with pride.* **3** N-VAR You use **heart** when you are talking about someone's character and attitude toward other people, especially when they are kind and generous. [APPROVAL] ◻ *She loved his brilliance and his generous heart.* **4** N-SING The **heart of** something is the most central and important part of it. ◻ *The heart of the problem is supply and demand.* **5** N-SING The **heart** of a place is its center. ◻ *...a busy dentists' practice in the heart of the city.* **6** N-COUNT A **heart** is a shape that is used as a symbol of love: ♥. ◻ *...heart-shaped chocolates.* **7** N-UNCOUNT-COLL **Hearts** is one of the four suits in a deck of playing cards. Each card in the suit is marked with one or more symbols in the shape of a heart. • N-COUNT A **heart** is a playing card of this suit. ◻ *West had to decide whether to play a heart.* **8** → See feature box at **body**; See also color supplement

---
COLLOCATIONS

heart
NOUN
① **2**
verb + **heart**: touch, warm; capture, win
① **3**
adjective + **heart**: generous, good, kind, warm; heavy

---

② **heart** ✦✧ /hɑrt/ (**hearts**) **1** PHRASE If you feel or believe something **with all** your **heart**, you feel or believe it very strongly. [EMPHASIS] ◻ *My own family I loved with all my heart.* **2** PHRASE If you say that someone is a particular kind of person **at heart**, you mean that that is what they are really like, even though they may seem very different. ◻ *He was a very gentle boy at heart.* **3** PHRASE If you say that someone has your interests or your welfare **at heart**, you mean that they are concerned about you and that is why they are doing something. ◻ *She told him she only had his interests at heart.* **4** PHRASE If someone **breaks** your **heart**, they make you very sad and unhappy, usually because they end a love affair or close relationship with you. [LITERARY] ◻ *I fell in love on vacation but the girl broke my heart.* **5** PHRASE If something **breaks** your **heart**, it makes you feel very sad and depressed, especially because people are suffering but you can do nothing to help them. ◻ *It really breaks my heart to see them this way.* **6** PHRASE If you know something such as a poem **by heart**, you have learned it so well that you can remember it without having to read it. ◻ *Mack knew this passage by heart.* **7** PHRASE If someone has a **change of heart**, their attitude toward something changes. ◻ *Several brokers have had a change of heart about prospects for the company.* **8** PHRASE If something such as a subject or project is **close to** your **heart** or **near to** your **heart**, it is very important to you and you are very interested in it and concerned about it. ◻ *This is a subject very close to my heart.* **9** PHRASE If you can do something **to** your **heart's content**, you can do it as much as you want. ◻ *I was delighted to be able to eat my favorite dishes to my heart's content.* **10** CONVENTION You can say '**cross my heart**' when you want someone to believe that you are telling the truth. You can also ask '**cross your heart?**' when you are asking someone if they are really telling the truth. [SPOKEN] ◻ *And I won't tell any of the other girls anything you tell me about it. I promise, cross my heart.* **11** PHRASE If you say something **from the heart** or **from the bottom of** your **heart**, you sincerely mean what you say. ◻ *He spoke with confidence, from the heart.* **12** PHRASE If you want to do something but do **not have the heart** to do it, you do not do it because you know it will make someone unhappy or disappointed. ◻ *We knew all along but didn't have the heart to tell her.* **13** PHRASE If you believe or know something **in** your **heart of hearts**, that is what you really believe or think, even though it may sometimes seem that you do not. ◻ *I know in my heart of hearts that I am the right man for that mission.* **14** PHRASE If your **heart isn't in** the thing you are doing, you have very little enthusiasm for it, usually because you are depressed or are thinking about something else. ◻ *I tried to learn some lines but my heart wasn't really in it.* **15** PHRASE If you **lose heart**, you become sad and depressed and are no longer interested in something, especially because it is not progressing as you would like. ◻ *He appealed to his countrymen not to lose heart.* **16** PHRASE If your **heart is in** your **mouth**, you feel very excited, worried, or frightened. ◻ *My heart was in my mouth when I walked into her office.* **17** PHRASE If you **open** your **heart** or **pour out** your **heart** to someone, you tell them your most private thoughts and feelings. ◻ *She opened her heart to millions yesterday and told how she came close to suicide.* **18** PHRASE If you say that someone's **heart is in the right place**, you mean that they are kind, considerate, and generous, although you may disapprove of other aspects of their character. ◻ *He's rich, handsome, funny, and his heart is in the right place.* **19** PHRASE If you have **set** your **heart on** something, you want it very much or want to do it very much. ◻ *He had always set his heart on a career in the fine arts.* **20** PHRASE If you **take heart** from something, you are encouraged and made to feel optimistic by it. ◻ *Investors and dealers also took heart from the better than expected industrial production figures.* **21** PHRASE If you **take** something **to heart**, for example someone's behavior, you are deeply affected and upset by it. ◻ *If someone says something critical I take it to heart.*

heart|ache /hɑrteɪk/ (**heartaches**) N-VAR **Heartache** is very great sadness and emotional suffering. ◻ *...after suffering the heartache of her divorce from her first husband.*

heart at|tack (**heart attacks**) N-COUNT If someone has a **heart attack**, their heart begins to beat very irregularly or stops completely. ◻ *He died of a heart attack brought on by overwork.*

heart|beat /hɑrtbit/ N-SING Your **heartbeat** is the regular movement of your heart as it pumps blood around your body. ◻ *Your baby's heartbeat will be monitored continuously.*

heart|break /hɑrtbreɪk/ (**heartbreaks**) N-VAR **Heartbreak** is very great sadness and emotional suffering, especially after the end of a love affair or close relationship. ◻ *...suffering and heartbreak for those close to the victims.*

heart|breaking /hɑrtbreɪkɪŋ/ ADJ Something that is **heartbreaking** makes you feel extremely sad and upset. ◻ *This year we won't even be able to buy presents for our grandchildren. It's heartbreaking.*

heart|broken /hɑrtbroʊkən/ ADJ Someone who is **heartbroken** is very sad and emotionally upset. ◻ *Was your daddy heartbroken when they got a divorce?*

heart|burn /hɑrtbɜrn/ N-UNCOUNT **Heartburn** is a painful burning sensation in your chest, caused by indigestion.

-hearted /-hɑrtɪd/ COMB IN ADJ **-hearted** combines with adjectives such as 'kind' or 'cold' to form adjectives which indicate that someone has a particular character or personality or is in a particular mood. ◻ *They are now realizing just how much they owe to kind-hearted strangers.*

heart|en /hɑrtən/ (**heartens, heartening, heartened**) V-T If someone **is heartened** by something, it encourages them and makes them cheerful. ◻ *The news heartened everybody.*
• **heart|ened** ADJ [v-link ADJ] ◻ *I feel heartened by her progress.*
• **heart|en|ing** ADJ ◻ *It is heartening news.*

heart fail|ure N-UNCOUNT **Heart failure** is a serious medical condition in which someone's heart does not work as well as it should, sometimes stopping completely so that they die. ◻ *He remained in a critical condition after suffering heart failure.*

heart|felt /hɑrtfɛlt/ ADJ **Heartfelt** is used to describe a deep or sincere feeling or wish. ◻ *My heartfelt sympathy goes out to all the relatives.*

hearth /hɑrθ/ (**hearths**) N-COUNT The **hearth** is the floor of a fireplace, which sometimes extends into the room. ◻ *It was winter and there was a huge fire roaring in the hearth.*

hearth rug (**hearth rugs**) also **hearthrug** N-COUNT A **hearth rug** is a rug which is put in front of a fireplace.

heart|land /hɑrtlænd/ (**heartlands**) **1** N-COUNT Journalists use **heartland** or **heartlands** to refer to the area or region where a particular set of activities or beliefs is most significant. ◻ *...his six-day bus tour around the industrial heartland of America.* **2** N-COUNT The most central area of a country or continent can be referred to as its **heartland** or **heartlands**. [WRITTEN] ◻ *For many, the essence of French living is to be found in the rural heartlands.*

heart|less /hɑrtlɪs/ ADJ If you describe someone as **heartless**, you mean that they are cruel and unkind, and have no sympathy for anyone or anything. ◻ *I couldn't believe they were so heartless.*

heart|rending /hɑrtrɛndɪŋ/ also **heart-rending** ADJ [usu ADJ n] You use **heartrending** to describe something that causes you to feel great sadness and pity. ◻ *...heartrending pictures of refugees.*

heart|sick /hɑ́rtsɪk/ ADJ Someone who is **heartsick** is very sad or depressed. ❑ *I was heartsick, for I felt that the splendid years of my carefree childhood had come to an end.*

heart-stopping also **heartstopping** **1** ADJ [usu ADJ n] A **heart-stopping** moment is one that makes you anxious or frightened because it seems that something bad is likely to happen. ❑ *There was a heart-stopping moment when she lost her balance and fell backwards.* **2** ADJ [usu ADJ n] A **heart-stopping** event or sight is very impressive or exciting. ❑ *...worth a visit for both the radical cooking and the heart-stopping sea view.*

heart|strings /hɑ́rtstrɪŋz/ N-PLURAL [oft with poss] If you say that someone or something pulls or tugs at your **heartstrings**, you mean that they cause you to feel strong emotions, usually sadness or pity. ❑ *She knows exactly how to tug at readers' heartstrings.*

heart|throb /hɑ́rtθrɒb/ (**heartthrobs**) N-COUNT If you describe someone, especially a man, as a **heartthrob**, you mean that they are physically very attractive, so that a lot of people fall in love with them.

heart-to-heart (**heart-to-hearts**) N-COUNT [oft N n] A **heart-to-heart** is a conversation between two people, especially close friends, in which they talk freely about their feelings or personal problems. ❑ *I've had a heart-to-heart with him.*

heart|warming /hɑ́rtwɔrmɪŋ/ also **heart-warming** ADJ Something that is **heartwarming** causes you to feel happy, usually because something nice has happened to people. ❑ *...the heartwarming story of enemies who discover a shared humanity.*

hearty /hɑ́rti/ (**heartier**, **heartiest**) **1** ADJ **Hearty** people or actions are loud, cheerful, and energetic. ❑ *Wade was a hearty, athletic sort of guy.* • **hearti|ly** ADV [ADV after v] ❑ *He laughed heartily.* **2** ADJ **Hearty** feelings or opinions are strongly felt or strongly held. ❑ *With the last sentiment, Arnold was in hearty agreement.* • **hearti|ly** ADV ❑ *Most people here are heartily sick of war.* **3** ADJ A **hearty** meal is large and very satisfying. ❑ *The men ate a hearty breakfast.* • **hearti|ly** ADV [ADV after v] ❑ *He ate heartily but would drink only beer.*

heat ✦✧ /hít/ (**heats**, **heating**, **heated**) **1** V-T When you **heat** something, you raise its temperature, for example, by using a flame or a special piece of equipment. ❑ *Meanwhile, heat the tomatoes and oil in a pan.* **2** N-UNCOUNT **Heat** is warmth or the quality of being hot. ❑ *The seas store heat and release it gradually during cold periods.* **3** N-UNCOUNT [also the N] The **heat** is very hot weather. ❑ *As an asthmatic, he cannot cope with the heat and humidity.* **4** N-UNCOUNT The **heat** of something is the temperature of something that is warm or that is being heated. ❑ *Adjust the heat of the barbecue by opening and closing the air vents.* **5** N-SING You use **heat** to refer to a source of heat, for example a burner on a stove or the heating system of a house. ❑ *Immediately remove the pan from the heat.* **6** N-UNCOUNT You use **heat** to refer to a state of strong emotion, especially of anger or excitement. ❑ *It was all done in the heat of the moment and I have certainly learned by my mistake.* **7** N-SING The **heat of** a particular activity is the point when there is the greatest activity or excitement. ❑ *People say all kinds of things in the heat of an argument.* **8** N-COUNT A **heat** is one of a series of races or competitions. The winners of a heat take part in another race or competition, against the winners of other heats. ❑ *...the heats of the men's 100 meter breaststroke.* **9** → See feature box at **global warming**
▶ **heat up** **1** PHRASAL VERB When you **heat** something **up**, especially food which has already been cooked and allowed to go cold, you make it hot. ❑ *Freda heated up a pie for me but I couldn't eat it.* **2** PHRASAL VERB When a situation **heats up**, things start to happen much more quickly and with increased interest and excitement among the people involved. ❑ *Then in the last couple of years, the movement for democracy began to heat up.* **3** PHRASAL VERB When something **heats up**, it gradually becomes hotter. ❑ *In the summer her mobile home heats up like an oven.*

SYNONYMS

heat
VERB **1**
warm (up): *All that she had to do was warm up the dessert.*
cook: *I have to go and cook the dinner.*
boil: *Boil the water in the saucepan and add the sage.*
fry: *Fry the breadcrumbs until golden brown.*
roast: *I personally would rather roast a chicken whole.*

---

heat|ed /hítɪd/ **1** ADJ A **heated** discussion or quarrel is one where the people involved are angry and excited. ❑ *It was a very heated argument and they were shouting at each other.* **2** ADJ [v-link ADJ about/over n] If someone gets **heated about** something, they get angry and excited about it. ❑ *You will understand that people get a bit heated about issues such as these.* • **heat|ed|ly** ADV [ADV with v] ❑ *The crowd continued to argue heatedly about the best way to tackle the problem.* **3** → See feature box at **debate**

heat|er /hítər/ (**heaters**) N-COUNT A **heater** is a piece of equipment or a machine which is used to raise the temperature of something, especially of the air inside a room or a car. ❑ *There's an electric heater in the bedroom.*

hea|then /híðən/ (**heathens**) **1** ADJ [usu ADJ n] **Heathen** means having no religion, or belonging to a religion that is not Christianity, Judaism, or Islam. [OLD-FASHIONED] • N-PLURAL [the N] The **heathen** are heathen people. ❑ *They first set out to convert the heathen.* **2** N-COUNT People sometimes refer to other people who have no religion as **heathens**, especially if they do not like the way they behave as a result of this. [OLD-FASHIONED, DISAPPROVAL]

heath|er /hɛ́ðər/ N-UNCOUNT **Heather** is a low, spreading plant with small purple, pink, or white flowers that grows wild on high land with poor soil.

heat|ing /hítɪŋ/ **1** N-UNCOUNT **Heating** is the process of heating a building or room, considered especially from the point of view of how much this costs. ❑ *We wanted to reduce the cost of heating and air-conditioning.* **2** N-UNCOUNT **Heating** is the system and equipment that is used to heat a building. ❑ *I wish I knew how to turn on the heating.* **3** → see also **central heating**

heat-seeking ADJ [ADJ n] A **heat-seeking** missile or device is one that is able to detect a source of heat. ❑ *The Italian government has said in a preliminary report that the plane was hit by a heat-seeking missile.* ❑ *A helicopter with heat-seeking equipment has been called in to help search for a missing man.*

heat|stroke /hítstroʊk/ also **heat-stroke** N-UNCOUNT **Heatstroke** is the same as **sunstroke**.

heat|wave /hítweɪv/ (**heatwaves**) also **heat wave** **1** N-COUNT A **heatwave** is a period of time during which the weather is much hotter than usual. **2** → See feature box at **hot**

heave /hív/ (**heaves**, **heaving**, **heaved**) **1** V-T If you **heave** something heavy or difficult to move somewhere, you push, pull, or lift it using a lot of effort. ❑ *It took five strong men to heave it up a ramp and lower it into place.* • N-COUNT **Heave** is also a noun. ❑ *It took only one heave to hurl him into the river.* **2** V-I If something **heaves**, it moves up and down with large regular movements. ❑ *His chest heaved, and he took a deep breath.* **3** V-I If you **heave**, or if your stomach **heaves**, you vomit or feel as if you are about to vomit. ❑ *He gasped and heaved again.* ❑ *The greasy food made her stomach heave.* **4** V-T If you **heave** a sigh, you give a big sigh. ❑ *Mr. Collier heaved a sigh and got to his feet.* **5** V-I [usu cont] If a place **is heaving** or if it **is heaving with** people, it is full of people. [mainly BRIT, INFORMAL] ❑ *The Happy Bunny club was heaving.* ❑ *Father Auberon's Academy Club positively heaved with dashing young men.* **6 to heave a sigh of relief** → see **sigh**

heav|en ✦✧ /hɛ́vən/ (**heavens**) **1** N-PROPER In some religions, **heaven** is said to be the place where God lives, where good people go when they die, and where everyone is always happy. It is usually imagined as being high up in the sky. ❑ *I believed that when I died I would go to heaven and see God.* **2** N-UNCOUNT You can use **heaven** to refer to a place or situation that you like very much. [INFORMAL] ❑ *I would go to movies in the afternoon or to ball games in the evening. It was heaven.* **3** EXCLAM You say '**Good heavens!**' or '**Heavens!**' to express surprise or to emphasize that you agree or disagree with someone. [SPOKEN, FEELINGS] ❑ *Good Heavens! That explains a lot!* **4** PHRASE You say '**Heaven help** someone' when you are worried that something bad is going to happen to them, often because you disapprove of what they are doing or the way they are behaving. [SPOKEN, DISAPPROVAL] ❑ *If this makes sense to our leaders, then heaven help us all.* **5** PHRASE You can say '**Heaven knows**' to emphasize that you do not know something, or that you find something very surprising. [SPOKEN, EMPHASIS] ❑ *Heaven knows what they put in it.* **6** PHRASE You can say '**Heaven knows**' to emphasize something that you feel or believe very strongly. [SPOKEN, EMPHASIS] ❑ *Heaven knows they have enough money.* **7** PHRASE If **the heavens open**, it suddenly starts raining very heavily. ❑ *The match had just begun when the heavens opened and play was suspended.* **8 for heaven's sake** → see **sake** **9 thank heavens** → see **thank**

heav|en|ly /hɛvənli/ **1** ADJ **Heavenly** things are things that are connected with the religious idea of heaven. ❑ *...heavenly beings whose function it is to serve God.* **2** ADJ Something that is **heavenly** is very pleasant and enjoyable. [INFORMAL] ❑ *The idea of spending two weeks with him may seem heavenly.*

heav|en|ly body (heavenly bodies) N-COUNT A **heavenly body** is a planet, star, moon, or other natural object in space.

heaven-sent also **heaven sent** ADJ [usu ADJ n] You use **heaven-sent** to describe something such as an opportunity which is unexpected, but which is very welcome because it occurs at just the right time. ❑ *It will be a heaven-sent opportunity to prove himself.*

heav|en|ward /hɛvənwərd/ also **heavenwards** ADV [ADV after v] **Heavenward** means toward the sky or to heaven. [WRITTEN] ❑ *He rolled his eyes heavenward in disgust.*

heavi|ly /hɛvɪli/ **1** ADV [ADV after v] If someone says something **heavily**, they say it in a slow way which shows a feeling such as sadness, tiredness, or annoyance. ❑ *"I didn't even think about her," he said heavily.* **2** → see also **heavy**

heavy ✦✦◇ /hɛvi/ (heavier, heaviest, heavies) **1** ADJ Something that is **heavy** weighs a lot. ❑ *These scissors are awfully heavy.* • **heavi|ness** N-UNCOUNT ❑ *...a sensation of warmth and heaviness in the muscles.* **2** ADJ You use **heavy** to ask or talk about how much someone or something weighs. ❑ *How heavy are you?* **3** ADJ **Heavy** means great in amount, degree, or intensity. ❑ *Heavy fighting has been going on.* ❑ *He worried about her heavy drinking.* • **heavi|ly** ADV ❑ *It has been raining heavily all day.* • **heavi|ness** N-UNCOUNT ❑ *...the heaviness of the blood loss.* **4** ADJ A **heavy** meal is large in amount and often difficult to digest. ❑ *He had been feeling drowsy, the effect of an unusually heavy meal.* **5** ADJ [v-link ADJ with n] Something that is **heavy with** things is full of them or loaded with them. [LITERARY] ❑ *The air is heavy with moisture.* **6** ADJ If a person's breathing is **heavy**, it is very loud and deep. ❑ *Her breathing became slow and heavy.* • **heavi|ly** ADV [ADV after v] ❑ *She sank back on the pillow and closed her eyes, breathing heavily as if asleep.* **7** ADJ [ADJ n] A **heavy** movement or action is done with a lot of force or pressure. ❑ *...a heavy blow on the back of the skull.* • **heavi|ly** ADV [ADV after v] ❑ *I sat down heavily on the ground beside the road.* **8** ADJ [ADJ n] A **heavy** machine or piece of military equipment is very large and very powerful. ❑ *...government militia backed by tanks and heavy artillery.* **9** ADJ If you describe a period of time or a schedule as **heavy**, you mean it involves a lot of work. ❑ *It's been a heavy day and I'm tired.* **10** ADJ **Heavy** work requires a lot of strength or energy. ❑ *The business is thriving and Philippa employs two full-timers for the heavy work.* **11** ADJ [v-link ADJ on n] If you say that something is **heavy on** another thing, you mean that it uses a lot of that thing or too much of that thing. ❑ *Tanks are heavy on fuel, destructive to roads and difficult to park.* **12** ADJ Air or weather that is **heavy** is unpleasantly still, hot, and damp. ❑ *The outside air was heavy and moist and sultry.* **13** ADJ A situation that is **heavy** is serious and difficult to cope with. [INFORMAL] ❑ *I don't want any more of that heavy stuff.* **14** N-COUNT A **heavy** is a large strong man who is employed to protect a person or place, often by using violence. You can also use **heavy** to refer to a male character who represents such a man in a movie or play. [INFORMAL] ❑ *They had employed heavies to evict squatters from neighboring sites.* ❑ *In 1943, he received his first role as a heavy in "Double Indemnity."*

heavy cream N-UNCOUNT **Heavy cream** is very thick cream. [AM]

heavy-duty ADJ A **heavy-duty** piece of equipment is very strong and can be used a lot. ❑ *...a heavy-duty plastic bag.*

heavy-handed ADJ If you say that someone's behavior is **heavy-handed**, you mean that they are too forceful or too rough. [DISAPPROVAL] ❑ *...heavy-handed police tactics.*

heavy in|dus|try (heavy industries) N-VAR **Heavy industry** is industry in which large machines are used to produce raw materials or to make large objects. ❑ *...the policy of redirecting investment to heavy industries like steel and energy.*

heavy met|al (heavy metals) **1** N-UNCOUNT [oft N n] **Heavy metal** is a type of very loud rock music with a fast beat. ❑ *...a German heavy metal band named The Scorpions.* **2** N-COUNT A **heavy metal** is a metallic element with a high density. Many heavy metals are poisonous. [TECHNICAL]

heavy|set /hɛvisɛt/ **1** ADJ Someone who is **heavyset** has a large solid body. **2** → See feature box at **appearance**

heavy|weight /hɛviweɪt/ (heavyweights) **1** N-COUNT A **heavyweight** is a boxer weighing more than 175 pounds and therefore in the heaviest class. **2** N-COUNT If you refer to a person or organization as a **heavyweight**, you mean that they have a lot of influence, experience, and importance in a particular field, subject, or activity. ❑ *He was a political heavyweight.*

He|brew /hibru/ **1** N-UNCOUNT **Hebrew** is a language that was spoken by Jews in former times. A modern form of Hebrew is spoken now in Israel. ❑ *He is a fluent speaker of Hebrew.* **2** ADJ **Hebrew** means belonging to or relating to the Hebrew language or people. ❑ *...the respected Hebrew newspaper Haarez.*

heck /hɛk/ **1** EXCLAM People sometimes say '**heck!**' when they are slightly irritated or surprised. [INFORMAL, FEELINGS] ❑ *Heck, if you don't like it, don't vote for him.* **2** PHRASE [PHR n] People use **a heck of** to emphasize how big something is or how much of it there is. [INFORMAL, EMPHASIS] ❑ *They're spending a heck of a lot of money.* ❑ *The truth is, I'm in one heck of a mess.* **3** PHRASE [quest PHR] You use **the heck** in expressions such as '**what the heck**' and '**how the heck**' in order to emphasize a question, especially when you are puzzled or annoyed. [INFORMAL, EMPHASIS] ❑ *What the heck's that?* ❑ *The question was, where the heck was he?* **4** PHRASE [PHR with cl] You say '**what the heck**' to indicate that you do not care about a bad aspect of an action or situation. [INFORMAL, FEELINGS] ❑ *What the heck, I thought, I'll give it a whirl.*

heck|le /hɛkəl/ (heckles, heckling, heckled) V-T/V-I If people in an audience **heckle** public speakers or performers, they interrupt them, for example by making rude remarks. ❑ *They heckled him and interrupted his address with angry questions.* • N-COUNT **Heckle** is also a noun. ❑ *The offending comment was in fact a heckle from an audience member.* • **heck|ling** N-UNCOUNT ❑ *The ceremony was disrupted by unprecedented heckling and slogan-chanting.* • **heck|ler** /hɛklər/ (hecklers) N-COUNT ❑ *As he began his speech, a heckler called out asking for his opinion on gun control.*

hec|tare /hɛktɛər/ (hectares) N-COUNT A **hectare** is a measurement of an area of land which is equal to 10,000 square meters, or 2.471 acres.

hec|tic /hɛktɪk/ ADJ A **hectic** situation is one that is very busy and involves a lot of rushed activity. ❑ *Despite his hectic work schedule, Benny has rarely suffered poor health.*

hec|tor /hɛktər/ (hectors, hectoring, hectored) V-T If you say that someone **is hectoring** you, you do not like the way they are trying to make you do something by bothering you and talking to you aggressively. [DISAPPROVAL] ❑ *I suppose you'll hector me until I phone him.* • **hec|tor|ing** ADJ [usu ADJ n] ❑ *In a loud, hectoring tone, Alan told us that he wasn't going to waste time discussing nonsense.*

he'd /hid, STRONG hid/ **1 He'd** is the usual spoken form of '**he had**,' especially when '**had**' is an auxiliary verb. ❑ *He'd never learned to read.* **2 He'd** is a spoken form of '**he would**.' ❑ *He'd come into the clubhouse every day.*

hedge /hɛdʒ/ (hedges, hedging, hedged) **1** N-COUNT A **hedge** is a row of bushes or small trees, usually along the edge of a lawn, garden, field, or road. **2** V-I If you **hedge against** something unpleasant or unwanted that might affect you, especially losing money, you do something which will protect you from it. ❑ *You can hedge against illness with insurance.* **3** N-COUNT Something that is a **hedge against** something unpleasant will protect you from its effects. ❑ *Gold is traditionally a hedge against inflation.* **4** PHRASE If you **hedge your bets**, you reduce the risk of losing a lot by supporting more than one person or thing in a situation where they are opposed to each other. ❑ *The company tried to hedge its bets by diversifying into other fields.*

hedge fund (hedge funds) N-COUNT A **hedge fund** is an investment fund that invests large amounts of money using methods that involve a lot of risk. [BUSINESS]

hedge|hog /hɛdʒhɔg/ (hedgehogs) N-COUNT A **hedgehog** is a small brown animal with sharp spikes covering its back.

hedge|row /hɛdʒroʊ/ (hedgerows) N-VAR A **hedgerow** is a row of bushes, trees, and plants, usually growing along a bank bordering a country road or between fields. ❑ *He crouched behind a low hedgerow.*

he|don|ism /hidᵊnɪzəm/ N-UNCOUNT **Hedonism** is the belief that gaining pleasure is the most important thing in life. [FORMAL] ❑ *...the life of hedonism that she embraced in her youth.*

he|don|ist /hidᵊnɪst/ (hedonists) N-COUNT A **hedonist** is someone who believes that having pleasure is the most important thing in life. [FORMAL]

he|don|is|tic /hidᵊnɪstɪk/ ADJ **Hedonistic** means relating to hedonism. [FORMAL] ❑ *...an eccentric and flamboyant aristocrat with a hedonistic lifestyle.*

heed /hid/ (heeds, heeding, heeded) **1** V-T If you **heed** someone's advice or warning, you pay attention to it and do what they suggest. [FORMAL] ❑ *But few at the conference in London last week heeded his warning.* **2** PHRASE If you **take heed of** what someone says or if you **pay heed to** them, you pay attention to them and consider carefully what they say. [FORMAL] ❑ *But what if the government takes no heed?*

heed|less /hidlɪs/ ADJ [oft ADJ of n] If you are **heedless** of someone or something, you do not take any notice of them. [FORMAL] ❑ *Heedless of time or any other consideration, they began to search the underwater cave.* ❑ *She was rummaging through the letters, scattering them about the table in her heedless haste.*

heel /hil/ (heels) **1** N-COUNT Your **heel** is the back part of your foot, just below your ankle. ❑ *He had an operation on his heel last week.* **2** N-COUNT The **heel** of a shoe is the raised part on the bottom at the back. ❑ *...the shoes with the high heels.* **3** N-PLURAL **Heels** are women's shoes that are raised very high at the back. ❑ *She was dressed in heels and a clingy dress.* **4** PHRASE If you **dig** your **heels in** or **dig in** your **heels**, you refuse to do something such as change your opinions or plans, especially when someone is trying very hard to make you do so. ❑ *It was really the British who, by digging their heels in, prevented any last-minute deal.* **5** PHRASE If you say that one event follows **hard on the heels of** another or **hot on the heels of** another, you mean that one happens very quickly or immediately after another. ❑ *Unfortunately, bad news has come hard on the heels of good.* **6** PHRASE If you say that someone is **hot on** your **heels**, you are emphasizing that they are chasing you and are not very far behind you. [EMPHASIS] ❑ *They sped through the southwest with the law hot on their heels.* **7 head over heels** → see **head** ③ **8 to drag your heels** → see **drag** **9** → See feature box at **body**

heft /hɛft/ (hefts, hefting, hefted) **1** V-T If you **heft** something, you lift it upward. ❑ *Emmy straightened, hefting her burden.* ❑ *He hefted the heavy camera up onto his shoulder.* **2** N-UNCOUNT The **heft** of something is its weight or bulk. ❑ *...a friendly wireless Internet gadget about the size and heft of a thick pork chop.* **3** N-UNCOUNT If something such as an idea or argument has **heft**, it has the power to influence or impress people. ❑ *Goldstone wished Tom Hill were there to add heft to his argument.* ❑ *The 155-page American edition of the book packs the intellectual heft of a much longer text.*

hefty /hɛfti/ (heftier, heftiest) **1** ADJ **Hefty** means large in size, weight, or amount. [INFORMAL] ❑ *She was quite a hefty woman.* **2** ADJ A **hefty** movement is done with a lot of force. [INFORMAL] ❑ *He would give the swing doors in the corridor a hefty push.*

he|gemo|ny /hɪdʒɛməni/ N-UNCOUNT **Hegemony** is a situation in which one country, organization, or group has more power, control, or importance than others. [FORMAL]

heh /hɛ/ EXCLAM You can use **heh**, especially in electronic communication, to show that you are amused by something. ❑ *Great comments on this site so far, especially about Bob (heh heh)!*

heif|er /hɛfər/ (heifers) N-COUNT A **heifer** is a young cow that has not yet had a calf.

height ✦◇◇ /haɪt/ (heights) **1** N-VAR The **height** of a person or thing is their size or length from the bottom to the top. ❑ *Her weight is about normal for her height.* ❑ *I am nearly 6 foot in height.* **2** N-UNCOUNT **Height** is the quality of being tall. ❑ *She admits that her height is intimidating for some people.* **3** N-VAR A particular **height** is the distance that something is above the ground or above something else mentioned. ❑ *At the speed and height at which he was moving, he was never more than half a second from disaster.* **4** N-COUNT A **height** is a high position or place above the ground. ❑ *I'm not afraid of heights.* **5** N-SING When an activity, situation, or organization is **at its height**, it is at its most successful, powerful, or intense. ❑ *At its height, the antiwar movement drew supporters from nearly every political camp.* **6** N-SING If you say that something is **the height of** a particular quality, you are emphasizing that it has that quality to the greatest degree possible. [EMPHASIS] ❑ *The hip-hugging black and white polka-dot dress was the height of fashion.* **7** N-PLURAL If something reaches great **heights**, it becomes very extreme or intense. ❑ *...the mid-1980s, when prices rose to absurd heights.* **8** → See feature box at **polite**

─── COLLOCATIONS ───
height
NOUN
1
adjective + **height**: full, maximum, minimum; average, medium, varying
height + be + adjective: adjustable
verb + **height**: adjust, lower, measure
7
adjective + **heights**: dizzying, giddy, heady, lofty; great, new, unprecedented
verb + **height**: achieve, hit, reach, scale

height|en /haɪtᵊn/ (heightens, heightening, heightened) V-T/V-I If something **heightens** a feeling or if the feeling **heightens**, the feeling increases in degree or intensity. ❑ *The move has heightened tension in the state.* ❑ *Cross's interest heightened.*

hei|nous /heɪnəs/ ADJ [usu ADJ n] If you describe something such as a crime as **heinous**, you mean that it is extremely evil or horrible. [FORMAL] ❑ *They are capable of the most heinous acts.*

heir /ɛər/ (heirs) N-COUNT An **heir** is someone who has the right to inherit a person's money, property, or title when that person dies. ❑ *...the heir to the throne.*

heir ap|par|ent (heirs apparent) N-COUNT [usu sing, oft the N to n, poss N] The **heir apparent** to a particular job or position is the person who is expected to have it after the person who has it now. [JOURNALISM]

heir|ess /ɛərɪs/ (heiresses) N-COUNT An **heiress** is a woman or girl who has the right to inherit property or a title, or who has inherited it, especially when this involves great wealth. ❑ *...the heiress to a jewelry empire.*

heir|loom /ɛərlum/ (heirlooms) N-COUNT An **heirloom** is an ornament or other object that has belonged to a family for a very long time and that has been handed down from one generation to another.

heist /haɪst/ (heists) N-COUNT [oft n N] A **heist** is a robbery, especially one in which money, jewelry, or art is stolen. [JOURNALISM]

held /hɛld/ **Held** is the past tense and past participle of **hold**.

heli|cop|ter ✦◇◇ /hɛlɪkɒptər/ (helicopters) N-COUNT A **helicopter** is an aircraft with long blades on top that go around very fast. It is able to stay still in the air and to move straight upward or downward.

heli|cop|ter gun|ship (helicopter gunships) N-COUNT A **helicopter gunship** is a helicopter with large guns attached to it.

heli|cop|ter par|ent (helicopter parents) N-COUNT If you say someone is a **helicopter parent**, you mean that they are too closely involved with their child's life and try to control every part of it. [DISAPPROVAL] ❑ *You don't want a helicopter parent hovering over your every move.*

heli|pad /hɛlɪpæd/ (helipads) N-COUNT A **helipad** is a place where helicopters can land and take off. ❑ *Each house had a helipad for a fast evacuation.*

heli|port /hɛlɪpɔrt/ (heliports) N-COUNT A **heliport** is an airport for helicopters.

he|lium /hiliəm/ N-UNCOUNT **Helium** is a very light gas that is colorless and has no smell.

he|lix /híːlɪks/ (**helixes**) N-COUNT A **helix** is a spiral shape or form. [TECHNICAL]

HELL
① NOUN USES
② PHRASES
---

① **hell** ♦♢♢ /hɛl/ (**hells**) **1** N-PROPER; N-COUNT In some religions, **hell** is the place where the Devil lives, and where wicked people are sent to be punished when they die. Hell is usually imagined as being under the ground and full of flames. ❑ *I've never believed. Not in heaven or hell or God or Satan until now.* **2** N-VAR If you say that a particular situation or place is **hell**, you are emphasizing that it is extremely unpleasant. [EMPHASIS] ❑ *...the hell of the Siberian labor camps.* **3** EXCLAM **Hell** is used by some people when they are angry or excited, or when they want to emphasize what they are saying. This use could cause offense. [EMPHASIS] ❑ *"Hell, no!" the doctor snapped.*

② **hell** ♦♢♢ /hɛl/ **1** PHRASE You can use **as hell** after adjectives or some adverbs to emphasize the adjective or adverb. [INFORMAL, EMPHASIS] ❑ *The men might be armed, but they sure as hell weren't trained.* **2** PHRASE If someone does something **for the hell of it**, or **just for the hell of it**, they do it for fun or for no particular reason. [INFORMAL] ❑ *I started shouting in German, just for the hell of it.* **3** PHRASE You can use **from hell** after a noun when you are emphasizing that something or someone is extremely unpleasant or evil. [INFORMAL, EMPHASIS] ❑ *He's a child from hell.* **4** PHRASE If you tell someone to **go to hell**, you are angrily telling them to go away and leave you alone. [INFORMAL, VULGAR, FEELINGS] ❑ *"Well, you can go to hell!" He swept out of the room.* **5** PHRASE If you say that someone can **go to hell**, you are emphasizing angrily that you do not care about them and that they will not stop you doing what you want. [INFORMAL, VULGAR, EMPHASIS] ❑ *Peter can go to hell. It's my money and I'll leave it to who I want.* **6** PHRASE If you say that someone is going **hell for leather**, you are emphasizing that they are doing something or are moving very quickly and perhaps carelessly. [INFORMAL, EMPHASIS] ❑ *The first horse often goes hell for leather, hits a few fences but gets away with it.* **7** PHRASE Some people say **like hell** to emphasize that they strongly disagree with you or are strongly opposed to what you say. [INFORMAL, EMPHASIS] ❑ *"I'll go myself."—"Like hell you will!"* **8** PHRASE Some people use **like hell** to emphasize how strong an action or quality is. [INFORMAL, EMPHASIS] ❑ *It hurts like hell.* **9** PHRASE If you say that **all hell breaks loose**, you are emphasizing that a lot of arguing or fighting suddenly starts. [INFORMAL, EMPHASIS] ❑ *He had an affair, I found out and then all hell broke loose.* **10** PHRASE If you talk about **a hell of a lot** of something, or **one hell of a lot** of something, you mean that there is a large amount of it. [INFORMAL, EMPHASIS] ❑ *The manager took a hell of a lot of money out of the club.* **11** PHRASE Some people use **a hell of** or **one hell of** to emphasize that something is very good, very bad, or very big. [INFORMAL, EMPHASIS] ❑ *Whatever the outcome, it's going to be one hell of a fight.* **12** PHRASE Some people use **the hell out of** for emphasis after verbs such as 'scare,' 'irritate,' and 'beat.' [INFORMAL, EMPHASIS] ❑ *I patted the top of her head in the condescending way I knew irritated the hell out of her.* **13** PHRASE If you say **there'll be hell to pay**, you are emphasizing that there will be serious trouble. [INFORMAL, EMPHASIS] ❑ *There would be hell to pay when Ferguson and Tony found out about it.* **14** PHRASE To **play hell** with something means to have a bad effect on it or cause great confusion. [INFORMAL] ❑ *The rain had played hell with business.* **15** PHRASE People sometimes use **the hell** for emphasis in questions, after words such as 'what,' 'where,' and 'why,' often in order to express anger. [INFORMAL, VULGAR, EMPHASIS] ❑ *Where the hell have you been?* **16** PHRASE If you **go through hell**, or if someone **puts** you **through hell**, you have a very difficult or unpleasant time. [INFORMAL] ❑ *All of you seem to have gone through hell making this record.* **17** PHRASE If you say you **hope to hell** or **wish to hell** that something is true, you are emphasizing that you strongly hope or wish it is true. [INFORMAL, EMPHASIS] ❑ *I hope to hell you're right.* **18** PHRASE You can say '**what the hell**' when you decide to do something in spite of the doubts that you have about it. [INFORMAL, FEELINGS] ❑ *What the hell, I thought, at least it will give the lazy old man some exercise.* **19** PHRASE If you say '**to hell with**' something, you are emphasizing that you do not care about something and that it will not stop you from doing what you want to do. [INFORMAL, EMPHASIS] ❑ *To hell with this, I'm getting out of here.*

he'll /hɪl, hil/ **He'll** is the usual spoken form of 'he will.' ❑ *By the time he's twenty he'll know everyone worth knowing in Washington.*

hell-bent also **hellbent** ADJ If you say that someone is **hell-bent** on doing something, you are emphasizing that they are determined to do it, even if this causes problems or difficulties for other people. [EMPHASIS] ❑ *He accused the company of being hell-bent on achieving its cuts by whatever means.*

Hel|len|ic /hɛlɛnɪk, -liː-/ ADJ [usu ADJ n] **Hellenic** is used to describe the people, language, and culture of Ancient Greece.

hell|hole /hɛlhoʊl/ (**hellholes**) N-COUNT If you call a place a **hellhole**, you mean that it is extremely unpleasant, usually because it is dirty and uncomfortable. ❑ *...stuck in this hellhole of a jail.*

hell|ish /hɛlɪʃ/ ADJ You describe something as **hellish** to emphasize that it is extremely unpleasant. [INFORMAL, EMPHASIS] ❑ *The atmosphere in Washington is hellish.*

hel|lo ♦♢♢ /hɛloʊ/ (**hellos**) also **hallo, hullo 1** CONVENTION You say '**Hello**' to someone when you meet them. [FORMULAE] ❑ *Hello, Trish. I won't shake hands, because I'm filthy.* • N-COUNT **Hello** is also a noun. ❑ *The salesperson greeted me with a warm hello.* **2** CONVENTION You say '**Hello**' to someone at the beginning of a telephone conversation, either when you answer the phone or before you give your name or say why you are phoning. [FORMULAE] ❑ *A moment later, Cohen picked up the phone. "Hello?"* **3** CONVENTION You can call '**hello**' to attract someone's attention. ❑ *Very softly, she called out: "Hello? Who's there?"*

hell-raiser (**hell-raisers**) N-COUNT If you describe someone as a **hell-raiser**, you mean that they often behave in a wild and unacceptable way, especially because they have drunk too much alcohol. [INFORMAL]

hell|uva /hɛləvə/ ADJ [a/one ADJ n] Some people say **a helluva** or **one helluva** to emphasize that something is very good, very bad, or very big. [INFORMAL, EMPHASIS] ❑ *It taught me a helluva lot about myself.* ❑ *The man did one helluva job.*

helm /hɛlm/ (**helms**) **1** N-COUNT [usu sing] The **helm** of a boat or ship is the part that is used to steer it. **2** N-SING [the N] You can say that someone is **at the helm** when they are leading or running a country or organization. ❑ *Some of the directors felt that a man of only 30 was too young to be at the helm of so large an internationally recognized company.*

hel|met /hɛlmɪt/ (**helmets**) N-COUNT A **helmet** is a hat made of a strong material which you wear to protect your head.

helms|man /hɛlmzmən/ (**helmsmen**) N-COUNT The **helmsman** of a boat is the man who is steering it.

helms|woman /hɛlmzwʊmən/ (**helmswomen**) N-COUNT The **helmswoman** of a boat is the woman who is steering it.

help ♦♦♦ /hɛlp/ (**helps, helping, helped**) **1** V-T/V-I If you **help** someone, you make it easier for them to do something, for example by doing part of the work for them or by giving them advice or money. ❑ *He has helped to raise a lot of money.* ❑ *You can of course help by giving them a donation directly.* • N-UNCOUNT **Help** is also a noun. ❑ *Thanks very much for your help.* **2** V-T/V-I If you say that something **helps**, you mean that it makes something easier to do or get, or that it improves a situation to some extent. ❑ *The right style of swimsuit can help to hide, minimize, or emphasize what you want it to.* ❑ *Building more bypasses will help the environment by reducing pollution and traffic jams in towns and cities.* ❑ *If it would help, I'd be happy to take photographs.* **3** V-I If you **help** someone go somewhere or move in some way, you give them support so that they can move more easily. ❑ *Martin helped Tanya over the rail.* **4** N-SING [a N, also no det] If you say that someone or something has been **a help** or has been some **help**, you mean that they have helped you to solve a problem. ❑ *Thank you. You've been a great help already.* **5** N-UNCOUNT **Help** is action taken to rescue a person who is in danger. You shout '**help!**' when you are in danger in order to attract someone's attention so that they can come and rescue you. ❑ *He was screaming for help.* **6** N-UNCOUNT In computing, **help**, or the **help menu**, is a file that gives you information and advice, for example about how to use a particular program. [COMPUTING] ❑ *If you get stuck, click on Help.* **7** V-T If you **help** yourself to something, you serve yourself or you take it for yourself. If someone tells you to **help** yourself, they are telling you politely to serve yourself anything you want or to take anything you want. ❏ *There's bread on the table. Help yourself.* ▌8▐ V-T If someone **helps** themselves **to** something, they steal it. [INFORMAL] ❏ *Two men forced the clerks to flee before helping themselves to the cash register.* ▌9▐ PHRASE If you **can't help** the way you feel or behave, you cannot control it or stop it from happening. You can also say that you **can't help** yourself. ❏ *I can't help feeling sorry for the poor man.* ▌10▐ PHRASE If you say you **can't help** thinking something, you are expressing your opinion in an indirect way, often because you think it seems rude. [VAGUENESS] ❏ *I can't help feeling that this may just be another of her schemes.* ▌11▐ PHRASE If someone or something **is of help**, they make a situation easier or better. ❏ *Can I be of help to you?* ▶ **help out** PHRASAL VERB If you **help out** or **help** someone **out**, you help them by doing some work for them or by lending them some money. ❏ *I help out with the accounts.* ❏ *All these presents came to more money than I had, and my mother had to help me out.*

SYNONYMS

help
VERB ▌1▐
aid: *...a software system to aid managers in advanced decision-making.*
assist: *Julia was assisting him to prepare his speech.*
abet: *We shall strike hard, without flinching, at terrorists and those who abet them.*

COLLOCATIONS

help
NOUN
▌1▐
adjective + **help**: big, enormous, great, tremendous; considerable; financial, medical, psychiatric, psychological, technical; expert, professional
verb + **help**: ask for, enlist, seek; need; offer, provide; get, receive
▌5▐
verb + **help**: summon; call for, scream for, shout for
VERB ▌2▐
help + *adverb*: enormously, immeasurably

help desk (help desks) N-COUNT A **help desk** is a special service that you can telephone or email in order to get information about a particular product or subject. ❏ *Some modern vehicles are so complicated these days, but our help desk can sort any problem out.*

help|er /hɛlpər/ (helpers) N-COUNT A **helper** is a person who helps another person or group with a job they are doing. ❏ *Phyllis and her helpers provided us with refreshment.*

help|ful /hɛlpfʊl/ ▌1▐ ADJ If you describe someone as **helpful**, you mean that they help you in some way, such as doing part of your job for you or by giving you advice or information. ❏ *The staff in the branch office are helpful but only have limited information.* • **help|ful|ly** ADV [ADV with v] ❏ *They had helpfully provided us with instructions on how to find the house.* ▌2▐ ADJ If you describe information or advice as **helpful**, you mean that it is useful for you. ❏ *The catalog includes helpful information on the different bike models available.* ▌3▐ ADJ Something that is **helpful** makes a situation more pleasant or more easy to tolerate. ❏ *It is often helpful to have your spouse in the room when major news is expected.*

help|ing /hɛlpɪŋ/ (helpings) ▌1▐ N-COUNT A **helping** of food is the amount of it that you get in a single serving. ❏ *She gave them extra helpings of ice cream.* ▌2▐ N-COUNT [N of n, usu adj N of n] You can refer to an amount of something, especially a quality, as a **helping** of that thing. [INFORMAL] ❏ *There are large helpings of escapism in these movies.*

help|less /hɛlplɪs/ ADJ If you are **helpless**, you do not have the strength or power to do anything useful or to control or protect yourself. ❏ *Parents often feel helpless, knowing that all the hugs in the world won't stop the tears.* • **help|less|ly** ADV ❏ *She could only watch helplessly as the taxi drove off.* • **help|less|ness** N-UNCOUNT ❏ *I remember my feelings of helplessness.*

help|line /hɛlplaɪn/ (helplines) N-COUNT A **helpline** is a special telephone service that people can call to get advice about a particular subject. ❏ *...a 24-hour telephone helpline for people needing medical advice of all kinds.*

help|mate /hɛlpmeɪt/ (helpmates) N-COUNT A person's **helpmate** is someone who helps them in their life or work, especially their husband or wife. [OLD-FASHIONED]

helter-skelter /hɛltər skɛltər/ ADJ [ADJ n] You use **helter-skelter** to describe something that is hurried and disorganized, especially when things happen very quickly, one after the other. ❏ *He now faces another crisis in his helter-skelter existence.* • ADV [ADV after v] **Helter-skelter** is also an adverb. ❏ *...a panic-stricken crowd running helter-skelter to get away from the tear gas.*

hem /hɛm/ (hems, hemming, hemmed) ▌1▐ N-COUNT A **hem** on something such as a piece of clothing is an edge that is folded over and stitched down to prevent threads coming loose. The **hem** of a skirt or dress is the bottom edge. ❏ *She lifted the hem of her dress and brushed her knees.* ▌2▐ → See feature box at **sewing**
▶ **hem in** ▌1▐ PHRASAL VERB If a place **is hemmed in** by mountains or by other places, it is surrounded by them. ❏ *The canyon is hemmed in by towering walls of rock.* ▌2▐ PHRASAL VERB If someone **is hemmed in** or if someone **hems** them **in**, they are prevented from moving or changing, for example because they are surrounded by people or obstacles. ❏ *The company's competitors complain that they are hemmed in by rigid legal contracts.*

he-man (he-men) N-COUNT A **he-man** is a strong and very masculine man. [INFORMAL]

hema|tol|ogy /himəˈtɒlədʒi/ N-UNCOUNT **Hematology** is the branch of medicine that is concerned with diseases of the blood. ❏ *...the American Society of Hematology.*

hemi|sphere /hɛmɪsfɪər/ (hemispheres) N-COUNT A **hemisphere** is one half of the earth. ❏ *...the depletion of the ozone layer in the northern hemisphere.*

hem|line /hɛmlaɪn/ (hemlines) N-COUNT The **hemline** of a dress or skirt is its lower edge. People sometimes use **hemline** to talk about how long a dress or skirt is. ❏ *Mickey favored tight skirts with a hemline at the knee.*

hem|lock /hɛmlɒk/ N-UNCOUNT **Hemlock** is a poisonous plant.

hemo|glo|bin /himəˈgloʊbɪn/ N-UNCOUNT **Hemoglobin** is the red substance in blood, which combines with oxygen and carries it around the body.

hemo|philia /himəˈfɪliə/ N-UNCOUNT **Hemophilia** is a medical condition in which a person's blood does not thicken or clot properly when they are injured, so they continue bleeding.

hemo|phili|ac /himəˈfɪliæk/ (hemophiliacs) N-COUNT A **hemophiliac** is a person who has hemophilia. ❏ *...a hemophiliac who contracted the AIDS virus through a blood transfusion.*

hem|or|rhage /hɛmərɪdʒ/ (hemorrhages, hemorrhaging, hemorrhaged) ▌1▐ N-VAR A **hemorrhage** is serious bleeding inside a person's body. ❏ *Shortly after his admission into the hospital he had a massive brain hemorrhage and died.* ▌2▐ V-I If someone **is hemorrhaging**, there is serious bleeding inside their body. ❏ *I hemorrhaged badly after the birth of all three of my sons.* • **hem|or|rhag|ing** N-UNCOUNT ❏ *A post mortem showed he died from shock and hemorrhaging.*

hem|or|rhoid /hɛmərɔɪd/ (hemorrhoids) N-COUNT [usu pl] **Hemorrhoids** are painful swellings that can appear in the veins inside the anus. [MEDICAL]

hemp /hɛmp/ N-UNCOUNT **Hemp** is a plant used for making rope or the drug marijuana.

hen /hɛn/ (hens) N-COUNT A **hen** is a female chicken. People often keep hens in order to eat or sell their eggs.

hence /hɛns/ ▌1▐ ADV [ADV cl/group] You use **hence** to indicate that the statement you are about to make is a consequence of what you have just said. [FORMAL] ❏ *The trade imbalance is likely to rise again in five years' time. Hence a new set of policy actions will be required soon.* ▌2▐ ADV [amount ADV] You use **hence** in expressions such as '**several years hence**' or '**six months hence**' to refer to a time in the future, especially a long time in the future. [FORMAL] ❏ *The gases that may be warming the planet will have their main effect many years hence.*

hence|forth /hɛnsfɔrθ/ ADV [ADV with cl] **Henceforth** means from this or that time onward. [FORMAL] ❏ *Henceforth all branches of the naval officer corps were equal to one another.*

hence|forward /hɛnsfɔrwərd/ ADV [ADV with cl] **Henceforward** means from this or that time on. [FORMAL] ❑ *Henceforward Utah and Idaho had a common interest.*

hench|man /hɛntʃmən/ (henchmen) N-COUNT [usu poss N] If you refer to someone as another person's **henchman**, you mean that they work for or support the other person, especially by doing unpleasant, violent, or dishonest things on their behalf. [DISAPPROVAL]

hen|house /hɛnhaʊs/ (henhouses) N-COUNT A **henhouse** is a special building where hens are kept.

hen|na /hɛnə/ N-UNCOUNT **Henna** is a reddish brown dye that is made from the leaves of a shrub. It is used especially for coloring hair or skin.

hen|pecked /hɛnpɛkt/ also **hen-pecked** ADJ [usu ADJ n] You use **henpecked** to describe a man when you disapprove of the fact that someone, often his partner, is always telling him what to do or telling him that he has done something wrong. [INFORMAL, DISAPPROVAL]

hepa|ti|tis /hɛpətaɪtɪs/ N-UNCOUNT **Hepatitis** is a serious disease which affects the liver.

hep|tath|lon /hɛptæθlɒn/ (heptathlons) N-COUNT The **heptathlon** is a track and field competition for women in which each athlete competes in seven different events.

her ♦♦♦ /hər, STRONG hɜr/

Her is a third person singular pronoun. **Her** is used as the object of a verb or a preposition. **Her** is also a possessive determiner.

◼ PRON-SING [V PRON, prep PRON] You use **her** to refer to a woman, girl, or female animal. ❑ *I went in the room and told her I had something to say to her.* • DET **Her** is also a possessive determiner. ❑ *Liz traveled around the world for a year with her boyfriend James.* ◼ PRON-SING [V PRON, prep PRON] In written English, **her** is sometimes used to refer to a person without saying whether that person is a man or a woman. Many people prefer to use 'him or her' or 'them' as an alternative to 'her.' ❑ *Talk to your baby, play games, and show her how much you enjoy her company.* • DET **Her** is also a possessive determiner. ❑ *The non-drinking, non-smoking model should do nothing to risk her reputation.* ◼ PRON-SING [V PRON, prep PRON] **Her** is sometimes used to refer to a country or nation. [FORMAL OR WRITTEN] • DET **Her** is also a possessive determiner. ❑ *America and her partners are helping to rebuild roads and bridges and buildings.* ◼ PRON-SING [V PRON, prep PRON] People sometimes use **her** to refer to a car, machine, or ship. Some people think it is better to refer to these things as 'it.' ❑ *Kemp got out of his truck. "Just fill her up, thanks."* • DET **Her** is also a possessive determiner. ❑ *This dramatic photograph was taken from Carpathia's deck by one of her passengers.*

her|ald /hɛrəld/ (heralds, heralding, heralded) ◼ V-T Something that **heralds** a future event or situation is a sign that it is going to happen or appear. [FORMAL] ❑ *...the sultry evening that heralded the end of the baking hot summer.* ◼ N-COUNT Something that is a **herald** of a future event or situation is a sign that it is going to happen or appear. [FORMAL] ❑ *I welcome the report as a herald of more freedom.* ◼ V-T [usu passive] If an important event or action **is heralded** by people, announcements are made about it so that it is publicly known and expected. [FORMAL] ❑ *Her new album has been heralded by a massive media campaign.*

he|ral|dic /hərældɪk/ ADJ [ADJ n] **Heraldic** means relating to heraldry. ❑ *...religious and heraldic symbols.*

her|ald|ry /hɛrəldri/ N-UNCOUNT **Heraldry** is the study of coats of arms and of the history of the families who have them.

herb /ɜrb/ (herbs) N-COUNT A **herb** is a plant whose leaves are used in cooking to add flavor to food, or as a medicine. ❑ *...beautiful, fragrant herbs such as basil and coriander.*

her|ba|ceous /hɜrbeɪʃəs, 3r-/ ADJ [ADJ n] **Herbaceous** plants have green stems, not hard, woody stems.

herb|al /ɜrbəl, 3r-/ ADJ [ADJ n] **Herbal** means made from or using herbs. ❑ *...herbal remedies for colds.*

herb|al|ism /ɜrbəlɪzəm, 3r-/ N-UNCOUNT **Herbalism** is the practice of using herbs to treat illnesses.

herb|al|ist /ɜrbəlɪst, 3r-/ (herbalists) N-COUNT A **herbalist** is a person who grows or sells herbs that are used in medicine.

herbi|cide /hɜrbɪsaɪd, 3r-/ (herbicides) N-MASS A **herbicide** is a chemical that is used to destroy plants, especially weeds.

her|bi|vore /hɜrbɪvɔr, 3r-/ (herbivores) N-COUNT A **herbivore** is an animal that only eats plants.

her|bi|vo|rous /hɜrbɪvərəs, 3r-/ ADJ **Herbivorous** animals only eat plants.

her|cu|lean /hɜrkyuliən/ also **Herculean** ADJ [usu ADJ n] A **herculean** task or ability is one that requires extremely great strength or effort. [LITERARY] ❑ *...his herculean efforts to bring peace to our troubled island.*

herd /hɜrd/ (herds, herding, herded) ◼ N-COUNT A **herd** is a large group of animals of one kind that live together. ❑ *Chobe is also renowned for its large herds of elephant and buffalo.* ◼ N-SING If you say that someone has joined **the herd** or follows **the herd**, you are criticizing them because you think that they behave just like everyone else and do not think for themselves. [DISAPPROVAL] ❑ *They are individuals; they will not follow the herd.* ◼ V-T If you **herd** people somewhere, you make them move there in a group. ❑ *He began to herd the prisoners out.* ◼ V-T If you **herd** animals, you make them move along as a group. ❑ *Stefano used a motorcycle to herd the sheep.* ◼ → See feature box at **farming**

herd|er /hɜrdər/ (herders) N-COUNT A **herder** is a person who looks after a herd of animals such as cattle or goats.

herd immunity N-UNCOUNT **Herd immunity** is immunity from a disease that occurs when a whole population is immune. [MEDICAL] ❑ *The risk of the disease reemerging starts to increase because the population no longer has herd immunity.*

here ♦♦♦ /hɪər/ ◼ ADV You use **here** when you are referring to the place where you are. ❑ *I'm here all by myself and I know I'm going to get lost.* ❑ *Well, I can't stand here chatting all day.* ◼ ADV You use **here** when you are pointing toward a place that is near you, in order to draw someone else's attention to it. ❑ *...if you will just sign here.* ◼ ADV You use **here** in order to indicate that the person or thing that you are talking about is near you or is being held by you. ❑ *My friend here writes for radio.* ◼ ADV [be ADV to-inf] If you say that you are **here** to do something, that is your role or function. ❑ *I'm here to help you.* ◼ ADV You use **here** in order to draw attention to something or someone who has just arrived in the place where you are, or to draw attention to the place you have just arrived at. ❑ *"Here's the taxi," she said politely.* ◼ ADV You use **here** to refer to a particular point or stage of a situation or subject that you have come to or that you are dealing with. ❑ *It's here that we come up against the difference of approach.* ◼ ADV You use **here** to refer to a period of time, a situation, or an event that is present or happening now. ❑ *Economic recovery is here.* ◼ ADV [ADV be n/wh] You use **here** at the beginning of a sentence in order to draw attention to something or to introduce something. ❑ *Now here's what I want you to do.* ◼ ADV [ADV be n] You use **here** when you are offering or giving something to someone. ❑ *Here's your coffee, just the way you like it.* ❑ *Here are some letters I want you to sign.* ◼ CONVENTION You say '**here we are**' when you have just found something that you have been looking for. ❑ *I rummaged through the drawers and came up with Amanda's folder. "Here we are."* ◼ CONVENTION You say '**here goes**' when you are about to do or say something difficult or unpleasant. ❑ *Dr. Culver nervously muttered "Here goes," and gave the little girl an injection.* ◼ PHRASE You use expressions such as '**here we go**' and '**here we go again**' in order to indicate that something is happening again in the way that you expected, especially something unpleasant. [INFORMAL] ❑ *"Police! Open up!"—"Oh well," I thought, "here we go."* ◼ PHRASE You use **here and now** to emphasize that something is happening at the present time, rather than in the future or past, or that you would like it to happen at the present time. [EMPHASIS] ❑ *I'm a practicing physician trying to help people here and now.* ◼ PHRASE If something happens **here and there**, it happens in several different places. ❑ *I do a bit of teaching here and there.* ◼ CONVENTION You use expressions such as '**here's to us**' and '**here's to your new job**' before drinking a toast in order to wish someone success or happiness. [FORMULAE] ❑ *He raised his glass. "Here's to neighbors."*

> **USAGE**
>
> **here**
> Don't use 'to' in front of **here**. Don't say, for example, 'We can come to here at any time.' Say 'We can come **here** at any time.'

here|abouts /hɪərəbaʊts/ ADV [ADV after v, n ADV] You use **hereabouts** to indicate that you are talking about something near you or in the same area as you. ◻ *It's a bit chilly and empty hereabouts.*

here|after /hɪəræftər/ **1** ADV [ADV with cl] **Hereafter** means from this time onward. [FORMAL, WRITTEN] ◻ *I realized how hard life was going to be for me hereafter.* **2** ADV [ADV with cl] In legal documents and in written English, **hereafter** is used to introduce information about an abbreviation that will be used in the rest of the text to refer to the person or thing just mentioned. ◻ *Michel Foucault (1972), The Archaeology of Knowledge; hereafter this text will be abbreviated as AK.* **3** N-SING [usu the N] The **hereafter** is sometimes used to refer to the time after you have died, or to the life which some people believe you have after you died. ◻ *...belief in the hereafter.* • ADJ [n ADJ] **Hereafter** is also an adjective. ◻ *...the life hereafter.*

here|by /hɪərbaɪ/ ADV [ADV before v] You use **hereby** when officially or formally saying what you are doing. [FORMAL] ◻ *I hereby consent for my son/daughter to take this personality test.*

he|red|itary /hɪrɛdɪtəri/ **1** ADJ A **hereditary** characteristic or illness is passed on to a child from its parents before it is born. ◻ *Cystic fibrosis is the commonest fatal hereditary disease.* **2** ADJ A title or position in society that is **hereditary** is one that is passed on as a right from parent to child. ◻ *The position of the head of state is hereditary.*

he|red|ity /hɪrɛdɪti/ N-UNCOUNT **Heredity** is the process by which features and characteristics are passed on from parents to their children before the children are born. ◻ *Heredity is not a factor in causing the cancer.*

here|in /hɪərɪn/ **1** ADV [ADV after v, n ADV] **Herein** means in this document, text, or book. [FORMAL, WRITTEN] ◻ *The statements and views expressed herein are those of the author and are not necessarily those of the publisher.* **2** ADV [ADV cl] You can use **herein** to refer back to the situation or fact you have just mentioned, when saying it is something such as a problem or reason for something. [FORMAL, WRITTEN] ◻ *The point is that people grew unaccustomed to thinking and acting in a responsible and independent way. Herein lies another big problem.*

her|esy /hɛrɪsi/ (**heresies**) **1** N-VAR **Heresy** is a belief or action that most people think is wrong, because it disagrees with beliefs that are generally accepted. ◻ *It might be considered heresy to suggest such a notion.* **2** N-VAR **Heresy** is a belief or action which seriously disagrees with the principles of a particular religion. ◻ *He said it was a heresy to suggest that women should not conduct services.*

her|etic /hɛrɪtɪk/ (**heretics**) **1** N-COUNT A **heretic** is someone whose beliefs or actions are considered wrong by most people, because they disagree with beliefs that are generally accepted. ◻ *He was considered a heretic and was ridiculed and ostracized for his ideas.* **2** N-COUNT A **heretic** is a person who belongs to a particular religion, but whose beliefs or actions seriously disagree with the principles of that religion.

he|reti|cal /hɪrɛtɪkəl/ **1** ADJ A belief or action that is **heretical** is one that most people think is wrong because it disagrees with beliefs that are generally accepted. ◻ *I made the then heretical suggestion that it might be cheaper to design new machines.* **2** ADJ A belief or action that is **heretical** is one that seriously disagrees with the principles of a particular religion. ◻ *The Church regards spirit mediums and people claiming to speak to the dead as heretical.*

here|to|fore /hɪərtəfɔr/ ADV **Heretofore** means 'before this time' or 'up to now.' [mainly AM, FORMAL] ◻ *They reported that clouds are an important and heretofore uninvestigated contributor to the climate.*

here|with /hɪərwɪθ, -wɪð/ ADV **Herewith** means with this document, text, or book. You can use **herewith** in a letter to say that you are enclosing something with it. [FORMAL, WRITTEN] ◻ *...the 236 revolutionary prisoners whose names are listed herewith.* ◻ *I return herewith your papers.*

her|it|age /hɛrɪtɪdʒ/ (**heritages**) N-VAR A country's **heritage** is all the qualities, traditions, or features of life there that have continued over many years and have been passed on from one generation to another. ◻ *The historic building is as much part of our heritage as the paintings.*

her|maph|ro|dite /hɜrmæfrədaɪt/ (**hermaphrodites**) N-COUNT A **hermaphrodite** is a person, animal, or flower that has both male and female reproductive organs.

her|met|ic /hɜrmɛtɪk/ **1** ADJ [ADJ n] If a container has a **hermetic** seal, the seal is very tight so that no air can get in or out. [TECHNICAL] • **her|meti|cal|ly** /hɜrmɛtɪkli/ ADV ◻ *The batteries are designed to be leak-proof and hermetically sealed.* **2** ADJ You use **hermetic** to describe something which you disapprove of because it seems to be totally separate from other people and things in society. [WRITTEN, DISAPPROVAL] ◻ *Its film industry operates in its own curiously hermetic way.* ◻ *...the composer's hermetic musical world.*

her|mit /hɜrmɪt/ (**hermits**) N-COUNT A **hermit** is a person who lives alone, away from people and society. ◻ *I've spent the past ten years living like a hermit.*

her|nia /hɜrniə/ (**hernias**) N-VAR A **hernia** is a medical condition which is often caused by strain or injury. It results in one of your internal organs sticking through a weak point in the surrounding tissue.

hero ♦◇◇ /hɪəroʊ/ (**heroes**) **1** N-COUNT The **hero** of a book, play, movie, or story is the main male character, who usually has good qualities. ◻ *The hero of Doctor Zhivago dies in 1929.* **2** N-COUNT A **hero** is someone who has done something brave, new, or good, and who is therefore greatly admired by a lot of people. ◻ *He called Mr. Mandela a hero who had inspired millions.* **3** N-COUNT If you describe someone as your **hero**, you mean that you admire them a great deal, usually because of a particular quality or skill that they have. ◻ *My boyhood hero was Kit Carson.*

he|ro|ic /hɪroʊɪk/ (**heroics**) **1** ADJ If you describe a person or their actions as **heroic**, you admire them because they show extreme bravery. ◻ *His heroic deeds were celebrated in every corner of India.* • **he|roi|cal|ly** /hɪroʊɪkli/ ADV [ADV with v] ◻ *He had acted heroically during the liner's evacuation.* **2** ADJ If you describe an action or event as **heroic**, you admire it because it involves great effort or determination to succeed. [APPROVAL] ◻ *The company has made heroic efforts at cost reduction.* • **he|roi|cal|ly** ADV ◻ *Single parents cope heroically in doing the job of two people.* **3** ADJ **Heroic** means being or relating to the hero or heroine of a story. ◻ *...the book's central, heroic figure.* **4** N-PLURAL **Heroics** are actions involving bravery, courage, or determination. ◻ *...the man whose aerial heroics helped save the helicopter pilot.* **5** N-PLURAL If you describe someone's actions or plans as **heroics**, you think that they are foolish or dangerous because they are too difficult or brave for the situation in which they occur. [SPOKEN, DISAPPROVAL] ◻ *He said his advice was: "No heroics, stay within the law."*

hero|in /hɛroʊɪn/ N-UNCOUNT **Heroin** is a powerful drug which some people take for pleasure, but which they can become addicted to.

hero|ine /hɛroʊɪn/ (**heroines**) **1** N-COUNT The **heroine** of a book, play, movie, or story is the main female character, who usually has good qualities. ◻ *The heroine is a senior TV executive.* **2** N-COUNT A **heroine** is a woman who has done something brave, new, or good, and who is therefore greatly admired by a lot of people. ◻ *The national heroine of the day was Xing Fen, winner of the first gold medal of the Games.* **3** N-COUNT If you describe a woman as your **heroine**, you mean that you admire her greatly, usually because of a particular quality or skill that she has. ◻ *My heroine was Elizabeth Taylor.*

hero|ism /hɛroʊɪzəm/ N-UNCOUNT **Heroism** is great courage and bravery. ◻ *...individual acts of heroism.*

her|on /hɛrən/ (**herons**) N-COUNT A **heron** is a large bird which has long legs and a long beak, and which eats fish.

hero-worship (**hero-worships, hero-worshiping, hero-worshiped**)

> The noun is spelled **hero worship**.

1 N-UNCOUNT **Hero worship** is a very great admiration of someone and a belief that they are special or perfect. ◻ *Of course your attempts to make me happy sprang not from* hero-worship but from insecurity. **2** V-T If you **hero-worship** someone, you admire them a great deal and think they are special or perfect. ☐ *He was amused by the way younger actors started to hero-worship and copy him.*

her|pes /hɜrpiz/ N-UNCOUNT **Herpes** is a disease which causes painful red spots to appear on the skin.

her|ring /hɛrɪŋ/ (**herring, herrings**) N-VAR A **herring** is a long silver-colored fish. Herring live in large groups in the ocean. ☐ *...a shoal of herring.* • N-UNCOUNT **Herring** is a piece of this fish eaten as food. ☐ *...a can of herring.*

herring|bone /hɛrɪŋboʊn/ N-UNCOUNT [oft N n] **Herringbone** is a pattern used in fabrics or brickwork which looks like parallel rows of zigzag lines.

hers /hɜrz/

Hers is a third person possessive pronoun.

1 PRON-POSS You use **hers** to indicate that something belongs or relates to a woman, girl, or female animal. ☐ *His hand as it shook hers was warm and firm.* ☐ *Professor Camm was a great friend of hers.* **2** PRON-POSS In written English, **hers** is sometimes used to refer to a person without saying whether that person is a man or a woman. Many people prefer to use 'his or hers' or 'theirs' as an alternative to 'hers.' ☐ *The author can report other people's results which more or less agree with hers.*

her|self ♦♦♦ /hɜrsɛlf/

Herself is a third person singular reflexive pronoun. Herself is used when the object of a verb or preposition refers to the same person as the subject of the verb, except in meaning **3**.

1 PRON-REFL [V PRON, prep PRON] You use **herself** to refer to a woman, girl, or female animal ☐ *She let herself out of the room.* ☐ *Jennifer believes she will move out on her own when she is financially able to support herself.* **2** PRON-REFL In written English, **herself** is sometimes used to refer to a person without saying whether that person is a man or a woman. Many people prefer to use 'himself or herself' or 'themselves' as an alternative to 'herself.' ☐ *How can anyone believe stories for which she feels herself to be in no way responsible?* **3** PRON-REFL-EMPH You use **herself** to emphasize the person or thing that you are referring to. **Herself** is sometimes used instead of 'her' as the object of a verb or preposition. [EMPHASIS] ☐ *She herself was not a keen gardener.*

he's /hiz, STRONG hiz/ **He's** is the usual spoken form of 'he is' or 'he has,' especially when 'has' is an auxiliary verb. ☐ *He's working maybe twenty-five hours a week.*

hesi|tant /hɛzɪtənt/ ADJ If you are **hesitant** about doing something, you do not do it quickly or immediately, usually because you are uncertain, embarrassed, or worried. ☐ *She was hesitant about coming forward with her story.* • **hesi|tan|cy** /hɛzɪtənsi/ N-UNCOUNT ☐ *A trace of hesitancy showed in Dr. Stockton's eyes.* • **hesi|tant|ly** ADV [ADV with v] ☐ *"Would you do me a favor?" she asked hesitantly.*

hesi|tate /hɛzɪteɪt/ (**hesitates, hesitating, hesitated**) **1** V-I If you **hesitate**, you do not speak or act for a short time, usually because you are uncertain, embarrassed, or worried about what you are going to say or do. ☐ *The telephone rang. Catherine hesitated, debating whether to answer it.* • **hesi|ta|tion** /hɛzɪteɪʃ°n/ (**hesitations**) N-VAR ☐ *Asked if he would go back, Mr. Searle said after some hesitation, "I'll have to think about that."* **2** V-T If you **hesitate to do** something, you delay doing it or are unwilling to do it, usually because you are not certain it would be right. If you do not **hesitate** to do something, you do it immediately. ☐ *Some parents hesitate to take these steps because they suspect that their child is exaggerating.* **3** V-T [only imper, with neg] You can use **hesitate** in expressions such as '**don't hesitate to call me**' or '**don't hesitate to contact us**' when you are telling someone that they should do something as soon as it needs to be done and should not worry about disturbing other people. ☐ *In the event of difficulties, please do not hesitate to contact our Customer Service Department.*

hesi|ta|tion /hɛzɪteɪʃ°n/ (**hesitations**) **1** N-VAR **Hesitation** is an unwillingness to do something, or a delay in doing it, because you are uncertain, worried, or embarrassed about it. ☐ *He promised there would be no more hesitations in pursuing reforms.*

2 → see also **hesitate** **3** PHRASE If you say that you **have no hesitation** in doing something, you are emphasizing that you will do it immediately or willingly because you are certain that it is the right thing to do. [EMPHASIS] ☐ *The board said it had no hesitation in unanimously rejecting the offer.* **4** PHRASE If you say that someone does something **without hesitation**, you are emphasizing that they do it immediately and willingly. [EMPHASIS] ☐ *The great majority of players would, of course, sign the contract without hesitation.*

hes|sian /hɛʃən/ N-UNCOUNT **Hessian** is the same as **burlap**. [mainly BRIT]

hetero|dox /hɛtərədɒks/ ADJ **Heterodox** beliefs, opinions, or ideas are different from the accepted or official ones. [FORMAL]

hetero|geneous /hɛtərədʒiniəs, -dʒinyəs/ ADJ [usu ADJ n] A **heterogeneous** group consists of many different types of things or people. [FORMAL] ☐ *...a rather heterogeneous collection of studies from diverse origins.*

hetero|nor|ma|tive /hɛtəroʊnɔrmətɪv/ ADJ [usu ADJ n] **Heteronormative** means regarding heterosexual relationships and behavior as normal. ☐ *...alternatives to the heteronormative family unit.* ☐ *Lesbian, gay, bisexual and trans people have higher rates of such problems because of the challenges of living within a heteronormative world.*

hetero|sex|ual /hɛtəroʊsɛkʃuəl/ (**heterosexuals**) **1** ADJ A **heterosexual** relationship is a sexual relationship between a man and a woman. ☐ *An increasing number of people are becoming infected with HIV through heterosexual sex.* **2** ADJ Someone who is **heterosexual** is sexually attracted to people of the opposite sex. ☐ *It doesn't matter whether people are heterosexual or homosexual.* • N-COUNT **Heterosexual** is also a noun. ☐ *There the age of consent is fifteen for both heterosexuals and homosexuals.* • **hetero|sex|ual|ity** /hɛtəroʊsɛkʃuælɪti/ N-UNCOUNT ☐ *In the film, he goes to every length to prove his heterosexuality.*

het up /hɛt ʌp/ ADJ [v-link ADJ] If you get **het up** about something, you get very excited, angry, or anxious about it. [BRIT, INFORMAL]

heu|ris|tic /hyʊrɪstɪk/ **1** ADJ A **heuristic** method of learning involves discovery and problem solving, using reasoning and past experience. [TECHNICAL] **2** ADJ A **heuristic** computer program uses rules based on previous experience in order to solve a problem, rather than using a mathematical procedure. [COMPUTING] **3** → see also **algorithm**

hew /hyu/ (**hews, hewing, hewed** or **hewn**) **1** V-T If you **hew** stone or wood, you cut it, for example with an ax. [OLD-FASHIONED] ☐ *He felled, peeled, and hewed his own timber.* **2** V-T [usu passive] If something **is hewn** from stone or wood, it is cut from stone or wood. [LITERARY, OLD-FASHIONED] ☐ *...the rock from which the lower chambers and subterranean passageways have been hewn.* ☐ *...medieval monasteries hewn out of the rockface.* **3** → see also **rough-hewn**

hex /hɛks/ (**hexes, hexing, hexed**) **1** N-COUNT [oft N on n] If you say that there is a **hex** on someone or something, you mean that there seems to be a supernatural power causing unpleasant things to happen to them. ☐ *It's almost as if there is a hex on my family.* **2** V-T If a person such as a witch or a wizard **hexes** someone, they put a hex on them. ☐ *...shamans who could hex someone at a distance.*

hexa|gon /hɛksəgɒn/ (**hexagons**) N-COUNT A **hexagon** is a shape that has six straight sides.

hex|ago|nal /hɛksæɡən°l/ ADJ A **hexagonal** object or shape has six straight sides.

hey /heɪ/ **1** CONVENTION In informal situations, you say or shout '**hey**' to attract someone's attention, or to show surprise, interest, or annoyance. [FEELINGS] ☐ *"Hey! Look out!" shouted Patty.* **2** CONVENTION In informal situations, you can say '**hey**' to greet someone. ☐ *She watched as he smiled, opened his mouth, and said, "Hey, Kate."*

hey|day /heɪdeɪ/ N-SING Someone's **heyday** is the time when they are most powerful, successful, or popular. ☐ *In its heyday, the studio's boast was that it had more stars than there are in heaven.*

HFC /eɪtʃ ɛf si/ (**HFCs**) N-COUNT **HFC** is a type of gas used in refrigerators and aerosols. **HFC** is an abbreviation for 'hydrofluorocarbon.'

HGH /eɪtʃ dʒi eɪtʃ/ **HGH** is an abbreviation for **human growth hormone**.

hi ✦✦✦ /haɪ/ CONVENTION In informal situations, you say 'hi' to greet someone. [FORMULAE] ❑ *"Hi, Liz," she said shyly.*

hi|atus /haɪeɪtəs/ N-SING A **hiatus** is a pause in which nothing happens, or a gap where something is missing. [FORMAL] ❑ *Diplomatic efforts to reach a settlement resume today after a two-week hiatus.*

hi|ber|nate /haɪbərneɪt/ (hibernates, hibernating, hibernated) V-I Animals that **hibernate** spend the winter in a state like a deep sleep. ❑ *Dormice hibernate from October to May.*

hi|bis|cus /haɪbɪskəs/ (hibiscus) N-VAR A **hibiscus** is a tropical bush that has large, brightly colored bell-shaped flowers.

hic|cup /hɪkʌp/ (hiccups, hiccuping or hiccupping, hiccuped or hiccupped) also **hiccough** ◼ N-COUNT You can refer to a small problem or difficulty as a **hiccup**, especially if it does not last very long or is easily corrected. ❑ *A recent sales hiccup is nothing to panic about.* ◼ N-UNCOUNT [also the N] When you have **hiccups**, you make repeated sharp sounds in your throat, often because you have been eating or drinking too quickly. ❑ *A baby may frequently get a bout of hiccups during or soon after a feeding.* ◼ V-I When you **hiccup**, you make repeated sharp sounds in your throat. ❑ *She was still hiccuping from the egg she had swallowed whole.*

hick /hɪk/ (hicks) N-COUNT [oft N n] If you refer to someone as a **hick**, you are saying in a rude way that you think they are uneducated and unsophisticated because they come from the countryside. [INFORMAL, DISAPPROVAL]

hickey /hɪki/ (hickeys) N-COUNT A **hickey** is a mark which someone has on their body as a result of being bitten by their partner when they were kissing or making love. [AM, INFORMAL] ❑ *She gave me a large hickey.*

hicko|ry /hɪkəri/ (hickories) N-VAR A **hickory** is a tree which has large leaves, greenish flowers, and nuts with smooth shells. ❑ *It would have meant cutting down over 200 trees, including oaks and hickories.* • N-UNCOUNT **Hickory** is the wood of this tree. ❑ *The first skis were long, thin strips of hickory.*

hid /hɪd/ **Hid** is the past tense of **hide**.

hid|den /hɪdən/ ◼ **Hidden** is the past participle of **hide**. ◼ ADJ **Hidden** facts, feelings, activities, or problems are not easy to notice or discover. ❑ *Under all the innocent fun, there are hidden dangers, especially for children.* ◼ ADJ A **hidden** place is difficult to find. ❑ *As you descend, suddenly you see at last the hidden waterfall.*

hid|den agen|da (hidden agendas) N-COUNT If you say that someone has a **hidden agenda**, you are criticizing them because you think they are secretly trying to achieve or cause a particular thing, while they appear to be doing something else. [DISAPPROVAL] ❑ *He accused foreign nations of having a hidden agenda to harm French influence.*

hide ✦✦✦ /haɪd/ (hides, hiding, hid, hidden) ◼ V-T If you **hide** something or someone, you put them in a place where they cannot easily be seen or found. ❑ *He hid the bicycle in the hawthorn hedge.* ◼ V-T/V-I If you **hide** or if you **hide** yourself, you go somewhere where you cannot easily be seen or found. ❑ *At their approach the little boy scurried and hid.* ◼ V-T If you **hide** your face, you press your face against something or cover your face with something, so that people cannot see it. ❑ *She hid her face under the collar of his jacket and started to cry.* ◼ V-T If you **hide** what you feel or know, you keep it a secret, so that no one knows about it. ❑ *Lee tried to hide his excitement.* ◼ V-T If something **hides** an object, it covers it and prevents it from being seen. ❑ *The man's heavy mustache hid his upper lip completely.* ◼ N-VAR A **hide** is the skin of a large animal such as a cow, horse, or elephant, which can be used for making leather. ❑ *...the process of tanning animal hides.* ◼ → see also **hidden**, **hiding**

hide-and-seek N-UNCOUNT **Hide-and-seek** is a children's game in which one player covers his or her eyes until the other players have hidden themselves, and then he or she tries to find them.

hide|away /haɪdəweɪ/ (hideaways) N-COUNT A **hideaway** is a place where you go to hide or to get away from other people. ❑ *The bandits fled to a remote mountain hideaway.*

hide|bound /haɪdbaʊnd/ ADJ [oft ADJ by n] If you describe someone or something as **hidebound**, you are criticizing them for having old-fashioned ideas or ways of doing things and being unwilling or unlikely to change. [DISAPPROVAL] ❑ *The men are hidebound and reactionary.* ❑ *The economy was hidebound by public spending and private monopolies.*

hid|eous /hɪdiəs/ ◼ ADJ If you say that someone or something is **hideous**, you mean that they are very ugly or unattractive. ❑ *She saw a hideous face at the window and screamed.* ◼ ADJ You can describe an event, experience, or action as **hideous** when you mean that it is very unpleasant, painful, or difficult to bear. ❑ *His family was subjected to a hideous attack by the gang.*

hid|eous|ly /hɪdiəsli/ ◼ ADV You use **hideously** to emphasize that something is very ugly or unattractive. [EMPHASIS] ❑ *Everything is hideously ugly.* ◼ ADV [ADV adj/-ed] You can use **hideously** to emphasize that something is very unpleasant or unacceptable. [EMPHASIS] ❑ *...a hideously complex program.*

hide|out /haɪdaʊt/ (hideouts) N-COUNT A **hideout** is a place where someone goes secretly because they do not want anyone to find them, for example if they are running away from the police.

hid|ing /haɪdɪŋ/ N-UNCOUNT If someone is in **hiding**, they have secretly gone somewhere where they cannot be seen or found. ❑ *He is thought to be in hiding near the France-Italy border.*

hid|ing place (hiding places) N-COUNT A **hiding place** is a place where someone or something can be hidden, or where they are hiding.

hi|er|ar|chi|cal /haɪərɑrkɪkəl/ ADJ A **hierarchical** system or organization is one in which people have different ranks or positions, depending on how important they are. ❑ *...the traditional hierarchical system of military organization.*

hi|er|ar|chy /haɪərɑrki/ (hierarchies) ◼ N-VAR A **hierarchy** is a system of organizing people into different ranks or levels of importance, for example in society or in a company. ❑ *Like most other American companies with a rigid hierarchy, workers and managers had strictly defined duties.* ◼ N-COUNT-COLL The **hierarchy** of an organization is the group of people who manage and control it. ❑ *The church hierarchy today feels the church should reflect the social and political realities of the country.*

hi|ero|glyph /haɪərəglɪf/ (hieroglyphs) N-COUNT **Hieroglyphs** are symbols in the form of pictures, which are used in some writing systems, especially those of ancient Egypt.

hi|ero|glyph|ics /haɪərəglɪfɪks/ N-PLURAL **Hieroglyphics** are symbols in the form of pictures which are used in some writing systems, for example those of ancient Egypt.

hi-fi /haɪ faɪ/ (hi-fis) N-VAR A **hi-fi** is a set of equipment on which you play CDs and tapes, and which produces stereo sound of very good quality. [OLD-FASHIONED]

higgledy-piggledy /hɪgəldi pɪgəldi/ ADJ If you say that things are **higgledy-piggledy**, you mean that they are very disorganized and untidy. [INFORMAL] ❑ *Books are often stacked in higgledy-piggledy piles on the floor.* • ADV [ADV after v] **Higgledy-piggledy** is also an adverb. ❑ *...a whole valley of boulders tossed higgledy-piggledy as though by some giant.*

high ✦✦✦ /haɪ/ (higher, highest, highs) ◼ ADJ Something that is **high** extends a long way from the bottom to the top when it is upright. You do not use **high** to describe people, animals, or plants. ❑ *...a house with a high wall all around it.* ❑ *Mount Marcy is the highest mountain in the Adirondacks.* • ADV [ADV after v] **High** is also an adverb. ❑ *...wagons packed high with bureaus, bedding, and cooking pots.* ◼ ADJ You use **high** to talk or ask about how much something upright measures from the bottom to the top. ❑ *...an elegant bronze horse only nine inches high.* ❑ *The grass in the yard was a foot high.* ◼ ADJ If something is **high**, it is a long way above the ground, above sea level, or above a person or thing. ❑ *I looked down from the high window.* ❑ *The sun was high in the sky, blazing down on us.* • ADV [ADV after v] **High** is also an adverb. ❑ *...being able to run faster or jump higher than other people.* • PHRASE If something is **high up**, it is a long way above the ground, above sea level, or above a person or thing. ❑ *His farm was high up in the hills.* ◼ ADJ You can use **high** to indicate that something is great in amount, degree, or intensity. ❑ *...the European country with the highest birth rate.* ❑ *Official reports said casualties were high.* • ADV [ADV after v] **High** is also an adverb. ❑ *He expects the unemployment figures to rise even higher in coming months.* • PHRASE You can use phrases such as '**in the high 80s**' to indicate that a number or level is, for example, more than 85 but not as much as 90. ◼ ADJ [v-link ADJ in n] If a food or other substance is **high in** a particular ingredient, it contains a large amount of that ingredient. ❑ *Don't indulge in rich sauces, fried food, and thick pastry as these are high in fat.* ◼ N-COUNT [oft N of amount] If something reaches a **high** of a particular amount or degree, that is the greatest it has ever been. ❑ *Traffic crossing the border is down to a dozen loaded trucks a day, compared with a high of 200 a day.* ◼ ADJ If you say that something is a **high** priority or is **high** on your list, you mean that you consider it to be one of the most important things you have to do or deal with. ❑ *The party has not made the issue a high priority.* ◼ ADJ [v-link ADJ in n, ADJ n] Someone who is **high** in a particular profession or society, or has a **high** position, has a very important position and has great authority and influence. ❑ *Was there anyone particularly high in the administration who was an advocate of a different policy?* ❑ *...corruption in high places.* • PHRASE Someone who is **high up** in a profession or society has a very important position. ❑ *His cousin is somebody quite high up in the navy.* ◼ ADV [ADV after v] If you aim **high**, you try to obtain or to achieve the best that you can. ❑ *You should not be afraid to aim high in the quest for an improvement in your income.* ◼ ADJ If someone has a **high** reputation, or people have a **high** opinion of them, people think they are very good in some way, for example at their work. ❑ *People have such high expectations of you.* ◼ ADJ If the quality or standard of something is **high**, it is extremely good. ❑ *This is high quality stuff.* ◼ ADJ A **high** sound or voice is close to the top of a particular range of notes. ❑ *Her high voice really irritated Maria.* ◼ ADJ If your spirits are **high**, you feel happy and excited. ❑ *Her spirits were high with the hope of seeing Nick in minutes rather than hours.* ◼ ADJ [v-link ADJ] If someone is **high** on alcohol or drugs, they are affected by the alcoholic drink or drugs they have taken. [INFORMAL] ❑ *He was too high on drugs and alcohol to remember them.* ◼ N-COUNT A **high** is a feeling or mood of great excitement or happiness. [INFORMAL] ❑ *"I'm still on a high," she said after the show.* ◼ PHRASE If you say that something came from **on high**, you mean that it came from a person or place of great authority. ❑ *Orders had come from on high that extra care was to be taken during this week.* ◼ PHRASE If you say that you were left **high and dry**, you are emphasizing that you were left in a difficult situation and were unable to do anything about it. [EMPHASIS] ❑ *Schools with better reputations will be flooded with applications while poorer schools will be left high and dry.* ◼ PHRASE If you refer to the **highs and lows** of someone's life or career, you are referring to both the successful or happy times, and the unsuccessful or bad times. ❑ *Here, she talks about the highs and lows of her life.* ◼ PHRASE If you say that you looked **high and low** for something, you are emphasizing that you looked for it in every place that you could think of. [EMPHASIS] ❑ *...and I rambled around the apartment looking high and low for an aspirin or painkiller.* ◼ → See feature box at **nutrition, storm, weather**

COLLOCATIONS

high
NOUN
◼
noun + **high**: career, season
adjective + **high**: all-time, new, record
verb + **high**: hit, reach, set
◼
adjective + **high**: emotional, exhilarating, tremendous
verb + **high**: experience, get

-high /-haɪ/ COMB IN ADJ **-high** combines with words such as 'knee' or 'shoulder' to indicate that someone or something reaches as high as the point that is mentioned. ❑ *The grass was knee-high.*

high-and-mighty ADJ If you describe someone as **high-and-mighty**, you disapprove of them because they consider themselves to be very important and are confident that they are always right. [DISAPPROVAL] ❑ *I think you're a bit too high-and-mighty yourself.*

high|ball /ˈhaɪbɔl/ (highballs) N-COUNT A **highball** is an alcoholic drink consisting of liquor such as whiskey or brandy mixed with soda water or ginger ale and served with ice in a tall glass. [AM] ❑ *...a bourbon highball.*

high beams N-PLURAL A vehicle's **high beams** are its headlights when they are set to shine their brightest. [AM] ❑ *Claire switched on her high beams for a better look at the trees across the road.*

high|boy /ˈhaɪbɔɪ/ (highboys) N-COUNT A **highboy** is a high chest of drawers consisting of two sections which are placed one on top of the other. [AM] ❑ *She saw him methodically searching the drawers of a highboy.*

high|brow /ˈhaɪbraʊ/ ◼ ADJ If you say that a book or discussion is **highbrow**, you mean that it is intellectual, academic, and is often difficult to understand. ❑ *He presents his own highbrow literary program.* ◼ ADJ [usu ADJ n] If you describe someone as **highbrow**, you mean that they are interested in serious subjects of a very intellectual nature, especially when these are difficult to understand. ❑ *Highbrow critics sniff that the program was "too sophisticated" to appeal to most viewers.*

high chair (high chairs) also **highchair** ◼ N-COUNT A **high chair** is a chair with long legs for a very young child to sit in while they are eating. ◼ → See also color supplement

high-class ADJ If you describe something as **high-class**, you mean that it is of very good quality or of superior social status. ❑ *...a high-class jeweler.*

high com|mand (high commands) N-COUNT-COLL [oft supp n] The **high command** is the group that consists of the most senior officers in a nation's armed forces.

High Com|mis|sion (High Commissions) N-COUNT [oft the adj N] A **High Commission** is the office where a High Commissioner and his or her staff work, or the group of officials who work there.

High Com|mis|sion|er (High Commissioners) ◼ N-COUNT [oft the adj N] A **High Commissioner** is a senior representative who is sent by a High Commission to fulfill a duty. ◼ N-COUNT [supp N] A **High Commissioner** is the head of an international commission. ❑ *...the United Nations High Commissioner for Refugees.*

high-defi|ni|tion also **high definition** ADJ [usu ADJ n] **High-definition** television or technology is a digital system that gives a much clearer picture than traditional television systems. ❑ *...high-definition TV, with its sharper images and better sound.* • N-UNCOUNT **High definition** is also a noun. ❑ *These games are more popular now that they are available in high definition.*

high-end ◼ ADJ **High-end** products, especially electronic products, are the most expensive of their kind. ❑ *...high-end personal computers and computer workstations.* ◼ → See feature box at **fashion**

high|er edu|ca|tion N-UNCOUNT **Higher education** is education at universities and colleges. ❑ *...students in higher education.*

higher-up (higher-ups) also **high-up** N-COUNT A **higher-up** is an important person who is at a senior level in an organization. [AM, INFORMAL] ❑ *Sherman recommended that Clarke be disciplined, but higher-ups rejected the idea.*

high ex|plo|sive (high explosives) N-VAR **High explosive** is an extremely powerful explosive substance.

high|fa|lu|tin /ˌhaɪfəˈluːtən/ ADJ People sometimes use **highfalutin** to describe something that they think is being made to sound complicated or important in order to impress people. [INFORMAL, OLD-FASHIONED, DISAPPROVAL] ❑ *This isn't highfalutin art-about-art. It's marvelous and adventurous stuff.*

high fi|del|ity also **high-fidelity** N-UNCOUNT [usu N n] **High fidelity** is the use of electronic equipment to reproduce a sound or image with very little distortion or loss of quality. ❑ *...a new, high-fidelity audio technology system.*

high five (high fives) also **high-five** N-COUNT If you give someone a **high five** or **high fives**, you put your hand up and hit their open hand with yours, especially after a victory or as a greeting.

high|flier /ˈhaɪflaɪər/ (highfliers) also **highflyer** N-COUNT A **highflier** is someone who has a lot of ability and is likely to be very successful in their career.

high-flown ADJ [usu ADJ n] **High-flown** language is very grand, formal, or literary. [DISAPPROVAL]

high|flyer /ˈhaɪflaɪər/ → see **highflier**

high-flying ADJ A **high-flying** person is successful or is likely to be successful in their career. ❑ *...her high-flying newspaper-editor husband.*

high ground N-SING [the N, oft the adj N] If a person or organization has **the high ground** in an argument or dispute, that person or organization has an advantage. [JOURNALISM] ❑ *The president must seek to regain the high ground in the political debate.* ◧ PHRASE [PHR after v] If you say that someone has taken the **moral high ground**, you mean that they consider that their policies and actions are morally superior to the policies and actions of their rivals. ❑ *The Republicans took the moral high ground with the message that they were best equipped to manage the authority.*

high-handed ADJ If you say that someone is **high-handed**, you disapprove of them because they use their authority in an unnecessarily forceful way without considering other people's feelings. [DISAPPROVAL] ❑ *He wants to be seen as less bossy and high-handed.* • **high-handedness** N-UNCOUNT ❑ *They have been accused of secrecy and high-handedness in their dealings.*

high-heeled ADJ [ADJ n] **High-heeled** shoes are women's shoes that have high heels.

high heels N-PLURAL You can refer to high-heeled shoes as **high heels**.

high-impact ◧ ADJ [usu ADJ n] **High-impact** exercise puts a lot of stress on your body. ❑ *...high-impact aerobics.* ◨ ADJ [usu ADJ n] **High-impact** materials are very strong. ❑ *The durable high-impact plastic case is water resistant to 100 feet.*

high jinks also **hijinks** N-UNCOUNT-COLL **High jinks** is lively, excited behavior in which people do things for fun. [INFORMAL, OLD-FASHIONED]

high jump N-SING [usu the N] The **high jump** is a track and field event which involves jumping over a raised bar.

high|lands /ˈhaɪləndz/ N-PLURAL **Highlands** are mountainous areas of land.

high life N-SING [also no det] You use the **high life** to refer to an exciting and luxurious way of living that involves a great deal of entertainment, going to parties, and eating good food. ❑ *...the Hollywood high life.*

high|light ✦✧ /ˈhaɪlaɪt/ (highlights, highlighting, highlighted) ◧ V-T If someone or something **highlights** a point or problem, they emphasize it or make you think about it. ❑ *Last year Collins wrote a moving ballad which highlighted the plight of the homeless.* ◨ V-T To **highlight** a piece of text means to mark it in a different color, either with a special type of pen or on a computer screen. ❑ *Highlight the chosen area by clicking and holding down the left mouse button.* ◩ N-COUNT The **highlights** of an event, activity, or period of time are the most interesting or exciting parts of it. ❑ *...a match that is likely to prove one of the highlights of the tournament.*

SYNONYMS

highlight
VERB ◧
emphasize: *We discussed pollution, emphasizing how nice a clean street or park looks.*
stress: *They also stress the need for improved employment opportunities.*
accentuate: *His shaved head accentuates his large, round face.*
NOUN ◩
high point: *The high point of this trip was a day at the races.*
climax: *Reaching the final was the climax of her career.*
peak: *His career was at its peak at the time of his death.*

high|light|er /ˈhaɪlaɪtər/ (highlighters) ◧ N-COUNT A **highlighter** is a pen with brightly colored ink that is used to mark parts of a document. ◨ N-MASS **Highlighter** is a pale-colored cosmetic that someone puts above their eyes or on their cheeks to emphasize the shape of their face.

high|ly ✦✦✧ /ˈhaɪli/ ◧ ADV [ADV adj] **Highly** is used before some adjectives to mean 'very.' ❑ *Mr. Singh was a highly successful salesman.* ❑ *It seems highly unlikely that she ever existed.* ◨ ADV [ADV -ed] You use **highly** to indicate that someone has an important position in an organization or set of people. ❑ *...a highly placed government advisor.* ◩ ADV [ADV -ed] If someone is **highly** paid, they receive a large salary. ❑ *...the 30 most highly paid athletes in the world.* ◪ ADV If you think **highly** of something or someone, you think they are extremely good. ❑ *Daphne and Michael thought highly of the school.*

SYNONYMS

highly
ADV ◧
extremely: *My smartphone is extremely useful.*
immensely: *Windsurfing can be strenuous, but immensely exciting.*
deeply: *Our meetings and conversations left me deeply depressed.*
tremendously: *The business is tremendously profitable.*
remarkably: *The labor market has been remarkably successful in absorbing the extra graduates.*

high-maintenance also **high maintenance** ADJ If you describe something or someone as **high-maintenance**, you mean that they require a lot of time, money, or effort. ❑ *Small gardens can be high maintenance.* ❑ *...a high-maintenance individual who needs to be the centre of attention.*

high mass also **High Mass** N-UNCOUNT **High mass** is a church service held in a Catholic church in which there is more ceremony than in an ordinary mass.

high-minded ADJ If you say that someone is **high-minded**, you think they have strong moral principles. ❑ *The president's hopes for the country were high-minded, but too vague.*

High|ness /ˈhaɪnɪs/ (Highnesses) N-VOC Expressions such as 'Your **Highness**' or 'Her **Highness**' are used to address or refer to a member of a royal family other than a king or queen. [POLITENESS] ❑ *That would be best, Your Highness.*

high noon ◧ N-UNCOUNT **High noon** means the same as noon. [LITERARY] ◨ N-UNCOUNT Journalists sometimes use **high noon** to refer to a crisis or event which is likely to decide finally what is going to happen in a conflict or situation. ❑ *With the coming of the Internet age, it looked like high noon for the nation's movie theaters.*

high-octane ◧ ADJ [ADJ n] You can use **high-octane** to emphasize that something is very exciting or intense. [JOURNALISM] ❑ *...a high-octane performance.* ◨ → see octane

high-performance ADJ [ADJ n] A **high-performance** car or other product goes very fast or does a lot. ❑ *...the thrill of taking an expensive high-performance car to its limits.*

high-pitched ADJ A **high-pitched** sound is shrill and high in pitch. ❑ *A woman squealed in a high-pitched voice.*

high point (high points) N-COUNT The **high point** of an event or period of time is the most exciting or enjoyable part of it. ❑ *The high point of this trip was a day at the beach.*

high-powered ◧ ADJ A **high-powered** machine or piece of equipment is very powerful and efficient. ❑ *...high-powered lasers.* ◨ ADJ Someone who is **high-powered** or has a **high-powered** job has a very important and responsible job which requires a lot of ability. ❑ *...a high-powered lawyer.*

high priest (high priests) N-COUNT [usu N of n] If you call a man the **high priest** of a particular thing, you are saying in a slightly mocking way that he is considered by people to be expert in that thing. ❑ *...the high priest of cheap periodical fiction.*

high priest|ess (high priestesses) N-COUNT [usu N of n] If you call a woman the **high priestess** of a particular thing, you are saying that she is considered by people to be expert in that thing. ❑ *...the American high priestess of wit.*

high-profile ADJ A **high-profile** person or a **high-profile** event attracts a lot of attention or publicity. ❑ *...a high-profile criminal defense lawyer*

high-ranking ADJ [ADJ n] A **high-ranking** person has an important position in a particular organization. ❑ *...a high-ranking officer in the medical corps.*

high-rise (high-rises) ADJ [ADJ n] **High-rise** buildings are modern buildings which are very tall and have many levels or floors. ❑ *...high-rise office buildings.* • N-COUNT A **high-rise** is a high-rise building. ❑ *That big high-rise above us is where Brian lives.*

high road (high roads) ◧ N-SING [usu the N] If you say that someone is taking the **high road** in a situation, you mean that they are taking the most positive and careful course of action. [mainly AM] ❑ *U.S. diplomats say the president is likely to take the high road in his statements about trade.* ◨ N-COUNT A **high road** is a main road. [BRIT]

in AM, use **highway**

high roller (high rollers) also **high-roller** N-COUNT High rollers are people who are very rich and who spend money in an extravagant or risky way, especially by gambling. [JOURNALISM]

high school ♦♦♦ (high schools) N-VAR; N-IN-NAMES A **high school** is a school for children usually aged between fourteen and eighteen. ❑ ...an 18-year-old inner-city kid who dropped out of high school.

high seas N-PLURAL [the N] The **high seas** is used to refer to the ocean. [LITERARY] ❑ ...battles on the high seas.

high so|ci|ety N-UNCOUNT You can use **high society** to refer to people who come from rich and important families.

high-sounding ADJ [usu ADJ n] You can use **high-sounding** to describe language and ideas which seem very grand and important, especially when you think they are not really important. [DISAPPROVAL] ❑ ...high-sounding decrees designed to impress foreigners and attract foreign capital.

high-speed ◼ ADJ [ADJ n] A **high-speed** vehicle or piece of equipment moves or operates very quickly. ❑ Japan's high-speed trains travel a long way in a short time. ◼ ADJ [ADJ n] A **high-speed** accident happens when the vehicles involved are traveling very fast. ❑ They were killed in a high-speed crash in a tunnel in Paris. ◼ ADJ [ADJ n] A **high-speed** internet connection allows users to access websites very quickly. ❑ Most of our customers have now upgraded to a high-speed broadband connection.

high-spirited ADJ Someone who is **high-spirited** is very lively and easily excited.

high spot (high spots) N-COUNT [oft N of n] The **high spot** of an event or activity is the most exciting or enjoyable part of it. ❑ Rough weather would have denied us a landing on the island, for me the high spot of the entire cruise.

high-stakes ADJ [ADJ n] A **high-stakes** game or contest is one in which the people involved can gain or lose a great deal. ❑ ...a high-stakes poker game. ❑ ...the high-stakes political battle over the New Jersey Senate campaign.

high street (high streets) N-COUNT; N-IN-NAMES The **high street** of a town is the main street where most of the stores and banks are. [mainly BRIT]

in AM, use **main street**

high-strung also **highly-strung** ADJ If someone is **high-strung**, they are very nervous and easily upset. ❑ The strain was pushing the high-strung foreign minister over the edge.

high sum|mer N-UNCOUNT **High summer** is the middle of summer.

high-tech /ˌhaɪ tɛk/ also **high tech, hi tech** ADJ **High-tech** activities or equipment involve or result from the use of high technology. ❑ ...such high-tech industries as computers or telecommunications.

high tech|nol|ogy N-UNCOUNT **High technology** is the practical use of advanced scientific research and knowledge, especially in relation to electronics and computers, and the development of new advanced machines and equipment. ❑ ...a limited war using high technology.

high-tension ADJ [ADJ n] A **high-tension** electricity cable is one which is able to carry a very powerful current.

high tide N-UNCOUNT At the coast, **high tide** is the time when the sea is at its highest level because the tide is in.

high trea|son N-UNCOUNT **High treason** is a very serious crime which involves putting your country or its head of state in danger.

high-up (high-ups) → see higher-up

high wa|ter N-UNCOUNT **High water** is the time at which the water in a river or sea is at its highest level as a result of the tide. ❑ Fishing is possible for a couple of hours either side of high water.

high-water mark also **high water mark** ◼ N-SING [the N] The **high-water mark** is the level reached in a particular place by the ocean at high tide or by a river in flood. ◼ N-SING [with supp, oft N of/for n] The **high-water mark** of a process is its highest or most successful stage of achievement. ❑ This was almost certainly the high-water mark of her career.

high|way ♦♦◊ /ˈhaɪweɪ/ (highways) N-COUNT A **highway** is a main road, especially one that connects towns or cities. [mainly AM] ❑ I crossed the highway, dodging the traffic.

high|way|man /ˈhaɪweɪmən/ (highwaymen) N-COUNT In former times, **highwaymen** were people who stopped travelers and robbed them.

high|way pa|trol (highway patrols) N-COUNT [usu sing; oft N n] In the United States, the **highway patrol** is the part of the police force within a particular state that is responsible for making sure that the roads are safe and for dealing with drivers who break the law. ❑ The Florida Highway Patrol shut down the 20-mile stretch of the interstate. ❑ ...highway patrol officers.

high wire (high wires) also **high-wire** ◼ N-COUNT A **high wire** is a length of rope or wire stretched tight high above the ground and used for balancing acts. ◼ N-SING [oft N n] Journalists talk about a person being on a **high wire** or performing a **high-wire** act when he or she is dealing with a situation in which it would be easy to do the wrong thing. ❑ The incident has swiftly turned into a high-wire act in which he must reassure neighboring countries without destroying his own conservative base.

hi|jab /hɪˈdʒæb, hɪˈdʒɑːb/ (hijabs) ◼ N-COUNT A **hijab** is a scarf that some Muslim women wear, which covers their hair and neck. ◼ N-UNCOUNT **Hijab** is traditional Muslim dress for women, and the rules concerning this. ❑ We can choose to wear hijab, we can practice our faith freely.

hi|jabi /hɪˈdʒæbi, hɪˈdʒɑːbi/ (hijabis) N-COUNT A **hijabi** is a Muslim woman who wears a hijab, a scarf that covers her face and neck. ❑ She was the first hijabi to ever win a gold medal.

hi|jack /ˈhaɪdʒæk/ (hijacks, hijacking, hijacked) ◼ V-T If someone **hijacks** a plane or other vehicle, they illegally take control of it by force while it is traveling from one place to another. ❑ Two men tried to hijack a plane on a flight from Riga to Murmansk. • N-COUNT **Hijack** is also a noun. ❑ Every minute during the hijack seemed like a week. • **hi|jack|ing** (hijackings) N-COUNT ❑ Car hijackings are running at a rate of nearly 50 a day. ◼ V-T If you say that someone **has hijacked** something, you disapprove of the way in which they have taken control of it when they had no right to do so. [DISAPPROVAL] ❑ A peaceful demonstration had been hijacked by anarchists intent on causing trouble.

hi|jack|er /ˈhaɪdʒækər/ (hijackers) N-COUNT A **hijacker** is a person who hijacks a plane or other vehicle.

hike /haɪk/ (hikes, hiking, hiked) ◼ N-COUNT A **hike** is a long walk in the country, especially one that you go on for pleasure. ❑ The site is reached by a 30-minute hike through dense forest. ◼ V-I If you **hike**, you go for a long walk in the country. ❑ You could hike through the Fish River Canyon – it's entirely up to you. • **hik|ing** N-UNCOUNT ❑ ...some harder, more strenuous hiking on cliff pathways. ◼ N-COUNT A **hike** is a sudden or large increase in prices, rates, taxes, or quantities. [INFORMAL] ❑ ...a sudden 1.75 percent hike in interest rates. ◼ V-T To **hike** prices, rates, taxes, or quantities means to increase them suddenly or by a large amount. [INFORMAL] ❑ It has now been forced to hike its rates by 5.25 percent. • PHRASAL VERB **Hike up** means the same as **hike**. ❑ The insurers have started hiking up premiums by huge amounts. ◼ → See feature box at **leisure**

hik|er /ˈhaɪkər/ (hikers) N-COUNT A **hiker** is a person who is going for a long walk in the countryside for pleasure.

hi|lari|ous /hɪˈlɛəriəs/ ◼ ADJ If something is **hilarious**, it is extremely funny and makes you laugh a lot. ❑ We thought it was hilarious when we first heard about it. • **hi|lari|ous|ly** ADV ❑ She found it hilariously funny. ◼ → See feature box at **humor**

hi|lar|ity /hɪˈlærɪti, -ˈlɛər-/ N-UNCOUNT **Hilarity** is great amusement and laughter.

hill ♦♦◊ /hɪl/ (hills) ◼ N-COUNT; N-IN-NAMES A **hill** is an area of land that is higher than the land that surrounds it. ❑ ...the shady street that led up the hill to the office building. ◼ PHRASE If you say that someone is **over the hill**, you are saying rudely that they are old and no longer fit, attractive, or capable of doing useful work. [INFORMAL, DISAPPROVAL] ❑ He doesn't take kindly to suggestions that he is over the hill.

hill|bil|ly /ˈhɪlbɪli/ (hillbillies) N-COUNT If you refer to someone as a **hillbilly**, you are saying in a fairly rude way that you think they are uneducated and unsophisticated because they come from the countryside. [AM, INFORMAL, DISAPPROVAL]

hill|ock /ˈhɪlək/ (hillocks) N-COUNT A **hillock** is a small hill.

hill|side /ˈhɪlsaɪd/ (hillsides) N-COUNT A **hillside** is the sloping side of a hill.

hill|top /hɪltɒp/ (hilltops) N-COUNT [oft N n] A **hilltop** is the top of a hill.

hilly /hɪli/ (hillier, hilliest) ADJ A **hilly** area has many hills. ❑ *The areas where the fighting is taking place are hilly and densely wooded.*

hilt /hɪlt/ (hilts) **1** N-COUNT The **hilt** of a sword, dagger, or knife is its handle. **2** PHRASE [usu PHR after v] **To the hilt** and **up to the hilt** mean to the maximum extent possible or as fully as possible. [INFORMAL, EMPHASIS] ❑ *The men who wield the power are certainly backing him to the hilt.*

him ✦✧✧ /hɪm/

Him is a third person singular pronoun. **Him** is used as the object of a verb or a preposition.

1 PRON-SING [V PRON, prep PRON] You use **him** to refer to a man, boy, or male animal. ❑ *John's aunt died suddenly and left him a surprisingly large sum.* ❑ *Is Sam there? Let me talk to him.* **2** PRON-SING [V PRON, prep PRON] In written English, **him** is sometimes used to refer to a person without saying whether that person is a man or a woman. Many people prefer to use 'him or her' or 'them' as an alternative to 'him.' ❑ *If the child encounters "hear," we should show him that this is the base word in "hearing" and "hears."*

him|self ✦✦✦ /hɪmsɛlf/

Himself is a third person singular reflexive pronoun. **Himself** is used when the object of a verb or preposition refers to the same person as the subject of the verb, except in meaning **3**.

1 PRON-REFL [V PRON, prep PRON] You use **himself** to refer to a man, boy, or male animal. ❑ *He poured himself a whiskey and sat down in the chair.* ❑ *William went away muttering to himself.* **2** PRON-REFL [V PRON, prep PRON] In written English, **himself** is sometimes used to refer to a person without saying whether that person is a man or a woman. Many people prefer to use 'himself or herself' or 'themselves' as an alternative to 'himself.' ❑ *There is nothing more dangerous than someone who thinks of himself as a victim.* **3** PRON-REFL-EMPH You use **himself** to emphasize the person or thing that you are referring to. **Himself** is sometimes used instead of 'him' as the object of a verb or preposition. [EMPHASIS] ❑ *The president himself is on a visit to Beijing.*

hind /haɪnd/ ADJ [ADJ n] An animal's **hind** legs are at the back of its body. ❑ *Suddenly the cow kicked up its hind legs.*

hin|der /hɪndər/ (hinders, hindering, hindered) **1** V-T If something **hinders** you, it makes it more difficult for you to do something or make progress. ❑ *Further investigation was hindered by the loss of all documentation on the case.* **2** V-T If something **hinders** your movement, it makes it difficult for you to move forward or move around. ❑ *A thigh injury increasingly hindered her mobility.*

Hin|di /hɪndi/ N-UNCOUNT **Hindi** is a language that is spoken by people in northern India. It is also one of the official languages of India.

hind|quarters /haɪndkwɔrtərz/ also **hind quarters** N-PLURAL [oft with poss] The **hindquarters** of a four-legged animal are its back part, including its two back legs.

hin|drance /hɪndrəns/ (hindrances) N-COUNT A **hindrance** is a person or thing that makes it more difficult for you to do something. ❑ *The higher rates have been a hindrance to economic recovery.*

hind|sight /haɪndsaɪt/ N-UNCOUNT **Hindsight** is the ability to understand and realize something about an event after it has happened, although you did not understand or realize it at the time. ❑ *With hindsight, we'd all do things differently.*

Hin|du /hɪndu/ (Hindus) **1** N-COUNT A **Hindu** is a person who believes in Hinduism and follows its teachings. **2** ADJ **Hindu** is used to describe things that belong or relate to Hinduism. ❑ *...a Hindu temple.*

Hin|du|ism /hɪnduɪzəm/ N-UNCOUNT **Hinduism** is an Indian religion. It has many gods and teaches that people have another life on earth after they die.

hinge /hɪndʒ/ (hinges, hinging, hinged) N-COUNT A **hinge** is a piece of metal, wood, or plastic that is used to join a door to its frame or to join two things together so that one of them can swing freely. ❑ *The top swung open on well-oiled hinges.* ▶ **hinge on** PHRASAL VERB Something that **hinges on** one thing or event depends entirely on it. ❑ *The plan hinges on a deal being struck with a new company.*

hinged /hɪndʒd/ ADJ Something that is **hinged** is joined to another thing, or joined together, by means of a hinge or hinges. ❑ *The mirror was hinged to a surrounding frame.*

hint ✦✧✧ /hɪnt/ (hints, hinting, hinted) **1** N-COUNT A **hint** is a suggestion about something that is made in an indirect way. ❑ *I'd dropped a hint about having an exhibition of his work up here.* • PHRASE If you **take a hint**, you understand something that is suggested to you indirectly. ❑ *"I think I hear the telephone ringing."—"Okay, I can take a hint."* **2** V-I If you **hint** at something, you suggest it in an indirect way. ❑ *She hinted at the possibility of a treat of some sort.* **3** N-COUNT A **hint** is a helpful piece of advice, usually about how to do something. ❑ *Here are some helpful hints to make your journey easier.* **4** N-SING A **hint** of something is a very small amount of it. ❑ *She added only a hint of vermouth to the gin.*

hinter|land /hɪntərlænd/ (hinterlands) **1** N-COUNT [usu pl] **Hinterlands** are remote areas of land far away from cities or towns. ❑ *There's lots of cheap land in the hinterlands.* **2** N-COUNT [usu sing, usu with supp] The **hinterland** of a stretch of coast or a large river is the area of land behind it or around it.

hip ✦✧✧ /hɪp/ (hips) **1** N-COUNT Your **hips** are the two areas at the sides of your body between the tops of your legs and your waist. ❑ *Tracey put her hands on her hips and sighed.* **2** N-COUNT You refer to the bones between the tops of your legs and your waist as your **hips**. ❑ *Eventually, surgeons replaced both hips and both shoulders.* **3** ADJ If you say that someone is **hip**, you mean that they are very modern and follow all the latest fashions, for example in clothes and ideas. [INFORMAL] ❑ *...a hip young character with tight-cropped blond hair and stylish glasses.* **4** EXCLAM If a large group of people want to show their appreciation or approval of someone, one of them says '**Hip hip**' and they all shout '**hooray.**' **5** PHRASE If you say that someone **shoots from the hip**, you mean that they react to situations or give their opinion very quickly, without stopping to think. ❑ *Judges don't have to shoot from the hip. They have the leisure to think, to decide.*

hip flask (hip flasks) N-COUNT A **hip flask** is a small metal container in which brandy, whiskey, or other spirits can be carried.

hip-hop N-UNCOUNT [oft N n] **Hip-hop** is a form of popular culture which started among young Black people in the United States in the 1980s. It includes rap music and graffiti art.

hip|hug|gers /hɪphʌgərz/ N-PLURAL **Hiphuggers** are pants which are designed so that the highest part of them is around your hips, rather than around your waist. [AM] ❑ *He wore white hiphuggers.*

hip|pie /hɪpi/ (hippies) also **hippy** N-COUNT **Hippies** were young people in the 1960s and 1970s who rejected conventional ways of living, dressing, and behaving, and tried to live a life based on peace and love. Hippies often had long hair and many took drugs.

hip|po /hɪpoʊ/ (hippos) N-COUNT A **hippo** is a hippopotamus. [INFORMAL]

Hip|po|crat|ic oath /hɪpəkrætɪk oʊθ/ N-SING [the N] The **Hippocratic oath** is a formal promise made by new doctors that they will follow the standards set by their profession and try to preserve life.

hippo|pota|mus /hɪpəpɒtəməs/ (hippopotamuses) **1** N-COUNT A **hippopotamus** is a very large African animal with short legs and thick, hairless skin. Hippopotamuses live in and near rivers. **2** → See feature box at **animal**

━━━━ **WORD HISTORY** ━━━━

hippopotamus
A **hippopotamus** is literally a 'water horse.' The word comes from Greek *hippos*, meaning 'horse,' and *potamos*, meaning 'river.'

hip|py /hɪpi/ → see hippie

hip|ster /hɪpstər/ (hipsters) **1** N-COUNT If you refer to someone as a **hipster**, you mean that they are very fashionable, often in a way that you think is silly. [HUMOROUS] **2** N-PLURAL [mainly BRIT] → see **hiphuggers** **3** → See feature box at **town**

hire ♦♢♢ /haɪər/ (hires, hiring, hired) **1** V-T/V-I If you **hire** someone, you employ them or pay them to do a particular job for you. ❑ *Sixteen of the contestants have hired lawyers and are suing the organizers.* ❑ *He will be in charge of all hiring and firing at the company.* **2** V-T If you **hire** something, you pay money to the owner so that you can use it for a period of time. [mainly BRIT]

> in AM, usually use **rent**

3 N-UNCOUNT You use **hire** to refer to the activity or business of hiring something. [mainly BRIT]

> in AM, usually use **rental**

4 PHRASE If something is **for hire**, it is available for you to hire. [mainly BRIT]

> in AM, usually use **for rent**

▶ **hire out** PHRASAL VERB If you **hire out** a person's services, you allow them to be used in return for payment. ❑ *...employment agencies which hire out personnel to foreign companies.*

> **SYNONYMS**
>
> **hire**
> VERB
> **1**
> **employ:** *The company employs 18 staff.*
> **take on:** *They decided to take Jack on as an office assistant.*
> **engage:** *He had been able to engage some staff.*
> **appoint:** *It made sense to appoint a banker to this job.*
> **2**
> **rent:** *He left his hotel in a rented car.*
> **charter:** *She chartered a jet to fly her home from California to Switzerland.*

> **COLLOCATIONS**
>
> **hire**
> VERB **1**
> **hire** + noun: consultant, staff, worker; detective, investigator, lawyer

hire|ling /haɪərlɪŋ/ (hirelings) N-COUNT If you refer to someone as a **hireling**, you disapprove of them because they do not care who they work for and they are willing to do illegal or immoral things as long as they are paid. [DISAPPROVAL]

hire pur|chase N-UNCOUNT [oft N n] **Hire purchase** is a way of buying goods gradually. You make regular payments until you have paid the full price and the goods belong to you. The abbreviation **HP** is often used. [BRIT]

> in AM, use **installment plan**

hir|sute /hɜːrsuːt/ ADJ Someone who is **hirsute** is hairy. [FORMAL]

his ♦♦♦

> The determiner is pronounced /hɪz/. The pronoun is pronounced /hɪz/.

> **His** is a third person singular possessive determiner. **His** is also a possessive pronoun.

DET You use **his** to indicate that something belongs or relates to a man, boy, or male animal. ❑ *Brian splashed water on his face, then brushed his teeth.* ❑ *He spent a large part of his career in Hollywood.* • PRON-POSS **His** is also a possessive pronoun. ❑ *Staff say the decision was his.*

His|pan|ic /hɪspænɪk/ (Hispanics) ADJ A **Hispanic** person is a citizen of the United States of America who originally came from Latin America, or whose family originally came from Latin America. ❑ *...a group of Hispanic doctors in Washington.* • N-COUNT A **Hispanic** is someone who is Hispanic. ❑ *About 80 percent of Hispanics here are U.S. citizens.*

hiss /hɪs/ (hisses, hissing, hissed) **1** V-I To **hiss** means to make a sound like a long 's.' ❑ *The tires of Lenny's bike hissed over the wet pavement as he slowed down.* ❑ *My cat hissed when I stepped on its tail.* • N-COUNT **Hiss** is also a noun. ❑ *...the hiss of water running into the burned pan.* • **hiss|ing** N-UNCOUNT ❑ *...a silence broken only by a steady hissing from above my head.* **2** V-I If people **hiss** at

someone such as a performer or a person making a speech, they express their disapproval or dislike of that person by making long loud 's' sounds. ❑ *One had to listen hard to catch the words of the president's speech as the delegates booed and hissed.* • N-COUNT **Hiss** is also a noun. ❑ *She was greeted with boos and hisses.*

his|to|rian /hɪstɔːriən/ (historians) N-COUNT A **historian** is a person who specializes in the study of history, and who writes books and articles about it.

his|tor|ic ♦♢♢ /hɪstɒrɪk/ ADJ Something that is **historic** is important in history, or likely to be considered important at some time in the future. ❑ *...the historic changes in Eastern Europe.*

his|tori|cal ♦♢♢ /hɪstɒrɪkəl/ **1** ADJ [ADJ n] **Historical** people, situations, or things existed in the past and are considered to be a part of history. ❑ *...an important historical figure.* ❑ *...the historical impact of Western capitalism on the world.* • **his|tori|cal|ly** ADV ❑ *Historically, royal marriages have been cold, calculating affairs.* **2** ADJ [ADJ n] **Historical** books, movies, or pictures describe or represent people, situations, or things that existed in the past. ❑ *He is writing a historical novel about nineteenth-century France.* **3** ADJ [ADJ n] **Historical** information, research, and discussion is related to the study of history. ❑ *...historical records.* **4** → See feature box at **research**

> **SYNONYMS**
>
> **historical**
> ADJ **1**
> **past:** *...a return to the turbulence of past centuries.*
> **former:** *...a former monastery.*
> **bygone:** *The book recalls other memories of a bygone age.*

> **VOCABULARY IN CONTEXT**
>
>
>
> **History**
>
> During the **reigns** of the first three kings of the Plantagenet **dynasty**, Henry II, Richard I, and John, the power and wealth of the **monarchy** increased considerably, and so did taxes. When Richard I was **captured** and held for **ransom** by Duke Leopold of Austria, the country had to pay the modern-day equivalent of £6.5 trillion. To add to the financial pressures, John was an incredibly unpopular **ruler**, considered to be untrustworthy, mean, and cruel. In 1212, an attempt to **assassinate** him failed, but within three years, the **feudal barons** had reached the point where they were ready to go to war. The only way to avert the **crisis** was for John to sign the **treaty** that became known as the Magna Carta. This agreement guaranteed, for the first time, the **rights** of individuals in the face of the wishes of the King.

his|to|ry ♦♦♦ /hɪstəri, -tri/ (histories) **1** N-UNCOUNT You can refer to the events of the past as **history**. You can also refer to the past events which concern a particular topic or place as its **history**. ❑ *The Catholic Church has played a prominent role throughout Polish history.* ❑ *...the most evil mass killer in history.* • PHRASE Someone who **makes history** does something that is considered to be important and significant in the development of the world or of a particular society. ❑ *Willy Brandt made history* by visiting East Germany in 1970. • PHRASE If someone or something **goes down in history**, people in the future remember them because of particular actions that they have done or because of particular events that have happened. ❏ *Bradley will go down in history as Los Angeles' longest serving mayor.* **2** N-UNCOUNT **History** is a subject studied in schools, colleges, and universities that deals with events that have happened in the past. ❏ *...a lecturer in history at Birmingham University.* **3** N-COUNT A **history** is an account of events that have happened in the past. ❏ *...his magnificent history of broadcasting in Canada.* **4** N-COUNT If a person or a place has a **history** of something, it has been very common or has happened frequently in their past. ❏ *He had a history of drinking problems.* **5** N-COUNT Someone's **history** is the set of facts that are known about their past. ❏ *He couldn't get a new job because of his medical history.* **6** PHRASE If you are telling someone about an event and say **the rest is history**, you mean that you do not need to tell them what happened next because everyone knows about it already. ❏ *We met in college, the rest is history.*

COLLOCATIONS

history
NOUN
4
adjective + **history**: checkered, fascinating, long
5
noun + **history**: family
adjective + **history**: medical, personal
verb + **history**: trace

his|tri|on|ic /hɪstriɒnɪk/ ADJ [usu ADJ n] If you refer to someone's behavior as **histrionic**, you are critical of it because it is very dramatic, exaggerated, and insincere. [DISAPPROVAL] ❏ *Dorothea let out a histrionic groan.*

his|tri|on|ics /hɪstriɒnɪks/ N-PLURAL If you disapprove of someone's dramatic and exaggerated behavior, you can describe it as **histrionics**. [DISAPPROVAL] ❏ *When I explained everything to my mom and dad, there were no histrionics.*

hit ♦♦♦ /hɪt/ (hits, hitting)

The form **hit** is used in the present tense and is the past and present participle.

→ Please look at meanings **11** - **14** to see if the expression you are looking for is shown under another headword.

1 V-T If you **hit** someone or something, you deliberately touch them with a lot of force, with your hand or an object held in your hand. ❏ *Find the exact grip that allows you to hit the ball hard.* **2** V-T When one thing **hits** another, it touches it with a lot of force. ❏ *The car had apparently hit a traffic sign before skidding out of control.* **3** V-T If a bomb or missile **hits** its target, it reaches it. ❏ *...multiple-warhead missiles that could hit many targets at a time.* • N-COUNT **Hit** is also a noun. ❏ *First a house took a direct hit and then the rocket exploded.* **4** V-T If something **hits** a person, place, or thing, it affects them very badly. [JOURNALISM] ❏ *The plan to charge motorists to use the freeway is going to hit me hard.* ❏ *About two hundred people died in the earthquake which hit the north of the country.* **5** V-T When a feeling or an idea **hits** you, it suddenly affects you or comes into your mind. ❏ *It hit me that I had a choice.* **6** V-T If you **hit** a particular high or low point on a scale of something such as success or health, you reach it. [JOURNALISM] ❏ *He admits to having hit the lowest point in his life.* **7** N-COUNT If a song, movie, or play is a **hit**, it is very popular and successful. ❏ *The song became a massive hit in 1945.* **8** N-COUNT A **hit** is a single visit to a website. [COMPUTING] ❏ *Our small company has had 78,000 hits on its internet pages.* **9** N-COUNT If someone who is searching for information on the internet gets a **hit**, they find a website where there is that information. **10** PHRASE If two people **hit it off**, they like each other and become friendly as soon as they meet. [INFORMAL] ❏ *Dad and Walter hit it off straight away.* **11** to **hit the headlines** → see **headline 12** to **hit home** → see **home** ① **13** to **hit the nail on the head** → see **nail 14** to **hit the roof** → see **roof 15** → See feature box at **accident**

▶ **hit on** also **hit upon 1** PHRASAL VERB If you **hit on** an idea or a solution to a problem, or **hit upon** it, you think of it. ❏ *After running through the numbers in every possible combination, we finally hit on a solution.* **2** PHRASAL VERB If someone **hits on** you, they speak or behave in a way that shows they want to have a sexual relationship with you. [INFORMAL] ❏ *She was hitting on me and I was surprised and flattered.*

▶ **hit up** PHRASAL VERB If you **hit** somebody **up** for something, especially for money, you ask them for it. [AM, INFORMAL] ❏ *They hit up Hector for the last $250.*

SYNONYMS

hit
VERB
1
strike: *She took two quick steps forward and struck him across the mouth.*
punch: *He punched the wall angrily, then spun around to face her.*
slap: *He would push or slap her once in a while.*
thump: *He thumped my shoulder affectionately, nearly knocking me over.*
whack: *You really have to whack the ball.*
2
collide: *Racing up the stairs, he almost collided with Daisy.*
bump: *He bumped his head on the low beams of the house.*
knock: *Isabel rose so abruptly that she knocked over her chair.*
crash: *The door swung inwards to crash against a chest of drawers behind it.*

hit-and-miss also **hit and miss** ADJ If something is **hit-and-miss** or **hit-or-miss**, it is sometimes successful and sometimes not. ❏ *Farming can be very much a hit-and-miss affair.*

hit-and-run 1 ADJ [ADJ n] A **hit-and-run** accident is an accident in which the driver of a vehicle hits someone and then drives away without stopping. ❏ *...the victim of a hit-and-run accident.* **2** ADJ [ADJ n] A **hit-and-run** attack on an enemy position relies on surprise and speed for its success. ❏ *The rebels appear to be making hit-and-run guerrilla style attacks on military targets.*

hitch /hɪtʃ/ (hitches, hitching, hitched) **1** N-COUNT A **hitch** is a slight problem or difficulty which causes a short delay. ❏ *After some technical hitches the show finally got under way.* **2** V-T/V-I If you **hitch**, **hitch** a lift, or **hitch** a ride, you hitchhike. [INFORMAL] ❏ *There was no garage in sight, so I hitched a lift into town.* **3** V-T If you **hitch** something to something else, you hook it or fasten it there. ❏ *Last night we hitched the horse to the cart and moved here.*

hitch|hike /hɪtʃhaɪk/ (hitchhikes, hitchhiking, hitchhiked) also **hitch-hike** V-I If you **hitchhike**, you travel by getting rides from passing vehicles without paying. ❏ *Neff hitchhiked to New York during his Christmas vacation.* • **hitch|hik|er** (hitchhikers) N-COUNT ❏ *On my way to Vancouver one Friday night I picked up a hitchhiker.*

hi tech → see **high-tech**

hith|er /hɪðər/ **1** ADV [ADV after v] **Hither** means to the place where you are. [OLD-FASHIONED] ❏ *He has sent hither swarms of officers to harass our people.* **2** PHRASE [PHR after v] **Hither and thither** means in many different directions or places, and in a disorganized way. The expression **hither and yon** is sometimes also used. ❏ *Refugees run hither and thither in search of safety.* ❏ *...the awful amount of time I spend moving things hither and yon every year!*

hith|er|to /hɪðərtuː/ ADV You use **hitherto** to indicate that something was true up until the time you are talking about, although it may no longer be the case. [FORMAL] ❏ *The ruling party is likely to be opened up to let in people hitherto excluded.*

hit list (hit lists) **1** N-COUNT If someone has a **hit list** of people or things, they are intending to take action concerning those people or things. ❏ *Some banks also have a hit list of people whom they threaten to sue for damages.* **2** N-COUNT A **hit list** is a list that someone makes of people they intend to have killed. ❏ *...a group of killers instructed by the deputy minister to attack people on his hit list.*

hit|man /hɪtmæn/ (hitmen) also **hit man** N-COUNT A **hitman** is a man who is hired by someone in order to kill another person.

hit-or-miss → see **hit-and-miss**

hit pa|rade N-SING [the N] The **hit parade** is the list of CDs which have sold the most copies over the previous week or month. [OLD-FASHIONED]

hit|ter /hɪtər/ (hitters) **1** N-COUNT [adj N] In sports, you can use **hitter** to say how good someone is at hitting the ball. ❑ *The Georgian, aged 19, is not one of the game's big hitters.* **2** N-COUNT [adj N] If you refer to someone such as a politician or a businessperson as a heavy **hitter** or a big **hitter**, you mean that they are powerful and influential. ❑ *He has certainly got some heavy hitters on board.*

HIV ♦⬦⬦ /eɪtʃ aɪ vi/ **1** N-UNCOUNT HIV is a virus which reduces people's resistance to illness and can cause AIDS. HIV is an abbreviation for 'human immunodeficiency virus.' **2** PHRASE If someone is **HIV positive**, they are infected with the HIV virus, and may develop AIDS. If someone is **HIV negative**, they are not infected with the virus.

hive /haɪv/ (hives) **1** N-COUNT A **hive** is a structure in which bees are kept, which is designed so that the beekeeper can collect the honey that they produce. **2** N-COUNT If you describe a place as a **hive** of activity, you approve of the fact that there is a lot of activity there or that people are busy working there. [APPROVAL] ❑ *In the morning the house was a hive of activity.*

hiya /haɪyə/ CONVENTION You can say '**hiya**' when you are greeting someone. [INFORMAL, FORMULAE] ❑ *Hiya. How are you?*

h'm also **hm** H'm is used in writing to represent a noise that people make when they are hesitating, for example because they are thinking about something.

HMO /eɪtʃ em oʊ/ (HMOs) N-COUNT An **HMO** is an organization to which you pay a fee and that allows you to use only doctors and hospitals which belong to the organization. HMO is an abbreviation for **health maintenance organization**. [AM] ❑ *How do we go about choosing a good HMO?*

ho /hoʊ/ (hos) N-COUNT A **ho** is a prostitute or a woman who has many sexual partners. [AM, VERY OFFENSIVE]

hoa|gie /hoʊgi/ (hoagies) N-COUNT A **hoagie** is a sandwich made with a long, narrow bread roll.

hoard /hɔrd/ (hoards, hoarding, hoarded) **1** V-T If you **hoard** things such as food or money, you save or store them, often in secret, because they are valuable or important to you. ❑ *They've begun to hoard food and gasoline and save their money.* **2** N-COUNT A **hoard** is a store of things that you have saved and that are valuable or important to you and you do not want other people to have. ❑ *The case involves a hoard of silver and jewels valued at up to $40m.*

hoard|ing /hɔrdɪŋ/ (hoardings) N-COUNT A **hoarding** is a very large board at the side of a road or on the side of a building, which is used for displaying advertisements and posters. [BRIT]

▸ in AM, use **billboard**

hoarse /hɔrs/ (hoarser, hoarsest) ADJ If your voice is **hoarse** or if you are **hoarse**, your voice sounds rough and unclear, for example because your throat is sore. ❑ *"So what do you think?" she said in a hoarse whisper.* ● **hoarse|ly** ADV ❑ *"Thank you," Maria said hoarsely.*

hoary /hɔri/ (hoarier, hoariest) ADJ [usu ADJ n] If you describe a problem or subject as **hoary**, you mean that it is old and familiar. ❑ *...the hoary old myth that increased competition will drive up standards.*

hoax /hoʊks/ (hoaxes) N-COUNT A **hoax** is a trick in which someone tells people a lie, for example that there is a bomb somewhere when there is not, or that a picture is genuine when it is not. ❑ *He denied making the hoax call but was convicted after a short trial.*

hob /hɒb/ (hobs) N-COUNT A **hob** is a surface on top of a stove or set into a work surface, which can be heated in order to cook things on it. [BRIT]

▸ in AM, use **cooktop**

hob|ble /hɒbəl/ (hobbles, hobbling, hobbled) V-I If you **hobble**, you walk in an awkward way with small steps, for example because your foot is injured. ❑ *He got up slowly and hobbled over to the coffee table.*

hob|by /hɒbi/ (hobbies) N-COUNT A **hobby** is an activity that you enjoy doing in your spare time. ❑ *My hobbies are letter writing, music, photography, and tennis.*

hobby|horse /hɒbihɔrs/ (hobbyhorses) also **hobby-horse** N-COUNT You describe a subject or idea as your **hobbyhorse** if you have strong feelings on it and like talking about it whenever you have the opportunity. ❑ *Honesty is a favorite hobbyhorse for Courau.*

hob|by|ist /hɒbiɪst/ (hobbyists) N-COUNT You can refer to person who is very interested in a particular hobby and spends a lot of time on it as a **hobbyist**.

hob|nob /hɒbnɒb/ (hobnobs, hobnobbing, hobnobbed) V-I If someone is spending a lot of time with a group of people, especially rich and powerful people, you can say that he or she **is hobnobbing** with them. [INFORMAL] ❑ *This gave Bill an opportunity to hobnob with the company's president, board chairman, and leading executives.*

hobo /hoʊboʊ/ (hobos or hoboes) N-COUNT A **hobo** is a person who has no home, especially one who travels from place to place and gets money by begging. [AM]

hock /hɒk/ (hocks) **1** V-T If you **hock** something you own, you pawn it. ❑ *He even hocked his wife's wedding ring.* **2** N-COUNT [usu n N] A **hock** is a piece of meat from above the foot of an animal, especially a pig. **3** PHRASE If someone is **in hock**, they are in debt. ❑ *Are consumers too deep in hock? A lot of observers think so.* **4** PHRASE [v-link PHR n] If you are **in hock to** someone, you feel you have to do things for them because they have given you money or support. ❑ *It is almost impossible for the prime minister to stand above the factions. He always seems in hock to one or another.*

hock|ey /hɒki/ **1** N-UNCOUNT **Hockey** is a game played on ice between two teams of 11 players who use long curved sticks to hit a small rubber disk, called a puck, and try to score goals. [mainly AM] ❑ *...a new hockey arena.* **2** N-UNCOUNT **Hockey** is an outdoor game played between two teams of 11 players who use long curved sticks to hit a small ball and try to score goals. [mainly BRIT]

▸ in AM, usually use **field hockey**

3 → See also color supplement

hocus-pocus /hoʊkəs poʊkəs/ N-UNCOUNT If you describe something as **hocus-pocus**, you disapprove of it because you think it is false and intended to trick or deceive people. [DISAPPROVAL]

hod /hɒd/ (hods) N-COUNT A **hod** is a container that is used by a building worker for carrying bricks.

hodge|podge /hɒdʒpɒdʒ/ also **hodge-podge** N-SING A **hodgepodge** is a mixture of all sorts of different things. [mainly AM, INFORMAL] ❑ *...a hodgepodge of maps, small tools, and notebooks.*

hoe /hoʊ/ (hoes, hoeing, hoed) **1** N-COUNT A **hoe** is a gardening tool with a long handle and a small square blade, which you use to remove small weeds and break up the surface of the soil. **2** V-T If you **hoe** a field or crop, you use a hoe on the weeds or soil there. ❑ *I have to feed the chickens and hoe the potatoes.* **3** → See also color supplement

hog /hɒg/ (hogs, hogging, hogged) **1** N-COUNT A **hog** is a pig. ❑ *We picked the corn by hand and we fed it to the hogs and the cows.* **2** V-T If you **hog** something, you take all of it in a greedy or impolite way. [INFORMAL] ❑ *Are you done hogging the bathroom?* **3** PHRASE If you **go whole hog** or **go the whole hog**, you do something bold or extravagant in the most complete way possible. [INFORMAL] ❑ *Well, I thought, I've already lost half my job, I might as well go the whole hog and lose it completely.*

hog-tie /hɒgtaɪ/ (hog-ties, hog-tying, hog-tied) also **hogtie** **1** V-T If someone **hog-ties** an animal or a person, they tie their legs together, or they tie their arms and legs together. [AM] ❑ *The cops come in, hog-tie him, chuck him in the back of an ambulance.* **2** V-T If you **are hog-tied** by something, it restricts you or stops you from doing something. [AM] ❑ *She had been hog-tied by the system but she had never lost her compassion.*

hog|wash /hɒgwɒʃ/ N-UNCOUNT If you describe what someone says as **hogwash**, you think it is nonsense. [INFORMAL, DISAPPROVAL] ❑ *Kevin said it was a "load of hogwash" that he was not interested in football.*

ho ho also **ho ho ho** EXCLAM **Ho ho** is used in writing to represent the sound that people make when they laugh. ❑ *"Ha ha, ho ho," he chortled.*

ho hum also **ho-hum** **1** PHRASE You can use **ho hum** when you want to show that you think something is not

hoi polloi

interesting, remarkable, or surprising in any way. [INFORMAL, FEELINGS] ❑ *My general reaction to this news might be summed up as "ho-hum."* ▨ EXCLAM You can say **ho hum** to show that you accept an unpleasant situation because it is not very serious. [INFORMAL, FEELINGS] ❑ *Ho hum, another nice job down the drain.*

hoi pol|loi /hɔɪ pəlɔɪ/ N-PLURAL If someone refers to the **hoi polloi**, they are referring in a humorous or rather rude way to ordinary people, in contrast to rich, well-educated, or upper-class people. ❑ *Monstrously inflated costs are designed to keep the hoi polloi at bay.*

hoist /hɔɪst/ (hoists, hoisting, hoisted) ◨ V-T If you **hoist** something heavy somewhere, you lift it or pull it up there. ❑ *Hoisting my suitcase on to my shoulder, I turned and headed toward my hotel.* ◨ V-T If something heavy **is hoisted** somewhere, it is lifted there using a machine such as a crane. ❑ *A twenty-foot steel pyramid is to be hoisted into position on top of the tower.* ◨ N-COUNT A **hoist** is a machine for lifting heavy things. ❑ *He uses a hydraulic hoist to unload two empty barrels.* ◨ V-T If you **hoist** a flag or a sail, you pull it up to its correct position by using ropes. ❑ *A group forced their way through police cordons and hoisted their flag on top of the disputed monument.*

ho|kum /hoʊkəm/ N-UNCOUNT If you describe something as **hokum**, you think it is nonsense. [INFORMAL] ❑ *The book is enjoyable hokum.*

HOLD

① PHYSICALLY TOUCHING, SUPPORTING, OR CONTAINING
② HAVING OR DOING
③ CONTROLLING OR REMAINING
④ PHRASES
⑤ PHRASAL VERBS

---

① **hold** ♦♦♦ /hoʊld/ (holds, holding, held) ◨ V-T When you **hold** something, you carry or support it, using your hands or your arms. ❑ *Hold the knife at an angle.* • N-COUNT **Hold** is also a noun. ❑ *He released his hold on the camera.* ◨ N-UNCOUNT **Hold** is used in expressions such as **grab hold of**, **catch hold of**, and **get hold of**, to indicate that you close your hand tightly around something, for example to stop something moving or falling. ❑ *I was woken up by someone grabbing hold of my sleeping bag.* ❑ *A doctor and a nurse caught hold of his arms.* ◨ V-T When you **hold** someone, you put your arms around them, usually because you want to show them how much you like them or because you want to comfort them. ❑ *If only he would hold her close to him.* ◨ V-T If you **hold** someone in a particular position, you use force to keep them in that position and stop them from moving. ❑ *He then held the man in an armlock until police arrived.* ◨ N-COUNT A **hold** is a particular way of keeping someone in a position using your own hands, arms, or legs. ❑ *The man wrestled him to the ground, locked in a hold he couldn't escape.* ◨ V-T When you **hold** a part of your body, you put your hand on or against it, often because it hurts. ❑ *Soon she was crying bitterly about the pain and was holding her throat.* ◨ V-T When you **hold** a part of your body in a particular position, you put it into that position and keep it there. ❑ *Hold your hands in front of your face.* ◨ V-T If one thing **holds** another in a particular position, it keeps it in that position. ❑ *...the wooden wedge which held the heavy door open.* ◨ V-T If one thing is used to **hold** another, it is used to store it. ❑ *Two knife racks hold her favorite knives.* ◨ N-COUNT In a ship or airplane, a **hold** is a place where cargo or luggage is stored. ❑ *A fire had been reported in the cargo hold.* ◨ V-T If a place **holds** something, it keeps it available for reference or for future use. ❑ *The company holds an enormous amount of information on any business project.* ◨ V-T [no cont] If something **holds** a particular amount of something, it can contain that amount. ❑ *...servers capable of holding 50 terabytes of data.* ◨ → See feature box at **work**

SYNONYMS

hold
VERB ① ◨
carry: *He was carrying a briefcase.*
grip: *She gripped the rope.*
grasp: *He grasped both my hands.*
clutch: *She was clutching a photograph.*
clasp: *She clasped the children to her.*

---

② **hold** ♦♦♦ /hoʊld/ (holds, holding, held)

> **Hold** is often used to indicate that someone or something has the particular thing, characteristic, or attitude that is mentioned. Therefore it takes most of its meaning from the word that follows it.

◨ V-T [no cont] **Hold** is used with words and expressions indicating an opinion or belief, to show that someone has a particular opinion or believes that something is true. ❑ *He held firm opinions which usually conflicted with my own.* ❑ *Current thinking holds that obesity is more a medical than a psychological problem.* ◨ V-T [no passive] **Hold** is used with words such as 'fear' or 'mystery' to indicate someone's feelings toward something, as if those feelings were a characteristic of the thing itself. ❑ *Death doesn't hold any fear for me.* ◨ V-T **Hold** is used with nouns such as 'office,' 'power,' and 'responsibility' to indicate that someone has a particular position of power or authority. ❑ *She has never held an elected office.* ◨ V-T **Hold** is used with nouns such as 'permit', 'degree,' or 'ticket' to indicate that someone has a particular document that allows them to do something. ❑ *Applicants should normally hold a good degree.* ❑ *He did not hold a firearms license.* ◨ V-T **Hold** is used with nouns such as 'party,' 'meeting,' 'talks,' 'election,' and 'trial' to indicate that people are organizing a particular activity. ❑ *The country will hold democratic elections within a year.* • **hold|ing** N-UNCOUNT ❑ *They also called for the holding of multi-party general elections.* ◨ V-RECIP **Hold** is used with nouns such as 'conversation,' 'interview,' and 'talks' to indicate that two or more people meet and discuss something. ❑ *The prime minister is holding consultations with his colleagues to finalize the deal.* ❑ *The engineer and his son held frequent meetings concerning technical problems.* ◨ V-T **Hold** is used with nouns such as 'shares' and 'stock' to indicate that someone owns a particular proportion of a business. ❑ *The group said it continues to hold 1,774,687 shares in the company.* ◨ → see also **holding** ◨ V-T **Hold** is used with nouns such as 'attention' or 'interest' to indicate that what you do or say keeps someone interested or listening to you. ❑ *If you want to hold someone's attention, look them directly in the eye but don't stare.* ◨ V-T If you **hold** someone responsible, liable, or accountable for something, you will blame them if anything goes wrong. ❑ *It's impossible to hold any individual responsible.*

③ **hold** ♦♦♦ /hoʊld/ (holds, holding, held) ◨ V-T If someone **holds** you in a place, they keep you there as a prisoner and do not allow you to leave. ❑ *The inside of a van was as good a place as any to hold a kidnap victim.* ❑ *Somebody is holding your wife hostage.* ◨ V-T If people such as an army or a violent crowd **hold** a place, they control it by using force. ❑ *Demonstrators have been holding the square since Sunday.* ◨ N-SING If you have a **hold** over someone, you have power or control over them, for example because you know something about them you can use to threaten them or because you are in a position of authority. ❑ *He had ordered his officers to keep an exceptionally firm hold over their men.* ◨ V-T/V-I [no passive] If you ask someone to **hold**, or to **hold the line**, when you are answering a telephone call, you are asking them to wait for a short time, for example so that you can find the person they want to speak to. ❑ *Could you hold the line and I'll just get my pen?* ◨ V-T If you **hold** telephone calls for someone, you do not allow people who phone to speak to that person, but take messages instead. ❑ *He tells his secretary to hold his calls.* ◨ V-T/V-I If something **holds** at a particular value or level, or **is held** there, it is kept at that value or level. ❑ *OPEC production is holding at around 21.5 million barrels a day.* ◨ V-T If you **hold** a sound or musical note, you continue making it. ❑ *...a voice which hit and held every note with perfect ease and clarity.* ◨ V-T If you **hold** something such as a train or an elevator, you delay it. ❑ *A spokesman defended the decision to hold the train until police arrived.* ◨ V-I If an offer or invitation still **holds**, it is still available for you to accept. ❑ *Does your offer still hold?* ◨ V-I If a good situation **holds**, it continues and does not get worse or fail. ❑ *Our luck couldn't hold forever.* ◨ V-I If an argument or theory **holds**, it is true or valid, even after close examination. ❑ *Today, most people think that argument no longer holds.* • PHRASAL VERB **Hold up** means the same as **hold**. ❑ *Democrats say arguments against the bill won't hold up.* ◨ V-I If part of a structure **holds**, it does not fall or break although there is a lot of force or pressure on it. ❑ *How long would the roof hold?* ◨ V-I If laws or rules **hold**, they exist and remain in force. ❑ *These laws also hold for universities.* **14** V-I If you **hold to** a promise or to high standards of behavior, you keep that promise or continue to behave according to those standards. [FORMAL] ❑ *Will the president be able to hold to this commitment?* **15** V-T If someone or something **holds** you **to** a promise or to high standards of behavior, they make you keep that promise or those standards. ❑ *"I won't make you marry him." — "I'll hold you to that."*

④ **hold** ♦♦♦ /hoʊld/ (holds, holding, held)

→ Please look at meanings **12** – **18** to see if the expression you are looking for is shown under another headword.

1 PHRASE If you **hold forth** on a subject, you speak confidently and for a long time about it, especially to a group of people. ❑ *Barry was holding forth on something.* **2** PHRASE If you **get hold of** an object or information, you obtain it, usually after some difficulty. ❑ *It is hard to get hold of guns in this country.* **3** PHRASE If you **get hold of** someone, you manage to contact them. ❑ *The only electrician we could get hold of was miles away.* **4** CONVENTION If you say '**Hold it**,' you are telling someone to stop what they are doing and to wait. ❑ *Hold it! Don't move!* **5** PHRASE If you put something **on hold**, you decide not to do it, deal with it, or change it now, but to leave it until later. ❑ *He put his retirement on hold to work 16 hours a day, seven days a week to find a solution.* **6** PHRASE If you **hold** your **own**, you are able to resist someone who is attacking or opposing you. ❑ *The Frenchman held his own against the challenger.* **7** PHRASE If you can do something well enough to **hold** your **own**, you do not appear foolish when you are compared with someone who is generally thought to be very good at it. ❑ *She can hold her own against almost any player.* **8** PHRASE If you **hold still**, you do not move. ❑ *Can't you hold still for a second?* **9** PHRASE If something **takes hold**, it gains complete control or influence over a person or thing. ❑ *She felt a strange excitement taking hold of her.* **10** PHRASE If you **hold tight**, you put your hand around or against something in order to prevent yourself from falling over. A bus driver might say '**Hold tight!**' to you if you are standing on a bus when it is about to move. ❑ *He held tight to the rope.* **11** PHRASE If you **hold tight**, you do not immediately start a course of action that you have been planning or thinking about. ❑ *The advice for individual investors is to hold tight.* **12 to hold something at bay** → see **bay 13 to hold something in check** → see **check 14 to hold fast** → see **fast 15 to hold the fort** → see **fort 16 to hold your ground** → see **ground** ③ **17 to hold someone for ransom** → see **ransom 18 to hold sway** → see **sway**

⑤ **hold** ♦♦♦ /hoʊld/ (holds, holding, held)

▶ **hold against** PHRASAL VERB If you **hold** something **against** someone, you let their actions in the past influence your present attitude toward them and cause you to deal severely or unfairly with them. ❑ *That was a mistake, but I don't hold it against you.*

▶ **hold back 1** PHRASAL VERB If you **hold back** or if something **holds** you **back**, you hesitate before you do something because you are not sure whether it is the right thing to do. ❑ *The administration had several reasons for holding back.* **2** PHRASAL VERB To **hold** someone or something **back** means to prevent someone from doing something, or to prevent something from happening. ❑ *Stagnation in home sales is holding back economic recovery.* **3** PHRASAL VERB If you **hold** something **back**, you keep it in reserve to use later. ❑ *Farmers apparently hold back produce in the hope that prices will rise.* **4** PHRASAL VERB If you **hold** something **back**, you do not include it in the information you are giving about something. ❑ *You seem to be holding something back.* **5** PHRASAL VERB If you **hold back** something such as tears or laughter, or if you **hold back**, you make an effort to stop yourself from showing how you feel. ❑ *She kept trying to hold back her tears.* **6** PHRASAL VERB If a teacher **holds** a student **back**, they keep them in the same grade instead of promoting them to a higher grade, because their work is not good enough. ❑ *16 percent of eighth-graders were held back for poor performance.*

▶ **hold down 1** PHRASAL VERB If you **hold down** a job or a place on a team, you manage to keep it. ❑ *He never could hold down a job.* **2** PHRASAL VERB If you **hold** someone **down**, you keep them under control and do not allow them to have much freedom or power or many rights. ❑ *Everyone thinks there is some vast conspiracy wanting to hold down the younger generation.* **3** → See feature box at **work**

▶ **hold off 1** PHRASAL VERB If you **hold off** doing something, you delay doing it or delay making a decision about it. ❑ *The hospital staff held off taking Rosenbaum in for an X-ray.* **2** PHRASAL VERB If you **hold off** a challenge in a race or competition, you do not allow someone to pass you. ❑ *Between 1987 and 1990, Steffi Graf largely held off Navratilova's challenge for the crown.*

▶ **hold on** also **hold onto 1** PHRASAL VERB If you **hold on**, or **hold onto** something, you keep your hand on it or around it, for example to prevent the thing from falling or to support yourself. ❑ *His right arm was extended up beside his head, still holding on to a coffee cup.* ❑ *He was struggling to hold onto a rock on the face of the cliff.* **2** PHRASAL VERB If you **hold on**, you manage to achieve success or avoid failure in spite of great difficulties or opposition. ❑ *The Rams held on to defeat the Nevada Wolf Pack in Reno, 32-28.* **3** PHRASAL VERB If you ask someone to **hold on**, you are asking them to wait for a short time. [SPOKEN] ❑ *The manager asked him to hold on while he investigated.*

▶ **hold out 1** PHRASAL VERB If you **hold out** your hand or something you have in your hand, you move your hand away from your body, for example to shake hands with someone. ❑ *"I'm Nancy Drew," she said, holding out her hand.* **2** PHRASAL VERB If you **hold out** for something, you refuse to accept something which you do not think is good enough or large enough, and you continue to demand more. ❑ *I should have held out for a better deal.* **3** PHRASAL VERB If you say that someone **is holding out** on you, you think that they are refusing to give you information that you want. [INFORMAL] ❑ *He had always believed that kids could sense it when you held out on them.* **4** PHRASAL VERB If you **hold out**, you manage to resist an enemy or opponent in difficult circumstances and refuse to give in. ❑ *One prisoner was still holding out on the roof of the jail.* **5** PHRASAL VERB If you **hold out** hope of something happening, you hope that in the future something will happen as you want it to. ❑ *He still holds out hope that they could be a family again.*

▶ **hold up 1** PHRASAL VERB If you **hold up** your hand or something you have in your hand, you move it upward into a particular position and keep it there. ❑ *She held up her hand stiffly.* **2** PHRASAL VERB If one thing **holds up** another, it is placed under the other thing in order to support it and prevent it from falling. ❑ *Mills have iron pillars all over the place holding up the roof.* **3** PHRASAL VERB To **hold up** a person or process means to make them late or delay them. ❑ *Why were you holding everyone up?* **4** PHRASAL VERB If someone **holds up** a place such as a bank or a store, they point a weapon at someone there to make them give them money or valuable goods. ❑ *When his money was gone he held up a gas station with a toy gun.* **5** PHRASAL VERB If you **hold up** something such as someone's behavior, you make it known to other people, so that they can criticize or praise it. ❑ *He had always been held up as an example to the younger ones.* **6** PHRASAL VERB If something such as a type of business **holds up** in difficult conditions, it stays in a reasonably good state. ❑ *Children's wear is one area that is holding up well in the recession.* **7** PHRASAL VERB If an argument or theory **holds up**, it is true or valid, even after close examination. ❑ *I'm not sure if the argument holds up, but it's stimulating.* **8** → see also **holdup**

hold|all /hoʊldɔl/ (holdalls) also **hold-all** N-COUNT A **holdall** is a strong bag which you use to carry your clothes and other things, for example when you are traveling. [mainly BRIT]

in AM, usually use **carryall**

hold|er ♦⃝⃝ /hoʊldər/ (holders) **1** N-COUNT A **holder** is someone who owns or has something. ❑ *This season the club has had 73,500 season-ticket holders.* **2** N-COUNT A **holder** is a container in which you put an object, usually in order to protect it or to keep it in place. ❑ *...a toothbrush holder.*

hold|ing /hoʊldɪŋ/ (holdings) N-COUNT If you have a **holding** in a company, you own shares in it. [BUSINESS] ❑ *That would increase our holding to 35%.*

hold|ing com|pa|ny (holding companies) N-COUNT A **holding company** is a company that has enough shares in one or more other companies to be able to control the other companies. [BUSINESS] ❑ *...a Montreal-based holding company with interests in telecommunications, gas, and natural resources.*

hold|ing pat|tern (holding patterns) **1** N-COUNT [usu sing; in a N] If an aircraft is put in a **holding pattern**, it is instructed to continue flying while waiting for permission to land. ❑ *As a result, planes were kept in a holding pattern, sometimes three or four miles apart, until they were cleared to land.* **2** N-COUNT [usu sing; in a N] If something or someone is in a **holding pattern**, they remain in the same state or continue to do the same thing while waiting for something to happen. ❑ *This news brings a better tone to the market, which has been in a kind of holding pattern, said one trader.* ❑ *I have lost a total of 19 pounds and have been pretty much in a holding pattern for the past three to four weeks.*

hold|out /hoʊldaʊt/ (**holdouts**) N-COUNT A **holdout** is someone who refuses to agree or act with other people in a particular situation and by doing so stops the situation from progressing or being resolved. [AM] ❑ *France has been the holdout in trying to negotiate an end to the dispute.*

hold|over /hoʊldoʊvər/ (**holdovers**) N-COUNT [oft N from n] A **holdover** from an earlier time is a person or thing which existed or occurred at that time and which still exists or occurs today. [AM] ❑ *Most of the U.S. attorneys are holdovers from Republican days.*

holdup /hoʊldʌp/ (**holdups**) also **hold-up** **1** N-COUNT A **holdup** is a situation in which someone is threatened with a weapon in order to make them hand over money or valuables. ❑ *What could have happened? A hold-up? There'd been no gunshot or scream.* **2** N-COUNT A **holdup** is a delay. ❑ *...bureaucratic holdups and legal wrangles over the contract.* **3** N-COUNT A **holdup** is the stopping or very slow movement of traffic, sometimes caused by an accident which happened earlier. ❑ *They arrived late due to a freeway holdup.*

hole ✦✦◇ /hoʊl/ (**holes**) **1** N-COUNT A **hole** is a hollow space in something solid, with an opening on one side. ❑ *He took a shovel, dug a hole, and buried his once-prized possessions.* **2** N-COUNT A **hole** is an opening in something that goes right through it. ❑ *...kids with holes in the knees of their jeans.* **3** N-COUNT A **hole** is the home or hiding place of a mouse, rabbit, or other small animal. ❑ *...a rabbit hole.* **4** N-COUNT A **hole** in a law, theory, or argument is a fault or weakness that it has. ❑ *There were some holes in that theory, some unanswered questions.* **5** N-COUNT A **hole** is also one of the nine or eighteen sections of a golf course. ❑ *I played nine holes with Gary today.* **6** PHRASE If you say that you are **in a hole**, you mean that you are in a difficult or embarrassing situation. [INFORMAL] ❑ *We were in a hole, but I was proud with the way we came back.* **7** PHRASE If a person or organization is **in the hole**, they owe money to someone else. [AM, INFORMAL] ❑ *Some estimates show next year's budget could be $2.5 billion in the hole.* **8** PHRASE If you get **a hole in one** in golf, you get the golf ball into the hole with a single stroke. ❑ *All they ever dream about is getting a hole in one.* **9** PHRASE If you **pick holes in** an argument or theory, you find weak points in it so that it is no longer valid. [INFORMAL] ❑ *He then goes on to pick holes in the article before reaching his conclusion.*

COLLOCATIONS

hole
NOUN
1
adjective + **hole**: deep, gaping, huge, massive
verb + **hole**: dig, drill; fill
2
adjective + **hole**: tiny
noun + **hole**: bullet
verb + **hole**: burn, cut, punch; plug

holed up ADJ [v-link ADJ] If you are **holed up** somewhere, you are hiding or staying there, usually so that other people cannot find or disturb you. [INFORMAL] ❑ *If he had another well-stocked hideaway like this, he could stay holed up for months.*

hole-in-the-wall **1** N-SING A **hole-in-the-wall** business is a business, especially a restaurant, that operates from very small premises. ❑ *It's a neighborhood hole-in-the-wall joint, so don't expect anything fancy.* **2** N-SING A **hole-in-the-wall** machine is a machine built into the wall of a bank or other building, which allows people to take out money from their bank account by using a special card. [BRIT, INFORMAL]

in AM, use **ATM**

holi|day ✦✦◇ /hɒlɪdeɪ/ (**holidays, holidaying, holidayed**) **1** N-COUNT A **holiday** is a day when people do not go to work or school because of a religious or national celebration. ❑ *New Year's Day is a public holiday.* **2** → see also **bank holiday** **3** N-COUNT A **holiday** is a period of time during which you relax and enjoy yourself away from home. People sometimes refer to their holiday as their **holidays**. [BRIT]

in AM, use **vacation**

4 N-PLURAL The **holidays** are the time when children do not have to go to school. [BRIT]

in AM, use **vacation**

5 N-UNCOUNT If you have a particular number of days' or weeks' **holiday**, you do not have to go to work for that number of days or weeks. [BRIT]

in AM, use **vacation**

6 V-I If you **are holidaying** in a place away from home, you are on holiday there. [BRIT]

in AM, use **vacation**

7 → See feature box at **leisure**

holi|day|maker /hɒlɪdeɪmeɪkər/ (**holidaymakers**) N-COUNT A **holidaymaker** is a person who is away from their home on holiday. [BRIT]

in AM, use **vacationer**

holier-than-thou ADJ If you describe someone as **holier-than-thou**, you disapprove of them because they seem to believe that they are more religious or have better moral qualities than anyone else. [DISAPPROVAL] ❑ *He has always sounded holier-than-thou.*

ho|li|ness /hoʊlɪnɪs/ **1** N-UNCOUNT [usu with supp] **Holiness** is the state or quality of being holy. ❑ *We were immediately struck by this city's holiness.* **2** N-VOC You say **Your Holiness** or **His Holiness** when you address or refer respectfully to the Pope or to leaders of some other religions. [POLITENESS] ❑ *The president received His Holiness at the White House.*

ho|lism /hoʊlɪzəm/ N-UNCOUNT **Holism** is the belief that everything in nature is connected in some way. [FORMAL] ❑ *Nature by itself, he writes, runs on "principles of balance and holism."*

ho|lis|tic /hoʊlɪstɪk/ ADJ **Holistic** means based on the principles of holism. [FORMAL] ❑ *...practitioners of holistic medicine.*

hol|ler /hɒlər/ (**hollers, hollering, hollered**) V-T/V-I If you **holler**, you shout loudly. [mainly AM, INFORMAL] ❑ *The audience whooped and hollered.* ❑ *"Watch out!" he hollered.* • N-COUNT **Holler** is also a noun. ❑ *She spun round as the man, with a holler, burst through the door.* • PHRASAL VERB **Holler out** means the same as **holler**. ❑ *I hollered out the names.*

hol|low /hɒloʊ/ (**hollows, hollowing, hollowed**) **1** ADJ Something that is **hollow** has a space inside it, as opposed to being solid all the way through. ❑ *...a hollow tree.* **2** ADJ A surface that is **hollow** curves inward. ❑ *He looked young, dark and sharp-featured, with hollow cheeks.* **3** N-COUNT A **hollow** is an area that is lower than the surrounding surface. ❑ *Below him the town lay warm in the hollow of the hill.* **4** ADJ If you describe a statement, situation, or person as **hollow**, you mean they have no real value, worth, or effectiveness. ❑ *Any threat to bring in the police is a hollow one.* • **hol|low|ness** N-UNCOUNT ❑ *One month before the deadline we see the hollowness of these promises.* **5** ADJ [ADJ n] If someone gives a **hollow** laugh, they laugh in a way that shows that they do not really find something amusing. ❑ *Murray Pick's hollow laugh had no mirth in it.* **6** ADJ [ADJ n] A **hollow** sound is dull and echoing. ❑ *...the hollow sound of a gunshot.* **7** V-T [usu passive] If something **is hollowed**, its surface is made to curve inward or downward. ❑ *The mule's back was hollowed by the weight of its burden.*

hol|ly /hɒli/ (**hollies**) N-VAR **Holly** is an evergreen tree or shrub which has hard, shiny leaves with sharp points, and red berries in winter.

Hol|ly|wood /hɒliwʊd/ N-PROPER [oft N n] You use **Hollywood** to refer to the movie industry that is based in Hollywood, California. ❑ *...a major Hollywood studio.*

holo|caust /hɒləkɔːst, hoʊlə-/ (**holocausts**) **1** N-VAR A **holocaust** is an event in which there is a lot of destruction and many people are killed, especially one caused by war.

❏ *A nuclear holocaust seemed a very real possibility in the '50s.* **2** N-SING **The Holocaust** is used to refer to the killing by the Nazis of millions of Jews during the Second World War. ❏ *...an Israeli-based fund for survivors of the Holocaust and their families.*

holo|gram /hɒləgræm, hoʊlə-/ (**holograms**) N-COUNT A **hologram** is a three-dimensional photographic image created by laser beams.

hol|ster /hoʊlstər/ (**holsters**) N-COUNT A **holster** is a holder for a small gun, which is worn on a belt around someone's waist or on a strap around their shoulder.

holy ♦◇◇ /hoʊli/ (**holier, holiest**) ADJ If you describe something as **holy**, you mean that it is considered to be special because it is connected with God or a particular religion. ❏ *To them, as to all Poles, this is a holy place.*

Holy Com|mun|ion N-UNCOUNT **Holy Communion** is the most important religious service in the Christian Church, in which people share bread and wine as a symbol of the Last Supper and the death of Christ.

Holy Father N-PROPER [*the* N] In the Catholic Church, **the Holy Father** is the Pope.

Holy Ghost N-PROPER [*the* N] **The Holy Ghost** is the same as the **Holy Spirit**.

Holy Land N-SING [*the* N] People sometimes refer to the part of the Middle East where most of the Bible is set as the **Holy Land**. ❏ *...one of the most sacred sites in the Holy Land.*

holy of holies /hoʊli əv hoʊliz/ N-SING A **holy of holies** is a place that is so sacred that only particular people are allowed to enter; often used in informal English to refer humorously to a place where only a few special people can go. ❏ *...the holy of holies in the Temple.*

holy or|ders also **Holy Orders** N-PLURAL Someone who is in **holy orders** is a member of the Christian clergy. ❏ *He took holy orders in 1935.*

Holy See N-PROPER [*the* N] The **Holy See** is the same as **the Vatican**. ❏ *...the Irish ambassador to the Holy See.*

Holy Spir|it N-PROPER [*the* N] In the Christian religion, **the Holy Spirit** is one of the three aspects of God, together with God the Father and God the Son.

holy war (**holy wars**) N-COUNT A **holy war** is a war that people fight in order to defend or support their religion. ❏ *He called for a holy war against imperialism.*

Holy Week N-UNCOUNT In the Christian religion, **Holy Week** is the week before Easter, when Christians remember the events leading up to the death of Christ.

hom|age /hɒmɪdʒ, ɒm-/ N-UNCOUNT [usu N *to* n] **Homage** is respect shown toward someone or something you admire, or to a person in authority. ❏ *...two marvelous films that pay homage to our literary heritage.*

HOME
① NOUN, ADJECTIVE, AND ADVERB USES
② PHRASAL VERB USES
---

① **home** ♦♦♦ /hoʊm/ (**homes**) **1** N-COUNT [oft poss N, also *at* N] Someone's **home** is the house or apartment where they live. ❏ *Last night they stayed at home and watched TV.* ❏ *The general divided his time between his shabby offices and his home in Hampstead.* **2** N-UNCOUNT You can use **home** to refer in a general way to the house, town, or country where someone lives now or where they were born, often to emphasize that they feel they belong in that place. ❏ *She gives frequent performances of her work, both at home and abroad.* ❏ *His father worked away from home for much of Jim's first five years.* **3** ADV **Home** means to or at the place where you live. ❏ *His wife wasn't feeling too well and she wanted to go home.* ❏ *I'll call you as soon as I get home.* **4** ADJ [ADJ n] **Home** means made or done in the place where you live. ❏ *...cheap but healthy home cooking.* **5** ADJ [ADJ n] **Home** means relating to your own country as opposed to foreign countries. ❏ *Europe's software companies still have a growing home market.* **6** N-COUNT A **home** is a large house or institution where a number of people live and are cared for, instead of living in their own houses or apartments. They usually live there because they are too old or ill to take care of themselves or for their families to care for them. ❏ *It's going to be a home for vulnerable adults.* **7** N-COUNT You can refer to a family unit as a **home**. ❏ *She had, at any rate, provided a peaceful and loving home for Harriet.* **8** N-SING If you refer to the **home** of something, you mean the place where it began or where it is most typically found. ❏ *This southwest region of France is the home of claret.* **9** N-COUNT If you find a **home** for something, you find a place where it can be kept. ❏ *The equipment itself is getting smaller, neater and easier to find a home for.* **10** ADV [ADV after v] If you press, drive, or hammer something **home**, you explain it to people as forcefully as possible. ❏ *It is now up to all of us to debate this issue and press home the argument.* **11** N-UNCOUNT When a sports team plays at **home**, they play a game on their own field, rather than on the opposing team's field. ❏ *I scored in both games; we tied at home and beat them away.* • ADJ [ADJ n] **Home** is also an adjective. ❏ *All three are fans, and attend all home games together.* **12** PHRASE If you feel **at home**, you feel comfortable in the place or situation that you are in. ❏ *He spoke very good English and appeared pleased to see us, and we soon felt quite at home.* **13** PHRASE To **bring** something **home** to someone means to make them understand how important or serious it is. ❏ *Their sobering conversation brought home to everyone present the serious and worthwhile work the Red Cross does.* **14** PHRASE If you say that someone is **home free** you mean that they have been successful or that they are certain to be successful. ❏ *Just when she thought she was home free, her father spoke from behind her.* **15** PHRASE If a situation or what someone says **hits home** or **strikes home**, people accept that it is real or true, even though it may be painful for them to realize. ❏ *Did the reality of war finally hit home?* **16** PHRASE You can say **a home away from home** to refer to a place in which you are as comfortable as in your own home. [APPROVAL] ❏ *The café seems to be her home away from home these days.* **17** CONVENTION If you say to a guest '**Make yourself at home**,' you are making them feel welcome and inviting them to behave in an informal, relaxed way. [POLITENESS] ❏ *Take off your jacket and make yourself at home.* **18** PHRASE If you say that something is **nothing to write home about**, you mean that it is not very interesting or exciting. [INFORMAL] ❏ *I see growth slightly up, but nothing to write home about.* **19** PHRASE If something that is thrown or fired **strikes home**, it reaches its target. [WRITTEN] ❏ *Only two torpedoes struck home.* **20** → See also color supplement

---
USAGE

house or **home**?
You don't usually say 'I am going to my house' or 'She was in her house.' You say 'I am going **home**' or 'She was **at home**.' *I'll finish the report at home.*
---

② **home** /hoʊm/ (**homes, homing, homed**)
▶ **home in** **1** PHRASAL VERB If you **home in** on one particular aspect of something, you give all your attention to it. ❏ *The critics immediately homed in on the group's essential members.* **2** PHRASAL VERB If something such as a missile **homes in on** something else, it is aimed at that thing and moves toward it. ❏ *Two rockets homed in on it from behind without a sound.*

home birth (**home births**) N-VAR If a woman has a **home birth**, she gives birth to her baby at home rather than in a hospital.

home|body /hoʊmbɒdi/ (**homebodies**) N-COUNT If you describe someone as a **homebody**, you mean that they enjoy being at home and spend most of their time there. ❏ *We're both homebodies. We don't feel good going to Hollywood parties.*

home|boy /hoʊmbɔɪ/ (**homeboys**) N-COUNT A **homeboy** is a boy or man from the same area as you, especially one from the same social group as you. [AM, INFORMAL]

home brew N-UNCOUNT **Home brew** is beer or wine that is made in someone's home, rather than in a brewery or a winery.

home|coming /hoʊmkʌmɪŋ/ (**homecomings**) **1** N-VAR Your **homecoming** is your return to your home or your country after being away for a long time. ❏ *Her homecoming was tinged with sadness.* **2** N-UNCOUNT **Homecoming** is a day or weekend each year when former students of a particular school, college, or university go back to it to meet each other again and go to parties and sports events. [AM] ❏ *...a recent Penn State graduate who was back for Homecoming weekend.*

home eco|nom|ics N-UNCOUNT **Home economics** is a school subject dealing with how to run a house well and efficiently.

home field (home fields) N-COUNT A sports team's **home field** is their own playing field, as opposed to that of other teams. [AM]

home front N-SING [the N] If something is happening on the **home front**, it is happening within the country where you live. ❑ *The Democrats are trying desperately to change the subject to the home front, to talk about domestic issues.*

home|girl /hoʊmɡɜrl/ (homegirls) N-COUNT A **homegirl** is a girl or woman from the same area as you, especially one from the same social group as you. [AM, INFORMAL]

home ground (home grounds) **1** PHRASE If you say that someone is **on home ground**, you mean that they are in or near where they work or live, and feel confident and secure because of this. ❑ *Although he was on home ground, his campaign had been rocked by adultery allegations.* **2** N-VAR A sports team's **home ground** is their own playing field, as opposed to that of other teams. [BRIT]

in AM, use **home field**

home|grown /hoʊmɡroʊn/ ADJ **Homegrown** fruit and vegetables have been grown in your garden, rather than on a farm, or in your country rather than abroad. ❑ *The menu features delicious homegrown local or organic produce.*

home|land /hoʊmlænd/ (homelands) **1** N-COUNT Your **homeland** is your native country. [mainly WRITTEN] ❑ *Many are planning to return to their homeland.* **2** N-COUNT The **homelands** were regions within South Africa in which Black South Africans had a limited form of self-government.

home|less ✦✧✧ /hoʊmlɪs/ **1** ADJ **Homeless** people have nowhere to live. ❑ *...the growing number of homeless families.* • N-PLURAL The **homeless** are people who are homeless. ❑ *...shelters for the homeless.* • **home|less|ness** N-UNCOUNT ❑ *The only way to solve homelessness is to provide more homes.* **2** → See feature box at **poverty**

home|ly /hoʊmli/ (homelier, homeliest) **1** ADJ If you say that someone is **homely**, you mean that they are not very attractive to look at. [AM] ❑ *The man was homely, overweight, and probably only two or three years younger than Lou.* **2** ADJ If you describe a room or house as **homely**, you like it because you feel comfortable and relaxed there. [BRIT, APPROVAL]

in AM, use **homey**

home|made /hoʊmmeɪd/ ADJ Something that is **homemade** has been made in someone's home, rather than in a store or factory. ❑ *The bread, pastry and mayonnaise are homemade.*

home|maker /hoʊmmeɪkər/ (homemakers) N-COUNT A **homemaker** is someone who spends a lot of time taking care of their home and family. You usually use the word to refer to someone who does not have a job outside the home.

home of|fice (home offices) N-COUNT A **home office** is a room in your home that you use as an office. ❑ *Also overlooking the living space is a study area suitable for use as a home office.*

homeo|path /hoʊmioʊpæθ/ (homeopaths) N-COUNT A **homeopath** is someone who treats illness by homeopathy. ❑ *The homeopath will test various strengths of remedies on the patient.*

homeo|path|ic /hoʊmioʊpæθɪk/ ADJ **Homeopathic** means relating to or used in homeopathy. ❑ *...homeopathic remedies.*

homeopa|thy /hoʊmɪpəθi/ N-UNCOUNT **Homeopathy** is a way of treating an illness in which the patient is given very small amounts of a drug that produces signs of the illness in healthy people.

home|own|er /hoʊmoʊnər/ (homeowners) also **home-owner** N-COUNT A **homeowner** is a person who owns the house or apartment that they live in.

home page (home pages) N-COUNT On the internet, a person's or organization's **home page** is the main page of information about them, which often contains links to other pages about them. ❑ *...the home page of a new sex education website.*

home plate N-UNCOUNT In baseball, **home plate** is the piece of rubber or other material that the batter stands beside. It is the last of the four bases that a runner must touch in order to score a run. ❑ *He severely injured his ankle in a collision at home plate.*

hom|er /hoʊmər/ (homers) N-COUNT A **homer** is the same as a **home run**. [mainly AM, INFORMAL] ❑ *Then, he hit a second homer - his longest ever.*

home|room /hoʊmrum/ (homerooms) N-VAR In a school, **homeroom** is the class or room where students in the same grade meet to get general information and be checked for attendance. [AM] ❑ *Oct. 24, 8:15 A.M. I'm sitting in homeroom and I'm the first person here.*

home rule N-UNCOUNT If a country or region has **home rule**, it has its own independent government and laws.

home run (home runs) N-COUNT In baseball, a **home run** is a hit that allows the batter to run around all four bases and score a run. ❑ *Ruth hit sixty home runs that year.*

home|school ✦✧✧ /hoʊmskul/ (homeschools, homeschooling, homeschooled) VERB If you **homeschool** children, you educate them completely at home instead of sending them to school. ❑ *We decided to homeschool our three children.* ❑ *There are many reasons why parents choose to homeschool.* • **home|school|ing** N-UNCOUNT ❑ *There has been an incredible growth in homeschooling in the past decade.*

home school|ing also **home-schooling** N-UNCOUNT **Home schooling** is the practice of educating your child at home rather than in a school. [mainly AM] ❑ *All fifty American states and the District of Columbia permit home schooling.*

home shop|ping N-UNCOUNT [oft N n] **Home shopping** is shopping that people do by ordering goods from their homes, usually either online or through television channels ❑ *...America's most successful home-shopping channel.*

home|sick /hoʊmsɪk/ ADJ If you are **homesick**, you feel unhappy because you are away from home and are missing your family, friends, and home very much. ❑ *She's feeling a little homesick.* • **home|sick|ness** N-UNCOUNT ❑ *There were inevitable bouts of homesickness.*

home|spun /hoʊmspʌn/ **1** ADJ [usu ADJ n] You use **homespun** to describe opinions or ideas that are simple and not based on special knowledge. ❑ *The book is simple homespun philosophy.* **2** N-UNCOUNT [usu N n] **Homespun** clothes are made from cloth that has been made at home, rather than in a factory.

home|stead /hoʊmstɛd/ (homesteads) **1** N-COUNT A **homestead** is a farmhouse, together with the land around it. **2** N-COUNT In United States history, a **homestead** was a piece of government land in the west, which was given to someone so they could settle there and develop a farm. [AM]

home|stretch /hoʊmstrɛtʃ/ also **home stretch** **1** N-SING [the N] The **homestretch** is the last part of a race. ❑ *Easy Goer overtook Clever Trevor in the homestretch.* **2** N-SING [the N] You can refer to the last part of any activity that lasts for a long time as the **homestretch**, especially if the activity is difficult or boring. ❑ *The Oscars race will enter the homestretch after this weekend.*

home|town /hoʊmtaʊn/ (hometowns) also **home town** N-COUNT [with poss] Someone's **hometown** is the town where they live or the town that they come from.

home|ward /hoʊmwərd/ also **homewards** **1** ADJ [ADJ n] If you are on a **homeward** trip, you are on a trip toward your home. ❑ *She's ready for the homeward trip.* **2** ADV [ADV after v] If you are traveling **homeward** or **homewards**, you are traveling toward your home. ❑ *John drove homeward.*

home|ward bound ADJ People or things that are **homeward bound** are on their way home. ❑ *I'd be homeward bound even before Grant arrived.*

home|work /hoʊmwɜrk/ **1** N-UNCOUNT **Homework** is schoolwork that teachers give to students to do at home in the evening or on the weekend. ❑ *Have you done your homework, Gemma?* **2** N-UNCOUNT If you do your **homework**, you find out what you need to know in preparation for something. ❑ *Before you go near a stockbroker, do your homework.*

home|work|ing ✦✧✧ /hoʊmwɜrkɪŋ/ N-UNCOUNT **Homeworking** is the activity of doing paid work from home, especially when you usually travel to work. ❑ *The growth in homeworking has been huge.* • **home|worker** (homeworkers) N-COUNT ❑ *Some homeworkers have a dedicated office with a separate phone line.*

homey /hoʊmi/ (homier, homiest) ADJ If you describe a room or house as **homey**, you like it because you feel comfortable and relaxed there. [mainly AM, INFORMAL, APPROVAL] ❑ ...*a large, homey dining room.*

homi|ci|dal /hɒmɪsaɪdᵊl, hoʊmɪ-/ ADJ **Homicidal** is used to describe someone who is dangerous because they are likely to kill someone. ❑ *That man is a homicidal maniac.*

homi|cide /hɒmɪsaɪd, hoʊmɪ-/ (**homicides**) N-VAR **Homicide** is the killing of a person. ❑ *The police arrived at the scene of the homicide.*

homi|ly /hɒmɪli/ (**homilies**) N-COUNT A **homily** is a speech or piece of writing in which someone complains about the state of something or tells people how they ought to behave. [FORMAL] ❑ ...*a receptive audience for his homily on moral values.*

hom|ing /hoʊmɪŋ/ **1** ADJ [ADJ n] A weapon or piece of equipment that has a **homing** system is able to guide itself to a target or to give out a signal that guides people to it. ❑ *All the cars are fitted with electronic homing devices.* **2** ADJ [ADJ n] An animal that has a **homing** instinct has the ability to remember and return to a place where it has been in the past. ❑ *Then the pigeons flew into thick fog, and the famous homing instinct failed.*

hom|ing pi|geon (**homing pigeons**) N-COUNT A **homing pigeon** is a pigeon that is trained to return to a particular place, especially in races with other pigeons.

homi|ny /hɒmɪni/ N-UNCOUNT **Hominy** is a food made from maize that has been crushed and boiled with milk or water. ❑ ...*trays of salted hominy.*

homoeo|path /hoʊmiəpæθ/ [BRIT] → see **homeopath**
homoeo|path|ic /hoʊmiəpæθɪk/ [BRIT] → see **homeopathic**
homoeopa|thy /hoʊmɪppəθi/ [BRIT] → see **homeopathy**

homo|erot|ic /hoʊmoʊɪrɒtɪk/ ADJ **Homoerotic** is used to describe things such as movies, literature, and images intended to be sexually appealing to gay people.

homo|genei|ty /hoʊmoʊdʒəniɪti/ N-UNCOUNT **Homogeneity** is the quality of being homogeneous. [FORMAL]

homo|geneous /hoʊmoʊdʒiniəs/ also **homogenous** ADJ **Homogeneous** is used to describe a group or thing which has members or parts that are all the same. [FORMAL] ❑ *The unemployed are not a homogeneous group.*

ho|mog|enize /həmɒdʒənaɪz/ (**homogenizes, homogenizing, homogenized**)

in BRIT, also use **homogenise**

V-T If something **is homogenized**, it is changed so that all its parts are similar or the same, especially in a way that is undesirable. [DISAPPROVAL] ❑ *He sees television as the force that homogenizes the world.*

ho|mog|enized /həmɒdʒənaɪzd/

in BRIT, also use **homogenised**

ADJ **Homogenized** milk is milk where the fat has been broken up so that it is evenly distributed.

ho|mog|enous /həmɒdʒənəs/ ADJ **Homogenous** means the same as **homogeneous**.

ho|mo|phobe /hoʊməfoʊb/ (**homophobes**) N-COUNT A **homophobe** is someone who fears or hates gay people. [DISAPPROVAL] ❑ *He claims that he is no homophobe and that he has gay friends.*

homo|pho|bia /hoʊməfoʊbiə/ N-UNCOUNT **Homophobia** is a strong and unreasonable dislike of gay people.

ho|mo|pho|bic /hoʊməfoʊbɪk/ ADJ **Homophobic** means involving or related to a strong and unreasonable dislike of gay people, especially gay men. ❑ *I'm not homophobic in any way and certainly don't condemn gay relationships.*

homo|phone /hoʊmoʊfoʊn/ (**homophones**) N-COUNT In linguistics, **homophones** are words with different meanings which are pronounced in the same way but are spelled differently. For example, 'write' and 'right' are homophones.

homo sa|pi|ens /hoʊmoʊ sæpiɛnz/ N-UNCOUNT **Homo sapiens** is used to refer to modern human beings as a species, in contrast to other species of ape or animal, or earlier forms of human. [TECHNICAL] ❑ *What distinguishes homo sapiens from every other living creature is the mind.*

homo|sex|ual /hoʊmoʊsɛkʃuəl/ (**homosexuals**) **1** ADJ A **homosexual** relationship is a sexual relationship between people of the same sex. ❑ ...*partners in a homosexual relationship.* **2** ADJ Someone who is **homosexual** is sexually attracted to people of the same sex. • N-COUNT **Homosexual** is also a noun. ❑ *The judge said that discrimination against homosexuals is deplorable.* • **homo|sex|ual|ity** /hoʊmoʊsɛkʃuælɪti/ N-UNCOUNT ❑ ...*a place where people could openly discuss homosexuality.*

Hon. /ɒn/ N-TITLE **Hon.** is an abbreviation for **honorable** and **honorary** when they are used as part of a person's title.

hon|cho /hɒntʃoʊ/ (**honchos**) N-COUNT A **honcho** is one of the people in charge of a company or organization. [mainly AM, INFORMAL] ❑ *As head honcho in the UK, he is responsible for 1500 employees and ensuring that the company's entire UK operations are in keeping with the overall business strategy.*

hone /hoʊn/ (**hones, honing, honed**) V-T If you **hone** something, for example a skill, technique, idea, or product, you carefully develop it over a long period of time so that it is exactly right for your purpose. ❑ *Leading companies spend time and money on honing the skills of senior managers.*

hon|est /ɒnɪst/ **1** ADJ If you describe someone as **honest**, you mean that they always tell the truth, and do not try to deceive people or break the law. ❑ *I know she's honest and reliable.* • **hon|est|ly** ADV [ADV after v] ❑ *She fought honestly for a just cause and for freedom.* **2** ADJ If you are **honest** in a particular situation, you tell the complete truth or give your sincere opinion, even if this is not very pleasant. ❑ *I was honest about what I was doing.* ❑ *He had been honest with her and she had tricked him!* • **hon|est|ly** ADV [ADV with v] ❑ *It came as a shock to hear an old friend speak so honestly about Ted.* **3** ADV [ADV with cl] You say '**honest**' before or after a statement to emphasize that you are telling the truth and that you want people to believe you. [INFORMAL, EMPHASIS] ❑ *I'm not sure, honest.* **4** PHRASE Some people say '**honest to God**' to emphasize their feelings or to emphasize that something is really true. [INFORMAL, EMPHASIS] ❑ *I wish we weren't doing this, Lillian, honest to God, I really do.* **5** PHRASE You can say '**to be honest**' before or after a statement to indicate that you are telling the truth about your own opinions or feelings, especially if you think these will disappoint the person you are talking to. [FEELINGS] ❑ *To be honest the house is not quite our style.*

hon|est bro|ker (**honest brokers**) N-COUNT [usu sing] If a person or country acts as an **honest broker**, they try to help people resolve a dispute or arrange a deal by talking to all sides and finding out what they want, without favoring any one side. ❑ *He doubts whether we could be an honest broker in the peace talks.*

hon|est|ly /ɒnɪstli/ **1** ADV [ADV before v] You use **honestly** to emphasize that you are referring to your, or someone else's, true beliefs or feelings. [EMPHASIS] ❑ *But did you honestly think we wouldn't notice?* **2** ADV [ADV with cl] You use **honestly** to emphasize that you are telling the truth and that you want people to believe you. [SPOKEN, EMPHASIS] ❑ *Honestly, I don't know anything about it.* **3** ADV [ADV with cl] You use **honestly** to indicate that you are annoyed or impatient. [SPOKEN, FEELINGS] ❑ *Honestly, Nev! Must you be so crude!* **4** → see also **honest**

hon|es|ty /ɒnɪsti/ N-UNCOUNT **Honesty** is the quality of being honest. ❑ *They said the greatest virtues in a politician were integrity, correctness, and honesty.* • PHRASE You say **in all honesty** when you are saying something that might be disappointing or upsetting, and you want to soften its effect by emphasizing your sincerity. [EMPHASIS]

hon|ey /hʌni/ (**honeys**) **1** N-VAR **Honey** is a sweet, sticky, yellowish substance that is made by bees. **2** N-VOC You call someone **honey** as a sign of affection. [mainly AM] ❑ *Honey, I don't really think that's a good idea.*

honey|bee /hʌnibi/ (**honeybees**) N-COUNT A **honeybee** is a bee that makes honey.

honey|comb /hʌnikoʊm/ (**honeycombs**) N-VAR A **honeycomb** is a wax structure consisting of rows of six-sided spaces where bees store their honey.

hon|eyed /hʌnid/ **1** ADJ [usu ADJ n] You can describe someone's voice or words as **honeyed** when they are very pleasant to listen to, especially if you want to suggest that they are insincere. ☐ *His gentle manner and honeyed tones reassured Andrew.* **2** ADJ [usu ADJ n] You can describe something as **honeyed** when it tastes or smells of honey, or is the pale yellowish color of honey. [LITERARY] ☐ *I could smell the honeyed ripeness of melons and peaches.* ☐ *...a warm, honeyed light.*

honey|moon /hʌnimun/ (honeymoons, honeymooning, honeymooned) **1** N-COUNT A **honeymoon** is a vacation taken by two people who have just gotten married. ☐ *The next time I went abroad was on my honeymoon.* **2** V-I When a recently married couple **honeymoon** somewhere, they go there on their honeymoon. ☐ *They honeymooned in Venice.* **3** N-COUNT You can use **honeymoon** to refer to a period of time after the start of a new job or when a newly elected official takes office when everyone is pleased with the person or people concerned and is nice to them. ☐ *Brett is enjoying a honeymoon period with both press and public.*

honey|pot /hʌnipɒt/ (honeypots) **1** N-COUNT If you describe someone as a **honeypot**, you mean that they are very attractive. **2** N-COUNT A **honeypot** is a source of money or income.

honey|suckle /hʌnisʌkəl/ (honeysuckles) N-VAR **Honeysuckle** is a climbing plant with sweet-smelling yellow, pink, or white flowers.

honey|trap /hʌnitræp/ (honeytraps) N-COUNT A **honeytrap** is a situation in which someone is tricked into immoral or illegal sexual behavior so that their behavior can be publicly exposed.

honk /hɒŋk/ (honks, honking, honked) V-T/V-I If you **honk** the horn of a vehicle or if the horn **honks**, you make the horn produce a short loud sound. ☐ *Drivers honked their horns in solidarity with the peace marchers.* ☐ *Horns honk. An angry motorist shouts.* • N-COUNT **Honk** is also a noun. ☐ *She pulled to the right with a honk.*

honky-tonk /hɒŋki tɒŋk/ (honky-tonks) **1** N-COUNT [oft N n] A **honky-tonk** is a cheap bar or nightclub. [AM] ☐ *...little honky-tonk bars in Texas.* **2** N-UNCOUNT [oft N n] **Honky-tonk** is the kind of piano music played in honky-tonks. ☐ *...the beat of honky-tonk pianos.*

hon|or ♦◇◇ /ɒnər/ (honors, honoring, honored)

in BRIT, use **honour**

1 N-UNCOUNT **Honor** means doing what you believe to be right and being confident that you have done what is right. ☐ *For me it was a question of integrity and honor.* **2** N-COUNT An **honor** is a special award that is given to someone, usually because they have done something good or because they are greatly respected. ☐ *He was showered with honors – among them an Oscar.* **3** V-T [usu passive] If someone **is honored**, they are given public praise or an award for something they have done. ☐ *It's nice to be honored with an award like this.* **4** N-SING If you describe doing or experiencing something as an **honor**, you mean you think it is something special and desirable. ☐ *Five other cities had been competing for the honor of staging the Games.* **5** V-T PASSIVE If you say that you would **be honored** to do something, you are saying very politely and formally that you would be pleased to do it. If you say that you **are honored** by something, you are saying that you are grateful for it and pleased about it. [POLITENESS] ☐ *Ms. Payne said she was honored to accept the appointment and looked forward to its challenges.* **6** V-T To **honor** someone means to treat them or regard them with special attention and respect. ☐ *They honored him with a seat at the head of the table.* **7** V-T If you **honor** an arrangement or promise, you do what you said you would do. ☐ *The two sides agreed to honor a new ceasefire.* **8** N-VOC [poss N; PRON: poss PRON] Judges and mayors are sometimes called **your honor** or referred to as **his honor** or **her honor**. ☐ *I bring this up, your honor, because I think it is important to understand the background of the defendant.* **9** PHRASE If something is arranged **in honor of** a particular event, it is arranged in order to celebrate that event. ☐ *The Foundation is holding a dinner at the Museum of American Art in honor of the opening of its new show.* **10** PHRASE If something is arranged or happens **in** someone's **honor**, it is done specially to show appreciation of them. ☐ *The President will attend an outdoor concert in his honor.*

SYNONYMS

honor
NOUN **1**
integrity: *I have always regarded him as a man of integrity.*
morality: *...standards of morality and justice in society.*
decency: *His sense of decency forced him to resign.*
VERB **6**
respect: *I want him to respect me as a career woman.*
esteem: *I greatly esteem your message in the midst of our hard struggle.*
admire: *He admired the way she had coped with life.*
revere: *Today, he's still revered as the father of the nation.*

hon|or|able /ɒnərəbəl/

in BRIT, use **honourable**

ADJ If you describe people or actions as **honorable**, you mean that they are good and deserve to be respected and admired. ☐ *He argued that the only honorable course of action was to resign.* • **hon|or|ably** /ɒnərəbli/ ADV ☐ *He also felt she had not behaved honorably in the leadership election.*

hon|or|able men|tion (honorable mentions)

in BRIT, use **honourable mention**

N-VAR If something that you do in a competition is given an **honorable mention**, it receives special praise from the judges although it does not actually win a prize. [AM] ☐ *Sometimes his designs received honorable mentions, and were reproduced in architectural journals.*

hono|rar|ium /ɒnərɛəriəm/ (honoraria /ɒnərɛəriə/ or honorariums) N-COUNT An **honorarium** is a fee that someone receives for doing something which is not a normal part of their job, for example giving a talk.

hon|or|ary /ɒnərɛri/ **1** ADJ [ADJ n] An **honorary** title or membership of a group is given to someone without their needing to have the necessary qualifications, usually because of their public achievements. ☐ *Harvard awarded him an honorary degree.* **2** ADJ [ADJ n] **Honorary** is used to describe an official job that is done without payment. ☐ *...the honorary secretary of the Beekeepers' Association.*

hon|or guard N-SING An **honor guard** is a group of troops who formally greet or accompany someone special such as a visiting head of state. [AM]

in BRIT, use **guard of honour**

hon|or|if|ic /ɒnərɪfɪk/ (honorifics) ADJ [ADJ n] An **honorific** title or way of talking is used to show respect or honor to someone. [FORMAL] ☐ *He was given the honorific title of national chairman.* • N-COUNT **Honorific** is also a noun. ☐ *The title "colonel" was an honorific.*

hon|or roll (honor rolls) N-COUNT An **honor roll** is a list of the names of people who are admired or respected for something they have done, such as doing very well in a sport or in school. [AM] ☐ *If you study hard, you can make the honor roll.*

hon|or sys|tem N-SING If a service such as an arrangement for buying something is based on an **honor system**, people are trusted to use the service honestly and without cheating or lying. [AM] ☐ *Until now, those guns have been sold primarily on an honor system, wherein the purchasers ensure the sellers they are legally entitled to buy firearms.*

hon|our /ɒnər/ [BRIT] → see **honor**

hon|our|able /ɒnərəbəl/ [BRIT] → see **honorable**

hooch /huːtʃ/ N-UNCOUNT **Hooch** is strong alcoholic drink. [INFORMAL]

hood /hʊd/ (hoods) **1** N-COUNT A **hood** is a part of a coat which you can pull up to cover your head. It is in the shape of a triangular bag attached to the neck of the coat at the back. ☐ *She threw back the hood of her cloak.* **2** N-COUNT The **hood** of a car is the metal cover over the engine at the front. [AM] ☐ *He raised the hood of McKee's truck.* **3** → See also color supplement

hood|ed /hʊdɪd/ **1** ADJ A **hooded** piece of clothing or furniture has a hood. ☐ *...a blue hooded sweatshirt.* **2** ADJ [ADJ n] A **hooded** person is wearing a hood or a piece of clothing pulled down over their face, so they are difficult to recognize. ☐ *The class was held hostage by a hooded gunman.*

hood|ie /hʊdi/ (hoodies) also **hoody** N-COUNT A **hoodie** is a type of casual jacket with a hood. [INFORMAL] ☐ *She wore jeans and a hoodie.*

hood|lum /hʊdləm/ (hoodlums) N-COUNT A **hoodlum** is a violent criminal, especially one who is a member of a group. [INFORMAL]

hood|wink /hʊdwɪŋk/ (hoodwinks, hoodwinking, hoodwinked) V-T If someone **hoodwinks** you, they trick or deceive you. ☐ *People expect others to be honest, which is why conmen find it so easy to hoodwink people.*

hoo|ey /hui/ N-UNCOUNT If you say that an idea or statement is **hooey**, you mean that it is foolish or wrong. [INFORMAL, DISAPPROVAL] ☐ *It's nice to say that knowledge is power, but of course that's a bunch of hooey!*

hoof /huf, huːf/ (hoofs or hooves) N-COUNT The **hooves** of an animal such as a horse are the hard lower parts of its feet. ☐ *The horses' hooves often could not get a proper grip.*

hoof|er /hʊfər, huː-/ (hoofers) N-COUNT A **hoofer** is a dancer, especially one who dances in musicals. [INFORMAL]

hoo-ha /huːhɑː/ N-SING [also no det] If there is a **hoo-ha**, there is a lot of fuss about something. [INFORMAL] ☐ *Schulman is a little tired of the hoo-ha about the all-women team.*

hook ♦♢♢ /hʊk/ (hooks, hooking, hooked) **1** N-COUNT A **hook** is a bent piece of metal or plastic that is used for catching or holding things, or for hanging things up. ☐ *One of his jackets hung from a hook.* **2** V-T/V-I If you **hook** one thing to another, you attach it there using a hook. If something **hooks** somewhere, it can be hooked there. ☐ *Paul hooked his tractor to the car and pulled it to safety.* **3** V-T If you **hook** your arm, leg, or foot round an object, you place it like a hook round the object in order to move it or hold it. ☐ *She latched on to his arm, hooking her other arm around a tree.* **4** V-T If you **hook** a fish, you catch it with a hook on the end of a line. ☐ *At the first cast I hooked a huge fish, probably a tench.* **5** N-COUNT A **hook** is a short sharp blow with your fist that you make with your elbow bent, usually in a boxing match. ☐ *This seemed to anger the champion, who retaliated with a left hook that sent the 32-year-old back on his heels.* **6** V-T/V-I If you **are hooked into** something, or **hook into** something, you get involved with it. [mainly AM] ☐ *I'm guessing again now because I'm not hooked into the political circles.* **7** PHRASE If someone gets **off the hook** or is let **off the hook**, they manage to get out of the awkward or unpleasant situation that they are in. [INFORMAL] ☐ *Officials accused of bribery and corruption get off the hook with monotonous regularity.* **8** PHRASE If you take a phone **off the hook**, you take the receiver off the part that it normally rests on, so that the phone will not ring. ☐ *I'd taken my phone off the hook in order to get some sleep.* **9** PHRASE If your phone **is ringing off the hook**, so many people are trying to telephone you that it is ringing constantly ☐ *Since war broke out, the phones at donation centers have been ringing off the hook.* **10** → See feature box at **DIY**
▶ **hook up** **1** PHRASAL VERB If someone **hooks up** with another person, they begin a sexual or romantic relationship with that person. You can also say that two people **hook up**. [INFORMAL] ☐ *I could be about to hook up with this incredibly intelligent, beautiful girl.* ☐ *We haven't exactly hooked up yet.* **2** PHRASAL VERB If you **hook up** with someone, you meet them and spend time with them. You can also say that two people **hook up**. [mainly AM, INFORMAL] ☐ *He hooked up with fellow cycling enthusiasts and joined several clubs.* ☐ *This afternoon Iz and Jude and Chris hooked up.* **3** PHRASAL VERB When someone **hooks up** a computer or other electronic machine, they connect it to other similar machines or to a central power supply. ☐ *...technicians who hook up computer systems and networks.* ☐ *He brought it down, hooked it up, and we got the generator going.*

hooked /hʊkt/ **1** ADJ If you describe something as **hooked**, you mean that it is shaped like a hook. ☐ *He was thin and tall, with a hooked nose.* **2** ADJ [v-link ADJ] If you are **hooked** on something, you enjoy it so much that it takes up a lot of your interest and attention. ☐ *Many of the leaders have become hooked on power and money.* **3** ADJ [v-link ADJ] If you are **hooked** on a drug, you are addicted to it. [INFORMAL] ☐ *He spent a number of years hooked on cocaine, heroin, and alcohol.*

hook|er /hʊkər/ (hookers) N-COUNT A **hooker** is a prostitute. [mainly AM, INFORMAL]

hook|up /hʊkʌp/ (hookups) also **hook-up** N-COUNT [usu supp N] A **hookup** is a connection between two places, systems, or pieces of equipment. ☐ *Water and electric hook-ups are available and facilities are good.*

hooky /hʊki/ also **hookey** PHRASE If a child **plays hooky**, they stay away from school without permission. [mainly AM, INFORMAL]

hoo|li|gan /huːlɪgən/ (hooligans) N-COUNT If you describe people, especially young people, as **hooligans**, you are critical of them because they behave in a noisy and violent way in a public place. [DISAPPROVAL] ☐ *...the problem of soccer hooligans.*

hoo|li|gan|ism /huːlɪgənɪzəm/ N-UNCOUNT **Hooliganism** is the behavior and actions of hooligans. ☐ *Officials dismiss these incidents as simple hooliganism.*

hoop /huːp/ (hoops) **1** N-COUNT A **hoop** is a ring made of wood, metal, or plastic. ☐ *A boy came towards them, rolling an iron hoop.* **2** N-COUNT A basketball **hoop** is the ring that players try to throw the ball into in order to score points for their team. **3** PHRASE If someone makes you **jump through hoops**, they make you do lots of difficult or boring things in order to please them or achieve something. ☐ *He had the receptionist almost jumping through hoops for him. But to no avail.*

hoop|la /huːplɑː/ N-UNCOUNT **Hoopla** is great fuss or excitement. [mainly AM, INFORMAL] ☐ *Despite all the hoopla, Palo Alto's 100th birthday party is actually designed to be a simple, down-to-earth affair.*

hoo|ray /hʊreɪ/ also **hurray** **1** EXCLAM People sometimes shout '**Hooray!**' when they are very happy and excited about something. **2 hip hip hooray** → see **hip**

hoot /huːt/ (hoots, hooting, hooted) **1** V-I If you **hoot**, you make a loud high-pitched noise when you are laughing or showing disapproval. ☐ *My guests have been hooted at and had obscene gestures made at them.* • N-COUNT **Hoot** is also a noun. ☐ *His confession was greeted with derisive hoots.* **2** PHRASE If you say that you **don't give a hoot** or **don't care two hoots** about something, you are emphasizing that you do not care at all about it. [INFORMAL, EMPHASIS] ☐ *Alan doesn't care two hoots about politics.* **3** V-T/V-I If you **hoot** the horn on a vehicle or if it **hoots**, it makes a loud noise on one note. [mainly BRIT]

in AM, usually use **honk**

4 → See feature box at **sound**

hooves /huːvz/ **Hooves** is a plural of **hoof**.

hop /hɒp/ (hops, hopping, hopped) **1** V-I If you **hop**, you move along by jumping on one foot. ☐ *I hopped down three steps.* • N-COUNT **Hop** is also a noun. ☐ *"This really is a catching rhythm, huh?" he added, with a few little hops.* **2** V-I When birds and some small animals **hop**, they move along by jumping on both or all four feet. ☐ *A small brown fawn hopped across the trail in front of them.* • N-COUNT **Hop** is also a noun. ☐ *The rabbit got up, took four hops and turned around.* **3** V-I If you **hop** somewhere, you move there quickly or suddenly. [INFORMAL] ☐ *My wife and I were the first to arrive and hopped on board.* **4** N-COUNT A **hop** is a short, quick trip, usually by plane. [INFORMAL] ☐ *It is a three-hour flight but can be reached by a 20-minute hop in a private helicopter.* **5** N-COUNT **Hops** are flowers that are dried and used for making beer.

hope ♦♦♦ /hoʊp/ (hopes, hoping, hoped) **1** V-T/V-I If you **hope** that something is true, or if you **hope** for something, you want it to be true or to happen, and you usually believe that it is possible or likely. ☐ *She had decided she must go on as usual, follow her normal routine, and hope and pray.* ☐ *He hesitates before leaving, almost as though he had been hoping for conversation.* **2** V-T/V-I [with brd-neg] If you say that you cannot **hope** for something, or if you talk about the only thing that you can **hope** to get, you mean that you are in a bad situation, and there is very little chance of improving it. ☐ *Things aren't ideal, but that's the best you can hope for.* • N-VAR **Hope** is also a noun. ☐ *The only hope of saving my life lay in operating immediately.* **3** N-UNCOUNT **Hope** is a feeling of desire and expectation that things will go well in the future. ☐ *Now that he has become president, many people once again have hope for genuine changes in the system.* ☐ *But Kevin hasn't given up hope of getting in shape.* **4** N-COUNT If someone wants something to happen, and considers it likely or possible, you can refer to their **hopes** of that thing, or to their **hope** that it will happen. ☐ *They have hopes of increasing trade between the two*

hoped-for

regions. ❏ *My hope is that, in the future, I will go over there and marry her.* **5** N-COUNT If you think that the help or success of a particular person or thing will cause you to be successful or to get what you want, you can refer to them as your **hope**. ❏ *...an advertising campaign claiming that biotechnology offered the best hope of achieving sustainable food production.* **6** PHRASE If you are in a difficult situation and do something and **hope for the best**, you hope that everything will happen in the way you want, although you know that it may not. ❏ *Some companies are cutting costs and hoping for the best.* **7** PHRASE If you tell someone not to **get** their **hopes up**, or not to **build** their **hopes up**, you are warning them that they should not become too confident of progress or success. ❏ *There is no reason for people to get their hopes up over this mission.* **8** PHRASE If you say that someone has **not** got **a hope in hell** of doing something, you are emphasizing that they will not be able to do it. [INFORMAL, EMPHASIS] ❏ *Everybody knows they haven't got a hope in hell of forming a government anyway.* **9** PHRASE If you have **high hopes** or **great hopes** that something will happen, you are confident that it will happen. ❏ *I had high hopes that Derek Randall might play an important part.* **10** PHRASE If you **hope against hope** that something will happen, you hope that it will happen, although it seems impossible. ❏ *She glanced about the hall, hoping against hope that Richard would be waiting for her.* **11** PHRASE You use '**I hope**' in expressions such as '**I hope you don't mind**' and '**I hope I'm not disturbing you**,' when you are being polite and want to make sure that you have not offended someone or disturbed them. [POLITENESS] ❏ *I hope you don't mind me coming to see you.* **12** PHRASE You say '**I hope**' when you want to warn someone not to do something foolish or dangerous. ❏ *You're not trying to see him, I hope?* **13** PHRASE If you do one thing **in the hope** of another thing happening, you do it because you think it might cause or help the other thing to happen, which is what you want. ❏ *He was studying in the hope of being admitted to an engineering college.* **14** PHRASE If you **live in hope** that something will happen, you continue to hope that it will happen, although it seems unlikely, and you realize that you are being foolish. ❏ *I just live in hope that one day she'll talk to me.*

USAGE

hope
If someone asks you whether something is true, or whether something will happen, you can answer 'yes' by saying '**I hope so**,' or 'no' by saying '**I hope not**.' Don't say 'I hope it' or 'I don't hope so.' *'Have you lost the ticket?'—'I hope not.'*

COLLOCATIONS

hope
NOUN **3**
adjective + **hope**: faint, false, forlorn, slim, vain; high; realistic
verb + **hope**: dash; raise; harbor; express; give up, lose
hope + be + adjective: alive

---

hoped-for ADJ [ADJ n] **Hoped-for** is used to describe something that people would like to happen, and which they usually think is likely or possible. [JOURNALISM] ❏ *The hoped-for economic recovery did not arrive.*

hope|ful /hóʊpfəl/ (**hopefuls**) **1** ADJ If you are **hopeful**, you are fairly confident that something that you want to happen will happen. ❏ *I am hopeful this misunderstanding will be rectified very quickly.* • **hope|ful|ly** ADV [ADV with v] ❏ *"Am I welcome?" He smiled hopefully, leaning on the door.* **2** ADJ If something such as a sign or event is **hopeful**, it makes you feel that what you want to happen will happen. ❏ *The result of the election is yet another hopeful sign that peace could come to the Middle East.* **3** ADJ [ADJ n] A **hopeful** action is one that you do in the hope that you will get what you want to get. ❏ *We've chartered the aircraft in the hopeful anticipation that the government will allow them to leave.* **4** N-COUNT If you refer to someone as a **hopeful**, you mean that they are hoping and trying to achieve success in a particular career, election, or competition. ❏ *His skills continue to be put to good use in his job as coach to young hopefuls.*

hope|ful|ly /hóʊpfəli/ ADV [ADV with cl/group] You say **hopefully** when mentioning something that you hope will happen. Some careful speakers of English think that this use

of **hopefully** is not correct, but it is very frequently used. ❏ *Hopefully, you won't have any problems after reading this.*

hope|less /hóʊplɪs/ **1** ADJ If you feel **hopeless**, you feel very unhappy because there seems to be no possibility of a better situation or success. ❏ *He had not heard her cry before in this uncontrolled, hopeless way.* • **hope|less|ly** ADV ❏ *I looked around hopelessly.* • **hope|less|ness** N-UNCOUNT ❏ *She had a feeling of hopelessness about the future.* **2** ADJ Someone or something that is **hopeless** is certain to fail or be unsuccessful. ❏ *I don't believe your situation is as hopeless as you think. If you love each other, you'll work it out.* **3** ADJ If someone is **hopeless** at something, they are very bad at it. [INFORMAL] ❏ *I'd be hopeless at working for somebody else.* **4** ADJ You use **hopeless** to emphasize how bad or inadequate something or someone is. [EMPHASIS] ❏ *Our economic policies were a hopeless mess.* • **hope|less|ly** ADV ❏ *Harry was hopelessly lost.* **5** → See feature box at **emotion**

hop|per /hɒpər/ (**hoppers**) N-COUNT A **hopper** is a large cone-shaped device into which substances such as grain, coal, or animal food can be put and from which they can be released when required.

hop|scotch /hɒpskɒtʃ/ N-UNCOUNT **Hopscotch** is a children's game which involves jumping between squares which are drawn on the ground or a sidewalk.

horde /hɔrd/ (**hordes**) N-COUNT If you describe a crowd of people as a **horde**, you mean that the crowd is very large and excited and, often, rather frightening or unpleasant. ❏ *This attracts hordes of tourists to Las Vegas.*

ho|ri|zon /həráɪzən/ (**horizons**) **1** N-SING The **horizon** is the line in the far distance where the sky seems to meet the land or the sea. ❏ *In the distance, the dot of a boat appeared on the horizon.* **2** N-COUNT Your **horizons** are the limits of what you want to do or of what you are interested or involved in. ❏ *As your horizons expand, these new ideas can give a whole new meaning to life.* **3** PHRASE If something is **on the horizon**, it is almost certainly going to happen or be done quite soon. ❏ *With breast cancer, as with many common diseases, there is no obvious breakthrough on the horizon.*

hori|zon|tal /hɔrɪzɒntəl/ ADJ Something that is **horizontal** is flat and level with the ground, rather than at an angle to it. ❏ *The board consists of vertical and horizontal lines.* • N-SING **Horizontal** is also a noun. ❏ *Do not raise your left arm above the horizontal.* • **hori|zon|tal|ly** ADV ❏ *The wind was cold and drove the snow at him almost horizontally.*

hor|mo|nal /hɔrmóʊnəl/ ADJ **Hormonal** means relating to or involving hormones. ❏ *...our individual hormonal balance.*

hor|mone /hɔrmoʊn/ (**hormones**) N-COUNT A **hormone** is a chemical, usually occurring naturally in your body, that makes an organ of your body do something. ❏ *...the male sex hormone testosterone.*

hor|mone re|place|ment thera|py N-UNCOUNT If a woman has **hormone replacement therapy**, she takes the hormone estrogen, usually in order to control the symptoms of menopause. The abbreviation **HRT** is often used.

horn /hɔrn/ (**horns**) **1** N-COUNT On a vehicle such as a car, the **horn** is the device that makes a loud noise as a signal or warning. ❏ *He sounded the car horn.* **2** N-COUNT The **horns** of an animal such as a cow or deer are the hard pointed things that grow from its head. ❏ *A mature cow has horns.* **3** N-COUNT A **horn** is a musical instrument of the brass family. It is a long circular metal tube, wide at one end, which you play by blowing. ❏ *He started playing the horn when he was eight.* **4** N-COUNT A **horn** is a simple musical instrument consisting of a metal tube that is wide at one end and narrow at the other. You play it by blowing into it. ❏ *...a hunting horn.* **5** PHRASE If two people **lock horns**, they argue about something. ❏ *During his six years in office, Seidman has often locked horns with lawmakers.* **6** → See feature box at **endanger**; See also color supplement

horned /hɔrnd/ ADJ [usu ADJ n] **Horned** animals have horns, or parts of their bodies that look like horns. ❏ *...horned cattle.* ❏ *...the call of a horned lark.*

hor|net /hɔrnɪt/ (**hornets**) **1** N-COUNT A **hornet** is a large wasp. Hornets live in nests and have a powerful sting. **2** PHRASE [usu PHR after v] If you say that someone has stirred up **a hornet's nest**, you mean that they have done something which has caused a lot of argument or trouble.

horn-rimmed ADJ [ADJ n] **Horn-rimmed** glasses have plastic frames that look as though they are made of horn.

horny /hɔrni/ (**hornier, horniest**) **1** ADJ If you describe someone as **horny**, you mean that they are sexually aroused or that they easily become sexually aroused. [INFORMAL] ❑ ...horny adolescent boys. **2** ADJ Something that is **horny** is hard, strong, and made of horn or of a hard substance like horn. ❑ His fingernails had grown long and horny.

horo|scope /hɔrəskoup/ (**horoscopes**) N-COUNT Your **horoscope** is a prediction of events which some people believe will happen to you in the future. Horoscopes are based on the position of the stars when you were born. ❑ I always read my horoscope and follow the advice.

hor|ren|dous /hɔrɛndəs, hə-/ **1** ADJ Something that is **horrendous** is very unpleasant or shocking. ❑ He described it as the most horrendous experience of his life. **2** ADJ Some people use **horrendous** to describe something that is so big or great that they find it extremely unpleasant. [INFORMAL] ❑ ...the usually horrendous traffic jams. ● **hor|ren|dous|ly** ADV ❑ The man in the photo was horrendously fat.

hor|ri|ble /hɔrɪbəl, hɒr-/ **1** ADJ If you describe something or someone as **horrible**, you do not like them at all. [INFORMAL] ❑ Her voice sounds horrible. ● **hor|ri|bly** /hɔrɪbli, hɒr-/ ADV [ADV with v] ❑ When trouble comes they behave selfishly and horribly. **2** ADJ You can call something **horrible** when it causes you to feel great shock, fear, and disgust. ❑ Still the horrible shrieking came out of his mouth. ● **hor|ri|bly** ADV [ADV with v] ❑ A two-year-old boy was horribly murdered. **3** ADJ [ADJ n] **Horrible** is used to emphasize how bad something is. [EMPHASIS] ❑ That seems like a horrible mess that will drag on for years. ● **hor|ri|bly** ADV ❑ Our plans have gone horribly wrong.

hor|rid /hɔrɪd, hɒr-/ **1** ADJ If you describe something as **horrid**, you mean that it is extremely unpleasant. [INFORMAL] ❑ What a horrid smell! **2** ADJ If you describe someone as **horrid**, you mean that they behave in a very unpleasant way toward other people. [INFORMAL] ❑ I must have been a horrid little girl.

hor|rif|ic /hɔrɪfɪk, hɒ-, hə-/ **1** ADJ If you describe a physical attack, accident, or injury as **horrific**, you mean that it is very bad, so that people are shocked when they see it or think about it. ❑ I have never seen such horrific injuries. ● **hor|rifi|cal|ly** ADV ❑ He had been horrifically assaulted before he died. **2** ADJ If you describe something as **horrific**, you mean that it is so big that it is extremely unpleasant. ❑ ...piling up horrific extra amounts of money on top of your original debt. ● **hor|rifi|cal|ly** ADV [ADV adj] ❑ Opera productions are horrifically expensive.

hor|ri|fy /hɔrɪfaɪ, hɒr-/ (**horrifies, horrifying, horrified**) V-T If someone **is horrified**, they feel shocked or disgusted, usually because of something that they have seen or heard. ❑ His family was horrified by the change.

hor|ri|fy|ing /hɔrɪfaɪɪŋ, hɒr-/ ADJ If you describe something as **horrifying**, you mean that it is shocking or disgusting. ❑ These were horrifying experiences.

hor|ror ✦◇◇ /hɔrər, hɒr-/ (**horrors**) **1** N-UNCOUNT **Horror** is a feeling of great shock, fear, and worry caused by something extremely unpleasant. ❑ I felt numb with horror. **2** N-SING If you have a **horror** of something, you are afraid of it or dislike it very much. ❑ ...his horror of death. **3** N-SING The **horror** of something, especially something that hurts people, is its very great unpleasantness. ❑ ...the horror of this most bloody of civil wars. **4** N-COUNT You can refer to extremely unpleasant or frightening experiences as **horrors**. ❑ Can you possibly imagine all the horrors we have undergone since I last wrote you? **5** ADJ [ADJ n] A **horror** movie or story is intended to be very frightening. ❑ ...a psychological horror movie. **6** ADJ [ADJ n] You can refer to an account of a very unpleasant experience or event as a **horror** story. ❑ ...a horror story about lost luggage while flying.

---- SYNONYMS ----

horror
NOUN **1**
hatred: Her hatred of them would never lead her to murder.
disgust: He spoke of his disgust at the incident.
loathing: She looked at him with loathing
aversion: Many people have a natural and emotional aversion to insects.
revulsion: ...their revulsion at the act of desecration.

horror-stricken ADJ **Horror-stricken** means the same as **horror-struck**.

horror-struck ADJ If you describe someone as **horror-struck** or **horror-stricken**, you mean that they feel very great horror at something that has happened. ❑ "What is the matter with Signora Anna?" he whispered, horror-struck at her vacant face.

hors d'oeu|vre /ɔrdɜrv/ (**hors d'oeuvres**) N-VAR **Hors d'oeuvres** are small amounts of food that are served before the main part of a meal.

horse ✦◆◇ /hɔrs/ (**horses, horsing, horsed**) **1** N-COUNT A **horse** is a large animal which people can ride. Some horses are used for pulling plows and carts. ❑ A small man on a gray horse had appeared. **2** PHRASE If you hear something **from the horse's mouth**, you hear it from someone who knows that it is definitely true. ❑ He has got to hear it from the horse's mouth. Then he can make a judgment as to whether his policy is correct or not.
▶ **horse around** PHRASAL VERB If you **horse around**, you play roughly and carelessly, so that you could hurt someone or damage something. [INFORMAL] ❑ My friends and I would horse around and try to push each other.

horse|back /hɔrsbæk/ **1** N-UNCOUNT If you do something on **horseback**, you do it while riding a horse. ❑ In remote mountain areas, voters arrived on horseback. **2** ADJ [ADJ n] A **horseback** ride is a ride on a horse. ❑ ...a horseback ride into the mountains. ● ADV **Horseback** is also an adverb. ❑ Many people in this area ride horseback.

horse|back rid|ing N-UNCOUNT **Horseback riding** is the activity of riding a horse, especially for enjoyment or as a form of exercise. [AM]

horse chest|nut (**horse chestnuts**) also **horse-chestnut** **1** N-COUNT A **horse chestnut** is a large tree which has leaves with several pointed parts and shiny reddish brown nuts that grow in cases with points on them. **2** N-COUNT **Horse chestnuts** are the nuts of a horse chestnut tree.

horse-drawn also **horsedrawn** ADJ [ADJ n] A **horse-drawn** carriage, cart, or other vehicle is one that is pulled by one or more horses. ❑ ...a horse-drawn open-topped carriage.

horse|hair /hɔrshɛər/ N-UNCOUNT [oft N n] **Horsehair** is hair from the tails or manes of horses and was used in the past to fill mattresses and furniture such as armchairs.

horse|man /hɔrsmən/ (**horsemen**) N-COUNT A **horseman** is a man who is riding a horse, or who rides horses well. ❑ Gerald was a fine horseman.

horse|man|ship /hɔrsmənʃɪp/ N-UNCOUNT **Horsemanship** is the ability to ride horses well.

horse|play /hɔrspleɪ/ N-UNCOUNT **Horseplay** is rough play in which people push and hit each other, or behave in a silly way. [OLD-FASHIONED]

horse|power /hɔrspaʊər/ N-UNCOUNT **Horsepower** is a unit of power used for measuring how powerful an engine is. ❑ ...a 300-horsepower engine.

horse rac|ing also **horse-racing, horseracing** N-UNCOUNT **Horse racing** is a sport in which horses ridden by people called jockeys run in races.

horse|radish /hɔrsrædɪʃ/ **1** N-UNCOUNT **Horseradish** is a plant with a long white root. It has a very strong sharp taste and is often made into a sauce. **2** N-UNCOUNT **Horseradish** or **horseradish sauce** is a sauce made from horseradish. It is often eaten with beef.

horse rid|ing also **horse-riding** → see horseback riding

horse|shoe /hɔrsʃu/ (**horseshoes**) **1** N-COUNT A **horseshoe** is a piece of metal shaped like a U, which is fixed with nails to the bottom of a horse's foot in order to protect it. **2** N-COUNT A **horseshoe** is an object in the shape of a horseshoe which is used as a symbol of good luck.

horse show (**horse shows**) N-COUNT A **horse show** is a sports event in which people riding horses compete in order to demonstrate their skill and control.

horse-trading also **horsetrading** N-UNCOUNT When negotiation or bargaining is forceful and shows clever and careful judgment, you can describe it as **horse-trading**. [AM] ❑ Some frenzied horse-trading is likely to take place in the next few weeks, as parties jockey for a place in a ruling coalition.

horse trail|er (horse trailers) N-COUNT A **horse trailer** is a vehicle which is used to take horses from one place to another. [AM]

horse|whip /hɔrswɪp/ (horsewhips, horsewhipping, horsewhipped) also **horse-whip** ◻ N-COUNT A **horsewhip** is a long, thin piece of leather on the end of a short, stiff handle. It is used to train and control horses. ◻ V-T If someone **horsewhips** an animal or a person, they hit them several times with a horsewhip in order to hurt or punish them. ◻ *These criminals deserve to be horse-whipped.*

horse|woman /hɔrswʊmən/ (horsewomen) N-COUNT A **horsewoman** is a woman who is riding a horse, or who rides horses well. ◻ *She developed into an excellent horsewoman.*

horsey /hɔrsi/ also **horsy** ◻ ADJ Someone who is **horsey** likes horses a lot and spends a lot of time with them. [INFORMAL] ◻ *...a very horsey family.* ◻ ADJ If you describe a woman as **horsey**, you are saying in a rather rude way that her face reminds you of a horse. [DISAPPROVAL]

hor|ti|cul|tur|al /hɔrtɪkʌltʃərəl/ ADJ **Horticultural** means concerned with horticulture. ◻ *...the seeds and young plants sold in most horticultural centers.*

hor|ti|cul|tur|al|ist /hɔrtɪkʌltʃərəlɪst/ (horticulturalists) N-COUNT A **horticulturalist** is a person who grows flowers, fruit, and vegetables, especially as their job.

hor|ti|cul|ture /hɔrtɪkʌltʃər/ N-UNCOUNT **Horticulture** is the study and practice of growing plants.

hose /hoʊz/ (hoses, hosing, hosed) ◻ N-COUNT A **hose** is a long, flexible pipe made of rubber or plastic. Water is directed through a hose in order to do things such as put out fires, clean cars, or water gardens. ◻ *You've left the garden hose on.* ◻ N-COUNT A **hose** is a pipe made of rubber or plastic, along which a liquid or gas flows, for example from one part of an engine to another. ◻ *Water in the engine compartment is sucked away by a hose.* ◻ V-T If you **hose** something, you wash or water it using a hose. ◻ *We wash our cars and hose our gardens without even thinking of the water that uses.* ◻ → See also color supplement

ho|siery /hoʊʒəri/ N-UNCOUNT You use **hosiery** to refer to stockings, socks, and tights, especially when they are on sale in stores. [FORMAL]

hos|pice /hɒspɪs/ (hospices) ◻ N-COUNT; N-IN-NAMES A **hospice** is a special hospital for people who are dying, where their practical and emotional needs are dealt with as well as their medical needs. ◻ *...a hospice for cancer patients.* ◻ ADJ [ADJ n] **Hospice** care is medical care that is provided for people, either in a hospice or in their own home, when they are dying. ◻ *He was diagnosed with colon cancer last year and had been under hospice care for the past few weeks.* ◻ *...a hospice nurse.*

hos|pi|table /hɒspɪtəbəl, hɒspɪt-/ ◻ ADJ A **hospitable** person is friendly, generous, and welcoming to guests or people they have just met. ◻ *The locals are hospitable and welcoming.* ◻ ADJ A **hospitable** climate or environment is one that encourages the existence or development of particular people or things. ◻ *Even in summer this place did not look exactly hospitable: in winter, conditions must have been exceedingly harsh.*

hos|pi|tal ✦✦✦ /hɒspɪtəl/ (hospitals) N-VAR A **hospital** is a place where people who are ill are cared for by nurses and doctors. ◻ *...a children's hospital with 120 beds.*

hos|pi|tal|ity /hɒspɪtælɪti/ ◻ N-UNCOUNT **Hospitality** is friendly, welcoming behavior toward guests or people you have just met. ◻ *Every visitor to Georgia is overwhelmed by the kindness, charm, and hospitality of the people.* ◻ N-UNCOUNT **Hospitality** is the food, drink, and other privileges which some companies provide for their visitors or clients at major sports events or other public events. ◻ *...corporate hospitality tents.*

hos|pi|tal|ize /hɒspɪtəlaɪz/ (hospitalizes, hospitalizing, hospitalized)

in BRIT, also use **hospitalise**

V-T [usu passive] If someone **is hospitalized**, they are sent or admitted to a hospital. ◻ *Most people do not have to be hospitalized for asthma or pneumonia.* • **hos|pi|tali|za|tion** /hɒspɪtɪləzeɪʃən/ N-UNCOUNT ◻ *Occasionally hospitalization is required to combat dehydration.*

host ✦✦✦ /hoʊst/ (hosts, hosting, hosted) ◻ N-COUNT The **host** at a party is the person who has invited the guests and provides the food, drink, or entertainment. ◻ *Apart from my host, I didn't know a single person there.* ◻ V-T If someone **hosts** a party, dinner, or other function, they have invited the guests and provide the food, drink, or entertainment. ◻ *Tonight she hosts a ball for 300 guests.* ◻ N-COUNT A country, city, or organization that is the **host** of an event provides the facilities for that event to take place. ◻ *Atlanta was chosen to be host of the 1996 Olympic games.* ◻ V-T If a country, city, or organization **hosts** an event, they provide the facilities for the event to take place. ◻ *New Bedford hosts a number of lively festivals throughout the summer months.* ◻ PHRASE If a person or country **plays host to** an event or an important visitor, they host the event or the visit. ◻ *Bush played host to Russian President Vladimir Putin.* ◻ N-COUNT The **host** of a radio or television show is the person who introduces it and talks to the people who appear in it. ◻ *I am host of a live radio program.* ◻ V-T The person who **hosts** a radio or television show introduces it and talks to the people who appear in it. ◻ *She also hosts a show on St. Petersburg Radio.* ◻ QUANT A **host** of things is a lot of them. ◻ *A host of problems may delay the opening of the new bridge.* ◻ N-COUNT A **host** or a **host computer** is the main computer in a network of computers, which controls the most important files and programs. ◻ *The virus searches for email addresses on the host computer's hard drive.* ◻ → See feature box at **Olympic Games**

hos|tage ✦✦◆ /hɒstɪdʒ/ (hostages) ◻ N-COUNT A **hostage** is someone who has been captured by a person or organization and who may be killed or injured if people do not do what that person or organization demands. ◻ *It is hopeful that two hostages will be freed in the next few days.* ◻ PHRASE If someone **is taken hostage** or **is held hostage**, they are captured and kept as a hostage. ◻ *He was taken hostage while on his first foreign assignment as a television journalist.* ◻ N-VAR If you say you are **hostage to** something, you mean that your freedom to take action is restricted by things that you cannot control. ◻ *Wine growers say they've been held hostage to the interests of cereal farmers.*

host|ess /hoʊstɪs/ (hostesses) N-COUNT The **hostess** at a party is the woman who has invited the guests and provides the food, drink, or entertainment. ◻ *The hostess introduced them.*

hos|tile /hɒstəl/ ◻ ADJ If you are **hostile** to another person or an idea, you disagree with them or disapprove of them, often showing this in your behavior. ◻ *Many people felt he would be hostile to the idea of foreign intervention.* ◻ *The West has gradually relaxed its hostile attitude to this influential state.* ◻ ADJ Someone who is **hostile** is unfriendly and aggressive. ◻ *Being competitive can lead you into becoming increasingly aggressive and hostile in your interaction with others.* ◻ ADJ **Hostile** situations and conditions make it difficult for you to achieve something. ◻ *...some of the most hostile climatic conditions in the world.* ◻ ADJ A **hostile** takeover bid is one that is opposed by the company that is being bid for. [BUSINESS] ◻ *Soon after he arrived, Kingfisher launched a hostile bid for Dixons.* ◻ ADJ [ADJ n] In a war, you use **hostile** to describe your enemy's forces, organizations, weapons, land, and activities. ◻ *The city is encircled by a hostile army.*

hos|til|ities /hɒstɪlɪtiz/ N-PLURAL You can refer to fighting between two countries or groups who are at war as **hostilities**. [FORMAL] ◻ *The authorities have urged people to stock up on fuel in case hostilities break out.*

hos|til|ity /hɒstɪlɪti/ ◻ N-UNCOUNT **Hostility** is unfriendly or aggressive behavior toward people or ideas. ◻ *...the age-old hostility towards all things English.* ◻ N-UNCOUNT Your **hostility** to something you do not approve of is your opposition to it. ◻ *There is hostility among traditionalists to this method of teaching history.*

hot ✦✦◆ /hɒt/ (hotter, hottest) ◻ ADJ Something that is **hot** has a high temperature. ◻ *When the oil is hot, add the sliced onion.* ◻ *What he needed was a hot bath and a good sleep.* ◻ ADJ **Hot** is used to describe the weather or the air in a room or building when the temperature is high. ◻ *It was too hot even for a gentle stroll.* ◻ ADJ If you are **hot**, you feel as if your body is at an unpleasantly high temperature. ◻ *I was too hot and tired to eat more than a few mouthfuls.* ◻ ADJ You can say that food is **hot** when it has a strong, burning taste caused by chilies, pepper, or other spices. ❑ ...hot curries. **5** ADJ A **hot** issue or topic is one that is very important at the present time and is receiving a lot of publicity. [JOURNALISM] ❑ The role of women in war has been a hot topic of debate since the Gulf conflict. **6** ADJ **Hot** news is new, recent, and fresh. [INFORMAL] ❑ ...eight pages of the latest movies, video releases, and the hot news from Tinseltown. **7** ADJ You can use **hot** to describe something that is very exciting and that many people want to see, use, obtain, or become involved with. [INFORMAL] ❑ When I was in Chicago in 1990 a friend got me a ticket for the hottest show in town: the Monet Exhibition at the Art Institute. **8** ADJ A **hot** contest is one that is intense and involves a great deal of activity and determination. [INFORMAL] ❑ It took hot competition from abroad, however, to show us just how good our product really is. **9** ADJ [ADJ n] If a person or team is the **hot** favorite, people think that they are the one most likely to win a race or competition. ❑ Atlantic City is the hot favorite to stage the fight. **10** ADJ Someone who has a **hot** temper gets angry very quickly and easily. ❑ His hot temper was making it increasingly difficult for others to work with him. **11** ADJ If you describe someone as **hot**, you mean that they are sexually attractive or sexually desirable. [INFORMAL] ❑ "He's great," Caroline said, "hot." ❑ If a hot chick comes on to you, smile and walk away. **12** PHRASE If someone **blows hot and cold**, they keep changing their attitude toward something, sometimes being very enthusiastic and at other times expressing no interest at all. ❑ The media, meanwhile, has blown hot and cold over the affair. **13** PHRASE If you are **hot and bothered**, you are so worried and anxious that you cannot think clearly or behave sensibly. ❑ Ray was getting very hot and bothered about the idea. **14** PHRASE If you say that one person **has the hots for** another, you mean that they feel a strong sexual attraction to that person. [INFORMAL] ❑ I've had the hots for him ever since he arrived.

VOCABULARY IN CONTEXT

Hot or cold?

Are you a hot weather person or a cold weather person? Most people have a preference for one or the other. For some, a **blizzard** will have them dreaming of escaping to a hot, sandy beach with **azure skies**. They will hide themselves away like hibernating bears to wait for the **thaw**. Meanwhile, others find **heatwaves stifling** and pray for a **cool** wind to bring some **relief**. **Wind, rain, sleet,** and **snow** are generally thought to make us more miserable than hotter weather conditions, but recent research shows that extreme hot weather may actually make us more miserable than extreme cold weather. If you think about it, it is logical. After all, in chilly weather, we can **wrap up** against a **gale**, but there are only so many layers of clothes we can take off when the sun is **blazing** down.

hot air N-UNCOUNT If you say that someone's claims or promises are just **hot air**, you are criticizing them because they are made mainly to impress people and have no real value or meaning. [INFORMAL, DISAPPROVAL] ❑ His justification for the merger was just hot air.

hot-air bal|loon (hot-air balloons) N-COUNT A **hot-air balloon** is a large balloon with a basket underneath in which people can travel. The balloon is filled with hot air in order to make it float in the air.

hot|bed /hɒtbed/ (hotbeds) N-COUNT [with supp, usu N of n] If you say that somewhere is a **hotbed** of an undesirable activity, you are emphasizing that a lot of the activity is going on there or being started there. [EMPHASIS] ❑ This area has long been a hotbed of militant activity.

hot-blooded ADJ [usu ADJ n] If you describe someone as **hot-blooded**, you mean that they are very quick to express their emotions, especially anger and love. ❑ Both of these dancers knew why they attracted the attentions of two hot-blooded young men.

hot but|ton (hot buttons) N-COUNT [oft N n] A **hot button** is a subject or problem that people have very strong feelings about. [mainly AM, JOURNALISM] ❑ Abortion is still one of the hot button issues of U.S. life.

hotch-potch /hɒtʃ pɒtʃ/ [BRIT] → see hodgepodge

hot-desk (hot-desks, hot-desking, hot-desked) V-I If employees **hot-desk**, they are not assigned particular desks and work at any desk that is available. [BUSINESS] ❑ Some employees will have to hot-desk until more accommodation can be found. ● **hot-desking** N-UNCOUNT ❑ I think that very few employees prefer hot-desking to having a fixed desk.

hot dog (hot dogs) N-COUNT A **hot dog** is a long bun with a hot sausage inside it. You can also use **hot dog** to refer to the sausage inside the bun.

ho|tel ✦✦◊ /hoʊtel/ (hotels) **1** N-COUNT A **hotel** is a building where people stay, for example on vacation, paying for their rooms and meals. **2** → See feature box at **tourism**

COLLOCATIONS

hotel
NOUN **1**
noun + **hotel**: boutique, budget, luxury; airport, resort
adjective + **hotel**: exclusive, expensive, luxurious; five-star, four-star, three-star
verb + **hotel**: book; run

ho|tel|ier /oʊtelyeɪ/ (hoteliers) N-COUNT A **hotelier** is a person who owns or manages a hotel.

hot flash (hot flashes) N-COUNT A **hot flash** is a sudden hot feeling which women often experience at menopause. [AM]

hot flush (hot flushes) N-COUNT A **hot flush** is the same as a **hot flash**. [mainly BRIT]

hot|foot /hɒtfʊt/ (hotfoots, hotfooting, hotfooted) also **hot-foot** V-T If you **hotfoot** it somewhere, you go there in a hurry. [INFORMAL] ❑ ...a group of actors hotfooting it for the bar.

hot|head /hɒthed/ (hotheads) N-COUNT If you refer to someone as a **hothead**, you are criticizing them for acting too quickly, without thinking of the consequences. [DISAPPROVAL]

hot|headed /hɒthedɪd/ ADJ If you describe someone as **hotheaded**, you are criticizing them for acting too quickly, without thinking of the consequences. [DISAPPROVAL]

hot|house /hɒthaʊs/ (hothouses) **1** N-COUNT A **hothouse** is a heated building, usually made of glass, in which plants and flowers can be grown. **2** N-COUNT [oft N n, N of n] You can refer to a situation or place as a **hothouse** when there is intense activity, especially intellectual or emotional activity. ❑ ...the reputation of the college as a hothouse of novel ideas.

hot key (hot keys) N-COUNT A **hot key** is a key, or a combination of keys, on a computer keyboard that you can press in order to make something happen, without having to type the full instructions. [COMPUTING] ❑ All macros can be set to run when a hot key is pressed.

hot|line /hɒtlaɪn/ (hotlines) also **hot line** **1** N-COUNT A **hotline** is a telephone line that the public can use to contact an organization about a particular subject. Hotlines allow people to obtain information from an organization or to give the organization information. ❑ ...a telephone hotline for gardeners seeking advice. **2** N-COUNT A **hotline** is a special, direct telephone line between the heads of government in different countries. ❑ They have discussed setting up a military hotline between Hanoi and Bangkok.

hot link (hot links) N-COUNT A **hot link** is a word or phrase in a hypertext document that can be selected in order to access additional information. [COMPUTING] ❑ *Each of these pages has hot links to other documents throughout the network.*

hot|ly /hɒtli/ **1** ADV [ADV with v] If people discuss, argue, or say something **hotly**, they speak in a lively or angry way, because they feel strongly. ❑ *The bank hotly denies any wrongdoing.* **2** ADV [ADV with v] If you are being **hotly** pursued, someone is trying hard to catch you and is close behind you. ❑ *He'd snuck out of the U.S. hotly pursued by the CIA.*

hot pants N-PLURAL [also *a pair of* N] **Hot pants** are very brief, tight shorts, worn by women. ❑ *...a couple of long-legged models in hot pants.*

hot|plate /hɒtpleɪt/ (hotplates) N-COUNT A **hotplate** is a portable device that you use for cooking food or keeping it warm.

hot po|ta|to (hot potatoes) N-COUNT If you describe a problem or issue as a **hot potato**, you mean that it is very difficult and nobody wants to deal with it. [INFORMAL]

hot rod (hot rods) N-COUNT A **hot rod** is a fast car used for racing, especially an old car fitted with a new engine. [INFORMAL]

hot seat PHRASE [usu *in/into* PHR] If you are in **the hot seat**, you are responsible for making important and difficult decisions. [INFORMAL] ❑ *He is to remain in the hot seat as chief executive.*

hot|shot /hɒtʃɒt/ (hotshots) N-COUNT [oft N n] If you refer to someone as a **hotshot**, you mean they are very good at a particular job and are going to be very successful. ❑ *...a bunch of corporate hotshots.*

hot spot (hot spots) also **hotspot 1** N-COUNT You can refer to an exciting place where there is a lot of activity or entertainment as a **hot spot**. [INFORMAL] ❑ *...a popular and lively package tour hotspot.* **2** N-COUNT You can refer to an area where there is fighting or serious political trouble as a **hot spot**. [JOURNALISM] ❑ *There were many hot spots in the region, where fighting had been going on.*

hot stuff N-UNCOUNT If you think that someone or something is **hot stuff**, you find them exciting or sexually attractive. [INFORMAL] ❑ *His love letters were hot stuff, apparently.*

hot take (hot takes) N-COUNT A **hot take** is a piece of journalism or other writing in which someone gives their opinion very forcefully, but does not give any evidence for that opinion. [INFORMAL] ❑ *Several reviewers took to the keyboards to express in a series of hot takes just how upset they were.*

hot-tempered ADJ If you describe someone as **hot-tempered**, you think they get angry very quickly and easily.

hot tub (hot tubs) N-COUNT A **hot tub** is a very large, round bath which several people can sit in together.

hot-water bot|tle (hot-water bottles) also **hot water bottle** N-COUNT A **hot-water bottle** is a rubber container that you fill with hot water and put in a bed to make it warm.

hot-wire (hot-wires, hot-wiring, hot-wired) V-T If someone, especially a thief, **hot-wires** a car, they start its engine using a piece of wire rather than the key. ❑ *A youth was inside the car, attempting to hot-wire it.*

hou|mous /hʊməs/ → see hummus

hound /haʊnd/ (hounds, hounding, hounded) **1** N-COUNT A **hound** is a type of dog that is often used for hunting or racing. ❑ *His chief interest in life is hunting with hounds.* **2** V-T If someone **hounds** you, they constantly disturb or speak to you in an annoying or upsetting way. ❑ *Newcomers are constantly hounding them for advice.* **3** V-T [usu passive] If someone **is hounded** out of a job or place, they are forced to leave it, often because other people are constantly criticizing them. ❑ *There is a general view around that he has been hounded out of office by the press.*

hour ♦♦♦ /aʊər/ (hours) **1** N-COUNT An **hour** is a period of sixty minutes. ❑ *They waited for about two hours.* ❑ *I only slept about half an hour that night.* **2** N-PLURAL People say that something takes or lasts **hours** to emphasize that it takes or lasts a very long time, or what seems like a very long time. [EMPHASIS] ❑ *Getting there would take hours.* **3** N-SING A clock that strikes **the hour** strikes when it is exactly one o'clock, two o'clock, and so on. ❑ *She'd heard a clock somewhere strike the hour as she'd slipped from her room.* **4** N-SING You can refer to a particular time or moment as a particular **hour**. [LITERARY] ❑ *His father lay ill, feverish and troubled as the hour of the birth approached.* **5** N-COUNT If you refer, for example, to someone's **hour** of need or **hour** of happiness, you are referring to the time in their life when they are or were experiencing that condition or feeling. [LITERARY] ❑ *He recalled her devotion to her husband during his hour of need.* **6** N-PLURAL You can refer to the period of time during which something happens or operates each day as the **hours** during which it happens or operates. ❑ *...the hours of darkness.* ❑ *Phone us on this number during office hours.* **7** N-PLURAL If you refer to the **hours** involved in a job, you are talking about how long you spend each week doing it and when you do it. ❑ *I worked quite irregular hours.* **8** → see also **rush hour 9** PHRASE If you do something **after hours**, you do it outside normal business hours or the time when you are usually at work. ❑ *...a local restaurant where steel workers unwind after hours.* **10** PHRASE If you say that something happens **at all hours** of the day or night, you disapprove of it happening at the time that it does or as often as it does. [DISAPPROVAL] ❑ *She didn't want her fourteen-year-old daughter coming home at all hours of the morning.* **11** PHRASE If something happens **in the early hours**, **in the small hours**, or **in the wee hours**, it happens in the early morning after midnight. ❑ *Gibbs was arrested in the early hours of yesterday morning.* **12** PHRASE If something happens **on the hour**, it happens every hour at, for example, nine o'clock, ten o'clock, and so on, and not at any number of minutes past an hour. ❑ *During this war in the Persian Gulf, NPR will have newscasts every hour on the hour.*

hour|glass /aʊərɡlæs/ (hourglasses) also **hour glass 1** N-COUNT An **hourglass** is a device that was used to measure the passing of an hour. It has two round glass sections linked by a narrow channel, and contains sand which takes an hour to flow from the top section into the lower one. **2** → See also color supplement

hour|ly /aʊərli/ **1** ADJ [ADJ n] An **hourly** event happens once every hour. ❑ *He flipped on the radio to get the hourly news broadcast.* • ADV [ADV after v] **Hourly** is also an adverb. ❑ *The hospital issued press releases hourly.* **2** ADJ [ADJ n] Your **hourly** earnings are the money that you earn in one hour. ❑ *They have little prospect of finding new jobs with the same hourly pay.*

house ♦♦♦ (houses, housing, housed)

> The noun and adjective are pronounced /haʊs/. The verb is pronounced /haʊz/. The form **houses** is pronounced /haʊzɪz/.

1 N-COUNT A **house** is a building in which people live, usually the people belonging to one family. ❑ *She has moved to a small house and is living off her meager savings.* **2** N-SING You can refer to all the people who live together in a house as the **house**. ❑ *If he set his alarm clock for midnight, it would wake the whole house.* **3** N-COUNT **House** is used in the names of types of places where people go to eat and drink. ❑ *...a steak house.* **4** N-COUNT **House** is used in the names of types of companies, especially ones which publish books, lend money, or design clothes. ❑ *Many of the clothes come from the world's top fashion houses.* **5** N-COUNT You can refer to one of the two bodies of the U.S. Congress as a **House**. The House of Representatives is sometimes referred to as the **House**. ❑ *Some members of the House and Senate worked all day yesterday.* **6** ADJ [ADJ n] A restaurant's **house** wine is the cheapest wine it sells, which is not listed by name on the wine list. ❑ *Tweed ordered a carafe of the house wine.* **7** V-T To **house** someone means to provide a house or apartment for them to live in. ❑ *...homes that house up to nine people.* **8** V-T [no cont] A building or container that **houses** something is the place where it is located or from where it operates. ❑ *The building is open to the public and houses a museum of motorcycles and cars.* **9** V-T [no cont] If you say that a building **houses** a number of people, you mean that is the place where they live or where they are staying. ❑ *The building will house twelve boys and eight girls.* **10** → see also **clearinghouse, White House 11** PHRASE If a person or their performance or speech **brings the house down**, the audience claps, laughs, or shouts loudly because the performance or speech is very impressive or amusing. [INFORMAL] ❑ *It's really an amazing dance. It just always brings the house down.* **12** PHRASE If two people **get on like a house on fire**, they quickly become close friends, for example because they have many interests in common. [INFORMAL] ❑ *I went over and struck up a conversation, and we got on like a house on fire.* **13** PHRASE If you are given something in a restaurant or bar **on the house**, you do not have to pay for it.

The owner knew about the engagement and brought them glasses of champagne on the house. **14** PHRASE If someone **gets** their **house in order**, **puts** their **house in order**, or **sets** their **house in order**, they arrange their affairs and solve their problems. ❑ He's got his house in order and made some tremendous decisions. **15** → See feature box at **humor**

SYNONYMS

house
NOUN **1**
home: ...his home in Hampstead.
residence: ...hotels and private residences.
dwelling: Some 3,500 new dwellings are planned for the area.
abode: I walked around the streets and found his new abode.

VOCABULARY IN CONTEXT

Types of houses

While some people dream of owning a **mansion** with huge **columns** framing the **doorway** and dozens of rooms inside, others are embracing the tiny house movement, building houses that are less than 46 square metres, and often **portable**.

Creating a tiny house requires some ingenuity. Beds are usually up on a **mezzanine** level or in the **loft**, and all the space is used. Even the **staircase** has pull-out drawers for **storage**. Windows and **skylights** help to give the impression of more space, while wooden **shutters** can provide privacy.

Need a little more space? You can put decking on a flat roof to make a garden, or use the space outdoors to add a **porch**.

Still need persuading? Most tiny-house **dwellers** have no **mortgage** at all.

USAGE

house or **home?**
You don't usually say 'I am going to my house' or 'She was in her house.' You say 'I am going **home**' or 'She was at **home**.' I'll finish the report **at home**.

house ar|rest N-UNCOUNT If someone is under **house arrest**, they are officially ordered not to leave their home, because they are suspected of being involved in an illegal activity. ❑ The main opposition leaders had been arrested or placed under house arrest.

house|boat /haʊsboʊt/ (houseboats) **1** N-COUNT A **houseboat** is a small boat on a river or canal which people live in. **2** → See also color supplement

house|bound /haʊsbaʊnd/ ADJ [usu v-link ADJ] Someone who is **housebound** is unable to go out of their house, usually because they are ill or cannot walk far. ❑ He just hates being housebound.

house|boy /haʊsbɔɪ/ (houseboys) N-COUNT A **houseboy** is a man or boy who cleans and does other jobs in someone else's house. [OLD-FASHIONED]

house|break|er /haʊsbreɪkər/ (housebreakers) N-COUNT A **housebreaker** is someone who enters another person's house by force, for example by breaking the locks or windows, in order to steal their possessions.

house|break|ing /haʊsbreɪkɪŋ/ N-UNCOUNT **Housebreaking** is the crime of entering another person's house by force, for example by breaking the locks or windows, in order to steal their possessions.

house|coat /haʊskoʊt/ (housecoats) N-COUNT A **housecoat** is a long loose piece of clothing that some women wear over their underwear or nightclothes when they are at home during the day.

house|guest /haʊsgest/ (houseguests) N-COUNT A **houseguest** is a person who is staying at someone's house for a period of time.

house|hold ✦◇◇ /haʊshoʊld/ (households) **1** N-COUNT A **household** is all the people in a family or group who live together in a house. ❑ ...growing up in a male-only household. **2** N-SING The **household** is your home and everything that is connected with taking care of it. ❑ ...household chores. **3** ADJ [ADJ n] Someone or something that is a **household** name or word is very well known. ❑ Today, fashion designers are household names.

VOCABULARY IN CONTEXT

Household items

Ever wondered just who first came up with the idea for all those everyday **household** items? Some, like **brooms** or **tweezers**, have been around so long that no-one knows, but for others, the inventor was known, but their names have now been almost forgotten. For example, the **mop** was invented by Manuel Jalón Corominas as recently as the 1950s, and the **toaster** was first dreamt up by Charles Strite in 1919.

Did you know that the **ironing board** was invented by African-American inventor Sarah Boone? Another female inventor, Josephine Cochrane, designed and engineered the first dishwasher, another **appliance** that most of us now couldn't live without.

It's not clear exactly when the **sieve** was invented – probably several thousand years ago – but we do know that the **grater** was invented by Francois Bouillier in the 1540s, and the first **can opener** was designed by Ezra Warner in 1858 (almost 50 years after the tin can was invented).

We may not be familiar with these inventors, but their **devices** certainly make our lives easier.

house|holder /haʊshoʊldər/ (householders) N-COUNT The **householder** is the person who owns or rents a particular house. ❑ Officials appealed to householders to open their homes to the thousands of persons made homeless by the storm.

house|husband /haʊshʌzbənd/ (househusbands) also **house husband** N-COUNT A **househusband** is a man who does not have a paid job, but instead takes care of his home and children.

house|keeper /haʊskiːpər/ (housekeepers) N-COUNT A **housekeeper** is a person whose job is to cook, clean, and take care of a house for its owner.

house|keeping /ha͞uskēpiNG/ N-UNCOUNT **Housekeeping** is the work and organization involved in running a home, including the shopping and cleaning. ❏ *I thought that cooking and housekeeping were unimportant, easy tasks.*

house|lights /ha͞uslīts/ N-PLURAL [the N] In a theater, when the **houselights** dim or go down, the lights where the audience sits are switched off. When the **houselights** come up, the lights are switched on.

house|maid /ha͞usmād/ (housemaids) N-COUNT A **housemaid** is a female servant who does cleaning and other work in someone's house.

house|man /ha͞usmən/ (housemen) ▮ N-COUNT A **houseman** is a doctor who has a junior post in a hospital and usually sleeps there. [BRIT, OLD-FASHIONED] ❷ N-COUNT A **houseman** is a man who is a servant in a house. [AM]

house|mate /ha͞usmāt/ (housemates) N-COUNT [usu poss N] Your **housemate** is someone who shares a house with you. You do not use 'housemate' to refer to members of your family or your boyfriend or girlfriend.

house of cards N-SING [usu a N] If you say that a system, organization, or plan is a **house of cards**, you mean that it is likely to fail or collapse. ❏ *The film is a house of cards. If one scene fails to hold, the entire credibility of the film comes crashing down.*

house of God (houses of God) N-COUNT A Christian church is sometimes referred to as a **house of God**.

House of Rep|re|senta|tives N-PROPER The House of Representatives is the larger of the two parts of Congress in the United States, or the equivalent part of the system of government in some other countries. ❏ *The House of Representatives approved a new budget.*

house own|er (house owners) also **house-owner** N-COUNT A **house owner** is a person who owns a house.

house par|ty (house parties) N-COUNT A **house party** is a party held at a big house in the country, usually on a weekend, where the guests stay for a few days.

house plant (house plants) also **houseplant** N-COUNT A **house plant** is a plant which is grown in a pot indoors.

house-sit (house-sits, house-sitting, house-sat) V-I If someone **house-sits** for you, they stay at your house and look after it while you are away. ❏ *Otherwise I might just have gone straight back to Connecticut, where Will was house-sitting for me.*

house-to-house also **house to house** ADJ [ADJ n] A **house-to-house** activity involves going to all the houses in an area one after another. ❏ *Security officers have carried out a number of house-to-house searches.* • ADV [ADV after v] **House-to-house** is also an adverb. ❏ *They're going house to house, rounding up the residents.*

house|wares /ha͞uswe(ə)rz/ N-PLURAL Some stores and manufacturers refer to objects on sale for use in your house as **housewares**, especially objects related to cooking and cleaning.

house|warm|ing /ha͞uswôrmiNG/ (housewarmings) N-COUNT [oft N n] A **housewarming** is a party that you give for friends when you have just moved to a new house. ❏ *I'm so sorry I missed the housewarming.* ❏ *...a housewarming party.*

house|wife /ha͞uswīf/ (housewives) N-COUNT A **housewife** is a married woman who does not have a paid job, but instead takes care of her home and children. ❏ *Married at nineteen, she was a traditional housewife and mother of four children.*

house|work /ha͞uswûrk/ N-UNCOUNT **Housework** is the work such as cleaning, washing, and ironing that you do in your home. ❏ *Men are doing more housework nowadays.*

hous|ing ✦✧✧ /ha͞uziNG/ ▮ N-UNCOUNT You refer to the buildings in which people live as **housing** when you are talking about their standard, price, or availability. ❏ *...a shortage of affordable housing.* ❷ → See feature box at **banking, poverty, town**

SYNONYMS

housing
NOUN
accommodation: *The government will provide temporary accommodation for up to three thousand people.*
homes: *...the allocation of land for new homes.*
dwellings: *Some 3,500 new dwellings are planned for the area.*

VOCABULARY IN CONTEXT

Housework

According to research, couples spend 40 minutes a day arguing over household **chores**. Leaving clothes **strewn** on the floor causes the most arguments, closely followed by the correct way to **load the dishwasher**. As well as arguing about who does the dishes, couples also disagree about whether it is necessary to **rinse** the soap off the plates.

Most people don't mind **dusting** and **polishing**, but many couples argue about who does the heavier work of **vacuuming**.

Hiding or covering up spills and **stains** rather than immediately **scrubbing** them clean is something which infuriates many of us. And putting off small jobs like changing light bulbs or fixing household **appliances** also drives us crazy.

hous|ing de|vel|op|ment (housing developments) N-COUNT A **housing development** is a large number of houses or apartments built close together at the same time.

hous|ing proj|ect (housing projects) N-COUNT A **housing project** is a group of homes for poorer families which is funded and controlled by the local government. [AM]

hov|el /hŭvəl/ (hovels) ▮ N-COUNT A **hovel** is a small hut, especially one which is dirty or needs a lot of repair. ❏ *They lived in a squalid hovel for the next five years.* ❷ N-COUNT You can describe a house, room, or apartment as a **hovel** to express your disapproval or dislike of it because it is dirty, untidy, and in poor condition. [DISAPPROVAL] ❏ *The room I was given was a hovel.*

hov|er /hŭvər/ (hovers, hovering, hovered) ▮ V-I To **hover** means to stay in the same position in the air without moving forward or backward. Many birds and insects can hover by moving their wings very quickly. ❏ *Beautiful butterflies hovered above the wild flowers.* ❷ V-I If you **hover**, you stay in one place and move slightly in a nervous way, for example because you cannot decide what to do. ❏ *Judith was hovering in the doorway.* ❸ V-I If you **hover**, you are in an uncertain situation or state of mind. ❏ *She hovered on the brink of death for three months as doctors battled to save her.* ❹ V-I If something such as a price, value, or score **hovers** around a particular level, it stays at more or less that level and does not change much. ❏ *In September 1989 the exchange rate hovered around 140 yen to the dollar.*

hover|craft /hŭvərkraft/ (hovercraft) N-COUNT [also by N] A **hovercraft** is a vehicle that can travel across land and water. It floats above the land or water on a cushion of air. ❏ *Traveling at speeds of up to thirty five knots, these hovercraft can easily outpace most boats.*

how ✦✦✦ /ha͞u/

The conjunction is pronounced /ha͞u/.

▮ QUEST You use **how** to ask about the way in which something happens or is done. ❏ *How do I make payments into my account?* ❏ *How do you manage to keep the place so neat?* • CONJ **How** is also a conjunction. ❏ *I don't want to know how he died.* ❷ CONJ You use **how** after certain adjectives and verbs to introduce a statement or fact, often something that you remember or expect other people to know about. ❏ *It's amazing how people collect so much stuff over the years.* ❏ *It's funny how I never seem to get a thing done on my day off.* ❸ QUEST You use **how** to ask questions about the quantity or degree of something. ❏ *How much money are we talking about?* ❏ *How many full-time staff have we got?* ❏ *How long will you be staying?* ❏ *How old is your son now?* ❹ QUEST You use **how** when you are asking someone whether something was successful or enjoyable. ❏ *How was your trip down to Orlando?* ❏ *How did your date go?* ❺ QUEST You use **how** to ask about someone's health or to find out someone's news. ❏ *Hi! How are you doing?* ❏ *How's Rosie?* ❻ ADV [ADV adj/adv] You use **how** to emphasize the degree to which something is true. [EMPHASIS] ❏ *I didn't realize how heavy that bag was going to be.* ❼ ADV [ADV adj/adv/cl] You use **how** in exclamations to emphasize an adjective, adverb, or statement. [EMPHASIS] ❏ *How strange that something so simple as a walk on the beach could suddenly mean so much.* ❽ QUEST [QUEST can/could] You use **how** in expressions such as '**How can you...**' and '**How could you...**' to indicate that you disapprove of what someone has done or that you find it hard to believe. [DISAPPROVAL] ❏ *How can you drink so much beer, Luke?* ❾ QUEST You use **how** in expressions such as '**How about...**' or '**How would you like...**' when you are making an offer or a suggestion. ❏ *How about a cup of coffee?* ❿ CONVENTION If you ask someone '**How about you?**' you are asking them what they think or want. ❏ *Well, I enjoyed that. How about you two?* ⓫ PHRASE You use **how about** to introduce a new subject which you think is relevant to the conversation you have been having. ❏ *Are your products and services competitive? How about marketing?* ⓬ PHRASE You ask '**How come?**' or '**How so?**' when you are surprised by something and are asking why it happened or was said. [INFORMAL] ❏ *"They don't say a single word to each other."—"How come?"*

USAGE

how
Don't use 'how' to ask what kind of person someone is. For example, if you are asking someone what kind of boss they have, don't say 'How is your boss?' Say '**What** is your boss **like?**' *What's his mother **like**?*

how|dy /haʊdi/ CONVENTION '**Howdy**' is an informal way of saying 'Hello.' [AM, DIALECT, FORMULAE]
how|ever ♦♦♦ /haʊevər/ ❶ ADV [ADV with cl] You use **however** when you are adding a comment which is surprising or which contrasts with what has just been said. ❏ *This was not an easy decision. It is, however, a decision that we feel is dictated by our duty.* ❷ ADV You use **however** before an adjective or adverb to emphasize that the degree or extent of something cannot change a situation. [EMPHASIS] ❏ *You should always strive to achieve more, however well you have done before.* ❏ *However hard she tried, nothing seemed to work.* ❸ CONJ You use **however** when you want to say that it makes no difference how something is done. ❏ *However we adopt healthcare reform, it isn't going to save major amounts of money.* ❹ ADV You use **however** in expressions such as **or however long it takes** and **or however many there were** to indicate that the figure you have just mentioned may not be accurate. [VAGUENESS] ❏ *Wait 30 to 60 minutes or however long it takes.* ❺ QUEST You can use **however** to ask in an emphatic way how something has happened which you are very surprised about. Some speakers of English think that this form is incorrect and prefer to use 'how ever.' [EMPHASIS] ❏ *However did you find this place in such weather?*

SYNONYMS

however
ADV ❶
nevertheless: *One in three marriages fail. Nevertheless, people continue to get married.*
still: *I'm average for my height. But, I still feel fat.*
yet: *It is completely waterproof, yet light and comfortable.*

how|itz|er /haʊtsər/ (**howitzers**) N-COUNT A **howitzer** is a large gun with a short barrel, which fires shells high up into the air so that they will drop down onto the target.
howl /haʊl/ (**howls, howling, howled**) ❶ V-I If an animal such as a wolf or a dog **howls**, it makes a long, loud, crying sound. ❏ *Somewhere a dog suddenly howled, baying at the moon.* • N-COUNT **Howl** is also a noun. ❏ *The dog let out a savage howl and, wheeling round, flew at him.* ❷ V-I If a person **howls**, they make a long, loud cry expressing pain, anger, or unhappiness. ❏ *He howled like a wounded animal as blood spurted from the gash.* • N-COUNT **Howl** is also a noun. ❏ *With a howl of rage, he grabbed the neck of a broken bottle and advanced.* ❸ V-I When the wind **howls**, it blows hard and makes a loud noise. ❏ *The wind howled all night, but I slept a little.* ❹ V-T If you **howl** something, you say it in a very loud voice. [INFORMAL] ❏ *"Get away, get away, get away!" he howled.* ❺ V-I If you **howl** with laughter, you laugh very loudly. ❏ *Joe, Pink, and Booker howled with delight.* • N-COUNT **Howl** is also a noun. ❏ *His stories caused howls of laughter.* ❻ → See feature box at **humor, onomatopoeia**
howl|er /haʊlər/ (**howlers**) N-COUNT A **howler** is a stupid mistake. [INFORMAL] ❏ *I felt as if I had made an outrageous howler.*
how-to ADJ [ADJ n] A **how-to** book provides instructions on how to do or make a particular thing, especially something that you do or make as a hobby. ❏ *...a simple how-to book that explains each step in taking a photo.*
hp /eɪtʃ piː/ **hp** is an abbreviation for **horsepower**.
HP /eɪtʃ piː/ N-UNCOUNT [oft on N] **HP** is an abbreviation for **hire purchase**. [BRIT] ❏ *I have never bought anything on HP.*
HQ /eɪtʃ kjuː/ (**HQs**) N-VAR **HQ** is an abbreviation for **headquarters**. ❏ *The regimental HQ is a tiny office manned by two retired officers.*
hr (**hrs**) **hr** is a written abbreviation for **hour**. ❏ *Let this cook on low for another 1 hr 15 mins.*
HR /eɪtʃ ɑːr/ N-UNCOUNT In a company or other organization, the **HR** department is the department with responsibility for the recruiting, training, and welfare of the staff. **HR** is an abbreviation for **human resources**. [BUSINESS]
HRT /eɪtʃ ɑːr tiː/ N-UNCOUNT **HRT** is given to women and involves taking the hormone estrogen, usually in order to control the symptoms of menopause. **HRT** is an abbreviation for **hormone replacement therapy**.
HTML /eɪtʃ tiː ɛm ɛl/ N-UNCOUNT **HTML** is a system of codes for producing documents for the internet. **HTML** is an abbreviation for 'hypertext markup language.' [COMPUTING] ❏ *...HTML documents.*
HTTP /eɪtʃ tiː tiː piː/ N-UNCOUNT **HTTP** is a way of formatting and transmitting messages on the internet. **HTTP** is an abbreviation for 'hypertext transfer protocol.' [COMPUTING]
hub /hʌb/ (**hubs**) ❶ N-COUNT You can describe a place as a **hub** of an activity when it is a very important center for that activity. ❏ *The island's social hub is the Cafe Sport.* ❷ N-COUNT The **hub** of a wheel is the part at the center. ❸ N-COUNT A **hub** or a **hub airport** is a large airport from which you can travel to many other airports. ❏ *...a campaign to secure Heathrow's place as Europe's main international hub.* ❹ → See also color supplement
hub|bub /hʌbʌb/ (**hubbubs**) ❶ N-VAR [oft N of n] A **hubbub** is a noise made by a lot of people all talking or shouting at the same time. [WRITTEN] ❏ *There was a hubbub of excited conversation from over a thousand people.* ❷ N-SING [also no det] You can describe a situation where there is great confusion or excitement as a **hubbub**. ❏ *In all the hubbub over the election, one might be excused for missing yesterday's announcement.*
hub|by /hʌbi/ (**hubbies**) N-COUNT [usu poss n] You can refer to someone's husband as their **hubby**. [INFORMAL, OLD-FASHIONED]
hub|cap /hʌbkæp/ (**hubcaps**) also **hub cap** ❶ N-COUNT A **hubcap** is a metal or plastic disk that covers and protects the center of a wheel on a car, truck, or other vehicle. ❷ → See also color supplement
hu|bris /hjuːbrɪs/ N-UNCOUNT If you accuse someone of **hubris**, you are accusing them of arrogant pride. [FORMAL] ❏ *...a tale of how an honorable man pursuing honorable goals was afflicted with hubris and led his nation toward catastrophe.*
huck|ster /hʌkstər/ (**hucksters**) N-COUNT If you refer to someone as a **huckster**, you are criticizing them for trying to sell useless or worthless things in a dishonest or aggressive way. [AM, DISAPPROVAL]
hud|dle /hʌdəl/ (**huddles, huddling, huddled**) ❶ V-I If you **huddle** somewhere, you sit, stand, or lie there holding your arms and legs close to your body, usually because you are cold or frightened. ❏ *Mr. Pell huddled in a corner with his notebook on his*

hue knees. **2** V-I If people **huddle** together or **huddle** around something, they stand, sit, or lie close to each other, usually because they all feel cold or frightened. ☐ *Tired and lost, we huddled together.* **3** V-RECIP If people **huddle** in a group, they gather together to discuss something quietly or secretly. ☐ *Off to one side, Sticht, Macomber, Jordan, and Kreps huddled to discuss something.* ☐ *The president has been huddling with his most senior aides.* **4** N-COUNT A **huddle** is a small group of people or things that are standing very close together or lying on top of each other, usually in a disorganized way. ☐ *We lay there: a huddle of bodies, gasping for air.*

hue /hyu/ (hues) **1** N-COUNT A **hue** is a color. [LITERARY] ☐ *The same hue will look different in different light.* **2** PHRASE If people raise a **hue and cry** about something, they protest angrily about it. [WRITTEN] ☐ *Just as the show ended, he heard a huge hue and cry outside.*

huff /hʌf/ (huffs, huffing, huffed) **1** V-T If you **huff**, you indicate that you are annoyed or offended about something, usually by the way that you say something. ☐ *"This," he huffed, "was discrimination."* **2** PHRASE If someone is **in a huff**, they are behaving in a bad-tempered way because they are annoyed and offended. [INFORMAL] ☐ *He was so disappointed that he drove off in a huff.*

huffy /hʌfi/ ADJ Someone who is **huffy** is obviously annoyed or offended about something. [INFORMAL] ☐ *I became embarrassed and huffy and told her to take the money back.* • **huffi|ly** /hʌfɪli/ ADV [ADV with v] ☐ *"I appreciate your concern for my feelings," Bess said huffily, "but I'm a big girl now."*

hug /hʌg/ (hugs, hugging, hugged) **1** V-RECIP When you **hug** someone, you put your arms around them and hold them tightly, for example because you like them or are pleased to see them. You can also say that two people **hug** each other or that they **hug**. ☐ *She had hugged him exuberantly and invited him to dinner the next day.* • N-COUNT **Hug** is also a noun. ☐ *She leapt out of the back seat, and gave him a hug.* **2** V-T If you **hug** something, you hold it close to your body with your arms tightly around it. ☐ *Shaerl trudged toward them, hugging a large box.* **3** V-T Something that **hugs** the ground or a stretch of land or water stays very close to it. [WRITTEN] ☐ *The road hugs the coast for hundreds of miles.*

huge ♦♦◊ /hyudʒ/ (huger, hugest) **1** ADJ Something or someone that is **huge** is extremely large in size. ☐ *...a tiny little woman with huge black glasses.* **2** ADJ Something that is **huge** is extremely large in amount or degree. ☐ *I have a huge number of ties because I never throw them away.* • **huge|ly** ADV ☐ *In summer this hotel is a hugely popular venue for wedding receptions.* **3** ADJ Something that is **huge** exists or happens on a very large scale, and involves a lot of different people or things. ☐ *Another team is looking at the huge problem of debts between companies.*

-hugging /-hʌgɪŋ/ COMB IN ADJ [usu ADJ n] **-hugging** combines with nouns to form adjectives which describe an item of clothing that fits very tightly and clearly reveals the shape of your body. ☐ *...a figure-hugging dress.*

huh /hʌ, hʒ/ **Huh** is used in writing to represent a noise that people make at the end of a question if they want someone to agree with them or if they want someone to repeat or explain what they have just said. **Huh** is also used to show that someone is surprised or not impressed. ☐ *Can we just get on with it, huh?*

hula /hulə/ N-SING [oft N n] The **hula** is a dance from Hawaii, performed by women. ☐ *...a hula dancer.*

hulk /hʌlk/ (hulks) **1** N-COUNT [oft N of n] The **hulk** of something is the large, ruined remains of it. ☐ *...the ruined hulk of the old church tower.* **2** N-COUNT [usu with supp] You use **hulk** to describe anything which is large and seems threatening to you. ☐ *I followed his big hulk into the house.*

hulk|ing /hʌlkɪŋ/ ADJ [ADJ n] You use **hulking** to describe a person or object that is extremely large, heavy, or slow-moving, especially when they seem threatening in some way. ☐ *When I woke up there was a hulking figure staring down at me.*

hull /hʌl/ (hulls) N-COUNT The **hull** of a boat or tank is the main body of it. ☐ *The hull had suffered extensive damage to the starboard side.*

hul|la|ba|loo /hʌləbəlu/ N-SING A **hullabaloo** is a lot of noise or fuss made by people who are angry or excited about something. [INFORMAL] ☐ *I was scared by the hullabaloo over my arrival.*

hul|lo /hʌlou/ → see **hello**

hum /hʌm/ (hums, humming, hummed) **1** V-I If something **hums**, it makes a low continuous noise. ☐ *The birds sang, the bees hummed.* • N-SING **Hum** is also a noun. ☐ *...the hum of traffic.* **2** V-T/V-I When you **hum**, or **hum** a tune, you sing a tune with your lips closed. ☐ *She was humming a merry little tune.* **3** V-I If you say that a place **hums**, you mean that it is full of activity. ☐ *The place is really beginning to hum.*

hu|man ♦♦♦ /hyumən/ (humans) **1** ADJ [ADJ n] **Human** means relating to or concerning people. ☐ *...the human body.* **2** N-COUNT You can refer to people as **humans**, especially when you are comparing them with animals or machines. ☐ *Like humans, cats and dogs are omnivores.* **3** ADJ **Human** feelings, weaknesses, or errors are ones that are typical of humans rather than machines. ☐ *...an ever-growing risk of human error.* **4** → See feature box at **genetics**

SYNONYMS

human
ADJ **3**
fallible: *They are only human and all too fallible.*
imperfect: *Human beings are imperfect.*

---

hu|man be|ing (human beings) N-COUNT A **human being** is a human child or adult.

hu|mane /hyumeɪn/ **1** ADJ **Humane** people act in a kind, sympathetic way toward other people and animals, and try to do them as little harm as possible. ☐ *In the mid-nineteenth century, Dorothea Dix began to campaign for humane treatment of the mentally ill.* • **hu|mane|ly** ADV [ADV with v] ☐ *Suffering animals should be humanely euthanized on the farm.* **2** ADJ **Humane** values and societies encourage people to act in a kind and sympathetic way toward others, even toward people they do not agree with or like. ☐ *...the humane values of socialism.*

hu|man growth hor|mone (human growth hormones) N-VAR **Human growth hormone** is a hormone that is used to help short people, especially short children, to grow taller. The abbreviation **HGH** is also used.

hu|man in|ter|est N-UNCOUNT [oft N n] If something such as a news story has **human interest**, people are likely to find it interesting because it gives interesting details about the person or people involved. ☐ *...a human interest story.*

hu|man|ism /hyumənɪzəm/ N-UNCOUNT **Humanism** is the belief that people can achieve happiness and live well without religion. • **hu|man|ist** (humanists) N-COUNT ☐ *He is a practical humanist, who believes in the dignity of mankind.*

hu|man|is|tic /hyumənɪstɪk/ ADJ [usu ADJ n] A **humanistic** idea, condition, or practice relates to humanism. ☐ *Religious values can often differ greatly from humanistic morals.*

hu|mani|tar|ian /hyumænɪtɛəriən/ ADJ If a person or society has **humanitarian** ideas or behavior, they try to avoid making people suffer or they help people who are suffering. ☐ *Air bombardment raised criticism on the humanitarian grounds that innocent civilians might suffer.*

hu|mani|tari|an|ism /hyumænɪtɛəriənɪzəm/ N-UNCOUNT **Humanitarianism** is humanitarian ideas or actions.

hu|man|ity /hyumænɪti/ (humanities) **1** N-UNCOUNT All the people in the world can be referred to as **humanity**. ☐ *They face charges of committing crimes against humanity.* **2** N-UNCOUNT A person's **humanity** is their state of being a human being, rather than an animal or an object. [FORMAL] ☐ *He was under discussion and it made him feel deprived of his humanity.* **3** N-UNCOUNT **Humanity** is the quality of being kind, thoughtful, and sympathetic toward others. ☐ *Her speech showed great maturity and humanity.* **4** N-PLURAL The **humanities** are the subjects such as history, philosophy, and literature which are concerned with human ideas and behavior. ☐ *The number of students majoring in the humanities has declined by about half.*

hu|man|ize /hyumənaɪz/ (humanizes, humanizing, humanized)

in BRIT, also use **humanise**

V-T If you **humanize** a situation or condition, you improve it by changing it in a way which makes it more suitable and pleasant for people. ☐ *...an effort to humanize our buildings and public places.*

human|kind /hyˈumənkaɪnd/ N-UNCOUNT **Humankind** is the same as **mankind**.

hu|man|ly /hyˈumənli/ PHRASE If something is **humanly** possible, it is possible for people to do it. ❏ *She has gained a reputation for creating books as perfect as is humanly possible.*

hu|man na|ture N-UNCOUNT **Human nature** is the natural qualities and ways of behavior that most people have. ❏ *It seems to be human nature to worry.*

hu|man|oid /hyˈumənɔɪd/ (humanoids) **1** ADJ Something that is **humanoid** looks or acts like a human being, although it is not human. ❏ *...humanoid robots that could mimic a range of human activities.* **2** N-COUNT A **humanoid** is a nonhuman creature that looks or acts like a human being, for example, in science fiction. ❏ *...a spaceship whose only occupants are humanoids killed in mysterious circumstances.*

hu|man race N-SING The **human race** is the same as **mankind**. ❏ *Can the human race carry on expanding and growing the same way that it is now?*

hu|man re|sources N-UNCOUNT In a company or other organization, the department of **human resources** is the department with responsibility for the recruiting, training, and welfare of the staff. The abbreviation **HR** is often used. [BUSINESS] ❏ *...our head of human resources.*

hu|man rights ♦◇◇ N-PLURAL **Human rights** are basic rights which many societies believe that all people should have. ❏ *In the treaty both sides pledge to respect human rights.*

hu|man shield N-SING If a group of people are used as a **human shield** in a battle or war, they are put in a particular place so that the enemy will be unwilling to attack that place and harm them.

hum|ble /hʌmbᵊl/ (humbler, humblest, humbles, humbling, humbled) **1** ADJ A **humble** person is not proud and does not believe that they are better than other people. ❏ *He gave a great performance, but he was very humble.* • **hum|bly** ADV [ADV with v] ❏ *"I'm a lucky man, undeservedly lucky," he said humbly.* **2** ADJ People with low social status are sometimes described as **humble**. ❏ *He started his career as a humble fisherman.* **3** ADJ A **humble** place or thing is ordinary and not special in any way. ❏ *There are restaurants, both humble and expensive, that specialize in noodles.* **4** ADJ People use **humble** in a phrase such as **in my humble opinion** as a polite way of emphasizing what they think, even though they do not feel humble about it. [POLITENESS] ❏ *It is, in my humble opinion, perhaps the best steak restaurant in the city.* • **hum|bly** ADV [ADV before v] ❏ *So may I humbly suggest we all do something next time.* **5** PHRASE If you **eat humble pie**, you speak or behave in a way which tells people that you admit you were wrong about something. ❏ *Anson was forced to eat humble pie and publicly apologize to her.* **6** V-T If you **humble** someone who is more important or powerful than you, you defeat them easily. ❏ *...the team that humbled the league champions a week ago.* **7** V-T If something or someone **humbles** you, they make you realize that you are not as important or good as you thought you were. ❏ *Ted's words humbled me.* • **hum|bling** ADJ ❏ *Giving up an addiction is a humbling experience.*

hum|ble|brag /hʌmbᵊlbræɡ/ (humblebrags, humblebragging, humblebragged) VERB If you **humblebrag**, you say something or write something on the internet that appears to be modest or critical of yourself, but is actually a way of boasting about your own success. [INFORMAL, DISAPPROVAL] ❏ *"I don't know why they like my stupid book so much," he humblebrags.* • N-COUNT **Humblebrag** is also a noun. [INFORMAL, DISAPPROVAL] ❏ *It was one of those classic humblebrags about not having studied at all and then acing all your tests.*

hum|bug /hʌmbʌɡ/ N-UNCOUNT If you describe someone's language or behavior as **humbug**, you mean that it is dishonest or insincere. [DISAPPROVAL] ❏ *There was all the usual humbug and obligatory compliments from ministers.*

hum|ding|er /hʌmdɪŋər/ (humdingers) N-COUNT [usu sing, oft *a* N *of* n] If you describe someone or something as a **humdinger**, you mean that they are very impressive, exciting, or enjoyable. [INFORMAL, APPROVAL] ❏ *It should be a humdinger of a match.* ❏ *His latest novel is a humdinger.*

hum|drum /hʌmdrʌm/ ADJ If you describe someone or something as **humdrum**, you mean that they are ordinary, dull, or boring. [DISAPPROVAL] ❏ *...her lawyer husband, trapped in a humdrum but well-paid job.*

hu|mid /hyˈumɪd/ ADJ You use **humid** to describe an atmosphere or climate that is very damp, and usually very hot. ❏ *Visitors can expect hot and humid conditions.*

hu|midi|fi|er /hyuˈmɪdɪfaɪər/ (humidifiers) N-COUNT A **humidifier** is a machine for increasing the amount of moisture in the air.

hu|mid|ity /hyuˈmɪdɪti/ **1** N-UNCOUNT You say there is **humidity** when the air feels very heavy and damp. ❏ *The heat and humidity were insufferable.* **2** N-UNCOUNT **Humidity** is the amount of water in the air. ❏ *The humidity is relatively low.* **3** → See feature box at **weather**

hu|mili|ate /hyuˈmɪlieɪt/ (humiliates, humiliating, humiliated) V-T To **humiliate** someone means to say or do something which makes them feel ashamed or stupid. ❏ *She had been beaten and humiliated by her husband.* • **hu|mili|at|ed** ADJ ❏ *I have never felt so humiliated in my life.*

hu|mili|at|ing /hyuˈmɪlieɪtɪŋ/ ADJ If something is **humiliating**, it embarrasses you and makes you feel ashamed and stupid. ❏ *The Democrats have suffered a humiliating defeat.*

hu|milia|tion /hyuˌmɪlieɪʃᵊn/ (humiliations) **1** N-UNCOUNT **Humiliation** is the embarrassment and shame you feel when someone makes you appear stupid, or when you make a mistake in public. ❏ *She faced the humiliation of discussing her husband's affair.* **2** N-COUNT A **humiliation** is an occasion or a situation in which you feel embarrassed and ashamed. ❏ *The result is a humiliation for the president.*

hu|mil|ity /hyuˈmɪlɪti/ N-UNCOUNT Someone who has **humility** is not proud and does not believe they are better than other people. ❏ *...a deep sense of humility.*

humming|bird /hʌmɪŋbɜrd/ (hummingbirds) N-COUNT A **hummingbird** is a small brightly colored bird found in North, Central and South America. It has a long thin beak and narrow powerful wings that can move very fast.

hum|mock /hʌmək/ (hummocks) N-COUNT A **hummock** is a small raised area of ground, like a very small hill.

hum|mus /hʊməs/ also **houmous, houmous** N-UNCOUNT **Hummus** is a smooth food made from chickpeas which people usually eat with bread or vegetables.

hu|mong|ous /hyuˈmʌŋɡəs, -mʌn-/ also **humungous** ADJ If you describe something or someone as **humongous**, you are emphasizing that they are very large or important. [INFORMAL, EMPHASIS] ❏ *We had a humongous fight just because she left.* ❏ *She is such a humongous star.*

hu|mor ♦◇◇ /hyˈumər/ (humors, humoring, humored)

in BRIT, use **humour**

1 N-UNCOUNT You can refer to the amusing things that people say as their **humor**. ❏ *Her humor and determination were a source of inspiration to others.* **2** → see also **sense of humor** **3** N-UNCOUNT **Humor** is a quality in something that makes you laugh, for example in a situation, in someone's words or actions, or in a book or movie. ❏ *She felt sorry for the man but couldn't ignore the humor of the situation.* **4** N-VAR If you are in a good **humor**, you feel cheerful and happy, and are pleasant to people. If you are in a bad **humor**, you feel bad-tempered and unhappy, and are unpleasant to people. ❏ *Christina was still not clear why he had been in such ill humor.* **5** N-UNCOUNT If you do something with good **humor**, you do it cheerfully and pleasantly. ❏ *Hugo bore his illness with great courage and good humor.* **6** V-T If you **humor** someone who is behaving strangely, you try to please them or pretend to agree with them, so that they will not become upset. ❏ *She disliked Dido but was prepared to tolerate her for a weekend in order to humor her husband.* **7** → See also feature box on next page

---

COLLOCATIONS

humor
NOUN
1
noun + **humor**: gallows, schoolboy, slapstick, toilet
adjective + **humor**: black, dark, dry, wry; gentle, self-deprecating
4
adjective + **humor**: bad, good, ill

VOCABULARY IN CONTEXT

Humor

As our local **comedy festival** continues, we've reviewed some of the highlights. Hurry while tickets last!

Comedy troupe Ace, performing nightly, will **amuse** the entire family. As they unfold their series of **slapstick** sketches, you'll hear kids **giggle** and adults **guffaw**. Their act is **farcical**, and we guarantee you'll find it **funny**.

Newcomer and rising star Dilly Disco is a **stand-up comedian** who **brings the house down** every night. Her unique brand of **irony** and ability to **improvise** may not appeal to everyone, but if you appreciate a **dry sense of humor**, you'll find it **side-splitting**. Dilly is sure to become a regular on the **comedy circuit**.

Comedy duo Gavvo & Savvo are back with a show that will make you **howl with laughter**. Building on last year's success, they've refined their **jokes** with **hilarious** results. The **punchlines** are **witty** and memorable. They're our top pick for **quips** and **puns**.

hu|mor|ist /hyu̱mərɪst/ (humorists) N-COUNT A **humorist** is a writer who specializes in writing amusing things. ❑ ...a political humorist.

hu|mor|less /hyu̱mərlɪs/
in BRIT, use **humourless**
ADJ If you accuse someone of being **humorless**, you mean that they are very serious about everything and do not find things amusing. [DISAPPROVAL] ❑ He was stubborn, humorless and ruthlessly ambitious.

hu|mor|ous /hyu̱mərəs/ ADJ If someone or something is **humorous**, they are amusing, especially in a clever or witty way. ❑ He was quite humorous, and I liked that about him. • **hu|mor|ous|ly** ADV ❑ He looked at me humorously as he wrestled with the door.

hu|mour /hyu̱mər/ [BRIT] → see **humor**

hump /hʌ̱mp/ (humps) **1** N-COUNT A **hump** is a small hill or raised area. ❑ The path goes over a large hump by a tree before running near a road. **2** N-COUNT A camel's **hump** is the large lump on its back. ❑ Camels rebuild fat stores in their hump. **3** PHRASE [v-link PHR] If you are **over the hump** in an unpleasant or difficult situation, you are past the worst part of it. ❑ It has been a traumatic week, but they are over the hump.

hump|back /hʌ̱mpbæk/ (humpbacks) N-COUNT A **humpback** or a **humpback whale** is a large whale with a curved back.

humped /hʌ̱mpt/ ADJ If someone is **humped**, their back is bent so that their shoulders are further forward than usual and their head hangs down. ❑ I was humped like an old lady.

hu|mung|ous /hyumʌ̱ŋgəs/ → see **humongous**

hu|mus /hyu̱məs/ N-UNCOUNT **Humus** is the part of soil which consists of dead plants that have begun to decay.

hunch /hʌ̱ntʃ/ (hunches, hunching, hunched) **1** N-COUNT If you have a **hunch** about something, you are sure that it is correct or true, even though you do not have any proof. [INFORMAL] ❑ I had a hunch that Susan and I would work well together.
2 V-I If you **hunch** forward, you raise your shoulders, put your head down, and lean forward, often because you are cold, ill, or unhappy. ❑ He got out his map and hunched over it to read the small print. **3** V-T If you **hunch** your shoulders, you raise them and lean forward slightly. ❑ Wes hunched his shoulders and leaned forward on the edge of the counter.

hunch|back /hʌ̱ntʃbæk/ (hunchbacks) N-COUNT A **hunchback** is someone who has a large lump on their back because their spine is curved. [OFFENSIVE, OLD-FASHIONED]

hunched /hʌ̱ntʃt/ ADJ If you are **hunched**, or **hunched up**, you are leaning forward with your shoulders raised and your head down, often because you are cold, ill, or unhappy. ❑ A solitary hunched figure emerged from the house.

hun|dred ♦♦♦ /hʌ̱ndrɪd/ (hundreds)

The plural form is **hundred** after a number, or after a word or expression referring to a number, such as 'several' or 'a few.'

1 NUM A **hundred** or one **hundred** is the number 100. ❑ According to one official more than a hundred people have been arrested. **2** QUANT [QUANT of pl-n] If you refer to **hundreds of** things or people, you are emphasizing that there are very many of them. [EMPHASIS] ❑ Hundreds of tree species face extinction. • PRON You can also use **hundreds** as a pronoun. ❑ Hundreds have been killed in the fighting and thousands made homeless. **3** PHRASE You can use **a hundred percent** or **one hundred percent** to emphasize that you agree completely with something or that it is completely right or wrong. [INFORMAL, EMPHASIS] ❑ Are you a hundred percent sure it's your neighbor?

hun|dredth ♦♦◊ /hʌ̱ndrɪdθ/ (hundredths) **1** ORD The **hundredth** item in a series is the one that you count as number one hundred. ❑ The bank celebrates its hundredth anniversary in December. **2** FRACTION A **hundredth** of something is one of a hundred equal parts of it. ❑ Mitchell beat Lewis by three-hundredths of a second.

hundred|weight /hʌ̱ndrɪdweɪt/ (hundredweights)

The plural form is **hundredweight** after a number.

N-COUNT [oft N of n] A **hundredweight** is a unit of weight that is equal to 100 pounds. ❑ ...a hundredweight of coal.

hung /hʌ̱ŋ/ **1** **Hung** is the past tense and past participle of most of the senses of **hang**. **2** ADJ A **hung** jury is the situation that occurs when a jury is unable to reach a decision because there is not a clear majority of its members in favor of any one decision. ❑ His first trial ended in a hung jury.

Hun|gar|ian /hʌŋge̱əriən/ (Hungarians) **1** ADJ [usu ADJ n] **Hungarian** means belonging or relating to Hungary, or to its people, language, or culture. ❑ ...the Hungarian government. **2** N-COUNT [usu pl] A **Hungarian** is a Hungarian citizen, or a person of Hungarian origin. **3** N-UNCOUNT **Hungarian** is the language spoken by people who live in Hungary.

hun|ger /hʌ̱ŋgər/ (hungers, hungering, hungered) **1** N-UNCOUNT **Hunger** is the feeling of weakness or discomfort that you get when you need something to eat. ❑ Hunger is the body's signal that levels of blood sugar are too low. **2** N-UNCOUNT **Hunger** is a severe lack of food which causes suffering or death. ❑ Three hundred people in this town are dying of hunger every day. **3** N-SING [also no det] If you have a **hunger** for something, you want or need it very much. [WRITTEN] ❑ He has a hunger for success that seems bottomless. **4** V-I If you say that someone **hungers** for something or **hungers** after it, you are emphasizing that they want it very much. [FORMAL, EMPHASIS] ❑ But Jules was not eager for classroom learning, he hungered for adventure.

hun|ger strike (hunger strikes) N-VAR If someone goes on **hunger strike** or goes on a **hunger strike**, they refuse to eat as a way of protesting about something. ❑ The protesters have been on hunger strike for 17 days.

hung|over /hʌ̱ŋoʊvər/ also **hung-over, hung over** ADJ [usu v-link ADJ] Someone who is **hungover** is unwell because they drank too much alcohol on the previous day. ❑ He was still hungover on the 25-minute bus ride to work the following morning.

hun|gry /hʌ̱ŋgri/ (hungrier, hungriest) **1** ADJ When you are **hungry**, you want some food because you have not eaten for some time and have an uncomfortable or painful feeling in your stomach. ❑ *My friend was hungry, so we drove to a shopping mall to get some food.* • **hun|gri|ly** /hˈʌŋgrɪli/ ADV [ADV with v] ❑ *James ate hungrily.* **2** PHRASE If people **go hungry**, they do not have enough food to eat. ❑ *They brought her meat so that she never went hungry.* **3** ADJ If you say that someone is **hungry** for something, you are emphasizing that they want it very much. [LITERARY, EMPHASIS] ❑ *I was hungry to be heard by my contemporaries.* • COMB IN ADJ **Hungry** is also a combining form. ❑ *...power-hungry politicians.* • **hun|gri|ly** ADV [ADV with v] ❑ *Other companies were also eyeing the market hungrily.*

hung up ADJ [v-link ADJ] If you say that someone is **hung up** about a particular person or thing, you are criticizing them for thinking or worrying too much about that person or thing. [INFORMAL, DISAPPROVAL] ❑ *It was a time when people weren't so hung up about health.*

hunk /hˈʌŋk/ (hunks) **1** N-COUNT A **hunk** of something is a large piece of it. ❑ *...a thick hunk of bread.* **2** N-COUNT If you refer to a man as a **hunk**, you mean that he is big, strong, and sexually attractive. [INFORMAL, APPROVAL] ❑ *...a blond, blue-eyed hunk.*

hunk|er /hˈʌŋkər/ (hunkers, hunkering, hunkered) ▶ **hunker down** **1** PHRASAL VERB If you **hunker down**, you bend your knees so that you are in a low position, balancing on your feet. [AM] ❑ *Betty hunkered down on the floor.* ❑ *He ended up hunkering down beside her.* **2** PHRASAL VERB If you say that someone **hunkers down**, you mean that they are trying to avoid doing things that will make them noticed or put them in danger. [AM] ❑ *Their strategy for the moment is to hunker down and let the fuss die down.*

hunky /hˈʌŋki/ ADJ If you describe a man as **hunky**, you mean that he is big, strong, and sexually attractive. [INFORMAL, APPROVAL] ❑ *...a hunky young doctor.* ❑ *He's 26 and really hunky.*

hunt ✦✧✧ /hˈʌnt/ (hunts, hunting, hunted) **1** V-I If you **hunt** for something or someone, you try to find them by searching carefully or thoroughly. ❑ *A forensic team was hunting for clues.* • N-COUNT **Hunt** is also a noun. ❑ *The couple had helped in the hunt for the toddlers.* **2** V-T If you **hunt** a criminal or an enemy, you search for them in order to catch or harm them. ❑ *Detectives have been hunting him for seven months.* • N-COUNT **Hunt** is also a noun. ❑ *Despite a nationwide hunt for the kidnap gang, not a trace of them was found.* **3** V-T/V-I When people or animals **hunt**, or **hunt** something, they chase and kill wild animals for food or as a sport. ❑ *As a child I learned to hunt and fish.* • N-COUNT **Hunt** is also a noun. ❑ *He set off for a nineteen-day moose hunt in Nova Scotia.* **4** PHRASE If a team or competitor is **in the hunt** for something, they still have a chance of winning it. ❑ *Six teams were still in the hunt for the team title.* **5** → See feature box at **endanger**
▶ **hunt down** PHRASAL VERB If you **hunt down** a criminal or an enemy, you find them after searching for them. ❑ *Last December they hunted down and killed one of the gangsters.*

COLLOCATIONS

hunt
NOUN **2**
noun + **hunt**: murder
adjective + **hunt**: nationwide, worldwide
hunt + be + adjective: underway
verb + **hunt**: launch, spark; join, lead

---

hunt|er ✦✧✧ /hˈʌntər/ (hunters) **1** N-COUNT A **hunter** is a person who hunts for animals or food as a sport. ❑ *The hunters stalked their prey.* **2** N-COUNT People who are searching for things of a particular kind are often referred to as **hunters**. ❑ *...job-hunters.* **3** → see also **headhunter**

hunter-gatherer (hunter-gatherers) N-COUNT **Hunter-gatherers** were people who lived by hunting and collecting food rather than by farming. There are still groups of hunter-gatherers living in some parts of the world.

hunt|ing /hˈʌntɪŋ/ **1** N-UNCOUNT **Hunting** is the chasing and killing of wild animals by people or other animals, for food or as a sport. ❑ *He'd gone deer hunting with his cousins.* **2** N-UNCOUNT **Hunting** is the activity of searching for a particular thing. ❑ *This was the fourth straight day that I had been out apartment hunting.* • COMB IN N-UNCOUNT **Hunting** is also a combining form. ❑ *Make job-hunting a full-time job until you find one.*

hunt|ing ground (hunting grounds) **1** N-COUNT [oft N *for* n] If you say that a place is a good **hunting ground** for something, you mean that people who have a particular interest are likely to find something that they want there. ❑ *Other people's weddings are the perfect hunting ground for ideas.* **2** N-COUNT A **hunting ground** is an area where people or animals chase and kill wild animals for food or as a sport.

hunts|man /hˈʌntsmən/ (huntsmen) N-COUNT A **huntsman** is a man who hunts wild animals, especially one who hunts foxes on horseback using dogs.

hunts|woman /hˈʌntswʊmən/ (huntswomen) N-COUNT A **huntswoman** is a woman who hunts wild animals, especially one who hunts foxes on horseback using dogs.

hur|dle /hˈɜrdəl/ (hurdles, hurdling, hurdled) **1** N-COUNT A **hurdle** is a problem, difficulty, or part of a process that may prevent you from achieving something. ❑ *Two-thirds of candidates fail at this first hurdle and are sent home.* **2** N-COUNT-COLL **Hurdles** is a race in which people have to jump over a number of obstacles that are also called hurdles. You can use **hurdles** to refer to one or more races. ❑ *Davis won the 400 meter hurdles in a new Olympic time of 49.3 sec.* **3** V-T/V-I If you **hurdle**, you jump over something while you are running. ❑ *He crossed the lawn and hurdled the short fence.*

hur|dler /hˈɜrdlər/ (hurdlers) N-COUNT A **hurdler** is an athlete who takes part in hurdles races.

hurl /hˈɜrl/ (hurls, hurling, hurled) **1** V-T If you **hurl** something, you throw it violently and with a lot of force. ❑ *Groups of angry youths hurled stones at police.* ❑ *Simon caught the grenade and hurled it back.* **2** V-T If you **hurl** abuse or insults at someone, you shout insults at them aggressively. ❑ *How would you handle being locked in the back of a cab while the driver hurled abuse at you?*

hurly-burly /hˈɜrli bˈɜrli/ N-SING [usu the N, oft N *of* n] If you talk about the **hurly-burly** of a situation, you are emphasizing how noisy or busy it is. [EMPHASIS] ❑ *No one expects him to get involved in the hurly-burly of campaigning.*

hur|ray /hʊreɪ/ also **hurrah** → see **hooray**

hur|ri|cane /hˈɜrɪkeɪn, hˈʌrɪkən/ (hurricanes) **1** N-COUNT A **hurricane** is an extremely violent storm that begins over ocean water. **2** → See feature box at **storm**

hur|ried /hˈɜrid, hˈʌr-/ **1** ADJ A **hurried** action is done quickly, because you do not have much time to do it in. ❑ *...a hurried breakfast.* • **hur|ried|ly** ADV [ADV with v] ❑ *...students hurriedly taking notes.* **2** ADJ A **hurried** action is done suddenly, in reaction to something that has just happened. ❑ *There had been a hurried overnight redrafting of the text.* • **hur|ried|ly** ADV [ADV with v] ❑ *The moment she saw it, she blushed and hurriedly left the room.* **3** ADJ Someone who is **hurried** does things more quickly than they should because they do not have much time to do them. ❑ *Parisians on the street often looked worried, hurried, and unfriendly.*

hur|ry /hˈɜri, hˈʌr-/ (hurries, hurrying, hurried) **1** V-I If you **hurry** somewhere, you go there as quickly as you can. ❑ *Claire hurried along the road.* **2** V-T If you **hurry** to do something, you start doing it as soon as you can, or try to do it quickly. ❑ *Mrs. Hardie hurried to make up for her tactlessness by asking her guest about his holiday.* **3** N-SING If you are in a **hurry** to do something, you need or want to do something quickly. If you do something in a **hurry**, you do it quickly or suddenly. ❑ *Kate was in a hurry to grow up, eager for knowledge and experience.* **4** V-T To **hurry** something means the same as to **hurry up** something. ❑ *...the president's attempt to hurry the process of independence.* **5** V-T If you **hurry** someone to a place or into a situation, you try to make them go to that place or get into that situation quickly. ❑ *They say they are not going to be hurried into any decision.* **6** PHRASE If you say to someone 'There's no hurry' or 'I'm in no hurry' you are telling them that there is no need for them to do something immediately. ❑ *I'll need to talk with you, but there's no hurry.* **7** PHRASE If you are **in no hurry** to do something, you are very unwilling to do it. ❑ *I love it here so I'm in no hurry to go anywhere.*
▶ **hurry along** → see **hurry up 2**
▶ **hurry up** **1** PHRASAL VERB If you tell someone to **hurry up**, you are telling them to do something more quickly than they were doing it. ❑ *Franklin told Howe to hurry up and take his bath; otherwise, they'd miss their train.* **2** PHRASAL VERB If you **hurry** something **up** or **hurry** it **along**, you make it happen faster or sooner than it would otherwise have done. ❑ *...if you're not a traditionalist and you want to hurry up the process.*

hurt /hɜrt/ (hurts, hurting, hurt) **1** V-T If you **hurt** yourself or **hurt** a part of your body, you feel pain because you have injured yourself. ◻ Yasin had seriously hurt himself while trying to escape from the police. **2** V-I If a part of your body **hurts**, you feel pain there. ◻ His collar bone only hurt when he lifted his arm. **3** ADJ If you are **hurt**, you have been injured. ◻ His comrades asked him if he was hurt. **4** V-T/V-I If you **hurt** someone, you cause them to feel pain. ◻ I didn't mean to hurt the kid, but I caught him on the ankle with my studs. ◻ That hurts! **5** V-T/V-I If someone **hurts** you, they say or do something that makes you unhappy. ◻ He is afraid of hurting Bessy's feelings. ◻ What hurts most is the betrayal. **6** ADJ If you are **hurt**, you are upset because of something that someone has said or done. ◻ She was deeply hurt and shocked by what Smith had said. **7** V-I [only cont] If you say that you **are hurting**, you mean that you are experiencing emotional pain. ◻ I am lonely and I am hurting. **8** V-T To **hurt** someone or something means to have a bad effect on them or prevent them from succeeding. ◻ The combination of hot weather and decreased water supplies is hurting many industries. **9** N-VAR A feeling of **hurt** is a feeling that you have when you think that you have been treated badly or judged unfairly. ◻ I was full of jealousy and hurt. **10** PHRASE If you say '**It won't hurt** to do something' or '**It never hurts** to do something,' you are recommending an action which you think is helpful or useful. [INFORMAL] ◻ It never hurts to ask.

SYNONYMS

hurt
VERB **1**
injure: Several police officers were injured in the clashes.
damage: The sun can damage your skin.
wound: The driver of an evacuation bus was wounded by shrapnel.

---

hurt|ful /hɜrtfəl/ ADJ If you say that someone's comments or actions are **hurtful**, you mean that they are unkind and upsetting. ◻ Her comments can only be very hurtful to Mrs. Green's family.

hur|tle /hɜrtᵊl/ (hurtles, hurtling, hurtled) V-I If someone or something **hurtles** somewhere, they move there very quickly, often in a rough or violent way. ◻ A pretty young girl came hurtling down the stairs.

hus|band /hʌzbənd/ (husbands) N-COUNT Someone's **husband** is the man they are married to. ◻ Eva married her husband Jack in 1957.

hus|band|ry /hʌzbəndri/ N-UNCOUNT **Husbandry** is the raising of farm animals and plants.

hush /hʌʃ/ (hushes, hushing, hushed) **1** CONVENTION You say '**Hush!**' to someone when you are asking or telling them to be quiet. ◻ Hush, my love, it's all right. **2** V-T/V-I If you **hush** someone or if they **hush**, they stop speaking or making a noise. ◻ She tried to hush her noisy father. **3** N-SING [also no det] You say there is a **hush** in a place when everything is quiet and peaceful, or suddenly becomes quiet. ◻ A hush fell over the crowd and I knew something terrible had happened.
▶ **hush up** PHRASAL VERB If someone **hushes** something **up**, they prevent other people from knowing about it. ◻ I thought it would reflect badly on me so I tried to hush the whole thing up.

hushed /hʌʃt/ **1** ADJ A **hushed** place is peaceful and much quieter and calmer than usual. ◻ The house seemed muted, hushed, as if it had been deserted. **2** ADJ A **hushed** voice or **hushed** conversation is very quiet. ◻ At first we spoke in hushed voices and crept about in order not to alarm them.

hush-hush ADJ Something that is **hush-hush** is secret and not to be discussed with other people. [INFORMAL] ◻ Apparently there's a very hush-hush project under way up north.

hush mon|ey N-UNCOUNT If a person is paid **hush money**, someone gives them money to not reveal information they have which could be damaging or embarrassing. [INFORMAL]

husk /hʌsk/ (husks) N-COUNT A **husk** is the outer covering of a grain or a seed.

husky /hʌski/ (huskier, huskiest, huskies) **1** ADJ If someone's voice is **husky**, it is low and somewhat rough, often in an attractive way. ◻ His voice was husky with grief. ◻ ...Dietrich's deep, husky voice. ● **huski|ly** ADV [ADV after v] ◻ "Ready?" I asked huskily. **2** ADJ [usu ADJ n] If you describe someone, especially a man, as **husky**, you think that they are tall, big, and strong. [INFORMAL] ◻ ...a very husky young man, built like a football player. **3** N-COUNT A **husky** is a strong, furry dog, which is used to pull sleds across snow.

hus|sy /hʌsi, hʌzi/ (hussies) N-COUNT If someone refers to a girl or woman as a **hussy**, they are criticizing her for behaving in a sexually immoral way. [HUMOROUS, OLD-FASHIONED, DISAPPROVAL]

hus|tle /hʌsᵊl/ (hustles, hustling, hustled) **1** V-T If you **hustle** someone, you try to make them go somewhere or do something quickly, for example by pulling or pushing them along. ◻ The guards hustled Harry out of the car. **2** V-I If you **hustle**, you go somewhere or do something as quickly as you can. ◻ You'll have to hustle if you're to get home for supper. **3** V-I If someone **hustles**, they try hard to earn money or to gain an advantage from a situation. [mainly AM] ◻ I like it here. It forces you to hustle and you can earn money. ◻ Hustling for social contacts isn't something that just happens. You have to make it happen. **4** V-T If someone **hustles** you, or if they **hustle** something, they try hard to get something, often by using dishonest or illegal means. [mainly AM] ◻ Two teenage boys asked us for money, saying they were forming a baseball team. Anna said they were hustling us. ◻ He hustled several daytime jobs and finished his education at night. **5** N-UNCOUNT **Hustle** is busy, noisy activity. ◻ ...the hustle and bustle of New York.

hus|tler /hʌslər/ (hustlers) **1** N-COUNT If you refer to someone as a **hustler**, you mean that they try to earn money or gain an advantage from situations they are in by using dishonest or illegal methods. [INFORMAL, DISAPPROVAL] ◻ ...an insurance hustler. **2** N-COUNT A **hustler** is a prostitute, especially a male prostitute. [INFORMAL]

hut /hʌt/ (huts) **1** N-COUNT A **hut** is a small house with only one or two rooms, especially one which is made of wood, mud, grass, or stones. **2** N-COUNT A **hut** is a small wooden building in someone's garden, or a temporary building used by builders or repair workers. [BRIT]

in AM, use **shed**

hutch /hʌtʃ/ (hutches) **1** N-COUNT A **hutch** is a wooden structure that rabbits or other small pet animals are kept in. **2** N-COUNT A **hutch** is a type of cabinet with shelves. [mainly AM]

hya|cinth /haɪəsɪnθ/ (hyacinths) N-COUNT A **hyacinth** is a plant with a lot of small, sweet-smelling flowers growing closely around a single stem. It grows from a bulb and the flowers are usually blue, pink, or white.

hy|brid /haɪbrɪd/ (hybrids) **1** N-COUNT A **hybrid** is an animal or plant that has been bred from two different species of animal or plant. [TECHNICAL] ◻ All these brightly colored hybrids are so lovely in the garden. ● ADJ [ADJ n] **Hybrid** is also an adjective. ◻ ...the hybrid corn seed. **2** N-COUNT A **hybrid** or a **hybrid car** is a car that can be powered by either gasoline or electricity. ◻ Hybrids, unlike pure electric cars, never need to be plugged in. ◻ Hybrid cars can go almost 600 miles between refueling. **3** N-COUNT You can use **hybrid** to refer to anything that is a mixture of other things, especially two other things. ◻ ...a hybrid of solid and liquid fuel. ● ADJ [ADJ n] **Hybrid** is also an adjective. ◻ ...a hybrid system.

hy|brid|ize /haɪbrɪdaɪz/ (hybridizes, hybridizing, hybridized)

in BRIT, also use **hybridise**

V-RECIP If one species of plant or animal **hybridizes** with another, the species reproduce together to make a hybrid. You can also say that you **hybridize** one species of plant or animal with another. [TECHNICAL] ◻ Marine and freshwater stickleback can hybridize in contact zones. ◻ Wild boar readily hybridizes with the domestic pig.

hy|drant /haɪdrənt/ (hydrants) → see **fire hydrant**

hy|drate /haɪdreɪt/ (hydrates, hydrating, hydrated) **1** N-MASS [usu n/adj n] A **hydrate** is a chemical compound that contains water. ◻ ...aluminum hydrate. **2** V-T If a substance **hydrates** your skin, it makes it softer and less dry. ◻ After-sun products will cool and hydrate your skin.

hy|drau|lic /haɪdrɔlɪk, -drɒl-/ ADJ [ADJ n] **Hydraulic** equipment or machinery involves or is operated by a fluid that is under pressure, such as water or oil. ◻ The boat has no fewer than five hydraulic pumps.

hy|drau|lics /haɪdrɔ̱lɪks, -drɒl-/ N-UNCOUNT **Hydraulics** is the study and use of systems that work using hydraulic pressure.

hydro|car|bon /ha͟ɪdroʊkɑːrbən/ (**hydrocarbons**) N-COUNT A **hydrocarbon** is a chemical compound that is a mixture of hydrogen and carbon.

hydro|chlo|ric acid /ha͟ɪdrəklɔːrɪk æ̱sɪd/ N-UNCOUNT **Hydrochloric acid** is a colorless, strong acid containing hydrogen and chlorine.

hydro|elec|tric /ha͟ɪdroʊɪle̱ktrɪk/ also **hydro-electric** ADJ [ADJ n] **Hydroelectric** means relating to or involving electricity made from the energy of running water.

hydro|elec|tric|ity /ha͟ɪdroʊɪlektrɪ̱sɪti/ N-UNCOUNT **Hydroelectricity** is electricity made from the energy of running water.

hydro|fluoro|car|bon /ha͟ɪdroʊflʊərəʊkɑːrbən/ (**hydrofluorocarbons**) N-COUNT **Hydrofluorocarbons** are a type of gas used in refrigerators and aerosols. ❏ *Hydrofluorocarbons can contribute to global warming.* ❏ *Such fridges are far less harmful to the environment than the hydrofluorocarbon units in general use.*

hydro|foil /ha͟ɪdrəfɔɪl/ (**hydrofoils**) **1** N-COUNT A **hydrofoil** is a boat which can travel partly out of the water on a pair of flat parts like wings. You can also refer to the flat parts as **hydrofoils**. **2** → See also color supplement

hydro|gen /ha͟ɪdrədʒən/ N-UNCOUNT **Hydrogen** is a colorless gas that is the lightest and commonest element in the universe.

hydro|gen bomb (**hydrogen bombs**) N-COUNT A **hydrogen bomb** is a nuclear bomb in which energy is released from hydrogen atoms.

hydro|gen per|ox|ide N-UNCOUNT **Hydrogen peroxide** is a chemical that is often used to make hair lighter or to kill germs.

hydro|log|ic cy|cle /ha͟ɪdrəlɒdʒɪk sa͟ɪkəl/ N-SING [the N] The **hydrologic cycle** is the process by which the Earth's water is circulated from the surface to the atmosphere through evaporation and back to the surface through rainfall. [TECHNICAL]

hydro|plane /ha͟ɪdrəpleɪn/ (**hydroplanes**) N-COUNT A **hydroplane** is a speedboat which rises out of the water when it is traveling fast.

hydro|pon|ics /ha͟ɪdrəpɒnɪks/ N-UNCOUNT **Hydroponics** is a method of growing plants without the use of soil, by using water through which nutrients are pumped. ❏ *So, is hydroponics a cheaper way of producing food?* • **hydro|pon|ic** /ha͟ɪdrəpɒnɪk/ ADJ ❏ *...hydroponic farms.* ❏ *...hydroponic strawberries.* • **hydro|poni|cal|ly** /ha͟ɪdrəpɒnɪkli/ ADV [ADV after v] ❏ *All crops will be grown hydroponically, in a shallow solution of water and minerals.*

hydro|thera|py /ha͟ɪdroʊθe̱rəpi/ N-UNCOUNT **Hydrotherapy** is a method of treating people with some diseases or injuries by making them swim or do exercises in water.

hy|ena /haɪi̱nə/ (**hyenas**) N-COUNT A **hyena** is an animal that looks like a dog and makes a sound which is similar to a human laugh. Hyenas live in Africa and Asia.

hy|giene /ha͟ɪdʒiːn/ N-UNCOUNT **Hygiene** is the practice of keeping yourself and your surroundings clean, especially in order to prevent illness or the spread of diseases. ❏ *Be extra careful about personal hygiene.*

hy|gien|ic /haɪdʒi̱nɪk/ ADJ Something that is **hygienic** is clean and unlikely to cause illness. ❏ *...a white, clinical-looking kitchen that was easy to keep clean and hygienic.*

hy|gien|ist /haɪdʒi̱nɪst/ (**hygienists**) N-COUNT A **hygienist** or a **dental hygienist** is a person who is trained to clean people's teeth and to give them advice on how to take care of their teeth and gums.

hy|men /ha͟ɪmən/ (**hymens**) N-COUNT A **hymen** is a piece of skin that covers the entrance to a girl's or woman's vagina and breaks, usually when she has sex for the first time. [MEDICAL]

hymn /hɪm/ (**hymns**) **1** N-COUNT A **hymn** is a religious song that Christians sing in church. ❏ *I like singing hymns.* **2** N-COUNT If you describe a movie, book, or speech as a **hymn to something**, you mean that it praises or celebrates that thing. [mainly JOURNALISM] ❏ *...a hymn to freedom and rebellion.*

hym|nal /hɪ̱mnəl/ (**hymnals**) N-COUNT A **hymnal** is a book of hymns. [FORMAL]

hype /ha͟ɪp/ (**hypes, hyping, hyped**) **1** N-UNCOUNT **Hype** is the use of a lot of publicity and advertising to make people interested in something such as a product. [DISAPPROVAL] ❏ *We are certainly seeing a lot of hype by some companies.* **2** V-T To **hype** a product means to advertise or praise it a lot. [DISAPPROVAL] ❏ *We had to hype the film to attract the financiers.* • PHRASAL VERB **Hype up** means the same as **hype**. ❏ *The media seems obsessed with hyping up individuals or groups.*

hyped up also **hyped-up** ADJ If someone is **hyped up** about something, they are very excited or anxious about it. [INFORMAL] ❏ *We were both so hyped up about buying the house, we could not wait to get in there.*

hy|per /ha͟ɪpər/ ADJ [usu v-link ADJ] If someone is **hyper**, they are very excited and energetic. [INFORMAL] ❏ *I was incredibly hyper. I couldn't sleep.*

PREFIX

hyper-
forms adjectives that refer to people or things that have a large amount of, or too much of, a particular quality. For example, someone who is **hypersensitive** becomes annoyed or offended very easily.

---

hyper|ac|tive /ha͟ɪpəræ̱ktɪv/ ADJ Someone who is **hyperactive** is unable to relax and is always moving around or doing things. ❏ *His research was used in planning treatments for hyperactive children.*

hyper|bo|le /haɪpɜːrbəli/ N-UNCOUNT If someone uses **hyperbole**, they say or write things that make something sound much more impressive than it really is. [FORMAL] ❏ *...the hyperbole that portrays him as one of the greatest visionaries in the world.*

hyper|bol|ic /ha͟ɪpərbɒlɪk/ ADJ [usu ADJ n] If you describe language as **hyperbolic**, you mean that it makes something sound much more impressive than it really is. [FORMAL]

hyper|con|nec|tiv|ity /ha͟ɪpərkɒnektɪ̱vɪti/ N-UNCOUNT **Hyperconnectivity** is the use of many systems and devices so that you are always connected to social networks and other sources of information. ❏ *The team is studying the effects of hyperconnectivity on the brain.*

hyper|in|fla|tion /ha͟ɪpərɪnfle͟ɪʃən/ N-UNCOUNT **Hyperinflation** is very severe inflation. ❏ *In the hyperinflation of 1922-23 a dollar could be bought for 4.2 billion marks.*

hyper|link /ha͟ɪpərlɪŋk/ (**hyperlinks, hyperlinking, hyperlinked**) **1** N-COUNT In an HTML document, a **hyperlink** is a link to another part of the document or to another document. Hyperlinks are shown as words with a line under them. [COMPUTING] ❏ *...Web pages full of hyperlinks.* **2** V-T [usu passive] If a document or file **is hyperlinked**, it contains hyperlinks. [COMPUTING] ❏ *The database is fully hyperlinked both within the database and to thousands of external links.*

hyper|sen|si|tive /ha͟ɪpərse̱nsɪtɪv/ **1** ADJ [oft ADJ to/about n] If you say that someone is **hypersensitive**, you mean that they get annoyed or offended very easily. ❏ *Student teachers were hypersensitive to any criticism of their performance.* **2** ADJ [oft ADJ to n] Someone who is **hypersensitive** is extremely sensitive to certain drugs or chemicals. [MEDICAL]

hyper|son|ic /ha͟ɪpərsɒnɪk/ ADJ [usu ADJ n] A **hypersonic** rocket or missile travels at five times the speed of sound or faster. ❏ *The university has been working on hypersonic technology for nearly 16 years.* ❏ *...his first experiments on hypersonic flight.*

hyper|ten|sion /ha͟ɪpərte̱nʃən/ N-UNCOUNT **Hypertension** is a medical condition in which a person has very high blood pressure.

hyper|text /ha͟ɪpərtekst/ N-UNCOUNT In computing, **hypertext** is a way of connecting pieces of text so that you can go quickly and directly from one to another. [COMPUTING] ❏ *...information embroidered with colorful graphics and tied together by hypertext links.*

hyper|ven|ti|late /ha͟ɪpərve̱ntɪleɪt/ (**hyperventilates, hyperventilating, hyperventilated**) V-I If someone **hyperventilates**, they begin to breathe very fast in an uncontrollable way, usually because they are very frightened, tired, or excited. ❏ *I hyperventilate when they come near me with the needle.* • **hyper|ven|ti|la|tion** /ha͟ɪpərventɪle͟ɪʃən/ N-UNCOUNT ❏ *Several notable researchers are studying the effects of hyperventilation.*

hy|phen /haɪfᵊn/ (hyphens) N-COUNT A **hyphen** is the punctuation sign used to join words together to make a compound, as in 'left-handed.' People also use a hyphen to show that the rest of a word is on the next line.

hy|phen|at|ed /haɪfəneɪtɪd/ ADJ A word that is **hyphenated** is written with a hyphen between two or more of its parts. ❑ ...hyphenated names such as Wong-Shong or Li-Wong.

hyp|no|sis /hɪpnoʊsɪs/ **1** N-UNCOUNT **Hypnosis** is a state in which a person seems to be asleep but can still see, hear, or respond to things said to them. ❑ Bevin is now an adult and has re-lived her birth experience under hypnosis. **2** N-UNCOUNT **Hypnosis** is the art or practice of hypnotizing people.

hyp|no|thera|pist /hɪpnoʊθɛrəpɪst/ (hypnotherapists) N-COUNT A **hypnotherapist** is a person who treats people by using hypnotherapy.

hyp|no|thera|py /hɪpnoʊθɛrəpi/ N-UNCOUNT **Hypnotherapy** is the practice of hypnotizing people in order to help them with a mental or physical problem, for example to help them give up smoking.

hyp|not|ic /hɪpnɒtɪk/ **1** ADJ If someone is in a **hypnotic** state, they have been hypnotized. ❑ The hypnotic state actually lies somewhere between being awake and being asleep. **2** ADJ Something that is **hypnotic** holds your attention or makes you feel sleepy, often because it involves repeated sounds, pictures, or movements. ❑ His songs are often both hypnotic and reassuringly pleasant.

hyp|no|tism /hɪpnətɪzəm/ N-UNCOUNT **Hypnotism** is the practice of hypnotizing people. ❑ Dulcy also saw a psychiatrist who used hypnotism to help her deal with her fear. ● **hyp|no|tist** (hypnotists) N-COUNT ❑ He was put into a trance by a police hypnotist.

hyp|no|tize /hɪpnətaɪz/ (hypnotizes, hypnotizing, hypnotized)

in BRIT, also use **hypnotise**

1 V-T If someone **hypnotizes** you, they put you into a state in which you seem to be asleep but can still see, hear, or respond to things said to you. ❑ A hypnotherapist will hypnotize you and will stop you from smoking. **2** V-T [usu passive] If you **are hypnotized** by someone or something, you are so fascinated by them that you cannot think of anything else. ❑ He's hypnotized by that black hair and that white face.

hypo|chon|dria /haɪpəkɒndriə/ N-UNCOUNT If someone has **hypochondria**, they continually worry about their health and imagine that they are ill, although there is really nothing wrong with them.

hypo|chon|dri|ac /haɪpəkɒndriæk/ (hypochondriacs) N-COUNT A **hypochondriac** is a person who continually worries about their health, although there is really nothing wrong with them.

hy|poc|ri|sy /hɪpɒkrɪsi/ (hypocrisies) N-VAR If you accuse someone of **hypocrisy**, you mean that they pretend to have qualities, beliefs, or feelings that they do not really have. [DISAPPROVAL] ❑ He accused newspapers of hypocrisy in their treatment of the story.

hypo|crite /hɪpəkrɪt/ (hypocrites) N-COUNT If you accuse someone of being a **hypocrite**, you mean that they pretend to have qualities, beliefs, or feelings that they do not really have. [DISAPPROVAL] ❑ The magazine wrongly suggested he was a liar and a hypocrite.

hypo|criti|cal /hɪpəkrɪtɪkᵊl/ ADJ If you accuse someone of being **hypocritical**, you mean that they pretend to have qualities, beliefs, or feelings that they do not really have. [DISAPPROVAL] ❑ It would be hypocritical to say I travel at 70 mph simply because that is the law.

hypo|der|mic /haɪpədɜrmɪk/ (hypodermics) ADJ [ADJ n] A **hypodermic** needle or syringe is a medical instrument with a hollow needle, which is used to give injections. ● N-COUNT **Hypodermic** is also a noun. ❑ He held up a hypodermic to check the dosage.

hy|pot|enuse /haɪpɒtənus/ (hypotenuses) N-COUNT [usu the N] The **hypotenuse** of a right-angled triangle is the side opposite its right angle. [TECHNICAL]

hypo|thala|mus /haɪpoʊθæləməs/ (hypothalami) N-COUNT [usu the N] The **hypothalamus** is the part of the brain that controls functions such as hunger and thirst. [MEDICAL] ❑ The stress response is controlled by the hypothalamus.

hypo|ther|mia /haɪpoʊθɜrmiə/ N-UNCOUNT If someone has **hypothermia**, their body temperature has become dangerously low as a result of being in severe cold for a long time. [MEDICAL]

hy|poth|esis /haɪpɒθɪsɪs/ (hypotheses) **1** N-VAR A **hypothesis** is an idea which is suggested as a possible explanation for a particular situation or condition, but which has not yet been proved to be correct. [FORMAL] ❑ Work will now begin to test the hypothesis in rats. **2** → See feature box at **experiment, research**

hy|poth|esize /haɪpɒθɪsaɪz/ (hypothesizes, hypothesizing, hypothesized)

in BRIT, also use **hypothesise**

V-T If you **hypothesize** that something will happen, you say that you think that thing will happen because of various facts you have considered. [FORMAL] ❑ To explain this, they hypothesize that galaxies must contain a great deal of missing matter which cannot be detected. ❑ I have long hypothesized a connection between these factors.

hypo|theti|cal /haɪpəθɛtɪkᵊl/ ADJ If something is **hypothetical**, it is based on possible ideas or situations rather than actual ones. ❑ Let's look at a hypothetical situation in which Carol, a recovering alcoholic, gets invited to a party. ● **hypo|theti|cal|ly** /haɪpəθɛtɪkli/ ADV ❑ He was invariably willing to discuss the possibilities hypothetically.

hys|ter|ec|to|my /hɪstərɛktəmi/ (hysterectomies) N-COUNT A **hysterectomy** is a surgical operation to remove a woman's uterus. ❑ I had to have a hysterectomy.

hys|te|ria /hɪstɛriə/ N-UNCOUNT **Hysteria** among a group of people is a state of uncontrolled excitement, anger, or panic. ❑ No one could help getting carried away by the hysteria.

hys|teri|cal /hɪstɛrɪkᵊl/ **1** ADJ Someone who is **hysterical** is in a state of uncontrolled excitement, anger, or panic. ❑ Police and bodyguards had to form a human shield around him as the almost hysterical crowds struggled to approach him. ● **hys|teri|cal|ly** /hɪstɛrɪkli/ ADV ❑ "What's that?" the child screamed hysterically. **2** ADJ **Hysterical** laughter is loud and uncontrolled. [INFORMAL] ❑ The young woman burst into hysterical laughter. ● **hys|teri|cal|ly** ADV [ADV with v] ❑ We looked at each other and just started to laugh hysterically. **3** ADJ If you describe something or someone as **hysterical**, you think that they are very funny and they make you laugh a lot. [INFORMAL] ❑ It was absolutely hysterical, and we had a great day. ● **hys|teri|cal|ly** ADV [ADV adj] ❑ It wasn't supposed to be a comedy but I found it hysterically funny.

hys|ter|ics /hɪstɛrɪks/ **1** N-PLURAL If someone is in **hysterics** or is having **hysterics**, they are in a state of uncontrolled excitement, anger, or panic. [INFORMAL] ❑ For once I ignored her hysterics. **2** N-PLURAL You can say that someone is in **hysterics** or is having **hysterics** when they are laughing loudly in an uncontrolled way. [INFORMAL] ❑ He'd often have us all in absolute hysterics.

I i

I also **i** /aɪ/ (**I's, i's**) N-VAR **I** is the ninth letter of the English alphabet.

I ♦♦♦ /aɪ/ PRON-SING [PRON v] A speaker or writer uses **I** to refer to himself or herself. **I** is a first person singular pronoun. **I** is used as the subject of a verb. ❑ *Jim and I are getting married.*

-ian → see **-an**

ibid. CONVENTION **Ibid.** is used in books and journals to indicate that a piece of text taken from somewhere else is from the same source as the previous piece of text.

SUFFIX
-ibility
replaces *-ible* at the end of adjectives to form nouns referring to the state or quality described by the adjective. *For example,* **responsibility** *is the state of being responsible.*

SUFFIX
-ible
forms adjectives that indicate what someone or something can have done to them. *For example, if a number is* **divisible***, it is possible to divide it.*

SUFFIX
-ic
forms adjectives that indicate that something or someone is connected with a particular thing. *For example,* **photographic** *equipment is equipment connected with photography.*

SUFFIX
-ication
forms nouns that refer to a state or process, or to an instance of that process. *For example,* **multiplication** *is the process of multiplying numbers.*

ice ♦♦◊ /aɪs/ (**ices, icing, iced**) **1** N-UNCOUNT **Ice** is frozen water. ❑ *Glaciers are moving rivers of ice.* **2** V-T If you **ice** a cake, you cover it with icing. [BRIT] ❑ *I've made the cake. I've iced and decorated it.* **3** → see also **iced, icing** **4** PHRASE If you **break the ice** at a party or meeting, or in a new situation, you say or do something to make people feel relaxed and comfortable. ❑ *That sort of approach should go a long way toward breaking the ice.* **5** PHRASE If you say that something **cuts no ice** with you, you mean that you are not impressed or influenced by it. ❑ *That sort of romantic attitude cuts no ice with moneymen.* **6** PHRASE If someone puts a plan or project **on ice**, they delay doing it. ❑ *There would be a three-month delay while the deal would be put on ice.* **7** PHRASE If you say that someone is **on thin ice** or **is skating on thin ice**, you mean that they are doing something risky that may have serious or unpleasant consequences. ❑ *I had skated on thin ice on many assignments and somehow had gotten away with it.*

Ice Age N-PROPER [the N] **The Ice Age** was a period of time lasting many thousands of years, during which a lot of the Earth's surface was covered with ice.

ice|berg /ˈaɪsbɜrɡ/ (**icebergs**) **1** N-COUNT An **iceberg** is a large tall mass of ice floating in the sea. **2 the tip of the iceberg** → see **tip**

WORD HISTORY
iceberg
The word **iceberg** comes from the Dutch word *ijsberg, ijs* meaning 'ice,' and *berg* meaning 'mountain.'

ice-blue COLOR **Ice-blue** is a very pale blue color. [LITERARY]

ice|box /ˈaɪsbɒks/ (**iceboxes**) also **ice-box** N-COUNT An **icebox** is the same as a **refrigerator**. [AM, OLD-FASHIONED]

ice|breaker /ˈaɪsbreɪkər/ (**icebreakers**) **1** N-COUNT An **icebreaker** is a large ship that sails through frozen waters, breaking the ice as it goes, in order to create a passage for other ships. **2** N-COUNT An **icebreaker** is something that someone says or does in order to make it easier for people who have never met before to talk to each other. ❑ *This exercise can be quite a useful icebreaker for new groups.*

ice buck|et (**ice buckets**) N-COUNT An **ice bucket** is a container that holds ice cubes or cold water and ice. You can use it to provide ice cubes to put in drinks, or to put bottles of wine in and keep the wine cool.

ice cap (**ice caps**) also **icecap** N-COUNT [usu the N] **The ice caps** are the thick layers of ice and snow that cover the North and South Poles.

ice-cold **1** ADJ If you describe something as **ice-cold**, you are emphasizing that it is very cold. ❑ *...delicious ice-cold beer.* **2** ADJ If you describe someone as **ice-cold**, you are emphasizing that they do not allow their emotions to affect them or that they lack feeling and friendliness. ❑ *...the gunman's ice-cold stare.*

ice cream (**ice creams**) also **ice-cream** **1** N-MASS **Ice cream** is a very cold sweet food made from frozen cream or a substance like cream and has a flavor such as vanilla, chocolate, or strawberry. ❑ *I'll get you some ice cream.* **2** N-COUNT An **ice cream** is an amount of ice cream sold in a small container or a cone made of a thin cookie. ❑ *Do you want an ice cream?*

ice cube (**ice cubes**) N-COUNT An **ice cube** is a small square block of ice that you put into a drink in order to make it cold.

iced /aɪst/ **1** ADJ [ADJ n] An **iced** drink has been made very cold, often by putting ice in it. ❑ *...iced tea.* **2** ADJ An **iced** cake is covered with a layer of icing.

ice floe (**ice floes**) N-COUNT An **ice floe** is a large area of ice floating in the sea.

ice hock|ey N-UNCOUNT **Ice hockey** is a game played on ice between two teams of 11 players who use long curved sticks to hit a small rubber disk, called a puck, and try to score goals.

in AM, usually use **hockey**

Ice|land|er /ˈaɪslændər/ (**Icelanders**) N-COUNT An **Icelander** is a person who comes from Iceland.

Ice|land|ic /aɪsˈlændɪk/ **1** ADJ Something that is **Icelandic** belongs or relates to Iceland, to its people, or to its language. **2** N-UNCOUNT **Icelandic** is the official language of Iceland.

ice lol|ly (**ice lollies**) N-COUNT An **ice lolly** is the same as a Popsicle. [BRIT]

ice pack (**ice packs**) N-COUNT An **ice pack** is a bag full of ice that is used to cool parts of the body when they are injured or painful.

ice pick (**ice picks**) also **icepick** N-COUNT An **ice pick** is a small pointed tool that you use for breaking ice.

ice rink (**ice rinks**) N-COUNT An **ice rink** is a level area of ice, usually inside a building, that has been made artificially and kept frozen so that people can skate on it.

ice sheet (**ice sheets**) N-COUNT An **ice sheet** is a large thick area of ice, especially one that exists for a long time.

ice skate (**ice skates, ice skating, ice skated**) **1** N-COUNT **Ice skates** are boots with a thin metal blade underneath that people wear to move quickly on ice. **2** V-I If you **ice skate**, you move around on ice wearing ice skates. ❑ We never learned to ice skate or ski. • **ice skat|ing** N-UNCOUNT ❑ I love watching ice skating on television. ❑ We went ice skating on a frozen lake.

ice skat|er (ice skaters) N-COUNT An **ice skater** is someone who skates on ice.

ice tea (ice teas) also **iced tea** N-VAR **Ice tea** or **iced tea** is a drink made from tea without milk but with sugar and sometimes fruit flavorings, drunk cold.

ice wa|ter N-UNCOUNT **Ice water** is very cold water served as a drink. [AM]

ici|cle /aɪsɪkᵊl/ (icicles) N-COUNT An **icicle** is a long pointed piece of ice hanging down from a surface. It forms when water comes slowly off the surface, and freezes as it falls.

ic|ing /aɪsɪŋ/ **1** N-UNCOUNT **Icing** is a sweet substance made from powdered sugar that is used to cover and decorate cakes. ❑ Paul made five-year-old Michelle a birthday cake with yellow icing. **2** PHRASE If you describe something as **icing on the cake** or **the icing on the cake**, you mean that it makes a good thing even better, but it is not essential. ❑ Qualifying was my only goal, so winning is icing on the cake.

ic|ing sug|ar N-UNCOUNT **Icing sugar** is the same as confectioners' sugar. [BRIT]

SUFFIX
-icity
replaces *-ic* at the end of adjectives to form nouns referring to the state, quality, or behavior described by the adjective. *For example, if someone disputes the* **authenticity** *of the document, they are saying that they do not think it is authentic.*

---

icky /ɪki/ **1** ADJ If you describe a substance as **icky**, you mean that it is disgustingly sticky. [mainly AM, INFORMAL, DISAPPROVAL] ❑ She could feel something icky on her fingers. **2** ADJ If you describe something as **icky**, you mean that it is too emotional or sentimental. [mainly AM, INFORMAL, DISAPPROVAL] ❑ ...a ballad whose sentiment some people might describe as icky.

icon /aɪkɒn/ (icons) also **ikon 1** N-COUNT If you describe something or someone as an **icon**, you mean that they are important as a symbol of a particular thing. ❑ ...only Marilyn has proved as enduring a fashion icon. **2** N-COUNT An **icon** is a picture of Christ, his mother, or a saint painted on a wooden panel. ❑ ...a painter of religious icons. **3** N-COUNT An **icon** is a picture on a computer screen representing a particular computer function. If you want to use it, you move the cursor onto the icon using a mouse. [COMPUTING] ❑ Kate clicked on the mail icon on her computer screen.

icon|ic /aɪkɒnɪk/ ADJ An **iconic** image or thing is important or impressive because it seems to be a symbol of something. [FORMAL] ❑ The ads helped Nike to achieve iconic status.

icono|clast /aɪkɒnəklæst/ (iconoclasts) N-COUNT If you describe someone as an **iconoclast**, you mean that they often criticize beliefs and things that are generally accepted by society. [FORMAL]

icono|clas|tic /aɪkɒnəklæstɪk/ ADJ If you describe someone or their words or ideas as **iconoclastic**, you mean that they contradict established beliefs. [FORMAL] ❑ ...his iconoclastic views of American society.

ico|no|gra|phy /aɪkənɒgrəfi/ N-UNCOUNT The **iconography** of a group of people consists of the symbols, pictures, and objects that represent their ideas and way of life. ❑ ...the iconography of revolutionary posters. ❑ ...religious iconography.

ICU /aɪ si yu/ (ICUs) N-COUNT An **ICU** is a part of a hospital where patients who are dangerously ill are looked after constantly. **ICU** is an abbreviation for 'intensive care unit.' ❑ Some patients in the ICU had to be manually ventilated.

icy /aɪsi/ (icier, iciest) **1** ADJ If you describe something as **icy** or **icy cold**, you mean that it is extremely cold. ❑ An icy wind blew hard across the open spaces. **2** ADJ An **icy** road has ice on it. ❑ The roads were icy. **3** ADJ If you describe a person or their behavior as **icy**, you mean that they are not affectionate or friendly, and they show their dislike or anger in a quiet, controlled way. [DISAPPROVAL] ❑ His response was icy.

ID /aɪ di/ (IDs) N-VAR If you have **ID** or an **ID**, you are carrying a document such as an identity card or driver's license that tells who you are. ❑ I had no ID on me so the police couldn't establish that I was the owner of the car.

I'd /aɪd/ **1 I'd** is the usual spoken form of 'I had,' especially when 'had' is an auxiliary verb. ❑ I felt absolutely certain that I'd seen her before. **2 I'd** is the usual spoken form of 'I would.' ❑ There are some questions I'd like to ask.

ID card (ID cards) N-COUNT An **ID card** is the same as an identity card, identification card. ❑ ...a proposal to introduce ID cards.

idea ◆◆◆ /aɪdiə/ (ideas) **1** N-COUNT An **idea** is a plan, suggestion, or possible course of action. ❑ It's a good idea to have your blood pressure checked regularly. ❑ I really like the idea of helping people. **2** N-COUNT An **idea** is an opinion or belief about what something is like or should be like. ❑ Some of his ideas about democracy are entirely his own. **3** N-SING If someone gives you an **idea of** something, they give you information about it without being very exact or giving a lot of detail. ❑ This table will give you some idea of how levels of ability in a foreign language can be measured. **4** N-SING If you have an **idea of** something, you know about it to some extent. ❑ No one has any real idea how much the company will make next year. ❑ We had no idea what was happening. **5** N-SING If you have an **idea** that something is the case, you think that it may be the case, although you are not certain. [VAGUENESS] ❑ I had an idea that he joined the army later, after college, but I may be wrong. **6** N-SING The **idea** of an action or activity is its aim or purpose. ❑ The idea is to get industry to be more efficient in the way it uses energy. **7** N-COUNT If you have the **idea of** doing something, you intend to do it. ❑ He sent for a number of books he admired with the idea of rereading them.

COLLOCATIONS
idea
NOUN
1
adjective + **idea**: bright, brilliant, good; creative, novel, original, radical
verb + **idea**: like, support; abandon, dismiss, reject; develop
3
adjective + **idea**: general, rough

---

ideal ◆◇◇ /aɪdiəl/ (ideals) **1** N-COUNT An **ideal** is a principle, idea, or standard that seems very good and worth trying to achieve. ❑ Here is a man who has stayed true to his ideals. **2** N-SING Your **ideal** of something is the person or thing that seems to you to be the best possible example of it. ❑ ...people who don't fit into our society's ideal of beauty. **3** ADJ The **ideal** person or thing for a particular task or purpose is the best possible person or thing for it. ❑ She decided that I was the ideal person to take over the job. **4** ADJ [ADJ n] An **ideal** society or world is the best possible one that you can imagine. ❑ We do not live in an ideal world.

SYNONYMS
ideal
NOUN **1**
principle: ...moral principles.
morals: They have no morals.
scruple: ...a man with no moral scruples.
standard: My father has always had high moral standards.
ADJ **3**
perfect: Hiring a nanny has turned out to be the perfect solution.
ultimate: He is the ultimate English gentleman.
model: As a girl she had been a model student.

---

ideal|ism /aɪdiəlɪzəm/ N-UNCOUNT **Idealism** is the beliefs and behavior of someone who has ideals and who tries to base their behavior on these ideals. ❑ She never lost her respect for the idealism of the 1960s. • **ideal|ist** (idealists) N-COUNT ❑ He is not such an idealist that he cannot see the problems.

ideal|is|tic /aɪdiəlɪstɪk, aɪdiə-/ **1** ADJ If you describe someone as **idealistic**, you mean that they have ideals, and base their behavior on these ideals, even though this may be impractical. ❑ Idealistic young people died for the cause. **2** → See feature box at **quality**

ideal|ize /aɪdiəlaɪz/ (idealizes, idealizing, idealized)
in BRIT, also use **idealise**
V-T If you **idealize** something or someone, you think of them,

or represent them to other people, as being perfect or much better than they really are. ❑ *People idealize the past.*

ideal|ly /aɪdiəli/ **1** ADV [ADV with cl/group] If you say that **ideally** a particular thing should happen or be done, you mean that this is what you would like to happen or be done, but you know that this may not be possible or practical. ❑ *People should, ideally, be persuaded to eat a diet with much less fat or oil.* **2** ADV If you say that someone or something is **ideally** suited, **ideally** located, or **ideally** qualified, you mean that they are as well suited, located, or qualified as they could possibly be. ❑ *They were an extremely happy couple, ideally suited.*

iden|ti|cal /aɪdɛntɪkəl/ ADJ Things that are **identical** are exactly the same. ❑ *The three bombs were virtually identical.* • **iden|ti|cal|ly** /aɪdɛntɪkli/ ADV ❑ *...nine identically dressed female dancers.*

iden|ti|cal twin (identical twins) N-COUNT [usu pl] **Identical twins** are twins of the same sex who look exactly the same.

iden|ti|fi|able /aɪdɛntɪfaɪəbəl/ ADJ Something or someone that is **identifiable** can be recognized. ❑ *In the corridor were four dirty, ragged bundles, just identifiable as human beings.*

iden|ti|fi|ca|tion /aɪdɛntɪfɪkeɪʃən/ (identifications) **1** N-VAR The **identification** of something is the recognition that it exists, is important, or is true. ❑ *Early identification of a disease can prevent death and illness.* **2** N-VAR The **identification** of a particular person or thing is the ability to name them because you know them or recognize them. ❑ *Officials are awaiting positive identification before charging the men with war crimes.* **3** N-UNCOUNT If someone asks you for some **identification**, they want to see something such as a driver's license, that proves who you are. ❑ *He did not have any identification when he arrived at the hospital.* **4** N-VAR The **identification** of one person or thing with another is the close association of one with the other. ❑ *...the identification of Spain with Catholicism.* **5** N-UNCOUNT **Identification with** someone or something is the feeling of sympathy and support for them. ❑ *Marilyn had an intense identification with animals.*

iden|ti|fi|ca|tion card (identification cards) N-COUNT An **identification card** is the same as an **identity card**. The abbreviation **ID card** is also used. [mainly AM]

iden|ti|fy ♦♦◊ /aɪdɛntɪfaɪ/ (identifies, identifying, identified) **1** V-T If you can **identify** someone or something, you are able to recognize them or distinguish them from others. ❑ *There are a number of distinguishing characteristics by which you can identify a Hollywood epic.* **2** V-T If you **identify** someone or something, you name them or say who or what they are. ❑ *Police have already identified 10 murder suspects.* **3** V-T If you **identify** something, you discover or notice its existence. ❑ *Scientists claim to have identified chemicals produced by certain plants which have powerful cancer-fighting properties.* **4** V-T If a particular thing **identifies** someone or something, it makes them easy to recognize, by making them different in some way. ❑ *She wore a little nurse's hat on her head to identify her.* **5** V-I If you **identify with** someone or something, you feel that you understand them or their feelings and ideas. ❑ *She would only play a role if she could identify with the character.* **6** V-T If you **identify** one person or thing **with** another, you think that they are closely associated or involved in some way. ❑ *Moore really hates to play the sweet, passive women that audiences have identified her with.*

────── **SYNONYMS** ──────
identify
VERB **1**
recognize: *He did not think she could recognize his car in the snow.*
place: *It was a voice he recognized, though he could not immediately place it.*
name: *One of the victims has been named as a twenty-year-old New Yorker.*
remember: *I can remember where and when I bought each one.*
put your finger on: *Amy couldn't quite put her finger on the reason.*
pinpoint: *It was almost impossible to pinpoint the cause of death.*

iden|ti|ty ♦♦◊ /aɪdɛntɪti/ (identities) **1** N-COUNT Your **identity** is who you are. ❑ *Abu is not his real name, but it's one he uses to disguise his identity.* **2** N-VAR The **identity** of a person or place is the characteristics that distinguish them from others. ❑ *I wanted a sense of my own identity.*

iden|tity card (identity cards) N-COUNT An **identity card** is a card with a person's name, photograph, date of birth, and other information on it. In some countries, people are required to carry identity cards in order to prove who they are. The abbreviation **ID card** is also used.

iden|tity cri|sis (identity crises) N-COUNT [usu sing: an N] If you say that someone or something is having an **identity crisis**, you mean that it is not clear what kind of person or thing they are, or what kind of person or thing they would like to be. ❑ *After Terminator 2, however, Arnie suffered a mid-career identity crisis and got mixed up in comedy.* ❑ *...another organization with an identity crisis; its very existence is a matter of dispute.*

iden|tity pa|rade (identity parades) N-COUNT An **identity parade** is the same as a **line-up**. [BRIT]

iden|tity poli|tics N-UNCOUNT **Identity politics** is political activity aimed at promoting the welfare of a particular social group to which you see yourself as belonging. ❑ *This disempowering rivalry was never what identity politics was supposed to be about.*

iden|tity theft **1** N-UNCOUNT **Identity theft** is the crime of getting personal information about another person without their knowledge, for example, in order to gain access to their bank account. ❑ *Protecting yourself from identity theft is a matter of treating all your personal and financial documents as top secret information.* **2** → See feature box at **crime**

ideo|gram /ɪdiəgræm/ (ideograms) **1** N-COUNT An **ideogram** is a sign or symbol that represents a particular idea or thing rather than a word. The writing systems of Japan and China, for example, use ideograms. **2** N-COUNT In languages such as English which are written using letters and words, an **ideogram** is a sign or symbol that can be used to represent a particular word. %, @, and & are examples of ideograms.

ideo|logi|cal /aɪdiəlɒdʒɪkəl, ɪdi-/ ADJ **Ideological** means relating to principles or beliefs. ❑ *Others left the party for ideological reasons.* • **ideo|logi|cal|ly** ADV ❑ *...an ideologically sound organization.*

ideolo|gist /aɪdiɒlədʒɪst/ (ideologists) N-COUNT An **ideologist** is someone who develops or supports a particular ideology.

ideo|logue /aɪdiəlɒg, ɪdi-, aɪdi-/ (ideologues) N-COUNT An **ideologue** is the same as an **ideologist**. [FORMAL]

ideol|ogy /aɪdiɒlədʒi, ɪdi-/ (ideologies) N-VAR An **ideology** is a set of beliefs, especially the political beliefs on which people, parties, or countries base their actions. ❑ *...capitalist ideology.*

id|io|cy /ɪdiəsi/ (idiocies) N-VAR [oft N of n/-ing] If you refer to something as **idiocy**, you mean that it is very stupid. ❑ *...the idiocy of continuing government subsidies for environmentally damaging activities.*

idi|om /ɪdiəm/ (idioms) N-COUNT An **idiom** is a group of words that have a different meaning when used together from the one they would have if you took the meaning of each word separately. [TECHNICAL] ❑ *...familiar idioms and metaphors, such as "turning over a new leaf."*

idio|mat|ic /ɪdiəmætɪk/ ADJ [usu ADJ n] **Idiomatic** language uses words in a way that sounds natural to native speakers of the language. ❑ *...her remarkable command of idiomatic English.*

idio|syn|cra|sy /ɪdiəsɪŋkrəsi/ (idiosyncrasies) N-VAR [usu with poss] If you talk about the **idiosyncrasies** of someone or something, you are referring to their rather unusual habits or characteristics. ❑ *Everyone has a few little idiosyncrasies.*

idio|syn|crat|ic /ɪdiəʊsɪŋkrætɪk/ ADJ If you describe someone's actions or characteristics as **idiosyncratic**, you mean that they are somewhat unusual. ❑ *...a highly idiosyncratic personality.*

id|iot /ɪdiət/ (idiots) N-COUNT If you call someone an **idiot**, you are showing that you think they are very stupid or have done something very stupid. [DISAPPROVAL] ❑ *I knew I'd been an idiot to stay there.*

idi|ot|ic /ɪdiɒtɪk/ ADJ If you call someone or something **idiotic**, you mean that they are very stupid or silly. [DISAPPROVAL] ❑ *What an idiotic thing to say!* • **idi|oti|cal|ly** /ɪdiɒtɪkli/ ADV ❑ *...his idiotically romantic views.*

idle /aɪdᵊl/ (**idles, idling, idled**) **1** ADJ [v-link ADJ] If people who were working are **idle**, they have no jobs or work. ❑ *4,000 workers have been idle for 12 of the first 27 weeks of this year.* **2** ADJ [v-link ADJ] If machines or factories are **idle**, they are not working or being used. ❑ *Now the machine is lying idle.* **3** ADJ If you say that someone is **idle**, you disapprove of them because they are not doing anything and you think they should be. [DISAPPROVAL] ❑ *...idle bureaucrats who spent the day reading newspapers.* • **idly** ADV [ADV with v] ❑ *We were not idly sitting around.* **4** ADJ [ADJ n] **Idle** is used to describe something that you do for no particular reason, often because you have nothing better to do. ❑ *Brian kept up the idle chatter for another five minutes.* • **idly** ADV ❑ *We talked idly about magazines and baseball.* **5** ADJ [ADJ n] You refer to an **idle** threat or boast when you do not think the person making it will or can do what they say. ❑ *It was more of an idle threat than anything.* **6** V-I If an engine or vehicle **is idling**, the engine is running slowly and quietly because it is not in gear, and the vehicle is not moving. ❑ *Beyond a stand of trees a small plane idled.*

idler /ˈaɪdlər/ (**idlers**) N-COUNT If you describe someone as an **idler**, you are criticizing them because you think they are lazy and should be working. [DISAPPROVAL] ❑ *This man was no idler - he worked harder than anyone I knew.*

idol /ˈaɪdᵊl/ (**idols**) **1** N-COUNT If you refer to someone such as a movie, pop, or sports star as an **idol**, you mean that they are greatly admired or loved by their fans. ❑ *A great cheer went up from the crowd as they caught sight of their idol.* **2** N-COUNT An **idol** is a statue or other object that is worshipped by people who believe that it is a god.

idola|try /aɪˈdɒlətri/ **1** N-UNCOUNT Someone who practices **idolatry** worships idols. [FORMAL] **2** N-UNCOUNT If you refer to someone's admiration for a particular person as **idolatry**, you think it is too great and uncritical. [FORMAL, DISAPPROVAL] ❑ *Their affection for her soon increased almost to idolatry.*

idol|ize /ˈaɪdəlaɪz/ (**idolizes, idolizing, idolized**)

in BRIT, also use **idolise**

V-T If you **idolize** someone, you admire them very much. ❑ *Naomi idolized her father as she was growing up.*

id|yll /ˈaɪdᵊl/ (**idylls**)

in AM, also use **idyl**

N-COUNT If you describe a situation as an **idyll**, you mean that it is idyllic. ❑ *She finds that the sleepy town she moves to isn't the rural idyll she imagined.*

idyl|lic /aɪˈdɪlɪk/ ADJ If you describe something as **idyllic**, you mean that it is extremely pleasant, simple, and peaceful without any difficulties or dangers. ❑ *...an idyllic setting for a summer romance.*

i.e. /ˈaɪ ˈiː/ **i.e.** is used to introduce a word or sentence that makes what you have just said clearer or gives details. ❑ *...an artificial intelligence system, i.e. a computer program.*

IED /ˈaɪ iː ˈdiː/ (**IEDs**) N-COUNT An **IED** is a simple bomb that is made and used by someone who is not in the army, often using materials that are not usually used for making bombs. IED is an abbreviation for 'improvised explosive device.' ❑ *The soldiers were killed by a roadside IED.*

-ied → see -ed

-ier → see -er

-iest → see -est

if ✦✦✦ /ɪf/

Often pronounced /ɪf/ at the beginning of the sentence.

1 CONJ You use **if** in conditional sentences to introduce the circumstances in which an event or situation might happen, might be happening, or might have happened. ❑ *She gets very upset if I exclude her from anything.* ❑ *You can go if you want.* **2** CONJ You use **if** in indirect questions where the answer is either 'yes' or 'no.' ❑ *He asked if I had left with you, and I said no.* **3** CONJ You use **if** to suggest that something might be slightly different from what you are stating in the main part of the sentence, for example, that there might be slightly more or less of a particular quality. ❑ *Sometimes that standard is quite difficult, if not impossible, to achieve.* **4** CONJ You use **if**, usually with 'can,' 'could,' 'may,' or 'might,' in a conversation when you are politely trying to make a point, change the subject, or interrupt another speaker. ❑ *If I could just make another small point about the weightlifters in the Olympics.* **5** CONJ You use **if** at or near the beginning of a clause when politely asking someone to do something. [POLITENESS] ❑ *I wonder if you'd be kind enough to give us some information, please?* **6** PHRASE You use **if not** in front of a word or phrase to indicate that your statement does not apply to that word or phrase, but to something closely related to it that you also mention. ❑ *She understood his meaning, if not his words, and took his advice.* **7** CONJ You use **if** to introduce a subordinate clause in which you admit a fact that you regard as less important than the statement in the main clause. ❑ *If there was any disappointment it was probably temporary.* **8** PHRASE You use **if ever** with past tenses when you are introducing a description of a person or thing, to emphasize how appropriate it is. [EMPHASIS] ❑ *I became a distraught, worried mother, a useless role if ever there was one.* **9** PHRASE You use **if only** with past tenses to introduce what you think is a fairly good reason for doing something, although you realize it may not be a very good one. ❑ *She always writes me once a month, if only to scold me because I haven't answered her last letter yet.* **10** PHRASE You use **if only** to express a wish or desire, especially one that cannot be fulfilled. [FEELINGS] ❑ *If only you had told me that some time ago.* **11** PHRASE You use **as if** when you are making a judgment about something that you see or notice. Your belief or impression might be correct, or it might be wrong. ❑ *It looked as if she had forgotten how to breathe.* **12** PHRASE You use **as if** to describe something or someone by comparing them with another thing or person. ❑ *He points two fingers at his head, as if he were holding a gun.* **13** PHRASE You use **as if** to emphasize that something is not true. [SPOKEN, EMPHASIS] ❑ *Getting my work done! My God! As if it mattered.*

if|fy /ˈɪfi/ (**iffier, iffiest**) **1** ADJ If something is **iffy**, it is uncertain. [INFORMAL] ❑ *His political future has looked iffy for most of this year.* **2** ADJ If you say that something is **iffy**, you mean that it is not very good in some way. [INFORMAL] ❑ *If your next record's a bit iffy, you're forgotten.*

SUFFIX

-ify
is used at the end of verbs that refer to making something or someone different in some way. For example, 'More needs to be done to **simplify** the process of registering to vote.'

---

ig|loo /ˈɪgluː/ (**igloos**) N-COUNT **Igloos** are dome-shaped houses built from blocks of snow by the Inuit people.

ig|ne|ous /ˈɪgniəs/ ADJ [ADJ n] In geology, **igneous** rocks are rocks that were once so hot that they were liquid. [TECHNICAL]

ig|nite /ɪgˈnaɪt/ (**ignites, igniting, ignited**) **1** V-T/V-I When you **ignite** something or when it **ignites**, it starts burning or explodes. ❑ *The bombs ignited a fire which destroyed some 60 houses.* **2** V-T If something or someone **ignites** your feelings, they cause you to have very strong feelings about something. [LITERARY] ❑ *There was one teacher who really ignited my interest in words.*

ig|ni|tion /ɪgˈnɪʃᵊn/ (**ignitions**) **1** N-VAR In a car engine, the **ignition** is the part where the fuel is ignited. ❑ *The device automatically disconnects the ignition.* **2** N-SING Inside a car, the **ignition** is the part where you turn the key so that the engine starts. ❑ *Abruptly he turned the ignition key and started the engine.* **3** N-UNCOUNT **Ignition** is the process of something starting to burn. ❑ *The ignition of methane gas killed eight men.*

ig|no|ble /ɪgˈnoʊbᵊl/ ADJ If you describe something as **ignoble**, you mean that it is bad and something to be ashamed of. [FORMAL, DISAPPROVAL] ❑ *...ignoble thoughts.*

ig|no|mini|ous /ˌɪgnəˈmɪniəs/ ADJ If you describe an experience or action as **ignominious**, you mean it is embarrassing because it shows a great lack of success. [FORMAL] ❑ *...their ignominious defeat.* • **ig|no|mini|ous|ly** ADV [ADV with v] ❑ *Even if her contract was cancelled, and she was ignominiously dismissed, she would not see that as a disaster.*

ig|no|miny /ˈɪgnəmɪni/ N-UNCOUNT [oft N *of* n/-ing] **Ignominy** is shame or public disgrace. [FORMAL] ❑ *...the ignominy of being fired.*

ig|no|ra|mus /ˌɪgnəˈreɪməs/ (**ignoramuses**) N-COUNT If you describe someone as an **ignoramus**, you are being critical of them because they do not have the knowledge you think they ought to have. [FORMAL, DISAPPROVAL]

ig|no|rance /ɪgnərəns/ N-UNCOUNT **Ignorance** of something is lack of knowledge about it. ❑ *I am beginning to feel embarrassed by my complete ignorance of world history.*

ig|no|rant /ɪgnərənt/ **1** ADJ If you describe someone as **ignorant**, you mean that they do not know things they should know. If someone is **ignorant** of a fact, they do not know it. ❑ *People don't like to ask questions for fear of appearing ignorant.* **2** ADJ People are sometimes described as **ignorant** when they do something that is not polite or kind. ❑ *I met some ignorant people who called me all kinds of names.*

ig|nore ♦♦◇ /ɪgnɔr/ (**ignores, ignoring, ignored**) **1** V-T If you **ignore** someone or something, you pay no attention to them. ❑ *She said her husband ignored her.* **2** V-T If you say that an argument or theory **ignores** an important aspect of a situation, you are criticizing it because it fails to consider that aspect or to take it into account. ❑ *Such arguments ignore the question of where ultimate responsibility lay.*

SYNONYMS
ignore
VERB **1**
neglect: *The woman denied that she had neglected her child.*
disregard: *He disregarded the advice of his executives.*
discount: *However, traders tended to discount the rumor.*
take no notice of: *They took no notice of him.*
overlook: *...a fact that we all tend to overlook.*

igua|na /ɪgwɑnə/ (**iguanas**) N-COUNT An **iguana** is a type of large lizard found in Central and South America.

PREFIX
il-
can be added to some words to form words that have the opposite meaning. For example, if an activity is **illegal**, it is not legal.

ilk /ɪlk/ N-SING [supp N] If you talk about people or things of the same **ilk**, you mean people or things of the same type as a person or thing that has been mentioned. ❑ *Let the politicians and their ilk rant and rave, we must maintain a discreet silence.* ❑ *Finding and talking to others of your ilk is easy through online communities.*

ill ♦♦◇ /ɪl/ (**ills**) **1** ADJ Someone who is **ill** is suffering from a disease or a health problem. ❑ *In November 1941 Payne was seriously ill with pneumonia.* • N-PLURAL People who are ill in some way can be referred to as, for example, the terminally **ill**. ❑ *The hospice provides care for the terminally ill.* **2** N-COUNT Difficulties and problems are sometimes referred to as **ills**. [FORMAL] ❑ *His critics maintain that he's responsible for many of Algeria's ills.* **3** ADJ [ADJ n] You can use **ill** in front of some nouns to indicate that you are referring to something harmful or unpleasant. [FORMAL] ❑ *She had brought ill luck into her family.* **4** N-UNCOUNT **Ill** is evil or harm. [LITERARY] ❑ *They say they mean you no ill.* **5** ADV [ADV with v] **Ill** means the same as 'badly.' [FORMAL] ❑ *The company's conservative instincts sit ill with competition.* **6** PHRASE If you say that someone **can ill afford** to do something, or **can ill afford** something, you mean that they must prevent it from happening because it would be harmful or embarrassing to them. [FORMAL] ❑ *It's possible he won't play but I can ill afford to lose him.* **7** PHRASE If you **fall ill** or **are taken ill**, you suddenly become ill. ❑ *Shortly before Christmas, he was mysteriously taken ill.* **8 to speak ill of someone** → see **speak**

USAGE
ill
Don't use 'ill' or 'sick' to say that someone has received an injury. Say that they are **injured** or **hurt**. *Two people were injured and taken to the hospital after the car crash.*

ill- /ɪl-/ COMB IN ADJ **Ill-** is added to words, especially adjectives and past participles, to add the meaning 'badly' or 'inadequately.' For example, 'ill-suited' means badly suited. ❑ *...ill-disciplined children.*

I'll /aɪl/ **I'll** is the usual spoken form of 'I will' or 'I shall.' ❑ *I'll be leaving town in a few weeks.*

ill-advised ADJ [oft ADJ to-inf] If you describe something that someone does as **ill-advised**, you mean that it is not sensible or wise. ❑ *They would be ill-advised to do this.*

ill at ease also **ill-at-ease** → see **ease**

ill-bred ADJ If you say that someone is **ill-bred**, you mean that they have bad manners. [DISAPPROVAL]

ill-conceived ADJ If you describe a plan or action as **ill-conceived**, you mean that it is likely to fail or have bad consequences because it has not been thought about carefully enough. ❑ *...an ill-conceived plan to close the coal mine.*

ill-considered ADJ If you describe something that someone says or does as **ill-considered**, you mean that it is not sensible or not appropriate. ❑ *He made some ill-considered remarks about the cost.*

ill-defined ADJ If you describe something as **ill-defined**, you mean that its exact nature or extent is not as clear as it should be or could be. ❑ *...staff with ill-defined responsibilities.*

ill ef|fects also **ill-effects** N-PLURAL If something has **ill effects**, it causes problems or damage. ❑ *Some people are still suffering ill effects from the contamination of their water.*

il|legal ♦◇ /ɪliɡəl/ (**illegals**) **1** ADJ If something is **illegal**, the law says that it is not allowed. ❑ *It is illegal to intercept radio messages.* ❑ *...illegal drugs.* • **il|legal|ly** ADV [ADV with v] ❑ *He was convicted of illegally using a handgun.* **2** ADJ [ADJ n] **Illegal** immigrants or workers have traveled into a country or are working without official permission. • N-COUNT Illegal immigrants or workers are sometimes referred to as **illegals**. ❑ *...a clothing factory where many other illegals also worked.*

il|leg|ible /ɪlɛdʒɪbəl/ ADJ Writing that is **illegible** is so unclear that you cannot read it.

il|legiti|ma|cy /ɪlɪdʒɪtɪməsi/ N-UNCOUNT **Illegitimacy** is the state of being born of parents who were not married to each other. ❑ *In those days illegitimacy was a terrible stigma.*

il|legiti|mate /ɪlɪdʒɪtɪmɪt/ **1** ADJ A person who is **illegitimate** was born of parents who were not married to each other. ❑ *They discovered he had an illegitimate child.* **2** ADJ **Illegitimate** is used to describe activities and institutions that are not in accordance with the law or with accepted standards of what is right. ❑ *He realized that, otherwise, the election would have been dismissed as illegitimate by the international community.*

ill-equipped ADJ Someone who is **ill-equipped** to do something does not have the ability, the qualities, or the equipment necessary to do it. ❑ *The government is ill-equipped to handle work by private contractors.*

ill-fated ADJ If you describe something as **ill-fated**, you mean that it ended or will end in an unsuccessful or unfortunate way. ❑ *...the glacier where the explorer trained for his ill-fated Antarctic expedition.*

ill-fitting ADJ [ADJ n] An **ill-fitting** piece of clothing does not fit the person who is wearing it properly. ❑ *He wore an ill-fitting green corduroy suit.*

ill-founded ADJ Something that is **ill-founded** is not based on any proper proof or evidence. ❑ *Suspicion and jealousy, however ill-founded, can poison a marriage.*

ill-gotten gains N-PLURAL **Ill-gotten gains** are things that someone has obtained in a dishonest or illegal way. ❑ *But many leaders have invested their ill-gotten gains in several different countries.*

ill health N-UNCOUNT Someone who suffers from **ill health** has an illness or keeps being ill. ❑ *He was forced to retire because of ill health.*

il|lib|er|al /ɪlɪbərəl/ ADJ If you describe someone or something as **illiberal**, you are critical of them because they do not allow or approve of much freedom or choice of action. [DISAPPROVAL] ❑ *...illiberal legislation.*

il|lic|it /ɪlɪsɪt/ ADJ An **illicit** activity or substance is not allowed by law or the social customs of a country. ❑ *Dante clearly condemns illicit love.*

il|lit|era|cy /ɪlɪtərəsi/ N-UNCOUNT **Illiteracy** is the state of not knowing how to read or write.

il|lit|er|ate /ɪlɪtərɪt/ (**illiterates**) ADJ Someone who is **illiterate** does not know how to read or write. ❑ *A large percentage of the population is illiterate.* • N-COUNT An **illiterate** is someone who is illiterate. ❑ *The number of illiterates has fallen considerably.*

ill-mannered ADJ If you describe someone as **ill-mannered**, you are critical of them because they are impolite or rude. [FORMAL, DISAPPROVAL] ❏ *Chantal would have considered it ill-mannered to show surprise.*

ill|ness ✦✧ /ɪlnɪs/ (**illnesses**) **1** N-UNCOUNT **Illness** is the fact or experience of being ill. ❏ *If your child shows any signs of illness, take her to the doctor.* **2** N-COUNT An **illness** is a particular disease such as measles or pneumonia. ❏ *She returned to her family home to recover from an illness.*

COLLOCATIONS

illness
NOUN
1
adjective + **illness**: mental, physical; serious, severe
verb + **illness**: cause; battle, feign
2
noun + **illness**: childhood, mystery, stomach
adjective + **illness**: chronic, debilitating, life-threatening, terminal; long, short; psychiatric, stress-related
verb + **illness**: contract, suffer; cure, diagnose, treat; prevent

VOCABULARY IN CONTEXT

Illness

If you wake up feeling ill, when should you **call in sick** to work or school? It partly depends on how bad you're feeling, but also on whether or not your **symptoms** are **contagious**. If your head is **throbbing** and you've got a slightly raised **temperature**, the chances are that a couple of **painkillers** are all it takes for you to be well enough to work. Contrary to popular belief, **food poisoning** can be **catching**. Whatever the case, if you're **vomiting** or you've got **diarrhea** because of either a **bacterial infection** or a **viral stomach bug**, your colleagues won't thank you for exposing them to your **germs**. If you've got a **rash**, maybe it's just an **allergic reaction** to something, but it could be more serious – though probably not **life-threatening**. It's tempting to **diagnose** yourself from the internet, but it's probably best to get a doctor to check it out before you come into contact with your colleagues or classmates.

il|logi|cal /ɪlɒdʒɪkᵊl/ ADJ If you describe an action, feeling, or belief as **illogical**, you are critical of it because you think that it does not result from a logical and ordered way of thinking. [DISAPPROVAL] ❏ *It was absurd and illogical to go out into such a storm.*

ill-prepared ADJ If you are **ill-prepared** for something, you have not made the correct preparations for it, for example, because you are not expecting it to happen. ❏ *The government was ill-prepared for the problems it now faces.*

ill-starred ADJ [usu ADJ n] If you describe something or someone as **ill-starred**, you mean that they were unlucky or unsuccessful. [LITERARY] ❏ *...his ill-starred mission to the Middle East.*

ill-suited ADJ [v-link ADJ] If something is **ill-suited** to a particular purpose, it is not right or appropriate for that purpose. If someone is **ill-suited** to a particular job, they are not right or appropriate for that job. ❏ *In its contemporary form, western democracy is held to be ill-suited to our country's cultural traditions.* ❏ *I was ill-suited to work in the mental health field.*

ill-tempered ADJ If you describe someone as **ill-tempered**, you mean they are angry or hostile, and you may be implying that this is unreasonable. [FORMAL] ❏ *It was a day of tense and often ill-tempered debate.*

ill-timed ADJ If you describe something as **ill-timed**, you mean that it happens or is done at the wrong time, so that it is damaging or rude. ❏ *He argued that the tax cut was ill-timed.*

ill-treat (**ill-treats, ill-treating, ill-treated**) V-T If someone **ill-treats** you, they treat you badly or cruelly. ❏ *They thought Mr. Smith had been ill-treating his wife.*

ill-treatment N-UNCOUNT **Ill-treatment** is harsh or cruel treatment. ❏ *...allegations of ill-treatment by the police.*

il|lu|mi|nate /ɪlumɪneɪt/ (**illuminates, illuminating, illuminated**) **1** V-T To **illuminate** something means to shine light on it and to make it brighter and more visible. [FORMAL] ❏ *No streetlights illuminated the street.* **2** V-T If you **illuminate** something that is unclear or difficult to understand, you make it clearer by explaining it carefully or giving information about it. [FORMAL] ❏ *Instead of formulas and charts, the two instructors use games and drawings to illuminate their subject.* • **il|lu|mi|nat|ing** ADJ ❏ *It would be illuminating to hear the views of the club vice-chairman.* **3** → See feature box at **light**

il|lu|mi|nat|ed /ɪlumɪneɪtɪd/ ADJ Something that is **illuminated** is lit up, usually by electric lighting. ❏ *...an illuminated sign.*

il|lu|mi|na|tion /ɪlumɪneɪʃᵊn/ N-UNCOUNT **Illumination** is the lighting that a place has. [FORMAL] ❏ *The only illumination came from a small window high in the opposite wall.*

il|lu|mine /ɪlumɪn/ (**illumines, illumining, illumined**) V-T To **illumine** something means the same as to **illuminate** it. [LITERARY] ❏ *The interchange of ideas illumines the debate.* ❏ *By night, the perimeter wire was illumined by lights.*

il|lu|sion /ɪluʒᵊn/ (**illusions**) **1** N-VAR An **illusion** is a false idea or belief. ❏ *No one really has any illusions about winning the war.* **2** N-COUNT An **illusion** is something that appears to exist or be a particular thing but does not actually exist or is in reality something else. ❏ *Floor-to-ceiling windows can look stunning, giving the illusion of extra height.*

il|lu|sion|ist /ɪluʒənɪst/ (**illusionists**) N-COUNT An **illusionist** is a performer who makes it seem that strange or impossible things are happening, for example, that a person has disappeared or been cut in half.

il|lu|so|ry /ɪluzəri, -səri/ ADJ If you describe something as **illusory**, you mean that although it seems true or possible, it is in fact false or impossible. ❏ *His freedom is illusory.*

il|lus|trate ✦✧ /ɪləstreɪt/ (**illustrates, illustrating, illustrated**) **1** V-T If you say that something **illustrates** a situation that you are drawing attention to, you mean that it shows that the situation exists. ❏ *The example of the United States illustrates this point.* ❏ *The situation illustrates how vulnerable the president is.* **2** V-T If you use an example, story, or diagram to **illustrate** a point, you use it to show that what you are saying is true or to make your meaning clearer. ❏ *Let me give another example to illustrate this difficult point.* • **il|lus|tra|tion** N-UNCOUNT ❏ *Here, by way of illustration, are some extracts from our new catalog.* **3** V-T If you **illustrate** a book, you put pictures, photographs, or diagrams into it. ❏ *She went on to art school and is now illustrating a book.* • **il|lus|tra|tion** N-UNCOUNT ❏ *...the world of children's book illustration.*

SYNONYMS

illustrate
VERB **1**
demonstrate: *The study also demonstrated a direct link between obesity and diabetes.*
show: *Research shows that a high-fiber diet may protect you from colon cancer.*
exemplify: *The style of the room exemplifies the designer's ideal of 'beauty and practicality.'*

il|lus|tra|tion ✦✧ /ɪləstreɪʃᵊn/ (**illustrations**) **1** N-COUNT An **illustration** is an example or a story that is used to make a point clear. ❏ *An illustration of China's dynamism is that a new* company is formed in Shanghai every 11 seconds. **2** N-COUNT An **illustration** in a book is a picture, design, or diagram. ❏ *She looked like a princess in a nineteenth-century illustration.* **3** → see also **illustrate**

SYNONYMS

illustration
NOUN **2**
picture: *...drawing a small picture with colored chalks.*
drawing: *She did a drawing of me.*
image: *...photographic images of young children.*
painting: *...a large oil-painting of Queen Victoria.*
representation: *...a lifelike representation of the leader.*

---

il|lus|tra|tive /ɪləstrətɪv/ ADJ [oft ADJ of n] If you use something as an **illustrative** example, or for **illustrative** purposes, you use it to show that what you are saying is true or to make your meaning clearer. [FORMAL] ❏ *The charts in this article are for illustrative purposes only.*

il|lus|tra|tor /ɪləstreɪtər/ (**illustrators**) N-COUNT An **illustrator** is an artist who draws pictures and diagrams for books and magazines.

il|lus|tri|ous /ɪlʌstriəs/ ADJ If you describe someone as an **illustrious** person, you mean that they are extremely well known because they have a high position in society or they have done something impressive. ❏ *...the most illustrious scientists of the century.*

ill will also ill-will N-UNCOUNT **Ill will** is unfriendly or hostile feelings that you have toward someone. ❏ *He didn't bear anyone any ill will.*

ill wind N-SING [usu a n] You can describe an unfortunate event as an **ill wind** if someone benefits from it. The expression occurs in the proverb 'It's an ill wind that blows nobody any good.' ❏ *But it's an ill wind; I recovered and married one of my nurses from that hospital.*

IM /aɪ ɛm/ (**IMs**) **1** N-UNCOUNT **IM** is an abbreviation for **instant messaging.** ❏ *The device permits multitasking, letting you, for example, simultaneously surf the Web and chat via IM.* **2** N-COUNT **IM** is an abbreviation for **instant message.**

PREFIX

im-
can be added to some words to form words that have the opposite meaning. *For example, if someone is* **impatient**, *they are not patient.*

I'm /aɪm/ **I'm** is the usual spoken form of 'I am.' ❏ *I'm sorry.*

im|age ♦♦◇ /ɪmɪdʒ/ (**images**) **1** N-COUNT If you have an **image** of something or someone, you have a picture or idea of them in your mind. ❏ *The image of art theft as a gentleman's crime is outdated.* **2** N-COUNT The **image** of a person, group, or organization is the way that they appear to other people. ❏ *...the government's negative public image.* **3** N-COUNT An **image** is a picture of someone or something. [FORMAL] ❏ *...photographic images of young children.* **4** N-COUNT An **image** is a poetic description of something. [FORMAL] ❏ *The natural images in the poem are meant to be suggestive of realities beyond themselves.* **5** PHRASE If you **are the image of** someone else, you look very much like them. ❏ *Marianne's son was the image of his father.* **6 spitting image** → see **spit**

SYNONYMS

image
NOUN
1
impression: *What were your first impressions of college?*
perception: *So how do our perceptions of death affect the way we live?*
idea: *My idea of physical perfection is to be very slender.*
vision: *Turning that vision into a practical reality is not easy.*
2
mask: *His mask of detachment cracked, and she saw, fleetingly, an angry man.*
persona: *...the contradictions between her private life and the public persona.*
facade: *They hid the troubles plaguing their marriage behind a facade of family togetherness.*

---

im|age|ry /ɪmɪdʒri/ **1** N-UNCOUNT You can refer to the descriptions in something such as a poem or song, and the pictures they create in your mind, as its **imagery.** [FORMAL] ❏ *...the nature imagery of the ballad.* **2** N-UNCOUNT You can refer to pictures and representations of things as **imagery**, especially when they act as symbols. [FORMAL] ❏ *This is an ambitious and intriguing movie, full of striking imagery.*

im|agi|nable /ɪmædʒɪnəbəl/ **1** ADJ You use **imaginable** after a superlative such as 'best' or 'worst' to emphasize that something is extreme in some way. [EMPHASIS] ❏ *...their imprisonment under some of the most horrible circumstances imaginable.* **2** ADJ [ADJ n, n ADJ] You use **imaginable** after a word like 'every' or 'all' to emphasize that you are talking about all the possible examples of something. You use **imaginable** after 'no' to emphasize that something does not have the quality mentioned. [EMPHASIS] ❏ *Parents encourage every activity imaginable.* ❏ *...a place of no imaginable strategic value.*

im|agi|nary /ɪmædʒɪnɛri/ ADJ An **imaginary** person, place, or thing exists only in your mind or in a story, and not in real life. ❏ *Lots of children have imaginary friends.*

im|agi|na|tion ♦♦◇ /ɪmædʒɪneɪʃən/ (**imaginations**) **1** N-VAR Your **imagination** is the ability that you have to form pictures or ideas in your mind of things that are new and exciting, or things that you have not experienced. ❏ *Latanya is a woman with a vivid imagination.* **2** N-COUNT Your **imagination** is the part of your mind that allows you to form pictures or ideas of things that do not necessarily exist in real life. ❏ *Long before I ever went there, Africa was alive in my imagination.* **3** PHRASE If you say that someone or something **captured** your **imagination,** you mean that you thought they were interesting or exciting when you saw them or heard them for the first time. ❏ *Their music continues to capture the imagination of the American public.* **4 not by any stretch of the imagination** → see **stretch**

SYNONYMS

imagination
NOUN **1**
creativity: *American art reached a peak of creativity in the '50s and '60s.*
inventiveness: *He has surprised us before with his inventiveness.*
inspiration: *My inspiration comes from poets like Baudelaire and Jacques Prévert.*
originality: *He was capable of writing things of startling originality.*

---

im|agi|na|tive /ɪmædʒɪnətɪv/ ADJ If you describe someone or their ideas as **imaginative,** you are praising them because they are easily able to think of or create new or exciting things. [APPROVAL] ❏ *...an imaginative writer.* • im|agi|na|tive|ly ADV [ADV with v] ❏ *The hotel is decorated imaginatively and attractively.*

im|ag|ine ♦♦◇ /ɪmædʒɪn/ (**imagines, imagining, imagined**) **1** V-T If you **imagine** something, you think about it and your mind forms a picture or idea of it. ❏ *He could not imagine a more peaceful scene.* ❏ *She couldn't imagine living in a place like that.* **2** V-T If you **imagine** that something is the case, you think that it is the case. ❏ *I imagine you're referring to Jean-Paul Sartre.* **3** V-T If you **imagine** something, you think that you have seen, heard, or experienced that thing, although actually you have not. ❏ *Looking back on it now, I realized that I must have imagined the whole thing.*

im|ag|ing /ɪmɪdʒɪŋ/ N-UNCOUNT **Imaging** is the process of forming images that represent things such as sound waves, temperature, chemicals, or electrical activity. [TECHNICAL] ❏ *...thermal imaging cameras.*

im|ag|in|ings /ɪmædʒɪnɪŋz/ N PLURAL **Imaginings** are things that you think you have seen or heard, although actually you have not. [LITERARY]

imam /ɪmɑm/ (**imams**) N-COUNT In Islam, an **imam** is a religious leader, especially the leader of a Muslim community or the person who leads the prayers in a mosque.

IMAX /aɪmæks/ N-UNCOUNT [oft N n] **IMAX** is a system for showing movies on very large screens with very clear sound and pictures. [TRADEMARK] ❏ *...a new IMAX cinema.*

im|bal|ance /ɪmbæləns/ (**imbalances**) N-VAR If there is an **imbalance** in a situation, the things involved are not the same size, or are not the right size in proportion to each other. ❏ *...the imbalance between the two sides in this war.*

im|bal|anced /ɪmbælənst/ ADJ If you describe a situation as **imbalanced**, you mean that the elements within it are not evenly or fairly arranged. ❑ ...the present imbalanced structure of world trade.

im|be|cile /ɪmbɪsᵊl/ (**imbeciles**) **1** N-COUNT If you call someone an **imbecile**, you are showing that you think they are stupid or have done something stupid. [DISAPPROVAL] ❑ I don't want to deal with these imbeciles any longer. **2** ADJ [ADJ n] **Imbecile** means stupid. ❑ It was an imbecile thing to do.

im|bibe /ɪmbaɪb/ (**imbibes, imbibing, imbibed**) **1** V-T/V-I To **imbibe** alcohol means to drink it. [FORMAL, often HUMOROUS] ❑ They were used to imbibing enormous quantities of alcohol. ❑ No one believes that current nondrinkers should be encouraged to start imbibing. **2** V-T If you **imbibe** ideas or arguments, you listen to them, accept them, and believe that they are right or true. [FORMAL] ❑ As a clergyman's son he'd imbibed a set of mystical beliefs from the cradle.

im|bro|glio /ɪmbroʊliou/ (**imbroglios**) N-COUNT [usu with supp] An **imbroglio** is a very confusing or complicated situation. [LITERARY]

im|bue /ɪmbyu/ (**imbues, imbuing, imbued**) V-T If someone or something **is imbued** with an idea, feeling, or quality, they become filled with it. [FORMAL] ❑ The film is imbued with the star's rebellious spirit.

IMF /aɪ ɛm ɛf/ N-PROPER The **IMF** is an international agency that tries to promote trade and improve economic conditions in poorer countries, sometimes by lending them money. **IMF** is an abbreviation for 'International Monetary Fund.'

IMHO **IMHO** is the written abbreviation for 'in my humble opinion,' mainly used in text messages and e-mails. [COMPUTING]

imi|tate /ɪmɪteɪt/ (**imitates, imitating, imitated**) **1** V-T If you **imitate** someone, you copy what they do or produce. ❑ ...a genuine German musical that does not try to imitate the American model. **2** V-T If you **imitate** a person or animal, you copy the way they speak or behave, usually because you are trying to be funny. ❑ Clarence screws up his face and imitates the Colonel again.

imi|ta|tion /ɪmɪteɪʃᵊn/ (**imitations**) **1** N-COUNT An **imitation** of something is a copy of it. ❑ ...the most accurate imitation of Chinese architecture in Europe. **2** N-UNCOUNT **Imitation** means copying someone else's actions. ❑ They discussed important issues in imitation of their elders. **3** ADJ [ADJ n] **Imitation** things are not genuine but are made to look as if they are. ❑ ...a complete set of Dickens bound in imitation leather. **4** N-COUNT If someone does an **imitation** of another person, they copy the way they speak or behave, sometimes in order to be funny. ❑ One boy did an imitation of a soldier with a loudspeaker.

imi|ta|tive /ɪmɪteɪtɪv/ ADJ People and animals who are **imitative** copy others' behavior. ❑ Babies of eight to twelve months are generally highly imitative.

imi|ta|tor /ɪmɪteɪtər/ (**imitators**) N-COUNT An **imitator** is someone who copies what someone else does, or copies the way they speak or behave. ❑ He doesn't take chances; that's why he's survived and most of his imitators haven't. ❑ ...the Beatles and their many imitators.

im|macu|late /ɪmækyulɪt/ **1** ADJ If you describe something as **immaculate**, you mean that it is extremely clean, tidy, or neat. ❑ Her kitchen was kept immaculate. • **im|macu|late|ly** ADV ❑ As always he was immaculately dressed. **2** ADJ If you say that something is **immaculate**, you are emphasizing that it is perfect, without any mistakes or bad parts at all. [EMPHASIS] ❑ The goalie's performance was immaculate. • **im|macu|late|ly** ADV [ADV with v] ❑ The orchestra plays immaculately.

im|ma|nent /ɪmənənt/ ADJ If you say that a quality is **immanent** in a particular thing, you mean that the thing has that quality, and cannot exist or be imagined without it. [FORMAL] ❑ Modern capitalist economy follows its own immanent laws.

im|ma|teri|al /ɪmətɪəriəl/ ADJ [v-link ADJ] If you say that something is **immaterial**, you mean that it is not important or not relevant. ❑ Whether we like him or not is immaterial.

im|ma|ture /ɪmətʃʊər, -tʊər/ **1** ADJ Something or someone that is **immature** is not yet completely grown or fully developed. ❑ She is emotionally immature. **2** ADJ If you describe someone as **immature**, you are being critical of them because they do not behave in a sensible or responsible way. [DISAPPROVAL] ❑ She's just being childish and immature.

im|meas|ur|able /ɪmɛʒərəbᵊl/ ADJ If you describe something as **immeasurable**, you are emphasizing how great it is. [FORMAL, EMPHASIS] ❑ His contribution is immeasurable.

im|meas|ur|ably /ɪmɛʒərəbli/ ADV [ADV with v, ADV adj] You use **immeasurably** to emphasize the degree or extent of a process or quality. [FORMAL, EMPHASIS] ❑ They have improved immeasurably since their arrival.

im|medi|acy /ɪmidiəsi/ N-UNCOUNT [oft N of n] The **immediacy** of an event or situation is the quality that makes it seem important or exciting because it is happening at the present time. ❑ Do they understand the immediacy of the crisis?

im|medi|ate ✦◇◇ /ɪmidiɪt/ **1** ADJ An **immediate** result, action, or reaction happens or is done without any delay. ❑ These tragic incidents have had an immediate effect. **2** ADJ **Immediate** needs and concerns exist at the present time and must be dealt with quickly. ❑ Relief agencies say the immediate problem is not a lack of food, but transportation. **3** ADJ [ADJ n] The **immediate** person or thing comes just before or just after another person or thing in a sequence. ❑ In the immediate aftermath of the riots, a mood of hope and reconciliation sprang up. **4** ADJ [ADJ n] You use **immediate** to describe an area or position that is next to or very near a particular place or person. ❑ Only a handful had returned to work in the immediate vicinity. **5** ADJ [ADJ n] Your **immediate** family are the members of your family who are most closely related to you, such as your parents, children, brothers, and sisters. ❑ The presence of his immediate family is obviously having a calming effect on him.

im|medi|ate|ly ✦◇ /ɪmidiɪtli/ **1** ADV [ADV with v] If something happens **immediately**, it happens without any delay. ❑ He immediately flung himself to the floor. **2** ADV [ADV adj] If something is **immediately** obvious, it can be seen or understood without any delay. ❑ The cause of the accident was not immediately apparent. **3** ADV [ADV adj/-ed] **Immediately** is used to indicate that someone or something is closely and directly involved in a situation. ❑ The man immediately responsible for this misery is the province's governor. **4** ADV [ADV prep/adj] **Immediately** is used to emphasize that something comes next, or is next to something else. ❑ They wish to begin immediately after dinner.

SYNONYMS

immediately
ADV **1**
at once: I have to go, I really must, at once.
instantly: The man was killed instantly.
right away: I should go and see a doctor right away.
promptly: Sister Francesca entered the chapel, took her seat, and promptly fell asleep.

im|memo|ri|al /ɪmɪmɔriəl/ PHRASE If you say that something has been happening **since time immemorial** or **from time immemorial**, you are emphasizing that it has been happening for many centuries. [LITERARY, EMPHASIS] ❑ It has remained virtually unchanged since time immemorial.

im|mense /ɪmɛns/ ADJ If you describe something as **immense**, you mean that it is extremely large or great. ❑ ...an immense cloud of smoke.

im|mense|ly /ɪmɛnsli/ ADV You use **immensely** to emphasize the degree or extent of a quality, feeling, or process. [EMPHASIS] ❑ I enjoyed this movie immensely.

im|merse /ɪmɜrs/ (**immerses, immersing, immersed**) **1** V-T If you **immerse** yourself in something that you are doing, you become completely involved in it. ❑ Their commitments do not permit them to immerse themselves in current affairs as fully as they might wish. • **im|mersed** ADJ [v-link ADJ in n] ❑ He's really becoming immersed in his work. **2** V-T [usu passive] If something **is immersed** in a liquid, someone puts it into the liquid so that it is completely covered. ❑ The electrodes are immersed in liquid.

im|mer|sion /ɪmɜrʒᵊn, -ʃᵊn/ **1** N-UNCOUNT [N in n] Someone's **immersion in** a subject is their complete involvement in it. ❑ ...long-term assignments that allowed them total immersion in their subjects. **2** N-UNCOUNT [oft N in n] **Immersion** of something in a liquid means putting it into the liquid so that it is completely covered. ❑ The wood had become swollen from prolonged immersion.

im|mi|grant /ɪmɪgrənt/ (**immigrants**) N-COUNT An **immigrant** is a person who has come to live in a country from some other country. Compare **emigrant**. ❑ *...illegal immigrants.*

im|mi|grate /ɪmɪgreɪt/ (**immigrates, immigrating, immigrated**) V-I [no passive] If someone **immigrates** to a particular country, they come to live or work in that country, after leaving the country where they were born. ❑ *...a Russian-born professor who had immigrated to the United States.* ❑ *He immigrated from India at age 18.* ❑ *10,000 people are expected to immigrate in the next two years.*

im|mi|gra|tion /ɪmɪgreɪʃ°n/ ■ N-UNCOUNT **Immigration** is the coming of people into a country in order to live and work there. ❑ *The government has decided to tighten its immigration policy.* ■ N-UNCOUNT **Immigration** or **immigration control** is the place at a port, airport, or international border where officials check the passports of people who wish to come into the country. ❑ *First, you have to go through immigration and customs.*

im|mi|nent /ɪmɪnənt/ ADJ If you say that something is **imminent**, especially something unpleasant, you mean it is almost certain to happen very soon. ❑ *There appeared no imminent danger.*

im|mo|bile /ɪmoʊb°l/ ■ ADJ [usu v-link ADJ] Someone or something that is **immobile** is completely still. ❑ *Joe remained immobile, as if he had been carved out of stone.* • **im|mo|bil|ity** /ɪmoʊbɪlɪti/ N-UNCOUNT ❑ *Hector maintained the rigid immobility of his shoulders.* ■ ADJ [usu v-link ADJ] Someone or something that is **immobile** is unable to move or unable to be moved. ❑ *A riding accident left him immobile.* • **im|mo|bil|ity** N-UNCOUNT ❑ *Again, the pain locked me into immobility.*

im|mo|bi|lize /ɪmoʊbɪlaɪz/ (**immobilizes, immobilizing, immobilized**)

in BRIT, also use **immobilise**

V-T To **immobilize** something or someone means to stop them from moving or operating. ❑ *...a car alarm system that immobilizes the engine.*

im|mo|bi|liz|er /ɪmoʊbɪlaɪzər/ (**immobilizers**)

in BRIT, also use **immobiliser**

N-COUNT An **immobilizer** is a device on a car that prevents it from starting unless a special key is used, so that no one can steal the car.

im|mod|er|ate /ɪmɒdərət/ ADJ [usu ADJ n] If you describe something as **immoderate**, you disapprove of it because it is too extreme. [FORMAL, DISAPPROVAL] ❑ *He launched an immoderate tirade on Turner.*

im|mod|est /ɪmɒdɪst/ ■ ADJ [usu ADJ n] If you describe someone's behavior as **immodest**, you mean that it shocks or embarrasses you because you think that it is rude or indecent. ❑ *Students should avoid any immodest behavior, on or off campus.* ■ ADJ [usu v-link ADJ] If you say that someone is **immodest**, you disapprove of the way in which they often say how good, important, or clever they are. [DISAPPROVAL] ❑ *At the risk of being immodest, I was a great salesman.*

im|mor|al /ɪmɒrəl/ ADJ If you describe someone or their behavior as **immoral**, you believe that their behavior is morally wrong. [DISAPPROVAL] ❑ *...those who think that birth control and abortion are immoral.*

im|mor|tal /ɪmɔrt°l/ (**immortals**) ■ ADJ Someone or something that is **immortal** is famous and likely to be remembered for a long time. ❑ *...Wuthering Heights, Emily Brontë's immortal love story.* • N-COUNT An **immortal** is someone who will be remembered for a long time. ❑ *...the players considered to be the immortals of the game.* • **im|mor|tal|ity** /ɪmɔrtælɪti/ N-UNCOUNT ❑ *Some people want to achieve immortality through their works.* ■ ADJ Someone or something that is **immortal** will live or last forever and never die or be destroyed. ❑ *The pharaohs, after all, were considered gods and therefore immortal.* • N-COUNT An **immortal** is an immortal being. ❑ *...porcelain figurines of the Chinese immortals.* • **im|mor|tal|ity** N-UNCOUNT ❑ *The Greeks accepted belief in the immortality of the soul.* ■ ADJ [ADJ n] If you refer to someone's **immortal** words, you mean that what they said is well-known, and you are usually about to quote it. ❑ *Everyone knows Teddy Roosevelt's immortal words, "Speak softly and carry a big stick."*

im|mor|tal|ize /ɪmɔrt°laɪz/ (**immortalizes, immortalizing, immortalized**)

in BRIT, also use **immortalise**

V-T If someone or something **is immortalized** in a story, movie, or work of art, they appear in it, and will be remembered for it. [WRITTEN] ❑ *His original interior design is immortalized in at least seven movies and television shows.*

im|mov|able /ɪmuːvəb°l/ ■ ADJ [usu ADJ n] An **immovable** object is fixed and cannot be moved. ■ ADJ [usu v-link ADJ] If someone is **immovable** in their attitude to something, they will not change their mind. ❑ *On one issue, however, she was immovable.*

im|mune /ɪmyuːn/ ■ ADJ [v-link ADJ] If you are **immune** to a particular disease, you cannot be affected by it. ❑ *About 93 percent of U.S. residents are immune to measles either because they were vaccinated or they had the disease as a child.* • **im|mun|ity** /ɪmyuːnɪti/ N-UNCOUNT ❑ *Birds in outside cages develop immunity to airborne bacteria.* ■ ADJ [v-link ADJ] If you are **immune** to something that happens or is done, you are not affected by it. ❑ *Higher education is no longer immune to state budget cuts.* ■ ADJ [v-link ADJ] Someone or something that is **immune** from a particular process or situation is able to escape it. ❑ *People with diplomatic passports are immune from criminal prosecution.* • **im|mun|ity** N-UNCOUNT ❑ *The police are offering immunity to witnesses who help identify the murderers.*

SYNONYMS

immune
ADJ ■
exempt: *Men in college were exempt from military service.*
be excused from: *She is usually excused from her school duties during the summer vacation.*

---

im|mune sys|tem (**immune systems**) N-COUNT Your **immune system** consists of all the organs and processes in your body that protect you from illness and infection. ❑ *His immune system completely broke down and he became very ill.*

im|mun|ize /ɪmyənaɪz/ (**immunizes, immunizing, immunized**)

in BRIT, also use **immunise**

V-T [usu passive] If people or animals **are immunized**, they are made immune to a particular disease, often by being given an injection. ❑ *We should require that every student is immunized against hepatitis B.* ❑ *Healthy children over five were among the last to be immunized.* • **im|mun|iza|tion** /ɪmyənaɪzeɪʃ°n/ (**immunizations**) N-VAR ❑ *...universal immunization against childhood diseases.*

im|mu|no|de|fi|cien|cy /ɪmyənoʊdɪfɪʃ°nsi/ N-UNCOUNT [usu N n] **Immunodeficiency** is a weakness in a person's immune system, or the failure of a person's immune system. [MEDICAL] ❑ *...a type of immunodeficiency disease totally unrelated to AIDS.*

im|mu|table /ɪmyuːtəb°l/ ADJ Something that is **immutable** will never change or cannot be changed. [FORMAL] ❑ *...the eternal and immutable principles of right and wrong.*

imp /ɪmp/ (**imps**) ■ N-COUNT In fairy stories, an **imp** is a small, magical creature that often causes trouble in a playful way. ■ N-COUNT People sometimes refer to a naughty child as an **imp**. [INFORMAL]

im|pact (**impacts, impacting, impacted**)

The noun is pronounced /ɪmpækt/. The verb is pronounced /ɪmpækt/ or /ɪmpækt/.

■ N-COUNT The **impact** that something has on a situation, process, or person is a sudden and powerful effect that it has on them. ❑ *They say they expect the meeting to have a marked impact on the future of the country.* ■ N-VAR An **impact** is the action of one object hitting another, or the force with which one object hits another. ❑ *Most of the meteorite was destroyed on impact.* ■ V-T/V-I To **impact** a situation, process, or person means to affect them. ❑ *Such schemes mean little unless they impact people.* ■ V-T/V-I If one object **impacts** on another, it hits it with great force. [FORMAL] ❑ *...the sharp tinkle of metal impacting on stone.* ■ → See feature box at **disaster, recycle**

COLLOCATIONS

impact
NOUN

1
adjective + **impact**: dramatic, immediate, major, potential; economic, environmental, psychological; adverse, negative, positive
verb + **impact**: achieve, create, have, make; assess, consider, examine

2
adjective + **impact**: full, initial
verb + **impact**: absorb, cushion, lessen, soften; feel
VERB **3**
impact + noun: community, economy, market
impact + adverb: adversely, negatively, severely, significantly

---

SYNONYMS

impact
NOUN **1**
effect: *Parents worry about the effect of music on their adolescent's behavior.*
influence: *Van Gogh had a major influence on the development of modern painting.*
consequence: *An economic crisis may have tremendous consequences for our global security.*
repercussions: *It was an effort which would have painful repercussions.*

---

im|pair /ɪmpɛər/ (impairs, impairing, impaired) v-T If something **impairs** something such as an ability or the way something works, it damages it or makes it worse. [FORMAL] ❏ *Consumption of alcohol impairs your ability to drive a car or operate machinery.* • **im|paired** ADJ ❏ *The blast left him with permanently impaired hearing.*

-impaired /-ɪmpɛərd/ COMB IN ADJ You use **-impaired** in adjectives where you are describing someone with a particular disability. For example, someone who is **hearing-impaired** has a disability affecting their hearing, and someone who is **visually-impaired** has a disability affecting their sight. ❏ *More than 1 in 20 people are hearing-impaired to some extent.* • COMB IN N-PLURAL [the N] **The hearing-impaired** or **the visually-impaired** are people with disabilities affecting their hearing or sight. This use could cause offense. ❏ *...giving a voice to the speech-impaired.*

im|pair|ment /ɪmpɛərmənt/ (impairments) N-VAR If someone has an **impairment**, they have a condition that prevents their eyes, ears, limbs or brain from working properly. ❏ *He has a visual impairment in the right eye.*

im|pale /ɪmpeɪl/ (impales, impaling, impaled) v-T To **impale** something on a pointed object means to cause the point to go into it or through it. ❏ *Researchers observed one bird impale a rodent on a cactus.*

im|part /ɪmpɑrt/ (imparts, imparting, imparted) **1** v-T If you **impart** information to people, you tell it to them. [FORMAL] ❏ *The ability to impart knowledge and command respect is the essential qualification for teachers.* **2** v-T To **impart** a particular quality to something means to give it that quality. [FORMAL] ❏ *She managed to impart great elegance to the unpretentious dress she was wearing.*

im|par|tial /ɪmpɑrʃəl/ ADJ Someone who is **impartial** is not directly involved in a particular situation, and is therefore able to give a fair opinion or decision about it. ❏ *Career counselors offer impartial advice, guidance and information to all pupils.* • **im|par|tial|ity** /ɪmpɑrʃiælɪti/ N-UNCOUNT ❏ *...a justice system lacking impartiality by democratic standards.* • **im|par|tial|ly** ADV [ADV with v] ❏ *He has vowed to oversee the elections impartially.*

im|pass|able /ɪmpæsəbəl/ ADJ If a road, path, or route is **impassable**, it is impossible to travel over because it is blocked or in bad condition.

im|passe /ɪmpæs/ N-SING If people are in a difficult position in which it is impossible to make any progress, you can refer to the situation as an **impasse**. ❏ *The company says it has reached an impasse in negotiations with the union.*

im|pas|sioned /ɪmpæʃənd/ ADJ An **impassioned** speech or piece of writing is one in which someone expresses their strong feelings about an issue in a forceful way. [WRITTEN] ❏ *He made an impassioned appeal for peace.*

im|pas|sive /ɪmpæsɪv/ ADJ If someone is **impassive** or their face is **impassive**, they are not showing any emotion. [WRITTEN] ❏ *He searched Hill's impassive face for some indication that he understood.* • **im|pas|sive|ly** ADV [ADV with v] ❏ *The lawyer looked impassively at him and said nothing.*

im|pa|tient /ɪmpeɪʃənt/ **1** ADJ [v-link ADJ] If you are **impatient**, you are annoyed because you have to wait too long for something. ❏ *Investors are growing impatient with promises of improved earnings.* • **im|pa|tient|ly** ADV [ADV with v] ❏ *People have been waiting impatiently for a chance to improve the situation.* • **im|pa|tience** N-UNCOUNT ❏ *There is considerable impatience with the slow pace of political change.* **2** ADJ If you are **impatient**, you are easily irritated by things. ❏ *Beware of being too impatient with others.* • **im|pa|tient|ly** ADV [ADV with v] ❏ *"Come on, David," Harry said impatiently.* • **im|pa|tience** N-UNCOUNT ❏ *There was a hint of impatience in his tone.* **3** ADJ [v-link ADJ] If you are **impatient** to do something or **impatient for** something to happen, you are eager to do it or for it to happen and do not want to wait. ❏ *He didn't want to tell Mr. Morrisson why he was impatient to get home.* • **im|pa|tience** N-UNCOUNT ❏ *She showed impatience to continue the climb.*

im|peach /ɪmpitʃ/ (impeaches, impeaching, impeached) v-T If a court or a group in authority **impeaches** a president or other senior official, it charges them with committing a crime that makes them unfit for office. ❏ *...an opposition move to impeach the president.*

im|peach|ment /ɪmpitʃmənt/ (impeachments) N-VAR The **impeachment** of a senior official is the process of charging them with a crime that makes them unfit for office. ❏ *There are grounds for impeachment.*

im|pec|cable /ɪmpɛkəbəl/ **1** ADJ If you describe something such as someone's behavior or appearance as **impeccable**, you are emphasizing that it is perfect and has no faults. [EMPHASIS] ❏ *She had impeccable taste in clothes.* • **im|pec|cably** /ɪmpɛkəbli/ ADV ❏ *He was charming, considerate and impeccably mannered.* **2** → See feature box at **polite**

im|pede /ɪmpid/ (impedes, impeding, impeded) v-T If you **impede** someone or something, you make their movement, development, or progress difficult. [FORMAL] ❏ *Debris and fallen rock are impeding the progress of the rescue workers.*

im|pedi|ment /ɪmpɛdɪmənt/ (impediments) **1** N-COUNT Something that is an **impediment** to a person or thing makes their movement, development, or progress difficult. [FORMAL] ❏ *He was satisfied that there was no legal impediment to the marriage.* **2** N-COUNT Someone who has a speech **impediment** has a disability that makes speaking difficult. ❏ *John's slight speech impediment made it difficult for his mother to understand him.* **3** → See feature box at **speak**

im|pel /ɪmpɛl/ (impels, impelling, impelled) v-T When something such as an emotion **impels** you to do something, it affects you so strongly that you feel forced to do it. ❏ *...the courage and competitiveness which impels him to take risks.*

im|pend|ing /ɪmpɛndɪŋ/ ADJ [ADJ n] An **impending** event is one that is going to happen very soon. [FORMAL] ❏ *On the morning of the expedition, I awoke with a feeling of impending disaster.*

im|pen|etrable /ɪmpɛnɪtrəbəl/ **1** ADJ If you describe something such as a barrier or a forest as **impenetrable**, you mean that it is impossible or very difficult to get through. ❏ *...the Caucasus range, an almost impenetrable barrier between Europe and Asia.* **2** ADJ If you describe something such as a book or a theory as **impenetrable**, you are emphasizing that it is impossible or very difficult to understand. [EMPHASIS] ❏ *His philosophical work is notoriously impenetrable.*

im|pera|tive /ɪmpɛrətɪv/ (imperatives) **1** ADJ If it is **imperative** that something be done, that thing is extremely important and must be done. [FORMAL] ❏ *It was imperative that he act as naturally as possible.* **2** N-COUNT An **imperative** is something that is extremely important and must be done. [FORMAL] ❏ *The most important political imperative is to limit the number of casualties.* **3** N-SING In grammar, a clause that is in **the imperative**, or in **the imperative** mood, contains the base form of a verb and usually has no subject. Examples are 'Go away' and 'Please be careful.' Clauses of this kind are typically used to tell someone to do something. **4** N-COUNT An **imperative** is a verb in the base form that is used, usually without a subject, in an imperative clause.

im|per|cep|tible /ɪmpərsɛptɪbəl/ ADJ Something that is **imperceptible** is so small that it is not noticed or cannot be seen. ❏ *Brian's hesitation was almost imperceptible.* • **im|per|cep|tibly** ADV ❏ *The disease develops gradually and imperceptibly.*

im|per|fect /ɪmpɜrfɪkt/ ADJ Something that is **imperfect** has faults and is not exactly as you would like it to be. [FORMAL] ❏ *We live in an imperfect world.*

im|per|fec|tion /ɪmpərfɛkʃən/ (imperfections) **1** N-VAR An **imperfection** in someone or something is a fault, weakness, or undesirable feature that they have. ❏ *He concedes that there are imperfections in the system.* **2** N-COUNT An **imperfection** in something is a small mark or damaged area that may spoil its appearance. ❏ *Optical scanners ensure that imperfections in the cloth are located and removed.*

im|peri|al /ɪmpɪəriəl/ ADJ [ADJ n] **1 Imperial** is used to refer to things or people that are or were connected with an empire. ❏ *...the Imperial Palace in Tokyo.* **2** ADJ [ADJ n] The **imperial** system of measurement uses inches, feet, yards and miles to measure length, ounces and pounds to measure weight, and pints, quarts and gallons to measure volume.

im|peri|al|ism /ɪmpɪəriəlɪzəm/ N-UNCOUNT **Imperialism** is a system in which a rich and powerful country controls other countries, or a desire for control over other countries. ❏ *...nations or groups which have been victims of imperialism.*

im|peri|al|ist /ɪmpɪəriəlɪst/ (imperialists) ADJ **Imperialist** means relating to or based on imperialism. ❏ *The developed nations have all benefited from their imperialist exploitation.* • N-COUNT An **imperialist** is someone who has imperialist views. ❏ *He claims that imperialists are trying to re-establish colonial rule in the country.*

im|peri|al|is|tic /ɪmpɪəriəlɪstɪk/ ADJ If you describe a country as **imperialistic**, you disapprove of it because it wants control over other countries. [DISAPPROVAL]

im|per|il /ɪmpɛrɪl/ (imperils, imperiling or imperilling, imperiled or imperilled) V-T Something that **imperils** you puts you in danger. [FORMAL] ❏ *You imperiled the lives of other road users by your driving.*

im|peri|ous /ɪmpɪəriəs/ ADJ If you describe someone as **imperious**, you mean that they have a proud manner and expect to be obeyed. [WRITTEN] ❏ *Her attitude is imperious at times.* • **im|peri|ous|ly** ADV [ADV with v] ❏ *Imperiously she beckoned me out of the room.*

im|per|ish|able /ɪmpɛrɪʃəbəl/ ADJ Something that is **imperishable** cannot disappear or be destroyed. [LITERARY] ❏ *My memories are within me, imperishable.*

im|per|ma|nent /ɪmpɜrmənənt/ ADJ Something that is **impermanent** does not last forever. [FORMAL] ❏ *We are reminded just how small and how impermanent we are.* • **im|per|ma|nence** /ɪmpɜrmənəns/ N-UNCOUNT ❏ *He was convinced of the impermanence of his work.*

im|per|meable /ɪmpɜrmiəbəl/ ADJ Something that is **impermeable** will not allow fluid to pass through it. [FORMAL] ❏ *The canoe is made from an impermeable wood.*

im|per|son|al /ɪmpɜrsənəl/ **1** ADJ If you describe a place, organization, or activity as **impersonal**, you mean that it is not very friendly and makes you feel unimportant because it involves or is used by a large number of people. [DISAPPROVAL] ❏ *Before then many children were cared for in large impersonal orphanages.* **2** ADJ If you describe someone's behavior as **impersonal**, you mean that they do not show any emotion about the person they are dealing with. ❏ *We must be as impersonal as a surgeon with his knife.* **3** ADJ An **impersonal** room or statistic does not give any information about the character of the person to whom it belongs or relates. ❏ *The rest of the room was neat and impersonal.*

im|per|son|ate /ɪmpɜrsəneɪt/ (impersonates, impersonating, impersonated) V-T If someone **impersonates** a person, they pretend to be that person, either to deceive people or to make people laugh. ❏ *He was returned to prison in 1977 for impersonating a police officer.* • **im|per|sona|tion** /ɪmpɜrsəneɪʃən/ (impersonations) N-COUNT ❏ *She excelled at impersonations of his teachers, which provided great amusement for him.*

im|per|sona|tor /ɪmpɜrsəneɪtər/ (impersonators) N-COUNT An **impersonator** is a stage performer who impersonates famous people.

im|per|ti|nence /ɪmpɜrtənəns/ (impertinences) N-VAR If someone talks or behaves in a rather impolite and disrespectful way, you can call this behavior **impertinence** or an **impertinence**. ❏ *He was punished for his impertinence.*

im|per|ti|nent /ɪmpɜrtənənt/ ADJ If someone talks or behaves in a rather impolite and disrespectful way, you can say that they are being **impertinent**. ❏ *Would it be impertinent to ask where exactly you were?*

im|per|turb|able /ɪmpərtɜrbəbəl/ ADJ If you describe someone as **imperturbable**, you mean that they remain calm, even in disturbing or dangerous situations. [WRITTEN] ❏ *Thomas, of course, was cool and aloof and imperturbable.*

im|per|vi|ous /ɪmpɜrviəs/ **1** ADJ [usu v-link ADJ, usu ADJ to n] If you are **impervious** to someone's actions, you are not affected or influenced by them. ❏ *She seems almost impervious to the criticism from all sides.* **2** ADJ [oft ADJ to n] Something that is **impervious** to water, heat, or a particular object is able to resist it or stop it from passing through it. ❏ *This also makes the painting impervious to water.*

im|petu|os|ity /ɪmpɛtʃuɒsɪti/ N-UNCOUNT **Impetuosity** is the quality of being impetuous. ❏ *With characteristic impetuosity, he announced he was leaving school.*

im|petu|ous /ɪmpɛtʃuəs/ ADJ If you describe someone as **impetuous**, you mean that they are likely to act quickly and suddenly without thinking or being careful. ❏ *He was young and impetuous.*

im|petus /ɪmpɪtəs/ N-UNCOUNT [also an N, oft N for n] Something that gives a process **impetus** or an **impetus** makes it happen or progress more quickly. ❏ *The impetus for change came from lawyers.*

im|pinge /ɪmpɪndʒ/ (impinges, impinging, impinged) V-I Something that **impinges** on you affects you to some extent. [FORMAL] ❏ *...the cuts in defense spending that have impinged on two of the region's largest employers.*

im|pi|ous /ɪmpiəs, -paɪ-/ ADJ If you describe someone as **impious**, you mean that they show a lack of respect for religious things. [FORMAL]

imp|ish /ɪmpɪʃ/ ADJ If you describe someone or their behavior as **impish**, you mean that they are disrespectful or naughty in a playful way. ❏ *He is well known for his impish sense of humor.* • **imp|ish|ly** ADV ❏ *He smiled at me impishly.*

im|plac|able /ɪmplækəbəl/ ADJ If you say that someone is **implacable**, you mean that they have very strong feelings of hostility or disapproval that nobody can change. ❏ *...the threat of invasion by a ruthless and implacable enemy.* • **im|plac|ably** ADV ❏ *...two implacably hostile groups.*

im|plant (implants, implanting, implanted)

The verb is pronounced /ɪmplænt/. The noun is pronounced /ɪmplænt/.

1 V-T To **implant** something into a person's body means to put it there, usually by means of a medical operation. ❏ *Two days later, they implanted the fertilized eggs back inside me.* **2** N-COUNT An **implant** is something that is implanted into a person's body. ❏ *They felt a woman had a right to choose to have a breast implant.* **3** V-I When an egg or embryo **implants** in the womb, it becomes established there and can then develop. ❏ *Non-identical twins are the result of two fertilized eggs implanting in the uterus at the same time.* **4** V-T If you **implant** an idea or attitude in people, you make it become accepted or believed. ❏ *The diagram implanted a dangerous prejudice firmly in the minds of countless economics students.*

im|plau|sible /ɪmplɔzɪbəl/ ADJ If you describe something as **implausible**, you believe that it is unlikely to be true. ❏ *I had to admit it sounded like an implausible excuse.* • **im|plau|sibly** ADV ❏ *...an implausibly optimistic theory.*

im|ple|ment ◆◇◇ (implements, implementing, implemented)

The verb is pronounced /ɪmplɪment/ or /ɪmplɪmənt/. The noun is pronounced /ɪmplɪmənt/.

1 V-T If you **implement** something such as a plan, you ensure that what has been planned is done. ❏ *The government promised*

implicate 656 **important**

to implement a new system to control financial loan institutions. • **im|ple|men|ta|tion** /ɪmplɪmənteɪʃ°n, -men-/ N-UNCOUNT ❑ Very little has been achieved in the implementation of the peace agreement signed last January. **2** N-COUNT An **implement** is a tool or other piece of equipment. [FORMAL] ❑ ...writing implements.

SYNONYMS

implement
NOUN **2**
tool: I find the best tool for the purpose is a pair of shears.
device: ...an electronic device that protects your vehicle 24 hours a day.
instrument: ...a thin tube-like optical instrument.
gadget: ...kitchen gadgets, including toasters, kettles, and percolators.
utensil: ...utensils such as bowls, steamers, and frying pans.

COLLOCATIONS

implement
VERB **1**
implement + noun: changes, measures, proposals, recommendations, reforms; plan, policy, scheme, strategy; program; change
implement + adverb: correctly, effectively, fully, properly, successfully; immediately, speedily, urgently

---

im|pli|cate /ɪmplɪkeɪt/ (implicates, implicating, implicated) V-T To **implicate** someone means to show or claim that they were involved in something wrong or criminal. ❑ He was obliged to resign when one of his own aides was implicated in a financial scandal. • **im|pli|ca|tion** /ɪmplɪkeɪʃ°n/ N-UNCOUNT ❑ Implication in a murder finally brought him to jail.

im|pli|cat|ed /ɪmplɪkeɪtɪd/ **1** ADJ [v-link ADJ] If someone or something is **implicated** in a crime or a bad situation, they are involved in it or responsible for it. ❑ The president was implicated in the cover-up and forced to resign. **2** → see also **implicate**

im|pli|ca|tion ✦✧ /ɪmplɪkeɪʃ°n/ (implications) **1** N-COUNT The **implications** of something are the things that are likely to happen as a result. ❑ The Attorney General was aware of the political implications of his decision to prosecute. **2** N-COUNT The **implication** of a statement, event, or situation is what it implies or suggests is the case. ❑ The implication was obvious: vote for us or it will be very embarrassing for you. • PHRASE If you say that something is the case **by implication**, you mean that a statement, event, or situation implies that it is the case. ❑ Now his authority and, by implication, that of the whole management team are under threat as never before. **3** → see also **implicate**

SYNONYMS

implication
NOUN **2**
suggestion: There are suggestions that he might be supported by the Socialists.
hint: The statement gave no hint as to what the measures would be.
overtone: It's a quite profound story, with powerful religious overtones.
intimation: I did not have any intimation that he was going to resign.

---

im|plic|it /ɪmplɪsɪt/ **1** ADJ Something that is **implicit** is expressed in an indirect way. ❑ He gave an implicit warning against precipitate military action. • **im|plic|it|ly** ADV [ADV with v] ❑ The jury implicitly criticized the government by their verdict. **2** ADJ [v-link ADJ in n] If a quality or element is **implicit** in something, it is involved in it or is shown by it. [FORMAL] ❑ Trust is implicit in the system. **3** ADJ If you say that someone has an **implicit** belief or faith in something, you mean that they have complete faith in it and no doubts at all. ❑ He had implicit faith in the noble intentions of the Emperor. • **im|plic|it|ly** ADV [ADV after v] ❑ I trust him implicitly.

im|plode /ɪmploʊd/ (implodes, imploding, imploded) **1** V-I If something implodes, it collapses into itself in a sudden and violent way. ❑ The engine imploded. **2** V-I If something such as an organization or a system **implodes**, it suddenly ends completely because it cannot deal with the problems it is experiencing. ❑ Will the mayor let the city's desperate health care system implode?

im|plore /ɪmplɔr/ (implores, imploring, implored) V-T If you **implore** someone to do something, you ask them to do it in a forceful, emotional way. ❑ We will implore both parties to stay at the negotiating table.

im|plor|ing /ɪmplɔrɪŋ/ ADJ [ADJ n] An **imploring** look, cry, or letter shows that you want someone to do something very much and are afraid they may not do it. ❑ Frank looked at Jim with imploring eyes. • **im|plor|ing|ly** ADV [ADV after v] ❑ Michael looked at him imploringly, eyes brimming with tears.

im|ply ✦✧ /ɪmplaɪ/ (implies, implying, implied) **1** V-T If you **imply** that something is the case, you say something that indicates that it is the case in an indirect way. ❑ "Are you implying that I have something to do with those attacks?" she asked coldly. **2** V-T If an event or situation **implies** that something is the case, it makes you think that it is the case. ❑ Exports in June rose 1.5%, implying that the economy was stronger than many investors had realized.

SYNONYMS

imply
VERB **1**
suggest: It is wrong to suggest that there are easy alternatives.
insinuate: Are you insinuating that I smell?
hint: The President hinted he might make some changes in his Cabinet.
indicate: Mr Rivers has indicated that he may resign.
intimate: She intimated that she was contemplating a shake-up of the company.

---

im|po|lite /ɪmpəlaɪt/ **1** ADJ If you say that someone is **impolite**, you mean that they are rather rude and do not have good manners. ❑ The Count acknowledged the two newcomers as briefly as was possible without being impolite. **2** → See feature box at **polite**

im|pon|der|able /ɪmpɒndərəb°l/ (imponderables) N-COUNT An **imponderable** is something unknown about which it is difficult or impossible to estimate or make correct guesses. ❑ They are speculating on the imponderables of the future.

im|port ✦✧ (imports, importing, imported)

The verb is pronounced /ɪmpɔrt/ or /ɪmpɔrt/. The noun is pronounced /ɪmpɔrt/.

1 V-T/V-I To **import** products or raw materials means to buy them from another country for use in your own country. ❑ Rich countries benefited from importing Indonesia's timber. ❑ ...our decision to import from the US. • N-UNCOUNT [also N in pl] **Import** is also a noun. ❑ Germany, however, insists on restrictions on the import of Polish coal. • **im|por|ta|tion** /ɪmpɔrteɪʃ°n/ N-UNCOUNT ❑ ...restrictions concerning the importation of birds. **2** N-COUNT **Imports** are products or raw materials bought from another country for use in your own country. ❑ ...cheap imports from other countries. **3** N-UNCOUNT The **import** of something is its importance. [FORMAL] ❑ Such arguments are of little import. **4** V-T If you **import** files or information into one type of software from another type, you open them in a format that can be used in the new software. [COMPUTING] ❑ Users can import files made in other packages.

im|por|tance ✦✧ /ɪmpɔrt°ns/ **1** N-UNCOUNT The **importance** of something is its quality of being significant, valued, or necessary in a particular situation. ❑ China has been stressing the importance of its ties with third world countries. **2** N-UNCOUNT **Importance** means having influence, power, or status. ❑ Obviously a man of his importance is going to be missed.

SYNONYMS

importance
NOUN **1**
significance: Ideas about the social significance of religion have changed over time.
worth: He had never had a woman of her worth as a friend.
consequence: Where he is from is of no consequence to me.
substance: It's questionable whether anything of substance has been achieved.

---

im|por|tant ✦✦✦ /ɪmpɔrt°nt/ **1** ADJ Something that is **important** is very significant, is highly valued, or is necessary. ❑ The most important thing in my life was my career.

❏ It's important to answer her questions as honestly as you can. ● im|por|tant|ly ADV ❏ I was hungry, and, more importantly, my children were hungry. ❷ ADJ Someone who is **important** has influence or power within a society or a particular group. ❏ ...an important figure in the media world.

USAGE

important
Don't use 'important' to say that an amount or quantity is very large. Don't talk, for example, about 'an important sum of money.' Use a word such as **considerable** or **significant**. A considerable amount of rain had fallen.

im|port|er /ɪmpɔrtər/ (**importers**) N-COUNT An **importer** is a country, company, or person that buys goods from another country for use in their own country. ❏ Japan is the biggest importer of U.S. beef.

im|por|tu|nate /ɪmpɔrtʃənɪt/ ADJ If you describe someone as **importunate**, you think they are annoying because they keep trying to get something from you. [FORMAL, DISAPPROVAL] ❏ His secretary shielded him from importunate visitors.

im|por|tune /ɪmpɔrtun/ (**importunes, importuning, importuned**) V-T If someone **importunes** another person, they ask them for something or ask them to do something, in an annoying way. [FORMAL, DISAPPROVAL] ❏ One can no longer walk the streets without seeing beggars importuning passersby.

im|pose ✦✧ /ɪmpoʊz/ (**imposes, imposing, imposed**) ❶ V-T If you **impose** something on people, you use your authority to force them to accept it. ❏ Fines are imposed on retailers who sell tobacco to minors. ❏ A third of companies reviewing pay since last August have imposed a pay freeze of up to a year. ● **im|po|si|tion** /ɪmpəzɪʃ°n/ N-UNCOUNT ❏ The imposition of sanctions against persistent offenders will make them change their practices. ❷ V-T If you **impose** your opinions or beliefs on other people, you try and make people accept them as a rule or as a model to copy. ❏ Parents should beware of imposing their own tastes on their children. ❸ V-T If something **imposes** strain, pressure, or suffering on someone, it causes them to experience it. ❏ The filming imposed an additional strain on her. ❹ V-I If someone **imposes** on you, they unreasonably expect you to do something for them which you do not want to do. ❏ I was afraid you'd feel we were imposing on you. ● **im|po|si|tion** N-COUNT ❏ I know this is an imposition. But please hear me out. ❺ V-T If someone **imposes** themselves on you, they force you to accept their company although you may not want to. ❏ I didn't want to impose myself on my married friends. ❻ → See feature box at **legal**

SYNONYMS

impose
VERB ❶
inflict: Rebels say they have inflicted heavy casualties on government forces.
enforce: They struggled to limit the cost by enforcing a low-tech specification.
force: To force this agreement on the nation is wrong
foist: I don't see my role as foisting my beliefs on them.

im|pos|ing /ɪmpoʊzɪŋ/ ADJ If you describe someone or something as **imposing**, you mean that they have an impressive appearance or manner. ❏ He was an imposing man.

im|pos|sible ✦✧ /ɪmpɒsɪb°l/ ❶ ADJ Something that is **impossible** cannot be done or cannot happen. ❏ It was impossible for anyone to get in because no one knew the password. ❏ He thinks the tax is impossible to administer. ● N-SING **The impossible** is something that is impossible. ❏ They were expected to do the impossible. ● **im|pos|sibly** ADV [ADV adj] ❏ Mathematical physics is an almost impossibly difficult subject. ● **im|pos|sibil|ity** /ɪmpɒsɪbɪlɪti/ (**impossibilities**) N-VAR ❏ ...the impossibility of knowing absolute truth. ❷ ADJ [ADJ n] An **impossible** situation or an **impossible** position is one that is very difficult to deal with. ❏ I think he was in an impossible position. ❸ ADJ If you describe someone as **impossible**, you are annoyed that their bad behavior or strong views make them difficult to deal with. [DISAPPROVAL] ❏ The woman is impossible, thought Francesca.

im|pos|tor /ɪmpɒstər/ (**impostors**) also **imposter** N-COUNT Someone who is an **impostor** is dishonestly pretending to be someone else in order to gain an advantage. ❏ He was an imposter who masqueraded as a doctor.

im|pos|tor syn|drome N-UNCOUNT If you have **impostor syndrome**, you feel that you do not deserve your status or success. ❏ It's a classic case of imposter syndrome: having achieved great wealth, she feels as though she doesn't deserve it.

im|po|tence /ɪmpətəns/ ❶ N-UNCOUNT **Impotence** is a lack of power to influence people or events. ❏ ...a sense of impotence in the face of deplorable events. ❷ N-UNCOUNT **Impotence** is a man's sexual problem in which his penis fails to get hard or stay hard. ❏ Impotence affects 10 million men in the U.S. alone.

im|po|tent /ɪmpətənt/ ❶ ADJ If someone feels **impotent**, they feel that they have no power to influence people or events. ❏ The aggression of a bully leaves people feeling hurt, angry and impotent. ❷ ADJ If a man is **impotent**, his penis fails to get hard or stay hard. ❏ At the age of 40, 1.9 percent of men are impotent.

im|pound /ɪmpaʊnd/ (**impounds, impounding, impounded**) V-T If something **is impounded** by police officers, customs officers, or other officials, they officially take possession of it because a law or rule has been broken. ❏ The ship was impounded under the terms of the UN trade embargo.

im|pov|er|ish /ɪmpɒvərɪʃ/ (**impoverishes, impoverishing, impoverished**) ❶ V-T Something that **impoverishes** a person or a country makes them poor. ❏ We need to reduce the burden of taxes that impoverish the economy. ● **im|pov|er|ished** ADJ ❏ The goal is to lure businesses into impoverished areas by offering them tax breaks. ❷ V-T A person or thing that **impoverishes** something makes it worse in quality. ❏ A top dressing of fertilizer should be added to improve growth as mint impoverishes the soil quickly.

im|pov|er|ish|ment /ɪmpɒvərɪʃmənt/ N-UNCOUNT **Impoverishment** is the state or process of being impoverished. ❏ National isolation can only cause economic and cultural impoverishment.

im|prac|ti|cable /ɪmpræktɪkəb°l/ ADJ [usu v-link ADJ] If something such as a course of action is **impracticable**, it is impossible to do. ❏ Such measures would be highly impracticable and almost impossible to apply.

im|prac|ti|cal /ɪmpræktɪk°l/ ❶ ADJ If you describe an object, idea, or course of action as **impractical**, you mean that it is not sensible or realistic, and does not work well in practice. ❏ Once there were regularly scheduled airlines, it became impractical to make a business trip by ocean liner. ❷ ADJ If you describe someone as **impractical**, you mean that they do not have the abilities or skills to do practical work such as making, repairing, or organizing things. ❏ Geniuses are supposed to be difficult, eccentric and hopelessly impractical.

im|pre|ca|tion /ɪmprɪkeɪʃ°n/ (**imprecations**) N-VAR An **imprecation** is something rude, angry, or hostile that is said to or about someone. [FORMAL]

im|pre|cise /ɪmprɪsaɪs/ ADJ Something that is **imprecise** is not clear, accurate, or precise. ❏ The charges were vague and imprecise.

im|pre|ci|sion /ɪmprɪsɪʒ°n/ N-UNCOUNT **Imprecision** is the quality of being imprecise. ❏ This served to hide the confusion and imprecision in their thinking.

im|preg|nable /ɪmprɛgnəb°l/ ❶ ADJ If you describe a building or other place as **impregnable**, you mean that it cannot be broken into or captured. ❏ The old Dutch fort with its thick high walls looks virtually impregnable. ❷ ADJ If you say that a person or group is **impregnable**, or their position is **impregnable**, you think they cannot be defeated by anyone. ❏ ...the company's impregnable market position.

im|preg|nate /ɪmprɛgneɪt/ (**impregnates, impregnating, impregnated**) ❶ V-T If someone or something **impregnates** a thing with a substance, they make the substance spread through it and stay in it. ❏ Impregnating clothes with insect repellent is effective. ● **-impregnated** COMB IN ADJ ❏ ...a block of plastic impregnated with a light absorbing dye. ❷ V-T When a man or a male animal **impregnates** a woman or female animal, he makes her pregnant. [FORMAL] ❏ They impregnate the cow and take the calf once it is born.

im|pre|sa|rio /ɪmprɪsɑrioʊ/ (**impresarios**) N-COUNT An **impresario** is a person who arranges for plays, concerts, and other entertainments to be performed.

im|press /ɪmprɛs/ (impresses, impressing, impressed) **1** V-T/V-I If something **impresses** you, you feel great admiration for it. ❑ *What impressed him most was their speed.* • **im|pressed** ADJ [v-link ADJ] ❑ *I was very impressed by one young man at my lectures.* **2** V-T If you **impress** something on someone, you make them understand its importance or degree. ❑ *I had always impressed upon the children that if they worked hard they would succeed in life.* ❑ *I've impressed upon them the need for more professionalism.* **3** V-T If something **impresses** itself on your mind, you notice and remember it. ❑ *But this change has not yet impressed itself on the minds of the public.* **4** V-T If someone or something **impresses** you as a particular thing, usually a good one, they give you the impression of being that thing. ❑ *It didn't impress me as a good place to live.*

im|pres|sion /ɪmprɛʃən/ (impressions) **1** N-COUNT Your **impression** of a person or thing is what you think they are like, usually after having seen or heard them. Your **impression** of a situation is what you think is going on. ❑ *What were your first impressions of college?* ❑ *My impression is that they are totally out of control.* **2** N-SING If someone gives you a particular **impression**, they cause you to believe that something is the case, often when it is not. ❑ *I don't want to give the impression that I'm running away from the charges.* **3** N-COUNT An **impression** is an amusing imitation of someone's behavior or way of talking, usually someone well-known. ❑ *I did an impression of daddy saying "do as I say, not as I do."* **4** N-COUNT An **impression** of an object is a mark or outline that it has left after being pressed hard onto a surface. ❑ *...the world's oldest fossil impressions of plant life.* **5** PHRASE If someone or something **makes an impression**, they have a strong effect on people or a situation. ❑ *The type of aid coming in makes no immediate impression on the horrific death rates.* **6** PHRASE If you are **under the impression** that something is the case, you believe that it is the case, usually when it is not actually the case. ❑ *He had apparently been under the impression that a military coup was in progress.*

im|pres|sion|able /ɪmprɛʃənəbəl/ ADJ Someone who is **impressionable**, usually a young person, is not very critical and is therefore easy to influence. ❑ *The law is intended to protect young and impressionable viewers.*

Im|pres|sion|ism /ɪmprɛʃənɪzəm/ N-UNCOUNT **Impressionism** is a style of painting developed in France between 1870 and 1900 that concentrated on showing the effects of light and color rather than on clear and exact detail.

im|pres|sion|ist /ɪmprɛʃənɪst/ (impressionists) N-COUNT An **impressionist** is an entertainer who does amusing imitations of well-known people.

Im|pres|sion|ist (Impressionists) **1** N-COUNT An **Impressionist** is an artist who painted in the style of Impressionism. ❑ *...the French Impressionists.* **2** ADJ [ADJ n] An **Impressionist** painting is by an Impressionist or is in the style of Impressionism.

im|pres|sion|is|tic /ɪmprɛʃənɪstɪk/ ADJ An **impressionistic** work of art or piece of writing shows the artist's or writer's impressions of something rather than giving clear details. ❑ *His paintings had become more impressionistic as his eyesight dimmed.*

im|pres|sive /ɪmprɛsɪv/ ADJ Something that is **impressive** impresses you, for example, because it is great in size or degree, or is done with a lot of skill. ❑ *It is an impressive achievement.* • **im|pres|sive|ly** ADV ❑ *...an impressively bright and energetic woman called Cathie Gould.*

─── SYNONYMS ───

impressive
ADJ
striking: *...her striking good looks.*
grand: *...this grand building in the center of town.*
powerful: *...a powerful new style of dance-theater.*
dramatic: *Their arrival was dramatic and exciting.*
awe-inspiring: *...a museum with an awe-inspiring display of jewelry.*

im|pri|ma|tur /ɪmprɪmɑtər/ (imprimaturs) N-COUNT [usu poss N] If something such as a position, policy, or course of action has someone's **imprimatur**, that person has given it their official approval, for example, by allowing their name to be associated with it. ❑ *...a project bearing the president's imprimatur.*

im|print (imprints, imprinting, imprinted)

The noun is pronounced /ɪmprɪnt/. The verb is pronounced /ɪmprɪnt/.

1 N-COUNT If something leaves an **imprint** on a place or on your mind, it has a strong and lasting effect on it. ❑ *World War I left an indelible imprint on the twentieth-century world.* **2** V-T When something **is imprinted** on your memory, it is firmly fixed in your memory so that you will not forget it. ❑ *As I arrived, the shimmering skyline of domes and minarets was imprinted on my memory.* **3** N-COUNT An **imprint** is a mark or outline made by the pressure of one object on another. ❑ *She could see the imprint of her fingers on his pale face.* **4** V-T [usu passive] If a surface **is imprinted** with a mark or design, that mark or design is printed on the surface or pressed into it. ❑ *The company carries a variety of binders that can be imprinted with your message or logo.*

im|pris|on /ɪmprɪzən/ (imprisons, imprisoning, imprisoned) V-T If someone **is imprisoned**, they are locked up or kept somewhere, usually in prison, as a punishment for a crime or for political opposition. ❑ *He was imprisoned for 18 months on charges of theft.*

im|pris|on|ment /ɪmprɪzənmənt/ N-UNCOUNT **Imprisonment** is the state of being imprisoned. ❑ *She was sentenced to seven years' imprisonment.*

im|prob|able /ɪmprɒbəbəl/ **1** ADJ Something that is **improbable** is unlikely to be true or to happen. ❑ *Ordered arrangements of large groups of atoms and molecules are highly improbable.* • **im|prob|abil|ity** /ɪmprɒbəbɪlɪti/ (improbabilities) N-VAR ❑ *...the improbability of such an outcome.* **2** ADJ If you describe something as **improbable**, you mean it is strange, unusual, or ridiculous. ❑ *On the face of it, their marriage seems an improbable alliance.* • **im|prob|ably** ADV ❑ *The sea is an improbably pale turquoise.*

im|promp|tu /ɪmprɒmptu/ ADJ An **impromptu** action is one that you do without planning or organizing it in advance. ❑ *This afternoon the Palestinians held an impromptu press conference.*

im|prop|er /ɪmprɒpər/ **1** ADJ **Improper** activities are illegal or dishonest. [FORMAL] ❑ *25 officers were investigated following allegations of improper conduct.* • **im|prop|er|ly** ADV [ADV with v] ❑ *I acted neither fraudulently nor improperly.* **2** ADJ [ADJ n] **Improper** conditions or methods of treatment are not suitable or good enough for a particular purpose. [FORMAL] ❑ *The improper use of medicine could lead to severe adverse reactions.* • **im|prop|er|ly** ADV [ADV with v] ❑ *The study confirmed many reports that doctors were improperly trained.* **3** ADJ If you describe someone's behavior as **improper**, you mean it is rude or shocking or in some way socially unacceptable. ❑ *Such improper behavior and language from a young lady left me momentarily incapable of speech.* • **im|prop|er|ly** ADV [ADV with v] ❑ *The company turns down people who show up at job interviews improperly dressed.*

im|pro|pri|ety /ɪmprəpraɪɪti/ (improprieties) N-VAR **Impropriety** is improper behavior. [FORMAL] ❑ *He resigned amid allegations of financial impropriety.*

im|prov /ɪmprɒv/ N-UNCOUNT **Improv** is acting, comedy, singing, or music in which someone creates what they say, sing, or play as they are doing it. [INFORMAL]

im|prove /ɪmpruv/ (improves, improving, improved) **1** V-T/V-I If something **improves** or if you **improve** it, it gets better. ❑ *Within a month, both the texture and condition of your hair should improve.* **2** V-T/V-I If a skill you have **improves** or you **improve** a skill, you get better at it. ❑ *Their French has improved enormously.* **3** V-I If you **improve** after an illness or an injury, your health gets better or you get stronger. ❑ *He had improved so much the doctor had cut his dosage.* **4** V-I If you **improve** on a previous achievement of your own or of someone else's, you achieve a better standard or result. ❑ *We need to improve on our previous performance.*

─── COLLOCATIONS ───

improve
VERB **1**
improve + noun: efficiency, performance, quality, safety; condition, health; relations; service, standards
improve + adverb: considerably, greatly, markedly, significantly, substantially; dramatically, enormously, massively

im|prove|ment /ɪmpruːvmənt/ (**improvements**) **1** N-VAR If there is an **improvement** in something, it becomes better. If you make **improvements** to something, you make it better. ❏ ...the dramatic improvements in organ transplantation in recent years. **2** N-COUNT If you say that something is an **improvement** on a previous thing or situation, you mean that it is better than that thing. ❏ The new governor is an improvement on his predecessor.

im|pro|vise /ɪmprəvaɪz/ (**improvises, improvising, improvised**) **1** V-T/V-I If you **improvise**, you make or do something using whatever you have or without having planned it in advance. ❏ You need a wok with a steaming rack for this; if you don't have one, improvise. ❏ The vet had improvised a harness. **2** V-T/V-I When performers **improvise**, they invent music or words as they play, sing, or speak. ❏ I asked her what the piece was and she said, "Oh, I'm just improvising." ❏ Uncle Richard read a chapter from the Bible and improvised a prayer. **3** → See feature box at **humor**

im|pru|dent /ɪmpruːdənt/ ADJ If you describe someone's behavior as **imprudent**, you think it is not sensible or carefully thought out. [FORMAL] ❏ ...an imprudent investment.

im|pu|dent /ɪmpyədənt/ ADJ If you describe someone as **impudent**, you mean they are rude or disrespectful, or do something they have no right to do. [FORMAL, DISAPPROVAL] ❏ Some of them spoke pleasantly and were well behaved, while others were impudent and insulting.

im|pugn /ɪmpyuːn/ (**impugns, impugning, impugned**) V-T If you **impugn** something such as someone's motives or integrity, you imply that they are not entirely honest or honorable. [FORMAL] ❏ The Secretary's letter impugns my motives.

im|pulse /ɪmpʌls/ (**impulses**) **1** N-COUNT An **impulse** is a sudden desire to do something. ❏ Unable to resist the impulse, he glanced at the sea again. **2** N-COUNT An **impulse** is a short electrical signal that is sent along a wire or nerve or through the air, usually as one of a series. ❏ It works by sending a series of electrical impulses which are picked up by hi-tech sensors. **3** ADJ [ADJ n] An **impulse** buy or **impulse** purchase is something that you decide to buy when you see it, although you had not planned to buy it. ❏ The curtains were an impulse buy. **4** PHRASE If you do something **on impulse**, you suddenly decide to do it, without planning it. ❏ Sean's a fast thinker, and he acts on impulse. **5** → See feature box at **brain**

im|pul|sive /ɪmpʌlsɪv/ ADJ If you describe someone as **impulsive**, you mean that they do things suddenly without thinking about them carefully first. ❏ He is too impulsive to be a responsible manager. ● **im|pul|sive|ly** ADV [ADV with v] ❏ He studied her face for a moment, then said impulsively: "Let's get married."

im|pu|nity /ɪmpyuːnɪti/ PHRASE [PHR after v] If you say that someone does something **with impunity**, you disapprove of the fact that they are not punished for doing something bad. [DISAPPROVAL] ❏ These gangs operate with apparent impunity.

im|pure /ɪmpyʊər/ ADJ A substance that is **impure** is not of good quality because it has other substances mixed with it. ❏ ...diarrhea, dysentery and other diseases borne by impure water.

im|pu|rity /ɪmpyʊərɪti/ (**impurities**) N-COUNT **Impurities** are substances that are present in small quantities in another substance and make it dirty or of an unacceptable quality. ❏ The air in the factory is filtered to remove impurities.

im|pute /ɪmpyuːt/ (**imputes, imputing, imputed**) V-T If you **impute** something such as blame or a crime to someone, you say that they are responsible for it or are the cause of it. [FORMAL] ❏ It is grossly unfair to impute blame to the United Nations.

IN

① POSITION OR MOVEMENT
② INCLUSION OR INVOLVEMENT
③ TIME AND NUMBERS
④ STATES AND QUALITIES
⑤ OTHER USES AND PHRASES

---

① **in** ✦✦✦

The preposition is pronounced /ɪn/. The adverb is pronounced /ɪn/.

In addition to the uses shown below, **in** is used after some verbs, nouns, and adjectives in order to introduce extra information. **In** is also used with verbs of movement such as 'walk' and 'push,' and in phrasal verbs such as 'give in' and 'dig in.'

1 PREP Someone or something that is **in** something else is enclosed by it or surrounded by it. If you put something **in** a container, you move it so that it is enclosed by the container. ❏ He was in his car. **2** PREP If something happens **in** a place, it happens there. ❏ ...spending a few days in a hotel. **3** ADV [be ADV] If you are **in**, you are present at your home or place of work. ❏ My roommate was in at the time. **4** ADV [ADV after v] When someone comes **in**, they enter a room or building. ❏ She looked up anxiously as he came in. **5** ADV If a train, boat, or plane has come **in** or is **in**, it has arrived at a station, port, or airport. ❏ ...every plane coming in from Melbourne. **6** ADV When the sea or tide comes **in**, the sea moves toward the shore rather than away from it. ❏ She thought of the tide rushing in, covering the wet sand. **7** PREP Something that is **in** a window, especially a store window, is just behind the window so that you can see it from outside. ❏ There was a camera for sale in the window. **8** PREP When you see something **in** a mirror, the mirror shows an image of it. ❏ I couldn't bear to see my reflection in the mirror. **9** PREP If you are dressed **in** a piece of clothing, you are wearing it. ❏ He was a big man, dressed in a suit and tie. **10** PREP Something that is covered or wrapped **in** something else has that thing over or around its surface. ❏ His legs were covered in mud. **11** PREP If there is something such as a crack or hole **in** something, there is a crack or hole on its surface. ❏ There was a deep crack in the ceiling above him.

② **in** ✦✦✦ /ɪn/ **1** PREP If something is **in** a book, movie, play, or picture, you can read it or see it there. ❏ Don't stick too precisely to what it says in the book. **2** PREP If you are **in** something such as a play or a race, you are one of the people taking part. ❏ Alfredo offered her a part in the play he was directing. **3** PREP Something that is **in** a group or collection is a member of it or part of it. ❏ The New England team is the worst in the league. **4** PREP You use **in** to specify a general subject or field of activity. ❏ ...those working in the defense industry.

③ **in** ✦✦✦ /ɪn/ **1** PREP If something happens **in** a particular year, month, or other period of time, it happens during that time. ❏ ...that early spring day in April 1949. ❏ Export orders improved in the last month. **2** PREP If something happens **in** a particular situation, it happens while that situation is going on. ❏ His father had been badly wounded in the last war. **3** PREP [PREP amount] If you do something **in** a particular period of time, that is how long it takes you to do it. ❏ He walked two hundred and sixty miles in eight days. **4** PREP [PREP amount] If something will happen **in** a particular length of time, it will happen after that length of time. ❏ I'll have some breakfast ready in a few minutes. **5** PREP [PREP poss pl-num] You use **in** to indicate roughly how old someone is. For example, if someone is **in** their fifties, they are between 50 and 59 years old. ❏ ...young people in their twenties. **6** PREP You use **in** to indicate roughly how many people or things do something. ❏ ...men who came there in droves. **7** PREP [num PREP num] You use **in** to express a ratio, proportion, or probability. ❏ One in three fourth-graders couldn't find their state on a map of the U.S.

④ **in** ✦✦✦ /ɪn/ **1** PREP [v-link PREP n] If something or someone is **in** a particular state or situation, that is their present state or situation. ❏ The economy was in trouble. ❏ Dave was in a hurry to get back to work. **2** PREP You use **in** to indicate the feeling or desire that someone has when they do something, or which causes them to do it. ❏ Simpson looked at them in surprise. **3** PREP If a particular quality or ability is **in** you, you naturally have it. ❏ Violence is not in his nature. **4** PREP You use **in** when saying that someone or something has a particular quality. ❏ He had all the qualities I was looking for in a partner. **5** PREP You use **in** to indicate how someone is expressing something. ❏ Information is given to the patient verbally and in writing. **6** PREP You use **in** in expressions such as **in a row** or **in a ball** to describe the arrangement or shape of something. ❏ The cards need to be laid out in two rows. **7** PREP If something is **in** a particular color, it has that color. ❏ ...white flowers edged in pink. **8** PREP You use **in** to specify which feature or aspect of something you are talking about. ❏ The movie is nearly two hours in length. ❏ There is a big difference in the amounts that banks charge.

⑤ **in** (**ins**)

Pronounced /ɪn/ for meanings **1** and **3** to **8**, and /ɪn/ for meaning **2**.

1 ADJ If you say that something is **in**, or is the **in** thing, you mean it is fashionable or popular. [INFORMAL] ❑ *A few years ago jogging was the in thing.* **2** PREP [PREP -ing] You use **in** with a present participle to indicate that when you do something, something else happens as a result. ❑ *He shifted uncomfortably on his feet. In doing so he knocked over Steven's briefcase.* **3** PHRASE If you say that someone **is in for** a shock or a surprise, you mean that they are going to experience it. ❑ *You might be in for a shock at the sheer hard work involved.* **4** PHRASE If someone **has it in for** you, they dislike you and try to cause problems for you. [INFORMAL] ❑ *The other kids had it in for me.* **5** PHRASE If you are **in on** something, you are involved in it or know about it. ❑ *I don't know. I wasn't in on that particular argument.* **6** PHRASE If you **are in with** a person or group, they like you and accept you, and are likely to help you. [INFORMAL] **7** PHRASE You use **in that** to introduce an explanation of a statement you have just made. ❑ *I'm lucky in that I've got four sisters.* **8** PHRASE The **ins and outs** of a situation are all the detailed points and facts about it. ❑ *...the ins and outs of high finance.*

PREFIX

in-
can be added to some words to form words that have the opposite meaning. For example, someone who is **independent** is not dependent on anyone.

in|abil|ity /ɪnəbɪlɪti/ N-UNCOUNT If you refer to someone's **inability** to do something, you are referring to the fact that they are unable to do it. ❑ *Her inability to concentrate could cause an accident.*

in|ac|ces|sible /ɪnəksɛsɪbəl/ **1** ADJ An **inaccessible** place is very difficult or impossible to reach. ❑ *...people living in remote and inaccessible parts of China.* **2** ADJ If something is **inaccessible**, you are unable to see, use, or buy it. ❑ *Ninety-five percent of its magnificent collection will remain inaccessible to the public.* **3** ADJ Someone or something that is **inaccessible** is difficult or impossible to understand or appreciate. [DISAPPROVAL] ❑ *...language that is inaccessible to working people.*

in|ac|cu|ra|cy /ɪnækyərəsi/ (**inaccuracies**) N-VAR The **inaccuracy** of a statement or measurement is the fact that it is not accurate or correct. ❑ *He was disturbed by the inaccuracy of the answers.*

in|ac|cu|rate /ɪnækyərɪt/ ADJ If a statement or measurement is **inaccurate**, it is not accurate or correct. ❑ *The book is both inaccurate and exaggerated.*

in|ac|tion /ɪnækʃən/ N-UNCOUNT If you refer to someone's **inaction**, you disapprove of the fact that they are doing nothing. [DISAPPROVAL] ❑ *He is bitter about the inaction of the other political parties.*

in|ac|tive /ɪnæktɪv/ ADJ Someone or something that is **inactive** is not doing anything or is not working. ❑ *He certainly was not politically inactive.* • **in|ac|tiv|ity** /ɪnæktɪvɪti/ N-UNCOUNT ❑ *The players have comparatively long periods of inactivity.*

in|ad|equa|cy /ɪnædɪkwəsi/ (**inadequacies**) **1** N-VAR The **inadequacy** of something is the fact that there is not enough of it, or that it is not good enough. ❑ *...the inadequacy of the water supply.* **2** N-UNCOUNT If someone has feelings of **inadequacy**, they feel that they do not have the qualities and abilities necessary to do something or to cope with life in general. ❑ *...his deep-seated sense of inadequacy.*

in|ad|equate /ɪnædɪkwɪt/ **1** ADJ If something is **inadequate**, there is not enough of it or it is not good enough. ❑ *Supplies of food and medicines are inadequate.* • **in|ad|equate|ly** ADV [ADV with v] ❑ *The projects were inadequately funded.* **2** ADJ If someone feels **inadequate**, they feel that they do not have the qualities and abilities necessary to do something or to cope with life in general. ❑ *I still feel inadequate, useless and mixed up.* **3** → See feature box at **review**

in|ad|mis|si|ble /ɪnədmɪsɪbəl/ **1** ADJ **Inadmissible** evidence cannot be used in a court of law. ❑ *The judge ruled that the evidence was inadmissible.* **2** ADJ [USU V-LINK ADJ] If you say that something someone says or does is **inadmissible**, you think that it is totally unacceptable. [DISAPPROVAL] ❑ *He said the use of force would be inadmissible.*

in|ad|vert|ent /ɪnədvɜrtənt/ ADJ An **inadvertent** action is one that you do without realizing what you are doing. ❑ *The government has said it was an inadvertent error.* • **in|ad|vert|ent|ly** ADV [ADV with v] ❑ *You may have inadvertently pressed the wrong button.*

in|ad|vis|able /ɪnədvaɪzəbəl/ ADJ A course of action that is **inadvisable** should not be carried out because it is not wise or sensible. ❑ *For three days last week, it was inadvisable to leave the harbor.*

in|al|ien|able /ɪneɪlyənəbəl/ ADJ [usu ADJ n] If you say that someone has an **inalienable** right to something, you are emphasizing that they have a right to it that cannot be changed or taken away. [FORMAL, EMPHASIS] ❑ *He said the republic now had an inalienable right to self-determination.*

in|ane /ɪneɪn/ ADJ If you describe someone's behavior or actions as **inane**, you think they are very silly or stupid. [DISAPPROVAL] ❑ *He always had this inane grin.* • **in|ane|ly** ADV [ADV after v] ❑ *He lurched through the bar, smiling inanely.* • **in|an|ity** /ɪnænɪti/ N-UNCOUNT ❑ *...the inanity of the conversation.*

in|ani|mate /ɪnænɪmɪt/ ADJ An **inanimate** object is one that has no life. ❑ *Many children become attached to some inanimate object, such as a blanket or soft toy.*

in|ap|pli|cable /ɪnæplɪkəbəl/ ADJ Something that is **inapplicable** to what you are talking about is not relevant or appropriate to it. ❑ *His theory was inapplicable to many underdeveloped economies.*

in|ap|pro|pri|ate /ɪnəproʊpriɪt/ **1** ADJ Something that is **inappropriate** is not useful or suitable for a particular situation or purpose. ❑ *There is no suggestion that clients have been sold inappropriate policies.* **2** ADJ If you say that someone's speech or behavior in a particular situation is **inappropriate**, you are criticizing it because you think it is not suitable for that situation. [DISAPPROVAL] ❑ *I feel the remark was inappropriate for such a serious issue.*

in|ar|ticu|late /ɪnɑrtɪkyʊlət/ ADJ If someone is **inarticulate**, they are unable to express themselves easily or well in speech. ❑ *Inarticulate and rather shy, he had always dreaded speaking in public.*

in|as|much as /ɪnəzmʌtʃ æz/ PHRASE You use **inasmuch as** to introduce a statement that explains something you have just said, and adds to it. [FORMAL] ❑ *We were doubly lucky inasmuch as my friend was living on the island and spoke Greek fluently.*

in|at|ten|tion /ɪnətɛnʃən/ N-UNCOUNT A person's **inattention** is their lack of attention. ❑ *Vital evidence had been lost through a moment's inattention.*

in|at|ten|tive /ɪnətɛntɪv/ ADJ Someone who is **inattentive** is not paying complete attention to a person or thing, which often causes an accident or problems.

in|aud|ible /ɪnɔdɪbəl/ ADJ If a sound is **inaudible**, you are unable to hear it. ❑ *His voice was almost inaudible.*

in|augu|ral /ɪnɔgyərəl/ ADJ [ADJ n] An **inaugural** meeting or speech is the first meeting of a new organization or the first speech by the new leader of an organization or a country. ❑ *In his inaugural address, the president appealed for national unity.*

in|augu|rate /ɪnɔgyʊreɪt/ (**inaugurates, inaugurating, inaugurated**) **1** V-T [usu passive] When a new leader is **inaugurated**, they are formally given their new position at an official ceremony. ❑ *The new president will be inaugurated on January 20th.* • **in|augu|ra|tion** /ɪnɔgyʊreɪʃən/ (**inaugurations**) N-VAR ❑ *...the inauguration of the new Governor.* **2** V-T [usu passive] When a new building or institution **is inaugurated**, it is declared open in a formal ceremony. ❑ *A Mafia Museum was inaugurated in Corleone.* • **in|augu|ra|tion** N-COUNT ❑ *They later attended the inauguration of the University.* **3** V-T If you **inaugurate** a new system or service, you start it. [FORMAL] ❑ *The new proprietor formed a band and inaugurated healthy exercise in the form of dancing.*

in|aus|pi|cious /ɪnɔspɪʃəs/ ADJ [usu ADJ n] An **inauspicious** event is one that gives signs that success is unlikely. [FORMAL] ❑ *The meeting got off to an inauspicious start when he was late.*

in|authen|tic /ɪnɔθɛntɪk/ ADJ Something that is **inauthentic** is false or copied, often in a way that does not follow tradition. ❑ *...an inauthentic but tasty paella recipe.*

in|board /ɪnbɔrd/ ADJ [ADJ n] An **inboard** motor or engine is inside a boat rather than attached to the outside.

in|born /ɪnbɔrn/ ADJ [usu ADJ n] **Inborn** qualities are natural ones that you are born with. ❑ *He had an inborn talent for languages.*

in|bound /ɪnbaʊnd/ ADJ [usu ADJ n] An **inbound** flight is one that is arriving from another place. ❑ *...a special inbound flight from Honduras.*

in|bounds /ɪnbaʊndz/ ADJ [ADJ n] In basketball, an **inbounds** pass is a throw from outside the playing area to a player who is inside the court. [AM] ❑ *Webber made a shot over Shawn Kemp after an inbounds pass to win it for the Kings.*

in|box /ɪnbɒks/ (**inboxes**) also **in-box** ■ N-COUNT An **inbox** is a shallow container used in offices to put letters and documents in before they are dealt with. [AM]

☐ in BRIT, use **in tray**

■ N-COUNT On a computer, your **inbox** is the part of your mailbox which stores e-mails that have arrived for you. ❑ *I returned home and checked my inbox.*

in|bred /ɪnbrɛd/ ■ ADJ **Inbred** means the same as **inborn**. ❑ *...behavior patterns that are inbred.* ■ ADJ [usu v-link ADJ] People who are **inbred** have ancestors who are all closely related to each other. ❑ *The whole population is so inbred that no genetic differences remain.*

in|breed|ing /ɪnbridɪŋ/ N-UNCOUNT **Inbreeding** is the repeated breeding of closely related animals or people. ❑ *In the 19th century, inbreeding nearly led to the extinction of the royal family.*

in|built /ɪnbɪlt/ also **in-built** ADJ [usu ADJ n] An **inbuilt** quality is one that someone has from the time they were born or that something has from the time it was produced. [mainly BRIT]

☐ in AM, usually use **built-in**

inc. In written advertisements, **inc.** is an abbreviation for **including**. ❑ *The hotel offers a two-night stay for $210 per person, inc. breakfast and dinner.*

Inc. ✦✧ /ɪŋk/ [AM] **Inc.** is an abbreviation for **Incorporated** when it is used after a company's name. [BUSINESS] ❑ *...Sun Microsystems Inc.*

in|cal|cu|lable /ɪnkælkjələbᵊl/ ADJ Something that is **incalculable** cannot be calculated or estimated because it is so great. ❑ *He warned that the effects of any war would be incalculable.*

in|can|des|cent /ɪnkændɛsᵊnt/ ■ ADJ **Incandescent** substances or devices give out a lot of light when heated. [TECHNICAL] ❑ *...incandescent gases.* ■ ADJ [usu ADJ n] If you describe someone or something as **incandescent**, you mean that they are very lively and impressive. [LITERARY] ❑ *Kerrie Mae had an extraordinary, incandescent personality.* • **in|can|des|cence** N-UNCOUNT ❑ *...the incandescence of his later works.*

in|can|ta|tion /ɪnkæntɛɪʃᵊn/ (**incantations**) N-COUNT An **incantation** is a series of words that a person says or sings as a magic spell. [FORMAL] ❑ *...strange prayers and incantations.*

in|ca|pable /ɪnkeɪpəbᵊl/ ■ ADJ [v-link ADJ of ing/n] Someone who is **incapable of** doing something is unable to do it. ❑ *She seemed incapable of making the decision.* ■ ADJ An **incapable** person is weak or stupid. ❑ *He lost his job for allegedly being incapable.*

in|ca|paci|tate /ɪnkəpæsɪteɪt/ (**incapacitates, incapacitating, incapacitated**) V-T If something **incapacitates** you, it weakens you in some way, so that you cannot do certain things. [FORMAL] ❑ *A broken toe had briefly incapacitated him.* • **in|ca|paci|tat|ed** ADJ [usu v-link ADJ] ❑ *He is incapacitated and can't work.*

in|ca|pac|ity /ɪnkəpæsɪti/ N-UNCOUNT The **incapacity** of a person, society, or system to do something is their inability to do it. [FORMAL] ❑ *...Europe's incapacity to take collective action.*

in-car ADJ [ADJ n] **In-car** devices are ones that are designed to be used in a car. [BRIT]

☐ in AM, use **on board**

in|car|cer|ate /ɪnkɑrsəreɪt/ (**incarcerates, incarcerating, incarcerated**) V-T If people **are incarcerated**, they are kept in a prison or other place. [FORMAL] ❑ *They were incarcerated for the duration of the war.* • **in|car|cera|tion** /ɪnkɑrsəreɪʃᵊn/ N-UNCOUNT ❑ *...her mother's incarceration in a psychiatric hospital.*

in|car|nate (**incarnates, incarnating, incarnated**)

The adjective is pronounced /ɪnkɑrnɪt/. The verb is pronounced /ɪnkɑrneɪt/.

■ ADJ [n ADJ] If you say that someone is a quality **incarnate**, you mean that they represent that quality or are typical of it in an extreme form. ❑ *She is evil incarnate.* ■ ADJ [v-link ADJ] You use **incarnate** to say that something, especially a god or spirit, is represented in human form. ❑ *Why should God become incarnate as a male?* ■ V-T If you say that a quality **is incarnated** in a person, you mean that they represent that quality or are typical of it in an extreme form. ❑ *The iniquities of the regime are incarnated in one man.* ❑ *...a writer who incarnates the changing consciousness of the Americas.* ■ V-T [usu passive] If you say that someone or something **is incarnated** in a particular form, you mean that they appear on earth in that form. ❑ *The god Vishnu was incarnated on earth as a king.*

in|car|na|tion /ɪnkɑrneɪʃᵊn/ (**incarnations**) ■ N-COUNT If you say that someone is the **incarnation of** a particular quality, you mean that they represent that quality or are typical of it in an extreme form. ❑ *The regime was the very incarnation of evil.* ■ N-COUNT An **incarnation** is an instance of being alive on earth in a particular form. Some religions believe that people have several incarnations in different forms. ❑ *She began recalling a series of previous incarnations.*

in|cau|tious /ɪnkɔʃəs/ ADJ [usu ADJ n] If you say that someone is **incautious**, you are criticizing them because they do or say something without thinking or planning. [FORMAL, DISAPPROVAL] • **in|cau|tious|ly** ADV ❑ *Incautiously, Crook had asked where she was.*

in|cen|di|ary /ɪnsɛndiɛri/ (**incendiaries**) ■ ADJ [ADJ n] **Incendiary** weapons or attacks are ones that cause large fires. ❑ *Five incendiary devices were found in her house.* ■ N-COUNT An **incendiary** is an incendiary bomb. ❑ *A shower of incendiaries struck the Opera House.* ■ ADJ If you accuse someone of saying or doing **incendiary** things, you mean that what they say or do is likely to make people react very angrily. [DISAPPROVAL] ❑ *...incendiary slogans such as "Hospital closures kill more than car bombs."*

in|cense (**incenses, incensing, incensed**)

The noun is pronounced /ɪnsɛns/. The verb is pronounced /ɪnsɛns/.

■ N-UNCOUNT **Incense** is a substance that is burned for its sweet smell, often as part of a religious ceremony. ■ V-T If you say that something **incenses** you, you mean that it makes you extremely angry. ❑ *This proposal will incense conservation campaigners.* • **in|censed** ADJ ❑ *Mom was incensed at his lack of compassion.*

in|cen|tive /ɪnsɛntɪv/ (**incentives**) N-VAR If something is an **incentive** to do something, it encourages you to do it. ❑ *There is little or no incentive to adopt such measures.*

in|cep|tion /ɪnsɛpʃᵊn/ N-UNCOUNT [with poss] The **inception** of an institution or activity is the start of it. [FORMAL] ❑ *Since its inception the company has produced 53 different aircraft designs.*

in|ces|sant /ɪnsɛsᵊnt/ ADJ An **incessant** process or activity is one that continues without stopping. ❑ *Incessant rain made conditions almost intolerable.* • **in|ces|sant|ly** ADV ❑ *Dee talked incessantly about herself.*

in|cest /ɪnsɛst/ N-UNCOUNT **Incest** is the crime of two members of the same family having sexual intercourse, such as a father and daughter, or a brother and sister. ❑ *Oedipus, according to ancient Greek legend, killed his father and committed incest with his mother.*

in|ces|tu|ous /ɪnsɛstʃuəs/ ■ ADJ An **incestuous** relationship is one involving sexual intercourse between two members of the same family, such as a father and daughter, or a brother and sister. ❑ *They accused her of an incestuous relationship with her father.* ■ ADJ If you describe a group of people as **incestuous**, you disapprove of the fact that they are not interested in ideas or people from outside the group. [DISAPPROVAL] ❑ *Its inhabitants are a close and incestuous bunch.*

inch ✦✧ /ɪntʃ/ (**inches, inching, inched**) ■ N-COUNT An **inch** is an imperial unit of length, approximately equal to 2.54 centimeters. There are twelve inches in a foot. ❑ *...18 inches below the surface.* ■ V-T/V-I To **inch** somewhere means to move there very slowly and carefully, or to make something do this.

inchoate

□ ...a climber inching up a vertical wall of rock. □ He inched the van forward. **3** PHRASE If you say that someone looks **every inch** a certain type of person, you are emphasizing that they look exactly like that kind of person. [EMPHASIS] □ He looks every inch the businessman, with his gray suit, dark blue shirt and blue tie.

in|cho|ate /ɪnkoʊɪt/ ADJ If something is **inchoate**, it is recent or new, and vague or not yet properly developed. [FORMAL] □ His dreams were senseless and inchoate.

in|ci|dence /ɪnsɪdəns/ (incidences) N-VAR The **incidence** of something, especially something bad such as a disease, is the frequency with which it occurs, or the occasions when it occurs. □ The incidence of breast cancer increases with age.

in|ci|dent ✦✧ /ɪnsɪdənt/ (incidents) N-COUNT [also without N] An **incident** is something that happens, often something that is unpleasant. [FORMAL] □ These incidents were the latest in a series of disputes between the two nations.

in|ci|den|tal /ɪnsɪdɛntəl/ ADJ If one thing is **incidental** to another, it is less important than the other thing or is not a major part of it. □ The playing of music proved to be incidental to the main business of the evening.

in|ci|den|tal|ly /ɪnsɪdɛntli/ **1** ADV [ADV with cl] You use **incidentally** to introduce a point that is not directly relevant to what you are saying, often a question or extra information that you have just thought of. □ "I didn't ask you to come. Incidentally, why have you come?" **2** ADV [ADV with v] If something occurs only **incidentally**, it is less important than another thing or is not a major part of it. □ The letter mentioned my great aunt and uncle only incidentally.

in|ci|den|tal mu|sic N-UNCOUNT In a movie, play, or television program, **incidental music** is music that is played to create a particular atmosphere.

in|cin|er|ate /ɪnsɪnəreɪt/ (incinerates, incinerating, incinerated) V-T When authorities **incinerate** garbage or waste material, they burn it completely in a special container. □ They were incinerating hazardous waste without a license. ● **in|cin|era|tion** /ɪnsɪnəreɪʃən/ N-UNCOUNT □ South Pacific nations have protested against the incineration of the weapons.

in|cin|era|tor /ɪnsɪnəreɪtər/ (incinerators) N-COUNT An **incinerator** is a special large container for burning garbage at a very high temperature.

in|cipi|ent /ɪnsɪpiənt/ ADJ [ADJ n] An **incipient** situation or quality is one that is starting to happen or develop. [FORMAL] □ ...an incipient economic recovery.

in|cise /ɪnsaɪz/ (incises, incising, incised) V-T [usu passive] If an object **is incised** with a design, the design is carefully cut into the surface of the object with a sharp instrument. [FORMAL] □ After the surface is polished, a design is incised or painted. □ ...a set of chairs incised with Grecian scrolls.

in|ci|sion /ɪnsɪʒən/ (incisions) N-COUNT An **incision** is a sharp cut made in something, for example, by a surgeon who is operating on a patient. □ The technique involves making a tiny incision in the skin.

in|ci|sive /ɪnsaɪsɪv/ ADJ You use **incisive** to describe a person, their thoughts, or their speech when you approve of their ability to think and express their ideas clearly, briefly, and forcefully. [APPROVAL] □ He is a very shrewd operator with an incisive mind.

in|ci|sor /ɪnsaɪzər/ (incisors) **1** N-COUNT Your **incisors** are the teeth at the front of your mouth that you use for biting into food. **2** → See also color supplement

in|cite /ɪnsaɪt/ (incites, inciting, incited) V-T If someone **incites** people to behave in a violent or illegal way, they encourage people to behave in that way, usually by making them excited or angry. □ He incited his fellow citizens to take their revenge. □ The party agreed not to incite its supporters to violence.

in|cite|ment /ɪnsaɪtmənt/ (incitements) N-VAR If someone is accused of **incitement** to violent or illegal behavior, they are accused of encouraging people to behave in that way. □ Insults can lead to the incitement of violence.

incl. **1** In written advertisements, **incl.** is an abbreviation for **including** or **included**. □ ...blood pressure monitor with batteries, case and 1 year warranty incl. **2** In written advertisements, **incl.** is an abbreviation for **inclusive**. □ Open July 19th - September 6th, Sun. to Thurs. incl.

in|clem|ent /ɪnklɛmənt/ ADJ **Inclement** weather is unpleasantly cold or stormy. [FORMAL]

in|cli|na|tion /ɪnklɪneɪʃən/ (inclinations) N-VAR An **inclination** is a feeling that makes you want to act in a particular way. □ He had neither the time nor the inclination to think of other things. □ She showed no inclination to go.

in|cline (inclines, inclining, inclined)

> The noun is pronounced /ɪnklaɪn/. The verb is pronounced /ɪnklaɪn/.

1 N-COUNT An **incline** is land that slopes at an angle. [FORMAL] □ He came to a halt at the edge of a steep incline. **2** V-T If you **incline** your head, you bend your neck so that your head is leaning forward. [WRITTEN] □ Jack inclined his head very slightly. **3** V-T If you **incline** to think or act in a particular way, or if something **inclines** you to it, you are likely to think or act in that way. [FORMAL] □ ...the factors that incline us toward particular beliefs. □ Those who fail incline to blame the world for their failure.

in|clined /ɪnklaɪnd/ **1** ADJ [v-link ADJ] If you are **inclined** to behave in a particular way, you often behave in that way, or you want to do so. □ Nobody felt inclined to argue with Smith. □ He was inclined to self-pity. **2** ADJ [v-link ADJ to-inf] If you say that you are **inclined** to have a particular opinion, you mean that you hold this opinion but you are not expressing it strongly. [VAGUENESS] □ I am inclined to agree with Alan. **3** ADJ [adv ADJ] Someone who is mathematically **inclined** or artistically **inclined**, for example, has a natural talent for mathematics or art. □ ...the needs of academically inclined pupils. **4** → see also **incline**

in|clude ✦✧✧ /ɪnklud/ (includes, including, included) **1** V-T If one thing **includes** another thing, it has the other thing as one of its parts. □ The trip has been extended to include a few other events. **2** V-T If someone or something **is included** in a large group, system, or area, they become a part of it or are considered a part of it. □ I had worked hard to be included in a project like this.

in|clud|ed ✦✧✧ /ɪnkludɪd/ ADJ [n ADJ, v-link ADJ] You use **included** to emphasize that a person or thing is part of the group of people or things that you are talking about. [EMPHASIS] □ Many runners, myself included, are loners.

in|clud|ing ✦✧✧ /ɪnkludɪŋ/ PREP [PREP n/-ing] You use **including** to introduce examples of people or things that are part of the group of people or things that you are talking about. □ Thousands were killed, including many women and children.

in|clu|sion /ɪnkluʒən/ (inclusions) N-VAR **Inclusion** is the act of making a person or thing part of a group or collection. □ ...a confident performance that justified his inclusion in the team.

in|clu|sive /ɪnklusɪv/ **1** ADJ If you describe a group or organization as **inclusive**, you mean that it allows all kinds of people to belong to it, rather than just one kind of person. □ The academy is far more inclusive now than it used to be. **2** ADJ [n ADJ] After stating the first and last item in a set of things, you can add **inclusive** to make it clear that the items stated are included in the set. □ You are also invited to join us on our prayer days (this year, June 6 to June 14 inclusive). **3** ADJ If a price is **inclusive**, it includes all the charges connected with the goods or services offered. If a price is **inclusive** of shipping and handling, it includes the charge for this. □ ...all prices are inclusive of delivery. ● ADV [amount ADV] **Inclusive** is also an adverb. □ The outpatient program costs $105 per day, all inclusive.

in|cog|ni|to /ɪnkɒgniːtoʊ/ ADJ [v-link ADJ, ADJ after v] Someone who is **incognito** is using a false name or wearing a disguise, in order not to be recognized or identified. □ Hotel inspectors have to travel incognito.

in|co|her|ent /ɪnkoʊhɪərənt/ **1** ADJ If someone is **incoherent**, they are talking in a confused and unclear way. □ The man was almost incoherent with fear. **2** ADJ If you say that something such as a policy is **incoherent**, you are criticizing it because the different parts of it do not fit together properly. [DISAPPROVAL] □ ...an incoherent set of objectives.

in|come ✦✦✧ /ɪnkʌm/ (incomes) **1** N-VAR A person's or organization's **income** is the money that they earn or receive, as opposed to the money that they have to spend or pay out. [BUSINESS] □ Many families on low incomes will be unable to afford to buy their own home. **2** → See feature box at **finance**

SYNONYMS

income
NOUN
earnings: *Average weekly earnings rose by 1.5% in July.*
revenue: *The theater has seen record advertising revenue and ticket sales.*
proceeds: *The proceeds from the concert will go towards famine relief.*
receipts: *He was tallying the day's receipts.*
takings: *Their takings were fifteen to twenty thousand dollars a week.*

in|come tax (income taxes) N-VAR **Income tax** is a part of your income that you have to pay regularly to the government. [BUSINESS] ❏ *You pay income tax on all your earnings, not just your salary.*

in|com|ing /ɪnkʌmɪŋ/ **1** ADJ [ADJ n] An **incoming** message or phone call is one that you receive. ❏ *He wasn't able to receive any incoming calls.* **2** ADJ [ADJ n] An **incoming** plane or passenger is one that is arriving at a place. ❏ *The airport was closed for incoming flights.* **3** ADJ [ADJ n] An **incoming** official or government is one that has just been appointed or elected. ❏ *...the problems confronting the incoming government.*

in|com|mu|ni|ca|do /ɪnkəmjunɪkɑːdoʊ/ **1** ADJ [usu v n ADJ] If someone is being kept **incommunicado**, they are not allowed to talk to anyone outside the place where they are. ❏ *He was held incommunicado in prison for ten days before being released without charge.* **2** ADJ [v-link ADJ] If someone is **incommunicado**, they do not want to be disturbed, or are in a place where they cannot be contacted. ❏ *Yesterday she was incommunicado, putting the finishing touches to her autobiography.*

in|com|pa|rable /ɪnkɒmpərəbəl/ **1** ADJ If you describe someone or something as **incomparable**, you mean that they are extremely good or impressive. ❏ *...the incomparable Tony Bennet singing "It had to be you."* **2** ADJ [ADJ n] You use **incomparable** to emphasize that someone or something has a good quality to a great degree. [FORMAL, EMPHASIS] ❏ *...an area of incomparable beauty.*

in|com|pa|rably /ɪnkɒmpərəbli/ ADV [ADV compar] You can use **incomparably** to emphasize that someone or something has a good quality to a great degree. [FORMAL, EMPHASIS] ❏ *...his incomparably brilliant love songs.*

in|com|pat|ible /ɪnkəmpætɪbəl/ **1** ADJ If one thing or person is **incompatible** with another, they are very different in important ways, and do not suit each other or agree with each other. ❏ *They feel strongly that their religion is incompatible with the political system.* • **in|com|pat|ibil|ity** /ɪnkəmpætɪbɪlɪti/ N-UNCOUNT ❏ *Incompatibility between the mother's and the baby's blood groups may cause jaundice.* **2** ADJ If one type of computer or computer system is **incompatible** with another, they cannot use the same programs or be linked up. ❏ *This made its mini-computers incompatible with its mainframes.*

in|com|pe|tence /ɪnkɒmpɪtəns/ N-UNCOUNT If you refer to someone's **incompetence**, you are criticizing them because they are unable to do their job or a task properly. [DISAPPROVAL] ❏ *The incompetence of government officials is appalling.*

in|com|pe|tent /ɪnkɒmpɪtənt/ (incompetents) **1** ADJ If you describe someone as **incompetent**, you are criticizing them because they are unable to do their job or a task properly. [DISAPPROVAL] ❏ *He wants the power to fire incompetent employees.* • N-COUNT An **incompetent** is someone who is incompetent. ❏ *The president turned furiously on his staff. "I'm surrounded by incompetents!"* **2** → See feature box at **service**

in|com|plete /ɪnkəmpliːt/ ADJ Something that is **incomplete** is not yet finished, or does not have all the parts or details that it needs. ❏ *The clearing of garbage and drains is still incomplete.*

in|com|pre|hen|sible /ɪnkɒmprɪhɛnsɪbəl/ ADJ Something that is **incomprehensible** is impossible to understand. ❏ *He spent his time devising incomprehensible mathematics puzzles.*

in|com|pre|hen|sion /ɪnkɒmprɪhɛnʃən/ N-UNCOUNT **Incomprehension** is the state of being unable to understand something or someone. ❏ *Rosie had a look of incomprehension on her face.*

in|con|ceiv|able /ɪnkənsiːvəbəl/ ADJ If you describe something as **inconceivable**, you think it is very unlikely to happen or be true. ❏ *It was inconceivable to me that Toby could have been my attacker.*

in|con|clu|sive /ɪnkənkluːsɪv/ **1** ADJ If research or evidence is **inconclusive**, it has not proved anything. ❏ *Research has so far proved inconclusive.* **2** ADJ If a contest or conflict is **inconclusive**, it is not clear who has won or who is winning. ❏ *The past two elections were inconclusive.*

in|con|gru|ity /ɪnkɒŋgruːɪti/ (incongruities) N-VAR [oft N of n] The **incongruity** of something is its strangeness when considered together with other aspects of a situation. [FORMAL] ❏ *She smiled at the incongruity of the question.*

in|con|gru|ous /ɪnkɒŋgruəs/ ADJ Someone or something that is **incongruous** seems strange when considered together with other aspects of a situation. [FORMAL] ❏ *To me this formality seemed both incongruous and irritating against the background of our ramshackle and poverty-stricken home.* • **in|con|gru|ous|ly** ADV ❏ *...a town of Western-style buildings perched incongruously in a high green valley.*

in|con|sequen|tial /ɪnkɒnsɪkwɛnʃəl/ ADJ Something that is **inconsequential** is not important. ❏ *...a constant reminder of just how insignificant and inconsequential their lives were.*

in|con|sid|er|able /ɪnkənsɪdərəbəl/ ADJ [with neg, usu ADJ n] If you describe an amount or quality as **not inconsiderable**, you are emphasizing that it is, in fact, large or present to a large degree. [EMPHASIS] ❏ *The production costs are a not inconsiderable $8 million.*

in|con|sid|er|ate /ɪnkənsɪdərɪt/ ADJ If you accuse someone of being **inconsiderate**, you mean that they do not take enough care over how their words or actions will affect other people. [DISAPPROVAL] ❏ *It's a bit inconsiderate of her not to let you know when she expects to arrive.*

in|con|sist|en|cy /ɪnkənsɪstənsi/ (inconsistencies) **1** N-UNCOUNT If you refer to someone's **inconsistency**, you are criticizing them for not behaving in the same way every time a similar situation occurs. [DISAPPROVAL] ❏ *His worst fault was his inconsistency.* **2** N-VAR If there are **inconsistencies** between two statements, one cannot be true if the other is true. ❏ *We were asked to investigate the alleged inconsistencies in his evidence.*

in|con|sist|ent /ɪnkənsɪstənt/ **1** ADJ If you describe someone as **inconsistent**, you are criticizing them for not behaving in the same way every time a similar situation occurs. [DISAPPROVAL] ❏ *You are inconsistent and unpredictable.* **2** ADJ Someone or something that is **inconsistent** does not stay the same, being sometimes good and sometimes bad. ❏ *We had a terrific start to the season, but recently we've been inconsistent.* **3** ADJ If two statements are **inconsistent**, one cannot possibly be true if the other is true. ❏ *The evidence given in court was inconsistent with what he had previously told them.* **4** ADJ [v-link ADJ with n] If something is **inconsistent with** a set of ideas or values, it does not fit in well with them or match them. ❏ *This legislation is inconsistent with what they call Free Trade.*

in|con|sol|able /ɪnkənsoʊləbəl/ ADJ If you say that someone is **inconsolable**, you mean that they are very sad and cannot be comforted. ❏ *When my mother died I was inconsolable.*

in|con|spicu|ous /ɪnkənspɪkjuəs/ **1** ADJ Someone who is **inconspicuous** does not attract attention to themselves. ❏ *I'll try to be as inconspicuous as possible.* • **in|con|spicu|ous|ly** ADV [ADV after v] ❏ *I sat inconspicuously in a corner.* **2** ADJ Something that is **inconspicuous** is not easily seen or does not attract attention because it is small, ordinary, or hidden away. ❏ *...an inconspicuous gray building.*

in|con|ti|nence /ɪnkɒntɪnəns/ N-UNCOUNT **Incontinence** is the inability to control urine or feces from coming out of your body. ❏ *Incontinence is not just a condition of old age.*

in|con|ti|nent /ɪnkɒntɪnənt/ ADJ Someone who is **incontinent** is unable to control urine or feces from coming out of their body. ❏ *His diseased bladder left him incontinent.*

in|con|tro|vert|ible /ɪnkɒntrəvɜːrtɪbəl/ ADJ **Incontrovertible** evidence or facts are absolutely certain and cannot be shown to be wrong. ❏ *We have incontrovertible evidence of what took place.* • **in|con|tro|vert|ibly** ADV ❏ *No solution is incontrovertibly right.*

in|con|ven|ience /ɪnkənviːnjəns/ (inconveniences, inconveniencing, inconvenienced) **1** N-VAR If someone or something causes **inconvenience**, they cause problems or difficulties. ❏ *We apologize for any inconvenience caused during the* repairs. **2** V-T If someone **inconveniences** you, they cause problems or difficulties for you. ❑ *He promised to be quick so as not to inconvenience them any further.*

in|con|ven|ient /ɪnkənviːniənt/ ADJ Something that is **inconvenient** causes problems or difficulties for someone. ❑ *Can you come at 10:30? I know it's inconvenient, but I have to see you.*

in|cor|po|rate /ɪnkɔːrpəreɪt/ (**incorporates, incorporating, incorporated**) **1** V-T If one thing **incorporates** another thing, it includes the other thing. [FORMAL] ❑ *The new cars will incorporate a number of major improvements.* **2** V-T If someone or something **is incorporated** into a large group, system, or area, they become a part of it. [FORMAL] ❑ *The agreement would allow the rebels to be incorporated into a new national police force.*

In|cor|po|rated /ɪnkɔːrpəreɪtɪd/ ADJ [n ADJ] **Incorporated** is used after a company's name to show that it is a legally established company. [AM, BUSINESS] ❑ *...MCA Incorporated.*

in|cor|rect /ɪnkərɛkt/ **1** ADJ Something that is **incorrect** is wrong and untrue. ❑ *He denied that his evidence about the telephone call was incorrect.* • **in|cor|rect|ly** ADV [ADV with v] ❑ *The magazine suggested, incorrectly, that he was planning to announce his retirement.* **2** ADJ Something that is **incorrect** is not the thing that is required or is most suitable in a particular situation. ❑ *...injuries caused by incorrect posture.* • **in|cor|rect|ly** ADV [ADV with v] ❑ *He was told that the doors had been installed incorrectly.*

in|cor|ri|gible /ɪnkɔːrɪdʒəbəl/ ADJ If you tell someone they are **incorrigible**, you are saying, often in a humorous way, that they have faults that will never change. ❑ *"Sunita, you are incorrigible!" he said.* ❑ *They are incorrigible optimists.*

in|cor|rupt|ible /ɪnkərʌptɪbəl/ ADJ If you describe someone as **incorruptible**, you approve of the fact that they cannot be persuaded or paid to do things that they should not do. [APPROVAL] ❑ *He was a sound businessman, totally reliable and incorruptible.*

in|crease ✦✦✦ (**increases, increasing, increased**)

The verb is pronounced /ɪnkriːs/. The noun is pronounced /ɪnkriːs/.

1 V-T/V-I If something **increases** or you **increase** it, it becomes greater in number, level, or amount. ❑ *The population continues to increase.* ❑ *Japan's industrial output increased by 2%.* **2** N-COUNT If there is an **increase** in the number, level, or amount of something, it becomes greater. ❑ *...a sharp increase in productivity.* **3** PHRASE If something is **on the increase**, it is happening more often or becoming greater in number or intensity. ❑ *Crime is on the increase.*

── SYNONYMS ──

increase
VERB **1**
expand: *We have to expand the size of the image.*
rise: *The number of business failures has risen.*
raise: *The Republic of Ireland is expected to raise interest rates.*
boost: *The move is designed to boost sales during the peak booking months.*
extend: *This year they have introduced three new products to extend their range.*
grow: *Opposition grew, and the government agreed to negotiate.*
NOUN **2**
growth: *The area has seen a rapid population growth.*
rise: *...the prospect of another rise in interest rates.*
boost: *It would get the economy going and give us the boost that we need.*
expansion: *...the rapid expansion of private health insurance.*
development: *...an ideal system for studying the development of the embryo.*

in|creas|ing|ly ✦✦◇ /ɪnkriːsɪŋli/ ADV You can use **increasingly** to indicate that a situation or quality is becoming greater in intensity or more common. ❑ *He was finding it increasingly difficult to make decisions.* ❑ *The U.S. has increasingly relied on Japanese capital.*

── SYNONYMS ──

increasingly
ADV
progressively: *Her symptoms became progressively worse.*
more and more: *Bob became more and more furious.*

in|cred|ible ✦◇◇ /ɪnkrɛdɪbəl/ **1** ADJ If you describe something or someone as **incredible**, you like them very much or are impressed by them, because they are extremely or unusually good. [APPROVAL] ❑ *The wildflowers will be incredible after this rain.* • **in|cred|ibly** /ɪnkrɛdɪbli/ ADV [ADV adj/adv] ❑ *Their father was incredibly good-looking.* **2** ADJ If you say that something is **incredible**, you mean that it is very unusual or surprising, and you cannot believe it is really true, although it may be. ❑ *It seemed incredible that people would still want to play football during a war.* • **in|cred|ibly** ADV ❑ *Incredibly, some people don't like the name.* **3** ADJ You use **incredible** to emphasize the degree, amount, or intensity of something. [EMPHASIS] ❑ *I work an incredible amount of hours.* • **in|cred|ibly** ADV [ADV adj/adv] ❑ *It was incredibly hard work.*

in|cre|du|lity /ɪnkrɪdjuːlɪti/ N-UNCOUNT If someone reacts with **incredulity** to something, they are unable to believe it because it is very surprising or shocking. [WRITTEN] ❑ *The announcement has been met with incredulity.*

in|credu|lous /ɪnkrɛdʒələs/ ADJ If someone is **incredulous**, they are unable to believe something because it is very surprising or shocking. ❑ *"He made you do it?" Her voice was incredulous.* • **in|credu|lous|ly** ADV [ADV with v] ❑ *"You told Pete?" Rachel said incredulously. "I can't believe it!"*

in|cre|ment /ɪnkrɪmənt/ (**increments**) **1** N-COUNT An **increment** in something or in the value of something is an amount by which it increases. [FORMAL] ❑ *The average yearly increment in productivity was 4.5 per cent.* **2** N-COUNT An **increment** is an amount by which your salary automatically increases after a fixed period of time. [BRIT, FORMAL]

in AM, use **raise**

in|cre|men|tal /ɪnkrɪmɛntəl/ ADJ [usu ADJ n] **Incremental** is used to describe something that increases in value or worth, often by a regular amount. [FORMAL] ❑ *...our ability to add production capacity at relatively low incremental cost.*

in|crimi|nate /ɪnkrɪmɪneɪt/ (**incriminates, incriminating, incriminated**) V-T If something **incriminates** you, it suggests that you are responsible for something bad, especially a crime. ❑ *He claimed that the drugs had been planted to incriminate him.* • **in|crimi|nat|ing** ADJ ❑ *Police had reportedly searched his house and found incriminating evidence.*

in|cu|bate /ɪnkjəbeɪt, ɪŋ/ (**incubates, incubating, incubated**) V-T/V-I When birds **incubate** their eggs, or when they **incubate**, they keep the eggs warm until the baby birds come out. ❑ *The birds returned to their nests and continued to incubate the eggs.* ❑ *They lay eggs that incubate through the winter.* • **in|cu|ba|tion** /ɪnkjəbeɪʃən, ɪŋ/ N-UNCOUNT ❑ *Male albatrosses share in the incubation of eggs.*

in|cu|ba|tor /ɪnkjəbeɪtər/ (**incubators**) **1** N-COUNT An **incubator** is a piece of hospital equipment that helps weak or small babies to survive. It consists of a transparent container in which the oxygen and temperature levels can be controlled. **2** N-COUNT An **incubator** is a piece of equipment used to keep eggs or bacteria at the correct temperature for them to develop.

in|cul|cate /ɪnkʌlkeɪt/ (**inculcates, inculcating, inculcated**) V-T If you **inculcate** an idea or opinion in someone's mind, you teach it to them by repeating it until it is fixed in their mind. [FORMAL] ❑ *We have tried to inculcate a feeling of citizenship in youngsters.* ❑ *The aim is to inculcate businesspeople with an appreciation of different cultures.* ❑ *Great care was taken to inculcate the values of nationhood and family.*

in|cum|bent /ɪnkʌmbənt/ (**incumbents**) **1** N-COUNT An **incumbent** is someone who holds an official post at a particular time. [FORMAL] ❑ *In general, incumbents have a 94 percent chance of being re-elected.* • ADJ [ADJ n] **Incumbent** is also an adjective. ❑ *...the only candidate who defeated an incumbent senator.* **2** ADJ If it is **incumbent** on or upon you to do something, it is your duty or responsibility to do it. [FORMAL] ❑ *She felt it was incumbent on herself to act immediately.*

in|cur /ɪnkɜːr/ (**incurs, incurring, incurred**) V-T If you **incur** something unpleasant, it happens to you because of something you have done. [WRITTEN] ❑ *The government had also incurred huge debts.*

in|cur|able /ɪnkjʊərəbəl/ **1** ADJ If someone has an **incurable** disease, they cannot be cured of it. ❑ *He is suffering from an* incurable skin disease. • **in|cur|ably** /ɪnkyʊərəbli/ ADV [ADV adj] ❏ ...youngsters who are incurably ill. **2** ADJ [ADJ n] You can use **incurable** to indicate that someone has a particular quality or attitude and will not change. ❏ Poor old Willy is an incurable romantic. • **in|cur|ably** ADV [ADV adj] ❏ I know you think I'm incurably nosy, but the truth is I'm concerned about you.

in|cur|sion /ɪnkɜrʒ³n, -ʃ³n/ (**incursions**) **1** N-COUNT [oft N into n] If there is an **incursion** into a country, enemy soldiers suddenly enter it. [FORMAL] ❏ ...armed incursions into border areas by rebel forces. **2** N-COUNT [oft N of n] If someone or something enters an area where you would not expect them to be, or where they have not been found before, you can call this an **incursion**, especially when you disapprove of their presence. [FORMAL] ❏ ...her disastrous incursion into the property market.

in|debt|ed /ɪndetɪd/ **1** ADJ [v-link ADJ to n] If you say that you are **indebted** to someone for something, you mean that you are very grateful to them for something. ❏ I am deeply indebted to him for his help. **2** ADJ **Indebted** countries, organizations, or people are ones that owe money to other countries, organizations, or people. ❏ The treasury secretary identified the most heavily indebted countries.

in|de|cen|cy /ɪndis³nsi/ (**indecencies**) **1** N-UNCOUNT If you talk about the **indecency** of something or someone, you are indicating that you find them morally or sexually offensive. ❏ ...the indecency of their language. **2** N-COUNT In law, an **indecency** is an illegal sexual act. ❏ ...sexual indecencies.

in|de|cent /ɪndis³nt/ **1** ADJ If you describe something as **indecent**, you mean that it is shocking and offensive, usually because it relates to sex or nakedness. ❏ He accused Mrs. Moore of making an indecent suggestion. • **in|de|cent|ly** ADV ❏ ...an indecently short skirt. **2** ADJ If you describe the speed or amount of something as **indecent**, you are indicating, often in a humorous way, that it is much quicker or larger than is usual or desirable. ❏ She finished her first glass of wine with indecent haste. • **in|de|cent|ly** ADV ❏ ...an indecently large office.

in|de|cent as|sault N-UNCOUNT **Indecent assault** is the crime of attacking someone in a way that involves touching or threatening them sexually, but not forcing them to have sexual intercourse.

in|de|cent ex|po|sure N-UNCOUNT **Indecent exposure** is a criminal offense that is committed when someone exposes their genitals in public.

in|de|ci|pher|able /ɪndɪsaɪfərəb³l/ ADJ If writing or speech is **indecipherable**, you cannot understand what the words are. ❏ Majid's writing was virtually indecipherable. ❏ He uttered little indecipherable sounds.

in|de|ci|sion /ɪndɪsɪʒ³n/ N-UNCOUNT If you say that someone suffers from **indecision**, you mean that they find it very difficult to make decisions. ❏ After months of indecision, the government gave the plan the go-ahead on Monday.

in|de|ci|sive /ɪndɪsaɪsɪv/ **1** ADJ If you say that someone is **indecisive**, you mean that they find it very difficult to make decisions. ❏ He was criticized as a weak and indecisive leader. **2** ADJ An **indecisive** result in a contest or election is one that is not clear or definite. ❏ The outcome of the battle was indecisive.

in|deed ♦♦◊ /ɪndid/ **1** ADV You use **indeed** to confirm or agree with something that has just been said. [EMPHASIS] ❏ Later, he admitted that the payments had indeed been made. ❏ "Did you know him?"—"I did indeed." **2** ADV [ADV with cl] You use **indeed** to introduce a further comment or statement that strengthens the point you have already made. [EMPHASIS] ❏ We have nothing against diversity; indeed, we want more of it. **3** ADV [adj ADV] You use **indeed** at the end of a clause to give extra force to the word 'very,' or to emphasize a particular word. [EMPHASIS] ❏ The results are often strange indeed.

in|de|fati|gable /ɪndɪfætɪgəb³l/ ADJ You use **indefatigable** to describe someone who never gets tired of doing something. [FORMAL] ❏ His indefatigable spirit helped him to cope with his illness. • **in|de|fati|gab|ly** /ɪndɪfætɪgəbli/ ADV [ADV with v, ADV adj] ❏ She worked indefatigably to interest children in music.

in|de|fen|sible /ɪndɪfensɪb³l/ **1** ADJ If you say that a statement, action, or idea is **indefensible**, you mean that it cannot be justified or supported because it is completely wrong or unacceptable. ❏ She described the new policy as "morally indefensible." **2** ADJ Places or buildings that are **indefensible** cannot be defended if they are attacked. ❏ The checkpoint was abandoned as militarily indefensible.

in|de|fin|able /ɪndɪfaɪnəb³l/ ADJ An **indefinable** quality or feeling cannot easily be described. [WRITTEN] ❏ There was something indefinable in her eyes.

in|defi|nite /ɪndefɪnɪt/ **1** ADJ If you describe a situation or period as **indefinite**, you mean that people have not decided when it will end. ❏ The trial was adjourned for an indefinite period. **2** ADJ Something that is **indefinite** is not exact or clear. ❏ ...at some indefinite time in the future.

in|defi|nite ar|ti|cle (**indefinite articles**) N-COUNT The words 'a' and 'an' are sometimes called the **indefinite article**.

in|defi|nite|ly /ɪndefɪnɪtli/ ADV [ADV with v] If a situation will continue **indefinitely**, it will continue forever or until someone decides to change it or end it. ❏ The visit has now been postponed indefinitely.

in|defi|nite pro|noun (**indefinite pronouns**) N-COUNT An **indefinite pronoun** is a pronoun such as 'someone,' 'anything,' or 'nobody,' that you use to refer in a general way to a person or thing.

in|del|ible /ɪndelɪb³l/ **1** ADJ [usu ADJ n] If you say that something leaves an **indelible** impression, you mean that it is very unlikely to be forgotten. ❏ My visit to India in 2017 left an indelible impression on me. • **in|del|ibly** ADV [ADV with v] ❏ The horrors he experienced are imprinted, perhaps indelibly, in his brain. **2** ADJ [usu ADJ n] **Indelible** ink or an **indelible** stain cannot be removed or washed out. ❏ It leaves indelible stains on clothes. ❏ The message was written in indelible ink.

in|deli|cate /ɪndelɪkɪt/ ADJ If something or someone is **indelicate**, they are rude or embarrassing. [FORMAL] ❏ She really could not touch upon such an indelicate subject.

in|dem|ni|fy /ɪndemnɪfaɪ/ (**indemnifies, indemnifying, indemnified**) V-T To **indemnify** someone against something bad happening means to promise to protect them, especially financially, if it happens. [FORMAL] ❏ They agreed to indemnify the taxpayers against any loss.

in|dem|nity /ɪndemnɪti/ N-UNCOUNT If something provides **indemnity**, it provides insurance or protection against damage or loss. [FORMAL] ❏ Political exiles had not been given indemnity from prosecution.

in|dent /ɪndent/ (**indents, indenting, indented**) V-T When you **indent** a line of writing, you start it further away from the edge of the paper than all the other lines. ❏ Indent the second line.

in|den|ta|tion /ɪndenteɪʃ³n/ (**indentations**) **1** N-COUNT An **indentation** is the space at the beginning of a line of writing when it starts further away from the edge of the paper than all the other lines. **2** N-COUNT An **indentation** is a shallow hole or cut in the surface or edge of something. ❏ Using a knife, make slight indentations around the edges of the pastry.

in|dent|ed /ɪndentɪd/ ADJ If something is **indented**, its edge or surface is uneven because parts of it have been worn away or cut away.

in|den|tured /ɪndentʃərd/ ADJ [usu ADJ n] In the past, an **indentured** servant was one who was forced to work for someone for a period of time, because of an agreement made by people in authority or to settle a debt.

in|de|pend|ence ♦♦◊ /ɪndɪpendəns/ **1** N-UNCOUNT If a country has or gains **independence**, it has its own government and is not ruled by any other country. ❏ In 1816, Argentina declared its independence from Spain. **2** N-UNCOUNT Someone's **independence** is the fact that they do not rely on other people. ❏ He was afraid of losing his independence.

SYNONYMS

independence
NOUN **1**
freedom: Today we have the freedom to decide our own futures.
liberty: Such a system would be a fundamental blow to our rights and liberties.
autonomy: Activists stepped up their demands for local autonomy last month.
sovereignty: Britain's concern to protect national sovereignty is far from new.

In|de|pend|ence Day N-UNCOUNT A country's **Independence Day** is the day on which its people celebrate their independence from another country that ruled them in the past. In the United States, Independence Day is celebrated each year on the 4th of July. ☐ *He died on Independence Day, 1831.*

in|de|pend|ent ♦♦♦ /ɪndɪpɛndənt/ (**independents**) **1** ADJ If one thing or person is **independent** of another, the two things are separate and not connected, so the first one is not affected or influenced by the second. ☐ *Your questions should be independent of each other.* ☐ *We're going independent from the university and setting up our own group.* • **in|de|pen|dent|ly** ADV ☐ *...several people working independently in different areas of the world.* **2** ADJ If someone is **independent**, they do not need help or money from anyone else. ☐ *Phil was now much more independent of his parents.* • **in|de|pen|dent|ly** ADV ☐ *...helping students with disabilities to live and study as independently as possible.* **3** ADJ **Independent** countries and states are not ruled by other countries but have their own government. ☐ *Papua New Guinea became independent from Australia in 1975.* **4** ADJ [ADJ n] An **independent** organization or other body is one that controls its own finances and operations, rather than being controlled by someone else. ☐ *...an independent television station.* **5** ADJ [ADJ n] An **independent** inquiry or opinion is one that involves people who are not connected with a particular situation, and should therefore be fair. ☐ *There were calls in Congress for an independent inquiry.* **6** ADJ An **independent** politician is one who does not represent any political party. ☐ *There's been a late surge of support for an independent candidate.* • N-COUNT An **independent** is an independent politician. ☐ *Standing as an independent, he succeeded in convincing a significant number of voters of his argument.*

in-depth ADJ [usu ADJ n] An **in-depth** analysis or study of something is a very detailed and complete study of it. ☐ *...an in-depth look at censorship in the music business.*

in|de|scrib|able /ɪndɪskraɪbəbəl/ ADJ You use **indescribable** to emphasize that a quality or condition is very intense or extreme, and therefore cannot be properly described. [EMPHASIS] ☐ *...her indescribable joy when it was confirmed her son was alive.* • **in|de|scrib|ably** /ɪndɪskraɪbəbli/ ADV [ADV adj] ☐ *...indescribably filthy conditions.*

in|de|struct|ible /ɪndɪstrʌktɪbəl/ ADJ If something is **indestructible**, it is very strong and cannot be destroyed. ☐ *This type of plastic is almost indestructible.*

in|de|ter|mi|na|cy /ɪndɪtɜrmɪnəsi/ N-UNCOUNT The **indeterminacy** of something is its quality of being uncertain or vague. [FORMAL] ☐ *...the indeterminacy of language.*

in|de|ter|mi|nate /ɪndɪtɜrmɪnɪt/ ADJ [usu ADJ n] If something is **indeterminate**, you cannot say exactly what it is. ☐ *I hope to carry on for an indeterminate period.*

in|dex ♦♢♢ /ɪndɛks/ (**indices, indexes, indexing, indexed**)

The usual plural is **indexes**, but the form **indices** can be used for meaning **1**.

1 N-COUNT An **index** is a system by which changes in the value of something and the rate at which it changes can be recorded, measured, or interpreted. ☐ *...the consumer price index.* **2** N-COUNT An **index** is an alphabetical list that is printed at the back of a book and tells you on which pages important topics are referred to. ☐ *There's even a special subject index.* **3** V-T If you **index** a book or a collection of information, you make an alphabetical list of the items in it. ☐ *A quarter of this vast archive has been indexed and made accessible to researchers.* **4** V-T [usu passive] If a quantity or value **is indexed** to another, a system is arranged so that it increases or decreases whenever the other one increases or decreases. ☐ *Minimum benefits and wages are to be indexed to inflation.* **5** → see also **card index** **6** → See feature box at **research**

in|dex card (**index cards**) N-COUNT An **index card** is a small card on which you can write information. Index cards are often kept in a box, arranged in order.

in|dex fin|ger (**index fingers**) N-COUNT Your **index finger** is the finger that is next to your thumb.

In|dian /ɪndiən/ (**Indians**) **1** ADJ [usu ADJ n] **Indian** means belonging or relating to India, or to its people or culture. ☐ *...the Indian government.* **2** N-COUNT An **Indian** is an Indian citizen, or a person of Indian origin. **3** N-COUNT **Indians** are the people who lived in North, South, or Central America before Europeans arrived, or people living today who are descended from them. The usual name for these groups of people is **Native American**.

In|dian sum|mer (**Indian summers**) N-COUNT You can refer to a period of unusually warm and sunny weather during the fall as an **Indian summer**.

in|di|cate ♦♦♢ /ɪndɪkeɪt/ (**indicates, indicating, indicated**) **1** V-T If one thing **indicates** another, the first thing shows that the second is true or exists. ☐ *A survey of retired people has indicated that most are independent and enjoying life.* ☐ *Our vote today indicates a change in United States policy.* **2** V-T If you **indicate** an opinion, an intention, or a fact, you mention it in an indirect way. ☐ *Mr. Rivers has indicated that he may resign.* **3** V-T If you **indicate** something to someone, you show them where it is, especially by pointing to it. [FORMAL] ☐ *He indicated a chair. "Sit down."* **4** V-T If one thing **indicates** something else, it is a sign of that thing. ☐ *Dreams can help indicate your true feelings.* **5** V-T If a technical instrument **indicates** something, it shows a measurement or reading. ☐ *...an instrument used to indicate wind direction.* **6** V-T/V-I When drivers **indicate**, they make lights flash on one side of their vehicle to show that they are going to turn in that direction. [mainly BRIT]

in AM, use **signal**

in|di|ca|tion ♦♢♢ /ɪndɪkeɪʃən/ (**indications**) N-VAR An **indication** is a sign that suggests, for example, what people are thinking or feeling. ☐ *He gave no indication that he was ready to compromise.*

── SYNONYMS ──
indication
NOUN
sign: *His face and movements rarely betrayed a sign of nerves.*
evidence: *Ganley said he'd seen no evidence of widespread fraud.*
signal: *Leaders saw the visit as an important signal of support.*
suggestion: *There is absolutely no suggestion of any mainstream political party involvement.*

in|dica|tive /ɪndɪkətɪv/ ADJ If one thing is **indicative** of another, it suggests what the other thing is likely to be. [FORMAL] ☐ *His action is indicative of growing concern about the shortage of skilled labor.*

in|di|ca|tor /ɪndɪkeɪtər/ (**indicators**) **1** N-COUNT An **indicator** is a measurement or value that gives you an idea of what something is like. ☐ *...vital economic indicators, such as inflation, growth and the trade gap.* **2** N-COUNT A car's **indicators** are the flashing lights that tell you when it is going to turn left or right. [mainly BRIT]

in AM, use **turn signals**

in|di|ces /ɪndɪsiz/ **Indices** is a plural form of **index**.

in|dict /ɪndaɪt/ (**indicts, indicting, indicted**) V-T [usu passive] If someone **is indicted** for a crime, they are officially charged with it. [mainly AM, LEGAL] ☐ *He was later indicted on corruption charges.*

in|dict|ment /ɪndaɪtmənt/ (**indictments**) **1** N-COUNT If you say that one thing is an **indictment** of another thing, you mean that it shows how bad the other thing is. ☐ *The movie is an indictment of Hollywood.* **2** N-VAR An **indictment** is a formal accusation that someone has committed a crime. [mainly AM, LEGAL] ☐ *Prosecutors may soon seek an indictment on racketeering and fraud charges.*

in|die /ɪndi/ (**indies**) **1** ADJ [ADJ n] **Indie** music refers to rock or pop music produced by new bands working with small, independent record companies. ☐ *...a promising indie band.* • N-COUNT An **indie** is an indie band or record company. ☐ *The fact was that the indies were selling a lot more CDs than the major record labels.* **2** ADJ [ADJ n] **Indie** movies are produced by small independent companies rather than by major studios. ☐ *...the most successful indie movie of all time.* • N-COUNT An **indie** is an indie film or film company. ☐ *The indies convert their digital movies to film.*

in|dif|fer|ence /ɪndɪfərəns/ N-UNCOUNT If you accuse someone of **indifference** to something, you mean that they have a complete lack of interest in it. ☐ *...his callous indifference to the plight of his son.*

in|dif|fer|ent /ɪndɪfərənt/ **1** ADJ If you accuse someone of being **indifferent** to something, you mean that they have a complete lack of interest in it. ❏ *People have become indifferent to the suffering of others.* • **in|dif|fer|ent|ly** ADV [ADV after v] ❏ *"Not that it matters," said Trujillo indifferently.* **2** ADJ If you describe something or someone as **indifferent**, you mean that their standard or quality is not very good, and often quite bad. ❏ *She had starred in several very indifferent movies.* • **in|dif|fer|ent|ly** ADV [ADV with v] ❏ *...a shoddy piece of work, poorly written, indifferently performed.*

in|dig|enous /ɪndɪdʒɪnəs/ ADJ **Indigenous** people or things belong to the country in which they are found, rather than coming there or being brought there from another country. [FORMAL] ❏ *...the country's indigenous population.*

in|di|gent /ɪndɪdʒənt/ ADJ Someone who is **indigent** is very poor. [FORMAL]

in|di|gest|ible /ɪndɪdʒɛstɪbəl, -daɪ-/ **1** ADJ Food that is **indigestible** cannot be digested easily. ❏ *In our body, some food is indigestible.* **2** ADJ If you describe facts or ideas as **indigestible**, you mean that they are difficult to understand, complicated, and dull. [DISAPPROVAL] ❏ *...a dense, indigestible and wordy book.*

in|di|ges|tion /ɪndɪdʒɛstʃən, -daɪ-/ N-UNCOUNT If you have **indigestion**, you have pains in your stomach and chest that are caused by difficulties in digesting food.

in|dig|nant /ɪndɪgnənt/ ADJ If you are **indignant**, you are shocked and angry, because you think that something is unjust or unfair. ❏ *He is indignant at suggestions that they were secret agents.* ❏ *He was indignant that his rival was offered the job.* • **in|dig|nant|ly** ADV [ADV with v] ❏ *"That is not true," Erica said indignantly.*

in|dig|na|tion /ɪndɪgneɪʃən/ N-UNCOUNT **Indignation** is a feeling of shock and anger when you think that something is unjust or unfair. ❏ *She was filled with indignation at the conditions under which miners were forced to work.*

in|dig|nity /ɪndɪgnɪti/ (**indignities**) N-VAR If you talk about the **indignity** of doing something, you mean that it makes you feel embarrassed or unimportant. [FORMAL] ❏ *Later, he suffered the indignity of having to flee angry protesters.*

in|di|go /ɪndɪgoʊ/ COLOR Something that is **indigo** is dark purplish blue in color.

in|di|rect /ɪndaɪrɛkt, -dɪr-/ **1** ADJ An **indirect** result or effect is not caused immediately and obviously by a thing or person, but happens because of something else that they have done. ❏ *Businesses are feeling the indirect effects from the recession that's going on elsewhere.* • **in|di|rect|ly** ADV ❏ *There is clear evidence that cellphone usage has been indirectly responsible for a number of accidents.* **2** ADJ An **indirect** route or journey does not use the shortest or easiest way between two places. ❏ *He took an indirect route back home.* **3** ADJ **Indirect** remarks and information suggest something or refer to it, without actually mentioning it or stating it clearly. ❏ *His remarks amounted to an indirect appeal for economic aid.* • **in|di|rect|ly** ADV [ADV with v] ❏ *He referred indirectly to the territorial dispute.*

in|di|rect dis|course N-UNCOUNT **Indirect discourse** is speech that tells you what someone said, but does not use the person's actual words; for example, 'They said you didn't like it.,' 'I asked him what his plans were.,' and 'Citizens complained about the smoke.'

in|di|rect ob|ject (**indirect objects**) N-COUNT An **indirect object** is an object that is used with a transitive verb to indicate who benefits from an action or gets something as a result. For example, in 'She gave him her address.,' 'him' is the indirect object. Compare **direct object**.

in|di|rect ques|tion (**indirect questions**) N-COUNT An **indirect question** is the same as a **reported question**. [mainly BRIT]

in|di|rect speech N-UNCOUNT **Indirect speech** is the same as **indirect discourse**.

in|di|rect tax (**indirect taxes**) N-COUNT An **indirect tax** is a tax on goods and services that is added to their price before they reach the consumer. Compare **direct tax**. [BUSINESS]

in|di|rect taxa|tion N-UNCOUNT **Indirect taxation** is a system in which a government raises money by means of indirect taxes.

in|dis|ci|pline /ɪndɪsɪplɪn/ N-UNCOUNT If you refer to **indiscipline** in a group or team, you disapprove of the fact that they do not behave in a controlled way as they should. [DISAPPROVAL] ❏ *There is growing evidence of indiscipline among the troops.*

in|dis|creet /ɪndɪskriːt/ ADJ If you describe someone as **indiscreet**, you mean that they do or say things in public that they should only do or say secretly or in private. ❏ *He is notoriously indiscreet about his private life.*

in|dis|cre|tion /ɪndɪskrɛʃən/ (**indiscretions**) N-VAR If you talk about someone's **indiscretion**, you mean that they have done or said something that is risky, careless, or likely to upset people. ❏ *Occasionally they paid for their indiscretion with their lives.*

in|dis|crimi|nate /ɪndɪskrɪmɪnɪt/ ADJ If you describe an action as **indiscriminate**, you are critical of it because it does not involve any careful thought or choice. [DISAPPROVAL] ❏ *The indiscriminate use of fertilizers is damaging to the environment.* • **in|dis|crimi|nate|ly** ADV ❏ *The men opened fire indiscriminately.*

in|dis|pen|sable /ɪndɪspɛnsəbəl/ ADJ If you say that someone or something is **indispensable**, you mean that they are absolutely essential and other people or things cannot function without them. ❏ *She was becoming indispensable to him.*

in|dis|posed /ɪndɪspoʊzd/ ADJ [usu v-link ADJ] If you say that someone is **indisposed**, you mean that they are not available because they are ill, or for a reason that you do not want to reveal. [FORMAL] ❏ *The speaker was regrettably indisposed.*

in|dis|put|able /ɪndɪspyuːtəbəl/ ADJ If you say that something is **indisputable**, you are emphasizing that it is true and cannot be shown to be untrue. [EMPHASIS] ❏ *It is indisputable that birds are harboring this illness.*

in|dis|tinct /ɪndɪstɪŋkt/ **1** ADJ Something that is **indistinct** is unclear and difficult to see, hear, or recognize. ❏ *The lettering is fuzzy and indistinct.* • **in|dis|tinct|ly** ADV [ADV after v] ❏ *Teddy mumbled indistinctly.* **2** → See feature box at **speak**

in|dis|tin|guish|able /ɪndɪstɪŋgwɪʃəbəl/ ADJ If one thing is **indistinguishable** from another, the two things are so similar that it is difficult to know which is which. ❏ *Replica weapons are indistinguishable from the real thing.*

in|di|vid|ual ✦✧ /ɪndɪvɪdʒuəl/ (**individuals**) **1** ADJ [ADJ n] **Individual** means relating to one person or thing, rather than to a large group. ❏ *...waiting for the group to decide rather than making individual decisions.* • **in|di|vid|ual|ly** ADV ❏ *...individually crafted tiles.* **2** N-COUNT An **individual** is a person. ❏ *...anonymous individuals who are doing good things within our community.* **3** ADJ If you describe someone or something as **individual**, you mean that you admire them because they are very unusual and do not try to imitate other people or things. [APPROVAL] ❏ *It was really all part of her very individual personality.*

SYNONYMS

individual
ADJ **3**
special: *So you didn't notice anything special about him?*
unique: *Each person's signature is unique.*
original: *It is one of the most original works of imagination in the language.*
distinctive: *His voice was very distinctive.*

---

in|di|vid|ual|ism /ɪndɪvɪdʒuəlɪzəm/ **1** N-UNCOUNT You use **individualism** to refer to the behavior of someone who likes to think and do things in their own way, rather than imitating other people. ❏ *He is struck by what he calls the individualism of American officers.* **2** N-UNCOUNT **Individualism** is the belief that people should have the greatest possible personal freedom. ❏ *...the strong individualism in their political culture.*

in|di|vid|ual|ist /ɪndɪvɪdʒuəlɪst/ (**individualists**) **1** N-COUNT If you describe someone as an **individualist**, you mean that they like to think and do things in their own way, rather than imitating other people. ❏ *Individualists say that you should be able to wear what you want.* **2** ADJ [usu ADJ n] **Individualist** means relating to the belief that people should have the greatest possible personal freedom. ❏ *...a party committed to individualist values.* • N-COUNT An **individualist** is a person with individualist views. ❏ *They share with earlier individualists a fear of collectivism.*

in|di|vidu|al|is|tic /ɪndɪvɪdʒuəlɪstɪk/ ADJ If you say that someone is **individualistic**, you mean that they like to think and do things in their own way, rather than imitating other people. You can also say that a society is **individualistic** if it encourages people to behave in this way. ❏ *Most artists are very individualistic.*

in|di|vidu|al|ity /ɪndɪvɪdʒuælɪti/ N-UNCOUNT The **individuality** of a person or thing consists of the qualities that make them different from other people or things. ❏ *People should be free to express their individuality.*

in|di|vidu|al|ize /ɪndɪvɪdʒuəlaɪz/ (**individualizes, individualizing, individualized**)

in BRIT, also use **individualise**

V-T To **individualize** a thing or person means to make them different from other things or people and to give them a recognizable identity. [FORMAL] ❏ *You can individualize a document by adding comments in the margins.*
• **in|di|vidu|al|ized** ADJ ❏ *Doctors feel that a more individualized approach to patients should now be adopted.*

in|di|vis|ible /ɪndɪvɪzɪbəl/ ADJ If you say that something is **indivisible**, you mean that it cannot be divided into different parts. ❏ *Far from being separate, the mind and body form an indivisible whole.*

PREFIX

Indo-
combines with nationality adjectives to form adjectives which describe something as connected with both India and another country. For example, **Indo-Pakistani** talks take place between representatives from both India and Pakistan.

---

in|doc|tri|nate /ɪndɒktrɪneɪt/ (**indoctrinates, indoctrinating, indoctrinated**) V-T If people **are indoctrinated**, they are taught a particular belief with the aim that they will reject other beliefs. [DISAPPROVAL] ❏ *They have been completely indoctrinated.* ❏ *I wouldn't say that she was trying to indoctrinate us.* • **in|doc|tri|na|tion** /ɪndɒktrɪneɪʃən/ N-UNCOUNT ❏ *...political indoctrination classes.*

in|do|lence /ɪndələns/ N-UNCOUNT **Indolence** means laziness. [FORMAL]

in|do|lent /ɪndələnt/ ADJ Someone who is **indolent** is lazy. [FORMAL]

in|domi|table /ɪndɒmɪtəbəl/ ADJ If you say that someone has an **indomitable** spirit, you admire them because they never give up or admit that they have been defeated. [FORMAL, APPROVAL] ❏ *...a woman of indomitable will.*

In|do|nesian /ɪndəniʒən/ (**Indonesians**) ◼ ADJ **Indonesian** means belonging or relating to Indonesia, or to its people or culture. ◼ N-COUNT An **Indonesian** is an Indonesian citizen, or a person of Indonesian origin. ◼ N-UNCOUNT **Indonesian** is the national language of Indonesia.

in|door /ɪndɔr/ ADJ [ADJ n] **Indoor** activities or things are ones that happen or are used inside a building and not outside. ❏ *No smoking in any indoor facilities.*

in|doors /ɪndɔrz/ ADV If something happens **indoors**, it happens inside a building. ❏ *I think perhaps we should go indoors.*

in|du|bi|table /ɪndubɪtəbəl/ ADJ You use **indubitable** to describe something when you want to emphasize that it is definite and cannot be doubted. [FORMAL, EMPHASIS] ❏ *His brilliance renders this film an indubitable classic.*
• **in|du|bi|tably** ADV ❏ *His behavior was indubitably ill-judged.*

in|duce /ɪndus/ (**induces, inducing, induced**) ◼ V-T To **induce** a state or condition means to cause it. ❏ *Doctors said surgery could induce a heart attack.* ◼ V-T If you **induce** someone to do something, you persuade or influence them to do it. ❏ *More than 4,000 teachers were induced to take early retirement.* ◼ → See feature box at **birth**

-induced /-ɪndust/ COMB IN ADJ **-induced** combines with nouns to form adjectives that indicate that a state, condition, or illness is caused by a particular thing. ❏ *...stress-induced disorders.* ❏ *...a drug-induced hallucination.*

in|duce|ment /ɪndusmənt/ (**inducements**) N-COUNT If someone is offered an **inducement** to do something, they are given or promised gifts or benefits in order to persuade them to do it. ❏ *They offer every inducement to foreign businesses to invest in their states.*

in|duct /ɪndʌkt/ (**inducts, inducting, inducted**) V-T If someone **is inducted** into a particular job, rank, honor, or position, they are given the job, rank, honor, or position in a formal ceremony. [FORMAL] ❏ *In 1987, he was inducted into the Rock and Roll Hall of Fame.* ❏ *She inducts Nina into the cult.*

in|duc|tion /ɪndʌkʃən/ (**inductions**) N-VAR **Induction** is a procedure or ceremony for introducing someone to a new job, organization, or way of life. ❏ *...his induction as president.*

in|dulge /ɪndʌldʒ/ (**indulges, indulging, indulged**) ◼ V-T/V-I If you **indulge** in something or if you **indulge** yourself, you allow yourself to have or do something that you know you will enjoy. ❏ *Only rarely will she indulge in a glass of wine.* ❏ *He returned to Ohio so that he could indulge his passion for football.* ◼ V-T If you **indulge** someone, you let them have or do what they want, even if this is not good for them. ❏ *He did not agree with indulging children.*

in|dul|gence /ɪndʌldʒəns/ (**indulgences**) N-VAR **Indulgence** means treating someone with special kindness, often when it is not a good thing. ❏ *The king's indulgence toward his sons angered the business community.*

in|dul|gent /ɪndʌldʒənt/ ADJ If you are **indulgent**, you treat a person with special kindness, often in a way that is not good for them. ❏ *His indulgent mother was willing to let him do anything he wanted.* • **in|dul|gent|ly** ADV ❏ *Najib smiled at him indulgently and said, "Come on over when you feel like it."*

in|dus|trial ✦✧ /ɪndʌstriəl/ ◼ ADJ You use **industrial** to describe things that relate to or are used in industry. ❏ *...industrial machinery and equipment.* ◼ ADJ An **industrial** city or country is one in which industry is important or highly developed. ❏ *...leading western industrial countries.*

in|dus|trial es|tate (**industrial estates**) N-COUNT An **industrial estate** is the same as an **industrial park**. [BRIT]

in|dus|tri|al|ism /ɪndʌstriəlɪzəm/ N-UNCOUNT **Industrialism** is the state of having an economy based on industry.

in|dus|tri|al|ist /ɪndʌstriəlɪst/ (**industrialists**) N-COUNT An **industrialist** is a powerful businessperson who owns or controls large industrial companies or factories. ❏ *...prominent Japanese industrialists.*

in|dus|tri|al|ize /ɪndʌstriəlaɪz/ (**industrializes, industrializing, industrialized**)

in BRIT, also use **industrialise**

V-T/V-I When a country **industrializes** or **is industrialized**, it develops a lot of industries. ❏ *Energy consumption rises as countries industrialize.* • **in|dus|tri|ali|za|tion** /ɪndʌstriəlɪzeɪʃən/ N-UNCOUNT ❏ *Industrialization began early in Spain.*

in|dus|tri|al|ized ✦✧ /ɪndʌstriəlaɪzd/ ADJ [ADJ n] An **industrialized** area or place is one that has a lot of industries. ❏ *Industrialized countries must reduce carbon dioxide emissions.*

in|dus|trial park (**industrial parks**) N-COUNT An **industrial park** is an area that has been specially planned for a lot of factories. [AM]

in BRIT, use **industrial estate**

in|dus|trial re|la|tions N-PLURAL **Industrial relations** refers to the relationship between employers and employees in industry, and the political decisions and laws that affect it. [BUSINESS] ❏ *The offer is seen as an attempt to improve industrial relations.*

in|dus|tri|ous /ɪndʌstriəs/ ADJ If you describe someone as **industrious**, you mean they work very hard. ❏ *She was an industrious and willing worker.* • **in|dus|tri|ous|ly** ADV [ADV with v] ❏ *Peggy paints industriously all through the summer.*

in|dus|try ✦✦✦ /ɪndəstri/ (**industries**) ◼ N-UNCOUNT **Industry** is the work and processes involved in collecting raw materials, and making them into products in factories. ❏ *Our industry suffers through insufficient investment in research.* ◼ N-COUNT A particular **industry** consists of all the people and activities involved in making a particular product or providing a particular service. ❑ ...*the motor vehicle and textile industries.* ❸ N-COUNT If you refer to a social or political activity as an **industry**, you are criticizing it because you think it involves a lot of people in unnecessary or useless work. [DISAPPROVAL] ❑ ...*the industry of western capitalism.* ❹ N-UNCOUNT **Industry** is the fact of working very hard. [FORMAL] ❑ *No one doubted his ability, his industry or his integrity.* ❺ → see also **cottage industry**, **service industry**

---SYNONYMS---

industry
NOUN ❶
business: ...*young people seeking a career in business.*
manufacturing: ...*management headquarters for manufacturing.*
trade: ...*negotiations on a new international trade agreement.*
commerce: *They have made their fortunes from commerce.*
production: *That model won't go into production before late 2019.*

---

ine|bri|at|ed /ɪnɪbrieɪtɪd/ ADJ Someone who is **inebriated** has drunk too much alcohol. [FORMAL] ❑ *Scott was obviously inebriated by the time the dessert was served.*

in|ed|ible /ɪnɛdɪbəl/ ADJ If you say that something is **inedible**, you mean you cannot eat it, for example, because it tastes bad or is poisonous. ❑ *Detainees complained of being given inedible food.*

in|ef|fable /ɪnɛfəbəl/ ADJ [usu ADJ n] You use **ineffable** to say that something is so great or extreme that it cannot be described in words. [FORMAL] ❑ ...*the ineffable sadness of many of the portraits.* • **in|ef|fably** /ɪnɛfəbli/ ADV [usu ADV adj] ❑ ...*his ineffably powerful brain.*

in|ef|fec|tive /ɪnɪfɛktɪv/ ADJ If you say that something is **ineffective**, you mean that it has no effect on a process or situation. ❑ *Economic reform will continue to be painful and ineffective.*

in|ef|fec|tual /ɪnɪfɛktʃuəl/ ADJ If someone or something is **ineffectual**, they fail to do what they are expected to do or are trying to do. ❑ *The mayor had become ineffectual in the struggle to clamp down on drugs.* • **in|ef|fec|tu|al|ly** ADV ❑ *Her voice trailed off ineffectually.*

in|ef|fi|cient /ɪnɪfɪʃənt/ ADJ **Inefficient** people, organizations, systems, or machines do not use time, energy, or other resources in the best way. ❑ *Their communication systems are inefficient in the extreme.* • **in|ef|fi|cien|cy** (**inefficiencies**) N-VAR ❑ *The inefficiency of the distribution system has led to the loss of millions of tons of food.* • **in|ef|fi|cient|ly** ADV [ADV with v] ❑ *Energy prices have been kept low, so energy is used inefficiently.*

in|el|egant /ɪnɛlɪgənt/ ADJ If you say that something is **inelegant**, you mean that it is not attractive or graceful. ❑ *The grand piano has been replaced with a small, inelegant electric model.*

in|eli|gible /ɪnɛlɪdʒəbəl/ ADJ If you are **ineligible** for something, you are not qualified for it or entitled to it. [FORMAL] ❑ *They were ineligible to remain in the U.S.*

in|eluc|table /ɪnɪlʌktəbəl/ ADJ [usu ADJ n] You use **ineluctable** to describe something that cannot be stopped, escaped, or ignored. [FORMAL] ❑ ...*the ineluctable tendency of populations to exceed resources.*

in|ept /ɪnɛpt/ ADJ If you say that someone is **inept**, you are criticizing them because they do something with a complete lack of skill. [DISAPPROVAL] ❑ *He was inept and lacked the intelligence to govern.*

in|epti|tude /ɪnɛptɪtud/ N-UNCOUNT If you refer to someone's **ineptitude**, you are criticizing them because they do something with a complete lack of skill. [DISAPPROVAL] ❑ ...*the tactical ineptitude of the allied commander.*

in|equal|ity /ɪnɪkwɒlɪti/ (**inequalities**) N-VAR **Inequality** is the difference in social status, wealth, or opportunity between people or groups. ❑ *People are concerned about corruption and social inequality.*

in|equi|table /ɪnɛkwɪtəbəl/ ADJ If you say that something is **inequitable**, you are criticizing it because it is unfair or unjust. [FORMAL, DISAPPROVAL] ❑ *The welfare system is grossly inequitable and inefficient.*

in|equi|ty /ɪnɛkwɪti/ (**inequities**) N-VAR If you refer to the **inequity** of something, it lacks balance or fairness. [FORMAL, DISAPPROVAL] ❑ *Social imbalance worries him more than inequity of income.*

in|eradi|cable /ɪnɪrædɪkəbəl/ ADJ [usu ADJ n] You use **ineradicable** to emphasize that a quality, fact, or situation is permanent and cannot be changed. [FORMAL, EMPHASIS] ❑ *Divorce is a permanent, ineradicable fact of modern life.*

in|ert /ɪnɜrt/ ❶ ADJ Someone or something that is **inert** does not move at all. ❑ *He covered the inert body with a blanket.* ❷ ADJ If you describe something as **inert**, you are criticizing it because it is not very lively or interesting. [DISAPPROVAL] ❑ *The novel itself remains oddly inert.* ❸ ADJ An **inert** substance is one that does not react with other substances. [TECHNICAL] ❑ ...*inert gases like neon and argon.*

in|er|tia /ɪnɜrʃə/ ❶ N-UNCOUNT If you have a feeling of **inertia**, you feel very lazy and unwilling to move or be active. ❑ *He resented her inertia, her lack of energy and self-direction.* ❷ N-UNCOUNT **Inertia** is the tendency of a physical object to remain still or to continue moving, unless a force is applied to it. [TECHNICAL]

in|es|cap|able /ɪnɪskeɪpəbəl/ ADJ If you describe a fact, situation, or activity as **inescapable**, you mean that it is difficult not to notice it or be affected by it. ❑ *The inescapable conclusion is that he was trying to avenge the death of his friend.* • **in|es|cap|ably** /ɪnɪskeɪpəbli/ ADV ❑ ...*the inescapably dreary hopelessness of the universe.*

in|es|sen|tial /ɪnɪsɛnʃəl/ ADJ If something is **inessential**, you do not need it. [FORMAL] ❑ *We have omitted footnotes which we judged inessential to the text.*

in|es|ti|mable /ɪnɛstɪməbəl/ ADJ [usu ADJ n] If you describe the value, benefit, or importance of something as **inestimable**, you mean that it is extremely great and cannot be calculated. [FORMAL] ❑ *Human life is of inestimable value.*

in|evi|tabil|ity /ɪnɛvɪtəbɪlɪti/ (**inevitabilities**) N-VAR The **inevitability** of something is the fact that it is certain to happen and cannot be prevented or avoided. ❑ *We are all bound by the inevitability of death.*

in|evi|table ✦✧✧ /ɪnɛvɪtəbəl/ ADJ If something is **inevitable**, it is certain to happen and cannot be prevented or avoided. ❑ *If the case succeeds, it is inevitable that other trials will follow.* • N-SING The **inevitable** is something that is inevitable. ❑ *"It's just delaying the inevitable," he said.*

---SYNONYMS---

inevitable
ADJ
unavoidable: *Managers said the job losses were unavoidable.*
inescapable: *The economic logic of reform is inescapable.*
certain: *Victory looked certain.*
inexorable: ...*the seemingly inexorable rise in unemployment.*

---

in|evi|tably /ɪnɛvɪtəbli/ ADV If something will **inevitably** happen, it is certain to happen and cannot be prevented or avoided. ❑ *Technological changes will inevitably lead to unemployment.*

in|ex|act /ɪnɪgzækt/ ADJ Something that is **inexact** is not precise or accurate. ❑ *Forecasting was an inexact science.*

in|ex|cus|able /ɪnɪkskyuzəbəl/ ADJ If you say that something is **inexcusable**, you are emphasizing that it cannot be justified or tolerated because it is extremely bad. [EMPHASIS] ❑ *He said the killing of innocent people was inexcusable.* • **in|ex|cus|ably** /ɪnɪkskyuzəbli/ ADV ❑ *She had been inexcusably careless.*

in|ex|haust|ible /ɪnɪgzɔstəbəl/ ADJ If there is an **inexhaustible** supply of something, there is so much of it that it cannot all be used up. ❑ *She has an inexhaustible supply of enthusiasm.*

in|exo|rable /ɪnɛksərəbəl/ ADJ You use **inexorable** to describe a process that cannot be prevented from continuing or progressing. [FORMAL] ❑ ...*the seemingly inexorable rise in unemployment.* • **in|exo|rably** /ɪnɛksərəbli/ ADV [ADV with v] ❑ *Spending on health is growing inexorably.*

in|ex|pen|sive /ɪnɪkspɛnsɪv/ ADJ Something that is **inexpensive** does not cost very much. ❑ *There is a large variety of good, inexpensive restaurants.*

in|ex|pe|ri|ence /ɪnɪkspɪəriəns/ N-UNCOUNT If you refer to someone's **inexperience**, you mean that they have little knowledge or experience of a particular situation or activity. ❑ *Critics attacked the youth and inexperience of his staff.*

in|ex|pe|ri|enced /ˌɪnɪkspɪəriənst/ ADJ If you are **inexperienced**, you have little knowledge or experience of a particular situation or activity. ❑ *Routine tasks are often delegated to inexperienced young doctors.*

in|ex|pert /ɪnˈɛkspɜrt/ ADJ If you describe someone or something as **inexpert**, you mean that they show a lack of skill. ❑ *He was too inexperienced and too inexpert to succeed.* ❑ *...inexpert needlework.*

in|ex|pli|cable /ˌɪnɛksˈplɪkəbəl, ɪnɪkˈsplɪk-/ ADJ If something is **inexplicable**, you cannot explain why it happens or why it is true. ❑ *His behavior was extraordinary and inexplicable.* • **in|ex|pli|cably** /ˌɪnɛksˈplɪkəbli, ɪnɪkˈsplɪk-/ ADV ❑ *She suddenly and inexplicably announced her retirement.*

in|ex|press|ible /ˌɪnɪkˈsprɛsɪbəl/ ADJ An **inexpressible** feeling cannot be expressed in words because it is so strong. [FORMAL] ❑ *He felt a sudden inexpressible loneliness.*

in ex|tre|mis PHRASE [PHR with v] If someone or something is **in extremis**, they are in a very difficult situation and have to use extreme methods. [FORMAL] ❑ *The use of antibiotics is permitted only in extremis.*

in|ex|tri|cable /ˌɪnɛkˈstrɪkəbəl, ɪnɪkˈstrɪk-/ ADJ If there is an **inextricable** link between things, they cannot be considered separately. [FORMAL] ❑ *Meetings are an inextricable part of business.*

in|ex|tri|cably /ˌɪnɛkˈstrɪkəbli, ɪnɪkˈstrɪk-/ ADV [ADV with v] If two or more things are **inextricably** linked, they cannot be considered separately. [FORMAL] ❑ *Our survival is inextricably linked to the survival of the rainforest.*

in|fal|lible /ɪnˈfælɪbəl/ ADJ If a person or thing is **infallible**, they are never wrong. ❑ *Although he was experienced, he was not infallible.* • **in|fal|libil|ity** /ɪnˌfælɪˈbɪlɪti/ N-UNCOUNT ❑ *...exaggerated views of the infallibility of science.*

in|fa|mous /ˈɪnfəməs/ ADJ **Infamous** people or things are well-known because of something bad. [FORMAL] ❑ *He was infamous for his anti-feminist attitudes.*

in|fa|my /ˈɪnfəmi/ N-UNCOUNT **Infamy** is the state of being infamous. [FORMAL] ❑ *...one of the greatest acts of infamy in history.*

in|fan|cy /ˈɪnfənsi/ ❶ N-UNCOUNT **Infancy** is the period of your life when you are a very young child. ❑ *...the development of the mind from infancy onwards.* ❷ N-UNCOUNT If something is in its **infancy**, it is new and has not developed very much. ❑ *Computing science was still in its infancy.*

in|fant /ˈɪnfənt/ (infants) ❶ N-COUNT An **infant** is a baby or very young child. [FORMAL] ❑ *...holding the infant in his arms.* ❑ *They are saying that he is tiring of playing daddy to their infant son.* ❷ ADJ [ADJ n] **Infant** means designed especially for very young children. [BRIT]

in AM, use **baby**

❸ ADJ [ADJ n] An **infant** organization or system is new and has not developed very much. ❑ *The infant company was based in Nebraska.*

--- WORD HISTORY ---

infant
An **infant** is literally a child who is too young to have learned to talk. The word comes from Latin *infans*, meaning 'unable to speak,' from *in-*, meaning 'not,' and *fārī*, meaning 'speak.'

in|fan|ti|cide /ɪnˈfæntɪsaɪd/ N-UNCOUNT **Infanticide** is the crime of killing a baby.

in|fan|tile /ˈɪnfəntaɪl/ ❶ ADJ [ADJ n] **Infantile** behavior or illnesses are typical of babies or very young children. [FORMAL] ❑ *...infantile aggression.* ❷ ADJ If you accuse someone or something of being **infantile**, you think that they are foolish and childish. [DISAPPROVAL] ❑ *This kind of humor is infantile and boring.*

in|fan|try /ˈɪnfəntri/ N-UNCOUNT-COLL **Infantry** are soldiers who fight on foot rather than in tanks or on horses. ❑ *...an infantry division.*

infantry|man /ˈɪnfəntrimən/ (infantrymen) N-COUNT An **infantryman** is a male soldier who fights on foot.

infantry|woman /ˈɪnfəntriwʊmən/ (infantrywomen) N-COUNT An **infantrywoman** is a female soldier who fights on foot.

in|fatu|at|ed /ɪnˈfætʃueɪtɪd/ ADJ [oft ADJ with n] If you are **infatuated** with a person or thing, you have strong feelings of love or passion for them that make you unable to think clearly or sensibly about them. ❑ *He was utterly infatuated with her.*

in|fatu|a|tion /ɪnˌfætʃuˈeɪʃən/ (infatuations) N-VAR If you have an **infatuation** for a person or thing, you have strong feelings of love or passion for them that make you unable to think clearly or sensibly about them. ❑ *...his infatuation with bullfighting.*

in|fect ♦◇◇ /ɪnˈfɛkt/ (infects, infecting, infected) ❶ V-T To **infect** people, animals, or plants means to cause them to have a disease or illness. ❑ *A single mosquito can infect a large number of people.* ❑ *...objects used by an infected person.* • **in|fec|tion** /ɪnˈfɛkʃən/ N-UNCOUNT ❑ *...plants that are resistant to infection.* ❷ V-T To **infect** a substance or area means to cause it to contain harmful germs or bacteria. ❑ *The birds infect the milk.* ❸ V-T When people, places, or things **are infected** by a feeling or influence, it spreads to them. ❑ *For an instant I was infected by her fear.* ❑ *He thought they might infect others with their bourgeois ideas.* ❹ V-T If a virus **infects** a computer, it damages or destroys files or programs. [COMPUTING] ❑ *This virus infected thousands of computers across the U.S. and Europe within days.*

in|fect|ed /ɪnˈfɛktɪd/ ADJ [ADJ n] An **infected** place is one where germs or bacteria are causing a disease to spread among people or animals. ❑ *In heavily infected areas, half the population become blind.*

in|fec|tion ♦◇◇ /ɪnˈfɛkʃən/ (infections) ❶ N-COUNT An **infection** is a disease caused by germs or bacteria. ❑ *Ear infections are common in preschool children.* ❷ → see also **infect** ❸ → See feature box at **illness**

--- COLLOCATIONS ---

infection
NOUN
noun + **infection**: chest, ear, kidney, lung, throat
adjective + **infection**: bacterial, fungal, respiratory, viral; acute, life-threatening, recurrent, serious, severe
verb + **infection**: acquire, contract

--- SYNONYMS ---

infection
NOUN
disease: *...the rapid spread of disease in the area.*
illness: *She returned to her family home to recover from an illness.*
ailment: *The pharmacist can assist you with the treatment of common ailments.*
complaint: *Eczema is a skin complaint which often runs in families.*
virus: *There are many different strains of the flu virus.*

in|fec|tious /ɪnˈfɛkʃəs/ ❶ ADJ A disease that is **infectious** can be caught by being near a person who has it. Compare **contagious**. ❑ *...infectious diseases such as measles.* ❷ ADJ If a feeling is **infectious**, it spreads to other people. ❑ *She radiates an infectious enthusiasm for everything she does.*

in|fec|tive /ɪnˈfɛktɪv/ ADJ [usu ADJ n] **Infective** means related to infection or likely to cause infection. [FORMAL] ❑ *...a mild and very common infective disease of children.*

in|fer /ɪnˈfɜr/ (infers, inferring, inferred) ❶ V-T If you **infer** that something is the case, you deduce that it is true on the basis of information that you already have. ❑ *I inferred from what she said that you have not been well.* ❷ V-T Some people use **infer** to mean 'imply,' but this use is incorrect. ❑ *The police inferred, though they didn't exactly say it, that they found her behavior rather suspicious.*

in|fer|ence /ˈɪnfərəns/ (inferences) ❶ N-COUNT An **inference** is a conclusion that you draw about something by using information that you already have about it. ❑ *There were two inferences to be drawn from her letter.* ❷ N-UNCOUNT **Inference** is the act of drawing conclusions about something on the basis of information that you already have. ❑ *It had an extremely tiny head and, by inference, a tiny brain.*

in|fe|ri|or /ɪnˈfɪəriər/ (inferiors) ❶ ADJ Something that is **inferior** is not as good as something else. ❑ *The gloves were of inferior quality.* ❑ *This resulted in overpriced and often inferior products.* ❷ ADJ If one person is regarded as **inferior** to another, they are regarded as less important because they have less status or ability. ❑ *He preferred the company of those who were intellectually inferior to himself.* • N-COUNT **Inferior** is also a noun. ❑ *It was a gentleman's duty always to be civil, even to his inferiors.* • **in|fe|ri|or|ity** /ɪnfɪəriɒrɪti/ N-UNCOUNT ❑ *I found it difficult to shake off a sense of social inferiority.*

in|fe|ri|or|ity com|plex (inferiority complexes) N-COUNT Someone who has an **inferiority complex** feels that they are of less worth or importance than other people.

in|fer|nal /ɪnfɜrnəl/ **1** ADJ [ADJ n] **Infernal** is used to emphasize that something is very annoying or unpleasant. [OLD-FASHIONED, EMPHASIS] ❑ *What is that infernal noise.* **2** ADJ [ADJ n] **Infernal** is used to describe things that relate to hell. [LITERARY] ❑ *...the goddess of the infernal regions.*

in|fer|no /ɪnfɜrnoʊ/ (infernos) N-COUNT [usu sing] If you refer to a fire as an **inferno**, you mean that it is burning fiercely and causing great destruction. [JOURNALISM] ❑ *Rescue workers fought to get to victims inside the inferno.*

in|fer|tile /ɪnfɜrtəl/ **1** ADJ A person or animal that is **infertile** is unable to produce babies. ❑ *According to one survey, one woman in eight is infertile.* • **in|fer|til|ity** /ɪnfɜrtɪlɪti/ N-UNCOUNT ❑ *Male infertility is becoming commonplace.* **2** ADJ **Infertile** soil is of poor quality because it lacks substances that plants need. ❑ *The land was barren and infertile.*

in|fest /ɪnfɛst/ (infests, infesting, infested) **1** V-T When creatures such as insects or rats **infest** plants or a place, they are present in large numbers and cause damage. ❑ *...pests like aphids which infest cereal crops.* • **in|fest|ed** ADJ ❑ *The prison is infested with rats.* **2** V-T If you say that people or things you disapprove of or regard as dangerous **are infesting** a place, you mean that there are large numbers of them in that place. [DISAPPROVAL] ❑ *Crime and drugs are infesting the inner cities.* • **in|fest|ed** ADJ ❑ *The road further south was infested with bandits.*

in|fi|del /ɪnfɪdəl/ (infidels) N-COUNT If one person refers to another as an **infidel**, the first person is hostile toward the second person because that person has a different religion or has no religion. [LITERARY, DISAPPROVAL] ❑ *...a holy war, to drive the infidels and the nonbelievers out of this holy land.* • ADJ [ADJ n] **Infidel** is also an adjective. ❑ *He promised to continue the fight against infidel forces.*

in|fi|del|ity /ɪnfɪdɛlɪti/ (infidelities) N-VAR **Infidelity** occurs when a person who is married or in a long-term relationship has sex with another person. ❑ *George turned a blind eye to his partner's infidelities.*

in|field /ɪnfild/ (infields) **1** N-COUNT [usu sing, the N] In baseball, the **infield** is the part of the playing field that is inside the area marked by the four bases. ❑ *He put six fielders on the right side of the infield.* **2** ADV [ADV after v] In sports such as soccer and rugby, if players move **infield**, they move toward the center of the playing field. ❑ *Farrell raced up the right touchline, dodged infield and curled a shot with his left foot.*

in|fight|ing /ɪnfaɪtɪŋ/ also **in-fighting** N-UNCOUNT **Infighting** is quarreling and competition between members of the same group or organization. ❑ *...in-fighting between right-wingers and moderates in the party.*

in|fill /ɪnfɪl/ (infills, infilling, infilled) V-T To **infill** a hollow place or gap means to fill it. [mainly BRIT]

in AM, use **fill in**

in|fil|trate /ɪnfɪltreɪt/ (infiltrates, infiltrating, infiltrated) **1** V-T/V-I If people **infiltrate** a place or organization, or **infiltrate** into it, they enter it secretly in order to spy on it or influence it. ❑ *Activists had infiltrated the student movement.* • **in|fil|tra|tion** /ɪnfɪltreɪʃən/ (infiltrations) N-VAR ❑ *...an inquiry into alleged infiltration by the far left group.* **2** V-T To **infiltrate** people **into** a place or organization means to get them into it secretly in order to spy on it or influence it. ❑ *He claimed that some countries have been trying to infiltrate their agents into the republic.*

in|fil|tra|tor /ɪnfɪltreɪtər/ (infiltrators) N-COUNT An **infiltrator** is a person who has infiltrated a place or organization.

infin. is an abbreviation for **infinitive**.

in|fi|nite /ɪnfɪnɪt/ **1** ADJ If you describe something as **infinite**, you are emphasizing that it is extremely great in amount or degree. [EMPHASIS] ❑ *...an infinite variety of landscapes.* ❑ *With infinite care, John shifted position.* • **in|fi|nite|ly** ADV [ADV adj/adv] ❑ *His design was infinitely better than anything I could have done.* **2** ADJ Something that is **infinite** has no limit, end, or edge. ❑ *...an infinite number of atoms.* • **in|fi|nite|ly** ADV [ADV with v] ❑ *A centimeter can be infinitely divided into smaller units.*

in|fini|tesi|mal /ɪnfɪnɪtɛsɪməl/ ADJ Something that is **infinitesimal** is extremely small. [FORMAL] ❑ *...mineral substances present in infinitesimal amounts in the soil.*

in|fini|tive /ɪnfɪnɪtɪv/ (infinitives) N-COUNT The **infinitive** of a verb is the basic form, for example, 'do,' 'be,' 'take,' and 'eat.' The infinitive is often used with 'to' in front of it.

in|fi|ni|tum /ɪnfɪnaɪtəm/ → see **ad infinitum**

in|fin|ity /ɪnfɪnɪti/ **1** N-UNCOUNT [also a N of n] **Infinity** is a number that is larger than any other number and can never be given an exact value. ❑ *These permutations multiply toward infinity.* **2** N-UNCOUNT **Infinity** is a point that is further away than any other point and can never be reached. ❑ *...the darkness of a starless night stretching to infinity.*

in|firm /ɪnfɜrm/ ADJ A person who is **infirm** is weak or ill, and usually old. [FORMAL] ❑ *...her aging, infirm husband.* • N-PLURAL The **infirm** are people who are infirm. ❑ *We are here to protect and assist the weak and infirm.*

in|fir|ma|ry /ɪnfɜrməri/ (infirmaries) N-COUNT An **infirmary** is a place in a school or other institution that is used to take care of people who are sick or injured.

in|flame /ɪnfleɪm/ (inflames, inflaming, inflamed) V-T If something **inflames** a situation or **inflames** people's feelings, it makes people feel even more strongly about something. [JOURNALISM] ❑ *They are responsible for inflaming the situation.*

in|flamed /ɪnfleɪmd/ ADJ If part of your body is **inflamed**, it is red or swollen, usually as a result of an infection, injury, or illness. ❑ *Symptoms include red, itchy and inflamed skin.*

in|flam|mable /ɪnflæməbəl/ ADJ An **inflammable** material or chemical catches fire and burns easily. ❑ *A highly inflammable liquid escaped into the drilling equipment.*

in|flam|ma|tion /ɪnfləmeɪʃən/ (inflammations) N-VAR An **inflammation** is a painful redness or swelling of a part of your body that results from an infection, injury, or illness. ❑ *The drug can cause inflammation of the liver.*

in|flam|ma|tory /ɪnflæmətɔri/ ADJ If you accuse someone of saying or doing **inflammatory** things, you mean that what they say or do is likely to make people react very angrily. [DISAPPROVAL] ❑ *...nationalist policies that are too drastic and inflammatory.* **2** ADJ [ADJ n] An **inflammatory** condition or disease is one in which the patient suffers from inflammation. [FORMAL] ❑ *...the inflammatory reactions that occur in asthma.*

in|flat|able /ɪnfleɪtəbəl/ (inflatables) **1** ADJ An **inflatable** object is one that you fill with air when you want to use it. ❑ *The children were playing on the inflatable castle.* **2** N-COUNT An **inflatable** is an inflatable object, especially a small boat. ❑ *...floats, tubes and other inflatables.*

in|flate /ɪnfleɪt/ (inflates, inflating, inflated) **1** V-T/V-I If you **inflate** something such as a balloon or tire, or if it **inflates**, it becomes bigger as it is filled with air or a gas. ❑ *Stuart jumped into the sea and inflated the liferaft.* **2** V-T/V-I If you say that someone **inflates** the price of something, or that the price **inflates**, you mean that the price increases. ❑ *The promotion of a big release can inflate a film's final cost.* • **in|flat|ed** ADJ ❑ *They had to buy everything at inflated prices at the ranch store.* **3** V-T If someone **inflates** the amount or effect of something, they say it is bigger, better, or more important than it really is, usually so that they can profit from it. ❑ *They inflated their clients' medical injuries and treatment to defraud insurance companies.*

in|fla|tion ✦✧✧ /ɪnfleɪʃən/ N-UNCOUNT **Inflation** is a general increase in the prices of goods and services in a country. [BUSINESS] ❑ *...rising unemployment and high inflation.*

COLLOCATIONS

inflation
NOUN
noun + **inflation**: consumer price, food, house price, wage
adjective + **inflation**: rampant, rising; high, low
verb + **inflation**: stoke; control, curb, reduce; outpace

in|fla|tion|ary /ɪnfleɪʃənəri/ ADJ **Inflationary** means connected with inflation or causing inflation. [BUSINESS] ❑ *The bank is worried about mounting inflationary pressures.*

in|flect /ɪnflɛkt/ (**inflects, inflecting, inflected**) V-I [V] If a word **inflects**, its ending or form changes in order to show its grammatical function. If a language **inflects**, it has words in it that inflect. ● **in|flect|ed** ADJ ❑ *...Sanskrit, a highly inflected language.*

-inflected /-ɪnflɛktɪd/ ◼ COMB IN ADJ **-inflected** is used to form adjectives describing someone's voice or accent. [LITERARY] ❑ *...a Yiddish-inflected New York accent.* ◻ COMB IN ADJ **-inflected** is used to form adjectives describing the style of a piece of music or a performance. [JOURNALISM] ❑ *...his attacking, gospel-inflected vocal style.*

in|flec|tion /ɪnflɛkʃən/ (**inflections**) N-VAR An **inflection** in someone's voice is a change in its tone or pitch as they are speaking. [WRITTEN] ❑ *...the upward inflection of her voice.*

in|flex|ible /ɪnflɛksɪbəl/ ◼ ADJ Something that is **inflexible** cannot be altered in any way, even if the situation changes. ❑ *Workers insisted the new system was too inflexible.* ● **in|flex|ibil|ity** /ɪnflɛksɪbɪlɪti/ N-UNCOUNT ❑ *The system's inflexibility was highlighted by several recent failures.* ❑ *Marvin's father was exceptional for the inflexibility of his rules.* ◻ ADJ If you say that someone is **inflexible**, you are criticizing them because they refuse to change their mind or alter their way of doing things. [DISAPPROVAL] ❑ *His opponents viewed him as stubborn, dogmatic, and inflexible.* ● **in|flex|ibil|ity** N-UNCOUNT ❑ *Joyce was irritated by the inflexibility of her colleagues.*

in|flex|ion /ɪnflɛkʃən/ [mainly BRIT] → see **inflection**

in|flict /ɪnflɪkt/ (**inflicts, inflicting, inflicted**) V-T To **inflict** harm or damage on someone or something means to make them suffer it. ❑ *...the damage being inflicted on industries by the recession.*

in-flight also **inflight** ADJ [ADJ n] **In-flight** services are ones that are provided on board an airplane. ❑ *...an inflight magazine.*

in|flow /ɪnfloʊ/ (**inflows**) N-COUNT [usu N of n] If there is an **inflow** of money or people into a place, a large amount of money or people move into a place. ❑ *The Swiss wanted to discourage an inflow of foreign money.*

in|flu|ence ◆◇◇ /ɪnfluəns/ (**influences, influencing, influenced**) ◼ N-UNCOUNT **Influence** is the power to make other people agree with your opinions or do what you want. ❑ *He used his influence to get his son into medical school.* ❑ *He denies exerting any political influence over them.* ◻ V-T If you **influence** someone, you use your power to make them agree with you or do what you want. ❑ *He is trying to improperly influence a witness.* ◾ N-COUNT To have an **influence** on people or situations means to affect what they do or what happens. ❑ *Van Gogh had a major influence on the development of modern painting.* ❹ V-T If someone or something **influences** a person or situation, they have an effect on that person's behavior or that situation. ❑ *We became the best of friends and he influenced me deeply.* ❺ N-COUNT Someone or something that is a good or bad **influence** on people has a good or bad effect on them. ❑ *I thought Sonny would be a good influence on you.* ❻ PHRASE If you are **under the influence of** someone or something, you are being affected or controlled by them. ❑ *He was arrested on suspicion of driving under the influence of alcohol.*

in|flu|encer /ɪnfluənsər/ (**influencers**) N-COUNT An **influencer** is someone who is able to persuade a lot of other people, for example their followers on social media, to do, buy, or use the same things that they do. They are often paid or given free products in exchange for doing this. ❑ *They invited a lot of minor celebrities and Instagram influencers to the launch party.*

in|flu|en|tial /ɪnfluɛnʃəl/ ADJ Someone or something that is **influential** has a lot of influence over people or events. ❑ *It helps to have influential friends.* ❑ *He had been influential in shaping economic policy.*

in|flu|en|za /ɪnfluɛnzə/ N-UNCOUNT **Influenza** is the same as **flu**. [FORMAL]

in|flux /ɪnflʌks/ (**influxes**) N-COUNT An **influx** of people or things into a place is their arrival there in large numbers. ❑ *...the first large influx of immigrants to arrive on these shores.*

info /ɪnfoʊ/ N-UNCOUNT **Info** is information. [INFORMAL] ❑ *For more info call 414-3935.*

in|fo|mer|cial /ɪnfoʊmɜrʃəl/ (**infomercials**) N-COUNT An **infomercial** is a television program that gives detailed information about a company's products or services. The word is formed from 'information' and 'commercial.'

in|form ◆◇◇ /ɪnfɔrm/ (**informs, informing, informed**) ◼ V-T If you **inform** someone of something, you tell them about it. ❑ *They would inform him of any progress they had made.* ❑ *My daughter informed me that she was pregnant.* ◻ V-I If someone **informs on** a person, they give information about the person to the police or another authority, which causes the person to be suspected or proved guilty of doing something bad. ❑ *Thousands of American citizens have informed on these organized crime syndicates.* ◾ V-T If a situation or activity **is informed** by an idea or a quality, that idea or quality is very noticeable in it. [FORMAL] ❑ *All great songs are informed by a certain sadness and tension.*

in|for|mal /ɪnfɔrməl/ ◼ ADJ **Informal** speech or behavior is relaxed and friendly rather than serious, very correct, or official. ❑ *She is refreshingly informal.* ● **in|for|mal|ly** ADV [ADV after v] ❑ *She was always there at half past eight, chatting informally to the children.* ● **in|for|mal|ity** /ɪnfɔrmælɪti/ N-UNCOUNT ❑ *He was overwhelmed by their friendly informality.* ◻ ADJ An **informal** situation is one that is relaxed and friendly and not very serious or official. ❑ *The house has an informal atmosphere.* ● **in|for|mal|ity** N-UNCOUNT ❑ *She enjoyed the relative informality of island life.* ◾ ADJ **Informal** clothes are casual and suitable for wearing when you are relaxing, but not on formal occasions. ❑ *For lunch, dress is informal.* ● **in|for|mal|ly** ADV ❑ *Everyone dressed informally in shorts or faded jeans, and baggy sweatshirts.* ❹ ADJ You use **informal** to describe something that is done unofficially or casually without planning. ❑ *The two leaders will retire to Camp David for informal discussions.* ● **in|for|mal|ly** ADV ❑ *He began informally to handle Ted's tax affairs for him.*

in|form|ant /ɪnfɔrmənt/ (**informants**) ◼ N-COUNT An **informant** is someone who gives another person a piece of information. [FORMAL] ❑ *On the basis of data furnished by her informants, Mead concluded that adolescents in Samoa had complete sexual freedom.* ◻ N-COUNT An **informant** is the same as an **informer**.

in|for|ma|tion ◆◆◇ /ɪnfərmeɪʃən/ ◼ N-UNCOUNT **Information** about someone or something consists of facts about them. ❑ *Pat refused to give her any information about Sarah.* ❑ *Each center would provide information on technology and training.* ◻ N-UNCOUNT **Information** consists of the facts and figures that are stored and used by a computer program. [COMPUTING] ❑ *Pictures are scanned into a form of digital information that computers can recognize.* ◾ N-UNCOUNT **Information** is a service that you can telephone to find out someone's telephone number. [AM] ❑ *He called information, and they gave him the number.*

in BRIT, use **directory enquiries**

❹ → See feature box at **research**

USAGE

information

◼ '**Information**' is an uncountable noun. Don't talk about 'an information' or 'informations.' You can talk about a **piece of information**. *I wondered how to use this piece of information.*

◻ Don't use 'tell.' Don't say, for example, 'Pat did not tell her any information about Sarah.' You say that you **give** people information, for example, say 'Pat did not **give** her any information about Sarah.'

---

in|for|ma|tion|al /ɪnfərmeɪʃənəl/ ADJ [ADJ n] **Informational** means relating to information. [JOURNALISM] ❑ *...the informational needs of school-age children.*

in|for|ma|tion tech|nol|ogy N-UNCOUNT **Information technology** is the theory and practice of using computers to store and analyze information. The abbreviation **IT** is often used. ❑ *...the information technology industry.*

in|forma|tive /ɪnfɔrmətɪv/ ADJ Something that is **informative** gives you useful information. ❑ *Both men termed the meeting friendly and informative.*

in|formed /ɪnfɔrmd/ ◼ ADJ Someone who is **informed** knows about a subject or what is happening in the world. ❑ *Informed*

informer people know the company is shaky. **2** → see also **well-informed** **3** ADJ [ADJ n] When journalists talk about **informed** sources, they mean people who are likely to give correct information because of their private or special knowledge. ❑ *According to informed sources, those taken into custody include at least one major-general.* **4** ADJ [ADJ n] An **informed** guess or decision is one that is likely to be good, because it is based on definite knowledge or information. ❑ *Science is now enabling us to make more informed choices about how we use common drugs.* **5** → see also **inform**

in|form|er /ɪnfɔrmər/ (**informers**) N-COUNT An **informer** is a person who tells the police that someone has done something illegal. ❑ *...two men suspected of being police informers.*

info|tain|ment /ɪnfoʊteɪnmənt/ N-UNCOUNT **Infotainment** is used to refer to radio or television programs that are intended both to entertain people and to give information. The word is formed from 'information' and 'entertainment.' ❑ *The network offers a buffet of food-related infotainment.*

in|frac|tion /ɪnfrækʃən/ (**infractions**) N-COUNT [oft N of n] An **infraction** of a rule or law is an instance of breaking it. ❑ *...an infraction of school rules.* ❑ *...parents of kids who committed minor infractions.*

infra|red /ɪnfrərɛd/ also **infra-red** **1** ADJ [ADJ n] **Infrared** radiation is similar to light but has a longer wavelength, so we cannot see it without special equipment. **2** ADJ [ADJ n] **Infrared** equipment detects infrared radiation. ❑ *...searching with infrared scanners for weapons and artillery.*

infra|struc|ture /ɪnfrəstrʌktʃər/ (**infrastructures**) N-VAR The **infrastructure** of a country, society, or organization consists of the basic facilities such as transportation, communications, power supplies, and buildings, which enable it to function. ❑ *...improvements in the country's infrastructure.*

in|fre|quent /ɪnfrikwənt/ ADJ If something is **infrequent**, it does not happen often. ❑ *...John's infrequent visits to Topeka.* • **in|fre|quent|ly** ADV [usu ADV with v, also ADV with cl/group] ❑ *The bridge is used infrequently.*

in|fringe /ɪnfrɪndʒ/ (**infringes, infringing, infringed**) **1** V-T If someone **infringes** a law or a rule, they break it or do something that disobeys it. ❑ *The film exploited his image and infringed his copyright.* **2** V-T/V-I If something **infringes** people's rights, or **infringes** on them, it interferes with these rights and does not allow people the freedom they are entitled to. ❑ *They rob us, they infringe our rights, they kill us.*

in|fringe|ment /ɪnfrɪndʒmənt/ (**infringements**) **1** N-VAR An **infringement** is an action or situation that interferes with your rights and the freedom you are entitled to. ❑ *...infringement of privacy.* **2** N-VAR An **infringement** of a law or rule is the act of breaking it or disobeying it. ❑ *There might have been an infringement of the rules.*

in|furi|ate /ɪnfyʊərieɪt/ (**infuriates, infuriating, infuriated**) V-T If something or someone **infuriates** you, they make you extremely angry. ❑ *His manner infuriated him.*

in|furi|at|ing /ɪnfyʊərieɪtɪŋ/ ADJ Something that is **infuriating** annoys you very much. ❑ *A man of indecision is infuriating to watch.*

in|fuse /ɪnfyuz/ (**infuses, infusing, infused**) V-T To **infuse** a quality into someone or something, or to **infuse** them with a quality, means to fill them with it. [FORMAL] ❑ *Many of the girls seemed to be infused with excitement on seeing the snow.*

in|fu|sion /ɪnfyuʒən/ (**infusions**) N-VAR [usu N of n] If there is an **infusion** of one thing into another, the first thing is added to the other thing and makes it stronger or better. [FORMAL] ❑ *He brought a tremendous infusion of hope to the people.*

SUFFIX

-ing

1 is added to verbs to make the *-ing* form, or present participle. Present participle forms are often used as adjectives describing a person or thing who is doing something. For example, a *sleeping* baby is a baby that is sleeping and an *amusing* joke is a joke that amuses people.

2 is also added to verbs to make present participle forms which are used as nouns that refer to activities. For example, if you say you like *dancing*, you mean that you like to dance.

---

in|gen|ious /ɪndʒinyəs/ ADJ Something that is **ingenious** is very clever and involves new ideas, methods, or equipment. ❑ *...a truly ingenious invention.*

in|ge|nue /ænʒənu/ (**ingenues**) also **ingénue** N-COUNT [usu sing] An **ingenue** is a young, innocent girl in a play or movie, or an actress who plays the part of young, innocent girls. [FORMAL] ❑ *I don't want any more ingenue roles.*

in|genu|ity /ɪndʒənuɪti/ N-UNCOUNT **Ingenuity** is skill at working out how to achieve things or skill at inventing new things. ❑ *Inspecting the nest can be difficult and may require some ingenuity.*

in|genu|ous /ɪndʒɛnyuəs/ ADJ If you describe someone as **ingenuous**, you mean that they are innocent, trusting, and honest. [FORMAL] ❑ *He seemed too ingenuous for a reporter.* • **in|genu|ous|ly** ADV [ADV with v, ADV adj] ❑ *Somewhat ingenuously, he explains how the crime may be accomplished.*

in|gest /ɪndʒɛst/ (**ingests, ingesting, ingested**) V-T When animals or plants **ingest** a substance, they take it into themselves, by eating or absorbing it. ❑ *...side effects occurring in fish that ingest this substance.* • **in|ges|tion** /ɪndʒɛstʃən/ N-UNCOUNT ❑ *Every ingestion of food can affect our mood or thinking processes.*

in|glo|ri|ous /ɪnglɔriəs/ ADJ [usu ADJ n] If you describe something as **inglorious**, you mean that it is something to be ashamed of. ❑ *He wouldn't have accepted such an inglorious outcome.* • **in|glo|ri|ous|ly** ADV ❑ *If fighting worsens, the troops might be reinforced, or ingloriously withdrawn.*

in|got /ɪŋgət/ (**ingots**) N-COUNT [oft n N] An **ingot** is a lump of metal, usually shaped like a brick. ❑ *...gold ingots.*

in|grained /ɪŋgreɪnd/ ADJ **Ingrained** habits and beliefs are difficult to change or remove. ❑ *Morals tend to be deeply ingrained.*

in|gra|ti|ate /ɪŋgreɪʃieɪt/ (**ingratiates, ingratiating, ingratiated**) V-T If someone tries to **ingratiate** themselves with you, they do things to try and make you like them. [DISAPPROVAL] ❑ *Many politicians are trying to ingratiate themselves with her.*

in|gra|ti|at|ing /ɪŋgreɪʃieɪtɪŋ/ ADJ If you describe someone or their behavior as **ingratiating**, you mean that they try to make people like them. [DISAPPROVAL] ❑ *He said this with an ingratiating smile.*

in|grati|tude /ɪŋgrætɪtud/ N-UNCOUNT **Ingratitude** is a lack of gratitude for something that has been done for you. ❑ *...the ingratitude of people toward their military forces in peacetime.*

in|gre|di|ent ♦◇◇ /ɪŋgridiənt/ (**ingredients**) **1** N-COUNT **Ingredients** are the things that are used to make something, especially all the different foods you use when you are cooking a particular dish. ❑ *Mix in the remaining ingredients.* **2** N-COUNT An **ingredient** of a situation is one of the essential parts of it. ❑ *The meeting had all the ingredients of high political drama.*

SYNONYMS

ingredient
NOUN **2**
component: *The management plan has four main components.*
element: *This was one of the key elements of the U.N.'s peace plan.*
feature: *Patriotic songs have long been a feature of Kuwaiti life.*
aspect: *He was interested in all aspects of the work here.*
part: *Respect is a very important part of any relationship.*

---

in|grown /ɪŋgroʊn/ ADJ An **ingrown** toenail is one that is growing into your toe, often causing you pain.

in|hab|it /ɪnhæbɪt/ (**inhabits, inhabiting, inhabited**) V-T If a place or region **is inhabited** by a group of people or a species of animal, those people or animals live there. ❑ *The valley is inhabited by the Dani tribe.* ❑ *...the people who inhabit these islands.*

in|hab|it|ant /ɪnhæbɪtənt/ (**inhabitants**) N-COUNT The **inhabitants** of a place are the people who live there. ❑ *...the inhabitants of Boise.*

in|ha|la|tion /ɪnhəleɪʃən/ (**inhalations**) **1** N-VAR **Inhalation** is the process or act of breathing in, taking air and sometimes other substances into your lungs. [FORMAL] ❑ *They were taken to the hospital suffering from smoke inhalation.* ❑ *Take several deep* inhalations. **2** N-COUNT An **inhalation** is a treatment for colds and other illnesses in which you dissolve substances in hot water and breathe in the vapor. ❑ *Inhalations can soothe and control the cough.*

in|hale /ɪnheɪl/ (**inhales, inhaling, inhaled**) V-T/V-I When you **inhale**, you breathe in. When you **inhale** something such as smoke, you take it into your lungs when you breathe in. ❑ *He took a long slow breath, inhaling deeply.*

in|hal|er /ɪnheɪlər/ (**inhalers**) N-COUNT An **inhaler** is a small device that helps you to breathe more easily if you have asthma or a bad cold. You put it in your mouth and breathe in deeply, and it sends a small amount of a drug into your lungs.

in|her|ent /ɪnhɛrənt, -hɪər-/ ADJ The **inherent** qualities of something are the necessary and natural parts of it. ❑ *Stress is an inherent part of dieting.* ● **in|her|ent|ly** ADV ❑ *There is nothing inherently wrong in this situation.*

in|her|it /ɪnhɛrɪt/ (**inherits, inheriting, inherited**) **1** V-T If you **inherit** money or property, you receive it from someone who has died. ❑ *He has no son to inherit his land.* **2** V-T If you **inherit** something such as a task, problem, or attitude, you get it from the people who used to have it, for example, because you have taken over their job or been influenced by them. ❑ *The government inherited an impossibly difficult situation from its predecessors.* **3** V-T If you **inherit** a characteristic or quality, you are born with it, because your parents or ancestors also had it. ❑ *We inherit from our parents many of our physical characteristics.* ❑ *Her children have inherited her love of sports.*

in|her|it|ance /ɪnhɛrɪtəns/ (**inheritances**) **1** N-VAR An **inheritance** is money or property that you receive from someone who has died. ❑ *She feared losing her inheritance to her stepmother.* **2** N-COUNT If you get something such as a job, problem, or attitude from someone who used to have it, you can refer to this as an **inheritance**. ❑ *...starvation and disease over much of Europe and Asia, which was Truman's inheritance as president.* **3** N-SING Your **inheritance** is the particular characteristics or qualities that your family or ancestors had and that you are born with. ❑ *Eye color shows more than your genetic inheritance.*

in|her|it|ance tax (**inheritance taxes**) N-COUNT An **inheritance tax** is a tax paid on the money and property of someone who has died.

in|heri|tor /ɪnhɛrɪtər/ (**inheritors**) N-COUNT [usu pl, usu N of n] The **inheritors** of something such as a tradition are the people who live or arrive after it has been established and are able to benefit from it. ❑ *...the proud inheritors of the Prussian military tradition.*

in|hib|it /ɪnhɪbɪt/ (**inhibits, inhibiting, inhibited**) **1** V-T If something **inhibits** an event or process, it prevents it or slows it down. ❑ *The high cost of borrowing is inhibiting investment by industry in new equipment.* **2** V-T To **inhibit** someone from doing something means to prevent them from doing it, although they want to do it or should be able to do it. ❑ *Officers will be inhibited from doing their duty.*

in|hib|it|ed /ɪnhɪbɪtɪd/ ADJ If you say that someone is **inhibited**, you mean that they find it difficult to behave naturally and show their feelings, and that you think this is a bad thing. [DISAPPROVAL] ❑ *The sad truth is that men are far less inhibited about their bodies than women.*

in|hi|bi|tion /ɪnɪbɪʃən/ (**inhibitions**) N-VAR **Inhibitions** are feelings of fear or embarrassment that make it difficult for you to behave naturally. ❑ *The whole point about dancing is to stop thinking and lose all your inhibitions.*

in|hos|pi|table /ɪnhɒspɪtəbəl/ ADJ [usu ADJ n] An **inhospitable** place is unpleasant to live in. ❑ *...the Earth's most inhospitable regions.* **2** ADJ If someone is **inhospitable**, they do not make people welcome when they visit.

in-house ADJ **In-house** work or activities are done by employees of an organization or company, rather than by workers outside the organization or company. ❑ *A lot of companies do in-house training.* ● ADV **In-house** is also an adverb. ❑ *The magazine is still produced in-house.*

in|hu|man /ɪnhyumən/ **1** ADJ If you describe treatment or an action as **inhuman**, you mean that it is extremely cruel. ❑ *The detainees are often held in cruel and inhuman conditions.* **2** ADJ If you describe someone or something as **inhuman**, you mean that they are strange or bad because they do not seem human in some way. ❑ *...inhuman screams and moans.*

in|hu|mane /ɪnhyumeɪn/ ADJ If you describe something as **inhumane**, you mean that it is extremely cruel. ❑ *He was kept under inhumane conditions.*

in|hu|man|ity /ɪnhyumænɪti/ (**inhumanities**) N-UNCOUNT [also N in pl, oft N of n] You can describe extremely cruel actions as **inhumanity**. ❑ *...the inhumanity of war.*

in|imi|cal /ɪnɪmɪkəl/ ADJ Conditions that are **inimical** to something make it difficult for that thing to exist or do well. [FORMAL] ❑ *...goals inimical to Western interests.*

in|imi|table /ɪnɪmɪtəbəl/ ADJ [usu ADJ n] You use **inimitable** to describe someone, especially a performer, when you like or admire them because of their special qualities. [FORMAL, APPROVAL] ❑ *He makes his own point in his own inimitable way.*

in|iqui|tous /ɪnɪkwɪtəs/ ADJ [usu ADJ n] If you describe something as **iniquitous**, you mean that it is very unfair or morally bad. [FORMAL] ❑ *...an iniquitous fine.*

in|iq|uity /ɪnɪkwɪti/ (**iniquities**) N-VAR You can refer to wicked actions or very unfair situations as **iniquity**. [FORMAL] ❑ *He rails against the iniquities of capitalism.*

ini|tial ♦◇◇ /ɪnɪʃəl/ (**initials, initialing** or **initialling, initialed** or **initialled**) **1** ADJ [ADJ n] You use **initial** to describe something that happens at the beginning of a process. ❑ *The initial reaction has been excellent.* **2** N-COUNT **Initials** are the capital letters that begin each word of a name. For example, if your full name is Michael Dennis Stocks, your initials are M.D.S. ❑ *...a silver Porsche with her initials JB on the side.* **3** V-T If someone **initials** an official document, they write their initials on it, to show that they have seen it or that they accept or agree with it. ❑ *Would you mind initialing this voucher?*

───── SYNONYMS ─────

initial
ADJ **1**
opening: *...the opening day of the fifth international conference.*
first: *She lost 16 pounds in the first month of her diet.*
early: *...the early hours of Saturday morning.*
introductory: *...just on the shelves at an introductory price of $2.99.*

ini|tial|ly ♦◇◇ /ɪnɪʃəli/ ADV **Initially** means soon after the beginning of a process or situation, rather than in the middle or at the end of it. ❑ *Forecasters say the storms may not be as bad as they initially predicted.*

───── SYNONYMS ─────

initially
ADV
at first: *At first, he seemed surprised by my questions.*
first: *I met him first at his house, where we had a chat.*
originally: *France originally refused to sign the treaty.*
to begin with: *It was great to begin with, but now it's difficult.*

ini|ti|ate /ɪnɪʃieɪt/ (**initiates, initiating, initiated**) **1** V-T If you **initiate** something, you start it or cause it to happen. ❑ *They wanted to initiate a discussion on economics.* **2** V-T If you **initiate** someone into something, you introduce them to a particular skill or type of knowledge and teach them about it. ❑ *He initiated her into the study of other cultures.* **3** V-T If someone **is initiated** into something such as a religion, secret society, or social group, they become a member of it by taking part in special ceremonies. ❑ *In many societies, young people are formally initiated into their adult roles.*

ini|tia|tion /ɪnɪʃieɪʃən/ (**initiations**) **1** N-UNCOUNT The **initiation** of something is the starting of it. ❑ *...the initiation of a rural development program.* **2** N-VAR Someone's **initiation** into a particular group is the act or process by which they officially become a member, often involving special ceremonies. ❑ *This was my initiation into the peace movement.*

ini|tia|tive ♦◇◇ /ɪnɪʃiətɪv, -ʃətɪv/ (**initiatives**) **1** N-COUNT An **initiative** is an important act or statement that is intended to solve a problem. ❑ *Local initiatives to help young people have been inadequate.* **2** N-SING In a fight or contest, if you have **the initiative**, you are in a better position than your opponents to decide what to do next. ❑ *We have the initiative; we intend to keep it.*

3 N-UNCOUNT If you have **initiative**, you have the ability to decide what to do next and to do it, without needing other people to tell you what to do. ◻ *She was disappointed by his lack of initiative.* **4** N-COUNT An **initiative** is a political procedure in which a group of citizens propose a new law or a change to the law, which all voters can then vote on. [mainly AM] ◻ *If they reject or ignore the initiative, the public will vote on it in November.* **5** PHRASE If you **take the initiative** in a situation, you are the first person to act, and are therefore able to control the situation. ◻ *We are the only power willing to take the initiative in the long struggle to end the war.*

ini|tia|tor /ɪnˈʃieɪtər/ (**initiators**) N-COUNT [oft N *of* n] The **initiator** of a plan or process is the person who was responsible for thinking of it or starting it. ◻ *...one of the major initiators of the tumultuous changes in Eastern Europe.*

in|ject /ɪndʒɛkt/ (**injects, injecting, injected**) **1** V-T To **inject** a substance such as a medicine into someone means to put it into their body using a device with a needle called a syringe. ◻ *He was injected with a sedative and discharged the same day.* ◻ *The technique consists of injecting healthy cells into the weakened muscles.* **2** V-T If you **inject** a new, exciting, or interesting quality into a situation, you add it. ◻ *She kept trying to inject a little fun into their relationship.* **3** V-T If you **inject** money or resources into a business or organization, you provide more money or resources for it. [BUSINESS] ◻ *The insurance fund would inject $750 million into the banks.*

in|jec|tion /ɪndʒɛkʃən/ (**injections**) **1** N-COUNT [also *by* N] If you have an **injection**, a doctor or nurse puts a medicine into your body using a device with a needle called a syringe. ◻ *They gave me an injection to help me sleep.* **2** N-COUNT An **injection** of money or resources into an organization is the act of providing it with more money or resources, to help it become more efficient or profitable. [BUSINESS] ◻ *An injection of cash is needed to fund some of these projects.*

in|ju|di|cious /ɪndʒudɪʃəs/ ADJ If you describe a person or something that they have done as **injudicious**, you are critical of them because they have shown very poor judgment. [FORMAL, DISAPPROVAL] ◻ *...a hasty and injudicious marriage.*

in|junc|tion /ɪndʒʌŋkʃən/ (**injunctions**) **1** N-COUNT An **injunction** is a court order, usually one telling someone not to do something. [LEGAL] ◻ *He took out a court injunction against the newspaper demanding the return of the document.* **2** N-COUNT An **injunction** to do something is an order or strong request to do it. [FORMAL] ◻ *We hear endless injunctions to managers to build commitment and a sense of community among their staff.*

in|jure /ɪndʒər/ (**injures, injuring, injured**) V-T If you **injure** a person or animal, you damage some part of their body. ◻ *A number of bombs have exploded, seriously injuring at least five people.*

in|jured ◆◇◇ /ɪndʒərd/ **1** ADJ An **injured** person or animal has physical damage to part of their body, usually as a result of an accident or fighting. ◻ *The other injured man had a superficial stomach wound.* • N-PLURAL **The injured** are people who are injured. ◻ *Army helicopters tried to evacuate the injured.* **2** ADJ If you have **injured** feelings, you feel upset because you believe someone has been unfair or unkind to you. ◻ *...a look of injured pride.*

--- SYNONYMS ---
injured
ADJ **1**
hurt: *His comrades asked him if he was hurt.*
wounded: *The two wounded men were taken to a nearby hospital.*
---

in|jured par|ty (**injured parties**) N-COUNT [usu *the* N] The **injured party** in a court case or dispute is the person who says they were unfairly treated. [LEGAL] ◻ *The injured party got some compensation.*

in|ju|ri|ous /ɪndʒʊəriəs/ ADJ [oft ADJ *to* n] Something that is **injurious** to someone or to their health or reputation is harmful or damaging to them. [FORMAL] ◻ *...substances that are injurious to health.*

in|ju|ry ◆◆◇ /ɪndʒəri/ (**injuries**) **1** N-VAR An **injury** is damage done to a person's or an animal's body. ◻ *Four police officers sustained serious injuries in the explosion.* **2** N-VAR If someone suffers **injury** to their feelings, they are badly upset by something. If they suffer **injury** to their reputation, their reputation is seriously harmed. [LEGAL] ◻ *She was awarded $3,500 for injury to her feelings.* **3 to add insult to injury** → see **insult**

--- SYNONYMS ---
injury
NOUN **1**
wound: *The wound is healing nicely.*
bruise: *How did you get that bruise on your cheek?*
cut: *...cuts and bruises.*
gash: *There was an inch-long gash just above his right eye.*
---

in|ju|ry time N-UNCOUNT **Injury time** is the period of time added to the end of a soccer game because play was stopped during the game when players were injured.

in|jus|tice /ɪndʒʌstɪs/ (**injustices**) **1** N-VAR **Injustice** is a lack of fairness in a situation. ◻ *They'll continue to fight injustice.* **2** N-COUNT An **injustice** is an action or statement in which someone judges you or treats you unfairly. ◻ *Calling them a bunch of capricious kids with half-formed ideas does them an injustice.*

ink /ɪŋk/ (**inks**) N-MASS **Ink** is the colored liquid used for writing or printing. ◻ *The letter was handwritten in black ink.*

ink|ling /ɪŋklɪŋ/ (**inklings**) N-COUNT [usu sing, usu N *of* n/wh, N *that*/wh] If you have an **inkling** of something, you have a vague idea about it. ◻ *I had no inkling of his real purpose until much later.*

ink|well /ɪŋkwɛl/ (**inkwells**) N-COUNT An **inkwell** is a container for ink on a desk.

inky /ɪŋki/ **1** ADJ [usu ADJ n] **Inky** means black or very dark blue. [LITERARY] ◻ *The moon was rising in the inky sky.* • COMB IN COLOR **Inky** is also a combining form. ◻ *...looking out over an inky blue ocean.* **2** ADJ If something is **inky**, it is covered in ink. ◻ *...inky fingers.*

in|laid /ɪnleɪd/ ADJ An object that is **inlaid** has a design on it that is made by putting materials such as wood, gold, or silver into the surface of the object. ◻ *...a box inlaid with little triangles.*

in|land

The adverb is pronounced /ɪnlænd/ or /ɪnlənd/. The adjective is pronounced /ɪnlənd/.

1 ADV If something is situated **inland**, it is away from the coast, toward or near the middle of a country. If you go **inland**, you go away from the coast, toward the middle of a country. ◻ *The vast majority live further inland.* ◻ *It's about 15 minutes' drive inland from Pensacola.* **2** ADJ [ADJ n] **Inland** areas, lakes, and places are not on the coast, but in or near the middle of a country. ◻ *...a rather quiet inland town.*

in-laws N-PLURAL Your **in-laws** are the parents and close relatives of your husband or wife. ◻ *...meals with the in-laws.*

in|lay /ɪnleɪ/ (**inlays**) N-VAR An **inlay** is a design or pattern on an object made by putting materials such as wood, gold, or silver into the surface of the object. ◻ *...an inlay of medieval glass.*

in|let /ɪnlɛt, -lɪt/ (**inlets**) N-COUNT An **inlet** is a narrow strip of water that goes from a sea or lake into the land. ◻ *A tiny fishing village by a rocky inlet.*

in-line skate (**in-line skates**) N-COUNT [usu plural] An **in-line skate** is a type of roller-skate with a single line of wheels along the bottom. ◻ *...a teenager on in-line skates.*

in|mate /ɪnmeɪt/ (**inmates**) **1** N-COUNT The **inmates** of a prison or psychiatric hospital are the prisoners or patients who are living there. ◻ *...education for prison inmates.* **2** → See feature box at **prison**

in|most /ɪnmoʊst/ ADJ [ADJ n] **Inmost** means the same as **innermost**. ◻ *He knew in his inmost heart that he was behaving badly.*

inn /ɪn/ (**inns**) N-COUNT; N-IN-NAMES An **inn** is a hotel, bar, or restaurant, often one in the country. ◻ *...the Waterside Inn.*

in|nards /ɪnərdz/ N-PLURAL [usu with poss] The **innards** of a person or animal are the organs inside their body. [INFORMAL]

in|nate /ɪneɪt/ ADJ An **innate** quality or ability is one that a person is born with. ◻ *We have an innate sense of fairness.* • **in|nate|ly** ADV [ADV adj] ◻ *I believe everyone is innately psychic.*

in|ner ◆◇◇ /ɪnər/ **1** ADJ [ADJ n] The **inner** parts of something are the parts contained or enclosed inside the other parts, closest to the center. ◻ *She got up and went into an inner office.*

2 ADJ [ADJ n] Your **inner** feelings are feelings that you have but do not show to other people. ❑ *Loving relationships that a child makes will give him an inner sense of security.*

in|ner child N-SING [oft poss N] Some people refer to a person's childish feelings as his or her **inner child**. ❑ *For me, recovery has been all about finding my inner child and accepting her.*

in|ner cir|cle (**inner circles**) **1** N-COUNT An **inner circle** is a small group of people within a larger group who have a lot of power, influence, or special information. ❑ *...the inner circle of company executives.* **2** → See feature box at **relationship**

in|ner ci|ty (**inner cities**) **1** N-COUNT You use **inner city** to refer to the areas in or near the center of a large city where people live and where there are often social and economic problems. ❑ *No one could deny that problems of crime in the inner city exist.* **2** → See feature box at **town**

inner|most /ɪnərmoʊst/ **1** ADJ [ADJ n] Your **innermost** thoughts and feelings are your most personal and secret ones. ❑ *...revealing a company's innermost secrets.* **2** ADJ [ADJ n] The **innermost** thing is the one that is nearest to the center. ❑ *...the innermost part of the eye.*

in|ner tube (**inner tubes**) N-COUNT An **inner tube** is a rubber tube containing air that is inside a car tire or a bicycle tire.

in|ning ♦◇◇ /ɪnɪŋ/ (**innings**) N-COUNT An **inning** is one of the nine periods that a standard baseball game is divided into. Each team is at bat once in each inning.

inn|keeper /ɪnkipər/ (**innkeepers**) N-COUNT An **innkeeper** is someone who owns or manages an inn.

in|no|cence /ɪnəsəns/ **1** N-UNCOUNT **Innocence** is the quality of having no experience or knowledge of the more complex or unpleasant aspects of life. ❑ *...the sweet innocence of youth.* **2** N-UNCOUNT If someone proves their **innocence**, they prove that they are not guilty of a crime. ❑ *He claims he has evidence which could prove his innocence.*

in|no|cent ♦◇◇ /ɪnəsənt/ (**innocents**) **1** ADJ If someone is **innocent**, they did not commit a crime that they have been accused of. ❑ *He was sure that the man was innocent of any crime.* **2** ADJ If someone is **innocent**, they have no experience or knowledge of the more complex or unpleasant aspects of life. ❑ *They seemed so young and innocent.* • N-COUNT An **innocent** is someone who is innocent. ❑ *She had always regarded Greg as a hopeless innocent where women were concerned.* • **in|no|cent|ly** ADV ❑ *The baby gurgled innocently on the bed.* **3** ADJ **Innocent** people are those who are not involved in a crime or conflict, but are injured or killed as a result of it. ❑ *All those wounded were innocent victims.* **4** ADJ An **innocent** question, remark, or comment is not intended to offend or upset people, even if it does so. ❑ *It was probably an innocent question, but Michael got flustered anyway.*

SYNONYMS

innocent
ADJ **2**
naïve: *It's naïve to think that teachers are always tolerant.*
trusting: *Perhaps I was too trusting.*
gullible: *I'm so gullible that I would have believed him.*
unworldly: *She was so young, so unworldly.*

---

in|no|cent|ly /ɪnəsəntli/ **1** ADV [ADV with v] If you say that someone does or says something **innocently**, you mean that they are pretending not to know something about a situation. ❑ *"What do you mean?" Annie asked innocently.* **2** → see also **innocent**

in|nocu|ous /ɪnɒkyuəs/ ADJ Something that is **innocuous** is not at all harmful or offensive. [FORMAL] ❑ *Both mushrooms look innocuous but are in fact deadly.*

in|no|vate /ɪnəveɪt/ (**innovates, innovating, innovated**) V-I To **innovate** means to introduce changes and new ideas in the way something is done or made. ❑ *What sets him apart from most engineers is his constant desire to innovate and experiment.*

in|no|va|tion /ɪnəveɪʃən/ (**innovations**) **1** N-COUNT An **innovation** is a new thing or a new method of doing something. ❑ *They produced the first vegetarian beanburger – an innovation which was rapidly exported.* **2** N-UNCOUNT **Innovation** is the introduction of new ideas, methods, or things. ❑ *We must promote originality, inspire creativity and encourage innovation.*

in|no|va|tive /ɪnəveɪtɪv/ **1** ADJ Something that is **innovative** is new and original. ❑ *...products which are cheaper, more innovative and more reliable than those of their competitors.* **2** ADJ An **innovative** person introduces changes and new ideas. ❑ *He was one of the most creative and innovative engineers of his generation.* **3** → See feature box at **upcycle**

in|no|va|tor /ɪnəveɪtər/ (**innovators**) N-COUNT An **innovator** is someone who introduces changes and new ideas. ❑ *He is an innovator in this field.*

in|nu|en|do /ɪnyuɛndoʊ/ (**innuendoes** or **innuendos**) N-VAR **Innuendo** is indirect reference to something rude or unpleasant. ❑ *The report was based on rumors, speculation, and innuendo.*

in|nu|mer|able /ɪnumərəbəl/ ADJ **Innumerable** means very many, or too many to be counted. [FORMAL] ❑ *He has invented innumerable excuses, told endless lies.*

in|ocu|late /ɪnɒkyəleɪt/ (**inoculates, inoculating, inoculated**) V-T To **inoculate** a person or animal means to inject a weak form of a disease into their body as a way of protecting them against the disease. ❑ *...a program to inoculate every child in the state.* ❑ *His dogs were inoculated against rabies.* • **in|ocu|la|tion** /ɪnɒkyəleɪʃən/ (**inoculations**) N-VAR [oft N against n] ❑ *This may eventually lead to routine inoculation of children.*

in|of|fen|sive /ɪnəfɛnsɪv/ ADJ If you describe someone or something as **inoffensive**, you mean that they are not unpleasant or unacceptable in any way, but are perhaps rather dull. ❑ *He's a mild, inoffensive man.*

in|op|er|able /ɪnɒpərəbəl/ ADJ An **inoperable** medical condition is one that cannot be cured by a surgical operation. [FORMAL] ❑ *He was diagnosed with inoperable lung cancer.*

in|op|era|tive /ɪnɒpərətɪv/ ADJ An **inoperative** rule, principle, or tax is one that does not work any more or that cannot be made to work. [FORMAL]

in|op|por|tune /ɪnɒpərtun/ ADJ If you describe something as **inopportune** or if you say that it happens at an **inopportune** time, you mean that it happens at an unfortunate or unsuitable time, and causes trouble or embarrassment because of this. ❑ *The dismissals came at an inopportune time.*

in|or|di|nate /ɪnɔrdənɪt/ ADJ If you describe something as **inordinate**, you are emphasizing that it is unusually or excessively great in amount or degree. [FORMAL, EMPHASIS] ❑ *They spend an inordinate amount of time talking.* • **in|or|di|nate|ly** ADV ❑ *He is inordinately proud of his wife's achievements.*

in|or|gan|ic /ɪnɔrgænɪk/ ADJ **Inorganic** substances are substances such as stone and metal that do not come from living things. ❑ *...roofing made from organic and inorganic fibers.*

in|patient /ɪnpeɪʃənt/ (**inpatients**) also **in-patient** N-COUNT An **inpatient** is someone who stays in a hospital while they receive their treatment. • ADJ [ADJ n] **Inpatient** is also an adjective. ❑ *...inpatient hospital care.*

in|put /ɪnpʊt/ (**inputs, inputting**)

> The form **input** is used in the present tense and is the past tense and past participle.

1 N-VAR **Input** consists of information or resources that a group or project receives. ❑ *It's up to the teacher to provide a variety of types of input in the classroom.* **2** N-UNCOUNT **Input** is information that is put into a computer. [COMPUTING] ❑ *The x-ray detectors feed the input into computer programs.* **3** V-T If you **input** information into a computer, you feed it in, for example, by typing it on a keyboard. [COMPUTING] ❑ *The computer acts as a word processor where the text of a speech can be input at any time.*

in|put de|vice (**input devices**) N-COUNT An **input device** is a piece of computer equipment such as a keyboard that enables you to put information into a computer. [COMPUTING] ❑ *The officers use stylus pen-based input devices to write their reports onto touch-sensitive screens.*

input/output **1** N-UNCOUNT **Input/output** refers to the information that is passed into or out of a computer. [COMPUTING] ❑ *...input/output delays.* **2** N-UNCOUNT **Input/output** refers to the hardware or software that controls the passing of information into or out of a computer. [COMPUTING] ❑ *...an input/output system.*

in|quest /ɪnkwest/ (inquests) **1** N-COUNT When an **inquest** is held, a public official hears evidence about someone's death in order to find out the cause. ▫ *The inquest into their deaths opened yesterday in Little Rock.* **2** N-COUNT You can refer to an investigation by the people involved in a defeat or failure as an **inquest**. ▫ *His plea came last night as party chiefs held an inquest into the election disaster.*

in|quire /ɪnkwaɪər/ (inquires, inquiring, inquired) also **enquire 1** V-T/V-I If you **inquire** about something, you ask for information about it. [FORMAL] ▫ *"What are you doing there?" she inquired.* ▫ *He called them several times to inquire about job possibilities.* **2** V-I If you **inquire into** something, you investigate it carefully. ▫ *Inspectors were appointed to inquire into the affairs of the company.*

in|quir|er /ɪnkwaɪərər/ (inquirers) also **enquirer 1** N-COUNT An **inquirer** is a person who asks for information about something or someone. [FORMAL] ▫ *I write personally to each inquirer.* **2** N-IN-NAMES [the supp N] **Inquirer** is used in the names of some newspapers and magazines. ▫ *...the Philadelphia Inquirer.*

in|quir|ing /ɪnkwaɪərɪŋ/ also **enquiring 1** ADJ [ADJ n] If you have an **inquiring** mind, you have a great interest in learning new things. ▫ *All this helps children to develop an inquiring attitude to learning.* **2** ADJ [ADJ n] If someone has an **inquiring** expression on their face, they are showing that they want to know something. [WRITTEN] ▫ *"That's right," she said in reply to his inquiring glance.* • **in|quir|ing|ly** ADV ▫ *She looked at me inquiringly. "Well?"*

in|quiry ✦✧✧ /ɪnkwaɪəri, ɪŋkwɪri/ (inquiries) also **enquiry 1** N-COUNT An **inquiry** is a question you ask in order to get some information. ▫ *He made some inquiries and discovered she had gone to Connecticut.* **2** N-COUNT An **inquiry** is an official investigation. ▫ *...a shocking murder inquiry.* **3** N-UNCOUNT **Inquiry** is the process of asking about or investigating something in order to find out more about it. ▫ *The investigation has suddenly switched to a new line of inquiry.*

─── COLLOCATIONS ───

inquiry
NOUN **2**
noun + **inquiry**: competition, corruption; police; murder
adjective + **inquiry**: independent, internal, official, public; congressional, judicial, parliamentary
inquiry + be + adjective: underway
verb + **inquiry**: launch, order, set up; carry out, chair, conduct, hold

─── SYNONYMS ───

inquiry
NOUN **1**
question: *The President refused to answer further questions on the subject.*
query: *If you have any queries, please contact the helpline.*
investigation: *He ordered an investigation into the affair.*

in|qui|si|tion /ɪnkwɪzɪʃən/ (inquisitions) N-COUNT An **inquisition** is an official investigation, especially one that is very thorough and uses harsh methods of questioning.

in|quisi|tive /ɪnkwɪzɪtɪv/ ADJ An **inquisitive** person likes finding out about things, especially secret things. ▫ *Barrow had an inquisitive nature.*

in|quisi|tor /ɪnkwɪzɪtər/ (inquisitors) N-COUNT An **inquisitor** is someone who asks someone else a series of questions, especially in a hostile way or as part of an inquisition.

in|quisi|to|rial /ɪnkwɪzɪtɔriəl/ ADJ If you describe something or someone as **inquisitorial**, you mean they resemble things or people in an inquisition. ▫ *The next hearings will be structured differently in order to minimize the inquisitorial atmosphere.*

in|roads /ɪnroʊdz/ PHRASE If one thing **makes inroads** into another, the first thing starts affecting or destroying the second. ▫ *In Italy, as elsewhere, television has made deep inroads into movies.*

in|sane /ɪnseɪn/ **1** ADJ Someone who is **insane** is severely mentally ill. ▫ *Some people simply can't take it and they just go insane.* **2** ADJ If you describe a decision or action as **insane**, you think it is very foolish or excessive. [DISAPPROVAL] ▫ *He asked me what I thought and I said, "Listen, this is completely insane."* • **in|sane|ly** ADV ▫ *I would be insanely jealous if Bill left me for another woman.*

in|sani|tary /ɪnsænɪtri/ [BRIT] → see **unsanitary**

in|san|ity /ɪnsænɪti/ **1** N-UNCOUNT **Insanity** is the state of being insane. ▫ *...a psychiatrist who specialized in diagnosing insanity.* **2** N-UNCOUNT If you describe a decision or an action as **insanity**, you think it is very foolish. [DISAPPROVAL] ▫ *...the final financial insanity of the 1980s.*

in|sa|tiable /ɪnseɪʃəbəl, -ʃiə-/ ADJ If someone has an **insatiable** desire for something, they want as much of it as they can possibly get. ▫ *A section of the reading public has an insatiable appetite for dirty stories about the famous.*

in|scribe /ɪnskraɪb/ (inscribes, inscribing, inscribed) **1** V-T If you **inscribe** words on an object, you write or carve the words on the object. ▫ *Some galleries commemorate donors by inscribing their names on the walls.* **2** V-T If you **inscribe** something in the front of a book or on a photograph, you write it there, often before giving it to someone. ▫ *On the back I had inscribed the words: "Here's to Great Ideas! John."*

in|scrip|tion /ɪnskrɪpʃən/ (inscriptions) **1** N-COUNT An **inscription** is writing carved into something made of stone or metal, such as a gravestone or medal. ▫ *The medal bears the inscription "For distinguished service."* **2** N-COUNT An **inscription** is something written by hand in the front of a book or on a photograph. ▫ *The inscription reads: "To Emma, with love from Harry."*

in|scru|table /ɪnskrutəbəl/ ADJ If a person or their expression is **inscrutable**, it is very hard to know what they are really thinking or what they mean. ▫ *In public he remained inscrutable.*

in|sect /ɪnsekt/ (insects) **1** N-COUNT An **insect** is a small animal that has six legs. Most insects have wings. Ants, flies, butterflies, and beetles are all insects. **2** → See also color supplement

in|sec|ti|cide /ɪnsektɪsaɪd/ (insecticides) N-MASS **Insecticide** is a chemical substance that is used to kill insects. ▫ *Spray the plants with insecticide.*

in|se|cure /ɪnsɪkyʊər/ **1** ADJ If you are **insecure**, you lack confidence because you think that you are not good enough or are not loved. ▫ *Most mothers are insecure about their performance as mothers.* • **in|secu|rity** /ɪnsɪkyʊərɪti/ (insecurities) N-VAR ▫ *She is always assailed by self-doubt and emotional insecurity.* **2** ADJ Something that is **insecure** is not safe or protected. ▫ *...low-paid, insecure jobs.* • **in|secu|rity** N-UNCOUNT ▫ *...the increase in crime, which has created feelings of insecurity in the population.*

in|semi|nate /ɪnsemɪneɪt/ (inseminates, inseminating, inseminated) **1** V-T To **inseminate** a woman or female animal means to put sperm into her in order to make her pregnant. ▫ *The gadget is used to artificially inseminate cows.* • **in|semi|na|tion** /ɪnsemɪneɪʃən/ N-UNCOUNT ▫ *The sperm sample is checked under the microscope before insemination is carried out.* **2** → see also **artificial insemination**

in|sen|si|tive /ɪnsensɪtɪv/ **1** ADJ If you describe someone as **insensitive**, you are criticizing them for being unaware of or unsympathetic to other people's feelings. [DISAPPROVAL] ▫ *I feel my husband is very insensitive about my problem.* • **in|sen|si|tiv|ity** /ɪnsensɪtɪvɪti/ N-UNCOUNT ▫ *I was ashamed and appalled at my clumsiness and insensitivity toward her.* **2** ADJ Someone who is **insensitive** to a situation or to a need does not think or care about it. ▫ *...women's and Latino organizations that say he is insensitive to civil rights.* • **in|sen|si|tiv|ity** N-UNCOUNT ▫ *...insensitivity to the environmental consequences.* **3** ADJ Someone who is **insensitive** to a physical sensation is unable to feel it. ▫ *He had become insensitive to cold.*

in|sep|arable /ɪnsepərəbəl/ **1** ADJ If one thing is **inseparable** from another, the things are so closely connected that they cannot be considered separately. ▫ *He firmly believes liberty is inseparable from social justice.* • **in|sepa|rably** ADV ▫ *In his mind, religion and politics were inseparably intertwined.* **2** ADJ If you say that two people are **inseparable**, you are emphasizing that they are very good friends and spend a lot of time together. [EMPHASIS] ▫ *She and Kristin were inseparable.* **3** → See feature box at **relationship**

insert

in|sert (inserts, inserting, inserted)

The verb is pronounced /ɪnsɜrt/. The noun is pronounced /ˈɪnsɜrt/.

1 V-T If you **insert** an object into something, you put the object inside it. ❏ *He took a small key from his pocket and slowly inserted it into the lock.* • **in|ser|tion** /ɪnsɜrʃən/ (**insertions**) N-VAR ❏ *...the first experiment involving the insertion of a new gene into a human being.* **2** V-T If you **insert** a comment into a piece of writing or a speech, you add it. ❏ *They joined with the monarchists to insert a clause calling for a popular vote on the issue.* • **in|ser|tion** N-VAR ❏ *...an item for insertion in the program.* **3** N-COUNT An **insert** is something that is inserted somewhere, especially an advertisement on a piece of paper that is placed between the pages of a book or magazine. ❏ *Sunday is the preferred day for advertising inserts in newspapers.*

in-service ADJ [ADJ n] If people working in a particular profession are given **in-service** training, they attend special courses to improve their skills or to learn about new developments in their field. ❏ *...in-service courses for people such as doctors, teachers, and civil servants.*

in|set /ˈɪnsɛt/ (**insets**) **1** ADJ Something that is **inset** with a decoration or piece of material has the decoration or material set inside it. ❏ *...a gold pendant, inset with a diamond.* **2** N-COUNT An **inset** is a small picture, diagram, or map that is inside a larger one. ❏ *I frequently paint between 10 and 20 insets for my murals.*

in|shore

The adverb is pronounced /ɪnʃɔr/. The adjective is pronounced /ˈɪnʃɔr/.

ADV [be ADV, ADV after v] If something is **inshore**, it is in the sea but quite close to the land. If something moves **inshore**, it moves from the sea toward the land. ❏ *A barge was close inshore about a hundred yards away.* • ADJ [ADJ n] **Inshore** is also an adjective. ❏ *...inshore reefs and islands.*

in|side ♦♦◊ /ɪnˈsaɪd/ (**insides**)

The preposition and adverb are usually pronounced /ɪnˈsaɪd/.

The form **inside of** can also be used as a preposition in American English.

1 PREP Something or someone that is **inside** a place, container, or object is in it or is surrounded by it. ❏ *Inside the passport was a folded slip of paper.* • ADV **Inside** is also an adverb. ❏ *The couple chatted briefly on the doorstep before going inside.* • ADJ [ADJ n] **Inside** is also an adjective. ❏ *...an inside wall.* **2** N-COUNT The **inside** of something is the part or area that its sides surround or contain. ❏ *The doors were locked from the inside.* • ADJ [ADJ n] **Inside** is also an adjective. ❏ *The popular papers all have photo features on their inside pages.* • ADV [adj ADV] **Inside** is also an adverb. ❏ *The potato cakes can be shallow or deep-fried until crisp outside and meltingly soft inside.* **3** ADJ [ADJ n] **Inside** information is obtained from someone who is involved in a situation and therefore knows a lot about it. ❏ *Sloane used inside diplomatic information to make himself rich.* ❏ *I cannot claim any inside knowledge of government policies.* **4** PREP If you are **inside** an organization, you belong to it. ❏ *75 percent of chief executives come from inside the company.* • ADJ [ADJ n] **Inside** is also an adjective. ❏ *...a recent book about the inside world of pro football.* • N-SING **Inside** is also a noun. ❏ *McAvoy was convinced he could control things from the inside but he lost control.* **5** ADV You can say that someone is **inside** when they are in prison. [INFORMAL] ❏ *They've both done prison time – he's been inside three times.* **6** N-PLURAL Your **insides** are your internal organs, especially your stomach. [INFORMAL] ❏ *Every pill made my insides turn upside down.* **7** ADV If you say that someone has a feeling **inside**, you mean that they have it but have not expressed it. ❏ *There is nothing left inside – no words, no anger, no tears.* • PREP **Inside** is also a preposition. ❏ *He felt a great weight of sorrow inside him.* • N-SING **Inside** is also a noun. ❏ *What is needed is a change from the inside, a real change in outlook and attitude.* **8** PREP [PREP amount] If you do something **inside** a particular time, you do it before the end of that time. ❏ *They should have everything working inside an hour.* **9** PHRASE If something such as a piece of clothing is **inside out**, the part that is normally inside now faces outward. ❏ *Her umbrella blew inside out.* **10** PHRASE If you say that you know something or someone **inside out**, you are emphasizing that you know them extremely well. [EMPHASIS] ❏ *He knew the game inside out.*

in|sid|er /ɪnˈsaɪdər/ (**insiders**) N-COUNT An **insider** is someone who is involved in a situation and who knows more about it than other people. ❏ *An insider said, "Katharine has told friends it is time to end her career."*

in|sid|er trad|ing N-UNCOUNT **Insider trading** is the illegal buying or selling of a company's stock by someone who has secret or private information about the company. [BUSINESS] ❏ *He is accused of insider trading in shares of his own company.*

in|sidi|ous /ɪnˈsɪdiəs/ ADJ Something that is **insidious** is unpleasant or dangerous and develops gradually without being noticed. ❏ *The changes are insidious, and will not produce a noticeable effect for 15 to 20 years.*

in|sight /ˈɪnsaɪt/ (**insights**) **1** N-VAR If you gain **insight** or an **insight** into a complex situation or problem, you gain an accurate and deep understanding of it. ❏ *The project would give scientists new insights into what is happening to the Earth's atmosphere.* **2** N-UNCOUNT If someone has **insight**, they are able to understand complex situations. ❏ *He was a man of forceful character, with considerable insight and diplomatic skills.*

in|sight|ful ♦♦◊ /ɪnˈsaɪtfʊl/ ADJ If you describe a person or their remarks as **insightful**, you mean that they show a very good understanding of people and situations. [APPROVAL] ❏ *She offered some really interesting, insightful observations.*

in|sig|nia /ɪnˈsɪgniə/ (**insignia**) N-COUNT An **insignia** is a design or symbol that shows that a person or object belongs to a particular organization, often a military one. ❏ *The red star was the national insignia of the USSR.*

in|sig|nifi|cance /ˌɪnsɪgˈnɪfɪkəns/ N-UNCOUNT **Insignificance** is the quality of being insignificant. ❏ *These prices pale into insignificance when compared with what was paid for two major works by the late Alfred Stieglitz.*

in|sig|nifi|cant /ˌɪnsɪgˈnɪfɪkənt/ ADJ Something that is **insignificant** is unimportant, especially because it is very small. ❏ *In 1949 Bonn was a small, insignificant city.*

in|sin|cere /ˌɪnsɪnˈsɪər/ ADJ If you say that someone is **insincere**, you are being critical of them because they say things they do not really mean, usually pleasant, admiring, or encouraging things. [DISAPPROVAL] ❏ *Some people are so terribly insincere you can never tell if they are telling the truth.*

in|sinu|ate /ɪnˈsɪnyueɪt/ (**insinuates, insinuating, insinuated**) **1** V-T If you say that someone **insinuates** that something bad is the case, you mean that they say it in an indirect way. [DISAPPROVAL] ❏ *The libel claim followed an article that insinuated the president was lying.* • **in|sinu|ation** /ɪnˌsɪnyuˈeɪʃən/ (**insinuations**) N-VAR ❏ *He speaks with rage of insinuations that there's a "gay mafia" in Hollywood.* **2** V-T If you say that someone **insinuates** themselves into a particular situation, you mean that they manage very cleverly, and perhaps dishonestly, to get into that situation. [DISAPPROVAL] ❏ *He gradually insinuated himself into her life.*

in|sinu|at|ing /ɪnˈsɪnyueɪtɪŋ/ ADJ If you describe someone's words or voice as **insinuating**, you mean that they are saying something disapproving in an indirect way. [DISAPPROVAL] ❏ *Cletus kept making insinuating remarks.*

in|sip|id /ɪnˈsɪpɪd/ **1** ADJ If you describe food or drink as **insipid**, you dislike it because it has very little taste. [DISAPPROVAL] ❏ *It tasted indescribably bland and insipid, like warmed cardboard.* **2** ADJ If you describe someone or something as **insipid**, you mean they are dull and boring. [DISAPPROVAL] ❏ *On the surface she seemed meek, rather insipid.*

in|sist ♦♦◊ /ɪnˈsɪst/ (**insists, insisting, insisted**) **1** V-T/V-I If you **insist** that something should be done, you say so very firmly and refuse to give in about it. If you **insist** on something, you say firmly that it must be done or provided. ❏ *My family insisted that I should not give in, but stay and fight.* ❏ *She insisted on being present at all the interviews.* **2** V-T/V-I If you **insist** that something is the case, you say so very firmly and refuse to say otherwise, even though other people do not believe you. ❏ *The president insisted that he was acting out of compassion, not political opportunism.* ❏ *"It's not that difficult," she insists.* ❏ *He insisted on his innocence.*

in|sist|ence /ɪnsɪstəns/ N-UNCOUNT Someone's **insistence** on something is the fact that they insist that it should be done or insist that it is the case. ◻ ...*her insistence on personal privacy.*

in|sist|ent /ɪnsɪstənt/ **1** ADJ Someone who is **insistent** keeps insisting that a particular thing should be done or is the case. ◻ *Stalin was insistent that the war would be won and lost in the machine shops.* • **in|sist|ent|ly** ADV [ADV with v] ◻ *"What is it?" his wife asked again, gently but insistently.* **2** ADJ An **insistent** noise or rhythm keeps going on for a long time and holds your attention. ◻ *...the insistent rhythms of the Caribbean and Latin America.*

in situ /ɪn sɪtu/ also **in-situ** ADV [ADV after v] If something remains **in situ**, especially while something is done to it, it remains where it is. [FORMAL] ◻ *Major works of painting, sculpture, mosaic and architecture were examined in situ in Venice.* • ADJ [ADJ n] **In-situ** is also an adjective. ◻ *...technical data derived from laboratory and in-situ experimentation.*

in|so|far as /ɪnsəfɑr æz, ɪnsoʊ-/ PHRASE You use **insofar as** to introduce a statement that explains and adds to something you have just said. [FORMAL] ◻ *Looking back helps insofar as it helps you learn from your mistakes.*

in|sole /ɪnsoʊl/ (**insoles**) N-COUNT [usu pl] The **insoles** of a pair of shoes are the soft layer of material inside each one, which the soles of your feet rest on.

in|so|lent /ɪnsələnt/ ADJ If you say that someone is being **insolent**, you mean they are being rude to someone they ought to be respectful to. ◻ *...her insolent stare.*

in|sol|uble /ɪnsɒlyəbəl/ **1** ADJ An **insoluble** problem is so difficult that it is impossible to solve. ◻ *I pushed the problem aside; at present it was insoluble.* **2** ADJ If a substance is **insoluble**, it does not dissolve in a liquid. ◻ *Carotenes are insoluble in water and soluble in oils and fats.*

in|sol|ven|cy /ɪnsɒlvənsi/ (**insolvencies**) N-VAR **Insolvency** is the state of not having enough money to pay your debts. [FORMAL, BUSINESS] ◻ *...eight mortgage companies, seven of which are on the brink of insolvency.*

in|sol|vent /ɪnsɒlvənt/ ADJ A person or organization that is **insolvent** does not have enough money to pay their debts. [FORMAL, BUSINESS] ◻ *Two years later, the bank was declared insolvent.*

in|som|nia /ɪnsɒmniə/ N-UNCOUNT Someone who suffers from **insomnia** finds it difficult to sleep.

in|som|ni|ac /ɪnsɒmniæk/ (**insomniacs**) N-COUNT An **insomniac** is a person who finds it difficult to sleep.

in|sou|ci|ance /ɪnsusiəns/ N-UNCOUNT **Insouciance** is lack of concern shown by someone about something that they are expected to take more seriously. [FORMAL] ◻ *He replied with characteristic insouciance: "So what?"*

in|sou|ci|ant /ɪnsusiənt/ ADJ An **insouciant** action or quality shows someone's lack of concern about something that they are expected to take more seriously. [FORMAL] ◻ *Television producers seem irresponsibly insouciant about churning out violence.*

Insp. N-TITLE **Insp.** is the written abbreviation for **Inspector** when it is used as a title. ◻ *...Insp. John Downs.*

in|spect ♦◇◇ /ɪnspɛkt/ (**inspects, inspecting, inspected**) **1** V-T If you **inspect** something, you look at every part of it carefully in order to find out about it or check that it is all right. ◻ *Elaine went outside to inspect the playing field.* • **in|spec|tion** /ɪnspɛkʃən/ (**inspections**) N-VAR ◻ *"Excellent work," he said when he had completed his inspection of the painted doors.* **2** V-T When an official **inspects** a place or a group of people, they visit it and check it carefully, for example, in order to find out whether regulations are being obeyed. ◻ *The Public Utilities Commission inspects us once a year.* • **in|spec|tion** N-VAR ◻ *Officers making a routine inspection of the vessel found fifty kilograms of cocaine.*

SYNONYMS

inspect
VERB **1**
examine: *He examined her passport and stamped it.*
check: *It's worth checking each item for obvious flaws.*
survey: *He pushed himself to his feet and surveyed the room.*
scrutinize: *Their results were carefully scrutinized.*
scan: *She scanned the advertisement pages of the newspapers.*

---

in|spec|tor ♦◇◇ /ɪnspɛktər/ (**inspectors**) **1** N-COUNT An **inspector** is a person, usually employed by a government agency, whose job is to find out whether people are obeying official regulations. ◻ *The mill was finally shut down by state safety inspectors.* **2** N-COUNT; N-TITLE; N-VOC An **inspector** is an officer in the police who is next in rank to a superintendent or police chief. ◻ *...San Francisco police inspector Tony Camileri.*

in|spec|tor|ate /ɪnspɛktərɪt/ (**inspectorates**) N-COUNT [usu with supp] An **inspectorate** is a group of inspectors who work on the same issue or area. ◻ *...the UN weapons inspectorate.*

in|spi|ra|tion /ɪnspɪreɪʃən/ (**inspirations**) **1** N-UNCOUNT **Inspiration** is a feeling of enthusiasm you get from someone or something, that gives you new and creative ideas. ◻ *My inspiration comes from poets like Baudelaire and Jacques Prévert.* **2** N-SING If you describe someone or something good as an **inspiration**, you mean that they make you or other people want to do or achieve something. [APPROVAL] ◻ *Powell's unusual journey to high office is an inspiration to millions.* **3** N-SING If something or someone is the **inspiration** for a particular book, work of art, or action, they are the source of the ideas in it or act as a model for it. ◻ *India's myths and songs are the inspiration for her books.* **4** N-COUNT If you suddenly have an **inspiration**, you suddenly think of an idea of what to do or say. ◻ *She had an inspiration, "Could we take Janice?"*

in|spi|ra|tion|al /ɪnspɪreɪʃənəl/ ADJ Something that is **inspirational** provides you with inspiration. [APPROVAL] ◻ *Gandhi was an inspirational figure.*

in|spire /ɪnspaɪər/ (**inspires, inspiring, inspired**) **1** V-T If someone or something **inspires** you to do something new or unusual, they make you want to do it. ◻ *Our challenge is to motivate those voters and inspire them to join our cause.* **2** V-T If someone or something **inspires** you, they give you new ideas and a strong feeling of enthusiasm. ◻ *In the 1960s, the electric guitar virtuosity of Jimi Hendrix inspired a generation.* **3** V-T [usu passive] If a book, work of art, or action **is inspired** by something, that thing is the source of the idea for it. ◻ *The book was inspired by a real person, namely Tamara de Treaux.* • **-inspired** COMB IN ADJ ◻ *...Mediterranean-inspired ceramics in bright yellow and blue.* **4** V-T Someone or something that **inspires** a particular emotion or reaction in people makes them feel that emotion or reaction. ◻ *The car's performance is effortless and its handling is precise and quickly inspires confidence.*

in|spir|ing /ɪnspaɪərɪŋ/ ADJ Something or someone that is **inspiring** is exciting and makes you feel strongly interested and enthusiastic. ◻ *She was a very strong, impressive character and one of the most inspiring people I've ever met.*

Inst. **Inst.** is a written abbreviation for **Institute** or **Institution**. ◻ *...the Cambridge Research Inst.*

in|stabil|ity /ɪnstəbɪlɪti/ N-UNCOUNT **Instability** is the quality of being unstable. ◻ *...unpopular policies, which resulted in social discontent and political instability.*

in|stall ♦◇◇ /ɪnstɔl/ (**installs, installing, installed**)

in BRIT, also use **instal**

1 V-T If you **install** a piece of equipment, you put it somewhere so that it is ready to be used. ◻ *They had installed a new phone line in the apartment.* • **in|stal|la|tion** N-UNCOUNT ◻ *Hundreds of lives could be saved if the installation of alarms was more widespread.* **2** V-T If you **install** a a program, you put it onto a computer or cell phone so that you can use it. ◻ *I installed a podcasting app on my smartphone.* **3** V-T If someone **is installed** in a new job or important position, they are officially given the job or position, often in a special ceremony. ◻ *A temporary government was installed.* ◻ *He was formally installed as president last Thursday.* • **in|stal|la|tion** N-UNCOUNT ◻ *He sent a letter inviting Naomi to attend his installation as chief of his tribe.* **4** V-T If you **install** yourself or someone else in a particular place, you settle there and make yourself or them comfortable. [FORMAL] ◻ *Before her husband's death she had installed herself in a modern villa.*

in|stal|la|tion /ɪnstəleɪʃən/ (**installations**) **1** N-COUNT An **installation** is a place that contains equipment and machinery that are being used for a particular purpose. ◻ *The building was turned into a secret military installation.* **2** → see also **install**

in|stal|ler ♦◇◇ /ɪnstɔlər/ (**installers**) also **instaler** **1** N-COUNT An **installer** is a person who puts a piece of equipment

installment

somewhere so it is ready to be used. ▫ *He works as a cable TV installer.* **2** N-COUNT An **installer** is a piece of software that installs a program on a computer. ▫ *Get the installer to write the game to the D drive.*

in|stall|ment /ɪnstɔ́lmənt/ (**installments**)

in BRIT, use **instalment**

1 N-COUNT If you pay for something in **installments**, you pay small sums of money at regular intervals over a period of time, rather than paying the whole amount at once. ▫ *Upper-bracket taxpayers who elected to pay their tax increase in installments must pay the third installment by April 15.* **2** N-COUNT An **installment** of a story or plan is one of its parts that are published or carried out separately one after the other. ▫ *The next installment of this four-part series deals with the impact of the war on the continent of Africa.*

in|stall|ment plan (**installment plans**) N-COUNT An **installment plan** is a way of buying products gradually. You make regular payments to the seller until, after some time, you have paid the full price. [AM]

in BRIT, use **hire purchase**

in|stance ◆◇◇ /ɪ́nstəns/ (**instances**) **1** PHRASE You use **for instance** to introduce a particular event, situation, or person that is an example of what you are talking about. ▫ *There was, for instance, almost no damage to the house.* **2** N-COUNT An **instance** is a particular example or occurrence of something. ▫ *…an investigation into a serious instance of corruption.* **3** PHRASE You say **in the first instance** to mention something that is the first step in a series of actions. [INFORMAL] ▫ *In the first instance your child will be seen by an ear, nose and throat specialist.*

SYNONYMS

instance
NOUN **2**
example: *The doctors gave numerous examples of patients being expelled from the hospital.*
case: *In extreme cases, insurance companies can prosecute for fraud.*
occurrence: *Complaints seemed to be an everyday occurrence.*
occasion: *Mr Davis has been asked on a number of occasions.*

in|stant ◆◇◇ /ɪ́nstənt/ (**instants**) **1** N-COUNT An **instant** is an extremely short period of time. ▫ *For an instant, Barney was tempted to flee.* **2** N-SING If you say that something happens at a particular **instant**, you mean that it happens at exactly the time you have been referring to, and you are usually suggesting that it happens quickly or immediately. ▫ *At that instant the museum was plunged into total darkness.* **3** PHRASE To do something **the instant** something else happens means to do it immediately. [EMPHASIS] ▫ *I bolted the door the instant I saw the bat.* **4** ADJ You use **instant** to describe something that happens immediately. ▫ *Mr. Porter's book was an instant hit.* ● **in|stant|ly** ADV ▫ *The man was killed instantly.* **5** ADJ [ADJ n] **Instant** food is food that you can prepare very quickly, for example, by just adding water. ▫ *He stirred instant coffee into a mug of hot water.*

SYNONYMS

instant
NOUN **1**
moment: *In a moment, he was gone.*
second: *Within seconds, the other soldiers began firing, too.*
flash: *It was done in a flash.*
split second: *Her gaze met Michael's for a split second.*
ADJ **4**
immediate: *These tragic incidents have had an immediate effect.*
prompt: *It is not too late, but prompt action is needed.*
instantaneous: *The bitter wind brought instantaneous tears to his eyes.*

in|stan|ta|neous /ɪ̀nstəntéɪniəs/ ADJ Something that is **instantaneous** happens immediately and very quickly. ▫ *Death was not instantaneous because none of the bullets hit the heart.* ● **in|stan|ta|neous|ly** ADV [ADV with v] ▫ *Airbags inflate instantaneously on impact to form a cushion between the driver and the steering column.*

in|stant mes|sage (**instant messages**) N-COUNT An **instant message** is a written messages that is sent from one computer to another. The message appears immediately on the screen of the computer you send it to, provided the computer is using the service. The abbreviation **IM** is also used. ▫ *Instructors answer student questions by email, instant message, phone or fax.*

in|stant mes|sag|ing N-UNCOUNT [oft N n] **Instant messaging** is the sending of written messages from one computer to another. The message appears immediately on the screen of the computer you send it to, provided the computer is using the service. The abbreviation **IM** is also used. ▫ *…users of the instant-messaging services of Yahoo, Microsoft and other rivals.*

in|stant re|play (**instant replays**) N-COUNT An **instant replay** is a repeated showing, usually in slow motion, of an event that has just been on television. [AM]

in BRIT, use **action replay**

in|stead ◆◇◇ /ɪnstéd/ **1** PHRASE If you do one thing **instead of** another, you do the first thing and not the second thing, as the result of a choice or a change of behavior. ▫ *They raised prices and cut production, instead of cutting costs.* **2** ADV [ADV with cl] If you do not do something, but do something else **instead**, you do the second thing and not the first thing, as the result of a choice or a change of behavior. ▫ *I decided to forget about dieting and eat normally instead.*

in|step /ɪ́nstep/ (**insteps**) N-COUNT Your **instep** is the middle part of your foot, where it arches upward.

in|sti|gate /ɪ́nstɪgeɪt/ (**instigates, instigating, instigated**) V-T Someone who **instigates** an event causes it to happen. ▫ *He did not instigate the coup or even know of it beforehand.* ● **in|sti|ga|tion** /ɪ̀nstɪgéɪʃən/ N-UNCOUNT ▫ *The talks are taking place at the instigation of Germany.*

in|sti|ga|tor /ɪ́nstɪgeɪtər/ (**instigators**) N-COUNT The **instigator** of an event is the person who causes it to happen. ▫ *He was accused of being the main instigator of the coup.*

in|still /ɪnstɪ́l/ (**instills, instilling, instilled**)

in BRIT, use **instil**

V-T If you **instill** an idea or feeling in someone, especially over a period of time, you make them think it or feel it. ▫ *The tough thing is trying to instill a winning attitude in the kids.*

in|stinct /ɪ́nstɪŋkt/ (**instincts**) **1** N-VAR **Instinct** is the natural tendency that a person or animal has to behave or react in a particular way. ▫ *I didn't have as strong a maternal instinct as some other mothers.* **2** N-COUNT If you have an **instinct** for something, you are naturally good at it or able to do it. ▫ *He seems to have an instinct for smart advertising and marketing.* **3** N-VAR If it is your **instinct** to do something, you feel that it is right to do it. ▫ *I should've gone with my first instinct, which was not to do the interview.* **4** N-VAR **Instinct** is a feeling, rather than an opinion or idea based on facts, that something is the case. ▫ *There is scientific evidence to support our instinct that being surrounded by plants is good for health.*

in|stinc|tive /ɪnstɪ́ŋktɪv/ ADJ An **instinctive** feeling, idea, or action is one that you have or do without thinking or reasoning. ▫ *It's an instinctive reaction – if a child falls you pick it up.* ● **in|stinc|tive|ly** ADV [ADV with v] ▫ *Jane instinctively knew all was not well with her 10-month old son.*

in|stinc|tual /ɪnstɪ́ŋktʃuəl/ ADJ An **instinctual** feeling, action, or idea is one based on instinct. [WRITTEN] ▫ *The relationship between a parent and a child is instinctual and stems from basic human nature.*

in|sti|tute ◆◇◇ /ɪ́nstɪtut/ (**institutes, instituting, instituted**) **1** N-COUNT; N-IN-NAMES An **institute** is an organization set up to do a particular type of work, especially research or teaching. You can also use **institute** to refer to the building the organization occupies. ▫ *…the National Cancer Institute.* **2** V-T If you **institute** a system, rule, or course of action, you start it. [FORMAL] ▫ *We will institute a number of measures to better safeguard the public.*

institution | 681 | insubordinate

SYNONYMS
institute
NOUN **1**
establishment: ...a scientific research establishment.
body: ...the Chairman of the police representative body, the Police Federation.
organization: Most of these specialized schools are provided by volunteer organizations.
institution: ...the Institution of Civil Engineers.
association: Research associations are often linked to a particular industry.

in|sti|tu|tion ✦✧✧ /ɪnstɪtjuːʃ°n/ (**institutions**) **1** N-COUNT; N-IN-NAMES An **institution** is a large important organization such as a university, church, or bank. ◻ ...financial institutions. **2** N-COUNT; N-IN-NAMES An **institution** is a building where certain people are cared for, such as people who are mentally ill or children who have no parents. ◻ Larry has been in an institution since he was four. **3** N-COUNT An **institution** is a custom or system that is considered an important or typical feature of a particular society or group, usually because it has existed for a long time. ◻ I believe in the institution of marriage. **4** N-UNCOUNT The **institution** of a new system is the act of starting it or bringing it in. ◻ There was never an official institution of censorship in Albania. **5** → See feature box at **prison**

SYNONYMS
institution
NOUN **1**
establishment: ...a scientific research establishment.
body: ...the main trade union body, COSATU, Congress of South African Trade Unions.
organization: ...a report by the International Labor Organization.

in|sti|tu|tion|al /ɪnstɪtjuːʃ°nəl/ **1** ADJ [ADJ n] **Institutional** means relating to a large organization, such as a university, bank, or church. ◻ NATO remains the United States' chief institutional anchor in Europe. **2** ADJ [ADJ n] **Institutional** means relating to a building where people are cared for or held. ◻ Outside the protected environment of institutional care he could not survive. **3** ADJ [ADJ n] An **institutional** value or quality is considered an important and typical feature of a particular society or group, usually because it has existed for a long time. ◻ ...social and institutional values. **4** ADJ [usu ADJ n] If someone accuses an organization of **institutional** racism or sexism, they mean that the organization is deeply racist or sexist and has been so for a long time. ◻ It is important that we continue to call out privilege and institutional racism for what it is. • **in|sti|tu|tion|al|ly** /ɪnstɪtjuːʃ°nəli/ ADV [ADV adj] ◻ The government's policy still appeared to be institutionally racist.

in|sti|tu|tion|al|ize /ɪnstɪtjuːʃ°nəlaɪz/ (**institutionalizes, institutionalizing, institutionalized**)

in BRIT, also use **institutionalise**

1 V-T [usu passive] If someone such as a sick, mentally ill, or old person **is institutionalized**, they are sent to stay in a special hospital or home, usually for a long period. ◻ She became seriously ill and had to be institutionalized for a lengthy period. **2** V-T To **institutionalize** something means to establish it as part of a culture, social system, or organization. ◻ The goal is to institutionalize family planning into community life.

in-store also **instore** ADJ [usu ADJ n] **In-store** facilities are facilities that are available within a department store, supermarket, or other large store. ◻ ...in-store banking. ◻ ...an instore bakery. • ADV [ADV after v] **In-store** is also an adverb. ◻ Ask in-store for details.

in|struct /ɪnstrʌkt/ (**instructs, instructing, instructed**) **1** V-T If you **instruct** someone to do something, you formally tell them to do it. [FORMAL] ◻ A doctor will often instruct patients to exercise. ◻ "Go and have a word with her, Ken," Wojtowicz instructed. **2** V-T Someone who **instructs** people in a subject or skill teaches it to them. ◻ He instructed family members in nursing techniques.

in|struc|tion ✦✧✧ /ɪnstrʌkʃ°n/ (**instructions**) **1** N-COUNT An **instruction** is something that someone tells you to do. ◻ Two lawyers were told not to leave the building but no reason for this instruction was given. **2** N-UNCOUNT If someone gives you **instruction** in a subject or skill, they teach it to you. [FORMAL] ◻ Each candidate is given instruction in safety. **3** N-PLURAL **Instructions** are clear and detailed information on how to do something. ◻ This book gives instructions for making a wide range of skin and hand creams.

SYNONYMS
instruction
NOUN **1**
order: As darkness fell, Clinton gave orders for his men to rest.
command: The tanker failed to respond to a command to stop.
rule: Strictly speaking, this was against the rules.
ruling: He tried to have the court ruling overturned.
demand: He grew ever more fierce in his demands.
direction: Do not throw away the directions until we've finished cooking.

in|struc|tion|al /ɪnstrʌkʃ°nəl/ ADJ [usu ADJ n] **Instructional** books or films are meant to teach people something or to offer them help with a particular problem. ◻ ...instructional material designed to help you with your lifestyle.

in|struc|tive /ɪnstrʌktɪv/ ADJ Something that is **instructive** gives useful information. ◻ ...an entertaining and instructive documentary.

in|struc|tor /ɪnstrʌktər/ (**instructors**) N-COUNT An **instructor** is someone who teaches a skill such as driving or skiing. An **instructor** can also be used to refer to a schoolteacher or to a university teacher of low rank. ◻ ...a fitness instructor.

in|stru|ment ✦✧✧ /ɪnstrəmənt/ (**instruments**) **1** N-COUNT An **instrument** is a tool or device that is used to do a particular task, especially a scientific task. ◻ ...instruments for cleaning and polishing teeth. **2** N-COUNT A musical **instrument** is an object such as a piano, guitar, or flute, which you play in order to produce music. ◻ Learning a musical instrument introduces a child to an understanding of music. **3** N-COUNT An **instrument** is a device that is used for making measurements of something such as speed, height, or sound, for example, on a ship or plane or in a car. ◻ The design of crucial instruments on the control panel will have to be improved. **4** N-COUNT Something that is an **instrument** for achieving a particular aim is used by people to achieve that aim. ◻ The veto has been a traditional instrument of diplomacy for centuries.

SYNONYMS
instrument
NOUN **1**
tool: I find the best tool for the purpose is a pair of shears.
device: ...an electronic device that protects your vehicle 24 hours a day.
implement: ...knives and other useful implements.
gadget: ...kitchen gadgets, including toasters, kettles, and percolators.
utensil: The best carving utensil is a long, sharp, flexible knife.

in|stru|men|tal /ɪnstrəmɛnt°l/ (**instrumentals**) **1** ADJ Someone or something that is **instrumental** in a process or event helps to make it happen. ◻ In his first years as chairman he was instrumental in raising the company's wider profile. **2** ADJ [ADJ n] **Instrumental** music is performed by instruments and not by voices. ◻ ...a CD of vocal and instrumental music. • N-COUNT **Instrumentals** are pieces of instrumental music. ◻ After a couple of brief instrumentals, he puts his guitar down.

in|stru|men|tal|ist /ɪnstrəmɛnt°lɪst/ (**instrumentalists**) N-COUNT An **instrumentalist** is someone who plays a musical instrument.

in|stru|men|ta|tion /ɪnstrəmɛnteɪʃ°n/ N-UNCOUNT **Instrumentation** is a group or collection of instruments, usually ones that are part of the same machine. ◻ Basic flight instrumentation was similar on both planes.

in|stru|ment pan|el (**instrument panels**) N-COUNT The **instrument panel** of a plane, car, or machine is the panel where the dials and switches are located.

in|sub|or|di|nate /ɪnsəbɔːrdɪnɪt/ ADJ If you say that someone is **insubordinate**, you mean that they do not obey someone of higher rank. [FORMAL] ◻ In industry, a worker who is grossly insubordinate is threatened with discharge.

in|sub|or|di|na|tion /ɪnsəbɔːrdᵊneɪʃᵊn/ N-UNCOUNT **Insubordination** is a refusal to obey someone of higher rank. [FORMAL] ❑ Hansen and his partner were fired for insubordination.

in|sub|stan|tial /ɪnsəbstænʃᵊl/ ADJ Something that is **insubstantial** is not large, solid, or strong. ❑ Mars has an insubstantial atmosphere, consisting almost entirely of carbon dioxide.

in|suf|fer|able /ɪnsʌfərəbᵊl/ ADJ If you say that someone or something is **insufferable**, you are emphasizing that they are very unpleasant or annoying. [FORMAL, EMPHASIS] ❑ He was an insufferable bore. ● **in|suf|fer|ably** /ɪnsʌfrəbli/ ADV [ADV adj] ❑ His letters are insufferably dull.

in|suf|fi|cient /ɪnsəfɪʃᵊnt/ ADJ Something that is **insufficient** is not large enough in amount or degree for a particular purpose. [FORMAL] ❑ He decided there was insufficient evidence to justify criminal proceedings. ● **in|suf|fi|cient|ly** ADV [ADV adj/-ed] ❑ Food that is insufficiently cooked can lead to food poisoning.

in|su|lar /ɪnsələr/ ADJ If you say that someone is **insular**, you are being critical of them because they are unwilling to meet new people or to consider new ideas. [DISAPPROVAL] ❑ They were an insular family. ● **in|su|lar|ity** /ɪnsəlærɪti/ N-UNCOUNT ❑ But at least they have started to break out of their old insularity.

in|su|late /ɪnsəleɪt/ (insulates, insulating, insulated) ◼ V-T To **insulate** something such as a building means to protect it from cold, heat, or noise by placing a layer of other material around it or inside it. ❑ People should insulate their homes to conserve energy. ❑ Is there any way we can insulate our home from the noise? ◼ V-T If a piece of equipment **is insulated**, it is covered with rubber or plastic to prevent electricity from passing through it and giving the person using it an electric shock. ❑ In order to make it safe, the element is electrically insulated. ◼ V-T If a person or group **is insulated** from the rest of society or from outside influences, they are protected from them. ❑ They wonder if their community is no longer insulated from big city problems. ● **in|su|la|tion** N-UNCOUNT ❑ They lived in happy insulation from brutal facts.

in|su|la|tion /ɪnsəleɪʃᵊn/ ◼ N-UNCOUNT **Insulation** is a thick layer of a substance that keeps something warm, especially a building. ❑ High electricity bills point to a poor heating system or bad insulation. ◼ → see also **insulate**

in|su|la|tor /ɪnsəleɪtər/ (insulators) N-COUNT [usu sing] An **insulator** is a material that insulates something. ❑ Fat is an excellent insulator against the cold.

in|su|lin /ɪnsəlɪn/ N-UNCOUNT **Insulin** is a substance that most people produce naturally in their body and that controls the level of sugar in their blood. ❑ Sufferers from the more severe form of diabetes have faulty insulin-producing cells.

in|sult (insults, insulting, insulted)

The verb is pronounced /ɪnsʌlt/. The noun is pronounced /ɪnsʌlt/.

◼ V-T If someone **insults** you, they say or do something that is rude or offensive. ❑ I did not mean to insult you. ● **in|sult|ed** ADJ ❑ I mean, I was a bit insulted that they thought I needed bribing to shut up. ◼ N-COUNT An **insult** is a rude remark, or something a person says or does which insults you. ❑ Their behavior was an insult to the people they represent. ◼ PHRASE You say **to add insult to injury** when mentioning an action or fact that makes an unfair or unacceptable situation even worse. ❑ It is the victim who is often put on trial and, to add insult to injury, she is presumed guilty until proven innocent of provoking the rape.

in|sult|ing /ɪnsʌltɪŋ/ ADJ Something that is **insulting** is rude or offensive. ❑ ...insulting language.

in|su|per|able /ɪnsuːpərəbᵊl/ ADJ A problem that is **insuperable** cannot be dealt with successfully. [FORMAL] ❑ ...an insuperable obstacle to negotiations.

in|sup|port|able /ɪnsəpɔːrtəbᵊl/ ADJ If you say that something is **insupportable**, you mean that it cannot be coped with or accepted. [FORMAL] ❑ Too much spending on rearmament would place an insupportable burden on the nation's productive capacity. ❑ The thought was somehow insupportable.

in|sur|ance ✦✧ /ɪnʃʊərəns/ (insurances) ◼ N-VAR **Insurance** is an arrangement in which you pay money to a company, and they pay you if something unpleasant happens to you, for example, if your property is stolen or damaged, or if you get a serious illness. ❑ The house was a total loss and the insurance company promptly paid us the policy limit. ◼ N-VAR If you do something as **insurance** against something unpleasant happening, you do it to protect yourself in case the unpleasant thing happens. ❑ Attentive proofreading is the only insurance against the kind of omissions described in this section.

COLLOCATIONS

insurance
NOUN ◼
noun + **insurance**: car, health, home, life, travel
verb + **insurance**: buy, take out

SYNONYMS

insurance
NOUN ◼
assurance: ...endowment assurance.
cover: Make sure that the firm's insurance cover is adequate.
protection: This is believed to be the first scheme to offer protection against illness.
indemnity: They were charged with failing to have professional indemnity coverage.

---

in|sur|ance ad|just|er (insurance adjusters) N-COUNT An **insurance adjuster** is the same as a **claims adjuster**. [AM, BUSINESS]

in BRIT, use **loss adjuster**

in|sure /ɪnʃʊər/ (insures, insuring, insured) ◼ V-T/V-I If you **insure** yourself or your property, you pay money to an insurance company so that, if you become ill or if your property is damaged or stolen, the company will pay you a sum of money. ❑ For protection against unforeseen emergencies, you insure your house, your furnishings and your car. ❑ While many people insure against death, far fewer take precautions against long-term loss of income because of sickness. ◼ V-T If you **insure** yourself against something unpleasant that might happen in the future, you do something to protect yourself in case it happens, or to prevent it from happening. ❑ All the electronics in the world cannot insure people against accidents, though.

in|sured /ɪnʃʊərd/ (insured) N-COUNT [usu sing, the N] **The insured** is the person who is insured by a particular policy. [LEGAL] ❑ Once the insured has sold his policy, he naturally loses all rights to it.

in|sur|er /ɪnʃʊərər/ (insurers) N-COUNT An **insurer** is a company that sells insurance. [BUSINESS]

in|sur|gen|cy /ɪnsɜːrdʒᵊnsi/ (insurgencies) N-VAR An **insurgency** is a violent attempt to oppose a country's government carried out by citizens of that country. [FORMAL] ❑ Both countries were threatened with communist insurgencies in the 1960s.

in|sur|gent /ɪnsɜːrdʒᵊnt/ (insurgents) N-COUNT [usu pl] **Insurgents** are people who are fighting against the government or army of their own country. [FORMAL] ❑ By early yesterday, the insurgents had taken control of the country's main military air base.

in|sur|mount|able /ɪnsərmaʊntəbᵊl/ ADJ A problem that is **insurmountable** is so great that it cannot be dealt with successfully. ❑ The crisis doesn't seem like an insurmountable problem.

in|sur|rec|tion /ɪnsərɛkʃᵊn/ (insurrections) N-VAR An **insurrection** is violent action that is taken by a large group of people against the rulers of their country, usually in order to remove them from office. [FORMAL] ❑ They were plotting to stage an armed insurrection if negotiations with the government should fail.

int. **Int.** is an abbreviation for **internal** or for **international**.

in|tact /ɪntækt/ ADJ Something that is **intact** is complete and has not been damaged or changed. ❑ Customs men put dynamite in the water to destroy the cargo, but most of it was left intact.

in|take /ɪnteɪk/ (intakes) ◼ N-SING Your **intake** of a particular kind of food, drink, or air is the amount that you eat, drink, or breathe in. ❑ Your intake of alcohol should not exceed two units per day. ◼ N-COUNT The people who are accepted into an organization or place at a particular time are referred to as a particular **intake**. [BRIT] ❑ ...one of this year's intake of students.

in|tan|gible /ɪntændʒɪbəl/ (**intangibles**) ADJ Something that is **intangible** is abstract or is hard to define or measure. ☐ *...the intangible and non-material dimensions of our human and social existence.* • N-PLURAL You can refer to intangible things as **intangibles**. ☐ *That approach fails to take into consideration intangibles such as pride of workmanship, loyalty and good work habits.*

in|te|ger /ɪntɪdʒər/ (**integers**) N-COUNT In mathematics, an **integer** is an exact whole number such as 1, 7, or 24 as opposed to a number with fractions or decimals. [TECHNICAL]

in|te|gral /ɪntɪgrəl/ ADJ Something that is an **integral** part of something is an essential part of that thing. ☐ *Rituals, celebrations, and festivals form an integral part of every society.*

in|te|grate ✦◇◇ /ɪntɪgreɪt/ (**integrates, integrating, integrated**) **1** V-T/V-I If someone **integrates** into a social group, or **is integrated** into it, they behave in such a way that they become part of the group or are accepted into it. ☐ *He didn't integrate successfully into the Italian way of life.* ☐ *Integrating the kids with the community is essential.* • **in|te|grat|ed** ADJ ☐ *He thinks we are living in a fully integrated, supportive society.* • **in|te|gra|tion** /ɪntɪgreɪʃən/ N-UNCOUNT ☐ *Americans overwhelmingly support the integration of people with disabilities into mainstream society.* **2** V-T/V-I When races **integrate** or when schools and organizations **are integrated**, people who belong to ethnic minorities can join others in their schools and organizations. [AM] ☐ *The Marine Corps was the last service to integrate.* • **in|te|grat|ed** ADJ [ADJ n] ☐ *...a Black honor student in Chicago's integrated Lincoln Park High School.* • **in|te|gra|tion** N-UNCOUNT ☐ *Lots of people in Chicago see progress toward integration.* **3** V-RECIP If you **integrate** one thing with another, or one thing **integrates** with another, the two things become closely linked or form part of a whole idea or system. You can also say that two things **integrate**. ☐ *Writing about a topic helps you integrate new knowledge with what you already know.* ☐ *...historic landmarks that integrate with the community.* • **in|te|grat|ed** ADJ ☐ *There is, he said, a lack of an integrated national transportation policy.* • **in|te|gra|tion** N-UNCOUNT ☐ *With Germany, France has been the prime mover behind closer European integration.*

---SYNONYMS---
integrate
VERB **3**
combine: *Different states or groups can combine to enlarge their markets.*
unite: *The two parties have been trying to unite since the New Year.*
blend: *...a band that blended jazz, folk, and classical music.*
incorporate: *The party vowed to incorporate environmental considerations into all its policies.*
merge: *He sees sense in merging the two agencies while both are new.*

---

in|te|grat|ed /ɪntɪgreɪtɪd/ **1** ADJ An **integrated** institution is intended for use by all races or religious groups. ☐ *We believe that students of integrated schools will have more tolerant attitudes.* **2** → see also **integrate**

in|te|grat|ed cir|cuit (**integrated circuits**) N-COUNT An **integrated circuit** is a very small electronic circuit printed on a single silicon chip. [TECHNICAL]

in|teg|rity /ɪntɛgrɪti/ **1** N-UNCOUNT If you have **integrity**, you are honest and firm in your moral principles. ☐ *I have always regarded him as a man of integrity.* **2** N-UNCOUNT The **integrity** of something such as a group of people or a text is its state of being a united whole. [FORMAL] ☐ *Separatist movements are a threat to the integrity of the nation.*

in|tel /ɪntɛl/ **1** N-UNCOUNT **Intel** is military information collected about an enemy's secret plans. [INFORMAL] ☐ *What makes this intel credible?* **2** N-UNCOUNT **Intel** is information. [INFORMAL]

in|tel|lect /ɪntɪlɛkt/ (**intellects**) **1** N-VAR **Intellect** is the ability to understand or deal with ideas and information. ☐ *Do the emotions develop in parallel with the intellect?* **2** N-VAR **Intellect** is the quality of being intelligent. ☐ *She is famed for her intellect.*

in|tel|lec|tual ✦◇◇ /ɪntɪlɛktʃuəl/ (**intellectuals**) **1** ADJ [ADJ n] **Intellectual** means involving a person's ability to think and to understand ideas and information. ☐ *High levels of lead could damage the intellectual development of children.* • **in|tel|lec|tual|ly** ADV ☐ *...intellectually satisfying work.* **2** N-COUNT An **intellectual** is someone who spends a lot of time studying and thinking about complicated ideas. ☐ *Teachers, artists and other intellectuals urged political parties to launch a united movement against the government.* • ADJ **Intellectual** is also an adjective. ☐ *They were very intellectual and witty.*

---SYNONYMS---
intellectual
ADJ **1**
cerebral: *Hannah preferred more cerebral activities, such as reading and discussing philosophy.*
scholarly: *He was a scholarly man.*
learned: *He is a serious scholar, a genuinely learned man.*
academic: *The system is failing most disastrously among less academic children.*
erudite: *He was never dull, always erudite and well informed.*

---

in|tel|lec|tu|al|ize /ɪntɪlɛktʃuəlaɪz/ (**intellectualizes, intellectualizing, intellectualized**)

in BRIT, also use **intellectualise**

V-T If someone **intellectualizes** a subject or issue, they consider it in an intellectual way, often when this is not appropriate. ☐ *I tended to mistrust my emotions and intellectualize everything.*

in|tel|lec|tual prop|er|ty N-UNCOUNT **Intellectual property** is something such as an invention or a copyright which is officially owned by someone. ☐ *...music and films that are defined as intellectual property and owned by named individuals or companies.*

in|tel|li|gence ✦◇◇ /ɪntɛlɪdʒəns/ **1** N-UNCOUNT **Intelligence** is the quality of being intelligent or clever. ☐ *She's a woman of exceptional intelligence.* **2** N-UNCOUNT **Intelligence** is the ability to think, reason, and understand instead of doing things automatically or by instinct. ☐ *Nerve cells, after all, do not have intelligence of their own.* **3** N-UNCOUNT **Intelligence** is information that is gathered by the government or the army about their country's enemies and their activities. ☐ *Why was military intelligence so lacking?*

in|tel|li|gent ✦◇◇ /ɪntɛlɪdʒənt/ **1** ADJ A person or animal that is **intelligent** has the ability to think, understand, and learn things quickly and well. ☐ *Susan's a very bright and intelligent woman who knows her own mind.* • **in|tel|li|gent|ly** ADV ☐ *They are incapable of thinking intelligently about politics.* **2** ADJ Something that is **intelligent** can think and understand instead of doing things automatically or by instinct. ☐ *Intelligent computers will soon be an indispensable diagnostic tool for every doctor.*

---SYNONYMS---
intelligent
ADJ **1**
clever: *My sister was always a lot cleverer than I was.*
smart: *He thinks he's smarter than Sarah is.*
bright: *I was convinced that he was brighter than average.*
brainy: *I don't think of myself as being very intelligent or brainy.*

---

in|tel|li|gent|sia /ɪntɛlɪdʒɛntsiə/ N-SING-COLL [usu the N] The **intelligentsia** in a country or community are the most educated people there, especially those interested in the arts, philosophy, and politics.

in|tel|li|gi|ble /ɪntɛlɪdʒɪbəl/ ADJ Something that is **intelligible** can be understood. ☐ *The language of Darwin was intelligible to experts and non-experts alike.*

in|tem|per|ate /ɪntɛmpərɪt/ ADJ If you describe someone's words as **intemperate**, you are critical of them because they are too forceful and uncontrolled. [FORMAL, DISAPPROVAL] ☐ *The tone of the article is intemperate.*

in|tend ✦✦◇ /ɪntɛnd/ (**intends, intending, intended**) **1** V-T If you **intend** to do something, you have decided or planned to do it. ☐ *Maybe he intends to leave her.* ☐ *What do you intend doing when you get to this place?* **2** V-T [usu passive] If something **is intended** for a particular purpose, it has been planned to fulfill that purpose. If something **is intended** for a particular person, it has been planned to be used by that person or to affect them in some way. ☐ *This money is intended for the development of the tourist industry.* ☐ *Columns are usually intended in architecture to add grandeur and status.* **3** V-T If you **intend** a particular idea or feeling in something that you say or do, you want to express it or want it to be understood. ❑ *He didn't intend any sarcasm.* ❑ *Barzun's response seemed a little patronizing, though he undoubtedly hadn't intended it that way.*

SYNONYMS

intend
VERB **1**
plan: *He planned to leave Baghdad on Monday.*
aim: *...an appeal which aims to raise funds for children with special needs.*
mean: *I didn't mean to hurt you.*
propose: *And where do you propose building such a huge thing?*
seek: *He also denied that he would seek to annex the country.*

---

in|tend|ed /ɪntɛndɪd/ ADJ [ADJ n] You use **intended** to describe the thing you are trying to achieve or the person you are trying to affect. ❑ *The intended target had been a military building.*

in|tense ♦◇◇ /ɪntɛns/ **1** ADJ **Intense** is used to describe something that is very great or extreme in strength or degree. ❑ *He was sweating from the intense heat.* ❑ *Stevens's murder was the result of a deep-seated and intense hatred.* • **in|tense|ly** ADV ❑ *The fast-food business is intensely competitive.* • **in|ten|sity** /ɪntɛnsɪti/ (**intensities**) N-VAR ❑ *The attack was anticipated but its intensity came as a shock.* **2** ADJ If you describe an activity as **intense**, you mean that it is very serious and concentrated, and often involves doing a lot in a short time. ❑ *The battle for third place was intense.* **3** ADJ If you describe the way someone looks at you as **intense**, you mean that they look at you very directly and seem to know what you are thinking or feeling. ❑ *I felt so self-conscious under Luke's mother's intense gaze.* • **in|tense|ly** ADV [ADV with v] ❑ *He sipped his drink, staring intensely at me.* **4** ADJ If you describe a person as **intense**, you mean that they appear to concentrate very hard on everything that they do, and they feel their emotions very strongly. ❑ *I know he's an intense player, but he does enjoy what he's doing.* • **in|ten|sity** N-UNCOUNT ❑ *His intensity and the ferocity of his feelings alarmed me.*

SYNONYMS

intense
ADJ **1**
extreme: *...people living in extreme poverty.*
great: *I'll take great care of it.*
severe: *I suffered from severe bouts of depression.*
deep: *I had a deep admiration for Sartre.*
powerful: *...tiny creamy flowers with a powerful scent.*
profound: *Anna's patriotism was profound.*

---

in|ten|si|fi|er /ɪntɛnsɪfaɪər/ (**intensifiers**) N-COUNT In grammar, an **intensifier** is a word such as 'very' or 'extremely' that you can put in front of an adjective or adverb in order to make its meaning stronger. [TECHNICAL]

in|ten|si|fy /ɪntɛnsɪfaɪ/ (**intensifies, intensifying, intensified**) V-T/V-I If you **intensify** something or if it **intensifies**, it becomes greater in strength, amount, or degree. ❑ *I jump, intensifying the pain in all my muscles.*

in|ten|sive /ɪntɛnsɪv/ **1** ADJ **Intensive** activity involves concentrating a lot of effort or people on one particular task in order to try to achieve a lot in a short time. ❑ *...after several days and nights of intensive negotiations.* • **in|ten|sive|ly** ADV [ADV with v] ❑ *Caitlin's parents opted to educate her intensively at home.* **2** ADJ **Intensive** farming involves producing as many crops or animals as possible from your land, usually with the aid of chemicals. ❑ *...intensive methods of rearing poultry.* • **in|ten|sive|ly** ADV [ADV with v] ❑ *Will they farm the rest of their land less intensively?* **3** → See feature box at **farming, global warming**

-intensive /-ɪntɛnsɪv/ COMB IN ADJ **-intensive** combines with nouns to form adjectives that indicate that an industry or activity involves the use of a lot of a particular thing. ❑ *...the development of capital-intensive farming.*

in|ten|sive care N-UNCOUNT If someone is in **intensive care**, they are being looked after constantly in a hospital because they are extremely ill or very badly injured. ❑ *She spent the night in intensive care after the operation.*

in|ten|sive care unit (**intensive care units**) N-COUNT An **intensive care unit** is a part of a hospital where patients who are extremely ill or very badly injured are looked after constantly. The abbreviation **ICU** is often used. ❑ *He spent three days in the intensive care unit.*

in|tent /ɪntɛnt/ (**intents**) **1** ADJ [v-link ADJ on/upon -ing/n] If you are **intent** on doing something, you are eager and determined to do it. ❑ *The rebels are obviously intent on keeping up the pressure.* **2** ADJ If someone does something in an **intent** way, they pay great attention to what they are doing. [WRITTEN] ❑ *She looked from one intent face to another.* • **in|tent|ly** ADV [ADV after v] ❑ *He listened intently, then slammed down the phone.* **3** N-VAR A person's **intent** is their intention to do something. [FORMAL] ❑ *The timing of this strong statement of intent on arms control is crucial.* **4** PHRASE You say **to all intents and purposes** to suggest that a situation is not exactly as you describe it but the effect is the same as if it were. ❑ *To all intents and purposes he was my father.*

in|ten|tion ♦◇◇ /ɪntɛnʃ°n/ (**intentions**) **1** N-VAR An **intention** is an idea or plan of what you are going to do. ❑ *The company has every intention of keeping the share price high.* ❑ *It is my intention to remain in my position until a successor is elected.* **2** PHRASE If you say that you **have no intention of** doing something, you are emphasizing that you are not going to do it. If you say that you **have every intention of** doing something, you are emphasizing that you intend to do it. [EMPHASIS] ❑ *I have no intention of allowing you to continue living here alone.*

SYNONYMS

intention
NOUN **1**
aim: *...a research program that has largely failed to achieve its principal aims.*
plan: *The project is part of a United Nations plan for refugees.*
idea: *The idea is to encourage people to get to know their neighbors.*
goal: *The goal is to raise as much money as possible.*
wish: *She was sincere in her wish to make amends for the past.*
objective: *His objective was to play golf and win.*

---

in|ten|tion|al /ɪntɛnʃən°l/ ADJ Something that is **intentional** is deliberate. ❑ *Women who are the victims of intentional discrimination will be able to get compensation.* • **in|ten|tion|al|ly** ADV ❑ *I've never intentionally hurt anyone.*

in|ter /ɪntɜr/ (**inters, interring, interred**) V-T When a dead person **is interred**, they are buried. [FORMAL] ❑ *The team of archaeologists found the spot where his bones were originally interred.*

PREFIX

inter-
forms adjectives that refer to things that move, exist, or happen between two or more people or things. For example, *inter-city* trains travel between cities.

---

inter|act /ɪntəræct/ (**interacts, interacting, interacted**) **1** V-RECIP When people **interact** with each other or **interact**, they communicate as they work or spend time together. ❑ *While the other children interacted and played together, Ted ignored them.* • **inter|ac|tion** /ɪntəræsʃ°n/ (**interactions**) N-VAR ❑ *...superficial interactions with other people.* **2** V-I When people **interact** with computers, or when computers **interact** with other machines, information or instructions are exchanged. ❑ *...new, simplified ways of interacting with a computer.* • **inter|ac|tion** N-VAR ❑ *...experts on human-computer interaction.* **3** V-RECIP When one thing **interacts** with another or two things **interact**, the two things affect each other's behavior or condition. ❑ *You have to understand how cells interact.* • **inter|ac|tion** N-VAR ❑ *...the interaction between physical and emotional illness.* **4** → See feature box at **medicine, service, socialize**

inter|ac|tive /ɪntəræktɪv/ **1** ADJ An **interactive** computer program or electronic device is one that allows direct communication between the user and the machine. ❑ *This will make computer games more interactive than ever.* • **inter|ac|tiv|ity** /ɪntəræktɪvɪti/ N-UNCOUNT ❑ *...digital television, with more channels and interactivity.* **2** ADJ If you describe a group of people or their activities as **interactive**, you mean that the people communicate with each other. ❑ *There is little evidence that this encouraged flexible, interactive teaching in the classroom.*

in|ter alia /ɪntər eɪliə/ PHRASE [PHR with cl] You use **inter alia**, meaning 'among other things,' when you want to say that there are other things involved apart from the one you are mentioning. [FORMAL] ◻ ...*a collector who had, inter alia, 900 engraved gems, 59 marble busts, and over 2,500 coins and medals.*

inter|cede /ɪntərsid/ **(intercedes, interceding, interceded)** V-I If you **intercede** with someone, you try to persuade them to forgive someone or end their disagreement with them. [FORMAL] ◻ *They asked my father to intercede with the king on their behalf.* ◻ *It has also asked Britain and the United States to intercede.*

inter|cept /ɪntərsɛpt/ **(intercepts, intercepting, intercepted)** V-T If you **intercept** someone or something that is traveling from one place to another, you stop them before they get to their destination. ◻ *Gunmen intercepted him on his way to the airport.* • **inter|cep|tion** /ɪntərsɛpʃən/ **(interceptions)** N-VAR ◻ *...the interception of a ship off the coast of Oregon.*

inter|cep|tor /ɪntərsɛptər/ **(interceptors)** N-COUNT An **interceptor** is an aircraft or ground-based missile system designed to intercept and attack enemy planes.

inter|ces|sion /ɪntərsɛʃən/ **(intercessions)** N-VAR **Intercession** is the act of interceding with someone. [FORMAL] ◻ *His intercession could be of help to the tribe.*

inter|change (interchanges, interchanging, interchanged)

The noun is pronounced /ɪntərtʃeɪndʒ/. The verb is pronounced /ɪntərtʃeɪndʒ/.

1 N-VAR If there is an **interchange** of ideas or information among a group of people, each person talks about his or her ideas or gives information to the others. ◻ *What made the meeting exciting was the interchange of ideas from different disciplines.* **2** V-RECIP If you **interchange** one thing with another, or you **interchange** two things, each thing takes the place of the other or is exchanged for the other. You can also say that two things **interchange**. ◻ *You cannot interchange a "male" with a "female" electric plug.* ◻ *Your task is to interchange words so that the sentence makes sense.* • N-VAR **Interchange** is also a noun. ◻ *...the interchange of matter and energy at atomic or sub-atomic levels.* **3** N-COUNT An **interchange** on a highway, freeway, or road is a place where it joins a main road or another highway or freeway. ◻ *...Sudley Road in Manassas, near the interchange with Interstate 66.*

inter|change|able /ɪntərtʃeɪndʒəbəl/ ADJ Things that are **interchangeable** can be exchanged with each other without it making any difference. ◻ *His greatest innovation was the use of interchangeable parts.* • **inter|change|ably** ADV [ADV after v] ◻ *These expressions are often used interchangeably, but they do have different meanings.*

inter|col|legi|ate /ɪntərkəlidʒɪt, -dʒiɪt/ ADJ [ADJ n] **Intercollegiate** means involving or related to more than one college or university. [AM] ◻ *...the first intercollegiate gymnastics team championship.*

inter|com /ɪntərkɒm/ **(intercoms)** N-COUNT An **intercom** is a small box with a microphone that is connected to a loudspeaker in another room. You use it to talk to the people in the other room. ◻ *I pushed a button on my intercom and told Viktor Ilyushin that I needed to see him.*

inter|con|nect /ɪntərkənɛkt/ **(interconnects, interconnecting, interconnected)** V-RECIP Things that **interconnect** or **are interconnected** are connected to or with each other. You can also say that one thing **interconnects** with another. ◻ *The causes are many and may interconnect.*

inter|con|nec|tion /ɪntərkənɛkʃən/ **(interconnections)** N-VAR If you say that there is an **interconnection** between two or more things, you mean that they are very closely connected. [FORMAL] ◻ *We can now fully understand the interconnections between politics, economy, and society.*

inter|con|ti|nen|tal /ɪntərkɒntɪnɛntəl/ ADJ [ADJ n] **Intercontinental** is used to describe something that exists or happens between continents. ◻ *...intercontinental flights.*

inter|course /ɪntərkɔrs/ **1** N-UNCOUNT **Intercourse** is the act of having sex. [FORMAL] ◻ *...sexual intercourse.* **2** N-UNCOUNT Social **intercourse** is communication between people as they spend time together. [OLD-FASHIONED] ◻ *There was social intercourse between the old and the young.*

inter|cut /ɪntərkʌt/ **(intercuts, intercutting)**

The form **intercut** is used in the present tense and is the past tense and past participle.

V-T If a film **is intercut with** particular images, those images appear regularly throughout the film. [TECHNICAL] ◻ *The film is set in a night club and intercut with images of gangland Chicago.* ◻ *He intercuts scenes of Rex getting more and more desperate with scenes of the abductor with his family.*

inter|de|pend|ence /ɪntərdɪpɛndəns/ N-UNCOUNT **Interdependence** is the condition of a group of people or things that all depend on each other. ◻ *...the interdependence of nations.*

inter|de|pend|ent /ɪntərdɪpɛndənt/ ADJ People or things that are **interdependent** all depend on each other. ◻ *We live in an increasingly interdependent world.*

inter|dict /ɪntərdɪkt/ **(interdicts, interdicting, interdicted)** V-T If an armed force **interdicts** something or someone, they stop them and prevent them from moving. If they **interdict** a route, they block it or cut it off. [AM, FORMAL] ◻ *Troops could be ferried in to interdict drug shipments.*

inter|dis|ci|pli|nary /ɪntərdɪsɪplɪnɛri/ ADJ [usu ADJ n] **Interdisciplinary** means involving more than one academic subject. ◻ *...interdisciplinary courses combining psychology, philosophy and linguistics.*

in|ter|est ✦✦✦ /ɪntrɪst, -tərɪst/ **(interests, interesting, interested)** **1** N-UNCOUNT [also a N] If you have an **interest** in something, you want to learn or hear more about it. ◻ *There has been a lively interest in the elections in the last two weeks.* ◻ *She'd liked him at first, but soon lost interest.* **2** N-COUNT Your **interests** are the things that you enjoy doing. ◻ *Encourage your child in her interests and hobbies.* **3** V-T If something **interests** you, it attracts your attention so that you want to learn or hear more about it or continue doing it. ◻ *Your financial problems do not interest me.* **4** V-T If you are trying to persuade someone to buy or do something, you can say that you are trying to **interest** them in it. ◻ *Can I interest you in a new car?* **5** N-COUNT If something is in the **interests** of a particular person or group, it will benefit them in some way. ◻ *Did those directors act in the best interests of their club?* **6** N-COUNT You can use **interests** to refer to groups of people who you think use their power or money to benefit themselves. ◻ *The government accused unnamed "foreign interests" of inciting the trouble.* **7** N-COUNT A person or organization that has an **interest** in an area, a company, a property or in a particular type of business owns stock in it. [BUSINESS] ◻ *My father had many business interests in Vietnam.* **8** N-COUNT If a person, country, or organization has an **interest** in a possible event or situation, they want that event or situation to happen because they are likely to benefit from it. ◻ *He had an interest in pushing for the company to be floated.* **9** N-UNCOUNT **Interest** is extra money that you receive if you have invested a sum of money. **Interest** is also the extra money that you pay if you have borrowed money or are buying something on credit. ◻ *Does your checking account pay interest?* **10** → see also **interested, interesting, compound interest, self-interest, vested interest** **11** PHRASE If you do something **in the interests of** a particular result or situation, you do it in order to achieve that result or maintain that situation. ◻ *...a call for all businessmen to work together in the interests of national stability.* **12 to have someone's interests at heart** → see **heart** ② **13** → See feature box at **finance**

COLLOCATIONS

interest
NOUN
1
adjective + **interest**: keen
verb + **interest**: express, show, take; arouse, attract; lose
5
verb + **interest**: defend, protect, safeguard

---

in|ter|est|ed ✦✦ /ɪntərɛstɪd, -trɪstɪd/ **1** ADJ If you are **interested** in something, you think it is important and want to learn more about it or spend time doing it. ◻ *I thought she might be interested in Paula's proposal.* **2** ADJ [ADJ n] An **interested** party or group of people is affected by or involved in a particular event or situation. ◻ *The success was only possible because all the interested parties eventually agreed to the idea.* **3** ADJ [usu v-link ADJ in n] If you say that one person is **interested** in another person, you mean that the first person would like to have a romantic or sexual relationship with the other person. ❏ *I heard there are a lot of guys interested in her.*

SYNONYMS

interested
ADJ **1**
curious: *Children are naturally curious.*
fascinated: *A new generation of scientists became fascinated by dinosaurs.*
keen: *I wasn't too keen on physics and chemistry.*
gripped: *The nation is gripped by the dramatic story.*
intent: *Rodney had been intent on his work.*

interest-free ADJ An **interest-free** loan has no interest charged on it. ❏ *He was offered a $10,000 interest-free loan.* • ADV [ADV after v] **Interest-free** is also an adverb. ❏ *Customers allowed the banks to use their money interest-free.*

in|ter|est|ing ♦◇◇ /ɪntərestɪŋ, -trɪstɪŋ/ ADJ If you find something **interesting**, it attracts your attention, for example, because you think it is exciting or unusual. ❏ *It was interesting to be in a different environment.*

SYNONYMS

interesting
ADJ
absorbing: *Children will find other exhibits equally absorbing.*
fascinating: *Madagascar is the most fascinating place I have ever been to.*
compelling: *...a frighteningly-violent yet compelling film.*
gripping: *The film turned out to be a gripping thriller.*
curious: *There is a curious thing about her writings in this period.*
intriguing: *This intriguing book is both thoughtful and informative.*

in|ter|est|ing|ly /ɪntərestɪŋli, -trɪstɪŋli/ ADV [ADV with cl] You use **interestingly** to introduce a piece of information that you think is interesting or unexpected. ❏ *Interestingly enough, a few weeks later, Benjamin remarried.*

in|ter|est rate (interest rates) **1** N-COUNT The **interest rate** is the amount of interest that must be paid. It is expressed as a percentage of the amount that is borrowed or gained as profit. [BUSINESS] ❏ *The Federal Reserve lowered interest rates by half a point.* **2** → See feature box at **finance**

inter|face /ɪntərfeɪs/ (interfaces, interfacing, interfaced)
1 N-COUNT The **interface** between two subjects or systems is the area in which they affect each other or have links with each other. ❏ *...a witty exploration of that interface between bureaucracy and the working world.* **2** N-COUNT The user **interface** of a particular piece of computer software is its presentation on the screen and how easy it is to operate. [COMPUTING] ❏ *...the development of better user interfaces.* **3** V-RECIP If one thing **interfaces** with another, or if two things **interface**, they have connections with each other. If you **interface** one thing with another, you connect the two things. [FORMAL] ❏ *...the way we interface with the environment.* ❏ *He had interfaced all this machinery with a master computer.*

inter|faith /ɪntərfeɪθ/ ADJ [usu ADJ n] **Interfaith** means involving more than one religion. ❏ *He took part in an interfaith conference.*

inter|fere /ɪntərfɪər/ (interferes, interfering, interfered)
1 V-I If you say that someone **interferes** in a situation, you mean they get involved in it although it does not concern them and their involvement is not wanted. [DISAPPROVAL] ❏ *I wish everyone would stop interfering and just leave me alone.*
2 V-I Something that **interferes with** a situation, activity, or process has a damaging effect on it. ❏ *Drinks such as tea, coffee and cola, all of which contain caffeine, may interfere with your ability to sleep.*

inter|fer|ence /ɪntərfɪərəns/ **1** N-UNCOUNT **Interference** by a person or group is their unwanted or unnecessary involvement in something. [DISAPPROVAL] ❏ *Airlines will be able to set cheap fares without further interference from the government.*
2 N-UNCOUNT When there is **interference**, a radio signal is affected by other radio waves or electrical activity so that it cannot be received properly. ❏ *...electrical interference.*

inter|fer|ing /ɪntərfɪərɪŋ/ ADJ [ADJ n] If you describe someone as **interfering**, you are criticizing them because they try to get involved in other people's affairs or to give them advice, especially when the advice is not wanted. [DISAPPROVAL] ❏ *...interfering neighbors.*

inter|ga|lac|tic /ɪntərgəlæktɪk/ ADJ [ADJ n] **Intergalactic** space travel is travel between different galaxies. ❏ *Intergalactic travel remains just a nice idea.*

in|ter|im ♦◇◇ /ɪntərɪm/ **1** ADJ [ADJ n] **Interim** is used to describe something that is intended to be used until something permanent is done or established. ❏ *She was sworn in as head of an interim government in March.* **2** PHRASE **In the interim** means until a particular thing happens or until a particular thing happened. [FORMAL] ❏ *But, in the interim, we obviously have a duty to maintain law and order.*

SYNONYMS

interim
ADJ **1**
temporary: *His job here is only temporary.*
provisional: *...the possibility of setting up a provisional coalition government.*
makeshift: *...the cardboard boxes and makeshift shelters of the homeless.*
acting: *...the new, acting President.*
stopgap: *This would be no more than a stopgap measure.*

in|te|ri|or ♦◇◇ /ɪntɪəriər/ (interiors) **1** N-COUNT The **interior** of something is the inside part of it. ❏ *The interior of the house was furnished with heavy, old-fashioned pieces.* **2** ADJ [ADJ n] You use **interior** to describe something that is inside a building or vehicle. ❏ *The interior walls were painted green.* **3** N-SING The **interior** of a country or continent is the central area of it.
❏ *The Yangtze River would give access to much of China's interior.* **4** ADJ [ADJ n] An **interior** minister, ministry, or department in some countries deals with affairs within that country, such as law and order. ❏ *The French Interior Minister has intervened in a scandal over the role of a secret police force.*

SYNONYMS

interior
NOUN **1**
inside: *I painted the inside of the house.*
center: *A large, wooden table dominates the center of the room.*
heart: *...a busy, dentists' practice in the heart of London's West End.*
middle: *Howard stood in the middle of the room, sipping a cup of coffee.*
core: *...the earth's core.*

in|te|ri|or deco|ra|tion N-UNCOUNT **Interior decoration** is the decoration of the inside of a house.

in|te|ri|or deco|ra|tor (interior decorators) N-COUNT An **interior decorator** is a person who is employed to decorate the inside of people's houses.

in|te|ri|or de|sign N-UNCOUNT **Interior design** is the art or profession of designing the decoration for the inside of a house.

in|te|ri|or de|sign|er (interior designers) N-COUNT An **interior designer** is a person who is employed to design the decoration for the inside of people's houses.

inter|ject /ɪntərdʒɛkt/ (interjects, interjecting, interjected)
V-T/V-I If you **interject**, or **interject** something, you say it and interrupt someone else who is speaking. [FORMAL] ❏ *"Surely there's something we can do?" interjected Wahid.* ❏ *He listened thoughtfully, interjecting only the odd word.*

inter|jec|tion /ɪntərdʒɛkʃən/ (interjections) **1** N-COUNT An **interjection** is something you say that interrupts someone else who is speaking. ❏ *...the moronic and insensitive interjections of the disc jockey.* **2** N-COUNT In grammar, an **interjection** is a word or expression that expresses a strong feeling such as surprise, pain, or horror.

inter|laced /ɪntərleɪst/ ADJ [oft ADJ with n] If things are **interlaced**, parts of one thing go over, under, or between parts of another. [WRITTEN] ❏ *During my whole report, he sat with his eyes closed and his fingers interlaced.* ❏ *...a pattern of flowers interlaced with vines.*

inter|link /ɪntərlɪŋk/ (interlinks, interlinking, interlinked)
V-RECIP Things that **are interlinked** or **interlink** are linked with each other in some way. ❏ *Those two processes are very closely interlinked.* ❏ *The question to be addressed is interlinked with the*

question of human rights. ❑ ...a more integrated transportation network, with bus, rail, and ferry services all interlinking.

inter|lock /ɪntərlɒk/ (interlocks, interlocking, interlocked) **1** V-RECIP Things that **interlock** or **are interlocked** go between or through each other so that they are linked. ❑ *The parts interlock.* ❑ *Interlock your fingers behind your back.* **2** V-RECIP If systems, situations, or plans **are interlocked** or **interlock**, they are very closely connected. ❑ *...a time when the destinies of all participating nations are interlocked.* ❑ *The tragedies begin to interlock.* ❑ *Your girlfriend's fear seems to interlock with your fear.*

inter|locu|tor /ɪntərlɒkyətər/ (interlocutors) **1** N-COUNT [oft poss N] Your **interlocutor** is the person with whom you are having a conversation. [FORMAL] ❑ *Orion had the habit of staring motionlessly at his interlocutor.* **2** N-COUNT If a person or organization has a role as an **interlocutor** in talks or negotiations, they take part or act as a representative of them. [FORMAL] ❑ *...key interlocutors in the Middle East conference.*

inter|lop|er /ɪntərloʊpər/ (interlopers) N-COUNT If you describe someone as an **interloper**, you mean that they have come into a situation or a place where they are not wanted or do not belong. [DISAPPROVAL] ❑ *She had no wish to share her father with any outsider and regarded us as interlopers.*

inter|lude /ɪntərlud/ (interludes) N-COUNT An **interlude** is a short period of time when an activity or situation stops and something else happens.

inter|mar|riage /ɪntərmærɪdʒ/ N-UNCOUNT **Intermarriage** is marriage between people from different social, racial, or religious groups. ❑ *...intermarriage between members of the old and new ruling classes.*

inter|mar|ry /ɪntərmæri/ (intermarries, intermarrying, intermarried) V-RECIP When people from different social, racial, or religious groups **intermarry**, they marry each other. You can also say that one group **intermarries** with another group. ❑ *They were allowed to intermarry.* ❑ *Some of the traders settled and intermarried with local women.*

inter|medi|ary /ɪntərmidieri/ (intermediaries) N-COUNT An **intermediary** is a person who passes messages or proposals between two people or groups. ❑ *She wanted him to act as an intermediary in the dispute with Moscow.*

inter|medi|ate /ɪntərmidiɪt/ (intermediates) **1** ADJ An **intermediate** stage, level, or position is one that occurs between two other stages, levels, or positions. ❑ *Do you make any intermediate stops between your home and work?* **2** ADJ **Intermediate** learners of something have some knowledge or skill but are not yet advanced. ❑ *Students are categorized as novice, intermediate, or advanced.* • N-COUNT An **intermediate** is an intermediate learner. ❑ *The ski school coaches beginners, intermediates, and advanced skiers.*

in|ter|ment /ɪntɜrmənt/ (interments) N-VAR The **interment** of a dead person is their burial. [FORMAL]

in|ter|mi|nable /ɪntɜrmɪnəbəl/ ADJ If you describe something as **interminable**, you are emphasizing that it continues for a very long time and indicating that you wish it was shorter or would stop. [EMPHASIS] ❑ *...an interminable meeting.* • **in|ter|mi|nably** ADV ❑ *He talked to me interminably about his first wife.*

inter|min|gle /ɪntərmɪŋgəl/ (intermingles, intermingling, intermingled) V-RECIP When people or things **intermingle**, they mix with each other. [FORMAL] ❑ *This allows the two cultures to intermingle without losing their separate identities.* ❑ *...an opportunity for them to intermingle with the citizens of other countries.* • **inter|min|gled** ADJ [usu v-link ADJ] ❑ *The ethnic populations are so intermingled that there's bound to be conflict.*

inter|mis|sion /ɪntərmɪʃən/ (intermissions) **1** N-COUNT An **intermission** is a short break between two parts of a concert, show, or movie. ❑ *...during the intermission of the musical "Steppin' Out."* **2** N-COUNT You can use **intermission** to refer to a short break between two parts of a game, or say that something happens at, after, or during the **intermission**. ❑ *Fraser did not perform until after the intermission.*

inter|mit|tent /ɪntərmɪtənt/ ADJ Something that is **intermittent** happens occasionally rather than continuously. ❑ *After three hours of intermittent rain, the game was abandoned.* • **inter|mit|tent|ly** ADV ❑ *The talks went on intermittently for three years.*

in|tern (interns, interning, interned)

The verb is pronounced /ɪntɜrn/. The noun is pronounced /ɪntɜrn/.

1 V-T [usu passive] If someone **is interned**, they are put in prison or in a prison camp for political reasons. ❑ *He was interned as an enemy alien at the outbreak of the Second World War.* **2** N-COUNT An **intern** is an advanced student or a recent graduate, especially in medicine, who is being given practical training under supervision. [AM] ❑ *...a medical intern.*

in|ter|nal ✦◇◇ /ɪntɜrnəl/ **1** ADJ [ADJ n] **Internal** is used to describe things that exist or happen inside a country or organization. ❑ *The country stepped up internal security.* ❑ *...Russia's Ministry of Internal Affairs.* • **in|ter|nal|ly** ADV ❑ *The state is not a unified and internally coherent entity.* **2** ADJ [ADJ n] **Internal** is used to describe things that exist or happen inside a particular person, object, or place. ❑ *The doctor said the internal bleeding had been massive.* • **in|ter|nal|ly** ADV ❑ *Evening primrose oil is used on the skin as well as taken internally.*

━━━━━ **SYNONYMS** ━━━━━
internal
ADJ **2**
inner: *She got up and went into an inner office.*
inside: *...four-berth inside cabins with en-suite bathroom and shower.*
interior: *The interior walls were painted green.*

in|ter|nal com|bus|tion en|gine (internal combustion engines) N-COUNT An **internal combustion engine** is an engine, used in many cars, that creates its energy by burning fuel inside itself.

in|ter|nal|ize /ɪntɜrnəlaɪz/ (internalizes, internalizing, internalized)

in BRIT, also use **internalise**

V-T If you **internalize** something such as a belief or a set of values, you make it become part of your attitude or way of thinking. [FORMAL] ❑ *Over time she internalized her parents' attitudes.* • **in|ter|nali|za|tion** /ɪntɜrnəlɪzeɪʃən/ N-UNCOUNT [usu with poss] ❑ *...my internalization of hatred, disgust and fear.*

In|ter|nal Rev|enue Ser|vice N-PROPER [the N] **The Internal Revenue Service** is the U.S. government authority that collects taxes. The abbreviation **IRS** is often used.

inter|nation|al ✦✦✦ /ɪntərnæʃənəl/ **1** ADJ **International** means between or involving different countries. ❑ *...an international agreement against exporting arms to that country.* • **inter|na|tion|al|ly** ADV ❑ *...internationally agreed-upon rules.* **2** → See feature box at **space**

inter|na|tion|al|ism /ɪntərnæʃənəlɪzəm/ N-UNCOUNT **Internationalism** is the belief that countries should work with, help, and be friendly with one another.

Inter|na|tion|al|ist /ɪntərnæʃənəlɪst/ (internationalists) ADJ If someone has **internationalist** beliefs or opinions, they believe that countries should work with, help, and be friendly with one another. ❑ *...a more genuinely internationalist view of U.S. participation in peacekeeping.*

inter|na|tion|al|ize /ɪntərnæʃənəlaɪz/ (internationalizes, internationalizing, internationalized)

in BRIT, also use **internationalise**

V-T If an issue or a crisis is **internationalized**, it becomes the concern of many nations throughout the world. [JOURNALISM] ❑ *A danger exists of the conflict becoming internationalized.* ❑ *The administration is on the right course by helping to internationalize the problem.* • **inter|na|tion|ali|za|tion** /ɪntərnæʃənəlɪzeɪʃən/ N-UNCOUNT ❑ *...the increasing internationalization of business.*

inter|na|tion|al re|la|tions N-PLURAL The political relationships between different countries are referred to as **international relations**. ❑ *...peaceful and friendly international relations.*

inter|necine /ɪntərnisin, -nesin/ ADJ [ADJ n] An **internecine** conflict, war, or fight is one which takes place between opposing groups within a country or organization. [FORMAL]

in|ter|nee /ɪntɜrni/ (internees) N-COUNT An **internee** is a person who has been put in prison for political reasons.

in|ter|net /ˈɪntərnɛt/ also **Internet** **1** N-PROPER The **internet** is the network that allows computer users to connect with computers all over the world, and that carries email. **2** → See feature box at **email**

in|ter|net café (internet cafés) N-COUNT An **internet café** is a café with computers where people can pay to use the internet.

in|tern|ist /ˈɪntɜrnɪst/ (internists) N-COUNT An **internist** is a doctor who specializes in the nonsurgical treatment of disorders occurring inside people's bodies. [AM] ❑ *I've been to see an internist, a nutritionist, and a chiropractor.*

in|tern|ment /ɪntˈɜrnmənt/ N-UNCOUNT **Internment** is the practice of putting people in prison for political reasons. ❑ *They called for the return of internment without trial for terrorists.*

in|tern|ship /ˈɪntɜrnʃɪp/ (internships) N-COUNT An **internship** is the position held by an intern, or the period of time when someone is an intern. [AM] ❑ *...an internship in surgery in New York.*

inter|per|son|al /ˌɪntərpˈɜrsənəl/ ADJ [ADJ n] **Interpersonal** means relating to relationships between people. ❑ *Training in interpersonal skills is essential.*

inter|plan|etary /ˌɪntərplˈænɪtɛri/ ADJ [ADJ n] **Interplanetary** space travel is travel between different planets. ❑ *...an unmanned rocket scheduled to head toward the sun, to a point in interplanetary space a million miles away.*

inter|play /ˈɪntərpleɪ/ N-UNCOUNT [usu N between/of pl-n] The **interplay** between two or more things or people is the way that they have an effect on each other or react to each other. ❑ *...the interplay of political, economic, social and cultural factors.*

in|ter|po|late /ɪntˈɜrpəleɪt/ (interpolates, interpolating, interpolated) **1** V-T If you **interpolate** a comment into a conversation or some words into a piece of writing, you put it in as an addition. [FORMAL] ❑ *He started humming a tune, then interpolated the odd word as though having difficulty remembering.* ❑ *These odd assertions were interpolated into the manuscript some time after 1400.* **2** V-T/V-I To **interpolate** means to estimate the value of a function between two known values. [TECHNICAL]

in|ter|po|la|tion /ɪntˌɜrpəlˈeɪʃən/ (interpolations) N-COUNT An **interpolation** is an addition to a piece of writing. [FORMAL] ❑ *The interpolation appears to have been inserted very soon after the original text was finished.*

inter|pose /ˌɪntərpˈoʊz/ (interposes, interposing, interposed) V-T If you **interpose** something between two people or things, you place it between them. [FORMAL] ❑ *Police had to interpose themselves between the two rival groups.* ❑ *What happens if you interpose a glass plate between two mirrors?*

in|ter|pret /ɪntˈɜrprɪt/ (interprets, interpreting, interpreted) **1** V-T If you **interpret** something in a particular way, you decide that this is its meaning or significance. ❑ *The fact that they had decided to come was interpreted as a positive sign.* ❑ *The judge quite rightly says that he has to interpret the law as it's been passed.* **2** V-T/V-I If you **interpret** what someone is saying, you translate it immediately into another language. ❑ *The chambermaid spoke little English, so her husband came with her to interpret.*

in|ter|pre|ta|tion /ɪntˌɜrprɪtˈeɪʃən/ (interpretations) **1** N-VAR An **interpretation** of something is an opinion about what it means. ❑ *Professor Wolfgang gives the data a very different interpretation.* **2** N-COUNT A performer's **interpretation** of something such as a piece of music or a role in a play is the particular way in which they choose to perform it. ❑ *...a pianist celebrated for his interpretation of Chopin.*

in|ter|pret|er /ɪntˈɜrprɪtər/ (interpreters) N-COUNT An **interpreter** is a person whose job is to translate what someone is saying into another language. ❑ *Speaking through an interpreter, Aristide said that Haitians had hoped coups were behind them.*

in|ter|pre|tive /ɪntˈɜrprɪtɪv/ ADJ [ADJ n] You use **interpretive** to describe something that provides an interpretation. [FORMAL] ❑ *History is an interpretive process.*

inter|reg|num /ˌɪntərrˈɛgnəm/ N-SING An **interregnum** is a period between the end of one person's time as ruler or leader and the coming to power of the next ruler or leader. [FORMAL]

inter|re|late /ˌɪntərrɪlˈeɪt/ (interrelates, interrelating, interrelated) V-RECIP If two or more things **interrelate**, there is a connection between them and they have an effect on each other. ❑ *The body and the mind interrelate.* ❑ *Each of these cells have their specific jobs to do, but they also interrelate with each other.* ❑ *...the way in which we communicate and interrelate with others.* ❑ *All things are interrelated.*

inter|re|la|tion|ship /ˌɪntərrɪlˈeɪʃənʃɪp/ (interrelationships) N-COUNT [oft N between/of pl-n] An **interrelationship** is a close relationship between two or more things or people. ❑ *...the interrelationships between unemployment, crime, and imprisonment.*

in|ter|ro|gate /ɪntˈɛrəgeɪt/ (interrogates, interrogating, interrogated) V-T If someone, especially a police officer, **interrogates** someone, they question them thoroughly for a long time in order to get some information from them. ❑ *I interrogated everyone even slightly involved.*

in|ter|ro|ga|tion /ɪntˌɛrəgˈeɪʃən/ (interrogations) N-VAR An **interrogation** is the act of interrogating someone. ❑ *...the right to silence in police interrogations.*

in|ter|roga|tive /ˌɪntərrˈɒgətɪv/ (interrogatives) **1** ADJ [usu ADJ n] An **interrogative** gesture or tone of voice shows that you want to know the answer to a question. [WRITTEN] ❑ *He made a further interrogative noise.* **2** N-SING [the N] In grammar, a clause that is in **the interrogative**, or in the **interrogative** mood, has its subject following 'do,' 'be,' 'have,' or a modal verb. Examples are 'When did she get back?' and 'Are you all right?' Clauses of this kind are typically used to ask questions. **3** N-COUNT In grammar, an **interrogative** is a word such as 'who,' 'how,' or 'why,' which can be used to ask a question.

in|ter|rupt /ˌɪntərˈʌpt/ (interrupts, interrupting, interrupted) **1** V-T/V-I If you **interrupt** someone who is speaking, you say or do something that causes them to stop. ❑ *Turkin tapped him on the shoulder. "Sorry to interrupt, Colonel."* • **in|ter|rup|tion** /ˌɪntərˈʌpʃən/ (interruptions) N-VAR ❑ *The sudden interruption stopped Justin in mid-sentence.* **2** V-T If someone or something **interrupts** a process or activity, they stop it for a period of time. ❑ *People kept nosing around the place, interrupting my work.* • **in|ter|rup|tion** N-VAR ❑ *...interruptions in the supply of food and fuel.* **3** V-T If something **interrupts** a line, surface, or view, it stops it from being continuous or makes it look irregular. ❑ *Taller plants interrupt the views from the house.*

inter|sect /ˌɪntərsˈɛkt/ (intersects, intersecting, intersected) **1** V-RECIP If two or more lines or roads **intersect**, they meet or cross each other. You can also say that one line or road **intersects** another. ❑ *The orbit of this comet intersects the orbit of the Earth.* **2** V-RECIP If one thing **intersects** with another or if two things **intersect**, the two things connect at a particular point. ❑ *...the ways in which historical events intersect with individual lives.*

inter|sec|tion /ˌɪntərsˈɛkʃən/ (intersections) N-COUNT An **intersection** is a place where roads or other lines meet or cross. ❑ *We crossed at a busy intersection.*

inter|sec|tion|al /ˌɪntərsˈɛkʃənəl/ ADJ **Intersectional** problems result from a person belonging to a number of social groups according to, for example, their race, gender, or class, which combine to create disadvantage or discrimination ❑ *This is about the intersectional oppression suffered each and every day by people from the LGBTQ community.*

inter|sex /ˈɪntərsɛks/ ADJ An **intersex** person has genitals or other sexual characteristics that do not clearly fit the usual definition for a male or female body. ❑ *...the controversy surrounding intersex athletes.*

inter|sperse /ˌɪntərspˈɜrs/ (intersperses, interspersing, interspersed) V-T If you **intersperse** one group of things with another or **among** another, you put or include the second things between or among the first things. ❑ *Originally the intention was to intersperse the historical scenes with modern ones.*

inter|spersed /ˌɪntərspˈɜrst/ ADJ [v-link ADJ prep] If one group of things is **interspersed with** another or **interspersed among** another, the second things occur between or among the first things. ❑ *...a series of bursts of gunfire, interspersed with single shots.*

inter|state /ˈɪntərsteɪt/ (interstates) **1** ADJ [ADJ n] **Interstate** means between states, especially the states of the United States. ❑ *...interstate commerce.* **2** N-COUNT [also N num] An **interstate** or **interstate highway** is a major road linking states. ❑ *...the southbound lane of Interstate 75.*

inter|stel|lar /ˌɪntərstˈɛlər/ ADJ [ADJ n] **Interstellar** means between the stars. [FORMAL] ❑ *...interstellar space.*

inter|twine /ɪntətwaɪn/ (intertwines, intertwining, intertwined) ◼ V-RECIP If two or more things **are intertwined** or **intertwine**, they are closely connected with each other in many ways. ❑ *Their destinies are intertwined.* ❑ *Three major narratives intertwine within Foucault's text, "Madness and Civilization."* ❑ *An attempt was made to intertwine the amusing with the educational.* ❑ *Her fate intertwined with his.* ◼ V-RECIP If two things **intertwine**, they are twisted together or go over and under each other. ❑ *Trees, undergrowth and creepers intertwined, blocking our way.* ❑ *The towels were embroidered with their intertwined initials.*

inter|val /ɪntəvəl/ (intervals) ◼ N-COUNT An **interval** between two events or dates is the period of time between them. ❑ *The process is repeated after a short interval of time.* ◼ N-COUNT An **interval** during a concert, show, movie, or game is a short break between two of the parts. [mainly BRIT]

> in AM, usually use **intermission**

◼ PHRASE If something happens **at intervals**, it happens several times with gaps or pauses in between. ❑ *She woke him for his medicines at intervals throughout the night.* ◼ PHRASE If things are placed **at** particular **intervals**, there are spaces of a particular size between them. ❑ *Several red and white barriers marked the road at intervals of about a mile.*

inter|vene /ɪntəvin/ (intervenes, intervening, intervened) ◼ V-I If you **intervene** in a situation, you become involved in it and try to change it. ❑ *The situation calmed down when police intervened.* ◼ V-I If you **intervene**, you interrupt a conversation in order to add something to it. ❑ *Hernandez intervened and told me to stop it.* ◼ V-I If an event **intervenes**, it happens suddenly in a way that stops, delays, or prevents something from happening. ❑ *The mailboat arrived on Friday mornings unless bad weather intervened.*

inter|ven|ing /ɪntəvinɪŋ/ ◼ ADJ [ADJ n] An **intervening** period of time is one that separates two events or points in time. ❑ *During those intervening years Bridget had married her husband Robert.* ◼ ADJ [ADJ n] An **intervening** object or area comes between two other objects or areas. ❑ *They had scoured the intervening miles of desert.*

inter|ven|tion ✦◇◇ /ɪntəvɛnʃən/ (interventions) N-VAR **Intervention** is the act of intervening in a situation. ❑ *...the role of the United States and its intervention in the internal affairs of many countries.*

inter|ven|tion|ist /ɪntəvɛnʃənɪst/ (interventionists) ADJ **Interventionist** policies are policies that show an organization's desire to become involved in a problem or a crisis that does not concern it directly. [JOURNALISM] ❑ *...Roosevelt's interventionist policy.* • N-COUNT An **interventionist** is someone who supports interventionist policies. [JOURNALISM]

inter|view ✦◆◇ /ɪntəvyu/ (interviews, interviewing, interviewed) ◼ N-VAR An **interview** is a formal meeting at which someone is asked questions in order to find out if they are suitable for a job or school. ❑ *The interview went well.* ◼ V-T [usu passive] If you **are interviewed** for a particular job or school, someone asks you questions about yourself to find out if you are suitable for it. ❑ *When Wardell was interviewed, he was impressive, and on that basis, he was hired.* ◼ N-COUNT An **interview** is a conversation in which a journalist puts questions to someone such as a famous person or politician. ❑ *The trouble began when Allan gave an interview to the Chicago Tribune last month.* ◼ V-T When a journalist **interviews** someone such as a famous person, they ask them a series of questions. ❑ *I'd interviewed him often in the past.* ◼ V-T When the police **interview** someone, they ask them questions about a crime that has been committed. ❑ *The police interviewed the driver, but had no evidence to go on.* ◼ → See feature box at **research**

inter|view|ee /ɪntəvyui/ (interviewees) N-COUNT An **interviewee** is a person who is being interviewed. ❑ *Is there any interviewee who stands out as memorable?*

inter|view|er ✦◇◇ /ɪntəvyuər/ (interviewers) N-COUNT An **interviewer** is the person who is asking someone questions at an interview. ❑ *Being a good interviewer, however, requires much preparation and skill.*

inter|weave /ɪntəwiv/ (interweaves, interweaving, interwove, interwoven) V-RECIP If two or more things **are interwoven** or **interweave**, they are very closely connected or are combined with each other. ❑ *For these people, land is inextricably interwoven with life itself.* ❑ *Complex family relationships interweave successfully with a murder plot in this ambitious new novel.* ❑ *The program successfully interweaves words and pictures.* ❑ *Social structures are not discrete objects; they overlap and interweave.*

in|tes|ti|nal /ɪntɛstɪnəl/ ADJ [ADJ n] **Intestinal** means relating to the intestines. [FORMAL]

in|tes|tine /ɪntɛstɪn/ (intestines) ◼ N-COUNT Your **intestines** are the tubes in your body through which food passes when it has left your stomach. ❑ *This area is always tender to the touch if the intestines are not functioning properly.* ◼ → See feature box at **body**; See also color supplement

in|ti|ma|cy /ɪntɪməsi/ ◼ N-UNCOUNT **Intimacy** between two people is a very close personal relationship between them. ❑ *...a means of achieving intimacy with another person.* ◼ N-UNCOUNT People sometimes use **intimacy** to refer to sex or a sexual relationship. ❑ *He did not feel like intimacy with anyone.*

in|ti|mate (intimates, intimating, intimated)

> The adjective is pronounced /ɪntɪmət/. The verb is pronounced /ɪntɪmeɪt/.

◼ ADJ If you have an **intimate** friendship with someone, you know them very well and like them a lot. ❑ *I discussed with my intimate friends whether I would immediately have a baby.* • **in|ti|mate|ly** ADV ❑ *He did not feel he had gotten to know them intimately.* ◼ ADJ If two people are in an **intimate** relationship, they are involved with each other in a loving or sexual way. ❑ *...their intimate moments with their boyfriends.* • **in|ti|mate|ly** ADV [ADV after v] ❑ *You have to be willing to get to know yourself and your partner intimately.* ◼ ADJ An **intimate** conversation or detail, for example, is very personal and private. ❑ *He wrote about the intimate details of his family life.* • **in|ti|mate|ly** ADV [ADV after v] ❑ *It was the first time they had attempted to talk intimately.* ◼ ADJ If you use **intimate** to describe an occasion or the atmosphere of a place, you like it because it is quiet and pleasant, and seems suitable for close conversations between friends. [APPROVAL] ❑ *...an intimate candlelit dinner for two.* ◼ ADJ An **intimate** connection between ideas or organizations, for example, is a very strong link between them. ❑ *...an intimate connection between madness and wisdom.* • **in|ti|mate|ly** ADV [ADV after v] ❑ *Scientific research and conservation are intimately connected.* ◼ ADJ An **intimate** knowledge of something is a deep and detailed knowledge of it. ❑ *He surprised me with his intimate knowledge of Kierkegaard and Schopenhauer.* • **in|ti|mate|ly** ADV ❑ *...a golden age of musicians whose work she knew intimately.* ◼ V-T If you **intimate** something, you say it in an indirect way. [FORMAL] ❑ *He went on to intimate that he was indeed contemplating a shake-up of the company.* ◼ → See feature box at **relationship**

in|ti|ma|tion /ɪntɪmeɪʃən/ (intimations) N-COUNT [usu N of n, N that] An **intimation** is an indirect suggestion or sign that something is likely to happen or be true. [FORMAL] ❑ *I did not have any intimation that he was going to resign.*

in|timi|date /ɪntɪmɪdeɪt/ (intimidates, intimidating, intimidated) V-T If you **intimidate** someone, you deliberately make them frightened enough to do what you want them to do. ❑ *Jones had set out to intimidate and dominate Paul.* • **in|timi|da|tion** /ɪntɪmɪdeɪʃən/ N-UNCOUNT ❑ *...an inquiry into allegations of intimidation during last week's vote.*

in|timi|dat|ed /ɪntɪmɪdeɪtɪd/ ADJ Someone who feels **intimidated** feels frightened and lacks confidence because of the people they are with or the situation they are in. ❑ *Some individuals have claimed to feel intimidated as they walk or cycle past the protests.*

in|timi|dat|ing /ɪntɪmɪdeɪtɪŋ/ ADJ If you describe someone or something as **intimidating**, you mean that they are frightening and make people lose confidence. ❑ *He was a huge, intimidating figure.*

into ✦✦✦

> Pronounced /ɪntu/ or /ɪntʊ/, particularly before pronouns and for meaning 14.

> In addition to the uses shown below, **into** is used after some verbs and nouns in order to introduce extra information. **Into** is also used with verbs of movement, such as 'walk' and 'push,' and in phrasal verbs such as 'enter into' and 'talk into.'

1 PREP If you put one thing **into** another, you put the first thing inside the second. ❑ *Combine the remaining ingredients and put them into a dish.* **2** PREP If you go **into** a place or vehicle, you move from being outside it to being inside it. ❑ *I have no idea how he got into Iraq.* **3** PREP If one thing goes **into** another, the first thing moves from the outside to the inside of the second thing, by breaking or damaging the surface of it. ❑ *The blade missed his kidney, but went into his bowel.* **4** PREP If one thing gets **into** another, the first thing enters the second and becomes part of it. ❑ *Poisonous chemicals got into the water supply.* **5** PREP If you are walking or driving a vehicle and you bump **into** something or crash **into** something, you hit it accidentally. ❑ *A train from New Jersey plowed into the barrier at the end of the track.* **6** PREP When you get **into** a piece of clothing, you put it on. ❑ *She could change into a different outfit in two minutes.* **7** PREP [v PREP n, n PREP n] If someone or something gets **into** a particular state, they start being in that state. ❑ *I slid into a depression.* **8** PREP [v n PREP n/-ing] If you talk someone **into** doing something, you persuade them to do it. ❑ *They sweet-talked him into selling the farm.* **9** PREP If something changes **into** something else, it then has a new form, shape, or nature. ❑ *...to turn a nasty episode into a joke.* **10** PREP If something is cut or split **into** a number of pieces or sections, it is divided so that it becomes several smaller pieces or sections. ❑ *Sixteen teams are taking part, divided into four groups.* **11** PREP [n PREP n] An investigation **into** a subject or event is concerned with that subject or event. ❑ *It would provide hundreds of millions of dollars for research into alternative energy sources.* **12** PREP If you move or go **into** a particular career or business, you start working in it. ❑ *In the early 1980s, it was easy to get into the rental business.* **13** PREP If something continues **into** a period of time, it continues until after that period of time has begun. ❑ *He had three children, and lived on into his sixties.* **14** PREP [v-link PREP n] If you are very interested in something and like it very much, you can say that you are **into** it. [INFORMAL] ❑ *I'm into electronics myself.*

in|tol|er|able /ɪntɒlərəbᵊl/ ADJ If you describe something as **intolerable**, you mean that it is so bad or extreme that no one can bear it or tolerate it. ❑ *They felt this would put intolerable pressure on them.* ● **in|tol|er|ably** /ɪntɒlərəbli/ ADV ❑ *...intolerably cramped conditions.*

in|tol|er|ance /ɪntɒlərəns/ N-UNCOUNT **Intolerance** is unwillingness to let other people act in a different way or hold different opinions from you. [DISAPPROVAL] ❑ *...his intolerance of any opinion other than his own.*

in|tol|er|ant /ɪntɒlərənt/ ADJ If you describe someone as **intolerant**, you mean that they do not accept behavior and opinions that are different from their own. [DISAPPROVAL] ❑ *...intolerant attitudes towards people of other cultures and religious beliefs.*

in|to|na|tion /ɪntəneɪʃᵊn/ (intonations) N-VAR Your **intonation** is the way that your voice rises and falls as you speak. ❑ *His voice had a very slight German intonation.*

in|tone /ɪntoʊn/ (intones, intoning, intoned) V-T If you **intone** something, you say it in a slow and serious way. [WRITTEN] ❑ *He quietly intoned several prayers.*

in|toxi|cat|ed /ɪntɒksɪkeɪtɪd/ **1** ADJ Someone who is **intoxicated** is drunk. [FORMAL] ❑ *He appeared intoxicated, police said.* **2** ADJ [v-link ADJ by/with n] If you are **intoxicated by** or **with** something such as a feeling or an event, you are so excited by it that you find it hard to think clearly and sensibly. [LITERARY] ❑ *My cousins seem to have become intoxicated by their success.*

in|toxi|cat|ing /ɪntɒksɪkeɪtɪŋ/ **1** ADJ [usu ADJ n] **Intoxicating** drink contains alcohol and can make you drunk. [FORMAL] ❑ *...intoxicating liquor.* **2** ADJ If you describe something as **intoxicating**, you mean that it makes you feel a strong sense of excitement or happiness. [LITERARY] ❑ *...the intoxicating fragrance of lilies.*

in|toxi|ca|tion /ɪntɒksɪkeɪʃᵊn/ **1** N-UNCOUNT **Intoxication** is the state of being drunk. [FORMAL] ❑ *Intoxication interferes with memory and thinking, speech and coordination.* **2** N-UNCOUNT [oft N of n] You use **intoxication** to refer to a quality of something that makes you feel very excited. [LITERARY] ❑ *...the intoxication of greed and success.*

in|trac|table /ɪntræktəbᵊl/ **1** ADJ **Intractable** people are very difficult to control or influence. [FORMAL] ❑ *What may be done to reduce the influence of intractable opponents?* **2** ADJ **Intractable** problems or situations are very difficult to deal with. [FORMAL] ❑ *The economy still faces intractable problems.*

intra|mu|ral /ɪntrəmyʊərəl/ ADJ [ADJ n] **Intramural** activities happen within one school, college, or university, rather than between different ones. [AM] ❑ *...a comprehensive, well-supported program of intramural sports.*

in|tra|net /ɪntrənɛt/ (intranets) N-COUNT An **intranet** is a network of computers, similar to the internet, within a particular company or organization.

in|tran|si|gence /ɪntrænsɪdʒᵊns/ N-UNCOUNT If you talk about someone's **intransigence**, you mean that they refuse to behave differently or to change their attitude to something. [FORMAL, DISAPPROVAL] ❑ *He often appeared angry and frustrated by the intransigence of both sides.*

in|tran|si|gent /ɪntrænsɪdʒᵊnt/ ADJ If you describe someone as **intransigent**, you mean that they refuse to behave differently or to change their attitude to something. [FORMAL, DISAPPROVAL] ❑ *...Sami's opinionated and intransigent father.*

in|tran|si|tive /ɪntrænsɪtɪv/ ADJ An **intransitive** verb does not have an object.

intra|venous /ɪntrəviːnəs/ ADJ [ADJ n] **Intravenous** foods or drugs are put into people's bodies through their veins, rather than their mouths. [MEDICAL] ❑ *...an intravenous drip.* ● **intra|venous|ly** ADV [ADV after v] ❑ *Premature babies have to be fed intravenously.*

in tray (in trays) also **in-tray** N-COUNT An **in tray** is a shallow container used in offices to put letters and documents in before they are dealt with. Compare **out tray**. [mainly BRIT]

in AM, usually use **inbox**

in|trep|id /ɪntrɛpɪd/ ADJ An **intrepid** person acts in a brave way. ❑ *...an intrepid space traveler.*

in|tri|ca|cy /ɪntrɪkəsi/ N-UNCOUNT **Intricacy** is the state of being made up of many small parts or details. ❑ *The price depends on the intricacy of the work.*

in|tri|cate /ɪntrɪkət/ ADJ You use **intricate** to describe something that has many small parts or details. ❑ *...the production of carpets with highly intricate patterns.* ● **in|tri|cate|ly** ADV ❑ *...intricately carved sculptures.*

in|trigue (intrigues, intriguing, intrigued)

The noun is pronounced /ɪntriːg/. The verb is pronounced /ɪntriːg/.

1 N-VAR **Intrigue** is the making of secret plans to harm or deceive people. ❑ *...political intrigue.* **2** V-T If something, especially something strange, **intrigues** you, it interests you and you want to know more about it. ❑ *The novelty of the situation intrigued him.*

in|trigued /ɪntriːgd/ ADJ If you are **intrigued** by something, especially something strange, it interests you and you want to know more about it. ❑ *I would be intrigued to hear others' views.*

in|tri|guing /ɪntriːgɪŋ/ ADJ If you describe something as **intriguing**, you mean that it is interesting or strange. ❑ *This intriguing book is both thoughtful and informative.* ● **in|tri|guing|ly** ADV ❑ *...the intriguingly-named newspaper Le Canard enchaîné (The Chained Duck).*

in|trin|sic /ɪntrɪnsɪk/ ADJ [ADJ n] If something has **intrinsic** value or **intrinsic** interest, it is valuable or interesting because of its basic nature or character, and not because of its connection with other things. [FORMAL] ❑ *Diamonds have little intrinsic value and their price depends almost entirely on their scarcity.* ● **in|trin|si|cal|ly** /ɪntrɪnsɪkli/ ADV ❑ *Sometimes I wonder if people are intrinsically evil.*

in|tro ♦♦◇ /ɪntroʊ/ (intros) N-COUNT [oft N to n] The **intro** to a song, program, or book is the first part, which comes before the main part. [INFORMAL] ❑ *...the keyboard intro to The Who's "Won't Get Fooled Again."*

intro|duce ♦♦◇ /ɪntrədjuːs/ (introduces, introducing, introduced) **1** V-T To **introduce** something means to cause it to enter a place or exist in a system for the first time. ❑ *MGM introduced a new system for hiring writers.* ● **intro|duc|tion**

N-UNCOUNT ❑ *What he is better remembered for is the introduction of the moving assembly-line in Detroit in 1913.* ▪ V-T If you **introduce** one person to another, or you **introduce** two people, you tell them each other's names, so that they can get to know each other. If you **introduce** yourself to someone, you tell them your name. ❑ *Tim, may I introduce you to my uncle's secretary, Mary Waller?* ❑ *We haven't been introduced. My name is Nero Wolfe.* • **intro|duc|tion** (**introductions**) N-VAR ❑ *With considerable shyness, Elaine performed the introductions.* ▪ V-T If you **introduce** someone **to** something, you cause them to learn about it or experience it for the first time. ❑ *He introduced us to the delights of natural food.* • **intro|duc|tion** N-SING ❑ *His introduction to fieldwork was a series of expeditions.* ▪ V-T The person who **introduces** a television or radio program speaks at the beginning of it, and often between the different items in it, in order to explain what the program or the items are about. ❑ *...talk shows introduced by women.*

SYNONYMS

introduce
VERB ▪
bring in: *The government brought in a controversial tax reform.*
establish: *The U.N. has established detailed criteria for who should be allowed to vote.*
set up: *The two sides agreed to set up a commission to investigate claims.*
pioneer: *...the folk-tale writing style pioneered by Marquez.*
initiate: *They wanted to initiate a discussion on economics.*
launch: *The police have launched an investigation into the incident.*

intro|duc|tion /ɪntrədʌkʃən/ (**introductions**) ▪ N-COUNT The **introduction** to a book or talk is the part that comes at the beginning and tells you what the rest of the book or talk is about. ❑ *Ellen Malos, in her introduction to "The Politics of Housework," provides a summary of the debates.* ▪ N-COUNT If you refer to a book as an **introduction** to a particular subject, you mean that it explains the basic facts about that subject. ❑ *The book is a friendly, down-to-earth introduction to physics.* ▪ N-COUNT You can refer to a new product as an **introduction** when it becomes available in a place for the first time. ❑ *There are two among their recent introductions that have greatly impressed me.* ▪ → see also **introduce**

intro|duc|tory /ɪntrədʌktəri/ ▪ ADJ [ADJ n] An **introductory** remark, talk, or part of a book gives a small amount of general information about a particular subject, often before a more detailed explanation. ❑ *...an introductory course in religion and theology.* ▪ ADJ [ADJ n] An **introductory** offer or price on a new product is something such as a free gift or a low price that is meant to attract new customers. [BUSINESS] ❑ *...a special introductory offer.*

intro|spec|tion /ɪntrəspɛkʃən/ ▪ N-UNCOUNT **Introspection** is the examining of your own thoughts, ideas, and feelings. ❑ *He had always had his moments of quiet introspection.* ▪ → See feature box at **personality**

intro|spec|tive /ɪntrəspɛktɪv/ ADJ **Introspective** people spend a lot of time examining their own thoughts, ideas, and feelings. You can also use **introspective** to describe music or writing that has these characteristics.

intro|vert /ɪntrəvɜrt/ (**introverts**) ▪ N-COUNT An **introvert** is a quiet, shy person who finds it difficult to talk to people.
▪ → See feature box at **personality**

intro|vert|ed /ɪntrəvɜrtɪd/ ADJ **Introverted** people are quiet and shy and find it difficult to talk to other people. ❑ *Machen was a lonely, introverted child.*

in|trude /ɪntrud/ (**intrudes, intruding, intruded**) ▪ V-I If you say that someone **is intruding** into a particular place or situation, you mean that they are not wanted or welcome there. ❑ *The press has been blamed for intruding into people's personal lives in an unacceptable way.* ▪ V-I If something **intrudes** on your mood or your life, it disturbs it or has an unwanted effect on it. ❑ *Do you feel anxious when unforeseen incidents intrude on your day?* ▪ V-I If someone **intrudes** into a place, they go there even though they are not allowed to be there. ❑ *An American officer on the scene said no one had intruded into the space he was defending.*

in|trud|er /ɪntrudər/ (**intruders**) N-COUNT An **intruder** is a person who goes into a place where they are not supposed to be. ❑ *He owned a gun for scaring off intruders.*

in|tru|sion /ɪntruʒən/ (**intrusions**) ▪ N-VAR If someone disturbs you when you are in a private place or having a private conversation, you can call this event an **intrusion**. ❑ *I hope you don't mind this intrusion, Jon.* ▪ N-VAR An **intrusion** is something that disturbs your mood or your life in a way you do not like. ❑ *I felt it was a grotesque intrusion into our lives.*

in|tru|sive /ɪntrusɪv/ ADJ Something that is **intrusive** disturbs your mood or your life in a way you do not like.
❑ *The cameras were not an intrusive presence.*

in|tu|it /ɪntuɪt/ (**intuits, intuiting, intuited**) V-T If you **intuit** something, you guess what it is on the basis of your intuition or feelings, rather than on the basis of knowledge. [FORMAL]
❑ *They would confidently intuit your very thoughts.* ❑ *He intuited that the old priest was hiding information.*

in|tui|tion /ɪntuɪʃən/ (**intuitions**) N-VAR Your **intuition** or your **intuitions** are unexplained feelings that something is true even when you have no evidence or proof of it. ❑ *Her intuition was telling her that something was wrong.*

in|tui|tive /ɪntuɪtɪv/ ADJ If you have an **intuitive** idea or feeling about something, you feel that it is true although you have no evidence or proof of it. ❑ *A positive pregnancy test soon confirmed her intuitive feelings.* • **in|tui|tive|ly** ADV ❑ *He seemed to know intuitively that I must be missing my mother.*

Inu|it /ɪnyuɪt/ (**Inuits** or **Inuit**) N-COUNT The **Inuit** are the people descended from the original people of Alaska, Eastern Canada, and Greenland.

in|un|date /ɪnʌndeɪt/ (**inundates, inundating, inundated**)
▪ V-T If you say that you **are inundated** with things such as letters, demands, or requests, you are emphasizing that you receive so many of them that you cannot deal with them all. [EMPHASIS] ❑ *Her office was inundated with requests for tickets.* ▪ V-T [usu passive] If an area of land **is inundated**, it becomes covered with water. ❑ *Their neighborhood is being inundated by the rising waters of the Colorado River.*

in|ured /ɪnyʊərd/ ADJ [v-link ADJ to n] If you are **inured** to something unpleasant, you have become used to it so that it no longer affects you. [FORMAL] ❑ *Doctors can become inured to death.*

in|vade /ɪnveɪd/ (**invades, invading, invaded**) ▪ V-T/V-I To **invade** a country means to enter it by force with an army.
❑ *In autumn 1944 the Allies invaded the Italian mainland at Anzio and Salerno.* ▪ V-T If you say that people or animals **invade** a place, you mean that they enter it in large numbers, often in a way that is unpleasant or difficult to deal with. ❑ *People invaded the streets in victory processions almost throughout the day.*

in|vad|er /ɪnveɪdər/ (**invaders**) ▪ N-COUNT **Invaders** are soldiers who are invading a country. ❑ *The city was destroyed by foreign invaders.* ▪ N-COUNT You can refer to a country or army that has invaded or is about to invade another country as an **invader**. ❑ *...action against a foreign invader.*

in|va|lid (**invalids**)

The noun is pronounced /ɪnvəlɪd/. The adjective is pronounced /ɪnvælɪd/ and is hyphenated in|val|id.

▪ N-COUNT An **invalid** is someone who needs to be cared for because they have an illness or disability. ❑ *I hate being treated as an invalid.* ▪ ADJ If an action, procedure, or document is **invalid**, it cannot be accepted, because it breaks the law or some official rule. ❑ *The trial was stopped and the results declared invalid.* ▪ ADJ An **invalid** argument or conclusion is wrong because it is based on a mistake. ❑ *We think that those arguments are rendered invalid by the facts.*

in|vali|date /ɪnvælɪdeɪt/ (**invalidates, invalidating, invalidated**) V-T If something **invalidates** something such as a law, contract, or election, it causes it to be considered illegal. ❑ *An official decree invalidated the vote in the capital.*

in|va|lid|ity /ɪnvəlɪdɪti/ N-UNCOUNT **Invalidity** is the state of being an invalid. ❑ *An error could lead to 70,000 pensioners receiving an incorrect level of invalidity allowance .*

in|valu|able /ɪnvælyuəbəl/ ADJ If you describe something as **invaluable**, you mean that it is extremely useful. ❑ *I was able to gain invaluable experience over that year.*

in|vari|able /ɪnvɛəriəbəl/ ADJ [usu ADJ n] You use **invariable** to describe something that never changes. ☐ *There are no absolute, invariable moral rules.*

in|vari|ably /ɪnvɛəriəbli/ ADV If something **invariably** happens or is **invariably** true, it always happens or is always true. ☐ *They almost invariably get it wrong.*

in|va|sion ✦✧ /ɪnveɪʒən/ (**invasions**) ◼ N-VAR If there is an **invasion** of a country, a foreign army enters it by force. ☐ *...seven years after the Roman invasion of Britain.* ◻ N-VAR If you refer to the arrival of a large number of people or things as an **invasion**, you are emphasizing that they are unpleasant or difficult to deal with. ☐ *...this year's annual invasion of flies, wasps and ants.* ◼ N-VAR If you describe an action as an **invasion**, you disapprove of it because it affects someone or something in a way that is not wanted. [DISAPPROVAL] ☐ *Is reading a child's diary always a gross invasion of privacy?*

in|va|sive /ɪnveɪsɪv/ ◼ ADJ You use **invasive** to describe something undesirable that spreads very quickly and that is very difficult to stop from spreading. ☐ *They found invasive cancer during a routine examination.* ◻ ADJ An **invasive** medical procedure involves operating on a patient or examining the inside of their body. ☐ *Many people find the idea of any kind of invasive surgery unbearable.*

in|vec|tive /ɪnvɛktɪv/ N-UNCOUNT [usu with supp] **Invective** is rude and unpleasant things that people shout at other people they hate or are angry with. [FORMAL] ☐ *A woman had hurled racist invective at the family.*

in|veigh /ɪnveɪ/ (**inveighs, inveighing, inveighed**) V-I If you **inveigh against** something, you criticize it strongly. [FORMAL] ☐ *A lot of his writings inveigh against luxury and riches.*

in|vei|gle /ɪnveɪɡəl/ (**inveigles, inveigling, inveigled**) V-T If you **inveigle** someone **into** doing something, you cleverly persuade them to do it when they do not really want to. [FORMAL] ☐ *She inveigles Paco into a plot to swindle Tania out of her savings.*

in|vent /ɪnvɛnt/ (**invents, inventing, invented**) ◼ V-T If you **invent** something such as a machine or process, you are the first person to think of it or make it. ☐ *He invented the first electric clock.* ◻ V-T If you **invent** a story or excuse, you try to make other people believe that it is true when in fact it is not. ☐ *I stood still, trying to invent a plausible excuse.*

in|ven|tion /ɪnvɛnʃən/ (**inventions**) ◼ N-COUNT An **invention** is a machine, device, or system that has been invented by someone. ☐ *The spinning wheel was a Chinese invention.* ◻ N-UNCOUNT **Invention** is the act of inventing something that has never been made or used before. ☐ *...the invention of the telephone.* ◼ N-VAR If you refer to someone's account of something as an **invention**, you think that it is untrue and that they have made it up. ☐ *The story was certainly a favorite one, but it was undoubtedly pure invention.* ◻ N-UNCOUNT **Invention** is the ability to invent things or to have clever and original ideas. ☐ *Perhaps, with such powers of invention and mathematical ability, he will be offered a job in computers.*

in|ven|tive /ɪnvɛntɪv/ ADJ An **inventive** person is good at inventing things or has clever and original ideas. ☐ *It inspired me to be more inventive with my own cooking.* • **in|ven|tive|ness** N-UNCOUNT ☐ *He has surprised us before with his inventiveness.*

in|ven|tor /ɪnvɛntər/ (**inventors**) N-COUNT An **inventor** is a person who has invented something, or whose job is to invent things. ☐ *...Alexander Graham Bell, the inventor of the telephone.*

in|ven|tory /ɪnvəntɔri/ (**inventories**) ◼ N-VAR An **inventory** is a supply or stock of something. [AM] ☐ *...one inventory of twelve sails for each yacht.* ◻ N-COUNT An **inventory** is a written list of all the objects in a particular place such as all the merchandise in a store. ☐ *Before starting, he made an inventory of everything that was to stay.*

in|verse /ɪnvɜrs/ ◼ ADJ [usu ADJ n] If there is an **inverse** relationship between two things, one of them becomes larger as the other becomes smaller. ☐ *The tension grew in inverse proportion to the distance from their final destination.* • **in|verse|ly** ADV ☐ *The size of the nebula at this stage is inversely proportional to its mass.* ◻ N-SING [the N, usu N of n] The **inverse** of something is its exact opposite. [FORMAL] ☐ *There is no sign that you bothered to consider the inverse of your logic.* • ADJ [ADJ n] **Inverse** is also an adjective. ☐ *The hologram can be flipped to show the inverse image.*

in|ver|sion /ɪnvɜrʒən, -ʃən/ (**inversions**) N-VAR [usu N of n] When there is an **inversion** of something, it is changed into its opposite. [FORMAL] ☐ *...a scandalous inversion of the truth.*

in|vert /ɪnvɜrt/ (**inverts, inverting, inverted**) V-T If you **invert** something, you turn it upside down or inside out. [FORMAL] ☐ *Invert the cake onto a serving plate.*

in|ver|te|brate /ɪnvɜrtɪbrɪt/ (**invertebrates**) N-COUNT An **invertebrate** is a creature that does not have a spine such as an insect, a worm, or an octopus. [TECHNICAL] • ADJ **Invertebrate** is also an adjective. ☐ *...invertebrate creatures.*

in|vert|ed com|mas N-PLURAL **Inverted commas** are punctuation marks that are used in writing to show where speech or a quotation begins and ends. They are usually written or printed as ' ' or " ". Inverted commas are also sometimes used around the titles of books, plays, or songs, or around a word or phrase that is being discussed. [BRIT]

in AM, use **quotation marks**

in|vest ✦✧ /ɪnvɛst/ (**invests, investing, invested**) ◼ V-T/V-I If you **invest** in something, or if you **invest** a sum of money, you use your money in a way that you hope will increase its value, for example, by putting it in a bank, or buying securities or property. ☐ *Many people don't like to invest in stocks.* ☐ *I'm tired of watching you invest our money in insane projects.* ◻ V-T/V-I If you **invest in** something useful, you buy it, because it will help you to do something more efficiently or more cheaply. ☐ *The company has invested a six-figure sum in an electronic order-control system which is used to keep stores stocked.* ◼ V-T/V-I When a government or organization **invests** in something, it gives or lends money for a purpose that it considers useful or profitable. ☐ *...the need to invest in new technology.* ☐ *Government agencies must invest more funds in training and development programs.* ◻ V-T If you **invest** time or energy in something, you spend a lot of time or energy on it because you think it will be useful or successful. ☐ *I would rather invest time in Rebecca than in the kitchen.* ◼ V-T To **invest** someone **with** rights or responsibilities means to give them those rights or responsibilities legally or officially. [FORMAL] ☐ *The constitution invested him with certain powers.*

---- COLLOCATIONS ----

invest
VERB
◼
invest + *noun*: cash, fund, money, sum; capital, profit; billions, millions
invest + *adverb*: directly, heavily; wisely; abroad, overseas, offshore
◻
noun + **invest**: company, firm, government, organization
◼
invest + *noun*: effort, time

in|ves|ti|gate ✦✧ /ɪnvɛstɪɡeɪt/ (**investigates, investigating, investigated**) ◼ V-T/V-I If someone, especially an official, **investigates** an event, situation, or claim, they try to find out what happened or what is the truth. ☐ *They're still investigating the accident.* • **in|ves|ti|ga|tion** /ɪnvɛstɪɡeɪʃən/ (**investigations**) N-VAR ☐ *He ordered an investigation into the affair.* ◻ → See feature box at **legal**

---- COLLOCATIONS ----

investigate
VERB
investigate + *noun*: allegation, claim, complaint; case, crime, death, incident
noun + **investigate**: authority, detective, officer, police
investigate + *adverb*: fully, properly, thoroughly

in|ves|ti|ga|tive /ɪnvɛstɪɡeɪtɪv/ ADJ **Investigative** work, especially journalism, involves investigating things. ☐ *...an investigative reporter.*

in|ves|ti|ga|tor /ɪnvɛstɪɡeɪtər/ (**investigators**) N-COUNT An **investigator** is someone who carries out investigations, especially as part of their job. ☐ *...an undercover investigator.*

in|ves|ti|ga|tory /ɪnvɛstɪɡətɔri/ ADJ [ADJ n] **Investigatory** means the same as **investigative**. ☐ *At no time did I make an attempt to impede any investigatory effort.*

in|ves|ti|ture /ɪnvɛstɪtʃər/ (**investitures**) N-COUNT An **investiture** is a ceremony in which someone is given an official title. ❑ ...her investiture as a member of the National Institute for Arts and Letters.

in|vest|ment ✦✦◇ /ɪnvɛstmənt/ (**investments**) ◼ N-UNCOUNT **Investment** is the activity of investing money. ❑ He said the government must introduce tax incentives to encourage investment. ◻ N-VAR An **investment** is an amount of money that you invest, or the thing that you invest it in. ❑ ...an investment of twenty-eight million dollars. ◼ N-COUNT If you describe something you buy as an **investment**, you mean that it will be useful, especially because it will help you to do a task more cheaply or efficiently. ❑ When selecting boots, fine, quality leather will be a wise investment. ◼ N-UNCOUNT **Investment** of time or effort is the spending of time or effort on something in order to make it a success. ❑ I worry about this big investment of time not working. ◼ → See feature box at **banking**, **business**

── COLLOCATIONS ──
investment
NOUN
◼
noun + **investment**: business, capital, property
adjective + **investment**: foreign, overseas; heavy
verb + **investment**: attract, boost, consider, encourage, promote; need, require
◼
adjective + **investment**: fixed, long-term, minimum; sound
verb + **investment**: make
◼
adjective + **investment**: wise, worthwhile

in|ves|tor ✦✦◇ /ɪnvɛstər/ (**investors**) ◼ N-COUNT An **investor** is a person or organization that buys securities or property in order to receive a profit. ❑ The main investor in the project is the French bank Credit National. ◻ → See feature box at **banking**

── COLLOCATIONS ──
investor
NOUN
noun + **investor**: bond, equity, real estate
adjective + **investor**: cautious, nervous, unhappy, wary; foreign, overseas; wealthy; institutional, private
verb + **investor**: attract; reassure; spook

in|vet|er|ate /ɪnvɛtərɪt/ ADJ [ADJ n] If you describe someone as, for example, an **inveterate** liar or smoker, you mean that they have lied or smoked for a long time and are not likely to stop doing it. ❑ ...an inveterate gambler.

in|vidi|ous /ɪnvɪdiəs/ ◼ ADJ If you describe a task or job as **invidious**, you mean that it is unpleasant because it is likely to make you unpopular. ❑ The local authority could find itself in the invidious position of having to refuse. ◻ ADJ An **invidious** comparison or choice between two things is an unfair one because the two things are very different or are equally good or bad. ❑ Police officers fear invidious comparisons.

in|vig|or|ate /ɪnvɪgəreɪt/ (**invigorates**, **invigorating**, **invigorated**) ◼ V-T If something **invigorates** you, it makes you feel more energetic. ❑ Take a deep breath in to invigorate you. ● **in|vig|or|at|ed** ADJ [usu v-link ADJ] ❑ She seemed invigorated, full of life and energy. ◻ V-T To **invigorate** a situation or a process means to make it more efficient or more effective. ❑ ...the promise that they would invigorate the economy.

in|vig|or|at|ing /ɪnvɪgəreɪtɪŋ/ ADJ If you describe something as **invigorating**, you mean that it makes you feel more energetic. ❑ ...the invigorating northern air.

in|vin|cible /ɪnvɪnsɪbəl/ ◼ ADJ If you describe an army or sports team as **invincible**, you believe that they cannot be defeated. ❑ You couldn't help feeling the military's fire power was invincible. ◻ ADJ If someone has an **invincible** belief or attitude, it cannot be changed. ❑ He also had an invincible faith in the medicinal virtues of garlic.

in|vio|lable /ɪnvaɪələbəl/ ◼ ADJ If a law or principle is **inviolable**, you must not break it. [FORMAL] ❑ The game had a single inviolable rule: obstacles were to be overcome, not circumvented. ◻ ADJ If a country says its borders are **inviolable**, it means they must not be changed or crossed without permission.

[FORMAL] ❑ Yesterday's resolution says the present border is "inviolable." ● **in|vio|labil|ity** /ɪnvaɪələbɪlɪti/ N-UNCOUNT ❑ ...the inviolability of U.S. territory.

in|vio|late /ɪnvaɪəlɪt/ ADJ If something is **inviolate**, it has not been or cannot be harmed or affected by anything. [FORMAL] ❑ We believed our love was inviolate.

in|vis|ible /ɪnvɪzɪbəl/ ◼ ADJ If you describe something as **invisible**, you mean that it cannot be seen, for example, because it is transparent, hidden, or very small. ❑ The lines were so finely etched as to be invisible from a distance. ● **in|vis|ibly** /ɪnvɪzɪbli/ ADV [ADV with v] ❑ A thin coil of smoke rose almost invisibly into the sharp, bright sky. ◻ ADJ [ADJ n] You can use **invisible** when you are talking about something that cannot be seen but has a definite effect. In this sense, **invisible** is often used before a noun that refers to something visible. ❑ All the time you are in doubt about the cause of your illness, you are fighting against an invisible enemy. ● **in|vis|ibly** ADV [ADV with v] ❑ ...the tradition that invisibly shapes things in the present. ◼ ADJ If you say that you feel **invisible**, you are complaining that you are being ignored by other people. If you say that a particular problem or situation is **invisible**, you are complaining that it is not being considered or dealt with. ❑ It was strange, how invisible a clerk could feel. ● **in|vis|ibil|ity** /ɪnvɪzɪbɪlɪti/ N-UNCOUNT ❑ She takes up the issue of the invisibility of women and women's concerns in society. ◼ ADJ In stories, **invisible** people or things have a magic quality that makes people unable to see them. ❑ ...The Invisible Man. ◼ ADJ [ADJ n] In economics, **invisible** earnings are the money that a country makes as a result of services such as banking and tourism, rather than by producing goods. [BUSINESS] ❑ The revenue from tourism is the biggest single item in the country's invisible earnings.

in|vi|ta|tion ✦◇◇ /ɪnvɪteɪʃən/ (**invitations**) ◼ N-COUNT An **invitation** is a written or spoken request to come to an event such as a party, a meal, or a meeting. ❑ ...an invitation to lunch. ❑ We had accepted an invitation to attend a friend's seventieth birthday party. ◻ N-COUNT An **invitation** is the card or paper on which an invitation is written or printed. ❑ Hundreds of invitations are being sent out this week. ◼ N-SING If you believe that someone's action is likely to have a particular result, especially a bad one, you can refer to the action as an **invitation to** that result. ❑ Don't leave your shopping on the back seat of your car – it's an open invitation to a thief.

in|vi|ta|tion|al /ɪnvɪteɪʃənəl/ (**invitationals**) ADJ [ADJ n] An **invitational** tournament or event is a sports competition in which only players who have been asked to take part can compete. ❑ After all, The Masters is an invitational tournament. ● N-COUNT **Invitational** is also a noun. ❑ ...a 59-team invitational for field and running events.

in|vite ✦✦◇ (**invites**, **inviting**, **invited**)

The verb is pronounced /ɪnvaɪt/. The noun is pronounced /ɪnvaɪt/.

◼ V-T If you **invite** someone to something such as a party or a meal, you ask them to come to it. ❑ She invited him to her 26th birthday party in New Jersey. ❑ Barron invited her to accompany him to the races. ◻ V-T If you **are invited** to do something, you are formally asked or given permission to do it. ❑ At a future date, managers will be invited to apply for a management buy-out. ❑ He invited me to go into partnership with him. ◼ V-T If you say or do **invites** trouble or criticism, it makes trouble or criticism more likely. ❑ Their refusal to compromise will inevitably invite more criticism from the UN. ◼ N-COUNT An **invite** is an invitation to something such as a party or a meal. [INFORMAL] ❑ She tried to wangle an invite to the party. ◼ → See feature box at **socialize**

in|vit|ing /ɪnvaɪtɪŋ/ ADJ If you say that something is **inviting**, you mean that it has good qualities that attract you or make you want to experience it. ❑ The February air was soft, cool, and inviting. ● **in|vit|ing|ly** ADV ❑ The waters of the tropics are invitingly clear. ◻ → see also **invite**

in vi|tro /ɪn viːtroʊ/ ADJ [ADJ n] **In vitro** fertilization is a method of helping a woman to have a baby in which an egg is removed from one of her ovaries, fertilized outside her body, and then replaced in her womb.

in|vo|ca|tion /ɪnvəkeɪʃən/ (**invocations**) ◼ N-VAR [oft N prep] An **invocation** is a request for help or forgiveness made to a

invoice god. [FORMAL] □ ...an invocation for divine guidance. **2** N-COUNT An **invocation** is a prayer at a public meeting, usually at the beginning. [AM]

in|voice /ɪnvɔɪs/ (**invoices, invoicing, invoiced**) **1** N-COUNT An **invoice** is a document that lists goods that have been supplied or services that have been done, and says how much money you owe for them. □ We will then send you an invoice for the total course fees. **2** V-T If you **invoice** someone, you send them a bill for goods or services you have provided them with. □ The agency invoices the client who then pays the full amount to the agency.

in|voke /ɪnvoʊk/ (**invokes, invoking, invoked**) **1** V-T If you **invoke** a law, you state that you are taking a particular action because that law allows or tells you to. □ The judge invoked an international law that protects refugees. **2** V-T If you **invoke** something such as a principle, a saying, or a famous person, you refer to them in order to support your argument. □ ...economists who invoke the principle of "consumer sovereignty" to support their arguments. **3** V-T If something such as a piece of music **invokes** a feeling or an image, it causes someone to have the feeling or to see the image. Many people consider this use to be incorrect because **evoke** is the correct word for this. □ "Appalachian Spring" by Aaron Copland invoked the atmosphere of the wide open spaces of the prairies.

in|vol|un|tary /ɪnvɒləntɛri/ **1** ADJ If you make an **involuntary** movement or exclamation, you make it suddenly and without intending to because you are unable to control yourself. □ Another surge of pain in my ankle caused me to give an involuntary shudder. ● **in|vol|un|tari|ly** /ɪnvɒləntɛərɪli/ ADV [ADV with v] □ His left eyelid twitched involuntarily. **2** ADJ You use **involuntary** to describe an action or situation that is forced on someone. □ ...insurance policies that cover death, accident, sickness and involuntary unemployment.

in|volve ♦♦◊ /ɪnvɒlv/ (**involves, involving, involved**) **1** V-T If a situation or activity **involves** something, that thing is a necessary part or consequence of it. □ Running a kitchen involves lots of discipline and speed. **2** V-T If a situation or activity **involves** someone, they are taking part in it. □ If there was a cover-up, it involved people at the very highest levels of government. **3** V-T If you say that someone **involves** themselves **in** something, you mean that they take part in it, often in a way that is unnecessary or unwanted. □ I seem to have involved myself in something I don't understand. **4** V-T If you **involve** someone **in** something, you get them to take part in it. □ Nasser and I do everything together, he involves me in everything. **5** V-T If one thing **involves** you **in** another thing, especially something unpleasant or inconvenient, the first thing causes you to do or deal with the second. □ I don't want to do anything that will involve me in a long-term commitment.

SYNONYMS
involve
VERB **1**
entail: The job entails teaching dancers the technique and performance of dance movements.
mean: Managing well means communicating well.
demand: The task would demand much patience, hard work, and sacrifice.
require: This isn't the kind of crisis that requires us to drop everything else.

in|volved ♦♦◊ /ɪnvɒlvd/ **1** ADJ [v-link ADJ] If you are **involved** in a situation or activity, you are taking part in it or have a strong connection with it. □ If she were involved in business, she would make a strong chief executive. **2** ADJ [v-link ADJ] If you are **involved** in something, you give a lot of time, effort, or attention to it. □ The family was deeply involved in Jewish culture. **3** ADJ [v-link ADJ] The things **involved** in something such as a job or system are the necessary parts or consequences of it. □ We believe the time and hard work involved in completing such an assignment are worthwhile. **4** ADJ If a situation or activity is **involved**, it has a lot of different parts or aspects, often making it difficult to understand, explain, or do. □ The operations can be quite involved, requiring many procedures in order to restructure the anatomy. **5** ADJ If one person is **involved** with another, especially someone they are not married to, they are having a sexual or romantic relationship. □ During a visit to Kenya in 1928 he became romantically involved with a married woman.

in|volve|ment ♦◊◊ /ɪnvɒlvmənt/ (**involvements**) **1** N-UNCOUNT Your **involvement** in or with something is the fact that you are taking part in it. □ She disliked his involvement with the group and disliked his friends. **2** N-UNCOUNT **Involvement** is the enthusiasm that you feel when you care deeply about something. □ Ben has always felt a deep involvement with animals. **3** N-VAR An **involvement** is a close relationship between two people, especially if they are not married to each other. □ They were very good friends but there was no romantic involvement.

in|vul|ner|able /ɪnvʌlnərəbəl/ ADJ [oft ADJ to n] If someone or something is **invulnerable**, they cannot be harmed or damaged. □ Many daughters assume that their mothers are invulnerable. ● **in|vul|ner|abil|ity** /ɪnvʌlnərəbɪlɪti/ N-UNCOUNT □ They have a sense of invulnerability to disease.

in|ward /ɪnwərd/ **1** ADJ [ADJ n] Your **inward** thoughts or feelings are the ones that you do not express or show to other people. □ I sighed with inward relief. ● **in|ward|ly** ADV □ Sara was inwardly furious. **2** ADJ [ADJ n] An **inward** movement is one toward the inside or center of something. □ ...a sharp, inward breath like a gasp. **3** ADV [ADV after v] If something moves or faces **inward**, it moves or faces toward the inside or center of something. □ He pushed open the front door, which swung inward with a groan.

inward-looking ADJ If you describe a people or society as **inward-looking**, you mean that they are more interested in themselves than in other people or societies. [DISAPPROVAL] □ ...an insular and inward-looking community.

in|wards /ɪnwərdz/ also **inward** ADV [ADV after v] If something moves or faces **inwards**, it moves or faces towards the inside or center of something. □ She pressed back against the door until it swung inwards. □ Keeping your heels on the ground, turn your feet inwards.

in-your-face ADJ [usu ADJ n] Someone who has an **in-your-face** attitude seems determined to behave in a way that is unusual or shocking, and does not care what people think of them. [INFORMAL] □ It's in-your-face feminism, and it's meant to shock.

iodine /aɪədaɪn/ N-UNCOUNT **Iodine** is a dark-colored substance used in medicine and photography.

ion /aɪən, aɪɒn/ (**ions**) N-COUNT [usu pl] **Ions** are electrically charged atoms. [TECHNICAL]

-ion → see -ation

ion|iz|er /aɪənaɪzər/ (**ionizers**)

in BRIT, also use **ioniser**

N-COUNT An **ionizer** is a device that is meant to make the air in a room more healthy by removing positive ions.

iota /aɪoʊtə/ **1** QUANT [with brd-neg, QUANT of n-uncount] If you say that there is not **an iota** or not **one iota** of something, you are emphasizing that there is not even a very small amount of it. [EMPHASIS] □ He's never shown an iota of interest in any kind of work. **2** PHRASE [with brd-neg, PHR after v] You can use **an iota** or **one iota** to emphasize a negative statement. **Not an iota** or **not one iota** means not even to a small extent or degree. [EMPHASIS] □ Our credit standards haven't changed one iota.

IOU /aɪ oʊ yu/ (**IOUs**) N-COUNT An **IOU** is a written promise that you will pay back some money that you have borrowed. **IOU** is an abbreviation for 'I owe you.'

IP ad|dress /aɪ pi ædrɛs/ (**IP addresses**) N-COUNT An **IP address** is a series of numbers that identify which particular computer or network is connected to the internet. **IP** is an abbreviation for 'Internet Protocol.' [COMPUTING] □ Every connection that you make to the network is stamped with your IP address.

iPod /aɪpɒd/ (**iPods**) N-COUNT An **iPod** is a portable MP3 player that can play music downloaded from the internet. [COMPUTING, TRADEMARK]

ipso fac|to /ɪpsoʊ fæktoʊ/ ADV [ADV with cl/group] If something is **ipso facto** true, it must be true, because of a fact that has been mentioned. □ If a crime occurs then there is, ipso facto, a guilty party.

IQ /aɪ kyu/ (**IQs**) N-VAR Your **IQ** is your level of intelligence, as indicated by a special test that you do. **IQ** is an abbreviation for 'intelligence quotient.' Compare **EQ**. □ His IQ is above average.

PREFIX

ir- can be added to some words to form words that have the opposite meaning. For example, if something is **irreplaceable** it cannot be replaced.

IRA /aɪ ɑr eɪ/ (**IRAs**) N-COUNT An **IRA** is a type of savings account where the money you put in and the interest you earn is not taxable until you retire. **IRA** is an abbreviation for 'Individual Retirement Account.' [AM] ❑ ...periodic distributions from an IRA on or after attainment of age 59.

Ira|nian /ɪreɪniən/ (**Iranians**) **1** ADJ **Iranian** means belonging or relating to Iran, or to its people or culture. **2** N-COUNT An **Iranian** is an Iranian citizen, or a person of Iranian origin.

Ira|qi /ɪræki, ɪrɒki/ (**Iraqis**) **1** ADJ **Iraqi** means belonging or relating to Iraq, or to its people or culture. **2** N-COUNT An **Iraqi** is an Iraqi citizen, or a person of Iraqi origin.

iras|cible /ɪræsɪbəl/ ADJ If you describe someone as **irascible**, you mean that they become angry very easily. [WRITTEN] ❑ He had an irascible temper.

irate /aɪreɪt/ ADJ If someone is **irate**, they are very angry about something. ❑ The owner was so irate he almost threw me out of the place.

IRC /aɪ ɑr si/ N-UNCOUNT **IRC** is a way of having conversations with people who are using the internet, especially people you do not know. **IRC** is an abbreviation for 'Internet Relay Chat.' ❑ Not long ago, just being in IRC was enough to forge bonds between chatters.

ire /aɪər/ N-UNCOUNT **Ire** is anger. [FORMAL] ❑ Their ire was directed mainly at the government.

iri|des|cent /ɪrɪdɛsənt/ ADJ Something that is **iridescent** has many bright colors that seem to keep changing. [LITERARY] ❑ ...iridescent bubbles.

iris /aɪrɪs/ (**irises**) **1** N-COUNT The **iris** is the round colored part of a person's eye. **2** → See also color supplement

Irish /aɪrɪʃ/ **1** ADJ **Irish** means belonging or relating to Ireland, or to its people, language, or culture. **Irish** sometimes refers to the whole of Ireland, and sometimes only to the Republic of Ireland. **2** N-PLURAL [usu the N] The **Irish** are the people of Ireland, or of the Republic of Ireland. **3** N-UNCOUNT **Irish** is a Celtic language spoken by people who live in Ireland, especially in the Republic of Ireland.

Irish|man /aɪrɪʃmən/ (**Irishmen**) N-COUNT An **Irishman** is a man who is an Irish citizen or is of Irish origin.

Irish|woman /aɪrɪʃwʊmən/ (**Irishwomen**) N-COUNT An **Irishwoman** is a woman who is an Irish citizen or is of Irish origin.

irk /ɜrk/ (**irks, irking, irked**) V-T If something **irks** you, it irritates or annoys you. ❑ The rehearsal process also irked him increasingly. ❑ I must admit it irks me to see this guy get all this free publicity. ❑ It irks them that some people have more of a chance than others for their voices to be heard. ● **irked** ADJ [v-link ADJ] ❑ Clem had seemed a little irked when he left.

irk|some /ɜrksəm/ ADJ If something is **irksome**, it irritates or annoys you. [FORMAL] ❑ ...the irksome regulations.

iron ✦✧✧ /aɪərn/ (**irons, ironing, ironed**) **1** N-UNCOUNT **Iron** is an element that usually takes the form of a hard, dark gray metal. It is used to make steel, and also forms part of many tools, buildings, and vehicles. Very small amounts of iron occur in your blood and in food. ❑ The huge, iron gate was locked. ❑ ...the highest grade iron ore deposits in the world. **2** N-COUNT An **iron** is an electrical device with a flat metal base. You heat it until the base is hot, then rub it over clothes to remove creases. **3** V-T If you **iron** clothes, you remove the creases from them using an iron. ❑ Ryan said he would iron his pants, shirt and my dress._ ● **iron|ing** N-UNCOUNT ❑ I managed to get all the ironing done this morning. **4** ADJ [ADJ n] You can use **iron** to describe the character or behavior of someone who is very firm in their decisions and actions, or who can control their feelings well. ❑ ...a man of icy nerve and iron will. **5** ADJ [ADJ n] **Iron** is used in expressions such as **an iron hand** and **iron discipline** to describe strong, harsh, or unfair methods of control that do not allow people much freedom. ❑ He died in 1985 after ruling Albania with an iron fist for 40 years. **6** PHRASE If someone has a lot of **irons in the fire**, they are involved in several different activities or have several different plans. ❑ Too many irons in the fire can sap your energy and prevent you from seeing which path to take. **7** → See also color supplement
▶ **iron out** PHRASAL VERB If you **iron out** difficulties, you resolve them and bring them to an end. ❑ "It was in the beginning, when we were still ironing out problems," a company spokesman said.

Iron Age N-PROPER [the N] The **Iron Age** was a period of time that began when people started making things from iron about three thousand years ago. ❑ ...the remains of an Iron Age fort.

iron|clad /aɪərnklæd/ also **iron-clad** ADJ If you describe a guarantee or plan as **ironclad**, you are emphasizing that it has been carefully put together, and that you think it is absolutely certain to work or be successful. [EMPHASIS] ❑ ...ironclad guarantees of safe passage.

Iron Cur|tain N-PROPER [the N] People referred to the border that separated the Soviet Union and the communist countries of Eastern Europe from the Western European countries as **the Iron Curtain**.

iron|ic /aɪrɒnɪk/ also **ironical** /aɪrɒnɪkəl/ **1** ADJ When you make an **ironic** remark, you say the opposite of what you really mean, as a joke. ❑ At the most solemn moments he will flash a mocking smile or make an ironic remark. **2** ADJ If you say that it is **ironic** that something happens, you mean that it is odd or amusing because it involves a contrast. ❑ It is ironic that so many women are anti-feminist.

ironi|cal|ly /aɪrɒnɪkli/ **1** ADV [ADV with cl] You use **ironically** to draw attention to a situation that is odd or amusing because it involves a contrast. ❑ Ironically, for a man who hated war, he would have made a superb war cameraman. **2** ADV [ADV with v] If you say something **ironically**, you say the opposite of what you really mean, as a joke. ❑ Classmates at West Point had ironically dubbed him Beauty.

iron|ing board (**ironing boards**) **1** N-COUNT An **ironing board** is a long narrow table covered with cloth on which you iron clothes. **2** → See feature box at **household**

iron|monger /aɪərnmʌŋgər/ (**ironmongers**) **1** N-COUNT An **ironmonger** is a storekeeper who sells articles for the house and garden such as tools, nails, and machine parts. [BRIT]

in AM, usually use **hardware dealer**

2 N-COUNT [oft the N] An **ironmonger** or an **ironmonger's** is a store where articles for the house and garden such as tools, nails, and pans are sold. [BRIT]

in AM, usually use **hardware store**

iron|mongery /aɪərnmʌŋgəri, -mɒŋgəri/ N-UNCOUNT **Ironmongery** is articles for the house and garden such as tools, nails, and machine parts that are sold in a hardware store. [BRIT]

in AM, usually use **hardware**

iron|work /aɪərnwɜrk/ N-UNCOUNT **Iron** objects or structures are referred to as **ironwork**. ❑ ...the ironwork on the doors.

iro|ny /aɪrəni, aɪər-/ (**ironies**) **1** N-UNCOUNT **Irony** is a subtle form of humor that involves saying things that are the opposite of what you really mean. ❑ His tone was tinged with irony. **2** N-VAR If you talk about the **irony** of a situation, you mean that it is odd or amusing because it involves a contrast. ❑ The irony is that many officials in Washington agree in private that their policy is inconsistent. **3** → See feature box at **humor**

ir|ra|di|ate /ɪreɪdieɪt/ (**irradiates, irradiating, irradiated**) V-T If someone or something is **irradiated**, they are exposed to a large amount of radioactivity. [TECHNICAL] ❑ ...the Chernobyl disaster, which irradiated large parts of Europe. ● **ir|ra|dia|tion** /ɪreɪdieɪʃən/ N-UNCOUNT ❑ ...the harmful effects of irradiation and pollution.

ir|ra|tion|al /ɪræʃənəl/ ADJ If you describe someone's feelings and behavior as **irrational**, you mean they are not based on logical reasons or clear thinking. ❑ ...an irrational fear of science. ● **ir|ra|tion|al|ly** ADV ❑ My husband is irrationally jealous over my past loves. ● **ir|ra|tion|al|ity** /ɪræʃənælɪti/ N-UNCOUNT ❑ ...the irrationality of his behavior.

ir|rec|on|cil|able /ɪrɛkənsaɪləbəl/ **1** ADJ If two things such as opinions or proposals are **irreconcilable**, they are so different from each other that it is not possible to believe or have both of them. [FORMAL] ❑ *These old concepts are irreconcilable with modern life.* **2** ADJ An **irreconcilable** disagreement or conflict is so serious that it cannot be settled. [FORMAL] ❑ *...an irreconcilable clash of personalities.*

ir|re|deem|able /ɪrɪdiːməbəl/ ADJ If someone or something has an **irredeemable** fault, it cannot be corrected. [FORMAL] ❑ *There seems to be no one they consider irredeemable.* • **ir|re|deem|ably** /ɪrɪdiːməbli/ ADV [ADV adj/-ed] ❑ *The applicant was irredeemably incompetent.*

ir|re|duc|ible /ɪrɪdyuːsɪbəl/ ADJ [usu ADJ n] **Irreducible** things cannot be made simpler or smaller. [FORMAL] ❑ *...the irreducible complexity of human life.*

ir|refu|table /ɪrɪfyuːtəbəl/ ADJ **Irrefutable** evidence, statements, or arguments cannot be shown to be incorrect or unsatisfactory. [FORMAL] ❑ *The pictures provide irrefutable evidence of the incident.*

ir|regu|lar /ɪrɛgyələr/ (**irregulars**) **1** ADJ If events or actions occur at **irregular** intervals, the periods of time between them are of different lengths. ❑ *Cars passed at irregular intervals.* ❑ *She was taken to a hospital suffering from an irregular heartbeat.* • **ir|regu|lar|ly** ADV [ADV with v] ❑ *He was eating irregularly, steadily losing weight.* • **ir|regu|lar|ity** /ɪrɛgyəlærɪti/ (**irregularities**) N-VAR ❑ *...a dangerous irregularity in her heartbeat.* **2** ADJ Something that is **irregular** is not smooth or straight, or does not form a regular pattern. ❑ *He had bad teeth, irregular and discolored.* • **ir|regu|lar|ly** ADV ❑ *Located off-center in the irregularly shaped lake was a fountain.* • **ir|regu|lar|ity** N-VAR ❑ *...treatment of abnormalities or irregularities of the teeth.* **3** ADJ **Irregular** behavior is dishonest or not in accordance with the normal rules. ❑ *...irregular business practices.* • **ir|regu|lar|ity** N-VAR ❑ *He faced charges arising from alleged financial irregularities.* **4** ADJ An **irregular** verb, noun, or adjective has different forms from most other verbs, nouns, or adjectives in the language. For example, 'break' is an irregular verb because its past form is 'broke,' not 'breaked.'

ir|rel|evance /ɪrɛlɪvəns/ (**irrelevances**) **1** N-UNCOUNT If you talk about the **irrelevance** of something, you mean that it is irrelevant. ❑ *...the utter irrelevance of the debate.* **2** N-COUNT If you describe something as an **irrelevance**, you have a low opinion of it because it is not important in a situation. ❑ *The party has been a political irrelevance since it was abandoned by its foreign backers.*

ir|rel|evan|cy /ɪrɛlɪvənsi/ (**irrelevancies**) N-COUNT If you describe something as an **irrelevancy**, you have a low opinion of it because it is not important in a situation. ❑ *Why was he wasting her time with these irrelevancies?*

ir|rel|evant /ɪrɛlɪvənt/ **1** ADJ If you describe something such as a fact or remark as **irrelevant**, you mean that it is not connected with what you are discussing or dealing with. ❑ *...irrelevant details.* **2** ADJ If you say that something is **irrelevant**, you mean that it is not important in a situation. ❑ *The choice of subject matter is irrelevant.*

ir|re|li|gious /ɪrɪlɪdʒəs/ ADJ An **irreligious** person does not accept the beliefs of any religion or opposes all religions.

ir|re|medi|able /ɪrɪmiːdiəbəl/ ADJ If a bad situation or change is **irremediable**, the situation cannot be improved. [FORMAL] ❑ *His memory suffered irremediable damage.*

ir|repa|rable /ɪrɛpərəbəl/ ADJ **Irreparable** damage or harm is so bad that it cannot be repaired or corrected. [FORMAL] ❑ *The move would cause irreparable harm to the organization.* • **ir|repa|rably** /ɪrɛpərəbli/ ADV [ADV with v, ADV -ed] ❑ *Her heart was irreparably damaged by a virus.*

ir|re|place|able /ɪrɪpleɪsəbəl/ ADJ **Irreplaceable** things are so special that they cannot be replaced if they are lost or destroyed. ❑ *...a rare and irreplaceable jewel.*

ir|re|press|ible /ɪrɪprɛsɪbəl/ ADJ An **irrepressible** person is lively and energetic and never seems to be depressed. ❑ *Jared's exuberance was irrepressible.* • **ir|re|press|ibly** /ɪrɪprɛsɪbli/ ADV [usu ADV adj/-ed] ❑ *Ginny was irrepressibly rebellious.*

ir|re|proach|able /ɪrɪproʊtʃəbəl/ ADJ If you say that someone's character or behavior is **irreproachable**, you mean that they behave so well that they cannot be criticized. ❑ *She welcomed her unexpected visitor with irreproachable politeness.*

ir|re|sist|ible /ɪrɪzɪstɪbəl/ **1** ADJ If you describe something such as a desire or force as **irresistible**, you mean that it is so powerful that it makes you act in a certain way, and there is nothing you can do to prevent this. ❑ *It proved an irresistible temptation to Bob to go back.* • **ir|re|sist|ibly** /ɪrɪzɪstɪbli/ ADV [ADV with v] ❑ *I found myself irresistibly drawn to Steve's world.* **2** ADJ If you describe something or someone as **irresistible**, you mean that they are so good or attractive that you cannot stop yourself from liking them or wanting them. [INFORMAL] ❑ *The music is irresistible.* • **ir|re|sist|ibly** ADV [ADV adj] ❑ *She had a charm that men found irresistibly attractive.*

ir|re|so|lute /ɪrɛzəluːt/ ADJ Someone who is **irresolute** cannot decide what to do. [FORMAL] ❑ *The worst reason to launch an attack would be a fear of seeming irresolute.*

ir|re|spec|tive /ɪrɪspɛktɪv/ PHRASE If you say that something happens or should happen **irrespective of** a particular thing, you mean that it is not affected or should not be affected by that thing. [FORMAL] ❑ *...their commitment to a society based on equality for all citizens irrespective of ethnic origin.*

ir|re|spon|sible /ɪrɪspɒnsɪbəl/ ADJ If you describe someone as **irresponsible**, you are criticizing them because they do things without properly considering their possible consequences. [DISAPPROVAL] ❑ *I felt that it was irresponsible to advocate the legalization of drugs.* • **ir|re|spon|sibly** /ɪrɪspɒnsɪbli/ ADV ❑ *They resent the implication that they have behaved irresponsibly.* • **ir|re|spon|sibil|ity** /ɪrɪspɒnsɪbɪlɪti/ N-UNCOUNT ❑ *I can only wonder at the irresponsibility of people who advocate such destruction to our environment.*

ir|re|triev|able /ɪrɪtriːvəbəl/ ADJ If you talk about **irretrievable** damage or an **irretrievable** situation, you mean that the damage or situation is so bad that there is no possibility of correcting it. [FORMAL] ❑ *...a country in irretrievable decline.* • **ir|re|triev|ably** /ɪrɪtriːvəbli/ ADV [usu ADV with v] ❑ *Eventually her marriage broke down irretrievably.*

ir|rev|er|ent /ɪrɛvərənt/ ADJ If you describe someone as **irreverent**, you mean that they do not show respect for people or things that are generally respected. [APPROVAL] ❑ *Taylor combined great knowledge with an irreverent attitude to history.* • **ir|rev|er|ence** N-UNCOUNT ❑ *His irreverence for authority marks him out as a troublemaker.*

ir|re|vers|ible /ɪrɪvɜrsɪbəl/ ADJ If a change is **irreversible**, things cannot be changed back to the way they were before. ❑ *She could suffer irreversible brain damage if she is not treated within seven days.*

ir|revo|cable /ɪrɛvəkəbəl/ ADJ If a decision, action, or change is **irrevocable**, it cannot be changed or reversed. [FORMAL] ❑ *He said the decision was irrevocable.* • **ir|revo|cably** /ɪrɛvəkəbli/ ADV ❑ *My relationships with friends have been irrevocably altered by their reactions to my illness.*

ir|ri|gate /ɪrɪgeɪt/ (**irrigates, irrigating, irrigated**) V-T To **irrigate** land means to supply it with water in order to help crops grow. ❑ *None of the water from Lake Powell is used to irrigate the area.* • **ir|ri|ga|tion** /ɪrɪgeɪʃən/ N-UNCOUNT ❑ *The agricultural land is hilly and the irrigation poor.*

ir|ri|table /ɪrɪtəbəl/ ADJ If you are **irritable**, you are easily annoyed. ❑ *He had been waiting for over an hour and was beginning to feel irritable.* • **ir|ri|tably** /ɪrɪtəbli/ ADV [ADV with v] ❑ *"Why are you whispering?" he asked irritably.* • **ir|ri|tabil|ity** /ɪrɪtəbɪlɪti/ N-UNCOUNT ❑ *Patients usually suffer from memory loss, personality changes, and increased irritability.*

ir|ri|tant /ɪrɪtənt/ (**irritants**) **1** N-COUNT If you describe something as an **irritant**, you mean that it keeps annoying you. [FORMAL] ❑ *He said the issue was not a major irritant.* **2** N-COUNT An **irritant** is a substance that causes a part of your body to itch or become sore. [FORMAL] ❑ *Many pesticides are irritants.*

ir|ri|tate /ɪrɪteɪt/ (**irritates, irritating, irritated**) **1** V-T If something **irritates** you, it keeps annoying you. ❑ *Their attitude irritates me.* • **ir|ri|tat|ed** ADJ ❑ *Not surprisingly, her teacher is getting irritated with her.* **2** V-T If something **irritates** a part of your body, it causes it to itch or become sore. ❑ *Wear rubber gloves while chopping chilies as they can irritate the skin.*

ir|ri|tat|ing /ɪrɪteɪtɪŋ/ **1** ADJ Something that is **irritating** keeps annoying you. ❑ *They also have the irritating habit of interrupting.* • **ir|ri|tat|ing|ly** ADV ❑ *They can be irritatingly*

irritation

indecisive at times. **2** ADJ An **irritating** substance can cause your body to itch or become sore. ❏ *In heavy concentrations, ozone is irritating to the eyes, nose and throat.*

ir|ri|ta|tion /ɪrɪteɪʃᵊn/ (**irritations**) **1** N-UNCOUNT **Irritation** is a feeling of annoyance, especially when something is happening that you cannot easily stop or control. ❏ *He tried not to let his irritation show as he blinked in the glare of the television lights.* **2** N-COUNT An **irritation** is something that keeps annoying you. ❏ *Don't allow a minor irritation in the workplace to mar your ambitions.* **3** N-VAR **Irritation** in a part of your body is a feeling of slight pain and discomfort there. ❏ *These oils may cause irritation to sensitive skins.*

IRS /aɪ ɑr ɛs/ N-PROPER The **IRS** is the federal government authority that collects taxes. **IRS** is an abbreviation for **Internal Revenue Service**.

is /ɪz/ **Is** is the third person singular of the present tense of **be**. **Is** is often added to other words and shortened to **-'s**.

ISDN /aɪ ɛs di ɛn/ N-UNCOUNT **ISDN** is a telephone network that can send voice and computer messages. **ISDN** is an abbreviation for 'Integrated Service Digital Network.' ❏ *...an ISDN phone line.*

SUFFIX

-ise
Verbs that can end in either *-ise* or *-ize* are dealt with in this dictionary at the *-ize* spelling. Many verbs ending in *-ise* describe processes by which things or people are brought into a new state. For example, 'The dispute could **jeopardise** the negotiations.'

SUFFIX

-ish
1 forms words that indicate that a particular time or age mentioned is approximate. For example, if someone is **fortyish**, they are about forty years old.
2 also forms adjectives that indicate that someone or something has a quality to a small extent. For example, something that is **yellowish** is slightly yellow in color.

Is|lam ◆◇◇ /ɪslɑm/ **1** N-UNCOUNT **Islam** is the religion of the Muslims, which was started by Mohammed. ❏ *He converted to Islam at the age of 16.* **2** N-UNCOUNT Some people use **Islam** to refer to all the countries where Islam is the main religion. ❏ *...relations between Islam and the West.*

Is|lam|ic ◆◇◇ /ɪslæmɪk, -lɑ-/ ADJ [ADJ n] **Islamic** means belonging or relating to Islam. ❏ *...Islamic law.*

Is|lam|ist /ɪzləmɪst/ (**Islamists**) N-COUNT [oft N n] An **Islamist** is someone who believes strongly in Islamic ideas and laws. ❏ *It was clear that there was significant support for the Islamists.*

is|land ◆◆◇ /aɪlənd/ (**islands**) **1** N-COUNT; N-IN-NAMES An **island** is a piece of land that is completely surrounded by water. ❏ *...the Canary Islands.* **2** → See feature box at **ocean**

COLLOCATIONS

island
NOUN
noun + **island**: paradise, resort; coral
adjective + **island**: remote, uninhabited; tropical, volcanic

---

is|land|er /aɪləndər/ (**islanders**) N-COUNT **Islanders** are people who live on an island. ❏ *The islanders endured centuries of exploitation.*

isle /aɪl/ (**isles**) N-COUNT; N-IN-NAMES An **isle** is an island; often used as part of an island's name, or in literary English. ❏ *...the Isle of Pines.*

is|let /aɪlɪt/ (**islets**) N-COUNT An **islet** is a small island. [LITERARY]

SUFFIX

-ism
forms nouns that refer to particular beliefs, or to behavior based on these beliefs. For example, **professionalism** is behavior that is professional.

---

isn't /ɪzᵊnt/ **Isn't** is the usual spoken form of 'is not.'

iso|late /aɪsəleɪt/ (**isolates, isolating, isolated**) **1** V-T To **isolate** a person or organization means to cause them to lose

issue

their friends or supporters. ❏ *This policy could isolate the country from the other permanent members of the United Nations Security Council.* ● **iso|lat|ed** ADJ ❏ *They are finding themselves increasingly isolated within the teaching profession.* ● **iso|la|tion** /aɪsəleɪʃᵊn/ N-UNCOUNT ❏ *Diplomatic isolation could lead to economic disaster.* **2** V-T If you **isolate** yourself, or if something **isolates** you, you become physically or socially separated from other people. ❏ *She seemed determined to isolate herself from everyone, even him.* ❏ *His radicalism and refusal to compromise isolated him.* **3** V-T If you **isolate** something such as an idea or a problem, you separate it from others that it is connected with, so that you can concentrate on it or consider it on its own. ❏ *Our anxieties can also be controlled by isolating thoughts, feelings and memories.* **4** V-T To **isolate** a substance means to obtain it by separating it from other substances using scientific processes. [TECHNICAL] ❏ *We can use genetic engineering techniques to isolate the gene that is responsible.* **5** V-T To **isolate** a sick person or animal means to keep them apart from other people or animals, so that their illness does not spread. ❏ *Patients will be isolated from other people for between three days and one month after treatment.* ● **iso|la|tion** N-UNCOUNT [oft N n] ❏ *Hayley contracted tuberculosis and had to be put in an isolation ward.*

iso|lat|ed /aɪsəleɪtɪd/ **1** ADJ An **isolated** place is a long way away from large towns and is difficult to reach. ❏ *Many of the refugee villages are in isolated areas.* **2** ADJ If you feel **isolated**, you feel lonely and without friends or help. ❏ *Some patients may become very isolated and depressed.* **3** ADJ [ADJ n] An **isolated** example is an example of something that is not very common. ❏ *They said the allegations related to an isolated case of cheating.*

iso|la|tion /aɪsəleɪʃᵊn/ **1** N-UNCOUNT **Isolation** is the state of feeling alone and without friends or help. ❏ *Many deaf people have feelings of isolation and loneliness.* **2** → see also **isolate** **3** PHRASE If something is considered **in isolation** from other things that it is connected with, it is considered separately, and those other things are not considered. ❏ *Punishment cannot, therefore, be discussed in isolation from social and political theory.* **4** PHRASE If someone does something **in isolation**, they do it without other people present or without their help. ❏ *Malcolm, for instance, works in isolation but I have no doubts about his abilities.*

iso|la|tion|ism /aɪsəleɪʃənɪzəm/ N-UNCOUNT If you refer to **isolationism**, you are referring to a country's policy of avoiding close relationships with other countries and of not taking sides in disputes between other countries. ❏ *...the perils of isolationism.* ● **iso|la|tion|ist** (**isolationists**) N-COUNT [oft N n] ❏ *The government had to overcome isolationist opposition to the plan.*

iso|met|rics /aɪsəmɛtrɪks/

The form **isometric** is used as a modifier.

N-PLURAL **Isometrics** or **isometric** exercises are exercises in which you make your muscles work against each other or against something else, for example, by pressing your hands together.

iso|tope /aɪsətoʊp/ (**isotopes**) N-COUNT **Isotopes** are atoms that have the same number of protons and electrons but different numbers of neutrons and therefore have different physical properties. [TECHNICAL] ❏ *...tritium, a radioactive isotope of hydrogen.*

ISP /aɪ ɛs pi/ (**ISPs**) N-COUNT An **ISP** is a company that provides internet and email services. **ISP** is an abbreviation for 'Internet service provider.'

Is|rae|li /ɪzreɪli/ (**Israelis**) **1** ADJ **Israeli** means belonging or relating to Israel, or to its people or culture. **2** N-COUNT An **Israeli** is an Israeli citizen, or a person of Israeli origin.

is|sue ◆◆◆ /ɪʃu/ (**issues, issuing, issued**) **1** N-COUNT An **issue** is an important subject that people are arguing about or discussing. ❏ *Agents will raise the issue of prize-money for next year's world championships.* ❏ *A key issue for higher education is the need for greater diversity of courses.* **2** N-SING If something is **the issue**, it is the thing you consider to be the most important part of a situation or discussion. ❏ *I was earning a lot of money, but that was not the issue.* ❏ *Do not draw it on the chart, however, as this will confuse the issue.* **3** N-COUNT An **issue** of something such as a magazine or newspaper is the version of it that is published, for example, in a particular month or on a particular day.

❏ *The growing problem is underlined in the latest issue of the Scientific American.* ◳ V-T If you **issue** a statement or a warning, you make it known formally or publicly. ❏ *Last night he issued a statement denying the allegations.* ❏ *The government issued a warning that the strikers should end their action or face dismissal.* ◳ V-T [usu passive] If you **are issued with** something, it is officially given to you. ❏ *On your appointment you will be issued with a written statement of particulars of employment.* • N-UNCOUNT **Issue** is also a noun. ❏ *...a standard army issue rifle.* ◳ PHRASE The question or point **at issue** is the question or point that is being argued about or discussed. ❏ *The problems of immigration were not the question at issue.* ◳ PHRASE If you **make an issue of** something, you try to make other people think about it or discuss it, because you are concerned or annoyed about it. ❏ *It seemed the Colonel had no desire to make an issue of the affair.* ◳ PHRASE If you **take issue with** someone or something they said, you disagree with them, and start arguing about it. ❏ *I will not take issue with the fact that we have a recession.* ◳ PHRASE [oft PHR with/about n] If someone **has issues** with a particular aspect of their life, they have problems connected with it. ❏ *Parents automatically go to a book when they have issues with their children.*

is|sue price (issue prices) N-COUNT The **issue price** of shares is the price at which they are offered for sale when they first become available to the public. [BUSINESS] ❏ *Shares in the company slipped below their issue price on their first day of trading.*

SUFFIX

-ist
◳ forms nouns that refer to people who play a particular musical instrument, often as their job. *For example, a* **guitarist** *is someone who plays the guitar.*
◳ also forms nouns that refer to people who do a particular kind of work. *For example, a* **scientist** *is someone whose work is connected with science.*

isth|mus /ˈɪsməs/ (isthmuses) N-COUNT [oft in names] An **isthmus** is a narrow piece of land connecting two large areas of land. ❏ *...the Isthmus of Panama.*

it ✦✦✦ /ɪt/

It is a third person singular pronoun. **It** is used as the subject or object of a verb, or as the object of a preposition.

◳ PRON-SING You use **it** to refer to an object, animal, or other thing that has already been mentioned. ❏ *It's a wonderful city, really. I'll show it to you if you want.* ❏ *My wife has become crippled by arthritis. She is embarrassed to ask the doctor about it.* ◳ PRON-SING You use **it** to refer to a child or baby whose sex you do not know or whose sex is not relevant to what you are saying. ❏ *She could compel him to support the child after it was born.* ◳ PRON-SING You use **it** to refer in a general way to a situation that you have just described. ❏ *He was through with sports, not because he had to be but because he wanted it that way.* ◳ PRON-SING You use **it** before certain nouns, adjectives, and verbs to introduce your feelings or point of view about a situation. ❏ *It was nice to see Steve again.* ❏ *It's a pity you're going away.* ◳ PRON-SING You use **it** in passive clauses that report a situation or event. ❏ *It has been said that stress causes cancer.* ◳ PRON-SING You use **it** with some verbs that need a subject or object, although there is no noun that 'it' refers to. ❏ *Of course, as it turned out, three-fourths of the people in the group were psychiatrists.* ◳ PRON-SING You use **it** as the subject of 'be' to say what the time, day, or date is. ❏ *It's three o'clock in the morning.* ❏ *It was a Monday, so she was at home.* ◳ PRON-SING You use **it** as the subject of a linking verb to describe the weather, the light, or the temperature. ❏ *It was very wet and windy the day I drove over the hill to Del Norte.* ◳ PRON-SING You use **it** when you are telling someone who you are, or asking them who they are, especially at the beginning of a phone call. You also use **it** in statements and questions about the identity of other people. ❏ *"Who is it?" he called.—"It's your neighbor."* ◳ PRON When you are emphasizing or drawing attention to something, you can put that thing immediately after **it** and a form of the verb 'be.' [EMPHASIS] ❏ *It's really the poor countries that don't have an economic base that have the worst environmental records.* ◳ PHRASE You use **it** in expressions such as **it's not that** or **it's not just that** when you are giving a reason for something and are suggesting that there are several other reasons. ❏ *It's not that I didn't want to be with my family.* ◳ **if it wasn't for** → see **be** ②

USAGE

it
Don't use 'it' with a linking verb and a noun phrase to say that something exists or is present. Don't say, for example, '~~It's a lot of traffic on this road tonight.~~' Say '**There's** a lot of traffic on this road tonight.' *There's a teacher at my school called Miss Large.*

IT ✦✦✦ /ˌaɪ ˈtiː/ **IT** is an abbreviation for **information technology**. ❏ *...people with IT skills.*

Ital|ian /ɪˈtæliən/ (Italians) ◳ ADJ **Italian** means belonging or relating to Italy, or to its people, language, or culture. ◳ N-COUNT An **Italian** is an Italian citizen, or a person of Italian origin. ◳ N-UNCOUNT **Italian** is the language spoken in Italy, and in parts of Switzerland.

ital|ic /ɪˈtælɪk/ (italics) ◳ N-PLURAL **Italics** are letters that slope to the right. Italics are often used to emphasize a particular word or sentence. The examples in this dictionary are printed in italics. ❏ *The title is printed in italics.* ◳ ADJ [ADJ n] **Italic** letters slope to the right. ❏ *She addressed them by hand in her beautiful italic script.*

itch /ɪtʃ/ (itches, itching, itched) ◳ V-I When a part of your body **itches**, you have an unpleasant feeling on your skin that makes you want to scratch. ❏ *When someone has hay fever, the eyes and nose will stream and itch.* • N-COUNT **Itch** is also a noun. ❏ *Scratch my back – I've got an itch.* • **itch|ing** N-UNCOUNT ❏ *It may be that the itching is caused by contact with irritant material.* ◳ V-T/V-I [usu cont] If you **are itching** to do something, you are very eager or impatient to do it. [INFORMAL] ❏ *I was itching to get involved.* • N-SING **Itch** is also a noun. ❏ *...cable TV viewers with an insatiable itch to switch from channel to channel.*

itchy /ˈɪtʃi/ ◳ ADJ If a part of your body or something you are wearing is **itchy**, you have an unpleasant feeling on your skin that makes you want to scratch. [INFORMAL] ❏ *...itchy, sore eyes.* ◳ PHRASE If you have **itchy feet**, you have a strong desire to leave a place and to travel. [INFORMAL] ❏ *The thought gave me really itchy feet so within a couple of months I decided to leave.*

it'd /ˈɪtəd/ ◳ **It'd** is a spoken form of 'it would.' ❏ *It'd be better for a place like this to remain closed.* ◳ **It'd** is a spoken form of 'it had,' especially when 'had' is an auxiliary verb. ❏ *Marcie was watching the news. It'd just started.*

item ✦✦◊ /ˈaɪtəm/ (items) ◳ N-COUNT An **item** is one of a collection or list of objects. ❏ *The most valuable item on show will be a Picasso drawing.* ◳ N-COUNT An **item** is one of a list of things for someone to do, deal with, or talk about. ❏ *The other item on the agenda is the tour.* ◳ N-COUNT An **item** is a report or article in a newspaper or magazine, or on television or radio. ❏ *There was an item in the paper about him.* ◳ N-SING If you say that two people are an **item**, you mean that they are having a romantic or sexual relationship. [INFORMAL] ❏ *She and Gino were an item.*

COLLOCATIONS

item
NOUN
◳
noun + **item**: fashion, food, grocery, household; auction, novelty
adjective + **item**: essential, luxury, valuable; electrical; personal
verb + **item**: buy
◳
noun + **item**: news, newspaper

item|ize /ˈaɪtəmaɪz/ (itemizes, itemizing, itemized)
in BRIT, also use **itemise**
V-T If you **itemize** a number of things, you make a list of them. ❏ *The report will itemize the cost of various improvements.*

It-girl (It-girls) also **It girl** N-COUNT Journalists sometimes use **It-girl** to describe a young woman who is well-known because she goes to the most fashionable places and events and knows famous people. [INFORMAL, JOURNALISM] ❏ *She is being heralded as fashion's new It-girl.*

itin|er|ant /aɪˈtɪnərənt/ (itinerants) ◳ ADJ [ADJ n] An **itinerant** worker travels around a region, working for short periods in

itinerary

different places. [FORMAL] ❏ ...*the author's experiences as an itinerant musician.* **2** N-COUNT An **itinerant** is someone whose way of life involves traveling around, usually someone who is poor and homeless. [FORMAL]

itin|er|ary /aɪtɪnəreri/ (**itineraries**) N-COUNT An **itinerary** is a plan of a trip, including the route and the places that you will visit. ❏ *The next place on our itinerary was Sedona.*

it'll /ɪtᵊl/ **It'll** is a spoken form of 'it will.' ❏ *It's been a while since I've seen her so it'll be nice to meet her in town on Thursday.*

its ◆◆◆ /ɪts/

| **Its** is a third person singular possessive determiner. |

DET You use **its** to indicate that something belongs or relates to a thing, place, or animal that has just been mentioned or whose identity is known. You can use **its** to indicate that something belongs or relates to a child or baby. ❏ *He held the knife by its blade.*

it's /ɪts/ **1** **It's** is the usual spoken form of 'it is.' ❏ *It's the best news I've heard in a long time.* **2** **It's** is the usual spoken form of 'it has,' especially when 'has' is an auxiliary verb. ❏ *It's been such a long time since I played.*

it|self ◆◆◆ /ɪtsɛlf/ **1** PRON-REFL [V PRON, prep PRON] **Itself** is used as the object of a verb or preposition when it refers to something that is the same thing as the subject of the verb. ❏ *Scientists have discovered remarkable new evidence showing how the body rebuilds itself while we sleep.* **2** PRON-REFL-EMPH You use **itself** to emphasize the thing you are referring to. [EMPHASIS] ❏ *I think life itself is a learning process.* **3** PRON-REFL-EMPH [n PRON] If you say that someone is, for example, politeness **itself** or kindness **itself**, you are emphasizing that they are extremely polite or extremely kind. [EMPHASIS] ❏ *He is rarely satisfied with anything less than perfection itself.*

SUFFIX

-ity
forms nouns that refer to a particular state or quality. For example, **simplicity** is the quality of being simple.

IUD /aɪ yu di/ (**IUDs**) N-COUNT An **IUD** is a piece of plastic or metal that is put inside a woman's womb so that she does not become pregnant. **IUD** is an abbreviation for 'intrauterine device.'

IV /aɪ vi/ (**IVs**) **1** N-COUNT An **IV** or an **IV drip** is a piece of medical equipment by which a liquid is slowly passed through a tube into a patient's blood. ❏ *She was muzzled with an oxygen mask and tethered to an IV.* ❏ ...*patients hooked up to IV drips and heart monitors.* **2** ADJ [ADJ n] **IV** is an abbreviation for **intravenous**. ❏ ...*the spread of AIDS among IV drug users.*

I've /aɪv/ **I've** is the usual spoken form of 'I have,' especially when 'have' is an auxiliary verb. ❏ *I've been invited to meet with the ambassador.*

IVF /aɪ vi ɛf/ N-UNCOUNT **IVF** is a method of helping a woman to have a baby in which an egg is removed from one of her ovaries, fertilized outside her body, and then replaced in her womb. **IVF** is an abbreviation for 'in vitro fertilization.' ❏ *When she first underwent IVF it was still a relatively new procedure.*

ivo|ry /aɪvəri/ **1** N-UNCOUNT **Ivory** is a hard cream-colored substance that forms the tusks of elephants and some other animals. It is valuable and can be used for making carved ornaments. ❏ ...*the international ban on the sale of ivory.* **2** COLOR **Ivory** is a creamy-white color. ❏ ...*small ivory flowers.* **3** → See feature box at **endanger**

ivo|ry tow|er (**ivory towers**) N-COUNT [usu prep N, N n] If you describe someone as living in an **ivory tower**, you mean that they have no knowledge or experience of the practical problems of everyday life. [DISAPPROVAL] ❏ *They don't really, in their ivory towers, understand how pernicious drug crime is.*

ivy /aɪvi/ (**ivies**) N-VAR **Ivy** is an evergreen plant that grows up walls or along the ground.

Ivy League N-PROPER [the N; oft N n] **The Ivy League** is a group of eight universities in the northeastern part of the United States, that have high academic and social status. ❏ ...*an Ivy League college.*

SUFFIX

-ize
Verbs that can end in either *-ize* or *-ise* are dealt with in this dictionary at the *-ize* spelling. Many verbs ending in *-ize* describe processes by which things or people are brought into a new state. For example, 'The dispute could **jeopardize** the negotiations.'

Jj

J also **j** /dʒeɪ/ (**J's, j's**) N-VAR J is the tenth letter of the English alphabet.

jab /dʒæb/ (**jabs, jabbing, jabbed**) **1** V-T/V-I If you **jab** one thing into another, you push it there with a quick, sudden movement and with a lot of force. ❑ *He saw her jab her thumb on a red button – a panic button.* ❑ *Stern jabbed at me with his glasses.* **2** N-COUNT A **jab** is a sudden, sharp punch. ❑ *He was simply too powerful for his opponent, rocking him with a steady supply of left jabs.*

jab|ber /dʒæbər/ (**jabbers, jabbering, jabbered**) V-I If you say that someone **is jabbering**, you mean that they are talking very quickly and excitedly, and you cannot understand them. [DISAPPROVAL] ❑ *The girl jabbered incomprehensibly.* ❑ *After a minute or two I left them there jabbering away.*

jack /dʒæk/ (**jacks**) **1** N-COUNT A **jack** is a device for lifting a heavy object, such as a car, off the ground. **2** N-COUNT A **jack** is a playing card whose value is between a ten and a queen. A jack is usually represented by a picture of a young man. ❑ *...the jack of spades.*

jack|al /dʒækəl, -ɔl/ (**jackals**) N-COUNT A **jackal** is a wild animal that looks like a dog, has long legs and pointed ears, and lives in Africa and southern Asia.

jack|ass /dʒækæs/ (**jackasses**) N-COUNT [oft N n] If you call someone a **jackass**, you mean they are very stupid or they have done something very stupid. [INFORMAL, VULGAR, DISAPPROVAL] ❑ *Paul is a tedious, self-absorbed jackass who neglects his girlfriend.* ❑ *I hate to talk bad about my government, but it is a jackass government.*

jack|boot /dʒækbut/ (**jackboots**) N-COUNT [usu pl] **Jackboots** are heavy boots that come up to the knee, such as the ones worn by some soldiers.

jack|daw /dʒækdɔ/ (**jackdaws**) N-COUNT A **jackdaw** is a large black and gray bird that is similar to a crow, and lives in Europe and Asia.

jack|et♦◇◇ /dʒækɪt/ (**jackets**) **1** N-COUNT A **jacket** is a short coat with long sleeves. ❑ *...a black leather jacket.* **2** N-COUNT The **jacket** of a book is the paper cover that protects the book. [mainly AM] ❑ *A beautiful girl gazes from the jacket of this book.* **3** → see also **dinner jacket, straitjacket**

jack|fruit /dʒækfrut/ (**jackfruit**) N-VAR **Jackfruit** is the large fruit of a tropical tree. **Jackfruit** is the flesh of this fruit eaten as food. ❑ *These delicious Indonesian fritters are made from jackfruit, sweet potato, spring onion, fresh coriander and a hint of chilli.*

jack|ham|mer /dʒækhæmər/ (**jackhammers**) N-COUNT A **jackhammer** is a large hammer, powered by compressed air, that is used for breaking up rocks and other hard material. ❑ *Outside a jackhammer was pounding away at a particularly stubborn piece of concrete.*

jack-in-the-box (**jack-in-the-boxes**) N-COUNT A **jack-in-the-box** is a child's toy that consists of a box with a doll inside that jumps out when the lid is opened.

jack|knife /dʒæknaɪf/ (**jackknifes, jackknifing, jackknifed**) V-I If a truck that is in two parts **jackknifes**, the back part swings around at a sharp angle to the front part in an uncontrolled way as the truck is moving. ❑ *Traffic on the Pacific Highway near Yatala was delayed early yesterday after a semi-trailer jackknifed and left the road.*

jack-of-all-trades (**jacks-of-all-trades**) also **jack of all trades** N-COUNT If you refer to someone as a **jack-of-all-trades**, you mean that they are able to do a variety of different jobs. You are also often suggesting that they are not very good at any of these jobs.

jack-o'-lantern /dʒæk ə læntərn/ (**jack-o'-lanterns**) also **jack o'lantern** N-COUNT A **jack-o'-lantern** is a lantern made from a hollow pumpkin that has been carved to look like a face. [AM] ❑ *Her children have lighted their jack-o'-lantern, even though there are still two days before Halloween.*

jack|pot /dʒækpɒt/ (**jackpots**) **1** N-COUNT A **jackpot** is the most valuable prize in a game or lottery, especially when the game involves increasing the value of the prize until someone wins it. ❑ *A nurse who gambled $5 in a slot machine walked away with the biggest ever jackpot of more than $5 million.* **2** PHRASE If you **hit the jackpot**, you have a great success, for example by winning a lot of money or having a piece of good luck. [INFORMAL] ❑ *Tennis player Michael Stich hit the jackpot yesterday when he won $2 million.*

jack|rab|bit /dʒækræbɪt/ (**jackrabbits**) N-COUNT A **jackrabbit** is a type of hare with long back legs and large ears. ❑ *He braked suddenly as a jackrabbit darted into the bright cones of light.*

Jaco|bean /dʒækəbiən/ ADJ [usu ADJ n] A **Jacobean** building, piece of furniture, or work of art was built or produced in Britain in the style of the period between 1603 and 1625.

Ja|cuz|zi /dʒəkuzi/ (**Jacuzzis**) N-COUNT A **Jacuzzi** is a large circular bath fitted with a device that makes the water move around. [TRADEMARK]

jade /dʒeɪd/ **1** N-UNCOUNT **Jade** is a hard stone, usually green in color, that is used for making jewelry and ornaments. ❑ *The Burmese jade choker in the catalog was very beautiful.* **2** COLOR Something that is **jade** or **jade green** is bright green in color. ❑ *Amy had bought a soft, jade green cashmere jacket for Helen.*

jad|ed /dʒeɪdɪd/ ADJ If you are **jaded**, you feel bored, tired, and not enthusiastic, because you have had too much of the same thing. ❑ *We had both become jaded and disillusioned.*

jag /dʒæg/ (**jags**) N-COUNT [n n] If you have a crying **jag** or a coughing **jag**, you have a period of uncontrolled crying or coughing. [INFORMAL] ❑ *I don't know how long my crying jag lasted.* ❑ *Laughing again, she was seized by a sudden coughing jag.*

jag|ged /dʒægɪd/ ADJ Something that is **jagged** has a rough, uneven shape or edge with lots of sharp points. ❑ *...jagged black cliffs.*

jagu|ar /dʒægwɑr/ (**jaguars**) N-COUNT A **jaguar** is a large animal of the cat family with dark spots on its back.

jai alai /haɪ əlaɪ/ N-UNCOUNT **Jai alai** is a game that is played in Spain, North America, and the Philippines, in which the players hit a ball against a wall using a long basket tied to their wrist.

jail♦◇◇ /dʒeɪl/ (**jails, jailing, jailed**)

[in BRIT, also use **gaol**]

1 N-VAR A **jail** is a place where criminals are kept in order to punish them, or where people waiting to be tried are kept. ❑ *Three prisoners escaped from a jail.* **2** V-T [usu passive] If someone **is jailed**, they are put into jail. ❑ *He was jailed for twenty years.*

jail|bird /dʒeɪlbɜrd/ (**jailbirds**) N-COUNT If you refer to someone as a **jailbird**, you mean that they are in prison, or have been in prison. [INFORMAL, OLD-FASHIONED]

jail|break /dʒeɪlbreɪk/ (**jailbreaks**) N-COUNT A **jailbreak** is an escape from jail.

jail|er /dʒeɪlər/ (**jailers**)

[in BRIT, also use **gaoler**]

N-COUNT A **jailer** is a person who is in charge of a jail and the prisoners in it. [OLD-FASHIONED]

jail|house /dʒeɪlhaʊs/ (jailhouses) N-COUNT A **jailhouse** is a small prison. [AM]

jala|peño /hɑləpeɪnyoʊ/ (jalapeños) also **jalapeno** N-COUNT **Jalapeños** are small hot green peppers that are often used in Mexican cooking.

jam /dʒæm/ (jams, jamming, jammed) **1** V-T If you **jam** something somewhere, you push or put it there roughly. ❏ *Pete jammed his hands into his pockets.* **2** V-T/V-I If something such as a part of a machine **jams**, or if something **jams** it, the part becomes fixed in position and is unable to move freely or work properly. ❏ *The second time he fired his gun jammed.* ❏ *A rope jammed the boat's propeller.* **3** V-T If vehicles **jam** a road, there are so many of them that they cannot move. ❏ *Hundreds of departing motorists jammed roads that had been closed during the height of the storm.* • N-COUNT **Jam** is also a noun. ❏ *400 trucks may sit in a jam for ten hours waiting to cross the limited number of bridges.* • **jammed** ADJ ❏ *Nearby roads and the dirt track to the beach were jammed with cars.* **4** V-T/V-I If a lot of people **jam** a place, or **jam** into a place, they are pressed tightly together so that they can hardly move. ❏ *Hundreds of people jammed the boardwalk to watch.* • **jammed** ADJ ❏ *The stadium was jammed and they had to turn away hundreds of disappointed fans.* **5** V-T To **jam** a radio or electronic signal means to interfere with it and prevent it from being received or heard clearly. ❏ *They will try to jam the transmissions electronically.* • **jam|ming** N-UNCOUNT ❏ *The plane is used for electronic jamming and radar detection.* **6** V-T If callers **are jamming** telephone lines, there are so many callers that the people answering the telephones find it difficult to deal with them all. ❏ *Hundreds of callers jammed the switchboard for more than an hour.* **7** N-MASS **Jam** is a sweet food consisting of pieces of fruit cooked with a large amount of sugar until it is thickened. It is usually spread on bread. [mainly BRIT]

in AM, use **jelly**

Ja|mai|can /dʒəmeɪkən/ (Jamaicans) **1** ADJ **Jamaican** means belonging or relating to Jamaica or to its people or culture. **2** N-COUNT A **Jamaican** is a person who comes from Jamaica.

jamb /dʒæm/ (jambs) N-COUNT [usu n N] A **jamb** is a post that forms the side or upright part of a door frame or window frame.

jam|bo|ree /dʒæmbəri/ (jamborees) N-COUNT [usu sing] A **jamboree** is a party, celebration, or other gathering where there are a large number of people and a lot of excitement, fun, and enjoyment.

jam-packed ADJ [oft ADJ *with* n] If somewhere is **jam-packed**, it is so full of people or things that there is no room for any more. [INFORMAL] ❏ *His room was jam-packed with fruit, flowers, and gifts.*

Jan. Jan. is a written abbreviation for **January**.

Jane Doe /dʒeɪn doʊ/ (Jane Does) N-COUNT **Jane Doe** is used to refer to a woman whose real name is not known or cannot be revealed, for example, for legal reasons. [AM] ❏ *The new action, filed in the Manhattan federal court, is on behalf of a woman named only as Jane Doe.*

jan|gle /dʒæŋɡəl/ (jangles, jangling, jangled) V-T/V-I When objects strike against each other and make a ringing noise, you can say that they **jangle** or **are jangled**. ❏ *Her bead necklaces and bracelets jangled as she walked.*

jani|tor /dʒænɪtər/ (janitors) N-COUNT A **janitor** is a person whose job is to take care of a building. [mainly AM] ❏ *Ed Roberts had been a school janitor for a long time.*

jan|ky /dʒæŋki/ (jankier, jankiest) ADJ If you describe something, especially computer equipment, as **janky**, you think it is of bad quality. [AM, INFORMAL]

Janu|ary ♦♦♦ /dʒænyueri/ (Januaries) N-VAR **January** is the first month of the year in the Western calendar. ❏ *We always have snow in January.*

Japa|nese /dʒæpəniːz/ (Japanese) **1** ADJ **Japanese** means belonging or relating to Japan, or to its people, language, or culture. **2** N-PLURAL The **Japanese** are the people of Japan. **3** N-UNCOUNT **Japanese** is the language spoken in Japan.

jar /dʒɑr/ (jars, jarring, jarred) **1** N-COUNT A **jar** is a glass container with a lid that is used for storing food. ❏ *...cucumbers in glass jars.* **2** N-COUNT You can use **jar** to refer to a jar and its contents, or to the contents only. ❏ *She opened up a jar of plums.* **3** V-T/V-I If something **jars**, or **jars** you, you find it unpleasant, disturbing, or shocking. ❏ *...televised congressional hearings that jarred the nation's faith in the presidency.* • **jar|ring** ADJ ❏ *In the context of this chapter, Dore's comments strike a jarring note.* **4** V-T/V-I If an object **jars**, or if something **jars** it, the object moves with a fairly hard shaking movement. ❏ *The ship jarred a little.* ❏ *The sudden movement jarred the box and it fell off the table.* **5** → See feature box at **recycle**

jar|gon /dʒɑrɡən/ N-UNCOUNT You use **jargon** to refer to words and expressions that are used in special or technical ways by particular groups of people, often making the language difficult to understand. ❏ *The manual is full of the jargon and slang of self-improvement courses.*

jas|mine /dʒæzmɪn/ (jasmines) N-VAR **Jasmine** is a plant with small white or yellow flowers that have a pleasant smell.

jaun|dice /dʒɔndɪs/ N-UNCOUNT **Jaundice** is an illness that makes your skin and eyes become yellow.

jaun|diced /dʒɔndɪst/ ADJ [usu ADJ n] If someone has a **jaundiced** view of something, they can see only the bad aspects of it. ❏ *The financial markets are taking a jaundiced view of the Government's motives.*

jaunt /dʒɔnt/ (jaunts) N-COUNT A **jaunt** is a short trip for pleasure or excitement.

jaun|ty /dʒɔnti/ (jauntier, jauntiest) ADJ If you describe someone or something as **jaunty**, you mean that they are full of confidence and energy. ❏ *...a jaunty little man.* • **jaun|ti|ly** /dʒɔntɪli/ ADV ❏ *He walked jauntily into the café.*

java /dʒɑvə/ N-UNCOUNT **Java** is another word for coffee. [AM, INFORMAL] ❏ *...a steaming cup of java.*

Java /dʒɑvə/ N-UNCOUNT **Java** is a computer programming language. It is used especially in creating websites. [TRADEMARK] ❏ *...applications written in Java.*

jave|lin /dʒævlɪn/ (javelins) **1** N-COUNT A **javelin** is a long spear that is used in sports competitions. Competitors try to throw the javelin as far as possible. **2** N-SING You can refer to the competition in which the javelin is thrown as **the javelin**. ❏ *...Steve Backley who won the javelin.*

jaw /dʒɔ/ (jaws) **1** N-COUNT Your **jaw** is the lower part of your face below your mouth. The movement of your jaw is sometimes considered to express a particular emotion. For example, if your **jaw drops**, you are very surprised. ❏ *He thought for a moment, stroking his well-defined jaw.* **2** N-COUNT A person's or animal's **jaws** are the two bones in their head that their teeth are attached to. ❏ *...a forest rodent with powerful jaws.* **3** N-PLURAL If you talk about the **jaws of** something unpleasant such as death or hell, you are referring to a dangerous or unpleasant situation. ❏ *A family dog rescued a newborn boy from the jaws of death.* **4** → See feature box at **appearance**

jaw|bone /dʒɔboʊn/ (jawbones) also **jaw bone** **1** N-COUNT A **jawbone** is the bone in the lower jaw of a person or animal. **2** → See feature box at **body**

jaw-dropping ADJ Something that is **jaw-dropping** is extremely surprising, impressive, or shocking. [INFORMAL, JOURNALISM] ❏ *One insider who has seen the report said it was pretty jaw-dropping stuff.*

jaw|line /dʒɔlaɪn/ (jawlines) also **jaw line** N-COUNT [usu sing] Your **jawline** is the part of your lower jaw that forms the outline of the bottom of your face. ❏ *...high cheekbones and a strong jawline.*

jay /dʒeɪ/ (jays) **1** N-COUNT In North America, a **jay** is a noisy bird with blue or gray feathers. **2** N-COUNT In Europe and Asia, a **jay** is a brownish-pink bird with blue and black wings.

jay|walk|ing /dʒeɪwɔkɪŋ/ N-UNCOUNT **Jaywalking** is the act of walking across a street in a careless and dangerous way, or not at the proper place.

jazz ♦◇◇ /dʒæz/ N-UNCOUNT **Jazz** is a style of music that was invented by African American musicians in the early part of the twentieth century. Jazz music has very strong rhythms and often involves improvisation. ❏ *The club has live jazz on Sundays.*

jazzy /dʒæzi/ (jazzier, jazziest) ADJ [usu ADJ n] If you describe something as **jazzy**, you mean that it is colorful and modern. ❏ *...a jazzy tie.*

jeal|ous /dʒɛləs/ **1** ADJ If someone is **jealous**, they feel angry or bitter because they think that another person is trying to take a lover or friend, or a possession, away from them. ❑ *She got insanely jealous and there was a terrible fight.* • **jeal|ous|ly** ADV [ADV with v] ❑ *The formula is jealously guarded.* **2** ADJ If you are **jealous** of another person's possessions or qualities, you feel angry or bitter because you do not have them. ❑ *She was jealous of his wealth.* • **jeal|ous|ly** ADV [ADV after v] ❑ *Gloria eyed them jealously.*

jeal|ousy /dʒɛləsi/ **1** N-UNCOUNT **Jealousy** is the feeling of anger or bitterness that someone has when they think that another person is trying to take a lover or friend, or a possession, away from them. ❑ *At first his jealousy only showed in small ways – he didn't mind me talking to other guys.* **2** N-UNCOUNT **Jealousy** is the feeling of anger or bitterness that someone has when they wish that they could have the qualities or possessions that another person has. ❑ *Her beauty causes envy and jealousy.*

jeans /dʒiːnz/ N-PLURAL [also a pair of N] **Jeans** are casual pants that are usually made of strong cotton cloth called denim. ❑ *...a young man in jeans and a worn T-shirt.*

Jeep /dʒiːp/ (**Jeeps**) N-COUNT A **Jeep** is a type of car that can travel over rough ground. [TRADEMARK] ❑ *...a U.S. Army Jeep.*

jeer /dʒɪər/ (**jeers, jeering, jeered**) **1** V-T/V-I To **jeer** at someone means to say or shout rude and insulting things to them to show that you do not like or respect them. ❑ *Marchers jeered at passers-by, but there was no violence, nor any arrests.* ❑ *Demonstrators jeered the mayor as he arrived for a week-long visit.* • **jeer|ing** N-UNCOUNT ❑ *There was constant jeering and interruption from the floor.* **2** N-COUNT **Jeers** are rude and insulting things that people shout to show they do not like or respect someone. ❑ *...the heckling and jeers of his audience.*

Jeez /dʒiːz/ EXCLAM Some people say **Jeez** when they are shocked or surprised about something, or to introduce a remark or response. **Jeez** is short for 'Jesus.' This use could cause offense. [INFORMAL] ❑ *Jeez, I wish they'd tell us what the hell is going on.*

jeg|gings /dʒɛɡɪŋz/ N-PLURAL **Jeggings** are women's leggings that are designed to look like tight jeans. ❑ *Flats work fabulously with this season's jeggings and a longline vest.*

Je|ho|vah /dʒɪhoʊvə/ N-PROPER **Jehovah** is the name given to God in the Old Testament.

Je|ho|vah's Wit|ness (**Jehovah's Witnesses**) N-COUNT A **Jehovah's Witness** is a member of a religious organization that accepts some Christian ideas and believes that the world is going to end very soon.

je|june /dʒɪdʒuːn/ **1** ADJ If you describe something or someone as **jejune**, you are criticizing them for being very simple and unsophisticated. [FORMAL, DISAPPROVAL] ❑ *...jejune generalizations.* **2** ADJ If you describe something or someone as **jejune**, you mean they are dull and boring. [OLD-FASHIONED] ❑ *We knew we were in for a pretty long, jejune evening.*

jell /dʒɛl/ (**jells, jelling, jelled**) also **gel** **1** V-I If people **jell** with each other, or if two groups of people **jell**, they work well together because their skills and personalities fit together well. ❑ *"It takes a team a while to jell,"* Mike Piazza said. **2** V-I If a vague shape, thought, or creation **jells**, it becomes clearer or more definite. ❑ *Results from those studies and others began to jell into a new theory.*

jel|lied /dʒɛlɪd/ ADJ [ADJ n] **Jellied** food is prepared and eaten in a jelly. ❑ *...jellied eels.*

Jell-O N-UNCOUNT **Jell-O** is a transparent, usually colored food that is eaten as a dessert. It is made from gelatin, fruit juice, and sugar. [AM, TRADEMARK] ❑ *...a bowl of Jell-O.*

in BRIT, use **jelly**

jel|ly /dʒɛli/ (**jellies**) **1** N-MASS **Jelly** is a sweet food that is made by cooking fruit or fruit juice with a large amount of sugar until it is thickened. It is usually spread on bread. ❑ *I had two peanut butter and jelly sandwiches.* **2** N-VAR **Jelly** is the same as Jell-O. [BRIT]

jel|ly bean (**jelly beans**) also **jellybean** N-COUNT [usu pl] **Jelly beans** are small colored candies that are hard on the outside and soft inside.

jel|ly|fish /dʒɛlifɪʃ/ (**jellyfish**) N-COUNT A **jellyfish** is a sea creature that has a clear soft body and can sting you.

jel|ly roll (**jelly rolls**) N-VAR A **jelly roll** is a cake made from a thin, flat cake covered with jelly or cream on one side, then rolled up. [AM]

in BRIT, use **swiss roll**

jeop|ard|ize /dʒɛpərdaɪz/ (**jeopardizes, jeopardizing, jeopardized**)

in BRIT, also use **jeopardise**

V-T To **jeopardize** a situation or activity means to do something that may destroy it or cause it to fail. ❑ *He has jeopardized his future career.*

jeop|ardy /dʒɛpərdi/ PHRASE If someone or something is **in jeopardy**, they are in a dangerous situation where they might fail, be lost, or be destroyed. ❑ *A series of setbacks have put the whole project in jeopardy.*

jerk /dʒɜːrk/ (**jerks, jerking, jerked**) **1** V-T/V-I If you **jerk** something or someone in a particular direction, or they **jerk** in a particular direction, they move a short distance very suddenly and quickly. ❑ *Mr. Griffin jerked forward in his chair.* ❑ *"This is Brady Coyne,"* said Sam, jerking his head in my direction. • N-COUNT **Jerk** is also a noun. ❑ *He indicated the bedroom with a jerk of his head.* **2** N-COUNT If you call someone a **jerk**, you are insulting them because you think they are stupid or you do not like them. [INFORMAL, OFFENSIVE, DISAPPROVAL] ❑ *The guy is such a jerk! He only cares about himself.*

jer|kin /dʒɜːrkɪn/ (**jerkins**) N-COUNT A **jerkin** is a sleeveless jacket worn by men or women. [OLD-FASHIONED]

jerky /dʒɜːrki/ (**jerkier, jerkiest**) ADJ **Jerky** movements are very sudden and quick, and do not flow smoothly. ❑ *Mr. Griffin made a jerky gesture.* • **jerki|ly** /dʒɜːrkɪli/ ADV [ADV with v] ❑ *Using his cane heavily, he moved jerkily toward the car.*

jerry-built /dʒɛri bɪlt/ ADJ If you describe houses or apartments as **jerry-built**, you are critical of the fact that they have been built very quickly and cheaply, without much care for safety or quality. [DISAPPROVAL] ❑ *...jerry-built equipment.* ❑ *The place is a bit jerry-built.*

jer|sey ♦◇◇ /dʒɜːrzi/ (**jerseys**) **1** N-COUNT A **jersey** is a knitted piece of clothing that covers the upper part of your body and your arms and does not open at the front. Jerseys are usually worn over a shirt or blouse. [OLD-FASHIONED] ❑ *...a sports jersey.* **2** N-UNCOUNT **Jersey** is a knitted, slightly stretchy fabric used especially to make women's clothing. ❑ *Sheila had come to dinner in a black jersey top.* **3** N-COUNT A **jersey** is a shirt that you wear when playing football, soccer, or some other sports.

Jer|sey /dʒɜːrzi/ (**Jerseys**) N-COUNT [oft N n] A **Jersey cow** or a **Jersey** is a light brown cow that produces very creamy milk.

Je|ru|sa|lem ar|ti|choke /dʒərusələm ɑːrtɪtʃoʊk/ (**Jerusalem artichokes**) N-VAR **Jerusalem artichokes** are small, yellowish-white vegetables that grow underground and look like potatoes.

jest /dʒɛst/ (**jests, jesting, jested**) **1** N-COUNT A **jest** is something you say that is intended to be amusing. [FORMAL] ❑ *It was a jest rather than a reproach.* • PHRASE [PHR after v] If you say something **in jest**, you do not mean it seriously, but want to be amusing. ❑ *Don't say that, even in jest.* **2** V-I If you **jest**, you tell jokes or say amusing things. [FORMAL] ❑ *He enjoyed drinking and jesting with his cronies.*

jest|er /dʒɛstər/ (**jesters**) N-COUNT In the courts of kings and queens in medieval Europe, the **jester** was the person whose job was to do silly things in order to make people laugh.

Jesu|it /dʒɛʒuɪt/ (**Jesuits**) N-COUNT A **Jesuit** is a Catholic priest who belongs to the Society of Jesus.

Jesus ♦◇◇ /dʒiːzəs/ **1** N-PROPER **Jesus** or **Jesus Christ** is the name of the man who Christians believe was the son of God, and whose teachings are the basis of Christianity. **2** EXCLAM **Jesus** is used by some people to express surprise, shock, or annoyance. This use could cause offense. [FEELINGS]

jet ♦◇◇ /dʒɛt/ (**jets, jetting, jetted**) **1** N-COUNT [oft by N] A **jet** is an aircraft that is powered by jet engines. ❑ *Her private jet landed in the republic on the way to Japan.* ❑ *He had arrived from Key West by jet.* **2** V-I If you **jet** somewhere, you travel there in a fast plane. ❑ *The president will be jetting off to Germany today.* **3** N-COUNT A **jet** of liquid or gas is a strong, fast, thin stream of it. ❑ *A jet of water poured through the windows.*

jet air|craft (jet aircraft) N-COUNT A **jet aircraft** is an aircraft that is powered by one or more jet engines.

jet black also **jet-black** ADJ Something that is **jet black** is a very intense black. ❑ ...jet-black hair.

jet en|gine (jet engines) N-COUNT A **jet engine** is an engine in which hot air and gases are forced out at the back. Jet engines are used for most modern aircraft.

jet lag

in BRIT, also use **jetlag**

N-UNCOUNT If you have **jet lag**, you feel tired and slightly confused after a long trip by airplane, especially after traveling between places that have a time difference of several hours. ❑ ...the best way to avoid jet lag.

jet-lagged ADJ [usu v-link ADJ] Someone who is **jet-lagged** has jet lag. ❑ I'm still a little jet-lagged.

jet|liner /dʒɛtlaɪnər/ (jetliners) N-COUNT A **jetliner** is a large aircraft, especially one that carries passengers. [AM]

jet|sam /dʒɛtsəm/ → see flotsam

jet set N-SING [usu the N] You can refer to rich and successful people who live in a luxurious way as the **jet set**. ❑ The winter sports bring the jet set to town.

jet-setting ADJ [ADJ n] You use **jet-setting** to describe people who are rich and successful and who have a luxurious lifestyle. ❑ ...the international jet-setting elite.

Jet Ski (Jet Skis) also **jet ski, jet-ski** N-COUNT A **Jet Ski** is a small machine like a motorcycle that is powered by a jet engine and can travel on the surface of water. [TRADEMARK] ❑ I watched as they got on the jet ski. • **jet ski|ing** N-UNCOUNT ❑ I like jet skiing, being out on boats, doing stuff like that.

jet stream (jet streams) N-COUNT The **jet stream** is a very strong wind that blows high in the Earth's atmosphere and has an important influence on the weather.

jet|ti|son /dʒɛtɪsən, -zən/ (jettisons, jettisoning, jettisoned) ◼ V-T If you **jettison** something, such as an idea or a plan, you deliberately reject it or decide not to use it. ❑ The governor seems to have jettisoned the plan. ◼ V-T To **jettison** something that is not needed or wanted means to throw it away or get rid of it. ❑ The crew jettisoned excess fuel and made an emergency landing.

jet|ty /dʒɛti/ (jetties) ◼ N-COUNT A **jetty** is a wide stone wall or wooden platform where boats stop to let people get on or off, or to load or unload goods. ◼ N-COUNT A **jetty** is a structure that is built at the edge of a shore in order to protect a harbor or to reduce the force of currents and waves.

Jew ✦◇◇ /dʒu/ (Jews) N-COUNT A **Jew** is a person who believes in and practices the religion of Judaism.

jew|el /dʒuəl/ (jewels) ◼ N-COUNT A **jewel** is a precious stone used to decorate valuable things that you wear, such as rings or necklaces. ❑ ...a golden box containing precious jewels. ◼ N-COUNT If you describe something or someone as a **jewel**, you mean that they are better, more beautiful, or more special than other similar things or than other people. ❑ ...a small jewel of a theater. ◼ PHRASE If you refer to an achievement or thing as the **jewel** in someone's **crown**, you mean that it is considered to be their greatest achievement or the thing they can be most proud of. ❑ His achievement is astonishing and this book is the jewel in his crown.

jew|el case (jewel cases) ◼ N-COUNT A **jewel case** is a box for keeping jewels in. ◼ N-COUNT A **jewel case** is the plastic box in which a compact disc is kept.

jew|eled /dʒuəld/

in BRIT, use **jewelled**

ADJ **Jeweled** items and ornaments are decorated with precious stones.

jew|el|er /dʒuələr/ (jewelers)

in BRIT, use **jeweller**

◼ N-COUNT A **jeweler** is a person who makes, sells, and repairs jewelry and watches. ◼ N-COUNT A **jeweler** is a store where jewelry and watches are made, sold, and repaired. ❑ ...a jeweler on Fifth Avenue that sells Rolex.

jew|el|ry /dʒuəlri/

in BRIT, use **jewellery**

N-UNCOUNT **Jewelry** is ornaments that people wear, such as rings, bracelets, and necklaces. It is often made of a valuable metal such as gold, and sometimes decorated with precious stones. ❑ Discover a full selection of fine watches and jewelry at these two Upper Manhattan stores.

jew|el|ry box (jewelry boxes) N-COUNT A **jewelry box** is a box for keeping jewels in.

Jew|ish ✦◇◇ /dʒuɪʃ/ ADJ **Jewish** means belonging or relating to the religion of Judaism, or to Jews as an ethnic group. ❑ ...the Jewish festival of Passover.

Jew|ish|ness /dʒuɪʃnɪs/ N-UNCOUNT [oft with poss] Someone's **Jewishness** is the fact that they are a Jew.

Jew|ry /dʒuri/ N-UNCOUNT [usu adj N] **Jewry** is all the people, or all the people in a particular place, who believe in and practice the religion of Judaism. [FORMAL] ❑ There could be no better way to strengthen the unity of world Jewry.

jib /dʒɪb/ (jibs) N-COUNT [usu the N in sing] The **jib** is the small triangular sail that is sometimes used at the front of a sailing boat.

jibe /dʒaɪb/ (jibes, jibing, jibed)

The spelling **gibe** is also used for meanings ◼ and ◼.

◼ N-COUNT A **jibe** is a rude or insulting remark about someone that is intended to make them look foolish. ❑ ...a cheap jibe about his loss of hair. ◼ V-T To **jibe** means to say something rude or insulting that is intended to make another person look foolish. [WRITTEN] ❑ "No doubt he'll give me the chance to fight him again," he jibed. ◼ V-RECIP If numbers, statements, or events **jibe**, they are exactly the same as each other or they are consistent with each other. [mainly AM] ❑ The numbers don't jibe.

jif|fy /dʒɪfi/ PHRASE [PHR after v] If you say that you will do something **in a jiffy**, you mean that you will do it very quickly or very soon. [INFORMAL]

jig /dʒɪg/ (jigs, jigging, jigged) ◼ N-COUNT A **jig** is a lively dance. ❑ She danced an Irish jig. ◼ V-T To **jig** means to dance or move energetically, especially bouncing up and down. ❑ His son, Louis, laughed and jigged around to the music.

jig|ger /dʒɪgər/ (jiggers) N-COUNT [oft N of n] A **jigger** of a drink such as whiskey or gin is the amount of it you are given when you order it in a bar. [mainly AM] ❑ ...a jigger of brandy.

jig|gle /dʒɪgᵊl/ (jiggles, jiggling, jiggled) ◼ V-T If you **jiggle** something, you move it quickly up and down or from side to side. [INFORMAL] ❑ He jiggled the doorknob noisily. ◼ V-I To **jiggle** around means to move quickly up and down or from side to side. [INFORMAL] ❑ He tapped his feet, hummed tunes and jiggled around.

jig|saw /dʒɪgsɔ/ (jigsaws) ◼ N-COUNT A **jigsaw** or **jigsaw puzzle** is a picture on cardboard or wood that has been cut up into odd shapes. You have to make the picture again by putting the pieces together correctly. ❑ Both her children did jigsaw puzzles easily. ◼ N-COUNT You can describe a complicated situation as a **jigsaw**. ❑ ...the jigsaw of high-level diplomacy.

ji|had /dʒɪhɑd/ ◼ N-SING A **jihad** is a holy war in which Muslims fight against those who threaten Islam. ◼ N-SING **Jihad** is used to talk about the fight against evil within an individual person.

jilt /dʒɪlt/ (jilts, jilting, jilted) V-T If someone **is jilted**, the person they are having a romantic relationship with suddenly ends the relationship in a surprising and upsetting way. [INFORMAL] ❑ She was jilted by her first fiancé. ❑ Driven to distraction, he murdered the woman who jilted him.

Jim Crow /dʒɪm kroʊ/ N-UNCOUNT [oft N n] The policy of segregating Black people from White people that used to be practiced in the United States is sometimes referred to as **Jim Crow**. The use of this word could cause offense. [AM] ❑ ...those who were conducting the struggle against Jim Crow. ❑ Jim Crow laws were strongest in the south.

jin|gle /dʒɪŋgᵊl/ (jingles, jingling, jingled) ◼ V-T/V-I When something **jingles** or when you **jingle** it, it makes a gentle ringing noise, like small bells. ❑ Brian put his hands in his pockets and jingled some change. • N-SING **Jingle** is also a noun. ❑ ...the jingle of money in a man's pocket. ◼ N-COUNT A **jingle** is a short, simple tune, often with words, that is used to advertise a product or program on radio or television. ❑ ...advertising jingles.

jin|go|ism /dʒɪŋgoʊɪzəm/ N-UNCOUNT **Jingoism** is a strong and unreasonable belief in the superiority of your own country. [DISAPPROVAL]

jin|go|is|tic /dʒɪŋgoʊɪstɪk/ ADJ [usu ADJ n] **Jingoistic** behavior shows a strong and unreasonable belief in the superiority of your own country. [DISAPPROVAL] ❑ *The press continued its jingoistic display.*

jinx /dʒɪŋks/ (jinxes) N-COUNT [usu sing] You can call something or someone that is considered to be unlucky or to bring bad luck a **jinx**. ❑ *He was beginning to think he was a jinx.*

jinxed /dʒɪŋkst/ ADJ If something is **jinxed**, it seems that it is unlucky or that it cannot possibly succeed.

jit|ters /dʒɪtərz/ N-PLURAL If you have the **jitters**, you feel extremely nervous, for example because you have to do something important or because you are expecting important news. [INFORMAL] ❑ *This only increased market jitters.*

jit|tery /dʒɪtəri/ ADJ If someone is **jittery**, they feel nervous or are behaving nervously. [INFORMAL] ❑ *International investors have become jittery about the country's economy.*

jive /dʒaɪv/ (jives, jiving, jived) **1** V-I If you **jive**, you dance energetically, especially to rock and roll or swing music. [INFORMAL] ❑ *I learned to jive there when they got the jukebox.* **2** N-UNCOUNT **Jive** is rock and roll or swing music that you jive to. **3** N-UNCOUNT **Jive** or **jive talk** is a kind of informal language used by some African Americans. [AM]

Jnr [BRIT] → see **Jr.**

job ✦✦✦ /dʒɒb/ (jobs) **1** N-COUNT A **job** is the work that someone does to earn money. ❑ *Once I'm in Miami I can get a job.* ❑ *Thousands have lost their jobs.* **2** N-COUNT A **job** is a particular task. ❑ *He said he hoped that the job of putting together a coalition wouldn't take too much time.* **3** N-COUNT The **job** of a particular person or thing is their duty or function. ❑ *Their main job is to preserve health rather than treat illness.* ❑ *His first job will be to try and get talks going between the two sides.* **4** N-SING If you say that someone is doing a good **job**, you mean that they are doing something well. ❑ *We could do a far better job of managing it than we have.* **5** N-SING If you say that you have a **job** doing something, you are emphasizing how difficult it is. [EMPHASIS] ❑ *He may have a hard job selling that argument to investors.* **6** PHRASE If someone is **on the job**, they are actually doing a particular job or task. ❑ *She reached the top pay scale after five years on the job.* **7 the job in hand** → see **hand** ① **8** → See feature box at **work**

job ac|tion (job actions) N-COUNT A **job action** is an action such as a strike in which workers join together and do something to show that they are unhappy with their pay or working conditions. [AM] ❑ *Experts say the cost of the job action will be hundreds of thousands of dollars or more.* ❑ *Strikes and other job actions by public employees are still illegal.*

in BRIT, use **industrial action**

job de|scrip|tion (job descriptions) N-COUNT A **job description** is a written account of all the duties and responsibilities involved in a particular job or position. ❑ *...the job description for the position of division general manager.*

job|less /dʒɒbləs/ ADJ Someone who is **jobless** does not have a job, although they would like one. ❑ *He has turned his back on millions of jobless Americans.* • N-PLURAL **The jobless** are people who are jobless. ❑ *They joined the ranks of the jobless.*

job lot (job lots) N-COUNT A **job lot** is a number of cheap things of low quality that are sold together, for example, at an auction.

job sat|is|fac|tion **1** N-UNCOUNT **Job satisfaction** is the pleasure that you get from doing your job. ❑ *I doubt I'll ever get rich, but I get job satisfaction.* **2** → See feature box at **work**

job seek|er (job seekers) N-COUNT A **job seeker** is an unemployed person who is trying to get a job.

job share (job shares, job sharing, job shared) V-I If two people **job share**, they share the same job by working part-time, for example, one person working in the mornings and the other in the afternoons. ❑ *They both want to job share.*

jock /dʒɒk/ (jocks) **1** N-COUNT A **jock** is a young man who is enthusiastic about a particular sport and spends a lot of time playing it. Some people use this term to suggest that the person has few other interests and is not very clever. [INFORMAL] ❑ *...an all-American football jock.* **2** N-COUNT A **jock** is the same as a **disk jockey**. [INFORMAL] ❑ *...the foolish radio jock who had dismissed the album.*

jock|ey /dʒɒki/ (jockeys, jockeying, jockeyed) **1** N-COUNT A **jockey** is someone who rides a horse in a race. **2** PHRASE If you say that someone **is jockeying** for something, you mean that they are using whatever methods they can in order to get it or do it before their competitors can get it or do it. ❑ *The rival political parties are already jockeying for power.* • PHRASE If someone **is jockeying for position**, they are using whatever methods they can in order to get into a better position than their rivals.

Jock|ey shorts N-PLURAL [also *a pair of* N] **Jockey shorts** are a type of men's underpants. [TRADEMARK]

jock|strap /dʒɒkstræp/ (jockstraps) N-COUNT A **jockstrap** is a piece of underwear worn by men to support their genitals when they are playing sports.

jocu|lar /dʒɒkyələr/ ADJ If you say that someone has a **jocular** manner, you mean that they are cheerful and often make jokes or try to make people laugh. [FORMAL] ❑ *He was in a less jocular mood than usual.*

jodh|purs /dʒɒdpərz/

The form **jodhpur** is used as a modifier.

N-PLURAL [oft *a pair of* N] **Jodhpurs** are pants that people wear when they ride a horse. Jodhpurs are usually loose above the knee and tight below the knee. ❑ *...a boy in jodhpurs.*

jog /dʒɒg/ (jogs, jogging, jogged) **1** V-I If you **jog**, you run slowly, often as a form of exercise. ❑ *I got up early the next morning to jog.* • N-COUNT **Jog** is also a noun. ❑ *He went for another early morning jog.* • **jog|ging** N-UNCOUNT ❑ *It isn't the walking and jogging that got his weight down.* **2** V-T If you **jog** something, you push or bump it slightly so that it moves. ❑ *Avoid jogging the camera.* **3** PHRASE If something or someone **jogs** your **memory**, they cause you to suddenly remember something that you had forgotten. ❑ *Police have planned a reconstruction of the crime tomorrow in the hope that this will jog the memory of passersby.*

jog|ger /dʒɒgər/ (joggers) N-COUNT A **jogger** is a person who jogs as a form of exercise.

john /dʒɒn/ (johns) N-COUNT A **john** is a toilet or bathroom. [AM, INFORMAL] ❑ *I've got to go to the john.*

John Doe /dʒɒn doʊ/ (John Does) N-COUNT **John Doe** is used to refer to a man whose real name is not known or cannot be revealed, for example, for legal reasons. [AM] ❑ *In fact he's not John Doe anymore, we have an ID.*

joie de vi|vre /ʒwɑ də vivrə/ N-UNCOUNT **Joie de vivre** is a feeling of happiness and enjoyment of life. [LITERARY] ❑ *He has plenty of joie de vivre.*

join ✦✦✦ /dʒɔɪn/ (joins, joining, joined) **1** V-T If one person **joins** another, they move or go to the same place, for example, so that both of them can do something together. ❑ *His wife and children moved to join him in their new home.* **2** V-T If you **join** an organization, you become a member of it or start work as an employee of it. ❑ *He joined the Army five years ago.* **3** V-T/V-I If you **join** an activity that other people are doing, you take part in it or become involved with it. ❑ *The United States joined the war in April 1917.* ❑ *The pastor requested the women present to join him in prayer.* ❑ *Nine Republicans joined in supporting the measure.* **4** V-T If you **join** a line, you stand at the end of it so that you are part of it. ❑ *It is advised that fans seeking autographs join the line before practice starts.* **5** V-T To **join** two things means to attach or fasten them together. ❑ *The opened link is used to join the two ends of the chain.* ❑ *...the conjunctiva, the skin which joins the eye to the lid.* **6** V-T If something such as a line or path **joins** two things, it connects them. ❑ *...a global highway of cables joining all the continents together.* **7** V-RECIP If two roads or rivers **join**, they meet or come together at a particular point. ❑ *Do you know the highway to Tulsa? The airport road joins it.* **8 join forces** → see **force** ②

▶ **join in** PHRASAL VERB If you **join in** an activity, you take part in it or become involved in it. ❑ *I hope everyone will join in the fun.*

▶ **join up** **1** PHRASAL VERB If someone **joins up**, they become a member of the army, the navy, or the air force. ❑ *When hostilities* broke out he joined up. **2** PHRASAL VERB If one person or organization **joins up** with another, they start doing something together. ❏ *Dwight decided to withdraw from the committee and join up with the opposition.*

COLLOCATIONS

join
VERB **2**
join + noun: club, group, party, union; squad, team; board, company, firm

---

join|er /dʒɔɪnər/ (joiners) N-COUNT A **joiner** is a person who makes the wooden parts of a building such as window frames, door frames, doors, and stairs. [mainly BRIT]

join|ery /dʒɔɪnəri/ N-UNCOUNT **Joinery** is the skill and work of a joiner. [mainly BRIT]

joint ◆◇◇ /dʒɔɪnt/ (joints) **1** ADJ [ADJ n] **Joint** means shared by or belonging to two or more people. ❏ *She and Frank had never gotten around to opening a joint account.* • **joint|ly** ADV [ADV with v] ❏ *The Port Authority is an agency jointly run by New York and New Jersey.* **2** N-COUNT A **joint** is a part of your body such as your elbow or knee where two bones meet and are able to move together. ❏ *Her joints ache if she exercises.* **3** N-COUNT A **joint** is the place where two things are fastened or joined together. ❏ *...the joint between the inner and outer panels.* **4** N-COUNT You can refer to a cheap place where people go for some form of entertainment as a **joint**. [INFORMAL] ❏ *They had come to the world's most famous pick-up joint.* **5** N-COUNT A **joint** is a cigarette that contains cannabis or marijuana. [INFORMAL] ❏ *He's smoking a joint.* **6** PHRASE If something puts someone's **nose out of joint**, it upsets or offends them because it makes them feel less important or less valued. [INFORMAL] ❏ *Barry had his nose put out of joint by Lucy's aloof sophistication.*

COLLOCATIONS

joint
NOUN **4**
noun + **joint**: burger, hamburger, fast food, pizza

SYNONYMS

joint
ADJ **1**
shared: *Most hostel guests would prefer single to shared rooms.*
mutual: *The East and the West can work together for their mutual benefit and progress.*
common: *Moldavians and Romanians share a common language.*
combined: *This was due to the combined efforts of these two organizations.*
concerted: *It's time for concerted action by world leaders.*

---

joint|ed /dʒɔɪntɪd/ ADJ Something that is **jointed** has joints that move. ❏ *The glass cover for this is jointed in the middle.*

joint-stock com|pa|ny (joint-stock companies) N-COUNT A **joint-stock company** is a company that is owned by the people who have bought shares in that company and who are responsible for its debts. [BUSINESS]

joint ven|ture (joint ventures) N-COUNT A **joint venture** is a business or project in which two or more companies or individuals have invested, with the intention of working together. [BUSINESS] ❏ *It will be sold to a joint venture created by Dow Jones and Westinghouse Broadcasting.*

joist /dʒɔɪst/ (joists) N-COUNT **Joists** are long thick pieces of metal, wood, or concrete that form part of the structure of a building, usually to support a floor or ceiling.

jo|jo|ba /həʊhoʊbə/ N-UNCOUNT **Jojoba** or **jojoba oil** is made from the seeds of the jojoba plant. It is used in many cosmetics such as shampoos.

joke ◆◇◇ /dʒoʊk/ (jokes, joking, joked) **1** N-COUNT A **joke** is something that is said or done to make you laugh, such as a funny story. ❏ *No one told worse jokes than Claus.* **2** V-I If you **joke**, you tell funny stories or say amusing things. ❏ *She would joke about her appearance.* ❏ *Luanne was laughing and joking with Tritt.* **3** N-COUNT A **joke** is something untrue that you tell another person in order to amuse yourself. ❏ *It was probably just a joke to them, but it wasn't funny to me.* **4** V-I If you **joke**, you tell someone something that is not true in order to amuse yourself. ❏ *Don't get defensive, Charlie. I was only joking.* **5** N-SING If you say that something or someone is **a joke**, you think they are ridiculous and do not deserve respect. [INFORMAL, DISAPPROVAL] ❏ *It's ridiculous, it's pathetic, it's a joke.* **6** PHRASE If you **make a joke of** something, you laugh at it even though it is in fact serious or sad. ❏ *I wish I had your courage, Michael, to make a joke of it like that.* **7** PHRASE If you describe a situation as **no joke**, you are emphasizing that it is very difficult or unpleasant. [INFORMAL, EMPHASIS] ❏ *Eight hours on a bus is no joke, is it?* **8** PHRASE If you say that **the joke is on** a particular person, you mean that they have been made to look very foolish by something. ❏ *"For once," he said, "the joke's on me. And it's not very funny."* **9** CONVENTION You say **you're joking** or **you must be joking** to someone when they have just told you something that is so surprising or unreasonable that you find it difficult to believe. [SPOKEN, FEELINGS] ❏ *You're joking. Are you serious?* **10** → See feature box at **humor**

jok|er /dʒoʊkər/ (jokers) **1** N-COUNT Someone who is a **joker** likes making jokes or doing amusing things. ❏ *He is, by nature, a joker, a witty man with a sense of fun.* **2** N-COUNT The **joker** in a deck of playing cards is the card that does not belong to any of the four suits. **3** N-COUNT You can call someone a **joker** if you think they are behaving in a stupid or dangerous way. [INFORMAL, DISAPPROVAL] ❏ *Keep your eye on these jokers, you never know what they will come up with.*

jok|ey /dʒoʊki/ (jokier, jokiest) ADJ [usu ADJ n] If someone behaves in a **jokey** way, they do things in a way that is intended to be amusing, rather than serious. [INFORMAL] ❏ *Bruno doesn't have his younger brother's jokey manner.*

jok|ing|ly /dʒoʊkɪŋli/ ADV [ADV with v] If you say or do something **jokingly**, you say or do it with the intention of amusing someone, rather than with any serious meaning or intention. ❏ *We sometimes jokingly refer to him as "the teenager from hell."*

jol|lity /dʒɒlɪti/ N-UNCOUNT **Jollity** is cheerful behavior. [OLD-FASHIONED] ❏ *...the singing and jollity of the celebration.*

jol|ly /dʒɒli/ (jollier, jolliest) **1** ADJ Someone who is **jolly** is happy and cheerful in their appearance or behavior. ❏ *She was a jolly, kindhearted woman.* **2** ADJ A **jolly** event is lively and enjoyable. ❏ *She had a very jolly time in Canada.*

jolt /dʒoʊlt/ (jolts, jolting, jolted) **1** V-T/V-I If something **jolts** or if something **jolts** it, it moves suddenly and quite violently. ❏ *The wagon jolted again.* ❏ *The train jolted into motion.* • N-COUNT **Jolt** is also a noun. ❏ *We were worried that one tiny jolt could worsen her injuries.* **2** V-T If something **jolts** someone, it gives them an unpleasant surprise or shock. ❏ *A stinging slap across the face jolted her.* • N-COUNT **Jolt** is also a noun. ❏ *Then my husband left me. It gave me the jolt I needed.*

Joneses /dʒoʊnzɪz/ also **Jones** PHRASE If you say that someone is **keeping up with the Joneses**, you mean that they are doing something in order to show that they have as much money as other people, rather than because they really want to do it. ❏ *Many people were holding down three jobs just to keep up with the Joneses.*

Jor|da|nian /dʒɔrdeɪniən/ (Jordanians) **1** ADJ **Jordanian** means belonging or relating to the country of Jordan, or to its people or culture. **2** N-COUNT A **Jordanian** is a Jordanian citizen, or a person of Jordanian origin.

jos|tle /dʒɒsəl/ (jostles, jostling, jostled) **1** V-T/V-I If people **jostle** you, they bump against you or push you in a way that annoys you, usually because you are in a crowd and they are trying to get past you. ❏ *You get 2,000 people jostling each other and bumping into furniture.* ❏ *We spent an hour jostling with the crowds as we did our shopping.* **2** V-I If people or things **are jostling for** something such as attention or a reward, they are competing with other people or things in order to get it. ❏ *...the contenders who have been jostling for the top job.*

jot /dʒɒt/ (jots, jotting, jotted) V-T If you **jot** something short such as an address somewhere, you write it down so that you will remember it. ❏ *Could you just jot his name on there?* • PHRASAL VERB **Jot down** means the same as **jot**. ❏ *Christine uses her journal to jot down ideas and lists of things to do.*

jot|ting /dʒɒtɪŋ/ (jottings) N-COUNT [usu pl] **Jottings** are brief, informal notes that you write down.

joule /dʒuːl/ (joules) N-COUNT In physics, a **joule** is a unit of energy or work. [TECHNICAL]

jour|nal /dʒɜːrnᵊl/ (journals) **1** N-COUNT A **journal** is a magazine, especially one that deals with a specialized subject. ▫ *All our results are published in scientific journals.* **2** N-COUNT A **journal** is a daily or weekly newspaper. The word 'journal' is often used in the name of the paper. ▫ *...ads in The New York Times, the Wall Street Journal and other publications.* **3** N-COUNT A **journal** is an account that you write of your daily activities. ▫ *Sara confided to her journal.* **4** → See feature box at **research**

jour|nal|ese /dʒɜːrnəliːz/ N-UNCOUNT People sometimes refer to the style of writing regarded as typical of journalists as **journalese**, especially when they think it is superficial or contains a lot of clichés. [DISAPPROVAL] ▫ *His humanity and charm come through in this book despite the author's sometimes grating journalese.*

jour|nal|ism /dʒɜːrnəlɪzəm/ **1** N-UNCOUNT **Journalism** is the job of collecting news and writing about it for newspapers, magazines, television, or radio. ▫ *He began a career in journalism, working for the Rocky Mountain News.* **2** → See feature box at **press**

jour|nal|ist /dʒɜːrnəlɪst/ (journalists) N-COUNT A **journalist** is a person whose job is to collect news and write about it for newspapers, magazines, television, or radio.

SYNONYMS

journalist
NOUN
reporter: *...a trainee sports reporter*
correspondent: *...our Diplomatic Correspondent, Mark Brayne.*
columnist: *Clarence Page is a columnist for the Chicago Tribune.*
hack: *...tabloid hacks, always eager to find victims in order to sell newspapers.*

---

jour|nal|is|tic /dʒɜːrnəlɪstɪk/ ADJ [ADJ n] **Journalistic** means relating to journalism, or produced by or typical of a journalist. ▫ *He began his journalistic career in the early eighties in Australia.*

jour|ney /dʒɜːrni/ (journeys, journeying, journeyed) **1** N-COUNT When you make a **journey**, you travel from one place to another. [FORMAL] ▫ *There is an express service from Paris that completes the journey to Bordeaux in under 4 hours.* **2** N-COUNT You can refer to a person's experience of changing or developing from one state of mind to another as a **journey**. ▫ *My films try to describe a journey of discovery, both for myself and the viewer.* **3** V-I If you **journey** somewhere, you travel there. [FORMAL] ▫ *In February 1935, Naomi journeyed to the United States for the first time.*

SYNONYMS

journey
NOUN **1**
trip: *On the Thursday, we took a day trip.*
tour: *It was week five of my tour of the major cities of Europe.*
excursion: *In Bermuda, Sam's father took him on an excursion to a coral reef.*
expedition: *...Byrd's 1928 expedition to Antarctica.*
travels: *He also collects unusual things on his travels abroad.*

---

journey|man /dʒɜːrnimən/ (journeymen) N-COUNT [oft N n] A **journeyman** plumber or electrician is one who is qualified, experienced, and reliable at their job.

joust /dʒaʊst/ (jousts, jousting, jousted) **1** V-RECIP When two or more people or organizations **joust**, they compete to see who is better. [LITERARY] ▫ *Lawyers for the two parties joust in the courtroom.* ▫ *Companies jousted with one another for lead position in the market.* **2** V-RECIP In medieval times, when two knights on horseback **jousted**, they fought against each other using long spears called lances. ▫ *Knights joust and frolic.* • **joust|ing** N-UNCOUNT ▫ *...medieval jousting tournaments.*

jo|vial /dʒoʊviəl/ ADJ If you describe a person as **jovial**, you mean that they are happy and behave in a cheerful way. [WRITTEN] ▫ *Father Whittaker appeared to be in a jovial mood.* • **jo|vi|al|ity** /dʒoʊviælɪti/ N-UNCOUNT ▫ *...his old expansive joviality.* • **jo|vi|al|ly** ADV [ADV with v] ▫ *"No problem," he said jovially.*

jowl /dʒaʊl/ (jowls) **1** N-COUNT [usu pl] You can refer to someone's lower cheeks as their **jowls**, especially when they hang down toward their jaw. [LITERARY] **2** PHRASE If you say that people or things are **cheek by jowl** with each other, you are indicating that they are very close to each other. ▫ *She and her family have to live cheek by jowl with these people.*

jowly /dʒaʊli/ (jowlier, jowliest) ADJ Someone who is **jowly** has fat cheeks that hang down towards their jaw.

joy /dʒɔɪ/ (joys) **1** N-UNCOUNT **Joy** is a feeling of great happiness. ▫ *Salter shouted with joy.* **2** N-COUNT A **joy** is something or someone that makes you feel happy or gives you great pleasure. ▫ *Spending evenings outside is one of the joys of summer.* **3** PHRASE If you say that someone **is jumping for joy**, you mean that they are very pleased or happy about something. ▫ *He jumped for joy on being told the news.* **4** → See feature box at **emotion**

SYNONYMS

joy
NOUN **1**
delight: *To my great delight, it worked perfectly.*
happiness: *I think mostly she was looking for happiness.*
ecstasy: *...the agony and ecstasy of college romance.*
bliss: *It was a scene of such domestic bliss.*
euphoria: *There was euphoria after the elections.*

---

joy|ful /dʒɔɪfəl/ **1** ADJ Something that is **joyful** causes happiness and pleasure. [FORMAL] ▫ *A wedding is a joyful celebration of love.* **2** ADJ Someone who is **joyful** is extremely happy. [FORMAL] ▫ *We're a very joyful people; we're very musical people and we love music.* • **joy|ful|ly** ADV ▫ *They greeted him joyfully.*

joy|less /dʒɔɪlɪs/ ADJ Something that is **joyless** produces no happiness or pleasure. [FORMAL] ▫ *Life seemed joyless.* ▫ *...a joyless marriage, dominated by duty and morality.*

joy|ous /dʒɔɪəs/ ADJ **Joyous** means extremely happy. [LITERARY] ▫ *She had made their childhood so joyous and carefree.* • **joy|ous|ly** ADV ▫ *Sarah accepted joyously.*

joy|ride /dʒɔɪraɪd/ (joyrides) N-COUNT If someone goes on a **joyride**, they steal a car and drive around in it at high speed.

joy|rider /dʒɔɪraɪdər/ (joyriders) N-COUNT A **joyrider** is someone who steals cars in order to drive around in them at high speed. ▫ *...a car crash caused by joyriders.*

joy|riding /dʒɔɪraɪdɪŋ/ N-UNCOUNT **Joyriding** is the crime of stealing a car and driving around in it at high speed.

joy|stick /dʒɔɪstɪk/ (joysticks) N-COUNT In some computer games, the **joystick** is the lever that the player uses in order to control the direction of the things on the screen.

JP /dʒeɪ piː/ (JPs) N-COUNT A **JP** is a Justice of the Peace.

JPEG /dʒeɪpɛɡ/ (JPEGs) also **Jpeg 1** N-UNCOUNT **JPEG** is a standard file format for compressing pictures so they can be stored or sent by email more easily. **JPEG** is an abbreviation for 'Joint Photographic Experts Group.' [COMPUTING] ▫ *...JPEG images.* **2** N-COUNT A **JPEG** is a JPEG file or picture. ▫ *You can add edge enhancement or smoothness to a Jpeg, or vary the color depth.*

Jr. Jr. is a written abbreviation for **Junior**. It is used after a man's name to distinguish him from an older member of his family, usually his father, with the same name. ▫ *...Harry Connick Jr.*

in BRIT, use **Jr**

ju|bi|lant /dʒuːbɪlənt/ ADJ If you are **jubilant**, you feel extremely happy because of a success. ▫ *The team were greeted by thousands of jubilant supporters.*

ju|bi|la|tion /dʒuːbɪleɪʃᵊn/ N-UNCOUNT **Jubilation** is a feeling of great happiness and pleasure, because of a success. [FORMAL] ▫ *His resignation was greeted by jubilation in the office.*

ju|bi|lee /dʒuːbɪliː/ (jubilees) N-COUNT A **jubilee** is a special anniversary of an event, especially the 25th or 50th anniversary. ▫ *...Queen Victoria's jubilee.*

Ju|da|ic /dʒuːdeɪɪk/ ADJ [ADJ n] **Judaic** means belonging or relating to Judaism. [FORMAL]

Ju|da|ism /dʒuːdiːɪzəm, -deɪ-/ N-UNCOUNT **Judaism** is the religion of the Jewish people. It is based on the Old Testament of the Bible and the Talmud.

Judas /dʒuːdəs/ (Judases) N-COUNT If you accuse someone of being a **Judas**, you are accusing them of being deceitful and betraying their friends or country. [DISAPPROVAL]

judge /dʒʌdʒ/ (judges, judging, judged) **1** N-COUNT; N-TITLE A **judge** is the person in a court of law who decides how the law should be applied, for example how criminals should be punished. ❑ *The judge adjourned the hearing until next Tuesday.* **2** N-COUNT A **judge** is a person who decides who will be the winner of a competition. ❑ *A panel of judges is now selecting the finalists.* **3** V-T If you **judge** something such as a competition, you decide who or what is the winner. ❑ *He was asked to judge a literary competition.* **4** V-T If you **judge** something or someone, you form an opinion about them after you have examined the evidence or thought carefully about them. ❑ *It will take a few more years to judge the impact of these ideas.* ❑ *I am ready to judge any book on its merits.* ❑ *It's for other people to judge how much I have improved.* **5** V-T If you **judge** something, you guess its amount, size, or value or you guess what it is. ❑ *It is important to judge the weight of your washing load correctly.* ❑ *I judged him to be about forty.* **6** N-COUNT If someone is a good **judge** of something, they understand it and can make sensible decisions about it. If someone is a bad **judge** of something, they cannot do this. ❑ *I'm a pretty good judge of character.* **7** PHRASE You use **judging by**, **judging from**, or **to judge from** to introduce the reasons why you believe or think something. ❑ *Judging by the opinion polls, he seems to be succeeding.* ❑ *Judging from the way he laughed as he told it, it was meant to be humorous.*

judg|ment /dʒʌdʒmənt/ (judgments)

in BRIT, also use **judgement**

1 N-VAR A **judgment** is an opinion that you have or express after thinking carefully about something. ❑ *In your judgment, what has changed over the past few years?* **2** N-UNCOUNT **Judgment** is the ability to make sensible guesses about a situation or sensible decisions about what to do. ❑ *I respect his judgment and I'll follow any advice he gives me.* **3** N-VAR A **judgment** is a decision made by a judge or by a court of law. ❑ *We are awaiting a judgment from the Supreme Court.* **4** PHRASE If something is **against** your **better judgment**, you believe that it would be more sensible or better not to do it. ❑ *Against our better judgment, we buy the products of manufacturers whose claims seem too good to be true.* **5** PHRASE If you **pass judgment** on someone or something, you give your opinion about it, especially if you are making a criticism. ❑ *They won't pass judgment on their friends or family.* **6** PHRASE If you **reserve judgment** on something, you refuse to give an opinion about it until you know more about it. ❑ *I think I'd have to reserve judgment on whether it'll make any difference until I see some of those key details.*

SYNONYMS

judgment
NOUN
1
opinion: *Most who expressed an opinion spoke favorably of Thomas.*
view: *I take the view that she should be stopped as soon as possible.*
belief: *It is our belief that improvements in health care will lead to a stronger economy.*
conviction: *It is our firm conviction that a step forward has been taken.*
3
verdict: *The jury returned a unanimous guilty verdict.*
finding: *The government hopes the court will announce its findings before the end of the month.*
ruling: *Goodwin tried to have the court ruling overturned.*
decision: *A decision was taken to discipline Marshall.*

judg|men|tal /dʒʌdʒmentəl/ ADJ If you say that someone is **judgmental**, you are critical of them because they form opinions of people and situations very quickly, when it would be better for them to wait until they know more about the person or situation. [DISAPPROVAL] ❑ *We tried not to seem critical or judgmental while giving advice that would protect him from ridicule.*

judg|ment call (judgment calls) N-COUNT If you refer to a decision as a **judgment call**, you mean that there are no firm rules or principles that can help you make it, so you have to rely on your own judgment and instinct. ❑ *Well, physicians make judgment calls every day.*

ju|di|cial /dʒudɪʃəl/ ADJ [ADJ n] **Judicial** means relating to the legal system and to judgments made in a court of law.
❑ *...an independent judicial system.* ❑ *...efforts to manipulate the judicial process.* ● **ju|di|cial|ly** ADV [ADV with v] ❑ *Even if the amendment is passed it can be defeated judicially.*

ju|di|ci|ary /dʒudɪʃieri/ N-SING **The judiciary** is the branch of authority in a country that is concerned with law and the legal system. [FORMAL] ❑ *The judiciary must think very hard before jailing nonviolent offenders.*

ju|di|cious /dʒudɪʃəs/ ADJ If you describe an action or decision as **judicious**, you approve of it because you think that it shows good judgment and sense. [FORMAL, APPROVAL] ❑ *The president authorizes the judicious use of military force to protect our citizens.* ● **ju|di|cious|ly** ADV [ADV with v] ❑ *Modern fertilizers should be used judiciously.*

judo /dʒudoʊ/ N-UNCOUNT **Judo** is a sport in which two people fight without weapons and try to throw each other to the ground. ❑ *He was also a black belt in judo.*

jug /dʒʌg/ (jugs) **1** N-COUNT A **jug** is a cylindrical container with a handle and is used for holding and pouring liquids. **2** N-COUNT You can use **jug** to refer to the jug and its contents, or to the contents only. ❑ *...a jug of water.*

jug|ger|naut /dʒʌgərnɔt/ (juggernauts) **1** N-COUNT If you describe an organization or group as a **juggernaut**, you are critical of them because they are large and extremely powerful, and you think they are not being controlled properly. [DISAPPROVAL] ❑ *The group became a sales juggernaut in the commodity options business.* **2** N-COUNT A **juggernaut** is a very large truck. [mainly BRIT]

jug|gle /dʒʌgəl/ (juggles, juggling, juggled) **1** V-T If you **juggle** lots of different things, such as your work and your family, you try to give enough time or attention to all of them. ❑ *The management team meets several times a week to juggle budgets and resources.* **2** V-T/V-I If you **juggle**, you entertain people by throwing things into the air, catching each one, and throwing it up again so that there are several of them in the air at the same time. ❑ *Soon she was juggling five eggs.* ● **jug|gling** N-UNCOUNT ❑ *He can perform an astonishing variety of acts, including mime and juggling.*

jug|gler /dʒʌglər/ (jugglers) N-COUNT A **juggler** is someone who juggles in order to entertain people.

jug|gling act (juggling acts) N-COUNT If you say that a situation is a **juggling act**, you mean that someone is trying to do two or more things at once, and that they are finding it difficult to do those things properly. ❑ *Trying to continue with a demanding career and manage a child or two is an impossible juggling act.*

jugu|lar /dʒʌgyələr/ (jugulars) **1** N-COUNT A **jugular** or **jugular vein** is one of the three important veins in your neck that carry blood from your head back to your heart. **2** PHRASE If you say that someone **went for the jugular**, you mean that they strongly attacked another person's weakest points in order to harm them. [INFORMAL] ❑ *Mr. Black went for the jugular, asking personal questions.*

juice /dʒus/ (juices, juicing, juiced) **1** N-MASS **Juice** is the liquid that can be obtained from a fruit or vegetable. ❑ *...fresh orange juice.* **2** N-PLURAL The **juices** of a piece of meat are the liquid that comes out of it when you cook it. ❑ *When cooked, drain off the juices and put the meat in a processor.*
▶ **juice up** PHRASAL VERB If you **juice up** a place or event, you do something to make it more lively or exciting. [AM, INFORMAL] ❑ *Look at the ads for Chamber of Secrets, and you'll see that the filmmakers are doing all they can to juice up the formula.*

juiced /dʒust/ also **juiced up** ADJ Someone who is **juiced** or **juiced up** is excited. [INFORMAL] ❑ *Script editors are all juiced up over the humorous potential.* ❑ *Even small eclipses get him juiced and should be fascinating to any amateur astronomer.*

juic|er /dʒusər/ (juicers) N-COUNT A **juicer** is an electrical appliance for extracting juice from fruit and vegetables. ❑ *This powerful electric juicer automatically separates the pulp from the juice.*

juicy /dʒusi/ (juicier, juiciest) **1** ADJ If food is **juicy**, it has a lot of juice in it and is very enjoyable to eat. ❑ *...a thick, juicy steak.* **2** ADJ **Juicy** gossip or stories contain details about people's lives, especially details that are normally kept private. [INFORMAL] ❑ *It provided some juicy gossip for a few days.*

juke|box /dʒukbɒks/ (jukeboxes) N-COUNT A **jukebox** is a machine that plays music in a place such as a bar. You put

Jul. money in and choose the song you want to hear. ❑ *My favorite song is on the jukebox.*

Jul. Jul. is a written abbreviation for **July**.

July ♦♦♦ /dʒʊlaɪ/ (**Julys**) N-VAR **July** is the seventh month of the year in the Western calendar. ❑ *In July 1969, Neil Armstrong walked on the moon.*

jum|ble /dʒʌmbəl/ (**jumbles, jumbling, jumbled**) **1** N-COUNT A **jumble** of things is a lot of different things that are all mixed together in a disorganized or confused way. ❑ *The shoreline was made up of a jumble of huge boulders.* **2** V-T/V-I If you **jumble** things, they become mixed together so that they are untidy or are not in the correct order. ❑ *He's making a new film by jumbling together bits of his other movies.* • PHRASAL VERB To **jumble up** means the same as to **jumble**. ❑ *They had jumbled it all up into a heap.* ❑ *The bank scrambles all that money together, jumbles it all up and lends it out to hundreds and thousands of borrowers.*

jum|bled /dʒʌmbəld/ ADJ If you describe things or ideas as **jumbled**, you mean that they are mixed up and not in order. ❑ *These jumbled priorities should be no cause for surprise.*

jum|ble sale (**jumble sales**) N-COUNT A **jumble sale** is the same as a **rummage sale**. [BRIT]

jum|bo /dʒʌmboʊ/ (**jumbos**) **1** ADJ [ADJ n] **Jumbo** means very large; used mainly in advertising and in the names of products. ❑ *...a jumbo box of tissues.* **2** N-COUNT A **jumbo** or a **jumbo jet** is a very large jet aircraft that can carry several hundred passengers.

---WORD HISTORY---

jumbo

Jumbo was the name of a famous and very large 19th-century African elephant that was used to give rides to children at London Zoo, before being sold in 1882 to Barnum and Bailey's circus.

---

jump ♦♦◇ /dʒʌmp/ (**jumps, jumping, jumped**) **1** V-T/V-I If you **jump**, you bend your knees, push against the ground with your feet, and move quickly upward into the air. ❑ *I jumped over the fence.* ❑ *I'd jumped seventeen feet six in the long jump, which was a school record.* • N-COUNT **Jump** is also a noun. ❑ *The longest jumps by a man and a woman were witnessed in Sestriere, Italy, yesterday.* **2** V-T/V-I If you **jump** from something above the ground, you deliberately push yourself into the air so that you drop toward the ground. ❑ *I jumped the last six feet down to the deck.* ❑ *He jumped out of a third-floor window.* **3** V-T If you **jump** something such as a fence, you move quickly up and through the air over or across it. ❑ *He jumped the first fence beautifully.* **4** V-I If you **jump** somewhere, you move there quickly and suddenly. ❑ *Adam jumped from his seat at the girl's cry.* **5** V-I If something makes you **jump**, it makes you make a sudden movement because you are frightened or surprised. ❑ *The phone shrilled, making her jump.* **6** V-T/V-I If an amount or level **jumps**, it suddenly increases or rises by a large amount in a short time. ❑ *Sales jumped from $94 million to over $101 million.* ❑ *The number of crimes jumped by ten percent last year.* ❑ *The firm's shares jumped 12 % on the news.* • N-COUNT **Jump** is also a noun. ❑ *A big jump in energy conservation could be achieved without much disruption of anyone's standard of living.* **7** V-I [no cont] If you **jump at** an offer or opportunity, you accept it quickly and eagerly. ❑ *Members of the public would jump at the chance to become part owners of the corporation.* **8** V-I If someone **jumps on** you, they quickly criticize you for doing something that they do not approve of. ❑ *A lot of people jumped on me about that, you know.* **9** V-T If someone **jumps** you, they attack you suddenly or unexpectedly. [mainly AM, INFORMAL] ❑ *Half a dozen sailors jumped him.* **10** PHRASE If you **get a jump on** something or someone or **get the jump on** them, you gain an advantage over them. [AM] ❑ *Helicopters helped fire crews get a jump on the blaze.* **11 to jump on the bandwagon** → see **bandwagon** **12 to jump bail** → see **bail** **13 to jump the gun** → see **gun** **14 to jump for joy** → see **joy**

---COLLOCATIONS---

jump
VERB **6**
noun + **jump**: earnings, prices, profits, rate, sales, shares
jump + adverb: dramatically, sharply

---

jump ball (**jump balls**) N-COUNT In basketball, a **jump ball** is a ball that the referee throws into the air between two players from opposing teams in order to continue a game after it has stopped. It is also a play in which the referee throws the ball into the air. ❑ *Chevon Troutman forces a jump ball with Ben Gordon with 1.2 seconds left.*

jump|er /dʒʌmpər/ (**jumpers**) **1** N-COUNT If you refer to a person or a horse as a particular kind of **jumper**, you are describing how good they are at jumping or the way that they jump. ❑ *He is a terrific athlete and a brilliant jumper.* **2** N-COUNT A **jumper** is a sleeveless dress that is worn over a blouse or sweater. [AM] ❑ *She wore a checkered jumper and had ribbons in her hair.*

in BRIT, use **pinafore**

3 N-COUNT A **jumper** is a warm knitted piece of clothing that covers the upper part of your body and your arms. [BRIT]

in AM, use **sweater**

jump|er ca|bles N-PLURAL **Jumper cables** are the thick wires that can be used to start a car when its battery does not have enough power. Jumper cables are used to connect the battery to the battery of another car that is working properly. [AM]

in BRIT, use **jump leads**

jumping-off point /dʒʌmpɪŋ ɒf pɔɪnt/ N-SING A **jumping-off point** or a **jumping-off place** is a place, situation, or occasion that you use as the starting point for something. ❑ *The base will serve as a jumping-off point for troops going out into the country areas.*

jump jet (**jump jets**) N-COUNT A **jump jet** is a jet aircraft that can take off and land vertically.

jump jock|ey (**jump jockeys**) N-COUNT A **jump jockey** is someone who rides horses in races such as steeplechases, where the horses have to jump over obstacles. [BRIT]

jump leads /dʒʌmp liːdz/ N-PLURAL **Jump leads** are the same as **jumper cables**. [BRIT]

jump rope (**jump ropes**) N-COUNT A **jump rope** is a piece of rope, usually with handles at each end. You exercise with it by turning it around and around and jumping over it. [AM]

in BRIT, use **skipping rope**

jump|start /dʒʌmpstɑːrt/ (**jumpstarts, jumpstarting, jumpstarted**) **1** V-T To **jumpstart** a vehicle that has a dead battery means to make the engine start by getting power from the battery of another vehicle, using special cables called jumper cables. ❑ *He was huddled with John trying to jumpstart his car.* • N-COUNT **Jumpstart** is also a noun. ❑ *I drove out to give him a jumpstart because his battery was dead.* **2** V-T To **jumpstart** a system or process that has stopped working or progressing means to do something that will make it start working quickly or effectively. ❑ *The EU is trying to jumpstart the peace process.* • N-COUNT **Jumpstart** is also a noun. ❑ *...attempts to give the industry a jumpstart.*

jump|suit /dʒʌmpsuːt/ (**jumpsuits**) N-COUNT A **jumpsuit** is a piece of clothing in the form of a top and pants in one continuous piece.

jumpy /dʒʌmpi/ ADJ [usu v-link ADJ] If you are **jumpy**, you are nervous or worried about something. [INFORMAL] ❑ *I told myself not to be so jumpy.* ❑ *When he spoke his voice was jumpy.*

Jun. Jun. is a written abbreviation for **June**.

junc|tion /dʒʌŋkʃən/ (**junctions**) N-COUNT; N-IN-NAMES A **junction** is a place where roads or railroad lines join. [BRIT]

in AM, usually use **intersection**

junc|ture /dʒʌŋktʃər/ (**junctures**) N-COUNT At a particular **juncture** means at a particular point in time, especially when it is a very important time in a process or series of events. ❑ *What's important at this juncture is the ability of the three republics to work together.*

June ♦♦♦ /dʒuːn/ (**Junes**) N-VAR **June** is the sixth month of the year in the Western calendar. ❑ *He spent two and a half weeks with us in June 2006.* ❑ *I am moving out on June 5th.*

jun|gle /dʒʌŋɡəl/ (**jungles**) **1** N-VAR A **jungle** is a forest in a tropical country where large numbers of tall trees and plants grow very close together. ❑ *...the mountains and jungles of Papua*

New Guinea. **2** N-SING If you describe a place as a **jungle**, you are emphasizing that it is full of lots of things and very messy. [EMPHASIS] ☐ *...a jungle of stuffed sofas, stuffed birds, knick-knacks, potted plants.* **3** N-SING If you describe a situation as a **jungle**, you dislike it because it is complicated and difficult to get what you want from it. [DISAPPROVAL] ☐ *Social Security law and procedure remain a jungle of complex rules.*

jun|ior ✦✦✧ /dʒ<u>u</u>niər/ (**juniors**) **1** ADJ A **junior** official or employee holds a low-ranking position in an organization or profession. ☐ *A handful of junior officers were made to bear responsibility for the incident.* • N-COUNT **Junior** is also a noun. ☐ *He has said legal aid work is for juniors when they start out in the law.* **2** N-SING If you are someone's **junior**, you are younger than they are. ☐ *She had fallen in love with a truck driver ten years her junior.* **3** N-COUNT In the United States, a student in the third year of high school or college is called a **junior**. ☐ *Their youngest daughter Amy's a junior at the University of Evansville in Indiana.* **4** N-IN-NAMES **Junior** is sometimes used after the name of the younger of two men in a family who have the same name, sometimes in order to prevent confusion. The abbreviation **Jr.** is also used. [AM] ☐ *Their first son, Bobby junior, was born the following year.*

jun|ior col|lege (**junior colleges**) N-COUNT In the United States, a **junior college** is a college that provides a two-year course that is usually equivalent to the first two years of a regular undergraduate course. ☐ *He went to a junior college and majored in computer programming.*

jun|ior high school (**junior high schools**) also **junior high** N-VAR; N-IN-NAMES A **junior high school** or a **junior high** is a school for students from 7th through 9th or 10th grade. [AM] ☐ *He dropped out of junior high school.* ☐ *...Benjamin Franklin Junior High.*

ju|ni|per /dʒ<u>u</u>nɪpər/ (**junipers**) N-VAR A **juniper** is an evergreen bush with purple berries which can be used in cooking and medicine.

junk /dʒʌŋk/ (**junks, junking, junked**) **1** N-UNCOUNT **Junk** is old and used things that have little value and that you do not want any more. ☐ *Rose finds her furniture in junk shops.* **2** V-T If you **junk** something, you get rid of it or stop using it. [INFORMAL] ☐ *Consumers will not have to junk their old disks to use the new format.*

junk bond (**junk bonds**) N-COUNT If a company issues **junk bonds**, it borrows money from investors, usually at a high rate of interest, in order to finance a particular deal that is risky. [BUSINESS]

jun|ket /dʒʌŋkɪt/ (**junkets**) N-COUNT If you describe a trip or visit by an official or businessperson as a **junket**, you disapprove of it because it is expensive, unnecessary, and often has been paid for with public money. [INFORMAL, DISAPPROVAL]

junk food (**junk foods**) N-MASS If you refer to food as **junk food**, you mean that it is quick and easy to prepare but is not good for your health. ☐ *Sharon fears that her love of junk food may have contributed to her cancer.*

junkie /dʒʌŋki/ (**junkies**) **1** N-COUNT A **junkie** is a drug addict. [INFORMAL] ☐ *...those desperate junkies who have tried every known drug.* **2** N-COUNT You can use **junkie** to refer to someone who is very interested in a particular activity, especially when they spend a lot of time on it. [INFORMAL] ☐ *...a computer junkie.*

junk mail **1** N-UNCOUNT **Junk mail** is advertisements and publicity materials in your mail that you have not asked for and that you do not want. ☐ *We still get junk mail for the previous occupants.* **2** → See feature box at **email**

junk|yard /dʒʌŋkyɑrd/ (**junkyards**) N-COUNT A **junkyard** is a place where old machines such as cars or ships are destroyed and where useful parts are saved. [mainly AM]

in BRIT, usually use **scrapyard**

jun|ta /dʒʌntə, hʊntə/ (**juntas**) N-COUNT-COLL A **junta** is a military government that has taken power by force, and not through elections.

ju|ris|dic|tion /dʒʊərɪsdɪkʃən/ (**jurisdictions**) **1** N-UNCOUNT **Jurisdiction** is the power that a court of law or an official has to carry out legal judgments or to enforce laws. [FORMAL] ☐ *The British police have no jurisdiction over foreign bank accounts.*

2 N-COUNT A **jurisdiction** is a state or other area in which a particular court and system of laws has authority. [LEGAL] ☐ *In most European jurisdictions, there is a right to strike.*

ju|ris|pru|dence /dʒʊərɪsprudəns/ N-UNCOUNT **Jurisprudence** is the study of law and the principles on which laws are based. [FORMAL]

ju|rist /dʒʊərɪst/ (**jurists**) N-COUNT A **jurist** is a person who is an expert on law. [FORMAL]

ju|ror /dʒʊərər/ (**jurors**) N-COUNT A **juror** is a member of a jury. ☐ *The foreman was asked by the clerk whether the jurors had reached verdicts on which they all agreed.*

jury ✦✦✧ /dʒʊəri/ (**juries**) **1** N-COUNT-COLL [also by n] In a court of law, the **jury** is the group of people who have been chosen from the general public to listen to the facts about a crime and to decide whether the person accused is guilty or not. ☐ *The jury convicted him of all offenses.* **2** N-COUNT-COLL A **jury** is a group of people who choose the winner of a competition. ☐ *I am not surprised that the jury chose to award this novel the prize.* **3** PHRASE If you say that **the jury is out** or **the jury is still out** on a particular subject, you mean that people in general have still not made a decision or formed an opinion about that subject. ☐ *The jury is out on whether or not this is true.* **4** → See feature box at **legal**

> ### JUST
> ① ADVERB USES
> ② ADJECTIVE USE

①**just** ✦✦✦ /dʒʌst/

→ Please look at meanings **17** – **19** to see if the expression you are looking for is shown under another headword.

1 ADV [ADV before v] You use **just** to say that something happened a very short time ago, or is starting to happen at the present time. For example, if you say that someone **just arrived** or **has just arrived**, you mean that they arrived a very short time ago. ☐ *I've just bought a new house.* ☐ *I just had the most awful dream.* **2** ADV If you say that you are **just** doing something, you mean that you are doing it now and will finish it very soon. If you say that you are **just about to** do something, or **just going to** do it, you mean that you will do it very soon. ☐ *I'm just making the sauce for the cauliflower.* ☐ *I'm just going to go mail a letter.* **3** ADV You can use **just** to emphasize that something is happening at exactly the moment of speaking or at exactly the moment that you are talking about. [EMPHASIS] ☐ *Randall would just now be getting the Sunday paper.* ☐ *Just then the phone rang.* **4** ADV [ADV group/cl] You use **just** to indicate that something is no more important, interesting, or difficult, for example, than you say it is, especially when you want to correct a wrong idea that someone may get or has already gotten. [EMPHASIS] ☐ *It's just a suggestion.* ☐ *It's not just a financial matter.* **5** ADV [ADV n] You use **just** to emphasize that you are talking about a small part, not the whole of an amount. [EMPHASIS] ☐ *That's just one example of the kind of experiments you can do.* **6** ADV [ADV amount] You use **just** to emphasize how small an amount is or how short a length of time is. [EMPHASIS] ☐ *Stephanie and David redecorated a room in just three days.* **7** ADV [ADV before v] You can use **just** in front of a verb to indicate that the result of something is unfortunate or undesirable and is likely to make the situation worse rather than better. ☐ *By doing what they did, they just hurt the people in their community.* **8** ADV You use **just** to indicate that what you are saying is the case, but only by a very small degree or amount. ☐ *Her hand was just visible in the dimly lit room.* ☐ *I arrived just in time for my flight to London.* **9** ADV [ADV with modal] You use **just** with 'might,' 'may,' and 'could,' when you mean that there is a small chance of something happening, even though it is not very likely. ☐ *It's an old trick but it just might work.* **10** ADV You use **just** to emphasize the following word or phrase, in order to express feelings such as annoyance, admiration, or certainty. [EMPHASIS] ☐ *She just won't relax.* **11** ADV [ADV n] You use **just** in expressions such as **just a minute** and **just a moment** to ask someone to wait for a short time. [SPOKEN] ☐ *"Let me in, Di."—"Okay. Just a minute."* **12** ADV [ADV n] You can use **just** in expressions such as **just a second** and **just a moment** to interrupt someone, for example, in order to disagree with them, explain something, or calm them down. [SPOKEN] ❑ *Well, now just a second, I don't altogether agree.* **13** ADV [ADV before v] If you say that you can **just** see or hear something, you mean that it is easy for you to imagine seeing or hearing it. ❑ *I can just hear her telling her friends, "Well, I blame his mother!"* **14** ADV You use **just** in expressions such as **just like**, **just as...as**, and **just the same** when you are emphasizing the similarity between two things or two people. [EMPHASIS] ❑ *Behind the facade they are just like the rest of us.* ❑ *He worked just as hard as anyone.* **15** PHRASE You use **just about** to indicate that what you are talking about is so close to being the case that it can be regarded as being the case. ❑ *There are those who believe that he is just about the best golfer in the world.* **16** PHRASE You use **just about** to indicate that what you are talking about is in fact the case, but only by a very small degree or amount. ❑ *I can just about tolerate it at the moment.* **17 not just** → see **not** **18 just now** → see **now** **19 it just goes to show** → see **show** ①

②**just** /dʒʌst/ ADJ If you describe a situation, action, or idea as **just**, you mean that it is right or acceptable according to particular moral principles, such as respect for all human beings. [FORMAL] ❑ *They believe that they are fighting a just war.*
• **just|ly** ADV [ADV with v] ❑ *They were not treated justly in the past.*

jus|tice ✦✧ /dʒʌstɪs/ (**justices**) **1** N-UNCOUNT **Justice** is fairness in the way that people are treated. ❑ *He has a good overall sense of justice and fairness.* ❑ *He only wants freedom, justice and equality.* **2** N-UNCOUNT The **justice** of a cause, claim, or argument is its quality of being reasonable, fair, or right. ❑ *We are a minority and must convince people of the justice of our cause.* **3** N-UNCOUNT **Justice** is the legal system that a country uses in order to deal with people who break the law. ❑ *Many in the community feel that the justice system does not treat them fairly.* **4** N-COUNT A **justice** is a judge. [AM] ❑ *She will be sworn in today as a justice on the Supreme Court.* **5** N-TITLE **Justice** is used before the names of judges. ❑ *A preliminary hearing was due to start today before Justice Carter, but was adjourned.* **6** PHRASE If a criminal is **brought to justice**, he or she is punished for a crime by being arrested and tried in a court of law. ❑ *They demanded that those responsible be brought to justice.* **7** PHRASE To **do justice** to a person or thing means to reproduce them accurately and show how good they are. ❑ *The photograph I had seen didn't do her justice.* **8** PHRASE If you **do justice** to someone or something, you deal with them properly and completely. ❑ *No one article can ever do justice to the topic of fraud.* **9** PHRASE If you **do yourself justice**, you do something as well as you are capable of doing it. ❑ *I don't think he did himself justice in the game today.*

---SYNONYMS---

justice
NOUN **1**
fairness: *...concern about the fairness of the election campaign.*
equity: *We base this call on the grounds of social justice and equity.*
impartiality: *...a justice system lacking impartiality by democratic standards.*

Jus|tice of the Peace (**Justices of the Peace**) N-COUNT In some states in the United States, a **Justice of the Peace** is an official who can carry out some legal tasks, such as settling minor cases in court or performing marriages. The abbreviation **JP** is also used.

jus|ti|fi|able /dʒʌstɪfaɪəbəl/ ADJ An action, situation, emotion, or idea that is **justifiable** is acceptable or correct because there is a good reason for it. ❑ *The violence of the revolutionary years was justifiable on the grounds of political necessity.* • **jus|ti|fi|ably** /dʒʌstɪfaɪəbli/ ADV ❑ *He was justifiably proud of his achievements.*

jus|ti|fi|ca|tion /dʒʌstɪfɪkeɪʃən/ (**justifications**) N-VAR A **justification** for something is an acceptable reason or explanation for it. ❑ *To me the only justification for a zoo is educational.*

jus|ti|fied /dʒʌstɪfaɪd/ **1** ADJ If you describe a decision, action, or idea as **justified**, you think it is reasonable and acceptable. ❑ *In my opinion, the decision was wholly justified.* **2** ADJ [v-link ADJ in -ing] If you think that someone is **justified in** doing something, you think that their reasons for doing it are good and valid. ❑ *He's absolutely justified in resigning. He was treated shamefully.*

jus|ti|fy ✦✧ /dʒʌstɪfaɪ/ (**justifies, justifying, justified**) **1** V-T To **justify** a decision, action, or idea means to show or prove that it is reasonable or necessary. ❑ *No argument can justify a war.* **2** V-T To **justify** printed text means to adjust the spaces between the words so that each line of type is exactly the same length. ❑ *Click on this icon to align or justify text at both the left and right margins.* **3** → see also **left-justify**, **right-justify**

---SYNONYMS---

justify
VERB **1**
warrant: *The allegations are serious enough to warrant an investigation.*
excuse: *That doesn't excuse my mother's behavior.*
vindicate: *Ministers and officials are confident their decision will be vindicated.*

---

just|ly /dʒʌstli/ **1** ADV You use **justly** to show that you approve of someone's attitude toward something, because it seems to be based on truth or reality. [APPROVAL] ❑ *Australians are justly proud of their native wildlife.* **2** → see also **just** ②

jut /dʒʌt/ (**juts, jutting, jutted**) **1** V-I If something **juts** out, it sticks out above or beyond a surface. ❑ *The northern end of the island juts out like a long, thin finger into the sea.* **2** V-T/V-I If you **jut** a part of your body, especially your chin, or if it **juts**, you push it forward in an aggressive or determined way. ❑ *His jaw jutted stubbornly forward; he would not be denied.* ❑ *Gwen jutted her chin forward, her nose in the air, and did not bother to answer the teacher.*

jute /dʒuːt/ N-UNCOUNT **Jute** is a substance that is used to make cloth and rope. It comes from a plant that grows mainly in southeast Asia.

ju|venile /dʒuːvənəl, -naɪl/ (**juveniles**) **1** N-COUNT A **juvenile** is a child or young person who is not yet old enough to be regarded as an adult. [FORMAL] ❑ *The number of juveniles in the general population has fallen by a fifth in the past 10 years.* **2** ADJ [ADJ n] **Juvenile** activity or behavior involves young people who are not yet adults. ❑ *Juvenile crime is increasing at a terrifying rate.*

ju|venile court (**juvenile courts**) N-VAR A **juvenile court** is a court that deals with crimes committed by young people who are not yet old enough to be considered as adults.

ju|venile de|lin|quen|cy N-UNCOUNT **Juvenile delinquency** is destruction of property and other criminal behavior that is committed by young people who are not old enough to be legally considered as adults.

ju|venile de|lin|quent (**juvenile delinquents**) N-COUNT A **juvenile delinquent** is a young person who is guilty of committing crimes, especially destruction of property or violence.

jux|ta|pose /dʒʌkstəpoʊz/ (**juxtaposes, juxtaposing, juxtaposed**) V-T If you **juxtapose** two contrasting objects, images, or ideas, you place them together or describe them together, so that the differences between them are emphasized. [FORMAL] ❑ *The technique Mr. Wilson uses most often is to juxtapose things for dramatic effect.* ❑ *Contemporary photographs are juxtaposed with a sixteenth century, copper Portuguese mirror.*

jux|ta|po|si|tion /dʒʌkstəpəzɪʃən/ (**juxtapositions**) N-VAR The **juxtaposition** of two contrasting objects, images, or ideas is the fact that they are placed together or described together, so that the differences between them are emphasized. [FORMAL] ❑ *This juxtaposition of brutal reality and lyrical beauty runs through Park's stories.*

Kk

K also **k** /keɪ/ (**K's, k's**) N-VAR **K** is the eleventh letter of the English alphabet.

K-12 /keɪ twelv/ ADJ **K-12** education is education for children from kindergarten through twelfth grade. [AM] ❑ ...all of the state's 11,000 K-12 schools.

ka|bob /kəbɒb/ (**kabobs**) → see kebab

kaffee|klatch /kɑfiklɑtʃ, -klætʃ, kɒfi-/ (**kaffeeklatches**) also **kaffee klatch** → see coffee klatch

kaf|tan /kæftæn/ (**kaftans**) → see caftan

Kal|ash|ni|kov /kəlæʃnɪkɒf/ (**Kalashnikovs**) N-COUNT A **Kalashnikov** is a type of rifle that is made in Russia.

kale /keɪl/ N-UNCOUNT **Kale** is a vegetable that is similar to a cabbage.

ka|lei|do|scope /kəlaɪdəskoʊp/ (**kaleidoscopes**) **1** N-COUNT A **kaleidoscope** is a toy in the shape of a tube with a small hole at one end. If you look through the hole and turn the other end of the tube, you can see a pattern of colors which changes as you turn the tube around. **2** N-SING You can describe something that is made up of a lot of different and frequently changing colors or elements as a **kaleidoscope**. ❑ ...the vivid kaleidoscope of colors displayed in the plumage of the peacock.

ka|lei|do|scop|ic /kəlaɪdəskɒpɪk/ ADJ [ADJ n] If you describe something as **kaleidoscopic**, you mean that it consists of a lot of very different parts, such as different colors, patterns, or shapes. ❑ ...a kaleidoscopic study of the shifting ideas and symbols of nationhood.

ka|mi|ka|ze /kæmɪkɑzi/ ADJ [ADJ n] If someone such as a soldier or terrorist performs a **kamikaze** act, they attack the enemy knowing that they will be killed doing it. ❑ ...kamikaze pilots ready to bomb nuclear installations.

kan|ga|roo /kæŋgəru/ (**kangaroos**) N-COUNT A **kangaroo** is a large Australian animal which moves by jumping on its back legs. Female kangaroos carry their babies in a pouch on their stomach.

kan|ga|roo court (**kangaroo courts**) N-COUNT If you refer to a court or a meeting as a **kangaroo court**, you disapprove of it because it is unofficial or unfair, and is intended to find someone guilty. [DISAPPROVAL]

ka|put /kəpʊt/ ADJ [usu v-link ADJ] If you say that something is **kaput**, you mean that it is completely broken, useless, or finished. [INFORMAL] ❑ "What's happened to your car?"—"It's kaput." ❑ He finally admitted that his film career was kaput.

kara|oke /kæriouki/ N-UNCOUNT **Karaoke** is a form of entertainment in which a machine plays the tunes of songs, and people take turns singing the words.

kar|at /kærət/ COMB IN ADJ **Karat** is used after a number to indicate how pure gold is. The purest gold is 24-karat gold. [AM] ❑ ...a twenty-four-karat gold necklace.

in BRIT, use **carat**

ka|ra|te /kərɑti/ N-UNCOUNT **Karate** is a Japanese sport or way of fighting in which people fight using their hands, elbows, feet, and legs.

kar|ma /kɑrmə/ N-UNCOUNT In religions such as Hinduism and Buddhism, **karma** is the belief that your actions in this life affect all your future lives.

kart /kɑrt/ (**karts**) N-COUNT A **kart** is the same as a **go-kart**.

kay|ak /kaɪæk/ (**kayaks**) **1** N-COUNT A **kayak** is a narrow boat like a canoe, used by the Inuit people and in the sport of kayaking. **2** → See also color supplement

ka|zoo /kəzu/ (**kazoos**) N-COUNT A **kazoo** is a small musical instrument that consists of a pipe with a hole in the top. You play the kazoo by blowing into it while making sounds.

Kb also **kb** **Kb** or **kb** is a written abbreviation for **kilobit** or **kilobits**.

KB **KB** is a written abbreviation for **kilobyte** or **kilobytes**.

Kbps also **kbps** **Kbps** is a unit for measuring the speed of a modem. **Kbps** is a written abbreviation for 'kilobits per second.' [COMPUTING] ❑ ...a 28.8 Kbps modem.

ke|bab /kəbɒb/ (**kebabs**) also **kabob** N-VAR A **kebab** is pieces of meat or vegetables grilled on a long thin stick, or slices of grilled meat served in pita bread.

ked|geree /kɛdʒəri/ N-UNCOUNT **Kedgeree** is a cooked dish consisting of rice, fish, and eggs.

keel /kil/ (**keels, keeling, keeled**) **1** N-COUNT The **keel** of a boat is the long, specially shaped piece of wood or steel along the bottom of it. ❑ The keel hit the rock first. **2** PHRASE If you say that someone or something is **on an even keel**, you mean that they are working or progressing smoothly and steadily, without any sudden changes. ❑ Jason had helped him out with a series of loans, until he could get back on an even keel. **3** → See also color supplement
▶ **keel over** PHRASAL VERB If someone **keels over**, they collapse because they are tired or ill. [INFORMAL] ❑ He then keeled over and fell flat on his back.

keen ♦◇◇ /kin/ (**keener, keenest**) **1** ADJ [ADJ n] If you say that someone has a **keen** mind, you mean that they are very clever and aware of what is happening around them. ❑ They described him as a man of keen intellect. ● **keen|ly** ADV ❑ They're keenly aware that whatever they decide will set a precedent. **2** ADJ If you have a **keen** eye or ear, you are able to notice things that are difficult to detect. ❑ ...an amateur artist with a keen eye for detail. ● **keen|ly** ADV [ADV with v] ❑ Charles listened keenly. **3** ADJ A **keen** interest or emotion is one that is very intense. [mainly BRIT] ❑ He had retained a keen interest in the progress of the work. ● **keen|ly** ADV ❑ She remained keenly interested in international affairs. **4** ADJ [v-link ADJ] If you are **keen** on doing something, you very much want to do it. ❑ You're not keen on going, are you? ● **keen|ness** N-UNCOUNT ❑ ...Doyle's keenness to please. **5** ADJ [v-link ADJ on n] If you are **keen on** something, you like it a lot and are very enthusiastic about it. ❑ I wasn't too keen on physics and chemistry. **6** ADJ You use **keen** to indicate that someone has a lot of enthusiasm for a particular activity and spends a lot of time doing it. ❑ She was a keen amateur photographer. **7** ADJ A **keen** fight or competition is one in which the competitors are all trying very hard to win, and it is not easy to predict who will win. [mainly BRIT] ● **keen|ly** ADV ❑ The contest should be very keenly fought.

KEEP

① REMAIN, STAY, OR CONTINUE TO HAVE/DO
② STOP OR PREVENT
③ SUPPORT, PROVIDE FOR
④ NOUN USE
⑤ PHRASAL VERBS

---

① **keep** ♦♦♦ /kip/ (**keeps, keeping, kept**)

→ Please look at meanings 18 – 26 to see if the expression you are looking for is shown under another headword.

1 V-LINK If someone **keeps** or **is kept** in a particular state, they remain in it. ❑ The noise kept him awake. ❑ People had to burn these trees to keep warm during harsh winters. **2** V-T/V-I If you **keep** or you **are kept** in a particular position or place, you remain in it. ▫ *Keep away from the doors while the train is moving.* ▫ *He kept his head down, hiding his features.* **3** V-I If you **keep** off something or **keep** away from it, you avoid it. If you **keep** out of something, you avoid getting involved in it. ▫ *I managed to stick to the diet and keep off sweet foods.* **4** V-T If you **keep** doing something, you do it repeatedly or continue to do it. ▫ *I keep forgetting it's December.* • PHRASAL VERB **Keep on** means the same as **keep**. ▫ *Did he give up or keep on trying?* **5** V-T **Keep** is used with some nouns to indicate that someone does something for a period of time or continues to do it. For example, if you **keep a grip** on something, you continue to hold or control it. ▫ *Until last year, the regime kept a tight grip on the country.* **6** V-T If you **keep** something, you continue to have it in your possession and do not throw it away, give it away, or sell it. ▫ *We must decide what to keep and what to give away.* **7** V-T If you **keep** something in a particular place, you always have it or store it in that place so that you can use it whenever you need it. ▫ *She kept her money under the mattress.* **8** V-T When you **keep** something such as a promise or an appointment, you do what you said you would do. ▫ *I'm hoping you'll keep your promise to come for a long visit.* **9** V-T If you **keep** a record of a series of events, you write down details of it so that they can be referred to later. ▫ *Eleanor began to keep a diary.* **10** V-I If food **keeps** for a certain length of time, it stays fresh and suitable to eat for that time. ▫ *Whatever is left over may be put into the refrigerator, where it will keep for 2-3 weeks.* **11** V-I [only cont] You can say or ask how someone **is keeping** as a way of saying or asking whether they are well. ▫ *She hasn't been keeping too well lately.* **12** PHRASE If you **keep at it**, you continue doing something that you have started, even if you are tired and would prefer to stop. ▫ *It may take a number of attempts, but it is worth keeping at it.* **13** PHRASE If you **keep going**, you continue moving along or doing something that you have started, even if you are tired and would prefer to stop. ▫ *She forced herself to keep going.* **14** PHRASE If one thing is **in keeping** with another, it is suitable in relation to that thing. If one thing is **out of keeping** with another, you mean that it is not suitable in relation to that thing. ▫ *This is not in keeping with our objective of representing the community.* **15** PHRASE If you **keep it up**, you continue working or trying as hard as you have been in the past. ▫ *There are fears that he will not be able to keep it up when he gets to the particularly demanding third year.* **16** PHRASE If you **keep** something **to** yourself, you do not tell anyone else about it. ▫ *I have to tell someone. I can't keep it to myself.* **17** PHRASE If you **keep to** yourself, you stay on your own most of the time and do not mix socially with other people. ▫ *He was a quiet man who always kept to himself.* **18** **to keep someone company** → see **company** **19** **to keep a straight face** → see **face** ① **20** **to keep your head** → see **head** ③ **21** **to keep pace** → see **pace** **22** **to keep the peace** → see **peace** **23** **keep quiet about sth/keep sth quiet** → see **quiet** **24** **to keep a secret** → see **secret** **25** **to keep time** → see **time** ④ **26** **to keep track** → see **track**

② **keep** ♦♦♦ /kip/ (keeps, keeping, kept) **1** V-T If someone or something **keeps** you from a particular action, they prevent you from doing it. ▫ *Embarrassment has kept me from doing all sorts of things.* **2** V-T If someone or something **keeps** you, they delay you and make you late. ▫ *Sorry to keep you, Jack.* **3** V-T If you **keep** something from someone, you do not tell them about it. ▫ *She knew that Gabriel was keeping something from her.*

③ **keep** ♦♦♦ /kip/ (keeps, keeping, kept) **1** N-SING Someone's **keep** is the cost of food and other things that they need in their daily life. ▫ *Ray will earn his keep on local farms while studying.* **2** V-T If you **keep** animals, you own them and take care of them. ▫ *I've brought you some eggs. We keep chickens.* **3** V-T If you **keep** yourself or **keep** someone else, you support yourself or the other person by earning enough money to provide food, clothing, money, and other necessary things. [mainly BRIT] ▫ *She could just about afford to keep her five kids.* ▫ *I just cannot afford to keep myself.*

④ **keep** /kip/ (keeps) N-COUNT A **keep** is the main tower of a medieval castle, in which people lived. ▫ *...the first stone-built castle keep in Britain.*

⑤ **keep** /kip/ (keeps, keeping, kept)
▶ **keep down** **1** PHRASAL VERB If you **keep** the number, size, or amount of something **down**, you do not let it get bigger or go higher. ▫ *The prime aim is to keep inflation down.* **2** PHRASAL VERB If someone **keeps** a group of people **down**, they prevent them from getting power and status and being completely free. ▫ *No matter what a woman tries to do to improve her situation, there is some barrier or attitude to keep her down.* **3** PHRASAL VERB If you **keep** food or drink **down**, you manage to swallow it properly and not vomit, even though you feel sick. ▫ *I tried to give her something to drink but she couldn't keep it down.*
▶ **keep on** **1** → see **keep** ① 4 **2** PHRASAL VERB If you **keep** someone **on**, you continue to employ them, for example after other employees have lost their jobs. ▫ *They concluded that firing him would be more damaging than keeping him on.*
▶ **keep to** **1** PHRASAL VERB If you **keep to** a rule, plan, or agreement, you do exactly what you are expected or supposed to do. ▫ *You've got to keep to the speed limit.* **2** PHRASAL VERB If you **keep to** something such as a path or river, you do not move away from it as you go somewhere. ▫ *Please keep to the paths.* **3** PHRASAL VERB If you **keep to** a particular subject, you talk only about that subject, and do not talk about anything else. ▫ *Let's keep to the subject, or you'll get me too confused.* **4** PHRASAL VERB If you **keep** something **to** a particular number or quantity, you limit it to that number or quantity. ▫ *Keep costs to a minimum.*
▶ **keep up** **1** PHRASAL VERB If you **keep up** with someone or something that is moving near you, you move at the same speed. ▫ *He lengthened his stride to keep up with his father.* **2** PHRASAL VERB To **keep up** with something that is changing means to be able to cope with the change, usually by changing at the same rate. ▫ *The union called the strike to press for wage increases which keep up with inflation.* **3** PHRASAL VERB If you **keep up** with your work or with other people, you manage to do or understand all your work, or to do or understand it as well as other people. ▫ *Penny tended to work through her lunch hour in an effort to keep up with her work.* **4** PHRASAL VERB If you **keep up** with what is happening, you make sure that you know about it. ▫ *She did not bother to keep up with the news.* **5** PHRASAL VERB If you **keep** something **up**, you continue to do it or provide it. ▫ *I was so hungry all the time that I could not keep the diet up for longer than a month.* **6** PHRASAL VERB If you **keep** something **up**, you prevent it from growing less in amount, level, or degree. ▫ *The riders had to keep their pace up.* **7** → see also **keep** ① 15

keep|er /kipər/ (keepers) **1** N-COUNT In football, a **keeper** is a play in which the quarterback keeps the ball. [AM] **2** N-COUNT A **keeper** at a zoo is a person who takes care of the animals. **3** N-COUNT A **keeper** is something or someone that you value and that you feel is worth keeping. [AM, INFORMAL] ▫ *The show's a keeper–daring, imaginative and provocative.* ▫ *His sweet nature and kindness made him a keeper, she said.*

keep|sake /kipseɪk/ (keepsakes) N-COUNT A **keepsake** is a small present that someone gives you so that you will not forget them.

keg /kɛg/ (kegs) N-COUNT [oft n n] A **keg** is a small barrel used for storing something such as beer or other alcoholic drinks.

kelp /kɛlp/ N-UNCOUNT **Kelp** is a type of flat brown seaweed.

ken /kɛn/ PHRASE [usu v-link PHR] If something is **beyond your ken**, you do not have enough knowledge to be able to understand it. ▫ *The subject matter was so technical as to be beyond the ken of the average layman.*

ken|nel /kɛnəl/ (kennels) **1** N-COUNT A **kennel** is a place where dogs are bred and trained, or cared for when their owners are away. ▫ *Once you have chosen a kennel, make a booking for your pet.* **2** N-COUNT A **kennel** is a small building made especially for a dog to sleep in. [mainly BRIT]

in AM, usually use **doghouse**

Ken|yan /kɛnyən/ (Kenyans) **1** ADJ **Kenyan** means belonging or relating to Kenya, or to its people or culture. **2** N-COUNT A **Kenyan** is a Kenyan citizen, or a person of Kenyan origin.

kept /kɛpt/ **Kept** is the past tense and past participle of **keep**.

kerb /kɜrb/ [BRIT] → see **curb** 3

ker|chief /kɜrtʃɪf/ (kerchiefs) N-COUNT A **kerchief** is a piece of cloth that you can wear on your head or around your neck. [OLD-FASHIONED]

ker|nel /kɜrnəl/ (kernels) **1** N-COUNT The **kernel** of a nut is the part that is inside the shell. **2** N-COUNT The **kernel** of a cereal crop such as wheat is the seed that is inside the hard husk. **3** N-COUNT [usu sing, usu N *of* n] The **kernel** of something is the central and most important part of it. ☐ *The kernel of that message was that peace must not be a source of advantage or disadvantage for anyone.* ◨ N-COUNT [usu sing, usu N *of* n] A **kernel** of something is a small element of it. ☐ *For all I know, there may be a kernel of truth in what he says.*

kero|sene /kɛrəsin/ N-UNCOUNT **Kerosene** is a clear, strong-smelling liquid which is used as a fuel, for example in heaters and lamps. [mainly AM] ☐ *...a kerosene lamp.*

in BRIT, usually use **paraffin**

kes|trel /kɛstrəl/ (kestrels) N-COUNT A **kestrel** is a small bird of prey.

ketch /kɛtʃ/ (ketches) N-COUNT A **ketch** is a type of sailing ship that has two masts.

ketch|up /kɛtʃəp, kætʃ-/ also **catsup** N-UNCOUNT **Ketchup** is a thick, cold sauce, usually made from tomatoes, that is sold in bottles.

ket|tle /kɛtᵊl/ (kettles) ◨ N-COUNT A **kettle** is a covered container that you use for boiling water. It has a handle, and a spout for the water to come out of. ☐ *I'll put the kettle on and make us some tea.* ◨ N-COUNT A **kettle** of water is the amount of water contained in a kettle. ☐ *Pour a kettle of boiling water over the onions.*

in AM, also use **teakettle**

◨ PHRASE If you say that something is **a different kettle of fish**, you mean that it is very different from another related thing that you are talking about. [INFORMAL] ☐ *Banking today is a very different kettle of fish from the industry of the past.*

kettle|drum /kɛtᵊldrʌm/ (kettledrums) N-COUNT A **kettledrum** is a large bowl-shaped drum which can be tuned to play a particular note.

key ✦✧◇ /ki/ (keys, keying, keyed) ◨ N-COUNT A **key** is a specially shaped piece of metal that you place in a lock and turn in order to open or lock a door, or to start or stop the engine of a vehicle. ☐ *They put the key in the door and entered.* ◨ N-COUNT The **keys** on a computer keyboard or typewriter are the buttons that you press in order to operate it. ☐ *Finally, press the Delete key.* ◨ N-COUNT The **keys** of a piano or organ are the long narrow pieces of wood or plastic that you press in order to play it. ☐ *...the black and white keys on a piano keyboard.* ◨ N-VAR In music, a **key** is a scale of musical notes that starts on one specific note. ☐ *...the key of A minor.* ◨ N-COUNT The **key** on a map or diagram or in a technical book is a list of the symbols or abbreviations used and their meanings. ☐ *You will find a key at the front of the book.* ◨ ADJ [ADJ n] The **key** person or thing in a group is the most important one. ☐ *He is expected to be the key witness at the trial.* ◨ N-COUNT The **key** to a desirable situation or result is the way in which it can be achieved. ☐ *The key to success is to be ready from the start.* ◨ N-COUNT A **key** is a small low island or reef, especially one in the Gulf of Mexico. ☐ *...the Florida Keys.*

▶ **key in** PHRASAL VERB If you **key** something **in**, you put information into a computer or you give the computer a particular instruction by typing the information or instruction on the keyboard. ☐ *Brian keyed in his personal code.*

═══ SYNONYMS ═══

key
NOUN ◨
answer: *Legislation is only part of the answer.*
secret: *The secret of success is honesty and fair dealing.*
solution: *...the ability to sort out simple, effective solutions to practical problems.*
formula: *He offered this simple formula for a long and happy life.*

key|board /kibɔrd/ (keyboards) ◨ N-COUNT The **keyboard** of a computer or typewriter is the set of keys that you press in order to operate it. ☐ *He was in his office, battering the keyboard of his computer as if it were an old manual typewriter.* ◨ N-COUNT The **keyboard** of a piano or organ is the set of black and white keys that you press in order to play it. ☐ *Tanya's hands rippled over the keyboard.* ◨ N-COUNT People sometimes refer to musical instruments that have a keyboard as **keyboards**. ☐ *...Sean O'Hagan on keyboards.* ◨ → See feature box at **computer**; See also color supplement

key|board|er /kibɔrdər/ (keyboarders) N-COUNT A **keyboarder** is a person whose job is typing information into a computer.

key|board|ing /kibɔrdɪŋ/ N-UNCOUNT **Keyboarding** is the activity of typing information into a computer.

key|board|ist /kibɔrdɪst/ (keyboardists) N-COUNT A **keyboardist** is someone who plays keyboard instruments, especially in popular music.

key card (key cards) N-COUNT A **key card** is a small plastic card which you can use instead of a key to open a door or barrier, for example in some hotels and parking lots. ☐ *The electronic key card to Julie's room would not work.*

keyed up /kid ʌp/ ADJ [v-link ADJ] If you are **keyed up**, you are very excited or nervous before an important or dangerous event. ☐ *I wasn't able to sleep that night, I was so keyed up.*

key|hole /kihoʊl/ (keyholes) N-COUNT A **keyhole** is the hole in a lock that you put a key in. ☐ *I looked through the keyhole.*

key|hole sur|gery N-UNCOUNT **Keyhole surgery** is a surgical technique in which the surgeon inserts the instruments through small cuts in the patient's body, using as a guide an image provided by equipment inserted into the patient's body. [MEDICAL]

key|note /kinoʊt/ (keynotes) N-COUNT [usu sing, oft N n] The **keynote** of a policy, speech, or idea is the main theme of it or the part of it that is emphasized the most. ☐ *He would be setting out his plans for the party in a keynote speech.*

key|pad /kipæd/ (keypads) N-COUNT The **keypad** on a telephone is the set of buttons that you press in order to operate it. Some other machines, such as ATMs, also have a keypad. ☐ *...an elevator's push-button keypad.*

key play|er (key players) N-COUNT The **key players** in a particular organization, event, or situation are the most important people or things involved in it. ☐ *The former chairman was a key player in the deals that pushed the bank to the top.*

key ring (key rings) also **keyring** N-COUNT A **key ring** is a metal ring which you use to keep your keys together. You pass the ring through the holes in your keys.

key|stone /kistoʊn/ (keystones) ◨ N-COUNT A **keystone** of a policy, system, or process is an important part of it, which is the basis for later developments. ☐ *The government's determination to beat inflation has so far been the keystone of its economic policy.* ◨ N-COUNT A **keystone** is a stone at the top of an arch, which keeps the other stones in place by its weight and position. [TECHNICAL]

key|stroke /kistroʊk/ (keystrokes) N-COUNT A **keystroke** is one touch of one of the keys on a computer or typewriter keyboard. ☐ *With a few keystrokes, Rebecca was connected to her computer at Liberty Air Service.*

key|word /kiwɜrd/ (keywords) also **key word** ◨ N-COUNT [oft the N] You can refer to a word or phrase as the **keyword** when you want to emphasize how important it is. ☐ *Collaboration was the keyword: editors, designers, picture researchers and production staff worked closely together.* ☐ *...codes of conduct and ethical trading – the new keywords of the fair trade movement.* ◨ N-COUNT A **keyword** is a word or phrase that is associated with a particular document or that describes the contents of a particular document, for example, in internet searches. ☐ *Users therefore can search by title, by author, by subject, and often by keyword.*

kg kg is a written abbreviation for **kilogram** or **kilograms**.

kha|ki /kæki/ ◨ N-UNCOUNT **Khaki** is a strong material of a beige color, used especially to make uniforms for some soldiers. ☐ *On each side of me was a figure in khaki.* ◨ COLOR Something that is **khaki** is beige in color. ☐ *He was dressed in khaki trousers.*

kHz kHz is a written abbreviation for **kilohertz**. It is often written on radios beside a series of numbers to help you find a particular radio station.

kib|butz /kɪbʊts/ (kibbutzim /kɪbʊtsim/) N-COUNT A **kibbutz** is a place of work in Israel, for example a farm or factory, where the workers live together and share all the duties and income.

ki|bosh /ˈkaɪbɒʃ/ PHRASE If someone or something **puts the kibosh on** your plans or activities, they cause them to fail or prevent them from continuing. [mainly BRIT, INFORMAL] ❑ *Rattray, however, personally showed up at the meeting to try and put the kibosh on their plans.* ❑ *...software that puts the kibosh on pop-up ads if a user doesn't want them.*

kick ✦✧✧ /kɪk/ (kicks, kicking, kicked) **1** V-T/V-I If you **kick** someone or something, you hit them forcefully with your foot. ❑ *He kicked the door hard.* ❑ *He threw me to the ground and started to kick.* • N-COUNT **Kick** is also a noun. ❑ *He suffered a kick to the knee.* **2** V-T When you **kick** a ball or other object, you hit it with your foot so that it moves through the air. ❑ *I went to kick the ball and I completely missed it.* ❑ *He kicked the ball away.* • N-COUNT **Kick** is also a noun. ❑ *He missed an easy kick.* **3** V-T/V-I If you **kick** or if you **kick** your legs, you move your legs with very quick, small, and forceful movements, once or repeatedly. ❑ *They were dragged away struggling and kicking.* ❑ *First he kicked the left leg, then he kicked the right.* • PHRASAL VERB **Kick out** means the same as **kick**. ❑ *As its rider tried to free it, the horse kicked out and rolled over, crushing her.* **4** V-T If you **kick** your legs, you lift your legs up very high one after the other, for example when you are dancing. ❑ *...kicking his legs like a cancan dancer.* **5** V-T If you **kick** a habit, you stop doing something that is bad for you and that you find difficult to stop doing. [INFORMAL] ❑ *She's kicked her drug habit and learned that her life has value.* **6** N-SING If something gives you **a kick**, it makes you feel very excited or very happy for a short period of time. [INFORMAL] ❑ *I got a kick out of seeing my name in print.* **7** PHRASE If you say that someone **kicks** you **when you are down**, you think they are behaving unfairly because they are attacking you when you are in a weak position. ❑ *In the end I just couldn't kick Jimmy when he was down.* **8** PHRASE If you say that someone does something **for kicks**, you mean that they do it because they think it will be exciting. [INFORMAL] ❑ *They made a few small bets for kicks.* **9** PHRASE If you say that someone is dragged **kicking and screaming** into a particular course of action, you are emphasizing that they are very unwilling to do what they are being made to do. [EMPHASIS] ❑ *He had to be dragged kicking and screaming into action.* **10** PHRASE If you describe an event as **a kick in the teeth**, you are emphasizing that it is very disappointing and upsetting. [INFORMAL, EMPHASIS] ❑ *We've been struggling for years and it's a real kick in the teeth to see a new band make it ahead of us.* **11 to kick up a fuss** → see **fuss**

▶ **kick around** PHRASAL VERB If you **kick around** ideas or suggestions, you discuss them informally. ❑ *We kicked a few ideas around.* ❑ *They started to kick around the idea of going to Brazil next week.*

▶ **kick off** **1** PHRASAL VERB In soccer or football, when the players **kick off**, they start a game by kicking the ball. ❑ *They kicked off an hour ago.* **2** PHRASAL VERB In football, when the players **kick off**, they resume a game by kicking the ball. **3** PHRASAL VERB If an event, game, series, or discussion **kicks off**, or **is kicked off**, it begins. ❑ *The shows kick off on October 24th.* ❑ *The mayor kicked off the party.* **4** PHRASAL VERB If you **kick off** your shoes, you shake your feet so that your shoes come off. ❑ *She stretched out on the sofa and kicked off her shoes.* **5** PHRASAL VERB To **kick** someone **off** an area of land means to force them to leave it. [INFORMAL] ❑ *We can't kick them off the island.*

▶ **kick out** **1** PHRASAL VERB To **kick** someone **out of** a place or an organization means to force them to leave it. [INFORMAL] ❑ *The country's leaders kicked five foreign journalists out of the country.* **2** → see also **kick 3**

kick-ass **1** ADJ [usu ADJ n] Some people use **kick-ass** to describe people or things that they think are tough or aggressive. [AM, INFORMAL, VULGAR] ❑ *...a kick-ass businesswoman.* ❑ *...streamlined, kick-ass rock'n'roll.* **2** ADJ [usu ADJ n] Some people use **kick-ass** to describe something that they think is very good or impressive. [AM, INFORMAL, VULGAR] ❑ *...the most kick-ass skateboarding crew the world ever saw.*

kick|back /ˈkɪkbæk/ (kickbacks) N-COUNT A **kickback** is a sum of money that is paid to someone illegally, for example money which a company pays someone to arrange for the company to be chosen to do an important job. ❑ *...alleged kickbacks and illegal party financing.*

kick box|ing also **kickboxing** N-UNCOUNT **Kick boxing** is a type of boxing in which the opponents are allowed to kick as well as punch each other.

kick|er /ˈkɪkər/ (kickers) N-COUNT In sports such as football and rugby, the **kicker** is a player whose role includes kicking the ball. [AM] ❑ *Redskins kicker Chip Lohmiller missed two field-goal attempts.*

kick|off /ˈkɪkɔf/ (kickoffs)

in BRIT, use **kick-off**

1 N-VAR In football or soccer, the **kickoff** is the time at which a particular game starts. ❑ *It was about 10 hours before kickoff and I still didn't know if I was playing.* **2** N-COUNT In football, a **kickoff** is the kick that begins a play, for example at the beginning of a half or after a touchdown or goal has been scored. [AM] ❑ *They fumbled the opening kickoff, leading to a Tennessee touchdown.* **3** N-SING The **kickoff** of an event or activity is its beginning. [INFORMAL] ❑ *Memorial Day weekend marks the kickoff of the summer vacation season.*

kick|stand /ˈkɪkstænd/ (kickstands) N-COUNT A **kickstand** is a metal bar attached to a bicycle or motorcycle that holds it upright when it is not being used. ❑ *He waved back, put down the kickstand, and took off his helmet.*

kick-start (kick-starts, kick-starting, kick-started) also **kickstart** **1** V-T To **kick-start** a process that has stopped working or progressing is to take a course of action that will quickly start it going again. ❑ *The president has chosen to kick-start the economy by slashing interest rates.* • N-COUNT **Kick-start** is also a noun. ❑ *The housing market needs a kick-start.* **2** V-T If you **kick-start** a motorcycle, you press the lever that starts it with your foot. ❑ *He lifted the bike off its stand and kick-started it.*

kid ✦✦✧ /kɪd/ (kids, kidding, kidded) **1** N-COUNT You can refer to a child as a **kid**. [INFORMAL] ❑ *They've got three kids.* **2** V-I [usu cont] If you **are kidding**, you are saying something that is not really true, as a joke. [INFORMAL] ❑ *I'm not kidding, Frank. There's a cow out there, just standing around.* ❑ *I'm just kidding.* **3** V-T If you **kid** someone, you tease them. ❑ *He liked to kid Ingrid a lot.* **4** V-T If people **kid** themselves, they allow themselves to believe something that is not true because they wish that it was true. ❑ *We're kidding ourselves, Bill. We're not winning, we're not even doing well.* **5** N-COUNT A **kid** is a young goat. **6** PHRASE You can say '**you've got to be kidding**' or '**you must be kidding**' to someone if they have said something that you think is ridiculous or completely untrue. [INFORMAL, FEELINGS] ❑ *You've got to be kidding! I can't live here!*

kid|die /ˈkɪdi/ (kiddies) also **kiddy** **1** N-COUNT [usu N n] A **kiddie** is a very young child. [INFORMAL] ❑ *I had dinner with my girl and the kiddies.* **2** ADJ [ADJ n] **Kiddie** things are suitable for, or intended for, young children. [INFORMAL] ❑ *...Saturday morning kiddie shows on television.*

kid|do /ˈkɪdoʊ/ (kiddos) N-VOC You can call someone **kiddo**, especially someone who is younger than you, as a sign of affection. [mainly AM, INFORMAL] ❑ *I'll miss you, kiddo.*

kid gloves N-PLURAL [oft with N] If you treat someone or something with the **kid gloves**, or if you give them the **kid glove** treatment, you are very careful in the way you deal with them. ❑ *In presidential campaigns, foreign policy is treated with kid gloves.*

kid|nap /ˈkɪdnæp/ (kidnaps, kidnaping or kidnapping, kidnaped or kidnapped) **1** V-T/V-I To **kidnap** someone is to take them away illegally and by force, and usually to hold them prisoner in order to demand something from their family, employer, or government. ❑ *Police in Brazil uncovered a plot to kidnap him.* ❑ *They were middle-class university students, intelligent and educated, yet they chose to kidnap and kill.* • **kid|nap|per** (kidnappers) N-COUNT ❑ *The kidnappers repeated demands for $1.5 billion and the release of two local leaders.* • **kid|nap|ping** (kidnappings) N-VAR ❑ *Two youngsters have been arrested and charged with kidnapping.* **2** N-VAR **Kidnap** or a **kidnap** is the crime of taking someone away by force. ❑ *Stewart denies attempted murder and kidnap.* **3** → See feature box at **crime**

kid|ney /ˈkɪdni/ (kidneys) **1** N-COUNT Your **kidneys** are the organs in your body that take waste matter from your blood and send it out of your body as urine. ❑ *...a kidney transplant.* **2** N-VAR **Kidneys** are the kidneys of an animal, for example a lamb, calf, or pig, that are eaten as meat. ❑ *...lambs' kidneys.* **3** → See feature box at **body**; See also color supplement

kid|ney bean (kidney beans) N-COUNT [usu pl] **Kidney beans** are small, reddish-brown beans that are eaten as a vegetable. They are the seeds of a bean plant.

kill /kɪl/ (kills, killing, killed) **1** V-T/V-I If a person, animal, or other living thing **is killed**, something or someone causes them to die. ❑ *More than 1,000 people have been killed by the armed forces.* ❑ *He had attempted to kill himself on several occasions.* ❑ *Drugs can kill.* • **killing** N-UNCOUNT ❑ *There is tension in the region following the killing of seven civilians.* **2** N-COUNT The act of killing an animal after hunting it is referred to as the **kill**. ❑ *After the kill the men and old women collect in an open space and eat a meal of whale meat.* **3** V-T If someone or something **kills** a project, activity, or idea, they completely destroy or end it. ❑ *His objective was to kill the space station project altogether.* • PHRASAL VERB **Kill off** means the same as **kill**. ❑ *He would soon launch a second offensive, killing off the peace process.* **4** V-T If something **kills** pain, it weakens it so that it is no longer as strong as it was. ❑ *He was forced to take opium to kill the pain.* **5** V-T [only cont] If you say that something **is killing** you, you mean that it is causing you physical or emotional pain. [INFORMAL] ❑ *My feet are killing me.* **6** V-T If you say that you **kill** yourself to do something, you are emphasizing that you make a great effort to do it, even though it causes you a lot of trouble or suffering. [INFORMAL, EMPHASIS] ❑ *I'm killing myself to get my work done.* **7** V-T If you say that you will **kill** someone for something they have done, you are emphasizing that you are extremely angry with them. [EMPHASIS] ❑ *Tell Richard I'm going to kill him when I get hold of him.* **8** V-T If you say that something will not **kill** you, you mean that it is not really as difficult or unpleasant as it might seem. [INFORMAL] ❑ *Three or four more weeks won't kill me!* **9** V-T If you **are killing** time, you are doing something because you have some time available, not because you really want to do it. ❑ *I'm just killing time until I can talk to the other witnesses.* **10** PHRASE If you say that you will do something **if it kills** you, you are emphasizing that you are determined to do it even though it is extremely difficult or painful. [EMPHASIS] ❑ *I'll make this marriage work if it kills me.* **11** PHRASE If you say that you **killed** yourself **laughing**, you are emphasizing that you laughed a lot because you thought something was extremely funny. [INFORMAL, EMPHASIS] ❑ *I eventually got to the top about an hour after everyone else, and they were all killing themselves laughing.* **12** PHRASE If you **move in for the kill** or if you **close in for the kill**, you take advantage of a changed situation in order to do something that you have been preparing to do. ❑ *Seeing his chance, Dennis moved in for the kill.* **13 to be killed outright** → see **outright** **14** → See feature box at **time**
▶ **kill off 1** → see **kill 3** **2** PHRASAL VERB If you say that a group or an amount of something **has been killed off**, you mean that all of them or all of it have been killed or destroyed. ❑ *Their natural predators have been killed off.* ❑ *It is an effective treatment for the bacteria and does kill it off.*

kill|er ◆◇◇ /kɪlər/ (killers) **1** N-COUNT A **killer** is a person who has killed someone, or who intends to kill someone. ❑ *The police are searching for his killers.* **2** N-COUNT You can refer to something that causes death or is likely to cause death as a **killer**. ❑ *Heart disease is the biggest killer of men in developed countries.*

kill|er bee (killer bees) N-COUNT A **killer bee** is a type of bee which is very aggressive and likely to attack and sting people.

kill|er in|stinct (killer instincts) N-VAR If you say that an athlete or politician has the **killer instinct**, you admire them for their toughness and determination to succeed. [APPROVAL] ❑ *He quit the sport when he realized he didn't have the killer instinct.*

kill|er whale (killer whales) N-COUNT A **killer whale** is a type of black and white whale.

kill|ing ◆◇◇ /kɪlɪŋ/ (killings) **1** N-COUNT A **killing** is an act of deliberately killing a person. ❑ *This is a brutal killing.* **2** PHRASE If you **make a killing**, you make a large profit very quickly and easily. [INFORMAL] ❑ *They have made a killing on the deal.*

SYNONYMS

killing
NOUN **1**
murder: *...brutal murders.*
massacre: *Maria lost her 62-year-old mother in the massacre.*
slaughter: *...the slaughter of seal pups on the east coast of Canada.*
execution: *Execution by lethal injection is scheduled for July 30th.*

COLLOCATIONS

killing
NOUN **1**
noun + **killing**: gangland, honor, revenge
adjective + **killing**: brutal, cold-blooded, gruesome, senseless; sectarian, targeted; indiscriminate, mass, random

---

kill|ing fields N-PLURAL [oft with poss] People sometimes refer to a battlefield or a place where many people have been killed as that place's **killing fields**.

kill|joy /kɪldʒɔɪ/ (killjoys) N-COUNT If you call someone a **killjoy**, you are critical of them because they stop other people from enjoying themselves, often by reminding them of something unpleasant. [DISAPPROVAL] ❑ *Don't be such a killjoy!*

kiln /kɪln/ (kilns) N-COUNT A **kiln** is an oven that is used to bake pottery and bricks in order to make them hard.

kilo /kiːloʊ/ (kilos) N-COUNT A **kilo** is the same as a **kilogram**. ❑ *He'd lost ten kilos in weight.*

PREFIX

kilo-
forms words that refer to things that have a thousand parts. *For example, a kilometer is a thousand meters.*

---

kilo|bit /kɪləbɪt/ (kilobits) N-COUNT In computing, a **kilobit** is 1,024 bits of data. ❑ *...a 256-kilobit chip.*

kilo|byte /kɪləbaɪt/ (kilobytes) N-COUNT In computing, a **kilobyte** is one thousand bytes of data.

kilo|gram /kɪləgræm/ (kilograms)

in BRIT, also use **kilogramme**

N-COUNT A **kilogram** is a metric unit of weight. One kilogram is a thousand grams, or a thousandth of a metric ton, and is equal to around 2.2 pounds. ❑ *...a parcel weighing around 4.5 kilograms.*

kilo|hertz /kɪləhɜrts/ (kilohertz)

Kilohertz is both the singular and the plural form.

N-COUNT A **kilohertz** is a unit of measurement of radio waves. One kilohertz is a thousand hertz. ❑ *Their instruments detected very faint radio waves at a frequency of 3 kilohertz.*

kilo|meter ◆◇◇ /kɪləmɪtər, kɪlɒmɪtər/ (kilometers)

in BRIT, use **kilometre**

N-COUNT A **kilometer** is a unit of distance or length. One kilometer is a thousand meters and is equal to around 0.62 miles. ❑ *...only one kilometer from the border.*

kilo|watt /kɪləwɒt/ (kilowatts) N-COUNT A **kilowatt** is a unit of power. One kilowatt is a thousand watts. ❑ *...a prototype system which produces 25 kilowatts of power.*

kilowatt-hour (kilowatt-hours) N-COUNT A **kilowatt-hour** is a unit of energy that is equal to the energy provided by a thousand watts in one hour.

kilt /kɪlt/ (kilts) N-COUNT A **kilt** is a skirt with a lot of vertical folds, traditionally worn by Scottish men. Kilts can also be worn by women and children.

kil|ter /kɪltər/ **1** PHRASE [oft v-link PHR] If something or someone is **out of kilter** or **off kilter**, they are not completely right. ❑ *Ignoring feelings of tiredness knocks our body clocks out of kilter.* **2** PHRASE [oft v-link PHR with n] If one thing is **out of kilter** with another, the first thing does not agree with or fit in with the second. ❑ *Her lifestyle was out of kilter with her politics*

ki|mo|no /kɪmoʊnə, -noʊ/ (kimonos) N-COUNT A **kimono** is an item of Japanese clothing. It is long, shaped like a coat, and has wide sleeves.

kin /kɪn/ **1** N-PLURAL Your **kin** are your relatives. [DIALECT or OLD-FASHIONED] **2** → see also **next of kin**

KIND

① NOUN USES AND PHRASES
② ADJECTIVE USES

---

① **kind** ◆◆◇ /kaɪnd/ (kinds) **1** N-COUNT If you talk about a particular **kind** of thing, you are talking about one of the types or sorts of that thing. ❑ *The party needs a different kind of* leadership. ❑ *Had Jamie ever been in any kind of trouble?* **2** N-COUNT If you refer to someone's **kind**, you are referring to all the other people that are like them or that belong to the same class or set. [DISAPPROVAL] ❑ *I can take care of your kind.* **3** PHRASE You can use **all kinds of** to emphasize that there are a great number and variety of particular things or people. [EMPHASIS] ❑ *Adoption can fail for all kinds of reasons.* **4** PHRASE You use **kind of** when you want to say that something or someone can be roughly described in a particular way. [SPOKEN, VAGUENESS] ❑ *It was kind of sad, really.* **5** PHRASE If you refer to someone or something as **one of a kind**, you mean that there is nobody or nothing else like them. [APPROVAL] ❑ *She's a very unusual woman, one of a kind.* **6** PHRASE If you refer, for example, to **two**, **three**, or **four of a kind**, you mean two, three, or four similar people or things that seem to go well or belong together. ❑ *They were two of a kind, from the same sort of background.* **7** PHRASE If you respond **in kind**, you react to something that someone has done to you by doing the same thing to them. ❑ *They hurled defiant taunts at the riot police, who responded in kind.* **8** PHRASE If you pay a debt **in kind**, you pay it in the form of goods or services and not money. ❑ *...benefits in kind.* **9** PHRASE You can use **of a kind** to indicate that something is not as good as it might be expected to be, but that it seems to be the best that is possible or available. [mainly BRIT] ❑ *She finds solace of a kind in alcohol.*

② **kind** /kaɪnd/ (kinder, kindest) **1** ADJ Someone who is **kind** behaves in a gentle, caring, and helpful way toward other people. ❑ *I must thank you for being so kind to me.* • **kind|ly** ADV [ADV after v] ❑ *"You seem tired this morning, Jenny," she said kindly.* **2** ADJ [v-link ADJ] You can use **kind** in expressions such as **please be so kind as to** and **would you be kind enough to** in order to ask someone to do something in a firm but polite way. [POLITENESS] ❑ *Please be so kind as to see to it that all the alterations are made at once!* **3** → see also **kindly**, **kindness**

kinda /kaɪndə/ **Kinda** is used in written English to represent the words 'kind of' when they are pronounced informally. ❑ *I'd kinda like to have a sheep farm in New Mexico.*

kin|der|gar|ten /kɪndərgɑrtᵊn/ (kindergartens) N-COUNT [also in/to/at N] A **kindergarten** is a school or class for children aged 4 to 6 years old. It prepares them to go into the first grade. ❑ *She's in kindergarten now.*

kind-hearted ADJ If you describe someone as **kind-hearted**, you mean that they are kind, caring, and generous. ❑ *He was a warm, generous and kind-hearted man.*

kin|dle /kɪndᵊl/ (kindles, kindling, kindled) **1** V-T If something **kindles** a particular emotion in someone, it makes them start to feel it. ❑ *The Second World War kindled his enthusiasm for politics.* **2** V-T If you **kindle** a fire, you light paper or wood in order to start it. ❑ *I came in and kindled a fire in the stove.*

kin|dling /kɪndlɪŋ/ N-UNCOUNT **Kindling** is small pieces of dry wood and other materials that you use to start a fire.

kind|ly /kaɪndli/ (kindlier, kindliest) **1** ADJ A **kindly** person is kind, caring, and sympathetic. ❑ *He was a stern critic but an extremely kindly man.* **2** ADV [ADV before v] If someone **kindly** does something for you, they act in a thoughtful and helpful way. ❑ *She kindly offered to go and fetch him some beer.* **3** ADV [ADV before v] If someone asks you to **kindly** do something, they are asking you in a way which shows that they have authority over you, or that they are angry with you. [FORMAL] ❑ *Will you kindly obey the instructions I am about to give?* **4** → see also **kind** ②

kind|ness /kaɪndnɪs/ N-UNCOUNT **Kindness** is the quality of being gentle, caring, and helpful. ❑ *We have been treated with such kindness by everybody.*

kin|dred /kɪndrɪd/ **1** N-UNCOUNT [with poss] Your **kindred** are your family, and all the people who are related to you. [DIALECT OR OLD-FASHIONED] **2** ADJ [usu ADJ N] **Kindred** things are similar to each other. [FORMAL] ❑ *I recall many discussions with her on these and kindred topics.*

kin|dred spir|it (kindred spirits) N-COUNT A **kindred spirit** is a person who has the same view of life or the same interests as you.

ki|net|ic /kɪnɛtɪk/ ADJ [usu ADJ n] In physics, **kinetic** is used to describe something that is concerned with movement. [TECHNICAL]

ki|net|ic en|er|gy N-UNCOUNT In physics, **kinetic energy** is the energy that is produced when something moves. [TECHNICAL]

kin|folk /kɪnfoʊk/ also **kinsfolk** N-PLURAL [oft poss N] Your **kinfolk** or **kinsfolk** are the people who are related to you. [LITERARY] ❑ *I sent my other son to the country to stay with kinfolk.* ❑ *Poor Emily. Her kinsfolk should come to her.*

king ♦♦◇ /kɪŋ/ (kings) **1** N-TITLE; N-COUNT A **king** is a man who is the most important member of the royal family of his country, and who is considered to be the head of state of that country. ❑ *...the king and queen of Spain.* **2** N-COUNT If you describe a man as **the king of** something, you mean that he is the most important person doing that thing or he is the best at doing it. ❑ *He was the king of the cowboys.* **3** N-COUNT A **king** is a playing card with a picture of a king on it. ❑ *...the king of diamonds.* **4** N-COUNT In chess, the **king** is the most important piece. When you are in a position to capture your opponent's king, you win the game.

king|dom /kɪŋdəm/ (kingdoms) **1** N-COUNT A **kingdom** is a country or region that is ruled by a king or queen. ❑ *The kingdom's power declined.* **2** N-SING All the animals, birds, and insects in the world can be referred to together as the animal **kingdom**. All the plants can be referred to as the plant **kingdom**. ❑ *The animal kingdom is full of fine and glorious creatures.*

king|fisher /kɪŋfɪʃər/ (kingfishers) N-COUNT A **kingfisher** is a brightly colored bird which lives near rivers and lakes and catches fish.

king|ly /kɪŋli/ ADJ [usu ADJ n] **Kingly** means like a king, or related to the duties of a king. [LITERARY] ❑ *...a noble man, kingly in stature.* ❑ *They thought that he should resume his kingly duties.*

king|maker /kɪŋmeɪkər/ (kingmakers) N-COUNT A **kingmaker** is a person or group who has control over which people are chosen for positions of authority, for example, in an election. ❑ *He will not run for office if he thinks he could lose but will instead seek to be a kingmaker.*

king|pin /kɪŋpɪn/ (kingpins) N-COUNT [oft N of n, n N] If you describe someone as the **kingpin** of an organization, you mean that they are the most important person involved in it. [JOURNALISM] ❑ *...one of the alleged kingpins of Colombia's largest drug ring.*

king|ship /kɪŋʃɪp/ N-UNCOUNT **Kingship** is the fact or position of being a king. ❑ *...the duties of kingship.*

king-size also **king-sized** ADJ [usu ADJ n] A **king-size** or **king-sized** version of something is a larger size than the standard version, and may be the largest size available. ❑ *...a king-size bed.* ❑ *...king-size cigarettes.*

kink /kɪŋk/ (kinks, kinking, kinked) **1** N-COUNT [oft N in n] A **kink** is a curve or twist in something which is otherwise or normally straight. ❑ *...a tiny black kitten with tufted ears and a kink in her tail.* **2** V-T/V-I If something **kinks** or **is kinked**, it has, or it develops, a curve or twist in it. ❑ *...her wet hair kinking in the breeze.* ❑ *Care is needed when loading the roll to prevent kinking the film.*

kinky /kɪŋki/ (kinkier, kinkiest) ADJ If you describe something, usually a sexual practice or preference, as **kinky**, you mean that it is unusual and would be considered strange by many people. [INFORMAL] ❑ *He had been engaging in some kind of kinky sexual activity.*

kins|folk /kɪnzfoʊk/ → see **kinfolk**

kin|ship /kɪnʃɪp/ **1** N-UNCOUNT **Kinship** is the relationship between members of the same family. ❑ *The ties of kinship may have helped the young man find his way in life.* **2** N-UNCOUNT If you feel **kinship** with someone, you feel close to them, because you have a similar background or similar feelings or ideas. ❑ *She evidently felt a sense of kinship with the woman.*

kins|man /kɪnzmən/ (kinsmen) N-COUNT [oft with poss] Someone's **kinsman** is their male relative. [LITERARY OR WRITTEN]

kins|woman /kɪnzwʊmən/ (kinswomen) N-COUNT [oft poss N] Someone's **kinswoman** is their female relative. [LITERARY OR WRITTEN]

ki|osk /kiɒsk/ (kiosks) N-COUNT A **kiosk** is a small structure with an open window at which people can buy things like newspapers, pay an attendant at a parking lot, or get information about something. ❑ *I was getting cigarettes at the kiosk.* ❑ *...an information kiosk.*

kip|per /kɪpər/ (kippers) N-COUNT A **kipper** is a fish, usually a herring, which has been preserved by being hung in smoke.

kirsch /kɪərʃ/ also **Kirsch** N-UNCOUNT **Kirsch** is a strong, colorless, alcoholic drink made from cherries which is usually drunk after a meal.

kis|met /kɪzmɪt, -mɛt/ N-UNCOUNT **Kismet** is the force which some people believe controls the things that happen to you in your life. ❑ *Omar and I were meant for each other. It was kismet.*

kiss ✦◇◇ /kɪs/ (kisses, kissing, kissed) ❶ V-RECIP If you **kiss** someone, you touch them with your lips to show affection or sexual desire, or to greet them or say goodbye. ❑ *She leaned up and kissed him on the cheek.* ❑ *Her parents kissed her goodbye as she set off from their home.* • N-COUNT **Kiss** is also a noun. ❑ *I put my arms around her and gave her a kiss.* ❷ V-T If you say that something **kisses** another thing, you mean that it touches that thing very gently. ❑ *The wheels of the aircraft kissed the runway.* ❸ PHRASE If you **blow** someone **a kiss** or **blow a kiss**, you touch the palm of your hand lightly with your lips, and then blow across your hand toward the person, in order to show them your affection. ❑ *Maria blew him a kiss.* ❹ PHRASE If you say that you **kiss** something **goodbye** or **kiss goodbye to** something, you accept the fact that you are going to lose it, although you do not want to. [INFORMAL] ❑ *I felt sure I'd have to kiss my dancing career goodbye.*

kiss-and-tell ADJ [ADJ n] If someone who has had a love affair with a famous person tells the story of that affair in public, for example in a newspaper or book, you can refer to this as a **kiss-and-tell** story. ❑ *...intimate photographs and kiss-and-tell revelations.*

kiss|er /kɪsər/ (kissers) N-COUNT [adj N] Someone who is a good **kisser** is good at kissing. Someone who is a bad **kisser** is not very good at kissing. ❑ *She's a great kisser.*

kiss of death N-SING [usu the N, oft N for/to n] If you say that a particular event is the **kiss of death** for something, you mean that it is certain to make it fail or be a disaster. ❑ *Trying to please an audience is the kiss of death for an artist.*

kiss of life N-SING [the N] The **kiss of life** is the same as mouth-to-mouth resuscitation. [BRIT]

kit /kɪt/ (kits) ❶ N-COUNT A **kit** is a group of items that are kept together, often in the same container, because they are all used for similar purposes. ❑ *Make sure you keep a well-stocked first aid kit ready to deal with any emergency.* ❷ N-COUNT A **kit** is a set of parts that can be put together in order to make something. ❑ *Her popular potholder is also available in do-it-yourself kits.* ❸ N-UNCOUNT **Kit** is special clothing and equipment that you use when you take part in a particular activity, especially a sport. [mainly BRIT]

in AM, usually use **gear**

kitch|en ✦◇◇ /kɪtʃən/ (kitchens) ❶ N-COUNT A **kitchen** is a room that is used for cooking and for household jobs such as washing dishes. ❷ → See also color supplement

kitch|en cabi|net (kitchen cabinets) N-COUNT [usu singular] The unofficial advisers of a president or a prime minister are sometimes referred to as the **kitchen cabinet**. [DISAPPROVAL]

kitch|en|ette /kɪtʃɪnɛt/ (kitchenettes) N-COUNT A **kitchenette** is a small kitchen, or a part of a larger room that is used for cooking.

kitch|en gar|den (kitchen gardens) N-COUNT A **kitchen garden** is a garden, or part of a garden, in which vegetables, herbs, and fruit are grown.

kitchen|ware /kɪtʃənwɛər/ N-UNCOUNT **Kitchenware** is pots and pans, knives and forks, and other utensils that you use in the kitchen. ❑ *She has a huge amount of Victorian kitchenware.*

kite /kaɪt/ (kites) ❶ N-COUNT A **kite** is an object, usually used as a toy, which is flown in the air. It consists of a light frame covered with paper or cloth and has a long string attached which you hold while the kite is flying. ❑ *Willy asks if I've ever flown a kite before.* ❷ PHRASE If you say that someone is **as high as a kite**, you mean that they are very excited or that they are greatly affected by alcohol or drugs. ❑ *The steroids made me feel so strange. I was as high as a kite some of the time.*

kith and kin /kɪθ ən kɪn/ N-PLURAL You can refer to your friends and family as your **kith and kin**. [OLD-FASHIONED]

kitsch /kɪtʃ/ N-UNCOUNT You can refer to a work of art or an object as **kitsch** if it is showy and thought by some people to be in bad taste. ❑ *...a hideous ballgown verging on the kitsch.* • ADJ **Kitsch** is also an adjective. ❑ *Blue and green eyeshadow has long been considered kitsch.*

kit|ten /kɪt°n/ (kittens) N-COUNT A **kitten** is a very young cat.

kit|ty /kɪti/ (kitties) ❶ N-COUNT A **kitty** is an amount of money gathered from several people, which is meant to be spent on things that these people will share or use together. ❑ *You haven't put any money in the kitty for three weeks.* ❷ N-COUNT A **kitty** is the total amount of money which is bet in a gambling game, and which is taken by the winner or winners. ❑ *Each month the total prize kitty is $13.5 million.* ❸ N-COUNT A **kitty** is a cat, especially a young cat. [INFORMAL] ❑ *...a cute little kitty.* ❑ *...kitty litter made of wood shavings.* ❹ N-COUNT **Kitty** is sometimes used as an affectionate way of referring to a cat or a kitten. [INFORMAL] ❑ *"Gertie!" the kids were calling into the yard. "Here kitty, kitty, kitty!"*

kitty-corner ADJ [AM] → see **catty-corner**

kiwi /kiwi/ (kiwis) A **kiwi** is the same as a **kiwi fruit**.

kiwi fruit (kiwi fruits)

Kiwi fruit can also be used as the plural form.

N-VAR A **kiwi fruit** is a fruit with a brown hairy skin and green flesh.

KKK /keɪ keɪ keɪ/ N-PROPER-COLL **KKK** is an abbreviation for **Ku Klux Klan**.

Klans|man /klænzmən/ (Klansmen) N-COUNT A **Klansman** is a man who is a member of the **Ku Klux Klan**.

klatch /klætʃ/ (klatches) also **klatsch** N-COUNT [n N] A **coffee klatch** or **kaffee klatsch** is an informal social event at which people talk and drink coffee. [AM]

Kleen|ex /klinɛks/ (Kleenex) N-COUNT A **Kleenex** is a piece of thin soft paper that is used as a handkerchief. [TRADEMARK] ❑ *...a box of Kleenex.*

klep|to|ma|ni|ac /klɛptəmeɪniæk/ (kleptomaniacs) N-COUNT A **kleptomaniac** is a person who cannot control their desire to steal things, usually because of a medical condition.

kludge /klʌdʒ/ (kludges) N-COUNT You can refer to an unsophisticated but fairly effective solution to a problem as a **kludge**. **Kludge** is used especially to talk about solutions to computing problems.

klutz /klʌts/ (klutzes) N-COUNT You can refer to someone who is very clumsy as a **klutz**. [mainly AM, INFORMAL, DISAPPROVAL]

km (kms) **km** is a written abbreviation for **kilometer**.

knack /næk/ (knacks) N-COUNT A **knack** is a particularly clever or skillful way of doing something successfully, especially something which most people find difficult. ❑ *He's got the knack of getting people to listen.*

knap|sack /næpsæk/ (knapsacks) also **backpack** N-COUNT A **knapsack** is a cloth or leather bag that you carry on your back or over your shoulder, for example when you are walking in the countryside.

knave /neɪv/ (knaves) N-COUNT If someone calls a man a **knave**, they mean that he is dishonest and should not be trusted. [OLD-FASHIONED, DISAPPROVAL]

knead /nid/ (kneads, kneading, kneaded) ❶ V-T When you **knead** dough or other food, you press and squeeze it with your hands so that it becomes smooth and ready to bake. ❑ *Lightly knead the mixture on a floured surface.* ❷ V-T If you **knead** a part of someone's body, you press or squeeze it with your fingers. ❑ *She felt him knead the aching muscles.*

knee ✦◇◇ /ni/ (knees, kneeing, kneed) ❶ N-COUNT Your **knee** is the place where your leg bends. ❑ *He will receive physical therapy on his damaged left knee.* ❷ N-COUNT If something or someone is on your **knee** or on your **knees**, they are resting or sitting on the upper part of your legs when you are sitting down. ❑ *He sat with the package on his knees.* ❸ N-PLURAL If you are on your **knees**, your legs are bent and your knees are on the ground. ❑ *She fell to the ground on her knees and prayed.* ❹ V-T If you **knee** someone, you hit them using your knee. ❑ *Ian kneed him in the groin.* ❺ PHRASE If a country or organization **is brought to its knees**, it is almost completely destroyed by someone or something. ❑ *The country was being brought to its knees by the loss of 2.4 million manufacturing jobs.* ❻ **on bended knee** → see **bended**

knee|cap /ni̱kæp/ (kneecaps) also **knee-cap** N-COUNT Your kneecaps are the bones at the front of your knees.

knee-capping (knee-cappings) also **kneecapping** N-VAR Knee-capping is the act of shooting someone in the knee and is carried out by some terrorist organizations as a form of punishment.

knee-deep **1** ADJ Something that is **knee-deep** is as high as your knees. ❏ *The water was only knee-deep.* **2** ADJ If a person or a place is **knee-deep** in something such as water, the level of the water comes up to a person's knees. ❏ *They spent much of their time knee-deep in mud.* **3** ADJ [v-link ADJ in n] If you say that you are **knee-deep** in something, you are emphasizing that you have a lot of it to deal with, and that it is taking up a lot of your time and attention. [INFORMAL, EMPHASIS] ❏ *The promised money won't help those students already knee-deep in debt.* ❏ *He was knee-deep in other people's problems.*

knee-high ADJ Something that is **knee-high** is as tall or high as an adult's knees.

knee-jerk ADJ [ADJ n] If you call someone's response to a question or situation a **knee-jerk** reaction, you mean that they react in a very predictable way, without thinking. [DISAPPROVAL] ❏ *The knee-jerk reaction to this is to call for proper security in all hospitals.*

kneel /ni̱l/ (kneels, kneeling, kneeled or knelt) V-I When you **kneel**, you bend your legs so that your knees are touching the ground. ❏ *She knelt by the bed and prayed.* ❏ *Other people were kneeling, but she just sat.* • PHRASAL VERB **Kneel down** means the same as **kneel**. ❏ *She kneeled down beside him.*

knell /ne̱l/ → see **death knell**

knelt /ne̱lt/ Knelt is a past tense and past participle of **kneel**.

knew /nu̱/ Knew is the past tense of **know**.

knick|ers /ni̱kərz/

The form **knicker** is used as a modifier.

N-PLURAL [also *a pair of* N] **Knickers** are the same as **panties**. [BRIT]

knick|knacks /ni̱knæks/ also **knick-knacks** N-PLURAL Knickknacks are small objects which people keep as ornaments or toys, rather than for a particular use. ❏ *Knickknacks filled three display cases and covered all the table tops.*

knife ♦◊◊ /na̱ɪf/ (knives, knifes, knifing, knifed)

Knives is the plural form of the noun and knifes is the third person singular of the present tense of the verb.

1 N-COUNT A **knife** is a tool for cutting or a weapon and consists of a flat piece of metal with a sharp edge on the end of a handle. ❏ *...a knife and fork.* **2** V-T To **knife** someone means to attack and injure them with a knife. ❏ *Dawson takes revenge on the man by knifing him to death.* **3** PHRASE If you **twist the knife in someone's wound**, you do or say something to make an unpleasant situation they are in even more unpleasant. ❏ *Hearing his own plans was like having a knife twisted in his wound.*

knife-edge also **knife edge 1** PHRASE [oft v-link PHR] To be **on a knife-edge** means to be in a situation in which nobody knows what is going to happen next, or in which one thing is just as likely to happen as another. ❏ *The game is poised on a knife-edge. One mistake or one piece of good luck could decide it.* **2** ADJ [ADJ n] You can use **knife-edge** to refer to something that is very exciting or tense because you do not know what is going to happen next. ❏ *Tonight's knife-edge vote could be uncomfortably close.*

knife|point /na̱ɪfpɔɪnt/ also **knife-point** PHRASE [PHR after v] If you are attacked or robbed **at knifepoint**, someone threatens you with a knife while they attack or steal from you. [JOURNALISM] ❏ *A 15-year-old girl was attacked at knifepoint in a subway.*

knif|ing /na̱ɪfɪŋ/ (knifings) **1** N-COUNT A **knifing** is an incident in which someone is attacked and injured with a knife. **2** → see also **knife**

knight /na̱ɪt/ (knights, knighting, knighted) **1** N-COUNT In medieval times, a **knight** was a man of noble birth, who served his king or lord in battle. ❏ *...King Arthur's faithful knight, Gawain.* **2** V-T [usu passive] If someone **is knighted**, they are given a knighthood. ❏ *He was knighted in June 1988.* **3** N-COUNT In chess, a **knight** is a piece which is shaped like a horse's head. **4** PHRASE If you refer to someone as a **knight in shining armor**, you mean that they are kind and brave, and likely to rescue you from a difficult situation. ❏ *The love songs tricked us all into believing in happy endings and knights in shining armor.*

knight|hood /na̱ɪthʊd/ (knighthoods) N-COUNT A **knighthood** is a title that is given to a man by a British king or queen for his achievements or his service to his country. A man who has been given a knighthood can put 'Sir' in front of his name instead of 'Mr.' ❏ *When he finally received his knighthood in 1975 Chaplin was 85.*

knit /ni̱t/ (knits, knitting, knitted) **1** V-T/V-I If you **knit** something, especially an article of clothing, you make it from wool or a similar thread by using two knitting needles or a machine. ❏ *I had endless hours to knit and sew.* ❏ *I have already started knitting baby clothes.* • COMB IN ADJ [ADJ n] **Knit** is also a combining form. ❏ *Ferris wore a heavy knit sweater.* **2** V-T If someone or something **knits** things or people together, they make them fit or work together closely and successfully. ❏ *The best thing about sports is that they knit the whole family close together.* • COMB IN ADJ **Knit** is also a combining form. ❏ *...a closer-knit family.* **3** V-I When broken bones **knit**, the broken pieces grow together again. ❏ *The bone hasn't knitted together properly.*

knit|ting /ni̱tɪŋ/ **1** N-UNCOUNT **Knitting** is something, such as an article of clothing, that is being knitted. ❏ *She had been sitting with her knitting at her fourth-floor window.* **2** N-UNCOUNT **Knitting** is the action or process of knitting. ❏ *Take up a relaxing hobby, such as knitting.*

knit|ting nee|dle (knitting needles) N-COUNT **Knitting needles** are thin plastic or metal rods which you use when you are knitting.

knit|wear /ni̱twɛər/ N-UNCOUNT **Knitwear** is clothing that has been knitted. ❏ *...expensive Italian knitwear.*

knives /na̱ɪvz/ Knives is the plural of **knife**.

knob /nɒ̱b/ (knobs) **1** N-COUNT A **knob** is a round handle on a door or drawer which you use in order to open or close it. ❏ *He turned the knob and pushed against the door.* **2** N-COUNT A **knob** is a round switch on a piece of machinery or equipment. ❏ *...the volume knob.*

knob|by /nɒ̱bi/ also **knobbly** /nɒ̱bli/ (knobbier or knobblier, knobbiest or knobbliest) ADJ Something that is **knobby** or **knobbly** has lumps on it which stick out and make the surface uneven. ❏ *...knobby knees.*

knock ♦◊◊ /nɒ̱k/ (knocks, knocking, knocked) **1** V-I If you **knock** on something such as a door or window, you hit it, usually several times, to attract someone's attention. ❏ *She went directly to Simon's apartment and knocked on the door.* • N-COUNT **Knock** is also a noun. ❏ *They heard a knock at the front door.* • **knock|ing** N-SING [also no det] ❏ *They were wakened by a loud knocking at the door.* **2** V-T If you **knock** something, you touch or hit it roughly, especially so that it falls or moves. ❏ *She accidentally knocked the glass off the shelf.* • N-COUNT **Knock** is also a noun. ❏ *The bags have tough exterior materials to protect against knocks, rain, and dust.* **3** V-T To **knock** someone into a particular position or condition means to hit them very hard so that they fall over or become unconscious. ❏ *The third wave was so strong it knocked me backwards.* **4** V-T [no cont] To **knock** a particular quality or characteristic out of someone means to make them lose it. ❏ *The school system is designed to knock passion out of people.* **5** V-T If you **knock** something or someone, you criticize them and say unpleasant things about them. [INFORMAL] ❏ *I'm not knocking them: if they want to do it, it's up to them.* **6** N-COUNT If someone receives a **knock**, they have an unpleasant experience which prevents them from achieving something or which causes them to change their attitudes or plans. **7 to knock someone or something into shape** → see **shape**

▶ **knock around**

in BRIT, also use **knock about**

1 PHRASAL VERB If someone **knocks around** somewhere, they spend time there, experiencing different situations or just passing time. ❏ *...reporters who knock around in troubled parts of the world.* ❏ *They knock around on weekends in grubby sweaters and pants.* **2** PHRASAL VERB If someone **knocks** you **around**, they hit or kick you several times. [INFORMAL] ❏ *He lied to me constantly and started knocking me around.*

knock down ◼ PHRASAL VERB To **knock down** a building or part of a building means to demolish it. ❑ *Why doesn't he just knock the wall down?* ◼ PHRASAL VERB To **knock down** a price or amount means to decrease it. [mainly AM] ❑ *The market might abandon the stock, and knock down its price.*

in BRIT, usually use **bring down**

◼ PHRASAL VERB If someone **is knocked down** or **is knocked over** by a vehicle or its driver, they are hit by a car and fall to the ground, and are often injured or killed. [mainly BRIT] ❑ *He was knocked down by a drunken driver in Miami.* ❑ *A drunk driver knocked down and killed two girls.* ❑ *A car knocked him over.*

in AM, usually use **hit**

▶ **knock off** ◼ PHRASAL VERB To **knock off** an amount from a price, time, or level means to reduce it by that amount. ❑ *We have knocked 10% off admission prices.* ◼ PHRASAL VERB When you **knock off**, you finish work at the end of the day or before a break. [INFORMAL] ❑ *If I get this report finished I'll knock off early.*
▶ **knock out** ◼ PHRASAL VERB To **knock** someone **out** means to cause them to become unconscious or to go to sleep. ❑ *The three drinks knocked him out.* ◼ PHRASAL VERB If a person or team **is knocked out** of a competition, they are defeated in a game, so that they take no more part in the competition. ❑ *He got knocked out in the first inning.* ◼ → see also **knockout**
◼ PHRASAL VERB If something is **knocked out** by enemy action or bad weather, it is destroyed or stops functioning because of it. ❑ *Our bombers have knocked out the mobile launchers.*
▶ **knock over** → see **knock down** 3
▶ **knock up** ◼ PHRASAL VERB If you **knock** something **up**, you make it or build it very quickly, using whatever materials are available. [BRIT, INFORMAL] ◼ PHRASAL VERB [usu passive] If a woman **is knocked up** by a man, she is made pregnant by him. [INFORMAL, VULGAR] ❑ *When I got knocked up, the whole town knew it.*

knock|down /nɒkdaʊn/ also **knock-down** ADJ [ADJ n] A **knockdown** price is much lower than it would be normally. [INFORMAL] ❑ *...the chance to buy it now at a knockdown price.*

knock|er /nɒkər/ (knockers) ◼ N-COUNT A **knocker** is a piece of metal on the front door of a building, which you use to hit the door in order to attract the attention of the people inside. ◼ → See feature box at **DIY**

knock-kneed ADJ Someone who is **knock-kneed** has legs which turn inward at the knees.

knock|off /nɒkɔːf/ (knockoffs) N-COUNT [oft N n] A **knockoff** is a cheap copy of a well-known product. [INFORMAL] ❑ *Frilly dresses are out; Chanel knockoffs are in.* ❑ *You can buy a nice knockoff watch from them.*

knock-on ◼ ADJ [ADJ n] If there is a **knock-on** effect, one action or event causes several other events to happen one after the other. [mainly BRIT] ❑ *The cut in new car prices has had a knock-on effect on the price of used cars.* ❑ *...a knock-on boost to the economy.*
◼ → See feature box at **endanger**

knock|out /nɒkaʊt/ (knockouts) also **knock-out** ◼ N-COUNT [also by N] In boxing, a **knockout** is a situation in which a boxer wins the fight by making his or her opponent fall to the ground and be unable to stand up before the referee has counted to ten. ❑ *I had 27 fights of which I won 25 by knockout.*
◼ ADJ [ADJ n] A **knockout** blow is an action or event that completely defeats an opponent. ❑ *He delivered a knockout blow to all of his rivals.* ◼ ADJ [ADJ n] A **knockout** competition is one in which the players or teams that win continue playing until there is only one winner left. [mainly BRIT]

in AM, use **elimination**

◼ N-SING If you describe someone as a **knockout**, you think that they are extremely attractive or impressive. [INFORMAL, APPROVAL] ❑ *Jill was a knockout with her biker leathers and t-shirt.*

knoll /noʊl/ (knolls) N-COUNT; N-IN-NAMES A **knoll** is a low hill with gentle slopes and a rounded top. [LITERARY] ❑ *...a grassy knoll.*

knot /nɒt/ (knots, knotting, knotted) ◼ N-COUNT If you tie a **knot** in a piece of string, rope, cloth, or other material, you pass one end or part of it through a loop and pull it tight. ❑ *One lace had broken and been tied in a knot.* ◼ V-T If you **knot** a piece of string, rope, cloth, or other material, you pass one end or part of it through a loop and pull it tight. ❑ *He knotted the laces securely together.* ❑ *He knotted the bandanna around his neck.* ◼ N-COUNT If you feel a **knot** in your stomach, you get an uncomfortable tight feeling in your stomach, usually because you are afraid or excited. ❑ *There was a knot of tension in his stomach.* ◼ V-T/V-I If your stomach **knots** or if something **knots** it, it feels tight because you are afraid or excited. ❑ *I felt my stomach knot with apprehension.* ◼ V-I If part of your face or your muscles **knot**, they become tense, usually because you are worried or angry. ❑ *His forehead knotted in a frown.* ◼ N-COUNT A **knot** in a piece of wood is a small hard area where a branch grew. ❑ *A carpenter often rejects half his wood because of knots or cracks.* ◼ N-COUNT A **knot** is a unit of speed. The speed of ships, aircraft, and wind is measured in knots. ❑ *They travel at speeds of up to 30 knots.*

knot|ty /nɒti/ (knottier, knottiest) ◼ ADJ [usu ADJ n] A **knotty** problem is complicated and difficult to solve. ❑ *The new management faces some knotty problems.* ◼ ADJ [usu ADJ n] **Knotty** wood has a lot of small hard areas on it where branches once grew.

KNOW
① VERB USES
② PHRASES

① **know** ♦♦♦ /noʊ/ (knows, knowing, knew, known) ◼ V-T/V-I [no cont] If you **know** a fact, a piece of information, or an answer, you have it correctly in your mind. ❑ *I don't know the name of the place.* ❑ *"People like doing things for nothing."—"I know they do."* ❑ *I don't know what happened to her husband.* ❑ *"How did we meet your mother?"—"I don't know."* ◼ V-T [no cont] If you **know** someone, you are familiar with them because you have met them and talked to them before. ❑ *Gifford was a friend. I'd known him for nine years.* ◼ V-T [no cont] If you say that you **know** of something, you mean that you have heard about it but you do not necessarily have a lot of information about it. ❑ *We know of the incident but have no further details.* ❑ *The president admitted that he did not know of any rebels having surrendered so far.* ◼ V-I [no cont] If you **know** about a subject, you have studied it or taken an interest in it, and understand part or all of it. ❑ *Hire someone with experience, someone who knows about real estate.* ❑ *She didn't know anything about music.* ◼ V-T [no cont] If you **know** a language, you have learned it and can understand it. ❑ *It helps to know French and Creole if you want to understand some of the lyrics.* ◼ V-T [no cont] If you **know** something such as a place, a work of art, or an idea, you have visited it, seen it, read it, or heard about it, and so you are familiar with it. ❑ *No matter how well you know this city, it is easy to get lost.* ◼ V-T [no cont] If you **know** how to do something, you have the necessary skills and knowledge to do it. ❑ *The health authorities now know how to deal with the disease.* ◼ V-T [no cont] You can say that someone **knows** that something is happening when they become aware of it. ❑ *Then I saw a gun under the hall table so I knew that something was wrong.* ◼ V-T [no cont] If you **know** something or someone, you recognize them when you see them or hear them. ❑ *Would she know you if she saw you on the street?* ◼ V-T [no cont] If someone or something is **known** as a particular name, they are called by that name. ❑ *The disease is more commonly known as Mad Cow Disease.* ❑ *...Peter and his wife Antonella (also known as Tony).* ◼ V-T If you **know** someone or something as a person or thing that has particular qualities, you consider that they have those qualities. ❑ *Lots of people know her as a very kind woman.* ◼ → see also **knowing, known**

② **know** /noʊ/ (knows, knowing, knew, known)
→ Please look at meanings ◼ – ◼ to see if the expression you are looking for is shown under another headword.

◼ PHRASE If you talk about a thing or system **as we know it**, you are referring to the form in which it exists now and which is familiar to most people. ❑ *He planned to end the welfare system as we know it.* ◼ PHRASE If you **get to know** someone, you find out what they are like by spending time with them. ❑ *The new neighbors were getting to know each other.* ◼ PHRASE People use expressions such as **goodness knows**, **Heaven knows**, and **God knows** when they do not know something and want to suggest that nobody could possibly know it. [INFORMAL] ❑ *"Who's he?"—"God knows."* ◼ CONVENTION You say '**I know**' to show that you agree with what has just been said. ❑ *"This country is so awful."—"I know, I know."* ◼ PHRASE You can

know-all

use **I don't know** to indicate that you do not completely agree with something or do not really think that it is true. ☐ *"He should quite simply resign."—"I don't know about that."* **6** PHRASE You can say '**I don't know about you**' to indicate that you are going to give your own opinion about something and you want to find out if someone else feels the same. ☐ *I don't know about the rest of you, but I'm hungry.* **7** PHRASE You use **I don't know** in expressions which indicate criticism of someone's behavior. For example, if you say that you **do not know how** someone can do something, you mean that you cannot understand or accept them doing it. [DISAPPROVAL] ☐ *I don't know how he could do this to his own daughter.* **8** PHRASE If you are **in the know** about something, especially something that is not known about or understood by many people, you have information about it. ☐ *It was gratifying to be in the know about important people.* **9** CONVENTION You can use expressions such as **you know what I mean** and **if you know what I mean** to suggest that the person listening to you understands what you are trying to say, and so you do not have to explain any more. [SPOKEN] ☐ *None of us stayed long. I mean, the atmosphere wasn't – well, you know what I mean.* **10** CONVENTION You say '**You never know**' or '**One never knows**' to indicate that it is not definite or certain what will happen in the future, and to suggest that there is some hope that things will turn out well. [VAGUENESS] ☐ *You never know, I might get lucky.* **11** CONVENTION You say '**Not that I know of**' when someone has asked you whether or not something is true and you think the answer is 'no' but you cannot be sure because you do not know all the facts. [VAGUENESS] ☐ *"Is he married?"—"Not that I know of."* **12** CONVENTION You use **you know** to emphasize or to draw attention to what you are saying. [SPOKEN, EMPHASIS] ☐ *The conditions in there are awful, you know.* **13** PHRASE You can say '**You don't know**' in order to emphasize how strongly you feel about the remark you are going to make. [SPOKEN, EMPHASIS] ☐ *You don't know how good it is to speak to somebody from home.* **14 to know best** → see **best 15 to know better** → see **better** ① **16 to know something for a fact** → see **fact 17 as far as I know** → see **far** ② **18 not to know the first thing about something** → see **first 19 to know full well** → see **full** ② **20 to let someone know** → see **let 21 to know your own mind** → see **mind** ① **22 to know the ropes** → see **rope**

know-all (know-alls) N-COUNT A **know-all** is the same as a **know-it-all**. [BRIT, INFORMAL, DISAPPROVAL]

know-how ✦◇◇ N-UNCOUNT **Know-how** is knowledge of the methods or techniques of doing something, especially something technical or practical. [INFORMAL] ☐ *He hasn't got the know-how to run a farm.*

know|ing /ˈnoʊɪŋ/ ADJ A **knowing** gesture or remark is one that shows that you understand something, for example the way that someone is feeling or what they really mean, even though it has not been mentioned directly. ☐ *Ron gave her a knowing smile.* • **know|ing|ly** ADV ☐ *He smiled knowingly.*

know|ing|ly /ˈnoʊɪŋli/ ADV [ADV before v] If you **knowingly** do something wrong, you do it even though you know it is wrong. ☐ *He repeated that he had never knowingly taken illegal drugs.*

know-it-all (know-it-alls) N-COUNT If you say that someone is a **know-it-all**, you are critical of them because they think that they know a lot more than other people. [AM, INFORMAL, DISAPPROVAL] ☐ *Don't act like a know-it-all. You listen to your mother.*

in BRIT, use **know-all**

knowl|edge ✦✦◇ /ˈnɒlɪdʒ/ N-UNCOUNT **1 Knowledge** is information and understanding about a subject which a person has, or which all people have. ☐ *She disclaims any knowledge of her husband's business concerns.* **2** PHRASE If you say that something is true **to your knowledge** or **to the best of your knowledge**, you mean that you believe it to be true but it is possible that you do not know all the facts. ☐ *Alec never carried a gun to my knowledge.*

═══════ SYNONYMS ═══════

knowledge
NOUN **1**
understanding: *They have a basic understanding of computers.*
awareness: *The 1980s brought an awareness of green issues.*
grasp: *They have a good grasp of foreign languages.*
appreciation: *They have a stronger appreciation of the importance of economic incentives.*

knowl|edge|able /ˈnɒlɪdʒəbəl/ also **knowledgable** ADJ Someone who is **knowledgeable** has or shows a clear understanding of many different facts about the world or about a particular subject. ☐ *Do you think you are more knowledgeable about life than your parents were at your age?*

known /noʊn/ **1 Known** is the past participle of **know**. **2** ADJ You use **known** to describe someone or something that is clearly recognized by or familiar to all people or to a particular group of people. ☐ *...He was a known drug dealer.* **3** ADJ [v-link ADJ for n/-ing] If someone or something is **known for** a particular achievement or feature, they are familiar to many people because of that achievement or feature. ☐ *He is better known for his film and TV work.* **4** PHRASE If you **let it be known** that something is the case, or you **let** something **be known**, you make sure that people know it or can find out about it. ☐ *The president has let it be known that he is against it.*

knuck|le /ˈnʌkəl/ (knuckles) **1** N-COUNT Your **knuckles** are the rounded pieces of bone that form lumps on your hands where your fingers join your hands, and where your fingers bend. ☐ *Brenda's knuckles were white as she gripped the arms of the chair.* **2 to rap sb's knuckles, to rap sb on/over the knuckles** → see **rap**

knuck|le-duster (knuckle-dusters) also **knuckleduster** N-COUNT A **knuckle-duster** is the same as '**brass knuckles**.' [mainly BRIT]

KO /ˌkeɪ ˈoʊ/ (KO's) N-COUNT **KO** is an abbreviation for **knockout**. ☐ *Thirty-four of his wins were KO's.*

koa|la /koʊˈɑːlə/ (koalas) N-COUNT A **koala** or a **koala bear** is an Australian animal which looks like a small bear with gray fur and lives in trees.

kohl /koʊl/ N-UNCOUNT **Kohl** is a cosmetic used to make a dark line along the edges of someone's eyelids.

kohl|ra|bi /koʊlˈrɑːbi/ (kohlrabi) N-VAR **Kohlrabi** is a green vegetable that has a round ball of leaves like a cabbage. It has a thick stem that you boil in water before eating.

kom|bucha /kɒmˈbuːtʃə/ N-UNCOUNT **Kombucha** is a sweet drink made by allowing tea, sugar, bacteria, and yeast to ferment. It is believed to be good for your health. ☐ *The taste of kombucha can be an acquired one.*

kook /kuːk/ (kooks) N-COUNT You can refer to someone who you think is slightly strange or eccentric as a **kook**. [mainly AM, INFORMAL]

kooky /ˈkuːki/ (kookier, kookiest) ADJ Someone or something that is **kooky** is slightly strange or eccentric, but often in a way which makes you like them. [INFORMAL] ☐ *It's slightly kooky, but I love it.* ☐ *She's been mocked for her kooky ways.*

Ko|ran /kɔːˈrɑːn/ N-PROPER **The Koran** is the sacred book on which the religion of Islam is based.

Ko|ran|ic /kɔːˈrænɪk/ ADJ [ADJ n] **Koranic** is used to describe something which belongs or relates to the Koran. ☐ *...Koranic schools.*

Ko|rean /kəˈriːən/ (Koreans) **1** ADJ **Korean** means belonging or relating to North or South Korea, or to their people, language, or culture. **2** N-COUNT A **Korean** is a North or South Korean citizen, or a person of North or South Korean origin. **3** N-UNCOUNT **Korean** is the language spoken by people who live in North and South Korea.

ko|sher /ˈkoʊʃər/ **1** ADJ Something, especially food, that is **kosher** is approved of or allowed by the dietary laws of Judaism. ☐ *...a kosher butcher.* **2** ADJ Something that is **kosher** is generally approved of or considered to be correct. [INFORMAL] ☐ *Acting was not a kosher trade for an upper-class girl.*

kow|tow /ˌkaʊˈtaʊ/ (kowtows, kowtowing, kowtowed) also **kow-tow** V-I If you say that someone **kowtows** to someone else, you are criticizing them because they are too eager to obey or be polite to someone in authority. [INFORMAL, DISAPPROVAL] ☐ *See how stupidly they kow-tow to persons higher in the hierarchy.*

kph /ˌkeɪ piː ˈeɪtʃ/ **kph** is written after a number to indicate the speed of something such as a vehicle. **kph** is an abbreviation for 'kilometers per hour.'

Krem|lin ✦◇◇ /ˈkrɛmlɪn/ N-PROPER [the N] **The Kremlin** is the building in Moscow where Russian government business takes place. You can also use **the Kremlin** to refer to the central government of Russia and of the former Soviet Union.

❏ *...a two hour meeting in the Kremlin.* ❏ *The Kremlin is still insisting on a diplomatic solution to the crisis.*

krill /krɪl/ N-UNCOUNT **Krill** are animals similar to small shrimps that live in the ocean and are the main food of some whales. ❏ *Thousands of penguins have already died from a shortage of krill.*

kryp|ton /krɪptɒn/ N-UNCOUNT **Krypton** is an element that is found in the air in the form of a gas. It is used in fluorescent lights and lasers.

ku|dos /kudoʊz, -doʊs/ N-UNCOUNT **Kudos** is admiration or recognition that someone or something gets as a result of a particular action or achievement. ❏ *...a new hotel chain that has won kudos for the way it treats guests.*

Ku Klux Klan /ku klʌks klæn/ N-PROPER-COLL [oft *the* N] The **Ku Klux Klan** is a secret organization of White Protestant men in the United States which promotes violence against Black people, Jews, and other minorities.

kung fu /kʌŋ fu/ N-UNCOUNT **Kung fu** is a Chinese way of fighting in which people use only their bare hands and feet.

Kurd /kɜrd/ (**Kurds**) N-COUNT A **Kurd** is a member of a race of people who live mainly in parts of Turkey, Iran, and Iraq. ❏ *...a group of Iraqi Kurds.* ❏ *...Kurd women.*

Kur|dish /kɜrdɪʃ/ **1** ADJ **Kurdish** means belonging or relating to the Kurds, or to their language or culture. ❏ *...a thriving modern Kurdish society.* **2** N-UNCOUNT **Kurdish** is the language spoken by Kurds. ❏ *...schoolchildren speaking Kurdish with their friends.*

Ku|wai|ti /kʊweɪti/ (**Kuwaitis**) **1** ADJ **Kuwaiti** means belonging or relating to Kuwait, or to its people or culture. **2** N-COUNT A **Kuwaiti** is a Kuwaiti citizen, or a person of Kuwaiti origin.

kvetch /kvɛtʃ/ (**kvetches, kvetching, kvetched**) **1** V-I If someone **kvetches** about something, they complain about it in a bad-tempered way. [AM, INFORMAL, DISAPPROVAL] ❏ *Denverites often kvetch about sleep disrupted by the Denver Police Department's helicopter orbiting overhead.* ❏ *I just really love to kvetch.* **2** N-COUNT A **kvetch** is someone who kvetches. [AM, INFORMAL, DISAPPROVAL] ❏ *I'm sorry. I don't mean to be a kvetch.*

kW also **KW** kW is a written abbreviation for **kilowatt**.

Ll

L also **l** /ɛl/ (**L's, l's**) N-VAR **L** is the twelfth letter of the English alphabet.

L8R **L8R** is the written abbreviation for 'later,' mainly used in text messages and e-mails. [COMPUTING]

lab /læb/ (**labs**) N-COUNT A **lab** is the same as a **laboratory**.

la|bel ♦◇◇ /leɪbəl/ (**labels, labeling** or **labelling, labeled** or **labelled**) **1** N-COUNT A **label** is a piece of paper or plastic that is attached to an object in order to give information about it. ◻ *He peered at the label on the bottle.* **2** V-T [usu passive] If something **is labeled**, a label is attached to it giving information about it. ◻ *It requires foreign frozen-food imports to be clearly labeled.* ◻ *The produce was labeled "Made in China."* **3** V-T [usu passive] If you say that someone or something **is labeled** as a particular thing, you mean that people generally describe them that way and you think that this is unfair. [DISAPPROVAL] ◻ *It won't be labeled in any way as a military expedition.* ◻ *It does not matter whether these duties are labeled "duties" or "tasks."*

la|bor ♦♦♦ /leɪbər/ (**labors, laboring, labored**)

| in BRIT, use **labour** |

1 N-UNCOUNT [also N in pl] **Labor** is very hard work, usually physical work. ◻ *...the labor of hauling the rocks away.* **2** V-I Someone who **labors** works hard using their hands. ◻ *He will be laboring 14 hundred meters below ground.* **3** V-T/V-I If you **labor** to do something, you do it with difficulty. ◻ *Scientists labored for months to unravel the mysteries of Neptune and still remain baffled.* ◻ *We're laboring under an unfair disadvantage.* **4** N-UNCOUNT **Labor** is used to refer to the workers of a country or industry, considered as a group. ◻ *We have a problem of skilled labor.* ◻ *Employers want cheap labor and consumers want cheap houses.* **5** N-UNCOUNT The work done by a group of workers or by a particular worker is referred to as their **labor**. ◻ *He exhibits a profound humility in the low rates he pays himself for his labor.* **6** N-UNCOUNT **Labor** is the last stage of pregnancy, in which the baby is gradually pushed out of the womb by the mother. ◻ *Her labor had lasted ten hours before the doctor arranged a Cesarean section.* **7** → See feature box at **birth, working**

COLLOCATIONS

labor
NOUN
1
adjective + **labor**: hard, manual; forced, unpaid
4
noun + **labor**: child, immigrant, migrant, slave
adjective + **labor**: semiskilled, skilled, unskilled; organized; cheap

la|bora|tory ♦◇◇ /læbrətɔri/ (**laboratories**) **1** N-COUNT A **laboratory** is a building or a room where scientific experiments, analyses, and research are carried out. ◻ *...a brain research laboratory at Columbia University.* **2** N-COUNT A **laboratory** in a school, college, or university is a room containing scientific equipment where students are taught science subjects such as chemistry. ◻ *...my old school chemistry laboratory.*

la|bor camp (**labor camps**)

| in BRIT, use **labour camp** |

N-COUNT A **labor camp** is a kind of prison, where the prisoners are forced to do hard, physical work, usually outdoors.

La|bor Day N-UNCOUNT In the United States, **Labor Day** is a national holiday in honor of working people. It is the first Monday in September.

la|bored /leɪbərd/

| in BRIT, use **laboured** |

1 ADJ If someone's breathing is **labored**, it is slow and seems to take a lot of effort. ◻ *She could hear Max's harsh, labored breathing.* **2** ADJ If something such as someone's writing or speech is **labored**, they have put too much effort into it so it seems awkward and unnatural. ◻ *...his characters' labored musings about love and death and morality.*

la|bor|er /leɪbərər/ (**laborers**)

| in BRIT, use **labourer** |

N-COUNT A **laborer** is a person who does a job which involves a lot of hard physical work. ◻ *She still lives on the farm where he worked as a laborer.*

la|bor force (**labor forces**)

| in BRIT, use **labour force** |

N-COUNT The **labor force** consists of all the people who are able to work in a country or area, or all the people who work for a particular company. [BUSINESS] ◻ *He says the reduction of the labor force could be significant.*

labor-intensive

| in BRIT, use **labour-intensive** |

ADJ **Labor-intensive** industries or methods of making things involve a lot of workers. Compare **capital-intensive**. [BUSINESS] ◻ *For labor-intensive businesses like garments, factory labor is cheap.*

la|bo|ri|ous /ləbɔriəs/ ADJ If you describe a task or job as **laborious**, you mean that it takes a lot of time and effort. ◻ *Keeping the yard tidy all year round can be a laborious task.* ● **la|bo|ri|ous|ly** ADV [ADV with v] ◻ *...the embroidery she'd worked on so laboriously during the long winter nights.*

la|bor mar|ket (**labor markets**)

| in BRIT, use **labour market** |

N-COUNT When you talk about the **labor market**, you are referring to all the people who are able to work and want jobs in a country or area, in relation to the number of jobs there are available in that country or area. [BUSINESS] ◻ *In a tight labor market, demand by employers exceeds the available supply of workers.*

la|bor re|la|tions

| in BRIT, use **labour relations** |

N-PLURAL **Labor relations** refers to the relationship between employers and employees in industry, and the political decisions and laws that affect it. ◻ *We have to balance good labor relations against the need to cut costs.*

labor-saving

| in BRIT, use **labour-saving** |

ADJ [usu ADJ n] A **labor-saving** device or idea makes it possible for you to do something with less effort than usual. ◻ *...labor-saving devices such as washing machines.*

la|bor un|ion (**labor unions**) N-COUNT A **labor union** is an organization that represents the rights and interests of workers to their employers, for example in order to improve working conditions or wages. [AM] ◻ *...NYSUT, the state's largest labor union.*

| in BRIT, use **trade union** |

la|bour /leɪbər/ [BRIT] → see labor
la|boured /leɪbərd/ [BRIT] → see labored
la|bour|er /leɪbərər/ [BRIT] → see laborer
lab|ra|dor /læbrədɔr/ (**labradors**) also **labrador retriever**, **Labrador retriever** N-COUNT A **labrador** or **labrador retriever** is a type of large dog with short, thick black or gold hair.
la|bur|num /ləbɜrnəm/ (**laburnums**) N-VAR A **laburnum** or a **laburnum tree** is a small tree which has long stems of yellow flowers.
laby|rinth /læbɪrɪnθ/ (**labyrinths**) **1** N-COUNT If you describe a place as a **labyrinth**, you mean that it is made up of a complicated series of paths or passages, through which it is difficult to find your way. [LITERARY] ❑ ...*the labyrinth of corridors.* **2** N-COUNT If you describe a situation, process, or area of knowledge as a **labyrinth**, you mean that it is very complicated. [FORMAL] ❑ ...*a labyrinth of conflicting political and sociological interpretations.*
laby|rin|thine /læbɪrɪnθɪn, -θɪn/ **1** ADJ [usu ADJ n] If you describe a place as **labyrinthine**, you mean that it is like a labyrinth. [FORMAL] ❑ *The streets of the Old City are narrow and labyrinthine.* **2** ADJ [usu ADJ n] If you describe a situation, process, or field of knowledge as **labyrinthine**, you mean that it is very complicated and difficult to understand. [FORMAL] ❑ ...*his failure to understand the labyrinthine complexities of the situation.*
lace /leɪs/ (**laces, lacing, laced**) **1** N-UNCOUNT **Lace** is a very delicate cloth which is made with a lot of holes in it. It is made by twisting together very fine threads of cotton to form decorative patterns. ❑ *She finally found the perfect gown, a beautiful creation trimmed with lace.* **2** N-COUNT **Laces** are thin pieces of material that are put through special holes in some types of clothing, especially shoes. The laces are tied together in order to tighten the clothing. ❑ *Barry was sitting on the bed, tying the laces of an old pair of running shoes.* **3** V-T If you **lace** something such as a pair of shoes, you tighten the shoes by pulling the laces through the holes, and usually tying them together. ❑ *I have a good pair of skates, but no matter how tightly I lace them, my ankles wobble.* • PHRASAL VERB **Lace up** means the same as **lace**. ❑ *He sat on the steps, and laced up his boots.* **4** V-T To **lace** food or drink with a substance such as alcohol or a drug means to put a small amount of the substance into the food or drink. ❑ *She laced his food with sleeping pills.*
lac|er|ate /læsəreɪt/ (**lacerates, lacerating, lacerated**) V-T If something **lacerates** your skin, it cuts it badly and deeply. ❑ *Its claws lacerated his thighs.* • **lac|er|ated** ADJ ❑ *She was suffering from a badly lacerated hand.*
lac|era|tion /læsəreɪʃən/ (**lacerations**) N-COUNT [usu pl, oft N prep] **Lacerations** are deep cuts on your skin. ❑ *He had lacerations on his back and thighs.*
lach|ry|mose /lækrɪmoʊs/ ADJ Someone who is **lachrymose** cries very easily and very often. [LITERARY] ❑ ...*the tears of lachrymose mourners.*
lack /læk/ (**lacks, lacking, lacked**) **1** N-UNCOUNT [also a N, usu N of n] If there is a **lack** of something, there is not enough of it or it does not exist at all. ❑ *Despite his lack of experience, he got the job.* ❑ *The charges were dropped for lack of evidence.* **2** V-T/V-I If you say that someone or something **lacks** a particular quality or that a particular quality is lacking in them, you mean that they do not have any or enough of it. ❑ *It lacked the power of the Italian cars.* ❑ *He lacked the judgment and political acumen for the post of chairman.* **3** PHRASE If you say there is **no lack of** something, you are emphasizing that there is a great deal of it. [EMPHASIS] ❑ *He said there was no lack of things for them to talk about.*

COLLOCATIONS

lack
NOUN **1**
adjective + **lack**: apparent, distinct, general, relative; appalling, chronic, severe, woeful; complete, profound, total
verb + **lack**: bemoan, blame, criticize, lament; cite, expose, indicate, show
VERB **2**
lack + noun: confidence, experience, power, skill; credibility, discipline, imagination; resources, support

---

lacka|dai|si|cal /lækədeɪzɪkəl/ ADJ If you say that someone is **lackadaisical**, you mean that they are rather lazy and do not show much interest or enthusiasm in what they do. ❑ *Dr. Jonsen seemed a little lackadaisical at times.* ❑ ...*the lackadaisical attitude of a number of the principal players.*
lack|ey /læki/ (**lackeys**) N-COUNT If you describe someone as a **lackey**, you are critical of them because they follow someone's orders completely, without ever questioning them. [DISAPPROVAL]
lack|ing /lækɪŋ/ ADJ [v-link ADJ] If something or someone is **lacking in** a particular quality, they do not have any of it or enough of it. ❑ ...*if your hair is lacking in luster and feeling dry.* ❑ *She felt nervous, increasingly lacking in confidence about herself.*
lack|luster /læklʌstər/

in BRIT, use **lacklustre**

ADJ If you describe something or someone as **lackluster**, you mean that they are not exciting or energetic. ❑ *He has already been blamed for his party's lackluster performance during the election campaign.*
la|con|ic /ləkɒnɪk/ ADJ If you describe someone as **laconic**, you mean that they use very few words to say something, so that they seem casual or unfriendly. ❑ *Usually so laconic in the office, Dr. Lahey seemed less guarded, more relaxed.*
lac|quer /lækər/ (**lacquers**) N-MASS **Lacquer** is a special liquid which is painted on wood or metal in order to protect it and to make it shiny. ❑ *We put on the second coating of lacquer.*
lac|quered /lækərd/ ADJ [ADJ n] **Lacquered** is used to describe things that have been coated or sprayed with lacquer. ❑ ...*17th-century lacquered cabinets.*
la|crosse /ləkrɒs/ N-UNCOUNT **Lacrosse** is an outdoor game in which players use long sticks with nets at the end to catch and throw a small ball, in order to try to score goals.
lac|ta|tion /lækteɪʃən/ N-UNCOUNT **Lactation** is the production of milk by women and female mammals during the period after they give birth. [FORMAL]
lac|tic acid /læktɪk æsɪd/ N-UNCOUNT **Lactic acid** is a type of acid which is found in sour milk and is also produced by your muscles when you have been exercising a lot.
lac|tose /læktoʊs/ N-UNCOUNT **Lactose** is a type of sugar which is found in milk and which is sometimes added to food.
la|cu|na /ləkyunə/ (**lacunae**) N-COUNT If you say that there is a **lacuna** in something such as a document or a person's argument, you mean that it does not deal with an important issue and is therefore not effective or convincing. [FORMAL]
lacy /leɪsi/ (**lacier, laciest**) ADJ **Lacy** things are made from lace or have pieces of lace attached to them. ❑ ...*lacy nightgowns.*
lad /læd/ (**lads**) N-COUNT; N-VOC A **lad** is a young man or boy. [OLD-FASHIONED] ❑ *When I was a lad his age I would laugh at the strangest things.*
lad|der /lædər/ (**ladders**) **1** N-COUNT A **ladder** is a piece of equipment used for climbing up something or down from something. It consists of two long pieces of wood, metal, or rope with steps fixed between them. ❑ *He climbed the ladder to the next deck.* **2** N-SING You can use the **ladder** to refer to something such as a society, organization, or system which has different levels that people can progress up or drop down. ❑ *If they want to climb the ladder of success they should be given that opportunity.* **3** N-COUNT A **ladder** is a hole or torn part in a pair of stockings or tights, where some of the vertical threads have broken, leaving only the horizontal threads. [BRIT]

in AM, use **run**

lad|en /leɪdən/ **1** ADJ If someone or something is **laden** with a lot of heavy things, they are holding or carrying them. [LITERARY] ❑ *I came home laden with cardboard boxes.* ❑ *The following summer the peach tree was laden with fruit.* **2** ADJ [v-link ADJ with n] If you describe a person or thing as **laden with** something, particularly something bad, you mean that they have a lot of it. ❑ *We're so laden with guilt.*
-laden /-leɪdən/ COMB IN ADJ [usu ADJ n] **-laden** combines with nouns to form adjectives which indicate that something has a lot of a particular thing or quality. ❑ ...*a fat-laden meal.* ❑ ...*smoke-laden air.* ❑ ...*a technology-laden military.*

la-di-da /lɑ di dɑ/ also **lah-di-dah** ADJ If you describe someone as **la-di-da**, you mean that they have an upper-class way of behaving, which you think seems unnatural and is only done to impress people. [OLD-FASHIONED, DISAPPROVAL] ❑ I wouldn't trust them in spite of all their la-di-da manners.

ladies' man N-SING [usu a N] If you say that a man is a **ladies' man**, you mean that he enjoys spending time socially with women and that women find him attractive. [OLD-FASHIONED]

ladies' room (ladies' rooms) N-COUNT [usu the N] Some people refer to a public toilet for women as **the ladies' room**.

la|dle /leɪdəl/ (ladles, ladling, ladled) **1** N-COUNT A **ladle** is a large, round, deep spoon with a long handle, used for serving soup, stew, or sauce. **2** V-T If you **ladle** food such as soup or stew, you serve it, especially with a ladle. ❑ Barry held the bowls while Liz ladled soup into them. ❑ Mrs. King went to the big black stove and ladled out steaming soup.

lady ♦♦◊ /leɪdi/ (ladies) **1** N-COUNT You can use **lady** when you are referring to a woman, especially when you are showing politeness or respect. ❑ ...a cream-colored lady's shoe. **2** N-VOC '**Lady**' is sometimes used by men as a form of address when they are talking to a woman that they do not know, especially in stores and on the street. [AM, INFORMAL, POLITENESS] ❑ What seems to be the trouble, lady? **3** N-TITLE In Britain, **Lady** is a title used in front of the names of some female members of the nobility, or the wives of knights.

lady|bird /leɪdibɜːd/ [BRIT] → see ladybug

lady|bug /leɪdibʌg/ (ladybugs) N-COUNT A **ladybug** is a small round beetle that is red with black spots. [AM]

in BRIT, use **ladybird**

lady friend (lady friends) N-COUNT [usu poss N] Someone's **lady friend** is the woman with whom they are having a romantic or sexual relationship. [OLD-FASHIONED]

lady-in-waiting (ladies-in-waiting) N-COUNT A **lady-in-waiting** is a woman whose job is to help a queen or princess.

lady-killer (lady-killers) N-COUNT If you refer to a man as a **lady-killer**, you mean that you think he is very successful at attracting women but quickly leaves them. [OLD-FASHIONED]

lady|like /leɪdilaɪk/ ADJ If you say that a woman or girl is **ladylike**, you mean that she behaves in a polite, dignified, and graceful way. ❑ I hate to be blunt, Frankie, but she just didn't strike me as being very ladylike. ❑ She crossed the room with quick, ladylike steps.

lag /læg/ (lags, lagging, lagged) **1** V-I If one thing or person **lags** behind another thing or person, their progress is slower than that of the other thing or person. ❑ Western banks still lag behind financial institutions in most other regions of the country. ❑ The restructuring of the pattern of consumption also lagged behind. **2** N-COUNT A time **lag** or a **lag** of a particular length of time is a period of time between one event and another related event. ❑ There's a time lag between infection with HIV and developing AIDS.

lag|gard /lægərd/ (laggards) N-COUNT If you describe a country, company, or product as **laggard**, you mean that it is not performing as well as its competitors. ❑ The company has developed a reputation as a technological laggard in the personal-computer arena. • ADJ **Laggard** is also an adjective. ❑ ...laggard product lines such as Jif peanut butter.

la|goon /ləgun/ (lagoons) N-COUNT A **lagoon** is an area of calm sea water that is separated from the ocean by a line of rock or sand.

lah-di-dah /lɑ di dɑ/ → see la-di-da

laid /leɪd/ **Laid** is the past tense and past participle of **lay**.

laid-back ADJ If you describe someone as **laid-back**, you mean that they behave in a calm relaxed way as if nothing will ever worry them. [INFORMAL] ❑ Everyone here has a really laid-back attitude.

lain /leɪn/ **Lain** is the past participle of **lie**.

lair /lɛər/ (lairs) **1** N-COUNT [usu with poss] A **lair** is a place where a wild animal lives, usually a place which is underground or well-hidden. ❑ ...a fox's lair. **2** N-COUNT [usu with poss] Someone's **lair** is the particular room or hiding place that they go to, especially when they want to get away from other people. [INFORMAL] ❑ The village was once a pirates' lair.

laissez-faire /leɪseɪ fɛər, lɛs-/ N-UNCOUNT **Laissez-faire** is the policy which is based on the idea that governments and the law should not interfere with business, finance, or the conditions of people's working lives. [BUSINESS] ❑ ...the doctrine of laissez-faire and unbridled individualism.

la|ity /leɪɪti/ N-SING-COLL [also no det] The **laity** are all the people involved in the work of a church who are not members of the clergy, monks, or nuns. ❑ The church and the laity were increasingly active in charity work. ❑ Clergy and laity alike are divided in their views.

lake ♦♦◊ /leɪk/ (lakes) **1** N-COUNT A **lake** is a large area of fresh water, surrounded by land. ❑ They can go fishing in the lake. **2** → See feature box at **water**

lake|front /leɪkfrʌnt/ also **lake front, lake-front** N-SING [oft N n] The **lakefront** is the area of land around the edge of a lake. [mainly AM] ❑ ...a cabin down on the lakefront. ❑ ...54 acres of wooded lakefront property beside Lake Geneva.

lake|side /leɪksaɪd/ N-SING The **lakeside** is the area of land around the edge of a lake. ❑ They were out by the lakeside a lot. ❑ ...the picturesque lakeside town of Lugano.

La-La land /lɑ lɑ lænd/ also **La La land, la-la land** **1** N-UNCOUNT People sometimes use **La-La land** to mean an imaginary place. [INFORMAL] ❑ If these politicians think we'll fix anything with more money, they're in la-la land. **2** N-UNCOUNT People sometimes refer to Los Angeles, in particular the Hollywood district of Los Angeles, as **La-La land**. [HUMOROUS, INFORMAL] ❑ ...her position as La-La land's premiere hairdresser.

lam /læm/ PHRASE If someone is **on the lam** or if they go **on the lam**, they are trying to escape or hide from someone such as the police or an enemy. [mainly AM, INFORMAL] ❑ He was on the lam for seven years.

lama ♦◊◊ /lɑmə/ (lamas) N-COUNT; N-TITLE A **lama** is a Buddhist priest or monk in Tibet or Mongolia.

lamb /læm/ (lambs) N-COUNT A **lamb** is a young sheep. • N-UNCOUNT **Lamb** is the flesh of a lamb eaten as food. ❑ Laura was basting the leg of lamb.

lam|baste /læmbeɪst/ (lambastes, lambasting, lambasted) also **lambast** V-T If you **lambaste** someone, you criticize them severely, usually in public. [FORMAL] ❑ And you can be sure that when the referee cheats our boys, I'll be ready to lambaste him.

lamb|ing /læmɪŋ/ N-UNCOUNT [oft N n] **Lambing** is the time in the spring when female sheep give birth to lambs. ❑ ...the lambing season.

lame /leɪm/ (lamer, lamest) **1** ADJ If someone is **lame**, they are unable to walk properly because of damage to one or both of their legs. ❑ I could see that she was lame in one leg. • N-PLURAL **The lame** are people who are lame. This use could cause offense. ❑ ...a place where the old, the blind and the lame would gather to beg. **2** ADJ If you describe an excuse, argument, or remark as **lame**, you mean that it is poor or weak. ❑ He mumbled some lame excuse about having gone to sleep. • **lame|ly** ADV [ADV with v] ❑ "Lovely house," I said lamely.

lamé /læmeɪ/ N-UNCOUNT [usu supp N] **Lamé** is cloth that has threads of gold or silver woven into it, which make it reflect light. ❑ ...a silver lamé dress.

lame duck (lame ducks) **1** N-COUNT [usu N n] If you refer to a politician or a government as a **lame duck**, you mean that they have little real power, for example, because their period of office is coming to an end. ❑ ...a lame duck government. **2** N-COUNT [oft N n] If you describe someone or something as a **lame duck**, you are critical of them because they are not successful and need to be helped a lot. [DISAPPROVAL] ❑ ...lame-duck industries.

la|ment /ləmɛnt/ (laments, lamenting, lamented) **1** V-T/V-I If you **lament** something, you express your sadness, regret, or disappointment about it. [mainly FORMAL or WRITTEN] ❑ Ken began to lament the death of his only son. ❑ He laments that people in Villa El Salvador are suspicious of the police. **2** N-COUNT Someone's **lament** is an expression of their sadness, regret, or disappointment about something. [mainly FORMAL or WRITTEN] ❑ She spoke of the professional woman's lament that a woman's judgment is questioned more than a man's. **3** N-COUNT A **lament** is a poem, song, or piece of music which expresses sorrow that someone has died. ❑ ...Shelley's lament for the death of Keats.

lam|en|table /læməntəbəl, ləmɛnt-/ ADJ If you describe something as **lamentable**, you mean that it is very unfortunate or disappointing. [LITERARY, FEELINGS] ❑ *This lamentable state of affairs lasted until 1947.* ❑ *His command of English was lamentable.* • **lam|en|tably** /læməntəbli, lamɛnt-/ ADV ❑ *There are still lamentably few women surgeons.* ❑ *They have failed lamentably.*

la|men|ta|tion /læmɛnteɪʃⁿn/ (lamentations) N-VAR A **lamentation** is an expression of great sorrow. [FORMAL] ❑ *It was a time for mourning and lamentation.* ❑ *...special prayers and lamentations.*

lami|nate /læmɪneɪt/ (laminates) N-MASS A **laminate** is a tough material that is made by sticking together two or more layers of a particular substance.

lami|nat|ed /læmɪneɪtɪd/ ◼ ADJ [usu ADJ n] Material such as wood or plastic that is **laminated** consists of several thin sheets or layers that are stuck together. ❑ *Modern windshields are made from laminated glass.* ◼ ADJ [usu ADJ n] A product that is **laminated** is covered with a thin sheet of something, especially clear or colored plastic, in order to protect it. ❑ *The photographs were mounted on laminated cards.* ❑ *...laminated work surfaces.*

lamp /læmp/ (lamps) N-COUNT A **lamp** is a light that works by using electricity or by burning oil or gas. ❑ *She switched on the bedside lamp.*

lamp|light /læmplaɪt/ N-UNCOUNT **Lamplight** is the light produced by a lamp. ❑ *Her cheeks glowed red in the lamplight.*

lam|poon /læmpun/ (lampoons, lampooning, lampooned) ◼ V-T If you **lampoon** someone or something, you criticize them very strongly, using humorous means. ❑ *He was lampooned for his short stature and political views.* ◼ N-VAR A **lampoon** is a piece of writing or speech which criticizes someone or something very strongly, using humorous means. ❑ *...his scathing lampoons of consumer culture.* ❑ *The style Shelley is using here is that of popular lampoon.*

lamp|post /læmppoʊst/ (lampposts) also **lamp post** N-COUNT A **lamppost** is a tall metal or concrete pole that is fixed beside a road and has a light at the top.

lamp|shade /læmpʃeɪd/ (lampshades) N-COUNT A **lampshade** is a covering that is fitted around or over an electric light bulb in order to protect it or decorate it, or to make the light less harsh.

LAN /læn/ (LANs) N-COUNT A **LAN** is a group of personal computers and associated equipment that are linked by cable, for example in an office building, and that share a communications line. **LAN** is an abbreviation for **local area network**. [COMPUTING] ❑ *You can take part in multiplayer games either on a LAN network or via the Internet.*

lance /læns/ (lances, lancing, lanced) ◼ V-T [usu passive] If a boil on someone's body **is lanced**, a small cut is made in it so that the liquid inside comes out. [MEDICAL] ❑ *It is a painful experience having the boil lanced.* ◼ N-COUNT A **lance** is a long spear used in former times by soldiers on horseback. ❑ *...the clang of lances striking armor.*

land ✦✦✦ /lænd/ (lands, landing, landed) ◼ N-UNCOUNT **Land** is an area of ground, especially one that is used for a particular purpose such as farming or building. ❑ *Good agricultural land is in short supply.* ❑ *...160 acres of land.* ◼ N-COUNT You can refer to an area of land which someone owns as their **land** or their **lands**. ❑ *Their home is on his father's land.* ◼ N-SING If you talk about **the land**, you mean farming and the way of life in farming areas, in contrast to life in the cities. ❑ *Living off the land was hard enough at the best of times.* ◼ N-UNCOUNT [also the N] **Land** is the part of the world that consists of ground, rather than sea or air. ❑ *It isn't clear whether the plane went down over land or sea.* ◼ N-COUNT You can use **land** to refer to a country in a poetic or emotional way. [LITERARY] ❑ *...America, land of opportunity.* ◼ V-I When someone or something **lands**, they come down to the ground after moving through the air or falling. ❑ *He was sent flying into the air and landed 20 feet away.* ◼ V-T/V-I When someone **lands** a plane, ship, or spacecraft, or when it **lands**, it arrives somewhere after a journey. ❑ *The jet landed after a flight of just under three hours.* ❑ *He landed his troops on the western shore.* ◼ V-T/V-I If you **land** in an unpleasant situation or place or if something **lands** you in it, something causes you to be in it. [INFORMAL] ❑ *He landed in a psychiatric ward.* ◼ V-I If something **lands** somewhere, it arrives there unexpectedly, often causing problems. [INFORMAL] ❑ *Two days later the book had already landed on his desk.* ◼ **to land on your feet** → see **foot** ① ◼ → See feature box at **farming**

land|ed /lændɪd/ ADJ [ADJ n] **Landed** means owning or including a large amount of land, especially land that has belonged to the same family for several generations. ❑ *Most of them were the nobility and the landed gentry.*

land|fall /lændfɔl/ (landfalls) N-VAR **Landfall** is the act of arriving somewhere after a journey at sea, or the land that you arrive at. ❑ *By the time we had made landfall the boat looked ten years older!*

land|fill /lændfɪl/ (landfills) ◼ N-UNCOUNT **Landfill** is a method of getting rid of very large amounts of garbage by burying it in a large deep hole. ❑ *...the environmental costs of landfill.* ◼ N-COUNT A **landfill** is a large deep hole in which very large amounts of garbage are buried. ❑ *The rubbish in modern landfills does not rot.*

land|form /lændfɔrm/ (landforms) also **land form** N-COUNT A **landform** is any natural feature of the Earth's surface, such as a hill, a lake, or a beach. ❑ *This small country has an amazing variety of landforms.* ❑ *...glacial land forms.*

land|ing /lændɪŋ/ (landings) ◼ N-COUNT In a house or other building, the **landing** is the area at the top of the staircase which has rooms leading off it. ❑ *I ran out onto the landing.* ◼ N-VAR A **landing** is an act of bringing an aircraft or spacecraft down to the ground. ❑ *I had to make a controlled landing into the sea.* ◼ N-COUNT When a **landing** takes place, troops are unloaded from boats or aircraft at the beginning of a military invasion or other operation. ❑ *American forces have begun a big landing.*

land|ing craft (landing craft) N-COUNT A **landing craft** is a small boat designed for the landing of troops and equipment on the shore.

land|ing gear N-UNCOUNT The **landing gear** of an aircraft is its wheels and the structures that support the wheels.

land|ing page (landing pages) N-COUNT The **landing page** is the page you see first when you enter a website. ❑ *The landing page asks for a user name and email address.*

land|ing strip (landing strips) N-COUNT A **landing strip** is a long flat piece of land from which aircraft can take off and land, especially one used only by private or military aircraft.

land|lady /lændleɪdi/ (landladies) N-COUNT Someone's **landlady** is the woman who allows them to live or work in a building which she owns, in return for rent. ❑ *There was a note under the door from my landlady.*

land|less /lændlɪs/ ADJ Someone who is **landless** is prevented from owning the land that they farm. ❑ *...landless peasants.* • N-PLURAL [the N] The **landless** are people who are landless. ❑ *We are giving an equal area of land to the landless.*

land|line /lændlaɪn/ (landlines) ◼ N-COUNT A **landline** is the phone connection that comes into a particular building using cables, rather than a cellphone connection. ❑ *One in five people no longer uses a landline.* ◼ → See feature box at **telephone**

land|locked /lændlɒkt/ also **land-locked** ADJ [usu ADJ n] A **landlocked** country is surrounded by other countries and does not have its own ports. ❑ *...the landlocked West African nation of Mali.*

land|lord /lændlɔrd/ (landlords) N-COUNT Someone's **landlord** is the man who allows them to live or work in a building which he owns, in return for rent. ❑ *His landlord doubled the rent.*

land|lubber /lændlʌbər/ (landlubbers) N-COUNT A **landlubber** is someone who is not used to or does not like traveling by boat, and has little knowledge of boats and the sea. [OLD-FASHIONED]

land|mark /lændmɑrk/ (landmarks) ◼ N-COUNT A **landmark** is a building or feature which is easily noticed and can be used to judge your position or the position of other buildings or features. ❑ *The Menger Hotel is a San Antonio landmark.* ◼ N-COUNT You can refer to an important stage in the development of something as a **landmark**. ❑ *...a landmark arms control treaty.*

land mass (land masses) also **landmass** N-COUNT A **land mass** is a very large area of land such as a continent. ❑ *...the Antarctic landmass.* ❑ *...the country's large land mass of 768 million hectares.*

land|mine /lændmaɪn/ (landmines) also **land mine** N-COUNT A **landmine** is an explosive device which is placed on or under the ground and explodes when a person or vehicle touches it.

land of|fice (land offices) N-COUNT In the United States, a **land office** is a government office where records are kept about the sale of public land, including information about who owns it. [AM] ❑ *Line-ups formed daily at the land offices as township after township was opened for settlement.*

land|owner /lændoʊnər/ (landowners) N-COUNT A **landowner** is a person who owns land, especially a large amount of land. ❑ *...rural communities involved in conflicts with large landowners.*

land|own|ing /lændoʊnɪŋ/ ADJ [ADJ n] **Landowning** is used to describe people who own a lot of land, especially when they are considered as a group within society. ❑ *The large estates were confiscated from the landowning families.*

land re|form (land reforms) N-VAR **Land reform** is a change in the system of land ownership, especially when it involves giving land to the people who actually farm it and taking it away from people who own large areas for profit. ❑ *...the new land reform policy under which thousands of peasant families are to be resettled.*

land|scape ♦◇◇ /lændskeɪp/ (landscapes, landscaping, landscaped) ■ N-VAR The **landscape** is everything you can see when you look across an area of land, including hills, rivers, buildings, trees, and plants. ❑ *...Arizona's desert landscape.* ■ N-COUNT A **landscape** is all the features that are important in a particular situation. ❑ *June's events completely altered the political landscape.* ■ N-COUNT A **landscape** is a painting which shows a scene in the countryside. ❑ *His latest series of landscapes is on show at the gallery.* ■ V-T If an area of land **is landscaped**, it is changed to make it more attractive, for example, by adding streams or ponds and planting trees and bushes. ❑ *The gravel pits have been landscaped and planted to make them attractive to wildfowl.* ❑ *They had landscaped their property with trees, shrubs, and lawns.* • **land|scap|ing** N-UNCOUNT ❑ *The landowner insisted on a high standard of landscaping.* ■ N-UNCOUNT [oft N n] If a sheet of paper is in **landscape** format or mode, the longer edge of the paper is horizontal and the shorter edge is vertical. ❑ *Most PowerPoint presentations are prepared for screens in landscape format.* ■ → See feature box at **fine art**, **garden**

COLLOCATIONS

landscape
NOUN
■
noun + **landscape**: desert
adjective + **landscape**: barren, bleak, flat, lunar; lush, natural, rugged, rural; urban
verb + **landscape**: dominate
■
adjective + **landscape**: cultural, musical, political; ever-changing, familiar, traditional
verb + **landscape**: alter, change, transform; dominate

SYNONYMS

landscape
NOUN ■
scenery: *Sometimes they just drive slowly down the lane, enjoying the scenery.*
countryside: *We are surrounded by lots of beautiful countryside.*
terrain: *The terrain changed quickly from arable land to desert.*
country: *...some of the best walking country in the Sierras.*

---

land|scape archi|tect (landscape architects) N-COUNT A **landscape architect** is the same as a **landscape gardener**.

land|scape gar|den|er (landscape gardeners) N-COUNT A **landscape gardener** is a person who designs gardens or parks so that they look attractive.

land|slide /lændslaɪd/ (landslides) ■ N-COUNT A **landslide** is a victory in an election in which a person or political party gets far more votes or seats than their opponents. ❑ *He won last month's presidential election by a landslide.* ■ N-COUNT A **landslide** is a large amount of earth and rocks falling down a cliff or the side of a mountain. ❑ *The storm caused landslides and flooding in Savona.*

land|ward /lændwərd/ ADJ [ADJ n] The **landward** side of something is the side nearest to the land or facing the land, rather than the sea. ❑ *Rebels surrounded the city's landward sides.*

lane ♦◇◇ /leɪn/ (lanes) ■ N-COUNT A **lane** is a narrow road, especially in the country. ❑ *...a quiet country lane.* ■ N-IN-NAMES **Lane** is also used in the names of roads, either in cities or in the country. ❑ *They had a house on Spring Park Lane in East Hampton.* ■ N-COUNT A **lane** is a part of a main road which is marked by the edge of the road and a painted line, or by two painted lines. ❑ *The truck was traveling at 20 mph in the slow lane.* ■ N-COUNT At a swimming pool, athletics track, or bowling alley, a **lane** is a long narrow section which is separated from other sections, for example by lines or ropes. ❑ *...after being disqualified for running out of his lane in the 200 meters.* ■ N-COUNT A **lane** is a route that is frequently used by aircraft or ships. ❑ *The collision took place in one of the busiest shipping lanes in the world.*

lan|guage ♦♦◇ /læŋgwɪdʒ/ (languages) ■ N-COUNT A **language** is a system of communication which consists of a set of sounds and written symbols which are used by the people of a particular country or region for talking or writing. ❑ *...the English language.* ❑ *Students are expected to master a second language.* ■ N-UNCOUNT **Language** is the use of a system of communication which consists of a set of sounds or written symbols. ❑ *Students examined how children acquire language.* ■ N-UNCOUNT You can refer to the words used in connection with a particular subject as the **language** of that subject. ❑ *...the language of business.* ■ N-UNCOUNT You can refer to someone's use of rude words or swearing as **bad language** when you find it offensive. ❑ *Television companies tend to censor bad language in feature films.* ■ N-UNCOUNT The **language** of a piece of writing or speech is the style in which it is written or spoken. ❑ *...a booklet summarizing it in plain language.* ❑ *The tone of his language was diplomatic and polite.* ■ N-VAR You can use **language** to refer to various means of communication involving recognizable symbols, nonverbal sounds, or actions. ❑ *The monks used a complex sign language.* ❑ *...the digital language of computers.* ■ → See feature box at **speak**

lan|guage la|bora|tory (language laboratories) N-COUNT A **language laboratory** is a classroom equipped with tape recorders or computers where people can practice listening to and speaking foreign languages.

lan|guid /læŋgwɪd/ ADJ If you describe someone as **languid**, you mean that they show little energy or interest and are very slow and casual in their movements. [LITERARY] ❑ *He's a large, languid man with a round and impassive face.* • **lan|guid|ly** ADV ❑ *We sat about languidly after dinner.*

lan|guish /læŋgwɪʃ/ (languishes, languishing, languished) ■ V-I If someone **languishes** somewhere, they are forced to remain and suffer in an unpleasant situation. ❑ *She continues to languish in prison.* ■ V-I If something **languishes**, it is not successful, often because of a lack of effort or because of a lot of difficulties. ❑ *Without the founder's drive and direction, the company gradually languished.*

lan|guor /læŋgər/ N-UNCOUNT **Languor** is a pleasant feeling of being relaxed and not having any energy or interest in anything. [LITERARY] ❑ *How easy it is for even an energetic person to lapse into a pleasant languor.*

lan|guor|ous /læŋgərəs/ ADJ [usu ADJ n] If you describe an activity as **languorous**, you mean that it is lazy, relaxed, and not energetic, usually in a pleasant way. [LITERARY] ❑ *...languourous morning coffees on the terrace.*

lank /læŋk/ ADJ If someone's hair is **lank**, it is long and perhaps greasy and hangs in a dull and unattractive way.

lanky /læŋki/ (lankier, lankiest) ADJ If you describe someone as **lanky**, you mean that they are tall and thin and move rather awkwardly. ❑ *He was six feet four, all lanky and leggy.*

lan|tern /læntərn/ (lanterns) N-COUNT A **lantern** is a lamp in a metal frame with glass sides and with a handle on top so you can carry it.

Lao|tian /leɪoʊʃən/ (Laotians) ■ ADJ **Laotian** means belonging or relating to Laos, or its people, language, or culture. ■ N-COUNT A **Laotian** is a Laotian citizen, or a person of Laotian origin. ■ N-UNCOUNT **Laotian** is the language spoken by people who live in Laos.

lap ♦◇ /læp/ (laps, lapping, lapped) **1** N-COUNT If you have something on your **lap** when you are sitting down, it is on top of your legs and near to your body. ☐ *She waited quietly with her hands in her lap.* **2** N-COUNT In a race, a competitor completes a **lap** when they have gone around a course once. ☐ *...that last lap of the race.* **3** V-T In a race, if you **lap** another competitor, you go past them while they are still on the previous lap. ☐ *He then built a 10-bike lead before lapping his first rider on lap 14.* **4** N-COUNT A **lap** of a long journey is one part of it, between two points where you stop. ☐ *I had thought we might travel as far as Oak Valley, but we only managed the first lap of the journey.* **5** V-I When water **laps** against something such as the shore or the side of a boat, it touches it gently and makes a soft sound. [WRITTEN] ☐ *...the water that lapped against the pillars of the boathouse.* ☐ *With a rising tide the water was lapping at his chin before rescuers arrived.* • **lap|ping** N-UNCOUNT ☐ *The only sound was the lapping of the waves.* **6** V-T When an animal **laps** a drink, it uses short quick movements of its tongue to take liquid up into its mouth. ☐ *It lapped milk from a dish.* • PHRASAL VERB **Lap up** means the same as **lap**. ☐ *She poured some water into a plastic bowl. Faust, her Great Dane, lapped it up with relish.*
▶ **lap up 1** PHRASAL VERB If you say that someone **laps up** something such as information or attention, you mean that they accept it eagerly, usually when you think they are being foolish for believing that it is sincere. ☐ *Their audience will lap up whatever they throw at them.* **2** → see lap 6

lap danc|ing N-UNCOUNT **Lap dancing** is a type of entertainment in a bar or club in which a woman who is wearing very few clothes dances in a sexy way close to customers or sitting on their laps. • **lap danc|er (lap dancers)** N-COUNT ☐ *...a club full of lap dancers.*

la|pel /ləpɛl/ (lapels) N-COUNT The **lapels** of a jacket or coat are the two top parts at the front that are folded back on each side and join on to the collar. ☐ *He sports a small red flower in his lapel.*

la|pis lazu|li /læpɪs læzyəli, -laɪ, læʒə-/ **1** N-UNCOUNT **Lapis lazuli** is a bright blue stone, used especially in making jewelry. **2** → See also color supplement

lapse /læps/ (lapses, lapsing, lapsed) **1** N-COUNT A **lapse** is a moment or instance of bad behavior by someone who usually behaves well. ☐ *On Friday he showed neither decency nor dignity. It was an uncommon lapse.* **2** N-COUNT A **lapse** of something such as concentration or judgment is a temporary lack of that thing, which can often cause you to make a mistake. ☐ *I had a little lapse of concentration in the middle of the race.* ☐ *He was a genius and because of it you could accept lapses of taste.* **3** V-I If you **lapse** into a quiet or inactive state, you stop talking or being active. ☐ *She muttered something unintelligible and lapsed into silence.* **4** V-I If someone **lapses** into a particular way of speaking, or behaving, they start speaking or behaving in that way, usually for a short period. ☐ *She lapsed into a little girl voice to deliver a nursery rhyme.* • N-COUNT **Lapse** is also a noun. ☐ *Her lapse into German didn't seem peculiar. After all, it was her native tongue.* **5** N-SING A **lapse** of time is a period that is long enough for a situation to change or for people to have a different opinion about it. ☐ *...the restoration of diplomatic relations after a lapse of 24 years.* **6** V-I If a period of time **lapses**, it passes. ☐ *New products and production processes are transferred to the developing countries only after a substantial amount of time has lapsed.* **7** V-I If a situation or legal contract **lapses**, it is allowed to end rather than being continued, renewed, or extended. ☐ *The terms of the treaty lapsed in 1987.* **8** V-I If a member of a particular religion **lapses**, they stop believing in it or stop following its rules and practices. ☐ *I lapsed in my 20s, returned to it, then lapsed again, while writing the life of historical Jesus.*

lap|top /læptɒp/ (laptops) **1** N-COUNT A **laptop** or a **laptop computer** is a small portable computer. ☐ *She used to work at her laptop until four in the morning.* **2** → See feature box at **computer**

lap|wing /læpwɪŋ/ (lapwings) N-COUNT A **lapwing** is a small dark green bird which has a white breast and feathers sticking up on its head.

lar|ceny /lɑrsəni/ N-UNCOUNT **Larceny** is the crime of stealing. [LEGAL] ☐ *He now faces two to 20 years in prison on grand larceny charges.*

larch /lɑrtʃ/ (larches) N-VAR A **larch** is a tree with needle-shaped leaves.

lard /lɑrd/ N-UNCOUNT **Lard** is soft white fat obtained from pigs. It is used in cooking.

lar|der /lɑrdər/ (larders) N-COUNT A **larder** is a room or large cupboard in a house, usually near the kitchen, in which food is kept. [mainly BRIT]

in AM, usually use **pantry**

large ♦♦♦ /lɑrdʒ/ (larger, largest) **1** ADJ A **large** thing or person is greater in size than usual or average. ☐ *The pike lives mainly in large rivers and lakes.* ☐ *In the largest room about a dozen children and seven adults are sitting on the carpet.* **2** ADJ A **large** amount or number of people or things is more than the average amount or number. ☐ *The gang finally fled with a large amount of cash and jewelry.* ☐ *There are a large number of centers where you can take full-time courses.* **3** ADJ **Large** is used to indicate that a problem or issue which is being discussed is very important or serious. ☐ *...the already large problem of under-age drinking.* **4** PHRASE You use **at large** to indicate that you are talking in a general way about most of the people mentioned. ☐ *I think the chances of getting reforms accepted by the community at large remain extremely remote.* **5** PHRASE If you say that a dangerous person, thing, or animal is **at large**, you mean that they have not been captured or made safe. ☐ *The man who tried to have her killed is still at large.* **6 to a large extent** → see **extent**

SYNONYMS

large
ADJ **1**
big: *Australia's a big country.*
substantial: *That is a very substantial improvement in the present situation.*
great: *The room had a great bay window.*
considerable: *Vets' fees can be considerable, even for routine visits.*
bulky: *...bulky items, like lawn mowers.*

---

large|ly ♦♦◇ /lɑrdʒli/ **1** ADV You use **largely** to say that a statement is not completely true but is mostly true. ☐ *The fund is largely financed through government borrowing.* ☐ *I largely work with people who already are motivated.* **2** ADV [ADV prep] **Largely** is used to introduce the main reason for a particular event or situation. ☐ *Retail sales dipped 6/10ths of a percent last month, largely because Americans were buying fewer cars.*

SYNONYMS

largely
ADV **1**
mainly: *The birds live mainly on nectar.*
mostly: *Cars are mostly metal.*
generally: *This is generally true.*
primarily: *...a book aimed primarily at high-energy physicists.*
chiefly: *His response to attacks on his work was chiefly bewilderment.*

---

large-scale also **large scale 1** ADJ [ADJ n] A **large-scale** action or event happens over a very wide area or involves a lot of people or things. ☐ *...a large scale military operation.* **2** ADJ [ADJ n] A **large-scale** map or diagram represents a small area of land or a building or machine on a scale that is large enough for small details to be shown. ☐ *...a large-scale map of the county.*

lar|gesse /lɑrdʒɛs, lɑrʒɛs/ also **largess** N-UNCOUNT **Largesse** is a generous gift of money or a generous act of kindness. [FORMAL] ☐ *...grateful recipients of their largesse.* ☐ *...his most recent act of largesse.*

larg|ish /lɑrdʒɪʃ/ ADJ [usu ADJ n] **Largish** means fairly large. ☐ *...a largish modern city.*

lar|go /lɑrɡoʊ/ (largos) **1** ADV [ADV after v] **Largo** written above a piece of music means that it should be played slowly. **2** N-COUNT A **largo** is a piece of music, especially part of a longer piece, that is played slowly.

lark /lɑrk/ (larks) N-COUNT A **lark** is a small brown bird which makes a pleasant sound.

lar|va /lɑrvə/ (larvae /lɑrvi/) N-COUNT A **larva** is an insect at the stage of its life after it has developed from an egg and before it changes into its adult form. ☐ *The eggs quickly hatch into larvae.*

lar|val /lɑːrvəl/ ADJ [ADJ n] **Larval** means concerning insect larvae or in the state of being an insect larva.

lar|yn|gi|tis /lærɪndʒaɪtɪs/ N-UNCOUNT **Laryngitis** is an infection of the throat in which your larynx becomes swollen and painful, making it difficult to speak.

lar|ynx /lærɪŋks/ (larynxes) **1** N-COUNT Your **larynx** is the top part of the passage that leads from your throat to your lungs and contains your vocal cords. [MEDICAL] **2** → See also color supplement

la|sa|gne /ləzɑːnyə/ (lasagnes) also **lasagna** N-VAR **Lasagne** is a food dish that consists of layers of pasta, tomato sauce, and a filling such as meat or cheese, baked in an oven.

las|civi|ous /ləsɪviəs/ ADJ If you describe someone as **lascivious**, you disapprove of them because they show a very strong interest in sex. [DISAPPROVAL] ▫ *The man was lascivious, sexually perverted and insatiable.* ▫ *...their lewd and lascivious talk.*

la|ser /leɪzər/ (lasers) N-COUNT A **laser** is a narrow beam of concentrated light produced by a special machine. It is used for cutting very hard materials, and in many technical fields such as surgery and telecommunications. ▫ *...new laser technology.*

la|ser print|er (laser printers) N-COUNT A **laser printer** is a computer printer that produces clear words and pictures by using laser beams.

lash /læʃ/ (lashes, lashing, lashed) **1** N-COUNT Your **lashes** are the hairs that grow on the edge of your upper and lower eyelids. ▫ *...somber gray eyes, with unusually long lashes.* **2** V-T If you **lash** two or more things together, you tie one of them firmly to the other. ▫ *Secure the anchor by lashing it to the rail.* ▫ *The shelter is built by lashing poles together to form a small dome.* **3** V-T/V-I If wind, rain, or water **lashes** someone or something, it hits them violently. [WRITTEN] ▫ *The worst winter storms of the century lashed the east coast of North America.* **4** V-T/V-I If someone **lashes** you or **lashes** into you, they speak very angrily to you, criticizing you or saying you have done something wrong. ▫ *She went quiet for a moment while she summoned up the words to lash him.* **5** N-COUNT A **lash** is a blow with a whip, especially a blow on someone's back as a punishment. ▫ *The villagers sentenced one man to five lashes for stealing a ham from his neighbor.*

▶ **lash out** **1** PHRASAL VERB If you **lash out**, you attempt to hit someone quickly and violently with a weapon or with your hands or feet. ▫ *Riot police fired in the air and lashed out with clubs to disperse hundreds of demonstrators.* **2** PHRASAL VERB If you **lash out** at someone or something, you speak to them or about them very angrily or critically. ▫ *As a politician Jefferson frequently lashed out at the press.*

lash|ing /læʃɪŋ/ (lashings) **1** N-COUNT [usu pl] **Lashings** are ropes or cables that are used to tie one thing to another. ▫ *We made a tour of the yacht, checking lashings and emergency gear.* **2** N-COUNT If you refer to someone's comments as a **lashing**, you mean that they are very critical and angry. ▫ *He never grew used to the lashings he got from the critics.* **3** N-COUNT A **lashing** is a punishment in which a person is hit with a whip.

Lasik /leɪsɪk/ also **LASIK** N-UNCOUNT [oft N n] **Lasik** is a form of eye surgery that uses lasers to improve or correct people's eyesight. **Lasik** is an abbreviation for 'laser-assisted in situ keratomileusis.' ▫ *Lasik is best for moderate, not severe, vision problems.* ▫ *Weir had Lasik surgery about 2 years ago.*

lass /læs/ (lasses) N-COUNT; N-VOC A **lass** is a young woman or girl. [OLD-FASHIONED] ▫ *Anne is a Lancashire lass from Longton, near Preston.*

las|si|tude /læsɪtuːd/ N-UNCOUNT **Lassitude** is a state of tiredness, laziness, or lack of interest. [FORMAL] ▫ *Symptoms of anemia include general fatigue and lassitude.*

las|so /læsoʊ, læsuː/ (lassoes, lassoing, lassoed) **1** N-COUNT A **lasso** is a long rope with a loop at one end, used especially by cowboys for catching cattle. **2** V-T If you **lasso** an animal, you catch it by throwing a lasso around its neck and pulling it tight. ▫ *Cowboys drove covered wagons and rode horses, lassoing cattle.*

last ✦✦✦ /læst/ (lasts, lasting, lasted) **1** DET You use **last** in expressions such as **last Friday**, **last night**, and **last year** to refer, for example, to the most recent Friday, night, or year. ▫ *I got married last July.* ▫ *He never made it home at all last night.* **2** ADJ [det ADJ] The **last** event, person, thing, or period of time is the most recent one. ▫ *Much has changed since my last visit.* ▫ *I split up with my last boyfriend three years ago.* • PRON **Last** is also a pronoun. ▫ *The next tide, it was announced, would be even higher than the last.* **3** ADV [ADV with v] If something **last** happened on a particular occasion, that is the most recent occasion on which it happened. ▫ *When were you there last?* ▫ *The house is a little more dilapidated than when I last saw it.* **4** ORD The **last** thing, person, event, or period of time is the one that happens or comes after all the others of the same kind. ▫ *...the last three pages of the chapter.* • PRON **Last** is also a pronoun. ▫ *It wasn't the first time that this particular difference had divided them and it wouldn't be the last.* **5** ADV [ADV after v] If you do something **last**, you do it after everyone else does, or after you do everything else. ▫ *I testified last.* ▫ *I was always picked last for the football team at school.* **6** PRON [PRON to-inf] If you are the **last** to do or know something, everyone else does or knows it before you. ▫ *She was the last to go to bed.* **7** ADJ [det ADJ] **Last** is used to refer to the only thing, person, or part of something that remains. ▫ *Jed nodded, finishing off the last piece of pizza.* • N-SING **Last** is also a noun. ▫ *He finished off the last of the wine.* **8** ADJ [det ADJ] You can use **last** to indicate that something is extremely undesirable or unlikely. [EMPHASIS] ▫ *The last thing I wanted to do was teach.* • PRON [PRON to-inf] **Last** is also a pronoun. ▫ *I would be the last to say that science has explained everything.* **9** PRON [the PRON that] **The last** you see of someone or **the last** you hear of them is the final time that you see them or talk to them. ▫ *She disappeared shouting, "To the river, to the river!" And that was the last we saw of her.* **10** V-T/V-I If an event, situation, or problem **lasts** for a particular length of time, it continues to exist or happen for that length of time. ▫ *The marriage had lasted for less than two years.* ▫ *The games lasted only half the normal time.* **11** V-T/V-I If something **lasts** for a particular length of time, it continues to be able to be used for that time, for example, because there is some of it left or because it is in good enough condition. ▫ *You only need a very small blob of glue, so one tube lasts for ages.* ▫ *The repaired sail lasted less than 24 hours.* **12** → see also **lasting** **13** PHRASE If you say that something has happened **at last** or **at long last**, you mean it has happened after you have been hoping for it for a long time. ▫ *I'm so glad that we've found you at last!* ▫ *Here, at long last, was the moment he had waited for.* **14** PHRASE You use expressions such as **the night before last**, **the election before last** and **the leader before last** to refer to the period of time, event, or person that came immediately before the most recent one in a series. ▫ *It was the dog he'd heard the night before last.* **15** PHRASE You can use expressions such as **the last I heard** and **the last she heard** to introduce a piece of information that is the most recent that you have on a particular subject. ▫ *The last I heard, Joe and Irene were still happily married.* **16** PHRASE If you **leave** something or someone **until last**, you delay using, choosing, or dealing with them until you have used, chosen, or dealt with all the others. ▫ *I have left my best wine until last.* **17** **the last straw** → see **straw** **18** **last thing** → see **thing** ②

USAGE

last
Don't use 'the' before 'last' with this meaning. Don't say, for example, 'I saw him the last week.' Say 'I saw him **last week**.'

COLLOCATIONS

last
VERB **8**
last + *noun*: hour, minute, month, year
noun + **last**: marriage, match, meeting, trial; effect
last + *adverb*: forever

---

last-ditch ADJ [ADJ n] A **last-ditch** action is done only because there are no other ways left to achieve something or to prevent something from happening. It is often done without much hope that it will succeed. ▫ *...a last-ditch attempt to prevent civil war.*

last hur|rah (last hurrahs) N-COUNT [usu sing] Someone's **last hurrah** is the last occasion on which they do something, especially at the end of their career. ▫ *I haven't even begun to think about quitting, or having a last hurrah, or allowing my career to wind down.*

last|ing /læstɪŋ/ **1** ADJ You can use **lasting** to describe a situation, result, or agreement that continues to exist or have an effect for a very long time. ❏ *We are well on our way to a lasting peace.* **2** → see also **last**

Last Judg|ment

in BRIT, also use **Last Judgement**

N-PROPER [the N] In the Christian religion, **the Last Judgment** is the last day of the world when God will judge everyone who has died and decide whether they will go to heaven or hell.

last|ly /læstli/ **1** ADV [ADV with cl/group] You use **lastly** when you want to make a final point, ask a final question, or mention a final item that is connected with the other ones you have already asked or mentioned. ❏ *Lastly, I would like to ask about your future plans.* **2** ADV [ADV cl] You use **lastly** when you are saying what happens after everything else in a series of actions or events. ❏ *They wash their hands, arms and faces, and lastly, they wash their feet.*

last-minute → see minute ① 6

last rites N-PLURAL [the N] **The last rites** is a religious ceremony performed by a Christian priest for a dying person. ❏ *Father Stephen Lea administered the last rites to the dying men.*

latch /lætʃ/ (**latches, latching, latched**) **1** N-COUNT A **latch** is a fastening on a door or gate. It consists of a metal bar which you lift in order to open the door. ❏ *You left the latch off the gate and the dog escaped.* **2** N-COUNT A **latch** is a lock on a door which locks automatically when you shut the door, so that you need a key in order to open it from the outside. ❏ *...a key clicked in the latch of the front door.*

▶ **latch onto** also **latch on** **1** PHRASAL VERB If someone **latches onto** a person or an idea or **latches on**, they become very interested in the person or idea, often finding them so useful that they do not want to leave them. [INFORMAL] ❏ *Rob had latched onto me. He followed me around and sat beside me at lunch.* **2** PHRASAL VERB If one thing **latches onto** another, or if it **latches on**, it attaches itself to it and becomes part of it. ❏ *These are substances which specifically latch onto the protein on the cell membrane.*

latch|key /lætʃki/ also **latch-key** ADJ [ADJ n] If you refer to a child as a **latchkey** kid, you disapprove of the fact that they have to let themselves into their home when returning from school because their parents are out at work. [DISAPPROVAL]

late ♦♦♦ /leɪt/ (**later, latest**) **1** ADV **Late** means near the end of a day, week, year, or other period of time. ❏ *It was late in the afternoon.* ❏ *His autobiography was written late in life.* • ADJ [ADJ n] **Late** is also an adjective. ❏ *The talks eventually broke down in late spring.* ❏ *He was in his late 20s.* **2** ADJ [v-link ADJ] If it is **late**, it is near the end of the day or it is past the time that you feel something should have been done. ❏ *It was very late and the streets were deserted.* • **late|ness** N-UNCOUNT ❏ *A large crowd had gathered despite the lateness of the hour.* **3** ADV **Late** means after the time that was arranged or expected. ❏ *Steve arrived late.* ❏ *The talks began some fifteen minutes late.* • ADJ **Late** is also an adjective. ❏ *His campaign got off to a late start.* ❏ *The train was 40 minutes late.* • **late|ness** N-UNCOUNT ❏ *He apologized for his lateness.* **4** ADV [ADV after v] **Late** means after the usual time that a particular event or activity happens. ❏ *We went to bed very late.* • ADJ [ADJ n] **Late** is also an adjective. ❏ *They had a late lunch in a café.* **5** ADJ [det ADJ] You use **late** when you are talking about someone who is dead, especially someone who has died recently. ❏ *...my late husband.* **6** → see also **later, latest** **7** PHRASE If an action or event is **too late**, it is useless or ineffective because it occurs after the best time for it. ❏ *It was too late to turn back.* **8 a late night** → see **night**

SYNONYMS

late
ADJ **2**
overdue: *I'll go home and pay an overdue visit to my mother.*
tardy: *I was as tardy as ever for the afternoon appointments.*
belated: *a belated birthday present.*

---

late|comer /leɪtkʌmər/ (**latecomers**) N-COUNT A **latecomer** is someone who arrives after the time that they should have done, or later than others. ❏ *A few latecomers were still arriving.*

late|ly /leɪtli/ ADV You use **lately** to describe events in the recent past, or situations that started a short time ago. ❏ *Dad's health hasn't been too good lately.* ❏ *"Have you talked to her lately?"—"Not lately, really."*

late-night **1** ADJ [ADJ n] **Late-night** is used to describe events, especially entertainments, that happen late in the evening or late at night. ❏ *He used to make late-night phone calls to his wife back home.* ❏ *...late-night drinking parties.* **2** ADJ [ADJ n] **Late-night** is used to describe services that are available late at night and do not close when most commercial activities finish. ❏ *Saturday night was a late-night shopping night.* ❏ *...late-night trains.*

la|tent /leɪtᵊnt/ ADJ **Latent** is used to describe something which is hidden and not obvious at the moment, but which may develop further in the future. ❏ *Advertisements attempt to project a latent meaning behind an overt message.*

lat|er ♦♦♦ /leɪtər/ **1** **Later** is the comparative of **late**. **2** ADV You use **later** to refer to a time or situation that is after the one that you have been talking about or after the present one. ❏ *He resigned ten years later.* • PHRASE You use **later on** to refer to a time or situation that is after the one that you have been talking about or after the present one. ❏ *Later on I'll be speaking to Patty Davis.* **3** ADJ [ADJ n, the ADJ, the ADJ of n] You use **later** to refer to an event, period of time, or other thing which comes after the one that you have been talking about or after the present one. ❏ *At a later news conference, he said differences should not be dramatized.* ❏ *The competition should have been re-scheduled for a later date.* **4** ADJ [ADJ n] You use **later** to refer to the last part of someone's life or career or the last part of a period of history. ❏ *He found happiness in later life.* ❏ *...the later part of the 20th century.* **5** → see also **late**

lat|er|al /lætərəl/ ADJ **Lateral** means relating to the sides of something, or moving in a sideways direction. ❏ *McKinnon estimated the lateral movement of the bridge to be between four and six inches.*

lat|est ♦♦◊ /leɪtɪst/ **1** **Latest** is the superlative of **late**. **2** ADJ You use **latest** to describe something that is the most recent thing of its kind. ❏ *...her latest book.* **3** ADJ You can use **latest** to describe something that is very new and modern and is better than older things of a similar kind. ❏ *Crooks are using the latest laser photocopiers to produce millions of fake banknotes.* ❏ *I got to drive the latest model.* **4** → see also **late** **5** PHRASE You use **at the latest** in order to indicate that something must happen at or before a particular time and not after that time. [EMPHASIS] ❏ *She should be back by ten o'clock at the latest.*

la|tex /leɪteks/ N-UNCOUNT **Latex** is a substance obtained from some kinds of trees, which is used to make products like paint, rubber, and glue.

lathe /leɪð/ (**lathes**) N-COUNT A **lathe** is a machine which is used for shaping wood or metal.

lath|er /lɒðər, læðər/ (**lathers, lathering, lathered**) **1** N-SING A **lather** is a white mass of bubbles which is produced by mixing a substance such as soap or detergent with water. ❏ *...the sort of water that easily makes a lather with soap.* ❏ *He wiped off the remains of the lather with a towel.* **2** V-I When a substance such as soap or detergent **lathers**, it produces a white mass of bubbles because it has been mixed with water. ❏ *The shampoo lathers and foams so much it's very hard to rinse it all out.* **3** V-T If you **lather** something, you rub a substance such as soap or detergent on it until a lather is produced, in order to clean it. ❏ *Lather your hair as normal.* ❏ *For super-soft skin, lather on a light body lotion before you bathe.*

Lat|in ♦♦◊ /lætɪn, -tᵊn/ **1** N-UNCOUNT **Latin** is the language which the ancient Romans used to speak. **2** ADJ **Latin** countries are countries where Spanish, or perhaps Portuguese, Italian, or French, is spoken. You can also use **Latin** to refer to things and people that come from these countries. ❏ *...in Mexico and other Latin countries.*

La|ti|na /lætiːnə/ (**Latinas**) N-COUNT [oft N n] A **Latina** is an American girl or woman who originally came from Latin America, or whose family originally came from Latin America. [mainly AM] ❏ *More Latinos and Latinas are running for office in California than ever before.* ❏ *...a young, poor Latina girl.*

Lat|in Ameri|can /lætɪn əmɛrɪkən/ ADJ **Latin American** means belonging or relating to the countries of South America, Central America, and Mexico. **Latin American** also means belonging or relating to the people or culture of these countries. ❏ *Leaders of eight Latin American countries are meeting in Caracas, Venezuela, today.*

Latino

La|ti|no /lætiːnoʊ/ (**Latinos**) also **latino** **1** N-COUNT [oft N n] A **Latino** is an American boy or man who originally came from Latin America, or whose family originally came from Latin America. [mainly AM] ❑ *He was a champion for Latinos and Blacks within the educational system.* ❑ *...the city's office of Latino Affairs.* **2** ADJ **Latino** means belonging or relating to Latino people or their culture.

lati|tude /lætɪtuːd/ (**latitudes**) **1** N-VAR The **latitude** of a place is its distance from the equator. Compare **longitude**. ❑ *In the middle to high latitudes rainfall has risen steadily over the last 20-30 years.* • ADJ **Latitude** is also an adjective. ❑ *The army must cease military operations above 36° latitude north.* **2** N-UNCOUNT **Latitude** is freedom to choose the way in which you do something. [FORMAL] ❑ *He would be given every latitude in forming a new government.*

la|trine /lətriːn/ (**latrines**) N-COUNT A **latrine** is a structure, usually consisting of a hole in the ground, that is used as a toilet, for example, in a military camp.

lat|te /lɑːteɪ/ (**lattes**) N-UNCOUNT **Latte** is strong coffee made with hot milk. • N-COUNT A **latte** is a cup of latte.

lat|ter ✦✧✧ /lætər/ **1** PRON [the PRON] When two people, things, or groups have just been mentioned, you can refer to the second of them as **the latter**. ❑ *He tracked down his cousin and uncle. The latter was sick.* • ADJ [ADJ n] **Latter** is also an adjective. ❑ *There are the people who speak after they think and the people who think while they're speaking. Mike definitely belongs in the latter category.* **2** ADJ [ADJ n] You use **latter** to describe the later part of a period of time or event. ❑ *He is getting into the latter years of his career.*

latter-day ADJ [ADJ n] **Latter-day** is used to describe someone or something that is a modern equivalent of a person or thing in the past. ❑ *He holds the belief that he is a latter-day prophet.*

lat|ter|ly /lætərli/ ADV [ADV with cl/group] You can use **latterly** to indicate that a situation or event is the most recent one. [WRITTEN] ❑ *He was to remain active in the association, latterly as vice president, for the rest of his life.*

lat|tice /lætɪs/ (**lattices**) N-COUNT A **lattice** is a pattern or structure made of strips of wood or another material which cross over each other diagonally leaving holes in between. ❑ *We were crawling along the narrow steel lattice of the bridge.*

lat|ticed /lætɪst/ ADJ Something that is **latticed** is decorated with or is in the form of a lattice. ❑ *...latticed doors.* ❑ *The surface of the brain is pinky-gray and latticed with tiny blood vessels.*

lat|tice|work /lætɪswɜːrk/ N-UNCOUNT **Latticework** is any structure that is made in the form of a lattice. ❑ *...latticework chairs.*

laud /lɔːd/ (**lauds, lauding, lauded**) V-T If people **laud** someone, they praise and admire them. [JOURNALISM] ❑ *He lauded the work of the UN High Commissioner for Refugees.* ❑ *They lauded the former president as a hero.* ❑ *Dickens was lauded for his social and moral sensitivity.* • **laud|ed** ADJ ❑ *...the most lauded actress in New York.*

laud|able /lɔːdəbəl/ ADJ Something that is **laudable** deserves to be praised or admired. [FORMAL] ❑ *One of Emma's less laudable characteristics was her jealousy.*

lau|da|num /lɔːdənəm/ N-UNCOUNT **Laudanum** was a medicine containing opium that was used in the past as a painkiller. ❑ *By the 19th century, vials of laudanum and raw opium were freely available.*

lauda|tory /lɔːdətɔːri/ ADJ [usu ADJ n] A **laudatory** piece of writing or speech expresses praise or admiration for someone. [FORMAL] ❑ *The New York Times has this very laudatory article about your retirement.* ❑ *Beth spoke of Dr. Hammer in laudatory terms.*

laugh ✦✦✧ /læf/ (**laughs, laughing, laughed**) **1** V-T/V-I When you **laugh**, you make a sound with your throat while smiling and show that you are happy or amused. People also sometimes laugh when they feel nervous or are being unfriendly. ❑ *He was about to offer an explanation, but she was beginning to laugh.* ❑ *I just couldn't laugh at his jokes the way I used to.* ❑ *"We could do with some help from our friends," he laughed.* • N-COUNT **Laugh** is also a noun. ❑ *Lysenko gave a deep rumbling laugh at his own joke.* **2** V-I If people **laugh at** someone or something, they mock them or make jokes about them. ❑ *I thought they were laughing at me because I was ugly.* **3** PHRASE If you do something **for a laugh** or **for laughs**, you do it as a joke or for fun. ❑ *They were persuaded onstage for a laugh.* **4** PHRASE If you describe a

launch

situation as **a laugh** or **a good laugh**, you think that it is fun and do not take it too seriously. [INFORMAL] ❑ *Working there's great. It's a good laugh.* **5 laugh one's head off** → see **head** ③
▶ **laugh off** PHRASAL VERB If you **laugh off** a difficult or serious situation, you try to suggest that it is amusing and unimportant, for example, by making a joke about it. ❑ *Frank tried to laugh off his aunt's worry.*

COLLOCATIONS

laugh
VERB **1**
laugh + *adverb*: heartily, hysterically, loudly, uproariously; nervously, softly

---

laugh|able /læfəbəl/ ADJ [usu v-link ADJ] If you say that something such as an idea or suggestion is **laughable**, you mean that it is so silly or stupid as to be funny and not worth serious consideration. ❑ *The idea that TV shows like "Dallas" or "Dynasty" represent typical American life is laughable.* • **laugh|ably** ADV [usu ADV adj] ❑ *To an outsider, the issues that we fight about would seem almost laughably petty.*

laugh|ing gas N-UNCOUNT **Laughing gas** is a type of anesthetic gas which sometimes has the effect of making people laugh uncontrollably.

laugh|ing|ly /læfɪŋli/ ADV [ADV with v] If you **laughingly** refer to something with a particular name or description, the description is not appropriate and you think that this is either amusing or annoying. ❑ *I spent much of what I laughingly call "the vacations" working through 621 pages of typescript.*

laugh|ing stock (**laughing stocks**) also **laughing-stock** N-COUNT If you say that a person or an organization has become a **laughing stock**, you mean that they are supposed to be important or serious but have been made to seem ridiculous. ❑ *The truth must never get out. If it did she would be a laughing-stock.* ❑ *His policies became the laughing stock of the financial community.*

laugh lines N-PLURAL **Laugh lines** are wrinkles which some older people have at the outside corners of their eyes. [AM] ❑ *He had long laugh lines that creased from the corners of his eyes all the way down to his narrow strip of beard.*

laugh|ter ✦✧✧ /læftər/ **1** N-UNCOUNT **Laughter** is the sound of people laughing, for example, because they are amused or happy. ❑ *Their laughter filled the corridor.* ❑ *He delivered the line perfectly, and everybody roared with laughter.* **2** → See feature box at **humor**

COLLOCATIONS

laughter
NOUN **1**
adjective + **laughter**: helpless, hysterical, raucous, uncontrollable; derisive, hollow, nervous; canned
laughter + *be* + *adjective*: contagious, infectious
verb + **laughter**: draw, prompt, provoke

---

laugh|ter lines N-PLURAL **Laughter lines** are the same as **laugh lines**. [BRIT]

in AM, use **laugh lines**

launch ✦✦✧ /lɔːntʃ/ (**launches, launching, launched**) **1** V-T To **launch** a rocket, missile, or satellite means to send it into the air or into space. ❑ *NASA plans to launch a satellite to study cosmic rays.* • N-VAR **Launch** is also a noun. ❑ *This morning's launch of the space shuttle Columbia has been delayed.* **2** V-T To **launch** a ship or a boat means to put it into water, often for the first time after it has been built. ❑ *There was no time to launch the lifeboats because the ferry capsized with such alarming speed.* • N-COUNT **Launch** is also a noun. ❑ *The launch of a ship was a big occasion.* **3** V-T To **launch** a large and important activity, for example, a military attack, means to start it. ❑ *A group of 80 attackers launched an all-out assault just before dawn.* ❑ *The police have launched an investigation into the incident.* • N-COUNT **Launch** is also a noun. ❑ *...the launch of a campaign to restore law and order.* **4** V-T If a company **launches** a new product, it makes it available to the public. ❑ *...powerful allies to help the company launch a low-cost "network computer."* • N-COUNT **Launch** is also a noun. ❑ *The company's spending has also risen following the launch of a new Sunday magazine.* **5** → See feature box at **travel**
▶ **launch into** PHRASAL VERB If you **launch into** something

such as a speech, task, or fight, you enthusiastically start it. ❏ *Horrigan launched into a speech about the importance of new projects.*

COLLOCATIONS

launch
VERB
1
launch + noun: missile, rocket
3
launch + noun: assault, attack, offensive, raid; inquiry, investigation, probe; appeal, bid, campaign
4
launch + noun: product, range, service
NOUN **4**
noun + launch: album, book, manifesto, product

SYNONYMS

launch
VERB
1
propel: *The rocket, attached to the spacecraft, propels it toward Mars.*
fire: *Soldiers fired rubber bullets to disperse crowds.*
discharge: *Lewis was tried for unlawfully and dangerously discharging a weapon.*
3
open: *They are now ready to open negotiations.*
initiate: *They wanted to initiate a discussion on economics.*
instigate: *Jenkinson instigated a refurbishment of the old gallery.*

---

launch|er /lɔntʃər/ (launchers) **1** N-COUNT [usu with supp] A missile **launcher** or a grenade **launcher** is a device that is used for firing missiles or grenades. ❏ *...a mobile missile launcher.* ❏ *The Marines fired back with a grenade launcher.* **2** → see also rocket launcher

launch pad (launch pads) **1** N-COUNT A **launch pad** or **launching pad** is a platform from which rockets, missiles, or satellites are launched. **2** N-COUNT A **launch pad** or **launching pad** is a situation, for example, a job, which you can use in order to go forward to something better or more important. ❏ *The Café de la Gare was considered a first-rate training ground and launch pad for young comedians.*

laun|der /lɔndər/ (launders, laundering, laundered) **1** V-T To **launder** money that has been obtained illegally means to process it through a legitimate business or to send it abroad to a foreign bank, so that when it comes back nobody knows that it was illegally obtained. ❏ *The House voted today to crack down on banks that launder drug money.* • **laun|der|er** (launderers) N-COUNT ❏ *...a businessman and self-described money launderer.* **2** V-T When you **launder** clothes, sheets, and towels, you wash and iron them. [FORMAL] ❏ *How many guests who expect clean towels every day in a hotel launder their own every day at home?*

Laun|der|ette /lɔndərɛt/ (Launderettes) also **laundrette** N-COUNT A **Launderette** is the same as a **Laundromat**. [mainly BRIT, TRADEMARK]

Laun|dro|mat /lɔndrəmæt/ (laundromats) N-COUNT A **Laundromat** is a place where people can pay to use machines to wash and dry their clothes. [AM, TRADEMARK]

in BRIT, use **Launderette**

laun|dry /lɔndri/ (laundries) **1** N-UNCOUNT **Laundry** is used to refer to clothes, sheets, and towels that are about to be washed, are being washed, or have just been washed. ❏ *I'll do your laundry.* ❏ *...the room where I hang the laundry.* **2** N-COUNT A **laundry** is a business that washes and irons clothes, sheets, and towels for people. ❏ *We had to have the washing done at the laundry.* **3** N-COUNT A **laundry** or a **laundry room** is a room in a house, hotel, or institution where clothes, sheets, and towels are washed. ❏ *He worked in the laundry at Oxford prison.*

laun|dry list (laundry lists) N-COUNT [usu N of n] If you describe something as a **laundry list** of things, you mean that it is a long list of them. ❏ *...a laundry list of reasons why shareholders should reject the bid.*

lau|rel /lɔrᵊl/ (laurels) **1** N-VAR A **laurel** or a **laurel tree** is a small evergreen tree with shiny leaves. The leaves are sometimes used to make decorations such as wreaths. **2** PHRASE If someone is **resting on** their **laurels**, they appear to be satisfied with the things they have achieved and have stopped putting effort into what they are doing. [DISAPPROVAL] ❏ *The committee's chairman accused NASA of resting on its laurels after making it to the moon.*

lava /lɑvə, lævə/ (lavas) **1** N-MASS **Lava** is the very hot liquid rock that comes out of a volcano. ❏ *Mexico's Mount Colima began spewing lava and ash last night.* **2** → See also color supplement

lava|tory /lævətɔri/ (lavatories) N-COUNT A **lavatory** is a toilet or a room with a toilet in it. [mainly BRIT] ❏ *...the ladies' lavatory.*

lav|en|der /lævɪndər/ N-UNCOUNT **Lavender** is a garden plant with sweet-smelling, bluish-purple flowers.

lav|ish /lævɪʃ/ (lavishes, lavishing, lavished) **1** ADJ If you describe something as **lavish**, you mean that it is very elaborate and impressive and a lot of money has been spent on it. ❏ *...a lavish party to celebrate Bryan's fiftieth birthday.* ❏ *He staged the most lavish productions of Mozart.* • **lav|ish|ly** ADV [ADV with v] ❏ *The apartment building was lavishly decorated.* **2** ADJ If you say that spending, praise, or the use of something is **lavish**, you mean that someone spends a lot or that something is praised or used a lot. ❏ *Critics attack his lavish spending and flamboyant style.* **3** ADJ If you say that someone is **lavish** in the way they behave, you mean that they give, spend, or use a lot of something. ❏ *Reviewers are lavish in their praise of this book.* • **lav|ish|ly** ADV [ADV with v] ❏ *Entertaining in style needn't mean spending lavishly.* **4** V-T If you **lavish** money, affection, or praise on someone or something, you spend a lot of money on them or give them a lot of affection or praise. ❏ *He lavished praise on his opponents.*

law ♦♦♦ /lɔ/ (laws) **1** N-SING **The law** is a system of rules that a society or government develops in order to deal with crime, business agreements, and social relationships. You can also use **the law** to refer to the people who work in this system. ❏ *Obscene and threatening phone calls are against the law.* ❏ *They are beginning criminal proceedings against him for breaking the law on financing political parties.* ❏ *The book analyses why women kill and how the law treats them.* **2** N-UNCOUNT **Law** is used to refer to a particular branch of the law, such as **criminal law** or **business law**. ❏ *He was a professor of criminal law at Harvard University law school.* ❏ *Under international law, diplomats living in foreign countries are exempt from criminal prosecution.* **3** N-COUNT A **law** is one of the rules in a system of law which deals with a particular type of agreement, relationship, or crime. ❏ *...the country's liberal political asylum law.* **4** N-PLURAL The **laws** of an organization or activity are its rules, which are used to organize and control it. ❏ *...the laws of the Catholic Church.* **5** N-COUNT A **law** is a rule or set of rules for good behavior which is considered right and important by the majority of people for moral, religious, or emotional reasons. ❏ *...inflexible moral laws.* **6** N-COUNT A **law** is a natural process in which a particular event or thing always leads to a particular result. ❏ *The laws of nature are absolute.* **7** N-COUNT A **law** is a scientific rule that someone has invented to explain a particular natural process. ❏ *the law of gravity.* **8** N-UNCOUNT **Law** or **the law** is all the professions which deal with advising people about the law, representing people in court, or giving decisions and punishments. ❏ *A career in law is becoming increasingly attractive to young people.* **9** N-UNCOUNT **Law** is the study of systems of law and how laws work. ❏ *He studied law.* **10** PHRASE If you accuse someone of thinking they are **above the law**, you criticize them for thinking that they are so clever or important that they do not need to obey the law. [DISAPPROVAL] ❏ *He accuses the government of wanting to be above the law.* **11** PHRASE If you have to do something **by law** or if you are not allowed to do something **by law**, the law states that you have to do it or that you are not allowed to do it. ❏ *By law all restaurants must display their prices outside.* **12** → See feature box at **working**

SYNONYMS

law
NOUN **3**
constitution: *...the United States Constitution.*
legislation: *...a letter calling for legislation to protect women's rights.*
code: *...Article 159 of the state's penal code.*
charter: *...Article 50 of the United Nations Charter.*
act: *...an Act of Parliament.*

law-abiding ADJ A **law-abiding** person always obeys the law and is considered to be good and honest because of this. ❑ *We believe that the law should protect decent law-abiding citizens and their property.*

law and or|der N-UNCOUNT When there is **law and order** in a country, the laws are generally accepted and obeyed, so that society there functions normally. ❑ *If there were a breakdown of law and order, the army might be tempted to intervene.*

law-breaker (law-breakers) also **lawbreaker** N-COUNT A **law-breaker** is someone who breaks the law.

law-breaking also **law breaking** N-UNCOUNT **Law-breaking** is any kind of illegal activity. ❑ *Civil disobedience, violent or non-violent, is intentional law breaking.*

law en|force|ment N-UNCOUNT [usu n n] **Law enforcement** agencies or officials are responsible for catching people who break the law. [mainly AM] ❑ *We need to restore respect for the law enforcement agencies.*

law|ful /lɔ:fəl/ ADJ If an activity, organization, or product is **lawful**, it is allowed by law. [FORMAL] ❑ *The detention of the fugitive was lawful.* ● **law|ful|ly** ADV [ADV with v] ❑ *He found Donna had acted lawfully in all dealings.*

law|less /lɔ:lɪs/ **1** ADJ **Lawless** actions break the law, especially in a wild and violent way. ❑ *The government recognized there were problems in urban areas but these could never be an excuse for lawless behavior.* ● **law|less|ness** N-UNCOUNT ❑ *Lawlessness is a major problem.* **2** ADJ A **lawless** place or time is one where people do not respect the law. ❑ *...lawless inner-city streets plagued by muggings, thefts, assaults and even murder.*

law|maker /lɔ:meɪkər/ (lawmakers) N-COUNT A **lawmaker** is someone such as a politician who is responsible for proposing and passing new laws. [AM]

law|man /lɔ:mæn/ (lawmen) **1** N-COUNT **Lawmen** are men such as policemen or lawyers, whose work involves the law. [JOURNALISM] ❑ *...the 61-year-old lawman who headed the inquiry.* **2** N-COUNT In former times in western North America, a **lawman** was a sheriff or deputy sheriff. [AM]

lawn /lɔ:n/ (lawns) **1** N-VAR A **lawn** is an area of grass that is kept cut short and is usually part of someone's yard, or part of a park. ❑ *They were sitting on the lawn under a large beech tree.* **2** → See feature box at **garden**

lawn bowl|ing N-UNCOUNT **Lawn bowling** is a game in which players try to roll large wooden balls as near as possible to a small wooden ball. Lawn bowling is usually played outdoors on grass. [AM] ❑ *...a revival of lawn bowling in the U.S.*

lawn chair (lawn chairs) N-COUNT A **lawn chair** is a simple chair with a folding frame. Lawn chairs are usually used outdoors. [AM] ❑ *Men set up folding tables and lawn chairs in the shade of giant pine trees.*

lawn|mow|er /lɔ:nmoʊər/ (lawnmowers) **1** N-COUNT A **lawnmower** is a machine for cutting grass on lawns. **2** → See also color supplement

lawn ten|nis N-UNCOUNT **Lawn tennis** is the same as **tennis**.

law|suit ♦♦◊ /lɔ:su:t/ (lawsuits) N-COUNT A **lawsuit** is a case in a court of law which concerns a dispute between two people or organizations. [FORMAL] ❑ *The dispute culminated last week in a lawsuit against the government.*

law|yer ♦♦◊ /lɔ:iər, lɔɪər/ (lawyers) N-COUNT A **lawyer** is a person who is qualified to advise people about the law and represent them in court. ❑ *Prosecution and defense lawyers are expected to deliver closing arguments next week.*

SYNONYMS

lawyer
NOUN
attorney: *...a prosecuting attorney.*
solicitor: *You will need advice from the town's solicitor.*
counsel: *Singleton's counsel said after the trial that he would appeal.*
advocate: *The court will appoint a public advocate to represent your son.*

---

lax /læks/ (laxer, laxest) ADJ If you say that a person's behavior or a system is **lax**, you mean they are not careful or strict about maintaining high standards. ❑ *One of the problem areas is lax security for airport personnel.* ❑ *There have been allegations from* survivors that safety standards had been lax. ● **lax|ity** N-UNCOUNT ❑ *The laxity of export control authorities has made a significant contribution to the problem.*

laxa|tive /læksətɪv/ (laxatives) N-MASS A **laxative** is something you eat or drink that makes you go to the toilet. ❑ *Foods that ferment quickly in the stomach are excellent natural laxatives.*

LAY
① VERB AND NOUN USES
② ADJECTIVE USES

---

① **lay** ♦♦◊ /leɪ/ (lays, laying, laid)

In standard English, the form **lay** is also the past tense of the verb **lie** in some meanings. In informal English, people sometimes use the word **lay** instead of **lie** in those meanings.

→ Please look at meanings **7** – **10** to see if the expression you are looking for is shown under another headword.

1 V-T If you **lay** something somewhere, you put it there in a careful, gentle, or neat way. ❑ *Lay a sheet of newspaper on the floor.* ❑ *Mothers routinely lay babies on their backs to sleep.* **2** V-T If you **lay** something such as carpets, cables, or foundations, you put them into their permanent position. ❑ *A man came to lay the carpet.* **3** V-T/V-I When a female bird **lays**, or **lays** an egg, it produces an egg by pushing it out of its body. ❑ *My canary has laid an egg.* **4** V-T **Lay** is used with some nouns to talk about making official preparations for something. For example, if you **lay the basis** for something or **lay plans** for it, you prepare it carefully. ❑ *Diplomats meeting in Chile have laid the groundwork for far-reaching environmental regulations.* **5** V-T **Lay** is used with some nouns in expressions about accusing or blaming someone. For example, if you **lay the blame** for a mistake on someone, you say it is their fault, or if the police **lay charges** against someone, they officially accuse that person of a crime. ❑ *She refused to lay the blame on any one party.* **6** V-T If you **lay** the table or **lay** the places at a table, you arrange the knives, forks, and other things that people need on the table before a meal. [OLD-FASHIONED] ❑ *The butler always laid the table.* **7** to lay something at someone's door → see **door** **8** to lay a finger on someone → see **finger** **9** to lay your hands on something → see **hand** ① **10** to lay siege to something → see **siege**

▶ **lay aside** **1** PHRASAL VERB If you **lay aside** a feeling or belief, you reject it or give it up in order to progress with something. ❑ *Perhaps the opposed parties will lay aside their sectional interests and rise to this challenge.* **2** PHRASAL VERB If you **lay** something **aside**, you put it down, usually because you have finished using it or want to save it to use later. [BRIT] ❑ *He finished the tea and laid the cup aside.*

▶ **lay down** **1** PHRASAL VERB If you **lay** something **down**, you put it down, usually because you have finished using it. ❑ *Daniel finished the article and laid the newspaper down on his desk.* **2** PHRASAL VERB If rules or people in authority **lay down** what people should do or must do, they officially state what they should or must do. ❑ *Not all companies lay down written guidelines and rules.* **3** PHRASAL VERB If someone **lays down** their weapons, they stop fighting a battle or war and make peace. ❑ *The drug-traffickers have offered to lay down their arms.*

▶ **lay off** **1** PHRASAL VERB If workers **are laid off**, they are told by their employers to leave their job, usually because there is no more work for them to do. [BUSINESS] ❑ *100,000 federal workers will be laid off to reduce the deficit.* **2** → see also **layoff** **3** → See feature box at **work**

▶ **lay on** PHRASAL VERB If you **lay on** something such as food, entertainment, or a service, you provide or supply it, especially in a generous or grand way. [mainly BRIT] ❑ *They laid on a superb evening.*

▶ **lay out** **1** PHRASAL VERB If you **lay out** a group of things, you spread them out and arrange them neatly, for example, so that they can all be seen clearly. ❑ *Grace laid out the knives and forks on the table.* **2** PHRASAL VERB To **lay out** ideas, principles, or plans means to explain or present them clearly, for example, in a document or a meeting. ❑ *Maxwell listened closely as Johnson laid out his plan.* **3** → see also **layout**

▶ **lay up** PHRASAL VERB [usu passive] If someone **is laid up** with an illness, the illness makes it necessary for them to stay in bed. [INFORMAL] ❏ *She was in the hospital for a week and laid up for a month after that.* ❏ *Powell ruptured a disc in his back and was laid up for a year.*

② **lay** /leɪ/ **1** ADJ [ADJ n] You use **lay** to describe people who are involved with a Christian church but are not members of the clergy or are not monks or nuns. ❏ *Edwards is a Methodist lay preacher and social worker.* **2** ADJ [ADJ n] You use **lay** to describe people who are not experts or professionals in a particular subject or activity. ❏ *It is difficult for a lay person to gain access to medical libraries.*

lay|about /leɪəbaʊt/ (**layabouts**) N-COUNT If you say that someone is a **layabout**, you disapprove of them because they do not work and you think they are lazy. [DISAPPROVAL]

lay-by (**lay-bys**) N-COUNT A **lay-by** is a short strip of road by the side of a main road, where cars can stop for a while. [BRIT] ❏ *I left my car in a lay-by and set off on foot.*

lay|er ✦◇◇ /leɪər/ (**layers, layering, layered**) **1** N-COUNT A **layer** of a material or substance is a quantity or piece of it that covers a surface or that is between two other things. ❏ *...the depletion of the ozone layer.* **2** N-COUNT If something such as a system or an idea has many **layers**, it has many different levels or parts. ❏ *Critics and the public puzzle out the layers of meaning in his photos.* **3** V-T If you **layer** something, you arrange it in layers. ❏ *Layer half the onion slices on top of the potatoes.*

lay|ered /leɪərd/ ADJ Something that is **layered** is made or exists in layers. ❏ *Maria wore a layered white dress that rustled when she moved.*

lay|man /leɪmən/ (**laymen**) N-COUNT A **layman** is a person who is not trained, qualified, or experienced in a particular subject or activity. ❏ *The mere mention of the words "heart failure" can conjure up, to the layman, the prospect of imminent death.*

lay|off /leɪɔf/ (**layoffs**) N-COUNT When there are **layoffs** in a company, people become unemployed because there is no more work for them in the company. [BUSINESS] ❏ *It will close more than 200 stores nationwide resulting in the layoffs of an estimated 2,000 employees.*

lay|out /leɪaʊt/ (**layouts**) N-COUNT The **layout** of a park, building, or piece of writing is the way in which the parts of it are arranged. ❏ *He tried to recall the layout of the farmhouse.*

lay|over /leɪoʊvər/ (**layovers**) N-COUNT A **layover** is a short stay in a place in between parts of a journey, especially a plane journey. [AM] ❏ *She booked a plane for Denver with a layover in Dallas.*

lay|person /leɪpɜrsən/ (**laypersons** or **laypeople**) also **lay person** N-COUNT A **layperson** is a person who is not trained, qualified, or experienced in a particular subject or activity.

lay|woman /leɪwʊmən/ (**laywomen**) N-COUNT A **laywoman** is a woman who is not trained, qualified, or experienced in a particular subject or activity. ❏ *Information is not out there for the laywoman as far as symptoms or how it's treated.*

laze /leɪz/ (**lazes, lazing, lazed**) V-I If you **laze** somewhere for a period of time, you relax and enjoy yourself, not doing any work or anything else that requires effort. ❏ *Fred lazed in an easy chair.* ❏ *They used the swimming pool, rode, lazed in the deep shade of the oaks in the heat of the day.* • PHRASAL VERB **Laze around** or **laze about** means the same as **laze**. ❏ *He went to Spain for nine months, to laze around and visit relations.* ❏ *I was happy enough to laze about on the beach.*

lazy /leɪzi/ (**lazier, laziest**) **1** ADJ If someone is **lazy**, they do not want to work or make any effort to do anything. ❏ *Lazy and incompetent police officers are letting the public down.* • **la|zi|ness** N-UNCOUNT ❏ *Current employment laws will be changed to reward effort and punish laziness.* **2** ADJ [ADJ n] You can use **lazy** to describe an activity or event in which you are very relaxed and which you do or take part in without making much effort. ❏ *Her latest novel is perfect for a lazy summer's afternoon's reading.* • **la|zi|ly** /leɪzɪli/ ADV [ADV with v] ❏ *Liz went back into the kitchen, stretching lazily.*

lb (**lbs**) **lb** is a written abbreviation for **pound**, when it refers to weight. ❏ *The baby was born three months early at 3 lbs 5 oz.*

LCD /ɛl si di/ (**LCDs**) N-COUNT An **LCD** is a display of information on a screen, which uses liquid crystals that become visible when electricity is passed through them. **LCD** is an abbreviation for **liquid crystal display**. ❏ *...a color LCD screen.*

LEAD
① BEING AHEAD OR TAKING SOMEONE SOMEWHERE
② SUBSTANCES

① **lead** ✦✦✦ /liːd/ (**leads, leading, led**)
→ Please look at meanings **13** and **19** to see if the expression you are looking for is shown under another headword.

1 V-T If you **lead** a group of people, you walk or ride in front of them. ❏ *The president and vice president led the mourners.* ❏ *He walks with a stick but still leads his soldiers into battle.* **2** V-T If you **lead** someone to a particular place or thing, you take them there. ❏ *He took Dickon by the hand to lead him into the house.* ❏ *She confessed to the killing and led police to his remains.* **3** V-I If a road, gate, or door **leads** somewhere, you can get there by following the road or going through the gate or door. ❏ *...the door that led to the yard.* ❏ *...a hallway leading to the living room.* **4** V-I If you are **leading** at a particular point in a race or competition, you are winning at that point. ❏ *He's leading in the presidential race.* ❏ *So far Fischer leads by five wins to two.* **5** N-SING If you have the **lead** or are in the **lead** in a race or competition, you are winning. ❏ *Harvard took the lead and remained unperturbed by the repeated challenges.* **6** V-T If one company or country **leads** others in a particular activity such as scientific research or business, it is more successful or advanced than they are in that activity. ❏ *In 1920, the United States led the world in iron and steel manufacturing.* **7** V-T If you **lead** a group of people, an organization, or an activity, you are in control or in charge of the people or the activity. ❏ *He led the country between 1949 and 1984.* **8** N-COUNT If you take the **lead**, you do something new or develop new ideas or methods that other people consider to be a good example or model to follow. ❏ *The American and Japanese navies took the lead in the development of naval aviation.* **9** V-T You can use **lead** when you are saying what kind of life someone has. For example, if you **lead** a busy life, your life is busy. ❏ *She led a normal, happy life with her sister and brother.* **10** V-I If something **leads** to a situation or event, usually an unpleasant one, it begins a process which causes that situation or event to happen. ❏ *Ethnic tensions among the republics could lead to civil war.* **11** V-T If something **leads** you to do something, it influences or affects you in such a way that you do it. ❏ *His involvement in his family's restaurant business and led him to study classical French cooking at culinary school.* **12** V-T You can say that one point or topic in a discussion or piece of writing **leads** you to another in order to introduce a new point or topic that is linked with the previous one. ❏ *Well, I think that leads me to the real point.* **13** N-COUNT A **lead** is a piece of information or an idea which may help people to discover the facts in a situation where many facts are not known, for example, in the investigation of a crime or in a scientific experiment. ❏ *The inquiry team is also following up possible leads after receiving 400 calls from the public.* **14** N-COUNT A dog's **lead** is a long, thin chain or piece of leather which you attach to the dog's collar so that you can control the dog. [BRIT]

in AM, use **leash**

15 N-COUNT A **lead** in a piece of equipment is a piece of wire covered in plastic which supplies electricity to the equipment or carries it from one part of the equipment to another. ❏ *...a lead that plugs into a socket on the laptop.* **16** N-COUNT The **lead** in a play, film, or show is the most important part in it. The person who plays this part can also be called the **lead**. ❏ *...the ballet stars who dance the leads.* ❏ *Neve Campbell is the lead, playing one of the dancers.* **17** → see also **leading 18 to lead someone astray** → see **astray 19 to lead the way** → see **way** ③

▶ **lead up to 1** PHRASAL VERB The events that **led up to** a particular event happened one after the other until that event occurred. ❏ *Alan Tomlinson has reconstructed the events that led up to the deaths.* **2** PHRASAL VERB If someone **leads up to** a particular subject, they gradually guide a conversation to a point where they can introduce it. ❏ *I'm leading up to something quite important.*

② **lead** /lɛd/ (**leads**) **1** N-UNCOUNT **Lead** is a soft, gray, heavy metal. ❏ *...drinking water supplied by old-fashioned lead pipes.* **2** N-COUNT The **lead** in a pencil is the center part of it which makes a mark on paper. ❏ *He grabbed a pencil, and the lead immediately broke.* **3** → See also color supplement

lead|ed /lɛdɪd/ **1** ADJ [ADJ n] **Leaded** gasoline has had lead added to it. ❑ *Arco says 20% of West Coast drivers want leaded gasoline.* **2** ADJ [ADJ n] **Leaded** windows are made of small pieces of glass held together by strips of lead.

lead|en /lɛdᵊn/ **1** ADJ A **leaden** sky or sea is dark gray and has no movement of clouds or waves. [LITERARY] ❑ *The weather was at its worst; bitterly cold, with leaden skies that gave minimum visibility.* **2** ADJ A **leaden** conversation or piece of writing is not very interesting. ❑ *...a leaden English translation from the Latin.* **3** ADJ If your movements are **leaden**, you move slowly and heavily, usually because you are tired. [LITERARY] ❑ *He heard the father's leaden footsteps move down the stairs.*

lead|er ♦♦♦ /liːdər/ (**leaders**) **1** N-COUNT The **leader** of a group of people or an organization is the person who is in control of it or in charge of it. ❑ *We now need a new leader of the party and a new style of leadership.* **2** N-COUNT The **leader** at a particular point in a race or competition is the person who is winning at that point. ❑ *The leaders came in two minutes clear of the field.*

COLLOCATIONS

leader
NOUN **1**
noun + **leader**: church, community, council, team, union; opposition, party, world; business, industry; division, group, league
adjective + **leader**: military, political, religious, spiritual, tribal; deputy
verb + **leader**: appoint, choose, elect

SYNONYMS

leader
NOUN **1**
boss: *Occasionally, I have to go and ask the boss for a raise.*
chief: *...a commission appointed by the police chief.*
head: *...the head waiter.*
captain: *...Mike Thomas, the captain of the university rugby club.*
commander: *The commander and some of the men had been released.*
director: *...the director of the intensive care unit at Guy's Hospital.*

---

lead|er|board /liːdərbɔːrd/ N-SING The **leaderboard** is a board that shows the names and positions of the leading competitors in a competition, especially a golf tournament. ❑ *I'm delighted to be on top of the leaderboard in a tournament that has so many star names playing.*

lead|er|ship ♦♦◊ /liːdərʃɪp/ (**leaderships**) **1** N-COUNT You refer to people who are in control of a group or organization as the **leadership**. ❑ *He is expected to hold talks with both leaderships.* **2** N-UNCOUNT Someone's **leadership** is their position or state of being in control of a group of people. ❑ *He praised her leadership during the crisis.*

lead-free /lɛd friː/ ADJ Something such as gasoline or paint which is **lead-free**, is made without lead, or has no lead added to it.

lead-in /liːd ɪn/ (**lead-ins**) N-COUNT A **lead-in** is something that is said or done as an introduction before the main subject or event, especially before a radio or television program.

lead|ing ♦♦◊ /liːdɪŋ/ **1** ADJ [ADJ n] The **leading** person or thing in a particular area is the one which is most important or successful. ❑ *...a leading member of the city's Sikh community.* **2** ADJ [ADJ n] The **leading** role in a play or movie is the main role. A **leading** lady or man is an actor who plays this role. ❑ *...an offer to play the leading role in an Arthur Miller play.* **3** ADJ [ADJ n] The **leading** group, vehicle, or person in a race or procession is the one that is at the front. ❑ *The leading car came to a halt.*

SYNONYMS

leading
ADJ **1**
top: *The President met this afternoon with his top military advisers.*
main: *...one of the main tourist areas of Amsterdam.*
chief: *The job went to one of her chief rivals.*
major: *Exercise has a major part to play in preventing and combatting disease.*
foremost: *He was one of the world's foremost scholars of ancient Indian culture.*

---

lead|ing edge N-SING The **leading edge** of a particular area of research or development is the area of it that seems most advanced or sophisticated. ❑ *I think Israel tends to be at the leading edge of technological development.* ● **leading-edge** ADJ ❑ *...leading-edge technology.*

lead|ing light (**leading lights**) N-COUNT If you say that someone is a **leading light** in an organization, campaign, or community, you mean that they are one of the most important, active, enthusiastic, and successful people in it.

lead|ing ques|tion (**leading questions**) N-COUNT A **leading question** is expressed in such a way that it suggests what the answer should be.

lead sing|er /liːd sɪŋər/ (**lead singers**) N-COUNT The **lead singer** of a pop group is the person who sings most of the songs.

lead time /liːd taɪm/ (**lead times**) **1** N-COUNT **Lead time** is the time between the original design or idea for a particular product and its actual production. [BUSINESS] ❑ *...a 16-month lead time from concept to production.* **2** N-COUNT **Lead time** is the period of time that it takes for goods to be delivered after someone has ordered them. [BUSINESS] ❑ *Lead times on new equipment orders can run as long as three years.*

lead-up /liːd ʌp/ N-SING [usu the N to n] The **lead-up** to an event is the things connected to that event that happen before it. ❑ *The lead-up to the wedding was extremely interesting.*

leaf ♦◊◊ /liːf/ (**leaves, leafs, leafing, leafed**) **1** N-COUNT [usu pl, also in/into n] The **leaves** of a tree or plant are the parts that are flat, thin, and usually green. Many plants and trees lose their leaves in the winter and grow new leaves in the spring. ❑ *In the garden, the leaves of the horse chestnut had already fallen.* **2** N-COUNT A **leaf** is one of the pieces of paper of which a book is made. ❑ *He flattened the wrappers and put them between the leaves of his book.* **3** PHRASE If you say that you are going to **turn over a new leaf**, you mean that you are going to start to behave in a better or more acceptable way. ❑ *He realized he was in the wrong and promised to turn over a new leaf.* **4** → See also color supplement
▶ **leaf through** PHRASAL VERB If you **leaf through** something such as a book or magazine, you turn the pages without reading or looking at them very carefully. ❑ *Most patients derive enjoyment from leafing through old picture albums.*

leaf|less /liːflɪs/ ADJ If a tree or plant is **leafless**, it has no leaves.

leaf|let /liːflɪt/ (**leaflets**) N-COUNT A **leaflet** is a little book or a piece of paper containing information about a particular subject. ❑ *Campaigners handed out leaflets on passive smoking.*

leaf mold N-UNCOUNT **Leaf mold** is a substance consisting of decayed leaves that is used to improve the soil.

leafy /liːfi/ **1** ADJ **Leafy** trees and plants have lots of leaves on them. ❑ *His two-story brick home was surrounded by tall, leafy trees.* **2** ADJ You say that a place is **leafy** when there are lots of trees and plants there. ❑ *...a gate leading to the narrow leafy streets at the top of the hill.*

league ♦♦◊ /liːg/ (**leagues**) **1** N-COUNT A **league** is a group of people, clubs, or countries that have joined together for a particular purpose, or because they share a common interest. ❑ *...the League of Nations.* **2** N-COUNT A **league** is a group of teams that play the same sport or activity against each other. ❑ *...the American League series between the Boston Red Sox and World Champion Oakland Athletics.* **3** N-COUNT You use **league** to make comparisons between different people or things, especially in terms of their quality. ❑ *Her success has taken her out of my league.* **4** PHRASE If you say that someone is **in league** with another person to do something bad, you mean that they are working together to do that thing. ❑ *There is no evidence that the broker was in league with the fraudulent vendor.*

league ta|ble (**league tables**) N-COUNT A **league table** is a list that shows how successful an organization such as a sports team or a business is when it is compared to other similar organizations. [BRIT]

leak ♦◊◊ /liːk/ (**leaks, leaking, leaked**) **1** V-T/V-I If a container **leaks**, there is a hole or crack in it which lets a substance such as liquid or gas escape. You can also say that a container **leaks** a substance such as liquid or gas. ❑ *The roof leaked.* ❑ *The pool's fiberglass sides had cracked and the water had leaked out.*

• N-COUNT **Leak** is also a noun. ❑ *It's thought a gas leak may have caused the blast.* ◪ N-COUNT A **leak** is a crack, hole, or other gap that a substance such as a liquid or gas can pass through. ❑ *...a leak in the radiator.* ◪ V-T/V-I If a secret document or piece of information **leaks** or **is leaked**, someone lets the public know about it. ❑ *Mr. Ashton accused police of leaking information to the press.* ❑ *We don't know how the transcript leaked.* • N-COUNT **Leak** is also a noun. ❑ *More serious leaks, possibly involving national security, are likely to be investigated by the police.* • PHRASAL VERB **Leak out** means the same as **leak**. ❑ *More details are now beginning to leak out.*

COLLOCATIONS

leak
NOUN
◪
noun + **leak**: gas, oil, radiation, water; minor
adjective + **leak**: radioactive, toxic
verb + **leak**: investigate; cause, spring; isolate, prevent, stop
◪
adjective + **leak**: damaging, embarrassing, serious; alleged, apparent
VERB
◪
leak + noun: gas, oil, water
noun + leak: pipe, roof, tap, valve
◪
leak + noun: details, information, security; document, email, memo
leak + adverb: accidentally, allegedly, deliberately

---

leak|age /líkɪdʒ/ (**leakages**) N-VAR A **leakage** is an amount of liquid or gas that is escaping from a pipe or container by means of a crack, hole, or other fault. ❑ *A leakage of kerosene has polluted water supplies.*

leak|er /líkər/ (**leakers**) N-COUNT A **leaker** is someone who lets people know secret information. [JOURNALISM] ❑ *He found no direct evidence to identify a leaker.*

leaky /líki/ (**leakier, leakiest**) ADJ Something that is **leaky** has holes, cracks, or other faults which allow liquids and gases to pass through. ❑ *They were very worried about the cost of repairing the leaky roof.*

lean ✦✧✧ /lín/ (**leans, leaning, leaned, leaner, leanest**) ◪ V-I When you **lean** in a particular direction, you bend your body in that direction. ❑ *Eileen leaned across and opened the passenger door.* ◪ V-T/V-I If you **lean** on or against someone or something, you rest against them so that they partly support your weight. If you **lean** an object on or against something, you place the object so that it is partly supported by that thing. ❑ *She was feeling tired and was glad to lean against him.* ❑ *Lean the plants against a wall and cover the roots with peat.* ◪ ADJ If you describe someone as **lean**, you mean that they are thin but look strong and healthy. [APPROVAL] ❑ *Like most athletes, she was lean and muscular.* ◪ ADJ If meat is **lean**, it does not have very much fat. ❑ *It is a beautiful meat, very lean and tender.* ◪ ADJ If you describe an organization as **lean**, you mean that it has become more efficient and less wasteful by getting rid of staff, or by dropping projects which were unprofitable. ❑ *...reforms which turned us into a lean and competitive nation.* ◪ ADJ If you describe periods of time as **lean**, you mean that people have less of something such as money or are less successful than they used to be. ❑ *My parents lived through the lean years of the 1930s.*
▶ **lean on** also **lean upon** PHRASAL VERB If you **lean on** someone or **lean upon** them, you depend on them for support and encouragement. ❑ *She leaned on him to help her to solve her problems.*

SYNONYMS

lean
VERB ◪
bend: *I bent over and kissed her cheek.*
tip: *He moved away from her, and she had to tip her head back to see him.*
incline: *Jack inclined his head very slightly.*

---

lean|ing /línɪŋ/ (**leanings**) N-COUNT [usu pl, with supp, oft N toward n] Your particular **leanings** are the beliefs, ideas, or aims you hold or a tendency you have toward them. ❑ *Many companies are wary of their socialist leanings.* ❑ *I always had a leaning toward sports.*

lean manu|fac|tur|ing N-UNCOUNT **Lean manufacturing** is a manufacturing method which aims to reduce wastage, for example, by keeping stocks low and by working more flexibly. [BUSINESS] ❑ *...efficiency-raising techniques such as lean manufacturing.*

lean pro|duc|tion N-UNCOUNT **Lean production** is the same as **lean manufacturing**. [BUSINESS] ❑ *...Japanese-style lean production techniques.*

lean-to (**lean-tos**) N-COUNT A **lean-to** is a building such as a shed or garage which is attached to one wall of a larger building, and which usually has a sloping roof.

leap ✦✧✧ /líp/ (**leaps, leaping, leaped** or **leapt**) ◪ V-T/V-I If you **leap**, you jump high in the air or jump a long distance. ❑ *He leaped in the air and waved his fists to the fans as he ran out of the stadium.* ❑ *Frederick leaped over 22 feet on his second attempt.* • N-COUNT **Leap** is also a noun. ❑ *The suspect took a leap out of a third-story window.* ◪ V-I If you **leap** somewhere, you move there suddenly and quickly. ❑ *The two men leaped into the jeep and roared off.* ◪ V-I If a vehicle **leaps** somewhere, it moves there in a short sudden movement. ❑ *The car leaped forward.* ◪ N-COUNT A **leap** is a large and important change, increase, or advance. [JOURNALISM] ❑ *The result has been a giant leap in productivity.* ❑ *...the leap in the unemployed from 35,000 to 75,000.* ◪ V-I If you **leap** to a particular place or position, you make a large and important change, increase, or advance. ❑ *The President's approval rating leaped to an astounding 88 percent.*

leap|frog /lípfrɔg/ (**leapfrogs, leapfrogging, leapfrogged**) ◪ N-UNCOUNT **Leapfrog** is a game which children play, in which a child bends over, while others jump over their back. ❑ *The kids were playing leapfrog and doing somersaults in the backyard.* ◪ V-T/V-I If one group of people **leapfrogs** into a particular position or **leapfrogs** someone else, they use the achievements of another person or group in order to make advances of their own. ❑ *It is already obvious that all four American systems have leapfrogged over the European versions.*

leap of faith (**leaps of faith**) N-COUNT [a N in sing] If you take a **leap of faith**, you do something even though you are not sure it is right or will succeed. ❑ *Take a leap of faith and trust them.*

leapt /lɛpt, lípt/ **Leapt** is a past tense and past participle of **leap**.

leap year (**leap years**) N-COUNT A **leap year** is a year which has 366 days. The extra day is February 29th. There is a leap year every four years.

learn ✦✦✦ /lɜrn/ (**learns, learning, learned**) ◪ V-T/V-I If you **learn** something, you obtain knowledge or a skill through studying or training. ❑ *Their children were going to learn English.* ❑ *He is learning to play the piano.* ❑ *It's going to be tough, but these guys learn quickly.* • **learn|ing** N-UNCOUNT ❑ *...a bilingual approach to the learning of English.* ◪ V-T/V-I If you **learn** of something, you find out about it. ❑ *It wasn't until after his death that I learned about the poverty and abuse he suffered as a child.* ❑ *It didn't come as a shock to learn that the fuel and cooling systems are the most common causes of breakdown.* ◪ V-T If people **learn** to behave or react in a particular way, they gradually start to behave in that way as a result of a change in attitudes. ❑ *You have to learn to face your problem.* ◪ V-T/V-I If you **learn** from an unpleasant experience, you change the way you behave so that it does not happen again or so that, if it happens again, you can deal with it better. ❑ *I am convinced that he has learned from his mistakes.* ❑ *I just hope we all learn some lessons from this.* ◪ V-T If you **learn** something such as a poem or a role in a play, you study or repeat the words so that you can remember them. ❑ *He learned this song as an inmate at a Texas prison.* ◪ → see also **learned, learning** ◪ **to learn the ropes** → see **rope** ◪ → See feature box at **study**

learn|ed /lɜ́rnɪd/ ADJ A **learned** person has gained a lot of knowledge by studying. ❑ *He is a scholar, a genuinely learned man.*

learn|er /lɜ́rnər/ (**learners**) N-COUNT A **learner** is someone who is learning about a particular subject or how to do something. ❑ *Clinton proved to be a quick learner and soon settled into serious struggles over cutting the budget.*

learn|er's per|mit (**learner's permits**) N-COUNT A **learner's permit** is a license that allows you to drive a vehicle before

learning

you have passed your driving test. [AM] ❑ *She took some friends for a ride in the family car when she only had her learner's permit.*

learn|ing /lɜrnɪŋ/ ◼ N-UNCOUNT **Learning** is the process of gaining knowledge through studying. ❑ *The brochure described the library as the focal point of learning on the campus.* ◼ → see also **learn** ◼ → See feature box at **study**

VOCABULARY IN CONTEXT

Online learning

The internet has revolutionized teaching and learning, with millions of people now **signing up** for **online courses**. A recent statistic showed that over 58 million students were enrolled on MOOCs (Massive Online Open Courses) worldwide. These **virtual classrooms** mean that geography is no barrier to attending classes at any time – day or night. While instructor-led lessons are available, most people access the **course** in their own time. Self-paced learning is just one of the advantages. As students work **autonomously** through the course content, there are usually practice activities they can do to check their **comprehension**. Since these feature **automated grading**, students instantly know where they need to reinforce their learning. They also have the benefit of **peer review**, discussion groups, and forums. **E-learning** is widely incorporated into higher education for tutorials and seminars, too. Blended learning is very popular for its collaborative and flexible approach.

learn|ing curve (learning curves) N-COUNT [usu sing] A **learning curve** is a process where people develop a skill by learning from their mistakes. A steep learning curve involves learning very quickly. ❑ *They are on a steep learning curve.*

learn|ing dif|fi|cul|ty (learning difficulties) N-COUNT If someone has a **learning difficulty**, they have a condition that makes it difficult for them to learn as quickly or in the same way as most other people. ❑ *The method helps people with coordination problems and learning difficulties, such as dyslexia.*

lease ♦◊◊ /lis/ (leases, leasing, leased) ◼ N-COUNT A **lease** is a legal agreement by which the owner of a building, a piece of land, or something such as a car allows someone else to use it for a period of time in return for money. ❑ *He took up a 10-year lease on the house.* ◼ V-T If you **lease** property or something such as a car from someone or if they **lease** it to you, they allow you to use it in return for regular payments of money. ❑ *He went to Toronto, where he leased an apartment.* ❑ *She hopes to lease the building to students.* ◼ PHRASE If you say that someone or something has been given **a new lease of life**, you are emphasizing that they are much more lively or successful than they have been in the past. ❑ *The operation has given me a new lease of life.* ◼ → See feature box at **upcycle**

lease|hold /lishoʊld/ ADJ If a building or land is described as **leasehold**, it is allowed to be used in return for payment according to the terms of a lease. ❑ *If they were prevented from exploring the leasehold acreage that they've got, some of it would come to market.*

lease|holder /lishoʊldər/ (leaseholders) N-COUNT A **leaseholder** is a person who is allowed to use a property according to the terms of a lease. [mainly BRIT]

leash /liʃ/ (leashes) N-COUNT A dog's **leash** is a long thin piece of leather or a chain, which you attach to the dog's collar so that you can keep the dog under control. ❑ *All dogs in public places should be on a leash.*

least ♦♦♦ /list/

Least is often considered to be the superlative form of **little**.

◼ PHRASE You use **at least** to say that a number or amount is the smallest that is possible or likely and that the actual number or amount may be greater. The forms **at the least** and **at the very least** are also used. ❑ *Aim to have at least half a pint of milk each day.* ❑ *About two-thirds of adults consult their doctor at least once a year.* ◼ PHRASE You use **at least** to say that something is the minimum that is true or possible. The forms **at the least** and **at the very least** are also used. ❑ *She could take a nice vacation at least.* ❑ *His possession of classified documents in his home was, at the very least, a violation of navy security regulations.* ◼ PHRASE You use **at least** to indicate an advantage that exists in spite of the disadvantage or bad situation that has just been mentioned. ❑ *We've no idea what his state of health is but at least we know he is still alive.* ◼ PHRASE You use **at least** to indicate that you are correcting or changing something that you have just said. ❑ *It's not difficult to get money for research or at least it's not always difficult.* ◼ ADJ [the ADJ n] You use **the least** to mean a smaller amount than anyone or anything else, or the smallest amount possible. ❑ *I try to offend the least amount of people possible.* • PRON [the PRON] **Least** is also a pronoun. ❑ *On education funding, Japan performs best but spends the least per student.* • ADV [the ADV after v] **Least** is also an adverb. ❑ *Damming the river may end up benefiting those who need it the least.* ◼ ADV [ADV adj/adv] You use **least** to indicate that someone or something has less of a particular quality than most other things of its kind. ❑ *He was one of the least warm human beings I had ever met.* ◼ ADJ [the ADJ n] You use **the least** to emphasize the smallness of something, especially when it hardly exists at all. [EMPHASIS] ❑ *I don't have the least idea of what you're talking about.* ◼ ADV [ADV with v] You use **least** to indicate that something is true or happens to a smaller degree or extent than anything else or at any other time. ❑ *He had a way of throwing Helen off guard with his charm when she least expected it.* ◼ ADJ [ADJ of def-n] You use **least** in structures where you are emphasizing that a particular situation or event is much less important or serious than other possible or actual ones. [EMPHASIS] ❑ *Having to get up at three o'clock every morning was the least of her worries.* ◼ PRON [the PRON cl] You use **the least** in structures where you are stating the minimum that should be done in a situation, and suggesting that more should really be done. ❑ *Well, the least you can do, if you won't help me yourself, is to tell me where to go instead.*

least|ways /listweɪz/ also **leastwise** /listwaɪz/ ADV You use **leastways** to indicate that you are correcting or changing something you have just said. [AM, SPOKEN] ❑ *Well, I don't imagine that will be necessary. Leastways, I hope not.* ❑ *"Your granddaddy don't care for 'em, neither," he threw in. "Not that I know of, leastwise."*

leath|er ♦◊◊ /lɛðər/ (leathers) N-MASS **Leather** is treated animal skin, usually from cows, which is used for making shoes, clothes, bags, and furniture. ❑ *He wore a leather jacket and dark trousers.*

leath|ery /lɛðəri/ ADJ If the texture of something, for example, someone's skin, is **leathery**, it is tough and hard, like leather.

LEAVE
① VERB USES
② NOUN USE
③ PHRASES AND PHRASAL VERBS

① **leave** ♦♦♦ /liv/ (leaves, leaving, left) ◼ V-T/V-I If you **leave** a place or person, you go away from that place or person. ❑ *He would not be allowed to leave the country.* ❑ *My flight leaves in less than an hour.* ◼ V-T/V-I If you **leave** an institution, group, or job, you permanently stop attending that institution, being a member of that group, or doing that job. ❑ *He left* school with no qualifications. ▫ *I am leaving to concentrate on writing fiction.* **3** V-T/V-I If you **leave** your husband, wife, or some other person with whom you have had a close relationship, you stop living with them or you end the relationship. ▫ *He'll never leave you. You needn't worry.* **4** V-T If you **leave** something or someone in a particular place, you let them remain there when you go away. If you **leave** something or someone with a person, you let them remain with that person so they are safe while you are away. ▫ *I left my bags in the car.* ▫ *From the moment that Philippe had left her in the bedroom at the hotel, she had heard nothing of him.* **5** V-T If you **leave** a message or an answer, you write it, record it, or give it to someone so that it can be found or passed on. ▫ *You can leave a message on our answering machine.* ▫ *I left my phone number with several people.* **6** V-T If you **leave** someone doing something, they are doing that thing when you go away from them. ▫ *Salter drove off, leaving Callendar surveying the scene.* **7** V-T If you **leave** someone to do something, you go away from them so that they do it on their own. If you **leave** someone to himself or herself, you go away from them and allow them to be alone. ▫ *I'll leave you to get to know each other.* ▫ *Diana took the hint and left them to it.* **8** V-T To **leave** an amount of something means to keep it available after the rest has been used or taken away. ▫ *He always left a little food for the next day.* **9** V-T To **leave** someone with something, especially when that thing is unpleasant or difficult to deal with, means to make them have it or make them deal with it. ▫ *...a crash which left him with a broken collar-bone.* **10** V-T If an event **leaves** people or things in a particular state, they are in that state when the event has finished. ▫ *...violent disturbances which have left at least ten people dead.* **11** V-T If you **leave** food or drink, you do not eat or drink it, often because you do not like it. ▫ *If you don't like the cocktail you ordered, just leave it and try a different one.* **12** V-T If something **leaves** a mark, effect, or sign, it causes that mark, effect, or sign to remain as a result. ▫ *A muscle tear will leave a scar after healing.* **13** V-T If you **leave** something in a particular state, position, or condition, you let it remain in that state, position, or condition. ▫ *He left the album open on the table.* ▫ *I've left the car lights on.* **14** V-T If you **leave** a space or gap in something, you deliberately make that space or gap. ▫ *Leave a gap at the top and bottom so air can circulate.* **15** V-T If you **leave** a job, decision, or choice to someone, you give them the responsibility for dealing with it or making it. ▫ *Affix the blue airmail label and leave the rest to us.* ▫ *The judge should not have left it to the jury to decide.* **16** V-T To **leave** someone with a particular course of action or the opportunity to do something means to let it be available to them, while restricting them in other ways. ▫ *He was left with no option but to resign.* **17** V-T If you **leave** something until a particular time, you delay doing it or dealing with it until then. ▫ *Don't leave it all until the last minute.* • PHRASE If you **leave** something **too late**, you delay doing it so that when you eventually do it, it is useless or ineffective. **18** V-T If you **leave** a particular subject, you stop talking about it and start discussing something else. ▫ *I think we'd better leave the subject of nationalism.* **19** V-T If you **leave** property or money to someone, you arrange for it to be given to them after you have died. ▫ *He died two and a half years later, leaving everything to his wife.* **20** V-T If you **leave** something somewhere, you forget to bring it with you. ▫ *I left my purse back there on the gas pump.* **21** → see also **left** ①

② **leave** ✦✦✦ /liːv/ **1** N-UNCOUNT **Leave** is a period of time when you are not working at your job, because you are on vacation, or for some other reason. If you are **on leave**, you are not working at your job. ▫ *Why don't you take a few days' leave?* ▫ *...maternity leave.* **2** → See feature box at **working**

③ **leave** ✦✦✦ /liːv/ (leaves, leaving, left)
→ Please look at meaning **3** to see if the expression you are looking for is shown under another headword.

1 PHRASE If you **leave** someone or something **alone**, or if you **leave** them **be**, you do not pay them any attention or bother them. ▫ *Some people need to confront a traumatic past; others find it better to leave it alone.* **2** PHRASE If something continues from where it **left off**, it starts happening again at the point where it had previously stopped. ▫ *As soon as the police disappear the violence will take up from where it left off.* **3** **take it or leave it**
→ see **take** ②

▶ **leave behind** **1** PHRASAL VERB If you **leave** someone or something **behind**, you go away permanently from them. ▫ *"I'd go and live there and leave Kentucky behind," says Brown.* **2** PHRASAL VERB If you **leave behind** an object or a situation, it remains after you have left a place. ▫ *I don't want to leave anything behind.* **3** PHRASAL VERB If a person, country, or organization **is left behind**, they remain at a lower level than others because they are not as quick at understanding things or developing. ▫ *We're going to be left behind by the rest of the world.* ▫ *People are concerned about getting left behind right now.*
▶ **leave off** PHRASAL VERB If someone or something **is left off** a list, they are not included on that list. ▫ *She has been deliberately left off the guest list.*
▶ **leave out** PHRASAL VERB If you **leave** someone or something **out** of an activity, collection, discussion, or group, you do not include them in it. ▫ *Some would question the wisdom of leaving her out of the team.* ▫ *If you prefer mild flavors reduce or leave out the chili.*

-leaved /-liːvd/ also **-leafed** COMB IN ADJ **-leaved** or **-leafed** combines with adjectives to form other adjectives which describe the type of leaves a tree or plant has. ▫ *...broad-leaved trees.* ▫ *...very dense and small-leafed maples.*

leav|en /lɛvᵊn/ (leavens, leavening, leavened) V-T If a situation or activity **is leavened** by or with something, it is made more interesting or cheerful. ▫ *His interest in science and technology was leavened by a genuine passion for architectural history and theory.* ▫ *He found congenial officers who knew how to leaven war's rigors with riotous enjoyment.*

leav|ened /lɛvᵊnd/ ADJ [usu ADJ n] **Leavened** bread or dough is made with yeast. ▫ *...a loaf of leavened bread.*

leave of ab|sence (leaves of absence) N-VAR If you have **leave of absence** you have permission to be away from work for a certain period.

leaves /liːvz/ **Leaves** is the plural form of **leaf**, and the third person singular form of **leave**.

Leba|nese /lɛbəniːz/ (Lebanese) **1** ADJ **Lebanese** means belonging or relating to Lebanon, or to its people or culture. **2** N-COUNT A **Lebanese** is a Lebanese citizen, or a person of Lebanese origin.

lech|er /lɛtʃər/ (lechers) N-COUNT If you describe a man as a **lecher**, you disapprove of him because you think he behaves in a way that shows he is only interested in other people sexually. [INFORMAL, DISAPPROVAL]

lech|er|ous /lɛtʃərəs/ ADJ [usu ADJ n] If you describe someone as **lecherous**, you disapprove of them because they behave in a way that shows they are only interested in other people sexually. [DISAPPROVAL]

lech|ery /lɛtʃəri/ N-UNCOUNT **Lechery** is the behavior of men who are only interested in other people sexually. [DISAPPROVAL] ▫ *His lechery made him the enemy of every self-respecting husband and father in the county.*

lec|tern /lɛktərn/ (lecterns) N-COUNT A **lectern** is a high sloping desk on which someone puts their notes when they are standing up and giving a lecture.

lec|ture ✦◇◇ /lɛktʃər/ (lectures, lecturing, lectured) **1** N-COUNT A **lecture** is a talk someone gives in order to teach people about a particular subject, usually at a university or college. ▫ *...a series of lectures by Professor Eric Robinson.* **2** V-I If you **lecture** on a particular subject, you give a lecture or a series of lectures about it. ▫ *She then invited him to Atlanta to lecture on the history of art.* **3** V-T If someone **lectures** you about something, they criticize you or tell you how they think you should behave. ▫ *He used to lecture me about getting too much sun.* ▫ *Chuck would lecture me, telling me to get a haircut.* • N-COUNT **Lecture** is also a noun. ▫ *Our captain gave us a stern lecture on safety.* **4** → See feature box at **university**

═════════ SYNONYMS ═════════

lecture
NOUN **1**
talk: *I attended a talk on ancient Rome.*
speech: *She is due to make a speech on the economy next week.*
seminar: *We attended a series of half-day seminars on information technology.*

lec|tur|er /lɛktʃərər/ (**lecturers**) ◼ N-COUNT A **lecturer** is a teacher at a university or college. ❑ ...a lecturer in law. ◼ N-COUNT A **lecturer** is a person who gives lectures.

lec|ture|ship /lɛktʃərʃɪp/ (**lectureships**) N-COUNT A **lectureship** is the position of lecturer at a university or college.

led /lɛd/ **Led** is the past tense and past participle of **lead**.

-led /-lɛd/ ◼ COMB IN ADJ [usu ADJ n] **-led** combines with nouns to form adjectives which indicate that something is organized, directed, or controlled by a particular person or group. ❑ ...the student-led democracy movement. ❑ ...a German-led European consortium. ◼ COMB IN ADJ **-led** combines with nouns to form adjectives which indicate that something is mainly caused or influenced by a particular factor. ❑ Their prosperity depends on export-led growth. ❑ ...a market-led economy.

ledge /lɛdʒ/ (**ledges**) ◼ N-COUNT A **ledge** is a piece of rock on the side of a cliff or mountain, which is in the shape of a narrow shelf. ❑ ...like a wounded bird seeking refuge on a mountain ledge. ◼ N-COUNT A **ledge** is a narrow shelf along the bottom edge of a window. ❑ Dorothy had climbed onto the ledge outside his window.

ledg|er /lɛdʒər/ (**ledgers**) N-COUNT A **ledger** is a book in which a company or organization writes down the amounts of money it spends and receives. [BUSINESS]

lee ✦◇◇ /li/ ◼ N-SING [with poss] The **lee** of a place is the shelter that it gives from the wind or bad weather. [LITERARY] ❑ ...the cathedral, which nestles in the lee of a hill beneath the town. ◼ ADJ [ADJ n] In sailing, the **lee** side of a ship is the one that is away from the wind. [TECHNICAL]

leech /litʃ/ (**leeches**) ◼ N-COUNT A **leech** is a small animal which looks like a worm and lives in water. Leeches feed by attaching themselves to other animals and sucking their blood. ◼ N-COUNT If you describe someone as a **leech**, you disapprove of them because they deliberately depend on other people, often making money out of them. [DISAPPROVAL] ❑ They're just a bunch of leeches living off others!

leek /lik/ (**leeks**) N-VAR **Leeks** are long thin vegetables which smell like onions. They are white at one end, have long light green leaves, and are eaten cooked.

leer /lɪər/ (**leers, leering, leered**) V-I If someone **leers** at you, they smile in an unpleasant way, usually because they are sexually interested in you. [DISAPPROVAL] ❑ ...men standing around, swilling beer and occasionally leering at passing females.

leery /lɪəri/ ◼ ADJ If you are **leery** of something, you are cautious and suspicious about it and try to avoid it. [INFORMAL] ❑ Executives say they are leery of the proposed system. ❑ They were leery about investing in a company controlled by a single individual. ◼ ADJ If someone looks or smiles at you in a **leery** way, they look or smile at you in an unpleasant way, usually because they are sexually interested in you. [DISAPPROVAL] ❑ ...a leery grin.

lee|way /liweɪ/ N-UNCOUNT **Leeway** is the freedom that someone has to take the action they want to or to change their plans. ❑ Rarely do schoolteachers have leeway to teach classes the way they want.

LEFT

① REMAINING
② DIRECTION AND POLITICAL GROUPINGS

---

① **left** ✦◇◇ /lɛft/ ◼ **Left** is the past tense and past participle of **leave**. ◼ ADJ [v-link ADJ, v n ADJ] If there is a certain amount of something **left**, or if you have a certain amount of it **left**, it remains when the rest has gone or been used. ❑ Is there any gin left? ❑ They still have six games left to play. • PHRASE If there is a certain amount of something **left over**, or if you have it **left over**, it remains when the rest has gone or been used. ❑ So much income is devoted to monthly mortgage payments that nothing is left over.

② **left** ✦✦✦ /lɛft/

The spelling **Left** is also used for meanings ◼ and ◼.

◼ N-SING The **left** is one of two opposite directions, sides, or positions. If you are facing north and you turn to the left, you will be facing west. In the word 'to,' the 't' is to the left of the 'o.' ❑ Go back to the last fork in the road and take a left. ❑ ...the brick wall to the left of the conservatory. • ADV [ADV after v] **Left** is also an adverb. ❑ Turn left at the crossroads into Clay Lane. ◼ ADJ [ADJ n] Your **left** arm, leg, or ear, for example, is the one which is on the left side of your body. Your **left** shoe or glove is the one which is intended to be worn on your left foot or hand. ❑ He landed awkwardly and twisted his left leg. ◼ N-SING-COLL In the U.S., **the left** refers to people who want to use legislation and the tax system to improve social conditions. In most other countries, **the left** refers to people who support the ideas of socialism. ❑ ...the traditional parties of the Left. ◼ N-SING If you say that a person or political party has moved to the **left**, you mean that their political beliefs have become more left-wing. ❑ After 1979, the party moved sharply to the left.

left-click (**left-clicks, left-clicking, left-clicked**) V-I To **left-click** or to **left-click** on something means to press the left-hand button on a computer mouse. [COMPUTING] ❑ When the menu has popped up you should left-click on one of the choices to make it operate.

left field ◼ N-SING [usu prep N] If you say that someone or something has come out of **left field** or is out in **left field**, you mean that they are untypical, unusual, or strange in some way. ❑ The question came out of left field, but Mary Ann wasn't really surprised. ❑ He is, like most theorists, out there in left field, ignoring the experimental evidence. ◼ N-UNCOUNT In baseball, **left field** is the left-hand part of the playing field. ❑ Ichiro's opening single to left field began a string of six straight hits.

left-hand ADJ [ADJ n] If something is on the **left-hand** side of something, it is positioned on the left of it. ❑ The Japanese drive on the left-hand side of the road.

left-handed ADJ Someone who is **left-handed** uses their left hand rather than their right hand for activities such as writing and sports and for picking things up. ❑ There is a store in town that supplies practically everything for left-handed people.

left-hander (**left-handers**) N-COUNT You can describe someone as a **left-hander** if they use their left hand rather than their right hand for activities such as writing and sports and for picking things up.

left|ism /lɛftɪzəm/ N-UNCOUNT **Leftism** refers to the beliefs and behavior of people who support the ideas of the political left.

left|ist /lɛftɪst/ (**leftists**) N-COUNT A **leftist** is someone who supports the ideas of the political left. ❑ Two of the men were leftists and two were centrists.

left-justify (**left-justifies, left-justifying, left-justified**) V-T If printed text is **left-justified**, each line begins at the same distance from the left-hand edge of the page or column. ❑ The data in the cells should be left-justified.

left-of-center

in BRIT, use **left-of-centre**

ADJ [usu ADJ n] **Left-of-center** people or political parties support the ideals of the political left.

left|over /lɛftoʊvər/ (**leftovers**) ◼ N-PLURAL You can refer to food that has not been eaten after a meal as **leftovers**. ❑ Refrigerate any leftovers. ◼ ADJ [ADJ n] You use **leftover** to describe an amount of something that remains after the rest of it has been used or eaten. ❑ ...leftover pieces of wallpaper.

left|ward /lɛftwərd/ also **leftwards** ADJ [ADJ n] **Leftward** or **leftwards** means on or towards the ideals of the political left. ❑ Their success does not necessarily reflect a leftward shift in politics. • ADV [ADV after v] **Leftward** or **leftwards** is also an adverb. ❑ He seemed to move leftwards as he grew older.

left-wing also **left wing** ◼ ADJ **Left-wing** people support the ideas of the political left. ❑ They said they would not be voting for him because he was too left-wing. ◼ N-SING The **left wing** of a group of people, especially a political party, consists of the members of it whose beliefs are closer to those of the political left than are those of its other members. ❑ She belongs on the left wing of the Democratic Party.

left-winger (**left-wingers**) N-COUNT A **left-winger** is someone whose political beliefs are close to those of the political left, or closer to them than most of the other people in the same group or party. ❑ The pro-life movement has right-wingers and left-wingers.

lefty /lɛfti/ (**lefties**) also **leftie** ◼ N-COUNT A **lefty** is someone who is left-handed. [mainly AM, INFORMAL] ◼ N-COUNT [oft N n]

If you refer to someone as a **lefty**, you mean that they support the ideals of the political left. [BRIT, INFORMAL, DISAPPROVAL]

leg ♦♦◊ /lɛg/ (**legs**) **1** N-COUNT A person or animal's **legs** are the long parts of their body that they use to stand on. ❑ *He was tapping his walking stick against his leg.* **2** N-COUNT The **legs** of a pair of pants are the parts that cover your legs. ❑ *He moved on through wet grass that soaked the legs of his pants.* **3** N-COUNT A **leg** of lamb, pork, chicken, or other meat is a piece of meat that consists of the animal's or bird's leg, especially the thigh. ❑ *...a chicken leg.* **4** N-COUNT The **legs** of a table, chair, or other piece of furniture are the parts that rest on the floor and support the furniture's weight. ❑ *His ankles were tied to the legs of the chair.* **5** N-COUNT A **leg** of a long journey is one part of it, usually between two points where you stop. ❑ *The first leg of the journey was by boat to Lake Naivasha in Kenya.* **6** N-COUNT A **leg** of a sports competition is one of a series of games that are played to find an overall winner. [mainly BRIT] **7** PHRASE If you **are pulling** someone's **leg**, you are teasing them by telling them something shocking or worrying as a joke. [INFORMAL] ❑ *Of course I won't tell them; I was only pulling your leg.* **8** → See also color supplement

lega|cy /lɛgəsi/ (**legacies**) **1** N-COUNT A **legacy** is money or property which someone leaves to you when they die. ❑ *You could make a real difference to someone's life by leaving them a generous legacy.* **2** N-COUNT A **legacy** of an event or period of history is something which is a direct result of it and which continues to exist after it is over. ❑ *...a program to overcome the legacy of inequality and injustice created by Apartheid.*

le|gal ♦♦◊ /liːgəl/ **1** ADJ [ADJ n] **Legal** is used to describe things that relate to the law. ❑ *He vowed to take legal action.* ❑ *...the legal system* ● **le|gal|ly** ADV ❑ *It could be a bit problematic, legally speaking.* **2** ADJ An action or situation that is **legal** is allowed or required by law. ❑ *What I did was perfectly legal.*

SYNONYMS

legal
ADJ **2**
lawful: *It was lawful for the doctors to treat her in the way they considered best.*
allowed: *Gifts like chocolates or flowers are allowed.*
authorized: *Entry into this area is for authorized personnel only.*

VOCABULARY IN CONTEXT

The legal system

If you've been the **victim** of a **crime**, you have the right to ask for updates on the **investigation**. The police should tell you if someone has been arrested, **charged**, **set free**, or let out on **bail**. Once the investigation has been concluded, the police will pass the **case** to the District Attorney or prosecutor who will decide whether the **defendant** should be **prosecuted**.

Some criminal cases start in a **magistrate's court**; more serious **offenses** are passed on to a higher court, where there will be a **trial by jury**. In both cases, the defendant is asked to enter a **plea**. If they **plead guilty**, or are found guilty, the magistrate or judge will **impose a sentence**. If they are **acquitted** or found not guilty, they are free to go.

---

le|gal aid N-UNCOUNT **Legal aid** is money given by the government or another organization to people who cannot afford to pay for a lawyer.

le|gal high (**legal highs**) N-COUNT A **legal high** is a drug that is taken because of its pleasant effects, but which is not illegal. ❑ *The girl suffered a dangerous reaction after taking a legal high.*

le|gal|is|tic /liːgəlɪstɪk/ ADJ [usu ADJ n] If you say that someone's language or ideas are **legalistic**, you are criticizing them for paying too much attention to legal details. [DISAPPROVAL] ❑ *...complicated legalistic language.* ❑ *...his fussily legalistic mind.*

le|gal|ity /liːgælɪti/ N-UNCOUNT If you talk about the **legality** of an action or situation, you are talking about whether it is legal or not. ❑ *The auditor has questioned the legality of the contracts.*

le|gal|ize /liːgəlaɪz/ (**legalizes**, **legalizing**, **legalized**)

in BRIT, also use **legalise**

V-T If something **is legalized**, a law is passed that makes it legal. ❑ *Divorce was legalized in 1981.*

le|gal ten|der N-UNCOUNT **Legal tender** is money, especially a particular coin or banknote, which is officially part of a country's currency at a particular time. ❑ *The French franc was no longer legal tender after midnight that night.*

leg|ate /lɛgɪt/ (**legates**) N-COUNT A **legate** is a person who is the official representative of another person, especially the Pope's official representative in a particular country. [FORMAL]

le|ga|tion /lɪgeɪʃən/ (**legations**) **1** N-COUNT [usu supp N] A **legation** is a group of government officials and diplomats who work in a foreign country and represent their government in that country. ❑ *...a member of the U.S. legation.* **2** N-COUNT A **legation** is the building in which a legation works.

leg|end /lɛdʒənd/ (**legends**) **1** N-VAR A **legend** is a very old and popular story that may be true. ❑ *...the legends of ancient Greece.* **2** N-COUNT If you refer to someone as a **legend**, you mean that they are very famous and admired by a lot of people. [APPROVAL] ❑ *...blues legends John Lee Hooker and B.B. King.*

leg|end|ary /lɛdʒənderi/ **1** ADJ If you describe someone or something as **legendary**, you mean that they are very famous and that many stories are told about them. ❑ *...the legendary Jazz singer Adelaide Hall.* **2** ADJ A **legendary** person, place, or event is mentioned or described in an old legend. ❑ *The hill is supposed to be the resting place of the legendary King Lud.*

leg|gings /lɛgɪŋz/ N-PLURAL [also a pair of N] **Leggings** are close-fitting pants, usually made out of a stretchy fabric. ❑ *She is wearing tight black leggings and a baggy green jersey.*

leg|gy /lɛgi/ (**leggier**, **leggiest**) ADJ If you describe someone as **leggy**, you mean that they have very long legs and usually that you find this attractive. ❑ *I am no tall, leggy blonde.*

leg|ible /lɛdʒɪbəl/ ADJ **Legible** writing is clear enough to read. ❑ *My handwriting isn't very legible.* ❑ *...a barely legible sign.*

le|gion /liːdʒən/ (**legions**) N-COUNT A **legion** is a large group of soldiers who form one section of an army. ❑ *...the commander of the Arab Legion.*

leg|is|late /lɛdʒɪsleɪt/ (**legislates**, **legislating**, **legislated**) V-T/V-I When a government or state **legislates**, it passes a new law. [FORMAL] ❑ *Most member countries have already legislated against excessive overtime.* ❑ *You cannot legislate to change attitudes.*

leg|is|la|tion ♦◊◊ /lɛdʒɪsleɪʃən/ N-UNCOUNT **Legislation** consists of a law or laws passed by a government. [FORMAL] ❑ *...a letter calling for legislation to protect women's rights.*

leg|is|la|tive /lɛdʒɪsleɪtɪv/ ADJ [ADJ n] **Legislative** means involving or relating to the process of making and passing laws. [FORMAL] ❑ *Today's hearing was just the first step in the legislative process.*

leg|is|la|tor /lɛdʒɪsleɪtər/ (**legislators**) N-COUNT A **legislator** is a person who is involved in making or passing laws. [FORMAL] ❑ *...an attempt to get U.S. legislators to change the system.*

leg|is|la|ture /lɛdʒɪsleɪtʃər/ (**legislatures**) N-COUNT The **legislature** of a particular state or country is the group of people in it who have the power to make and pass laws. [FORMAL] ❑ *The proposals before the legislature include the creation of two special courts to deal exclusively with violent crimes.*

le|git /lədʒɪt/ ADJ [usu v-link ADJ] If you describe a person or thing as **legit**, you mean that they are in accordance with

le|giti|mate /lɪdʒɪtɪmɪt/ **1** ADJ Something that is **legitimate** is acceptable according to the law. ❑ *The French government has condemned the coup in Haiti and has demanded the restoration of the legitimate government.* ● **le|giti|ma|cy** /lɪdʒɪtəmɪsi/ N-UNCOUNT ❑ *The opposition parties do not recognize the political legitimacy of his government.* ● **le|giti|mate|ly** ADV [ADV with v] ❑ *The government has been legitimately elected by the people.* **2** ADJ If you say that something such as a feeling or claim is **legitimate**, you think that it is reasonable and justified. ❑ *That's a perfectly legitimate fear.* ● **le|giti|ma|cy** N-UNCOUNT ❑ *Sampras beat Carl-Uwe Steeb by 6-1, 6-2, 6-1 to underline the legitimacy of his challenge for the title.* ● **le|giti|mate|ly** ADV [ADV with v] ❑ *They could quarrel quite legitimately with some of my choices.*

le|giti|mize /lɪdʒɪtɪmaɪz/ (legitimizes, legitimizing, legitimized) also **legitimatize**

in BRIT, also use **legitimise**

V-T To **legitimize** something, especially something bad, means to officially allow it, approve it, or make it seem acceptable. [FORMAL] ❑ *They will accept no agreement that legitimizes the ethnic division of the country.*

leg|room /lɛgrʊm/ also **leg room** N-UNCOUNT **Legroom** is the amount of space, especially in a car or other vehicle, that is available in front of your legs. ❑ *Tall drivers won't have enough legroom.*

leg|ume /lɛgyum, lɪgyum/ (legumes) **1** N-COUNT Some seeds that can be cooked and eaten are called **legumes**, for example, peas, beans, and lentils. [AM]

in BRIT, use **pulses**

2 → See feature box at **nutrition**

leg|work /lɛgwɜrk/ N-UNCOUNT You use **legwork** to refer to work that involves physical activity such as interviewing people or gathering information, especially when this work forms the basis of other, more intellectual work. ❑ *He assisted in unofficial ways with the routine legwork in various investigations.*

lei|sure /liʒər, lɛʒ-/ **1** N-UNCOUNT **Leisure** is the time when you are not working and you can relax and do things that you enjoy. ❑ *...a relaxing way to fill my leisure time.* **2** PHRASE If someone does something **at leisure** or **at their leisure**, they enjoy themselves by doing it when they want to, without hurrying. ❑ *You will be able to stroll at leisure through the gardens.*

lei|sured /liʒərd, lɛʒ-/ **1** ADJ [ADJ n] **Leisured** people are people who do not work, usually because they are rich. ❑ *...the leisured classes.* **2** ADJ **Leisured** activities are done in a relaxed way or do not involve work. ❑ *...this leisured life of reading and writing.*

lei|sure|ly /liʒərli, lɛʒ-/ ADJ A **leisurely** action is done in a relaxed and unhurried way. ❑ *Lunch was a leisurely affair.* ● ADV [ADV with v] **Leisurely** is also an adverb. ❑ *We walked leisurely into the hotel.*

leisure|wear /liʒərwɛər, lɛʒ-/ N-UNCOUNT **Leisurewear** is informal clothing which you wear when you are not working, for example, on weekends or on vacation. [WRITTEN] ❑ *Their range of leisurewear is aimed at fashion-conscious 13 to 25 year-olds.*

leit|mo|tif /laɪtmoʊtif/ (leitmotifs) also **leitmotiv** N-COUNT A **leitmotif** in something such as a book or movie or in a person's life is an idea or an object which occurs again and again. [FORMAL] ❑ *The title of one of Dietrich's best-known songs could serve as the leitmotif for her life.*

lem|ming /lɛmɪŋ/ (lemmings) **1** N-COUNT A **lemming** is an animal that looks like a large rat with thick fur. Lemmings live in cold northern regions and sometimes travel in very large numbers. **2** N-COUNT [usu pl] If you say that a large group of people are acting like **lemmings**, you are critical of them because they all follow each other into an action without thinking about it. [DISAPPROVAL] ❑ *You have to ask yourself why people line up, like lemmings, to take part in this peculiar sport.*

lem|on /lɛmən/ (lemons) N-VAR A **lemon** is a bright yellow fruit with very sour juice. Lemons grow on trees in warm countries. ❑ *...a slice of lemon.* ❑ *...oranges, lemons and other citrus fruits.*

VOCABULARY IN CONTEXT

Leisure pursuits

In Britain, the Victorian period was the first great age of leisure. Although conditions in the factories were hard by today's standards, the 1833 Factory Act cut back on working hours and established **public holidays**, leaving more time for leisure **pursuits** and **pastimes**.

Excursions and day trips to the beach or country became popular, as people escaped the pollution of the cities by **hiking**, fishing, or boating.

A better **standard of living** (itself a Victorian phrase) meant that the **middle class**, as well as their **spending** power, expanded. Richer people, who didn't have to do their own **time-consuming** housework, had plenty of time to take up the new sports invented in the Victorian period, such as lawn tennis and badminton. Shopping also became a **recreational** activity for the first time, as new department stores encouraged **browsing** and **window shopping**.

lem|on|ade /lɛməneɪd/ N-UNCOUNT **Lemonade** is a drink that is made from lemons, sugar, and water. ❑ *He was pouring ice and lemonade into tall glasses.*

lem|on curd N-UNCOUNT **Lemon curd** is a thick yellow food made from lemons. You spread it on bread or use it to fill cakes or pastries.

lem|on|grass /lɛməngræs/ N-UNCOUNT **Lemongrass** is a type of grass that grows in warm countries. It is used as a flavoring in food.

lem|ony /lɛməni/ ADJ Something that smells or tastes of lemons can be described as **lemony**.

lem|on yel|low also **lemon-yellow** COLOR **Lemon yellow** or **lemon** is used to describe things that are pale yellow in color.

le|mur /limər/ (lemurs) N-COUNT A **lemur** is an animal that looks like a small monkey and has a long tail and a face similar to that of a fox.

lend ♦◇◇ /lɛnd/ (lends, lending, lent) **1** V-T/V-I When people or organizations such as banks **lend** you money, they give it to you and you agree to pay it back at a future date, often with an extra amount as interest. ❑ *The bank is reassessing its criteria for lending money.* ❑ *The government will lend you money at incredible rates, between zero percent and 3 percent.* ● **lend|ing** N-UNCOUNT ❑ *...a financial institution that specializes in the lending of money.* **2** V-T If you **lend** something that you own, you allow someone to have it or use it for a period of time. ❑ *Will you lend me your jacket for a little while?* **3** V-T If you **lend** your support to someone or something, you help them with what they are doing or with a problem that they have. ❑ *He was approached by the organizers to lend support to a benefit concert.* **4** V-T If something **lends** itself to a particular activity or result, it is easy for it to be used for that activity or to achieve that result. ❑ *The room lends itself well to summer eating with its light, airy atmosphere.* **5** → see also **lent 6 to lend a hand** → see **hand** ①

SYNONYMS

lend
VERB **1**
loan: *He had kindly offered to loan us all the plants required for the exhibit.*
advance: *The bank advanced $1.2 billion to help the country with debt repayments.*

---

lend|er /lɛndər/ (lenders) N-COUNT A **lender** is a person or an institution that lends money to people. [BUSINESS] ❑ *...the six leading mortgage lenders.*

lend|ing li|brary (lending libraries) N-COUNT A **lending library** is a library from which the public are allowed to borrow books.

lend|ing rate (lending rates) N-COUNT The **lending rate** is the rate of interest that you have to pay when you are repaying a loan. [BUSINESS] ❑ *The bank left its lending rates unchanged.*

length ♦♦◊ /lɛŋθ/ (lengths) **1** N-VAR The **length** of something is the amount that it measures from one end to the other along the longest side. ❑ *It is about a meter in length.* ❑ *...the length of the fish.* **2** N-VAR The **length** of something such as a piece of writing is the amount of writing that is contained in it. ❑ *...a book of at least 100 pages in length.* **3** N-VAR The **length** of an event, activity, or situation is the period of time from beginning to end for which something lasts or during which something happens. ❑ *The exact length of each period may vary.* **4** N-COUNT A **length** of rope, cloth, wood, or other material is a piece of it that is intended to be used for a particular purpose or that exists in a particular situation. ❑ *...a 30 feet length of rope.* **5** N-UNCOUNT The **length** of something is its quality of being long. ❑ *Many have been surprised at the length of time it has taken him to make up his mind.* **6** → see also **full-length** **7** at arm's length → see arm ①

-length /-lɛŋθ/ **1** COMB IN ADJ **-length** combines with nouns to form adjectives that describe something that is of a certain length, or long enough to reach the point indicated by the noun. ❑ *...shoulder-length hair.* ❑ *...knee-length boots.* ❑ *...a feature-length film.* **2** → see also **full-length**

length|en /lɛŋθən/ (lengthens, lengthening, lengthened) **1** V-T/V-I When something **lengthens** or when you **lengthen** it, it increases in length. ❑ *The evening shadows were lengthening.* **2** V-T/V-I When something **lengthens** or when you **lengthen** it, it lasts for a longer time than it did previously. ❑ *Vacations have lengthened and the work week has shortened.*

length|wise /lɛŋθwaɪz/ also **lengthways** /lɛŋθweɪz/ ADV [ADV after v] **Lengthwise** or **lengthways** means in a direction or position along the length of something. ❑ *She tore off two sections of paper towel and folded them lengthwise.*

lengthy /lɛŋθi/ (lengthier, lengthiest) **1** ADJ You use **lengthy** to describe an event or process which lasts for a long time. ❑ *The board members held a lengthy meeting to decide future policy.* **2** ADJ A **lengthy** report, article, book, or document contains a lot of speech, writing, or other material. ❑ *Friedman's lengthy report quoted an unnamed source.*

le|ni|en|cy /liniənsi, linyən-/ N-UNCOUNT [oft N to/toward n] **Leniency** is a lenient attitude or lenient behavior. ❑ *The judge rejected pleas for leniency and sentenced him to a year in prison.*

le|ni|ent /liniənt, linyənt/ ADJ When someone in authority is **lenient**, they are not as strict or severe as expected. ❑ *He believes the government already is lenient with drug traffickers.* ● **le|ni|ent|ly** ADV [ADV after v] ❑ *Many people believe reckless drivers are treated too leniently.*

lens ♦◊◊ /lɛnz/ (lenses) **1** N-COUNT A **lens** is a thin curved piece of glass or plastic used in things such as cameras, telescopes, and pairs of glasses. You look through a lens in order to make things look larger, smaller, or clearer. ❑ *...a camera lens.* **2** N-COUNT In your eye, the **lens** is the part behind the pupil that focuses light and helps you to see clearly. ❑ *...degenerative changes in the lens of the eye.* **3** → see also **contact lens** **4** → See also color supplement

lent /lɛnt/ **Lent** is the past tense and past participle of **lend**.

Lent /lɛnt/ N-UNCOUNT **Lent** is the period of forty days before Easter, during which some Christians give up something that they enjoy.

len|til /lɛntɪl, -tᵊl/ (lentils) N-COUNT [usu pl] **Lentils** are the seeds of a lentil plant. They are usually dried and are used to make soups and stews.

Leo /liou/ (Leos) **1** N-UNCOUNT **Leo** is one of the twelve signs of the zodiac. Its symbol is a lion. People who are born between approximately the 23rd of July and the 22nd of August come under this sign. **2** N-COUNT A **Leo** is a person whose sign of the zodiac is Leo.

leo|nine /liənaɪn/ ADJ [usu ADJ n] **Leonine** means like a lion, and is used especially to describe men with a lot of hair on their head, or with big beards. [LITERARY] ❑ *...a tall leonine gray-haired man.*

leop|ard /lɛpərd/ (leopards) N-COUNT A **leopard** is a type of large, wild cat. Leopards have yellow fur and black spots, and live in Africa and Asia.

leo|tard /liətɑrd/ (leotards) N-COUNT A **leotard** is a tight-fitting piece of clothing, covering the body but not the legs, that some people wear when they practice dancing or do exercise.

lep|er /lɛpər/ (lepers) **1** N-COUNT **Leper** is an old-fashioned and offensive word for a person who has leprosy. **2** N-COUNT If you refer to someone as a **leper**, you mean that people in their community avoid them because they have done something that has shocked or offended people. ❑ *The newspaper article had branded her a social leper not fit to be seen in company.*

lep|re|chaun /lɛprəkɒn/ (leprechauns) N-COUNT In Irish folklore, a **leprechaun** is an imaginary creature that looks like a little old man. ❑ *You could search forever in Ireland, but you'd never find a leprechaun.*

lep|ro|sy /lɛprəsi/ N-UNCOUNT **Leprosy** is an infectious disease that damages people's flesh.

les|bian ♦◊◊ /lɛzbiən/ (lesbians) ADJ **Lesbian** is used to describe gay women. ❑ *...a woman who had contacts in the homosexual and lesbian community.* ● N-COUNT A **lesbian** is a woman who is lesbian. ❑ *...a youth group for lesbians and bisexuals.*

les|bi|an|ism /lɛzbiənɪzəm/ N-UNCOUNT **Lesbianism** refers to homosexual relationships between women or the preference that a woman shows for sexual relationships with women. ❑ *...today's increased public awareness of lesbianism.*

le|sion /liʒᵊn/ (lesions) N-COUNT A **lesion** is an injury or wound to someone's body. [MEDICAL] ❑ *...skin lesions.*

less ♦♦♦ /lɛs/

> **Less** is often considered to be the comparative form of **little**.

1 DET You use **less** to indicate that there is a smaller amount of something than before or than average. You can use 'a little,' 'a lot,' 'a bit,' 'far,' and 'much' in front of **less**. ❑ *People should eat less fat to reduce the risk of heart disease.* ❑ *...a dishwasher that uses less water and electricity than older machines.* ● PRON **Less** is also a pronoun. ❑ *Borrowers are striving to ease their financial position by spending less and saving more.* ● QUANT **Less** is also a quantifier. ❑ *Last year less of the money went into high-technology companies.* **2** PHRASE You use **less than** before a number or amount to say that the actual number or amount is smaller than this. ❑ *...a country whose entire population is less than 12 million.* **3** ADV You use **less** to indicate that something or someone has a smaller amount of a quality than they used to or than is average or usual. ❑ *I often think about those less fortunate than me.* ❑ *Other amenities, less commonly available, include a library and exercise room.* **4** ADV If you say that something is **less** one thing than another, you mean that it is like the second thing rather than the first. ❑ *At first sight it looked less like a capital city than a mining camp.* **5** ADV [ADV with v] If you do something **less** than before or **less** than someone else, you do it to a smaller extent or not as often. ❑ *We are eating more and exercising less.* **6** PREP When you are referring to amounts, you use **less** in front of a number or quantity to indicate that it is to be subtracted from another number or quantity already mentioned. ❑ *You will pay between ten and twenty five percent, less tax.* **7** PHRASE You use **less than** to say that something does not have a particular quality. For example, if you describe something as **less than** perfect, you mean that it is not perfect at all. [EMPHASIS] ❑ *Her greeting was less than enthusiastic.* **8** couldn't care less → see care **9** more or less → see more

lessee

SUFFIX

-less forms adjectives that indicate that someone or something does not have a particular thing. *For example, someone who is jobless does not have a job.*

les|see /lɛsi/ (lessees) N-COUNT A **lessee** is a person who has taken out a lease on something such as a house or piece of land. [LEGAL]

less|en /lɛsᵊn/ (lessens, lessening, lessened) V-T/V-I If something **lessens** or you **lessen** it, it becomes smaller in size, amount, degree, or importance. ❏ *He is used to a lot of attention from his wife, which will inevitably lessen when the baby is born.* • **less|en|ing** N-UNCOUNT ❏ *...increased trade and a lessening of tension on the border.*

less|er /lɛsər/ ■ ADJ [ADJ n, the ADJ of n] You use **lesser** in order to indicate that something is smaller in extent, degree, or amount than another thing that has been mentioned. ❏ *No medication works in isolation but is affected to a greater or lesser extent by many other factors.* • ADV [ADV -ed] *Lesser* is also an adverb. ❏ *...lesser known works by famous artists.* ❷ ADJ [ADJ n, the ADJ of n] You can use **lesser** to refer to something or someone that is less important than other things or people of the same type. ❏ *They pleaded guilty to lesser charges of criminal damage.* ❸ **the lesser of two evils** → see **evil**

les|son ♦⟨⟩ /lɛsᵊn/ (lessons) ■ N-COUNT A **lesson** is a fixed period of time when people are taught about a particular subject or taught how to do something. ❏ *It would be his last French lesson for months.* ❷ N-COUNT You use **lesson** to refer to an experience which acts as a warning to you or an example from which you should learn. ❏ *There's still one lesson to be learned from the crisis – we all need to better understand the thinking of the other side.* • PHRASE If you say that you are going to **teach** someone **a lesson**, you mean that you are going to punish them for something that they have done so that they do not do it again.

COLLOCATIONS

lesson
NOUN
■
noun + **lesson**: driving, English, piano, swimming
adjective + **lesson**: compulsory, free, private; one-hour
verb + **lesson**: give, offer
❷
noun + **lesson**: life
adjective + **lesson**: hard, harsh; important, salutary, valuable
verb + **lesson**: learn; teach

les|sor /lɛsɔr/ (lessors) N-COUNT A **lessor** is a person who owns something such as a house or piece of land and leases it to someone else. [LEGAL]

lest /lɛst/ CONJ If you do something **lest** something unpleasant should happen, you do it to try to prevent the unpleasant thing from happening. [FORMAL] ❏ *I was afraid to open the door lest he should follow me.* ❏ *And, lest we forget, Einstein wrote his most influential papers while working as a clerk.*

let ♦♦♦ /lɛt/ (lets, letting)

> The form **let** is used in the present tense and is the past tense and past participle.

■ V-T If you **let** something happen, you allow it to happen without doing anything to stop or prevent it. ❏ *People said we were interfering with nature, and that we should just let the animals die.* ❏ *I can't let myself be distracted by those things.* ❷ V-T If you **let** someone do something, you give them your permission to do it. ❏ *I love candy but Mom doesn't let me have it very often.* ❸ V-T If you **let** a person or an animal into, out of, or through a place, you allow them to enter, leave, or go through it, for example, by opening a door or making room for them. ❏ *I had to let them into the building because they had lost their keys.* ❹ V-T [only imper] You use **let me** when you are introducing something you want to say. ❏ *Let me tell you what I saw last night.* ❏ *Let me explain why.* ❺ V-T [only imper] You use **let me** when you are offering politely to do something. [POLITENESS] ❏ *Let me take your coat.* ❻ V-T [only imper] You say **let's** or, in more formal English, **let**

742

let

us, to direct the attention of the people you are talking to toward the subject that you want to consider next. ❏ *Let us look at these views in more detail.* ❼ V-T [only imper] You say **let's** or, in formal English, **let us**, when you are making a suggestion that involves both you and the person you are talking to, or when you are agreeing to a suggestion of this kind. ❏ *I'm bored. Let's go home.* ❽ V-T [only imper] Someone in authority, such as a teacher, can use **let's** or, in more formal English, **let us**, in order to give a polite instruction to another person or group of people. [POLITENESS] ❏ *Let's have some quiet, please.* ❾ V-T [only imper] You can use **let** when you are saying what you think someone should do, usually when they are behaving in a way that you think is unreasonable or wrong. ❏ *Let him get his own cup of tea.* ❿ V-T If you **let** your house or land to someone, you allow them to use it in exchange for money that they pay you regularly. [mainly BRIT]

> in AM, use **rent**

• PHRASAL VERB **Let out** means the same as **let**. ❏ *I couldn't sell the apartment, so I let it out.* ⓫ PHRASE **Let alone** is used after a statement, usually a negative one, to indicate that the statement is even more true of the person, thing, or situation that you are going to mention next. [EMPHASIS] ❏ *It is incredible that the 12-year-old managed to even reach the pedals, let alone drive the car.* ⓬ PHRASE If you **let go** of someone or something, you stop holding them. ❏ *She let go of Mona's hand and took a sip of her drink.* ⓭ PHRASE If you **let** someone or something **go**, you allow them to leave or escape. ❏ *They held him for three hours and they let him go.* ⓮ PHRASE When someone leaves a job, either because they are told to or because they want to, the employer sometimes says that they are **letting** that person **go**. [BUSINESS] ❏ *I've assured him I have no plans to let him go.* ⓯ PHRASE If you say that you did not know what you were **letting** yourself **in for** when you decided to do something, you mean you did not realize how difficult, unpleasant, or expensive it was going to be. ❏ *He got the impression that Miss Hawes had no idea of what she was letting herself in for.* ⓰ PHRASE If you **let** someone **know** something, you tell them about it or make sure that they know about it. ❏ *They want to let them know that they are safe.* ⓱ **to let fly** → see **fly** ⓲ **to let your hair down** → see **hair** ⓳ **to let someone off the hook** → see **hook** ⓴ **to let it be known** → see **known**

▶ **let down** ■ PHRASAL VERB If you **let** someone **down**, you disappoint them, by not doing something that you have said you will do or that they expected you to do. ❏ *Don't worry, Xiao, I won't let you down.* • **let down** ADJ [v-link ADJ] ❏ *The company now has a large number of workers who feel badly let down.* ❷ PHRASAL VERB If something **lets** you **down**, it is the reason you are not as successful as you could have been. ❏ *Many believe it was his shyness and insecurity which let him down.*

▶ **let in** PHRASAL VERB If an object **lets in** something such as air, light, or water, it allows air, light, or water to get into it, for example, because the object has a hole in it. ❏ *...balconies shaded with lattice-work which lets in air but not light.*

▶ **let off** ■ PHRASAL VERB If someone in authority **lets** you **off** a task or duty, they give you permission not to do it. ❏ *I realized that having a new baby lets you off going to boring dinner parties.* ❷ PHRASAL VERB If you **let** someone **off**, you give them a lighter punishment than they expect or no punishment at all. ❏ *Because he was a Christian, the judge let him off.* ❸ PHRASAL VERB If you **let off** an explosive or a gun, you explode or fire it. ❏ *A resident of his neighborhood had let off fireworks to celebrate the revolution.*

▶ **let on** PHRASAL VERB If you do not **let on** that something is true, you do not tell anyone that it is true, and you keep it a secret. [INFORMAL] ❏ *She never let on that anything was wrong.* ❏ *I didn't let on to the staff what my conversation was.* ❏ *He knows the culprit but is not letting on.*

▶ **let out** ■ PHRASAL VERB If something or someone **lets** water, air, or breath **out**, they allow it to flow out or escape. ❏ *It lets sunlight in but doesn't let heat out.* ❷ PHRASAL VERB If you **let out** a particular sound, you make that sound. [WRITTEN] ❏ *When she saw him, she let out a cry of horror.* ❸ PHRASAL VERB If you **let out** a dress or pair of pants, you make it larger by undoing the seams and sewing closer to the edge of the material. ❏ *I'll have to let this dress out a bit before the wedding next week.* ❹ → see also **let 10**

▶ **let up** PHRASAL VERB If an unpleasant, continuous process **lets up**, it stops or becomes less intense. ❏ *The traffic in this city never lets up, even at night.*

SYNONYMS

let
VERB **2**
allow: *Smoking will not be allowed.*
grant: *Permission was granted a few weeks ago.*
permit: *He can let the court's decision stand and permit the execution.*
authorize: *We are willing to authorize the President to use force if necessary.*

---

let-down (**let-downs**) also **letdown** N-VAR A **let-down** is a disappointment that you suffer, usually because something has not happened in the way in which you expected it to happen. ❏ *The band's performance that night at the Seattle Center Coliseum was a letdown.* ❏ *The sense of let-down today is all the greater because in the past doctors have been over-confident about these treatments.*

le|thal /liːθəl/ **1** ADJ A substance that is **lethal** can kill people or animals. ❏ *...a lethal dose of sleeping pills.* **2** ADJ If you describe something as **lethal**, you mean that it is capable of causing a lot of damage. ❏ *Amorality and intelligence is probably the most lethal combination to be found within one personality.*

le|thar|gic /lɪθɑːrdʒɪk/ ADJ If you are **lethargic**, you do not have much energy or enthusiasm. ❏ *He felt too miserable and lethargic to get dressed.*

leth|ar|gy /lɛθərdʒi/ N-UNCOUNT **Lethargy** is the condition or state of being lethargic. ❏ *Symptoms include tiredness, paleness, and lethargy.*

let's ◆◇◇ /lɛts/ **Let's** is the usual spoken form of 'let us.'

let|ter ◆◆◆ /lɛtər/ (**letters, lettering, lettered**) **1** N-COUNT [also by N] If you write a **letter** to someone, you write a message on paper and send it to them, usually through the mail. ❏ *I had received a letter from a very close friend.* ❏ *...a letter of resignation.* **2** N-COUNT **Letters** are written symbols which represent one of the sounds in a language. ❏ *...the letters of the alphabet.* **3** V-I If a student **letters** in sports or athletics by being part of the university or college team, they are entitled to wear on their jacket the initial letter of the name of their university or college. [AM] ❏ *Burkoth lettered in soccer.* **4** → see also **covering letter, newsletter**

COLLOCATIONS

letter
NOUN **1**
noun + **letter**: reference, rejection, resignation, warning; love, thank-you
adjective + **letter**: anonymous, handwritten, open

---

let|ter bomb (**letter bombs**) N-COUNT A **letter bomb** is a small bomb which is disguised as a letter or package and sent to someone through the mail. It is designed to explode when it is opened.

let|ter|box /lɛtərbɒks/ (**letterboxes**) also **letter box** **1** N-COUNT A **letterbox** is a rectangular hole in a door or a small box at the entrance to a building into which letters and small packages are delivered. Compare **postbox**. [mainly BRIT]

in AM, usually use **mailbox**

2 ADJ If something is displayed on a television or computer screen in **letterbox** format, it is displayed across the middle of the screen with dark bands at the top and bottom of the screen.

let|ter car|ri|er (**letter carriers**) N-COUNT A **letter carrier** is a person whose job is to collect and deliver letters and parcels that are sent by mail. [AM]

let|tered /lɛtərd/ ADJ Something that is **lettered** is covered or decorated with letters or words. ❏ *...a crudely lettered cardboard sign.*

let|ter|head /lɛtərhɛd/ (**letterheads**) N-COUNT A **letterhead** is the name and address of a person, company, or organization which is printed at the top of their writing paper. ❏ *Colleagues at work enjoy having a letterhead with their name at the top.*

let|ter|ing /lɛtərɪŋ/ N-UNCOUNT **Lettering** is writing, especially when you are describing the type of letters used. ❏ *...a small blue sign with white lettering.*

let|ter of cred|it (**letters of credit**) **1** N-COUNT A **letter of credit** is a letter written by a bank authorizing another bank to pay someone a sum of money. Letters of credit are often used by importers and exporters. [BUSINESS] **2** N-COUNT A **letter of credit** is a written promise from a bank stating that they will repay bonds to lenders if the borrowers are unable to pay them. [BUSINESS] ❏ *The project is being backed by a letter of credit from Lasalle Bank.*

let|tuce /lɛtɪs/ (**lettuces**) N-VAR A **lettuce** is a plant with large green leaves that is the basic ingredient of many salads.

let-up N-UNCOUNT [also *a* N, usu with brd-neg] If there is no **let-up** in something, usually something unpleasant, there is no reduction in the intensity of it. ❏ *There was no let-up in the battle on the money markets yesterday.*

leu|ke|mia /luːkiːmiə/

in BRIT, use **leukaemia**

N-UNCOUNT **Leukemia** is a disease of the blood in which the body produces too many white blood cells.

levee /lɛvi/ (**levees**) N-COUNT A **levee** is a raised bank alongside a river. [AM] ❏ *Water poured over a levee and flooded about 75 percent of Montegut.*

lev|el ◆◆◆ /lɛvəl/ (**levels, leveling** or **levelling, leveled** or **levelled**) **1** N-COUNT A **level** is a point on a scale, for example, a scale of amount, quality, or difficulty. ❏ *If you don't know your cholesterol level, it's a good idea to have it checked.* ❏ *We do have the lowest level of inflation for some years.* **2** N-SING The **level** of a river, lake, or ocean or the **level** of liquid in a container is the height of its surface. ❏ *The water level of the Mississippi River is already 6.5 feet below normal.* **3** → see also **sea level** **4** N-SING If something is at a particular **level**, it is at that height. ❏ *Liz sank down until the water came up to her chin and the bubbles were at eye level.* **5** N-COUNT A **level** of a building is one of its different stories, which is situated above or below other stories. ❏ *Thurlow and Brown's rooms were on the second level, to the rear of the building.* **6** N-COUNT A **level** is a device for testing to see if a surface is level. It consists of a plastic, wood, or metal frame containing a glass tube of liquid with an air bubble in it. [AM] **7** ADJ [v-link ADJ] If one thing is **level** with another thing, it is at the same height as it. ❏ *He leaned over the counter so his face was almost level with the boy's.* **8** ADJ When something is **level**, it is completely flat with no part higher than any other. ❏ *The floor was level, but the ceiling sloped toward his head.* **9** ADV [ADV after v] If you draw **level** with someone or something, you get closer to them until you are by their side. ❏ *Just before we drew level with the gates, he slipped out of the jeep and disappeared.* • ADJ [v-link ADJ] **Level** is also an adjective. ❏ *He waited until they were level with the door before he turned more sharply.* **10** V-T If someone or something such as a violent storm **levels** a building or area of land, they destroy it completely or make it completely flat. ❏ *The storm was the most powerful to hit Hawaii this century. It leveled sugar plantations and destroyed homes.* **11** V-T If an accusation or criticism is **leveled** at someone, they are accused of doing wrong or they are criticized for something they have done. ❏ *Allegations of corruption were leveled at him and his family.* **12 a level playing field** → see **playing field** **13** → See also color supplement
▶ **level off** also **level out** **1** PHRASAL VERB If a changing number or amount **levels off** or **levels out**, it stops increasing or decreasing at such a fast speed. ❏ *The figures show evidence that murders in the nation's capital are beginning to level off.* **2** PHRASAL VERB If an aircraft **levels off** or **levels out**, it travels horizontally after having been traveling in an upward or downward direction. ❏ *The aircraft leveled out at about 30,000 feet.*

lev|el cross|ing (**level crossings**) N-COUNT A **level crossing** is a place where a railroad track crosses a road at the same level. [BRIT]

in AM, use **grade crossing**

lev|el|er /lɛvələr/ (**levelers**) also **leveller** N-COUNT [usu sing, oft adj N] If you describe something as a **leveler**, you mean that it makes all people seem the same, in spite of their differences in, for example, age or social status. ☐ *But the war has been a great leveler. Everyone is equal because everyone is poor.*

level-headed ADJ If you describe a person as **level-headed**, you mean that they are calm and sensible even in difficult situations. ☐ *Simon is level-headed and practical.* ☐ *His level-headed approach suggests he will do what is necessary.*

lev|er /lɛvər, lɛv-/ (**levers, levering, levered**) **1** N-COUNT A **lever** is a handle or bar that is attached to a piece of machinery and which you push or pull in order to operate the machinery. ☐ *Push the tiny lever on the lock and let the door lock itself.* **2** → see also **gear lever 3** N-COUNT A **lever** is a long bar, one end of which is placed under a heavy object so that when you press down on the other end you can move the object. ☐ *He examined the machine, worked a lever that lifted the lid.* **4** V-T If you **lever** something in a particular direction, you move it there, especially by using a lot of effort. ☐ *Neighbors eventually levered open the door with a crowbar.*

lev|er|age /lɛvərɪdʒ/ (**leverages, leveraging, leveraged**) **1** N-UNCOUNT **Leverage** is the ability to influence situations or people so that you can control what happens. ☐ *His position as mayor gives him leverage to get things done.* **2** V-T To **leverage** a company or investment means to use borrowed money in order to buy it or pay for it. [BUSINESS] ☐ *He might feel that leveraging the company at a time when he sees tremendous growth opportunities would be a mistake.*

le|via|than /lɪvaɪəθən/ (**leviathans**) N-COUNT [usu sing] A **leviathan** is something which is extremely large and difficult to control, and which you find rather frightening. [LITERARY] ☐ *Democracy survived the Civil War and the developing industrial leviathan and struggled on into the twentieth century.*

Levi's /liːvaɪz/ also **Levis** N-PLURAL [also a pair of N] **Levi's** are a type of jeans. [TRADEMARK]

levi|tate /lɛvɪteɪt/ (**levitates, levitating, levitated**) V-T/V-I If someone or something **levitates**, they appear to rise and float in the air without any support from other people or objects. ☐ *He has claimed he can levitate.* ☐ *Nina can, apparently, levitate a small ball between her hands.* • **levi|ta|tion** /lɛvɪteɪʃən/ N-UNCOUNT ☐ *...such magical powers as levitation, prophecy, and healing.*

lev|ity /lɛvɪti/ N-UNCOUNT **Levity** is behavior that shows a tendency to treat serious matters in a nonserious way. [LITERARY] ☐ *At the time, Arnold had disapproved of such levity.*

levy /lɛvi/ (**levies, levying, levied**) **1** N-COUNT A **levy** is a sum of money that you have to pay, for example, as a tax to the government. ☐ *...an annual levy on all drivers.* **2** V-T If a government or organization **levies** a tax or other sum of money, it demands it from people or organizations. ☐ *They levied religious taxes on Christian commercial transactions.*

lewd /luːd/ ADJ If you describe someone's behavior as **lewd**, you are critical of it because it is sexual in a rude and unpleasant way. [DISAPPROVAL] ☐ *Drew spends all day eyeing the women and making lewd comments.* • **lewd|ness** N-UNCOUNT ☐ *The critics condemned the play for lewdness.*

lexi|cal /lɛksɪkəl/ ADJ [usu ADJ n] **Lexical** means relating to the words of a language. ☐ *We chose a few of the commonest lexical items in the languages.*

lexi|cog|ra|phy /lɛksɪkɒgrəfi/ N-UNCOUNT **Lexicography** is the activity or profession of writing dictionaries. • **lexi|cog|ra|pher** (**lexicographers**) N-COUNT ☐ *A lexicographer's job is to describe the language.*

lexi|con /lɛksɪkɒn, -kən/ (**lexicons**) **1** N-SING [with supp] The **lexicon** of a particular subject is all the terms associated with it. The **lexicon** of a person or group is all the words they commonly use. ☐ *...the lexicon of management.* ☐ *Chocolate equals sin in most people's lexicon.* **2** N-COUNT A **lexicon** is an alphabetical list of the words in a language or the words associated with a particular subject.

lex|is /lɛksɪs/ N-UNCOUNT In linguistics, the words of a language can be referred to as the **lexis** of that language. [TECHNICAL]

LGBT /ɛl dʒi bi ti/ **LGBT** is an abbreviation for 'lesbian, gay, bisexual, and transgender.'

LGBTI /ɛl dʒi bi ti aɪ/ **LGBTI** is an abbreviation for 'lesbian, gay, bisexual, transgender, and intersex.'

LGBTQ+ /ɛl dʒi bi ti kyu plʌs/ **LGBTQ+** is an abbreviation for lesbian, gay, bisexual, transgender, and queer (or questioning), plus other sexual and gender identities.

lia|bil|ity /laɪəbɪlɪti/ (**liabilities**) **1** N-COUNT If you say that someone or something is a **liability**, you mean that they cause a lot of problems or embarrassment. ☐ *As the president's prestige continues to fall, they're clearly beginning to consider him a liability.* **2** N-COUNT A company's or organization's **liabilities** are the sums of money which it owes. [BUSINESS OR LEGAL] ☐ *The company had assets of $138 million and liabilities of $120.5 million.* **3** → see also **liable**

lia|ble /laɪəbəl/ **1** PHRASE When something **is liable to** happen, it is very likely to happen. ☐ *When challenged about his behavior, David was liable to dissolve in tears.* **2** ADJ [v-link ADJ to n] If people or things are **liable to** something unpleasant, they are likely to experience it or do it. ☐ *She will grow into a woman particularly liable to depression.* **3** ADJ [v-link ADJ] If you are **liable** for something such as a debt, you are legally responsible for it. ☐ *The airline's insurer is liable for damages to the victims' families.* • **lia|bil|ity** N-UNCOUNT ☐ *The company does not accept liability for fragile, valuable or perishable articles.*

li|aise /lieɪz/ (**liaises, liaising, liaised**) V-RECIP When organizations or people **liaise**, or when one organization **liaises** with another, they work together and keep each other informed about what is happening. [mainly BRIT] ☐ *Detectives are liaising with police following the bomb explosion early today.*

liai|son /lieɪzɒn/ (**liaisons**) **1** N-UNCOUNT **Liaison** is cooperation and the exchange of information between different organizations or between different sections of an organization. ☐ *Liaison between police forces and the art world is vital to combat art crime.* **2** N-VAR [also a N, oft N with n] If someone acts as **liaison** with a particular group, or between two or more groups, their job is to encourage co-operation and the exchange of information. ☐ *He is acting as liaison with the film crew.* ☐ *She acts as a liaison between patients and staff.*

liar /laɪər/ (**liars**) **1** N-COUNT If you say that someone is a **liar**, you mean that they tell lies. ☐ *He was a liar and a cheat.* **2** → See feature box at **truth**

lib /lɪb/ **1** N-UNCOUNT **Lib** is used in the names of some movements that are concerned with achieving social and legal freedom for particular groups in society. **Lib** is an abbreviation for **liberation**. ☐ *...Women's Lib.* **2** → see also **ad-lib**

li|ba|tion /laɪbeɪʃən/ (**libations**) N-COUNT In ancient Greece and Rome, a **libation** was an alcoholic drink that was offered to the gods. [LITERARY]

li|bel /laɪbəl/ (**libels, libeling** or **libelling, libeled** or **libelled**) **1** N-VAR **Libel** is a written statement which wrongly accuses someone of something, and which is therefore against the law. Compare **slander**. [LEGAL] ☐ *Warren sued him for libel over the remarks.* **2** V-T To **libel** someone means to write or print something in a book, newspaper, or magazine which wrongly damages that person's reputation and is therefore against the law. [LEGAL] ☐ *The newspaper which libeled him had already offered compensation.*

li|bel|ous /laɪbələs/ also **libellous** ADJ If a statement in a book, newspaper, or magazine is **libelous**, it wrongly accuses someone of something, and is therefore against the law. ☐ *...stories that are inaccurate or outright libelous.*

lib|er|al /lɪbərəl, lɪbrəl/ (**liberals**) **1** ADJ Someone who has **liberal** views believes people should have a lot of freedom in deciding how to behave and think. ☐ *He has liberal views on immigration and the environment.* • N-COUNT **Liberal** is also a noun. ☐ *...a nation of free-thinking liberals.* **2** ADJ A **liberal** system allows people or organizations a lot of political or economic freedom. ☐ *...a liberal democracy with a multiparty political system.* • N-COUNT **Liberal** is also a noun. ☐ *These kinds of price controls go against all the financial principles of the free market liberals.* **3** ADJ [ADJ n] A **Liberal** politician or voter is a member of a Liberal Party or votes for a Liberal Party. ☐ *She withdrew because she did not wish to split the Liberal vote.* • N-COUNT **Liberal** is also a noun. ☐ *The Liberals hold twenty-three seats.* **4** ADJ **Liberal** means giving, using, or taking a lot of something, or existing in large quantities. ☐ *As always he is liberal with his jokes.* • **lib|er|al|ly** ADV [ADV with v] ☐ *Chemical products were used liberally over agricultural land.*

lib|er|al arts N-PLURAL At a university or college, **liberal arts** courses are on subjects such as history or literature rather than science, law, medicine, or business. [AM]

lib|er|al|ism /lɪbərəlɪzəm, lɪbrəl-/ **1** N-UNCOUNT **Liberalism** is a belief in gradual social progress by changing laws, rather than by revolution. ❑ ...*a democrat who has decided that economic liberalism is the best way to secure change.* ❑ ...*the tradition of nineteenth-century liberalism.* **2** N-UNCOUNT **Liberalism** is the belief that people should have a lot of political and individual freedom. ❑ *He was concerned over growing liberalism in the church.*

lib|er|al|ize /lɪbərəlaɪz, lɪbrəl-/ (**liberalizes**, **liberalizing**, **liberalized**)

> in BRIT, also use **liberalise**

V-T/V-I When a country or government **liberalizes**, or **liberalizes** its laws or its attitudes, it becomes less strict and allows people more freedom in their actions. ❑ ...*authoritarian states that have only now begun to liberalize.* • **lib|er|ali|za|tion** /lɪbərəlɪzeɪʃən, lɪbrəl-/ N-UNCOUNT ❑ ...*the liberalization of divorce laws in the late 1960s.*

lib|er|ate ♦◇◇ /lɪbəreɪt/ (**liberates**, **liberating**, **liberated**) **1** V-T To **liberate** a place or the people in it means to free them from the political or military control of another country, area, or group of people. ❑ *They planned to march on and liberate the city.* • **lib|era|tion** /lɪbəreɪʃən/ N-UNCOUNT ❑ ...*a mass liberation movement.* **2** V-T To **liberate** someone from something means to help them escape from it or overcome it, and lead a better way of life. ❑ *He asked how committed the leadership was to liberating its people from poverty.* • **lib|er|at|ing** ADJ ❑ *If you have the chance to spill your problems out to a therapist it can be a very liberating experience.* • **lib|era|tion** N-UNCOUNT ❑ ...*the women's liberation movement.*

> **SYNONYMS**
>
> **liberate**
> VERB **2**
> **free:** *They are set to free more prisoners.*
> **set free:** *Most of the prisoners were set free.*
> **rescue:** *He had rescued her from a horrible life.*
> **let out:** *I'd better go and let the dog out.*
> **release:** *He was released from custody the next day.*

lib|er|at|ed /lɪbəreɪtɪd/ ADJ If you describe someone as **liberated**, you mean that they do not accept their society's traditional values or restrictions on behavior. [APPROVAL] ❑ *She was determined that she would become a liberated businesswoman.*

lib|era|tion theo|ol|ogy N-UNCOUNT **Liberation theology** is the belief that the Christian Church should be actively involved in politics in order to bring about social change.

lib|era|tor /lɪbəreɪtər/ (**liberators**) N-COUNT A **liberator** is someone who sets people free from a system, situation, or set of ideas that restricts them in some way. [FORMAL] ❑ *For some people, the operation is a liberator from years of pain and discomfort.*

Li|berian /laɪbɪəriən/ (**Liberians**) **1** ADJ **Liberian** means belonging or relating to Liberia, its people, or its culture. **2** N-COUNT A **Liberian** is a person who comes from Liberia, or a person of Liberian origin.

lib|er|tar|ian /lɪbərtɛəriən/ (**libertarians**) ADJ If someone is **libertarian** or has **libertarian** attitudes, they believe in or support the idea that people should be free to think and behave in the way that they want. [FORMAL] ❑ ...*the libertarian argument that people should be allowed to choose.* • N-COUNT A **libertarian** is someone with libertarian views. ❑ *Libertarians argue that nothing should be censored.*

lib|er|tine /lɪbərtin/ (**libertines**) N-COUNT If you refer to someone as a **libertine**, you mean that they are sexually immoral and do not care about the effect their behavior has on other people. [LITERARY, DISAPPROVAL]

lib|er|ty ♦◇◇ /lɪbərti/ (**liberties**) **1** N-VAR **Liberty** is the freedom to live your life in the way that you want, without interference from other people or the authorities. ❑ ...*the ideal of equality and the appreciation of liberty.* **2** N-UNCOUNT **Liberty** is the freedom to go wherever you want, which you lose when you are a prisoner. ❑ *Why not say that three convictions before court for stealing cars means three months' loss of liberty.* **3** PHRASE If someone is **at liberty** to do something, they have been given permission to do it. ❑ *The island's in the Pacific Ocean; I'm not at liberty to say exactly where, because we're still negotiating for its purchase.* **4** → See feature box at **prison**

> **SYNONYMS**
>
> **liberty**
> NOUN **1**
> **freedom:** *They want greater political freedom.*
> **emancipation:** *They fought for the emancipation of women.*
> **independence:** *In 1816, Argentina declared its independence from Spain.*

li|bidi|nous /lɪbɪdənəs/ ADJ People who are **libidinous** have strong sexual feelings and express them in their behavior. [LITERARY] ❑ *Anderson let his libidinous imagination run away with him.*

li|bi|do /lɪbidoʊ/ (**libidos**) N-VAR A person's **libido** is the part of their personality that is considered to cause their emotional, especially sexual, desires. ❑ *Lack of sleep is a major factor in loss of libido.*

Li|bra /librə/ (**Libras**) **1** N-UNCOUNT **Libra** is one of the twelve signs of the zodiac. Its symbol is a pair of scales. People who are born between approximately the 23rd of September and the 22nd of October come under this sign. **2** N-COUNT A **Libra** is a person whose sign of the zodiac is Libra. ❑ *My brother-in-law is a Libra.*

li|brar|ian /laɪbrɛəriən/ (**librarians**) N-COUNT A **librarian** is a person who is in charge of a library or who has been specially trained to work in a library. ❑ *The new librarian is a friend of mine.*

li|brary ♦◇◇ /laɪbrɛri/ (**libraries**) **1** N-COUNT A public **library** is a building where things such as books, newspapers, and music are kept for people to read, use, or borrow. ❑ ...*the local library.* **2** N-COUNT A private **library** is a collection of things such as books or music, that is normally only used with the permission of the owner. ❑ *The company owns a very diverse library of Arabic music.* **3** N-COUNT A **library** is a public building or a room, for example in a school or hospital, where things such as books, newspapers, videos, and music are kept for people to read, use, or borrow. **4** N-COUNT In some large houses the **library** is the room where most of the books are kept. ❑ *Guests were rarely entertained in the library.*

li|bret|tist /lɪbrɛtɪst/ (**librettists**) N-COUNT A **librettist** is a person who writes the words that are used in an opera or musical play.

li|bret|to /lɪbrɛtoʊ/ (**librettos** or **libretti**) N-COUNT The **libretto** of an opera is the words that are sung in it. ❑ ...*the author of one or two opera librettos.*

Liby|an /lɪbiən/ (**Libyans**) **1** ADJ **Libyan** means belonging or relating to Libya, or to its people or culture. **2** N-COUNT A **Libyan** is a Libyan citizen, or a person of Libyan origin.

lice /laɪs/ **Lice** is the plural of **louse**.

li|cence /laɪsəns/ [BRIT] → see **license**

li|cense ♦◇◇ /laɪsəns/ (**licenses**, **licensing**, **licensed**)

> in BRIT, use **licence** for meanings **1** and **2**

1 N-COUNT A **license** is an official document which gives you permission to do, use, or own something. ❑ *The judge fined the man and suspended his license.* ❑ *The company has applied to the FDA for a license to sell the drug.* **2** N-UNCOUNT [also a N, N to-inf] If you say that something gives someone **license** or a **license** to act in a particular way, you mean that it gives them an excuse to behave in an irresponsible or excessive way. [DISAPPROVAL] ❑ *Partition would give license to other aggressors in other conflicts.* **3** V-T To **license** a person or activity means to give official permission for the person to do something or for the activity to take place. ❑ ...*a proposal that would require the state to license guns the way it does cars.*

> **COLLOCATIONS**
>
> **license**
> NOUN **1**
> *noun* + **license**: banking, driver's, fishing; marriage; exploration, export, firearms
> *adjective* + **license**: provisional; invalid, valid
> *verb* + **license**: award, grant, issue, renew; revoke, suspend; obtain, require

SYNONYMS

license
NOUN **1**
permit: *The majority of foreign nationals working here have work permits.*
certificate: *You will need to bring your birth certificate.*
document: *The police officer wanted to see all our documents.*

li|censed /laɪsᵊnst/ **1** ADJ If you are **licensed** to do something, you have official permission from the government or from the authorities to do it. ❑ *There were about 250 people on board, about 100 more than the ferry was licensed to carry.* **2** ADJ If something that you own or use is **licensed**, you have official permission to own it or use it. ❑ *While searching the house they discovered an unlicensed shotgun and a licensed rifle.*

li|cen|see /laɪsᵊnsi/ (**licensees**) N-COUNT A **licensee** is a person or organization that has been given a license. [FORMAL]

li|cense num|ber (**license numbers**) N-COUNT The **license number** of a car or other road vehicle is the series of letters and numbers shown on the back, and in many places also on the front, of a vehicle. [AM] ❑ *Police have asked people to leave detailed messages about the incidents they report, including each car's license number.*

in BRIT, use **registration number**

li|cense plate (**license plates**) **1** N-COUNT A **license plate** is a sign on the back, and in some places also on the front, of a vehicle that shows its license number. [AM] ❑ *...a car with Austrian license plates.*

in BRIT, use **number plate**

2 → See also color supplement

li|cen|tious /laɪsɛnʃəs/ ADJ If you describe a person as **licentious**, you mean that they are very immoral in their sexual behavior. [FORMAL, DISAPPROVAL] ❑ *...alarming stories of licentious behavior.* ● **li|cen|tious|ness** N-UNCOUNT ❑ *...moral licentiousness.*

li|chen /laɪkən/ (**lichens**) N-MASS **Lichen** is a group of tiny plants that looks like moss and grows on the surface of things such as rocks, trees, and walls.

lick /lɪk/ (**licks, licking, licked**) **1** V-T When people or animals **lick** something, they move their tongue across its surface. ❑ *She folded up her letter, licking the envelope flap with relish.* ● N-COUNT **Lick** is also a noun. ❑ *It's incredible how long a cat can go without more than a lick of milk or water.* **2** N-COUNT [usu N of n] A **lick** of something is a small amount of it. [INFORMAL] ❑ *It could do with a lick of paint to brighten up its premises.* **3 to lick into shape** → see **shape**

lickety-split /lɪkəti splɪt/ ADV If you do something **lickety-split**, you do it very quickly. [mainly AM, INFORMAL] ❑ *Obligingly, the waiter returned lickety-split with the orders of ribs.*

lick|ing /lɪkɪŋ/ (**lickings**) N-COUNT [usu sing] A **licking** is a severe defeat by someone in a fight, battle, or competition. ❑ *They gave us a hell of a licking.*

lico|rice /lɪkərɪʃ, -ɪs/ also **liquorice** N-UNCOUNT **Licorice** is a firm black substance with a strong taste. It is used for making candy which may be black or red.

lid /lɪd/ (**lids**) N-COUNT A **lid** is the top of a box or other container which can be removed or raised when you want to open the container. ❑ *She lifted the lid of the box and displayed the contents.*

lid|ded /lɪdɪd/ **1** ADJ [ADJ n] **Lidded** is used to describe a container that has a lid. ❑ *...a lidded saucepan.* **2** ADJ When someone has **lidded** eyes, their eyelids are partly or fully closed. [LITERARY] ❑ *Julie squinted at her through lidded eyes.*

LIE
① POSITION OR SITUATION
② THINGS THAT ARE NOT TRUE

① **lie** ✦✧✧ /laɪ/ (**lies, lying, lay, lain**)
→ Please look at meanings **8** and **9** to see if the expression you are looking for is shown under another headword.

1 V-I If you **are lying** somewhere, you are in a horizontal position and are not standing or sitting. ❑ *There was a child lying on the ground.* **2** V-I If an object **lies** in a particular place, it is in a flat position in that place. ❑ *...a newspaper lying on a nearby couch.* **3** V-I If you say that a place **lies** in a particular position or direction, you mean that it is situated there. ❑ *The islands lie at the southern end of the Kurile chain.* **4** V-LINK You can use **lie** to say that something is or remains in a particular state or condition. For example, if something **lies forgotten**, it has been and remains forgotten. ❑ *The picture lay hidden in the archives for over 40 years.* **5** V-I You can talk about where something such as a problem, solution, or fault **lies** to say what you think it consists of, involves, or is caused by. ❑ *The problem lay with the family and the school system rather than with television.* **6** V-I You use **lie** in expressions such as **lie ahead**, **lie in store**, and **lie in wait** when you are talking about what someone is going to experience in the future, especially when it is something unpleasant or difficult. ❑ *She'd need all her strength and bravery to cope with what lay in store.* **7** V-T/V-I You can use **lie** to say what position a competitor or team is in during a competition. [BRIT] ❑ *I was going well and was lying fourth.* **8 to lie in state** → see **state** **9 to take something lying down** → see **take** ②

COLLOCATIONS

lie
VERB ① **5**
noun + **lie**: blame, fault, problem, responsibility; answer, solution; interest, strength
lie + adverb: elsewhere

▶ **lie around** PHRASAL VERB If things are left **lying around**, they are not put away but left casually somewhere where they can be seen. ❑ *People should be careful about their possessions and not leave them lying around.*
▶ **lie behind** PHRASAL VERB If you refer to what **lies behind** a situation or event, you are referring to the reason the situation exists or the event happened. ❑ *It seems that what lay behind the clashes was disagreement over the list of candidates.*
▶ **lie down** PHRASAL VERB When you **lie down**, you move into a horizontal position, usually in order to rest or sleep. ❑ *Why don't you go upstairs and lie down for a bit?*

② **lie** ✦✧✧ /laɪ/ (**lies, lying, lied**) **1** N-COUNT A **lie** is something that someone says or writes which they know is untrue. ❑ *"Who else do you work for?"—"No one."—"That's a lie."* ❑ *I've had enough of your lies.* **2** V-I If someone **is lying**, they are saying something which they know is not true. ❑ *I know he's lying.* ● **ly|ing** N-UNCOUNT ❑ *Lying is something that I will not tolerate.* **3** → see also **lying**

COLLOCATIONS

lie
NOUN ② **1**
adjective + **lie**: blatant, downright, outright
verb + **lie**: peddle, spread, tell; expose

SYNONYMS

lie
NOUN ② **1**
falsehood: *He accused them of knowingly spreading falsehoods about him.*
fabrication: *This story is total fabrication.*
deception: *You've been the victim of a rather cruel deception.*
untruth: *The Advertising Standards Authority accused real estate agents of using blatant untruths.*

lie de|tec|tor (**lie detectors**) N-COUNT [oft N n] A **lie detector** is an electronic machine used mainly by the police to find out whether a suspect is telling the truth. ❑ *...the results of a lie detector test.*

lieu /lu/ **1** PHRASE If you do, get, or give one thing **in lieu of** another, you do, get, or give it instead of the other thing, because the two things are considered to have the same value or importance. [FORMAL] ❑ *He left what little furniture he owned to his landlord in lieu of rent.* **2** PHRASE If you do, get, or give something **in lieu**, you do, get, or give it instead of something else, because the two things are considered to have the same value or importance. [FORMAL] ❑ *...an increased salary or time off in lieu.*

Lieut. **Lieut.** is a written abbreviation for **lieutenant** when it is a person's title. ❑ *...Lieut. J. J. Doughty.*

lieu|ten|ant /lutɛnənt/ (**lieutenants**) N-COUNT; N-TITLE A **lieutenant** is a person who holds a junior officer's rank in the army, navy, marines, or air force, or in the U.S. police force. ☐ *Lieutenant Campbell ordered the man at the wheel to steer for the gunboat.*

lieu|ten|ant gov|er|nor (**lieutenant governors**) **1** N-COUNT A **lieutenant governor** is an elected official who acts as the deputy of a state governor in the United States. [AM] **2** N-COUNT A **lieutenant governor** is an official elected by the Canadian government to act as a representative of the British king or queen in a province of Canada.

life ✦✦✦ /laɪf/ (**lives** /laɪvz/) **1** N-UNCOUNT **Life** is the quality which people, animals, and plants have when they are not dead, and which objects and substances do not have. ☐ *...a baby's first minutes of life.* ☐ *These guidelines were essential to protect the public's right to life.* **2** N-UNCOUNT You can use **life** to refer to things or groups of things which are alive. ☐ *Is there life on Mars?* **3** N-COUNT If you refer to someone's **life**, you mean their state of being alive, especially when there is a risk or danger of them dying. ☐ *Your life is in danger.* ☐ *A nurse began to try to save his life.* **4** N-COUNT Someone's **life** is the period of time during which they are alive. ☐ *He spent the last fourteen years of his life in retirement.* **5** N-COUNT You can use **life** to refer to a period of someone's life when they are in a particular situation or job. ☐ *Interior designers spend their working lives keeping up to date with the latest trends.* **6** N-COUNT You can use **life** to refer to particular activities which people regularly do during their lives. ☐ *My personal life has had to take second place to my career.* **7** N-UNCOUNT You can use **life** to refer to the things that people do and experience that are characteristic of a particular place, group, or activity. ☐ *How did you adjust to college life?* ☐ *He abhors the wheeling-and-dealing associated with conventional political life.* **8** N-UNCOUNT A person, place, book, or movie that is full of **life** gives an impression of excitement, energy, or cheerfulness. [APPROVAL] ☐ *The town itself was full of life and character.* **9** N-UNCOUNT If someone is sentenced to **life**, they are sentenced to stay in prison for the rest of their life or for a very long time. [INFORMAL] ☐ *He could get life in prison, if convicted.* **10** N-COUNT The **life** of something such as a machine, organization, or project is the period of time that it lasts for. ☐ *The repairs did not increase the value or the life of the equipment.* **11** PHRASE If you **bring** something **to life** or if it **comes to life**, it becomes interesting or exciting. ☐ *The cold, hard cruelty of two young men is vividly brought to life in this true story.* **12** PHRASE If you say that someone **is fighting for** their **life**, you mean that they are in a very serious condition and may die as a result of an accident or illness. [JOURNALISM] ☐ *...a horrifying robbery that left a man fighting for his life.* **13** PHRASE **For life** means for the rest of a person's life. ☐ *He was jailed for life in 1966 for the murder of three policemen.* ☐ *She may have been scarred for life.* **14** PHRASE If someone **takes** another person's **life**, they kill them. If someone **takes** their own **life**, they kill themselves. [FORMAL] ☐ *He is a killer, who has taken the lives of three people and wounded many others.* **15** PHRASE You can use expressions such as **to come to life**, **to spring to life**, and **to roar into life** to indicate that a machine or vehicle suddenly starts working or moving. [LITERARY] ☐ *To his great relief the engine came to life.* **16 a matter of life and death** → see **death**

life-affirming ADJ [usu ADJ n] A **life-affirming** activity or attitude emphasizes the positive aspects of life. [APPROVAL] ☐ *The exhibition is an enjoyable and, ultimately, life-affirming experience.*

life-and-death → see **death**

life|belt /laɪfbɛlt/ (**lifebelts**) N-COUNT A **lifebelt** is a large ring, usually made of a light substance such as cork, which someone who has fallen into deep water can use to float. [BRIT]

> in AM, use **life preserver**

life|blood /laɪfblʌd/ also **life-blood** N-SING [usu with poss] The **lifeblood** of an organization, area, or person is the most important thing that they need in order to exist, develop, or be successful. ☐ *Small businesses are the lifeblood of the economy.* ☐ *Coal and steel were the region's lifeblood.*

life|boat /laɪfboʊt/ (**lifeboats**) **1** N-COUNT A **lifeboat** is a medium-sized boat that is sent out from a port or harbor in order to rescue people who are in danger at sea. **2** N-COUNT A **lifeboat** is a small boat that is carried on a ship, which people on the ship use to escape when the ship is in danger of sinking. ☐ *The captain ordered all passengers and crew into lifeboats.* **3** → See also color supplement

life coach (**life coaches**) N-COUNT A **life coach** is someone whose job involves helping people to improve their lives by doing challenging or worthwhile things. • **life coach|ing** N-UNCOUNT ☐ *...life-coaching workshops.*

life cy|cle (**life cycles**) **1** N-COUNT The **life cycle** of an animal or plant is the series of changes and developments that it passes through from the beginning of its life until its death. ☐ *...a plant that completes its life cycle in a single season.* **2** N-COUNT The **life cycle** of something such as an idea, product, or organization is the series of developments that take place in it from its beginning until the end of its usefulness. ☐ *Each new product would have a relatively long life cycle.*

life-enhancing ADJ If you describe something as **life-enhancing**, you mean that it makes you feel happier and more content. ☐ *...a life-enhancing and exciting trip.* ☐ *His letters, like his poetry, are life-enhancing and a delight.*

life ex|pec|tan|cy **1** N-UNCOUNT [also N in pl] The **life expectancy** of a person, animal, or plant is the length of time that they are normally likely to live. ☐ *The average life expectancy was 40.* **2** → See feature box at **population**

life force also **life-force** N-UNCOUNT **Life force** is energy that some people believe exists in all living things and keeps them alive.

life form (**life forms**) N-COUNT [with supp] A **life form** is any living thing such as an animal or plant.

life|guard /laɪfgɑrd/ (**lifeguards**) N-COUNT A **lifeguard** is a person who works at a beach or swimming pool and rescues people when they are in danger of drowning.

life his|to|ry (**life histories**) N-COUNT The **life history** of a person is all the things that happen to them during their life. ☐ *Some people give you their life history without much prompting.*

life im|pris|on|ment N-UNCOUNT If someone is sentenced to **life imprisonment**, they are sentenced to stay in prison for the rest of their life, or for a very long period of time.

life in|sur|ance N-UNCOUNT **Life insurance** is a form of insurance in which a person makes regular payments to an insurance company, in return for a sum of money to be paid to them after a period of time, or to their family if they die. ☐ *I have also taken out a life insurance policy on him just in case.*

life jack|et (**life jackets**) also **lifejacket** N-COUNT A **life jacket** is a sleeveless jacket which helps you to float when you have fallen into deep water.

life|less /laɪflɪs/ **1** ADJ If a person or animal is **lifeless**, they are dead, or are so still that they appear to be dead. ☐ *Their cold-blooded killers had then dragged their lifeless bodies upstairs to the bathroom.* **2** ADJ If you describe an object or a machine as **lifeless**, you mean that they are not living things, even though they may resemble living things. ☐ *It was made of plaster, hard and white and lifeless, bearing no resemblance to human flesh.* **3** ADJ A **lifeless** place or area does not have anything living or growing there at all. ☐ *Dry stone walls may appear stark and lifeless, but they provide a valuable habitat for plants and animals.*

life|like /laɪflaɪk/ ADJ Something that is **lifelike** has the appearance of being alive. ☐ *...a lifelike doll.*

life|line /laɪflaɪn/ (**lifelines**) N-COUNT A **lifeline** is something that enables an organization or group to survive or to continue with an activity. ☐ *Information about the job market can be a lifeline for those who are out of work.*

life|long /laɪflɔŋ/ ADJ [ADJ n] **Lifelong** means existing or happening for the whole of a person's life. ☐ *...her lifelong friendship with Naomi.*

life mem|ber (**life members**) also **lifetime member** N-COUNT [oft N of n] If you are a **life member** of a club or organization, you have paid or been chosen to be a member for the rest of your life.

life pre|serv|er (**life preservers**) N-COUNT A **life preserver** is something such as a jacket, belt, or ring, which helps you to float when you have fallen into deep water. [AM]

lif|er /laɪfər/ (**lifers**) N-COUNT A **lifer** is a criminal who has been given a life sentence. [INFORMAL]

life raft (life rafts) also **life-raft** N-COUNT A **life raft** is a small rubber boat carried on an aircraft or large boat which can be filled with air and used in an emergency.

life|saver /laɪfseɪvər/ (lifesavers) N-COUNT If you say that something is a **lifesaver**, you mean that it helps people in a very important way, often in a way that is important to their health. ❑ *The cervical smear test is a lifesaver.*

life|saving /laɪfseɪvɪŋ/ **1** ADJ [usu ADJ n] A **lifesaving** drug, operation, or action is one that saves someone's life or is likely to save their life. ❑ *...lifesaving drugs such as antibiotics.* ❑ *She decided her child should go to America for lifesaving treatment.* **2** N-UNCOUNT You use **lifesaving** to refer to the skills and activities connected with rescuing people, especially people who are drowning.

life sci|ence (life sciences) N-COUNT [usu pl] The **life sciences** are sciences such as zoology, botany, and anthropology which are concerned with human beings, animals, and plants.

life sen|tence (life sentences) N-COUNT If someone receives a **life sentence**, they are sentenced to stay in prison for the rest of their life, or for a very long period of time. ❑ *Some were serving life sentences for murder.*

life-size also **life-sized** ADJ A **life-size** representation of someone or something, for example a painting or sculpture, is the same size as the person or thing that they represent. ❑ *...a life-size statue of an Indian boy.*

life|span /laɪfspæn/ (lifespans) also **life span** **1** N-VAR The **lifespan** of a person, animal, or plant is the period of time for which they live or are normally expected to live. ❑ *A 15-year lifespan is not uncommon for a dog.* **2** N-COUNT The **lifespan** of a product, organization, or idea is the period of time for which it is expected to work properly or to last. ❑ *Most boilers have a lifespan of 15 to 20 years.*

life|style /laɪfstaɪl/ (lifestyles) also **life-style, life style** **1** N-VAR The **lifestyle** of a particular person or group of people is the living conditions, behavior, and habits that are typical of them or are chosen by them. ❑ *They enjoyed an income and lifestyle that many people would envy.* **2** ADJ [ADJ n] **Lifestyle** magazines, television programs, and products are aimed at people who wish to be associated with glamorous and successful lifestyles. ❑ *This year people are going for luxury and buying lifestyle products.* **3** ADJ [ADJ n] **Lifestyle** drugs are drugs that are intended to improve people's quality of life rather than to treat particular medical disorders. ❑ *"I see anti-depressants as a lifestyle drug," says Dr. Charlton.*

life sup|port N-UNCOUNT [oft on N] **Life support** is a system that is used to keep a person alive when they are very ill and cannot breathe without help. ❑ *She was kept on life support through the afternoon so family and friends could say goodbye.*

life-support ma|chine (life-support machines) N-COUNT A **life-support machine** is the equipment that is used to keep a person alive when they are very ill and cannot breathe without help. [mainly BRIT] ❑ *He is in a coma and on a life-support machine.*

life's work N-SING [usu poss N] Someone's **life's work** or **life work** is the main activity that they have been involved in during their life, or their most important achievement. ❑ *An exhibition of his life's work is being shown in the garden of his home.* ❑ *My father's life work was devoted to the conservation of the Longleat estate.*

life-threatening **1** ADJ [oft adv ADJ] If someone has a **life-threatening** illness or is in a **life-threatening** situation, there is a strong possibility that the illness or the situation will kill them. ❑ *Caitlin was born with a life-threatening heart abnormality.* **2** → See feature box at **illness**

life|time /laɪftaɪm/ (lifetimes) N-COUNT A **lifetime** is the length of time that someone is alive. ❑ *During my lifetime I haven't got around to much traveling.* ❑ *...a trust fund to be administered throughout his wife's lifetime.*

life|time mem|ber (lifetime members) → see **life member**

lift ✦✦◇ /lɪft/ (lifts, lifting, lifted) **1** V-T If you **lift** something, you move it to another position, especially upward. ❑ *The colonel lifted the phone and dialed his superior.* • PHRASAL VERB **Lift up** means the same as **lift**. ❑ *She put her arms around him and lifted him up.* **2** V-T If you **lift** your eyes or your head, you look up, for example, when you have been reading and someone comes into the room. ❑ *When he finished he lifted his eyes and looked out the window.* **3** V-T If people in authority **lift** a law or rule that prevents people from doing something, they end it. ❑ *The European Commission has urged France to lift its ban on imports of British beef.* **4** V-T/V-I If something **lifts** your spirits or your mood, or if they **lift**, you start feeling more cheerful. ❑ *He used his incredible sense of humor to lift my spirits.* **5** N-COUNT If you give someone a **lift** somewhere, you take them there in your car as a favor to them. ❑ *He had a car and often gave me a lift home.* **6** N-UNCOUNT **Lift** is the force that makes an aircraft leave the ground and stay in the air. ❑ *An airplane has to reach a certain speed before there is enough lift to get it off the ground.* **7** V-T If a government or organization **lifts** people or goods in or out of an area, it transports them there by aircraft, especially when there is a war. ❑ *The army lifted people off rooftops where they had climbed to escape the flooding.* **8** V-T To **lift** something means to increase its amount or to increase the level or the rate at which it happens. [BRIT] **9** N-COUNT A **lift** is a device that carries people or goods up and down inside tall buildings. [BRIT]

in AM, use **elevator**

10 to lift a finger → see **finger**

COLLOCATIONS

lift
NOUN **5**
verb + **lift**: catch, hitch, thumb
VERB
3
lift + noun: ban, embargo, restrictions, sanctions
4
lift + noun: mood, spirits

---

lift-off (lift-offs) **1** N-VAR **Lift-off** is the beginning of a rocket's flight into space, when it leaves the ground. ❑ *The lift-off was delayed about seven minutes.* ❑ *The rocket tumbled out of control shortly after lift-off.* **2** → See feature box at **travel**

liga|ment /lɪgəmənt/ (ligaments) N-COUNT A **ligament** is a band of strong tissue in a person's body which connects bones. ❑ *He suffered torn ligaments in his knee.*

LIGHT
① BRIGHTNESS OR ILLUMINATION
② NOT GREAT IN WEIGHT, AMOUNT, OR INTENSITY
③ UNIMPORTANT OR NOT SERIOUS

---

① **light** ✦✦◇ /laɪt/ (lights, lighting, lit or lighted, lighter, lightest)

→ Please look at meaning **10** to see if the expression you are looking for is shown under another headword.

1 N-UNCOUNT [also the N] **Light** is the brightness that lets you see things. Light comes from sources such as the sun, moon, lamps, and fire. ❑ *Cracks of light filtered through the shutters.* ❑ *...ultraviolet light.* **2** N-COUNT A **light** is something such as an electric lamp which produces light. ❑ *The janitor comes around to turn the lights out.* **3** N-PLURAL You can use **lights** to refer to a set of traffic lights. ❑ *...the heavy city traffic with its endless delays at lights and crosswalks.* **4** V-T If a place or object **is lit** by something, it has light shining on it. ❑ *It was dark and a giant moon lit the road so brightly you could see the landscape clearly.* ❑ *The room was lit by only the one light.* **5** ADJ If it is **light**, the sun is providing light at the beginning or end of the day. ❑ *It was still light when we arrived at Lalong Creek.* **6** ADJ If a room or building is **light**, it has a lot of natural light in it, for example, because it has large windows. ❑ *It is a light room with tall windows.* • **light|ness** N-UNCOUNT ❑ *The dark green spare bedroom is in total contrast to the lightness of the large main bedroom.* **7** V-T/V-I If you **light** something such as a cigarette or fire, or if it **lights**, it starts burning. ❑ *Stephen hunched down to light a cigarette.* ❑ *If the charcoal does fail to light, use a special liquid spray and light it with a long taper.* **8** N-COUNT If something is presented in a particular **light**, it is presented so that you think about it in a particular way or so that it appears to be of a particular nature. ❑ *He has worked hard in recent months to portray New York in a better light.* **9** → see also **lighter, lighting** **10** PHRASE If something **comes to light** or **is brought to light**, it becomes obvious or is made known to a lot of people. ❑ *Nothing about this sum has come to light.* **11** PHRASE If someone in authority gives you **a green light**, they give you permission to do something. ❑ *The food industry was given a green light to extend the use of these chemicals.* **12** PHRASE If something is possible **in the light of** particular information, it is only possible because you have this information. ❑ *In the light of this information it is now possible to identify a number of key issues.* **13** PHRASE To **shed light on**, **throw light on**, or **cast light on** something means to make it easier to understand, because more information is known about it. ❑ *A new approach offers an answer, and may shed light on an even bigger question.* **14** PHRASE If you **set light to** something, you make it start burning. [mainly BRIT]

in AM, usually use **set fire to**

15 **all sweetness and light** → see **sweetness**
▶ **light up** **1** PHRASAL VERB If you **light** something **up** or if it **lights up**, it becomes bright, usually when you shine light on it. ❑ *...a keypad that lights up when you pick up the handset.* **2** PHRASAL VERB If your face or your eyes **light up**, you suddenly look very surprised or happy. ❑ *Sue's face lit up with surprise.*
② **light** ✦✧ /laɪt/ (**lighter**, **lightest**) **1** ADJ Something that is **light** does not weigh very much, or weighs less than you would expect it to. ❑ *Modern tennis rackets are now apparently 20 per cent lighter.* ❑ *...weight training with light weights.* • **light|ness** N-UNCOUNT [usu with supp] ❑ *The toughness, lightness, strength, and elasticity of whalebone gave it a wide variety of uses.* **2** ADJ Something that is **light** is not very great in amount, degree, or intensity. ❑ *It's a Sunday like any other with the usual light traffic in the city.* ❑ *Trading was very light ahead of yesterday's auction.* • **light|ly** ADV ❑ *Put the onions in the pan and cook until lightly browned.* **3** ADJ Something that is **light** is very pale in color. ❑ *He is light haired with gray eyes.* • COMB IN COLOR **Light** is also a combining form. ❑ *We know he has a light green van.* **4** ADJ [ADJ n] A **light** sleep is one that is easily disturbed and in which you are often aware of the things around you. If you are a **light** sleeper, you are easily woken when you are asleep. ❑ *She had drifted into a light sleep.* • **light|ly** ADV [ADV after v] ❑ *He was dozing lightly in his chair.* **5** ADJ A **light** meal consists of food that is easy

Light

Originating in Southeast Asia, but now celebrated by millions of people across the world, Diwali is a five-day festival celebrating the triumph of light over darkness and good over evil. Held in October or November, the festival begins with everyone cleaning their houses until they **sparkle**. It is also traditional to buy and wear new clothes in **dazzlingly** bright colors.

The streets are decorated with strings of **flickering** lights and everywhere **glimmers** and **gleams**. Firework displays **illuminate** the night sky.

People's houses are also adorned with hundreds of **twinkling** candles, or earthenware oil lamps, called 'diyas'. It is traditionally believed that their **glow** will encourage the Goddess Lakshmi, bringer of wealth, to enter each home.

to digest. ❑ *...a light, healthy lunch.* • **light|ly** ADV [ADV after v] ❑ *She found it impossible to eat lightly.* **6** ADJ **Light** work does not involve much physical effort. ❑ *He was on the training field for some light work yesterday.* **7** ADJ If you describe the result of an action or a punishment as **light**, you mean that it is less serious or severe than you expected. ❑ *She confessed her astonishment at her light sentence when her father visited her at the jail.* • **light|ly** ADV [ADV after v] ❑ *One of the accused got off lightly in exchange for pleading guilty to withholding information from Congress.* **8** ADJ Movements and actions that are **light** are graceful or gentle and are done with very little force or effort. ❑ *Use a light touch when applying cream or makeup.* • **light|ly** ADV [ADV with v] ❑ *He kissed her lightly on the mouth.* • **light|ness** N-UNCOUNT ❑ *She danced with a grace and lightness that were breathtaking.* **9** ADJ **Light** is used to describe foods or drinks that contain few calories or low amounts of sugar, fat, or alcohol. ❑ *There's been a flood of low-fat and light ice creams on the market.* ❑ *They refreshed themselves with cans of light beer.*

③ **light** ✦✧ /laɪt/ (**lighter**, **lightest**) **1** ADJ If you describe things such as books, music, and movies as **light**, you mean that they entertain you without making you think very deeply. ❑ *He doesn't like me reading light novels.* ❑ *...light classical music.* **2** ADJ If you say something in a **light** way, you sound as if you think that something is not important or serious. ❑ *Talk to him in a friendly, light way about the relationship.* • **light|ly** ADV [ADV after v] ❑ *"Once a detective, always a detective," he said lightly.* • **light|ness** N-UNCOUNT ❑ *I'm not an authority on them,* Jessica said with forced lightness. **3** PHRASE If you **make light of** something, you treat it as though it is not serious or important, when in fact it is. ❑ *Roberts attempted to make light of his discomfort.*

light air|craft (**light aircraft**) N-COUNT A **light aircraft** is a small airplane that is designed to carry a small number of passengers or a small amount of cargo.

light bulb (**light bulbs**) N-COUNT A **light bulb** or **bulb** is the round glass part of an electric light or lamp which light shines from.

light cream N-UNCOUNT **Light cream** is thin cream that does not have a lot of fat in it. [AM]

in BRIT, use **single cream**

light|en /ˈlaɪtən/ (**lightens**, **lightening**, **lightened**) **1** V-T/V-I When something **lightens** or when you **lighten** it, it becomes less dark in color. ❑ *The sky began to lighten.* **2** V-T If someone **lightens** a situation, they make it less serious or less boring. ❑ *Anthony felt the need to lighten the atmosphere.* **3** V-T/V-I If your attitude or mood **lightens**, or if someone or something **lightens** it, they make you feel more cheerful, happy, and relaxed. ❑ *As they approached the outskirts of the city, Ella's mood visibly lightened.*

light|er /ˈlaɪtər/ (**lighters**) N-COUNT A **lighter** is a small device that produces a flame which you can use to light cigarettes, cigars, and pipes.

light-fingered ADJ If you say that someone is **light-fingered**, you mean that they steal things. [INFORMAL]

light|headed /ˌlaɪtˈhɛdɪd/

in BRIT, use **light-headed**

ADJ [usu v-link ADJ] If you feel **lightheaded**, you feel somewhat unsteady and strange, for example, because you are ill or because you have drunk too much alcohol.

light|hearted /ˌlaɪtˈhɑːrtɪd/

in BRIT, use **light-hearted**

1 ADJ Someone who is **lighthearted** is cheerful and happy. ❑ *I was amazingly lighthearted and peaceful.* **2** ADJ Something that is **lighthearted** is intended to be entertaining or amusing, and not at all serious. ❑ *There have been many attempts, both lighthearted and serious, to locate the Loch Ness Monster.*

light heavy|weight (**light heavyweights**) N-COUNT A **light heavyweight** is a professional boxer who weighs between 160 and 175 pounds, or an amateur boxer who weighs between 165 and 179 pounds.

light|house /ˈlaɪthaʊs/ (**lighthouses**) N-COUNT A **lighthouse** is a tower containing a powerful flashing lamp that is built on the coast or on a small island. Lighthouses are used to guide ships or to warn them of danger.

light in|dus|try (light industries) N-VAR **Light industry** is industry in which only small items are made, for example, household goods and clothes. ❑ *State and local officials are hoping to bring some light industry to the site.*

light|ing /laɪtɪŋ/ **1** N-UNCOUNT The **lighting** in a place is the way that it is lit, for example, by electric lights, by candles, or by windows, or the quality of the light in it. ❑ *...the bright fluorescent lighting of the laboratory.* ❑ *The whole room is bathed in soft lighting.* **2** → See feature box at **theater**

light|ning /laɪtnɪŋ/ **1** N-UNCOUNT **Lightning** is the very bright flashes of light in the sky that happen during thunderstorms. ❑ *One man died when he was struck by lightning.* ❑ *Another flash of lightning lit up the cave.* **2** ADJ [ADJ n] **Lightning** describes things that happen very quickly or last for only a short time. ❑ *Driving today demands lightning reflexes.* **3** → See feature box at **electricity**

light|ning bug (lightning bugs) N-COUNT A **lightning bug** is a type of beetle that produces light from its body. [AM]

light|ning rod (lightning rods)

in BRIT, use **lightning conductor**

1 N-COUNT A **lightning rod** is a long thin piece of metal on top of a building that attracts lightning and allows it to reach the ground safely. [AM] **2** PHRASE [PHR n] If you say that someone **is a lightning rod** for something, you mean that they attract that thing to themselves. [AM] ❑ *He is a lightning rod for controversy.*

light|ship /laɪtʃɪp/ (lightships) N-COUNT A **lightship** is a small ship that stays in one place and has a powerful flashing lamp. Lightships are used to guide ships or to warn them of danger.

light|weight /laɪtweɪt/ (lightweights) also **light-weight** **1** ADJ Something that is **lightweight** weighs less than most other things of the same type. ❑ *...lightweight denim.* **2** N-UNCOUNT **Lightweight** is a category in some sports, such as boxing, judo, or rowing, based on the weight of the athlete. ❑ *By the age of sixteen he was the junior lightweight champion of Poland.* **3** N-COUNT If you describe someone as a **lightweight**, you are critical of them because you think that they are not very important or skillful in a particular area of activity. [DISAPPROVAL] ❑ *Brian considered Sam a lightweight, a real amateur.* • ADJ **Lightweight** is also an adjective. ❑ *Some of the discussion in the book is lightweight and unconvincing.*

light year (light years) **1** N-COUNT A **light year** is the distance that light travels in a year. ❑ *...a star system millions of light years away.* **2** N-COUNT You can say that two things are **light years** apart to emphasize a very great difference or a very long distance or period of time between them. [INFORMAL, EMPHASIS] ❑ *She says the French education system is light years ahead of the English one.*

lik|able /laɪkəbəl/ also **likeable** ADJ Someone or something that is **likable** is pleasant and easy to like. ❑ *He was a bright guy, a likable guy.*

LIKE
① PREPOSITION AND CONJUNCTION USES
② VERB USES
③ NOUN USES AND PHRASES

---

① **like** ✦✦✦ /laɪk/ **1** PREP If you say that one person or thing is **like** another, you mean that they share some of the same qualities or features. ❑ *He looks like Father Christmas.* ❑ *It's a bit like going to the dentist; it's never as bad as you fear.* ❑ *It's nothing like what happened in the mid-Seventies.* **2** PREP If you talk about what something or someone is **like**, you are talking about their qualities or features. ❑ *What was Bulgaria like?* ❑ *What did she look like?* **3** PREP [n PREP n/-ing] You can use **like** to introduce an example of the set of things or people that you have just mentioned. ❑ *The neglect that large cities like New York have received over the past 12 years is tremendous.* **4** PREP You can use **like** to say that someone or something is in the same situation as another person or thing. ❑ *It also moved those who, like me, are too young to have lived through the war.* **5** PREP [v PREP n] If you say that someone is behaving **like** something or someone else, you mean that they are behaving in a way that is typical of that kind of thing or person. **Like** is used in this way in many fixed expressions, for example, **to cry like a baby** and **to watch someone like a hawk**. ❑ *I was shaking all over, trembling like a leaf.* **6** CONJ **Like** is sometimes used as a conjunction in order to say that something appears to be the case when it is not. Some people consider this use to be incorrect. ❑ *His arms look like they might snap under the weight of his gloves.* **7** CONJ **Like** is sometimes used as a conjunction in order to indicate that something happens or is done in the same way as something else. Some people consider this use to be incorrect. ❑ *People are strolling, buying ice cream for their children, just like they do every Sunday.* ❑ *He spoke exactly like I did.* **8** PREP [with neg] You can use **like** in negative expressions such as **nothing like it** and **no place like it** to emphasize that there is nothing as good as the situation, thing, or person mentioned. [EMPHASIS] ❑ *There's nothing like candlelight for creating a romantic mood.* **9** PREP [with neg] You can use **like** in expressions such as **nothing like** to make an emphatic negative statement. [EMPHASIS] ❑ *Three hundred million dollars will be nothing like enough.*

② **like** ✦✦✦ /laɪk/ (likes, liking, liked) **1** V-T [no cont] If you **like** something or someone, you think they are interesting, enjoyable, or attractive. ❑ *He likes baseball.* ❑ *I just didn't like being in crowds.* ❑ *Do you like to go swimming?* **2** V-T [no cont, no passive] If you ask someone how they **like** something, you are asking them for their opinion of it and whether they enjoy it or find it pleasant. ❑ *How do you like America?* **3** V-T [no cont, no passive] If you say that you **like** to do something or that you **like** something to be done, you mean that you prefer to do it or prefer it to be done as part of your normal life or routine. ❑ *I like to get to airports in good time.* **4** V-T [no cont, no passive] If you say that you would **like** something or would **like** to do something, you are indicating a wish or desire that you have. ❑ *I'd like a bath.* **5** V-T [no cont, no passive] If you ask someone if they **would like** something or **would like** to do something, you are making a polite offer or invitation. [POLITENESS] ❑ *Here's your change. Would you like a bag?* ❑ *Perhaps while you wait you would like a drink at the bar.* **6** V-T [no cont, no passive] If you say to someone that you **would like** something or you **would like** them to do something, or ask them if they **would like** to do it, you are politely telling them what you want or what you want them to do. [POLITENESS] ❑ *I'd like an explanation.* ❑ *We'd like you to look around and tell us if anything is missing.*

USAGE

like
You say '**Would you like**...' followed by a *to*-infinitive when you are inviting someone to do something. Don't say '~~Do you like to meet him~~?' *Would you like to meet him?*
Use **like it** in front of a clause beginning with **when** or **if**. Don't say '~~I like when I can go home early~~.' *I like it when I can go home early.*
You must put **very much** after the person or thing that you like. Don't say, for example, '~~I like very much driving~~.' Say 'I like driving **very much**.'

---

③ **like** ✦✦✦ /laɪk/ (likes) **1** N-UNCOUNT You can use **like** in expressions such as **like attracts like**, when you are referring to two or more people or things that have the same or similar characteristics. ❑ *You have to make sure you're comparing like with like.* **2** N-PLURAL Someone's **likes** are the things that they enjoy or find pleasant. ❑ *I thought that I knew everything about Jemma: her likes and dislikes, her political viewpoints.* **3** → see also **liking** **4** PHRASE You say **if you like** when you are making or agreeing to an offer or suggestion in a casual way. ❑ *You can stay here if you like.* **5** PHRASE You say **like this, like that,** or **like so** when you are showing someone how something is done. ❑ *It opens and closes, like this.* **6** PHRASE You use **like this** or **like that** when you are drawing attention to something that you are doing or that someone else is doing. ❑ *I'm sorry to intrude on you like this.* **7** PHRASE You use the expression **something like** with an amount, number, or description to indicate that it is approximately accurate. ❑ *They can get something like $3,000 a year.*

-like /-laɪk/ COMB IN ADJ **-like** combines with nouns to form adjectives which describe something as being similar to the thing referred to by the noun. ❏ ...*beautiful purple-red petunia-like flowers.* ❏ ...*a tiny worm-like creature.*

like|able /laɪkəbᵊl/ → see likable

like|li|hood /laɪklihʊd/ **1** N-UNCOUNT The **likelihood** of something happening is how likely it is to happen. ❏ *The likelihood of infection is minimal.* **2** N-SING If something is a **likelihood**, it is likely to happen. ❏ *But the likelihood is that people would be willing to pay if they were certain that their money was going to a good cause.*

like|ly ✦✦✦ /laɪkli/ (**likelier, likeliest**) **1** ADJ You use **likely** to indicate that something is probably the case or will probably happen in a particular situation. ❏ *Experts say a "yes" vote is still the likely outcome.* ❏ *If this is your first baby, it's far more likely that you'll get to the hospital too early.* • ADV **with cl/group**] **Likely** is also an adverb. ❏ *Profit will most likely have risen by about $25 million.* **2** ADJ [v-link ADJ to-inf] If someone or something is **likely** to do a particular thing, they will very probably do it. ❏ *In the meantime the war of nerves seems likely to continue.*

▬▬▬ SYNONYMS ▬▬▬

likely
ADJ **1**
probable: *It is probable that the medication will suppress the symptoms.*
expected: *Their expected time of arrival is 6 o'clock.*
anticipated: *The long-anticipated study drew criticism from the tobacco industry.*

like-minded ADJ **Like-minded** people have similar opinions, ideas, attitudes, or interests. ❏ ...*the opportunity to mix with hundreds of like-minded people.*

lik|en /laɪkən/ (**likens, likening, likened**) V-T If you **liken** one thing or person **to** another thing or person, you say that they are similar. ❏ *The bookseller likens his job to a treasure hunt.*

like|ness /laɪknɪs/ (**likenesses**) **1** N-SING If two things or people have a **likeness** to each other, they are similar to each other. ❏ *These myths have a startling likeness to one another.* **2** N-COUNT A **likeness** of someone is a picture or sculpture of them. ❏ *The museum displays wax likenesses of every U.S. president.* **3** N-COUNT If you say that a picture of someone is a good **likeness**, you mean that it looks just like them. ❏ *She says the artist's impression is an excellent likeness of her abductor.*

like|wise /laɪkwaɪz/ **1** ADV You use **likewise** when you are comparing two methods, states, or situations and saying that they are similar. ❏ *What is fair for homeowners likewise should be fair to businesses.* **2** ADV [ADV after v] If you do something and someone else does **likewise**, they do the same or a similar thing. ❏ *He lent money, made donations and encouraged others to do likewise.*

lik|ing /laɪkɪŋ/ **1** N-SING If you have a **liking** for something or someone, you like them. ❏ *She had a liking for good clothes.* ❏ *He bought me CDs to encourage my liking for music.* **2** PHRASE If something is, for example, too fast **for** your **liking**, you would prefer it to be slower. If it is not fast enough **for** your **liking**, you would prefer it to be faster. ❏ *He had become too powerful for their liking.* **3** PHRASE If something is **to** your **liking**, it suits your interests, tastes, or wishes. ❏ *London was more to his liking than Rome.*

li|lac /laɪlak, -læk, -lək/ (**lilacs**)

Lilac can also be used as the plural form.

1 N-VAR A **lilac** or a **lilac tree** is a small tree which has sweet-smelling purple, pink, or white flowers in large, cone-shaped groups. ❏ *Lilacs grew against the side wall.* **2** COLOR Something that is **lilac** is pale pinkish-purple in color. ❏ *All shades of mauve, lilac, lavender and purple were fashionable.*

lilt /lɪlt/ N-SING If someone's voice has a **lilt** in it, the pitch of their voice rises and falls in a pleasant way, as if they were singing. ❏ *Her voice is child-like, with a West Country lilt.*

lilt|ing /lɪltɪŋ/ ADJ [usu ADJ n] A **lilting** voice or song rises and falls in pitch in a pleasant way. ❏ *He had a pleasant, lilting northern accent.*

lily /lɪli/ (**lilies**) N-VAR A **lily** is a plant with large flowers that are often white.

lily of the val|ley (**lilies of the valley** or **lily of the valley**) N-VAR **Lily of the valley** are small plants with large leaves and small, white, bell-shaped flowers.

lima bean /liːmə biːn/ (**lima beans**) N-COUNT [usu pl] **Lima beans** are flat round beans that are light green in color and are eaten as a vegetable. They are the seeds of a plant that grows in tropical areas.

limb /lɪm/ (**limbs**) **1** N-COUNT Your **limbs** are your arms and legs. ❏ *She would be able to stretch out her cramped limbs and rest for a few hours.* **2** PHRASE If someone goes **out on a limb**, they do something they strongly believe in even though it is risky or extreme, and is likely to fail or be criticized by other people. ❏ *They can see themselves going out on a limb, voting for a very controversial energy bill.*

-limbed /-lɪmd/ COMB IN ADJ **-limbed** combines with adjectives to form other adjectives which indicate that a person or animal has limbs of a particular type or appearance. ❏ *He was long-limbed and dark-eyed.*

lim|ber /lɪmbər/ (**limbers, limbering, limbered**) ADJ Someone who is **limber** is able to move or bend their body easily. ❏ *Active people stay more limber.*
▶ **limber up** PHRASAL VERB If you **limber up**, you prepare for an energetic physical activity such as a sport by moving and stretching your body. ❏ *Next door, 200 girls are limbering up for their ballet exams.* ❏ *A short walk will limber up the legs.*

lim|bo /lɪmboʊ/ N-UNCOUNT If you say that someone or something is in **limbo**, you mean that they are in a situation where they seem to be caught between two stages and it is unclear what will happen next. ❏ *The negotiations have been in limbo since mid-December.*

lime /laɪm/ (**limes**) **1** N-VAR A **lime** is a green fruit that tastes like a lemon. Limes grow on trees in tropical countries. ❏ ...*peeled slices of lime.* **2** N-UNCOUNT **Lime** is a substance containing calcium. It is found in soil and water. ❏ *If your soil is very acidic, add lime.*

lime green also **lime-green** COLOR Something that is **lime green** is light yellowish-green in color.

lime|light /laɪmlaɪt/ N-UNCOUNT If someone is in the **limelight**, a lot of attention is being paid to them, because they are famous or because they have done something very unusual or exciting. ❏ *Tony has now been thrust into the limelight, with a high-profile job.*

lim|er|ick /lɪmərɪk/ (**limericks**) N-COUNT A **limerick** is a humorous poem which has five lines.

lime|stone /laɪmstoʊn/ (**limestones**) **1** N-MASS **Limestone** is a whitish-colored rock which is used for building and for making cement. ❏ ...*high limestone cliffs.* **2** → See also color supplement

lim|ey /laɪmi/ (**limeys**) N-COUNT Some Americans refer to British people as **limeys**. Some people consider this use offensive. [INFORMAL]

lim|it ✦✦◇ /lɪmɪt/ (**limits, limiting, limited**) **1** N-COUNT A **limit** is the greatest amount, extent, or degree of something that is possible. ❏ *Her love for him was being tested to its limits.* **2** There is no limit to how much fresh fruit you can eat in a day. **2** N-COUNT A **limit** of a particular kind is the largest or smallest amount of something such as time or money that is allowed because of a rule, law, or decision. ❏ *The three month time limit will be up in mid-June.* **3** N-COUNT The **limit** of an area is its boundary or edge. ❏ ...*the city limits of Baghdad.* **4** N-PLURAL The **limits** of a situation are the facts involved in it which make only some actions or results possible. ❏ *She has to work within the limits of a fairly tight budget.* **5** V-T If you **limit** something, you prevent it from becoming greater than a particular amount or degree. ❏ *He limited payments on the country's foreign debt.* **6** V-T If you **limit** yourself to something, or if someone or something **limits** you, the number of things that you have or do is reduced. ❏ *Please limit letters to 125 words or less.* • **lim|it|ing** ADJ ❏ *The conditions laid down to me were not too limiting.* **7** V-T [usu passive] If something **is limited** to a particular place or group of people, it exists only in that place, or is had or done only by that group. ❏ *The protests were not limited to New York.* **8** → see also **limited** **9** PHRASE If an area or a place is **off limits**, you are not allowed to go there. ❏ *A one-mile area around the wreck is still off limits.*

limitation 752 **line**

COLLOCATIONS

limit
NOUN **2**
noun + **limit**: age, height, size; speed, time; alcohol
adjective + **limit**: legal, statutory; lower, upper; acceptable, reasonable, recommended, strict
verb + **limit**: impose, set; break, exceed

SYNONYMS

limit
NOUN
3
boundary: *The Bow Brook forms the western boundary of the woods.*
edge: *We were on a hill, right on the edge of town.*
confines: *The movie is set entirely within the confines of the abandoned factory.*
4
restriction: *The relaxation of travel restrictions means they are free to travel and work.*
constraint: *Water shortages in the area will be the main constraint on development.*
limitation: *There is to be no limitation on the number of opposition parties.*
VERB **5**
restrict: *There is talk of raising the admission requirements to restrict the number of students on campus.*
control: *The federal government tried to control rising health care costs.*
check: *A free press will help to check corruption.*
curb: *Inflation needs to be curbed.*

---

limi|ta|tion /lɪmɪteɪʃ°n/ (limitations) **1** N-UNCOUNT The **limitation** of something is the act or process of controlling or reducing it. ▫ *All the talk had been about the limitation of nuclear weapons.* **2** N-VAR A **limitation** on something is a rule or decision which prevents that thing from growing or extending beyond certain limits. ▫ *...a limitation on the tax deductions for people who make more than $100,000 a year.* **3** N-PLURAL If you talk about the **limitations** of someone or something, you mean that they can only do some things and not others, or cannot do something very well. ▫ *I realized how possible it was to overcome your limitations, to achieve well beyond what you believe yourself capable of.* **4** N-VAR A **limitation** is a fact or situation that allows only some actions and makes others impossible. ▫ *This drug has one important limitation. Its effects only last six hours.* **5** → See feature box at **review**

lim|it|ed ♦◇◇ /lɪmɪtɪd/ **1** ADJ Something that is **limited** is not very great in amount, range, or degree. ▫ *They may only have a limited amount of time to get their points across.* **2** ADJ A **limited** company is one whose owners are legally responsible for only a part of any money that it may owe if it goes bankrupt. [BRIT, CANADIAN, BUSINESS]

in AM, use **incorporated**

lim|it|ed edi|tion (limited editions) N-COUNT A **limited edition** is a work of art, such as a book, which is only produced in very small numbers, so that each one will be valuable in the future. ▫ *This strictly limited edition of four fine art prints has been specially produced under the close supervision of the artist.*

lim|it|less /lɪmɪtlɪs/ ADJ If you describe something as **limitless**, you mean that there is or appears to be so much of it that it will never be exhausted. ▫ *...a cheap and potentially limitless supply of energy.*

limo /lɪmoʊ/ (limos) N-COUNT [also by N] A **limo** is a limousine. [INFORMAL]

lim|ou|sine /lɪməziːn/ (limousines) **1** N-COUNT A **limousine** is a large and very comfortable car. Limousines are usually driven by a chauffeur and often hired for important occasions. **2** → See also color supplement

limp /lɪmp/ (limps, limping, limped, limper, limpest) **1** V-I If a person or animal **limps**, they walk with difficulty or in an uneven way because one of their legs or feet is hurt. ▫ *I wasn't badly hurt, but I injured my thigh and had to limp.* ● N-COUNT **Limp** is also a noun. ▫ *A stiff knee following surgery forced her to walk with a limp.* **2** V-I If you say that something such as an organization, process, or vehicle **limps** along, you mean that it continues slowly or with difficulty, for example because it has been weakened or damaged. ▫ *In recent years the newspaper had been limping along on limited resources.* **3** ADJ If you describe something as **limp**, you mean that it is soft or weak when it should be firm or strong. ▫ *She was told to reject applicants with limp handshakes.* ● **limp|ly** ADV [ADV with v] ▫ *Flags and bunting hung limply in the still, warm air.* **4** ADJ If someone is **limp**, their body has no strength and is not moving, for example, because they are asleep or unconscious. ▫ *He carried her limp body into the room and laid her on the bed.*

lim|pet /lɪmpɪt/ (limpets) N-COUNT A **limpet** is a small sea animal with a cone-shaped shell which attaches itself tightly to rocks.

lim|pid /lɪmpɪd/ **1** ADJ If you say that something is **limpid**, you mean that it is very clear and transparent. [LITERARY] ▫ *...limpid blue eyes.* ▫ *...limpid rock pools.* **2** ADJ If you describe speech, writing, or music as **limpid**, you like it because it is clear, simple, and flowing. [LITERARY, APPROVAL] ▫ *He thought the speech a model of its kind, limpid and unaffected.*

linch|pin /lɪntʃpɪn/ (linchpins) also **lynchpin** N-COUNT [with supp, usu N of n] If you refer to a person or thing as the **linchpin** of something, you mean that they are the most important person or thing involved in it. ▫ *He's the linchpin of our team and crucial to my long-term plans.*

lin|den /lɪndən/ (lindens) N-VAR A **linden** or a **linden tree** is a large tree with pale green leaves which is often planted in parks in towns and cities.

LINE
① NOUN USES
② PHRASES
③ VERB USES
④ PHRASAL VERB

---

① **line** ♦♦♦ /laɪn/ (lines) **1** N-COUNT A **line** is a long thin mark which is drawn or painted on a surface. ▫ *Draw a line down that page's center.* ▫ *...a dotted line.* **2** N-COUNT The **lines** on someone's skin, especially on their face, are long thin marks that appear there as they grow older. ▫ *He has a large, generous face with deep lines.* **3** N-COUNT A **line** of people or things is a number of them arranged one behind the other or side by side. ▫ *The sparse line of spectators noticed nothing unusual.* **4** N-COUNT A **line** of people or vehicles is a number of them that are waiting one behind another, for example, in order to buy something or to go in a particular direction. ▫ *Children clutching empty bowls form a line.* **5** N-COUNT A **line** of a piece of writing is one of the rows of words, numbers, or other symbols in it. ▫ *The next line should read: Five days, 23.5 hours.* **6** N-COUNT A **line** of a poem, song, or play is a group of words that are spoken or sung together. If an actor **learns** his or her **lines** for a play or film, they learn what they have to say. ▫ *...a line from Shakespeare's Othello: "one that loved not wisely but too well."* ▫ *Every time I say that line, I have to compete with that darn trombone!* **7** N-VAR You can refer to a long piece of wire, string, or cable as a **line** when it is used for a particular purpose. ▫ *She put her washing on the line.* ▫ *...a piece of fishing-line.* **8** N-COUNT A **line** is a connection which makes it possible for two people to speak to each other on the telephone. ▫ *The telephone lines went dead.* ▫ *It's not a very good line. Shall we call you back Susan?* **9** N-COUNT You can use **line** to refer to a telephone number which you can call in order to get information or advice. ▫ *...the 24-hour information line.* **10** N-COUNT A **line** is a route, especially a dangerous or secret one, along which people move or send messages or supplies. ▫ *The North American continent's geography severely limited the lines of attack.* ▫ *Negotiators say they're keeping communication lines open.* **11** N-COUNT The **line** in which something or someone moves is the particular route that they take, especially when they keep moving straight ahead. ▫ *Walk in a straight line.* **12** N-COUNT A **line** is a particular route, involving the same stations, roads, or stops along which a train or bus service regularly operates. ▫ *They've got to ride all the way to the end of the line.* **13** N-COUNT A railroad **line** consists of the pieces of metal and wood which form the track that the trains travel along. ▫ *Floods washed out much of the railroad* line. ◨ N-COUNT A shipping, air, or bus **line** is a company which provides services for transporting people or goods by sea, air, or bus. [BUSINESS] ❏ *...the country's biggest shipping lines.* ◨ N-COUNT A state or county **line** is a boundary between two states or counties. [AM] ❏ *...the California state line.* ◨ N-COUNT You can use **lines** to refer to the set of physical defenses or the soldiers that have been established along the boundary of an area occupied by an army. ❏ *Their unit was shelling the German lines only seven miles away.* ◨ N-COUNT The particular **line** that a person has toward a problem is the attitude that they have toward it. For example, if someone takes a **hard line** on something, they have a firm strict policy which they refuse to change. ❏ *Forty members of the governing Conservative party rebelled, voting against the government line.* ◨ N-COUNT You can use **line** to refer to the way in which someone's thoughts or activities develop, particularly if it is logical. ❏ *Our discussion in the previous chapter continues this line of thinking.* ◨ N-PLURAL If you say that something happens along particular **lines**, or on particular **lines**, you are giving a general summary or approximate account of what happens, which may not be correct in every detail. ❏ *There followed an assortment of praise for the coffee along the lines of "Hey, this coffee is fantastic!"* ❏ *He'd said something on those lines already.* ◨ N-PLURAL If something is organized on particular **lines**, or along particular **lines**, it is organized according to that method or principle. ❏ *...so-called autonomous republics based on ethnic lines.* ◨ N-COUNT Your **line** of business or work is the kind of work that you do. [BUSINESS] ❏ *So what was your father's line of business?* ◨ N-COUNT In a factory, a **line** is an arrangement of workers or machines where a product passes from one worker to another until it is finished. ❏ *...a production line capable of producing three different products.* ◨ N-COUNT You can use **line** when you are referring to a number of people who are ranked according to status. ❏ *He was seventh in the line of succession to the throne.* ◨ N-COUNT A particular **line** of people or things is a series of them that has existed over a period of time, when they have all been similar in some way, or done similar things. ❏ *We were part of a long line of artists.* ◨ → see also **bottom line, front line, picket line**

② **line** ♦♦♦ /laɪn/
→ Please look at meaning ◨ to see if the expression you are looking for is shown under another headword.
◨ PHRASE If you say that someone has **crossed the line** or has **stepped over the line**, you mean that they have behaved in a way that is considered unacceptable. ❏ *He has crossed the line, and it must stop.* ❏ *Sometimes, I think the administration steps over the line when they make these kinds of accusations.* ◨ PHRASE If you **draw the line** at a particular activity, you refuse to do it, because you disapprove of it or because it is more extreme than what you normally do. ❏ *I'll pretty much give anything a go, but I draw the line at eating offal.* ◨ PHRASE If you do something or if it happens to you **in the line of duty**, you do it or it happens as part of your regular work or as a result of it. ❏ *More than 3,000 police officers were wounded in the line of duty last year.* ◨ PHRASE If you refer to a method as **the first line of**, for example, defense or treatment, you mean that it is the first or most important method to be used in dealing with a problem. ❏ *Residents have the responsibility of being the first line of defense against wildfires.* ◨ PHRASE If one object is **in line** with others, or moves **into line** with others, they are arranged in a line. You can also say that a number of objects are **in line** or move **into line**. ❏ *The device itself was right under the vehicle, almost in line with the gear lever.* ◨ PHRASE If one thing is **in line** with another, or is brought **into line** with it, the first thing is, or becomes, similar to the second, especially in a way that has been planned or expected. ❏ *The structure of our schools is now broadly in line with the major countries of the world.* ❏ *This brings the law into line with most medical opinion.* ◨ PHRASE If you keep someone **in line** or bring them **into line**, you make them obey you, or you make them behave in the way you want them to. ❏ *All this was just designed to frighten me and keep me in line.* ◨ PHRASE If a machine or piece of equipment comes **on line**, it starts operating. If it is **off line**, it is not operating. ❏ *The new machine will go on line in June 2006.* ◨ PHRASE If you do something **on line**, you do it using a computer or a computer network. ❏ *They can order their requirements on line.* ◨ → see also **online**
◨ **to sign on the dotted line** → see **dotted**

③ **line** ♦♦♦ /laɪn/ (**lines, lining, lined**) ◨ V-T If people or things **line** a road, room, or other place, they are present in large numbers along its edges or sides. ❏ *Thousands of local people lined the streets and clapped as the procession went by.* ◨ V-T If you **line** a wall, container, or other object, you put a layer of something such as leaves or paper on the inside surface of it in order to make it stronger, warmer, or cleaner. ❏ *Line the basket with a bright checkered napkin just before adding the cookies.* ◨ → see also **lining** ◨ → See feature box at **telephone, theater**

④ **line** ♦♦♦ /laɪn/ (**lines, lining, lined**)
▶ **line up** ◨ PHRASAL VERB If people **line up** or if you **line** them **up**, they move so that they are standing in a line. ❏ *The senior leaders lined up behind him in orderly rows.* ❏ *The gym teachers lined us up against the cement walls.* ◨ PHRASAL VERB If you **line** things **up**, you move them into a straight row. ❏ *I would line up my toys on this windowsill and play.* ◨ PHRASAL VERB If you **line** one thing **up** with another, or one thing **lines up** with another, the first thing is moved into its correct position in relation to the second. You can also say that two things **line up**, or **are lined up**. ❏ *You have to line the car up with the ones beside you.* ❏ *The plane circled twice, trying in vain to line up with the runway.* ◨ PHRASAL VERB If you **line up** an event or activity, you arrange for it to happen. If you **line** someone **up** for an event or activity, you arrange for them to be available for that event or activity. ❏ *She lined up executives, politicians and educators to serve on the board of directors.* ◨ → see also **lineup**

lin|eage /lɪniɪdʒ/ (**lineages**) N-VAR Someone's **lineage** is the series of families from which they are directly descended. [FORMAL] ❏ *They can trace their lineage back to the 18th century.*

lin|eal /lɪniəl/ ADJ [ADJ n] A **lineal** descendant of a particular person or family is someone in a later generation who is directly related to them. [FORMAL]

lin|ear /lɪniər/ ◨ ADJ A **linear** process or development is one in which something changes or progresses straight from one stage to another, and has a starting point and an ending point. ❏ *...decisions that lead the story in various directions, rather than follow traditional linear storytelling.* ◨ ADJ A **linear** shape or form consists of straight lines. ❏ *...the sharp, linear designs of the Seventies and Eighties.* ◨ ADJ **Linear** movement or force occurs in a straight line rather than in a curve. ❏ *...linear movement toward a goal.*

line|back|er /laɪnbækər/ (**linebackers**) N-COUNT In football, a **linebacker** is a player who tries to stop members of the other team from scoring by tackling them.

lined /laɪnd/ ◨ ADJ If someone's face or skin is **lined**, it has lines on it as a result of old age, tiredness, worry, or illness. ❏ *His lined face was that of an old man.* ◨ ADJ **Lined** paper has lines printed across it to help you write neatly. ◨ → see also **line** ③, **line** ④

line danc|ing N-UNCOUNT **Line dancing** is a style of dancing in which people move across the floor in a line, accompanied by country and western music.

line draw|ing (**line drawings**) N-COUNT A **line drawing** is a drawing which consists only of lines.

line drive (**line drives**) N-COUNT In baseball, a **line drive** is a ball that is hit hard and travels straight and close to the ground. [AM] ❏ *Perez led off the third with a line drive into the left-field corner.*

line|man /laɪnmən/ (**linemen**) N-COUNT In football, a **lineman** is one of the players on the line of scrimmage at the start of each play. [AM] ❏ *Green is a defensive lineman for the Atlanta Falcons.*

line man|ag|er (**line managers**) N-COUNT Your **line manager** is the person at work who is in charge of your department, group, or project. [mainly BRIT, BUSINESS] ❏ *Speak to your line manager and ask if there any opportunities for promotion.*

lin|en /lɪnɪn/ (**linens**) ◨ N-MASS **Linen** is a kind of cloth that is made from a plant called flax. It is used for making clothes and things such as tablecloths and sheets. ❏ *...a white linen suit.* ◨ N-UNCOUNT [also N in pl] **Linen** is tablecloths, sheets, pillowcases, and similar things made of cloth that are used in the home. ❏ *...embroidered bed linen.*

line of cred|it (**lines of credit**) N-COUNT A **line of credit** is the same as a **credit line**. [mainly AM]

line of scrim|mage N-SING In football, the **line of scrimmage** is an imaginary line on either side of which the

line of sight

offense and defense line up. ❑ *The Bears stacked the line of scrimmage with extra defenders to stop the run.*

line of sight (lines of sight) N-COUNT [usu sing, oft with poss] Your **line of sight** is an imaginary line that stretches between your eye and the object that you are looking at. ❑ *He was trying to keep out of the bird's line of sight.*

line of vi|sion N-SING [usu with poss] Your **line of vision** is the same as your **line of sight**. ❑ *Any crack in a car windshield always seems to be right in the driver's line of vision.*

lin|er /laɪnər/ (liners) N-COUNT A **liner** is a large ship in which people travel long distances, especially on vacation. ❑ *...luxury ocean liners.*

lin|er note (liner notes) N-COUNT [usu pl] The **liner notes** on CD jackets are short pieces of writing that tell you something about the CD or the musicians playing on the CD. [AM]

in BRIT, use **sleeve notes**

lines|man /laɪnzmən/ (linesmen) N-COUNT A **linesman** is an official who assists the referee or umpire in games such as football and tennis by indicating when the ball goes over the lines around the edge of the field or court.

line|up /laɪnʌp/ (lineups) **1** N-COUNT A **lineup** is a group of people or a series of things that have been gathered together to be part of a particular event. ❑ *For tickets and to view the complete lineup to date, visit the website.* **2** N-COUNT At a **lineup**, a witness to a crime tries to identify the criminal from among a line of people. ❑ *He failed to identify Graham from photographs, but later picked him out of a police lineup.*

lin|ger /lɪŋɡər/ (lingers, lingering, lingered) **1** V-I When something such as an idea, feeling, or illness **lingers**, it continues to exist for a long time, often much longer than expected. ❑ *The scent of her perfume lingered on in the room.* ❑ *He was ashamed. That feeling lingered, and he was never comfortable in church after that.* **2** V-I If you **linger** somewhere, you stay there for a longer time than is necessary, for example, because you are enjoying yourself. ❑ *Customers are welcome to linger over coffee until around midnight.*

lin|gerie /lɑnʒəreɪ, læn-/ N-UNCOUNT **Lingerie** is women's underwear and nightclothes. ❑ *...a new range of lingerie.*

lin|go /lɪŋɡoʊ/ (lingos) **1** N-COUNT [usu sing] People sometimes refer to a foreign language, especially one that they do not speak or understand, as a **lingo**. [INFORMAL] ❑ *I don't speak the lingo.* **2** N-UNCOUNT [also a N] A **lingo** is a range of words or a style of language which is used in a particular situation or by a particular group of people. [INFORMAL] ❑ *In music-business lingo, that means he wanted to buy the rights to the song and market it.* ❑ *...an author who writes in a lurid lingo, freely punctuated with crude expletives.*

lin|gua fran|ca /lɪŋɡwə fræŋkə/ N-SING A **lingua franca** is a language or way of communicating which is used between people who do not speak one another's native language. [FORMAL] ❑ *English is rapidly becoming the lingua franca of Asia.*

lin|gui|ne /lɪŋɡwini/ also **linguini** N-UNCOUNT **Linguine** is a kind of pasta in the shape of thin, flat strands. ❑ *The linguine was great.*

lin|guist /lɪŋɡwɪst/ (linguists) **1** N-COUNT A **linguist** is someone who is good at speaking or learning foreign languages. ❑ *He had a scholarly air and was an accomplished linguist.* **2** N-COUNT A **linguist** is someone who studies or teaches linguistics. ❑ *Many linguists have looked at language in this way.*

lin|guis|tic /lɪŋɡwɪstɪk/ (linguistics) **1** ADJ **Linguistic** abilities or ideas relate to language or linguistics. ❑ *...linguistic skills.* **2** N-UNCOUNT **Linguistics** is the study of the way in which language works. ❑ *Modern linguistics emerged as a distinct field in the nineteenth century.*

lini|ment /lɪnɪmənt/ (liniments) N-MASS **Liniment** is a liquid that you rub into your skin in order to reduce pain or stiffness.

lin|ing /laɪnɪŋ/ (linings) **1** N-VAR The **lining** of something such as a piece of clothing or a curtain is a layer of cloth attached to the inside of it in order to make it thicker or warmer, or in order to make it hang better. ❑ *...a padded satin jacket with quilted lining.* **2** N-COUNT The **lining** of your stomach or other organ is a layer of tissue on the inside of it. ❑ *...a bacterium that attacks the lining of the stomach.* **3** → see also **line** ③, **line** ④

linkage

link ♦♦◊ /lɪŋk/ (links, linking, linked) **1** N-COUNT If there is a **link** between two things or situations, there is a relationship between them, for example, because one thing causes or affects the other. ❑ *...the link between smoking and lung cancer.* **2** V-T If someone or something **links** two things or situations, there is a relationship between them, for example, because one thing causes or affects the other. ❑ *The U.N. Security Council has linked any lifting of sanctions to compliance with the ceasefire terms.* ❑ *The study further strengthens the evidence linking smoking with early death.* **3** N-COUNT A **link** between two things or places is a physical connection between them. ❑ *...the railroad link between Boston and New York.* ❑ *Drivers ran into a field of weeds at the state border, where no link with the neighboring state had yet been planned.* **4** V-T If two places or objects **are linked** or something **links** them, there is a physical connection between them. ❑ *...the Rama Road, which links the capital, Managua, with the Caribbean coast.* ❑ *Seven miles of track were installed to link the hotel to the golf course.* **5** N-COUNT A **link** between two people, organizations, or places is a friendly or business connection between them. ❑ *He hopes to cement close links between Northern Ireland and India.* ❑ *He also emphasized that there must be a close link between the prison and the community which it serves.* **6** N-COUNT A **link** to another person or organization is something that allows you to communicate with them or have contact with them. ❑ *She was my only link with the past.* ❑ *The Red Cross was created to provide a link between soldiers in battle and their families at home.* **7** V-T If you **link** one person or thing to another, you claim that there is a relationship or connection between them. ❑ *Evidence she uncovers leads her to link the crime to a series of other unsolved murders.* ❑ *They've linked her with various men, including a publishing magnate.* **8** N-COUNT In computing, a **link** is a connection between different documents, or between different parts of the same document, using hypertext. ❑ *Available in English, French, German and Italian, it has links to other relevant tourism sites.* • V-T **Link** is also a verb. ❑ *...the method of using HTML to link pages together.* **9** N-COUNT A **link** is one of the rings in a chain. ❑ *...a chain of heavy gold links.* **10** V-T If you **link** one thing with another, you join them by putting one thing through the other. ❑ *She linked her arm through his.* • PHRASE If two or more people **link arms**, or if one person **links arms** with another, they stand next to each other, and each person puts their arm around the arm of the person next to them. ❑ *It was so slippery that some of the walkers linked arms and proceeded very carefully.* **11** → see also **linkup** **12** → See feature box at **commute**

▶ **link up 1** PHRASAL VERB If you **link up** with someone, you join them for a particular purpose. ❑ *They linked up with a series of local anti-nuclear and anti-apartheid groups.* **2** PHRASAL VERB If one thing **is linked up to** another, the two things are connected to each other. ❑ *The television screens of the next century will be linked up to an emerging world telecommunications grid.*

─────── **COLLOCATIONS** ───────

link
NOUN **1**
adjective + **link**: close, direct, strong; tenuous, weak; causal
verb + **link**: build, create, establish, forge; break, cut, sever; maintain, retain
VERB **2**
link + adverb: closely, directly

─────── **SYNONYMS** ───────

link
NOUN **1**
connection: *The police say he had no connection with the security forces.*
relationship: *There is a relationship between diet and cancer.*
association: *Black was considered inappropriate because of its associations with death.*
VERB **4**
connect: *You can connect the machine to your computer.*
join: *The parking lots are joined by a footpath.*
unite: *The vast majority of nations have agreed to unite their efforts to bring peace.*
attach: *The gadget can be attached to any vertical surface.*

link|age /lɪŋkɪdʒ/ (linkages) **1** N-VAR [oft N between/with/of N] A **linkage** between two things is a link or connection between them. The **linkage** of two things is the act of linking or connecting them. ❑ *No one disputes the direct linkage between the unemployment rate and crime.* ❑ *We're trying to establish linkages between these groups and financial institutions.* ❑ *...the creation of new research materials by the linkage of previously existing sources.* **2** N-UNCOUNT [oft N between/with n] **Linkage** is an arrangement where one country agrees to do something only if another country agrees to do something in return. ❑ *There is no formal linkage between the two agreements.* ❑ *He insisted that there could be no linkage with other Mideast problems.*

link|ing verb (linking verbs) N-COUNT A **linking verb** is a verb which links the subject of a clause and a complement. 'Be,' 'seem,' and 'become' are linking verbs.

link|ing word (linking words) N-COUNT A **linking word** is a word which shows a connection between clauses or sentences. 'However' and 'so' are linking words.

link|up /lɪŋkʌp/ (linkups) **1** N-COUNT A **linkup** is a connection between two machines or communication systems. ❑ *...a live satellite linkup with Berlin.* **2** N-COUNT A **linkup** is a relationship or partnership between two organizations. ❑ *...new linkups between school and commerce.*

li|no|leum /lɪnoʊliəm/ N-UNCOUNT [oft N n] **Linoleum** is a floor covering which is made of cloth covered with a hard shiny substance. ❑ *...a gray linoleum floor.* ❑ *...black and white squares of linoleum.*

lin|seed oil /lɪnsid ɔɪl/ N-UNCOUNT **Linseed oil** is an oil made from seeds of the flax plant. It is used to make paints and inks, or to rub into wooden surfaces to protect them.

lint /lɪnt/ **1** N-UNCOUNT **Lint** is small unwanted threads or fibers that collect on clothes. [mainly AM] **2** N-UNCOUNT **Lint** is cotton or linen fabric which you can put on your skin if you have a cut. [BRIT]

lin|tel /lɪntəl/ (lintels) N-COUNT A **lintel** is a piece of stone or wood over a door or window which supports the bricks above the door or window.

lion /laɪən/ (lions) N-COUNT A **lion** is a large wild member of the cat family that is found in Africa. Lions have yellowish fur, and male lions have long hair on their head and neck.

li|on|ess /laɪənes/ (lionesses) N-COUNT A **lioness** is a female lion.

li|on|ize /laɪənaɪz/ (lionizes, lionizing, lionized)

in BRIT, also use **lionise**

V-T If someone **is lionized**, they are treated as if they are very important or special by a particular group of people, often when they do not really deserve to be. [FORMAL] ❑ *By the 1920s, he was lionized by literary New York.* ❑ *The press began to lionize him enthusiastically.* ❑ *In 1936, Max Schmeling had been lionized as boxing's great hope.*

lion's share N-SING If a person, group, or project gets the **lion's share** of something, they get the largest part of it, leaving very little for other people. ❑ *Military and nuclear research have received the lion's share of public funding.*

lip ✦✧✧ /lɪp/ (lips) N-COUNT Your **lips** are the two outer parts of the edge of your mouth. ❑ *Wade stuck the cigarette between his lips.*

COLLOCATIONS

lip
NOUN
adjective + **lip**: pouting; quivering, trembling; pursed
verb + **lip**: curl; bite

---

lip gloss (lip glosses) N-MASS **Lip gloss** is a clear or very slightly colored substance that is put on the lips to make them shiny.

lipo|suc|tion /lɪpoʊsʌkʃən, laɪpoʊ-/ N-UNCOUNT **Liposuction** is a form of cosmetic surgery where fat is removed from a particular area of the body by dissolving it with special chemicals and then sucking it out with a tube.

-lipped /-lɪpt/ **1** COMB IN ADJ **-lipped** combines with adjectives to form other adjectives which describe the sort of lips that someone has. ❑ *A thin-lipped smile spread over the captain's face.* ❑ *...his full-lipped mouth.* **2** → see also **tight-lipped**

lip-read (lip-reads, lip-reading)

The form **lip-read** is pronounced /lɪprid/ when it is the present tense, and /lɪprɛd/ when it is the past tense and past participle.

V-I If someone can **lip-read**, they are able to understand what someone else is saying by looking at the way the other person's lips move as they speak, without actually hearing any of the words. ❑ *They are not given hearing aids or taught to lip-read.* • **lip read|ing** N-UNCOUNT ❑ *The teacher should not move around too much as this makes lip reading more difficult.*

lip ser|vice N-UNCOUNT [usu N to n/-ing] If you say that someone pays **lip service** to an idea, you are critical of them because they say they are in favor of it, but they do not do anything to support it. [DISAPPROVAL] ❑ *Unhappily, he had done no more than pay lip service to their views.*

lip|stick /lɪpstɪk/ (lipsticks) N-MASS **Lipstick** is a colored substance in the form of a stick which people put on their lips. ❑ *She was wearing red lipstick.*

liq|ue|fy /lɪkwɪfaɪ/ (liquefies, liquefying, liquefied) When a gas or solid substance **liquefies** or **is liquefied**, it changes its form and becomes liquid. ❑ *Heat the jam until it liquefies.* ❑ *You can liquefy the carbon dioxide to separate it from the other constituents.* ❑ *...a truck carrying liquefied petroleum gas.*

li|queur /lɪkɜr, -kyʊər/ (liqueurs) N-MASS A **liqueur** is a strong alcoholic drink with a sweet taste. You drink it after a meal. ❑ *...liqueurs such as Grand Marnier and Kirsch.*

liq|uid /lɪkwɪd/ (liquids) **1** N-MASS A **liquid** is a substance which is not solid but which flows and can be poured, for example, water. ❑ *Drink plenty of liquid.* ❑ *Boil for 20 minutes until the liquid has reduced by half.* **2** ADJ A **liquid** substance is in the form of a liquid rather than being solid or a gas. ❑ *Wash in warm water with liquid detergent.* ❑ *The tanker was carrying liquid nitrogen.* **3** ADJ **Liquid** assets are the things that a person or company owns which can be quickly turned into cash if necessary. [BUSINESS] ❑ *The bank had sufficient liquid assets to continue operations.*

liq|ui|date /lɪkwɪdeɪt/ (liquidates, liquidating, liquidated) **1** V-T To **liquidate** a company is to close it down and sell all its assets, usually because it is in debt. [BUSINESS] ❑ *A unanimous vote was taken to liquidate the company.* • **liq|ui|da|tion** /lɪkwɪdeɪʃən/ (liquidations) N-VAR ❑ *The company went into liquidation.* **2** V-T If a company **liquidates** its assets, its property such as buildings or machinery is sold in order to get money. [BUSINESS] ❑ *The company closed down operations and began liquidating its assets in January.*

liq|ui|da|tor /lɪkwɪdeɪtər/ (liquidators) N-COUNT A **liquidator** is a person who is responsible for settling the affairs of a company that is being liquidated. [BUSINESS] ❑ *...the failed company's liquidators.*

liq|uid crys|tal (liquid crystals) N-COUNT A **liquid crystal** is a liquid that has some of the qualities of crystals, for example, reflecting light from different directions in different ways.

liq|uid crys|tal dis|play (liquid crystal displays) also **liquid-crystal display** N-COUNT A **liquid crystal display** is a display of information on a screen, which uses liquid crystals that become visible when electricity is passed through them.

li|quid|ity /lɪkwɪdɪti/ N-UNCOUNT In finance, a company's **liquidity** is the amount of cash or liquid assets it has easily available. [BUSINESS] ❑ *The company maintains a high degree of liquidity.*

liq|uid|ize /lɪkwɪdaɪz/ (liquidizes, liquidizing, liquidized)

in BRIT, also use **liquidise**

V-T If you **liquidize** food, you process it using an electrical appliance in order to make it liquid.

liq|uid|iz|er /lɪkwɪdaɪzər/ (liquidizers)

in BRIT, also use **liquidiser**

N-COUNT A **liquidizer** is the same as a **blender**. [BRIT]

liq|uor /lɪkər/ (liquors) N-MASS Strong alcoholic drinks such as whiskey, vodka, and gin can be referred to as **liquor**. [AM] ❑ *The room was filled with cases of liquor.*

in BRIT, use **spirits**

liquo|rice /lɪkərɪʃ, -ɪs/ → see **licorice**

liq|uor store (liquor stores) N-COUNT A **liquor store** is a store which sells beer, wine, and other alcoholic drinks. [AM]

in BRIT, use **off-licence**

lira /lɪərə/ (lire /lɪərə/) N-COUNT [usu num N] The **lira** was the unit of money that was used in Italy before it was replaced by the euro. ❑ *Coin-operated telephones took 100, 200 and 500 lire coins.* • N-SING [the N] The **lira** was also used to refer to the Italian currency system, and it also sometimes refers to the currency system of other countries which use the lira.

lisp /lɪsp/ (lisps, lisping, lisped) **1** N-COUNT [usu sing] If someone has a **lisp**, they pronounce the sounds 's' and 'z' as if they were 'th.' For example, they say 'thing' instead of 'sing.' ❑ *He has a slight lisp.* **2** V-T/V-I If someone **lisps**, they say something with a lisp or speak with a lisp. ❑ *The little man, upset, was lisping badly.* ❑ *Bochmann lisped his congratulations.* ❑ *...her low, lisping voice.*

list ✦✦✦ /lɪst/ (lists, listing, listed) **1** N-COUNT A **list** of things such as names or addresses is a set of them which all belong to a particular category, written down one below the other. ❑ *We are making a list of the top ten men we would not want to be married to.* ❑ *There were six names on the list.* **2** → see also **hit list, mailing list, waiting list** **3** N-COUNT A **list** of things is a set of them that you think of as being in a particular order. ❑ *High on the list of public demands is to end military control of broadcasting.* ❑ *The criminal judicial system always comes up at the top of the list of voters' concerns in focus groups.* **4** V-T To **list** several things such as reasons or names means to write or say them one after another, usually in a particular order. ❑ *The pupils were asked to list the sports they loved most and hated most.* **5** V-T To **list** something in a particular way means to include it in that way in a list or report. ❑ *A medical examiner has listed the deaths as homicides.* **6** V-T/V-I If a company **is listed**, or if it **lists**, on a stock exchange, it obtains an official quotation for its shares so that people can buy and sell them. [BUSINESS] ❑ *...a basket of blue chip stocks listed on the American Exchange.* **7** → see also **listed company**

SYNONYMS

list
NOUN **1**
record: *Keep a record of all the payments.*
inventory: *Before starting, he made an inventory of everything that was to stay.*
catalogue: *This is the world's biggest seed catalogue.*
register: *She calls the register for her class of thirty 12-year-olds.*
VERB **4**
catalogue: *The Royal Greenwich Observatory was founded to observe and catalogue the stars.*
itemize: *Itemize your gear and mark major items with your name and zip code.*
record: *You can buy software packages which record the details of your photographs.*

---

list|ed com|pa|ny (listed companies) N-COUNT A **listed company** is a company whose shares are quoted on a stock exchange. [BUSINESS] ❑ *Some of Australia's largest listed companies are expected to announce huge interim earnings this week.*

lis|ten ✦✦✦ /lɪsən/ (listens, listening, listened) **1** V-I If you **listen** to someone who is talking or to a sound, you give your attention to them or it. ❑ *He spent his time listening to the radio.* • **lis|ten|er** (listeners) N-COUNT ❑ *One or two listeners had fallen asleep while the president was speaking.* **2** V-I If you **listen** for a sound, you keep alert and are ready to hear it if it occurs. ❑ *We listen for footsteps approaching.* **3** V-I If you **listen** to someone, you do what they advise you to do, or you believe them. ❑ *Anne, you need to listen to me this time.* **4** CONVENTION You say **listen** when you want someone to pay attention to you because you are going to say something important. ❑ *Listen, I finish at one.*
▶ **listen in** PHRASAL VERB If you **listen in** to a private conversation, you secretly listen to it. ❑ *He assigned federal agents to listen in on Martin Luther King's phone calls.*

COLLOCATIONS

listen
VERB **1**
listen + *adverb:* attentively, carefully, hard, intently; patiently, politely

---

lis|ten|able /lɪsənəbəl/ ADJ If something is **listenable**, it is very pleasant to listen to. ❑ *It's an eminently listenable album.*

lis|ten|er /lɪsnər, lɪsnər/ (listeners) **1** N-COUNT A **listener** is a person who listens to the radio or to a particular radio program. ❑ *I'm a regular listener to her show.* **2** N-COUNT If you describe someone as a good **listener**, you mean that they listen carefully and sympathetically to you when you talk, for example, about your problems. ❑ *Dr. Brian was a good listener.* **3** → see also **listen**

lis|te|ria /lɪstɪəriə/ N-UNCOUNT **Listeria** is a serious form of food poisoning caused by bacteria in food. You can also refer to the bacteria itself as **listeria**. ❑ *...an outbreak of listeria.* ❑ *Tests showed it was contaminated by listeria and other bacteria.*

list|ing /lɪstɪŋ/ (listings) N-COUNT A **listing** is a published list, or an item in a published list. ❑ *A full listing of the companies will be published quarterly.*

list|less /lɪstlɪs/ ADJ Someone who is **listless** has no energy or enthusiasm. ❑ *He was listless and pale and wouldn't eat much.* • **list|less|ly** ADV [ADV with v] ❑ *Usually, you would just sit listlessly, too hot to do anything else.*

list price (list prices) N-COUNT The **list price** of an item is the price which the manufacturer suggests that a store should charge for it. ❑ *...a small car with a list price of $18,000.*

list|serv /lɪstsɜrv/ (listservs) N-COUNT A **listserv** is a computerized list of names and email addresses that a company or organization keeps, so that they can send people emails containing information or advertisements. [AM]

lit /lɪt/ **Lit** is a past tense and past participle of **light**.

lita|ny /lɪtəni/ (litanies) **1** N-COUNT If you describe what someone says as a **litany** of things, you mean that you have heard it many times before, and you think it is boring or insincere. [DISAPPROVAL] ❑ *She remained in the doorway, listening to his litany of complaints against her client.* **2** N-COUNT A **litany** is part of a church service in which the priest says a set group of words and the people reply, also using a set group of words.

lite /laɪt/ ADJ **Lite** is used to describe foods or drinks that contain few calories or low amounts of sugar, fat, or alcohol. ❑ *...lite beer.* ❑ *...lite yogurt.*

li|ter /lɪtər/ (liters)

in BRIT, use **litre**

N-COUNT A **liter** is a metric unit of volume that is a thousand cubic centimeters. It is equal to 2.11 pints. ❑ *...a 13-thousand liter water tank.* ❑ *It is sold to the public at eight cents a liter.*

lit|era|cy /lɪtərəsi/ N-UNCOUNT **Literacy** is the ability to read and write. ❑ *Many adults have problems with literacy and numeracy.*

lit|er|al /lɪtərəl/ **1** ADJ The **literal** sense of a word or phrase is its most basic sense. ❑ *In many cases, the people there are fighting, in a literal sense, for their homes.* **2** ADJ A **literal** translation is one in which you translate each word of the original work rather than giving the meaning of each expression or sentence using words that sound natural. ❑ *A literal translation of the name Tapies is "walls."*

lit|er|al|ly /lɪtərəli/ **1** ADV You can use **literally** to emphasize an exaggeration. Some careful speakers of English think that this use is incorrect. [EMPHASIS] ❑ *We've got to get the economy under control or it will literally eat us up.* **2** ADV You use **literally** to emphasize that what you are saying is true, even though it seems exaggerated or surprising. [EMPHASIS] ❑ *Putting on an opera is a tremendous enterprise involving literally hundreds of people.* **3** ADV If a word or expression is translated **literally**, its most simple or basic meaning is translated. ❑ *The word "volk" translates literally as "folk."*

lit|er|ary ✦◇◇ /lɪtəreri/ **1** ADJ **Literary** means concerned with or connected with the writing, study, or appreciation of literature. ❑ *Her literary criticism focuses on the way great literature suggests ideas.* ❑ *She's the literary editor of the "Sunday Review."*
2 ADJ **Literary** words and expressions are often unusual in some way and are used to create a special effect in a piece of writing such as a poem, speech, or novel. ❑ *...archaic, literary words from the Tang dynasty.* **3** → See feature box at **book**

lit|er|ary criti|cism N-UNCOUNT **Literary criticism** is the academic study of the techniques used in the creation of literature.

lit|er|ate /lɪtərɪt/ ADJ Someone who is **literate** is able to read and write. ❑ *Over one-quarter of the adult population are not fully literate.* ❷ → see also **computer-literate** ❸ → See feature box at **finance**

lit|era|ti /lɪtərɑːti/ N-PLURAL **Literati** are well-educated people who are interested in literature. ❑ *...the Australian storyteller who was loved by readers but disdained by the literati.*

lit|era|ture ✦✧ /lɪtərətʃər, -tʃʊr/ (**literatures**) ❶ N-VAR Novels, plays, and poetry are referred to as **literature**, especially when they are considered to be good or important. ❑ *...classic works of literature.* ❑ *I have spent my life getting to know diverse literatures of different epochs.* ❷ N-UNCOUNT The **literature** on a particular subject of study is all the books and articles that have been published about it. ❑ *...the literature on immigration policy.* ❸ N-UNCOUNT **Literature** is written information produced by people who want to sell you something or give you advice. ❑ *I am sending you literature from two other companies that provide a similar service.*

lithe /laɪð/ ADJ A **lithe** person is able to move and bend their body easily and gracefully. ❑ *...a lithe young gymnast.* ❑ *His walk was lithe and graceful.*

litho|graph /lɪθəɡræf, -ɡrɑːf/ (**lithographs**) N-COUNT A **lithograph** is a printed picture made by the method of lithography.

li|thog|ra|phy /lɪθɒɡrəfi/ N-UNCOUNT **Lithography** is a method of printing in which a piece of stone or metal is specially treated so that ink sticks to some parts of it and not to others. • **litho|graph|ic** ADJ ❑ *The book's 85 color lithographic plates look staggeringly fresh and bold.*

Lithua|nian /lɪθjueɪniən/ (**Lithuanians**) ❶ ADJ **Lithuanian** means belonging or relating to Lithuania, or to its people, language, or culture. ❷ N-COUNT A **Lithuanian** is a Lithuanian citizen, or a person of Lithuanian origin. ❸ N-UNCOUNT **Lithuanian** is the language spoken by people who live in Lithuania.

liti|gant /lɪtɪɡənt/ (**litigants**) N-COUNT A **litigant** is a person who is involved in a civil legal case, either because they are making a formal complaint about someone, or because a complaint is being made about them. [LEGAL]

liti|gate /lɪtɪɡeɪt/ (**litigates**, **litigating**, **litigated**) V-T/V-I To **litigate** means to take legal action. [LEGAL] ❑ *...the cost of litigating personal injury claims in the county court.* ❑ *If we have to litigate, we will.*

liti|ga|tion /lɪtɪɡeɪʃən/ N-UNCOUNT **Litigation** is the process of fighting or defending a case in a civil court of law. ❑ *The settlement ends more than four years of litigation on behalf of the residents.*

liti|ga|tor /lɪtɪɡeɪtər/ (**litigators**) N-COUNT A **litigator** is a lawyer who helps someone take legal action. [LEGAL]

li|Li|gious /lɪtɪdʒəs/ ADJ Someone who is **litigious** often makes formal complaints about people to a civil court of law. [FORMAL]

lit|mus test /lɪtməs tɛst/ (**litmus tests**) N-COUNT [usu sing, usu N of/for n] If you say that something is a **litmus test** of something, you mean that it is an effective and definite way of proving it or measuring it. ❑ *Ending the fighting must be the absolute priority, the litmus test of the agreement's validity.* ❑ *The success of wind power represents a litmus test for renewable energy.*

li|tre /liːtər/ [BRIT] → see **liter**

lit|ter /lɪtər/ (**litters**, **littering**, **littered**) ❶ N-UNCOUNT **Litter** is garbage or trash that is left lying around outside. ❑ *If you see litter in the corridor, pick it up.* ❷ V-T If a number of things **litter** a place, they are scattered around it or over it. ❑ *Glass from broken bottles litters the sidewalk.* • **lit|tered** ADJ [v-link ADJ prep] ❑ *The entrance hall is littered with toys.* ❸ ADJ [v-link ADJ with n] If something is **littered with** things, it contains many examples of it. ❑ *History is littered with men and women spurred into achievement by a father's disregard.* ❹ N-COUNT A **litter** is a group of animals born to the same mother at the same time. ❑ *...a litter of pups.* ❺ → See feature box at **urban**

lit|ter bin (**litter bins**) N-COUNT A **litter bin** is the same as a **trash can**. [BRIT]

lit|ter|bug /lɪtərbʌɡ/ (**litterbugs**) N-COUNT If you accuse someone of being a **litterbug**, you mean that you disapprove of the fact that they drop litter in public places. [DISAPPROVAL] ❑ *...a city full of litterbugs.*

LITTLE
① DETERMINER, QUANTIFIER, AND ADVERB USES
② ADJECTIVE USES

① **lit|tle** ✦✦✦ /lɪtəl/ ❶ DET You use **little** to indicate that there is only a very small amount of something. You can use 'so', 'too', and 'very' in front of **little**. ❑ *I had little money and little free time.* ❑ *I find that I need very little sleep these days.* • QUANT [QUANT of def-n] **Little** is also a quantifier. ❑ *Little of the existing housing is of good enough quality.* • PRON **Little** is also a pronoun. ❑ *He ate little, and drank less.* ❑ *In general, employers do little to help the single working mother.* ❷ ADV [ADV with v] **Little** means not very often or to only a small extent. ❑ *On their way back to Marseille they spoke very little.* ❸ DET **A little** of something is a small amount of it, but not very much. You can also say **a very little**. ❑ *Mrs. Caan needs a little help getting her groceries home.* ❑ *A little food would do us all some good.* • PRON **Little** is also a pronoun. ❑ *They get paid for it. Not much. Just a little.* • QUANT **Little** is also a quantifier. ❑ *Pour a little of the sauce over the chicken.* ❹ ADV [ADV after v] If you do something **a little**, you do it for a short time. ❑ *He walked a little by himself in the garden.* ❺ ADV **A little** or **a little bit** means to a small extent or degree. ❑ *He complained a little of a nagging pain between his shoulder blades.* ❑ *He was a little bit afraid of his father's reaction.*

② **lit|tle** ✦✦✦ /lɪtəl/ (**littler**, **littlest**)

The comparative **littler** and the superlative **littlest** are sometimes used in spoken English for meanings ❶, ❸, and ❹, but otherwise the comparative and superlative forms of the adjective **little** are not used.

❶ ADJ **Little** things are small in size. **Little** is slightly more informal than **small**. ❑ *We sat around a little table, eating and drinking wine.* ❷ ADJ [ADJ n] You use **little** to indicate that someone or something is small, in a pleasant and attractive way. ❑ *She's got the nicest little house not far from the library.* ❑ *...a little old lady.* ❸ ADJ [ADJ n] Your **little** sister or brother is younger than you are. ❑ *Whenever Daniel's little sister was asked to do something she always had a naughty reply.* ❹ ADJ [ADJ n] A **little** distance, period of time, or event is short in length. ❑ *Just go down the road a little way, turn left, and cross the bridge.* ❑ *Why don't we just wait a little while and see what happens.* ❺ ADJ [ADJ n] A **little** sound or gesture is quick. ❑ *I had a little laugh to myself.* ❻ ADJ [ADJ n] You use **little** to indicate that something is not serious or important. ❑ *...irritating little habits.*

SYNONYMS
little
ADJ ① ❶
small: *She is small for her age.*
tiny: *The living room is tiny.*
minute: *Only a minute amount is needed.*
compact: *...my compact office in Washington.*
diminutive: *She noticed a diminutive figure standing at the entrance.*

lit|tle fin|ger (**little fingers**) N-COUNT Your **little finger** is the smallest finger on your hand.

Lit|tle League N-PROPER The **Little League** is an organization of children's baseball teams that compete against each other in the United States.

lit|to|ral /lɪtərəl/ (**littorals**) N-COUNT [usu sing, usu the N, N n] In geography, the **littoral** means the coast. [TECHNICAL] ❑ *...the countries of the north African littoral.* ❑ *...the littoral countries of the Persian Gulf.*

li|tur|gi|cal /lɪtɜːrdʒɪkəl/ ADJ [usu ADJ n] **Liturgical** things are used in or relate to church services. [FORMAL]

lit|ur|gy /lɪtərdʒi/ (**liturgies**) N-VAR A **liturgy** is a particular form of religious service, usually one that is set and approved by a branch of the Christian Church. ❑ *A clergyman read the liturgy from the prayer-book.* ❑ *...the many similarities in ministry, liturgy and style between the two churches.*

LIVE
① VERB USES
② ADJECTIVE USES

① **live** ♦♦♦ /lɪv/ (lives, living, lived)
→ Please look at meaning **8** to see if the expression you are looking for is shown under another headword.

1 V-I If someone **lives** in a particular place or with a particular person, their home is in that place or with that person. ❑ *She has lived here for 10 years.* ❑ *Where do you live?* **2** V-T/V-I If you say that someone **lives** in particular circumstances or that they **live** a particular kind of life, you mean that they are in those circumstances or that they have that kind of life. ❑ *We lived quite grandly.* ❑ *Compared to people living only a few generations ago, we have greater opportunities to have a good time.* **3** V-I If you say that someone **lives for** a particular thing, you mean that it is the most important thing in their life. ❑ *He lived for his work.* **4** V-T/V-I To **live** means to be alive. If someone **lives** to a particular age, they stay alive until they are that age. ❑ *He's got a terrible disease and will not live long.* ❑ *He lived to be 103.* **5** V-I [no cont] If people **live by** doing a particular activity, they get the money, food, or clothing they need by doing that activity. ❑ *...the last indigenous people to live by hunting.* **6** → see also **living** **7** PHRASE If you **live it up**, you have a very enjoyable and exciting time, for example by going to lots of parties or going out drinking with friends. [INFORMAL] ❑ *There is no reason why you couldn't live it up once in a while.* **8** to **live hand to mouth** → see **hand** ①

▶ **live down** PHRASAL VERB If you are unable to **live down** a mistake, failure, or bad reputation, you are unable to make people forget about it. ❑ *It was unable to live down its reputation as the party of high taxes.*

▶ **live off** PHRASAL VERB If you **live off** another person, you rely on them to provide you with money. ❑ *...a man who all his life had lived off his father.*

▶ **live on** also **live off** **1** PHRASAL VERB If you **live on** or **live off** a particular amount of money, you have that amount of money to buy things. ❑ *...people trying to live on $100 a week.* **2** PHRASAL VERB If you **live on** or **live off** a particular source of income, that is where you get the money that you need. ❑ *The proportion of Americans living on welfare rose.* **3** PHRASAL VERB If an animal **lives on** or **lives off** a particular food, this is the kind of food that it eats. ❑ *The fish live on the plankton.*

▶ **live on** PHRASAL VERB If someone **lives on**, they continue to be alive for a long time after a particular point in time or after a particular event. ❑ *I know my life has been cut short by this terrible virus but Daniel will live on after me.*

▶ **live up to** PHRASAL VERB If someone or something **lives up to** what they were expected to be, they are as good as they were expected to be. ❑ *Sales have not lived up to expectations this year.*

SYNONYMS

live
VERB ① **1**
dwell: *They are concerned for the fate of the forest and the Indians who dwell in it.*
lodge: *...the story of the farming family she lodged with as a young teacher.*
inhabit: *...the people who inhabit these islands.*
reside: *Margaret resides with her mother in a London suburb.*

② **live** ♦♦♦ /laɪv/ **1** ADJ [ADJ n] **Live** animals or plants are alive, rather than being dead or artificial. ❑ *...a protest against the company's tests on live animals.* **2** ADJ A **live** television or radio program is one in which an event or performance is broadcast at exactly the same time as it happens, rather than being recorded first. ❑ *Murray was a guest on a live radio show.* • ADV [ADV after v] **Live** is also an adverb. ❑ *It was broadcast live in 50 countries.* **3** ADJ A **live** performance is given in front of an audience, rather than being recorded and then broadcast or shown in a movie. ❑ *The venue has just started hosting live music on a weekly basis in the last few months.* ❑ *A live audience will pose the questions.* • ADV [ADV after v] **Live** is also an adverb. ❑ *She has been playing live with her new band.* **4** ADJ A **live** wire or piece of electrical equipment is directly connected to a source of electricity. ❑ *The plug broke, exposing live wires.* **5** ADJ **Live** bullets are made of metal, rather than rubber or plastic, and are intended to kill people rather than injure them. ❑ *They trained in the jungle using live ammunition.*

live|blog /laɪvblɒg/ (liveblogs, liveblogging, liveblogged) **1** N-COUNT A **liveblog** is a blog in which you write about an event as it happens. ❑ *She provided a liveblog from the conflict area.* **2** V-T/V-I If you **liveblog**, or **liveblog** an event, you write on your blog about an event as it happens. ❑ *Several people were liveblogging from the scene.*

live-in ♦♦♦ /lɪv ɪn/ **1** ADJ [ADJ n] A **live-in** partner is someone who lives in the same house as the person they are having a sexual relationship with, but is not married to them. ❑ *She shared the apartment with her live-in partner.* **2** ADJ [ADJ n] A **live-in** servant or other domestic worker sleeps and eats in the house where they work. ❑ *I have a live-in nanny for my youngest daughter.*

live|li|hood /laɪvlihʊd/ (livelihoods) N-VAR Your **livelihood** is the job or other source of income that gives you the money to buy the things you need. ❑ *...fishermen who depend on the seas for their livelihood.*

live|ly /laɪvli/ (livelier, liveliest) **1** ADJ You can describe someone as **lively** when they behave in an enthusiastic and cheerful way. ❑ *She had a sweet, lively personality.* • **live|li|ness** N-UNCOUNT ❑ *Amy could sense his liveliness even from where she stood.* **2** ADJ A **lively** event or a **lively** discussion, for example, has lots of interesting and exciting things happening or being said in it. ❑ *It turned out to be a very interesting session with a lively debate.* • **live|li|ness** N-UNCOUNT ❑ *Some may enjoy the liveliness of such a restaurant for a few hours a day or week.* **3** ADJ Someone who has a **lively** mind is intelligent and interested in a lot of different things. ❑ *She was a very well educated girl with a lively mind, a girl with ambition.*

liv|en /laɪvən/ (livens, livening, livened)
▶ **liven up** **1** PHRASAL VERB If a place or event **livens up**, or if something **livens** it **up**, it becomes more interesting and exciting. ❑ *How could we decorate the room to liven it up?* ❑ *The multicolored rag rug was chosen to liven up the gray carpet.* **2** PHRASAL VERB If people **liven up**, or if something **livens** them **up**, they become more cheerful and energetic. ❑ *Talking about her daughters livens her up.*

liv|er /lɪvər/ (livers) **1** N-COUNT Your **liver** is a large organ in your body which processes your blood and helps to clean unwanted substances out of it. ❑ *Three weeks ago, it was discovered the cancer had spread to his liver.* **2** N-VAR **Liver** is the liver of some animals, especially lambs, pigs, and cows, which is cooked and eaten. ❑ *...grilled calves' liver.* **3** → See feature box at **body**; See also color supplement

liv|eried /lɪvərid/ ADJ [ADJ n] A **liveried** servant is one who wears a special uniform. ❑ *The tea was served to guests by liveried footmen.*

liv|ery /lɪvəri/ (liveries) **1** N-COUNT [usu with poss] The **livery** of a particular company is the special design or set of colors associated with it that is put on its products and possessions. [BRIT] ❑ *...buffet cars in the railway company's bright red and yellow livery.* **2** N-VAR The **livery** of someone such as a soldier or servant is the special uniform that he or she wears. ❑ *...attendants in red and black livery.*

liv|ery sta|ble (livery stables) also **livery stables** N-COUNT A **livery stable** or **livery stables** is a building where horses are kept and hired out to people.

lives

Pronounced /laɪvz/ for meaning 1, and /lɪvz/ for meaning 2.

1 **Lives** is the plural of **life**. **2** **Lives** is the third person singular form of **live**.

live|stock /laɪvstɒk/ **1** N-UNCOUNT-COLL Animals such as cattle and sheep which are kept on a farm are referred to as **livestock**. ❑ *The heavy rains and flooding killed scores of livestock.* **2** → See feature box at **farming**, **global warming**

live|stream /laɪvstrim/ (livestreams, livestreaming, livestreamed) **1** V-T If someone **livestreams** an event, they broadcast it on the internet while it is happening. ❑ *The designer was one of the first to livestream his fashion shows.* **2** N-VAR A **livestream** of an event is an internet broadcast of it while it

live wire /laɪv waɪər/ (**live wires**) N-COUNT If you describe someone as a **live wire**, you mean that they are lively and energetic. [INFORMAL]

liv|id /lɪvɪd/ ADJ Someone who is **livid** is extremely angry. [INFORMAL] ❑ *I am absolutely livid about it.*

liv|ing ✦✧✧ /lɪvɪŋ/ (**livings**) **1** N-COUNT The work that you do for a **living** is the work that you do in order to earn the money that you need. ❑ *Father never talked about what he did for a living.* **2** N-UNCOUNT You use **living** when you are talking about the quality of people's daily lives. ❑ *Olivia has always been a model of healthy living.* **3** ADJ [ADJ n] You use **living** to talk about the places where people relax when they are not working. ❑ *The spacious living quarters were on the second floor.* **4** → See feature box at **ecosystem, work**

liv|ing room (**living rooms**) also **living-room** N-COUNT The **living room** in a house is the room where people sit and relax. ❑ *We were sitting on the couch in the living room watching TV.*

liv|ing stand|ard (**living standards**) N-COUNT [usu pl] **Living standards** or **living standard** is used to refer to the level of comfort in which people live, which usually depends on how much money they have. ❑ *Cheaper housing would vastly improve the living standards of ordinary people.* ❑ *Critics say his reforms have caused the fall in living standards.*

liv|ing wage N-SING [usu a N] A **living wage** is a wage which is just enough to enable you to buy food, clothing, and other necessary things. ❑ *Many farmers have to depend on subsidies to make a living wage.*

liv|ing wall (**living walls**) N-COUNT A **living wall** is the same as a **green wall**.

liv|ing will (**living wills**) N-COUNT A **living will** is a document in which you say what medical or legal decisions you want people to make for you if you become too ill to make these decisions yourself.

liz|ard /lɪzərd/ (**lizards**) N-COUNT A **lizard** is a reptile with short legs and a long tail.

-'ll /-əl/ **-'ll** is the usual spoken form of 'will.' It is added to the end of the pronoun which is the subject of the verb. For example, 'you will' can be shortened to 'you'll.'

lla|ma /lɑmə/ (**llamas**) N-COUNT A **llama** is a South American animal with thick hair, which looks like a small camel without a hump.

lo /loʊ/ CONVENTION **Lo and behold** or **lo** is used to emphasize a surprising event that is about to be mentioned, or to emphasize in a humorous way that something is not surprising at all. [HUMOROUS OR LITERARY, EMPHASIS] ❑ *He called the Minister of the Interior and, lo and behold, within about an hour, the prisoners were released.* ❑ *I looked and lo! every one of the fifteen men who had been standing with me had disappeared.*

load ✦✧✧ /loʊd/ (**loads, loading, loaded**) **1** V-T If you **load** a vehicle or a container, you put a large quantity of things into it. ❑ *The three men seemed to have finished loading the truck.* ❑ *Mr. Dambar had loaded his plate with lasagne.* **2** N-COUNT A **load** is something, usually a large quantity or heavy object, which is being carried. ❑ *He drove by with a big load of hay.* **3** QUANT If you refer to **a load of** people or things or **loads of** them, you are emphasizing that there are a lot of them. [INFORMAL, EMPHASIS] ❑ *I've got loads of money.* ❑ *...a load of kids.* **4** V-T When someone **loads** a weapon such as a gun, they put a bullet or missile in it so that it is ready to use. ❑ *I knew how to load and handle a gun.* ❑ *He carried a loaded gun.* **5** V-T To **load** a camera or other piece of equipment means to put film, tape, or data into it so that it is ready to use. ❑ *A photographer from the newspaper was loading his camera with film.* **6** N-COUNT You can refer to the amount of work you have to do as a **load**. ❑ *She's taking some of the load off the secretaries.* **7** N-COUNT The **load** of a system or piece of equipment, especially a supply system supplying electricity or a computer, is the extent to which it is being used at a particular time. ❑ *An efficient bulb may lighten the load of power stations.* **8** N-SING The **load** on something is the amount of weight that is pressing down on it or the amount of strain that it is under. ❑ *Some of these chairs have flattened feet which spread the load on the ground.* **9** → see also **loaded** **10** **a load off your mind** → see **mind** ① **11** → See feature box at **housework**

▶ **load down** PHRASAL VERB If you **load** someone **down** with things, especially heavy things, you give them a large number of them or put a large number of them on them. ❑ *She loaded me down with around a dozen books.* ❑ *They had come up from London loaded down with six suitcases.*

▶ **load up** PHRASAL VERB **Load up** means the same as **load**. ❑ *I've just loaded my truck up.* ❑ *The giggling couple loaded up their red sports car and drove off.*

╺━━━━━━ SYNONYMS ━━━━━━╸

load
VERB **1**
pack: *When I was 17, I packed my bags and left home.*
stuff: *He grabbed my purse, opened it, and stuffed it full, then gave it back to me.*
pile: *He was piling clothes into the suitcase.*

-load /-loʊd/ (**-loads**) COMB IN N-COUNT **-load** combines with nouns referring to a vehicle or container to form nouns that refer to the total amount of something that the vehicle or container mentioned can hold or carry. ❑ *The first plane-loads of food, children's clothing and medical supplies began arriving.* ❑ *Let's bring in a truck-load of lumber and start building tomorrow.*

load|ed /loʊdɪd/ **1** ADJ A **loaded** question or word has more meaning or purpose than it appears to have, because the person who uses it hopes it will cause people to respond in a particular way. ❑ *That's a loaded question.* **2** ADJ If something is **loaded** with a particular characteristic, it has that characteristic to a very great degree. ❑ *The president's visit is loaded with symbolic significance.* **3** ADJ If a place or object is **loaded** with things, it has very many of them in it or it is full of them. ❑ *...a tray loaded with cups.* ❑ *The second store you enter is loaded with jewelry.* **4** ADJ If you say that something is **loaded** in favor of someone, you mean it works unfairly to their advantage. If you say it is **loaded** against them, you mean it works unfairly to their disadvantage. [DISAPPROVAL] ❑ *The press is loaded in favor of this present government.* **5** ADJ If someone is **loaded**, they are intoxicated as a result of drinking alcohol or taking drugs. [INFORMAL] ❑ *We gather as a group once or twice a year, for old times' sake, and get loaded.*

loaf /loʊf/ (**loaves, loafs, loafing, loafed**) **1** N-COUNT A **loaf** of bread is bread which has been shaped and baked in one piece. It is usually large enough for more than one person and can be cut into slices. ❑ *...a loaf of crusty bread.* **2** V-I If you **loaf**, you spend time in a lazy way, doing nothing in particular, especially when you should be working. ❑ *There were always a lot of men loafing in the shop.*

loaf|er /loʊfər/ (**loafers**) **1** N-COUNT **Loafers** are flat leather shoes with no straps or laces. [mainly AM] **2** → See also color supplement

loam /loʊm/ N-UNCOUNT **Loam** is soil that is good for growing crops and plants in because it contains a lot of decayed vegetable matter and does not contain too much sand or clay.

loan ✦✦✧ /loʊn/ (**loans, loaning, loaned**) **1** N-COUNT A **loan** is a sum of money that you borrow. ❑ *The country has no access to foreign loans or financial aid.* ❑ *The president wants to make it easier for small businesses to get bank loans.* **2** → see also **bridge loan, soft loan** **3** N-SING If someone gives you a **loan of** something, you borrow it from them. ❑ *I am in need of a loan of a bike for a few weeks.* **4** V-T If you **loan** something to someone, you lend it to them. ❑ *He had kindly offered to loan us all the plants required for the exhibit.* ● PHRASAL VERB **Loan out** means the same as **loan**. ❑ *It is common practice for clubs to loan out players to sides in the lower divisions.* **5** PHRASE If something is **on loan**, it has been borrowed. ❑ *...impressionist paintings on loan from the National Gallery.* **6** → See feature box at **finance, university**

╺━━━━━━ SYNONYMS ━━━━━━╸

loan
NOUN **1**
advance: *She was paid a $100,000 advance for her next two novels.*
credit: *The group can't get credit to buy farming machinery.*
mortgage: *There has been an increase in mortgage rates.*
VERB **4**
advance: *I advanced him some money, which he would repay on our way home.*
lend: *I had to lend him ten dollars to take his children to the movies.*

loan shark (loan sharks) N-COUNT If you describe someone as a **loan shark**, you disapprove of them because they lend money to people and charge them very high rates of interest on the loan. [INFORMAL, DISAPPROVAL]

loath /loʊθ/ also **loth** ADJ [v-link ADJ to-inf] If you are **loath** to do something, you do not want to do it. ❑ *Sensing he held the advantage, Mr. Danbar was loath to change the subject.*

loathe /loʊð/ (loathes, loathing, loathed) V-T If you **loathe** something or someone, you dislike them very much. ❑ *The two men loathe each other.*

loath|ing /loʊðɪŋ/ N-UNCOUNT **Loathing** is a feeling of great dislike and disgust. ❑ *She looked at him with loathing.*

loath|some /loʊðsəm/ ADJ If you describe someone or something as **loathsome**, you are indicating how much you dislike them or how much they disgust you. ❑ *...the loathsome spectacle we were obliged to witness.*

loaves /loʊvz/ **Loaves** is the plural of **loaf**.

lob /lɒb/ (lobs, lobbing, lobbed) V-T If you **lob** something, you throw it so that it goes quite high in the air. ❑ *I lobbed the ball back over the net.*

lob|by ✦✧✧ /lɒbi/ (lobbies, lobbying, lobbied) **1** V-T/V-I If you **lobby** someone such as a member of a government or council, you try to persuade them that a particular law should be changed or that a particular thing should be done. ❑ *The Wilderness Society lobbied Congress to authorize the Endangered Species Act.* **2** N-COUNT A **lobby** is a group of people who represent a particular organization or campaign, and try to persuade a government or council to help or support them. ❑ *Agricultural interests are some of the most powerful lobbies in Washington.* **3** N-COUNT In a hotel or other large building, the **lobby** is the area near the entrance that usually has corridors and staircases leading off it. ❑ *I met her in the lobby of the museum.* **4** → See feature box at **politics**

lob|by|ist /lɒbiɪst/ (lobbyists) N-COUNT A **lobbyist** is someone who tries actively to persuade a government or council that a particular law should be changed or that a particular thing should be done.

lobe /loʊb/ (lobes) **1** N-COUNT The **lobe** of your ear is the soft, fleshy part at the bottom. **2** N-COUNT [usu with supp] A **lobe** is a rounded part of something, for example, one of the sections of your brain or lungs, or one of the rounded sections along the edges of some leaves. ❑ *...damage to the temporal lobe of the brain.*

lo|boto|my /ləbɒtəmi/ (lobotomies) N-VAR A **lobotomy** is a surgical operation in which some of the nerves in the brain are cut in order to treat severe mental illness. Lobotomies are now rarely carried out. [MEDICAL]

lob|ster /lɒbstər/ (lobsters) N-VAR A **lobster** is a sea creature that has a hard shell, two large claws, and eight legs. ❑ *She sold me a couple of live lobsters.* • N-UNCOUNT **Lobster** is the flesh of a lobster eaten as food. ❑ *...lobster on a bed of fresh vegetables.*

lob|ster pot (lobster pots) N-COUNT A **lobster pot** is a trap used for catching lobsters. It is in the shape of a basket.

lo|cal ✦✦✦ /loʊkəl/ (locals) **1** ADJ [ADJ n] **Local** means existing in or belonging to the area where you live, or to the area that you are talking about. ❑ *We'd better check on the game in the local paper.* ❑ *Some local residents joined the students' protest.* • N-COUNT The **locals** are local people. ❑ *Camping is a great way to meet the locals as the Portuguese themselves are enthusiastic campers.* • **lo|cal|ly** ADV ❑ *We've got cards which are drawn and printed and designed by someone locally.* **2** ADJ **Local** government is elected by people in one area of a country and controls aspects such as education, housing, and transportation within that area. ❑ *Education comprises two-thirds of all local government spending.* **3** ADJ A **local** anesthetic or condition affects only a small area of your body. [MEDICAL] ❑ *The procedure was done under local anesthetic in the physician's office.*

lo|cal area net|work (local area networks) N-COUNT A **local area network** is a group of computers and associated equipment that are linked by cable, for example, in an office building, and that share a communications line. The abbreviation **LAN** is also used. [COMPUTING] ❑ *Users can easily move files between PCs connected by local area networks or the Internet.*

lo|cal author|ity ✦✧✧ (local authorities) N-COUNT A **local authority** is the same as a **local government**.

lo|cal col|or

in BRIT, use **local colour**

N-UNCOUNT **Local color** is used to refer to customs, traditions, dress, and other things which give a place or period of history its own particular character. ❑ *There are many corners of America that are bright with local color.*

lo|cale /loʊkæl/ (locales) N-COUNT A **locale** is a small area, for example, the place where something happens or where the action of a book or movie is set. [FORMAL] ❑ *An amusement park is the perfect locale for youngsters to have all sorts of adventures.*

lo|cal gov|ern|ment (local governments) **1** N-UNCOUNT **Local government** is the system of electing representatives to be responsible for the administration of public services and facilities in a particular area. ❑ *...careers in local government.* **2** N-COUNT A **local government** is an organization that is officially responsible for all the public services and facilities in a particular area. [AM]

in BRIT, use **local authority**

lo|cal|ism /loʊkəlɪzəm/ N-UNCOUNT **Localism** is a particular way of acting or speaking in a specific area.

lo|cal|ity /loʊkælɪti/ (localities) N-COUNT A **locality** is a small area of a country or city. [FORMAL] ❑ *Following the discovery of the explosives the president canceled his visit to the locality.*

lo|cal|ize /loʊkəlaɪz/ (localizes, localizing, localized)

in BRIT, also use **localise**

1 V-T If you **localize** something, you identify precisely where it is. ❑ *Examine the painful area carefully in an effort to localize the most tender point.* **2** V-T If you **localize** something, you limit the size of the area that it affects and prevent it from spreading. ❑ *Few officers thought that the war could be localized.*

lo|cal|ized /loʊkəlaɪzd/

in BRIT, also use **localised**

ADJ Something that is **localized** remains within a small area and does not spread. ❑ *She had localized breast cancer and both of her doctors had advised surgery.*

lo|cal time N-UNCOUNT **Local time** is the official time in a particular region or country. ❑ *It will arrive in Tokyo around noon Saturday local time.*

lo|cate /loʊkeɪt/ (locates, locating, located) **1** V-T If you **locate** something or someone, you find out where they are. [FORMAL] ❑ *The scientists want to locate the position of the gene on a chromosome.* **2** V-T If you **locate** something in a particular place, you put it there or build it there. [FORMAL] ❑ *Atlanta was voted the best city in which to locate a business by more than 400 chief executives.* **3** V-I If you **locate** in a particular place, you move there or open a business there. [mainly AM, BUSINESS] ❑ *...tax breaks for businesses that locate in run-down neighborhoods.*

lo|cat|ed /loʊkeɪtɪd/ ADJ [v-link ADJ prep, adv ADJ] If something is **located** in a particular place, it is present or has been built there. [FORMAL] ❑ *A boutique and beauty salon are conveniently located within the grounds.*

lo|ca|tion ✦✧✧ /loʊkeɪʃən/ (locations) **1** N-COUNT A **location** is the place where something happens or is situated. ❑ *The first thing he looked at was his office's location.* **2** N-COUNT The **location** of someone or something is their exact position. ❑ *She knew the exact location of The Eagle's headquarters.* **3** N-VAR A **location** is a place away from a studio where a movie or part of a movie is made. ❑ *...an art movie with dozens of exotic locations.*

loch /lɒx, lɒk/ (lochs) N-COUNT A **loch** is a large area of water in Scotland that is completely or almost completely surrounded by land. ❑ *...twenty miles north of Loch Ness.*

loci /loʊsaɪ, loʊkaɪ/ **Loci** is the plural of **locus**.

lock ✦✧✧ /lɒk/ (locks, locking, locked) **1** V-T When you **lock** something such as a door, drawer, or case, you fasten it, usually with a key, so that other people cannot open it. ❑ *Are you sure you locked the front door?* **2** N-COUNT The **lock** on something such as a door or drawer is the device which is used to keep it shut and prevent other people from opening it. Locks are opened with a key. ❑ *At that moment he heard Gill's*

lockdown

key turning in the lock of the door. ◼3 V-T If you **lock** something or someone in a place, room, or container, you put them there and fasten the lock. ❑ *Her maid locked the case in the safe.* ◼4 V-T/V-I If you **lock** something in a particular position, or if it **locks** there, it is held or fitted firmly in that position. ❑ *He leaned back in the swivel chair and locked his fingers behind his head.* ◼5 N-COUNT On a canal or river, a **lock** is a place where walls have been built with gates at each end so that boats can move to a higher or lower section of the canal or river, by gradually changing the water level inside the gates. ❑ *As the lock filled, the ducklings rejoined their mother to wait for another vessel to go through.* ◼6 N-COUNT A **lock** of hair is a small bunch of hairs on your head that grow together and curl or curve in the same direction. ❑ *She brushed a lock of hair off his forehead.*

▶ **lock away** ◼1 PHRASAL VERB If you **lock** something **away** in a place or container, you put or hide it there and fasten the lock. ❑ *She meticulously cleaned the gun and locked it away in its case.* ◼2 PHRASAL VERB To **lock** someone **away** means to put them in prison or a secure psychiatric hospital. ❑ *Locking them away is not sufficient, you have to give them treatment.*

▶ **lock out** ◼1 PHRASAL VERB If someone **locks** you **out** of a place, they prevent you entering it by locking the doors. ❑ *His wife locked him out of their bedroom after the argument.* ◼2 PHRASAL VERB In an industrial dispute, if a company **locks** its workers **out**, it closes the factory or office in order to prevent the employees coming to work. [BUSINESS] ❑ *The company locked out the workers, and then the rest of the work force went on strike.*

▶ **lock up** ◼1 PHRASAL VERB If you **lock** something **up** in a place or container, you put or hide it there and fasten the lock. ❑ *Give away any food you have on hand, or lock it up and give the key to the neighbors.* ◼2 PHRASAL VERB To **lock** someone **up** means to put them in prison or a secure psychiatric hospital. ❑ *Mr. Milner persuaded the federal prosecutors not to lock up his client.* ◼3 PHRASAL VERB When you **lock up** a building or car or **lock up**, you make sure that all the doors and windows are locked so that nobody can get in. ❑ *Don't forget to lock up.*

lock|down /lɒkdaʊn/ (lockdowns) ◼1 N-VAR If there is a **lockdown** in a building or the building is **on lockdown**, nobody is allowed to enter or leave because of a dangerous situation. ❑ *The lockdown lasted for about an hour until the intruder was arrested.* ❑ *The prison was put on lockdown after riots broke out.* ◼2 N-VAR If there is a **lockdown**, people must stay at home unless they need to go out for certain reasons, such as going to work, buying food, or taking exercise. ❑ *The lockdown can only be relaxed once infection rates fall.* ❑ *One third of the global population is on lockdown.*

locked ◆∞ /lɒkt/ ADJ [v-link ADJ in n] If you say that people are **locked in** conflict or in battle, you mean they are arguing or fighting in a fierce or determined way, and neither side seems likely to stop.

lock|er /lɒkər/ (lockers) N-COUNT A **locker** is a small metal or wooden cabinet with a lock, where you can put your personal possessions, for example in a school, place of work, or sports club.

lock|er room (locker rooms) ◼1 N-COUNT A locker room is a room containing lockers at a gymnasium, stadium, or school where people can change their clothes, often to get ready to do sport. ❑ *In the locker room, Amanda changed quickly.* ◼2 N-COUNT The **locker room** is the room where a team of sportsmen or sportswomen get ready to play a match, and where they go afterwards. ❑ *We went inside the Broncos' locker room moments after one of the most embarrassing defeats in their history.*

lock|et /lɒkɪt/ (lockets) N-COUNT A **locket** is a piece of jewelry containing something such as a picture, which a woman wears on a chain around her neck.

lock|out (lockouts)

in BRIT, use **lock-out**

N-COUNT A **lockout** is a situation in which employers close a place of work and prevent workers from entering it until the workers accept the employer's new proposals on pay or conditions of work. [BUSINESS] ❑ *The lockout could resume if no new contract agreement is signed*

lock|smith /lɒksmɪθ/ (locksmiths) N-COUNT A **locksmith** is a person whose job is to make or repair locks.

lock|step /lɒkstɛp/ also lock-step, lock step ◼1 N-UNCOUNT [usu in n] When members of the armed forces march in **lockstep**, they march very close to each other. [AM] ❑ *Navy officers marched in lockstep to lay flowers at the base of the new monument.* ◼2 PHRASE [after v; oft PHR with n] If people or things move **in lockstep**, or if they move **in lockstep with** each other, they act in a similar way. [mainly AM] ❑ *After years of moving in lockstep, France and Germany are growing apart at an alarming rate.* ❑ *In the end, the 1987 collapse suggested, the economy doesn't move in lockstep with stock prices.*

lock-up (lock-ups) also **lockup** N-COUNT A **lock-up** is the same as a **jail**. [AM, INFORMAL]

lo|co|mo|tion /loʊkəmoʊʃən/ N-UNCOUNT **Locomotion** is the ability to move and the act of moving from one place to another. [FORMAL] ❑ *Flight is the form of locomotion that puts the greatest demands on muscles.*

lo|co|mo|tive /loʊkəmoʊtɪv/ (locomotives) N-COUNT A **locomotive** is a large vehicle that pulls a train. [FORMAL]

lo|cus /loʊkəs/ (loci) N-COUNT [usu sing, N of n] The **locus of** something is the place where it happens or the most important area or point with which it is associated. [FORMAL] ❑ *Barcelona is the locus of Spanish industry.*

lo|cust /loʊkəst/ (locusts) N-COUNT **Locusts** are large insects, similar to grasshoppers, that live mainly in hot areas and often cause serious damage to crops. ❑ *...a swarm of locusts.*

lodge /lɒdʒ/ (lodges, lodging, lodged) ◼1 N-COUNT A **lodge** is a house or hotel in the country or in the mountains where people stay on vacation, especially when they want to hunt or fish. ❑ *...a Victorian hunting lodge.* ◼2 N-COUNT A **lodge** is a small house at the entrance to the grounds of a large house. ❑ *I drove out of the gates, past the keeper's lodge.* ◼3 V-T If you **lodge** a complaint, protest, accusation, or claim, you officially make it. ❑ *He has four weeks in which to lodge an appeal.* ◼4 V T/V I If you **lodge** somewhere, such as in someone else's house or if you **are lodged** there, you live there, usually paying rent. ❑ *...the story of the farming family she lodged with as a young teacher.* ◼5 V-I If an object **lodges** somewhere, it becomes stuck there. ❑ *The bullet lodged in the sergeant's leg, shattering his thigh bone.* ◼6 → see also **lodging**

lodg|er /lɒdʒər/ (lodgers) N-COUNT A **lodger** is a person who pays money to live in someone else's house, usually in their own room. ❑ *Jennie took in a lodger to help with the mortgage.*

lodg|ing /lɒdʒɪŋ/ (lodgings) N-UNCOUNT [also N in pl] If you are provided with **lodging** or **lodgings**, you are provided with a place to stay for a period of time. You can use **lodgings** to refer to one or more of these places. ❑ *He was given free lodging.*

lodg|ing house [BRIT] → see **rooming house**

loft /lɔft/ (lofts) ◼1 N-COUNT A **loft** is the space inside the sloping roof of a house or other building, where things are sometimes stored. ❑ *A loft conversion can add considerably to the value of a house.* ◼2 N-COUNT A **loft** is an apartment in the upper part of a building, especially a building such as a warehouse or factory that has been converted for people to live in. Lofts are usually large and not divided into separate rooms. ❑ *...Andy Warhol's New York loft.* ◼3 → See feature box at **house**

lofty /lɔfti/ (loftier, loftiest) ◼1 ADJ A **lofty** ideal or ambition is noble, important, and admirable. ❑ *It was a bank that started out with grand ideas and lofty ideals.* ◼2 ADJ A **lofty** building or room is very high. [FORMAL] ❑ *...a light, lofty apartment in the suburbs of Salzburg.* ◼3 ADJ If you say that someone behaves in a **lofty** way, you are critical of them for behaving in a proud and somewhat overbearing way, as if they think they are very important. [DISAPPROVAL] ❑ *...the lofty disdain he often expresses for his profession.*

log /lɒg/ (logs, logging, logged) ◼1 N-COUNT A **log** is a piece of a thick branch or of the trunk of a tree that has been cut so that it can be used for fuel or for making things. ❑ *He dumped the logs on the big stone hearth.* ◼2 N-COUNT A **log** is an official written account of what happens each day, for example, on board a ship. ❑ *The family made an official complaint to a ship's officer, which was recorded in the log.* ◼3 V-T If you **log** an event or fact, you record it officially in writing or on a computer. ❑ *They log everyone and everything that comes in and out of here.*

▶ **log in** also **log on** PHRASAL VERB When someone **logs in** or **logs on**, or **logs into** a computer system, they start using the system, usually by typing their name or identity code and a password. ☐ *Customers pay to log on and gossip with other users.*

▶ **log out** also **log off** PHRASAL VERB When someone who is using a computer system **logs out** or **logs off**, they finish using the system by typing a particular command. ☐ *If a computer user fails to log off, the system is accessible to all.*

logan|berry /lóʊɡənbɛri/ (**loganberries**) N-COUNT A **loganberry** is a purplish red fruit that is similar to a raspberry.

loga|rithm /lɔ́ɡərɪðəm/ (**logarithms**) N-COUNT In mathematics, the **logarithm** of a number is a number that it can be represented by in order to make a difficult multiplication or division sum simpler.

log book (**log books**) N-COUNT A **log book** is a book in which someone records details and events relating to something, for example, a journey or period of their life, or a vehicle.

log|ger /lɔ́ɡər/ (**loggers**) N-COUNT A **logger** is someone whose job is to cut down trees. [AM]

in BRIT, use **lumberjack**

log|ger|heads /lɔ́ɡərhɛdz/ PHRASE If two or more people or groups are **at loggerheads**, they disagree very strongly with each other. ☐ *For months dentists and the health department have been at loggerheads over fees.* ☐ *Are mothers and teens inevitably at loggerheads?*

log|gia /lɒ́dʒə, loʊ-/ (**loggias**) N-COUNT A **loggia** is a roofed area attached to a house. [FORMAL]

log|ging /lɔ́ɡɪŋ/ N-UNCOUNT [oft N n] **Logging** is the activity of cutting down trees in order to sell the wood. ☐ *Logging companies would have to leave a central area of the forest before the end of the year.*

log|ic /lɒ́dʒɪk/ **1** N-UNCOUNT **Logic** is a method of reasoning that involves a series of statements, each of which must be true if the statement before it is true. ☐ *Apart from criminal investigation techniques, students learn forensic medicine, philosophy and logic.* **2** N-UNCOUNT The **logic** of a conclusion or an argument is its quality of being correct and reasonable. ☐ *I don't follow the logic of your argument.* **3** N-UNCOUNT A particular kind of **logic** is the way of thinking and reasoning about things that is characteristic of a particular type of person or particular field of activity. ☐ *The plan was based on sound commercial logic.*

logi|cal /lɒ́dʒɪk°l/ **1** ADJ In a **logical** argument or method of reasoning, each step must be true if the step before it is true. ☐ *Only when each logical step has been checked by other mathematicians will the proof be accepted.* ● **logi|cal|ly** /lɒ́dʒɪkli/ ADV ☐ *My professional training has taught me to look at things logically.* **2** ADJ The **logical** conclusion or result of a series of facts or events is the only one which can come from it, according to the rules of logic. ☐ *If the climate gets drier, then the logical conclusion is that even more drought will occur.* ● **logi|cal|ly** ADV [ADV with v] ☐ *From that it followed logically that he would not be meeting Hildegarde.* **3** ADJ Something that is **logical** seems reasonable or sensible in the circumstances. ☐ *Connie suddenly struck her as a logical candidate.* ☐ *There was a logical explanation.* ● **logi|cal|ly** ADV ☐ *This was the one possibility I hadn't taken into consideration, though logically I should have.*

-logical → see -ological

log|ic bomb (**logic bombs**) N-COUNT A **logic bomb** is an unauthorized program that is inserted into a computer system so that when it is started it affects the operation of the computer. [COMPUTING] ☐ *Viruses and logic bombs can doubtless do great damage under some circumstances.*

lo|gi|cian /loʊdʒɪ́ʃ°n/ (**logicians**) N-COUNT A **logician** is a person who is a specialist in logic.

-logist → see -ologist

lo|gis|tic /loʊdʒɪ́stɪk/ also **logistical** /loʊdʒɪ́stɪk°l/ ADJ [ADJ n] **Logistic** or **logistical** means relating to the organization of something complicated. ☐ *Logistical problems may be causing the delay.* ☐ *She described the distribution of food and medical supplies as a logistical nightmare.* ● **lo|gis|ti|cal|ly** /loʊdʒɪ́stɪkli/ ADV ☐ *Some women find breast-feeding logistically difficult because of work.* ☐ *It is about time that the U.N. considers logistically deploying additional military resources.* ☐ *Logistically it is very difficult to value unit-linked policies.*

lo|gis|tics /loʊdʒɪ́stɪks/ N-UNCOUNT-COLL If you refer to the **logistics** of doing something complicated that involves a lot of people or equipment, you are referring to the skillful organization of it so that it can be done successfully and efficiently. ☐ *The skills and logistics of getting such a big show on the road pose enormous practical problems.*

log|jam /lɒ́ɡdʒæm/ (**logjams**) N-COUNT [usu sing] To break the **logjam** means to change or deal with a difficult situation which has existed for a long time. [JOURNALISM] ☐ *A new initiative was needed to break the logjam.*

logo /loʊɡoʊ/ (**logos**) N-COUNT The **logo** of a company or organization is the special design or way of writing its name that it puts on all its products, stationery, or advertisements. ☐ *...the famous MGM logo of the roaring lion.*

log-rolling also **logrolling** N-UNCOUNT If you accuse politicians of **log-rolling**, you mean that they make private agreements with each other, so that, for example, they give each other help or vote for each other's bills. [AM, DISAPPROVAL] ☐ *Often, such projects are the result of legislative log-rolling.*

-logy → see -ology

loin /lɔ́ɪn/ (**loins**) **1** N-VAR **Loin** or a **loin** is a piece of meat which comes from the back or sides of an animal, near the tail end. ☐ *Heat the honey and brush it on to the outside of the loin.* ☐ *...roast loin of venison.* **2** N-PLURAL Someone's **loins** are the front part of their body between their waist and legs, especially their genitals. [LITERARY, OLD-FASHIONED]

loin|cloth /lɔ́ɪnklɒθ/ (**loincloths**) N-COUNT A **loincloth** is a piece of cloth sometimes worn by men in order to cover their genitals, especially in countries when it is too hot to wear anything else.

loi|ter /lɔ́ɪtər/ (**loiters, loitering, loitered**) V-I If you **loiter** somewhere, you remain there or walk up and down without any real purpose. ☐ *Unemployed young men loiter at the entrance of the factory.*

LOL LOL is a written abbreviation for 'laughing out loud' or 'lots of love,' often used in email and text messages.

loll /lɒ́l/ (**lolls, lolling, lolled**) **1** V-I If you **loll** somewhere, you sit or lie in a very relaxed position. ☐ *He was lolling on the sofa in the shadows near the fire...* ☐ *He lolled back in his comfortable chair.* **2** V-I If something fairly heavy, especially someone's head or tongue, **lolls**, it hangs down in a loose, uncontrolled way. ☐ *When he let go the head lolled sideways.* ☐ *Tongue lolling, the dog came back from the forest.*

lol|li|pop /lɒ́lipɒp/ (**lollipops**) N-COUNT A **lollipop** is a candy consisting of a hard disk or ball of a sugary substance on the end of a stick.

lone /loʊn/ ADJ [ADJ n] If you talk about a **lone** person or thing, you mean that they are alone. ☐ *A lone woman motorist waited for six hours for help yesterday because of a name mix-up.*

lone|li|ness /loʊnlinɪs/ N-UNCOUNT **Loneliness** is the unhappiness that is felt by someone because they do not have any friends or do not have anyone to talk to. ☐ *I have so many friends, but deep down, underneath, I have a fear of loneliness.*

lone|ly /loʊnli/ (**lonelier, loneliest**) **1** ADJ Someone who is **lonely** is unhappy because they are alone or do not have anyone they can talk to. ☐ *...lonely people who just want to talk.* **2** ADJ A **lonely** situation or period of time is one which you feel unhappy because you are alone or do not have anyone to talk to. ☐ *I desperately needed something to occupy me during those long, lonely nights.* **3** ADJ A **lonely** place is one where very few people come. ☐ *It felt like the loneliest place in the world.*

lone|ly hearts ADJ [ADJ n] A **lonely hearts** section in a newspaper or a **lonely hearts** club is used by people who are trying to find a lover or friend. [OLD-FASHIONED]

lon|er /loʊnər/ (**loners**) N-COUNT If you describe someone as a **loner**, you mean they prefer to be alone rather than with a group of people. ☐ *I'm very much a loner – I never go out.*

lone|some /loʊnsəm/ **1** ADJ [usu v-link ADJ] Someone who is **lonesome** is unhappy because they do not have any friends or do not have anyone to talk to. [mainly AM] ☐ *I've grown so lonesome, thinking of you.* **2** ADJ A **lonesome** place is one which very few people come to and which is a long way from places where people live. [AM] ☐ *He was finding the river lonesome.*

LONG
① TIME
② DISTANCE AND SIZE
③ PHRASES
④ VERB USES

① **long** ♦♦♦ /lɒŋ/ (longer /lɒŋɡər/, longest /lɒŋɡɪst/) **1** ADV **Long** means a great amount of time or for a great amount of time. ❑ *Repairs to the cable did not take too long.* ❑ *Have you known her parents long?* ❑ *I learned long ago to avoid these invitations.* • PHRASE The expression **for long** is used to mean 'for a great amount of time.' ❑ *"Did you live there?"—"Not for long."* **2** ADJ A **long** event or period of time lasts for a great amount of time or takes a great amount of time. ❑ *We had a long meeting with the attorney general.* ❑ *She is planning a long vacation in Europe.* **3** ADJ You use **long** to ask or talk about amounts of time. ❑ *How long have you lived around here?* ❑ *He has been on a diet for as long as any of his friends can remember.* • ADJ [how ADJ, amount ADJ] **Long** is also an adjective. ❑ *So how long is your commute?* **4** ADJ A **long** speech, book, movie, or list contains a lot of information or a lot of items and takes a lot of time to listen to, read, watch, or deal with. ❑ *He was making quite a long speech.* **5** ADJ If you describe a period of time or work as **long**, you mean it lasts for more hours or days than is usual, or seems to last for more time than it actually does. ❑ *Go to sleep. I've got a long day tomorrow.* ❑ *She was a TV reporter and worked long hours.* **6** ADJ If someone has a **long** memory, they are able to remember things that happened far back in the past. ❑ *Mr. Assad, who has a long memory, will not have forgotten that meeting.* **7** ADV [n ADV] **Long** is used in expressions such as **all year long**, **the whole day long**, and **your whole life long** to say and emphasize that something happens for the whole of a particular period of time. [EMPHASIS] ❑ *We played that CD all night long.*

SYNONYMS
long
ADJ **2**
prolonged: *...a prolonged drought.*
lengthy: *...a lengthy meeting.*
protracted: *...a protracted civil war.*

② **long** ♦♦♦ /lɒŋ/ (longer /lɒŋɡər/, longest /lɒŋɡɪst/) **1** ADJ Something that is **long** measures a great distance from one end to the other. ❑ *...a long table.* ❑ *Lucy was 27, with long dark hair.* **2** ADJ A **long** distance is a great distance. A **long** journey or route covers a great distance. ❑ *These people were a long way from home.* ❑ *The long journey tired him.* **3** ADJ [ADJ n] A **long** piece of clothing covers the whole of someone's legs or more of their legs than usual. Clothes with **long** sleeves cover the whole of someone's arms. ❑ *She is wearing a long black dress.* **4** ADJ You use **long** to talk or ask about the distance something measures from one end to the other. ❑ *An eight-week-old embryo is only an inch long.* ❑ *How long is the tunnel?* • COMB IN ADJ **Long** is also a combining form. ❑ *...a three-foot-long gash in the tanker's side.*

③ **long** ♦♦♦ /lɒŋ/ (longer /lɒŋɡər/)
→ Please look at meanings **6** – **10** to see if the expression you are looking for is shown under another headword.

1 PHRASE If you say that something is the case **as long as** or **so long as** something else is the case, you mean that it is only the case if the second thing is the case. ❑ *He said he would still support them, as long as they didn't break the rules.* **2** PHRASE If you say that someone **won't be long**, you mean that you think they will arrive or be back soon. If you say that it **won't be long** before something happens, you mean that you think it will happen soon. ❑ *"What's happened to her?"—"I'm sure she won't be long."* **3** PHRASE If you say that something will happen or happened **before long**, you mean that it will happen or it happened soon. ❑ *German interest rates will come down before long.* **4** PHRASE Something that is **no longer** the case used to be the case but is not the case now. You can also say that something is not the case **any longer**. ❑ *Food shortages are no longer a problem.* ❑ *She could no longer afford to keep him at school.* **5** PHRASE You can say **so long** as an informal way of saying goodbye. ❑ *Well, so long, pal, see you around.* **6** at long last → see last **7** in the long run → see run ③ **8** a long shot → see shot **9** in the long term → see term **10** to go a long way → see way ③

④ **long** /lɒŋ/ (longs, longing, longed) **1** v T/v-I If you **long for** something, you want it very much. ❑ *Steve longed for the good old days.* ❑ *I'm longing to meet her.* **2** → see also **longing**

SYNONYMS
long
VERB **1**
desire: *She had remarried and desired a child with her new husband.*
crave: *You may be craving some fresh air.*
covet: *She coveted his job so openly that conversations between them were tense.*
hanker: *I hankered after a floor-length, brown, suede coat.*

long-awaited ADJ [ADJ n] A **long-awaited** event or thing is one that someone has been waiting for for a long time. ❑ *...the long-awaited signing of a peace agreement.*

long-distance 1 ADJ [ADJ n] **Long-distance** is used to describe travel between places that are far apart. ❑ *Trains are reliable, cheap and best for long-distance travel.* **2** ADJ **Long-distance** is used to describe communication that takes place between people who are far apart. ❑ *He received a long-distance phone call from his girlfriend in Colorado.* **3** → See feature box at **telephone**

long drawn out also **long-drawn-out** ADJ [usu ADJ n] A **long drawn out** process or conflict lasts an unnecessarily long time or an unpleasantly long time. ❑ *...a long drawn out election campaign.*

longed-for ADJ [ADJ n] A **longed-for** thing or event is one that someone wants very much. ❑ *...the wet weather that prevents your longed-for picnic.*

lon|gev|ity /lɒndʒɛvɪti/ N-UNCOUNT **Longevity** is long life. [FORMAL] ❑ *Human longevity runs in families.* ❑ *The main characteristic of the strike has been its longevity.*

long|hand /lɒŋhænd/ N-UNCOUNT [usu in N] If you write something down in **longhand**, you write it by hand using complete words and normal letters rather than typing it or using shortened forms or special symbols.

long-haul 1 ADJ [ADJ n] **Long-haul** is used to describe things that involve transporting passengers or goods over long distances. Compare **short-haul**. ❑ *...learning how to avoid the unpleasant side-effects of long-haul flights.* **2** → see also **haul**

long|ing /lɒŋɪŋ/ (longings) N-VAR If you feel **longing** or a **longing** for something, you have a rather sad feeling because you want it very much. ❑ *He felt a longing for the familiar.*

long|ing|ly /lɒŋɪŋli/ ADV [ADV with v] If you look **longingly** at something you want, or think **longingly** about it, you look at it or think about it with a feeling of desire. ❑ *Claire looked longingly at the sunlit gardens outside the window.*

long|ish /lɒŋɪʃ/ ADJ [usu ADJ n] **Longish** means fairly long. ❑ *She's about my age, with longish hair.*

lon|gi|tude /lɒndʒɪtud/ (longitudes) N-VAR The **longitude** of a place is its distance to the west or east of a line passing through Greenwich, England. Compare **latitude**. ❑ *He noted the latitude and longitude, then made a mark on the admiralty chart.* • ADJ **Longitude** is also an adjective. ❑ *A similar feature is found at 13 degrees north between 230 degrees and 250 degrees longitude.*

lon|gi|tu|di|nal /lɒndʒɪtudənəl/ ADJ [ADJ n] A **longitudinal** line or structure goes from one end of an object to the other rather than across it from side to side.

long johns N-PLURAL [also *a pair of* N] **Long johns** are warm underpants with long legs.

long jump N-SING [*the* N] The **long jump** is a track and field contest which involves jumping as far as you can from a marker which you run up to.

long-lasting (longer-lasting, longest-lasting) also **long lasting** ADJ Something that is **long-lasting** lasts for a long time. ❑ *One of the long-lasting effects of the infection is damage to a valve in the heart.*

long-life ADJ [ADJ n] **Long-life** light bulbs and batteries are manufactured so that they last longer than ordinary ones. **Long-life** fruit juice and milk have been specially treated so that they last a long time.

long-list (long-lists, long-listing, long-listed) also **longlist 1** N-COUNT A **long-list** for something such as a job or a prize is a large group that has been chosen from all the people who applied for the job, or all the people or things that are competing for the prize. The successful ones from this group are chosen to go on the **shortlist**. ❑ *There are 27 riders on the long-list.* **2** V-T If someone or something **is long-listed** for a job or a prize, they are put on a long-list of those to be considered for that job or prize. ❑ *She was long-listed for the senior team last year.*

long-lived also **long lived** ADJ Something that is **long-lived** lives or lasts for a long time. ❑ *The flowers may only last a day but the plants are long-lived.* ❑ *...huge piles of long-lived radioactive material.*

long-lost ADJ [ADJ n] You use **long-lost** to describe someone or something that you have not seen for a long time. ❑ *For me it was like meeting a long-lost sister. We talked, and talked, and talked.*

long-range ■ ADJ A **long-range** piece of military equipment or vehicle is able to hit or detect a target a long way away or to travel a long way in order to do something. ❑ *He is eager to reach agreement with the U.S. on reducing long-range nuclear missiles.* ■ ADJ A **long-range** plan or prediction relates to a period extending a long time into the future. ❑ *Eisenhower was intensely aware of the need for long-range planning.*

long-running (longest-running) ADJ [ADJ n] Something that is **long-running** has been in existence, or has been performed, for a long time. ❑ *...a long-running trade dispute.*

long|shore|man /lɔŋʃɔrmən/ (**longshoremen**) N-COUNT A **longshoreman** is a person who works in the docks, loading and unloading ships. [AM]

| in BRIT, use **docker** |

long-sighted ADJ **Long-sighted** is the same as **farsighted**. [BRIT]

long-standing ADJ A **long-standing** situation has existed for a long time. ❑ *They are on the brink of resolving their long-standing dispute over money.*

long-suffering ADJ Someone who is **long-suffering** patiently puts up with a lot of trouble or unhappiness, especially when it is caused by someone else. ❑ *His long-suffering mother was at a loss about what to do with him.*

long-term ♦♦◊ ■ ADJ Something that is **long-term** has continued for a long time or will continue for a long time in the future. ❑ *They want their parents to have access to affordable long-term care.* ■ N-SING When you talk about what happens in **the long term**, you are talking about what happens over a long period of time, either in the future or after a particular event. ❑ *In the long term the company hopes to open in Moscow and other major cities.*

long-time ♦◊◊ ADJ [ADJ n] You use **long-time** to describe something that has existed or been a particular thing for a long time. ❑ *Newcomers had to pay far more in taxes than long-time land owners.*

long wave N-UNCOUNT **Long wave** is a range of radio waves which are used for broadcasting. ❑ *...broadcasting on long wave.* ❑ *...1500m on long wave.*

long-winded ADJ [usu v-link ADJ] If you describe something that is written or said as **long-winded**, you are critical of it because it is longer than necessary. [DISAPPROVAL] ❑ *The manifesto is long-winded, repetitious and often ambiguous or poorly drafted.* ❑ *I hope I'm not being too long-winded.*

loo|fah /luːfə/ (**loofahs**) N-COUNT A **loofah** is a long rough sponge-like piece of plant fiber which you use to scrub your body.

LOOK
① USING YOUR EYES OR YOUR MIND
② APPEARANCE

① **look** ♦♦♦ /lʊk/ (**looks, looking, looked**)
→ Please look at meaning ⑫ to see if the expression you are looking for is shown under another headword.

■ V-I If you **look** in a particular direction, you direct your eyes in that direction, especially so that you can see what is there or see what something is like. ❑ *I looked down the hallway to room number nine.* ❑ *If you look, you'll see what was a lake.* • N-SING **Look** is also a noun. ❑ *Lucille took a last look in the mirror.* ② V-I If you **look at** a book, newspaper, or magazine, you read it fairly quickly or read part of it. ❑ *You've just got to look at the last bit of Act Three.* • N-SING **Look** is also a noun. ❑ *A quick look at Monday's newspapers shows that there's plenty of interest in foreign news.* ③ V-I If you **look at** someone in a particular way, you look at them with your expression showing what you are feeling or thinking. ❑ *She looked at him earnestly. "You don't mind?"* • N-COUNT **Look** is also a noun. ❑ *He gave her a blank look, as if he had no idea who she was.* ④ V-I If you **look** for something, for example, something that you have lost, you try to find it. ❑ *I'm looking for a child.*

VOCABULARY IN CONTEXT

Looking and seeing

Eye contact is central to human communication. We know that at just two days old, babies prefer looking at faces that **gaze** back at them, and there is a strong belief that by **staring** into someone's eyes, it is possible to **glimpse** their true nature.

However, the 'rules' about eye contact vary from culture to culture. In some countries, people are taught that it is polite to 'look someone in the eye'. If you frequently **blink** or **glance** away, people may assume that you have something to hide. However, in other cultures, direct eye contact is not the norm, and **focusing** on a superior's face could be seen as a sign of disrespect. Making eye contact with the opposite sex may also be interpreted as flirting, or '**eyeing someone up**'.

The messages we give with our eyes may not involve words, but can certainly communicate a great deal.

I believe your husband can help me find her. ❑ *I looked everywhere for ideas.* • N-SING **Look** is also a noun. ❑ *Go and have another look.* ⑤ V-I If you are **looking for** something such as the solution to a problem or a new method, you want it and are trying to obtain it or think of it. ❑ *The working group will be looking for practical solutions to the problems faced by doctors.* ⑥ V-I If you **look at** a subject, problem, or situation, you think about it or study it, so that you know all about it and can perhaps consider what should be done in relation to it. ❑ *Next term we'll be looking at the Second World War period.* ❑ *Anne Holker looks at the pros and cons of making changes to your property.* • N-SING **Look** is also a noun. ❑ *A close look at the statistics reveals a troubling picture.* ⑦ V-I If you **look at** a person, situation, or subject from a particular point of view, you judge them or consider them from that point of view. ❑ *Brian had learned to look at her with new respect.* ⑧ CONVENTION You say **look** when you want someone to pay attention to you because you are going to say something important. ❑ *Look, I'm sorry. I didn't mean it.* ⑨ V-T/V-I [only imper] You can use **look** to draw attention to a particular situation, person, or thing, for example because you find it very surprising, significant, or annoying. ❑ *Hey, look at the time! We'll talk about it tonight. All right?* ❑ *I mean, look at how many people watch television and how few read books.* ❑ *Look what you've done!* ⑩ V-I If something such as a building or window **looks** somewhere, it has a view of a particular place. ❑ *The castle looks over private parkland.* • PHRASAL VERB **Look out** means the same as **look**. ❑ *Nine windows looked out over the sculpture gardens.* ⑪ EXCLAM If you say or shout '**look out!**' to someone, you are warning them that they are in danger. ❑ *"Look out!" somebody shouted, as the truck started to roll toward the sea.* ⑫ **to look down your nose at someone** → see **nose**

▶ **look after** ■ PHRASAL VERB If you **look after** someone or something, you do what is necessary to keep them healthy, safe, or in good condition. ❑ *I love looking after the children.* ② PHRASAL VERB If you **look after** something, you are responsible for it and deal with it or make sure it is all right, especially because it is your job to do so. ❑ *...the farm manager who looks after the day-to-day organization.*

▶ **look around** PHRASAL VERB If you **look around** or **look round** a building or place, you walk round it and look at the different parts of it. ❑ *She left Annie and Cooper looking around the store and headed back onto the street.*

▶ **look back** PHRASAL VERB If you **look back**, you think about things that happened in the past. ❑ *Looking back, I am staggered how easily it was all arranged.*

▶ **look down on** PHRASAL VERB To **look down on** someone means to consider that person to be inferior or unimportant, usually when this is not true. ❑ *I wasn't successful, so they looked down on me.*

▶ **look forward to** ◼ PHRASAL VERB If you **look forward to** something that is going to happen, you want it to happen because you think you will enjoy it. ❑ *He was looking forward to working with the new manager.* ◼ PHRASAL VERB If you say that someone **is looking forward** to something useful or positive, you mean they expect it to happen. ❑ *He says that he's looking forward to increased sales.*

▶ **look in** PHRASAL VERB If you **look in** on a person, you visit that person for a short time to check on their health or safety. ❑ *Could I look in on Sam?* ❑ *I think I'll look in on my parents on the way home from work.*

▶ **look into** PHRASAL VERB If a person or organization **is looking into** a possible course of action, a problem, or a situation, they are finding out about it and examining the facts relating to it. ❑ *He had once looked into buying his own island off Nova Scotia.*

▶ **look on** PHRASAL VERB If you **look on** while something happens, you watch it happening without taking part yourself. ❑ *About 150 local people looked on in silence as the two coffins were taken into the church.*

▶ **look on** also **look upon** PHRASAL VERB If you **look on** or **look upon** someone or something in a particular way, you think of them in that way. ❑ *A lot of people looked on him as a healer.* ❑ *A lot of people look on it like that.*

▶ **look out** → see look ① 10

▶ **look out for** PHRASAL VERB If you **look out for** something, you pay attention to things so that you notice it if or when it occurs. ❑ *Look out for special deals.*

▶ **look over** PHRASAL VERB If you **look** something **over**, you examine it in order to get an idea of what it is like. ❑ *They presented their draft to the president, who looked it over, nodded and signed it.*

▶ **look round** → see look around

▶ **look through** ◼ PHRASAL VERB If you **look through** a group of things, you examine each one so that you can find or choose the one that you want. ❑ *Peter starts looking through the mail as soon as the door shuts.* ◼ PHRASAL VERB If you **look through** something that has been written or printed, you read it. ❑ *He happened to be looking through the medical book "Gray's Anatomy" at the time.*

▶ **look to** ◼ PHRASAL VERB If you **look to** someone or something for a particular thing that you want, you expect or hope that they will provide it. ❑ *He runs the team because he commands their respect. The kids really look to him.* ◼ PHRASAL VERB If you **look to** something that will happen in the future, you think about it. ❑ *Looking to the future, though, we asked him what the prospects are for a vaccine to prevent infection in the first place.*

▶ **look up** ◼ PHRASAL VERB If you **look up** a fact or a piece of information, you find it out by looking in something such as a reference book or a list. ❑ *I looked your address up in the personnel file.* ◼ PHRASAL VERB If you **look** someone **up**, you visit them after not having seen them for a long time. ❑ *I'll try to look him up, ask him a few questions.*

▶ **look up to** PHRASAL VERB If you **look up to** someone, especially someone older than you, you respect and admire them. ❑ *You're a popular girl, Grace, and a lot of the younger ones look up to you.*

COLLOCATIONS

look
NOUN
① ◼
adjective + **look**: close, good, hard, long, quick
verb + **look**: get, have, take
① ◼
adjective + **look**: blank, dirty, funny, puzzled, quizzical

---

② **look** ✦✦✦ /lʊk/ (looks, looking, looked) ◼ V-LINK You use **look** when describing the appearance of a person or thing or the impression that they give. ❑ *Sheila was looking miserable.* ❑ *They look like stars to the naked eye.* ❑ *He looked as if he was going to smile.* ◼ N-SING If someone or something has a particular **look**, they have a particular appearance or expression. ❑ *She had the look of someone deserted and betrayed.* ❑ *When he came to decorate the kitchen, Kenneth opted for a friendly rustic look.* ◼ N-PLURAL When you refer to someone's **looks**, you are referring to how beautiful or ugly they are, especially how beautiful they are. ❑ *I never chose people just because of their looks.* ◼ V-LINK You use **look** when indicating what you think will happen in the future or how a situation seems to you. ❑ *He had lots of time to think about the future, and it didn't look good.* ❑ *So far it looks like Warner Brothers' gamble is paying off.* ❑ *The Europeans had hoped to win, and, indeed, had looked like they would win.* ◼ PHRASE You use expressions such as **by the look of her** and **by the looks of it** when you want to indicate that you are giving an opinion based on the appearance of someone or something. ❑ *He was not a well man by the look of him.* ◼ PHRASE If you **don't like the look of** something or someone, you feel that they may be dangerous or cause problems. ❑ *I don't like the look of those clouds.* ◼ PHRASE If you ask **what** someone or something **looks like**, you are asking for a description of them. ◼ → See feature box at **appearance**

look|alike /lʊkəlaɪk/ (lookalikes) also **look-alike** N-COUNT [usu n-proper N] A **lookalike** is someone who has a very similar appearance to another person, especially a famous person. ❑ *...a Marilyn Monroe look-alike.*

look|er /lʊkər/ (lookers) N-COUNT You can refer to an attractive man or woman as a **looker** or a **good looker**. [INFORMAL] ❑ *I was quite a looker when I was younger.*

look|ing glass (looking glasses) also **looking-glass** N-COUNT A **looking glass** is a mirror. [OLD-FASHIONED]

look|out /lʊkaʊt/ (lookouts) ◼ N-COUNT A **lookout** is a place from which you can see clearly in all directions. ❑ *Troops tried to set up a lookout post inside a refugee camp.* ◼ N-COUNT A **lookout** is someone who is watching for danger in order to warn other people about it. ❑ *His girlfriend helped plan the botched burglary and acted as a lookout.* ◼ PHRASE If someone **keeps a lookout**, especially on a boat, they look around all the time in order to make sure there is no danger. ❑ *He denied that he'd failed to keep a proper lookout that night.*

loom /luːm/ (looms, looming, loomed) ◼ V-I If something **looms** over you, it appears as a large or unclear shape, often in a frightening way. ❑ *Vincent loomed over me, as pale and gray as a tombstone.* ◼ V-I If a worrying or threatening situation or event **is looming**, it seems likely to happen soon. [JOURNALISM] ❑ *Another government spending crisis is looming in the United States.* ❑ *The threat of renewed civil war looms ahead.* ◼ N-COUNT A **loom** is a machine that is used for weaving thread into cloth.

loony /luːni/ (loonies) ◼ N-COUNT If you refer to someone as a **loony**, you mean that they behave in a way that seems crazy, strange, or eccentric. [INFORMAL, OFFENSIVE, DISAPPROVAL] ❑ *At first they all thought I was a loony.* ◼ ADJ If you describe someone's behavior or ideas as **loony**, you mean that they seem mad, strange, or eccentric. Some people consider this use offensive. [INFORMAL, OFFENSIVE] ❑ *What's she up to? She's as loony as her brother!*

loop /luːp/ (loops, looping, looped) ◼ N-COUNT A **loop** is a curved or circular shape in something long, for example, in a piece of string. ❑ *Mrs. Morrell reached for a loop of garden hose.* ◼ V-T If you **loop** something such as a piece of rope around an object, you tie a length of it in a loop around the object, for example, in order to fasten it to the object. ❑ *He looped the rope over the wood.* ◼ V-I If something **loops** somewhere, it goes there in a circular direction that makes the shape of a loop. ❑ *The enemy was looping around the south side.*

loop|hole /luːphoʊl/ (loopholes) N-COUNT A **loophole** in the law is a small mistake which allows people to do something that would otherwise be illegal. ❑ *It is estimated that 60,000 businesses are exploiting a loophole in the law to avoid prosecution.*

loose ✦✧✧ /luːs/ (looser, loosest) ◼ ADJ Something that is **loose** is not firmly held or fixed in place. ❑ *If a tooth feels very loose, your dentist may recommend that it's taken out.* ❑ *Two wooden beams had come loose from the ceiling.* • **loose|ly** ADV [ADV with v] ❑ *Tim clasped his hands together and held them loosely in front of* his belly. **2** ADJ Something that is **loose** is not attached to anything, or held or contained in anything. ❑ *Frank emptied a handful of loose change on the table.* **3** ADJ If people or animals break **loose** or are set **loose**, they are no longer held, tied, or kept somewhere and can move around freely. ❑ *She broke loose from his embrace and crossed to the window.* **4** ADJ Clothes that are **loose** are somewhat large and do not fit closely. ❑ *A pistol wasn't that hard to hide under a loose shirt.* • **loose|ly** ADV ❑ *His shirt hung loosely over his thin shoulders.* **5** ADJ If your hair is **loose**, it hangs freely around your shoulders and is not tied back. ❑ *She was still in her nightgown, with her hair hanging loose over her shoulders.* **6** ADJ A **loose** grouping, arrangement, or organization is flexible rather than strictly controlled or organized. ❑ *Murray and Alison came to some sort of loose arrangement before he went home.* • **loose|ly** ADV [ADV with v] ❑ *The investigation had aimed at a loosely organized group of criminals.* **7** PHRASE If a person or an animal is **on the loose**, they are free because they have escaped from a person or place. ❑ *Up to a thousand prisoners may be on the loose inside the jail.* **8** **a loose cannon** → see **cannon** **9** **all hell breaks loose** → see **hell** ②

loose end (loose ends) **1** N-COUNT A **loose end** is part of a story, situation, or crime that has not yet been explained. ❑ *There are some annoying loose ends in the plot.* **2** PHRASE If you are **at loose ends**, you are bored because you do not have anything to do and cannot think of anything that you want to do. [INFORMAL] ❑ *She had woken feeling at loose ends.*

loose-fitting also **loose fitting** ADJ [usu ADJ n] **Loose-fitting** clothes are somewhat large and do not fit tightly on your body.

loos|en /lˈuːsᵊn/ (loosens, loosening, loosened) **1** V-T If someone **loosens** restrictions or laws, for example, they make them less strict or severe. ❑ *Many business groups have been pressing the Federal Reserve to loosen interest rates.* • **loos|en|ing** N-SING ❑ *Domestic conditions did not justify a loosening of monetary policy.* **2** V-T/V-I If someone or something **loosens** the ties between people or groups of people, or if the ties **loosen**, they become weaker. ❑ *The Federal Republic must loosen its ties with the United States.* ❑ *The deputy leader is cautious about loosening the links with the unions.* **3** V-T If you **loosen** your clothing or something that is tied or fastened, you undo it slightly so that it is less tight or less firmly held in place. ❑ *He reached up to loosen the scarf around his neck.* ❑ *Loosen the bolt so the bars can be turned.* **4** V-T/V-I If you **loosen** your grip on something, or if your grip **loosens**, you hold it less tightly. ❑ *Jane tried to pry open the dog's mouth but it wouldn't loosen its grip.* **5** V-T/V-I If a government or organization **loosens** its grip on a group of people or an activity, or if its grip **loosens**, it begins to have less control over it. ❑ *There is no sign that the party will loosen its grip on the country.*

▶ **loosen up** **1** PHRASAL VERB If a person or situation **loosens up**, they become more relaxed and less tense. ❑ *Relax, smile; loosen up in mind and body.* ❑ *Things loosened up, in politics and the economy.* **2** PHRASAL VERB If you **loosen up** your body, or if it **loosens up**, you do simple exercises to get your muscles ready for a difficult physical activity, such as running or playing sports. ❑ *Squeeze the foot with both hands to loosen up tight muscles.*

loot /lˈuːt/ (loots, looting, looted) **1** V-T/V-I If people **loot**, or **loot** stores or houses, they steal things from them, for example, during a war or riot. ❑ *The trouble began when gangs began breaking windows and looting shops.* • **loot|ing** N-UNCOUNT ❑ *In the country's largest cities there has been rioting and looting.* **2** V-T If someone **loots** things, they steal them, for example, during a war or riot. ❑ *The town has been plagued by armed thugs who have looted food supplies and terrorized the population.*

loot|er /lˈuːtər/ (looters) N-COUNT A **looter** is a person who steals things from stores, for example, during a war or riot.

lop /lˈɒp/ (lops, lopping, lopped)
▶ **lop off** **1** PHRASAL VERB If you **lop** something **off**, you cut it away from what it was attached to, usually with a quick, strong stroke. ❑ *Somebody lopped the heads off our tulips.* ❑ *...men with axes, lopping off branches.* ❑ *His ponytail had been lopped off.* **2** PHRASAL VERB If you **lop** an amount of money or time **off** something such as a budget or a schedule, you reduce the budget or schedule by that amount. [INFORMAL] ❑ *The Air France plane lopped over four hours off the previous best time.* ❑ *More than 100 million dollars will be lopped off the prison building program.*

lope /lˈoʊp/ (lopes, loping, loped) V-I If a person or animal **lopes** somewhere, they run in an easy and relaxed way, taking long steps. ❑ *He was loping across the sand toward Nancy.* ❑ *Matty saw him go loping off.* • **lop|ing** ADJ [ADJ n] ❑ *She turned and walked away with long, loping steps.*

lop|sided /lˈɒpsaɪdɪd/ ADJ Something that is **lopsided** is uneven because one side is lower or heavier than the other. ❑ *His suit had shoulders that made him look lopsided.*

lo|qua|cious /loʊkwˈeɪʃəs/ ADJ If you describe someone as **loquacious**, you mean that they talk a lot. [FORMAL] ❑ *The normally loquacious Mr. O'Reilly has said little.*

lord ♦♦♢ /lˈɔːrd/ (lords) **1** N-COUNT; N-TITLE A **lord** is a man who has a high rank in the nobility, for example, an earl, a viscount, or a marquis. ❑ *She married a lord and lives in this huge house in the Cotswolds.* **2** N-PROPER [usu the N; N-VOC] In the Christian church, people refer to God and to Jesus Christ as the **Lord**. ❑ *I know the Lord will look after him.* ❑ *She prayed now. "Lord, help me to find courage."* **3** EXCLAM **Lord** is used in exclamations such as '**good Lord**!' and '**oh Lord**!' to express surprise, shock, frustration, or annoyance about something. [FEELINGS] ❑ *"Good lord, that's what he is: he's a policeman."*

lord|ly /lˈɔːrdli/ **1** ADJ [usu ADJ n] If you say that someone's behavior is **lordly**, you are critical of them because they treat other people in a proud and arrogant way. [DISAPPROVAL] ❑ *...their usual lordly indifference to patients.* **2** ADJ [ADJ n] **Lordly** means impressive and suitable for a lord. ❑ *...the site of a lordly mansion.*

Lord|ship /lˈɔːrdʃɪp/ (Lordships) N-VOC; PRON [poss PRON] You use the expressions **Your Lordship**, **His Lordship**, or **Their Lordships** when you are addressing or referring to a judge, a bishop, or a male member of the British nobility. [POLITENESS] ❑ *My name is Richard Savage, your Lordship.* ❑ *His Lordship expressed the hope that the Law Commission might look at the subject.*

Lord's Prayer N-PROPER [the N] The **Lord's Prayer** is a Christian prayer that was originally taught by Jesus Christ to his followers.

lore /lˈɔːr/ N-UNCOUNT [with supp] The **lore** of a particular country or culture is its traditional stories and history. ❑ *...the Book of the Sea, which was stuffed with sailors' lore.* ❑ *...ancient Catalan lore.*

lor|ry /lˈɒri/ (lorries) N-COUNT A **lorry** is the same as a **truck**. [BRIT]

lose ♦♦♦ /lˈuːz/ (loses, losing, lost) **1** V-T/V-I If you **lose** a contest, a fight, or an argument, you do not succeed because someone does better than you and defeats you. ❑ *The Golden Bears have lost three games this season.* ❑ *The government lost the argument over the pace of reform.* ❑ *No one likes to lose.* **2** V-T If you **lose** something, you do not know where it is, for example, because you have forgotten where you put it. ❑ *I lost my keys.* **3** V-T You say that you **lose** something when you no longer have it because it has been taken away from you or destroyed. ❑ *I lost my job when the company moved to another state.* ❑ *He lost his license for six months.* **4** V-T If someone **loses** a quality, characteristic, attitude, or belief, they no longer have it. ❑ *He lost all sense of reason.* ❑ *The government had lost all credibility.* **5** V-T If you **lose** an ability, you stop having that ability because of something such as an accident. ❑ *They lost their ability to hear.* **6** V-T If someone or something **loses** heat, their temperature becomes lower. ❑ *Babies lose heat much faster than adults.* **7** V-T If you **lose** blood or fluid from your body, it leaves your body so that you have less of it. ❑ *The victim suffered a dreadful injury and lost a lot of blood.* **8** V-T If you **lose** weight, you become less heavy, and usually look thinner. ❑ *I have lost a lot of weight.* **9** V-T If someone **loses** their life, they die. ❑ *...the ferry disaster in 1987, in which 192 people lost their lives.* **10** V-T If you **lose** a close relative or friend, they die. ❑ *My Grandma lost her brother in the war.* **11** V-T [usu passive] If things **are lost**, they are destroyed in a disaster. ❑ *...the famous Nanjing pottery that was lost in a shipwreck off the coast of China.* **12** V-T If you **lose** time, something slows you down so that you do not make as much progress as you hoped. ❑ *They claim that police lost valuable time in the early part of the investigation.* **13** V-T If you **lose** an opportunity, you do not take advantage of it. ❑ *If you don't do it soon you're going to lose the opportunity.* ❑ *They did not lose the opportunity to say what they thought of events.* **14** V-T If you **lose** yourself in something or if you **are lost** in it, you give a lot of attention to it and do not think about anything else.

❏ *Michael held on to her arm, losing himself in the music.* ▣ V-T If a business **loses** money, it earns less money than it spends, and is therefore in debt. [BUSINESS] ❏ *His stores stand to lose millions of dollars.* ▣ V-T If something **loses** you a contest or **loses** you something that you had, it causes you to fail or to no longer have what you had. ❏ *My own stupidity lost me the match.* ▣ → see also **lost** ▣ PHRASE If you **lose** your **way**, you become lost when you are trying to go somewhere. ❏ *The men lost their way in a sandstorm.* ▣ **to lose your balance** → see **balance** ▣ **to lose contact** → see **contact** ▣ **to lose face** → see **face** ① ▣ **to lose your grip** → see **grip** ▣ **to lose your head** → see **head** ③ ▣ **to lose heart** → see **heart** ② ▣ **to lose your mind** → see **mind** ① ▣ **to lose your nerve** → see **nerve** ▣ **to lose sight of** → see **sight** ▣ **to lose your temper** → see **temper** ▣ **to lose touch** → see **touch** ② ▣ **to lose track of** → see **track**
▶ **lose out** PHRASAL VERB If you **lose out**, you suffer a loss or disadvantage because you have not succeeded in what you were doing. ❏ *We both lost out.* ❏ *Laura lost out to Tom.*

▬▬▬▬ COLLOCATIONS ▬▬▬▬

lose
VERB ▣
lose + *noun*: confidence, faith, interest; control

los|er /lúːzər/ (**losers**) ▣ N-COUNT The **losers** of a game, contest, or struggle are the people who are defeated or beaten. ❏ *...the winners and losers of this year's Super Bowl.* • PHRASE If someone is a **good loser**, they accept that they have lost a game or contest without complaining. If someone is a **bad loser**, they hate losing and complain about it. ❏ *I'm a great winner and I try to be a good loser.* ▣ N-COUNT If you refer to someone as a **loser**, you have a low opinion of them because you think they are always unsuccessful. [INFORMAL, DISAPPROVAL] ❏ *They've only been trained to compete with other men, so a successful woman can make them feel like a real loser.* ▣ N-COUNT People who are **losers** as the result of an action or event, are in a worse situation because of it or do not benefit from it. ❏ *Some of the top business successes of the 1980s became the country's greatest losers in the recession.* ▣ → See feature box at **competition**

loss ✦✦✦ /lɒs/ (**losses**) ▣ N-VAR **Loss** is the fact of no longer having something or having less of it than before. ❏ *...loss of sight.* ❏ *...hair loss.* ▣ N-VAR **Loss** of life occurs when people die. ❏ *...a terrible loss of human life.* ▣ N-UNCOUNT The **loss** of a relative or friend is their death. ❏ *They took the time to talk about the loss of Thomas and how their grief was affecting them.* ▣ N-UNCOUNT **Loss** is the feeling of sadness you experience when someone or something you like is taken away from you. ❏ *Talk to others about your feelings of loss and grief.* ▣ N-COUNT A **loss** is the disadvantage you suffer when a valuable and useful person or thing leaves or is taken away. ❏ *She said his death was a great loss to herself.* ▣ N-UNCOUNT The **loss** of something such as heat, blood, or fluid is the gradual reduction of it or of its level in a system or in someone's body. ❏ *...blood loss.* ❏ *...a rapid loss of heat from the body.* ▣ N-VAR If a business makes a **loss**, it earns less than it spends. [BRIT] ❏ *The company said it made a loss of $4.9 billion (3.6 billion euros) last year.* ❏ *They will stop producing fertilizer next year because of continued losses.* ▣ PHRASE If a business produces something **at a loss**, they sell it at a price which is less than it cost them to produce it or buy it. [BUSINESS] ❏ *Timber owners have often produced lumber at a loss and survived these down cycles in demand.* ▣ PHRASE If you say that you are **at a loss**, you mean that you do not know what to do in a particular situation. ❏ *I was at a loss for what to do next.* ▣ → See feature box at **disaster**

▬▬▬▬ COLLOCATIONS ▬▬▬▬

loss
NOUN
▣
noun + **loss**: hair, hearing, memory, weight
adjective + **loss**: heavy, huge, massive
▣
adjective + **loss**: heartbreaking, sad, tragic
verb + **loss**: mourn, suffer
▣
adjective + **loss**: attributable; net, pre-tax
verb + **loss**: incur; record, report; offset

loss ad|just|er (**loss adjusters**) also **loss adjustor**
▣ N-COUNT A **loss adjuster** is someone who is employed by an insurance company to decide how much money should be paid to a person making a claim. [BRIT, BUSINESS] ▣ → see also **claims adjuster**, **insurance adjuster**

loss lead|er (**loss leaders**) also **loss-leader** N-COUNT A **loss leader** is an item that is sold at such a low price that it makes a loss in the hope that customers will be attracted by it and buy other products at the same store. [BUSINESS] ❏ *Hoskins does not expect a huge profit from the cookies, viewing them more as a loss leader.*

lost ✦✦✦ /lɒst/ ▣ **Lost** is the past tense and past participle of **lose**. ▣ ADJ If you are **lost** or if you get **lost**, you do not know where you are or are unable to find your way. ❏ *Barely had I set foot in the street when I realized I was lost.* ▣ ADJ If something is **lost**, or gets **lost**, you cannot find it, for example, because you have forgotten where you put it. ❏ *...a lost book.* ❏ *He was scrabbling for his pen, which had got lost somewhere under the sheets of paper.* ▣ ADJ If you feel **lost**, you feel very uncomfortable because you are in an unfamiliar situation. ❏ *Of the funeral he remembered only the cold, the waiting, and feeling very lost.* ▣ ADJ If you describe something as **lost**, you mean that you no longer have it or it no longer exists. ❏ *...their lost homeland.* ❏ *The sense of community is lost.* ▣ ADJ [ADJ n] You use **lost** to refer to a period or state of affairs that existed in the past and no longer exists. ❏ *He seemed to pine for his lost youth.* ❏ *They are links to a lost age.* ▣ ADJ If something is **lost**, it is not used properly and is considered wasted. ❏ *Smith is not bitter about the lost opportunity to compete in the games.*

lost and found ▣ N-SING **Lost and found** is the place where lost property is kept. [AM] ❏ *Excuse me, can you tell me where the lost and found is?*

in BRIT, use **lost property**

▣ ADJ **Lost-and-found** things are things which someone has lost and which someone else has found. ❏ *...the shelf where they stored lost-and-found articles.*

lost cause (**lost causes**) N-COUNT If you refer to something or someone as a **lost cause**, you mean that people's attempts to change or influence them have no chance of succeeding. ❏ *They do not want to expend energy in what, to them, is a lost cause.*

lost prop|er|ty [BRIT] ▣ N-UNCOUNT **Lost property** consists of things that people have lost or accidentally left in a public place, for example, on a train or in a school. ❏ *Lost property should be handed to the driver.* ▣ → see **lost and found**

lost soul (**lost souls**) N-COUNT If you call someone a **lost soul**, you mean that they seem unhappy, and unable to fit in with any particular group of people in society. ❏ *They just clung to each other like two lost souls.*

lot ✦✦✦ /lɒt/ (**lots**) ▣ QUANT [QUANT of n] **A lot of** something or **lots of** it is a large amount of it. **A lot of** people or things, or **lots of** them, is a large number of them. ❏ *A lot of our land is used to grow crops for export.* ❏ *He drank lots of milk.* • PRON **Lot** is also a pronoun. ❏ *I personally prefer to be in a town where there's lots going on.* ❏ *I learned a lot from him about how to run a band.* ▣ ADV **A lot** means to a great extent or degree. ❏ *Matthew's out quite a lot doing his research.* ❏ *I like you, a lot.* ▣ ADV [ADV after v] If you do something **a lot**, you do it often or for a long time. ❏ *They went out a lot, to restaurants and bars.* ▣ N-COUNT You can use **lot** to refer to a set or group of things or people. ❏ *He bought two lots of 1,000 shares in the company during August and September.* ▣ N-SING You can refer to a specific group of people as a particular **lot**. [INFORMAL] ❏ *Future generations are going to think that we were a pretty boring lot.* ▣ N-SING You can use **the lot** to refer to the whole of an amount that you have just mentioned. [INFORMAL] ❏ *This may turn out to be the best football game of the lot.* ▣ N-SING Your **lot** is the kind of life you have or the things that you have or experience. ❏ *She tried to accept her marriage as her lot in life but could not.* ▣ N-COUNT A **lot** is a small area of land that belongs to a person or company. [AM] ❏ *If oil or gold are discovered under your lot, you can sell the mineral rights.* ▣ → see also **parking lot** ▣ N-COUNT A **lot** in an auction is one of the objects or groups of objects that are being sold. ❏ *The receivers are keen to sell the stores as one lot.* ▣ PHRASE If people **draw lots** to decide who will do something, they each take a piece of paper from a container. One or more pieces of paper is marked, and the people who take marked pieces are chosen. ❑ *For the first time in the World Cup finals, lots had to be drawn to decide who would finish second and third.*

loth /loʊθ/ → see **loath**

lo|tion /loʊʃⁿn/ (**lotions**) N-MASS A **lotion** is a liquid that you use to clean, improve, or protect your skin or hair. ❑ *...suntan lotion.*

lot|tery /lɒtəri/ (**lotteries**) **1** N-COUNT A **lottery** is a type of gambling game in which people buy numbered tickets. Several numbers are then chosen, and the people who have those numbers on their tickets win a prize. ❑ *...the national lottery.* **2** N-SING If you describe something as **a lottery**, you mean that what happens depends entirely on luck or chance. ❑ *The stock market is a lottery.*

lo|tus /loʊtəs/ (**lotuses**) N-COUNT A **lotus** or a **lotus flower** is a type of water lily that grows in Africa and Asia.

lo|tus po|si|tion N-SING [usu the N] If someone doing meditation or yoga is in the **lotus position**, they are sitting with their legs crossed and each foot resting on top of the opposite thigh.

louche /luːʃ/ ADJ If you describe a person or place as **louche**, you mean that they are unconventional and not respectable, but often in a way that people find rather attractive. [WRITTEN] ❑ *...that section of society which somehow managed to be louche and fashionable at the same time.*

loud ♦♦♢ /laʊd/ (**louder, loudest**) **1** ADJ If a noise is **loud**, the level of sound is very high and it can be easily heard. Someone or something that is **loud** produces a lot of noise. ❑ *Suddenly there was a loud bang.* ❑ *His voice became harsh and loud.* • ADV [ADV after v] **Loud** is also an adverb. ❑ *She wonders whether Paul's hearing is OK because he turns the television up very loud.* • **loud|ly** ADV [ADV with v] ❑ *His footsteps echoed loudly in the tiled hall.* **2** ADJ If you describe something, especially a piece of clothing, as **loud**, you dislike it because it has very bright colors or very large, bold patterns which look unpleasant. [DISAPPROVAL] ❑ *He liked to shock with his gold chains and loud clothes.* **3** PHRASE If you say or read something **out loud**, you say it or read it so that it can be heard, rather than just thinking it. ❑ *Even Ford, who seldom smiled, laughed out loud a few times.*

SYNONYMS

loud
ADJ **1**
noisy: *...my noisy old typewriter.*
deafening: *...the deafening roar of fighter jets taking off.*
ear-splitting: *...ear-splitting screams.*

---

loud|hail|er /laʊdheɪlər/ (**loudhailers**) also **loud-hailer** N-COUNT A **loudhailer** is the same as a **bullhorn**. [BRIT]

loud|mouth /laʊdmaʊθ/ (**loudmouths** /laʊdmaʊðz/) N-COUNT If you describe someone as a **loudmouth**, you are critical of them because they talk a lot, especially in an unpleasant, offensive, or stupid way. [DISAPPROVAL]

loud|mouthed /laʊdmaʊθt/ ADJ [usu ADJ n] If you describe someone as **loudmouthed**, you are critical of them because they talk a lot, especially in an unpleasant, offensive, or stupid way. [DISAPPROVAL] ❑ *...a loud-mouthed oaf with very little respect for women.*

loud|speak|er /laʊdspiːkər/ (**loudspeakers**) also **loud speaker** **1** N-COUNT A **loudspeaker** is a piece of electronic equipment that forms part of a public address system and transmits sound. ❑ *The loudspeaker announced the arrival of the train.* **2** N-COUNT A **loudspeaker** is a piece of equipment, for example, part of a radio or hi-fi system, through which sound comes out. [BRIT]

lounge /laʊndʒ/ (**lounges, lounging, lounged**) **1** N-COUNT In a hotel, club, or other public place, a **lounge** is a room where people can sit and relax. ❑ *I spoke to her in the lounge of a big Johannesburg hotel where she was attending a union meeting.* **2** N-COUNT In an airport, a **lounge** is a very large room where people can sit and wait for aircraft to arrive or leave. ❑ *Instead of taking me to the departure lounge they took me right to my seat on the plane.* **3** N-COUNT In a house, a **lounge** is a room where people sit and relax. [BRIT]

in AM, use **family room**

4 V-I If you **lounge** somewhere, you sit or lie there in a relaxed or lazy way. ❑ *They ate and drank and lounged in the shade.*

louse /laʊs/ (**lice**) N-COUNT **Lice** are small insects that live on the bodies of people or animals and bite them in order to feed off their blood.

lousy /laʊzi/ (**lousier, lousiest**) **1** ADJ If you describe something as **lousy**, you mean that it is of very bad quality or that you do not like it. [INFORMAL] ❑ *He blamed Fiona for a lousy weekend.* ❑ *...a café where the menu is limited and the food is lousy.* **2** ADJ If you describe someone as **lousy**, you mean that they are very bad at something they do. [INFORMAL] ❑ *I was a lousy secretary.* **3** ADJ If you describe the number or amount of something as **lousy**, you mean it is smaller than you think it should be. [INFORMAL] ❑ *The pay is lousy.* **4** ADJ [feel/look ADJ] If you feel **lousy**, you feel very ill. [INFORMAL] ❑ *I wasn't actually sick but I felt lousy.*

lout /laʊt/ (**louts**) N-COUNT If you describe someone as a **lout**, you are critical of them because they behave in an impolite or aggressive way. [DISAPPROVAL] ❑ *...a drunken lout.*

lout|ish /laʊtɪʃ/ ADJ [usu ADJ n] If you describe someone as **loutish**, you are critical of them because their behavior is impolite and aggressive. [DISAPPROVAL] ❑ *I was appalled by the loutish behavior.*

lou|ver /luːvər/ (**louvers**)

in BRIT, use **louvre**

N-COUNT [oft N n] A **louver** is a door or window with narrow, flat, sloping pieces of wood or glass across its frame.

lov|able /lʌvəbᵊl/ ADJ If you describe someone as **lovable**, you mean that they have attractive qualities, and are easy to like. ❑ *His vulnerability makes him even more lovable.*

love ♦♦♦ /lʌv/ (**loves, loving, loved**) **1** V-T If you **love** someone, you feel romantically or sexually attracted to them, and they are very important to you. ❑ *Oh, Amy, I love you.* **2** N-UNCOUNT **Love** is a very strong feeling of affection toward someone who you are romantically or sexually attracted to. ❑ *Our love for each other has been increased by what we've been through together.* ❑ *...an old-fashioned love story.* **3** V-T You say that you **love** someone when their happiness is very important to you, so that you behave in a kind and caring way toward them. ❑ *You'll never love anyone the way you love your baby.* **4** N-UNCOUNT **Love** is the feeling that a person's happiness is very important to you, and the way you show this feeling in your behavior toward them. ❑ *My love for all my children is unconditional.* **5** V-T If you **love** something, you like it very much. ❑ *We loved the food so much, especially the fish dishes.* ❑ *...one of these people that loves to be in the outdoors.* **6** V-T You can say that you **love** something when you consider that it is important and want to protect or support it. ❑ *I love my country as you love yours.* **7** N-UNCOUNT **Love** is a strong liking for something, or a belief that it is important. ❑ *This is no way to encourage a love of literature.* **8** N-COUNT Your **love** is someone or something that you love. ❑ *"She is the love of my life," he said.* **9** V-T If you **would love** to have or do something, you very much want to have it or do it. ❑ *I would love to play for England again.* ❑ *I would love a hot bath and clean clothes.* **10** NUM In tennis, **love** is a score of zero. ❑ *He beat Thomas Muster of Austria three sets to love.* **11** CONVENTION You can use expressions such as **love**, **love from**, and **all my love**, followed by your name, as an informal way of ending a letter to a friend or relative. ❑ *...with love from Grandma and Grandpa.* **12** N-UNCOUNT If you send someone your **love**, you ask another person, who will soon be speaking or writing to them, to tell them that you are thinking about them with affection. ❑ *Please give her my love.* **13** → see also **loving** **14** PHRASE If you **fall in love** with someone, you start to be in love with them. ❑ *I fell in love with him because of his kind nature.* **15** PHRASE If you **fall in love** with something, you start to like it very much. ❑ *I fell in love with the movies.* **16** PHRASE If you **are in love** with someone, you feel romantically or sexually attracted to them, and they are very important to you. ❑ *Laura had never before been in love.* **17** PHRASE If you are **in love** with something, you like it very much. ❑ *He had always been in love with the enchanted landscape of the West.* **18** PHRASE When two people **make love**, they have sex. ❑ *Have you ever made love to a girl before?*

COLLOCATIONS

love
VERB **1**
love + *adverb*: dearly, unconditionally
NOUN **2**
adjective + **love**: true, unconditional, undying, unrequited; passionate, romantic

love af|fair (love affairs) **1** N-COUNT A **love affair** is a romantic and usually sexual relationship between two people who love each other but who are not married or living together. ❑ ...*a stressful love affair with a married man*. **2** N-SING If you refer to someone's **love affair** with something, you mean that they like it a lot and are very enthusiastic about it. ❑ ...*the American love affair with firearms*.

love|birds /lʌvbɜrdz/ N-PLURAL You can refer to two people as **lovebirds** when they are obviously very much in love. [HUMOROUS]

love bite [BRIT] → see hickey

love child (love children) N-COUNT If journalists refer to someone as a **love child**, they mean that the person was born as a result of a love affair between two people who have never been married to each other. ❑ *Eric has a secret love child*.

-loved /-lʌvd/ COMB IN ADJ [usu ADJ n] **-loved** combines with adverbs to form adjectives that describe how much someone or something is loved. ❑ *The similarities between the much-loved father and his son are remarkable*. ❑ ...*two of Mendelssohn's best-loved works*.

love-hate re|la|tion|ship (love-hate relationships) N-COUNT [usu sing] If you have a **love-hate relationship** with someone or something, your feelings toward them change suddenly and often from love to hate. ❑ ...*a book about the close love-hate relationship between two boys*.

love|less /lʌvlɪs/ ADJ [usu ADJ n] A **loveless** relationship or situation is one where there is no love. ❑ *She is in a loveless relationship*.

love let|ter (love letters) N-COUNT A **love letter** is a letter that you write to someone in order to tell them that you love them.

love life (love lives) N-COUNT Someone's **love life** is the part of their life that consists of their romantic and sexual relationships. ❑ *His love life was complicated, and involved intense relationships*.

love|lorn /lʌvlɔrn/ ADJ [usu ADJ n] **Lovelorn** means the same as **lovesick**. ❑ *He was acting like a lovelorn teenager*.

love|ly ♦♢♢ /lʌvli/ (lovelier, loveliest) **1** ADJ If you describe someone or something as **lovely**, you mean that they are very beautiful and therefore pleasing to look at or listen to. ❑ *You look lovely, Marcia*. ❑ *He had a lovely voice*. • **love|li|ness** N-UNCOUNT ❑ *You are a vision of loveliness*. **2** ADJ If you describe something as **lovely**, you mean that it gives you pleasure. [mainly SPOKEN] ❑ *Mary! How lovely to see you!* ❑ *It's a lovely day*.

SYNONYMS

lovely
ADJ **1**
beautiful: *New England is beautiful*.
appealing: *There was a sense of humor in what he did that I found very appealing*.
attractive: *The creamy, white flowers are attractive in the spring*.
charming: ...*a charming, little, fishing village*.
adorable: *We have three adorable children*.

love|making /lʌvmeɪkɪŋ/ N-UNCOUNT **Lovemaking** refers to sexual activities that take place between two people, especially between people who love each other. ❑ *Their lovemaking became less and less frequent*.

love nest (love nests) N-COUNT [usu sing] A **love nest** is a house or apartment where two people who are having a love affair live or meet. [JOURNALISM]

lov|er ♦♢♢ /lʌvər/ (lovers) **1** N-COUNT Someone's **lover** is someone who they are having a sexual relationship with but are not married to. ❑ *Every Thursday she would meet her lover Leon*. **2** N-COUNT If you are a **lover** of something such as animals or

the arts, you enjoy them very much and take great pleasure in them. ❑ *She is a great lover of horses and horse racing*.

love|sick /lʌvsɪk/ ADJ [usu ADJ n] If you describe someone as **lovesick**, you mean that they are so in love with someone who does not love them, that they are behaving in a strange and foolish way. ❑ ...*a lovesick boy consumed with self-pity*.

love sto|ry (love stories) N-COUNT A **love story** is something such as a novel or movie about a love affair.

love-stricken also **lovestruck** ADJ If you describe someone as **love-stricken**, you mean that they are so much in love that they are behaving in a strange and foolish way.

love tri|an|gle (love triangles) N-COUNT [usu sing] A **love triangle** is a relationship in which three people are each in love with at least one other person in the relationship. [JOURNALISM]

lovey-dovey /lʌvi dʌvi/ ADJ You can use **lovey-dovey** to describe, in a humorous or slightly disapproving way, lovers who show their affection for each other very openly. [INFORMAL, DISAPPROVAL] ❑ *All my friends were either lovey-dovey couples or wild, single girls*.

lov|ing /lʌvɪŋ/ **1** ADJ Someone who is **loving** feels or shows love to other people. ❑ *Jim was a most loving husband and father*. • **lov|ing|ly** ADV ❑ *Brian gazed lovingly at Mary Ann*. **2** ADJ **Loving** actions are done with great enjoyment and care. ❑ *The house has been restored with loving care*. • **lov|ing|ly** ADV ❑ *I lifted the box and ran my fingers lovingly over the top*.

low ♦♦♦ /loʊ/ (lower, lowest, lows) **1** ADJ Something that is **low** measures only a short distance from the bottom to the top, or from the ground to the top. ❑ ...*the low garden wall that separated the front garden from next door*. ❑ *The country, with its low, rolling hills was beautiful*. **2** ADJ If something is **low**, it is close to the ground, to sea level, or to the bottom of something. ❑ *He bumped his head on the low beams*. ❑ *It was late afternoon and the sun was low in the sky*. **3** ADJ When a river is **low**, it contains less water than usual. ❑ ...*pumps that guarantee a constant depth of water even when the supplying river is low*. **4** ADJ You can use **low** to indicate that something is small in amount or that it is at the bottom of a particular scale. You can use phrases such as **in the low 80s** to indicate that a number or level is less than 85 but not as little as 80. ❑ *Casualties remained remarkably low*. ❑ *They are still having to live on very low incomes*. **5** ADJ **Low** is used to describe people who are not considered to be very important because they are near the bottom of a particular scale or system. ❑ *She refused to promote Colin above the low rank of "legal adviser."* **6** N-COUNT If something reaches a **low** of a particular amount or degree, that is the smallest it has ever been. ❑ *Prices dropped to a low of about $1.12 in December*. **7** ADJ If the quality or standard of something is **low**, it is very poor. ❑ *A school would not accept low-quality work from any student*. ❑ *The inquiry team criticizes staff at the psychiatric hospital for the low standard of care*. **8** ADJ [v-link ADJ in n] If a food or other substance is **low in** a particular ingredient, it contains only a small amount of that ingredient. ❑ *They look for foods that are low in calories*. • COMB IN ADJ **Low** is also a combining form. ❑ ...*low-sodium tomato sauce*. **9** ADJ If you have a **low** opinion of someone or something, you disapprove of them or dislike them. ❑ *The majority of sex offenders have a low opinion of themselves*. **10** ADJ You can use **low** to describe negative feelings and attitudes. ❑ *We are all very tired and morale is low*. **11** ADJ If a sound or noise is **low**, it is deep. ❑ *Then suddenly she gave a low, choking moan and began to tremble violently*. **12** ADJ If someone's voice is **low**, it is quiet or soft. ❑ *Her voice was so low he had to strain to catch it*. **13** ADJ A light that is **low** is not bright or strong. ❑ *Their eyesight is poor in low light*. **14** ADJ If a radio, oven, or light is on **low**, it has been adjusted so that only a small amount of sound, heat, or light is produced. ❑ *She turned her little kitchen radio on low*. ❑ *Buy a dimmer switch and keep the light on low, or switch it off altogether*. **15** ADJ [v-link ADJ] If you are **low** on something or if a supply of it is **low**, there is not much of it left. ❑ *We're a bit low on bed linen*. **16** ADJ If you are **low**, you are depressed. [INFORMAL] ❑ *"I didn't ask for this job, you know," he tells friends when he is low*. **17** → see also **lower 18 to look high and low** → see **high 19 low profile** → see **profile 20 to be running low** → see **run** ③

COLLOCATIONS

low
NOUN [6]
adjective + **low**: all-time, historic, new, record
verb + **low**: hit, plumb, reach

low|brow /loʊbraʊ/ also **low-brow** ADJ If you say that something is **lowbrow**, you mean that it is easy to understand or appreciate rather than intellectual and is therefore perhaps inferior. ☐ *His choice of subject matter has been regarded as lowbrow.* ☐ *...low-brow novels.*

low-cal ADJ [usu ADJ n] **Low-cal** food is food that contains only a few calories. People who are trying to lose weight eat low-cal food.

low-cut ADJ [usu ADJ n] **Low-cut** dresses and blouses do not cover the top part of a woman's chest.

low|down /loʊdaʊn/ [1] N-SING [the N, oft N on n] If someone gives you the **lowdown** on a person or thing, they tell you all the important information about them. [INFORMAL] ☐ *We want you to give us the lowdown on your teammates.* [2] ADJ [ADJ n] You can use **lowdown** to emphasize how bad, dishonest, or unfair you consider a particular person or their behavior to be. [INFORMAL, EMPHASIS] ☐ *...a lowdown, evil drunkard.* ☐ *They will stoop to every lowdown trick.*

low-emission ADJ [ADJ n] A **low-emission** vehicle is one that does not produce much pollution. A **low-emission** zone is an area where vehicles that produce pollution are not allowed or have to pay to enter. ☐ *They have created a new generation of low-emission buses.*

low-end ADJ **Low-end** products, especially electronic products, are the least expensive of their kind. ☐ *...a low-end laser printer.*

low|er ♦⬦ /loʊər/ (lowers, lowering, lowered) [1] ADJ [ADJ n, the ADJ, the ADJ of n] You can use **lower** to refer to the bottom one of a pair of things. ☐ *She bit her lower lip.* ☐ *...the lower of the two holes.* [2] ADJ [ADJ n] You can use **lower** to refer to the bottom part of something. ☐ *Use a small cushion to help give support to the lower back.* [3] ADJ [ADJ n, the ADJ] You can use **lower** to refer to people or things that are less important than similar people or things. ☐ *Already the awards are causing resentment in the lower ranks of council officers.* ☐ *The nation's highest court reversed the lower court's decision.* [4] V-T If you **lower** something, you move it slowly downward. ☐ *Two reporters had to help lower the coffin into the grave.* ☐ *Sokolowski lowered himself into the black leather chair.* • **low|er|ing** N-UNCOUNT ☐ *...the extinguishing of the Olympic flame and the lowering of the flag.* [5] V-T If you **lower** something, you make it less in amount, degree, value, or quality. ☐ *The Central Bank has lowered interest rates by 2 percent.* • **low|er|ing** N-UNCOUNT ☐ *...a package of social measures which included the lowering of the retirement age.* [6] V-T If someone **lowers** their head or eyes, they look downward, for example, because they are sad or embarrassed. ☐ *She lowered her head and brushed past photographers as she went back inside.* [7] V-T [oft with brd-neg] If you say that you would not **lower** yourself by doing something, you mean that you would not behave in a way that would make you or other people respect you less. ☐ *Don't lower yourself, don't be the way they are.* [8] V-T/V-I If you **lower** your voice or if your voice **lowers**, you speak more quietly. ☐ *The man moved closer, lowering his voice.* [9] → see also **low** [10] → See feature box at **water**

SYNONYMS

lower
VERB [5]
lessen: *Make sure that your immunizations are up to date to lessen the risk of serious illness.*
cut: *The first priority is to cut costs.*
reduce: *Consumption is being reduced by 25 percent.*

low|er|case also **lower-case, lower case** N-UNCOUNT **Lowercase** letters are small letters, not capital letters. ☐ *It was printed in lowercase.*

low|er class (lower classes) also **lower-class** N-COUNT-COLL [usu pl] Some people use the **lower class** or the **lower classes** to refer to the division of society that they consider to have the lowest social status. ☐ *Education now offers the lower classes access to job opportunities.* • ADJ **Lower class** is also an adjective. ☐ *...lower-class families.*

low|er house (lower houses) also **Lower House** N-COUNT; N-PROPER In countries where the legislature or parliament is divided into two groups of members, the **lower house** is usually the larger and more representative group. ☐ *At least 15 different parties have won seats in the lower house of the Parliament.*

low|est com|mon de|nomi|na|tor (lowest common denominators) [1] N-COUNT [usu sing] If you describe a plan or policy as the **lowest common denominator**, you are critical of it because it has been deliberately made too simple so that nobody will disagree. [DISAPPROVAL] ☐ *Although the plan received unanimous approval, this does not mean that it represents the lowest common denominator.* [2] N-COUNT [usu sing] If you say that something is designed to appeal to the **lowest common denominator**, you are critical of it because it is designed to be liked by the majority of people. [DISAPPROVAL] ☐ *Tabloid newspapers pander to the lowest common denominator.* [3] N-COUNT In mathematics, the **lowest common denominator** is the smallest number that all the numbers on the bottom of a particular group of fractions can be divided into. [TECHNICAL]

low-flying ADJ [ADJ n] **Low-flying** aircraft or birds are flying very close to the ground, or lower than normal.

low-impact [1] ADJ [usu ADJ n] **Low-impact** exercise does not put a lot of stress on your body. [2] ADJ [usu ADJ n] **Low-impact** projects, developments, and activities such as vacations are designed to cause minimum harm to the environment. ☐ *...sensitive, enlightened, low-impact ecotourism.*

low-key ADJ If you say that something is **low-key**, you mean that it is on a small scale rather than involving a lot of activity or being made to seem impressive or important. ☐ *The wedding will be a very low-key affair.*

low|lands /loʊləndz/ also **lowland**

The form **lowland** is also used as a modifier.

N-PLURAL [usu the N] **Lowlands** are an area of low, flat land. ☐ *...the coastal lowlands of East Africa.* ☐ *...the fever-haunted old town on the lowland across the lake.* ☐ *...lowland areas.*

low life also **low-life, lowlife** N-UNCOUNT [oft N n] People sometimes use **low life** to refer in a disapproving way to people who are involved in criminal, dishonest, or immoral activities, or to these activities. [DISAPPROVAL] ☐ *...the sort of low-life characters who populate this film.*

low|ly /loʊli/ (lowlier, lowliest) ADJ If you describe someone or something as **lowly**, you mean they are low in rank, status, or importance. ☐ *...lowly bureaucrats pretending to be senators.*

low-lying ADJ [usu ADJ n] **Low-lying** land is at, near, or below sea level. ☐ *Sea walls collapsed, and low-lying areas were flooded.*

low-maintenance also **low maintenance** ADJ If you describe something or someone as **low-maintenance**, you mean that they require very little time, money, or effort to look after them. ☐ *...a secluded, low-maintenance yard.* ☐ *I'm probably the most low-maintenance, easygoing person ever.*

low-paid ADJ If you describe someone or their job as **low-paid**, you mean that their work earns them very little money. ☐ *...low-paid workers.*

low-pitched [1] ADJ A sound that is **low-pitched** is deep. ☐ *With a low-pitched rumbling noise, the propeller began to rotate.* [2] ADJ A voice that is **low-pitched** is very soft and quiet. ☐ *He kept his voice low-pitched in case someone was listening.*

low-rent [1] ADJ If someone lives in a **low-rent** house, they only have to pay a small amount of money to live there. ☐ *...a low-rent housing development.* [2] ADJ You can use **low-rent** to describe something that is of poor quality, especially when it is compared with something else. [DISAPPROVAL] ☐ *...a low-rent horror movie.*

low-rise (low-rises) ADJ [ADJ n] **Low-rise** buildings are modern buildings which have only a few stories. ☐ *...low-rise apartment buildings.* • N-COUNT A **low-rise** is a low-rise building. ☐ *...a mix of low-rises, town houses and single-family homes.*

low sea|son [1] N-SING The **low season** is the same as the **off season**. [BRIT] [2] → See feature box at **tourism**

low-slung ADJ [usu ADJ n] **Low-slung** chairs or cars are very low, so that you are close to the ground when you are sitting in them.

low-tech /loʊ tɛk/ ADJ **Low-tech** machines or systems are ones that do not use modern or sophisticated technology. □ ...a simple form of low-tech electric propulsion.

low tide (low tides) N-VAR [oft at N] At the coast, **low tide** is the time when the sea is at its lowest level because the tide is out. □ The causeway to the island is only accessible at low tide.

low wa|ter N-UNCOUNT **Low water** is the same as **low tide**.

lox /lɒks/ N-UNCOUNT **Lox** is salmon that has been smoked and is eaten raw. [mainly AM]

loy|al /lɔɪəl/ ADJ Someone who is **loyal** remains firm in their friendship or support for a person or thing. [APPROVAL] □ They had remained loyal to the president. ● **loy|al|ly** ADV [ADV with v] □ They have loyally supported their party and their leader.

loy|al|ist /lɔɪəlɪst/ (loyalists) N-COUNT A **loyalist** is a person who remains firm in their support for a government or ruler. □ Party loyalists responded as they always do, waving flags and carrying placards.

loy|al|ty /lɔɪəlti/ (loyalties) **1** N-UNCOUNT **Loyalty** is the quality of staying firm in your friendship or support for someone or something. □ I have sworn an oath of loyalty to the monarchy. **2** N-COUNT **Loyalties** are feelings of friendship, support, or duty toward someone or something. □ She had developed strong loyalties to the Manet family. **3** → See feature box at **service**

loy|al|ty card (loyalty cards) N-COUNT A **loyalty card** is a plastic card that some stores give to regular customers. Each time the customer buys something from the store, points are electronically stored on their card and can be exchanged later for goods or services.

loz|enge /lɒzɪndʒ/ (lozenges) **1** N-COUNT **Lozenges** are sweet tablets which you can suck to make a cough or sore throat better. □ ...throat lozenges. **2** N-COUNT A **lozenge** is a shape with four corners. The two corners that point up and down are further away than the two pointing sideways.

LP /ɛl piː/ (LPs) N-COUNT An **LP** is a record which usually has about 25 minutes of music or speech on each side. **LP** is an abbreviation for 'long-playing record.' □ As a solo artist, he released 18 LPs.

LPG /ɛl piː dʒiː/ N-UNCOUNT **LPG** is a type of fuel consisting of hydrocarbon gases in liquid form. **LPG** is an abbreviation for 'liquefied petroleum gas.'

LPN /ɛl piː ɛn/ (LPNs) N-COUNT An **LPN** is a nurse who is trained to provide patients with basic care under the supervision of a doctor or a registered nurse. **LPN** is an abbreviation for 'licensed practical nurse.' [AM] □ Having worked as an LPN, I knew well the appearance of a dead body.

LSAT /ɛlsæt/ (LSATs) N-PROPER The **LSAT** is an examination which is often taken by students who wish to enter a law school. **LSAT** is an abbreviation for 'Law School Admission Test.' [AM] □ He had cheated on the LSAT to get into law school.

LSD /ɛl ɛs diː/ N-UNCOUNT **LSD** is a very powerful illegal drug which makes the user see things that only exist in their mind.

Lt. Lt. is a written abbreviation for **lieutenant**. □ He was replaced by Lt. Frank Fraser.

lub|ri|cant /luːbrɪkənt/ (lubricants) **1** N-MASS A **lubricant** is a substance which you put on the surfaces or parts of something, especially something mechanical, to make the parts move smoothly. □ Its nozzle was smeared with some kind of lubricant. □ ...industrial lubricants. **2** N-COUNT [usu supp N] If you refer to something as a **lubricant** in a particular situation, you mean that it helps to make things happen without any problems. □ I think humor is a great lubricant for life.

lu|bri|cate /luːbrɪkeɪt/ (lubricates, lubricating, lubricated) V-T If you **lubricate** something such as a part of a machine, you put a substance such as oil on it so that it moves smoothly. [FORMAL] □ Mineral oils are used to lubricate machinery. ● **lu|bri|ca|tion** /luːbrɪkeɪʃən/ N-UNCOUNT □ Use a touch of linseed oil for lubrication.

lu|cid /luːsɪd/ **1** ADJ **Lucid** writing or speech is clear and easy to understand. □ ...a lucid account of the history of mankind. ● **lu|cid|ly** ADV [ADV with v] □ Both of them had the ability to present complex matters lucidly. ● **lu|cid|ity** /luːsɪdɪti/ N-UNCOUNT □ His writings were marked by an extraordinary lucidity and elegance of style. **2** ADJ If someone is **lucid**, they are thinking clearly again after a period of illness or confusion. [FORMAL] □ He wasn't very lucid, he didn't quite know where he was. ● **lu|cid|ity** N-UNCOUNT □ The pain had lessened in the night, but so had his lucidity.

luck ♦◇◇ /lʌk/ (lucks, lucking, lucked) **1** N-UNCOUNT **Luck** or **good luck** is success or good things that happen to you, that do not come from your own abilities or efforts. □ I knew I needed a bit of luck to win. □ The Sri Lankans have been having no luck with the weather. **2** N-UNCOUNT **Bad luck** is lack of success or bad things that happen to you, that have not been caused by yourself or other people. □ I had a lot of bad luck during the first half of this season. **3** CONVENTION If you ask someone the question '**Any luck?**' or '**No luck?**,' you want to know if they have been successful in something they were trying to do. [INFORMAL] □ "Any luck?"—"No." **4** CONVENTION You can say '**Bad luck**' or '**Hard luck**' to someone when you want to express sympathy to them. [INFORMAL, FORMULAE] □ Bad luck, man, just bad luck. **5** CONVENTION If you say '**Good luck**' or '**Best of luck**' to someone, you are telling them that you hope they will be successful in something they are trying to do. [INFORMAL, FORMULAE] □ He kissed her on the cheek. "Best of luck!" **6** PHRASE You can say someone **is in luck** when they are in a situation where they can have what they want or need. □ You're in luck. The doctor's still in. **7** PHRASE If you say that someone **is out of luck**, you mean that they cannot have something which they can normally have. □ "What do you want, Roy? If it's money, you're out of luck."
▶ **luck out** PHRASAL VERB If you **luck out**, you get some advantage or are successful because you have good luck. □ Was he born to be successful, or did he just luck out?

luck|i|ly /lʌkɪli/ ADV [ADV with cl] You add **luckily** to a statement to indicate that it is good that a particular thing happened or is the case because otherwise the situation would have been difficult or unpleasant. □ Luckily, we both love football.

luck|less /lʌklɪs/ ADJ [usu ADJ n] If you describe someone or something as **luckless**, you mean that they are unsuccessful or unfortunate. [WRITTEN] □ ...the luckless parent of an extremely difficult child.

lucky ♦◇◇ /lʌki/ (luckier, luckiest) **1** ADJ You say that someone is **lucky** when they have something that is very desirable or when they are in a very desirable situation. □ I am luckier than most. I have a job. □ He is incredibly lucky to be alive. **2** ADJ Someone who is **lucky** seems to always have good luck. □ Some people are born lucky, aren't they? **3** ADJ If you describe an action or experience as **lucky**, you mean that it was good or successful, and that it happened by chance and not as a result of planning or preparation. □ They admit they are now desperate for a lucky break. **4** ADJ A **lucky** object is something that people believe helps them to be successful. □ He did not have on his other lucky charm, a pair of green socks. **5** PHRASE If you say that someone **will be lucky** to do or get something, you mean that they are very unlikely to do or get it, and will definitely not do or get any more than that. □ You'll be lucky if you get any breakfast. □ Those remaining in work will be lucky to get the smallest of pay increases.

lu|cra|tive /luːkrətɪv/ **1** ADJ A **lucrative** activity, job, or business deal is very profitable. □ Thousands of ex-army officers have found lucrative jobs in private security firms. **2** → See feature box at **crime**

lu|cre /luːkər/ N-UNCOUNT People sometimes refer to money or profit as **lucre**, especially when they think that it has been obtained by dishonest means. [HUMOROUS or OLD-FASHIONED, DISAPPROVAL] □ ...so they can feel less guilty about their piles of filthy lucre.

Lud|dite /lʌdaɪt/ (Luddites) **1** N-COUNT [oft N n] If you refer to someone as a **Luddite**, you are criticizing them for opposing changes in technology or working methods, especially the introduction of new machines and modern methods. [DISAPPROVAL] □ The majority have a built-in Luddite mentality; they are resistant to change. **2** → See feature box at **technology**

lu|di|crous /luːdɪkrəs/ ADJ If you describe something as **ludicrous**, you are emphasizing that you think it is foolish, unreasonable, or unsuitable. [EMPHASIS] □ It was ludicrous to suggest that the visit could be kept secret. ● **lu|di|crous|ly** ADV □ This is just another ludicrously over-hyped product.

lug /lʌg/ (lugs, lugging, lugged) V-T If you **lug** a heavy or awkward object somewhere, you carry it there with difficulty. [INFORMAL] □ Nobody wants to lug around huge suitcases full of clothes.

luge /luʒ/ (luges) N-COUNT A **luge** is an object that is used for racing downhill over snow or ice. Riders lie on their backs and travel with their feet pointing toward the front of the luge.

lug|gage /lʌgɪdʒ/ N-UNCOUNT **Luggage** is the suitcases and bags that you take with you when travel. ☐ *Leave your luggage in the hotel.*

lug|gage rack (luggage racks) **1** N-COUNT A **luggage rack** is a shelf for putting luggage on, on a vehicle such as a train or bus. **2** N-COUNT A **luggage rack** is a metal frame that is fixed on top of a car and used for carrying large objects. [AM]

in BRIT, use **roof rack**

lu|gu|bri|ous /luːguːbriəs/ ADJ If you say that someone or something is **lugubrious**, you mean that they are sad rather than lively or cheerful. [LITERARY] ☐ *...a tall, thin man with a long and lugubrious face.* ☐ *He plays some passages so slowly that they become lugubrious.* • **lu|gu|bri|ous|ly** ADV [ADV with v, ADV adj] ☐ *The dog gazed at us lugubriously for a few minutes.*

luke|warm /luːkwɔːrm/ **1** ADJ Something, especially a liquid, that is **lukewarm** is only slightly warm. ☐ *Wash your face with lukewarm water.* **2** ADJ If you describe a person or their attitude as **lukewarm**, you mean that they are not showing much enthusiasm or interest. ☐ *Economists have never been more than lukewarm toward him.*

lull /lʌl/ (lulls, lulling, lulled) **1** N-COUNT A **lull** is a period of quiet or calm in a longer period of activity or excitement. ☐ *There was a lull in political violence after the election of the current president.* **2** V-T If you **are lulled** into feeling safe, someone or something causes you to feel safe at a time when you are not safe. ☐ *It is easy to be lulled into a false sense of security.* ☐ *I had been lulled into thinking the publicity would be a trivial matter.*

lulla|by /lʌləbaɪ/ (lullabies) **1** N-COUNT A **lullaby** is a quiet song which is intended to be sung to babies and young children to help them go to sleep. **2** → See feature box at **music**

lum|ba|go /lʌmbeɪgoʊ/ N-UNCOUNT If someone has **lumbago**, they have pains in the lower part of their back.

lum|bar /lʌmbər/ ADJ [ADJ n] **Lumbar** means relating to the lower part of your back. [MEDICAL] ☐ *Lumbar support is very important if you're driving a long way.*

lum|ber /lʌmbər/ (lumbers, lumbering, lumbered) **1** N-UNCOUNT **Lumber** consists of trees and large pieces of wood that have been roughly cut up. [mainly AM] ☐ *It was made of soft lumber, spruce by the look of it.* **2** V-I If someone or something **lumbers** from one place to another, they move there very slowly and clumsily. ☐ *He lumbered back to his chair.*

lumber|jack /lʌmbərdʒæk/ (lumberjacks) N-COUNT A **lumberjack** is a person whose job is to cut down trees.

lumber|man /lʌmbərmən/ (lumbermen) N-COUNT A **lumberman** is a man who sells timber. [AM]

lumber|yard /lʌmbəryɑːrd/ (lumberyards) also **lumber yard** N-COUNT A **lumberyard** is a place where wood is stored and sold. [AM]

in BRIT, use **timber yard**

lu|mi|nary /luːmɪneri/ (luminaries) N-COUNT If you refer to someone as a **luminary**, you mean that they are an expert in a particular subject or activity. [LITERARY] ☐ *...the political opinions of such luminaries as Sartre or de Beauvoir.*

lu|mi|nes|cence /luːmɪnɛsəns/ N-UNCOUNT **Luminescence** is a soft, glowing light. [LITERARY] ☐ *Lights reflected off dust-covered walls creating a ghostly luminescence.*

lu|mi|nos|ity /luːmɪnɒsɪti/ **1** N-UNCOUNT The **luminosity** of a star or sun is how bright it is. [TECHNICAL] ☐ *For a few years its luminosity flared up to about 10,000 times the present-day luminosity of the Sun.* **2** N-UNCOUNT You can talk about the **luminosity** of someone's skin when it has a healthy glow. ☐ *Ultrafine powder with a rosy tinge gives the skin warmth and luminosity.*

lu|mi|nous /luːmɪnəs/ ADJ Something that is **luminous** shines or glows in the dark. ☐ *The luminous dial on the clock showed five minutes to seven.*

lump /lʌmp/ (lumps, lumping, lumped) **1** N-COUNT A **lump** of something is a solid piece of it. ☐ *The potter shaped and squeezed the lump of clay into a graceful shape.* ☐ *...a lump of wood.* **2** N-COUNT A **lump** on or in someone's body is a small, hard swelling that has been caused by an injury or an illness. ☐ *I've got a lump on my shoulder.* **3** N-COUNT A **lump** of sugar is a small cube of it. ☐ *...a nugget of rough gold about the size of a lump of sugar.* **4** → see also **lump sum** **5** PHRASE If you say that you have a **lump in your throat**, you mean that you have a tight feeling in your throat because of a strong emotion such as sorrow or gratitude. ☐ *I stood there with a lump in my throat and tried to fight back tears.*

▶ **lump together** PHRASAL VERB If a number of different people or things **are lumped together**, they are considered as a group rather than separately. ☐ *Policemen and prostitutes, bankers and butchers are all lumped together in the service sector.*

lum|pec|to|my /lʌmpɛktəmi/ (lumpectomies) N-COUNT A **lumpectomy** is an operation in which a woman has a lump such as a tumor removed from one of her breasts, rather than having the whole breast removed.

lump sum (lump sums) N-COUNT A **lump sum** is an amount of money that is paid as a large amount on a single occasion rather than as smaller amounts on several separate occasions. ☐ *...a tax-free lump sum of $50,000.*

lumpy /lʌmpi/ (lumpier, lumpiest) **1** ADJ Something that is **lumpy** contains lumps or is covered with lumps. ☐ *When the rice isn't cooked properly it goes lumpy and gooey.* **2** → See feature box at **snow**

lu|na|cy /luːnəsi/ **1** N-UNCOUNT If you describe someone's behavior as **lunacy**, you mean that it seems very strange or foolish. [DISAPPROVAL] ☐ *...the lunacy of the times we live in.* ☐ *It remains lunacy to produce yet more coal to add to power stations' stockpiles.* **2** N-UNCOUNT **Lunacy** is severe mental illness. [OLD-FASHIONED]

lu|nar /luːnər/ ADJ [ADJ n] **Lunar** means relating to the moon. ☐ *The vast volcanic slope was eerily reminiscent of a lunar landscape.*

lu|na|tic /luːnətɪk/ (lunatics) **1** N-COUNT If you describe someone as a **lunatic**, you think they behave in a dangerous, stupid, or annoying way. [INFORMAL, DISAPPROVAL] ☐ *Her son thinks she's an absolute raving lunatic.* **2** ADJ If you describe someone's behavior or ideas as **lunatic**, you think they are very foolish and possibly dangerous. [DISAPPROVAL] ☐ *...the operation of the market taken to lunatic extremes.* **3** N-COUNT People who were mentally ill used to be called **lunatics**. [OLD-FASHIONED, OFFENSIVE] ☐ *...the lunatics in the Bedlam asylum.*

lu|na|tic asy|lum (lunatic asylums) N-COUNT A **lunatic asylum** was a place where mentally disturbed people used to be locked up. [OLD-FASHIONED, OFFENSIVE]

lu|na|tic fringe N-SING [usu the N] If you refer to a group of people as the **lunatic fringe**, you mean that they are very extreme in their opinions or behavior. ☐ *Demands for a separate Siberia are confined for now to the lunatic fringe.*

lunch ♦♦◊ /lʌntʃ/ (lunches, lunching, lunched) **1** N-VAR **Lunch** is the meal that you have in the middle of the day. ☐ *Shall we meet somewhere for lunch?* ☐ *He did not enjoy business lunches.* **2** V-I When you **lunch**, you have lunch, especially at a restaurant. [FORMAL] ☐ *Only the extremely rich could afford to lunch here.*

lunch|box /lʌntʃbɒks/ (lunchboxes) N-COUNT A **lunchbox** is a small container with a lid. You put food such as sandwiches in it to eat for lunch at work or at school.

lunch break (lunch breaks) also **lunchbreak** N-COUNT [usu poss N] Your **lunch break** is the period in the middle of the day when you stop work in order to have a meal.

lunch coun|ter (lunch counters) N-COUNT A **lunch counter** is an informal café or a counter in a store where people can buy and eat meals. [AM]

lunch|eon /lʌntʃən/ (luncheons) N-COUNT A **luncheon** is a formal lunch, for example, to celebrate an important event or to raise money for charity. ☐ *Earlier this month, a luncheon for former U.N. staff was held in Vienna.*

lunch|eon|ette /lʌntʃənɛt/ (luncheonettes) N-COUNT A **luncheonette** is a small restaurant that serves light meals. [AM]

lunch hour (lunch hours) N-COUNT [usu poss N] Your **lunch hour** is the period in the middle of the day when you stop working, usually for one hour, in order to have a meal.

lunch meat (lunch meats) N-VAR **Lunch meat** is meat that you eat in a sandwich or salad, and that is usually cold and either sliced or formed into rolls. [AM]

lunch|room /lʌntʃrum/ (lunchrooms) also **lunch room** N-COUNT A **lunchroom** is the room in a school or company where you buy and eat your lunch. [AM]

lunch|time /lʌntʃtaɪm/ (lunchtimes) also **lunch time** N-VAR **Lunchtime** is the period of the day when people have their lunch. ❑ *Could we meet at lunchtime?*

lung /lʌŋ/ (lungs) **1** N-COUNT Your **lungs** are the two organs inside your chest which fill with air when you breathe in. ❑ *...a smoker who died of lung cancer.* **2** → See feature box at **body**; See also color supplement

lunge /lʌndʒ/ (lunges, lunging, lunged) V-I If you **lunge** in a particular direction, you move in that direction suddenly and clumsily. ❑ *He lunged at me, grabbing me violently.* • N-COUNT **Lunge** is also a noun. ❑ *The attacker knocked on their door and made a lunge for Wendy when she answered.*

lung|ful /lʌŋfʊl/ (lungfuls) N-COUNT [usu N of n] If someone takes a **lungful** of something such as fresh air or smoke, they breathe in deeply so that their lungs feel as if they are full of that thing. [WRITTEN] ❑ *I bobbed to the surface and gasped a lungful of air.*

lurch /lɜrtʃ/ (lurches, lurching, lurched) **1** V-I To **lurch** means to make a sudden movement, especially forward, in an uncontrolled way. ❑ *As the car sped over a pothole she lurched forward.* ❑ *Henry looked, stared, and lurched to his feet.* • N-COUNT **Lurch** is also a noun. ❑ *The car took a lurch forward.* **2** V-I If you say that a person or organization **lurches** from one thing to another, you mean they move suddenly from one course of action or attitude to another in an uncontrolled way. [DISAPPROVAL] ❑ *The state government has lurched from one budget crisis to another.* • N-COUNT **Lurch** is also a noun. ❑ *The property sector was another casualty of the lurch toward higher interest rates.*

lure /lʊər/ (lures, luring, lured) **1** V-T To **lure** someone means to trick them into a particular place or to trick them into doing something that they should not do. ❑ *He lured her to his apartment by claiming that he had left his money there.* ❑ *They did not realize that they were being lured into a trap.* **2** N-COUNT A **lure** is an object which is used to attract animals, especially fish, so that they can be caught. **3** N-COUNT A **lure** is an attractive quality that something has, or something that you find attractive. ❑ *Plans like these will without doubt act as a lure to potential investors.*

lu|rid /lʊərɪd/ **1** ADJ If you say that something is **lurid**, you are critical of it because it involves a lot of violence, sex, or shocking detail. [DISAPPROVAL] ❑ *...lurid accounts of Claire's sexual exploits.* **2** ADJ If you describe something as **lurid**, you do not like it because it is very brightly colored. [DISAPPROVAL] ❑ *She took care to paint her toe nails a lurid red or orange.*

lurk /lɜrk/ (lurks, lurking, lurked) **1** V-I If someone **lurks** somewhere, they wait there secretly so that they cannot be seen, usually because they intend to do something bad. ❑ *He thought he saw someone lurking above the chamber during the address.* **2** V-I If something such as a danger, doubt, or fear **lurks** somewhere, it exists but is not obvious or easily recognized. ❑ *Hidden dangers lurk in every family home.*

lus|cious /lʌʃəs/ **1** ADJ If you describe a person or something about them as **luscious**, you mean that you find them or this thing sexually attractive. ❑ *...a luscious young blonde.* **2** ADJ **Luscious** food is juicy and very good to eat. ❑ *...a small apricot tree which bore luscious fruit.*

lush /lʌʃ/ (lushes, lusher, lushest) **1** ADJ **Lush** fields or gardens have a lot of very healthy grass or plants. ❑ *...the lush green meadows bordering the river.* **2** ADJ [v-link ADJ] If you describe a place or thing as **lush**, you mean that it is very luxurious. ❑ *The Carlton-intercontinental hotel is lush, plush, and very non-backpacker.* **3** N-COUNT If you describe someone as a **lush**, you mean that they drink too much alcohol. **4** → See feature box at **ecosystem**

lust /lʌst/ **1** N-UNCOUNT **Lust** is a feeling of strong sexual desire for someone. ❑ *His relationship with Angie was the first which combined lust with friendship.* **2** N-UNCOUNT A **lust** for something is a very strong and eager desire to have it. ❑ *It was Fred's lust for glitz and glamour that was driving them apart.*

lus|ter /lʌstər/
in BRIT, use **lustre**

1 N-UNCOUNT **Luster** is gentle shining light that is reflected from a surface, for example from polished metal. ❑ *These pearls had a fine luster.* **2** N-UNCOUNT **Luster** is the qualities that something has that make it interesting and exciting. ❑ *...a brand that has lost its luster.*

lust|ful /lʌstfʊl/ ADJ [usu ADJ n] **Lustful** means feeling or expressing strong sexual desire. ❑ *...lustful thoughts.*

lus|tre /lʌstər/ [BRIT] → see **luster**

lus|trous /lʌstrəs/ ADJ Something that is **lustrous** shines brightly and gently, because it has a smooth or shiny surface. ❑ *...a head of thick, lustrous, wavy brown hair.*

lusty /lʌsti/ (lustier, lustiest) ADJ [usu ADJ n] If you say that something is **lusty**, you mean that it is healthy and full of strength and energy. ❑ *...plants with large, lusty roots.* ❑ *...remembering his lusty singing in the open park.* • **lusti|ly** ADV ❑ *Bob ate lustily.*

lute /lut/ (lutes) N-VAR [oft the N] A **lute** is a stringed instrument with a rounded body that is similar to a guitar and is played with the fingers.

Lu|ther|an /luθərən/ (Lutherans) **1** ADJ **Lutheran** means belonging or relating to a Protestant church, founded on the teachings of Martin Luther, which emphasizes the importance of faith and of the authority of the Bible. ❑ *...the city's premier Lutheran church.* ❑ *...a Lutheran hymn.* **2** N-COUNT A **Lutheran** is a member of the Lutheran church. ❑ *...a junior high school in Hong Kong run by Lutherans.*

luxu|ri|ant /lʌgʒʊəriənt/ **1** ADJ [usu ADJ n] **Luxuriant** plants, trees, and gardens are large, healthy, and growing well. ❑ *There were two very large oak trees in front of our house with wide spreading branches and luxuriant foliage.* **2** ADJ If you describe someone's hair as **luxuriant**, you mean that it is very thick and healthy. ❑ *Hair that's thick and luxuriant needs regular trimming.*

luxu|ri|ate /lʌgʒʊərieɪt/ (luxuriates, luxuriating, luxuriated) V-I If you **luxuriate in** something, you relax in it and enjoy it very much, especially because you find it comfortable and luxurious. ❑ *Lie back and luxuriate in the scented oil.* ❑ *Ralph was luxuriating in the first real vacation he'd had in years.*

luxu|ri|ous /lʌgʒʊəriəs/ **1** ADJ If you describe something as **luxurious**, you mean that it is very comfortable and expensive. ❑ *Our honeymoon was two days in Las Vegas at a luxurious hotel called Le Mirage.* • **luxu|ri|ous|ly** ADV ❑ *The dining-room is luxuriously furnished and carpeted.* **2** ADJ **Luxurious** means feeling or expressing great pleasure and comfort. ❑ *Amy tilted her wine in her glass with a luxurious sigh.* • **luxu|ri|ous|ly** ADV [ADV after v] ❑ *Liz laughed, stretching luxuriously.*

luxu|ry ♦◇◇ /lʌkʃəri, lʌgʒə-/ (luxuries) **1** N-UNCOUNT **Luxury** is very great comfort, especially among beautiful and expensive surroundings. ❑ *By all accounts he leads a life of considerable luxury.* **2** N-COUNT A **luxury** is something expensive which is not necessary but which gives you pleasure. ❑ *A week by the sea is a luxury they can no longer afford.* **3** ADJ [ADJ n] A **luxury** item is something expensive which is not necessary but which gives you pleasure. ❑ *He could not afford luxury food on his pay.* **4** N-SING A **luxury** is a pleasure which you do not often have the opportunity to enjoy. ❑ *Hot baths are my favorite luxury.*

luxury goods N-PLURAL **Luxury goods** are things which are not necessary, but which give you pleasure or make your life more comfortable. ❑ *...increased taxes on luxury goods, such as boats and expensive cars.*

LW LW is a written abbreviation for **long wave**.

SUFFIX

-ly forms adverbs that indicate how something is done. For example, if someone speaks **cheerfully**, they speak in a cheerful way.

---

ly|chee /liːtsi/ (lychees) N-VAR **Lychees** are Chinese fruit which have white flesh and a large seed inside and a pinkish-brown skin.

Ly|cra /laɪkrə/ N-UNCOUNT **Lycra** is a type of stretchy fabric, similar to elastic, which is used to make tight-fitting garments such as tights and swimsuits. [TRADEMARK]

ly|ing /laɪɪŋ/ **Lying** is the present participle of **lie**.

lymph node /lɪmf noʊd/ (lymph nodes) N-COUNT [usu pl] **Lymph nodes** or **lymph glands** are small masses of tissue in your body where white blood cells are formed.

lynch /lɪntʃ/ (lynches, lynching, lynched) V-T If an angry crowd of people **lynch** someone, they kill that person by hanging them, without letting them have a trial, because they believe that that person has committed a crime. ❑ *They were about to lynch him when reinforcements from the army burst into the room and rescued him.* • **lynch|ing** (lynchings) N-VAR ❑ *Some towns found that lynching was the only way to drive away bands of outlaws.*

lynch mob (lynch mobs) **1** N-COUNT A **lynch mob** is an angry crowd of people who want to kill someone without a trial, because they believe that person has committed a crime. **2** N-COUNT You can refer to a group of people as a **lynch mob** if they are very angry with someone because they believe that person has done something bad or wrong.

lynch|pin /lɪntʃpɪn/ → see linchpin

lynx /lɪŋks/ (lynxes) N-COUNT A **lynx** is a wild animal similar to a large cat.

lyre /laɪər/ (lyres) N-COUNT A **lyre** is a stringed instrument that looks like a small harp.

lyr|ic /lɪrɪk/ (lyrics) **1** ADJ [ADJ n] **Lyric** poetry is written in a simple and direct style, and usually expresses personal emotions such as love. ❑ *...Lawrence's splendid short stories and lyric poetry.* **2** N-COUNT The **lyrics** of a song are its words. ❑ *...Kurt Weill's Broadway opera with lyrics by Langston Hughes.* **3** → See feature box at **music**

lyri|cal /lɪrɪkəl/ ADJ Something that is **lyrical** is poetic and romantic. ❑ *His paintings became more lyrical.* ❑ *...its remarkable free-flowing and often lyrical style.*

lyri|cism /lɪrɪsɪzəm/ N-UNCOUNT **Lyricism** is gentle and romantic emotion, often expressed in writing, poetry, or music. ❑ *...a natural lyricism which can be expressed through dance and music.*

lyri|cist /lɪrɪsɪst/ (lyricists) N-COUNT A **lyricist** is someone who writes the words for modern songs or for musicals.

Visual Dictionary

Sometimes it's much easier to understand the meaning of a word if you are shown a picture of it. This supplement helps you by presenting some vocabulary in a visual format. The first section contains images which show '**types of**' a particular area of vocabulary, for example 'boats' or 'devices.' The images in the second section show '**parts of**' something, for example 'parts of a bicycle' or 'parts of the skeleton.' You may find it helpful to study the colorful images in the supplement – learning vocabulary sets through images can be particularly helpful for memorizing words.

'TYPES OF'

This section shows you groups of related vocabulary items. Studying the images together is helpful in understanding the difference between words which are used for items belonging to a particular set. The groups of related vocabulary items that have been illustrated are:

architecture	cars	footwear	metals
bags	chairs	gardening tools	nuts
bats, sticks, and rackets	clocks	gemstones	rocks
beds	cups and glasses	hats	ships
bikes	devices	homes	woodworking tools
boats	DIY	kitchen utensils	

ARCHITECTURE

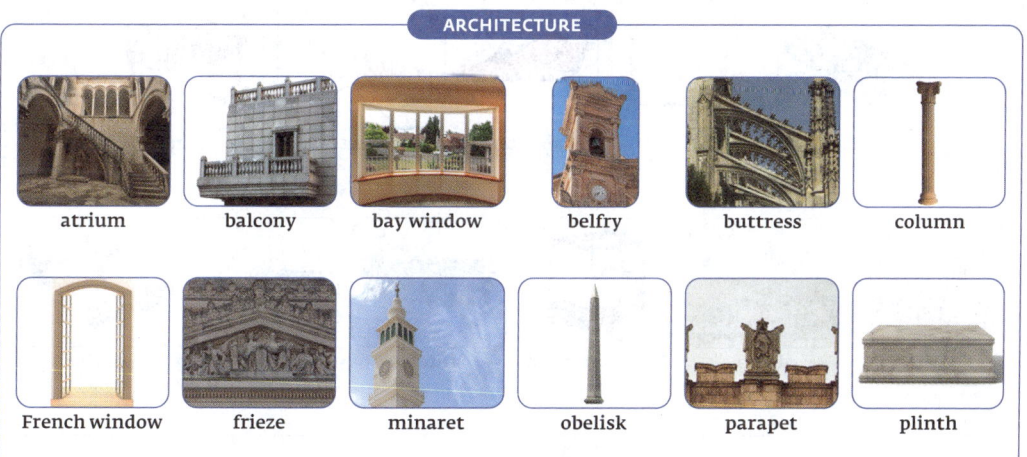

atrium · balcony · bay window · belfry · buttress · column
French window · frieze · minaret · obelisk · parapet · plinth

BAGS

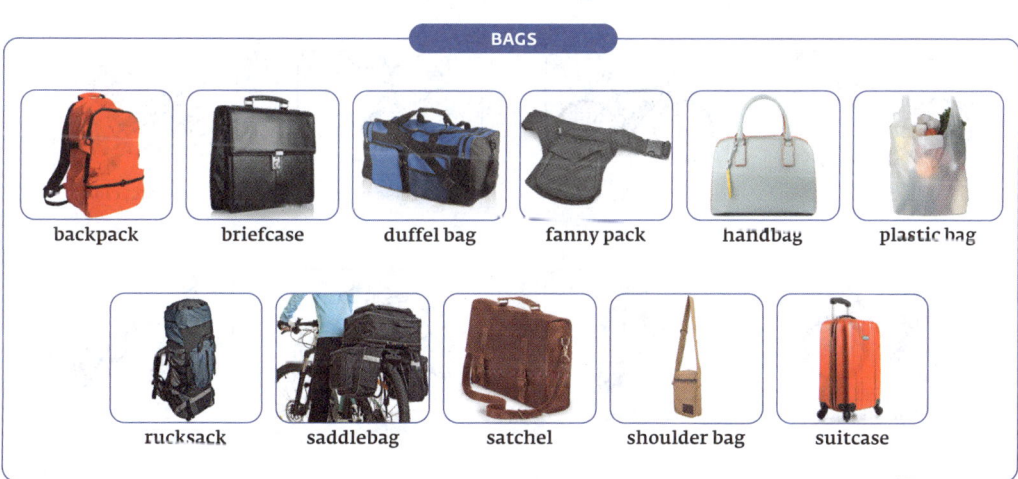

backpack · briefcase · duffel bag · fanny pack · handbag · plastic bag
rucksack · saddlebag · satchel · shoulder bag · suitcase

BATS, STICKS, AND RACKETS

badminton racket

baseball bat

cricket bat

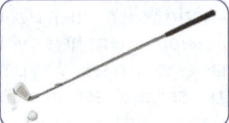
golf club

hockey stick

pool cue

table tennis paddle

tennis racket

BEDS

airbed

bunk bed

chaise longue

cot

cradle

crib

divan

four-poster bed

futon

hammock

sofa bed

BIKES

bicycle

e-bike

exercise bike

motorcycle

mountain bike

scooter

tandem

tricycle

BOATS

 barge
 canoe
 catamaran
 dinghy
 gondola
 houseboat

 kayak
 lifeboat
 motorboat
 raft
 rowboat
 yacht

CARS

 coupe
 hatchback
 limousine
 minivan
 motor home

 roadster
 sport utility vehicle
 sports car
 station wagon
 stock car

CHAIRS

 armchair
 bench
 bucket seat
 deck chair
 easy chair

 high chair
 pew
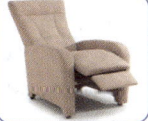 recliner
 rocking chair
 stool
 throne

VISUAL DICTIONARY

CLOCKS

 digital clock

 grandfather clock

 hourglass

 phone

 stopwatch

 sundial

 watch

CUPS AND GLASSES

 chalice

 cup

 goblet

 mug

 tankard

 teacup

 tumbler

 water bottle

 wine glass

DEVICES

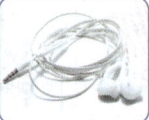 binoculars

 earphones

 headphones

 megaphone

 metronome

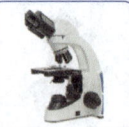 microphone

 microscope

 periscope

 remote control

 stethoscope

 telescope

USB stick

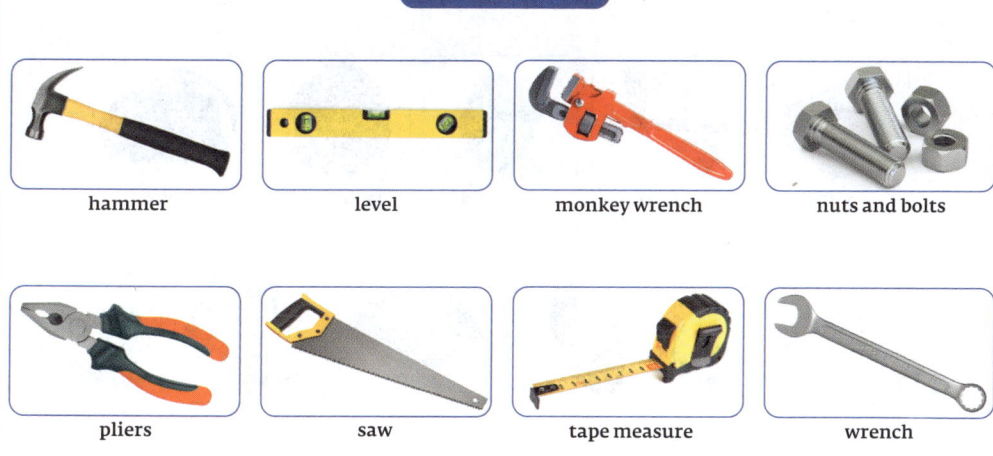

VISUAL DICTIONARY

GEMSTONES

amethyst — diamond — emerald — lapis lazuli — onyx

opal — quartz — ruby — sapphire — topaz — turquoise

HATS

bearskin — beret — bonnet — cloth cap — fez

hard hat — ski mask — sou'wester — top hat — turban

HOMES

apartment — bungalow — cabin — castle — chalet — cottage

farmhouse — mansion — manufactured home — palace — villa

KITCHEN UTENSILS

can opener — garlic crusher — grater — masher — mortar and pestle — nutcracker

  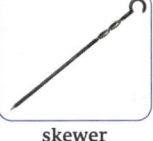  

peeler — scale — skewer — spatula — whisk

METALS

aluminum — copper — gold — iron — lead — mercury

nickel — platinum — silver — tin — titanium — zinc

NUTS

  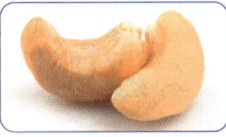

almonds — brazil nuts — cashews

hazelnuts — peanuts — pecans — walnuts

VISUAL DICTIONARY

ROCKS

 basalt
 coal
 flint
 granite
 lava

 limestone
 marble
 pumice
 sandstone
 shale
 slate

SHIPS

 aircraft carrier
 cruise ship
 ferry
 frigate
 galleon
 hydrofoil

 sailing ship
 steamboat
 submarine
 supertanker
 tanker
 trawler

WOODWORKING TOOLS

 chisel
 circular saw
 drill
 hacksaw
 nail
 plane

 sander
 sandpaper
 screw
 screwdriver
 vise

washers

VISUAL DICTIONARY

'PARTS OF'

This section presents one image together with a list of important words associated with that image. Learning the words related to a particular item or topic is a useful way of building up vocabulary. The vocabulary items that have been illustrated here are thematically grouped:

computer	fish	volcano	heart
airplane	flower	water cycle	organs
bike	insect	wind turbine	respiratory system
car	compass points	digestive system	skeleton
ship	continents	ear	teeth
bird	greenhouse effect	eye	

COMPUTER

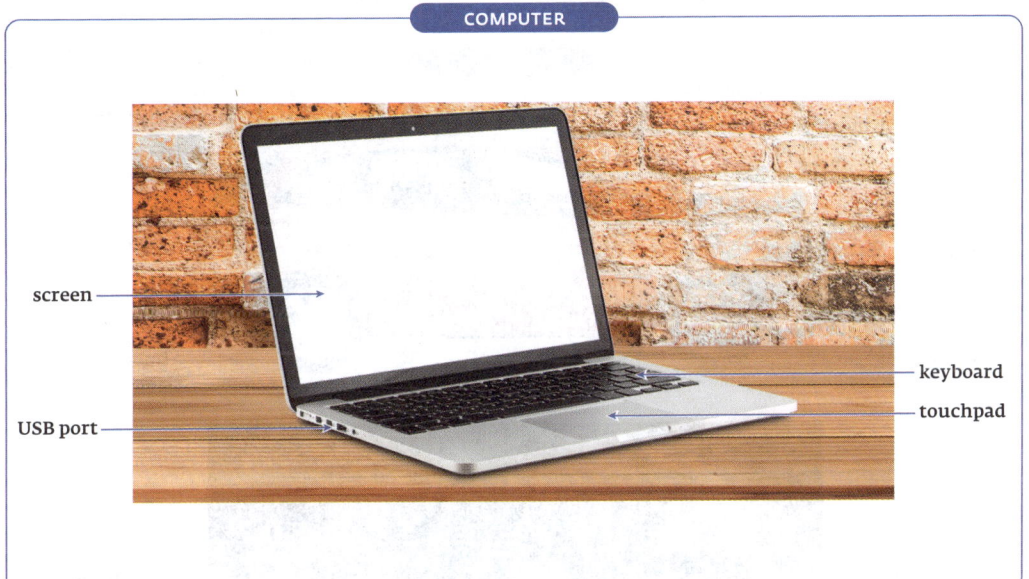

AIRPLANE

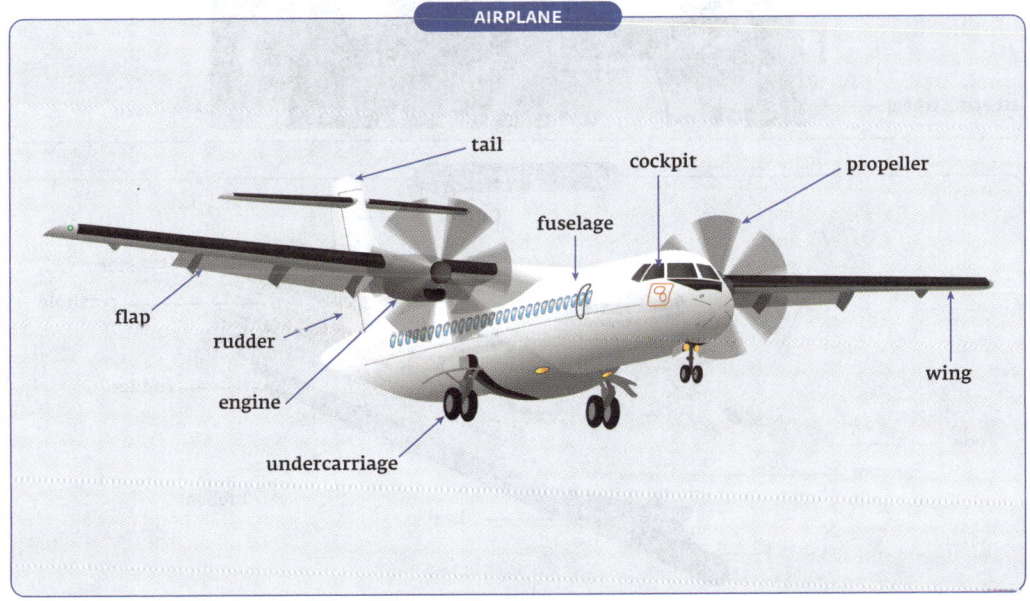

VISUAL DICTIONARY

VISUAL DICTIONARY

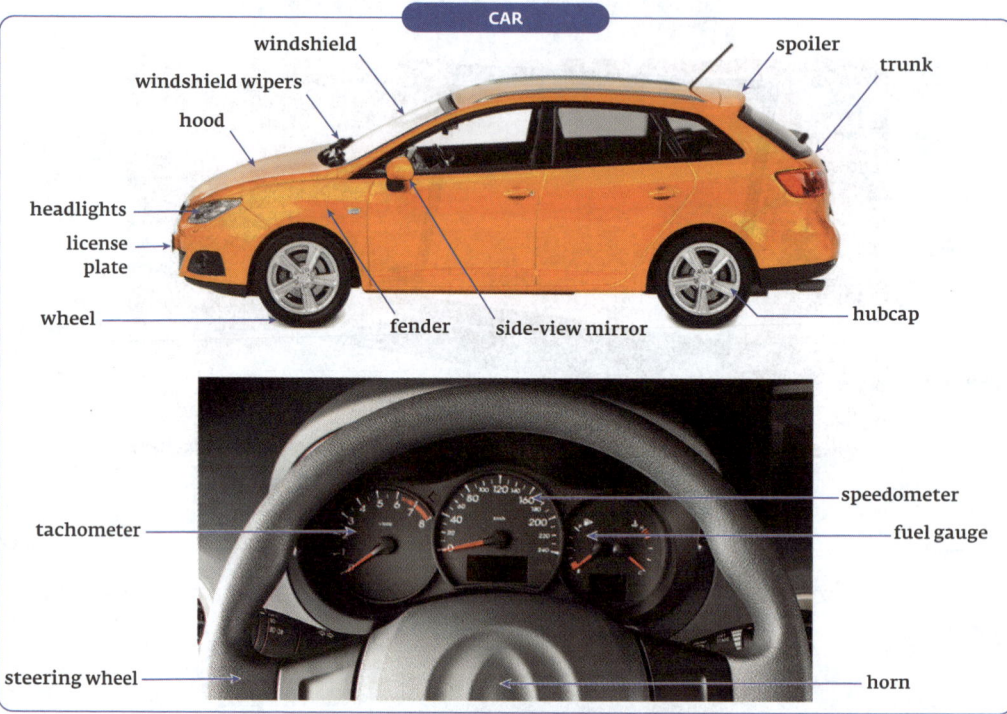

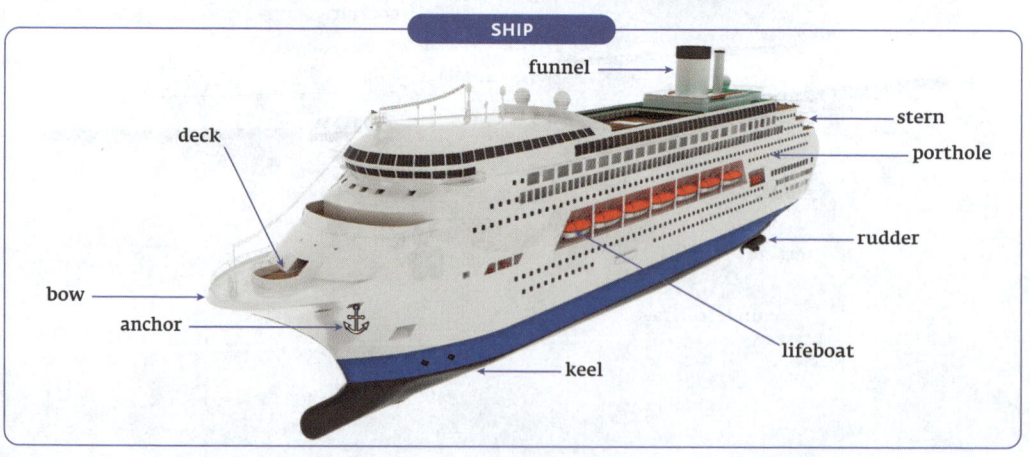

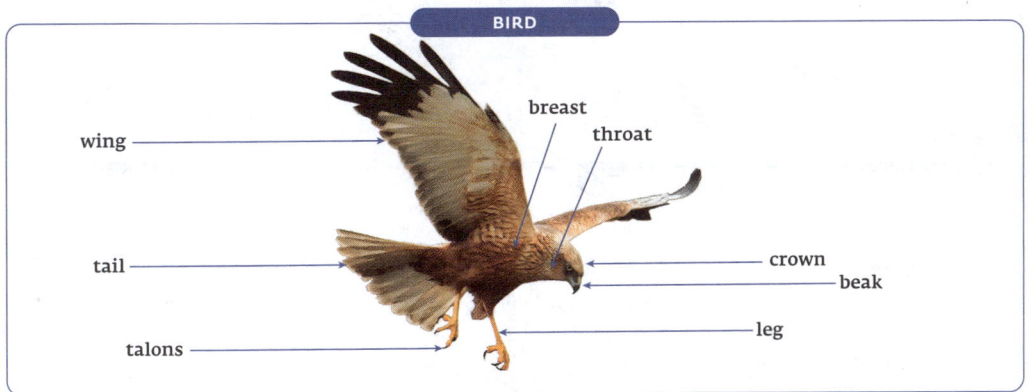

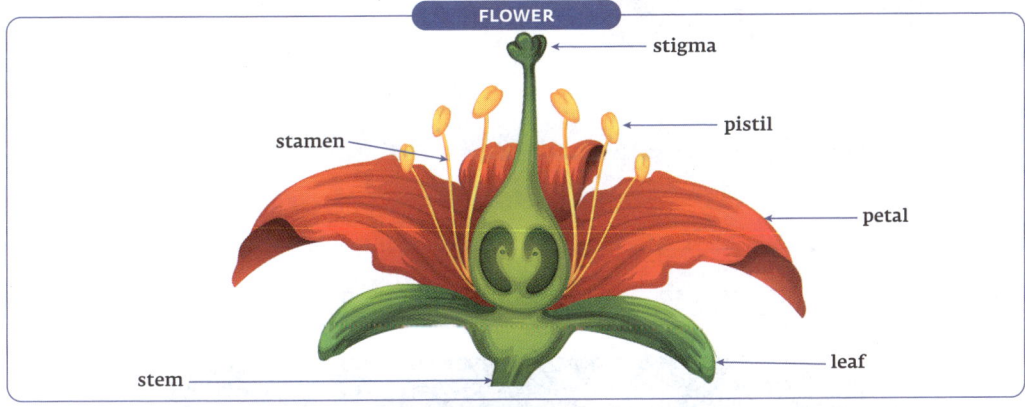
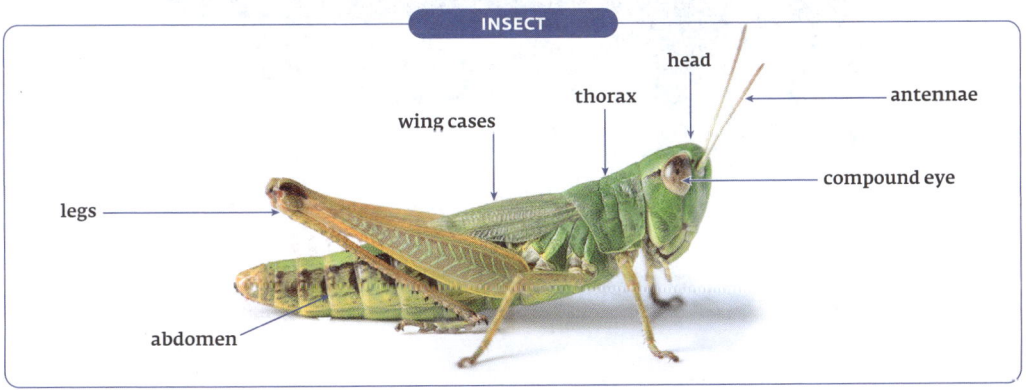

VISUAL DICTIONARY

COMPASS POINTS

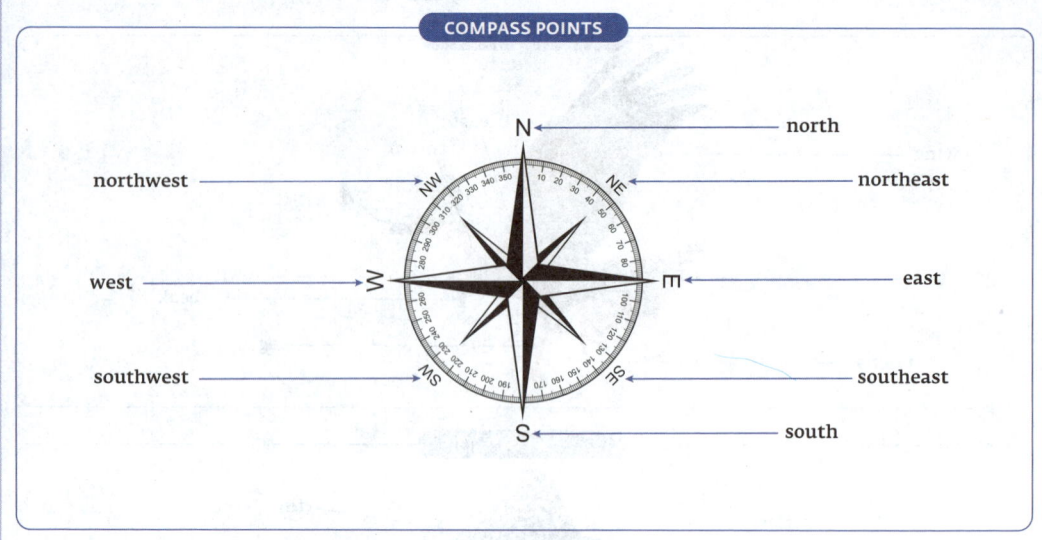

CONTINENTS

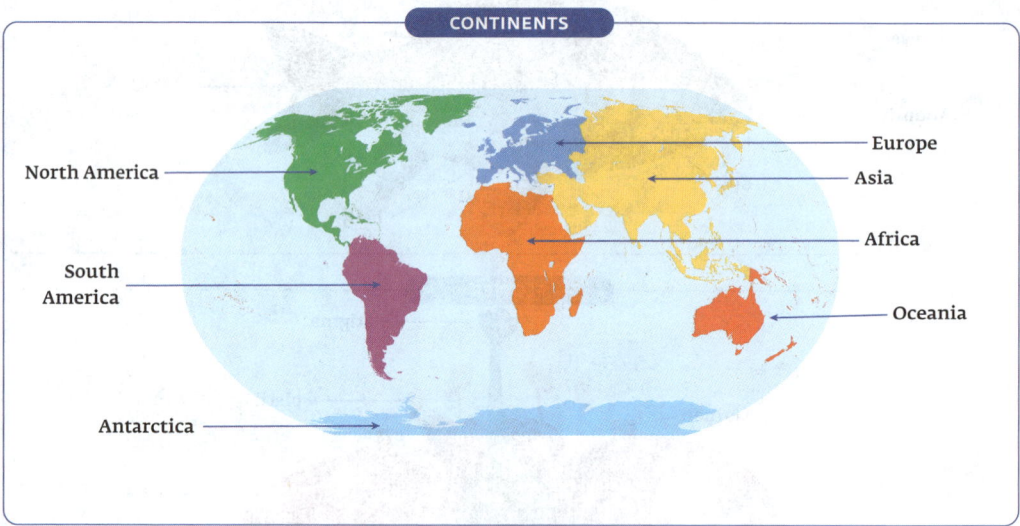

GREENHOUSE EFFECT

VOLCANO

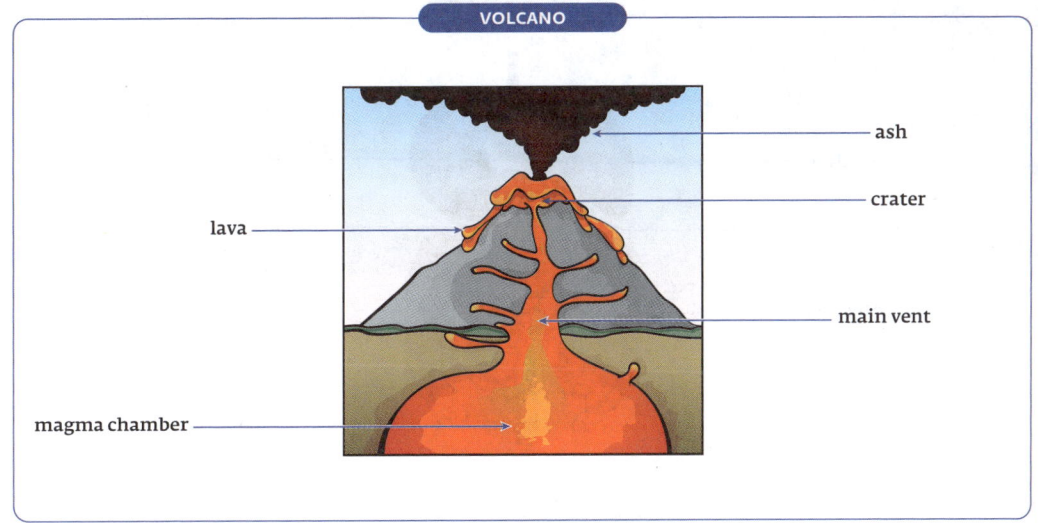

WATER CYCLE

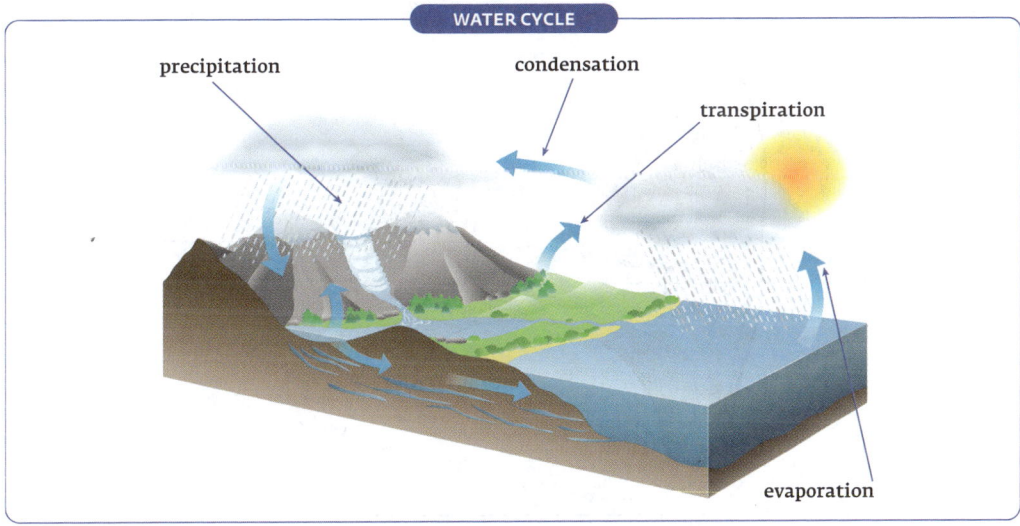

WIND TURBINE

VISUAL DICTIONARY

DIGESTIVE SYSTEM

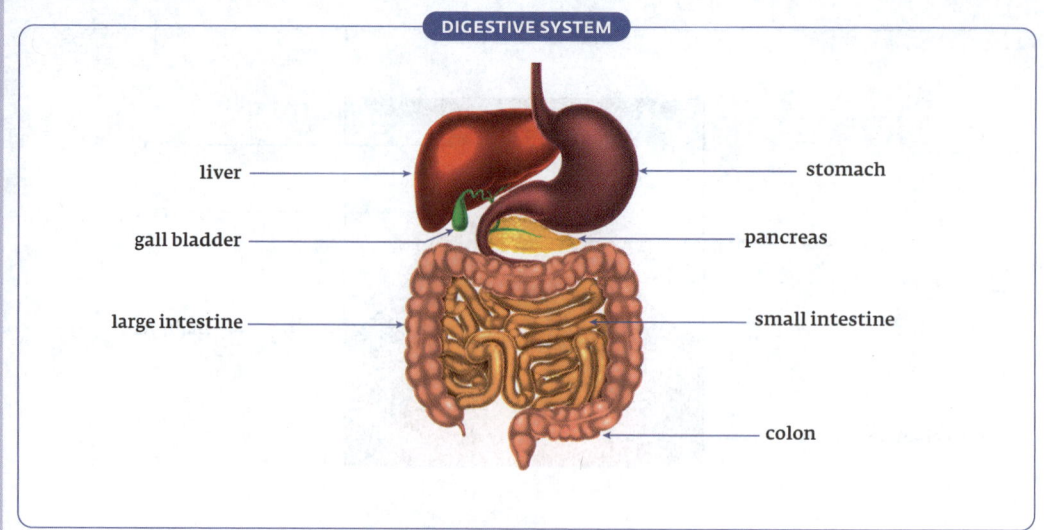

EAR

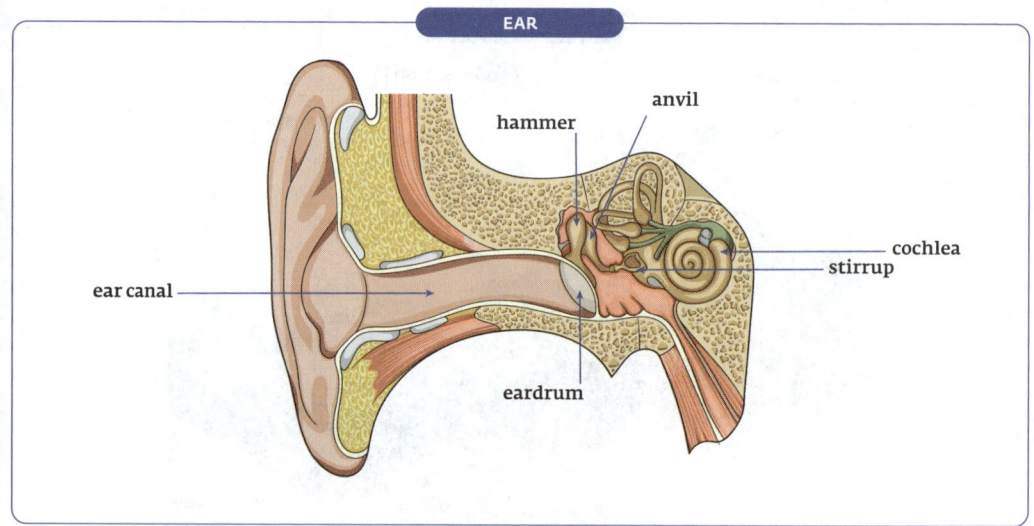

EYE

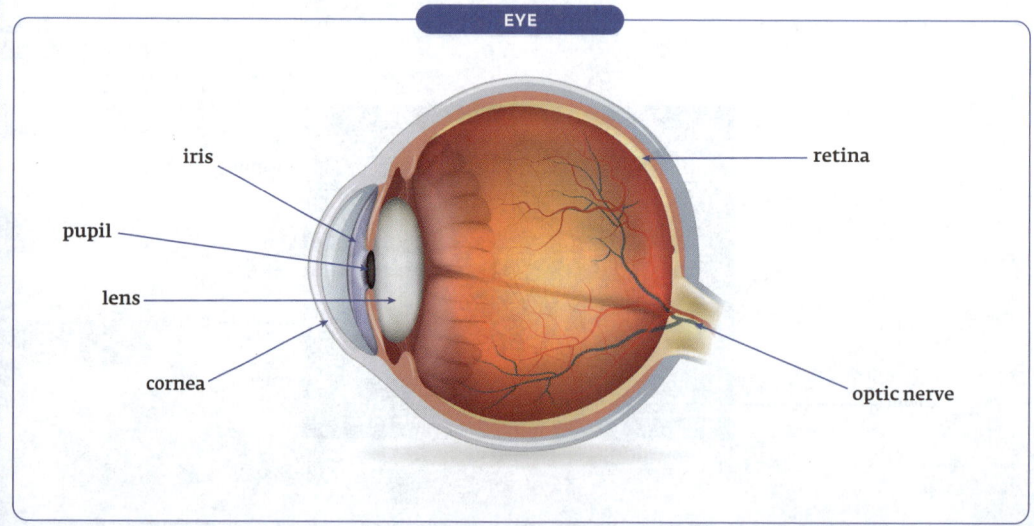

HEART

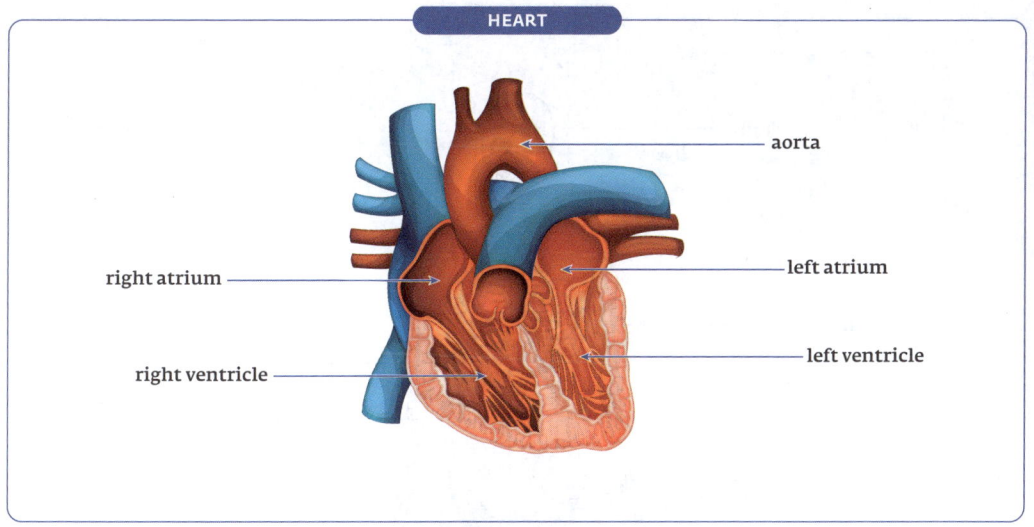

ORGANS

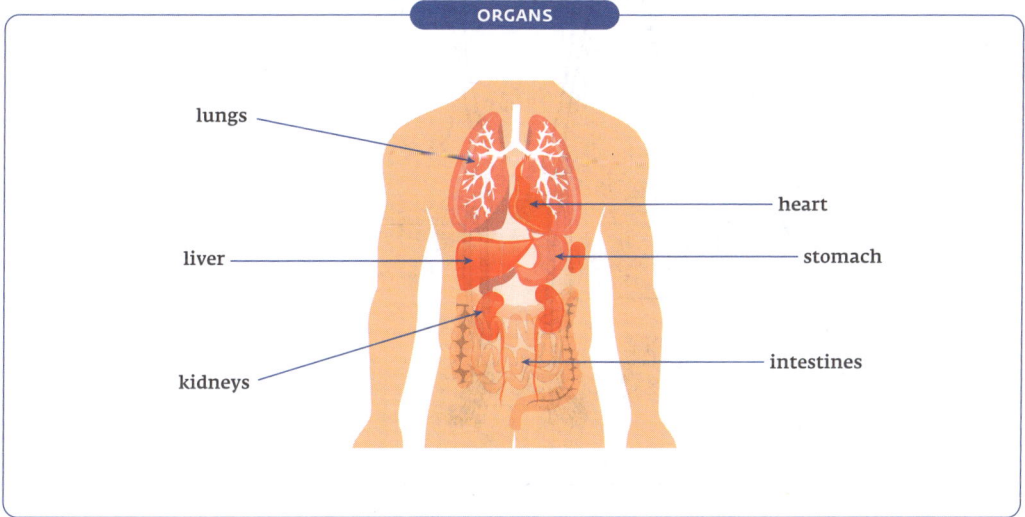

RESPIRATORY SYSTEM

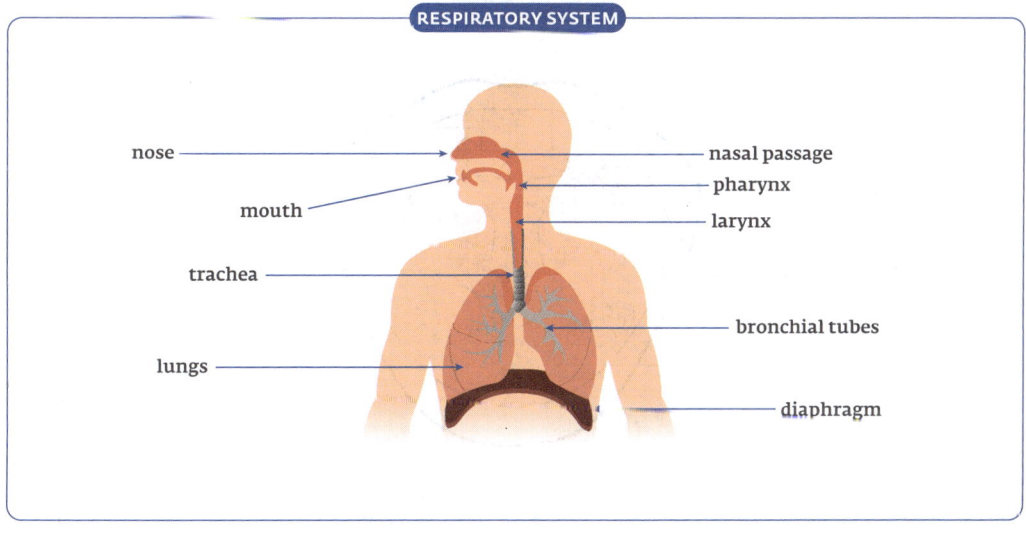

VISUAL DICTIONARY

SKELETON

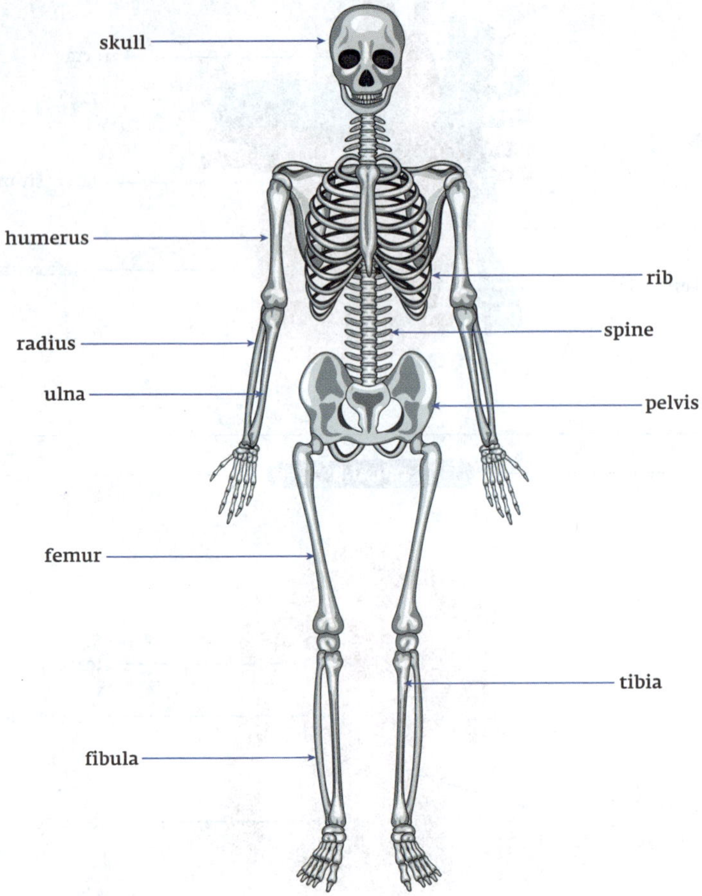

- skull
- humerus
- rib
- radius
- spine
- ulna
- pelvis
- femur
- tibia
- fibula

TEETH

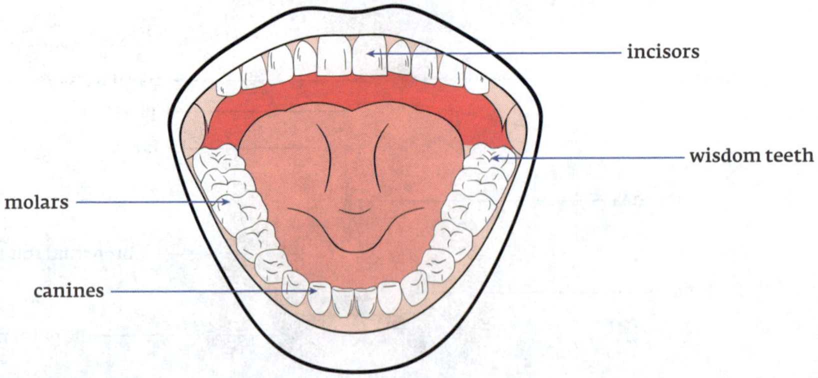

- incisors
- wisdom teeth
- molars
- canines

VISUAL DICTIONARY

Mm

M also **m** /ɛm/ (**M's, m's**) N-VAR **M** is the thirteenth letter of the English alphabet.

-'m /-m/ **'m** is the usual spoken form of 'am,' used after 'I' in 'I'm.'

ma /mɑ/ (**mas**) N-FAMILY Some people refer to or address their mother as **ma**. [INFORMAL] ❑ *Ma was still at work when I got back.*

MA /ɛm eɪ/ (**MAs**) also **M.A.** N-COUNT An **MA** is a master's degree in an arts or social science subject. **MA** is an abbreviation for **Master of Arts**. ❑ *He has an MA in English Literature from Louisiana State University.*

ma'am /mæm/ N-VOC People sometimes say **ma'am** as a polite way of addressing a woman whose name they do not know, especially in the American South. [mainly AM, POLITENESS] ❑ *Would you repeat that please, ma'am?*

ma|ca|bre /məkɑbrə/ ADJ You describe something such as an event or story as **macabre** when it is strange and horrible or upsetting, usually because it involves death or injury. ❑ *Police have made a macabre discovery.*

maca|ro|ni /mækəroʊni/ N-UNCOUNT **Macaroni** is a kind of pasta made in the shape of short, hollow tubes.

maca|ro|ni and cheese

in BRIT, use **macaroni cheese**

N-UNCOUNT **Macaroni and cheese** is a dish made from macaroni and cheese sauce.

maca|roon /mækərun/ (**macaroons**) N-COUNT **Macaroons** are cookies that are made with egg whites and flavored with coconut or almond.

mace /meɪs/ (**maces**) **1** N-COUNT A **mace** is an ornamental stick carried by an official or placed somewhere as a symbol of authority. **2** N-UNCOUNT **Mace** is a substance that causes tears and sickness, and that is used in sprays as a defense against rioters or attackers. [TRADEMARK]

mac|er|ate /mæsəreɪt/ (**macerates, macerating, macerated**) V-T/V-I If you **macerate** food, or if it **macerates**, you soak it in a liquid for a period of time so that it absorbs the liquid. ❑ *I like to macerate the food in liqueur for a few minutes before serving.* ❑ *Cognac is also used to macerate and flavor ingredients and casseroles.* ❑ *Seal tightly then leave for four to five days to macerate.*

Mach /mɑk/ N-UNCOUNT [N n/num] **Mach** is used as a unit of measurement in stating the speed of a moving object in relation to the speed of sound. For example, if an aircraft is traveling at Mach 1, it is traveling at exactly the speed of sound. [TECHNICAL]

ma|chete /məʃɛti/ (**machetes**) N-COUNT A **machete** is a large knife with a broad blade.

Machia|vel|lian /mækiəvɛliən/ ADJ [usu ADJ n] If you describe someone as **Machiavellian**, you are critical of them because they often make clever and secret plans to achieve their aims and are not honest with people. [DISAPPROVAL] ❑ *...Machiavellian republicans plotting to destabilize the throne.* ❑ *A Machiavellian plot was suspected.*

machi|na|tions /mækɪneɪʃənz, mæʃ-/ N-PLURAL [usu with supp] You use **machinations** to describe secret and complicated plans, especially to gain power. [DISAPPROVAL] ❑ *...the political machinations that brought him to power.*

ma|chine ♦♢♢ /məʃin/ (**machines, machining, machined**) **1** N-COUNT [also by n] A **machine** is a piece of equipment that uses electricity or an engine in order to do a particular kind of work. ❑ *I put the coin in the machine and pulled the lever.* **2** N-COUNT You can use **machine** to refer to a large and well-controlled system or organization. ❑ *...Nazi Germany's military machine.* **3** → see also **vending machine** **4** V-T [usu passive] If you **machine** something, you make it or work on it using a machine. ❑ *The material is machined in a factory.* ❑ *...machined brass zinc alloy gears.*

> **SYNONYMS**
>
> **machine**
> NOUN **1**
> **appliance:** *He could also learn to use other household appliances.*
> **device:** *It is an electronic device that protects your vehicle 24 hours a day.*
> **apparatus:** *One of the boys had to be rescued by firefighters wearing breathing apparatus.*

ma|chine code N-UNCOUNT **Machine code** is a way of expressing instructions and information in the form of numbers which can be understood by a computer or microchip. [COMPUTING]

ma|chine gun (**machine guns**) N-COUNT A **machine gun** is a gun which fires a lot of bullets one after the other very quickly. ❑ *Attackers fired machine guns at the convoy.*

ma|chin|ery /məʃinəri/ **1** N-UNCOUNT You can use **machinery** to refer to machines in general, or machines that are used in a factory or on a farm. ❑ *...quality tools and machinery.* **2** N-SING The **machinery** of a government or organization is the system and all the procedures that it uses to deal with things. ❑ *The machinery of democracy could be created quickly.*

ma|chine tool (**machine tools**) N-COUNT A **machine tool** is a machine driven by power that cuts, shapes, or finishes metal or other materials.

ma|chin|ist /məʃinɪst/ (**machinists**) N-COUNT A **machinist** is a person whose job is to operate a machine, especially in a factory. ❑ *His father is a machinist in an aerospace plant.*

ma|chis|mo /mɑtʃizmoʊ, mə-/ N-UNCOUNT You use **machismo** to refer to men's behavior or attitudes when they are very conscious and proud of their masculinity. ❑ *Charlie, naturally, has to prove his machismo by going on the scariest rides twice.*

macho /mɑtʃoʊ/ ADJ You use **macho** to describe men who are very conscious and proud of their masculinity. [INFORMAL] ❑ *...displays of macho bravado.*

mac|in|tosh /mækɪntɒʃ/ → see **mackintosh**

macke|rel /mækərəl, mækrəl/ (**mackerel**)

Mackerel is both the singular and the plural form.

N-VAR A **mackerel** is a sea fish with a dark, patterned back. ❑ *Almiro's boat had sailed out to the middle of the bay to fish for mackerel.* ● N-UNCOUNT **Mackerel** is this fish eaten as food. ❑ *...piles of smoked mackerel.*

mack|in|tosh /mækɪntɒʃ/ (**mackintoshes**) N-COUNT A **mackintosh** is a raincoat, especially one made from a particular kind of waterproof cloth. [mainly BRIT]

macro /mækroʊ/ (**macros**) **1** ADJ [usu ADJ n] You use **macro** to indicate that something relates to a general area, rather than being detailed or specific. [TECHNICAL] ❑ *...coordinated programs of regulation of the economy both at the macro level and at the micro level.* **2** N-COUNT A **macro** is a shortened version of a computer command which makes the computer carry out a set of actions. [COMPUTING]

macrobiotic | magic

PREFIX

macro- is added to words in order to form new words that are technical and that refer to things which are large or involve the whole of something. *For example,* **macroeconomic** *policies relate to the economic system of a whole country.*

macro|bi|ot|ic /mækroʊbaɪɒtɪk/ ADJ [usu ADJ n] **Macrobiotic** food consists of whole grains and vegetables that are grown without chemicals. [TECHNICAL] ❑ *...a strict macrobiotic diet.*

macro|bi|ot|ics /mækroʊbaɪɒtɪks/ N-UNCOUNT **Macrobiotics** is the practice of eating macrobiotic food. [TECHNICAL]

macro|cosm /mækrəkɒzəm/ N-SING [usu the N] A **macrocosm** is a complex organized system such as the universe or a society, considered as a single unit. [FORMAL] ❑ *The macrocosm of the universe is mirrored in the microcosm of the mind.*

macro|eco|nom|ics /mækroʊekənɒmɪks, -ikə-/ also **macro-economics** N-UNCOUNT **Macroeconomics** is the branch of economics that is concerned with the major, general features of a country's economy, such as the level of inflation, unemployment, or interest rates. [BUSINESS] ❑ *Too many politicians forget the importance of macroeconomics.* ● **macro|eco|nom|ic** /mækroʊekənɒmɪk, -ikə-/ ADJ [usu ADJ n] ❑ *...the attempt to substitute low inflation for full employment as a goal of macroeconomic policy.*

mad ♦◇◇ /mæd/ (**madder, maddest**) **1** ADJ If you say that someone is **mad**, you mean that they are very angry. [INFORMAL] ❑ *You're just mad at me because I don't want to go.* **2** ADJ You use **mad** to describe people or things that you think are very foolish. [DISAPPROVAL] ❑ *You'd be mad to work with him again.* ● **mad|ness** N-UNCOUNT ❑ *It is political madness.* **3** ADJ Someone who is **mad** has a mind that does not work in a normal way, with the result that their behavior is very strange. ❑ *She was afraid of going mad.* ● **mad|ness** N-UNCOUNT ❑ *He was driven to the brink of madness.* **4** ADJ [v-link ADJ about/on n] If you are **mad about** something or someone, you like them very much. [INFORMAL] ❑ *She's not as mad about sports as I am.* ❑ *He's mad about you.* ● COMB IN ADJ **Mad** is also a combining form. [mainly BRIT] ❑ *...his football-mad son.* **5** ADJ **Mad** behavior is wild and uncontrolled. ❑ *You only have an hour to complete the game so it's a mad dash against the clock.* ● **mad|ly** ADV [ADV with v] ❑ *Down in the streets people were waving madly.* **6** PHRASE If you say that someone or something **drives** you **mad**, you mean that you find them extremely annoying. [INFORMAL] ❑ *There are certain things he does that drive me mad.* **7** PHRASE If you do something **like mad**, you do it very energetically or enthusiastically. [INFORMAL] ❑ *He was weight training like mad.* **8** → see also **madly**

mad|am /mædəm/ also **Madam** N-VOC People sometimes say **Madam** as a very formal and polite way of addressing a woman whose name they do not know. For example, a store clerk might address a woman customer as **Madam**. [POLITENESS] ❑ *Try them on, madam.*

mad|cap /mædkæp/ ADJ [usu ADJ n] A **madcap** plan or scheme is very foolish and not likely to succeed. [INFORMAL] ❑ *The politicians simply flitted from one madcap scheme to another.*

mad cow dis|ease N-UNCOUNT **Mad cow disease** is a disease which affects the nervous system of cattle and causes death.

mad|den /mædᵊn/ (**maddens, maddening, maddened**) V-T To **madden** a person or animal means to make them very angry. ❑ *The deer were maddening farmers by eating their crops.*

mad|den|ing /mædnɪŋ/ ADJ If you describe something as **maddening**, you mean that it makes you feel angry, irritated, or frustrated. ❑ *Shopping during sales can be maddening.* ● **mad|den|ing|ly** ADV ❑ *The service is maddeningly slow.*

made /meɪd/ **1 Made** is the past tense and past participle of **make**. **2** ADJ [v-link ADJ of/out of n] If something is **made of** or **made out of** a particular substance, that substance was used to build it. ❑ *The top of the table is made of glass.* **3** PHRASE If you say that someone **has it made** or **has got it made**, you mean that they are certain to be rich or successful. [INFORMAL] ❑ *When I was at school, I thought I had it made.*

-made /-meɪd/ COMB IN ADJ [usu ADJ n] **-made** combines with words such as 'factory' to make adjectives that indicate that something has been made or produced in a particular place or in a particular way. ❑ *...an American-made car.* ❑ *...factory-made goods.*

made-to-meas|ure ADJ [usu ADJ n] A **made-to-measure** suit, shirt, or other item of clothing is one that is made by a tailor to fit you exactly, rather than one that you buy already made in a store.

made to or|der also **made-to-order** ADJ If something is **made to order**, it is made according to someone's special requirements. ❑ *The curving glass wall was made to order by Jeff Bell.* ❑ *...a maker of made-to-order jewelry.*

made-up ♦◇◇ also **made up 1** ADJ [v-link ADJ] If you are **made-up**, you are wearing makeup such as powder or eye shadow. ❑ *She was beautifully made up, beautifully groomed.* **2** ADJ A **made-up** word, name, or story is invented, rather than really existing or being true. ❑ *It looks like a made-up word.*

mad|house /mædhaʊs/ (**madhouses**) N-COUNT [usu sing] If you describe a place or situation as a **madhouse**, you mean that it is full of confusion and noise. ❑ *That place is a madhouse.*

mad|ly /mædli/ ADV You can use **madly** to indicate that one person loves another a great deal. ❑ *She has fallen madly in love with him.*

mad|man /mædmæn, -mən/ (**madmen**) N-COUNT A **madman** is a man who is insane. ❑ *He wanted to jump up and run outside, screaming like a madman.*

Ma|don|na /mədɒnə/ N-PROPER [the N] Catholics and other Christians sometimes call Mary, the mother of Jesus Christ, the Madonna.

mad|ri|gal /mædrɪgᵊl/ (**madrigals**) N-COUNT A **madrigal** is a song sung by several singers without any musical instruments. Madrigals were popular in England in the sixteenth century.

mad|woman /mædwʊmən/ (**madwomen**) N-COUNT A **madwoman** is a woman who is insane. [INFORMAL]

mael|strom /meɪlstrəm/ (**maelstroms**) N-COUNT [usu sing, usu with supp, oft N of n] If you describe a situation as a **maelstrom**, you mean that it is very confused or violent. [LITERARY] ❑ *...the maelstrom of ethnic hatreds and vendetta politics.* ❑ *Inside, she was a maelstrom of churning emotions.*

maes|tro /maɪstroʊ/ (**maestros**) N-COUNT; N-VOC A **maestro** is a skilled and well-known musician or conductor. ❑ *...the urbane maestro's delightful first show.*

Ma|fia /mɑfiə/ (**Mafias**) also **mafia 1** N-COUNT-COLL [the N] The **Mafia** is a criminal organization that makes money illegally, especially by threatening people and dealing in drugs. ❑ *The Mafia is by no means ignored by Italian television.* **2** N-COUNT [usu with supp] You can use **mafia** to refer to an organized group of people who you disapprove of because they use unfair or illegal means in order to get what they want. [DISAPPROVAL] ❑ *They are well-connected with the education-reform mafia.*

mag /mæg/ (**mags**) N-COUNT A **mag** is the same as a magazine. [INFORMAL] ❑ *...a well-known glossy mag.*

maga|zine ♦◇◇ /mægəzin, -zɪn/ (**magazines**) **1** N-COUNT A **magazine** is a publication with a paper cover which is issued regularly, usually every week or every month, and which contains articles, stories, photographs, and advertisements. ❑ *Her face is on the cover of a dozen or more magazines.* **2** N-COUNT In an automatic gun, the **magazine** is the part that contains the bullets. ❑ *The corporal ignored him, sliding the empty magazine from his weapon and replacing it with a fresh one.*

ma|gen|ta /mədʒentə/ (**magentas**) COLOR **Magenta** is used to describe things that are dark reddish purple in color.

mag|got /mægət/ (**maggots**) N-COUNT **Maggots** are creatures that look like very small worms and turn into flies.

mag|ic ♦◇◇ /mædʒɪk/ **1** N-UNCOUNT **Magic** is the power to use supernatural forces to make impossible things happen, such as making people disappear or controlling events in nature. ❑ *They believe in magic.* ❑ *...the use of magic to combat any adverse powers or influences.* **2** N-UNCOUNT You can use **magic** when you are referring to an event that is so wonderful, strange, or unexpected that it seems as if supernatural powers have caused it. You can also say that something happens **as if by**

magical — **magnificent**

magic or like magic. ▫ *All this was supposed to work like magic.* **3** ADJ [ADJ n] You use **magic** to describe something that does things, or appears to do things, by magic. ▫ *So it's a magic potion?* **4** N-UNCOUNT **Magic** is the art and skill of performing mysterious tricks to entertain people, for example by making things appear and disappear. ▫ *His secret hobby: performing magic tricks.* **5** N-UNCOUNT If you refer to the **magic** of something, you mean that it has a special mysterious quality which makes it seem wonderful and exciting to you and which makes you feel happy. ▫ *It infected them with some of the magic of a lost age.* • ADJ **Magic** is also an adjective. ▫ *Then came those magic moments in the rose garden.* **6** N-UNCOUNT If you refer to a person's **magic**, you mean a special talent or ability that they have, which you admire or consider very impressive. ▫ *The 32-year-old Jamaican-born fighter believes he can still regain some of his old magic.* **7** ADJ [ADJ n] You can use expressions such as **the magic number** and **the magic word** to indicate that a number or word is the one which is significant or desirable in a particular situation. ▫ *...their quest to gain the magic number of 270 electoral votes on Election Day.* **8** ADJ [ADJ n, with neg] **Magic** is used in expressions such as **there is no magic formula** and **there is no magic solution** to say that someone will have to make an effort to solve a problem, because it will not solve itself. ▫ *There is no magic formula for producing winning products.*

magi|cal /mǽdʒɪkəl/ **1** ADJ Something that is **magical** seems to use magic or to be able to produce magic. ▫ *...the story of Sin-Sin, a little boy who has magical powers.* • **magi|cal|ly** /mǽdʒɪkli/ ADV [ADV with v] ▫ *During the holiday season the town is magically transformed into a Christmas wonderland.* **2** ADJ You can say that a place or object is **magical** when it has a special mysterious quality that makes it seem wonderful and exciting. ▫ *The beautiful island of Bermuda is a magical place to get married.*

mag|ic bul|let (magic bullets) **1** N-COUNT In medicine, a **magic bullet** is a drug or treatment that can cure a disease quickly and completely. **2** N-COUNT A **magic bullet** is an easy solution to a difficult problem. [INFORMAL] ▫ *A lot of people are looking for some sort of magic bullet that will solve this problem.*

mag|ic car|pet (magic carpets) N-COUNT In stories, a **magic carpet** is a special carpet that can carry people through the air.

ma|gi|cian /mədʒɪʃən/ (magicians) N-COUNT A **magician** is a person who entertains people by doing magic tricks.

Mag|ic Mark|er (Magic Markers) N-VAR A **Magic Marker** is a pen with a thick piece of fiber at the end that the ink comes through. Magic markers are often used for writing on flip charts and whiteboards. [TRADEMARK] ▫ *Using a Magic Marker, he wrote seven digits on the poster-size banner.* ▫ *...huge drawings in green Magic Marker.*

mag|ic mush|room (magic mushrooms) N-COUNT [usu pl] **Magic mushrooms** are a type of mushroom which contain a drug and may make the person who eats them believe they are seeing things which are not real.

mag|ic re|al|ism also **magical realism** N-UNCOUNT **Magic realism** is a style of writing or painting which sometimes describes dreams as though they were real, and real events as though they were dreams.

mag|ic wand (magic wands) **1** N-COUNT A **magic wand** or a **wand** is a long, thin rod that magicians and fairies wave when they are performing tricks and magic. **2** N-COUNT [usu with brd-neg] You use **magic wand**, especially in the expression **there is no magic wand**, to indicate that someone is dealing with a difficult problem which cannot be solved quickly and easily. ▫ *There is no magic wand to secure a just peace.*

mag|is|te|rial /mædʒɪstɪəriəl/ ADJ [usu ADJ n] If you describe someone's behavior or work as **magisterial**, you mean that they show great authority or ability. [FORMAL] ▫ *...his magisterial voice and bearing.* ▫ *The World History of Human Disease is a magisterial work.*

mag|is|trate /mǽdʒɪstreɪt/ (magistrates) **1** N-COUNT A **magistrate** is an official who acts as a judge in law courts which deal with minor crimes or disputes. ▫ *She will face a local magistrate on Tuesday.* **2** → See feature box at **legal**

mag|ma /mǽgmə/ **1** N-UNCOUNT **Magma** is molten rock that is formed in very hot conditions inside the earth. [TECHNICAL] ▫ *The volcano threw new showers of magma and ash into the air.* **2** → See also color supplement

mag|na|nim|ity /mægnənɪmɪti/ N-UNCOUNT **Magnanimity** is kindness and generosity toward someone, especially after defeating them or being treated badly by them. [FORMAL] ▫ *The father of one victim spoke with remarkable magnanimity.*

mag|nani|mous /mægnǽnɪməs/ ADJ If you are **magnanimous**, you behave kindly and generously toward someone, especially after defeating them or being treated badly by them. ▫ *I was prepared to be magnanimous, prepared to feel compassion for him.* • **mag|nani|mous|ly** ADV [usu ADV with v] ▫ *"You were right, and we were wrong," he said magnanimously.*

mag|nate /mǽgneɪt, -nɪt/ (magnates) N-COUNT A **magnate** is someone who has earned a lot of money from a particular business or industry. ▫ *...a multimillionaire shipping magnate.*

mag|ne|sium /mægniːziəm/ N-UNCOUNT **Magnesium** is a light, silvery white metal which burns with a bright white flame.

mag|net /mǽgnɪt/ (magnets) **1** N-COUNT If you say that something is a **magnet** or is like a **magnet**, you mean that people are very attracted by it and want to go to it or look at it. ▫ *Prospect Park, with its vast lake, is a magnet for all health freaks.* **2** N-COUNT A **magnet** is a piece of iron or other material which attracts iron toward it. ▫ *It's possible to hang a nail from a magnet and then use that nail to pick up another nail.*

mag|net|ic /mægnétɪk/ **1** ADJ If something metal is **magnetic**, it acts like a magnet. ▫ *...magnetic particles.* **2** ADJ You use **magnetic** to describe something that is caused by or relates to the force of magnetism. ▫ *The electrically charged gas particles are affected by magnetic forces.* **3** ADJ You use **magnetic** to describe tapes and other objects which have a coating of a magnetic substance and contain coded information that can be read by computers or other machines. ▫ *...her magnetic-strip ID card.* **4** ADJ If you describe something as **magnetic**, you mean that it is very attractive to people because it has unusual, powerful, and exciting qualities. ▫ *...the magnetic effect of the prosperous American economy on would-be immigrants.*

mag|net|ic field (magnetic fields) N-COUNT A **magnetic field** is an area around a magnet, or something functioning as a magnet, in which the magnet's power to attract things is felt.

mag|net|ic tape (magnetic tapes) N-VAR **Magnetic tape** is plastic tape covered with iron oxide or a similar magnetic substance. It is used for recording sounds, film, or computer information.

mag|net|ism /mǽgnɪtɪzəm/ **1** N-UNCOUNT Someone or something that has **magnetism** has unusual, powerful, and exciting qualities which attract people to them. ▫ *There was no doubting the animal magnetism of the man.* **2** N-UNCOUNT **Magnetism** is the natural power of some objects and substances, especially iron, to attract other objects toward them. ▫ *...his research in electricity and magnetism.*

mag|net|ize /mǽgnɪtaɪz/ (magnetizes, magnetizing, magnetized)

in BRIT, also use **magnetise**

V-T If you **magnetize** something, you make it magnetic. ▫ *Make a Mobius strip out of a ribbon of mild steel and magnetize it.* ▫ *...a small metal chessboard with magnetized playing pieces.*

mag|net school (magnet schools) N-COUNT A **magnet school** is a school attended by students outside the local area who want to study special subjects.

mag|ni|fi|ca|tion /mægnɪfɪkeɪʃən/ (magnifications) **1** N-UNCOUNT **Magnification** is the act or process of magnifying something. ▫ *The man was tall, his figure shortened by the magnification of Lenny's binoculars.* **2** N-VAR **Magnification** is the degree to which a lens, mirror, or other device can magnify an object, or the degree to which the object is magnified. ▫ *The electron microscope uses a beam of electrons to produce images at high magnifications.*

mag|nifi|cent /mægnɪfɪsənt/ ADJ If you say that something or someone is **magnificent**, you mean that you think they are extremely good, beautiful, or impressive. ▫ *...a magnificent country house in wooded grounds.* • **mag|nifi|cence** N-UNCOUNT ▫ *I shall never forget the magnificence of the Swiss mountains and the* beauty of the lakes. • **mag|nifi|cent|ly** ADV ❑ *The team played magnificently throughout the competition.*

mag|ni|fy /mǽgnɪfaɪ/ (magnifies, magnifying, magnified) **1** V-T To **magnify** an object means to make it appear larger than it really is, by means of a special lens or mirror. ❑ *This version of the Digges telescope magnifies images 11 times.* ❑ *A lens would magnify the picture so it would be like looking at a large TV screen.* **2** V-T To **magnify** something means to increase its effect, size, loudness, or intensity. ❑ *Poverty and human folly magnify natural disasters.* **3** V-T If you **magnify** something, you make it seem more important or serious than it really is. ❑ *They do not grasp the broad situation and spend their time magnifying ridiculous details.*

mag|ni|fy|ing glass (magnifying glasses) N-COUNT A **magnifying glass** is a piece of glass which makes objects appear bigger than they actually are.

mag|ni|tude /mǽgnɪtud/ **1** N-UNCOUNT If you talk about the **magnitude** of something, you are talking about its great size, scale, or importance. ❑ *An operation of this magnitude is going to be difficult.* **2** PHRASE You can use **order of magnitude** when you are giving an approximate idea of the amount or importance of something. ❑ *America and Russia do not face a problem of the same order of magnitude as Japan.*

mag|no|lia /mægnóʊlyə/ (magnolias) N-COUNT A **magnolia** is a kind of tree with white, pink, yellow, or purple flowers.

mag|num /mǽgnəm/ (magnums) N-COUNT [oft N of n] A **magnum** is a wine bottle holding the equivalent of two normal bottles, approximately 1.5 liters. ❑ *...a magnum of champagne.*

mag|num opus N-SING [oft poss N] A **magnum opus** is the greatest or most important work produced by a writer, artist, musician, or academic. ❑ *...Gadamer's magnum opus "Truth and Method."*

mag|pie /mǽgpaɪ/ (magpies) N-COUNT A **magpie** is a large black and white bird with a long tail.

ma|ha|ra|ja /mɑhərɑ́dʒə, -ʒə/ (maharajas) also **maharajah** N-COUNT A **maharaja** is the head of one of the royal families that used to rule parts of India.

ma|hoga|ny /məhɒ́gəni/ N-UNCOUNT **Mahogany** is a dark reddish brown wood that is used to make furniture. ❑ *...mahogany tables and chairs.*

maid /meɪd/ (maids) N-COUNT A **maid** is a woman who works as a servant in a hotel or private house. ❑ *A maid brought me breakfast at nine o'clock.*

maid|en /meɪdᵊn/ (maidens) **1** N-COUNT A **maiden** is a young girl or woman. [LITERARY] ❑ *...stories of noble princes and their brave deeds on behalf of beautiful maidens.* **2** ADJ [ADJ n] The **maiden** voyage or flight of a ship or aircraft is the first official journey that it makes. ❑ *In 1912, the Titanic sank on her maiden voyage.*

maid|en aunt (maiden aunts) N-COUNT A **maiden aunt** is an aunt who is not married. [OLD-FASHIONED]

maid|en name (maiden names) N-COUNT A married woman's **maiden name** is her parents' surname, which she used before she got married and started using her husband's surname. ❑ *The marriage broke up and she took back her maiden name of Boreman.*

maid of hon|or (maids of honor)

in BRIT, use **maid of honour**

N-COUNT A **maid of honor** is the chief bridesmaid at a wedding.

mail ✦✧✧ /meɪl/ (mails, mailing, mailed) **1** N-SING [the N, also by N] The **mail** is the public service or system by which letters and packages are collected and delivered. ❑ *Your check is in the mail.* **2** N-UNCOUNT [also the N] You can refer to letters and packages that are delivered to you as **mail**. ❑ *There was no mail except the usual junk addressed to the occupant.* **3** V-T If you **mail** a letter or package to someone, you send it to them by putting it in a mailbox or taking it to a post office. [mainly AM] ❑ *Last year, he mailed the documents to French journalists.* ❑ *He mailed me the contract.*

in BRIT, usually use **post**

4 V-T To **mail** a message to someone means to send it to them by means of email or a computer network. • N-COUNT **Mail** is also a noun. ❑ *If you have any problems then send me a mail.* **5** → see also **airmail, electronic mail, email, junk mail, mailing, surface mail**

COLLOCATIONS

mail
NOUN **2**
noun + **mail**: bulk, fan, hate, junk, snail
adjective + **mail**: first-class; undelivered, unopened, unsolicited
verb + **mail**: deliver, forward, redirect, send; receive

---

mail|bag /meɪlbæg/ (mailbags) N-COUNT A **mailbag** is a large bag that is used by postal workers for carrying mail.

mail|box /meɪlbɒks/ (mailboxes) **1** N-COUNT A **mailbox** is a box outside your house where your letters are delivered. [AM] ❑ *The next day there was a letter in her mailbox.* **2** N-COUNT A **mailbox** is a metal box in a public place, where you put letters and small packages to be collected. They are then sorted and delivered. [mainly AM] ❑ *And with a trembling hand, he dropped the letters into the mailbox.*

in BRIT, use **postbox**

3 N-COUNT On a computer, your **mailbox** is the file where your email is stored. ❑ *If spam does reach your mailbox, try complaining to the sender's ISP.*

mail car|ri|er (mail carriers) N-COUNT A **mail carrier** is a person whose job is to collect and deliver letters and parcels that are sent by post. [AM]

in BRIT, usually use **postman** or **postwoman**

mail|er /meɪlər/ (mailers) **1** N-COUNT A **mailer** is a box, large envelope, or other container for mailing things. [AM] ❑ *Complete the attached self-addressed, postage-paid mailer and send it back to us.* **2** N-COUNT A **mailer** is a letter advertising something or appealing for money for a particular charity. Mailers are sent out to a large number of people at once. [AM] ❑ *Now, thousands of mailers, catalogs and sales pitches go straight into the trash.* **3** N-COUNT [usu with supp] A **mailer** is a company that sends out mail. [AM] ❑ *...the Association for Postal Commerce, a trade group for bulk mailers.*

mail|ing /meɪlɪŋ/ (mailings) **1** N-UNCOUNT [also N in pl] **Mailing** is the activity of sending things to people through the postal service. ❑ *The newsletter was printed toward the end of June and ready for mailing July 1.* **2** N-COUNT A **mailing** is something that is sent to people through the postal service. ❑ *Most of Mahony's expenses were for mass mailings to conservatives across the state.*

mail|ing list (mailing lists) N-COUNT A **mailing list** is a list of names and addresses that a company or organization keeps, so that they can send people information or advertisements. ❑ *Place your name on our mailing list now.*

mail|man /meɪlmæn/ (mailmen) N-COUNT A **mailman** is a man whose job is to collect and deliver letters and parcels that are sent by mail. [AM]

in BRIT, usually use **postman**

mail merge N-UNCOUNT **Mail merge** is a word processing procedure which was used to combine a document with a data file, for example a list of names and addresses, so that copies of the document were different for each person it was sent to. [COMPUTING] ❑ *Using mail-merge software, she makes sure each card goes out on time.*

mail or|der (mail orders) **1** N-UNCOUNT **Mail order** is a system of buying and selling goods. You choose the goods you want from a company by looking at their catalog, and the company sends them to you by mail. ❑ *The toys are available by mail order from the following address.* **2** N-COUNT **Mail orders** are goods that have been ordered by mail order. [mainly AM] ❑ *I supervise the packing of all mail orders.*

maim /meɪm/ (maims, maiming, maimed) V-T To **maim** someone means to injure them so badly that part of their body is permanently damaged. ❑ *Mines have been scattered in rice paddies and jungles, maiming and killing civilians.*

main ✦✦✦ /meɪn/ (mains) **1** ADJ [det ADJ] The **main** thing is the most important one of several similar things in a particular situation. ❑ *...one of the main tourist areas of San*

Francisco. ❑ *My main concern now is to protect the children.* ◼2 PHRASE If you say that something is true **in the main**, you mean that it is generally true, although there may be exceptions. ❑ *Tourists are, in the main, sympathetic people.* ◼3 N-COUNT The **mains** are the pipes which supply gas or water to buildings, or which take sewage away from them. ❑ *...the water supply from the mains.*

main clause (**main clauses**) N-COUNT A **main clause** is a clause that can stand alone as a complete sentence. Compare **subordinate clause**.

main drag N-SING [the N] The **main drag** in a town or city is its main street. [mainly AM, INFORMAL]

main|frame /meɪnfreɪm/ (**mainframes**) N-COUNT A **mainframe** or **mainframe computer** is a large, powerful computer which can be used by many people at the same time and which can do very large or complicated tasks. ❑ *I downloaded the whole thing into the hospital mainframe before I left work today.*

main|land /meɪnlænd/ N-SING You can refer to the largest part of a country or continent as **the mainland** when contrasting it with the islands around it. ❑ *She was going to Nanaimo to catch the ferry to the mainland.*

main|line /meɪnlaɪn/ (**mainlines, mainlining, mainlined**) ◼1 ADJ [ADJ n] You can use **mainline** to describe people, ideas, and activities that belong to the most central, conventional, and normal part of a tradition, institution, or business. ❑ *We observe a striking shift away from a labor theory among all mainline economists.* ◼2 V-T/V-I [usu cont] If people **mainline** a drug or if they **mainline**, they inject an illegal drug into themselves. [INFORMAL] ❑ *We see him snorting and mainlining cocaine.*

main|ly ♦♦♢ /meɪnli/ ◼1 ADV You use **mainly** when mentioning the main reason or thing involved in something. ❑ *The stock market scandal is refusing to go away, mainly because there's still no consensus over how it should be dealt with.* ◼2 ADV [ADV with group] You use **mainly** when you are referring to a group and stating something that is true of most of it. ❑ *The African half of the audience was mainly from Senegal or Mali.*

SYNONYMS

mainly
ADV ◼1
chiefly: *His response to attacks on his work was chiefly bewilderment.*
mostly: *I am working with mostly highly-motivated people.*
largely: *The French Empire had expanded largely through military conquest.*
generally: *As women, we generally say and feel too much about these things.*
primarily: *He believes that violent crime is primarily an urban problem.*

---

main road (**main roads**) N-COUNT A **main road** is an important road that leads from one town or city to another. ❑ *Troops had barricaded the main road from the airport.*

main|spring /meɪnsprɪŋ/ (**mainsprings**) N-COUNT [usu sing, usu the N of n] If you say that an idea, emotion, or other factor is the **mainspring** of something, you mean that it is the most important reason or motive for that thing. [WRITTEN] ❑ *My life has been music, and a constant search for it has been the mainspring of my life.* ❑ *You begin to understand what actions were the mainspring of the story.*

main|stay /meɪnsteɪ/ (**mainstays**) N-COUNT [usu the N of n] If you describe something as the **mainstay** of a particular thing, you mean that it is the most basic part of it. ❑ *Fish and rice were the mainstays of the country's diet.* ❑ *This principle of collective bargaining has been a mainstay in labor relations in this country.*

main|stream /meɪnstrim/ (**mainstreams**) N-COUNT People, activities, or ideas that are part of the **mainstream** are regarded as the most typical, normal, and conventional because they belong to the same group or system as most others of their kind. ❑ *...people outside the economic mainstream.*

main|stream me|dia ◼1 N-SING [with sing or pl verb] The **mainstream media** refers to conventional newspapers, television and other news sources that most people know about and regard as reliable. ❑ *We have seen how the mainstream media uniformly supports the official government line on this.* ❑ *The story got little mainstream media coverage.* ◼2 → See feature box at **press**

Main Street ◼1 N-PROPER In small towns in the United States, the street where most of the stores are is often called **Main Street**. ❑ *Almost all the stores and restaurants along Main Street were shut for the season.* ◼2 N-UNCOUNT **Main Street** is used by journalists to refer to ordinary Americans who live in small towns rather than big cities or are not very rich. [AM] ❑ *This financial crisis had a much greater impact on Main Street.*

main|tain ♦♦♢ /meɪnteɪn/ (**maintains, maintaining, maintained**) ◼1 V-T If you **maintain** something, you continue to have it, and do not let it stop or grow weaker. ❑ *France maintained close contacts with Jordan during the Gulf War.* ◼2 V-T If you say that someone **maintains** that something is true, you mean that they have stated their opinion strongly but not everyone agrees with them or believes them. ❑ *He has maintained that the money was donated for international purposes.* ❑ *"Not all feminism has to be like this," Jo maintains.* ◼3 V-T If you **maintain** something at a particular rate or level, you keep it at that rate or level. ❑ *The government was right to maintain interest rates at a high level.* ◼4 V-T If you **maintain** a road, building, vehicle, or machine, you keep it in good condition by regularly checking it and repairing it when necessary. ❑ *The house costs a fortune to maintain.* ◼5 V-T If you **maintain** someone, you provide them with money and other things that they need. ❑ *...the basic costs of maintaining a child.* ◼6 → See feature box at **urban**

SYNONYMS

maintain
VERB
◼1
retain: *The interior of the shop still retains a nineteenth century atmosphere.*
preserve: *We will do everything to preserve peace.*
sustain: *The parameters within which life can be sustained on Earth are extraordinarily narrow.*
keep up: *There will be a major incentive among TV channels to keep standards up.*
◼2
assert: *The defendants, who continue to assert their innocence, are expected to appeal.*
state: *'Our relationship is totally platonic,' she stated.*
claim: *He claimed that it was all a conspiracy against him.*
contend: *The government contends that he is fundamentalist.*
profess: *Why do organizations profess that they care?*

---

main|te|nance /meɪntɪnəns/ ◼1 N-UNCOUNT The **maintenance** of a building, vehicle, road, or machine is the process of keeping it in good condition by regularly checking it and repairing it when necessary. ❑ *Workmen work on government buildings.* ❑ *The window had been replaced last week during routine maintenance.* ◼2 N-UNCOUNT **Maintenance** is money that someone gives regularly to another person to pay for the things that the person needs. ❑ *...the government's plan to make absent fathers pay maintenance for their children.* ◼3 N-UNCOUNT If you ensure the **maintenance** of a state or process, you make sure that it continues. ❑ *...the maintenance of peace and stability in Asia.*

mai|tre d' /meɪtrə di, meɪtər-/ (**maitre d's** or **maitres d'**) N-COUNT [usu sing] At a restaurant, the **maitre d'** is the head waiter. ❑ *We found a table and the maitre d' assured us that we would be served quickly.*

maize /meɪz/ N-UNCOUNT **Maize** is the same as **corn**. [BRIT]

Maj. N-TITLE **Maj.** is a written abbreviation for **Major** when it is used as a title. ❑ *...Maj. John Cane.*

ma|jes|tic /mədʒɛstɪk/ ADJ If you describe something or someone as **majestic**, you think they are very beautiful, dignified, and impressive. ❑ *...a majestic country home that once belonged to the Astor family.* • **ma|jes|ti|cal|ly** /mədʒɛstɪkli/ ADV ❑ *She rose majestically to her feet.*

maj|es|ty /mædʒɪsti/ (**majesties**) ◼1 N-VOC; PRON [POSS PRON] You use majesty in expressions such as **Your Majesty** or **Her Majesty** when you are addressing or referring to a king or queen. [POLITENESS] ❑ *His Majesty requests your presence in the*

major royal chambers. **2** N-UNCOUNT **Majesty** is the quality of being beautiful, dignified, and impressive. ❑ ...the majesty of the mainland mountains.

ma|jor ♦♦♦ /meɪdʒər/ (majors, majoring, majored) **1** ADJ [ADJ n] You use **major** when you want to describe something that is more important, serious, or significant than other things in a group or situation. ❑ The major factor in the decision to stay or to leave was usually professional. ❑ Drug abuse has long been a major problem for the authorities there. **2** N-COUNT; N-TITLE; N-VOC A **major** is an officer who is one rank above captain in the United States Army, Air Force, or Marines. ❑ I was a major in the war, you know. **3** N-COUNT At a university or college in the United States, a student's **major** is the main subject that they are studying. **4** N-COUNT At a university or college in the United States, if a student is, for example, a geology **major**, geology is the main subject they are studying. ❑ She was a history major at the University of Oklahoma. **5** V-I If a student at a university or college in the United States **majors** in a particular subject, that subject is the main one they study. ❑ He majored in finance at Claremont Men's College in California. **6** ADJ [n ADJ, ADJ n] In music, a **major** scale is one in which the third note is two tones higher than the first. ❑ The orchestra played Mozart's Symphony No. 35 in D Major. **7** N-PLURAL The **majors** are groups of professional sports teams that compete against each other, especially in baseball. [mainly AM] ❑ I knew what I could do in the minor leagues, I just wanted a chance to prove myself in the majors. **8** N-COUNT A **major** is an important sports competition, especially in golf or tennis. ❑ Sarazen became the first golfer to win all four majors. **9** → See feature box at **global warming**

SYNONYMS

major
ADJ **1**
vital: The port is vital to supply relief to millions of drought victims.
critical: He says setting priorities is of critical importance.
important: The planned general strike represents an important economic challenge to the government.
significant: I think it was significant that he never knew his own father.

ma|jor|ette /meɪdʒərɛt/ (majorettes) N-COUNT A **majorette** is one of a group of girls or young women who march at the front of a musical band in a procession.

ma|jor gen|er|al (major generals) N-COUNT; N-TITLE; N-VOC In the United States, a **major general** is a senior officer in the army, air force, or marines, one rank above brigadier general.

ma|jor|ity ♦♦◇ /mədʒɔrɪti/ (majorities) **1** N-SING-COLL The **majority** of people or things in a group is more than half of them. ❑ The majority of my patients come to me from out of town. • PHRASE If a group is **in a majority** or **in the majority**, they form more than half of a larger group. ❑ Surveys indicate that supporters of the treaty are still in the majority. **2** N-COUNT A **majority** is the difference between the number of votes or seats in a legislature or parliament that the winner gets in an election, and the number of votes or seats that the next person or party gets. ❑ Members of parliament approved the move by a majority of ninety-nine. **3** ADJ [ADJ n] **Majority** is used to describe opinions, decisions, and systems of government that are supported by more than half the people involved. ❑ ...her continuing disagreement with the majority view. **4** N-UNCOUNT **Majority** is the state of legally being an adult. In most states in the United States, people reach their majority at the age of eighteen. ❑ Although she had reached the age of majority, her mother refused her permission to go.

ma|jor league (major leagues) **1** N-PLURAL The **major leagues** are groups of professional sports teams that compete against each other, especially in baseball. ❑ Chandler was instrumental in making Jackie Robinson the first Black player in the major leagues. **2** ADJ **Major league** means connected with the major leagues in baseball. ❑ I'm doomed to live in a town with no major league baseball. **3** ADJ **Major-league** people or institutions are important or successful. ❑ James Hawes's books have achieved cult status, and his first film boasts major-league stars. **4** PHRASE If someone **moves into the major league** or **makes it into the major league**, they become very successful in their career.

[JOURNALISM] ❑ Once a model has made it into the major league every detail is mapped out by her agency.

MAKE
① CARRYING OUT AN ACTION
② CAUSING OR CHANGING
③ CREATING OR PRODUCING
④ LINK VERB USES
⑤ ACHIEVING OR REACHING
⑥ STATING AN AMOUNT OR TIME
⑦ PHRASAL VERBS
---

① **make** ♦♦♦ /meɪk/ (makes, making, made)

Make is used in a large number of expressions which are explained under other words in this dictionary. For example, the expression 'to make sense' is explained at 'sense.'

1 V-T You can use **make** with a wide range of nouns to indicate that someone performs an action or says something. For example, if you **make** a suggestion, you suggest something. ❑ I'd just like to make a comment. ❑ I made a few phone calls. **2** V-T You can use **make** with certain nouns to indicate that someone does something well or badly. For example, if you **make** a success of something, you do it successfully, and if you **make** a mess of something, you do it very badly. ❑ Apparently he made a mess of his audition. **3** V-T/V-I If you **make** as if to do something or **make** to do something, you behave in a way that makes it seem that you are just about to do it. [WRITTEN] ❑ Mary made as if to protest, then hesitated. **4** PHRASE If you **make do** with something, you use or have it instead of something else that you do not have, although it is not as good. ❑ Why make do with a copy if you can afford the genuine article?

② **make** ♦♦♦ /meɪk/ (makes, making, made)

→ Please look at meaning **10** to see if the expression you are looking for is shown under another headword.

1 V-T If something **makes** you do something, it causes you to do it. ❑ Dirt from the highway made him cough. ❑ The white tips of his shirt collar made him look like a choirboy. **2** V-T If you **make** someone do something, you force them to do it. ❑ You can't make me do anything. **3** V-T You use **make** to talk about causing someone or something to be a particular thing or to have a particular quality. For example, to **make** someone a star means to cause them to become a star, and to **make** someone angry means to cause them to become angry. ❑ ...James Bond, the role that made him a star. ❑ She made life very difficult for me. **4** V-T If you say that one thing or person **makes** another seem, for example, small, stupid, or good, you mean that they cause them to seem small, stupid, or good in comparison, even though they are not. ❑ They live in fantasy worlds which make Disneyland seem uninventive. **5** V-T If you **make** yourself understood, heard, or known, you succeed in getting people to understand you, hear you, or know that you are there. ❑ He learned enough Spanish to make himself understood. **6** V-T If you **make** someone something, you appoint them to a particular job, role, or position. ❑ He made her a director in his numerous companies. **7** V-T If you **make** something into something else, you change it in some way so that it becomes that other thing. ❑ We made it into a beautiful home. **8** V-T To **make** a total or score a particular amount means to increase it to that amount. ❑ This makes the total cost of the bulb and energy $27. **9** V-T When someone **makes** a friend or an enemy, someone becomes their friend or their enemy, often because of a particular thing they have done. ❑ Lorenzo was a natural leader who made friends easily. **10 to make friends** → see **friend**

③ **make** ♦♦♦ /meɪk/ (makes, making, made) **1** V-T To **make** something means to produce, construct, or create it. ❑ She made her own bread. ❑ Having curtains made professionally can be costly. **2** V-T If you **make** a note or list, you write something down in that form. ❑ Mr. Perry made a note in his book. **3** V-T If you **make** rules or laws, you decide what these should be. ❑ The police don't make the laws, they merely enforce them. **4** V-T If you **make** money, you get it by working for it, by selling something, or by winning it. ❑ I think every business's goal is to make money. **5** V-T If you **make** a case for something, you try to establish or prove that it is the best thing to do. ❑ You could certainly make a case for this point of view. **6** N-COUNT The **make** of something such as a car or radio is the name of the company that made it. ☐ *The only car parked outside is a black Saab – a different make.*

④ **make** ♦♦♦ /meɪk/ (makes, making, made) **1** V-LINK You can use **make** to say that someone or something has the right qualities for a particular task or role. For example, if you say that someone will **make** a good politician, you mean that they have the right qualities to be a good politician. ☐ *She'll make a good actress, if she gets the right training.* ☐ *You've a very good idea there. It will make a good book.* **2** V-LINK If people **make** a particular pattern such as a line or a circle, they arrange themselves in this way. ☐ *A group of people made a circle around the Pentagon.* **3** V-LINK You can use **make** to say what two numbers add up to. ☐ *Four twos make eight.*

⑤ **make** ♦♦♦ /meɪk/ (makes, making, made) **1** V-T If someone **makes** a particular team or **makes** a particular high position, they do so well that they are put in that team or get that position. ☐ *The athletes are just happy to make the team.* **2** V-T If you **make** a place in or by a particular time, you get there in or by that time, often with some difficulty. ☐ *The engine is gulping two tons of fuel an hour in order to make New Orleans by nightfall.* **3** PHRASE If you **make it** somewhere, you succeed in getting there, especially in time to do something. ☐ *So you did make it to America, after all.* ☐ *...the hostages who never made it home.* **4** PHRASE If you **make it**, you are successful in achieving something difficult, or in surviving through a very difficult period. ☐ *I believe I have the talent to make it.* **5** PHRASE If you cannot **make it**, you are unable to attend an event that you have been invited to. ☐ *He hadn't been able to make it to our dinner.*

⑥ **make** ♦♦♦ /meɪk/ (makes, making, made) **1** V-T You use **make it** when saying what you calculate or guess an amount to be. ☐ *"How many shots has she got left?"—"I make it two."* **2** V-T You use **make** it when saying what time your watch says it is. ☐ *I make it nearly nine o'clock.*

⑦ **make** ♦♦♦ /meɪk/ (makes, making, made)
▶ **make for 1** PHRASAL VERB If you **make for** a place, you move toward it. ☐ *He rose from his seat and made for the door.* **2** PHRASAL VERB If something **makes for** another thing, it causes or helps to cause that thing to happen or exist. [INFORMAL] ☐ *A happy parent makes for a happy child.*
▶ **make of** PHRASAL VERB If you ask a person what they **make of** something, you want to know what their impression, opinion, or understanding of it is. ☐ *Nancy wasn't sure what to make of Mick's apology.*
▶ **make off** PHRASAL VERB If you **make off**, you leave somewhere as quickly as possible, often in order to escape. ☐ *They broke free and made off in a stolen car.*
▶ **make off with** PHRASAL VERB If you **make off with** something, you steal it and take it away with you. ☐ *Otto made off with the last of the brandy.*
▶ **make out 1** PHRASAL VERB If you **make** something **out**, you manage with difficulty to see or hear it. ☐ *I could just make out a tall, pale, shadowy figure tramping through the undergrowth.* ☐ *She thought she heard a name. She couldn't make it out, though.* **2** PHRASAL VERB If you try to **make** something **out**, you try to understand it or decide whether or not it is true. ☐ *I couldn't make it out at all.* ☐ *It is hard to make out what criteria are used.* **3** PHRASAL VERB If you **make out** that something is the case or **make** something **out** to be the case, you try to cause people to believe that it is the case. ☐ *They were trying to make out that I'd actually done it.* ☐ *I don't think it was as glorious as everybody made it out to be.* **4** PHRASAL VERB When you **make out** a check, receipt, or order form, you write all the necessary information on it. ☐ *I'll make the check out to you and put it in the mail this afternoon.* **5** PHRASAL VERB If two people **are making out**, they are engaged in sexual activity. [mainly AM, INFORMAL] ☐ *...pictures of the couple making out on the beach.*
▶ **make up 1** PHRASAL VERB The people or things that **make up** something are the members or parts that form that thing. ☐ *The Chinese make up the largest single ethnic group in the city's public classrooms.* ☐ *Women officers make up 13 percent of the police force.* **2** PHRASAL VERB If you **make up** something such as a story or excuse, you invent it, sometimes in order to deceive people. ☐ *I think it's very unkind of you to make up stories about him.* **3** PHRASAL VERB If you **make up** an amount, you add something to it so that it is as large as it should be. ☐ *Less than half of the money that students receive is in the form of grants, and loans have made up the difference.* **4** PHRASAL VERB If you **make up** time or hours, you work some extra hours because you have previously taken some time off work. ☐ *They'll have to make up time lost during the strike.* **5** PHRASAL VERB If a student **makes up** an examination or course they have failed or missed, they take the examination or course again. [AM] ☐ *Everyone gets a chance to make up tests.* **6** PHRASAL VERB If two people **make up** after a quarrel or disagreement, they become friends again. ☐ *She came back and they made up.* **7** PHRASAL VERB If you **make up** something such as food or medicine, you prepare it by mixing or putting different things together. ☐ *Prepare the soufflé dish before making up the soufflé mixture.* **8** PHRASAL VERB If you **make up** a bed, you put sheets and blankets on it so that someone can sleep there. ☐ *Her mother made up a bed in her old room.*

make-believe 1 N-UNCOUNT If someone is living in a **make-believe** world, they are pretending that things are better, different, or more exciting than they really are instead of facing up to reality. [DISAPPROVAL] ☐ *...the glamorous make-believe world of show business.* **2** N-UNCOUNT You use **make-believe** to refer to the activity involved when a child plays a game in which they pretend something, for example that they are someone else. ☐ *She used to play games of make-believe with her elder sister.* ☐ *...his make-believe playmate.* **3** ADJ You use **make-believe** to describe things, for example in a play or movie, that imitate or copy something real, but which are not what they appear to be. ☐ *The violence in those films was too unreal, it was make-believe.*

make|over /meɪkoʊvər/ (makeovers) **1** N-COUNT If a person or room is given a **makeover**, their appearance is improved, usually by an expert. ☐ *She received a cosmetic makeover at a beauty salon as a birthday gift.* **2** N-COUNT If an organization or system is given a **makeover**, important changes are made in order to improve it. ☐ *The biggest makeover has been in TV drama.*

mak|er ♦♦◊ /meɪkər/ (makers) **1** N-COUNT The **maker** of a product is the company that manufactures it. ☐ *...Japan's two largest car makers.* **2** N-COUNT You can refer to the person who makes something as its **maker**. ☐ *...the makers of news and current affairs programs.*

SYNONYMS

maker
NOUN **1**
manufacturer: *...the world's largest doll manufacturer.*
producer: *The estate is generally a producer of high quality wines.*
creator: *I have always believed that a garden dies with its creator.*

---

make|shift /meɪkʃɪft/ ADJ **Makeshift** things are temporary and usually of poor quality, but they are used because there is nothing better available. ☐ *...the cardboard boxes and makeshift shelters of the homeless.*

make|up ♦♦◊ /meɪkʌp/ **1** N-UNCOUNT **Makeup** consists of things such as lipstick, eye shadow, and powder which some women put on their faces to make themselves look more attractive or which actors use to change or improve their appearance. ☐ *Normally she wore little makeup, but this evening was clearly an exception.* **2** N-UNCOUNT Someone's **makeup** is their nature and the various qualities in their character. ☐ *There was some fatal flaw in his makeup, and at times went on he lapsed into long silences or became off-hand.* **3** N-UNCOUNT The **makeup** of something consists of its different parts and the way these parts are arranged. ☐ *The ideological makeup of the unions is now radically different from what it had been.*

make|weight /meɪkweɪt/ (makeweights) N-COUNT If you describe someone or something as a **makeweight**, you think that they are not good or valuable and that they have been included in an activity in order to fill up a gap. [DISAPPROVAL] ☐ *He has not been signed to the team as a makeweight to fill out the numbers.*

mak|ing /meɪkɪŋ/ (makings) **1** N-UNCOUNT The **making** of something is the act or process of producing or creating it. ☐ *...Salamon's book about the making of this movie.* **2** PHRASE If you describe a person or thing as something **in the making**, you mean that they are going to become known or recognized as that thing. ☐ *Her drama teacher is confident Julie is a star in the making.* **3** PHRASE If something **is the making of** a person or thing, it is the reason that they become successful or become very much better than they used to be. ☐ *This discovery may yet be the making of him.* ▪ PHRASE If you say that a person or thing has **the makings of** something, you mean it seems possible or likely that they will become that thing, as they have the necessary qualities. ☐ *Godfrey had the makings of a successful journalist.* ▪ PHRASE If you say that something such as a problem you have is **of** your **own making**, you mean you have caused or created it yourself. ☐ *Some of the university's financial troubles are of its own making.*

PREFIX

mal-
forms words that refer to things that are bad or unpleasant, or that are unsuccessful or imperfect. *For example, malware is a type of computer program that damages a computer.*

---

mal|ad|just|ed /mælədʒʌstɪd/ ADJ If you describe a person as **maladjusted**, you mean that they have psychological problems and behave in a way which is not acceptable to society. ☐ *...a school for maladjusted children.*

mal|ad|min|is|tra|tion /mælædmɪnɪstreɪʃən/ N-UNCOUNT **Maladministration** is the act or process of running a system or organization incorrectly. [FORMAL] ☐ *...a request to investigate a claim about maladministration.*

mala|droit /mælədrɔɪt/ ADJ If you describe someone as **maladroit**, you mean that they are clumsy or handle situations badly. [FORMAL] ☐ *Some of his first interviews with the press were rather maladroit.*

mala|dy /mælədi/ (maladies) ▪ N-COUNT A **malady** is an illness or disease. [OLD-FASHIONED] ☐ *He was stricken at twenty-one with a crippling malady.* ▪ N-COUNT In written English, people sometimes use **maladies** to refer to serious problems in a society or situation. ☐ *He believes many of our social maladies spring from dysfunctional families.*

ma|laise /mæleɪz/ ▪ N-UNCOUNT **Malaise** is a state in which there is something wrong with a society or group, for which there does not seem to be a quick or easy solution. [FORMAL] ☐ *There is no easy short-term solution to the country's chronic economic malaise.* ▪ N-UNCOUNT **Malaise** is a state in which people feel dissatisfied or unhappy but feel unable to change, usually because they do not know what is wrong. [FORMAL] ☐ *He complained of depression, headaches, and malaise.*

ma|laria /məlɛəriə/ N-UNCOUNT **Malaria** is a serious disease carried by mosquitoes, which causes periods of fever.

WORD HISTORY

malaria
The word **malaria** come from early Italian *mal*, meaning 'bad' and *aria*, meaning 'air.' People used to think that the bad air coming from the swamps around Rome caused this particular fever. We now know that it's the mosquitoes that inhabit this type of area which are to blame.

---

ma|lar|ial /məlɛəriəl/ ADJ [usu ADJ n] You can use **malarial** to refer to things connected with malaria or areas which are affected by malaria. ☐ *...malarial parasites.*

Ma|lay /məleɪ, meɪleɪ/ (Malays) ▪ ADJ [usu ADJ n] **Malay** means belonging or relating to the people, language, or culture of the largest racial group in Malaysia. ▪ N-COUNT A **Malay** is a member of the largest racial group in Malaysia. ▪ N-UNCOUNT **Malay** is a language that is spoken in Malaysia and in parts of Indonesia.

Ma|lay|sian /məleɪʒən/ (Malaysians) ADJ Something that is **Malaysian** belongs or relates to Malaysia or to its people. • N-COUNT **Malaysians** are people who are Malaysian.

mal|con|tent /mælkəntɛnt/ (malcontents) N-COUNT [usu pl] You can describe people as **malcontents** when you disapprove of the fact that they are dissatisfied with a situation and want it to change. [FORMAL, DISAPPROVAL] ☐ *Five years ago a band of malcontents, mainly high-educated radicals, seized power.*

male ♦♦◊ /meɪl/ (males) ▪ ADJ Someone who is **male** is a man or a boy. ☐ *From 1995 to 2002, the total number of male prisoners nationwide in state and federal prisons grew 27 percent.* ☐ *The company has engaged two male dancers from the Bolshoi.* ▪ N-COUNT Men and boys are sometimes referred to as **males** when they are being considered as a type. ☐ *...the remains of a Caucasian male, aged 65-70.* ▪ ADJ [ADJ n] **Male** means relating to, belonging to, or affecting men rather than women. ☐ *Massive male unemployment has diminished the status of men in the family.* ☐ *...the rise of female comics who have appropriated male humor.* ▪ N-COUNT You can refer to any creature that belongs to the sex that cannot lay eggs or have babies as a **male**. ☐ *Males and females take turns brooding the eggs.* • ADJ **Male** is also an adjective. ☐ *After mating, the male wasps tunnel through the sides of their nursery.*

male chau|vin|ism N-UNCOUNT If you accuse a man of **male chauvinism**, you disapprove of him because his beliefs and behavior show that he thinks men are naturally superior to women. [DISAPPROVAL]

male chau|vin|ist (male chauvinists) ADJ [usu ADJ n] If you describe an attitude or remark as **male chauvinist**, you are critical of it because you think it is based on the belief that men are naturally superior to women. [DISAPPROVAL] ☐ *The male chauvinist attitude of some people in the company could get you down.* • N-COUNT A **male chauvinist** is a man who has male chauvinist views. ☐ *I'm not a male chauvinist.*

male-dominated ADJ [usu ADJ n] A **male-dominated** society, organization, or area of activity is one in which men have most of the power and influence. ☐ *...the male-dominated world of journalism.*

mal|efac|tor /mælɪfæktər/ (malefactors) N-COUNT A **malefactor** is someone who has done something bad or illegal. [FORMAL] ☐ *...a well-known criminal lawyer who had saved many a malefactor from going to jail.*

ma|levo|lent /məlɛvələnt/ ADJ A **malevolent** person deliberately tries to cause harm or evil. [FORMAL] ☐ *Her stare was malevolent, her mouth a thin line.* • **ma|levo|lence** N-UNCOUNT ☐ *...a rare streak of malevolence.* • **ma|levo|lent|ly** ADV ☐ *Mark watched him malevolently.*

mal|for|ma|tion /mælfɔrmeɪʃən/ (malformations) N-COUNT A **malformation** in a person's body is a part which does not have the proper shape or form, especially when it has been like this since birth. [WRITTEN] ☐ *...babies with a high incidence of congenital malformations.*

mal|formed /mælfɔrmd/ ADJ If people or parts of their body are **malformed**, they do not have the shape or form that they are supposed to, especially when they have been like this since birth. [FORMAL] ☐ *...malformed babies.* ☐ *More rarely, the tubes have been malformed from birth.*

mal|func|tion /mælfʌŋkʃən/ (malfunctions, malfunctioning, malfunctioned) V-I If a machine or part of the body **malfunctions**, it fails to work properly. [FORMAL] ☐ *The radiation can damage microprocessors and computer memories, causing them to malfunction.* • N-COUNT **Malfunction** is also a noun. ☐ *There must have been a computer malfunction.*

mal|ice /mælɪs/ N-UNCOUNT **Malice** is behavior that is intended to harm people or their reputations, or cause them embarrassment and upset. ☐ *There was a strong current of malice in many of his portraits.*

ma|li|cious /məlɪʃəs/ ▪ ADJ If you describe someone's words or actions as **malicious**, you mean that they are intended to harm people or their reputation, or cause them embarrassment and upset. ☐ *That might merely have been malicious gossip.* • **ma|li|cious|ly** ADV ☐ *...his maliciously accurate imitation of Hubert de Burgh.* ▪ → See feature box at **truth**

ma|lign /məlaɪn/ (maligns, maligning, maligned) ▪ V-T If you **malign** someone, you say unpleasant and untrue things about them. [FORMAL] ☐ *We maligned him dreadfully when you come to think of it.* ▪ ADJ [ADJ n] If something is **malign**, it causes harm. [FORMAL] ☐ *...the malign influence jealousy had on their lives.* ▪ → see also **much-maligned**

ma|lig|nan|cy /məlɪgnənsi/ (malignancies) N-VAR A tumor or disease in a state of **malignancy** is out of control and is likely to cause death. [MEDICAL] ☐ *Tissue that is removed during the operation is checked for signs of malignancy.*

ma|lig|nant /məlɪgnənt/ ▪ ADJ A **malignant** tumor or disease is out of control and likely to cause death. [MEDICAL] ☐ *She developed a malignant breast tumor.* ▪ ADJ If you say that someone is **malignant**, you think that they are cruel and like to cause harm. ☐ *He said that we were evil, malignant, and mean.*

ma|lin|ger /məlɪŋgər/ (malingers, malingering, malingered) V-I [usu cont] If someone **is malingering**, they pretend to be ill in order to avoid working. [DISAPPROVAL] ❑ *She was told by her doctor that she was malingering.*

mall /mɔl/ (malls) N-COUNT A **mall** is a very large, enclosed shopping area.

mal|lard /mælərd/ (mallards) N-COUNT A **mallard** is a kind of wild duck that is very common.

mal|le|able /mæliəbəl/ **1** ADJ If you say that someone is **malleable**, you mean that they are easily influenced or controlled by other people. [WRITTEN] ❑ *She was young enough to be malleable.* **2** ADJ A substance that is **malleable** is soft and can easily be made into different shapes. ❑ *Gold is the most malleable of all metals.*

mal|let /mælɪt/ (mallets) N-COUNT A **mallet** is a wooden hammer with a square head.

mall rat (mall rats) N-COUNT **Mall rats** are young people who spend a lot of time hanging around in shopping malls with their friends. [AM, DISAPPROVAL]

mal|nour|ished /mælnɜrɪʃt/ ADJ [usu v-link ADJ] If someone is **malnourished**, they are physically weak because they do not eat enough food or do not eat the right kind of food. ❑ *About thirty percent of the country's children were malnourished.*

mal|nu|tri|tion /mælnutrɪʃən/ **1** N-UNCOUNT If someone is suffering from **malnutrition**, they are physically weak and extremely thin because they have not eaten enough food. ❑ *Infections are more likely in those suffering from malnutrition.* **2** → See feature box at **poverty**

mal|odor|ous /mæloʊdərəs/ ADJ [usu ADJ n] Something that is **malodorous** has an unpleasant smell. [LITERARY] ❑ *...tons of malodorous garbage bags.*

mal|prac|tice /mælpræktɪs/ (malpractices) N-VAR If you accuse someone of **malpractice**, you are accusing them of being careless or of breaking the law or the rules of their profession. [FORMAL] ❑ *There were only one or two serious allegations of malpractice.*

malt /mɔlt/ (malts) **1** N-UNCOUNT **Malt** is a substance made from grain that has been soaked in water and then dried in a hot oven. Malt is used in the production of whiskey, beer, and other alcoholic drinks. ❑ *German beer has traditionally been made from just four ingredients – hops, malt, yeast, and water.* **2** N-COUNT A **malt** is a drink made from malted milk powder, milk, ice cream, and sometimes other flavorings. [AM] ❑ *...a chocolate malt.*

malt|ed /mɔltɪd/ ADJ [ADJ n] **Malted** barley has been soaked in water and then dried in a hot oven. It is used in the production of whiskey, beer, and other alcoholic drinks.

Mal|tese /mɔltiz/ (Maltese) **1** ADJ [usu ADJ n] **Maltese** means belonging or relating to Malta, or to its people, language, or culture. **2** N-COUNT A **Maltese** is a Maltese citizen or a person of Maltese origin. **3** N-UNCOUNT **Maltese** is a language spoken by people who live in Malta.

mal|treat /mæltrit/ (maltreats, maltreating, maltreated) V-T [usu passive] If a person or animal **is maltreated**, they are treated badly, especially by being hurt. ❑ *He said that he was not tortured or maltreated during his detention.*

mal|treat|ment /mæltrɪtmənt/ N-UNCOUNT [oft N of n] **Maltreatment** is cruel behavior, especially involving hurting a person or animal. ❑ *2,000 prisoners died as a result of torture and maltreatment.*

malt whis|key (malt whiskies) N-MASS **Malt whiskey** or **malt** is whiskey that is made from malt.

in BRIT, use **malt whisky**

mal|ware /mælwɛər/ **1** N-UNCOUNT **Malware** is a type of computer program that is designed to damage or disrupt a computer. [COMPUTING] ❑ *Hackers conceal malware in pop-up windows.* **2** → See feature box at **email**

mama /mɑmə, məmɑ/ (mamas) also **mamma** N-FAMILY **Mama** means the same as **mother**. [OLD-FASHIONED]

mam|bo /mɑmboʊ/ (mambos) N-COUNT [oft the N] The **mambo** is a lively dance that comes from Cuba. ❑ *The 1940s and '50s were the golden age of the mambo, the rumba and the chachacha.* ❑ *mambo music.*

mam|mal /mæməl/ (mammals) **1** N-COUNT **Mammals** are animals such as humans, dogs, lions, and whales. Most female mammals give birth to babies rather than laying eggs, and all female mammals feed their young with milk. **2** → See feature box at **animal**

mam|ma|lian /mæmeɪliən, -meɪlyən/ ADJ [ADJ n] In zoology, **mammalian** means relating to mammals. [TECHNICAL] ❑ *The disease can spread from one mammalian species to another.*

mam|ma|ry /mæməri/ ADJ [ADJ n] **Mammary** means relating to the breasts. [TECHNICAL] ❑ *...the mammary glands.*

mam|mo|gram /mæməgræm/ (mammograms) N-COUNT A **mammogram** is a test that uses x-rays to check for breast cancer.

mam|mog|ra|phy /mæmɒgrəfi/ N-UNCOUNT **Mammography** is the use of X-rays to examine women's breasts in order to detect cancer. ❑ *...poorer countries, where mammography is not routinely available.*

Mam|mon /mæmən/ also **mammon** N-UNCOUNT You can use **Mammon** to refer to money and business activities if you want to show your disapproval of people who think that becoming rich is the most important thing in life. [LITERARY, DISAPPROVAL] ❑ *It is not every day that one meets a businessperson who is not obsessed with Mammon.*

mam|moth /mæməθ/ (mammoths) **1** ADJ You can use **mammoth** to emphasize that a task or change is very large and needs a lot of effort to achieve. [EMPHASIS] ❑ *...the mammoth task of relocating the library.* **2** N-COUNT A **mammoth** was an animal like an elephant, with very long tusks and long hair, that lived a long time ago but no longer exists.

man ♦♦♦ /mæn/ (men, mans, manning, manned) **1** N-COUNT A **man** is an adult male human being. ❑ *He had not expected the young man to reappear before evening.* ❑ *I have always regarded him as a man of integrity.* **2** N-VAR **Man** and **men** are sometimes used to refer to all human beings, including both males and females. Many people prefer to avoid this use. ❑ *The chick initially has no fear of man.* **3** N-COUNT If you say that a **man** is, for example, a gambling **man** or an outdoors **man**, you mean that he likes gambling or outdoor activities. ❑ *I thought you were a sailing man.* **4** N-COUNT If you say that a man is, for example, a Harvard **man** or a Yale **man**, you mean that he went to that university. ❑ *Stewart, a Yale man, was invited to stay on and write the script.* **5** N-COUNT If you refer to a particular company's or organization's **man**, you mean a man who works for or represents that company or organization. [JOURNALISM] ❑ *...the Chicago Tribune's man in Abu Dhabi.* **6** N-SING Some people refer to a person's husband, lover, or boyfriend as their **man**. [INFORMAL] ❑ *...if they see your man cuddle you in the kitchen or living room.* **7** N-VOC In very informal social situations, **man** is sometimes used as a greeting or form of address to a man. [FORMULAE] ❑ *Hey wow, man! Where d'you get those boots?* **8** V-T If you **man** something such as a place or machine, you operate it or are in charge of it. ❑ *French soldiers manned roadblocks in the capital city.* ❑ *...the person manning the phone at the complaint department.* **9** → see also **manned**, **no-man's land** **10** PHRASE If you say that a man is **man enough** to do something, you mean that he has the necessary courage or ability to do it. ❑ *I told him that he should be man enough to admit he had done wrong.* **11** PHRASE If you describe a man as **a man's man**, you mean that he has qualities which make him popular with other men rather than with women. ❑ *Very much a man's man, he enjoyed drinking and jesting with his cronies.* **12** PHRASE If you say that a man **is his own man**, you approve of the fact that he makes his decisions and his plans himself, and does not depend on other people. [APPROVAL] ❑ *Be your own man. Make up your own mind.* **13** PHRASE If you say that a group of men are, do, or think something **to a man**, you are emphasizing that every one of them is, does, or thinks that thing. [EMPHASIS] ❑ *To a man, the survivors blamed the government.*

▶ **man up** PHRASAL VERB If you **man up**, you start to be braver in the way that you deal with a situation. ❑ *You need to man up and confront them.*

-man /-mæn, -mən/ COMB IN ADJ [ADJ n] **-man** combines with numbers to make adjectives which indicate that something involves or is intended for that number of people. ❑ *The four-man crew on board the fishing trawler.* ❑ *...a two-man tent.*

mana|cle /mænəkəl/ (manacles, manacling, manacled) **1** N-COUNT [usu pl] **Manacles** are metal devices attached to a prisoner's wrists or legs in order to prevent him or her from moving or escaping. **2** V-T [usu passive] If a prisoner is

manacled, their wrists or legs are put in manacles in order to prevent them from moving or escaping. ❑ *His hands were manacled behind his back.* ❑ *He was manacled by the police.*

man|age ✦✦◇ /mǽnɪdʒ/ (**manages, managing, managed**) **1** V-T If you **manage** an organization, business, or system, or the people who work in it, you are responsible for controlling them. ❑ *Within two years he was managing the store.* ❑ *There is a lack of confidence in the government's ability to manage the economy.* **2** V-T If you **manage** time, money, or other resources, you deal with them carefully and do not waste them. ❑ *In a busy world, managing your time is increasingly important.* **3** V-T If you **manage** to do something, especially something difficult, you succeed in doing it. ❑ *Somehow, he'd managed to persuade Kay to buy one for him.* ❑ *I managed to pull myself up onto a wet, sloping ledge.* **4** V-I If you **manage**, you succeed in coping with a difficult situation. ❑ *She had managed perfectly well without medication for three years.* **5** V-T If you say that you can **manage** an amount of time or money for something, you mean that you can afford to spend that time or money on it. ❑ *I try to manage about five hours a week on my bike.* **6** V-T If you say that someone **managed** a particular response, such as a laugh or a greeting, you mean that it was difficult for them to do it because they were feeling sad or upset. ❑ *He looked dazed as he spoke to reporters, managing only a weak smile.* **7** CONVENTION You say '**I can manage**' or '**I'll manage**' as a way of refusing someone's offer of help and insisting on doing something by yourself. ❑ *I know you mean well, but I can manage by myself.*

man|age|able /mǽnɪdʒəbᵊl/ ADJ Something that is **manageable** is of a size, quantity, or level of difficulty that people are able to deal with. ❑ *He will now try to cut down the task to a manageable size.*

man|aged care N-UNCOUNT **Managed care** is a method of controlling the cost of medical care by fixing a doctor's fees and limiting a patient's choice of doctors and hospitals. [AM] ❑ *There's no evidence that managed care is effective at containing health care costs.*

man|age|ment ✦✦◇ /mǽnɪdʒmənt/ (**managements**) **1** N-UNCOUNT **Management** is the control and organizing of a business or other organization. ❑ *The charity needed better management rather than more money.* ❑ *The dispute is about wages, working conditions, and the management of the mining industry.* **2** N-VAR-COLL You can refer to the people who control and organize a business or other organization as the **management**. [BUSINESS] ❑ *The management is doing its best to improve the situation.* ❑ *We need to get more women into top management.* **3** N-UNCOUNT **Management** is the way people control different parts of their lives. ❑ *...her management of her professional life.*

man|age|ment buy|out (**management buyouts**) N-COUNT A **management buyout** is the buying of a company by its managers. The abbreviation **MBO** is also used. [BUSINESS] ❑ *Dozens of company boards are now discreetly sounding out venture capitalists to see if they will support management buyouts.*

man|age|ment con|sult|ant (**management consultants**) N-COUNT A **management consultant** is someone whose job is to advise companies on the most efficient ways to run their business. [BUSINESS] ❑ *...a leading firm of management consultants.*

man|ag|er ✦✦◇ /mǽnɪdʒər/ (**managers**) **1** N-COUNT A **manager** is a person who is responsible for running part of or the whole of a business organization. ❑ *The chef, staff, and managers are all Chinese.* **2** N-COUNT The **manager** of a pop star or other entertainer is the person who takes care of their business interests. ❑ *...the star's manager and agent.* **3** N-COUNT The **manager** of a baseball team is the person responsible for training the players and organizing the way they play. In other sports, **coach** is used instead. ❑ *The team expects to have a new manager before spring training.*

SYNONYMS

manager
NOUN **1**
supervisor: *She has a full-time job as a supervisor at a factory.*
head: *He was the head waiter.*
director: *He works as the director of the intensive care unit at Guy's Hospital.*
boss: *He cannot stand his boss.*

---

man|ag|er|ess /mǽnɪdʒərɪs/ (**manageresses**) N-COUNT The **manageress** of a store, restaurant, or other small business is the woman who is responsible for running it. Some people dislike this word and prefer the term 'manager.' [BRIT, OLD-FASHIONED]

mana|ge|rial /mænɪdʒɪəriəl/ ADJ **Managerial** means relating to the work of a manager. ❑ *...his managerial skills.* ❑ *...a managerial career.*

man|ag|ing di|rec|tor (**managing directors**) N-COUNT The **managing director** of a company is the most important working director, and is in charge of the way the company is managed. [mainly BRIT, BUSINESS]

mana|tee /mǽnəti/ (**manatees**) N-COUNT A **manatee** is a mammal which lives in the sea and looks like a small whale with a broad, flat tail.

man|da|rin /mǽndərɪn/ (**mandarins**) **1** N-UNCOUNT **Mandarin** is the official language of China. **2** N-COUNT A **mandarin** or a **mandarin orange** is a small orange whose skin comes off easily. **3** N-COUNT A **mandarin** was, in former times, an important government official in China.

man|date /mǽndeɪt/ (**mandates, mandating, mandated**) **1** N-COUNT If a government or other elected body has a **mandate** to carry out a particular policy or task, they have the authority to carry it out as a result of winning an election or vote. ❑ *The president and his supporters are almost certain to read this vote as a mandate for continued economic reform.* **2** N-COUNT If someone is given a **mandate** to carry out a particular policy or task, they are given the official authority to do it. ❑ *How much longer does the independent prosecutor have a mandate to pursue this investigation?* **3** N-COUNT You can refer to the fixed length of time that a country's leader or government remains in office as their **mandate**. [FORMAL] ❑ *...his intention to leave politics once his mandate ends.* **4** V-T [usu passive] When someone **is mandated** to carry out a particular policy or task, they are given the official authority to do it. [FORMAL] ❑ *He'd been mandated by the West African Economic Community to go in and to enforce a ceasefire.* **5** V-T To **mandate** something means to make it mandatory. [AM] ❑ *The proposed initiative would mandate a reduction of carbon dioxide of 40%.* ❑ *Sixteen years ago, Quebec mandated that all immigrants send their children to French schools.*

man|da|tory /mǽndətɔri/ **1** ADJ If an action or procedure is **mandatory**, people have to do it, because it is a rule or a law. [FORMAL] ❑ *...the mandatory retirement age of 65.* **2** ADJ If a crime carries a **mandatory** punishment, that punishment is fixed by law for all cases, in contrast to crimes for which the judge or magistrate has to decide the punishment for each particular case. [FORMAL] ❑ *...the mandatory life sentence for murder.*

man|di|ble /mǽndɪbᵊl/ (**mandibles**) **1** N-COUNT A **mandible** is the bone in the lower jaw of a person or animal. [TECHNICAL] **2** N-COUNT [usu pl] An insect's **mandibles** are the two parts of its mouth which it uses for biting, similar to an animal's jaws. [TECHNICAL]

man|do|lin /mǽndəlɪn, -lɪn/ (**mandolins**) N-VAR [oft the N] A **mandolin** is a musical instrument that looks like a small guitar and has four pairs of strings.

mane /meɪn/ (**manes**) N-COUNT The **mane** on a horse or lion is the long, thick hair that grows from its neck. ❑ *The horse's mane can be washed at the same time as his body.*

man-eating ADJ [ADJ n] A **man-eating** animal is one that has killed and eaten human beings, or that people think might do so. ❑ *...man-eating lions.*

ma|neu|ver /mənúvər/ (**maneuvers, maneuvering, maneuvered**)

in BRIT, use **manoeuvre**

1 V-T/V-I If you **maneuver** something into or out of an awkward position, you skillfully move it there. ❑ *That will allow them to maneuver the satellite into the shuttle's cargo bay.* ❑ *I maneuvered my way among the tables to the back corner of the place.* • N-VAR **Maneuver** is also a noun. ❑ *The chopper shot upward in a maneuver matched by the other pilot.* **2** V-T/V-I If you **maneuver** a situation, you change it in a clever and skillful way so that you can benefit from it. ❑ *The president has tried to maneuver the* campaign away from himself. • N-COUNT **Maneuver** is also a noun. ❑ *The company announced a series of maneuvers to raise cash and reduce debt.* **3** N-PLURAL Military **maneuvers** are training exercises which involve the movement of soldiers and equipment over a large area. ❑ *Allied troops begin maneuvers tomorrow to show how quickly forces could be mobilized in case of a new invasion.*

ma|neu|ver|able /mənuvərəbᵊl/

in BRIT, use **manoeuvrable**

ADJ Something that is **maneuverable** can be easily moved into different positions. ❑ *Soviet fighter planes were extremely maneuverable.* ❑ *...a light, maneuverable cart.*

man|ful|ly /mænfᵊli/ ADV [ADV with v] If you say that someone does something **manfully**, you mean that they do it in a very determined or brave way. ❑ *They stuck to their task manfully.*

man|ga /mæŋgə/ N-UNCOUNT [oft N n] **Manga** is a style of drawing, originally from Japan, that is used in comic books with adult themes. ❑ *Known as manga, Japanese comic art has grown into a cult here.* ❑ *...the sharp, stylized characters of Japanese manga comics.*

man|ga|nese /mæŋgəniz/ N-UNCOUNT **Manganese** is a grayish white metal that is used in making steel.

man|ger /meɪndʒər/ (mangers) N-COUNT A **manger** is a low, open container which cows, horses, and other animals feed from when indoors. [OLD-FASHIONED]

mange|tout /mɒndʒtu/ (mangetout or mangetouts) also **mange-tout** N-COUNT **Mangetout** are the same as **snow peas**. [BRIT]

man|gle /mæŋgᵊl/ (mangles, mangling, mangled) V-T [usu passive] If a physical object **is mangled**, it is crushed or twisted very forcefully, so that it is difficult to see what its original shape was. ❑ *His body was crushed and mangled beyond recognition.*

man|go /mæŋgoʊ/ (mangoes or mangos) N-VAR A **mango** is a large, sweet, yellowish fruit which grows on a tree in hot areas. ❑ *Peel, stone, and dice the mango.* • N-COUNT A **mango** is the tree that this fruit grows on. ❑ *...orchards of lime and mango trees.*

man|grove /mæŋgroʊv/ (mangroves) N-COUNT [oft N n] A **mangrove** or **mangrove tree** is a tree with roots which are above the ground and that grows along coasts or on the banks of large rivers in hot areas. ❑ *...mangrove swamps.*

man|gy /meɪndʒi/ (mangier, mangiest) ADJ [usu ADJ n] A **mangy** animal looks dirty, uncared for, or ill. ❑ *...mangy old dogs.*

man|han|dle /mænhændᵊl/ (manhandles, manhandling, manhandled) **1** V-T If someone **is manhandled**, they are physically held or pushed, for example when they are being taken somewhere. ❑ *Foreign journalists were manhandled by armed police, and told to leave.* ❑ *A porter arrived, manhandled me into a wheelchair and took me to another room for X-rays.* **2** V-T If you **manhandle** something big or heavy somewhere, you move it there by hand. ❑ *The three of us manhandled the uncovered dinghy out of the shed.*

man|hole /mænhoʊl/ (manholes) N-COUNT A **manhole** is a large hole in a road or path, covered by a metal plate that can be removed. Workers climb down through manholes when they want to examine or clean the drains.

man|hood /mænhʊd/ N-UNCOUNT **Manhood** is the state of being a man rather than a boy. ❑ *They were failing lamentably to help their sons grow from boyhood to manhood.*

man-hour (man-hours) N-COUNT A **man-hour** is the average amount of work that one person can do in an hour. **Man-hours** are used to estimate how long jobs take, or how many people are needed to do a job in a particular time. ❑ *The restoration took almost 4,000 man-hours over five years.*

man|hunt /mænhʌnt/ (manhunts) N-COUNT [oft N for n] A **manhunt** is a major search for someone who has escaped or disappeared.

ma|nia /meɪniə/ (manias) **1** N-COUNT If you say that a person or group has a **mania** for something, you mean that they enjoy it very much or spend a lot of time on it. ❑ *The mania for dinosaurs began in the late 1800s.* **2** N-UNCOUNT [also N in pl] **Mania** is a mental illness which causes the sufferer to become very worried or concerned about something. ❑ *...the treatment of mania.*

ma|ni|ac /meɪniæk/ (maniacs) **1** N-COUNT A **maniac** is a crazy person who is violent and dangerous. ❑ *The cabin looked as if a maniac had been let loose there.* **2** ADJ [ADJ n] If you describe someone's behavior as **maniac**, you are emphasizing that it is extremely foolish and uncontrolled. [EMPHASIS] ❑ *He could not maintain his maniac speed for much longer.* **3** N-COUNT If you call someone, for example, a religious **maniac** or a sports **maniac**, you are critical of them because they have such a strong interest in religion or sports. [DISAPPROVAL] ❑ *My mom is turning into a religious maniac.*

ma|nia|cal /mənaɪəkᵊl/ ADJ If you describe someone's behavior as **maniacal**, you mean that it is extreme, violent, or very determined, as if the person were insane. [DISAPPROVAL] ❑ *He was almost maniacal in his pursuit of sporting records.* ❑ *She is hunched forward over the wheel with a maniacal expression.* • **ma|nia|cal|ly** /mənaɪəkli/ ADV ❑ *He was last seen striding maniacally to the hotel reception.*

man|ic /mænɪk/ **1** ADJ If you describe someone as **manic**, you mean that they do things extremely quickly or energetically, often because they are very excited or anxious about something. ❑ *He was really manic.* • **man|ic|al|ly** /mænɪkli/ ADV ❑ *We cleaned the house manically over the weekend.* **2** ADJ If you describe someone's smile, laughter, or sense of humor as **manic**, you mean that it seems excessive or strange, as if they were insane. ❑ *...a manic grin.*

man|ic de|pres|sion N-UNCOUNT **Manic depression** is a medical condition in which a person sometimes feels excited and confident and at others feels very depressed. People now use the term **bipolar disorder** to refer to this condition. [OLD-FASHIONED] ❑ *Going off the medication for her manic depression was a mistake.*

manic-depressive (manic-depressives) also **manic depressive** ADJ If someone is **manic-depressive**, they have a medical condition in which they sometimes feel excited and confident and at other times very depressed. People now use the term **bipolar** to refer to someone with this condition. [OLD-FASHIONED] ❑ *She told them that her daughter-in-law was manic-depressive.* • N-COUNT A **manic-depressive** is someone who is manic-depressive. ❑ *Her mother is a manic-depressive.*

mani|cure /mænɪkyʊər/ (manicures, manicuring, manicured) V-T If you **manicure** your hands or nails, you care for them by softening your skin and cutting and polishing your nails. ❑ *He chose this moment to begin manicuring his hands after his own unostentatious fashion.* • N-COUNT **Manicure** is also a noun. ❑ *I have a manicure occasionally.*

mani|cured /mænɪkyʊərd/ **1** ADJ [oft adv ADJ] A **manicured** lawn, park, or garden has very short, neatly cut grass. [WRITTEN] ❑ *...the manicured lawns of the White House.* **2** → See feature box at **garden**

mani|cur|ist /mænɪkyʊərɪst/ (manicurists) N-COUNT A **manicurist** is a person whose job is manicuring people's hands and nails.

mani|fest /mænɪfɛst/ (manifests, manifesting, manifested) **1** ADJ If you say that something is **manifest**, you mean that it is clearly true and that nobody would disagree with it if they saw it or considered it. [FORMAL] ❑ *...the manifest failure of the policies.* • **mani|fest|ly** ADV ❑ *She manifestly failed to last the mile-and-a-half of the race.* **2** V-T If you **manifest** a particular quality, feeling, or illness, or if it **manifests** itself, it becomes visible or obvious. [FORMAL] ❑ *He manifested a pleasing personality on stage.* ❑ *The virus needs two weeks to manifest itself.* • ADJ **Manifest** is also an adjective. ❑ *The same alarm is manifest everywhere.*

mani|fes|ta|tion /mænɪfɛsteɪʃᵊn/ (manifestations) N-COUNT A **manifestation** of something is one of the different ways in which it can appear. [FORMAL] ❑ *Different animals in the colony had different manifestations of the disease.*

mani|fes|to /mænɪfɛstoʊ/ (manifestos or manifestoes) N-COUNT A **manifesto** is a statement published by a person or group of people, especially a political party, or a government,

manifold /mænɪfoʊld/ ADJ Things that are **manifold** are of many different kinds. [LITERARY] ❑ *Gaelic can be heard here in manifold forms.*

ma|nila /mənɪlə/ also **manilla** ADJ [ADJ n] A **manila** envelope or folder is made from a strong paper that is usually light brown.

ma|nipu|late /mənɪpyəleɪt/ (manipulates, manipulating, manipulated) ◼ V-T If you say that someone **manipulates** people, you disapprove of them because they skillfully force or persuade people to do what they want. [DISAPPROVAL] ❑ *He lies, cheats and shamelessly manipulates people to get what he wants.* • **ma|nipu|la|tion** /mənɪpyəleɪʃ³n/ (manipulations) N-VAR ❑ *...repeated criticism or manipulation of our minds.* ◼ V-T If you say that someone **manipulates** an event or situation, you disapprove of them because they use or control it for their own benefit, or cause it to develop in the way they want. [DISAPPROVAL] ❑ *She was unable, for once, to control and manipulate events.* • **ma|nipu|la|tion** N-VAR ❑ *...accusations of political manipulation.* ◼ V-T If you **manipulate** something that requires skill, such as a complicated piece of equipment or a difficult idea, you operate it or process it. ❑ *The technology uses a pen to manipulate a computer.* • **ma|nipu|la|tion** N-VAR ❑ *...science that requires only the simplest of mathematical manipulations.* ◼ V-T If someone **manipulates** your bones or muscles, they skillfully move and press them with their hands in order to push the bones into their correct position or make the muscles less stiff. ❑ *The way he can manipulate my leg has helped my arthritis so much.* • **ma|nipu|la|tion** N-VAR ❑ *A permanent cure will only be effected by acupuncture, chiropractic, or manipulation.*

ma|nipu|la|tive /mənɪpyəleɪtɪv, -lətɪv/ ADJ If you describe someone as **manipulative**, you disapprove of them because they skillfully force or persuade people to act in the way that they want. [DISAPPROVAL] ❑ *She described him as cold, calculating, and manipulative.*

ma|nipu|la|tor /mənɪpyʊleɪtər/ (manipulators) N-COUNT If you describe someone as a **manipulator**, you mean that they skillfully control events, situations, or people, often in a way that other people disapprove of. ❑ *Jean Brodie is a manipulator. She cons everybody.*

man|kind /mænkaɪnd/ N-UNCOUNT You can refer to all human beings as **mankind** when considering them as a group. Some people dislike this use. ❑ *...the evolution of mankind.*

man|ly /mænli/ (manlier, manliest) ADJ If you describe a man's behavior or appearance as **manly**, you mean it shows qualities that are considered typical of a man, such as strength or courage. [APPROVAL] ❑ *He set himself manly tasks and expected others to follow his example.* • **man|li|ness** N-UNCOUNT ❑ *He has no doubts about his manliness.*

man-made also **manmade** ADJ **Man-made** things are created or caused by people, rather than occurring naturally. ❑ *Man-made and natural disasters have disrupted the government's economic plans.* ❑ *...man-made lakes.*

man|na /mænə/ PHRASE [oft v-link PHR] If you say that something unexpected is **manna from heaven**, you mean that it is good and happened just at the time that it was needed. ❑ *Downloading music from the Internet has been manna from heaven for some consumers.*

manned /mænd/ ◼ ADJ A **manned** vehicle such as a spacecraft has people in it who are operating its controls. ❑ *In thirty years from now the United States should have a manned spacecraft on Mars.* ◼ → see also **man 8** ◼ → See feature box at **travel**

man|ne|quin /mænɪkɪn/ (mannequins) N-COUNT A **mannequin** is a life-sized model of a person which is used to display clothes, especially in shop windows.

man|ner ✦✦✦ /mænər/ (manners) ◼ N-SING The **manner** in which you do something is the way that you do it. ❑ *She smiled again in a friendly manner.* ❑ *I'm a professional and I have to conduct myself in a professional manner.* ◼ N-SING Someone's **manner** is the way in which they behave and talk when they are with other people, for example whether they are polite, confident, or bad-tempered. ❑ *His manner was self-assured and brusque.* • **-mannered** COMB IN ADJ ❑ *Forrest was normally mild-mannered, affable, and untalkative.* ◼ N-PLURAL If someone has **good manners**, they are polite and observe social customs. If someone has **bad manners**, they are impolite and do not observe these customs. ❑ *He dressed well and had impeccable manners.* ❑ *The manners of many doctors were appalling.* ◼ → See feature box at **polite**

SYNONYMS

manner
NOUN ◼
style: *Sam celebrated in fine style.*
way: *Freezing isn't a bad way of preserving food.*
fashion: *There is another drug called DHE that works in a similar fashion.*
method: *This method of treatment became the basis of modern psychotherapy.*
means: *The move is a means to fight crime.*

---

man|nered /mænərd/ ◼ ADJ [usu ADJ n] If you describe someone's behavior or a work of art as **mannered**, you dislike it because it is elaborate or formal, and therefore seems false or artificial. [DISAPPROVAL] ❑ *...Naomi's mannered voice.* ❑ *If you arrange your picture too systematically the results can look very mannered and artificial.* ◼ ADJ **Mannered** behavior is polite and observes social customs. ❑ *Its intention is to restore pride in the past and create a more mannered society.*

man|ner|ism /mænərɪzəm/ (mannerisms) N-COUNT Someone's **mannerisms** are the gestures or ways of speaking that are very characteristic of them, and which they often use. ❑ *His mannerisms are more those of a preoccupied math professor.*

man|nish /mænɪʃ/ ADJ [usu ADJ n] If you describe a woman's appearance or behavior as **mannish**, you mean it is more like a man's appearance or behavior than a woman's. ❑ *She shook hands in a mannish way, her grip dry and firm.* ❑ *...a mannish pantsuit.*

ma|noeu|vrable /mənuːvərəb³l/ [BRIT] → see **maneuverable**

ma|noeu|vre /mənuːvər/ [BRIT] → see **maneuver**

man|power /mænpaʊər/ N-UNCOUNT Workers are sometimes referred to as **manpower** when they are being considered as a part of the process of producing goods or providing services. ❑ *...the shortage of skilled manpower in the industry.*

man|qué /mɒŋkeɪ/ ADJ [n ADJ] You use **manqué** to describe someone who has never had the type of job indicated, although they had the ability for it or wanted it. [FORMAL] ❑ *...his inescapable feeling that he is a great actor manqué.*

manse /mæns/ (manses) N-COUNT A **manse** is the same as a **rectory**. [mainly BRIT]

man|sion /mænʃ³n/ (mansions) ◼ N-COUNT A **mansion** is a very large house. ❑ *...an eighteenth-century mansion in New Hampshire.* ◼ → See feature box at **house**; See also color supplement

man|slaughter /mænslɔːtər/ N-UNCOUNT **Manslaughter** is the illegal killing of a person by someone who did not intend to kill them. [LEGAL] ❑ *A judge accepted her plea that she was guilty of manslaughter, not murder.*

man|tel /mænt³l/ (mantels) N-COUNT A **mantel** is a mantelpiece. [OLD-FASHIONED]

mantel|piece /mænt³lpiːs/ (mantelpieces) also **mantelpiece** N-COUNT A **mantelpiece** is a wood or stone shelf which is the top part of a border around a fireplace. ❑ *On the mantelpiece are a pair of bronze Ming vases.*

man|tle /mænt³l/ (mantles) ◼ N-SING [the N of n] If you take on the **mantle** of something such as a profession or an important job, you take on the responsibilities and duties which must be fulfilled by anyone who has this profession or job. [WRITTEN] ❑ *We have the rare opportunity to seize the mantle of national leadership.* ◼ N-COUNT [with supp] A **mantle** of something is a layer of it covering a surface, for example a layer of snow on the ground. [WRITTEN] ❑ *The parks and squares looked grim under a mantle of soot and ash.* ◼ N-SING [the N] In geology, the **mantle** is the part of the earth that lies between the crust and the core. It is divided into the upper mantle and the lower mantle. [TECHNICAL] ◼ → see also **mantel**

mantle|piece /mænt³lpis/ → see **mantelpiece**
man-to-man → see **man**
man|tra /mæntrə/ (**mantras**) **1** N-COUNT A **mantra** is a word or phrase repeated by Buddhists and Hindus when they meditate, or to help them feel calm. **2** N-COUNT You can use **mantra** to refer to a statement or a principle that people repeat very often because they think it is true, especially when you think that it is not true or is only part of the truth. ❏ *Listening to customers is now part of the mantra of new management in public services.*
manu|al /mænyuəl/ (**manuals**) **1** ADJ **Manual** work is work in which you use your hands or your physical strength rather than your mind. ❏ *...skilled manual workers.* **2** ADJ [ADJ n] **Manual** is used to talk about movements which are made by someone's hands. [FORMAL] ❏ *...toys designed to help develop manual dexterity.* **3** ADJ [ADJ n] **Manual** means operated by hand, rather than by electricity or a motor. ❏ *There is a manual pump to get rid of the water.* • **manu|al|ly** ADV [ADV with v] ❏ *The device is manually operated, using a simple handle.* **4** N-COUNT A **manual** is a book which tells you how to do something or how a piece of machinery works. ❏ *...the instruction manual.*
manu|fac|ture ✦✧✧ /mænyəfæktʃər/ (**manufactures, manufacturing, manufactured**) **1** V-T To **manufacture** something means to make it in a factory, usually in large quantities. [BUSINESS] ❏ *They manufacture the class of plastics known as thermoplastic materials.* ❏ *The first three models are being manufactured at the factory in Dayton.* • N-UNCOUNT **Manufacture** is also a noun. ❏ *...the manufacture of nuclear weapons.* • **manu|fac|tur|ing** N-UNCOUNT ❏ *...management headquarters for manufacturing in China.* **2** N-COUNT In economics, **manufactures** are goods or products which have been made in a factory. [BUSINESS] ❏ *...a long-term rise in the share of manufactures in non-oil exports.* **3** V-T If you say that someone **manufactures** information, you are criticizing them because they invent information that is not true. [DISAPPROVAL] ❏ *According to the prosecution, the officers manufactured an elaborate story.* **4** → See feature box at **recycle**

SYNONYMS

manufacture
VERB **1**
make: *They now make cars at two plants in Europe.*
build: *Workers at the plant build the F-16 jet fighter.*
produce: *The company produced circuitry for communications systems.*
construct: *The boxes should be constructed from rough-sawn timber.*

---

manu|fac|tured home (**manufactured homes**) **1** N-COUNT A **manufactured home** is a house built with parts which have been made in a factory and then quickly put together at the place where the house was built. [AM] **2** → See also color supplement
manu|fac|tur|er ✦✧✧ /mænyəfæktʃərər/ (**manufacturers**) N-COUNT A **manufacturer** is a business or company which makes goods in large quantities to sell. [BUSINESS] ❏ *...the world's largest doll manufacturer.*
ma|nure /mənʊər/ (**manures**) N-MASS **Manure** is animal feces, sometimes mixed with chemicals, that is spread on the ground in order to make plants grow healthy and strong. ❏ *...bags of manure.*
manu|script /mænyəskrɪpt/ (**manuscripts**) N-COUNT [also in N] A **manuscript** is a handwritten or typed document, especially a writer's first version of a book before it is published. ❏ *He had seen a manuscript of the book.*
Manx /mæŋks/ ADJ **Manx** is used to describe people or things that belong to or concern the Isle of Man and the people who live there.
many ✦✦✦ /mɛni/ **1** DET You use **many** to indicate that you are talking about a large number of people or things. ❏ *I don't think many people would argue with that.* ❏ *Not many films are made in Finland.* • PRON **Many** is also a pronoun. ❏ *We stood up, thinking through the possibilities. There weren't many.* • QUANT [QUANT of def-pl-n] **Many** is also a quantifier. ❏ *More couples now live together before getting married.* ❏ *It seems there are not very many of them left in the sea.* • ADJ **Many** is also an adjective. ❏ *Among his many hobbies was the breeding of fine horses.* **2** ADV [ADV as reply] You use **many** in expressions such as 'not many,' 'not very many,' and 'too many' when replying to questions about numbers of things or people. ❏ *"How many of the songs that dealt with this theme became hit songs?"—"Not very many."* **3** PREDET You use **many** followed by 'a' and a noun to emphasize that there are a lot of people or things involved in something. [EMPHASIS] ❏ *Many a mother tries to act out her unrealized dreams through her daughter.* **4** DET You use **many** after 'how' to ask questions about numbers or quantities. You use **many** after 'how' in reported clauses to talk about numbers or quantities. ❏ *How many years have you been here?* • PRON [how PRON] **Many** is also a pronoun. ❏ *The roses are a pound each. How many do you want to send?* **5** DET You use **many** with 'as' when you are comparing numbers of things or people. ❏ *I've always entered as many photo competitions as I can.* • PRON [as PRON] **Many** is also a pronoun. ❏ *Let the child try on as many as she likes.* **6** PRON You use **many** to mean 'many people.' ❏ *Iris Murdoch was regarded by many as a supremely good and serious writer.* **7** N-SING **The many** means a large group of people, especially the ordinary people in society, considered as separate from a particular small group. ❏ *The printing press gave power to a few to change the world for the many.* **8** PHRASE You use **as many as** before a number to suggest that it is surprisingly large. [EMPHASIS] ❏ *As many as 4 million people watched today's parade.*
Mao|ri /maʊri/ (**Maoris**) **1** ADJ **Maori** means belonging to or relating to the race of people who have lived in New Zealand and the Cook Islands since before Europeans arrived. **2** N-COUNT The **Maori** or the **Maoris** are people who are Maori.
map ✦✧✧ /mæp/ (**maps, mapping, mapped**) **1** N-COUNT A **map** is a drawing of a particular area such as a city, a country, or a continent, showing its main features as they would appear if you looked at them from above. ❏ *He unfolded the map and set it on the floor.* **2** V-T To **map** an area means to make a map of it. ❏ *...a spacecraft which is using radar to map the surface of Venus.*
▶ **map out** PHRASAL VERB If you **map out** something that you are intending to do, you work out in detail how you will do it. ❏ *I went home and mapped out my strategy.* ❏ *I cannot conceive of anybody writing a play by sitting down and mapping it out.*
ma|ple /meɪp³l/ (**maples**) N-VAR A **maple** or a **maple tree** is a tree with five-pointed leaves which turn bright red or gold in the fall. • N-UNCOUNT **Maple** is the wood of this tree. ❏ *...a solid maple worktop.*
ma|ple syr|up N-UNCOUNT **Maple syrup** is a sweet, sticky, brown liquid made from the sap of maple trees, that can be eaten with pancakes or used to make desserts.
mar /mɑr/ (**mars, marring, marred**) V-T To **mar** something means to spoil or damage it. ❏ *A number of problems marred the smooth running of this event.*
Mar. **Mar.** is a written abbreviation for **March**.
mara|thon /mærəθɒn/ (**marathons**) **1** N-COUNT A **marathon** is a race in which people run a distance of just over 26 miles, which is about 42 km. ❏ *...running in his first marathon.* **2** ADJ [ADJ n] If you use **marathon** to describe an event or task, you are emphasizing that it takes a long time and is very tiring. [EMPHASIS] ❏ *People make marathon journeys to buy glass here.*
ma|raud|er /mərɔdər/ (**marauders**) N-COUNT If you describe a group of people or animals as **marauders**, you mean they are unpleasant and dangerous, because they wander around looking for opportunities to steal or kill. [LITERARY] ❏ *They were raided by roaming bands of marauders.*
ma|raud|ing /mərɔdɪŋ/ ADJ [ADJ n] If you talk about **marauding** groups of people or animals, you mean they are unpleasant and dangerous, because they wander around looking for opportunities to steal or kill. [LITERARY] ❏ *Marauding gangs of armed men have been looting food relief supplies.*
mar|ble /mɑrb³l/ (**marbles**) **1** N-UNCOUNT **Marble** is a type of very hard rock which feels cold when you touch it and which shines when it is cut and polished. Statues and parts of buildings are sometimes made of marble. ❏ *The house has a superb staircase made from oak and marble.* **2** N-COUNT **Marbles** are sculptures made of marble. ❏ *...marbles and bronzes from the Golden Age of Athens.* **3** N-UNCOUNT **Marbles** is a children's game played with small balls, usually made of colored glass. You roll a ball along the ground and try to hit an opponent's

ball with it. ◻ *On the far side of the street, two boys were playing marbles.* **4** N-COUNT A **marble** is one of the small balls used in the game of marbles. ◻ *...a glass marble.* **5** → See also color supplement

mar|bled /mɑrbᵊld/ ADJ Something that is **marbled** has a pattern or coloring like that of marble. ◻ *...green marbled soap.*

march ✦✧ /mɑrtʃ/ (**marches, marching, marched**) **1** V-T/V-I When soldiers **march** somewhere, or when a commanding officer **marches** them somewhere, they walk there with very regular steps, as a group. ◻ *A U.S. infantry battalion was marching down the street.* ◻ *Captain Ramirez called them to attention and marched them off to the main camp.* • N-COUNT **March** is also a noun. ◻ *After a short march, the column entered the village.* **2** V-I When a large group of people **march** for a cause, they walk somewhere together in order to express their ideas or to protest about something. ◻ *The demonstrators then marched through the capital chanting slogans and demanding free elections.* • N-COUNT **March** is also a noun. ◻ *Organizers expect up to 300,000 protesters to join the march.* • **march|er** (**marchers**) N-COUNT ◻ *Fights between police and marchers lasted for three hours.* **3** V-I If you say that someone **marches** somewhere, you mean that they walk there quickly and in a determined way, for example because they are angry. ◻ *He marched into the kitchen without knocking.* **4** V-T If you **march** someone somewhere, you force them to walk there with you, for example by holding their arm tightly. ◻ *They were marched through a crocodile-infested area and, if they slowed down, were beaten with sticks.* **5** N-SING The **march** of something is its steady development or progress. ◻ *It is easy to feel trampled by the relentless march of technology.* **6** N-COUNT A **march** is a piece of music with a regular rhythm that you can march to. ◻ *A military band played Russian marches and folk tunes at the parade last Sunday.*

March ✦✦✦ /mɑrtʃ/ (**Marches**) N-VAR **March** is the third month of the year in the Western calendar. ◻ *I flew to Milwaukee in early March.* ◻ *She was born in Austria on March 6, 1920.*

march|ing band (**marching bands**) N-COUNT A **marching band** is a group of musicians who play music as they march along the street or march as part of a ceremony.

mar|chion|ess /mɑrʃənɪs, -nɛs/ (**marchionesses**) N-COUNT; N-TITLE A **marchioness** is the wife of a marquis, or a woman with the same rank as a marquis.

Mar|di Gras /mɑrdi grɑ/ N-UNCOUNT **Mardi Gras** is the Christian festival of Shrove Tuesday, the day before Lent, which people in some places celebrate by wearing colorful costumes and dancing through the streets.

mare /mɛər/ (**mares**) N-COUNT A **mare** is an adult female horse.

mar|ga|rine /mɑrdʒərɪn/ (**margarines**) N-MASS **Margarine** is a yellow substance made from vegetable oil that is similar to butter. You spread it on bread or use it for cooking.

mar|ga|ri|ta /mɑrɡəritə/ (**margaritas**) N-COUNT A **margarita** is an alcoholic drink containing tequila and lime or lemon juice. ◻ *The margarita was the best I have ever had.*

mar|gin ✦✧ /mɑrdʒɪn/ (**margins**) **1** N-COUNT A **margin** is the difference between two amounts, especially the difference in the number of votes or points between the winner and the loser in an election or other contest. ◻ *They could end up with a 50-point winning margin.* **2** N-COUNT The **margin** of a written or printed page is the empty space at the side of the page. ◻ *She added her comments in the margin.* **3** N-VAR If there is a **margin** for something in a situation, there is some freedom to choose what to do or decide how to do it. ◻ *The money is collected in a straightforward way with little margin for error.* **4** N-COUNT The **margin** of a place or area is the extreme edge of it. ◻ *...the low coastal plain along the western margin.* **5** N-PLURAL To be on the **margins** of a society, group, or activity means to be among the least typical or least important parts of it. ◻ *Students have played an important role in the past, but for the moment, they're on the margins.* **6** → see also **profit margin**

> **COLLOCATIONS**
>
> **margin**
> NOUN **1**
> adjective + **margin**: narrow, slender, slim, thin, tight; comfortable, considerable, wide; winning
> verb + **margin**: cut, erode, narrow, reduce, shrink; extend, improve, stretch, widen

> **SYNONYMS**
>
> **margin**
> NOUN
> **1**
> **gap:** *Britain needs to bridge the technology gap between academia and industry.*
> **difference:** *The difference between the numbers is 8,532.*
> **4**
> **edge:** *Daniel stepped in front of his desk and sat down on its edge.*
> **side:** *Coyne slid his legs over the side of the bed.*
> **limit:** *... the city limits of Baghdad.*
> **border:** *...a grade 2 listed residence on the outer borders of the city.*

mar|gin|al /mɑrdʒɪnᵊl/ **1** ADJ If you describe something as **marginal**, you mean that it is small or not very important. ◻ *This is a marginal improvement on October.* **2** ADJ If you describe people as **marginal**, you mean that they are not involved in the main events or developments in society because they are poor or have no power. ◻ *The tribunals were established for the well-integrated members of society and not for marginal individuals.* **3** ADJ **Marginal** activities, costs, or taxes are not the main part of a business or an economic system, but often make the difference between its success or failure, and are therefore important to control. [BUSINESS] ◻ *The analysts applaud the cuts in marginal businesses, but insist the company must make deeper sacrifices.*

mar|gin|al|ize /mɑrdʒɪnᵊlaɪz/ (**marginalizes, marginalizing, marginalized**)

in BRIT, also use **marginalise**

V-T To **marginalize** a group of people means to make them feel isolated and unimportant. ◻ *We've always been marginalized, exploited, and constantly threatened.*

mar|gin|al|ly /mɑrdʒɪnᵊli/ ADV **Marginally** means to only a small extent. ◻ *Sales last year were marginally higher than the year before.*

mari|achi /mæriɑtʃi/ N-UNCOUNT [usu N n] In Mexico, a **mariachi** band is a small group of musicians who play music in the street. ◻ *My father was a singer in a mariachi band.* ◻ *...passionate, joyous mariachi music.*

mari|gold /mærɪgoʊld/ (**marigolds**) N-VAR A **marigold** is a type of yellow or orange flower.

ma|ri|jua|na /mærɪwɑnə/ N-UNCOUNT **Marijuana** is a drug which is made from the dried leaves and flowers of the hemp plant, and which can be smoked.

ma|ri|na /mərinə/ (**marinas**) N-COUNT A **marina** is a small harbor for small boats that are used for leisure.

mari|nade /mærɪneɪd/ (**marinades, marinading, marinaded**) **1** N-COUNT A **marinade** is a sauce of oil, vinegar, spices, and herbs, which you pour over meat or fish before you cook it, in order to add flavor, or to make the meat or fish softer. ◻ *Fish is already tender and moist, so a marinade is just added for flavor.* **2** V-T/V-I To **marinade** means the same as to **marinate**. ◻ *Leave to marinade for 24 hours.*

mari|nate /mærɪneɪt/ (**marinates, marinating, marinated**) V-T/V-I If you **marinate** meat or fish, or if it **marinates**, you keep it in a mixture of oil, vinegar, and herbs before cooking it, so that it can develop a special flavor. ◻ *Marinate the chicken for at least 4 hours.*

ma|rine ✦✧ /mərin/ (**marines**) **1** N-COUNT A **marine** is a member of an armed force, for example the U.S. Marine Corps or the Royal Marines, who are specially trained for military duties at sea as well as on land. ◻ *A small number of Marines were wounded.* **2** ADJ [ADJ n] **Marine** is used to describe things relating to the sea or to the animals and plants that live in the sea. ◻ *...breeding grounds for marine life.* **3** ADJ [ADJ n] **Marine** is used to describe things relating to ships and their movement at sea. ◻ *...a lawyer specializing in marine law.*

mari|ner /mærɪnər/ (**mariners**) N-COUNT A **mariner** is a sailor. [LITERARY]

mari|on|ette /mæriənɛt/ (**marionettes**) N-COUNT A **marionette** is a puppet whose different parts you can move using strings or wires.

mari|tal /mærɪtᵊl/ ADJ [ADJ n] **Marital** is used to describe

marital status things relating to marriage. ❑ *Caroline was hoping to make her marital home in Pittsburgh to be near her family.*

mari|tal sta|tus N-UNCOUNT Your **marital status** is whether you are married, single, or divorced. [FORMAL] ❑ *How well off you are in old age is largely determined by race, sex, and marital status.*

mari|time /mærɪtaɪm/ ADJ [ADJ n] **Maritime** is used to describe things relating to the sea and to ships. ❑ *...the largest maritime museum of its kind.*

mar|jo|ram /mɑrdʒərəm/ N-UNCOUNT **Marjoram** is a kind of herb.

mark ✦✧✧ /mɑrk/ (marks, marking, marked) **1** N-COUNT A **mark** is a small area of something such as dirt that has accidentally gotten onto a surface or piece of clothing. ❑ *The dogs are always rubbing against the wall and making dirty marks.* **2** V-T/V-I If something **marks** a surface, or if the surface **marks**, the surface is damaged by marks or a mark. ❑ *Leather overshoes were put on the horses' hooves to stop them from marking the turf.* **3** N-COUNT A **mark** is a written or printed symbol, for example a letter of the alphabet. ❑ *He made marks with a pencil.* **4** V-T If you **mark** something with a particular word or symbol, you write that word or symbol on it. ❑ *The bank marks the check "certified."* ❑ *Mark them with a symbol.* **5** N-COUNT A **mark** is a point that is given for a correct answer or for doing something well in an exam or competition. A **mark** can also be a written symbol such as a letter that indicates how good a student's or competitor's work or performance is. ❑ *...a simple scoring device of marks out of 10, where "1" equates to "Very poor performance."* **6** N-PLURAL If someone gets good or high **marks** for doing something, they have done it well. If they get poor or low **marks**, they have done it badly. ❑ *You have to give her top marks for moral guts.* **7** V-T When a teacher **marks** a student's work, the teacher decides how good it is and writes a number or letter on it to indicate this opinion. ❑ *He was marking essays in his small study.* • **marking** N-UNCOUNT ❑ *For the rest of the lunch break I do my marking.* **8** N-COUNT A particular **mark** is a particular number, point, or stage which has been reached or might be reached, especially a significant one. ❑ *Unemployment is rapidly approaching the one million mark.* **9** N-COUNT The **mark** of something is the characteristic feature that enables you to recognize it. ❑ *The mark of a civilized society is that it looks after its weakest members.* **10** N-SING If you say that a type of behavior or an event is a **mark** of a particular quality, feeling, or situation, you mean it shows that that quality, feeling, or situation exists. ❑ *It was a mark of his unfamiliarity with Hollywood that he didn't understand that an agent was paid out of his client's share.* **11** V-T If something **marks** a place or position, it shows where something else is or where it used to be. ❑ *A huge crater marks the spot where the explosion happened.* **12** V-T An event that **marks** a particular stage or point is a sign that something different is about to happen. ❑ *The announcement marks the end of an extraordinary period in European history.* **13** V-T If you do something to **mark** an event or occasion, you do it to show that you are aware of the importance of the event or occasion. ❑ *Hundreds of thousands of people took to the streets to mark the occasion.* **14** V-T Something that **marks** someone as a particular type of person indicates that they are that type of person. ❑ *Her opposition to abortion and feminism marks her as a convinced traditionalist.* **15** → see also **marked, marking, punctuation mark, question mark** **16** PHRASE If someone or something **leaves** their **mark** or **leaves a mark**, they have a lasting effect on another person or thing. ❑ *Years of conditioning had left their mark on her, and she never felt inclined to talk to strange men.* **17** PHRASE If you **make** your **mark** or **make a mark**, you become noticed or famous by doing something impressive or unusual. ❑ *She made her mark in the film industry in the 1960s.* **18** PHRASE If something such as a claim or estimate is **wide of the mark**, it is incorrect or inaccurate. ❑ *That comparison isn't as wide of the mark as it seems.*

▶ **mark down 1** PHRASAL VERB To **mark** an item **down** or **mark** its price **down** means to reduce its price. ❑ *A toy store has marked down the latest computer games.* **2** PHRASAL VERB If you **mark** something **down**, you write it down. ❑ *I tend to forget things unless I mark them down.*

▶ **mark off** PHRASAL VERB If you **mark off** a piece or length of something, you make it separate, for example by putting a line on it or around it. ❑ *He used a rope to mark off the circle.*

▶ **mark up 1** PHRASAL VERB If you **mark** something **up**, you increase its price. ❑ *You can sell it to them at a set wholesale price, allowing them to mark it up for retail.* **2** → see also **markup**

SYNONYMS

mark
NOUN **1**
spot: *The leaves have yellow areas on the top and underneath are powdery, orange spots.*
stain: *Remove stains by soaking in a mild solution of bleach.*
smudge: *There was a dark smudge on his forehead.*
blotch: *His face was covered in red blotches, seemingly a nasty case of acne.*

---

mark|down /mɑrkdaʊn/ (markdowns) N-COUNT A **markdown** is a reduction in the price of something. ❑ *Customers know that our sales offer genuine markdowns across the store.*

marked ✦✧✧ /mɑrkt/ ADJ A **marked** change or difference is very obvious and easily noticed. ❑ *There has been a marked increase in crimes against property.* • **mark|ed|ly** /mɑrkɪdli/ ADV ❑ *The current economic downturn is markedly different from previous recessions.*

mark|er /mɑrkər/ (markers) **1** N-COUNT A **marker** is an object which is used to show the position of something, or is used to help someone remember something. ❑ *He put a marker in his book and followed her out.* **2** N-COUNT A **marker** or a **marker pen** is a pen with a thick tip made of felt, which is used for drawing and for coloring things. ❑ *Draw your child's outline with a heavy black marker or crayon.*

mar|ket ✦✦✦ /mɑrkɪt/ (markets, marketing, marketed) **1** N-COUNT A **market** is a place where goods are bought and sold, usually outdoors. ❑ *He sold boots at a market stall.* **2** N-COUNT The **market** for a particular type of thing is the number of people who want to buy it, or the area of the world in which it is sold. [BUSINESS] ❑ *The foreign market was increasingly crucial.* **3** N-SING The **market** refers to the total amount of a product that is sold each year, especially when you are talking about the competition between the companies who sell that product. [BUSINESS] ❑ *The two big companies control 72% of the market.* **4** ADJ [ADJ n] If you talk about a **market** economy, or the **market** price of something, you are referring to an economic system in which the prices of things depend on how many are available and how many people want to buy them, rather than prices being fixed by governments. [BUSINESS] ❑ *...the development of a market economy.* ❑ *He must sell the house for the current market value.* **5** V-T To **market** a product means to organize its sale, by deciding on its price, where it should be sold, and how it should be advertised. [BUSINESS] ❑ *...if you marketed our music the way you market pop music.* **6** N-SING **The job market** or **the labor market** refers to the people who are looking for work and the jobs available for them to do. [BUSINESS] ❑ *Every year, 250,000 people enter the job market.* **7** N-SING The stock market is sometimes referred to as **the market**. [BUSINESS] ❑ *The market collapsed last October.* **8** → see also **black market, market forces, open market** **9** PHRASE If you say that it is **a buyer's market**, you mean that it is a good time to buy a particular thing, because there is a lot of it available, so its price is low. If you say that it is **a seller's market**, you mean that very little of it is available, so its price is high. [BUSINESS] ❑ *Don't be afraid to haggle: for the moment, it's a buyer's market.* **10** PHRASE If you are **in the market for** something, you are interested in buying it. ❑ *If you're in the market for a new radio, you'll see that the latest models are very different.* **11** PHRASE If something is **on the market**, it is available for people to buy. If it comes **onto the market**, it becomes available for people to buy. [BUSINESS] ❑ *...putting more empty offices on the market.* **12** PHRASE If you **price** yourself **out of the market**, you try to sell goods or services at a higher price than other people, with the result that no one buys them from you. [BUSINESS] ❑ *At $250,000 for a season, he really is pricing himself out of the market.* **13** → See feature box at **business**

mar|ket|able /mɑrkɪtəbəl/ ADJ Something that is **marketable** is able to be sold because people want to buy it. [BUSINESS] ❑ *What began as an attempt at artistic creation has turned into a marketable commodity.*

mar|ket|eer /mɑrkɪtɪər/ (marketeers) **1** N-COUNT A **marketeer** is the same as a **marketer**. [BUSINESS] **2** → see also **free-marketeer**

mar|ket|er /mɑrkɪtər/ (marketers) N-COUNT A **marketer** is someone whose job involves marketing. [BUSINESS] ❑ *As a marketer I understood what makes people buy things.*

mar|ket forces N-PLURAL When politicians and economists talk about **market forces**, they mean the economic factors that affect the availability of goods and the demand for them, without any help or control by governments. [BUSINESS] ❑ *...opening the economy to market forces and increasing the role of private enterprise.*

mar|ket|ing ✦◇◇ /mɑrkɪtɪŋ/ N-UNCOUNT **Marketing** is the organization of the sale of a product, for example, deciding on its price, the areas it should be supplied to, and how it should be advertised. [BUSINESS] ❑ *...expert advice on production and marketing.*

― SYNONYMS ―
marketing
NOUN
promotion: *The company spent a lot of money on advertising and promotion.*
advertising: *We need a bigger advertising budget.*
PR: *It will be good PR.*

mar|ket|ing mix N-SING A company's **marketing mix** is the combination of marketing activities it uses in order to promote a particular product or service. [BUSINESS] ❑ *The key focus of the marketing mix will be on price and distribution.*

mar|ket lead|er (market leaders) N-COUNT A **market leader** is a company that sells more of a particular product or service than most of its competitors do. [BUSINESS] ❑ *We are becoming one of the market leaders in the fashion industry.*

market|place /mɑrkɪtpleɪs/ (marketplaces) **1** N-COUNT The **marketplace** refers to the activity of buying and selling products. [BUSINESS] ❑ *It's our hope that we will play an increasingly greater role in the marketplace and, therefore, supply more jobs.* **2** N-COUNT A **marketplace** is a small area in a town or city where goods are bought and sold, often outdoors. ❑ *The marketplace was jammed with a noisy crowd of buyers and sellers.*

mar|ket re|search N-UNCOUNT **Market research** is the activity of collecting and studying information about what people want, need, and buy. [BUSINESS] ❑ *A new all-woman market research company has been set up to find out what women think about major news and issues.*

mar|ket share (market shares) N-VAR A company's **market share** in a product is the proportion of the total sales of that product that is produced by that company. [BUSINESS] ❑ *A falling market share might suggest that a product needs a redesign or a new marketing campaign.*

mar|ket test (market tests, market testing, market tested) **1** N-COUNT If a company carries out a **market test**, it asks a group of people to try a new product or service and give their opinions on it. [BUSINESS] ❑ *Results from market tests in the U.S. and Europe show little enthusiasm for the product.* **2** V-T If a new product or service **is market tested**, a group of people are asked to try it and then asked for their opinions on it. [BUSINESS] ❑ *These nuts have been market tested and found to be most suited to the Australian palate.* • **mar|ket test|ing** N-UNCOUNT ❑ *They learned a lot from the initial market testing exercise.*

mar|ket town (market towns) N-COUNT A **market town** is a town, especially in a country area, that has or used to have a market in it.

mark|ing /mɑrkɪŋ/ (markings) **1** N-COUNT **Markings** are colored lines, shapes, or patterns on the surface of something, which help to identify it. ❑ *A plane with Danish markings was over-flying his vessel.* **2** → see also **mark**

marks|man /mɑrksmən/ (marksmen) N-COUNT A **marksman** is a man who can shoot very accurately. ❑ *Police marksmen opened fire.*

marks|man|ship /mɑrksmənʃɪp/ N-UNCOUNT **Marksmanship** is the ability to shoot accurately.

marks|woman /mɑrkswʊmən/ (markswomen) N-COUNT A **markswoman** is a woman who can shoot very accurately. ❑ *A skilled markswoman, the bow and arrow is her weapon of choice.*

mark|up /mɑrkʌp/ (markups) N-COUNT A **markup** is an increase in the price of something, for example the difference between its cost and the price that it is sold for. ❑ *We all know that most wine in restaurants is over-priced: a markup of 200 percent on cost is considered normal.*

mar|ma|lade /mɑrməleɪd/ (marmalades) N-MASS **Marmalade** is a food made from oranges, lemons, or grapefruit that is similar to jam. It is eaten on bread or toast at breakfast.

mar|mo|set /mɑrməzɛt/ (marmosets) N-COUNT A **marmoset** is a type of small monkey.

ma|roon /mərun/ (maroons, marooning, marooned) **1** COLOR Something that is **maroon** is dark reddish purple in color. ❑ *...maroon velvet curtains.* **2** V-T [usu passive] If someone **is marooned** somewhere, they are left in a place that is difficult for them to escape from. ❑ *He was marooned for a year in Jamaica.*

ma|rooned /mərund/ ADJ If you say that you are **marooned**, you mean that you feel alone and helpless and you cannot escape from the place or situation you are in. ❑ *...families marooned in decaying inner-city areas.*

marque /mɑrk/ (marques) N-COUNT A **marque** is the name of a famous company that makes motor vehicles, or the vehicles it produces. ❑ *...a marque long associated with motor racing success, Alfa Romeo.*

mar|quee /mɑrki/ (marquees) **1** N-COUNT A **marquee** is a cover over the entrance of a building, for example a hotel or a theater. [AM] **2** N-COUNT A **marquee** is a large tent which is used at a fair, garden party, or other outdoor event, usually for eating and drinking in.

mar|quis /mɑrkwɪs/ (marquises) also **marquess** N-COUNT; N-TITLE A **marquis** is a male member of the nobility who has a rank between duke and earl.

mar|riage ✦✦◇ /mærɪdʒ/ (marriages) **1** N-COUNT A **marriage** is the relationship between a person and their husband or wife. ❑ *In a good marriage, both husband and wife work hard to solve any problems that arise.* ❑ *When I was 35 my marriage broke up.* **2** N-VAR A **marriage** is the act of marrying someone, or the ceremony at which this is done. ❑ *I opposed her marriage to Darryl.*

― COLLOCATIONS ―
marriage
NOUN
1
adjective + **marriage**: broken, failed, loveless, unhappy; happy, successful; first, previous, second
verb + **marriage**: contemplate, propose; dissolve, end, fail; save
2
adjective + **marriage**: civil, gay, same-sex; sham
verb + **marriage**: celebrate; oppose

mar|riage|able /mærɪdʒəbəl/ ADJ [usu ADJ n] If you describe someone as **marriageable**, you mean that they are suitable for marriage, especially that they are the right age to marry. [OLD-FASHIONED] ❑ *...girls of marriageable age.* ❑ *...a marriageable daughter.*

mar|riage li|cense (marriage licenses) N-COUNT A **marriage license** is an official document that you need in order to get married. [AM] ❑ *She was 15 years old at the time and lied about her age to get a marriage license.*

mar|ried ✦◇◇ /mærid/ **1** ADJ If you are **married**, you have a husband or wife. ❑ *We have been married for 14 years.* ❑ *She is married to an Englishman.* **2** ADJ [ADJ n] **Married** means relating to marriage or to people who are married. ❑ *For the first ten years of our married life we lived in a farmhouse.* **3** ADJ [v-link ADJ to n] If you say that someone is **married to** their work or another activity, you mean that they are very involved with it and have little interest in anything else. ❑ *"Sam was married to his job," McWhorter said.*

mar|row /mæroʊ/ (marrows) **1** N-UNCOUNT **Marrow** is the same as **bone marrow**. ❑ *The marrow donor is her 14-month-old sister.* **2** N-SING [the N, usu N of n] The **marrow** of something is the most important and basic part of it. ❑ *We're getting into the marrow of the film.* **3** N-VAR A **marrow** is a long, thick, green vegetable with soft white flesh that is eaten cooked. [BRIT]

in AM, use **squash**

marrow|bone /mæroʊboʊn/ (marrowbones) N-VAR **Marrowbones** are the bones of certain animals, especially cows, that contain a lot of bone marrow. They are used in cooking and in dog food.

mar|ry ♦♦◊ /mæri/ (marries, marrying, married) **1** V-RECIP When two people **get married** or **marry**, they legally take each other as partners in a special ceremony. **Get married** is less formal and more commonly used than **marry**. ❑ *I thought he would change after we got married.* ❑ *They married a month after they met.* ❑ *He wants to marry her.* **2** V-T When a priest or official **marries** two people, he or she conducts the ceremony in which the two people legally take each other as partners in marriage. ❑ *The minister has agreed to marry us in the college chapel.*

USAGE
marry
You don't usually use 'marry' without a following noun. Don't say, for example, '~~She married~~.' Use **get married**. *I'm getting married next month.*

marsh /mɑrʃ/ (marshes) **1** N-VAR A **marsh** is a wet, muddy area of land. **2** → See feature box at **water**

mar|shal /mɑrʃəl/ (marshals, marshaling or marshalling, marshaled or marshalled) **1** V-T If you **marshal** people or things, you gather them together and arrange them for a particular purpose. ❑ *The company turned its attention to marshaling its creditors' approval.* **2** N-COUNT A **marshal** is an official who helps to supervise a public event, especially a sports event. ❑ *The grand prix is controlled by well-trained marshals.* **3** N-COUNT In the United States and some other countries, a **marshal** is a police officer, often one who is responsible for a particular area. ❑ *A federal marshal was killed in a shoot-out.* **4** N-COUNT A **marshal** is an officer in a fire department. [AM] ❑ *She was ordered out of her home by a fire marshal because the house next door had an explosion from a leaking gas main.*

marsh|land /mɑrʃlænd/ (marshlands) N-UNCOUNT [also N in pl] **Marshland** is land with a lot of wet, muddy areas.

marsh|mal|low /mɑrʃmɛloʊ, -mæloʊ/ (marshmallows) **1** N-UNCOUNT **Marshmallow** is a soft, sweet food that is used in some cakes, puddings, and candies. **2** N-COUNT **Marshmallows** are candies made from marshmallow.

marshy /mɑrʃi/ (marshier, marshiest) ADJ [usu ADJ n] **Marshy** land is always wet and muddy. ❑ *The low, marshy land runs out for miles toward the gulf.*

mar|su|pial /mɑrsupiəl/ (marsupials) N-COUNT A **marsupial** is an animal such as a kangaroo or an opossum. Female marsupials carry their babies in a pouch on their stomach.

mart /mɑrt/ (marts) N-COUNT A **mart** is a place such as a market where things are bought and sold. [AM] ❑ *...the flower mart.*

mar|tial /mɑrʃəl/ **1** ADJ **Martial** is used to describe things relating to soldiers or war. [FORMAL] ❑ *The paper was actually twice banned under the martial regime.* **2** → see also **court martial**

mar|tial art (martial arts) N-COUNT A **martial art** is one of the methods of fighting, often without weapons, that come from the Far East, for example kung fu, karate, or judo.

mar|tial law N-UNCOUNT **Martial law** is control of an area by soldiers, not the police. ❑ *The military leadership has lifted martial law in several more towns.*

Mar|tian /mɑrʃən/ (Martians) **1** N-COUNT A **Martian** is an imaginary creature from the planet Mars. ❑ *Orson Welles managed to convince many Americans that they were being invaded by Martians.* **2** ADJ [usu ADJ n] Something that is **Martian** exists on or relates to the planet Mars. ❑ *The Martian atmosphere contains only tiny amounts of water.*

mar|tin /mɑrtən/ (martins) N-COUNT A **martin** is a small bird with a forked tail.

mar|ti|net /mɑrtɪnɛt/ (martinets) N-COUNT If you say that someone is a **martinet**, you are criticizing them because they are very strict and demand that people obey their rules and orders. [FORMAL, DISAPPROVAL] ❑ *He's a retired lieutenant colonel and a bit of a martinet.*

mar|ti|ni /mɑrtini/ (martinis) also **Martini** N-COUNT **Martini** is a cocktail made from gin and vermouth. A **martini** is a glass of martini. ❑ *Tell him I had three martinis that evening.*

mar|tyr /mɑrtər/ (martyrs, martyring, martyred) **1** N-COUNT A **martyr** is someone who is killed or made to suffer greatly because of their religious or political beliefs, and is admired and respected by people who share those beliefs. ❑ *...a glorious martyr to the cause of liberty.* **2** V-T [usu passive] If someone **is martyred**, they are killed or made to suffer greatly because of their religious or political beliefs. ❑ *St. Pancras was martyred in 304 A.D.* **3** N-COUNT If you refer to someone as a **martyr**, you disapprove of the fact that they pretend to suffer, or exaggerate their suffering, in order to get sympathy or praise from other people. [DISAPPROVAL] ❑ *When are you going to quit acting like a martyr?* **4** N-COUNT If you say that someone is a **martyr** to something, you mean that they suffer as a result of it. ❑ *Edgar was a martyr to his sense of honor and responsibility.*

mar|tyr|dom /mɑrtərdəm/ **1** N-UNCOUNT If someone suffers **martyrdom**, they are killed or made to suffer greatly because of their religious or political beliefs. ❑ *...the martyrdom of Bishop Feliciano.* ❑ *He suffered martyrdom by stoning.* **2** N-UNCOUNT If you describe someone's behavior as **martyrdom**, you are critical of them because they are exaggerating their suffering in order to gain sympathy or praise. [DISAPPROVAL] ❑ *She sat picking at her small plate of rice salad with an air of martyrdom.*

mar|tyred /mɑrtərd/ ADJ [ADJ n] If you describe a person or their behavior as **martyred**, you mean that they often exaggerate their suffering in order to gain sympathy or praise. [LITERARY, DISAPPROVAL] ❑ *"As usual," muttered his martyred wife.* ❑ *You put on your martyred expression, sigh and say, "If you really, really want to..."*

mar|vel /mɑrvəl/ (marvels, marveling or marvelling, marveled or marvelled) **1** V-I If you **marvel** at something, you express your great surprise, wonder, or admiration. ❑ *Her fellow members marveled at her seemingly infinite energy.* ❑ *Sara and I read the story and marveled.* **2** N-COUNT You can describe something or someone as a **marvel** to indicate that you think that they are wonderful. ❑ *The whale, like the dolphin, has become a symbol of the marvels of creation.*

mar|vel|ous /mɑrvələs/
in BRIT, use **marvellous**

ADJ If you describe someone or something as **marvelous**, you are emphasizing that they are very good. ❑ *It's the most marvelous piece of music.* ● **mar|vel|ous|ly** ADV ❑ *We want people to think he's doing marvelously.*

Marx|ism /mɑrksɪzəm/ N-UNCOUNT **Marxism** is a political philosophy based on the writings of Karl Marx which stresses the importance of the struggle between different social classes.

Marx|ist /mɑrksɪst/ (Marxists) **1** ADJ **Marxist** means based on Marxism or relating to Marxism. ❑ *...a Marxist state.* **2** N-COUNT A **Marxist** is a person who believes in Marxism or who is a member of a Marxist party. ❑ *...a 78-year-old former Marxist.*

mar|zi|pan /mɑrzɪpæn/ N-UNCOUNT **Marzipan** is a paste made of almonds, sugar, and eggs which is sometimes put on top of cakes and used in making candies.

masc. Masc. is a written abbreviation of **masculine**.

mas|cara /mæskærə/ (mascaras) N-MASS **Mascara** is a substance used as makeup to make eyelashes darker. ❑ *...water-resistant mascaras.*

mas|car|pone /mæskərpoʊni/ N-UNCOUNT **Mascarpone** is a soft white cheese traditionally made in Italy. It is used to make desserts.

mas|cot /mæskɒt/ (mascots) N-COUNT A **mascot** is an animal, toy, or symbol which is associated with a particular organization or event, and which is thought to bring good luck. ❑ *...the official mascot of the Detroit Tigers.*

mas|cu|line /mæskyəlɪn/ **1** ADJ **Masculine** qualities and things relate to or are considered typical of men, in contrast to women. ❑ *...masculine characteristics like a husky voice and facial hair.* **2** ADJ If you say that someone or something is **masculine**, you mean that they have qualities such as strength or confidence which are considered typical of men. ❑ *She has a deep, rather masculine laugh.* **3** ADJ In some languages, a **masculine** noun, pronoun, or adjective has a different form from a feminine or neuter one, or behaves in a different way.

mas|cu|lin|ity /mæskjəlɪnɪti/ ◼ N-UNCOUNT A man's **masculinity** is the fact that he is a man. ❑ ...*a project on the link between masculinity and violence.* ◼ N-UNCOUNT **Masculinity** means the qualities that are considered to be typical of men. ❑ *The old ideas of masculinity do not work for most men.*

mas|cu|lin|ize /mæskjəlɪnaɪz/ (masculinizes, masculinizing, masculinized)

in BRIT, also use **masculinise**

V-T [usu passive] To **masculinize** something means to make it into something that involves mainly men or is thought suitable for or typical of men. [FORMAL] ❑ *Not all factory work has been masculinized.*

mash /mæʃ/ (mashes, mashing, mashed) V-T If you **mash** food that is solid but soft, you crush it so that it forms a soft mass. ❑ *Mash the bananas with a fork.*

mash|er /mæʃər/ (mashers) ◼ N-COUNT A **masher** is a special tool used for crushing potatoes to make them into a soft mass. ❑ ...*a potato masher.* ◼ → See also color supplement

mask ♦♢ /mæsk/ (masks, masking, masked) ◼ N-COUNT A **mask** is a piece of cloth or other material, which you wear over your face so that people cannot see who you are, or so that you look like someone or something else. ❑ *The gunman, whose mask had slipped, fled.* ◼ N-COUNT A **mask** is a piece of cloth or other material that you wear over all or part of your face to protect you from germs or harmful substances. ❑ *You must wear goggles and a mask that will protect you against the fumes.* ◼ N-COUNT If you describe someone's behavior as a **mask**, you mean that they do not show their real feelings or character. ❑ *His mask of detachment cracked, and she saw for an instant an angry and violent man.* ◼ N-COUNT A **mask** is a thick cream or paste made of various substances, which you spread over your face and leave for some time in order to improve your skin. ❑ *This mask leaves your complexion feeling soft and supple.* ◼ V-T If you **mask** your feelings, you deliberately do not show them in your behavior, so that people cannot know what you really feel. ❑ *Dina lit a cigarette, trying to mask her agitation.* ◼ V-T If one thing **masks** another, it prevents people from noticing or recognizing the other thing. ❑ *He was squinting through the smoke that masked the enemy.* ◼ → see also **gas mask**

COLLOCATIONS

mask
NOUN ◼
noun + **mask**: eye, face, ski
adjective + **mask**: protective, respiratory, surgical
verb + **mask**: remove, wear
VERB ◼
mask + noun: feeling
noun + **mask**: smile

---

masked /mæskt/ ADJ If someone is **masked**, they are wearing a mask. ❑ *Masked youths threw stones and firebombs.*

mask|ing tape ◼ N-UNCOUNT **Masking tape** is plastic or paper tape which is sticky on one side and is used, for example, to protect part of a surface that you are painting. ◼ → See feature box at **DIY**

maso|chism /mæsəkɪzəm/ ◼ N-UNCOUNT **Masochism** is behavior in which someone gets sexual pleasure from their own pain or suffering. ❑ *The tendency toward masochism is however always linked with elements of sadism.* • **maso|chist** (masochists) N-COUNT ❑ ...*consensual sexual masochists.*
◼ N-UNCOUNT If you describe someone's behavior as **masochism**, you mean that they seem to be trying to get into a situation which causes them suffering or great difficulty. ❑ *Once you have tasted life in southern California, it takes a peculiar kind of masochism to return to a British winter.* • **maso|chist** N-COUNT ❑ *Anybody who enjoys this is a masochist.*

maso|chis|tic /mæsəkɪstɪk/ ◼ ADJ **Masochistic** behavior involves a person getting sexual pleasure from their own pain or suffering. ❑ ...*his masochistic tendencies.* ◼ ADJ If you describe someone's behavior as **masochistic**, you mean that they seem to be trying to get into a situation which causes them suffering or great difficulty. ❑ *It seems masochistic, somehow.*

ma|son /meɪsən/ (masons) N-COUNT A **mason** is a person who is skilled at making things or building things with stone or bricks.

Ma|son|ic /məsɒnɪk/ ADJ [ADJ n] **Masonic** is used to describe things relating to the organization of Freemasons. ❑ ...*a Masonic lodge on Main Street.*

ma|son jar (mason jars) also **Mason jar** N-COUNT A **mason jar** is a glass jar with a lid that you screw on, which is used for preserving food. [AM]

ma|son|ry /meɪsənri/ N-UNCOUNT **Masonry** is bricks or pieces of stone which have been stuck together with cement as part of a wall or building. ❑ ...*a huge blast that sent pieces of masonry flying through the air.*

mas|quer|ade /mæskəreɪd/ (masquerades, masquerading, masqueraded) ◼ V-I To **masquerade as** someone or something means to pretend to be that person or thing, particularly in order to deceive other people. ❑ *He masqueraded as a doctor and fooled everyone.* ◼ N-COUNT A **masquerade** is an attempt to deceive people about the true nature or identity of something. ❑ *He told a news conference that the elections would be a masquerade.*

mass ♦♦♢ /mæs/ (masses, massing, massed) ◼ N-SING A **mass of** things is a large number of them grouped together. ❑ *On his desk is a mass of books and papers.* ◼ N-SING A **mass** of something is a large amount of it. ❑ *She had a mass of auburn hair.* ◼ QUANT **Masses of** something means a great deal of it. [INFORMAL] ❑ *There's masses of work for her to do.* ◼ ADJ [ADJ n] **Mass** is used to describe something which involves or affects a very large number of people. ❑ ...*ideas on combating mass unemployment.* ❑ *All the lights went off, and mass hysteria broke out.*
◼ N-COUNT A **mass** of a solid substance, a liquid, or a gas is an amount of it, especially a large amount which has no definite shape. ❑ ...*before it cools and sets into a solid mass.*
◼ N-PLURAL If you talk about **the masses**, you mean the ordinary people in society, in contrast to the leaders or the highly educated people. ❑ *His music is commercial. It is aimed at the masses.* ◼ N-SING The **mass** of people are most of the people in a country, society, or group. ❑ *The 1939-45 world war involved the mass of the population.* ◼ V-T/V-I When people or things **mass**, or when you **mass** them, they gather together into a large crowd or group. ❑ *Shortly after the workers went on strike, police began to mass at the shipyard.* ◼ N-SING If you say that something is a **mass of** things, you mean that it is covered with them or full of them. ❑ *His body was a mass of sores.*
◼ N-VAR In physics, the **mass** of an object is the amount of physical matter that it has. [TECHNICAL] ❑ *Astronomers know that Pluto and Triton have nearly the same size, mass, and density.*
◼ N-VAR **Mass** is a Christian church ceremony, especially in a Roman Catholic or Orthodox church, during which people eat bread and drink wine in order to remember the last meal of Jesus Christ. ❑ *She attended a convent school and went to Mass each day.* ◼ → see also **massed**

mas|sa|cre /mæsəkər/ (massacres, massacring, massacred) ◼ N-VAR A **massacre** is the killing of a large number of people at the same time in a violent and cruel way. ❑ *Maria lost her 62-year-old mother in the massacre.* ◼ V-T If people **are massacred**, a large number of them are attacked and killed in a violent and cruel way. ❑ *300 civilians are believed to have been massacred by the rebels.*

mas|sage /məsɑːʒ/ (massages, massaging, massaged)
◼ N-VAR **Massage** is the action of squeezing and rubbing someone's body, as a way of making them relax or reducing their pain. ❑ *Alex asked me if I wanted a massage.* ◼ V-T If you **massage** someone or a part of their body, you squeeze and rub their body, in order to make them relax or reduce their pain. ❑ *She continued massaging her right foot, which was bruised and aching.* ◼ V-T If you say that someone **massages** statistics, figures, or evidence, you are criticizing them for changing or presenting the facts in a way that misleads people. [DISAPPROVAL] ❑ *Their governments have no reason to "massage" the statistics.*

mas|sage par|lor (massage parlors)

in BRIT, use **massage parlour**

N-COUNT A **massage parlor** is a place where people go and pay for a massage. Some places that are called **massage parlors** are in fact places where people pay to have sex.

masse /mæs/ → see **en masse**

massed /mæst/ ADJ [ADJ n] **Massed** is used to describe a large number of people who have been brought together for a particular purpose. ❏ *He could not escape the massed ranks of newsmen who spotted him crossing the lawn.*

mas|seur /mæsɜːr/ (masseurs) N-COUNT A **masseur** is a man whose job is to give massages.

mas|seuse /mæsʊz/ (masseuses) N-COUNT A **masseuse** is a woman whose job is to give massages.

mas|sif /mæsif/ (massifs) N-COUNT [oft in names] A **massif** is a group of mountains that form part of a mountain range.

mas|sive ♦⃟ /mæsɪv/ ◻ ADJ Something that is **massive** is very large in size, quantity, or extent. [EMPHASIS] ❏ *There was evidence of massive fraud.* ❏ *...massive air attacks.* • **mas|sive|ly** ADV ❏ *...a massively popular game.* ◪ ADJ [ADJ n] If you describe a medical condition as **massive**, you mean that it is extremely serious. ❏ *He died six weeks later of a massive heart attack.*

SYNONYMS

massive
ADJ ◻
huge: *...a tiny, little woman with huge, black glasses.*
enormous: *The main bedroom is enormous.*
gigantic: *...gigantic rocks.*
vast: *...those farmers who own vast stretches of land.*
immense: *...an immense cloud of smoke.*

---

mass mar|ket (mass markets) ◻ N-COUNT **Mass market** is used to refer to the large numbers of people who want to buy a particular product. [BUSINESS] ❏ *They now have access to the mass markets of China, Japan and the U.K.* ◪ ADJ [ADJ n] **Mass-market** products are designed and produced for selling to large numbers of people. [BUSINESS] ❏ *...mass-market paperbacks.*

mass me|dia N-SING-COLL You can use the **mass media** to refer to the various ways, especially television, radio, newspapers, and magazines, by which information and news is given to large numbers of people. ❏ *...mass media coverage of the issue.*

mass mur|der (mass murders) N-VAR **Mass murder** is the deliberate illegal killing of a large number of people by a person or an organization.

mass mur|der|er (mass murderers) N-COUNT A **mass murderer** is someone who deliberately kills a large number of people illegally.

mass noun (mass nouns) ◻ N-COUNT A **mass noun** is a noun such as 'wine' which is usually uncount but is used with 'a' or 'an' or used in the plural when it refers to types of that substance, as in 'a range of Australian wines.' ◪ N-COUNT In some descriptions of grammar, a **mass noun** is the same as an **uncount noun**.

mass-produce (mass-produces, mass-producing, mass-produced) V-T If someone **mass-produces** something, they make it in large quantities, usually by machine. This means that the product can be sold cheaply. [BUSINESS] ❏ *...the invention of machinery to mass-produce footwear.* • **mass-produced** ADJ [ADJ n] ❏ *In 1981 it launched the first mass-produced mountain bike.*

mass pro|duc|tion N-UNCOUNT **Mass production** is the production of something in large quantities, especially by machine. [BUSINESS] ❏ *...equipment that would allow the mass production of baby food.*

mass tran|sit N-UNCOUNT [oft N n] **Mass transit** is the transportation of people by means of buses, trains, or other vehicles running on fixed routes. [AM] ❏ *The president wants to spend $105 billion over the next five years to improve the nation's highways and mass transit systems.*

in BRIT, use **public transport**

mast /mæst/ (masts) ◻ N-COUNT The **masts** of a boat are the tall, upright poles that support its sails. ◪ N-COUNT A radio **mast** is a tall upright structure that is used to transmit radio or television signals.

mas|tec|to|my /mæstɛktəmi/ (mastectomies) N-VAR A **mastectomy** is a surgical operation to remove a woman's breast.

mas|ter ♦♦⃟ /mæstər/ (masters, mastering, mastered)
◻ N-COUNT A servant's **master** is the man that he or she works for. ❏ *My master ordered me not to deliver the message except in private.* ◪ N-COUNT If you say that someone is a **master** of a particular activity, you mean that they are extremely skilled at it. ❏ *She was a master of the English language.* • ADJ [ADJ n] **Master** is also an adjective. ❏ *...a master craftsman.* ◨ N-VAR If you are **master** of a situation, you have complete control over it. ❏ *Jackson remained calm and always master of his passions.* ◩ V-T If you **master** something, you learn how to do it properly or you succeed in understanding it completely. ❏ *Duff soon mastered the skills of radio production.* ◰ V-T If you **master** a difficult situation, you succeed in controlling it. ❏ *When you have mastered one situation you have to go on to the next.* ◱ → see also **headmaster** ◲ N-COUNT A famous male painter of the past is often called a **master**. ❏ *...a portrait by the Dutch master, Vincent Van Gogh.* ◳ ADJ [ADJ n] A **master** copy of something, such as a film or a tape recording, is an original copy that can be used to produce other copies. ❏ *Keep one as a master copy for your own reference and circulate the others.* ◴ N-SING A **master's degree** can be referred to as a **master's**. ❏ *I've got a master's in economics.*

SYNONYMS

master
NOUN ◻
ruler: *He was a weak-willed and indecisive ruler.*
boss: *He cannot stand his boss.*
employer: *He had been sent to Rome by his employer.*

COLLOCATIONS

master
VERB ◩
master + *noun*: art, basics, skill, technique; language, technology
master + *adverb*: completely, successfully

---

mas|ter bed|room (master bedrooms) N-COUNT The **master bedroom** in a house is the largest bedroom.

mas|ter class (master classes) N-COUNT A **master class** is a lesson where someone who is an expert at something such as dancing or music gives advice to a group of good students. Master classes usually take place in public or are broadcast on television.

mas|ter|ful /mæstərfəl/ ◻ ADJ If you describe someone as **masterful**, you mean they behave in a way which shows that they are in control of a situation and can tell other people what to do. [APPROVAL] ❏ *Big, successful moves need bold, masterful managers.* ◪ ADJ If you describe someone's behavior or actions as **masterful**, you mean that they show great skill. ❏ *...a masterful performance of boxing and punching skills.*

mas|ter key (master keys) N-COUNT A **master key** is a key which will open all the locks in a set, even though each lock has its own different key.

mas|ter|ly /mæstərli/ ADJ If you describe something as **masterly**, you admire it because it has been done extremely well or shows the highest level of ability and skill. [APPROVAL] ❏ *Malcolm Hebden gives a masterly performance.*

master|mind /mæstərmaɪnd/ (masterminds, masterminding, masterminded) ◻ V-T If you **mastermind** a difficult or complicated activity, you plan it in detail and then make sure that it happens successfully. ❏ *There are many theories as to who masterminded the attacks.* ◪ N-COUNT The **mastermind** behind a difficult or complicated plan, often a criminal one, is the person who is responsible for planning and organizing it. ❏ *He was the mastermind behind the plan to acquire the explosives.*

Mas|ter of Arts N-SING A **Master of Arts** degree is the same as an **MA** degree.

mas|ter of cer|emo|nies (masters of ceremonies) N-COUNT At events such as formal dinners, award ceremonies, and variety shows, the **master of ceremonies** is the person who introduces the speakers or performers, and who announces what is going to happen next.

Mas|ter of Sci|ence N-SING A **Master of Science** degree is the same as an **M.S.** or **M.Sc.** degree.

master|piece /mæstərpis/ (masterpieces) ◻ N-COUNT A **masterpiece** is an extremely good painting, novel, movie, or

master plan other work of art. ❏ *His book, I must add, is a masterpiece.* **2** N-COUNT An artist's, writer's, or composer's **masterpiece** is the best work that they have ever produced. ❏ *"Man's Fate," translated into sixteen languages, is probably his masterpiece.* **3** N-COUNT A **masterpiece** is an extremely clever or skillful example of something. ❏ *The whole thing was a masterpiece of crowd management.* **4** → See feature box at **fine art**

mas|ter plan (master plans) N-COUNT A **master plan** is a thorough plan that is intended to help someone succeed in a very difficult or important task. ❏ *...the master plan for the reform of the economy.*

mas|ter's de|gree (master's degrees) also **Master's degree** N-COUNT A **master's degree** is a university degree such as an M.A. or an M.S. which is of a higher level than a bachelor's degree and usually takes one or two years to complete.

master|stroke /mæstərstroʊk/ (masterstrokes) N-COUNT [usu sing] A **masterstroke** is something you do which is unexpected but very skillful and which helps you to achieve something. ❏ *His promise during the campaign to try to bring the war to an end was a political masterstroke.*

master|work /mæstərwɜrk/ (masterworks) N-COUNT [oft poss N, N of N] If you describe something such as a book or a painting as a **masterwork**, you think it is extremely good or the best that someone has produced. ❏ *They endure as masterworks of American musical theater.*

mas|tery /mæstəri/ N-UNCOUNT If you show **mastery** of a particular skill or language, you show that you have learned or understood it completely and have no difficulty using it. ❏ *He doesn't have mastery of the basic rules of grammar.*

mast|head /mæsthɛd/ (mastheads) **1** N-COUNT A ship's **masthead** is the highest part of its mast. **2** N-COUNT [usu sing, usu with poss] A newspaper's **masthead** is the part at the top of the front page where its name appears in big letters.

mas|ti|cate /mæstɪkeɪt/ (masticates, masticating, masticated) V-T/V-I When you **masticate** food, you chew it. [FORMAL] ❏ *Hines slowly masticated a shrimp.* ❏ *Don't gulp everything down without masticating.* • **mas|ti|ca|tion** /mæstɪkeɪʃən/ N-UNCOUNT ❏ *Poor digestion can be caused by defective mastication of the food in the mouth.*

mas|tiff /mæstɪf/ (mastiffs) N-COUNT A **mastiff** is a large, powerful, short-haired dog.

mas|tur|bate /mæstərbeɪt/ (masturbates, masturbating, masturbated) V-I If someone **masturbates**, they stroke or rub their own genitals in order to get sexual pleasure. ❏ *Do women masturbate as often as men?*

mat /mæt/ (mats) **1** N-COUNT A **mat** is a small piece of something such as cloth, card, or plastic which you put on a table to protect it from plates or cups. ❏ *The food is served on polished tables with mats.* **2** N-COUNT A **mat** is a small piece of carpet or other thick material which is put on the floor for protection, decoration, or comfort. ❏ *There was a letter on the mat.* **3** → see also **matte**

mata|dor /mætədɔr/ (matadors) N-COUNT A **matador** is the person in a bullfight who is supposed to kill the bull.

match ♦♦♦ /mætʃ/ (matches, matching, matched) **1** N-COUNT A **match** is an organized game of tennis, soccer, cricket, or some other sport. ❏ *He was watching a soccer match.* **2** N-COUNT A **match** is a small wooden stick with a substance on one end that produces a flame when you rub it along the rough side of a matchbox or a matchbook. ❏ *...a pack of cigarettes and a book of matches.* **3** V-RECIP If something of a particular color or design **matches** another thing, they have the same color or design, or have a pleasing appearance when they are used together. ❏ *"The shoes are too tight."—"Well, they do match your dress."* ❏ *All the chairs matched.* • PHRASAL VERB **Match up** means the same as **match**. ❏ *The pillow cover can match up with the sheets.* **4** V-RECIP If something such as an amount or a quality **matches** with another amount or quality, they are both the same or equal. If you **match** two things, you make them the same or equal. ❏ *Their strengths in memory and spatial skills matched.* ❏ *Our value system does not match with their value system.* **5** V-RECIP If one thing **matches** another, they are connected or suit each other in some way. ❏ *The students are asked to match*

794

material the books with the authors. ❏ *It can take time and effort to match buyers and sellers.* • PHRASAL VERB **Match up** means the same as **match**. ❏ *The consultant seeks to match up jobless professionals with small companies in need of expertise.* ❏ *They compared the fat intake of groups of vegetarians and meat eaters, and matched their diets up with levels of harmful blood fats.* **6** N-SING If a combination of things or people is a good **match**, they have a pleasing effect when placed or used together. ❏ *Helen's choice of lipstick was a good match for her skin tone.* **7** V-T If you **match** something, you are as good as it or equal to it, for example in speed, size, or quality. ❏ *They played some fine offensive football, but I think we matched them in every department.* **8** → see also **matched, matching**

USAGE

match

Don't use 'matches to.' For example, don't say '~~Do these shoes match to my dress?~~' You say that the first thing **matches** the other thing, for example, 'Do these shoes match my dress?'

---

match|book /mætʃbʊk/ (matchbooks) N-COUNT A **matchbook** is a folded piece of cardboard with paper matches inside. [mainly AM]

match|box /mætʃbɒks/ (matchboxes) N-COUNT A **matchbox** is a small box that you buy with matches in it.

matched /mætʃt/ **1** ADJ [adv ADJ] If you say that two people are well **matched**, you mean that they have qualities that will enable them to have a good relationship. ❏ *My parents were not very well matched.* **2** ADJ [adv ADJ] In sports and other competitions, if the two opponents or teams are well **matched**, they are both of the same standard in strength or ability. ❏ *Two well-matched sides conjured up an entertaining game.*

match|ing /mætʃɪŋ/ ADJ [ADJ n] **Matching** is used to describe things that are of the same color or design. ❏ *...a coat and a matching handbag.*

match|less /mætʃlɪs/ ADJ [usu ADJ n] You can use **matchless** to emphasize that you think something is extremely good. [EMPHASIS] ❏ *A timeless comic actor – his simplicity and his apparent ease are matchless.* ❏ *The Savoy provides a matchless hotel experience.*

match|maker /mætʃmeɪkər/ (matchmakers) N-COUNT A **matchmaker** is someone who tries to encourage people they know to form a romantic relationship or to get married. ❏ *Some friends played matchmaker and had us both over to dinner.*

match|making /mætʃmeɪkɪŋ/ N-UNCOUNT **Matchmaking** is the activity of encouraging people you know to form relationships or get married.

match play N-UNCOUNT [usu N n] **Match play** is a form of golf where the game is scored by the number of holes someone wins rather than the number of strokes it takes them to complete the course.

match point (match points) N-VAR In a game of tennis, **match point** is the situation when the player who is in the lead can win the whole match if they win the next point.

match|stick /mætʃstɪk/ (matchsticks) N-COUNT A **matchstick** is the wooden part of a match.

mate ♦◊◊ /meɪt/ (mates, mating, mated) **1** N-COUNT Someone's wife, husband, or sexual partner can be referred to as their **mate**. ❏ *He has found his ideal mate.* **2** N-COUNT An animal's **mate** is its sexual partner. ❏ *The males guard their mates zealously.* **3** V-RECIP When animals **mate**, a male and a female have sex in order to produce young. ❏ *This allows the pair to mate properly and stops the hen from staying in the nest.* ❏ *They want the males to mate with wild females.* **4** → see also **classmate, roommate, running mate**

ma|teri|al ♦♦◊ /mətɪəriəl/ (materials) **1** N-VAR A **material** is a solid substance. ❏ *...electrons in a conducting material such as a metal.* **2** N-MASS **Material** is cloth. ❏ *...the thick material of her skirt.* **3** N-PLURAL **Materials** are the things that you need for a particular activity. ❏ *The builders ran out of materials.* **4** N-UNCOUNT Ideas or information that are used as a basis for a book, play, or film can be referred to as **material**. ❏ *In my version of the story, I added some new material.* **5** ADJ **Material** things are related to possessions or money, rather than to more abstract things such as ideas or values. ❏ *Every room must have been stuffed with material things.* • **ma|teri|al|ly** ADV

materialism ❑ He has tried to help this child materially and spiritually. **6** ADJ [ADJ n] **Material** evidence or information is directly relevant and important in a legal or academic argument. [FORMAL] ❑ The nature and availability of material evidence was not to be discussed. **7** → See feature box at **recycle**

SYNONYMS

material
NOUN
1
substance: The substance that's causing the problem comes from the barley.
matter: They feed mostly on decaying vegetable matter.
stuff: I don't object to the powdered stuff if it's all you've got.
2
cloth: She began cleaning the wound with a piece of cloth.
fabric: ...small squares of red, cotton fabric.
textile: ...decorative textiles for the home.

---

ma|teri|al|ism /mətɪəriəlɪzəm/ **1** N-UNCOUNT **Materialism** is the attitude of someone who attaches a lot of importance to money and wants to possess a lot of material things. ❑ ...the rising consumer materialism in society at large. **2** N-UNCOUNT **Materialism** is the belief that only physical matter exists, and that there is no spiritual world. ❑ Scientific materialism thus triumphed over ignorance and superstition.

ma|teri|al|ist /mətɪəriəlɪst/ ADJ [usu ADJ n] **Materialist** is used to describe things relating to the philosophy of materialism. ❑ ...the materialist view of nature and society.

ma|teri|al|is|tic /mətɪəriəlɪstɪk/ ADJ If you describe a person or society as **materialistic**, you are critical of them because they attach too much importance to money and material possessions. [DISAPPROVAL] ❑ During the 1980s the U.S. became a very materialistic society.

ma|teri|al|ize /mətɪəriəlaɪz/ (materializes, materializing, materialized)
in BRIT, also use **materialise**
1 V-I [usu with brd-neg] If a possible or expected event does not **materialize**, it does not happen. ❑ A rebellion by radicals failed to materialize. **2** V-I If a person or thing **materializes**, they suddenly appear, after they have been invisible or in another place. ❑ A moment later Jane materialized, coming in the front door.

ma|ter|nal /mətɜrnᵊl/ **1** ADJ **Maternal** is used to describe feelings or actions which are typical of those of a kind mother toward her child. ❑ She had little maternal instinct. **2** ADJ [ADJ n] **Maternal** is used to describe things that relate to the mother of a baby. ❑ Maternal smoking can damage the unborn child. **3** ADJ [ADJ n] A **maternal** relative is one who is related through a person's mother rather than their father. ❑ Her maternal grandfather was mayor of Karachi.

ma|ter|nity /mətɜrnɪti/ **1** ADJ [ADJ n] **Maternity** is used to describe things relating to the help and medical care given to a woman when she is pregnant and when she gives birth. ❑ Your job will be kept open for your return after maternity leave. **2** → See feature box at **working**

math /mæθ/ N-UNCOUNT **Math** is the same as **mathematics**. [AM] ❑ He studied math in college.
in BRIT, use **maths**

math|emati|cal /mæθəmætɪkᵊl/ **1** ADJ [ADJ n] Something that is **mathematical** involves numbers and calculations. ❑ ...mathematical calculations. • **math|emati|cal|ly** /mæθəmætɪkli/ ADV ❑ ...a mathematically complicated formula. **2** ADJ If you have **mathematical** abilities or a **mathematical** mind, you are good at doing calculations or understanding problems that involve numbers. ❑ ...a mathematical genius. • **math|emati|cal|ly** ADV [ADV -ed/adj] ❑ Anyone can be an astrologer as long as they are mathematically minded.

math|ema|ti|cian /mæθəmətɪʃᵊn/ (mathematicians) **1** N-COUNT A **mathematician** is a person who is trained in the study of numbers and calculations. ❑ The risks can be so complex that banks hire mathematicians to assess them. **2** N-COUNT A **mathematician** is a person who is good at doing calculations and using numbers. ❑ I'm not a very good mathematician.

math|emat|ics /mæθəmætɪks/ **1** N-UNCOUNT **Mathematics** is the study of numbers, quantities, or shapes. ❑ ...a professor of mathematics at Boston College. **2** N-UNCOUNT The **mathematics** of a problem is the calculations that are involved in it. ❑ Once you understand the mathematics of debt you can work your way out of it.

maths /mæθs/ N-UNCOUNT **Maths** is the same as **mathematics**. [BRIT]

mati|nee /mætᵊneɪ/ (matinees) N-COUNT A **matinee** is a performance of a play or a showing of a movie which takes place in the afternoon.

ma|tri|arch /meɪtriɑrk/ (matriarchs) **1** N-COUNT A **matriarch** is a woman who rules in a society in which power passes from mother to daughter. **2** N-COUNT A **matriarch** is an old and powerful female member of a family, for example a grandmother.

ma|tri|ar|chal /meɪtriɑrkᵊl/ **1** ADJ A **matriarchal** society, family, or system is one in which the rulers are female and power or property is passed from mother to daughter. ❑ ...the 3,000 years of the matriarchal Sumerian society. **2** ADJ [usu ADJ n] If you describe a woman as **matriarchal**, you mean that she has authority and power within her family or group. ❑ ...the matriarchal figure of his grandmother.

ma|tri|ar|chy /meɪtriɑrki/ (matriarchies) N-VAR A **matriarchy** is a system in which power or property is passed from mother to daughter.

ma|tri|ces /meɪtrɪsiz/ **Matrices** is the plural of **matrix**.

ma|tricu|late /mətrɪkyəleɪt/ (matriculates, matriculating, matriculated) V-I In some countries, if you **matriculate**, you register formally as a student at a university, or you satisfy the academic requirements necessary for registration for a course. ❑ He matriculated in the English Literature Department at the Tokyo Imperial University. • **ma|tricu|la|tion** /mətrɪkyəleɪʃᵊn/ N-UNCOUNT ❑ In secondary schools across South Africa, students are taking matriculation exams.

mat|ri|mo|nial /mætrɪmoʊniəl/ ADJ [usu ADJ n] **Matrimonial** means concerning marriage or married people. [FORMAL] ❑ ...the matrimonial home.

mat|ri|mo|ny /mætrɪmoʊni/ N-UNCOUNT **Matrimony** is marriage. [FORMAL] ❑ ...the bonds of matrimony.

ma|trix /meɪtrɪks/ (matrices) **1** N-COUNT A **matrix** is the environment or context in which something such as a society develops and grows. [FORMAL] ❑ ...the matrix of their culture. **2** N-COUNT In mathematics, a **matrix** is an arrangement of numbers, symbols, or letters in rows and columns which is used in solving mathematical problems.

ma|tron /meɪtrən/ (matrons) **1** N-COUNT People sometimes refer to middle-aged women as **matrons**. [OLD-FASHIONED or WRITTEN] **2** N-COUNT The **matron** in a hospital or other institution is the woman who is in charge of domestic matters. **Matron** is also used to refer to a female officer in a prison. [AM, OLD-FASHIONED]

ma|tron|ly /meɪtrənli/ ADJ You can use **matronly** to describe a woman who is fairly fat and looks middle-aged, especially if you think the clothes she is wearing are not fashionable or attractive. ❑ ...a matronly woman with an air of authority.

ma|tron of hon|or (matrons of honor)
in BRIT, use **matron of honour**
N-COUNT A **matron of honor** is a married woman who serves as the chief bridesmaid at a wedding. ❑ The groom's sister Karla Walton was the matron of honor.

matte /mæt/ also **matt, mat** ADJ A **matte** color, paint, or surface is dull rather than shiny. ❑ ...a creamy white matte emulsion.

mat|ted /mætɪd/ ADJ If you describe someone's hair as **matted**, you mean that it has become a thick and tangled mass, often because it is wet or dirty. ❑ She had matted hair and torn, dusty clothes.

mat|ter ✦✦✦ /mætər/ (matters, mattering, mattered) **1** N-COUNT A **matter** is a task, situation, or event which you have to deal with or think about, especially one that involves problems. ❑ It was clear that she wanted to discuss some private matter. ❑ Business matters drew him to Louisville. **2** N-PLURAL [no det] You use **matters** to refer to the situation you are talking about, especially when something is affecting the situation in some way. ❑ We have no objection to this change, but doubt that it will significantly improve matters. ◻ If it would facilitate matters, I would be happy to come to New York. **3** N-SING If you say that a situation is a **matter** of a particular thing, you mean that that is the most important thing to be done or considered when you are involved in the situation or explaining it. ◻ History is always a matter of interpretation. ◻ Observance of the law is a matter of principle for us. **4** N-UNCOUNT Printed **matter** consists of books, newspapers, and other texts that are printed. Reading **matter** consists of things that are suitable for reading, such as books and newspapers. ◻ ...the government's plans to place a tax on printed matter. **5** N-UNCOUNT **Matter** is the physical part of the universe consisting of solids, liquids, and gases. ◻ A proton is an elementary particle of matter that possesses a positive charge. **6** N-UNCOUNT You use **matter** to refer to a particular type of substance. ◻ ...waste matter from industries. **7** N-SING You use **matter** in expressions such as '**What's the matter?**' or '**Is anything the matter?**' when you think that someone has a problem and you want to know what it is. ◻ Carole, what's the matter? You don't seem happy. **8** N-SING You use **matter** in expressions such as '**a matter of weeks**' when you are emphasizing how small an amount is or how short a period of time is. [EMPHASIS] ◻ Within a matter of days she was back at work. **9** V-T/V-I [no cont, usu with brd-neg] If you say that something does not **matter**, you mean that it is not important to you because it does not have an effect on you or on a particular situation. ◻ A lot of the food goes on the floor but that doesn't matter. ◻ As long as staff members are well-groomed, it does not matter how long their hair is. **10** → see also **subject matter** **11** PHRASE If you say that something is **another matter** or **a different matter**, you mean that it is very different from the situation that you have just discussed. ◻ Being responsible for one's own health is one thing, but being responsible for another person's health is quite a different matter. **12** PHRASE If you are going to do something **as a matter of** urgency or priority, you are going to do it as soon as possible, because it is important. ◻ Your doctors can help a great deal and you need to talk about it with them as a matter of urgency. **13** PHRASE If something is **no easy matter**, it is difficult to do it. ◻ Choosing the color for the living-room walls was no easy matter. **14** PHRASE If someone says **that's the end of the matter** or **that's an end to the matter**, they mean that a decision that has been taken must not be changed or discussed any more. ◻ "He's moving in here," Maria said. "So that's the end of the matter." **15** PHRASE You use **the fact of the matter is** or **the truth of the matter is** to introduce a fact which supports what you are saying or which is not widely known, for example because it is a secret. ◻ The fact of the matter is that most people consume far more protein than they actually need. **16** CONVENTION You say '**it doesn't matter**' to tell someone who is apologizing to you that you are not angry or upset, and that they should not worry. ◻ "Did I wake you?"—"Yes, but it doesn't matter." **17** PHRASE If you say that something **makes matters worse**, you mean that it makes a difficult situation even more difficult. ◻ Don't let yourself despair; this will only make matters worse. **18** PHRASE You use **no matter** in expressions such as '**no matter how**' and '**no matter what**' to say that something is true or happens in all circumstances. ◻ No matter what your age, you can lose weight by following this program. **19 a matter of life and death** → see **death 20 as a matter of course** → see **course 21 as a matter of fact** → see **fact**

USAGE

matter
You can say **What's the matter?** to ask about a problem or difficulty. Don't use 'the matter' with this meaning in other types of sentence. Don't say, for example, '~~The matter is that we don't know where she is.~~' Say **the problem** or **the trouble**. What's **the matter?** You seem unhappy. **The problem** is that she can't cook.

mat|ter-of-fact ADJ If you describe a person as **matter-of-fact**, you mean that they show no emotions such as enthusiasm, anger, or surprise, especially in a situation where you would expect them to be emotional. ◻ John was doing his best to give Francis the news in a matter-of-fact way.
● **matter-of-factly** ADV [ADV after v] ◻ "She thinks you're a spy," Scott said matter-of-factly.

mat|ting /mætɪŋ/ N-UNCOUNT **Matting** is strong, thick material, usually made from a material like rope, straw, or rushes, which is used as a floor covering.

mat|tress /mætrɪs/ (mattresses) N-COUNT A **mattress** is the large, flat object which is put on a bed to make it comfortable to sleep on.

matu|ra|tion /mætʃəreɪʃ^ən/ **1** N-UNCOUNT The **maturation** of something such as wine or cheese is the process of its being left for a time to become mature. [FORMAL] ◻ The period of maturation is determined by the cellar master. **2** N-UNCOUNT The **maturation** of a young person's body is the process of it becoming like an adult's. [FORMAL]

ma|ture /mətyʊər, -tʊər, -tʃʊər/ (matures, maturing, matured, maturer, maturest) **1** V-I When a child or young animal **matures**, it becomes an adult. ◻ You will learn what to expect as your child matures physically. **2** V-I When something **matures**, it reaches a state of complete development. ◻ When the trees matured they were cut. **3** V-I If someone **matures**, they become more fully developed in their personality and emotional behavior. ◻ They have matured way beyond their age. **4** ADJ If you describe someone as **mature**, you think that they are fully developed and balanced in their personality and emotional behavior. [APPROVAL] ◻ They are emotionally mature and should behave responsibly. **5** V-T/V-I If something such as wine or cheese **matures** or **is matured**, it is left for a time to allow its full flavor or strength to develop. ◻ Unlike wine, brandy matures only in wood, not glass. **6** ADJ **Mature** cheese or wine has been left for a time to allow its full flavor or strength to develop. ◻ Grate some mature cheddar cheese. **7** V-I When an investment such as an insurance policy or bond **matures**, it reaches the stage when the company pays you back the money you have saved, and the interest your money has earned. [BUSINESS] ◻ These bonuses will be paid when your savings plan matures in ten years' time. **8** ADJ If you say that someone is **mature** or of **mature** years, you are saying politely that they are middle-aged or old. [POLITENESS] ◻ ...a man of mature years who had been in the job for longer than most of the members could remember.

ma|ture stu|dent (mature students) N-COUNT A **mature student** is a person who begins their studies at a university or college a number of years after leaving school, so that they are older than most of the people who are studying with. [BRIT]

in AM, usually use **adult student**

ma|tur|ity /mətyʊərɪti, -tʊər-, -tʃʊər-/ (maturities) **1** N-UNCOUNT **Maturity** is the state of being fully developed or adult. ◻ Humans experience a delayed maturity; we arrive at all stages of life later than other mammals. **2** N-UNCOUNT Someone's **maturity** is their quality of being fully developed in their personality and emotional behavior. ◻ Her speech showed great maturity and humanity. **3** N-VAR When an investment such as an insurance policy or bond reaches **maturity**, it reaches the stage when the company pays you back the money you have saved, and the interest your money has earned. [BUSINESS] ◻ Customers are told what their policies will be worth on maturity, not what they are worth today.

maud|lin /mɔdlɪn/ **1** ADJ If you describe someone as **maudlin**, you mean that they are being sad and sentimental in a foolish way, perhaps because of drinking alcohol. ◻ Jimmy turned maudlin after three drinks. ◻ ...maudlin self-pity. **2** ADJ If you describe a song, book, or movie as **maudlin**, you are criticizing it for being very sentimental. [DISAPPROVAL] ◻ ...the most maudlin song of all time.

maul /mɔl/ (mauls, mauling, mauled) V-T If you **are mauled** by an animal, you are violently attacked by it and badly injured. ◻ He had been mauled by a bear.

Maun|dy Thurs|day /mɔndi θɜrzdeɪ, θɜrzdi/ N-UNCOUNT **Maundy Thursday** is the Thursday before Easter Sunday.

Mau|ri|tian /mɔrɪʃ^ən/ (Mauritians) **1** ADJ **Mauritian** means belonging or relating to Mauritius, or to its people or culture. **2** N-COUNT A **Mauritian** is a Mauritian citizen, or a person of Mauritian origin.

mau|so|leum /mɔzəliəm/ (mausoleums) N-COUNT A **mausoleum** is a building which contains the grave of a famous person or the graves of a rich family.

mauve /moʊv/ (mauves) COLOR Something that is **mauve** is of a pale purple color. ◻ It bears clusters of mauve flowers in early summer.

ma|ven /meɪvᵊn/ (**mavens**) N-COUNT [oft with supp] A **maven** is a person who is an expert on a particular subject. [AM] ❑ ...*the gossip columnists and fashion mavens of New York City.*

mav|er|ick /mævərɪk/ (**mavericks**) N-COUNT If you describe someone as a **maverick**, you mean that they are unconventional and independent, and do not think or behave in the same way as other people. ❑ *He was too much of a maverick ever to hold high office.* • ADJ [ADJ n] **Maverick** is also an adjective. ❑ ...*a maverick group of scientists, who oppose the prevailing medical opinion on the disease.*

maw /mɔː/ (**maws**) N-COUNT [usu sing, usu with supp] If you describe something as a **maw**, you mean that it is like a big open mouth which swallows everything near it. [LITERARY] ❑ *They were helping to chop wood to feed the red maw of the stove.*

mawk|ish /mɔːkɪʃ/ ADJ You can describe something as **mawkish** when you think it is sentimental and silly. [DISAPPROVAL] ❑ *A sordid, sentimental plot unwinds, with an inevitable mawkish ending.*

max /mæks/ (**maxes, maxing, maxed**)
▶ **max out** PHRASAL VERB If you **max out** something such as money or credit, you use it all up. [INFORMAL] ❑ *He claimed his wife had drained his bank account and maxed out all his credit cards.* ❑ *I have so much credit-card debt; I maxed them out to pay for my training.*

max. /mæks/ ADJ [num ADJ, ADJ n] **Max.** is the abbreviation for maximum. ❑ *I'll give him eight out of 10, max.*

max|im /mæksɪm/ (**maxims**) N-COUNT A **maxim** is a rule for good or sensible behavior, especially one in the form of a saying. ❑ *I believe in the maxim "if it ain't broke, don't fix it."*

max|im|ize /mæksɪmaɪz/ (**maximizes, maximizing, maximized**)

| in BRIT, also use **maximise** |

1 V-T If you **maximize** something, you make it as great in amount or importance as you can. ❑ *In order to maximize profit, the firm would seek to maximize output.* **2** V-T If you **maximize** a window on a computer screen, you make it as large as possible. ❑ *Click on the square icon to maximize the window.*

maxi|mum ♦◇◇ /mæksɪməm/ **1** ADJ [ADJ n] You use **maximum** to describe an amount which is the largest that is possible, allowed, or required. ❑ *Under planning law the maximum height for a fence or hedge is 6 feet.* • N-SING **Maximum** is also a noun. ❑ *The law provides for a maximum of two years in prison.* **2** ADJ [ADJ n] You use **maximum** to indicate how great an amount is. ❑ *I need the maximum amount of information you can give me.* ❑ *It was achieved with minimum fuss and maximum efficiency.* **3** ADV [amount ADV] If you say that something is a particular amount **maximum**, you mean that this is the greatest amount it should be or could possibly be, although a smaller amount is acceptable or very possible. ❑ *We need an extra 6 grams a day maximum.*

may ♦♦♦ /meɪ/

| **May** is a modal verb. It is used with the base form of a verb. |

1 MODAL You use **may** to indicate that something will possibly happen or be true in the future, but you cannot be certain. [VAGUENESS] ❑ *We may have some rain today.* ❑ *I may be back next year.* **2** MODAL You use **may** to indicate that there is a possibility that something is true, but you cannot be certain. [VAGUENESS] ❑ *Civil rights officials say there may be hundreds of other cases of racial violence.* **3** MODAL You use **may** to indicate that something is sometimes true or is true in some circumstances. ❑ *A vegetarian diet may not provide enough calories for a child's normal growth.* **4** MODAL You use **may have** with a past participle when suggesting that it is possible that something happened or was true, or when giving a possible explanation for something. [VAGUENESS] ❑ *He may have been to some of those places.* **5** MODAL You use **may** in statements where you are accepting the truth of a situation, but contrasting it with something that is more important. ❑ *I may be almost 50, but there's not much I've forgotten.* **6** MODAL You use **may** when you are mentioning a quality or fact about something that people can make use of if they want to. ❑ *The bag has narrow straps, so it may be worn over the shoulder or carried in the hand.* **7** MODAL You use **may** to indicate that someone is allowed to do something, usually because of a rule or law. You use **may not** to indicate that someone is not allowed to do something. ❑ *In the US, any two persons may marry provided that both persons are at least 16 years of age on the day of their marriage.* **8** MODAL You use **may** when you are giving permission to someone to do something, or when asking for permission. [FORMAL] ❑ *Mr. Hobbs? May we come in?* **9** MODAL You use **may** when you are making polite requests. [FORMAL, POLITENESS] ❑ *I'd like the use of your living room, if I may.* **10** MODAL You use **may** when you are mentioning the reaction or attitude that you think someone is likely to have to something you are about to say. ❑ *You know, Brian, whatever you may think, I work hard for a living.* **11** MODAL If you do something so that a particular thing may happen, you do it so that there is an opportunity for that thing to happen. ❑ ...*the need for an increase in the numbers of surgeons so that patients may be treated as soon as possible.* **12** **may as well** → see **well** ③

May ♦♦♦ /meɪ/ (**Mays**) N-VAR **May** is the fifth month of the year in the Western calendar. ❑ *Graduation ceremonies are held in early May.*

may|be ♦♦◇ /meɪbi/ **1** ADV [ADV with cl/group] You use **maybe** to express uncertainty, for example when you do not know that something is definitely true, or when you are mentioning something that may possibly happen in the future in the way you describe. [VAGUENESS] ❑ *Maybe she is in love.* ❑ *I do think about having children, maybe when I'm 40.* **2** ADV [ADV with cl/group] You use **maybe** when you are making suggestions or giving advice. **Maybe** is also used to introduce polite requests. [POLITENESS] ❑ *Maybe we can go to the movies or something.* ❑ *Maybe you'd better tell me what this is all about.* **3** ADV [ADV cl] You use **maybe** to indicate that, although a comment is partly true, there is also another point of view that should be considered. ❑ *Maybe there is jealousy, but I think the envy is more powerful.* **4** ADV [ADV as reply] You can say **maybe** as a response to a question or remark, when you do not want to agree or disagree. ❑ *"Is she coming back?" "Maybe. No one hears from her."* **5** ADV [ADV amount] You use **maybe** when you are making a rough guess at a number, quantity, or value, rather than stating it exactly. [VAGUENESS] ❑ *The men were maybe a hundred feet away and coming closer.* **6** ADV [ADV with cl/group] People use **maybe** to mean 'sometimes,' particularly in a series of general statements about what someone does, or about something that regularly happens. ❑ *They'll come to the bar for a year, or maybe even two, then they'll find another favorite spot.*

May|day /meɪdeɪ/ (**Maydays**) N-COUNT If someone in a plane or ship sends out a **Mayday** or a **Mayday** message, they send out a radio message calling for help because they are in serious difficulty. ❑ *He raced to pick up the life jackets while his stepmother sent out a Mayday call.*

May Day N-UNCOUNT **May Day** is the 1st of May, which in many countries is celebrated as a public holiday, especially as one in honor of working people.

may|fly /meɪflaɪ/ (**mayflies**) N-COUNT A **mayfly** is an insect which lives near water and only lives for a very short time as an adult.

may|hem /meɪhem/ N-UNCOUNT You use **mayhem** to refer to a situation that is not controlled or ordered, when people are behaving in a disorganized, confused, and often violent way. ❑ *Their arrival caused mayhem as crowds of refugees rushed towards them.*

mayn't /meɪənt/ **Mayn't** is a spoken form of 'may not.' [OLD-FASHIONED]

mayo /meɪoʊ/ N-UNCOUNT **Mayo** is the same as **mayonnaise**. [INFORMAL]

may|on|naise /meɪəneɪz/ N-UNCOUNT **Mayonnaise** is a thick, pale sauce made from egg yolks and oil. It is put on food such as salad and sandwiches.

mayor ♦◇◇ /meɪər, meər/ (**mayors**) N-COUNT The **mayor** of a town or city is the person who has been elected for a fixed period of time to run its government. ❑ ...*the new mayor of New York.*

mayor|al /meɪərəl/ ADJ [ADJ n] **Mayoral** activities or things relate or belong to a mayor. ❑ ... *the former New York mayoral candidate.*

may've /meɪəv/ **May've** is a spoken form of 'may have,' especially when 'have' is an auxiliary verb.

maze /meɪz/ (mazes) **1** N-COUNT A **maze** is a complex system of passages or paths between walls or hedges and is designed to confuse people who try to find their way through it, often as a form of amusement. ❑ *The palace has extensive gardens, a maze, and tennis courts.* **2** N-COUNT A **maze** of streets, rooms, or tunnels is a large number of them that are connected in a complicated way, so that it is difficult to find your way through them. ❑ *The children lead me through the maze of alleys to the edge of the city.* **3** N-COUNT You can refer to a set of ideas, topics, or rules as a **maze** when a large number of them are related to each other in a complicated way that makes them difficult to understand. ❑ *The book tries to steer you through the maze of alternative therapies.*

M.B.A. /ɛm bi eɪ/ (**M.B.A.s**) also **MBA** N-COUNT An **M.B.A.** is a master's degree in business administration. You can also refer to a person who has this degree as an **M.B.A.** **M.B.A.** is an abbreviation for 'Master of Business Administration.'

MBO /ɛm bi oʊ/ (**MBOs**) N-COUNT **MBO** is an abbreviation for **management buyout**. [BUSINESS] ❑ *...the largest MBO ever undertaken by Australian financial investors.*

MC /ɛm si/ (**MCs**) N-COUNT; N-TITLE An **MC** is the same as a **master of ceremonies**.

McCoy /məkɔɪ/ PHRASE If you describe someone or something as **the real McCoy**, you mean that they really are what they claim to be and are not an imitation. [INFORMAL]

M.D. /ɛm di/ (**M.D.s**) N-COUNT **M.D.** is an abbreviation for 'medical doctor.' You can also refer to a person who has this degree as an **M.D.**

me ✦✦✦ /mi, STRONG mi/ PRON-SING [V PRON, prep PRON] A speaker or writer uses **me** to refer to himself or herself. **Me** is a first person singular pronoun. **Me** is used as the object of a verb or a preposition. ❑ *I had to make important decisions that would affect me for the rest of my life.* ❑ *He asked me to go to California with him.*

USAGE
me or myself?
Don't use '**me**' when the person who is speaking is both the subject and the object of the verb. Don't say, for example, '~~I got me a drink~~.' Say 'I got **myself** a drink.' *I made **myself** some breakfast.*

mead /miːd/ N-UNCOUNT In former times, **mead** was an alcoholic drink made of honey, spices, and water.

mead|ow /mɛdoʊ/ (**meadows**) N-COUNT A **meadow** is a field which has grass and flowers growing in it.

mea|ger /miːgər/
in BRIT, use **meagre**
ADJ If you describe an amount or quantity of something as **meager**, you are critical of it because it is very small or not enough. [DISAPPROVAL] ❑ *The rations that they gave us were meager and inadequate.*

meal ✦◊◊ /mil/ (**meals**) **1** N-COUNT A **meal** is an occasion when people sit down and eat, usually at a regular time. ❑ *She sat next to him throughout the meal.* **2** N-COUNT A **meal** is the food you eat during a meal. ❑ *The waiter offered him red wine or white wine with his meal.* **3** PHRASE If you have a **square meal**, you have a large, healthy meal. ❑ *The troops are very tired. They haven't had a square meal for four or five days.*

meals on wheels also **Meals on Wheels** N-UNCOUNT **Meals on wheels** is a service that delivers hot meals to people who are too old or too sick to cook for themselves.

meal tick|et N-SING [usu a N] If you say that something or someone is a **meal ticket**, you mean that they provide a person with money or a lifestyle which they would not otherwise have. ❑ *His chosen field was unlikely to be a meal ticket for life.* ❑ *I don't intend to be a meal ticket for anyone.*

meal|time /miltaɪm/ (**mealtimes**) N-VAR [usu pl] **Mealtimes** are occasions when you eat breakfast, lunch, or dinner. ❑ *At mealtimes he would watch her eat.*

mealy /mili/ ADJ Food that is dry and powdery can be described as **mealy**. ❑ *The boiled potato was mealy.*

mealy-mouthed ADJ If you say that someone is being **mealy-mouthed**, you are critical of them for being unwilling to speak in a simple or open way because they want to avoid talking directly about something unpleasant. [DISAPPROVAL] ❑ *He repeated that he did not intend to be mealy-mouthed with the country's leaders.*

MEAN
① VERB USES
② ADJECTIVE USES
③ NOUN USE
---

① **mean** ✦✦✦ /min/ (**means, meaning, meant**) **1** V-T [no cont] If you want to know what a word, code, signal, or gesture **means**, you want to know what it refers to or what its message is. ❑ *"Credible" means "believable."* ❑ *What does "evidence" mean?* **2** V-T [no cont] If you ask someone what they **mean**, you are asking them to explain exactly what or who they are referring to or what they are intending to say. ❑ *Do you mean me?* ❑ *Let me illustrate what I mean with an old story.* **3** V-T [no cont] If something **means** something to you, it is important to you in some way. ❑ *The idea that she witnessed this shameful incident meant nothing to him.* **4** V-T [no cont] If one thing **means** another, it shows that the second thing exists or is true. ❑ *An enlarged prostate does not necessarily mean cancer.* **5** V-T [no cont] If one thing **means** another, the first thing leads to the second thing happening. ❑ *It would almost certainly mean the end of NATO.* **6** V-T If doing one thing **means** doing another, it involves doing the second thing. ❑ *Children universally prefer to live in peace and security, even if that means living with only one parent.* **7** V-T [no cont] If you say that you **mean** what you are saying, you are telling someone that you are serious about it and are not joking, exaggerating, or just being polite. ❑ *He says you're fired if you're not back at work on Friday. And I think he meant it.* **8** V-T [no cont] If you say that someone **meant** to do something, you are saying that they did it deliberately. ❑ *I didn't mean to hurt you.* ❑ *If that sounds harsh, it is meant to.* **9** V-T [no cont, with brd-neg] If you say that someone did not **mean** any harm, offense, or disrespect, you are saying that they did not intend to upset or offend people or to cause problems, even though they may in fact have done so. ❑ *I'm sure he didn't mean any harm.* **10** V-T [no cont] If you **mean** to do something, you intend or plan to do it. ❑ *Summer is the perfect time to catch up on the new books you meant to read.* **11** V-T [usu passive, no cont] If you say that something **was meant** to happen, you believe that it was made to happen by God or fate, and did not just happen by chance. ❑ *John was constantly reassuring me that we were meant to be together.* **12** PHRASE You say '**I mean**' when making clearer something that you have just said. [SPOKEN] ❑ *It was his idea. Gordon's, I mean.* **13** PHRASE You can use '**I mean**' to introduce a statement, especially one that justifies something that you have just said. [SPOKEN] ❑ *I'm sure he wouldn't mind. I mean, I was the one who asked him.* **14** PHRASE You say **I mean** when correcting something that you have just said. [SPOKEN] ❑ *It was law or classics – I mean English or classics.* **15** PHRASE If you **know what it means** to do something, you know everything that is involved in a particular activity or experience, especially the effect that it has on you. ❑ *I know what it means to lose a child under such tragic circumstances.* **16** PHRASE If a name, word, or phrase **means something to** you, you have heard it before and you know what it refers to. ❑ *"Oh, Gairdner," he said, as if that meant something to him.* **17** PHRASE You use '**you mean**' in a question to check that you have understood what someone has said. ❑ *What accident? You mean Christina's?* **18** → see also **meaning, means, meant 19 you know what I mean** → see **know** ②

USAGE
mean
Don't use '**mean**' when you are talking about people's opinions or beliefs. Use **think** or **believe**. Don't say, for example, '~~Most of the directors mean he should resign.~~' Say 'Most of the directors **think** he should resign.' *Scientists **believe** that life began four billion years ago.*

② **mean** /min/ (**meaner, meanest**) **1** ADJ If someone is being **mean**, they are being unkind to another person, for example by not allowing them to do something. ❑ *The little girls had locked themselves in the room because Mack had been mean to them.*

2 ADJ If you describe a person or animal as **mean**, you are saying that they are very bad-tempered and cruel. [mainly AM] ❑ *The state's former commissioner of prisons once called Leonard the meanest man he'd ever seen.* **3** ADJ If you describe someone as **mean**, you are being critical of them because they are unwilling to spend much money or to use very much of a particular thing. [BRIT, DISAPPROVAL]

in AM, use **cheap**

③ **mean** /miːn/ **1** N-SING The **mean** is a number that is the average of a set of numbers. ❑ *Take a hundred and twenty values and calculate the mean.* **2** → see also **means**

me|ander /miændər/ (meanders, meandering, meandered) **1** V-I If a river or road **meanders**, it has a lot of bends, rather than going in a straight line from one place to another. ❑ *We took a gravel road that meandered through farmland.* ❑ *We crossed a small iron bridge over a meandering stream.* **2** V-I If you **meander** somewhere, you move slowly and not in a straight line. ❑ *We meandered through a landscape of mountains, rivers, and vineyards.*

mean|ing ◆◇◇ /miːnɪŋ/ (meanings) **1** N-VAR The **meaning** of a word, expression, or gesture is the thing or idea that it refers to or represents and which can be explained using other words. ❑ *I hadn't a clue as to the meaning of "activism."* **2** N-VAR The **meaning** of what someone says or of something such as a book or film is the thoughts or ideas that are intended to be expressed by it. ❑ *Unsure of the meaning of this remark, Ryle chose to remain silent.* **3** N-UNCOUNT If an activity or action has **meaning**, it has a purpose and is worthwhile. ❑ *Art has real meaning when it helps people to understand themselves.*

mean|ing|ful /miːnɪŋfəl/ **1** ADJ If you describe something as **meaningful**, you mean that it is serious, important, or useful in some way. ❑ *She believes these talks will be the start of a constructive and meaningful dialogue.* **2** ADJ [ADJ n] A **meaningful** look or gesture is one that is intended to express something, usually to a particular person, without anything being said. ❑ *Upon the utterance of this word, Dan and Harry exchanged a quick, meaningful look.* ● **mean|ing|ful|ly** ADV ❑ *He glanced meaningfully at the other policeman, then he went up the stairs.*

mean|ing|ful|ly /miːnɪŋfəli/ **1** ADV [ADV after v] You use **meaningfully** to indicate that someone has deliberately chosen their words in order to express something in a way which is not obvious but which is understood by the person they are talking to. ❑ *"I have a knack for making friends, you know," she added meaningfully.* **2** → see also **meaningful**

mean|ing|less /miːnɪŋlɪs/ **1** ADJ If something that someone says or writes is **meaningless**, it has no meaning, or appears to have no meaning. ❑ *The sentence "kicked the ball the man" is meaningless.* **2** ADJ Something that is **meaningless** in a particular situation is not important or relevant. ❑ *Fines are meaningless to guys earning millions.* **3** ADJ If something that you do is **meaningless**, it has no purpose and is not at all worthwhile. ❑ *They seek strong sensations to dull their sense of a meaningless existence.*

means ◆◆◇ /miːnz/ (means) **1** N-COUNT A **means** of doing something is a method, instrument, or process which can be used to do it. **Means** is both the singular and the plural form for this use. ❑ *The move is a means to fight crime.* ❑ *The army had perfected the use of terror as a means of controlling the population.* **2** N-PLURAL You can refer to the money that someone has as their **means**. [FORMAL] ❑ *...a person of means.* **3** PHRASE If someone is living **beyond** their **means**, they are spending more money than they can afford. If someone is living **within** their **means**, they are not spending more money than they can afford. ❑ *The more gifts she received, the more she craved, until he was living beyond his means.* ❑ *It is far better to pay off old debts steadily by living within your means.* **4** PHRASE If you do something **by means of** a particular method, instrument, or process, you do it using that method, instrument, or process. ❑ *This is a two-year course taught by means of lectures and seminars.* **5** CONVENTION You can say **'by all means'** to tell someone that you are very willing to allow them to do something. [FORMULAE] ❑ *"Can I come and have a look at your house?"—"Yes, by all means."* **6** → See feature box at **finance**

> **SYNONYMS**
>
> **means**
> NOUN **1**
> **method:** *...new teaching methods.*
> **mechanism:** *There's no mechanism for punishing arms exporters who break the rules.*
> **way:** *Freezing isn't a bad way of preserving food.*
> **process:** *The best way to proceed is by a process of elimination.*

means test (means tests) N-COUNT [usu sing] A **means test** is a test in which your income is calculated in order to decide whether you qualify for a grant or benefit from the government.

means-tested ADJ A grant or benefit that is **means-tested** varies in amount depending on a means test. ❑ *...means-tested benefits.*

meant /mɛnt/ **1** **Meant** is the past tense and past participle of **mean**. **2** ADJ [v-link ADJ to-inf] You use **meant to** to say that something or someone was intended to be or do a particular thing, especially when they have failed to be or do it. ❑ *I can't say any more, it's meant to be a big secret.* ❑ *Everything is meant to be businesslike.* **3** ADJ [v-link ADJ for n] If something **is meant for** particular people or for a particular situation, it is intended for those people or for that situation. ❑ *Fairy tales weren't just meant for children.* ❑ *The seeds were not meant for human consumption.* **4** PHRASE If you say that something **is meant to** happen, you mean that it is expected to happen or that it ought to happen. ❑ *The peculiar thing about getting engaged is that you're meant to announce it to everyone.* **5** PHRASE If you say that something **is meant to** have a particular quality or characteristic, you mean that it has a reputation for being like that. ❑ *The Spurs are meant to be one of the top teams in the league.*

mean|time /miːntaɪm/ **1** PHRASE **In the meantime** or **meantime** means in the period of time between two events. ❑ *Eventually your child will leave home to lead her own life, but in the meantime she relies on your support.* **2** PHRASE **For the meantime** means for a period of time from now until something else happens. ❑ *Some of her stuff is stored for the meantime with her children.*

mean|while ◆◆◇ /miːnwaɪl/ **1** ADV [ADV with cl] **Meanwhile** means while a particular thing is happening. ❑ *Brush the eggplant with oil, add salt and pepper, and bake till soft. Meanwhile, heat the remaining oil in a heavy pan.* **2** ADV [ADV with cl] **Meanwhile** means in the period of time between two events. ❑ *You needn't worry; I'll be ready to greet them. Meanwhile, I'm off to discuss the Fowlers' party with Felix.* **3** ADV [ADV with cl] You use **meanwhile** to introduce a different aspect of a particular situation, especially one that is completely opposite to the one previously mentioned. ❑ *He had always found his wife's mother a bit annoying. The mother-daughter relationship, meanwhile, was close.*

mea|sles /miːzəlz/ N-UNCOUNT [also the N] **Measles** is an infectious illness that gives you a high temperature and red spots on your skin.

mea|sly /miːzli/ ADJ If you describe an amount, quantity, or size as **measly**, you are critical of it because it is very small or inadequate. [INFORMAL, DISAPPROVAL] ❑ *The company offered what he considered a measly amount.* ❑ *...a measly twelve-year-old like me.*

meas|ur|able /mɛʒərəbəl/ **1** ADJ If you describe something as **measurable**, you mean that it is large enough to be noticed or to be significant. [FORMAL] ❑ *Both leaders seemed to expect measurable progress.* **2** ADJ Something that is **measurable** can be measured. ❑ *Economists emphasize measurable quantities – the number of jobs, the per capita income.*

meas|ure ◆◆◇ /mɛʒər/ (measures, measuring, measured) **1** V-T If you **measure** the quality, value, or effect of something, you discover or judge how great it is. ❑ *I continued to measure his progress against the charts in the doctor's office.* **2** V-T If you **measure** a quantity that can be expressed in numbers, such as the length of something, you discover it using a particular instrument or device, for example a ruler. ❑ *Measure the length and width of the gap.* **3** V-T [no cont] If something **measures** a particular length, width, or amount, that is its size or intensity, expressed in numbers. ❑ *It measures 20 yards from side* to side. **4** N-SING A **measure of** a particular quality, feeling, or activity is a fairly large amount of it. [FORMAL] ❑ *With the exception of Juan, each attained a measure of success.* **5** N-SING If you say that one aspect of a situation is a **measure of** that situation, you mean that it shows that the situation is very serious or has developed to a very great extent. ❑ *That is a measure of how bad things have become at the bank.* **6** N-COUNT When someone, usually a government or other authority, takes **measures** to do something, they carry out particular actions in order to achieve a particular result. [FORMAL] ❑ *The government warned that police would take tougher measures to contain the trouble.* **7** N-COUNT A **measure** of a strong alcoholic drink such as brandy or whiskey is an amount of it in a glass. In bars, a **measure** is an official standard amount. [BRIT] ❑ *He poured himself another generous measure of whiskey.* **8** N-COUNT In music, a **measure** is one of the several short parts of the same length into which a piece of music is divided. [AM] ❑ *Malcolm wanted to mix the beginning of a sonata, then add Beethoven for a few measures, then go back to Bach.*

in BRIT, use **bar**

9 → see also **tape measure** **10** PHRASE If you say that something has changed or that it has affected you **beyond measure**, you are emphasizing that it has done this to a great extent. [EMPHASIS] ❑ *Mankind's knowledge of the universe has increased beyond measure.* **11** → See feature box at **sewing**
▶ **measure up** PHRASAL VERB If you do not **measure up** to a standard or to someone's expectations, you are not good enough to achieve the standard or fulfill the person's expectations. ❑ *It was fatiguing sometimes to try to measure up to her standard of perfection.*

SYNONYMS

measure
VERB **1**
monitor: *You need feedback to monitor progress.*
follow: *She was following Laura's progress closely.*
keep track of: *They had become so numerous I hadn't been able to keep track of them.*

meas|ured /mɛʒərd/ ADJ [usu ADJ n] You use **measured** to describe something that is careful and deliberate. ❑ *The men spoke in soft, measured tones.* ❑ *Her more measured response will appeal to voters.*

meas|ure|ment /mɛʒərmənt/ (**measurements**) **1** N-COUNT A **measurement** is a result, usually expressed in numbers, that you obtain by measuring something. ❑ *We took lots of measurements.* **2** N-VAR **Measurement** of something is the process of measuring it in order to obtain a result expressed in numbers. ❑ *Tests include measurement of height, weight, and blood pressure.* **3** N-VAR The **measurement** of the quality, value, or effect of something is the activity of deciding how great it is. ❑ *The measurement of intelligence has been the greatest achievement of twentieth-century scientific psychology.* **4** N-PLURAL Your **measurements** are the size of your waist, chest, hips, and other parts of your body, which you need to know when you are buying clothes. ❑ *I know all her measurements and find it easy to buy stuff she likes.*

meas|ur|ing /mɛʒərɪŋ/ ADJ [ADJ n] A **measuring** cup or spoon is specially designed for measuring quantities, especially in cooking.

meat ✦◇◇ /mit/ (**meats**) N-MASS **Meat** is flesh taken from a dead animal that people cook and eat. ❑ *Meat and fish are relatively expensive.* ❑ *...imported meat products.*

meat|ball /mitbɔl/ (**meatballs**) N-COUNT [usu pl] **Meatballs** are small balls of ground meat. They are usually eaten with a sauce.

meat grind|er (**meat grinders**) N-COUNT A **meat grinder** is a machine which cuts meat into very small pieces by forcing it through very small holes. [AM]

in BRIT, use **mincer**

meat|less /mitlɪs/ **1** ADJ **Meatless** dishes, meals, and diets do not contain meat. ❑ *Even fast-food outlets are offering more meatless dishes.* ❑ *Try making one day a week meatless.* **2** ADJ **Meatless** food looks and tastes like meat but does not contain any meat.

meat loaf (**meat loaves**) also **meatloaf** N-VAR **Meat loaf** is ground meat made into the shape of a loaf of bread and baked.

meat|pack|ing /mitpækɪŋ/ also **meat-packing, meat packing** N-UNCOUNT [usu N n] **Meatpacking** is the processing and packaging of meat for sale. [AM] ❑ *...the local meatpacking plant.*

meaty /miti/ (**meatier, meatiest**) **1** ADJ Food that is **meaty** contains a lot of meat. ❑ *...a pleasant lasagna with a meaty sauce.* **2** ADJ You can describe something such as a piece of writing or a part in a movie as **meaty** if it contains a lot of interesting or important material. ❑ *The short, meaty reports are those he likes best.*

mec|ca /mɛkə/ (**meccas**) **1** N-PROPER **Mecca** is a city in Saudi Arabia, which is the holiest city in Islam because the Prophet Mohammed was born there. All Muslims face toward Mecca when they pray. **2** N-COUNT [usu sing, with supp] If you describe a place as a **mecca** or **Mecca** for a particular thing or activity, you mean that many people who are interested in it go there. ❑ *Thailand has become the tourist mecca of Asia.*

me|chan|ic /mɪkænɪk/ (**mechanics**) **1** N-COUNT A **mechanic** is someone whose job is to repair and maintain machines and engines, especially car engines. ❑ *If you smell something unusual (gas fumes or burning, for instance), take the car to your mechanic.* **2** N-PLURAL The **mechanics** of a process, system, or activity are the way in which it works or the way in which it is done. ❑ *What are the mechanics of this new process?* **3** N-UNCOUNT **Mechanics** is the part of physics that deals with the natural forces that act on moving or stationary objects. ❑ *He has not studied mechanics or engineering.*

me|chani|cal /mɪkænɪkᵊl/ **1** ADJ A **mechanical** device has parts that move when it is working, often using power from an engine or from electricity. ❑ *...a small mechanical device that taps out the numbers.* ❑ *This is the oldest working mechanical clock in the world.* ● **me|chani|cal|ly** /mɪkænɪkli/ ADV [ADV with v] ❑ *The air was circulated mechanically.* **2** ADJ [ADJ n] **Mechanical** means relating to machines and engines and the way they work. ❑ *...mechanical engineering.* ● **me|chani|cal|ly** ADV [ADV adj/-ed] ❑ *The car was mechanically sound, he decided.* **3** ADJ If you describe a person as **mechanical**, you mean they are naturally good at understanding how machines work. ❑ *He was a very mechanical person, who knew a lot about sound.* ● **me|chani|cal|ly** ADV [ADV -ed] ❑ *I'm not mechanically minded.* **4** ADJ If you describe someone's action as **mechanical**, you mean that they do it automatically, without thinking about it. ❑ *It is real prayer, and not mechanical repetition.* ● **me|chani|cal|ly** ADV [ADV with v] ❑ *He nodded mechanically, his eyes fixed on the girl.*

mecha|nism ✦◇◇ /mɛkənɪzəm/ (**mechanisms**) **1** N-COUNT In a machine or piece of equipment, a **mechanism** is a part, often consisting of a set of smaller parts, which performs a particular function. ❑ *...the locking mechanism.* **2** N-COUNT A **mechanism** is a special way of getting something done within a particular system. ❑ *There's no mechanism for punishing arms exporters who break the rules.* **3** N-COUNT A **mechanism** is a part of your behavior that is automatic and that helps you to survive or to cope with a difficult situation. ❑ *...a survival mechanism, a means of coping with intolerable stress.*

SYNONYMS

mechanism
NOUN **1**
workings: *These computer systems mimic the workings of the brain.*
motor: *She got in and started the motor.*
machinery: *Farmers import most of their machinery and materials.*

mecha|nis|tic /mɛkənɪstɪk/ ADJ If you describe a view or explanation of something as **mechanistic**, you are criticizing it because it describes a natural or social process as if it were a machine. [DISAPPROVAL] ❑ *...a mechanistic view of things that ignores the emotional realities in people's lives.* ❑ *Most of my colleagues in biology are still very mechanistic in their thinking.*

mecha|nize /mɛkənaɪz/ (**mechanizes, mechanizing, mechanized**)

in BRIT, also use **mechanise**

medal

v-t If someone **mechanizes** a process, they cause it to be done by a machine or machines, when it was previously done by people. ❑ *Only gradually are technologies being developed to mechanize the task.* ● **mecha|ni|za|tion** /mɛkənɪzeɪʃᵊn/ N-UNCOUNT ❑ *Mechanization happened years ago on the farms of Islay.*

med|al ✦◇ /mɛdᵊl/ (**medals**) N-COUNT A **medal** is a small metal disk which is given as an award for bravery or as a prize in a sports event. ❑ *Dufour was awarded his country's highest medal for bravery.*

med|al|ist /mɛdᵊlɪst/ (**medalists**) **1** N-COUNT [usu supp N] A **medalist** is a person who has won a medal in sports. [JOURNALISM] ❑ *...the gold medalists.* **2** → See feature box at **Olympic Games**

me|dal|lion /mɪdælyən/ (**medallions**) N-COUNT A **medallion** is a round metal disk which some people wear as an ornament, especially on a chain around their neck.

Med|al of Hon|or (**Medals of Honor**) N-COUNT [usu the N] The **Medal of Honor** is a medal that is given to members of the U.S. armed forces who have shown special courage or bravery in battle. ❑ *He won the Medal of Honor for his actions in 1943.*

med|dle /mɛdᵊl/ (**meddles, meddling, meddled**) v-i If you say that someone **meddles** in something, you are criticizing the fact that they try to influence or change it without being asked. [DISAPPROVAL] ❑ *Already some people are asking whether scientists have any right to meddle in such matters.* ❑ *If only you hadn't felt compelled to meddle.*

med|dle|some /mɛdᵊlsəm/ ADJ If you describe a person as **meddlesome**, you are criticizing them because they try to influence or change things that do not concern them. [DISAPPROVAL] ❑ *...a meddlesome member of the public.*

me|dia ✦◇ /midiə/ **1** N-SING-COLL You can refer to television, radio, newspapers, and magazines as **the media**. ❑ *It is hard work and not a glamorous job as portrayed by the media.* ❑ *They are wondering whether bias in the news media contributed to the president's defeat.* **2** → see also **mass media, multimedia 3 Media** is a plural of **medium**. **4** → See feature box at **press**

me|dia cir|cus (**media circuses**) N-COUNT If an event is described as a **media circus**, a large group of people from the media are there to report on it and take photographs. [DISAPPROVAL] ❑ *The couple married in the Caribbean to avoid a media circus.*

me|di|aeval /mɛdiivᵊl, mɪdivᵊl/ [BRIT] → see **medieval**

me|dian /midiən/ (**medians**) **1** ADJ [ADJ n] The **median** value of a set of values is the middle one when they are arranged in order. For example, if a group of five students take a test and their scores are 5, 7, 7, 8, and 10, the median score is 7. [TECHNICAL] **2** N-COUNT A **median** is the same as a **median strip**. [AM]

me|dian strip (**median strips**) N-COUNT The **median strip** is the strip of ground, often covered with grass, that separates the two sides of a major road. [AM]

in BRIT, use **central reservation**

me|di|ate /midieɪt/ (**mediates, mediating, mediated**) v-T/v-I If someone **mediates** between two groups of people, or **mediates** an agreement between them, they try to settle an argument between them by talking to both groups and trying to find things that they can both agree to. ❑ *My mom was the one who mediated between Zelda and her mom.* ❑ *United Nations officials have mediated a series of peace meetings between the two sides.* ● **me|dia|tion** /midieɪʃᵊn/ N-UNCOUNT ❑ *The agreement provides for United Nations mediation between the two sides.* ● **me|dia|tor** (**mediators**) N-COUNT ❑ *An archbishop has been acting as mediator between the rebels and the authorities.*

med|ic /mɛdɪk/ (**medics**) **1** N-COUNT A **medic** is a doctor or medical student. [INFORMAL] **2** N-COUNT A **medic** is a doctor who works with the armed forces, as part of a medical corps. [AM] ❑ *A navy medic was wounded by sniper fire.*

Medi|caid /mɛdɪkeɪd/ N-UNCOUNT [oft N n] In the United States, **Medicaid** is a government program that helps to pay medical costs for people. ❑ *For her medical care, the family was forced to turn to Medicaid.* ❑ *Some doctors won't accept Medicaid patients.*

medicine

medi|cal ✦◇ /mɛdɪkᵊl/ (**medicals**) **1** ADJ [ADJ n] **Medical** means relating to illness and injuries and to their treatment or prevention. ❑ *Several police officers received medical treatment for cuts and bruises.* ● **medi|cal|ly** /mɛdɪkli/ ADV ❑ *Therapists cannot prescribe drugs as they are not necessarily medically qualified.* **2** N-COUNT A **medical** is a thorough examination of your body by a doctor, for example before you start a new job. [mainly BRIT]

in AM, use **physical**

medi|cal ex|am|in|er (**medical examiners**) **1** N-COUNT A **medical examiner** is a medical expert who is responsible for investigating the deaths of people who have died in a sudden, violent, or unusual way. [AM] **2** N-COUNT A **medical examiner** is a doctor whose job is to examine people, for example when they apply for a job or for health insurance. [AM]

Medi|care /mɛdɪkɛər/ N-UNCOUNT [oft N n] In the United States, **Medicare** is a government program that provides health insurance to cover medical costs for people aged 65 and older. ❑ *...cuts in services like Medicare.*

medi|cat|ed /mɛdɪkeɪtɪd/ ADJ [usu ADJ n] A **medicated** soap or shampoo contains substances which are intended to kill bacteria and therefore make your skin or hair healthier.

medi|ca|tion /mɛdɪkeɪʃᵊn/ (**medications**) N-VAR **Medication** is medicine that is used to treat and cure illness. ❑ *When somebody comes for treatment I always ask them if they are on any medication.*

me|dici|nal /mədɪsənᵊl/ ADJ **Medicinal** substances or substances with **medicinal** effects can be used to treat and cure illnesses. ❑ *...medicinal plants.*

medi|cine ✦◇ /mɛdɪsɪn/ (**medicines**) **1** N-UNCOUNT **Medicine** is the treatment of illness and injuries by doctors and nurses. ❑ *He pursued a career in medicine.* ❑ *I was interested in alternative medicine and becoming an aromatherapist.* **2** N-MASS **Medicine** is a substance that you drink or swallow in order to cure an illness. ❑ *People in hospitals are dying because of shortages of medicine.*

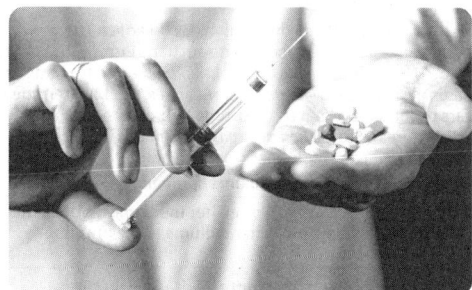

VOCABULARY IN CONTEXT

Medicine

Medicine advances because of the work of researchers and doctors, but no progress would be made if it weren't for ordinary people. New drugs have to undergo years of **clinical trials** on volunteers before they can be **prescribed** to patients. During the trials, researchers look for potential **side-effects**, or for **interactions** with other drugs. The most reliable investigations follow a **double-blind** procedure, where neither the volunteer nor the researcher knows who has been given the actual drug and who has been given a **placebo**. **Genetic** testing is a newer, more controversial advance in medicine, but it also takes years of research before these tests can be used to **diagnose** diseases, to **screen** people for tendencies towards certain medical conditions, or to help doctors decide which **treatment** is best for a patient. Whatever **health care** you receive, remember the volunteers that made it possible.

SYNONYMS

medicine
NOUN **2**
remedy: ...natural remedies to help overcome winter infections.
drug: The drug will be useful to hundreds of thousands of infected people.
medication: She stopped taking the prescribed medications.

me|di|eval /mɪdiːvəl, mɪdiːvəl/

in BRIT, also use **mediaeval**

ADJ Something that is **medieval** relates to or was made in the period of European history between the end of the Roman Empire in AD 476 and about AD 1500. ❑ ...a medieval castle.

me|dio|cre /miːdioʊkər/ ADJ If you describe something as **mediocre**, you mean that it is of average quality but you think it should be better. [DISAPPROVAL] ❑ His school record was mediocre.

me|di|oc|rity /miːdiɒkrɪti/ N-UNCOUNT If you refer to the **mediocrity** of something, you mean that it is of average quality but you think it should be better. [DISAPPROVAL] ❑ ...the mediocrity of most contemporary literature.

medi|tate /mɛdɪteɪt/ (meditates, meditating, meditated) **1** V-I If you **meditate on** something, you think about it very carefully and deeply for a long time. ❑ On the day her son began school, she meditated on the uncertainties of his future. **2** V-I If you **meditate** you remain in a silent and calm state for a period of time, as part of a religious training or so that you are more able to deal with the problems and difficulties of everyday life. ❑ I was meditating, and reached a higher state of consciousness.

medi|ta|tion /mɛdɪteɪʃən/ N-UNCOUNT **Meditation** is the act of remaining in a silent and calm state for a period of time, as part of a religious training, or so that you are more able to deal with the problems of everyday life. ❑ Many busy executives have begun to practice yoga and meditation.

medi|ta|tive /mɛdɪteɪtɪv/ ADJ [ADJ n] **Meditative** describes things that are related to the act of meditating or the act of thinking very deeply about something. ❑ Music can induce a meditative state. ● **medi|ta|tive|ly** ADV [ADV after v] ❑ Martin rubbed his chin meditatively.

Medi|ter|ra|nean /mɛdɪtəreɪniən/ **1** N-PROPER **The Mediterranean** is the sea between southern Europe and North Africa. ❑ You have the choice of night fishing in the Mediterranean, or windsurfing on a lake in Switzerland. **2** N-PROPER **The Mediterranean** refers to the southern part of Europe, which is next to the Mediterranean Sea. ❑ Barcelona has become one of the most dynamic and prosperous cities in the Mediterranean.

me|dium ✦✧ /miːdiəm/ (mediums or media)

The plural of the noun can be either **mediums** or **media** for meanings **4** and **5**. The form **mediums** is the plural for meaning **6**.

1 ADJ If something is of **medium** size, it is neither large nor small, but approximately halfway between the two. ❑ A medium dose produces severe nausea within hours. **2** ADJ You use **medium** to describe something that is average in degree or amount, or approximately halfway along a scale between two extremes. ❑ Foods that contain only medium levels of sodium are bread, cakes, milk, butter, and margarine. ● ADV [ADV adj] **Medium** is also an adverb. ❑ Toast by stirring in a medium-hot skillet for a few minutes. **3** COMB IN COLOR If something is of a **medium** color, it is neither light nor dark, but approximately halfway between the two. ❑ Andrea has medium brown hair, gray eyes, and very pale skin. **4** N-COUNT A **medium** is a way or means of expressing your ideas or of communicating with people. ❑ In Sierra Leone, English is used as the medium of instruction for all primary education. **5** N-COUNT A **medium** is a substance or material which is used for a particular purpose or in order to produce a particular effect. ❑ Blood is the medium in which oxygen is carried to all parts of the body. **6** N-COUNT A **medium** is a person who claims to be able to contact and speak to people who are dead, and to pass messages between them and people who are still alive. ❑ He says he has been talking to his late father through a medium.
7 → see also **media**

SYNONYMS

medium
ADJ **1**
average: ...a woman of average height.
mean: ...the mean score for 26-year-olds.
middling: ...a man of middling height.

me|dium dry ADJ **Medium dry** wine or sherry is not very sweet.
medium-sized also **medium size** ADJ [usu ADJ n] **Medium-sized** means neither large nor small, but approximately halfway between the two. ❑ ...a medium-sized saucepan. ❑ ...medium-sized accountancy firms.

medium-term **1** ADJ Something that is **medium-term** has continued for a few months or years beyond the present time, in contrast with the short term or the long term. ❑ Economists had been arguing that the medium-term economic prospects remained poor. **2** N-SING When you talk about what happens in **the medium term**, you are talking about what happens over a few months or years, either in the future or after a particular event. ❑ She risks losing her salary in the medium-term and damaging her long-term career prospects.

med|ley /mɛdli/ (medleys) **1** N-COUNT [oft N of n] In music, a **medley** is a collection of different tunes or songs that are played one after the other as a single piece of music. ❑ ...a medley of traditional songs. **2** N-COUNT [oft supp N] In sports, a **medley** is a swimming race in which the four main strokes are used one after the other. ❑ Japan won the Men's 200 meter individual medley.

meek /miːk/ (meeker, meekest) ADJ If you describe a person as **meek**, you think that they are gentle and quiet, and likely to do what other people say. ❑ He was a meek, mild-mannered fellow. ● **meek|ly** ADV [ADV with v] ❑ Most have meekly accepted such advice.

meet ✦✦✦ /miːt/ (meets, meeting, met) **1** V-RECIP If you **meet** someone, you happen to be in the same place as them and start talking to them. You may know the other person, but be surprised to see them, or you may not know them at all. ❑ I have just met the man I want to spend the rest of my life with. ❑ He's the kindest and sincerest person I've ever met. ● PHRASAL VERB **Meet up** means the same as **meet**. ❑ Last night, when he was parking my car, he met up with a buddy he had at Stanford. **2** V-RECIP If two or more people **meet**, they go to the same place, which they have earlier arranged to do, so that they can talk or do something together. ❑ We could meet for a drink after work. ● PHRASAL VERB **Meet up** means the same as **meet**. ❑ We tend to meet up for lunch once a week. **3** V-T If you **meet** someone, you are introduced to them and begin talking to them and getting to know them. ❑ Hey, Terry, come and meet my Dad. **4** V-T You use **meet** in expressions such as '**Pleased to meet you**' and '**Nice to have met you**' when you want to politely say hello or goodbye to someone you have just met for the first time. [FORMULAE] ❑ "Jennifer," Miss Mallory said, "this is Leigh Taylor."— "Pleased to meet you," Jennifer said. **5** V-T If you **meet** someone at or off their train, plane, or bus, you go to the station, airport, or bus stop in order to be there when they arrive. ❑ Mama met me at the station. ❑ Lili and my father met me off the boat. **6** V-I When a group of people such as a committee **meet**, they gather together for a particular purpose. ❑ Officials from the two countries will meet again soon to resume negotiations. **7** V-I If you **meet with** someone, you have a meeting with them. [mainly AM] ❑ Most of the lawmakers who met with the president yesterday said they backed the mission. **8** V-T/V-I If something such as a suggestion, proposal, or new book **meets with** or **is met with** a particular reaction, it gets that reaction from people. ❑ The idea met with a cool response from various quarters. ❑ We hope today's offer will meet with your approval too. **9** V-T If something **meets** a need, requirement, or condition, it is good enough to do what is required. ❑ He suggested that the current arrangements for the care of severely mentally ill people are inadequate to meet their needs. **10** V-T If you **meet** something such as a problem or challenge, you deal with it satisfactorily or do what is required. ❑ Manufacturing failed to meet the crisis of the 1970s. **11** V-T If you **meet** the cost of something, you provide the money that is needed for it. ❑ The government said it will help meet some of the cost of the damage. **12** V-T If you **meet** a situation, attitude, or

problem, you experience it or become aware of it. ☐ *I honestly don't know how I will react the next time I meet a potentially dangerous situation.* **13** V-I You can say that someone **meets with** success or failure when they are successful or unsuccessful. ☐ *Attempts to find civilian volunteers have met with embarrassing failure.* **14** V-RECIP When a moving object **meets** another object, it hits or touches it. ☐ *He held the lighter so it met the tip of his cigarette.* **15** V-RECIP If your eyes **meet** someone else's, you both look at each other at the same time. [WRITTEN] ☐ *Nina's eyes met her sister's across the table.* **16** V-RECIP If two areas **meet**, especially two areas of land or sea, they are next to one another. ☐ *It is one of the rare places in the world where the desert meets the sea.* **17** V-RECIP The place where two lines **meet** is the place where they join together. ☐ *Parallel lines will never meet no matter how far extended.* **18 to make ends meet** → see **end** ① **19 to meet someone halfway** → see **halfway**
▶ **meet up** → see meet 1, 2

SYNONYMS

meet
VERB
1
encounter: *Did you encounter anyone in the building?*
come across: *I came across a group of children playing.*
run into: *He ran into Krettner in the corridor a few minutes later.*
2
gather: *In the evenings, we gathered around the fireplace.*
assemble: *There wasn't even a convenient place for students to assemble between classes.*
get together: *This is the only forum where East and West can get together.*
congregate: *Visitors congregated on Sunday afternoons to view public exhibitions.*

meet|ing ◆◆◆ /mitɪŋ/ (**meetings**) **1** N-COUNT A **meeting** is an event in which a group of people come together to discuss things or make decisions. ☐ *Can we have a meeting to discuss that?* • N-SING You can also refer to the people at a meeting as **the meeting**. ☐ *The meeting decided that further efforts were needed.* **2** N-COUNT When you meet someone, either by chance or by arrangement, you can refer to this event as a **meeting**. ☐ *In January, 37 years after our first meeting, I was back in the studio with Dennis.*

meeting|house /mitɪŋhaʊs/ (**meetinghouses**) N-COUNT A **meetinghouse** is a building in which certain groups of Christians, for example Quakers, meet in order to worship together.

meet|ing place (**meeting places**) N-COUNT A **meeting place** is a place where people meet.

mega /mɛgə/ **1** ADV [usu ADV adj/adv] Young people sometimes use **mega** in front of adjectives or adverbs in order to emphasize them. [INFORMAL, EMPHASIS] ☐ *He has become mega rich.* **2** ADJ [ADJ n] Young people sometimes use **mega** in front of nouns in order to emphasize that the thing they are talking about is very good, very large, or very impressive. [INFORMAL, EMPHASIS] ☐ *...the mega superstar Madonna.*

PREFIX

mega-
forms words that refer to units which are a million times bigger. *For example, a* **megabyte** *is a million bytes.*

mega|bit /mɛgəbɪt/ (**megabits**) N-COUNT In computing, a **megabit** is one million bits. ☐ *They promise to deliver broadband connections of 100 megabits per second.*

mega|byte /mɛgəbaɪt/ (**megabytes**) N-COUNT In computing, a **megabyte** is one million bytes of data. ☐ *Large computer files, such as image files, are measured in megabytes.*

mega|hertz /mɛgəhɜrts/ (**megahertz**) N-COUNT [num N] A **megahertz** is a unit of frequency, used especially for radio frequencies. One megahertz equals one million cycles per second. ☐ *...UHF frequencies of around 900 megahertz.*

mega|lo|ma|nia /mɛgəloʊmeɪniə/ N-UNCOUNT **Megalomania** is the belief that you are more powerful and important than you really are. Megalomania is sometimes a mental illness.

mega|lo|ma|ni|ac /mɛgəloʊmeɪniæk/ (**megalomaniacs**) N-COUNT [oft N n] If you describe someone as a **megalomaniac**, you are criticizing them because they enjoy being powerful, or because they believe that they are more powerful or important than they really are. [DISAPPROVAL]

mega|lo|po|lis /mɛgəlɒpəlɪs/ (**megalopolises** or **megalopoli**) N-COUNT [usu sing] A **megalopolis** is a very large city, or an urban area that consists of several towns and cities. ☐ *...the densely populated megalopolis that stretches down the East Coast from Boston to Washington.*

mega|phone /mɛgəfoʊn/ (**megaphones**) **1** N-COUNT A **megaphone** is a cone-shaped device for making your voice sound louder in the open air. **2** → see also **bullhorn** **3** → See also color supplement

mega|pixel /mɛgəpɪksᵊl/ (**megapixels**) N-COUNT A **megapixel** is a unit for measuring the quality of a picture created by a digital camera, scanner, or other piece of digital equipment. One **megapixel** is equivalent to a million pixels.

mega|store /mɛgəstɔr/ (**megastores**) N-COUNT A **megastore** is an extremely large supermarket or store, usually selling one particular type of product. ☐ *Small independent stores are threatened by out-of-town malls and megastores.*

mega|ton /mɛgətʌn/ (**megatons**) N-COUNT [num N] You can use **megaton** to refer to the power of a nuclear weapon. A one megaton bomb has the same power as one million tons of TNT.

mega|watt /mɛgəwɒt/ (**megawatts**) N-COUNT [num N, oft N of n] A **megawatt** is a unit of power. One megawatt is a million watts. ☐ *The project is designed to generate around 30 megawatts of power for the national grid.*

meh /mɛ/ EXCLAM You can say **meh** to show that you do not care about something. [INFORMAL] ☐ *If I'm wrong about any of this, meh.*

-meister /-maɪstər/ (**-meisters**) COMB IN N-COUNT **-meister** combines with nouns to form nouns which refer to someone who is extremely good at a particular activity. ☐ *The film – directed by horror-meister Sam Raimi – is almost assured an Oscar nomination.*

mel|an|cho|lia /mɛlənkoʊliə/ N-UNCOUNT **Melancholia** is a feeling of great sadness, especially one that lasts a long time. [LITERARY] ☐ *He sank into deep melancholia.*

mel|an|chol|ic /mɛlənkɒlɪk/ ADJ If you describe someone or something as **melancholic**, you mean that they are very sad. [LITERARY] ☐ *...his gentle, melancholic songs.*

mel|an|choly /mɛlənkɒli/ ADJ You describe something that you see or hear as **melancholy** when it gives you an intense feeling of sadness. ☐ *The only sounds were the distant, melancholy cries of the sheep.*

me|lange /meɪlɒndʒ/ (**melanges**) also **mélange** N-COUNT [with supp, oft N of n] A **melange** of things is a mixture of them, especially when this is attractive or exciting. [WRITTEN] ☐ *...a successful melange of music styles, from soul and rhythm and blues to rap.* ☐ *...a wonderful mélange of flavors.*

mela|nin /mɛlənɪn/ N-UNCOUNT **Melanin** is a dark substance in the skin, eyes, and hair of people and animals, which gives them color and can protect them against strong sunlight.

mela|no|ma /mɛlənoʊmə/ (**melanomas**) N-VAR A **melanoma** is an area of cancer cells in the skin which is caused by very strong sunlight.

meld /mɛld/ (**melds, melding, melded**) **1** V-I If several things **meld**, or if something **melds** them, they combine or blend in a pleasant or useful way. [FORMAL] ☐ *She sang the first verse again, listening to the way the words melded with the music.* ☐ *Leave for 30 minutes for the flavors to meld.* **2** V-I If several things **meld** into another thing, or if they **are melded** into another thing, they combine and become the other thing. [FORMAL] ☐ *The white smoke and cannon's glare melded into a smear of horror before his eyes.* ☐ *The second major change at McCormick Place was that two unions were melded into one group.* **3** N-COUNT [usu sing: a N of n] A **meld** of things is a mixture or combination of them that is useful or pleasant. [FORMAL] ☐ *...a perfect meld of art and social comment.*

me|lee /meɪleɪ/ (**melees**) also **mêlée** **1** N-COUNT [usu sing] A **melee** is a noisy, confusing fight between the people in a

mellifluous · memorial

crowd. [WRITTEN] ❑ *A policeman was killed and scores of people were injured in the melee.* **2** N-SING [usu N *of* n] A **melee** of things is a large, confusing, disorganized group of them. [WRITTEN] ❑ *...the melee of streets around the waterfront.*

mel|lif|lu|ous /mɪlɪfluəs/ ADJ [usu ADJ n] A **mellifluous** voice or piece of music is smooth and gentle and very pleasant to listen to. [FORMAL] ❑ *I grew up around people who had wonderful, mellifluous voices.*

mel|low /mɛloʊ/ (mellower, mellowest, mellows, mellowing, mellowed) **1** ADJ **Mellow** is used to describe things that have a pleasant, soft, rich color, usually red, orange, yellow, or brown. ❑ *...the softer, mellower light of evening.* **2** ADJ A **mellow** sound or flavor is pleasant, smooth, and rich. ❑ *His voice was deep and mellow and his speech had a soothing and comforting quality.* **3** V-T/V-I If someone **mellows** or if something **mellows** them, they become kinder or less extreme in their behavior, especially as a result of growing older. ❑ *He became a taciturn man, a man not easy to live with. Later, when the older children married and had children of their own, he mellowed a little.* • ADJ **Mellow** is also an adjective. ❑ *Is she more mellow and tolerant?*
▶ **mellow out** PHRASAL VERB If someone **mellows out**, they become very relaxed. [INFORMAL] ❑ *Until the moment everyone started telling me to mellow out, I had never been tense for a single moment in my life.*

me|lod|ic /mɪlɒdɪk/ **1** ADJ [usu ADJ n] **Melodic** means relating to melody. ❑ *...Schubert's effortless gift for melodic invention.* • **me|lodi|cal|ly** /mɪlɒdɪkli/ ADV ❑ *...the third of Tchaikovsky's ten operas, and melodically one of his richest scores.* **2** ADJ Music that is **melodic** has beautiful tunes in it. ❑ *Wonderfully melodic and tuneful, his songs have made me weep.* • **me|lodi|cal|ly** ADV [ADV after v] ❑ *The leader has also learned to play more melodically.*

me|lo|dious /mɪloʊdiəs/ ADJ A **melodious** sound is pleasant to listen to. [LITERARY] ❑ *She spoke in a quietly melodious voice.*

melo|dra|ma /mɛlədrɑːmə/ (melodramas) N-VAR A **melodrama** is a story or play in which there are a lot of exciting or sad events and in which people's emotions are very exaggerated.

melo|dra|mat|ic /mɛlədrəmætɪk/ ADJ **Melodramatic** behavior is behavior in which someone treats a situation as much more serious than it really is. ❑ *"Don't you think you're being slightly melodramatic?" Jane asked.*

melo|dy /mɛlədi/ (melodies) **1** N-COUNT A **melody** is a tune. [FORMAL] ❑ *I whistle melodies from Beethoven and Vivaldi and the more popular classical composers.* **2** → See feature box at **music**

mel|on /mɛlən/ (melons) N-VAR A **melon** is a large fruit which is sweet and juicy inside and has a hard green or yellow skin. ❑ *...some juicy slices of melon.*

melt /mɛlt/ (melts, melting, melted) **1** V-T/V-I When a solid substance **melts** or when you **melt** it, it changes to a liquid, usually because it has been heated. ❑ *The snow had melted, but the lake was still frozen solid.* ❑ *Meanwhile, melt the white chocolate in a bowl suspended over simmering water.* **2** V-I If something such as your feelings **melt**, they suddenly disappear and you no longer feel them. [LITERARY] ❑ *His anxiety about the outcome melted, only to return later.* **3** PHRASAL VERB **Melt away** means the same as **melt**. ❑ *When he heard these words, Scot felt his inner doubts melt away.* **4** V-I If a person or thing **melts into** something such as darkness or a crowd of people, they become difficult to see, for example because they are moving away from you or are the same color as the background. [LITERARY] ❑ *The youths dispersed and melted into the darkness.*

melt|down /mɛltdaʊn/ (meltdowns) **1** N-VAR If there is **meltdown** in a nuclear reactor, the fuel rods start melting because of a failure in the system, and radiation starts to escape. ❑ *Scientists warned that emergency cooling systems could fail and a reactor meltdown could occur.* **2** N-UNCOUNT The **meltdown** of a company, organization, or system is its sudden and complete failure. [JOURNALISM] ❑ *Urgent talks are going on to prevent the market going into financial meltdown during the summer.*

melt|ing point (melting points) N-COUNT [oft with poss] The **melting point** of a substance is the temperature at which it melts when you heat it.

melt|ing pot (melting pots) N-COUNT A **melting pot** is a place or situation in which people or ideas of different kinds gradually get mixed together. ❑ *The republic is a melting pot of different nationalities.*

mem|ber ✦✦✦ /mɛmbər/ (members) **1** N-COUNT A **member** of a group is one of the people, animals, or things belonging to that group. ❑ *He refused to name the members of staff involved.* ❑ *Their lack of training could put members of the public at risk.* **2** N-COUNT A **member** of an organization such as a club or a political party is a person who has officially joined the organization. ❑ *The support of our members is of great importance to the association.* **3** ADJ [ADJ n] A **member country** or **member state** is one of the countries that has joined an international organization or group. ❑ *...the member countries of the North American Free Trade Association.* **4** N-COUNT A **member** or **Member** is a person who has been elected to a legislature or parliament. ❑ *He was elected to Parliament as the Member for Leeds.*

Mem|ber of Con|gress (Members of Congress) N-COUNT A **Member of Congress** is a person who has been elected to the United States Congress. ❑ *...the party's only Black member of Congress.*

Mem|ber of Par|lia|ment (Members of Parliament) N-COUNT A **Member of Parliament** is a person who has been elected by the people in a particular area to represent them in a country's parliament. The abbreviation **MP** is often used. ❑ *...the Member of Parliament for Torbay.*

mem|ber|ship ✦◇◇ /mɛmbərʃɪp/ (memberships) **1** N-UNCOUNT **Membership** in an organization is the state of being a member of it. ❑ *...his membership in the Communist Party.* **2** N-VAR-COLL The **membership** of an organization is the people who belong to it, or the number of people who belong to it. ❑ *By 1890 the organization had a membership of 409,000.*

mem|brane /mɛmbreɪn/ (membranes) N-COUNT A **membrane** is a thin piece of skin that connects or covers parts of a person's or animal's body. ❑ *...inflammation of the thin membrane that lines the heart.*

meme /miːm/ (memes) N-COUNT A **meme** is something such as a video, picture, or phrase that a lot of people send to each other on the internet. ❑ *The image quickly became a meme.*

me|men|to /mɪmɛntoʊ/ (mementos or mementoes) N-COUNT [oft N *of* n] A **memento** is an object which you keep because it reminds you of a person or a special occasion. ❑ *Inside the folder were photographs, cards, letters and other mementos of her sister.*

memo /mɛmoʊ/ (memos) N-COUNT A **memo** is a short official note that is sent by one person to another within the same company or organization. ❑ *He sent out a memo expressing his disagreement with their decisions.*

mem|oir /mɛmwɑr/ (memoirs) N-COUNT A **memoir** is a book or article that you write about yourself or someone who you have known well. [FORMAL] ❑ *He has just published a memoir in honor of his captain.*

mem|oirs /mɛmwɑrz/ N-PLURAL [usu with poss] A person's **memoirs** are a written account of the people who they have known and events that they remember. ❑ *In retirement he published his memoirs.*

memo|ra|bilia /mɛmərəbɪliə/ N-PLURAL **Memorabilia** are things that you collect because they are connected with a person or organization in which you are interested. ❑ *...the country's leading dealer in Beatles memorabilia.*

memo|rable /mɛmərəbəl/ ADJ Something that is **memorable** is worth remembering or likely to be remembered, because it is special or very enjoyable. ❑ *...the perfect setting for a nostalgic memorable day.*

memo|ran|dum /mɛmərændəm/ (memoranda or memorandums) **1** N-COUNT A **memorandum** is a written report that is prepared for a person or committee in order to provide them with information about a particular matter. ❑ *...a memorandum from the Department of Defense on its role.* **2** N-COUNT A **memorandum** is a short official note that is sent by one person to another within the same company or organization. [FORMAL] ❑ *...a memorandum sent to all senior UN personnel.*

me|mo|rial /mɪmɔriəl/ (memorials) **1** N-COUNT A **memorial** is a structure built in order to remind people of a famous person or event. ❑ *Building a memorial to Columbus has been his lifelong dream.* **2** ADJ [ADJ n] A **memorial** event, object, or prize is in honor of someone who has died, so that they will be remembered. ❑ *A memorial service is being held for her at St. Paul's Church.* ❸ N-COUNT If you say that something will be a **memorial to** someone who has died, you mean that it will continue to exist and remind people of them. ❑ *The museum will serve as a memorial to the millions who passed through Ellis Island.*

Me|mo|rial Day N-UNCOUNT In the United States, **Memorial Day** is a public holiday when people honor the memory of Americans who have died in wars. Memorial Day is celebrated in most states on the last Monday in May.

me|mo|ri|al|ize /mɪmɔːriəlaɪz/ (**memorializes, memorializing, memorialized**)

in BRIT, also use **memorialise**

V-T If a person or event **is memorialized**, something is produced that will continue to exist and remind people of them. ❑ *He was praised in print and memorialized in stone throughout the South.* ❑ *When she died in 1946, her friends wanted to memorialize her in some significant way.*

memo|rize /mɛməraɪz/ (**memorizes, memorizing, memorized**)

in BRIT, also use **memorise**

V-T If you **memorize** something, you learn it so that you can remember it exactly. ❑ *He studied his map, trying to memorize the way to Rose's street.*

memo|ry ♦♦◇ /mɛməri/ (**memories**) ❶ N-VAR Your **memory** is your ability to remember things. ❑ *All the details of the meeting are fresh in my memory.* ❑ *But locals with long memories thought this was fair revenge for the injustice of 1961.* ❑ *He had a good memory for faces.* ❷ N-COUNT A **memory** is something that you remember from the past. ❑ *She cannot bear to watch the film because of the bad memories it brings back.* ❑ *Her earliest memoir is of singing at the age of four to wounded soldiers.* ❸ N-COUNT A computer's **memory** is the part of the computer where information is stored, especially for a short time before it is transferred to something else. [COMPUTING] ❑ *The data are stored in the computer's memory.* ❹ N-SING If you talk about the **memory** of someone who has died, especially someone who was loved or respected, you are referring to the thoughts, actions, and ceremonies by which they are remembered. ❑ *She remained devoted to his memory.* ❺ PHRASE If you say that someone is taking a walk or trip **down memory lane**, you mean that they are talking, writing, or thinking about something that happened to them a long time ago. [INFORMAL] ❑ *His 1998 memoir is a delightful trip down memory lane.* ❻ PHRASE If you do something **from memory**, for example speak the words of a poem or play a piece of music, you do it without looking at it, because you know it very well. ❑ *Many members of the church sang from memory.* ❼ PHRASE If you say that something is, for example, the best, worst, or first thing of its kind **in living memory**, you are emphasizing that it is the only thing of that kind that people can remember. [EMPHASIS] ❑ *The floods are the worst in living memory.* ❽ PHRASE If you **lose your memory**, you forget things that you used to know. ❑ *His illness caused him to lose his memory.* ❾ **to commit something to memory** → see **commit**

memo|ry card (**memory cards**) N-COUNT A **memory card** is a type of card containing computer memory that is used in digital cameras and other devices. [COMPUTING]

memo|ry chip (**memory chips**) N-COUNT In a computer, the **memory chip** is the microchip in which information is stored.

memo|ry stick (**memory sticks**) N-COUNT A **memory stick** is a small device that connects to a computer and allows you to store and copy information. [COMPUTING] ❑ *I'll bring my presentation on a memory stick.*

men /mɛn/ **Men** is the plural of **man**.

men|ace /mɛnɪs/ (**menaces, menacing, menaced**) ❶ N-COUNT If you say that someone or something is a **menace to** other people or things, you mean that person or thing is likely to cause serious harm. ❑ *In my view, you are a menace to the public.* ❷ N-COUNT You can refer to someone or something as a **menace** when you want to say that they cause you trouble or annoyance. [INFORMAL] ❑ *You're a menace to my privacy, Kenton.* ❸ N-UNCOUNT **Menace** is a quality or atmosphere that gives you the feeling that you are in danger or that someone wants to harm you. ❑ *There is a pervading sense of menace.* ❹ V-T If you say that one thing **menaces** another, you mean that the first thing is likely to cause the second thing serious harm. ❑ *They seem determined to menace the United States and its allies.*

men|ac|ing /mɛnɪsɪŋ/ ADJ If someone or something looks **menacing**, they give you a feeling that they are likely to cause you harm or put you in danger. ❑ *The strong, dark eyebrows give his face an oddly menacing look.* ● **men|ac|ing|ly** ADV ❑ *A group of men suddenly emerged from a doorway and moved menacingly forward to block her way.*

me|nage /meɪnɑːʒ/ also **ménage** N-SING [usu with supp] A **menage** is a group of people living together in one house. [FORMAL]

me|nage a trois /meɪnɑːʒ ɑ trwɑː/ (**menages a trois**) also **ménage à trois** N-COUNT [usu sing] A **menage a trois** is a situation where three people live together, especially when one of them is having a sexual relationship with both of the others.

me|nag|erie /mənædʒəri/ (**menageries**) ❶ N-COUNT A **menagerie** is a collection of wild animals. ❷ N-COUNT [usu sing: N of n] A **menagerie** of things is a collection of them. ❑ *Many children have a menagerie of stuffed animals in their rooms.*

mend /mɛnd/ (**mends, mending, mended**) ❶ V-T If you **mend** a tear or a hole in a piece of clothing, you repair it by sewing it. ❑ *We mended our clothes and darned socks.* ❷ V-T/V-I If a person or a part of their body **mends** or **is mended**, they get better after they have been ill or have had an injury. ❑ *I'm feeling a lot better. The cut aches, but it's mending.* ❸ V-T If you try to **mend** divisions between people, you try to end the disagreements or quarrels between them. ❑ *He sent Evans as his personal envoy to discuss ways to mend relations between the two countries.* ❹ V-T If you **mend** something that is broken or not working, you repair it, so that it works properly or can be used. [mainly BRIT] ❑ *They took a long time to mend the roof.* ❺ PHRASE If a relationship or situation is **on the mend** after a difficult or unsuccessful period, it is improving. [INFORMAL] ❑ *More evidence that the economy was on the mend was needed.* ❻ PHRASE If you are **on the mend** after an illness or injury, you are recovering from it. [INFORMAL] ❑ *The baby had been ill but seemed to be on the mend.* ❼ PHRASE If someone who has been behaving badly **mends** their **ways**, they begin to behave well. ❑ *He has promised drastic disciplinary action if they do not mend their ways.* ❽ → See feature box at **sewing**

men|da|cious /mɛndeɪʃəs/ ADJ A **mendacious** person is someone who tells lies. A **mendacious** statement is one that is a lie. [FORMAL]

men|dac|ity /mɛndæsɪti/ N-UNCOUNT **Mendacity** is lying, rather than telling the truth. [FORMAL] ❑ *...an astonishing display of cowardice and mendacity.*

mend|ing /mɛndɪŋ/ ❶ N-UNCOUNT **Mending** is the sewing and repairing of clothes that have gotten holes in them. [OLD-FASHIONED] ❑ *Who will then do the cooking, the washing, the mending?* ❷ → see also **mend**

men|folk /mɛnfoʊk/ N-PLURAL [usu poss N] When women refer to their **menfolk**, they mean the men in their family or society. [INFORMAL]

me|nial /miːniəl, mɪnyəl/ ADJ **Menial** work is very boring, and the people who do it have a low status and are usually badly paid. ❑ *...low-paid menial jobs, such as cleaning and domestic work.*

men|in|gi|tis /mɛnɪndʒaɪtɪs/ N-UNCOUNT **Meningitis** is a serious infectious illness which affects your brain and spinal cord.

Men|no|nite /mɛnənaɪt/ (**Mennonites**) ❶ N-COUNT **Mennonites** are members of a Protestant sect within the Christian church who do not baptize their children and who are opposed to military service. ❷ ADJ **Mennonite** means relating to the religious beliefs or practices of Mennonites. ❑ *...Pennsylvania's Amish and Mennonite communities.*

meno|pause /mɛnəpɔːz/ N-SING **Menopause** is the time during which a woman gradually stops menstruating, usually when she is about fifty years old. ❑ *...alternative therapies to fight the symptoms of menopause.*

in BRIT, sometimes use **the menopause**

• **meno|pau|sal** ADJ ❏ *A menopausal woman of average build and height requires 1600 – 2400 calories daily.*

me|no|rah /mənərə, -nourə/ (menorahs) N-COUNT A **menorah** is a candelabra consisting of seven or sometimes eight branches. It is a symbol of Judaism. ❏ *We lit the menorah.*

men's room (men's rooms) N-COUNT [usu the N in sing] The **men's room** is a toilet for men in a public building. [mainly AM]

men|strual /mɛnstruəl/ ADJ [ADJ n] **Menstrual** means relating to menstruation. ❏ *...the menstrual cycle.*

men|stru|ate /mɛnstrueɪt/ (menstruates, menstruating, menstruated) V-I When a woman **menstruates**, a flow of blood comes from her uterus. Women usually menstruate once a month unless they are pregnant or have reached menopause. [FORMAL] ❏ *Lean, hard-training women athletes may menstruate less frequently or not at all.* • **men|strua|tion** /mɛnstrueɪʃən/ N-UNCOUNT ❏ *Menstruation may cease when a woman is anywhere between forty-five and fifty years of age.*

mens|wear /mɛnzwɛər/ N-UNCOUNT **Menswear** is clothing for men. ❏ *...the menswear industry.*

SUFFIX

-ment

forms nouns that refer to the process of making or doing something, or to the result of this process. For example, **replacement** is the process of replacing something or the thing that replaces it.

men|tal ♦◇◇ /mɛntəl/ ADJ [ADJ n] **Mental** means relating to the process of thinking. ❏ *The intellectual environment has a significant influence on the mental development of the children.* • **men|tal|ly** ADV ❏ *I think you are mentally tired.* ◾ ADJ [ADJ n] **Mental** means relating to the state or the health of a person's mind. ❏ *The mental state that had created her psychosis was no longer present.* ❏ *...mental health problems.* • **men|tal|ly** ADV ❏ *...an inmate who is mentally disturbed.* ◾ ADJ [ADJ n] A **mental** act is one that involves only thinking and not physical action. ❏ *Practice mental arithmetic when you go out shopping.* • **men|tal|ly** ADV [ADV with v] ❏ *This technique will help people mentally organize information.* ◾ → See feature box at **poverty**

men|tal age (mental ages) N-COUNT [usu sing] A person's **mental age** is the age which they are considered to have reached in their ability to think or reason.

men|tal hos|pi|tal (mental hospitals) N-COUNT A **mental hospital** is a hospital for people who are mentally ill. [OLD-FASHIONED, OFFENSIVE]

men|tal|ity /mɛntælɪti/ (mentalities) N-COUNT Your **mentality** is your attitudes and your way of thinking. ❏ *...a criminal mentality.*

men|thol /mɛnθɒl/ N-UNCOUNT **Menthol** is a substance that smells a bit like peppermint and is used to flavor things such as cigarettes and toothpaste. It is also used in some medicines, especially for curing colds.

men|tion ♦♦◇ /mɛnʃən/ (mentions, mentioning, mentioned) ◾ V-T If you **mention** something, you say something about it, usually briefly. ❏ *She did not mention her mother's absence.* ❏ *I may not have mentioned it to her.* ❏ *I had mentioned that I didn't really like contemporary music.* ◾ N-VAR A **mention** is a reference to something or someone. ❏ *The statement made no mention of government casualties.* ◾ V-T [usu passive] If someone is **mentioned** in writing, a reference is made to them by name, often to criticize or praise something that they have done. ❏ *I was absolutely outraged that I could be even mentioned in an article of this kind.* ◾ N-VAR A special or honorable **mention** is formal praise that is given for an achievement that is very good, although not usually the best of its kind. ❏ *Several groups and individuals also deserve special mention for their help.* ◾ CONVENTION People sometimes say '**don't mention it**' as a polite reply to someone who has just thanked them for doing something. [FORMULAE] ❏ *"Thank you very much."—"Don't mention it."*

men|tor /mɛntɔr/ (mentors, mentoring, mentored) ◾ N-COUNT A person's **mentor** is someone who gives them help and advice over a period of time, especially help and advice related to their job. ❏ *She was my mentor and my friend.* ◾ V-T To **mentor** someone means to give them help and advice over a period of time, especially help and advice related to their job. ❏ *He had mentored scores of younger doctors.*

menu /mɛnyu/ (menus) ◾ N-COUNT In a restaurant or café or at a formal meal, the **menu** is a list of the meals and drinks that are available. ❏ *A waiter offered him the menu.* ◾ N-COUNT A **menu** is the food that you serve at a meal. ❏ *Try out the menu on a few friends.* ◾ N-COUNT On a computer screen, a **menu** is a list of choices. Each choice represents something that you can do using the computer. ❏ *Hold down the shift key and press F7 to display the print menu.*

meow /miau/ (meows, meowing, meowed)

in BRIT, usually use **miaow**

◾ N-COUNT; SOUND **Meow** is used to represent the noise that a cat makes. ❏ *...the meow of a cat.* • V-I **Meow** is also a verb. ❏ *...a cute and furry life-sized toy kitty that could meow and purr and walk.* ◾ → See feature box at **onomatopoeia**

MEP /ɛm i pi/ (MEPs) N-COUNT An **MEP** is a person who has been elected to the European Parliament. **MEP** is an abbreviation for 'Member of the European Parliament.' ❏ *...Tuesday's secret ballot of Europe's MEPs.*

mer|can|tile /mɜrkəntaɪl/ ADJ [ADJ n] **Mercantile** means relating to or involved in trade. [FORMAL] ❏ *...the emergence of a new mercantile class.*

mer|ce|nary /mɜrsənɛri/ (mercenaries) ◾ N-COUNT A **mercenary** is a soldier who is paid to fight by a country or group that they do not belong to. ❏ *...the recruitment of foreign mercenaries.* ◾ ADJ If you describe someone as **mercenary**, you are criticizing them because you think that they are only interested in the money that they can get from a particular person or situation. [DISAPPROVAL] ❏ *"I hate to sound mercenary,"* Labane said, *"but am I getting paid to be in this play of yours?"*

mer|chan|dise /mɜrtʃəndaɪz, -daɪs/ N-UNCOUNT **Merchandise** is products that are bought, sold, or traded. [FORMAL] ❏ *...a mail-order company that provides merchandise for people suffering from allergies.*

mer|chan|dis|er /mɜrtʃəndaɪzər/ (merchandisers) N-COUNT A **merchandiser** is a person or company that sells products to the public. [AM, BUSINESS] ❏ *In 1979, Liquor Barn thrived as a discount merchandiser.*

in BRIT, use **retailer**

mer|chan|dis|ing /mɜrtʃəndaɪzɪŋ/ ◾ N-UNCOUNT **Merchandising** is used to refer to the way stores and businesses organize the sale of their products, for example the way they are displayed and the prices that are chosen. [mainly AM, BUSINESS] ❏ *Company executives say revamped merchandising should help the store's earnings to grow.* ◾ N-UNCOUNT **Merchandising** consists of goods such as toys and clothes that are linked with something such as a movie, sports team, or pop group. ❏ *We are selling the full range of World Cup merchandising.*

mer|chant ♦◇◇ /mɜrtʃənt/ (merchants) ◾ N-COUNT A **merchant** is a person who buys or sells goods in large quantities, especially one who imports and exports them. ❏ *Any knowledgeable wine merchant would be able to advise you.* ◾ N-COUNT A **merchant** is a person who owns or runs a store, or other business. [AM] ❏ *The family was forced to live on credit from local merchants.*

in BRIT, usually use **retailer**

◾ ADJ [ADJ n] **Merchant** seamen or ships are involved in carrying goods for trade. ❏ *There's been a big reduction in the size of the merchant fleet in recent years.*

SYNONYMS

merchant
NOUN ◾
trader: *...a fur trader.*
dealer: *...an antique dealer.*
broker: *We sell through a broker.*
supplier: *...Hillsdown Holdings, one of the U.K.'s biggest food suppliers.*

mer|chant bank (merchant banks) N-COUNT A **merchant bank** is the same as an **investment bank**.

mer|ci|ful /mɜrsɪfəl/ ◾ ADJ If you describe God or a person in a position of authority as **merciful**, you mean that they show kindness and forgiveness to people. ❏ *We can only hope the court is merciful.* ❷ ADJ If you describe an event or situation as **merciful**, you mean that it is a good thing, especially because it stops someone's suffering or discomfort. ❏ *Eventually the session came to a merciful end.*

mer|ci|ful|ly /mˈɜrsɪfəli/ ADV You can use **mercifully** to show that you are glad that something good has happened, or that something bad has not happened or has stopped. [FEELINGS] ❏ *Mercifully, a friend came to the rescue.*

mer|ci|less /mˈɜrsɪlɪs/ ADJ If you describe someone as **merciless**, you mean that they are very cruel or determined and do not show any concern for the effect their actions have on other people. ❏ *...the merciless efficiency of a modern police state.* • **mer|ci|less|ly** ADV ❏ *We teased him mercilessly.*

mer|cu|rial /mɜrkjˈʊəriəl/ ADJ If you describe someone as **mercurial**, you mean that they frequently change their mind or mood without warning. [LITERARY] ❏ *...his mercurial temperament.*

mer|cu|ry /mˈɜrkjəri/ ❶ N-UNCOUNT **Mercury** is a silver-colored liquid metal that is used especially in thermometers and barometers. ❷ → See also color supplement

mer|cy /mˈɜrsi/ (**mercies**) ❶ N-UNCOUNT If someone in authority shows **mercy**, they choose not to harm someone they have power over, or they forgive someone they have the right to punish. ❏ *Neither side took prisoners or showed any mercy.* ❷ ADJ [ADJ n] **Mercy** is used to describe a special journey to help someone in great need, such as people who are sick or made homeless by war. [JOURNALISM] ❏ *She vanished nine months ago while on a mercy mission to West Africa.* ❸ N-COUNT If you refer to an event or a situation as a **mercy**, you mean that it makes you feel happy or relieved, usually because it stops something unpleasant from happening. ❏ *It really was a mercy that he'd gone so rapidly at the end.* ❹ PHRASE If one person or thing is **at the mercy of** another, the first person or thing is in a situation where they cannot prevent themselves from being harmed or affected by the second. ❏ *Buildings are left to decay at the mercy of vandals and the weather.*

mer|cy kill|ing (**mercy killings**) N-VAR A **mercy killing** is an act of killing someone who is very ill, in order to stop them from suffering any more pain.

mere♦◊◊ /mˈɪər/ (**merest**)

> **Mere** does not have a comparative form. The superlative form **merest** is used to emphasize how small something is, rather than in comparisons.

❶ ADJ [ADJ n] You use **mere** to emphasize how unimportant or inadequate something is, in comparison to the general situation you are describing. [EMPHASIS] ❏ *...successful exhibitions which go beyond mere success.* ❏ *There is more to good health than the mere absence of disease.* ❷ ADJ [ADJ n] You use **mere** to indicate that a quality or action that is usually unimportant has a very important or strong effect. ❏ *The mere mention of food had triggered off hunger pangs.* ❸ ADJ [a ADJ amount] You use **mere** to emphasize how small a particular amount or number is. [EMPHASIS] ❏ *While there are many women teaching at intermediate levels at this school, a mere five percent occupy the upper professor positions.*

mere|ly♦◊◊ /mˈɪərli/ ❶ ADV You use **merely** to emphasize that something is only what you say and not better, more important, or more exciting. [EMPHASIS] ❏ *Michael is now merely a good friend.* ❏ *Francis Watson was far from being merely a furniture expert.* ❷ ADV [ADV amount] You use **merely** to emphasize that a particular amount or quantity is very small. [EMPHASIS] ❏ *The brain accounts for merely three percent of body weight.* ❸ PHRASE You use **not merely** before the less important of two contrasting statements, as a way of emphasizing the more important statement. [EMPHASIS] ❏ *The team needs players who want to play for Canada, not merely any country that will have them.*

mer|etri|cious /mɛrɪtrˈɪʃəs/ ADJ If you describe something as **meretricious**, you disapprove of it because although it looks attractive it is actually of little value. [FORMAL, DISAPPROVAL] ❏ *...vulgar, meretricious, and shabby souvenirs.*

merge /mˈɜrdʒ/ (**merges, merging, merged**) ❶ V-RECIP If one thing **merges** with another, or **is merged** with another, they combine or come together to make one whole thing. You can also say that two things **merge**, or **are merged**. ❏ *Bank of America merged with a rival bank.* ❏ *The rivers merge just north of a vital irrigation system.* ❏ *The two countries merged into one.* ❷ V-RECIP If one sound, color, or object **merges** into another, the first changes so gradually into the second that you do not notice the change. ❏ *Like a chameleon, he could merge unobtrusively into the background.* ❏ *His features merged with the darkness.*

mer|ger♦◊◊ /mˈɜrdʒər/ (**mergers**) N-COUNT A **merger** is the joining together of two separate companies or organizations so that they become one. [BUSINESS] ❏ *...a merger between two of America's biggest trade unions.*

SYNONYMS

merger
NOUN
union: *The majority in this province voted for union with Romania.*
fusion: *His final reform was the fusion of regular and reserve forces.*

---

me|rid|ian /mərˈɪdiən/ (**meridians**) N-COUNT A **meridian** is an imaginary line from the North Pole to the South Pole. Meridians are drawn on maps to help you describe the position of a place.

me|ringue /məræŋ/ (**meringues**) N-VAR **Meringue** is a mixture of beaten egg whites and sugar which is baked in the oven.

mer|it /mˈɛrɪt/ (**merits, meriting, merited**) ❶ N-UNCOUNT If something has **merit**, it has good or worthwhile qualities. ❏ *The argument seemed to have considerable merit.* ❷ N-PLURAL The **merits** of something are its advantages or other good points. ❏ *They have been persuaded of the merits of peace.* ❸ V-T If someone or something **merits** a particular action or treatment, they deserve it. [FORMAL] ❏ *He said he had done nothing wrong to merit a criminal investigation.*

meri|toc|ra|cy /mɛrɪtˈɒkrəsi/ (**meritocracies**) N-VAR A **meritocracy** is a society or social system in which people get status or rewards because of what they achieve, rather than because of their wealth or social status.

meri|to|crat|ic /mɛrɪtəkrˈætɪk/ ADJ [usu ADJ n] A **meritocratic** society or social system gives people status or rewards because of what they achieve, rather than because of their wealth or social position.

meri|to|ri|ous /mɛrɪtˈɔriəs/ ADJ If you describe something as **meritorious**, you approve of it for its good or worthwhile qualities. [FORMAL, APPROVAL] ❏ *I had been promoted for what was called gallant and meritorious service.*

mer|maid /mˈɜrmeɪd/ (**mermaids**) N-COUNT In fairy tales and legends, a **mermaid** is a woman with a fish's tail instead of legs, who lives in the sea.

mer|ri|ly /mˈɛrɪli/ ❶ ADV [ADV with v] If you say that someone **merrily** does something, you are critical of the fact that they do it without realizing that there are a lot of problems which they have not thought about. [DISAPPROVAL] ❏ *There they were, merrily describing their 16-hour working days while claiming to be happily married.* ❷ ADV [ADV with v] If you say that something is happening **merrily**, you mean that it is happening fairly quickly, and in a pleasant or satisfactory way. ❏ *The ferry cut merrily through the water.*

mer|ri|ment /mˈɛrɪmənt/ N-UNCOUNT **Merriment** means laughter. [OLD-FASHIONED]

mer|ry /mˈɛri/ (**merrier, merriest**) ❶ ADJ If you describe someone's character or behavior as **merry**, you mean that they are happy and cheerful. [OLD-FASHIONED] ❏ *From the house come bursts of merry laughter.* • **mer|ri|ly** ADV [ADV after v] ❏ *Chris threw back his head and laughed merrily.* ❷ CONVENTION Just before Christmas and on Christmas Day, people say '**Merry Christmas**' to other people to express the hope that they will have a happy time. [FORMULAE] ❏ *Merry Christmas, everyone.*

merry-go-round (**merry-go-rounds**) ❶ N-COUNT A **merry-go-round** is a circular platform at a carnival or amusement park on which there are model animals or vehicles for people to ride on as it turns around. ❷ N-COUNT [usu sing, oft N of n] You can refer to a continuous series of activities as a **merry-go-round**. ❏ *...a merry-go-round of parties, dances, musical events, and the like.*

merry-making N-UNCOUNT **Merry-making** is the activities of people who are enjoying themselves together in a lively way, for example by eating, drinking, or dancing. ❏ ...*a time of merry-making, feasting, and visiting friends.*

MERS /mɛrz/ N-UNCOUNT **MERS** is an infectious disease that affects the breathing and is caused by a virus. **MERS** is short for 'Middle East respiratory syndrome.' ❏ *MERS was first identified in Saudi Arabia in September 2012.*

me|sa /meɪsə/ (mesas) N-COUNT A **mesa** is a large hill with a flat top and steep sides; used mainly of hills in the southwestern United States. [AM]

mesh /mɛʃ/ (meshes, meshing, meshed) **1** N-VAR **Mesh** is material like a net made from wire, thread, or plastic. ❏ *The ground-floor windows are obscured by wire mesh.* **2** V-RECIP If two things or ideas **mesh** or **are meshed**, they go together well or fit together closely. ❏ *Their senses of humor meshed perfectly.* ❏ *This of course meshes with the economic philosophy of those on the right.* **3** → See feature box at **experiment**

mes|mer|ize /mɛzməraɪz/ (mesmerizes, mesmerizing, mesmerized)

> in BRIT, also use **mesmerise**

V-T If you **are mesmerized** by something, you are so interested in it or so attracted to it that you cannot think about anything else. ❏ *He was absolutely mesmerized by Pavarotti on television.*

mess ✦✧✧ /mɛs/ (messes, messing, messed) **1** N-SING [also no det] If you say that something is a **mess** or in a **mess**, you think that it is not neat. ❏ *The house is a mess.* **2** N-VAR If you say that a situation is a **mess**, you mean that it is full of trouble or problems. You can also say that something is in a **mess**. ❏ *I've made such a mess of my life.* ❏ *...the many reasons why the economy is in such a mess.* **3** N-VAR A **mess** is something liquid or sticky that has been accidentally dropped on something. ❏ *I'll clear up the mess later.* **4** N-COUNT The **mess** at a military base or military barracks is the building in which members of the armed forces can eat or relax. ❏ *...a party at the officers' mess.*

▶ **mess around**

> in BRIT, also use **mess about**

1 PHRASAL VERB If you **mess around**, you spend time doing things without any particular purpose or without achieving anything. ❏ *We were just messing around playing with paint.* **2** PHRASAL VERB If you say that someone **is messing around with** something, you mean that they are interfering with it in a harmful way. ❏ *"Don't be stupid," Max snapped. "You don't want to go messing around with bears."* **3** PHRASAL VERB If someone **is messing around**, they are behaving in a joking or silly way. ❏ *I thought she was messing around.*

▶ **mess up 1** PHRASAL VERB If you **mess** something **up** or if you **mess up**, you cause something to fail or be spoiled. [INFORMAL] ❏ *When politicians mess things up, it is the people who pay the price.* ❏ *He had messed up one career.* **2** PHRASAL VERB If you **mess up** a place or a thing, you make it dirty or not neat. [INFORMAL] ❏ *I hope they haven't messed up your room.*

▶ **mess with** PHRASAL VERB If you tell someone not to **mess with** a person or thing, you are warning them not to get involved with that person or thing. ❏ *You are messing with people's religion and they don't like that.*

---SYNONYMS---

mess
NOUN **1**
disorder: *Inside all was disorder: drawers fallen out, shoes and boots scattered.*
clutter: *Caroline prefers her desk to be clear of clutter.*
disarray: *He found the room in disarray, with food dumped on the floor and drawers pulled open.*

---

mes|sage ✦✦✧ /mɛsɪdʒ/ (messages, messaging, messaged) **1** N-COUNT A **message** is a piece of information or a request that you send to someone or leave for them when you cannot speak to them directly. ❏ *I got a message you were trying to reach me.* **2** N-COUNT The **message** that someone is trying to communicate, for example in a book or play, is the idea or point that they are trying to communicate. ❏ *The report's message was unequivocal.* ❏ *I no longer want to be friends with her but I don't know how to get the message across.* **3** V-T/V-I If you

message someone, you send them a message electronically using a computer or another device such as a cellphone. ❏ *People who message a lot feel unpopular if they don't get many back.*

---SYNONYMS---

message
NOUN
1
note: *I'll have to leave a note for Karen.*
communication: *The ambassador has brought a communication from the President.*
memo: *Did you get the memo about opening hours?*
2
point: *The following tale will clearly illustrate this point.*
meaning: *Unsure of the meaning of this remark, Ryle chose to remain silent.*
theme: *The need to strengthen the family has been a recurrent theme for the Prime Minister.*
import: *I have already spoken about the import of his speech.*

---

mes|sage board (message boards) N-COUNT In computing, a **message board** is a system that allows users to send and receive messages of general interest. [COMPUTING] ❏ *Have your say on our message board by clicking here.*

mes|sag|ing /mɛsɪdʒɪŋ/ N-UNCOUNT **Messaging** is the sending of written or spoken messages using a computer or another electronic device such as a cellphone. ❏ *...services such as messaging, games and music.*

mes|sen|ger /mɛsɪndʒər/ (messengers) N-COUNT [also by N] A **messenger** takes a message to someone, or takes messages regularly as their job. ❏ *There will be a messenger at the airport to collect the photographs from our courier.*

mes|sen|ger boy (messenger boys) N-COUNT A **messenger boy** is a boy who is employed to take messages to people.

mess hall (mess halls) N-COUNT A **mess hall** is a large room where a particular group of people, especially members of the armed forces, eat meals together.

mes|si|ah /mɪsaɪə/ (messiahs) also **Messiah 1** N-PROPER For Jews, **the Messiah** is the King of the Jews, who will be sent to them by God. **2** N-PROPER For Christians, **the Messiah** is Jesus Christ. **3** N-COUNT [usu with supp] If you refer to someone as a **messiah**, you mean that they are expected to do wonderful things, especially to rescue people from a very difficult or dangerous situation, or that they are thought to have done these things. ❏ *People saw Mandela as their messiah.* ❏ *He was somehow destined to become a rock messiah.*

mes|si|an|ic /mɛsiænɪk/ also **Messianic 1** ADJ [ADJ n] **Messianic** means relating to a divine being who has been born, or who will be born, and who will change the world. ❏ *The cult leader saw himself as a messianic figure.* **2** ADJ [usu ADJ n] **Messianic** means relating to the belief that there will be a complete change in the social order in a country or in the world. ❏ *The defeated radicals of the French Revolution were the first to have this messianic vision in 1794.*

Messrs. /mɛsərz/

> in BRIT, use **Messrs**

N-TITLE You use **Messrs.** before the names of two or more men as the plural of **Mr.** [FORMAL, WRITTEN] ❏ *I cannot allow the remarks made by Messrs. Fortt and Wyre to remain unchallenged.*

messy /mɛsi/ (messier, messiest) **1** ADJ A **messy** person or activity makes things dirty or not neat. ❏ *She was a good, if messy, cook.* **2** ADJ Something that is **messy** is dirty or not neat. ❏ *Don't worry if this first coat of paint looks messy.* **3** ADJ If you describe a situation as **messy**, you are emphasizing that it is confused or complicated, and therefore unsatisfactory. ❏ *John had been through a messy divorce himself.*

met /mɛt/ **Met** is the past tense and past participle of **meet**.

meta|bol|ic /mɛtəbɒlɪk/ ADJ [ADJ n] **Metabolic** means relating to a person's or animal's metabolism. ❏ *People who have inherited a low metabolic rate will gain weight.*

me|tabo|lism /mɪtæbəlɪzəm/ (metabolisms) N-VAR Your **metabolism** is the way that chemical processes in your body cause food to be used in an efficient way, for example to make new cells and to give you energy. ❏ *If you skip breakfast, your metabolism slows down.*

me|tabo|lize /mɪtǽbəlaɪz/ (metabolizes, metabolizing, metabolized)

> in BRIT, also use **metabolise**

V-T When you **metabolize** a substance, it is affected by chemical processes in your body so that, for example, it is broken down, absorbed, and used. [TECHNICAL] ☐ *Diabetics cannot metabolize glucose properly.*

met|al ♦◇◇ /mɛ́t°l/ (metals) **1** N-MASS **Metal** is a hard substance such as iron, steel, gold, or lead. ☐ *...pieces of furniture in wood, metal, and glass.* **2** → See feature box at **recycle**; See also color supplement

meta|lan|guage /mɛ́təlæŋgwɪdʒ/ (metalanguages) N-VAR In linguistics, the words and expressions that people use to describe or refer to language can be called **metalanguage**. [TECHNICAL]

me|tal|lic /mətǽlɪk/ **1** ADJ A **metallic** sound is like the sound of one piece of metal hitting another. ☐ *There was a metallic click and the gates swung open.* **2** ADJ **Metallic** paint or colors shine like metal. ☐ *He had painted all the wood with metallic silver paint.* **3** ADJ Something that tastes **metallic** has a bitter, unpleasant taste. ☐ *There was a metallic taste at the back of his throat.* **4** ADJ **Metallic** means consisting entirely or partly of metal. ☐ *Even the smallest metallic object, whether a nail file or cigarette lighter, is immediately confiscated.*

met|al|lur|gist /mɛ́t°lɜrdʒɪst/ (metallurgists) N-COUNT A **metallurgist** is an expert in metallurgy.

met|al|lur|gy /mɛ́t°lɜrdʒi/ N-UNCOUNT **Metallurgy** is the scientific study of the properties and uses of metals.

metal|work /mɛ́t°lwɜrk/ **1** N-UNCOUNT **Metalwork** is the activity of making objects out of metal in a skillful way. ☐ *He was a craftsman in metalwork from Dresden.* **2** N-UNCOUNT The **metalwork** is the metal part of something. ☐ *Rust and flaking paint mean the metalwork is in poor condition.*

meta|morph|ic /mɛtəmɔ́rfɪk/ ADJ **Metamorphic** rocks are rocks that have had their original structure changed by pressure and heat. [TECHNICAL]

meta|mor|phose /mɛ́təmɔrfoʊz/ (metamorphoses, metamorphosing, metamorphosed) **1** VERB To **metamorphose** or **be metamorphosed** means to develop and change into something completely different. [FORMAL] ☐ *...hysterical laughter which gradually metamorphoses into convulsive sobs.* ☐ *The tadpoles metamorphose and emerge onto land.* ☐ *She had been metamorphosed by the war.* **2** → see also **metamorphosis**

meta|mor|pho|sis /mɛtəmɔ́rfəsɪs/ (metamorphoses) N-VAR When a **metamorphosis** occurs, a person or thing develops and changes into something completely different. [FORMAL] ☐ *...his metamorphosis from a Republican to a Democrat.*

meta|phor /mɛ́təfɔr/ (metaphors) **1** N-VAR A **metaphor** is an imaginative way of describing something by referring to something else which is the same in a particular way. For example, if you want to say that someone is very shy and frightened of things, you might say that they are a mouse. ☐ *...the avoidance of violent expressions and metaphors like "kill two birds with one stone."* **2** N-VAR If one thing is a **metaphor** for another, it is intended or regarded as a symbol of it. ☐ *The divided family remains a powerful metaphor for a society that continued to tear itself apart.* **3** PHRASE If you **mix** your **metaphors**, you use two conflicting metaphors. People do this accidentally, or sometimes deliberately as a joke. ☐ *To mix yet more metaphors, you were trying to run before you could walk, and I've clipped your wings.*

meta|phori|cal /mɛtəfɔ́rɪk°l/ ADJ You use the word **metaphorical** to indicate that you are not using words with their ordinary meaning, but are describing something by means of an image or symbol. ☐ *It turns out Levy is talking in metaphorical terms.* ● **meta|phori|cal|ly** ADV ☐ *You're speaking metaphorically, I hope.*

meta|physi|cal /mɛtəfɪ́zɪk°l/ ADJ [usu ADJ n] **Metaphysical** means relating to metaphysics. ☐ *...metaphysical questions like personal responsibility for violence.*

meta|phys|ics /mɛtəfɪ́zɪks/ N-UNCOUNT **Metaphysics** is a part of philosophy which is concerned with understanding reality and developing theories about what exists and how we know that it exists.

me|tas|ta|size /mətǽstəsaɪz/ (metastasizes, metastasizing, metastasized)

> in BRIT, also use **metastasise**

V-I If cancer cells **metastasize**, they spread to another part of the body. [MEDICAL] ☐ *A checkup revealed a small tumor on the left lower lobe of his lung, but it had not yet metastasized.* ☐ *...when diagnosis is delayed until cancer has metastasized to other parts of the body.*

mete /mit/ (metes, meting, meted)
▶ **mete out** PHRASAL VERB To **mete out** a punishment means to order that someone should be punished in a certain way. [FORMAL] ☐ *This provided an illustrative example of how justice was meted out to the local population at the time.*

me|teor /mítiər/ (meteors) N-COUNT A **meteor** is a piece of rock or metal that burns very brightly when it enters the Earth's atmosphere from space.

me|teor|ic /mitiɔ́rɪk/ ADJ If you use **meteoric** when you are describing someone's career, you mean that they achieved success very quickly. ☐ *...his meteoric rise to fame.*

me|teor|ite /mítiəraɪt/ (meteorites) N-COUNT A **meteorite** is a large piece of rock or metal from space that has landed on Earth.

me|teoro|logi|cal /mitiərəlɒ́dʒɪk°l/ ADJ [ADJ n] **Meteorological** means relating to meteorology. ☐ *...adverse meteorological conditions.*

me|teor|ol|ogy /mitiərɒ́lədʒi/ N-UNCOUNT **Meteorology** is the study of the processes in the Earth's atmosphere that cause particular weather conditions, especially in order to predict the weather. ● **me|teor|olo|gist** /mitiərɒ́lədʒɪst/ (meteorologists) N-COUNT ☐ *Meteorologists have predicted mild rains for the next few days.*

me|ter /mítər/ (meters, metering, metered) **1** N-COUNT A **meter** is a device that measures and records something such as the amount of gas or electricity that you have used. ☐ *He was there to read the electricity meter.* **2** V-T To **meter** something such as gas or electricity means to use a meter to measure how much of it people use, usually in order to calculate how much they have to pay. ☐ *Only a third of these households thought it reasonable to meter water.* **3** N-COUNT A **meter** is the same as a **parking meter**. **4** N-COUNT A **meter** is a metric unit of length equal to 100 centimeters. [AM] ☐ *She's running the 1,500 meters here.*

> in BRIT, use **metre**

metha|done /mɛ́θədoʊn/ N-UNCOUNT **Methadone** is a drug that is sometimes prescribed to heroin addicts as a substitute for heroin. ☐ *...the danger of patients overdosing on methadone.*

me|thane /mɛ́θeɪn/ N-UNCOUNT **Methane** is a colorless gas that has no smell. Natural gas consists mostly of methane.

metha|nol /mɛ́θənɒl/ N-UNCOUNT **Methanol** is a colorless, poisonous liquid, used as a solvent and fuel. ☐ *...so-called alternative fuels such as ethanol and methanol.*

meth|od ♦♦◇ /mɛ́θəd/ (methods) N-COUNT A **method** is a particular way of doing something. ☐ *This method of treatment became the basis of modern psychotherapy.*

SYNONYMS

method
NOUN
means: *The move is a means to fight crime.*
mechanism: *There's no mechanism for punishing arms exporters who break the rules.*
way: *Freezing isn't a bad way of preserving food.*
process: *The best way to proceed is by a process of elimination.*

me|thodi|cal /məθɒ́dɪk°l/ ADJ If you describe someone as **methodical**, you mean that they do things carefully, thoroughly, and in order. ☐ *Da Vinci was methodical in his research, carefully recording his observations and theories.* ● **me|thodi|cal|ly** /məθɒ́dɪkli/ ADV [ADV with v] ☐ *She methodically put the things into her suitcase.*

Meth|od|ism /mɛ́θədɪzəm/ N-UNCOUNT **Methodism** is the beliefs and practices of Methodists.

Meth|od|ist /mɛ́θədɪst/ (Methodists) N-COUNT **Methodists** are Protestant Christians who follow the teachings of John

Wesley and who have their own branch of the Christian church and their own form of worship.

meth|od|ol|ogy /mɛθədɒlədʒi/ (**methodologies**) N-VAR A **methodology** is a system of methods and principles for doing something, for example for teaching or for carrying out research. [FORMAL] ❑ *Teaching methodologies vary according to the topic.* ● **meth|odo|logi|cal** /mɛθədəlɒdʒɪkəl/ ADJ ❑ *...theoretical and methodological issues raised by the study of literary texts.*

me|ticu|lous /mətɪkyələs/ ADJ If you describe someone as **meticulous**, you mean that they do things very carefully and with great attention to detail. ❑ *He was so meticulous about everything.* ● **me|ticu|lous|ly** ADV ❑ *The flat had been meticulously cleaned.*

me|ti|er /mɛtyeɪ/ (**metiers**) also **métier** N-COUNT [usu with poss] Your **metier** is the type of work that you have a natural talent for and do well. [FORMAL] ❑ *It was as the magazine's business manager that he found his true metier.*

me|tre ♦◊◊ /mitər/ [BRIT] → see **meter**

met|ric /mɛtrɪk/ ADJ **Metric** means relating to the metric system. ❑ *Around 180,000 metric tons of food aid is required.*

met|ric sys|tem N-SING [the N] The **metric system** is the system of measurement that uses meters, grams, and liters.

met|ric ton (**metric tons**) N-COUNT [num N, oft N of N] A **metric ton** is 1,000 kilograms. ❑ *The Wall Street Journal uses 220,000 metric tons of newsprint each year.*

met|ro /mɛtroʊ/ (**metros**) also **Metro** N-COUNT The **metro** is the subway system in some cities, for example in Washington or Paris. ❑ *A new metro runs under the square, carrying hundreds of thousands who used to cycle to work.*

met|ro|nome /mɛtrənoʊm/ (**metronomes**) **1** N-COUNT A **metronome** is a device which is used to indicate how quickly a piece of music should be played. It can be adjusted to make regular sounds at different speeds. **2** → See also color supplement

me|tropo|lis /mətrɒpəlɪs/ (**metropolises**) N-COUNT A **metropolis** is the largest, busiest, and most important city in a country or region. ❑ *Even Lhasa was a small provincial town compared to the bustling metropolis of Chengdu.*

met|ro|poli|tan /mɛtrəpɒlɪtən/ ADJ [ADJ n] **Metropolitan** means belonging to or typical of a large, busy city. ❑ *...the metropolitan district of Miami.* ❑ *...a dozen major metropolitan hospitals.*

met|ro|sex|ual /mɛtroʊsɛkʃuəl/ ADJ A man who is **metrosexual** spends a lot of time and money on his appearance, and often his home. ❑ *My metrosexual husband has so many shirts that he needs more wardrobe space.*

met|tle /mɛtəl/ N-UNCOUNT [usu poss N] Someone's **mettle** is their ability to do something well in difficult circumstances. ❑ *His first important chance to show his mettle came when he opened the new session of the legislature.*

mew /myu/ (**mews, mewing, mewed**) V-I When a cat **mews**, it makes a soft, high-pitched noise. ❑ *From somewhere, the kitten mewed.*

Mexi|can /mɛksɪkən/ (**Mexicans**) **1** ADJ **Mexican** means belonging or relating to Mexico, or to its people or culture. **2** N-COUNT A **Mexican** is a Mexican citizen, or a person of Mexican origin.

Mexi|can wave (**Mexican waves**) N-COUNT If a crowd of people do a **Mexican wave**, each person in the crowd stands up and puts their arms in the air after the person to one side of them, creating a continuous wave-like motion through the crowd. [BRIT]

in AM, use **wave**

mez|za|nine /mɛzənin/ (**mezzanines**) **1** N-COUNT A **mezzanine** is a small floor which is built between two main floors of a building. ❑ *...the dining room on the mezzanine.* **2** N-COUNT [oft the N] The **mezzanine** is the lowest balcony in a theater, or the front rows in the lowest balcony. [AM]

in BRIT, usually use **dress circle**

3 → See feature box at **house**

mez|zo /mɛtsoʊ/ (**mezzos**) N-COUNT A **mezzo** is the same as a **mezzo-soprano**.

mezzo-soprano (**mezzo-sopranos**) N-COUNT A **mezzo-soprano** is a female singer who sings with a higher range than a contralto but a lower range than a soprano. ❑ *She became a professional mezzo-soprano.* ❑ *...her remarkable mezzo-soprano voice.*

mg mg is a written abbreviation for **milligram** or **milligrams**. ❑ *...300 mg of calcium.*

Mgr. **1** Mgr. is a written abbreviation for **Monsignor**. **2** mgr. is a written abbreviation for **manager**.

MHz MHz is a written abbreviation for **megahertz**.

MIA /ɛm aɪ eɪ/ ADJ MIA is used to describe members of the armed forces who do not return from a military operation but who are not known to have been killed or captured. MIA is an abbreviation for 'missing in action.' [mainly AM] ❑ *He was listed as MIA.*

miaow /miaʊ/ (**miaows, miaowing, miaowed**) → see **meow**

mi|as|ma /maɪæzmə, mi-/ (**miasmas**) N-VAR You can describe something bad or confused that seems to be in the air all around you as a **miasma**. [LITERARY] ❑ *He had lived most of his life in a miasma of uncertainty.*

mic /maɪk/ (**mics**) N-COUNT A **mic** is the same as a **microphone**. [INFORMAL]

mica /maɪkə/ (**micas**) N-MASS **Mica** is a hard mineral which is found as small, flat crystals in rocks. It has a great resistance to heat and electricity.

mice /maɪs/ **Mice** is the plural of **mouse**.

Mickey Mouse ADJ You use **Mickey Mouse** to show that you think something is silly, childish, easy, or worthless. [DISAPPROVAL] ❑ *This is not a Mickey Mouse course where every player has a chance.*

mi|cro /maɪkroʊ/ ADJ [usu ADJ n] You use **micro** to indicate that something relates to a specific area, rather than a general one. [mainly TECHNICAL] ❑ *The vital task was to allow the economy to operate freely at a micro level.*

PREFIX

micro-
forms nouns that have small as part of their meaning. For example, a **microorganism** is a very small living thing that you cannot see with your eyes alone.

---

mi|crobe /maɪkroʊb/ (**microbes**) N-COUNT A **microbe** is a very small, living thing, which you can only see if you use a microscope. ❑ *...a type of bacteria that include the microbes responsible for tuberculosis and leprosy.*

mi|cro|bial /maɪkroʊbiəl/ ADJ [ADJ n] **Microbial** means relating to or caused by microbes. ❑ *...the question of whether microbial life exists, or once existed, on Mars.* ❑ *Microbial infections now kill 17m people a year.*

micro|bio|logi|cal /maɪkroʊbaɪəlɒdʒɪkəl/ ADJ [ADJ n] **Microbiological** refers to studies or tests relating to very small living things such as bacteria and their effects on people. ❑ *...microbiological testing.*

micro|bi|ol|ogy /maɪkroʊbaɪɒlədʒi/ N-UNCOUNT **Microbiology** is the branch of biology which is concerned with very small living things such as bacteria and their effects on people. ❑ *...a professor of microbiology and immunology.* ● **micro|bi|olo|gist** (**microbiologists**) N-COUNT ❑ *...a microbiologist at Columbia University.*

micro|brewery /maɪkroʊbruəri/ (**microbreweries**) N-COUNT A **microbrewery** is a type of small brewery where beer is produced using traditional methods.

micro|chip /maɪkroʊtʃɪp/ (**microchips**) N-COUNT A **microchip** is a very small piece of silicon inside a computer. It has electronic circuits on it and can hold large quantities of information or perform mathematical and logical operations.

micro|com|put|er /maɪkroʊkəmpyutər/ (**microcomputers**) N-COUNT A **microcomputer** is a small computer, especially one used for writing documents.

micro|cosm /maɪkrəkɒzəm/ (**microcosms**) N-COUNT [oft N of n, also in N] A **microcosm** is a small society, place, or activity which has all the typical features of a much larger one and so seems like a smaller version of it. [FORMAL] ❑ *Kitchell says the city was a microcosm of all American culture during the '60s.*

micro|cred|it /maɪkroʊkrɛdɪt/ N-UNCOUNT **Microcredit** is credit in the form of small loans offered to local businesses, especially in developing countries. [BUSINESS] ❑ *One tool to fight poverty is the use of microcredit loans.*

micro|eco|nom|ics /maɪkroʊɛkənɒmɪks, -ik-/ also **micro-economics** N-UNCOUNT **Microeconomics** is the branch of economics that is concerned with individual areas of economic activity, such as those within a particular company or relating to a particular market. [BUSINESS] ❑ *He has 250 students in his microeconomics course.* ● **micro|eco|nom|ic** /maɪkroʊɛkənɒmɪk, -ik-/ ADJ [usu ADJ n] ❑ *...an important flaw in microeconomic theory.* ❑ *It is possible to have a microeconomic success and a macroeconomic failure, as Britain did in the late eighties.*

micro|elec|tron|ics /maɪkroʊɪlɛktrɒnɪks/

The form **microelectronic** is used as a modifier.

N-UNCOUNT **Microelectronics** is the branch of electronics that deals with miniature electronic circuits.

micro|fiber /maɪkroʊfaɪbər/ (**microfibers**)

in BRIT, use **microfibre**

N-VAR **Microfibers** are extremely light, artificial fibers that are used to make cloth. ❑ *...woven in great looking and durable microfiber.*

micro|fiche /maɪkrəfiʃ/ (**microfiches**) N-VAR A **microfiche** is a small sheet of film on which writing or other information is stored, greatly reduced in size.

micro|film /maɪkrəfɪlm/ (**microfilms**) N-VAR **Microfilm** is film that is used for photographing information and storing it in a reduced form.

micro|fi|nance /maɪkroʊfaɪnæns/ N-UNCOUNT **Microfinance** is the same as **microcredit**. [BUSINESS] ❑ *The work of microfinance institutions and development organizations is essential in helping the poorest in society.*

micro|or|gan|ism /maɪkroʊɔːrgənɪzəm/ (**microorganisms**) N-COUNT A **microorganism** is a very small living thing which you can only see if you use a microscope.

micro|phone /maɪkrəfoʊn/ (**microphones**) ◻ N-COUNT A **microphone** is a device that is used to make sounds louder or to record them on a tape recorder. ◼ → See also color supplement

micro|pro|ces|sor /maɪkroʊprɒsɛsər/ (**microprocessors**) N-COUNT In a computer, the **microprocessor** is the main microchip, which controls its most important functions. [COMPUTING]

micro|scope /maɪkrəskoʊp/ (**microscopes**) ◻ N-COUNT A **microscope** is a scientific instrument which makes very small objects look bigger so that more detail can be seen. ◼ → See also color supplement

micro|scop|ic /maɪkrəskɒpɪk/ ◻ ADJ **Microscopic** objects are extremely small, and usually can be seen only through a microscope. ❑ *Microscopic fibers of protein were visible.* ◼ ADJ [ADJ n] A **microscopic** examination is done using a microscope. ❑ *Microscopic examination of a cell's chromosomes can reveal the sex of the fetus.* ◻ → See feature box at **brain**

micro|sec|ond /maɪkroʊsɛkənd/ (**microseconds**) N-COUNT A **microsecond** is one millionth of a second.

micro|sur|gery /maɪkroʊsɜːrdʒəri/ N-UNCOUNT **Microsurgery** is a form of surgery where doctors repair or remove parts of the body that are so small that they can only be seen clearly using a microscope.

micro|wave /maɪkroʊweɪv/ (**microwaves, microwaving, microwaved**) ◻ N-COUNT A **microwave** or a **microwave oven** is an oven which cooks food very quickly by electromagnetic radiation rather than by heat. ◼ V-T To **microwave** food or drink means to cook or heat it in a microwave oven. ❑ *Steam or microwave the vegetables until tender.*

micro|wave|able /maɪkroʊweɪvəbəl/ also **microwavable** ADJ **Microwaveable** food can be cooked in a microwave.

PREFIX

mid- forms nouns and adjectives that refer to the middle part of a particular period of time, or the middle part of a particular place. For example, *mid-June* is the middle of June.

---

mid|air also **mid-air** /mɪdɛər/ N-UNCOUNT If something happens in **midair**, it happens in the air, rather than on the ground. ❑ *The bird stopped and hovered in mid-air.*

mid-Atlantic ADJ If you describe someone's accent as **mid-Atlantic**, you mean that it is a mixture of British and American accents. ❑ *For himself, he had cultivated a mid-Atlantic accent.*

mid|day /mɪddeɪ/ ◻ N-UNCOUNT **Midday** is twelve o'clock in the middle of the day. ❑ *At midday everyone would go down to Reg's Café.* ◼ N-UNCOUNT **Midday** is the middle part of the day, from late morning to early afternoon. ❑ *People were beginning to tire in the midday heat.*

mid|dle ♦♦♦ /mɪdəl/ (**middles**) ◻ N-COUNT The **middle** of something is the part of it that is farthest from its edges, ends, or outside surface. ❑ *Howard stood in the middle of the room sipping a cup of coffee.* ❑ *They had a volleyball court in the middle of the courtyard.* ◼ **the middle of nowhere** → see **nowhere** ◼ ADJ [ADJ n] The **middle** object in a row of objects is the one that has an equal number of objects on each side. ❑ *The middle button of his uniform jacket was strained over his belly.* ◼ N-SING The **middle** of an event or period of time is the part that comes after the first part and before the last part. ❑ *I woke up in the middle of the night and could hear a tapping on the window.* ● ADJ [ADJ n] **Middle** is also an adjective. ❑ *Many classical violinists and pianists become conductors in their middle years.* ◼ PHRASE If you are **in the middle of** doing something, you are busy doing it. ❑ *It's a bit hectic. I'm in the middle of cooking for nine people.*

mid|dle age N-UNCOUNT **Middle age** is the period in your life when you are no longer young but have not yet become old. Middle age is usually considered to take place between the ages of 40 and 60. ❑ *Men tend to put on weight in middle age.*

middle-aged ◻ ADJ If you describe someone as **middle-aged**, you mean that they are neither young nor old. People between the ages of 40 and 60 are usually considered to be middle-aged. ❑ *...middle-aged, married businessmen.* ◼ ADJ If you describe someone's activities or interests as **middle-aged**, you are critical of them because you think they are typical of a middle-aged person, for example by being conventional or old-fashioned. [DISAPPROVAL] ❑ *Her novels are middle-aged and boring.*

Mid|dle Ages N-PLURAL [the N] In European history, **the Middle Ages** was the period between the end of the Roman Empire in A.D. 476 and about A.D. 1500, especially the later part of this period.

Mid|dle Ameri|ca ◻ N-UNCOUNT Journalists use **Middle America** to refer to middle class people in the United States who are believed not to like change. ❑ *People in the United States want the president to pay attention to Middle America.* ◼ N-PROPER **Middle America** is the same as the **Midwest**.

middle|brow /mɪdəlbraʊ/ ADJ [usu ADJ n] If you describe a piece of entertainment such as a book or movie as **middlebrow**, you mean that although it may be interesting and enjoyable, it does not require much thought. ❑ *This program disproves the theory that TV, a middlebrow medium, is neither as smart as the smartest movies nor as dumb as the dumbest.*

mid|dle class ♦◇◇ (**middle classes**) ◻ N-COUNT-COLL The **middle class** or **middle classes** are the people in a society who are not working class or upper class. Business people, managers, doctors, lawyers, and teachers are usually regarded as middle class. ❑ *...the expansion of the middle class in the late 19th century.* ● ADJ **Middle class** is also an adjective. ❑ *He is rapidly losing the support of blue-collar voters and of middle-class conservatives.* ◼ → See feature box at **leisure**

mid|dle dis|tance ◻ N-SING [the N, usu into/in the N] If you are looking into the **middle distance**, you are looking at a place that is neither near nor far away. ❑ *He stares detachedly into the middle distance, toward nothing in particular.* ◼ ADJ [ADJ n] A **middle-distance** runner is someone who takes part in races of medium length, for example 800 meters.

Mid|dle East ♦♦◇ N-PROPER The **Middle East** is the area around the eastern Mediterranean that includes Iran and all the countries in Asia to the west and southwest of Iran. ❑ *The two great rivers of the Middle East rise in the mountains of Turkey.*

Mid|dle East|ern ADJ [ADJ n] **Middle Eastern** means relating to the Middle East. ❑ *Most Middle Eastern countries have extremely high rates of population growth.*

middleman · middweek

middle|man /mɪdᵊlmæn/ (**middlemen**) **1** N-COUNT A **middleman** is a person or company which buys things from the people who produce them and sells them to the people who want to buy them. [BUSINESS] ❑ *Why don't they cut out the middleman and let us do it ourselves?* **2** N-COUNT A **middleman** is a person who helps in negotiations between people who are unwilling to meet each other directly. ❑ *The two sides would only meet indirectly, through middlemen.*

mid|dle man|age|ment N-UNCOUNT **Middle management** refers to managers who are below the top level of management, and who are responsible for controlling and running an organization rather than making decisions about how it operates. [BUSINESS] ❑ *The proportion of women in middle management has risen to 40%.*

mid|dle name (**middle names**) **1** N-COUNT [usu poss N] Your **middle name** is the name that comes between your first name and your surname. ❑ *His middle name is Justin.* **2** N-COUNT [usu poss N] You can use **middle name** in expressions such as '**discretion was her middle name**' and '**his middle name is loyalty**' to indicate that someone always behaves with a great deal of a particular quality. [HUMOROUS] ❑ *He's a gambler, and chance is his middle name.*

middle-of-the-road **1** ADJ If you describe someone's opinions or policies as **middle-of-the-road**, you mean that they are neither left wing nor right wing, and not at all extreme. ❑ *Consensus need not be weak, nor need it result in middle-of-the-road policies.* **2** ADJ If you describe something or someone as **middle-of-the-road**, you mean that they are ordinary or unexciting. ❑ *I actually don't want to be a middle-of-the-road person, married with a mortgage.*

middle-ranking ADJ [ADJ n] A **middle-ranking** person has a fairly important or responsible position in a particular organization, but is not one of the most important people in it. ❑ *...middle-ranking army officers.*

mid|dle school (**middle schools**) N-VAR A **middle school** is a school for children in the fifth to eighth grades, between the ages of 10 and 13. ❑ *...Harlem Park Middle School.*

Mid|dle West N-PROPER [the N] The **Middle West** is the central part of the United States.

mid|dling /mɪdlɪŋ/ ADJ [usu ADJ n] If you describe a quality such as the size of something as **middling**, you mean that it is average. ❑ *The Beatles enjoyed only middling success until 1963.* ❑ *...a man of middling height.*

mid|field /mɪdfiːld/ N-UNCOUNT [oft N n] In football and soccer, the **midfield** is the central area of the playing field between the two goals, or the players whose usual position is in this area. ❑ *In the last two years, I played a lot of games in midfield.* ❑ *We need to try and get the midfield scoring more goals.* ❑ *...the best midfield player in the world.*

mid|field|er /mɪdfiːldər/ (**midfielders**) N-COUNT In soccer, a **midfielder** is a player whose usual position is in the midfield. ❑ *The young French midfielder has yet to score.*

midge /mɪdʒ/ (**midges**) N-COUNT **Midges** are very small insects which bite.

midg|et /mɪdʒɪt/ (**midgets**) N-COUNT People who are very short are sometimes referred to as **midgets**. [OFFENSIVE]

MIDI /mɪdi/ also **Midi** N-UNCOUNT [usu N n] **MIDI** is a computer system that allows you to record the output of a musical instrument such as an electric guitar or synthesizer, so that the recording is in a digital form. **MIDI** is an abbreviation for 'musical instrument digital interface.' [COMPUTING] ❑ *...a MIDI keyboard.*

mid|life cri|sis /mɪdlaɪf kraɪsɪs/ (**midlife crises**) N-COUNT [usu sing] A **midlife crisis** is a period of doubt and anxiety that some people experience in middle age, when they think about whether their life is the kind of life that they want. ❑ *I went through my midlife crisis about four or five years ago, when I was forty.*

mid|night ✦✧✧ /mɪdnaɪt/ **1** N-UNCOUNT **Midnight** is twelve o'clock in the middle of the night. ❑ *It was well after midnight by the time Anne returned to her apartment.* **2** ADJ [ADJ n] **Midnight** is used to describe something that happens or appears at midnight or in the middle of the night. ❑ *It is totally out of the question to postpone the midnight deadline.* **3** PHRASE If someone **is burning the midnight oil**, they are staying up very late in order to study or do some other work. ❑ *Chris is asleep after burning the midnight oil trying to finish his article.*

mid|night blue COLOR Something that is **midnight blue** is a very dark blue color, almost black.

mid|point /mɪdpɔɪnt/ also **mid-point** **1** N-SING [oft N between/of n] The **midpoint** between two things is the point that is the same distance from both things. ❑ *...the midpoint between New York and Chicago.* **2** N-SING [oft N of n] The **midpoint** of an event is the time halfway between the beginning and the end of it. ❑ *She has not yet reached the midpoint of her life.*

mid-range also **midrange** ADJ [ADJ n] You can use **mid-range** to describe products or services which are neither the most expensive nor the cheapest of their type. ❑ *...the price of a mid-range family car.*

mid|riff /mɪdrɪf/ (**midriffs**) N-COUNT [usu sing] Someone's **midriff** is the middle part of their body, between their waist and their chest. ❑ *...the girl with the bare midriff.*

mid|ship|man /mɪdʃɪpmən/ (**midshipmen**) N-COUNT; N-TITLE A **midshipman** is a cadet who is training to become a junior officer in the navy. ❑ *He had become a midshipman at age sixteen.* ❑ *...midshipman Edward Brooke of the U.S. Navy.*

mid|sized /mɪdsaɪzd/ also **mid-sized, midsize** ADJ [ADJ n] You use **midsized** or **midsize** to describe products, cities, companies, and other things that are neither large nor small. ❑ *...a low-cost midsized car.* ❑ *...a midsize city.*

midst /mɪdst/ **1** PHRASE If you are **in the midst of** doing something, you are doing it at the moment. ❑ *We are in the midst of one of the worst recessions for many, many years.* **2** PHRASE If something happens **in the midst of** an event, it happens during it. ❑ *Eleanor arrived in the midst of a blizzard.* **3** PHRASE If someone or something is **in the midst of** a group of people or things, they are among them or surrounded by them. ❑ *Many were surprised to see him exposed like this in the midst of a large crowd.*

mid|stream /mɪdstriːm/ **1** N-UNCOUNT [oft in n] Someone or something that is in **midstream** is in the middle of a river, where the current is strongest. ❑ *Their boat had capsized in midstream.* • ADV **Midstream** is also an adverb. ❑ *Some of them got caught midstream by the tide.* **2** N-UNCOUNT [oft in n] If someone who has been doing something such as talking stops or pauses in **midstream**, they stop doing it, often before continuing. ❑ *I was cut off in midstream.* • ADV [ADV after v] **Midstream** is also an adverb. ❑ *The most difficult thing in a fast game of basketball is to change course midstream.*

mid|sum|mer /mɪdsʌmər/ N-UNCOUNT **Midsummer** is the period in the middle of the summer. ❑ *In midsummer every Cape Cod town is impossibly crowded.* ❑ *It was a lovely midsummer morning.*

Mid|sum|mer's Day N-PROPER **Midsummer's Day** or **Midsummer Day** is the 24th of June. [BRIT]

mid|term /mɪdtɜːrm/ (**midterms**) **1** ADJ [ADJ n] A **midterm** election is an election that takes place approximately halfway through a president's or a government's term of office. ❑ *The Republican Party faces a tough challenge in midterm congressional elections in November.*

> in BRIT, usually use **mid-term**

2 N-COUNT A **midterm** or a **midterm exam** is a test which a student takes in the middle of a school or college term. ❑ *She was about to walk into a midterm exam for a subject she knew very little about.*

mid|town /mɪdtaʊn/ ADJ [ADJ n] **Midtown** places are in the center of a city. [AM] ❑ *...a midtown Manhattan hotel.* • N-UNCOUNT **Midtown** is also a noun. ❑ *He drove around midtown, singing.*

mid|way /mɪdweɪ/ **1** ADV [ADV prep] If something is **midway** between two places, it is between them and the same distance from each of them. ❑ *The studio is midway between his aunt's old home and his cottage.* • ADJ [ADJ n] **Midway** is also an adjective. ❑ *Fresno is close to the midway point between LA and San Francisco.* **2** ADV If something happens **midway** through a period of time, it happens during the middle part of it. ❑ *He crashed midway through the race.* • ADJ [ADJ n] **Midway** is also an adjective. ❑ *They were denied an obvious penalty before the midway point of the first half.*

mid|week /mɪdwiːk/ ADJ [ADJ n] **Midweek** describes something that happens in the middle of the week. ❑ *Enjoy the peace and* beauty of midweek walks in the park. • ADV **Midweek** is also an adverb. ❏ *They'll be able to go up to Washington midweek.*

Mid|west /mɪdwɛst/ N-PROPER [usu the N] The **Midwest** is the region in the central part of the United States and north of Texas. ❏ *...farmers in the Midwest.* ❏ *...the Midwest states.*

Mid|west|ern /mɪdwɛstərn/ ADJ [usu ADJ n] **Midwestern** means belonging or relating to the Midwest. ❏ *...the Midwestern plains.* ❏ *...traditional Midwestern values.*

mid|wife /mɪdwaɪf/ (**midwives**) ■ N-COUNT A **midwife** is a nurse who is trained to deliver babies and to advise pregnant women. ❏ *You don't have to call the midwife as soon as labor starts.* ■ → See feature box at **birth**

mid|wife|ry /mɪdwɪfəri, -waɪfə-/ N-UNCOUNT **Midwifery** is the work of delivering babies and advising pregnant women.

mid|win|ter /mɪdwɪntər/ N-UNCOUNT **Midwinter** is the period in the middle of winter. ❏ *...the bleak midwinter.* ❏ *...the cold midwinter weather.*

mien /min/ N-SING [usu poss N] Someone's **mien** is their general appearance and manner, especially the expression on their face, which shows what they are feeling or thinking. [LITERARY] ❏ *It was impossible to tell from his mien whether he was offended.* ❏ *...his mild manner and aristocratic mien.*

miffed /mɪft/ ADJ [usu v-link ADJ] If you are **miffed**, you are slightly annoyed and hurt because of something that someone has said or done to you. [INFORMAL] ❏ *I was a little miffed about that.*

MIGHT
① MODAL USES
② NOUN USES
---

① **might** ✦✦✦ /maɪt/

Might is a modal verb. It is used with the base form of a verb.

→ Please look at meaning ⓫ to see if the expression you are looking for is shown under another headword.

■ MODAL You use **might** to indicate that something will possibly happen or be true in the future, but you cannot be certain. [VAGUENESS] ❏ *There's a report today that smoking might be banned in most buildings.* ❏ *I might well regret it later.* ❷ MODAL You use **might** to indicate that there is a possibility that something is true, but you cannot be certain. [VAGUENESS] ❏ *She and Robert's father had not given up hope that he might be alive.* ❏ *You might be right.* ❸ MODAL You use **might** to indicate that something could happen or be true in particular circumstances. [VAGUENESS] ❏ *America might sell more cars to the islands if they were made with the steering wheel on the right.* ❹ MODAL You use **might have** with a past participle to indicate that it is possible that something happened or was true, or when giving a possible explanation for something. ❏ *I heard what might have been an explosion.* ❺ MODAL You use **might have** with a past participle to indicate that something was a possibility in the past, although it did not actually happen. ❏ *If she had had to give up riding she might have taken up sailing competitively.* ❻ MODAL You use **might** in statements where you are accepting the truth of a situation, but contrasting it with something that is more important. ❏ *They might not have two cents to rub together, but at least they have a kind of lifestyle that is different.* ❼ MODAL You use **might** when you are saying emphatically that someone ought to do the thing mentioned, especially when you are annoyed because they have not done it. [EMPHASIS] ❏ *You might have told me that before!* ❽ MODAL You use **might** to make a suggestion or to give advice in a very polite way. [POLITENESS] ❏ *They might be wise to stop advertising on television.* ❾ MODAL You use **might** as a polite way of interrupting someone, asking a question, making a request, or introducing what you are going to say next. [FORMAL, SPOKEN, POLITENESS] ❏ *Might I make a suggestion?* ❏ *Might I ask what you're doing here?* ❿ MODAL You use **might** in expressions such as **I might have known** and **I might have guessed** to indicate that you are not surprised at a disappointing event or fact. ❏ *I might have known she'd be late.* ⓫ **might as well** → see **well** ③

② **might** /maɪt/ ■ N-UNCOUNT **Might** is power or strength. [FORMAL] ❏ *The might of the army could prove a decisive factor.* ❷ PHRASE If you do something **with all** your **might**, you do it using all your strength and energy. ❏ *Kai had hold of his wrists now, and was pulling with all his might.*

mighti|ly /maɪtɪli/ ADV **Mightily** means to a great extent or degree. [OLD-FASHIONED, EMPHASIS] ❏ *He had given a mightily impressive performance.* ❏ *She strove mightily to put Mike from her thoughts.*

mightn't /maɪtᵊnt/ **Mightn't** is a spoken form of 'might not.'

might've /maɪtəv/ **Might've** is the usual spoken form of 'might have,' especially when 'have' is an auxiliary verb.

mighty /maɪti/ (**mightier, mightiest**) ■ ADJ **Mighty** is used to describe something that is very large or powerful. [LITERARY] ❏ *There was a flash and a mighty bang.* ❷ ADV [ADV adj/adv] **Mighty** is used in front of adjectives and adverbs to emphasize the quality that they are describing. [mainly AM, INFORMAL, EMPHASIS] ❏ *It's something you'll be mighty proud of.* ❸ → see also **high-and-mighty**

mi|graine /maɪgreɪn/ (**migraines**) N-VAR A **migraine** is an extremely painful headache that makes you feel very ill. ❏ *Her mother suffered from migraines.*

WORD HISTORY

migraine
Migraine comes via French from Latin *hēmicrānia*, meaning 'pain in half the head,' from Greek *hemi-*, meaning 'half,' and *kranion*, meaning 'cranium' or 'skull.'
---

mi|grant /maɪgrənt/ (**migrants**) ■ N-COUNT A **migrant** is a person who moves from one place to another, especially in order to find work. ❏ *The government divides asylum seekers into economic migrants and genuine refugees.* ❷ N-COUNT **Migrants** are birds, fish, or animals that migrate from one part of the world to another. ❏ *Migrant birds shelter in the reeds.*

mi|grate /maɪgreɪt/ (**migrates, migrating, migrated**) ■ V-I If people **migrate**, they move from one place to another, especially in order to find work or to live somewhere for a short time. ❏ *People migrate to cities like Jakarta in search of work.* • **mi|gra|tion** /maɪgreɪʃᵊn/ (**migrations**) N-VAR ❏ *...a mass migration of twentysomethings back to their family homes during the pandemic.* ❷ V-I When birds, fish, or animals **migrate**, they move at a particular season from one part of the world or from one part of a country to another, usually in order to breed or to find new feeding grounds. ❏ *Most birds have to fly long distances to migrate.* • **mi|gra|tion** N-VAR ❏ *...the migration of animals in the Serengeti.*

mi|gra|tory /maɪgrətɔri/ ■ ADJ [usu ADJ n] A **migratory** bird, fish, or animal is one that migrates every year. ❷ ADJ [ADJ n] **Migratory** means relating to the migration of people, birds, fish, or animals. ❏ *...migratory farm labor.*

mike /maɪk/ (**mikes**) N-COUNT A **mike** is the same as a microphone. [INFORMAL]

mil /mɪl/ (**mil**) NUM **Mil** means the same as **million**. [INFORMAL] ❏ *Zhamnov, 22, signed for $1.25 mil over three years.*

mild ✦◇◇ /maɪld/ (**milder, mildest**) ■ ADJ **Mild** is used to describe something such as a feeling, attitude, or illness that is not very strong or severe. ❏ *Teddy turned to Mona with a look of mild confusion.* • **mild|ly** ADV ❏ *Josephine must have had the disease very mildly as she showed no symptoms.* ❷ ADJ A **mild** person is gentle and does not get angry easily. ❏ *He is a mild man, who is reasonable almost to the point of blandness.* • **mild|ly** ADV [ADV after v] ❏ *"I'm not meddling," Ken said mildly, "I'm just curious."* ❸ ADJ **Mild** weather is pleasant because it is neither extremely hot nor extremely cold. ❏ *The area is famous for its very mild winter climate.* ❹ ADJ You describe food as **mild** when it does not taste or smell strong, sharp, or bitter, especially when you like it because of this. ❏ *This cheese has a soft, mild flavor.* ❺ → see also **mildly**

mil|dew /mɪldu/ N-UNCOUNT **Mildew** is a soft, smelly fungus that grows in damp places. ❏ *The room smelled of mildew.*

mil|dewed /mɪldud/ ADJ Something that is **mildewed** has mildew growing on it.

mild|ly /maɪldli/ ■ → see **mild** ❷ PHRASE You use **to put it mildly** to indicate that you are describing something in language that is much less strong, direct, or critical than what you really think. ❏ *But not all the money, to put it mildly, has been used wisely.*

mild-mannered also **mild mannered** ADJ If you describe someone as **mild mannered**, you approve of them because they are gentle, kind, and polite. [APPROVAL]

mile ✦✧ /maɪl/ (**miles**) **1** N-COUNT A **mile** is a unit of distance equal to 1760 yards or approximately 1.6 kilometers. ❑ *They drove 600 miles across the desert.* ❑ *She lives just half a mile away.* **2** N-PLURAL **Miles** is used, especially in the expression **miles away**, to refer to a long distance. ❑ *If you enroll at a gym that's miles away, you won't be visiting it as often as you should.* **3** N-COUNT **Miles** or **a mile** is used with the meaning 'very much' in order to emphasize the difference between two things or qualities, or the difference between what you aimed to do and what you actually achieved. [INFORMAL, EMPHASIS] ❑ *You're miles better than most of the performers we see nowadays.* ❑ *With a Democratic candidate in place they won by a mile.*

WORD HISTORY

mile
In Roman times, a **mile** was equal to a thousand paces. In Latin, 'one thousand paces' is *milia passuum*, from *mille*, meaning 'a thousand' (the same Latin word as is found in English words such as 'millennium' and 'millimeter').

mile|age /maɪlɪdʒ/ **1** N-UNCOUNT **Mileage** refers to the distance that you have traveled, measured in miles. ❑ *While most of their mileage may be in and around town, they still want highways for longer trips.* **2** N-UNCOUNT The **mileage** of a vehicle is the number of miles that it can travel using one gallon or liter of fuel. ❑ *They are willing to pay up to $500 more for cars that get better mileage.* **3** N-UNCOUNT The **mileage** in a particular course of action is its usefulness in getting you what you want. ❑ *It's obviously important to get as much mileage out of the convention as possible.*

mile|stone /maɪlstoʊn/ (**milestones**) N-COUNT A **milestone** is an important event in the history or development of something or someone. ❑ *He said the launch of the party represented a milestone in Zambian history.*

mi|lieu /mɪlyu, mil-/ (**milieux** or **milieus**) N-COUNT Your **milieu** is the group of people or activities that you live among or are familiar with. [FORMAL] ❑ *They stayed, safe and happy, within their own social milieu.*

mili|tant ✦✧ /mɪlɪtənt/ (**militants**) **1** ADJ You use **militant** to describe people who believe in something very strongly and are active in trying to bring about political or social change, often in extreme ways that other people find unacceptable. ❑ *Militant mine workers in the Ukraine have voted for a one-day stoppage next month.* • N-COUNT **Militant** is also a noun. ❑ *Even now we could not be sure that the militants would not find some new excuse to call a strike the following winter.* • **mili|tan|cy** N-UNCOUNT ❑ *...the rise of labor union militancy.* **2** → See feature box at **politics**

SYNONYMS

militant
ADJ
aggressive: *Some children are much more aggressive than others.*
belligerent: *...the belligerent statements from both sides which have led to fears of war.*
warring: *The warring factions have not yet turned in all their heavy weapons.*
combative: *He conducted the meeting in his usual combative style, refusing to admit any mistakes.*

mili|ta|rism /mɪlɪtərɪzəm/ N-UNCOUNT **Militarism** is a country's desire to strengthen their armed forces in order to make themselves more powerful. [DISAPPROVAL] ❑ *The country slipped into a dangerous mixture of nationalism and militarism.*

mili|ta|rist /mɪlɪtərɪst/ (**militarists**) **1** N-COUNT [oft N n] If you describe someone as a **militarist**, you mean that they want their country's armed forces to be strengthened in order to make it more powerful. [DISAPPROVAL] **2** ADJ [usu ADJ n] **Militarist** means the same as **militaristic**. [DISAPPROVAL] ❑ *...militarist policies.*

mili|ta|ris|tic /mɪlɪtərɪstɪk/ ADJ **Militaristic** is used to describe groups, ideas, or policies which support the strengthening of the armed forces of their country in order to make it more powerful. [DISAPPROVAL] ❑ *...aggressive militaristic governments.*

mili|ta|rized /mɪlɪtəraɪzd/

in BRIT, also use **militarised**

1 ADJ [usu ADJ n] A **militarized** area or region has members of the armed forces and military equipment in it. ❑ *...the militarized zone that separates the faction leaders' areas of control.* **2** ADJ You can use **militarized** to show disapproval of something that has many military characteristics, for example the quality of being aggressive or strict. [DISAPPROVAL] ❑ *...a militarized style of politics.*

mili|tary ✦✦✦ /mɪlɪteri/ (**militaries**) **1** ADJ **Military** means relating to the armed forces of a country. ❑ *Military action may become necessary.* ❑ *The president is sending in almost 20,000 military personnel to help with the relief efforts.* • **mili|tari|ly** /mɪlɪtɛərɪli/ ADV ❑ *They remain unwilling to intervene militarily in what could be an unending war.* **2** N-COUNT-COLL The **military** are the armed forces of a country, especially officers of high rank. ❑ *The bombing has been far more widespread than the military will admit.* **3** ADJ **Military** means well organized, controlled, or neat, in a way that is typical of a soldier. ❑ *Your working day will need to be organized with military precision.*

mili|tary po|lice **1** N-SING-COLL The **military police** are the part of an army, navy, or air force that act as its police force. ❑ *The government has said it will reform the military police.* **2** N-PLURAL **Military police** are men and women who are members of the part of an army, navy, or air force that act as its police force. ❑ *The camp is surrounded by razor-wire fences and guarded by military police.*

mili|tary police|man (**military policemen**) N-COUNT A **military policeman** is a male member of the military police.

mili|tary police|woman (**military policewomen**) N-COUNT A **military policewoman** is a female member of the military police.

mili|tary ser|vice **1** N-UNCOUNT If someone does **military service** they spend a period of time in the armed forces. [AM] **2** N-UNCOUNT [oft with poss] **Military service** is a period of service in the armed forces that every man in certain countries has to do. ❑ *Many conscripts resent having to do their military service.*

mili|tate /mɪlɪteɪt/ (**militates, militating, militated**) V-I To **militate against** something means to make it less possible or likely. To **militate against** someone means to prevent them from achieving something. [FORMAL] ❑ *Her background militates against her.* ❑ *We can never promise to sail anywhere in particular, because the weather might militate against it.*

mi|li|tia /mɪlɪʃə/ (**militias**) N-COUNT A **militia** is an organization that operates like an army but whose members are not professional soldiers. ❑ *The troops will not attempt to disarm the warring militias.*

mi|li|tia|man /mɪlɪʃəmən/ (**militiamen**) N-COUNT A **militiaman** is a member of a militia.

milk ✦✧ /mɪlk/ (**milks, milking, milked**) **1** N-UNCOUNT **Milk** is the white liquid produced by cows, goats, and some other animals, which people drink and use to make butter, cheese, and yogurt. ❑ *He stepped out to buy a quart of milk.* **2** V-T If someone **milks** a cow or goat, they get milk from it, using either their hands or a machine. ❑ *Farm workers milked cows by hand.* **3** N-UNCOUNT **Milk** is the white liquid produced by women to feed their babies. ❑ *Milk from the mother's breast is a perfect food for the human baby.* **4** N-MASS Liquid products for cleaning your skin or making it softer are sometimes referred to as **milks**. ❑ *Sales of cleansing milks, creams, and gels have doubled over the past decade.* **5** V-T If you say that someone **milks** something, you mean that they get as much benefit or profit as they can from it, without caring about the effects this has on other people. [DISAPPROVAL] ❑ *A few people tried to milk the insurance companies.* **6** → see also **skim milk**

milk choco|late N-UNCOUNT **Milk chocolate** is chocolate that has been made with milk. It is lighter in color and has a creamier taste than dark chocolate.

milk|maid /mɪlkmeɪd/ (**milkmaids**) N-COUNT In former times, a **milkmaid** was a woman who milked cows and made butter and cheese on a farm.

milk|man /mɪlkmæn/ (**milkmen**) N-COUNT A **milkman** is a man who delivers milk to people's homes.

milk prod|uct (milk products) N-COUNT [usu pl] Milk products are foods made from milk, for example butter, cheese, and yogurt.

milk shake (milk shakes) also **milkshake** N-COUNT A milk shake is a cold drink made by mixing milk with a flavoring or fruit, and sometimes ice cream. ❑ ...*a strawberry milk shake.*

milk tooth (milk teeth) N-COUNT [usu pl] Your milk teeth are the first teeth that grow in your mouth, which later fall out and are replaced by a second set.

milk white COLOR You can use milk white to describe things that are a milky white color. [LITERARY] ❑ *Mist was rising, and trees and shrubs began to disappear in a milk-white haze.*

milk|woman /mɪlkwʊmən/ (milkwomen) N-COUNT A milkwoman is a woman who delivers milk to people's homes.

milky /mɪlki/ (milkier, milkiest) **1** ADJ If you describe something as milky, you mean that it is pale white in color. You can describe other colors as milky when they are very pale. ❑ *A milky mist filled the valley.* **2** ADJ Drinks or food that are milky contain a lot of milk. ❑ ...*his big cup of milky coffee.*

Milky Way N-PROPER [the N] The Milky Way is the pale strip of light consisting of many stars that you can see stretched across the sky at night.

mill ♦◇◇ /mɪl/ (mills, milling, milled) **1** N-COUNT A mill is a building in which grain is crushed to make flour. ❑ *There was an old mill that really did grind corn.* **2** N-COUNT A mill is a small device used for grinding something such as coffee beans or pepper into powder. ❑ ...*a pepper mill.* **3** N-COUNT A mill is a factory used for making and processing materials such as steel, wool, or cotton. ❑ ...*a steel mill.* **4** V-T To mill something such as wheat or pepper means to grind it in a mill. ❑ *They do not have the capacity to mill the grain.*
▶ **mill around**

in BRIT, also use **mill about**

PHRASAL VERB When a crowd of people mill around, they move around a place or area without any clear purpose. ❑ *Quite a few people were milling around, but nothing was happening.*

mil|len|nium /mɪlɛniəm/ (millenniums or millennia) **1** N-COUNT A millennium is a period of one thousand years, especially one which begins and ends with a year ending in '000,' for example the period from the year 1000 to the year 2000. [FORMAL] ❑ ...*the dawn of a new millennium.* **2** N-SING Many people refer to the year 2000 as the Millennium. ❑ ...*the eve of the Millennium.*

mil|ler /mɪlər/ (millers) N-COUNT A miller is a person who owns or operates a mill in which grain is crushed to make flour.

mil|let /mɪlɪt/ (millets) N-MASS Millet is a cereal crop that is grown for its seeds or hay.

PREFIX

milli-
forms nouns that refer to units that are a thousand times smaller. *For example, a millimeter is a thousandth of a meter.*

mil|li|gram /mɪlɪgræm/ (milligrams)

in BRIT, also use **milligramme**

N-COUNT A milligram is a unit of weight that is equal to a thousandth of a gram. ❑ ...*0.5 milligrams of mercury.*

mil|li|li|ter /mɪlɪlitər/ (milliliters)

in BRIT, use **millilitre**

N-COUNT A milliliter is a unit of volume for liquids and gases that is equal to a thousandth of a liter. ❑ ...*100 milliliters of blood.*

mil|li|meter /mɪlɪmitər/ (millimeters)

in BRIT, use **millimetre**

N-COUNT A millimeter is a metric unit of length that is equal to a tenth of a centimeter or a thousandth of a meter. ❑ *The creature is a tiny centipede, just 10 millimeters long.*

mil|li|ner /mɪlɪnər/ (milliners) N-COUNT A milliner is a person whose job is making or selling women's hats.

mil|li|nery /mɪlɪnɛri/ N-UNCOUNT [oft N n] Millinery is used to refer to women's hats. [OLD-FASHIONED, FORMAL] ❑ ...*her aunt's modest millinery shop.*

mill|ing /mɪlɪŋ/ ADJ [ADJ n] The people in a milling crowd move around within a particular place or area, so that the movement of the whole crowd looks very confused. ❑ *They moved purposefully through the milling crowd.*

mil|lion ♦♦♦ /mɪlyən/ (millions)

The plural form is **million** after a number, or after a word or expression referring to a number, such as 'several' or 'a few.'

1 NUM A million or one million is the number 1,000,000. ❑ *Up to five million people a year visit the county.* **2** QUANT-PLURAL [QUANT of pl-n] If you talk about millions of people or things, you mean that there is a very large number of them but you do not know or do not want to say exactly how many. ❑ *The program was viewed on television in millions of homes.*

USAGE

million
Don't add '-s' to the word million when you put another number in front of it. Don't say, for example, 'five millions dollars.' Say 'five million dollars.' *Over six million people visit the country every year.*

mil|lion|aire /mɪlyənɛər/ (millionaires) N-COUNT A millionaire is a very rich person who has money or property worth at least a million dollars. ❑ *By the time he died, he was a millionaire.*

mil|lion|air|ess /mɪlyənɛərɪs/ (millionairesses) N-COUNT A millionairess is a woman who has money or property worth at least a million dollars.

mil|lionth ♦◇◇ /mɪlyənθ/ (millionths) **1** ORD The millionth item in a series is the one you count as number one million. ❑ *Last year the millionth truck rolled off the assembly line.* **2** FRACTION A millionth of something is one of a million equal parts of it. ❑ *The bomb must explode within less than a millionth of a second.*

mil|li|pede /mɪlɪpid/ (millipedes) N-COUNT A millipede is a small creature with a long, narrow body and a lot of legs.

mil|li|sec|ond /mɪlɪsɛkənd/ (milliseconds) N-COUNT A millisecond is a unit of time equal to one thousandth of a second.

mill|stone /mɪlstoʊn/ (millstones) **1** N-COUNT A millstone is a large, flat, round stone which is one of a pair of stones used to grind grain into flour. **2** PHRASE [usu v-link PHR] If you describe something as a millstone or a millstone around your neck, you mean that it is a very unpleasant problem or responsibility that you cannot escape from. [DISAPPROVAL] ❑ *For today's politicians, the treaty is becoming a millstone.* ❑ *That contract proved to be a millstone around his neck.*

mime /maɪm/ (mimes, miming, mimed) **1** N-VAR Mime is the use of movements and gestures in order to express something or tell a story without using speech. ❑ *Music, mime, and strong visual imagery play a strong part in the productions.* **2** V-T/V-I If you mime something, you describe or express it using mime rather than speech. ❑ *It featured a solo dance in which a woman mimed a lot of dainty housework.* **3** V-T/V-I If you mime, you pretend to be singing or playing an instrument, although the music is in fact coming from a CD or cassette. [BRIT]

in AM, use **lip-synch**

mi|met|ic /mɪmɛtɪk/ ADJ [usu ADJ n] Mimetic movements or activities are ones in which you imitate something. [FORMAL] ❑ *Both realism and naturalism are mimetic systems or practices of representation.*

mim|ic /mɪmɪk/ (mimics, mimicking, mimicked) **1** V-T If you mimic the actions or voice of a person or animal, you imitate them, usually in a way that is meant to be amusing or entertaining. ❑ *He could mimic anybody, and he often reduced Isabel to helpless laughter.* **2** V-T If someone or something mimics another person or thing, they try to be like them. ❑ *The computer doesn't mimic human thought; it reaches the same ends by different means.* **3** N-COUNT A mimic is a person who is able to mimic people or animals. ❑ *At school I was a good mimic.*

mim|ic|ry /mɪmɪkri/ N-UNCOUNT **Mimicry** is the action of mimicking someone or something. ☐ *One of his few strengths was his skill at mimicry.*

mi|mo|sa /mɪmoʊsə/ (mimosas) N-COUNT A **mimosa** is a drink made from champagne and orange juice.

min. **Min.** is a written abbreviation for **minimum**, or for **minutes** or **minute**.

mina|ret /mɪnərɛt/ (minarets) **1** N-COUNT A **minaret** is a tall, thin tower which is part of a mosque. **2** → See also color supplement

mince /mɪns/ (minces, mincing, minced) **1** V-T If you **mince** food such as meat or vegetables, you cut or grind it up into very small pieces, usually in a machine. ☐ *Perhaps I'll buy lean meat and mince it myself.* **2** N-UNCOUNT **Mince** is meat which has been cut or ground up into very small pieces using a machine. [BRIT]

in AM, use **ground beef**

mince|meat /mɪnsmit/ **1** N-UNCOUNT **Mincemeat** is a sticky mixture of small pieces of dried fruit. It is usually cooked in pastry to make mincemeat pies. **2** N-UNCOUNT **Mincemeat** is the same as **mince**. [mainly BRIT]

in AM, use **ground beef**

3 PHRASE If you **make mincemeat of** someone or **make mincemeat out of** them, you defeat them completely in an argument, fight, or competition. ☐ *I can imagine a defense lawyer making mincemeat of him if we ever put him up in court.*

mince pie (mince pies) N-COUNT **Mince pies** are small pies containing a sticky mixture of small pieces of dried fruit. Mince pies are usually eaten at Christmas.

minc|er /mɪnsər/ (mincers) N-COUNT A **mincer** is a machine which cuts meat into very small pieces by forcing it through very small holes. [BRIT]

in AM, use **meat grinder**

MIND
① NOUN USES
② VERB USES

① **mind** ✦✦✦ /maɪnd/ (minds)

→ Please look at meaning 壓 to see if the expression you are looking for is shown under another headword.

1 N-COUNT You refer to someone's **mind** when talking about their thoughts. For example, if you say that something is **in your mind**, you mean that you are thinking about it, and if you say that something is **at the back of your mind**, you mean that you are aware of it, although you are not thinking about it very much. ☐ *I'm trying to clear my mind of all this.* ☐ *There was no doubt in his mind that the man was serious.* **2** N-COUNT Your **mind** is your ability to think and reason. ☐ *You have a good mind.* ☐ *Studying stretched my mind and got me thinking about things.* **3** N-COUNT If you have a particular type of **mind**, you have a particular way of thinking which is part of your character, or a result of your education or professional training. ☐ *Andrew, you have a very suspicious mind.* ☐ *The key to his success is his logical mind.* **4** N-COUNT You can refer to someone as a particular kind of **mind** as a way of saying that they are smart, intelligent, or imaginative. ☐ *She moved to New York, meeting some of the best minds of her time.* **5** → see also **frame of mind**, **state of mind** **6** PHRASE If you tell someone to **bear** something **in mind** or to **keep** something **in mind**, you are reminding or warning them about something important which they should remember. ☐ *Bear in mind that gas stations are scarce in the more remote areas.* **7** PHRASE If you **cast** your **mind back** to a time in the past, you think about what happened then. ☐ *Cast your mind back to 1978, when Forest won the title.* **8** PHRASE If you **change** your **mind**, or if someone or something **changes** your **mind**, you change a decision you have made or an opinion that you had. ☐ *I was going to vote for him, but I changed my mind.* **9** PHRASE If something **comes to mind** or **springs to mind**, you think of it without making any effort. ☐ *Integrity and honesty are words that spring to mind when talking of the man.* **10** PHRASE If you say that an idea or possibility never **crossed** your **mind**, you mean that you did not think of it. ☐ *It had never crossed his mind that there might be a problem.* **11** PHRASE If you **see** something **in** your **mind's eye**, you imagine it and have a clear picture of it in your mind. ☐ *In his mind's eye, he can imagine the effect he's having.* **12** PHRASE If you say that you **have a good mind to** do something or **have half a mind to** do it, you are threatening or announcing that you have a strong desire to do it, although you probably will not do it. ☐ *He raged on about how he had a good mind to resign.* **13** PHRASE If you ask someone what they **have in mind**, you want to know in more detail about an idea or wish they have. ☐ *"Maybe we could celebrate tonight."—"What did you have in mind?"* **14** PHRASE If you do something **with** a particular thing **in mind**, you do it with that thing as your aim or as the reason or basis for your action. ☐ *These families need support. With this in mind a group of 35 specialists met last weekend.* **15** PHRASE If you say that something such as an illness is all **in the mind**, you mean that it relates to someone's feelings or attitude, rather than having any physical cause. ☐ *It could be a virus, or it could be all in the mind.* **16** PHRASE If you **know** your **own mind**, you are sure about your opinions, and are not easily influenced by other people. ☐ *She knows her own mind and won't let anyone talk her into something she doesn't want to do.* **17** PHRASE If you say that someone **is losing** their **mind**, you mean that they are becoming mad. ☐ *Sometimes I feel like I'm losing my mind.* **18** PHRASE If you **make up** your **mind** or **make** your **mind up**, you decide which of a number of possible things you will have or do. ☐ *Once he made up his mind to do something, there was no stopping him.* **19** PHRASE If a number of people are **of one mind**, **of like mind**, or **of the same mind**, they all agree about something. ☐ *Contact with other disabled yachtsmen of like mind would be helpful.* **20** PHRASE If you say that something that happens is **a load off** your **mind** or **a weight off** your **mind**, you mean that it causes you to stop worrying, for example because it solves a problem that you had. ☐ *Knowing that she had medical insurance took a great load off her mind.* **21** PHRASE If something is **on** your **mind**, you are worried or concerned about it and think about it a lot. ☐ *This game has been on my mind all week.* **22** PHRASE If your **mind is on** something or you **have** your **mind on** something, you are thinking about that thing. ☐ *At school I was always in trouble – my mind was never on my work.* **23** PHRASE If you have **an open mind**, you avoid forming an opinion or making a decision until you know all the facts. ☐ *It's hard to see it any other way, though I'm trying to keep an open mind.* **24** PHRASE If something **opens** your **mind** to new ideas or experiences, it makes you more willing to accept them or try them. ☐ *She also stimulated his curiosity and opened his mind to other cultures.* **25** PHRASE If you say that someone is **out of their mind**, you mean that they are mad or very foolish. [INFORMAL, DISAPPROVAL] ☐ *What are you doing? Are you out of your mind?* **26** PHRASE If you say that someone is **out of their mind** with a feeling such as worry or fear, you are emphasizing that they are extremely worried or afraid. [INFORMAL, EMPHASIS] ☐ *I was out of my mind with fear. I didn't know what to do.* **27** PHRASE If you say that someone is, for example, **bored out of** their **mind**, **scared out of** their **mind**, or **stoned out of** their **mind**, you are emphasizing that they are extremely bored, scared, or affected by drugs. [INFORMAL, EMPHASIS] ☐ *That was one of the most depressing experiences of my life. I was bored out of my mind after five minutes.* **28** PHRASE If you **put** your **mind to** something, you start making an effort to do it. ☐ *You could do fine in the world if you put your mind to it.* **29** PHRASE If you can **read** someone's **mind**, you know what they are thinking without them saying anything. ☐ *Don't expect others to read your mind.* **30** PHRASE To **put** someone's **mind at rest** or **set** their **mind at rest** means to stop them from worrying about something. ☐ *It may be advisable to have a blood test to put your mind at rest.* **31** PHRASE If you say that nobody **in** their **right mind** would do a particular thing, you are emphasizing that it is an irrational thing to do and you would be surprised if anyone did it. [EMPHASIS] ☐ *No one in her right mind would make such a major purchase without asking questions.* **32** PHRASE If you **set** your **mind on** something or **have** your **mind set on** it, you are determined to do it or obtain it. ☐ *When my wife sets her mind on something, she invariably finds a way to achieve it.* **33** PHRASE If something **slips** your **mind**, you forget it. ☐ *I was going to mention it, but it slipped my mind.* **34** PHRASE If you **speak** your **mind**, you say firmly and honestly what you think about a situation, even if this may offend or upset people. ☐ *The tennis star has never been afraid to speak her mind.*

38 PHRASE If something **sticks in** your **mind**, it remains firmly in your memory. ❑ *I've always been fond of poetry and one piece has always stuck in my mind.* **36 PHRASE** If something **takes** your **mind off** a problem or unpleasant situation, it helps you to forget about it for a while. ❑ *"How about a game of tennis?" suggested Alan. "That'll take your mind off things."* **37 PHRASE** You say or write **to my mind** to indicate that the statement you are making is your own opinion. ❑ *There are scenes in this play which, to my mind, are incredibly violent.* **38 PHRASE** If you are **of two minds**, you are uncertain about what to do, especially when you have to choose between two courses of action. ❑ *He was of two minds about this plan.* **39 to give someone a piece of your mind** → see **piece**

COLLOCATIONS

mind
NOUN
① **1**
verb + **mind**: clear; concentrate, focus; occupy
① **2**
adjective + **mind**: good, healthy, sound; conscious, subconscious, unconscious; human, young
mind + be + adjective: blank
① **3**
adjective + **mind**: inquiring, open, suspicious; brilliant, creative; criminal

---
SYNONYMS

mind
NOUN
① **1**
brain: *Once you stop using your brain, you soon go stale.*
psyche: *'It probably reveals a deeply immature part of my psyche,' he confesses.*
head: *I can't get that song out of my head.*
① **2**
intelligence: *Nerve cells, after all, do not have intelligence of their own.*
reason: *...a conflict between emotion and reason.*
intellect: *Do the emotions develop in parallel with the intellect?*

---

② **mind** ✦✧✧ /maɪnd/ (**minds, minding, minded**) **1** V-T/V-I [usu with brd-neg] If you do not **mind** something, you are not annoyed or bothered by it. ❑ *I don't mind the noise during the day.* ❑ *I hope you don't mind me stopping in like this, without an appointment.* ❑ *I lit a cigarette and nobody seemed to mind.* **2** V-T/V-I You use **mind** in the expressions **'do you mind?'** and **'would you mind?'** as a polite way of asking permission or asking someone to do something. [POLITENESS] ❑ *Do you mind if I ask you one more thing?* ❑ *Would you mind waiting outside for a moment?* **3** V-T [with brd-neg] If someone does not **mind** what happens or what something is like, they do not have a strong preference for any particular thing. ❑ *I don't mind what we play, really.* **4** V-T If you **mind** a child or something such as a store or luggage, you take care of it, usually while the person who owns it or is usually responsible for it is somewhere else. ❑ *Jim Coulters will mind the store while I'm away.* **5** PHRASE People use the expression **if you don't mind** when they are rejecting an offer or saying that they do not want to do something, especially when they are annoyed. [FEELINGS] ❑ *"Sit down."—"I prefer standing for a while, if you don't mind."* **6** PHRASE You use **mind you** to emphasize a piece of information that you are adding, especially when the new information explains what you have said or contrasts with it. Some people use **mind** in a similar way. [EMPHASIS] ❑ *They pay full rates. Mind you, they can afford it.* **7** CONVENTION You say **never mind** when you are emphasizing that something is not serious or important, especially when someone is upset about it or is saying they are sorry. [EMPHASIS] ❑ *Her voice trembled. "Oh, Sylvia, I'm so sorry."—"Never mind."* **8** PHRASE You use **never mind** to tell someone that they need not do something or worry about something, because it is not important or because you will do it yourself. ❑ *"Was his name David?"—"No I don't think it was, but never mind, go on."* ❑ *Dorothy, come on. Never mind your shoes. They'll soon dry off.* **9** PHRASE You use **never mind** after a statement, often a negative one, to indicate that the statement is even more true of the person, thing, or situation that you are going to mention next. [EMPHASIS] ❑ *I'm not going to believe it* myself, never mind convince anyone else. **10** PHRASE If you say that you **wouldn't mind** something, you mean that you would quite like it. ❑ *I wouldn't mind a coffee.* **11** V-T If you tell someone to **mind** something, you are warning them to be careful not to hurt themselves or other people, or damage something. [mainly BRIT]

in AM, usually use **watch**

12 V-T You use **mind** when you are reminding someone to do something or telling them to be careful not to do something. [mainly BRIT]

in AM, usually use **make sure**

13 → See feature box at **weather**

SYNONYMS

mind
VERB
②
object: *A lot of people will object to the book.*
resent: *I resent being dependent on her.*
disapprove: *Most people disapprove of such violent tactics.*

---

mind-altering also **mind altering** ADJ [usu ADJ n] A **mind-altering** drug is one that produces mood changes in the person who has taken it.

mind-bending also **mind bending** **1** ADJ [usu ADJ n] If you describe something as **mind-bending**, you mean that it is difficult to understand or think about. ❑ *...mind-bending debates about the nature of life.* **2** ADJ [usu ADJ n] **Mind-bending** means the same as **mind-altering**. ❑ *...mind-bending drugs.*

mind-blowing also **mind blowing** ADJ If you describe something as **mind-blowing**, you mean that it is extremely impressive or surprising. [INFORMAL] ❑ *...a mind-blowing array of treatments.*

mind-boggling also **mind boggling** ADJ If you say that something is **mind-boggling**, you mean that it is so large, complicated, or extreme that it is very hard to imagine. [INFORMAL] ❑ *The amount of paperwork involved is mind-boggling.*

-minded /-maɪndɪd/ **1** COMB IN ADJ **-minded** combines with adjectives to form words that describe someone's character, attitude, opinions, or intelligence. ❑ *These are evil-minded people.* ❑ *He is famous for his tough-minded professionalism.* **2** COMB IN ADJ **-minded** combines with adverbs to form adjectives that indicate that someone is interested in a particular subject or is able to think in a particular way. ❑ *I am not an academically-minded person.* **3** COMB IN ADJ **-minded** combines with nouns to form adjectives that indicate that someone thinks a particular thing is important or cares a lot about it. ❑ *He is seen as more business-minded than his predecessor.* ❑ *We weren't career-minded like girls are today.*

mind|er /maɪndər/ (**minders**) N-COUNT A **minder** is a person whose job is to protect someone, especially someone famous. [mainly BRIT, INFORMAL]

in AM, use **bodyguard**

mind|ful /maɪndfəl/ ADJ [v-link ADJ] If you are **mindful** of something, you think about it and consider it when taking action. [FORMAL] ❑ *We must be mindful of the consequences of selfishness.*

mind|ful|ness /maɪndfəlnəs/ N-UNCOUNT **Mindfulness** is a way of training your mind to concentrate on the present, in order to feel calm and improve your mental state. ❑ *We have started teaching mindfulness techniques to our pupils.*

mind|less /maɪndləs/ **1** ADJ If you describe a violent action as **mindless**, you mean that it is done without thought and will achieve nothing. [DISAPPROVAL] ❑ *...a plot that mixes blackmail, extortion and mindless violence.* **2** ADJ If you describe a person or group as **mindless**, you mean that they are stupid or do not think about what they are doing. [DISAPPROVAL] ❑ *She wasn't at all the mindless little wife so many people perceived her to be.*
● **mind|less|ly** ADV [ADV with v] ❑ *I was annoyed with myself for having so quickly and mindlessly lost thirty dollars.* **3** ADJ If you describe an activity as **mindless**, you mean that it is so dull that people do it or take part in it without thinking. [DISAPPROVAL] ❑ *...the mindless repetitiveness of some tasks.*
● **mind|less|ly** ADV [ADV with v] ❑ *I spent many hours mindlessly banging a tennis ball against the wall.*

mind-numbing also **mind numbing** ADJ If you describe an event or experience as **mind-numbing**, you mean that it is so bad, boring, or great in extent that you are unable to think about it clearly. ☐ *It was another day of mind-numbing tedium.* • **mind-numbingly** ADV [ADV adj] ☐ *...a mind-numbingly boring sport.*

mind|set /maɪndsɛt/ (**mindsets**) also **mind-set** N-COUNT If you refer to someone's **mindset**, you mean their general attitudes and the way they typically think about things. ☐ *I can't understand the mindset of these people.*

MINE
① PRONOUN USE
② NOUN AND VERB USES
---

① **mine** ◆◆◆ /maɪn/ PRON-POSS **Mine** is the first person singular possessive pronoun. A speaker or writer uses **mine** to refer to something that belongs or relates to himself or herself. ☐ *Her right hand is inches from mine.* ☐ *That wasn't his fault, it was mine.*

② **mine** /maɪn/ (**mines, mining, minded**) **1** N-COUNT A **mine** is a place where deep holes and tunnels are dug under the ground in order to obtain a mineral such as coal, diamonds, or gold. ☐ *...coal mines.* **2** V-T [usu passive] When a mineral such as coal, diamonds, or gold **is mined**, it is obtained from the ground by digging deep holes and tunnels. ☐ *The pit is being shut down because it no longer has enough coal that can be mined economically.* **3** N-COUNT A **mine** is a bomb which is hidden in the ground or in water and which explodes when people or things touch it. **4** V-T If an area of land or water **is mined**, mines are placed there which will explode when people or things touch them. ☐ *The approaches to the garrison have been heavily mined.* **5** → see also **mining**

mine|field /maɪnfiːld/ (**minefields**) **1** N-COUNT A **minefield** is an area of land or water where explosive mines have been hidden. **2** N-COUNT If you describe a situation as a **minefield**, you are emphasizing that there are a lot of hidden dangers or problems, and people need to behave with care because things could easily go wrong. [EMPHASIS] ☐ *The whole subject is a political minefield.*

min|er ◆◇◇ /maɪnər/ (**miners**) N-COUNT A **miner** is a person who works underground in mines in order to obtain minerals such as coal, diamonds, or gold.

min|er|al /mɪnərəl/ (**minerals**) **1** N-COUNT A **mineral** is a substance such as tin, salt, or sulfur that is formed naturally in rocks and in the earth. Minerals are also found in small quantities in food and drink. **2** → See feature box at **nutrition**

min|er|al wa|ter (**mineral waters**) N-MASS **Mineral water** is water that comes out of the ground naturally and is considered healthy to drink.

min|estro|ne /mɪnɪstroʊni/ N-UNCOUNT **Minestrone** soup is a type of soup made from meat stock that contains small pieces of vegetables and pasta.

mine|sweeper /maɪnswiːpər/ (**minesweepers**) also **mine sweeper** N-COUNT A **minesweeper** is a ship that is used to clear away explosive mines in the sea.

min|gle /mɪŋɡəl/ (**mingles, mingling, mingled**) **1** V-RECIP If things such as sounds, smells, or feelings **mingle**, they become mixed together but are usually still recognizable. ☐ *Now the cheers and applause mingled in a single sustained roar.* **2** V-RECIP At a party, if you **mingle** with the other people there, you move around and talk to them. ☐ *Go out of your way to mingle with others at the wedding.* ☐ *Guests ate and mingled.* **3** → See feature box at **socialize**

mini /mɪni/ (**minis**) N-COUNT A **mini** is the same as a **miniskirt**.

PREFIX

mini-
forms nouns that refer to things that are a smaller version of something else. For example, a **minibus** is a small bus.
---

minia|ture /mɪniətʃər, -tʃʊər/ (**miniatures**) **1** ADJ [ADJ n] **Miniature** is used to describe something that is very small, especially a smaller version of something which is normally much bigger. ☐ *The farm has been selling miniature roses since 1979.* **2** PHRASE If you describe one thing as another thing **in miniature**, you mean that it is much smaller in size or scale than the other thing, but is otherwise exactly the same. ☐ *Ecuador provides a perfect introduction to South America; it's a continent in miniature.* **3** N-COUNT A **miniature** is a very small, detailed painting, often of a person.

minia|tur|ize /mɪniɪtʃəraɪz, mɪnɪ-/ (**miniaturizes, miniaturizing, miniaturized**)

in BRIT, also use **miniaturise**

V-T If you **miniaturize** something such as a machine, you produce a very small version of it. ☐ *...the problems of further miniaturizing the available technologies.* ☐ *...miniaturized amplifiers and receivers.* • **minia|turi|za|tion** /mɪniɪtʃərɪzeɪʃən, mɪnɪ-/ N-UNCOUNT ☐ *...increasing miniaturization in the computer industry.*

mini|bar /mɪnibɑːr/ (**minibars**) N-COUNT In a hotel room, a **minibar** is a small refrigerator containing alcoholic drinks.

mini|bus /mɪnibʌs/ (**minibuses**) also **mini-bus** N-COUNT [also by N] A **minibus** is a large van which has seats in the back for passengers, and windows along its sides. ☐ *He was then taken by minibus to the military base.*

mini|cam /mɪnikæm/ (**minicams**) N-COUNT A **minicam** is a very small television camera.

mini|dish /mɪnidɪʃ/ (**minidishes**) N-COUNT A **minidish** is a small satellite dish that can receive signals from communications satellites for media such as television programs and the internet.

min|im /mɪnɪm/ (**minims**) N-COUNT A **minim** is the same as a **half note**. [BRIT]

mini|mal /mɪnɪməl/ ADJ Something that is **minimal** is very small in quantity, value, or degree. ☐ *The cooperation between the two is minimal.*

mini|mal|ism /mɪnɪməlɪzəm/ N-UNCOUNT **Minimalism** is a style in which a small number of very simple things are used to create a particular effect. ☐ *In her own home, she replaced austere minimalism with cosy warmth and color.*

mini|mal|ist /mɪnɪməlɪst/ (**minimalists**) **1** N-COUNT A **minimalist** is an artist or designer who uses minimalism. ☐ *He was influenced by the minimalists in the 1970s.* **2** ADJ **Minimalist** is used to describe ideas, artists, or designers that are influenced by minimalism. ☐ *The two designers settled upon a minimalist approach.*

mini|mal|istic /mɪnɪməlɪstɪk/ ADJ A **minimalistic** style is simple and plain, without any decoration. ☐ *The modern trend is minimalistic with simple, square components.*

mini|mize /mɪnɪmaɪz/ (**minimizes, minimizing, minimized**)

in BRIT, also use **minimise**

1 V-T If you **minimize** a risk, problem, or unpleasant situation, you reduce it to the lowest possible level, or prevent it from increasing beyond that level. ☐ *Concerned people want to minimize the risk of developing cancer.* **2** V-T If you **minimize** something, you make it seem smaller or less significant than it really is. ☐ *Some have minimized the importance of ideological factors.* **3** V-T If you **minimize** a window on a computer screen, you make it very small, because you do not want to use it. ☐ *Click the square icon again to minimize the window.*

mini|mum ◆◇◇ /mɪnɪməm/ **1** ADJ [ADJ n] You use **minimum** to describe an amount which is the smallest that is possible, allowed, or required. ☐ *He was only five feet nine, the minimum height for a policeman.* • N-SING **Minimum** is also a noun. ☐ *This will take a minimum of one hour.* **2** ADJ [ADJ n] You use **minimum** to state how small an amount is. ☐ *The basic needs of life are available with minimum effort.* • N-SING **Minimum** is also a noun. ☐ *With a minimum of fuss, she produced the grandson he had so desperately wished for.* **3** ADV [amount ADV] If you say that something is a particular amount **minimum**, you mean that this is the smallest amount it should be or could possibly be, although a larger amount is acceptable or very possible. ☐ *You're talking over a thousand dollars minimum for one course.*

mini|mum se|cu|rity pris|on (**minimum security prisons**) N-COUNT A **minimum security prison** is a prison where there are fewer restrictions on prisoners than in a normal prison. [mainly AM]

in BRIT, use **open prison**

mini|mum wage ◼ N-SING The **minimum wage** is the lowest wage that an employer is allowed to pay an employee, according to a law or agreement. ❑ *Some of them earn below the minimum wage.* ◼ → See feature box at **working**

min|ing /maɪnɪŋ/ N-UNCOUNT **Mining** is the industry and activities connected with getting valuable or useful minerals from the ground, for example coal, diamonds, or gold. ❑ *...traditional industries such as coal mining and steel making.*

min|ion /mɪnyən/ (minions) N-COUNT [usu pl, usu poss N] If you refer to someone's **minions**, you are referring to people who have to do what that person tells them to do, especially unimportant or boring tasks. [LITERARY, DISAPPROVAL] ❑ *She delegated the job to one of her minions.*

mini|series /mɪnisɪəriːz/ (miniseries) N-COUNT A **miniseries** is a drama shown on television in two or three parts, usually in one week.

mini|skirt /mɪniskɜːrt/ (miniskirts) N-COUNT A **miniskirt** is a very short skirt.

min|is|ter ✦✦✦ /mɪnɪstər/ (ministers) ◼ N-COUNT A **minister** is a member of the clergy, especially in Protestant churches. ❑ *His father was a Baptist minister.* ◼ N-COUNT A **minister** is a person who officially represents their government in a foreign country and has a lower rank than an ambassador. ❑ *He concluded a deal with the Danish minister in Washington.* ◼ N-COUNT In some countries outside the United States, a **minister** is a person who is in charge of a particular government department. ❑ *When the government came to power, he was named minister of culture.*

min|is|terial /mɪnɪstɪəriəl/ ADJ [ADJ n] You use **ministerial** to refer to people, events, or jobs that are connected with government ministers. ❑ *The prime minister's initial ministerial appointments haven't pleased all his supporters.*

mini|stra|tions /mɪnɪstreɪʃənz/ N-PLURAL [usu with poss] A person's **ministrations** are the things they do to help or care for someone in a particular situation, especially someone who is weak or ill. [HUMOROUS OR LITERARY] ❑ *...the tender ministrations of the buxom woman who cut his hair.*

min|is|try ✦✦◇ /mɪnɪstri/ (ministries) N-COUNT In many countries, a **ministry** is a government department which deals with a particular thing or area of activity, for example trade, defense, or transportation. ❑ *...the Ministry of Justice.*

mini|van /mɪnivæn/ (minivans) ◼ N-COUNT A **minivan** is a large, family car whose seats can be moved or removed, for example, so that it can carry large loads. [AM] ❑ *A minivan drove by, five faces peering at the window.* ◼ → See also color supplement

mink /mɪŋk/ (minks)

> Mink can also be used as the plural form.

◼ N-COUNT A **mink** is a small animal with highly valued fur. ❑ *...a proposal for a ban on the hunting of foxes, mink, and hares.* • N-UNCOUNT **Mink** is the fur of a mink. ❑ *...a mink coat.* ◼ N-COUNT A **mink** is a coat or other garment made from the fur of a mink. ❑ *Some people like to dress up in minks and diamonds.*

min|now /mɪnoʊ/ (minnows) N-COUNT A **minnow** is a very small fish that lives in lakes and rivers.

mi|nor ✦◇◇ /maɪnər/ (minors) ◼ ADJ You use **minor** when you want to describe something that is less important, serious, or significant than other things in a group or situation. ❑ *She is known in Italy for a number of minor roles in films.* ◼ ADJ A **minor** illness or operation is not likely to be dangerous to someone's life or health. ❑ *Sarah had been plagued continually by a series of minor illnesses since her mid teens.* ◼ N-COUNT A **minor** is a person who is still legally a child. In most states in the United States, people are minors until they reach the age of eighteen. ❑ *The approach has virtually ended cigarette sales to minors.* ◼ ADJ A **minor** scale is one in which the third note is three semitones higher than the first. ❑ *...the unfinished sonata movement in F minor.*

---SYNONYMS---

minor
ADJ ◼
unimportant: *It was an unimportant job, and paid very little.*
insignificant: *In 1949, Bonn was a small, insignificant city.*
trivial: *The director tried to wave aside these issues as trivial details.*

mi|nor|ity ✦✦◇ /mɪnɔrɪti, maɪ-/ (minorities) ◼ N-SING If you talk about a **minority** of people or things in a larger group, you are referring to a number of them that forms less than half of the larger group, usually much less than half. ❑ *Local authority child-care provision covers only a tiny minority of working mothers.* • PHRASE If people are **in a minority** or **in the minority**, they belong to a group of people or things that form less than half of a larger group. ❑ *Even in the 1960s, politically active students and academics were in a minority.* ◼ N-COUNT A **minority** is a group of people of the same race, culture, or religion who live in a place where most of the people around them are of a different race, culture, or religion. ❑ *...the region's ethnic minorities.*

mi|nor league (minor leagues) ◼ N-COUNT [oft N n] In baseball, a **minor league** is a professional league that is not one of the major leagues. [AM] ❑ *In 1952, there were 43 minor leagues and 324 teams nationwide.* ❑ *After military service he played some minor league baseball.* ◼ ADJ **Minor-league** people are not very important or not very successful. [mainly AM] ❑ *...minor-league celebrities.* ❑ *His economic team is minor-league compared with the heavy hitters of previous years.*

min|strel /mɪnstrəl/ (minstrels) N-COUNT In medieval times, a **minstrel** was a singer and musician who traveled around and entertained noble families.

mint /mɪnt/ (mints, minting, minted) ◼ N-UNCOUNT **Mint** is an herb with fresh-tasting leaves. ❑ *Garnish with mint sprigs.* ◼ N-COUNT A **mint** is a candy with a peppermint flavor. Some people suck mints in order to make their breath smell fresher. ❑ *She popped a mint into her mouth.* ◼ N-COUNT The **mint** is the place where the official coins of a country are made. ❑ *In 1965 the mint stopped putting silver in dimes.* ◼ V-T To **mint** coins or medals means to make them in a mint. ❑ *...the right to mint coins.*

mint|ed /mɪntɪd/ ADJ [usu ADJ n, adv ADJ] If you describe something as **newly minted** or **freshly minted**, you mean that it is very new, and that it has just been produced or completed. ❑ *He seemed to be pleased by this newly minted vehicle.* ❑ *...the movie's freshly minted script.*

minu|et /mɪnyuɛt/ (minuets) ◼ N-COUNT In the music of the seventeenth and eighteenth centuries, a **minuet** is a piece of music with three beats in a bar which is played at moderate speed. ◼ N-COUNT A **minuet** is a slow and formal dance which was popular in the seventeenth and eighteenth centuries.

mi|nus /maɪnəs/ (minuses) ◼ CONJ You use **minus** to show that one number or quantity is being subtracted from another. ❑ *One minus one is zero.* ◼ ADJ [ADJ amount] **Minus** before a number or quantity means that the number or quantity is less than zero. ❑ *The aircraft was subjected to temperatures of minus 65 degrees and plus 120 degrees.* ◼ ADJ Teachers use **minus** in grading work in schools and colleges. 'B minus' is not as good as 'B,' but is a better grade than 'C.' ❑ *I'm giving him a B minus.* ◼ PREP To be **minus** something means not to have that thing. ❑ *The film company collapsed, leaving Chris jobless and minus his life savings.* ◼ N-COUNT A **minus** is a disadvantage. [INFORMAL] ❑ *The minuses far outweigh that possible gain.*

mi|nus|cule /mɪnɪskyuːl/ ADJ If you describe something as **minuscule**, you mean that it is very small. ❑ *The film was shot in 17 days, a minuscule amount of time.*

mi|nus sign (minus signs) N-COUNT A **minus sign** is the sign - which is put between two numbers in order to show that the second number is being subtracted from the first one. It is also put before a number to show that the number is less than zero.

---MINUTE---
① NOUN AND VERB USES
② ADJECTIVE USE

① **min|ute** ✦✦✦ /mɪnɪt/ (minutes, minuting, minuted) ◼ N-COUNT A **minute** is one of the sixty parts that an hour is divided into. People often say 'a minute' or 'minutes' when they mean a short length of time. ❑ *The pizza will then take about twenty minutes to cook.* ❑ *Bye Mom, see you in a minute.* ◼ N-PLURAL The **minutes** of a meeting are the written records of the things that are discussed or decided at it. ☐ *He'd been reading the minutes of the last meeting.* ■3 V-T When someone **minutes** something that is discussed or decided at a meeting, they make a written record of it. ☐ *You don't need to minute that.* ■4 CONVENTION People often use expressions such as **wait a minute** or **just a minute** when they want to stop you doing or saying something. ☐ *Wait a minute, folks, something is wrong here.* ■5 PHRASE If you say that something will or may happen **at any minute** or **any minute now**, you are emphasizing that it is likely to happen very soon. [EMPHASIS] ☐ *It looked as though it might rain at any minute.* ■6 PHRASE A **last-minute** action is one that is done at the latest time possible. ☐ *He will probably wait until the last minute.* ■7 PHRASE If you say that something happens **the minute** something else happens, you are emphasizing that it happens immediately after the other thing. [EMPHASIS] ☐ *The minute you do this, you'll lose control.*

② **mi|nute** /maɪnuːt/ (**minutest**) ADJ If you say that something is **minute**, you mean that it is very small. ☐ *Only a minute amount is needed.*

mi|nute|ly /maɪnuːtli/ ■1 ADV [ADV with v] You use **minutely** to indicate that something is done in great detail. ☐ *The metal is then minutely examined to ensure there are no cracks.* ■2 ADV [usu ADV adj/-ed] You use **minutely** to indicate that the size or extent of something is very small. ☐ *The benefit of an x-ray far outweighs the minutely increased risk of cancer.*

mi|nu|tiae /mɪnuːʃiː/ N-PLURAL [usu the N of n] The **minutiae** of something such as someone's job or life are the very small details of it. [FORMAL] ☐ *Much of his early work is concerned with the minutiae of rural life.*

mira|cle /mɪrəkəl/ (**miracles**) ■1 N-COUNT If you say that a good event is a **miracle**, you mean that it is very surprising and unexpected. ☐ *It is a miracle no one was killed.* ■2 ADJ [ADJ n] A **miracle** drug or product does something that was thought almost impossible. [JOURNALISM] ☐ *...the miracle drugs that keep his 94-year-old mother healthy.* ■3 N-COUNT A **miracle** is a wonderful and surprising event that is believed to be caused by God. ☐ *...Jesus's ability to perform miracles.*

mira|cle work|er (**miracle workers**) N-COUNT If you describe someone as a **miracle worker**, you mean that they have achieved or are able to achieve success in something that other people have found very difficult. [APPROVAL] ☐ *At work he was regarded as a miracle worker, the man who took risks and could not lose.*

mi|racu|lous /mɪrækjələs/ ■1 ADJ If you describe a good event as **miraculous**, you mean that it is very surprising and unexpected. ☐ *The horse made a miraculous recovery to finish a close third.* ● **mi|racu|lous|ly** ADV ☐ *Miraculously, the guards escaped death or serious injury.* ■2 ADJ If someone describes a wonderful event as **miraculous**, they believe that the event was caused by God. ☐ *...miraculous healing.*

mi|rage /mɪrɑːʒ/ (**mirages**) ■1 N-COUNT A **mirage** is something that you see when it is extremely hot, for example in the desert, and which appears to be quite near but is actually a long way away or does not really exist. ☐ *It hovered before his eyes like the mirage of an oasis.* ■2 N-COUNT [usu sing] If you describe something as a **mirage**, you mean that it is not real or true, although it may seem to be. ☐ *The girl was a mirage, cast up by his troubled mind.*

mire /maɪər/ ■1 N-SING [oft N of n] You can refer to an unpleasant or difficult situation as a **mire** of some kind. [LITERARY] ☐ *...a mire of poverty and ignorance.* ■2 N-UNCOUNT **Mire** is dirt or mud. [LITERARY] ☐ *...the muck and mire of sewers and farmyards.*

mir|ror◆◇◇ /mɪrər/ (**mirrors, mirroring, mirrored**) ■1 N-COUNT A **mirror** is a flat piece of glass which reflects light, so that when you look at it you can see yourself reflected in it. ☐ *He went into the bathroom absent-mindedly and looked at himself in the mirror.* ■2 V-T If something **mirrors** something else, it has similar features to it, and therefore seems like a copy or representation of it. ☐ *Despite the fact that I have tried to be objective, the book inevitably mirrors my own interests and experiences.* ■3 V-T If you see something reflected in water, you can say that the water **mirrors** it. [LITERARY] ☐ *...the sudden glitter where a newly flooded field mirrors the sky.*

COLLOCATIONS

mirror
NOUN ■1
noun + **mirror**: bathroom, hand, shaving, vanity; rearview, side
adjective + **mirror**: full-length, two-way

SYNONYMS

mirror
VERB ■2
copy: *Children can be seen to copy the behavior of others whom they admire or identify with.*
reflect: *Concern for the economic situation was reflected in the government's budget.*
show: *These figures show an increase of over one million in unemployment.*

mir|ror im|age (**mirror images**) N-COUNT [oft N of n] If something is a **mirror image** of something else, it is like a reflection of it, either because it is exactly the same or because it is the same but reversed. ☐ *I saw in him a mirror image of myself.*

mir|ror site (**mirror sites**) N-COUNT A **mirror site** is a website which is the same as another website operated by the same person or organization but has a slightly different address. Mirror sites are designed to make it easier for more people to visit a popular website.

mirth /mɜːrθ/ N-UNCOUNT **Mirth** is amusement which you express by laughing. [LITERARY] ☐ *That caused considerable mirth among students and coaches alike.*

mirth|less /mɜːrθlɪs/ ADJ [usu ADJ n] If someone gives a **mirthless** laugh or smile, it is obvious that they are not really amused. [WRITTEN]

PREFIX

mis-
forms verbs and nouns that refer to something being done badly or wrongly. For example, **misbehavior** is bad behavior.

mis|ad|ven|ture /mɪsədvɛntʃər/ (**misadventures**) N-VAR A **misadventure** is an unfortunate incident. [FORMAL] ☐ *...a series of misadventures.*

mis|an|thrope /mɪsənθroʊp, mɪz-/ (**misanthropes**) N-COUNT A **misanthrope** is a person who does not like other people. [FORMAL]

mis|an|throp|ic /mɪsənθrɒpɪk, mɪz-/ ADJ If you describe a person or their feelings as **misanthropic**, you mean that they do not like other people. [FORMAL]

mis|an|thro|py /mɪsænθrəpi, mɪz-/ N-UNCOUNT **Misanthropy** is a general dislike of people. [FORMAL]

mis|ap|pli|ca|tion /mɪsæplɪkeɪʃən/ (**misapplications**) N-VAR [usu N of n] If you talk about the **misapplication** of something, you mean it is used for a purpose it was not intended for. ☐ *He's charged with conspiracy, misapplication of funds and other crimes.* ☐ *...a common misapplication of the law.*

mis|ap|ply /mɪsəplaɪ/ (**misapplies, misapplying, misapplied**) V-T [usu passive] If something **is misapplied**, it is used for a purpose for which it is not intended or not suitable. ☐ *Many lines from Shakespeare's plays are misquoted and misapplied.* ☐ *The law had been misapplied.*

mis|ap|pre|hen|sion /mɪsæprɪhɛnʃən/ (**misapprehensions**) N-VAR [oft N that, under n] A **misapprehension** is a wrong idea or impression that you have about something. ☐ *Many here seem to be labouring under the misapprehension that grapes are alien to India.*

mis|ap|pro|pri|ate /mɪsəproʊprieɪt/ (**misappropriates, misappropriating, misappropriated**) V-T If someone **misappropriates** money which does not belong to them, they take it without permission and use it for their own purposes. ☐ *I took no money for personal use and have not misappropriated any funds whatsoever.* ● **mis|ap|pro|pria|tion** /mɪsəproʊprieɪʃən/ N-UNCOUNT [usu N of n] ☐ *He pleaded guilty to charges of misappropriation of bank funds.*

mis|be|have /mɪsbɪheɪv/ (**misbehaves, misbehaving, misbehaved**) V-I If someone, especially a child, **misbehaves**,

misbehavior

they behave in a way that is not acceptable to other people. ❏ *When the children misbehaved she was unable to cope.*

mis|be|hav|ior /mɪsbɪheɪvyər/

in BRIT, use **misbehaviour**

N-UNCOUNT **Misbehavior** is behavior that is not acceptable to other people. [FORMAL] ❏ *Another couple attributed their son's misbehavior to his small size.*

mis|cal|cu|late /mɪskælkyəleɪt/ (**miscalculates, miscalculating, miscalculated**) V-T/V-I If you **miscalculate**, you make a mistake in judging a situation or in making a calculation. ❏ *It's clear that he has badly miscalculated the mood of the people.* • **mis|cal|cu|la|tion** /mɪskælkyəleɪʃ°n/ (**miscalculations**) N-VAR ❏ *The coup failed because of miscalculations by the plotters.*

mis|car|riage /mɪskærɪdʒ, -kær-/ (**miscarriages**) ◼ N-VAR If a pregnant woman has a **miscarriage**, her baby is born before it is properly formed, and it dies. ❏ *No one had any idea she had had a miscarriage.* ◼ → See feature box at **birth**

mis|car|riage of jus|tice (**miscarriages of justice**) N-VAR A **miscarriage of justice** is a wrong decision made by a court, as a result of which an innocent person is punished. ❏ *I can imagine no greater miscarriage of justice than the execution of an innocent man.*

mis|car|ry /mɪskæri, -kæri/ (**miscarries, miscarrying, miscarried**) V-I If a woman **miscarries**, she has a miscarriage. ❏ *Many women who miscarry eventually have healthy babies.*

mis|cast /mɪskæst/ ADJ [usu v-link ADJ] If someone who is acting in a play or movie is **miscast**, the role that they have is not suitable for them, so that they appear silly or unconvincing to the audience.

mis|cel|la|neous /mɪsəleɪniəs/ ADJ [ADJ n] A **miscellaneous** group consists of many different kinds of things or people that are difficult to put into a particular category. ❏ *...a hoard of miscellaneous junk.*

mis|cel|la|ny /mɪsəleɪni/ (**miscellanies**) N-COUNT [oft N of n] A **miscellany** of things is a collection or group of many different kinds of things. [WRITTEN] ❏ *...glass cases filled with a miscellany of objects.*

mis|chief /mɪstʃɪf/ ◼ N-UNCOUNT **Mischief** is playing harmless tricks on people or doing things you are not supposed to do. It can also refer to the desire to do this. ❏ *The little boy was a real handful. He was always up to mischief.* ◼ N-UNCOUNT **Mischief** is behavior that is intended to cause trouble for people. It can also refer to the trouble that is caused. ❏ *The more sinister explanation is that he is about to make mischief in the Middle East again.*

mis|chief-maker (**mischief-makers**) N-COUNT If you say that someone is a **mischief-maker**, you are criticizing them for saying or doing things which are intended to cause trouble between people. [DISAPPROVAL] ❏ *The letter had come from an unknown mischief-maker.*

mis|chie|vous /mɪstʃɪvəs/ ◼ ADJ A **mischievous** person likes to have fun by playing harmless tricks on people or doing things they are not supposed to do. ❏ *She rocks back and forth on her chair like a mischievous child.* • **mis|chie|vous|ly** ADV ❏ *Kathryn winked mischievously.* ◼ ADJ A **mischievous** act or suggestion is intended to cause trouble. ❏ *"I have a few mischievous plans," says Zevon.* • **mis|chie|vous|ly** ADV ❏ *That does not require "massive" military intervention, as some have mischievously claimed.*

mis|com|mu|ni|ca|tion /mɪskəmyunɪkeɪʃ°n/ (**miscommunications**) N-VAR A **miscommunication** is a failure to communicate effectively. ❏ *Don't let your marriage fall apart because of a simple miscommunication.*

mis|con|ceived /mɪskənsivd/ ADJ If you describe a plan or method as **misconceived**, you mean it is not the right one for dealing with a particular problem or situation. ❏ *The teachers say the tests for 14-year-olds are misconceived.* ❏ *...Lawrence's worthy but misconceived idea.*

mis|con|cep|tion /mɪskənsɛpʃ°n/ (**misconceptions**) N-COUNT A **misconception** is an idea that is not correct. ❏ *It is a misconception that Peggy was fabulously wealthy.*

mis|con|duct /mɪskɒndʌkt/ N-UNCOUNT **Misconduct** is bad or unacceptable behavior, especially by a professional person. ❏ *A psychologist was found guilty of serious professional misconduct yesterday.*

misery

mis|con|strue /mɪskənstru/ (**misconstrues, misconstruing, misconstrued**) V-T If you **misconstrue** something that has been said or something that happens, you interpret it wrongly. [FORMAL] ❏ *An outsider might misconstrue the nature of the relationship.*

mis|cre|ant /mɪskriənt/ (**miscreants**) N-COUNT A **miscreant** is someone who has done something illegal or behaved badly. [LITERARY] ❏ *Local people demanded that the police apprehend the miscreants.*

mis|cue /mɪskyu/ (**miscues, miscueing, miscued**) ◼ N-COUNT In sports such as football, baseball, and billiards, a **miscue** is an instance of failing to kick, hit, or strike the ball properly. [AM] ◼ V-T/V-I In soccer, if a player **miscues** a shot, or if he **miscues**, he fails to kick the ball properly. ❏ *He could have levelled within a minute but miscued his shot.* ❏ *He miscued from six yards.* • N-COUNT **Miscue** is also a noun. ❏ *To be sure, the visitors also had plenty of miscues.*

mis|deed /mɪsdid/ (**misdeeds**) N-COUNT A **misdeed** is a bad or evil act. [FORMAL] ❏ *...the alleged financial misdeeds of his government.*

mis|de|mean|or /mɪsdɪminər/ (**misdemeanors**)

in BRIT, use **misdemeanour**

◼ N-COUNT A **misdemeanor** is an act that some people consider to be wrong or unacceptable. [FORMAL] ❏ *Paul appeared before the faculty to account for his various misdemeanors.* ◼ N-COUNT In the United States and other countries where the legal system distinguishes between very serious crimes and less serious ones, a **misdemeanor** is a less serious crime. [LEGAL] ❏ *He was charged with a misdemeanor last fall when he got into a brawl outside his hotel.*

mis|di|rect /mɪsdɪrɛkt, -daɪ-/ (**misdirects, misdirecting, misdirected**) ◼ V-I [usu passive] If resources or efforts are **misdirected**, they are used in the wrong way or for the wrong purposes. ❏ *Many of the aid projects in the developing world have been misdirected in the past.* • **mis|di|rect|ed** ADJ ❏ *...a misdirected effort to mollify the bishop.* ◼ V-T If you **misdirect** someone, you send them in the wrong direction. ❏ *He had deliberately misdirected the reporters.*

mi|ser /maɪzər/ (**misers**) N-COUNT If you say that someone is a **miser**, you disapprove of them because they seem to hate spending money, and to spend as little as possible. [DISAPPROVAL] ❏ *I'm married to a miser.*

mis|er|able /mɪzərəb°l/ ◼ ADJ If you are **miserable**, you are very unhappy. ❏ *I took a series of badly paid secretarial jobs which made me really miserable.* • **mis|er|ably** /mɪzərəbli/ ADV ❏ *He looked miserably down at his plate.* ◼ ADJ If you describe a place or situation as **miserable**, you mean that it makes you feel unhappy or depressed. ❏ *There was nothing at all in this miserable place to distract him.* ◼ ADJ If you describe the weather as **miserable**, you mean that it makes you feel depressed, because it is raining or dull. ❏ *On a gray, wet, miserable day our teams congregated in Port Townsend.* ◼ ADJ [ADJ n] If you describe someone as **miserable**, you mean that you do not like them because they are bad-tempered or unfriendly. ❏ *He always was a miserable man. He never spoke to me nor anybody else, not even to pass the time of day.* ◼ ADJ You can describe a quantity or quality as **miserable** when you think that it is much smaller or worse than it ought to be. [EMPHASIS] ❏ *Our speed over the ground was a miserable 2.2 knots.* • **mis|er|ably** ADV [ADV adj] ❏ *...the miserably inadequate supply of books now provided for schools.* ◼ ADJ [ADJ n] A **miserable** failure is a very great one. [EMPHASIS] ❏ *The film was a miserable commercial failure both in Italy and in the United States.* • **mis|er|ably** ADV [ADV with v] ❏ *Some manage it. Some fail miserably.*

mi|ser|ly /maɪzərli/ ◼ ADJ If you describe someone as **miserly**, you disapprove of them because they seem to hate spending money, and to spend as little as possible. [DISAPPROVAL] ❏ *He is miserly with both his time and his money.* ◼ ADJ [usu ADJ n] If you describe an amount of something as **miserly**, you are critical of it because it is very small. [DISAPPROVAL] ❏ *Being a student today with miserly grants and limited career prospects is difficult.*

mis|ery /mɪzəri/ (**miseries**) ◼ N-VAR **Misery** is great unhappiness. ❏ *All that money brought nothing but sadness and misery and tragedy.* ◼ N-UNCOUNT **Misery** is the way of life and

misfire /mɪsfaɪər/ (misfires, misfiring, misfired) **1** V-I If a plan **misfires**, it goes wrong and does not have the results that you intend it to have. ❑ *Some of their policies had misfired.* **2** V-I If an engine **misfires**, the fuel fails to start burning when it should. ❑ *The boat's engine misfired after he tried to start it up.* **3** V-I If a gun **misfires**, the bullet is not sent out as it should be when the gun is fired. ❑ *The gun misfired after one shot and jammed.*

misfit /mɪsfɪt/ (misfits) N-COUNT A **misfit** is a person who is not easily accepted by other people, often because their behavior is very different from that of everyone else. ❑ *I have been made to feel a social and psychological misfit for not wanting children.*

misfortune /mɪsfɔːrtʃən/ (misfortunes) N-VAR A **misfortune** is something unpleasant or unlucky that happens to someone. ❑ *She seemed to enjoy the misfortunes of others.*

misgender /mɪsdʒɛndər/ (misgenders, misgendering, misgendered) VERB If someone **misgenders** a person, they refer to them using words, especially pronouns, that do not reflect that person's gender identity. ❑ *Currently, newspapers either misgender people, or include both male and female pronouns to navigate the problem.*

misgiving /mɪsgɪvɪŋ/ (misgivings) N-VAR If you have **misgivings** about something that is being suggested or done, you feel that it is not quite right, and are worried that it may have unwanted results. ❑ *She had some misgivings about what she was about to do.*

misguided /mɪsgaɪdɪd/ ADJ If you describe an opinion or plan as **misguided**, you are critical of it because you think it is based on an incorrect idea. You can also describe people as misguided. [DISAPPROVAL] ❑ *In a misguided attempt to be funny, he manages only offensiveness.*

mishandle /mɪshændəl/ (mishandles, mishandling, mishandled) V-T If you say that someone has **mishandled** something, you are critical of them because you think they have dealt with it badly. [DISAPPROVAL] ❑ *She completely mishandled an important project purely through lack of attention.* • **mishandling** N-UNCOUNT ❑ *...the government's mishandling of the economy.*

mishap /mɪshæp/ (mishaps) N-VAR A **mishap** is an unfortunate but not very serious event that happens to someone. ❑ *After a number of mishaps she did manage to get back to Germany.*

mishear /mɪshɪər/ (mishears, mishearing, misheard) V-T/V-I If you **mishear** what someone says, you hear it incorrectly, and think they said something different. ❑ *You misheard me, Frank.* ❑ *She must have misheard.*

mishmash /mɪʃmæʃ, -mɑʃ/ also **mish-mash** N-SING [usu a N of n] If you say that something is a **mishmash**, you are criticizing it because it is a confused mixture of different types of things. [DISAPPROVAL] ❑ *You end up with a mishmash of policies rather than a consistent national approach.*

misinform /mɪsɪnfɔːrm/ (misinforms, misinforming, misinformed) V-T If you **are misinformed**, you are told something that is wrong or inaccurate. ❑ *He has been misinformed by members of his own party.* ❑ *The president accused the media of misinforming the people.*

misinformation /mɪsɪnfərmeɪʃən/ N-UNCOUNT **Misinformation** is wrong information which is given to someone, often in a deliberate attempt to make them believe something that is not true. ❑ *This was a deliberate piece of misinformation.*

misinterpret /mɪsɪntɜːrprɪt/ (misinterprets, misinterpreting, misinterpreted) V-T If you **misinterpret** something, you understand it wrongly. ❑ *He was amazed that he'd misinterpreted the situation so completely.* • **misinterpretation** /mɪsɪntɜːrprɪteɪʃən/ (misinterpretations) N-VAR ❑ *...a misinterpretation of the aims and ends of socialism.*

misjudge /mɪsdʒʌdʒ/ (misjudges, misjudging, misjudged) V-T If you say that someone **has misjudged** a person or situation, you mean that they have formed an incorrect idea or opinion about them, and often that they have made a wrong decision as a result of this. ❑ *Perhaps I had misjudged him, and he was not so predictable after all.*

misjudgment /mɪsdʒʌdʒmənt/ (misjudgments)

in BRIT, also use **misjudgement**

N-VAR A **misjudgment** is an incorrect idea or opinion that is formed about someone or something, especially when a wrong decision is made as a result of this. ❑ *...a misjudgment in foreign policy which had far-reaching consequences.* ❑ *Many accidents were due to pilot misjudgment.*

miskick (miskicks, miskicking, miskicked)

The verb is pronounced /mɪskɪk/. The noun is pronounced /mɪskɪk/.

VERB To **miskick** the ball in a game such as football means to kick it badly so that it does not go in the direction you want it to. [JOURNALISM] ❑ *He miskicked the ball twice at the edge of the penalty box.* ❑ *He miskicked completely as he lost his footing.* • N-COUNT **Miskick** is also a noun. ❑ *A miskick gave her a clear shot at goal.*

mislay /mɪsleɪ/ (mislays, mislaying, mislaid) V-T If you **mislay** something, you put it somewhere and then forget where you have put it. ❑ *I appear to have mislaid my sweater.*

mislead /mɪsliːd/ (misleads, misleading, misled) V-T If you say that someone or something **has misled** you, you mean that they have made you believe something that is not true, either by telling you a lie or by giving you a wrong idea or impression. ❑ *It's this legend which has misled scholars.*

misleading /mɪsliːdɪŋ/ ADJ If you describe something as **misleading**, you mean that it gives you a wrong idea or impression. ❑ *It would be misleading to say that we were friends.* • **misleadingly** ADV ❑ *The data had been presented misleadingly.*

misled /mɪslɛd/ **Misled** is the past tense and past participle of **mislead**.

mismanage /mɪsmænɪdʒ/ (mismanages, mismanaging, mismanaged) V-T To **mismanage** something means to manage it badly. ❑ *75% of voters think the president has mismanaged the economy.*

mismanagement /mɪsmænɪdʒmənt/ N-UNCOUNT Someone's **mismanagement** of a system or organization is the bad way they have dealt with it or organized it. ❑ *His gross mismanagement left the company desperately in need of restructuring.*

mismatch (mismatches, mismatching, mismatched)

The noun is pronounced /mɪsmætʃ/. The verb is pronounced /mɪsmætʃ/.

1 N-COUNT [oft N between/of pl-n, N of pl-n] If there is a **mismatch** between two or more things or people, they do not go together well or are not suitable for each other. ❑ *There is a mismatch between the skills offered by people and the skills needed by industry.* ❑ *...an unfortunate mismatch of styles.* **2** V-T To **mismatch** things or people means to put them together although they do not go together well or are not suitable for each other. ❑ *She was deliberately mismatching articles of clothing.* • **mismatched** ADJ ❑ *The two opponents are mismatched.*

misnamed /mɪsneɪmd/ V-T PASSIVE If you say that something or someone **is misnamed**, you mean that they have a name that describes them incorrectly. ❑ *...a high school teacher who was misnamed Mr. Witty.* ❑ *...the misnamed Grand Hotel.* ❑ *The truth is that junk bonds were misnamed, and therefore misunderstood.*

misnomer /mɪsnoʊmər/ (misnomers) N-COUNT [usu a N in sing] If you say that a word or name is a **misnomer**, you mean that it describes something incorrectly. ❑ *Herbal "tea" is something of a misnomer because these drinks contain no tea at all.*

mi|sogy|nist /mɪsɒdʒɪnɪst/ (**misogynists**) **1** N-COUNT A **misogynist** is someone who dislikes women. **2** ADJ [usu ADJ n] **Misogynist** attitudes or actions are ones that involve or show a strong dislike of women.

miso|gyn|is|tic /mɪsɒdʒɪnɪstɪk/ ADJ **Misogynistic** means the same as **misogynist**.

mi|sogy|ny /mɪsɒdʒɪni/ N-UNCOUNT **Misogyny** is a strong dislike of women.

mis|per|cep|tion /mɪspərsɛpʃən/ (**misperceptions**) N-COUNT A **misperception** is an idea or impression that is not correct. [AM] ❑ *There's a misperception that the tenants here don't care and don't have an investment in the city.*

in BRIT, use **misconception**

mis|place /mɪspleɪs/ (**misplaces, misplacing, misplaced**) V-T If you **misplace** something, you lose it, usually only temporarily. ❑ *Somehow the suitcase with my clothes was misplaced.*

mis|placed /mɪspleɪst/ ADJ If you describe a feeling or action as **misplaced**, you are critical of it because you think it is inappropriate, or directed towards the wrong thing or person. [DISAPPROVAL] ❑ *A telling sign of misplaced priorities is the concentration on health, not environmental issues.*

mis|print /mɪsprɪnt/ (**misprints**) N-COUNT A **misprint** is a mistake in the way something is printed, for example a spelling mistake.

mis|pro|nounce /mɪsprənaʊns/ (**mispronounces, mispronouncing, mispronounced**) V-T If you **mispronounce** a word, you pronounce it wrongly. ❑ *He repeatedly mispronounced words and slurred his speech.* • **mis|pro|nun|cia|tion** /mɪsprənʌnsieɪʃən/ N-VAR ❑ *...Dwight's mispronunciation of Taos Square.* ❑ *The teacher notes reading errors such as mispronunciations.*

mis|quote /mɪskwoʊt/ (**misquotes, misquoting, misquoted**) V-T If someone **is misquoted**, something that they have said or written is repeated incorrectly. ❑ *He claimed that he had been misquoted and he threatened to sue the magazine for libel.*

mis|read /mɪsriːd/ (**misreads, misreading**)

The form **misread** is used in the present tense, and is the past tense and past participle, when it is pronounced /mɪsrɛd/.

1 V-T If you **misread** a situation or someone's behavior, you do not understand it properly. ❑ *The administration largely misread the mood of the electorate.* • **mis|read|ing** (**misreadings**) N-COUNT ❑ *...a misreading of opinion in France.* **2** V-T If you **misread** something that has been written or printed, you look at it and think that it says something that it does not say. ❑ *His chauffeur misread his route and took a wrong turn.*

mis|re|mem|ber /mɪsrɪmɛmbər/ (**misremembers, misremembering, misremembered**) V-T If you **misremember** something, you remember it incorrectly. [mainly AM] ❑ *He proved overconfident on the witness stand, misremembering a key piece of evidence.*

mis|rep|re|sent /mɪsrɛprɪzɛnt/ (**misrepresents, misrepresenting, misrepresented**) V-T If someone **misrepresents** a person or situation, they give a wrong or inaccurate account of what the person or situation is like. ❑ *He said that the press had misrepresented him as arrogant and bullying.* ❑ *Hollywood films misrepresented us as drunks, maniacs, and murderers.* • **mis|rep|re|sen|ta|tion** /mɪsrɛprɪzɛnteɪʃən/ (**misrepresentations**) N-VAR ❑ *I wish to point out your misrepresentation of the facts.*

mis|rule /mɪsruːl/ N-UNCOUNT If you refer to someone's government of a country as **misrule**, you are critical of them for governing their country badly or unfairly. [DISAPPROVAL] ❑ *He was arrested last December, accused of corruption and misrule.*

miss ✦✦◇ /mɪs/ (**misses, missing, missed**)
→ Please look at meaning **11** to see if the expression you are looking for is shown under another headword.

1 V-T/V-I If you **miss** something, you fail to hit it, for example when you have thrown something at it or you have shot a bullet at it. ❑ *She tossed the ashtray across the room, narrowly missing my head.* ❑ *When I'd missed a few times, he suggested I rest the rifle on a rock to steady it.* • N-COUNT **Miss** is also a noun. ❑ *After more misses, they finally put two arrows into the lion's chest.* **2** V-T/V-I In sports, if you **miss** a shot, you fail to get the ball in the goal, net, or hole. ❑ *He scored four of the baskets but missed a free throw.* ❑ *He dived for the ball and missed.* • N-COUNT **Miss** is also a noun. ❑ *Snow made his first basket of the game after eight misses.* **3** V-T If you **miss** something, you fail to notice it. ❑ *From this vantage point he watched, his searching eye never missing a detail.* **4** V-T If you **miss** the meaning or importance of something, you fail to understand or appreciate it. ❑ *One ABC correspondent had totally missed the point of the question.* **5** V-T If you **miss** a chance or opportunity, you fail to take advantage of it. ❑ *It was too good an opportunity to miss.* **6** V-T If you **miss** someone who is no longer with you or who has died, you feel sad and wish that they were still with you. ❑ *Your mama and I are going to miss you at Christmas.* **7** V-T If you **miss** something, you feel sad because you no longer have it or are no longer doing or experiencing it. ❑ *I could happily move back into an apartment if it wasn't for the fact that I'd miss my garden.* **8** V-T If you **miss** something such as a plane or train, you arrive too late to catch it. ❑ *He missed the last bus home and had to stay with a friend.* **9** V-T If you **miss** something such as a meeting or an activity, you do not go to it or take part in it. ❑ *It's a pity Martha and I had to miss our class last week.* ❑ *You won't be missing much on TV tonight apart from the usual repeats.* **10** → see also **missing** **11 to miss the boat** → see **boat**

▶ **miss out** **1** PHRASAL VERB If you **miss out** on something that would be enjoyable or useful to you, you are not involved in it or do not take part in it. ❑ *We're missing out on a tremendous opportunity.* **2** PHRASAL VERB If you **miss out** something or someone, you fail to include them. [BRIT]

in AM, use **leave out**

Miss ✦✦◇ /mɪs/ (**Misses**) N-TITLE You use **Miss** in front of the name of a girl or unmarried woman when you are speaking to her or referring to her. Many people prefer the title 'Ms.' [FORMAL] ❑ *It was nice talking to you, Miss Ellis.*

mis|shap|en /mɪsʃeɪpən/ ADJ If you describe something as **misshapen**, you think that it does not have a normal or natural shape. ❑ *...misshapen vegetables.* ❑ *Her hands were misshapen by arthritis.*

mis|sile ✦◇◇ /mɪsəl/ (**missiles**) **1** N-COUNT A **missile** is a tube-shaped weapon that travels long distances through the air and explodes when it reaches its target. ❑ *The authorities offered to stop firing missiles if the rebels agreed to stop attacking civilian targets.* **2** N-COUNT Anything that is thrown as a weapon can be called a **missile**. ❑ *The football fans began throwing missiles, one of which hit the referee.*

miss|ing ✦◇◇ /mɪsɪŋ/ **1** ADJ If something is **missing** or has gone **missing**, it is not in its usual place, and you cannot find it. ❑ *It was only an hour or so later that I discovered that my gun was missing.* **2** ADJ If a part of something is **missing**, it has been removed or has come off, and has not been replaced. ❑ *Three buttons were missing from his shirt.* **3** ADJ If you say that something is **missing**, you mean that it has not been included, and you think that it should have been. ❑ *She had given me an incomplete list. One name was missing from it.* **4** ADJ Someone who is **missing** cannot be found, and it is not known whether they are alive or dead. ❑ *Five people died in the explosion and more than one thousand were injured. One person is still missing.* • PHRASE If a member of the armed forces is **missing in action**, they have not returned from a battle, their body has not been found, and they are not thought to have been captured.

miss|ing link (**missing links**) N-COUNT [usu sing] The **missing link** in a situation is the piece of information or evidence that you need in order to make your knowledge or understanding of something complete. ❑ *We're dealing with probably the biggest missing link in what we know about human evolution.*

miss|ing per|son (**missing persons**) N-COUNT A **missing person** has suddenly left their home without telling their family where they are going, and it is not known whether they are alive or dead.

mis|sion ✦✦◇ /mɪʃən/ (**missions**) **1** N-COUNT A **mission** is an important task that people are given to do, especially one that involves traveling to another country. ❑ *Salisbury sent him on a diplomatic mission to North America.* **2** N-COUNT A **mission** is a group of people who have been sent to a foreign country to carry out an official task. ❑ *...a senior member of a diplomatic* mission. **3** N-COUNT A **mission** is a special journey made by a military airplane or spacecraft. ❏ *...a bomber that crashed during a training mission in the west Texas mountains.* **4** N-SING If you say that you have a **mission**, you mean that you have a strong commitment and sense of duty to do or achieve something. ❏ *He viewed his mission in life as protecting the weak from the evil.* **5** N-COUNT A **mission** is the activities of a group of Christians who have been sent to a place to teach people about Christianity. ❏ *They say God spoke to them and told them to go on a mission to the poorest country in the Western Hemisphere.* **6** N-COUNT A **mission** is a building or group of buildings in which missionary work is carried out. ❏ *I reside at the mission at St. Michael's.* **7** → See feature box at **travel**

mis|sion|ary /mɪʃəneri/ (**missionaries**) **1** N-COUNT A **missionary** is a Christian who has been sent to a foreign country to teach people about Christianity. ❏ *My mother would still like me to be a missionary in Africa.* **2** ADJ [ADJ n] **Missionary** is used to describe the activities of missionaries. ❏ *You should be in missionary work.* **3** ADJ [ADJ n] If you refer to someone's enthusiasm for an activity or belief as **missionary** zeal, you are emphasizing that they are very enthusiastic about it. [EMPHASIS] ❏ *She had a kind of missionary zeal about bringing culture to the masses.*

mis|sion|ary po|si|tion N-SING [usu the N] The **missionary position** is a position for sexual intercourse in which the man lies on top of the woman and they are facing each other.

mis|sion con|trol N-UNCOUNT **Mission control** is the group of people on Earth who are in charge of a flight by a spacecraft, or the place where these people work.

mis|sion state|ment (**mission statements**) N-COUNT A company's or organization's **mission statement** is a document which states what they aim to achieve and the kind of service they intend to provide. [BUSINESS] ❏ *Our mission statement is to be the best design firm in the world.*

mis|sive /mɪsɪv/ (**missives**) N-COUNT A **missive** is a letter or other message that someone sends. [HUMOROUS OR LITERARY] ❏ *...the customary missive from your dear mother.*

mis|spell /mɪsspɛl/ (**misspells, misspelling, misspelled**) V-T If someone **misspells** a word, they spell it wrongly. ❏ *Sorry I misspelled your last name.* • **mis|spell|ing** (**misspellings**) N-COUNT ❏ *...a misspelling of the writer's name.*

mis|spend /mɪsspɛnd/ (**misspends, misspending, misspent**) V-T If you say that time or money **has been misspent**, you disapprove of the way in which it has been spent. [DISAPPROVAL] ❏ *Much of the money was grossly misspent.*

mis|state /mɪsstɛɪt/ (**misstates, misstating, misstated**) V-T If you **misstate** something, you state it incorrectly or give false information about it. [mainly AM] ❏ *Look at the false police reports that omitted or misstated crucial facts.* ❏ *The amount was misstated in the table because of an error by regulators.*

mis|state|ment /mɪsstɛɪtmənt/ (**misstatements**) N-COUNT A **misstatement** is an incorrect statement, or the giving of false information. [mainly AM] ❏ *He finally corrected his misstatement and offered to reduce the fee.* ❏ *This booklet is filled with misstatements of fact.*

mis|step /mɪsstɛp/ (**missteps**) N-COUNT A **misstep** is a mistake. [AM] ❏ *Las Vegas police committed a string of costly missteps.*

mis|sus /mɪsɪz/ also **missis** N-SING [poss/the N] Some people refer to someone's wife as their **missus**. [INFORMAL] ❏ *I do a little shopping for the missus.*

mist /mɪst/ (**mists, misting, misted**) **1** N-VAR **Mist** consists of a large number of tiny drops of water in the air, which make it difficult to see very far. ❏ *Thick mist made flying impossible.* **2** V-T/V-I If a piece of glass **mists** or **is misted**, it becomes covered with tiny drops of moisture, so that you cannot see through it easily. ❏ *The windows misted, blurring the stark streetlight.* • PHRASAL VERB **Mist over** means the same as **mist**. ❏ *The front windshield was misting over.*

mis|take ♦♦◊ /mɪsteɪk/ (**mistakes, mistaking, mistook, mistaken**) **1** N-COUNT [oft N of -ing, also by N] If you make a **mistake**, you do something which you did not intend to do, or which produces a result that you do not want. ❏ *They made the big mistake of thinking they could seize its border with a relatively small force.* ❏ *There must be some mistake.* **2** N-COUNT A **mistake** is something or part of something that is incorrect or not right. ❏ *Her mother sighed and rubbed out another mistake in the crossword puzzle.* **3** V-T If you **mistake** one person or thing **for** another, you wrongly think that they are the other person or thing. ❏ *When may fever first occurs it is often mistaken for a summer cold.* **4** V-T If you **mistake** something, you fail to recognize or understand it. ❏ *The administration completely mistook the feeling of the country.* **5** PHRASE You can say **there is no mistaking** something when you are emphasizing that you cannot fail to recognize or understand it. [EMPHASIS] ❏ *There's no mistaking the eastern flavor of the food.*

USAGE
---

mistake
Don't say that someone 'does' a mistake or an error. Don't say, for example, 'He did a terrible mistake.' You say that someone makes a mistake or does something **by mistake** or, in more formal English, **in error**. Don't say 'in mistake' or 'by error.' *I went into the wrong room by mistake.*

mis|tak|en /mɪsteɪkən/ **1** ADJ [v-link ADJ] If you are **mistaken** about something, you are wrong about it. ❏ *I see I was mistaken about you.* • PHRASE You use expressions such as **if I'm not mistaken** and **unless I'm very much mistaken** as a polite way of emphasizing the statement you are making, especially when you are confident that it is correct. [EMPHASIS] ❏ *I think Alfred wanted to marry Jennifer, if I am not mistaken.* **2** ADJ [ADJ n] A **mistaken** belief or opinion is incorrect. ❏ *I had a mistaken view of what was happening.* • **mis|tak|en|ly** ADV [ADV with v] ❏ *He says they mistakenly believed the standard licenses they held were sufficient.*

mis|tak|en iden|tity N-UNCOUNT When someone incorrectly thinks that they have found or recognized a particular person, you refer to this as a case of **mistaken identity**. ❏ *The dead man could have been the victim of mistaken identity.*

mis|ter /mɪstər/ N-VOC Men are sometimes addressed as **mister**, especially by children and especially when the person talking to them does not know their name. [INFORMAL] ❏ *Look, Mister, we know our job, so don't try to tell us what to do.*

mis|time /mɪstaɪm/ (**mistimes, mistiming, mistimed**) V-T If you **mistime** something, you do it at the wrong time, so that it is not successful. ❏ *You're bound to mistime a tackle every so often.* ❏ *...a certain mistimed comment.*

mis|tle|toe /mɪsəltoʊ/ N-UNCOUNT **Mistletoe** is a plant with pale berries that grows on the branches of some trees. Mistletoe is used in the United States as a Christmas decoration, and people often kiss under it.

mis|took /mɪstʊk/ **Mistook** is the past tense of **mistake**.

mis|treat /mɪstriːt/ (**mistreats, mistreating, mistreated**) V-T If someone **mistreats** a person or an animal, they treat them badly, especially by making them suffer physically. ❏ *She has been mistreated by men in the past.*

mis|treat|ment /mɪstriːtmənt/ N-UNCOUNT **Mistreatment** of a person or animal is cruel behavior towards them, especially by making them suffer physically. ❏ *...issues like police brutality and mistreatment of people in prisons.*

mis|tress /mɪstrɪs/ (**mistresses**) N-COUNT A married man's **mistress** is a woman who is not his wife and with whom he is having a sexual relationship. [OLD-FASHIONED] ❏ *Tracy was his mistress for three years.*

mis|tri|al /mɪstraɪəl/ (**mistrials**) **1** N-COUNT A **mistrial** is a legal trial that is conducted unfairly, for example because not all the evidence is considered, so that there must be a new trial. ❏ *The past has been scarred by countless mistrials and perversions of justice.* **2** N-COUNT A **mistrial** is a legal trial which ends without a verdict, for example because the jury cannot agree on one. [AM] ❏ *The judge said he would declare a mistrial if the jury did not reach its verdict today.*

mis|trust /mɪstrʌst/ (**mistrusts, mistrusting, mistrusted**) **1** N-UNCOUNT **Mistrust** is the feeling that you have toward someone who you do not trust. ❏ *There was mutual mistrust between the two men.* **2** V-T If you **mistrust** someone or something, you do not trust them. ❏ *It frequently appears that Bell mistrusts all journalists.*

mis|trust|ful /mɪstrʌstfəl/ ADJ [oft ADJ of n] If you are **mistrustful** of someone, you do not trust them. ❏ *He had always been mistrustful of women.*

misty /mɪsti/ (mistier, mistiest) ADJ On a **misty** day, there is a lot of mist in the air. ❏ *It's a little misty this morning.*

misty-eyed ADJ [usu v-link ADJ] If you say that something makes you **misty-eyed**, you mean that it makes you feel so happy or sentimental, especially about the past, that you feel as if you are going to cry. ❏ *They got misty-eyed listening to records of Ruby Murray singing "Danny Boy."*

mis|under|stand /mɪsʌndərstænd/ (misunderstands, misunderstanding, misunderstood) **1** V-T/V-I If you **misunderstand** someone or something, you do not understand them properly. ❏ *I misunderstood you.* ❏ *They have simply misunderstood what rock and roll is.* • CONVENTION You can say **don't misunderstand me** when you want to correct a wrong impression that you think someone may have gotten about what you are saying. **2** → see also **misunderstood**

mis|under|stand|ing /mɪsʌndərstændɪŋ/ (misunderstandings) **1** N-VAR A **misunderstanding** is a failure to understand something properly, for example a situation or a person's remarks. ❏ *There has been some misunderstanding of our publishing aims.* **2** N-COUNT You can refer to a disagreement or slight quarrel as a **misunderstanding**. [FORMAL] ❏ *There was a little misunderstanding with the police and he was arrested.*

mis|under|stood /mɪsʌndərstʊd/ **1** Misunderstood is the past tense and past participle of **misunderstand**. **2** ADJ If you describe someone or something as **misunderstood**, you mean that people do not understand them and have a wrong impression or idea of them. ❏ *Eric is very badly misunderstood.*

mis|use (misuses, misusing, misused)

The noun is pronounced /mɪsyus/. The verb is pronounced /mɪsyuz/.

1 N-VAR The **misuse** of something is incorrect, careless, or dishonest use of it. ❏ *...the misuse of power and privilege.* **2** V-T If someone **misuses** something, they use it incorrectly, carelessly, or dishonestly. ❏ *Inspectors were thought to be misusing their position in order to seek work in a consultancy capacity.* ❏ *Tess would like a dollar for every time she had heard that word misused by television journalists.*

mite /maɪt/ (mites) N-COUNT Mites are very tiny creatures that live on plants, for example, or in animals' fur. ❏ *...an itching skin disorder caused by parasitic mites.*

miti|gate /mɪtɪgeɪt/ (mitigates, mitigating, mitigated) V-T To **mitigate** something means to make it less unpleasant, serious, or painful. [FORMAL] ❏ *...ways of mitigating the effects of an explosion.*

miti|gat|ing /mɪtɪgeɪtɪŋ/ ADJ [ADJ n] **Mitigating** circumstances or factors make a bad action, especially a crime, easier to understand and excuse, and may result in the person responsible being punished less severely. [LEGAL] ❏ *The judge found that in her case there were mitigating circumstances.*

miti|ga|tion /mɪtɪgeɪʃən/ **1** PHRASE [PHR with cl] If someone, especially in a court, is told something **in mitigation**, they are told something that makes a crime or fault easier to understand and excuse. [FORMAL] ❏ *The prosecutor told the judge in mitigation that the offenses had been at the lower end of the scale.* **2** N-UNCOUNT **Mitigation** is a reduction in the unpleasantness, seriousness, or painfulness of something. [FORMAL] ❏ *...the mitigation or cure of a physical or mental condition.*

mitt /mɪt/ (mitts) **1** N-COUNT You can refer to a person's hands as their **mitts**. [INFORMAL] ❏ *I pressed a dime into his grubby mitt.* **2** N-COUNT [usu supp n] A baseball **mitt** is a large glove worn by a player whose job involves catching the ball.

mit|ten /mɪtən/ (mittens) N-COUNT [usu pl] **Mittens** are gloves which have one section that covers your thumb and another section that covers your four fingers together.

mix ♦♦♢ /mɪks/ (mixes, mixing, mixed) **1** V-RECIP If two substances **mix** or if you **mix** one substance with another, you stir or shake them together, or combine them in some other way, so that they become a single substance. ❏ *Oil and water don't mix.* ❏ *A quick stir will mix them thoroughly.* ❏ *Mix the cinnamon with the rest of the sugar.* **2** V-T If you **mix** something, you prepare it by mixing other things together. ❏ *He had spent several hours mixing cement.* **3** N-VAR A **mix** is a powder containing all the substances that you need in order to make something such as a cake or a sauce. When you use

it, you add liquid. ❏ *For speed we used packets of pizza dough mix.* **4** N-COUNT A **mix** of different things or people is two or more of them together. ❏ *The story is a magical mix of fantasy and reality.* **5** V-RECIP [usu with brd-neg] If two things or activities do not **mix**, it is not a good idea to have them or do them together, because the result would be unpleasant or dangerous. ❏ *Politics and sports don't mix.* ❏ *Some of these pills don't mix with drink.* **6** V-RECIP If you **mix** with other people, you meet them and talk to them. You can also say that people **mix**. ❏ *I ventured the idea that the secret of staying young was to mix with older people.* ❏ *People are supposed to mix, do you understand?* **7** → see also **mixed** **8** **to mix your metaphors** → see **metaphor**
▶ **mix up** **1** PHRASAL VERB If you **mix up** two things or people, you confuse them, so that you think that one of them is the other one. ❏ *People often mix me up with other actors.* ❏ *Depressed people may mix up their words.* **2** PHRASAL VERB If you **mix up** a number of things, you put things of different kinds together or place things so that they are not in order. ❏ *I like to mix up designer clothes.* ❏ *Take the cards and mix them up.* **3** → see also **mixed up**

COLLOCATIONS

mix
NOUN **4**
adjective + **mix**: diverse, eclectic; heady, intoxicating, potent; toxic; fascinating, interesting; curious, odd, strange; explosive; rich, vibrant; complex

mixed ♦♢♢ /mɪkst/ **1** ADJ If you have **mixed** feelings about something or someone, you feel uncertain about them because you can see both good and bad points about them. ❏ *I came home from the meeting with mixed feelings.* **2** ADJ A **mixed** group of people consists of people of many different types. ❏ *I found a very mixed group of individuals, some of whom I could relate to and others with whom I had very little in common.* **3** ADJ **Mixed** is used to describe something that involves people from two or more different races. ❏ *Sally had attended a racially mixed school.* **4** ADJ **Mixed** education or accommodations are intended for both males and females. ❏ *Girls who have always been at a mixed school know how to stand up for themselves.* **5** ADJ [ADJ n] **Mixed** is used to describe something which includes or consists of different things of the same general kind. ❏ *...a teaspoon of mixed herbs.*

mixed bag N-SING [usu a N, oft N of n] If you describe a situation or a group of things or people as a **mixed bag**, you mean that it contains some good items, features, or people and some bad ones. ❏ *Research on athletes and ordinary human subjects has yielded a mixed bag of results.* ❏ *This autumn's collections are a very mixed bag.*

mixed dou|bles N-UNCOUNT [also the N] In some sports, such as tennis and badminton, **mixed doubles** is a match in which a man and a woman play as partners against another man and woman.

mixed econo|my (mixed economies) N-COUNT A **mixed economy** is an economic system in which some companies are owned by the state and some are not. [BUSINESS] ❏ *Naturally, this argument was also deployed against those who advocated a mixed economy, combining public ownership with a market system.*

mixed mar|riage (mixed marriages) N-COUNT A **mixed marriage** is a marriage between two people who are not of the same race or religion.

mixed mar|tial arts N-UNCOUNT **Mixed martial arts** is a sport in which two people fight by hitting, kicking, and holding each other, both in a standing position and on the ground. ❏ *It's a movie about the world of mixed martial arts.*

mixed up **1** ADJ If you are **mixed up**, you are confused, often because of emotional or social problems. ❏ *I think he's a rather mixed up kid.* **2** ADJ [v-link ADJ in/with n] To be **mixed up** in something bad, or with someone you disapprove of, means to be involved in it or with them. ❏ *Why did I ever get mixed up with you?*

mix|er /mɪksər/ (mixers) **1** N-COUNT A **mixer** is a machine used for mixing things together. ❏ *...an electric mixer.* **2** N-COUNT A **mixer** is a nonalcoholic drink such as fruit juice or soda that you mix with strong alcohol such as gin. ❏ *At the Tropicana you order ice and mixers from the waiters at the table.*

3 N-COUNT If you say that someone is a good **mixer**, you mean that they are good at talking to people and making friends. ❑ *Cooper was a good mixer, he was popular.* **4** N-COUNT A **mixer** is a piece of equipment that is used to make changes to recorded music or film. ❑ *...a three-channel audio mixer.*

mix|ing bowl (mixing bowls) N-COUNT A **mixing bowl** is a large bowl used for mixing ingredients.

mix|ture ✦✧ /mɪkstʃər/ (mixtures) **1** N-SING A **mixture** of things consists of several different things together. ❑ *They looked at him with a mixture of horror, envy, and awe.* **2** N-COUNT A **mixture** is a substance that consists of other substances which have been stirred or shaken together. ❑ *...a mixture of water and sugar and salt.*

mix-up (mix-ups) N-COUNT A **mix-up** is a mistake or a failure in the way that something has been planned. [INFORMAL] ❑ *...a mix-up over travel arrangements.*

ml ml is a written abbreviation for **milliliter** or **milliliters**. ❑ *Boil the sugar and 100 ml of water.*

mm ✦✧ mm is a written abbreviation for **millimeter** or **millimeters**. ❑ *...a 135mm lens.*

MMR /ɛm ɛm ɑr/ N-UNCOUNT [oft N N] **MMR** is a vaccine that is given to young children to protect them against certain diseases. **MMR** is an abbreviation for 'measles, mumps, and rubella.' ❑ *...the MMR vaccine.*

mne|mon|ic /nɪmɒnɪk/ (mnemonics) N-COUNT [oft N N] A **mnemonic** is a word, short poem, or sentence that is intended to help you remember things such as scientific rules or spelling rules. For example, 'i before e, except after c' is a mnemonic to help people remember how to spell words like 'believe' and 'receive.' ❑ *...mnemonic devices.*

moan /moʊn/ (moans, moaning, moaned) **1** V-T/V-I If you **moan**, you make a low sound, usually because you are unhappy or in pain. ❑ *Tony moaned in his sleep and then turned over on his side.* • N-COUNT **Moan** is also a noun. ❑ *Suddenly she gave a low, choking moan and began to tremble violently.* **2** V-I To **moan** means to complain or speak in a way which shows that you are very unhappy. [DISAPPROVAL] ❑ *I used to moan if I didn't get at least six hours' sleep at night.* ❑ *...moaning about the weather.* **3** N-COUNT A **moan** is a complaint. [INFORMAL] ❑ *They have been listening to people's moans and praise.*

moan|er /moʊnər/ (moaners) N-COUNT If you refer to someone as a **moaner**, you are critical of them because they often complain about things. [INFORMAL, DISAPPROVAL] ❑ *Film critics are dreadful moaners.*

moat /moʊt/ (moats) N-COUNT A **moat** is a deep, wide channel dug around a place such as a castle and filled with water, in order to protect the place from attack.

mob /mɒb/ (mobs, mobbing, mobbed) **1** N-COUNT A **mob** is a large, disorganized, and often violent crowd of people. ❑ *The inspectors watched a growing mob of demonstrators gathering.* **2** N-SING You can refer to the people involved in organized crime as **the Mob**. [INFORMAL] ❑ *He makes ends meet by working as a forger for the Mob.* **3** N-SING People sometimes use **the mob** to refer in a disapproving way to the majority of people in a country or place, especially when these people are behaving in a violent or uncontrolled way. [mainly BRIT, DISAPPROVAL] ❑ *If they continue like this there is a danger of the mob taking over.* **4** V-T [usu passive] If you say that someone is being **mobbed** by a crowd of people, you mean that the people are trying to talk to them or get near them in an enthusiastic or threatening way. ❑ *Her car was mobbed by the media.*

mo|bile ✦✧ /moʊbəl/ (mobiles) **1** ADJ You use **mobile** to describe something large that can be moved easily from place to place. ❑ *...the four-hundred seat mobile theater.* **2** ADJ If you are **mobile**, you can move or travel easily from place to place, for example because you do not have a physical disability or because you have your own transportation. ❑ *I'm still very mobile.* • **mo|bil|ity** /moʊbɪlɪti/ N-UNCOUNT ❑ *Two cars gave them the freedom and mobility to go their separate ways.* **3** ADJ In a **mobile** society, people move easily from one job, home, or social class to another. ❑ *We are a very mobile society and can't resist trying to take everything with us.* • **mo|bil|ity** N-UNCOUNT ❑ *Prior to the nineteenth century, there were almost no channels of social mobility.* **4** N-COUNT A **mobile** is a decoration that you hang from a ceiling. It usually consists of several small objects which move as the air around them moves. **5** N-COUNT A **mobile** is the same as a **mobile phone**. [mainly BRIT]

mo|bile home (mobile homes) N-COUNT A **mobile home** is a large trailer that people live in and that usually remains in the same place, but which can be pulled to another place using a car or van.

mo|bile phone (mobile phones) N-COUNT A **mobile phone** is a telephone that you can carry with you and use to make or receive calls wherever you are. [BRIT]

in AM, use **cellphone**

mo|bi|lize /moʊbɪlaɪz/ (mobilizes, mobilizing, mobilized)

in BRIT, also use **mobilise**

1 V-T/V-I If you **mobilize** support or **mobilize** people to do something, you succeed in encouraging people to take action, especially political action. If people **mobilize**, they prepare to take action. ❑ *The best hope is that we will mobilize international support and get down to action.* • **mo|bi|li|za|tion** /moʊbɪlɪzeɪʃən/ N-UNCOUNT ❑ *...the rapid mobilization of international opinion in support of the revolution.* **2** V-T If you **mobilize** resources, you start to use them or make them available for use. ❑ *If you could mobilize the resources, you could get it done.* • **mo|bi|li|za|tion** N-UNCOUNT ❑ *...the mobilization of resources for education.* **3** V-T/V-I If a country **mobilizes**, or **mobilizes** its armed forces, or if its armed forces **mobilize**, they are given orders to prepare for a conflict. [JOURNALISM or MILITARY] ❑ *The country even threatened to mobilize in response to the ultimatums.* • **mo|bi|li|za|tion** N-UNCOUNT ❑ *...a demand for full-scale mobilization to defend the republic.*

mob|ster /mɒbstər/ (mobsters) N-COUNT A **mobster** is someone who is a member of an organized group of violent criminals.

moc|ca|sin /mɒkəsɪn/ (moccasins) N-COUNT **Moccasins** are soft leather shoes that have a low heel and a raised seam around the top of the front part.

mo|cha /moʊkə/ (mochas) **1** N-VAR **Mocha** is a drink that is a mixture of coffee and chocolate. A **mocha** is a cup of mocha. ❑ *...a cup of mocha.* ❑ *...the opportunity to choose between a latte and a mocha.* **2** N-UNCOUNT **Mocha** is a type of strong coffee.

mock /mɒk/ (mocks, mocking, mocked) **1** V-T If someone **mocks** you, they show or pretend that they think you are foolish or inferior, for example by saying something funny about you, or by imitating your behavior. ❑ *I thought you were mocking me.* **2** ADJ [ADJ N] You use **mock** to describe something which is not real or genuine, but which is intended to be very similar to the real thing. ❑ *"It's tragic!" swoons Jeffrey in mock horror.*

mock|ery /mɒkəri/ **1** N-UNCOUNT If someone mocks you, you can refer to their behavior or attitude as **mockery**. ❑ *Was there a glint of mockery in his eyes?* **2** N-SING If something makes a **mockery** of something, it makes it appear worthless and foolish. ❑ *This action makes a mockery of the administration's continuing protestations of concern.*

mock|ing /mɒkɪŋ/ ADJ A **mocking** expression or **mocking** behavior indicates that you think someone or something is stupid or inferior. ❑ *She gave a mocking smile.*

mocking|bird /mɒkɪŋbɜrd/ (mockingbirds) N-COUNT A **mockingbird** is a gray bird with a long tail that is found in North America. Mockingbirds are able to copy the songs of other birds.

mock-up (mock-ups) N-COUNT [oft N of n] A **mock-up** of something such as a machine or building is a model of it which is used in tests or to show people what it will look like. ❑ *There's a mock-up of the main street where the Goodwins go shopping.*

mod|al /moʊdəl/ (modals) N-COUNT In grammar, a **modal** or a **modal auxiliary** is a word such as 'can' or 'would' which is used with a main verb to express ideas such as possibility, intention, or necessity. [TECHNICAL]

mode /moʊd/ (modes) **1** N-COUNT A **mode** of life or behavior is a particular way of living or behaving. [FORMAL] ❑ *...the capitalist mode of production.* **2** N-COUNT A **mode** is a particular style in art, literature, or dress. ❑ *...a slightly more elegant and formal mode of dress.* **3** N-COUNT On some cameras or electronic devices, the different **modes** available are the different programs or settings that you can choose when you use them. ❏ ...*when the camera is in manual mode.*

mod|el ♦♦◇ /mɒdəl/ (**models, modeling** or **modelling, modeled** or **modelled**) **1** N-COUNT A **model** of an object is a physical representation that shows what it looks like or how it works. The model is often smaller than the object it represents. ❏ ...*an architect's model of a wooden house.* ❏ *I made a model out of paper and glue.* • ADJ [ADJ N] **Model** is also an adjective. ❏ ...*a model railway.* **2** N-COUNT A **model** is a system that is being used and that people might want to copy in order to achieve similar results. [FORMAL] ❏ ...*the Chinese model of economic reform.* **3** N-COUNT A **model** of a system or process is a theoretical description that can help you understand how the system or process works, or how it might work. [FORMAL] ❏ *Darwin eventually put forward a model of biological evolution.* **4** V-T If someone such as a scientist **models** a system or process, they make an accurate theoretical description of it in order to understand or explain how it works. [FORMAL] ❏ *I have moved from trying to model and understand the distribution and evolution of water vapor.* **5** N-COUNT If you say that someone or something is a **model** of a particular quality, you are showing approval of them because they have that quality to a large degree. [APPROVAL] ❏ *A model of good manners, he has conquered any inward fury.* **6** ADJ [ADJ N] You use **model** to express approval of someone when you think that they perform their role or duties extremely well. [APPROVAL] ❏ *As a girl she had been a model student.* **7** V-T If one thing **is modeled** on another, the first thing is made so that it is like the second thing in some way. ❏ *The quota system was modeled on those operated in America and continental Europe.* **8** V-T If you **model** yourself **on** someone, you copy the way that they do things, because you admire them and want to be like them. ❏ *You have been modeling yourself on others all your life.* **9** N-COUNT A particular **model** of a machine is a particular version of it. ❏ *To keep the cost down, opt for a basic model.* **10** N-COUNT An artist's **model** is a person who stays still in a particular position so that the artist can make a picture or sculpture of them. ❏ ...*the model for his portrait of Mary Magdalene, the Marchesa Attavanti.* **11** V-I If someone **models** for an artist, they stay still in a particular position so that the artist can make a picture or sculpture of them. ❏ *Tullio has been modeling for Sandra for eleven years.* **12** N-COUNT A fashion **model** is a person whose job is to display clothes by wearing them. ❏ ...*Paris's top fashion model.* **13** V-T/V-I If someone **models**, or **models** clothes, they display them by wearing them. ❏ *She began modeling in Paris at age 15.* • **mod|el|ing** N-UNCOUNT ❏ *She was being offered a modeling contract.* **14** V-T/V-I If you **model** in a substance such as clay or wood, or **model** shapes or figures, you make them out of that substance. ❏ *There she began to model in clay.* **15** → see also **role model**

COLLOCATIONS

model
NOUN
2
noun + **model**: business; computer
verb + **model**: adopt, develop
adjective + **model**: mathematical
12
noun + **model**: fashion, runway

mod|el|er /mɒdələr/ (**modelers**)

in BRIT, sometimes in AM, use **modeller**

1 N-COUNT A **modeler** is someone who makes objects or figures out of substances such as wood or clay. **2** N-COUNT [usu supp N] A **modeler** is someone who makes theoretical descriptions of systems or processes in order to understand them and be able to predict how they will develop. ❏ ...*climate modelers.*

mo|dem /moʊdəm, -dɛm/ (**modems**) N-COUNT [also by N] A **modem** is a device which uses a telephone line to connect computers or computer systems. [COMPUTING] ❏ *He sent his work to his publishers by modem.*

mod|er|ate ♦◇◇ (**moderates, moderating, moderated**)

The adjective and noun are pronounced /mɒdərɪt/. The verb is pronounced /mɒdəreɪt/.

1 ADJ **Moderate** political opinions or policies are not extreme. ❏ *He was an easygoing man of very moderate views.* **2** ADJ You use **moderate** to describe people or groups who have moderate political opinions or policies. ❏ ...*a moderate Democrat.* • N-COUNT A **moderate** is someone with moderate political opinions. ❏ *If he presents himself as a radical he risks scaring off the moderates whose votes he so desperately needs.* **3** ADJ You use **moderate** to describe something that is neither large nor small in amount or degree. ❏ *While a moderate amount of stress can be beneficial, too much stress can exhaust you.* • **mod|er|ate|ly** ADV ❏ *Both are moderately large insects, with a wingspan of around four centimeters.* **4** ADJ A **moderate** change in something is a change that is not great. ❏ *Most drugs offer either no real improvement or, at best, only moderate improvements.* • **mod|er|ate|ly** ADV [ADV after v] ❏ *Share prices on the Tokyo Exchange declined moderately.* **5** V-T/V-I If you **moderate** something or if it **moderates**, it becomes less extreme or violent and easier to deal with or accept. ❏ *They are hoping that once in office he can be persuaded to moderate his views.* • **mod|era|tion** /mɒdəreɪʃən/ N-UNCOUNT ❏ *A moderation in food prices helped to offset the first increase in energy prices.*

SYNONYMS

moderate
ADJ
1
mild: *Teddy turned to Mona with a look of mild confusion.*
limited: *They may only have a limited amount of time to get their points across.*
restrained: *Caroline's greeting seemed a little restrained.*
3
reasonable: *They will need a reasonable amount of desk space and good light.*
average: ...*a woman of average height.*
acceptable: *We've made an acceptable start, but it could've been better.*

mod|era|tion /mɒdəreɪʃən/ **1** N-UNCOUNT If you say that someone's behavior shows **moderation**, you approve of them because they act in a way that you think is reasonable and not extreme. [APPROVAL] ❏ *The United Nations Secretary General called on all parties to show moderation.* • PHRASE If you say that someone does something such as eat, drink, or smoke **in moderation**, you mean that they do not eat, drink, or smoke too much or more than is reasonable. **2** → see also **moderate**

mod|era|tor /mɒdəreɪtər/ (**moderators**) **1** N-COUNT In debates and negotiations, the **moderator** is the person who is in charge of the discussion and makes sure that it is conducted in a fair and organized way. [FORMAL] **2** N-COUNT In some Protestant churches, a **moderator** is a senior member of the clergy who is in charge at large and important meetings. ❏ ...*a former moderator of the General Assembly of the Presbyterian Church.*

mod|ern ♦♦◇ /mɒdərn/ **1** ADJ [ADJ N] **Modern** means relating to the present time, for example the present decade or present century. ❏ *We had a long talk about the problem of materialism in modern society.* **2** ADJ Something that is **modern** is new and involves the latest ideas or equipment. ❏ *In many ways, it was a very modern school for its time.* **3** ADJ People are sometimes described as **modern** when they have opinions or ways of behaving that have not yet been accepted by most people in a society. ❏ *She is very modern in outlook.* **4** ADJ [ADJ N] **Modern** is used to describe styles of art, dance, music, and architecture that have developed in recent times, in contrast to classical styles. ❏ *She'd been a dancer with a modern dance company in New York.* **5** → See feature box at **upcycle**

modern-day ADJ [ADJ N] **Modern-day** is used to refer to the new or modern aspects of a place, an activity, or a society. ❏ ...*modern-day America.* ❏ ...*the by-products of modern-day living.*

mod|ern|ism /mɒdərnɪzəm/ **1** N-UNCOUNT **Modernism** was a movement in the arts in the first half of the twentieth century that rejected traditional values and techniques, and emphasized the importance of individual experience. **2** → see also **postmodernism**

mod|ern|ist /mɒdərnɪst/ **1** ADJ [usu ADJ N] **Modernist** means relating to the ideas and methods of modern art. ❏ ...*modernist architecture.* ❏ ...*modernist art.* **2** → see also **postmodernist**

mod|ern|is|tic /mɒdɜːnɪstɪk/ ADJ A **modernistic** building or piece of furniture looks very modern.

mod|ern|ize /mɒdənaɪz/ (modernizes, modernizing, modernized)

| in BRIT, also use **modernise** |

V-T To **modernize** something such as a system or a factory means to change it by replacing old equipment or methods with new ones. ▫ ...plans to modernize the refinery. • **mod|erni|za|tion** /mɒdənaɪzeɪʃən/ N-UNCOUNT ▫ ...a five-year modernization program.

mod|ern|iz|er /mɒdənaɪzər/ (modernizers)

| in BRIT, also use **moderniser** |

N-COUNT A **modernizer** is someone who replaces old equipment or methods with new ones.

mod|ern lan|guages N-PLURAL **Modern languages** refers to the modern European languages, for example French, German, and Russian, which are studied at school or college. ▫ ...head of modern languages at a local high school.

mod|est ♦◊◊ /mɒdɪst/ **1** ADJ A **modest** house or other building is not large or expensive. ▫ They had spent the night at a modest hotel. **2** ADJ You use **modest** to describe something such as an amount, rate, or improvement which is fairly small. ▫ Unemployment rose to the still modest rate of 0.7%. • **mod|est|ly** ADV ▫ The nation's balance of payments improved modestly last month. **3** ADJ If you say that someone is **modest**, you approve of them because they do not talk much about their abilities or achievements. [APPROVAL] ▫ He's modest, as well as being a great player. • **mod|est|ly** ADV [ADV with v] ▫ "You really must be very good at what you do."—"I suppose I am," Kate said modestly.

---SYNONYMS---

modest
ADJ **1**
simple: He ate a simple dinner of rice and beans.
unpretentious: The establishment is both comfortable and unpretentious.

---

mod|es|ty /mɒdɪsti/ **1** N-UNCOUNT Someone who shows **modesty** does not talk much about their abilities or achievements. [APPROVAL] ▫ His modesty does him credit, for the food he produces speaks for itself. **2** N-UNCOUNT You can refer to the **modesty** of something such as a place or amount when it is fairly small. ▫ The modesty of the town itself comes as something of a surprise. **3** N-UNCOUNT If someone, especially a woman, shows **modesty**, they are cautious about the way they dress and behave because they are aware that other people may view them in a sexual way. ▫ There were shrieks of embarrassment, mingled with giggles, from some of the girls as they struggled to protect their modesty.

modi|cum /mɒdɪkəm/ QUANT [QUANT of n-uncount] A **modicum** of something, especially something that is good or desirable, is a reasonable but not large amount of it. [FORMAL] ▫ I'd like to think I've had a modicum of success. ▫ ...a modicum of privacy.

modi|fi|er /mɒdɪfaɪər/ (modifiers) N-COUNT A **modifier** is a word or group of words that describes, classifies, or restricts the meaning of another word or group. In some descriptions of grammar, only words that are used before a noun are called **modifiers**.

modi|fy /mɒdɪfaɪ/ (modifies, modifying, modified) V-T If you **modify** something, you change it slightly, usually in order to improve it. ▫ The club members did agree to modify their recruitment policy. • **modi|fi|ca|tion** /mɒdɪfɪkeɪʃən/ (modifications) N-VAR ▫ Relatively minor modifications were required.

mod|ish /moʊdɪʃ/ ADJ Something that is **modish** is fashionable. [LITERARY] ▫ ...a short checklist of much that is modish at the moment. ▫ ...modish young women from New York society.

modu|lar /mɒdʒələr/ **1** ADJ **Modular** means relating to a part of a machine, especially a computer, which performs a particular function. ▫ Its modular architecture allows modules to be swapped out and in depending on the processor and operating system. **2** ADJ In building, **modular** means relating to the construction of buildings in parts called modules. ▫ They ended up buying a modular home on a two-acre lot.

modu|late /mɒdʒəleɪt/ (modulates, modulating, modulated) **1** V-T If you **modulate** your voice or a sound, you change or vary its loudness, pitch, or tone in order to create a particular effect. [WRITTEN] ▫ He carefully modulated his voice. **2** V-T To **modulate** an activity or process means to alter it so that it is more suitable for a particular situation. [FORMAL] ▫ These chemicals modulate the effect of potassium. • **modu|la|tion** /mɒdʒəleɪʃən/ (modulations) N-VAR ▫ The famine turned the normal modulation of climate into disaster.

mod|ule /mɒdʒuːl/ (modules) **1** N-COUNT A **module** is a part of a machine, especially a computer, which performs a particular function. **2** N-COUNT A **module** is a part of a spacecraft which can operate by itself, often away from the rest of the spacecraft. ▫ A rescue plan could be achieved by sending an unmanned module to the space station.

mo|dus op|eran|di /moʊdəs ɒpərændi, -daɪ/ N-SING A **modus operandi** is a particular way of doing something. [FORMAL] ▫ An example of her modus operandi was provided during a terse exchange with the defendant.

mo|dus vi|ven|di /moʊdəs vɪvɛndi, -daɪ/ N-SING A **modus vivendi** is an arrangement which allows people who have different attitudes to live or work together. [FORMAL] ▫ After 1940, a modus vivendi between church and state was achieved.

mo|gul /moʊɡəl/ (moguls) **1** N-COUNT A **Mogul** was a Muslim ruler in India in the sixteenth to eighteenth centuries. **2** N-COUNT [usu supp N] A **mogul** is an important, rich, and powerful businessman, especially one in the news, movie, or television industry. ▫ ...an international media mogul. ▫ ...Hollywood movie moguls.

mo|hair /moʊhɛər/ N-UNCOUNT [oft N n] **Mohair** is a type of very soft wool. ▫ ...a brown mohair dress.

moist /mɔɪst/ (moister, moistest) ADJ Something that is **moist** is slightly wet. ▫ The soil is reasonably moist after the September rain.

mois|ten /mɔɪsən/ (moistens, moistening, moistened) V-T To **moisten** something means to make it slightly wet. ▫ She took a sip of water to moisten her dry throat.

mois|ture /mɔɪstʃər/ **1** N-UNCOUNT **Moisture** is tiny drops of water in the air, on a surface, or in the ground. ▫ When the soil is dry, more moisture is lost from the plant. **2** → See feature box at **weather**

mois|tur|ize /mɔɪstʃəraɪz/ (moisturizes, moisturizing, moisturized)

| in BRIT, also use **moisturise** |

V-T If you **moisturize** your skin, you rub cream into it to make it softer. If a cream **moisturizes** your skin, it makes it softer. ▫ ...products to moisturize, protect, and firm your skin.

moist|ur|iz|er /mɔɪstʃəraɪzər/ (moisturizers)

| in BRIT, also use **moisturiser** |

N-MASS A **moisturizer** is a cream that you put on your skin to make it feel softer and smoother.

mo|ji|to /məhiːtoʊ/ (mojitos) N-COUNT A **mojito** is a drink consisting of rum, sugar, lime, mint, and soda water. ▫ Marina remained faithful to the local taste by ordering a mojito.

mo|jo /moʊdʒoʊ/ N-SING People use **mojo** to mean magic, or a magic spell or magic charm. [MAINLY AM, INFORMAL] ▫ I don't know what mojo is working with this team, but it's not a good one right now. ▫ ...the best sign that Congress got its mojo working.

mo|lar /moʊlər/ (molars) **1** N-COUNT Your **molars** are the large, flat teeth toward the back of your mouth that you use for chewing food. **2** → See also color supplement

mo|las|ses /məlæsɪz/ N-UNCOUNT **Molasses** is a thick, dark brown syrup which is produced when sugar is processed. It is used in cooking.

mold /moʊld/ (molds, molding, molded)

| in BRIT, use **mould** |

1 N-COUNT A **mold** is a hollow container that you pour liquid into. When the liquid becomes solid, it takes the same shape as the mold. ▫ He makes plastic reusable molds. **2** N-COUNT If a person fits into or is cast in a **mold** of a particular kind, they have the characteristics, attitudes, behavior, or lifestyle that are typical of that type of person. ▫ He could never be accused of

molder

fitting the mold. • PHRASE If you say that someone **breaks the mold**, you mean that they do completely different things from what has been done before or from what is usually done. ◻ **3** V-T If you **mold** a soft substance such as plastic or clay, you make it into a particular shape or into an object. ◻ *He would dampen the clay and begin to mold it into an entirely different shape.* **4** V-T To **mold** someone or something means to change or influence them over a period of time so that they develop in a particular way. ◻ *It was a very safe, long childhood with Diane, and she really molded my ideas a lot.* **5** V-T/V-I When something **molds** to an object or when you **mold** it there, it fits around the object tightly so that the shape of the object can still be seen. ◻ *It looked as though the plastic wrap was molded to the fruit.* **6** N-MASS **Mold** is a soft gray, green, or blue substance that sometimes forms in spots on old food or on damp walls or clothes. ◻ *She discovered black and green mold growing in her hall closet.*

mold|er /moʊldər/ (**molders, moldering, moldered**)

in BRIT, use **moulder**

V-I [usu cont] If something **is moldering**, it is decaying slowly where it has been left. ◻ *These toys are moldering in warehouses all over the country.* ◻ *It is clear that such ideas will be left to molder.*

mold|ing /moʊldɪŋ/ (**moldings**)

in BRIT, use **moulding**

N-COUNT A **molding** is a strip of plaster or wood along the top of a wall or around a door, which has been made into an ornamental shape or decorated with a pattern.

moldy /moʊldi/ (**moldier, moldiest**)

in BRIT, use **mouldy**

ADJ Something that is **moldy** is covered with mold. ◻ *...moldy bread.* ◻ *Oranges can be kept for a long time without getting moldy.*

mole /moʊl/ (**moles**) **1** N-COUNT A **mole** is a natural dark spot or small dark lump on someone's skin. ◻ *Researchers studied moles on those aged between 12 and 50.* **2** N-COUNT A **mole** is a small animal with black fur that lives underground. **3** N-COUNT A **mole** is a member of a government or other organization who gives secret information to the press or to a rival organization. ◻ *He had been recruited by the Russians as a mole and trained in Moscow.*

mo|lecu|lar /məlɛkyələr/ ADJ [ADJ n] **Molecular** means relating to or involving molecules. ◻ *...the molecular structure of fuel.*

mo|lecu|lar bi|ol|ogy N-UNCOUNT **Molecular biology** is the study of the structure and function of the complex chemicals that are found in living things. • **mo|lecu|lar bi|olo|gist** (**molecular biologists**) N-COUNT ◻ *This substance has now been cloned by molecular biologists.*

mol|ecule /mɒlɪkyuːl/ (**molecules**) **1** N-COUNT A **molecule** is the smallest amount of a chemical substance which can exist by itself. ◻ *...the hydrogen bonds between water molecules.* **2** → See feature box at **genetics**

mole|hill /moʊlhɪl/ (**molehills**) **1** N-COUNT A **molehill** is a small pile of earth made by a mole digging a tunnel. **2** PHRASE If you say that someone is **making a mountain out of a molehill**, you are critical of them for making an unimportant fact or difficulty seem like a serious one. [DISAPPROVAL] ◻ *The press, making a mountain out of a molehill, precipitated an unnecessary economic crisis.*

mo|lest /məlɛst/ (**molests, molesting, molested**) V-T A person who **molests** someone, especially a child, commits a sexual assault against them. ◻ *It is alleged the girl was molested in her bedroom.*

mol|li|fy /mɒlɪfaɪ/ (**mollifies, mollifying, mollified**) V-T If you **mollify** someone, you do or say something to make them less upset or angry. [FORMAL] ◻ *The investigation was undertaken primarily to mollify pressure groups.*

mol|lusk /mɒləsk/ (**mollusks**)

in BRIT, use **mollusc**

N-COUNT A **mollusk** is an animal such as a snail, clam, or octopus which has a soft body. Many types of mollusk have hard shells to protect them.

moment of truth

molly|coddle /mɒlikɒdəl/ (**mollycoddles, mollycoddling, mollycoddled**) V-T If you accuse someone of **mollycoddling** someone else, you are critical of them for doing too many things for the other person and protecting them too much from unpleasant experiences. [DISAPPROVAL] ◻ *Christopher accused me of mollycoddling Andrew.*

Molotov cock|tail /mɒlətɒf kɒkteɪl/ (**Molotov cocktails**) N-COUNT A **Molotov cocktail** is a simple bomb made by putting gasoline and cloth into a bottle. It is exploded by setting fire to the cloth.

molt /moʊlt/ (**molts, molting, molted**)

in BRIT, use **moult**

V-I When an animal or bird **molts**, it gradually loses its coat or feathers so that a new coat or feathers can grow. ◻ *Like most aquatic insects, mayflies molt as they grow.*

mol|ten /moʊltən/ ADJ **Molten** rock, metal, or glass has been heated to a very high temperature and has become a hot, thick liquid. ◻ *The molten metal is poured into the mold.*

mom ♦◇◇ /mɒm/ (**moms**) N-FAMILY Your **mom** is your mother. [AM, INFORMAL] ◻ *We waited for Mom and Dad to get home.*

in BRIT, use **mum**

mo|ment ♦♦♦ /moʊmənt/ (**moments**) **1** N-COUNT You can refer to a very short period of time, for example a few seconds, as a **moment** or **moments**. ◻ *In a moment he was gone.* ◻ *In moments, I was asleep once more.* **2** N-COUNT A particular **moment** is the point in time at which something happens. ◻ *At this moment a car stopped at the house.* **3** PHRASE If you say that something will or may happen **at any moment** or **any moment now**, you are emphasizing that it is likely to happen very soon. [EMPHASIS] ◻ *He'll be here to see you any moment now.* **4** PHRASE You use expressions such as **at the moment**, **at this moment**, and **at the present moment** to indicate that a particular situation exists at the time when you are speaking. ◻ *At the moment, no one is talking to me.* ◻ *He's touring South America at this moment in time.* **5** PHRASE You use **for the moment** to indicate that something is true now, even if it will not be true in the future. ◻ *For the moment, a potential crisis appears to have been averted.* **6** PHRASE If you say that someone or something has their **moments**, you are indicating that there are times when they are successful or interesting, but that this does not happen very often. ◻ *The film has its moments.* **7** PHRASE If someone does something at **the last moment**, they do it at the latest time possible. ◻ *They changed their minds at the last moment and refused to go.* **8** PHRASE You use the expression **the next moment**, or expressions such as '**one moment** he was there, **the next** he was gone,' to emphasize that something happens suddenly, especially when it is very different from what was happening before. [EMPHASIS] ◻ *He is unpredictable, weeping one moment, laughing the next.* **9** PHRASE You use **of the moment** to describe someone or something that is or was especially popular at a particular time, especially when you want to suggest that their popularity is unlikely to last long or did not last long. ◻ *He's the man of the moment, isn't he?* **10** PHRASE If you say that something happens **the moment** something else happens, you are emphasizing that it happens immediately after the other thing. [EMPHASIS] ◻ *The moment I closed my eyes, I fell asleep.* **11 spur of the moment** → see **spur**

COLLOCATIONS

moment
NOUN **2**
adjective + **moment**: crucial, key; defining, memorable, pivotal, proud; anxious, rare
verb + **moment**: capture, seize

---

mo|men|tari|ly /moʊməntɛrɪli/ **1** ADV **Momentarily** means for a short time. ◻ *She paused momentarily when she saw them.* **2** ADV **Momentarily** means very soon. [AM] ◻ *"My husband will be here momentarily," Sophia informed them.*

mo|men|tary /moʊməntɛri/ ADJ Something that is **momentary** lasts for a very short period of time, for example for a few seconds or less. ◻ *...a momentary lapse of concentration.*

mo|ment of truth (**moments of truth**) N-COUNT If you refer to a time or event as the **moment of truth**, you mean that it is an important time when you must make a decision quickly, and whatever you decide will have important consequences in the future. □ *Both men knew the moment of truth had arrived.*

mo|men|tous /moʊmɛntəs/ ADJ If you refer to a decision, event, or change as **momentous**, you mean that it is very important, often because of the effects that it will have in the future. □ *...the momentous decision to send in the troops.*

mo|men|tum /moʊmɛntəm/ ◪ N-UNCOUNT If a process or movement gains **momentum**, it keeps developing or happening more quickly and keeps becoming less likely to stop. □ *This campaign is really gaining momentum.* ◪ N-UNCOUNT In physics, **momentum** is the mass of a moving object multiplied by its speed in a particular direction. [TECHNICAL]

mom|ma /mɒmə/ (**mommas**) N-FAMILY **Momma** means the same as **mommy**. [AM, INFORMAL]

mom|my /mɒmi/ (**mommies**) N-FAMILY Some people, especially young children, call their mother **mommy**. [AM, INFORMAL] □ *Be very good and very quiet and help your mommy.*

in BRIT, use **mummy**

Mon. **Mon.** is a written abbreviation for **Monday**. □ *...Mon., Oct. 19.*

mon|arch /mɒnərk, -ɑrk/ (**monarchs**) N-COUNT The **monarch** of a country is the king, queen, emperor, or empress.

mo|nar|chi|cal /mənɑrkɪkəl/ ADJ [usu ADJ n] **Monarchical** means relating to a monarch or monarchs. □ *...a monarchical system of government.*

mon|ar|chist /mɒnərkɪst/ (**monarchists**) ADJ If someone has **monarchist** views, they believe that their country should have a monarch, such as a king or queen. □ *A monarchist party is running in the forthcoming elections.* • N-COUNT A **monarchist** is someone with monarchist views. □ *The queen's responses to Mr. Chretien will be studied by republicans and monarchists alike here.*

mon|ar|chy /mɒnərki/ (**monarchies**) ◪ N-VAR A **monarchy** is a system in which a country has a monarch. □ *...a serious debate on the future of the monarchy.* ◪ N-COUNT A **monarchy** is a country that has a monarch. □ *Britain is a constitutional monarchy.* ◪ N-COUNT The **monarchy** is used to refer to the monarch and his or her family. □ *The monarchy has to create a balance between its public and private lives.* ◪ → See feature box at **history**

mon|as|tery /mɒnəstəri/ (**monasteries**) N-COUNT A **monastery** is a building or collection of buildings in which monks live.

mo|nas|tic /mənæstɪk/ ADJ [usu ADJ n] **Monastic** means relating to monks or to a monastery. □ *He was drawn to the monastic life.*

Mon|day ✦✦✦ /mʌndeɪ, -di/ (**Mondays**) N-VAR **Monday** is the day after Sunday and before Tuesday. □ *I went back to work on Monday.* □ *The first meeting of the group took place last Monday.*

mon|etar|ism /mɒnɪtərɪzəm/ N-UNCOUNT **Monetarism** is an economic policy that involves controlling the amount of money that is available and in use in a country at any one time. [BUSINESS]

mon|etar|ist /mɒnɪtərɪst/ (**monetarists**) ADJ **Monetarist** policies or views are based on the theory that the amount of money that is available and in use in a country at any one time should be controlled. [BUSINESS] □ *...tough monetarist policies.* • N-COUNT A **monetarist** is someone with monetarist views. □ *Such a policy, monetarists claim, encourages steady growth and price stability.*

mon|etary ✦◇◇ /mɒnɪtəri/ ADJ [ADJ n] **Monetary** means relating to money, especially the total amount of money in a country. [BUSINESS] □ *Some countries tighten monetary policy to avoid inflation.*

mon|e|tize /mɒnɪtaɪz/ (**monetizes, monetizing, monetized**)

in BRIT, also use **monetise**

V-T If you **monetize** an activity or something you own, you find a way to make money from it. □ *The websites have been getting a large number of hits and the company is hoping to monetize that traffic.* • **mon|e|ti|za|tion** /mɒnɪtaɪzeɪʃən, [AM] -tɪz-/ N-UNCOUNT □ *She can advise artists on the monetization of their brand.*

mon|ey ✦✦✦ /mʌni/ (**monies** or **moneys**) ◪ N-UNCOUNT **Money** is the coins or bank notes that you use to buy things, or the sum that you have in a bank account. □ *A lot of the money that you pay at the movies goes back to the film distributors.* □ *Players should be allowed to earn money from advertising.* ◪ N-PLURAL **Monies** is used to refer to several separate sums of money that form part of a larger amount that is received or spent. [FORMAL] □ *We drew up a schedule of payments for the rest of the monies owed.* ◪ → see also **pocket money** ◪ PHRASE If you say that someone **has money to burn**, you mean that they have more money than they need, or that they spend their money on things that you think are unnecessary. □ *He was a high-earning broker with money to burn.* ◪ PHRASE If you are **in the money**, you have a lot of money to spend. [INFORMAL] □ *If you are one of the lucky callers chosen to play, you could be in the money.* ◪ PHRASE If you **make money**, you obtain money by earning it or by making a profit. □ *...the only part of the firm that consistently made money.* ◪ PHRASE If you say that you want someone to **put** their **money where** their **mouth is**, you want them to spend money to improve a bad situation, instead of just talking about improving it. □ *The government might be obliged to put its money where its mouth is to prove its commitment.* ◪ PHRASE If you say that the **smart money** is on a particular person or thing, you mean that people who know a lot about it think that this person will be successful, or this thing will happen. [JOURNALISM] □ *With Japan not playing, the smart money was on the Canadians.* ◪ PHRASE If you say that **money talks**, you mean that if someone has a lot of money, they also have a lot of power. □ *The formula in Hollywood is simple – money talks.* ◪ PHRASE If you say that someone is **throwing money at** a problem, you are critical of them for trying to improve it by spending money on it, instead of doing more thoughtful and practical things to improve it. [DISAPPROVAL] □ *The governor's answer to the problem has been to throw money at it.* ◪ PHRASE If you get your **money's worth**, you get something which is worth the money that it costs or the effort you have put in. □ *The fans get their money's worth.* ◪ **to give someone a run for their money** → see **run** ③

mon|eyed /mʌnid/ also **monied** ADJ A **moneyed** person has a lot of money. [FORMAL] □ *Fear of crime among Japan's new moneyed classes is rising rapidly.*

mon|ey laun|der|ing N-UNCOUNT **Money laundering** is the crime of processing stolen money through a legitimate business or sending it abroad to a foreign bank, to hide the fact that the money was illegally obtained. □ *Investigators are looking at what they believe may be the largest money-laundering scandal in history.*

money|lender /mʌnilɛndər/ (**moneylenders**) N-COUNT A **moneylender** is a person who lends money which has to be paid back at a high rate of interest.

money|maker /mʌnimeɪkər/ (**moneymakers**) N-COUNT If you say that a business, product, or investment is a **moneymaker**, you mean that it makes a big profit. [BUSINESS] □ *The drug is a big moneymaker for them.*

mon|ey mar|ket (**money markets**) N-COUNT A country's **money market** consists of all the banks and other organizations that deal with short-term loans, capital, and foreign exchange. [BUSINESS] □ *On the money markets the dollar was weaker against European currencies.*

mon|ey or|der (**money orders**) N-COUNT A **money order** is a piece of paper representing a sum of money which you can buy at a post office or a bank and send to someone as a way of sending them money by mail. [AM] □ *I sent them a money order for $40.*

in BRIT, use **postal order**

mon|ey pit (**money pits**) N-COUNT You can refer to a place or project as a **money pit** if you keep having to spend large amounts of money on it. □ *Make sure the property you buy isn't going to turn into a money pit.*

mon|ey sup|ply N-UNCOUNT The **money supply** is the total amount of money in a country's economy at any one time. [BUSINESS] □ *They believed that controlling the money supply would reduce inflation.*

Mon|gol /mɒŋgəl/ (**Mongols**) ◪ N-COUNT The **Mongols** were an Asian people who, led by Genghis Khan and Kublai Khan, took control of large areas of China and Central Asia in the

12th and 13th centuries A.D. **2** ADJ [ADJ n] **Mongol** means belonging or relating to the Mongols. ◻ ...*the Mongol invasions of the 13th century.*

Mon|go|lian /mɒŋgoʊliən/ (**Mongolians**) **1** ADJ **Mongolian** means belonging or relating to Mongolia, or to its people, language, or culture. **2** N-COUNT A **Mongolian** is a Mongolian citizen, or a person of Mongolian origin. **3** N-UNCOUNT **Mongolian** is the language that is spoken in Mongolia.

mon|grel /mʌŋgrəl, mɒŋ-/ (**mongrels**) N-COUNT A **mongrel** is a dog that is a mixture of different breeds.

mon|ied /mʌnid/ → see moneyed

moni|ker /mɒnɪkər/ (**monikers**) N-COUNT The **moniker** of a person or thing is their name, especially when they have changed it. [INFORMAL] ◻ *She's the author of three detective novels under the moniker of Janet Neel.*

moni|tor ◆◇◇ /mɒnɪtər/ (**monitors, monitoring, monitored**) **1** V-T If you **monitor** something, you regularly check its development or progress, and sometimes comment on it. ◻ *Officials had not been allowed to monitor the voting.* **2** V-T If someone **monitors** radio broadcasts from other countries, they record them or listen carefully to them in order to obtain information. ◻ *Peter Murray is in Washington and has been monitoring reports out of Monrovia.* **3** N-COUNT A **monitor** is a machine that is used to check or record things, for example processes or substances inside a person's body. ◻ *The heart monitor shows low levels of consciousness.* **4** N-COUNT A **monitor** is a screen which is used to display certain kinds of information, for example on a computer, in airports, or in television studios. ◻ *He was watching a game of tennis on a television monitor.* **5** N-COUNT You can refer to a person who checks that something is done correctly, or that it is fair, as a **monitor**. ◻ *Government monitors will continue to accompany reporters.* **6** → See feature box at **urban**

SYNONYMS

monitor
ADJ **1**
measure: *I continued to measure his progress against the charts in the doctor's office.*
follow: *She was following Laura's progress closely.*
keep track of: *They had become so numerous I hadn't been able to keep track of them.*
supervise: *He supervised and trained more than 400 volunteers.*

---

monk /mʌŋk/ (**monks**) N-COUNT A **monk** is a member of a male religious community that is usually separated from the outside world. ◻ ...*saffron-robed Buddhist monks.*

mon|key /mʌŋki/ (**monkeys**) **1** N-COUNT A **monkey** is an animal with a long tail which lives in hot countries and climbs trees. **2** N-COUNT If you refer to a child as a **monkey**, you are saying in an affectionate way that he or she is very lively and naughty. [FEELINGS] ◻ *She's such a little monkey.*

mon|key bars N-PLURAL **Monkey bars** are metal or wooden bars that are joined together to form a structure for children to climb and play on. [AM]

in BRIT, use **climbing frame**

mon|key wrench (**monkey wrenches**) **1** N-COUNT A **wrench** is an adjustable metal tool used for tightening or loosening metal nuts of different sizes. **2** → See also color supplement

mono /mɒnoʊ/ ADJ **Mono** is used to describe a system of playing music in which all the sound is directed through one speaker only. Compare **stereo**. ◻ *This model has a mono soundtrack.*

PREFIX

mono-
forms nouns and adjectives that have 'one' or 'single' as part of their meaning. *For example, a monochromatic picture uses only one color.*

---

mono|chrome /mɒnəkroʊm/ **1** ADJ [usu ADJ n] A **monochrome** film, photograph, or television shows black, white, and shades of gray, but no other colors. ◻ ...*color and monochrome monitors.* **2** ADJ [usu ADJ n] A **monochrome** picture uses only one color in various shades. ◻ ...*an old monochrome etching of a brewery.*

mono|cle /mɒnəkəl/ (**monocles**) N-COUNT A **monocle** is a glass lens which people wore in former times in front of one of their eyes to improve their ability to see with that eye.

mo|noga|mous /mənɒgəməs/ **1** ADJ Someone who is **monogamous** or who has a **monogamous** relationship has a sexual relationship with only one partner. ◻ *Do you believe that men are not naturally monogamous?* **2** ADJ **Monogamous** animals have only one sexual partner during their lives or during each mating season. ◻ *Only about five percent of mammals are monogamous.*

mo|noga|my /mənɒgəmi/ **1** N-UNCOUNT **Monogamy** is the practice of having a sexual relationship with only one partner. ◻ *People still opt for monogamy and marriage.* **2** N-UNCOUNT **Monogamy** is the state or custom of being married to only one person at a particular time. ◻ *In many non-Western societies, however, monogamy has never dominated.*

mono|gram /mɒnəgræm/ (**monograms**) N-COUNT A **monogram** is a design based on the first letters of a person's names, which is put on things they own, such as their clothes.

mono|grammed /mɒnəgræmd/ ADJ **Monogrammed** means marked with a design based on the first letters of a person's names. ◻ ...*a monogrammed handkerchief.*

mono|graph /mɒnəgræf/ (**monographs**) N-COUNT [oft N on n] A **monograph** is a book which is a detailed study of only one subject. [FORMAL] ◻ ...*a monograph on her favorite author, John Updike.*

mono|lin|gual /mɒnəlɪŋgwəl/ ADJ [usu ADJ n] **Monolingual** means involving, using, or speaking one language. ◻ ...*a largely monolingual country such as Great Britain.*

mono|lith /mɒnəlɪθ/ (**monoliths**) **1** N-COUNT A **monolith** is a very large, upright piece of stone, especially one that was put in place in ancient times. **2** N-COUNT If you refer to an organization or system as a **monolith**, you are critical of it because it is very large and very slow to change, and it does not seem to have different parts with different characters. [DISAPPROVAL] ◻ *A deal between the two powerful institutions would have created a banking monolith.*

mono|lith|ic /mɒnəlɪθɪk/ **1** ADJ If you refer to an organization or system as **monolithic**, you are critical of it because it is very large and very slow to change, and does not seem to have different parts with different characters. [DISAPPROVAL] ◻ ...*an authoritarian and monolithic system.* **2** ADJ If you describe something such as a building as **monolithic**, you do not like it because it is very large and plain with no character. [DISAPPROVAL] ◻ ...*a huge monolithic concrete building.*

mono|logue /mɒnəlɔg/ (**monologues**) also **monolog** **1** N-COUNT If you refer to a long speech by one person during a conversation as a **monologue**, you mean it prevents other people from talking or expressing their opinions. ◻ *Morris ignored the question and continued his monologue.* **2** N-VAR A **monologue** is a long speech which is spoken by one person as an entertainment, or as part of an entertainment such as a play. ◻ ...*a monologue based on the writing of Quentin Crisp.*

mono|nu|cleo|sis /mɒnoʊnuːkliˈoʊsɪs/ N-UNCOUNT **Mononucleosis** is a disease which causes swollen glands, fever, and a sore throat. [mainly AM]

in BRIT, usually use **glandular fever**

mo|nopo|lis|tic /mənɒpəlɪstɪk/ ADJ [usu ADJ n] If you refer to a business or its practices as **monopolistic**, you mean that it tries to control as much of an industry as it can and does not allow fair competition.

mo|nopo|lize /mənɒpəlaɪz/ (**monopolizes, monopolizing, monopolized**)

in BRIT, also use **monopolise**

1 V-T If you say that someone **monopolizes** something, you mean that they have a very large share of it and prevent other people from having a share. ◻ *They are controlling so much cocoa that they are virtually monopolizing the market.* ● **mo|nopo|li|za|tion** /mənɒpəlaɪzeɪʃən/ N-UNCOUNT ◻ ...*the monopolization of a market by a single supplier.* **2** V-T If something or someone **monopolizes** you, they demand a lot of your time and attention, so that there is very little time left for anything or anyone else. ◻ *He would monopolize her totally, to the exclusion of her brothers and sisters.*

mo|nopo|ly /mənɒpəli/ (monopolies) **1** N-VAR If a company, person, or state has a **monopoly** on something such as an industry, they have complete control over it, so that it is impossible for others to become involved in it. [BUSINESS] ❑ ...*a state monopoly on the import and milling of wheat.* **2** N-COUNT A **monopoly** is a company which is the only one providing a particular product or service. [BUSINESS] ❑ ...*a state-owned monopoly.* **3** N-SING If you say that someone does not have a **monopoly** on something, you mean that they are not the only person who has that thing. ❑ *Women do not have a monopoly on feelings of betrayal.*

mono|rail /mɒnoʊreɪl/ (monorails) N-COUNT [also by N] A **monorail** is a system of transportation in which small trains travel along a single rail that is usually high above the ground.

mono|so|dium glu|ta|mate /mɒnəsoʊdiəm glutəmeɪt/ N-UNCOUNT **Monosodium glutamate** is a substance which is sometimes added to food to make it taste better. The abbreviation **MSG** is also used.

mono|syl|lab|ic /mɒnoʊsɪlæbɪk/ ADJ If you refer to someone or the way they speak as **monosyllabic**, you mean that they say very little, usually because they do not want to have a conversation. ❑ *He could be gruff and monosyllabic.*

mono|syl|la|ble /mɒnəsɪləbəl/ (monosyllables) N-COUNT [usu in N in pl] If you say that someone speaks in **monosyllables**, you mean that they speak very little or they only use words consisting of one syllable, such as 'yes,' 'no,' or 'I don't know,' usually because they do not want to have a conversation. ❑ *A taciturn man, he replied to my questions in monosyllables.*

mono|theism /mɒnəθiɪzəm/ N-UNCOUNT **Monotheism** is the belief that there is only one God. ❑ *He recommended monotheism but believed in reincarnation.*

mono|theis|tic /mɒnəθiɪstɪk/ ADJ **Monotheistic** religions believe that there is only one God. ❑ ...*all the major monotheistic religions.*

mono|tone /mɒnətoʊn/ (monotones) **1** N-COUNT [usu sing, also in N] If someone speaks in a **monotone**, their voice does not vary at all in tone or loudness and so it is not interesting to listen to. ❑ *The evidence was read out to the court in a dull monotone.* **2** ADJ [usu adj n] A **monotone** sound or surface does not have any variation in its tone or color. ❑ *He was seen on TV delivering platitudes about the crisis in a monotone voice.*

mo|noto|nous /mənɒt^ənəs/ ADJ Something that is **monotonous** is very boring because it has a regular, repeated pattern which never changes. ❑ *It's monotonous work, like most factory jobs.*

mo|noto|ny /mənɒt^əni/ N-UNCOUNT [oft N *of* n] The **monotony** of something is the fact that it never changes and is boring. ❑ *A night on the town may help to break the monotony of the week.*

mon|ox|ide /mənɒksaɪd/ → see **carbon monoxide**

Mon|sig|nor /mɒnsiːnyər/ (Monsignors) N-TITLE; N-COUNT [usu sing] **Monsignor** is the title of a priest of high rank in the Catholic Church. ❑ *Monsignor Jaime Goncalves was also there.*

mon|soon /mɒnsuːn/ (monsoons) **1** N-COUNT The **monsoon** is the season in Southern Asia when there is a lot of very heavy rain. ❑ ...*the end of the monsoon.* **2** N-PLURAL **Monsoon** rains are sometimes referred to as the **monsoons**. ❑ *In Bangladesh, the monsoons have started.*

mon|ster /mɒnstər/ (monsters) **1** N-COUNT A **monster** is a large imaginary creature that looks very ugly and frightening. ❑ *Both movies are about a monster in the bedroom closet.* **2** N-COUNT A **monster** is something which is extremely large, especially something that is difficult to manage or which is unpleasant. ❑ ...*the monster which is now the Boston marathon.* **3** ADJ [ADJ n] **Monster** means extremely and surprisingly large. [INFORMAL, EMPHASIS] ❑ ...*a monster weapon.* **4** N-COUNT If you describe someone as a **monster**, you mean that they are cruel, frightening, or evil. ❑ *She said that her husband was a depraved monster who threatened and humiliated her.*

mon|stros|ity /mɒnstrɒsɪti/ (monstrosities) N-COUNT If you describe something, especially something large, as a **monstrosity**, you mean that it is extremely ugly. [DISAPPROVAL] ❑ *Most of the older buildings have been torn down and replaced by modern monstrosities.*

mon|strous /mɒnstrəs/ **1** ADJ If you describe a situation or event as **monstrous**, you mean that it is extremely shocking or unfair. ❑ *She endured the monstrous behavior for years.* • **mon|strous|ly** ADV [ADV after v] ❑ *Your husband's family has behaved monstrously.* **2** ADJ If you describe an unpleasant thing as **monstrous**, you mean that it is extremely large in size or extent. [EMPHASIS] ❑ *A group of men are erecting a monstrous copper edifice.* • **mon|strous|ly** ADV [ADV adj/-ed] ❑ *It would be monstrously unfair.* **3** ADJ If you describe something as **monstrous**, you mean that it is extremely frightening because it appears unnatural or ugly. ❑ ...*the film's monstrous fantasy figure.*

mon|tage /mɒntɑːʒ/ (montages) N-COUNT A **montage** is a picture, film, or piece of music which consists of several different items that are put together, often in an unusual combination or sequence. ❑ ...*a photo montage of some of Italy's top television stars.*

month ♦♦♦ /mʌnθ/ (months) **1** N-COUNT A **month** is one of the twelve periods of time that a year is divided into, for example January or February. ❑ *The trial is due to begin next month.* ❑ ...*an exhibition which opens this month at the Guggenheim Museum.* **2** N-COUNT A **month** is a period of about four weeks. ❑ *She was here for a month.* ❑ *Over the next several months I met most of her family.*

month|ly ♦◊◊ /mʌnθli/ (monthlies) **1** ADJ [ADJ n] A **monthly** event or publication happens or appears every month. ❑ *Many people are now having trouble making their monthly house payments.* ❑ *Kidscape runs monthly workshops for teachers.* • ADV [ADV after v] **Monthly** is also an adverb. ❑ *In some areas the property price can rise monthly.* **2** N-COUNT You can refer to a publication that is published monthly as a **monthly**. ❑ ...*a satirical monthly.* **3** ADJ [ADJ n] **Monthly** quantities or rates relate to a period of one month. ❑ *Consumers are charged a monthly fee above their basic cable costs.*

monu|ment /mɒnyəmənt/ (monuments) **1** N-COUNT A **monument** is a large structure, usually made of stone, which is built to remind people of an event in history or of a famous person. ❑ ...*a newly restored monument commemorating a 119-year-old tragedy.* **2** N-COUNT A **monument** is something such as a castle or bridge that was built a very long time ago and is regarded as an important part of a country's history. ❑ ...*the ancient monuments of Mexico and Peru.* **3** N-COUNT If you describe something as a **monument** to someone's qualities, you mean that it is a very good example of the results or effects of those qualities. ❑ *By his international achievements he leaves a fitting monument to his beliefs.*

monu|men|tal /mɒnyəmɛnt^əl/ **1** ADJ You can use **monumental** to emphasize the large size or extent of something. [EMPHASIS] ❑ *It had been a monumental blunder to give him the assignment.* **2** ADJ If you describe a book or musical work as **monumental**, you are emphasizing that it is very large and impressive, and is likely to be important for a long time. [EMPHASIS] ❑ ...*his monumental work on Chinese astronomy.* **3** ADJ [ADJ n] A **monumental** building or sculpture is very large and impressive. ❑ *I take no real interest in monumental sculpture.*

moo /muː/ (moos, mooing, mooed) V-I When cattle, especially cows, **moo**, they make the long, low sound that cattle typically make. ❑ ...*a sound like a cow mooing.* • N-COUNT; SOUND **Moo** is also a noun. ❑ *The cow says "moo-moo."*

MOOC /muːk/ (MOOCs) **1** N-COUNT A **MOOC** is a free online course that many people can study. **MOOC** is an abbreviation for 'massive open online course.' ❑ *The university has developed a MOOC in clinical psychology.* **2** → See feature box at **learning**

mooch /muːtʃ/ (mooches, mooching, mooched) V-T/V-I If someone **mooches** food, money, or help off of you, or if they **mooch** off of you, they ask you for food, money, or help, and succeed in getting it. [AM, INFORMAL] ❑ *I didn't want Ron coming over trying to mooch off of me like he always does.*

in BRIT, use **cadge**

▶ **mooch around**

in BRIT, also use **mooch about**

mood PHRASAL VERB If you **mooch around** a place, you move around there slowly with no particular purpose.

mood ✦✧ /muːd/ (moods) **1** N-COUNT Your **mood** is the way you are feeling at a particular time. If you are in a good mood, you feel cheerful. If you are in a bad mood, you feel angry and impatient. ▪ *He is clearly in a good mood today.* ▪ *Lily was in one of her aggressive moods.* • PHRASE If you say that you are **in the mood** for something, you mean that you want to do it or have it. If you say that you are **in no mood** to do something, you mean that you do not want to do it or have it. ▪ *After a day of air and activity, you should be in the mood for a good meal.* **2** N-COUNT If someone is in a **mood**, the way they are behaving shows that they are feeling angry and impatient. ▪ *She was obviously in a mood.* **3** N-SING The **mood** of a group of people is the way that they think and feel about an idea, event, or question at a particular time. ▪ *The government seemed to be in tune with the popular mood.* **4** N-COUNT The **mood** of a place is the general impression that you get of it. ▪ *First set the mood with music.*

moody /ˈmuːdi/ (moodier, moodiest) **1** ADJ If you describe someone as **moody**, you mean that their feelings and behavior change frequently, and in particular that they often become depressed or angry without any warning. ▪ *David's mother was unstable and moody.* • **moodily** /ˈmuːdɪli/ ADV ▪ *He sat and stared moodily out the window.* • **moodiness** N-UNCOUNT ▪ *His moodiness may have been caused by his poor health.* **2** ADJ If you describe a picture, movie, or piece of music as **moody**, you mean that it suggests particular emotions, especially sad ones. ▪ *...moody black and white photographs.*

moon ✦✧ /muːn/ (moons) **1** N-SING [usu the N, also *full/new* N] The **moon** is the object that you can often see in the sky at night. It goes around the earth once every four weeks, and as it does so its appearance changes from a circle to part of a circle. ▪ *...the first man on the moon.* **2** N-COUNT A **moon** is an object similar to a small planet that travels around a planet. ▪ *...Neptune's large moon.* **3** → See feature box at **emotion**

moon|beam /ˈmuːnbiːm/ (moonbeams) N-COUNT A moonbeam is a ray of light from the moon.

moon|less /ˈmuːnlɪs/ ADJ A moonless sky or night is dark because there is no moon.

moon|light /ˈmuːnlaɪt/ (moonlights, moonlighting, moonlighted) **1** N-UNCOUNT **Moonlight** is the light that comes from the moon at night. ▪ *They walked along the road in the moonlight.* **2** V-I If someone **moonlights**, they have a second job in addition to their main job, often without informing their main employers or the tax office. ▪ *...an engineer who was moonlighting as a taxi driver.*

moon|lit /ˈmuːnlɪt/ ADJ [usu ADJ n] Something that is **moonlit** is lit by moonlight. ▪ *...a beautiful moonlit night.*

moon|shine /ˈmuːnʃaɪn/ **1** N-UNCOUNT **Moonshine** is whiskey that is made illegally. [mainly AM] **2** N-UNCOUNT If you say that someone's thoughts, ideas, or comments are **moonshine**, you think they are foolish and not based on reality. [DISAPPROVAL] ▪ *The story is pure moonshine.*

moor /mʊər/ (moors, mooring, moored) **1** N-VAR A **moor** is an area of open and usually high land with poor soil that is covered mainly with grass and heather. [mainly BRIT] ▪ *Colliford is higher, right up on the moors.* **2** V-T/V-I If you **moor**, or **moor** a boat somewhere, you stop and tie it to the land with a rope or chain so that it cannot move away. ▪ *She had moored her barge on the right bank of the river.* ▪ *I decided to moor near some tourist boats.* **3** N-COUNT The **Moors** were a Muslim people who established a civilization in North Africa and Spain between the 8th and the 15th centuries A.D. **4** → see also **mooring**

moor|ing /ˈmʊərɪŋ/ (moorings) **1** N-COUNT A **mooring** is a place where a boat can be tied so that it cannot move away, or the object it is tied to. ▪ *Free moorings will be available.* **2** N-PLURAL **Moorings** are the ropes, chains, and other objects used to moor a boat. ▪ *He cut the engine and grabbed the mooring lines.*

Moor|ish /ˈmʊərɪʃ/ ADJ [usu ADJ n] Something that is **Moorish** belongs to or is characteristic of the Muslim civilization in North Africa and Spain between the 8th and the 15th centuries A.D. ▪ *...a medieval Moorish palace.*

moor|land /ˈmʊərlænd/ (moorlands) N-UNCOUNT [also N in pl] **Moorland** is land which consists of moors. [mainly BRIT] ▪ *...rugged Yorkshire moorland.*

moose /muːs/ (moose)

Moose is both the singular and the plural form.

N-COUNT A **moose** is a large type of deer. Moose have big flat horns called antlers and are found in Northern Europe, Asia, and North America. Some people use **moose** to refer to the North American variety of this animal, and **elk** to refer to the European and Asian varieties.

moot /muːt/ (moots, mooting, mooted) **1** V-T [usu passive] If a plan, idea, or subject **is mooted**, it is suggested or introduced for discussion. [FORMAL] ▪ *Plans have been mooted for a 450,000-strong army.* **2** ADJ If something is a **moot** point or question, people cannot agree about it. ▪ *How long he'll be able to do so is a moot point.* **3** ADJ If a subject or question is **moot**, it has no practical importance. [AM] ▪ *For Layton, the question was moot right now.*

mop /mɒp/ (mops, mopping, mopped) **1** N-COUNT A **mop** is a piece of equipment for washing floors. It consists of a sponge or many pieces of string attached to a long handle. **2** V-T If you **mop** a surface such as a floor, you clean it with a mop. ▪ *There was a woman mopping the stairs.* **3** V-T If you **mop** sweat from your forehead or **mop** your forehead, you wipe it with a piece of cloth. ▪ *He mopped perspiration from his forehead.* **4** → See feature box at **household**
▶ **mop up** **1** PHRASAL VERB If you **mop up** a liquid, you clean it with a cloth so that the liquid is absorbed. ▪ *A waiter mopped up the mess as best he could.* ▪ *When the washing machine spurts out water at least we can mop it up.* **2** PHRASAL VERB If you **mop up** something that you think is undesirable or dangerous, you remove it or deal with it so that it is no longer a problem. ▪ *The infantry divisions mopped up remaining centers of resistance.*

mope /moʊp/ (mopes, moping, moped) V-I If you **mope**, you feel miserable and do not feel interested in doing anything. ▪ *Get on with life and don't sit back and mope.*

mo|ped /ˈmoʊpɛd/ (mopeds) N-COUNT A **moped** is a small motorcycle which can also pedal like a bicycle.

MOR /ɛm oʊ ɑːr/ N-UNCOUNT [oft n n] **MOR** is a type of pop music which is pleasant and not extreme or unusual. **MOR** is an abbreviation of **middle-of-the-road**. ▪ *...MOR singer Daniel O'Donnell.*

mor|al ✦✧ /ˈmɔːrəl/ (morals) **1** N-PLURAL **Morals** are principles and beliefs concerning right and wrong behavior. ▪ *...Western ideas and morals.* **2** ADJ [ADJ n] **Moral** means relating to beliefs about what is right or wrong. ▪ *She describes her own moral dilemma in making the film.* • **mor|al|ly** ADV ▪ *When, if ever, is it morally justifiable to allow a patient to die?* **3** ADJ [ADJ n] **Moral** courage or duty is based on what you believe is right or acceptable, rather than on what the law says should be done. ▪ *The government had a moral, if not a legal, duty to pay compensation.* **4** ADJ A **moral** person behaves in a way that is believed by most people to be good and right. ▪ *The people who will be on the committee are moral, cultured, competent people.* • **mor|al|ly** ADV [ADV with v] ▪ *Art is not there to improve you morally.* **5** ADJ [ADJ n] If you give someone **moral** support, you encourage them in what they are doing by expressing approval. ▪ *Moral as well as financial support is what the West should provide.* **6** N-COUNT The **moral** of a story or event is what you learn from it about how you should or should not behave. ▪ *I think the moral of the story is let the buyer beware.* **7** moral victory → see victory

═══════ SYNONYMS ═══════

moral
NOUN **1**
principle: *It's not just a matter of principle.*
belief: *He refuses to compete on Sundays because of his religious beliefs.*
morality: *...standards of morality and justice in society.*
integrity: *I have always regarded him as a man of integrity.*
ADJ **3**
ethical: *...the ethical schools in the school.*
just: *She fought honestly for a just cause and for freedom.*
principled: *She was a strong, principled woman.*
good: *The president is a good man.*

mo|rale /mərǽl/ N-UNCOUNT **Morale** is the amount of confidence and cheerfulness that a group of people have. ☐ *Many pilots are suffering from low morale.*

mo|rale boost|er (**morale boosters**) N-COUNT [usu sing] You can refer to something that makes people feel more confident and cheerful as a **morale booster**. ☐ *This win has been a great morale booster.*

morale-boosting ADJ [usu ADJ n] A **morale-boosting** action or event makes people feel more confident and cheerful. ☐ *...the president's morale-boosting visit to the troops.*

mor|al fi|ber

in BRIT, use **moral fibre**

N-UNCOUNT **Moral fiber** is the quality of being determined to do what you think is right. ☐ *Raeder was also at pains to see that each nominee was of strong moral fiber.*

mor|al|ist /mɒrəlɪst/ (**moralists**) N-COUNT A **moralist** is someone who has strong ideas about right and wrong behavior, and who tries to make other people behave according to these ideas.

mor|al|is|tic /mɒrəlɪstɪk/ ADJ If you describe someone or something as **moralistic**, you are critical of them for making harsh judgments of other people on the basis of their own ideas about what is right and wrong. [DISAPPROVAL] ☐ *He has become more moralistic.*

mor|al|ity /mərǽlɪti/ (**moralities**) **1** N-UNCOUNT **Morality** is the belief that some behavior is right and acceptable and that other behavior is wrong. ☐ *...standards of morality and justice in society.* **2** N-COUNT A **morality** is a system of principles and values concerning people's behavior, which is generally accepted by a society or by a particular group of people. ☐ *...a morality that is sexist.* **3** N-UNCOUNT The **morality** of something is how right or acceptable it is. ☐ *...the arguments about the morality of blood sports.*

mor|al|ize /mɒrəlaɪz/ (**moralizes, moralizing, moralized**)

in BRIT, also use **moralise**

V-I If you say that someone **is moralizing**, you are critical of them for telling people what they think is right or wrong, especially when they have not been asked their opinion. [DISAPPROVAL] ☐ *As a dramatist, I hate to moralize.* • **mor|al|iz|ing** N-UNCOUNT ☐ *We have tried to avoid any moralizing.*

mor|al ma|jor|ity N-SING-COLL; N-PROPER-COLL [the N] If there is a large group in society that holds strong, conservative opinions on matters of morality and religion, you can refer to these people as the **moral majority**. In the United States, there is an organized group called **the Moral Majority**. ☐ *...unless the writers begin to write decent comedy and stop pandering to the moral majority.*

mo|rass /mərǽs/ (**morasses**) N-COUNT [usu sing, with supp, oft N of n] If you describe an unpleasant or confused situation as a **morass**, you mean that it seems impossible to escape from or resolve, because it has become so serious or so complicated. ☐ *I tried to drag myself out of the morass of despair.* ☐ *...the economic morass.*

mora|to|rium /mɒrətɔriəm/ (**moratoriums** or **moratoria**) N-COUNT A **moratorium** on a particular activity or process is the stopping of it for a fixed period of time, usually as a result of an official agreement. ☐ *The House voted to impose a one-year moratorium on nuclear testing.*

mor|bid /mɔrbɪd/ ADJ If you describe a person or their interest in something as **morbid**, you mean that they are very interested in unpleasant things, especially death, and you think this is strange. [DISAPPROVAL] ☐ *Some people have a morbid fascination with crime.* • **mor|bid|ly** ADV ☐ *There's something morbidly fascinating about the thought.*

mor|dant /mɔrdᵊnt/ ADJ [usu ADJ n] **Mordant** humor is very critical and often mocks someone or something. [FORMAL] ☐ *A wicked, mordant sense of humor has come to the fore in Blur's world.*

more ✦✦✦ /mɔr/

More is often considered to be the comparative form of **much** and **many**.

1 DET You use **more** to indicate that there is a greater amount of something than before or than average, or than something else. You can use 'a little,' 'a lot,' 'a bit,' 'far,' and 'much' in front of **more**. ☐ *More and more people are surviving heart attacks.* ☐ *He spent more time perfecting his dance moves instead of gym work.* • PRON **More** is also a pronoun. ☐ *As the level of work increased from light to heavy, workers ate more.* • QUANT [QUANT of def-n] **More** is also a quantifier. ☐ *Employees may face increasing pressure to take on more of their own medical costs in retirement.* **2** PHRASE You use **more than** before a number or amount to say that the actual number or amount is even greater. ☐ *The Afghan authorities say the airport had been closed for more than a year.* **3** ADV [ADV adj/adv] You use **more** to indicate that something or someone has a greater amount of a quality than they used to or than is average or usual. ☐ *Weather conditions have become more brutal.* **4** ADV If you say that something is **more** one thing than another, you mean that it is like the first thing rather than the second. ☐ *He's more like a movie star than a lifeguard, really.* ☐ *Sue screamed, not loudly, more in surprise than terror.* **5** ADV [ADV with v] If you do something **more** than before or **more** than someone else, you do it to a greater extent or more often. ☐ *When we are tired, tense, depressed, or unwell, we feel pain much more.* **6** ADV [ADV after v] You can use **more** to indicate that something continues to happen for a further period of time. ☐ *Things might have been different if I'd talked a bit more.* • PHRASE You can use **some more** to indicate that something continues to happen for a further period of time. **7** ADV You use **more** to indicate that something is repeated. For example, if you do something 'once more,' you do it again once. ☐ *This train would stop twice more in the suburbs before rolling southeast toward Baltimore.* **8** DET You use **more** to refer to an additional thing or amount. You can use 'a little,' 'a lot,' 'a bit,' 'far,' and 'much' in front of **more**. ☐ *They needed more time to consider whether to hold an inquiry.* • ADJ [ADJ n] **More** is also an adjective. ☐ *We stayed in Danville two more days.* • PRON **More** is also a pronoun. ☐ *Oxfam has appealed to western nations to do more to help the refugees.* **9** ADV [ADV adv/adj] You use **more** in conversations when you want to draw someone's attention to something interesting or important that you are about to say. ☐ *More seriously for him, there are members who say he is wrong on this issue.* **10** PHRASE You can use **more and more** to indicate that something is becoming greater in amount, extent, or degree all the time. ☐ *Her life was heading more and more where she wanted it to go.* **11** PHRASE If something is **more or less** true, it is true in a general way, but is not completely true. [VAGUENESS] ☐ *The conference is more or less over.* **12** PHRASE If something is **more than** a particular thing, it has greater value or importance than this thing. ☐ *He's more than a coach, he's a friend.* **13** PHRASE You use **more than** to say that something is true to a greater degree than is necessary or than average. ☐ *The company has more than enough cash available to refinance the loan.* **14** PHRASE You can use **what is more** or **what's more** to introduce an extra piece of information which supports or emphasizes the point you are making. [EMPHASIS] ☐ *Many more institutions, especially banks, were allowed to lend money for mortgages, and what was more, banks could lend out more money than they actually held.* **15** → see also **anymore 16 all the more** → see **all** ②

USAGE

more

Don't use **more** with adjectives that have only one syllable. Don't say, for example, 'more tall.' Instead, add *-er* to the end of the adjective. *Krish is taller than me.*

---

more|over ✦◇◇ /mɔroʊvər/ ADV You use **moreover** to introduce a piece of information that adds to or supports the previous statement. [FORMAL] ☐ *She saw that there was indeed a man immediately behind her. Moreover, he was observing her strangely.*

SYNONYMS

moreover
ADV
furthermore: *Furthermore, they claim that any interference is completely ineffective.*
in addition: *In addition, students can take classes computing.*
also: *He is an asthmatic who was also anaemic.*
besides: *Besides, I'd grown fond of our little, rented house.*

mo|res /mɔreɪz/ N-PLURAL [usu with supp] The **mores** of a particular place or group of people are the customs and behavior that are typically found in that place or group. [FORMAL] ❑ ...the accepted mores of society.

morgue /mɔrg/ (morgues) N-COUNT A **morgue** is a building or a room in a hospital where dead bodies are kept before they are buried or cremated, or before they are identified or examined.

mori|bund /mɔrɪbʌnd/ ADJ If you describe something as **moribund**, you mean that it is in a very bad condition. [FORMAL] ❑ ...the moribund economy.

Mor|mon /mɔrmən/ (Mormons) ADJ **Mormon** means relating to the Church of Jesus Christ of Latter-day Saints, a religion started by Joseph Smith in the United States. ❑ ...the Mormon church. • N-COUNT **Mormons** are people who are Mormon.

morn /mɔrn/ N-SING [also no det] **Morn** means the same as morning. [LITERARY] ❑ ...one cold February morn.

morn|ing ✦✦✦ /mɔrnɪŋ/ (mornings) **1** N-VAR The **morning** is the part of each day between the time that people usually wake up and 12 o'clock noon or lunchtime. ❑ During the morning your guide will take you around the city. ❑ On Sunday morning Bill was woken by the telephone. **2** N-SING If you refer to a particular time in the **morning**, you mean a time between 12 o'clock midnight and 12 o'clock noon. ❑ I often stayed up until two or three in the morning. **3** PHRASE If you say that something will happen **in the morning**, you mean that it will happen during the morning of the following day. ❑ I'll fly it to St Louis in the morning. **4** PHRASE If you say that something happens **morning, noon and night**, you mean that it happens all the time. ❑ You get fit by playing the game, day in, day out, morning, noon and night.

morning-after pill (morning-after pills) N-COUNT [usu the N in sing] The **morning-after pill** is a pill that a woman can take some hours after having sex to prevent herself from becoming pregnant.

morn|ing dress N-UNCOUNT **Morning dress** is a suit that is worn by men for very formal occasions such as weddings. It consists of a gray or black coat that is longer at the back than the front, gray pants, a white shirt, a gray tie, and often a top hat. [mainly BRIT]

morn|ing sick|ness N-UNCOUNT If a pregnant woman has **morning sickness**, she feels sick or is sick, often in the morning. **2** → See feature box at **birth**

morn|ing star N-SING [the N] The **morning star** is the planet Venus, which can be seen shining in the sky just after the sun rises.

Mo|roc|can /mərɒkən/ (Moroccans) **1** ADJ **Moroccan** means belonging or relating to Morocco or to its people or culture. **2** N-COUNT A **Moroccan** is a Moroccan citizen, or a person of Moroccan origin.

mor|on /mɔrɒn/ (morons) N-COUNT If you refer to someone as a **moron**, you think that they are very stupid. [OFFENSIVE, DISAPPROVAL] ❑ I used to think that he was a moron.

mo|ron|ic /mərɒnɪk/ ADJ If you say that a person or their behavior is **moronic**, you think that they are very stupid. [OFFENSIVE, DISAPPROVAL] ❑ It was wanton, moronic vandalism.

mo|rose /mərous/ ADJ Someone who is **morose** is miserable, bad-tempered, and not willing to talk very much to other people. ❑ She was morose, pale, and reticent. • **mo|rose|ly** ADV ❑ One elderly man sat morosely at the bar.

morph /mɔrf/ (morphs, morphing, morphed) V-I If one thing **morphs** into another thing, especially something very different, the first thing changes into the second. [INFORMAL] ❑ Mild-mannered Stanley morphs into a confident, grinning hero.

mor|pheme /mɔrfim/ (morphemes) N-COUNT A **morpheme** is the smallest unit of meaning in a language. The words 'the', 'in', and 'girl' consist of one morpheme. The word 'girls' consists of two morphemes: 'girl' and 's.'

mor|phine /mɔrfin/ N-UNCOUNT **Morphine** is a drug used to relieve pain.

morph|ing /mɔrfɪŋ/ N-UNCOUNT **Morphing** is a technique that involves using a computer to make an image on film or television appear to change shape or change into something else.

mor|phol|ogy /mɔrfɒlədʒi/ N-UNCOUNT The **morphology** of something is its form and structure. In linguistics, **morphology** refers to the way words are constructed with stems, prefixes, and suffixes. [TECHNICAL]

mor|row /mɔrou/ **1** N-SING [the N, oft on the N] The **morrow** means the next day or tomorrow. [LITERARY or OLD-FASHIONED] ❑ We do depart for home on the morrow. **2** CONVENTION **Good morrow** means the same as 'good morning.' [LITERARY or OLD-FASHIONED] ❑ Good morrow to you, my lord.

morse code /mɔrs koud/ also **Morse code** N-UNCOUNT **Morse code** or **morse** is a code used for sending messages. It represents each letter of the alphabet using short and long sounds or flashes of light, which can be written down as dots and dashes.

mor|sel /mɔrsəl/ (morsels) N-COUNT A **morsel** is a very small amount of something, especially a very small piece of food. ❑ ...a delicious little morsel of meat.

mor|tal /mɔrtəl/ (mortals) **1** ADJ If you refer to the fact that people are **mortal**, you mean that they have to die and cannot live forever. ❑ A man is deliberately designed to be mortal. He grows, he ages, and he dies. • **mor|tal|ity** /mɔrtælɪti/ N-UNCOUNT ❑ She has suddenly come face to face with her own mortality. **2** N-COUNT You can describe someone as a **mortal** when you want to say that they are an ordinary person. ❑ Tickets seem unobtainable to the ordinary mortal. **3** ADJ [ADJ n] You can use **mortal** to show that something is very serious or may cause death. ❑ The police were defending themselves and others against mortal danger. • **mor|tal|ly** ADV ❑ He falls, mortally wounded. **4** ADJ [ADJ n] You can use **mortal** to emphasize that a feeling is extremely great or severe. [EMPHASIS] ❑ When self-esteem is high, we lose our mortal fear of jealousy. • **mor|tal|ly** ADV [ADV -ed/adj/adv] ❑ Candace admits to having been "mortally embarrassed."

mor|tal|ity /mɔrtælɪti/ N-UNCOUNT The **mortality** in a particular place or situation is the number of people who die. ❑ The nation's infant mortality rate has reached a record low.

mor|tal sin (mortal sins) N-VAR In the Roman Catholic Church, a **mortal sin** is an extremely serious sin. Catholics believe the person who has committed it will be punished after death unless they are forgiven by the Church.

mor|tar /mɔrtər/ (mortars) **1** N-COUNT A **mortar** is a big gun that fires missiles high into the air over a short distance. ❑ The two sides exchanged fire with mortars and small arms. **2** N-UNCOUNT **Mortar** is a mixture of sand, water, and cement or lime which is put between bricks to hold them together. ❑ ...the mortar between the bricks. **3** N-COUNT A **mortar** is a bowl in which you can crush things such as herbs, spices, or grain using a rod called a pestle. ❑ Use a mortar and pestle to crush the shells and claws. **4** → See also color supplement

mor|tar|board (mortarboards) N-COUNT A **mortarboard** is a stiff, black cap which has a flat, square top with a bunch of threads attached to it. In the United States, mortarboards are worn by students at graduation ceremonies at high schools, colleges, and universities.

mort|gage ✦✦ /mɔrgɪdʒ/ (mortgages, mortgaging, mortgaged) **1** N-COUNT A **mortgage** is a loan of money which you get from a bank or savings and loan association in order to buy a house. ❑ ...an increase in mortgage rates. **2** V-T If you **mortgage** your house or land, you use it as a guarantee to a company in order to borrow money from them. ❑ They had to mortgage their home to pay the bills. **3** → See feature box at **banking, finance, house**

mor|tice lock /mɔrtɪs lɒk/ → see **mortise lock**

mor|ti|cian /mɔrtɪʃən/ (morticians) N-COUNT A **mortician** is a person whose job is to deal with the bodies of people who have died and to arrange funerals. [mainly AM]

mor|ti|fi|ca|tion /mɔrtɪfɪkeɪʃən/ N-UNCOUNT [oft poss N] **Mortification** is a strong feeling of shame and embarrassment. ❑ The chairman tried to disguise his mortification.

mor|ti|fied /mɔrtɪfaɪd/ ADJ [usu v-link ADJ] If you say that someone is **mortified**, you mean that they feel extremely offended, ashamed, or embarrassed. ❑ If I reduced somebody to tears I'd be mortified.

mor|ti|fy /mɔrtɪfaɪ/ (mortifies, mortifying, mortified) V-T [no cont] If you say that something **mortifies** you, you mean that

mor|ti|fy|ing /mɔrtɪfaɪɪŋ/ ADJ If you say that something is mortifying, you mean that it makes you feel extremely ashamed or embarrassed. ❑ *She felt it would be utterly mortifying to be seen in such company as his by anyone.*

mor|tise lock /mɔrtɪs lɒk/ (mortise locks) also **mortice lock** N-COUNT A **mortise lock** is a type of lock which fits into a hole cut into the edge of a door rather than being attached to one side of it.

mor|tu|ary /mɔrtʃuɛri/ (mortuaries) N-COUNT A **mortuary** is a building or a room in a hospital where dead bodies are kept before they are buried or cremated, or before they are identified or examined.

mo|sa|ic /moʊzeɪɪk/ (mosaics) N-VAR A **mosaic** is a design which consists of small pieces of colored glass, pottery, or stone set in concrete or plaster. ❑ *...a Roman villa which once housed a fine collection of mosaics.*

mo|sey /moʊzi/ (moseys, moseying, moseyed) V-I If you **mosey** somewhere, you go there slowly, often without any particular purpose. [INFORMAL] ❑ *He usually moseys into town for no special reason.*

mosh /mɒʃ/ (moshes, moshing, moshed) V-I If people at a rock concert **mosh**, they jump up and down together in front of the stage, often pushing each other. ❑ *Moshing down the front, crushed against the stage in a sweat-drenched T-shirt, is all part of the gig experience.*

mosh|pit /mɒʃpɪt/ (moshpits) also **mosh pit** N-COUNT The **moshpit** at a rock concert is the area in front of the stage where people jump up and down.

Mos|lem /mɒzləm, mʊzlɪm/ → see Muslim

mosque /mɒsk/ (mosques) N-COUNT A **mosque** is a building where Muslims go to worship.

mos|qui|to /məskitoʊ/ (mosquitoes or mosquitos) N-COUNT **Mosquitos** are small flying insects which bite people and animals in order to suck their blood.

mos|qui|to net (mosquito nets) N-COUNT A **mosquito net** is a curtain made of very fine cloth which is hung around a bed in order to keep mosquitoes and other insects away from a person while they are sleeping.

moss /mɒs/ (mosses) N-MASS **Moss** is a very small, soft, green plant which grows on damp soil, or on wood or stone. ❑ *...ground covered over with moss.*

mossy /mɒsi/ (mossier, mossiest) ADJ A **mossy** surface is covered with moss. ❑ *...a mossy wall.*

most ♦♦♦ /moʊst/

Most is often considered to be the superlative form of **much** and **many**.

1 QUANT [QUANT of def-n] You use **most** to refer to the majority of a group of things or people or the largest part of something. ❑ *Most of the houses in the capital don't have indoor plumbing.* ❑ *By stopping smoking you are undoing most of the damage smoking has caused.* ❑ *Most people think the queen has done a good job over the last 50 years.* • PRON **Most** is also a pronoun. ❑ *Seventeen civilians were hurt. Most are students who had been attending a twenty-first birthday party.* **2** ADJ [the ADJ n] You use **the most** to mean a larger amount than anyone or anything else, or the largest amount possible. ❑ *The president himself won the most votes.* • PRON **Most** is also a pronoun. ❑ *The most they earn in a day is a hundred dollars.* **3** ADV [ADV with v] You use **most** to indicate that something is true or happens to a greater degree or extent than anything else. ❑ *What she feared most was becoming like her mother.* ❑ *...Professor Morris, the person he most hated.* • PHRASE You use **most of all** to indicate that something is true to a greater extent than anything else. **4** ADV [ADV adj/adv] You use **most** to indicate that someone or something has a greater amount of a particular quality than most other things of its kind. ❑ *Her children had the best, most elaborate birthday parties in the neighborhood.* ❑ *He was one of the most influential performers of modern jazz.* **5** ADV [the ADV after v] If you do something **the most**, you do it to the greatest extent possible or with the greatest frequency. ❑ *What question are you asked the most?* **6** ADV [ADV adv/adj] You use **most** in conversations when you want to draw someone's attention to something very interesting or important that you are about to say. ❑ *Most surprisingly, quite a few said they don't intend to vote at all.* **7** PHRASE You use **at most** or **at the most** to say that a number or amount is the maximum that is possible and that the actual number or amount may be smaller. ❑ *Poach the pears in apple juice or water and sugar for ten minutes at most.* **8** PHRASE If you **make the most of** something, you get the maximum use or advantage from it. ❑ *Happiness is the ability to make the most of what you have.*

SUFFIX

-most

is added to adjectives in order to form other adjectives that describe something as being further in a particular direction than other things of the same kind. For example, 'the **northernmost** suburbs of Chicago' are the suburbs that are furthest north of the city of Chicago.

---

most|ly ♦◊◊ /moʊstli/ ADV [ADV with cl/group] You use **mostly** to indicate that a statement is generally true, for example true about the majority of a group of things or people, true most of the time, or true in most respects. ❑ *I am working with mostly highly motivated people.* ❑ *Cars are mostly metal.*

mo|tel /moʊtɛl/ (motels) N-COUNT A **motel** is a hotel intended for people who are traveling by car.

moth /mɔθ/ (moths) N-COUNT A **moth** is an insect like a butterfly which usually flies around at night.

moth|ball /mɔθbɔl/ (mothballs, mothballing, mothballed) **1** N-COUNT A **mothball** is a small ball made of a special chemical, which you can put among clothes or blankets in order to keep moths away. **2** V-T If someone in authority **mothballs** a plan, factory, or piece of equipment, they decide to stop developing or using it, perhaps temporarily. [JOURNALISM] ❑ *...the decision to mothball the Bataan Nuclear Power Plant, for safety and political reasons.*

moth-eaten 1 ADJ **Moth-eaten** clothes look very old and have holes in them. **2** ADJ If you describe something as **moth-eaten**, you mean that it seems unattractive or useless because it is old or has been used too much. [DISAPPROVAL] ❑ *We drove through a somewhat moth-eaten deer park.* ❑ *This strategy looks increasingly moth-eaten.*

moth|er ♦♦♦ /mʌðər/ (mothers, mothering, mothered) **1** N-FAMILY Your **mother** is the woman who gave birth to you. You can also call someone your **mother** if she brings you up as if she was this woman. ❑ *She sat on the edge of her mother's bed.* ❑ *She's an English teacher and a mother of two children.* **2** V-T If a woman **mothers** a child, she takes care of it and brings it up, usually because she is its mother. ❑ *Colleen had dreamed of mothering a large family.* **3** V-T If you **mother** someone, you treat them with great care and affection, as if they were a small child. ❑ *Stop mothering me.* **4** → See feature box at **birth**

moth|er|board /mʌðərbɔrd/ (motherboards) N-COUNT In a computer, the **motherboard** is the main electronic circuit board to which the microchips that perform important functions are attached.

moth|er coun|try (mother countries) also **Mother Country 1** N-COUNT [oft with poss] Someone's **mother country** is the country in which they or their ancestors were born and to which they still feel emotionally linked, even if they live somewhere else. ❑ *Dr Kengerli looks to Turkey as his mother country.* **2** N-SING [usu the N] If you refer to **the mother country** of a particular state or country, you are referring to the very powerful country that used to control its affairs. ❑ *Australia, New Zealand, and Canada had no colonial conflict with the mother country.*

moth|er fig|ure (mother figures) N-COUNT If you regard someone as a **mother figure**, you think of them as having the role of a mother and being the person you can turn to for help, advice, or support.

moth|er|fuck|er /mʌðərfʌkər/ (motherfuckers) N-COUNT If someone calls a person a **motherfucker**, they are insulting them in a very unpleasant way. [mainly AM, OFFENSIVE, VULGAR, DISAPPROVAL]

moth|er|hood /mʌðərhʊd/ N-UNCOUNT **Motherhood** is the state of being a mother. ❑ *...women who combine work and motherhood.*

mother-in-law (mothers-in-law) N-COUNT Someone's mother-in-law is the mother of their husband or wife.

moth|er|land /mʌðərlænd/ also **Motherland** N-SING [usu the N] The **motherland** is the country in which you or your ancestors were born and to which you still feel emotionally linked, even if you live somewhere else. ❑ ...love for the motherland.

moth|er|less /mʌðərlɪs/ ADJ You describe children as **motherless** if their mother has died or does not live with them. ❑ ...Michael's seven motherless children.

moth|er|ly /mʌðərli/ ADJ **Motherly** feelings or actions are like those of a kind mother. ❑ It was an incredible display of motherly love and forgiveness.

Moth|er Na|ture N-UNCOUNT **Mother Nature** is sometimes used to refer to nature, especially when it is being considered as a force that affects human beings. ❑ ...when Mother Nature created Iceland out of volcanic lava and glaciers.

Moth|er of God N-PROPER In Christianity, **the Mother of God** is another name for the Virgin Mary, the mother of Jesus Christ.

mother-of-pearl also **mother of pearl** N-UNCOUNT **Mother-of-pearl** is the shiny layer on the inside of some shells. It is used to make buttons or to decorate things.

Moth|er's Day N-UNCOUNT **Mother's Day** is a special day on which children give cards and presents to their mothers as a sign of their love for them. In the United States, Mother's Day is the second Sunday in May.

Moth|er Su|peri|or (Mother Superiors) N-COUNT A **Mother Superior** is a nun who is in charge of the other nuns in a convent.

mother-to-be (mothers-to-be) N-COUNT A **mother-to-be** is a woman who is pregnant, especially for the first time.

moth|er tongue (mother tongues) N-COUNT [oft poss N] Your **mother tongue** is the language that you learn when you are a baby.

mo|tif /moʊtiːf/ (motifs) **1** N-COUNT A **motif** is a design which is used as a decoration or as part of an artistic pattern. ❑ ...a rose motif. **2** N-COUNT A **motif** is a theme or idea that is frequently repeated throughout a piece of literature or music. ❑ Shipwrecks are a recurring motif in her writings.

mo|tion ♦♢♢ /moʊʃən/ (motions, motioning, motioned) **1** N-UNCOUNT **Motion** is the activity or process of continually changing position or moving from one place to another. ❑ ...the laws governing light, sound, and motion. ❑ One group of muscles sets the next group in motion. **2** N-COUNT A **motion** is an action, gesture, or movement. ❑ He made a neat chopping motion with his hand. **3** N-COUNT A **motion** is a formal proposal or statement in a meeting, debate, or trial, which is discussed and then voted on or decided on. ❑ The conference is now debating the motion and will vote on it shortly. ❑ Opposition parties are likely to bring a no-confidence motion against the government. **4** V-T/V-I If you **motion** to someone, you move your hand or head as a way of telling them to do something or telling them where to go. ❑ She motioned for the locked front doors to be opened. ❑ He stood aside and motioned Don to the door. **5** → see also **slow motion** **6** PHRASE If you say that someone **is going through the motions**, you think they are only saying or doing something because it is expected of them without being interested, enthusiastic, or sympathetic. ❑ "You really don't care, do you?" she said quietly. "You're just going through the motions." **7** PHRASE If a process or event is **in motion**, it is happening. If it is **set in motion**, it is happening or beginning to happen. ❑ The current chain of events was set in motion by that kidnapping. **8** PHRASE If someone **sets the wheels in motion**, they take the necessary action to make something start happening. ❑ I have set the wheels in motion to sell their Arizona ranch.

---SYNONYMS---

motion
NOUN **1**
movement: Movement is a big challenge for him since he broke his hip.
action: As always, Peter had a reason for his action.
mobility: Two cars gave them the freedom and mobility to go their separate ways.

2
gesture: Sarah made a menacing gesture with her fist.
sign: They gave Lavalle the thumbs-up sign.
wave: Steve stopped him with a wave of the hand.
signal: As soon as it was dark, Mrs Evans gave the signal.

mo|tion|less /moʊʃənlɪs/ ADJ Someone or something that is **motionless** is not moving at all. ❑ He has this ability of being able to remain as motionless as a statue, for hours on end.

mo|tion pic|ture (motion pictures) N-COUNT A **motion picture** is a movie made for movie theaters. [mainly AM, FORMAL] ❑ It was there that I saw my first motion picture.

mo|ti|vate ♦♢♢ /moʊtɪveɪt/ (motivates, motivating, motivated) **1** V-T If you **are motivated** by something, especially an emotion, it causes you to behave in a particular way. ❑ They are motivated by a need to achieve. ● **mo|ti|vat|ed** ADJ ❑ ...highly motivated employees. ● **mo|ti|va|tion** /moʊtɪveɪʃən/ N-UNCOUNT ❑ His poor performance may be attributed to lack of motivation rather than to reading difficulties. **2** V-T If someone **motivates** you to do something, they make you feel determined to do it. ❑ How do you motivate people to work hard and efficiently? ● **mo|ti|va|tion** N-UNCOUNT ❑ Given parental motivation, we are optimistic about the ability of people to change.

mo|ti|va|tion /moʊtɪveɪʃən/ (motivations) N-COUNT Your **motivation** for doing something is what causes you to want to do it. ❑ Money is my motivation.

mo|ti|va|tion|al /moʊtɪveɪʃənəl/ ADJ Something that is **motivational** provides you with motivation. [APPROVAL] ❑ ...a veteran Italian mountaineer and motivational speaker.

mo|tive /moʊtɪv/ (motives) N-COUNT Your **motive** for doing something is your reason for doing it. ❑ Police have ruled out robbery as a motive for the killing.

mot|ley /mɒtli/ ADJ [ADJ n] You can describe a group of things as a **motley** collection if you think they seem strange together because they are all very different. ❑ ...a motley collection of vans, old buses, cattle trucks, and even a fire engine.

mo|tor ♦♢♢ /moʊtər/ (motors) **1** N-COUNT The **motor** in a machine, vehicle, or boat is the part that uses electricity or fuel to produce movement, so that the machine, vehicle, or boat can work. ❑ She got in and started the motor. **2** ADJ [ADJ n] **Motor** vehicles and boats have a gasoline or diesel engine. ❑ Theft of motor vehicles is up by 15.9%. **3** ADJ **Motor** is used to describe activities relating to vehicles such as cars and buses. [mainly BRIT]

in AM, usually use **automotive**

4 → see also **motoring**

motor|bike /moʊtərbaɪk/ (motorbikes) N-COUNT A **motorbike** is a lighter, less powerful motorcycle. [AM]

motor|boat /moʊtərboʊt/ (motorboats) **1** N-COUNT A **motorboat** is a boat that is driven by an engine. **2** → See also color supplement

motor|cade /moʊtərkeɪd/ (motorcades) N-COUNT A **motorcade** is a line of slow-moving cars carrying important people, usually as part of a public ceremony. ❑ At times the president's motorcade slowed to a crawl.

motor|cycle /moʊtərsaɪkəl/ (motorcycles) **1** N-COUNT A **motorcycle** is a vehicle with two wheels and an engine. **2** → See also color supplement

motor|cyclist /moʊtərsaɪklɪst/ (motorcyclists) N-COUNT A **motorcyclist** is a person who rides a motorcycle.

motor home (motor homes) **1** N-COUNT A **motor home** is a large vehicle containing beds and equipment for cooking and washing. Motor homes can be used for vacations or long trips. **2** → See also color supplement

mo|tor|ing /moʊtərɪŋ/ ADJ **Motoring** means relating to cars and driving. [mainly BRIT]

in AM, usually use **driving**

mo|tor|ised /moʊtəraɪzd/ [BRIT] → see **motorized**

mo|tor|ist /moʊtərɪst/ (motorists) **1** N-COUNT A **motorist** is a person who drives a car. ❑ Police urged motorists to take extra care on the roads. **2** → See feature box at **drive**

mo|tor|ized /moʊtəraɪzd/

in BRIT, also use **motorised**

motormouth

1 ADJ A **motorized** vehicle has an engine. ❑ *Around 1910 motorized carriages were beginning to replace horse-drawn cabs.* **2** ADJ A **motorized** group of soldiers is equipped with motor vehicles. ❑ *...motorized infantry and artillery.*

motor|mouth /moʊtərmaʊθ/ N-SING If you describe someone as a **motormouth**, you mean that they talk a lot, especially in a loud or aggressive way. [INFORMAL, DISAPPROVAL]

mo|tor neu|ron dis|ease N-UNCOUNT **Motor neuron disease** is a disease which destroys the part of a person's nervous system that controls movement.

in BRIT, use **motor neurone disease**

motor|way /moʊtərweɪ/ (motorways) N-VAR A **motorway** is a major road that has been specially built for fast travel over long distances. Motorways have several lanes and special places where traffic gets on and leaves. [BRIT]

in AM, usually use **freeway**

mot|tled /mɒtld/ ADJ Something that is **mottled** is covered with patches of different colors which do not form a regular pattern. ❑ *...mottled green and yellow leaves.*

mot|to /mɒtoʊ/ (mottoes or mottos) N-COUNT A **motto** is a short sentence or phrase that expresses a rule for sensible behavior, especially a way of behaving in a particular situation. ❑ *"Stay true to yourself" has always been his motto.*

mould /moʊld/ [BRIT] → see **mold**

moult /moʊlt/ [BRIT] → see **molt**

mound /maʊnd/ (mounds) **1** N-COUNT A **mound** of something is a large, rounded pile of it. ❑ *The bulldozers piled up huge mounds of dirt.* **2** N-COUNT In baseball, the **mound** is the raised area where the pitcher stands when he or she throws the ball. ❑ *He went to the mound to talk with a struggling pitcher who spoke only Spanish.*

mount ♦◇◇ /maʊnt/ (mounts, mounting, mounted) **1** V-T If you **mount** a campaign or event, you organize it and make it take place. ❑ *The party announced it was mounting a major campaign of mass political protests.* **2** V-I If something **mounts**, it increases in intensity. ❑ *For several hours, tension mounted.* **3** V-I If something **mounts**, it increases in quantity. ❑ *The uncollected garbage mounts in city streets.* • PHRASAL VERB To **mount up** means the same as to **mount**. ❑ *Her medical bills mounted up.* **4** V-T If you **mount** the stairs or a platform, you go up the stairs or go up onto the platform. [FORMAL] ❑ *Larry was mounting the stairs up into the attic.* **5** V-T If you **mount** a horse or motorcycle, you climb on to it so that you can ride it. ❑ *A man in a crash helmet was mounting a motorcycle.* **6** V-T If you **mount** an object on something, you fix it there firmly. ❑ *Her husband mounts the work on velour paper and makes the frame.* • **-mounted** COMB IN ADJ ❑ *She installed a wall-mounted electric fan.* **7** V-T If you **mount** an exhibition or display, you organize and present it. ❑ *The gallery has mounted an exhibition of art by Irish women painters.* **8** N-IN-NAMES **Mount** is used as part of the name of a mountain. ❑ *...Mount Everest.* **9** → see also **mounted**

─── SYNONYMS ───

mount
VERB **2**
increase: *We are experiencing an increasing number of problems.*
build: *Pressure built yesterday for postponement of the ceremony.*
grow: *Opposition grew, and the government agreed to negotiate.*
intensify: *Groups of refugees are on the move following intensified fighting in the region.*
escalate: *The protests escalated into five days of rioting.*

─── COLLOCATIONS ───

mount
VERB
1
mount + noun: attack, bid, campaign, challenge; defense; investigation, operation, search
2
noun + mount: concern, fear, pressure, tension; anger, criticism; speculation
mount + adverb: steadily
3
noun + mount: debts, evidence

mouse pad

moun|tain ♦♦◇ /maʊntən/ (mountains) **1** N-COUNT A **mountain** is a very high area of land with steep sides. ❑ *Mt. McKinley, in Alaska, is the highest mountain in North America.* **2** QUANT If you talk about a **mountain** of something, or **mountains** of something, you are emphasizing that there is a large amount of it. [INFORMAL, EMPHASIS] ❑ *They are faced with a mountain of bureaucracy.* **3** PHRASE If you say that someone has **a mountain to climb**, you mean that it will be difficult for them to achieve what they want to achieve. [JOURNALISM] ❑ *"We had a mountain to climb after the second goal went in," said Crosby.*

moun|tain bike (mountain bikes) **1** N-COUNT A **mountain bike** is a type of bicycle that is suitable for riding over rough ground. It has a strong frame and thick tires. **2** → See also color supplement

moun|tain|eer /maʊntənɪər/ (mountaineers) N-COUNT A **mountaineer** is a person who is skillful at climbing the steep sides of mountains.

moun|tain|eer|ing /maʊntənɪərɪŋ/ N-UNCOUNT **Mountaineering** is the activity of climbing the steep sides of mountains as a hobby or sport.

moun|tain lion (mountain lions) N-COUNT A **mountain lion** is a wild animal that is a member of the cat family. Mountain lions have brownish gray fur and live in mountain regions of North and South America. [mainly AM]

in BRIT, usually use **puma**

moun|tain|ous /maʊntənəs/ **1** ADJ A **mountainous** place has a lot of mountains. ❑ *...the mountainous region of New Mexico.* **2** ADJ [ADJ n] You use **mountainous** to emphasize that something is great in size, quantity, or degree. [EMPHASIS] ❑ *The plan is designed to reduce some of the company's mountainous debt.*

moun|tain|side /maʊntənsaɪd/ (mountainsides) N-COUNT A **mountainside** is one of the steep sides of a mountain. ❑ *The couple trudged up the dark mountainside.*

mount|ed /maʊntɪd/ **1** ADJ [ADJ n] **Mounted** police or soldiers ride horses when they are on duty. ❑ *A dozen mounted police rode into the square.* **2** → see also **mount**

mourn /mɔrn/ (mourns, mourning, mourned) **1** V-T/V-I If you **mourn** someone who has died or **mourn** for them, you are very sad that they have died and show your sorrow in the way that you behave. ❑ *Joan still mourns her father.* ❑ *He mourned for his valiant men.* **2** V-T/V-I If you **mourn** something or **mourn** for it, you regret that you no longer have it and show your regret in the way that you behave. ❑ *We mourned the loss of our cities.*

mourn|er /mɔrnər/ (mourners) N-COUNT A **mourner** is a person who attends a funeral, especially as a relative or friend of the dead person. ❑ *Weeks after his death, mourners still gather outside the house.*

mourn|ful /mɔrnfəl/ **1** ADJ If you are **mournful**, you are very sad. ❑ *He looked mournful, even near to tears.* • **mourn|ful|ly** ADV ❑ *He stood mournfully at the gate waving bye bye.* **2** ADJ A **mournful** sound seems very sad. ❑ *...the mournful wail of bagpipes.*

mourn|ing /mɔrnɪŋ/ **1** N-UNCOUNT **Mourning** is behavior in which you show sadness about a person's death. ❑ *Expect to feel angry, depressed, and confused. It's all part of the mourning process.* **2** PHRASE [usu v-link PHR] If you are **in mourning**, you are dressed or behaving in a particular way because someone you love or respect has died. ❑ *Yesterday the whole of Greece was in mourning.*

mouse /maʊs/ (mice) **1** N-COUNT A **mouse** is a small, furry animal with a long tail. ❑ *...a mouse running in a wheel in its cage.* **2** N-COUNT A **mouse** is a device that is connected to a computer. By moving it over a flat surface and pressing its buttons, you can move the cursor around the screen and do things without using the keyboard. ❑ *Her message had been written; all she had to do was click the mouse.*

mouse mat (mouse mats) also **mousemat** N-COUNT A **mouse mat** is the same as a **mouse pad**. [BRIT]

mouse pad (mouse pads) also **mousepad** N-COUNT A **mouse pad** is a flat piece of plastic or some other material that you rest the mouse on while using a computer. [mainly AM]

in BRIT, usually use **mouse mat**

mouse|trap /maʊstræp/ (**mousetraps**) N-COUNT A mousetrap is a small device that catches or kills mice.

mous|sa|ka /musɑkə/ (**moussakas**) N-VAR Moussaka is a Greek dish consisting of layers of meat and eggplant.

mousse /mus/ (**mousses**) **1** N-VAR Mousse is a sweet, light food made from eggs and cream. It is often flavored with fruit or chocolate. ▫ ...a rich chocolate mousse. **2** N-MASS Mousse is a soft substance containing a lot of tiny bubbles, for example one that you can put in your hair to make it easier to shape into a particular style. ▫ He had even put mousse in his hair.

mous|tache /mʊstæʃ/ [BRIT] → see mustache

mous|ta|chi|oed /məstæʃioʊd/ also **mustachioed** ADJ A moustachioed man has a moustache. [HUMOROUS or WRITTEN]

mousy /maʊsi/ (**mousier, mousiest**) also **mousey** **1** ADJ [usu ADJ n] Mousy hair is a dull, light brown color. ▫ He was aged between 25 and 30, with a medium build and collar-length mousy hair. **2** ADJ [usu ADJ n] If you describe someone as **mousy**, you mean that they are quiet and shy and that people do not notice them. ▫ The inspector remembered her as a small, mousy woman, invariably worried.

mouth ✦✦◇ (**mouths, mouthing, mouthed**)

> The noun is pronounced /maʊθ/. The verb is pronounced /maʊð/. The plural of the noun and the third person singular of the verb are both pronounced /maʊðz/.

1 N-COUNT Your **mouth** is the area of your face where your lips are, or the space behind your lips where your teeth and tongue are. ▫ She clamped her hand against her mouth. • **-mouthed** /-maʊðd/ COMB IN ADJ ▫ He straightened up and looked at me, open-mouthed. **2** N-COUNT You can say that someone has a particular kind of **mouth** to indicate that they speak in a particular kind of way or that they say particular kinds of things. ▫ I've always had a loud mouth, I refuse to be silenced. • **-mouthed** COMB IN ADJ ▫ ...Sam, their smart-mouthed teenage son. **3** N-COUNT The **mouth** of a cave, hole, or bottle is its entrance or opening. ▫ By the mouth of the tunnel he bent to retie his shoelace. • **-mouthed** COMB IN ADJ ▫ He put the flowers in a wide-mouthed blue vase. **4** N-COUNT The **mouth** of a river is the place where it flows into the sea. ▫ ...the town at the mouth of the River Fox. **5** V-T If you **mouth** something, you form words with your lips without making any sound. ▫ I mouthed a goodbye and hurried in behind Momma. **6** PHRASE If you have a number of **mouths to feed**, you have the responsibility of earning enough money to feed and take care of that number of people. ▫ He had to feed his family on the equivalent of seven hundred dollars a month and, with five mouths to feed, he found this very hard. **7** PHRASE If you say that someone does not **open** their **mouth**, you are emphasizing that they never say anything at all. [EMPHASIS] ▫ Sometimes I hardly dare open my mouth. **8** PHRASE If you **keep** your **mouth shut** about something, you do not talk about it, especially because it is a secret. ▫ You wouldn't be here now if she'd kept her mouth shut. **9 to live hand to mouth → see hand ① 10 heart in your mouth →** see **heart ② 11 from the horse's mouth →** see **horse 12 to put your money where your mouth is →** see **money 13 word of mouth →** see **word ② 14 →** See also color supplement

mouth|ful /maʊθfʊl/ (**mouthfuls**) **1** N-COUNT A **mouthful** of drink or food is the amount that you put or have in your mouth. ▫ She gulped down a mouthful of coffee. **2** N-SING If you describe a long word or phrase as **a mouthful**, you mean that it is difficult to say. [INFORMAL] ▫ It's called the Pan-Caribbean Disaster Preparedness and Prevention Project, which is quite a mouthful.

mouth|piece /maʊθpis/ (**mouthpieces**) **1** N-COUNT The **mouthpiece** of a telephone is the part that you speak into. ▫ He shouted into the mouthpiece. **2** N-COUNT The **mouthpiece** of a musical instrument or other device is the part that you put into your mouth. ▫ He showed him how to blow into the ivory mouthpiece. **3** N-COUNT The **mouthpiece** of an organization or person is someone who informs other people of the opinions and policies of that organization or person. ▫ Their mouthpiece is the vice president.

mouth-to-mouth re|sus|ci|ta|tion also **mouth-to-mouth** N-UNCOUNT If you give someone who has stopped breathing **mouth-to-mouth resuscitation**, you breathe into their mouth to make them start breathing again.

mouth|wash /maʊθwɒʃ/ (**mouthwashes**) N-MASS Mouthwash is a liquid that you put in your mouth and then spit out in order to clean your mouth and make your breath smell pleasant.

mouth-watering also **mouthwatering** **1** ADJ Mouth-watering food looks or smells extremely nice. ▫ ...hundreds of cheeses, in a mouth-watering variety of shapes, textures and tastes. **2** ADJ If you describe something as **mouth-watering**, you are emphasizing that it is very attractive. [JOURNALISM, EMPHASIS] ▫ Prizes worth a mouth-watering $16 million are unclaimed.

mov|able /muvəbəl/ also **moveable** ADJ Something that is **movable** can be moved from one place or position to another. ▫ It's a vinyl doll with movable arms and legs.

MOVE

① VERB AND NOUN USES
② PHRASES
③ PHRASAL VERBS

---

① move ✦✦✦ /muv/ (**moves, moving, moved**) **1** V-T/V-I When you **move** something or when it **moves**, its position changes and it does not remain still. ▫ She moved the sheaf of papers into position. ▫ A traffic policeman asked him to move his car. ▫ The train began to move. **2** V-I When you **move**, you change your position or go to a different place. ▫ She waited for him to get up, but he didn't move. ▫ He moved around the room, putting his possessions together. • N-COUNT **Move** is also a noun. ▫ The doctor made a move toward the door. **3** V-I If you **move**, you act or you begin to do something. ▫ Firms will have to move fast to comply with the new guidelines. **4** N-COUNT A **move** is an action that you take in order to achieve something. ▫ The one-point cut in interest rates was a wise move. ▫ It may also be a good move to suggest she talks things over. **5** V-I If a person or company **moves**, they leave the building where they have been living or working, and they go to live or work in a different place, taking their possessions with them. ▫ Two people in love are at home wherever they are, no matter how often they move. ▫ She had often considered moving to Seattle. • N-COUNT **Move** is also a noun. ▫ Modigliani announced his move to Montparnasse in 1909. **6** V-T If people in authority **move** someone, they make that person go from one place or job to another one. ▫ His superiors moved him to another parish. **7** V-I If you **move** from one job or interest to another, you change to it. ▫ He moved from being a part-time tutor to being a lecturer in social history. • N-COUNT **Move** is also a noun. ▫ His move to the chairmanship means he will take a less active role in day-to-day management. **8** V-I If you **move** to a new topic in a conversation, you start talking about something different. ▫ Let's move to another subject, Dan. **9** V-T If you **move** an event or the date of an event, you change the time at which it happens. ▫ The club has moved its meeting to Saturday, January 22nd. **10** V-I If you **move** toward a particular state, activity, or opinion, you start to be in that state, do that activity, or have that opinion. ▫ The Labour Party has moved to the right and become like your Democratic Party. • N-COUNT **Move** is also a noun. ▫ His move to the left was not a sudden leap but a natural working out of ideas. **11** V-I [usu cont] If a situation or process **is moving**, it is developing or progressing, rather than staying still. ▫ Events are moving fast. **12** V-T [usu passive] If you say that you will not **be moved**, you mean that you have come to a decision and nothing will change your mind. ▫ Everyone thought I was crazy to go back, but I wouldn't be moved. **13** V-T If something **moves** you to do something, it influences you and causes you to do it. ▫ It was punk that first moved him to join a band seriously. **14** V-T If something **moves** you, it has an effect on your emotions and causes you to feel sadness or sympathy for another person. ▫ These stories surprised and moved me. • **moved** ADJ [v-link ADJ] ▫ Those who listened to him were deeply moved. **15** V-I If you say that someone **moves in** a particular society, circle, or world, you mean that they know people in a particular social class or group and spend most of their time with them. ▫ She moves in high-society circles in Palm Beach. **16** V-T/V-I At a meeting, if you **move** for something or **move** that something should happen, you formally suggest it so that everyone present can vote on it. ▫ Somebody needs to move for an adjournment. **17** N-COUNT A **move** is an act of putting a chess piece or other counter in a different position on a board

moveable when it is your turn to do so in a game. ☐ *With no idea of what to do for my next move, my hand hovered over the board.*

② **move** ♦♦♦ /mu̱v/ (moves, moving, moved)
→ Please look at meaning ⑤ to see if the expression you are looking for is shown under another headword.
1 PHRASE If you say that one **false move** will cause a disaster, you mean that you or someone else must not make any mistakes because the situation is so difficult or dangerous. ☐ *He knew one false move would end in disaster.* **2** PHRASE If you **make a move**, you prepare or begin to leave one place and go somewhere else. ☐ *He glanced at his wristwatch. "I suppose we'd better make a move."* **3** PHRASE If you **make a move**, you take a course of action. ☐ *The week before the deal was supposed to close, fifteen Japanese banks made a move to pull out.* **4** PHRASE If you are **on the move**, you are going from one place to another. ☐ *Jack never wanted to stay in one place for very long, so they were always on the move.* **5** to move a muscle → see **muscle**

③ **move** ♦♦♦ /mu̱v/ (moves, moving, moved)
▶ **move in** **1** PHRASAL VERB When you **move in** somewhere, you begin to live there as your home. ☐ *Her house was in perfect order when she moved in.* ☐ *Her husband had moved in with a younger woman.* **2** PHRASAL VERB If police, soldiers, or attackers **move in**, they go toward a place or person in order to deal with or attack them. ☐ *There were violent and chaotic scenes when police moved in to disperse the crowd.* **3** PHRASAL VERB If someone **moves in** on an area of activity which was previously only done by a particular group of people, they start becoming involved with it for the first time. ☐ *I don't want another guy moving in on my territory, you know?*
▶ **move off** PHRASAL VERB When you **move off**, you start moving away from a place. ☐ *Gil waved his hand and the car moved off.*
▶ **move on** **1** PHRASAL VERB When you **move on** somewhere, you leave the place where you have been staying or waiting and go there. ☐ *Mr. Brooke moved on from LA to Phoenix.* **2** PHRASAL VERB If someone such as a police officer **moves** you **on**, they order you to stop standing in a particular place and to go somewhere else. ☐ *Eventually the police were called to move them on.* **3** PHRASAL VERB If you **move on**, you finish or stop one activity and start doing something different. ☐ *She ran this shop for ten years before deciding to move on to fresh challenges.*
▶ **move out** PHRASAL VERB If you **move out**, you stop living in a particular house or place and go to live somewhere else. ☐ *The harassment had become too much to tolerate and he decided to move out.*
▶ **move over** **1** PHRASAL VERB If you **move over** to a new system or way of doing something, you change to it. ☐ *The government is having to introduce some difficult changes, particularly in moving over to a market economy.* **2** PHRASAL VERB If someone **moves over**, they leave their job or position in order to let someone else have it. ☐ *Mr. Jenkins should make balanced programs or move over and let someone else who can.* **3** PHRASAL VERB If you **move over**, you change your position in order to make room for someone else. ☐ *Move over and let me drive.*
▶ **move up** **1** PHRASAL VERB If you **move up**, you change your position, especially in order to be nearer someone or to make room for someone else. ☐ *Move up, John, and let the lady sit down.* **2** PHRASAL VERB If someone or something **moves up**, they go to a higher level, grade, or class. ☐ *Share prices moved up.*

move|able /mu̱vəbəl/ → see **movable**

move|ment ♦♦◊ /mu̱vmənt/ (movements) **1** N-COUNT A **movement** is a group of people who share the same beliefs, ideas, or aims. ☐ *It's part of a broader nationalist movement that's gaining strength throughout the country.* **2** N-VAR **Movement** involves changing position or going from one place to another. ☐ *They actually monitor the movement of the fish going up river.* ☐ *There was movement behind the window in the back door.* **3** N-VAR A **movement** is a planned change in position that an army makes during a battle or military exercise. ☐ *There are reports of fresh troop movements across the border.* **4** N-VAR **Movement** is a gradual development or change of an attitude, opinion, or policy. ☐ *...the movement toward democracy in Latin America.* **5** N-PLURAL Your **movements** are everything that you do or plan to do during a period of time. ☐ *I want a full account of your movements the night Mr. Gower was killed.*

COLLOCATIONS

movement
NOUN
1
noun + **movement**: civil rights, independence, protest, trade union
adjective + **movement**: environmental, revolutionary
verb + **movement**: join, support
5
verb + **movement**: monitor, track

SYNONYMS

movement
NOUN **1**
group: *Members of an environmental group are staging a protest inside a chemical plant.*
party: *...a member of the Labor party.*
organization: *...a report by the International Labor Organization.*

---

mov|er /mu̱vər/ (movers) PHRASE The **movers and shakers** in a place or area of activity are the people who have the most power or influence. ☐ *It is the movers and shakers of the record industry who will decide which bands make it.*

movie ♦♦◊ /mu̱vi/ (movies) **1** N-COUNT A **movie** is a series of moving pictures that have been recorded so that they can be shown in a theater or on television. A movie tells a story, or shows a real situation. ☐ *In the first movie Tony Curtis ever made he played a grocery clerk.* **2** N-PLURAL You can talk about **the movies** when you are talking about seeing a movie in a movie theater. [mainly AM] ☐ *He took her to the movies.*
  in BRIT, usually use **the cinema**

movie|goer /mu̱vigoʊər/ (moviegoers) N-COUNT A **moviegoer** is a person who often goes to the movies. [AM] ☐ *What is it about Tom Hanks that moviegoers find so appealing?*
  in BRIT, usually use **cinema-goer**

movie house (movie houses) N-COUNT A **movie house** is the same as a **movie theater**. [AM, OLD-FASHIONED]

movie star (movie stars) N-COUNT A **movie star** is a famous actor or actress who appears in movies. [mainly AM]
  in BRIT, usually use **film star**

movie thea|ter (movie theaters) N-COUNT A **movie theater** is a place where people go to watch movies for entertainment. [AM]
  in BRIT, use **cinema**

mov|ing /mu̱vɪŋ/ **1** ADJ If something is **moving**, it makes you feel an emotion such as sadness, pity, or sympathy very strongly. ☐ *It is very moving to see how much strangers can care for each other.* ● **mov|ing|ly** ADV [ADV with v] ☐ *You write very movingly of your sister Amy's suicide.* **2** ADJ [ADJ n] A **moving** model or part of a machine moves or is able to move. ☐ *It also means there are no moving parts to break down.*

mov|ing pic|ture (moving pictures) N-COUNT A **moving picture** is a movie. [OLD-FASHIONED]

mow /moʊ/ (mows, mowing, mowed, mown)
  The past participle can be either **mowed** or **mown**.
V-T/V-I If you **mow** an area of grass, you cut it using a machine called a lawn mower. ☐ *He continued to mow the lawn and do other routine chores.*
▶ **mow down** PHRASAL VERB If someone **is mowed down**, they are killed violently by a vehicle or gunfire. ☐ *She was mowed down on a pedestrian crossing.*

mow|er /moʊər/ (mowers) **1** N-COUNT A **mower** is the same as a **lawnmower**. **2** N-COUNT A **mower** is a machine that has sharp blades for cutting something such as corn or wheat.

moz|za|rel|la /mɒtsərelə, moʊt-/ (mozzarellas) N-MASS **Mozzarella** is a type of white Italian cheese, often used as a topping for pizzas. ☐ *...layers of fresh mozzarella.*

MP3 /ɛm pi θri̱/ N-UNCOUNT **MP3** is a kind of technology that enables you to record and play music from the internet.

MP3 play|er (MP3 players) N-COUNT An **MP3 player** is a machine on which you can play music downloaded from the internet.

MPEG /ɛmpɛg/ N-UNCOUNT **MPEG** is a standard file format for compressing video images so that they can be stored or sent by email more easily. **MPEG** is an abbreviation for 'Motion Picture Experts Group.' [COMPUTING]

mpg also **m.p.g.** **mpg** is written after a number to indicate how many miles a vehicle can travel using one gallon of fuel. **mpg** is an abbreviation for 'miles per gallon.' ◻ *Fuel consumption is 38 mpg around town, 55 mpg on the open road.*

mph also **m.p.h.** **mph** is written after a number to indicate the speed of something such as a vehicle. **mph** is an abbreviation for 'miles per hour.' ◻ *Inside these zones, traffic speeds are restricted to 20 mph.*

Mr. ♦♦♦ /mɪstər/

in BRIT, use **Mr**

1 N-TITLE **Mr.** is used before a man's name when you are speaking or referring to him. ◻ *...Mr. Grant.* ◻ *...Mr. Bob Price.* **2** N-VOC **Mr.** is sometimes used in front of words such as 'president' and 'chairman' to address the man who holds the position mentioned. ◻ *Mr. President, you're aware of the system.* **3** → see also **Messrs.**

MRI /ɛm ɑr aɪ/ N-UNCOUNT **MRI** is a method by which medical staff can get a picture of soft parts inside a patient's body, using a powerful magnetic field. **MRI** is an abbreviation for 'magnetic resonance imaging.'

Mrs. ♦♦♦ /mɪsɪz/

in BRIT, use **Mrs**

N-TITLE **Mrs.** is used before the name of a married woman when you are speaking or referring to her. Many people prefer the title 'Ms.' ◻ *Hello, Mrs. Miles.* ◻ *...Mrs. Anne Pritchard.*

MRSA /ɛm ɑr ɛs eɪ/ N-UNCOUNT **MRSA** is a bacterium that is resistant to most antibiotics. **MRSA** is an abbreviation for 'methicillin-resistant Staphylococcus aureus.' ◻ *...the problem of MRSA in hospitals.*

MS /ɛm ɛs/ N-UNCOUNT **MS** is a serious disease of the nervous system, which gradually makes a person weaker, and sometimes affects their sight or speech. **MS** is an abbreviation for **multiple sclerosis**. ◻ *She says she has battled MS for 19 years.*

ms. (**mss**) **ms.** is a written abbreviation for **manuscript**.

Ms. ♦♦♦ /mɪz/

in BRIT, use **Ms**

N-TITLE **Ms.** is used, especially in written English, before a woman's name when you are speaking or referring to her. If you use **Ms.**, you are not specifying if the woman is married or not. ◻ *...Ms. Brown.*

M.S. /ɛm ɛs/ (**M.S.s**) also **MS** N-COUNT An **M.S.** or **MS** is a master's degree in a science subject. **M.S.** or **MS** is an abbreviation for **Master of Science**. **M.S.** or **MS** is also written after someone's name to indicate that they have an M.S. [AM] ◻ *...Joyce Hanna, M.A., M.S.*

M.Sc. /ɛm ɛs si/ (**M.Sc.s**) also **MSc** N-COUNT An **M.Sc.** is the same as an **M.S.**

MSG /ɛm ɛs dʒi/ N-UNCOUNT **MSG** is an abbreviation for **monosodium glutamate**.

Msgr. also **Msgr** **Msgr.** is a written abbreviation for **Monsignor**.

Mt. (**Mts.**) also **Mt** **Mt.** is a written abbreviation for **Mount** or **Mountain**. ◻ *...Mt. Everest.* ◻ *...the Rocky Mts.*

much ♦♦♦ /mʌtʃ/ **1** ADV [ADV after v] You use **much** to indicate the great intensity, extent, or degree of something such as an action, feeling, or change. **Much** is usually used with 'so,' 'too,' and 'very,' and in negative clauses with this meaning. ◻ *She laughs too much.* ◻ *Thank you very much.* **2** ADV If something does not happen **much**, it does not happen very often. ◻ *He said that his father never talked much about the war.* ◻ *Gwen had not seen her dad all that much, because mostly he worked on the ships.* **3** ADV You use **much** in front of 'too' or comparative adjectives and adverbs in order to emphasize that there is a large amount of a particular quality. [EMPHASIS] ◻ *The skin is much too delicate.* **4** ADV If one thing is **much** the same as another thing, it is very similar to it. ◻ *The day ended much as it began.* **5** DET You use **much** to indicate that you are referring to a large amount of a substance or thing. ◻ *They are grown on the hillsides in full sun, without much water.* ◻ *The government has been reluctant to offer much aid to Nepal.* • PRON **Much** is also a pronoun. ◻ *...eating too much and drinking too much.* • QUANT **Much** is also a quantifier. ◻ *Much of the time we do not notice that we are solving problems.* **6** ADV [ADV as reply] You use **much** in expressions such as **not much**, **not very much**, and **too much** when replying to questions about amounts. ◻ *"Can you hear it where you live?" He shook his head. "Not much."* **7** QUANT [with brd-neg, QUANT of n-proper/pron] If you do not see **much of** someone, you do not see them very often. ◻ *I don't see much of Tony nowadays.* **8** DET You use **much** in the expression **how much** to ask questions about amounts or degrees, and also in reported clauses and statements to give information about the amount or degree of something. ◻ *How much money can I afford?* • ADV **Much** is also an adverb. ◻ *She knows how much this upsets me but she persists in doing it.* • PRON [how PRON] **Much** is also a pronoun. ◻ *How much do you earn?* **9** DET You use **much** in the expression **as much** when you are comparing amounts. ◻ *I shall try, with as much patience as is possible, to explain yet again.* ◻ *Their aim will be to produce as much milk as possible.* **10** PHRASE You use **much as** to introduce a fact which makes something else you have just said or will say rather surprising. ◻ *Much as they hope to go home tomorrow, they're resigned to staying on until the end of the year.* **11** PHRASE You use **much** in expressions such as '**I thought as much**' and '**I guessed as much**' after you have just been told something and you want to say that you already believed or expected it to be true. ◻ *You're waiting for a woman – I thought as much.* **12** PHRASE You use **as much as** before an amount to suggest that it is surprisingly large. [EMPHASIS] ◻ *The organizers hope to raise as much as $6m for charity.* **13** PHRASE You use **much less** after a statement, often a negative one, to indicate that the statement is more true of the person, thing, or situation that you are going to mention next. ◻ *They are always short of water to drink, much less to bathe in.* **14** PHRASE If you say that something is not **so much** one thing **as** another, you mean that it is more like the second thing than the first. ◻ *I don't really think of her as a daughter so much as a very good friend.* **15** PHRASE You use **so much so** to indicate that your previous statement is true to a very great extent, and therefore it has the result mentioned. ◻ *He himself believed in freedom, so much so that he would rather die than live without it.* **16** PHRASE If a situation or action is **too much** for you, it is so difficult, tiring, or upsetting that you cannot cope with it. ◻ *His inability to stay at one job for long had finally proved too much for her.* **17** PHRASE You use **very much** to emphasize that someone or something has a lot of a particular quality, or that the description you are about to give is particularly accurate. [EMPHASIS] ◻ *...a man very much in charge of himself.* **18 a bit much** → see **bit**

USAGE

much

1 You don't usually use 'much' as an object pronoun in positive sentences. Instead you use **a lot**. For example, don't say 'He knows much about butterflies.' Say 'He knows **a lot** about butterflies.' *She talks a lot about music.*
2 In positive sentences, don't use 'much' without 'very.' Don't say, for example, 'I enjoyed it much' or 'We much agree' Say 'I enjoyed it **very much**' or 'We **very much** agree.'

much- /mʌtʃ-/ COMB IN ADJ **Much-** combines with past participles to form adjectives which emphasize the intensity of the specified state or action. [EMPHASIS] ◻ *I'm having a much needed rest* ◻ *a much-improved version of last season's model.*

much-maligned ADJ [usu ADJ n] If you describe someone or something as **much-maligned**, you mean that they are often criticized by people, but you think the criticism is unfair or exaggerated because they have good qualities too. ◻ *I'm happy for James. He's a much-maligned player but has tremendous spirit.*

much-traveled

in BRIT, sometimes in AM, use **much-travelled**

ADJ A **much-traveled** person has traveled a lot in foreign countries.

muck /mʌk/ N-UNCOUNT **Muck** is dirt or some other unpleasant substance. [INFORMAL] ◻ *This congealed muck was interfering with the filter and causing the flooding.*

muck|raking /mʌkreɪkɪŋ/ N-UNCOUNT If you accuse someone of **muckraking**, you are criticizing them for finding and spreading unpleasant or embarrassing information about someone, especially a public figure. [DISAPPROVAL] ▫ *The senator accused opposition leaders of muckraking.*

mucky /mʌki/ (muckier, muckiest) ADJ Something that is **mucky** is very dirty. [INFORMAL]

mu|cous mem|brane /myuːkəs mɛmbreɪn/ (mucous membranes) N-COUNT A **mucous membrane** is skin that produces mucus to prevent itself from becoming dry. It covers delicate parts of the body such as the inside of your nose. [TECHNICAL]

mu|cus /myuːkəs/ N-UNCOUNT **Mucus** is a thick liquid that is produced in some parts of your body, for example the inside of your nose. ▫ *...the thin layer of mucus that helps protect the delicate lining of the rectum.*

mud /mʌd/ N-UNCOUNT **Mud** is a sticky mixture of earth and water. ▫ *His uniform was crumpled, untidy, splashed with mud.*

mud|dle /mʌdᵊl/ (muddles, muddling, muddled) **1** N-VAR If people or things are in a **muddle**, they are in a state of confusion or disorder. ▫ *My thoughts are all in a muddle.* ▫ *We are going to get into a hopeless muddle.* **2** V-T If you **muddle** things or people, you get them mixed up, so that you do not know which is which. ▫ *Already, one or two critics have begun to muddle the two names.* • PHRASAL VERB **Muddle up** means the same as **muddle**. ▫ *The question muddles up three separate issues.*
• **mud|dled up** ADJ ▫ *I know that I am getting my words muddled up.*
▶ **muddle through** PHRASAL VERB If you **muddle through**, you manage to do something even though you do not have the proper equipment or do not really know how to do it. ▫ *We will muddle through and just play it day by day.* ▫ *They may be able to muddle through the next five years like this.*
▶ **muddle up** → see **muddle 2**

mud|dled /mʌdᵊld/ ADJ If someone is **muddled**, they are confused about something. ▫ *I'm afraid I'm a little muddled. I'm not exactly sure where to begin.*

mud|dy /mʌdi/ (muddier, muddiest, muddies, muddying, muddied) **1** ADJ Something that is **muddy** contains mud or is covered in mud. ▫ *...a muddy track.* **2** V-T If you **muddy** something, you cause it to be muddy. ▫ *The ground still smelled of rain and they muddied their shoes.* **3** V-T If someone or something **muddies** a situation or issue, they cause it to seem less clear and less easy to understand. ▫ *It's difficult enough without muddying the issue with religion.* • PHRASE If someone or something **muddies the waters**, they cause a situation or issue to seem less clear and less easy to understand.

mud|flap /mʌdflæp/ (mudflaps) N-COUNT [usu pl] The **mudflaps** of a vehicle are heavy pieces of rubber that hang down behind the tires to prevent splashing.

mud|flats /mʌdflæts/ also **mud flats** N-PLURAL **Mudflats** are areas of flat empty land at the coast which are covered by the sea only when the tide is in.

mud|guard /mʌdgɑːrd/ [BRIT] → see **mudflap**

mud|slide /mʌdslaɪd/ (mudslides) N-COUNT A **mudslide** is a large amount of mud sliding down a mountain, usually causing damage or destruction.

mud|slinging /mʌdslɪŋɪŋ/ N-UNCOUNT If you accuse someone of **mudslinging**, you are accusing them of making insulting, unfair, and damaging remarks about their opponents. [DISAPPROVAL] ▫ *Voters are disillusioned with the mudslinging campaigns run by many candidates in recent years.*

mues|li /myuːzli/ (mueslis) N-MASS **Muesli** is a breakfast cereal made from chopped nuts, dried fruit, and grains.

mu|ez|zin /muɛzɪn/ (muezzins) N-COUNT A **muezzin** is an official who calls from the tower of a mosque when it is time for Muslims to pray.

muff /mʌf/ (muffs, muffing, muffed) **1** V-T If you **muff** something, you do it badly or you make a mistake while you are doing it, so that it is not successful. [INFORMAL] ▫ *He muffed his opening speech.* **2** N-COUNT A **muff** is a piece of fur or thick cloth shaped like a short, hollow cylinder. You wear a muff on your hands to keep them warm in cold weather.

muf|fin /mʌfɪn/ (muffins) **1** N-COUNT **Muffins** are small, round, sweet cakes, usually with fruit or bran inside. They are often eaten for breakfast. [AM] ▫ *...breakfasts of pancakes, blueberry muffins, eggs, and bacon.* **2** N-COUNT **Muffins** are small, flat, bread rolls that you eat hot with butter. [BRIT]

in AM, use **English muffins**

muf|fle /mʌfᵊl/ (muffles, muffling, muffled) V-T If something **muffles** a sound, it makes it quieter and more difficult to hear. ▫ *Blake held his handkerchief over the mouthpiece to muffle his voice.*

muf|fled /mʌfᵊld/ ADJ [usu v-link ADJ] If you are **muffled**, you are wearing a lot of heavy clothes so that very little of your body or face is visible. ▫ *...children muffled in scarves and woolly hats.*

muf|fler /mʌflər/ (mufflers) **1** N-COUNT A **muffler** is a device on a car exhaust that makes it quieter. [AM]

in BRIT, use **silencer**

2 N-COUNT A **muffler** is a long scarf that you wear around your neck to keep warm.

mug /mʌg/ (mugs, mugging, mugged) **1** N-COUNT A **mug** is a large, deep cup with straight sides and a handle, used for hot drinks. ▫ *He spooned instant coffee into two of the mugs.* **2** N-COUNT You can use **mug** to refer to the mug and its contents, or to the contents only. ▫ *He had been drinking mugs of coffee to keep himself awake.* **3** N-COUNT Someone's **mug** is their face. [INFORMAL] ▫ *He managed to get his ugly mug on TV.* **4** V-T If someone **mugs** you, they attack you in order to steal your money. ▫ *I was walking out to my car when this guy tried to mug me.*
• **mug|ging** (muggings) N-VAR ▫ *Bank robberies, burglaries, and muggings are reported almost daily in the press.* **5** → See feature box at **crime**; See also color supplement

mug|ger /mʌgər/ (muggers) N-COUNT A **mugger** is a person who attacks someone violently in a street in order to steal money from them. ▫ *...hiding places for muggers and thieves.*

mug|gy /mʌgi/ ADJ **Muggy** weather is unpleasantly warm and damp. ▫ *It was muggy and overcast.*

mug shot (mug shots) N-COUNT A **mug shot** is a photograph of someone, especially a photograph of a criminal which has been taken by the police. [INFORMAL]

mul|berry /mʌlbɛri/ (mulberries) N-VAR A **mulberry** or a **mulberry tree** is a tree that has small purple berries which you can eat. • N-COUNT **Mulberries** are the fruit of a mulberry tree.

mulch /mʌltʃ/ (mulches, mulching, mulched) **1** N-MASS A **mulch** is a layer of something such as old leaves, small pieces of wood, or manure which you put on the soil around plants in order to protect them and help them to grow. **2** V-T To **mulch** plants means to put a mulch around them to protect them and help them to grow. ▫ *In May, mulch the bed with garden compost.*

mule /myuːl/ (mules) **1** N-COUNT A **mule** is an animal whose parents are a horse and a donkey. **2** N-COUNT A **mule** is a shoe or slipper which is open around the heel.

mull /mʌl/ (mulls, mulling, mulled) V-T If you **mull** something, you think about it for a long time before deciding what to do. [AM] ▫ *Last month, a federal grand jury began mulling evidence in the case.*
▶ **mull over** PHRASAL VERB If you **mull** something **over**, you think about it for a long time before deciding what to do. ▫ *McLaren had been mulling over an idea to make a movie.*

mul|lah /mʊlə, mʌlə/ (mullahs) N-COUNT; N-TITLE A **mullah** is a Muslim who is a religious teacher or leader.

mulled /mʌld/ ADJ [ADJ n] **Mulled** wine has sugar and spice added to it and is then heated.

mul|let /mʌlɪt/ (mullets or mullet) N-VAR A **mullet** is a small sea fish that people cook and eat. • N-UNCOUNT **Mullet** is this fish eaten as food.

PREFIX

multi-
forms adjectives that refer to something that consists of many things of a particular kind. *For example, a multi-colored object has many different colors.*

multi|col|ored /mʌltikʌlərd/

in BRIT, use **multicoloured, multi-coloured**

ADJ [usu ADJ n] A **multicolored** object has many different colors. ❑ ...a sea of multicolored umbrellas.

multi|cul|tur|al /mʌltikʌltʃərəl/ ADJ **Multicultural** means consisting of or relating to people of many different nationalities and cultures. ❑ ...children growing up in a multicultural society.

multi|cul|tur|al|ism /mʌltikʌltʃərəlɪzəm/ N-UNCOUNT **Multiculturalism** is a situation in which all the different cultural or racial groups in a society have equal rights and opportunities, and none is ignored or regarded as unimportant.

multi|fac|et|ed /mʌltifæsɪtɪd/ ADJ [usu ADJ n] **Multifaceted** means having a variety of different and important features or elements. ❑ Webb is a multifaceted performer. ❑ Her job is multifaceted.

multi|fari|ous /mʌltɪfɛəriəs/ ADJ If you describe things as **multifarious**, you mean that they are many in number and of many different kinds. [LITERARY] ❑ Spain is a composite of multifarious traditions and people. ❑ The reasons for closure are multifarious.

multi|grain /mʌltigreɪn/ ADJ [usu ADJ n] **Multigrain** bread or flour contains more than one type of grain. ❑ Start the day with a slice of multigrain toast and peanut butter.

multi|lat|er|al /mʌltilætərəl/ ADJ **Multilateral** means involving at least three different groups of people or nations. ❑ Many want to abandon the multilateral trade talks in Geneva.

multi-level mar|ket|ing N-UNCOUNT **Multi-level marketing** is a business structure in which an individual seller earns a commission from direct sales and the sales of the seller's recruits, of those recruited by the seller's recruits, and so on [BUSINESS] ❑ If the scheme appears to be a multi-level marketing situation, have nothing to do with it.

multi|lin|gual /mʌltilɪŋgwəl/ ❶ ADJ [usu ADJ n] **Multilingual** means involving several different languages. ❑ ...a multilingual country. ❑ ...multilingual dictionaries. ❷ ADJ A **multilingual** person is able to speak more than two languages very well. ❑ He recruited two multilingual engineers.

multi|media /mʌltimidiə/ ❶ N-UNCOUNT You use **multimedia** to refer to computer programs and products which involve sound, pictures, and film, as well as text. ❑ ...the case of an insurance company using multimedia to improve customer service in its branches. ❷ N-UNCOUNT In education, **multimedia** is the use of television and other different media in a lesson, as well as books. ❑ I am making a multimedia presentation for my science project.

multi|mil|lion|aire /mʌltɪmɪliənɛər/ (**multimillionaires**) N-COUNT A **multimillionaire** is a very rich person who has money or property worth several million dollars.

multi|na|tion|al /mʌltinæʃənᵊl/ (**multinationals**) ❶ ADJ A **multinational** company has branches or owns companies in many different countries. • N-COUNT **Multinational** is also a noun. ❑ ...multinationals such as Ford and IBM. ❷ ADJ **Multinational** armies, organizations, or other groups involve people from several different countries. ❑ The U.S. troops would be part of a multinational force. ❸ ADJ **Multinational** countries or regions have a population that is made up of people of several different nationalities. ❑ We live in a multinational country.

multi|play|er /mʌltipleɪər/ ADJ A **multiplayer** computer or video game is played by more than one player at one time. [COMPUTING] ❑ Internet multiplayer games are responsible for much of the increase in broadband use.

multi|ple /mʌltɪpᵊl/ (**multiples**) ❶ ADJ You use **multiple** to describe things that consist of many parts, involve many people, or have many uses. ❑ He died of multiple injuries. ❷ N-COUNT If one number is a **multiple** of a smaller number, it can be exactly divided by that smaller number. ❑ Their numerical system, derived from the Babylonians, was based on multiples of the number six.

multi|ple choice ADJ In a **multiple choice** test or question, you have to choose the answer that you think is right from several possible answers that are listed on the question paper. ❑ The multiple-choice questions must be answered within a strict time limit.

multi|ple scle|ro|sis N-UNCOUNT **Multiple sclerosis** is a serious disease of the nervous system, which gradually makes a person weaker, and sometimes affects their sight or speech. The abbreviation **M.S.** is also used.

multi|plex (**multiplexes** /mʌltɪplɛks/) N-COUNT A **multiplex** is a movie theater complex with several screens.

multi|pli|ca|tion /mʌltɪplɪkeɪʃᵊn/ ❶ N-UNCOUNT **Multiplication** is the process of calculating the total of one number multiplied by another. ❑ There will be simple tests in addition, subtraction, multiplication, and division. ❷ N-UNCOUNT The **multiplication** of things of a particular kind is the process or fact of them increasing in number or amount. ❑ Increasing gravity is known to speed up the multiplication of cells.

multi|pli|ca|tion sign (**multiplication signs**) N-COUNT A **multiplication sign** is the sign x which is put between two numbers to show that they are being multiplied.

multi|pli|ca|tion ta|ble (**multiplication tables**) N-COUNT A **multiplication table** is a list of the multiplications of numbers between one and twelve. Children usually have to learn multiplication tables in school.

multi|plic|ity /mʌltɪplɪsɪti/ QUANT [QUANT of pl-n] A **multiplicity** of things is a large number or a large variety of them. [FORMAL] ❑ ...a writer who uses a multiplicity of styles.

multi|pli|er /mʌltɪplaɪər/ (**multipliers**) N-COUNT When you multiply a number by another number, the second number is the **multiplier**. [TECHNICAL] ❑ Were the government to use a multiplier of five instead of three, the proportion of the population below the poverty line would rise to more than 24 percent.

multi|ply /mʌltɪplaɪ/ (**multiplies, multiplying, multiplied**) ❶ V-T/V-I When something **multiplies** or when you **multiply** it, it increases greatly in number or amount. ❑ Such disputes multiplied in the eighteenth and nineteenth centuries. ❷ V-I When animals and insects **multiply**, they increase in number by giving birth to large numbers of young. ❑ These creatures can multiply quickly. ❸ V-T If you **multiply** one number by another, you add the first number to itself as many times as is indicated by the second number. For example 2 multiplied by 3 is equal to 6. ❑ What do you get if you multiply six by nine?

multi|pur|pose /mʌltipɜrpəs/ ADJ [usu ADJ n] A **multipurpose** object can be used for several different purposes. ❑ ...a multipurpose tool that folded out to provide everything from pliers to screwdrivers to a small saw.

multi|ra|cial /mʌltireɪʃᵊl/ ADJ **Multiracial** means consisting of or involving people of many different races. ❑ We live in a multiracial society.

multi|skilled /mʌltiskɪld/ ADJ **Multiskilled** employees have a number of different skills, enabling them to do more than one kind of work. ❑ ...a more adaptable, multiskilled workforce.

multi|skill|ing /mʌltiskɪlɪŋ/ N-UNCOUNT **Multiskilling** is the practice of training employees to do a number of different tasks. ❑ He said restructuring at the station would lead to increased multiskilling among staff.

multi|story /mʌltistɔri/ also **multistoried**

in BRIT, also use **multi-storey, multistorey, multi-storeyed**

ADJ [usu ADJ n] A **multistory** building has several floors at different levels above the ground. ❑ ...the Moskovski Department Store, a vast multistory complex near the city's center. ❑ ...a multistory parking garage.

multi|task /mʌltitæsk/ (**multitasks, multitasking, multitasked**) V-I If a person or a computer **multitasks**, they do several things at the same time. • **multi|task|ing** /mʌltitæskɪŋ/ N-UNCOUNT ❑ The big advantage of multitasking is that all equipment is used most of the time. ❑ Multitasking makes us feel efficient, but it actually slows down our thinking.

multi|tude /mʌltɪtud/ (**multitudes**) ❶ QUANT [QUANT of pl-n] A **multitude of** things or people is a very large number of them. ❑ There are a multitude of small, quiet roads to cycle along. ❑ Addiction to drugs can bring a multitude of other problems. • PHRASE If you say that something covers or hides **a multitude of sins**, you mean that it hides something unattractive or does not reveal the true nature of something. ❷ N-COUNT You can refer to a very large number of people as a **multitude**. [WRITTEN] ❑ ...surrounded by a noisy multitude. ❸ N-COUNT-COLL You can refer to the great majority of people in a particular country or situation as **the multitude** or **the multitudes**. ❑ *The hideous truth was hidden from the multitude.*

multi|vita|min /mʌltivaɪtəmɪn/ (**multivitamins**) also **multi-vitamin** N-COUNT **Multivitamins** are pills that contain several different vitamins.

mum ♦◇◇ /mʌm/ (**mums**) N-FAMILY Your **mum** is your mother. [BRIT, INFORMAL]

in AM, use **mom**

mum|ble /mʌmbəl/ (**mumbles, mumbling, mumbled**) ◼ V-T/V-I If you **mumble**, you speak very quietly and not at all clearly with the result that the words are difficult to understand. ❑ *Her grandmother mumbled in her sleep.* ❑ *He mumbled a few words.* • N-COUNT **Mumble** is also a noun. ❑ *He could hear the low mumble of Navarro's voice.* ◼ → See feature box at **speak**

mum|bo jum|bo /mʌmboʊ dʒʌmboʊ/ also **mumbo-jumbo** N-UNCOUNT If you describe ideas or words, especially religious or technical ones, as **mumbo jumbo**, you mean that they are nonsense. [INFORMAL, DISAPPROVAL] ❑ *It's all full of psychoanalytic mumbo-jumbo.*

mum|mi|fy /mʌmɪfaɪ/ (**mummifies, mummifying, mummified**) V-T [usu passive] If a dead body **is mummified**, it is preserved, for example by rubbing it with special oils, and wrapping it in cloth. ❑ *In the United States, people are paying up to $150,000 to be mummified after death.* ❑ *...the mummified pharaoh.*

mum|my /mʌmi/ (**mummies**) ◼ N-COUNT A **mummy** is a dead body which was preserved long ago by being rubbed with special oils and wrapped in cloth. ❑ *...an Egyptian mummy.* ◼ N-FAMILY **Mummy** is the same as **mommy**. [BRIT, INFORMAL]

mumps /mʌmps/ N-UNCOUNT **Mumps** is a disease caught mostly by children. It causes a mild fever and painful swelling of the glands in the neck.

munch /mʌntʃ/ (**munches, munching, munched**) V-T/V-I If you **munch** food, you eat it by chewing it slowly, thoroughly, and rather noisily. ❑ *Luke munched the chicken sandwiches.* ❑ *Across the table, his son Benjie munched appreciatively.*

mun|chies /mʌntʃiz/ ◼ N-PLURAL [the N] If someone gets **the munchies**, they suddenly feel a strong desire to eat a snack or something sweet, especially when they have been taking drugs. [INFORMAL] ❑ *...an attack of the munchies.* ◼ N-PLURAL **Munchies** are small snacks. [INFORMAL] ❑ *He foraged in the refrigerator for munchies.*

mun|dane /mʌndeɪn/ ADJ Something that is **mundane** is very ordinary and not at all interesting or unusual. ❑ *Be willing to do mundane tasks with good grace.* • N-SING You can refer to mundane things as **the mundane**. ❑ *It's an attitude that turns the mundane into something more interesting and exciting.*

mu|nici|pal /mjuːnɪsɪpəl/ ADJ [ADJ n] **Municipal** means associated with or belonging to a city or town that has its own local government. ❑ *The municipal authorities gave the go-ahead for the march.* ❑ *...next month's municipal elections.*

mu|nici|pal|ity /mjuːnɪsɪpælɪti/ (**municipalities**) N-COUNT A **municipality** is a city or town that is incorporated and can elect its own government, which is also called a **municipality**.

mu|nifi|cent /mjuːnɪfɪsənt/ ADJ A **munificent** person is very generous. [FORMAL] ❑ *...one of the country's most munificent artistic benefactors.* ❑ *...a munificent donation.*

mu|ni|tions /mjuːnɪʃənz/ N-PLURAL **Munitions** are military equipment and supplies, especially bombs, shells, and guns. ❑ *...the shortage of men and munitions.*

mu|ral /mjʊərəl/ (**murals**) N-COUNT A **mural** is a picture painted on a wall. ❑ *...a mural of San Francisco Bay.*

mur|der ♦♦◇ /mɜrdər/ (**murders, murdering, murdered**) ◼ N-VAR **Murder** is the deliberate and illegal killing of a person. ❑ *The three accused, aged between 19 and 20, are charged with attempted murder.* ❑ *She refused to testify, unless the murder charge against her was dropped.* ◼ V-T To **murder** someone means to commit the crime of killing them deliberately. ❑ *...a thriller about two men who murder a third to see if they can get away with it.* ◼ PHRASE If you say that someone **gets away with murder**, you are complaining that they can do whatever they like without anyone trying to control them or punish them. [INFORMAL, DISAPPROVAL] ❑ *His charm and the fact that he is so likeable often allows him to get away with murder.*

mur|der|er /mɜrdərər/ (**murderers**) N-COUNT A **murderer** is a person who has murdered someone. ❑ *One of these men may have been the murderer.*

mur|der|ess /mɜrdərɪs/ (**murderesses**) N-COUNT A **murderess** is a woman who has murdered someone. [OLD-FASHIONED]

mur|der|ous /mɜrdərəs/ ◼ ADJ [usu ADJ n] Someone who is **murderous** is likely to murder someone and may already have murdered someone. ❑ *This murderous lunatic could kill them both without a second thought.* ◼ ADJ [usu ADJ n] A **murderous** attack or other action is very violent and intended to result in someone's death. ❑ *He made a murderous attack on his wife that evening.*

mur|der|ous|ly /mɜrdərəsli/ ADV [ADV adj, ADV with v] You use **murderously** to indicate that something is extremely unpleasant or threatening. ❑ *Beauchamp glared at her murderously.*

murk /mɜrk/ N-SING [usu the N] The **murk** is darkness, dark water, or thick mist that is very difficult to see through. ❑ *All of a sudden a tall old man in a black cloak loomed out of the murk.*

murky /mɜrki/ (**murkier, murkiest**) ◼ ADJ A **murky** place or time of day is dark and rather unpleasant because there is not enough light. ❑ *The large lamplit room was murky with wood smoke.* ◼ ADJ **Murky** water or fog is so dark and dirty that you cannot see through it. ❑ *...the deep, murky waters of Loch Ness.* ◼ ADJ If you describe something as **murky**, you mean that the details of it are not clear or that it is difficult to understand. ❑ *The law here is a little bit murky.*

mur|mur /mɜrmər/ (**murmurs, murmuring, murmured**) ◼ V-T If you **murmur** something, you say it very quietly, so that not many people can hear what you are saying. ❑ *He turned and murmured something to the professor.* ❑ *"How lovely," she murmured.* ◼ N-COUNT A **murmur** is something that is said but can hardly be heard. ❑ *They spoke in low murmurs.* ◼ N-SING A **murmur** is a continuous low sound, like the noise of a river or of voices far away. ❑ *The piano music mixes with the murmur of conversation.* • VERB **Murmur** is also a verb. ❑ *The only noise was a delightful backdrop of voices murmuring.* ◼ N-COUNT A **murmur** of a particular emotion is a quiet expression of it. ❑ *The promise of some basic working rights draws murmurs of approval.* ◼ N-COUNT A **murmur** is an abnormal sound which is made by the heart and which shows that there is probably something wrong with it. ❑ *The doctor said James had now developed a heart murmur.* ◼ PHRASE If someone does something **without a murmur**, they do it without complaining. ❑ *Then came the bill and my friend paid up without a murmur.* ◼ → See feature box at **onomatopoeia, speak**

mur|mur|ings /mɜrmərɪŋz/ N-PLURAL [usu N of n] If there are **murmurings** of, for example, approval or disapproval, people are expressing their approval or disapproval of something in a quiet way. ❑ *For some time there have been murmurings of discontent over this administration's policy on inflation.* ❑ *At this point there were murmurings of approval from the experts.*

Murphy's Law /mɜrfiz lɔ/ N-PROPER **Murphy's Law** is the idea that whatever can go wrong in a situation will go wrong.

mus|cle ♦◇◇ /mʌsəl/ (**muscles, muscling, muscled**) ◼ N-VAR A **muscle** is a piece of tissue inside your body that connects two bones and which you use when you make a movement. ❑ *Keeping your muscles strong and in tone helps you to avoid back problems.* ◼ N-UNCOUNT If you say that someone has **muscle**, you mean that they have power and influence, which enables them to do difficult things. ❑ *Eisenhower used his muscle to persuade Congress to change the law.* ◼ PHRASE If a group, organization, or country **flexes** its **muscles**, it does something to impress or frighten people, in order to show them that it has power and is considering using it. ❑ *The Fair Trade Commission has of late been flexing its muscles, cracking down on cases of corruption.* ◼ PHRASE If you say that someone did not **move a muscle**, you mean that they stayed absolutely still. ❑ *He stood without moving a muscle, unable to believe what his eyes saw so plainly.*
▶ **muscle in** PHRASAL VERB If someone **muscles in** on something, they force their way into a situation where they have no right to be and where they are not welcome, in order to gain some advantage for themselves. [DISAPPROVAL] ❑ *Cohen complained that Kravis was muscling in on his deal.*

muscle|bound /mʌsəlbaʊnd/ also **muscle-bound** ADJ If you describe someone as **musclebound**, you mean that their muscles are well developed, usually in an unattractive way. ❏ ...a musclebound Hollywood action hero.

mus|cu|lar /mʌ́skyələr/ **1** ADJ [ADJ n] **Muscular** means involving or affecting your muscles. ❏ As a general rule, all muscular effort is enhanced by breathing in as the effort is made. **2** ADJ If a person or their body is **muscular**, they are very fit and strong, and have firm muscles which are not covered with a lot of fat. ❏ Like most female athletes, she was lean and muscular.

mus|cu|lar dys|tro|phy N-UNCOUNT **Muscular dystrophy** is a serious disease in which your muscles gradually weaken.

mus|cu|la|ture /mʌ́skyʊlətʃər, -tʃʊər/ N-UNCOUNT [oft with poss] **Musculature** is used to refer to all the muscles in your body, or to a system of muscles that you use to perform a particular type of action. [FORMAL]

muse /myuz/ (muses, musing, mused) V-T/V-I If you **muse** on something, you think about it, usually saying or writing what you are thinking at the same time. [WRITTEN] ❏ Many of the papers muse on the fate of the president. ❏ "As a whole," she muses, "the 'organized church' turns me off." ● **mus|ing** (musings) N-COUNT ❏ His musings were interrupted by Montagu who came and sat down next to him.

mu|seum ✦✦◇ /myuzíəm/ (museums) N-COUNT A **museum** is a building where a large number of interesting and valuable objects, such as works of art or historical items, are kept, studied, and displayed to the public. ❏ For months Malcolm had wanted to visit the New York art museums.

mu|seum piece (museum pieces) N-COUNT If you describe an object or building as a **museum piece**, you mean that it is old and unusual. ❏ One day these are multimillion-dollar war machines and the next they are museum pieces.

mush /mʌʃ/ (mushes, mushing, mushed) **1** N-VAR [also a N] **Mush** is a thick, soft paste. ❏ Be very careful not to overcook them or they will turn to mush. **2** N-UNCOUNT If you describe something such as a movie or book as **mush**, you mean that it is very sentimental. [DISAPPROVAL] ❏ Whenever famous actresses get together to make a "woman's film" you can bet on an overload of sentimental mush. **3** V-T If you **mush** something, you make it into a mush. ❏ ...mushed-up potatoes and cauliflower.

mush|room /mʌ́ʃrum/ (mushrooms, mushrooming, mushroomed) **1** N-VAR **Mushrooms** are fungi that you can eat. They have short stems and round tops. ❏ There are many types of wild mushrooms. **2** V-I If something such as an industry or a place **mushrooms**, it grows or comes into existence very quickly. ❏ The media training industry has mushroomed over the past decade.

mush|room cloud (mushroom clouds) N-COUNT A **mushroom cloud** is an extremely large cloud caused by a nuclear explosion.

mushy /mʌ́ʃi/ **1** ADJ Vegetables and fruit that are **mushy** are soft and have lost most of their shape. ❏ When the fruit is mushy and cooked, remove from the heat. **2** ADJ If you describe someone or something as **mushy**, you mean that they are very sentimental. [DISAPPROVAL] ❏ Don't go getting all mushy and sentimental. **3** → See feature box at snow

mu|sic ✦✦✦ /myúzɪk/ N-UNCOUNT **Music** is the pattern of sounds produced by people singing or playing instruments. ❏ ...classical music. **2** N-UNCOUNT **Music** is the art of creating or performing music. ❏ He went on to study music, specializing in the clarinet. **3** N-UNCOUNT **Music** is the symbols written on paper which represent musical sounds. ❏ He's never been able to read music. **4** PHRASE If something that you hear is **music to your ears**, it makes you feel very happy. [FEELINGS] ❏ Popular support – it's music to the ears of any politician. **5** PHRASE If you **face the music**, you put yourself in a position where you will be criticized or punished for something you have done. ❏ Sooner or later, I'm going to have to face the music.

mu|si|cal ✦◇◇ /myúzɪkəl/ (musicals) **1** ADJ [ADJ n] You use **musical** to indicate that something is connected with playing or studying music. ❏ We have a wealth of musical talent in this region. ● **mu|si|cal|ly** /myúzɪkli/ ADV ❏ Musically there is a lot to enjoy. **2** N-COUNT A **musical** is a play or movie that uses singing and dancing in the story. ❏ ...the smash hit musical, Miss Saigon. **3** ADJ Someone who is **musical** has a natural ability and interest in music. ❏ I came from a musical family. **4** ADJ Sounds that are **musical** are light and pleasant to hear. ❏ He had a soft, almost musical voice.

VOCABULARY IN CONTEXT

Music

Human beings have always **made music**. From our primitive beginnings in caves to all the advanced technologies of the 21st century, performing and listening to music has consistently been part of the human condition. As children, we are soothed by the soft **notes** of a **lullaby**. While exercising, earbuds in place, we power our workout to the fast **rhythm** of **upbeat tunes**. Falling in love or falling out of love, who hasn't believed that the **lyrics** of every **ballad** were written just for them? Songs and musical **compositions** have deep associations for many of us. We hear the first **chord**, then the **melody**, and we are instantly transported back to a particular memory. If you want to reduce stress, try listening to a great **choral** piece. Allow yourself to be transported by the **harmonies** and the extraordinary power of the human voice. **Sing along**, if you wish!

mu|si|cal chairs **1** N-UNCOUNT **Musical chairs** is a game that children play at parties. They run around a row of chairs while music plays and try to sit down on one when the music stops. **2** N-UNCOUNT If you describe the situation within a particular organization or area of activity as **musical chairs**, you are critical of the fact that people in that organization or area exchange jobs or positions very often. [DISAPPROVAL] ❏ It was musical chairs. Creative people would switch jobs just to get more money.

mu|si|cal com|edy (musical comedies) N-VAR **Musical comedy** is a type of play or movie that has singing and dancing as part of the story and that is humorous and entertaining.

mu|si|cal di|rec|tor (musical directors) N-COUNT A **musical director** is the same as a **music director**.

mu|si|cal in|stru|ment (musical instruments) N-COUNT A **musical instrument** is an object such as a piano, guitar, or violin which you play in order to produce music. ❏ The drum is one of the oldest musical instruments.

mu|sic box (music boxes) N-COUNT A **music box** is a box that plays a tune when you open the lid.

mu|sic di|rec|tor (music directors) N-COUNT The **music director** of an orchestra or other group of musicians is the person who decides what they will play and where, and usually conducts them as well.

mu|sic hall [BRIT] → see vaudeville

mu|si|cian ✦◇◇ /myuzɪ́ʃən/ (musicians) N-COUNT A **musician** is a person who plays a musical instrument as their job or hobby. ❏ He was a brilliant musician.

mu|si|cian|ship /myuzɪ́ʃənʃɪp/ N-UNCOUNT **Musicianship** is the skill involved in performing music. ❏ Her musicianship is excellent.

mu|sic stand (music stands) N-COUNT A **music stand** is a device that holds pages of music in position while you play a musical instrument.

musk /mʌsk/ N-UNCOUNT **Musk** is a substance with a strong smell that is used in making perfume.

mus|ket /mʌskɪt/ (muskets) N-COUNT A **musket** was an early type of gun with a long barrel, which was used before rifles were invented.

musky /mʌski/ (muskier, muskiest) ADJ A **musky** smell is strong, warm, and sweet. ❑ *She dabbed a drop of the musky perfume behind each ear.*

Mus|lim ✦✦ /mʌzlɪm, mʊs-/ (Muslims) **1** N-COUNT A **Muslim** is someone who believes in Islam and lives according to its rules. **2** ADJ **Muslim** means relating to Islam or Muslims. ❑ *...Iran and other Muslim countries.*

mus|lin /mʌzlɪn/ (muslins) N-MASS **Muslin** is very thin, cotton cloth. ❑ *...white muslin curtains.*

muso /myuzoʊ/ (musos) **1** N-COUNT A **muso** is a musician. [INFORMAL] ❑ *...country muso Shania Twain.* **2** ADJ **Muso** means the same as **musical**. [INFORMAL] ❑ *...the Chicago muso scene.*

muss /mʌs/ (musses, mussing, mussed) V-T To **muss** something, especially someone's hair, or to **muss** it **up**, means to make it messy. [mainly AM] ❑ *He reached out and mussed my hair.* ❑ *His clothes were all mussed up.*

mus|sel /mʌsᵊl/ (mussels) N-COUNT **Mussels** are a kind of shellfish that you can eat from their shells.

must ✦✦✦ /məst, STRONG mʌst/ (musts)

The noun is pronounced /mʌst/.

Must is a modal verb. It is followed by the base form of a verb.

1 MODAL You use **must** to indicate that you think it is very important or necessary for something to happen. You use **must not** or **mustn't** to indicate that you think it is very important or necessary for something not to happen. ❑ *What you wear should be stylish and clean, and must definitely fit well.* ❑ *You are going to have to take a certain amount of criticism, but you must cope with it.* **2** MODAL You use **must** to indicate that it is necessary for something to happen, usually because of a rule or law. ❑ *Candidates must satisfy the general conditions for admission.* ❑ *Mr. Allen must pay Mr. Farnham's legal costs.* **3** MODAL You use **must** to indicate that you are fairly sure that something is the case. ❑ *At 29 Russell must be one of the youngest ever international referees.* ❑ *Claire's car wasn't there, so she must have gone to her mother's.* **4** MODAL You use **must**, or **must have** with a past participle, to indicate that you believe that something is the case, because of the available evidence. ❑ *"You must be Emma," said the visitor.* ❑ *Miss Holloway had a weak heart. She must have had a heart attack.* **5** MODAL If you say that one thing **must have** happened in order for something else to happen, you mean that it is necessary for the first thing to have happened before the second thing can happen. ❑ *In order to take that job, you must have left another job.* **6** MODAL You use **must** to express your intention to do something. ❑ *I must be getting back.* ❑ *I must telephone my parents.* **7** MODAL You use **must** to make suggestions or invitations very forcefully. ❑ *You must see a doctor, Frederick.* **8** MODAL You use **must** in remarks and comments where you are expressing sympathy. ❑ *This must be a very difficult job for you.* **9** MODAL You use **must** in conversation in expressions such as '**I must say**' and '**I must admit**' in order to emphasize a point that you are making. [EMPHASIS] ❑ *This came as a surprise, I must say.* ❑ *I must admit I like looking feminine.* **10** MODAL You use **must** in expressions such as '**it must be noted**' and '**it must be remembered**' in order to draw the reader's or listener's attention to what you are about to say. ❑ *It must be noted, however, that not all British and American officers carried out orders.* **11** MODAL You use **must** in questions to express your anger or irritation about something that someone has done, usually because you do not understand their behavior. [FEELINGS] ❑ *Why must she interrupt?* **12** MODAL You use **must** in exclamations to express surprise or shock. [EMPHASIS] ❑ *"Go! Please go."—"You must be joking!"* ❑ *I really must be quite mad!* **13** N-COUNT If you refer to something as a **must**, you mean that it is absolutely necessary. [INFORMAL] ❑ *Taking out travel insurance may seem an unnecessary expense, but it is a must.* **14** PHRASE You say '**if you must**' when you know that you cannot stop someone doing something that you think is wrong or stupid. ❑ *If you must be in the sunlight, use the strongest sunscreen you can get.* **15** PHRASE You say '**if you must know**' when you tell someone something that you did not want them to know and you want to suggest that you think they were wrong to ask you about it. ❑ *It scared the hell out of her, if you must know. And me, too.*

must- /mʌst-/ COMB IN ADJ; N-COUNT **Must-** is added to verbs such as 'see,' 'have,' or 'read' to form adjectives and nouns which describe things that you think people should see, have, or read. For example, a **must-have** is something which you think people should get, and a **must-win** game is one which a team needs to win. [INFORMAL] ❑ *...a list of must-see movies.*

mus|tache /mʌstæʃ/ (mustaches) also **moustache** N-COUNT A **mustache** is the hair that grows on someone's upper lip. If a man has a long mustache, it is sometimes referred to as his **mustaches**. ❑ *The thick beard had gone, replaced by a bushy mustache.*

mus|tachioed /məstæʃioʊd/ A **mustachioed** man has a mustache. [HUMOROUS or WRITTEN]

mus|tang /mʌstæŋ/ (mustangs) N-COUNT A **mustang** is a small, wild horse that lives on the plains of North America.

mus|tard /mʌstərd/ (mustards) **1** N-MASS **Mustard** is a yellow or brown paste usually eaten with meat. It tastes hot and spicy. ❑ *...a jar of mustard.* **2** COLOR **Mustard** is used to describe things that are brownish yellow in color. ❑ *I sat in my father's chair, a mustard-colored recliner.* **3** PHRASE If someone does not **cut the mustard**, their work or their performance is not as good as it should be or as good as it is expected to be. [INFORMAL] ❑ *He just wasn't a good student. He wasn't cutting the mustard and we let him go.*

mus|tard gas N-UNCOUNT **Mustard gas** is a gas which burns the skin and was used in war as a weapon.

mus|tard pow|der N-UNCOUNT **Mustard powder** is a yellow powder. You add hot water to it in order to make mustard.

mus|ter /mʌstər/ (musters, mustering, mustered) **1** V-T If you **muster** something such as support, strength, or energy, you gather as much of it as you can in order to do something. ❑ *He traveled around West Africa trying to muster support for his movement.* **2** V-T/V-I When soldiers **muster** or **are mustered**, they gather together in one place in order to take part in a military action. ❑ *The men mustered before their clan chiefs.*

must-have (must-haves) N-COUNT A **must-have** is something that many people want to have. ❑ *The cellular phone is now a must-have for children.* • ADJ **Must-have** is also an adjective. ❑ *...a must-have fashion accessory.*

mustn't /mʌsᵊnt/ **Mustn't** is the usual spoken form of 'must not.'

must've /mʌstəv/ **Must've** is the usual spoken form of 'must have,' especially when 'have' is an auxiliary verb.

mus|ty /mʌsti/ ADJ Something that is **musty** smells old and damp. ❑ *...that terrible musty smell.*

mu|tant /myutᵊnt/ (mutants) N-COUNT A **mutant** is an animal or plant that is physically different from others of the same species because of a change in its genes. ❑ *New species are merely mutants of earlier ones.*

mu|tate /myuteɪt/ (mutates, mutating, mutated) **1** V-T/V-I If an animal or plant **mutates**, or something **mutates** it, it develops different characteristics as the result of a change in its genes. ❑ *The virus mutates in the carrier's body.* ❑ *HIV has proven to possess an ability to mutate into drug-resistant forms.* • **mu|ta|tion** /myuteɪʃᵊn/ (mutations) N-VAR ❑ *Scientists have found a genetic mutation that appears to be the cause of Huntington's disease.* **2** V-I If something **mutates into** something different, it changes into that thing. ❑ *Overnight, the gossip begins to mutate into headlines.*

mute /myut/ (mutes, muting, muted) **1** ADJ Someone who is **mute** is silent for a particular reason and does not speak. ❑ *He was mute, distant, and indifferent.* • ADV [ADV after v] **Mute** is also an adverb. ❑ *He could watch her standing mute by the phone.* **2** ADJ Someone who is **mute** is unable to speak. [OFFENSIVE] ❑ *Marianna, the duke's daughter, became mute after a shock.* **3** V-T If someone **mutes** something such as their feelings or their activities, they reduce the strength or intensity of them. ❑ *The corruption does not seem to have muted the country's prolonged economic boom.* • **mut|ed** ADJ ❑ *The threat contrasted starkly with his administration's previous muted criticism.* **4** V-T If you **mute** a noise or sound, you lower its volume or make it less distinct.

❑ They begin to mute their voices, not be as assertive. • **mut|ed** ADJ ❑ "Yes," he muttered, his voice so muted I hardly heard his reply.

mut|ed /myutɪd/ ADJ **Muted** colors are soft and gentle, not bright and strong. ❑ ...painted in subtle, muted colors.

mu|ti|late /myutᵊleɪt/ (**mutilates, mutilating, mutilated**)
1 V-T If a person or animal **is mutilated**, their body is severely damaged, usually by someone who physically attacks them. ❑ More than 30 horses have been mutilated in the last nine months. ❑ He tortured and mutilated six young men. • **mu|ti|la|tion** /myutᵊleɪʃᵊn/ (**mutilations**) N-VAR ❑ Amnesty International chronicles cases of torture and mutilation. **2** V-T If something **is mutilated**, it is deliberately damaged or spoiled. ❑ Brecht's verdict was that his screenplay had been mutilated.

mu|ti|neer /myutᵊnɪər/ (**mutineers**) N-COUNT A **mutineer** is a person who takes part in a mutiny.

mu|ti|nous /myutᵊnəs/ ADJ If someone is **mutinous**, they are strongly dissatisfied with a person in authority and are likely to stop obeying them. ❑ His own army, stung by defeats, is mutinous.

mu|ti|ny /myutᵊni/ (**mutinies, mutinying, mutinied**) **1** N-VAR A **mutiny** is a refusal by people, usually soldiers or sailors, to continue obeying a person in authority. ❑ A series of coup attempts and mutinies within the armed forces destabilized the regime. **2** V-I If a group of people, usually soldiers or sailors, **mutiny**, they refuse to continue obeying a person in authority. ❑ Units stationed around the capital mutinied because they had received no pay for nine months.

mutt /mʌt/ (**mutts**) N-COUNT A **mutt** is the same as a **mongrel**. [INFORMAL]

mut|ter /mʌtər/ (**mutters, muttering, muttered**) **1** V-T/V-I If you **mutter**, you speak very quietly so that you cannot easily be heard, often because you are complaining about something. ❑ "God knows," she muttered, "what's happening in that madman's mind." ❑ She can hear the old woman muttering about consideration. • N-COUNT **Mutter** is also a noun. ❑ They make no more than a mutter of protest. • **mut|ter|ing** (**mutterings**) N-VAR ❑ He heard muttering from the front of the crowd. **2** → See feature box at **speak**

mut|ton /mʌtᵊn/ N-UNCOUNT **Mutton** is meat from an adult sheep that is eaten as food. ❑ ...a leg of mutton.

mu|tu|al ♦♢♢ /myutʃuəl/ **1** ADJ You use **mutual** to describe a situation, feeling, or action that is experienced, felt, or done by both of two people mentioned. ❑ The East and the West can work together for their mutual benefit and progress. • **mu|tu|al|ly** ADV ❑ Attempts to reach a mutually agreed solution had been fruitless. **2** → see **exclusive** **3** ADJ You use **mutual** to describe something such as an interest which two or more people share. ❑ They do, however, share a mutual interest in design. **4** ADJ [ADJ n] If an insurance company or savings bank has **mutual** status, it is not owned by shareholders but by its customers, who receive a share of the profits. [BUSINESS] ❑ ...a mutual company based in Columbus, Ohio.

---- SYNONYMS ----

mutual
ADJ **1**
common: Moldavians and Romanians share a common language.
joint: Jackie and Ben came to a joint decision as to where they would live.
reciprocal: They expected a reciprocal gesture before more hostages could be freed.

---

mu|tu|al fund (**mutual funds**) N-COUNT A **mutual fund** is an organization which invests money in many different kinds of business and which offers units for sale to the public as an investment. [AM, BUSINESS]

in BRIT, use **unit trust**

Mu|zak /myuzæk/ also **muzak** **1** N-UNCOUNT **Muzak** is recorded music that is played as background music in stores or restaurants. [TRADEMARK] **2** N-UNCOUNT If you describe music as **muzak**, you dislike it because you think it is dull or unnecessary. [DISAPPROVAL]

muz|zle /mʌzᵊl/ (**muzzles, muzzling, muzzled**) **1** N-COUNT The **muzzle** of an animal such as a dog is its nose and mouth. ❑ The mongrel presented his muzzle for scratching. **2** N-COUNT A **muzzle** is an object that is put over a dog's nose and mouth so that it cannot bite people or make a noise. ❑ ...dogs like pit bulls, which have to wear a muzzle. **3** V-T If you **muzzle** a dog or other animal, you put a muzzle over its nose and mouth. ❑ He was convicted of failing to muzzle a pit bull. **4** V-T If you say that someone **is muzzled**, you are complaining that they are prevented from expressing their views freely. [DISAPPROVAL] ❑ He complained of being muzzled by the chairman. **5** N-COUNT The **muzzle** of a gun is the end where the bullets come out when it is fired. ❑ Mickey felt the muzzle of a rifle press hard against his neck.

MVP /ɛm vi pi/ (**MVPs**) N-COUNT [oft N n] The **MVP** is the player on a sports team who has performed best in a particular game or series of games. **MVP** is an abbreviation for 'most valuable player.' [AM] ❑ Brondello secured the MVP award by scoring 357 points.

MW **MW** is a written abbreviation for **megawatt**.

my ♦♦♦ /maɪ/

My is the first person singular possessive determiner.

1 DET A speaker or writer uses **my** to indicate that something belongs or relates to himself or herself. ❑ I invited him back to my apartment for coffee. **2** DET In conversations or in letters, **my** is used in front of a word like 'dear' or 'darling' to show affection. [FEELINGS] ❑ My sweet Freda. **3** DET **My** is used in phrases such as '**My God**' and '**My goodness**' to express surprise or shock. [SPOKEN, FEELINGS] ❑ My God, I've never seen you so nervous.

myo|pia /maɪoʊpiə/ N-UNCOUNT **Myopia** is the inability to see things properly when they are far away, because there is something wrong with your eyes. [FORMAL]

my|op|ic /maɪɒpɪk/ **1** ADJ If you describe someone as **myopic**, you are critical of them because they seem unable to realize that their actions might have negative consequences. [DISAPPROVAL] ❑ The government still has a myopic attitude to spending. **2** ADJ If someone is **myopic**, they are unable to see things that are far away from them. [FORMAL]

myr|iad /mɪriəd/ **1** QUANT [QUANT of pl-n] A **myriad** or **myriads** of people or things is a very large number or great variety of them. ❑ They face a myriad of problems bringing up children. **2** ADJ [ADJ n] **Myriad** means having a large number or great variety. ❑ The magazine has been celebrating pop in all its myriad forms.

my|self ♦♦♢ /maɪsɛlf/

Myself is the first person singular reflexive pronoun.

1 PRON-REFL [v PRON, prep PRON] A speaker or writer uses **myself** to refer to himself or herself. **Myself** is used as the object of a verb or preposition when the subject refers to the same person. ❑ I asked myself what I would have done in such a situation. **2** PRON-REFL-EMPH You use **myself** to emphasize a first person singular subject. In more formal English, **myself** is sometimes used instead of 'me' as the object of a verb or preposition, for emphasis. [EMPHASIS] ❑ I myself enjoy movies, poetry, eating out, and long walks. **3** PRON-REFL-EMPH If you say something such as 'I did it **myself**,' you are emphasizing that you did it, rather than anyone else. [EMPHASIS] ❑ "Where did you get that embroidery?"—"I made it myself."

---- USAGE ----

me or **myself?**
Don't use 'me' when the person who is speaking is both the subject and the object of the verb. Don't say, for example, '~~I got me a drink~~.' Say 'I got **myself** a drink.' I made **myself** some breakfast.

---

mys|teri|ous /mɪstɪəriəs/ **1** ADJ Someone or something that is **mysterious** is strange and is not known about or understood. ❑ He died in mysterious circumstances. ❑ A mysterious illness confined him to bed for over a month. • **mys|teri|ous|ly** ADV ❑ A couple of messages had mysteriously disappeared. **2** ADJ [v-link ADJ] If someone is **mysterious** about something, they deliberately do not talk much about it, sometimes because they want to make people more interested in it. ❑ As for his job – well, he was very mysterious about it. • **mys|teri|ous|ly** ADV [ADV after v] ❑ Asked what she meant, she said mysteriously: "Work it out for yourself."

mys|tery ♦♢♢ /mɪstəri, mɪstri/ (**mysteries**) **1** N-COUNT A **mystery** is something that is not understood or known about.

❑ *The source of the gunshots still remains a mystery.* ▢ N-UNCOUNT If you talk about the **mystery** of someone or something, you are talking about how difficult they are to understand or know about, especially when this gives them a rather strange or magical quality. ❑ *She's a lady of mystery.* ▢ ADJ [ADJ n] A **mystery** person or thing is one whose identity or nature is not known. ❑ *The mystery hero immediately alerted police after spotting a bomb.* ▢ N-COUNT A **mystery** is a story in which strange things happen that are not explained until the end. ❑ *His fourth novel is a murder mystery set in London.*

SYNONYMS

mystery
NOUN ▢
puzzle: *She was a puzzle – no one knew or understood her properly.*
riddle: *Scientists claimed yesterday to have solved the riddle of the birth of the Universe.*
enigma: *He was an enigma – his feelings hidden behind a wall of distrust.*
conundrum: *...this theological conundrum of the existence of evil and suffering in a world created by a good God.*

---

mys|tic /mɪstɪk/ (**mystics**) ▢ N-COUNT A **mystic** is a person who practices or believes in religious mysticism. ❑ *...an Indian mystic known as Bhagwan Shree Rajneesh.* ▢ ADJ [ADJ n] **Mystic** means the same as **mystical**. ❑ *...mystic union with God.*

mys|ti|cal /mɪstɪkəl/ ADJ Something that is **mystical** involves spiritual powers and influences that most people do not understand. ❑ *That was clearly a deep mystical experience.*

mys|ti|cism /mɪstɪsɪzəm/ N-UNCOUNT **Mysticism** is a religious practice in which people search for truth, knowledge, and closeness to God through meditation and prayer. ❑ *As a younger man Harrison was intrigued by Indian mysticism.*

mys|ti|fy /mɪstɪfaɪ/ (**mystifies, mystifying, mystified**) V-T If you **are mystified** by something, you find it impossible to explain or understand. ❑ *The audience must have been totally mystified by the plot.* • **mys|ti|fy|ing** ADJ ❑ *I find your attitude a little mystifying, Marilyn.*

mys|tique /mɪstiːk/ N-SING; N-UNCOUNT If there is a **mystique** about someone or something, they are thought to be special and people do not know much about them. ❑ *His book destroyed the mystique of monarchy.*

myth ✦◇◇ /mɪθ/ (**myths**) ▢ N-VAR A **myth** is a well-known story which was made up in the past to explain natural events or to justify religious beliefs or social customs. ❑ *There is a famous Greek myth in which Icarus flew too near to the Sun.* ▢ N-VAR If you describe a belief or explanation as a **myth**, you mean that many people believe it but it is actually untrue. ❑ *Contrary to the popular myth, women are not reckless spendthrifts.*

myth|ic /mɪθɪk/ ▢ ADJ [usu ADJ n] Someone or something that is **mythic** exists only in myths and is therefore imaginary. [LITERARY] ❑ *...the mythic figure of King Arthur.* ▢ ADJ [usu ADJ n] If you describe someone or something as **mythic**, you mean that they have become very famous or important. ❑ *...a team whose reputation has achieved mythic proportions.*

mythi|cal /mɪθɪkəl/ ▢ ADJ Something or someone that is **mythical** exists only in myths and is therefore imaginary. ❑ *...the Hydra, the mythical beast that had seven or more heads.* ▢ ADJ If you describe something as **mythical**, you mean that it is untrue or does not exist. ❑ *...the American West, not the mythical, romanticized West of cowboys and gunslingers, but the real West.*

my|thol|ogy /mɪθɒlədʒi/ (**mythologies**) ▢ N-VAR **Mythology** is a group of myths, especially all the myths from a particular country, religion, or culture. ❑ *In Greek mythology, the god Zeus took the form of a swan to seduce Leda.* • **mytho|logi|cal** /mɪθəlɒdʒɪkəl/ ADJ ❑ *...the mythological beast that was part lion and part goat.* ▢ N-VAR You can use **mythology** to refer to the beliefs or opinions that people have about something, when you think that they are false or untrue. ❑ *Altman strips away the pretense and mythology to expose the film industry as a business like any other, dedicated to the pursuit of profit.*

Nn

N also **n** /ɛn/ (**N's, n's**) N-VAR **N** is the fourteenth letter of the English alphabet.

'n' /ən/ CONJ The word 'and' is sometimes written as **'n'** between certain pairs of words, as in 'rock 'n' roll.' [INFORMAL] ❑ ...a country 'n' western song.

NA also **n/a** CONVENTION **NA** is a written abbreviation for **not applicable** or **not available**.

naan /nɑn/ (**naans**) also **nan** N-VAR **Naan** or **naan bread** is a type of bread that comes in a large, round, flat piece and is usually eaten with Indian food.

nab /næb/ (**nabs, nabbing, nabbed**) V-T If people in authority such as the police **nab** someone who they think has done something wrong, they catch them or arrest them. [INFORMAL] ❑ He killed 12 people before the authorities finally nabbed him. ❑ Soon he was back in the armed robbery business. Again, he got nabbed.

na|cho /nætʃoʊ/ (**nachos**) N-COUNT [usu pl] **Nachos** are a snack, originally from Mexico, consisting of pieces of tortilla, usually with a topping of cheese, salsa, and peppers. ❑ ...a plate of nachos.

na|dir /neɪdər/ ◼ N-SING [usu with poss] The **nadir** of something such as someone's career or the history of an organization is its worst time. [LITERARY] ❑ 1945 to 1946 was the nadir of Truman's presidency. ◼ N-SING [the N] In astronomy, **the nadir** is the point at which the sun or moon is directly below you, on the other side of the earth. [TECHNICAL]

nag /næg/ (**nags, nagging, nagged**) ◼ V-T/V-I If someone **nags** you, or if they **nag**, they keep asking you to do something you have not done yet or do not want to do. [DISAPPROVAL] ❑ The more Sarah nagged her, the more stubborn Cissie became. ❑ My boyfriend nagged me to cut my hair. • N-COUNT A **nag** is someone who nags. ❑ Aunt Molly is a nag about regular meals. • **nag|ging** N-UNCOUNT ❑ I gave up smoking a year ago after constant nagging from my kids. ◼ V-T/V-I If something such as a doubt or worry **nags** at you, or **nags** you, it keeps worrying you. ❑ He could be wrong about her. The feeling nagged at him. ❑ ...the anxiety that had nagged Amy all through lunch.

nag|ging /nægɪŋ/ ◼ ADJ [ADJ n] A **nagging** pain is not very severe but is difficult to cure. ❑ He complained of a nagging pain between his shoulder blades. ◼ → see also **nag**

nail /neɪl/ (**nails, nailing, nailed**) ◼ N-COUNT A **nail** is a thin piece of metal with one pointed end and one flat end. You hit the flat end with a hammer in order to push the nail into something such as a wall. ❑ A mirror hung on a nail above the sink. ◼ V-T If you **nail** something somewhere, you fasten it there using one or more nails. ❑ Frank put the first plank down and nailed it in place. ❑ They nail shut the front door. ◼ N-COUNT Your **nails** are the thin hard parts that grow at the ends of your fingers and toes. ❑ Keep your nails short and your hands clean. ◼ V-T To **nail** someone means to catch them and prove that they have been breaking the law. [INFORMAL] ❑ The prosecution still managed to nail him for robberies at the homes of leading industrialists. ◼ PHRASE If you say that someone **has hit the nail on the head**, you think they are exactly right about something. ❑ "I think it would help if they had decent conditions." —"I think you've hit the nail on the head." ◼ → See also color supplement

▶ **nail down** ◼ PHRASAL VERB If you **nail down** something unknown or uncertain, you find out exactly what it is. ❑ It would be useful if you could nail down the source of this tension. ◼ PHRASAL VERB If you **nail down** an agreement, you manage to reach a firm agreement with a definite result. ❑ The Secretary of State and his Russian counterpart met to try to nail down the elusive accord.

nail-biting ADJ If you describe something such as a story or a game as **nail-biting**, you mean that it makes you feel very excited or nervous because you do not know how it is going to end. ❑ ...the nail-biting legal thriller, "The Pelican Brief."

nail bomb (**nail bombs**) N-COUNT A **nail bomb** is a bomb which contains nails that are intended to cause a lot of damage and injury when the bomb goes off.

nail brush (**nail brushes**) also **nailbrush** N-COUNT A **nail brush** is a small brush that you use to clean your nails when washing your hands.

nail file (**nail files**) N-COUNT A **nail file** is a small strip of rough metal or cardboard that you rub across the ends of your nails to shorten them or shape them.

nail pol|ish (**nail polishes**) N-MASS **Nail polish** is a thick liquid that is used to decorate your fingernails or toenails.

nail scis|sors N-PLURAL [also a pair of N] **Nail scissors** are small scissors that you use for cutting your nails. ❑ Mishka got some nail scissors and started carefully trimming his fingernails.

nail var|nish (**nail varnishes**) N-MASS **Nail varnish** is the same as **nail polish**. [BRIT]

na|ive /nɑːiːv/ also **naïve** ADJ If you describe someone as **naive**, you think they lack experience and so expect things to be easy or people to be honest or kind. ❑ It's naive to think that teachers are always tolerant. ❑ Their view was that he had been politically naive. • **na|ive|ly** ADV ❑ ...naively applying Western solutions to Eastern problems. • **na|ive|ty** /nɑːiːvɪti/ N-UNCOUNT ❑ I was alarmed by his naivety and ignorance of international affairs.

na|ked /neɪkɪd/ ◼ ADJ Someone who is **naked** is not wearing any clothes. ❑ Kate throws a kimono over her naked body. ❑ They stripped me naked. • **na|ked|ness** N-UNCOUNT ❑ He had pulled the blanket over his body to hide his nakedness. ◼ ADJ If an animal or part of an animal is **naked**, it has no fur or feathers on it. ❑ The nest contained eight little mice that were naked and blind. ◼ ADJ You can describe an object as **naked** when it does not have its normal covering. ❑ ...a naked bulb dangling in a bare room. ◼ ADJ [ADJ n] You can use **naked** to describe unpleasant or violent actions and behavior which are not disguised or hidden in any way. [JOURNALISM] ❑ Naked aggression and an attempt to change frontiers by force could not go unchallenged. ❑ ...violence and the naked pursuit of power.

name ♦♦♦ /neɪm/ (**names, naming, named**) ◼ N-COUNT The **name** of a person, place, or thing is the word or group of words that is used to identify them. ❑ "What's his name?"— "Peter." ❑ I don't even know if Sullivan's his real name. ◼ V-T When you **name** someone or something, you give them a name, usually at the beginning of their life. ❑ My mother insisted on naming me Horace. ❑ ...a man named John T. Benson. ◼ V-T If you **name** someone or something after another person or thing, you give them the same name as that person or thing. ❑ Why haven't you named any of your sons after yourself? ◼ V-T If you **name** someone, you identify them by stating their name. ❑ It's nearly thirty years since a journalist was jailed for refusing to name a source. ◼ V-T If you **name** something such as a price, time, or place, you say what you want it to be. ❑ Call Marty, tell him to name his price. ◼ V-T If you **name** the person for a particular job, you say who you want to have the job. ❑ The CEO has named a new chief financial officer. ❑ When the chairman retired, I was named as his successor. ◼ N-COUNT You can refer to the reputation of a person or thing as their **name**. ❑ *He had a name for good judgement*. **8** N-COUNT You can refer to someone as, for example, a famous **name** or a great **name** when they are well known. [JOURNALISM] ❑ *...some of the most famous names in modeling and show business*. **9** → see also **brand name**, **Christian name**, **first name**, **maiden name 10** PHRASE If something is **in** someone's **name**, it officially belongs to them or is reserved for them. ❑ *The house is in my husband's name*. **11** PHRASE If someone does something **in the name of** a group of people, they do it as the representative of that group. ❑ *In the United States the majority governs in the name of the people*. **12** PHRASE If you do something **in the name of** an ideal or an abstract thing, you do it in order to preserve or promote that thing. ❑ *...one of those rare occasions in history when a political leader risked his own power in the name of the greater public good*. **13** PHRASE When you mention someone or something **by name**, or address someone **by name**, you use their name. ❑ *When he walks down 131st street, he greets most people he sees by name*. **14** PHRASE You can use **by name** or **by the name of** when you are saying what someone is called. [FORMAL] ❑ *In 1911 he met up with a young Australian by the name of Harry Busteed*. **15** PHRASE If someone **calls** you **names**, they insult you by saying unpleasant things to you or about you. ❑ *At my last school they called me names because I was so slow*. **16** PHRASE If you **make a name for** yourself or **make** your **name** as something, you become well known for that thing. ❑ *She was beginning to make a name for herself as a portrait photographer*.

name|check /neɪmtʃɛk/ (**namechecks, namechecking, namechecked**) also **name-check** N-COUNT If someone gets a **namecheck** in something such as an article or interview, their name is mentioned in it. ❑ *She has had many credits and name-checks in American Vogue*. • VERB **Namecheck** is also a verb. ❑ *Several bands have namechecked him in interviews*.

name-drop (**name-drops, name-dropping, name-dropped**) V-I If you say that someone **name-drops**, you disapprove of them referring to famous people they have met in order to impress people. [DISAPPROVAL] ❑ *He doesn't like to name-drop, but he has made a guitar for Jackson Browne*. • **name-dropping** N-UNCOUNT ❑ *He is a master at name-dropping and meaningless Hollywood double-talk*.

name|less /neɪmlɪs/ **1** ADJ [usu ADJ n] You describe people or things as **nameless** when you do not know their name or when they do not have a name. ❑ *They can have their cases rejected, without reasons being given, by nameless officials*. **2** ADJ [v-link ADJ] If you say that someone or something will remain **nameless**, you mean that you will not mention their name, often because you do not want to embarrass them. ❑ *A local friend who will remain nameless warned me that I was in for trouble soon*.

name|ly /neɪmli/ ADV You use **namely** to introduce detailed information about the subject you are discussing, or a particular aspect of it. ❑ *A district should serve its clientele, namely students, staff, and parents*.

name|plate /neɪmpleɪt/ (**nameplates**) N-COUNT A **nameplate** is a sign on a door, wall, or desk which shows the name of the person or organization that occupies a particular place.

name|sake /neɪmseɪk/ (**namesakes**) N-COUNT [usu poss N] Someone's or something's **namesake** has the same name as they do. [WRITTEN] ❑ *He is putting together a four-man team, including his son and namesake Tony O'Reilly Jr*. ❑ *The town of Breckenridge and its namesake ski area could prosper under the plan*.

nan|dro|lone /nændrəloʊn/ N-UNCOUNT **Nandrolone** is a type of drug that can improve performance in sports and is used illegally by some athletes.

nan|ny /næni/ (**nannies**) N-COUNT A **nanny** is a person who is paid by parents to take care of their child or children.

nan|ny|ing /næniɪŋ/ N-UNCOUNT **Nannying** is the job of being a nanny. ❑ *...low-paid jobs such as nannying*.

PREFIX

nano-
nouns and adjectives that refer to something that is so small that it can only be seen with a powerful microscope. For example, **nano-sized** particles are extremely small.

---

nano|tech|nol|ogy /næno͡ʊtɛknɒlədʒi, nɛno͡ʊ-/ N-UNCOUNT **Nanotechnology** is the science of making or working with things that are so small that they can only be seen using a powerful microscope.

nap /næp/ (**naps, napping, napped**) **1** N-COUNT If you take or have a **nap**, you have a short sleep, usually during the day. ❑ *I might take a little nap*. **2** V-I If you **nap**, you sleep for a short period of time, usually during the day. ❑ *An elderly person may nap during the day and then sleep only five hours a night*. **3** PHRASE If someone **is caught napping**, something happens when they are not prepared for it, although they should have been. [INFORMAL] ❑ *The security services were clearly caught napping*.

na|palm /neɪpɑːm/ (**napalms, napalming, napalmed**) **1** N-UNCOUNT **Napalm** is a substance containing gasoline which is used to make bombs that burn people, buildings, and plants. ❑ *The government has consistently denied using napalm*. **2** V-T If people **napalm** other people or places, they attack and burn them using napalm. ❑ *Why napalm a village now?*

nape /neɪp/ (**napes**) N-COUNT [usu sing, usu the N of n] The **nape** of your neck is the back of it. ❑ *...the way that his hair grew at the nape of his neck*.

nap|kin /næpkɪn/ (**napkins**) N-COUNT A **napkin** is a square of cloth or paper that you use when you are eating to protect your clothes, or to wipe your mouth or hands. ❑ *...taking tiny bites of a hot dog and daintily wiping my lips with a napkin*.

nap|kin ring (**napkin rings**) N-COUNT A **napkin ring** is a ring-shaped object which is used to hold a rolled-up napkin.

nap|py /næpi/ (**nappies**) N-COUNT A **nappy** is a piece of soft thick cloth or paper which is fastened around a baby's bottom in order to soak up its urine and feces. [BRIT]

in AM, use **diaper**

nar|ci|si /nɑːrsɪsaɪ/ **Narcissi** is a plural form of **narcissus**.

nar|ci|sism /nɑːrsɪsɪzəm/ N-UNCOUNT **Narcissism** is the habit of always thinking about yourself and admiring yourself. [FORMAL, DISAPPROVAL] ❑ *Those who suffer from narcissism become self-absorbed or chronic show-offs*.

nar|cis|sis|tic /nɑːrsɪsɪstɪk/ ADJ If you describe someone as **narcissistic**, you disapprove of them because they think about themselves a lot and admire themselves too much. [FORMAL, DISAPPROVAL] ❑ *He was insufferable at times – self-centred and narcissistic*.

nar|cis|sus /nɑːrsɪsəs/ (**narcissi** or **narcissus**) N-COUNT [usu pl] **Narcissi** are plants that appear in the spring and have yellow or white flowers with cone-shaped centers.

PREFIX

narco-
is added to words to form new words that relate to illegal narcotics. For example, **narco-trafficking** is the buying and selling of illegal drugs.

---

nar|co|lep|sy /nɑːrkəlɛpsi/ N-UNCOUNT **Narcolepsy** is a rare medical condition. It causes people who suffer from it to fall into a deep sleep at any time without any warning.

nar|cot|ic /nɑːrkɒtɪk/ (**narcotics**) **1** N-COUNT **Narcotics** are drugs such as opium or heroin which make you sleepy and stop you from feeling pain. You can also use **narcotics** to mean any kind of illegal drugs. ❑ *He was indicted for dealing in narcotics*. **2** ADJ If something, especially a drug, has a **narcotic** effect, it makes the person who uses it feel sleepy. ❑ *...hormones that have a narcotic effect on the immune system*.

nar|rate /næreɪt/ (**narrates, narrating, narrated**) **1** V-T If you **narrate** a story, you tell it from your own point of view. [FORMAL] ❑ *The three of them narrate the same events from three perspectives*. • **nar|ra|tion** /nəreɪʃən/ N-UNCOUNT ❑ *Its story-within-a-story method of narration is confusing*. • **nar|ra|tor** /næreɪtər/ (**narrators**) N-COUNT ❑ *Jules, the story's narrator, is an actress in her late thirties*. **2** V-T The person who **narrates** a film or program speaks the words which accompany the pictures, but does not appear in it. ❑ *She also narrated a documentary about the Kirov Ballet School*. • **nar|ra|tion** N-UNCOUNT ❑ *As soon as the crew gets back from lunch, we can put your narration on it right away*. • **nar|ra|tor** N-COUNT ❑ *...the narrator of the documentary*.

nar|ra|tive /nærətɪv/ (**narratives**) **1** N-COUNT A **narrative** is a story or an account of a series of events. ❑ *...a fast-moving narrative*. **2** N-UNCOUNT **Narrative** is the description of a series of events, usually in a novel. ❑ *Neither author was very strong on narrative*. **3** → See feature box at **book**

nar|row /nǽroʊ/ (narrower, narrowest, narrows, narrowing, narrowed) **1** ADJ Something that is **narrow** measures a very small distance from one side to the other, especially compared to its length or height. ❏ ...through the town's narrow streets. ❏ She had long, narrow feet. • **nar|row|ness** N-UNCOUNT ❏ ...the narrowness of the river mouth. **2** V-I If something **narrows**, it becomes less wide. ❏ The wide track narrows before crossing another stream. **3** V-T/V-I If your eyes **narrow** or if you **narrow** your eyes, you almost close them, for example because you are angry or because you are trying to concentrate on something. [WRITTEN] ❏ Coggins' eyes narrowed angrily. "You think I'd tell you?" **4** ADJ If you describe someone's ideas, attitudes, or beliefs as **narrow**, you disapprove of them because they are restricted in some way, and often ignore the more important aspects of an argument or situation. [DISAPPROVAL] ❏ ...a narrow and outdated view of family life. • **nar|row|ly** ADV ❏ They may define their contribution too narrowly. • **nar|row|ness** N-UNCOUNT ❏ ...the narrowness of their mental and spiritual outlook. **5** V-T/V-I If something **narrows** or if you **narrow** it, its extent or range becomes smaller. ❏ Most recent opinion polls suggest that the gap between the two main parties has narrowed. • **nar|row|ing** N-SING ❏ ...a narrowing of the gap between rich members and poor. **6** ADJ If you have a **narrow** victory, you succeed in winning but only by a small amount. ❏ Voters approved the plan by a narrow majority. • **nar|row|ly** ADV ❏ She narrowly failed to win enough votes. • **nar|row|ness** N-UNCOUNT ❏ The narrowness of the victory reflected deep division within the party. **7** ADJ [ADJ n] If you have a **narrow** escape, something unpleasant nearly happens to you. ❏ Two police officers had a narrow escape when rioters attacked their vehicles. • **nar|row|ly** ADV [ADV with v] ❏ Five firemen narrowly escaped death when a staircase collapsed beneath their feet.
▶ **narrow down** PHRASAL VERB If you **narrow down** a range of things, you reduce the number of things included in it. ❏ What's happened is that the new results narrow down the possibilities.

SYNONYMS

narrow
ADJ **1**
thin: A thin cable carries the signal to a computer.
fine: The heat scorched the fine hairs on her arms.
slender: He gazed at her slender neck.

nar|row|ly /nǽroʊli/ **1** ADV [ADV after v] If you look at someone **narrowly**, you look at them in a concentrated way, often because you think they are not giving you full information about something. ❏ He grimaced and looked narrowly at his colleague. **2** → see also **narrow**

narrow-minded ADJ If you describe someone as **narrow-minded**, you are criticizing them because they are unwilling to consider new ideas or other people's opinions. [DISAPPROVAL] ❏ ...a narrow-minded bigot.

NASA /nǽsə/ N-PROPER **NASA** is a U.S. government organization concerned with spacecraft and space travel. **NASA** is an abbreviation for 'National Aeronautics and Space Administration.'

na|sal /neɪzᵊl/ **1** ADJ [ADJ n] **Nasal** is used to describe things relating to the nose and the functions it performs. ❏ ...inflamed nasal passages. **2** ADJ If someone's voice is **nasal**, it sounds as if air is passing through their nose as well as their mouth while they are speaking. ❏ Her voice was nasal and penetrating. **3** → See also color supplement

NASCAR /nǽskɑr/ N-PROPER In the United States, **NASCAR** racing is motor racing that involves old cars which often crash into one another. **NASCAR** is an abbreviation for 'National Association for Stock Car Auto Racing.' ❏ ...NASCAR's longest and fastest track ❏ ...a NASCAR race.

nas|cent /nǽsᵊnt/ ADJ [ADJ n] **Nascent** things or processes are just beginning, and are expected to become stronger or to grow bigger. [FORMAL] ❏ ...the country's nascent democracy ❏ ...the still nascent science of psychology.

na|stur|tium /nǽstɜrʃəm/ (nasturtiums) N-COUNT **Nasturtiums** are low plants with large round leaves and orange, red, and yellow flowers.

nas|ty /nǽsti/ (nastier, nastiest) **1** ADJ Something that is **nasty** is very unpleasant to see, experience, or feel. ❏ ...an extremely nasty murder. • **nas|ti|ness** N-UNCOUNT ❏ ...the nastiness of war. **2** ADJ If you describe a person or their behavior as **nasty**, you mean that they behave in an unkind and unpleasant way. ❏ What nasty little snobs you all are. ❏ The guards looked really nasty. • **nas|ti|ly** ADV [ADV after v] ❏ She took the money and eyed me nastily. • **nas|ti|ness** N-UNCOUNT ❏ As the years went by his nastiness began to annoy his readers. **3** ADJ If you describe something as **nasty**, you mean it is unattractive, undesirable, or in bad taste. ❏ They should put warning labels on those nasty little devices. **4** ADJ A **nasty** problem or situation is very worrisome and difficult to deal with. ❏ A spokesman said this firm action had defused a very nasty situation. **5** ADJ If you describe an injury or a disease as **nasty**, you mean that it is serious or looks unpleasant. ❏ My little granddaughter caught her heel in the spokes of her bicycle – it was a very nasty wound.

natch /nǽtʃ/ ADV [ADV with cl/group] **Natch** is used to indicate that a particular fact or event is what you would expect and not at all surprising. [mainly JOURNALISM, INFORMAL] ❏ ...a bizarre, dreamy (but sarcastic, natch) ballad. ❏ Ina is a bad girl so, natch, ends up in prison.

na|tion /neɪʃᵊn/ (nations) **1** N-COUNT A **nation** is an individual country considered together with its social and political structures. ❏ Such policies would require unprecedented cooperation between nations. **2** N-SING The **nation** is sometimes used to refer to all the people who live in a particular country, or all the people who belong to a particular ethnic group. [JOURNALISM] ❏ It was a story that touched the nation's heart. ❏ ...the former chief of the Cherokee nation.

COLLOCATIONS

nation
NOUN
1
noun + **nation**: eurozone, member, sovereign; host; island
adjective + **nation**: developing, industrial, populous, rich; African, Arab, European, Western
verb + **nation**: lead, represent
2
adjective + **nation**: entire, whole
verb + **nation**: divide, unite; grip, shock

SYNONYMS

nation
NOUN **1**
country: ... the fifth most populous country in the world.
state: Mexico is a secular state.
kingdom: The kingdom's power declined.
land: ...this land of free speech.

na|tion|al /nǽʃᵊnᵊl/ (nationals) **1** ADJ **National** means relating to the whole of a country or nation rather than to part of it or to other nations. ❏ ...major national and international issues. • **na|tion|al|ly** ADV ❏ ...a nationally televised speech. **2** ADJ [ADJ n] **National** means typical of the people or customs of a particular country or nation. ❏ ...the national characteristics and history of the country. **3** N-COUNT You can refer to someone who is legally a citizen of a country as a **national** of that country. ❏ ...a Sri-Lankan national. **4** → See feature box at **press**

na|tion|al an|them (national anthems) N-COUNT [usu sing] A **national anthem** is a nation's official song which is played or sung on public occasions.

na|tion|al debt (national debts) N-COUNT [usu sing] A country's **national debt** is all the money that the government of the country has borrowed and still owes. ❏ He talked about the importance of reducing the national debt. ❏ No wonder then that the national debts of so many countries are reaching astronomical proportions.

Na|tion|al Guard (National Guards) N-COUNT [usu the N] In the United States, the **National Guard** is a military force within an individual state, which can be sent on a mission by either the state or national government if there is an emergency. ❏ ...the leader of the Arkansas National Guard

Na|tion|al Guards|man (National Guardsmen) N-COUNT A **National Guardsman** is a male member of the National Guard.

Na|tion|al Guards|woman (National Guardswomen) N-COUNT A **National Guardswoman** is a female member of the National Guard.

na|tion|al holi|day (national holidays) N-COUNT A **national holiday** is a day when people do not go to work or school because of a religious or national festival. ❑ *Today is a national holiday in Japan. It is Sports Day.*

na|tion|al|ism /næʃənəlɪzəm/ **1** N-UNCOUNT You can refer to a person's great love for their nation as **nationalism**. It is often associated with the belief that a particular nation is better than any other nation, and in this case is often used showing disapproval. ❑ *This kind of fierce nationalism is a powerful and potentially volatile force.* **2** N-UNCOUNT **Nationalism** is the desire for political independence of people who feel they are historically or culturally a separate group within a country. ❑ *The rising tide of nationalism may also help the party to win representation in parliament.*

na|tion|al|ist ♦⃝⃝ /næʃənəlɪst/ (nationalists) **1** ADJ [ADJ n] **Nationalist** means connected with the desire of a group of people within a country for political independence. ❑ *The crisis has set off a wave of nationalist feelings in Quebec.* • N-COUNT A **nationalist** is someone with nationalist views. ❑ *...demands by nationalists for an independent state.* **2** ADJ [ADJ n] **Nationalist** means connected with a person's great love for their nation. It is often associated with the belief that her nation is better than any other nation, and in this case is often used showing disapproval. ❑ *Political life has been infected by growing nationalist sentiment.* • N-COUNT A **nationalist** is someone with nationalist views. ❑ *The parliament is composed mainly of extreme nationalists.*

na|tion|al|is|tic /næʃənəlɪstɪk/ ADJ If you describe someone as **nationalistic**, you mean they are very proud of their nation. They also often believe that their nation is better than any other nation, and in this case it is often used showing disapproval. ❑ *Nationalistic fervor is running high.*

na|tion|al|ity /næʃənælɪti/ (nationalities) **1** N-VAR If you have the **nationality** of a particular country, you were born there or have the legal right to be a citizen. ❑ *Asked his nationality, he said American.* **2** N-COUNT You can refer to people who have the same racial origins as a **nationality**, especially when they do not have their own independent country. ❑ *...the many nationalities that comprise Ethiopia.*

na|tion|al|ize /næʃənəlaɪz/ (nationalizes, nationalizing, nationalized)

in BRIT, also use **nationalise**

V-T If a government **nationalizes** a private company or industry, that company or industry becomes owned by the state and controlled by the government. [BUSINESS] ❑ *...a proposal to inject federal money directly into certain banks, in effect partially nationalizing the banking system.* • **na|tion|ali|za|tion** /næʃənəlaɪzeɪʃən/ N-UNCOUNT ❑ *...the campaign for the nationalization of the coal mines.*

na|tion|al park (national parks) N-COUNT; N-IN-NAMES A **national park** is a large area of land which is protected by the government because of its natural beauty, plants, or animals, and which the public can usually visit. ❑ *Roads into Yosemite National Park are closed due to landslides.*

na|tion|al se|cu|rity N-UNCOUNT A country's **national security** is its ability to protect itself from the threat of violence or attack. ❑ *We must deal with threats to our national security regardless of the cost.*

na|tion|al ser|vice N-UNCOUNT **National service** is service in the armed forces, which young people in certain countries have to do by law. ❑ *Banks spent his national service in the Royal Navy.*

nation-building N-UNCOUNT [oft N n] **Nation-building** is sometimes used to refer to government policies that are designed to create a strong sense of national identity. [JOURNALISM] ❑ *...calling for reconciliation and nation-building after the bitter election campaign.* ❑ *This revolutionary expansion required energetic nation-building policies.*

na|tion|hood /neɪʃənhʊd/ N-UNCOUNT A country's **nationhood** is its status as a nation. ❑ *To them, the presidency is the special symbol of nationhood.*

nation-state (nation-states) also **nation state** N-COUNT A **nation-state** is an independent state which consists of people from one particular national group. ❑ *Albania is a small nation state of around 3 million people.*

nation|wide /neɪʃənwaɪd/ ADJ **Nationwide** activities or situations happen or exist in all parts of a country. ❑ *The rising number of car crimes is a nationwide problem.* • ADV **Nationwide** is also an adverb. ❑ *The figures show unemployment falling nationwide last month.*

na|tive ♦⃝⃝ /neɪtɪv/ (natives) **1** ADJ [ADJ n] Your **native** country or area is the country or area where you were born and brought up. ❑ *It was his first visit to his native country since 1948.* **2** N-COUNT A **native** of a particular country or region is someone who was born in that country or region. ❑ *Dr. Aubin is a native of St. Louis.* • ADJ [ADJ n] **Native** is also an adjective. ❑ *Joshua Halpern is a native Northern Californian.* **3** N-COUNT Some European people use **native** to refer to a person living in a non-Western country who belongs to the race or tribe that the majority of people there belong to. This use could cause offense. ❑ *They used force to banish the natives from the more fertile land.* • ADJ [ADJ n] **Native** is also an adjective. ❑ *Native people were allowed to retain some sense of their traditional culture and religion.* **4** ADJ [ADJ n] Your **native** language or tongue is the first language that you learned to speak when you were a child. ❑ *She spoke not only her native language, Swedish, but also English and French.* **5** ADJ [ADJ n, v-link ADJ to n] Plants or animals that are **native to** a particular region live or grow there naturally and were not brought there. ❑ *...a project to create a 50 acre forest of native Caledonian pines.* • N-COUNT **Native** is also a noun. ❑ *The coconut palm is a native of Malaysia.*

SYNONYMS

native
ADJ **1**
indigenous: *...the country's indigenous population.*
vernacular: *The play was written in vernacular language.*
original: *The inhabitants have voted to restore the city's original name.*

Na|tive Ameri|can (Native Americans) N-COUNT **Native Americans** are people from one of the many groups who were already living in North America before Europeans arrived, especially those groups in the continental United States. ❑ *The eagle is the animal most sacred to the Native Americans.* • ADJ [ADJ n] **Native American** is also an adjective. ❑ *...a gathering of Native American elders.*

na|tive speak|er (native speakers) N-COUNT A **native speaker** of a language is someone who speaks that language as their first language rather than having learned it as a foreign language. ❑ *She sat in the Spanish lab for hours, trying to acquire the accent of a native speaker.*

Na|tiv|ity /nətɪvɪti, neɪ-/ N-SING [the N] **The Nativity** is the birth of Jesus, which is celebrated by Christians at Christmas. ❑ *They admired the tableau of the Nativity.* ❑ *...the Nativity story.*

na|tiv|ity play (nativity plays) N-COUNT A **nativity play** is a play about the birth of Jesus, usually one performed by children at Christmas time.

NATO ♦⃝⃝ /neɪtoʊ/ N-PROPER **NATO** is an international organization which consists of the U.S., Canada, Britain, and other European countries, all of whom have agreed to support one another if they are attacked. **NATO** is an abbreviation for 'North Atlantic Treaty Organization.' ❑ *NATO says it will keep a reduced number of modern nuclear weapons to guarantee peace.*

nat|ter /nætər/ (natters, nattering, nattered) V-RECIP When people **natter**, they talk casually for a long time about unimportant things. [mainly BRIT, INFORMAL]

in AM, use **chat**

nat|ty /næti/ (nattier, nattiest) ADJ [usu ADJ n] If you describe clothes, especially men's clothes, as **natty**, you mean that they are fashionable and neat. [INFORMAL, APPROVAL]

natu|ral ♦⃝⃝ /nætʃərəl, nætʃrəl/ (naturals) **1** ADJ If you say that it is **natural** for someone to act in a particular way or for something to happen in that way, you mean that it is reasonable in the circumstances. ❑ *It is only natural for youngsters to crave the excitement of driving a fast car.* ❑ *It is only natural that he should resent you.* **2** ADJ **Natural** behavior is shared by all people or all animals of a particular type and has not been learned. ❑ *...the insect's natural instinct to feed.* **3** ADJ Someone with a

natural ability or skill was born with that ability and did not have to learn it. ❏ *She has a natural ability to understand the motives of others.* **4** N-COUNT If you say that someone is a **natural**, you mean that they do something very well and very easily. ❏ *He's a natural with any kind of engine.* **5** ADJ If someone's behavior is **natural**, they appear to be relaxed and are not trying to hide anything. ❏ *Bethan's sister was as friendly and natural as the rest of the family.* ● **natu|ral|ly** ADV [ADV after v] ❏ *For pictures of people behaving naturally, not posing for the camera, it is essential to shoot unnoticed.* ● **natu|ral|ness** N-UNCOUNT ❏ *The critics praised the reality of the scenery and the naturalness of the acting.* **6** ADJ [ADJ n] **Natural** things exist or occur in nature and are not made or caused by people. ❏ *The gigantic natural harbor is a haven for boats.* ● **natu|ral|ly** ADV ❏ *Nitrates are chemicals that occur naturally in water and the soil.* **7** PHRASE If someone dies of or from **natural causes**, they die because they are ill or old rather than because of an accident or violence. ❏ *Your brother died of natural causes.*

natu|ral child|birth N-UNCOUNT If a woman gives birth by **natural childbirth**, she does not take any drugs to relieve her pain or to put her to sleep.

natu|ral food (**natural foods**) N-VAR **Natural food** is food which has not been processed much and has not had artificial ingredients added to it. ❏ *Her diet consisted of natural food, uncontaminated by pesticides, salt or refined sugar.* ❏ *...the organic and natural foods movement.*

natu|ral gas N-UNCOUNT **Natural gas** is gas which is found underground or under the sea. It is collected and stored, and piped into people's homes to be used for cooking and heating.

natu|ral his|to|ry N-UNCOUNT [usu N n] **Natural history** is the study of animals and plants and other living things. ❏ *Schools regularly bring children to the beach for natural history lessons.*

natu|ral|ism /nætʃərəlɪzəm, nætʃrəl-/ N-UNCOUNT **Naturalism** is a theory in art and literature which states that people and things should be shown in a realistic way.

natu|ral|ist /nætʃərəlɪst, nætʃrəl-/ (**naturalists**) N-COUNT A **naturalist** is a person who studies plants, animals, insects, and other living things.

natu|ral|is|tic /nætʃərəlɪstɪk, nætʃrəl-/ **1** ADJ **Naturalistic** art or writing tries to show people and things in a realistic way. ❏ *These drawings are among his most naturalistic.* **2** ADJ **Naturalistic** means resembling something that exists or occurs in nature. ❏ *Further research is needed under rather more naturalistic conditions.*

natu|ral|ize /nætʃərəlaɪz, nætʃrəl-/ (**naturalizes, naturalizing, naturalized**)

in BRIT, also use **naturalise**

1 V-T/V-I To **naturalize** a species of plant means to start it growing in an area where it is not usually found. If a plant **naturalizes** in an area where it was not found before, it starts to grow there naturally. ❏ *A friend sent me a root from Mexico, and I hope to naturalize it.* ❏ *The plant naturalizes well in grass.* **2** V-T If the government of a country **naturalizes** someone, they allow a person who was not born in that country to become a citizen of it. ❏ *Immigration officials were allowed to enter the country and naturalize soldiers under the 1942 law.* ● **natu|rali|za|tion** /nætʃərəlɪzeɪʃən, nætʃrəl-/ N-UNCOUNT ❏ *They swore their allegiance to the U.S. and received their naturalization papers.* **3** → see also **naturalized**

natu|ral|ized /nætʃərəlaɪzd, nætʃrəl-/

in BRIT, also use **naturalised**

ADJ [ADJ n] A **naturalized** citizen of a particular country is someone who has legally become a citizen of that country, although they were not born there.

natu|ral|ly ✦✦✧ /nætʃərəli, nætʃrəli/ **1** ADV You use **naturally** to indicate that you think something is very obvious and not at all surprising under the circumstances. ❏ *When things go wrong, all of us naturally feel disappointed and frustrated.* ❏ *Naturally these comings and goings excited some curiosity.* **2** ADV [ADV after v] If one thing develops **naturally** from another, it develops as a normal consequence or result of it. ❏ *A study of yoga leads naturally to meditation.* **3** ADV [ADV adj] You can use **naturally** to talk about a characteristic of someone's personality when it is the way that they normally act. ❏ *He has a lively sense of humor and appears naturally confident.* **4** ADV [ADV adj] If someone is **naturally** good at something, they learn it easily and quickly and do it very well. ❏ *Some individuals are naturally good communicators.* **5** PHRASE If something **comes naturally** to you, you find it easy to do and quickly become good at it. ❏ *Humanitarian work comes naturally to them.* **6** → see also **natural**

╒══ SYNONYMS ══╕

naturally
ADV
1
obviously: *Obviously, they've had sponsorship from some big companies.*
of course: *Of course, there were lots of other interesting things at the exhibition.*
certainly: *Certainly, pets can help children develop friendship skills.*
4
inherently: *Airplanes are not inherently dangerous.*
instinctively: *Jane instinctively knew all was not well with her 10-month-old son.*
innately: *I believe everyone is innately psychic.*

natu|ral re|sources N-PLURAL **Natural resources** are all the land, forests, energy sources, and minerals existing naturally in a place that can be used by people. ❏ *Angola was a country rich in natural resources.*

natu|ral se|lec|tion N-UNCOUNT **Natural selection** is a process by which species of animals and plants that are best adapted to their environment survive and reproduce, while those that are less well adapted die out. ❏ *Natural selection ensures only the fittest survive to pass their genes on to the next generation.*

natu|ral wast|age N-UNCOUNT **Natural wastage** is the same as **attrition**. [mainly BRIT, BUSINESS]

na|ture ✦✦✧ /neɪtʃər/ (**natures**) **1** N-UNCOUNT **Nature** is all the animals, plants, and other things in the world that are not made by people, and all the events and processes that are not caused by people. ❏ *The most amazing thing about nature is its infinite variety.* ❏ *...grasses that grow wild in nature.* **2** N-SING The **nature** of something is its basic quality or character. ❏ *Mr. Sharp would not comment on the nature of the issues being investigated.* ❏ *The rise of a major power is both economic and military in nature.* **3** N-COUNT [with poss, also by N] Someone's **nature** is their character, which they show by the way they behave. ❏ *Just how do the managers harness their energy, rivalry and ambitious nature into winning teamwork?* ❏ *She trusted people. That was her nature.* **4** → see also **human nature** **5** PHRASE If you say that something has a particular characteristic **by** its **nature** or **by** its **very nature**, you mean that things of that type always have that characteristic. ❏ *Peacekeeping, by its nature, makes pre-planning difficult.* **6** PHRASE If you say that something is **in the nature of things**, you mean that you would expect it to happen in the circumstances mentioned. ❏ *In the nature of things, a town or village springs up around its local river.* **7** PHRASE If you say that one thing is **in the nature of** another, you mean that it is like the other thing. ❏ *There is movement toward, I think, something in the nature of a pluralistic system.* **8** PHRASE If a way of behaving is **second nature** to you, you do it almost without thinking because it is easy for you or obvious to you. ❏ *Planning ahead had always come as second nature to her.*

╒══ SYNONYMS ══╕

nature
NOUN
3
quality: *...the pretentious quality of the poetry.*
characteristics: *Genes determine the characteristics of every living thing.*
attribute: *Cruelty is a normal attribute of human behavior.*
4
character: *Perhaps there is a negative side to his character that you haven't seen yet.*
personality: *He has such a kind, friendly personality.*
temperament: *His impulsive temperament regularly got him into trouble.*

na|ture study N-UNCOUNT **Nature study** is the study of animals and plants by looking at them directly, for example when it is taught to young children.

na|ture trail (nature trails) N-COUNT A **nature trail** is a route through an area of countryside which has signs drawing attention to interesting animals, plants, or rocks.

naught /nɔːt/ → see nought

naugh|ty /nɔːti/ (naughtier, naughtiest) **1** ADJ If you say that a child is **naughty**, you mean that they behave badly or do not do what they are told. ▫ *Girls, you're being very naughty.* **2** ADJ You can describe books, pictures, or words as **naughty** when they are slightly vulgar or related to sex. ▫ *You know what little boys are like with naughty words.*

nau|sea /nɔːziə, -ʒə, -siə, -ʃə/ N-UNCOUNT **Nausea** is the condition of feeling sick and the feeling that you are going to vomit. ▫ *I was overcome with a feeling of nausea.*

nau|seam /nɔːziəm/ → see ad nauseam

nau|seate /nɔːzieɪt, -ʒi-, -si-, -ʃi-/ (nauseates, nauseating, nauseated) V-T If something **nauseates** you, it makes you feel as if you are going to vomit. ▫ *The smell of frying nauseated her.* ▫ *She could not eat anything without feeling nauseated.*

nau|seat|ing /nɔːzieɪtɪŋ, -ʒi-, -si-, -ʃi-/ ADJ If you describe someone's attitude or their behavior as **nauseating**, you mean that you find it extremely unpleasant and feel disgusted by it. [DISAPPROVAL] ▫ *The judge described the offenses as nauseating and unspeakable.* ▫ *For them to attack our views is nauseating hypocrisy.*

nau|seous /nɔːʃəs/ ADJ If you feel **nauseous**, you feel as if you want to vomit. ▫ *If patients are poorly nourished, the drugs make them feel nauseous.* ▫ *A nauseous wave of pain broke over her.*

nau|ti|cal /nɔːtɪkəl/ **1** ADJ **Nautical** means relating to ships and sailing. ▫ *...a nautical chart of the region you sail.* **2** → See feature box at **boat**

nau|ti|cal mile (nautical miles) N-COUNT A **nautical mile** is a unit of measurement used at sea. It is equal to 1,852 meters (about 6,076 feet).

na|val ◆◇◇ /neɪvəl/ ADJ [ADJ n] **Naval** means belonging to, relating to, or involving a country's navy. ▫ *He was the senior serving naval officer.*

nave /neɪv/ (naves) N-COUNT The **nave** of a church is the long central part where people gather to worship.

na|vel /neɪvəl/ (navels) N-COUNT Your **navel** is the small hollow near your waist at the front of your body. ▫ *...a girl with a ring in her navel.*

navel-gazing N-UNCOUNT If you refer to an activity as **navel-gazing**, you are critical of it because people are thinking about something for a long time but take no action on it. [DISAPPROVAL] ▫ *She dismisses the reform process as an exercise in collective navel-gazing.*

navi|gable /nævɪɡəbəl/ ADJ A **navigable** river is wide and deep enough for a boat to travel along safely. [FORMAL] ▫ *...the navigable portion of the Nile.*

navi|gate /nævɪɡeɪt/ (navigates, navigating, navigated) **1** V-T/V-I When someone **navigates** a ship or an aircraft somewhere, they decide which course to follow and steer it there. ▫ *Captain Cook was responsible for safely navigating his ship without accident for three long voyages.* ▫ *The purpose of the visit was to navigate into an ice-filled fiord.* • **navi|ga|tion** /nævɪɡeɪʃən/ (navigations) N-VAR ▫ *The expedition was wrecked by bad planning and poor navigation.* **2** V-T/V-I When a ship or boat **navigates** an area of water, it sails on or across it. ▫ *...a lock system to allow sea-going craft to navigate the upper reaches of the river.* ▫ *Such boats can navigate on the Hudson.* **3** V-I When someone in a car **navigates**, or they **navigate** their way, they decide what roads the car should be driven along in order to get somewhere. ▫ *When traveling on fast roads at night it is impossible to drive and navigate at the same time.* ▫ *...the relief at successfully navigating across the Golden Gate Bridge to arrive here.* **4** V-T When fish, animals, or insects **navigate** somewhere, they find the right direction to go and travel there. ▫ *In tests, the bees navigate back home after being placed in a field a mile away.* **5** V-T If you **navigate** an obstacle, you move carefully in order to avoid hitting the obstacle or hurting yourself. ▫ *He's got to learn how to navigate his way around the residence.*

navi|ga|tion /nævɪɡeɪʃən/ **1** N-UNCOUNT You can refer to the movement of ships as **navigation**. ▫ *Pack ice around Iceland was becoming a threat to navigation.* **2** → see also **navigate**

navi|ga|tion|al /nævɪɡeɪʃənəl/ ADJ [usu ADJ n] **Navigational** means relating to the act of navigating a ship or an aircraft. ▫ *The crash was a direct result of inadequate navigational aids.*

navi|ga|tor /nævɪɡeɪtər/ (navigators) N-COUNT The **navigator** on an aircraft or ship is the person whose job is to work out the direction in which the aircraft or ship should be traveling. ▫ *He became a navigator during the war.*

navy ◆◆◇ /neɪvi/ (navies) **1** N-COUNT A country's **navy** consists of the people it employs to fight at sea, and the ships they use. ▫ *The operation was organized by the US Navy.* ▫ *Her own son was also in the navy.* **2** COLOR Something that is **navy** or **navy-blue** is very dark blue. ▫ *When I was a fashion editor, I mostly wore white shirts and black or navy pants.*

nay /neɪ/ **1** CONVENTION **Nay** is sometimes used to mean 'no' when talking about people voting against something or refusing to give consent for something. ▫ *The board wants input from members before they all vote yea or nay.* **2** ADV [ADV with cl/group] You use **nay** in front of a stronger word or phrase which you feel is more correct than the one you have just used and helps to emphasize the point you are making. [FORMAL, EMPHASIS] ▫ *Long essays, nay, whole books have been written on this.* **3** CONVENTION **Nay** is an old-fashioned, literary, or dialect word for 'no.' [FORMULAE]

Nazi ◆◇◇ /nɑːtsi/ (Nazis) **1** N-COUNT The **Nazis** were members of the right-wing political party, led by Adolf Hitler, which held power in Germany from 1933 to 1945. **2** ADJ You use **Nazi** to say that something relates to the Nazis. ▫ *...the rise of the Nazi Party.*

Na|zism /nɑːtsɪzəm/ N-UNCOUNT **Nazism** was the political ideas and activities of the German Nazi Party.

NB /ɛn biː/ also **N.B.** You write **NB** or **N.B.** to draw someone's attention to what you are about to say or write. ▫ *NB: The opinions stated in this essay do not necessarily represent those of the Church of God Missionary Society.*

NBA /ɛn biː eɪ/ N-PROPER [the N] In the United States, the **NBA** is the organization responsible for professional basketball. **NBA** is an abbreviation for 'National Basketball Association.' ▫ *The Portland Trail Blazers had the best record in the NBA last year.* ▫ *...the new NBA champions.*

NCO /ɛn siː oʊ/ (NCOs) N-COUNT An **NCO** is a soldier who has a fairly low rank such as sergeant or corporal. **NCO** is an abbreviation for 'non-commissioned officer.' ▫ *Food for the ordinary Soviet troops and NCOs was very poor.*

SUFFIX

-nd is added to written numbers ending in 2, except for numbers ending in 12, in order to form ordinal numbers. For example, February **22nd** is day number 22 in the month of February.

NE **NE** is a written abbreviation for **northeast**. ▫ *...on the NE outskirts of the city.*

ne|an|der|thal /niændərθɔːl, -tɔːl/ (neanderthals) **1** ADJ [ADJ n] **Neanderthal** people lived in Europe between 35,000 and 70,000 years ago. ▫ *Neanderthal man was able to kill woolly mammoths and bears.* • N-COUNT [usu pl] You can refer to people from the Neanderthal period as **Neanderthals**. **2** ADJ [usu ADJ n] If you describe people's, especially men's, ideas or ways of behaving as **Neanderthal**, you disapprove of them because they are very old-fashioned and uncivilized. [DISAPPROVAL] ▫ *It is a peculiarity of modern sport that so many coaches persist in a Neanderthal approach.* **3** N-COUNT If you call a man a **neanderthal**, you disapprove of him because you think he behaves in a very uncivilized way. [DISAPPROVAL] ▫ *...drunken neanderthals.*

near ◆◆◆ /nɪər/ (nearer, nearest, nears, nearing, neared) **1** PREP If something is **near** a place, thing, or person, it is a short distance from them. ▫ *Don't come near me.* ▫ *He drew his chair nearer the fire.* • ADV **Near** is also an adverb. ▫ *He crouched as near to the door as he could.* ▫ *She took a step nearer to the barrier.* • ADJ [ADJ n, the ADJ of n] **Near** is also an adjective. ▫ *He collapsed into the nearest chair.* ▫ *The nearer of the two barges was perhaps a mile away.* **2** PHRASE If someone or something is **near to** a

nearby — particular state, they have almost reached it. □ *After the war, the firm came near to bankruptcy.* □ *The repairs to the Hafner machine were near to completion.* • PREP **Near** means the same as **near to**. □ *He was near tears.* □ *For almost a month he lay near death.* **3** PHRASE If something is similar to something else, you can say that it is **near to** it. □ *It combined with the resinous cedar smell of the logs to produce a sickening sensation that was near to nausea.* • PREP **Near** means the same as **near to**. □ *Often her feelings were nearer hatred than love.* **4** ADJ [the ADJ] n to n, the ADJ to n] You describe the thing most similar to something as the **nearest** thing **to** it when there is no example of the thing itself. □ *It would appear that the legal profession is the nearest thing to a recession-proof industry.* **5** ADV If a time or event draws **near**, it will happen soon. [WRITTEN] □ *The time for my departure from Japan was drawing nearer every day.* **6** PREP If something happens **near** a particular time, it happens just before or just after that time. □ *Performance is lowest between 3 a.m. and 5 a.m., and reaches a peak near midday.* □ *"Since I retired to this place," he wrote near the end of his life, "I have never been out of these mountains."* **7** PREP You use **near** to say that something is a little more or less than an amount or number stated. □ *...to increase manufacturing from about 2.5 million cars a year to nearer 4.75 million.* **8** PREP [with brd-neg] You can say that someone will not go **near** a person or thing when you are emphasizing that they refuse to see them or go there. [EMPHASIS] □ *He will absolutely not go near a hospital.* **9** ADJ [det ADJ n] The **near** one of two things is the one that is closer. □ *...a mighty beech tree on the near side of the little clearing.* **10** ADJ [ADJ n] You use **near** to indicate that something is almost the thing mentioned. □ *No one wants to live in near poverty for that length of time.* • ADV [ADV adj] **Near** is also an adverb. □ *...his near fatal accident two years ago.* **11** ADJ [ADJ n] In a contest, your **nearest** rival or challenger is the person or team that is most likely to defeat you. □ *He completed the lengthy course some three seconds faster than his nearest rival.* **12** V-T [no passive] When you **near** a place, you get quite near to it. [LITERARY] □ *As he neared the stable, he slowed the horse and patted it on the neck.* **13** V-T [no passive] When someone or something **nears** a particular stage or point, they will soon reach that stage or point. □ *His age was hard to guess – he must have been nearing fifty.* □ *You are nearing the end of your training and you haven't attempted any assessments yet.* **14** V-I You say that an important time or event **nears** when it is going to occur quite soon. [LITERARY] □ *As half time neared, the home team almost scored twice.* **15** PHRASE You use **near and far** to indicate that you are referring to a very large area or distance. □ *People would gather from near and far.* **16** PHRASE If you say that something will happen **in the near future**, you mean that it will happen quite soon. □ *The controversy regarding vitamin C is unlikely to be resolved in the near future.* **17** PHRASE You use **nowhere near** and **not anywhere near** to emphasize that something is not the case. [EMPHASIS] □ *They are nowhere near good enough.* □ *It was nowhere near as painful as David had expected.*

near|by ♦♢♢ /nɪərbaɪ/ ADV If something is **nearby**, it is only a short distance away. □ *He might easily have been seen by someone who lived nearby.* □ *The helicopter crashed to earth nearby.* • ADJ [ADJ n] **Nearby** is also an adjective. □ *At a nearby table a man was complaining in a loud voice.*

near-death ex|peri|ence (near-death experiences) N-COUNT A **near-death experience** is a strange experience that some people who have nearly died say they had when they were unconscious.

Near East N-PROPER [the N] The **Near East** is the same as the Middle East.

near|ly ♦♦♢ /nɪərli/ **1** ADV **Nearly** is used to indicate that something is not quite the case, or not completely the case. □ *Goldsworth stared at me in silence for nearly twenty seconds.* □ *Hunter knew nearly all of this already.* □ *The beach was nearly empty.* **2** ADV **Nearly** is used to indicate that something will soon be the case. □ *It was already nearly eight o'clock.* □ *I was nearly asleep.* □ *I've nearly finished the words for your song.*

SYNONYMS

nearly
ADV **1**
practically: *He'd known the old man practically all his life.*
almost: *The couple had been dating for almost three years.*
virtually: *Virtually all cooking was done over coal-fired ranges.*

near miss (near misses) also **near-miss** **1** N-COUNT You can say that there is a **near miss** when something is nearly hit by another thing, for example by a vehicle or a bomb. □ *Details have been given of a near miss between two passenger jets over Washington DC earlier this week.* □ *We've had a few near misses in the raids, as I expect you've noticed.* **2** N-COUNT A **near miss** is an attempt to do something which fails by a very small amount. □ *...a near miss by the United States in its quarterfinal loss to Germany.*

near|sight|ed /nɪərsaɪtɪd/ also **near-sighted** **1** ADJ Someone who is **nearsighted** cannot see distant things clearly. □ *As you get older, you may become farsighted or near-sighted.* **2** → See feature box at **eyesight**

neat ♦♢♢ /niːt/ (neater, neatest) **1** ADJ A **neat** place, thing, or person is organized and clean, and has everything in the correct place. □ *So they left her in the neat little house, alone with her memories.* □ *Everything was neat and tidy and gleamingly clean.* • **neat|ly** ADV [ADV with v] □ *He folded his paper neatly and sipped his coffee.* • **neat|ness** N-UNCOUNT □ *The grounds were a perfect balance between neatness and natural wildness.* **2** ADJ Someone who is **neat** keeps their home or possessions organized and clean, with everything in the correct place. □ *"That's not like Alf," he said, "leaving papers muddled like that. He's always so neat."* • **neat|ly** ADV [ADV with v] □ *I followed her into that room which her mother had maintained so neatly.* • **neat|ness** N-UNCOUNT □ *...a paragon of neatness, efficiency and reliability.* **3** ADJ A **neat** object, part of the body, or shape is quite small and has a smooth outline. □ *...neat handwriting.* **4** ADJ A **neat** movement or action is done accurately and skillfully, with no unnecessary movements. □ *"Did you have any trouble?" Byron asked, driving into a small parking lot and changing the subject in the same neat maneuver.* • **neat|ly** ADV [ADV with v] □ *He watched her peel and dissect a pear neatly, no mess, no sticky fingers.* **5** ADJ A **neat** way of organizing, achieving, explaining, or expressing something is clever and convenient. □ *It had been such a neat, clever plan.* □ *Neat solutions are not easily found to these issues.* • **neat|ly** ADV [ADV with v] □ *Real people do not fit neatly into these categories.* **6** ADJ If you say that something is **neat**, you mean that it is very good. [INFORMAL, APPROVAL] □ *He thought Mick was a really neat guy.* **7** ADJ When someone drinks strong alcohol **neat**, they do not add a weaker liquid such as water to it. [mainly BRIT]

in AM, usually use **straight**

SYNONYMS

neat
ADJ **1**
tidy: *Having a tidy desk can seem impossible if you have a busy, demanding job.*
orderly: *Their vehicles were parked in orderly rows.*
immaculate: *Her dining room was immaculate.*

nebu|la /nɛbyələ/ (nebulae /nɛbyəliː/) N-COUNT [oft in names] A **nebula** is a cloud of dust and gas in space. New stars are produced from nebulae.

nebu|lous /nɛbyələs/ ADJ If you describe something as **nebulous**, you mean that it is vague and not clearly defined or not easy to describe. □ *The notions we children were able to form of the great world beyond were exceedingly nebulous.* □ *Music is such a nebulous thing.*

nec|es|sari|ly ♦♢♢ /nɛsɪsɛrɪli/ **1** ADV If you say that something is not **necessarily** the case, you mean that it may not be the case or is not always the case. [VAGUENESS] □ *Anger is not necessarily the most useful or acceptable reaction to such events.* • CONVENTION If you reply '**Not necessarily**,' you mean that what has just been said or suggested may not be true. □ *"He was lying, of course."—"Not necessarily."* **2** ADV If you say that something **necessarily** happens or is the case, you mean that it has to happen or be the case and cannot be any different. □ *Designer goods necessarily command high prices.*

nec|es|sary ♦♦♢ /nɛsɪsɛri/ **1** ADJ Something that is **necessary** is needed in order for something else to happen. □ *I kept the engine running because it might be necessary to leave fast.* □ *Make the necessary arrangements.* **2** ADJ [ADJ n] A **necessary** consequence or connection must happen or exist, because of the nature of the things or events involved. □ *Scientific work is differentiated from art by its necessary connection with the idea of progress.*

ne|ces|si|tate /nɪsɛsɪteɪt/ (necessitates, necessitating, necessitated) v-t If something **necessitates** an event, action, or situation, it makes it necessary. [FORMAL] ❑ *A prolonged drought had necessitated the introduction of water rationing.*

ne|ces|sity /nɪsɛsɪti/ (necessities) ◼ N-UNCOUNT The **necessity** of something is the fact that it must happen or exist. ❑ *There is agreement on the necessity of reforms.* ❑ *As soon as the necessity for action is over the troops must be withdrawn.* • PHRASE If you say that something is **of necessity** the case, you mean that it is the case because nothing else is possible or practical under the circumstances. [FORMAL] ❑ *...large families where children, of necessity, shared a bed.* ◼ N-COUNT A **necessity** is something that you must have in order to live properly or do something. ❑ *Water is a basic necessity of life.* ◼ N-COUNT A situation or action that is a **necessity** is necessary and cannot be avoided. ❑ *The president pleaded that strong rule from the center was a necessity.*

neck ✦◇◇ /nɛk/ (necks) ◼ N-COUNT Your **neck** is the part of your body which joins your head to the rest of your body. ❑ *She threw her arms around his neck and hugged him warmly.* ◼ N-COUNT The **neck** of an article of clothing such as a shirt, dress, or sweater is the part which surrounds your neck. ❑ *...the low, ruffled neck of her blouse.* ◼ N-COUNT The **neck** of something such as a bottle or a guitar is the long narrow part at one end of it. ❑ *Catherine gripped the broken neck of the bottle.* ◼ PHRASE If you say that someone **is breathing down** your **neck**, you mean that they are watching you very closely and checking everything you do. ❑ *Most farmers have loan officers breathing down their necks.* ◼ PHRASE In a competition, especially an election, if two or more competitors are **neck and neck**, they are level with each other and have an equal chance of winning. ❑ *The latest polls indicate that the two main parties are neck and neck.* ◼ PHRASE If you **stick** your **neck out**, you bravely say or do something that might be criticized or might turn out to be wrong. [INFORMAL] ❑ *During my political life I've earned myself a reputation as someone who'll stick his neck out, a bit of a rebel.*

neck|er|chief /nɛkərtʃɪf, -tʃiːf/ (neckerchiefs) N-COUNT A **neckerchief** is a piece of cloth which is folded to form a triangle and worn around your neck.

neck|lace /nɛklɪs/ (necklaces) N-COUNT A **necklace** is a piece of jewelry such as a chain or a string of beads which someone wears around their neck. ❑ *...a diamond necklace and matching earrings.*

neck|line /nɛklaɪn/ (necklines) N-COUNT [oft supp N] The **neckline** of a dress, blouse, or other piece of clothing is the edge that goes around your neck, especially the front part of it. ❑ *...a dress with pale pink roses around the neckline.*

neck|tie /nɛktaɪ/ (neckties) N-COUNT A **necktie** is a narrow piece of cloth that is worn under a shirt collar and tied so that the ends hang down in front.

nec|ro|man|cy /nɛkrəmænsi/ N-UNCOUNT **Necromancy** is magic that some people believe brings a dead person back to this world so that you can talk to them. [FORMAL]

nec|ro|philia /nɛkrəfɪliə/ N-UNCOUNT **Necrophilia** is the act of having sexual intercourse with a dead body, or the desire to do this.

ne|cropo|lis /nəkrɒpəlɪs, nɛ-/ (necropolises) N-COUNT A **necropolis** is a place where dead people are buried. [FORMAL]

ne|cro|sis /nəkroʊsɪs, nɛ-/ N-UNCOUNT [usu supp N] **Necrosis** is the death of part of someone's body, for example because it is not getting enough blood. [MEDICAL] ❑ *...liver necrosis.*

nec|tar /nɛktər/ N-UNCOUNT **Nectar** is a sweet liquid produced by flowers, which bees and other insects collect.

nec|tar|ine /nɛktəriːn/ (nectarines) N-COUNT A **nectarine** is a round, juicy fruit which is similar to a peach but has a smooth skin.

née /neɪ/ also **nee** You use **née** after a married woman's name and before you mention the surname she had before she got married. [FORMAL] ❑ *...Lady Helen Taylor (née Windsor).*

need ✦✦✦ /niːd/ (needs, needing, needed)

> **Need** sometimes behaves like an ordinary verb, for example 'She needs to know' and 'She doesn't need to know' and sometimes like a modal, for example 'No-one need know,' 'She needn't know,' or, in more formal English, 'She need not know.'

◼ V-T [no cont] If you **need** something, or **need** to do something, you cannot successfully achieve what you want or live properly without it. ❑ *He desperately needed money.* ❑ *I need to make a phone call.* ❑ *I need you to do something for me.* ❑ *I need you here, Wally.* • N-COUNT **Need** is also a noun. ❑ *Charles has never felt the need to compete with anyone.* ❑ *...the child who never had his need for attention and importance satisfied.* ◼ V-T [no cont] If an object or place **needs** something done to it, that action should be done to improve the object or place. If a task **needs** doing, it should be done to improve a particular situation. ❑ *The building needs quite a few repairs.* ❑ *...a garden that needs tidying.* ◼ N-SING If there is a **need** for something, that thing would improve a situation or something cannot happen without it. ❑ *Mr. Forrest believes there is a need for other similar schools throughout the country.* ❑ *"I think we should see a specialist."—"I don't think there's any need for that."* ❑ *I felt a need to take care of my family.* ◼ V-T [with neg] If you say that someone does not **need** to do something, you are telling them not to do it, or advising or suggesting that they should not do it. ❑ *Well, for Heaven's sake, you don't need to apologize.* • MODAL [no cont, with neg] **Need** is also a modal. ❑ *"I'll put the key in the window."—"You needn't bother," he said gruffly.* ❑ *Look, you needn't shout.* ◼ V-T [no cont, with neg] If you tell someone that they don't **need** to do something, or that something **need** not happen, you are telling them that that thing is not necessary, in order to make them feel better. ❑ *He replied, with a reassuring smile, "Oh, you don't need to worry about them."* • MODAL [with brd-neg] **Need** is also a modal. ❑ *You needn't worry.* ❑ *We have learned that a market crash need not lead to economic disaster.* ◼ V-T [no cont] You use **don't need** to when you are giving someone permission not to do something. ❑ *You don't need to wait for me.* • MODAL [with neg] **Need** is also a modal. ❑ *You needn't come again, if you don't want to.* ◼ MODAL [with neg] If someone **needn't** have done something, they didn't need to do it. ❑ *She could have made the sandwich herself; her mother needn't have bothered to do anything.* ❑ *I was a little nervous when I announced my engagement to Grace, but I needn't have worried.* ◼ V-T [no cont, with neg] If someone **didn't need to** do something, it wasn't necessary or useful for them to do it, although they did it. ❑ *You didn't need to give me any more money you know, but thank you.* ◼ MODAL You use **need** in expressions such as **I need hardly say** and **I needn't add** to emphasize that the person you are talking to already knows what you are going to say. [EMPHASIS] ❑ *I needn't add that if you fail to do as I ask, you will suffer the consequences.* • V-T [no cont] **Need** is also a verb. ❑ *I hardly need to say that I have never lost contact with him.* ◼ PHRASE People **in need** do not have enough of essential things such as money, food, or good health. ❑ *The portable clinic will take doctors to children in need.* ◼ PHRASE If you are **in need of** something, you need it or ought to have it. ❑ *I was all right but in need of rest.* ❑ *He was badly in need of a shave.* ◼ PHRASE If you say that you will do something, especially an extreme action, **if need be**, you mean that you will do if it is necessary. ❑ *They will act as my legal advisers if need be.*

USAGE
---

need
Don't use **need** in the progressive form. Don't say, for example, 'I am needing money for food.' You say you **need** something. *I need money for food.*

need|ful /niːdfəl/ ADJ **Needful** means necessary. [OLD-FASHIONED] ❑ *The section of society most needful of such guidance is the young male.*

nee|dle /niːdəl/ (needles) ◼ N-COUNT A **needle** is a small, very thin piece of polished metal which is used for sewing. It has a sharp point at one end and a hole in the other for a thread to go through. ❑ *He took a needle and thread and sewed it up.* ◼ N-COUNT A **needle** is a thin hollow metal rod with a sharp point, which is part of a medical instrument called a syringe. It is used to put a drug into someone's body, or to take blood out. ❑ *...the transmission of the virus through dirty needles.* ◼ N-COUNT Knitting **needles** are thin sticks that are used for knitting. They are usually made of plastic or metal and have a point at one end. ❑ *...a pair of knitting needles.* ◼ N-COUNT A **needle** is a thin metal rod with a point which is put into a patient's body during acupuncture. ❑ *I gave Kevin* a course of acupuncture using six needles strategically placed on the scalp. ◻ N-COUNT On an instrument which measures something such as speed or weight, the **needle** is the long strip of metal or plastic on the dial that moves backward and forward, showing the measurement. ◻ *She kept looking at the dial on the boiler. The needle had reached 250 degrees.* ◻ N-COUNT The **needles** of a fir or pine tree are its thin, hard, pointed leaves. ◻ *The carpet of pine needles was soft underfoot.*

nee|dle ex|change (needle exchanges) also **needle-exchange** N-COUNT A **needle exchange** is a place where drug addicts are able to obtain new syringes in exchange for used ones. ◻ *There are needle exchanges where people can get clean needles.* ◻ *...needle exchange programs.*

need|less /ní:dlɪs/ ADJ Something that is **needless** is completely unnecessary. ◻ *But his death was so needless.*
• **need|less|ly** ADV ◻ *Half a million women die needlessly each year during childbirth.*

needle|work /ní:dəlwɜːrk/ ◻ N-UNCOUNT **Needlework** is sewing or stitching that is done by hand. ◻ *She did beautiful needlework and she embroidered table napkins.* ◻ N-UNCOUNT **Needlework** is the activity of sewing or stitching. ◻ *...watching my mother and grandmothers doing needlework.* ◻ → See feature box at **sewing**

needn't /ní:dənt/ **Needn't** is the usual spoken form of 'need not.'

needy /ní:di/ (needier, neediest) ADJ **Needy** people do not have enough food, medicine, or clothing, or adequate houses. ◻ *...a multinational force aimed at ensuring that food and medicine get to needy areas.* • N-PLURAL **The needy** are people who are needy. ◻ *There will be efforts to get larger amounts of food to the needy.*

ne|fari|ous /nɪfɛəriəs/ ADJ [usu ADJ n] If you describe an activity as **nefarious**, you mean that it is wicked and immoral. [LITERARY] ◻ *Why make a whole village prisoner if it was not to some nefarious purpose?*

neg. Neg. is a written abbreviation for **negative**.

ne|gate /nɪgeɪt/ (negates, negating, negated) ◻ V-T If one thing **negates** another, it causes that other thing to lose the effect or value that it had. [FORMAL] ◻ *These weaknesses negated his otherwise progressive attitude towards the staff.* ◻ V-T If someone **negates** something, they say that it does not exist. [FORMAL] ◻ *He warned that to negate the results of elections would only make things worse.*

ne|ga|tion /nɪgeɪʃən/ ◻ N-SING [N of n] The **negation** of something is its complete opposite or something which destroys it or makes it lose its effect. [FORMAL] ◻ *Badly written legislation is the negation of the rule of law and of democracy.* ◻ N-UNCOUNT **Negation** is disagreement, refusal, or denial. [FORMAL] ◻ *Irena shook her head, but in bewilderment, not negation.*

nega|tive ✦✧✧ /nɛgətɪv/ (negatives) ◻ ADJ A fact, situation, or experience that is **negative** is unpleasant, depressing, or harmful. ◻ *The news from overseas is overwhelmingly negative.*
• **nega|tive|ly** ADV [ADV with v] ◻ *This will negatively affect the result over the first half of the year.* ◻ ADJ If someone is **negative** or has a **negative** attitude, they consider only the bad aspects of a situation, rather than the good ones. ◻ *When asked for your views about your current job, on no account must you be negative about it.* • **nega|tive|ly** ADV ◻ *A few weeks later he said that maybe he viewed all his relationships rather negatively.* • **nega|tiv|ity** /nɛgətɪvɪti/ N-UNCOUNT ◻ *I loathe negativity. I can't stand people who moan.*
◻ ADJ A **negative** reply or decision indicates the answer 'no.' ◻ *The doctor gave a vague but negative response.* ◻ *Upon a negative decision, the applicant loses the protection offered by Belgian law.*
• **nega|tive|ly** ADV [ADV after v] ◻ *Sixty percent of people answered negatively.* ◻ N-COUNT A **negative** is a word, expression, or gesture that means 'no' or 'not.' ◻ *In the past we have heard only negatives when it came to following a healthy diet.* ◻ ADJ In grammar, a **negative** clause contains a word such as 'not,' 'never,' or 'no one.' ◻ ADJ If a medical test or scientific test is **negative**, it shows no evidence of the medical condition or substance that you are looking for. ◻ *So far 57 have taken the test and all have been negative.* ◻ **HIV negative** → see **HIV** ◻ N-COUNT In photography, a **negative** is an image that shows dark areas as light and light areas as dark. Negatives are made from camera film, and are used to print photographs. ◻ *...negatives of Diana's wedding dress.* ◻ ADJ A **negative** charge or current has the same electrical charge as an electron. ◻ *Stimulate the injury or site of greatest pain with a small negative current.* • **nega|tive|ly** ADV [ADV -ed] ◻ *As these electrons are negatively charged they will attempt to repel each other.* ◻ ADJ A **negative** number, quantity, or measurement is less than zero. ◻ *Difficult texts record a positive score and simple ones score negative numbers.* ◻ PHRASE If an answer is **in the negative**, it is 'no' or means 'no.' ◻ *The Council answered those questions in the negative.* ◻ → See feature box at **electricity**, **success**

SYNONYMS

negative
ADJ
◻
unpleasant: *The symptoms can be uncomfortable, unpleasant, and serious.*
damaging: *Is the recycling process in itself damaging to the environment?*
harmful: *...the harmful effects of smoking.*
◻
pessimistic: *Not everyone is so pessimistic about the future.*
cynical: *It's hard not to be cynical about reform.*
gloomy: *Miller is gloomy about the fate of the serious playwright in America.*

ne|glect /nɪglɛkt/ (neglects, neglecting, neglected) ◻ V-T If you **neglect** someone or something, you fail to take care of them properly. ◻ *The woman denied that she had neglected her child.* ◻ *Feed plants and they grow, neglect them and they suffer.* • N-UNCOUNT **Neglect** is also a noun. ◻ *The town's old quayside is collapsing after years of neglect.* ◻ V-T If you **neglect** someone or something, you fail to give them the amount of attention that they deserve. ◻ *He'd given too much to his career, worked long hours, neglected her.* • **ne|glect|ed** ADJ ◻ *The fact that she is not coming today makes her grandmother feel lonely and neglected.* ◻ *...a neglected aspect of the city's forgotten history.* ◻ V-T If you **neglect** to do something that you ought to do or **neglect** your duty, you fail to do it. ◻ *We often neglect to make proper use of our bodies.*

ne|glect|ful /nɪglɛktfəl/ ◻ ADJ If you describe someone as **neglectful**, you think they fail to do everything they should do to take care of someone or something properly. ◻ *...neglectful parents.* ◻ ADJ [oft v-link ADJ of n] If someone is **neglectful** of something, they do not give it the attention or consideration that it should be given. ◻ *Have I been neglectful of my friend, taking him for granted?*

neg|li|gee /nɛglɪʒeɪ/ (negligees) also **négligée** N-COUNT A **negligee** is a very thin garment which a woman wears over her nightclothes. ◻ *...a pink satin negligee.*

neg|li|gence /nɛglɪdʒəns/ N-UNCOUNT If someone is guilty of **negligence**, they have failed to do something which they ought to do. [FORMAL] ◻ *The soldiers were ordered to appear before a disciplinary council on charges of negligence.*

neg|li|gent /nɛglɪdʒənt/ ADJ If someone in a position of responsibility is **negligent**, they do not do something which they ought to do. ◻ *The jury determined that the airline was negligent in training and supervising the crew.* • **neg|li|gent|ly** ADV [ADV with v] ◻ *A manufacturer negligently made and marketed a car with defective brakes.*

neg|li|gible /nɛglɪdʒɪbəl/ ADJ An amount or effect that is **negligible** is so small that it is not worth considering or worrying about. ◻ *The pay that the soldiers received was negligible.*

ne|go|tiable /nɪgoʊʃiəbəl, -ʃəbəl/ ADJ Something that is **negotiable** can be changed or agreed upon when people discuss it. ◻ *He warned that his economic program for the country was not negotiable.*

ne|go|ti|ate ✦✧✧ /nɪgoʊʃieɪt/ (negotiates, negotiating, negotiated) ◻ V-RECIP If people **negotiate** with each other or **negotiate** an agreement, they talk about a problem or a situation such as a business arrangement in order to solve the problem or complete the arrangement. ◻ *It is not clear whether the president is willing to negotiate with the Democrats.* ◻ *When you have two adversaries negotiating, you need to be on neutral territory.* ◻ *The local government and the army negotiated a truce.* ◻ *Western governments have this week urged him to negotiate and avoid force.* ◻ V-T If you **negotiate** an area of land, a place,

negotiating table

or an obstacle, you successfully travel across it or around it. ☐ *Frank Mariano negotiates the desert terrain in his battered pickup.* ☐ *I negotiated the corner on my motorcycle and pulled to a stop.*

SYNONYMS

negotiate
VERB **1**
bargain: *They prefer to bargain with individual clients, for cash.*
debate: *At the moment we are debating what furniture to buy for the house.*
discuss: *The Cabinet met today to discuss how to respond to the ultimatum.*

---

ne|go|ti|at|ing ta|ble N-SING If you say that people are at the **negotiating table**, you mean that they are having discussions in order to settle a dispute or reach an agreement. ☐ *"We want to settle all matters at the negotiating table," he said.*

ne|go|tia|tion ♦♦◊ /nɪgoʊʃieɪʃᵊn/ (**negotiations**) N-VAR **Negotiations** are formal discussions between people who have different aims or intentions, especially in business or politics, during which they try to reach an agreement. ☐ *Warren said, "We have had meaningful negotiations and I believe we are very close to a deal."*

SYNONYMS

negotiation
NOUN
discussion: *There was a lot of discussion about the wording of the report.*
debate: *An intense debate is going on within the government.*
bargaining: *The government has called for sensible bargaining with the unions.*

---

ne|go|tia|tor /nɪgoʊʃieɪtər/ (**negotiators**) N-COUNT **Negotiators** are people who take part in political or financial negotiations. ☐ *On Thursday night the rebels' chief negotiator at the peace talks announced that dialogue had gone as far as it could go.*

Ne|gro /niːgroʊ/ (**Negroes**) N-COUNT **Negro** is a word that was used in the past to refer to someone with dark skin who comes from Africa or whose ancestors came from Africa. [OFFENSIVE, OLD-FASHIONED]

neigh /neɪ/ (**neighs, neighing, neighed**) **1** V-I When a horse **neighs**, it makes a loud sound with its mouth. ☐ *The mare neighed once more, and disappeared among the trees.* • N-COUNT **Neigh** is also a noun. ☐ *The horse gave a loud neigh.* **2** → See feature box at **sound**

neigh|bor ♦◊◊ /neɪbər/ (**neighbors**)

in BRIT, use **neighbour**

1 N-COUNT Your **neighbor** is someone who lives near you. ☐ *My neighbor spies on me through a crack in the fence.* **2** N-COUNT You can refer to the person who is standing or sitting next to you as your **neighbor**. ☐ *The woman prodded her neighbor and whispered urgently in his ear.* **3** N-COUNT You can refer to something which stands next to something else of the same kind as its **neighbor**. ☐ *...its big oil-rich neighbor.*

neigh|bor|hood ♦♦◊ /neɪbərhʊd/ (**neighborhoods**)

in BRIT, use **neighbourhood**

1 N-COUNT A **neighborhood** is one of the parts of a town where people live. ☐ *There is no neighborhood which is really safe.* **2** N-COUNT The **neighborhood** of a place or person is the area or the people around them. ☐ *...a suburban Boston neighborhood close to where I live.* **3** PHRASE **In the neighborhood of** a number means approximately that number. ☐ *The album's now sold something in the neighborhood of 2 million copies.* **4** PHRASE A place that is **in the neighborhood of** another place is near it. ☐ *Several people were arrested in the neighborhood of Bridgeport.*

neigh|bor|ing /neɪbərɪŋ/

in BRIT, use **neighbouring**

ADJ [ADJ n] **Neighboring** places or things are near other things of the same kind. ☐ *He is on his way back to Beijing after a tour of neighboring Asian capitals.*

neigh|bor|ly /neɪbərli/

in BRIT, use **neighbourly**

ADJ If the people who live near you are **neighborly**, they are friendly and helpful. If you live in a **neighborly** place, it has a friendly atmosphere. ☐ *The noise would have provoked alarm and neighborly concern.* ☐ *The older people had stopped being neighborly to each other.*

nei|ther ♦♦◊ /niːðər, naɪ-/ **1** CONJ You use **neither** in front of the first of two or more words or expressions when you are linking two or more things which are not true or do not happen. The other thing is introduced by 'nor.' ☐ *Her parents spoke neither English nor German.* **2** DET You use **neither** to refer to each of two things or people, when you are making a negative statement that includes both of them. ☐ *At first, neither man could speak.* • QUANT-NEG **Neither** is also a quantifier. ☐ *Neither of us felt like going out.* • PRON-NEG **Neither** is also a pronoun. ☐ *They both smiled; neither seemed likely to be aware of my absence for long.* **3** CONJ If you say that one person or thing does not do something and **neither** does another, what you say is true of all the people or things that you are mentioning. ☐ *I never learned to swim and neither did they.* **4** CONJ You use **neither** after a negative statement to emphasize that you are introducing another negative statement. [FORMAL] ☐ *I can't ever recall Dad hugging me. Neither did I sit on his knee.*

nem|esis /nɛmɪsɪs/ (**nemeses** /nɛmɪsiːz/) **1** N-UNCOUNT [oft with poss] The **nemesis** of a person or thing is a situation, event, or person which causes them to be seriously harmed, especially as a punishment. ☐ *The new mathematics test will become the nemesis of teachers.* **2** N-COUNT A person's **nemesis** is their opponent or rival, especially one who has been their opponent or rival for a long time. ☐ *The company has abandoned its legal fight and agreed to cooperate with its longtime nemesis.*

PREFIX

neo-
forms nouns and adjectives that refer to modern versions of styles and particular groups of the past. *For example,* **neo-classical** *architecture is based on ancient Greek or Roman architecture.*

---

neo|clas|si|cal /niːoʊklæsɪkᵊl/ ADJ **Neoclassical** architecture or art is from the late 18th century and uses designs from Roman and Greek architecture and art. ☐ *The building was erected between 1798 and 1802 in the neoclassical style of the time.*

neo|lib|er|al|ism /niːoʊlɪbərəlɪzəm/ N-UNCOUNT **Neoliberalism** is a form of liberalism that supports economic freedom and the free market. ☐ *The key tenets of neoliberalism include privatization and deregulation.*

Neo|lith|ic /niːəlɪθɪk/ also **neolithic** ADJ **Neolithic** is used to describe things relating to the period when people had started farming but still used stone for making weapons and tools. ☐ *...neolithic culture.* ☐ *The monument was Stone Age or Neolithic.*

ne|olo|gism /niːɒlədʒɪzəm/ (**neologisms**) N-COUNT A **neologism** is a new word or expression in a language, or a new meaning for an existing word or expression. [TECHNICAL] ☐ *The newspaper used the neologism "dinks," Double Income No Kids.*

neon /niːɒn/ **1** ADJ [ADJ n] **Neon** lights or signs are made from glass tubes filled with neon gas which produce a bright electric light. ☐ *In the city squares the neon lights flashed in turn.* **2** N-UNCOUNT **Neon** is a gas which occurs in very small amounts in the atmosphere. ☐ *Inert gases like neon and argon have eight electrons in their outer shell.*

neo|na|tal /niːoʊneɪtᵊl/ ADJ [ADJ n] **Neonatal** means relating to the first few days of life of a newborn baby. ☐ *...the neonatal intensive care unit.*

neo-Nazi (**neo-Nazis**) N-COUNT [oft N n] **Neo-Nazis** are people who admire Adolf Hitler and the beliefs of the right-wing party which he led in Germany from 1933 to 1945.

neo|phyte /niːəfaɪt/ (**neophytes**) N-COUNT A **neophyte** is someone who is new to a particular activity. [FORMAL] ☐ *...the self-proclaimed political neophyte Ross Perot.*

neph|ew /nɛfyu/ (nephews) N-COUNT Someone's **nephew** is the son of their sister or brother. ❑ *I am planning a 25th birthday party for my nephew.*

nepo|tism /nɛpətɪzəm/ N-UNCOUNT **Nepotism** is the unfair use of power in order to get jobs or other benefits for your family or friends. [DISAPPROVAL] ❑ *Many will regard his appointment as the kind of nepotism the banking industry ought to avoid.*

nerd /nɜrd/ (nerds) N-COUNT If you say that someone is a **nerd**, you mean that they are unpopular or boring, especially because they wear unfashionable clothes or show too much interest in computers or science. Some people consider this word offensive. [INFORMAL, DISAPPROVAL] ❑ *Mark claimed he was made to look a nerd.* ❑ *...the notion that users of the internet are all sad computer nerds.*

nerdy /nɜrdi/ (nerdier, nerdiest) ADJ If you describe someone as **nerdy**, you think that they are a nerd or look like a nerd. Some people consider this word offensive [INFORMAL, DISAPPROVAL] ❑ *...nerdy types who never exercise.* ❑ *...the Prince's nerdy hairstyle.*

nerve♦◊◊ /nɜrv/ (nerves) **1** N-COUNT **Nerves** are long thin fibers that transmit messages between your brain and other parts of your body. ❑ *...spinal nerves.* **2** N-PLURAL If you refer to someone's **nerves**, you mean their ability to cope with problems such as stress, worry, and danger. ❑ *Jill's nerves are stretched to breaking point.* **3** N-PLURAL You can refer to someone's feelings of anxiety or tension as **nerves**. ❑ *I just played badly. It wasn't nerves.* **4** N-UNCOUNT **Nerve** is the courage that you need in order to do something difficult or dangerous. ❑ *The brandy made him choke, but it restored his nerve.* **5** PHRASE If someone or something **gets on** your **nerves**, they annoy or irritate you. [INFORMAL] ❑ *Lately he hasn't done a thing and it's getting on my nerves.* **6** PHRASE If you say that someone **has a nerve** or **has the nerve** to do something, you are criticizing them for doing something which you feel they had no right to do. [INFORMAL, DISAPPROVAL] ❑ *He told his critics they had a nerve complaining about him.* **7** PHRASE If you **lose** your **nerve**, you suddenly panic and become too afraid to do something that you were about to do. ❑ *She lost her nerve and began to cry.* **8** → See feature box at **brain**

SYNONYMS

nerve
NOUN **4**
bravery: *He deserves the highest praise for his bravery.*
courage: *They do not have the courage to apologize for their actions.*
daring: *His daring may have cost him his life.*

---

nerve agent (nerve agents) N-MASS A **nerve agent** is a chemical weapon that affects people's nervous systems.

nerve cen|ter (nerve centers)
in BRIT, use **nerve centre**
N-COUNT [usu with poss] The **nerve center** of an organization is the place where its activities are controlled and where its leaders meet. ❑ *My office is the nerve center of the operation.*

nerve end|ing (nerve endings) N-COUNT [usu pl] Your **nerve endings** are the millions of points on the surface of your body and inside it which send messages to your brain when you feel sensations such as heat, cold, and pain.

nerve gas (nerve gases) N-MASS **Nerve gas** is a poisonous gas used in war as a weapon.

nerve-racking also **nerve-wracking** ADJ A **nerve-racking** situation or experience makes you feel very tense and worried. ❑ *The women and children spent a nerve-racking day outside waiting while fighting continued around them.* ❑ *It was nerve-racking to be in a big-league park.*

ner|vo|sa /nɜrvoʊsə/ → see **anorexia**, **bulimia**

nerv|ous♦◊◊ /nɜrvəs/ **1** ADJ If someone is **nervous**, they are frightened or worried about something that is happening or might happen, and show this in their behavior. ❑ *The party has become deeply nervous about its prospects of winning the next election.* • **nerv|ous|ly** ADV [ADV with v] ❑ *Brunhilde stood up nervously as the men came into the room.* • **nerv|ous|ness** N-UNCOUNT ❑ *I smiled warmly so he wouldn't see my nervousness.* **2** ADJ A **nervous** person is very tense and easily upset. ❑ *She was apparently a very nervous woman, and that affected her career.* **3** ADJ [ADJ n] A **nervous** illness or condition is one that affects your emotions and your mental state. ❑ *The number of nervous disorders was rising in the region.*

nerv|ous break|down (nervous breakdowns) N-COUNT If someone has a **nervous breakdown**, they become extremely depressed and cannot cope with their normal life. ❑ *His wife would not be able to cope and might suffer a nervous breakdown.*

nerv|ous sys|tem (nervous systems) N-COUNT Your **nervous system** consists of all the nerves in your body together with your brain and spinal cord. ❑ *So it is possible that the symptoms will not finally go until your nervous system is in a better state.*

nerv|ous wreck (nervous wrecks) N-COUNT If you say that someone is a **nervous wreck**, you mean that they are extremely nervous or worried about something. ❑ *She was a nervous wreck, crying when anyone asked her about her experience.*

nervy /nɜrvi/ (nervier, nerviest) ADJ If you say that someone is **nervy**, you mean that their behavior is bold or daring. [AM] ❑ *John liked him because he was a nervy guy.*

SUFFIX

-ness
forms nouns that refer to a particular state or quality. For example, **gentleness** is the state or quality of being gentle.

---

nest /nɛst/ (nests, nesting, nested) **1** N-COUNT A bird's **nest** is the home that it makes to lay its eggs in. ❑ *I can see an eagle's nest on the rocks.* **2** V-I When a bird **nests** somewhere, it builds a nest and settles there to lay its eggs. ❑ *Some species may nest in close proximity to each other.* **3** N-COUNT A **nest** is a home that a group of insects or other creatures make in order to live in and give birth to their young in. ❑ *Some solitary bees make their nests in burrows in the soil.*

nest egg (nest eggs) also **nest-egg** N-COUNT [usu sing] A **nest egg** is a sum of money that you are saving for a particular purpose. [INFORMAL] ❑ *They have a little nest egg tucked away somewhere for a rainy day.*

nes|tle /nɛsəl/ (nestles, nestling, nestled) **1** V-T/V-I If you **nestle** or **are nestled** somewhere, you move into a comfortable position, usually by pressing against someone or against something soft. ❑ *John took one child into the crook of each arm and let them nestle against him.* **2** V-I If something such as a building **nestles** somewhere, it is in that place and seems safe or sheltered. ❑ *Nearby, nestling in the hills, was the children's home.*

nest|ling /nɛstlɪŋ/ (nestlings) N-COUNT A **nestling** is a young bird that has not yet learned to fly.

NET

① NOUN AND VERB USES
② ADJECTIVE AND ADVERB USES

---

① **net**♦◊◊ /nɛt/ (nets, netting, netted) **1** N-UNCOUNT **Net** is a kind of cloth that you can see through. It is made of fine threads woven together so that there are small equal spaces between them. **2** N-COUNT A **net** is a piece of netting which is used as a protective covering for something, for example to protect vegetables from birds. ❑ *I threw aside my mosquito net, jumped out of bed and drew up the blind.* **3** N-COUNT A **net** is a piece of netting which is used for catching fish, insects, or animals. ❑ *Several fishermen sat on wooden barrels, tending their nets.* **4** V-T If you **net** a fish or other animal, you catch it in a net. ❑ *I'm quite happy to net a fish and then let it go.* **5** V-T If you **net** something, you manage to get it, especially by using skill. ❑ *Two fourth-quarter drives netted a grand total of 21 yards.* **6** V-T If you **net** a particular amount of money, you gain it as profit after all expenses have been paid. ❑ *He netted profit of $1.85 billion from three large sales of stock.* **7** N-SING **The Net** is the same as the **internet**. **8** → see also **safety net** **9** → See feature box at **recycle**

SYNONYMS

net
NOUN ① **1**
mesh: *The ground-floor windows are obscured by wire mesh.*
netting: *...mosquito netting.*
lattice: *We were crawling along the narrow steel lattice of the bridge.*

② **net** ✦◊ /nɛt/

in BRIT, also use **nett**

1 ADJ [ADJ n, v-link ADJ of n] A **net** amount is one which remains when everything that should be subtracted from it has been subtracted. ◻ ...*a rise in sales and net profit.* ◻ *What you actually receive is net of deductions.* • ADV **Net** is also an adverb. ◻ *Balances of $5,000 and above will earn 11 percent gross, 8.25 percent net.* ◻ *They pay him around $2 million net.* **2** ADJ [ADJ n] The **net** weight of something is its weight without its container or the material that has been used to wrap it. ◻ ...*350 mg net weight.* **3** ADJ [ADJ n] A **net** result is a final result after all the details have been considered or included. ◻ *There has been a net gain in jobs in our country.* **4** → See feature box at **ocean**

net|book /nɛtbʊk/ (netbooks) N-COUNT A **netbook** is a type of small computer that you can easily carry around with you. [COMPUTING]

net|head /nɛthɛd/ (netheads) N-COUNT If you call someone a **nethead**, you mean that they spend a lot of time using the internet. [INFORMAL]

neth|er /nɛðər/ ADJ [ADJ n] **Nether** means the lower part of a thing or place. [OLD-FASHIONED] ◻ *He was escorted back to the nether regions of Main Street.*

nether|world /nɛðərwɜrld/ N-SING [usu with supp] If you refer to a place as a **netherworld**, you mean that it is dangerous and full of poor people and criminals. ◻ *Waits sang about the boozy netherworld of urban America.*

neti|quette /nɛtɪkɪt, -kɛt/ N-UNCOUNT **Netiquette** is the set of rules and customs that it is considered polite to follow when you are communicating by means of email or the internet.

nett /nɛt/ [BRIT] → see net ②

net|ting /nɛtɪŋ/ N-UNCOUNT [oft supp N] **Netting** is a kind of material made of pieces of thread or metal wires. These are woven together so that there are equal spaces between them. ◻ ...*mosquito netting.* ◻ ...*wire netting.*

net|tle /nɛtᵊl/ (nettles, nettling, nettled) **1** N-COUNT **Nettles** are wild plants which have leaves covered with fine hairs that sting you when you touch them. ◻ *The nettles stung their legs.* **2** V-T If you **are nettled** by something, you are annoyed or offended by it. ◻ *He was nettled by her manner.*

net|work ✦✦ /nɛtwɜrk/ (networks, networking, networked) **1** N-COUNT A radio or television **network** is a company or group of companies that broadcast radio or television programs throughout an area. ◻ ...*a Spanish-language broadcast television network.* **2** N-COUNT A **network** of people or institutions is a large number of them that have a connection with each other and work together as a system. ◻ *Distribution of the food is going ahead using a network of local church people and other volunteers.* **3** N-COUNT A particular **network** is a system of things which are connected and which operate together. For example, a **computer network** consists of a number of computers that are part of the same system. ◻ ...*a computer network with 154 terminals.* **4** N-COUNT A **network** of lines, roads, veins, or other long thin things is a large number of them which cross each other or meet at many points. ◻ ...*Strasbourg, with its rambling network of medieval streets.* **5** V-I If you **network**, you try to meet new people who might be useful to you in your job. [BUSINESS] ◻ *In business, it is important to network with as many people as possible on a face to face basis.*

--- SYNONYMS ---

network
NOUN **4**
maze: *The children lead me through the maze of alleys to the edge of the city.*
warren: ...*a warren of narrow streets.*
labyrinth: ...*the labyrinth of corridors.*
system: ...*Australia's road and rail system.*
structure: *The feet are highly specialized structures made up of 26 small delicate bones.*
grid: ...*a grid of narrow streets.*

net|work card (network cards) also **network interface card** N-COUNT A **network card** or a **network interface card** is a card that connects a computer to a network. [COMPUTING]

net|work|ing /nɛtwɜrkɪŋ/ **1** N-UNCOUNT **Networking** is the process of trying to meet new people who might be useful to you in your job, often through social activities. [BUSINESS] ◻ *If executives fail to exploit the opportunities of networking they risk being left behind.* **2** N-UNCOUNT You can refer to the things associated with a computer system or the process of establishing such a system as **networking**. ◻ *Managers have learned to grapple with networking, artificial intelligence, computer-aided engineering and manufacturing.* **3** → See feature box at **personality**

net-zero ADJ [usu ADJ n] A **net-zero** amount or effect is nothing, after all the details have been considered and included. ◻ *They are investing in green energy and carbon offsets to achieve net-zero emissions.*

neu|ral /nʊərəl/ ADJ **Neural** means relating to a nerve or to the nervous system. [MEDICAL] ◻ ...*neural pathways in the brain.*

neu|ral|gia /nʊærældʒə/ N-UNCOUNT **Neuralgia** is very severe pain along the whole length of a nerve caused when the nerve is damaged or not working properly. [MEDICAL]

neu|ral net|work (neural networks) N-COUNT In computing, a **neural network** is a program or system which is modeled on the human brain and is designed to imitate the brain's method of functioning, particularly the process of learning.

--- PREFIX ---

neuro-
is used to form words that refer or relate to a nerve or the nervous system. *For example, a **neurotransmitter** is a chemical by which nerve cells communicate.*

neu|ro|di|ver|gent /nʊəroʊdaɪvɜrdʒənt/ ADJ **Neurodivergent** means the same as **neurodiverse**.

neu|ro|di|verse /nʊəroʊdaɪvɜrs/ ADJ People who are **neurodiverse** have brains that function in a different way to that usually considered as normal. ◻ *Businesses are starting to realize that neurodiverse conditions can bring creativity, innovation and real brilliance into the workplace.*

neu|ro|logi|cal /nʊərəlɒdʒɪkᵊl/ ADJ [ADJ n] **Neurological** means related to the nervous system. [MEDICAL] ◻ ...*neurological disorders such as Parkinson's disease.*

neu|rol|ogy /nʊərɒlədʒi/ N-UNCOUNT **Neurology** is the study of the structure, function, and diseases of the nervous system. [MEDICAL] ◻ *He trained in neurology at the National Hospital for Nervous Diseases.* • **neu|rolo|gist** (neurologists) N-COUNT ◻ *Someone with suspected MS should see a neurologist specializing in the disease.*

neu|ron /nʊərɒn/ (neurons)

in BRIT, usually use **neurone**

1 N-COUNT A **neuron** is a cell which is part of the nervous system. Neurons send messages to and from the brain. [TECHNICAL] ◻ *Information is transferred along each neuron by means of an electrical impulse.* **2** → see also **motor neuron disease** **3** → See feature box at **brain**

neu|ro|sis /nʊəroʊsɪs/ (neuroses /nʊəroʊsiːz/) N-VAR **Neurosis** is a mental condition which causes people to have unreasonable fears and worries over a long period of time. ◻ *He was anxious to the point of neurosis.* ◻ *She had a neurosis about chemicals and imagined them everywhere doing her harm.*

neu|rot|ic /nʊərɒtɪk/ (neurotics) ADJ If you say that someone is **neurotic**, you mean that they are always frightened or worried about things that you consider unimportant. [DISAPPROVAL] ◻ *He was almost neurotic about being followed.* • N-COUNT A **neurotic** is someone who is neurotic. ◻ *These patients are not neurotics.*

neu|ter /nutər/ (neuters, neutering, neutered) **1** V-T [usu passive] When an animal **is neutered**, its reproductive organs are removed so that it cannot create babies. ◻ *We ask the public to have their dogs neutered and keep them under close supervision.* **2** ADJ In some languages, a **neuter** noun, pronoun, or adjective has a different form from a masculine or feminine one, or behaves in a different way. **3** V-T To **neuter** an organization, group, or person means to make them powerless and ineffective. [JOURNALISM] ◻ ...*the Government's "hidden agenda" to neuter local authorities.* ◻ *Their air force had been neutered before the work began.*

neu|tral /nˈuːtrəl/ (neutrals) **1** ADJ If a person or country adopts a **neutral** position or remains **neutral**, they do not support anyone in a disagreement, war, or contest. ❑ *Let's meet on neutral territory.* • N-COUNT A **neutral** is someone who is neutral. ❑ *It was a good game to watch for the neutrals.* • **neu|tral|ity** /nuːtrˈælɪti/ N-UNCOUNT ❑ *...a reputation for political neutrality and impartiality.* **2** ADJ If someone speaks in a **neutral** voice or if the expression on their face is **neutral**, they do not show what they are thinking or feeling. ❑ *Isabel put her magazine down and said in a neutral voice, "You're very late, darling."* • **neu|tral|ity** N-UNCOUNT ❑ *I noticed, behind the neutrality of his gaze, a deep weariness.* **3** ADJ If you say that something is **neutral**, you mean that it does not have any effect on other things because it lacks any significant qualities of its own, or it is an equal balance of two or more different qualities, amounts, or ideas. ❑ *Three in every five interviewed felt that the budget was neutral and they would be no better off.* **4** N-UNCOUNT **Neutral** is the position between the gears of a vehicle such as a car, in which the gears are not connected to the engine. ❑ *Graham put the van in neutral and jumped out into the road.* **5** ADJ In an electrical device or system, the **neutral** wire is one of the three wires needed to complete the circuit so that the current can flow. The other two wires are called the ground wire and the live or positive wire. ❑ *The ground wire in the house is connected to the neutral wire.* **6** COLOR **Neutral** is used to describe things that have a pale color such as cream or gray, or that have no color at all. ❑ *At the horizon the land mass becomes a continuous pale neutral gray, almost blending with the sky.* **7** ADJ In chemistry, **neutral** is used to describe things that are neither acid nor alkaline. ❑ *Pure water is neutral with a pH of 7.*

neu|tral|ize /nˈuːtrəlaɪz/ (neutralizes, neutralizing, neutralized)

in BRIT, also use **neutralise**

1 V-T To **neutralize** something means to prevent it from having any effect or from working properly. ❑ *The U.S. is trying to neutralize the resolution in the UN Security Council.* **2** V-T When a chemical substance **neutralizes** an acid, it makes it less acid. ❑ *Antacids are alkaline and they relieve pain by neutralizing acid in the contents of the stomach.*

neu|tron /nˈuːtrɒn/ (neutrons) **1** N-COUNT A **neutron** is an atomic particle that has no electrical charge. ❑ *Each atomic cluster is made up of neutrons and protons.* **2** → See feature box at **brain**

neu|tron bomb (neutron bombs) N-COUNT A **neutron bomb** is a nuclear weapon that is designed to kill people and animals without a large explosion and without destroying buildings or causing serious radioactive pollution.

neu|tron star (neutron stars) N-COUNT A **neutron star** is a star that has collapsed under the weight of its own gravity.

nev|er ✦✦✦ /nˈɛvər/ **1** ADV **Never** means at no time in the past or at no time in the future. ❑ *I have never lost the weight I put on in my teens.* ❑ *Never had he been so free of worry.* ❑ *That was a mistake. We'll never do it again.* **2** ADV **Never** means 'not in any circumstances at all.' ❑ *I would never do anything to hurt him.* ❑ *Divorce is never easy for children.* **3** PHRASE **Never ever** is an emphatic way of saying 'never.' [EMPHASIS] ❑ *I never, ever sit around thinking, "What shall I do next?"* **4** ADV **Never** is used to refer to the past and means 'not'. ❑ *He never achieved anything.* ❑ *I never knew him.* **5 never mind** → see **mind** ②

USAGE

never

Don't use 'do' in front of **never**. Don't say, for example, '~~He does never write to me.~~' Say 'He **never writes** to me.' He **never complains**.

never-ending ADJ If you describe something bad or unpleasant as **never-ending**, you are emphasizing that it seems to last a very long time. [EMPHASIS] ❑ *...a never-ending series of scandals rocking the presidency.*

never-never land N-UNCOUNT [also a n] **Never-never land** is an imaginary place where everything is perfect and no one has any problems. [INFORMAL] ❑ *We became suspended in some stately never-never land of pleasure, luxury, and idleness.*

nev|er|the|less ✦◇◇ /nˌɛvərðəlˈɛs/ ADV [ADV with cl] You use **nevertheless** when saying something that contrasts with what has just been said. [FORMAL] ❑ *Although the market has been flat, residential property costs remain high. Nevertheless, the fall-off in demand has had an impact on resale values.*

SYNONYMS

nevertheless
ADV
even so: *The bus was only half full. Even so, a young man asked Nina if the seat next to her was taken.*
still: *Their luck had simply run out. Still, never fear.*
nonetheless: *There was still a long way to go. Nonetheless, some progress had been made.*
yet: *I don't eat much, yet I am a size 16.*

new ✦✦✦ /nˈuː/ (newer, newest) **1** ADJ Something that is **new** has been recently created, built, or invented or is in the process of being created, built, or invented. ❑ *They've just opened a new hotel in the area.* ❑ *These ideas are nothing new.* **2** ADJ Something that is **new** has not been used or owned by anyone. ❑ *That afternoon she went out and bought a new dress.* ❑ *There are many boats, new and used, for sale.* **3** ADJ You use **new** to describe something which has replaced another thing, for example because you no longer have the old one, or it no longer exists, or it is no longer useful. ❑ *Under the new rules, some factories will cut emissions by as much as 90 percent.* ❑ *I had to find somewhere new to live.* ❑ *Rachel has a new boyfriend.* **4** ADJ **New** is used to describe something that has only recently been discovered or noticed. ❑ *The new planet is about ten times the size of the earth.* **5** ADJ [ADJ n] A **new** day or year is the beginning of the next day or year. ❑ *The start of a new year is a good time to reflect on the many achievements of the past.* **6** ADJ [ADJ n] **New** is used to describe someone or something that has recently acquired a particular status or position. ❑ *...the usual exhaustion of a new mother.* **7** ADJ [v-link ADJ] If you are **new** to a situation or place, or if the situation or place is **new** to you, you have not previously seen it or had any experience with it. ❑ *She wasn't new to the company.* ❑ *His name was new to me then and it stayed in my mind.* **8** ADJ [ADJ n] **New** potatoes, carrots, or peas are produced early in the season for such vegetables and are usually small with a sweet flavor. ❑ *Serve with a salad and new potatoes.* **9** → see also **brand-new** **10 as good as new** → see **good** ①

new- /nˈuː-/ COMB IN ADJ [usu ADJ n] **New-** combines with the past participle of some verbs to form adjectives which indicate that an action has been done or completed very recently. ❑ *He loved the smell of new-mown grass.* ❑ *Gerald treasures his new-won independence.*

New Age ADJ [usu ADJ n] **New Age** is used to describe spiritual or nonscientific activities such as meditation, astrology, and alternative medicine, or people who are connected with such activities. ❑ *She was involved in many New Age activities such as yoga and healing.*

new|bie /nˈuːbi/ (newbies) N-COUNT A **newbie** is someone who is new to an activity, especially in computing or on the internet. ❑ *All newbies are offered an individually tailored training and development program.*

new blood N-UNCOUNT If people talk about bringing **new blood** into an organization or onto a sports team, they are referring to new people who are likely to improve the organization or team. ❑ *We'll get some new blood in there.*

new|born /nˈuːbɔrn/ ADJ A **newborn** baby or animal is one that has just been born. ❑ *The electronic sensor has been adapted to fit on a newborn baby.* • N-PLURAL **The newborn** are babies or animals who are newborn. ❑ *Mild jaundice in the newborn is common and often clears without treatment.*

new|comer /nˈuːkʌmər/ (newcomers) N-COUNT A **newcomer** is a person who has recently arrived in a place, joined an organization, or started a new activity. ❑ *He must be a newcomer to town and he obviously didn't understand our local customs.*

new face (new faces) N-COUNT Someone who is new in a particular public role can be referred to as a **new face**. [JOURNALISM] ❑ *All together there are six new faces in the cabinet.*

new|fangled /nˈuːfæŋɡəld/ ADJ [ADJ n] If someone describes a new idea or a new piece of equipment as **newfangled**, they mean that it is too complicated or is unnecessary. [OLD-

FASHIONED, DISAPPROVAL] ❏ *Mr. Goss does not believe in any of this newfangled nonsense about lean meat.* ❏ *...a newfangled tax structure.*

new|found /n**u**faʊnd/ ADJ [ADJ n] A **newfound** quality or ability is one that you have got recently. ❏ *His friends have a newfound sense of patriotism.*

new|ly ✦✧✧ /n**u**li/ ADV [ADV -ed/adj] **Newly** is used before a past participle or an adjective to indicate that a particular action is very recent, or that a particular state of affairs has very recently begun to exist. ❏ *She was young at the time, and newly married.*

SYNONYMS

newly
ADV
recently: *The bank recently opened a branch in Germany.*
lately: *Thomas has not been looking well lately.*
freshly: *...freshly cut grass.*
latterly: *Latterly, he has written extensively about alternative medicine.*

newly|wed /n**u**liwɛd/ (**newlyweds**) N-COUNT [usu pl] **Newlyweds** are two people who have very recently gotten married to each other. ❏ *Lavalais raised his glass to propose a toast to the newlyweds.*

new me|dia N-PLURAL **New media** are new technologies such as the internet, and digital television and radio. ❏ *...a company which specializes in new media.* ❏ *The new-media industry attracts young and creative people.*

new moon (**new moons**) N-COUNT [usu sing] A **new moon** is the moon when it first appears as a thin curved shape at the start of its four-week cycle. The **new moon** is also the time of the month when the moon appears in this way. ❏ *...the pale crescent of a new moon.* ❏ *The new moon was the occasion of festivals of rejoicing in Egypt.*

news ✦✦✦ /n**u**z/ ◼ N-UNCOUNT **News** is information about a recently changed situation or a recent event. ❏ *We waited and waited for news of him.* ❏ *They still haven't had any news about when they'll be able to go home.* ◼ N-UNCOUNT [also the N] **News** is information that is published in newspapers and broadcast on radio and television about recent events in the country or world or in a particular area of activity. ❏ *Foreign News is on page 16.* ❏ *Those are some of the top stories in the news.* ◼ N-SING **The news** is a television or radio broadcast which consists of information about recent events in the country or the world. ❏ *I heard all about the bombs on the news.* ◼ N-UNCOUNT If you say that someone or something is **news**, you mean that they are considered to be interesting and important at the moment, and that people want to hear about them on the radio and television and in newspapers. [INFORMAL] ❏ *A murder was big news.* ◼ PHRASE If you say that something is **bad news**, you mean that it will cause you trouble or problems. If you say that something is **good news**, you mean that it will be useful or helpful to you. ❏ *The drop in travel is bad news for the airline industry.* ◼ PHRASE If you say that something **is news to** you, you mean that you did not previously know what you have just been told, especially when you are surprised or annoyed about it. ❏ *I'd certainly tell you if I knew anything, but I don't. What you're saying is news to me.* ◼ → See feature box at **press**

USAGE

news
Don't talk about '<s>a news</s>.' You refer to a piece of information as **some news** or **a piece of news**. *I have some good news for you.*

news agen|cy ✦✧✧ (**news agencies**) N-COUNT A **news agency** is an organization that gathers news stories from a particular country or from all over the world and supplies them to journalists. ❏ *A correspondent for Reuters news agency says he saw a number of demonstrators being beaten.*

news|cast /n**u**zkæst/ (**newscasts**) N-COUNT A **newscast** is a news program that is broadcast on the radio or on television.

news|caster ✦✧✧ /n**u**zkæstər/ (**newscasters**) N-COUNT A **newscaster** is a person who reads the news on the radio or on television. [mainly AM] ❏ *...TV newscaster Barbara Walters.*

in BRIT, use **newsreader**

news con|fer|ence (**news conferences**) N-COUNT A **news conference** is a meeting held by a famous or important person in which they answer journalists' questions. ❏ *He is due to hold a news conference in about an hour.*

news|flash /n**u**zflæʃ/ (**newsflashes**) also **news flash** N-COUNT A **newsflash** is an important item of news that television or radio stations broadcast as soon as they receive it, often interrupting other programs to do so. ❏ *We interrupt our programs for a newsflash.*

news|group /n**u**zgrup/ (**newsgroups**) N-COUNT A **newsgroup** is an internet site where people can put information and opinions about a particular subject so they can be read by everyone who looks at the site. ❏ *This allows parents to prohibit access to specific websites, newsgroups, and bulletin boards.*

news|letter /n**u**zlɛtər/ (**newsletters**) N-COUNT A **newsletter** is one or more printed sheets of paper containing information about an organization that is sent regularly to its members. ❏ *The organization now has around 18,000 members who receive a quarterly newsletter.*

news|man /n**u**zmæn, -mən/ (**newsmen**) N-COUNT A **newsman** is a male journalist for a newspaper or for a television or radio news program. [JOURNALISM]

news|paper ✦✦✧ /n**u**zpeɪpər, n**u**s-/ (**newspapers**) ◼ N-COUNT A **newspaper** is a publication consisting of a number of large sheets of folded paper, on which news, advertisements, and other information is printed. ❏ *He was carrying a newspaper.* ❏ *They read their daughter's allegations in the newspaper.* ◼ N-COUNT A **newspaper** is an organization that produces a newspaper. ❏ *It is the nation's fastest growing national daily newspaper.* ◼ N-UNCOUNT **Newspaper** consists of pieces of old newspapers, especially when they are being used for another purpose such as wrapping things up. ❏ *He found two pots, each wrapped in newspaper.*

news|paper|man /n**u**zpeɪpərmæn, n**u**s-/ (**newspapermen**) N-COUNT A **newspaperman** is a male journalist who works for a newspaper.

news|paper|woman /n**u**zpeɪpərwʊmən, n**u**s-/ (**newspaperwomen**) N-COUNT A **newspaperwoman** is a female journalist who works for a newspaper.

news|print /n**u**zprɪnt/ ◼ N-UNCOUNT **Newsprint** is the cheap, fairly rough paper on which newspapers are printed. ❏ *...a newsprint warehouse.* ◼ N-UNCOUNT **Newsprint** is the text that is printed in newspapers. ❏ *...the acres of newsprint devoted to the crisis in the past seven days.* ◼ N-UNCOUNT **Newsprint** is the ink which is used to print newspapers and magazines. ❏ *They get their hands covered in newsprint.*

news|read|er /n**u**zridər/ (**newsreaders**) N-COUNT A **newsreader** is a person who reads the news on the radio or on television. [BRIT]

in AM, use **newscaster**

news|reel /n**u**zril/ (**newsreels**) N-COUNT [oft N n] A **newsreel** is a short film of national or international news events. In the past newsreels were made for showing in movie theaters.

news re|lease (**news releases**) N-COUNT A **news release** is a written statement about a matter of public interest which is given to the press by an organization concerned with the matter. [mainly AM] ❏ *In a news release, the company said it had experienced severe financial problems.*

in BRIT, use **press release**

news|room /n**u**zrum/ (**newsrooms**) N-COUNT A **newsroom** is an office in a newspaper, radio, or television organization where news reports are prepared before they are printed or broadcast.

news-sheet (**news-sheets**) N-COUNT A **news-sheet** is a small newspaper that is usually printed and distributed in small quantities by a local political or social organization.

news|stand /n**u**zstænd/ (**newsstands**) N-COUNT A **newsstand** is a stall in the street or a public place, which sells newspapers and magazines. ❏ *No new national newspapers have appeared on the newsstands recently.*

news|woman /n**u**zwʊmən/ (**newswomen**) N-COUNT A **newswoman** is a female journalist for a newspaper or for a television or radio news program. [mainly AM] ❑ ...*Rosanna Scotto (the TV newswoman).*

news|worthy /nj̵uːzwɜːrði/ ADJ An event, fact, or person that is **newsworthy** is considered to be interesting enough to be reported in newspapers or on the radio or television. ❑ *There is nothing newsworthy to report.*

newt /nj̵uːt/ (newts) N-COUNT A **newt** is a small creature that has four legs and a long tail and can live on land and in water.

New Tes|ta|ment N-PROPER [the N] **The New Testament** is the part of the Bible that deals with the life and teachings of Jesus Christ and with Christianity in the early Church.

new wave (new waves) N-COUNT In the arts or in politics, a **new wave** is a group or movement that deliberately introduces new or unconventional ideas instead of using traditional ones. ❑ *...the new wave of satirical comedy.*

New World N-PROPER [the N] **The New World** is used to refer to the continents of North and South America. ❑ *...the massive growth in imports of good wines from the New World and Australasia.*

New Year ❶ N-UNCOUNT [also the N] **New Year** or **the New Year** is the time when people celebrate the start of a year. ❑ *Happy New Year, everyone.* ❑ *The restaurant was closed over the New Year.*
❷ N-SING **The New Year** is the first few weeks of a year. ❑ *Isabel was expecting their baby in the New Year.*

New Year's N-UNCOUNT **New Year's** is another name for **New Year's Day** or **New Year's Eve**. [AM]

New Year's Day N-UNCOUNT **New Year's Day** is the first day of the year. In Western countries this is the 1st of January. ❑ *On New Year's Day in 1974, I started keeping a journal.*

New Year's Eve N-UNCOUNT **New Year's Eve** is the last day of the year, the day before New Year's Day. ❑ *On New Year's Eve I usually give a party, which is always chaotic.*

New Year's reso|lu|tion (New Year's resolutions) also **New Year resolution** N-COUNT If you make a **New Year's resolution**, you make a decision at the beginning of a year to start doing something or to stop doing something. ❑ *She made a New Year's resolution to get in shape.*

New Zea|land|er /nj̵uː ziːləndər/ (**New Zealanders**) N-COUNT A **New Zealander** is a citizen of New Zealand, or a person of New Zealand origin.

next ◆◆◆ /nɛkst/ ❶ ORD The **next** period of time, event, person, or thing is the one that comes immediately after the present one or after the previous one. ❑ *I got up early the next morning.* ❑ *...the next available flight.* ❑ *Who will be the next mayor?* ❷ DET You use **next** in expressions such as **next Friday, next day**, and **next year** to refer, for example, to the first Friday, day, or year that comes after the present or previous one. ❑ *Let's plan a big night next week.* ❑ *He retires next January.* • ADJ [n ADJ] **Next** is also an adjective. ❑ *I'll be 26 years old next Friday.* • PRON **Next** is also a pronoun. ❑ *He predicted that the region's economy would grow by about six percent both this year and next.* ❸ ADJ [det ADJ] The **next** place or person is the one that is nearest to you or that is the first one that you come to. ❑ *Grace sighed so heavily that Trish could hear it in the next room.* ❑ *The man in the next chair was asleep.*
❹ ADV The thing that happens **next** is the thing that happens immediately after something else. ❑ *Next, close your eyes then screw them up tight.* ❑ *I don't know what to do next.* ❺ ADV [ADV before v] When you **next** do something, you do it for the first time since you last did it. ❑ *I next saw him at his house in Vermont.*
❻ ADV [ADV adj-superl] You use **next** to say that something has more of a particular quality than all other things except one. For example, the thing that is **next** best is the one that is the best except for one other thing. ❑ *The one thing he didn't have was a son. I think he's felt that a grandson is the next best thing.* ❼ PHRASE You use **after next** in expressions such as **the week after next** to refer to a period of time after the next one. For example, when it is May, the month after next is July. ❑ *...the party's annual conference, to be held the week after next.* ❽ PHRASE If you say that you do something or experience something as much **as the next person**, you mean that you are no different from anyone else in the respect mentioned. [EMPHASIS] ❑ *I enjoy pleasure as much as the next person.* ❾ PHRASE If one thing is **next to** another thing, it is at the other side of it. ❑ *She sat down next to him on the sofa.* ❑ *...at the southern end of the Gaza Strip next to the Egyptian border.* ❿ PHRASE You use **next to** in order to give the most important aspect of something when comparing it with another aspect. ❑ *Her children were the number two priority in her life next to her career.* ⓫ PHRASE You use **next to** before a negative, or a word that suggests something negative, to mean almost, but not completely. ❑ *Johnson still knew next to nothing about tobacco.*

USAGE

next
Don't use 'next' simply to say that a particular thing is the closest one. Don't say, for example, 'They took him to the next hospital.' You say 'They took him to **the closest hospital**.' **The nearest town** is Brompton.

---

next door

The adjective is usually spelled **next-door**.

❶ ADV If a room or building is **next door**, it is the next one to the right or left. ❑ *I went next door to the bathroom.* ❑ *...the people who live next door.* • ADJ [ADJ n] **Next door** is also an adjective. ❑ *...a thud like a cellar door slamming shut in a next-door house.* ❷ PHRASE If a room or building is **next door to** another one, it is the next one to the left or right. ❑ *The kitchen is right next door to the dining room.* ❸ ADV [n ADV] The people **next door** are the people who live in the house or apartment to the right or left of yours. ❑ *The neighbors thought the family next door had moved.* • ADJ [ADJ n] **Next door** is also an adjective. ❑ *Even your next-door neighbor didn't see through your disguise.* ❹ PHRASE If you refer to someone as **the boy next door** or **the girl next door**, you mean that they are pleasant, respectable, and likeable. ❑ *He was dependable, straightforward, the boy next door.*

next of kin N-UNCOUNT-COLL **Next of kin** is sometimes used to refer to the person who is your closest relative, especially in official or legal documents. [FORMAL] ❑ *We have notified the next of kin.*

nex|us /nɛksəs/ (**nexus**) N-COUNT [usu with supp] A **nexus** is a connection or series of connections within a particular situation or system. [FORMAL] ❑ *...the nexus between the dominant class and the State.*

NFL /ɛn ɛf ɛl/ N-PROPER [the N] In the United States, the **NFL** is the organization responsible for professional football. **NFL** is an abbreviation for 'National Football League.' ❑ *...one of the best defensive backs in the NFL.* ❑ *...an NFL player.*

NGO /ɛn dʒiː oʊ/ (**NGOs**) N-COUNT An **NGO** is an organization which is not run by the government. **NGO** is an abbreviation for nongovernmental organization.

NHL /ɛn eɪtʃ ɛl/ N-PROPER [the N] In the United States, the **NHL** is the organization responsible for professional hockey. **NHL** is an abbreviation for 'National Hockey League.' ❑ *...the best goaltender in the NHL.* ❑ *...a former NHL player.*

nia|cin /naɪəsɪn/ N-UNCOUNT **Niacin** is a vitamin that occurs in milk, liver, yeast, and some other foods.

nib /nɪb/ (**nibs**) N-COUNT A **nib** is a pointed piece of metal at the end of some pens, which controls the flow of ink as you write.

nib|ble /nɪbəl/ (**nibbles, nibbling, nibbled**) ❶ V-T/V-I If you **nibble** food, you eat it by biting very small pieces of it, for example because you are not very hungry. ❑ *Linda lay face down on a living room couch, nibbling popcorn.* ❑ *She nibbled at a piece of dry toast.* • N-COUNT **Nibble** is also a noun. ❑ *We each took a nibble.*
❷ V-T/V-I If you **nibble** something, you bite it very gently. ❑ *John found he was kissing and nibbling her ear.* ❑ *Daniel nibbled on his pen.* ❸ V-T/V-I When an animal **nibbles** something, it takes small bites of it quickly and repeatedly. ❑ *A herd of goats was nibbling the turf around the base of the tower.* ❑ *The birds nibble at the brickwork.* • PHRASAL VERB **Nibble away** means the same as **nibble**. ❑ *The rabbits nibbled away on the herbaceous plants.* ❹ V-I If one thing **nibbles** at another, it gradually affects, harms, or destroys it. ❑ *It was all going according to plan, yet small doubts kept nibbling at the edges of his mind.* • PHRASAL VERB **Nibble away** means the same as **nibble**. ❑ *Several manufacturers have also been nibbling away at our traditional customer base.*

ni|cad /naɪkæd/ also **ni-cad** ADJ A **nicad** battery is a battery made from a combination of nickel and cadmium.

nice ◆◆◇ /naɪs/ (**nicer, nicest**) ❶ ADJ If you say that something is **nice**, you mean that you find it attractive, pleasant, or enjoyable. ❑ *I think silk ties can be quite nice.* ❑ *It's nice to be here together again.* • **nice|ly** ADV ❑ *He's just written a book, nicely illustrated and not too technical.* **2** ADJ If you say that it is **nice of** someone to say or do something, you are saying that they are being kind and thoughtful. This is often used as a way of thanking someone. ❑ *It's awfully nice of you to come all this way to see me.* ❑ *"How are your boys?"—"How nice of you to ask."* **3** ADJ If you say that someone is **nice**, you mean that you like them because they are friendly and pleasant. ❑ *I've met your father and he's rather nice.* **4** ADJ [v-link ADJ] If you are **nice** to people, you are friendly, pleasant, or polite toward them. ❑ *She met Mr. and Mrs. Ricciardi, who were very nice to her.* • **nice|ly** ADV [after v] ❑ *He treated you very nicely and acted like a decent guy.* **5** ADJ When the weather is **nice**, it is warm and pleasant. ❑ *He nodded to us and said, "Nice weather we're having."* **6** ADJ You can use **nice** to emphasize a particular quality that you like. [EMPHASIS] ❑ *With a nice dark color, the wine is medium to full bodied.* ❑ *I'll explain it nice and simply so you can understand.* **7** ADJ [it v-link ADJ to-inf] You can use **nice** when you are greeting people. For example, you can say '**Nice to meet you**,' '**Nice to have met you**,' or '**Nice to see you.**' [FORMULAE] ❑ *Good morning. Nice to meet you and thanks for being with us this weekend.* **8** → see also **nicely**

SYNONYMS

nice
ADJ
1
pleasant: *The weather is very pleasant today.*
delightful: *It was the most delightful garden I had ever seen.*
agreeable: *…an agreeable surprise.*
3
kind: *I must thank you for being so kind to me.*
helpful: *James is a very helpful and cooperative young man.*
obliging: *He is an extremely pleasant and obliging man.*
considerate: *I think he's the most charming, most considerate man I've ever known.*

---

nice-looking ADJ Someone who is **nice-looking** is physically attractive. ❑ *I saw this nice-looking man in a gray suit.* ❑ *We got on very well and she was very nice-looking.*

nice|ly /naɪsli/ **1** ADV [ADV with v] If something is happening or working **nicely**, it is happening or working in a satisfactory way or in the way that you want it to. ❑ *She has a bit of private money, so they manage quite nicely.* **2** → see also **nice** **3** PHRASE If someone or something is **doing nicely**, they are being successful. ❑ *…another hotel owner who is doing very nicely.*

ni|cety /naɪsɪti/ (**niceties**) N-COUNT [usu pl, oft the N of n, adj N] The **niceties** of a situation are its details, especially with regard to good manners or the appropriate behavior for that situation. ❑ *…the niceties of dinner party conversation.* ❑ *He wasted no time with social niceties.*

niche /nɪtʃ, niʃ/ (**niches**) **1** N-COUNT A **niche** in the market is a specific area of marketing which has its own particular requirements, customers, and products. [BUSINESS] ❑ *I think we have found a niche in the toy market.* **2** ADJ [ADJ n] **Niche** marketing is the practice of dividing the market into specialized areas for which particular products are made. A **niche** market is one of these specialized areas. [BUSINESS] ❑ *Many media experts see such all-news channels as part of a general move towards niche marketing.* **3** N-COUNT A **niche** is a hollow area in a wall which has been made to hold a statue, or a natural hollow part in a hill or cliff. ❑ *Above him, in a niche on the wall, sat a tiny veiled Ganesh, the elephant god.* **4** N-COUNT Your **niche** is the job or activity which is exactly suitable for you. ❑ *I suddenly felt that I'd been born to be an agony aunt: at last I'd found my true niche.* **5** → See feature box at **business**

nick /nɪk/ (**nicks, nicking, nicked**) **1** V-T If you **nick** something or **nick** yourself, you accidentally make a small cut in the surface of the object or your skin. ❑ *When I pulled out of the space, I nicked the rear bumper of the car in front of me.* ❑ *A sharp blade is likely to nick the skin and draw blood.* **2** N-COUNT A **nick** is a small cut made in the surface of something, usually in someone's skin. ❑ *The barbed wire had left only the tiniest nick just below my right eye.*

nick|el /nɪkəl/ (**nickels**) **1** N-UNCOUNT **Nickel** is a silver-colored metal that is used in making steel. **2** N-COUNT In the United States and Canada, a **nickel** is a coin worth five cents. ❑ *…a large glass jar filled with pennies, nickels, dimes, and quarters.* **3** → See also color supplement

nickel-and-dime (**nickels-and-dimes, nickel-and-diming** or **nickeling-and-diming, nickel-and-dimed** or **nickeled-and-dimed**) also **nickel and dime** **1** V-T If you accuse a person of **nickel-and-diming** someone or something, you are criticizing that person for weakening or exhausting them, for example, by continually taking small amounts of money away from them, or by continually making small changes or requests. [AM, INFORMAL, DISAPPROVAL] ❑ *A bad contractor may hide mistakes or blame someone else and nickel-and-dime you with extra charges.* ❑ *If you try to nickel-and-dime people, they are not going to be co-operative.* **2** ADJ If you describe someone or something as **nickel-and-dime**, you mean that they are not very important or they only function on a small scale. [AM, INFORMAL] ❑ *…a number of nickel-and-dime jobs – janitor, pastry chef, window washer.*

nick|name /nɪkneɪm/ (**nicknames, nicknaming, nicknamed**) **1** N-COUNT A **nickname** is an informal name for someone or something. ❑ *Red got his nickname for his red hair.* **2** V-T If you **nickname** someone or something, you give them an informal name. ❑ *When he got older I nicknamed him Little Alf.*

nico|tine /nɪkətin/ N-UNCOUNT **Nicotine** is the substance in tobacco that people can become addicted to. ❑ *Nicotine produces a feeling of well-being in the smoker.*

nico|tine patch (**nicotine patches**) N-COUNT A **nicotine patch** is a small piece of sticky material that you can stick to your skin if you are trying to give up smoking. The patch slowly releases nicotine into your bloodstream so that your desire for tobacco is reduced. ❑ *…a week's supply of nicotine patches.*

niece /nis/ (**nieces**) N-COUNT Someone's **niece** is the daughter of their sister or brother. ❑ *…his niece, the daughter of his eldest sister.*

nif|ty /nɪfti/ (**niftier, niftiest**) ADJ [usu ADJ n] If you describe something as **nifty**, you think it is neat and pleasing or cleverly done. [INFORMAL, APPROVAL] ❑ *Bridgeport was a pretty nifty place.* ❑ *It was a nifty arrangement, a perfect partnership.*

Ni|gerian /naɪdʒɪəriən/ (**Nigerians**) **1** ADJ **Nigerian** means belonging or relating to Nigeria, its people, or its culture. **2** N-COUNT A **Nigerian** is a Nigerian citizen, or a person of Nigerian origin.

nig|gard|ly /nɪgərdli/ ADJ If you describe someone as **niggardly**, you are criticizing them because they do not give or provide much of something. [DISAPPROVAL] ❑ *Officials say the EU, which is supposed to provide most of the food needs, is being particularly niggardly.* ❑ *…a niggardly supply of hot water.*

nig|ger /nɪgər/ (**niggers**) N-COUNT **Nigger** is an extremely offensive word for a Black person. [VERY OFFENSIVE]

nig|gle /nɪgəl/ (**niggles, niggling, niggled**) V-T/V-I If someone **niggles** you, they annoy you by continually criticizing you for what you think are small or unimportant things. ❑ *I don't react anymore when opponents try to niggle me.* • N-COUNT **Niggle** is also a noun. ❑ *The life we have built together is more important than any minor niggle either of us might have.*

nig|gling /nɪgəlɪŋ/ ADJ [usu ADJ n] A **niggling** injury or worry is small but bothers you over a long period of time. ❑ *Both players have been suffering from niggling injuries.* ❑ *…a niggling worry that the cheap car is also the one that will cause endless trouble.*

nigh /naɪ/ **1** ADV [be ADV] If an event is **nigh**, it will happen very soon. [OLD-FASHIONED] ❑ *The end of the world may be nigh, but do we really care?* **2** → see also **well-nigh** **3** PHRASE [PHR amount] **Nigh on** an amount, number, or age means almost that amount, number, or age. [OLD-FASHIONED] ❑ *I had to pay nigh on forty dollars for it.*

night ◆◆◆ /naɪt/ (**nights**) **1** N-VAR The **night** is the part of each day when the sun has set and it is dark outside, especially the time when people are sleeping. ❑ *The fighting began in the late afternoon and continued all night.* ❑ *Finally night fell.* **2** N-COUNT The **night** is the period of time between the end of the afternoon and the time that you go to bed, especially the time when you relax before going to bed. ❑ *So whose party was it last night?* **3** N-COUNT A particular **night** is a particular evening when a special event takes place, such as a show or a play. ❑ *The first night crowd packed the building.* **4** PHRASE If it is a particular time

at night, it is during the time when it is dark and is before midnight. ❏ *It's eleven o'clock at night in Moscow.* **5** PHRASE If something happens **at night**, it happens regularly during the evening or night. ❏ *He was going to college at night, in order to become an accountant.* **6** PHRASE If something happens **day and night** or **night and day**, it happens all the time without stopping. ❏ *Dozens of doctors and nurses have been working day and night for weeks.* **7** PHRASE If you have **an early night**, you go to bed early. If you have **a late night**, you go to bed late. ❏ *I've had a hell of a day, and all I want is an early night.* **8 morning, noon, and night** → see **morning**

night|cap /naɪtkæp/ (nightcaps) N-COUNT A **nightcap** is a drink that you have just before you go to bed, usually an alcoholic drink. ❏ *Perhaps you would join me for a nightcap?*

night|clothes /naɪtkloʊz, -kloʊðz/ N-PLURAL **Nightclothes** are clothes that you wear in bed.

night|club /naɪtklʌb/ (nightclubs) N-COUNT A **nightclub** is a place where people go late in the evening to drink and dance.

night|club|bing /naɪtklʌbɪŋ/ N-UNCOUNT **Nightclubbing** is the activity of going to nightclubs.

night|dress /naɪtdrɛs/ (nightdresses) N-COUNT A **nightdress** is the same as a **nightgown**.

night|fall /naɪtfɔl/ N-UNCOUNT **Nightfall** is the time of day when it starts to get dark. ❏ *I need to get to Houston by nightfall.*

night|gown /naɪtɡaʊn/ (nightgowns) N-COUNT A **nightgown** is a sort of loose dress that a woman or girl wears in bed.

in BRIT, use **nightdress**

nightie /naɪti/ (nighties) N-COUNT A **nightie** is the same as a nightgown. [INFORMAL]

night|in|gale /naɪtəngeɪl/ (nightingales) N-COUNT A **nightingale** is a small brown bird. The male, which can be heard at night, sings beautifully.

night|life /naɪtlaɪf/ **1** N-UNCOUNT **Nightlife** is all the entertainment and social activities that are available at night in cities and towns, such as nightclubs and theaters. ❏ *New York's energetic nightlife is second to none.* **2** → See feature box at **socialize**

night light (night lights) N-COUNT A **night light** is a light that is not bright and is kept on during the night, especially in a child's room.

night-long also **nightlong** ADJ [ADJ n] A **night-long** event is one that continues throughout the night. ❏ *...a night-long party.* ❏ *...a nightlong search.*

night|ly /naɪtli/ ADJ [ADJ n] A **nightly** event happens every night. ❏ *I'm sure we watched the nightly news, and then we turned on the movie.* • ADV **Nightly** is also an adverb. ❏ *She appears nightly on the television news.*

night|mare ✦◊◊ /naɪtmɛər/ (nightmares) **1** N-COUNT A **nightmare** is a very frightening dream. ❏ *All the victims still suffered nightmares.* **2** PHRASE If you refer to a situation as a **nightmare**, you mean that it is very frightening and unpleasant. ❏ *The years in prison were a nightmare.* **3** N-COUNT If you refer to a situation as a **nightmare**, you are saying in a very emphatic way that it is irritating because it causes you a lot of trouble. [EMPHASIS] ❏ *Taking my son Peter to a restaurant was a nightmare.*

> **WORD HISTORY**
>
> **nightmare**
> **Nightmare** comes from *night* and Old English *mare*, meaning 'evil spirit.'

night|mare sce|nar|io (nightmare scenarios) N-COUNT [usu sing] If you describe a situation or event as a **nightmare scenario**, you mean that it is the worst possible thing that could happen. ❏ *Discovering your child takes drugs is a nightmare scenario for most parents.*

night|mar|ish /naɪtmɛərɪʃ/ ADJ If you describe something as **nightmarish**, you mean that it is extremely frightening and unpleasant. ❏ *She described a nightmarish scene of dead bodies lying in the streets.*

night owl (night owls) N-COUNT A **night owl** is someone who regularly stays up late at night, or who prefers to work at night. [INFORMAL]

night school (night schools) N-VAR Someone who goes to **night school** takes educational classes in the evenings. ❏ *People can go out to work in the daylight hours and then come to night school in the evening.*

night|shirt /naɪtʃɜrt/ (nightshirts) N-COUNT A **nightshirt** is a long, loose shirt worn in bed.

night|spot /naɪtspɒt/ (nightspots) N-COUNT A **nightspot** is a nightclub. [INFORMAL] ❏ *...Harlem's most famous nightspot, the Cotton Club.*

night|stand /naɪtstænd/ (nightstands) N-COUNT A **nightstand** is a small table usually with shelves or drawers, that you have next to your bed. [AM]

in BRIT, use **bedside table**

night|stick /naɪtstɪk/ (nightsticks) N-COUNT A **nightstick** is a short thick club that is carried by police officers. [AM]

in BRIT, use **truncheon**

night ta|ble (night tables) N-COUNT A **night table** is the same as a **nightstand**. [AM]

night|time /naɪttaɪm/ N-UNCOUNT [oft N n] **Nighttime** is the period of time between when it gets dark and when the sun rises. ❏ *They wanted someone responsible to look after the place at nighttime.* ❏ *A twelve hour nighttime curfew is in force.*

night vi|sion N-UNCOUNT [usu N n] **Night vision** equipment enables people, for example soldiers or pilots, to see better at night. ❏ *...night vision goggles.*

night watch|man (night watchmen) N-COUNT A **night watchman** is a person whose job is to guard buildings at night.

ni|hil|ism /naɪɪlɪzəm/ N-UNCOUNT **Nihilism** is a belief which rejects all political and religious authority and current ideas in favor of the individual. • **ni|hil|ist** (nihilists) N-COUNT ❏ *Why wasn't Weber a nihilist?*

ni|hil|is|tic /naɪɪlɪstɪk/ ADJ If you describe someone as **nihilistic**, you mean they do not trust political and religious authority and place their faith in the individual. ❏ *She exhibited none of the narcissistic and nihilistic tendencies of her peers.*

nil /nɪl/ N-UNCOUNT If you say that something is **nil**, you mean that it does not exist at all. ❏ *Their legal rights are virtually nil.*

nim|ble /nɪmbəl/ (nimbler, nimblest) **1** ADJ Someone who is **nimble** is able to move their fingers, hands, or legs quickly and easily. ❏ *Everything had been stitched by Molly's nimble fingers.* **2** ADJ If you say that someone has a **nimble** mind, you mean they are clever and can think very quickly. ❏ *A nimble mind backed by a degree in economics gave him a firm grasp of financial matters.*

nim|bus /nɪmbəs/ N-SING [usu N n] A **nimbus** is a large gray cloud that brings rain or snow. [TECHNICAL] ❏ *...layers of cold nimbus clouds.*

NIMBY /nɪmbi/ also **Nimby** ADJ [usu ADJ n] If you say that someone has a **NIMBY** attitude, you are criticizing them because they do not want something such as a new road, public housing, or a prison built near to where they live. **NIMBY** is an abbreviation for 'not in my backyard.' [INFORMAL, DISAPPROVAL] ❏ *...the usual NIMBY protests from local residents.*

nine ✦◊◊ /naɪn/ (nines) NUM **Nine** is the number 9. ❏ *We still sighted nine yachts.*

999 /naɪn naɪn naɪn/ NUM **999** is the number that you call in Britain in order to contact the emergency services. ❏ *...a fire engine answering a 999 call.* ❏ *She dialled 999 on her mobile.*

9/11 /naɪn ɪlɛvən/ also **nine-eleven** N-PROPER **9/11** or **nine-eleven** is used to refer to the events that took place in the United States on September 11, 2001, when terrorists attacked the World Trade Center in New York and the Pentagon. ❏ *...the victims of 9/11.* ❏ *Everything changed after nine-eleven.*

911 /naɪn wʌn wʌn/ NUM **911** is the number that you call in the United States in order to contact the emergency services. ❏ *The women made their first 911 call about a prowler at 12:46 a.m.*

nine|teen ✦◊◊ /naɪntin/ (nineteens) NUM **Nineteen** is the number 19. ❏ *They have nineteen days to make up their minds.*

nine|teenth ✦◊◊ /naɪntinθ/ ORD The **nineteenth** item in a series is the one that you count as number nineteen. ❏ *...my nineteenth birthday.*

nine|ti|eth /naɪntiiθ/ ORD The **ninetieth** item in a series is the one that you count as number ninety. ❑ *He celebrates his ninetieth birthday on Friday.*

nine-to-five ADJ A **nine-to-five** job is one that you do during normal office hours, for example a job in a factory or an office. ❑ *She works a nine-to-five job.* • ADV **Nine to five** is also an adverb. ❑ *I wish I could go to work in a factory, nine to five.*

nine|ty /naɪnti/ (nineties) **1** NUM **Ninety** is the number 90. ❑ *It was decided she had to stay another ninety days.* **2** N-PLURAL When you talk about the **nineties**, you are referring to numbers between 90 and 99. For example, if you are **in your nineties**, you are aged between 90 and 99. If the temperature is **in the nineties**, the temperature is between 90 and 99 degrees. ❑ *By this time she was in her nineties and needed help more and more frequently.* **3** N-PLURAL **The nineties** is the decade between 1990 and 1999. ❑ *These trends only got worse as we moved into the nineties.*

nin|ny /nɪni/ (ninnies) N-COUNT If you refer to someone as a **ninny**, you think that they are foolish or silly. [INFORMAL, OLD-FASHIONED, DISAPPROVAL]

ninth /naɪnθ/ (ninths) **1** ORD The **ninth** item in a series is the one that you count as number nine. ❑ *...January the ninth.* ❑ *...students in the ninth grade.* **2** FRACTION A **ninth** is one of nine equal parts of something. ❑ *The dollar rose by a ninth of a cent.*

nip /nɪp/ (nips, nipping, nipped) **1** V-T If an animal or person **nips** you, they bite you lightly or squeeze a piece of your skin between their finger and thumb. ❑ *I have known cases where dogs have nipped babies.* • N-COUNT **Nip** is also a noun. ❑ *Incidents range from a nip, which fails to break the skin or draw blood, to serious injuries.* **2** N-COUNT A **nip** is a small amount of a strong alcoholic drink. ❑ *She had a habit of taking an occasional nip from a flask of cognac.* **3 to nip something in the bud** → see **bud**

nip|ple /nɪpᵊl/ (nipples) **1** N-COUNT The **nipples** on someone's body are the two small pieces of slightly hard flesh on their chest. Babies suck milk from their mothers' breasts through their mothers' nipples. ❑ *Sore nipples can inhibit the milk supply.* **2** N-COUNT A **nipple** is a piece of rubber or plastic which is attached to the top of a baby's bottle. ❑ *...a white plastic bottle with a rubber nipple.*

nip|py /nɪpi/ (nippier, nippiest) ADJ [usu v-link ADJ] If the weather is **nippy**, it is rather cold. [INFORMAL] ❑ *It could get suddenly nippy in the evenings.*

niqab /nɪkɑb/ (niqabs) N-COUNT A **niqab** is a piece of cloth that some Muslim women wear covering their face apart from their eyes.

nir|va|na /nɪrvɑnə, nɜr-/ **1** N-UNCOUNT In the Hindu and Buddhist religions, **Nirvana** is the highest spiritual state that can possibly be achieved. ❑ *Entering the realm of Nirvana is only possible for those who have become pure.* **2** N-UNCOUNT People sometimes refer to a state of complete happiness and peace as **nirvana**. ❑ *Many businessmen think that a world where relative prices never varied would be nirvana.*

Nissen hut /nɪsᵊn hʌt/ (Nissen huts) N-COUNT A **Nissen hut** is the same as a **Quonset hut**. [BRIT]

nit /nɪt/ (nits) N-COUNT [usu pl] **Nits** are the eggs of insects called lice which live in people's hair.

nite /naɪt/ (nites) N-VAR **Nite** is another spelling of **night**, used in less formal written English. [mainly AM] ❑ *...$50 per nite, $350 weekly.*

nit|pick /nɪtpɪk/ (nitpicks, nitpicking, nitpicked) V-I If someone **nitpicks**, they criticize small and unimportant details. [INFORMAL] ❑ *I looked hard for items to nitpick about, and couldn't find any. Altogether a great car.*

nit|pick|ing /nɪtpɪkɪŋ/ also **nit-picking** N-UNCOUNT If you refer to someone's opinion as **nitpicking**, you disapprove of the fact that it concentrates on small and unimportant details, especially to try and find fault with something. [DISAPPROVAL] ❑ *A lot of nit-picking was going on about irrelevant things.* ❑ *I can get down to nitpicking detail, I am pretty fussy about certain things.*

ni|trate /naɪtreɪt/ (nitrates) N-MASS **Nitrate** is a chemical compound that includes nitrogen and oxygen. Nitrates are used as fertilizers in agriculture. ❑ *High levels of nitrate occur in the Midwest because of the heavy use of fertilizers.*

ni|tric /naɪtrɪk/ ADJ [ADJ n] **Nitric** means relating to or containing nitrogen. ❑ *...nitric oxide.*

ni|tric acid N-UNCOUNT **Nitric acid** is a strong colorless acid containing nitrogen, hydrogen, and oxygen.

nitro- /naɪtroʊ-/ COMB IN N **Nitro-** combines with nouns to form other nouns referring to things which contain nitrogen and oxygen. ❑ *...highly corrosive substances such as nitro-phosphates.*

ni|tro|gen /naɪtrədʒən/ N-UNCOUNT **Nitrogen** is a colorless element that has no smell and is usually found as a gas. It forms about 78 percent of the Earth's atmosphere, and is found in all living things.

ni|tro|glyc|er|in /naɪtroʊglɪsərɪn/ also **nitroglycerine** N-UNCOUNT **Nitroglycerin** is a liquid that is used to make explosives and also in some medicines.

ni|trous /naɪtrəs/ ADJ [ADJ n] **Nitrous** means coming from, relating to, or containing nitrogen. ❑ *...nitrous oxides.*

nitty-gritty /nɪti grɪti/ also **nitty gritty** N-SING [usu the N] If people get down to the **nitty-gritty** of a matter, situation, or activity, they discuss the most important, basic parts of it or facts about it. [INFORMAL] ❑ *...the nitty gritty of everyday politics.*

nit|wit /nɪtwɪt/ (nitwits) N-COUNT If you refer to someone as a **nitwit**, you think they are stupid or silly. [INFORMAL, DISAPPROVAL] ❑ *You nitwit!*

nix /nɪks/ (nixes, nixing, nixed) V-T If you **nix** a plan or suggestion, you reject or forbid it. [AM, INFORMAL] ❑ *It only took a few minutes for me to nix this proposal.*

no /noʊ/ (noes or no's) **1** CONVENTION You use **no** to give a negative response to a question. ❑ *"Any problems?"—"No, I'm O.K."* **2** CONVENTION You use **no** to say that something someone has just said is not true. ❑ *"We thought you'd emigrated."—"No, no."* **3** CONVENTION You use **no** to refuse an offer or a request, or to refuse permission. ❑ *"Here, have mine."—"No, this is fine."* ❑ *"Can you just get the message through to Pete for me?"—"No, no I can't."* **4** EXCLAM You use **no** to indicate that you do not want someone to do something. ❑ *No. I forbid it. You cannot.* **5** CONVENTION You use **no** to acknowledge a negative statement or to show that you accept and understand it. ❑ *"We're not on the main campus."—"No."* ❑ *"It's not one of my favorite forms of music."—"No."* **6** CONVENTION You use **no** before correcting what you have just said. ❑ *I was twenty-two – no, twenty-one.* **7** EXCLAM You use **no** to express shock or disappointment at something you have just been told. [FEELINGS] ❑ *"We went with Sarah and the man she's currently seeing."—"Oh no."* **8** DET You use **no** to mean not any or not one person or thing. ❑ *He had no intention of paying the cash.* ❑ *No job has more influence on the future of the world.* **9** DET You use **no** to emphasize that someone or something is not the type of thing mentioned. [EMPHASIS] ❑ *He is no singer.* ❑ *I make it no secret that our worst consultants earn nothing.* **10** ADV [ADV compar] You can use **no** to make the negative form of a comparative. ❑ *The second report must be submitted no later than September.* ❑ *Yesterday no fewer than thirty climbers reached the summit.* **11** DET You use **no** in front of an adjective and noun to make the noun group mean its opposite. ❑ *Sometimes a bit of selfishness, if it leads to greater self-knowledge, is no bad thing.* **12** DET **No** is used in notices or instructions to say that a particular activity or thing is forbidden. ❑ *The captain turned out the "no smoking" signs.* ❑ *No talking after lights out.* **13** N-COUNT A **no** is a person who has answered 'no' to a question or who has voted against something. **No** is also used to refer to their answer or vote. ❑ *According to the latest opinion polls, the noes have 50 percent, the yeses 35 percent.* **14** PHRASE If you say **there is no** doing a particular thing, you mean that it is very difficult or impossible to do that thing. [EMPHASIS] ❑ *There is no going back to the life she had.* **15 not to take no for an answer** → see **answer** **16 no doubt** → see **doubt** **17 no longer** → see **long** ③ **18 in no way** → see **way** ③ **19 there's no way** → see **way** ④ **20 no way** → see **way** ④

No. (Nos) **No.** is a written abbreviation for **number**. ❑ *That year he was named the nation's No. 1 college football star.*

no-account ADJ [usu ADJ n] A **no-account** person or thing is one that you consider worthless. [AM, INFORMAL, DISAPPROVAL] ❑ *...a mongrelized, no-account place.*

Nobel Prize /noʊbəl praɪz/ (**Nobel Prizes**) N-COUNT [oft N for n] A **Nobel Prize** is one of a set of prizes that are awarded each year to people who have done important work in science, literature, or economics, or for world peace. ❑ ...the Nobel Prize for literature.

no|bil|ity /noʊbɪlɪti/ **1** N-SING-COLL The **nobility** of a society are all the people who have titles and belong to a high social class. ❑ They married into the nobility and entered the highest ranks of state administration. **2** N-UNCOUNT A person's **nobility** is their noble character and behavior. [FORMAL] ❑ ...his nobility of character, and his devotion to his country.

no|ble /noʊbəl/ (**nobler, noblest**) **1** ADJ If you say that someone is a **noble** person, you admire and respect them because they are unselfish and morally good. [APPROVAL] ❑ He was an upright and noble man who was always willing to help in any way he could. ● **no|bly** ADV [ADV with v] ❑ Eric's sister had nobly volunteered to help with the gardening. **2** ADJ If you say that something is a **noble** idea, goal, or action, you admire it because it is based on high moral principles. [APPROVAL] ❑ He had implicit faith in their noble intentions. ❑ We'll always justify our actions with noble sounding theories. **3** ADJ If you describe something as **noble**, you think that its appearance or quality is very impressive, making it superior to other things of its type. ❑ ...the great parks with their noble trees. **4** ADJ **Noble** means belonging to a high social class and having a title. ❑ ...rich and noble families.

noble|man /noʊbəlmən/ (**noblemen**) N-COUNT In former times, a **nobleman** was a man who was a member of the nobility. ❑ It had once been the home of a wealthy nobleman.

no|blesse oblige /noʊblɛs oʊbliːʒ/ N-UNCOUNT **Noblesse oblige** is the idea that people with advantages, for example those of a high social class, should help and do things for other people. [FORMAL] ❑ They did so without hope of further profit and out of a sense of noblesse oblige.

noble|woman /noʊbəlwʊmən/ (**noblewomen**) N-COUNT In former times, a **noblewoman** was a woman who was a member of the nobility.

no|body ✦✧ /noʊbɒdi, -bʌdi/ (**nobodies**) **1** PRON-INDEF-NEG **Nobody** means not a single person, or not a single member of a particular group or set. ❑ They were shut away in a little room where nobody could overhear. ❑ Nobody realizes how bad things are. **2** N-COUNT If someone says that a person is a **nobody**, they are saying in an unkind way that the person is not at all important. [DISAPPROVAL] ❑ A man in my position has nothing to fear from a nobody like you.

no-brainer /noʊ breɪnər/ (**no-brainers**) **1** N-COUNT If you describe a question or decision as a **no-brainer**, you mean that it is a very easy one to answer or make. [INFORMAL] ❑ If it's illegal for someone under 21 to drink, it should be illegal for them to drink and drive. That's a no-brainer. **2** N-COUNT If you describe a person or action as a **no-brainer**, you mean that they are stupid. [AM, INFORMAL, DISAPPROVAL]

no claims bo|nus also **no-claims bonus** ADJ [ADJ n] A **no claims bonus** is a reduction in the money that you have to pay for an insurance policy, which you get when you have not made any claims in the previous year. ❑ Motorists could lose their no-claims bonus, even if they are not at fault in an accident.

no-confidence **1** N-UNCOUNT [usu n of N, N n] If members of an organization pass a vote or motion of **no-confidence** in someone, they take a vote which shows that they no longer support that person or their ideas. ❑ A call for a vote of no-confidence was rejected. ❑ ...a no-confidence motion. **2** N-UNCOUNT [usu n of N] You can refer to something people say or do as **a vote of no-confidence** when it shows that they no longer support a particular person or organization. ❑ Many police officers view this action as a vote of no-confidence in their service.

noc|tur|nal /nɒktɜːrnəl/ **1** ADJ **Nocturnal** means occurring at night. ❑ The dog's main duty will be to accompany me on long nocturnal walks. **2** ADJ **Nocturnal** creatures are active mainly at night. ❑ When there is a full moon, this nocturnal rodent is careful to stay in its burrow.

noc|turne /nɒktɜːrn/ (**nocturnes**) N-COUNT [usu with supp] A **nocturne** is a short gentle piece of music, often one written to be played on the piano.

nod ✦✧ /nɒd/ (**nods, nodding, nodded**) **1** V-T/V-I [no passive] If you **nod**, you move your head downward and upward to show that you are answering 'yes' to a question, or to show agreement, understanding, or approval. ❑ "Are you okay?" I asked. She nodded and smiled. ❑ Jacques tasted one and nodded his approval. ● N-COUNT **Nod** is also a noun. ❑ She gave a nod and said, "I see." ❑ "Probably," agreed Hunter, with a slow nod of his head. **2** V-I [no passive] If you **nod** in a particular direction, you bend your head once in that direction in order to indicate something or to give someone a signal. ❑ "Does it work?" he asked, nodding at the piano. ❑ She nodded toward the dining room. "He's in there." **3** V-T/V-I [no passive] If you **nod**, you bend your head once, as a way of saying hello or goodbye. ❑ All the girls nodded and said "Hi." ❑ Both of them smiled and nodded at friends. ❑ Tom nodded a greeting. **4** → See feature box at **body language**
▶ **nod off** PHRASAL VERB If you **nod off**, you fall asleep, especially when you had not intended to. [INFORMAL] ❑ The judge appeared to nod off yesterday while a witness was being cross-examined.

node /noʊd/ (**nodes**) N-COUNT A **node** is a point, especially in the form of lump or swelling, where one thing joins another. ❑ Cut them off cleanly through the stem just below the node. ❑ ...nerve nodes.

nod|ule /nɒdʒuːl/ (**nodules**) **1** N-COUNT A **nodule** is a small round lump that can appear on your body and is a sign of an illness. [MEDICAL] **2** N-COUNT [oft n n] A **nodule** is a small round lump which is found on the roots of certain plants.

Noel /noʊɛl/ also **Noël** N-PROPER **Noel** is sometimes printed on Christmas cards and Christmas wrapping paper to mean 'Christmas.'

no-fly zone (**no-fly zones**) N-COUNT A **no-fly zone** is an area of sky where military and other aircraft are not allowed to fly, especially because of a war.

no-go area (**no-go areas**) **1** N-COUNT If you refer to a place as a **no-go area**, you mean that it has a reputation for violence and crime which makes people frightened to go there. ❑ ...a subway system whose reputation for violence and lawlessness makes it a no-go area for many natives of the city. **2** N-COUNT A **no-go area** is a place which is controlled by a group of people who use force to prevent other people from entering it. ❑ The area of the president's residence is a no-go area after six p.m.

noir /nwɑːr/ ADJ If you describe a film as **noir**, you mean it is in a style that shows the world as a dangerous or depressing place where many people suffer, especially because of the greed or cruelty of others. ❑ An NYPD officer is obsessed with tracking down his pregnant wife's unknown murderer in this 2008 noir action film. ❑ ...their 1930s noir adaptation of Macbeth.

noise ✦✧ /nɔɪz/ (**noises**) **1** N-UNCOUNT **Noise** is a loud or unpleasant sound. ❑ There was too much noise in the room and he needed peace. ❑ The noise of bombs and guns was incessant. **2** N-COUNT A **noise** is a sound that someone or something makes. ❑ Gerald made a small noise in his throat. ❑ ...birdsong and other animal noises. **3** N-PLURAL If someone **makes noises** of a particular kind about something, they say things that indicate their attitude to it in a rather indirect or vague way. ❑ The president took care to make encouraging noises about the future. **4** PHRASE If you say that someone **makes the right noises** or **makes all the right noises**, you think that they are showing concern or enthusiasm about something because they feel they ought to rather than because they really want to. ❑ But at the annual party conference he always made the right noises.

COLLOCATIONS

noise
NOUN **1**
adjective + **noise**: deafening, loud; ambient
noun + **noise**: aircraft, engine, road, traffic; background; crowd
verb + **noise**: minimize, reduce; muffle

---

noise|less /nɔɪzlɪs/ ADJ Something or someone that is **noiseless** does not make any sound. ❑ The snow was light and noiseless as it floated down. ● **noise|less|ly** ADV [ADV with v] ❑ I shut the door noiselessly behind me.

noi|some /nɔɪsəm/ ADJ [usu ADJ n] If you describe something or someone as **noisome**, you mean that you find them extremely unpleasant. [LITERARY] ❏ *Noisome vapors arise from the mud left in the docks.* ❏ *His noisome reputation for corruption had already begun to spread.*

noisy /nɔɪzi/ (**noisier**, **noisiest**) **1** ADJ A **noisy** person or thing makes a lot of loud or unpleasant noise. ❏ *...my noisy old typewriter.* • **nois|i|ly** ADV ❏ *The students on the grass bank cheered noisily.* **2** ADJ A **noisy** place is full of a lot of loud or unpleasant noise. ❏ *It's a noisy place with film clips showing constantly on one of the cafe's giant screens.* ❏ *The baggage hall was crowded and noisy.* **3** ADJ If you describe someone as **noisy**, you are critical of them for trying to attract attention to their views by frequently and forcefully discussing them. [DISAPPROVAL] ❏ *It might, at last, silence the small but noisy intellectual clique.*

no|mad /noʊmæd/ (**nomads**) N-COUNT A **nomad** is a member of a group of people who travel from place to place rather than living in one place all the time. ❏ *...a country of nomads who raise cattle and camels.*

no|mad|ic /noʊmædɪk/ **1** ADJ **Nomadic** people travel from place to place rather than living in one place all the time. ❏ *...the great nomadic tribes of the Western Sahara.* **2** ADJ If someone has a **nomadic** way of life, they travel from place to place and do not have a settled home. ❏ *The daughter of a railroad engineer, she at first had a somewhat nomadic childhood.*

no-man's land 1 N-UNCOUNT **No-man's land** is an area of land that is not owned or controlled by anyone, for example the area of land between two opposing armies. **2** N-SING If you refer to a situation as a **no-man's land** between different things, you mean that it seems unclear because it does not fit into any of the categories. ❏ *The play is set in the dangerous no-man's land between youth and adolescence.*

nom de guerre /nɒm də gɛər/ (**noms de guerre**) N-COUNT A **nom de guerre** is a false name which is sometimes used by people who belong to an unofficial military organization. [FORMAL] ❏ *His real name was Sabri al-Banna, but he became widely known by his nom de guerre, Abu Nidal.*

nom de plume /nɒm də pluːm/ (**noms de plume**) N-COUNT An author's **nom de plume** is a name that they use instead of their real name. [FORMAL] ❏ *She writes under the nom de plume of Alison Cooper.*

no|men|cla|ture /noʊmənkleɪtʃər/ N-UNCOUNT [also N in pl] The **nomenclature** of a particular set of things is the system of naming those things. [FORMAL] ❏ *...mistakes arising from ignorance of the nomenclature of woody plants.*

nomi|nal /nɒmɪnəl/ **1** ADJ You use **nominal** to indicate that someone or something is supposed to have a particular identity or status, but in reality does not have it. ❏ *As he was still not allowed to run a company, his wife became its nominal head.* • **nomi|nal|ly** ADV ❏ *The sultan was still nominally the chief of staff.* ❏ *The road is nominally under the control of UN peacekeeping troops.* **2** ADJ [ADJ n] A **nominal** price or sum of money is very small in comparison with the real cost or value of the thing that is being bought or sold. ❏ *I am prepared to sell my shares at a nominal price.* **3** ADJ [ADJ n] In economics, the **nominal** value, rate, or level of something is the one expressed in terms of current prices or figures, without taking into account general changes in prices that take place over time. ❏ *Inflation would be lower and so nominal rates would be more attractive in real terms.*

nomi|nal group (**nominal groups**) N-COUNT A **nominal group** is the same as a **noun group**.

nomi|nate /nɒmɪneɪt/ (**nominates**, **nominating**, **nominated**) **1** V-T If someone **is nominated** for a job or position, their name is formally suggested as a candidate for it. ❏ *This week one of them will be nominated by the Democratic Party for the presidency of the United States.* ❏ *The Security Council can nominate anyone for secretary-general.* **2** V-T If you **nominate** someone to a job or position, you formally choose them to hold that job or position. ❏ *In 1967 Johnson nominated Thurgood Marshall to the Supreme Court.* ❏ *She was nominated by the president as ambassador to Barbados.* **3** V-T If someone or something such as an actor or a movie **is nominated** for an award, someone formally suggests that they should be given that award. ❏ *Practically every movie he made was nominated for an Oscar.*

nomi|na|tion /nɒmɪneɪʃən/ (**nominations**) **1** N-COUNT A **nomination** is an official suggestion of someone as a candidate in an election or for a job. ❏ *...his candidacy for the Republican presidential nomination.* **2** N-COUNT A **nomination** for an award is an official suggestion that someone or something should be given that award. ❏ *They say he's certain to get a nomination for best supporting actor.* **3** N-VAR The **nomination** of someone to a particular job or position is their appointment to that job or position. ❏ *His transition to the political arena, leading to his nomination as Republican presidential candidate, was swift.*

nomi|na|tive /nɒmɪnətɪv/ N-SING [the N] In the grammar of some languages, **the nominative** or **the nominative case** is the case used for a noun when it is the subject of a verb. Compare **accusative**.

nomi|nee /nɒmɪniː/ (**nominees**) N-COUNT A **nominee** is someone who is nominated for a job, position, or award. ❏ *His nominee for vice president was elected only after a second ballot.*

PREFIX

non-
1 forms nouns that refer to situations where a particular action has not taken place. *For example, someone's **non-attendance** at a meeting is the fact that they did not go to the meeting.*
2 also forms nouns and adjectives that refer to people or things that do not have a particular quality or characteristic. *For example, a **non-fatal** accident is not fatal.*

---

non|ag|gres|sion /nɒnəgrɛʃən/
in BRIT, also use **non-aggression**
N-UNCOUNT [usu with supp] If a country adopts a policy of **nonaggression**, it declares that it will not attack or try to harm a particular country in any way. ❏ *A nonaggression pact will be signed this week between the two countries.*

non|al|co|hol|ic /nɒnælkəhɒlɪk/
in BRIT, also use **non-alcoholic**
ADJ [usu ADJ n] A **nonalcoholic** drink does not contain alcohol. ❏ *...bottles of nonalcoholic beer.*

non|aligned /nɒnəlaɪnd/
in BRIT, also use **non-aligned**
ADJ [usu ADJ n] **Nonaligned** countries did not support or were in no way linked to groups of countries headed by the United States or the former Soviet Union. ❏ *...a meeting of foreign ministers from nonaligned countries.*

non|align|ment /nɒnəlaɪnmənt/
in BRIT, also use **non-alignment**
N-UNCOUNT **Nonalignment** is the state or policy of being nonaligned. ❏ *The Afro-Asian nations had approved the basic general principles of nonalignment.*

nonbinary or **non-binary** /nɒnbaɪnəri/ ADJ A **nonbinary** person expresses themself in a way that is not traditionally considered completely male or completely female. ❏ *It can still be difficult for many nonbinary indiyiduals to be treated normally.*

non|cha|lant /nɒnʃələnt/ ADJ If you describe someone as **nonchalant**, you mean that they appear not to worry or care about things and that they seem very calm. ❏ *Clark's mother is nonchalant about her role in her son's latest work.* ❏ *Denis tried to look nonchalant and uninterested.* • **non|cha|lance** /nɒnʃələns/ N-UNCOUNT ❏ *Affecting nonchalance, I handed her two hundred dollar bills.* • **non|cha|lant|ly** ADV ❏ *"Does Will intend to return with us?" Joanna asked as nonchalantly as she could.*

non|com|bat|ant /nɒnkəmbætənt/ (**noncombatants**)
in BRIT, also use **non-combatant**
1 N-COUNT [usu N n] **Noncombatant** troops are members of the armed forces whose duties do not include fighting. ❏ *The general does not like noncombatant personnel near a scene of action.* **2** N-COUNT [usu pl] In a war, **noncombatants** are people who are not members of the armed forces. ❏ *The Red Cross has arranged two local ceasefires, allowing noncombatants to receive medical help.*

non|com|mis|sioned /nɒnkəmɪʃ³nd/

in BRIT, also use **non-commissioned**

ADJ [ADJ n] A **noncommissioned** officer in the armed forces is someone with a rank such as corporal or sergeant who used to have a lower rank, rather than an officer of higher rank who has been given a commission.

non|com|mit|tal /nɒnkəmɪt³l/

in BRIT, also use **non-committal**

ADJ [usu v-link ADJ] You can describe someone as **noncommittal** when they deliberately do not express their opinion or intentions clearly. ❏ *Mr. Hall is non-committal about the number of jobs that the development corporation has created.* ❏ *Sylvia's face was noncommittal.* ❏ *...a very bland noncommittal answer.* ● **non|com|mit|tal|ly** ADV ❏ *"I like some of his novels better than others," I said noncommittally.*

non|con|form|ist /nɒnkənfɔrmɪst/ (**nonconformists**)

in BRIT, also use **non-conformist**

ADJ If you say that someone's way of life or opinions are **nonconformist**, you mean that they are different from those of most people. ❏ *Their views are nonconformist and their political opinions are extreme.* ❏ *...a nonconformist lifestyle.* ● N-COUNT A **nonconformist** is someone who is nonconformist. ❏ *Victoria stood out as a dazzling nonconformist.*

non|con|form|ity /nɒnkənfɔrmɪti/

in BRIT, also use **non-conformity**

N-UNCOUNT **Nonconformity** is behavior or thinking which is different from that of most people. ❏ *You're deliberately unconventional. Even your choice of clothes is a statement of your nonconformity.* ❏ *Lovelock's principled nonconformity can be traced to his childhood.*

non|cus|to|dial /nɒnkʌstoʊdiəl/

in BRIT, also use **non-custodial**

ADJ [ADJ n] The **noncustodial** parent in a couple who are separated or divorced is the parent who does not live with the children. ❏ *More than half the children of divorce did not see the noncustodial parent on a regular basis.*

non|de|script /nɒndɪskrɪpt/ ADJ [usu ADJ n] If you describe something or someone as **nondescript**, you mean that their appearance is rather dull, and not at all interesting or attractive. ❏ *...hundreds of nondescript buildings.* ❏ *...a nondescript woman of uncertain age.*

none ♦♢ /nʌn/ ◼ QUANT [QUANT of def-n] **None of** something means not even a small amount of it. **None of** a group of people or things means not even one of them. ❏ *None of us knew how to treat her.* ● PRON-INDEF-NEG **None** is also a pronoun. ❏ *I searched bookstores and libraries for information, but found none.* ❏ *No one could imagine a great woman painter. None had existed yet* ◼ PHRASE If you say that someone **will have none of** something, or **is having none of** something, you mean that they refuse to accept it. [INFORMAL] ❏ *He knew his own mind and was having none of their attempts to keep him at home.* ◼ PHRASE You use **none too** in front of an adjective or adverb in order to emphasize that the quality mentioned is not present. [FORMAL, EMPHASIS] ❏ *He was none too thrilled to hear from me at that hour.* ◼ PHRASE You use **none the** to say that someone or something does not have any more of a particular quality than they did before. ❏ *You could end up none the wiser about managing your finances.* ◼ second to none → see second ②

non|en|tity /nɒnɛntɪti/ (**nonentities**) N-COUNT If you refer to someone as a **nonentity**, you mean that they are not special or important in any way. [DISAPPROVAL] ❏ *Amidst the current bunch of nonentities, he is a towering figure.* ❏ *She was written off then as a political nonentity.*

non|es|sen|tial /nɒnɪsɛnʃ³l/ (**nonessentials**)

in BRIT, also use **non-essential**

◼ ADJ [usu ADJ n] **Nonessential** means not absolutely necessary. ❏ *The crisis has led to the closure of a number of nonessential government services.* ❏ *...non-essential goods.* ◼ N-PLURAL **Nonessentials** are things that are not absolutely necessary. ❏ *In a recession, consumers could be expected to cut down on nonessentials like toys.*

none|the|less /nʌnðəlɛs/ ADV [ADV with cl] **Nonetheless** means the same as **nevertheless**. [FORMAL] ❏ *There was still a long way to go. Nonetheless, some progress had been made.*

non|event /nɒnɪvɛnt/ (**nonevents**)

in BRIT, also use **non-event**

N-COUNT If you say that something was a **nonevent**, you mean that it was disappointing or dull, especially when this was not what you had expected. ❏ *Unfortunately, the entire evening was a total nonevent.*

non|ex|ecu|tive /nɒnɪgzɛkyətɪv/

in BRIT, also use **non-executive**

ADJ [ADJ n] Someone who has a **nonexecutive** position in a company or organization gives advice but is not responsible for making decisions or ensuring that decisions are carried out. [BUSINESS] ❏ *...nonexecutive directors.*

non|ex|ist|ence /nɒnɪgzɪstəns/

in BRIT, also use **non-existence**

N-UNCOUNT **Nonexistence** is the fact of not existing. ❏ *I was left with puzzlement as to the existence or nonexistence of God.*

non|ex|ist|ent /nɒnɪgzɪstənt/

in BRIT, also use **non-existent**

ADJ If you say that something is **nonexistent**, you mean that it does not exist when you feel that it should. ❏ *Hygiene was nonexistent: no running water, no bathroom.*

non|fat /nɒnfæt/

in BRIT, also use **non-fat**

ADJ **Nonfat** foods have no fat in them. ❏ *...plain nonfat yogurt.*

non|fic|tion /nɒnfɪkʃ³n/

in BRIT, also use **non-fiction**

N-UNCOUNT [oft N n] **Nonfiction** is writing that gives information or describes real events, rather than telling a story. ❏ *The series will include both fiction and nonfiction.* ❏ *Lewis is the author of thirteen novels and ten nonfiction books.*

non|fi|nite /nɒnfaɪnaɪt/

in BRIT, also use **non-finite**

ADJ [usu ADJ n] A **nonfinite** clause is a clause which is based on an infinitive or a participle and has no tense.

non|gov|ern|men|tal or|gani|za|tion (**nongovernmental organizations**) or **non-governmental organization** N-COUNT A **nongovernmental organization** is the same as an **NGO**.

non|hu|man /nɒnhyumən/

in BRIT, also use **non-human**

ADJ **Nonhuman** means not human or not produced by humans. ❏ *Hostility towards outsiders is characteristic of both human and nonhuman animals.*

non|inter|ven|tion /nɒnɪntərvɛnʃ³n/

in BRIT, also use **non-intervention**

N-UNCOUNT **Nonintervention** is the practice or policy of not becoming involved in a dispute or disagreement between other people and of not helping either side. ❏ *Generally, I think the policy of nonintervention is the correct one.*

non|lin|ear /nɒnlɪniər/

in BRIT, also use **non-linear**

ADJ If you describe something as **nonlinear**, you mean that it does not progress or develop smoothly from one stage to the next in a logical way. Instead, it makes sudden changes, or seems to develop in different directions at the same time. ❏ *Environmental systems tend to be nonlinear, and therefore not easy to predict.*

non|mem|ber /nɒnmɛmbər/ (**nonmembers**)

in BRIT, also use **non-member**

N-COUNT [usu pl] **Nonmembers** of a club or organization are people who are not members of it.

❑ ...Cost: Members $10; Nonmembers $25. ❑ ...the problems of coffee sales to non-member countries.

non|nu|clear /nɒnnukliər/

in BRIT, also use **non-nuclear**

ADJ **Nonnuclear** means not using or involving nuclear weapons or nuclear power. ❑ *The agreement is the first postwar treaty to reduce nonnuclear weapons in Europe.*

no-no N-SING [a N] If you say that something is **a no-no**, you think it is undesirable or unacceptable. [INFORMAL] ❑ *We all know that cheating on our taxes is a no-no.*

no-nonsense ◼ ADJ If you describe someone as a **no-nonsense** person, you approve of the fact that they are efficient, direct, and quite tough. [APPROVAL] ❑ *She saw herself as a direct, no-nonsense, modern woman.* ◼ ADJ If you describe something as a **no-nonsense** thing, you approve of the fact that it is plain and does not have unnecessary parts. [APPROVAL] ❑ *You'll need no-nonsense boots for the jungle.*

non|par|ti|san /nɒnpɑrtɪzən/

in BRIT, also use **non-partisan**

ADJ A person or group that is **nonpartisan** does not support or help a particular political party or group. ❑ *...a nonpartisan organization that does economic research for business and labor groups.* ❑ *...the president called for a nonpartisan approach to the problem.*

non|pay|ment /nɒnpeɪmənt/

in BRIT, also use **non-payment**

N-UNCOUNT **Nonpayment** is a failure to pay a sum of money that you owe. ❑ *She faced an end to treatments because of nonpayment of her claim.*

non|plused /nɒnplʌst/ also **nonplussed** ADJ [usu v-link ADJ] If you are **nonplused**, you feel confused and unsure how to react. ❑ *She expected him to ask for a scotch and was rather nonplused when he asked her to mix him a martini.*

non|pre|scrip|tion /nɒnprɪskrɪpʃən/ ADJ [usu ADJ n] **Nonprescription** drugs are medicines that you can buy without the need for a doctor's prescription. ❑ *Aspirin is the most popular nonprescription drug on the market.*

in BRIT, also use **non-prescription**

non|prof|it /nɒnprɒfɪt/

in BRIT, also use **non-profit**

ADJ A **nonprofit** organization is one which is not run with the aim of making a profit. [BUSINESS] ❑ *Most of that money goes to nonprofit organizations that run programs for the poor.*

non|pro|lif|era|tion /nɒnprəlɪfəreɪʃən/

in BRIT, also use **non-proliferation**

N-UNCOUNT [usu N n] **Nonproliferation** is the limiting of the production and spread of something such as nuclear or chemical weapons. ❑ *...the Nuclear Nonproliferation Treaty.*

non|resi|dent /nɒnrɛzɪdənt/ (**non-residents**)

in BRIT, also use **non-resident**

ADJ A **nonresident** person is someone who is visiting a particular place but who does not live or stay there permanently. ❑ *The paper said that 100,000 nonresident workers would have to be sent back to their home villages.* • N-COUNT A **nonresident** is someone who is nonresident. ❑ *Both hotels have gardens and restaurants open to nonresidents.*

non|sense /nɒnsens, -səns/ ◼ N-UNCOUNT If you say that something spoken or written is **nonsense**, you mean that you consider it to be untrue or silly. [DISAPPROVAL] ❑ *Most orthodox doctors however dismiss this as complete nonsense.* ❑ *...all that poetic nonsense about love.* ◼ N-UNCOUNT [also a N, usu supp N] You can use **nonsense** to refer to something that you think is foolish or that you disapprove of. [DISAPPROVAL] ❑ *Surely it is an economic nonsense to deplete the world of natural resources.* ◼ N-UNCOUNT You can refer to spoken or written words that do not mean anything because they do not make sense as **nonsense**. ❑ *...a children's nonsense poem by Charles E Carryl.* ◼ → see also **no-nonsense** ◼ PHRASE To **make a nonsense of** something or to **make nonsense of** it means to make it seem ridiculous or pointless. ❑ *The fighting made a nonsense of peace pledges made last week.*

non|sen|si|cal /nɒnsɛnsɪkəl/ ADJ [usu v-link ADJ] If you say that something is **nonsensical**, you think it is stupid, ridiculous, or untrue. [DISAPPROVAL] ❑ *It seemed to me that Robert's arguments were nonsensical.* ❑ *There were no nonsensical promises about reviving the economy.*

non se|qui|tur /nɒn sɛkwɪtər/ (**non sequiturs**) N-VAR A **non sequitur** is a statement, remark, or conclusion that does not follow naturally or logically from what has just been said. [FORMAL] ❑ *Had she missed something important, or was this just a non sequitur?*

non|smok|er /nɒnsmoʊkər/ (**nonsmokers**)

in BRIT, also use **non-smoker**

N-COUNT A **nonsmoker** is someone who does not smoke. ❑ *People who smoked an average of one or more packs of cigarettes a day had 118 percent higher medical expenses than nonsmokers.*

non|smok|ing /nɒnsmoʊkɪŋ/

in BRIT, also use **non-smoking**

◼ ADJ A **nonsmoking** area in a public place is an area in which people are not allowed to smoke. ❑ *We've had complaints about smoking in non-smoking areas.* ◼ ADJ A **nonsmoking** person is a person who does not smoke. ❑ *The fertility of women who smoke is half that of nonsmoking women.*

non|spe|cif|ic /nɒnspɪsɪfɪk/

in BRIT, also use **non-specific**

◼ ADJ [usu ADJ n] **Nonspecific** medical conditions or symptoms have more than one possible cause. ❑ *...nonspecific headaches.* ◼ ADJ [usu ADJ n] Something that is **nonspecific** is general rather than precise or exact. ❑ *I intend to use these terms in a deliberately nonspecific and all-embracing way.*

non|stand|ard /nɒnstændərd/

in BRIT, also use **non-standard**

ADJ [usu ADJ n] **Nonstandard** things are different from the usual version or type of that thing. ❑ *The shop is completely out of nonstandard sizes.*

non|start|er /nɒnstɑrtər/ (**nonstarters**)

in BRIT, also use **non-starter**

N-COUNT If you describe a plan or idea as a **nonstarter**, you mean that it has no chance of success. [INFORMAL] ❑ *The United States is certain to reject the proposal as a nonstarter.*

non|stick /nɒnstɪk/

in BRIT, also use **non-stick**

ADJ **Nonstick** saucepans, frying pans, or baking pans have a special coating on the inside which prevents food from sticking to them. ❑ *Use a shallow nonstick baking pan.*

non|stop /nɒnstɒp/

in BRIT, also use **non-stop**

ADJ Something that is **nonstop** continues without any pauses or interruptions. ❑ *Many U.S. cities now have nonstop flights to Aspen.* ❑ *...80 minutes of nonstop music.* • ADV [ADV after v] **Nonstop** is also an adverb. ❑ *Amy had driven nonstop through Spain.*

non|un|ion /nɒnyunyən/ ADJ [usu ADJ n] **Nonunion** workers do not belong to a labor union. A **nonunion** company or organization does not employ workers who belong to a labor union. [BUSINESS] ❑ *The company originally intended to reopen the factory with nonunion workers.*

in BRIT, also use **non-union**

non|ver|bal /nɒnvɜrbəl/

in BRIT, also use **non-verbal**

◼ ADJ [usu ADJ n] **Nonverbal** communication consists of things such as the expression on your face, your arm movements, or your tone of voice, which show how you feel about something without using words. ◼ → See feature box at **body language**

non|vio|lent /nɒnvaɪələnt/

in BRIT, also use **non-violent**

◼ ADJ **Nonviolent** methods of bringing about change do not involve hurting people or causing damage. ❑ *King was a*

non-White (non-Whites) also **nonWhite** ADJ A **non-White** person is a member of a race of people who are not of European origin. This use could cause offense. ❑ *Non-White people are effectively excluded from certain jobs.* ❑ *Sixty percent of the population is non-White.* • N-COUNT **Non-White** is also a noun. This use could cause offense. ❑ *Not one non-White has ever been selected to play for the team.*

nooch /nutʃ/ N-UNCOUNT **Nooch** is a health food consisting of a type of yeast. **Nooch** is short for 'nutritional yeast.'

noo|dle /nud³l/ (noodles) N-COUNT **Noodles** are long, thin strips of pasta. They are used especially in Chinese and Italian cooking.

nook /nuk/ (nooks) **1** N-COUNT A **nook** is a small and sheltered place. ❑ *We found a seat in a little nook, and had some lunch.* **2** PHRASE If you talk about every **nook and cranny** of a place or situation, you mean every part or every aspect of it. [EMPHASIS] ❑ *Boxes are stacked in every nook and cranny at the factory.* ❑ *...Cole's vast knowledge of the nooks and crannies of US politics.*

nookie /nuki/ also **nooky** N-UNCOUNT You can refer to sexual intercourse as **nookie**. [INFORMAL, HUMOROUS]

noon /nun/ **1** N-UNCOUNT **Noon** is twelve o'clock in the middle of the day. ❑ *The long day of meetings started at noon.* **2** ADJ [ADJ n] **Noon** means happening or appearing in the middle part of the day. ❑ *The noon sun was fierce.* **3** **morning, noon, and night** → see morning

noon|day /nundeɪ/ ADJ [ADJ n] **Noonday** means happening or appearing in the middle part of the day. ❑ *It was hot, nearly 90 degrees in the noonday sun.*

no one ♦♦◊

in BRIT, also use **no-one**

PRON-INDEF-NEG **No one** means not a single person, or not a single member of a particular group or set. ❑ *Everyone wants to be a hero, but no one wants to die.*

――――― USAGE ―――――

no one
You don't usually use any other negative word after **no one** or **nobody**. Don't say, for example, 'No one didn't come.' Say 'No one came.' Similarly, don't use 'no one' or 'nobody' as the object of a sentence which already has a negative word in it. Don't say, for example, 'We didn't see no one.' You say 'We didn't see **anyone**' or 'We didn't see **anybody**.' You mustn't tell **anyone**.

noon|time /nuntaɪm/ also **noon-time, noon time** N-UNCOUNT [oft N n] **Noontime** is the middle part of the day. [AM] ❑ *There was a demonstration at noontime yesterday at the Chinese Embassy.* ❑ *The animals settled peacefully to their noontime meal.*

noose /nus/ (nooses) N-COUNT A **noose** is a circular loop at the end of a piece of rope or wire. A noose is tied with a knot that allows it to be tightened, and it is usually used to trap animals or hang people. ❑ *...a man swinging from a noose.*

nope /noʊp/ CONVENTION **Nope** is sometimes used instead of 'no' as a negative response. [INFORMAL, SPOKEN] ❑ *"Is she supposed to work today?"—"Nope, tomorrow."*

nor ♦♦◊ /nɔr/ **1** CONJ You use **nor** after 'neither' in order to introduce the second alternative or the last of a number of alternatives in a negative statement. ❑ *Neither Mr. Rose nor Mr. Woodhead was available for comment yesterday.* ❑ *I can give you neither an opinion nor any advice.* **2** CONJ You use **nor** after a negative statement in order to introduce another negative statement which adds information to the previous one. ❑ *Cooking up a quick dish doesn't mean you have to sacrifice flavor. Nor does fast food have to be junk food.* **3** CONJ You use **nor** after a negative statement in order to indicate that the negative statement also applies to you or to someone or something else. ❑ *"None of us has any idea how long we're going to be here."—"Nor do I."* ❑ *"If my husband has no future," she said, "then nor do my children."*

Nor|dic /nɔrdɪk/ ADJ [ADJ n] **Nordic** means relating to the Scandinavian countries of northern Europe. ❑ *...the Nordic countries.*

nor'east|er /nɔrist̬ər/ (nor'easters) N-COUNT A **nor'easter** is a storm or wind that blows from the north-east. ❑ *Sometimes a nor'easter can be worse than a hurricane.*

norm /nɔrm/ (norms) **1** N-COUNT **Norms** are ways of behaving that are considered normal in a particular society. ❑ *The actions taken depart from what she called the commonly accepted norms of democracy.* **2** N-SING If you say that a situation is **the norm**, you mean that it is usual and expected. ❑ *Families of six or seven are the norm here.* **3** N-COUNT A **norm** is an official standard or level that organizations are expected to reach. ❑ *About 32 percent of students meet national norms in reading.* **4** → See feature box at **polite**

nor|mal ♦♦◊ /nɔrm³l/ **1** ADJ Something that is **normal** is usual and ordinary, and is what people expect. ❑ *The two countries resumed normal diplomatic relations.* ❑ *Her height and weight are normal for her age.* **2** ADJ A **normal** person has no serious physical or mental health problems. ❑ *Statistics indicate that depressed patients are more likely to become ill than are normal people.*

nor|mal|cy /nɔrm³lsi/ N-UNCOUNT **Normalcy** is a situation in which everything is normal. ❑ *Underneath this image of normalcy, addiction threatened to rip this family apart.*

nor|mal|ity /nɔrmælɪti/ N-UNCOUNT **Normality** is a situation in which everything is normal. ❑ *A semblance of normality has returned with people going to work and shops reopening.*

nor|mal|ize /nɔrməlaɪz/ (normalizes, normalizing, normalized)

in BRIT, also use **normalise**

1 V-T/V-I When you **normalize** a situation or when it **normalizes**, it becomes normal. ❑ *Meditation tends to lower or normalize blood pressure.* **2** V-RECIP If people, groups, or governments **normalize** relations, or when relations **normalize**, they become normal or return to normal. ❑ *The two governments were close to normalizing relations.* ❑ *The United States says they are not prepared to join in normalizing ties with their former enemy.* • **nor|mali|za|tion** /nɔrməlɪzeɪʃ³n/ N-UNCOUNT ❑ *The two sides would like to see the normalization of diplomatic relations.*

nor|mal|ly ♦◊◊ /nɔrməli/ **1** ADV If you say that something **normally** happens or that you **normally** do a particular thing, you mean that it is what usually happens or what you usually do. ❑ *All airports in the country are working normally today.* ❑ *Social progress is normally a matter of struggles and conflicts.* **2** ADV [ADV after v] If you do something **normally**, you do it in the usual or conventional way. ❑ *...failure of the blood to clot normally.*

――――― SYNONYMS ―――――

normally
ADV **1**
usually: *Usually, the work is boring.*
generally: *It is generally true that the darker the fruit, the higher its iron content.*
commonly: *Parsley is probably the most commonly used of all herbs.*
typically: *It typically takes a day or two, depending on size.*

Nor|man /nɔrmən/ (Normans) **1** N-COUNT The **Normans** were the people who came from northern France and took control of England in 1066, or their descendants. **2** ADJ **Norman** is used to refer to the period of history in Britain from 1066 until around 1300, and in particular to the style of architecture of that period. ❑ *In Norman England, the greyhound was a symbol of nobility.* ❑ *...a Norman castle.*

nor|ma|tive /nɔrmətɪv/ ADJ [usu ADJ n] **Normative** means creating or stating particular rules of behavior. [FORMAL] ❑ *In some social circles, smoking remains normative behavior.* ❑ *...a normative model of teaching.*

Norse /nɔrs/ **1** ADJ **Norse** means belonging or relating to Scandinavian countries in medieval times. ❑ *In Norse* *mythology the moon is personified as male.* **2** N-UNCOUNT **Norse** is the language that was spoken in Scandinavian countries in medieval times.

Norse|man /nɔrsmən/ (**Norsemen**) N-COUNT The **Norsemen** were people who lived in Scandinavian countries in medieval times.

north ♦♦♦ /nɔrθ/ also **North** **1** N-UNCOUNT [also *the* N] The **north** is the direction which is on your left when you are looking toward the direction where the sun rises. ❏ *In the north the ground becomes very cold as the winter snow and ice cover the ground.* **2** N-SING The **north** of a place, country, or region is the part which is in the north. ❏ *The plan mostly benefits people in the North and Midwest.* **3** ADV [ADV after v] If you go **north**, you travel toward the north. ❏ *Anita drove north up Pacific Highway.* **4** ADV Something that is **north** of a place is positioned to the north of it. ❏ *...a little village a few miles north of Portland.* **5** ADJ [ADJ n] The **north** edge, corner, or part of a place or country is the part which is toward the north. ❏ *...the north side of the mountain.* **6** ADJ [ADJ n] **North** is used in the names of some countries, states, and regions in the north of a larger area. ❏ *There were demonstrations this weekend in cities throughout North America, Asia and Europe.* **7** ADJ [ADJ n] A **north** wind is a wind that blows from the north. ❏ *...a bitterly cold north wind.* **8** N-SING [*the* N] **The North** is used to refer to the richer, more developed countries of the world. ❏ *Malaysia has emerged as the toughest critic of the North's environmental attitudes.* **9** → See also color supplement

north|bound /nɔrθbaʊnd/ ADJ [ADJ n, n ADJ] **Northbound** roads or vehicles lead or are traveling toward the north. ❏ *The northbound lane should remain open at most times.* ❏ *Laguna Canyon Road was blocked off again northbound.*

north|east ♦♦◇ /nɔrθist/

in BRIT, also use **north-east**

1 N-UNCOUNT [also *the* N] The **northeast** is the direction which is halfway between north and east. ❏ *...the warm waters of Salt Springs Island to the northeast.* **2** N-SING **The northeast** of a place, country, or region is the part which is in the northeast. ❏ *The northeast has been particularly hard hit..* **3** ADV [ADV after v] If you go **northeast**, you travel toward the northeast. ❏ *"We're going northeast," Paula told them, before they started.* **4** ADV [ADV of n] Something that is **northeast of** a place is positioned to the northeast of it. ❏ *a village, twenty miles northeast of the capital.* **5** ADJ [ADJ n] The **northeast** edge, corner, or part of a place is the part which is toward the northeast. ❏ *...a climate like that of our northeast coast.* **6** → See also color supplement

north|easter|ly /nɔrθistərli/ ADJ [usu ADJ n] A **northeasterly** point, area, or direction is to the northeast or toward the northeast.

in BRIT, also use **north-easterly**

north|eastern /nɔrθistərn/

in BRIT, also use **north-eastern**

ADJ **Northeastern** means in or from the northeast of a region or country. ❏ *...on the northeastern coast of Florida.*

nor|ther|ly /nɔrðərli/ ADJ A **northerly** point, area, or direction is to the north or toward the north. ❏ *The storm is headed on a northerly path.*

north|ern ♦♦◇ /nɔrðərn/ also **Northern** ADJ [ADJ n] **Northern** means in or from the north of a region, state, or country. ❏ *Their two children were immigrants to Northern Ireland from Pennsylvania.*

north|ern|er /nɔrðərnər/ (**northerners**) N-COUNT A **northerner** is a person who was born in or who lives in the north of a place or country. ❏ *I like the openness of northerners.*

north|ern|most /nɔrðərnmoʊst/ ADJ [usu ADJ n] The **northernmost** part of an area or the **northernmost** place is the one that is farthest toward the north. ❏ *...the northernmost tip of Canada.* ❏ *The Chablis vineyard is the northernmost in Burgundy.*

North Pole N-PROPER [usu *the* N] **The North Pole** is the place on the surface of the earth which is farthest toward the north.

north|ward /nɔrθwərd/ also **northwards** ADV **Northward** or **northwards** means toward the north. ❏ *Tropical storm Marco was pushing northward up Florida's coast.* • ADJ [ADJ n] **Northward** is also an adjective. ❏ *The northward journey from Jalalabad was no more than 120 miles.*

north|west ♦♦◇ /nɔrθwɛst/

in BRIT, also use **north-west**

1 N-UNCOUNT [also *the* N] The **northwest** is the direction which is halfway between north and west. ❏ *...four miles to the northwest.* **2** N-SING The **northwest** of a place, country, or region is the part which is toward the northwest. ❏ *...in the extreme northwest of the country.* **3** ADV [ADV after v] If you go **northwest**, you travel toward the northwest. ❏ *Take the narrow lane going northwest parallel with the railroad line.* **4** ADV [ADV of n] Something that is **northwest of** a place is positioned to the northwest of it. ❏ *Just a couple of hours to the northwest of the capital is the wine-growing area of Hunter Valley.* **5** ADJ [ADJ n] The **northwest** part of a place, country, or region is the part which is toward the northwest. ❏ *...the northwest coast of the United States.* **6** → See also color supplement

north|wester|ly /nɔrθwɛstərli/

in BRIT, also use **north-westerly**

ADJ [usu ADJ n] A **northwesterly** point, area, or direction is to the northwest or toward the northwest.

north|western /nɔrθwɛstərn/

in BRIT, also use **north-western**

ADJ **Northwestern** means in or from the northwest of a region or country. ❏ *Virtually every river in northwestern Oregon was near flood stage.*

Nor|we|gian /nɔrwidʒən/ (**Norwegians**) **1** ADJ **Norwegian** means belonging or relating to Norway, or to its people, language, or culture. • N-COUNT A **Norwegian** is a person who comes from Norway. **2** N-UNCOUNT **Norwegian** is the language spoken by people who live in Norway.

nose ♦◇◇ /noʊz/ (**noses, nosing, nosed**) **1** N-COUNT Your **nose** is the part of your face which sticks out above your mouth. You use it for smelling and breathing. ❏ *She wiped her nose with a tissue.* **2** N-COUNT The **nose** of a vehicle such as an airplane or a boat is the front part of it. ❏ *They went over to the airplane and stood near its nose.* **3** N-COUNT You can refer to your sense of smell as your **nose**. ❏ *The river that runs through Middlesbrough became ugly on the eye and hard on the nose.* **4** V-T/V-I If a vehicle **noses** in a certain direction or if you **nose** it there, you move it slowly and carefully in that direction. ❏ *He could not see the driver as the car nosed forward.* ❏ *A motorboat nosed out of the mist and nudged into the branches of a tree.* **5** PHRASE If you **keep your nose clean**, you behave well and stay out of trouble. [INFORMAL] ❏ *If you kept your nose clean, you had a job for life.* **6** PHRASE If you **follow your nose** to get to a place, you go straight ahead or follow the most obvious route. ❏ *Just follow your nose and in about five minutes you're at the old railway.* **7** PHRASE If you **follow** your **nose**, you do something in a particular way because you feel it should be done like that, rather than because you are following any plan or rules. ❏ *You won't have to think, just follow your nose.* **8** PHRASE If you say that someone **has a nose for** something, you mean that they have a natural ability to find it or recognize it. ❏ *He had a nose for trouble and a brilliant tactical mind.* **9** PHRASE If you say that someone **looks down** their **nose** at something or someone, you mean that they believe they are superior to that person or thing and treat them with disrespect. [DISAPPROVAL] ❏ *I don't look down my nose at comedy.* **10** PHRASE If you say that you **paid through the nose** for something, you are emphasizing that you had to pay what you consider too high a price for it. [INFORMAL, EMPHASIS] ❏ *We don't like paying through the nose for our wine when eating out.* **11** PHRASE If someone **pokes** their **nose into** something or **sticks** their **nose into** something, they try to interfere with it even though it does not concern them. [INFORMAL, DISAPPROVAL] ❏ *We don't like strangers who poke their noses into our affairs.* **12** PHRASE To **rub** someone's **nose in** something that they do not want to think about, such as a failing or a mistake they have made, means to remind them repeatedly about it. [INFORMAL] ❏ *His enemies will attempt to rub his nose in past policy statements.* **13** PHRASE If you **turn up** your **nose** at something, you reject it because you think that it is not good enough for you. ❑ *I'm not in a financial position to turn up my nose at several hundred thousand dollars.* ◨ PHRASE If you do something **under** someone's **nose**, you do it right in front of them, without trying to hide it from them. ❑ *This had been happening right under my nose, and I had no idea.* ◨ PHRASE If vehicles are **nose to tail**, the front of one vehicle is close behind the back of another. [mainly BRIT]

in AM, use **bumper-to-bumper**

◨ **to put someone's nose out of joint** → see **joint** ◨ → See also color supplement

▶ **nose around** PHRASAL VERB If you **nose around**, you look around a place that belongs to someone else, to see if you can find something interesting. [INFORMAL] ❑ *I wondered what else he'd taken and nosed around his bureau.* ❑ *He had thought to just nose around, see what he could.*

nose|bleed /n**oʊ**zbliːd/ (**nosebleeds**) also **nose bleed** N-COUNT If someone has a **nosebleed**, blood comes out from inside their nose. ❑ *Whenever I have a cold I get a nosebleed.*

nose|dive /n**oʊ**zdaɪv/ (**nosedives, nosediving, nosedived**) also **nose-dive** ◨ V-I If prices, profits, or exchange rates **nosedive**, they suddenly fall by a large amount. [JOURNALISM] ❑ *The value of other shares nosedived by $2.6 billion.* • N-SING **Nosedive** is also a noun. ❑ *The bank yesterday revealed a 30 percent nosedive in profits.* ◨ V-I If something such as someone's reputation or career **nosedives**, it suddenly gets much worse. [JOURNALISM] ❑ *...at a time when the reputation of politicians has nosedived.* • N-SING **Nosedive** is also a noun. ❑ *He told the tribunal his career had "taken a nosedive" since his dismissal last year.*

nose job (**nose jobs**) N-COUNT A **nose job** is a surgical operation that some people have to improve the shape of their nose. [INFORMAL] ❑ *I've never had plastic surgery, though people always think I've had a nose job.*

nos|ey /n**oʊ**zi/ → see **nosy**

nosh /n**ɒ**ʃ/ (**noshes, noshing, noshed**) ◨ N-SING A **nosh** is a snack or light meal. [AM, INFORMAL] ◨ V-T/V-I If you **nosh**, you eat. [INFORMAL] ❑ *They take in a movie or nosh at a restaurant.* ❑ *Peter noshed bagels and cream cheese.*

no-show (**no-shows**) N-VAR If someone who is expected to go somewhere fails to go there, you can say that they are a **no-show**. ❑ *At my wife Lucy's fortieth there were two no-shows, and two people called up to cancel after the party had started.*

nos|tal|gia /nɒst**æ**ldʒə/ N-UNCOUNT **Nostalgia** is an affectionate feeling you have for the past, especially for a particularly happy time. ❑ *He might be influenced by nostalgia for the surroundings of his happy youth.*

nos|tal|gic /nɒst**æ**ldʒɪk/ ◨ ADJ **Nostalgic** things cause you to think affectionately about the past. ❑ *Although we still depict nostalgic snow scenes on Christmas cards, winters are now very much warmer.* ◨ ADJ If you feel **nostalgic**, you think affectionately about experiences you had in the past. ❑ *Many people were nostalgic for the good old days.* • **nos|tal|gi|cal|ly** /nɒst**æ**ldʒɪkli/ ADV ❑ *People look back nostalgically on the war period, simply because everyone pulled together.*

nos|tril /n**ɒ**strɪl/ (**nostrils**) N-COUNT Your **nostrils** are the two openings at the end of your nose. ❑ *Keeping your mouth closed, breathe in through your nostrils.*

nos|trum /n**ɒ**strəm/ (**nostrums**) ◨ N-COUNT [usu pl, oft N of n] You can refer to ideas or theories about how something should be done as **nostrums**, especially when you think they are old-fashioned or wrong in some way. [FORMAL] ❑ *...yesterday's failed socialist nostrums.* ◨ N-COUNT If you refer to a medicine as a **nostrum**, you mean that it is not effective or has not been tested in a proper scientific way. ❑ *...pills, tablets, and other nostrums claiming to be magic potions.*

nosy /n**oʊ**zi/ (**nosier, nosiest**) also **nosey** ADJ If you describe someone as **nosy**, you mean that they are interested in things which do not concern them. [INFORMAL, DISAPPROVAL] ❑ *He was having to whisper in order to avoid being overheard by their nosy neighbors.*

not ♦♦♦ /n**ɒ**t/

Not is often shortened to **n't** in spoken English, and added to the auxiliary or modal verb. For example, 'did not' is often shortened to 'didn't.'

◨ NEG You use **not** with verbs to form negative statements. ❑ *The sanctions are not working the way they were intended.* ❑ *I don't trust my father anymore.* ◨ NEG You use **not** to form questions to which you expect the answer 'yes.' ❑ *Haven't they got enough problems there already?* ❑ *Didn't I see you at the party last week?* ◨ NEG You use **not**, usually in the form **n't**, in questions which imply that someone should have done something, or to express surprise that something is not the case. ❑ *Why didn't you do it months ago?* ❑ *Why couldn't he listen to her?* ◨ NEG You use **not**, usually in the form **n't**, in question tags after a positive statement. ❑ *It's crazy, isn't it?* ❑ *I've been a great husband, haven't I?* ◨ NEG You use **not**, usually in the form **n't**, in polite suggestions. [POLITENESS] ❑ *Actually we do have a position in mind. Why don't you fill out our application?* ◨ NEG You use **not** to represent the negative of a word, group, or clause that has just been used. ❑ *"Have you found Paula?"—"I'm afraid not, Kate."* ◨ NEG You can use **not** in front of 'all' or 'every' when you want to say something that applies only to some members of the group that you are talking about. ❑ *Not all the money, to put it mildly, has been used wisely.* ◨ NEG If something is **not** always the case, you mean that sometimes it is the case and sometimes it is not. ❑ *He didn't always win the arguments, but he often was right.* ❑ *She couldn't always afford a babysitter.* ◨ NEG You can use **not** or **not even** in front of 'a' or 'one' to emphasize that there is none at all of what is being mentioned. [EMPHASIS] ❑ *...no office, no phone, not even a shelf on which to put my meager belongings.* ❑ *I sent report after report. But not one word was published.* ◨ NEG [NEG amount] You can use **not** in front of a word referring to a distance, length of time, or other amount to say that the actual distance, time, or amount is less than the one mentioned. ❑ *The tug crossed our stern not fifty yards away.* ❑ *...a large crowd not ten yards away waiting for a bus.* ◨ NEG You use **not** when you are contrasting something that is true with something that is untrue. You use this especially to indicate that people might think that the untrue statement is true. ❑ *He has his place in the team not because he is young but because he is good.* ❑ *Training is an investment not a cost.* ◨ NEG You use **not** in expressions such as 'not only,' 'not just,' and 'not simply' to emphasize that something is true, but it is not the whole truth. [EMPHASIS] ❑ *These movies were not only making money; they were also perceived to be original.* ❑ *What's it going to cost us, not just in terms of money, but in terms of lives?* ◨ PHRASE You use **not that** to introduce a negative clause that contradicts something that the previous statement implies. ❑ *His death took me a year to get over; not that you're ever really over it.* ◨ CONVENTION **Not at all** is an emphatic way of saying 'No' or of agreeing that the answer to a question is 'No.' [EMPHASIS] ❑ *"Sorry. I sound like Abby, don't I?"—"No. Not at all."* ◨ CONVENTION **Not at all** is a polite way of acknowledging a person's thanks. [FORMULAE] ❑ *"Thank you very much for speaking with us."—"Not at all."* ◨ **not half** → see **half** ◨ **if not** → see **if** ◨ **more often than not** → see **often**

no|table /n**oʊ**təbəl/ ADJ Someone or something that is **notable** is important or interesting. ❑ *The proposed new structure is notable not only for its height, but for its shape.* ❑ *Mo did not want to be ruled by anyone and it is notable that she never allowed the men in her life to eclipse her.*

no|tably /n**oʊ**təbli/ ◨ ADV [ADV group/cl] You use **notably** to specify an important or typical example of something that you are talking about. ❑ *The divorce would be granted when more important problems, notably the fate of the children, had been decided.* ◨ ADV [ADV adj/adv] You can use **notably** to emphasize a particular quality that someone or something has. [EMPHASIS] ❑ *Old established friends are notably absent, so it's a good opportunity to make new contacts.*

no|ta|ry /n**oʊ**təri/ (**notaries**) N-COUNT A **notary** or a **notary public** is a person, often a lawyer, who has legal authority to witness the signing of documents in order to make them legally valid.

no|ta|tion /noʊt**eɪ**ʃ°n/ (**notations**) N-VAR [usu supp N] A system of **notation** is a set of written symbols that are used to represent something such as music or mathematics. ❑ *Musical notation was conceived for the C major scale and each line and space represents a note in this scale.* ❑ *...some other abstract notation system like a computer language.*

notch /n**ɒ**tʃ/ (**notches, notching, notched**) ◨ N-COUNT You can refer to a level on a scale of measurement or achievement

as a **notch**. [JOURNALISM] ☐ *Average earnings in the economy moved up another notch in August.* ☐ *In this country the good players are pulled down a notch or two.* **2** V-T If you **notch** a success, especially in a sports contest, you achieve it. [JOURNALISM] ☐ *She has notched all of her three victories at this track.* **3** N-COUNT A **notch** is a small V-shaped or circular cut in the surface or edge of something. ☐ *It is a myth that gunslingers in the American west cut notches in the handle of their pistol for each man they shot.*
▶ **notch up** PHRASAL VERB If you **notch up** something such as a score or total, you achieve it. [JOURNALISM] ☐ *He had notched up more than 25 victories worldwide.*

note ◆◆◇ /n**oʊ**t/ (**notes**, **noting**, **noted**) **1** N-COUNT A **note** is a short letter. ☐ *Stevens wrote him a note asking him to come to his apartment.* **2** N-COUNT A **note** is something that you write down to remind yourself of something. ☐ *I knew that if I didn't make a note I would lose the thought so I asked to borrow a pen or pencil.* ☐ *She wasn't taking notes on the lecture.* **3** N-COUNT In a book or article, a **note** is a short piece of additional information. ☐ *See Note 16 on p. 223.* **4** N-COUNT A **note** is a short document that has to be signed by someone and that gives official information about something. ☐ *Since Mr. Bennett was going to need some time off work, he asked for a sick note.* **5** N-COUNT In music, a **note** is the sound of a particular pitch, or a written symbol representing this sound. ☐ *She has a deep voice and doesn't even try for the high notes.* **6** N-SING You can use **note** to refer to a particular quality in someone's voice that shows how they are feeling. ☐ *There is an unmistakable note of nostalgia in his voice when he looks back on the early years of the family business.* **7** N-SING You can use **note** to refer to a particular feeling, impression, or atmosphere. ☐ *Yesterday's testimony began on a note of passionate but civilized disagreement.* ☐ *Somehow he tells these stories without a note of horror.* **8** V-T If you **note** a fact, you become aware of it. ☐ *The White House has noted his promise to support any attack that was designed to enforce the UN resolutions.* ☐ *Suddenly, I noted that the rain had stopped.* **9** V-T If you tell someone to **note** something, you are drawing their attention to it. ☐ *Note the statue to Sallustio Bandini, a prominent Sienese.* **10** V-T If you **note** something, you mention it in order to draw people's attention to it. ☐ *The report notes that export and import volumes picked up in leading economies.* **11** V-T When you **note** something, you write it down as a record of what has happened. ☐ *"He has had his tonsils out and has been ill, too," she noted in her diary.* ☐ *They never noted the building's history of problems.* **12** N-COUNT You can refer to a banknote as a **note**. [mainly BRIT]

in AM, usually use **bill**

13 → see also **noted**, **promissory note** **14** PHRASE Someone or something that is **of note** is important, worth mentioning, or well-known. ☐ *...politicians of note.* **15** PHRASE If you **take note** of something, you pay attention to it because you think that it is important or significant. ☐ *Take note of the weather conditions.* **16** → See feature box at **music**
▶ **note down** PHRASAL VERB If you **note down** something, you write it down quickly, so that you have a record of it. ☐ *She had noted down the names and she told me the story simply and factually.* ☐ *If you find a name that's on the list I've given you, note it down.*

SYNONYMS

note
NOUN **1**
message: *I got a message you were trying to reach me.*
communication: *The ambassador has brought a communication from the President.*
memo: *Did you get the memo about opening hours?*
letter: *I had received a letter from a very close friend.*
VERB
9
notice: *Luckily, I'd noticed where you left the car.*
observe: *In 1664, Hooke observed a reddish spot on the surface of the planet.*
perceive: *'Precisely what other problems do you perceive?' she asked.*
11
write down: *On the morning before starting the fast, write down your starting weight.*
record: *...a place which has rarely suffered a famine in its recorded history.*
jot down: *Keep a pad handy to jot down queries as they occur.*

note|book /n**oʊ**tbʊk/ (**notebooks**) **1** N-COUNT A **notebook** is a small book for writing notes in. ☐ *He brought out a notebook and pen from his pocket.* **2** N-COUNT A **notebook computer** is a small personal computer. ☐ *...a range of notebook computers which allows all your important information to travel safely with you.*

not|ed ◆◇◇ /n**oʊ**tɪd/ ADJ To be **noted** for something you do or have means to be well known and admired for it. ☐ *...a television program noted for its attacks on organized crime.*

SYNONYMS

noted
ADJ
famous: *New Orleans is famous for its cuisine.*
celebrated: *He was soon one of the most celebrated young painters in England.*
well-known: *He surrounds himself with attractive, intelligent, or well-known people.*
prominent: *...a prominent member of the Law Society.*
renowned: *...Sir William Crookes, the renowned chemist.*

note|pad /n**oʊ**tpæd/ (**notepads**) N-COUNT A **notepad** is a pad of paper that you use for writing notes or letters on.

note|paper /n**oʊ**tpeɪpər/ N-UNCOUNT [oft supp N] **Notepaper** is paper that you use for writing letters on. ☐ *He had written letters on official notepaper to promote a relative's company.*

note|worthy /n**oʊ**twɜrði/ ADJ A fact or event that is **noteworthy** is interesting, remarkable, or significant in some way. [FORMAL] ☐ *It is noteworthy that the program has been shifted from its original August slot to July.* ☐ *I found nothing particularly noteworthy to report.* ☐ *The most noteworthy feature of the list is that there are no women on it.*

not-for-profit ADJ [usu ADJ n] A **not-for-profit** organization is one which is not run with the aim of making a profit. [mainly AM, BUSINESS] ☐ *...a not-for-profit foundation that brings technology into public schools.*

noth|ing ◆◆◆ /n**ʌ**θɪŋ/ (**nothings**) **1** PRON-INDEF-NEG **Nothing** means not a single thing, or not a single part of something. ☐ *I've done nothing much since this morning.* ☐ *There is nothing wrong with the car.* **2** PRON-INDEF-NEG You use **nothing** to indicate that something or someone is not important or significant. ☐ *Because he had always had money it meant nothing to him.* ☐ *Do our years together mean nothing?* ● N-COUNT **Nothing** is also a noun. ☐ *It is the picture itself that is the problem; so small, so dull. It's a nothing, really.* **3** PRON-INDEF-NEG If you say that something cost **nothing** or is worth **nothing**, you are indicating that it cost or is worth a surprisingly small amount of money. ☐ *The furniture was threadbare; he'd obviously picked it up for nothing.* **4** PRON-INDEF-NEG You use **nothing** before an adjective or 'to'-infinitive to say that something or someone does not have the quality indicated. ☐ *Around the lake the countryside generally is nothing special.* ☐ *There was nothing remarkable about him.* **5** PRON-INDEF-NEG You can use **nothing** before 'so' and an adjective or adverb, or before a comparative, to emphasize how strong or great a particular quality is. [EMPHASIS] ☐ *Youngsters learn nothing so fast as how to beat the system.* ☐ *I consider nothing more important in my life than songwriting.* **6** PHRASE You can use **all or nothing** to say that either something must be done fully and completely or else it cannot be done at all. ☐ *Either he went through with this thing or he did not; it was all or nothing.* **7** PHRASE If you say that something is **better than nothing**, you mean that it is not what is required, but that it is better to have that thing than to have nothing at all. ☐ *After all, 15 minutes of exercise is better than nothing.* **8** PHRASE You use **nothing but** in front of a noun, an infinitive without 'to,' or an '-ing' form to mean 'only.' ☐ *All that money brought nothing but sadness and misery and tragedy.* ☐ *It did nothing but make us ridiculous.* ☐ *He is focused on nothing but winning.* **9** CONVENTION People sometimes say '**It's nothing**' as a polite response after someone has thanked them for something they have done. [FORMULAE] ☐ *"Thank you for the wonderful dinner."—"It's nothing," Sarah said.* **10** PHRASE If you say about a story or report that there is **nothing to it**, you mean that it is untrue. ☐ *It's all superstition, and there's nothing to it.*

nothingness

11 PHRASE If you say about an activity that there is **nothing to it**, you mean that it is extremely easy. ❑ *If you've shied away from making pancakes in the past, don't be put off – there's really nothing to it!* **12** PHRASE **Nothing of the sort** is used when strongly contradicting something that has just been said. [EMPHASIS] ❑ *"We're going to talk this over in my office."—"We're going to do nothing of the sort."* **13 nothing to write home about** → see home ① **14 to stop at nothing** → see stop **15 to think nothing of** → see think ②

USAGE

nothing
You don't usually use any other negative word such as 'not' after **nothing**. Don't say, for example, '~~Nothing didn't happen.~~' You say '**Nothing happened.**' Similarly, don't use 'nothing' as the object of a sentence which already has a negative word in it. Don't say, for example, '~~I couldn't hear nothing.~~' Say 'I couldn't hear **anything**.' *I did not say anything.*

noth|ing|ness /nʌθɪŋnɪs/ **1** N-UNCOUNT **Nothingness** is the fact of not existing. ❑ *There might be something beyond the grave, you know, and not nothingness.* **2** N-UNCOUNT **Nothingness** means complete emptiness. ❑ *Her eyes, glazed with the drug, stared with half closed lids at nothingness.*

no|tice ♦♦◊ /noʊtɪs/ (**notices, noticing, noticed**) **1** V-T/V-I If you **notice** something or someone, you become aware of them. ❑ *He stressed that people should not hesitate to contact the police if they've noticed any strangers recently.* ❑ *I noticed that most academics were writing papers during the summer.* ❑ *Luckily, I'd noticed where you left the car.* ❑ *If he thought no one would notice, he's wrong.* **2** N-COUNT A **notice** is a written announcement in a place where everyone can read it. ❑ *Notices in the waiting room requested that you neither smoke nor spit.* ❑ *A few guest houses had "No Vacancies" notices in their windows.* **3** N-UNCOUNT If you give **notice** about something that is going to happen, you give a warning in advance that it is going to happen. ❑ *Interest is paid monthly. Three months' notice is required for withdrawals.* ❑ *The insured must be given at least 10 days' notice of cancellation.* **4** N-COUNT A **notice** is a formal announcement in a newspaper or magazine about something that has happened or is going to happen. ❑ *I spotted a notice in a local newspaper.* **5** N-COUNT A **notice** is one of a number of letters that are similar or exactly the same which an organization sends to people in order to give them information or ask them to do something. ❑ *Bonus notices were issued each year from head office to local agents.* **6** N-COUNT A **notice** is a written article in a newspaper or magazine in which someone gives their opinion of a play, movie, or concert. [BRIT]

in AM, use **review**

7 PHRASE **Notice** is used in expressions such as '**on short notice**,' '**at a moment's notice**,' or '**at twenty-four hours' notice**,' to indicate that something can or must be done within a short period of time. ❑ *There's no one available on such short notice to take her class.* ❑ *I live just a mile away, so I can usually be available on short notice.* **8** PHRASE If a situation is said to exist **until further notice**, it will continue for an uncertain length of time until someone changes it. ❑ *The bad news was that all flights had been canceled until further notice.* **9** PHRASE If an employer **gives** an employee **notice**, the employer tells the employee that he or she must leave his or her job within a short fixed period of time. [BUSINESS] ❑ *The next morning I telephoned him and gave him his notice.* **10** PHRASE If you **give notice** or **hand in notice** you tell your employer that you intend to leave your job soon, within a set period of time. You can also **hand in** your **notice**. [BUSINESS] ❑ *He handed in his notice at the bank and ruined his promising career.* **11** PHRASE If you **take notice** of a particular fact or situation, you behave in a way that shows that you are aware of it. ❑ *We want the government to take notice of what we think they should do for single parents.* **12** PHRASE If you **take no notice** of someone or something, you do not consider them to be important enough to affect what you think or what you do. ❑ *They took no notice of him, he did not stand out, he was in no way remarkable.* **13** → See feature box at **work**

COLLOCATIONS

notice
NOUN
3
adjective + **notice**: advance, prior; adequate, reasonable
verb + **notice**: give, serve
5
noun + **notice**: enforcement, eviction, infringement
verb + **notice**: circulate, issue; receive
VERB **1**
notice + noun: change, difference, increase

no|tice|able /noʊtɪsəbəl/ ADJ Something that is **noticeable** is very obvious, so that it is easy to see, hear, or recognize. ❑ *It is noticeable that women do not have the rivalry that men have.* ● **no|tice|ably** ADV ❑ *Standards of living were deteriorating rather noticeably.*

no|tice|board /noʊtɪsbɔrd/ (**noticeboards**) N-COUNT A **noticeboard** is a board which is usually attached to a wall in order to display notices giving information about something. [mainly BRIT]

in AM, usually use **bulletin board**

no|ti|fi|able /noʊtɪfaɪəbəl/ ADJ A **notifiable** disease or crime is one that must be reported to the authorities whenever it occurs, because it is considered to be dangerous to the community. ❑ *Many doctors fail to report cases, even though food poisoning is a notifiable disease.*

no|ti|fi|ca|tion /noʊtɪfɪkeɪʃən/ (**notifications**) N-VAR If you are given **notification** of something, you are officially informed of it. ❑ *Names of the dead and injured are being withheld pending notification of relatives.*

no|ti|fy /noʊtɪfaɪ/ (**notifies, notifying, notified**) V-T If you **notify** someone of something, you officially inform them about it. [FORMAL] ❑ *The skipper notified the coastguard of the tragedy.* ❑ *Earlier this year they were notified that their homes were to be cleared away.*

no|tion ♦◊◊ /noʊʃən/ (**notions**) **1** N-COUNT A **notion** is an idea or belief about something. ❑ *We each have a notion of just what kind of person we'd like to be.* ❑ *I reject absolutely the notion that privatization of our industry is now inevitable.* **2** N-PLURAL **Notions** are small articles for sewing, such as buttons, zips, and thread. [AM]

SYNONYMS

notion
NOUN **1**
idea: *Some of his ideas about democracy are entirely his own.*
view: *My own view is absolutely clear. What I did was right.*
opinion: *He held the opinion that a government should think before introducing a tax.*

no|tion|al /noʊʃənəl/ ADJ Something that is **notional** exists only in theory or as a suggestion or idea, but not in reality. [FORMAL] ❑ *...the notional value of state assets.* ● **no|tion|al|ly** ADV ❑ *...those who notionally supported the republic but did nothing in terms of action.* ❑ *That meant that he, notionally at least, outranked them all.*

no|to|ri|ety /noʊtəraɪɪti/ N-UNCOUNT To achieve **notoriety** means to become well known for something bad. ❑ *He achieved notoriety as chief counsel to the President in the Watergate break-in.*

no|to|ri|ous /noʊtɔriəs/ ADJ To be **notorious** means to be well known for something bad. ❑ *...an area notorious for drugs, crime and violence.* ● **no|to|ri|ous|ly** ADV ❑ *The train company is overstaffed and notoriously inefficient.* ❑ *He worked mainly in New York City where living space is notoriously at a premium.*

not|with|stand|ing /nɒtwɪθstændɪŋ, -wɪð-/ PREP If something is true **notwithstanding** something else, it is true in spite of that other thing. [FORMAL] ❑ *He despised William Pitt, notwithstanding the similar views they both held.* ● ADV [n ADV] **Notwithstanding** is also an adverb. ❑ *His relations with colleagues, differences of opinion notwithstanding, were unfailingly friendly.*

nou|gat /nuːgət/ N-UNCOUNT **Nougat** is a kind of firm candy, containing nuts and sometimes fruit.

nought /nɔːt/ (noughts) NUM Nought is the number 0. [mainly BRIT]

in AM, usually use **zero**

noun /naʊn/ (nouns) **1** N-COUNT A **noun** is a word such as 'car,' 'love,' or 'Anne' which is used to refer to a person or thing. **2** → see also **count noun, proper noun**

noun group (noun groups) N-COUNT A **noun group** is a noun or pronoun, or a group of words based on a noun or pronoun. In the sentence, 'She put the bottle of wine on the kitchen table,' 'She,' 'the bottle of wine,' and 'the kitchen table' are all noun groups.

noun phrase (noun phrases) N-COUNT A **noun phrase** is the same as a **noun group**.

nourish /nɜːrɪʃ/ (nourishes, nourishing, nourished) **1** V-T To **nourish** a person, animal, or plant means to provide them with the food that is necessary for life, growth, and good health. ❑ *The food she eats nourishes both her and the baby.* • **nourishing** ADJ ❑ *Most of these nourishing substances are in the yolk of the egg.* **2** → See feature box at **nutrition**

-nourished /-nɜːrɪʃt/ COMB IN ADJ **-nourished** is used with adverbs such as 'well' or 'under' to indicate how much food someone eats or whether it is the right kind of food. ❑ *To make sure the children are well nourished, vitamin drops are usually recommended.* ❑ *...undernourished and poorly dressed orphans.*

nourishment /nɜːrɪʃmənt/ **1** N-UNCOUNT If something provides a person, animal, or plant with **nourishment**, it provides them with the food that is necessary for life, growth, and good health. ❑ *The mother provides the embryo with nourishment and a place to grow.* **2** N-UNCOUNT The action of nourishing someone or something, or the experience of being nourished, can be referred to as **nourishment**. ❑ *Sugar gives quick relief to hunger but provides no lasting nourishment.*

nouveau riche /nuːvoʊ riːʃ/ (nouveau riche or nouveaux riches) **1** N-PLURAL [usu *the* N] The **nouveaux riches** are people who have only recently become rich and who have tastes and manners that some people consider vulgar. [DISAPPROVAL] ❑ *The nouveau riche have to find a way to be accepted.* **2** ADJ **Nouveau riche** means belonging or relating to the nouveaux riches. [DISAPPROVAL] ❑ *...critics who did not appreciate his nouveau riche taste.*

nouvelle cuisine /nuːvɛl kwɪziːn/ N-UNCOUNT **Nouvelle cuisine** is a style of cooking in which very fresh foods are lightly cooked and served in unusual combinations. You can also refer to food that has been cooked in this way as **nouvelle cuisine**. ❑ *Dining out is easy with everything from a hamburger to hyper-expensive nouvelle cuisine on your doorstep.*

Nov. Nov. is a written abbreviation for **November**. ❑ *The first ballot is on Tuesday Nov. 20.*

novel ♦♦◊ /nɒvəl/ (novels) **1** N-COUNT A **novel** is a long written story about imaginary people and events. ❑ *...a novel by Herman Hesse.* **2** ADJ **Novel** things are new and different from anything that has been done, experienced, or made before. ❑ *Protesters found a novel way of demonstrating against steeply rising oil prices.* **3** → See feature box at **book, upcycle**

─── SYNONYMS ───

novel
ADJ **2**
new: *...the introduction of new drugs to suppress the immune system.*
different: *This recipe is certainly interesting and different.*
original: *It is one of the most original works of imagination in the language.*
innovative: *...products which are more innovative than those of their competitors.*

novelist /nɒvəlɪst/ (novelists) N-COUNT A **novelist** is a person who writes novels. ❑ *The key to success as a romantic novelist is absolute belief in your story.*

novella /noʊvɛlə/ (novellas) N-COUNT A **novella** is a short novel or a long short story. ❑ *...an autobiographical novella from French writer Marguerite Duras.*

novelty /nɒvəlti/ (novelties) **1** N-UNCOUNT **Novelty** is the quality of being different, new, and unusual. ❑ *In the contemporary western world, rapidly changing styles cater to a desire for novelty and individualism.* **2** N-COUNT A **novelty** is something that is new and therefore interesting. ❑ *Stores really like orange cauliflower because it's a novelty, it's something different.* **3** N-COUNT **Novelties** are cheap toys, ornaments, or other objects that are sold as presents or souvenirs. ❑ *At Easter, we give them plastic eggs filled with small toys, novelties, and coins.*

November ♦♦♦ /noʊvɛmbər/ (Novembers) N-VAR **November** is the eleventh month of the year in the Western calendar. ❑ *He arrived in London in November 1939.*

novice /nɒvɪs/ (novices) **1** N-COUNT A **novice** is someone who has been doing a job or other activity for only a short time and so is not experienced at it. ❑ *I'm a novice at these things, Lieutenant. You're the professional.* **2** N-COUNT In a monastery or convent, a **novice** is a person who is preparing to become a monk or nun.

now ♦♦♦ /naʊ/ **1** ADV You use **now** to refer to the present time, often in contrast to a time in the past or the future. ❑ *She's a widow now.* ❑ *But we are now a much more fragmented society.* • PRON **Now** is also a pronoun. ❑ *Now is the time when we must all live as economically as possible.* **2** ADV [ADV after v] If you do something **now**, you do it immediately. ❑ *I'm sorry, but I must go now.* • PRON **Now** is also a pronoun. ❑ *Now is your chance to talk to him.* **3** CONJ You use **now** or **now that** to indicate that an event has occurred and as a result something else may or will happen. ❑ *Now you're settled, why don't you take up some serious study?* **4** ADV You use **now** to indicate that a particular situation is the result of something that has recently happened. ❑ *Mrs. Chandra has received one sweater for each of her five children and says that the winter will not be so hard now.* ❑ *She told me not to repeat it, but now I don't suppose it matters.* **5** ADV In stories and accounts of past events, **now** is used to refer to the particular time that is being written or spoken about. ❑ *She felt a little better now.* ❑ *It was too late now for Blake to lock his room door.* **6** ADV You use **now** in statements which specify the length of time up to the present that something has lasted. ❑ *They've been married now for 30 years.* ❑ *They have been missing for a long time now.* **7** ADV [ADV cl] You say '**Now**' or '**Now then**' to indicate to the person or people you are with that you want their attention, or that you are about to change the subject. [SPOKEN] ❑ *"Now then," Max said, "to get back to the point." ❑ Now then, what's the trouble?* **8** ADV [ADV with cl] You use **now** to give a slight emphasis to a request or command. [SPOKEN] ❑ *Come on now. You know you must be hungry.* ❑ *Come and sit down here, now.* **9** ADV [ADV cl] You can say '**Now**' to introduce information which is relevant to the part of a story or account that you have reached, and which needs to be known before you can continue. [SPOKEN] ❑ *My son went to Aspen, in Colorado. Now he and his wife are people who love a quiet vacation.* **10** ADV [ADV cl] You say '**Now**' to introduce something which contrasts with what you have just said. [SPOKEN] ❑ *Now, if it was me, I'd want to do more than just change the locks.* **11** PHRASE If you say that something happens **now and then** or **every now and again**, you mean that it happens sometimes but not very often or regularly. ❑ *My father has a collection of magazines to which I return every now and then.* **12** PHRASE If you say that something will happen **any day now, any moment now,** or **any time now**, you mean that it will happen very soon. ❑ *Jim expects to be sent to Europe any day now.* **13** PHRASE **Just now** means a very short time ago. [SPOKEN] ❑ *You looked pretty upset just now.* ❑ *I spoke just now of being in love.* **14** PHRASE You use **just now** when you want to say that a particular situation exists at the time when you are speaking, although it may change in the future. [SPOKEN] ❑ *I'm pretty busy just now.* **15** PHRASE People such as television hosts sometimes use **now for** when they are going to start talking about a different subject or start presenting a new activity. [SPOKEN] ❑ *And now for something completely different.*

─── SYNONYMS ───

now
ADV **1**
nowadays: *I don't see much of Tony nowadays.*
currently: *He currently has no strong rivals for power.*
at the moment: *At the moment, no one is talking to me.*
these days: *She is doing just fine these days.*

nowa|days /naʊədeɪz/ ADV [ADV with cl] **Nowadays** means at the present time, in contrast with the past. ❑ *Nowadays it's acceptable for women to be ambitious. But it wasn't then.*

no|where ♦◇◇ /noʊwɛər/ **1** ADV You use **nowhere** to emphasize that a place has more of a particular quality than any other place, or that it is the only place where something happens or exists. [EMPHASIS] ❑ *Nowhere is language a more serious issue than in Hawaii.* ❑ *This kind of forest exists nowhere else in the world.* **2** ADV You use **nowhere** when making negative statements to say that a suitable place of the specified kind does not exist. ❑ *There was nowhere to hide and nowhere to run.* ❑ *I have nowhere else to go, nowhere in the world.* **3** ADV You use **nowhere** to indicate that something or someone cannot be seen or found. ❑ *Michael glanced anxiously down the corridor, but Wilfred was nowhere to be seen.* ❑ *The escaped prisoner was nowhere in sight.* **4** ADV You can use **nowhere** to refer in a general way to small, unimportant, or uninteresting places. ❑ *...endless paths that led nowhere in particular.* **5** ADV [from/out of ADV] If you say that something or someone appears **from nowhere** or **out of nowhere**, you mean that they appear suddenly and unexpectedly. ❑ *A car came from nowhere, and I had to jump back into the hedge just in time.* **6** ADV You use **nowhere** to mean not in any part of a text, speech, or argument. [EMPHASIS] ❑ *He nowhere offers concrete historical background to support his arguments.* ❑ *Point taken, but nowhere did we suggest that this yacht's features were unique.* **7** PHRASE If you say that a place is **in the middle of nowhere**, you mean that it is a long way from other places. ❑ *At dusk we pitched camp in the middle of nowhere.* **8** PHRASE If you use **nowhere near** in front of a word or expression, you are emphasizing that the real situation is very different from, or has not yet reached, the state which that word or expression suggests. [EMPHASIS] ❑ *He's nowhere near recovered yet from his experiences.*

> **USAGE**
> **nowhere**
> You don't usually use another negative word with 'nowhere.' Don't say, for example, 'I couldn't find her nowhere.' You say 'I couldn't find her **anywhere**.' *I changed my mind and decided not to go **anywhere**.*

no-win ADJ [ADJ n] If you are in a **no-win** situation, any action you take will fail to benefit you in any way. ❑ *It was a no-win situation. Either she pretended she hated Ned and felt awful or admitted she loved him and felt even worse!*

nox|ious /nɒkʃəs/ **1** ADJ [usu ADJ n] A **noxious** gas or substance is poisonous or very harmful. ❑ *Many household products give off noxious fumes.* **2** ADJ [usu ADJ n] If you refer to someone or something as **noxious**, you mean that they are extremely unpleasant. [FORMAL] ❑ *...the heavy, noxious smell of burning sugar, butter, fats, and flour.* ❑ *Their behavior was noxious.*

noz|zle /nɒzəl/ (**nozzles**) N-COUNT The **nozzle** of a hose or pipe is a narrow piece attached to the end to control the flow of liquid or gas. ❑ *If he put his finger over the nozzle he could produce a forceful spray.*

NT /ɛn tiː/ **NT** is a written abbreviation for the **New Testament** of the Bible. Compare **OT**.

-n't /-ᵊnt/ → see **not**

nth /ɛnθ/ **1** ADJ [ADJ n] If you refer to the most recent item in a series of things as the **nth** item, you are emphasizing the number of times something has happened. [EMPHASIS] ❑ *The story was raised with me for the nth time two days before the article appeared.* **2** PHRASE [PHR after v, n PHR] If something is done **to the nth degree**, it is done to an extreme degree. [EMPHASIS] ❑ *You're a risk-taker to the nth degree.*

nu|ance /nuːɑːns/ (**nuances**) N-VAR A **nuance** is a small difference in sound, feeling, appearance, or meaning. ❑ *We can use our eyes and facial expressions to communicate virtually every subtle nuance of emotion there is.*

nub /nʌb/ N-SING [the N, usu N of n] The **nub** of a situation, problem, or argument is the central and most basic part of it. ❑ *That, I think, is the nub of the problem.* ❑ *Here we reach the nub of the argument.*

nu|bile /nuːbɪl, -baɪl/ ADJ [usu ADJ n] A **nubile** woman is young, physically mature, and sexually attractive. ❑ *What is this current television obsession with older men and nubile young women?*

nu|clear ♦♦◇ /nuːkliər/ **1** ADJ [ADJ n] **Nuclear** means relating to the nuclei of atoms, or to the energy released when these nuclei are split or combined. ❑ *...a nuclear power station.* ❑ *...nuclear energy.* **2** ADJ [ADJ n] **Nuclear** means relating to weapons that explode by using the energy released when the nuclei of atoms are split or combined. ❑ *They rejected a demand for the removal of all nuclear weapons.*

nu|clear ca|pa|bil|ity (**nuclear capabilities**) N-VAR If a country has **nuclear capability**, it is able to produce nuclear power and usually nuclear weapons.

nu|clear fami|ly (**nuclear families**) **1** N-COUNT A **nuclear family** is a family unit that consists of a father, mother, and children. **2** → See feature box at **family**

nuclear-free ADJ [usu ADJ n] A **nuclear-free** place is a place where nuclear energy or nuclear weapons are forbidden. ❑ *This is an important step toward a nuclear-free world.*

nu|clear fuel (**nuclear fuels**) N-VAR **Nuclear fuel** is fuel that provides nuclear energy, for example in power stations.

nu|clear re|ac|tor (**nuclear reactors**) N-COUNT A **nuclear reactor** is a machine which is used to produce nuclear energy or the place where this machine and other related machinery and equipment is kept. ❑ *The nuclear reactor was not damaged in the lightning storm that struck late last night.*

nu|clear win|ter N-VAR [also a N] **Nuclear winter** refers to the possible effects on the environment of a war in which large numbers of nuclear weapons are used. It is thought that there would be very low temperatures and very little light during a nuclear winter.

nu|cleic acid /nuːkliːɪk æsɪd, -kleɪ-/ (**nucleic acids**) N-MASS **Nucleic acids** are complex chemical substances, such as DNA, which are found in living cells. [TECHNICAL]

nu|cleus /nuːkliəs/ (**nuclei** /nuːkliaɪ/) **1** N-COUNT The **nucleus** of an atom or cell is the central part of it. ❑ *Neutrons and protons are bound together in the nucleus of an atom.* **2** N-COUNT The **nucleus** of a group of people or things is the small number of members which form the most important part of the group. ❑ *Matt Cummings and Liko Soules-Ono form the nucleus of the team.* **3** → See feature box at **electricity**

nude /nuːd/ (**nudes**) **1** ADJ A **nude** person is not wearing any clothes. ❑ *The occasional nude bather comes here.* • PHRASE If you do something **in the nude**, you are not wearing any clothes. If you paint or draw someone **in the nude**, they are not wearing any clothes. ❑ *Sleeping in the nude, if it suits you, is not a bad idea.* **2** N-COUNT A **nude** is a picture or statue of a person who is not wearing any clothes. A **nude** is also a person in a picture who is not wearing any clothes. ❑ *He was one of Australia's most distinguished artists, renowned for his portraits, landscapes, and nudes.*

nudge /nʌdʒ/ (**nudges, nudging, nudged**) **1** V-T If you **nudge** someone, you push them gently, usually with your elbow, in order to draw their attention to something. ❑ *I nudged Stan and pointed again.* • N-COUNT **Nudge** is also a noun. ❑ *She slipped her arm under his and gave him a nudge.* **2** V-T If you **nudge** someone or something into a place or position, you gently push them there. ❑ *Edna Swinson nudged him into the sitting room.* • N-COUNT **Nudge** is also a noun. ❑ *McKinnon gave the wheel another slight nudge to starboard.* **3** V-T If you **nudge** someone into doing something, you gently persuade them to do it. ❑ *Bit by bit Bob had nudged Fritz into selling his controlling interest.* ❑ *Foreigners must use their power not simply to punish the country but to nudge it toward greater tolerance.* • N-COUNT **Nudge** is also a noun. ❑ *I had a feeling that the challenge appealed to him. All he needed was a nudge.*

nud|ism /nuːdɪzəm/ N-UNCOUNT **Nudism** is the practice of not wearing any clothes on beaches and other areas specially set aside for this purpose. ❑ *Nudism, the council decided, was doing the resort more harm than good.* • **nud|ist** (**nudists**) N-COUNT [oft N n] ❑ *There are no nudist areas and topless sunbathing is only allowed on a few beaches.*

nu|dity /nuːdɪti/ N-UNCOUNT **Nudity** is the state of wearing no clothes. ❑ *...constant nudity and bad language on TV.*

nug|get /nʌɡɪt/ (**nuggets**) N-COUNT [oft n N, N of n] A **nugget** is a small lump of something, especially gold. ❑ *...pure high-grade gold nuggets.* ❑ *...a small nugget of butter.*

nui|sance /nuːsəns/ (**nuisances**) N-COUNT If you say that someone or something is a **nuisance**, you mean that they annoy you or cause you a lot of problems. ❑ *The rain has been*

nuke /nuːk/ (nukes, nuking, nuked) **1** N-COUNT A **nuke** is a nuclear weapon. [INFORMAL] ☐ *They have nukes, and if they're sufficiently pushed, they'll use them.* **2** V-T If one country **nukes** another, it attacks it using nuclear weapons. [INFORMAL] ☐ *He wanted to nuke the area.* **3** V-T If you **nuke** food, you cook it in a microwave oven. [AM, INFORMAL] ☐ *He put the sagging box in the microwave and nuked it.*

null /nʌl/ PHRASE If an agreement, a declaration, or the result of an election is **null and void**, it is not legally valid. ☐ *A spokeswoman said the agreement had been declared null and void.*

nul|li|fy /ˈnʌlɪfaɪ/ (nullifies, nullifying, nullified) **1** V-T To **nullify** a legal decision or procedure means to declare that it is not legally valid. [FORMAL] ☐ *They knew the courts could nullify the marriage before the ink was dry.* **2** V-T To **nullify** something means to make it have no effect. [FORMAL] ☐ *A missing or illegible name will nullify your vote.*

numb /nʌm/ (numbs, numbing, numbed) **1** ADJ If a part of your body is **numb**, you cannot feel anything there. ☐ *He could feel his fingers growing numb at their tips.* • **numb|ness** N-UNCOUNT ☐ *I have recently been suffering from pain and numbness in my hands.* **2** ADJ If you are **numb** with shock, fear, or grief, you are so shocked, frightened, or upset that you cannot think clearly or feel any emotion. ☐ *The mother, numb with grief, has trouble speaking.* • **numb|ness** N-UNCOUNT ☐ *Many men become more aware of emotional numbness in their 40s.* **3** V-T If an event or experience **numbs** you, you can no longer think clearly or feel any emotion. ☐ *For a while the shock of Philippe's letter numbed her.* • **numbed** ADJ ☐ *I'm so numbed with shock that I can hardly think.* **4** V-T If cold weather, a drug, or a blow **numbs** a part of your body, you can no longer feel anything in it. ☐ *The cold numbed my fingers.* ☐ *An injection of local anesthetic is usually given first to numb the area.*

num|ber ♦♦♦ /ˈnʌmbər/ (numbers, numbering, numbered) **1** N-COUNT A **number** is a word such as 'two', 'nine', or 'twelve', or a symbol such as 1, 3, or 47. You use numbers to say how many things you are referring to or where something comes in a series. ☐ *No, I don't know the room number.* ☐ *Stan Laurel was born at number 3, Argyll Street.* **2** N-COUNT You use **number** with words such as 'large' or 'small' to say approximately how many things or people there are. ☐ *Quite a considerable number of interviews are going on.* ☐ *I have had an enormous number of letters from single parents.* **3** N-SING If there are a **number** of things or people, there are several of them. If there are any **number** of things or people, there is a large quantity of them. ☐ *I seem to remember that Sam told a number of lies.* **4** N-UNCOUNT You can refer to someone's or something's position in a list of the most successful or most popular of a particular type of thing as, for example, **number** one or **number** two. ☐ *...the opportunity to play golf with the world number one.* ☐ *Before you knew it, the single was at number 90 in the U.S. singles charts.* **5** V-T If a group of people or things **numbers** a particular total, that is how many there are. ☐ *They told me that their village numbered 100.* **6** N-COUNT A **number** is the series of numbers that you dial when you are making a telephone call. ☐ *...a list of names and telephone numbers.* ☐ *My number is 414-3925.* **7** N-COUNT You can refer to a short piece of music, a song, or a dance as a **number**. ☐ *..."Unforgettable," a number that was written and performed in 1951.* **8** V-T If someone or something **is numbered** among a particular group, they are believed to belong in that group. [FORMAL] ☐ *Lech Walesa and Nelson Mandela are numbered among my personal heroes.* **9** V-T If you **number** something, you mark it with a number, usually starting at 1. ☐ *He cut his paper up into tiny squares, and he numbered each one.* **10** → see also **serial number**

num|ber crunch|er (number crunchers) N-COUNT [usu pl] If you refer to **number crunchers**, you mean people whose jobs involve dealing with numbers or mathematical calculations, for example in finance or statistics. [INFORMAL] ☐ *Even if the recovery is under way, it may be some time before the official number crunchers confirm it.*

num|ber crunch|ing N-UNCOUNT [oft N n] If you refer to **number crunching**, you mean activities or processes concerned with numbers or mathematical calculation, for example in finance, statistics, or computing. [INFORMAL] ☐ *The computer does most of the number crunching.*

num|ber|less /ˈnʌmbərlɪs/ ADJ [usu ADJ n] If there are **numberless** things, there are too many to be counted. [LITERARY] ☐ *...numberless acts of personal bravery by firefighters and rescue workers.*

num|ber one (number ones) **1** ADJ [ADJ n] **Number one** means better, more important, or more popular than anything else or anyone else of its kind. [INFORMAL] ☐ *The economy is the number one issue by far.* **2** N-COUNT In popular music, the **number one** is the best-selling recording in any one week, or the group or person who has made that recording. [INFORMAL] ☐ *Paula is the only artist to achieve four number ones from a debut album.*

num|ber plate (number plates) also **numberplate** N-COUNT A **number plate** is the same as a **license plate**. [BRIT]

num|bers game N-SING If you say that someone is playing the **numbers game**, you think that they are concentrating on the aspects of something which can be expressed in statistics, usually in order to mislead people. [DISAPPROVAL] ☐ *Regrettably, he resorts to the familiar numbers game when he boasts that fewer than 300 state enterprises currently remain in the public sector.*

numb|skull /ˈnʌmskʌl/ (numbskulls) N-COUNT If you refer to someone as a **numbskull**, you mean that they are very stupid. [INFORMAL, OLD-FASHIONED, DISAPPROVAL] ☐ *How were we to know that he was a numbskull?*

nu|mera|cy /ˈnuːmərəsi/ N-UNCOUNT [oft N n] **Numeracy** is the ability to do arithmetic. ☐ *Six months later John had developed literacy and numeracy skills, plus confidence.*

nu|mer|al /ˈnuːmərəl/ (numerals) N-COUNT **Numerals** are written symbols used to represent numbers. ☐ *...a flat, square wristwatch with classic Roman numerals.* ☐ *...the numeral 6.*

nu|mer|ate /ˈnuːmərɪt/ ADJ Someone who is **numerate** is able to do arithmetic. ☐ *Your children should be literate and numerate.*

nu|meri|cal /nuːˈmɛrɪkəl/ ADJ **Numerical** means expressed in numbers or relating to numbers. ☐ *Your job is to group them by letter and put them in numerical order.* • **nu|meri|cal|ly** ADV ☐ *...a numerically coded color chart.*

nu|mer|ol|ogy /ˌnuːməˈrɒlədʒi/ N-UNCOUNT **Numerology** is the study of particular numbers, such as a person's date of birth, in the belief that they may have special significance in a person's life.

nu|mero uno /ˌnuːməroʊ ˈuːnoʊ/ ADJ **Numero uno** means better, more important, or more popular than anything else or anyone else of its kind. [INFORMAL] ☐ *The company's chief operating officer was the numero-uno fund-raiser for the event.*

nu|mer|ous ♦◇◇ /ˈnuːmərəs/ ADJ If people or things are **numerous**, they exist or are present in large numbers. ☐ *Sex crimes were just as numerous as they are today.*

───── SYNONYMS ─────

numerous
ADJ
many: *Acting is a young person's profession in many ways.*
several: *I had lived two doors away from this family for several years.*
a lot of: *I remember a lot of things.*
countless: *She brought joy to countless people through her music.*

nu|mi|nous /ˈnuːmɪnəs/ ADJ Things that are **numinous** seem holy or spiritual and mysterious. [LITERARY] ☐ *The account of spiritual struggle that follows has a humbling and numinous power.*

nun /nʌn/ (nuns) N-COUNT A **nun** is a member of a female religious community. ☐ *Mr. Thomas was taught by the Catholic nuns whose school he attended to work and study hard.*

nun|cio /ˈnʌnsioʊ/ (nuncios) N-COUNT In the Roman Catholic church, a **nuncio** is an official who represents the Pope in a foreign country. ☐ *...the papal nuncio.*

nun|nery /ˈnʌnəri/ (nunneries) N-COUNT A **nunnery** is a group of buildings in which a community of nuns live together. [OLD-FASHIONED]

nup|tial /ˈnʌpʃəl/ (nuptials) **1** ADJ [usu ADJ n] **Nuptial** is used to refer to things relating to a wedding or to marriage.

[OLD-FASHIONED] ❑ *I went to the room which he had called the nuptial chamber.* ◻ N-PLURAL [usu with poss] Someone's **nuptials** are their wedding celebrations. [OLD-FASHIONED] ❑ *She became immersed in planning her nuptials.*

nurse ◆◇◇ /n₃rs/ (nurses, nursing, nursed) ◻ N-COUNT; N-TITLE; N-VOC A **nurse** is a person whose job is to care for people who are ill. ❑ *She had spent 29 years as a nurse.* ◻ V-T If you **nurse** someone, you care for them when they are ill. ❑ *All the years he was sick my mother had nursed him.* ◻ V-T If you **nurse** an illness or injury, you allow it to get better by resting as much as possible. ❑ *We're going to go home and nurse our colds.* ◻ V-T If you **nurse** an emotion or desire, you feel it strongly for a long time. ❑ *Jane still nurses the pain of rejection.*

COLLOCATIONS

nurse
NOUN ◻
noun + **nurse**: agency, practice, student, trainee
adjective + **nurse**: cardiac, dental, pediatric, psychiatric; veterinary; qualified, trained

---

nurse|maid /n₃rsmeɪd/ (nursemaids) N-COUNT A **nursemaid** is a woman or girl who is paid to take care of young children. [OLD-FASHIONED]

nurse prac|ti|tion|er (nurse practitioners) N-COUNT A **nurse practitioner** is a nurse with advanced training who provides some of the medical care usually provided by a doctor. ❑ *California law also permits nurse practitioners to furnish patients with prescriptions for most medications.*

nurse|ry /n₃rsəri/ (nurseries) ◻ N-COUNT A **nursery** is a room in a family home in which the young children of the family sleep or play. ❑ *He has painted murals in his children's nursery.* ◻ N-COUNT [also at/from/to N] A **nursery** is a place where children who are not old enough to go to school are cared for. ❑ *She puts her baby in this nursery and then goes back to work.* ◻ N-VAR **Nursery** is a school for very young children. [BRIT]

in AM, use **nursery school**

◻ N-COUNT A **nursery** is a place where plants are grown in order to be sold. ❑ *The garden, developed over the past 35 years, includes a nursery.*

nursery|man /n₃rsəriman/ (nurserymen) N-COUNT A **nurseryman** is a man who works in a place where young plants are grown in order to be sold.

nurse|ry rhyme (nursery rhymes) N-COUNT A **nursery rhyme** is a poem or song for young children, especially one that is old or well known.

nurse|ry school (nursery schools) N-VAR A **nursery school** is a school for very young children. ❑ *She began her professional career as a nursery school teacher.*

nursery|woman /n₃rsəriwʊmən/ (nurserywomen) N-COUNT A **nurserywoman** is a woman who works in a place where young plants are grown in order to be sold.

nurs|ing /n₃rsɪŋ/ N-UNCOUNT **Nursing** is the profession of caring for people who are ill. ❑ *She had no aptitude for nursing.*

nurs|ing bot|tle (nursing bottles) N-COUNT A **nursing bottle** is a plastic bottle with a special rubber top through which a baby can suck milk or another liquid. [AM]

nurs|ing home (nursing homes) N-COUNT A **nursing home** is a residence for old or sick people. ❑ *He died in a nursing home at the age of 87.*

nur|ture /n₃rtʃər/ (nurtures, nurturing, nurtured) ◻ V-T If you **nurture** something such as a young child or a young plant, you care for it while it is growing and developing. [FORMAL] ❑ *Parents want to know the best way to nurture and raise their child to adulthood.* ◻ V-T If you **nurture** plans, ideas, or people, you encourage them or help them to develop. [FORMAL] ❑ *She had always nurtured great ambitions for her son.* ❑ *...parents whose political views were nurtured in the sixties.* ◻ N-UNCOUNT **Nurture** is care and encouragement that is given to someone while they are growing up. ❑ *The human organism learns partly by nature, partly by nurture.*

nut /nʌt/ (nuts) ◻ N-COUNT The firm shelled fruit of some trees and bushes are called **nuts**. Some nuts can be eaten. ❑ *Nuts and seeds are good sources of vitamin E.* ◻ → see also **peanut**

◻ N-COUNT A **nut** is a thick metal ring which you screw onto a metal rod called a bolt. Nuts and bolts are used to hold things such as pieces of machinery together. ❑ *If you want to repair the wheels you just undo the four nuts.* ◻ N-COUNT If you describe someone as, for example, a baseball **nut** or a health **nut**, you mean that they are extremely enthusiastic about the thing mentioned. [INFORMAL] ❑ *...Annie, the girlfriend who was a true baseball nut.* ◻ ADJ [v-link ADJ about n] If you are **nuts** about something or someone, you like them very much. [INFORMAL, FEELINGS] ❑ *They're nuts about the car.* ◻ ADJ [v-link ADJ] If you say that someone **goes nuts** or is **nuts**, you mean that they go crazy or are very foolish. [INFORMAL] ❑ *You guys are nuts.* ◻ PHRASE If someone **goes nuts**, they become extremely angry. [INFORMAL] ❑ *My father would go nuts if he saw bruises on me.* ◻ → See also color supplement

nut-brown COLOR **Nut-brown** is used to describe things that are dark reddish brown in color.

nut|case /nʌtkeɪs/ (nutcases) also **nut case** N-COUNT If you refer to someone as a **nutcase**, you mean that they are mad or that their behavior is very strange. [INFORMAL, DISAPPROVAL] ❑ *The woman's a nutcase. She needs to be locked up.*

nut|cracker /nʌtkrækər/ (nutcrackers) ◻ N-COUNT A **nutcracker** is a device used to crack the shell of a nut. ◻ → See also color supplement

nut|meg /nʌtmeg/ N-UNCOUNT **Nutmeg** is a spice made from the seed of a tree that grows in hot countries. Nutmeg is usually used to flavor sweet food.

nu|tri|ent /nutriənt/ (nutrients) N-COUNT **Nutrients** are substances that help plants and animals to grow. ❑ *In her first book she explained the role of vegetable fibers, vitamins, minerals, and other essential nutrients.*

nu|tri|tion /nutrɪʃən/ N-UNCOUNT **Nutrition** is the process of taking food into the body and absorbing the nutrients in those foods. ❑ *There are alternative sources of nutrition to animal meat.*

VOCABULARY IN CONTEXT

Nutrition: is a vegan diet healthy?

The answer to this question depends on whether you are following a **balanced diet**. A vegan diet is naturally low in certain **minerals** and vitamins, so it's important to consider the **nutritional** value of what you eat. Provided you do this, vegan food can be both **nourishing** and cheap.

Dieticians recommend that nuts, **legumes**, and **soya** should be included in a vegan diet. Nuts contain **protein** and **fiber**. Although they are **fatty**, and therefore highly **calorific**, they are **high** in so-called 'good fats', which, unlike trans fats, are actually good for you. Legumes have the effect of lowering **cholesterol**, and soya is an excellent substitute for both meat and **dairy** products.

---

nu|tri|tion|al /nutrɪʃənəl/ ◻ ADJ The **nutritional** content of food is all the substances that are in it which help you to remain healthy. ❑ *It does sometimes help to know the nutritional content of foods.* • **nu|tri|tion|al|ly** ADV ❑ *...a nutritionally balanced diet.* ◻ → See feature box at **nutrition**

nu|tri|tion|ist /nutrɪʃənɪst/ (nutritionists) N-COUNT A **nutritionist** is a person whose job is to give advice on what you should eat to remain healthy. ❑ *Nutritionists say only 33 percent of our calorie intake should be from fat.*

nu|tri|tious /nutrıʃəs/ ADJ **Nutritious** food contains substances which help your body to be healthy. ❑ *It is always important to choose enjoyable, nutritious foods.*

nu|tri|tive /nutrıtıv/ ADJ [ADJ n] The **nutritive** content of food is all the substances that are in it which help you to remain healthy. ❑ *Coconut milk has little nutritive value.*

nut|shell /nʌtʃɛl/ PHRASE [usu PHR with cl] You can use **in a nutshell** to indicate that you are saying something in a very brief way, using few words. ❑ *In a nutshell, the owners thought they knew best.*

nut|ty /nʌti/ (nuttier, nuttiest) **1** ADJ If you describe food as **nutty**, you mean that it tastes of nuts, has the texture of nuts, or is made with nuts. ❑ *...nutty butter cookies.* ❑ *Chick peas have a distinctive, delicious, and nutty flavor.* **2** ADJ If you describe someone as **nutty**, you mean that their behavior is very strange or foolish. [INFORMAL, DISAPPROVAL] ❑ *He was undoubtedly a bit nutty.* ❑ *That's a nutty idea.*

nuz|zle /nʌzəl/ (nuzzles, nuzzling, nuzzled) V-T/V-I If you **nuzzle** someone or something, you gently rub your nose and mouth against them to show affection. ❑ *She nuzzled me and I cuddled her.* ❑ *The dog came and nuzzled up against me.*

NW NW is a written abbreviation for **northwest**. ❑ *...National Public Radio, 2025 M. Street NW, Washington, D.C.*

ny|lon /naılɒn/ (nylons) **1** N-UNCOUNT **Nylon** is a strong, flexible artificial fiber. ❑ *The chair is made of lightweight nylon.* **2** N-PLURAL **Nylons** are stockings made of nylon. [OLD-FASHIONED] ❑ *She wore a long skirt with pink pumps and black nylons.*

nymph /nımf/ (nymphs) **1** N-COUNT In Greek and Roman mythology, **nymphs** were spirits of nature who appeared as young women. **2** N-COUNT A **nymph** is the larva, or young form, of an insect such as a dragonfly.

nym|pho|ma|ni|ac /nımfəmeıniæk/ (nymphomaniacs) N-COUNT If someone refers to a woman as a **nymphomaniac**, they mean that she has sex or wants to have sex much more often than they consider normal or acceptable. [DISAPPROVAL]

Oo

O also **o** /<u>ou</u>/ (**O's, o's**) N-VAR **O** is the fifteenth letter of the English alphabet.

o' /ə/ **1** PREP **O'** is used in written English to represent the word 'of' pronounced without the 'f.' [INFORMAL] ❑ *Can we have a cup o' coffee, please?* **2** → see also **o'clock**

oaf /<u>ou</u>f/ (**oafs**) N-COUNT [oft adj N] If you refer to someone as an **oaf**, you think that they are impolite, clumsy, or aggressive. [DISAPPROVAL] ❑ *Leave the lady alone, you drunken oaf.*

oaf|ish /<u>ou</u>fɪʃ/ ADJ If you describe someone as **oafish**, you disapprove of their behavior because you think that it is impolite, clumsy, or aggressive. [DISAPPROVAL] ❑ *The bodyguards, as usual, were brave but oafish.* ❑ *...oafish humor.*

oak /<u>ou</u>k/ (**oaks**) N-VAR An **oak** or an **oak tree** is a large tree that often grows in forests and has strong, hard wood. ❑ *Many large oaks were felled during the war.* ● N-UNCOUNT **Oak** is the wood of this tree. ❑ *The cabinet was made of oak and was hand-carved.*

oar /<u>ɔ</u>r/ (**oars**) N-COUNT **Oars** are long poles with a wide, flat blade at one end which are used for rowing a boat.

oar|lock /<u>ɔ</u>rlɒk/ (**oarlocks**) N-COUNT The **oarlocks** on a rowboat are the U-shaped pieces of metal that keep the oars in position while you move them backward and forward. [AM]

in BRIT, use **rowlock**

oasis /ou<u>eɪ</u>sɪs/ (**oases** /ou<u>eɪ</u>siːz/) **1** N-COUNT An **oasis** is a small area in a desert where water and plants are found. **2** N-COUNT You can refer to a pleasant place or situation as an **oasis** when it is surrounded by unpleasant ones. ❑ *The immaculately tended gardens are an oasis in the midst of Cairo's urban sprawl.*

oath /<u>ou</u>θ/ (**oaths**) **1** N-COUNT An **oath** is a formal promise, especially a promise to be loyal to a person or country. ❑ *He took an oath of loyalty to the government.* **2** N-SING [the N, also on/under N] In a court of law, when someone takes the **oath**, they make a formal promise to tell the truth. You can say that someone is **under oath** when they have made this promise. ❑ *His girlfriend had gone into the witness box and taken the oath.* ❑ *Under oath, Andy finally admitted that he had lied.*

oat|meal /<u>ou</u>tmiːl/ **1** N-UNCOUNT [oft N n] **Oatmeal** is a kind of flour made by crushing oats. ❑ *...oatmeal cookies.* **2** N-UNCOUNT **Oatmeal** is a thick sticky food made from oats cooked in water or milk and eaten hot, especially for breakfast. [mainly AM]

in BRIT, usually use **porridge**

oats /<u>ou</u>ts/

The form **oat** is used as a modifier.

N-PLURAL **Oats** are a cereal crop or its grains, used for making cookies or a food called oatmeal, or for feeding animals. ❑ *Oats provide good, nutritious food for horses.*

ob|du|ra|cy /<u>ɒ</u>bdʊrəsi/ N-UNCOUNT If you accuse someone of **obduracy**, you think their refusal to change their decision or opinion is unreasonable. [FORMAL, DISAPPROVAL] ❑ *He shook his head in bewilderment at the obduracy of this man.*

ob|du|rate /<u>ɒ</u>bdʊrɪt/ ADJ If you describe someone as **obdurate**, you think that they are being unreasonable in their refusal to change their decision or opinion. [FORMAL, DISAPPROVAL] ❑ *Parts of the administration may be changing but others have been obdurate defenders of the status quo.*

obedi|ent /oub<u>iː</u>diənt/ ADJ A person or animal who is **obedient** does what they are told to do. ❑ *He was very respectful at home and obedient to his parents.* ● **obedi|ence** N-UNCOUNT ❑ *...unquestioning obedience to the law.* ● **obedi|ent|ly** ADV [ADV with v] ❑ *He was looking obediently at Keith, waiting for orders.*

obei|sance /oub<u>eɪ</u>səns/ (**obeisances**) **1** N-UNCOUNT [usu N to n] **Obeisance** to someone or something is great respect shown for them. [FORMAL] ❑ *While he was still young and strong all paid obeisance to him.* **2** N-VAR An **obeisance** is a physical gesture, especially a bow, that you make in order to show your respect for someone or something. [FORMAL] ❑ *One by one they came forward, mumbled grudging words of welcome, made awkward obeisances.*

ob|elisk /<u>ɒ</u>bəlɪsk/ (**obelisks**) **1** N-COUNT An **obelisk** is a tall stone pillar that has been built in honor of a person or an important event. **2** → See also color supplement

obese /oub<u>iː</u>s/ ADJ If someone is **obese**, they are extremely fat. ❑ *Obese people tend to have higher blood pressure than lean people.* ● **obesity** /oub<u>iː</u>sɪti/ N-UNCOUNT ❑ *...the excessive consumption of sugar that leads to problems of obesity.*

obey /oub<u>eɪ</u>/ (**obeys, obeying, obeyed**) V-T/V-I If you **obey** a person, a command, or an instruction, you do what you are told to do. ❑ *Cissie obeyed her mother without question.* ❑ *Most people obey the law.* ❑ *It was his duty to obey.*

ob|fus|cate /<u>ɒ</u>bfəskeɪt, ɒbfʌskeɪt/ (**obfuscates, obfuscating, obfuscated**) V-T/V-I To **obfuscate** something means to deliberately make it seem confusing and difficult to understand. [FORMAL, DISAPPROVAL] ❑ *They are obfuscating the issue, as only insurance companies can.* ❑ *It is language intended not to reveal but to conceal, not to communicate but to obfuscate.*

ob/gyn /<u>ou</u> biː dʒiː waɪ <u>ɛ</u>n/ (**ob/gyns**) also **ob-gyn, Ob-Gyn, OB/GYN 1** N-UNCOUNT **Ob/gyn** is the branch of medicine that deals with women's medical conditions, pregnancy, and birth. **Ob/gyn** is an abbreviation for 'obstetrics/gynecology.' [INFORMAL] ❑ *We are already having trouble getting needed services in surgery and ob/gyn.* **2** N-COUNT An **Ob/gyn** is a doctor who specializes in women's medical conditions, pregnancy, and birth. **Ob/gyn** is an abbreviation for 'obstetrician/gynecologist.' [INFORMAL] ❑ *My mom's an Ob/gyn and she works with high-risk pregnancies.*

obi|tu|ary /oub<u>ɪ</u>tʃueri/ (**obituaries**) N-COUNT Someone's **obituary** is an account of their life and character which is presented in a newspaper or broadcast soon after they die. ❑ *His obituary was published in one edition of his own newspaper before it was discovered that he was alive.*

ob|ject ✦✦◇ (**objects, objecting, objected**)

The noun is pronounced /<u>ɒ</u>bdʒɪkt/. The verb is pronounced /əbdʒ<u>ɛ</u>kt/.

1 N-COUNT An **object** is anything that has a fixed shape or form, that you can touch or see, and that is not alive. ❑ *He squinted his eyes as though he were studying an object on the horizon.* ❑ *...an object in the shape of a coconut.* **2** N-COUNT The **object** of what someone is doing is their aim or purpose. ❑ *The object of the exercise is to raise money for the charity.* **3** N-COUNT The **object of** a particular feeling or reaction is the person or thing it is directed toward or that causes it. ❑ *The object of her hatred was 24-year-old model Ros French.* ❑ *The object of great interest at the temple was a large marble tower built in memory of Buddha.* **4** N-COUNT In grammar, the **object** of a verb or a preposition is the word or phrase which completes the structure begun by the verb or preposition. **5** → see also **direct object, indirect object 6** V-T If you **object** to something, you express your dislike or disapproval of it. ❑ *A lot of people will object to the book.* ❑ *Cullen objected that his small staff would be unable to handle the added work.* ◾ PHRASE If you say that **money is no object** or **distance is no object**, you are emphasizing that you are willing or able to spend as much money as necessary or travel whatever distance is required. [EMPHASIS] ❑ *This was a very impressive program in which money seems to have been no object.*

ob|jec|tion /əbdʒɛkʃən/ (**objections**) ◾ N-VAR If you express or raise an **objection** to something, you say that you do not like it or agree with it. ❑ *Despite objections by the White House, the Senate voted today to cut off aid.* ◾ N-UNCOUNT If you say that you have no **objection** to something, you mean that you are not annoyed or bothered by it. ❑ *I have no objection to banks making money.*

ob|jec|tion|able /əbdʒɛkʃənəbəl/ ADJ If you describe someone or something as **objectionable**, you consider them to be extremely offensive and unacceptable. [FORMAL] ❑ *I don't like your tone; in fact I find it highly objectionable.*

ob|jec|tive ◆◇◇ /əbdʒɛktɪv/ (**objectives**) ◾ N-COUNT Your **objective** is what you are trying to achieve. ❑ *Our main objective was the recovery of the child safe and well.* ◾ ADJ [ADJ n] **Objective** information is based on facts. ❑ *He had no objective evidence that anything extraordinary was happening.* • **ob|jec|tive|ly** ADV ❑ *We simply want to inform people objectively about events.* • **ob|jec|tiv|ity** /ˌpbdʒɛktɪvɪti/ N-UNCOUNT ❑ *The poll, whose objectivity is open to question, gave the party a 39% share of the vote.* ◾ ADJ If someone is **objective**, they base their opinions on facts rather than on their personal feelings. ❑ *I believe that a journalist should be completely objective.* • **ob|jec|tive|ly** ADV ❑ *Try to view situations more objectively, especially with regard to work.* • **ob|jec|tiv|ity** N-UNCOUNT ❑ *The psychiatrist must learn to maintain an unusual degree of objectivity.*

SYNONYMS

objective
NOUN ◾
purpose: *The purpose of the occasion was to raise money for medical supplies.*
aim: *The aim of the festival is to increase awareness of Hindu culture and traditions.*
goal: *The goal is to raise as much money as possible.*
target: *He's won back his position too late to achieve his target of 20 goals this season.*

ADJ ◾
unbiased: *The researchers were expected to be unbiased.*
neutral: *Let's meet on neutral territory.*
impartial: *Career advisers offer impartial advice to all students.*

---

ob|ject les|son (**object lessons**) N-COUNT [oft N on/in n] If you describe an action, event, or situation as an **object lesson**, you think that it demonstrates the correct way to do something, or that it demonstrates the truth of a particular principle. ❑ *It was an object lesson in how to use television as a means of persuasion.*

ob|jec|tor /əbdʒɛktər/ (**objectors**) N-COUNT An **objector** is someone who states or shows that they oppose or disapprove of something. ❑ *The district council agreed with the objectors and turned down the application.* ◾ → see also **conscientious objector**

object-oriented ADJ [usu ADJ n] In computing, **object-oriented** programming involves dealing with code and data in blocks so that it is easier to change or do things with. ❑ *...object-oriented software.*

ob|jet d'art /ˌɒbʒeɪ dɑr/ (**objets d'art**) N-COUNT [usu pl] **Objets d'art** are ornaments that are considered to be attractive and of good quality. [FORMAL]

ob|li|gate /ˈɒblɪgeɪt/ (**obligates, obligating, obligated**) V-T If something **obligates** you to do a particular thing, it creates a situation where you have to do it. [FORMAL] ❑ *The ruling obligates airlines to release information about their flight delays.*

ob|li|gat|ed /ˈɒblɪgeɪtɪd/ ADJ [v-link ADJ] If you feel **obligated** to do something, you feel that it is your duty to do it. If you are **obligated to** someone, you feel that it is your duty to take care of them. [FORMAL] ❑ *I felt obligated to let him read the letter.* ❑ *He had gotten a girl pregnant and felt obligated to her and the child.*

ob|li|ga|tion /ˌɒblɪgeɪʃən/ (**obligations**) ◾ N-VAR If you have an **obligation** to do something, it is your duty to do that thing. ❑ *When teachers assign homework, students usually feel an obligation to do it.* ◾ N-VAR If you have an **obligation** to a person, it is your duty to take care of them or protect their interests. ❑ *The United States will do that which is necessary to meet its obligations to its own citizens.* ◾ PHRASE In advertisements, if a product or a service is available **without obligation**, you do not have to pay for that product or service until you have tried it and are satisfied with it. ❑ *If you are selling your property, why not call us for a free valuation without obligation.*

ob|liga|tory /əˈblɪgətɔri/ ADJ If something is **obligatory**, you must do it because of a rule or a law. ❑ *Most women will be offered an ultrasound scan during pregnancy, although it's not obligatory.*

oblige /əˈblaɪdʒ/ (**obliges, obliging, obliged**) ◾ V-T If you are **obliged** to do something, a situation, rule, or law makes it necessary for you to do that thing. ❑ *The storm got worse and worse. Finally, I was obliged to abandon the car and continue on foot.* ◾ V-T/V-I To **oblige** someone means to be helpful to them by doing what they have asked you to do. ❑ *Mr. Oakley has always been ready to oblige journalists with information.* ❑ *We called up three economists to ask how to eliminate the deficit and they obliged with very straightforward answers.* ◾ CONVENTION If you tell someone that you **would be obliged** or **should be obliged** if they would do something, you are telling them in a polite but firm way that you want them to do it. [FORMAL, POLITENESS] ❑ *I would be obliged if you could read it to us.*

oblig|ing /əˈblaɪdʒɪŋ/ ADJ If you describe someone as **obliging**, you think that they are willing and eager to be helpful. [OLD-FASHIONED or WRITTEN, APPROVAL] ❑ *He is an extremely pleasant and obliging man.* • **oblig|ing|ly** ADV [ADV with v] ❑ *Benedict obligingly held the door open.*

oblique /oʊˈblik/ ADJ If you describe a statement as **oblique**, you mean that is not expressed directly or openly, making it difficult to understand. ❑ *It was an oblique reference to his mother.* • **oblique|ly** ADV [ADV with v] ❑ *He obliquely referred to the U.S., Britain and Saudi Arabia.*

oblit|erate /əˈblɪtəreɪt/ (**obliterates, obliterating, obliterated**) ◾ V-T If something **obliterates** an object or place, it destroys it completely. ❑ *Their warheads are enough to obliterate the world several times over.* • **oblit|era|tion** /əˌblɪtəˈreɪʃən/ N-UNCOUNT ❑ *...the obliteration of three isolated rainforests.* ◾ V-T If you **obliterate** something such as a memory, emotion, or thought, you remove it completely from your mind. ❑ *There was time enough to obliterate memories of how things once were for him.*

obliv|ion /əˈblɪviən/ ◾ N-UNCOUNT **Oblivion** is the state of not being aware of what is happening around you, for example, because you are asleep or unconscious. ❑ *He just drank himself jovially into oblivion.* ◾ N-UNCOUNT **Oblivion** is the state of having been forgotten or of no longer being considered important. ❑ *It seems that the so-called new theory is likely to sink into oblivion.* ◾ N-UNCOUNT If you say that something is bombed or blasted **into oblivion**, you are emphasizing that it is completely destroyed. [EMPHASIS] ❑ *An entire poor section of town was bombed into oblivion.*

obliv|ious /əˈblɪviəs/ ADJ If you are **oblivious** to something or **oblivious** of it, you are not aware of it. ❑ *She lay motionless where she was, oblivious to pain.*

ob|long /ˈɒblɒŋ/ (**oblongs**) N-COUNT [oft N n] An **oblong** is a shape which has two long sides and two short sides and in which all the angles are right angles. ❑ *...an oblong table.*

ob|nox|ious /əbˈnɒkʃəs/ ◾ ADJ If you describe someone or their behavior as **obnoxious**, you think that they are very unpleasant because of being aggressive, loud, or offensive. [DISAPPROVAL] ❑ *The people at my table were so obnoxious I had to change my seat.* ◾ → See feature box at **polite**

obo In advertisements, **obo** is used after a price to indicate that the person who is selling something is willing to accept slightly less money than the sum they have mentioned. **obo** is a written abbreviation for 'or best offer.' [mainly AM] ❑ *Family boat. $6,000 obo.*

oboe /ˈoʊboʊ/ (**oboes**) N-VAR [oft the N] An **oboe** is a musical instrument shaped like a tube which you play by blowing through a double reed in the top end.

WORD HISTORY

oboe
Oboe comes from French *haut bois*, meaning 'high wood,' a reference to the instrument's high pitch compared to other instruments of the woodwind family.

obo|ist /o͡ʊbo͡ʊɪst/ (oboists) N-COUNT An **oboist** is someone who plays the oboe.

ob|scene /əbsin/ **1** ADJ If you describe something as **obscene**, you mean it offends you because it relates to sex or violence in a way that you think is unpleasant and shocking. ❑ *I'm not prudish but I think these photographs are obscene.* **2** ADJ In legal contexts, books, pictures, or movies which are judged **obscene** are illegal because they deal with sex or violence in a way that is offensive to the general public. ❑ *A city magistrate ruled that the novel was obscene and copies should be destroyed.* **3** ADJ If you describe something as **obscene**, you disapprove of it very strongly and consider it to be offensive or immoral. [DISAPPROVAL] ❑ *It was obscene to spend millions producing unwanted food.*

ob|scen|ity /əbsɛnɪti/ (obscenities) **1** N-UNCOUNT **Obscenity** is behavior, art, or language that is sexual and offends or shocks people. ❑ *He insisted these photographs were not art but obscenity.* **2** N-VAR An **obscenity** is a very offensive word or expression. ❑ *They shouted obscenities at us and smashed bottles on the floor.*

ob|scu|rant|ism /əbskyu͟ərəntɪzəm/ N-UNCOUNT **Obscurantism** is the practice or policy of deliberately making something vague and difficult to understand, especially in order to prevent people from finding out the truth. [FORMAL or WRITTEN] ❑ *...legalistic obscurantism.*

ob|scu|rant|ist /əbskyu͟ərəntɪst/ ADJ If you describe something as **obscurantist**, you mean that it is deliberately vague and difficult to understand, so that it prevents people from finding out the truth about it. [FORMAL or WRITTEN] ❑ *I think that a lot of poetry published today is obscurantist nonsense.*

ob|scure /əbskyu͟ər/ (obscures, obscuring, obscured) **1** ADJ If something or someone is **obscure**, they are unknown, or are known by only a few people. ❑ *The origin of the custom is obscure.* **2** ADJ Something that is **obscure** is difficult to understand or deal with, usually because it involves so many parts or details. ❑ *The contracts are written in obscure language.* **3** V-T If one thing **obscures** another, it prevents it from being seen or heard properly. ❑ *Trees obscured his vision; he couldn't see much of the square's southern half.* **4** V-T To **obscure** something means to make it difficult to understand. ❑ *...the jargon that frequently obscures educational writing.*

ob|scu|rity /əbskyu͟ərɪti/ (obscurities) **1** N-UNCOUNT **Obscurity** is the state of being known by only a few people. ❑ *For the lucky few, there's the chance of being plucked from obscurity and thrown into the glamorous world of modelling.* **2** N-VAR **Obscurity** is the quality of being difficult to understand. An **obscurity** is something that is difficult to understand. ❑ *"How can that be?" asked Hunt, irritated by the obscurity of Henry's reply.*

ob|se|qui|ous /əbsi͟kwiəs/ ADJ If you describe someone as **obsequious**, you are criticizing them because they are too eager to help or agree with someone more important than them. [DISAPPROVAL] ❑ *Barrow was positively obsequious to me until he learned that I too was the son of a laboring man.* ● **ob|se|qui|ous|ly** ADV [ADV with v] ❑ *He smiled and bowed obsequiously to Wilson.* ● **ob|se|qui|ous|ness** N-UNCOUNT ❑ *I told him to get lost and leave me alone and his tone quickly changed from obsequiousness to outright anger.*

ob|serv|able /əbzɜrvəbəl/ ADJ Something that is **observable** can be seen. ❑ *Mars is too faint and too low in the sky to be observable.*

ob|ser|vance /əbzɜrvəns/ (observances) N-VAR The **observance** of something such as a law or custom is the practice of obeying or following it. ❑ *County governments should use their powers to ensure strict observance of laws.*

ob|ser|vant /əbzɜrvənt/ ADJ Someone who is **observant** pays a lot of attention to things and notices more about them than most people do. ❑ *That's a good description, Mrs. Drummond. You're very observant.*

ob|ser|va|tion /ɒbzərveɪʃən/ (observations) **1** N-UNCOUNT **Observation** is the action or process of carefully watching someone or something. ❑ *...careful observation of the movement of the planets.* **2** N-COUNT An **observation** is something that you have learned by seeing or watching something and thinking about it. ❑ *This book contains observations about the causes of addictions.* **3** N-COUNT If a person makes an **observation**, they make a comment about something or someone, usually as a result of watching how they behave. ❑ *Is that a criticism or just an observation?* **4** N-UNCOUNT **Observation** is the ability to pay a lot of attention to things and to notice more about them than most people do. ❑ *She has good powers of observation.*

ob|ser|va|tion|al /ɒbzərveɪʃənəl/ ADJ **Observational** means relating to the watching of people or things, especially in order to learn something new. [FORMAL] ❑ *...observational humor. The observational work is carried out on a range of telescopes.*

ob|ser|va|tory /əbzɜrvətɔri/ (observatories) N-COUNT An **observatory** is a building with a large telescope from which scientists study things such as the planets by watching them.

ob|serve ✦✧✧ /əbzɜrv/ (observes, observing, observed) **1** V-T If you **observe** a person or thing, you watch them carefully, especially in order to learn something about them. ❑ *Olson also studies and observes the behavior of babies.* ❑ *Are there any classes I could observe?* **2** V-T If you **observe** someone or something, you see or notice them. [FORMAL] ❑ *In 1664 Hooke observed a reddish spot on the surface of the planet.* **3** V-T If you **observe** that something is the case, you make a remark or comment about it, especially when it is something you have noticed and thought about a lot. [FORMAL] ❑ *We observe that the first calls for radical transformation did not begin until the period of the industrial revolution.* **4** V-T If you **observe** something such as a law or custom, you obey it or follow it. ❑ *Imposing speed restrictions is easy, but forcing drivers to observe them is trickier.* ❑ *The army was observing a ceasefire.* **5** V-T If you **observe** an important day such as a holiday or anniversary, you do something special in order to honor or celebrate it. ❑ *...where he will observe Thanksgiving with family members.*

SYNONYMS

observe
VERB **1**
watch: *The man was standing in his doorway, watching him.*
study: *Debbie studied her friend's face for a moment.*
look at: *She turned to look at him.*

ob|serv|er ✦✧✧ /əbzɜrvər/ (observers) **1** N-COUNT You can refer to someone who sees or notices something as an **observer**. ❑ *A casual observer would have taken them to be three men out for an evening stroll.* **2** N-COUNT An **observer** is someone who studies current events and situations, especially in order to comment on them and predict what will happen next. [JOURNALISM] ❑ *Observers say the events of the weekend seem to have increased support for the opposition.* **3** N-COUNT An **observer** is a person who is sent to observe an important event or situation, especially in order to make sure it happens as it should, or to tell other people about it. ❑ *The president suggested that a UN observer should attend the conference.*

ob|sess /əbsɛs/ (obsesses, obsessing, obsessed) V-T/V-I If something **obsesses** you or if you **obsess** about something, you keep thinking about it and find it difficult to think about anything else. ❑ *A string of scandals is obsessing America.* ❑ *He stopped drinking but began obsessing about his eating habits.*

ob|sessed /əbsɛst/ ADJ If someone is **obsessed** with a person or thing, they keep thinking about them and find it difficult to think about anything else. ❑ *He was obsessed with gangster movies.*

ob|ses|sion /əbsɛʃən/ (obsessions) N-VAR If you say that someone has an **obsession** with a person or thing, you think they are spending too much time thinking about them. ❑ *She would try to forget her obsession with Christopher.*

ob|ses|sion|al /əbsɛʃənəl/ ADJ **Obsessional** means the same as **obsessive**. ❑ *He became almost obsessional about the way he looked.*

ob|ses|sive /əbsɛsɪv/ (obsessives) **1** ADJ If someone's behavior is **obsessive**, they cannot stop doing a particular thing or behaving in a particular way. ❑ *Williams is obsessive about motor racing.* ● **ob|ses|sive|ly** ADV ❑ *He couldn't help worrying* obsessively about what would happen. **2** N-COUNT An **obsessive** is someone who is obsessive about something or who behaves in an obsessive way.

obsessive-compulsive dis|or|der N-UNCOUNT If someone has **obsessive-compulsive disorder**, they cannot stop doing a particular thing, for example, washing their hands. The abbreviation **OCD** is also used.

ob|so|les|cence /ɒbsəlɛsəns/ N-UNCOUNT **Obsolescence** is the state of being no longer needed because something newer or more efficient has been invented. ▫ *The aircraft was nearing obsolescence by early 1942.*

ob|so|les|cent /ɒbsəlɛsənt/ ADJ If something is **obsolescent**, it is becoming out of date because something better has been invented. ▫ *...outmoded, obsolescent equipment.*

ob|so|lete /ɒbsəliːt/ ADJ Something that is **obsolete** is no longer needed because something better has been invented. ▫ *So much equipment becomes obsolete almost as soon as it's made.*

ob|sta|cle /ɒbstəkəl/ (obstacles) **1** N-COUNT An **obstacle** is an object that makes it difficult for you to go where you want to go, because it is in your way. ▫ *Most competition cars will only roll over if they hit an obstacle.* **2** N-COUNT You can refer to anything that makes it difficult for you to do something as an **obstacle**. ▫ *Overcrowding remains a large obstacle to improving conditions.* **3** → See feature box at **success**

ob|sta|cle course (obstacle courses) N-COUNT In a race, an **obstacle course** is a series of obstacles that people have to go over or around in order to complete the race.

ob|ste|tri|cian /ɒbstətrɪʃən/ (obstetricians) **1** N-COUNT An **obstetrician** is a doctor who is specially trained to deal with pregnancy and birth. [MEDICAL] **2** → See feature box at **birth**

ob|stet|rics /əbstɛtrɪks/ **1** N-UNCOUNT **Obstetrics** is the branch of medicine that is concerned with pregnancy and giving birth. [MEDICAL] ▫ *...the American College of Obstetrics and Gynecology.* **2** ADJ [ADJ n] **Obstetric** medicine and care is concerned with pregnancy and giving birth. [MEDICAL] ▫ *For a child to be born with this disability indicates a defect in obstetric care.*

ob|sti|nate /ɒbstɪnɪt/ **1** ADJ If you describe someone as **obstinate**, you are being critical of them because they are very determined to do what they want, and refuse to change their mind or be persuaded to do something else. [DISAPPROVAL] ▫ *He is obstinate and determined and will not give up.* ● **ob|sti|nate|ly** ADV [ADV with v] ▫ *I stayed obstinately in my room, sitting by the telephone.* ● **ob|sti|na|cy** N-UNCOUNT ▫ *I might have become a dangerous man with all that stubbornness and obstinacy built into me.* **2** ADJ You can describe things as **obstinate** when they are difficult to move, change, or destroy. ▫ *...rusted farm equipment strewn among the obstinate weeds.* ● **ob|sti|nate|ly** ADV [ADV with v] ▫ *...the door of the shop which obstinately stayed closed when he tried to push it open.*

ob|strep|er|ous /əbstrɛpərəs/ ADJ If you say that someone is **obstreperous**, you think that they are noisy and difficult to control. [DISAPPROVAL] ▫ *You know I have no intention of being awkward and obstreperous.*

ob|struct /əbstrʌkt/ (obstructs, obstructing, obstructed) **1** V-T If something **obstructs** a road or path, it blocks it, stopping people or vehicles getting past. ▫ *A knot of black and white cars obstructed the intersection.* **2** V-T To **obstruct** someone or something means to make it difficult for them to move forward by blocking their path. ▫ *A number of local people have been arrested for trying to obstruct trucks loaded with logs.* **3** V-T To **obstruct** progress or a process means to prevent it from happening properly. ▫ *The authorities are obstructing a United Nations investigation.* **4** V-T If someone or something **obstructs** your view, they are positioned between you and the thing you are trying to look at, stopping you from seeing it completely. ▫ *Claire positioned herself so as not to obstruct David's line of sight.*

ob|struc|tion /əbstrʌkʃən/ (obstructions) **1** N-COUNT An **obstruction** is something that blocks a road or path. ▫ *John was irritated by drivers parking near his house and causing an obstruction.* **2** N-VAR An **obstruction** is something that blocks a passage in your body. ▫ *The boy was suffering from a bowel obstruction.* **3** N-UNCOUNT **Obstruction** is the act of deliberately delaying something or preventing something from happening, usually in business, law, or government.
▫ *Mr. Anderson refused to let them in and now faces a criminal charge of obstruction.*

ob|struc|tion|ism /əbstrʌkʃənɪzəm/ N-UNCOUNT **Obstructionism** is the practice of deliberately delaying or preventing a process or change, especially in politics. ▫ *Obstructionism is generally most evident at the stage of implementing a law.*

ob|struc|tive /əbstrʌktɪv/ ADJ If you say that someone is being **obstructive**, you think that they are deliberately causing difficulties for other people. ▫ *Mr. Smith was obstructive and refused to follow correct procedure.*

ob|tain ♦♦◇ /əbteɪn/ (obtains, obtaining, obtained) V-T To **obtain** something means to get it or achieve it. [FORMAL] ▫ *Evans was trying to obtain a false passport and other documents.*

USAGE

obtain
You don't usually use 'get' in the passive. Don't say, for example, 'Maps can be got from the Tourist Office.' Say 'Maps **can be obtained** from the Tourist Office' or, in conversation, '**You can get** maps from the Tourist Office.' All the above items **can be obtained** from most supermarkets.

SYNONYMS

obtain
VERB
get: *I got a job at the sawmill.*
acquire: *I recently acquired some wood from a holly tree.*
gain: *Students can gain valuable experience by working on the campus radio or magazine.*
procure: *It remained very difficult to procure food, fuel, and other daily necessities.*

---

ob|tain|able /əbteɪnəbəl/ ADJ If something is **obtainable**, it is possible to get or achieve it. ▫ *The dried herb is obtainable from health shops.*

ob|trude /ɒbtruːd/ (obtrudes, obtruding, obtruded) V-T/V-I When something **obtrudes** or when you **obtrude** it, it becomes noticeable in an undesirable way. [LITERARY] ▫ *A 40 watt bulb would be quite sufficient and would not obtrude.* ▫ *Gertrude now clearly felt that she had obtruded her sorrow.* ▫ *He didn't want to obtrude on her privacy.*

ob|tru|sive /əbtruːsɪv/ ADJ If you say that someone or something is **obtrusive**, you think they are noticeable in an unpleasant way. ▫ *These heaters are less obtrusive and are easy to store away in the summer.* ● **ob|tru|sive|ly** ADV [ADV with v] ▫ *Hawke got up and walked obtrusively out of the building.*

ob|tuse /əbtuːs/ **1** ADJ An **obtuse** angle is between 90° and 180°. Compare **acute** angle. [TECHNICAL] **2** ADJ Someone who is **obtuse** has difficulty understanding things, or makes no effort to understand them. ▫ *I've been waiting for you to ask me the question yourself, and you're being obtuse and slow about it.*

ob|verse /ɒbvɜːrs/ N-SING [the N] The **obverse** of an opinion, situation, or argument is its opposite. [FORMAL] ▫ *The obverse of rising unemployment is continued gains in productivity.*

ob|vi|ate /ɒbvieɪt/ (obviates, obviating, obviated) V-T To **obviate** something such as a problem or a need means to remove it or make it unnecessary. [FORMAL] ▫ *The use of a lawyer trained as a mediator would obviate the need for independent legal advice.*

ob|vi|ous ♦♦◇ /ɒbviəs/ **1** ADJ If something is **obvious**, it is easy to see or understand. ▫ *...the need to rectify what is an obvious injustice.* **2** ADJ If you describe something that someone says as **obvious**, you are being critical of it because you think it is unnecessary or shows lack of imagination. [DISAPPROVAL] ▫ *Such an explanation seems too simple, and too obvious.* ● PHRASE If you say that someone **is stating the obvious**, you mean that they are saying something that everyone already knows and understands.

ob|vi|ous|ly ♦♦◇ /ɒbviəsli/ **1** ADV [ADV with cl] You use **obviously** when you are stating something that you expect the person who is listening to know already. [EMPHASIS] ▫ *Obviously, they've had sponsorship from some big companies.* **2** ADV [ADV with cl/group] You use **obviously** to indicate that something is easily noticed, seen, or recognized. ▫ *They obviously appreciate you very much.*

occasion

> **SYNONYMS**
>
> **obviously**
> ADV
> **1**
> **clearly:** *Clearly, the police cannot break the law in order to enforce it.*
> **evidently:** *The two Russians evidently knew each other.*
> **of course:** *Of course, there were lots of other interesting things at the exhibition.*
> **2**
> **plainly:** *The judge's conclusion was plainly wrong.*
> **patently:** *He made his displeasure patently obvious.*
> **unquestionably:** *He is unquestionably a star.*

oc|ca|sion ✦✧ /əkeɪʒªn/ (occasions) **1** N-COUNT An **occasion** is a time when something happens, or a case of it happening. ❑ *I often think fondly of an occasion some years ago in New Orleans.* **2** N-COUNT An **occasion** is an important event, ceremony, or celebration. ❑ *Taking her with me on official occasions has been a challenge.* **3** N-COUNT An **occasion for** doing something is an opportunity for doing it. [FORMAL] ❑ *It is an occasion for all the family to celebrate.* **4** PHRASE If you **have occasion to** do something, you have the opportunity to do it or have a need to do it. ❑ *Over the next few years many people had occasion to reflect on the truth of his warnings.* **5** PHRASE If you say that someone **rose to the occasion**, you mean that they did what was necessary to successfully overcome a difficult situation. ❑ *Colorado rose to the occasion with four players scoring 16 points or more.*

oc|ca|sion|al ✦✧ /əkeɪʒənªl/ ADJ **Occasional** means happening sometimes, but not regularly or often. ❑ *I've had occasional mild headaches all my life.* • **oc|ca|sion|al|ly** ADV ❑ *He still misbehaves occasionally.*

oc|ci|den|tal /ɒksɪdentªl/ ADJ [ADJ n] **Occidental** means relating to the countries of Europe and North and South America. [FORMAL]

oc|cult /əkʌlt, ɒkʌlt/ N-SING **The occult** is the knowledge and study of supernatural or magical forces. ❑ *Interest in the occult tended toward ceremonial magic rather than witchcraft.* • ADJ [ADJ n] **Occult** is also an adjective. ❑ *...paganism and occult practice.*

oc|cult|ist /əkʌltɪst/ (occultists) N-COUNT An **occultist** is a person who believes in the supernatural and the power of magic.

oc|cu|pan|cy /ɒkyəpənsi/ N-UNCOUNT **Occupancy** is the act of using a room, building, or area of land, usually for a fixed period of time. [FORMAL] ❑ *Hotel occupancy has been as low as 40%.*

oc|cu|pant /ɒkyəpənt/ (occupants) **1** N-COUNT The **occupants** of a building or room are the people who live or work there. ❑ *Most of the occupants had left before the fire broke out.* **2** N-PLURAL You can refer to the people who are in a place such as a room, vehicle, or bed at a particular time as the **occupants**. ❑ *He wanted the occupants of the vehicle to get out.*

oc|cu|pa|tion ✦✧ /ɒkyəpeɪʃªn/ (occupations) **1** N-COUNT Your **occupation** is your job or profession. ❑ *I suppose I was looking for an occupation which was going to be an adventure.* **2** N-COUNT An **occupation** is something that you spend time doing, either for pleasure or because it needs to be done. ❑ *Parachuting is a dangerous occupation.* **3** N-UNCOUNT The **occupation** of a country happens when it is entered and controlled by a foreign army. ❑ *...the occupation of Poland.*

> **SYNONYMS**
>
> **occupation**
> NOUN
> **1**
> **job:** *Once I'm in America, I can get a job.*
> **business:** *You can't mix business with pleasure.*
> **work:** *What kind of work do you do?*
> **career:** *She is now concentrating on a career as a fashion designer.*
> **2**
> **hobby:** *My hobbies are football, music, photography, and tennis.*
> **pastime:** *His favorite pastime is golf.*
> **diversion:** *Finger painting is very messy but an excellent diversion.*

oc|cu|pa|tion|al /ɒkyəpeɪʃənªl/ ADJ **Occupational** means relating to a person's job or profession. ❑ *Some received substantial occupational assistance in the form of low-interest loans.*

oc|cu|pa|tion|al haz|ard (occupational hazards) N-COUNT An **occupational hazard** is something unpleasant that people often suffer or experience as a result of doing a particular job or hobby. ❑ *Catching colds is unfortunately an occupational hazard in this profession.*

oc|cu|pa|tion|al health N-UNCOUNT **Occupational health** is the branch of medicine that deals with the health of people in their workplace or in relation to their job. ❑ *Experts in occupational health are puzzled by symptoms reported by office workers, including headache, nausea and fatigue.*

oc|cu|pa|tion|al thera|pist (occupational therapists) N-COUNT An **occupational therapist** is someone whose job involves helping people by means of occupational therapy.

oc|cu|pa|tion|al thera|py N-UNCOUNT **Occupational therapy** is a method of helping people who have been ill or injured to develop skills or get skills back by giving them certain activities to do. ❑ *She will now begin occupational therapy to regain the use of her hands.*

oc|cu|pi|er /ɒkyəpaɪər/ (occupiers) N-COUNT The **occupier** of a house, apartment, or piece of land is the person who lives or works there. [BRIT, FORMAL]

in AM, use **occupant**

oc|cu|py ✦✧ /ɒkyəpaɪ/ (occupies, occupying, occupied) **1** V-T The people who **occupy** a building or a place are the people who live or work there. ❑ *There were over 40 tenants, all occupying one wing of the building.* **2** V-T PASSIVE If a room or something such as a seat **is occupied**, someone is using it, so that it is not available for anyone else. ❑ *The hospital bed is occupied by his wife.* **3** V-T If a group of people or an army **occupies** a place or country, they move into it, using force in order to gain control of it. ❑ *U.S. forces now occupy a part of the country.* **4** V-T If someone or something **occupies** a particular place in a system, process, or plan, they have that place. ❑ *Many men still occupy more positions of power than women.* **5** V-T If something **occupies** you, or if you **occupy** yourself, your time, or your mind with it, you are busy doing that thing or thinking about it. ❑ *Her career occupies all of her time.* ❑ *He occupied himself with packing the car.* • **oc|cu|pied** ADJ [v-link ADJ] ❑ *Keep the brain occupied.* **6** V-T If something **occupies** you, it requires your efforts, attention, or time. ❑ *I had other matters to occupy me, during the day at least.* **7** V-T If something **occupies** a particular area or place, it fills or covers it, or exists there. ❑ *Even small aircraft occupy a lot of space.*

> **SYNONYMS**
>
> **occupy**
> VERB
> **1**
> **inhabit:** *The valley is inhabited by the Dani tribe.*
> **live in:** *She has lived in this house for ten years.*
> **reside:** *All single, full-time students must reside in university residence halls.*
> **3**
> **invade:** *The Romans and the Normans came to Britain as invading armies.*
> **take over:** *The Belgians took over Rwanda under a League of Nations mandate.*
> **capture:** *They now appear ready to capture more territory.*
> **seize:** *Troops have seized the airport and railroad stations.*

oc|cur ✦✧ /əkɜr/ (occurs, occurring, occurred) **1** V-I When something **occurs**, it happens. ❑ *If headaches only occur at night, lack of fresh air and oxygen is often the cause.* ❑ *The crash occurred when the crew shut down the wrong engine.* **2** V-I When something **occurs** in a particular place, it exists or is present there. ❑ *These snails do not occur on low-lying coral islands.* **3** V-I [no passive, no cont] If a thought or idea **occurs to** you, you suddenly think of it or realize it. ❑ *It did not occur to me to check my insurance policy.*

> **USAGE**
>
> **occur**
> Don't say that a planned event 'occurs' or 'happens.' Say that it **takes place**. *The first meeting of this committee took place on January 9th.*

SYNONYMS

occur
VERB **1**
happen: We cannot say for sure what will happen.
take place: The discussion took place in a famous villa on the lake's shore.
come about: That came about when we went to Glastonbury last year.

oc|cur|rence /əkɜrəns/ (occurrences) **1** N-COUNT An **occurrence** is something that happens. [FORMAL] ▫ Complaints seemed to be an everyday occurrence. **2** N-COUNT The **occurrence** of something is the fact that it happens or is present. ▫ The greatest occurrence of coronary heart disease is in those over 65.

OCD /oʊ si di/ **1** N-UNCOUNT OCD is a condition in which someone has repeated thoughts or worries that they cannot control, or cannot stop doing a particular thing such as washing their hands. OCD is an abbreviation for **obsessive-compulsive disorder**. **2** ADJ If you describe someone as OCD, you mean that they have the condition OCD or that they have a tendency to think or worry too much about a particular thing. [INFORMAL] ▫ They knew Jack was a bit OCD when he insisted on mopping up when tea dripped on to the table.

ocean ◆◇◇ /oʊʃən/ (oceans) **1** N-SING The **ocean** is the sea. ▫ There were few sights as beautiful as the calm ocean on a warm night. **2** N-COUNT An **ocean** is one of the five very large areas of sea on the Earth's surface. ▫ They spent many days cruising the northern Pacific Ocean. **3** N-COUNT If you say that there is an **ocean of** something, you are emphasizing that there is a very large amount of it. [INFORMAL, EMPHASIS] ▫ I had cried oceans of tears. **4** PHRASE If you say that something is **a drop in the ocean**, you mean that it is a very small amount which is unimportant compared to the cost of other things or is so small that it has very little effect on something. [EMPHASIS] ▫ His fee is a drop in the ocean compared with the real cost of broadcasting. **5** → See feature box at **water**

VOCABULARY IN CONTEXT

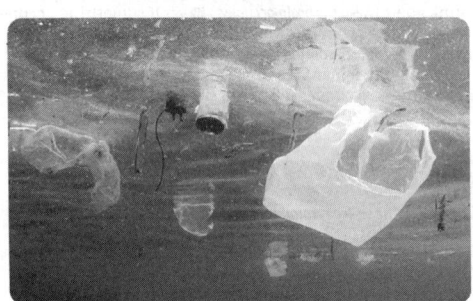

The ocean

Our oceans are facing a serious challenge: plastic pollution. **Deep-sea** animals encounter discarded plastic in many shapes and sizes, and the sheer quantity of plastic in the oceans has become a serious threat to **biodiversity**. We have all seen pictures of animals such as **turtles** and **seals** that have become entangled in plastic cord or discarded fishing **nets**. But the problem is far more extensive and far-reaching that that. Plastic microbeads found in cosmetics make their way through the water system into the ocean, where they settle on the **ocean floor** and the **coral reefs**. Fish and crustaceans swallow them, and the microbeads enter the food chain – a food chain that ends with us. All sorts of other plastic rubbish is swept up by the ocean **currents** onto **beaches** and **coastlines**, or far out to sea, where it forms huge, floating **islands** of plastic rubbish, which grow bigger week by week.

ocean-going ADJ [usu ADJ n] **Ocean-going** ships are designed for traveling on the sea rather than on rivers, canals, or lakes. ▫ At the height of his shipping career he owned about 60 ocean-going vessels.

ocean|ic /oʊʃiænɪk/ ADJ [ADJ n] **Oceanic** means belonging or relating to an ocean or to the sea. ▫ Many oceanic islands are volcanic.

ocean|og|ra|phy /oʊʃənɒgrəfi/ N-UNCOUNT **Oceanography** is the scientific study of ocean currents, the ocean floor, and the fish and animals that live in the sea. • **ocean|og|ra|pher** (oceanographers) N-COUNT ▫ ...an oceanographer working on an environmental protection program. • **oceano|graph|ic** /oʊʃənəɡræfɪk/ ADJ [ADJ n] ▫ ...oceanographic research.

ocher /oʊkər/ also **ochre** COLOR Something that is **ocher** is a yellowish orange color. ▫ For our dining room I have chosen ocher yellow walls.

o'clock ◆◇◇ /əklɒk/ ADV [num ADV] You use **o'clock** after numbers from one to twelve to say what time it is. For example, if you say that it is 9 o'clock, you mean that it is nine hours after midnight or nine hours after noon. ▫ The trouble began just after ten o'clock last night.

Oct. Oct. is a written abbreviation for **October**. ▫ ...Tuesday Oct. 25th.

oc|ta|gon /ɒktəgɒn/ (octagons) N-COUNT An **octagon** is a shape that has eight straight sides.

oc|tago|nal /ɒktægənəl/ ADJ Something that is **octagonal** has eight straight sides. ▫ ...a white octagonal box.

oc|tane /ɒkteɪn/ **1** N-UNCOUNT [usu with supp] **Octane** is a chemical substance that exists in gasoline. Higher octane fuel is of better quality. ▫ ...high octane fuel for cars. **2** → see also **high-octane**

oc|tave /ɒktɪv/ (octaves) N-COUNT An **octave** is a series of eight notes in a musical scale. It is also used to talk about the difference in pitch between the first and last notes in a musical scale.

oc|tet /ɒktɛt/ (octets) N-COUNT [oft in names] An **octet** is a group of eight singers or musicians. ▫ ...the Stan Tracey Octet.

Oc|to|ber ◆◆◇ /ɒktoʊbər/ (Octobers) N-VAR **October** is the tenth month of the year in the Western calendar. ▫ Most seasonal hiring is done in early October. ▫ The first plane is due to leave on October 2.

oc|to|genar|ian /ɒktədʒɪnɛəriən/ (octogenarians) N-COUNT An **octogenarian** is a person who is between eighty and eighty-nine years old.

oc|to|pus /ɒktəpəs/ (octopuses) N-VAR An **octopus** is a soft sea creature with eight long arms called tentacles which it uses to catch food. • N-UNCOUNT **Octopus** is this creature eaten as food. ▫ ...plates of octopus.

ocu|lar /ɒkyələr/ ADJ [ADJ n] **Ocular** means relating to the eyes or the ability to see. [MEDICAL] ▫ Other ocular signs include involuntary rhythmic movement of the eyeball.

OD /oʊ di/ (OD's, OD'ing, OD'd) V-I To **OD** means the same as to **overdose**. [INFORMAL] ▫ His son was a junkie; the kid OD'd a year ago. • N-COUNT **OD** is also a noun. ▫ "I had a friend who died of an OD," she said.

odd ◆◆◇ /ɒd/ (odder, oddest) **1** ADJ If you describe someone or something as **odd**, you think that they are strange or unusual. ▫ He'd always been odd, but not to this extent. ▫ What an odd coincidence that he should have known your family. • **odd|ly** ADV [ADV with v] ▫ ...an oddly shaped hill. **2** ADJ [det ADJ] You use **odd** before a noun to indicate that you are not mentioning the type, size, or quality of something because it is not important. ▫ ...moving from place to place where she could find the odd bit of work. ▫ He had various odd cleaning jobs around the place. **3** ADV [num ADV] You use **odd** after a number to indicate that it is only approximate. [INFORMAL] ▫ How many pages was it, 500 odd? ▫ He has now appeared in sixty odd films. **4** ADJ **Odd** numbers, such as 3 and 17, are those which cannot be divided exactly by the number two. ▫ The odd numbers are on the left as you walk up the street. **5** ADJ You say that two things are **odd** when they do not belong to the same set or pair. ▫ I'm wearing odd socks today by the way. **6** PHRASE **The odd man out**, **the odd woman out**, or **the odd one out** in a particular situation is a

oddball 887 **of**

person who is different from the other people in it. ❑ *The state was formerly the odd man out, the one republic not to hold democratic elections.* **7** → see also **odds**

SYNONYMS

odd
ADJ
1
strange: *Then a strange thing happened.*
peculiar: *Rachel thought it tasted peculiar.*
unusual: *They have replanted many areas with rare and unusual plants.*
weird: *That first day was weird.*
2
occasional: *I've had occasional mild headaches all my life.*
random: *...random variations of the wind.*
various: *The school has received various grants from the education department.*

---

odd|ball /ɒdbɔːl/ (**oddballs**) N-COUNT If you refer to someone as an **oddball**, you think they behave in a strange way. [INFORMAL] ❑ *His mother and father thought Jim was a bit of an oddball too.* • ADJ **Oddball** is also an adjective. ❑ *I came from a family that was decidedly oddball you know.*

odd|ity /ɒdɪti/ (**oddities**) N-COUNT An **oddity** is someone or something that is very strange. ❑ *Losing my hair made me feel an oddity.*

odd jobs N-PLURAL **Odd jobs** are various small jobs that have to be done in someone's home, such as cleaning or repairing things.

odd-looking ADJ If you describe someone or something as **odd-looking**, you think that they look strange or unusual. ❑ *They were an odd-looking couple.*

odd|ly /ɒdli/ **1** ADV You use **oddly** to indicate that what you are saying is true, but that it is not what you expected. ❑ *He said no and seemed oddly reluctant to talk about it.* ❑ *Oddly, Emma says she never considered her face to be attractive.* **2** → see also **odd**

odd|ment /ɒdmənt/ (**oddments**) N-COUNT **Oddments** are unimportant objects of any kind, usually ones that are old or left over from a larger group of things. ❑ *...searching street markets for interesting jewelry and oddments.*

odds /ɒdz/ **1** N-PLURAL You refer to how likely something is to happen as the **odds** that it will happen. ❑ *What are the odds of finding a parking space right outside the door?* **2** N-PLURAL In betting, **odds** are expressions with numbers such as '10 to 1' and '7 to 2' that show how likely something is thought to be, for example, how likely a particular horse is to lose or win a race. ❑ *We are offering odds of 6-1 on the fight ending in a knockout.* **3** PHRASE If someone is **at odds** with someone else, or if two people are **at odds**, they are disagreeing or arguing with each other. ❑ *He was at odds with the boss.* **4** PHRASE If you say that **the odds are against** something or someone, you mean that they are unlikely to succeed. ❑ *He reckons the odds are against the plan going ahead.* **5** PHRASE If something happens **against** all **odds**, it happens or succeeds although it seemed impossible or very unlikely. ❑ *...families in terrible circumstances, who have stayed together against all odds.* **6** PHRASE If you say that **the odds are in** someone's **favor**, you mean that they are likely to succeed, in what they are doing. ❑ *The troops will only engage in a ground battle when all the odds are in their favor.*

odds and ends N-PLURAL You can refer to a disorganized group of things of various kinds as **odds and ends**. [INFORMAL] ❑ *She put in some clothes, odds and ends, and make-up.*

odds-on also **odds on** ADJ If there is an **odds-on** chance that something will happen, it is very likely that it will happen. [INFORMAL] ❑ *Of the five companies bidding for the contract, Wall Street analysts have made Lockheed the odds-on favorite.* ❑ *It was odds-on that there was no killer.*

ode /oʊd/ (**odes**) N-COUNT An **ode** is a poem, especially one that is written in praise of a particular person, thing, or event. ❑ *...Keats' "Ode to a Nightingale."*

odi|ous /oʊdiəs/ ADJ If you describe people or things as **odious**, you think that they are hateful or disgusting. ❑ *Mr. Smith is certainly the most odious man I have ever met.*

odium /oʊdiəm/ N-UNCOUNT **Odium** is the extreme disapproval or hatred that people feel for a particular person, usually because of something that the person has done. [FORMAL] ❑ *The complainant has been exposed to public odium, scandal, and contempt.*

odom|eter /oʊdɒmɪtər/ (**odometers**) N-COUNT An **odometer** is a device in a vehicle which shows how far the vehicle has traveled. [mainly AM]

in BRIT, use **mileometer**

odor /oʊdər/ (**odors**)

in BRIT, use **odour**

N-VAR An **odor** is a particular and distinctive smell. ❑ *...the lingering odor of automobile exhaust.*

odor|less /oʊdərlɪs/

in BRIT, use **odourless**

ADJ An **odorless** substance has no smell. ❑ *...an odorless insect repellent.* ❑ *The gases are odorless.*

odour /oʊdər/ [BRIT] → see **odor**

od|ys|sey /ɒdɪsi/ (**odysseys**) N-COUNT An **odyssey** is a long exciting journey on which a lot of things happen. [LITERARY] ❑ *The march to Travnik was the final stretch of a 16-hour odyssey.*

Oedipus com|plex /ɛdɪpəs kɒmplɛks, iːd-/ N-SING If a boy or man has an **Oedipus complex**, he feels sexual desire for his mother and has hostile feelings toward his father.

OEM /oʊ iː ɛm/ (**OEMs**) N-COUNT [usu N n] An **OEM** is a manufacturer that produces goods for other companies to sell under their own name. **OEM** is an abbreviation for 'original equipment manufacturer.' ❑ *The company sells the PC under its own brand name and also supplies the PC to other manufacturers on an OEM basis.*

o'er /ɔːr/ PREP **O'er** means the same as 'over.' [LITERARY, OLD-FASHIONED] ❑ *As long as mist hangs o'er the mountains, the deeds of the brave will be remembered.*

oesopha|gus /iːsɒfəgəs/ [BRIT] → see **esophagus**

oes|tro|gen /iːstrədʒən/ [BRIT] → see **estrogen**

of ♦♦♦ /əv, STRONG ʌv/

In addition to the uses shown below, **of** is used after some verbs, nouns, and adjectives in order to introduce extra information. **Of** is also used in phrasal prepositions such as 'because of,' 'instead of,' and 'in spite of,' and in phrasal verbs such as 'make of' and 'dispose of.'

1 PREP [n PREP n] You use **of** to combine two nouns when the first noun identifies the feature of the second noun that you want to talk about. ❑ *The average age of the women interviewed was only 21.5.* ❑ *...the population of this town.* **2** PREP [n PREP n/-ing] You use **of** to combine two nouns, or a noun and a present participle, when the second noun or present participle defines or gives more information about the first noun. ❑ *She let out a little cry of pain.* ❑ *...the problem of having a national shortage of teachers.* **3** PREP [n PREP n] You use **of** after nouns referring to actions to specify the person or thing that is affected by the action or that performs the action. For example, 'the kidnapping of the child' refers to an action affecting a child; 'the arrival of the next train' refers to an action performed by a train. ❑ *It sets targets for reduction of greenhouse-gas emissions.* **4** PREP You use **of** after words and phrases referring to quantities or groups of things to indicate the substance or thing that is being measured. ❑ *...dozens of people.* ❑ *...a collection of short stories.* **5** PREP [n PREP n] You use **of** after the name of someone or something to introduce the institution or place they belong to or are connected with. ❑ *...the governor of Missouri.* **6** PREP [n PREP n] You use **of** after a noun referring to a container to form an expression referring to the container and its contents. ❑ *...a box of tissues.* ❑ *...a roomful of people.* **7** PREP [n PREP n] You use **of** after a countable noun and before an uncountable noun when you want to talk about an individual piece or item. ❑ *...a blade of grass.* ❑ *Marina ate only one slice of bread.* **8** PREP [n PREP n] You use **of** to indicate the materials or things that form something. ❑ *...local decorations of wood and straw.* ❑ *...loose-fitting garments of linen.* **9** PREP [n PREP n] You use **of** after a noun which specifies a particular part of something, to introduce the thing that it is a part of.

❑ ...*the other side of the square.* ❑ ...*the beginning of the year.* **10** PREP You use **of** after some verbs to indicate someone or something else involved in the action. ❑ *He'd been dreaming of her.* ❑ *Listen, I shall be thinking of you always.* **11** PREP [adj PREP n/-ing] You use **of** after some adjectives to indicate the person or thing that a feeling or quality relates to. ❑ *I have grown very fond of Alec.* ❑ *His father was quite naturally very proud of him.* **12** PREP You use **of** before a word referring to the person who performed an action when saying what you think about the action. ❑ *This has been so nice, so terribly kind of you.* **13** PREP [more/less PREP a n] If something is **more of** or **less of** a particular thing, it is that thing to a greater or smaller degree. ❑ *Your extra fat may be more of a health risk than you realize.* **14** PREP You use **of** to indicate a characteristic or quality that someone or something has. ❑ ...*the worth of their music.* ❑ *She is a woman of enviable beauty.* **15** PREP [n PREP amount] You use **of** to specify an amount, value, or age. ❑ *Last Thursday, Nick announced record revenues of $3.4 billion.* ❑ ...*young people under the age of 16 years.* **16** PREP [n PREP n/-ing] You use **of** after a noun such as 'month' or 'year' to indicate the length of time that some state or activity continues. ❑ ...*eight bruising years of war.* **17** PREP You can use **of** to say what time it is by indicating how many minutes there are before the hour mentioned. [AM] ❑ *At about a quarter of eight in the evening Joe Urber calls.*

in BRIT, use **to**

USAGE

of
Don't use 'of' in front of a personal pronoun such as 'me,' 'him,' or 'them' when you are talking about possession. Don't say, for example, '~~the sister of me~~.' Instead, you use a possessive determiner such as **my**, **his**, or **their**. *My sister visited us last week.*

of course ♦♦♦ **1** ADV [ADV with cl] You say **of course** to suggest that something is normal, obvious, or well-known, and should therefore not surprise the person you are talking to. [SPOKEN] ❑ *Of course there were lots of other interesting things at the exhibition.* ❑ *"I have read about you in the newspapers of course,"* Charlie said. **2** CONVENTION You use **of course** as a polite way of giving permission. [SPOKEN, FORMULAE] ❑ *"Can I just say something about the game on Saturday?"—"Yes, of course you can."* **3** ADV You use **of course** in order to emphasize a statement that you are making, especially when you are agreeing or disagreeing with someone. [SPOKEN, EMPHASIS] ❑ *"I guess you're right."—"Of course I'm right!"* ❑ *Of course I'm not afraid!* **4** CONVENTION **Of course not** is an emphatic way of saying no. [SPOKEN, EMPHASIS] ❑ *"You're not really seriously considering this thing, are you?"—"No, of course not."*

OFF
① AWAY FROM
② OTHER USES

① **off** ♦♦♦

The preposition is pronounced /ɒf/. The adverb is pronounced /ɔf/.

1 PREP If something is taken **off** something else or moves **off** it, it is no longer touching that thing. ❑ *He took his feet off the desk.* ❑ *I took the key for the room off a rack above her head.* • ADV [ADV after v] **Off** is also an adverb. ❑ *Lee broke off a small piece of orange and held it out to him.* **2** PREP When you get **off** a bus, train, or plane, you come out of it or leave it after you have been traveling on it. ❑ *Don't try to get on or off a moving train!* • ADV [ADV after v] **Off** is also an adverb. ❑ *At the next stop the man got off too and introduced himself.* **3** PREP If you keep **off** a street or piece of land, you do not step on it or go there. ❑ *Locking up men does nothing more than keep them off the streets.* • ADV **Off** is also an adverb. ❑ ...*a sign saying "Keep Off."* **4** PREP If something is situated **off** a place such as a coast, room, or road, it is near to it or next to it, but not exactly in it. ❑ *The boat was anchored off the northern coast of the peninsula.* ❑ *Lily lives in a penthouse just off Park Avenue.* **5** ADV If you go **off**, you leave a place. ❑ *He was just about to drive off when the secretary came running out.* ❑ *She was off again, to Kenya.* **6** ADV [ADV after v] When you take **off** clothing or jewelry that you are wearing, you remove it from your body. ❑ *He took off his spectacles and rubbed frantically at the lens.* **7** ADV If you have time **off** or a particular day **off**, you do not go to work or school, for example, because you are sick or it is a day when you do not usually work. ❑ *The rest of the men had the day off.* ❑ *I'm off tomorrow.* • PREP **Off** is also a preposition. ❑ *He could not get time off work to go on vacation.* **8** PREP If you keep **off** a subject, you deliberately avoid talking about it. ❑ *Keep off the subject of politics.* **9** PREP [amount PREP n] If there is money **off** something, its price is reduced by the amount specified. ❑ *20 per cent off all jackets this Saturday.* • ADV **Off** is also an adverb. ❑ *Take $5 off the regular price of any membership.* **10** ADV [n/amount ADV] If something is a long way **off**, it is a long distance away from you. ❑ *Florida was a long way off.* **11** ADV [n/amount ADV] If something is a long time **off**, it will not happen for a long time. ❑ *An end to the crisis seems a long way off.* **12** PREP If you get something **off** someone, you obtain it from them. [SPOKEN] ❑ *I don't really get a lot of information, and if I do I get it off Mark.*

② **off** ♦♦♦ **1** ADV If something such as an agreement or a sports event is **off**, it is canceled. ❑ *Until Pointon is completely happy, however, the deal's off.* **2** PREP If someone is **off** something harmful such as a drug, they have stopped taking or using it. ❑ *She felt better and the psychiatrist took her off antidepressants.* **3** PREP If you are **off** something, you have stopped liking it. ❑ *I'm off coffee at the moment.* **4** ADV When something such as a machine or electric light is **off**, it is not functioning or in use. When you switch it **off**, you stop it from functioning. ❑ *As he pulled into the driveway, he saw her bedroom light was off.* ❑ *We used sail power and turned the engine off to save our fuel.* **5** ADJ If food has gone **off**, it tastes and smells bad because it is no longer fresh enough to be eaten. [mainly BRIT]

in AM, usually use **spoiled**

6 PREP [v PREP n] If you live **off** a particular kind of food, you eat it in order to live. If you live **off** a particular source of money, you use it to live. ❑ *Her husband's memories are of living off roast chicken and drinking whiskey.* **7** PREP [v PREP n] If a machine runs **off** a particular kind of fuel or power, it uses that power in order to function. ❑ *The electric armor runs off the tank's power supply.* **8** PHRASE If something happens **on and off**, or **off and on**, it happens occasionally, or only for part of a period of time, not in a regular or continuous way. ❑ *I was still working on and off as a waitress to support myself.*

In addition to the uses shown here, **off** is used after some verbs and nouns in order to introduce extra information. **Off** is also used in phrasal verbs such as 'get off,' 'pair off,' and 'sleep off.'

off-air also **off air** ADV [ADV after v, be ADV] In radio or television, when a program goes **off-air** or when something happens **off-air**, it is not broadcast. • ADJ **Off-air** is also an adjective. [BRIT]

in AM, use **off the air**

of|fal /ˈɒfəl/ **N-UNCOUNT Offal** is the parts of animals' bodies that are thrown away after the animals have been butchered. ❑ ...*all the blood and offal the butchers shove down in the gutters.* **2** N-UNCOUNT **Offal** is the internal organs of animals, for example, their hearts and livers, when they are cooked and eaten.

off-balance also **off balance** **1** ADJ [v n ADJ, v-link ADJ] If someone or something is **off-balance**, they can easily fall or be knocked over because they are not standing firmly. ❑ *He tried to use his own weight to push his attacker off but he was off balance.* **2** ADJ If someone is caught **off-balance**, they are extremely surprised or upset by a particular event or piece of news they are not expecting. ❑ *Mullins knocked me off-balance with his abrupt change of subject.*

off|beat /ˈɒfbiːt/ also **off-beat** ADJ [usu ADJ n] If you describe something or someone as **offbeat**, you think that they are different from normal. ❑ ...*a wickedly offbeat imagination.*

off-Broadway /ˌɒfˈbrɔːdweɪ/ **1** ADJ [ADJ n] An **off-Broadway** theater is located close to Broadway, the main theater district in New York. **2** ADJ [ADJ n] An **off-Broadway** play is less commercial and often more unusual than those usually staged on Broadway.

off-center

in BRIT, use **off-centre**

1 ADJ [usu v-link ADJ] If something is **off-center**, it is not exactly in the middle of a space or surface. ❑ *Her mouth curved in an off-center smile.* **2** ADJ If you describe someone or something as **off-center**, you mean that they are less conventional than other people or things. ❑ *...her off-center interpretation of the "Star-Spangled Banner."* ❑ *Davies's writing is far too off-center to be commercial.*

off-chance also **off chance** PHRASE If you do something **on the off-chance**, you do it because you hope that it will succeed, although you think that this is unlikely. ❑ *He had taken a flight to Paris on the off-chance that he might be able to meet Francesca.*

off-color

in BRIT, use **off-colour**

ADJ An **off-color** joke or remark is rude or offensive. ❑ *He denies making off-color remarks about his colleagues.*

off day (off days) also **off-day** N-COUNT If someone has an **off day**, they do not perform as well as usual. [INFORMAL] ❑ *A teacher who merely has an off day in the classroom cannot be dismissed for incompetence.*

off-duty ADJ When someone such as a soldier or police officer is **off-duty**, they are not working. ❑ *The place is the haunt of off-duty policemen.*

of|fence /əfɛns/ [BRIT] → see **offense**

of|fend /əfɛnd/ (offends, offending, offended) **1** V-T/V-I If you **offend** someone, you say or do something rude which upsets or embarrasses them. ❑ *He apologizes for his comments and says he had no intention of offending the community.* ❑ *In the great effort not to offend, we end up saying nothing.* • **of|fend|ed** ADJ [v-link ADJ] ❑ *She is terribly offended, angered and hurt by this.* **2** V-I [no cont] If someone **offends**, they commit a crime. [FORMAL] ❑ *In Western countries girls are far less likely to offend than boys.*

of|fend|er /əfɛndər/ (offenders) **1** N-COUNT An **offender** is a person who has committed a crime. ❑ *This led to a large number of convicted offenders being released from prison.* **2** N-COUNT You can refer to someone or something that you think is causing a problem as an **offender**. ❑ *The plant's leaves can often turn brown, and I sometimes cut off the worst offenders.* **3** → See feature box at **prison**

of|fend|ing /əfɛndɪŋ/ **1** ADJ [the ADJ N] You can use **offending** to describe something that is causing a problem that needs to be dealt with. ❑ *The book was withdrawn for the offending passages to be deleted.* **2** N-UNCOUNT **Offending** is the act of committing a crime. ❑ *Ms. Mann is working with young offenders and trying to break cycles of offending.*

of|fense ✦✧✧ /əfɛns/ (offenses)

in BRIT, use **offence**

Pronounced /ɔfɛns/ for meaning 3.

1 N-COUNT An **offense** is a crime that breaks a particular law and requires a particular punishment. ❑ *A first offense carries a fine of $1,000.* **2** N-VAR **Offense** or an **offense** is behavior that causes people to be upset or embarrassed. ❑ *He said he didn't mean to give offense.* **3** N-SING [the N] In sports such as football or basketball, the **offense** is the team which has possession of the ball and is trying to score. [AM] ❑ *Between plays the coach was talking to the offense in the huddle.* **4** CONVENTION Some people say '**no offense**' to make it clear that they do not want to upset you, although what they are saying may seem rude. [FORMULAE] ❑ *"No offense," she said, "but your sister seems a little gloomy."* **5** PHRASE If someone **takes offense** at something you say or do, they feel upset, often unnecessarily, because they think you are being rude to them. ❑ *Instead of taking offense, the woman smiled.* **6** → See feature box at **legal**

SYNONYMS

offense
NOUN
1
crime: *He and Lieutenant Cassidy were checking the scene of the crime.*
wrong: *...a man who believes that he has done no wrong.*
sin: *Was it the sin of pride to have believed too much in themselves?*
wrongdoing: *The city attorney's office hasn't found any evidence of criminal wrongdoing.*

2
outrage: *The Treaty has failed to arouse genuine public outrage.*
anger: *Ellen felt both despair and anger at her mother.*
indignation: *No wonder he could hardly contain his indignation.*

of|fen|sive ✦✧✧ /əfɛnsɪv/ (offensives) **1** ADJ Something that is **offensive** upsets or embarrasses people because it is rude or insulting. ❑ *Some friends of his found the play horribly offensive.* **2** N-COUNT A military **offensive** is a carefully planned attack made by a large group of soldiers. ❑ *Its latest military offensive against rebel forces is aimed at re-opening important trade routes.* **3** N-COUNT If you conduct an **offensive**, you take strong action to show how angry you are about something or how much you disapprove of something. ❑ *Republicans acknowledged that they had little choice but to mount an all-out offensive on the Democratic nominee.* **4** PHRASE If you **go on the offensive**, **go over to the offensive**, or **take the offensive**, you begin to take strong action against people who have been attacking you. ❑ *The West African forces went on the offensive in response to attacks on them.* **5** → See feature box at **polite**

SYNONYMS

offensive
ADJ **1**
rude: *Unfair bosses and rude customers make us unhappy on the job.*
insulting: *One of the apprentices made an insulting remark to a passing officer.*
objectionable: *I find your tone highly objectionable.*
disrespectful: *They shouldn't treat their mother in this disrespectful way.*

of|fer ✦✦✦ /ɔfər/ (offers, offering, offered) **1** V-T If you **offer** something to someone, you ask them if they would like to have it or use it. ❑ *He has offered seats at the conference table to the Russian leader and the president of Kazakhstan.* ❑ *The number of companies offering them work increased.* **2** V-T If you **offer** to do something, you say that you are willing to do it. ❑ *Peter offered to teach them water-skiing.* **3** N-COUNT An **offer** is something that someone says they will give you or do for you. ❑ *The offer of talks with Moscow marks a significant change from the previous Western position.* ❑ *"I ought to reconsider her offer to move in," he mused.* **4** V-T If you **offer** someone information, advice, or praise, you give it to them, usually because you feel that they need it or deserve it. ❑ *They manage a company offering advice on mergers and acquisitions.* ❑ *She offered him emotional and practical support in countless ways.* **5** V-T If you **offer** someone something such as love or friendship, you show them that you feel that way toward them. ❑ *The president has offered his sympathy to the Georgian people.* ❑ *It must be better to be able to offer them love and security.* **6** V-T If people **offer** prayers, praise, or a sacrifice to God or a god, they speak to or give something to their god. ❑ *Church leaders offered prayers and condemned the bloodshed.* • PHRASAL VERB **Offer up** means the same as **offer**. ❑ *He should consider offering up a prayer to St. Lambert.* **7** V-T If an organization **offers** something such as a service or product, it provides it. ❑ *We have been successful because we are offering a quality service.* ❑ *The grocery store is offering customers 5 cents for each shopping bag re-used.* **8** N-COUNT [oft supp N, also *on* N] An **offer** in a store is a specially low price for a specific product or something extra that you get if you buy a certain product. ❑ *This month's offers include a pork loin and avocados.* ❑ *Today's special offer gives you a choice of three destinations.* **9** V-T If you **offer** a particular amount of money for something, you say that you will pay that much to buy it. ❑ *He is in a position to offer $825,000 for the bankrupt airline's assets.* ❑ *They are offering farmers $2.15 a bushel for corn.* **10** N-COUNT An **offer** is the amount of money that someone says they will pay to buy something. ❑ *The real estate agents say no one else will make me an offer.* **11** PHRASE If someone or something **has** something **to offer**, they have a quality or ability that makes them important, attractive, or useful. ❑ *In your free time, explore all that this incredible city has to offer.* **12** PHRASE If there is something **on offer**, it is available to be used or bought. ❑ *They are making trips to check out the merchandise on offer.* **13** PHRASE If you are **open to offers**, you are willing to do something if someone will pay you an amount of money that you think is reasonable. ❑ *It seems that while the Dodgers are eager to have him, he is still open to offers.* **14** → See feature box at **university**

offering

SYNONYMS

offer
NOUN **3**
proposal: *The Security Council has rejected the latest peace proposal.*
suggestion: *He followed her suggestion of a stroll to the river.*
proposition: *I want to make you a proposition.*

of|fer|ing ✦✦✦ /ˈɒfərɪŋ/ (offerings) **1** N-COUNT An **offering** is something that is being sold. ❑ *It was very, very good, far better than vegetarian offerings in many an expensive restaurant.* **2** N-COUNT An **offering** is a gift that people offer to their God or gods as a form of worship. ❑ *...the holiest of the Shinto rituals, where offerings are made at night to the great Sun.*

of|fer price (offer prices) **1** N-COUNT The **offer price** for a particular stock or share is the price that the person selling it says that they want for it. [BUSINESS] ❑ *The company stunned the technology world by increasing its offer price to $36.* **2** → see also **asking price, bid price**

off-grid also **off-the-grid** ADJ If a place is **off-grid**, it is not connected to the public electricity supply, and also perhaps other services such as water and gas. ❑ *...an off-grid campsite on the edge of a national park.* ❑ *They want to make the house completely off-grid.* • ADV; ADV GRADED [ADV after v] **Off-grid** is also an adverb. ❑ *They have lived off-grid for ages.*

off-guard ADJ [v n ADJ, v-link ADJ] If someone is caught **off-guard**, they are not expecting a surprise or danger that suddenly occurs. ❑ *The question caught her completely off-guard and she did not know how to reply.*

off|hand /ˌɒfˈhænd/ also **off-hand** **1** ADJ [usu v-link ADJ] If you say that someone is being **offhand**, you are critical of them for being unfriendly or impolite, and not showing any interest in what other people are doing or saying. [DISAPPROVAL] ❑ *Consumers found the attitude of its staff offhand and generally offensive to the paying customer.* **2** ADV [ADV after v] If you say something **offhand**, you say it without checking the details or facts of it. ❑ *"Have they done the repairs?"—"Can't say off-hand, but I doubt it."*

of|fice ✦✦✦ /ˈɒfɪs/ (offices) **1** N-COUNT An **office** is a room or a part of a building where people work sitting at desks. ❑ *By the time Flynn arrived at his office it was 5:30.* ❑ *Telephone their head office for more details.* **2** N-COUNT; N-IN-NAMES An **office** is a department of an organization, especially the government, where people deal with a particular kind of administrative work. ❑ *Thousands have registered with unemployment offices.* ❑ *...the Congressional Budget Office.* **3** N-COUNT An **office** is a small building or room where people can go for information, tickets, or a service of some kind. ❑ *The tourist office operates a useful room-finding service.* **4** N-COUNT A doctor's or dentist's **office** is a place where a doctor or dentist sees their patients. [AM] ❑ *The chance of getting AIDS at the doctor's or dentist's office is extremely low.*

in BRIT, use **surgery**

5 N-UNCOUNT If someone holds **office** in a government, they have an important job or position of authority. ❑ *The events to mark the president's four years in office went ahead as planned.* ❑ *The treasurer shall hold office for five years.* **6** → see also **box office, post office**

COLLOCATIONS

office
NOUN **5**
adjective + **office**: public
verb + **office**: assume, hold, take; leave

SYNONYMS

office
NOUN **2**
branch: *The local branch of Bank of America is handling the accounts.*
department: *He moved to the sales department.*
division: *...the bank's Latin American division.*

of|fice boy (office boys) N-COUNT An **office boy** is a young man, especially one who has just left school, who is employed in an office to do simple tasks. [OLD-FASHIONED]

of|fice build|ing (office buildings) N-COUNT An **office building** is a large building that contains offices. [AM] ❑ *...the world's second highest office building.*

of|fice girl (office girls) N-COUNT An **office girl** is a young woman, especially one who has just left school, who is employed in an office to do simple tasks. [OLD-FASHIONED]

office-holder (office-holders) also **office holder** N-COUNT An **office-holder** is a person who has an important official position in an organization or government. ❑ *They appear to be in a mood to vote against office-holders in the elections.*

of|fice hours N-PLURAL **Office hours** are the times when an office or similar place is open for business. For example, office hours in the United States and Britain are usually between 9 o'clock and 5 o'clock from Monday to Friday. ❑ *If you have any questions, please call Anne Fisher at 555-6203 during office hours.*

of|fic|er ✦✦✦ /ˈɒfɪsər/ (officers) **1** N-COUNT In the armed forces, an **officer** is a person who is in a position of authority. ❑ *...a retired army officer.* **2** N-COUNT Members of the police force can be referred to as **officers**. ❑ *The officer saw no obvious signs of a break-in.* ❑ *Officer Montoya was first on the scene.* **3** N-COUNT An **officer** is a person who has a responsible position in an organization, especially a government organization. ❑ *...a local authority education officer.* **4** → see also **police officer, probation officer**

of|fi|cial ✦✦✦ /əˈfɪʃəl/ (officials) **1** ADJ **Official** means approved by the government or by someone in authority. ❑ *According to the official figures, over one thousand people died during the revolution.* ❑ *An official announcement is expected in the next few days.* • **of|fi|cial|ly** ADV ❑ *The election results have still not been officially announced.* **2** ADJ [ADJ n] **Official** activities are carried out by a person in authority as part of their job. ❑ *The president is in Brazil for an official two-day visit.* **3** ADJ [ADJ n] **Official** things are used by a person in authority as part of their job. ❑ *...the official residence of the head of state.* **4** ADJ [ADJ n] If you describe someone's explanation or reason for something as the **official** explanation, you are suggesting that it is probably not true, but is used because the real explanation is embarrassing. ❑ *They realized that the official explanation left facts unexplained.* • **of|fi|cial|ly** ADV [ADV with cl/group] ❑ *Officially, the guard was to protect us. In fact, they were there to report on our movements.* **5** N-COUNT An **official** is a person who holds a position of authority in an organization. ❑ *A senior UN official hopes to visit Baghdad this month.* **6** N-COUNT An **official** at a sports event is a referee, umpire, or other person who checks that the players follow the rules. ❑ *Officials suspended the game because of safety concerns.*

SYNONYMS

official
ADJ **1**
authorized: *Only authorized personnel may enter the building.*
approved: *The approved method of cleaning is industrial sand-blasting.*
sanctioned: *The use of force is not sanctioned.*

of|fi|cial|dom /əˈfɪʃəldəm/ N-UNCOUNT **Officialdom** is used to refer to officials who work for the government or in other organizations, especially when you think that their rules are unhelpful. [DISAPPROVAL] ❑ *Officialdom has been against us from the start.*

of|fi|ci|ate /əˈfɪʃieɪt/ (officiates, officiating, officiated) **1** V-I When someone **officiates** at a ceremony or formal occasion, they are in charge and perform the official part of it. ❑ *Bishop Silvester officiated at the funeral.* ❑ *A memorial service was held yesterday; the Rev. Michael Logan officiated.* **2** V-I When someone **officiates** at a sports match or competition, they are in charge and make sure the players do not break the rules. ❑ *He will officiate at the next Bears game.* ❑ *They are the first women ever hired to officiate in a men's professional sport.*

of|fi|cious /əˈfɪʃəs/ ADJ If you describe someone as **officious**, you are critical of them because they are eager to tell people what to do when you think they should not. [DISAPPROVAL] ❑ *When people put on uniforms, their attitude becomes more confident and their manner more officious.* • **of|fi|cious|ly** ADV [ADV with v] ❑ *Corporal Williams officiously ordered them out.*

of|fing /ɔfɪŋ/ PHRASE [v-link PHR] If you say that something is **in the offing**, you mean that it is likely to happen soon. ❑ *A general amnesty for political prisoners may be in the offing.*

off-key ADJ When music is **off-key**, it is not in tune. ❑ *...wailing, off-key vocals and strangled guitars.* • ADV [ADV after v] Off-key is also an adverb. ❑ *Moe was having fun banging the drums and singing off-key.*

off-licence (off-licences) N-COUNT An **off-licence** is a store that sells beer, wine, and other alcoholic drinks. [BRIT]

in AM, use **liquor store**

off lim|its also **off-limits** ❶ ADJ If a place is **off limits** to someone, they are not allowed to go there. ❑ *Certain areas have been declared off limits to servicemen.* ❷ ADJ [v-link ADJ] If you say that an activity or a substance is **off limits** for someone, you mean that they are not allowed to do it or have it. ❑ *Fraternizing with the customers is off limits.*

off|line /ɔflaɪn/ ❶ ADJ If a computer is **offline**, it is not connected to the internet. Compare **online**. [COMPUTING] ❑ *Initially the system was offline for a number of days.* • ADV [ADV with v] Offline is also an adverb. ❑ *Most software programs allow you to compose e-mails offline.* ❷ **off line** → see **line** ②

off|load /ɔfloʊd/ (offloads, offloading, offloaded) ❶ V-T When goods **are offloaded**, they are removed from a container or vehicle and put somewhere else. ❑ *The cargo was due to be offloaded in Singapore three days later.* ❷ V-T If you **offload** something that you do not want, you get rid of it by giving it or selling it to someone else. [mainly BRIT]

in AM, usually use **unload**

off-message ADJ [usu v-link ADJ] If a politician is **off-message**, they say something that does not follow the official policy of their party.

off-peak ADJ [ADJ n] You use **off-peak** to describe something that happens or that is used at times when there is least demand for it. Prices at off-peak times are often lower than at other times. ❑ *Callers now pay 33 cents during peak hours and 30 cents during off-peak hours.* • ADV [ADV after v] Off-peak is also an adverb. ❑ *It lasts three minutes and costs 36 cents per minute off-peak and 48 cents at all other times.*

off-putting ADJ If you describe a quality or feature of something as **off-putting**, you mean that it makes you dislike that thing or not want to get involved with it. ❑ *However, many customers found the smell of this product distinctly off-putting.*

off-ramp (off-ramps) N-COUNT An **off-ramp** is a road which cars use to drive off a highway. [AM] ❑ *...the Embarcadero Road off-ramp from the freeway.*

off-roader (off-roaders) N-COUNT An **off-roader** is the same as an **off-road vehicle**. [INFORMAL]

off-roading N-UNCOUNT Off-roading is the activity of driving off-road vehicles over rough ground. ❑ *...training sessions for anyone who wants to go off-roading.*

off-road ve|hi|cle (off-road vehicles) N-COUNT An **off-road vehicle** is a vehicle that is designed to travel over rough ground.

off-screen also **offscreen** ADV [ADV with cl] You use **off-screen** to refer to the real lives of movie or television actors, in contrast with the lives of the characters they play. ❑ *He was immensely attractive to women, on-screen and off-screen.* ❑ *Off-screen, Kathy is under the watchful eye of her father Terry.* • ADJ [ADJ n] Off-screen is also an adjective. ❑ *They were quick to dismiss rumors of an off-screen romance.*

off sea|son also **off-season** ❶ N-SING [also no det, oft N n] The **off season** is the time of the year when not many people go on vacation and when things such as hotels and plane tickets are often cheaper. ❑ *It is possible to vacation at some of the more expensive resorts if you go in the off season.* ❑ *Although it was off season, the hotel was fully occupied.* ❑ *...off-season prices.* • ADV Off season is also an adverb. ❑ *Times become more flexible off-season, especially in the smaller provincial museums.* ❷ N-SING [oft N n] The **off season** is the time of the year when a particular sport is not played. ❑ *He has coached and played in Italy during the Australian off season.* ❑ *...intensive off-season training.* • ADV Off season is

also an adverb. ❑ *To stay fit off season, I play tennis or football.* ❑ *...the many problems that dominated baseball off season.*

off|set /ɔfsɛt/ (offsets, offsetting)

The form **offset** is used in the present tense and is the past tense and past participle of the verb.

V-T If one thing **is offset** by another, the effect of the first thing is reduced by the second, so that any advantage or disadvantage is canceled out. ❑ *The increase in pay costs was more than offset by higher productivity.*

off|shoot /ɔfʃut/ (offshoots) N-COUNT If one thing is an **offshoot** of another, it has developed from that other thing. ❑ *Psychology began as a purely academic offshoot of natural philosophy.*

off|shore /ɔfʃɔr/ ❶ ADJ [ADJ n] **Offshore** means situated or happening in the sea, near to the coast. ❑ *...the offshore oil industry.* • ADV Offshore is also an adverb. ❑ *One day a larger ship anchored offshore.* ❷ ADJ [ADJ n] Offshore investments or companies are located in a place, usually an island, which has fewer tax regulations than most other countries. [BUSINESS] ❑ *The island offers a wide range of offshore banking facilities.*

off|side /ɔfsaɪd/ also **off-side** ❶ ADJ In football, a player is **offside** if they cross the line of scrimmage before a play begins. ❷ ADJ In games such as soccer or hockey, when an attacking player is **offside**, they have broken the rules by being nearer to the goal than a defending player when the ball is passed to them. ❑ *The goal was disallowed because Wark was offside.* • ADV [ADV after v] Offside is also an adverb. ❑ *Yoon was standing at least ten yards offside.* • N-UNCOUNT Offside is also a noun. ❑ *Rush had a 45th-minute goal disallowed for offside.*

off-site → see **site**

off|spring /ɔfsprɪŋ/

Offspring is both the singular and the plural form.

N-COUNT You can refer to a person's children or to an animal's young as their **offspring**. [FORMAL] ❑ *Eleanor was now less anxious about her offspring than she had once been.*

off|stage /ɔfsteɪdʒ/ also **off-stage** ❶ ADV [ADV after v, n ADV] When an actor or entertainer goes **offstage**, they go into the area behind or to the side of the stage, so that the audience no longer sees them. ❑ *She ran offstage in tears.* ❑ *There was a lot of noise offstage.* ❷ ADJ [ADJ n] Offstage is used to describe the behavior of actors or entertainers in real life, when they are not performing. ❑ *...the tragedies of their off-stage lives.* • ADV [ADV with cl] Offstage is also an adverb. ❑ *Despite their bitter screen rivalry, off-stage they are close friends.*

off-the-cuff → see **cuff**
off-the-peg → see **peg**
off-the-rack → see **rack**
off-the-record → see **record**
off-the-shelf → see **shelf**

off-the-wall ❶ ADJ [usu ADJ n] If you describe something as **off-the-wall**, you mean that it is unusual and rather strange but in an amusing or interesting way. [INFORMAL] ❑ *surreal off-the-wall humor.* ❷ ADJ If you say that a person, their ideas, or their ways of doing something are **off-the-wall**, you are critical of them because you think they are crazy or very foolish. [INFORMAL, DISAPPROVAL] ❑ *It can be done without following some absurd, off-the-wall investment strategy.*

off top|ic also **off-topic** ADJ If you describe something that someone says or writes as **off topic**, you mean that it is not relevant to the current discussion; used especially of discussions on the internet. ❑ *Sometimes something that makes no sense, is completely off topic, or just utterly stupid gets the best laughs.*

off-white COLOR Something that is **off-white** is not pure white, but slightly gray or yellow.

off-year (off-years) N-COUNT [oft N n] An **off-year** is a year when no major political elections are held. [AM] ❑ *Election officials predict they'll set a new turnout record for an off-year election in Washington state.*

oft- /ɔft-/ COMB IN ADJ **Oft-** combines with past participles to form adjectives that mean that something happens or is done often. [LITERARY] ❑ *Her views on the treaty are well documented and oft-repeated.*

of|ten /ˈɒfᵊn/

Often is usually used before the verb, but it may be used after the verb when it has a word like 'less' or 'more' before it, or when the clause is negative.

1 ADV If something **often** happens, it happens many times or much of the time. ▫ *They often spent Christmas together.* ▫ *That doesn't happen very often.* **2** ADV You use **how often** to ask questions about frequency. You also use **often** in reported clauses and other statements to give information about the frequency of something. ▫ *How often do you brush your teeth?* **3** PHRASE If something happens **every so often**, it happens regularly, but with fairly long intervals between each occasion. ▫ *She's going to come back every so often.* **4** PHRASE If you say that something happens **as often as not**, or **more often than not**, you mean that it happens fairly frequently, and that this can be considered as typical. ▫ *Yet, as often as not, they find themselves the target of persecution rather than praise.*

SYNONYMS

often
ADV **1**
frequently: *Folic acid supplements are frequently given to pregnant women.*
generally: *We generally say and feel too much about these things.*
repeatedly: *Both men have repeatedly denied the allegations.*

USAGE

often
Don't use 'often' to talk about something that happens several times within a short period of time. Don't say, for example, 'I often phoned her yesterday.' You say 'I phoned her **several times** yesterday' or 'I kept phoning her yesterday.' *That fear was expressed **several times** last week.*

often|times /ˈɒfᵊntaɪmz/ ADV If something **oftentimes** happens, it happens many times or much of the time. [AM, OLD-FASHIONED] ▫ *Oftentimes, I wouldn't even return the calls.*

ogle /ˈoʊɡᵊl/ (**ogles, ogling, ogled**) V-T/V-I If one person **ogles** another, they stare continually at that person in a way that indicates a strong sexual interest. [DISAPPROVAL] ▫ *All she did was hang around ogling the men in the factory.* ▫ *Paula is not used to everyone ogling at her while she undresses backstage.*

ogre /ˈoʊɡər/ (**ogres**) N-COUNT If you refer to someone as an **ogre**, you are saying in a humorous way that they are very frightening. ▫ *Tax auditors do not really like being thought of as ogres.*

oh /oʊ/ **1** CONVENTION You use **oh** to introduce a response or a comment on something that has just been said. [SPOKEN] ▫ *"Had you seen the car before?"—"Oh yes, it was always in the driveway."* **2** EXCLAM You use **oh** to express a feeling such as surprise, pain, annoyance, or happiness. [SPOKEN, FEELINGS] ▫ *"Oh!" Kenny blinked. "Has everyone gone?"* **3** CONVENTION You use **oh** when you are hesitating while speaking, for example, because you are trying to estimate something, or because you are searching for the right word. [SPOKEN] ▫ *I've been here, oh, since the end of June.*

ohm /oʊm/ (**ohms**) N-COUNT An **ohm** is a unit which is used to measure electrical resistance. [TECHNICAL]

OHP /oʊ eɪtʃ piː/ (**OHPs**) N-COUNT An **OHP** is the same as an **overhead projector**.

oil /ɔɪl/ (**oils, oiling, oiled**) **1** N-MASS **Oil** is a smooth, thick liquid that is used as a fuel and for making the parts of machines move smoothly. Oil is found underground. ▫ *The company buys and sells about 600,000 barrels of oil a day.* ▫ *…the rapid rise in prices for oil and gasoline.* **2** V-T If you **oil** something, you put oil onto or into it, for example, to make it work smoothly or to protect it. ▫ *A crew of assistants oiled and adjusted the release mechanism until it worked perfectly.* **3** N-MASS **Oil** is a smooth, thick liquid made from plants and is often used for cooking. ▫ *Combine the beans, chopped mint, and oil in a large bowl.* **4** N-MASS **Oil** is a smooth, thick liquid, often with a pleasant smell, that you rub into your skin or add to your bath. ▫ *Try a hot bath with some relaxing bath oil.* **5** → see also **crude oil, olive oil** **6 to burn the midnight oil** → see **midnight**

oil|cloth /ˈɔɪlklɒθ/ (**oilcloths**) **1** N-UNCOUNT **Oilcloth** is a cotton fabric with a shiny waterproof surface. **2** N-COUNT An **oilcloth** is a covering made from oilcloth, such as a tablecloth.

oiled /ɔɪld/ **1** ADJ [usu ADJ n] Something that is **oiled** has had oil put into or onto it, for example, to make it work smoothly or to protect it. ▫ *Oiled wood is water-resistant and won't flake.* **2** → see also **well-oiled**

oil|field /ˈɔɪlfiːld/ (**oilfields**) also **oil field** N-COUNT An **oilfield** is an area of land or sea under which there is oil.

oil-fired ADJ [ADJ n] **Oil-fired** heating systems and power stations use oil as a fuel. ▫ *…an oil-fired furnace.*

oil|man /ˈɔɪlmæn/ (**oilmen**) also **oil man** N-COUNT An **oilman** is a man who owns an oil company or who works in the oil business. [JOURNALISM]

oil paint N-UNCOUNT [also N in pl] **Oil paint** is a thick paint used by artists. It is made from colored powder and linseed oil.

oil paint|ing (**oil paintings**) N-COUNT An **oil painting** is a picture which has been painted using oil paints. ▫ *Several magnificent oil paintings adorn the walls.*

oil pan (**oil pans**) N-COUNT An **oil pan** is the place under an engine that holds the engine oil. [mainly AM]

in BRIT, usually use **sump**

oil plat|form (**oil platforms**) N-COUNT An **oil platform** is a structure that is used when getting oil from the ground under the sea.

oil rig (**oil rigs**) N-COUNT An **oil rig** is a structure on land or in the sea that is used when getting oil from the ground.

oil|seed rape /ˈɔɪlsiːd reɪp/ also **oil-seed rape** N-UNCOUNT **Oilseed rape** is a plant with yellow flowers which is grown as a crop. Its seeds are crushed to make cooking oil. [BRIT]

in AM, use **rape**

oil|skins /ˈɔɪlskɪnz/ N-PLURAL **Oilskins** are a coat and a pair of pants made from thick waterproof cotton cloth.

oil slick (**oil slicks**) N-COUNT An **oil slick** is a layer of oil that is floating on the sea or on a lake because it has accidentally come out of a ship or container. ▫ *The oil slick is now 35 miles long.*

oil tank|er (**oil tankers**) N-COUNT An **oil tanker** is a ship that is used for transporting oil.

oil well (**oil wells**) N-COUNT An **oil well** is a deep hole which is made in order to get oil out of the ground.

oil|woman /ˈɔɪlwʊmən/ (**oilwomen**) also **oil woman** N-COUNT An **oilwoman** is a woman who owns an oil company or who works in the oil business. [JOURNALISM]

oily /ˈɔɪli/ (**oilier, oiliest**) **1** ADJ Something that is **oily** is covered with oil or contains oil. ▫ *He was wiping his hands on an oily rag.* **2** ADJ **Oily** means looking, feeling, tasting, or smelling like oil. ▫ *…traces of an oily substance.*

oint|ment /ˈɔɪntmənt/ (**ointments**) **1** N-MASS An **ointment** is a smooth thick substance that is put on sore skin or a wound to help it heal. ▫ *A range of ointments and creams is available for the treatment of eczema.* **2** PHRASE If you describe someone or something as a **fly in the ointment**, you think they spoil a situation and prevent it from being as successful as you had hoped. ▫ *Rachel seems to be the one fly in the ointment of Caroline's smooth life.*

OJ /oʊ dʒeɪ/ N-MASS **OJ** is the same as **orange juice**. [AM, INFORMAL] ▫ *…a glass of OJ.*

okay /ˌoʊˈkeɪ/ (**okays, okaying, okayed**) also **OK, O.K., ok** **1** ADJ If you say that something is **okay**, you find it satisfactory or acceptable. [INFORMAL] ▫ *…a shooting range where it's OK to use weapons.* ▫ *Is it okay if I come by myself?* • ADV [ADV after v] **Okay** is also an adverb. ▫ *We seemed to manage okay for the first year or so after David was born.* **2** ADJ [v-link ADJ] If you say that someone is **okay**, you mean that they are safe and well. [INFORMAL] ▫ *Check that the baby's okay.* **3** CONVENTION You can say '**Okay**' to show that you agree to something. [INFORMAL, FORMULAE] ▫ *"Just tell him I would like to talk to him."—"OK."* **4** CONVENTION You can say '**Okay?**' to check whether the person you are talking to understands what you have said and accepts it. [INFORMAL] ▫ *We'll get together next week, OK?* **5** CONVENTION You can use **okay** to indicate that you want to start talking about something else or doing something else. [INFORMAL] ▫ *OK. Now, let's talk some business.* **6** CONVENTION You can use **okay** to stop someone from arguing with you by showing that you accept the point they are making, though you do not necessarily regard it as very important. [INFORMAL] ▫ *Okay, there is a slight*

okey dokey

difference. **7** V-T If someone in authority **okays** something, they officially agree to it or allow it to happen. [INFORMAL] ❑ *His doctor wouldn't OK the trip.* • N-SING **Okay** is also a noun. ❑ *He gave the okay to issue a new press release.*

okey do|key /ˌoʊki ˈdoʊki/ also **okey doke** CONVENTION **Okey dokey** is used in the same way as 'OK' to show that you agree to something, or that you want to start talking about something else or doing something else. [INFORMAL, SPOKEN] ❑ *Okey dokey. I'll give you a call.*

okra /ˈoʊkrə/ N-UNCOUNT **Okra** is a vegetable that consists of long green parts containing seeds.

old ✦✦✦ /oʊld/ (**older**, **oldest**) **1** ADJ Someone who is **old** has lived for many years and is no longer young. ❑ *...a white-haired old man.* • N-PLURAL **The old** are people who are old. This use could cause offense. ❑ *...providing a caring response for the needs of the old.* **2** ADJ You use **old** to talk about how many days, weeks, months, or years someone or something has lived or existed. ❑ *He was abandoned by his father when he was three months old.* ❑ *How old are you now?* ❑ *Bill was six years older than David.* **3** ADJ Something that is **old** has existed for a long time. ❑ *She loved the big old house.* ❑ *These books must be very old.* **4** ADJ Something that is **old** is no longer in good condition because of its age or because it has been used a lot. ❑ *He took a bunch of keys from the pocket of his old corduroy trousers.* **5** ADJ [ADJ n] You use **old** to refer to something that is no longer used, that no longer exists, or that has been replaced by something else. ❑ *The old road had disappeared under grass and heather.* **6** ADJ [poss ADJ n] You use **old** to refer to something that used to belong to you, or to a person or thing that used to have a particular role in your life. ❑ *I'll make up the bed in your old room.* ❑ *I still have affection for my old school.* **7** ADJ [ADJ n] An **old** friend, enemy, or rival is someone who has been your friend, enemy, or rival for a long time. ❑ *I called my old friend John Horner.* ❑ *Mr. Brownson, I assure you, King's an old enemy of mine.* **8** ADJ You can use **old** to express affection when talking to or about someone you know. [BRIT, INFORMAL, FEELINGS] **9** PHRASE You use **any old** to emphasize that the quality or type of something is not important. If you say that a particular thing is not **any old** thing, you are emphasizing how special or famous it is. [INFORMAL, EMPHASIS] ❑ *Any old paper will do.* **10** PHRASE **In the old days** means in the past, before things changed. ❑ *In the old days, doctors made house calls.* **11** PHRASE When people refer to **the good old days**, they are referring to a time in the past when they think that life was better than it is now. ❑ *He remembers the good old days when everyone in his village knew him and you could leave your door open at night.* **12 good old** → see **good** ① **13 to settle an old score** → see **score**

───── SYNONYMS ─────

old
ADJ **1**
elderly: *...an elderly couple.*
aged: *She helps to look after an aged aunt.*
aging: *John lives with his aging mother.*
mature: *...a man of mature years.*

old age N-UNCOUNT Your **old age** is the period of years toward the end of your life. ❑ *They worry about how they will support themselves in their old age.*

old age pen|sion (**old age pensions**) also **old-age pension** N-COUNT An **old age pension** is a regular amount of money that people receive from the government when they have retired from work. [BRIT]

in AM, use **social security**

old bat (**old bats**) N-COUNT [usu sing] If someone refers to an old person, especially an old woman, as an **old bat**, they think that person is silly, annoying, or unpleasant. [INFORMAL, OFFENSIVE, DISAPPROVAL]

olde /oʊld/ ADJ [ADJ n] **Olde** is used in names of places and in advertising to make people think that something is very old and interesting. ❑ *I always feel at home at Ye Olde Starre Inn.*

old|en /ˈoʊldən/ **1** ADJ [ADJ n] If you refer to a period in the past as the **olden** days, you feel affection for it. [LITERARY] ❑ *We had a delightful time talking about the olden days on his farm.* ❑ *...the nicely painted railways of olden times.* **2 In the olden days**

old wives' tale

or **in olden days** means in the past. ❑ *In the olden days the girls were married young.*

old-fashioned 1 ADJ Something such as a style, method, or device that is **old-fashioned** is no longer used, done, or admired by most people, because it has been replaced by something that is more modern. ❑ *The house was dull, old-fashioned and in bad condition.* **2** ADJ **Old-fashioned** ideas, customs, or values are the ideas, customs, and values of the past. ❑ *She has some old-fashioned values and can be a strict disciplinarian.*

old flame (**old flames**) N-COUNT An **old flame** is someone with whom you once had a romantic relationship. ❑ *Sue was seen dating an old flame.*

Old Glo|ry N-UNCOUNT People sometimes refer to the flag of the United States as **Old Glory**. [AM]

old guard N-SING-COLL [usu the/poss N] If you refer to a group of people as the **old guard**, you mean that they have worked in a particular organization for a very long time and are unwilling to accept new ideas or practices. [DISAPPROVAL] ❑ *The old guard did not like the changes that Barros introduced.*

old hand (**old hands**) N-COUNT [oft N at n] If someone is an **old hand** at something, they are very skilled at it because they have been doing it for a long time. ❑ *An old hand at photography, Tim has been shooting wildlife as a hobby for the last 13 years.*

old hat → see **hat**

oldie /ˈoʊldi/ (**oldies**) N-COUNT You can refer to something such as an old song or movie as an **oldie**, especially when you think it is still good. [INFORMAL] ❑ *My favorite radio station plays Top 40 stuff and oldies.* • ADJ [ADJ n] **Oldie** is also an adjective. ❑ *During the festival, we'll be showing 13 classic oldie films.*

old lady N-SING [usu poss N] Some people refer to their wife, girlfriend, or mother as their **old lady**. This use could cause offense. [INFORMAL] ❑ *He had met his old lady when he was a house painter and she was a secretary.*

old maid (**old maids**) N-COUNT People sometimes refer to an old or middle-aged woman as an **old maid** when she has never married and they think that it is unlikely that she ever will marry. This word is likely to cause offense, and should not be used. [OLD-FASHIONED, DISAPPROVAL] ❑ *Alex is too young to be already thinking of herself as an old maid.*

old man N-SING [the/poss N] Some people refer to their father, husband, or boyfriend as their **old man**. This use could cause offense. [INFORMAL] ❑ *Her old man left her a few million when he died.*

old mas|ter (**old masters**) N-COUNT An **old master** is a painting by one of the famous European painters of the 16th, 17th, and 18th centuries. These painters can also be referred to as the Old Masters. ❑ *...his collection of old masters and modern art.* ❑ *...portraits by Gainsborough, Rubens and other Old Masters.*

old school tie N-SING [the N] When people talk about **the old school tie**, they are referring to the situation in which people who attended the same school or college use their positions of influence to help each other. [mainly BRIT] ❑ *Of course, the old school tie has been a help.*

old-style ADJ [ADJ n] You use **old-style** to describe something or someone of a type that was common or popular in the past but is not common or popular now. ❑ *...a proper barber shop with real old-style barber chairs.*

Old Tes|ta|ment N-PROPER [the N] **The Old Testament** is the first part of the Bible. It deals especially with the relationship between God and the Jewish people.

old-time ADJ [ADJ n] If you describe something as **old-time**, you mean that it was common or popular in the past but is not common or popular now. ❑ *...an old-time dance hall which still has a tea dance on Monday afternoons.*

old-timer (**old-timers**) **1** N-COUNT An old man is sometimes referred to as an **old-timer**. [AM, INFORMAL] **2** N-COUNT If you refer to someone as an **old-timer**, you mean that he or she has been living in a particular place or doing a particular job for a long time. [INFORMAL] ❑ *The old-timers and established families clutched the reins of power.*

old wives' tale (**old wives' tales**) N-COUNT An **old wives' tale** is a traditional belief, especially one which is incorrect. ❑ *Ann Bradley dispels the old wives' tales and gives the medical facts.*

old wom|an (old women) N-COUNT If you refer to someone as an **old woman**, you are critical of them because you think they are too anxious about things. [INFORMAL, DISAPPROVAL]

old world also **Old World, old-world** ADJ [ADJ n] **Old world** is used to describe places and things that are or seem to be from an earlier period of history, and that look interesting or attractive. ❑ *The newcomers to the Village were attracted by its winding streets and Old World charm.*

ole /<u>oʊ</u>l/ ADJ [ADJ n] **Ole** is used in written English to represent the word 'old' pronounced in a particular way. ❑ *"I started fixin' up ole bicycles fer poor kids."*

olean|der /<u>oʊ</u>liændər/ (**oleanders**) N-VAR An **oleander** is an evergreen tree or shrub that has white, pink, or purple flowers.

ol|fac|tory /ɒlfæktəri, -tri, oʊl-/ ADJ [ADJ n] **Olfactory** means concerned with the sense of smell. [FORMAL] ❑ *This olfactory sense develops in the womb.*

oli|gar|chy /<u>ɒ</u>lɪgɑrki/ (**oligarchies**) **1** N-COUNT An **oligarchy** is a small group of people who control and run a particular country or organization. You can also refer to a country which is governed in this way as an **oligarchy**. **2** N-UNCOUNT **Oligarchy** is a situation in which a country or organization is run by an oligarchy. ❑ *...a protest against imperialism and oligarchy in the region.*

ol|ive /<u>ɒ</u>lɪv/ (**olives**) **1** N-VAR **Olives** are small green or black fruits with a bitter taste. Olives are often pressed to make olive oil. ❑ *...a pile of black olives.* **2** N-COUNT An **olive tree** or an **olive** is a tree on which olives grow. ❑ *Olives look romantic on a hillside in Provence.* **3** COLOR Something that is **olive** is yellowish-green in color. ❑ *...glowing colors such as deep red, olive, saffron and ocher.* • COMB IN COLOR **Olive** is also a combining form. ❑ *She wore an olive-green T-shirt.* **4** ADJ If someone has **olive** skin, the color of their skin is yellowish brown. ❑ *They are handsome with dark, shining hair, olive skin and fine brown eyes.*

ol|ive branch (**olive branches**) N-COUNT [usu sing] If you offer an **olive branch** to someone, you say or do something in order to show that you want to end a disagreement or quarrel. ❑ *Clarke also offered an olive branch to critics in his party.*

ol|ive oil (**olive oils**) N-MASS **Olive oil** is oil that is obtained by pressing olives. It is used for putting on salads or in cooking.

SUFFIX

-ological
is used to replace -ology at the end of nouns in order to form adjectives that describe something as relating to a particular science or subject. For example, **biological** systems relate to biology.

SUFFIX

-ologist
is used to replace -ology at the end of nouns in order to form other nouns that refer to people who are concerned with a particular science or subject. For example, a **biologist** is someone who studies biology.

SUFFIX

-ology
is used at the end of some nouns that refer to a particular science or subject. For example, **geology** or **sociology**.

Olym|pian /əlɪmpiən/ (**Olympians**) **1** ADJ [usu ADJ n] **Olympian** means very powerful, large, or impressive. [FORMAL] ❑ *Getting his book into print has been an Olympian task in itself.* **2** N-COUNT An **Olympian** is a competitor in the Olympic Games. [TRADEMARK] ❑ *The importance of being an Olympian will vary from athlete to athlete.*

Olym|pic ♦◇◇ /əlɪmpɪk/ (**Olympics**) **1** ADJ [ADJ n] **Olympic** means relating to the Olympic Games. [TRADEMARK] ❑ *...the reigning Olympic champion.* **2** N-PROPER **The Olympics** are the Olympic Games. [TRADEMARK] ❑ *Have you been watching the Olympics?* **3** → See feature box at **Olympic Games**

Olym|pic Games N-PROPER-COLL The **Olympic Games** are a set of international sports competitions which take place every four years, each time in a different city. [TRADEMARK] ❑ *At the 1968 Olympic Games she had won gold medals in races at 200, 400, and 800 meters.*

VOCABULARY IN CONTEXT

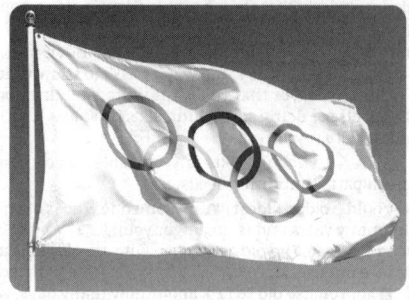

The Olympic Games®

It must be the best feeling ever. To be an Olympic **medalist**, to stand on the **podium** while the national anthem of your country is played; to be a winner in your **sport** at these **ancient games**. The Olympic Games are the oldest **sporting tournament** in the world. A different city **hosts** the games every four years, and **spectators** lucky enough to attend sometimes enjoy the privilege of seeing **world records** broken. Around the globe, millions watch on television. At the 2012 Olympic Games in London, 10,000 **athletes** were viewed by five billion people. The **opening ceremony** is always a spectacle of pageantry. Tradition deems that the **Olympic torch** is relayed from Greece to the site of the games, and the **Olympic flame** is kept burning until the closing ceremony. Although the Olympic Games have been mired in controversy, it has to be said that any event which brings 200 countries together is a worthy one.

---

om|buds|man /ɒmbʊdzmən/ (**ombudsmen**) N-COUNT The **ombudsman** is an independent official who has been appointed to investigate complaints that people make against the government or public organizations. ❑ *The leaflet explains how to complain to the banking ombudsman.*

om|buds|woman /ɒmbʊdzwʊmən/ (**ombudswomen**) N-COUNT The **ombudswoman** is an independent official who has been appointed to investigate complaints that people make against the government or public organizations. ❑ *The ombudswoman's report will set out recommendations for what the national framework should include.*

ome|let /ɒmlɪt, ɒməlɪt/ (**omelets**) also **omelette** N-COUNT An **omelet** is a type of food made by beating eggs and cooking them in a flat frying pan. ❑ *...a cheese omelet.*

omen /oʊmən/ (**omens**) N-COUNT If you say that something is an **omen**, you think it indicates what is likely to happen in the future and whether it will be good or bad. ❑ *Her appearance at this moment is an omen of disaster.*

OMG **OMG** is the written abbreviation for 'Oh my God!,' used especially in emails and text messages.

omi|nous /ɒmɪnəs/ ADJ If you describe something as **ominous**, you mean that it worries you because it makes you think that something bad is going to happen. ❑ *There was an ominous silence at the other end of the phone.* • **omi|nous|ly** ADV ❑ *The bar seemed ominously quiet.*

omis|sion /oʊmɪʃən/ (**omissions**) **1** N-COUNT An **omission** is something that has not been included or has not been done, either deliberately or accidentally. ❑ *He was surprised by his wife's omission from the guest list.* **2** N-VAR **Omission** is the act of not including a particular person or thing or of not doing something. ❑ *...the prosecution's seemingly malicious omission of recorded evidence.*

omit /oʊmɪt/ (**omits, omitting, omitted**) **1** V-T If you **omit** someone or something, you do not include them in an activity or piece of work, deliberately or accidentally. ❑ *Omit the salt in this recipe.* **2** V-T If you **omit** to do something, you do not do it. [FORMAL] ❑ *His new girlfriend had omitted to tell him she was married.*

om|ni|bus /ˈɒmnɪbʌs, -bəs/ (**omnibuses**) **1** N-COUNT An **omnibus** is a book which contains a large collection of stories or articles, often by a particular person or about a particular subject. ❑ *...a new omnibus edition of three Ruth Rendell chillers.* **2** ADJ [ADJ n] An **omnibus** bill is a piece of legislation which contains several different parts or which applies to a variety of different situations. [AM] ❑ *The money was part of an omnibus spending bill approved by Congress.*

om|nipo|tence /ɒmˈnɪpətəns/ N-UNCOUNT **Omnipotence** is the state of having total authority or power. [FORMAL] ❑ *...the omnipotence of love.*

om|nipo|tent /ɒmˈnɪpətənt/ ADJ Someone or something that is **omnipotent** has complete power over things or people. [FORMAL] ❑ *Doug lived in the shadow of his seemingly omnipotent father.*

om|ni|pres|ent /ˌɒmnɪˈprezənt/ ADJ Something that is **omnipresent** is present everywhere or seems to be always present. [FORMAL] ❑ *The sound of sirens was an omnipresent background noise in New York.*

om|nis|ci|ent /ɒmˈnɪʃənt/ ADJ If you describe someone as **omniscient**, you mean they know or seem to know everything. [FORMAL] ❑ *...a benevolent and omniscient deity.* ❑ *...the newspaper's omniscient data-gathering network.* ● **om|nis|ci|ence** N-UNCOUNT ❑ *...the divine attributes of omnipotence, benevolence and omniscience.*

om|niv|or|ous /ɒmˈnɪvərəs/ **1** ADJ An **omnivorous** person or animal eats all kinds of food, including both meat and plants. [FORMAL, TECHNICAL] ❑ *Brown bears are omnivorous, eating anything that they can get their paws on.* **2** ADJ **Omnivorous** means liking a wide variety of things of a particular type. [FORMAL] ❑ *As a child, Coleridge developed omnivorous reading habits.*

ON

① DESCRIBING POSITIONS AND LOCATIONS
② TALKING ABOUT HOW OR WHEN SOMETHING HAPPENS
③ OTHER USES
④ PHRASES

---

① **on** ✦✦✦

The preposition is pronounced /ɒn/. The adverb and the adjective are pronounced /ɒn/.

1 PREP If someone or something is **on** a surface or object, the surface or object is immediately below them and is supporting their weight. ❑ *He is sitting beside her on the sofa.* ❑ *On top of the cupboards are straw baskets.* **2** PREP If something is **on** a surface or object, it is stuck to it or attached to it. ❑ *I stared at the peeling paint on the ceiling.* ❑ *The clock on the wall showed one minute to twelve.* ● ADV [ADV after v] **On** is also an adverb. ❑ *I know how to sew a button on.* **3** PREP If you put, throw, or drop something **on** a surface, you move it or drop it so that it is then supported by the surface. ❑ *He got his winter jacket from the closet and dropped it on the sofa.* **4** PREP You use **on** to say what part of your body is supporting your weight. ❑ *He continued to lie on his back and look at clouds.* ❑ *He raised himself on his elbows, squinting into the sun.* **5** PREP You use **on** to say that someone or something touches a part of a person's body. ❑ *He leaned down and kissed her lightly on the mouth.* **6** PREP [n PREP n] If someone has a particular expression **on** their face, their face has that expression. ❑ *The maid looked at him, a nervous smile on her face.* **7** ADV [ADV after v] When you put a piece of clothing **on**, you place it over part of your body in order to wear it. If you have it **on**, you are wearing it. ❑ *He put his coat on while she opened the front door.* **8** PREP [PREP pron] You can say that you have something **on** you if you are carrying it in your pocket or in a purse. ❑ *I didn't have any money on me.* **9** PREP If someone's eyes are **on** you, they are looking or staring at you. ❑ *Everyone's eyes were fixed on him.* **10** PREP If you hurt yourself **on** something, you accidentally hit a part of your body against it and that thing causes damage to you. ❑ *Mr. Pendle hit his head on a wall as he fell.* **11** PREP If you are **on** an area of land, you are there. ❑ *He was able to spend only a few days on the island.* ❑ *You lived on the farm until you came back to America?* **12** PREP If something is situated **on** a place such as a road or coast, it forms part of it or is by the side of it. ❑ *Bergdorf Goodman has opened a men's store on Fifth Avenue.* ❑ *The hotel is on the coast.* **13** PREP If you get **on** a bus, train, or plane, you go into it in order to travel somewhere. If you are **on** it, you are traveling in it. ❑ *We waited till twelve and we finally got on the plane.* ● ADV [ADV after v] **On** is also an adverb. ❑ *He showed his ticket to the conductor and got on.* **14** PREP If there is something **on** a piece of paper, it has been written or printed there. ❑ *The writing on the back of the card was cramped but scrupulously neat.* **15** PREP If something is **on** a list, it is included in it. ❑ *I've seen your name on the list of deportees.*

② **on** ✦✦✦

The preposition is pronounced /ɒn/. The adverb and the adjective are pronounced /ɒn/.

1 PREP You use **on** to introduce the method, principle, or system which is used to do something. ❑ *...a television that we bought on credit two months ago.* ❑ *They want all groups to be treated on an equal basis.* **2** PREP If something is done **on** an instrument or a machine, it is done using that instrument or machine. ❑ *...songs that I could just sit down and play on the piano.* **3** PREP If information is, for example, **on** tape or **on** computer, that is the way that it is stored. ❑ *We've got her statement on tape.* **4** PREP If something is being broadcast, you can say that it is **on** the radio or television. ❑ *Every sporting event on television and satellite over the next seven days is listed.* ● ADJ [v-link ADJ] **On** is also an adjective. ❑ *...teenagers complaining there's nothing good on.* **5** ADJ [v-link ADJ] When an activity is taking place, you can say that it is **on**. ❑ *There's an exciting match on at Wimbledon right now.* **6** ADV You use **on** in expressions such as 'have a lot going on' and 'not have very much on' to indicate how busy someone is. [SPOKEN] ❑ *I have a lot on in the next week.* **7** PREP You use **on** to introduce an activity that someone is doing, particularly traveling. ❑ *I've always wanted to go on a cruise.* ❑ *We're going on a trip next month.* **8** PREP You can indicate when something happens by saying that it happens **on** a particular day, date, or part of the week. ❑ *This year's event will take place on June 19th, a week earlier than usual.* ❑ *I was born on Christmas Day.* ❑ *The highway is often lined with cars on the weekend.* **9** PREP [PREP n/-ing] You use **on** when mentioning an event that was followed by another one. ❑ *She waited in her hotel to welcome her children on their arrival from Vancouver.* **10** ADV [ADV after v] You use **on** to say that someone is continuing to do something. ❑ *They walked on in silence for a while.* ❑ *We worked on into the night.* **11** ADV [from n ADV] You use **on** in expressions such as **from now on** and **from then on** to indicate that something starts to happen at the time mentioned and continues to happen afterward. ❑ *Perhaps it would be best not to see much of you from now on.* ❑ *We can expect trouble from this moment on.* **12** ADV [adv ADV] You often use **on** after the adverbs 'early,' 'late,' 'far,' and their comparative forms, especially at the beginning or end of a sentence, or before a preposition. ❑ *The market square is a riot of color and animation from early on in the morning.* ❑ *Later on I learned how to read music.*

③ **on** ✦✦✦

The preposition is pronounced /ɒn/. The adverb and the adjective are pronounced /ɒn/.

1 PREP Books, discussions, or ideas **on** a particular subject are concerned with that subject. ❑ *They offer free counseling on legal matters.* ❑ *He declined to give any information on the presidential election.* **2** ADV When something such as a machine or an electric light is **on**, it is functioning or in use. When you switch it **on**, it starts functioning. ❑ *The light was on and the door was open.* ❑ *The heating's been turned off. I've turned it on again.* **3** PREP If you are **on** a committee or council, you are a member of it. ❑ *Claire and Alita were on the organizing committee.* **4** PREP Someone who is **on** a drug takes it regularly. ❑ *She was on antibiotics for an eye infection that wouldn't go away.* **5** PREP [v PREP n] If you live **on** a particular kind of food, you eat it. If a machine runs **on** a particular kind of power or fuel, it uses it in order to function. ❑ *The caterpillars feed on a wide range of trees, shrubs and plants.* ❑ *He lived on a diet of water and canned fish.* **6** PREP If you are **on** a particular income, that is the income that you have. [BRIT] ❑ *...young people who are unemployed or on low wages.* ❑ *He's on three hundred a week.* **7** PREP [n PREP n] Taxes or profits that are obtained from something are referred to as taxes or profits **on** it. ❑ *...a general strike to protest a tax on food and medicine.* **8** PREP [PREP n/-ing] When you buy something or pay for something, you spend money **on** it. ❑ *I resolved not to*

on board

waste money on a hotel. ❏ *He spent more on feeding the dog than he spent on feeding himself.* **9** PREP [PREP n/-ing] When you spend time or energy **on** a particular activity, you spend time or energy doing it. ❏ *People complain about how children spend so much time on computer games.* ❏ *You all know why I am here, so I won't waste time on preliminaries.*

④ **on** ✦✦✦ /ɒn/

→ Please look at meanings ❸ – ❻ to see if the expression you are looking for is shown under another headword.

1 PHRASE If you say that something happens **on and on**, you mean that it continues to happen for a very long time. ❏ *...designers, builders, fitters – the list goes on and on.* ❏ *Lobell drove on and on through the dense and blowing snow.* **2** PHRASE If you say that something is **not on** or is **just not on**, you mean that it is unacceptable or impossible. [BRIT, INFORMAL] **3 on behalf of** → see **behalf** **4 on and off** → see **off** ② **5 and so on** → see **so** **6 on top of** → see **top** ③

> In addition to the uses shown here, **on** is used after some verbs, nouns, and adjectives in order to introduce extra information. **On** is also used in phrasal verbs such as 'keep on' and 'sign on.'

on board also **onboard, on-board** **1** ADJ [v-link ADJ] If a person or group of people is **on board**, they support you and agree with what you are doing. ❏ *We want to see that everyone is on board for creating change.* ❏ *We were able to keep some moderate and conservative Democrats on board.* **2** → see also **board**

once ✦✦✦ /wʌns/ **1** ADV [ADV with v] If something happens **once**, it happens one time only. ❏ *I met Miquela once, briefly.* ❏ *Since that evening I haven't once slept through the night.* • PRON [the/this PRON] **Once** is also a pronoun. ❏ *"Have they been to visit you yet?"—"Just the once, yeah."* **2** ADV [ADV a n] You use **once** with 'a' and words like 'day,' 'week,' and 'month' to indicate that something happens regularly, one time in each day, week, or month. ❏ *Lung cells die and are replaced about once a week.* **3** ADV If something was **once** true, it was true at some time in the past, but is no longer true. ❏ *Her parents once ran a store.* ❏ *I lived there once myself, before I got married.* **4** ADV [ADV with v] If someone **once** did something, they did it at some time in the past. ❏ *I once went camping at Lake Michigan with a friend.* ❏ *We once walked across the frozen pond at two in the morning.* **5** CONJ If something happens **once** another thing has happened, it happens immediately afterward. ❏ *The decision had taken about 10 seconds once he'd read a market research study.* **6** PHRASE If something happens **at once**, it happens suddenly, often when you are not expecting it to happen. ❏ *All at once there was someone knocking on the door.* **7** PHRASE If you do something **at once**, you do it immediately. ❏ *I have to go at once.* ❏ *Remove from the heat, add the parsley, toss and serve at once.* **8** PHRASE If a number of different things happen **at once** or **all at once**, they all happen at the same time. ❏ *You can't be doing two things at once.* **9** PHRASE **For once** is used to emphasize that something happens on this particular occasion, that it has never happened before, and may never happen again. [EMPHASIS] ❏ *For once, Dad is not complaining.* **10** PHRASE If something happens **once again** or **once more**, it happens again. ❏ *Amy picked up the hairbrush and brushed her hair once more.* **11** PHRASE If something happens **once and for all**, it happens completely or finally. [EMPHASIS] ❏ *We have to resolve this matter once and for all.* **12** PHRASE If something happens **once in a while**, it happens sometimes, but not very often. ❏ *Your body, like any other machine, needs a full service once in a while.* **13** PHRASE If you have done something **once or twice**, you have done it a few times, but not very often. ❏ *I visited once or twice.* ❏ *Once or twice she had caught a flash of interest in William's eyes.*

once-over PHRASE [PHR after v] If you **give** something or someone **the once-over**, you quickly look at or examine them. [INFORMAL] ❏ *She gave the apartment the once-over.*

on|coming /ɒnkʌmɪŋ/ ADJ [ADJ n] **Oncoming** means moving toward you. ❏ *She was thrown from his car after it skidded into the path of an oncoming car.*

on-demand ADJ [usu ADJ n] An **on-demand** service is available at any time that you want to use it. ❏ *...a TV package offering thousands of on-demand programs and movies.* • ADV [ADV after v] **On-demand** is also an adverb. ❏ *Viewers increasingly choose to watch on-demand.*

one

ONE
① NUMBER
② PRONOUN, DETERMINER AND ADJECTIVE USES
③ PHRASES

① **one** ✦✦✦ /wʌn/ (**ones**) NUM **One** is the number 1. ❏ *They had three sons and one daughter.* ❏ *...one thousand years ago.*

USAGE
one
You can't use a plural form of 'one' in this kind of sentence. Don't say, for example, 'If you like grapes, I'll get you ones.' Say 'If you like grapes, I'll get you some.' If you want more staples, there are **some** in the stationery cupboard.

② **one** ✦✦✦ /wʌn/ (**ones**)

→ Please look at meaning ⓬ to see if the expression you are looking for is shown under another headword.

1 ADJ [det ADJ] If you say that someone or something is the **one** person or thing of a particular kind, you are emphasizing that they are the only person or thing of that kind. [EMPHASIS] ❏ *They had alienated the one man who knew the business.* **2** DET **One** can be used instead of 'a' to emphasize the following noun. [EMPHASIS] ❏ *There is one thing I would like to know – What is it about Tim that you find so irresistible?* **3** DET You can use **one** instead of 'a' to emphasize the following adjective or expression. [INFORMAL, EMPHASIS] ❏ *If we ever get married we'll have one terrific wedding.* **4** DET You can use **one** to refer to the first of two or more things that you are comparing. ❏ *Prices vary from one shop to another.* • ADJ [det ADJ] **One** is also an adjective. ❏ *The one thing that she accomplished was raising money to update our facilities.* • PRON **One** is also a pronoun. ❏ *The twins were dressed differently and one was thinner than the other.* **5** PRON You can use **one** or **ones** instead of a noun when it is clear what type of thing or person you are referring to and you are describing them or giving more information about them. ❏ *They are selling their house to move to a smaller one.* **6** PRON You use **ones** to refer to people in general. ❏ *We are the only ones who know.* **7** PRON [PRON of n, PRON that] You can use **one** instead of a noun group when you have just mentioned something and you want to describe it or give more information about it. ❏ *The issue of land reform was one that dominated Hungary's parliamentary elections.* **8** DET You can use **one** when you have been talking or writing about a group of people or things and you want to say something about a particular member of the group. ❏ *"A college degree isn't enough," said one honors student.* • PRON **One** is also a pronoun. ❏ *Some of them couldn't eat a thing. One couldn't even drink.* **9** QUANT [QUANT of adj-superl] You use **one** in expressions such as '**one of the biggest airports**' or '**one of the most experienced players**' to indicate that something or someone is bigger or more experienced than most other things or people of the same kind. ❏ *It is one of the smallest car makers in the world.* **10** DET You can use **one** when referring to a time in the past or in the future. For example, if you say that you did something **one day**, you mean that you did it on a day in the past. ❏ *How would you like to have dinner one night, just you and me?* **11** PRON You use **one** to make statements about people in general which also apply to themselves. **One** can be used as the subject or object of a sentence. [FORMAL] ❏ *If one looks at the bigger picture, a lot of positive things are happening.* ❏ *Where does one go from there?* ⓬ **one day** → see **day**

③ **one** ✦✦✦ /wʌn/

→ Please look at meanings ⓾ – ⓭ to see if the expression you are looking for is shown under another headword.

1 PHRASE You can use **for one** to emphasize that a particular person is definitely reacting or behaving in a particular way, even if other people are not. [EMPHASIS] ❏ *I, for one, hope you don't get the job.* **2** PHRASE You can use expressions such as **a hundred and one**, **a thousand and one**, and **a million and one** to emphasize that you are talking about a large number of things or people. [EMPHASIS] ❏ *There are a hundred and one ways in which you can raise money.* **3** PHRASE You can use **in one** to indicate that something is a single unit, but is made up of several different parts or has several different functions. ❏ *...a love story and an adventure all in one.* **4** PHRASE You use **one**

after the other or **one after another** to say that actions or events happen with very little time between them. ❑ *My three guitars broke one after the other.* **5** PHRASE **The one and only** can be used in front of the name of an actor, singer, or other famous person when they are being introduced on a show. ❑ *...one of the greatest ever rock performers, the one and only Tina Turner.* **6** PHRASE You can use **one by one** to indicate that people do things or that things happen in sequence, not all at the same time. ❑ *We went into the room one by one.* **7** PHRASE You use **one or other** to refer to one or more things or people in a group, when it does not matter which particular one or ones are thought of or chosen. ❑ *One or other of the two women was wrong.* **8** PHRASE **One or two** means a few. ❑ *We may make one or two changes.* ❑ *I've also sold one or two to a publisher.* **9** PHRASE If you try to get **one up on** someone, you try to gain an advantage over them. ❑ *...the competitive kind who will see this as the opportunity to be one up on you.* **10 one another** → see **another** **11 one thing after another** → see **another** **12 of one mind** → see **mind** ① **13 in one piece** → see **piece**

one-armed ban|dit (one-armed bandits) N-COUNT A **one-armed bandit** is a machine used for gambling. You put money into it and if a particular combination of symbols, especially fruit, appears, you win money.

one-horse 1 ADJ [ADJ n] If someone describes a town as a **one-horse** town, they mean it is very small, dull, and old-fashioned. [DISAPPROVAL] ❑ *Would you want to live in a small, one-horse town for your whole life?* **2** ADJ [ADJ n] If a contest is described as a **one-horse** race, it is thought that one person or thing will obviously win it. ❑ *He described the referendum as a one-horse race.*

one-liner (one-liners) N-COUNT A **one-liner** is a funny remark or a joke told in one sentence, for example, in a play or comedy show. [INFORMAL] ❑ *The book is witty and peppered with good one-liners.*

one-man 1 ADJ [ADJ n] A **one-man** performance is given by only one man, rather than by several people. ❑ *I saw him do his one-man show in Austin, which I loved.* **2** ADJ [ADJ n] A **one-man** organization, such as a business or type of government, is controlled by one person, rather than by several people. ❑ *It has grown from a one-man business to a multi-million dollar business with close to $10 million in assets.* ❑ *He established one-man rule in his country seven months ago.*

one-man band (one-man bands) N-COUNT A **one-man band** is a street entertainer who wears and plays a lot of different instruments at the same time.

one-night stand (one-night stands) N-COUNT A **one-night stand** is an occasion when two people have sex once and never again. [INFORMAL]

one-of-a-kind ADJ [ADJ n] You use **one-of-a-kind** to describe something that is special because there is nothing else exactly like it. [mainly AM] ❑ *...a small one-of-a-kind publishing house.*

one-off (one-offs) **1** N-COUNT You can refer to something as a **one-off** when it is made or happens only once. ❑ *Our survey revealed that these allergies were mainly one-offs.* **2** ADJ A **one-off** thing is made or happens only once. [mainly BRIT]

in AM, usually use **one-time**

one-on-one ADJ [usu ADJ n] A **one-on-one** situation, meeting, or contest involves only two people. ❑ *...a one-on-one therapy session.* • ADV [ADV after v] **One-on-one** is also an adverb. ❑ *Talking one-on-one with people is not his idea of fun.* • N-SING [oft N with n] **One-on-one** is also a noun. ❑ *Holloway was beaten in a one-on-one with Miklosko just before half-time.*

one-parent fami|ly (one-parent families) N-COUNT A **one-parent family** is a family that consists of one parent and his or her children living together. ❑ *Many children are now born into or raised in one-parent families.*

one-person ADJ [ADJ n] A **one-person** performance is given by only one person rather than by several people. ❑ *She has had many one-person shows and television appearances.*

one-piece (one-pieces) **1** ADJ [ADJ n] A **one-piece** article of clothing consists of one piece only, rather than two or more separate parts. ❑ *...a blue one-piece bathing suit.* **2** N-COUNT A **one-piece** is a type of woman's bathing suit that consists of one piece of material and which covers her from the top of the legs to the shoulders. ❑ *A one-piece is more flattering than a bikini.*

on|er|ous /ˈɒnərəs, ˈoʊnər-/ ADJ If you describe a task as **onerous**, you dislike having to do it because you find it difficult or unpleasant. [FORMAL] ❑ *...parents who have had the onerous task of bringing up a very difficult child.*

one's ◆◇◇ /wʌnz/ **1** DET Speakers and writers use **one's** to indicate that something belongs or relates to people in general, or to themselves in particular. [FORMAL] ❑ *...a feeling of responsibility for the welfare of others in one's community.* **2 One's** can be used as a spoken form of 'one is' or 'one has,' especially when 'has' is an auxiliary verb. ❑ *No one's going to hurt you.* → see **one** ①

one|self /wʌnˈsɛlf/

Oneself is a third person singular reflexive pronoun.

1 PRON-REFL **Oneself** is used to mean 'any person in general' as the object of a verb or preposition, when this refers to the same person as the subject of the verb. [FORMAL] ❑ *One must apply oneself to the present and keep one's eyes firmly fixed on one's future goals.* **2** PRON-REFL **Oneself** is used to mean 'any person in general' as the object of a verb or preposition, when 'one' is not present but is understood to be the subject of the verb. [FORMAL] ❑ *The historic feeling of the town makes it a pleasant place to base oneself for summer vacations.*

one-shot ADJ A **one-shot** thing is made or happens only once. [AM] ❑ *We have to have this money year after year. It's not a one-shot deal.* ❑ *This conclusion is unfounded because it depends on the results of a one-shot study.*

one-sided 1 ADJ If you say that an activity or relationship is **one-sided**, you think that one of the people or groups involved does much more than the other or is much stronger than the other. ❑ *The negotiating was completely one-sided.* **2** ADJ If you describe someone as **one-sided**, you are critical of what they say or do because you think it shows that they have considered only one side of an issue or event. [DISAPPROVAL] ❑ *The organization still believes the government is being one-sided.*

one|sie /ˈwʌnzi/ (onesies) N-COUNT A **onesie** is a single piece of clothing that combines a top with trousers. It is usually worn for sleeping or at home. ❑ *She came down to breakfast wearing a onesie.*

one-stop ADJ [ADJ n] A **one-stop** store or shop is a place where you can buy everything you need for a particular purpose. ❑ *A marvelous discovery for every bride-to-be, The Wedding Center is the ultimate one-stop shop.*

one-time also **onetime 1** ADJ [ADJ n] **One-time** is used to describe something which happened in the past, or something such as a job, position, or role which someone used to have. [JOURNALISM] ❑ *The legislative body had voted to oust the country's onetime rulers.* **2** ADJ [ADJ n] A **one-time** thing is made or happens only once. [mainly AM] ❑ *...a one-time charge.*

one-to-one 1 ADJ [ADJ n] In a **one-to-one** relationship, one person deals directly with only one other person. ❑ *...one-to-one training.* • ADV [ADV after v] **One-to-one** is also an adverb. ❑ *She would like to talk to people one to one.* **2** ADJ [ADJ n] If there is a **one-to-one** match between two sets of things, each member of one set matches a member of the other set. ❑ *In English, there is not a consistent one-to-one match between each written symbol and each distinct spoken sound.*

one-upmanship /wʌnˈʌpmənʃɪp/ N-UNCOUNT [oft supp N] If you refer to someone's behavior as **one-upmanship**, you disapprove of them trying to make other people feel inferior in order to make themselves appear more important. [DISAPPROVAL] ❑ *The two men are playing a game of political one-upmanship.*

one-way 1 ADJ [ADJ n] In **one-way** streets or traffic systems, vehicles can only travel along in one direction. ❑ *Gotham's maze of one-way streets.* **2** ADJ **One-way** describes trips which go to just one place, rather than to that place and then back again. ❑ *The trailers will be rented for one-way trips.* **3** ADJ A **one-way** ticket or fare is for a trip from one place to another, but not back again. [mainly AM] ❑ *...a one-way ticket from New York to*

one-woman ADJ [ADJ n] A **one-woman** performance or business is given or controlled by only one woman, rather than by several people. ❑ *She has already presented a one-woman show of her paintings.*

on|going /ɒngoʊɪŋ/ ADJ An **ongoing** situation has been happening for quite a long time and seems likely to continue for some time in the future. ❑ *There is an ongoing debate on the issue.*

on|ion /ʌnyən/ (onions) N-VAR An **onion** is a round vegetable with a light brown skin. It has many white layers on its inside which have a strong, sharp smell and taste. ❑ *You grind the onion and the raw cranberries together.*

on|line ♦♦♦ /ɒnlaɪn/ also **on-line** ◼ ADJ If a company goes **online**, its services become available on the internet. [BUSINESS, COMPUTING] ❑ *...the first bank to go online.* ❑ *...an online shopping center.* ◼ ADJ If you are **online**, your computer is connected to the internet. Compare **offline**. [COMPUTING] ❑ *You can chat to other people who are online.* • ADV [ADV after v] **Online** is also an adverb. ❑ *...the cool stuff you find online.* ◼ on line → see line ② ◼ → See feature box at **crime**, **learning**

on|look|er /ɒnlʊkər/ (onlookers) N-COUNT An **onlooker** is someone who watches an event take place but does not take part in it. ❑ *A handful of onlookers stand in the field watching.*

ONLY
① ADVERB AND ADJECTIVE USES
② CONJUNCTIONS
③ PHRASES
---

① **only** ♦♦♦ /oʊnli/

> In written English, **only** is usually placed immediately before the word it qualifies. In spoken English, however, you can use stress to indicate what **only** qualifies, so its position is not important.

◼ ADV You use **only** to indicate the one thing that is true, appropriate, or necessary in a particular situation, in contrast with all the other things that are not true, appropriate, or necessary. ❑ *Only the president could authorize the use of the atomic bomb.* ❑ *A business can only be built and expanded on a sound financial base.* ◼ ADV [ADV cl/prep] You use **only** to introduce the thing which must happen before the thing mentioned in the main part of the sentence can happen. ❑ *The lawyer is paid only if he wins.* ❑ *The Bank of England insists that it will cut interest rates only when it is ready.* ◼ ADJ [det ADJ] If you talk about the **only** person or thing involved in a particular situation, you mean there are no others involved in it. ❑ *She was the only woman in Shell's legal department.* ◼ ADJ [ADJ n] An **only** child is a child who has no brothers or sisters. ❑ *The actor, an only child, grew up in the Bronx.* ◼ ADV You use **only** to indicate that something is no more important, interesting, or difficult, for example, than you say it is, especially when you want to correct a wrong idea that someone has or may get. ❑ *At the moment it is only a theory.* ❑ *"I'm only a sergeant," said Clements.* ◼ ADV [ADV n/adv] You use **only** to emphasize how small an amount is or how short a length of time is. [EMPHASIS] ❑ *Child car seats only cost about $10 a week to rent.* ❑ *...spacecraft guidance systems weighing only a few grams.* ◼ ADV [ADV n] You use **only** to emphasize that you are talking about a small part of an amount or group, not the whole of it. [EMPHASIS] ❑ *These are only a few of the possibilities.* ◼ ADV [modal ADV inf] **Only** is used after 'can' or 'could' to emphasize that it is impossible to do anything except the rather inadequate or limited action that is mentioned. [EMPHASIS] ❑ *For a moment I could say nothing. I could only stand and look.* ◼ ADV [ADV before v] You can use **only** in the expressions **I only wish** or **I only hope** in order to emphasize what you are hoping or wishing. [EMPHASIS] ❑ *I only wish he were here now that things are getting better for me.* ◼ ADV [ADV to-inf] You can use **only** before an infinitive to introduce an event which happens immediately after one you have just mentioned, and which is surprising or unfortunate. ❑ *Ron tried the embassy, only to be told that Hugh was in a meeting.* ◼ ADV You can use **only** to emphasize how appropriate a certain course of action or type of behavior is. [EMPHASIS] ❑ *It's only fair to let her know that you intend to apply.* ◼ ADV [ADV before v] You can use **only** in front of a verb to indicate that the result of something is unfortunate or undesirable and is likely to make the situation worse rather than better. ❑ *The embargo would only hurt innocent civilians.*

② **only** ♦♦♦ /oʊnli/ ◼ CONJ **Only** can be used to add a comment which slightly changes or limits what you have just said. [INFORMAL] ❑ *It's just as dramatic as a movie, only it's real.* ❑ *It's a bit like my house, only nicer.* ◼ CONJ **Only** can be used after a clause with 'would' to indicate why something is not done. [SPOKEN] ❑ *I'd invite you to come with me, only it's such a long way.*

③ **only** ♦♦♦ /oʊnli/ ◼ PHRASE If you say you **only have to** do one thing in order to achieve or prove a second thing, you are emphasizing how easily the second thing can be achieved or proved. [EMPHASIS] ❑ *Any time you want a babysitter, dear, you only have to ask.* ◼ PHRASE You can say that something has **only just** happened when you want to emphasize that it happened a very short time ago. [EMPHASIS] ❑ *I've only just arrived.* ◼ PHRASE You use **only just** to emphasize that something is true, but by such a small degree that it is almost not true at all. [EMPHASIS] ❑ *For centuries farmers there have only just managed to survive.* ❑ *I am old enough to remember the War, but only just.* ◼ PHRASE You can use **only too** to emphasize that something is true or exists to a much greater extent than you would expect or like. [EMPHASIS] ❑ *I know only too well that plans can easily go wrong.* ◼ PHRASE You can say that you are **only too** happy to do something to emphasize how willing you are to do it. [EMPHASIS] ❑ *I'll be only too pleased to help them out with any questions.* ◼ if only → see if ◼ not only → see not ◼ the one and only → see one ③ ◼ → See feature box at **family**

on-message ADJ [usu v-link ADJ] If a politician is **on-message**, they say something that follows the official policy of their party.

ono|mato|poeia /ɒnəmætəpiə, -mɑtə-/ N-UNCOUNT **Onomatopoeia** refers to the use of words which sound like the noise they refer to. 'Hiss,' 'buzz,' and 'rat-a-tat-tat' are examples of onomatopoeia. [TECHNICAL]

VOCABULARY IN CONTEXT

Onomatopoeia

'Onomatopoeia' refers to words which, when spoken aloud, sound similar to the noise they describe. Some of the most common examples of onomatopoeia describe animal noises, such as '**meow**' for the sound of a cat, or '**woof**' for the sound a dog makes. Words that describe nature are also often onomatopoeic. For example, rain may **drip** or **splash**, a stream can **babble** or **murmur**, and waves may **crash** or **slap** onto the shore. Fires can **crackle**, **fizzle**, **spit**, or **sputter**, and the wind might **whisper**, **howl**, or **roar**.

Onomatopoeia is common in literature and poetry, and, used sparingly, can bring your writing alive.

---

ono|mato|poe|ic /ɒnəmætəpiːɪk, -mɑtə-/ ADJ **Onomatopoeic** words sound like the noise they refer to. 'Hiss,' 'buzz,' and 'rat-a-tat-tat' are examples of onomatopoeic words. [TECHNICAL]

on-ramp (on-ramps) N-COUNT An **on-ramp** is a road which cars use to drive onto a highway. [AM] ❑ *The expressway on-ramp lay just ahead.*

on|rush /ɒnrʌʃ/ N-SING [usu N *of* n] The **onrush** of something is its sudden development, which happens so quickly and forcefully that you are unable to control it. ❑ *The onrush of tears took me by surprise.* ❑ *She was screwing up her eyes against the onrush of air.*

on|rush|ing /ɒnrʌʃɪŋ/ ADJ [ADJ n] **Onrushing** describes something such as a vehicle that is moving forward so quickly or forcefully that it would be very difficult to stop. ❑ *He was killed by an onrushing locomotive.* ❑ *...the roar of the onrushing water.*

on-screen also **onscreen** **1** ADJ [ADJ n] **On-screen** means appearing on the screen of a television, movie theater, or computer. ❑ *Read the on-screen lyrics and sing along.* **2** ADJ [ADJ n] **On-screen** means relating to the roles played by film or television actors, in contrast with their real lives. ❑ *...her first on-screen kiss.* • ADV [ADV with cl] **On-screen** is also an adverb. ❑ *He was immensely attractive, on-screen and off-screen.*

on|set /ɒnset/ N-SING The **onset** of something is the beginning of it, used especially to refer to something unpleasant. ❑ *Most of the passes have been closed with the onset of winter.*

on|shore /ɒnʃɔr/ ADJ **Onshore** means happening on land, rather than at sea. ❑ *...Western Europe's biggest onshore oilfield.* • ADV [ADV after v] **Onshore** is also an adverb. ❑ *They missed the ferry and remained onshore.*

on|side /ɒnsaɪd/ **1** ADJ In games such as soccer and hockey, when an attacking player is **onside**, they have not broken the rules because at least two players from the opposing team are between them and the goal when the ball is passed to them. **2** ADJ [v-link ADJ] If a person or group of people is **onside**, they support you and agree with what you are doing. [BRIT]

in AM, use **on board**

on-site → see site

on|slaught /ɒnslɔt/ (onslaughts) **1** N-COUNT An **onslaught** on someone or something is a very violent, forceful attack against them. ❑ *The press launched another vicious onslaught on the president.* **2** N-COUNT If you refer to an **onslaught** of something, you mean that there is a large amount of it, often so that it is very difficult to deal with. ❑ *...the constant onslaught of ads on TV.*

on|stage /ɒnsteɪdʒ/ ADV When someone such as an actor or musician goes **onstage**, they go onto the stage in a theater to give a performance. ❑ *When she walked onstage she was given a standing ovation.*

on-the-job → see job

on-the-spot ADJ [ADJ n] **On-the-spot** things are done immediately and at the place where you are. ❑ *Rail travelers who try to avoid paying their fares could face on-the-spot fines.*

onto ✦✧ /ɒntu/

The spelling **on to** is also used.

In addition to the uses shown below, **onto** is used in phrasal verbs such as 'hold onto' and 'latch onto.'

1 PREP If something moves **onto** or is put **onto** an object or surface, it is then on that object or surface. ❑ *I took my bags inside, lowered myself onto the bed and switched on the TV.* **2** PREP You can sometimes use **onto** to mention the place or area that someone moves into. ❑ *The players jogged onto the field.* ❑ *At exactly 6:00 p.m., Marcia drove onto the freeway.* **3** PREP You can use **onto** to introduce the place toward which a light or someone's look is directed. ❑ *...the metal part of the door onto which the sun had been shining.* ❑ *The colors rotated around on a disc and were reflected onto the wall behind.* **4** PREP [v PREP n] If a door or room opens **onto** a place, that place is directly in front of it. ❑ *The door opened onto a well-lit hallway.* **5** PREP When you change the position of your body, you use **onto** to introduce the part of your body which is now supporting you. ❑ *As he stepped backwards she fell onto her knees, then onto her face.* ❑ *Puffing a little, Mabel shifted her weight onto her feet.* **6** PREP When you get **onto** a bus, train, or plane, you enter it in order to travel somewhere. ❑ *As he got on to the plane, he asked me how I was feeling.* **7** PREP **Onto** is used after verbs such as 'hold,' 'hang,' and 'cling' to indicate what someone is holding firmly or where something is being held firmly. ❑ *The reflector is held onto the sides of the spacecraft with a frame.* **8** PREP If people who are talking get **onto** a different subject, they begin talking about it. ❑ *Let's get on to more important matters.* **9** PREP You can sometimes use **onto** to indicate that something or someone becomes included as a part of a list or system. ❑ *The Macedonian question had failed to get on to the agenda.* ❑ *The pill itself has changed a lot since it first came onto the market.* **10** PREP [be PREP n] If someone **is onto** something, they are about to discover something important. [INFORMAL] ❑ *He leaned across the table and whispered to me, "I'm really onto something."* **11** PREP [be PREP n] If someone **is onto** you, they have discovered that you are doing something illegal or wrong. [INFORMAL] ❑ *I had told people what he had been doing, so now the police were onto him.*

on|tol|ogy /ɒntɒlədʒi/ N-UNCOUNT **Ontology** is the branch of philosophy that deals with the nature of existence. [TECHNICAL] • **on|to|logi|cal** /ɒntᵊlɒdʒɪkᵊl/ ADJ [usu ADJ n] ❑ *...the ontological question of the relationship between mind and body.*

onus /oʊnəs/ N-SING If you say that the **onus** is on someone to do something, you mean it is their duty or responsibility to do it. [FORMAL] ❑ *The onus is on companies and consumers to keep up with anti-virus updates.*

on|ward /ɒnwərd/

The form **onwards** can also be used as an adverb.

1 ADJ **Onward** means moving forward or continuing a journey. ❑ *American Airlines have two flights a day to Bangkok, and there are onward flights to Phnom Penh.* • ADV [ADV after v] **Onward** is also an adverb. ❑ *The bus continued onward.* **2** ADJ **Onward** means developing, progressing, or becoming more important over a period of time. ❑ *...the onward march of progress in the aircraft industry.* • ADV [ADV after v] **Onward** is also an adverb. ❑ *From here, it has been onward and upward all the way.* **3** ADV [from n ADV] If something happens from a particular time **onward** or **onwards**, it begins to happen at that time and continues to happen afterward. ❑ *From the turn of the century onward, she shared the life of the aborigines.*

onyx /ɒnɪks/ **1** N-UNCOUNT **Onyx** is a stone which can be various colors. It is used for making ornaments, jewelry, or furniture. **2** → See also color supplement

oo /u/ → see ooh

oodles /uːdᵊlz/ QUANT If you say that there are **oodles of** something, you are emphasizing that there is a very large quantity of it. [INFORMAL, EMPHASIS] ❑ *She's made oodles of money in investments.*

ooh /u/ also **oo** EXCLAM People say '**ooh**' when they are surprised, looking forward to something, or find something pleasant or unpleasant. [INFORMAL, FEELINGS] ❑ *All he wants is to give people food and hear them say "Ooh, that's so good."* ❑ *"Ooh, that hurts."*

oomph /ʊmf/ N-UNCOUNT If you say that someone or something has **oomph**, you mean that they are energetic and exciting. [INFORMAL, APPROVAL] ❑ *"There's no buzz, there's no oomph about the place," he complained.*

oops /ʊps, uːps/ EXCLAM You say '**oops**' to indicate that there has been a slight accident or mistake, or to apologize to someone for it. [INFORMAL, FEELINGS] ❑ *Today they're saying, "Oops, we made a mistake."*

ooze /uːz/ (oozes, oozing, oozed) **1** V-T/V-I When a thick or sticky liquid **oozes** from something or when something **oozes** it, the liquid flows slowly and in small quantities. ❑ *Blood was still oozing from the wound.* ❑ *The lava will just ooze gently out of the crater.* **2** V-T/V-I If you say that someone or something **oozes** a quality or characteristic, or **oozes** with it, you mean that they show it very strongly. ❑ *The Southern plantation house oozes charm.*

op /ɒp/ (ops) N-COUNT [usu pl] **Ops** are military operations. ❑ *Flt Lt Beamont had completed a 200 hour tour of ops in December 1941.*

op. In music, **op.** is a written abbreviation for **opus**. ❑ *...Beethoven's Op. 101 and 111 sonatas.*

opac|ity /oʊpæsɪti/ **1** N-UNCOUNT **Opacity** is the quality of being difficult to see through. [FORMAL] ❑ *Opacity of the eye lens can be induced by deficiency of certain vitamins.* **2** N-UNCOUNT If you refer to something's **opacity**, you mean that it is difficult to understand. [FORMAL] ☐ ...a stupefying verbal opacity.

opal /ˈoʊpəl/ (**opals**) **1** N-VAR An **opal** is a precious stone. Opals are colorless or white, but other colors are reflected in them. **2** → See also color supplement

opal|es|cent /ˌoʊpəˈlɛsənt/ ADJ **Opalescent** means colorless or white like an opal, or changing color like an opal. [LITERARY] ☐ Elaine turned her opalescent eyes on him. ☐ ...a sky which was still faintly opalescent. • **opal|es|cence** N-UNCOUNT ☐ The sunset was making great splashes of fiery opalescence across the sky.

opaque /oʊˈpeɪk/ **1** ADJ If an object or substance is **opaque**, you cannot see through it. ☐ You can always use opaque glass if you need to block a street view. **2** ADJ If you say that something is **opaque**, you mean that it is difficult to understand. ☐ ...the opaque language of the inspector's reports.

op. cit. /ˌɒp ˈsɪt/ In reference books, **op. cit.** is used after an author's name to refer to a book of theirs which has already been mentioned. [FORMAL] ☐ ...quoted in Iyer, op. cit., p. 332.

OPEC /ˈoʊpɛk/ N-PROPER **OPEC** is an organization of countries that produce oil. It tries to develop a common policy and system of prices. OPEC is an abbreviation for 'Organization of Petroleum-Exporting Countries.' ☐ Each member of OPEC would seek to maximize its own production.

op-ed /ˌɒp ˈɛd/ ADJ [ADJ n] In a newspaper, the **op-ed** page is a page containing articles in which people express their opinions about things. [AM, INFORMAL]

OPEN
① DESCRIBING A POSITION OR MOVEMENT
② ACCESSIBLE OR AVAILABLE; NOT HIDDEN, BLOCKED, ETC.
③ BEGIN, START
④ PHRASES AND PHRASAL VERBS
---

① **open** ♦♦♦ /ˈoʊpən/ (**opens, opening, opened**) **1** V-T/V-I If you **open** something such as a door, window, or lid, or if it **opens**, its position is changed so that it no longer covers a hole or gap. ☐ He opened the window and looked out. • ADJ **Open** is also an adjective. ☐ ...an open window. **2** V-T If you **open** something such as a bottle, box, parcel, or envelope, you move, remove, or cut part of it so you can take out what is inside. ☐ I opened the letter. • ADJ **Open** is also an adjective. ☐ ...an open bottle of milk. • PHRASAL VERB **Open up** means the same as **open**. ☐ He opened up a cage and lifted out a 6ft python. **3** V-T/V-I If you **open** something such as a book, an umbrella, or your hand, or if it **opens**, the different parts of it move away from each other so that the inside of it can be seen. ☐ He opened the heavy Bible. ☐ The flower opens to reveal a bee. • ADJ **Open** is also an adjective. ☐ Without warning, Bardo smacked his fist into his open hand. • PHRASAL VERB **Open out** means the same as **open**. ☐ Keith took a map from the dashboard and opened it out on his knees. **4** V-T If you **open** a computer file, you give the computer an instruction to display it on the screen. [COMPUTING] ☐ Double click on the icon to open the file. **5** V-T/V-I When you **open** your eyes or your eyes **open**, you move your eyelids upward, for example, when you wake up, so that you can see. ☐ When I opened my eyes I saw Melissa standing at the end of my bed. • ADJ **Open** is also an adjective. ☐ As soon as he saw that her eyes were open he sat up. **6** V-T If you **open** your arms, you stretch them wide apart in front of you, usually in order to put them around someone. ☐ She opened her arms and gave me a big hug. **7** V-T If you **open** your shirt or coat, you undo the buttons or pull down the zipper. ☐ I opened my coat and let him see the belt. • ADJ [ADJ n, v-link ADJ] **Open** is also an adjective. ☐ ...dressing informally in open shirt and cowboy boots.

USAGE
open
Opened is the past tense and past participle of the verb **open**. You only use it when you are describing the action of opening something. For example, 'A tall man *opened* the front door.' Don't describe the position of a door by saying that it 'is opened.' Say that it 'is open.' *The door was open, and the sunshine streamed in.*
---

② **open** ♦♦♦ /ˈoʊpən/ (**opens, opening, opened**) **1** V-T/V-I If people **open** something such as a blocked road or a border, or if it **opens**, people can then pass along it or through it. ☐ The rebels have opened the road to the capital. • ADJ **Open** is also an adjective. ☐ We were part of an entire regiment that had nothing else to do but to keep that highway open. • PHRASAL VERB **Open up** means the same as **open**. ☐ As rescue workers opened up roads today, it became apparent that some small towns were totally devastated. **2** V-I If a place **opens** into another, larger place, you can move from one directly into the other. ☐ The corridor opened into a low smoky room. • PHRASAL VERB **Open out** means the same as **open**. ☐ ...narrow streets opening out into charming squares. **3** ADJ An **open** area is a large area that does not have many buildings or trees in it. ☐ Officers will also continue their search of nearby open ground. **4** ADJ [ADJ n] An **open** structure or object is not covered or enclosed. ☐ Don't leave a child alone in a room with an open fire. **5** V-T/V-I When a store, office, or public building **opens** or **is opened**, its doors are unlocked and the public can go in. ☐ Banks closed on Friday afternoon and did not open again until Monday morning. ☐ I'd been waiting for him to open the shop. • ADJ **Open** is also an adjective. ☐ The gallery is open Monday through Friday, 9 am to 6 pm. **6** V-T/V-I When a public building, factory, or company **opens** or when someone **opens** it, it starts operating for the first time. ☐ The original station opened in 1954. ☐ The complex opens to the public tomorrow. **7** ADJ [v-link ADJ] If a factory or company remains **open**, it continues to operate. ☐ The government says it's no longer willing to spend $170 million a month to keep the pits open. ☐ ...any operating subsidy required to keep the airline open. • **open|ing** (**openings**) N-COUNT ☐ He was there, though, for the official opening. **8** ADJ If you describe a person or their character as **open**, you mean they are honest and do not want or try to hide anything or to deceive anyone. ☐ He had always been open with her and she always felt she would know if he lied. • **open|ness** N-UNCOUNT ☐ ...a relationship based on honesty and openness. **9** ADJ [ADJ n] If you describe a situation, attitude, or way of behaving as **open**, you mean it is not kept hidden or secret. ☐ The action is an open violation of the Vienna Convention. • **open|ness** N-UNCOUNT ☐ ...the new climate of political openness. **10** ADJ [v-link ADJ to n] If you are **open to** suggestions or ideas, you are ready and willing to consider or accept them. ☐ They are open to suggestions on how working conditions might be improved. **11** ADJ [v-link ADJ to n] If you say that a system, person, or idea is **open to** something such as abuse or criticism, you mean they might receive abuse or criticism because of their qualities, effects, or actions. ☐ The system, though well-meaning, is open to abuse. **12** ADJ If you say that a fact or question is **open** to debate, interpretation, or discussion, you mean that people are uncertain whether it is true, what it means, or what the answer is. ☐ Her interpretation of the facts may be open to doubt. **13** ADJ You can use **open** to describe something that anyone is allowed to take part in or accept. ☐ It's an open meeting, everybody's invited. ☐ ...an open invitation. **14** ADJ [v-link ADJ] If something such as an offer or job is **open**, it is available for someone to accept or apply for. ☐ The offer will remain open until further notice. **15** → see also **opening 6 16** ADJ [v-link ADJ to n] If an opportunity or choice **is open to** you, you are able to do a particular thing if you choose to. ☐ There are a wide range of career opportunities open to young people. **17** V-T To **open** opportunities or possibilities means the same as to **open** them **up**. ☐ The Chief of Naval Operations wants to open opportunities for women in the navy.

③ **open** ♦♦♦ /ˈoʊpən/ (**opens, opening, opened**) **1** V-T/V-I If something such as a meeting or series of talks **opens**, or if someone **opens** it, it begins. ☐ ...an emergency session of the Russian Parliament due to open later this morning. • **open|ing** N-SING ☐ ...a statement issued at the opening of the talks. **2** V-T/V-I If an event such as a meeting or discussion **opens** with a particular activity, that activity is the first thing that happens or is dealt with. You can also say that someone such as a speaker or singer **opens** by doing a particular thing. ☐ The service opened with a hymn. ☐ I opened by saying, "Honey, you look sensational." **3** V-I On the stock exchange, the price at which currencies, shares, or commodities **open** is their value at the start of that day's trading. [BUSINESS] ☐ Gold declined $2 in Zurich to open at $385.50. **4** V-I When a movie, play, or other public event **opens**, it begins to be shown, be performed, or take place for a limited period of time. ☐ A photographic exhibition opens at the

Smithsonian on Wednesday. • **open|ing** N-SING [the N of n] ▢ *He is due to attend the opening of the Asian Games on Saturday.* **5** V-T If you **open** an account with a bank or a commercial organization, you begin to use their services. ▢ *He tried to open an account at the branch of his bank nearest to his workplace.*

④ **open** ✦✦✦ /ˈoʊpən/ (opens, opening, opened)
→ Please look at meanings **6** – **14** to see if the expression you are looking for is shown under another headword.
1 PHRASE If you do something **in the open** or **out in the open**, you do it outdoors rather than in a house or other building. ▢ *Many are sleeping in the open because they have no shelter.* **2** PHRASE If an attitude or situation is **in the open** or **out in the open**, people know about it and it is no longer kept secret. ▢ *They had advised us to keep it a secret, but we wanted it out in the open.* **3** PHRASE If something is **wide open**, it is open to its full extent. ▢ *The child had left the inner door wide open.* **4** PHRASE If you say that a competition, race, or election is **wide open**, you mean that anyone could win in it, because there is no competitor who seems to be much better than the others. ▢ *The competition has been thrown wide open by the absence of the world champion.* **5 with open arms** → see **arm** ①   **6 to keep your eyes open** → see **eye** ①   **7 with your eyes open** → see **eye** ①   **8 to open your eyes** → see **eye** ①   **9 to open fire** → see **fire** ②   **10 to open your heart** → see **heart** ②   **11 the heavens open** → see **heaven**   **12 an open mind** → see **mind** ①   **13 to open your mind** → see **mind** ①   **14 to keep your options open** → see **option** **15** → See feature box at **debate**
▶ **open out** → see **open** ① 3, **open** ② 2
▶ **open up** **1** → see **open** ① 2, **open** ② 1   **2** PHRASAL VERB If a place, economy, or area of interest **opens up**, or if someone **opens** it **up**, more people can go there or become involved in it. ▢ *As the market opens up, I think people are going to be able to spend more money on consumer goods.* ▢ *He said he wanted to see how the country was opening up to the world.* **3** PHRASAL VERB If something **opens up** opportunities or possibilities, or if they **open up**, they are created. ▢ *It was also felt that the collapse of the system opened up new possibilities.* **4** PHRASAL VERB When you **open up** a building, you unlock and open the door so that people can get in. ▢ *Several customers were waiting when I arrived to open up the shop.* **5** PHRASAL VERB If someone **opens up**, they start to say exactly what they think or feel. ▢ *Lorna found that people were willing to open up to her.*

open ac|cess also **open-access 1** N-UNCOUNT If people have **open access** to a place or thing, they can go there or use it as much as they like. ▢ *There's 24-hour open access to computers in the library.* **2** ADJ An **open-access** place or thing can be used by anyone. ▢ *Its faculty buildings are well equipped, with banks of open-access computers.*

open-air also **open air 1** ADJ An **open-air** place or event is outside rather than in a building. ▢ *...an open air concert in brilliant sunshine.* **2** N-SING If you are in the **open air**, you are outside rather than in a building. ▢ *We sleep out under the stars, and eat our meals in the open air.*

open-and-shut ADJ [usu ADJ n] If you describe a dispute or a legal case as **open-and-shut**, you mean that is easily decided or solved because the facts are very clear. ▢ *It's an open-and-shut case. The hospital is at fault.*

open|cast /ˈoʊpənkæst/ also **open-cast** ADJ [ADJ n] At an **opencast** mine, the coal, metal, or minerals are near the surface and underground passages are not needed. [BRIT]

in AM, use **strip mine**

open day (open days) N-COUNT An **open day** is a day on which members of the public are encouraged to visit a particular school, university, or other institution to see what it is like. [BRIT]

in AM, use **open house**

open-door also **open door** ADJ [ADJ n] If a country or organization has an **open-door** policy toward people or goods, it allows them to come there freely, without any restrictions. ▢ *...reformers who have advocated an open door economic policy.*
• N-SING **Open door** is also a noun. ▢ *...an open door to further foreign investment.*

open-ended ADJ When people begin an **open-ended** discussion or activity, they do not start with any intention of achieving a particular decision or result. ▢ *...an open-ended commitment to the security of the Gulf.*

open|er /ˈoʊpənər/ (openers) **1** N-COUNT [usu n n] An **opener** is a tool which is used to open containers such as cans or bottles. ▢ *...a can opener.* **2** → see also **eye-opener**

open house (open houses) **1** N-VAR [also N n] An **open house** is a day on which members of the public are encouraged to visit a particular institution or place to see what it is like. [AM] ▢ *A week later, Sara and I attended open house at Ted's school.*

in BRIT, use **open day**

2 N-UNCOUNT If you say that someone keeps **open house**, you mean that they welcome friends or visitors to their house whenever they arrive and allow them to stay for as long as they want to. [BRIT]

open|ing ✦✧ /ˈoʊpənɪŋ/ (openings) **1** ADJ [ADJ n] The **opening** event, item, day, or week in a series is the first one. ▢ *They returned to play in the season's opening game.* **2** N-COUNT The **opening** of something such as a book, play, or concert is the first part of it. ▢ *The opening of the scene depicts Akhnaten and his family in a moment of intimacy.* **3** N-COUNT An **opening** is a hole or empty space through which things or people can pass. ▢ *He squeezed through a narrow opening in the fence.* **4** N-COUNT An **opening** in a forest is a small area where there are no trees or bushes. [mainly AM] ▢ *I glanced down at the beach as we passed an opening in the trees.*

in BRIT, usually use **clearing**

5 N-COUNT An **opening** is a good opportunity to do something, for example, to show people how good you are. ▢ *Her capabilities were always there; all she needed was an opening to show them.* **6** N-COUNT An **opening** is a job that is available. ▢ *We don't have any openings now, but we'll call you if something comes up.* **7** → see also **open** ①, **open** ②, **open** ③, **open** ④ **8** → See feature box at **Olympic Games**

open|ing hours N-PLURAL **Opening hours** are the times during which a shop, bank, library, or bar is open for business. [mainly BRIT]

in AM, use **business hours**

open|ing night (opening nights) **1** N-COUNT The **opening night** of a play or an opera is the first night on which a particular production is performed. **2** → See feature box at **theater**

open|ing time (opening times) **1** N-UNCOUNT [also the N] You can refer to the time that a store, bank, library, or bar opens for business as its **opening time**. ▢ *Shoppers began arriving long before the 10am opening time.* **2** N-PLURAL The **opening times** of a place such as a store, a restaurant, or a museum are the period during which it is open. [BRIT]

in AM, use **business hours**

open let|ter (open letters) N-COUNT An **open letter** is a letter that is published in a newspaper or magazine. It is addressed to a particular person but is intended for the general reader, usually in order to protest or give an opinion about something. ▢ *The Lithuanian parliament also sent an open letter to the United Nations.*

open|ly /ˈoʊpənli/ ADV If you do something **openly**, you do it without hiding any facts or hiding your feelings. ▢ *She openly criticized other athletes.*

open mar|ket N-SING Goods that are bought and sold on **the open market** are advertised and sold to anyone who wants to buy them. [BUSINESS] ▢ *On the open market, this would be worth much more.*

open mic also **open mike** (open mics) N-COUNT An **open mic** is an occasion when members of the public are invited to sing or do comedy. ▢ *...an open mic night.* ▢ *Are you brave enough to sing at the café's Thursday night open mike?*

open-minded ADJ If you describe someone as **open-minded**, you approve of them because they are willing to listen to and consider other people's ideas and suggestions. [APPROVAL] ▢ *He was very open-minded about other people's work.* • **open-mindedness** N-UNCOUNT ▢ *He was praised for his enthusiasm and his open-mindedness.*

open-mouthed ADJ If someone is looking **open-mouthed**, they are staring at something with their mouth wide open because it has shocked, frightened, or excited them. ☐ *They watched almost open-mouthed as the two men came toward them.* ☐ *The finale had 50,000 adults standing in open-mouthed wonderment.*

open-necked also **open-neck** ADJ [ADJ n] An **open-necked** shirt or blouse has no buttons at the top, or does not have the top button buttoned.

open pit (open pits) N-COUNT An **open pit** is a mine where the coal, metal, or minerals are near the surface and underground passages are not needed. [AM]

in BRIT, use **opencast mine**

open-plan ADJ An **open-plan** building, office, or room has no internal walls dividing it into smaller areas. ☐ *The firm's top managers share the same open-plan office.*

open pris|on (open prisons) N-COUNT [oft in names] An **open prison** is a prison where there are fewer restrictions on prisoners than in a normal prison. [BRIT]

in AM, use **minimum security prison**

open ques|tion (open questions) N-COUNT If something is an **open question**, people have different opinions about it and nobody can say which opinion is correct. ☐ *A UN official said he thought it was an open question whether sanctions would do any good.*

open sea|son N-UNCOUNT If you say that it is **open season** on someone or something, you mean that a lot of people are currently criticizing or attacking them. ☐ *"It's open season on smokers," I say.*

open se|cret (open secrets) N-COUNT If you refer to something as an **open secret**, you mean that it is supposed to be a secret, but many people know about it. ☐ *It's an open secret that the security service bugged telephones.*

open source also **open-source** ADJ **Open source** software is software that anyone is allowed to modify without asking permission from the company that developed it. [COMPUTING] ☐ *Supporters say open source software is more secure, cheaper to buy and maintain and easier to customize.*

open-top also **open-topped** ADJ [ADJ n] An **open-top** bus has no roof, so that the people sitting on the top level can see or be seen more easily. An **open-top** car has no roof or has a roof that can be removed. [mainly BRIT]

op|era ♦♦◇ /ɒpərə, ɒprə/ (operas)

Pronounced /ɒpərə/ or /oupərə/ for meaning 3.

1 N-VAR An **opera** is a play with music in which all the words are sung. ☐ *...a one-act opera about contemporary women in America.* ☐ *...an opera singer.* **2** → see also **soap opera** **3** **Opera** is an alternative plural of **opus**.

op|era house (opera houses) N-COUNT; N-IN-NAMES An **opera house** is a theater that is specially designed for the performance of operas. ☐ *...Sydney Opera House.*

op|eran|di /ɒpərændiː/ → see **modus operandi**

op|er|ate ♦♦♦ /ɒpəreɪt/ (operates, operating, operated)
1 V-T/V-I If you **operate** a business or organization, you work to keep it running. If a business or organization **operates**, it carries out its work. ☐ *Until his death in 1986 Greenwood owned and operated an enormous pear orchard.* ☐ *...allowing commercial banks to operate in the country.* ● **op|era|tion** /ɒpəreɪʃən/ N-UNCOUNT ☐ *Company finance is to provide funds for the everyday operation of the business.* **2** V-I The way that something **operates** is the way that it works or has a particular effect. ☐ *Ceiling and wall lights can operate independently.* ☐ *How do accounting records operate?* ● **op|era|tion** N-UNCOUNT ☐ *No money can be spent on the construction and operation of the streetcar.* **3** V-T/V-I When you **operate** a machine or device, or when it **operates**, you make it work. ☐ *A massive rock fall trapped the men as they operated a tunneling machine.* ● **op|era|tion** N-UNCOUNT ☐ *...over 1,000 dials monitoring every aspect of the operation of the airplane.* **4** V-I When surgeons **operate** on a patient in a hospital, they cut open a patient's body in order to remove, replace, or repair a diseased or damaged part. ☐ *In March 2005, surgeons operated on Max for a brain aneurysm.*

SYNONYMS

operate
VERB
1
run: *His stepfather ran a prosperous paint business.*
manage: *Within two years, he was managing the store.*
control: *He now controls the largest retail development empire in southern California.*
2
function: *The machine is functioning normally.*
work: *The pump doesn't work, and we have no running water.*
3
work: *Do you know how to work this washing machine?*
control: *...a computerized system to control the gates.*

---

op|er|at|ic /ɒpərætɪk/ ADJ **Operatic** means relating to opera. ☐ *...the local amateur operatic society.*

op|er|at|ing /ɒpəreɪtɪŋ/ ADJ [ADJ n] **Operating** profits and costs are the money that a company earns and spends in carrying out its ordinary trading activities, in contrast to such things as interest and investment. [BUSINESS] ☐ *The group made operating profits of $80M before interest.*

op|er|at|ing room (operating rooms) N-COUNT An **operating room** is a special room in a hospital where surgeons carry out medical operations.

in BRIT, use **operating theatre**

op|er|at|ing sys|tem (operating systems) **1** N-COUNT The **operating system** of a computer is its most basic program, which it needs in order to function and run other programs. [COMPUTING] ☐ *...Microsoft's Windows operating system.* **2** → See feature box at **computer**

op|er|at|ing ta|ble (operating tables) N-COUNT An **operating table** is a table which a patient in a hospital lies on during a surgical operation.

op|er|at|ing thea|tre (operating theatres) N-COUNT An **operating theatre** is the same as an **operating room**. [BRIT]

op|era|tion ♦♦♦ /ɒpəreɪʃən/ (operations) **1** N-COUNT An **operation** is a highly organized activity that involves many people doing different things. ☐ *The rescue operation began on Friday afternoon.* ☐ *The soldiers were engaged in a military operation close to the Ugandan border.* **2** N-COUNT A business or company can be referred to as an **operation**. [BUSINESS] ☐ *The company's electronics operation employs around 5,000 people.* **3** N-COUNT When a patient has an **operation**, a surgeon cuts open their body in order to remove, replace, or repair a diseased or damaged part. ☐ *Charles was at the clinic recovering from an operation on his arm.* **4** N-UNCOUNT If a system is in **operation**, it is being used. ☐ *...the free banking system that has been in operation since the early eighties.* **5** N-UNCOUNT If a machine or device is in **operation**, it is working. ☐ *There are three ski lifts in operation.* **6** → see also **operative** **7** PHRASE When a rule, system, or plan **comes into operation** or you **put** it **into operation**, you begin to use it. ☐ *The Financial Services Act came into operation four years ago.*

op|era|tion|al /ɒpəreɪʃənəl/ **1** ADJ A machine or piece of equipment that is **operational** is in use or is ready for use. ☐ *The whole system will be fully operational by December.* **2** ADJ **Operational** factors or problems relate to the working of a system, device, or plan. ☐ *The nuclear industry was required to prove that every operational and safety aspect had been fully researched.* ● **op|era|tion|al|ly** ADV ☐ *...goods which are economically or operationally impractical to transport.*

op|era|tive /ɒpərətɪv, -əreɪtɪv/ (operatives) **1** ADJ A system or service that is **operative** is working or having an effect. [FORMAL] ☐ *The commercial telephone service was no longer operative.* **2** N-COUNT An **operative** is a worker, especially one who does work with their hands. [FORMAL] ☐ *In an automated car plant there is not a human operative to be seen.* **3** N-COUNT An **operative** is someone who works for a government agency such as the intelligence service. [mainly AM] ☐ *Naturally the CIA wants to protect its operatives.* **4** PHRASE If you describe a word as **the operative word**, you want to draw attention to it because you think it is important or exactly true in a particular situation. ☐ *As long as the operative word is "greed," you can't count on people keeping the costs down.*

op|era|tor ✦✧✧ /ˈɒpəreɪtər/ (operators) **1** N-COUNT An **operator** is a person who connects telephone calls at a telephone exchange or in a place such as an office or hotel. ❑ *He dialed the operator and put in a call to Rome.* **2** N-COUNT An **operator** is a person who is employed to operate or control a machine. ❑ *...computer operators.* **3** N-COUNT An **operator** is a person or a company that runs a business. [BUSINESS] ❑ *...the nation's largest cable TV operator.* **4** N-COUNT If you call someone a smooth or shrewd **operator**, you mean that they are skillful at achieving what they want, often in a slightly dishonest way. [INFORMAL] ❑ *He is a smooth operator. Don't underestimate him.* **5** → See feature box at **telephone**

COLLOCATIONS

operator
NOUN
2
noun + **operator**: computer, machine, train
adjective + **operator**: experienced, skilled
3
noun + **operator**: hotel, network

---

op|er|et|ta /ˌɒpəˈrɛtə/ (operettas) N-VAR An **operetta** is a light-hearted opera which has some of the words spoken rather than sung.

-ophile /-əfaɪl/ (-ophiles) SUFFIX → see **-phile**

-ophobe /-əfoʊb/ (-ophobes) SUFFIX → see **-phobe**

-ophobia /-əˈfoʊbiə/ SUFFIX → see **-phobia**

-ophobic /-əˈfoʊbɪk/ SUFFIX → see **-phobic**

oph|thal|mic /ɒfˈθælmɪk/ ADJ [ADJ n] **Ophthalmic** means relating to or concerned with the medical care of people's eyes. [FORMAL] ❑ *Ophthalmic surgeons are now performing laser surgery to correct myopia.*

oph|thal|molo|gist /ˌɒfθælˈmɒlədʒɪst/ (ophthalmologists) N-COUNT An **ophthalmologist** is a medical doctor who specializes in diseases and problems affecting people's eyes.

oph|thal|mol|ogy /ˌɒfθælˈmɒlədʒi/ N-UNCOUNT **Ophthalmology** is branch of medicine concerned with people's eyes and the problems that affect them.

opi|ate /ˈoʊpiɪt/ (opiates) N-COUNT An **opiate** is a drug that contains opium. Opiates are used to reduce pain or to help people to sleep.

opine /oʊˈpaɪn/ (opines, opining, opined) V-T/V-I To **opine** means to express your opinion. [FORMAL] ❑ *"A house is a machine for living," opined Le Corbusier.* ❑ *He opined that the navy would need to start again from the beginning.*

opin|ion ✦✦✧ /əˈpɪnyən/ (opinions) **1** N-COUNT Your **opinion** about something is what you think or believe about it. ❑ *I wasn't asking for your opinion, Mike.* ❑ *He held the opinion that a government should think before introducing a tax.* **2** N-SING Your **opinion** of someone is your judgment of their character or ability. ❑ *That improved Mrs. Goole's already favorable opinion of him.* **3** N-UNCOUNT You can refer to the beliefs or views that people have as **opinion**. ❑ *Some, I suppose, might even be in positions to influence opinion.* **4** N-COUNT An **opinion** from an expert is the advice or judgment that they give you in the subject that they know a lot about. ❑ *Even if you have had a regular physical check-up recently, you should still seek a medical opinion.* **5** → see also **public opinion**, **second opinion** **6** PHRASE You add expressions such as '**in my opinion**' or '**in their opinion**' to a statement in order to indicate that it is what you or someone else thinks, and is not necessarily a fact. ❑ *The book is, in Henry's opinion, the best book on the subject.* **7** PHRASE If someone is **of the opinion** that something is the case, that is what they believe. [FORMAL] ❑ *Frank is of the opinion that Romero should have won.*

COLLOCATIONS

opinion
NOUN
1
adjective + **opinion**: objective, subjective; humble, strong; informed, valid; forthright, honest
verb + **opinion**: express, voice
opinion + verb: differ, vary

4
verb + **opinion**: divide, polarize, split
opinion + verb: shift, swing
adjective + **opinion**: legal, medical, scientific

opin|ion|at|ed /əˈpɪnyəneɪtɪd/ ADJ If you describe someone as **opinionated**, you mean that they have very strong opinions and refuse to accept that they may be wrong. ❑ *Sue is the extrovert in the family; opinionated, talkative and passionate about politics.*

opin|ion mak|er (opinion makers) N-COUNT **Opinion makers** are people who have a lot of influence over what the public thinks about things.

opin|ion poll (opinion polls) N-COUNT An **opinion poll** involves asking people's opinions on a particular subject, especially one concerning politics. ❑ *Nearly three-quarters of people questioned in an opinion poll agreed with the government's decision.*

opium /ˈoʊpiəm/ N-UNCOUNT **Opium** is a powerful drug made from the seeds of a type of poppy. Opium is used in medicines that relieve pain or help someone sleep.

opos|sum /əˈpɒsəm/ (opossums) N-VAR An **opossum** is a small animal that lives in America and Australia. It carries its young in a pouch on its body, and has thick fur and a long hairless tail.

op|po|nent ✦✧✧ /əˈpoʊnənt/ (opponents) **1** N-COUNT A politician's **opponents** are other politicians who belong to a different party or who have different aims or policies. ❑ *...Mr. Kennedy's opponent in the leadership contest.* **2** N-COUNT In a sports contest, your **opponent** is the person who is playing against you. ❑ *Norris twice knocked down his opponent in the early rounds of the fight.* **3** N-COUNT The **opponents** of an idea or policy do not agree with it and do not want it to be carried out. ❑ *...opponents of the spread of nuclear weapons.* **4** → See feature box at **competition**

SYNONYMS

opponent
NOUN **1**
adversary: *His political adversaries were creating trouble for him.*
rival: *He eliminated his rivals in a brutal struggle for power.*
enemy: *The Government's political enemies were quick to pick up on this mishap.*
opposition: *The main opposition parties boycotted the election.*

---

op|por|tune /ˌɒpərˈtun/ ADJ If something happens at an **opportune** time or is **opportune**, it happens at the time that is most convenient for someone or most likely to lead to success. [FORMAL] ❑ *I believe that I have arrived at a very opportune moment.* ❑ *The timing of the meetings was opportune.*

op|por|tun|ism /ˌɒpərˈtunɪzəm/ N-UNCOUNT If you refer to someone's behavior as **opportunism**, you are criticizing them for taking advantage of any opportunity that occurs in order to gain money or power, without thinking about whether their actions are right or wrong. [DISAPPROVAL] ❑ *The senator responded by saying that the opposition's concern for the environment was political opportunism.*

op|por|tun|ist /ˌɒpərˈtunɪst/ (opportunists) ADJ If you describe someone as **opportunist**, you are critical of them because they take advantage of any situation in order to gain money or power, without considering whether their actions are right or wrong. [DISAPPROVAL] ❑ *...corrupt and opportunist politicians.* ● N-COUNT An **opportunist** is someone who is opportunist. ❑ *Like most successful politicians, Sinclair was an opportunist.*

op|por|tun|is|tic /ˌɒpərtuˈnɪstɪk/ ADJ If you describe someone's behavior as **opportunistic**, you are critical of them because they take advantage of situations in order to gain money or power, without thinking about whether their actions are right or wrong. [DISAPPROVAL] ❑ *Many of the party's members joined only for opportunistic reasons.*

op|por|tu|nity ✦✦✧ /ˌɒpərˈtuniti/ (opportunities) N-VAR An **opportunity** is a situation in which it is possible for you to do something that you want to do. ❑ *I had an opportunity to go to New York and study.* ❑ *...equal opportunities in employment.*

> **SYNONYMS**
>
> **opportunity**
> NOUN
> **chance:** *The electoral council announced that all eligible people would get a chance to vote.*
> **opening:** *Her capabilities were always there; all she needed was an opening to show them.*
> **possibility:** *There were several possibilities open to each manufacturer.*

op|pose ✦✧✧ /əp<u>ou</u>z/ (**opposes**, **opposing**, **opposed**) V-T If you **oppose** someone or **oppose** their plans or ideas, you disagree with what they want to do and try to prevent them from doing it. ☐ *Mr. Taylor was not bitter toward those who had opposed him.*

op|posed ✦✧✧ /əp<u>ou</u>zd/ **1** ADJ [v-link ADJ to n/-ing] If you **are opposed to** something, you disagree with it or disapprove of it. ☐ *I am utterly opposed to any form of terrorism.* **2** ADJ You say that two ideas or systems are **opposed** when they are opposite to each other or very different from each other. ☐ *...people with policies almost diametrically opposed to his own.* **3** PHRASE You use **as opposed to** when you want to make it clear that you are talking about one particular thing and not something else. ☐ *We ate in the restaurant, as opposed to the bistro.*

> **SYNONYMS**
>
> **opposed**
> ADJ
> **1**
> **hostile:** *Many people felt he would be hostile to the idea of foreign intervention.*
> **averse:** *He's not averse to publicity, of the right kind.*
> **2**
> **conflicting:** *There are conflicting reports about the identity of the hostage.*
> **opposing:** *I have a friend who has the opposing view and felt that the war was immoral.*
> **contrary:** *This view is contrary to the aims of critical social research for a number of reasons.*

op|pos|ing /əp<u>ou</u>zɪŋ/ **1** ADJ [ADJ n] **Opposing** ideas or tendencies are totally different from each other. ☐ *I have a friend who has the opposing view and felt that the war was immoral.* **2** ADJ [ADJ n] **Opposing** groups of people disagree about something or are in competition with one another. ☐ *The Georgian leader said in a radio broadcast that he still favored dialogue between the opposing sides.* **3** → See feature box at **conflict**

op|po|site ✦✧✧ /<u>ɒ</u>pəzɪt/ (**opposites**) **1** PREP If one thing is **opposite** another, it is on the other side of a space from it. ☐ *Jennie had sat opposite her at breakfast.* • ADV **Opposite** is also an adverb. ☐ *He looked up at the buildings opposite, but could see no open window.* **2** ADJ [ADJ n] The **opposite** side or part of something is the side or part that is furthest away from you. ☐ *...the opposite corner of the room.* **3** ADJ **Opposite** is used to describe things of the same kind which are completely different in a particular way. For example, north and south are opposite directions, and winning and losing are opposite results in a game. ☐ *All the cars driving in the opposite direction had their headlights on.* **4** N-COUNT The **opposite** of someone or something is the person or thing that is most different from them. ☐ *Ritter was a very complex man but Marius was the opposite, a simple farmer.* ☐ *Well, whatever he says, you can bet he's thinking the opposite.*

op|po|site num|ber (**opposite numbers**) N-COUNT Your **opposite number** is a person who has the same job or rank as you, but works in a different department, firm, or organization. [mainly BRIT, JOURNALISM]

> in AM, usually use **counterpart**

op|po|site sex N-SING If you are talking about men and refer to **the opposite sex**, you mean women. If you are talking about women and refer to **the opposite sex**, you mean men. ☐ *Body language can also be used to attract members of the opposite sex.*

op|po|si|tion ✦✦✧ /<u>ɒ</u>pəzɪʃ^ən/ (**oppositions**) **1** N-UNCOUNT **Opposition** is strong, angry, or violent disagreement and disapproval. ☐ *There is bitter opposition from local business to the plan.* **2** N-COUNT-COLL The **opposition** is the political parties or groups that are opposed to a government. ☐ *The main opposition parties boycotted the election, saying it would not be conducted fairly.* **3** N-COUNT-COLL In countries with a parliament, such as Britain, the **opposition** refers to the politicians or political parties that form part of the parliament, but are not the government. ☐ *...the Leader of the Opposition.* **4** N-SING-COLL The **opposition** is the person or team you are competing against in a sports event. ☐ *The coach says his team is not underestimating the opposition.*

> **SYNONYMS**
>
> **opposition**
> NOUN **1**
> **resistance:** *Calls for cuts in agricultural export subsidies are meeting resistance.*
> **hostility:** *There is hostility among traditionalists to this method of teaching history.*
> **disapproval:** *His action had been greeted with almost universal disapproval.*

op|press /əpr<u>ɛ</u>s/ (**oppresses**, **oppressing**, **oppressed**) V-T To **oppress** people means to treat them cruelly, or to prevent them from having the same opportunities, freedom, and benefits as others. ☐ *These people often are oppressed by the governments of the countries they find themselves in.*

op|pressed /əpr<u>ɛ</u>st/ ADJ People who are **oppressed** are treated cruelly or are prevented from having the same opportunities, freedom, and benefits as others. ☐ *Before they took power, they felt oppressed by the rich elitists who controlled things.* • N-PLURAL **The oppressed** are people who are oppressed. ☐ *...a sense of community with the poor and oppressed.*

op|pres|sion /əpr<u>ɛ</u>ʃ^ən/ N-UNCOUNT **Oppression** is the cruel or unfair treatment of a group of people. ☐ *...an attempt to escape political oppression.*

op|pres|sive /əpr<u>ɛ</u>sɪv/ **1** ADJ If you describe a society, its laws, or customs as **oppressive**, you think they treat people cruelly and unfairly. ☐ *The new laws will be just as oppressive as those they replace.* **2** ADJ If you describe the weather or the atmosphere in a room as **oppressive**, you mean that it is unpleasantly hot and damp. ☐ *The oppressive afternoon heat had tired him out.* **3** ADJ An **oppressive** situation makes you feel depressed and uncomfortable. ☐ *...the oppressive sadness that weighed upon him like a physical pain.*

op|pres|sor /əpr<u>ɛ</u>sər/ (**oppressors**) N-COUNT [oft with poss] An **oppressor** is a person or group of people that is treating another person or group of people cruelly or unfairly. ☐ *Lacking leadership, they could organize no defense against their oppressors.*

op|pro|brium /əpr<u>ou</u>briəm/ N-UNCOUNT **Opprobrium** is open criticism or disapproval of something that someone has done. [FORMAL] ☐ *His political opinions have attracted the opprobrium of the Left.*

opt ✦✧✧ /<u>ɒ</u>pt/ (**opts**, **opting**, **opted**) V-T/V-I If you **opt for** something, or **opt** to do something, you choose it or decide to do it in preference to anything else. ☐ *Depending on your circumstances you can opt for one method or the other.*
▶ **opt out** PHRASAL VERB If you **opt out** of something, you choose to be no longer involved in it. ☐ *The rich can opt out of the public school system.*

op|tic /<u>ɒ</u>ptɪk/ **1** ADJ [ADJ n] **Optic** means relating to the eyes or to sight. ☐ *The optic nerve is a part of the brain.* **2** → See also color supplement

op|ti|cal /<u>ɒ</u>ptɪk^əl/ ADJ **Optical** devices, processes, and effects involve or relate to vision, light, or images. ☐ *...optical telescopes.* ☐ *...an optical scanner.*

op|ti|cal fi|ber (**optical fibers**)

> in BRIT, use **optical fibre**

N-VAR An **optical fiber** is a very thin thread of glass inside a protective coating. Optical fibers are used to carry information in the form of light.

op|ti|cal il|lu|sion (**optical illusions**) N-COUNT An **optical illusion** is something that tricks your eyes so that what you think you see is different from what is really there. ☐ *Sloping walls on the bulk of the building create an optical illusion.*

op|ti|cian /ɒptɪʃ³n/ (**opticians**) **1** N-COUNT An **optician** is someone whose job is to make and sell glasses and contact lenses. **2** N-COUNT An **optician** is someone whose job is to test people's eyesight. [BRIT]

> in AM, use **optometrist**

3 N-COUNT An **optician** is a store where you can have your eyes tested and buy glasses and contact lenses. **4** → See feature box at **eyesight**

op|tics /ɒptɪks/ **1** N-UNCOUNT **Optics** is the branch of science concerned with vision, sight, and light. **2** → see also **fiber optics**

op|ti|mal /ɒptɪm³l/ → see **optimum**

op|ti|mism /ɒptɪmɪzəm/ N-UNCOUNT **Optimism** is the feeling of being hopeful about the future or about the success of something in particular. ❏ *The Indian prime minister has expressed optimism about India's future relations with the U.S.*

op|ti|mist /ɒptɪmɪst/ (**optimists**) N-COUNT An **optimist** is someone who is hopeful about the future. ❏ *He has the upbeat manner of an eternal optimist.*

op|ti|mis|tic ✦◇◇ /ɒptɪmɪstɪk/ ADJ Someone who is **optimistic** is hopeful about the future or the success of something in particular. ❏ *The president says she is optimistic that an agreement can be worked out soon.* ● **op|ti|mis|ti|cal|ly** ADV [ADV with v] ❏ *Both sides have spoken optimistically about the talks.*

SYNONYMS

optimistic
ADJ
hopeful: *Surgeons were hopeful of saving the sight in Sara's left eye.*
positive: *Be positive about your future and get on with living a normal life.*
bright: *The boy was so bright and animated.*
cheerful: *Jack sounded quite cheerful about the idea.*

---

op|ti|mize /ɒptɪmaɪz/ (**optimizes, optimizing, optimized**)

> in BRIT, also use **optimise**

V-T To **optimize** a plan, system, or machine means to arrange or design it so that it operates as smoothly and efficiently as possible. [FORMAL] ❏ *The new systems have been optimized for running Microsoft Windows.*

op|ti|mum /ɒptɪməm/ also **optimal** ADJ The **optimum** or **optimal** level or state of something is the best level or state that it could achieve. [FORMAL] ❏ *Try to do some physical activity three times a week for optimum health.*

op|tion ✦✦◇ /ɒpʃ³n/ (**options**) **1** N-COUNT An **option** is something that you can choose to do in preference to one or more alternatives. ❏ *He's argued from the start that the US and its allies are putting too much emphasis on the military option.* **2** N-SING If you have the **option** of doing something, you can choose whether to do it or not. ❏ *Criminals are given the option of going to jail or facing public humiliation.* **3** N-COUNT In business, an **option** is an agreement or contract that gives someone the right to buy or sell something such as property or shares at a future date. [BUSINESS] ❏ *Each bank has granted the other an option on 19.9% of its shares.* **4** N-COUNT An **option** is one of a number of subjects which a student can choose to study as a part of his or her course. [mainly BRIT] ❏ *Several options are offered for the student's senior year.* **5** PHRASE If you **keep** your **options open** or **leave** your **options open**, you delay making a decision about something. ❏ *I am keeping my options open; I can decide in a few months.*

COLLOCATIONS

option
NOUN **1**
noun + **option**: career, treatment
adjective + **option**: attractive, cheap, easy, healthy; available, safe, viable
verb + **option**: choose, exercise, select; consider, discuss, explore

---
SYNONYMS

option
NOUN **1**
alternative: *New ways to treat arthritis may provide an alternative to painkillers.*
choice: *You've got three choices: small, medium, or large.*

---

op|tion|al /ɒpʃən³l/ ADJ If something is **optional**, you can choose whether or not you do it or have it. ❏ *Sex education is a sensitive area for some parents, and thus it should remain optional.*

op|tom|etrist /ɒptɒmətrɪst/ (**optometrists**) N-COUNT An **optometrist** is someone whose job is to test people's eyesight to see if they need glasses, and how strong their glasses should be. [mainly AM]

> in BRIT, usually use **optician**

opt-out (**opt-outs**) **1** N-COUNT You can refer to the action of choosing not to be involved in a particular part of an agreement as an **opt-out**. ❏ *...a list of demands, such as opt-outs from some parts of the treaty.* **2** ADJ [ADJ n] An **opt-out** clause in an agreement gives people the choice not to be involved in one part of that agreement. ❏ *...an opt-out clause.*

opu|lent /ɒpyələnt/ ADJ **Opulent** things or places look grand and expensive. [FORMAL] ❏ *Heavy silverplate adds an opulent touch to a formal dinner party.* ● **opu|lence** N-UNCOUNT ❏ *...the elegant opulence of the embassy.*

opus /oʊpəs/ (**opuses** or **opera**) **1** N-COUNT [usu N num] An **opus** is a piece of classical music by a particular composer. **Opus** is usually followed by a number which indicates at what point the piece was written. The abbreviation **op.** is also used. ❏ *...Beethoven's Piano Sonata in E minor, Opus 90.* **2** N-COUNT You can refer to an artistic work such as a piece of music or writing or a painting as an **opus**. ❏ *...the new opus from Peter Gabriel.* **3** → see also **magnum opus**

or ✦✦✦ /ər, STRONG ɔr/
→ Please look at meanings **9** to **12** to see if the expression you are looking for is shown under another headword.

1 CONJ You use **or** to link two or more alternatives. ❏ *"Tea or coffee?" John asked.* ❏ *He said he would try to write or call as soon as he reached the Canary Islands.* **2** CONJ You use **or** to give another alternative, when the first alternative is introduced by 'either' or 'whether.' ❏ *Items like bread, milk and meat were either unavailable or could be obtained only on the black market.* ❏ *Either you can talk to him, or I will.* **3** CONJ You use **or** between two numbers to indicate that you are giving an approximate amount. ❏ *Everyone benefited from limiting their intake of coffee to just one or two cups a day.* ❏ *When I was nine or ten someone explained to me that when you are grown up you have to work.* **4** CONJ You use **or** to introduce a comment which corrects or modifies what you have just said. ❏ *The man was a fool, he thought, or at least incompetent.* **5** CONJ If you say that someone should do something **or** something bad will happen, you are warning them that if they do not do it, the bad thing will happen. ❏ *She had to have the operation, or she would die.* **6** CONJ You use **or** to introduce something which is evidence for the truth of a statement you have just made. ❏ *He must have thought they were worth it or he wouldn't have wasted time on them, I suppose.* **7** PHRASE You use **or not** to emphasize that a particular thing makes no difference to what is going to happen. [EMPHASIS] ❏ *Like it or not, you're in charge.* **8** PHRASE You use **or no** between two occurrences of the same noun in order to say that whether something is true or not makes no difference to a situation. ❏ *The next day, rain or no rain, it was business as usual.* **9 or else** → see **else** **10 or other** → see **other** **11 or so** → see **so** **12 or something** → see **something**

SUFFIX

-or
forms nouns that refer to a person who performs a particular action, often because it is their job. For example, a **sailor** is someone who sails.

---

ora|cle /ɒrək³l/ (**oracles**) N-COUNT In ancient Greece, an **oracle** was a priest or priestess who made statements about future events or about the truth.

oral /ɔrəl/ (**orals**) **1** ADJ **Oral** communication is spoken rather than written. ❏ *...the written and oral traditions of ancient cultures.* ● **oral|ly** ADV [ADV after v] ❏ *...their ability to present ideas orally and in writing.* **2** N-COUNT An **oral** is an examination, especially in a foreign language, that is spoken rather than written. ❏ *I spoke privately to the candidate after the oral.* **3** ADJ You use **oral** to indicate that something is done with a person's mouth or relates to a person's mouth. ❏ *...good oral hygiene.*
● **oral|ly** ADV ❏ *...antibiotic tablets taken orally.*

o|ral his|to|ry (oral histories) N-VAR **Oral history** consists of spoken memories, stories, and songs, and the study of these, as a way of communicating and discovering information about the past.

o|ral sex N-UNCOUNT **Oral sex** is sexual activity involving contact between a person's mouth and their partner's genitals.

or|ange ♦♦◊ /ɔrɪndʒ/ (oranges) **1** COLOR Something that is **orange** is of a color between red and yellow. ◻ ...*men in bright orange uniforms.* **2** N-VAR An **orange** is a round juicy fruit with a thick, orange-colored skin. ◻ ...*orange trees.*

WORD HISTORY

orange
Did you know that the word **orange** comes from the Arabic *naranj*? The initial *n* sound was lost because it got confused with the indefinite article.

---

or|ange blos|som N-UNCOUNT The flowers of the orange tree are called **orange blossom**. Orange blossom is white and is traditionally associated with weddings in Europe and the U.S.

or|ang|ery /ɔrɪndʒri/ (orangeries) N-COUNT An **orangery** is a building with glass walls and roof which is used for growing orange trees and other plants which need to be kept warm.

or|angey /ɔrɪndʒi/ ADJ **Orangey** means slightly orange in color. • COMB IN COLOR **Orangey** is also a combining form. ◻ *The hall is decorated in bright orangey-red with black and gold woodwork.*

orang|utan /ɔræŋutæn/ (orangutans) N-COUNT An **orangutan** is an ape with long reddish hair that comes from Borneo and Sumatra.

ora|tion /ɔreɪʃᵊn/ (orations) N-COUNT [oft supp N] An **oration** is a formal speech made in public. [FORMAL] ◻ ...*a brief funeral oration.*

ora|tor /ɔrətər/ (orators) N-COUNT [oft adj N] An **orator** is someone who is skilled at making formal speeches, especially ones which affect people's feelings and beliefs. ◻ *He was a natural politician, a gifted orator who knew how to work a crowd.*

ora|tori|cal /ɔrətɔrɪkᵊl/ ADJ [ADJ N] **Oratorical** means relating to or using oratory. [FORMAL] ◻ *He reached oratorical heights which left him and some of his players in tears.*

ora|to|rio /ɔrətɔriou/ (oratorios) N-COUNT An **oratorio** is a long piece of music with a religious theme which is written for singers and an orchestra.

ora|tory /ɔrətɔri/ (oratories) **1** N-UNCOUNT **Oratory** is the art of making formal speeches which strongly affect people's feelings and beliefs. [FORMAL] ◻ *He displayed determination as well as powerful oratory.* **2** N-COUNT An **oratory** is a room or building where Christians go to pray. [mainly BRIT]

orb /ɔrb/ (orbs) **1** N-COUNT An **orb** is something that is shaped like a ball, for example, the sun or moon. [LITERARY] ◻ *The moon's round orb would shine high in the sky, casting its velvety light on everything.* **2** N-COUNT An **orb** is a small, ornamental ball with a cross on top that is carried by some kings or queens at important ceremonies.

or|bit /ɔrbɪt/ (orbits, orbiting, orbited) **1** N-COUNT [also in/into N] An **orbit** is the curved path in space that is followed by an object going around and around a planet, moon, or star. ◻ *Mars and Earth have orbits which change with time.* **2** V-T If something such as a satellite **orbits** a planet, moon, or sun, it moves around it in a continuous, curving path. ◻ *In 1957 the Soviet Union launched the first satellite to orbit the earth.* **3** → See feature box at **electricity, space, travel**

or|bit|al /ɔrbɪtᵊl/ **1** ADJ [ADJ N] **Orbital** describes things relating to the orbit of an object in space. ◻ *The newly discovered world followed an orbital path unlike that of any other planet.* **2** ADJ An **orbital** road goes all the way around a large city. [mainly BRIT]

in AM, use **beltway**

or|ca /ɔrkə/ (orcas or orca) N-COUNT An **orca** is a large black and white killer whale.

or|chard /ɔrtʃərd/ (orchards) N-COUNT An **orchard** is an area of land on which fruit trees are grown.

or|ches|tra /ɔrkɪstrə/ (orchestras) **1** N-COUNT An **orchestra** is a large group of musicians who play a variety of different instruments together. Orchestras usually play classical music. ◻ ...*the Los Angeles Philharmonic Orchestra.* **2** → see also **symphony orchestra** **3** N-SING The **orchestra** or the **orchestra seats** in a theater or concert hall are the seats on the first floor directly in front of the stage. [mainly AM] ◻ *With the balcony blocked off, patrons filled most of the orchestra seats.*

in BRIT, usually use **stalls**

or|ches|tral /ɔrkɛstrəl/ ADJ [ADJ N] **Orchestral** means relating to an orchestra and the music it plays. ◻ ...*an orchestral concert.*

or|ches|tra pit N-SING In a theater, the **orchestra pit** is the space reserved for the musicians playing the music for an opera, musical, or ballet, immediately in front of or below the stage.

or|ches|trate /ɔrkɪstreɪt/ (orchestrates, orchestrating, orchestrated) V-T If you say that someone **orchestrates** an event or situation, you mean that they carefully organize it in a way that will produce the result that they want. ◻ *The colonel was able to orchestrate a rebellion from inside an army jail.* • **or|ches|tra|tion** N-UNCOUNT ◻ ...*his skilful orchestration of latent nationalist feeling.*

or|ches|tra|tion /ɔrkɪstreɪʃᵊn/ (orchestrations) N-COUNT An **orchestration** is a piece of music that has been rewritten so that it can be played by an orchestra. ◻ *Mahler's own imaginative orchestration was heard in the same concert.*

or|chid /ɔrkɪd/ (orchids) N-COUNT **Orchids** are plants with brightly colored, unusually shaped flowers.

or|dain /ɔrdeɪn/ (ordains, ordaining, ordained) **1** V-T When someone **is ordained**, they are made a member of the clergy in a religious ceremony. ◻ *He was ordained a Catholic priest in 1982.* ◻ *Women have been ordained for many years in the Presbyterian Church.* **2** V-T If some authority or power **ordains** something, they decide that it should happen or be in existence. [FORMAL] ◻ *Nehru ordained that socialism should rule.* ◻ *His rule was ordained by heaven.*

or|deal /ɔrdil/ (ordeals) N-COUNT If you describe an experience or situation as an **ordeal**, you think it is difficult and stressful. ◻ ...*the painful ordeal of the last eight months.*

ORDER

① SUBORDINATING CONJUNCTION USES
② COMMANDS AND REQUESTS
③ ARRANGEMENTS, SITUATIONS, AND GROUPINGS

---

① **or|der** ♦♦◊ /ɔrdər/ **1** PHRASE If you do something **in order to** achieve a particular thing or **in order that** something can happen, you do it because you want to achieve that thing. ◻ *Most schools are extremely unwilling to cut down on staff in order to cut costs.* **2** PHRASE If someone must be in a particular situation **in order to** achieve something they want, they cannot achieve that thing if they are not in that situation. ◻ *We need to get rid of the idea that we must be liked all the time in order to be worthwhile.* **3** PHRASE If something must happen **in order for** something else to happen, the second thing cannot happen if the first thing does not happen. ◻ *In order for their computers to trace a person's records, they need both the name and address of the individual.*

② **or|der** ♦♦◊ /ɔrdər/ (orders, ordering, ordered)
→ Please look at meaning **12** to see if the expression you are looking for is shown under another headword.

1 V-T If a person in authority **orders** someone to do something, they tell them to do it. ◻ *Williams ordered him to leave.* **2** V-T If someone in authority **orders** something, they give instructions that it should be done. ◻ *The president has ordered a full investigation.* **3** N-COUNT If someone in authority gives you an **order**, they tell you to do something. ◻ *The activists were shot when they refused to obey an order to halt.* ◻ *As darkness fell, Clinton gave orders for his men to rest.* **4** N-COUNT A court **order** is a legal instruction stating that something must be done. ◻ *She has decided not to appeal against a court order banning her from keeping animals.* **5** V-T/V-I When you **order** something that you are going to pay for, you ask for it to be brought to you, sent to you, or obtained for you. ◻ *The couple ordered a new*

order book

set of sterling silver rings from Tiffany for $200 each. ❑ *The waiter appeared. "Are you ready to order?"* **6** N-COUNT An **order** is a request for something to be brought, made, or obtained for you in return for money. ❑ *The city is going to place an order for a hundred and eighty-eight buses.* **7** N-COUNT Someone's **order** is what they have asked to be brought, made, or obtained for them in return for money. ❑ *The waiter returned with their order and Graham signed the bill.* **8** → see also **mail order, postal order** **9** PHRASE Something that is **on order** at a store or factory has been asked for but has not yet been supplied. ❑ *The airlines still have 2,500 new planes on order.* **10** PHRASE If you do something **to order**, you do it whenever you are asked to do it. ❑ *She now makes wonderful dried flower arrangements to order.* **11** PHRASE If you are **under orders** to do something, you have been told to do it by someone in authority. ❑ *I am under orders not to discuss his mission or his location with anyone.* **12** **a tall order** → see **tall**

▶ **order around**

in BRIT, also use **order about**

PHRASAL VERB If you say that someone **is ordering** you **around**, you mean they are telling you what to do as if they have authority over you, and you dislike this. ❑ *When we're out he gets really bossy and starts ordering me around.*

③ **or|der** ✦✧✧ /ɔrdər/ (**orders, ordering, ordered**)

→ Please look at meanings **13** and **18** to see if the expression you are looking for is shown under another headword.

1 N-UNCOUNT [also a N] If a set of things are arranged or done in a particular **order**, they are arranged or done so one thing follows another, often according to a particular factor such as importance. ❑ *Write down (in order of priority) the qualities you'd like to have.* ❑ *Music shops should arrange their recordings in simple alphabetical order, rather than by category.* **2** N-UNCOUNT **Order** is the situation that exists when everything is in the correct or expected place, or happens at the correct or expected time. ❑ *The wish to impose order upon confusion is a kind of intellectual instinct.* **3** N-UNCOUNT **Order** is the situation that exists when people obey the law and do not fight or riot. ❑ *Troops were sent to the islands to restore order last November.* **4** N-SING When people talk about a particular **order**, they mean the way society is organized at a particular time. ❑ *The end of the Cold War has produced the prospect of a new world order based on international co-operation.* **5** V-T The way that something **is ordered** is the way that it is organized and structured. ❑ *...a society which is ordered by hierarchy.* ❑ *We know the French order things differently.* **6** N-COUNT A religious **order** is a group of monks or nuns who live according to a particular set of rules. ❑ *...the Benedictine order of monks.* **7** → see also **law and order** **8** PHRASE If you put or keep something **in order**, you make sure that it is neat or well organized. ❑ *Now he has a chance to put his life back in order.* **9** PHRASE If you think something is **in order**, you think it should happen or be provided. ❑ *Reforms are clearly in order.* **10** PHRASE You use **in the order of** or **on the order of** when mentioning an approximate figure. ❑ *They borrowed something in the order of $10 million.* **11** PHRASE If something is **in good order**, it is in good condition. ❑ *The vessel's safety equipment was not in good order.* **12** PHRASE A machine or device that is **in working order** is functioning properly and is not broken. ❑ *Only half of the spacecraft's six science instruments are still in working order.* **13** PHRASE A machine or device that is **out of order** is broken and does not work. ❑ *Their phone's out of order.* **14** PHRASE If you say that someone or their behavior is **out of order**, you mean that their behavior is unacceptable. [INFORMAL] ❑ *Kent, you're out of order.* **15** **to put your house in order** → see **house** **16** **order of magnitude** → see **magnitude**

SYNONYMS

order
VERB ② **1**
command: *He commanded his troops to attack.*
instruct: *'Go and have a word with her, Ken,' Webb instructed.*
direct: *The Bishop directed the faithful to stay at home.*
NOUN
② **3**
instruction: *They were told to leave, but no reason for this instruction was given.*
ruling: *Goodwin tried to have the court ruling overturned.*
demand: *They rejected the demand to remove U.S. troops.*
decree: *He issued a decree ordering all armed groups to disband.*

---

③ **2**
organization: *The organization of the book is not very well thought-out.*
system: *...a flexible and relatively-efficient filing system.*
arrangement: *...an arrangement of dark-blue armchairs around a coffee table.*
pattern: *A change in the pattern of his breathing became apparent.*
VERB ③ **5**
arrange: *He started to arrange the books in piles.*
group: *The fact sheets are grouped into seven sections.*
sort: *He sorted the materials into their folders.*
organize: *He began to organize his materials.*

---

or|der book (**order books**) N-COUNT When you talk about the state of a company's **order book** or **order books**, you are talking about how many orders for their goods the company has. [BRIT, BUSINESS]

or|dered /ɔrdərd/ ADJ [usu ADJ n] An **ordered** society or system is well-organized and has a clear structure. ❑ *An objective set of rules which we all agree to accept is necessary for any ordered society.*

or|der|ly /ɔrdərli/ (**orderlies**) **1** ADJ If something is done in an **orderly** fashion or manner, it is done in a well-organized and controlled way. ❑ *The organizers guided them in an orderly fashion out of the building.* **2** ADJ Something that is **orderly** is neat or arranged in a neat way. ❑ *It's a beautiful, clean and orderly city.* ● **or|der|li|ness** N-UNCOUNT ❑ *A balance is achieved in the painting between orderliness and unpredictability.* **3** N-COUNT An **orderly** is a person who works in a hospital and does jobs that do not require special medical training. ❑ *For most of his life, he was a hospital orderly.*

or|di|nal num|ber /ɔrdᵊnᵊl nʌmbər/ (**ordinal numbers**) N-COUNT An **ordinal number** or an **ordinal** is a word such as 'first,' 'third,' and 'tenth' that tells you where a particular thing occurs in a sequence of things. Compare **cardinal number**.

or|di|nance /ɔrdᵊnəns/ (**ordinances**) N-COUNT An **ordinance** is an official rule or order, especially from a local government. [FORMAL] ❑ *...ordinances that restrict building development.*

or|di|nari|ly /ɔrdᵊnɛrɪli/ ADV If you say what is **ordinarily** the case, you are saying what is normally the case. ❑ *The streets would ordinarily have been full of people, but now they were empty.*

or|di|nary ✦✧✧ /ɔrdᵊnɛri/ **1** ADJ **Ordinary** people or things are normal and not special or different in any way. ❑ *I strongly suspect that most ordinary people would agree with me.* ❑ *It has 25 calories less than ordinary ice cream.* **2** PHRASE Something that is **out of the ordinary** is unusual or different. ❑ *The boy's knowledge was out of the ordinary.*

or|di|nary shares N-PLURAL **Ordinary shares** are shares in a company that are owned by people who have a right to vote at the company's meetings and to receive part of the company's profits after the holders of preference shares have been paid. Compare **preference shares**. [BRIT, BUSINESS]

in AM, use **common stock**

or|di|na|tion /ɔrdᵊneɪʃᵊn/ (**ordinations**) N-VAR When someone's **ordination** takes place, they are made a minister, priest, or rabbi. ❑ *...supporters of the ordination of women.*

ord|nance /ɔrdnəns/ N-UNCOUNT **Ordnance** refers to military supplies, especially weapons. [FORMAL] ❑ *...a team clearing an area littered with unexploded ordnance.*

ore /ɔr/ (**ores**) N-MASS **Ore** is rock or earth from which metal can be obtained. ❑ *...a huge iron ore mine.*

orega|no /ərɛgənoʊ/ N-UNCOUNT **Oregano** is an herb that is used in cooking.

or|gan /ɔrgən/ (**organs**) **1** N-COUNT An **organ** is a part of your body that has a particular purpose or function, for example, your heart or lungs. ❑ *...damage to the muscles and internal organs.* ❑ *...the reproductive organs.* **2** N-COUNT An **organ** is a large musical instrument with pipes of different lengths through which air is forced. It has keys and pedals like a piano. ❑ *...the church organ.* **3** N-COUNT You refer to a newspaper or organization as the **organ** of the government or another group when it is used by them as a means of giving information or getting things done. ❑ *...according to the People's Daily, the* official organ of the Chinese communist party. ■ → See feature box at **body**, **brain**; See also color supplement

or|gan|dy /ˈɔrgəndi/ also **organdie** N-UNCOUNT [oft N n] Organdy is a thin, slightly stiff cotton fabric.

or|gan grind|er (organ grinders) also **organ-grinder** N-COUNT An **organ grinder** was an entertainer who played a barrel organ in the streets.

or|gan|ic /ɔrˈgænɪk/ ■ ADJ **Organic** methods of farming and gardening do not use pesticides, chemical fertilizers, growth hormones, or antibiotics, so that the food produced does not contain toxic chemicals. ❑ *Organic farming is expanding everywhere.* • **or|gani|cal|ly** ADV ❑ *...organically grown vegetables.* ■ ADJ **Organic** substances are produced by or found in living things. ❑ *Incorporating organic material into chalky soils will reduce the alkalinity.* ■ ADJ **Organic** change or development happens gradually and naturally rather than suddenly. [FORMAL] ❑ *...to manage the company and supervise its organic growth.* ■ → See feature box at **farming**

or|gani|sa|tion|al /ˌɔrgənaɪˈzeɪʃənəl/ [BRIT] → see **organizational**

or|gan|is|er /ˈɔrgənaɪzər/ [BRIT] → see **organizer**

or|gan|ism /ˈɔrgənɪzəm/ (organisms) ■ N-COUNT An **organism** is an animal or plant, especially one that is so small that you cannot see it without using a microscope. ❑ *Not all chemicals normally present in living organisms are harmless.* ■ → See feature box at **ecosystem**, **genetics**

or|gan|ist /ˈɔrgənɪst/ (organists) N-COUNT An **organist** is someone who plays the organ.

or|gani|za|tion ♦♦◇ /ˌɔrgənaɪˈzeɪʃən/ (organizations)

in BRIT, also use **organisation**

■ N-COUNT An **organization** is an official group of people, for example, a political party, a business, a charity, or a club. ❑ *Most of the food for the homeless is provided by voluntary organizations.* ■ N-UNCOUNT The **organization** of an event or activity involves making all the necessary arrangements for it. ❑ *...the exceptional attention to detail that goes into the organization of this event.* ■ N-UNCOUNT The **organization** of something is the way in which its different parts are arranged or relate to each other. ❑ *I am aware that the organization of the book leaves something to be desired.*

or|gani|za|tion|al /ˌɔrgənaɪˈzeɪʃənəl/

in BRIT, also use **organisational**

■ ADJ [ADJ n] **Organizational** abilities and methods relate to the way that work, activities, or events are planned and arranged. ❑ *Evelyn's excellent organizational skills were soon spotted by her employers.* ■ ADJ [ADJ n] **Organizational** means relating to the structure of an organization. ❑ *The police now recognize that big organizational changes are needed.* ■ ADJ [ADJ n] **Organizational** means relating to organizations, rather than individuals. ❑ *This problem needs to be dealt with at an organizational level.*

or|gan|ize ♦♦◇ /ˈɔrgənaɪz/ (organizes, organizing, organized)

in BRIT, also use **organise**

■ V-T If you **organize** an event or activity, you make sure that the necessary arrangements are made. ❑ *In the end, we all decided to organize a concert for Easter.* ❑ *...a two-day meeting organized by the United Nations.* ■ V-T If you **organize** something that someone wants or needs, you make sure that it is provided. ❑ *I will organize transportation.* ■ V-T If you **organize** a set of things, you arrange them in an ordered way or give them a structure. ❑ *He began to organize his materials.* ❑ *She took a hasty cup of coffee and tried to organize her scattered thoughts.* ■ V-T If you **organize** yourself, you plan your work and activities in an ordered, efficient way. ❑ *...changing the way you organize yourself.* ❑ *Go right ahead, I'm sure you don't need me to organize you.*

---- SYNONYMS ----

organize
VERB
■
arrange: *He arranged an appointment for Friday afternoon at 4.15.*
set up: *...an organization which sets up meetings about issues of interest to women.*
plan: *I had been planning a trip to the west coast.*

■
arrange: *He started to arrange the books in piles.*
group: *The fact sheets are grouped into seven sections.*
sort: *He sorted the materials into their folders.*
order: *...a carefully-ordered system in which everyone has a place.*

or|ga|nized ♦◇◇ /ˈɔrgənaɪzd/

in BRIT, also use **organised**

■ ADJ [ADJ n] An **organized** activity or group involves a number of people doing something together in a structured way, rather than doing it by themselves. ❑ *...organized groups of art thieves.* ❑ *...organized religion.* ■ ADJ Someone who is **organized** plans their work and activities efficiently. ❑ *These people are very efficient, very organized, and excellent time managers.*

-organized /-ˈɔrgənaɪzd/

in BRIT, also use **-organised**

COMB IN ADJ [ADJ n] **-organized** is added to nouns to form adjectives which indicate who organizes something. ❑ *...student-organized seminars.*

or|ga|nized crime

in BRIT, also use **organised crime**

N-UNCOUNT **Organized crime** refers to criminal activities which involve large numbers of people and are organized and controlled by a small group.

or|gan|iz|er ♦◇◇ /ˈɔrgənaɪzər/ (organizers)

in BRIT, also use **organiser**

■ N-COUNT The **organizer** of an event or activity is the person who makes sure that the necessary arrangements are made. ❑ *He became an organizer for the Democratic Party.* ■ → see also **personal organizer**

or|gano|phos|phate /ɔrˌgænoʊˈfɒsfeɪt/ (organophosphates) N-COUNT **Organophosphates** are toxic chemical substances that are used in pesticides and fertilizers.

or|gan|za /ɔrˈgænzə/ N-UNCOUNT [oft N n] **Organza** is a thin, stiff fabric made of silk, cotton, or an artificial fiber.

or|gasm /ˈɔrgæzəm/ (orgasms) N-VAR An **orgasm** is the moment of greatest pleasure and excitement in sexual activity. ❑ *...the ability to reach orgasm.*

or|gas|mic /ɔrˈgæzmɪk/ ■ ADJ [usu ADJ n] **Orgasmic** means relating to a sexual orgasm. ❑ *Testosterone does not increase their erectile or orgasmic ability.* ■ ADJ [usu ADJ n] Some people refer to things they find extremely enjoyable or exciting as **orgasmic**. [mainly JOURNALISM] ❑ *...jerking the neck of his guitar in orgasmic fits of ecstasy.*

or|gi|as|tic /ˌɔrdʒiˈæstɪk/ ADJ [ADJ n] An **orgiastic** event is one in which people enjoy themselves in an extreme, uncontrolled way. ❑ *...an orgiastic party.*

orgy /ˈɔrdʒi/ (orgies) N-COUNT An **orgy** is a party in which people behave in a very uncontrolled way, especially one involving sexual activity. ❑ *It was reminiscent of a scene from a Roman orgy.*

ori|ent /ˈɔriɛnt/ (orients, orienting, oriented) ■ V-T When you **orient** yourself to a new situation or course of action, you learn about it and prepare to deal with it. [FORMAL] ❑ *You will need the time to orient yourself to your new way of eating.* ■ → see also **oriented**

Ori|ent /ˈɔriənt/ N-PROPER [the N] The eastern part of Asia is sometimes referred to as **the Orient**. [LITERARY, OLD-FASHIONED]

ori|en|tal /ˌɔriˈɛntəl/ ADJ **Oriental** means coming from or associated with eastern Asia, especially China and Japan. ❑ *There were Oriental carpets on the floors.*

Ori|en|tal|ist /ˌɔriˈɛntəlɪst/ (Orientalists) also **orientalist** N-COUNT An **Orientalist** is someone who studies the language, culture, history, or customs of countries in eastern Asia.

ori|en|tate /ˈɔriənteɪt/ **Orientate** means the same as **orient**.

ori|en|tat|ed /ˈɔriənteɪtɪd/ **Orientated** means the same as **oriented**.

-orientated /-ˈɔriənteɪtɪd/ **-orientated** means the same as **-oriented**.

ori|en|ta|tion /ˌɔriənˈteɪʃən/ (orientations) ■ N-VAR If you talk about the **orientation** of an organization or country, you are talking about the kinds of aims and interests it has. ☐ ...a marketing orientation. ☐ To a society which has lost its orientation he has much to offer. **2** N-VAR Someone's **orientation** is their basic beliefs or preferences. ☐ ...legislation that would have made discrimination on the basis of sexual orientation illegal. **3** N-UNCOUNT **Orientation** is basic information or training that is given to people starting a new job, school, or course. ☐ They give their new employees a day or two of orientation. **4** N-COUNT The **orientation** of a structure or object is the direction it faces. ☐ Farnese had the orientation of the church changed so that the front would face a square.

ori|ent|ed /ɔ́riɛntɪd/ also **orientated** ADJ [v-link ADJ toward/to n] If someone **is oriented toward** or **oriented to** a particular thing or person, they are mainly concerned with that thing or person. ☐ It seems almost inevitable that these economies will still be primarily oriented toward Europe.

-oriented /-ɔ́riɛntɪd/ also **-orientated** COMB IN ADJ **-oriented** is added to nouns and adverbs to form adjectives which describe what someone or something is mainly interested in or concerned with. ☐ ...a market-oriented economy. ☐ ...family-oriented vacations.

ori|ent|eer|ing /ɔ̀riəntíərɪŋ/ N-UNCOUNT **Orienteering** is a sport in which people run from one place to another, using a compass and a map to guide them between points that are marked along the route.

ori|fice /ɔ́rɪfɪs/ (orifices) N-COUNT An **orifice** is an opening or hole, especially one in your body such as your mouth. [FORMAL] ☐ After a massive heart attack, he was strapped to a bed, with tubes in every orifice.

ori|ga|mi /ɔ̀rɪgɑ́mi/ N-UNCOUNT **Origami** is the craft of folding paper to make models of animals, people, and objects.

ori|gin ◆◇◇ /ɔ́rɪdʒɪn/ (origins) **1** N-COUNT You can refer to the beginning, cause, or source of something as its **origin** or **origins**. ☐ ...theories about the origin of life. ☐ Their medical problems are basically physical in origin. **2** N-COUNT [usu poss N, also of/in N] When you talk about a person's **origin** or **origins**, you are referring to the country, race, or living conditions of their parents or ancestors. ☐ Thomas has not forgotten his humble origins. ☐ ...people of Asian origin.

origi|nal ◆◆◇ /ərɪ́dʒɪnəl/ (originals) **1** ADJ [det ADJ] You use **original** when referring to something that existed at the beginning of a process or activity, or the characteristics that something had when it began or was made. ☐ The original plan was to go by bus. **2** N-COUNT If something such as a document, a work of art, or a piece of writing is an **original**, it is not a copy or a later version. ☐ When you have filled in the questionnaire, copy it and send the original to your employer. **3** ADJ An **original** document or work of art is not a copy. ☐ ...an original movie poster. **4** ADJ An **original** piece of writing or music was written recently and has not been published or performed before. ☐ ...with catchy original songs by Richard Warner. **5** ADJ If you describe someone or their work as **original**, you mean that they are very imaginative and have new ideas. [APPROVAL] ☐ It is one of the most original works of imagination in the language. • **origi|nal|ity** /ərɪ̀dʒɪnǽlɪti/ N-UNCOUNT ☐ He was capable of writing things of startling originality.

SYNONYMS

original
ADJ
1
first: ...the first few flakes of snow.
initial: The aim of this initial meeting is to clarify the issues.
aboriginal: Many would acknowledge that aboriginal people have had a bad deal.
5
fresh: These designers are full of fresh ideas.
novel: It will also be used to test novel ideas for data handling and workflow.
innovative: ...products which are more innovative than those of their competitors.

---

origi|nal|ly ◆◇◇ /ərɪ́dʒɪnəli/ ADV When you say what happened or was the case **originally**, you are saying what happened or was the case when something began or came into existence, often to contrast it with what happened later. ☐ The plane has been kept in service far longer than originally intended.

SYNONYMS

originally
ADV
initially: Initially, they were wary of Simon.
at first: At first, he seemed surprised by my questions.
first: I met him first at his house, where we had a chat.
firstly: Firstly, it is needed for hormone production.

---

origi|nal sin N-UNCOUNT According to some Christians, **original sin** is the wickedness that all human beings are born with, because the first human beings, Adam and Eve, disobeyed God.

origi|nate /ərɪ́dʒɪneɪt/ (originates, originating, originated) V-T/V-I When something **originates** or when someone **originates** it, it begins to happen or exist. [FORMAL] ☐ The disease originated in Africa. ☐ All carbohydrates originate from plants.

origi|na|tor /ərɪ́dʒɪneɪtər/ (originators) N-COUNT [usu with poss] The **originator** of something such as an idea or scheme is the person who first thought of it or began it. [FORMAL] ☐ ...the originator of the theory of relativity.

ori|ole /ɔ́rioʊl/ (orioles) N-COUNT An **oriole** is a bird which has black and yellow or orange feathers. There are several different sorts of oriole. ☐ ...a pair of golden orioles.

or|na|ment /ɔ́rnəmənt/ (ornaments) **1** N-COUNT An **ornament** is an attractive object that you display in your home or in your garden. ☐ ...a shelf containing a few photographs and ornaments. **2** N-UNCOUNT Decorations and patterns on a building or a piece of furniture can be referred to as **ornament**. [FORMAL] ☐ ...walls of glass overlaid with ornament.

or|na|men|tal /ɔ̀rnəméntəl/ ADJ Something that is **ornamental** is attractive and decorative. ☐ ...an ornamental fountain.

or|na|men|ta|tion /ɔ̀rnəmɛnteɪ́ʃən/ N-UNCOUNT Decorations and patterns can be referred to as **ornamentation**. [FORMAL] ☐ The chairs were comfortable, functional, and free of ornamentation.

or|na|ment|ed /ɔ́rnəmɛntɪd/ ADJ [oft ADJ with n] If something is **ornamented** with attractive objects or patterns, it is decorated with them. ☐ It had a high ceiling, ornamented with plaster fruits and flowers.

or|nate /ɔrneɪ́t/ ADJ An **ornate** building, piece of furniture, or object is decorated with complicated patterns or shapes. ☐ ...an ornate iron staircase.

or|nery /ɔ́rnəri/ ADJ If you describe someone as **ornery**, you mean that they are bad-tempered, difficult, and often do things that are mean. [AM, DISAPPROVAL] ☐ The old lady was still being ornery, but at least she had consented to this visit.

or|ni|thol|ogy /ɔ̀rnɪθɒ́lədʒi/ N-UNCOUNT **Ornithology** is the study of birds. [FORMAL] • **or|ni|tho|logi|cal** /ɔ̀rnɪθəlɒ́dʒɪkəl/ ADJ [ADJ n] ☐ ...a member of the Wilson Ornithological Society. • **or|ni|tholo|gist** (ornithologists) N-COUNT ☐ That area is an ornithologist's paradise.

or|phan /ɔ́rfən/ (orphans, orphaned) **1** N-COUNT An **orphan** is a child whose parents are dead. ☐ ...a young orphan girl brought up by peasants. **2** V-T PASSIVE [no cont] If a child **is orphaned**, their parents die, or their remaining parent dies. ☐ ...a fifteen-year-old boy left orphaned by the recent disaster.

or|phan|age /ɔ́rfənɪdʒ/ (orphanages) N-COUNT An **orphanage** is a place where orphans live and are cared for.

ortho|don|tist /ɔ̀rθədɒ́ntɪst/ (orthodontists) N-COUNT An **orthodontist** is a dentist who corrects the position of people's teeth.

ortho|dox /ɔ́rθədɒks/

The spelling **Orthodox** is also used for meanings **2** and **3**.

1 ADJ **Orthodox** beliefs, methods, or systems are ones which are accepted or used by most people. ☐ Many of these ideas are now being incorporated into orthodox medical treatment. **2** ADJ If you describe someone as **orthodox**, you mean that they hold the older and more traditional ideas of their religion or party.

☐ ...*Orthodox Jews*. **3** ADJ The **Orthodox** churches are Christian churches from Eastern Europe which separated from the western church in the eleventh century. ☐ ...*the Greek Orthodox Church*.

ortho|doxy /ɔ‍ːrθədɒksi/ (orthodoxies) **1** N-VAR An **orthodoxy** is an accepted view about something. ☐ *These ideas rapidly became the new orthodoxy in linguistics.* **2** N-UNCOUNT The old, traditional beliefs of a religion, political party, or philosophy can be referred to as **orthodoxy**. ☐ ...*a conflict between Nat's religious orthodoxy and Rube's belief that his mission is to make money*.

ortho|paedic [BRIT] → see orthopedic

ortho|pedic /ɔ‍ːrθəpiːdɪk/ ADJ [ADJ n] **Orthopedic** means relating to problems affecting people's joints and spines. [MEDICAL] ☐ ...*an orthopedic surgeon*. ☐ ...*orthopedic shoes*.

OS /oʊ ɛs/ (OS's) N-COUNT **OS** is an abbreviation for **operating system**. [COMPUTING] ☐ *The new OS can accommodate high-resolution color screens of 320 by 320 pixels*.

os|cil|late /ɒsɪleɪt/ (oscillates, oscillating, oscillated) **1** V-I If an object **oscillates**, it moves repeatedly from one position to another and back again, or keeps getting bigger and smaller. [FORMAL] ☐ *I checked to see if the needle indicating volume was oscillating.* ● **os|cil|la|tion** /ɒsɪleɪʃ°n/ (oscillations) N-VAR ☐ *Some oscillation of the fuselage had been noticed on early flights*. **2** V-I [no passive] If the level or value of something **oscillates**, it keeps going up and down. [FORMAL] ☐ *Oil markets oscillated on the day's reports from Geneva.* ☐ ...*an oscillating signal of microwave frequency*. ● **os|cil|la|tion** N-VAR ☐ *There have always been slight oscillations in world temperature.* **3** V-I [no passive] If you **oscillate** between two moods, attitudes, or types of behavior, you keep changing from one to the other and back again. [FORMAL] ☐ *The president of the republic oscillated between a certain audacity and a prudent realism.* ● **os|cil|la|tion** N-UNCOUNT ☐ ...*that perpetual oscillation between despair and distracted joy*.

OSHA /oʊ ɛs eɪtʃ eɪ/ N-PROPER **OSHA** is a government agency in the United States which is responsible for maintaining standards of health and safety in workplaces. **OSHA** is an abbreviation for 'Occupational Safety and Health Administration.' ☐ *Fuller says OSHA must target its resources as effectively as possible.*

os|mo|sis /ɒzmoʊsɪs, ɒs-/ **1** N-UNCOUNT **Osmosis** is the process by which a liquid passes through a thin piece of solid substance such as the roots of a plant. [TECHNICAL] ☐ ...*the processes of diffusion and osmosis.* **2** N-UNCOUNT [usu by/through n] If you say that people influence each other by **osmosis**, or that skills are gained by **osmosis**, you mean that this is done gradually and without any obvious effort. [FORMAL] ☐ *She allowed her life to be absorbed by his, taking on as if by osmosis his likes and dislikes.*

os|si|fy /ɒsɪfaɪ/ (ossifies, ossifying, ossified) V-T/V-I If an idea, system, or organization **ossifies** or if something **ossifies** it, it becomes fixed and difficult to change. [FORMAL, DISAPPROVAL] ☐ ...*conventions that threatened to ossify art.* ☐ ...*after 50 years in charge, the party has ossified.*

os|ten|sible /ɒstɛnsɪbəl/ ADJ [ADJ n] **Ostensible** is used to describe something that seems to be true or is officially stated to be true, but about which you or other people have doubts. [FORMAL] ☐ *The ostensible purpose of these meetings was to gather information on financial strategies.* ● **os|ten|sibly** /ɒstɛnsɪbli/ ADV ☐ ...*ostensibly independent organizations.*

os|ten|ta|tion /ɒstɛnteɪʃ°n/ N-UNCOUNT If you describe someone's behavior as **ostentation**, you are criticizing them for doing or buying things in order to impress people. [FORMAL, DISAPPROVAL] ☐ *On the whole she had lived modestly, with a notable lack of ostentation.*

os|ten|ta|tious /ɒstɛnteɪʃəs/ **1** ADJ If you describe something as **ostentatious**, you disapprove of it because it is expensive and is intended to impress people. [DISAPPROVAL] ☐ ...*his house, which, however elaborate, is less ostentatious than the preserves of other Dallas tycoons.* **2** ADJ If you describe someone as **ostentatious**, you disapprove of them because they want to impress people with their wealth or importance. [DISAPPROVAL] ☐ *Obviously he had plenty of money and was generous in its use without being ostentatious.* ● **os|ten|ta|tious|ly** ADV ☐ *Her servants were similarly, if less ostentatiously attired.* **3** ADJ You can describe an action or behavior as **ostentatious** when it is done in an exaggerated way to attract people's attention. ☐ *His wife was fairly quiet but she is not an ostentatious person anyway.* ● **os|ten|ta|tious|ly** ADV ☐ *Harry stopped under a street lamp and ostentatiously began inspecting the contents of his bag.*

os|teo|path /ɒstiəpæθ/ (osteopaths) N-COUNT An **osteopath** is a physician who treats painful conditions or illnesses by pressing and moving parts of the patient's body.

os|teo|po|ro|sis /ɒstioʊpərəʊsɪs/ N-UNCOUNT **Osteoporosis** is a condition in which your bones lose calcium and become more likely to break. [MEDICAL]

os|tra|cism /ɒstrəsɪzəm/ N-UNCOUNT **Ostracism** is the state of being ostracized or the act of ostracizing someone. [FORMAL] ☐ ...*those who have decided to risk social ostracism and stay on the wrong side of town.* ☐ ...*denunciation, tougher sanctions and ostracism from the civilized world.*

os|tra|cize /ɒstrəsaɪz/ (ostracizes, ostracizing, ostracized)

in BRIT, also use **ostracise**

V-T [usu passive] If someone **is ostracized**, people deliberately behave in an unfriendly way toward them and do not allow them to take part in any of their social activities. ☐ *She claims she's being ostracized by some members of her local community.*

os|trich /ɒstrɪtʃ/ (ostriches) N-COUNT An **ostrich** is a very large, long-necked African bird that cannot fly.

OT /oʊ tiː/ (OTs) **1** N-UNCOUNT In sports, **OT** is an abbreviation for **overtime**. [AM] ☐ *Mullin's team pulled out a one-point victory in OT for the championship.* **2** **OT** is a written abbreviation for the **Old Testament** of the Bible. Compare **NT**. ☐ *In OT times women were not members of the priesthood.* **3** N-UNCOUNT **OT** is an abbreviation for **occupational therapy**. **4** N-COUNT **OT** is an abbreviation for **occupational therapist**.

OTC /oʊ tiː siː/ ADJ [ADJ n] **OTC** is an abbreviation for **over-the-counter**. ☐ ...*the first OTC heartburn drug.*

oth|er ♦♦♦ /ʌðər/ (others)
→ Please look at meanings **7** to **8** to see if the expression you are looking for is shown under another headword.

When **other** follows the determiner **an**, it is written as one word: see **another**.

1 ADJ [det ADJ, ADJ n] You use **other** to refer to an additional thing or person of the same type as one that has been mentioned or is known about. ☐ *They were just like any other young couple.* ● PRON **Other** is also a pronoun. ☐ *Four crew members were killed, one other was injured.* **2** ADJ [det ADJ, ADJ n] You use **other** to indicate that a thing or person is not the one already mentioned, but a different one. ☐ *The authorities insist that the discussions must not be linked to any other issue.* ☐ *He would have to accept it; there was no other way.* ● PRON **Other** is also a pronoun. ☐ *This issue, more than any other, has divided her cabinet.* **3** ADJ [det ADJ] You use the **other** to refer to the second of two things or people when the identity of the first is already known or understood, or has already been mentioned. ☐ *The captain was at the other end of the room.* ☐ *You deliberately went in the other direction.* ● PRON-SING [the PRON] The **other** is also a pronoun. ☐ *Almost everybody had a cigarette in one hand and a martini in the other.* **4** ADJ [det ADJ, ADJ n] You use **other** at the end of a list or a group of examples, to refer generally to people or things like the ones just mentioned. ☐ *The new Station Center will have shops, restaurants and other amenities.* ● PRON **Other** is also a pronoun. ☐ *Descartes received his stimulus from the new physics and astronomy of Copernicus, Galileo, and others.* **5** ADJ [det ADJ] You use the **other** to refer to the rest of the people or things in a group, when you are talking about one particular person or thing. ☐ *When the other kids were taken to the zoo, he was left behind.* ● PRON [the PRON] The **others** is also a pronoun. ☐ *Aubrey's on his way here, with the others.* **6** ADJ [ADJ n] **Other** people are people in general, as opposed to yourself or a person you have already mentioned. ☐ *The suffering of other people appalls me.* ● PRON-PLURAL **Others** means the same as **other people**. ☐ *His humor depended on contempt for others.* **7** ADJ [the ADJ n] You use **other** in informal expressions of time such as **the other day**, **the other evening**, or **the other week** to refer to a day, evening, or week in the recent past. ☐ *I called her the* *other day and she said she'd like to come over.* **8** PHRASE You use expressions like **among other** things or **among others** to indicate that there are several more facts, things, or people like the one or ones mentioned, but that you do not intend to mention them all. [VAGUENESS] ❏ *He moved to Ohio in 2005 where, among other things, he worked as a journalist.* ❏ *His travels took him to Peru, among other places.* **9** PHRASE If something happens, for example, **every other day** or **every other month**, there is a day or month when it does not happen between each day or month when it happens. ❏ *Their food is adequate. It includes meat at least every other day, vegetables and fruit.* **10** PHRASE You use **every other** to emphasize that you are referring to all the rest of the people or things in a group. [EMPHASIS] ❏ *The same will apply in every other country.* **11** PHRASE You use **nothing other than** and **no other than** when you are going to mention a course of action, decision, or description and emphasize that it is the only one possible in the situation. [EMPHASIS] ❏ *Nothing other than an immediate custodial sentence could be justified.* ❏ *The rebels would not be happy with anything other than the complete removal of the current regime.* **12** PHRASE You use **or other** in expressions like **somehow or other** and **someone or other** to indicate that you cannot or do not want to be more precise about the information that you are giving. [VAGUENESS] ❏ *I was going to have him called away from the house on some pretext or other.* ❏ *The foundation is holding a dinner in honor of something or other.* **13** PHRASE You use **other than** after a negative statement to say that the person, item, or thing that follows is the only exception to the statement. ❏ *She makes no reference to any feminist work other than her own.* **14** each other → see **each** **15** one after the other → see **one** ③ **16** one or other → see one ③ **17** this, that, and the other → see **this** **18** in other words → see **word** ②

oth|er|ness /ˈʌðərnɪs/ N-UNCOUNT **Otherness** is the quality that someone or something has which is different from yourself or from the things that you have experienced. ❏ *She is interested in the otherness of men's minds and bodies.*

other|wise ♦◇◇ /ˈʌðərwaɪz/ **1** ADV [ADV with cl] You use **otherwise** after mentioning a situation or telling someone to do something, in order to say what the result or consequence would be if the situation did not exist or the person did not do as you say. ❏ *Make a note of the questions you want to ask; you will invariably forget some of them otherwise.* ❏ *I'm lucky that I'm interested in school work, otherwise I'd go crazy.* **2** ADV [ADV group] You use **otherwise** before stating the general condition or quality of something, when you are also mentioning an exception to this general condition or quality. ❏ *The decorations for the games have lent a splash of color to an otherwise drab city.* **3** ADV [ADV with v] You use **otherwise** to refer in a general way to actions or situations that are very different from, or the opposite to, your main statement. [WRITTEN] ❏ *Take approximately 60 mg up to four times a day, unless advised otherwise by a doctor.* ❏ *There is no way anything would ever happen between us, and believe me I've tried to convince myself otherwise.* **4** ADV [ADV before v] You use **otherwise** to indicate that other ways of doing something are possible in addition to the way already mentioned. ❏ *The studio could punish its players by keeping them out of work, and otherwise controlling their lives.* **5** PHRASE You use **or otherwise** or **and otherwise** to mention something that is not the thing just referred to or is the opposite of that thing. ❏ *It was for the police to assess the validity or otherwise of the evidence.*

other|worldly /ˌʌðərˈwɜːrldli/ ADJ [usu ADJ n] **Otherworldly** people, things, and places seem strange or spiritual, and not much connected with ordinary things. ❏ *They encourage an image of the region as an otherworldly sort of place.* ❏ *...a strange, otherworldly smile.*

ot|ter /ˈɒtər/ (**otters**) N-COUNT An **otter** is a small animal with brown fur, short legs, and a long tail. Otters swim well and eat fish.

ot|to|man /ˈɒtəmən/ (**ottomans**) **1** N-COUNT An **ottoman** is a low, padded seat similar to a couch but without a back or arms. **2** N-COUNT An **ottoman** is a low, padded stool that you can rest your feet on when you are sitting in a chair.

ouch /aʊtʃ/ EXCLAM '**Ouch!**' is used in writing to represent the noise that people make when they suddenly feel pain. ❏ *She was barefoot and stones dug into her feet. "Ouch, ouch!" she cried.*

ought ♦◇◇ /ɔːt/

Ought to is a phrasal modal verb. It is used with the base form of a verb.

1 PHRASE You use **ought to** to mean that it is morally right to do a particular thing or that it is morally right for a particular situation to exist, especially when giving or asking for advice or opinions. ❏ *Mark, you've got a good wife. You ought to take care of her.* ❏ *The people who already own a bit of money or land ought to have a voice in saying where it goes.* **2** PHRASE You use **ought to** when saying that you think it is a good idea and important for you or someone else to do a particular thing, especially when giving or asking for advice or opinions. ❏ *You don't have to be alone with him and I don't think you ought to be.* ❏ *You ought to ask a lawyer's advice.* **3** PHRASE You use **ought to** to indicate that you expect something to be true or to happen. ❏ *"This ought to be fun," he told Alex, eyes gleaming.* **4** PHRASE You use **ought to** to indicate that you think that something should be the case, but might not be. ❏ *They ought to win easily today, but nothing in life is certain.* **5** PHRASE You use **ought to** to indicate that you think that something has happened because of what you know about the situation, but you are not certain. [VAGUENESS] ❏ *He ought to have reached the house some time ago.* **6** PHRASE You use **ought to have** with a past participle to indicate that something was expected to happen or be the case, but it did not happen or was not the case. ❏ *Basically the system ought to have worked.* **7** PHRASE You use **ought to have** with a past participle to indicate that although it was best or correct for someone to do something in the past, they did not actually do it. ❏ *I realize I ought to have told you about it.* ❏ *I ought not to have asked you a thing like that. I'm sorry.* **8** PHRASE You use **ought to** when politely telling someone that you must do something, for example, that you must leave. [POLITENESS] ❏ *I really ought to be getting back now.*

oughtn't /ˈɔːtənt/ **Oughtn't** is a spoken form of 'ought not.'

Oui|ja board /ˈwiːdʒə bɔːrd, ˈwiːdʒi-/ (**Ouija boards**) N-COUNT A **Ouija board** is a board with the letters of the alphabet written on it. It is used to ask questions which some people believe are answered by the spirits of dead people. [TRADEMARK]

ounce /aʊns/ (**ounces**) **1** N-COUNT An **ounce** is a unit of weight used in the U.S. and Britain. There are sixteen ounces in a pound and one ounce is equal to 28.35 grams. ❏ *...four ounces of sugar.* **2** N-SING You can refer to a very small amount of something, such as a quality or characteristic, as an **ounce**. ❏ *If only my father had possessed an ounce of business sense.*

our ♦♦♦ /aʊər/

Our is the first person plural possessive determiner.

1 DET You use **our** to indicate that something belongs or relates both to yourself and to one or more other people. ❏ *We're expecting our first baby.* **2** DET A speaker or writer sometimes uses **our** to indicate that something belongs or relates to people in general. ❏ *We are all entirely responsible for our actions, and for our reactions.*

Our Lady N-PROPER Some Christians, especially Catholics, refer to Mary, the mother of Jesus Christ, as **Our Lady**. ❏ *Will you pray to Our Lady for me?*

Our Lord N-PROPER Christians refer to Jesus Christ as **Our Lord**. ❏ *Let us remember the words of Our Lord from the gospel of Mark.*

ours /aʊərz/

Ours is the first person plural possessive pronoun.

PRON-POSS You use **ours** to refer to something that belongs or relates both to yourself and to one or more other people. ❏ *That car is ours.* ❏ *There are few strangers in a town like ours.*

our|self /aʊərˈself/ PRON [v PRON, prep PRON] **Ourself** is sometimes used instead of 'ourselves' when it clearly refers to a singular subject. Some people consider this use to be incorrect. ❏ *...the way we think of ourself and others.*

our|selves ♦◇◇ /aʊərˈselvz/

Ourselves is the first person plural reflexive pronoun.

1 PRON-REFL [V PRON, prep PRON] You use **ourselves** to refer to yourself and one or more other people as a group. ❏ *We sat around the fire to keep ourselves warm.* **2** PRON-REFL [V PRON, prep

PRON] A speaker or writer sometimes uses **ourselves** to refer to people in general. **Ourselves** is used as the object of a verb or preposition when the subject refers to the same people. ❑ *We all know that when we exert ourselves our heart rate increases.* ◻ PRON-REFL-EMPH You use **ourselves** to emphasize a first person plural subject. In more formal English, **ourselves** is sometimes used instead of 'us' as the object of a verb or preposition, for emphasis. [EMPHASIS] ❑ *Others are feeling just the way we ourselves would feel in the same situation.* ◻ PRON-REFL-EMPH If you say something such as 'We did it **ourselves**,' you are indicating that the people you are referring to did it, rather than anyone else. ❑ *We villagers built that ourselves, we had no help from anyone.*

oust /aʊst/ (**ousts, ousting, ousted**) V-T If someone **is ousted** from a position of power, job, or place, they are forced to leave it. [JOURNALISM] ❑ *The leaders have been ousted from power by nationalists.* ❑ *The Republicans may oust him in November.* • **oust|er** (**ousters**) N-COUNT [usu sing with poss, AM] ❑ *The group has called for the ouster of the trust's board.* • **oust|ing** N-UNCOUNT ❑ *The ousting of his predecessor was one of the most dramatic coups the business world had seen in years.*

OUT

① ADVERB USES
② ADJECTIVE AND ADVERB USES
③ VERB USE
④ PREPOSITION USES

---

① **out** ✦✦✦ /aʊt/

Out is often used with verbs of movement, such as 'walk' and 'pull,' and also in phrasal verbs such as 'give out' and 'run out.'

◼ ADV [ADV after v] When something is in a particular place and you take it **out**, you remove it from that place. ❑ *I like the pop you get when you pull out a cork.* ❑ *He took out his notebook and flipped the pages.* ◻ ADV [ADV after v] You can use **out** to indicate that you are talking about the situation outside, rather than inside buildings. ❑ *It's hot out – very hot, very humid.* ◻ ADV If you are **out**, you are not at home or not at your usual place of work. ❑ *I tried to get in touch with you yesterday evening, but I think you were out.* ◻ ADV [ADV adv/prep] If you say that someone is **out** in a particular place, you mean that they are in a different place, usually one far away. ❑ *The police tell me they've finished their investigations out there.* ◻ ADV When the sea or tide goes **out**, the sea moves away from the shore. ❑ *The tide was out and they walked among the rock pools.* ◻ ADV [ADV n] If you are **out** a particular amount of money, you have that amount less than you should or than you did. [mainly AM, INFORMAL] ❑ *I'm out ten thousand dollars, with nothing to show for it!*

② **out** ✦✦✦ /aʊt/ ◼ ADJ [v-link ADJ] If a light or fire is **out** or goes **out**, it is no longer shining or burning. ❑ *All the lights were out in the house.* ◻ ADJ [v-link ADJ] If flowers are **out**, their petals have opened. ❑ *Well, the daffodils are out in the gardens and there's always a beautiful show.* • ADV [ADV after v] **Out** is also an adverb. ❑ *I usually put it in my diary when I see the wild flowers coming out.* ◻ ADJ [v-link ADJ] If something such as a book or CD is **out**, it is available for people to buy. ❑ *Their new album is out now.* • ADV [ADV after v] **Out** is also an adverb. ❑ *The French edition came out in early 2006.* ◻ ADJ [v-link ADJ] In a game or sport, if someone is **out**, they can no longer take part either because they are unable to or because they have been defeated. ◻ ADJ [v-link ADJ] In baseball, a player is **out** if they do not reach a base safely. When three players on a team are out in an inning, then the team is **out**. ◻ ADJ [v-link ADJ] If you say that a proposal or suggestion is **out**, you mean that it is unacceptable. ❑ *That idea is out, I'm afraid.* ◻ ADJ [v-link ADJ] If you say that a particular thing is **out**, you mean that it is no longer fashionable at the present time. ❑ *Romance is making a comeback. Reality is out.* ◻ ADJ [v-link ADJ] If you say that a calculation or measurement is **out**, you mean that it is incorrect. ❑ *When the two ends of the tunnel met in the middle they were only a few inches out.* ◻ ADJ [v-link ADJ to-inf] If someone is **out** to do something, they intend to do it. [INFORMAL] ❑ *Most companies these days are just out to make a quick profit.* ◻ ADJ [v-link ADJ] If news or information about something is **out**, information about it has been made public. ❑ *The word is out that she has fled the country.* ◻ ADJ [v-link ADJ] If a person is **out**, they are open about their sexuality or gender identity. • ADV [ADV after v] **Out** is also an adverb. ❑ *What is missing is for one professional football or hockey player to come out.*

③ **out** /aʊt/ (**outs, outing, outed**) V-T If a group of people **out** a public figure or famous person, they reveal that person's sexuality or gender identity against their wishes. ❑ *A New York gay action group recently outed an American Congressman.* • **out|ing** N-UNCOUNT ❑ *The gay and lesbian rights group, Stonewall, sees outing as completely unhelpful.*

④ **out** ✦✦✦ /aʊt/

Out of is used with verbs of movement, such as 'walk' and 'pull,' and also in phrasal verbs such as 'get out of' and 'grow out of.' **Out** is often used instead of **out of**, for example in 'He looked out the window.'

◼ PHRASE If you go **out of** a place, you leave it. ❑ *She let him out of the house.* ◻ PHRASE If you take something **out of** the container or place where it has been, you remove it so that it is no longer there. ❑ *I always took my key out of my bag and put it in my pocket.* ◻ PHRASE If you look or shout **out of** a window, you look or shout away from the room where you are toward the outside. ❑ *He went on staring out of the window.* ◻ PHRASE If you are **out of** the sun, the rain, or the wind, you are sheltered from it. ❑ *People can keep out of the sun to avoid skin cancer.* ◻ PHRASE If someone or something gets **out of** a situation, especially an unpleasant one, they are then no longer in it. If they keep **out of** it, they do not start being in it. ❑ *In the past army troops have relied heavily on air support to get them out of trouble.* ❑ *The economy is starting to climb out of recession.* ◻ PHRASE You can use **out of** to say that someone leaves an institution. ❑ *That is precisely what I came out of college thinking I was supposed to do.* ◻ PHRASE If you are **out of** range of something, you are beyond the limits of that range. ❑ *Shaun was in the bedroom, out of earshot, watching television.* ◻ PHRASE You use **out of** to say what feeling or reason causes someone to do something. For example, if you do something **out of** pity, you do it because you pity someone. ❑ *He took up office out of a sense of duty.* ◻ PHRASE If you get something such as information or work **out of** someone, you manage to make them give it to you, usually when they are unwilling to give it. ❑ *"Where is she being held prisoner?" I asked. "Did you get it out of him?"* ◻ PHRASE If you get pleasure or an advantage **out of** something, you get it as a result of being involved with that thing or making use of it. ❑ *Jenkins hasn't let the pressure take the fun out of the sport.* ◻ PHRASE If you are **out of** something, you no longer have any of it. ❑ *I can't find the sugar – and we're out of milk.* ◻ PHRASE If something is made **out of** a particular material, it consists of that material because it has been formed or constructed from it. ❑ *Would you advise people to make a building out of wood or stone?* ◻ PHRASE You use **out of** to indicate what proportion of a group of things something is true of. For example, if something is true of one **out of** five things, it is true of one fifth of all things of that kind. ❑ *Two out of five thought the business would be sold privately on their retirement or death.*

PREFIX

out-
You can use **out-** to form verbs that describe an action as being done better by one person than by another. *For example, if you can outswim someone, you can swim further or faster than they can.*

---

out|age /ˈaʊtɪdʒ/ (**outages**) N-COUNT An **outage** is a period of time when the electricity supply to a building or area is interrupted, for example, because of damage to the cables. [AM] ❑ *A windstorm in Washington is causing power outages throughout the region.*

in BRIT, use **power cut**

out-and-out ADJ [ADJ n] You use **out-and-out** to emphasize that someone or something has all the characteristics of a particular type of person or thing. [EMPHASIS] ❑ *Much of what has been written about us is out-and-out lies.*

out|back /ˈaʊtbæk/ N-SING The parts of Australia that are far away from towns are referred to as **the outback**. ❑ *Are there many people living in the outback?*

out|bid /aʊtbɪd/ (outbids, outbidding)

> The form **outbid** is used in the present tense and is the past tense and past participle.

V-T If you **outbid** someone, you offer more money than they do for something that you both want to buy. ▫ *The Museum has antagonized rivals by outbidding them for the world's greatest art treasures.*

out|board /aʊtbɔrd/ ADJ [ADJ n] An **outboard** motor is one that you can fix to the back of a small boat.

out|bound /aʊtbaʊnd/ ADJ An **outbound** flight is one that is leaving or about to leave a particular place. ▫ *Airport officials say at least 20 outbound flights were delayed.*

out|box /aʊtbɒks/ (outboxes) also **out-box** ◼ N-COUNT An **outbox** is a shallow container used in offices to put letters and documents in when they have been dealt with and are ready to be sent somewhere else. [AM] ▫ *He signed his name and placed the letter in his outbox.* ◼ N-COUNT On a computer, your **outbox** is the part of your mailbox which stores e-mails that you have not yet sent. ▫ *You'll get a dialogue box when exiting the program reminding you that there are still e-mails in your outbox.*

out|break /aʊtbreɪk/ (outbreaks) N-COUNT If there is an **outbreak** of something unpleasant, such as violence or a disease, it suddenly starts to happen. ▫ *The four-day festival ended a day early after an outbreak of violence involving hundreds of youths.* ▫ *...an outbreak of chickenpox.*

out|build|ing /aʊtbɪldɪŋ/ (outbuildings) N-COUNT [usu pl] **Outbuildings** are small buildings for keeping things in or working in which are near to a house or main building but separate from it.

out|burst /aʊtbɜrst/ (outbursts) ◼ N-COUNT An **outburst** of an emotion, especially anger, is a sudden strong expression of that emotion. ▫ *...a spontaneous outburst of cheers and applause.* ◼ N-COUNT An **outburst** of violent activity is a sudden period of this activity. ▫ *Five people were reported killed today in a fresh outburst of violence.*

out|cast /aʊtkæst/ (outcasts) N-COUNT An **outcast** is someone who is not accepted by a group of people or by society. ▫ *He had always been an outcast, unwanted and alone.*

out|class /aʊtklæs/ (outclasses, outclassing, outclassed) ◼ V-T If you **are outclassed** by someone, they are a lot better than you are at a particular activity. ▫ *Sanchez was totally outclassed by Monica Seles in the final.* ◼ V-T If one thing **outclasses** another thing, the first thing is of a much higher quality than the second thing. ▫ *Few city hotels can outclass the Hotel de Crillon.* ▫ *The story outclasses anything written by Forber.*

out|come ♦◇◇ /aʊtkʌm/ (outcomes) N-COUNT The **outcome** of an activity, process, or situation is the situation that exists at the end of it. ▫ *Mr. Singh said he was pleased with the outcome.* ▫ *It's too early to know the outcome of her illness.*

---- COLLOCATIONS ----

outcome
NOUN
noun + **outcome**: treatment; election, student
adjective + **outcome**: adverse, negative, positive, satisfactory; likely, possible, predictable, probable; eventual, final
verb + **outcome**: affect, decide, determine, influence; await, predict; achieve

---- SYNONYMS ----

outcome
NOUN
result: *These people have developed asthma as a direct result of their work.*
end: *The police force is being manipulated for political ends.*
consequence: *An economic crisis may have tremendous consequences for our global security.*

out|crop /aʊtkrɒp/ (outcrops) also **outcropping** N-COUNT An **outcrop** is a large area of rock sticking out of the ground. ▫ *...an outcrop of rugged granite.*

out|cry /aʊtkraɪ/ (outcries) N-VAR An **outcry** is a reaction of strong disapproval and anger shown by the public or media about a recent event. ▫ *The killing caused an international outcry.*

out|dat|ed /aʊtdeɪtɪd/ ADJ If you describe something as **outdated**, you mean that you think it is old-fashioned and no longer useful or relevant to modern life. ▫ *...outdated and inefficient factories.* ▫ *...outdated attitudes.*

out|did /aʊtdɪd/ **Outdid** is the past tense of **outdo**.

out|dis|tance /aʊtdɪstəns/ (outdistances, outdistancing, outdistanced) ◼ V-T If you **outdistance** someone, you are a lot better and more successful than they are at a particular activity over a period of time. ▫ *It didn't matter that Ingrid had outdistanced them as a movie star.* ◼ V-T If you **outdistance** your opponents in a contest of some kind, you beat them easily. ▫ *...a millionaire businessman who easily outdistanced his major rivals for the nomination.*

out|do /aʊtdu/ (outdoes, outdoing, outdid, outdone) ◼ V-T If you **outdo** someone, you are a lot more successful than they are at a particular activity. ▫ *It was important for me to outdo them, to feel better than they were.* ◼ PHRASE You use **not to be outdone** to introduce an action which someone takes in response to a previous action. ▫ *She wore a lovely tiara but the groom, not to be outdone, had on a very smart embroidered waistcoat.*

out|door /aʊtdɔr/ ADJ [ADJ n] **Outdoor** activities or things happen or are used outside and not in a building. ▫ *If you enjoy outdoor activities, this is the trip for you.*

out|doors /aʊtdɔrz/ ◼ ADV If something happens **outdoors**, it happens outside in the fresh air rather than in a building. ▫ *It was warm enough to be outdoors all afternoon.* ◼ N-SING You refer to **the outdoors** when talking about activities that take place outside away from buildings. ▫ *I'm a lover of the outdoors.*

out|doors|man /aʊtdɔrzmən/ (outdoorsmen) N-COUNT An **outdoorsman** is a man who spends a lot of time outdoors, doing things such as camping, hunting, or fishing. [AM]

out|er /aʊtər/ ADJ [ADJ n] The **outer** parts of something are the parts which contain or enclose the other parts, and which are furthest from the center. ▫ *He heard a voice in the outer room.*

outer|most /aʊtərmoʊst/ ADJ [ADJ n] The **outermost** thing in a group is the one that is farthest from the center. ▫ *...the outermost membrane covering the brain and spinal cord.*

out|er space N-UNCOUNT **Outer space** is the area outside the Earth's atmosphere where the other planets and stars are situated. ▫ *In 1957, the Soviets launched Sputnik 1 into outer space.*

outer|wear /aʊtərwɛər/ N-UNCOUNT **Outerwear** is clothing that is worn on top of indoor clothes in order to go outside. ▫ *...a line of outerwear that uses portable music technology in snowboarding jackets.*

out|fall /aʊtfɔl/ (outfalls) N-COUNT An **outfall** is a place where water or waste flows out of a drain, often into the sea. ▫ *During the winter months, great flocks of gulls gather at landfills and sewage outfalls.*

out|field /aʊtfild/ N-SING [the N] In baseball and cricket, the **outfield** is the part of the field that is farthest from the batting area.

out|field|er /aʊtfildər/ (outfielders) N-COUNT In baseball and cricket, the **outfielders** are the players in the part of the field that is farthest from the batting area.

out|fit /aʊtfɪt/ (outfits) ◼ N-COUNT An **outfit** is a set of clothes. ▫ *She was wearing an outfit she'd bought the previous day.* ◼ N-COUNT You can refer to an organization as an **outfit**. ▫ *He works for a private security outfit.*

out|fit|ter /aʊtfɪtər/ (outfitters) also **outfitters** ◼ N-COUNT An **outfitter** is a store or storekeeper that supplies people with equipment and guides for special purposes, such as hunting. [AM] ▫ *Jack Sumner was a guide and outfitter who ran a trading post in the Colorado Rockies.* ◼ N-COUNT An **outfitter** or an **outfitters** is a store that sells clothes. [BRIT]

out|flank /aʊtflæŋk/ (outflanks, outflanking, outflanked) ◼ V-T In a battle, when one group of soldiers **outflanks** another, it succeeds in moving past the other group in order to be able to attack it from the side. ▫ *...plans designed by the general to outflank them from the west.* ◼ V-T If you **outflank** someone, you succeed in getting into a position where you can defeat them, for example, in an argument. ▫ *He had tried to outflank them.*

out|flow /aʊtfloʊ/ (outflows) N-COUNT When there is an **outflow** of money or people, a large amount of money or people move from one place to another. ◻ *There was a net outflow of about $650m.*

out|fox /aʊtfɒks/ (outfoxes, outfoxing, outfoxed) V-T If you **outfox** someone, you defeat them in some way because you are more clever than they are. ◻ *There is no greater thrill than to bluff a man, trap him, and outfox him.*

out|going /aʊtgoʊɪŋ/ **1** ADJ [ADJ n] **Outgoing** things such as planes, mail, and passengers are leaving or being sent somewhere. ◻ *All outgoing flights were grounded.* **2** ADJ Someone who is **outgoing** is very friendly and likes meeting and talking to people. ◻ *She's very outgoing.* **3** ADJ [ADJ n] You use **outgoing** to describe a person in charge of something who is soon going to leave that position. ◻ *...the outgoing director of the International Folk Festival.* **4** → See feature box at **personality**

out|goings /aʊtgoʊɪŋz/ N-PLURAL Your **outgoings** are the regular amounts of money which you have to spend every week or every month, for example, in order to pay your rent or bills. [BRIT]

in AM, use **outlay**

out|grow /aʊtgroʊ/ (outgrows, outgrowing, outgrew, outgrown) **1** V-T If a child **outgrows** a piece of clothing, they grow bigger, so that it no longer fits them. ◻ *She outgrew her clothes so rapidly that Patsy was always having to buy new ones.* **2** V-T If you **outgrow** a particular way of behaving or thinking, you change and become more mature, so that you no longer behave or think in that way. ◻ *The girl may or may not outgrow her interest in fashion.*

out|growth /aʊtgroʊθ/ (outgrowths) N-COUNT [usu N of n] Something that is an **outgrowth** of another thing has developed naturally as a result of it. ◻ *Her first book is an outgrowth of an art project she began in 2003.*

out|guess /aʊtgɛs/ (outguesses, outguessing, outguessed) V-T If you **outguess** someone, you try to predict what they are going to do in order to gain some advantage. ◻ *Only by being him can you hope to outguess him.* ◻ *A very good investor will outguess the market.*

out|gun /aʊtgʌn/ (outguns, outgunning, outgunned) **1** V-T [usu passive] In a battle, if one army **is outgunned**, they are in a very weak position because the opposing army has more or better weapons. ◻ *The First Airborne Division was heavily outgunned by German forces.* **2** V-T If you **are outgunned** in a contest, you are beaten because your rival is stronger or better than you. ◻ *Clearly, the network is being outgunned by HBO's original drama.* ◻ *He soon hit top speed to outgun all his rivals in the opening qualifying session.*

out|house /aʊthaʊs/ (outhouses) **1** N-COUNT An **outhouse** is an outside toilet. [AM] **2** N-COUNT An **outhouse** is a small building attached to a house or very close to the house, used, for example, for storing things in.

out|ing /aʊtɪŋ/ (outings) **1** N-COUNT An **outing** is a short trip, usually with a group of people, away from your home, school, or place of work. ◻ *One evening, she made a rare outing to the local night club.* **2** → see also **out** ③

out|land|ish /aʊtlændɪʃ/ ADJ If you describe something as **outlandish**, you disapprove of it or find it funny because you think it is very unusual, strange, or unreasonable. [DISAPPROVAL] ◻ *This idea is not as outlandish as it sounds.*

out|last /aʊtlæst/ (outlasts, outlasting, outlasted) V-T [no passive] If one thing **outlasts** another, the first thing lives or exists longer than the second. ◻ *These naturally dried flowers will outlast a bouquet of fresh blooms.*

out|law /aʊtlɔː/ (outlaws, outlawing, outlawed) **1** V-T When something **is outlawed**, it is made illegal. ◻ *In some states gambling was outlawed.* ◻ *The German government has outlawed some fascist groups.* **2** N-COUNT An **outlaw** is a criminal who is hiding from the authorities. [OLD-FASHIONED] ◻ *Jesse was an outlaw, a bandit, a criminal.*

out|lay /aʊtleɪ/ (outlays) N-VAR **Outlay** is the amount of money that you have to spend in order to buy something or start a project. ◻ *Apart from the capital outlay of buying the machine, dishwashers can actually save you money.*

out|let /aʊtlɛt, -lɪt/ (outlets) **1** N-COUNT An **outlet** is a store or organization which sells the goods made by a particular manufacturer or at a discount price, often direct from the manufacturer. ◻ *...the largest retail outlet in the city.* ◻ *At the factory outlet you'll find discounted items at up to 75% off regular prices.* **2** N-COUNT If someone has an **outlet** for their feelings or ideas, they have a means of expressing and releasing them. ◻ *Her father had found an outlet for his ambition in his work.* **3** N-COUNT An **outlet** is a hole or pipe through which liquid or air can flow away. ◻ *...a warm air outlet.* **4** N-COUNT An **outlet** is a place, usually in a wall, where you can connect electrical devices to the electricity supply. [mainly AM] ◻ *Just plug it into any electric outlet.*

in BRIT, usually use **socket**

5 → See feature box at **press**

out|line /aʊtlaɪn/ (outlines, outlining, outlined) **1** V-T If you **outline** an idea or a plan, you explain it in a general way. ◻ *The mayor outlined his plan to clean up the town's image.* **2** N-COUNT [also in n] An **outline** is a general explanation or description of something. ◻ *Following is an outline of the survey findings.* **3** V-T PASSIVE You say that an object **is outlined** when you can see its general shape because there is light behind it. ◻ *The Ritz was outlined against the lights up there.* **4** N-COUNT The **outline** of something is its general shape, especially when it cannot be clearly seen. ◻ *He could see only the hazy outline of the goalposts.*

out|live /aʊtlɪv/ (outlives, outliving, outlived) V-T If one person **outlives** another, they are still alive after the second person has died. If one thing **outlives** another thing, the first thing continues to exist after the second has disappeared or been replaced. ◻ *I'm sure Rose will outlive many of us.*

out|look /aʊtlʊk/ (outlooks) **1** N-COUNT [usu sing, with supp, also in n] Your **outlook** is your general attitude toward life. ◻ *I adopted a positive outlook on life.* **2** N-SING The **outlook** for something is what people think will happen in relation to it. ◻ *The economic outlook is one of rising unemployment.*

out|ly|ing /aʊtlaɪɪŋ/ ADJ [ADJ n] **Outlying** places are far away from the main cities of a country. ◻ *Tourists can visit outlying areas like the Napa Valley Wine Country.*

out|ma|neu|ver /aʊtmənuːvər/ (outmaneuvers, outmaneuvering, outmaneuvered)

in BRIT, use **outmanoeuvre**

V-T If you **outmaneuver** someone, you gain an advantage over them in a particular situation by behaving in a clever and skillful way. ◻ *Again, Murphy had quietly outmaneuvered him.*

out|mod|ed /aʊtmoʊdɪd/ ADJ If you describe something as **outmoded**, you mean that you think it is old-fashioned and no longer useful or relevant to modern life. ◻ *The country badly needs aid to modernize its outmoded industries.* ◻ *The political system has become thoroughly outmoded.*

out|num|ber /aʊtnʌmbər/ (outnumbers, outnumbering, outnumbered) V-T If one group of people or things **outnumbers** another, the first group has more people or things in it than the second group. ◻ *...a town where men outnumber women four to one.*

out of → see **out** ④

out-of-body ADJ [ADJ n] An **out-of-body** experience is one in which you feel as if you are outside your own body, watching it and what is going on around it.

out-of-court → see **court** ① 6

out of date also **out-of-date** ADJ Something that is **out of date** is old-fashioned and no longer useful. ◻ *The regulations were out of date and confusing.*

out of doors also **out-of-doors** ADV [ADV after v, be ADV] If you are **out of doors**, you are outside a building rather than inside it. ◻ *Sometimes we eat out of doors.*

out-of-pocket 1 ADJ [ADJ n] **Out-of-pocket** expenses are those which you pay out of your own money on behalf of someone else, and which are often paid back to you later. **2** → see also **pocket**

out-of-state 1 ADJ [ADJ n] **Out-of-state** is used to describe people who do not live permanently in a particular state within a country, but have traveled there from somewhere else. ❑ *95% of our students are out-of-state students.* **2** ADJ [ADJ n] **Out-of-state** companies are based outside a particular state but conduct business within that state. ❑ *...the impact of new competition from out-of-state banks.*

out-of-the-way also **out of the way** ADJ **Out-of-the-way** places are difficult to reach and are therefore not often visited. ❑ *...an out-of-the-way location.*

out of touch **1** ADJ [v-link ADJ] Someone who is **out of touch** with a situation is not aware of recent changes in it. ❑ *They accuse politicians of being out of touch with ordinary people.* **2** ADJ [v-link ADJ] If you are **out of touch** with someone, you have not been in contact with them recently and are not familiar with their present situation. ❑ *James and I have been out of touch for years.*

out-of-town **1** ADJ [ADJ n] **Out-of-town** stores or facilities are situated away outside a town or city. ❑ *...shopping at cheaper, out-of-town supermarkets.* **2** ADJ [ADJ n] **Out-of-town** is used to describe people who do not live in a particular town or city, but have traveled there for a particular purpose. ❑ *...a deluxe hotel for out-of-town visitors.* **3** ADJ [be ADJ] If someone is **out of town**, they have left the town or city where they live for a short time, for example because they are on vacation. ❑ *She was out of town and unavailable for comment.* • ADV [after v] **Out of town** is also an adverb ❑ *I had to get out of town.*

out of work ADJ Someone who is **out of work** does not have a job. ❑ *...a town where half the men are usually out of work.*

out|pace /aʊtpeɪs/ (**outpaces, outpacing, outpaced**) V-T To **outpace** someone or something means to perform a particular action faster or better than they can. ❑ *These hovercrafts can easily outpace most boats.* ❑ *The Japanese economy will continue to outpace its foreign rivals for years to come.*

out|pa|tient /aʊtpeɪʃənt/ (**outpatients**) also **out-patient** N-COUNT An **outpatient** is someone who receives treatment at a hospital but does not spend the night there. ❑ *...the outpatient clinic.*

out|per|form /aʊtpərfɔːrm/ (**outperforms, outperforming, outperformed**) V-T If one person or thing **outperforms** another, the first is more successful or efficient than the second. [JOURNALISM] ❑ *In recent years their economy has outperformed most other industrial economies.*

out|place|ment /aʊtpleɪsmənt/ N-UNCOUNT An **outplacement** agency gives advice to managers and other professional people who have recently become unemployed, and helps them find new jobs. [BUSINESS] ❑ *...an outplacement firm in Denver.*

out|play /aʊtpleɪ/ (**outplays, outplaying, outplayed**) V-T In sports, if one person or team **outplays** an opposing person or team, they play much better than their opponents. ❑ *He was outplayed by the Swedish 21-year-old.*

out|point /aʊtpɔɪnt/ (**outpoints, outpointing, outpointed**) V-T In boxing, if one boxer **outpoints** another, they win the match by getting more points than their opponent. ❑ *Kane won the world title in 1938 when he outpointed Jackie Durich.*

out|post /aʊtpoʊst/ (**outposts**) **1** N-COUNT An **outpost** is a small group of buildings used for trading or military purposes, either in a distant part of your own country or in a foreign country. ❑ *...a remote mountain outpost, linked to the outside world by the poorest of roads.* **2** N-COUNT An **outpost** is a small settlement or community that is situated in a remote part of a country. ❑ *This rural outpost, 400 miles northeast of Helena, has one stoplight.*

out|pour|ing /aʊtpɔːrɪŋ/ (**outpourings**) N-COUNT [usu sing, usu N of n] An **outpouring** of something such as an emotion or a reaction is the expression of it in an uncontrolled way. ❑ *The news of his death produced an instant outpouring of grief.*

out|put ♦◇◇ /aʊtpʊt/ (**outputs**) **1** N-VAR **Output** is used to refer to the amount of something that a person or thing produces. ❑ *Government statistics show the largest drop in industrial output for ten years.* **2** N-VAR The **output** of a computer or word processor is the information that it displays on a screen or prints on paper as a result of a particular program. ❑ *You run the software, you look at the output, you make modifications.*

out|rage (**outrages, outraging, outraged**)

The verb is pronounced /aʊtreɪdʒ/. The noun is pronounced /aʊtreɪdʒ/.

1 V-T If you **are outraged** by something, it makes you extremely angry and shocked. ❑ *Many people have been outraged by some of the things that have been said.* • **out|raged** ADJ ❑ *He is truly outraged about what's happened to him.* **2** N-UNCOUNT **Outrage** is an intense feeling of anger and shock. ❑ *The decision provoked outrage from women and human rights groups.* **3** N-COUNT You can refer to an act or event that angers and shocks you as an **outrage**. ❑ *The latest outrage was to have been a coordinated gun and bomb attack on the station.*

out|ra|geous /aʊtreɪdʒəs/ ADJ If you describe something as **outrageous**, you are emphasizing that it is unacceptable or very shocking. [EMPHASIS] ❑ *By diplomatic standards, this was outrageous behavior.* • **out|ra|geous|ly** ADV ❑ *...outrageously expensive skin care items.*

out|ran /aʊtræn/ **Outran** is the past tense of **outrun**.

out|rank /aʊtræŋk/ (**outranks, outranking, outranked**) V-T If one person **outranks** another person, he or she has a higher position or grade within an organization than the other person. ❑ *The most junior executive officer outranked the senior engineer officer aboard ship.*

outré /uːtreɪ/ ADJ Something that is **outré** is very unusual and strange. [FORMAL] ❑ *...outré outfits designed by students at the College of Art.*

out|reach /aʊtriːtʃ/ N-UNCOUNT [usu N n] **Outreach** programs and plans try to find people who need help or advice rather than waiting for those people to come and ask for help. ❑ *Their brief is to undertake outreach work aimed at young African Americans.*

out|rid|er /aʊtraɪdər/ (**outriders**) N-COUNT [usu N n] **Outriders** are people such as police officers who ride on motorcycles or horses beside or in front of an official vehicle, in order to protect the people in the vehicle. ❑ *...a black Mercedes with motorcycle outriders provided by the city's police.*

out|right

The adjective is pronounced /aʊtraɪt/. The adverb is pronounced /aʊtraɪt/.

1 ADJ [ADJ n] You use **outright** to describe behavior and actions that are open and direct, rather than indirect. ❑ *Kawaguchi finally resorted to an outright lie.* • ADV [ADV after v] **Outright** is also an adverb. ❑ *Why are you so mysterious? Why don't you tell me outright?* **2** ADJ [ADJ n] **Outright** means complete and total. ❑ *She had failed to win an outright victory.* • ADV [ADV after v] **Outright** is also an adverb. ❑ *The peace plan wasn't rejected outright.* • PHRASE If someone **is killed outright**, they die immediately, for example, in an accident.

out|run /aʊtrʌn/ (**outruns, outrunning, outran**)

The form **outrun** is used in the present tense and is also the past participle of the verb.

1 V-T If you **outrun** someone, you run faster than they do, and therefore are able to escape from them or to arrive somewhere before they do. ❑ *There are not many players who can outrun me.* **2** V-T If one thing **outruns** another thing, the first thing develops faster than the second thing. ❑ *Spending could outrun the capacity of businesses to produce the goods.*

out|sell /aʊtsɛl/ (**outsells, outselling, outsold**) V-T If one product **outsells** another product, the first product is sold more quickly or in larger quantities than the second. [BUSINESS] ❑ *The team's products easily outsell those of other American baseball teams overseas.*

out|set /aʊtsɛt/ PHRASE If something happens **at the outset** of an event, process, or period of time, it happens at the beginning of it. If something happens **from the outset**, it happens from the beginning and continues to happen. ❑ *Decide at the outset what kind of learning program you want to follow.*

out|shine /aʊtʃaɪn/ (**outshines, outshining, outshone**) V-T If you **outshine** someone at a particular activity, you are much better at it than they are. ❑ *Jesse has begun to outshine me in sports.*

out|side ♦♦♦ /aʊtsaɪd/ (**outsides**)

The form **outside of** can also be used as a preposition.

outside ￭ N-COUNT The **outside** of something is the part which surrounds or encloses the rest of it. ❑ ...the outside of the building. • ADJ [ADJ n] **Outside** is also an adjective. ❑ ...high up on the outside wall. ￭ ADV If you are **outside**, you are not inside a building but are quite close to it. ❑ I stepped outside and pulled up my collar against the cold mist. ❑ Outside, the light was fading rapidly. • PREP **Outside** is also a preposition. ❑ The victim was outside a shop when he was attacked. • ADJ [ADJ n] **Outside** is also an adjective. ❑ ...the outside temperature. ￭ PREP If you are **outside** a room, you are not in it but are in the passage or area next to it. ❑ She'd sent him outside the classroom. • ADV **Outside** is also an adverb. ❑ They heard voices coming from outside in the corridor. ￭ ADJ [ADJ n] When you talk about the **outside** world, you are referring to things that happen or exist in places other than your own home, workplace, or community. ❑ ...a side of Morris's character she hid carefully from the outside world. • ADV [ADV after v] **Outside** is also an adverb. ❑ The scheme was good for the prisoners because it brought them outside into the community. ￭ PREP [n/-ed PREP n] People or things **outside** a country, town, or region are not in it. ❑ ...an old castle outside Budapest. • N-SING [the N] **Outside** is also a noun. ❑ Peace cannot be imposed from the outside by the United States or anyone else. ￭ ADJ [ADJ n] **Outside** people or organizations are not part of a particular organization or group. ❑ The company now makes much greater use of outside consultants. • PREP **Outside** is also a preposition. ❑ He is hoping to recruit a chairman from outside the company. ￭ PREP **Outside** a particular institution or field of activity means in other fields of activity or in general life. ❑ ...the largest merger ever to take place outside the oil industry. ￭ PREP Something that is **outside** a particular range of things is not included within it. ❑ It is a beautiful boat, but way, way outside my price range. ￭ PREP Something that happens **outside** a particular period of time happens at a different time from the one mentioned. ❑ They are open outside normal daily banking hours.

out|sid|er /aʊtsaɪdər/ (**outsiders**) ￭ N-COUNT An **outsider** is someone who does not belong to a particular group or organization. ❑ The most likely outcome may be to subcontract much of the work to an outsider. ￭ N-COUNT An **outsider** is someone who is not accepted by a particular group, or who feels that they do not belong in it. ❑ Malone, a cop, felt as much an outsider as any of them. ￭ N-COUNT In a competition, an **outsider** is a competitor who is unlikely to win. ❑ He was an outsider in the race to be the new UN Secretary-General.

out|size /aʊtsaɪz/ also **outsized** ADJ [usu ADJ n] **Outsize** or **outsized** things are much larger than usual or much larger than you would expect. ❑ ...an outsize pair of scissors.

out|skirts /aʊtskɜrts/ N-PLURAL The **outskirts** of a city or town are the parts of it that are farthest away from its center. ❑ Hours later we reached the outskirts of New York.

out|smart /aʊtsmɑrt/ (**outsmarts, outsmarting, outsmarted**) V-T If you **outsmart** someone, you defeat them or gain an advantage over them in a clever and sometimes dishonest way. ❑ Troy was very wise for his age and had already figured out ways to outsmart her.

out|sold /aʊtsoʊld/ **Outsold** is the past tense and past participle of **outsell**.

out|source /aʊtsɔrs/ (**outsources, outsourcing, outsourced**) V-T/V-I If a company **outsources** work or things, it pays workers from outside the company and often outside the country to do the work or supply the things. [BUSINESS] ❑ ...companies that outsource IT functions. ❑ The company began looking for ways to cut costs, which led to the decision to outsource. • **out|sourc|ing** N-UNCOUNT ❑ The concept of outsourcing to data centres is not new.

out|spo|ken /aʊtspoʊkən/ ADJ Someone who is **outspoken** gives their opinions about things openly and honestly, even if they are likely to shock or offend people. ❑ Some church leaders have been outspoken in their support for political reform. • **out|spo|ken|ness** N-UNCOUNT ❑ Their outspokenness on behalf of civil rights sometimes cost them their jobs.

out|stand|ing ♦◇◇ /aʊtstændɪŋ/ ￭ ADJ If you describe someone or something as **outstanding**, you think that they are very remarkable and impressive. ❑ Derartu is an outstanding athlete and deserved to win. ￭ ADJ Money that is **outstanding** has not yet been paid and is still owed to someone. ❑ The total debt outstanding is $70 billion. ￭ ADJ **Outstanding** issues or problems have not yet been resolved. ❑ We still have some outstanding issues to resolve before we'll have a treaty that is ready to sign. ￭ ADJ **Outstanding** means very important or obvious. ❑ The company is an outstanding example of a small business that grew into a big one.

> **SYNONYMS**
>
> **outstanding**
> ADJ ￭
> **remarkable:** It was a remarkable achievement.
> **extraordinary:** Rozhdestvensky is an extraordinary musician.
> **exceptional:** ...children with exceptional ability.

out|stand|ing|ly /aʊtstændɪŋli/ ADV [ADV adj/adv] You use **outstandingly** to emphasize how good, or occasionally how bad, something is. [EMPHASIS] ❑ Guatemala is an outstandingly beautiful place to visit.

out|stay /aʊtsteɪ/ (**outstays, outstaying, outstayed**) V-T If you say that someone **outstays** their welcome, you mean that they stay somewhere longer than they are wanted or expected to. ❑ After the kindness that had been shown to him, he didn't want to outstay his welcome.

out|stretched /aʊtstretʃt/ ADJ If a part of the body of a person or animal is **outstretched**, it is stretched out as far as possible. ❑ She was staring into the fire muttering, and holding her arms outstretched to warm her hands.

out|strip /aʊtstrɪp/ (**outstrips, outstripping, outstripped**) V-T If one thing **outstrips** another, the first thing becomes larger in amount, or more successful or important, than the second thing. ❑ In 1989 and 1990 demand outstripped supply, and prices went up by more than a third.

outta /aʊtə/ [AM] **Outta** is used in written English to represent the words 'out of' when they are pronounced informally. ❑ So go, get outta here.

out-take (**out-takes**) also **outtake** N-COUNT An **out-take** is a piece of film or a song that is not in the final version of a program, movie, or record, for example, because it contains a mistake.

out-there ADJ Someone or something that is **out-there** is very extreme or unusual. [INFORMAL] ❑ ...various artists with out-there names like Furry Green Lamppost.

out tray (**out trays**) also **out-tray** N-COUNT An **out tray** is a shallow container used in offices to put letters and documents in when they have been dealt with and are ready to be sent somewhere else. Compare **in tray**. [mainly BRIT]

> in AM, usually use **out box**

out|vote /aʊtvoʊt/ (**outvotes, outvoting, outvoted**) V-T If you are **outvoted**, more people vote against what you are suggesting than vote for it, so that your suggestion is defeated. ❑ They walked out in protest after being outvoted. ❑ Twice his colleagues have outvoted him.

out|ward /aʊtwərd/

> The form **outwards** can also be used for meanings ￭ and ￭.

￭ ADJ [ADJ n] The **outward** feelings, qualities, or attitudes of someone or something are the ones they appear to have rather than the ones that they actually have. ❑ In spite of my outward calm I was very shaken. ￭ ADJ [ADJ n] The **outward** features of something are the ones that you can see from the outside. ❑ Mark was lying unconscious but with no outward sign of injury. ￭ ADV [ADV after v] If something moves or faces **outward**, it moves or faces away from the place you are in or the place you are talking about. ❑ The top door opened outward. ￭ ADV [ADV after v] If you say that a person or a group of people, such as a government, looks **outward**, you mean that they turn their attention to another group that they are interested in or would like greater involvement with. ❑ Other poor countries looked outward, strengthening their ties to the economic superpowers. ￭ ADJ [ADJ n] An **outward** flight or journey is one that you make away from a place that you are intending to return to later.

out|ward|ly /aʊtwərdli/ ADV You use **outwardly** to indicate the feelings or qualities that a person or situation may appear to have, rather than the ones that they actually have. ❑ They may feel tired, and though outwardly calm, can be irritable.

out|wards /aʊtwərdz/ → see outward

out|weigh /aʊtweɪ/ (outweighs, outweighing, outweighed) **1** V-T If one thing **outweighs** another, the first thing is of greater importance, benefit, or significance than the second thing. [FORMAL] ❑ *The advantages of this deal largely outweigh the disadvantages.* **2** V-T If you **outweigh** someone, you are heavier than them. ❑ *Young outweighed her opponent by about 60 pounds.*

out|wit /aʊtwɪt/ (outwits, outwitting, outwitted) V-T If you **outwit** someone, you use your intelligence or a trick to defeat them or to gain an advantage over them. ❑ *To win the presidency he first had to outwit his rivals within the Socialist Party.*

out|with /aʊtwɪθ/ PREP In Scottish English, **outwith** means outside. ❑ *It is, however, necessary on occasion to work outwith these hours.*

out|worn /aʊtwɔrn/ ADJ If you describe a belief or custom as **outworn**, you mean that it is old-fashioned and no longer has any meaning or usefulness. ❑ *...an ancient nation irretrievably sunk in an outworn culture.*

ouzo /uzoʊ/ (ouzos) N-UNCOUNT **Ouzo** is a strong aniseed-flavored alcoholic drink that is made in Greece. • N-COUNT A glass of ouzo can be referred to as an **ouzo**.

ova /oʊvə/ **Ova** is the plural of **ovum**.

oval /oʊvəl/ (ovals) ADJ **Oval** things have a shape that is like a circle but is wider in one direction than the other. ❑ *...the small oval framed picture of a little boy.* • N-COUNT **Oval** is also a noun. ❑ *Using 2 spoons, form the cheese into small balls or ovals.*

Oval Of|fice N-UNCOUNT The **Oval Office** is the American president's private office in the White House. You can also use the **Oval Office** to refer to the American presidency itself. ❑ *...a meeting in the Oval Office.* ❑ *...his successors in the Oval Office.*

ovar|ian /oʊvɛəriən/ ADJ [ADJ n] **Ovarian** means in or relating to the ovaries. ❑ *My mother is undergoing treatment for ovarian cancer.*

ova|ry /oʊvəri/ (ovaries) N-COUNT A woman's **ovaries** are the two organs in her body that produce eggs. ❑ *...women who have had their ovaries removed.*

ova|tion /oʊveɪʃən/ (ovations) N-COUNT An **ovation** is a large amount of applause from an audience for a particular performer or speaker. [FORMAL] ❑ *They became civic heroes and received a tumultuous ovation on their appearance in New York City.*

oven /ʌvən/ (ovens) N-COUNT An **oven** is a device for cooking that is like a box with a door. You heat it and cook food inside it. ❑ *Put the onions and ginger in the oven and let them roast for thirty minutes.*

oven|proof /ʌvənpruf/ **1** ADJ [usu ADJ n] An **ovenproof** dish is one that has been specially made to be used in an oven without being damaged by the heat. **2** → See feature box at **cooking**

OVER
① POSITION AND MOVEMENT
② AMOUNTS AND OCCURRENCES
③ OTHER USES

① **over** ♦♦♦ /oʊvər/

In addition to the uses shown below, **over** is used after some verbs, nouns, and adjectives in order to introduce extra information. **Over** is also used in phrasal verbs such as 'hand over' and 'glaze over.'

1 PREP If one thing is **over** another thing or is moving **over** it, the first thing is directly above the second, either resting on it, or with a space between them. ❑ *He looked at himself in the mirror over the table.* • ADV [ADV after v] **Over** is also an adverb. ❑ *...planes flying over every 10 or 15 minutes.* **2** PREP If one thing is **over** another thing, it is supported by it and its ends are hanging down on each side of it. ❑ *A gray raincoat was folded over her arm.* **3** PREP If one thing is **over** another thing, it covers part or all of it. ❑ *Mix the ingredients and pour over the mushrooms.* ❑ *He was wearing a light-gray suit over a shirt.* • PREP [ADV after v] **Over** is also an adverb. ❑ *Heat this syrup and pour it over.* **4** PREP [V PREP n] If you lean **over** an object, you bend your body so that the top part of it is above the object. ❑ *They stopped to lean over a gate.* • ADV [ADV after v] **Over** is also an adverb. ❑ *Sam leaned over to open the door of the car.* **5** PREP If you look **over** or talk **over** an object, you look or talk across the top of it. ❑ *I went and stood beside him, looking over his shoulder.* **6** PREP [n PREP n, V PREP n] If a window has a view **over** an area of land or water, you can see the land or water through the window. ❑ *...a light and airy bar with a wonderful view over the river.* **7** PREP [V PREP n] If someone or something goes **over** a barrier, obstacle, or boundary, they get to the other side of it by going across it, or across the top of it. ❑ *I stepped over a broken piece of wood.* ❑ *Nearly one million people crossed over the river into Moldavia.* • ADV [ADV after v] **Over** is also an adverb. ❑ *I climbed over into the back seat.* **8** PREP If someone or something moves **over** an area or surface, they move across it, from one side to the other. ❑ *She ran swiftly over the lawn to the gate.* **9** PREP If something is on the opposite side of a road or river, you can say that it is **over** the road or river. ❑ *...a fashionable neighborhood, just over the river from Manhattan.* **10** ADV If you go **over** to a place, you go to that place. ❑ *I got out the car and drove over to Greg's place.* ❑ *I thought you might have invited her over.* **11** ADV You can use **over** to indicate a particular position or place a short distance away from someone or something. ❑ *He noticed Rolfe standing silently over by the window.* ❑ *John reached over and took Joanna's hand.* **12** ADV [ADV after v] You use **over** to say that someone or something falls toward or onto the ground, often suddenly or violently. ❑ *If he drinks more than two glasses of wine he falls over.* ❑ *She pushed past me, almost knocking me over.* **13** ADV [ADV after v] If something rolls **over** or is turned **over**, its position changes so that the part that was facing upward is now facing downward. ❑ *His car rolled over after a tire was punctured.* **14** PHRASE **All over** a place means in every part of it. ❑ *...doctors who work all over the country.* **15** PHRASE **Over here** means near you, or in the country you are in. ❑ *Why don't you come over here tomorrow evening.* **16** PHRASE **Over there** means in a place a short distance away from you, or in another country. ❑ *The cafe is just across the road over there.*

② **over** ♦♦♦ /oʊvər/ **1** PREP [PREP amount] If something is **over** a particular amount, measurement, or age, it is more than that amount, measurement, or age. ❑ *They say that tobacco will kill over 4 million people worldwide this year.* ❑ *His family have accumulated property worth well over $1 million.* • ADV [amount and ADV] **Over** is also an adverb. ❑ *...people aged 65 and over.* **2** PHRASE **Over and above** an amount, especially a normal amount, means more than that amount or in addition to it. ❑ *Expenditure on education has gone up by seven point eight per cent over and above inflation.* **3** ADV If you say that you have some food or money **over** or left **over**, you mean that it remains after you have used all that you need. ❑ *The company pay me well enough, but there's not much left over for luxuries.* **4** ADV [ADV after v] If you do something **over**, you do it again or start doing it again from the beginning. [AM] ❑ *She said if she had the chance to do it over, she would have hired a press secretary.* **5** PHRASE If you say that something happened **twice over**, **three times over** and so on, you are stating the number of times that it happened and emphasizing that it happened more than once. [mainly BRIT, EMPHASIS] ❑ *James had to have everything spelled out twice over for him.* **6** PHRASE If you do something **over again**, you do it again or start doing it again from the beginning. ❑ *If I could live my life over again, I would do things exactly the same way.* **7** PHRASE If you say that something is happening **all over again**, you are emphasizing that it is happening again, and you are suggesting that it is tiring, boring, or unpleasant. [EMPHASIS] ❑ *The whole process started all over again.* **8** PHRASE If you say that something happened **over and over** or **over and over again**, you are emphasizing that it happened many times. [EMPHASIS] ❑ *He plays the same songs over and over.*

③ **over** ♦♦♦ /oʊvər/ **1** ADJ [v-link ADJ] If an activity is **over** or all **over**, it is completely finished. ❑ *Warplanes that have landed there will be kept until the war is over.* ❑ *I am glad it's all over.* **2** PREP If you are **over** an illness or an experience, it has finished and you have recovered from its effects. ❑ *I'm glad that you're over the flu.* **3** PREP [n PREP n] If you have control of influence **over** someone or something, you are able to control them or influence them. ❑ *He's never had any influence over her.* **4** PREP [n PREP n, V PREP n] You use **over** to indicate what a disagreement or feeling relates to or is caused by. ❑ *...concern over recent events in the Dominican Republic.* ❑ *Staff at some air and sea ports are* beginning to protest over pay. **5** PREP If something happens **over** a particular period of time or **over** something such as a meal, it happens during that time or during the meal. ☐ *The number of attacks on the capital had gone down over the past week.* **6** PREP You use **over** to indicate that you give or receive information using a telephone, radio, or other piece of electrical equipment. ☐ *I'm not prepared to discuss this over the telephone.* ☐ *The head of state addressed the nation over the radio.* **7** PHRASE The presenter of a radio or television program says '**over to someone**' to indicate the person who will speak next. ☐ *With the rest of the sports news, over to Mike Martinez.* **8** CONVENTION When people such as the police or the army are using a radio to communicate, they say '**Over**' to indicate that they have finished speaking and are waiting for a reply. [FORMULAE]

PREFIX

over-
forms words that refer to a quality of action that exists or is done to too great an extent. *For example, if someone is being* **overcautious**, *they are being too cautious.*

---

over|achieve /oʊvərətʃiːv/ (**overachieves, overachieving, overachieved**) V-I If someone **overachieves** in something such as school work or a job, they work very hard because it is very important to them to do well and not because they enjoy what they are doing. ☐ *...emotions such as guilt, compulsion to please or overachieve, or depression.* • **over|achiev|er** (**overachievers**) N-COUNT *He comes from a family of overachievers.*

over|act /oʊvərækt/ (**overacts, overacting, overacted**) V-I If you say that someone **overacts**, you mean they exaggerate their emotions and movements, usually when acting in a play. ☐ *Sometimes he had overacted in his role as Prince.*

over|age /oʊvəreɪdʒ/ **1** ADJ If you are **overage**, you are officially too old to do something. ☐ *He was a couple of months overage for the youth team.* **2** ADJ [ADJ n] You use **overage** to describe someone who is doing something that is usually done by much younger people, and which therefore seems inappropriate or silly. [DISAPPROVAL] ☐ *...an overage nightclub singer.*

over|all ♦♦◊ (**overalls**)

The adjective and adverb are pronounced /oʊvərɔːl/. The noun is pronounced /oʊvərɔːl/.

1 ADJ [ADJ n] You use **overall** to indicate that you are talking about a situation in general or about the whole of something. ☐ *...the overall rise in unemployment.* • ADV [ADV with cl] **Overall** is also an adverb. ☐ *Overall I was disappointed.* **2** N-PLURAL [also *a pair of* N] **Overalls** are pants that are attached to a piece of cloth which covers your chest and which has straps going over your shoulders. [AM] ☐ *An elderly man dressed in faded overalls took the witness stand.*

in BRIT, use **dungarees**

3 N-PLURAL [also *a pair of* N] **Overalls** consist of a single piece of clothing that combines pants and a jacket. You wear overalls over your clothes in order to protect them while you are working. **4** → See feature box at DIY

SYNONYMS

overall
ADJ **1**
total: *The total cost of the project would be more than $240 million.*
general: *The figures represent a general decline in employment.*

---

over|all ma|jor|ity (**overall majorities**) N-COUNT [usu sing] If a political party wins an **overall majority** in an election or vote, they get more votes than the total number of votes or seats won by all their opponents together.

over|arch|ing /oʊvərɑːrtʃɪŋ/ ADJ [ADJ n] You use **overarching** to indicate that you are talking about something that includes or affects everything or everyone. [FORMAL] ☐ *The overarching question seems to be what happens when the U.S. pulls out?*

over|arm /oʊvərɑːrm/ ADJ [ADJ n] You use **overarm** to describe actions, such as throwing a ball, in which you stretch your arm over your shoulder. ☐ *...a single overarm stroke.*

over|awe /oʊvərɔː/ (**overawes, overawing, overawed**) V-T [usu passive] If you **are overawed** by something or someone,

you are very impressed by them and a little afraid of them. ☐ *Don't be overawed by people in authority, however important they are.*

over|bal|ance /oʊvərbæləns/ (**overbalances, overbalancing, overbalanced**) V-I If you **overbalance**, you fall over or nearly fall over, because you are not standing properly. ☐ *He overbalanced and fell head first.*

over|bear|ing /oʊvərbeərɪŋ/ ADJ An **overbearing** person tries to make other people do what he or she wants in an unpleasant and forceful way. [DISAPPROVAL] ☐ *My husband can be a little overbearing with our son.*

over|blown /oʊvərbloʊn/ ADJ Something that is **overblown** makes something seem larger, more important, or more significant than it really is. ☐ *Warnings of disaster may be overblown.* ☐ *The reporting of the story was fair, if sometimes overblown.*

over|board /oʊvərbɔːrd/ **1** ADV [ADV after v] If you fall **overboard**, you fall over the side of a boat into the water. ☐ *His sailing instructor fell overboard and nearly drowned during a lesson.* **2** PHRASE If you say that someone **goes overboard**, you mean that they do something to a greater extent than is necessary or reasonable. [INFORMAL] ☐ *People sometimes damage their skin by going overboard with abrasive cleansers.*

over|book /oʊvərbʊk/ (**overbooks, overbooking, overbooked**) **1** V-T/V-I If an organization such as an airline or a theater company **overbooks**, they sell more tickets than they have places for. ☐ *Planes are crowded, airlines overbook, and departures are almost never on time.* ☐ *It's the airline's policy not to overbook its flights.* **2** → See feature box at **tourism**

over|booked /oʊvərbʊkt/ ADJ [usu v-link ADJ] If something such as a hotel, bus, or aircraft is **overbooked**, more people have booked than the number of places that are available. ☐ *Sorry, the plane is overbooked.*

over|bur|dened /oʊvərbɜːrdənd/ **1** ADJ [oft ADJ with/by n] If a system or organization is **overburdened**, it has too many people or things to deal with and so does not function properly. ☐ *The city's hospitals are overburdened by casualties.* ☐ *...an overburdened air traffic control system.* **2** ADJ [oft ADJ with/by n] If you are **overburdened** with something such as work or problems, you have more of it than you can cope with. ☐ *Our boss dislikes being overburdened with insignificant detail.* ☐ *...overburdened teachers.*

over|came /oʊvərkeɪm/ **Overcame** is the past tense of **overcome**.

over|ca|pac|ity /oʊvərkəpæsɪti/ N-UNCOUNT If there is **overcapacity** in a particular industry or area, more goods have been produced than are needed, and the industry is therefore less profitable than it could be. [BUSINESS] ☐ *There is huge overcapacity in the world car industry.*

over|cast /oʊvərkæst/ **1** ADJ If it is **overcast**, or if the sky or the day is **overcast**, the sky is completely covered with cloud and there is not much light. ☐ *For three days it was overcast.* ☐ *The weather forecast is for showers and overcast skies.* **2** → See feature box at **weather**

over|charge /oʊvərtʃɑːrdʒ/ (**overcharges, overcharging, overcharged**) V-T If someone **overcharges** you, they charge you too much for their goods or services. ☐ *If you feel a taxi driver has overcharged you, say so.*

over|coat /oʊvərkoʊt/ (**overcoats**) N-COUNT An **overcoat** is a thick warm coat that you wear in winter.

over|come ♦◊ /oʊvərkʌm/ (**overcomes, overcoming, overcame**)

The form **overcome** is used in the present tense and is also the past participle.

1 V-T If you **overcome** a problem or a feeling, you successfully deal with it and control it. ☐ *Molly had fought and overcome her fear of flying.* **2** V-T If you **are overcome** by a feeling or event, it is so strong or has such a strong effect that you cannot think clearly. ☐ *The night before the test I was overcome by fear and despair.* **3** V-T [usu passive] If you **are overcome** by smoke or a poisonous gas, you become very ill or die from breathing it in. ☐ *The residents were trying to escape from the fire but were overcome by smoke.* **4** → See feature box at **challenge**

> **SYNONYMS**
>
> **overcome**
> VERB ❶
> **conquer:** *He has never conquered his addiction to smoking.*
> **master:** *His genius alone has mastered every crisis.*

over|crowd|ed /oʊvərkraʊdɪd/ ADJ An **overcrowded** place has too many things or people in it. ❏ *...a windswept, overcrowded, unattractive beach.*

over|crowd|ing /oʊvərkraʊdɪŋ/ N-UNCOUNT If there is a problem of **overcrowding**, there are more people living in a place than it was designed for. ❏ *Students were protesting at overcrowding in the dorms.*

over|do /oʊvərdu/ (overdoes, overdoing, overdid, overdone) ❶ V-T If someone **overdoes** something, they behave in an exaggerated or extreme way. ❏ *The extent of the rise might indicate that it had been overdone.* ❷ V-T If you **overdo** an activity, you try to do more than you can physically manage. ❏ *It is important never to overdo new exercises.* ❏ *It's important to study hard, but don't overdo it.*

over|done /oʊvərdʌn/ ❶ ADJ If food is **overdone**, it has been cooked for too long. ❏ *The meat was overdone and the vegetables soggy.* ❷ ADJ [usu v-link ADJ] If you say that something is **overdone**, you mean that you think it is excessive or exaggerated. ❏ *Everything about the party was overdone and silly: the band, the balloons, the paper hats.*

over|dose /oʊvərdoʊs/ (overdoses, overdosing, overdosed) ❶ N-COUNT If someone takes an **overdose** of a drug, they take more of it than is safe. ❏ *He was admitted to hospital after taking an overdose.* ❷ V-I If someone **overdoses** on a drug, they take more of it than is safe. ❏ *He'd overdosed on heroin.* ❸ N-COUNT You can refer to too much of something, especially something harmful, as an **overdose**. ❏ *An overdose of sun, sea, sand and chlorine can give lighter hair a green tinge.* ❹ V-I You can say that someone **overdoses** on something if they have or do too much of it. ❏ *The city, he concluded, had overdosed on design.*

over|draft /oʊvərdræft/ (overdrafts) N-COUNT If you have an **overdraft**, you have spent more money than you have in your bank account, and so you are in debt to the bank. ❏ *Her bank warned that unless she repaid the overdraft she could face legal action.*

over|drawn /oʊvərdrɔn/ ADJ If you are **overdrawn** or if your bank account is **overdrawn**, you have spent more money than you have in your account, and so you are in debt to the bank. ❏ *Nick's bank sent him a letter saying he was $500 overdrawn.*

over|dressed /oʊvərdrɛst/ ❶ ADJ If you say that someone is **overdressed**, you are criticizing them for wearing clothes that are not appropriate for the occasion because they are too formal. ❷ → See feature box at **fashion**

over|drive /oʊvərdraɪv/ (overdrives) ❶ N-COUNT [usu sing, oft N n] The **overdrive** in a vehicle is a very high gear that is used when you are driving at high speeds. ❷ PHRASE [PHR after v] If you go **into overdrive**, you begin to work very hard or perform a particular activity in a very intense way. ❏ *Once again, the press went into overdrive, with headlines such as "Butterfly Killing Corn."*

over|due /oʊvərdu/ ❶ ADJ If you say that a change or an event is **overdue**, you mean that you think it should have happened before now. ❏ *This debate is long overdue.* ❷ ADJ **Overdue** sums of money have not been paid, even though it is later than the date on which they should have been paid. ❏ *There is a 2% interest charge on overdue balances.* ❸ ADJ An **overdue** library book has not been returned to the library, even though the date on which it should have been returned has passed. ❏ *...a library book now weeks overdue.* ❹ → See feature box at **birth**

over easy also **over-easy** PHRASE [usu v n PHR] If a fried egg is served **over easy**, it is cooked on both sides. [AM] ❏ *We could handle a couple of eggs over easy, and coffee.*

over|eat /oʊvərit/ (overeats, overeating, overate, overeaten) V-I If you say that someone **overeats** than you mean they eat more than they need to or more than is healthy. ❏ *Unlike adults, children don't tend to overeat for emotional reasons.*

over|em|pha|sis /oʊvərɛmfəsɪs/ N-SING [also no det, usu N on n] If you say that there is an **overemphasis** on a particular thing, you mean that more importance or attention is given to it than is necessary. ❏ *He attributed the party's lack of success to an overemphasis on ideology and ideas.*

over|em|pha|size /oʊvərɛmfəsaɪz/ (overemphasizes, overemphasizing, overemphasized)

> in BRIT, also use **overemphasise**

❶ V-T If you say that someone **overemphasizes** something, you mean that they give it more importance than it deserves or than you consider appropriate. ❏ *Democrats will complain he overemphasizes punishment at the expense of prevention and treatment.* ❷ V-T [with brd-neg] If you say that something cannot **be overemphasized**, you are emphasizing that you think it is very important. [EMPHASIS] ❏ *The importance of education cannot be overemphasized.* ❏ *I can't overemphasize the cleanliness of this place.*

over|es|ti|mate (overestimates, overestimating, overestimated)

> The verb is pronounced /oʊvərɛstɪmeɪt/. The noun is pronounced /oʊvərɛstɪmɪt/.

❶ V-T/V-I If you say that someone **overestimates** something, you mean that they think it is greater in amount or importance than it really is. ❏ *He was overestimating their desire for peace.* ❏ *If they overestimate, they lose revenue.* • N-COUNT **Overestimate** is also a noun. ❏ *Twenty-five thousand turned out to be an overestimate.* ❷ V-T [with brd-neg] If you say that something cannot **be overestimated**, you are emphasizing that you think it is very important. [EMPHASIS] ❏ *The importance of the media in communicating antidrug messages cannot be overestimated.* ❸ V-T If you **overestimate** someone, you think that they have more of a skill or quality than they really have. ❏ *I think you overestimate me, Fred.*

over|excited /oʊvərɪksaɪtɪd/ ADJ [usu v-link ADJ] If you say that someone is **overexcited**, you mean that they are more excited than you think is desirable. ❏ *You'll need to provide continuous, organized entertainment or children may get overexcited.*

over|ex|posed /oʊvərɪkspoʊzd/ ADJ An **overexposed** photograph is of poor quality because the film has been exposed to too much light, either when the photograph was taken or during the developing process.

over|ex|tend|ed /oʊvərɪkstɛndɪd/ ADJ If a person or organization is **overextended**, they have become involved in more activities than they can financially or physically manage. ❏ *The company was overextended and faced bankruptcy.*

over|flight /oʊvərflaɪt/ (overflights) N-VAR An **overflight** is the passage of an aircraft from one country over another country's territory. ❏ *Nations react strongly to unauthorized overflights.*

over|flow (overflows, overflowing, overflowed)

> The verb is pronounced /oʊvərfloʊ/. The noun is pronounced /oʊvərfloʊ/.

❶ V-T/V-I [no passive] If a liquid or a river **overflows**, it flows over the edges of the container or place it is in. ❏ *Pour in some of the broth, but not all of it, because it will probably overflow.* ❏ *The rivers overflowed their banks.* ❷ V-I [usu cont] If a place or container **is overflowing** with people or things, it is too full of them. ❏ *Schreiber addressed an auditorium overflowing with journalists.* ❸ N-COUNT The **overflow** is the extra people or things that something cannot contain or deal with because it is not large enough. ❏ *Tents have been set up next to hospitals to handle the overflow.* ❹ PHRASE If a place or container is filled **to overflowing**, it is so full of people or things that no more can fit in. ❏ *The kitchen garden was full to overflowing with fresh vegetables.*

over|fly /oʊvərflaɪ/ (overflies, overflying, overflew, overflown) V-T When an aircraft **overflies** an area, it flies over it. [FORMAL] ❏ *Permission has not yet been granted for the airline to overfly Tanzania.*

over|grown /oʊvərgroʊn/ ❶ ADJ If a garden or other place is **overgrown**, it is covered with a lot of unruly plants because it has not been cared for. ❏ *We hurried on until we reached a courtyard overgrown with weeds.* ❷ ADJ [ADJ n] If you describe an adult as an **overgrown** child, you mean that their behavior and attitudes are like those of a child, and that you dislike this. [DISAPPROVAL] ❏ *...a bunch of overgrown kids.* ❸ → See feature box at **garden**

over|hang (overhangs, overhanging, overhung)

The verb is pronounced /ˌoʊvərˈhæŋ/. The noun is pronounced /ˈoʊvərhæŋ/.

1 V-T If one thing **overhangs** another, it sticks out over and above it. ◻ *Part of the rock wall overhung the path at one point.* **2** N-COUNT An **overhang** is the part of something that sticks out over and above something else. ◻ *A sharp overhang of rock gave them cover.*

over|haul (overhauls, overhauling, overhauled)

The verb is pronounced /ˌoʊvərˈhɔl/. The noun is pronounced /ˈoʊvərhɔl/.

1 V-T [usu passive] If a piece of equipment **is overhauled**, it is cleaned, checked thoroughly, and repaired if necessary. ◻ *They had ensured the plumbing was overhauled a year ago.* • N-COUNT **Overhaul** is also a noun. ◻ *...the overhaul of a cruiser.* **2** V-T If you **overhaul** a system or method, you examine it carefully and make many changes in it in order to improve it. ◻ *...proposals to overhaul bank regulations.* • N-COUNT **Overhaul** is also a noun. ◻ *The study says there must be a complete overhaul of air traffic control systems.*

over|head

The adjective and noun are pronounced /ˈoʊvərhɛd/. The adverb is pronounced /ˌoʊvərˈhɛd/.

1 ADJ [ADJ n] You use **overhead** to indicate that something is above you or above the place that you are talking about. ◻ *She turned on the overhead light and looked around the little room.* • ADV **Overhead** is also an adverb. ◻ *...planes passing overhead.* **2** N-UNCOUNT The **overhead** of a business is its regular and essential expenses, such as salaries, rent, electricity, and telephone bills. [BUSINESS] ◻ *Private insurers spend 27 cents of every dollar on overhead.*

in BRIT, use **overheads**

3 → See feature box at **business**

over|head pro|jec|tor (overhead projectors) N-COUNT An **overhead projector** is a machine that has a light inside it and makes the writing or pictures on a sheet of plastic appear on a screen or wall. The abbreviation **OHP** is also used.

over|hear /ˌoʊvərˈhɪər/ (overhears, overhearing, overheard) V-T If you **overhear** someone, you hear what they are saying when they are not talking to you and they do not know that you are listening. ◻ *I overheard two doctors discussing my case.*

over|heat /ˌoʊvərˈhit/ (overheats, overheating, overheated) **1** V-T/V-I If something **overheats** or if you **overheat** it, it becomes hotter than is necessary or desirable. ◻ *The engine was overheating and the car was not handling well.* • **over|heat|ed** ADJ ◻ *...that stuffy, overheated apartment.* **2** V-T/V-I If a country's economy **overheats** or if conditions **overheat** it, it grows so rapidly that inflation and interest rates rise very quickly. [BUSINESS] ◻ *The private sector is increasing its spending so sharply that the economy is overheating.* • **over|heat|ed** ADJ ◻ *...the disastrous consequences of an overheated market.*

over|heat|ed /ˌoʊvərˈhitɪd/ ADJ Someone who is **overheated** is very angry about something. ◻ *I think the reaction has been a little overheated.*

over|hung /ˌoʊvərˈhʌŋ/ **Overhung** is the past tense and past participle of **overhang**.

over|in|dulge /ˌoʊvərɪnˈdʌldʒ/ (overindulges, overindulging, overindulged) V-I If you **overindulge**, or **overindulge** in something that you like very much, usually food or drink, you allow yourself to have more of it than is good for you. ◻ *We all overindulge occasionally.* ◻ *Don't abuse your body by overindulging in alcohol.*

over|joyed /ˌoʊvərˈdʒɔɪd/ ADJ [v-link ADJ] If you are **overjoyed**, you are extremely happy about something. ◻ *Shelley was overjoyed to see me.*

over|kill /ˈoʊvərkɪl/ N-UNCOUNT You can say that something is **overkill** when you think that there is more of it than is necessary or appropriate. ◻ *Such security measures may be overkill.*

over|land /ˈoʊvərlænd/ ADJ [ADJ n] An **overland** journey is made across land rather than by ship or airplane. ◻ *...an overland journey through Iraq, Turkey, Iran and Pakistan.* • ADV [ADV after v] **Overland** is also an adverb. ◻ *They're traveling to Baghdad overland.*

over|lap (overlaps, overlapping, overlapped)

The verb is pronounced /ˌoʊvərˈlæp/. The noun is pronounced /ˈoʊvərlæp/.

1 V-RECIP If one thing **overlaps** another, or if you **overlap** them, a part of the first thing occupies the same area as a part of the other thing. You can also say that two things **overlap**. ◻ *When the bag is folded, the bottom overlaps one side.* ◻ *Overlap the slices carefully so there are no gaps.* **2** V-RECIP If one idea or activity **overlaps** another, or **overlaps** with another, they involve some of the same subjects, people, or periods of time. ◻ *Christian Holy Week overlaps with the beginning of the Jewish holiday of Passover.* ◻ *The needs of patients invariably overlap.* • N-VAR **Overlap** is also a noun. ◻ *...the overlap between civil and military technology.*

over|lay /ˌoʊvərˈleɪ/ (overlays, overlaying, overlaid) **1** V-T [usu passive] If something **is overlaid** with something else, it is covered by it. ◻ *The floor was overlaid with rugs of oriental design.* **2** V-T If something **is overlaid** with a feeling or quality, that feeling or quality is the most noticeable one, but there may be deeper and more important ones involved. [WRITTEN] ◻ *The party had been overlaid with a certain nervousness.* ◻ *...a surge of feeling which at this moment overlaid all others.*

over|leaf /ˈoʊvərlif/ ADV **Overleaf** is used in books and magazines to say that something is on the other side of the page you are reading. [FORMAL] ◻ *Answer the questionnaire overleaf.*

over|load (overloads, overloading, overloaded)

The verb is pronounced /ˌoʊvərˈloʊd/. The noun is pronounced /ˈoʊvərloʊd/.

1 V-T If you **overload** something such as a vehicle, you put more things or people into it than it was designed to carry. ◻ *Don't overload the boat or it will sink.* • **over|load|ed** ADJ ◻ *Some trains were so overloaded that their suspension collapsed.* **2** V-T To **overload** someone **with** work, problems, or information means to give them more work, problems, or information than they can cope with. ◻ *...an effective method that will not overload staff with yet more paperwork.* • N-UNCOUNT **Overload** is also a noun. ◻ *57 percent complained of work overload.* • **over|load|ed** ADJ ◻ *The bar waiter was already overloaded with orders.* **3** V-T If you **overload** an electrical system, you cause too much electricity to flow through it, and so damage it. ◻ *Never overload an electrical outlet.*

over|look /ˌoʊvərˈlʊk/ (overlooks, overlooking, overlooked) **1** V-T If a building or window **overlooks** a place, you can see the place clearly from the building or window. ◻ *Pretty and comfortable rooms overlook a flower-filled garden.* **2** V-T If you **overlook** a fact or problem, you do not notice it, or do not realize how important it is. ◻ *We overlook all sorts of warning signals about our own health.* **3** V-T If you **overlook** someone's faults or bad behavior, you forgive them and take no action. ◻ *...satisfying relationships that enable them to overlook each other's faults.*

over|lord /ˈoʊvərlɔrd/ (overlords) **1** N-COUNT [usu with supp] If you refer to someone as an **overlord**, you mean that they have great power and are likely to use it in a bad way. [WRITTEN] ◻ *We really don't want to be the overlords of the Palestinian population.* **2** N-COUNT In former times, an **overlord** was someone who had power over many people. ◻ *Henry II was the first king to be recognized as overlord of Ireland.*

over|ly /ˈoʊvərli/ ADV [ADV adj/adv/-ed] **Overly** means more than is normal, necessary, or reasonable. ◻ *Employers may become overly cautious about taking on new staff.*

over|manned /ˌoʊvərˈmænd/ ADJ If you say that a place or an industry is **overmanned**, you mean that you think there are more people working there or doing the work than is necessary. ◻ *Many factories were chronically overmanned.*

over|man|ning /ˌoʊvərˈmænɪŋ/ N-UNCOUNT If there is a problem of **overmanning** in an industry, there are more people working there or doing the work than is necessary.

over|much /ˌoʊvərˈmʌtʃ/ ADV If something happens **overmuch**, it happens too much or very much. [FORMAL] ◻ *He was not a man who thought overmuch about clothes.*

over|night ✦✧ /ˌoʊvərˈnaɪt/ **1** ADV [ADV after v] If something happens **overnight**, it happens throughout the night or at some point during the night. ❏ *The decision was reached overnight.* • ADJ [ADJ n] **Overnight** is also an adjective. ❏ *Travel and overnight accommodation are included.* ◻2 ADV [ADV after v] You can say that something happens **overnight** when it happens very quickly and unexpectedly. ❏ *The rules are not going to change overnight.* • ADJ [ADJ n] **Overnight** is also an adjective. ❏ *In 1970 he became an overnight success in America.* ◻3 ADJ [ADJ n] **Overnight** bags or clothes are ones that you take when you go and stay somewhere for one or two nights. ❏ *He realized he'd left his overnight bag at Mary's house.*

over|paid /oʊvərpeɪd/ ADJ If you say that someone is **overpaid**, you mean that you think they are paid more than they deserve for the work they do. ❏ *...grossly overpaid corporate lawyers.*

over|pass /oʊvərpæs/ (overpasses) N-COUNT An **overpass** is a structure which carries one road over the top of another one. [mainly AM] ❏ *...a $16 million highway overpass over Route 1.*

in BRIT, usually use **flyover**

over|pay /oʊvərpeɪ/ (overpays, overpaying, overpaid) ◻1 V-T/V-I If you **overpay** someone, or if you **overpay** for something, you pay more than is necessary or reasonable. ❏ *Management has to make sure it does not overpay its staff.* ❏ *The scheme will overpay some lawyers and underpay others.* ◻2 → see also **overpaid**

over|play /oʊvərpleɪ/ (overplays, overplaying, overplayed) ◻1 V-T If you say that someone **is overplaying** something such as a problem, you mean that they are making it seem more important than it really is. ❏ *I think the historical factor is overplayed, that it really doesn't mean much.* ◻2 PHRASE If someone **overplays** their hand, they act more confidently than they should because they believe that they are in a stronger position than they actually are. ❏ *The United States has to be careful it doesn't overplay its hand.*

over|popu|lat|ed /oʊvərpɒpyəleɪtɪd/ ADJ If an area is **overpopulated**, there are problems because it has too many people living there. ❏ *Environmentalists say parts of Arizona are already overpopulated.*

over|popu|la|tion /oʊvərpɒpyəleɪʃ°n/ N-UNCOUNT If there is a problem of **overpopulation** in an area, there are more people living there than can be supported properly. ❏ *...young people who are concerned about overpopulation in the world.*

over|pow|er /oʊvərpaʊər/ (overpowers, overpowering, overpowered) ◻1 V-T If you **overpower** someone, you manage to take hold of and keep hold of them, although they struggle a lot. ❏ *It took ten guardsmen to overpower him.* ◻2 V-T If a feeling **overpowers** you, it suddenly affects you very strongly. ❏ *A sudden dizziness overpowered him.* ◻3 V-T In a sports match, when one team or player **overpowers** the other, they play much better than the other and beat them easily. ❏ *Britain's tennis No 1 yesterday overpowered the reigning champion 7-6, 6-3.* ◻4 V-T If something such as a color or flavor **overpowers** another color or flavor, it is so strong that it makes the second one less noticeable. ❏ *A delicate wine will be overpowered by strong food.*

over|pow|er|ing /oʊvərpaʊərɪŋ/ ◻1 ADJ An **overpowering** feeling is so strong that you cannot resist it. ❏ *The desire for revenge can be overpowering.* ◻2 ADJ An **overpowering** smell or sound is so strong that you cannot smell or hear anything else. ❏ *There was an overpowering smell of alcohol.* ◻3 ADJ An **overpowering** person makes other people feel uncomfortable because they have such a strong personality. ❏ *Mrs. Winter was large and somewhat overpowering.*

over|priced /oʊvərpraɪst/ ADJ If you say that something is **overpriced**, you mean that you think it costs much more than it should. ❏ *I went and had an overpriced cup of coffee in the hotel cafeteria.*

over|ran /oʊvərræn/ **Overran** is the past tense of **overrun**.

over|rate /oʊvərreɪt/ (overrates, overrating, overrated) also **over-rate** V-T If you say that something or someone **is overrated**, you mean that people have a higher opinion of them than they deserve. ❏ *More people are finding out that the joys of work have been overrated.* • **over|rat|ed** ADJ ❏ *Life in the wild is vastly overrated.*

over|reach /oʊvərriːtʃ/ (overreaches, overreaching, overreached) V-T If you say that someone **overreaches** themselves, you mean that they fail at something because they are trying to do more than they are able to. ❏ *The company had overreached itself and made unwise investments.*

over|react /oʊvərriækt/ (overreacts, overreacting, overreacted) V-I If you say that someone **overreacts** to something, you mean that they have and show more of an emotion than is necessary or appropriate. ❏ *I overreact to anything sad.*

over|ride (overrides, overriding, overrode, overridden)

The verb is pronounced /oʊvərraɪd/. The noun is pronounced /oʊvərraɪd/.

◻1 V-T If one thing in a situation **overrides** other things, it is more important than they are. ❏ *The welfare of a child should always override the wishes of its parents.* ◻2 V-T If someone in authority **overrides** a person or their decisions, they cancel their decisions. ❏ *The president vetoed the bill, and the Senate failed by a single vote to override his veto.* ◻3 N-COUNT An **override** is an attempt to cancel someone's decisions by using your authority over them or by gaining more votes than they do in an election or contest. [AM] ❏ *The bill now goes to the House where an override vote is expected to fail.*

over|rid|ing /oʊvərraɪdɪŋ/ ADJ In a particular situation, the **overriding** factor is the one that is the most important. ❏ *My overriding concern is to raise the standards of state education.*

over|rule /oʊvərruːl/ (overrules, overruling, overruled) V-T If someone in authority **overrules** a person or their decision, they officially decide that the decision is incorrect or not valid. ❏ *Last year, the Court of Appeal overruled this decision.*

over|run /oʊvərrʌn/ (overruns, overrunning, overran) ◻1 V-T If an army or an armed force **overruns** a place, area, or country, it succeeds in occupying it very quickly. ❏ *A group of rebels overran the port area and most of the northern suburbs.* ◻2 ADJ [v-link ADJ] If you say that a place **is overrun** with things that you consider undesirable, you mean that there are a large number of them there. ❏ *The hotel has been ordered to close because it is overrun by mice and rats.* ◻3 V-T/V-I If costs **overrun**, they are higher than was planned or expected. [BUSINESS] ❏ *We should stop the nonsense of taxpayers trying to finance joint weapons whose costs always overrun hugely.* ❏ *Costs overran the budget by about 30%.* • N-COUNT **Overrun** is also a noun. ❏ *He was stunned to discover cost overruns of at least $1 billion.* ◻4 V-I If an event or meeting **overruns** by, for example, ten minutes, it continues for ten minutes longer than it was intended to. [BRIT]

over|seas ✦✧ /oʊvərsiːz/ ◻1 ADJ [ADJ n] You use **overseas** to describe things that involve or are in foreign countries, usually across a sea or an ocean. ❏ *He has returned to South Africa from his long overseas trip.* • ADV **Overseas** is also an adverb. ❏ *If you're staying for more than three months or working overseas, a full 10-year passport is required.* ◻2 ADJ [ADJ n] An **overseas** student or visitor comes from a foreign country, usually across a sea or an ocean. ❏ *Every year nine million overseas visitors come to the city.*

SYNONYMS

overseas
ADJ ◻1
foreign: *She was on her first foreign vacation without her parents.*
international: *...emergency aid from the international community.*

over|see /oʊvərsiː/ (oversees, overseeing, oversaw, overseen) V-T If someone in authority **oversees** a job or an activity, they make sure that it is done properly. ❏ *Use a surveyor or architect to oversee and inspect the different stages of the work.*

over|seer /oʊvərsɪər/ (overseers) ◻1 N-COUNT An **overseer** is someone whose job is to make sure that employees are working properly. ❏ *I was promoted to overseer at the tailor shop* ◻2 N-COUNT [usu with poss] If a person or organization is the **overseer** of a particular system or activity, they are responsible for making sure that the system or activity works well and is successful. ❏ *...the department's dual role as overseer of oil production and safety.*

oversell

over|sell /oʊvərsɛl/ (oversells, overselling, oversold) V-T If you say that something or someone **is oversold**, you mean that people say they are better or more useful than they really are. ❑ *The idea of being in a couple is certainly oversold.*

over|sexed /oʊvərsɛkst/ ADJ If you describe someone as **oversexed**, you mean that they are more interested in sex or more involved in sexual activities than you think they should be. [DISAPPROVAL]

over|shad|ow /oʊvərʃædoʊ/ (overshadows, overshadowing, overshadowed) ◼ V-T If an unpleasant event or feeling **overshadows** something, it makes it less happy or enjoyable. ❑ *Fears for the president's safety could overshadow his peace-making mission.* ◻ V-T [usu passive] If you **are overshadowed** by a person or thing, you are less successful, important, or impressive than they are. ❑ *Hester is overshadowed by her younger and more attractive sister.* ◼ V-T If one building, tree, or large structure **overshadows** another, it stands near it, is much taller than it, and casts a shadow over it. ❑ *She said stations should be in the open, near housing, not overshadowed by trees or walls.*

over|share /oʊvərʃɛər/ (overshares, oversharing, overshared) VERB If someone **overshares**, they tell other people too much about their personal life. [DISAPPROVAL] ❑ *Her tendency to overshare made her a reality TV star.*

over|shoot (overshoots, overshooting, overshot)

The verb is pronounced /oʊvərʃuːt/. The noun is pronounced /oʊvərʃuːt/.

◼ V-T If you **overshoot** a place that you want to get to, you go past it by mistake. ❑ *The plane apparently overshot the runway after landing.* ◻ V-T If a government or organization **overshoots** its budget, it spends more than it had planned to. ❑ *The government usually overshoot its original spending target.* • N-COUNT [usu supp N] **Overshoot** is also a noun. ❑ *...the 100 million dollar overshoot in the cost of building the hospital.*

over|sight /oʊvərsaɪt/ (oversights) ◼ N-COUNT If there has been an **oversight**, someone has forgotten to do something which they should have done. ❑ *William was angered and embarrassed by his oversight.* ◻ ADJ [ADJ n] An **oversight** committee or board is responsible for making sure that a process or system works efficiently and correctly. ❑ *The bill creates an oversight board with the authority to investigate and punish accounting firms.*

over|sim|pli|fy /oʊvərsɪmplɪfaɪ/ (oversimplifies, oversimplifying, oversimplified) V-T If you say that someone is **oversimplifying** something, you mean that they are describing or explaining it so simply that what they say is no longer true or reasonable. ❑ *One should not oversimplify the situation.* • **over|sim|pli|fied** ADJ [usu ADJ n] ❑ *...an oversimplified view of mathematics and the sciences.* • **over|sim|pli|fi|ca|tion** /oʊvərsɪmplɪfɪkeɪʃən/ (oversimplifications) N-VAR ❑ *There is an old saying that "we are what we eat." Obviously this is an oversimplification.*

over|size /oʊvərsaɪz/ also **oversized** ADJ [usu ADJ n] **Oversize** or **oversized** things are too big, or much bigger than usual. ❑ *...the oversize white sweater she had worn at school.* ❑ *...an oversized bed.*

over|sleep /oʊvərsliːp/ (oversleeps, oversleeping, overslept) V-I If you **oversleep**, you sleep longer than you should have. ❑ *I forgot to set my alarm and I overslept.*

over|spend (overspends, overspending, overspent)

The verb is pronounced /oʊvərspɛnd/. The noun is pronounced /oʊvərspɛnd/.

◼ V-I If you **overspend**, you spend more money than you can afford to. ❑ *Don't overspend on your home and expect to get the money back when you sell.* ◻ N-COUNT If an organization or business has an **overspend**, it spends more money than was planned or allowed in its budget. [BRIT, BUSINESS]

in AM, use **overrun**

over|spill /oʊvərspɪl/ (overspills) ◼ N-UNCOUNT [also a N, oft N n] **Overspill** is used to refer to people who live near a city because there is no room in the city itself. [BRIT] ❑ *...overspill council housing.*

in AM, use **overflow**

overthink

◻ N-UNCOUNT [also a N] You can use **overspill** to refer to things or people which there is no room for in the usual place because it is full. [BRIT] ❑ *An overspill from the museum's collection has been housed in a west London office block.*

in AM, use **overflow**

over|staffed /oʊvərstæft/ ADJ If you say that a place is **overstaffed**, you think there are more people working there than is necessary. ❑ *Many workers believe the factory is overstaffed.*

over|state /oʊvərsteɪt/ (overstates, overstating, overstated) V-T If you say that someone **is overstating** something, you mean they are describing it in a way that makes it seem more important or serious than it really is. ❑ *The authors no doubt overstated their case with a view to catching the public's attention.*

over|state|ment /oʊvərsteɪtmənt/ (overstatements) N-VAR If you refer to the way something is described as an **overstatement**, you mean it is described in a way that makes it seem more important or serious than it really is. ❑ *This may have been an improvement, but "breakthrough" was an overstatement.*

over|stay /oʊvərsteɪ/ (overstays, overstaying, overstayed) V-T [no passive] If you **overstay** your time, you stay somewhere for longer than you should. ❑ *Up to forty percent of the students had overstayed their visas.*

over|step /oʊvərstɛp/ (oversteps, overstepping, overstepped) V-T If you say that someone **oversteps** the limits of a system or situation, you mean that they do something that is not allowed or is not acceptable. ❑ *The commission is sensitive to accusations that it is overstepping its authority.* • PHRASE If someone **oversteps the mark**, they behave in a way that is considered unacceptable. [mainly BRIT]

in AM, use **go over the line**

over|stretch /oʊvərstrɛtʃ/ (overstretches, overstretching, overstretched) V-T/V-I If you **overstretch** something or someone or if they **overstretch**, you force them to do something they are not really capable of, and they may be harmed as a result. ❑ *Dr. Boutros Ghali said the operation would overstretch resources.* ❑ *Do what you know you can do well and don't overstretch yourself.* ❑ *Never force your legs to overstretch, or you can cause injuries.*

over|stretched /oʊvərstrɛtʃt/ ADJ If a system or organization is **overstretched**, it is being forced to work more than it is supposed to. ❑ *Analysts fear the overstretched air traffic control system could reach breaking point.*

over|sub|scribed /oʊvərsəbskraɪbd/ ADJ [usu v-link ADJ] If something such as an event or a service is **oversubscribed**, too many people apply to attend the event or use the service.

overt /oʊvɜrt/ ADJ An **overt** action or attitude is done or shown in an open and obvious way. ❑ *Although there is no overt hostility, Black and White students do not mix much.* • **overt|ly** ADV ❑ *He's written a few overtly political lyrics over the years.*

over|take /oʊvərteɪk/ (overtakes, overtaking, overtook, overtaken) ◼ V-T If someone or something **overtakes** a competitor, they become more successful than them. ❑ *Lung cancer has now overtaken breast cancer as a cause of death for women in the U.S.* ◻ V-T If a feeling **overtakes** you, it affects you very strongly. [LITERARY] ❑ *Something like panic overtook me in a flood.* ◼ V-T/V-I If you **overtake**, or **overtake** a vehicle or a person that is ahead of you and moving in the same direction, you pass them. [mainly BRIT]

in AM, usually use **pass**

over|tax /oʊvərtæks/ (overtaxes, overtaxing, overtaxed) ◼ V-T If you **overtax** someone or something, you force them to work harder than they can really manage, and may do them harm as a result. ❑ *...a contralto who has overtaxed her voice.* ◻ V-T If you say that a government **is overtaxing** its people, you mean that it is making them pay more tax than you think they should pay. ❑ *You can't help a country by overtaxing its people.*

over-the-counter → see **counter**

over the top → see **top** ③ 12

over|think /oʊvərθɪŋk/ (overthinks, overthinking, overthought) V-T/V-I If you **overthink**, or if you **overthink** a problem, you spend too much time thinking about it. ❑ *You overthink things and start worrying.*

over|throw (overthrows, overthrowing, overthrew, overthrown)

> The verb is pronounced /ouvərθrou/. The noun is pronounced /ouvərθrou/.

V-T When a government or leader **is overthrown**, they are removed from power by force. ❑ *That government was overthrown in a military coup three years ago.* • N-SING **Overthrow** is also a noun. ❑ *They were charged with plotting the overthrow of the state.*

over|time /ouvərtaɪm/ **1** N-UNCOUNT **Overtime** is time that you spend doing your job in addition to your normal working hours. ❑ *He would work overtime, without pay, to finish a job.* **2** PHRASE If you say that someone **is working overtime** to do something, you mean that they are using a lot of energy, effort, or enthusiasm trying to do it. [INFORMAL] ❑ *We had to battle very hard and our defense worked overtime to keep us in the game.* **3** N-UNCOUNT **Overtime** is an additional period of time that is added to the end of a sports game in which the score is tied, so that one team can score and win the game. ❑ *Denver had won the championship in overtime.* **4** → See feature box at **working**

over|tired /ouvərtaɪərd/ ADJ [usu v-link ADJ] If you are **overtired**, you are so tired that you feel unhappy or irritable, or feel that you cannot do things well.

over|tone /ouvərtoun/ (overtones) N-COUNT If something has **overtones** of a particular thing or quality, it suggests that thing or quality but does not openly express it. ❑ *The strike has taken on overtones of a civil rights campaign.*

over|took /ouvərtʊk/ **Overtook** is the past tense of **overtake**.

over|ture /ouvərtʃər, -tʃuər/ (overtures) N-COUNT; N-IN-NAMES An **overture** is a piece of music, often one that is the introduction to an opera or play. ❑ *...Wagner's Mastersingers Overture.*

over|turn /ouvərtɜrn/ (overturns, overturning, overturned) **1** V-T/V-I If something **overturns** or if you **overturn** it, it turns upside down or on its side. ❑ *The motorcycle veered out of control, overturned and smashed into a wall.* ❑ *Alex jumped up so violently that he overturned his glass of wine.* **2** V-T If someone in authority **overturns** a legal decision, they officially decide that that decision is incorrect or not valid. ❑ *When the courts overturned his decision, he backed down.*

over|use (overuses, overusing, overused)

> The verb is pronounced /ouvəryuz/. The noun is pronounced /ouvəryus/.

1 V-T If someone **overuses** something, they use more of it than necessary, or use it more often than necessary. ❑ *Don't overuse heated appliances on your hair.* • N-UNCOUNT **Overuse** is also a noun. ❑ *Supplies are under increasing threat from overuse and pollution.* **2** V-T If you say that people **overuse** a word or idea, you mean that they use it so often that it no longer has any real meaning or effect. ❑ *Which words or phrases do you most overuse?* • **over|used** ADJ ❑ *"Just Do It" has become one of the most overused catch phrases in recent memory.*

over|value /ouvərvælyu/ (overvalues, overvaluing, overvalued) V-T To **overvalue** something, often a cost or rate of exchange, means to place its value at too high a level compared with other similar things. ❑ *...a rate which does not overvalue the peso.* • **over|valu|ation** /ouvərvælyueɪʃ°n/ N-UNCOUNT [oft N of n] ❑ *These problems were aggravated by the overvaluation of the dollar.* • **over|valued** ADJ ❑ *It still can be argued that Japanese shares are overvalued in terms of the return they offer.*

over|view /ouvərvyu/ (overviews) N-COUNT An **overview** of a situation is a general understanding or description of it as a whole. ❑ *The central section of the book is a historical overview of drug use.*

over|ween|ing /ouvərwinɪŋ/ ADJ [usu ADJ n] If you want to emphasize your disapproval of someone's great ambition or pride, you can refer to their **overweening** ambition or pride. [FORMAL, DISAPPROVAL] ❑ *"Your modesty is a cover for your overweening conceit," she said.*

over|weight /ouvərweɪt/ ADJ Someone who is **overweight** weighs more than is considered healthy or attractive. ❑ *Being even moderately overweight increases your risk of developing high blood pressure.*

over|whelm /ouvərwɛlm/ (overwhelms, overwhelming, overwhelmed) **1** V-T If you **are overwhelmed** by a feeling or event, it affects you very strongly, and you do not know how to deal with it. ❑ *He was overwhelmed by a longing for times past.* ❑ *Sightseers may be a little overwhelmed by the crowds and noise.* **2** V-T If a group of people **overwhelm** a place or another group, they gain complete control or victory over them. ❑ *It was clear that one massive Allied offensive would overwhelm the weakened enemy.*

over|whelm|ing ✦✧ /ouvərwɛlmɪŋ/ **1** ADJ If something is **overwhelming**, it affects you very strongly, and you do not know how to deal with it. ❑ *The task won't feel so overwhelming if you break it down into small, easy-to-accomplish steps.* • **over|whelm|ing|ly** ADV [ADV adj] ❑ *The other women all seemed overwhelmingly confident.* **2** ADJ You can use **overwhelming** to emphasize that an amount or quantity is much greater than other amounts or quantities. [EMPHASIS] ❑ *The overwhelming majority of small businesses go broke within the first twenty-four months.* • **over|whelm|ing|ly** ADV ❑ *The people voted overwhelmingly for change.*

over|work /ouvərwɜrk/ (overworks, overworking, overworked) V-T/V-I If you **overwork** or if someone **overworks** you, you work too hard, and are likely to become very tired or sick. ❑ *He's overworking and has a lot on his mind.* • N-UNCOUNT **Overwork** is also a noun. ❑ *He died of a heart attack brought on by overwork.* • **over|worked** ADJ ❑ *...an overworked doctor.*

over|worked /ouvərwɜrkt/ ADJ If you describe a word, expression, or idea as **overworked**, you mean it has been used so often that it no longer has much effect or meaning. ❑ *"Ecological" has become one of the most overworked adjectives among manufacturers of garden supplies.*

over|wrought /ouvərrɔt/ ADJ Someone who is **overwrought** is extremely upset and emotional. ❑ *One overwrought member had to be restrained by friends.*

ovu|late /ɒvyəleɪt, ouv-/ (ovulates, ovulating, ovulated) V-I When a woman or female animal **ovulates**, an egg is produced from one of her ovaries. ❑ *Some girls may first ovulate even before they menstruate.* • **ovu|la|tion** /ɒvyəleɪʃ°n, ouv-/ N-UNCOUNT ❑ *By noticing these changes, the woman can tell when ovulation is about to occur.*

ovum /ouvəm/ (ova) N-COUNT An **ovum** is one of the eggs of a woman or female animal. [TECHNICAL]

ow /aʊ/ EXCLAM '**Ow!**' is used in writing to represent the noise that people make when they suddenly feel pain. ❑ *Ow! Don't do that!*

owe ✦✧ /oʊ/ (owes, owing, owed) **1** V-T If you **owe** money to someone, they have lent it to you and you have not yet paid it back. ❑ *The company owes money to more than 60 banks.* ❑ *Blake already owed him nearly $50.* **2** V-T [no passive] If someone or something **owes** a particular quality or their success to a person or thing, they only have it because of that person or thing. ❑ *I always suspected she owed her first job to her friendship with Roger.* ❑ *He owed his survival to his strength as a swimmer.* **3** V-I If you say that you **owe** a great deal to someone or something, you mean that they have helped you or influenced you a lot, and you feel very grateful to them. ❑ *As a musician I owe much to the radio station in my home town.* **4** V-T If you say that something **owes** a great deal to a person or thing, you mean that it exists, is successful, or has its particular form mainly because of them. ❑ *The island's present economy owes a good deal to tourism.* **5** V-T If you say that you **owe** someone gratitude, respect, or loyalty, you mean that they deserve it from you. ❑ *Perhaps we owe these people more respect.* ❑ *I owe you an apology; you must have found my attitude very annoying.* **6** V-T [no passive] If you say that you **owe it to** someone to do something, you mean that you should do that thing because they deserve it. ❑ *I can't go; I owe it to him to stay.* ❑ *You owe it to yourself to get some professional help.* **7** PHRASE You use **owing to** when you are introducing the reason for something. ❑ *Owing to staff shortages, there was no food on the plane.*

owl /aʊl/ (owls) N-COUNT An **owl** is a bird with a flat face, large eyes, and a small sharp beak. Most owls obtain their food by hunting small animals at night.

owl|ish /aʊlɪʃ/ ADJ [usu ADJ n] An **owlish** person looks like an owl, especially because they wear glasses, and seems to be very serious and smart. ❏ *With his owlish face, it is easy to understand why he was called "The Professor."*

own ♦♦♦ /oʊn/ (owns, owning, owned) **1** ADJ [poss ADJ] You use **own** to indicate that something belongs to a particular person or thing. ❏ *My wife decided I should have my own shop.* ❏ *He could no longer trust his own judgement.* • PRON [poss PRON] **Own** is also a pronoun. ❏ *He saw the major's face a few inches from his own.* **2** ADJ [poss ADJ] You use **own** to indicate that something is used by, or is characteristic of, only one person, thing, or group. ❏ *Jennifer insisted on her own room.* ❏ *Each nation has its own peculiarities when it comes to doing business.* • PRON [poss PRON] **Own** is also a pronoun. ❏ *This young lady has a sense of style that is very much her own.* **3** ADJ [poss ADJ] You use **own** to indicate that someone does something without any help from other people. ❏ *They enjoy making their own decisions.* • PRON [poss PRON] **Own** is also a pronoun. ❏ *There's no career structure; you have to create your own.* **4** V-T If you **own** something, it is your property. ❏ *His father owns a local diner.* **5** V-T If you **own** someone when playing a sport or computer game, you defeat them completely. [INFORMAL] ❏ *I just totally owned you!* **6** PHRASE If you have something you can **call** your **own**, it belongs only to you, rather than being controlled by or shared with someone else. ❏ *I would like a place I could call my own.* **7** PHRASE If someone or something **comes into** their **own**, they become very successful or start to perform very well because the circumstances are right. ❏ *Women are coming into their own in the new South Africa.* **8** PHRASE If you **get** your **own back** on someone, you have your revenge on them because of something bad that they have done to you. [BRIT, INFORMAL] **9** PHRASE If you say that someone has a particular thing **of** their **own**, you mean that that thing belongs or relates to them, rather than to other people. ❏ *He set out in search of ideas for starting a company of his own.* **10** PHRASE If someone or something has a particular quality or characteristic **of** their **own**, that quality or characteristic is especially theirs, rather than being shared by other things or people of that type. ❏ *The cries of the seagulls gave this part of the harbor a fascinating character of its own.* **11** PHRASE When you are **on** your **own**, you are alone. ❏ *He lives on his own.* ❏ *I felt pretty lonely last year being on my own.* **12** PHRASE If you do something **on** your **own**, you do it without any help from other people. ❏ *I work best on my own.* **13 to hold your own** → see **hold** ④
▶ **own up** PHRASAL VERB If you **own up** to something wrong that you have done, you admit that you did it. ❏ *The teacher is waiting for someone to own up to the graffiti.*

---- COLLOCATIONS ----

own
NOUN **4**
own + noun: business, company, share, stake; home, house, land, property
own + adverb: collectively, jointly, outright, partly; privately, publicly

---- SYNONYMS ----

own
VERB **4**
have: *Oscar had a new bicycle.*
possess: *He is said to possess a large fortune.*
keep: *This eccentric writer kept a lobster as a pet.*

own brand (own brands) N-COUNT **Own brands** are products which have the trademark or label of the store which sells them, especially a supermarket chain. They are normally cheaper than other popular brands. [BRIT, BUSINESS]

in AM, use **store brand**

-owned /-oʊnd/ COMB IN ADJ **-owned** combines with nouns, adjectives, and adverbs to form adjectives that indicate who owns something. ❏ *Many state-owned companies have been sold since the early 1980s.* ❏ *...a famous Japanese-owned hotel in Los Angeles.*

own|er ♦♦◊ /oʊnər/ (owners) N-COUNT If you are the **owner** of something, it belongs to you. ❏ *The owner of the store was sweeping his floor when I walked in.*

owner-occupier (owner-occupiers) N-COUNT An **owner-occupier** is a person who owns the house or apartment that they live in.

own|er|ship ♦◊◊ /oʊnərʃɪp/ N-UNCOUNT **Ownership** of something is the state of owning it. ❏ *On January 23rd, the U.S. decided to relax its rules on the foreign ownership of its airlines.* ❏ *...the growth of home ownership.*

own goal (own goals) **1** N-COUNT [usu sing] In sports, if someone scores an **own goal**, they accidentally score a goal for the team they are playing against. [BRIT] **2** N-COUNT [usu sing] If a course of action that someone takes harms their own interests, you can refer to it as an **own goal**. [BRIT]

own la|bel (own labels) N-COUNT **Own label** is the same as **own brand**. [BUSINESS] ❏ *People will trade down to own labels which are cheaper.*

ox /ɒks/ (oxen /ɒksən/) N-COUNT An **ox** is a bull that has been castrated. Oxen are used in some countries for pulling vehicles or carrying things.

ox|ford /ɒksfərd/ (oxfords) also **Oxford** **1** N-PLURAL **Oxfords** are low shoes with laces at the front. [mainly AM] ❏ *He had changed his boots for a pair of Oxfords.* **2** N-UNCOUNT [usu N n] **Oxford** or **oxford cloth** is a type of cotton fabric, used especially for men's shirts. [mainly AM] ❏ *This pure cotton Oxford shirt comes in three colors.* ❏ *I hugged him, smelling new oxford cloth and warm skin.* **3** → See also color supplement

oxi|da|tion /ɒksɪdeɪʃən/ N-UNCOUNT **Oxidation** is a process in which a chemical substance changes because of the addition of oxygen. [TECHNICAL]

ox|ide /ɒksaɪd/ (oxides) N-MASS [usu supp N] An **oxide** is a compound of oxygen and another chemical element.

oxi|dize /ɒksɪdaɪz/ (oxidizes, oxidizing, oxidized)

in BRIT, also use **oxidise**

V-T/V-I When a substance **is oxidized** or when it **oxidizes**, it changes chemically because of the effect of oxygen on it. ❏ *If the organic material decays or is oxidized, it will not form petroleum.* ❏ *The original white lead pigments have oxidized and turned black.*

ox|tail /ɒksteɪl/ (oxtails) N-VAR **Oxtail** is meat from the tail of a cow. It is used for making soups and stews. ❏ *...oxtail soup.*

oxy|gen /ɒksɪdʒən/ N-UNCOUNT **Oxygen** is a colorless gas that exists in large quantities in the air. All plants and animals need oxygen in order to live. ❏ *The human brain needs to be without oxygen for only four minutes before permanent damage occurs.*

oxy|gen|ate /ɒksɪdʒɪneɪt/ (oxygenates, oxygenating, oxygenated) V-T To **oxygenate** something means to mix or dissolve oxygen into it. ❏ *Previous attempts at filtering and oxygenating aquarium water had failed.* ❏ *...freshly oxygenated blood.*

oxy|gen mask (oxygen masks) N-COUNT An **oxygen mask** is a device that is connected to a cylinder of oxygen by means of a tube. It is placed over the nose and mouth of someone who is having difficulty in breathing in order to help them breathe more easily.

oxy|mo|ron /ɒksɪmɔːrɒn/ (oxymorons) N-COUNT If you describe a phrase as an **oxymoron**, you mean that what it refers to combines two opposite qualities or ideas and therefore seems impossible. [TECHNICAL] ❏ *This has made many Americans conclude that business ethics is an oxymoron.*

oys|ter /ɔɪstər/ (oysters) **1** N-COUNT An **oyster** is a large flat shellfish. Some oysters can be eaten and others produce valuable objects called pearls. ❏ *He had two dozen oysters and enjoyed every one of them.* **2** PHRASE If you say that **the world is** someone's **oyster**, you mean that they can do anything or go anywhere that they want to. ❏ *You're young, you've got a lot of opportunity. The world is your oyster.*

oys|ter bed (oyster beds) N-COUNT An **oyster bed** is a place where oysters breed and grow naturally or are kept for food or pearls.

oyster|catch|er /ɔɪstərkætʃər/ (oystercatchers) N-COUNT An **oystercatcher** is a black and white bird with a long red beak. It lives near the sea and eats small shellfish.

oz **Oz** is a written abbreviation for **ounce**. ❏ *Whisk 1 oz of butter into the sauce.*

ozone /oʊzoʊn/ N-UNCOUNT **Ozone** is a colorless gas which is a form of oxygen. There is a layer of ozone high above the Earth's surface, that protects us from harmful radiation from the sun. ❑ *What they find could provide clues to what might happen worldwide if ozone depletion continues.*

ozone-fri̱endly ADJ Ozone-friendly chemicals, products, or technology do not cause harm to the ozone layer. ❑ *...ozone-friendly chemicals for fridges and air conditioners.*

o̱zone lay|er ◼ N-SING The **ozone layer** is the part of the Earth's atmosphere that has the most ozone in it. The ozone layer protects living things from the harmful radiation of the sun. ❑ *...the hole in the ozone layer.* ◼ → See also color supplement

Pp

P also **p** /piː/ (**P's**, **p's**) N-VAR P is the sixteenth letter of the English alphabet.

pa /pɑː/ (**pas**) N-FAMILY Some people address or refer to their father as **pa**. [INFORMAL] ❑ *Pa used to be in the army.*

PA /piː eɪ/ (**PAs**) N-COUNT [usu the N in sing] If you refer to the **PA** or the **PA system** in a place, you are referring to the public address system. ❑ *A voice came booming over the PA.*

p.a. p.a. is a written abbreviation for **per annum**.

PAC /pæk/ (**PACs**) N-COUNT A **PAC** is an organization that campaigns for particular political policies, and that gives money to political parties or candidates who support those policies. PAC is an abbreviation for **political action committee**. [AM] ❑ *Something like $2 million of PAC money has flowed into his campaigns for the last 17 years.*

pace ◆◇◇ /peɪs/ (**paces**, **pacing**, **paced**) **1** N-SING [usu with supp] The **pace** of something is the speed at which it happens or is done. ❑ *Many people were not satisfied with the pace of change.* ❑ *They could not stand the pace or the workload.* **2** N-SING [usu with supp] Your **pace** is the speed at which you walk. ❑ *He moved at a brisk pace down the rue St. Antoine.* **3** N-COUNT [usu with supp] A **pace** is the distance that you move when you take one step. ❑ *He'd only gone a few paces before he stopped again.* **4** V-T/V-I If you **pace** a small area, you keep walking up and down in it, because you are anxious or impatient. ❑ *As they waited, Kravis paced the room nervously.* ❑ *He found John pacing around the house, unable to sleep.* **5** V-T If you **pace** yourself when doing something, you do it at a steady rate. ❑ *It was a tough race and I had to pace myself.* **6** PHRASE If something **keeps pace** with something else that is changing, it changes quickly in response to it. ❑ *The earnings of the average American have failed to keep pace with the rate of inflation.* **7** PHRASE If you **keep pace** with someone who is walking or running, you succeed in going as fast as them, so that you remain close to them. ❑ *With four laps to go, he kept pace with the leaders.* **8** PHRASE If you do something **at your own pace**, you do it at a speed that is comfortable for you. ❑ *The computer will give students the opportunity to learn at their own pace.* **9 at a snail's pace** → see **snail**

paced /peɪst/ ADJ [adv ADJ] If you talk about the way that something such as a movie or book is **paced**, you are referring to the speed at which the story is told. ❑ *This excellent thriller is fast paced and believable.*

pace|maker /peɪsmeɪkər/ (**pacemakers**) **1** N-COUNT A **pacemaker** is a device that is placed inside someone's body in order to help their heart beat in the right way. ❑ *She was fitted with a pacemaker after suffering serious heart trouble.* **2** N-COUNT A **pacemaker** is a competitor in a race whose task is to start the race very quickly in order to help the other runners achieve a very fast time. Pacemakers usually stop before the race is finished.

pace|setter /peɪssɛtər/ (**pacesetters**) **1** N-COUNT A **pacesetter** is someone who is in the lead during part of a race or competition and therefore decides the speed or standard of the race or competition for that time. ❑ *The two Americans are unlikely pacesetters.* ❑ *Hammond was the early pacesetter.* **2** N-COUNT A **pacesetter** is a person or a company that is considered to be the leader in a particular field or activity. ❑ *They were the pacesetter for political change in the region.*

pachy|derm /pækidɜrm/ (**pachyderms**) N-COUNT A **pachyderm** is a large thick-skinned animal such as an elephant or rhinoceros. [TECHNICAL]

pa|cif|ic /pəsɪfɪk/ ADJ [usu ADJ n] A **pacific** person, country, or course of action is peaceful or has the aim of bringing about peace. [FORMAL] ❑ *The statesman was less pacific than people thought.*

Pa|cif|ic **1** N-PROPER [the N] **The Pacific** or **the Pacific Ocean** is a very large sea to the west of North and South America, and to the east of Asia and Australia. ❑ *...an island in the Pacific.* **2** ADJ [ADJ n] **Pacific** is used to describe things that are in or that relate to the Pacific Ocean. ❑ *...the tiny Pacific island of Pohnpei.*

Pa|cif|ic Rim N-SING [the N] **The Pacific Rim** is the area on the western shores of the Pacific Ocean, including Japan, China, Korea, Thailand, and Malaysia. ❑ *...the growing need for energy which is now emerging in Asia and the Pacific Rim.* ❑ *...the economies of Pacific Rim countries.*

paci|fi|er /pæsɪfaɪər/ (**pacifiers**) N-COUNT A **pacifier** is a rubber or plastic object that you give to a baby to suck so that he or she feels comforted. [AM]

in BRIT, use **dummy**

paci|fism /pæsɪfɪzəm/ N-UNCOUNT **Pacifism** is the belief that war and violence are always wrong. ❑ *...a leading exponent of pacifism.*

paci|fist /pæsɪfɪst/ (**pacifists**) **1** N-COUNT A **pacifist** is someone who believes that violence is wrong and refuses to take part in wars. ❑ *Many protesters insist they are pacifists, opposed to war in all forms.* **2** ADJ If someone has **pacifist** views, they believe that war and violence are always wrong. ❑ *...his mother's pacifist ideals.*

paci|fy /pæsɪfaɪ/ (**pacifies**, **pacifying**, **pacified**) **1** V-T If you **pacify** someone who is angry, upset, or not pleased, you succeed in making them calm or pleased. ❑ *Is this a serious step, or is this just something to pacify the critics?* **2** V-T If the army or the police **pacify** a group of people, they use force to overcome their resistance or protests. ❑ *Government forces have found it difficult to pacify the rebels.* ● **paci|fi|ca|tion** /pæsɪfɪkeɪʃən/ N-UNCOUNT ❑ *...the pacification of the country.*

pack ◆◆◇ /pæk/ (**packs**, **packing**, **packed**) **1** V-T/V-I When you **pack**, or when you **pack** a bag, you put clothes and other things into it, because you are leaving a place or going on vacation. ❑ *When I was 17, I packed my bags and left home.* ❑ *I began to pack a few things for the trip.* ● **pack|ing** N-UNCOUNT ❑ *She left Frances to finish her packing.* **2** V-T When people **pack** things, for example, in a factory, they put them into containers or boxes so that they can be shipped and sold. ❑ *They offered me a job packing boxes in a warehouse.* ❑ *Machines now exist to pack olives in jars.* ● **pack|ing** N-UNCOUNT ❑ *The shipping and packing costs are passed along in the item price.* **3** V-T/V-I If people or things **pack into** a place or if they **pack** a place, there are so many of them that the place is full. ❑ *Hundreds of people packed into the mosque.* **4** N-COUNT A **pack** of things is a collection of them that is sold or given together in a box or bag. ❑ *The club will send a free information pack.* ❑ *...a pack of cigarettes.* **5** N-COUNT You can refer to a group of people who go around together as a **pack**, especially when it is a large group that you feel threatened by. ❑ *He thus avoided a pack of journalists eager to question him.* **6** N-COUNT A **pack** of wolves or dogs is a group of them that hunt together. ❑ *...a pack of stray dogs.* **7** N-COUNT A **pack** of playing cards is a complete set of playing cards. [mainly BRIT]

in AM, usually use **deck**

package

8 → see also **packed, packing** 9 PHRASE If you say that an account is **a pack of lies**, you mean that it is completely untrue. ❑ *You told me a pack of lies.* 10 PHRASE If you **send** someone **packing**, you make them go away. [INFORMAL] ❑ *I decided I wanted to live alone and I sent him packing.*

pack|age ✦✧✧ /pǽkɪdʒ/ (packages, packaging, packaged) 1 N-COUNT A **package** is something wrapped in paper, in a bag or large envelope, or in a box, usually so that it can be sent to someone by mail. ❑ *I tore open the package.* 2 N-COUNT A **package** is a small container in which a quantity of something is sold. Packages are either small boxes made of thin cardboard, or bags or envelopes made of paper or plastic. [mainly AM] ❑ *...a package of doughnuts.*

in BRIT, usually use **packet**

3 N-COUNT A **package** is a set of proposals that are made by a government or organization and that must be accepted or rejected as a group. ❑ *...a package of measures to help the movie industry.* 4 V-T [usu passive] When a product **is packaged**, it is put into containers to be sold. ❑ *The beans are then ground and packaged for sale as ground coffee.* 5 V-T [usu passive] If something **is packaged** in a particular way, it is presented or advertised in that way in order to make it seem attractive or interesting. ❑ *A city is like any product, it has to be packaged properly to be attractive to the consumer.* 6 N-COUNT A **package** tour is a vacation in which your travel and your accommodations are booked for you. ❑ *...package tours to Egypt.*

pack|age deal (package deals) N-COUNT [usu sing] A **package deal** is a set of offers or proposals that is made by a government or an organization that must be accepted or rejected as a whole.

pack|ag|ing /pǽkɪdʒɪŋ/ N-UNCOUNT **Packaging** is the container or covering that something is sold in. ❑ *It is selling very well, in part because the packaging is so attractive.*

pack ani|mal (pack animals) N-COUNT A **pack animal** is an animal such as a horse or donkey that is used to carry things.

packed /pækt/ 1 ADJ A place that is **packed** is very crowded. ❑ *The place is packed at lunchtime.* ❑ *...a packed meeting in Detroit.* 2 ADJ [v-link ADJ with n] Something that is **packed with** things contains a very large number of them. ❑ *The encyclopedia is packed with clear illustrations and over 250 recipes.* 3 → See feature box at **commute**

pack|er /pǽkər/ (packers) N-COUNT A **packer** is a worker whose job is to pack things into containers. ❑ *Norma Jones worked as a packer in a local chemical factory.*

pack|et /pǽkɪt/ (packets) 1 N-COUNT [with supp] An information **packet** is a set of information about a particular subject that is given to people who are interested in that subject. [AM] ❑ *Call us for a free information packet that tells you more.* ❑ *...a 23-page packet of topics to be discussed.*

in BRIT, use **pack**

2 N-COUNT A **packet** is a small container in which a quantity of something is sold. Packets are either small boxes made of thin cardboard, or bags or envelopes made of paper or plastic. [mainly BRIT] ❑ *...sugar packets.* 3 N-COUNT You can use **packet** to refer to a packet and its contents, or to the contents only. [mainly BRIT]

in AM, usually use **pack**

pack|et switch|ing also packet-switching N-UNCOUNT **Packet switching** is a method of sending computer data on telephone lines that automatically divides the data into short pieces in order to send it and puts it together again when it is received. [COMPUTING]

pack ice N-UNCOUNT **Pack ice** is an area of ice that is floating on the sea. It is made up of pieces of ice that have been pushed together.

pack|ing /pǽkɪŋ/ 1 N-UNCOUNT **Packing** is the paper, plastic, or other material that is put around things that are being sent somewhere to protect them. ❑ *My fingers shook as I pulled the packing from the box.* 2 → see also **pack**

pack|ing box (packing boxes) N-COUNT A **packing box** is the same as a **packing crate**. [mainly AM]

pack|ing case (packing cases) N-COUNT A **packing case** is the same as a **packing crate**. [mainly BRIT]

pack|ing crate (packing crates) N-COUNT A **packing crate** is a large wooden box in which things are put so that they can be stored or taken somewhere.

pack|ing plant (packing plants) N-COUNT A **packing plant** is a company that processes and packs food, especially meat, to be sold. [AM]

pact ✦✧✧ /pækt/ (pacts) N-COUNT A **pact** is a formal agreement between two or more people, organizations, or governments to do a particular thing or to help each other. ❑ *Last month he signed a new non-aggression pact with Germany.*

SYNONYMS

pact
NOUN
agreement: *The two countries signed an agreement to jointly launch satellites.*
deal: *The two sides tried and failed to come to a deal.*
treaty: *...the Treaty of Rome, which established the European Community.*
protocol: *...the Montreal Protocol to phase out use and production of CFCs.*

---

pad /pæd/ (pads, padding, padded) 1 N-COUNT A **pad** is a fairly thick, flat piece of a material such as cloth or rubber. Pads are used, for example, to clean things, to protect things, or to change their shape. ❑ *He withdrew the needle and placed a pad of cotton over the spot.* ❑ *...a scouring pad.* 2 N-COUNT A **pad** of paper is a number of pieces of paper attached together along the top or the side, so that each piece can be torn off when it has been used. ❑ *She wrote on a pad of paper.* ❑ *Have a pad and pencil ready and jot down some of your thoughts.* 3 V-I When someone **pads** somewhere, they walk there with steps that are fairly quick, light, and quiet. ❑ *Freddy speaks very quietly and pads around in soft velvet slippers.* ❑ *...a dog padding through the streets.* 4 N-COUNT A **pad** is a platform or an area of flat, hard ground where helicopters take off and land or rockets are launched. ❑ *...a little round helicopter pad.* ❑ *...a landing pad on the back of the ship.* 5 N-COUNT The **pads** of a person's fingers and toes or of an animal's feet are the soft, fleshy parts of them. ❑ *Tap your cheeks all over with the pads of your fingers.* 6 V-T If you **pad** something, you put something soft in it or over it in order to make it less hard, to protect it, or to give it a different shape. ❑ *Pad the back of a car seat with a pillow.* • **pad|ded** ADJ ❑ *...a padded jacket.* 7 V-T If you **pad** or **pad out** a piece of writing or a speech with unnecessary words or pieces of information, you include them to make it longer and hide the fact that you do not have very much to say. ❑ *Quotations should be used to make points, not to pad the essay.* ❑ *The reviewer padded out his review with a lengthy biography of the author.* 8 V-T If an employee with an expense account **pads** their expenses, they claim that their expenses are greater than they really are in order to get more money from their employer. ❑ *She was fired for padding her expenses.* 9 → see also **padding**
▶ **pad out** PHRASAL VERB → see **pad** 7

pad|ded cell (padded cells) N-COUNT A **padded cell** is a small room with padded walls in a psychiatric hospital or prison, where a person who may behave violently can be put so that they do not hurt themselves.

pad|ding /pǽdɪŋ/ N-UNCOUNT **Padding** is soft material put on something or inside it in order to make it less hard, to protect it, or to give it a different shape. ❑ *...the foam rubber padding on the headphones.* ❑ *Players must wear padding to protect them from injury.*

pad|dle /pǽdəl/ (paddles, paddling, paddled) 1 N-COUNT A **paddle** is a short pole with a wide flat part at one end or at both ends. You hold it in your hands and use it as an oar to move a small boat through water. ❑ *We might be able to push ourselves across with the paddle.* 2 V-T/V-I If you **paddle** a boat, you move it through water using a paddle. ❑ *...the skills you will use to paddle the canoe.* 3 N-COUNT A **paddle** is a specially shaped piece of wood that is used for hitting the ball in table tennis. [AM]

in BRIT, use **bat**

4 → See also color supplement

pad|dleboat (paddleboats) N-COUNT A **paddleboat** or a **paddle steamer** is a large boat that is pushed through the water by the movement of large wheels called paddle wheels that are attached to its sides.

pad|dock /pædək/ (paddocks) N-COUNT A **paddock** is a small field where horses are kept. ❑ *The family kept horses in the paddock in front of the house.*

pad|dy /pædi/ (paddies) N-COUNT A **paddy** or a **paddy field** is a field that is kept flooded with water and is used for growing rice. ❑ *...the paddy fields of China.*

pad|dy wag|on (paddy wagons) N-COUNT A **paddy wagon** is a van or truck which the police use for transporting prisoners or people who have been arrested. [mainly AM, INFORMAL] ❑ *The block was entirely barricaded by police, who began arresting the demonstrators and putting them in paddy wagons and buses.*

pad|lock /pædlɒk/ (padlocks, padlocking, padlocked)
■ N-COUNT A **padlock** is a lock that is used for fastening two things together. It consists of a block of metal with a U-shaped bar attached to it. One end of the bar is released by turning a key in the lock. ❑ *They had put a padlock on the door of his house.* ■ V-T If you **padlock** something, you lock it or fasten it to something else using a padlock. ❑ *Eddie parked his bicycle against a lamppost and padlocked it.*

pa|dre /pɑːdreɪ/ (padres) N-COUNT; N-VOC A **padre** is a Christian priest, especially one who works with the armed forces. [INFORMAL] ❑ *Could I speak to you in private a moment, padre?*

paean /piːən/ (paeans) N-COUNT [usu N to n] A **paean** is a piece of music, writing, or a movie that expresses praise, admiration, or happiness. [LITERARY] ❑ *...a paean to deep, passionate love.*

pa|el|la /paɪeɪlə, -eɪljə/ (paellas) N-VAR **Paella** is a dish cooked especially in Spain, that consists of rice mixed with small pieces of vegetables, shellfish, and chicken.

pa|gan /peɪgən/ (pagans) ■ ADJ **Pagan** beliefs and activities do not belong to any of the main religions of the world. They are older, or are believed to be older, than other religions. ❑ *The Christian church has adapted many pagan ideas over the centuries.* ■ N-COUNT In former times, **pagans** were people who did not believe in Christianity and whom many Christians considered to be inferior people. ❑ *The pagans used torchlight parades and bonfires to celebrate important events.*

pa|gan|ism /peɪgənɪzəm/ N-UNCOUNT **Paganism** is pagan beliefs and activities. ❑ *The country swayed precariously between Christianity and paganism.*

page ♦♦♦ /peɪdʒ/ (pages, paging, paged) ■ N-COUNT A **page** is one side of one of the pieces of paper in a book, magazine, or newspaper. Each page usually has a number printed at the top or bottom. ❑ *Take out your book and turn to page 4.* ❑ *...the front page of USA Today.* ■ N-COUNT The **pages** of a book, magazine, or newspaper are the pieces of paper it consists of. ❑ *He turned the pages of his notebook.* ■ N-COUNT You can refer to an important event or period of time as a **page** of history. [LITERARY] ❑ *...a new page in the country's political history.* ■ V-T If someone who is in a public place is **paged**, they receive a message, often over a speaker, telling them that someone is trying to contact them. ❑ *He was paged repeatedly as the flight was boarding.* ■ N-COUNT A **page** is a young person who takes messages or does small jobs for members of the United States Congress or state legislatures. [AM] ■ N-COUNT A **page** is a small boy who accompanies the bride at a wedding.

pag|eant /pædʒənt/ (pageants) ■ N-COUNT A **pageant** or a **beauty pageant** is a competition in which young women are judged to decide which one is the most beautiful. ❑ *...the Miss Universe beauty pageant.* ■ N-COUNT A **pageant** is a colorful public procession, show, or ceremony. Pageants are usually held outdoors and often celebrate events or people from history. ❑ *...a historical pageant of kings and queens.*

pag|eant|ry /pædʒəntri/ N-UNCOUNT People use **pageantry** to refer to the colorful and formal things that are done for special official or royal occasions, for example, the wearing of special clothes and the playing of special music. ❑ *...all the pageantry of an official state visit.*

page|boy /peɪdʒbɔɪ/ (pageboys) also **page-boy** N-COUNT A **pageboy** is a small boy who accompanies the bride at a wedding. [mainly BRIT]

in AM, usually use **page**

pag|er /peɪdʒər/ (pagers) N-COUNT A **pager** is a small electronic device that you can carry around with you and that gives you a number or a message when someone is trying to contact you. ❑ *Scores of messages on his pager have not been answered.*

page-turner (page-turners) N-COUNT You can refer to an exciting novel, such as a thriller, as a **page-turner**. ❑ *It's an extraordinarily compelling page-turner that also happens to be a major work of literature.*

pa|go|da /pəgoʊdə/ (pagodas) N-COUNT A **pagoda** is a building that is used for religious purposes, especially by Buddhists, in China, Japan, and Southeast Asia. Pagodas are usually very highly decorated.

paid /peɪd/ ■ **Paid** is the past tense and past participle of **pay**. ■ ADJ [ADJ n] **Paid** workers, or people who do **paid** work, receive money for the work that they do. ❑ *Apart from a small team of paid staff, the organization consists of unpaid volunteers.* ■ ADJ [ADJ n] If you are given **paid** vacation, you get your wages or salary even though you are not at work. ❑ *He agreed to hire her at slightly over minimum wage with two weeks' paid vacation.* ■ ADJ [adv ADJ] If you are well **paid**, you receive a lot of money for the work that you do. If you are badly **paid**, you do not receive much money. ❑ *...a well-paid accountant.* ❑ *The prospects for the worst-paid workers are poor.*

paid-up also **paid up** ■ ADJ [ADJ n] If a person or country is a **paid-up** member of a group, they are an enthusiastic member or are recognized by most people as being a member of it. ❑ *Despite a past in an inner-city housing project, I am a fully paid-up member of the middle classes now.* ■ ADJ [ADJ n] If someone is a **paid-up** member of an organization, they have paid the money needed to become an official member. ❑ *...a fully paid-up member of the National Geographic Society.*

pail /peɪl/ (pails) N-COUNT A **pail** is a bucket, usually made of metal or wood. [mainly AM]

pain ♦♦◊ /peɪn/ (pains, pained) ■ N-VAR **Pain** is the feeling of great discomfort you have, for example, when you have been hurt or when you are ill. ❑ *...back pain.* ❑ *To help ease the pain, heat can be applied to the area with a hot water bottle.* ❑ *I felt a sharp pain in my lower back.* • PHRASE If you are **in pain**, you feel pain in a part of your body because you are injured or ill. ❑ *She was writhing in pain, bathed in perspiration.* ■ N-UNCOUNT **Pain** is the feeling of unhappiness that you have when something unpleasant or upsetting happens. ❑ *...gray eyes that seemed filled with pain.* ■ V-T [no cont] If a fact or idea **pains** you, it makes you feel upset and disappointed. ❑ *This public acknowledgment of Ted's disability pained my mother.* ■ PHRASE In informal English, if you call someone or something **a pain** or **a pain in the neck**, you mean that they are very annoying or irritating. Expressions such as **a pain in the ass** and **a pain in the butt** are also used, but most people consider them offensive. [INFORMAL, DISAPPROVAL] ❑ *Getting rid of unwanted applications from your PC can be a real pain.* ■ PHRASE If you **take pains** to do something or **go to great pains** to do something, you try hard to do it, because you think it is important to do it. ❑ *He took great pains to see that he got it right.*

pained /peɪnd/ ADJ If you have a **pained** expression or look, you look upset, worried, or slightly annoyed. ❑ *Tanya put on a pained look, as though the subject was too delicate to be spoken about.*

pain|ful ♦◊◊ /peɪnfəl/ ■ ADJ If a part of your body is **painful**, it hurts because it is injured or because there is something wrong with it. ❑ *Her glands were swollen and painful.* ❑ *Her leg was too painful to ignore.* • **pain|ful|ly** ADV [ADV with v] ❑ *His tooth had started to throb painfully again.* ■ ADJ If something such as an illness, injury, or operation is **painful**, it causes you a lot of physical pain. ❑ *...a painful back injury.* • **pain|ful|ly** ADV [ADV with v] ❑ *...cracking his head painfully against the cupboard.* ■ ADJ Situations, memories, or experiences that are **painful** are difficult and unpleasant to deal with, and often make you feel sad and upset. ❑ *Remarks like that brought back painful memories.* ❑ *...the painful transition to democracy.* • **pain|ful|ly** ADV [ADV with v] ❑ *...their old relationship, which he had painfully broken off.*

painfully — pale

> **SYNONYMS**
>
> **painful**
> ADJ
> **1**
> **sore:** My chest is still sore from the surgery.
> **tender:** My tummy felt very tender.
> **excruciating:** I was in excruciating pain and one leg wouldn't move.
> **3**
> **distressing:** It is very distressing to see your baby attached to tubes and monitors.
> **unpleasant:** The symptoms can be uncomfortable, unpleasant, and serious.
> **upsetting:** Childhood illness can be upsetting for children and parents alike.

pain|ful|ly /peɪnfəli/ **1** ADV [ADV adv/adj] You use **painfully** to emphasize a quality or situation that is undesirable. [EMPHASIS] ◻ Things are moving painfully slowly. ◻ ...a painfully shy young man. **2** → see also **painful**

pain|killer /peɪnkɪlər/ (painkillers) **1** N-COUNT A **painkiller** is a drug that reduces or stops physical pain. **2** → See feature box at **illness**

pain|less /peɪnlɪs/ **1** ADJ If something such as a treatment is **painless** it causes no physical pain. ◻ Acupuncture treatment is gentle, painless, and relaxing. ◻ The operation itself is a brief, painless procedure. • **pain|less|ly** ADV [ADV with v] ◻ ...a technique to eliminate unwanted facial hair quickly and painlessly. **2** ADJ If a process or activity is **painless**, there are no difficulties involved, and you do not have to make a great effort or suffer in any way. ◻ The journey is relatively painless, even with children. • **pain|less|ly** ADV [ADV with v] ◻ ...a game for children that painlessly teaches essential pre-reading skills.

pains|taking /peɪnzteɪkɪŋ, peɪnsteɪ-/ ADJ A **painstaking** search, examination, or investigation is done extremely carefully and thoroughly. ◻ Forensic experts carried out a painstaking search of the debris. • **pains|taking|ly** ADV ◻ Broken bones were painstakingly pieced together and reshaped.

paint ✦✧ /peɪnt/ (paints, painting, painted) **1** N-MASS **Paint** is a colored liquid that you put onto a surface with a brush in order to protect the surface or to make it look nice, or that you use to produce a picture. ◻ ...a can of red paint. ◻ They saw some large letters in white paint. **2** N-SING On a wall or object, **the paint** is the covering of dried paint on it. ◻ The paint was peeling on the window frames. **3** V-T/V-I If you **paint** a wall or an object, you cover it with paint. ◻ They started to mend the woodwork and paint the walls. ◻ I had come here to paint. **4** V-T If you **paint** something or **paint** a picture of it, you produce a picture of it using paint. ◻ He is painting a huge volcano. ◻ Why do people paint pictures? **5** V-T When you **paint** a design or message on a surface, you put it on the surface using paint. ◻ ...a machine for painting white lines on roads. ◻ They went around painting rude slogans on cars. **6** V-T If you **paint** a grim or vivid picture of something, you give a description of it that is grim or vivid. ◻ The report paints a grim picture of life there. **7** → see also **gloss paint**, **oil paint**, **painting**

paint|box /peɪntbɒks/ (paintboxes) N-COUNT A **paintbox** is a small flat plastic or metal container with a number of little blocks of colored paint inside that can be made wet and used to paint a picture.

paint|brush /peɪntbrʌʃ/ (paintbrushes) N-COUNT A **paintbrush** is a brush that you use for painting.

paint|er /peɪntər/ (painters) **1** N-COUNT A **painter** is an artist who paints pictures. ◻ ...the French painter Claude Monet. **2** N-COUNT A **painter** is someone who paints walls, doors, and some other parts of buildings as their job. ◻ ...the son of a painter and decorator.

paint|er|ly /peɪntərli/ ADJ [usu ADJ n] **Painterly** means relating to or characteristic of painting or painters. ◻ ...his painterly talents. ◻ The film has a painterly eye.

paint|ing ✦✧ /peɪntɪŋ/ (paintings) **1** N-COUNT A **painting** is a picture that someone has painted. ◻ ...a large painting of Dwight Eisenhower. **2** N-UNCOUNT **Painting** is the activity of painting pictures. ◻ ...two hobbies she really enjoyed, painting and gardening. **3** N-UNCOUNT **Painting** is the activity of painting doors, walls, and some other parts of buildings. ◻ ...painting and decorating.

paint strip|per (paint strippers) N-MASS **Paint stripper** is a liquid that removes old paint from things such as doors or pieces of furniture.

paint|work /peɪntwɜrk/ N-UNCOUNT The **paintwork** of a building, room, or vehicle is the covering of paint on it, or the parts of it that are painted. [BRIT]

pair ✦✧ /pɛər/ (pairs, pairing, paired) **1** N-COUNT A **pair** of things are two things of the same size and shape that are used together or are both part of something, for example, shoes, earrings, or parts of the body. ◻ ...a pair of socks. ◻ ...earrings that cost $142.50 a pair. **2** N-COUNT Some objects that have two main parts of the same size and shape are referred to as a **pair**, for example, **a pair of pants** or **a pair of scissors**. ◻ ...a pair of faded jeans. **3** N-SING You can refer to two people as a **pair** when they are standing or walking together or when they have some kind of relationship with each other. ◻ A pair of teenage boys were smoking cigarettes. ◻ The pair admitted that their three-year-old marriage was going through "a difficult time." **4** V-T [usu passive] If one thing **is paired with** another, it is put with it or considered with it. ◻ The trainees will then be paired with experienced managers. **5** → see also **au pair**

> **COLLOCATIONS**
>
> **pair**
> NOUN
> **1**
> adjective + **pair**: identical, matching
> **3**
> adjective + **pair**: odd, unlikely
> **pair** + be + adjective: inseparable

pair|ing /pɛərɪŋ/ (pairings) N-COUNT Two people, especially athletes, actors, or musicians, who are working together as a pair can be referred to as a **pairing**. ◻ The two actors are an unlikely pairing.

pais|ley /peɪzli/ (paisleys) N-VAR **Paisley** is a special pattern of curving shapes and colors, used especially on fabric. ◻ He was elegantly dressed in a gray suit, blue shirt, and paisley tie.

pa|jam|as /pədʒɑməz/ N-PLURAL [also a pair of N] A pair of **pajamas** consists of loose pants and a top that people wear to bed. ◻ I don't want to get out of my pajamas in the morning.

in BRIT, use **pyjamas**

> **WORD HISTORY**
>
> **pajamas**
> Pajamas comes from Persian pāy jāma, meaning 'leg clothing.'

Pa|ki|stani /pækɪstæni, pɑkɪstɑni/ (Pakistanis) **1** ADJ **Pakistani** means belonging or relating to Pakistan, or to its people or culture. **2** N-COUNT [usu pl] A **Pakistani** is a Pakistani citizen, or a person of Pakistani origin.

pal /pæl/ (pals) N-COUNT Your **pals** are your friends. [INFORMAL, OLD-FASHIONED] ◻ They talked like old pals.

pal|ace ✦✧ /pælɪs/ (palaces) **1** N-COUNT A **palace** is a very large impressive house, especially one that is the official home of a king, queen, or president. ◻ ...Buckingham Palace. **2** → See also color supplement

pal|at|able /pælətəbəl/ **1** ADJ If you describe food or drink as **palatable**, you mean that it tastes pleasant. [FORMAL] ◻ ...flavorings and preservatives, designed to make the food look more palatable. **2** ADJ If you describe something such as an idea or method as **palatable**, you mean that people are willing to accept it. ◻ ...a palatable way of firing employees.

pal|ate /pælɪt/ (palates) **1** N-COUNT Your **palate** is the top part of the inside of your mouth. **2** N-COUNT You can refer to someone's **palate** as a way of talking about their ability to judge good food or drink. ◻ ...fresh pasta sauces to tempt more demanding palates.

pa|la|tial /pəleɪʃəl/ ADJ [usu ADJ n] A **palatial** house, hotel, or office building is very large and impressive. ◻ ...a palatial Hollywood mansion.

pale ✦✧ /peɪl/ (paler, palest, pales, paling, paled) **1** ADJ If something is **pale**, it is very light in color or almost white. ◻ Migrating birds filled the pale sky. ◻ As we age, our skin becomes paler. • COMB IN COLOR **Pale** is also a combining form. ◻ ...a pale blue sailor dress. **2** ADJ If someone looks **pale**, their face looks a lighter color than usual, usually because they are ill, frightened, or shocked. ▫ *She looked pale and tired.* **3** V-I If one thing **pales** in comparison with another, it is made to seem much less important, serious, or good by it. ▫ *When someone you love has a life-threatening illness, everything else pales in comparison.*

pale|on|tol|ogy /peɪliɒntɒlədʒi/
in BRIT, also use **palaeontology**
N-UNCOUNT **Paleontology** is the study of fossils as a guide to the history of life on earth. ● **pale|on|tolo|gist** (**paleontologists**) N-COUNT ▫ *...Harvard paleontologist Stephen Jay Gould.*

Pal|es|tin|ian /pæləstɪniən/ (**Palestinians**) **1** ADJ **Palestinian** means belonging or relating to the area between the River Jordan and the Mediterranean Sea that used to be called Palestine, or to the Arabs who come from this area. **2** N-COUNT [usu pl] A **Palestinian** is someone from Palestine.

pal|ette /pælɪt/ (**palettes**) **1** N-COUNT A **palette** is a flat piece of wood or plastic on which an artist mixes paints. ▫ *The painter's right hand holds the brush, the left the palette.* **2** N-COUNT You can refer to the range of colors that are used by a particular artist or group of artists as their **palette**. ▫ *He paints from a palette consisting almost exclusively of gray and mud brown.*

pal|ette knife (**palette knives**) N-COUNT A **palette knife** is a knife with a broad, flat, flexible blade used in cooking, or in painting to apply oil paint to a canvas or other surface.

pali|mo|ny /pælɪmoʊni/ N-UNCOUNT **Palimony** is money that a person pays to a partner they have lived with for a long time but not been married to and are now separated from. Compare **alimony**.

pal|in|drome /pælɪndroʊm/ (**palindromes**) N-COUNT A **palindrome** is a word or a phrase that is the same whether you read it backward or forward, for example, the word 'refer.'

pali|sade /pælɪseɪd/ (**palisades**) **1** N-COUNT A **palisade** is a fence of wooden posts that are driven into the ground in order to protect people from attack. **2** N-COUNT A **palisade** is a high cliff or a line of high cliffs, especially alongside a river or a coastline. [AM] ▫ *...the lofty palisade of black granite cliffs that ran parallel to the shore.* ▫ *We flew north up the Hudson with its purple palisades.*

pall /pɔl/ (**palls, palled**) **1** V-I [no cont] If something **palls**, it becomes less interesting or less enjoyable after a period of time. ▫ *Already the allure of meals in restaurants had begun to pall.* **2** N-COUNT [usu N of n] If a **pall** of smoke hangs over a place, there is a thick cloud of smoke above it. ▫ *A pall of oily black smoke drifted over the clifftop.* **3** PHRASE If something unpleasant **casts a pall over** an event or occasion, it makes it less enjoyable than it should be. ▫ *The unrest has cast a pall over what is usually a day of national rejoicing.*

pall|bearer /pɔlbɛərər/ (**pallbearers**) N-COUNT At a funeral, a **pallbearer** is a person who helps to carry the coffin or who walks beside it.

pal|let /pælɪt/ (**pallets**) **1** N-COUNT A **pallet** is a flat wooden or metal platform on which goods are stored so that they can be lifted and moved using a forklift truck. ▫ *The warehouse will hold more than 90,000 pallets storing 30 million Easter eggs.* **2** N-COUNT A **pallet** is a narrow mattress filled with straw that is put on the floor for someone to sleep on. **3** N-COUNT A **pallet** is a hard, narrow bed. ▫ *He was given only a wooden pallet with a blanket.*

pal|lia|tive /pæliətɪv, -iætɪv/ (**palliatives**) **1** N-COUNT A **palliative** is a drug or medical treatment that relieves suffering without treating the cause of the suffering. **2** N-COUNT A **palliative** is an action that is intended to make the effects of a problem less severe but does not actually solve the problem. [FORMAL] ▫ *The loan was a palliative, not a cure, for ever-increasing financial troubles.*

pal|lid /pælɪd/ **1** ADJ Someone or something that is **pallid** is pale in an unattractive or unnatural way. ▫ *...helpless grief on pallid faces.* **2** ADJ You can describe something such as a performance or book as **pallid** if it is weak or not at all exciting. ▫ *...a pallid government publication.*

pal|lor /pælər/ N-SING [usu with supp] If you refer to the **pallor** of someone's face or skin, you mean that it is pale and unhealthy. ▫ *The deathly pallor of her skin had been replaced by the faintest flush of color.*

pal|ly /pæli/ ADJ [oft ADJ with n] If you are **pally** with someone, you are friendly with them. [INFORMAL]

palm /pɑm/ (**palms**) **1** N-COUNT A **palm** or a **palm tree** is a tree that grows in hot countries. It has long leaves growing at the top, and no branches. ▫ *...golden sands and swaying palms.* **2** N-COUNT The **palm** of your hand is the inside part of your hand, between your fingers and your wrist. ▫ *Dornberg slapped the table with the palm of his hand.* **3** PHRASE If you have someone or something **in the palm of** your **hand**, you have control over them. ▫ *Johnson thought he had the board of directors in the palm of his hand.*

palm|cord|er /pɑmkɔrdər/ (**palmcorders**) N-COUNT A **palmcorder** is a small video camera that you can hold in the palm of your hand.

palm|is|try /pɑmɪstri/ N-UNCOUNT **Palmistry** is the practice and art of trying to find out what people are like and what will happen in their future by examining the lines on the palms of their hands.

palm oil N-UNCOUNT **Palm oil** is a yellow oil that comes from the fruit of certain palm trees and is used in making soap and sometimes as a fat in cooking.

Palm Sun|day N-UNCOUNT **Palm Sunday** is the Sunday before Easter. It is the day when Christians remember Jesus Christ's arrival in Jerusalem a few days before he was killed.

palo|mi|no /pæləminoʊ/ (**palominos**) N-COUNT A **palomino** is a horse that is yellowish or cream in color and has a white mane and tail.

pal|pable /pælpəbəl/ ADJ You describe something as **palpable** when it is obvious or intense and easily noticed. ▫ *The tension between Amy and Jim is palpable.* ● **pal|pably** /pælpəbli/ ADV [ADV with cl/group] ▫ *The scene was palpably intense to watch.*

pal|pi|tate /pælpɪteɪt/ (**palpitates, palpitating, palpitated**) **1** V-I If someone's heart **palpitates**, it beats very fast in an irregular way, because they are frightened or anxious. ▫ *He felt suddenly faint, and his heart began to palpitate.* **2** V-I If something **palpitates**, it shakes or seems to shake. [LITERARY] ▫ *She lay on the bed, her eyes closed and her bosom palpitating.*

pal|pi|ta|tion /pælpɪteɪʃən/ (**palpitations**) N-VAR When someone has **palpitations**, their heart beats very fast in an irregular way. ▫ *Caffeine can cause palpitations and headaches.*

pal|sy /pɔlzi/ **1** N-UNCOUNT **Palsy** is a medical condition in which a person is unable to move part of their body, or in which a part of their body shakes uncontrollably. **2** → see also **cerebral palsy**

pal|try /pɔltri/ (**paltrier, paltriest**) ADJ A **paltry** amount of money or of something else is one that you consider to be very small. ▫ *...a paltry fine of $150.*

pam|pas /pæmpəs, -əz/ N-SING [the N] The **pampas** is the large area of flat, grassy land in South America.

pam|per /pæmpər/ (**pampers, pampering, pampered**) V-T If you **pamper** someone, you make them feel comfortable by doing things for them or giving them expensive or luxurious things. ▫ *Why don't you let your mother pamper you for a while?* ▫ *Pamper yourself with our luxury gifts.* ● **pam|pered** ADJ ▫ *...today's pampered superstars.*

pam|phlet /pæmflɪt/ (**pamphlets**) N-COUNT A **pamphlet** is a very thin book with a paper cover that gives information about something. ▫ *...a pamphlet about smoking.*

pam|phlet|eer /pæmflɪtɪər/ (**pamphleteers**) N-COUNT A **pamphleteer** is a person who writes pamphlets, especially about political subjects.

pan ✦✧ /pæn/ (**pans, panning, panned**) **1** N-COUNT A **pan** is a round metal container with a long handle, that is used for cooking things in, usually on top of a stove. ▫ *Heat the butter and oil in a large pan.* **2** V-T [usu passive] If something such as a movie or a book **is panned** by journalists, they say it is very bad. [INFORMAL] ▫ *His first high-budget movie, called "Brain Donors," was panned by the critics.* **3** V-T/V-I If you **pan** a movie or television camera or if it **pans** somewhere, it moves slowly around so that a wide area is filmed. ▫ *The camera panned along the line of players.* ▫ *A television camera panned the stadium.*

PREFIX

pan-
is added to the beginning of adjectives and nouns to form other adjectives and nouns that describe something as being connected with all places or people of a particular kind. *For example, a **pan-European** defense system is designed to protect all of the countries in Europe.*

pana|cea /pænəsiə/ (panaceas) N-COUNT If you say that something is a **panacea** for a set of problems, you mean that it will solve all those problems. ▢ *Trade is not a panacea for the world's economic or social ills.*

pa|nache /pənæʃ/ N-UNCOUNT If you do something with **panache**, you do it in a confident, stylish, and elegant way. ▢ *The orchestra played with great panache.*

pana|ma hat /pænɑmɑ hæt/ (panama hats) N-COUNT A **panama hat** or a **panama** is a hat, worn especially by men, that is woven from the leaves of a palm-like plant and worn when it is sunny.

pan|cake /pænkeɪk/ (pancakes) N-COUNT A **pancake** is a thin, flat, circular piece of cooked batter made from milk, flour, and eggs. Pancakes are usually eaten for breakfast, with butter and syrup.

pan|cre|as /pæŋkriəs, pæn-/ (pancreases) **1** N-COUNT Your **pancreas** is an organ in your body that is situated behind your stomach. It produces insulin and substances that help your body digest food. **2** → See also color supplement

pan|cre|at|ic /pæŋkriætɪk, pæn-/ ADJ [ADJ n] **Pancreatic** means relating to or involving the pancreas. ▢ *...pancreatic juices.*

pan|da /pændə/ (pandas) N-COUNT A **panda** or a **giant panda** is a large animal like a bear that has black and white fur and lives in the bamboo forests of China.

pan|dem|ic /pændɛmɪk/ (pandemics) N-COUNT A **pandemic** is an occurrence of a disease that affects many people over a very wide area. [FORMAL] ▢ *They feared a new cholera pandemic.*

pan|de|mo|nium /pændɪmoʊniəm/ N-UNCOUNT If there is **pandemonium** in a place, the people there are behaving in a very noisy and uncontrolled way. ▢ *There was pandemonium in court as the judge gave his verdict.*

pan|der /pændər/ (panders, pandering, pandered) V-I If you **pander** to someone or to their wishes, you do everything that they want, often to get some advantage for yourself. [DISAPPROVAL] ▢ *He has offended the party's traditional base by pandering to the rich and the middle classes.*

Pandora /pændɔrə/ PHRASE If someone or something **opens Pandora's box** or **opens a Pandora's box**, they do something that causes a lot of problems to appear that did not exist or were not known about before.

pane /peɪn/ (panes) N-COUNT A **pane** of glass is a flat sheet of glass in a window or door. ▢ *I watch my reflection in a pane of glass.*

pan|egyr|ic /pænɪdʒɪrɪk/ (panegyrics) N-COUNT A **panegyric** is a speech or piece of writing that praises someone or something. [FORMAL] ▢ *The book is a panegyric on the intoxicating effects of marijuana.*

pan|el ✦✧✧ /pænəl/ (panels) **1** N-COUNT-COLL A **panel** is a small group of people who are chosen to do something, for example, to discuss something in public or to make a decision. ▢ *He assembled a panel of scholars to advise him.* ▢ *All the writers on the panel agreed that Quinn's book should be singled out for special praise.* **2** N-COUNT A **panel** is a flat rectangular piece of wood or other material that forms part of a larger object such as a door. ▢ *...the frosted glass panel set in the center of the door.* **3** N-COUNT [n n] A control **panel** or instrument **panel** is a board or surface that contains switches and controls used to operate a machine or piece of equipment. ▢ *The equipment was extremely sophisticated and was monitored from a central control panel.*

pan|eled /pænəld/ also **panelled** **1** ADJ A **paneled** room has decorative wooden panels covering its walls. ▢ *...their cozy paneled den.* • COMB IN ADJ **-paneled** combines with nouns to form adjectives that describe the way a room or wall is decorated or the way a door or window is made. ▢ *...an elegant wood-paneled library.* **2** ADJ A **paneled** wall, door, or window does not have a flat surface but has square or rectangular areas set into its surface. ▢ *...an oil landscape on the paneled wall.*

pan|el|ing /pænəlɪŋ/ also **panelling** N-UNCOUNT **Paneling** consists of boards or strips of wood covering a wall inside a building. ▢ *The walls were dark oak paneling.*

pan|el|ist /pænəlɪst/ (panelists)

in BRIT, use **panellist**

N-COUNT A **panelist** is a person who is a member of a panel and speaks in public, especially on a radio or television program.

pan|el truck (panel trucks) N-COUNT A **panel truck** is a small van, used especially for delivering goods. [AM] ▢ *At that instant, the rear doors of a panel truck some twenty yards away flew open.*

pan-fried ADJ **Pan-fried** food is food that has been cooked in hot fat or oil in a frying pan.

pang /pæŋ/ (pangs) N-COUNT A **pang** is a sudden strong feeling or emotion, for example, of sadness or pain. ▢ *For a moment she felt a pang of guilt about the way she was treating him.* ▢ *...hunger pangs.*

pan|han|dle /pænhændəl/ (panhandles, panhandling, panhandled) **1** N-COUNT A **panhandle** is a narrow strip of land joined to a larger area of land. [AM] ▢ *...the Texas panhandle.* **2** V-T/V-I If someone **panhandles**, they stop people in the street and ask them for money. [mainly AM, INFORMAL] ▢ *Many of these street people seemed to support themselves by panhandling and doing odd jobs.* ▢ *There was also a guy panhandling for quarters.*

in BRIT, usually use **beg**

• **pan|han|dling** N-UNCOUNT ▢ *Sergeant Rivero says arrests for panhandling take place every day.*

pan|han|dler /pænhændlər/ (panhandlers) N-COUNT A **panhandler** is a person who stops people in the street and asks them for money. [mainly AM, INFORMAL]

in BRIT, usually use **beggar**

pan|ic ✦✧✧ /pænɪk/ (panics, panicking, panicked) **1** N-VAR **Panic** is a very strong feeling of anxiety or fear that makes you act without thinking carefully. ▢ *An earthquake has hit the capital, causing damage to buildings and panic among the population.* **2** N-UNCOUNT [also a N] **Panic** or a **panic** is a situation in which people are affected by a strong feeling of anxiety. ▢ *There was a moment of panic as it became clear just how vulnerable the nation was.* ▢ *I'm in a panic about getting everything done in time.* **3** V-T/V-I If you **panic** or if someone **panics** you, you suddenly feel anxious or afraid, and act quickly and without thinking carefully. ▢ *Guests panicked and screamed when the bomb exploded.* ▢ *The unexpected and sudden memory briefly panicked her.*

SYNONYMS

panic
NOUN **1**
alarm: *She sat up in alarm.*
fear: *I was sitting on the floor, shivering with fear.*
terror: *I shook with terror whenever I was about to fly in an airplane.*
hysteria: *Several were hurt in the panic. 'It was mass hysteria,' said Walker.*

pan|ic buy (panic buys, panic buying, panic bought) VERB If people **panic buy**, they buy far more of something than they need because they are afraid supplies will run out. ▢ *If customers do not panic buy, we should have enough for everyone.* ▢ *People were panic buying pasta and toilet paper.* • **pan|ic buy|ing** N-UNCOUNT ▢ *Fears of shortages had led to panic buying.*

pan|icky /pænɪki/ ADJ A **panicky** feeling or **panicky** behavior is characterized by panic. ▢ *She suddenly felt panicky like a mouse cornered by a hungry cat.*

panic-stricken ADJ If someone is **panic-stricken** or is behaving in a **panic-stricken** way, they are so anxious or afraid that they may act without thinking carefully. ▢ *Panic-stricken travelers fled for the borders.*

pa|ni|ni /pəniːni/ (paninis) N-COUNT A **panini** is a type of Italian bread, usually served hot with a variety of fillings. ▢ *...a panini with smoked salmon and cream cheese.*

pan|ni|er /pænyər, -iər/ (panniers) **1** N-COUNT A **pannier** is a large basket or bag, usually one of two that are put over an animal and used for carrying loads. **2** N-COUNT A **pannier** is the same as a **saddlebag**. [BRIT]

pano|ply /pǽnəpli/ N-SING [usu N of n] A **panoply** of things is a wide range of them, especially one that is considered impressive. [FORMAL] ◻ *He was attended, as are all heads of state, by a full panoply of experts.*

pano|ra|ma /pæ̀nərɑ́mə, -rǽmə/ (panoramas) **1** N-COUNT A **panorama** is a view in which you can see a long way over a wide area of land, usually because you are on high ground. ◻ *Horton looked out over a panorama of fertile valleys and gentle hills.* **2** N-COUNT A **panorama** is a broad view of a state of affairs or of a constantly changing series of events. ◻ *The play presents a panorama of the history of communism.*

pano|ram|ic /pæ̀nərǽmɪk/ ADJ If you have a **panoramic** view, you can see a long way over a wide area. ◻ *The terrain's high points provide a panoramic view of Los Angeles.*

pan|sex|ual /pænsɛ́kʃuəl/ ADJ Someone who is **pansexual** is sexually attracted to people of any gender identity. ◻ *The singer gave an interview in which she identified herself as pansexual.*

pan|sy /pǽnzi/ (pansies) **1** N-COUNT A **pansy** is a small brightly colored garden flower with large round petals. **2** N-COUNT **Pansy** is an offensive word for a gay person. [INFORMAL, OLD-FASHIONED, OFFENSIVE]

pant /pǽnt/ (pants, panting, panted) **1** V-I If you **pant**, you breathe quickly and loudly with your mouth open, because you have been doing something energetic. ◻ *She climbed rapidly until she was panting with the effort.* **2** → see also **pants**

pan|ta|loons /pæ̀ntəlúːnz/ N-PLURAL **Pantaloons** are long pants with very wide legs, gathered at the ankle.

pan|theism /pǽnθiːɪzəm/ **1** N-UNCOUNT **Pantheism** is the religious belief that God is in everything in nature and the universe. **2** N-UNCOUNT **Pantheism** is a willingness to worship and believe in all gods.

pan|theis|tic /pæ̀nθiːɪ́stɪk/ ADJ [usu ADJ n] **Pantheistic** religions involve believing that God is in everything in nature and the universe.

pan|the|on /pǽnθiɒn, -ən/ (pantheons) N-COUNT [oft N of n] You can refer to a group of gods or a group of important people as a **pantheon**. [WRITTEN] ◻ *...the birthplace of Krishna, another god of the Hindu pantheon.*

pan|ther /pǽnθər/ (panthers) N-COUNT A **panther** is a large wild animal that belongs to the cat family. Panthers are usually black.

panties /pǽntiz/ N-PLURAL **Panties** are short, close-fitting underpants worn by women or girls. [mainly AM] ◻ *...a pair of white panties.*

in BRIT, usually use **pants**

pan|to|mime /pǽntəmaɪm/ N-SING If you say that a situation or a person's behavior is a **pantomime**, you mean that it is silly or exaggerated and that there is something false about it. [mainly BRIT] ◻ *They were made welcome with the usual pantomime of exaggerated smiles and gestures.*

pan|try /pǽntri/ (pantries) N-COUNT A **pantry** is a small room in a house, usually near the kitchen, where food is kept.

pants /pǽnts/ **1** N-PLURAL [also a pair of N] **Pants** are a piece of clothing that covers the lower part of your body and each leg. [AM] ◻ *She described him as wearing brown corduroy pants and a white cotton shirt.*

in BRIT, use **trousers**

2 N-PLURAL [also a pair of N] **Pants** are a piece of underwear which has two holes to put your legs through and elastic around the top to hold them up around your waist or hips. [BRIT]

in AM, usually use **panties, underpants**

USAGE

pants
Don't say 'a pants' or 'two shorts.' You can say **a pair of pants** or **two pairs of shorts**. *Make sure you pack a pair of shorts.*

---

pant|suit /pǽntsuːt/ (pantsuits) also **pants suit** N-COUNT A **pantsuit** is women's clothing consisting of a pair of pants and a jacket which are made from the same material. [AM] ◻ *Today she wore a red pantsuit that fit real well.*

pan|ty|hose /pǽntihoʊz/ also **panty hose** N-PLURAL [also a pair of N] **Pantyhose** are a piece of clothing which covers the hips, legs and feet. They are usually made of nylon. [mainly AM] ◻ *She told him her pantyhose were slipping.*

in BRIT, usually use **tights**

pap /pǽp/ **1** N-UNCOUNT If you describe something such as information, writing, or entertainment as **pap**, you mean that you consider it to be of no worth, value, or serious interest. [DISAPPROVAL] **2** N-UNCOUNT **Pap** is food that has been mashed or made soft so that it is suitable for babies and very old people. ◻ *He finally had a little pap and looks like he's going to sleep.*

papa /pɑ́pə/ (papas) N-FAMILY Some people refer to or address their father as **papa**. [OLD-FASHIONED] ◻ *He was so much older than me, older even than my papa.*

pa|pa|cy /péɪpəsi/ also **Papacy** N-SING [usu the N] The **papacy** is the position, power, and authority of the Pope, including the period of time that a particular person holds this position. ◻ *...the papacy of John Paul II.*

pa|pal /péɪp(ə)l/ ADJ [ADJ n] **Papal** is used to describe things relating to the Pope. ◻ *...the doctrine of papal infallibility.*

pa|pa|raz|zo /pæ̀pərǽtsoʊ/ (paparazzi /pæ̀pərǽtsi/) N-COUNT [usu pl] The **paparazzi** are photographers who follow famous people around, hoping to take interesting or shocking photographs of them that they can sell to a newspaper. ◻ *The paparazzi pursue Armani wherever he travels.*

pa|pa|ya /pəpɑ́jə/ (papayas) N-COUNT A **papaya** is a fruit with a green skin, sweet orange flesh, and small black seeds. Papayas grow on trees in hot countries.

pa|per ◆◆◆ /péɪpər/ (papers, papering, papered) **1** N-UNCOUNT **Paper** is a material that you write on or wrap things with. The pages of this book are made of paper. ◻ *He wrote his name down on a piece of paper for me.* ◻ *...a paper bag.* **2** N-COUNT A **paper** is a newspaper. ◻ *I might get a paper in the town.* **3** N-COUNT You can refer to newspapers in general as **the paper** or **the papers**. ◻ *You can't believe everything you read in the paper.* **4** N-PLURAL Your **papers** are sheets of paper with information on them that you might keep in a safe place at home. ◻ *After her death, her papers – including unpublished articles and correspondence – were deposited at the library.* **5** N-PLURAL Your **papers** are official documents, such as your passport or identity card, that prove who you are or that give you official permission to do something. ◻ *A young Moroccan stopped by police refused to show his papers.* **6** N-COUNT A **paper** is a long, formal piece of writing about an academic subject. ◻ *He just published a paper in the journal Nature analyzing the fires.* **7** N-COUNT A **paper** is an essay written by a student. [mainly AM] ◻ *...the ten common errors that appear most frequently in student papers.* **8** N-COUNT A **paper** prepared by a government or a committee is a report on a question they have been considering or a set of proposals for changes in the law. ◻ *...a new government paper on electoral reform.* **9** ADJ [ADJ n] **Paper** agreements, qualifications, or profits are ones that are stated by official documents to exist, although they may not really be effective or useful. ◻ *They expressed deep mistrust of the paper promises.* **10** V-T If you **paper** a wall, you put wallpaper on it. ◻ *We papered all four bedrooms.* ◻ *We have papered this bedroom in softest gray.* **11** PHRASE If you put your thoughts down **on paper**, you write them down. ◻ *It is important to get something down on paper.* **12** PHRASE If something seems to be the case **on paper**, it seems to be the case from what you read or hear about it, but it may not really be the case. ◻ *On paper, their country is a multi-party democracy.*

paper|back /péɪpərbæk/ (paperbacks) N-COUNT [also in N] A **paperback** is a book with a thin cardboard or paper cover. Compare **hardback**. ◻ *She said she would buy the book when it comes out in paperback.*

paper|boy /péɪpərbɔɪ/ (paperboys) N-COUNT A **paperboy** is a boy who delivers newspapers to people's homes.

pa|per clip (paper clips) also **paper-clip, paperclip** N-COUNT A **paper clip** is a small piece of bent wire that is used to hold papers together.

paper|girl /peɪpərgɜrl/ (papergirls) N-COUNT A **papergirl** is a girl who delivers newspapers to people's homes.

pa|per knife (paper knives) N-COUNT A **paper knife** is a tool shaped like a knife that is used for opening envelopes.

paper|less /peɪpərlɪs/ ADJ [ADJ n] **Paperless** is used to describe business or office work that is done by computer or telephone, rather than by writing things down. ❑ ...*the impact of paperless distribution on the design community.* ❑ ...*the paperless office.*

pa|per mon|ey N-UNCOUNT **Paper money** is money that is made of paper. Paper money is usually worth more than coins.

pa|per route (paper routes) N-COUNT A **paper route** is a job of delivering newspapers to houses along a particular route. [AM]

in BRIT, use **paper round**

paper-thin also **paper thin** ADJ If something is **paper-thin**, it is very thin. ❑ *Cut the onion into paper-thin slices.*

pa|per ti|ger (paper tigers) N-COUNT If you say that an institution, a country, or a person is a **paper tiger**, you mean that although they seem powerful they do not really have any power.

pa|per trail N-SING Documents that provide evidence of someone's activities can be referred to as a **paper trail**. [mainly AM] ❑ *Criminals are very reluctant to leave a paper trail.*

paper|weight /peɪpərweɪt/ (paperweights) N-COUNT A **paperweight** is a small heavy object that you place on papers to prevent them from being disturbed or blown away.

paper|work /peɪpərwɜrk/ N-UNCOUNT **Paperwork** is the routine part of a job that involves writing or dealing with letters, reports, and records. ❑ *At every stage in the production there will be paperwork—forms to fill in, permissions to obtain, letters to write.*

pa|pery /peɪpəri/ ADJ Something that is **papery** is thin and dry like paper. ❑ *Leave each garlic clove in its papery skin.*

papier-mâché /peɪpər məʃeɪ/ N-UNCOUNT [oft N n] **Papier-mâché** is a mixture of pieces of paper and glue. It can be made, while still damp, into objects such as bowls, ornaments, and models. ❑ ...*papier-mâché bowls.*

pa|pist /peɪpɪst/ (papists) also **Papist** N-COUNT Some Protestants refer to Catholics as **papists**. [OFFENSIVE]

pap|py /pæpi/ (pappies) N-FAMILY Some people refer to their father as their **pappy**. [AM, INFORMAL] ❑ *"Where do you get this stuff?" asks Leroy. "From your pappy?"*

pap|ri|ka /pəprɪkə, pæprɪkə/ N-UNCOUNT **Paprika** is a red powder used for flavoring meat and other food.

Pap smear (Pap smears) also **Pap test** N-COUNT A **Pap smear** is a medical test in which cells are taken from a woman's cervix and analyzed to see if any cancer cells are present.

pa|py|rus /pəpaɪrəs/ (papyri /pəpaɪri/) ◼ N-UNCOUNT **Papyrus** is a tall water plant that grows in Africa. ◼ N-UNCOUNT **Papyrus** is a type of paper made from papyrus stems that was used in ancient Egypt, Rome, and Greece. ◼ N-COUNT A **papyrus** is an ancient document that is written on papyrus.

par /pɑr/ ◼ PHRASE If you say that two people or things are **on a par with** each other, you mean that they are equally good or bad, or equally important. ❑ *The water park will be on a par with some of the best public swim facilities around.* ◼ N-UNCOUNT [N with num, under/over N] In golf, **par** is the number of strokes that a good player should take to get the ball into a hole or into all the holes on a particular golf course. ❑ *He was five under par after the first round.* ◼ PHRASE If you say that someone or something is **below par** or **under par**, you are disappointed in them because they are below the standard you expected. ❑ *His amateurish guitar playing is well below par.* ❑ *A teacher's job is relatively safe, even if they perform under par in the classroom.* ◼ PHRASE If you say that someone or something is not **up to par**, you are disappointed in them because they are below the standard you expected. ❑ *It's a constant struggle to try to keep them up to par.* ◼ PHRASE If you **feel below par** or **under par** or **not up to par**, you feel tired and unable to perform as well as you normally do. ❑ *After the birth of her baby she felt generally under par.*

para. /pærə/ (paras) **Para.** is a written abbreviation for paragraph. ❑ *See Chapter 9, para. 1.2.*

para|ble /pærəbl/ (parables) N-COUNT A **parable** is a short story, that is told in order to make a moral or religious point, like those in the Bible. ❑ ...*the parable of the Good Samaritan.*

pa|ra|bo|la /pəræbələ/ (parabolas) N-COUNT A **parabola** is a type of curve such as the path of something that is thrown up into the air and comes down in a different place. [TECHNICAL]

para|bol|ic /pærəbɒlɪk/ ADJ [usu ADJ n] A **parabolic** object or curve is shaped like a parabola. ❑ ...*a parabolic mirror.*

para|chute /pærəʃut/ (parachutes, parachuting, parachuted) ◼ N-COUNT A **parachute** is a device that enables a person to jump from an aircraft and float safely to the ground. It consists of a large piece of thin cloth attached to your body by strings. ❑ *They fell 41,000 ft. before opening their parachutes.* ❑ *U.N. troops could be landed by helicopter or even by parachute.* ◼ V-T/V-I If a person **parachutes** or someone **parachutes** them somewhere, they jump from an aircraft using a parachute. ❑ *He was a courier for the Polish underground and parachuted into Warsaw.* ◼ V-T To **parachute** something somewhere means to drop it somewhere by parachute. ❑ *Planes parachuted food, clothing, blankets, medicine, and water into the rugged mountainous border region.* ◼ V-T/V-I If a person **parachutes into** an organization or if they **are parachuted into** it, they are brought in suddenly in order to help it. ❑ ...*a consultant who parachutes into corporations and helps provide strategic thinking.* ❑ *Executives with political influence are parachuted into the company.*

para|chut|ing /pærəʃutɪŋ/ N-UNCOUNT **Parachuting** is the activity or sport of jumping from an aircraft with a parachute. ❑ *His hobby is freefall parachuting.*

para|chut|ist /pærəʃutɪst/ (parachutists) N-COUNT A **parachutist** is a person who jumps from an aircraft using a parachute. ❑ *He was an experienced parachutist who had done over 150 jumps.*

pa|rade /pəreɪd/ (parades, parading, paraded) ◼ N-COUNT A **parade** is a procession of people or vehicles moving through a public place in order to celebrate an important day or event. ❑ *A military parade marched slowly and solemnly down Pennsylvania Avenue.* ◼ V-I When people **parade** somewhere, they walk together in a formal group or a line, usually with other people watching them. ❑ *More than four thousand soldiers, sailors, and airmen paraded down the Champs Elysées.* ◼ N-VAR [oft on N] **Parade** is a formal occasion when soldiers stand in lines to be seen by an officer or important person, or march in a group. ❑ *He had them on parade at six o'clock in the morning.* ◼ V-T [usu passive] If you say that someone **parades** a person, you mean that they show that person to others only in order to gain some advantage for themselves. ❑ *Captured prisoners were paraded before television cameras.* ❑ *Five leading fighter pilots have been captured and paraded before the media.* ◼ V-T If people **parade** something, they show it in public so that it can be admired. ❑ *Valentino is eager to see celebrities parading his clothes at big occasions.* ◼ V-T/V-I If you say that something **parades as** or **is paraded as** a good or important thing, you mean that some people say that it is good or important but you think it probably is not. ❑ ...*all the fashions that parade as modern movements in art.*

pa|rade ground (parade grounds) N-COUNT A **parade ground** is an area of ground where soldiers practice marching and have parades.

para|digm /pærədaɪm/ (paradigms) N-VAR A **paradigm** is a model for something that explains it or shows how it can be produced. [FORMAL] ❑ ...*a new paradigm of production.*

para|dig|mat|ic /pærədɪgmætɪk/ ADJ You can describe something as **paradigmatic** if it acts as a model or example for something. [FORMAL] ❑ *Their great academic success was paraded as paradigmatic.*

para|dise /pærədaɪs/ (paradises) ◼ N-PROPER According to some religions, **paradise** is a wonderful place where people go after they die, if they have led good lives. ❑ *The Koran describes paradise as a place containing a garden of delight.* ◼ N-VAR You can refer to a place or situation that seems beautiful or perfect as **paradise** or **a paradise**. ❑ *Bali is one of the world's great natural paradises.*

para|dox /pærədɒks/ (paradoxes) ◼ N-COUNT You describe a situation as a **paradox** when it involves two or more facts or qualities that seem to contradict each other. ❑ *The paradox is that the region's most dynamic economies have the most primitive*

paradoxical   934   **paranoid**

financial systems. ❑ *The paradox of exercise is that while using a lot of energy it seems to generate more.* ▪ N-VAR A **paradox** is a statement in which it seems that if one part of it is true, the other part of it cannot be true. ❑ *The story contains many levels of paradox.*

para|doxi|cal /pærədɒksɪkəl/ ADJ If something is **paradoxical**, it involves two facts or qualities that seem to contradict each other. ❑ *Some sedatives produce the paradoxical effect of making the person more anxious.* ● **para|doxi|cal|ly** /pærədɒksɪkli/ ADV ❑ *Paradoxically, the less you have to do the more you may resent the work that does come your way.*

par|af|fin /pærəfɪn/ ▪ N-UNCOUNT **Paraffin** is a white wax obtained from petroleum or coal. It is used to make candles, to form seals, and in beauty treatments. ▪ N-UNCOUNT **Paraffin** is a strong-smelling liquid which is used as a fuel in heaters, lamps, and engines. [mainly BRIT]

in AM, use **kerosene**

para|glide /pærəglaɪd/ (paraglides, paragliding, paraglided) V-I If a person **paraglides**, they jump from an aircraft or off a hill or tall building while wearing a special parachute that allows them to control the way they float to the ground. ❑ *They planned to paraglide from Long Mountain.* ● **para|glid|ing** N-UNCOUNT ❑ *Hang gliding and paragliding are allowed from the top of Windy Hill.*

para|glid|er /pærəglaɪdər/ (paragliders) ▪ N-COUNT A **paraglider** is a special type of parachute that you use for paragliding. ▪ N-COUNT A **paraglider** is a person who paraglides.

para|gon /pærəgɒn/ (paragons) N-COUNT If you refer to someone as a **paragon**, you mean that they are perfect or have a lot of a good qualities. ❑ *We don't expect candidates to be paragons of virtue.* ❑ *Our administrator is a paragon of neatness, efficiency, and reliability.*

para|graph /pærəgræf/ (paragraphs) N-COUNT A **paragraph** is a section of a piece of writing. A paragraph always begins on a new line and contains at least one sentence. ❑ *The length of a paragraph depends on the information it conveys.*

para|keet /pærəkit/ (parakeets) N-COUNT A **parakeet** is a type of small parrot that is brightly colored and has a long tail.

para|le|gal /pærəligəl/ (paralegals) N-COUNT A **paralegal** is someone who is paid to help lawyers with their work but is not qualified as a lawyer. [AM]

par|al|lax /pærəlæks/ (parallaxes) N-VAR **Parallax** is when an object appears to change its position because the person or instrument observing it has changed their position. [TECHNICAL]

par|al|lel /pærəlɛl/ (parallels, paralleling, paralleled) ▪ N-COUNT If something has a **parallel**, it is similar to something else, but exists or happens in a different place or at a different time. If it has **no parallel** or is **without parallel**, it is not similar to anything else. ❑ *Readers familiar with military conflict will find a vague parallel to the Vietnam War.* ❑ *It's an ecological disaster with no parallel anywhere else in the world.* ▪ N-COUNT If there are **parallels** between two things, they are similar in some ways. ❑ *Detailed study of folk music from a variety of countries reveals many close parallels.* ❑ *There are significant parallels with the 1980s.* ▪ V-T If one thing **parallels** another, they happen at the same time or are similar, and often seem to be connected. ❑ *Often there are emotional reasons paralleling the financial ones.* ❑ *His remarks paralleled those of the president.* ▪ ADJ **Parallel** events or situations happen at the same time as one another, or are similar to one another. ❑ *...parallel talks between the two countries' foreign ministers.* ❑ *Their instincts do not always run parallel with ours.* ▪ ADJ If two lines, two objects, or two lines of movement are **parallel**, they are the same distance apart along their whole length. ❑ *...seventy-two ships, drawn up in two parallel lines.* ❑ *Remsen Street is parallel with Montague Street.* ▪ N-COUNT [usu the ord N] A **parallel** is an imaginary line round the earth that is parallel to the equator. Parallels are shown on maps. ❑ *...the area south of the 38th parallel.*

par|al|lel bars N-PLURAL **Parallel bars** consist of a pair of horizontal bars on posts, that are used for doing physical exercises.

par|al|lel|ism /pærəlɛlɪzəm/ N-UNCOUNT When there is **parallelism** between two things, there are similarities between them. [FORMAL] ❑ *The last thing we should do is make any parallelism between the murderers and their victims.*

par|al|lelo|gram /pærəlɛləgræm/ (parallelograms) N-COUNT A **parallelogram** is a four-sided shape in which each side is parallel to the side opposite it.

par|al|lel park (parallel parks, parallel parking, parallel parked) ▪ VERB If you **parallel park** a vehicle or **parallel park** somewhere, you drive the vehicle into a position parallel to the road in order to park it there. ❑ *Sit back, relax and let your car parallel park itself.* ▪ → See feature box at **drive**

par|al|lel pro|cess|ing N-UNCOUNT In computing, **parallel processing** is a system in which several instructions are carried out at the same time instead of one after the other.

para|lyse /pærəlaɪz/ [BRIT] → see **paralyze**

pa|raly|sis /pəræləsɪs/ ▪ N-UNCOUNT **Paralysis** is the loss of the ability to move and feel in all or part of your body. ❑ *...paralysis of the leg.* ▪ N-UNCOUNT **Paralysis** is the state of being unable to act or function properly. ❑ *The paralysis of the leadership leaves the army without its supreme command.*

para|lyt|ic /pærəlɪtɪk/ ADJ [usu ADJ n] **Paralytic** means related to paralysis. ❑ *...paralytic disease.*

para|lyze /pærəlaɪz/ (paralyzes, paralyzing, paralyzed)

in BRIT, use **paralyse**

▪ V-T If someone **is paralyzed** by an accident or an illness, they have no feeling in their body, or in part of their body, and are unable to move. ❑ *She is paralyzed from the waist down.* ● **para|lyzed** ADJ ❑ *A guy with paralyzed legs is not supposed to ride horses.* ▪ V-T If a person, place, or organization **is paralyzed** by something, they become unable to act or function properly. ❑ *The city has been virtually paralyzed by sudden snowstorms.* ❑ *She was paralyzed by fear and love.* ● **para|lyzed** ADJ ❑ *He sat in his chair, paralyzed with dread.*

para|med|ic /pærəmɛdɪk/ (paramedics) N-COUNT A **paramedic** is a person whose training is similar to that of a nurse and who helps to do medical work. ❑ *We intend to have a paramedic on every ambulance within the next three years.*

para|medi|cal /pærəmɛdɪkəl/ ADJ [ADJ n] **Paramedical** workers and services help doctors and nurses in medical work. ❑ *...doctors and paramedical staff.*

pa|ram|eter /pəræmɪtər/ (parameters) N-COUNT **Parameters** are factors or limits that affect the way something can be done or made. [FORMAL] ❑ *...some of the parameters that determine the taste of a wine.*

para|mili|tary /pærəmɪlɪtɛri/ (paramilitaries) ▪ ADJ [ADJ n] A **paramilitary** organization is organized like an army and performs either civil or military functions in a country. ❑ *Searches by the army and paramilitary forces have continued today.* ● N-COUNT **Paramilitaries** are members of a paramilitary organization. ❑ *Paramilitaries and army recruits patrolled the village.* ▪ ADJ [ADJ n] A **paramilitary** organization is an illegal group that is organized like an army. ❑ *...a law which said that all paramilitary groups must be disarmed.* ● N-COUNT **Paramilitaries** are members of an illegal paramilitary organization. ❑ *Paramilitaries were blamed for the shooting.*

para|mount /pærəmaʊnt/ ADJ Something that is **paramount** or of **paramount** importance is more important than anything else. ❑ *The children's welfare must be seen as paramount.*

par|amour /pærəmʊər/ (paramours) N-COUNT [oft poss N] Someone's **paramour** is their lover. [OLD-FASHIONED]

para|noia /pærənɔɪə/ ▪ N-UNCOUNT If you say that someone suffers from **paranoia**, you think that they are too suspicious and afraid of other people. ❑ *The mood is one of paranoia and expectation of war.* ▪ N-UNCOUNT In psychology, **paranoia** is when someone wrongly believes that other people are trying to harm them, or when they believe themselves to be much more important than they really are.

para|noi|ac /pærənɔɪæk/ ADJ **Paranoiac** means the same as **paranoid**. [FORMAL]

para|noid /pærənɔɪd/ (paranoids) ▪ ADJ If you say that someone is **paranoid**, you mean that they are extremely suspicious and afraid of other people. ❑ *I'm not going to get paranoid about it.* ❑ *...a paranoid politician who saw enemies all around him.* **2** ADJ Someone who is **paranoid** has the mental illness of paranoia. ❑ *...paranoid delusions.* • N-COUNT A **paranoid** is someone who is paranoid. ❑ *I think you're the opposite of a paranoid.*

para|nor|mal /pærənɔrməl/ ADJ [usu ADJ n] A **paranormal** event or power, such as the appearance of a ghost, cannot be explained by scientific laws and is thought to involve strange, unknown forces. ❑ *Science may be able to provide some explanations of paranormal phenomena.* • N-SING [the N] You can refer to paranormal events and matters as **the paranormal**. ❑ *We have been looking at the shadowy world of the paranormal.*

para|pet /pærəpɪt/ (parapets) **1** N-COUNT A **parapet** is a low wall along the edge of something high such as a bridge or roof. **2** → See also color supplement

para|pher|na|lia /pærəfərneɪlyə, -fəneɪl-/ N-UNCOUNT You can refer to a large number of objects that someone has with them or that are connected with a particular activity as **paraphernalia**. ❑ *...a large courtyard full of builders' paraphernalia.*

para|phrase /pærəfreɪz/ (paraphrases, paraphrasing, paraphrased) **1** V-T If you **paraphrase** someone or **paraphrase** something that they have said or written, you express what they have said or written in a different way. ❑ *To paraphrase the President, we must restore confidence in our economic sector.* ❑ *Baxter paraphrased the contents of the press release.* **2** N-COUNT A **paraphrase** of something written or spoken is the same thing expressed in a different way. ❑ *The last two clauses were an exact quote rather than a paraphrase of Mr. Forth's remarks.*

para|plegia /pærəplidʒə/ N-UNCOUNT **Paraplegia** is the condition of being unable to move the lower half of your body. [MEDICAL]

para|plegic /pærəplidʒɪk/ (paraplegics) N-COUNT A **paraplegic** is someone who cannot move the lower half of their body, for example, because of an injury to their spine. ❑ *Theoretically, such equipment could help paraplegics regain movement.* • ADJ **Paraplegic** is also an adjective. ❑ *A passenger was injured so badly he will be paraplegic for the rest of his life.*

para|psy|chol|ogy /pærəsaɪkɒlədʒi/ N-UNCOUNT **Parapsychology** is the study of strange mental abilities that cannot be explained by accepted scientific theories.

Para|quat /pærəkwæt/ also **para|quat** N-UNCOUNT **Paraquat** is a very poisonous substance that is used to kill weeds. [TRADEMARK]

para|site /pærəsaɪt/ (parasites) **1** N-COUNT A **parasite** is a small animal or plant that lives on or inside a larger animal or plant, and gets its food from it. ❑ *Kangaroos harbor a vast range of parasites.* **2** N-COUNT If you disapprove of someone because you think that they get money or other things from other people but do not do anything in return, you can call them a **parasite**. [DISAPPROVAL] ❑ *...a parasite, who produced nothing but lived on the work of others.* **3** → See feature box at **farming**

WORD HISTORY

parasite
Parasite comes from Greek *parasitos*, meaning 'someone who eats at someone else's table.'

para|sit|ic /pærəsɪtɪk/ also **parasitical** **1** ADJ **Parasitic** diseases are caused by parasites. ❑ *Will global warming mean the spread of tropical parasitic diseases?* **2** ADJ **Parasitic** animals and plants live on or inside larger animals or plants and get their food from them. ❑ *...tiny parasitic insects.* **3** ADJ If you describe a person or organization as **parasitic**, you mean that they get money or other things from people without doing anything in return. [DISAPPROVAL] ❑ *...a parasitic new class of consultants and experts.*

para|sol /pærəsɔl/ (parasols) N-COUNT A **parasol** is an object like an umbrella that provides shade from the sun.

para|troop|er /pærətrupər/ (paratroopers) N-COUNT **Paratroopers** are soldiers who are trained to be dropped by parachute into battle or into enemy territory.

para|troops /pærətrups/
The form **paratroop** is used as a modifier.
N-PLURAL **Paratroops** are soldiers who are trained to be dropped by parachute into battle or into enemy territory. ❑ *The airport is in the hands of French paratroops.*

par|boil /pɑrbɔɪl/ (parboils, parboiling, parboiled) V-T If you **parboil** food, especially vegetables, you boil it until it is partly cooked. ❑ *Roughly chop and parboil the potatoes.*

par|cel /pɑrsəl/ (parcels) **1** N-COUNT A **parcel** is something wrapped in paper, in a bag or large envelope, or in a box, usually so that it can be sent to someone by mail. ❑ *They also sent parcels of food and clothing.* **2** PHRASE If you say that something is **part and parcel** of something else, you are emphasizing that it is involved or included in it. [EMPHASIS] ❑ *Learning about life in a new culture is part and parcel of what newcomers to America face.*

par|cel post N-UNCOUNT [oft by N] **Parcel post** is a mail service for the delivery of packages. [mainly AM] ❑ *It is much quicker and handier than sending them by parcel post.*

parched /pɑrtʃt/ **1** ADJ If something, especially the ground or a plant, is **parched**, it is very dry, because there has been no rain. ❑ *The clouds gathered and showers poured down upon the parched earth.* **2** ADJ If your mouth, throat, or lips are **parched**, they are unpleasantly dry. ❑ *Her throat was parched, and she was exhausted from all the walking.* **3** ADJ [v-link ADJ] If you say that you are **parched**, you mean that you are very thirsty. [INFORMAL] ❑ *When I told them I was parched, they went and got me a bottle of mineral water.*

parch|ment /pɑrtʃmənt/ **1** N-UNCOUNT In former times, **parchment** was the skin of a sheep or goat that was used for writing on. ❑ *...old manuscripts written on parchment.* **2** N-UNCOUNT **Parchment** is a kind of thick yellowish paper. ❑ *...an old lamp with a parchment shade.*

par|don /pɑrdən/ (pardons, pardoning, pardoned) **1** CONVENTION You say **Pardon?**, **I beg your pardon?**, or **Pardon me?** when you want someone to repeat what they have just said because you have not heard or understood it. [SPOKEN, FORMULAE] ❑ *"Will you let me open it?"—"Pardon?"—"Can I open it?"* **2** CONVENTION People say '**I beg your pardon?**' when they are surprised or offended by something that someone has just said. [SPOKEN, FEELINGS] ❑ *"Would you get undressed, please?"—"I beg your pardon?"—"Will you get undressed?"* **3** CONVENTION You say '**I beg your pardon**' as a way of apologizing for accidentally doing something wrong, such as disturbing someone or making a mistake. [SPOKEN, FORMULAE] ❑ *I beg your pardon. I thought you were someone else.* **4** CONVENTION Some people say '**Pardon me**' instead of 'Excuse me' when they want to politely get someone's attention or interrupt them. [SPOKEN, FORMULAE] ❑ *Pardon me, are you finished, madam?* **5** V-T [usu passive] If someone who has been found guilty of a crime **is pardoned**, they are officially allowed to go free and are not punished. ❑ *Hundreds of political prisoners were pardoned and released.* • N-COUNT **Pardon** is also a noun. ❑ *They lobbied the government on his behalf and he was granted a presidential pardon.*

par|don|able /pɑrdənəbəl/ ADJ You describe someone's action or attitude as **pardonable** if you think it is wrong but you understand why they did that action or have that attitude. ❑ *"I have," he remarked with pardonable pride, "done what I set out to do."*

pare /pɛər/ (pares, paring, pared) **1** V-T When you **pare** something, or **pare** part of it off or away, you cut off its skin or its outer layer. ❑ *Pare the brown skin from the meat with a very sharp knife.* ❑ *He took out a slab of cheese, pared off a slice and ate it hastily.* **2** V-T If you **pare** something **down** or **back**, or if you **pare** it, you reduce it. ❑ *The governor's campaign fund could be pared down to $500.* ❑ *The luxury tax won't really do much to pare down the budget deficit.*

pared-down ADJ If you describe something as **pared-down**, you mean that it has no unnecessary features, and has been reduced to a very simple form. ❑ *Her style is pared-down and simple.*

par|ent ♦♦♦ /pɛərənt, pær-/ (parents) **1** N-COUNT Your **parents** are your mother and father. ❑ *Children need their parents.* ❑ *This is where a lot of parents go wrong.* **2** → see also **single parent** **3** ADJ [ADJ n] An organization's **parent** organization is the organization that created it and usually still controls it. ❑ *Each unit including the parent company has its own, local management.*

par|ent|age /pɛərəntɪdʒ, pær-/ N-UNCOUNT [oft of adj N] Your **parentage** is the identity and origins of your parents. For example, if you are of Greek **parentage**, your parents are Greek. ☐ ...children of mixed parentage.

pa|ren|tal /pərɛntəl/ ADJ **Parental** is used to describe something that relates to parents in general, or to one or both of the parents of a particular child. ☐ Medical treatment was sometimes given to children without parental consent.

pa|ren|tal leave N-UNCOUNT **Parental leave** is time away from work, usually without pay, that parents are allowed in order to care for their children. [BUSINESS] ☐ Parents are entitled to 13 weeks' parental leave to be taken during the first five years of a child's life.

pa|ren|thesis /pərɛnθəsɪs/ (**parentheses** /pərɛnθəsiːz/) N-COUNT **Parentheses** are a pair of curved marks that you put around words or numbers to indicate that they are additional, separate, or less important. (This sentence is in parentheses.)

par|en|the|ti|cal /pærənθɛtɪkəl/ ADJ [usu ADJ n] A **parenthetical** remark or section is put into something written or spoken but is not essential to it. ☐ Fox was making a long parenthetical remark about his travels on the border of the country. • **par|en|the|ti|cal|ly** ADV ☐ Well, parenthetically, I was trying to quit smoking at the time. ☐ And what, we may ask parenthetically, does it mean?

par|ent|hood /pɛərənthʊd, pær-/ N-UNCOUNT **Parenthood** is the state of being a parent. ☐ She may feel unready for the responsibilities of parenthood.

par|ent|ing /pɛərəntɪŋ, pær-/ N-UNCOUNT **Parenting** is the activity of bringing up and taking care of your child. ☐ Parenting is not fully valued by society.

parent-teacher as|so|cia|tion (**parent-teacher associations**) N-COUNT A **parent-teacher association** is the same as a **PTA**.

par ex|cel|lence /pɑːr ɛksəlɒns/ ADJ [n ADJ] You say that something is a particular kind of thing **par excellence** in order to emphasize that it is a very good example of that kind of thing. [EMPHASIS] ☐ He has been a meticulous manager, a manager par excellence. • ADV [ADV after v] **Par excellence** is also an adverb. ☐ Bresson is par excellence the Catholic filmmaker.

pa|ri|ah /pəraɪə/ (**pariahs**) N-COUNT If you describe someone as a **pariah**, you mean that other people dislike them so much that they refuse to associate with them. [DISAPPROVAL] ☐ His landlady had treated him like a dangerous criminal, a pariah.

par|ing /pɛərɪŋ/ (**parings**) N-COUNT [usu pl] **Parings** are thin pieces that have been cut off things such as fingernails, fruit, or vegetables. ☐ ...nail parings. ☐ ...vegetable parings.

par|ing knife (**paring knives**) N-COUNT A **paring knife** is a knife that is designed for peeling fruit and vegetables. ☐ Peel the skins with a paring knife.

par|ish /pærɪʃ/ (**parishes**) **1** N-COUNT A **parish** is part of a city or town that has its own Catholic church and priest. ☐ ...Good Shepherd, a parish of about 450 members. ☐ ...a parish priest. **2** N-COUNT In some parts of the United States, a **parish** is a small region within a state which has its own local government. [AM] ☐ ...the middle-class parishes of northern Louisiana.

pa|rish|ion|er /pərɪʃənər/ (**parishioners**) N-COUNT [usu pl] A priest's **parishioners** are the people who live in his or her parish, especially the ones who go to his or her church.

Pa|ris|ian /pərɪʒən, -rɪziən/ (**Parisians**) **1** ADJ [usu ADJ n] **Parisian** means belonging or relating to Paris. ☐ ...Parisian fashion. **2** N-COUNT A **Parisian** is a person who comes from Paris.

par|ity /pærɪti/ N-UNCOUNT If there is **parity** between two things, they are equal. [FORMAL] ☐ Women have yet to achieve wage or occupational parity in many fields.

park ✦✧✧ /pɑːrk/ (**parks, parking, parked**) **1** N-COUNT A **park** is a public area of land with grass and trees, usually in a town, where people go in order to relax and enjoy themselves. ☐ ...Central Park. ☐ ...a brisk walk with the dog around the park. **2** N-COUNT [supp N] You can refer to a place where a particular activity is carried out as a **park**. ☐ ...a science and technology park. **3** V-T/V-I When you **park** a vehicle or **park** somewhere, you drive the vehicle into a position where it can stay for a period of time, and leave it there. ☐ Greenfield turned into the next side street and parked. ☐ He found a place to park the car. **4** V-T If you **park yourself** somewhere, you sit there. [INFORMAL] ☐ Every Friday, I would park myself in front of the TV. **5** → see also **ballpark, national park** **6** → See feature box at **drive**

par|ka /pɑːrkə/ (**parkas**) N-COUNT A **parka** is a jacket or coat that has a thick lining and a hood with fur around the edge.

parked /pɑːrkt/ ADJ [v-link ADJ] If you are **parked** somewhere, you have parked your car there. ☐ My sister was parked down the road. ☐ We're parked out front.

park|ing /pɑːrkɪŋ/ **1** N-UNCOUNT **Parking** is the action of moving a vehicle into a place in a garage or by the side of the road where it can be left. ☐ In many towns parking is allowed only on one side of the street. **2** N-UNCOUNT **Parking** is space for parking a vehicle in. ☐ Cars allowed, but parking is limited.

park|ing gar|age (**parking garages**) N-COUNT A **parking garage** is a building where people can leave their cars. [AM] ☐ ...a multi-level parking garage.

in BRIT, use **car park**

park|ing light (**parking lights**) N-COUNT The **parking lights** on a vehicle are the small lights at the front that help other drivers to notice the vehicle and to judge its width. [AM]

in BRIT, use **sidelights**

park|ing lot (**parking lots**) N-COUNT A **parking lot** is an area of ground where people can leave their cars. [AM] ☐ A block up the street I found a parking lot.

in BRIT, use **car park**

park|ing me|ter (**parking meters**) N-COUNT A **parking meter** is a device that you put money into when you park in a parking space.

park|ing tick|et (**parking tickets**) N-COUNT A **parking ticket** is a piece of paper with instructions to pay a fine that is put on your car when you have parked it somewhere illegally.

park|land /pɑːrklænd/ (**parklands**) N-UNCOUNT [also N in pl] **Parkland** is land with grass and trees on it. ☐ Its beautiful gardens and parkland are also open to the public.

par|kour /pɑːrkʊər/ N-UNCOUNT **Parkour** is the activity of running through areas in a town, using skillful movements to jump over walls and other objects. ☐ He runs a parkour club for local kids.

park|way /pɑːrkweɪ/ (**parkways**) N-COUNT A **parkway** is a wide road with trees and grass on both sides. [mainly AM]

par|lance /pɑːrləns/ N-UNCOUNT [supp N, usu in N] You use **parlance** when indicating that the expression you are using is normally used by a particular group of people. [FORMAL] ☐ The phrase is common diplomatic parlance for spying. ☐ To put it in business parlance, it's a lose-lose situation.

par|ley /pɑːrli/ (**parleys, parleying, parleyed**) **1** N-VAR A **parley** is a discussion between two opposing people or groups in which both sides try to come to an agreement. [OLD-FASHIONED] **2** V-RECIP When two opposing people or groups **parley**, they meet to discuss something in order to come to an agreement. [HUMOROUS OR INFORMAL] ☐ ...a place where we meet and parley. ☐ I don't think you've ever tried parleying with Jorge, have you?

par|lia|ment ✦✧✧ /pɑːrləmənt/ (**parliaments**) also **Parliament** **1** N-COUNT; N-PROPER The **parliament** of some countries is the group of people who make or change its laws, and decide what policies the country should follow. ☐ The Bangladesh Parliament today approved the policy, but it has not yet become law. **2** → see also **Member of Parliament** **3** N-COUNT A particular **parliament** is a particular period of time in which a parliament is doing its work, between two elections or between two periods of vacation. ☐ The legislation is expected to be passed in the next parliament.

par|lia|men|tar|ian /pɑːrləmɛntɛəriən/ (**parliamentarians**) **1** N-COUNT **Parliamentarians** are members of a parliament; used especially to refer to a group who are dealing with a particular task. ☐ He's been meeting with British parliamentarians and government officials. **2** N-COUNT A **parliamentarian** is a

parliamentary

member of parliament who is an expert on the rules and procedures of parliament and takes an active part in debates. ❑ *He is a veteran parliamentarian whose views enjoy widespread respect.*

par|lia|men|ta|ry ✦◇◇ /pɑrləmɛntəri/ ADJ [ADJ n] **Parliamentary** is used to describe things that are connected with a parliament or with members of parliament. ❑ *He used his influence to make sure she was not selected as a parliamentary candidate.*

par|lor /pɑrlər/ (parlors)

in BRIT, use **parlour**

N-COUNT [n N] **Parlor** is used in the names of some types of stores that provide a service, rather than selling things. ❑ *...a funeral parlor.*

par|lor|maid /pɑrlərmeɪd/ (parlormaids)

in BRIT, use **parlourmaid**

N-COUNT In former times, a **parlormaid** was a female servant in a private house whose job involved serving people meals.

par|lous /pɑrləs/ ADJ [usu ADJ n] If something is in a **parlous** state, it is in a bad or dangerous condition. [FORMAL] ❑ *...the parlous state of our economy.*

Par|me|san /pɑrmɪzæn, -zən/ also **parmesan** N-UNCOUNT **Parmesan** or **Parmesan cheese** is a hard cheese with a strong flavour, often used in Italian cooking.

pa|ro|chial /pəroʊkiəl/ **1** ADJ If you describe someone as **parochial**, you are critical of them because you think they are too concerned with their own affairs and should be thinking about more important things. [DISAPPROVAL] ❑ *When her brother arrives home on a visit from Hong Kong, he sneers at her parochial existence.* **2** ADJ [ADJ n] **Parochial** is used to describe things that relate to the parish connected with a particular church. ❑ *She was a secretary on the local parochial church council.* ❑ *Their children attend a Jewish parochial school.*

pa|ro|chi|al|ism /pəroʊkiəlɪzəm/ N-UNCOUNT **Parochialism** is the quality of being parochial in your attitude. [DISAPPROVAL] ❑ *We have been guilty of parochialism, of resistance to change.*

pa|ro|chial school (parochial schools) N-COUNT A **parochial school** is a private school that is funded and controlled by a particular branch of the Christian Church. [AM] ❑ *My kids will probably go to parochial schools.*

paro|dy /pærədi/ (parodies, parodying, parodied) **1** N-VAR A **parody** is a humorous piece of writing, drama, or music that imitates the style of a well-known person or represents a familiar situation in an exaggerated way. ❑ *It was like a parody of the balcony scene from Romeo and Juliet.* **2** V-T When someone **parodies** a particular work, thing, or person, they imitate it in an amusing or exaggerated way. ❑ *...a sketch parodying the views of well-known politicians.*

pa|role /pəroʊl/ (paroles, paroling, paroled) **1** N-UNCOUNT If a prisoner is given **parole**, he or she is released before the official end of their prison sentence and has to promise to behave well. ❑ *Although sentenced to life, he will become eligible for parole after serving 10 years.* ❑ *...a parole violation.* • PHRASE If a prisoner is **on parole**, he or she is released before the official end of their prison sentence and will not be sent back to prison if their behavior is good. **2** V-T [usu passive] If a prisoner **is paroled**, he or she is given parole. ❑ *He faces at most 12 years in prison and could be paroled after eight years.*

par|ox|ysm /pærəksɪzəm/ (paroxysms) **1** N-COUNT [usu N of n] A **paroxysm** of emotion is a sudden, very strong occurrence of it. ❑ *He exploded in a paroxysm of rage.* **2** N-COUNT [usu N of n/-ing] A **paroxysm** is a series of sudden, violent, uncontrollable movements that your body makes because you are coughing, laughing, or in great pain. ❑ *He broke into a paroxysm of coughing.*

par|quet /pɑrkeɪ/ N-UNCOUNT [usu N n] **Parquet** is a floor covering made of small rectangular blocks of wood fitted together in a pattern. ❑ *...the polished parquet floors.*

par|rot /pærət/ (parrots, parroting, parroted) **1** N-COUNT A **parrot** is a tropical bird with a curved beak and brightly-colored or gray feathers. Parrots can be kept as pets. Some parrots are able to copy what people say. **2** V-T If you disapprove of the fact that someone is just repeating what someone else has

part

said, often without really understanding it, you can say that they **are parroting** it. [DISAPPROVAL] ❑ *Generations of students have learned to parrot the standard explanations.*

par|ry /pæri/ (parries, parrying, parried) **1** V-T If you **parry** a question or argument, you cleverly avoid answering it or dealing with it. ❑ *In an awkward press conference, Mr. Kurtz parried questions on the allegations.* **2** V-T/V-I If you **parry** a blow from someone who is attacking you, you push aside their arm or weapon so that you are not hurt. ❑ *I did not want to wound him, but to restrict myself to defense, to parry his attacks.* ❑ *I parried, and that's when my sword broke.*

parse /pɑrs/ (parses, parsing, parsed) V-T [V n] In grammar, if you **parse** a sentence, you examine each word and clause in order to work out their grammatical type. [TECHNICAL]

par|si|mo|ni|ous /pɑrsɪmoʊniəs/ ADJ [usu ADJ n] Someone who is **parsimonious** is very unwilling to spend money. [FORMAL, DISAPPROVAL]

par|si|mo|ny /pɑrsɪmoʊni/ N-UNCOUNT **Parsimony** is extreme unwillingness to spend money. [FORMAL, DISAPPROVAL] ❑ *Due to official parsimony only the one machine was built.*

pars|ley /pɑrsli/ N-UNCOUNT **Parsley** is a small plant with curly leaves that are used for flavoring or decorating food. ❑ *...rice with fresh parsley.*

pars|nip /pɑrsnɪp/ (parsnips) N-COUNT A **parsnip** is a long cream-colored root vegetable.

par|son /pɑrsᵊn/ (parsons) N-COUNT A **parson** is a minister in the Protestant Church.

par|son|age /pɑrsənɪdʒ/ (parsonages) N-COUNT A **parsonage** is the house where a parson or other minister lives. [OLD-FASHIONED]

PART
① NOUN USES, QUANTIFIER USES, AND PHRASES
② VERB USES

① **part** ✦✦✦ /pɑrt/ (parts)

→ Please look at meaning **18** to see if the expression you are looking for is shown under another headword.

1 N-COUNT A **part** of something is one of the pieces, sections, or elements that it consists of. ❑ *I like that part of Cape Town.* **2** N-COUNT A **part** for a machine or vehicle is one of the smaller pieces that are used to make it. ❑ *...spare parts for military equipment.* **3** QUANT **Part of** something is some of it. ❑ *It was a very severe accident and he lost part of his foot.* ❑ *Perry spent part of his childhood in Canada.* **4** ADV If you say that something is **part** one thing, **part** another, you mean that it is to some extent the first thing and to some extent the second thing. ❑ *The television producer today has to be part news person, part educator.* **5** N-COUNT You can use **part** when you are talking about the proportions of substances in a mixture. For example, if you are told to use five **parts** water to one **part** paint, the mixture should contain five times as much water as paint. ❑ *Use turpentine and linseed oil, three parts to two.* **6** N-COUNT A **part** in a play or movie is one of the roles in it which an actor can perform. ❑ *Alf Sjoberg offered her a large part in the play he was directing.* **7** N-SING [poss N in n] Your **part in** something that happens is your involvement in it. ❑ *If only he could conceal his part in the accident.* **8** N-UNCOUNT [also a N, N of n] If something or someone is **part of** a group or organization, they belong to it or are included in it. ❑ *Annie had never been part of the in-crowd.* **9** N-COUNT The **part** in someone's hair is the line running from the front to the back of their head where their hair lies in different directions. [AM] ❑ *The straight white part in her ebony hair seemed to divide the back of her head in half.*

in BRIT, use **parting**

10 PHRASE If something or someone **plays** a large or important **part** in an event or situation, they are very involved in it and have an important effect on what happens. ❑ *These days work plays an important part in a single woman's life.* **11** PHRASE If you **take part in** an activity, you do it together with other people. ❑ *Thousands of students have taken part in demonstrations.* **12** PHRASE If you **do** your **part**, you do something that, to a small or limited extent, helps to achieve something. ▫ *Each of you is going to have to do your part in keeping the community crime-free.* **13** PHRASE When you are describing people's thoughts or actions, you can say **for** her **part** or **for** my **part**, for example, to introduce what a particular person thinks or does. [FORMAL] ▫ *For my part, I feel elated and close to tears.* **14** PHRASE If you talk about a feeling or action **on** someone's **part**, you are referring to something that they feel or do. ▫ *...techniques on their part to keep us from knowing exactly what's going on.* ▫ *There is no need for any further instructions on my part.* **15** PHRASE You use **in part** to indicate that something exists or happens to some extent but not completely. [FORMAL] ▫ *The levels of blood glucose depend in part on what you eat and when you eat.* **16** part and parcel → see parcel

② **part** ✦✧✧ /pɑːt/ (parts, parting, parted) **1** V-T/V-I If things that are next to each other **part** or if you **part** them, they move in opposite directions, so that there is a space between them. ▫ *Her lips parted as if she were about to take a deep breath.* **2** V-T If you **part** your hair in the middle or at one side, you make it lie in two different directions so that there is a straight line running from the front of your head to the back. ▫ *Picking up a brush, Joanna parted her hair.* **3** V-RECIP When two people **part**, or if one person **parts from** another, they leave each other. [FORMAL] ▫ *He gave me the envelope and we parted.* **4** V-RECIP If you **are parted from** someone you love, you are prevented from being with them. ▫ *I don't believe Laverne and I will ever be parted.* **5** → see also **parting**

▶ **part with** PHRASAL VERB If you **part with** something that is valuable or that you would prefer to keep, you give it or sell it to someone else. ▫ *Buyers might require further assurances before parting with their cash.*

par|take /pɑːˈteɪk/ (partakes, partaking, partook, partaken) **1** V-I If you **partake of** food or drink, you eat or drink some of it. [FORMAL] ▫ *They were happy to partake of our feast, but not to share our company.* **2** V-I If you **partake in** an activity, you take part in it. [FORMAL] ▫ *You will probably be asked about whether you partake in very vigorous sports.*

par|tial /pɑːʃəl/ **1** ADJ You use **partial** to refer to something that is not complete or whole. ▫ *He managed to reach a partial agreement with both republics.* ▫ *...a partial ban on the use of cars in the city.* **2** ADJ [v-link ADJ to n/-ing] If you are **partial to** something, you like it. ▫ *He is also partial to golf, music and chocolate.* ▫ *Mollie confesses she is rather partial to pink.* **3** ADJ [v-link ADJ] Someone who is **partial** supports a particular person or thing, for example, in a competition or dispute, instead of being completely fair. ▫ *I might be accused of being partial.*

par|tial|ly /pɑːʃəli/ ADV [ADV with cl/group] If something happens or exists **partially**, it happens or exists to some extent, but not completely. ▫ *Lisa is deaf in one ear and partially blind.*

par|tici|pant /pɑːˈtɪsɪpənt/ (participants) N-COUNT The **participants** in an activity are the people who take part in it. ▫ *40 of the course participants are offered employment with the company.*

par|tici|pate ✦✧✧ /pɑːˈtɪsɪpeɪt/ (participates, participating, participated) V-I If you **participate** in an activity, you take part in it. ▫ *They expected him to participate in the ceremony.* ▫ *Over half the population of this country participate in sports.*
• **par|tici|pa|tion** /pɑːˌtɪsɪˈpeɪʃən/ N-UNCOUNT ▫ *...participation in religious activities.*

par|tici|pa|tive /pɑːˈtɪsɪpətɪv/ ADJ [usu ADJ n] **Participative** management or decision-making involves the participation of all the people engaged in an activity or affected by certain decisions. [FORMAL] ▫ *...a participative management style.*

par|tici|pa|tory /pɑːˌtɪsɪˈpeɪtəri/ ADJ [usu ADJ n] A **participatory** system, activity, or role involves a particular person or group of people taking part in it. ▫ *...participatory management styles.*

par|ti|cip|ial /pɑːˈtɪsɪpiəl/ ADJ In grammar, **participial** means relating to a participle.

par|ti|ci|ple /pɑːˈtɪsɪpəl/ (participles) N-COUNT In grammar, a **participle** is a form of a verb that can be used in compound tenses of the verb. There are two participles in English: the past participle, which usually ends in '-ed,' and the present participle, which ends in '-ing.'

par|ti|cle /pɑːˈtɪkəl/ (particles) **1** N-COUNT A **particle** of something is a very small piece or amount of it. ▫ *...a particle of hot metal.* ▫ *There is a particle of truth in his statement.* **2** N-COUNT In physics, a **particle** is a piece of matter smaller than an atom such as an electron or a proton. [TECHNICAL] ▫ *...the sub-atomic particles that make up matter.*

par|ti|cle ac|cel|era|tor (particle accelerators) N-COUNT A **particle accelerator** is a machine used for research in nuclear physics that can make particles smaller than atoms move very fast.

par|ti|cle phys|ics N-UNCOUNT **Particle physics** is the study of the particles that make up atoms and the way they behave and react.

par|ticu|lar ✦✦✧ /pɑːˈtɪkjələr/ **1** ADJ [ADJ n] You use **particular** to emphasize that you are talking about one thing or one kind of thing rather than other similar ones. [EMPHASIS] ▫ *I remembered a particular story about a mailman who was a murderer.* ▫ *I have to know exactly why it is I'm doing a particular job.* **2** ADJ [ADJ n] If a person or thing has a **particular** quality or possession, it is distinct and belongs only to them. ▫ *I have a particular responsibility to ensure I make the right decision.* **3** ADJ [ADJ n] You can use **particular** to emphasize that something is greater or more intense than usual. [EMPHASIS] ▫ *Particular emphasis will be placed on oral language training.* **4** ADJ If you say that someone is **particular**, you mean that they choose things and do things very carefully, and are not easily satisfied. ▫ *Ted was very particular about the colors he used.* **5** → see also **particulars** **6** PHRASE You use **in particular** to indicate that what you are saying applies especially to one thing or person. ▫ *The situation in Ethiopia in particular is worrisome.* ▫ *Why should he notice her car in particular?*

SYNONYMS

particular
ADJ

1
specific: *There are several specific problems to be dealt with.*
exact: *I don't remember the exact words.*
precise: *He was not clear on the precise nature of his mission.*

2
special: *Just to see him was something special.*
exceptional: *...children with exceptional ability.*
notable: *With a few notable exceptions, doctors are a pretty sensible bunch.*
remarkable: *It was a remarkable achievement.*

4
fussy: *He is not fussy about what he eats.*
demanding: *Ricky was a very demanding child.*
exacting: *Privately, they seem to have the same exacting standards.*
fastidious: *He was fastidious about his appearance.*

---

par|ticu|lar|ity /pɑːˌtɪkjəˈlærɪti/ (particularities) **1** N-VAR [also N in pl] The **particularity** of something is its quality of being different from other things. The **particularities** of something are the features that make it different. [FORMAL] ▫ *...the particularity of our societal system.* ▫ *...the particularities of each situation.* **2** N-UNCOUNT **Particularity** is the giving or showing of details. [FORMAL]

par|ticu|lar|ize /pɑːˈtɪkjələraɪz/ (particularizes, particularizing, particularized)

in BRIT, also use **particularise**

V-T/V-I If you **particularize** something that you have been talking about in a general way, you give details or specific examples of it. [FORMAL] ▫ *Mr. Johnson particularizes the general points he wants to make.* ▫ *A farmer is entitled to a certain particularized tax treatment.*

par|ticu|lar|ly ✦✦✧ /pɑːˈtɪkjələrli/ **1** ADV [ADV with cl/group] You use **particularly** to indicate that what you are saying applies especially to one thing or situation. ▫ *Keep your office space looking good, particularly your desk.* ▫ *More local employment will be created, particularly in service industries.* **2** ADV [ADV with cl/group] **Particularly** means more than usual or more than other things. [EMPHASIS] ▫ *Progress has been particularly disappointing.*

SYNONYMS

particularly
ADV **1**
especially: Reapply sunscreen every two hours, especially if you have been swimming.
specifically: We haven't specifically targeted school children.
in particular: Why should he notice her car in particular?

par|ticu|lars /pətɪkyələrz/ N-PLURAL The **particulars** of something or someone are facts or details about them that are written down and kept as a record. ❑ *You will find all the particulars in Chapter 9.*

par|ticu|late /pətɪkyʊlɪt/ (**particulates**) N-COUNT [oft N n] **Particulates** are very small particles of a substance, especially those that are produced when fuel is burned. [TECHNICAL] ❑ *...the particulate pollution in our atmosphere.*

part|ing /pɑrtɪŋ/ (**partings**) **1** N-VAR **Parting** is the act of leaving a particular person or place. A **parting** is an occasion when this happens. ❑ *Parting from any one of you for even a short time is hard.* **2** ADJ [ADJ n] Your **parting** words or actions are the things that you say or do as you are leaving a place or person. ❑ *Her parting words left him feeling empty and alone.* **3** N-COUNT The **parting** in someone's hair is the line running from the front to the back of their head where their hair lies in different directions. [BRIT]

in AM, use **part**

part|ing shot (**parting shots**) N-COUNT If someone makes a **parting shot**, they make an unpleasant or forceful remark at the end of a conversation, and then leave so that no one has the chance to reply. ❑ *He turned to face her for his parting shot. "You're one cold-hearted woman, you know that?"*

par|ti|san /pɑrtɪzən/ (**partisans**) **1** ADJ Someone who is **partisan** strongly supports a particular person or cause, often without thinking carefully about the matter. ❑ *He is clearly too partisan to be a referee.* **2** N-COUNT **Partisans** are ordinary people, rather than soldiers, who join together to fight enemy soldiers who are occupying their country. ❑ *He was rescued by some Italian partisans.*

par|ti|san|ship /pɑrtɪzənʃɪp/ N-UNCOUNT **Partisanship** is support for a person or group without fair consideration of the facts and circumstances. ❑ *His politics were based on loyal partisanship.*

par|ti|tion /pɑrtɪʃən/ (**partitions, partitioning, partitioned**) **1** N-COUNT A **partition** is a wall, screen, or divider that separates one part of a room, vehicle, or other space from another. ❑ *...new offices divided only by glass partitions.* **2** V-T If you **partition** a room, you separate one part of it from another by means of a partition. ❑ *Bedrooms have again been created by partitioning a single larger room.* **3** V-T If a country **is partitioned**, it is divided into two or more independent countries. ❑ *Korea was partitioned in 1945.* ❑ *...Churchill's plans to partition the German state.* • N-UNCOUNT **Partition** is also a noun. ❑ *...fighting which followed the partition of India.*

part|ly ✦✦◇ /pɑrtli/ ADV [ADV with cl/group] You use **partly** to indicate that something happens or exists to some extent, but not completely. ❑ *It's partly my fault.* ❑ *I have not worried so much this year, partly because I have had other things to think about.*

part|ner ✦✦◇ /pɑrtnər/ (**partners, partnering, partnered**) **1** N-COUNT Your **partner** is the person you are married to or are having a romantic or sexual relationship with. ❑ *Wanting other friends doesn't mean you don't love your partner.* **2** N-COUNT Your **partner** is the person you are doing something with, for example, dancing with or playing with in a game against two other people. ❑ *...to dance with a partner.* ❑ *Her partner for the game was Venus Williams.* **3** N-COUNT The **partners** in a firm or business are the people who share the ownership of it. [BUSINESS] ❑ *He's a partner in a Chicago law firm.* **4** N-COUNT The **partner** of a country or organization is another country or organization with which they work or do business. ❑ *Spain has been one of Cuba's major trading partners.* **5** V-T If you **partner** someone, you are their partner in a game or in a dance. ❑ *He had partnered the famous Russian ballerina.* ❑ *He will be partnered by Ian Baker, the defending champion.*

COLLOCATIONS

partner
NOUN
1
noun + **partner**: marriage
adjective + **partner**: civil, sexual; ideal, perfect, potential; former, long-term
verb + **partner**: find, seek
3
noun + **partner**: business
adjective + **partner**: junior, managing, senior; equal, full

part|ner|ship ✦◇◇ /pɑrtnərʃɪp/ (**partnerships**) N-VAR **Partnership** or a **partnership** is a relationship in which two or more people, organizations, or countries work together as partners. ❑ *...the partnership between Germany's banks and its businesses.*

COLLOCATIONS

partnership
NOUN
adjective + **partnership**: close, effective, solid, successful; joint, strategic
verb + **partnership**: create, develop, forge, form

SYNONYMS

partnership
NOUN
cooperation: *A deal with Japan could open the door to economic cooperation with East Asia.*
association: *...the company's six-year association with retailer J.C. Penney Co.*
alliance: *The two parties were still too much apart to form an alliance.*

part of speech (**parts of speech**) N-COUNT A **part of speech** is a particular grammatical class of word such as noun, adjective, or verb.

par|took /pɑrtʊk/ **Partook** is the past tense of **partake**.

par|tridge /pɑrtrɪdʒ/ (**partridges**) N-COUNT A **partridge** is a wild bird with brown feathers, a round body, and a short tail. • N-UNCOUNT **Partridge** is the flesh of this bird eaten as food. ❑ *...a main course of partridge.*

part-time

The adverb is also spelled **part time**.

1 ADJ If someone is a **part-time** worker or has a **part-time** job, they work for only part of each day or week. ❑ *Many businesses are cutting back by employing lower-paid part-time workers.* ❑ *Part-time work is generally hard to find.* • ADV [ADV after v] **Part-time** is also an adverb. ❑ *I want to work part-time.* **2** → See feature box at **working**

part-timer (**part-timers**) N-COUNT A **part-timer** is a person who works part-time. ❑ *Customer service departments are often staffed by part-timers.*

part way also **part-way** ADV **Part way** means part of the way or partly. ❑ *Local authorities will run out of money part way through the financial year.* ❑ *It might go part way to repaying the debt.*

par|ty ✦✦✦ /pɑrti/ (**parties, partying, partied**) **1** N-COUNT A **party** is a political organization whose members have similar aims and beliefs. Usually the organization tries to get its members elected to the legislature of a country. ❑ *...a member of the Republican Party.* ❑ *...opposition parties.* **2** N-COUNT A **party** is a social event, often in someone's home, at which people enjoy themselves doing things such as eating, drinking, dancing, talking, or playing games. ❑ *The couple met at a party.* ❑ *We threw a huge birthday party.* **3** V-I If you **party**, you enjoy yourself doing things such as going out to parties, drinking, dancing, and talking to people. ❑ *They come to eat and drink, to swim, to party.* **4** N-COUNT A **party** of people is a group of people who are doing something together, for example, traveling together. ❑ *They became separated from their party.* ❑ *...a party of sightseers.* **5** → see also **search party** **6** N-COUNT One of the people involved in a legal agreement or dispute can be referred to as a particular **party**. [LEGAL] ❑ *It has to be proved that they are the guilty party.* ❑ *...he was the injured party.* **7** PHRASE

Someone who **is a party to** or **is party to** an action or agreement is involved in it, and therefore partly responsible for it. ☐ *You were the one that brought up the idea of blackmail. I'd never be a party to such a thing.*

SYNONYMS

party
NOUN ②
get-together: *...a get-together I had at my home.*
celebration: *...his eightieth birthday celebrations.*
do: *A friend is having a do in Stoke.*

---

par|ty|goer /pɑːrtigoʊər/ (**partygoers**) N-COUNT A **partygoer** is someone who likes going to parties or someone who is at a particular party. ☐ *At least half the partygoers were under 15.*

par|ty line N-SING The **party line** on a particular issue is the official view taken by a political party, which its members are expected to support. ☐ *They ignored the official party line.*

par|ty poli|tics N-UNCOUNT **Party politics** is political activity involving political parties. ☐ *He thinks preachers should not identify themselves too closely with party politics.*

par|ty poop|er /pɑːrti puːpər/ (**party poopers**) N-COUNT You describe someone as a **party pooper** when you think that they spoil other people's fun and their enjoyment of something. [INFORMAL, DISAPPROVAL] ☐ *I hate to be a party pooper, but I am really tired.*

par|ty spir|it N-UNCOUNT If you talk about someone being in the **party spirit**, you mean that they are in the mood to enjoy a party or to have fun. ☐ *Sparkling wine can also put you in the party spirit.*

par|venu /pɑːrvənuː/ (**parvenus**) N-COUNT If you describe someone as a **parvenu**, you think that although they have acquired wealth or high status they are not very cultured or well-educated. [FORMAL, DISAPPROVAL]

pas de deux (pas de deux)

> **pas de deux** is both the singular and the plural form; both forms are pronounced /pɑː də dɜː/.

N-COUNT In ballet, a **pas de deux** is a dance sequence for two dancers.

pash|mi|na /pæʃmiːnə/ (**pashminas**) ◼ N-UNCOUNT **Pashmina** is very fine, soft wool made from the hair of goats. ☐ *...pashmina scarves.* ◼ N-COUNT A **pashmina** is a type of shawl made from pashmina.

PASS

① VERB USES
② NOUN USES
③ PHRASAL VERBS

---

① **pass** ♦♦♦ /pæs/ (passes, passing, passed)
→ Please look at meanings ㉑ and ㉒ to see if the expression you are looking for is shown under another headword.

◼ V-T/V-I To **pass** someone or something means to go past them without stopping. ☐ *As she passed the library door, the telephone began to ring.* ☐ *Jane stood aside to let her pass.* ◻ V-I When someone or something **passes** in a particular direction, they move in that direction. ☐ *He passed through the doorway into the kitchen.* ☐ *He passed down the tunnel.* ◻ V-I If something such as a road or pipe **passes** along a particular route, it goes along that route. ☐ *A dirt road passes through the town.* ◻ V-T If you **pass** something through, over, or around something else, you move or push it through, over, or around that thing. ☐ *She passed the needle through the rough cloth, back and forth.* ☐ *"I don't understand," the detective mumbled, passing a hand through his hair.* ◻ V-T If you **pass** something to someone, you take it in your hand and give it to them. ☐ *Ken passed the books to Sergeant Wong.* ◻ V-T/V-I If something **passes** or **is passed** from one person to another, the second person then has it instead of the first. ☐ *His mother's small estate had passed to him after her death.* ☐ *These powers were eventually passed to municipalities.* ◻ V-T If you **pass** information to someone, you give it to them because it concerns them. ☐ *Officials failed to pass vital information to their superiors.* • PHRASAL VERB **Pass on** means the same as **pass**. ☐ *I do not know what to do with the information if I cannot pass it on.* ☐ *From time to time he passed on confidential information to him.* ◻ V-T/V-I If you **pass**, or **pass** the ball to someone on your team in a game such as football or basketball, you throw it to them. ☐ *Your partner should then pass the ball back to you.* ◻ V-I When a period of time **passes**, it happens and finishes. ☐ *He couldn't imagine why he had let so much time pass without contacting her.* ☐ *As the years pass we can feel trapped by certain realities of marriage.* ◻ V-T If you **pass** a period of time in a particular way, you spend it in that way. ☐ *The children passed the time playing in the streets.* ◻ V-I If you **pass through** a stage of development or a period of time, you experience it. ☐ *The country was passing through a grave crisis.* ◻ V-T If an amount **passes** a particular total or level, it becomes greater than that total or level. ☐ *They became the first company in their field to pass the $2 billion turn-over mark.* ◻ V-T If someone or something **passes** a test, they are considered to be of an acceptable standard. ☐ *Kevin has just passed his driving test.* ☐ *...new drugs which have passed early tests to show that they are safe.* ◻ V-T If someone in authority **passes** a person or thing, they declare that they are of an acceptable standard or have reached an acceptable standard. ☐ *Several popular beaches were found unfit for swimming although the government passed them last year.* ◻ V-T When people in authority **pass** a new law or a proposal, they formally agree to it or approve it. ☐ *The Estonian parliament has passed a resolution declaring the republic fully independent.* ◻ V-T When a judge **passes** sentence on someone, he or she says what their punishment will be. ☐ *Passing sentence, the judge said it all had the appearance of a con trick.* ◻ V-I If someone or something **passes for** or **passes as** something that they are not, they are accepted as being that thing or mistaken for that thing. ☐ *Children's toy guns now look so realistic that they can often pass for the real thing.* ☐ *It is doubtful whether Ted, even with his fluent French, passed for one of the locals.* ◻ V-T If someone makes you an offer or asks you a question and you say that you will **pass** on it, you mean that you do not want to accept or answer it now. [INFORMAL] ☐ *I think I'll pass on the swimming.* ☐ *"You can join us if you like." Brad shook his head. "I'll pass, thanks."* ◻ V-I In some card games and other games, if you **pass**, you choose not to play at that stage in the game. ◻ V-T If you **pass** comment or **pass** a comment, you say something. [BRIT] ㉑ **to pass the buck** → see **buck** ㉒ **to pass judgment** → see **judgment** ㉓ → See feature box at **drive**

② **pass** ♦♦♦ /pæs/ (passes) ◼ N-COUNT A **pass** in an examination, test, or course is a successful result in it. ☐ *He's been allowed to re-take the exam, and he's going to get a pass.* ◻ N-COUNT A **pass** is a document that allows you to do something. ☐ *I got myself a pass into the barracks.* ◻ N-COUNT A **pass** in a game such as football or basketball is an act of throwing the ball to someone on your team. ☐ *Hirst rolled a short pass to Merson.* ◻ N-COUNT; N-IN-NAMES A **pass** is a narrow path or route between mountains. ☐ *The monastery is in a remote mountain pass.*

③ **pass** ♦♦♦ /pæs/ (passes, passing, passed)
▸ **pass away** PHRASAL VERB You can say that someone **passed away** to mean that they died, if you want to avoid using the word 'die' because you think it might upset or offend people. ☐ *He unfortunately passed away last year.*
▸ **pass off** PHRASAL VERB If an event **passes off** without any trouble, it happens and ends without any trouble. [BRIT]
▸ **pass off as** PHRASAL VERB If you **pass** something **off as** another thing, you convince people that it is that other thing. ☐ *He passed himself off as a senior psychologist.* ☐ *I've tried to pass off my accent as a New York one.*
▸ **pass on** ◼ PHRASAL VERB If you **pass** something **on** to someone, you give it to them so that they have it instead of you. ☐ *The winner is passing the money on to a selection of her favorite charities.* ☐ *The late governor passed on much of his fortune to his daughter.* ◻ PHRASAL VERB You can say that someone **passed on** to mean that they died, if you think it might upset or offend people to use the word 'die' because you think it might upset or offend people. ☐ *He passed on at the age of 72.* ◻ → see also **pass** ① 7
▸ **pass out** PHRASAL VERB If you **pass out**, you faint or collapse. ☐ *He felt sick and dizzy and then passed out.*
▸ **pass over** ◼ PHRASAL VERB If someone **is passed over** for a job or position, they do not get the job or position and someone younger or less experienced is chosen instead. ☐ *Other candidates, however, have been passed over for promotion inexplicably and almost certainly unfairly.* ◻ PHRASAL VERB If you **pass over** a topic in a conversation or speech, you do not talk

passable /pæsəbəl/ **1** ADJ [usu ADJ n] If something is a **passable** effort or of **passable** quality, it is satisfactory or fairly good. ❑ *Stan puffed out his thin cheeks in a passable imitation of his dad.* • **pass|ably** /pæsəbli/ ADV ❑ *She has always been quick to pick things up, doing passably well in school without really trying.* **2** ADJ [usu v-link ADJ] If a road is **passable**, it is not completely blocked, and people can still use it. ❑ *The airport road is passable today for the first time in a week.*

pas|sage ✧✧✧ /pæsɪdʒ/ (**passages**) **1** N-COUNT A **passage** is a long narrow space with walls or fences on both sides, that connects one place or room with another. ❑ *Harry stepped into the passage and closed the door behind him.* **2** N-COUNT A **passage** in a book, speech, or piece of music is a section of it that you are considering separately from the rest. ❑ *He read a passage from Emerson.* ❑ *...the passage in which the author speaks of the world of imagination.* **3** N-COUNT A **passage** is a long narrow hole or tube in your body, that air or liquid can pass along. ❑ *...cells that line the air passages.* **4** N-COUNT A **passage** through a crowd of people or things is an empty space that allows you to move through them. ❑ *He cleared a passage for himself through the crammed streets.* **5** N-UNCOUNT The **passage** of someone or something is their movement from one place to another. ❑ *Germany had not requested Franco's consent for the passage of troops through Spain.* **6** N-UNCOUNT The **passage** of someone or something is their progress from one situation or one stage in their development to another. ❑ *...to ease their passage to a market economy.* **7** N-UNCOUNT The **passage** of a bill is its progress through Congress so that it can become a law. ❑ *...a Medicare bill expected to get final passage in Congress today.* **8** N-SING The **passage** of a period of time is its passing. ❑ *...an asset that increases in value with the passage of time.* **9** N-COUNT A **passage** is a journey by ship. ❑ *We'd arrived the day before after a 10-hour passage from Anchorage.* **10** N-UNCOUNT If you are granted **passage** through a country or area of land, you are given permission to go through it. ❑ *Mr. Thomas would be given safe passage to and from Jaffna.*

── SYNONYMS ──
passage
NOUN **1**
corridor: *They walked down the corridor.*
hallway: *The living room was at the end of a long hallway.*
passageway: *There's an underground passageway that connects the five buildings.*

passage|way /pæsɪdʒweɪ/ (**passageways**) N-COUNT A **passageway** is a long narrow space with walls or fences on both sides, that connects one place or room with another. ❑ *Outside, in the passageway, I could hear people moving around.*

pass|book /pæsbʊk/ (**passbooks**) N-COUNT A **passbook** is a small book recording the amount of money you put in or take out of a savings account at a bank.

pas|sé /pæseɪ/ ADJ [usu v-link ADJ] If someone describes something as **passé**, they think that it is no longer fashionable or that it is no longer effective. [DISAPPROVAL] ❑ *Punk is passé.*

pas|sen|ger ✧✧✧ /pæsɪndʒər/ (**passengers**) **1** N-COUNT A **passenger** in a vehicle such as a bus, boat, or plane is a person who is traveling in it, but who is not driving it or working on it. ❑ *Mr. Fullemann was a passenger in the car when it crashed.* **2** ADJ [ADJ n] **Passenger** is used to describe something that is designed for passengers, rather than for drivers or freight. ❑ *I sat in the passenger seat.*

── SYNONYMS ──
passenger
NOUN **1**
traveler: *Many air travelers suffer puffy ankles and feet during long flights.*
commuter: *The number of commuters to London has dropped by 100,000.*

pass|er|by /pɑsərbaɪ, pæs-/ (**passersby**) also **passer-by** N-COUNT A **passerby** is a person who is walking past someone or something. ❑ *A passerby described what he saw moments after the car bomb had exploded.*

pas|sim /pæsəm/ ADV In indexes and notes, **passim** indicates that a particular name or subject occurs frequently throughout a particular piece of writing or section of a book. ❑ *...The Theories of their Relation (London, 1873), p. 8 and passim.*

pass|ing /pæsɪŋ/ **1** ADJ [ADJ n] A **passing** fashion, activity, or feeling lasts for only a short period of time and is not worth taking very seriously. ❑ *Hamnett does not believe environmental concern is a passing fad.* **2** N-SING The **passing** of something such as a time or system is the fact of its coming to an end. ❑ *It was an historic day, yet its passing was not marked by the slightest excitement.* **3** N-SING You can refer to someone's death as their **passing**, if you want to avoid using the word 'death' because you think it might upset or offend people. ❑ *His passing will be mourned by many people.* **4** N-SING The **passing of** a period of time is the fact or process of its going by. ❑ *The passing of time brought a sense of emptiness.* **5** ADJ [ADJ n] A **passing** mention or reference is brief and is made while you are talking or writing about something else. ❑ *It was just a passing comment, he didn't expand.* **6** → see also **pass** ①, **pass** ③ **7** PHRASE If you mention something **in passing**, you mention it briefly while you are talking or writing about something else. ❑ *The army is only mentioned in passing.*

pas|sion ✧✧✧ /pæʃən/ (**passions**) **1** N-UNCOUNT [also N in pl] **Passion** is strong sexual feelings toward someone. ❑ *...my passion for a dark-haired, slender boy named Josh.* ❑ *...the expression of love and passion.* **2** N-UNCOUNT [also N in pl] **Passion** is a very strong feeling about something or a strong belief in something. ❑ *He spoke with great passion.* **3** N-COUNT If you have a **passion for** something, you have a very strong interest in it and like it very much. ❑ *She had a passion for gardening.*

pas|sion|ate /pæʃənɪt/ **1** ADJ A **passionate** person has very strong feelings about something or a strong belief in something. ❑ *...his passionate commitment to peace.* ❑ *He is very passionate about the project.* • **pas|sion|ate|ly** ADV ❑ *I am passionately opposed to the death penalty.* **2** ADJ A **passionate** person has strong romantic or sexual feelings and expresses them in their behavior. ❑ *...a beautiful, passionate woman of twenty-six.* • **pas|sion|ate|ly** ADV ❑ *He was passionately in love with her.*

pas|sion fruit (**passion fruit**) also **passionfruit** N-VAR A **passion fruit** is a small, round, brown fruit that is produced by certain types of tropical flower.

pas|sion|less /pæʃənlɪs/ ADJ If you describe someone or something as **passionless**, you mean that they do not have or show strong feelings. ❑ *...a passionless academic.* ❑ *...their apparently passionless marriage.*

pas|sive /pæsɪv/ **1** ADJ If you describe someone as **passive**, you mean that they do not take action but instead let things happen to them. [DISAPPROVAL] ❑ *His passive attitude made things easier for me.* • **pas|sive|ly** ADV ❑ *He sat there passively, content to wait for his father to make the opening move.* **2** ADJ [ADJ n] A **passive** activity involves watching, looking at, or listening to things rather than doing things. ❑ *They want less passive ways of filling their time.* **3** ADJ [ADJ n] **Passive** resistance involves showing opposition to the people in power in your country by not cooperating with them and protesting in nonviolent ways. ❑ *They made it clear that they would only exercise passive resistance in the event of a military takeover.* **4** N-SING In grammar, **the passive** or **the passive voice** is formed using 'be' and the past participle of a verb. The subject of a passive clause does not perform the action expressed by the verb but is affected by it. For example, in 'She's been injured,' the verb is in the passive. Compare **active**.

pas|sive smok|ing N-UNCOUNT **Passive smoking** involves breathing in the smoke from other people's cigarettes because you happen to be near them. ❑ *...the dangers of passive smoking.*

Pass|over /pæsoʊvər/ N-UNCOUNT [also the N] **Passover** is a Jewish festival that begins in March or April and lasts for seven or eight days. Passover begins with a special meal that reminds Jewish people of how God helped their ancestors escape from Egypt.

pass|port /pæsport/ (passports) N-COUNT Your **passport** is an official document containing your name, photograph, and personal details, which you need to show when you enter or leave a country. ▫ *You should take your passport with you when changing money.*

pass|word /pæswɜrd/ (passwords) **1** N-COUNT A **password** is a secret word or phrase that you must know in order to be allowed to enter a place such as a military base, or to be allowed to use a computer system. ▫ *Advance and give the password.* **2** → See feature box at **email**

past ♦♦♦ /pæst/ (pasts)

In addition to the uses shown below, **past** is used in the phrasal verb 'run past.'

1 N-SING **The past** is the time before the present, and the things that have happened. ▫ *In the past, about a third of the babies born to women with diabetes died.* • PHRASE If you accuse someone of **living in the past**, you mean that they think too much about the past or believe that things are the same as they were in the past. [DISAPPROVAL] ▫ *What was the point in living in the past, thinking about what had or had not happened?* **2** N-COUNT Your **past** consists of all the things that you have done or that have happened to you. ▫ *...revelations about his past.* **3** ADJ [ADJ n] **Past** events and things happened or existed before the present time. ▫ *I knew from past experience that alternative therapies could help.* ▫ *...a return to the turbulence of past centuries.* **4** ADJ [det ADJ n] You use **past** to talk about a period of time that has just finished. For example, if you talk about the **past five years**, you mean the period of five years that has just finished. ▫ *Most stores have remained closed for the past three days.* **5** PREP [num PREP num] You use **past** when you are stating a time that is thirty minutes or less after a particular hour. For example, if it is **twenty past** six, it is twenty minutes after six o'clock. ▫ *It's ten past eleven.* • ADV [num ADV] **Past** is also an adverb. ▫ *I have my lunch at half past.* **6** PREP If it is **past** a particular time, it is later than that time. ▫ *It was past midnight.* **7** PREP If you go **past** someone or something, you go near them and keep moving, so that they are behind you. ▫ *I dashed past him and out of the door.* ▫ *A steady procession of people filed past the coffin.* • ADV **Past** is also an adverb. ▫ *An ambulance drove past.* **8** PREP [v PREP n] If you look or point **past** a person or thing, you look or point at something behind them. ▫ *She stared past Christine at the bed.* **9** PREP [v-link PREP n] If something is **past** a place, it is on the other side of it. ▫ *Go north on I-15 to the exit just past Barstow.* **10** PREP If someone or something is **past** a particular point or stage, they are no longer at that point or stage. ▫ *He was well past retirement age.*

COLLOCATIONS

past
NOUN
1
adjective + **past**: distant, recent
2
adjective + **past**: dark, murky, troubled, violent; colorful, glorious, rich

---
SYNONYMS

past
ADJ **4**
last: *She got married last July.*
recent: *Sales have fallen by more than 75 percent in recent years.*
previous: *It was a surprisingly dry day after the rain of the previous week.*

---

pas|ta /pɑstə/ (pastas) N-MASS **Pasta** is a type of food made from a mixture of flour, eggs, and water that is formed into different shapes and then boiled. Spaghetti, macaroni, and noodles are types of pasta.

paste /peɪst/ (pastes, pasting, pasted) **1** N-MASS **Paste** is a soft, wet, sticky mixture of a substance and a liquid, that can be spread easily. Some types of paste are used to stick things together. ▫ *Blend a little milk with the custard powder to form a paste.* **2** N-MASS **Paste** is a soft smooth mixture of crushed meat, fruit, or vegetables. You can, for example, spread it onto bread or use it in cooking. ▫ *...tomato paste.* **3** V-T If you **paste** something on a surface, you put glue or paste on it and stick it on the surface. ▫ *...pasting labels on bottles.*

pas|tel /pæstɛl/ (pastels) ADJ [ADJ n, ADJ color] **Pastel** colors are pale rather than dark or bright. ▫ *...delicate pastel shades.* ▫ *...pastel pink, blue, peach, and green.* • N-COUNT **Pastel** is also a noun. ▫ *The lobby is decorated in pastels.*

pas|teur|ized /pæstʃəraɪzd/

in BRIT, also use **pasteurised**

ADJ [usu ADJ n] **Pasteurized** milk, cream, or cheese has had bacteria removed from it by a special heating process to make it safer to eat or drink.

pas|tiche /pæstiʃ, pɑs-/ (pastiches) N-VAR A **pastiche** is something such as a piece of writing or music in which the style is copied from somewhere else, or which contains a mixture of different styles. [FORMAL] ▫ *His bathroom is a brilliant pastiche of expensive interior design.*

pas|tille /pæstɪl/ (pastilles) N-COUNT A **pastille** is a small, round sweet or piece of candy that has a fruit flavor. Some pastilles contain medicine and you can suck them if you have a sore throat or a cough.

pas|time /pæstaɪm/ (pastimes) **1** N-COUNT A **pastime** is something that you do in your spare time because you enjoy it or are interested in it. ▫ *His favorite pastime is golf.* **2** → See feature box at **leisure**

past mas|ter (past masters) N-COUNT [usu N at/in/of n] If you are a **past master** at something, you are very skillful at it because you have had a lot of experience doing it. ▫ *He was a past master at manipulating the media for his own ends.* ▫ *She is an adept rock-climber and a past master of the obstacle course.*

pas|tor /pæstər/ (pastors) N-COUNT A **pastor** is a member of the clergy in some churches, especially Protestant churches.

pas|to|ral /pæstərəl, pæstɔr-/ **1** ADJ [ADJ n] The **pastoral** duties of a priest or other religious leader involve looking after the people he or she has responsibility for, especially by helping them with their personal problems. ▫ *...the pastoral care of the sick.* **2** ADJ [ADJ n] A **pastoral** place, atmosphere, or idea is characteristic of peaceful country life and scenery. ▫ *...a tranquil pastoral scene.*

past par|ti|ci|ple (past participles) N-COUNT In grammar, the **past participle** of a verb is a form that is usually the same as the past form and so ends in '-ed.' A number of verbs have irregular past participles, for example, 'break' - past participle 'broken,' and 'come' - past participle 'come.' Past participles are used to form perfect tenses and the passive voice, and many of them can be used like an adjective in front of a noun.

past per|fect ADJ [ADJ n] In grammar, the **past perfect** tenses of a verb are the ones used to talk about things that happened before a specific time. The simple past perfect tense uses 'had' and the past participle of the verb, as in 'She had seen him before.' It is sometimes called the **pluperfect**.

pas|tra|mi /pəstrɑmi/ N-UNCOUNT **Pastrami** is strongly seasoned smoked beef.

pas|try /peɪstri/ (pastries) **1** N-UNCOUNT **Pastry** is a food made from flour, fat, and water that is mixed together, rolled flat, and baked in the oven. It is used, for example, for making pies. **2** N-COUNT A **pastry** is a small cake made with sweet pastry. ▫ *...a wide range of cakes and pastries.*

pas|ture /pæstʃər/ (pastures) N-VAR **Pasture** is land with grass growing on it for farm animals to eat. ▫ *The cows are out now, grazing in the pasture.*

pasty /peɪsti/ ADJ If you are **pasty** or if you have a **pasty** face, you look pale and unhealthy. ▫ *My complexion remained pale and pasty.*

pat /pæt/ (pats, patting, patted) **1** V-T If you **pat** something or someone, you tap them lightly, usually with your hand held flat. ▫ *"Don't you worry about any of this," she said, patting me on the knee.* ▫ *The landlady patted her hair nervously.* • N-COUNT **Pat** is also a noun. ▫ *He gave her an encouraging pat on the shoulder.* **2** N-COUNT A **pat** of butter or something else that is soft is a small lump of it. ▫ *Terreano put a pat of butter on his plate.* **3** PHRASE If you give someone **a pat on the back** or if you **pat** them **on the back**, you show them that you think they have done well and deserve to be praised. [APPROVAL] ▫ *The players deserve a pat on the back.*

patch /pætʃ/ (patches, patching, patched) **1** N-COUNT A **patch** on a surface is a part of it that is different in appearance from the area around it. ❑ ...the bald patch on the top of his head. ❑ There was a small patch of blue in the gray clouds. **2** N-COUNT A **patch** of land is a small area of land where a particular plant or crop grows. ❑ ...a patch of land covered in forest. ❑ ...the little vegetable patch in her backyard. **3** N-COUNT A **patch** is a piece of material that you use to cover a hole in something. ❑ ...jackets with patches on the elbows. **4** N-COUNT A **patch** is a small piece of material that you wear to cover an injured eye. ❑ She went to the hospital and found him lying down with a patch over his eye. **5** V-T If you **patch** something that has a hole in it, you repair it by fastening a patch over the hole. ❑ He and Walker patched the barn roof. ❑ One of the mechanics took off the damaged tire, and took it back to the station to be patched. **6** N-COUNT A **patch** is a piece of computer program code written as a temporary solution for dealing with a computer virus and distributed by the makers of the original program. [COMPUTING] ❑ Older machines will need a software patch to correct the date. **7** PHRASE If you have or go through **a rough patch**, you have a lot of problems for a time. ❑ His marriage was going through a rough patch.
▸ **patch up 1** PHRASAL VERB If you **patch up** an argument or relationship, you try to be friendly again and not to argue anymore. ❑ She has gone on vacation with her husband to try to patch up their marriage. ❑ France patched things up with New Zealand. **2** PHRASAL VERB If you **patch up** something that is damaged, you repair it or patch it. ❑ We can patch up those holes. **3** PHRASAL VERB If doctors **patch** someone **up** or **patch** their wounds **up**, they treat their injuries. ❑ ...the medical staff who patched her up after the accident.

patch|work /pætʃwɜrk/ ADJ [ADJ n] A **patchwork** quilt, cushion, or piece of clothing is made by sewing together small pieces of material of different colors or patterns. ❑ ...beds covered in patchwork quilts. • N-UNCOUNT **Patchwork** is also a noun. ❑ For centuries, quilting and patchwork have been popular needlecrafts.

patchy /pætʃi/ **1** ADJ A **patchy** substance or color exists in some places but not in others, or is thick in some places and thin in others. ❑ Thick patchy fog and irresponsible driving were to blame. ❑ ...the brown, patchy grass. **2** ADJ If something is **patchy**, it is not completely reliable or satisfactory because it is not always good. ❑ The evidence is patchy.

pate /peɪt/ (pates) N-COUNT Your **pate** is the top of your head. [OLD-FASHIONED] ❑ ...Bryan's bald pate.

pâté /pɑteɪ/ (pâtés) N-MASS **Pâté** is a soft mixture of meat, fish, or vegetables with various flavorings that is eaten cold.

pa|tent /pætənt/ (patents, patenting, patented) **1** N-COUNT A **patent** is an official right to be the only person or company allowed to make or sell a new product for a certain period of time. ❑ P&G applied for a patent on its cookies. ❑ He held a number of patents for his many innovations. **2** V-T If you **patent** something, you obtain a patent for it. ❑ He patented the idea that the atom could be split. ❑ The invention has been patented by the university. **3** ADJ You use **patent** to describe something, especially something bad, in order to indicate in an emphatic way that you think its nature or existence is clear and obvious. [EMPHASIS] ❑ This was patent nonsense. • **pa|tent|ly** ADV ❑ He made his displeasure patently obvious.

pa|tent leath|er N-UNCOUNT [oft N n] **Patent leather** is leather that has a shiny surface. It is used to make shoes, bags, and belts. ❑ He wore patent leather shoes.

pa|ter|nal /pətɜrnəl/ **1** ADJ **Paternal** is used to describe feelings or actions that are typical of those of a kind father toward his child. ❑ ...paternal love for his children. **2** ADJ [ADJ n] A **paternal** relative is one that is related through a person's father rather than their mother. ❑ ...my paternal grandparents.

pa|ter|nal|ism /pətɜrnəlɪzəm/ N-UNCOUNT **Paternalism** means making all the decisions for people you govern, employ, or are responsible for, so that they cannot do not have to make their own decisions. ❑ ...the company's reputation for paternalism.

pa|ter|nal|ist /pətɜrnəlɪst/ (paternalists) **1** N-COUNT A **paternalist** is a person who acts in a paternalistic way. ❑ He himself was a benevolent and sincere paternalist. **2** ADJ [usu

ADJ n] **Paternalist** means the same as **paternalistic**. ❑ ...a paternalist policy of state welfare for the deserving poor.

pa|ter|nal|is|tic /pətɜrnəlɪstɪk/ ADJ Someone who is **paternalistic** makes all the decisions for the people they govern, employ, or are responsible for. ❑ The doctor is being paternalistic. He's deciding what information the patient needs to know.

pa|ter|nity /pətɜrnɪti/ N-UNCOUNT **Paternity** is the state or fact of being the father of a particular child. [FORMAL] ❑ He was tricked into marriage by a false accusation of paternity.

pa|ter|nity leave /pətɜrnɪti liv/ N-UNCOUNT If a man has **paternity leave**, his employer allows him some time off work because his child has just been born. [BUSINESS] ❑ Paternity leave is rare and, where it does exist, it's unlikely to be for any longer than two weeks.

pa|ter|nity suit (paternity suits) N-COUNT If a woman starts or takes out a **paternity suit**, she asks a court of law to help her to prove that a particular man is the father of her child, often in order to claim financial support from him.

path ♦◇◇ /pæθ/ (paths) **1** N-COUNT A **path** is a long strip of ground that people walk along to get from one place to another. ❑ We followed the path along the clifftops. ❑ Feet had worn a path in the rock. **2** N-COUNT Your **path** is the space ahead of you as you move along. ❑ A group of reporters blocked his path. **3** N-COUNT The **path** of something is the line that it moves along in a particular direction. ❑ He stepped without looking into the path of a reversing car. ❑ ...people who live near airports or under the flight path of airplanes. **4** N-COUNT A **path** that you take is a particular course of action or way of achieving something. ❑ They appear to have chosen the path of cooperation rather than confrontation. **5** → See feature box at **work**

pa|thet|ic /pəθɛtɪk/ **1** ADJ If you describe a person or animal as **pathetic**, you mean that they are sad and weak or helpless, and they make you feel very sorry for them. ❑ ...a pathetic little dog with a curly tail. ❑ The small group of onlookers presented a pathetic sight. • **pa|theti|cal|ly** /pəθɛtɪkli/ ADV ❑ She was pathetically thin. **2** ADJ If you describe someone or something as **pathetic**, you mean that they make you feel impatient or angry, often because they are weak or not very good. [DISAPPROVAL] ❑ What pathetic excuses. ❑ Don't be so pathetic. • **pa|theti|cal|ly** ADV [ADV adj] ❑ Five women in a group of 18 people is a pathetically small number.

path|finder /pæθfaɪndər/ (pathfinders) N-COUNT A **pathfinder** is someone whose job is to find routes across areas.

patho|gen /pæθədʒən, -dʒɛn/ (pathogens) N-COUNT A **pathogen** is any organism that can cause disease in a person, animal, or plant. [TECHNICAL]

patho|gen|ic /pæθədʒɛnɪk/ ADJ [usu ADJ n] A **pathogenic** organism can cause disease in a person, animal, or plant. [TECHNICAL]

patho|logi|cal /pæθəlɒdʒɪkəl/ **1** ADJ You describe a person or their behavior as **pathological** when they behave in an extreme and unacceptable way, and have very powerful feelings that they cannot control. ❑ He experiences chronic, almost pathological jealousy. ❑ He's a pathological liar. **2** ADJ **Pathological** means relating to pathology or illness. [MEDICAL] ❑ ...pathological conditions in animals.

pa|tholo|gist /pəθɒlədʒɪst/ (pathologists) N-COUNT A **pathologist** is someone who studies or investigates diseases and illnesses, or who examines dead bodies in order to find out the cause of death.

pa|thol|ogy /pəθɒlədʒi/ N-UNCOUNT **Pathology** is the study of the way diseases and illnesses develop. [MEDICAL]

pa|thos /peɪθɒs/ N-UNCOUNT **Pathos** is a quality in a situation, movie, or play that makes people feel sadness and pity. ❑ ...the pathos of man's isolation.

path|way /pæθweɪ/ (pathways) **1** N-COUNT A **pathway** is a path that you can walk along or a route that you can take. ❑ Richard was coming up the pathway. **2** N-COUNT A **pathway** is a particular course of action or a way of achieving something. ❑ Diplomacy will smooth your pathway to success.

pa|tience /peɪʃəns/ **1** N-UNCOUNT If you have **patience**, you are able to stay calm and not get annoyed, for example, when something takes a long time, or when someone is not doing what you want them to do. ☐ *He doesn't have the patience to wait.* **2** PHRASE If someone **tries** your **patience** or **tests** your **patience**, they annoy you so much that it is very difficult for you to stay calm. ☐ *He tended to stutter whenever he spoke to her, which tried her patience.*

pa|tient /ˈpeɪʃᵊnt/ (**patients**) **1** N-COUNT A **patient** is a person who is receiving medical treatment from a doctor or hospital. A **patient** is also someone who is taken care of by a particular doctor. ☐ *The earlier the treatment is given, the better the patient's chances.* ☐ *She was tough but wonderful with her patients.* **2** → see also **customer** **3** ADJ If you are **patient**, you stay calm and do not get annoyed, for example, when something takes a long time, or when someone is not doing what you want them to do. ☐ *Please be patient – your check will arrive.*
• **pa|tient|ly** ADV [ADV with v] ☐ *She waited patiently for Frances to finish.*

SYNONYMS

patient
ADJ **2**
forbearing: *He was always very forbearing.*
understanding: *Her boss, who was very understanding, gave her time off.*
tolerant: *They need to be tolerant of different points of view.*
uncomplaining: *He was a cheerful and uncomplaining travel companion.*

---

pati|na /ˈpætɪnə, pəˈtiːnə/ **1** N-SING [with supp] A **patina** is a thin layer of something that has formed on the surface of something. ☐ *He allowed a fine patina of old coffee to develop around the inside of the mug.* **2** N-SING [with supp] The **patina** on an old object is an attractive soft shine that has developed on its surface, usually because it has been used a lot. ☐ *...a mahogany door that is golden brown with the patina of age.* **3** N-SING [with supp, oft N of N] If you say that someone has a **patina** of a quality or characteristic, you mean that they have a small but impressive amount of this quality or characteristic. ☐ *Except for a patina of charisma, he was like a thousand other bright young men in Toronto.*

pa|tio /ˈpætioʊ/ (**patios**) N-COUNT A **patio** is an area of flat blocks of stone or concrete next to a house, where people can sit and relax or eat.

pa|tio door (**patio doors**) N-COUNT **Patio doors** are glass doors that lead onto a patio.

pa|tis|serie /pəˈtiːsəri/ (**patisseries**) **1** N-COUNT A **patisserie** is a shop where cakes and pastries are sold. **2** N-UNCOUNT [also N in pl] **Patisserie** is cakes and pastries. ☐ *Blois is famous for patisserie.*

pat|ois (**patois**)

patois is both the singular and the plural form; the singular form is pronounced /ˈpætwɑː/, and the plural form is pronounced /ˈpætwɑːz/.

1 N-VAR A **patois** is a form of a language, especially French, that is spoken in a particular area of a country. ☐ *In France patois was spoken in rural, less developed regions.* **2** N-VAR A **patois** is a language that has developed from a mixture of other languages. ☐ *A substantial proportion of the population speak a French-based patois.*

pa|tri|arch /ˈpeɪtriɑːrk/ (**patriarchs**) **1** N-COUNT A **patriarch** is the male head of a family or tribe. ☐ *The patriarch of the house, Mr. Jawad, rules it with a ferocity renowned throughout the neighborhood.* **2** N-COUNT; N-TITLE A **patriarch** is the head of one of a number of Eastern Christian Churches.

pa|tri|ar|chal /ˌpeɪtriˈɑːrkᵊl/ ADJ [usu ADJ n] A **patriarchal** society, family, or system is one in which the men have all or most of the power and importance. ☐ *To feminists she is a classic victim of the patriarchal society.*

pa|tri|ar|chy /ˈpeɪtriɑːrki/ (**patriarchies**) **1** N-UNCOUNT **Patriarchy** is a system in which men have all or most of the power and importance in a society or group. ☐ *The main cause of women's and children's oppression is patriarchy.* **2** N-COUNT A **patriarchy** is a patriarchal society.

pa|tri|cian /pəˈtrɪʃᵊn/ (**patricians**) **1** N-COUNT A **patrician** is a person who comes from a family of high social rank. [FORMAL] ☐ *Cameron was a rich man, a patrician.* **2** ADJ If you

describe someone as **patrician**, you mean that they behave in a sophisticated way, and look as though they are from a high social rank. ☐ *He was a lean, patrician gent in his early sixties.*

pat|ri|mo|ny /ˈpætrɪmoʊni/ **1** N-SING Someone's **patrimony** is the possessions that they have inherited from their father or ancestors. [FORMAL] ☐ *I left my parents' house, relinquished my estate and my patrimony.* **2** N-SING A country's **patrimony** is its land, buildings, and works of art. [FORMAL] ☐ *These archeological findings are part of the national patrimony.*

pa|tri|ot /ˈpeɪtriət/ (**patriots**) N-COUNT Someone who is a **patriot** loves their country and feels very loyal toward it. ☐ *It has been suggested the founders were not true patriots but men out to protect their own interests.*

pat|ri|ot|ic /ˌpeɪtriˈɒtɪk/ ADJ Someone who is **patriotic** loves their country and feels very loyal toward it. ☐ *Winona is fiercely patriotic.*

pat|ri|ot|ism /ˈpeɪtriətɪzəm/ N-UNCOUNT **Patriotism** is love for your country and loyalty toward it. ☐ *He was a country boy who had joined the army out of a sense of patriotism and adventure.*

pa|trol /pəˈtroʊl/ (**patrols, patrolling, patrolled**) **1** V-T When soldiers, police, or guards **patrol** an area or building, they move around it in order to make sure that there is no trouble there. ☐ *Prison officers continued to patrol the grounds within the jail.* • N-COUNT **Patrol** is also a noun. ☐ *He failed to return from a patrol.* **2** PHRASE Soldiers, police, or guards who are **on patrol** are patrolling an area. ☐ *The army is now on patrol in Srinagar and a curfew has been imposed.* **3** N-COUNT A **patrol** is a group of soldiers or vehicles that are patrolling an area. ☐ *Guerrillas attacked a patrol with hand grenades.*

pa|trol car (**patrol cars**) N-COUNT A **patrol car** is a police car used for patrolling streets and roads.

patrol|man /pəˈtroʊlmən/ (**patrolmen**) N-COUNT A **patrolman** is a male police officer who patrols a particular area. [AM]

pa|trol wag|on (**patrol wagons**) N-COUNT A **patrol wagon** is a van or truck which the police use for transporting prisoners. [AM]

patrol|woman /pəˈtroʊlwʊmən/ (**patrolwomen**) N-COUNT A **patrolwoman** is a female police officer who patrols a particular area. [AM]

pa|tron /ˈpeɪtrən/ (**patrons**) **1** N-COUNT A **patron** is a person who supports and gives money to artists, writers, or musicians. ☐ *Catherine the Great was a patron of the arts and sciences.* **2** N-COUNT The **patron** of a charity, group, or campaign is an important person who allows his or her name to be used for publicity. ☐ *He has now become one of the patrons of the association.* **3** N-COUNT The **patrons** of a place such as a bar or hotel are its customers. ☐ *Few patrons of a high-priced hotel can be led to expect anything other than luxury service.*

pat|ron|age /ˈpeɪtrənɪdʒ, ˈpæt-/ N-UNCOUNT **Patronage** is the support and money given by someone to a person or a group such as a charity. ☐ *...government patronage of the arts in Europe.*

pa|tron|ess /ˈpeɪtrənɪs/ (**patronesses**) N-COUNT [usu with supp] A woman who is a patron of something can be described as a **patroness**.

pat|ron|ize /ˈpeɪtrənaɪz/ (**patronizes, patronizing, patronized**)

in BRIT, also use **patronise**

1 V-T If someone **patronizes** you, they speak or behave toward you in a way that seems friendly, but that shows that they think they are superior to you in some way. [DISAPPROVAL] ☐ *Don't you patronize me!* **2** V-T Someone who **patronizes** artists, writers, or musicians supports them and gives them money. [FORMAL] ☐ *The Japanese imperial family patronizes the Japanese Art Association.* **3** V-T If someone **patronizes** a place such as a bar, store, or hotel, they are one of its customers. ☐ *It also promotes French culture and is often patronized by prominent people.*

pat|ron|iz|ing /ˈpeɪtrənaɪzɪŋ/

in BRIT, also use **patronising**

ADJ If someone is **patronizing**, they speak or behave toward you in a way that seems friendly, but that shows that they think they are superior to you. [DISAPPROVAL] ☐ *The tone of the interview was unnecessarily patronizing.*

pa|tron saint (patron saints) N-COUNT [usu with poss] The **patron saint** of a place, an activity, or a group of people is a saint who is believed to give them special help and protection. ❑ ...St. Nicholas, patron saint of sailors.

pat|sy /pætsi/ (patsies) N-COUNT If you describe someone as a **patsy**, you mean that they are stupid and are easily tricked by other people, or can be made to take the blame for other people's actions. [AM, INFORMAL, DISAPPROVAL] ❑ Davis was nobody's patsy.

pat|ter /pætər/ (patters, pattering, pattered) **1** V-I If something **patters** on a surface, it hits it quickly several times, making quiet, tapping sounds. ❑ Rain pattered gently outside, dripping onto the roof from the pines. **2** N-SING A **patter** is a series of quick, quiet, tapping sounds. ❑ ...the patter of the driving rain on the roof. **3** N-SING Someone's **patter** is a series of things that they say quickly and easily, usually in order to entertain people or to persuade them to buy or do something. ❑ Women found him charming. It must have been his patter.

pat|tern ♦♦◇ /pætərn/ (patterns) **1** N-COUNT A **pattern** is the repeated or regular way in which something happens or is done. ❑ All three attacks followed the same pattern. **2** N-COUNT A **pattern** is an arrangement of lines or shapes, especially a design in which the same shape is repeated at regular intervals over a surface. ❑ ...a golden robe embroidered with red and purple thread stitched into a pattern of flames. **3** N-COUNT A **pattern** is a diagram or shape that you can use as a guide when you are making something such as a model or a piece of clothing. ❑ ...cutting out a pattern for slacks. ❑ Send for our free patterns to knit yourself.

COLLOCATIONS

pattern
NOUN
1
noun + **pattern**: breathing, sleep, speech, thought; shift, weather; behavior, migration, voting
adjective + **pattern**: familiar, normal, regular
verb + **pattern**: exhibit, follow, repeat, show; establish, set
2
adjective + **pattern**: complex, floral, geometric, intricate

---
SYNONYMS

pattern
NOUN
1
order: List the key headings and sort them into a logical order.
system: ...a flexible and relatively efficient filing system.
arrangement: ...an arrangement of dark-blue armchairs around a coffee table.
sequence: ...the color sequence yellow, orange, purple, blue, green, and white.
2
design: Their range of tableware is decorated with a blackberry design.
decoration: The only wall decorations are candles and a single mirror.

---

pat|terned /pætərnd/ **1** ADJ Something that is **patterned** is covered with a pattern or design. ❑ ...a plain carpet with a patterned border. **2** V-T PASSIVE If something new **is patterned** on something else that already exists, it is deliberately made so that it has similar features. [mainly AM] ❑ New York City announced a 10-point policy patterned on the federal bill of rights for taxpayers.

pat|tern|ing /pætərnɪŋ/ **1** N-UNCOUNT [usu with supp] **Patterning** is the forming of fixed ways of behaving or of doing things by constantly repeating something or copying other people. [FORMAL] ❑ ...social patterning. ❑ ...the patterning of behavior. **2** N-UNCOUNT [usu with supp] You can refer to lines, spots, or other patterns as **patterning**. ❑ ...geometric patterning. ❑ ...a jazzy patterning of lights.

pat|ty /pæti/ (patties) **1** N-COUNT A **patty** is an amount of ground food such as beef formed into a flat, round shape. **2** N-COUNT A **patty** is a small, round meat pie. [mainly AM]

pau|city /pɔsɪti/ N-SING [N of n] If you say that there is a **paucity of** something, you mean that there is not enough of it. [FORMAL] ❑ Even the film's impressive finale can't hide the first hour's paucity of imagination. ❑ ...the paucity of good women sprinters.

paunch /pɔntʃ/ (paunches) N-COUNT If someone has a **paunch**, they have a fat stomach. ❑ He finished his dessert and patted his paunch.

paunchy /pɔntʃi/ (paunchier, paunchiest) ADJ Someone who is **paunchy** has a fat stomach.

pau|per /pɔpər/ (paupers) N-COUNT A **pauper** is a very poor person. ❑ He did die a pauper and is buried in an unmarked grave.

pause ♦◇◇ /pɔz/ (pauses, pausing, paused) **1** V-I If you **pause** while you are doing something, you stop for a short period and then continue. ❑ "It's rather embarrassing," he began, and paused. ❑ He talked for two hours without pausing for breath. **2** N-COUNT A **pause** is a short period when you stop doing something before continuing. ❑ After a pause Al said sharply: "I'm sorry if I've upset you."

SYNONYMS

pause
NOUN **2**
delay: They claimed that such a delay wouldn't hurt anyone.
interval: There was a long interval of silence.
hesitation: ...the prime minister's hesitation to accept a ceasefire.

---

pave /peɪv/ (paves, paving, paved) V-T [usu passive] If a road or an area of ground **has been paved**, it has been covered with asphalt or concrete, so that it is suitable for walking or driving on. ❑ The avenue had never been paved, and deep mud made it impassable in winter.

pave|ment /peɪvmənt/ (pavements) **1** N-COUNT The **pavement** is the hard surface of a road. [AM] ❑ The tires of Lenny's bike hissed over the wet pavement. **2** N-COUNT A **pavement** is a path with a hard surface, usually by the side of a road. [BRIT]

in AM, use **sidewalk**

pav|er /peɪvər/ (pavers) N-COUNT **Pavers** are flat pieces of stone or concrete, usually square in shape, that are put on the ground, for example, to make a path.

pa|vil|ion /pəvɪlyən/ (pavilions) **1** N-COUNT A **pavilion** is a large temporary structure such as a tent that is used at outdoor public events. ❑ ...heading across the beautiful green lawn toward the International Pavilion. **2** N-COUNT A **pavilion** is an ornamental building in a garden or park. ❑ Despite persistent rain showers, the lawn and pavilion were packed with fans.

pav|ing /peɪvɪŋ/ N-UNCOUNT [oft supp N] **Paving** is flat blocks of stone or concrete covering an area. ❑ ...concrete paving.

pav|lo|va /pævlouvə/ (pavlovas) N-VAR A **pavlova** is a dessert which consists of a hard base made of egg whites and sugar with fruit and cream on top.

paw /pɔ/ (paws, pawing, pawed) **1** N-COUNT The **paws** of an animal such as a cat, dog, or bear are its feet, which have claws for gripping things and soft pads for walking on. ❑ The kitten was black with white front paws and a white splotch on her chest. **2** V-T/V-I If an animal **paws** something, or **paws** at it, it draws its foot over it or down it. ❑ Madigan's horse pawed the ground. **3** V-T/V-I If one person **paws** another, or **paws** at them, they touch or stroke them in a way that the other person finds offensive. [DISAPPROVAL]

pawn /pɔn/ (pawns, pawning, pawned) **1** V-T If you **pawn** something that you own, you leave it with a pawnbroker, who gives you money for it and who can sell it if you do not pay back the money before a certain time. ❑ He is contemplating pawning his watch. **2** N-COUNT In chess, a **pawn** is the smallest and least valuable playing piece. Each player has eight pawns at the start of the game. **3** N-COUNT If you say that someone is using you as a **pawn**, you mean that they are using you for their own advantage. ❑ It looks as though he is being used as a political pawn by the president.

▶ **pawn off** PHRASAL VERB If you **pawn off** something or someone that you do not want on another person, you persuade the person to accept them. [DISAPPROVAL] ❑ The factories produce hugely subsidized rubbish they can't pawn off on anybody but the Russians. ❑ Are you trying to pawn me off on somebody?

pawn|broker /pɔnbroʊkər/ (pawnbrokers) N-COUNT A **pawnbroker** is a person who lends people money. People give the pawnbroker something they own, which can be sold if they do not pay back the money before a certain time.

pawn|shop /pɔnʃɒp/ (pawnshops) N-COUNT A **pawnshop** is a pawnbroker's shop.

paw|paw /pɔpɔ/ (pawpaws) also **paw-paw** **1** N-COUNT A **pawpaw** is a tree that grows in the eastern United States or the oval yellow fruit of this tree. **2** N-VAR A **pawpaw** is another name for a **papaya**.

pay ◆◆◆ /peɪ/ (pays, paying, paid) **1** V-T/V-I When you **pay** an amount of money to someone, you give it to them because you are buying something from them or because you owe it to them. When you **pay** something such as a bill or a debt, you pay the amount that you owe. □ *Owners who have already paid for repairs will be reimbursed.* □ *The wealthier may have to pay a little more in taxes.* **2** V-T When you **are paid**, you get your wages or salary from your employer. □ *The lawyer was paid a huge salary.* □ *I get paid monthly.* **3** N-UNCOUNT Your **pay** is the money that you get from your employer as wages or salary. □ *...their complaints about their pay and conditions.* **4** V-T If you **are paid** to do something, someone gives you some money so that you will help them or perform some service for them. □ *There are people who are paid to sit around and play games.* **5** V-I If a government or organization makes someone **pay** for something, it makes them responsible for providing the money for it, for example, by increasing prices or taxes. □ *...a legally binding international treaty that establishes who must pay for environmental damage.* **6** V-T/V-I If a job, deal, or investment **pays** a particular amount, it brings you that amount of money. □ *We're stuck in jobs that don't pay very well.* □ *The banks don't pay interest on those accounts.* **7** V-I If a job, deal, or investment **pays**, it brings you a profit or earns you some money. □ *There are some agencies now specializing in helping older people to find jobs which pay.* **8** V-T/V-I If a course of action **pays**, it results in some advantage or benefit for you. □ *It pays to invest in protective clothing.* □ *We must demonstrate that aggression will not pay.* **9** V-T/V-I If you **pay** for something that you do or have, you suffer as a result of it. □ *He was to pay dearly for his lack of resolve.* □ *Why should I pay the penalty for somebody else's mistake?* **10** V-T If you **pay** money down when you are buying something, you pay only a part of the total cost. You then finish paying for it later, usually by paying a certain amount every month. [AM] □ *We paid $500 down and $100 a month after that.* **11** V-T You use **pay** with some nouns, such as in the expressions **pay a visit** and **pay attention**, to indicate that something is given or done. □ *Pay us a visit next time you're in Portland.* □ *He felt a heavy bump, but paid no attention to it.* **12** → see also **paid**, **sick pay** **13** PHRASE If something that you buy or invest in **pays for itself** after a period of time, the money you gain from it, or save because you have it, is greater than the amount you originally spent or invested. □ *...investments in energy efficiency that would pay for themselves within five years.* **14 to pay dividends** → see **dividend** **15 to pay through the nose** → see **nose**

▶ **pay back** **1** PHRASAL VERB If you **pay back** some money that you have borrowed or taken from someone, you give them an equal sum of money at a later time. □ *He burst into tears, begging her to forgive him and swearing to pay back everything he had stolen.* **2** PHRASAL VERB If you **pay** someone **back** for doing something unpleasant to you, you take your revenge on them or make them suffer for what they did. □ *Some day I'll pay you back for this!*

▶ **pay down** PHRASAL VERB If you **pay down** a debt, or **pay down** part of a debt, you give someone part of or all of the money that you owe them. [AM] □ *The Treasury plans to pay down about $1.58 billion on the federal debt.*

▶ **pay off** **1** PHRASAL VERB If you **pay off** a debt, you give someone all the money you owe them. □ *It would take him the rest of his life to pay off that loan.* **2** PHRASAL VERB If an action **pays off**, it is successful or profitable after a period of time. □ *Sandra was determined to become a doctor and her persistence paid off.* **3** → see also **payoff**

▶ **pay out** **1** PHRASAL VERB If you **pay out** money, usually a large amount, you spend it on something. □ *The insurance industry will pay out billions of dollars for damage caused by Hurricane Katrina.* **2** → see also **payout**

▶ **pay up** PHRASAL VERB If you **pay up**, you give someone the money that you owe them or that they are entitled to, even though you would prefer not to give it. □ *We claimed a refund from the association, but they would not pay up.*

USAGE

pay
You must use **for** after **pay** in sentences like this. Don't say 'Willie paid the drinks.' Say 'Willie **paid for** the drinks.'

---

pay|able /peɪəbəl/ **1** ADJ [v-link ADJ] If an amount of money is **payable**, it has to be paid or it can be paid. □ *The money is not payable until January 31.* **2** ADJ [v n ADJ, n ADJ, ADJ to n] If a check or money order is made **payable** to you, it has your name written on it to indicate that you are the person who will receive the money. □ *Make your check payable to "Stanford Alumni Association."*

pay-as-you-go also **pay as you go** ADJ **Pay-as-you-go** is a system in which a person or organization pays for the costs of something when they occur rather than before or afterward. □ *...a new pay-as-you-go telephone service.*

pay|back /peɪbæk/ (paybacks) **1** N-COUNT You can use **payback** to refer to the profit or benefit that you obtain from something that you have spent money, time, or effort on. [mainly AM] □ *There is a substantial payback in terms of employee and union relations.* **2** ADJ [ADJ n] The **payback** period of a loan is the time in which you are required or allowed to pay it back. □ *The payback period can be as short as seven years.* **3** PHRASE **Payback time** is when someone has to take the consequences of what they have done in the past. You can use this expression to talk about good or bad consequences. [INFORMAL] □ *This was payback time. I've proved once and for all I can become champion.*

pay|check /peɪtʃɛk/ (paychecks)

in BRIT, use **paycheque**

N-COUNT Your **paycheck** is a piece of paper that your employer gives you as your wages or salary, and which you can then cash at a bank. You can also use **paycheck** as a way of referring to your wages or salary. □ *I just get a small paycheck every month.* □ *He says his expenses are rising faster than his paycheck.*

pay|day /peɪdeɪ/ (paydays) N-UNCOUNT [also N in pl] **Payday** is the day of the week or month on which you receive your wages or salary. □ *Until next payday, I was literally without any money.*

pay|day lend|er (payday lenders) N-COUNT A **payday lender** is a company that lends small amounts of money for a short time, usually at a very high rate of interest. □ *There has been controversy over the sky-high interest rates charged by payday lenders.*

pay|day loan (payday loans) N-COUNT A **payday loan** is a small amount of money lent to someone for a short time, usually at a very high rate of interest.

pay|dirt /peɪdɜrt/ also **pay dirt** PHRASE If you say that someone **has struck paydirt** or **has hit paydirt**, you mean that they have achieved sudden success or gained a lot of money very quickly. [mainly AM, INFORMAL] □ *Howard Hawks hit paydirt with "Rio Bravo."*

payee /peɪi/ (payees) N-COUNT The **payee** of a check or similar document is the person who should receive the money. [FORMAL] □ *On the check, write the name of the payee and then sign your name.*

pay en|velope (pay envelopes) N-COUNT Your **pay envelope** is the envelope containing your wages that your employer gives you. [AM]

in BRIT, use **pay packet**

pay|er /peɪər/ (payers) **1** N-COUNT You can refer to someone as a **payer** if they pay a particular kind of bill or fee. For example, a mortgage **payer** is someone who pays a mortgage. □ *Lower interest rates pleased millions of mortgage payers.* **2** → see also **taxpayer** **3** N-COUNT A **good payer** pays you quickly or pays you a lot of money. A **bad payer** takes a long time to pay you, or does not pay you very much. □ *Small businesses, hit hard by the recession, blame the government, banks, and late payers.*

pay|load /peɪloʊd/ (payloads) **1** N-VAR The **payload** of an aircraft or spacecraft is the amount or weight of things or people that it is carrying. [TECHNICAL] □ *With these very large*

paymaster

passenger payloads one question looms above all others – safety. **2** N-VAR The **payload** of a missile or similar weapon is the quantity of explosives it contains. [MILITARY] ❑ *The missile can carry a 1,000kg payload up to 1,300 miles.*

pay|master /ˈpeɪmæstər/ (**paymasters**) **1** N-COUNT [oft with poss] A **paymaster** is a person or organization that pays and therefore controls another person or organization. ❑ *...the ruling party's paymasters in business and banking.* **2** N-COUNT A **paymaster** is an official in the armed forces who is responsible for the payment of wages and salaries. [MILITARY]

pay|ment ♦♦◊ /ˈpeɪmənt/ (**payments**) **1** N-COUNT A **payment** is an amount of money that is paid to someone, or the act of paying this money. ❑ *Thousands of its customers are behind with loans and mortgage payments.* **2** N-UNCOUNT **Payment** is the act of paying money to someone or of being paid. ❑ *He had sought to obtain payment of a sum which he had claimed was owed to him.* **3** → see also **balance of payments, down payment**

pay|ment card (**payment cards**) N-COUNT A **payment card** is a plastic card which you use like a credit card, but which takes the money directly from your bank account.

pay|off /ˈpeɪɒf/ (**payoffs**) also **pay-off** **1** N-COUNT The **payoff** from an action is the advantage or benefit that you get from it. ❑ *If such materials became generally available to the optics industry the payoffs from such a breakthrough would be enormous.* **2** N-COUNT A **payoff** is a payment made to someone, often secretly or illegally, so that they will not cause trouble. ❑ *Soldiers in both countries supplement their incomes with payoffs from drugs exporters.* **3** N-COUNT A **payoff** is a large payment made to someone by their employer when the person has been forced to leave their job. ❑ *The ousted chairman received a $1.5 million payoff from the loss-making oil company.*

pay|ola /peɪˈoʊlə/ N-UNCOUNT **Payola** is the illegal practice of paying radio broadcasters to play certain music, so that it will become more popular and therefore make more profits for the record company. [AM]

pay|out /ˈpeɪaʊt/ (**payouts**) N-COUNT A **payout** is a sum of money, especially a large one, that is paid to someone, for example, by an insurance company or as a prize. ❑ *...long delays in receiving insurance payouts.*

pay pack|et (**pay packets**) **1** N-COUNT Your **pay packet** is the envelope containing your wages that your employer gives you at the end of every week. [BRIT]

> in AM, use **pay envelope**

2 N-COUNT You can refer to someone's wages or salary as their **pay packet**. [BRIT]

> in AM, use **paycheck**

pay-per-click ADJ A **pay-per-click** system of payment is one in which a company has ads on someone else's website and pays the website owner each time someone clicks on the ad. ❑ *The site hosts several pay-per-click ads.*

pay-per-view N-UNCOUNT **Pay-per-view** is a cable or satellite television service in which you pay a fee to watch a particular program. The abbreviation **PPV** is also used. ❑ *The match appeared on pay-per-view television.*

pay|phone /ˈpeɪfoʊn/ (**payphones**) also **pay phone** N-COUNT A **payphone** is a telephone that you put coins or a card into before you can make a call. Payphones are usually in public places.

pay|roll /ˈpeɪroʊl/ (**payrolls**) N-COUNT The people on the **payroll** of a company or an organization are the people who work for it and are paid by it. [BUSINESS] ❑ *They had 87,000 employees on the payroll.*

pay|slip /ˈpeɪslɪp/ (**payslips**) also **pay slip** N-COUNT A **payslip** is the same as a **paystub**. [BRIT]

pay|stub /ˈpeɪstʌb/ (**paystubs**) also **pay stub** N-COUNT A **paystub** is a piece of paper given to an employee when he or she is paid stating how much money has been earned and how much has been taken from that sum for things such as tax. [AM]

> in BRIT, use **payslip**

pay tele|vi|sion also **pay-television** N-UNCOUNT **Pay television** is television that you can watch only if you pay a

peace

fee such as a subscription to a satellite or cable television company. ❑ *Pay television is beginning to produce the best original programming.* ❑ *...one of Europe's leading pay-television companies.*

pay-TV also **pay TV** N-UNCOUNT **Pay-TV** is the same as **pay television**. ❑ *...two struggling Spanish providers of pay-TV by satellite.*

pay|wall /ˈpeɪwɔl/ (**paywalls**) N-COUNT A **paywall** is a system that stops the user of a website from seeing other pages on that site if they do not pay. ❑ *Most of their data is behind the paywall.*

PBS /piː biː ɛs/ N-PROPER In the United States, **PBS** is an organization that broadcasts television programs and is not financed by advertising. **PBS** is an abbreviation for 'Public Broadcasting Service.' ❑ *...a five-part PBS special.*

PC /piː siː/ (**PCs**) **1** N-COUNT A **PC** is a computer that is used by one person at a time in a business, a school, or at home. **PC** is an abbreviation for **personal computer**. ❑ *The average price of a PC has dropped over the past few years.* **2** ADJ If you say that someone is **PC**, you mean that they are extremely careful not to offend or upset any group of people in society who have a disadvantage. **PC** is an abbreviation for **politically correct**. ❑ *And people who challenge PC views are often targeted with personal abuse.*

PCP /piː siː piː/ (**PCPs**) **1** N-UNCOUNT **PCP** is a drug that is used illegally for its hallucinogenic effects. **PCP** is an abbreviation for 'phencyclidine.' ❑ *Then she started doing PCP along with pot and coke.* **2** N-COUNT **PCP** is an abbreviation for 'primary-care physician.' ❑ *Your health care needs are coordinated by a physician you select called a Primary Care Physician (PCP).*

pd. pd. is a written abbreviation for **paid**. It is written on a bill to indicate that it has been paid.

PDA /piː diː eɪ/ (**PDAs**) N-COUNT A **PDA** is a handheld computer, used mainly for storing and accessing personal information such as addresses, telephone numbers, and memos. **PDA** is an abbreviation for 'personal digital assistant.' ❑ *A typical PDA can function as a cellphone and a personal organizer.*

PDF /piː diː ɛf/ N-UNCOUNT [usu n n] **PDF** files are computer documents which look exactly like the original documents, regardless of which software or operating system was used to create the original documents. **PDF** is an abbreviation for 'Portable Document Format.' [COMPUTING] ❑ *The leaflet is in PDF format.*

PE /piː iː/ N-UNCOUNT In schools, **PE** is the school subject in which students do physical exercises or take part in physical games and sports. **PE** is an abbreviation for **physical education**.

pea /piː/ (**peas**) N-COUNT **Peas** are round green seeds that grow in long thin cases and are eaten as a vegetable.

peace ♦♦♦ /piːs/ **1** N-UNCOUNT If countries or groups involved in a war or violent conflict are discussing **peace**, they are talking to each other in order to try to end the conflict. ❑ *Peace talks involving other rebel leaders and government representatives broke up without agreement last week, but are due to resume shortly.* ❑ *Leaders of some rival factions signed a peace agreement last week.* **2** N-UNCOUNT If there is **peace** in a country or in the world, there are no wars or violent conflicts going on. ❑ *The president spoke of a shared commitment to world peace and economic development.* **3** N-UNCOUNT If you disapprove of weapons, especially nuclear weapons, you can use **peace** to refer to campaigns and other activities intended to reduce their numbers or stop their use. ❑ *...two peace campaigners accused of causing damage to an E 11 nuclear bomber.* **4** N-UNCOUNT If you have **peace**, you are not being disturbed, and you are in calm, quiet surroundings. ❑ *All I want is to have some peace and quiet and spend a couple of nice days with my grandchildren.* **5** N-UNCOUNT If you have a feeling of **peace**, you feel contented and calm and not at all worried. You can also say that you are **at peace**. ❑ *I had a wonderful feeling of peace and serenity when I saw my husband.* **6** N-UNCOUNT If there is **peace** among a group of people, they live or work together in a friendly way and do not argue. You can also say that people live or work **in peace with** each other. ❑ *...a period of relative peace in the country's industrial relations.* **7** PHRASE If someone in authority, such as the army or the police, **keeps the peace**, they make sure that people behave and do not fight or quarrel with each other. ❑ *...the first U.N contingent assigned to help keep the peace in Cambodia.* **8** PHRASE If something gives you **peace of mind**, it stops you from worrying about a particular problem or difficulty. ❑ *The main appeal these bonds hold for individual investors is the safety and peace of mind they offer.*

peace|able /pisəbᵊl/ ADJ Someone who is **peaceable** tries to avoid arguing or fighting with other people. [WRITTEN] ❑ *...an attempt by ruthless people to impose their will on a peaceable majority.*

peace|ably /pisəbli/ ADV [ADV with v] If you do something **peaceably**, you do it quietly or peacefully, without violence or anger. [WRITTEN] ❑ *The rival guerrilla groups had agreed to stop fighting and settle their differences peaceably.*

Peace Corps N-PROPER [the N] The **Peace Corps** is a U.S. government organization that sends people to help with projects in developing countries.

peace divi|dend (peace dividends) N-COUNT [usu sing] The **peace dividend** is the economic benefit that was expected in the world after the end of the Cold War, as a result of money previously spent on defense and arms becoming available for other purposes.

peace|ful ✦✧✧ /pisfəl/ ■ ADJ **Peaceful** activities and situations do not involve war. ❑ *He has attempted to find a peaceful solution to the Ossetian conflict.* • **peace|ful|ly** ADV [ADV with v] ❑ *The U.S. military expects the matter to be resolved peacefully.* ■ ADJ **Peaceful** occasions happen without violence or serious disorder. ❑ *The farmers staged a noisy but peaceful protest outside the headquarters of the organization.* • **peace|ful|ly** ADV [ADV with v] ❑ *The governor asked the crowd of protestors to leave peacefully.* ■ ADJ **Peaceful** people are not violent and try to avoid arguing or fighting with other people. ❑ *...warriors who killed or enslaved the peaceful farmers.* • **peace|ful|ly** ADV [ADV with v] ❑ *They've been living and working peacefully with members of various ethnic groups.* ■ ADJ A **peaceful** place or time is quiet, calm, and free from disturbance. ❑ *...a peaceful house in the heart of the Ozarks.* • **peace|ful|ly** ADV [ADV after v] ❑ *Except for traffic noise the night passed peacefully.*

peace|ful|ly /pisfəli/ ■ ADV [ADV after v] If you say that someone died **peacefully**, you mean that they suffered no pain or violence when they died. ❑ *He died peacefully on December 10 after a short illness.* ■ → see also **peaceful**

peace|keep|er /piskipər/ (peacekeepers) ■ N-COUNT [usu pl, oft supp N] **Peacekeepers** are soldiers who are members of a peacekeeping force. ❑ *UN peacekeepers are trying to distribute supplies to 30,000 civilians.* ■ N-COUNT [usu sing] If you describe a country or an organization as a **peacekeeper**, you mean that it often uses its influence or armed forces to try to prevent wars or violent conflicts in the world. ❑ *They want the United Nations to play a bigger role as the world's peacekeeper.*

peace|keep|ing /piskipɪŋ/ also **peace-keeping** N-UNCOUNT [usu N N] A **peacekeeping** force is a group of soldiers that is sent to a country where there is war or fighting, in order to try to prevent more violence. Peacekeeping forces are usually made up of troops from several different countries. ❑ *...the possibilities of a UN peacekeeping force monitoring the ceasefire in the country.*

peace-loving ADJ [usu ADJ N] If you describe someone as **peace-loving**, you mean that they try to avoid arguing or fighting with other people. ❑ *By and large, these people are peace-loving, law-abiding citizens.*

peace|maker /pismeɪkər/ (peacemakers) N-COUNT You can describe an organization, a country, or a person as a **peacemaker** when they try to persuade countries or people to stop fighting or arguing. ❑ *...his vision of acting as a peacemaker and mediator.*

peace|making /pismeɪkɪŋ/ N-UNCOUNT [usu N N] **Peacemaking** efforts are attempts to persuade countries or groups to stop fighting with each other. ❑ *...the failure of international peacemaking efforts.* ❑ *They are taking a leading role in peace-making in the region.*

peace|nik /pisnɪk/ (peaceniks) N-COUNT If you describe someone as a **peacenik**, you mean that they are strongly opposed to war. [INFORMAL]

peace of|fer|ing (peace offerings) N-COUNT [usu sing] You can use **peace offering** to refer to something that you give someone to show that you want to end the disagreement between you. ❑ *"A peace offering," Roberts said as he handed the box of cigars to Cohen.*

peace pro|cess (peace processes) N-COUNT [usu sing, oft the N] A **peace process** consists of all the meetings, agreements, and negotiations in which people such as politicians are involved when they are trying to arrange peace between countries or groups that are fighting with each other.

peace|time /pistaɪm/ N-UNCOUNT [oft in N] **Peacetime** is a period of time during which a country is not at war. ❑ *We could afford to reduce defense spending in peacetime without excessive risk.*

peach /pitʃ/ (peaches) ■ N-COUNT A **peach** is a soft, round, slightly furry fruit with sweet yellow flesh and pinky-orange skin. Peaches grow in warm countries. ■ COLOR Something that is **peach** is pale pinky-orange in color. ❑ *...a peach silk blouse.*

peaches and cream ADJ [usu ADJ N] If you say that someone has a **peaches and cream complexion**, you mean that they have very clear, smooth, pale skin. [APPROVAL]

peachy /pitʃi/ (peachier, peachiest) ■ ADJ If you say that something is **peachy** or **peachy keen**, you mean that it is very nice. [AM, INFORMAL] ❑ *Everything in her life is just peachy.* ■ ADJ If you describe something as **peachy**, you mean that it tastes or smells like a peach or is similar in color to a peach. ❑ *...a rich, peachy dessert wine.* ❑ *...peachy pink.*

pea coat (pea coats) also **pea jacket** N-COUNT A **pea coat** or a **pea jacket** is a short, double-breasted overcoat made of wool and worn especially by sailors. ❑ *...a young man in a pea coat and sailor's hat.*

pea|cock /pikɒk/ (peacocks) N-COUNT A **peacock** is a large bird. The male has a very large tail covered with blue and green spots, which it can spread out like a fan. ❑ *...peacocks strutting slowly across the garden.* ❑ *...peacock feathers.*

pea|cock blue COLOR Something that is **peacock blue** is a deep, bright, greenish-blue in color.

peak ✦✧✧ /pik/ (peaks, peaking, peaked) ■ N-COUNT The **peak** of a process or an activity is the point at which it is at its strongest, most successful, or most fully developed. ❑ *The firm has slashed its workforce from a peak of 150,000 in 2000.* ❑ *...a flourishing career that was at its peak at the time of his death.* ■ V-I When something **peaks**, it reaches its highest value or its highest level. ❑ *Temperatures have peaked at over 90 degrees.* ■ ADJ [ADJ N] The **peak** level or value of something is its highest level or value. ❑ *Today's price is 59% lower than the peak level of $1.5 million.* ■ ADJ [ADJ N] **Peak** times are the times when there is most demand for something or most use of something. ❑ *It's always crowded at peak times.* ■ N-COUNT A **peak** is a mountain or the top of a mountain. ❑ *...the snow-covered peaks.* ■ → See feature box at **football**, **tourism**

peaked /pikt/ ADJ [ADJ N] A **peaked** cap has a pointed or rounded part that sticks out above your eyes. ❑ *...a man in a blue-gray uniform and peaked cap.*

peal /pil/ (peals, pealing, pealed) ■ V-I When bells **peal**, they ring one after another, making a musical sound. ❑ *Church bells pealed at the stroke of midnight.* • N-COUNT **Peal** is also a noun. ❑ *...the great peal of the abbey bells.* ■ N-COUNT A **peal** of laughter or thunder consists of a long, loud series of sounds. ❑ *I heard a peal of laughter.*

pea|nut /pinʌt, -nət/ (peanuts) ■ N-COUNT **Peanuts** are small nuts that grow under the ground. Peanuts are often eaten as a snack, especially roasted and salted, and their oil is used in cooking. ❑ *...a packet of peanuts.* ■ → See also color supplement

pea|nut but|ter N-UNCOUNT **Peanut butter** is a brown paste made out of crushed peanuts that you can spread on bread and eat.

pear /pɛər/ (pears) N-COUNT A **pear** is a sweet, juicy fruit that is narrow near its stalk, and wider and rounded at the bottom. Pears have white flesh and thin green, yellow, or brown skin.

pearl /pɜrl/ (pearls) ■ N-COUNT A **pearl** is a hard round object that is shiny and creamy white in color. Pearls grow inside the shell of an oyster and are used for making expensive jewelry. ❑ *She wore a string of pearls at her throat.* ■ ADJ **Pearl** is used to describe something that looks like a pearl. ❑ *...tiny pearl buttons.*

pearly /pɜrli/ ADJ [usu ADJ N] Something that is **pearly** is pale and shines softly, like a pearl. ❑ *...the pearly light of early morning.* • COMB IN COLOR **Pearly** is also a combining form. ❑ *...pearly pink lipstick.*

pear-shaped ❶ ADJ Something that is **pear-shaped** has a shape like a pear. ❑ ...her pear-shaped diamond earrings. ❷ ADJ If someone is **pear-shaped**, they are wider around their hips than around the top half of their body.

peas|ant /pɛzᵊnt/ (peasants) N-COUNT A **peasant** is a poor person of low social status who works on the land; used to refer to people who live in countries where farming is still a common way of life. ❑ ...the peasants in the Peruvian highlands.

peas|ant|ry /pɛzᵊntri/ N-SING-COLL [also no det, usu the N] You can refer to all the peasants in a particular country as the **peasantry**. ❑ The Russian peasantry stood on the brink of disappearance.

peat /piːt/ N-UNCOUNT **Peat** is decaying plant material that is found under the ground in some cool, wet regions. Peat can be added to soil to help plants grow, or can be burned to produce coal. ❑ ...a peat fire.

peaty /piːti/ (peatier, peatiest) ADJ [usu ADJ n] **Peaty** soil or land contains a large quantity of peat.

peb|ble /pɛbᵊl/ (pebbles) N-COUNT A **pebble** is a small, smooth, round stone which is found on beaches and at the bottom of rivers.

peb|bly /pɛbli, pɛbli/ (pebblier, pebbliest) ADJ [usu ADJ n] A **pebbly** beach is covered in pebbles.

pe|can /pikɒn, -kæn/ (pecans) ❶ N-COUNT **Pecans** are nuts with a thin, smooth shell that grow on trees in the southern United States and Central America and that you can eat. ❷ → See also color supplement

pec|ca|dil|lo /pɛkədɪloʊ/ (peccadilloes or peccadillos) N-COUNT [usu pl] **Peccadilloes** are small, unimportant sins or faults. [WRITTEN] ❑ People are not tolerant of extra-marital peccadilloes by public figures.

peck /pɛk/ (pecks, pecking, pecked) ❶ V-T/V-I If a bird **pecks at** something or **pecks** something, it moves its beak forward quickly and bites at it. ❑ It was winter and the sparrows were pecking at whatever they could find. ❑ Chickens pecked in the dust. ❑ It pecked his leg. ❷ V-T If you **peck** someone on the cheek, you give them a quick, light kiss. ❑ Elizabeth walked up to him and pecked him on the cheek. • N-COUNT **Peck** is also a noun. ❑ He gave me a little peck on the cheek.

peck|er /pɛkər/ (peckers) N-COUNT A man's **pecker** is his penis. [AM, INFORMAL, VULGAR]

peck|ing or|der (pecking orders) N-COUNT [usu sing] The **pecking order** of a group is the arrangement of people according to their status or power within the group. ❑ He knew his place in the pecking order.

peck|ish /pɛkɪʃ/ ADJ [usu v-link ADJ] If you say that you are feeling **peckish**, you mean that you are slightly hungry. [mainly BRIT, INFORMAL]

pecs /pɛks/ N-PLURAL **Pecs** are the same as **pectorals**. [INFORMAL]

pec|tin /pɛktɪn/ (pectins) N-MASS **Pectin** is a substance that is found in fruit. It is used when making jelly and jam to help it become firm.

pec|to|ral /pɛktərəl/ (pectorals) N-COUNT [usu pl] Your **pectorals** are the large chest muscles that help you to move your shoulders and your arms.

pe|cu|liar /pɪkjuːlyər/ ❶ ADJ If you describe someone or something as **peculiar**, you think that they are strange or unusual, sometimes in an unpleasant way. ❑ Mr. Kennet has a rather peculiar sense of humor. • **pe|cu|liar|ly** ADV ❑ His face had become peculiarly expressionless. ❷ ADJ If something is **peculiar** to a particular thing, person, or situation, it belongs or relates only to that thing, person, or situation. ❑ Punks, soldiers, hippies, and Sumo wrestlers all have distinct hair styles, peculiar to their group. • **pe|cu|liar|ly** ADV ❑ ...a peculiarly American habit.

pe|cu|li|ar|ity /pɪkjuːliærɪti/ (peculiarities) ❶ N-COUNT A **peculiarity** that someone or something has is a strange or unusual characteristic or habit. ❑ Joe's other peculiarity was that he was constantly munching hard candy. ❷ N-COUNT A **peculiarity** is a characteristic or quality that belongs or relates only to one person or thing. ❑ ...a strange peculiarity of the U.S. system.

pe|cu|ni|ary /pɪkjuːniɛri/ ADJ **Pecuniary** means concerning or involving money. [FORMAL] ❑ She denies obtaining a pecuniary advantage by deception.

peda|gog|ic /pɛdəgɒdʒɪk/ ADJ [ADJ n] **Pedagogic** means the same as **pedagogical**.

peda|gogi|cal /pɛdəgɒdʒɪkᵊl/ ADJ [ADJ n] **Pedagogical** means concerning the methods and theory of teaching. [FORMAL] ❑ The school district provides training to help teachers improve their pedagogical methods.

peda|gogue /pɛdəgɒg/ (pedagogues) N-COUNT If you describe someone as a **pedagogue**, you mean that they like to teach people things in a firm way as if they know more than anyone else. [FORMAL] ❑ De Gaulle was a born pedagogue.

peda|go|gy /pɛdəgoʊdʒi/ N-UNCOUNT **Pedagogy** is the study and theory of the methods and principles of teaching. [FORMAL]

ped|al /pɛdᵊl/ (pedals, pedaling or pedalling, pedaled or pedalled) ❶ N-COUNT The **pedals** on a bicycle are the two parts that you push with your feet in order to make the bicycle move. ❷ V-T/V-I When you **pedal** a bicycle, you push the pedals around with your feet to make it move. ❑ She climbed on her bike with a feeling of pride and pedaled the five miles home. ❸ N-COUNT A **pedal** in a car or on a machine is a lever that you press with your foot in order to control the car or machine. ❑ ...the brake or accelerator pedals. ❹ → See also color supplement

ped|ant /pɛdᵊnt/ (pedants) N-COUNT If you say that someone is a **pedant**, you mean that they are too concerned with unimportant details or traditional rules, especially in connection with academic subjects. [DISAPPROVAL]

pe|dan|tic /pɪdæntɪk/ ADJ If you say someone is **pedantic**, you mean that they are too concerned with unimportant details or traditional rules, especially in connection with academic subjects. [DISAPPROVAL] ❑ His lecture was so pedantic and uninteresting.

ped|ant|ry /pɛdᵊntri/ N-UNCOUNT If you accuse someone of **pedantry**, you mean that you disapprove of them because they pay too much attention to unimportant details or traditional rules, especially in connection with academic subjects. [DISAPPROVAL]

ped|dle /pɛdᵊl/ (peddles, peddling, peddled) ❶ V-T Someone who **peddles** things goes from place to place trying to sell them. ❑ His attempts to peddle his paintings around Laramie's tiny gallery scene proved unsuccessful. ❷ V-T Someone who **peddles** drugs sells illegal drugs. ❑ When a drug pusher offered the Los Angeles youngster $100 to peddle drugs, Jack refused. • **ped|dling** N-UNCOUNT ❑ The war against drug peddling is all about cash. ❸ V-T If someone **peddles** an idea or a piece of information, they try to get people to accept it. [DISAPPROVAL] ❑ They even set up their own news agency to peddle anti-isolationist propaganda.

ped|dler /pɛdlər/ (peddlers) ❶ N-COUNT A **peddler** is someone who goes from place to place in order to sell something. [AM] ❷ N-COUNT A **drug peddler** is a person who sells illegal drugs. ❸ N-COUNT [usu N of n] A **peddler** of information or ideas is someone who frequently expresses such ideas to other people. [DISAPPROVAL] ❑ ...the peddlers of fear.

ped|es|tal /pɛdɪstᵊl/ (pedestals) ❶ N-COUNT A **pedestal** is the base on which something such as a statue stands. ❑ ...a larger than life-sized bronze statue on a granite pedestal. ❷ N-COUNT If you put someone **on a pedestal**, you admire them very much and think that they cannot be criticized. If someone is knocked off a **pedestal** they are no longer admired. ❑ Since childhood, I put my own parents on a pedestal. I felt they could do no wrong.

pe|des|trian /pɪdɛstriən/ (pedestrians) ❶ N-COUNT A **pedestrian** is a person who is walking, especially in a town or city, rather than traveling in a vehicle. ❑ Ingrid was a walker, even in Los Angeles, where a pedestrian is a rare sight. ❷ ADJ If you describe something as **pedestrian**, you mean that it is ordinary and not at all interesting. [DISAPPROVAL] ❑ His style is so pedestrian that the book becomes a real bore.

pe|des|trian cross|ing (pedestrian crossings) N-COUNT A **pedestrian crossing** is a place where pedestrians can cross a street and where drivers must stop to let them cross. [BRIT]

in AM, use **crosswalk**

pe|des|tri|an|ized /pɪdɛstriənaɪzd/

in BRIT, also use **pedestrianised**

❶ ADJ [usu ADJ n] A **pedestrianized** area has been made into an area that is intended for pedestrians, not vehicles. ❑ ...pedestrianized streets. ❷ → See feature box at **town**

pe|des|trian mall (pedestrian malls) N-COUNT A **pedestrian mall** is a street or part of a town where vehicles are not allowed. [AM]

in BRIT, use **pedestrian precinct**

pe|dia|tri|cian /pidiətrɪʃⁿn/ (pediatricians)

in BRIT, use **paediatrician**

N-COUNT A **pediatrician** is a doctor who specializes in treating children.

pe|di|at|rics /pidiætrɪks/

The form **pediatric** is used as a modifier.

N-UNCOUNT **Pediatrics** is the area of medicine that is concerned with the treatment of children. ☐ ...a career in pediatrics.

pedi|cure /pɛdɪkyʊər/ (pedicures) N-COUNT If you have a **pedicure**, you have your toenails cut and polished and the skin on your feet softened.

pedi|gree /pɛdɪgri/ (pedigrees) **1** N-COUNT If a dog, cat, or other animal has a **pedigree**, its ancestors are known and recorded. An animal is considered to have a good pedigree when all its known ancestors are of the same type. ☐ 60 percent of dogs and ten percent of cats have pedigrees. **2** N-COUNT Someone's **pedigree** is their background or their ancestors. ☐ Hammer's business pedigree almost guaranteed him the acquaintance of presidents.

pedi|greed /pɛdɪgrid/ ADJ A **pedigreed** animal is descended from animals that have all been of a particular type, and is therefore considered to be of good quality.

pedi|ment /pɛdɪmənt/ (pediments) N-COUNT A **pediment** is a large triangular structure built over a door or window as a decoration.

ped|lar /pɛdlər/ [BRIT] → see peddler 1, 3

pe|dom|eter /pɪdɒmɪtər/ (pedometers) N-COUNT A **pedometer** is a device that measures the distance that someone has walked. ☐ ...a small pager with a built-in pedometer to count the number of steps its owner took.

pe|do|phile /pidəfaɪl/ (pedophiles)

in BRIT, use **paedophile**

N-COUNT A **pedophile** is a person who is sexually attracted to children.

pe|do|philia /pidəfɪliə/

in BRIT, use **paedophilia**

N-UNCOUNT **Pedophilia** is the condition of being sexually attracted to children. ☐ ...allegations of his pedophilia. ☐ He addressed the clinical aspects of pedophilia and abuse.

pee /pi/ (pees, peeing, peed) V-I When someone **pees**, they urinate. [INFORMAL] ☐ He needed to pee. • N-SING [a N] **Pee** is also a noun. ☐ The driver was probably taking a pee.

peek /pik/ (peeks, peeking, peeked) V-I If you **peek at** something or someone, you take a quick look at them, often secretly. ☐ On two occasions she had peeked at him through a crack in the wall. • N-COUNT **Peek** is also a noun. ☐ Companies have been paying outrageous fees for a peek at the technical data.

peeka|boo /pikəbu/ also **peek-a-boo** N-UNCOUNT; EXCLAM **Peekaboo** is a game you play with babies in which you cover your face with your hands or hide behind something and then suddenly show your face, saying 'peekaboo!'

peel /pil/ (peels, peeling, peeled) **1** N-VAR The **peel** of a fruit such as a lemon or an apple is its skin. You can also refer to a **peel**. ☐ ...grated lemon peel. ☐ ...a banana peel. **2** V-T When you **peel** fruit or vegetables, you remove their skins. ☐ She sat down in the kitchen and began peeling potatoes. **3** V-T/V-I If you **peel** off something that has been sticking to something or if it **peels** off, it comes away from the surface. ☐ One of the kids was peeling plaster off the wall. ☐ It took me two days to peel off the labels. ☐ Paint was peeling off the walls. **4** V-I [usu cont] If a surface **is peeling**, the paint on it is coming away. ☐ Its once-elegant white pillars are peeling. **5** V-I [usu cont] If you **are peeling** or if your skin **is peeling**, small pieces of skin are coming off, usually because you have been burned by the sun. ☐ His face was peeling from sunburn. **6** → See feature box at **cooking**

peel|er /pilər/ (peelers) **1** N-COUNT A **peeler** is a special tool used for removing the skin from fruit and vegetables. ☐ ...a potato peeler. **2** → See also color supplement

peel|ings /pilɪŋz/ N-PLURAL [usu supp N] **Peelings** are pieces of skin removed from vegetables and fruit. ☐ ...potato peelings.

peep /pip/ (peeps, peeping, peeped) **1** V-I If you **peep**, or **peep at** something, you take a quick look at it, often secretly and quietly. ☐ Children came to peep at him around the doorway. • N-SING [a N] **Peep** is also a noun. ☐ "Fourteen minutes," Chris said, taking a peep at his watch. **2** V-I If something **peeps** out from behind or under something, a small part of it is visible or becomes visible. ☐ Purple and yellow flowers peeped up between rocks. **3** PHRASE If you say that you **don't hear a peep** from someone, you mean that they do not say anything or make any noise. [INFORMAL] ☐ You don't hear a peep from her once she's gone to bed.

peep|hole /piphoʊl/ (peepholes) N-COUNT A **peephole** is a small hole in a door or wall through which you can look secretly at what is happening on the other side.

Peep|ing Tom (Peeping Toms) N-COUNT If you refer to someone as a **Peeping Tom**, you mean that they secretly watch other people, especially when those people are taking their clothes off. [DISAPPROVAL]

peeps /pips/ N-PLURAL **Peeps** is a spoken abbreviation for 'people.' [INFORMAL] ☐ So what do you think, peeps?

peep|show /pipʃoʊ/ (peepshows) N-COUNT A **peepshow** is box containing moving pictures that you can look at through a small hole. Peepshows used to be a form of entertainment at fairs.

peer ♦◇◇ /pɪər/ (peers, peering, peered) **1** V-I If you **peer at** something, you look at it very hard, usually because it is difficult to see clearly. ☐ I had been peering at a computer print-out that made no sense at all. **2** N-COUNT Your **peers** are the people who are the same age as you or who have the same status as you. ☐ His engaging personality made him popular with his peers. **3** → See feature box at **learning**

---SYNONYMS---
peer
VERB **1**
gaze: She stood gazing at herself in the mirror.
squint: The girl squinted at the photograph.
peek: On two occasions, she had peeked at him through a crack in the wall.
---

peer group (peer groups) N-COUNT Your **peer group** is the group of people you know who are the same age as you or who have the same social status as you. ☐ It is important for a manager to be able to get the support of his peer group.

peer|less /pɪərlɪs/ ADJ [usu ADJ n] Something that is **peerless** is so beautiful or wonderful that you feel that nothing can equal it. [FORMAL] ☐ ...two days of clear sunshine under peerless blue skies.

peer pres|sure N-UNCOUNT If someone does something because of **peer pressure**, they do it because other people in their social group do it. ☐ Naomi admits that it was peer pressure to be "cool" that drove her into having sex early.

peeve /piv/ (peeves) N-COUNT If something is your **peeve** or your **pet peeve**, it makes you particularly irritated or angry. [AM] ☐ The unsolicited ads appear prominently on the screen and are a pet peeve for many users. ☐ We all have our irrational peeves.

peeved /pivd/ ADJ [usu v-link ADJ] If you are **peeved** about something, you are annoyed about it. [INFORMAL] ☐ Susan couldn't help feeling a little peeved. ☐ ...complaints from peeved citizens who pay taxes.

peev|ish /pivɪʃ/ ADJ Someone who is **peevish** is bad-tempered. ☐ Aubrey had slept little and that always made him peevish. ☐ She glared down at me with a peevish expression on her face. • **peev|ish|ly** ADV [ADV with v, ADV adj] ☐ Brian sighed peevishly. ☐ She had grown ever more peevishly frustrated with him. • **peev|ish|ness** N-UNCOUNT ☐ He complained with characteristic peevishness.

peg ♦◇◇ /pɛg/ (pegs, pegging, pegged) **1** N-COUNT A **peg** is a small piece of wood or metal that is used for fastening something to something else. ☐ He builds furniture using wooden pegs instead of nails. **2** N-COUNT A **peg** is a small hook or knob that is attached to a wall or door and is used for hanging things on. ☐ His work jacket hung on the peg in the kitchen.

3 N-COUNT A **peg** is a small device that you use to fasten clothes to a clothes line. [mainly BRIT]

> in AM, usually use **clothespin**

4 V-T If you **peg** something somewhere or **peg** it down, you fix it there with pegs. ❑ *Peg down netting over the top to keep out leaves.* ❑ *...a tent pegged to the ground nearby for the kids.* **5** V-T If a price or amount of something **is pegged** at a particular level, it is fixed at that level. ❑ *Its currency is pegged to the dollar.* ❑ *The Bank wants to peg rates at 9%.* **6** → See feature box at **fashion**

pe|jo|ra|tive /pədʒɒrətɪv/ ADJ A **pejorative** word or expression is one that expresses criticism of someone or something. [FORMAL] ❑ *I agree I am ambitious, and I don't see that as a pejorative term.*

pe|kin|ese /piːkɪniːz/ (pekineses) also **pekingese** N-COUNT A **pekinese** is a type of small dog with long hair, short legs, and a short, flat nose.

peli|can /pɛlɪkən/ (pelicans) N-COUNT A **pelican** is a type of large water bird. It catches fish and keeps them in the bottom part of its beak which is shaped like a large bag.

pel|let /pɛlɪt/ (pellets) N-COUNT A **pellet** is a small ball of paper, mud, lead, or other material. ❑ *He was shot in the head by an air gun pellet.*

pell-mell /pɛl mɛl/ ADV [ADV after v] If you move **pell-mell** somewhere, you move there in a hurried, uncontrolled way. ❑ *All three of us rushed pell-mell into the kitchen.*

pel|lu|cid /pəluːsɪd/ ADJ Something that is **pellucid** is extremely clear. [LITERARY] ❑ *...her pellucid blue eyes.* ❑ *...the warm pellucid water.*

pel|met /pɛlmɪt/ [BRIT] → see **valance 1**

pe|lo|ta /pəlɒtə/ N-UNCOUNT **Pelota** is the same as **jai alai**.

pelt /pɛlt/ (pelts, pelting, pelted) **1** N-COUNT The pelt of an animal is its skin, which can be used to make clothing or rugs. ❑ *...a bed covered with beaver pelts.* **2** V-T If you **pelt** someone with things, you throw things at them. ❑ *Some of the younger men began to pelt one another with snowballs.* **3** V-I [usu cont] If the rain **is pelting down**, it is raining very hard. [INFORMAL] ❑ *The rain now was pelting down.*

pel|vic /pɛlvɪk/ ADJ [ADJ n] **Pelvic** means near or relating to your pelvis. ❑ *...an inflammation of the pelvic region.*

pel|vis /pɛlvɪs/ (pelvises) **1** N-COUNT Your **pelvis** is the wide, curved group of bones at the level of your hips. **2** → See also color supplement

pen ✦✧ /pɛn/ (pens, penning, penned) **1** N-COUNT A **pen** is a long thin object which you use to write in ink. **2** V-T If someone **pens** a letter, article, or book, they write it. [FORMAL] ❑ *I really intended to pen this letter to you early this morning.* **3** N-COUNT A **pen** is a small area with a fence around it in which farm animals are kept for a short time. ❑ *...a holding pen for sheep.* **4** V-T [usu passive] If people or animals **are penned** somewhere or **are penned up**, they are forced to remain in a very small area. ❑ *The cattle were penned for the night.* ❑ *The animals were penned up in cages.*

pe|nal /piːnəl/ **1** ADJ **Penal** means relating to the punishment of criminals. ❑ *...penal and legal systems.* **2** → See feature box at **prison**

pe|nal code (penal codes) N-COUNT The **penal code** of a country consists of all the laws that are related to crime and punishment. [FORMAL]

pe|nal|ize /piːnəlaɪz/ (penalizes, penalizing, penalized)

> in BRIT, also use **penalise**

V-T [usu passive] If a person or group **is penalized** for something, they are made to suffer in some way because of it. ❑ *Some of the players may, on occasion, break the rules and be penalized.*

pen|al|ty ✦✧ /pɛnəlti/ (penalties) **1** N-COUNT A **penalty** is a punishment that someone is given for doing something which is against a law or rule. ❑ *One of those arrested could face the death penalty.* **2** N-COUNT In sports such as soccer, football, and hockey, a **penalty** is a disadvantage forced on the team that breaks a rule. ❑ *Referee Michael Reed had no hesitation in awarding a penalty.* **3** N-COUNT The **penalty** that you pay for something you have done is something unpleasant that you experience as a result. ❑ *Why should I pay the penalty for somebody else's mistake?*

> **SYNONYMS**
> **penalty**
> NOUN **1**
> **punishment:** *The government is proposing tougher punishments for officials convicted of corruption.*
> **price:** *He's paying the price for working his body so hard.*
> **fine:** *She had to pay a fine.*

pen|al|ty area (penalty areas) N-COUNT In soccer, the **penalty area** is the rectangular area in front of the goal. Inside this area the goalkeeper is allowed to handle the ball, and if the defending team breaks a rule here, the opposing team gets a penalty.

pen|al|ty box (penalty boxes) **1** N-COUNT In ice hockey, the **penalty box** is an area in which players who have broken a rule have to sit for a period of time. **2** N-COUNT In soccer, the **penalty box** is the same as the **penalty area**. [mainly BRIT]

pen|al|ty shoot-out (penalty shoot-outs) N-COUNT In soccer, a **penalty shoot-out** is a way of deciding the result of a game that has ended in a draw. Players from each team try to score a goal in turn until one player fails to score and their team loses the game. [mainly BRIT]

pen|ance /pɛnəns/ (penances) N-VAR If you do **penance** for something wrong that you have done, you do something that you find unpleasant to show that you are sorry. ❑ *...a time of fasting, penance, and pilgrimage.*

pen and ink ADJ [usu ADJ n] A **pen and ink** drawing is done using a pen rather than a pencil.

pence /pɛns/ N-PLURAL **Pence** is the plural form of penny, a British coin worth one hundredth of a pound. ❑ *Matches cost only a few pence.*

pen|chant /pɒ̃ʃɒ̃/ N-SING If someone has a **penchant for** something, they have a special liking for it or a tendency to do it. [FORMAL] ❑ *...a stylish woman with a penchant for dark glasses.*

pen|cil /pɛnsəl/ (pencils) **1** N-COUNT [also in N] A **pencil** is an object that you write or draw with. It consists of a thin piece of wood with a rod of a black or colored substance through the middle. If you write or draw something **in pencil**, you do it using a pencil. ❑ *I found a pencil and some blank paper in her desk.* **2** → See feature box at **fine art**

pen|cil push|er (pencil pushers) N-COUNT If you call someone a **pencil pusher**, you mean that their work consists of writing or dealing with documents, and does not seem very useful or important. [AM, DISAPPROVAL] ❑ *...the pencil pushers who decide the course of people's lives.*

> in BRIT, use **pen-pusher**

pen|dant /pɛndənt/ (pendants) N-COUNT A **pendant** is an ornament on a chain that you wear around your neck.

pend|ing /pɛndɪŋ/ **1** ADJ If something such as a legal procedure is **pending**, it is waiting to be dealt with or settled. [FORMAL] ❑ *She had a libel action against the magazine pending.* ❑ *In 2006, the court had 600 pending cases.* **2** PREP If something is done **pending** a future event, it is done until that event happens. [FORMAL] ❑ *A judge has suspended the ban pending a full inquiry.* **3** ADJ Something that is **pending** is going to happen soon. [FORMAL] ❑ *A growing number of customers have been inquiring about the pending price rises.*

pen|du|lous /pɛndjʊləs/ ADJ Something that is **pendulous** hangs downward and moves loosely, usually in an unattractive way. [LITERARY] ❑ *...a stout, gloomy man with a pendulous lower lip.* ❑ *...pendulous cheeks.*

pen|du|lum /pɛndjʊləm/ (pendulums) **1** N-COUNT The **pendulum** of a clock is a rod with a weight at the end which swings from side to side in order to make the clock work. **2** N-SING You can use the idea of a **pendulum** and the way it swings regularly as a way of talking about regular changes in a situation or in people's opinions. ❑ *The political pendulum has swung in favor of the liberals.*

pen|etrate /pɛnɪtreɪt/ (penetrates, penetrating, penetrated) **1** V-T If something or someone **penetrates** a physical object or an area, they succeed in getting into it or passing through it. ❑ *X rays can penetrate many objects.* ● **pen|etra|tion** /pɛnɪtreɪʃən/ (penetrations) N-UNCOUNT [also N in pl] ❑ *The thick walls prevented penetration by debris from the hurricane.* **2** V-T If someone

penetrates an organization, a group, or a profession, they succeed in entering it although it is difficult to do so. ❑ ...*their continuing failure to penetrate the higher levels of engineering.* **3** V-T If someone **penetrates** an enemy group or a rival organization, they succeed in joining it in order to get information or cause trouble. ❑ *The CIA had requested our help to penetrate a drug ring operating out of Munich.* • **pen|etra|tion** N-UNCOUNT ❑ ...*the successful penetration by foreign spies of the intelligence service.* **4** V-T If a company or country **penetrates** a market or area, they succeed in selling their products there. [BUSINESS] ❑ *There have been around 15 attempts from outside Idaho to penetrate the market.* • **pen|etra|tion** N-UNCOUNT ❑ ...*import penetration across a broad range of heavy industries.*

pen|etrat|ing /pɛnɪtreɪtɪŋ/ **1** ADJ A **penetrating** sound is loud and usually high-pitched. ❑ *Mary heard the penetrating siren of an ambulance.* **2** ADJ If someone gives you a **penetrating** look, it makes you think that they know what you are thinking. ❑ *He gazed at me with a sharp, penetrating look that made my heart pound.*

pene|tra|tive /pɛnɪtreɪtɪv/ ADJ [ADJ n] If a man has **penetrative** sex with someone, he inserts his penis into his partner's vagina or anus.

pen-friend (pen-friends) also **penfriend** N-COUNT A **pen-friend** is the same as a **pen pal**. [BRIT]

pen|guin /pɛŋgwɪn/ (penguins) N-COUNT A **penguin** is a type of large black and white sea bird found mainly in the Antarctic. Penguins cannot fly but use their short wings for swimming.

peni|cil|lin /pɛnɪsɪlɪn/ N-UNCOUNT **Penicillin** is a drug that kills bacteria and is used to treat infections.

pe|nile /piːnaɪl/ ADJ [ADJ n] **Penile** means relating to a penis. [FORMAL] ❑ ...*penile cancer.*

pen|in|su|la /pənɪnsələ, -nɪnsyə-/ (peninsulas) N-COUNT A **peninsula** is a long narrow piece of land that sticks out from a larger piece of land and is almost completely surrounded by water. ❑ ...*the political situation in the Korean peninsula.*

pe|nis /piːnɪs/ (penises) N-COUNT A man's **penis** is the part of his body that he uses when he urinates and when he has sex.

peni|tence /pɛnɪtəns/ N-UNCOUNT **Penitence** is sincere regret for wrong or evil things that you have done.

peni|tent /pɛnɪtənt/ ADJ Someone who is **penitent** is very sorry for something wrong that they have done, and regrets their actions. [LITERARY] ❑ *Robert Gates sat before them, almost penitent about the past.* ❑ ...*penitent criminals.* • **peni|tent|ly** ADV ❑ *He sat penitently in his chair by the window.*

peni|ten|tial /pɛnɪtɛnʃəl/ ADJ [usu ADJ n] **Penitential** means expressing deep sorrow and regret at having done something wrong. [FORMAL] ❑ ...*penitential psalms.*

peni|ten|tia|ry /pɛnɪtɛnʃəri/ (penitentiaries) N-COUNT A **penitentiary** is a prison. [AM, FORMAL]

pen|knife /pɛnnaɪf/ (penknives) N-COUNT A **penknife** is a small knife with a blade that folds back into the handle.

pen|man|ship /pɛnmənʃɪp/ N-UNCOUNT **Penmanship** is the art and skill of writing by hand. [FORMAL]

pen name (pen names) N-COUNT A writer's **pen name** is the name that he or she uses on books and articles instead of his or her real name. ❑ ...*Baroness Blixen, also known by her pen name Isak Dinesen.*

pen|nant /pɛnənt/ (pennants) **1** N-COUNT A **pennant** is a long, narrow, triangular flag. ❑ *The second car was flying the Ghanaian pennant.* **2** N-COUNT In baseball, a **pennant** is a flag that is given each year to the top team in a league. The league championship is also called **the pennant.** [AM] ❑ *The Red Sox lost the pennant to Detroit by a single game.* ❑ ...*the grueling pennant race.*

pen|nies /pɛniz/ **Pennies** is the plural of **penny. Pennies** is mainly used to refer only to coins, rather than to amounts.

pen|ni|less /pɛnɪləs/ ADJ Someone who is **penniless** has hardly any money at all. ❑ *They'd soon be penniless and homeless if she couldn't find suitable work.*

pen|ny ◆◇◇ /pɛni/ (pennies, pence) **1** N-COUNT A **penny** is one cent, or a coin worth one cent. [AM, INFORMAL] ❑ *Unleaded gasoline rose more than a penny a gallon.* **2** N-SING If you say, for example, that you do not have **a penny**, or that something does not cost **a penny**, you are emphasizing that you do not have any money at all, or that something did not cost you any money at all. [EMPHASIS] ❑ *From the day you arrive at my house, you need not spend a single penny.*

penny-pinching **1** N-UNCOUNT **Penny-pinching** is the practice of trying to spend as little money as possible. [DISAPPROVAL] ❑ *Government penny-pinching is blamed for the decline in food standards.* **2** ADJ **Penny-pinching** people spend as little money as possible. [DISAPPROVAL] ❑ ...*small-minded penny-pinching administrators.*

pen|ny stocks N-PLURAL **Penny stocks** are stocks whose shares are offered for sale at a very low price. [BUSINESS]

pen pal (pen pals) also **pen-pal** N-COUNT A **pen pal** is someone you write friendly letters to and receive letters from, although the two of you may never have met.

pen|sion ◆◇◇ /pɛnʃən/ (pensions) N-COUNT Someone who has a **pension** receives a regular sum of money from a former employer because they have retired or because they are widowed or have a disability. ❑ ...*struggling by on a pension.*

---SYNONYMS---

pension
NOUN
allowance: *He lives on a single parent's allowance of £70 a week.*
benefit: *In order to get benefit payments, I had to answer some questions.*
annuity: *Their annuity provides most of their income.*

---

pen|sion|er /pɛnʃənər/ (pensioners) N-COUNT A **pensioner** is someone who receives a pension, especially a pension paid by the state to retired people. [mainly BRIT]

pen|sion plan (pension plans) N-COUNT A **pension plan** is an arrangement to receive a pension from an organization such as an insurance company or a former employer in return for making regular payments to them over a number of years. [BUSINESS] ❑ *I would have been much wiser to start my own pension plan when I was younger.*

pen|sion scheme (pension schemes) **1** N-COUNT A **pension scheme** is the same as a **pension plan**. [BUSINESS] ❑ *His company has the best pension scheme in the industry.* **2** → See feature box at **work**

pen|sive /pɛnsɪv/ ADJ If you are **pensive**, you are thinking deeply about something, especially something that worries you slightly. ❑ *He looked suddenly somber, pensive.* • **pen|sive|ly** ADV [ADV with v] ❑ *Angela stared pensively out of the window at the rain.*

pen|ta|gon /pɛntəgɒn/ (pentagons) N-COUNT A **pentagon** is a shape with five sides.

Pen|ta|gon N-PROPER **The Pentagon** is the main building of the U.S. Defense Department, in Washington DC. The U.S. Defense Department is often referred to as **the Pentagon.** ❑ ...*a news conference at the Pentagon.*

pen|tam|eter /pɛntæmɪtər/ (pentameters) N-COUNT A **pentameter** is a line of poetry that has five strong beats in it. [TECHNICAL]

pen|tath|lon /pɛntæθlɒn/ (pentathlons) N-COUNT [oft the N] A **pentathlon** is a track and field competition in which each person must compete in five different events.

Pen|tecost /pɛntɪkɒst/ **1** N-UNCOUNT **Pentecost** is a Christian festival that takes place on the seventh Sunday after Easter and celebrates the sending of the Holy Spirit to the first followers of Christ. **2** N-UNCOUNT **Pentecost** is a Jewish festival that takes place 50 days after Passover and celebrates the giving of the Ten Commandments.

Pen|tecos|tal /pɛntɪkɒstəl/ ADJ [ADJ n] **Pentecostal** churches are Christian churches that emphasize the work of the Holy Spirit and the exact truth of the Bible.

pent|house /pɛnthaʊs/ (penthouses) N-COUNT A **penthouse** or a **penthouse** apartment or suite is a luxurious apartment or set of rooms at the top of a tall building. ❑ ...*her swanky Manhattan penthouse.*

pent-up /pɛnt ʌp/ ADJ **Pent-up** emotions, energies, or forces have been held back and not expressed, used, or released. ❑ *He still had a lot of pent-up anger to release.*

pe|nul|ti|mate /pɪnʌltɪmət/ ADJ [det ADJ] The **penultimate** thing in a series of things is the second to the last. [FORMAL] ❑ ...*on the penultimate day of the Asian Games.*

pe|num|bra /pɪnʌmbrə/ (penumbras) N-COUNT A **penumbra** is an area of light shadow. [FORMAL]

penu|ry /pɛnyəri/ N-UNCOUNT **Penury** is the state of being extremely poor. [FORMAL] ▫ *He was brought up in penury, without education.*

peo|ny /piəni/ (peonies) N-COUNT A **peony** is a medium-sized garden plant that has large round flowers, usually pink, red, or white.

peo|ple ◆◆◆ /pipəl/ (peoples, peopling, peopled) ◼ N-PLURAL **People** are men, women, and children. **People** is normally used as the plural of **person**, instead of 'persons.' ▫ *Millions of people have lost their homes.* ▫ *...the people of Angola.* ◼ N-PLURAL **The people** is sometimes used to refer to ordinary men and women, in contrast to the government or the military. ▫ *...the will of the people.* ◼ N-COUNT-COLL A **people** is all the men, women, and children of a particular country or race. ▫ *...the native peoples of Central and South America.* ◼ V-T [usu passive] If a place or country **is peopled by** a particular group of people, that group of people live there. ▫ *It was peopled by a fiercely independent race of peace-loving Buddhists.*

peo|ple mov|er (people movers) also **people-mover** N-COUNT A **people mover** is a rapid transport system to move people. Moving sidewalks or driverless shuttles are examples of people movers. ▫ *The automated people mover carries 20 to 100 passengers and is used in places such as airports.*

peo|ple skills N-PLURAL **People skills** are the ability to deal with, influence, and communicate effectively with other people. [BUSINESS] ▫ *She has very good people skills and is able to manage a team.*

peo|ple smug|gling also **people trafficking** N-UNCOUNT [oft N n] **People smuggling** or **people trafficking** is the practice of bringing immigrants into a country illegally. ▫ *...a people-smuggling operation.*

pep /pɛp/ (peps, pepping, pepped) N-UNCOUNT **Pep** is liveliness and energy. [INFORMAL, OLD-FASHIONED] ▫ *Many say that, given a choice, they would opt for a vacation to put the pep back in their lives.*
▸ **pep up** PHRASAL VERB If you try to **pep** something **up**, you try to make it more lively, more interesting, or stronger. [INFORMAL] ▫ *The governor aired some ideas about pepping up trade in the region.* ▫ *How about pepping up a bland sauce with chilies?*

pep|per ◆◇◇ /pɛpər/ (peppers, peppering, peppered) ◼ N-UNCOUNT **Pepper** or **black pepper** is a hot-tasting spice used to flavor food. ▫ *Season with salt and pepper.* ◼ N-COUNT A **pepper**, or a **bell pepper**, is a hollow green, red, or yellow vegetable with seeds inside it. ▫ *...2 red or green peppers, sliced.* ◼ V-T [usu passive] If something **is peppered with** small objects, a lot of those objects hit it. ▫ *He was wounded in both legs and severely peppered with shrapnel.*

pepper|corn /pɛpərkɔrn/ (peppercorns) N-COUNT **Peppercorns** are the small berries that are dried and crushed to make pepper. They are sometimes used whole in cooking.

pep|per mill (pepper mills) also **peppermill** N-COUNT A **pepper mill** is a container in which peppercorns are crushed to make pepper. You turn the top of the container and the pepper comes out of the bottom.

pepper|mint /pɛpərmɪnt/ (peppermints) ◼ N-UNCOUNT **Peppermint** is a strong, sharp flavoring from the peppermint plant. ◼ N-COUNT A **peppermint** is a peppermint-flavored piece of candy.

pep|pero|ni /pɛpəroʊni/ N-UNCOUNT **Pepperoni** is a kind of spicy sausage that is often sliced and put on pizzas.

pep|per shak|er (pepper shakers) N-COUNT A **pepper shaker** is a small container with holes in the top, used for shaking pepper onto food. [mainly AM]

in BRIT, usually use **pepperpot**

pep|per spray (pepper sprays) N-VAR A **pepper spray** is a device that releases a substance which stings the skin, and that is used as a defense against rioters or attackers. ▫ *The officers blasted him with pepper spray.*

pep|pery /pɛpəri/ ADJ Food that is **peppery** has a strong, hot taste like pepper. ▫ *...a crisp green salad with a few peppery radishes.*

pep|py /pɛpi/ (peppier, peppiest) ADJ Someone or something that is **peppy** is lively and full of energy. [INFORMAL] ▫ *At the end of every day, jot down a brief note on how peppy or tired you felt.* ▫ *...peppy dance-numbers.*

pep ral|ly (pep rallies) N-COUNT A **pep rally** at a school, college, or university is a gathering to support a sports team. [AM]

pep talk (pep talks) also **pep-talk** N-COUNT A **pep talk** is a speech intended to encourage someone to make more effort or feel more confident. [INFORMAL] ▫ *Powell and Cheney spent the day giving pep talks to the troops.*

pep|tic ul|cer /pɛptɪk ʌlsər/ (peptic ulcers) N-COUNT A **peptic ulcer** is an ulcer that occurs in the digestive system.

per ◆◆◇ /pər, STRONG pɜr/ ◼ PREP [amount PREP n] You use **per** to express rates and ratios. For example, if something costs $50 per year, you must pay $50 each year for it. If a vehicle is traveling at 40 miles per hour, it travels 40 miles each hour. ▫ *...$6 per week for lunch.* ◼ **per head** → see **head** ③

per|am|bu|late /pəræmbyəleɪt/ (perambulates, perambulating, perambulated) V-I When someone **perambulates**, they walk around for pleasure. [OLD-FASHIONED]

per an|num /pər ænəm/ ADV [amount ADV] A particular amount **per annum** means that amount each year. ▫ *...a fee of $35 per annum.*

per|cale /pərkeɪl/ (percales) N-MASS [usu N n] **Percale** is a type of cotton fabric, used especially to make bed linen. ▫ *...percale pillowcases.*

per capi|ta /pər kæpɪtə/ ADJ [ADJ n] The **per capita** amount of something is the total amount of it in a country or area divided by the number of people in that country or area. ▫ *They have the world's largest per capita income.* • ADV [n ADV] **Per capita** is also an adverb. ▫ *Ethiopia has almost the lowest oil consumption per capita in the world.*

per|ceive /pərsiv/ (perceives, perceiving, perceived) ◼ V-T If you **perceive** something, you see, notice, or realize it, especially when it is not obvious. ▫ *Students must perceive for themselves the relationship between success and effort.* ◼ V-T If you **perceive** someone or something **as** doing or being a particular thing, it is your opinion that they do this thing or that they are that thing. ▫ *Stress is widely perceived as contributing to coronary heart disease.*

percent ◆◆◆ /pərsɛnt/ (percent) N-COUNT You use **percent** to talk about amounts. For example, if an amount is 10 percent (10%) of a larger amount, it is equal to 10 hundredths of the larger amount. ▫ *Sixteen percent of children live in poverty in this country.* ▫ *Sales of new homes fell by 1.4 percent in August.* • ADJ [ADJ n] **Percent** is also an adjective. ▫ *...a 15 percent increase in border patrols.* • ADV [ADV with v] **Percent** is also an adverb. ▫ *He predicted sales will fall 2 percent to 6 percent in the second quarter.*

in BRIT, usually use **per cent**

per|cent|age ◆◆◇ /pərsɛntɪdʒ/ (percentages) N-COUNT A **percentage** is a fraction of an amount expressed as a particular number of hundredths of that amount. ▫ *Only a few vegetable-origin foods have such a high percentage of protein.*

per|cent|age point (percentage points) N-COUNT A **percentage point** is one percent of something. ▫ *The Fed cut the rate a full percentage point to 3 percent.*

per|cen|tile /pərsɛntaɪl/ (percentiles) N-COUNT [usu with supp] A **percentile** is one of the equal divisions of an amount, expressed on a scale from 0 to 100. The 90th percentile of an amount is all amounts between zero percent and ninety percent. ▫ *She says Blacks who identify with the Democratic Party have fallen from the 90th percentile down to around 70 percent.*

per|cep|tible /pərsɛptɪbəl/ ADJ Something that is **perceptible** can barely be seen or noticed. ▫ *Pasternak gave him a barely perceptible smile.* • **per|cep|tibly** /pərsɛptɪbli/ ADV [ADV with v] ▫ *The tension was mounting perceptibly.*

per|cep|tion /pərsɛpʃən/ (perceptions) ◼ N-COUNT Your **perception** of something is the way that you think about it or the impression you have of it. ▫ *He is interested in how our perceptions of death affect the way we live.* ◼ N-UNCOUNT Someone who has **perception** realizes or notices things that are not obvious. ▫ *It did not require a lot of perception to realize the interview was over.* ◼ N-COUNT **Perception** is the recognition of things using your senses, especially the sense of sight.

per|cep|tive /pərsɛptɪv/ ADJ If you describe a person or their remarks or thoughts as **perceptive**, you think that they are good at noticing or realizing things, especially things that are not obvious. [APPROVAL] ❏ *He was one of the most perceptive U.S. political commentators.*

per|cep|tual /pərsɛptʃuəl/ ADJ [ADJ n] **Perceptual** means relating to the way people interpret and understand what they see or notice. [FORMAL] ❏ *Some children have more finely trained perceptual skills than others.*

perch /pɜrtʃ/ (perches, perching, perched)

The form **perch** is used for both the singular and plural in meaning ⓺.

❶ V-I If you **perch on** something, you sit down lightly on the very edge or tip of it. ❏ *He lit a cigarette and perched on the corner of the desk.* ❷ V-I To **perch** somewhere means to be on the top or edge of something. ❏ *...the vast slums that perch precariously on top of the hills around which the city was built.* ❸ V-T If you **perch** something **on** something else, you put or balance it on the top or edge of that thing. ❏ *The use of steel and concrete has allowed the builders to perch a light concrete dome on eight slender columns.* ❹ V-I When a bird **perches** on something such as a branch or a wall, it lands on it and stands there. ❏ *A blackbird flew down and perched on the parapet outside his window.* ❺ N-COUNT A **perch** is a short rod for a bird to stand on. ❏ *A small, yellow bird in a cage sat on its perch outside the house.* ❻ N-COUNT A **perch** is an edible fish. There are several kinds of perch.

per|chance /pərtʃæns/ ADV **Perchance** means perhaps. [LITERARY, OLD-FASHIONED]

per|co|late /pɜrkəleɪt/ (percolates, percolating, percolated) ❶ V-I If an idea, feeling, or piece of information **percolates** through a group of people or a thing, it spreads slowly through the group or thing. ❏ *New fashions took a long time to percolate down.* ❏ *All of these thoughts percolated through my mind.* ❷ V-T/V-I When you **percolate** coffee or when coffee **percolates**, you prepare it in a percolator. ❸ V-I To **percolate** somewhere means to pass slowly through something that has very small holes or gaps in it. ❏ *Rain water will only percolate through slowly.*

per|co|la|tor /pɜrkəleɪtər/ (percolators) N-COUNT A **percolator** is a piece of equipment for making and serving coffee, in which boiling water passes through crushed coffee beans.

per|cus|sion /pərkʌʃn/ N-UNCOUNT **Percussion** instruments are musical instruments that you hit, such as drums. ❏ *...a large orchestra, with a vast percussion section.*

per|cus|sion|ist /pərkʌʃnɪst/ (percussionists) N-COUNT A **percussionist** is a person who plays percussion instruments such as drums.

per|cus|sive /pərkʌsɪv/ ADJ [usu ADJ n] **Percussive** sounds are like the sound of drums. ❏ *...using all manner of percussive effects.*

per diem /pɜr diəm, pər/ N-SING A **per diem** is an amount of money that someone is given to cover their daily expenses while they are working. [mainly AM] ❏ *He received a per diem allowance to cover his travel expenses.*

per|di|tion /pərdɪʃn/ N-UNCOUNT [usu prep N] If you say that someone is on the road to **perdition**, you mean that their behavior is likely to lead them to failure and punishment. [LITERARY]

per|egrine fal|con /pɛrɪgrɪn fɔlkən, -fælkən/ (peregrine falcons) N-COUNT A **peregrine falcon** or a **peregrine** is a bird of prey.

per|emp|tory /pərɛmptəri/ ADJ [usu ADJ n] Someone who does something in a **peremptory** way does it in a way that shows that they expect to be obeyed immediately. [FORMAL, DISAPPROVAL] ❏ *With a brief, almost peremptory gesture he pointed to a chair.* • **per|emp|to|ri|ly** /pərɛmptərɪli/ ADV [ADV with v] ❏ *"Hello!" the voice said, more peremptorily. "Who is it? Who do you want?"*

per|en|nial /pərɛniəl/ (perennials) ❶ ADJ You use **perennial** to describe situations or states that keep occurring or that seem to exist all the time; used especially to describe problems or difficulties. ❏ *...the perennial urban problems of drugs and homelessness.* ❷ ADJ A **perennial** plant lives for several years and has flowers each year. ❏ *...a perennial herb with greenish-yellow flowers.* • N-COUNT **Perennial** is also a noun. ❏ *...a low-growing perennial.*

pe|re|stroi|ka /pɛrɪstrɔɪkə/ N-UNCOUNT **Perestroika** is a term which was used to describe the changing political and social structure of the former Soviet Union during the late 1980s.

per|fect ✧✧✧ (perfects, perfecting, perfected)

The adjective is pronounced /pɜrfɪkt/. The verb is pronounced /pərfɛkt/.

❶ ADJ Something that is **perfect** is as good as it could possibly be. ❏ *He spoke perfect English.* ❏ *Nobody is perfect.* ❷ ADJ If you say that something is **perfect** for a particular person, thing, or activity, you are emphasizing that it is very suitable for them or for that activity. [EMPHASIS] ❏ *The pool area is perfect for entertaining.* ❸ ADJ If an object or surface is **perfect**, it does not have any marks on it, or does not have any lumps, hollows, or cracks in it. ❏ *Use only clean, Grade A, perfect eggs.* ❹ ADJ [ADJ n] You can use **perfect** to give emphasis to the noun following it. [EMPHASIS] ❏ *She was a perfect fool.* ❏ *Some people are always coming up to perfect strangers and asking them what they do.* ❺ V-T If you **perfect** something, you improve it so that it becomes as good as it can possibly be. ❏ *We perfected a hand-signal system so that he could keep me informed of hazards.* ❏ *I removed the fibroid tumors, using the techniques that I have perfected.*

per|fec|tion /pərfɛkʃn/ ❶ N-UNCOUNT **Perfection** is the quality of being as good as it is possible for something of a particular kind to be. ❏ *His quest for perfection is relentless.* ❷ N-UNCOUNT **The perfection of** something such as a skill, system, or product involves making it as good as it could possibly be. ❏ *Madame Clicquot is credited with the perfection of this technique.*

per|fec|tion|ism /pərfɛkʃənɪzəm/ N-UNCOUNT **Perfectionism** is the attitude or behavior of a perfectionist.

per|fec|tion|ist /pərfɛkʃənɪst/ (perfectionists) N-COUNT Someone who is a **perfectionist** refuses to do or accept anything that is not as good as it could possibly be. ❏ *He was such a perfectionist that he published only those results that satisfied him completely.*

per|fect|ly ✧✧✧ /pɜrfɪktli/ ❶ ADV [ADV adj/adv] You can use **perfectly** to emphasize an adjective or adverb, especially when you think the person you are talking to might doubt what you are saying. [EMPHASIS] ❏ *There's no reason why you can't have a perfectly normal child.* ❏ *You know perfectly well what happened.* ❷ ADV [ADV with v] If something is done **perfectly**, it is done so well that it could not possibly be done better. ❏ *This ambitious adaptation perfectly captures the spirit of Kurt Vonnegut's acclaimed novel.*

---- SYNONYMS ----

perfectly
ADV ❶
completely: *Dozens of homes had been completely destroyed.*
totally: *The fire totally destroyed the top floor.*
absolutely: *There is absolutely no difference!*
quite: *It is quite clear that we were firing in self-defense.*

per|fect pitch N-UNCOUNT Someone who has **perfect pitch** is able to identify or sing musical notes correctly.

per|fect storm (perfect storms) N-COUNT [usu sing] A **perfect storm** is an unusual combination of events or things that produce an unusually bad or powerful result. ❏ *Investors are faced with the perfect storm of slowing economic growth, rising prices and an unstable housing market.*

per|fidi|ous /pərfɪdiəs/ ADJ [usu ADJ n] If you describe someone as **perfidious**, you mean that they have betrayed someone or cannot be trusted. [LITERARY] ❏ *Their feet will trample on the dead bodies of their perfidious aggressors.*

per|fi|dy /pɜrfɪdi/ N-UNCOUNT **Perfidy** is the action of betraying someone or behaving very badly toward someone. [LITERARY]

per|fo|rate /pɜrfəreɪt/ (perforates, perforating, perforated) V-T To **perforate** something means to make a hole or holes in it. ❏ *I refused to wear headphones because they can perforate your eardrums.* • **per|fo|rat|ed** ADJ [ADJ n] ❏ *Separate the ballot at the perforated line.*

per|fo|ra|tion /pɜrfəreɪʃ³n/ (perforations) N-COUNT [usu pl] **Perforations** are small holes that are made in something, especially in paper. ❑ *Tear off the form along the perforations and send it to Sales.*

per|force /pərfɔrs/ ADV **Perforce** is used to indicate that something happens or is the case because it cannot be prevented or avoided. [OLD-FASHIONED] ❑ *What is true for TV broadcasts will perforce also apply to print media.*

per|form ◆◆◇ /pərfɔrm/ (performs, performing, performed) **1** V-T When you **perform** a task or action, especially a complicated one, you do it. ❑ *We're looking for people of all ages who have performed outstanding acts of bravery, kindness, or courage.* ❑ *His council had had to perform miracles on a tiny budget.* **2** V-T If something **performs** a particular function, it has that function. ❑ *An engine has many parts, each performing a different function.* **3** V-T If you **perform** a play, a piece of music, or a dance, you do it in front of an audience. ❑ *Gardiner has pursued relentlessly high standards in performing classical music.* ❑ *This play was first performed in 411 BC.* **4** V-I If someone or something **performs well**, they work well or achieve a good result. If they **perform badly**, they work badly or achieve a poor result. ❑ *He had not performed well in his exams.* ❑ *State-owned industries will always perform poorly.*

───── SYNONYMS ─────

perform
VERB **1**
achieve: *We have achieved what we set out to do.*
carry out: *Commitments have been made with very little intention of carrying them out.*
effect: *Prospects for effecting real political change seemed to have taken a major step backwards.*
accomplish: *If we all work together, I think we could accomplish our goal.*

per|for|mance ◆◆◇ /pərfɔrməns/ (performances) **1** N-COUNT A **performance** involves entertaining an audience by doing something such as singing, dancing, or acting. ❑ *Inside the theater, they were giving a performance of Bizet's Carmen.* ❑ *...her performance as the betrayed Medea.* **2** N-VAR Someone's or something's **performance** is how successful they are or how well they do something. ❑ *That study looked at the performance of 18 surgeons.* ❑ *The poor performance has been blamed on the recession and cheaper sports car imports.* **3** N-SING The **performance** of a task is the fact or action of doing it. ❑ *He devoted in excess of seventy hours a week to the performance of his duties.*

───── COLLOCATIONS ─────

performance
NOUN
1
noun + **performance:** concert, dance, stage; matinee, evening
adjective + **performance:** dramatic, musical, vocal; impressive, outstanding, stellar, stunning; live
2
noun + **performance:** investment; team
adjective + **performance:** disappointing, dismal; consistent, solid, strong; all-round, overall
verb + **performance:** deliver, produce

───── SYNONYMS ─────

performance
NOUN **1**
production: *For this production, she has learned the role in Spanish.*
show: *How about going shopping and seeing a show in London?*

per|for|mance art N-UNCOUNT **Performance art** is a theatrical presentation that includes various art forms such as dance, music, painting, and sculpture.

performance-related pay N-UNCOUNT **Performance-related pay** is a rate of pay which is based on how well someone does their job. [BUSINESS] ❑ *...plans to introduce performance-related pay for teachers.*

per|form|er /pərfɔrmər/ (performers) **1** N-COUNT A **performer** is a person who acts, sings, or does other entertainment in front of audiences. ❑ *A performer plays classical selections on the violin.* **2** N-COUNT You can use **performer** when describing someone or something in a way that indicates how well they do a particular thing. ❑ *Until 1987, Canada's industry had been the star performer.*

per|form|ing arts N-PLURAL [usu the N] Dance, drama, music, and other forms of entertainment that are usually performed live in front of an audience are referred to as the **performing arts**.

per|fume /pɜrfyum, pərfyum/ (perfumes, perfuming, perfumed) **1** N-MASS **Perfume** is a pleasant-smelling liquid that you can put on your skin to make yourself smell nice. ❑ *The hall smelled of her mother's perfume.* ❑ *...a bottle of perfume.* **2** N-MASS **Perfume** is the ingredient that is added to some products to make them smell nice. ❑ *...a delicate white soap without perfume.* **3** V-T If something is used to **perfume** a product, it is added to the product to make it smell nice. ❑ *The oil is used to flavor and perfume soaps, foam baths, and scents.*

per|fumed /pɜrfyumd, pərfyumd/ **1** ADJ Something such as fruit or wine that is **perfumed** has a sweet pleasant smell. ❑ *Champenois wines can be particularly fragrant and perfumed.* **2** ADJ [usu ADJ n] **Perfumed** things have a sweet pleasant smell, either naturally or because perfume has been added to them. ❑ *She opened the perfumed envelope.*

per|fum|ery /pərfyuməri/ (perfumeries) **1** N-UNCOUNT [oft N n] **Perfumery** is the activity or business of producing perfume. ❑ *...the perfumery trade.* **2** N-COUNT A **perfumery** is a store or a department in a store where perfume is the main product sold.

per|func|tory /pərfʌŋktəri/ ADJ [usu ADJ n] A **perfunctory** action is done quickly and carelessly, and shows a lack of interest in what you are doing. ❑ *She gave the list only a perfunctory glance.* ❑ *Our interest was purely perfunctory.* ● **per|func|to|ri|ly** /pərfʌŋktərɪli/ ADV [ADV with v] ❑ *Melina was perfunctorily introduced to the men.*

per|go|la /pɜrgələ/ (pergolas) N-COUNT In a garden, a **pergola** is an arch or a structure with a roof over which climbing plants can be grown.

per|haps ◆◆◆ /pərhæps, præps/ **1** ADV [ADV with cl/group] You use **perhaps** to express uncertainty, for example, when you do not know that something is definitely true, or when you are mentioning something that may possibly happen in the future in the way you describe. [VAGUENESS] ❑ *In the end they lose millions, perhaps billions.* ❑ *Perhaps, in time, the message will get through.* **2** ADV [ADV with cl/group] You use **perhaps** in opinions and remarks to make them appear less definite or more polite. [VAGUENESS] ❑ *Perhaps the most important lesson is to be learned is that you simply cannot please everyone.* ❑ *His very last paintings are perhaps the most puzzling.* **3** ADV [ADV with cl] You use **perhaps** when you are making suggestions or giving advice. **Perhaps** is also used in formal English to introduce requests. [POLITENESS] ❑ *Perhaps I may be permitted a few suggestions.* ❑ *Well, perhaps you'll come and see us at our place?*

per|il /perɪl/ (perils) N-VAR **Perils** are great dangers. [FORMAL] ❑ *...the perils of the sea.* ❑ *In spite of great peril, I have survived.*

peri|lous /perɪləs/ ADJ Something that is **perilous** is very dangerous. [LITERARY] ❑ *...a perilous journey across the war zone.* ❑ *The road grew even steeper and more perilous.* ● **peri|lous|ly** ADV ❑ *The track snaked perilously upwards.*

pe|rim|eter /pərɪmɪtər/ (perimeters) N-COUNT The **perimeter** of an area of land is the whole of its outer edge or boundary. ❑ *...the perimeter of the airport.*

peri|na|tal /pɛrɪneɪt³l/ ADJ [ADJ n] **Perinatal** deaths, problems, or experiences happen at the time of a baby's birth or soon after the time of birth. [MEDICAL] ❑ *Premature birth is the main cause of perinatal mortality.*

pe|ri|od ◆◆◇ /pɪəriəd/ (periods) **1** N-COUNT [usu with supp] A **period** is a length of time. ❑ *This crisis might last for a long period of time.* ❑ *...a period of a few months.* **2** N-COUNT A **period** in the life of a person, organization, or society is a length of time that is remembered for a particular situation or activity. ❑ *...a period of economic good health and expansion.* ❑ *He went through a period of wanting to be accepted.* **3** N-COUNT A particular length of time in history is sometimes called a **period**. For example,

you can talk about **the Civil War period** or **the Prohibition period** in the U.S. ☐ *The novel is set in the Roman period.* ☐ *No reference to their existence appears in any literature of the period.*
4 ADJ [ADJ n] **Period** costumes, furniture, and instruments were made at an earlier time in history, or look as if they were made then. ☐ *The characters were dressed in full period costume.* **5** N-COUNT Exercise, training, or study **periods** are lengths of time that are set aside for exercise, training, or study. ☐ *They accompanied him during his exercise periods.*
6 N-COUNT A **period** is the punctuation mark . that you use at the end of a sentence when it is not a question or an exclamation. [AM]

> in BRIT, use **full stop**

7 N-COUNT When a woman has a **period**, she bleeds from her uterus. This usually happens once a month. ☐ *Can you get pregnant if you have sex during your period?*

SYNONYMS
period
NOUN **1**
time: *By this time he was thirty.*
term: *Premiums are guaranteed throughout the term of the policy.*
stretch: *...after an 18-month stretch in the army.*
phase: *The crisis is entering a crucial, critical phase.*

pe|ri|od|ic /pɪərɪɒdɪk/ ADJ **Periodic** events or situations happen occasionally, at fairly regular intervals. ☐ *Periodic checks are taken to ensure that high standards are maintained.*
pe|ri|odi|cal /pɪərɪɒdɪkəl/ (**periodicals**) **1** N-COUNT **Periodicals** are magazines, especially serious or academic ones, that are published at regular intervals. ☐ *The walls would be lined with books and periodicals.* **2** ADJ **Periodical** events or situations happen occasionally, at fairly regular intervals. ☐ *She made periodical visits to her dentist.* • **pe|ri|odi|cal|ly** /pɪərɪɒdɪkli/ ADV [ADV with v] ☐ *Meetings are held periodically to monitor progress on the case.*
pe|ri|od|ic ta|ble N-SING [the N] In chemistry, **the periodic table** is a table showing the chemical elements arranged according to their atomic numbers.
perio|don|tal /pɛrɪədɒntəl/ ADJ [ADJ n] **Periodontal** disease is disease of the gums. [TECHNICAL]
pe|ri|od pain (**period pains**) N-VAR **Period pain** is the pain that some women have when they menstruate.
pe|ri|od piece (**period pieces**) **1** N-COUNT A **period piece** is a play, book, or movie that is set at a particular time in history and describes life at that time. **2** → See feature box at **upcycle**
peri|pa|tet|ic /pɛrɪpətɛtɪk/ ADJ [usu ADJ n] If someone has a **peripatetic** life or career, they travel around a lot, living or working in places for short periods of time. [FORMAL] ☐ *Her father was in the army and the family led a peripatetic existence for most of her childhood.*
pe|riph|er|al /pərɪfərəl/ (**peripherals**) **1** ADJ A **peripheral** activity or issue is one that is not very important compared with other activities or issues. ☐ *Companies are increasingly eager to contract out peripheral activities like training.* ☐ *...peripheral and boring information.* **2** ADJ **Peripheral** areas of land are ones that are on the edge of a larger area. ☐ *...urban development in the outer peripheral areas of large towns.* **3** N-COUNT **Peripherals** are devices that can be attached to computers. [COMPUTING] ☐ *...peripherals to expand the use of our computers.*
pe|riph|ery /pərɪfəri/ (**peripheries**) N-COUNT If something is on the **periphery** of an area, place, or thing, it is on the edge of it. [FORMAL] ☐ *Taste buds are concentrated at the tip and rear of the tongue and around its periphery.*
peri|scope /pɛrɪskoʊp/ (**periscopes**) **1** N-COUNT A **periscope** is a vertical tube that people inside submarines can look through to see above the surface of the water. **2** → See also color supplement
per|ish /pɛrɪʃ/ (**perishes, perishing, perished**) V-I If people or animals **perish**, they die as a result of very harsh conditions or as the result of an accident. [WRITTEN] ☐ *Most of the butterflies perish in the first frosts of autumn.*
per|ish|able /pɛrɪʃəbəl/ ADJ Goods such as food that are **perishable** go bad after a short length of time. ☐ *...perishable food like fruit, vegetables, and meat.*

peri|to|ni|tis /pɛrɪtənaɪtɪs/ N-UNCOUNT **Peritonitis** is a disease in which the inside wall of your abdomen becomes swollen and very painful. [MEDICAL]
peri|win|kle /pɛrɪwɪŋkəl/ (**periwinkles**) **1** N-VAR **Periwinkle** is a plant that grows along the ground and has blue flowers. **2** N-COUNT **Periwinkles** are small sea snails that can be eaten.
per|jure /pɜrdʒər/ (**perjures, perjuring, perjured**) V-T If someone **perjures** themselves in a court of law, they lie, even though they have promised to tell the truth. ☐ *Witnesses lied and perjured themselves.*
per|jured /pɜrdʒərd/ ADJ [usu ADJ n] In a court of law, **perjured** evidence or **perjured** testimony is a false statement of events. ☐ *...information that was based on perjured testimony.*
per|jury /pɜrdʒəri/ N-UNCOUNT If someone who is giving evidence in a court of law commits **perjury**, they lie. [LEGAL] ☐ *This witness has committed perjury and no reliance can be placed on her evidence.*
perk /pɜrk/ (**perks, perking, perked**) N-COUNT **Perks** are special benefits that are given to people who have a particular job or belong to a particular group. ☐ *...a company car, health insurance and other perks.*
▶ **perk up** **1** PHRASAL VERB If something **perks** you **up** or if you **perk up**, you become cheerful and lively, after feeling tired, bored, or depressed. ☐ *He perks up and jokes with them.* **2** PHRASAL VERB If you **perk** something **up**, you make it more interesting. ☐ *To make the bland taste more interesting, the locals began perking it up with local produce.* **3** PHRASAL VERB If sales, prices, or economies **perk up**, or if something **perks** them **up**, they begin to increase or improve. [JOURNALISM] ☐ *House prices could perk up during the fall.*
perky /pɜrki/ (**perkier, perkiest**) ADJ If someone is **perky**, they are cheerful and lively. ☐ *He wasn't quite as perky as normal.*
perm /pɜrm/ (**perms, perming, permed**) **1** N-COUNT If you have a **perm**, your hair is curled and treated with chemicals so that it stays curly for several months. ☐ *...a middle-aged lady with a perm.* **2** V-T When a hairstylist **perms** someone's hair, they curl it and treat it with chemicals so that it stays curly for several months. ☐ *She had her hair permed.*
per|ma|frost /pɜrməfrɒst/ N-UNCOUNT **Permafrost** is land that is permanently frozen to a great depth.
per|ma|nent ✦✧✧ /pɜrmənənt/ (**permanents**) **1** ADJ Something that is **permanent** lasts forever. ☐ *Heavy drinking can cause permanent damage to the brain.* ☐ *...a permanent solution to the problem.* • **per|ma|nent|ly** ADV ☐ *His confidence had been permanently affected by the ordeal.* • **per|ma|nence** N-UNCOUNT ☐ *Anything which threatens the permanence of the treaty is a threat to stability and to peace.* **2** ADJ You use **permanent** to describe situations or states that keep occurring or that seem to exist all the time; used especially to describe problems or difficulties. ☐ *...a permanent state of tension.* ☐ *They feel under permanent threat.* • **per|ma|nent|ly** ADV ☐ *...the heavy, permanently locked gate.* **3** ADJ [ADJ n] A **permanent** employee is one who is employed for an unlimited length of time. ☐ *At the end of the probationary period you will become a permanent employee.* • **per|ma|nent|ly** ADV [ADV with v] ☐ *...permanently employed lifeguards.* **4** ADJ [ADJ n] Your **permanent** home or your **permanent** address is the one at which you spend most of your time or the one that you return to after having stayed in other places. ☐ *They had no permanent address.* **5** N-COUNT A **permanent** is a treatment in which a hairstylist curls your hair and treats it with a chemical so that it stays curly for several months. [AM] ☐ *Her hair had had a permanent, but it had grown out.*

SYNONYMS
permanent
ADJ **1**
lasting: *We are well on our way to a lasting peace.*
enduring: *...the start of an enduring friendship.*
eternal: *...the quest for eternal youth.*
everlasting: *...a message of peace and everlasting life.*

per|ma|nent wave (**permanent waves**) N-COUNT A **permanent wave** is the same as a **perm**. [OLD-FASHIONED]
per|me|able /pɜrmiəbəl/ ADJ If a substance is **permeable**, something such as water or gas can pass through it or soak

permeate

into it. ☐ *A number of products have been developed which are permeable to air and water.*

per|me|ate /pɜrmieɪt/ (permeates, permeating, permeated)
1 V-T If an idea, feeling, or attitude **permeates** a system or **permeates** society, it affects every part of it or is present throughout it. ☐ *Bias against women permeates every level of society.*
2 V-T If something **permeates** a place, it spreads throughout it. ☐ *The smell of roast beef permeated the air.*

per|mis|sible /pərmɪsəbəl/ ADJ If something is **permissible**, it is considered to be acceptable because it does not break any laws or rules. ☐ *Religious practices are permissible under the Constitution.*

per|mis|sion ♦⋄⋄ /pərmɪʃən/ N-UNCOUNT If someone who has authority over you gives you **permission** to do something, they say that they will allow you to do it. ☐ *He asked permission to leave the room.* ☐ *They cannot leave the country without permission.*

COLLOCATIONS

permission
NOUN
adjective + **permission**: express, prior, special; parental, written
verb + **permission**: give, grant, refuse; ask, need, obtain, seek

---

per|mis|sive /pərmɪsɪv/ ADJ A **permissive** person, society, or way of behaving allows or tolerates things that other people disapprove of. ☐ *The call for law and order replaced the "permissive tolerance" of the 1960s.* • **per|mis|sive|ness** N-UNCOUNT ☐ *...a culture of permissiveness.*

per|mit ♦⋄⋄ (permits, permitting, permitted)

The verb is pronounced /pərmɪt/. The noun is pronounced /pɜrmɪt/.

1 V-T If someone **permits** something, they allow it to happen. If they **permit** you to do something, they allow you to do it. [FORMAL] ☐ *He can let the court's decision stand and permit the extradition.* ☐ *The guards permitted me to bring my camera.*
2 N-COUNT A **permit** is an official document which says that you may do something. For example, you usually need a **permit** to work in a foreign country. ☐ *He has to apply for a permit, and we have to find him a job.* **3** V-T/V-I If a situation **permits** something, it makes it possible for that thing to exist, happen, or be done or it provides the opportunity for it. [FORMAL] ☐ *Try to go out for a walk at lunchtime, if the weather permits.* ☐ *This method of cooking also permits heat to penetrate evenly from both sides.*

per|mu|ta|tion /pɜrmyuteɪʃən/ (permutations) N-COUNT [usu pl] A **permutation** is one of the ways in which a number of things can be ordered or arranged. ☐ *Variation among humans is limited to the possible permutations of our genes.*

per|ni|cious /pərnɪʃəs/ ADJ If you describe something as **pernicious**, you mean that it is very harmful. [FORMAL] ☐ *Parents are blaming not only peer pressure but also the pernicious influence of the internet.*

per|ni|cious anemia N-UNCOUNT **Pernicious anemia** is a very severe blood disease.

per|nick|ety /pərnɪkɪti/ ADJ **Pernickety** is the same as **persnickety**. [BRIT]

pero|ra|tion /pɛrəreɪʃən/ (perorations) **1** N-COUNT A **peroration** is the last part of a speech, especially the part where the speaker sums up his or her argument. [FORMAL] **2** N-COUNT If someone describes a speech as a **peroration**, they mean that they dislike it because they think it is very long and not worth listening to. [FORMAL, DISAPPROVAL]

per|ox|ide /pərɒksaɪd/ (peroxides) **1** N-MASS **Peroxide** is a chemical that is often used for making hair lighter in color. It can also be used to kill germs. **2** → see also **hydrogen peroxide**

per|ox|ide blonde (peroxide blondes) also **peroxide blond** N-COUNT You can refer to someone whose hair has been artificially made lighter in color as a **peroxide blonde** or a **peroxide blond**, especially when you want to show that you disapprove of this, or that you think their hair looks unnatural or unattractive.

per|pen|dicu|lar /pɜrpəndɪkyələr/ **1** ADJ [usu ADJ n] A **perpendicular** line or surface points straight up, rather than being sloping or horizontal. ☐ *We made two slits for the eyes and a perpendicular line for the nose.* ☐ *The sides of the mountain are almost perpendicular.* **2** ADJ [usu v-link ADJ to n] If one thing is **perpendicular** to another, it is at an angle of 90 degrees to it. [FORMAL] ☐ *The left wing dipped until it was perpendicular to the ground.*

per|pe|trate /pɜrpɪtreɪt/ (perpetrates, perpetrating, perpetrated) V-T If someone **perpetrates** a crime or any other immoral or harmful act, they do it. [FORMAL] ☐ *A high proportion of crime in any country is perpetrated by young males in their teens and twenties.* • **per|pe|tra|tor** (perpetrators) N-COUNT ☐ *The perpetrator of the crime does not have to be traced before you can claim compensation.*

per|pet|ual /pərpɛtʃuəl/ **1** ADJ A **perpetual** feeling, state, or quality is one that never ends or changes. ☐ *...the creation of a perpetual union.* • **per|pet|ual|ly** ADV ☐ *They were all perpetually starving.* **2** ADJ A **perpetual** act, situation, or state is one that happens again and again and so seems never to end. ☐ *I thought her perpetual complaints were going to prove too much for me.* • **per|pet|ual|ly** ADV ☐ *He perpetually interferes in political affairs.*

per|pet|ual mo|tion also perpetual-motion N-UNCOUNT The idea of **perpetual motion** is the idea of something continuing to move forever without getting energy from anything else.

per|petu|ate /pərpɛtʃueɪt/ (perpetuates, perpetuating, perpetuated) V-T If someone or something **perpetuates** a situation, system, or belief, especially a bad one, they cause it to continue. ☐ *We must not perpetuate the religious divisions of the past.*

per|pe|tu|ity /pɜrpɪtuɪti/ PHRASE [PHR after v] If something is done **in perpetuity**, it is intended to last for ever. [FORMAL] ☐ *The U.S. government gave the land to the tribe in perpetuity.*

per|plex /pərplɛks/ (perplexes, perplexing, perplexed) V-T If something **perplexes** you, it confuses and worries you because you do not understand it or because it causes you difficulty. ☐ *It perplexed him because he was tackling it the wrong way.*

per|plexed /pərplɛkst/ ADJ If you are **perplexed**, you feel confused and slightly worried by something because you do not understand it. ☐ *She is perplexed about what to do for her daughter.*

per|plex|ing /pərplɛksɪŋ/ ADJ [usu ADJ n] If you find something **perplexing**, you do not understand it or do not know how to deal with it. ☐ *It took years to understand many perplexing diseases.*

per|plex|ity /pərplɛksɪti/ (perplexities) **1** N-UNCOUNT **Perplexity** is a feeling of being confused and frustrated because you do not understand something. ☐ *He began counting them and then, with growing perplexity, counted them a second time.* **2** N-COUNT [usu pl] The **perplexities** of something are those things about it that are difficult to understand because they are complicated. ☐ *...the perplexities of quantum mechanics.*

per|qui|site /pɜrkwɪzɪt/ (perquisites) N-COUNT A **perquisite** is the same as a **perk**. [FORMAL] ☐ *...long-distance calls, a perquisite of her employment.*

per se /pɜr seɪ, pər-/ ADV **Per se** means 'by itself' or 'in itself,' and is used when you are talking about the qualities of one thing considered on its own, rather than in connection with other things. ☐ *I don't work out per se, but I'm very active physically.*

per|secute /pɜrsɪkyut/ (persecutes, persecuting, persecuted) V-T If someone is **persecuted**, they are treated cruelly and unfairly, often because of their race or beliefs. ☐ *Mr. Weaver and his family have been persecuted by the authorities for their beliefs.* ☐ *They began by brutally persecuting the Catholic Church.*

per|secu|tion /pɜrsɪkyuʃən/ (persecutions) N-COUNT **Persecution** is cruel and unfair treatment of a person or group, especially because of their religious or political beliefs, or their race. ☐ *...the persecution of minorities.* ☐ *...victims of political persecution.*

per|secu|tor /pɜrsɪkyutər/ (persecutors) N-COUNT [usu pl] The **persecutors** of a person or group treat them cruelly and unfairly, especially because of their religious or political beliefs, or their race.

per|sever|ance /pɜrsɪvɪərəns/ N-UNCOUNT **Perseverance** is the quality of continuing with something even though it is difficult. ❑ *He has never stopped trying and showed great perseverance.*

per|severe /pɜrsɪvɪər/ (perseveres, persevering, persevered) V-I If you **persevere** with something, you keep trying to do it and do not give up, even though it is difficult. ❑ *This ability to persevere despite obstacles and setbacks is the quality people most admire in others.* ❑ *...a school with a reputation for persevering with difficult and disruptive children.*

Per|sian /pɜrʒən/ (Persians) **1** ADJ Something that is **Persian** belongs or relates to the ancient kingdom of Persia, or sometimes to the modern state of Iran. **2** N-COUNT **Persians** were the people who came from the ancient kingdom of Persia. **3** ADJ **Persian** carpets and rugs traditionally come from Iran. They are made by hand from silk or wool and usually have patterns in deep colors. **4** N-UNCOUNT **Persian** is the language that is spoken in Iran, and was spoken in the ancient Persian empire. Persian is also called **Farsi**.

Per|sian cat (Persian cats) N-COUNT A **Persian cat** is a type of cat which has a round face and long hair.

Per|sian Gulf N-PROPER [usu the N] The **Persian Gulf** is the area of sea between Saudi Arabia and Iran.

per|sim|mon /pɜrsɪmən/ (persimmons) N-COUNT A **persimmon** is a soft, orange fruit that looks like a large tomato. Persimmons grow on trees in warm areas including the southern U.S.

per|sist /pɜrsɪst/ (persists, persisting, persisted) **1** V-I If something undesirable **persists**, it continues to exist. ❑ *Contact your doctor if the cough persists.* **2** V-I If you **persist** in doing something, you continue to do it, even though it is difficult or other people are against it. ❑ *Why do people persist in begging for money in the street?* ❑ *He urged the United States to persist with its efforts to bring about peace.* **3** → See feature box at **success**

per|sis|tence /pɜrsɪstəns/ **1** N-UNCOUNT If you have **persistence**, you continue to do something even though it is difficult or other people are against it. ❑ *Skill comes only with practice, patience, and persistence.* **2** N-UNCOUNT The **persistence** of something, especially something bad, is the fact of its continuing to exist for a long time. ❑ *...an expression of concern at the persistence of inflation and high interest rates.*

per|sis|tent /pɜrsɪstənt/ **1** ADJ Something that is **persistent** continues to exist or happen for a long time; used especially about bad or undesirable states or situations. ❑ *Her position as national leader has been weakened by persistent fears of another coup attempt.* ❑ *His cough grew more persistent until it never stopped.* **2** ADJ Someone who is **persistent** continues trying to do something, even though it is difficult or other people are against it. ❑ *...a persistent critic of the president.*

per|sis|tent|ly /pɜrsɪstəntli/ **1** ADV If something happens **persistently**, it happens again and again or for a long time. ❑ *The allegations have been persistently denied by ministers.* **2** ADV [ADV with v] If someone does something **persistently**, they do it with determination even though it is difficult or other people are against it. ❑ *Rachel gently but persistently imposed her will on Doug.*

per|sis|tent veg|eta|tive state (persistent vegetative states) N-COUNT If someone is in a **persistent vegetative state**, they are unable to think, speak, or move because they have severe brain damage, and their condition is not likely to improve. [MEDICAL]

per|snick|ety /pɜrsnɪkɪti/ ADJ If you describe someone as **persnickety**, you think that they pay too much attention to small, unimportant details. [AM, INFORMAL, DISAPPROVAL] ❑ *He is a very rigorous man, very persnickety.*

in BRIT, use **pernickety**

per|son ♦♦♦ /pɜrsən/ (people or persons)

The usual word for 'more than one person' is **people**. The form **persons** is used as the plural in formal or legal language.

1 N-COUNT A **person** is a man, woman, or child. ❑ *At least one person died and several others were injured.* ❑ *They were both lovely, friendly people.* **2** N-PLURAL **Persons** is used as the plural of **person** in formal, legal, and technical writing. ❑ *...removal of the right of accused persons to remain silent.* **3** N-COUNT If you talk about someone **as a person**, you are considering them from the point of view of their real nature. ❑ *Robin didn't feel good about herself as a person.* **4** PHRASE If you do something **in person**, you do it yourself rather than letting someone else do it for you. ❑ *You must collect the mail in person and take along some form of identification.* **5** PHRASE If you meet, hear, or see someone **in person**, you are in the same place as them, rather than, for example, speaking to them on the telephone, writing to them, or seeing them online or on television. ❑ *It was the first time she had seen him in person.* **6** N-COUNT Your **person** is your body. [FORMAL] ❑ *The suspect had refused to give any details of his identity and had carried no documents on his person.* **7** N-COUNT In grammar, we use the term **first person** when referring to 'I' and 'we,' **second person** when referring to 'you,' and **third person** when referring to 'he,' 'she,' 'it,' 'they,' and all other noun groups. **Person** is also used like this when referring to the verb forms that go with these pronouns and noun groups.

-person /-pɜrsən/ (-people or -persons) **1** COMB IN ADJ [ADJ n] **-person** is added to numbers to form adjectives that indicate how many people are involved in something or can use something. **People** is not used in this way. ❑ *...two-person households.* ❑ *...the spa's 32-person staff.* ❑ *...his 1971 one-person exhibition.* **2** COMB IN N-COUNT **-person** is added to nouns to form other nouns that refer to someone who does a particular job or is in a particular group. **-person** is used by people who do not want to use a term that indicates whether someone is a man or a woman. **-people** can also be used in this way. ❑ *...Mrs. Sahana Pradhan, chairperson of the United Leftist Front.* ❑ *He had a staff of six salespeople working for him.*

per|so|na /pɜrsoʊnə/ (personas or personae /pɜrsoʊni/) N-COUNT Someone's **persona** is the aspect of their character or nature that they present to other people, perhaps in contrast to their real character or nature. [FORMAL] ❑ *The contradictions between his private life and the public persona are not always fully explored.*

per|son|able /pɜrsənəbəl/ ADJ Someone who is **personable** has a pleasant appearance and character. [APPROVAL] ❑ *The people I met were intelligent, mature, personable.*

per|son|age /pɜrsənɪdʒ/ (personages) **1** N-COUNT A **personage** is a famous or important person. [FORMAL] ❑ *...politicians, movie stars, and other important personages.* **2** N-COUNT A **personage** is a character in a play or book, or in history. [FORMAL] ❑ *There is no evidence for such a historical personage.*

per|son|al ♦♦♦ /pɜrsənəl/ **1** ADJ [ADJ n] A **personal** opinion, quality, or thing belongs or relates to one particular person rather than to other people. ❑ *He learned this lesson the hard way – from his own personal experience.* ❑ *That's my personal opinion.* **2** ADJ If you give something your **personal** care or attention, you deal with it yourself rather than letting someone else deal with it. ❑ *...a business that requires a lot of personal contact.* ❑ *...a personal letter from the president's secretary.* **3** ADJ **Personal** matters relate to your feelings, relationships, and health. ❑ *...teaching young people about marriage and personal relationships.* ❑ *You never allow personal problems to affect your performance.* **4** ADJ **Personal** comments refer to someone's appearance or character in an offensive way. ❑ *Newspapers resorted to personal abuse.* **5** ADJ [ADJ n] **Personal** care involves taking care of your body and appearance. ❑ *...people who take time and care over personal hygiene.* **6** ADJ A **personal** relationship is one that is not connected with your job or public life. ❑ *He was a great and valued personal friend whom I've known for many years.* **7** ADJ [ADJ n] If someone has a **personal** shopper or a **personal** trainer, they employ another person to shop for them or to help them keep fit. ❑ *Another way of escaping the crowds and the changing rooms is to employ a personal shopper.* ❑ *The best clubs also offer personal trainers to help motivate and ensure that exercises are properly performed.* **8** → see also **personals**

per|son|al as|sis|tant (personal assistants) N-COUNT A **personal assistant** is a person who does office work and administrative work for someone. The abbreviation **PA** is also used. [BUSINESS] ❑ *She started as a personal assistant to the CEO.*

per|son|al best (personal bests) N-COUNT [usu sing] An athlete's **personal best** is the highest score or fastest time that they have ever achieved. ❑ *She ran a personal best of 13.01 sec.*

per|son|al col|umn (personal columns) N-COUNT The **personal column** in a newspaper or magazine contains messages for individual people and advertisements of a private nature. [mainly BRIT]

> in AM, usually use **personals**

per|son|al com|put|er (personal computers) N-COUNT A **personal computer** is a computer that is used by one person at a time in a business, a school, or at home. The abbreviation **PC** is also used.

per|son|al ex|emp|tion (personal exemptions) N-COUNT Your **personal exemption** is the amount of money that is deducted from your gross income before you have to start paying income tax. [AM] ▢ *Changes for this year include an increase in the personal exemption.* ▢ *Income taxes skyrocketed and personal exemptions were lowered.*

per|son|al|ity ✦◇◇ /pɜrsənælɪti/ (personalities) **1** N-VAR Your **personality** is your whole character and nature. ▢ *She has such a kind, friendly personality.* ▢ *The contest was as much about personalities as it was about politics.* **2** N-VAR If someone has **personality** or is **a personality**, they have a strong and lively character. ▢ *...a woman of great personality.* **3** N-COUNT You can refer to a famous person, especially in entertainment, broadcasting, or sports, as a **personality**. ▢ *...the radio and television personality, Johnny Carson.*

SYNONYMS

personality
NOUN **1**
character: *Perhaps there is a negative side to his character that you haven't seen yet.*
temperament: *His impulsive temperament regularly got him into trouble.*
nature: *She trusted people. That was her nature.*
identity: *I wanted a sense of my own identity.*

VOCABULARY IN CONTEXT

Introvert and extrovert

It can look like the world of work is set up to the advantage of the **extrovert**. **Outgoing** people are ideally suited to **networking**, so they build business relationships easily. Happy to be **in the spotlight** – you might even call them attention-seekers – their naturally **chatty** nature means they're comfortable in most situations. They're also **assertive** about putting their ideas and arguments forward, so they find it easy to be heard in meetings. **Introverts**, on the other hand, are much more **reserved** and less likely to speak up. Their tendency toward **awkwardness** means they're more likely to be **hanging back** at conferences than making useful contacts. Being an introvert is not necessarily the same as being shy; instead, it's a preference for **contemplation** and **introspection**. In fact, their focus, objectivity, and attention to detail has meant that some of the world's most successful people are introverts, for example, Mark Zuckerberg, Bill Gates, Christina Aguilera, and J.K. Rowling. And don't forget Harry Potter himself!

---

per|son|al|ity dis|or|der (personality disorders) N-VAR A **personality disorder** is a mental disorder in which a person habitually behaves in ways considered likely to cause suffering to themself or others. [MEDICAL] ▢ *One forensic psychiatrist described him as having an incurable antisocial personality disorder.*

per|son|al|ize /pɜrsənºlaɪz/ (personalizes, personalizing, personalized)

> in BRIT, also use **personalise**

1 V-T [usu passive] If an object **is personalized**, it is marked with the name or initials of its owner. ▢ *Gift certificates are personalized with both the recipient and giver names.* ● **per|son|al|ized** ADJ [ADJ n] ▢ *The personalized license plate is 7698, Tiger's birthday.* **2** V-T If you **personalize** something, you do or design it specially according to the needs of an individual or to your own needs. ▢ *You can usually also personalize a computer dictionary.* ▢ *In a small company, you will receive more personalized service.* **3** V-T If you **personalize** an argument, discussion, idea, or issue, you consider it from the point of view of individual people and their characters or relationships, rather than considering the facts in a general or abstract way. ▢ *Anne Frank personalized the horrors of the Holocaust in her own words.* ▢ *From the beginning, the whole crisis was too personalized.*

per|son|al|ly ✦◇◇ /pɜrsənəli/ **1** ADV [ADV with cl] You use **personally** to emphasize that you are giving your own opinion. [EMPHASIS] ▢ *Personally I think it's a waste of time.* ▢ *You can disagree about them, and I personally do, but they are great ideas that have made people think.* **2** ADV [ADV with v] If you do something **personally**, you do it yourself rather than letting someone else do it. ▢ *He is returning to Paris to answer the allegations personally.* ▢ *When the great man arrived, the club's manager personally escorted him upstairs.* **3** ADV [ADV with v] If you meet or know someone **personally**, you meet or know them in real life, rather than knowing about them or knowing their work. ▢ *He did not know them personally, but he was familiar with their reputation.* **4** ADV You can use **personally** to say that something refers to an individual person rather than to other people. ▢ *He was personally responsible for all that people suffered under his rule.* **5** ADV You can use **personally** to show that you are talking about someone's private life rather than their professional or public life. ▢ *This has taken a great toll on me personally and professionally.* **6** PHRASE If you **take** someone's remarks **personally**, you are upset because you think that they are criticizing you in particular. ▢ *I take everything too personally.*

per|son|al or|gan|iz|er (personal organizers)

> in BRIT, also use **personal organiser**

N-COUNT A **personal organizer** is a book containing personal or business information, that you can add pages to or remove pages from to keep the information up-to-date. Small computers with a similar function are also called **personal organizers**.

per|son|al pro|noun (personal pronouns) N-COUNT A **personal pronoun** is a pronoun such as 'I,' 'you,' 'she,' or 'they' which is used to refer to the speaker or the person spoken to, or to a person or thing whose identity is clear, usually because they have already been mentioned.

per|son|al pro|tec|tive equip|ment N-UNCOUNT **Personal protective equipment** is equipment such as gloves, masks, and gowns worn by people who are at risk of injury or infection. The abbreviation **PPE** is often used. ▢ *We sell personal protective equipment for people like oil-rig workers.*

per|son|als /pɜrsənºlz/ N-PLURAL [usu the N] The section in a newspaper or magazine that contains messages for individual people and advertisements of a private nature is called the **personals**. [AM]

> in BRIT, usually use **personal column**

per|son|al space 1 N-UNCOUNT [oft poss N] If someone invades your **personal space**, they stand or lean too close to you, so that you feel uncomfortable. **2** N-UNCOUNT [oft poss N] If you need your **personal space**, you need time by yourself, with the freedom to do something that you want to do or to think about something. ▢ *Self confidence means being relaxed enough to allow your lover their personal space.*

per|son|al ste|reo (personal stereos) N-COUNT A **personal stereo** is a small cassette or CD player with very light headphones, that people used to carry around so that they could listen to music while doing something else.

per|so|na non gra|ta /pərsoʊnə nɒn grɑtə, -grætə/ (personae non gratae) PHRASE If someone becomes or is declared **persona non grata**, they become unwelcome or unacceptable because of something they have said or done. ❏ *The government has declared the French ambassador persona non grata and ordered him to leave the country.*

per|soni|fi|ca|tion /pərsɒnɪfɪkeɪʃ³n/ N-SING If you say that someone is the **personification** of a particular thing or quality, you mean that they are a perfect example of that thing or that they have a lot of that quality. ❏ *Janis Joplin was the personification of the '60s female rock singer.*

per|soni|fy /pərsɒnɪfaɪ/ (personifies, personifying, personified) V-T If you say that someone **personifies** a particular thing or quality, you mean that they seem to be a perfect example of that thing, or to have that quality to a very large degree. ❏ *She seemed to personify goodness and nobility.*

per|son|nel ✦✧✧ /pɜrsənel/ **1** N-PLURAL The **personnel** of an organization are the people who work for it. ❏ *The country has never dispatched military personnel abroad.* ❏ *There has been very little renewal of personnel in higher education.* **2** N-UNCOUNT **Personnel** is the department in a large company or organization that deals with employees, keeps their records, and helps with any problems they might have. [OLD-FASHIONED, BUSINESS] ❏ *Her first job was in personnel.*

per·son-to-per·son ADJ If you make a **person-to-person** call, you say that you want to talk to one person in particular. If that person cannot come to the telephone, you do not have to pay for the call.

per|spec|tive ✦✧✧ /pərspektɪv/ (perspectives) **1** N-COUNT A particular **perspective** is a particular way of thinking about something, especially one that is influenced by your beliefs or experiences. ❏ *He says the death of his father 18 months ago has given him a new perspective on life.* ❏ *...two different perspectives on the nature of adolescent development.* **2** PHRASE If you get something **in perspective** or **into perspective**, you judge its real importance by considering it in relation to everything else. If you get something **out of perspective**, you fail to judge its real importance in relation to everything else. ❏ *Remember to keep things in perspective.* ❏ *I let things get out of perspective.*

─── SYNONYMS ───
perspective
NOUN **1**
outlook: *The illness had a profound effect on his outlook.*
attitude: *...the general change in attitude towards people with disabilities.*
angle: *He was considering the idea from all angles.*

per|spi|ca|cious /pɜrspɪkeɪʃəs/ ADJ Someone who is **perspicacious** notices, realizes, and understands things quickly. [FORMAL] ❏ *...one of the most perspicacious and perceptive historians of that period.* • **per|spi|cac|ity** /pɜrspɪkæsɪti/ N-UNCOUNT ❏ *I congratulated her on her perspicacity.*

per|spi|ra|tion /pɜrspɪreɪʃ³n/ N-UNCOUNT **Perspiration** is the liquid that comes out on the surface of your skin when you are hot or frightened. [FORMAL] ❏ *His hands were wet with perspiration.*

per|spire /pərspaɪər/ (perspires, perspiring, perspired) V-I When you **perspire**, a liquid comes out on the surface of your skin because you are hot or frightened. [FORMAL] ❏ *He began to perspire heavily.* ❏ *...mopping their perspiring brows.*

per|suade ✦✧✧ /pərsweɪd/ (persuades, persuading, persuaded) **1** V-T If you **persuade** someone to do something, you cause them to do it by giving them good reasons for doing it. ❏ *My husband persuaded me to come.* ❏ *We're trying to persuade manufacturers to sell them here.* **2** V-T If something **persuades** someone to take a particular course of action, it causes them to take that course of action because it is a good reason for doing so. ❏ *It was the lack of privacy that eventually persuaded us to move after Ben was born.* **3** V-T If you **persuade** someone that something is true, you say things that eventually make them believe that it is true. ❏ *I've persuaded Mrs. Tennant* that it's time she retired. ❏ *We had managed to persuade them that it was worth working with us.*

per|sua|sion /pərsweɪʒ³n/ (persuasions) **1** N-UNCOUNT **Persuasion** is the act of persuading someone to do something or to believe that something is true. ❏ *Only after much persuasion from Ellis had she agreed to hold a show at all.* **2** N-COUNT If you are of a particular **persuasion**, you have a particular belief or set of beliefs. [FORMAL] ❏ *It is a national movement and has within it people of all political persuasions.*

per|sua|sive /pərsweɪsɪv/ ADJ Someone or something that is **persuasive** is likely to persuade a person to believe or do a particular thing. ❏ *What do you think were some of the more persuasive arguments on the other side?* ❏ *I can be very persuasive when I want to be.* • **per|sua|sive|ly** ADV [ADV with v] ❏ *...a trained lawyer who can present arguments persuasively.*

pert /pɜrt/ **1** ADJ If someone describes a young woman as **pert**, they mean that they like her because she is lively and not afraid to say what she thinks. This use could cause offense. ❏ *...a pert redhead in uniform.* ❏ *...pert replies by servant girls.* **2** ADJ If you say that someone has, for example, a **pert** nose, you mean that it is quite small and neat, and you think it is attractive. [APPROVAL]

per|tain /pərteɪn/ (pertains, pertaining, pertained) V-I If one thing **pertains** to another, it relates, belongs, or applies to it. [FORMAL] ❏ *...matters pertaining to naval district defense.*

per|ti|na|cious /pɜrt³neɪʃəs/ ADJ Someone who is **pertinacious** continues trying to do something difficult rather than giving up quickly. [FORMAL]

per|ti|nent /pɜrt³nənt/ ADJ Something that is **pertinent** is relevant to a particular subject. [FORMAL] ❏ *She had asked some pertinent questions.* ❏ *...name, address, and other pertinent information.*

per|turb /pərtɜrb/ (perturbs, perturbing, perturbed) **1** V-T If something **perturbs** you, it worries you quite a lot. [FORMAL] ❏ *What perturbs me is that magazine articles are so much shorter nowadays.* **2** → see also **perturbed**

per|tur|ba|tion /pɜrtərbeɪʃ³n/ (perturbations) **1** N-VAR A **perturbation** is a small change in the movement, quality, or behavior of something, especially an unusual change. [TECHNICAL] ❏ *...perturbations in Jupiter's gravitational field.* **2** N-UNCOUNT **Perturbation** is worry caused by some event. [FORMAL] ❏ *This message caused perturbation in the Middle East Headquarters.*

per|turbed /pərtɜrbd/ ADJ If someone is **perturbed** by something, they are worried or upset by it. [FORMAL] ❏ *He apparently was not perturbed by the prospect of a police officer coming to the door.* ❏ *Peter was quite perturbed at Randi's behavior, and threw her out three days later.*

per|tus|sis /pərtʌsɪs/ N-UNCOUNT **Pertussis** is the medical term for **whooping cough.**

pe|rus|al /pəruz³l/ N-UNCOUNT [also a N] **Perusal** of something such as a letter, article, or document is the action of reading it. [FORMAL] ❏ *They undertook to send each of us a sample contract for perusal.*

pe|ruse /pəruz/ (peruses, perusing, perused) V-T If you **peruse** something such as a letter, article, or document, you read it. [FORMAL] ❏ *We perused the company's financial statements for the past five years.*

Pe|ru|vian /pəruviən/ (Peruvians) ADJ **Peruvian** means belonging or relating to Peru, or to its people or culture. • N-COUNT A **Peruvian** is someone who is Peruvian.

per|vade /pərveɪd/ (pervades, pervading, pervaded) V-T If something **pervades** a place or thing, it is a noticeable feature throughout it. [FORMAL] ❏ *The smell of sawdust and glue pervaded the factory.*

per|va|sive /pərveɪsɪv/ ADJ Something, especially something bad, that is **pervasive** is present or felt throughout a place or thing. [FORMAL] ❏ *...the pervasive influence of the army in national life.*

per|verse /pərvɜrs/ ADJ Someone who is **perverse** deliberately does things that are unreasonable or that result in harm for themselves. [DISAPPROVAL] ❏ *It would be perverse to stop this healthy trend.* ❏ *He seemed to take a perverse pleasure in being disagreeable.* • **per|verse|ly** ADV ❏ *She was perversely pleased to be causing trouble.*

per|ver|sion /pərvɜːʳʒən, -ʃən/ (perversions) **1** N-VAR You can refer to a sexual desire or action that you consider to be abnormal and unacceptable as a **perversion**. [DISAPPROVAL] ❏ *The book was the authority on sexual perversions.* **2** N-VAR A **perversion** of something is a form of it that is bad or wrong, or the changing of it into this form. [DISAPPROVAL] ❏ *Critics say that the system is a dangerous perversion of democracy.*

per|vert (perverts, perverting, perverted)

> The verb is pronounced /pərvɜːʳt/. The noun is pronounced /pɜːʳvɜːʳt/.

1 V-T If you **pervert** something such as a process or society, you interfere with it so that it is not as good as it used to be or as it should be. [FORMAL, DISAPPROVAL] ❏ *Any reform will destroy and pervert our constitution.* **2** N-COUNT If you say that someone is a **pervert**, you mean that you consider their behavior, especially their sexual behavior, to be immoral or unacceptable. [DISAPPROVAL] ❏ *I hope the police track down these perverts and charge them with rape.*

per|vert|ed /pərvɜːʳtɪd/ **1** ADJ If you say that someone is **perverted**, you mean that you consider their behavior, especially their sexual behavior, to be immoral or unacceptable. [DISAPPROVAL] ❏ *You've been protecting sick and perverted men.* **2** ADJ You can use **perverted** to describe actions or ideas which you think are wrong, unnatural, or harmful. [DISAPPROVAL] ❏ *...a perverted form of knowledge.*

pesce|tar|ian /pɛskɪtɛəriən/ (pescetarians) ADJ A **pescetarian** diet includes fish but not meat. • N-COUNT A **pescetarian** is someone who is pescetarian. ❏ *Pescetarians eat fish in an otherwise vegetarian diet.*

pe|seta /pəseɪtə/ (pesetas) N-COUNT The **peseta** was the unit of money that was used in Spain before it was replaced by the euro.

pesky /pɛski/ ADJ [ADJ n] **Pesky** means annoying. [INFORMAL] ❏ *He was a pesky tourist asking silly questions.*

peso /peɪsoʊ/ (pesos) N-COUNT The **peso** is the unit of money that is used in Argentina, Chile, Colombia, Cuba, the Dominican Republic, Mexico, the Philippines, and Uruguay.

pes|sa|ry /pɛsəri/ (pessaries) **1** N-COUNT A **pessary** is a small block of a medicine or a contraceptive chemical that a woman puts in her vagina. **2** N-COUNT A **pessary** is a device that is put in a woman's vagina to support her uterus.

pes|si|mism /pɛsɪmɪzəm/ **1** N-UNCOUNT **Pessimism** is the belief that bad things are going to happen. ❏ *...universal pessimism about the economy.* **2** → See feature box at **quality**

pes|si|mist /pɛsɪmɪst/ (pessimists) N-COUNT A **pessimist** is someone who thinks that bad things are going to happen. ❏ *I'm a natural pessimist; I usually expect the worst.*

pes|si|mis|tic /pɛsɪmɪstɪk/ ADJ Someone who is **pessimistic** thinks that bad things are going to happen. ❏ *Not everyone is so pessimistic about the future.* ❏ *Hardy has often been criticized for an excessively pessimistic view of life.*

pest /pɛst/ (pests) **1** N-COUNT **Pests** are insects or small animals that damage crops or food supplies. ❏ *...crops which are resistant to some of the major insect pests and diseases.* ❏ *Each year ten percent of the crop is lost to a pest called corn rootworm.* **2** N-COUNT You can describe someone, especially a child, as a **pest** if they keep bothering you. [INFORMAL, DISAPPROVAL] ❏ *He climbed on the table, pulled my hair, and was generally a pest.*

pes|ter /pɛstəʳ/ (pesters, pestering, pestered) V-T If you say that someone **is pestering** you, you mean that they keep asking you to do something, or keep talking to you, and you find this annoying. [DISAPPROVAL] ❏ *I thought she'd stop pestering me, but it only seemed to make her worse.* ❏ *I know he gets fed up with people pestering him for money.*

pes|ti|cide /pɛstɪsaɪd/ (pesticides) **1** N-MASS **Pesticides** are chemicals that farmers put on their crops to kill harmful insects. **2** → See feature box at **farming**

pes|ti|lence /pɛstɪləns/ (pestilences) N-VAR **Pestilence** is any disease that spreads quickly and kills large numbers of people. [LITERARY]

pes|ti|len|tial /pɛstɪlɛnʃəl/ **1** ADJ [ADJ n] **Pestilential** is used to refer to things that cause disease or are caused by disease. [FORMAL] ❏ *...people who were dependent for their water supply on this pestilential stream.* ❏ *...a pestilential fever.* **2** ADJ [ADJ n] **Pestilential** animals destroy crops or exist in such large numbers that they cause harm. [FORMAL]

pes|tle /pɛsəl/ (pestles) **1** N-COUNT A **pestle** is a short rod with a thick round end. It is used for crushing things such as herbs, spices, or grain in a bowl called a mortar. **2** → See also color supplement

pes|to /pɛstoʊ/ N-UNCOUNT **Pesto** is an Italian sauce made from basil, garlic, pine nuts, cheese, and olive oil.

pet ✦✧✧ /pɛt/ (pets, petting, petted) **1** N-COUNT A **pet** is an animal that you keep in your home to give you company and pleasure. ❏ *It is plainly cruel to keep turtles as pets.* ❏ *...a bachelor living alone in a house with his pet dog.* **2** ADJ Someone's **pet** theory, project, or subject is one that they particularly support or like. ❏ *He would not stand by and let his pet project be killed off.* **3** V-T If you **pet** a person or animal, you touch them in an affectionate way. ❏ *The man reached down and petted the wolfhound.*

COLLOCATIONS

pet
NOUN **1**
verb + **pet**: pamper; adopt; abandon, dump
adjective + **pet**: beloved, much-loved; unwanted; domestic
noun + **pet**: family, household

---

pet|al /pɛtəl/ (petals) **1** N-COUNT The **petals** of a flower are the thin colored or white parts that together form the flower. ❏ *...bowls of dried rose petals.* **2** → See also color supplement

pe|ter /piːtəʳ/ (peters, petering, petered)
▶ **peter out** PHRASAL VERB If something **peters out**, it gradually comes to an end. ❏ *The six-month strike seemed to be petering out.*

Peter /piːtəʳ/ PHRASE If you say that someone **is robbing Peter to pay Paul**, you mean that they are transferring money from one group of people or place to another, rather than providing extra money. [DISAPPROVAL] ❏ *Sometimes he was moving money from one account to another, robbing Peter to pay Paul.*

pet|it bour|geois /pɛti buəʳʒwɑː/ also **petty bourgeois** ADJ Someone or something that is **petit bourgeois** belongs or relates to the lower middle class. [DISAPPROVAL] ❏ *He had a petit bourgeois mentality.*

pet|it bour|geoi|sie /pɛti buəʳʒwɑːzi/ also **petty bourgeoisie** N-SING-COLL [the N] The **petit bourgeoisie** are people in the lower middle class. [DISAPPROVAL]

pe|tite /pətiːt/ ADJ If you describe a woman as **petite**, you are saying that she is small and slim. ❏ *She was of below average height, petite and slender.*

pet|it four /pɛti fɔːʳ/ (petits fours or petit fours) N-COUNT [usu pl] **Petits fours** are very small sweet cakes. They are sometimes served with coffee at the end of a meal.

pe|ti|tion /pətɪʃən/ (petitions, petitioning, petitioned) **1** N-COUNT A **petition** is a document signed by a lot of people that asks a government or other official group to do a particular thing. ❏ *People feel so strongly that we recently presented the government with a petition signed by 4,500 people.* **2** N-COUNT A **petition** is a formal request made to a court of law for some legal action to be taken. [LEGAL] ❏ *His lawyers filed a petition for all charges to be dropped.* **3** V-T/V-I If you **petition** someone in authority, you make a formal request to them. [LEGAL] ❏ *...couples petitioning for divorce.* ❏ *All the attempts to petition Congress had failed.* **4** → See feature box at **politics**

pe|ti|tion|er /pətɪʃənəʳ/ (petitioners) **1** N-COUNT A **petitioner** is a person who presents or signs a petition. **2** N-COUNT A **petitioner** is a person who brings a legal case to a court of law. [LEGAL] ❏ *The judge awarded the costs of the case to the petitioners.*

pet name (pet names) N-COUNT A **pet name** is a special name that you use for a close friend or a member of your family instead of using their real name.

pet|rel /pɛtrəl/ (petrels) N-COUNT A **petrel** is a type of sea bird that often flies a long way from land. There are many kinds of petrel.

Pet|ri dish /piːtri dɪʃ/ (Petri dishes) N-COUNT A **Petri dish** is a shallow circular dish that is used in laboratories for producing groups of microorganisms. [TECHNICAL]

pet|ri|fied /pɛtrɪfaɪd/ **1** ADJ If you are **petrified**, you are extremely frightened, perhaps so frightened that you cannot think or move. ❏ *I've always been petrified of being alone.* **2** ADJ [ADJ n] A **petrified** plant or animal has died and has gradually turned into stone. ❏ *...a block of petrified wood.*

pet|ri|fy /pɛtrɪfaɪ/ (petrifies, petrifying, petrified) V-T If something **petrifies** you, it makes you feel very frightened. ❏ *Prison petrifies me and I don't want to go there.* • **pet|ri|fy|ing** ADJ ❏ *I found the climb absolutely petrifying.*

pet|ro|chemi|cal /pɛtroʊkɛmɪkəl/ (petrochemicals) also **petro-chemical** N-COUNT [usu pl] **Petrochemicals** are chemicals that are obtained from petroleum or natural gas.

pet|ro|dol|lars /pɛtroʊdɒlərz/ also **petro-dollars** N-PLURAL **Petrodollars** are a unit of money used to calculate how much a country has earned by exporting petroleum or natural gas.

pet|rol /pɛtrəl/ N-UNCOUNT **Petrol** is the same as **gasoline**. [BRIT]

pet|rol bomb (petrol bombs) N-COUNT A **petrol bomb** is a simple bomb consisting of a bottle full of gasoline with a cloth in it that is lit just before the bottle is thrown. [mainly BRIT]

in AM, use **Molotov cocktail**

pe|tro|leum /pətroʊliəm/ **1** N-UNCOUNT **Petroleum** is oil that is found under the surface of the earth or under the sea bed. Gasoline and kerosene are obtained from petroleum. **2** → See feature box at **global warming**

pe|tro|leum jel|ly N-UNCOUNT **Petroleum jelly** is a soft, clear substance obtained from oil or petroleum. It is put on the skin to protect or soften it, or put on surfaces to make them move against each other easily.

pet|ti|coat /pɛtɪkoʊt/ (petticoats) N-COUNT A **petticoat** is a piece of clothing like a thin skirt that is worn under a skirt or dress. [OLD-FASHIONED]

pet|ting /pɛtɪŋ/ **1** N-UNCOUNT **Petting** is when two people kiss and touch each other in a sexual way, but without having sexual intercourse. **2** N-UNCOUNT [N n] A **petting** zoo or a **petting** farm is a place with animals that small children can safely stroke or play with.

pet|ty /pɛti/ (pettier, pettiest) **1** ADJ You can use **petty** to describe things such as problems, rules, or arguments that you think are unimportant or relate to unimportant things. [DISAPPROVAL] ❏ *He was miserable all the time and fights would start over petty things.* ❏ *...endless rules and petty regulations.* **2** ADJ If you describe someone's behavior as **petty**, you mean that they care too much about small, unimportant things and perhaps that they are unnecessarily unkind. [DISAPPROVAL] ❏ *He was petty-minded and obsessed with detail.* • **pet|ti|ness** N-UNCOUNT ❏ *Never had she met such spite and pettiness.* **3** ADJ [ADJ n] **Petty** is used of people or actions that are less important, serious, or great than others. ❏ *...petty crime, such as purse-snatching and minor break-ins.* **4** → See feature box at **urban**

pet|ty bour|geois → see petit bourgeois

pet|ty bour|geoi|sie → see petit bourgeoisie

pet|ty cash N-UNCOUNT **Petty cash** is money that is kept in the office of a company, for making small payments in cash when necessary. [BUSINESS] ❏ *After having her expense claims overruled, she took the money from petty cash.*

pet|ty of|fic|er (petty officers) N-COUNT; N-TITLE A **petty officer** is an officer of low rank in the navy.

petu|lance /pɛtʃələns/ N-UNCOUNT **Petulance** is unreasonable, childish bad temper over something unimportant. ❏ *His petulance made her impatient.*

petu|lant /pɛtʃələnt/ ADJ Someone who is **petulant** is unreasonably angry and upset in a childish way. ❏ *His critics say he's just being silly and petulant.*

pe|tu|nia /pɪtunyə/ (petunias) N-COUNT A **petunia** is a type of garden plant with pink, white, or purple flowers shaped like short, wide cones.

pew /pyu/ (pews) **1** N-COUNT A **pew** is a long wooden seat with a back that people sit on in church. ❏ *Charlene sat in the front pew.* **2** → See also color supplement

pew|ter /pyutər/ N-UNCOUNT **Pewter** is a gray metal that is made by mixing tin and lead. Pewter was often used in former times to make ornaments or containers for eating and drinking. ❏ *...pewter plates.*

PG /pi dʒi/ In the United States, movies that are rated **PG** are not considered suitable for younger children to see without an adult being with them. **PG** is an abbreviation for 'parental guidance.'

PG-13 /pi dʒi θɜrtin/ Movies that are labeled **PG-13** are not considered suitable for children under the age of thirteen, but parents can decide whether or not to allow their children to see the movies. **PG** is an abbreviation for 'parental guidance.'

pH /pi eɪtʃ/ N-UNCOUNT [also a N] The **pH** of a solution indicates how acid or alkaline the solution is. A pH of less than 7 indicates that it is an acid, and a pH of more than 7 indicates that it is an alkali. ❏ *...the pH of sea water.* ❏ *Skin is naturally slightly acidic and has a pH of 5.5.*

phal|anx /feɪlæŋks, fæl-/ (phalanxes or phalanges /fəlændʒiz/) **1** N-COUNT A **phalanx** is a group of soldiers or police who are standing or marching close together ready to fight. [FORMAL] **2** N-COUNT [usu N of n] A **phalanx** of people is a large group who are brought together for a particular purpose. [FORMAL] ❏ *...a phalanx of waiters.*

phal|lic /fælɪk/ ADJ [usu ADJ n] Something that is **phallic** is shaped like an erect penis. Phallic can also mean relating to male sexual powers. ❏ *...a phallic symbol.*

phal|lus /fæləs/ (phalluses or phalli /fælaɪ/) **1** N-COUNT A **phallus** is a model of an erect penis, especially one used as a symbol in ancient religions. **2** N-COUNT A **phallus** is a penis. [TECHNICAL]

phan|tas|ma|gori|cal /fæntæzməgɒrɪkəl/ ADJ [usu ADJ n] **Phantasmagorical** means very strange, like something in a dream. [LITERARY]

phan|tom /fæntəm/ (phantoms) **1** N-COUNT A **phantom** is a ghost. ❏ *They vanished down the stairs like two phantoms.* **2** ADJ [ADJ n] You use **phantom** to describe something that you think you experience but that is not real. ❏ *...phantom pregnancies.* **3** ADJ [ADJ n] **Phantom** is used to describe business organizations, agreements, or goods that do not really exist, but that someone pretends do exist in order to cheat people. ❏ *A phantom trading scheme at a Wall Street investment bank went unnoticed for three years.*

phar|aoh /feəroʊ, færoʊ, feɪ-/ (pharaohs) N-COUNT; N-PROPER A **pharaoh** was a king of ancient Egypt. ❏ *...Rameses II, Pharaoh of All Egypt.*

Phari|sees /færɪsiz/ N-PROPER-PLURAL The **Pharisees** were a group of Jews, mentioned in the New Testament of the Bible, who believed in strictly obeying the laws of Judaism.

phar|ma|ceu|ti|cal /fɑrməsutɪkəl/ (pharmaceuticals) **1** ADJ [ADJ n] **Pharmaceutical** means connected with the industrial production of medicines. ❏ *...a Swiss pharmaceutical company.* **2** N-PLURAL **Pharmaceuticals** are medicines. ❏ *Antibiotics were of no use, neither were other pharmaceuticals.*

phar|ma|cist /fɑrməsɪst/ (pharmacists) N-COUNT A **pharmacist** is a person who is qualified to prepare and sell medicines. ❏ *Ask your pharmacist for advice.*

phar|ma|col|ogy /fɑrməkɒlədʒi/ N-UNCOUNT **Pharmacology** is the branch of science relating to drugs and medicines. • **phar|ma|co|logi|cal** /fɑrməkəlɒdʒɪkəl/ ADJ [ADJ n] ❏ *As little as 50 mg of caffeine can produce pharmacological effects.* • **phar|ma|colo|gist** (pharmacologists) N-COUNT ❏ *...a pharmacologist from the University of California.*

phar|ma|co|poeia /fɑrməkəpiə/ (pharmacopoeias) also **pharmacopeia** N-COUNT A **pharmacopoeia** is an official book that lists all the drugs that can be used to treat people in a particular country, and describes how to use them.

phar|ma|cy /fɑrməsi/ (pharmacies) **1** N-COUNT A **pharmacy** is a store or a department in a store where medicines are sold or given out. ❏ *Pick up the medicine from the pharmacy.* **2** N-UNCOUNT **Pharmacy** is the job or the science of preparing medicines. ❏ *He spent four years studying pharmacy.*

phase ✦✧ /feɪz/ (phases, phasing, phased) N-COUNT A **phase** is a particular stage in a process or in the gradual development of something. ❏ *This fall, 6000 residents will participate in the first phase of the project.* ❏ *The crisis is entering a crucial, critical phase.*

▶ **phase in** PHRASAL VERB If a new way of doing something **is phased in**, it is introduced gradually. ❏ *The reforms would be phased in over three years.*
▶ **phase out** PHRASAL VERB If something **is phased out**, people gradually stop using it. ❏ *They said the present system of military conscription should be phased out.*

SYNONYMS

phase
NOUN
stage: *Mr Cook has arrived in Greece on the final stage of his tour.*
point: *At this point, Diana arrived.*
period: *He went through a period of wanting to be accepted.*

Ph.D. /piː eɪtʃ diː/ (**Ph.D.s**) also **PhD** **1** N-COUNT A **Ph.D.** is a degree awarded to people who have done advanced research into a particular subject. Ph.D. is an abbreviation for Doctor of Philosophy. ❏ *He is more highly educated, with a Ph.D. in chemistry.* **2** Ph.D. is written after someone's name to indicate that they have a Ph.D. ❏ *...R.D. Combes, Ph.D.*

pheas|ant /fɛz³nt/ (**pheasants**)

Pheasant can also be used as the plural form.

N-COUNT A **pheasant** is a bird with a long tail. Pheasants are often shot as a sport and then eaten. • N-UNCOUNT **Pheasant** is the flesh of this bird eaten as food. ❏ *...roast pheasant.*

phe|no|bar|bi|tal /fiːnoʊbɑːrbɪtɔːl/ N-UNCOUNT **Phenobarbital** is a drug that is used to help people to sleep and as a treatment for epilepsy. [mainly AM] ❏ *...sleeping pills containing phenobarbital.*

phe|nom|ena /fɪnɒmɪnə/ **Phenomena** is the plural of phenomenon.

phe|nom|enal /fɪnɒmɪn³l/ ADJ Something that is **phenomenal** is unusually great or good. [EMPHASIS] ❏ *Exports of Australian wine are growing at a phenomenal rate.* • **phe|nom|enal|ly** ADV ❏ *Annie, 37, has recently re-launched her phenomenally successful singing career.*

phe|nom|enol|ogy /fɪnɒmɪnɒlədʒi/ N-UNCOUNT **Phenomenology** is a branch of philosophy that deals with consciousness, thought, and experience. • **phe|nom|eno|logi|cal** /fɪnɒmɪnəlɒdʒɪkəl/ ADJ [usu ADJ n] ❏ *...a phenomenological approach to the definition of "reality."*

phe|nom|enon /fɪnɒmɪnɒn/ (**phenomena**) N-COUNT A **phenomenon** is something that is observed to happen or exist. [FORMAL] ❏ *...scientific explanations of natural phenomena.*

phero|mone /fɛrəmoʊn/ (**pheromones**) N-COUNT Some animals and insects produce chemicals called **pheromones** that affect the behavior of other animals and insects of the same type, for example, by attracting them sexually. [TECHNICAL]

phew /fyuː/ EXCLAM **Phew** is used in writing to represent the soft whistling sound that you make when you breathe out quickly, for example, when you are relieved or shocked about something or when you are very hot. ❏ *Phew, what a relief!*

Phi Beta Kap|pa /fiː beɪtə kæpə/ N-PROPER [usu N n] In the United States, **Phi Beta Kappa** is an association of American college students who have achieved high academic success. ❏ *...Miss Harold, a Phi Beta Kappa graduate of the University of Illinois.* • ADV [after v] **Phi Beta Kappa** is also an adverb ❏ *Moving rapidly through school, he graduated Phi Beta Kappa from the University of Kentucky at age 18.*

phi|lan|der|er /fɪlændərər/ (**philanderers**) N-COUNT If you say that a man is a **philanderer**, you mean that he has a lot of casual sexual relationships. [DISAPPROVAL]

phi|lan|der|ing /fɪlændərɪŋ/ (**philanderings**) **1** ADJ [ADJ n] A **philandering** man has a lot of casual sexual relationships. [DISAPPROVAL] ❏ *...her philandering husband.* **2** N-UNCOUNT [also N in pl] **Philandering** means having a lot of casual sexual relationships. [DISAPPROVAL] ❏ *She intended to leave her husband because of his philandering.*

phil|an|throp|ic /fɪlənθrɒpɪk/ ADJ [usu ADJ n] A **philanthropic** person or organization freely gives money or other help to people who need it. ❏ *Some of the best services for the seniors are sponsored by philanthropic organizations.*

phi|lan|thro|pist /fɪlænθrəpɪst/ (**philanthropists**) N-COUNT A **philanthropist** is someone who freely gives money and help to people who need it.

phi|lan|thro|py /fɪlænθrəpi/ N-UNCOUNT **Philanthropy** is the giving of money to people who need it, without wanting anything in return. ❏ *...a retired banker well known for his philanthropy.*

phi|lat|elist /fɪlætəlɪst/ (**philatelists**) N-COUNT A **philatelist** is a person who collects and studies postage stamps. [FORMAL]

phi|lat|ely /fɪlætəli/ N-UNCOUNT **Philately** is the hobby of collecting and learning about postage stamps. [FORMAL]

SUFFIX

-phile, -ophile
occurs in words which refer to someone who has a very strong liking for people or things of a particular kind. For example, a *Francophile* admires France and the French.

---

phil|har|mon|ic /fɪlhɑːrmɒnɪk, fɪlər-/ (**philharmonics**) ADJ [ADJ n] A **philharmonic** orchestra is a large orchestra that plays classical music. ❏ *The Lithuanian Philharmonic Orchestra played Beethoven's Ninth Symphony.* • N-IN-NAMES **Philharmonic** is also a noun. ❏ *He will conduct the Los Angeles Philharmonic in the final concert of the season.*

Phil|ip|pine /fɪlɪpiːn/ ADJ **Philippine** means belonging or relating to the Philippines, or to their people or culture.

phil|is|tine /fɪlɪstiːn/ (**philistines**) **1** N-COUNT If you call someone a **philistine**, you mean that they do not care about or understand good art, music, or literature, and do not think that they are important. [DISAPPROVAL] **2** ADJ [ADJ n] You can use **philistine** to describe people or organizations who you think do not care about or understand the value of good art, music, or literature. [DISAPPROVAL] ❏ *...a philistine government that allowed the arts to decline.*

phil|is|tin|ism /fɪlɪstɪnɪzəm/ N-UNCOUNT **Philistinism** is the attitude or quality of not caring about, understanding, or liking good art, music, or literature. [DISAPPROVAL]

phi|lol|ogy /fɪlɒlədʒi/ N-UNCOUNT **Philology** is the study of words, especially the history and development of the words in a particular language or group of languages. • **phi|lolo|gist** (**philologists**) N-COUNT ❏ *He is a philologist, specializing in American poetry.*

phi|loso|pher /fɪlɒsəfər/ (**philosophers**) **1** N-COUNT A **philosopher** is a person who studies or writes about philosophy. ❏ *...the Greek philosopher Plato.* **2** N-COUNT If you refer to someone as a **philosopher**, you mean that they think deeply and seriously about life and other basic matters. ❏ *Carlos was something of a philosopher.*

philo|soph|ic /fɪləsɒfɪk/ ADJ **Philosophic** means the same as philosophical.

philo|sophi|cal /fɪləsɒfɪk³l/ **1** ADJ **Philosophical** means concerned with or relating to philosophy. ❏ *He was more accustomed to cocktail party chatter than to political or philosophical discussions.* • **philo|sophi|cal|ly** /fɪləsɒfɪkli/ ADV ❏ *Wilbur says he's not a coward, but that he's philosophically opposed to war.* **2** ADJ Someone who is **philosophical** does not get upset when disappointing or disturbing things happen. [APPROVAL] ❏ *Lewis has grown philosophical about life.* • **philo|sophi|cal|ly** ADV [ADV after v] ❏ *She says philosophically: "It could have been far worse."*

phi|loso|phize /fɪlɒsəfaɪz/ (**philosophizes, philosophizing, philosophized**)

in BRIT, also use **philosophise**

V-I If you say that someone **is philosophizing**, you mean that they are talking or thinking about important subjects, sometimes instead of doing something practical. ❏ *He philosophized, he admitted, not because he was certain of establishing the truth, but because it gave him pleasure.* ❏ *...a tendency to philosophize about racial harmony.* • **phi|loso|phiz|ing** N-UNCOUNT ❏ *The general was anxious to cut short the philosophizing and get down to more urgent problems.*

phi|loso|phy ♦◇◇ /fɪlɒsəfi/ (**philosophies**) **1** N-UNCOUNT **Philosophy** is the study or creation of theories about basic things such as the nature of existence, knowledge, and thought, or about how people should live. ❏ *He studied* philosophy and psychology at Yale. **2** N-COUNT A **philosophy** is a particular set of ideas that a philosopher has. ☐ ...the philosophies of Socrates, Plato, and Aristotle. **3** N-COUNT A **philosophy** is a particular theory that someone has about how to live or how to deal with a particular situation. ☐ The best philosophy is to change your food habits to a low-sugar diet.

phish|ing /fɪʃɪŋ/ **1** N-UNCOUNT **Phishing** is the practice of trying to trick people into giving secret financial information by sending emails that look as if they come from a bank, credit-card account, etc. The details are then used to steal people's money, or to steal their identity in order to commit crimes. [COMPUTING] **2** → See feature box at **crime, email**

phlegm /flɛm/ N-UNCOUNT **Phlegm** is the thick yellowish substance that develops in your throat and at the back of your nose when you have a cold.

phleg|mat|ic /flɛgmætɪk/ ADJ Someone who is **phlegmatic** stays calm even when upsetting or exciting things happen. [FORMAL]

SUFFIX

-phobe, -ophobe

occurs in words which refer to a very strong, irrational fear or hatred of people or things of a particular kind. For example, a **germophobe** has a strong fear of germs.

---

pho|bia /foʊbiə/ (phobias) N-COUNT A **phobia** is a very strong irrational fear or hatred of something. ☐ The man had a phobia about flying.

SUFFIX

-phobia, -ophobia

occurs in words which refer to someone who has a very strong, irrational fear or hatred of people or things of a particular kind. For example, someone who shows signs of **arachnophobia** has a strong fear of spiders.

---

pho|bic /foʊbɪk/ (phobics) **1** ADJ A **phobic** feeling or reaction results from or is related to a strong, irrational fear or hatred of something. ☐ Many children acquire a phobic horror of dogs. **2** ADJ Someone who is **phobic** has a strong, irrational fear or hatred of something. ☐ In years gone by, people were phobic about getting on trains. They weren't used to it. • N-COUNT **Phobic** is also a noun. ☐ Social phobics quake at the thought of meeting strangers.

SUFFIX

-phobic, -ophobic

occurs in words which refer to a very strong, irrational fear or hatred of people or things of a particular kind. For example, someone who is **technophobic** has a strong dislike of new technology.

---

phoe|nix /fiːnɪks/ (phoenixes) **1** N-COUNT [usu sing] A **phoenix** is an imaginary bird that, according to ancient stories, burns itself to ashes every five hundred years and is then born again. **2** N-SING If you describe someone or something as a **phoenix**, you mean that they return again after seeming to disappear or be destroyed. [LITERARY] ☐ Out of the ashes of the economic shambles, a phoenix of recovery can arise.

phone ✦✧ /foʊn/ (phones, phoning, phoned) **1** N-SING [usu the N, also by N] The **phone** is an electrical system that you use to talk to someone else in another place, by dialing a number on a piece of equipment and speaking into it. ☐ "I didn't tell you over the phone," she said. "I didn't know who might be listening." ☐ She looked forward to talking to her daughter by phone. **2** N-COUNT The **phone** is the piece of equipment that you use when you dial someone's phone number and talk to them. ☐ Two minutes later the phone rang. **3** → see also **cellular phone 4** N-SING If you say that someone picks up or puts down **the phone**, you mean that they lift or replace the receiver. ☐ She picked up the phone, and began to dial Maurice's number. **5** V-T/V-I When you **phone** someone, you dial their phone number and speak to them by phone. ☐ He'd phoned Laura to see if she was better. **6** PHRASE If you say that someone is **on the phone**, you mean that they are speaking to someone by phone. ☐ She's always on the phone, wanting to know what I've been up to. **7** → See also color supplement

▶ **phone in 1** PHRASAL VERB If you **phone in** to a radio or television show, you telephone the show in order to give your opinion on a matter that the show has raised. ☐ Listeners have been invited to phone in to pick the winner. **2** PHRASAL VERB If you **phone in** to a place, you make a telephone call to that place. ☐ He has phoned in to say he is thinking over his options. **3** PHRASAL VERB If you **phone in** an order for something, you place the order by telephone. ☐ Just phone in your order three or more days prior to departure.

▶ **phone up** PHRASAL VERB When you **phone** someone **up**, you dial their phone number and speak to them by phone. ☐ Phone him up and tell him to come and have dinner with you one night.

phone book (phone books) N-COUNT A **phone book** is a book that contains an alphabetical list of the names, addresses, and telephone numbers of the people and businesses in a town or area.

phone booth (phone booths) **1** N-COUNT A **phone booth** is a place in a station, hotel, or other public building where there is a public telephone. **2** N-COUNT A **phone booth** is a small shelter outdoors or in a building in which there is a public telephone. [AM]

phone box (phone boxes) N-COUNT A **phone box** is the same as a **phone booth** [BRIT]

phone call (phone calls) N-COUNT If you make a **phone call**, you dial someone's phone number and speak to them by phone. ☐ Wait there for a minute. I have to make a phone call.

phone|card /foʊnkɑːrd/ (phonecards) also **phone card** N-COUNT A **phonecard** is a plastic card that you can use instead of money to pay for telephone calls in some public telephones.

phone-in (phone-ins) N-COUNT A **phone-in** is a program on radio or television in which people telephone with questions or opinions and their calls are broadcast. ☐ She took part in a radio phone-in program.

pho|neme /foʊniːm/ (phonemes) N-COUNT A **phoneme** is the smallest unit of significant sound in a language. [TECHNICAL]

phone num|ber (phone numbers) N-COUNT Your **phone number** is the number that other people dial when they want to talk to you on the phone.

phone-tapping 1 N-UNCOUNT **Phone-tapping** is the activity of listening secretly to someone's phone conversations using special electronic equipment. In most cases phone-tapping is illegal. ☐ There have also been claims of continued phone-tapping and bugging. **2** → see also **tap 4**

pho|net|ics /fənɛtɪks/

The form **phonetic** is used as a modifier.

1 N-UNCOUNT In linguistics, **phonetics** is the study of speech sounds. **2** ADJ [usu ADJ n] **Phonetic** means relating to the sound of a word or to the sounds that are used in languages. ☐ ...the Japanese phonetic system, with its relatively few, simple sounds. • **pho|neti|cal|ly** /fənɛtɪkli/ ADV [ADV with v] ☐ ...phonetically learning how to spell things.

pho|ney /foʊni/ → see **phony**

phon|ic /fɒnɪk/ ADJ [usu ADJ n] In linguistics, **phonic** means relating to the sounds of speech. [TECHNICAL] ☐ ...the phonic system underlying a particular language.

phon|ics /fɒnɪks/ N-UNCOUNT **Phonics** is a method of teaching people to read by training them to associate written letters with their sounds. [TECHNICAL]

pho|no|graph /foʊnəgræf/ (phonographs) N-COUNT A **phonograph** is a record player. [AM]

pho|nol|ogy /fənɒlədʒi/ N-UNCOUNT In linguistics, **phonology** is the study of speech sounds in a particular language. [TECHNICAL]

pho|ny /foʊni/ (phonies, phonier, phoniest) also **phoney 1** ADJ If you describe something as **phony**, you disapprove of it because it is false rather than genuine. [INFORMAL, DISAPPROVAL] ☐ He'd telephoned with some phony excuse she didn't believe for a minute. **2** ADJ If you say that someone is **phony**, you disapprove of them because they are pretending to be someone that they are not in order to deceive people. [INFORMAL, DISAPPROVAL] ☐ The people are so phony. • N-COUNT **Phony** is also a noun. ☐ She's a phony, a fake.

phos|phate /fɒsfeɪt/ (phosphates) N-MASS A **phosphate** is a chemical compound that contains phosphorus. Phosphates are often used in fertilizers.

phos|pho|res|cence /fɒsfərɛsᵊns/ N-UNCOUNT
Phosphorescence is a glow or soft light that is produced in the dark without using heat.

phos|pho|res|cent /fɒsfərɛsᵊnt/ ADJ [usu ADJ n] A phosphorescent object or color glows in the dark with a soft light, but gives out little or no heat. ❑ ...phosphorescent paint.

phos|phor|ic acid /fɒsfɒrɪk æsɪd/ N-UNCOUNT Phosphoric acid is a type of acid that contains phosphorus. [TECHNICAL]

phos|pho|rus /fɒsfərəs/ N-UNCOUNT Phosphorus is a poisonous yellowish-white chemical element. It glows slightly, and burns when air touches it.

pho|to ✦✧✧ /foʊtoʊ/ (photos) N-COUNT A photo is the same as a photograph. ❑ Let's take a photo!

PREFIX

photo-
is added to nouns and adjectives in order to form other nouns and adjectives which refer or relate to photography, or to light. For example, *photosensitive* film is sensitive to light.

pho|to|bomb /foʊtoʊbɒm/ (photobombs, photobombing, photobombed) V-T If you photobomb someone, you spoil a photograph of them by stepping in front of or behind them as the photograph is taken, often doing something silly such as making a funny face. ❑ This is the one where my sister photobombed me.

photo|copi|er /foʊtəkɒpiər/ (photocopiers) N-COUNT A photocopier is a machine that quickly copies documents onto paper by photographing them.

photo|copy /foʊtəkɒpi/ (photocopies, photocopying, photocopied) **1** N-COUNT A photocopy is a copy of a document made using a photocopier. ❑ He was shown a photocopy of the certificate. **2** V-T If you photocopy a document, you make a copy of it using a photocopier. ❑ Staff photocopied the check before cashing it.

photo-finish (photo-finishes) also photo finish N-COUNT If the end of a race is a photo-finish, two or more of the competitors cross the finish line so close together that a photograph of the finish has to be examined to decide who has won. ❑ He was just beaten in a photo-finish.

photo|gen|ic /foʊtədʒɛnɪk/ ADJ Someone who is photogenic looks nice in photographs. ❑ I've got a million photos of my boy. He's very photogenic.

photo|graph ✦✦✧ /foʊtəgræf/ (photographs, photographing, photographed) **1** N-COUNT A photograph is a picture that is made using a camera. ❑ He wants to take some photographs of the house. **2** V-T When you photograph someone or something, you use a camera to obtain a picture of them. [FORMAL] ❑ She photographed the children. ❑ I hate being photographed.

pho|tog|ra|pher ✦✦✧ /fətɒgrəfər/ (photographers) N-COUNT A photographer is someone who takes photographs as a job or hobby. ❑ ...a professional photographer. ❑ ...an amateur photographer.

photo|graph|ic /foʊtəgræfɪk/ **1** ADJ Photographic means connected with photographs or photography. ❑ ...photographic equipment. **2** ADJ If you have a photographic memory, you are able to remember things in great detail after you have seen them. ❑ He had a photographic memory for maps.

pho|tog|ra|phy /fətɒgrəfi/ N-UNCOUNT Photography is the skill, job, or process of producing photographs. ❑ Photography is one of her hobbies.

photo|jour|nal|ism /foʊtoʊdʒɜrnᵊlɪzəm/ N-UNCOUNT Photojournalism is a form of journalism in which stories are presented mainly through photographs rather than words. ❑ ...some of the finest photojournalism of the Civil Rights era. • **photo|jour|nal|ist** (photojournalists) N-COUNT ❑ ...the agency for many international photojournalists, Magnum Photos.

pho|ton /foʊtɒn/ (photons) N-COUNT A photon is a particle of light. [TECHNICAL]

pho|to op|por|tu|nity (photo opportunities) N-COUNT If a politician or other public figure arranges a photo opportunity, they invite the newspapers and television to photograph them doing something that they think will interest or impress the public.

pho|to shoot (photo shoots) also photo-shoot N-COUNT A photo shoot is an occasion when a photographer takes pictures, especially of models or famous people, to be used in a newspaper or magazine. ❑ ...a long day of interviews and photo-shoots.

photo|syn|the|sis /foʊtoʊsɪnθəsɪs/ N-UNCOUNT Photosynthesis is the way that green plants make their food using sunlight. [TECHNICAL]

photovoltaic /foʊtoʊvɒlteɪk/ ADJ [ADJ n] A photovoltaic cell or panel is a device that uses sunlight to cause a chemical reaction which produces electricity. [TECHNICAL]

phras|al verb /freɪzᵊl vɜrb/ (phrasal verbs) N-COUNT A phrasal verb is a combination of a verb and an adverb or preposition, for example, 'shut up' or 'knock back,' which together have a particular meaning.

phrase ✦✧✧ /freɪz/ (phrases, phrasing, phrased) **1** N-COUNT A phrase is a short group of words that people often use as a way of saying something. The meaning of a phrase is often not obvious from the meaning of the individual words in it. ❑ He used a phrase I hate: "You have to be cruel to be kind." **2** N-COUNT A phrase is a small group of words that forms a unit, either on its own or within a sentence. ❑ A writer spends many hours going over and over a scene—changing a phrase here, a word there. **3** V-T If you phrase something in a particular way, you express it in words in that way. ❑ I would have phrased it quite differently. ❑ The speech was carefully phrased. **4** PHRASE If someone has a particular turn of phrase, they have a particular way of expressing themselves in words. ❑ ...Schwarzkopf's distinctive turn of phrase. **5** to coin a phrase → see coin

SYNONYMS

phrase
NOUN **1**
expression: She used some very coarse expressions.
saying: We also realize the truth of that old saying: Charity begins at home.
proverb: An old proverb says, 'The enemy of my enemy is my friend.'
idiom: Proverbs and idioms may become worn with overuse.

phrase book (phrase books) N-COUNT A phrase book is a book used by people traveling to a foreign country. It has lists of useful words and expressions, together with the translation of each word or expression in the language of that country. ❑ We bought a Danish phrase book.

phra|seol|ogy /freɪziɒlədʒi/ N-UNCOUNT [usu with supp] If something is expressed using a particular type of phraseology, it is expressed in words and expressions of that type. ❑ This phraseology is intended to appeal to various sides of the conflict.

phras|ing /freɪzɪŋ/ N-UNCOUNT [oft N of n] The phrasing of something that is said or written is the exact words that are chosen to express the ideas in it. ❑ The phrasing of the question was vague.

phre|nol|ogy /frɪnɒlədʒi/ N-UNCOUNT Phrenology is the study of the size and shape of people's heads in the belief that you can find out about their characters and abilities from this. Most people no longer believe in it.

phys ed /fɪz ɛd/ N-UNCOUNT Phys ed is the same as physical education. [AM, INFORMAL] ❑ ...Don, who taught phys ed at a junior high school.

physi|cal ✦✦✧ /fɪzɪkᵊl/ (physicals) **1** ADJ Physical qualities, actions, or things are connected with a person's body, rather than with their mind. ❑ ...the physical and mental problems caused by the illness. ❑ Physical activity promotes good health. • **physi|cal|ly** ADV ❑ You may be physically and mentally exhausted after a long flight. **2** ADJ Physical things are real things that can be touched and seen, rather than ideas or spoken words. ❑ Physical and ideological barriers had come down in Eastern Europe. ❑ ...physical evidence to support the story. • **physi|cal|ly** ADV ❑ ...physically cut off from every other country. **3** ADJ [ADJ n] Physical means relating to the structure, size, or shape of something that can be seen. ❑ ...the physical characteristics of the terrain. **4** ADJ [ADJ n] Physical means connected with physics or the laws of physics. ❑ ...the physical laws of combustion and thermodynamics. **5** ADJ Someone who is physical touches people a lot, either in an affectionate way or in a rough way. ❑ We decided that in the game we would be physical and aggressive. **6** ADJ [ADJ n] **Physical** is used in expressions such as **physical love** and **physical relationships** to refer to sexual relationships between people. ❏ *It had been years since they had shared any meaningful form of physical relationship.* **7** N-COUNT A **physical** is a medical examination by your doctor to make sure that there is nothing wrong with your health, or a medical examination to make sure you are fit enough to do a particular job. ❏ *Bob failed his physical.* **8** → See feature box at **appearance**

SYNONYMS

physical
ADJ **2**
material: *Every room must have been stuffed with material things.*
real: *No, it wasn't a dream. It was real.*
tangible: *There should be some tangible evidence that the economy is starting to recover.*

---

physi|cal edu|ca|tion N-UNCOUNT **Physical education** is the school subject in which students do physical exercises or take part in physical games and sports. The abbreviation **PE** is also used.

physi|cal|ity /fɪzɪkælɪti/ N-UNCOUNT If you refer to the **physicality** of something such as an artist's or a musician's work, you mean that their energy and enthusiasm is obvious in the work they produce. ❏ *There's not another guitarist to rival the sheer physicality of his work.*

physi|cal sci|ence (**physical sciences**) N-COUNT [usu pl] The **physical sciences** are branches of science such as physics, chemistry, and geology that are concerned with natural forces and with things that do not have life.

physi|cal thera|pist (**physical therapists**) N-COUNT A **physical therapist** is a person who treats people using physical therapy.

in BRIT, usually use **physiotherapist**

physi|cal thera|py N-UNCOUNT **Physical therapy** is medical treatment for problems of the joints, muscles, or nerves, which involves doing exercises or having part of your body massaged or warmed. [mainly AM] ❏ *He'll need intensive physical therapy.*

in BRIT, usually use **physiotherapy**

phy|si|cian /fɪzɪʃən/ (**physicians**) N-COUNT A **physician** is a medical doctor. [FORMAL] ❏ *...your family physician.*

phy|si|cian's as|sis|tant (**physician's assistants**) N-COUNT A **physician's assistant** is a person who is trained to do some of the same work that a doctor does but who is not a doctor. [AM] ❏ *In a few Minnesota communities, physician's assistants are being used in place of doctors.*

physi|cist /fɪzɪsɪst/ (**physicists**) N-COUNT A **physicist** is a person who does research connected with physics or who studies physics. ❏ *...a nuclear physicist.*

phys|ics /fɪzɪks/ N-UNCOUNT **Physics** is the scientific study of forces such as heat, light, sound, pressure, gravity, and electricity, and the way that they affect objects. ❏ *...the laws of physics.*

physi|og|no|my /fɪziɒgnəmi, -ɒnəmi/ (**physiognomies**) N-COUNT Your **physiognomy** is your face, especially when it is considered to show your real character. [FORMAL] ❏ *He was fascinated by her physiognomy – the prominent nose, brooding eyes, and thick hair.*

physi|ol|ogy /fɪziɒlədʒi/ **1** N-UNCOUNT **Physiology** is the scientific study of how people's and animals' bodies function, and of how plants function. ❏ *...the Nobel Prize for Medicine and Physiology.* **2** N-UNCOUNT The **physiology** of a human or animal's body or of a plant is the way that it functions. ❏ *...the physiology of respiration.* • **physio|logi|cal** /fɪziəlɒdʒɪkəl/ ADJ ❏ *...the physiological effects of stress.*

physio|thera|pist /fɪzioʊθɛrəpɪst/ (**physiotherapists**) N-COUNT A **physiotherapist** is the same as a **physical therapist**. [BRIT]

physio|thera|py /fɪzioʊθɛrəpi/ N-UNCOUNT **Physiotherapy** is the same as **physical therapy**. [BRIT]

phy|sique /fɪzik/ (**physiques**) N-COUNT Someone's **physique** is the shape and size of their body. ❏ *He has the physique and energy of a man half his age.*

pi /paɪ/ NUM **Pi** is a number, approximately 3.14, which is equal to the distance around a circle divided by its width. It is usually represented by the Greek letter π.

pia|nis|si|mo /piænɪsɪmoʊ/ ADV [ADV after v] A piece of music that is played **pianissimo** is played very quietly. [TECHNICAL]

pia|nist /piænɪst, piənɪst/ (**pianists**) N-COUNT A **pianist** is a person who plays the piano. ❏ *She was an accomplished pianist, a superb swimmer, and a gifted artist.*

pi|ano /piænoʊ, pyænoʊ/ (**pianos**) N-VAR A **piano** is a large musical instrument with a row of black and white keys. When you press these keys with your fingers, little hammers hit wire strings inside the piano which vibrate to produce musical notes. ❏ *I taught myself how to play the piano.* ❏ *He started piano lessons at the age of 7.*

pi|ano|for|te /piænoʊfɔrteɪ, -ti, piænoʊfɔrt/ (**pianofortes**) N-COUNT A **pianoforte** is a **piano**. [OLD-FASHIONED]

pia|no|la /piənoʊlə/ (**pianolas**) N-VAR A **pianola** is a type of mechanical piano. When you press the pedals, air is forced through holes in a roll of paper to press the keys and play a tune. [BRIT, TRADEMARK]

in AM, use **player piano**

pi|az|za /piæzə, -ætsə/ (**piazzas**) N-COUNT A **piazza** is a large open square in a town or city, especially in Italy. ❏ *...a piazza dotted with fountains.*

pic /pɪk/ (**pics**) **1** N-COUNT A **pic** is a photograph. [INFORMAL] ❏ *Photographer Weegee shot to fame with his shocking pics of New York crime in the 30s.* **2** N-COUNT A **pic** is a movie. [INFORMAL] ❏ *"Angels with Dirty Faces" is a Cagney gangster pic.*

pica|resque /pɪkərɛsk/ ADJ [usu ADJ n] A **picaresque** story is one in which a dishonest but likeable person travels around and has lots of exciting experiences. [LITERARY]

pic|co|lo /pɪkəloʊ/ (**piccolos**) N-VAR A **piccolo** is a small musical instrument that is like a flute but produces higher notes.

pick ♦♦◇ /pɪk/ (**picks, picking, picked**)

→ Please look at meanings **10** and **11** to see if the expression you are looking for is shown under another headword.

1 V-T If you **pick** a particular person or thing, you choose that one. ❏ *Mr. Nowell had picked ten people to interview for six sales jobs in Dallas.* **2** N-SING You can refer to the best things or people in a particular group as **the pick** of that group. ❏ *The boys here are the pick of the high school's soccer players.* **3** V-T When you **pick** flowers, fruit, or leaves, you break them off the plant or tree and collect them. ❏ *She used to pick flowers in the Adirondacks.* **4** V-T If you **pick** something from a place, you remove it from there with your fingers or your hand. ❏ *He picked the napkin from his lap and placed it alongside his plate.* **5** V-T If you **pick** your **nose** or **teeth**, you remove substances from inside your nose or between your teeth. ❏ *Edgar, don't pick your nose, dear.* **6** V-T If you **pick** a fight **with** someone, you deliberately cause one. ❏ *He picked a fight with a waiter and landed in jail.* **7** V-T If someone such as a thief **picks** a lock, they open it without a key, for example, by using a piece of wire. ❏ *He picked each lock deftly, and rifled the papers within each drawer.* **8** N-COUNT A **pick** is the same as a **pickax**. **9** PHRASE If you are told to **take** your **pick**, you can choose any one that you like from a group of things. ❏ *Accountants can take their pick of company cars.* **10 to pick holes in something** → see **hole** **11 to pick someone's pocket** → see **pocket**

▶ **pick on** PHRASAL VERB If someone **picks on** you, they repeatedly criticize you unfairly or treat you unkindly. [INFORMAL] ❏ *Bullies pick on younger children.*

▶ **pick out** **1** PHRASAL VERB If you **pick out** someone or something, you recognize them when it is difficult to see them, for example, because they are among a large group. ❏ *The detective picked out the words with difficulty.* **2** PHRASAL VERB If you **pick out** someone or something, you choose them from a group of people or things. ❏ *I have been picked out to represent the whole team.*

▶ **pick up** **1** PHRASAL VERB When you **pick** something **up**, you lift it up. ❏ *He picked his cap up from the floor and stuck it back on his head.* **2** PHRASAL VERB When you **pick** yourself **up** after you have fallen or been knocked down, you stand up rather slowly. ❏ *Tony picked himself up and set off along the track.* **3** PHRASAL VERB When you **pick up** someone or something that is waiting to be collected, you go to the place where they are and take them away, often in a car. ❏ *She was going over to her parents' house to pick up some clean clothes for Oskar.* ❹ PHRASAL VERB If someone **is picked up** by the police, they are arrested and taken to a police station. ❏ *Rawlings had been picked up by police at his office.* ❺ PHRASAL VERB If you **pick up** something such as a skill or an idea, you acquire it without effort over a period of time. [INFORMAL] ❏ *Where did you pick up your English?* ❻ PHRASAL VERB If you **pick up** someone you do not know, you talk to them and try to start a sexual relationship with them. [INFORMAL] ❏ *He had picked her up at a nightclub, where she worked behind the bar.* ❼ PHRASAL VERB If you **pick up** an illness, you get it from somewhere or something. ❏ *They've picked up a really nasty infection from something they've eaten.* ❽ PHRASAL VERB If a piece of equipment, for example, a radio or a microphone, **picks up** a signal or sound, it receives it or detects it. ❏ *We can pick up Mexican television.* ❾ PHRASAL VERB If you **pick up** something, such as a feature or a pattern, you discover or identify it. ❏ *Some groups of consumers are slow to pick up trends in the use of information technology.* ❿ PHRASAL VERB If someone **picks up** a point or topic that has already been mentioned, or if they **pick up on** it, they refer to it or develop it. ❏ *Can I just pick up that guy's point?* ⓫ PHRASAL VERB If trade or the economy of a country **picks up**, it improves. ❏ *Industrial production is beginning to pick up.* ⓬ PHRASAL VERB If you **pick up** a room or house, you tidy it. [AM] ❏ *She decided to start picking up the house from the top down.* ⓭ → see also **pickup** ⓮ PHRASE When a vehicle **picks up speed**, it begins to move more quickly. ❏ *Brian started the engine and pulled away slowly, but picked up speed once he entered Oakwood Drive.*

SYNONYMS

pick
VERB ❶
select: *Voters are selecting candidates for both U.S. Senate seats and for 52 congressional seats.*
choose: *They will be able to choose their own leaders in democratic elections.*
opt for: *You may wish to opt for one method or the other.*

pick|ax /pɪkæks/ (**pickaxes**) also **pickaxe** N-COUNT A **pickax** is a large tool consisting of a curved, pointed piece of metal with a long handle attached to the middle. Pickaxes are used for breaking up rocks or the ground.

pick|er /pɪkər/ (**pickers**) N-COUNT [usu supp N] A fruit **picker** or cotton **picker**, for example, is a person who picks fruit or cotton, usually for money.

pick|et /pɪkɪt/ (**pickets, picketing, picketed**) ❶ V-T/V-I When a group of people, usually labor union members, **picket**, or **picket** a place of work, they stand outside it in order to protest about something, to prevent people from going in, or to persuade the workers to join a strike. ❏ *A few dozen employees picketed the company's headquarters.* • N-COUNT **Picket** is also a noun. ❏ *...forty demonstrators who have set up a twenty-four-hour picket.* ❷ N-COUNT **Pickets** are people who are picketing a place of work. ❏ *The strikers agreed to remove their pickets and hold talks with the company.*

pick|et fence (**picket fences**) N-COUNT A **picket fence** is a fence made of pointed wooden sticks with pieces of wood nailed across them.

pick|et line (**picket lines**) N-COUNT A **picket line** is a group of pickets outside a place of work. ❏ *No one tried to cross the picket lines.*

pick|ings /pɪkɪŋz/ N-PLURAL [usu supp N] You can refer to the money that can be made easily in a particular place or area of activity as the **pickings**. ❏ *Traditional hiding places are easy pickings for experienced burglars.*

pick|le /pɪkəl/ (**pickles, pickling, pickled**) ❶ N-PLURAL **Pickles** are vegetables or fruit, sometimes cut into pieces, which have been kept in vinegar or salt water for a long time so that they have a strong, sharp taste. ❏ *...a bowl of sliced pickles in lemon juice.* ❷ N-MASS **Pickle** is a cold spicy sauce with pieces of vegetables and fruit in it. ❏ *...jars of pickle.* ❸ V-T When you **pickle** food, you keep it in vinegar or salt water so that it does not go bad and it develops a strong, sharp taste. ❏ *Select your favorite fruit or veg and pickle them while they are still fresh.*

pick|led /pɪkəld/ ADJ **Pickled** food, such as vegetables, fruit, and fish, has been kept in vinegar or salt water to preserve it. ❏ *...a jar of pickled fruit.*

pick-me-up (**pick-me-ups**) N-COUNT A **pick-me-up** is something that you have or do when you are tired or depressed in order to make you feel better. [INFORMAL] ❏ *A five day holiday in the Bahamas would be a great pick-me-up.*

pick|pocket /pɪkpɒkɪt/ (**pickpockets**) N-COUNT A **pickpocket** is a person who steals things from people's pockets or bags in public places. ❏ *Beware of pickpockets, especially when making a purchase.*

pick|up ♦◇◇ /pɪkʌp/ (**pickups**) ❶ N-COUNT A **pickup** or a **pickup truck** is a small truck with low sides that can be easily loaded and unloaded. ❷ N-SING A **pickup** in a country's economy is an improvement in it. ❏ *...a pickup in the housing market.* ❸ N-COUNT A **pickup** takes place when someone picks up a person or thing that is waiting to be collected. ❏ *The company had pickup points in most cities.*

picky /pɪki/ ADJ Someone who is **picky** is difficult to please and only likes a small range of things. [INFORMAL, DISAPPROVAL] ❏ *Some people are very picky about who they choose to share their lives with.*

pic|nic /pɪknɪk/ (**picnics, picnicking, picnicked**) ❶ N-COUNT When people have a **picnic**, they eat a meal outdoors, usually in a park or a forest, or at the beach. ❏ *We're going on a picnic tomorrow.* ❷ V-I When people **picnic** somewhere, they have a picnic. ❏ *Afterwards, we picnicked on the riverbank.*

pic|to|gram /pɪktəgræm/ also **pictograph** /pɪktəgræf, -grɑːf/ N-COUNT A **pictogram** is a simple drawing that represents something. Pictograms were used as the earliest form of writing.

pic|to|rial /pɪktɔːriəl/ ADJ **Pictorial** means using or relating to pictures. ❏ *...a pictorial history of the Jewish people.*

pic|ture ♦♦◇ /pɪktʃər/ (**pictures, picturing, pictured**)
❶ N-COUNT A **picture** consists of lines and shapes that are drawn, painted, or printed on a surface and show a person, thing, or scene. ❏ *...drawing a small picture with colored chalk.* ❷ N-COUNT A **picture** is a photograph. ❏ *The tourists have nothing to do but take pictures of each other.* ❸ N-COUNT Television **pictures** are the scenes that you see on a television screen. ❏ *...heartrending television pictures of human suffering.* ❹ V-T [usu passive] To **be pictured** somewhere, for example, in a newspaper or magazine, means to appear in a photograph or picture. ❏ *The golfer is pictured on many of the front pages, kissing his trophy as he holds it aloft.* ❏ *...a woman who claimed she had been pictured dancing with a celebrity in a nightclub.* ❺ N-COUNT You can refer to a movie as a **picture**. ❏ *...a director of epic action pictures.* ❻ N-COUNT If you have a **picture** of something in your mind, you have a clear idea or memory of it in your mind as if you were actually seeing it. ❏ *We are just trying to get our picture of the whole afternoon straight.* ❼ V-T If you **picture** something in your mind, you think of it and have such a clear memory or idea of it that you seem to be able to see it. ❏ *He pictured her with long black braided hair.* ❏ *He pictured Carrie sitting out in the car, waiting for him.* ❽ N A **picture** of something is a description of it or an indication of what it is like. ❏ *I'll try and give you a better picture of what the boys do.* ❾ N-SING When you refer to the **picture** in a particular place, you are referring to the situation there. ❏ *It's a similar picture across the border in Ethiopia.* ❿ PHRASE [v-link PHR, PHR after v] If you say that someone is **in the picture**, you mean that they are involved in the situation that you are talking about. If you say that they are **out of the picture**, you mean that they are not involved in the situation you are talking about. ❏ *Meyerson is back in the picture after disappearing in July.* ❏ *His dad had been out of the picture since he was eight.* ⓫ PHRASE If you **put** someone **in the picture**, you tell them about a situation which they need to know about. ❏ *Has anyone put you in the picture?*

pic|ture book (**picture books**) N-COUNT A **picture book** is a book with a lot of pictures in it and not much writing. Many picture books are intended for children.

pic|ture li|brary (**picture libraries**) N-COUNT [oft in names] A **picture library** is a collection of photographs that is held by a particular company or organization. Newspapers or publishers can pay to use the photographs in their publications.

pic|ture mes|sag|ing N-UNCOUNT [oft N n] **Picture messaging** is the sending of photographs or pictures from one cellphone to another. ☐ *...picture messaging on camera phones.*

pic|ture post|card (picture postcards) N-COUNT A **picture postcard** is a postcard with a photograph of a place on it. People often buy picture postcards of places they visit when on vacation.

pic|ture show (picture shows) N-COUNT A **picture show** is a movie or movie theater. [AM, OLD-FASHIONED]

pic|tur|esque /pɪktʃəresk/ ADJ A **picturesque** place is attractive and interesting, and has no ugly or modern buildings. ☐ *...a picturesque mountain village.* • N-SING You can refer to picturesque things as **the picturesque**. ☐ *...lovers of the picturesque.*

pic|ture win|dow (picture windows) N-COUNT A **picture window** is a window containing one large sheet of glass, so that people have a good view of what is outside.

pid|dle /pɪdᵊl/ (piddles, piddling, piddled) V-I To **piddle** means to urinate. [INFORMAL]

pid|dling /pɪdlɪŋ/ ADJ [usu ADJ n] **Piddling** means small or unimportant. [INFORMAL] ☐ *...arguing over piddling amounts of money.*

pidg|in /pɪdʒɪn/ (pidgins) **1** N-VAR **Pidgin** is a simple form of a language that speakers of a different language use to communicate. **Pidgin** is not anyone's first language. ☐ *He's at ease speaking pidgin with the factory workers and guys on the docks.* **2** ADJ [ADJ n] If someone is speaking their own language simply or another language badly and is trying to communicate, you can say that they are speaking, for example, **pidgin** English or **pidgin** Italian. ☐ *The restaurant owner could only speak pidgin English.*

pie /paɪ/ (pies) **1** N-VAR A **pie** consists of fruit, meat, or vegetables baked in pastry. ☐ *...a slice of apple pie.* **2 to eat humble pie** → see **humble**

pie|bald /paɪbɔld/ ADJ A **piebald** animal has patches of black and white on it. ☐ *...a piebald pony.*

piece ◆◆◇ /pis/ (pieces, piecing, pieced)
→ Please look at meanings **13** and **14** to see if the expression you are looking for is shown under another headword.
1 N-COUNT A **piece of** something is an amount of it that has been broken off, torn off, or cut off. ☐ *...a piece of cake.* ☐ *Cut the ham into pieces.* **2** N-COUNT A **piece** of an object is one of the individual parts or sections that it is made of, especially a part that can be removed. ☐ *...assembling objects out of standard pieces.* **3** N-COUNT A **piece of** land is an area of land. ☐ *People struggle to get the best piece of land.* **4** N-COUNT You can use **piece of** with many uncount nouns to refer to an individual thing of a particular kind. For example, you can refer to some advice as a **piece of advice**. ☐ *When I produced this piece of work, my lecturers were very critical.* ☐ *...an interesting piece of information.* **5** N-COUNT You can refer to an article in a newspaper or magazine, some music written by someone, a broadcast, or a play as a **piece**. ☐ *She wrote a piece on Gwyneth Paltrow for the New Yorker.* ☐ *...a vaguely familiar orchestral piece.* **6** N-COUNT You can refer to a work of art as a **piece**. [FORMAL] ☐ *Each piece is unique, an exquisite painting of a real person, done on ivory.* **7** N-COUNT You can refer to specific coins as **pieces**. For example, a 5 cent **piece** is a coin that is worth 5 cents. ☐ *...lots of 10 cent, 20 cent, and 50 cent pieces.* **8** N-COUNT The **pieces** that you use when you play a board game such as chess are the specially made objects that you move around on the board. ☐ *How many pieces does each player have in backgammon?* **9** PHRASE If you **give someone a piece of** your **mind**, you tell them very clearly what you think they have behaved badly. [INFORMAL] ☐ *How very thoughtless. I'll give him a piece of my mind.* **10** PHRASE If someone or something is still **in one piece** after a dangerous journey or experience, they are safe and not damaged or hurt. ☐ *...providing that my brother gets back alive and in one piece from his mission.* **11** PHRASE You use **to pieces** in expressions such as 'smash to pieces,' or 'take something to pieces,' when you are describing how something is broken or comes apart so that it is in separate pieces. **12** PHRASE If you **go to pieces**, you are so upset or nervous that you lose control of yourself and cannot do what you should. [INFORMAL] ☐ *She's a strong woman, but she nearly went to pieces when Arnie died.* **13 a piece of the action** → see **action 14 bits and pieces** → see **bit**

▶ **piece together** **1** PHRASAL VERB If you **piece together** the truth about something, you gradually discover it. ☐ *They've pieced together his movements for the last few days before his death.* ☐ *In the following days, Frankie was able to piece together what had happened.* **2** PHRASAL VERB If you **piece** something **together**, you gradually make it by joining several things or parts together. ☐ *This process is akin to piecing together a jigsaw puzzle.*

-piece /-pis/ COMB IN ADJ [ADJ n] **-piece** combines with numbers to form adjectives indicating that something consists of a particular number of items. ☐ *...a three-piece jazz band.*

pièce de ré|sis|tance /piɛs də reɪzistɒns/ N-SING The **pièce de résistance** of a collection or series of things is the most impressive thing in it. [FORMAL] ☐ *The pièce de résistance, however, was a gold evening gown.*

piece|meal /pismil/ ADJ If you describe a change or process as **piecemeal**, you disapprove of it because it happens gradually, usually at irregular intervals, and is probably not satisfactory. [DISAPPROVAL] ☐ *These piecemeal solutions won't work.* • ADV [ADV after v] **Piecemeal** is also an adverb. ☐ *It was built piecemeal over some 130 years.*

piece|work /pisw3rk/ N-UNCOUNT If you do **piecework**, you are paid according to the amount of work that you do rather than the length of time that you work. ☐ *The tobacco workers were paid on a piecework basis.*

pie chart (pie charts) N-COUNT A **pie chart** is a circle divided into sections to show the relative proportions of a set of things.

pied-à-terre /pieɪd ɑ tɛər/ (pieds-à-terre) N-COUNT A **pied-à-terre** is a small house or apartment, especially in a town, which you own or rent but only use occasionally.

pier /pɪər/ (piers) N-COUNT A **pier** is a platform sticking out into water that people walk along or use when getting onto or off boats. ☐ *...Chicago's Navy Pier.*

pierce /pɪərs/ (pierces, piercing, pierced) **1** V-T If a sharp object **pierces** something, or if you **pierce** something with a sharp object, the object goes into it and makes a hole in it. ☐ *One bullet pierced the left side of his chest.* **2** V-T If you have your ears or some other part of your body **pierced**, you have a small hole made through them so that you can wear a piece of jewelry in them. ☐ *I'm having my ears pierced on Saturday.* • **pierc|ing** (piercings) N-VAR ☐ *...health risks from needles used in piercing and tattooing.* ☐ *...barefoot girls with braids and piercings.*

pierc|ing /pɪərsɪŋ/ **1** ADJ A **piercing** sound or voice is high-pitched and very sharp and clear in an unpleasant way. ☐ *A piercing scream split the air.* **2** ADJ If someone has **piercing** eyes or a **piercing** stare, they seem to look at you very intensely. [WRITTEN] ☐ *...his sandy blond hair and piercing blue eyes.* **3** ADJ A **piercing** wind makes you feel very cold. ☐ *Warm clothing is recommended as the wind can be piercing.* **4** → see **pierce 2**

pi|eties /paɪɪtiz/ N-PLURAL You refer to statements about what is morally right as **pieties** when you think they are insincere or unrealistic. [DISAPPROVAL] ☐ *...politicians who constantly intone pieties about respect for the rule of law.*

pi|ety /paɪɪti/ N-UNCOUNT **Piety** is strong religious belief, or behavior that is religious or morally correct. ☐ *Known for her piety, she would walk miles to attend communion services in the neighboring villages.*

pif|fle /pɪfᵊl/ N-UNCOUNT If you describe what someone says as **piffle**, you think that it is nonsense. [INFORMAL, DISAPPROVAL] ☐ *He talks such a load of piffle.*

pif|fling /pɪflɪŋ/ ADJ [usu ADJ n] If you describe something as **piffling**, you are critical of it because it is very small or unimportant. [INFORMAL, DISAPPROVAL] ☐ *...some piffling dispute regarding visiting rights.*

pig /pɪg/ (pigs, pigging, pigged) **1** N-COUNT A **pig** is a pink or black animal with short legs and not much hair on its skin. Pigs are often kept on farms for their meat, which is called pork, ham, or bacon. ☐ *...the grunting of the pigs.* **2** → see **guinea pig 3** N-COUNT If you call someone a **pig**, you think that they are unpleasant in some way, especially that they are greedy or unkind. [INFORMAL, DISAPPROVAL] ☐ *These guys destroyed the company. They're all a bunch of greedy pigs.* **4** PHRASE If you say **'when pigs fly'** after someone has said that something might happen, you are emphasizing that you think it is very

pigeon

unlikely. [HUMOROUS, INFORMAL, EMPHASIS] ☐ *When would he be hired again? Perhaps, as the saying goes, when pigs fly.* **5** PHRASE If you say that someone is **making a pig of** themselves, you are criticizing them for eating a very large amount at one meal. [INFORMAL, DISAPPROVAL] ☐ *I'm afraid I made a pig of myself at dinner.*
▶ **pig out** PHRASAL VERB If you say that people **are pigging out**, you are criticizing them for eating a very large amount at one meal or over a short period of time. [INFORMAL, DISAPPROVAL] ☐ *Some are so accustomed to pigging out, they can't cut back.*

pi|geon /pɪdʒɪn/ (pigeons) N-COUNT A **pigeon** is a bird, usually gray in color, that has a fat body. Pigeons often live in cities and towns.

pigeon|hole /pɪdʒɪnhoʊl/ (pigeonholes, pigeonholing, pigeonholed) also **pigeon-hole** **1** N-COUNT A **pigeonhole** is one of the sections in a frame on a wall where letters and messages can be left for someone, or one of the sections in a writing desk where you can keep documents. **2** V-T To **pigeonhole** someone or something means to decide that they belong to a particular class or category, often without considering all their qualities or characteristics. ☐ *He felt they had pigeonholed him.*

pigeon-toed ADJ Someone who is **pigeon-toed** walks with their toes pointing slightly inward.

pig|gy /pɪgi/ (piggies) **1** N-COUNT A **piggy** is a child's word for a pig or a piglet. **2** ADJ [ADJ n] If someone has **piggy** eyes, their eyes are small and unattractive.

piggy|back /pɪgibæk/ (piggybacks, piggybacking, piggybacked) **1** N-COUNT If you give someone a **piggyback**, you carry them high on your back, supporting them under their knees. ☐ *They give each other piggyback rides.* • ADV [ADV after v] **Piggyback** is also an adverb. ☐ *My father carried me up the hill, piggyback.* **2** V-I If you **piggyback on** something that someone else has thought of or done, you use it to your advantage. ☐ *I was just piggybacking on Stokes's idea.* ☐ *They are piggybacking onto developed technology.*

pig|gy bank (piggy banks) also **piggybank** N-COUNT A **piggy bank** is a small container shaped like a pig, with a narrow hole in the top through which to put coins. Children often use piggy banks to save money.

pig|headed /pɪghɛdɪd/ ADJ If you describe someone as **pigheaded**, you are critical of them because they refuse to change their mind about things, and you think they are unreasonable. [DISAPPROVAL] ☐ *She, in her pigheaded way, insists that she is right and that everyone else is wrong.* • **pig|headed|ness** /pɪghɛdɪdnɪs/ N-UNCOUNT ☐ *I am not sure whether this was courage or pigheadedness.*

pig|let /pɪglɪt/ (piglets) N-COUNT A **piglet** is a young pig.

pig|ment /pɪgmənt/ (pigments) N-MASS A **pigment** is a substance that gives something a particular color. [FORMAL] ☐ *The Romans used natural pigments on their fabrics and walls.*

pig|men|ta|tion /pɪgməənteɪʃ°n/ N-UNCOUNT The **pigmentation** of a person's or animal's skin is its natural coloring. [FORMAL] ☐ *I have a skin disorder, it destroys the pigmentation in my skin.*

pig|ment|ed /pɪgmɛntɪd/ ADJ **Pigmented** skin has a lot of natural coloring. [FORMAL]

pig|my /pɪgmi/ → see pygmy

pig|pen /pɪgpɛn/ (pigpens) also **pig pen** N-COUNT A **pigpen** is the same as a **pigsty**. [mainly AM]

pig|skin /pɪgskɪn/ N-UNCOUNT [oft N n] **Pigskin** is leather made from the skin of a pig.

pig|sty /pɪgstaɪ/ (pigsties) also **pig sty** **1** N-COUNT A **pigsty** is an enclosed place where pigs are kept on a farm. **2** N-COUNT [usu sing] If you describe a room or a house as a **pigsty**, you are criticizing the fact that it is very dirty and messy. [INFORMAL, DISAPPROVAL] ☐ *The office is a pigsty.*

pig|swill /pɪgswɪl/ N-UNCOUNT **1** **Pigswill** is waste food that is fed to pigs. **2** N-UNCOUNT If you describe food as **pigswill**, you are criticizing it because it is of very poor quality. [INFORMAL, DISAPPROVAL]

pig|tail /pɪgteɪl/ (pigtails) N-COUNT If someone has a **pigtail** or **pigtails**, their hair is braided into one or two lengths. ☐ *...a little girl with pigtails.*

piling

pike /paɪk/ (pike)

The plural can also be **pikes**.

N-VAR A **pike** is a large fish that lives in rivers and lakes and eats other fish. • N-UNCOUNT **Pike** is this fish eaten as food. ☐ *...a mousse of pike.*

pi|laf /pɪlɑf/ (pilafs) also **pilaff** N-MASS **Pilaf** is rice flavored with spices, often mixed with pieces of meat or fish.

pi|las|ter /pɪlæstər/ (pilasters) N-COUNT [usu pl] **Pilasters** are shallow decorative pillars attached to a wall.

Pi|la|tes /pɪlɑtiz/ N-UNCOUNT **Pilates** is a type of exercise similar to yoga. ☐ *She'd never done Pilates before.*

pi|lau /pɪlaʊ/ (pilaus) N-MASS **Pilau** or **pilau rice** is the same as **pilaf**.

pil|chard /pɪltʃərd/ (pilchards) N-COUNT **Pilchards** are small fish that live in the sea. Pilchards can be eaten as food.

pile ♦◇◇ /paɪl/ (piles, piling, piled) **1** N-COUNT A **pile of** things is a mass of them that is high in the middle and has sloping sides. ☐ *...a pile of sand.* ☐ *...a little pile of crumbs.* **2** N-COUNT A **pile of** things is a quantity of things that have been put neatly somewhere so that each thing is on top of the one below. ☐ *...a pile of boxes.* ☐ *We sat in Sam's study, among the piles of books.* **3** V-T If you **pile** things somewhere, you put them there so that they form a pile. ☐ *He was piling clothes into the suitcase.* **4** V-T [usu passive] If something is **piled with** things, it is covered or filled with piles of things. ☐ *Tables were piled high with local produce.* **5** V-I If a group of people **pile into** or **out of** a vehicle, they all get into it or out of it in a disorganized way. ☐ *They all piled into Jerry's car.* **6** N-COUNT **Piles** are wooden, concrete, or metal posts that are pushed into the ground and on which buildings or bridges are built. Piles are often used in very wet areas so that the buildings do not flood. ☐ *...settlements of wooden houses, set on piles along the shore* **7** N-PLURAL **Piles** is an informal word meaning **hemorrhoids**. **8** N-SING The **pile of** a carpet or of a fabric such as velvet is its soft surface. It consists of a lot of little threads standing on end. ☐ *...the carpet's thick pile.* **9** PHRASE Someone who is **at the bottom of the pile** is low down in society or low down in an organization. Someone who is **at the top of the pile** is high up in society or high up in an organization. [INFORMAL] ☐ *These workers are fed up with being at the bottom of the pile when it comes to pay.*
▶ **pile up** **1** PHRASAL VERB If you **pile up** a quantity of things or if they **pile up**, they gradually form a pile. ☐ *Bulldozers piled up huge mounds of dirt.* **2** PHRASAL VERB If you **pile up** work, problems, or losses or if they **pile up**, you get more and more of them. ☐ *Problems were piling up at work.*

---- SYNONYMS ----

pile
NOUN **1**
heap: *...a heap of bricks.*
stack: *There were stacks of books on the nightstand and floor.*
mound: *The bulldozers piled up huge mounds of dirt.*

---

pile|up /paɪlʌp/ (pileups)

in BRIT, use **pile-up**

N-COUNT A **pileup** is a road accident in which a lot of vehicles crash into each other. ☐ *...a 54-car pileup.*

pil|fer /pɪlfər/ (pilfers, pilfering, pilfered) V-T/V-I If someone **pilfers**, they steal things, usually small cheap things. ☐ *The staff were pilfering behind the bar.* ☐ *When food stores close, they go to work, pilfering food for resale on the black market.* • **pil|fer|ing** N-UNCOUNT ☐ *Precautions had to be taken to prevent pilfering.*

pil|grim /pɪlgrɪm/ (pilgrims) N-COUNT **Pilgrims** are people who journey to a holy place for a religious reason. ☐ *This is where pilgrims to the abbey would pay their first devotions.*

pil|grim|age /pɪlgrɪmɪdʒ/ (pilgrimages) **1** N-COUNT If you make a **pilgrimage** to a holy place, you go there for a religious reason. ☐ *...the pilgrimage to Mecca.* **2** N-COUNT A **pilgrimage** is a trip that someone makes to a place that is very important to them. ☐ *...a private pilgrimage to family graves.*

pil|ing /paɪlɪŋ/ (pilings) N-COUNT [usu pl] **Pilings** are wooden, concrete, or metal posts that are pushed into the ground and on which buildings or bridges are built. Pilings are often used in very wet areas so that the buildings do not flood. ❏ ...bridges set on stone pilings.

pill ✦◇◇ /pɪl/ (pills) **1** N-COUNT **Pills** are small solid round masses of medicine or vitamins that you swallow without chewing. ❏ Why do I have to take all these pills? **2** N-SING If a woman is on **the pill**, she takes a pill that prevents her from becoming pregnant. ❏ She had been on the pill for three years. **3** PHRASE If a person or group has to accept a failure or an unpleasant piece of news, you can say that it was **a bitter pill** or **a bitter pill to swallow**. ❏ You're too old to be given a job. That's a bitter pill to swallow. **4** PHRASE If someone does something to **sweeten the pill**, they do it to make some unpleasant news or an unpleasant measure more acceptable. ❏ A few words of praise help to sweeten the pill of criticism.

pil|lage /pɪlɪdʒ/ (pillages, pillaging, pillaged) V-T If a group of people **pillage** a place, they steal property from it using violent methods. ❏ Soldiers went on a rampage, pillaging stores and shooting. • N-UNCOUNT **Pillage** is also a noun. ❏ There were no signs of violence or pillage. • **pil|lag|ing** N-UNCOUNT ❏ ...pillaging by people looking for something to eat.

pil|lar /pɪlər/ (pillars) **1** N-COUNT A **pillar** is a tall solid structure that is usually used to support part of a building. ❏ ...the pillars supporting the roof. **2** N-COUNT If something is the **pillar** of a system or agreement, it is the most important part of it or what makes it strong and successful. ❏ The pillar of her economic policy was keeping tight control over money supply. **3** N-COUNT If you describe someone as a **pillar** of society or as a **pillar** of the community, you approve of them because they play an important and active part in society or in the community. [APPROVAL] ❏ My father is a pillar of the community.

pil|lared /pɪlərd/ ADJ [usu ADJ n] A **pillared** building is a building that is supported by pillars.

pill|box /pɪlbɒks/ (pillboxes) also **pill box 1** N-COUNT A **pillbox** is a small box in which you can keep pills. **2** N-COUNT A **pillbox** is a small building made of concrete that is used to defend a place. **3** N-COUNT A **pillbox** or a **pillbox hat** is a small round hat for a woman.

pil|lion /pɪlyən/ (pillions) N-COUNT [oft N n] On a motorcycle, the **pillion** is the seat or part behind the rider. ❏ You must not carry a pillion passenger.

pil|lo|ry /pɪləri/ (pillories, pillorying, pilloried) V-T [usu passive] If someone is **pilloried**, a lot of people, especially journalists, criticize them and make them look stupid. ❏ A man has been forced to resign as a result of being pilloried by some of the press.

pil|low /pɪloʊ/ (pillows) N-COUNT A **pillow** is a rectangular cushion that you rest your head on when you are in bed.

pillow|case /pɪloʊkeɪs/ (pillowcases) also **pillow case** N-COUNT A **pillowcase** is a cover for a pillow that can be removed and washed.

pil|low talk N-UNCOUNT Conversations that people have when they are in bed together can be referred to as **pillow talk**, especially when they are about secret or private subjects.

pi|lot ✦◇◇ /paɪlət/ (pilots, piloting, piloted) **1** N-COUNT A **pilot** is a person who is trained to fly an aircraft. ❏ He spent seventeen years as an airline pilot. **2** N-COUNT A **pilot** is a person who steers a ship through a difficult stretch of water, for example, the entrance to a harbor. ❏ It seemed that the pilot had another ship to take up the river that evening. **3** V-T If someone **pilots** an aircraft or ship, they act as its pilot. ❏ He piloted his own plane part of the way to Washington. **4** ADJ A **pilot** plan or a **pilot** project is one that is used to test an idea before deciding whether to introduce it on a larger scale. ❏ The plan is to launch a pilot program next summer. **5** V-T If a government or organization **pilots** a program or project, they test it, before deciding whether to introduce it on a larger scale. ❏ Teachers are piloting a literature-based reading program.

pi|lot light (pilot lights) N-COUNT A **pilot light** is a small gas flame in a gas stove, furnace, or water heater. It burns all the time and lights the main large flame when the gas is turned fully on.

pi|men|to /pɪmɛntoʊ/ (pimentos) also **pimiento** N-VAR A **pimento** is a red pepper with thick flesh.

pimp /pɪmp/ (pimps, pimping, pimped) **1** N-COUNT A **pimp** is someone who gets clients for prostitutes and takes some of the money the prostitutes earn. **2** V-I Someone who **pimps** gets clients for prostitutes and takes some of the money the prostitutes earn. ❏ He stole, lied, deceived, and pimped his way out of poverty.

pim|per|nel /pɪmpərnɛl/ (pimpernels) N-VAR A **pimpernel** is a small wild plant that usually has red flowers.

pim|ple /pɪmp³l/ (pimples) N-COUNT **Pimples** are small raised spots, especially on the face. ❏ My brother's face was covered with pimples.

pim|ply /pɪmpli/ ADJ If someone is **pimply** or has a **pimply** face, they have a lot of pimples on their face. ❏ ...pimply teenagers. ❏ ...an old man with a pimply nose.

pin ✦◇◇ /pɪn/ (pins, pinning, pinned) **1** N-COUNT **Pins** are very small thin pointed pieces of metal. They are used in sewing to fasten pieces of material together until they have been sewn. ❏ ...a box of needles and pins. **2** V-T If you **pin** something on or to something, you attach it with a pin, a safety pin or a thumbtack. ❏ They pinned a notice to the door. ❏ Everyone was supposed to dance with the bride and pin money on her dress. **3** V-T If someone **pins** you to something, they press you against a surface so that you cannot move. ❏ I pinned him against the wall. ❏ I'd try to get away and he'd pin me down, saying he would kill me. **4** N-COUNT A **pin** is any long narrow piece of metal or wood that is not sharp, especially one that is used to fasten two things together. ❏ ...the 18-inch steel pin holding his left leg together. **5** V-T If someone tries to **pin** something **on** you or to **pin the blame on** you, they say, often unfairly, that you were responsible for something bad or illegal. ❏ They're trying to pin it on us. **6** V-T If you **pin** your hopes **on** something or **pin** your faith **on** something, you hope very much that it will produce the result you want. ❏ The Democrats are pinning their hopes on the next election. **7** N-COUNT A **pin** is something worn on your clothing, for example, as jewelry, which is fastened with a pointed piece of metal. [AM] ❏ ...necklaces, bracelets, and pins. **8** → see also **safety pin**
▶ **pin down 1** PHRASAL VERB If you try to **pin** something **down**, you try to discover exactly what, where, or when it is. ❏ It has taken until now to pin down its exact location. ❏ I can only pin it down to between 1936 and 1942. **2** PHRASAL VERB If you **pin** someone **down**, you force them to make a decision or to tell you what their decision is, when they have been trying to avoid doing this. ❏ She couldn't pin him down to a date.

PIN /pɪn/ N-SING [oft N n] Someone's **PIN** or **PIN number** is a secret number that they can use, for example, with a bank card to withdraw money from a cash machine or ATM. **PIN** is an abbreviation for 'personal identification number.' ❏ To use the service you'll need a PIN number.

pina co|la|da /piːnyə kəlɑːdə/ (pina coladas) N-COUNT A **pina colada** is a drink made from rum, coconut milk, and pineapple juice.

pina|fore /pɪnəfɔr/ (pinafores) N-COUNT A **pinafore** is a sleeveless dress. It is worn over a blouse or sweater.

pin|ball /pɪnbɔl/ N-UNCOUNT **Pinball** is a game in which a player presses two buttons on each side of a pinball machine in order to hit a small ball to the top of the machine. The aim of the game is to prevent the ball from rolling out of the bottom of the machine by pressing the buttons.

pin|ball ma|chine (pinball machines) N-COUNT A **pinball machine** is a machine on which pinball is played. It consists of a sloping table with objects that a ball hits as it rolls down.

pince-nez /pæns neɪ, -neɪz/ N-PLURAL [also a N] **Pince-nez** are old-fashioned glasses that consist of two lenses that fit tightly onto the top of your nose and do not have parts that rest on your ears.

pin|cer /pɪnsər/ (pincers) **1** N-PLURAL [also a pair of N] **Pincers** consist of two pieces of metal that are hinged in the middle. They are used as a tool for gripping things or for pulling things out. ❏ His surgical instruments were a knife and a pair of pincers. **2** N-COUNT The **pincers** of an animal such as a crab or a lobster are its front claws.

pin|cer move|ment (pincer movements) N-COUNT A **pincer movement** is an attack by an army or other group in which they attack their enemies in two places at once with the aim of surrounding them. ❏ They are moving in a pincer movement to cut the republic in two.

pinch /pɪntʃ/ (pinches, pinching, pinched) **1** V-T If you **pinch** a part of someone's body, you take a piece of their skin between your thumb and first finger and give it a short squeeze. ❑ *She pinched his arm as hard as she could.* • N-COUNT **Pinch** is also a noun. ❑ *She gave him a little pinch.* **2** N-COUNT A **pinch of** an ingredient such as salt is the amount of it that you can hold between your thumb and your first finger. ❑ *Put all the ingredients, including a pinch of salt, into a food processor.* **3** V-T To **pinch** something, especially something of little value, means to steal it. [INFORMAL] ❑ *Do you remember when I pinched your glasses?* **4** PHRASE If a person or company **is feeling the pinch**, they do not have as much money as they used to, and so they cannot buy the things they would like to buy. ❑ *Consumers are spending less and merchants are feeling the pinch.*

pinched /pɪntʃt/ ADJ If someone's face is **pinched**, it looks thin and pale, usually because they are ill or old. ❑ *Her face was pinched and drawn.*

pinch-hit (pinch-hits, pinch-hitting, pinch-hit) **1** V-I If you **pinch-hit** for someone, you do something for them because they are unexpectedly unable to do it. [AM] ❑ *The staff here can pinch-hit for each other when the hotel is busy.* **2** V-I In a game of baseball, if you **pinch-hit** for another player, you hit the ball instead of them. [AM] ❑ *Davalillo goes up to pinch-hit.* • **pinch-hitter** (pinch-hitters) N-COUNT ❑ *Pinch-hitter Francisco Cabrera lashed a single to left field.*

pin|cushion /pɪnkʊʃ°n/ (pincushions) N-COUNT A **pincushion** is a very small cushion that you stick pins and needles into so that you can get them easily when you need them.

pine /paɪn/ (pines, pining, pined) **1** N-VAR A **pine tree** or a **pine** is a tall tree that has very thin, sharp leaves called needles and a fresh smell. Pine trees have leaves all year round. ❑ *...high mountains covered in pine trees.* • N-UNCOUNT **Pine** is the wood of this tree. ❑ *...a big pine table.* **2** V-I If you **pine for** someone who has died or gone away, you want them to be with you very much and feel sad because they are not there. ❑ *She'd be sitting at home pining for her lost husband.* **3** V-I If you **pine for** something, you want it very much, especially when it is unlikely that you will be able to have it. ❑ *I pine for the countryside.*

pine|apple /paɪnæp°l/ (pineapples) N-VAR A **pineapple** is a large oval fruit that grows in hot countries. It is sweet, juicy, and yellow inside. It has a thick brownish skin.

pine cone (pine cones) N-COUNT A **pine cone** is one of the brown oval seed cases produced by a pine tree.

pine nee|dle (pine needles) N-COUNT [usu pl] **Pine needles** are very thin, sharp leaves that grow on pine trees.

pine nut (pine nuts) N-COUNT [usu pl] **Pine nuts** are small cream-colored seeds that grow on certain pine trees. They can be used in salads and other dishes.

pine|wood /paɪnwʊd/ (pinewoods)

> The spelling **pine wood** is also used for meaning **1**.

1 N-COUNT A **pinewood** is a forest that consists mainly of pine trees. ❑ *...the hilly pinewoods of northeast Georgia.* **2** N-UNCOUNT [usu N n] **Pinewood** is wood that has come from a pine tree. ❑ *...Italian pinewood furniture.*

ping /pɪŋ/ (pings, pinging, pinged) V-I If a bell or a piece of metal **pings**, it makes a short, high-pitched noise. ❑ *The elevator bell pinged at the fourth floor.* • N-COUNT **Ping** is also a noun. ❑ *...a metallic ping.*

Ping-Pong N-UNCOUNT **Ping-Pong** is the game of **table tennis**. [TRADEMARK]

pin|head /pɪnhɛd/ (pinheads) N-COUNT A **pinhead** is the small metal or plastic part on the top of a pin. ❑ *It may even be possible to make computers the size of a pinhead one day.*

pin|hole /pɪnhoʊl/ (pinholes) N-COUNT A **pinhole** is a tiny hole.

pin|ion /pɪnyən/ (pinions, pinioning, pinioned) V-T If you are **pinioned**, someone prevents you from moving or escaping, especially by holding or tying your arms. ❑ *His wrists were pinioned tightly behind his back.*

pink ◆◇◇ /pɪŋk/ (pinks, pinker, pinkest) **1** COLOR **Pink** is the color between red and white. ❑ *...pink lipstick.* ❑ *...white flowers edged in pink.* **2** ADJ **Pink** is used to refer to things relating to or connected with gay people. [BRIT]

pinkie /pɪŋki/ (pinkies) also **pinky** N-COUNT Your **pinkie** is the smallest finger on your hand. [INFORMAL] ❑ *He pushes his glasses up his nose with his pinkie.*

pinko /pɪŋkoʊ/ (pinkos or pinkoes) N-COUNT If you call someone a **pinko**, you mean that they have left-wing views. [INFORMAL, DISAPPROVAL]

pink slip (pink slips) N-COUNT If employees are given their **pink slips**, they are informed that they are no longer needed to do the job that they have been doing. [AM, INFORMAL] ❑ *It was his fourth pink slip in two years.* ❑ *Eastern Airlines shut down operations at midnight, and 18,000 employees were given their pink slips.*

pinky /pɪŋki/ → see **pinkie**

pin mon|ey N-UNCOUNT **Pin money** is small amounts of extra money that someone earns or gets in order to buy things that they want but that they do not really need. [INFORMAL] ❑ *She built it into a little business to earn pin money.*

pin|na|cle /pɪnək°l/ (pinnacles) **1** N-COUNT A **pinnacle** is a pointed piece of stone or rock that is high above the ground. ❑ *A walker broke his arms, legs, and pelvis yesterday when he plunged 80 feet from a rocky pinnacle.* **2** N-COUNT If someone reaches the **pinnacle of** their career or the **pinnacle of** a particular area of life, they are at the highest point of it. ❑ *She was still at the pinnacle of her career.*

pin|point /pɪnpɔɪnt/ (pinpoints, pinpointing, pinpointed) **1** V-T If you **pinpoint** the cause of something, you discover or explain the cause exactly. ❑ *It was almost impossible to pinpoint the cause of death.* ❑ *...if you can pinpoint exactly what the anger is about.* **2** V-T If you **pinpoint** something or its position, you discover or show exactly where it is. ❑ *I could pinpoint his precise location on a map.*

pin|prick /pɪnprɪk/ (pinpricks) N-COUNT [with supp] A very small spot of something can be described as a **pinprick**. ❑ *...a pinprick of light.*

pins and nee|dles N-UNCOUNT If you have **pins and needles** in part of your body, you feel small sharp pains there for a short period of time. It usually happens when that part of your body has been in an uncomfortable position. ❑ *I had pins and needles in the tips of my fingers.*

pin|stripe /pɪnstraɪp/ (pinstripes) also **pin-stripe** N-COUNT **Pinstripes** are very narrow vertical stripes found on certain types of clothing. Businessmen's suits often have pinstripes. ❑ *He wore an expensive, dark blue pinstripe suit.*

pin|striped /pɪnstraɪpt/ ADJ [usu ADJ n] A **pinstriped** suit is made of cloth that has very narrow vertical stripes.

pint /paɪnt/ (pints) N-COUNT A **pint** is a unit of measurement for liquids. It is equal to 473 cubic centimeters or one eighth of a gallon. ❑ *...a pint of ice cream.*

pin|to bean /pɪntoʊ bin/ (pinto beans) N-COUNT [usu pl] **Pinto beans** are a type of bean, similar to kidney beans, that are eaten as a vegetable. ❑ *My two sons share a favorite food – pinto beans.*

pint-sized ADJ [usu ADJ n] If you describe someone or something as **pint-sized**, you think they are smaller than is normal or smaller than they should be. [INFORMAL] ❑ *Two pint-sized kids emerged from a doorway.*

pin-up (pin-ups) also **pinup** N-COUNT A **pin-up** is an attractive man or woman who appears on posters, often wearing very few clothes. ❑ *...pin-up boys.*

pio|neer /paɪənɪər/ (pioneers, pioneering, pioneered) **1** N-COUNT Someone who is referred to as a **pioneer** in a particular area of activity is one of the first people to be involved in it and develop it. ❑ *...one of the leading pioneers of photojournalism.* **2** V-T Someone who **pioneers** a new activity, invention, or process is one of the first people to do it. ❑ *...Professor Alec Jeffreys, who invented and pioneered DNA tests.* **3** N-COUNT **Pioneers** are people who leave their own country or the place where they were living, and go and live in a place that has not been lived in before. ❑ *...abandoned settlements of early European pioneers.*

pio|neer|ing /paɪənɪərɪŋ/ ADJ **Pioneering** work or a **pioneering** individual does something that has not been done before, for example, by developing or using new methods or

pi|ous /paɪəs/ ADJ Someone who is **pious** is very religious and moral. ❑ *He was brought up by pious female relatives.* • **pi|ous|ly** ADV [ADV with v] ❑ *Conti kneeled and crossed himself piously.*

pipe ✦✧ /paɪp/ (**pipes**, **piping**, **piped**) **1** N-COUNT A **pipe** is a long, round, hollow object, usually made of metal or plastic, through which a liquid or gas can flow. ❑ *The liquid can't escape into the air, because it's inside a pipe.* **2** N-COUNT A **pipe** is an object that is used for smoking tobacco. You put the tobacco into the cup-shaped part at the end of the pipe, light it, and breathe in the smoke through a narrow tube. ❑ *Do you smoke a pipe?* **3** N-COUNT A **pipe** is a simple musical instrument in the shape of a tube with holes in it. You play a pipe by blowing into it while covering and uncovering the holes with your fingers. **4** N-COUNT An **organ pipe** is one of the long hollow tubes in which air vibrates and produces a musical note. **5** V-T If liquid or gas **is piped** somewhere, it is transferred from one place to another through a pipe. ❑ *The heated gas is piped through a coil surrounded by water.* ❑ *The Communists brought electricity to his village and piped in drinking water from the reservoir.* **6** → see also **piping**

COLLOCATIONS

pipe
NOUN **1**
noun + **pipe**: drainage, exhaust, overflow, sewage; gas, water; concrete, copper, lead, metal
adjective + **pipe**: burst, leaking
verb + **pipe**: lay, repair, replace

pipe bomb (**pipe bombs**) N-COUNT A **pipe bomb** is a small bomb in a narrow tube made by someone such as a terrorist.

pipe clean|er (**pipe cleaners**) N-COUNT A **pipe cleaner** is a piece of wire covered with a soft substance that is used to clean a tobacco pipe.

pipe dream (**pipe dreams**) N-COUNT A **pipe dream** is a hope or plan that you know will never really happen. ❑ *You could waste your whole life on a pipe dream.*

pipe|line /paɪplaɪn/ (**pipelines**) **1** N-COUNT A **pipeline** is a large pipe that is used for carrying oil or gas over a long distance, often underground. ❑ *A consortium plans to build a natural-gas pipeline from Russia to supply eastern Germany.* **2** PHRASE If something is **in the pipeline**, it has already been planned or begun. ❑ *Already in the pipeline is a 2.9 percent pay increase for teachers.*

pipe or|gan (**pipe organs**) N-COUNT A **pipe organ** is a large musical instrument with pipes of different lengths through which air is forced. It has keys and pedals like a piano.

pip|er /paɪpər/ (**pipers**) **1** N-COUNT A **piper** is a musician who plays the bagpipes. **2** PHRASE If you say '**He who pays the piper**' or '**He who pays the piper calls the tune,**' you mean that the person who provides the money for something decides what will be done, or has a right to decide what will be done.

pipe|work /paɪpwɜrk/ N-UNCOUNT **Pipework** consists of the pipes that are part of a machine, building, or structure. ❑ *The stainless steel pipework has been constructed, tested, and inspected to very high standards.*

pip|ing /paɪpɪŋ/ N-UNCOUNT **Piping** is metal, plastic, or another substance made in the shape of a pipe or tube. ❑ *...rolls of bright yellow plastic piping.*

pip|ing hot also **piping-hot** ADJ Food or water that is **piping hot** is very hot. ❑ *...large cups of piping-hot coffee.*

pi|quant /piːkənt, -kɑːnt, piːkɑːnt/ **1** ADJ Food that is **piquant** has a pleasantly spicy taste. [WRITTEN] ❑ *...a crisp mixed salad with an unusually piquant dressing.* • **pi|quan|cy** /piːkənsi/ N-UNCOUNT ❑ *A little mustard is served on the side to add further piquancy.* **2** ADJ Something that is **piquant** is interesting and exciting. [WRITTEN] ❑ *There may well have been a piquant novelty about her books when they came out.* • **pi|quan|cy** N-UNCOUNT ❑ *Sexual detail added piquancy to the story.*

pique /piːk/ (**piques**, **piquing**, **piqued**) **1** N-UNCOUNT **Pique** is the feeling of annoyance you have when you think someone has not treated you properly. ❑ *Mimi had gotten over her pique at Susan's refusal to accept the job.* **2** V-T If something **piques** your interest or curiosity, it makes you interested or curious. ❑ *This phenomenon piqued Dr. Morris' interest.* **3** PHRASE If someone does something **in a fit of pique**, they do it suddenly because they are annoyed at being not treated properly. ❑ *Lawrence, in a fit of pique, left the Army and took up a career in accounting.*

piqued /piːkt/ ADJ [usu v-link ADJ] If someone is **piqued**, they are offended or annoyed, often by something that is not very important. ❑ *Granny was astounded and a little piqued, I think, because it had all been arranged without her knowledge.* ❑ *She wrinkled her nose, piqued by his total lack of enthusiasm.*

pi|ra|cy /paɪrəsi/ **1** N-UNCOUNT **Piracy** is robbery at sea carried out by pirates. ❑ *Seven of the fishermen have been formally charged with piracy.* **2** N-UNCOUNT You can refer to the illegal copying of things such as DVDs and computer programs as **piracy**. ❑ *...protection against piracy of books, films, and other intellectual property.*

pi|ra|nha /pɪrɑːnə/ (**piranhas** or **piranha**) N-COUNT A **piranha** is a small, fierce fish of South America that sometimes attacks people or animals in the water.

pi|rate /paɪrɪt/ (**pirates**, **pirating**, **pirated**) **1** N-COUNT **Pirates** are sailors who attack other ships and steal property from them. ❑ *In the nineteenth century, pirates roamed the seas.* **2** V-T Someone who **pirates** CDs, DVDs, books, or computer programs copies and sells them when they have no right to do so. ❑ *Computer crimes include data theft and pirating software.* • **pi|rat|ed** ADJ ❑ *New technology makes it possible to make pirated copies of music and movies.* **3** ADJ [ADJ n] A **pirate** version of something is an illegal copy of it. ❑ *Pirate copies of the DVD are already being sold.*

pirou|ette /pɪruːet/ (**pirouettes**, **pirouetting**, **pirouetted**) **1** N-COUNT A **pirouette** is a movement in ballet dancing. The dancer stands on one foot and spins their body around fast. **2** V-I If someone **pirouettes**, they perform one or more pirouettes. ❑ *She pirouetted in front of the glass.*

Pi|sces /paɪsiːz/ **1** N-UNCOUNT **Pisces** is one of the twelve signs of the zodiac. Its symbol is two fish. People who are born approximately between the 19th of February and the 20th of March come under this sign. **2** N-SING [a N] A **Pisces** is a person whose sign of the zodiac is Pisces.

piss /pɪs/ (**pisses**, **pissing**, **pissed**) V-I To **piss** means to urinate. [INFORMAL, VULGAR] ❑ *A man pissed against a wall.*
▶ **piss off 1** PHRASAL VERB If someone or something **pisses** you **off**, they annoy you. [INFORMAL, VULGAR] ❑ *It pisses me off when they start moaning about going to war.* • **pissed off** ADJ ❑ *I was really pissed off.* **2** PHRASAL VERB If someone tells a person to **piss off**, they are telling the person in a rude way to go away. [INFORMAL, VULGAR]

pissed /pɪst/ ADJ [v-link ADJ] If you say that someone is **pissed**, you mean that they are annoyed. [AM, INFORMAL, VULGAR] ❑ *You know Molly's pissed at you.*

pis|ta|chio /pɪstæʃioʊ/ (**pistachios**) N-VAR **Pistachios** or **pistachio nuts** are small, green, edible nuts.

piste /piːst/ (**pistes**) N-COUNT A **piste** is a track of firm snow for skiing on. ❑ *...confident skiers who want to move off the piste.*

pis|til /pɪstɪl/ (**pistils**) **1** N-COUNT The **pistil** of a flower relates to the part in the middle which produces the seeds. [TECHNICAL] **2** → See also color supplement

pis|tol /pɪstəl/ (**pistols**) N-COUNT A **pistol** is a small gun.

pistol-whip (**pistol-whips**, **pistol-whipping**, **pistol-whipped**) V-T If someone **pistol-whips** another person, they hit them or beat them with the barrel of a handgun. [mainly AM] ❑ *Three of the victims were pistol-whipped and two were shot.* ❑ *He allegedly pistol-whipped a man he saw kissing his wife.*

pis|ton /pɪstən/ (**pistons**) N-COUNT A **piston** is a cylinder or metal disk that is part of an engine. Pistons slide up and down inside tubes and cause various parts of the engine to move.

pit ✦✧ /pɪt/ (**pits**, **pitting**, **pitted**) **1** N-COUNT A **pit** is the underground part of a mine, especially a coal mine. **2** N-COUNT A **gravel pit** or **clay pit** is a very large hole that is left where gravel or clay has been dug from the ground. ❑ *This area of former farmland was worked as a gravel pit until 1964.* **3** V-T [usu passive] If two opposing things or people **are pitted against** one another, they are in conflict. ❑ *You will be pitted*

pita

against two, three, or four people who are every bit as good as you are. ◨ N-COUNT A **pit** is a large hole that is dug in the ground. ❑ *Eric lost his footing and began to slide into the pit.* ◨ N-PLURAL In auto racing, the **pits** are the areas at the side of the track where drivers stop to get more fuel and to repair their cars during races. ❑ *He moved quickly into the pits and climbed rapidly out of the car.* ◨ N-COUNT A **pit** is the large hard seed of a fruit or vegetable. [AM] ❑ *...cherry pits.* ◨ → see also **orchestra pit, pitted** ◨ PHRASE If you **pit** your **wits against** someone, you compete with them in a test of knowledge or intelligence. ❑ *I'd like to manage at the very highest level and pit my wits against the best.* ◨ PHRASE If you have a feeling **in the pit of** your **stomach**, you have a tight or sick feeling in your stomach, usually because you are afraid or anxious. ❑ *I had a funny feeling in the pit of my stomach.* ◨ → See feature box at **cooking**

pita /piːtə/ (**pitas**) N-VAR **Pita** or **pita bread** is a type of bread in the shape of a flat oval. It can be split open and filled with food such as meat and vegetables. ❑ *...a wholesome filling for a whole-wheat pita.*

pit bull ter|ri|er (**pit bull terriers**) N-COUNT A **pit bull terrier** or a **pit bull** is a very fierce kind of dog. Some people train pit bull terriers to fight other dogs.

pitch ✦✧✧ /pɪtʃ/ (**pitches, pitching, pitched**) ◨ V-T If you **pitch** something somewhere, you throw it with some force, usually aiming it carefully. ❑ *Simon pitched the empty bottle into the lake.* ◨ V-T In the game of baseball, when you **pitch** the ball, you throw it to the batter for them to hit it. ❑ *We passed long, hot afternoons pitching a baseball.* ◨ V-T/V-I To **pitch** somewhere means to fall forward suddenly and with a lot of force. ❑ *The movement took him by surprise, and he pitched forward.* ❑ *Alan staggered sideways, pitched head-first over the low wall and fell into the lake.* ◨ V-T If someone **is pitched into** a new situation, they are suddenly forced into it. ❑ *They were being pitched into a new adventure in which they would have to fight the whole world.* ◨ N-UNCOUNT The **pitch** of a sound is how high or low it is. ❑ *He raised his voice to an even higher pitch.* ◨ V-T [usu passive] If a sound **is pitched at** a particular level, it is produced at the level indicated. ❑ *His cry is pitched at a level that makes it impossible to ignore.* ❑ *His voice was pitched high, the words muffled by his crying.* ◨ → see also **high-pitched** ◨ V-T If something **is pitched** at a particular level or degree of difficulty, it is set at that level. ❑ *While this is very important material I think it's probably pitched at too high a level for our students.* ◨ N-SING If something such as a feeling or a situation rises to a high **pitch**, it rises to a high level. ❑ *The public's feelings were at a high pitch of indignation.* ◨ V-T If someone **pitches** an idea for something such as a new product, they try to persuade people to accept the idea. ❑ *My agent has pitched the idea to my editor in New York.* ◨ N-COUNT A **pitch** is an area of ground that is marked out and used for playing a game such as soccer, cricket, or hockey. [BRIT]

in AM, use **field**

◨ PHRASE If someone **makes a pitch** for something, they try to persuade people to do or buy it. ❑ *The president speaks in New York today, making another pitch for his economic program.* ◨ → see also **sales pitch**

▶ **pitch for** PHRASAL VERB If someone is **pitching for** something, they are trying to persuade other people to give it to them. ❑ *It was middle-class votes they were pitching for.*

▶ **pitch in** PHRASAL VERB If you **pitch in**, you join in and help with an activity. [INFORMAL] ❑ *The agency says international relief agencies also have pitched in.*

SYNONYMS

pitch
NOUN ◨
ground: *...the city's sports ground.*
arena: *...the largest indoor sports arena in the world.*
field: *...a football field.*
stadium: *...a baseball stadium.*

---

pitch-black ADJ If a place or the night is **pitch-black**, it is completely dark. ❑ *...a cold pitch-black winter morning.*

pitch-dark also **pitch dark** ADJ **Pitch-dark** means the same as **pitch-black**.

pitched /pɪtʃt/ ◨ ADJ A **pitched** roof is one that slopes as opposed to one that is flat. ❑ *...a rather quaint lodge with a steeply-pitched roof.* ◨ → see also **high-pitched, low-pitched**

pity

pitched bat|tle (**pitched battles**) N-COUNT A **pitched battle** is a very fierce and violent fight involving a large number of people. ❑ *Pitched battles were fought with the police.*

pitch|er /pɪtʃər/ (**pitchers**) ◨ N-COUNT A **pitcher** is a cylindrical container with a handle and is used for holding and pouring liquids. [mainly AM] ❑ *My sister fetched a pitcher of iced water.* ◨ N-COUNT In baseball, the **pitcher** is the person who throws the ball to the batter, who tries to hit it.

pitch|fork /pɪtʃfɔːrk/ (**pitchforks**) N-COUNT A **pitchfork** is a tool with a long handle and three or four pointed parts that is used on a farm for lifting hay or cut grass.

pit|eous /pɪtiəs/ ADJ Something that is **piteous** is so sad that you feel great pity for the person involved. [WRITTEN] ❑ *As they pass by, a piteous wailing is heard.*

pit|fall /pɪtfɔːl/ (**pitfalls**) N-COUNT The **pitfalls** involved in a particular activity or situation are the things that may go wrong or may cause problems. ❑ *The pitfalls of working abroad are numerous.*

pith /pɪθ/ N-UNCOUNT [usu the N] The **pith** of an orange, lemon, or similar fruit is the white substance between the skin and the inside of the fruit.

pithy /pɪθi/ (**pithier, pithiest**) ADJ [usu ADJ n] A **pithy** comment or piece of writing is short, direct, and full of meaning. [WRITTEN] ❑ *His pithy advice to young painters was, "Above all, keep your colors fresh."* ❑ *Many of them made a point of praising the film's pithy dialogue.* ● **pith|i|ly** ADV ❑ *Louis Armstrong defined jazz pithily as "what I play for a living."*

piti|able /pɪtiəbəl/ ADJ Someone who is **pitiable** is in such a sad or weak state that you feel pity for them. [WRITTEN] ❑ *Her grandmother seemed to her a pitiable figure.* ● **piti|ably** /pɪtiəbli/ ADV [ADV with v, ADV adj] ❑ *...pitiably low pay.* ❑ *She found Irene lying on the bed crying pitiably.*

piti|ful /pɪtɪfəl/ ◨ ADJ Someone or something that is **pitiful** is so sad, weak, or small that you feel pity for them. ❑ *He sounded both pitiful and eager to get what he wanted.* ● **piti|ful|ly** ADV ❑ *His legs were pitifully thin compared to the rest of his bulk.* ◨ ADJ If you describe something as **pitiful**, you mean that it is completely inadequate. [DISAPPROVAL] ❑ *The choice is pitiful and the quality of some of the products is very low.* ● **piti|ful|ly** ADV ❑ *Clearly that constitutes a pitifully inadequate return on my investment.*

piti|less /pɪtɪlɪs/ ADJ Someone or something that is **pitiless** shows no pity or kindness. [LITERARY] ❑ *He saw the pitiless eyes of his enemy.* ● **piti|less|ly** ADV ❑ *She had scorned him pitilessly.*

pit|man /pɪtmən/ (**pitmen**) N-COUNT [usu pl] A **pitman** is a coal miner. ❑ *Many of the older pitmen may never work again.*

pit stop (**pit stops**) ◨ N-COUNT In auto racing, if a driver makes a **pit stop**, he or she stops in a special place at the side of the track to get more fuel and to make repairs. ❑ *He had to make four pit stops during the race.* ◨ N-COUNT If someone makes a **pit stop** during a trip, they stop somewhere for a short time, for example, in order to go to the bathroom or to eat or drink something. [INFORMAL] ❑ *There's a rest area partway up the mountain; we could make a pit stop there.* ❑ *I could use a pit stop.*

pit|tance /pɪtəns/ (**pittances**) N-COUNT [usu sing] If you say that you **receive** a **pittance**, you are emphasizing that you get only a very small amount of money, probably not as much as you think you deserve. [EMPHASIS] ❑ *Her secretaries work tirelessly for a pittance.*

pit|ted /pɪtɪd/ ◨ ADJ [ADJ n] **Pitted** fruits have had their pits removed. ❑ *...green and black pitted olives.* ◨ ADJ If the surface of something is **pitted**, it is covered with a lot of small, shallow holes. ❑ *Everywhere building facades are pitted with shell and bullet holes.*

pi|tui|tary gland /pɪtjuːɪteri glænd/ (**pituitary glands**) N-COUNT [usu sing] The **pituitary gland** or the **pituitary** is a gland that is attached to the base of the brain. It produces hormones that affect growth, sexual development, and other functions of the body. [TECHNICAL]

pity /pɪti/ (**pities, pitying, pitied**) ◨ N-UNCOUNT If you feel **pity** for someone, you feel very sorry for them. ❑ *He felt a sudden tender pity for her.* ◨ → see also **self-pity** ◨ V-T If you **pity** someone, you feel very sorry for them. ❑ *I don't know whether to hate or pity him.* ◨ N-SING If you say that it is **a pity** that something is the case, you mean that you feel disappointment or regret about it. [FEELINGS] ❑ *It is a great pity that all students in the city cannot have the same chances.* ❑ *It's a pity you've arrived so* late in the year. **5** N-UNCOUNT If someone shows **pity**, they do not harm or punish someone they have power over. ❑ *Noncommunist forces have some pity toward people here.* **6** PHRASE If you **take pity on** someone, you feel sorry for them and help them. ❑ *No woman had ever felt the need to take pity on him before.*

pity|ing /pɪtiɪŋ/ ADJ [usu ADJ n] A **pitying** look shows that someone feels pity and perhaps slight contempt. ❑ *She gave him a pitying look; that was the sort of excuse her father would use.*
• **pity|ing|ly** ADV [ADV after v] ❑ *Stasik looked at him pityingly and said nothing.*

piv|ot /pɪvət/ (pivots, pivoting, pivoted) **1** N-COUNT The **pivot** in a situation is the most important thing that everything else is based on or arranged around. ❑ *Forming the pivot of the exhibition is a large group of watercolors.* **2** V-I If something or someone **pivots**, they balance or turn on a central point. ❑ *The wheels pivot for easy maneuvering.* ❑ *He pivoted on his heels and walked on down the hall.* **3** N-COUNT A **pivot** is the pin or the central point on which something balances or turns. ❑ *The pedal had sheared off at the pivot.*

piv|ot|al /pɪvətəl/ ADJ A **pivotal** role, point, or figure in something is one that is very important and affects the success of that thing. ❑ *The elections may prove to be pivotal in Colombia's political history.*

pix /pɪks/ N-PLURAL **Pix** is an informal way of spelling **pics**, meaning 'photographs' or 'movies.' ❑ *...splendid pix by ace photographer Mike Goldwater.*

pix|el /pɪksəl/ (pixels) N-COUNT A **pixel** is the smallest area on a computer screen that can be given a separate color by the computer. [COMPUTING] ❑ *...a display screen that measures one million pixels.*

pixie /pɪksi/ (pixies) N-COUNT A **pixie** is an imaginary little creature like a fairy. Pixies have pointed ears and wear pointed hats.

piz|za /pi:tsə/ (pizzas) N-VAR A **pizza** is a flat, round piece of dough covered with tomatoes, cheese, and other toppings, and then baked in an oven. ❑ *...the last piece of pizza.*

piz|zazz /pɪzæz/ also **pizazz** N-UNCOUNT If you say that someone or something has **pizzazz**, you mean that they are very exciting, energetic, and stylish. [INFORMAL, APPROVAL] ❑ *...a young woman with a lot of energy and pizzazz.*

piz|ze|ria /pi:tsəriːə/ (pizzerias) N-COUNT A **pizzeria** is a place where pizza is made, sold, and eaten.

piz|zi|ca|to /pɪtsɪkɑːtoʊ/ (pizzicatos) ADV [ADV after v] If a stringed instrument is played **pizzicato**, it is played by pulling the strings with the fingers rather than with the bow. [TECHNICAL] • N-COUNT [oft N n] **Pizzicato** is also a noun. ❑ *...an extended pizzicato section.*

pjs /pi:dʒeɪz/ also **pj's** N-PLURAL **Pjs** are the same as **pajamas**. [AM, INFORMAL] ❑ *I work from home and live in my pjs most of the time.*

pkg. **Pkg.** is a written abbreviation for **package**.

pkt. **Pkt.** is a written abbreviation for **packet**.

pl. also **pl** **1** In addresses and on maps and signs, **Pl.** is often used as a written abbreviation for **Place**. ❑ *...1060 Colorado Pl., Palo Alto.* **2** In grammar, **pl.** is often used as a written abbreviation for **plural**.

plac|ard /plækɑːrd, -kərd/ (placards) N-COUNT A **placard** is a large notice that is carried in a march or displayed in a public place. ❑ *The protesters sang songs and waved placards.*

pla|cate /pleɪkeɪt/ (placates, placating, placated) V-T If you **placate** someone, you do or say something to make them stop feeling angry. [FORMAL] ❑ *He smiled, and made a gesture intended to placate me.*

placa|tory /pleɪkətɔːri, plæk-/ ADJ A **placatory** remark or action is intended to make someone stop feeling angry. [FORMAL] ❑ *When next he spoke he was more placatory.* ❑ *He raised a placatory hand. "All right, we'll see what we can do."*

PLACE
① NOUN USES
② VERB USES
③ PHRASES

---

① **place** ✦✦✦ /pleɪs/ (places) **1** N-COUNT A **place** is any point, building, area, town, or country. ❑ *...a list of museums and places of interest.* ❑ *We're going to a place called Platoro.* ❑ *The pain is always in the same place.* **2** N-SING You can use **the place** to refer to the point, building, area, town, or country that you have already mentioned. ❑ *Except for the remarkably tidy kitchen, the place was a mess.* **3** N-COUNT You can refer to somewhere that provides a service, such as a hotel, restaurant, or institution, as a particular kind of **place**. ❑ *He found a bed-and-breakfast place.* ❑ *My wife and I discovered some superb places to eat.* **4** PHRASE When something **takes place**, it happens, especially in a controlled or organized way. ❑ *The discussion took place in a famous villa on the lake's shore.* ❑ *She wanted Randy's wedding to take place quickly.* **5** N-SING **Place** can be used after 'any,' 'no,' 'some,' or 'every' to mean 'anywhere,' 'nowhere,' 'somewhere,' or 'everywhere.' [mainly AM, INFORMAL] ❑ *The poor guy obviously didn't have any place to go for Easter.* **6** ADV [ADV after v] If you **go places**, you visit pleasant or interesting places. [mainly AM] ❑ *I don't have money to go places.* **7** N-COUNT You can refer to the position where something belongs, or where it is supposed to be, as its **place**. ❑ *He returned the album to its place on the shelf.* **8** N-COUNT A **place** is a seat or position that is available for someone to occupy. ❑ *He walked back to the table and sat at the nearest of two empty places.* **9** N-COUNT Someone's or something's **place** in a society, system, or situation is their position in relation to other people or things. ❑ *They want to see more women take their place higher up the corporate or professional ladder.* **10** N-COUNT Your **place** in a race or competition is your position in relation to the other competitors. If you are in first place, you are ahead of all the other competitors. ❑ *He has risen to second place in the opinion polls.* **11** N-COUNT If you get a **place** on a team, on a committee, or in an institution, for example, you are accepted as a member of the team or committee or as a resident of the institution. ❑ *Derek had lost his place on the team.* ❑ *They should be in residential care but there are no places available.* **12** N-SING A good **place** to do something in a situation or activity is a good time or stage at which to do it. ❑ *It seemed an appropriate place to end somehow.* **13** N-COUNT Your **place** is the house or apartment where you live. [INFORMAL] ❑ *Let's all go back to my place!* **14** N-COUNT Your **place** in a book or speech is the point you have reached in reading the book or making the speech. ❑ *...her finger marking her place in the book.* **15** N-COUNT If you say how many decimal **places** there are in a number, you are saying how many numbers there are to the right of the decimal point. ❑ *A pocket calculator only works to eight decimal places.*

② **place** ✦✦✦ /pleɪs/ (places, placing, placed) **1** V-T If you **place** something somewhere, you put it in a particular position, especially in a careful, firm, or deliberate way. ❑ *Brand folded it in his handkerchief and placed it in the inside pocket of his jacket.* **2** V-T To **place** a person or thing in a particular state means to cause them to be in it. ❑ *Widespread protests have placed the president under serious pressure.* ❑ *The crisis could well place the relationship at risk.* **3** V-T You can use **place** instead of 'put' or 'lay' in certain expressions where the meaning is carried by the following noun. For example, if you **place emphasis** on something, you emphasize it, and if you **place the blame** on someone, you blame them. ❑ *He placed great emphasis on the importance of family life and ties.* ❑ *She seemed to be placing most of the blame on her mother.* **4** V-T If you **place** someone or something in a particular class or group, you label or judge them in that way. ❑ *The authorities have placed the drug in Class A, the same category as heroin and cocaine.* **5** V-T [usu passive] If a competitor in a race or competition **is placed** first, second, or third, they finish first, second or third. If a horse **is placed** in a race, it finishes second. ❑ *I had been placed 2nd and 3rd a few times but had never won.* **6** V-T If you **place an order** for a product or for a meal, you ask for it to be sent or brought to you. ❑ *It is a good idea to place your order well in advance as delivery can often take months rather than weeks.* **7** V-T If you **place an advertisement** in a newspaper, you arrange for the advertisement to appear in the newspaper. ❑ *They placed an advertisement in the local paper for a secretary.* **8** V-T If you **place a bet**, you bet money on something. ❑ *For this race, though, he had already placed a bet on one of the horses.* **9** V-T If an agency or organization **places** someone, it finds them a job or somewhere to live. ❑ *They managed to place fourteen women in paid positions.*

③ **place** ✦✦✦ /pleɪs/ **1** PHRASE If something is happening

all over the place, it is happening in many different places. ☐ *Businesses are closing down all over the place.* ◨ PHRASE If things are **all over the place**, they are spread over a very large area, usually in a disorganized way. ☐ *Our fingerprints are probably all over the place.* ◨ PHRASE If you **change places** with another person, you start being in their situation or role, and they start being in yours. ☐ *With his door key in his hand, knowing Millie and the kids awaited him, he wouldn't change places with anyone.* ◨ PHRASE If you have been trying to understand something puzzling and then everything **falls into place** or **clicks into place**, you suddenly understand how different pieces of information are connected and everything becomes clearer. ☐ *When the reasons behind the decision were explained, of course, it all fell into place.* ◨ PHRASE If things **fall into place**, events happen naturally to produce a situation you want. ☐ *Once the decision was made, things fell into place rapidly.* ◨ PHRASE If you say that someone **is going places**, you mean that they are showing a lot of talent or ability and are likely to become very successful. ☐ *You always knew Barbara was going places, she was different.* ◨ PHRASE People **in high places** are people who have powerful and influential positions in a government, society, or organization. ☐ *He had friends in high places.* ◨ PHRASE If something is **in place**, it is in its correct or usual position. If it is **out of place**, it is not in its correct or usual position. ☐ *Gary hastily pushed the drawer back into place.* ◨ PHRASE If something such as a law, a policy, or an administrative structure is **in place**, it is working or able to be used. ☐ *Similar legislation is already in place in Utah.* ◨ PHRASE If one thing or person is used or does something **in place of** another, they replace the other thing or person. ☐ *Cooked kidney beans can be used in place of French beans.* ◨ PHRASE If something has particular characteristics or features **in places**, it has them at several points within an area. ☐ *Even now the snow along the roadside was five or six feet deep in places.* ◨ PHRASE If you say what you would have done **in someone else's place**, you say what you would have done if you had been in their situation and had been experiencing what they were experiencing. ☐ *In her place I wouldn't have been able to resist it.* ◨ PHRASE You say **in the first place** when you are talking about the beginning of a situation or about the situation as it was before a series of events. ☐ *What brought you to Washington in the first place?* ◨ PHRASE You say **in the first place** and **in the second place** to introduce the first and second in a series of points or reasons. **In the first place** can also be used to emphasize a very important point or reason. ☐ *In the first place you are not old, Conway. And in the second place, you are a very strong and appealing man.* ◨ PHRASE If you say that **it is not** your **place** to do something, you mean that it is not right or appropriate for you to do it, or that it is not your responsibility to do it. ☐ *He says that it is not his place to comment on government commitment to further funds.* ◨ PHRASE If someone or something seems **out of place** in a particular situation, they do not seem to belong there or to be suitable for that situation. ☐ *I felt out of place in my suit and tie.* ◨ PHRASE If you **place** one thing **above**, **before**, or **over** another, you think that the first thing is more important than the second and you show this in your behavior. ☐ *He continued to place security above all other objectives.* ◨ PHRASE If you **put** someone **in** their **place**, you show them that they are less important or clever than they think they are. ☐ *In a few words she had put him in his place.* ◨ PHRASE If you say that someone should **be shown** their **place** or **be kept in** their **place**, you are saying, often in a humorous way, that they should be made aware of their low status. ☐ *...an uppity bartender who needs to be shown his place.* ◨ PHRASE If one thing **takes second place** to another, it is considered to be less important and is given less attention than the other thing. ☐ *My personal life has had to take second place to my career.* ◨ PHRASE If one thing or person **takes the place of** another or **takes** another's **place**, they replace the other thing or person. ☐ *Optimism was gradually taking the place of pessimism.*

Place /pleɪs/ N-IN-NAMES **Place** is used as part of the name of a square or short street in a town. ☐ *...1300 Brook Place, Mountain View.*

pla|cebo /pləsiːboʊ/ (**placebos**) ◨ N-COUNT A **placebo** is a substance with no chemical effects that a doctor gives to a patient instead of a drug. Placebos are used when testing new drugs or sometimes when a patient has imagined their illness. ◨ → See feature box at **medicine**

pla|cebo ef|fect (**placebo effects**) N-COUNT [usu the N in sing] The **placebo effect** is the fact that some patients' health improves after taking what they believe is an effective drug but which is in fact a placebo.

place card (**place cards**) N-COUNT A **place card** is a small card with a person's name on it that is put on a table at a formal meal to indicate where that person is to sit.

-placed /-pleɪst/ ◨ COMB IN ADJ **-placed** combines with adverbs to form adjectives that describe how well or badly someone is able to do a particular task. ☐ *As an expert on the Middle East, he is well-placed to comment.* ◨ COMB IN ADJ *Fund managers are poorly placed to monitor companies.* ◨ COMB IN ADJ **-placed** combines with adverbs to form adjectives that indicate how good or bad the position of a building or area is considered to be. ☐ *Chicago is perfectly-placed for exploring the U.S. by train.*

place|mat /pleɪsmæt/ (**placemats**) N-COUNT **Placemats** are mats that are put on a table before a meal for people to put their plates or bowls on.

place|ment /pleɪsmənt/ (**placements**) ◨ N-UNCOUNT The **placement** of something or someone is the act of putting them in a particular place or position. ☐ *The treatment involves the placement of twenty-two electrodes in the inner ear.* ◨ N-UNCOUNT The **placement** of someone in a job, home, or school is the act or process of finding them a job, home, or school. ☐ *The children were waiting for placement in a foster care home.* ◨ N-COUNT If someone gets a **placement**, they get a job for a short period of time to gain experience. ☐ *He spent a year studying Japanese in Tokyo, followed by a six-month work placement with the Japanese government.*

place|ment test (**placement tests**) N-COUNT A **placement test** is a test given by a school to determine the academic or skill level of a student, especially a new student, in order to place them in the correct class. ☐ *Students are required to take placement tests before registering.*

pla|cen|ta /pləsɛntə/ (**placentas**) N-COUNT [usu the N] The **placenta** is the mass of veins and tissue inside the uterus of a pregnant woman or animal, which the unborn baby is attached to. ☐ *The drug can be transferred to the baby via the placenta.*

place set|ting (**place settings**) ◨ N-COUNT A **place setting** is an arrangement of knives, forks, spoons, and glasses that has been laid out on a table for the use of one person at a meal. ◨ N-COUNT A **place setting** of china or of knives, forks, and spoons is a complete set of all the things that one person might use at a meal. ☐ *A seven-piece place setting costs about $45.*

plac|id /plæsɪd/ ◨ ADJ A **placid** person or animal is calm and does not easily become excited, angry, or upset. ☐ *She was a placid child who rarely cried.* ◨ ADJ A **placid** place, area of water, or life is calm and peaceful. ☐ *...the placid waters of Lake Erie.*

pla|gia|rism /pleɪdʒərɪzəm/ N-UNCOUNT **Plagiarism** is the practice of using or copying someone else's idea or work and pretending that you thought of it or created it. ☐ *Now he's in real trouble. He has been accused of plagiarism.*

pla|gia|rize /pleɪdʒəraɪz/ (**plagiarizes, plagiarizing, plagiarized**)

in BRIT, also use **plagiarise**

V-T If someone **plagiarizes** another person's idea or work, they use it or copy it and pretend that they thought of it or created it. ☐ *The students denied plagiarizing papers.*

plague /pleɪg/ (**plagues, plaguing, plagued**) ◨ N-UNCOUNT [also the N] **Plague** or **the plague** is a very infectious disease that usually results in death. The patient has a severe fever and swellings on his or her body. ☐ *...a fresh outbreak of plague.* ◨ N-COUNT A **plague of** unpleasant things is a large number of them that arrive or happen at the same time. ☐ *The city is under threat from a plague of rats.* ◨ V-T If you are **plagued** by unpleasant things, they continually cause you a lot of trouble or suffering. ☐ *She was plagued by weakness, fatigue, and dizziness.* ◨ → See feature box at **farming**

plaice /pleɪs/ (**plaice**)

Plaice is both the singular and the plural form.

plaid

N-VAR **Plaice** are a type of flat sea fish. • N-UNCOUNT **Plaice** is this fish eaten as food.

plaid /plæd/ (**plaids**) N-MASS [oft N n] **Plaid** is material with a check design on it. **Plaid** is also the design itself. ☐ *Eddie wore blue jeans and a plaid shirt.*

plain ✦✧✧ /pleɪn/ (**plainer, plainest, plains**) **1** ADJ A **plain** object, surface, or fabric is entirely in one color and has no pattern, design, or writing on it. ☐ *In general, a plain carpet makes a room look bigger.* ☐ *He placed the paper in a plain envelope.* **2** ADJ Something that is **plain** is very simple in style. ☐ *It was a plain, gray stone house.* • **plain|ly** ADV [ADV -ed] ☐ *He was very tall and plainly dressed.* **3** ADJ If a fact, situation, or statement is **plain**, it is easy to recognize or understand. ☐ *It was plain to him that I was having a nervous breakdown.* **4** ADJ If you describe someone as **plain**, you think they look ordinary and not at all beautiful. ☐ *...a shy, rather plain girl with a pale complexion.* **5** N-COUNT A **plain** is a large flat area of land with very few trees on it. ☐ *Once there were 70 million buffalo on the plains.* **6** PHRASE If a police officer is **in plain clothes**, he or she is wearing ordinary clothes instead of a police uniform. ☐ *Three officers in plain clothes told me to get out of the car.* **7** **plain sailing** → see **sailing**

COLLOCATIONS

plain
NOUN **5**
adjective + **plain**: alluvial; arid, barren, dusty; coastal; fertile; grassy; rolling
noun + **plain**: flood

---

plain choco|late N-UNCOUNT **Plain chocolate** is the same as **dark chocolate**. [BRIT]

plain|clothes /pleɪnkloʊz, -kloʊðz/ **1** ADJ [ADJ n] **Plainclothes** police officers wear ordinary clothes instead of a police uniform. ☐ *He was arrested by plainclothes detectives as he walked through the customs hall.* **2 in plain clothes** → see **plain**

plain flour N-UNCOUNT **Plain flour** is the same as **all-purpose flour**. [BRIT]

plain|ly /pleɪnli/ **1** ADV You use **plainly** to indicate that you believe something is obviously true, often when you are trying to convince someone else that it is true. [EMPHASIS] ☐ *The judge's conclusion was plainly wrong.* ☐ *Plainly, a more objective method of description must be adopted.* **2** ADV You use **plainly** to indicate that something is easily seen, noticed, or recognized. ☐ *He was plainly annoyed.* ☐ *I could plainly see him turning his head to the right and left.* **3** → see also **plain**

plain-spoken also **plainspoken** ADJ If you say that someone is **plain-spoken**, you mean that they say exactly what they think, even when they know that what they say may not please other people. [APPROVAL] ☐ *...a plain-spoken American full of scorn for pomp and pretense.*

plaint /pleɪnt/ (**plaints**) N-COUNT A **plaint** is a complaint or a sad cry. [LITERARY] ☐ *...a forlorn, haunting plaint.*

plain|tiff /pleɪntɪf/ (**plaintiffs**) N-COUNT A **plaintiff** is a person who brings a legal case against someone in a court of law. ☐ *The lead plaintiff of the lawsuit is the University of California.*

plain|tive /pleɪntɪv/ ADJ A **plaintive** sound or voice sounds sad. [LITERARY] ☐ *They lay on the firm sands, listening to the plaintive cry of the seagulls.*

plait /pleɪt/ (**plaits, plaiting, plaited**) **1** V-T If you **plait** three or more lengths of hair, rope, or other material together, you twist them over and under each other to make one thick length. [mainly BRIT]

in AM, usually use **braid**

2 N-COUNT A **plait** is a length of hair that has been plaited. [mainly BRIT]

in AM, usually use **braid**

plan ✦✦✦ /plæn/ (**plans, planning, planned**) **1** N-COUNT A **plan** is a method of achieving something that you have worked out in detail beforehand. ☐ *The three leaders had worked out a peace plan.* ☐ *He maintains that everything is going according to plan.* **2** V-T/V-I If you **plan** what you are going to do, you decide in detail what you are going to do, and you intend to do it. ☐ *If you plan what you're going to eat, you reduce your chances of overeating.* ☐ *He planned to leave Baghdad on Monday.* ☐ *Moderate Republicans gathered together to plan for the future.* **3** N-PLURAL If you have **plans**, you are intending to do a particular thing. ☐ *"I'm sorry," she said. "I have plans for tonight."* **4** V-T When you **plan** something that you are going to make, build, or create, you decide what the main parts of it will be and do a drawing of how it should be made. ☐ *It is no use trying to plan an 18-hole golf course on a 120-acre site if you have to ruin the environment to do it.* **5** N-COUNT A **plan** of something that is going to be built or made is a detailed diagram or drawing of it. ☐ *...when you have drawn a plan of the garden.* **6** → see also **planning**
▶ **plan on** PHRASAL VERB If you **plan on** doing something, you intend to do it. ☐ *They were planning on getting married.*

plane ✦✦✧ /pleɪn/ (**planes, planing, planed**) **1** N-COUNT A **plane** is a vehicle with wings and one or more engines that can fly through the air. ☐ *He had plenty of time to catch his plane.* ☐ *Her mother was killed in a plane crash.* **2** N-COUNT A **plane** is a flat, level surface that may be sloping at a particular angle. ☐ *...a building with angled planes.* **3** N-SING If a number of points are in the same **plane**, one line or one flat surface could pass through them all. ☐ *All the planets orbit the Sun in roughly the same plane, around its equator.* **4** N-COUNT A **plane** is a tool that has a flat bottom with a sharp blade in it. You move the plane over a piece of wood in order to remove thin pieces of its surface. **5** V-T If you **plane** a piece of wood, you make it smaller or smoother by using a plane. ☐ *She watches him plane the surface of a walnut board.* **6** N-COUNT A **plane** or a **plane tree** is the same as a **sycamore**. **7** → See also color supplement

plane|load /pleɪnloʊd/ (**planeloads**) N-COUNT [usu N of n] A **planeload** of people or freight is as many people or things as a plane can carry. ☐ *The Red Cross has sent four planeloads of relief supplies to the stricken areas.*

plan|et ✦✧✧ /plænɪt/ (**planets**) **1** N-COUNT A **planet** is a large, round object in space that moves around a star. The Earth is a planet. ☐ *The picture shows six of the nine planets in the solar system.* **2** N-SING The **planet** is used to refer to the world we live in, especially our natural environment. ☐ *They were trying to cut their carbon footprint and save the planet.* ☐ *They are among the few people on the planet who can afford to shop there.* **3** → See feature box at **space**

plan|etar|ium /plænɪtɛəriəm/ (**planetariums**) N-COUNT A **planetarium** is a building where lights are shone on the ceiling to represent the planets and the stars and to show how they appear to move.

plan|etary /plænɪtəri/ ADJ [ADJ n] **Planetary** means relating to or belonging to planets. ☐ *Within our own galaxy there are probably tens of thousands of planetary systems.*

plan|gent /plændʒənt/ ADJ A **plangent** sound is a deep, loud sound, which may be sad. [LITERARY] ☐ *...plangent violins.*

plank /plæŋk/ (**planks**) **1** N-COUNT A **plank** is a long, flat, rectangular piece of wood. ☐ *It was very strong, made of three solid planks of wood.* **2** N-COUNT The main **plank** of a particular group or political party is the main principle on which it bases its policy, or its main aim. [JOURNALISM] ☐ *The Saudi authorities have made agricultural development a central plank of policy to make the country less dependent on imports.*

plank|ing /plæŋkɪŋ/ N-UNCOUNT **Planking** is wood that has been cut into long flat pieces. It is used especially to make floors.

plank|ton /plæŋktən/ N-UNCOUNT **Plankton** is a mass of tiny animals and plants that live in the surface layer of the sea. ☐ *...its usual diet of plankton and other small organisms.*

plan|ner /plænər/ (**planners**) N-COUNT **Planners** are people whose job is to make decisions about what is going to be done in the future. For example, town planners decide how land should be used and what new buildings should be built. ☐ *...a panel that includes city planners, art experts, and historians.*

plan|ning ✦✧✧ /plænɪŋ/ **1** N-UNCOUNT **Planning** is the process of deciding in detail how to do something before you actually start to do it. ☐ *The trip needs careful planning.* **2** → see also **family planning** **3** N-UNCOUNT **Planning** is control by the local government of the way that land is used in an area and of what new buildings are built there. ☐ *New York City's Planning Commissions rejected the builder's proposals.*

plant

> **SYNONYMS**
>
> **planning**
> NOUN **1**
> **organization:** *Several projects have been delayed by poor organization.*
> **preparation:** *Behind any successful event lay months of preparation.*
> **arrangement:** *The staff is working frantically on final arrangements for the summit.*

plant ◆◆◇ /plænt/ (plants, planting, planted) **1** N-COUNT A **plant** is a living thing that grows in the earth and has a stem, leaves, and roots. ◻ *Water each plant as often as required.* **2** V-T When you **plant** a seed, plant, or young tree, you put it into the ground so that it will grow there. ◻ *He says he plans to plant fruit trees and vegetables.* • **plant|ing** N-UNCOUNT ◻ *Extensive flooding in the country has delayed planting and many crops are still under water.* **3** V-T When someone **plants** land with a particular type of plant or crop, they put plants, seeds, or young trees into the land to grow them there. ◻ *They plan to plant the area with grass and trees.* ◻ *Recently much of their energy has gone into planting a large vegetable garden.* **4** N-COUNT A **plant** is a factory or a place where power is produced. ◻ *...Ford's car assembly plants.* **5** N-UNCOUNT **Plant** is large machinery that is used in industrial processes. ◻ *Companies may start to invest in plant and equipment abroad where costs may be lower.* **6** V-T If you **plant** something somewhere, you put it there firmly. ◻ *She planted her feet wide and bent her knees slightly.* **7** V-T To **plant** something such as a bomb means to hide it somewhere so that it explodes or works there. ◻ *So far no one has admitted planting the bomb.* **8** V-T [oft passive] If something such as a weapon or drugs **is planted** on someone, it is put among their possessions or in their house so that they will be wrongly accused of a crime. ◻ *He always protested his innocence and claimed that the drugs had been planted to incriminate him.* **9** V-T If an organization **plants** someone somewhere, they send that person there so that they can get information or watch someone secretly. ◻ *Journalists informed police who planted an undercover detective to trap Smith.* **10** → See feature box at **garden, water**

> **SYNONYMS**
>
> **plant**
> VERB **3**
> **sow:** *Sow the seeds in a warm place in February/March.*
> **scatter:** *He began by scattering seeds and putting in plants.*
> **transplant:** *Farmers will be able to seed it directly, rather than having to transplant seedlings.*

plan|tain /ˈplæntɪn/ (plantains) **1** N-VAR A **plantain** is a type of green banana that can be cooked and eaten as a vegetable. **2** N-VAR A **plantain** is a wild plant with broad or narrow leaves and a head of tiny green flowers on a long stem.

plan|ta|tion /plænˈteɪʃ°n/ (plantations) **1** N-COUNT A **plantation** is a large piece of land, especially in a tropical country, where crops such as rubber, coffee, tea, or sugar are grown. ◻ *...banana plantations in Costa Rica.* **2** N-COUNT A **plantation** is a large number of trees that have been planted together. ◻ *...a plantation of almond trees.*

plant-based ADJ [ADJ n] A **plant-based** diet includes fruit and vegetables but no meat or animal products such as milk and eggs. ◻ *Increasing numbers of people are turning to a plant-based diet.*

plant|er /ˈplæntər/ (planters) **1** N-COUNT **Planters** are people who own or manage plantations. **2** N-COUNT A **planter** is a container for plants that people keep in their homes.

plaque /plæk/ (plaques) **1** N-COUNT A **plaque** is a flat piece of metal or stone with writing on it which is fixed to a wall or other structure to remind people of an important person or event. ◻ *The First Lady unveiled a commemorative plaque.* **2** N-UNCOUNT **Plaque** is a substance containing bacteria that forms on the surface of your teeth. ◻ *Deposits of plaque build up between the tooth and the gum.*

plas|ma /ˈplæzmə/ N-UNCOUNT **Plasma** is the clear liquid part of blood that contains the blood cells.

plas|ma screen (plasma screens) also **plasma display** N-COUNT A **plasma screen** is a type of thin television screen or computer screen that produces high-quality images. ◻ *...a 50-inch plasma screen.* ◻ *...flat-panel TVs using thin plasma displays.*

plas|ter /ˈplæstər/ (plasters, plastering, plastered) **1** N-UNCOUNT **Plaster** is a smooth paste made of sand, lime, and water that gets hard when it dries. Plaster is used to cover walls and ceilings and is also used to make sculptures. ◻ *There were huge cracks in the plaster, and the green shutters were faded.* **2** V-T If you **plaster** a wall or ceiling, you cover it with a layer of plaster. ◻ *The ceiling he had just plastered fell in and knocked him off his ladder.* **3** V-T If you **plaster** a surface or a place with posters or pictures, you stick a lot of them all over it. ◻ *He has plastered the city with posters proclaiming his qualifications and experience.* **4** V-T If you **plaster** yourself in some kind of sticky substance, you cover yourself in it. ◻ *She gets sunburned even when she plasters herself from head to toe in factor 7 sun lotion.* **5** N-COUNT A **plaster** is a strip of sticky material used for covering small cuts or sores on your body. [BRIT]

> in AM, usually use **Band-aid**

6 → see also **plastered** **7** → See feature box at **DIY**

plaster|board /ˈplæstərbɔːrd/ N-UNCOUNT **Plasterboard** is cardboard covered with plaster that is used for covering walls and ceilings instead of using plaster.

plas|ter cast (plaster casts) **1** N-COUNT A **plaster cast** is a cover made of plaster of Paris that is used to protect a broken bone by keeping part of the body stiff. **2** N-COUNT A **plaster cast** is a copy of a statue or other object, made from plaster of Paris. ◻ *...a plaster cast of the Venus de Milo.*

plas|tered /ˈplæstərd/ **1** ADJ [v-link ADJ prep/adv] If something is **plastered to** a surface, it is sticking to the surface. ◻ *His hair was plastered down to his scalp by the rain.* **2** ADJ [v-link ADJ] If something or someone is **plastered with** a sticky substance, they are covered with it. ◻ *My hands, boots, and pants were plastered with mud.* **3** ADJ [v-link ADJ prep/adv] If a story or photograph is **plastered all over** the front page of a newspaper, it is given a lot of space on the page and made very noticeable. ◻ *His picture was plastered all over the newspapers.* **4** ADJ [v-link ADJ] If someone gets **plastered**, they get very drunk. [INFORMAL] ◻ *I decided to get some beer. Seems a good night to get plastered.*

plas|ter|er /ˈplæstərər/ (plasterers) N-COUNT A **plasterer** is a person whose job it is to cover walls and ceilings with plaster.

plas|ter of Paris /ˌplæstər əv ˈpærɪs/ N-UNCOUNT **Plaster of Paris** is a type of plaster made from white powder and water that dries quickly. It is used to make plaster casts.

plas|tic ◆◇◇ /ˈplæstɪk/ (plastics) **1** N-MASS **Plastic** is a material that is produced from oil by a chemical process and that is used to make many objects. It is light in weight and does not break easily. ◻ *...a wooden crate, sheltered from rain by sheets of plastic.* ◻ *A lot of the plastics that carmakers are using cannot be recycled.* **2** ADJ If you describe something as **plastic**, you mean that you think it looks or tastes unnatural or not real. [DISAPPROVAL] ◻ *You wanted proper home-cooked meals, you said you had enough plastic hotel food and airline food.* **3** N-UNCOUNT If you use **plastic** or **plastic money** to pay for something, you pay for it with a credit card instead of using cash. [INFORMAL] ◻ *Using plastic to pay for an order is simplicity itself.* **4** ADJ Something that is **plastic** is soft and can easily be made into different shapes. ◻ *You can also enjoy mud packs with the natural mud, smooth, gray, soft, and plastic as butter.* **5** → See feature box at **recycle**

plas|tic bul|let (plastic bullets) N-COUNT A **plastic bullet** is a large bullet made of plastic that is intended to make people stop rioting, rather than to kill people.

plas|tic ex|plo|sive (plastic explosives) N-MASS **Plastic explosive** is a substance that explodes and that is used in making small bombs.

plas|tic sur|geon (plastic surgeons) N-COUNT A **plastic surgeon** is a doctor who performs operations to repair or replace skin that has been damaged, or to improve people's appearance.

plas|tic sur|gery N-UNCOUNT **Plastic surgery** is the practice of performing operations to repair or replace skin that has been damaged, or to improve people's appearance. ◻ *She even had plastic surgery to change the shape of her nose.*

plas|tic wrap N-UNCOUNT **Plastic wrap** is a thin, clear, stretchy plastic that you use to cover food to keep it fresh. [AM]

> in BRIT, use **clingfilm**

plate /pleɪt/ (**plates**) **1** N-COUNT A **plate** is a round or oval flat dish that is used to hold food. ❑ *Anita pushed her plate away; she had eaten virtually nothing.* **2** N-COUNT A **plate** of food is the amount of food on a plate. ❑ *...a huge plate of bacon and eggs.* **3** N-COUNT A **plate** is a flat piece of metal, especially on machinery or a building. ❑ *...a recess covered by a brass plate.* **4** N-COUNT A **plate** is a small, flat piece of metal with someone's name written on it, which you usually find beside the front door of an office or house. ❑ *...a brass plate by the front door bearing his name.* **5** N-PLURAL On a road vehicle, the **plates** are the panels on the front and back that display the license number. ❑ *...dusty-looking cars with New Jersey plates.* **6** → see also **license plate 7** N-COUNT A **plate** in a book is a picture or photograph that takes up a whole page and is usually printed on better quality paper than the rest of the book. ❑ *The book has 55 color plates.* **8** PHRASE If you **have enough on** your **plate** or **have a lot on** your **plate**, you have a lot of work to do or a lot of things to deal with. ❑ *We have enough on our plate. There is plenty of work to be done on what we have.*

plat|eau /plætoʊ/ (**plateaus** or **plateaux**) **1** N-COUNT A **plateau** is a large area of high and fairly flat land. ❑ *A broad valley opened up leading to a high, flat plateau of cultivated land.* **2** N-COUNT If you say that an activity or process has reached a **plateau**, you mean that it has reached a stage where there is no further change or development. ❑ *The U.S. heroin market now appears to have reached a plateau.* **3** → See feature box at **weather**

plat|ed /pleɪtɪd/ ADJ [v-link ADJ with n] If something made of metal is **plated with** a thin layer of another type of metal, it is covered with it. ❑ *...a range of jewelry, plated with 22-carat nickel-free gold.*

-plated /-pleɪtɪd/ COMB IN ADJ Something made of metal that is **plated** is covered with a thin layer of another type of metal such as gold and silver. ❑ *...a gold-plated watch.*

plate|ful /pleɪtfʊl/ (**platefuls**) N-COUNT [usu N of n] A **plateful** of food is an amount of food that is on a plate and fills it. ❑ *...a greasy plateful of bacon and eggs.*

plate glass also **plate-glass** N-UNCOUNT **Plate glass** is thick glass made in large, flat pieces, which is used especially to make large windows and doors.

plate|let /pleɪtlɪt/ (**platelets**) N-COUNT [usu pl] A **platelet** is a kind of blood cell. If you cut yourself and you are bleeding, platelets help to stop the bleeding. [TECHNICAL]

plate tec|ton|ics N-UNCOUNT **Plate tectonics** is the study of the way that large pieces of the Earth's surface move slowly around. [TECHNICAL]

plat|form ♦♦♢ /plætfɔrm/ (**platforms**) **1** N-COUNT A **platform** is a flat raised structure, usually made of wood, that people stand on when they make speeches or give a performance. ❑ *Nick finished what he was saying and jumped down from the platform.* **2** N-COUNT A **platform** is a flat raised structure or area, usually one that something can stand on or land on. ❑ *They found a spot on a rocky platform where they could pitch their tents.* **3** N-COUNT A **platform** is a structure built for people to work and live on when drilling for oil or gas at sea, or when extracting it. ❑ *The platform began to produce oil in 1994.* **4** N-COUNT A **platform** in a train or subway station is the area beside the tracks where you wait for or get off a train. ❑ *The train was about to leave and I was not even on the platform.* **5** N-COUNT The **platform** of a political party is what they say they will do if they are elected. ❑ *The party has announced a platform of political and economic reforms.* **6** N-COUNT If someone has a **platform**, they have an opportunity to tell people what they think or want. ❑ *The demonstration provided a platform for a broad cross-section of speakers.*

plat|ing /pleɪtɪŋ/ N-UNCOUNT **Plating** is a thin layer of metal on something, or a covering of metal plates. ❑ *The tanker began spilling oil the moment her outer plating ruptured.*

plati|num /plætɪnəm, plætnəm/ **1** N-UNCOUNT **Platinum** is a very valuable, silvery-gray metal. It is often used for making jewelry. **2** → See also color supplement

plati|tude /plætɪtud/ (**platitudes**) N-COUNT A **platitude** is a statement that is considered meaningless and boring because it has been made many times before in similar situations. [DISAPPROVAL] ❑ *Why couldn't he say something vital and original instead of just spouting the same old platitudes?*

pla|ton|ic /plətɒnɪk/ ADJ **Platonic** relationships or feelings of affection do not involve sex. ❑ *She values the platonic friendship she has had with Chris for ten years.*

pla|toon /plətun/ (**platoons**) N-COUNT A **platoon** is a small group of soldiers, usually one that is commanded by a lieutenant.

plat|ter /plætər/ (**platters**) **1** N-COUNT A **platter** is a large flat plate used for serving food. [mainly AM] ❑ *The food was being served on silver platters.* **2** N-COUNT A **platter** of food is the amount of food on a platter. ❑ *They were served platters of cheese and fruit.* **3** PHRASE If you say that someone has things **handed to** them **on a platter**, you disapprove of them because they get good things easily. [DISAPPROVAL] ❑ *Even the presidency was handed to him on a platter.*

plau|dits /plɔdɪts/ N-PLURAL If a person or a thing receives **plaudits** from a group of people, those people express their admiration for or approval of that person or thing. [FORMAL] ❑ *They won plaudits and prizes for their accomplished films.*

plau|sible /plɔzɪbəl/ **1** ADJ An explanation or statement that is **plausible** seems likely to be true or valid. ❑ *A more plausible explanation would seem to be that people are fed up with the administration.* • **plau|sibly** /plɔzɪbli/ ADV [ADV with v] ❑ *Having bluffed his way in without paying, he could not plausibly demand his money back.* • **plau|sibil|ity** /plɔzɪbɪlɪti/ N-UNCOUNT ❑ *...the plausibility of the theory.* **2** ADJ If you say that someone is **plausible**, you mean that they seem to be telling the truth and to be sincere and honest. ❑ *All I can say is that he was so plausible it wasn't just me that he conned.*

play ♦♦♦ /pleɪ/ (**plays, playing, played**)

→ Please look at meanings **15** to **21** to see if the expression you are looking for is shown under another headword.

1 V-I When children, animals, or adults **play**, they spend time doing enjoyable things, such as using toys and taking part in games. ❑ *...invite the children over to play.* ❑ *They played in the little garden.* • N-UNCOUNT **Play** is also a noun. ❑ *...a few hours of play until the babysitter puts them to bed.* **2** V-RECIP When you **play** a sport, game, or match, you take part in it. ❑ *While the twins played cards, Leona sat reading.* ❑ *I used to play basketball.* • N-UNCOUNT **Play** is also a noun. ❑ *They've got more exciting players and a more exciting style of play.* **3** V-T/V-I When one person or team **plays** another or **plays against** them, they compete against them in a sport or game. ❑ *Dallas will play Green Bay.* • N-UNCOUNT **Play** is also a noun. ❑ *Fischer won after 5 hours and 41 minutes of play.* **4** V-T If you **play** a joke or a trick on someone, you deceive them or give them a surprise in a way that you think is funny, but that often causes problems for them or annoys them. ❑ *Someone had played a trick on her, stretched a piece of string at the top of those steps.* **5** V-I If you **play with** an object or with your hair, you keep moving it or touching it with your fingers, perhaps because you are bored or nervous. ❑ *She stared at the floor, idly playing with the strap of her handbag.* **6** N-COUNT A **play** is a piece of writing performed in a theater, on the radio, or on television. ❑ *It's my favorite Shakespeare play.* **7** V-T If an actor **plays** a role or character in a play or movie, he or she performs the part of that character. ❑ *...Dr. Jekyll and Mr. Hyde, in which he played Hyde.* **8** V-LINK You can use **play** to describe how someone behaves, when they are deliberately behaving in a certain way or like a certain type of person. For example, to **play the innocent** means to pretend to be innocent, and to **play deaf** means to pretend not to hear something. ❑ *Hill tried to play the peacemaker.* ❑ *She was just playing the devoted mother.* **9** V-T You can describe how someone deals with a situation by saying that they **play it** in a certain way. For example, if someone **plays it cool**, they keep calm and do not show much emotion, and if someone **plays it straight**, they behave in an honest and direct way. ❑ *Investors are playing it cautious, and they're playing it smart.* **10** V-T/V-I If you **play** a musical instrument or **play** a tune on a musical instrument, or if a musical instrument **plays**, music is produced from it. ❑ *Nina had been playing the piano.* ❑ *He played for me.* **11** V-T If you **play** a record, a CD, or a DVD, you put it into a machine and sound and sometimes pictures are produced. If a record, CD, or DVD **is playing**, sound and sometimes pictures are being produced from it. ❑ *She played her records too loudly.* ❑ *There is classical music playing in the background.* **12** V-T/V-I If a musician or group of musicians **plays** or **plays** a concert, they perform music for

playable

people to listen or dance to. ◻ *A band was playing.* **13** PHRASE When something **comes into play** or **is brought into play**, it begins to be used or to have an effect. ◻ *The real existence of a military option will come into play.* **14** PHRASE If something or someone **plays a part** or **plays a role** in a situation, they are involved in it and have an effect on it. ◻ *They played a part in the life of their community.* ◻ *The U.N. would play a major role in monitoring a ceasefire.* **15 to play the fool** → see **fool 16 to play to the gallery** → see **gallery 17 to play hard to get** → see **hard 18 to play havoc** → see **havoc 19 to play hooky** → see **hooky 20 to play host** → see **host 21 to play safe** → see **safe**

▶ **play around 1** PHRASAL VERB If you **play around**, you behave in a silly way to amuse yourself or other people. [INFORMAL] ◻ *Stop playing around and eat!* ◻ *There was no doubt he was serious, it wasn't just playing around.* **2** PHRASAL VERB If you **play around with** a problem or an arrangement of objects, you try different ways of organizing it in order to find the best solution or arrangement. [INFORMAL] ◻ *I can play around with the pictures in all sorts of ways to make them more eye-catching.* **3** PHRASAL VERB If someone **plays around**, they have sex with people other than the person they are married to or having a serious relationship with. [INFORMAL] ◻ *I suspect that my partner may be playing around.* ◻ *Robert was playing around with another woman.*

▶ **play at 1** PHRASAL VERB [no passive] If you say that someone is **playing at** something, you disapprove of the fact that they are doing it casually and not very seriously. [DISAPPROVAL] ◻ *We were still playing at war – dropping leaflets instead of bombs.* **2** PHRASAL VERB [no passive] If someone, especially a child, **plays at** being someone or doing something, they pretend to be that person or do that thing as a game. ◻ *Ed played at being a pirate.* **3** PHRASAL VERB If you do not know what someone **is playing at**, you do not understand what they are doing or what they are trying to achieve. [INFORMAL] ◻ *She began to wonder what he was playing at.*

▶ **play back** PHRASAL VERB When you **play back** a tape or film, you listen to the sounds or watch the pictures after recording them. ◻ *He bought an answering machine that plays back his messages when he calls.* ◻ *Ted might benefit from hearing his own voice recorded and played back.*

▶ **play down** PHRASAL VERB If you **play down** something, you try to make people believe that it is not particularly important. ◻ *Western diplomats have played down the significance of the reports.*

▶ **play on** PHRASAL VERB If you **play on** someone's fears, weaknesses, or faults, you deliberately use them in order to persuade that person to do something, or to achieve what you want. ◻ *...a campaign which plays on the population's fear of change.*

▶ **play up** PHRASAL VERB If you **play up** something, you emphasize it and try to make people believe that it is important. ◻ *The media played up the prospects for a settlement.*

SYNONYMS

play
VERB
1
amuse yourself: *I need to amuse myself so I won't keep thinking about things.*
enjoy yourself: *I must say I am really enjoying myself at the moment.*
3
compete: *It is essential for all players who wish to compete that they earn computer ranking points.*
challenge: *We challenged a team who called themselves 'College Athletes.'*
take on: *I knew I couldn't take him on.*
7
act: *She confessed to her parents her desire to act.*
portray: *In 1975, he portrayed the king in a Los Angeles revival of 'Camelot.'*
perform: *This play was first performed in 411 BC.*
NOUN **6**
drama: *He acted in radio dramas.*
show: *A daily, one-hour news show can cost $250,000 to produce.*
performance: *We went to see Helen in a performance of 'Hamlet.'*

---

play|able /ˈpleɪəbəl/ ADJ GRADED; ADJ If a musical instrument or piece of music is **playable**, it can be played. ◻ *...the world's second-biggest playable guitar.* ◻ *They started to sell music downloads as MP3 files playable on any device.*

play|act /ˈpleɪækt/ (**playacts**, **playacting**, **playacted**) V-I [usu cont] If someone **is playacting**, they are pretending to have attitudes or feelings that they do not really have. ◻ *The "victim" revealed he was only playacting.*

play|act|ing /ˈpleɪæktɪŋ/ N-UNCOUNT **Playacting** is behavior where someone pretends to have attitudes or feelings that they do not really have. ◻ *It was just a piece of playacting.*

play|back /ˈpleɪbæk/ (**playbacks**) N-COUNT [usu sing] The **playback** of a tape is the operation of playing it on a machine in order to listen to the sound or watch the pictures recorded on it. ◻ *I heard a playback of one of the tapes.*

play|book /ˈpleɪbʊk/ (**playbooks**) N-COUNT You can use **playbook** to refer to the range of methods used by a person, organization, or country. ◻ *It is one of the oldest tricks in the Hollywood producer's playbook.* ◻ *The campaign managers stick to an outdated political playbook.*

play|boy /ˈpleɪbɔɪ/ (**playboys**) N-COUNT You can refer to a rich man who spends most of his time enjoying himself, for example, by having many sexual relationships, as a **playboy**. ◻ *Father was a rich playboy.* ◻ *...the playboy millionaire.*

play-by-play N-SING [oft N n] A **play-by-play** is a commentary on a sports game or other event that describes every part of it in great detail. [AM] ◻ *Gene Deckerhoff does radio play-by-play for Florida State.* ◻ *He also was the play-by-play announcer for the Chicago Fire soccer team.*

Play-Doh /ˈpleɪdoʊ/ N-UNCOUNT **Play-Doh** is a soft, colored substance like clay that children use for making models. [TRADEMARK]

play|er ◆◆◆ /ˈpleɪər/ (**players**) **1** N-COUNT A **player** in a sport or game is a person who takes part, either as a job or for fun. ◻ *...his greatness as a player.* ◻ *She was a good golfer and tennis player.* **2** N-COUNT You can use **player** to refer to a musician. For example, a **piano player** is someone who plays the piano. ◻ *...a professional trumpet player.* **3** N-COUNT If a person, country, or organization is a **player** in something, they are involved in it and important in it. ◻ *Big business has become a major player in the art market.* **4** N-COUNT You can refer to a person who spends a lot of time enjoying themselves, especially by having a lot of sexual relationships, as a **player**. [AM, INFORMAL] ◻ *He was a ladies' man. A cheater. A player.* **5** → see also **CD player**, **record player**

play|er pia|no (**player pianos**) N-COUNT A **player piano** is a type of mechanical piano that uses a special roll of paper to play itself. [mainly AM]

in BRIT, usually use **pianola**

play|ful /ˈpleɪfəl/ **1** ADJ A **playful** gesture or person is friendly or humorous. ◻ *...a playful kiss on the tip of his nose.* ◻ *...a playful fight.* ● **play|ful|ly** ADV ◻ *She pushed him away playfully.* ● **play|ful|ness** N-UNCOUNT ◻ *...the child's natural playfulness.* **2** ADJ A **playful** animal is lively and cheerful. ◻ *...a playful puppy.*

play|ground /ˈpleɪɡraʊnd/ (**playgrounds**) N-COUNT A **playground** is a piece of land, at school or in a public area, where children can play. ◻ *...a seven-year-old boy playing in a school playground.*

play|group /ˈpleɪɡruːp/ (**playgroups**) also **play group** N-COUNT [also prep N] A **playgroup** is an informal school for very young children, where they learn things by playing.

play|house /ˈpleɪhaʊs/ (**playhouses**) **1** N-COUNT A **playhouse** is a theater. ◻ *Auditions will be held at the Manhattan Playhouse.* **2** N-COUNT A **playhouse** is a small house made for children to play in. ◻ *My father built me a playhouse.*

play|ing card (**playing cards**) N-COUNT **Playing cards** are thin pieces of cardboard with numbers or pictures printed on them that are used to play various games. ◻ *...a deck of playing cards.*

play|ing field (**playing fields**) **1** N-COUNT A **playing field** is a large area of grass where people play sports. ◻ *Jefferson County has three grass playing fields for 18 varsity football teams.* **2** PHRASE You talk about **a level playing field** to mean a situation that is fair, because no competitor or opponent in it has an advantage over another. ◻ *American businessmen ask for a level playing field when they compete with foreign companies.*

play|list /pleɪlɪst/ (playlists) **1** N-COUNT A **playlist** is a list of songs, albums, and artists that a radio station broadcasts. ◻ *The radio station's playlist is dominated by top-selling youth-orientated groups.* **2** N-COUNT A **playlist** is a list of songs that someone makes on an app or on their computer so that they can listen to them. ◻ *I've made a playlist full of my all-time favourites.*

play|mate /pleɪmeɪt/ (playmates) N-COUNT A child's **playmate** is another child who often plays with him or her. ◻ *The young girl loved to play with her playmates.*

play|off ◆◇◇ /pleɪɒf/ (playoffs) **1** N-COUNT A **playoff** is an extra game that is played to decide the winner of a sports competition when two or more people have the same score. ◻ *Nick Faldo was beaten by Peter Baker in a playoff.* **2** N-COUNT You use **playoffs** to refer to a series of games that are played to decide the winner of a championship. ◻ *It's been a long time since these two teams faced each other in the playoffs.*

play on words (plays on words) N-COUNT [usu a N in sing] A **play on words** is the same as a **pun**.

play|pen /pleɪpɛn/ (playpens) N-COUNT A **playpen** is a small structure designed for a baby or young child to play safely in. It has bars or a net around the sides and is open at the top.

play|room /pleɪrum/ (playrooms) N-COUNT A **playroom** is a room in a house for children to play in.

play|thing /pleɪθɪŋ/ (playthings) N-COUNT A **plaything** is a toy or other object that a child plays with. ◻ *...an untidy garden scattered with children's playthings.*

play|time /pleɪtaɪm/ N-UNCOUNT In a school for young children, **playtime** is the period of time between lessons when they can play outside. ◻ *Any child who is caught will be kept in at playtime.*

play|wright /pleɪraɪt/ (playwrights) N-COUNT A **playwright** is a person who writes plays.

pla|za /plɑzə, plæzə/ (plazas) **1** N-COUNT A **plaza** is an open square in a city. ◻ *Across the busy plaza, vendors sell hot dogs and croissant sandwiches.* **2** N-COUNT A **plaza** is a group of stores or buildings that are joined together or share common areas. [AM] ◻ *...a new retail plaza.*

plea /pli/ (pleas) **1** N-COUNT A **plea** is an appeal or request for something, made in an intense or emotional way. [JOURNALISM] ◻ *Mr. Nicholas made his emotional plea for help in solving the killing.* **2** N-COUNT In a court of law, a person's **plea** is the answer that they give when they have been charged with a crime, saying whether or not they are guilty of that crime. ◻ *The judge questioned him about his guilty plea.* ◻ *We will enter a plea of not guilty.* **3** N-COUNT A **plea** is a reason given, to a court of law or to other people, as an excuse for doing something or for not doing something. ◻ *Phillips murdered his wife, but got off on a plea of insanity.* **4** → See feature box at **legal**

plea bar|gain (plea bargains, plea bargaining, plea bargained) **1** N-COUNT In some legal systems, a **plea bargain** is an agreement that, if an accused person says they are guilty, they will be charged with a less serious crime or will receive a less severe punishment. ◻ *A plea bargain was offered by the state assuring her that she would not go to prison.* **2** V-I If an accused person **plea bargains** or **plea-bargains**, they accept a plea bargain. ◻ *More and more criminals will agree to plea-bargain.* • **plea bar|gain|ing** N-UNCOUNT ◻ *...the introduction of a system of plea bargaining.*

plead /plid/ (pleads, pleading, pleaded or pled) **1** V-I If you **plead with** someone to do something, you ask them in an intense, emotional way to do it. ◻ *The woman pleaded with her daughter to come back home.* ◻ *He was kneeling on the floor pleading for mercy.* **2** V-I When someone charged with a crime **pleads guilty** or **not guilty** in a court of law, they officially state that they are guilty or not guilty of the crime. ◻ *Morris had pleaded guilty to robbery.* **3** V-T If you **plead the case** or **cause** of someone or something, you speak out in their support or defense. ◻ *He appeared before the committee to plead his case.* **4** V-T If you **plead** a particular thing as the reason for doing or not doing something, you give it as your excuse. ◻ *Mr. Giles pleads ignorance as his excuse.* **5** → See feature box at **legal**

plead|ing /plidɪŋ/ (pleadings) **1** ADJ A **pleading** expression or gesture shows someone that you want something very much. ◻ *...his pleading eyes.* ◻ *...the pleading expression on her face.* **2** N-UNCOUNT [also N in pl] **Pleading** is asking someone for something you want very much, in an intense or emotional way. ◻ *He simply ignored Sid's pleading.*

pleas|ant ◆◇◇ /plɛzənt/ (pleasanter, pleasantest) **1** ADJ Something that is **pleasant** is nice, enjoyable, or attractive. ◻ *I've got a pleasant little apartment.* • **pleas|ant|ly** ADV ◻ *We talked pleasantly of old times.* **2** ADJ Someone who is **pleasant** is friendly and likeable. ◻ *The woman had a pleasant face.*

pleas|ant|ry /plɛzəntri/ (pleasantries) N-COUNT [usu pl] **Pleasantries** are casual, friendly remarks that you make in order to be polite. ◻ *He exchanged pleasantries about his hotel and the weather.*

please ◆◆◇ /pliz/ (pleases, pleasing, pleased) **1** ADV [ADV with cl] You say **please** when you are politely asking or inviting someone to do something. [POLITENESS] ◻ *Can you help us please?* ◻ *Please come in.* ◻ *Can we have the bill please?* **2** ADV You say **please** when you are accepting something politely. [FORMULAE] ◻ *"Tea?"—"Yes, please."* **3** CONVENTION You can say **please** to indicate that you want someone to stop doing something or stop speaking. You would say this if, for example, what they are doing or saying makes you angry or upset. [FEELINGS] ◻ *Please, Mary, this is all so unnecessary.* **4** CONVENTION You can say **please** in order to attract someone's attention politely. [POLITENESS] ◻ *Please, Miss Smith, a moment.* **5** V-T/V-I If someone or something **pleases** you, they make you feel happy and satisfied. ◻ *More than anything, I want to please you.* ◻ *It pleased him to talk to her.* ◻ *He appeared anxious to please.* **6** PHRASE You use **please** in expressions such as **as she pleases**, **whatever you please**, and **anything he pleases** to indicate that someone can do or have whatever they want. ◻ *Women should be free to dress and act as they please.* ◻ *He does whatever he pleases.*

pleased ◆◇◇ /plizd/ **1** ADJ If you are **pleased**, you are happy about something or satisfied with something. ◻ *Felicity seemed pleased at the suggestion.* ◻ *I think he's going to be pleased that we identified the real problems.* **2** ADJ [v-link ADJ to-inf] If you say you will be **pleased** to do something, you are saying in a polite way that you are willing to do it. [POLITENESS] ◻ *We will be pleased to answer any questions you may have.* **3** ADJ [v-link ADJ] You can tell someone that you are **pleased** with something they have done in order to express your approval. [FEELINGS] ◻ *I'm pleased with the way things have been going.* ◻ *I am very pleased about the result.* ◻ *We are pleased that the problems have been resolved.* **4** ADJ [v-link ADJ to-inf] When you are about to give someone some news that you know will please them, you can say that you are **pleased** to tell them the news or that they will be **pleased** to hear it. ◻ *I'm pleased to say that he is now doing well.* **5** ADJ [v-link ADJ to-inf] In official letters, people often say they will be **pleased** to do something, as a polite way of introducing what they are going to do or inviting people to do something. [POLITENESS] ◻ *We will be pleased to delete the charge from the original invoice.* **6** PHRASE If someone seems very satisfied with something they have done, you can say that they are **pleased with** themselves, especially if you think they are more satisfied than they should be. ◻ *"Sophie was glad to see you," he said, pleased with himself again for having remembered her name.* **7** CONVENTION You can say **'Pleased to meet you'** as a polite way of greeting someone who you are meeting for the first time. [FORMULAE]

SYNONYMS

pleased
ADJ **1**
delighted: *He said that he was delighted with the public response.*
happy: *I'm just happy to be back running.*
contented: *Whenever he returns to this place, he is happy and contented.*
thrilled : *He's thrilled by the news.*

---

pleas|ing /plizɪŋ/ ADJ Something that is **pleasing** gives you pleasure and satisfaction. ◻ *This area of France has a pleasing climate in August.* ◻ *Such a view is pleasing.* • **pleas|ing|ly** ADV ◻ *The interior design is pleasingly simple.*

pleas|ur|able /plɛʒərəbəl/ ADJ **Pleasurable** experiences or sensations are pleasant and enjoyable. ◻ *The most pleasurable experience of the evening was the wonderful fireworks display.*

pleas|ure /plɛʒər/ (pleasures) **1** N-UNCOUNT If something gives you **pleasure**, you get a feeling of happiness, satisfaction, or enjoyment from it. □ *Watching sports gave him great pleasure.* □ *Everybody takes pleasure in eating.* **2** N-UNCOUNT **Pleasure** is the activity of enjoying yourself, especially rather than working or doing what you have a duty to do. □ *He mixed business and pleasure in a perfect and dynamic way.* **3** N-COUNT A **pleasure** is an activity, experience, or aspect of something that you find very enjoyable or satisfying. □ *Watching TV is our only pleasure.* □ *...the pleasure of seeing a smiling face.* **4** CONVENTION If you meet someone for the first time, you can say, as a way of being polite, that it is **a pleasure to meet** them. You can also ask for **the pleasure of** someone's **company** as a polite and formal way of inviting them somewhere. [POLITENESS] □ *"A pleasure to meet you, sir," he said.* **5** CONVENTION You can say **'It's a pleasure'** or **'My pleasure'** as a polite way of replying to someone who has just thanked you for doing something. [FORMULAE] □ *"Thanks very much anyhow."—"It's a pleasure."*

SYNONYMS

pleasure
NOUN **1**
enjoyment: *...her enjoyment of the beauty of the countryside.*
satisfaction: *She felt a small glow of satisfaction.*
bliss: *It was a scene of such domestic bliss.*
delight: *The views are a constant source of surprise and delight.*
happiness: *I think mostly she was looking for happiness.*

pleas|ure boat (pleasure boats) also **pleasure craft** N-COUNT A **pleasure boat** is a large boat that takes people for trips on rivers, lakes, or on the ocean for pleasure.

pleat /plit/ (pleats) N-COUNT A **pleat** in a piece of clothing is a permanent fold that is made in the cloth by folding one part over the other and sewing across the top end of the fold. □ *Her skirt hangs in perfect wide pleats.*

pleat|ed /plitɪd/ ADJ A **pleated** piece of clothing has pleats in it. □ *...a short white pleated skirt.*

ple|beian /pləbiən/ also **plebian 1** ADJ [usu ADJ n] A person, especially one from an earlier period of history, who is **plebeian**, comes from a low social class. **2** ADJ [usu ADJ n] If someone describes something as **plebeian**, they think that it is unsophisticated and connected with or typical of people from a low social class. [FORMAL, DISAPPROVAL] □ *...a philosophy professor with an alarmingly plebeian manner.*

plebi|scite /plɛbɪsaɪt, -sɪt/ (plebiscites) N-COUNT A **plebiscite** is a direct vote by the people of a country or region in which they say whether they agree or disagree with a particular policy, for example, whether a region should become an independent state.

pledge /plɛdʒ/ (pledges, pledging, pledged) **1** N-COUNT When someone makes a **pledge**, they make a serious promise that they will do something. □ *The meeting ended with a pledge to step up cooperation between the six states of the region.* **2** V-T When someone **pledges** to do something, they promise in a serious way to do it. When they **pledge** something, they promise to give it. □ *The Communists have pledged to support the opposition's motion.* □ *Philip pledges support and offers to help in any way that he can.* **3** V-T If you **pledge** a sum of money to an organization or activity, you promise to pay that amount of money to it at a particular time or over a particular period. □ *The French President is pledging $150 million in French aid next year.* • N-COUNT **Pledge** is also a noun. □ *...a pledge of forty-two million dollars a month.* **4** V-T If you **pledge** yourself to something, you commit yourself to following a particular course of action or to supporting a particular person, group, or idea. □ *The president pledged himself to increase taxes for the rich but not the middle classes.* **5** V-T If you **pledge** something such as a valuable possession or a sum of money, you leave it with someone as a guarantee that you will repay money that you have borrowed. □ *He asked her to pledge the house as security for a loan.*

SYNONYMS

pledge
NOUN **1**
promise: *If you make a promise, you should keep it.*
vow: *I took my marriage vows and kept them.*
oath: *She took an oath of loyalty to the government.*
guarantee: *California's state Constitution includes a guarantee of privacy.*

COLLOCATIONS

pledge
NOUN **1**
noun + **pledge:** election, manifesto, referendum
adjective + **pledge:** solemn
verb + **pledge:** make, sign; fulfill, honor

ple|na|ry /plinəri, plɛn-/ (plenaries) ADJ [ADJ n] A **plenary session** or **plenary meeting** is one that is attended by everyone who has the right to attend. [TECHNICAL] □ *...a plenary session of the Central Committee.* • N-COUNT **Plenary** is also a noun. □ *There'll be another plenary at the end of the afternoon after the workshop.*

pleni|po|ten|ti|ary /plɛnɪpətɛnʃiɛri/ (plenipotentiaries) also **Plenipotentiary 1** N-COUNT A **plenipotentiary** is a person who has full power to make decisions or take action on behalf of their government, especially in a foreign country. [FORMAL] □ *...the U.S. Plenipotentiary to the UN conference.* **2** ADJ [n ADJ] An **ambassador plenipotentiary** or **minister plenipotentiary** has full power or authority to represent their country. [FORMAL] **3** ADJ [ADJ n] If someone such as an ambassador has **plenipotentiary powers**, they have full power or authority to represent their country. [FORMAL]

pleni|tude /plɛnɪtud/ **1** N-UNCOUNT **Plenitude** is a feeling that an experience is satisfying because it is full or complete. [FORMAL] □ *The music brought him a feeling of plenitude and freedom.* **2** N-SING [usu N of n] If there is a **plenitude of** something, there is a great quantity of it. [FORMAL] □ *What is the use of a book about interior design without a plenitude of pictures in color?*

plen|ti|ful /plɛntɪfəl/ ADJ Things that are **plentiful** exist in such large amounts or numbers that there is enough for people's wants or needs. □ *Fish are plentiful in the lake.*

plen|ty /plɛnti/ QUANT If there is **plenty of** something, there is a large amount of it. If there are **plenty of** things, there are many of them. **Plenty** is used especially to indicate that there is enough of something, or more than you need. □ *There was still plenty of time to take Jill out for pizza.* □ *Most businesses face plenty of competition.* • PRON **Plenty** is also a pronoun. □ *I don't believe in long interviews. Fifteen minutes is plenty.*

ple|num /plinəm/ (plenums) N-COUNT A **plenum** is a meeting that is attended by all the members of a committee or conference. [TECHNICAL]

pletho|ra /plɛθərə/ N-SING A **plethora of** something is a large amount of it, especially an amount of it that is greater than you need, want, or can cope with. [FORMAL] □ *A plethora of new operators will be allowed to enter the market.*

pleu|ri|sy /plʊərɪsi/ N-UNCOUNT **Pleurisy** is a serious illness in which a person's lungs are sore and breathing is difficult.

Plexi|glas /plɛksɪglæs/ also **Plexiglass** N-UNCOUNT [oft N n] **Plexiglas** is a transparent plastic that is used to make things like plastic sheeting. [mainly AM, TRADEMARK] □ *...a Plexiglas window.*

plex|us /plɛksəs/ → see **solar plexus**

pli|able /plaɪəbəl/ ADJ If something is **pliable**, you can bend it easily without cracking or breaking it. □ *As your baby grows bigger, his bones become less pliable.*

pli|ant /plaɪənt/ **1** ADJ A **pliant** person can be easily influenced and controlled by other people. □ *She's proud and stubborn, you know, under that pliant exterior.* **2** ADJ If something is **pliant**, you can bend it easily without breaking it. □ *...pliant young willows.*

pli|ers /plaɪərz/ N-PLURAL [also *a pair of* N] **Pliers** are a tool with two handles at one end and two hard, flat, metal parts at the other. Pliers are used for holding or pulling out things such as nails, or for bending or cutting wire. **2** → See feature box at **DIY**; See also color supplement

plight /plaɪt/ (plights) N-COUNT If you refer to someone's **plight**, you mean that they are in a difficult or distressing situation that is full of problems. □ *The nation saw the plight of the farmers, whose crops had died.*

plinth /plɪnθ/ (plinths) **1** N-COUNT A **plinth** is a rectangular block of stone on which a statue or pillar stands. **2** → See also color supplement

plod /plɒd/ (plods, plodding, plodded) **1** V-I If someone **plods**, they walk slowly and heavily. □ *Crowds of people plodded around in yellow plastic raincoats.* **2** V-I If you say that someone **plods on**

plodder

or **plods along** with a job, you mean that the job is taking a long time. ❏ *He is plodding on with negotiations.*

plod|der /plɒdər/ (**plodders**) N-COUNT If you say that someone is a **plodder**, you have a low opinion of them because they work slowly and steadily but without showing enthusiasm or having new ideas. [INFORMAL, DISAPPROVAL] ❏ *He was quiet, conscientious, a bit of a plodder.*

plop /plɒp/ (**plops, plopping, plopped**) **1** N-COUNT; SOUND A **plop** is a soft, gentle sound, like the sound made by something dropping into water without disturbing the surface much. ❏ *Another drop of water fell with a soft plop.* **2** V-I If something **plops** somewhere, it drops there with a soft, gentle sound. ❏ *The ice cream plopped to the ground.*

plot ✦✧ /plɒt/ (**plots, plotting, plotted**) **1** N-COUNT A **plot** is a secret plan by a group of people to do something that is illegal or wrong, usually against a person or a government. ❏ *Security forces have uncovered a plot to overthrow the government.* **2** V-T If people **plot** to do something or **plot** something that is illegal or wrong, they plan secretly to do it. ❏ *Prosecutors in the trial allege the defendants plotted to overthrow the government.* ❏ *The military were plotting a coup.* **3** V-T When people **plot** a strategy or a course of action, they carefully plan each step of it. ❏ *Yesterday's meeting was intended to plot a survival strategy for the party.* **4** N-VAR The **plot** of a movie, novel, or play is the connected series of events which make up the story. ❏ *He began to tell me the plot of his new book.* **5** N-COUNT A **plot** of land is a small piece of land, especially one that has been measured or marked out for a special purpose, such as building houses or growing vegetables. ❏ *I thought that I'd buy myself a small plot of land and build a house on it.* **6** V-T When someone **plots** something on a graph, they mark certain points on it and then join the points up. ❏ *We plotted about eight points on the graph.* **7** V-T When someone **plots** the position or course of a plane or ship, they mark it on a map using instruments to obtain accurate information. ❏ *We were trying to plot the course of the submarine.* **8** V-T If someone **plots** the progress or development of something, they make a diagram or a plan which shows how it has developed in order to give some indication of how it will develop in the future. ❏ *They used a computer to plot the movements of everyone in the police station on that night.* **9** → See feature box at **book**

plot|line /plɒtlaɪn/ (**plotlines**) N-COUNT The **plotline** of a book, movie, or play is its plot and the way in which it develops. ❏ *The plotline is similar to that of many other movies.*

plot|ter /plɒtər/ (**plotters**) **1** N-COUNT [usu pl] A **plotter** is a person who secretly plans with others to do something that is illegal or wrong, usually against a person or government. ❏ *Coup plotters tried to seize power in Moscow.* **2** N-COUNT A **plotter** is a person or instrument that marks the position of something such as a ship on a map or chart.

plov|er /plʌvər, ploʊvər/ (**plovers**) N-COUNT A **plover** is a bird with a rounded body, a short tail, and a short beak that is found by the sea or by lakes.

plow /plaʊ/ (**plows, plowing, plowed**)

in BRIT, use **plough**

1 N-COUNT A **plow** is a large farming tool with sharp blades that is pulled across the soil to turn it over, usually before seeds are planted. ❏ *There are new tractors and new plows in the machinery lot.* **2** → see also **snowplow** **3** V-T When someone **plows** an area of land, they turn over the soil using a plow. ❏ *They were no longer using mules and horses to plow their fields.*
▶ **plow back** PHRASAL VERB [usu passive] If profits **are plowed back** into a business, they are used to increase the size of the business or to improve it. [BUSINESS] ❏ *...cash profits that are quickly plowed back into the market.*

plow|man /plaʊmən/ (**plowmen**)

in BRIT, use **ploughman**

N-COUNT A **plowman** is a man whose job it is to plow the land, especially with a plow pulled by horses or oxen.

plow|share /plaʊʃɛər/ (**plowshares**)

in BRIT, use **ploughshare**

PHRASE If you say that **swords have been turned into plowshares** or **beaten into plowshares**, you mean that a state

plugged

of conflict between two or more groups of people has ended and a period of peace has begun. [JOURNALISM]

ploy /plɔɪ/ (**ploys**) N-COUNT A **ploy** is a way of behaving that someone plans carefully and secretly in order to gain an advantage for themselves. ❏ *Christmas should be a time of excitement and wonder, not a cynical marketing ploy.*

pls. **Pls.** is a written abbreviation for **please**. ❏ *Have you moved yet? Pls. advise address, phone no., etc.*

pluck /plʌk/ (**plucks, plucking, plucked**) **1** V-T If you **pluck** a fruit, flower, or leaf, you take it between your fingers and pull it in order to remove it from its stalk where it is growing. [WRITTEN] ❏ *I plucked a lemon from the tree.* **2** V-T If you **pluck** something from somewhere, you take it between your fingers and pull it sharply from where it is. [WRITTEN] ❏ *He plucked the cigarette from his mouth and tossed it out into the street.* ❏ *He plucked the baby out of my arms.* **3** V-T If you **pluck** a guitar or other musical instrument, you pull the strings with your fingers and let them go, so that they make a sound. ❏ *Nell was plucking a harp.* **4** V-T If you **pluck** a chicken or other dead bird, you pull its feathers out to prepare it for cooking. ❏ *She looked relaxed as she plucked a chicken.* **5** V-T If a woman **plucks** her **eyebrows**, she pulls out some of the hairs using tweezers. ❏ *You've plucked your eyebrows at last!* **6** PHRASE If you **pluck up the courage** to do something that you feel nervous about, you make an effort to be brave enough to do it. ❏ *It took me about two hours to pluck up the courage to call.*

plucky /plʌki/ ADJ [usu ADJ n] If someone is described as **plucky**, it means that they face their difficulties with courage. [JOURNALISM, APPROVAL] ❏ *...a plucky kid struggling to rise from a squalid background.*

plug /plʌg/ (**plugs, plugging, plugged**) **1** N-COUNT A **plug** on a piece of electrical equipment is a small plastic object with two or three metal pins that fit into the holes of an electric outlet, connecting the equipment to the electricity supply. ❏ *I used to go around and take every plug out at night.* **2** N-COUNT A **plug** is an electric outlet. [INFORMAL] ❏ *Then Bob spotted the problem - the plug in the wall hadn't been switched on.* **3** N-COUNT A **plug** is a thick, circular piece of rubber or plastic that you use to block the hole in a bathtub or sink when it is filled with water. ❏ *She put the plug in the sink and filled it with cold water.* **4** N-COUNT A **plug** is a small, round piece of wood, plastic, or wax that is used to block holes. ❏ *A plug had been inserted in the drill hole.* **5** V-T If you **plug** a hole, you block it with something. ❏ *Crews are working to plug a major oil leak.* **6** V-T If someone **plugs** a commercial product, especially a book or a movie, they praise it in order to encourage people to buy it or see it because they have an interest in it doing well. ❏ *We did not want people on the show who are purely interested in plugging a book or movie.* • N-COUNT **Plug** is also a noun. ❏ *Let's do this show tonight and it'll be a great plug, a great promotion.* **7** PHRASE If someone in a position of power **pulls the plug on** a project or **on** someone's activities, they use their power to stop them from continuing. ❏ *The banks have the power to pull the plug on the project.*
▶ **plug in** also **plug into** **1** PHRASAL VERB If you **plug** a piece of electrical equipment **into** an electricity supply or if you **plug** it **in**, you push its plug into an electric outlet so that it can work. ❏ *They plugged in their equipment and left.* ❏ *I had a TV set but there was no place to plug it in.* **2** PHRASAL VERB If you **plug** one piece of electrical equipment **into** another or if you **plug** it **in**, you make it work by connecting the two. ❏ *They plugged their guitars into amplifiers.* **3** PHRASAL VERB If one piece of electrical equipment **plugs in** or **plugs into** another piece of electrical equipment, it works by being connected by an electrical cord or lead to an electricity supply or to the other piece of equipment. ❏ *The device plugs into the home television and stereo system.* ❏ *They plug into a laptop, desktop, or handheld computer.* **4** PHRASAL VERB If you **plug** something **into** a hole, you push it into the hole. ❏ *Her instructor plugged live bullets into the gun's chamber.* **5** → see also **plug-in**

plug-and-play ADJ [ADJ n] **Plug-and-play** is used to describe computer equipment, for example, a printer, that is ready to use immediately when you connect it to a computer. [COMPUTING] ❏ *...a plug-and-play USB camera.*

plugged /plʌgd/ also **plugged up** ADJ If something is **plugged** or **plugged up**, it is completely blocked so that nothing can get through it. ❏ *...a plugged toilet.* ❏ *His ears and nose were plugged up.*

plug|hole /pl∧ghoʊl/ (plugholes) N-COUNT A **plughole** is a small hole in a bathtub or sink that allows the water to flow away and into which you can put a plug. [BRIT]

> in AM, use **drain**

plug-in (plug-ins) **1** ADJ [ADJ n] A **plug-in** machine is a piece of electrical equipment that is operated by being connected to an electricity supply or to another piece of electrical equipment by means of a plug. ❑ ...a plug-in radio. **2** N-COUNT A **plug-in** is something such as a piece of software that can be added to a computer system to give extra features or functions. [COMPUTING] ❑ Some websites make it seem like you need to download a plug-in or program to access the site.

plum /pl∧m/ (plums) **1** N-COUNT A **plum** is a small, sweet fruit with a smooth purple, red, or yellow skin and a pit in the middle. **2** COLOR Something that is **plum** or **plum-colored** is a dark reddish-purple color. ❑ ...plum-colored silk.

plum|age /pluːmɪdʒ/ N-UNCOUNT A bird's **plumage** is all the feathers on its body.

plumb /pl∧m/ (plumbs, plumbing, plumbed) **1** V-T If you **plumb** something mysterious or difficult to understand, you succeed in understanding it. [LITERARY] ❑ She never abandoned her attempts to plumb my innermost emotions. **2** V-T When someone **plumbs** a building, they put in all the pipes for carrying water. ❑ She learned to wire and plumb the house herself. **3** PHRASE [oft PHR of n] If someone **plumbs the depths** of an unpleasant emotion or quality, they experience it or show it to an extreme degree. ❑ They frequently plumb the depths of loneliness, humiliation, and despair. **4** PHRASE [oft PHR of n] If you say that something **plumbs new depths**, you mean that it is worse than all the things of its kind that have existed before, even though some of them have been very bad. ❑ Relations between the two countries have plumbed new depths.

plumb|er /pl∧mər/ (plumbers) N-COUNT A **plumber** is a person whose job is to connect and repair things such as water and drainage pipes, bathtubs, and toilets.

plumb|ing /pl∧mɪŋ/ **1** N-UNCOUNT The **plumbing** in a building consists of the water and drainage pipes, bathtubs, and toilets in it. ❑ The wiring and the plumbing were sound but everything else had to be cleaned up. **2** N-UNCOUNT **Plumbing** is the work of connecting and repairing things such as water and drainage pipes, bathtubs, and toilets. ❑ She learned the rudiments of bricklaying, wiring, and plumbing.

plumb line (plumb lines) N-COUNT A **plumb line** is a piece of string with a weight attached to the end that is used to check that something such as a wall is vertical or that it slopes at the correct angle.

plume /pluːm/ (plumes) **1** N-COUNT A **plume** of smoke, dust, fire, or water is a large quantity of it that rises into the air in a column. ❑ The rising plume of black smoke could be seen all over Kabul. **2** N-COUNT A **plume** is a large, soft bird's feather. ❑ ...broad straw hats decorated with ostrich plumes.

plumed /pluːmd/ ADJ [usu ADJ n] **Plumed** means decorated with a plume or plumes. ❑ ...a young man wearing a plumed hat.

plum|met /pl∧mɪt/ (plummets, plummeting, plummeted) V-I If an amount, rate, or price **plummets**, it decreases quickly by a large amount. [JOURNALISM] ❑ In Tokyo share prices have plummeted for the sixth successive day. ❑ The president's popularity has plummeted to an all-time low in recent weeks.

plump /pl∧mp/ (plumper, plumpest, plumps, plumping, plumped) **1** ADJ You can describe someone or something as **plump** to indicate that they are somewhat fat or rounded. ❑ Maria was pretty, small and plump with a mass of curly hair. ❑ He pushed a plump little hand toward me. **2** V-T If you **plump** a pillow or cushion, you shake it and hit it gently so that it goes back into a rounded shape. ❑ She patted all the seats and plumped all the cushions. • PHRASAL VERB **Plump up** means the same as **plump**. ❑ "You need to rest," she told him reassuringly as she moved to plump up his pillows.

plum to|ma|to (plum tomatoes) N-VAR **Plum tomatoes** are long egg-shaped tomatoes.

plun|der /pl∧ndər/ (plunders, plundering, plundered) V-T If someone **plunders** a place or **plunders** things from a place, they steal things from it. [LITERARY] ❑ He plundered the palaces and ransacked the treasuries. ❑ She faces charges of helping to plunder her country's treasury of billions of dollars. • N-UNCOUNT **Plunder** is also a noun. ❑ ...a guerrilla group infamous for torture and plunder.

plunge ✦✧✧ /pl∧ndʒ/ (plunges, plunging, plunged) **1** V-I If something or someone **plunges** in a particular direction, especially into water, they fall, rush, or throw themselves in that direction. ❑ At least 50 people died when a bus plunged into a river. • N-COUNT **Plunge** is also a noun. ❑ ...a plunge into cold water. **2** V-T If you **plunge** an object into something, you push it quickly or violently into it. ❑ A soldier plunged a bayonet into his body. ❑ She plunged her face into a bowl of cold water. **3** V-T/V-I If a person or thing **is plunged** into a particular state or situation, or if they **plunge** into it, they are suddenly in that state or situation. ❑ The government's political and economic reforms threaten to plunge the country into chaos. ❑ Eddy found himself plunged into a world of brutal violence. • N-COUNT **Plunge** is also a noun. ❑ That peace often looked like a brief truce before the next plunge into war. **4** V-T/V-I If you **plunge into** an activity or **are plunged into** it, you suddenly get very involved in it. ❑ The two men plunged into discussion. ❑ The prince should be plunged into work. • N-COUNT **Plunge** is also a noun. ❑ His sudden plunge into the field of international diplomacy is a major surprise. **5** V-I If an amount or rate **plunges**, it decreases quickly and suddenly. ❑ His weight began to plunge. ❑ The Peso plunged to a new low on the foreign exchange markets yesterday. • N-COUNT **Plunge** is also a noun. ❑ The banks are in trouble because of bad loans and the stock market plunge. **6** PHRASE If you **take the plunge**, you decide to do something that you consider difficult or risky. ❑ If you have been thinking about buying mutual funds, now could be the time to take the plunge.

plung|er /pl∧ndʒər/ (plungers) N-COUNT A **plunger** is a device for clearing waste pipes. It consists of a rubber cup on the end of a stick which you press down several times over the end of the pipe.

plung|ing /pl∧ndʒɪŋ/ ADJ [ADJ n] A dress or blouse with a **plunging** neckline is cut in a very low V-shape at the front.

plunk /pl∧ŋk/ (plunks, plunking, plunked) **1** V-T If you **plunk** something somewhere, you put it there without great care. [AM, INFORMAL] ❑ Melanie plunked her cosmetic case down on a chair. ❑ She swept up a hat from where it had fallen on the ground, and plunked it on her hair.

> in BRIT, use **plonk**

2 V-T/V-I If you **plunk** yourself somewhere, or **plunk down**, you sit down heavily and clumsily. [AM, INFORMAL] ❑ I plunked down on one of the small metal chairs.

> in BRIT, use **plonk**

plu|per|fect /pluːpɜrfɪkt/ N-SING [the N] The **pluperfect** is the same as the **past perfect**.

plu|ral /plʊərəl/ (plurals) **1** ADJ The **plural** form of a word is the form that is used when referring to more than one person or thing. ❑ "Data" is the Latin plural form of "datum." **2** N-COUNT The **plural** of a noun is the form of it that is used to refer to more than one person or thing. ❑ What is the plural of "person"?

plu|ral|ism /plʊərəlɪzəm/ N-UNCOUNT If there is **pluralism** within a society, it has many different groups and political parties. [FORMAL] ❑ ...as the country shifts toward political pluralism.

plu|ral|ist /plʊərəlɪst/ ADJ [usu ADJ n] A **pluralist** society is one in which many different groups and political parties are allowed to exist. [FORMAL] ❑ ...an attempt to create a pluralist democracy.

plu|ral|is|tic /plʊərəlɪstɪk/ ADJ [usu ADJ n] **Pluralistic** means the same as **pluralist**. [FORMAL] ❑ Our objective is a free, open, and pluralistic society.

plu|ral|ity /plʊræliti/ (pluralities) **1** QUANT-PLURAL If there is a **plurality of** things, a number of them exist. [FORMAL] ❑ Federalism implies a plurality of political authorities, each with its own powers. **2** QUANT-PLURAL If a candidate, political party, or idea has the support of a **plurality of** people, they have more support than any other candidate, party, or idea. [FORMAL] ❑ 35% of the population, a plurality, believed that the economic reforms would result in only insignificant change. **3** N-COUNT A **plurality** in an election is the number of votes that the winner gets, when this is less than the total number of votes for all the other candidates. [AM] ❏ *He only got a plurality on November 3, just 49 percent.* ◳ N-COUNT A **plurality** in an election is the difference in the number of votes between the candidate who gets the most votes and the candidate who comes second. [AM] ❏ *Franklin had won with a plurality in electoral votes of 449 to 82.*

plus ♦♦◇ /plʌs/ (**pluses** or **plusses**) ◱ CONJ You say **plus** to show that one number or quantity is being added to another. ❏ *...$5 for a small locker, plus a $3 deposit.* ◲ ADJ [ADJ amount] **Plus** before a number or quantity means that the number or quantity is greater than zero. ❏ *The aircraft was subjected to temperatures of minus 65 degrees and plus 120 degrees.* ◳ CONJ You can use **plus** when mentioning an additional item or fact. [INFORMAL] ❏ *There's easily enough room for two adults and three children, plus a dog in the trunk.* ◴ ADJ [amount ADJ] You use **plus** after a number or quantity to indicate that the actual number or quantity is greater than the one mentioned. ❏ *There are only 35 staff to serve 30,000-plus customers.* ◵ ADJ Teachers use **plus** in grading work in schools and colleges. 'B plus' is a better grade than 'B,' but it is not as good as 'A.' ◶ N-COUNT A **plus** is an advantage or benefit. [INFORMAL] ❏ *Well-known figures would be a big plus for the new board.*

plus fours N-PLURAL [also *a pair of* N] **Plus fours** are short wide pants fastened below the knees that people used to wear when hunting or playing golf. [OLD-FASHIONED]

plush /plʌʃ/ (**plusher, plushest**) ADJ If you describe something as **plush**, you mean that it is very comfortable and expensive. ❏ *...their plush new training facility.*

plus sign (**plus signs**) N-COUNT A **plus sign** is the sign + that is put between two numbers in order to show that the second number is being added to the first. It can also be put before a number to show that the number is greater than zero (+3), and after a number to indicate a number that is more than a minimum number or amount (18+).

plu|toc|ra|cy /pluːtɒkrəsi/ (**plutocracies**) N-COUNT A **plutocracy** is a country that is ruled by its wealthiest people, or a class of wealthy people who rule a country. [FORMAL]

plu|to|crat /pluːtəkræt/ (**plutocrats**) N-COUNT If you describe someone as a **plutocrat**, you disapprove of them because you believe they are powerful only because they are rich. [FORMAL, DISAPPROVAL]

plu|to|nium /pluːtoʊniəm/ N-UNCOUNT **Plutonium** is a radioactive element used especially in nuclear weapons and as a fuel in nuclear power stations.

ply /plaɪ/ (**plies, plying, plied**) ◱ V-T If you **ply** someone with food or drink, you keep giving them more of it. ❏ *Elsie, who had been told that Maria wasn't well, plied her with food.* ◲ V-T If you **ply** someone with questions, you keep asking them questions. ❏ *Giovanni plied him with questions and comments with the deliberate intention of prolonging his stay.*

-ply /-plaɪ/ COMB IN ADJ [ADJ n] You use **-ply** after a number to indicate how many pieces are twisted or placed together to make a type of wool, rope, paper, or wood. ❏ *You need 3 balls of any 4-ply knitting wool.*

ply|wood /plaɪwʊd/ N-UNCOUNT **Plywood** is wood that consists of thin layers of wood stuck together. ❏ *...a sheet of plywood.*

p.m. /piː ɛm/ also **pm** ADV [num ADV] **p.m.** is used after a number to show that you are referring to a particular time between 12 noon and 12 midnight. Compare **a.m.** ❏ *The spa is open from 7:00 a.m. to 9:00 p.m. every day of the year.*

PMS /piː ɛm ɛs/ N-UNCOUNT **PMS** is an abbreviation for **premenstrual syndrome**.

pneu|mat|ic /nuːmætɪk/ ◱ ADJ [ADJ n] A **pneumatic drill** is operated by air under pressure and is very powerful. Pneumatic drills are often used for digging up roads. ❏ *...the sound of a pneumatic drill hammering away.* ◲ ADJ [ADJ n] **Pneumatic** means filled with air. ❏ *...pneumatic tires.*

pneu|mo|nia /nuːmoʊnyə, -moʊniə/ N-UNCOUNT **Pneumonia** is a serious disease that affects your lungs and makes it difficult for you to breathe. ❏ *She nearly died of pneumonia.*

PO /piː oʊ/ also **P.O.** **PO** is an abbreviation for **Post Office**.

poach /poʊtʃ/ (**poaches, poaching, poached**) ◱ V-T/V-I If someone **poaches** fish, animals, or birds, they illegally catch them on someone else's property. ❏ *Many national parks set up to provide a refuge for wildlife are regularly invaded by people poaching game.* • **poach|er** (**poachers**) N-COUNT ❏ *Security cameras have been installed to guard against poachers.* • **poach|ing** N-UNCOUNT ❏ *The poaching of elephants for their tusks could start to decline soon.* ◲ V-T If an organization **poaches** members or customers from another organization, they secretly or dishonestly persuade them to join them or become their customers. ❏ *Companies sometimes poach employees from one another.* • **poach|ing** N-UNCOUNT ❏ *The union was accused of poaching.* ◳ V-T If someone **poaches** an idea, they dishonestly or illegally use the idea. ❏ *They've poached all our best ideas.* ◴ V-T If you **poach** food such as fish, you cook it gently in boiling water, milk, or other liquid. ❏ *Poach the chicken until just cooked.* ❏ *...a pear poached in red wine.* • **poach|ing** N-UNCOUNT ❏ *You will need a pot of broth for poaching.*

PO Box /piː oʊ bɒks/ also **P.O. Box** **PO Box** is used before a number as a kind of address. The Post Office keeps letters addressed to the PO Box until they are collected by the person who has paid for the service. ❏ *Send your order and a check to PO Box 2855, Sunnyvale 94087.*

pocked /pɒkt/ ADJ **Pocked** means the same as **pockmarked**. ❏ *...a bus pocked with bullet holes.*

pock|et ♦◇◇ /pɒkɪt/ (**pockets, pocketing, pocketed**) ◱ N-COUNT A **pocket** is a kind of small bag that forms part of a piece of clothing, and that is used for carrying small things such as money or a handkerchief. ❏ *He took his flashlight from his jacket pocket and switched it on.* ◲ N-COUNT You can use **pocket** in a lot of different ways to refer to money that people have, get, or spend. For example, if someone gives or pays a lot of money, you can say that they **dig deep into** their **pocket**. If you approve of something because it is very cheap to buy, you can say that it **suits people's pockets**. ❏ *When you come to choosing a dining table, it really is worth digging deep into your pocket for the best you can afford.* ❏ *...fashions to suit all shapes, sizes, and pockets.* ◳ ADJ [ADJ n] You use **pocket** to describe something that is small enough to fit into a pocket, often something that is a smaller version of a larger item. ❏ *...a pocket calculator.* ◴ N-COUNT A **pocket** of something is a small area where something is happening, or a small area which has a particular quality, and which is different from the other areas around it. ❏ *Trapped in a pocket of air, they had only 40 minutes before the tide flooded the chamber.* ◵ V-T If someone who is in possession of something valuable such as a sum of money **pockets** it, they steal it or take it for themselves, even though it does not belong to them. ❏ *Banks have passed some of the savings on to customers and pocketed the rest.* ◶ V-T If you say that someone **pockets** something such as a prize or sum of money, you mean that they win or obtain it, often without needing to make much effort or in a way that seems unfair. [JOURNALISM] ❏ *He pocketed more money from this tournament than in his entire three years as a professional.* ◷ V-T If someone **pockets** something, they put it in their pocket, for example, because they want to steal it or hide it. ❏ *Anthony snatched his letters and pocketed them.* ◸ PHRASE If you say that a person or organization has **deep pockets**, you mean that they have a lot of money with which to pay for something. ❏ *The church will do anything to avoid scandal – and everyone knows it has deep pockets.* ❏ *...investors with deep pockets.* ◹ PHRASE If you are **out of pocket**, you have less money than you should have or than you intended, for example, because you have spent too much or because of a mistake. ❏ *Make sure you are not out of pocket for your expenses.* ◺ PHRASE If someone **picks** your **pocket**, they steal something from your pocket, usually without you noticing. ❏ *They were more in danger of having their pockets picked than being shot at.*

pocket|book /pɒkɪtbʊk/ (**pocketbooks**) ◱ N-COUNT You can use **pocketbook** to refer to people's concerns about the money they have or hope to earn. [AM, JOURNALISM] ❏ *People feel pinched in their pocketbooks and insecure about their futures.* ❏ *...the voters' concerns over pocketbook issues.* ◲ N-COUNT A **pocketbook** is a small bag that a woman uses to carry things such as her money and keys in when she goes out. [AM]

in BRIT, use **handbag**

pock|et knife (pocket knives) also **pocketknife** N-COUNT A **pocket knife** is a small knife with several blades that fold into the handle so that you can carry it around with you safely.

pock|et mon|ey N-UNCOUNT **Pocket money** is money for buying small things that you find you want or need. ❑ *They earned themselves a little pocket money by selling cigarettes.*

pocket-sized also **pocket-size** ADJ [usu ADJ n] If you describe something as **pocket-sized**, you approve of it because it is small enough to fit in your pocket. [APPROVAL] ❑ *...a handy pocket-sized reference book.*

pock|mark /pɒkmɑːk/ (pockmarks) N-COUNT [usu pl] **Pockmarks** are small hollows on the surface of something. ❑ *She has a poor complexion and pockmarks on her forehead.* ❑ *The pockmarks made by her bullets are still on the wall.*

pock|marked /pɒkmɑːkt/ ADJ [oft ADJ with n] If the surface of something is **pockmarked**, it has small hollow marks covering it. ❑ *He had a pockmarked face.* ❑ *The living room is pockmarked with bullet holes.*

pod /pɒd/ (pods) N-COUNT A **pod** is a seed container that grows on plants such as peas or beans. ❑ *...fresh peas in the pod.*

pod|cast /pɒdkæst/ (podcasts) N-COUNT A **podcast** is an audio file similar to a radio broadcast, that can be downloaded and listened to on a computer or iPod. ❑ *Now there are thousands of podcasts available daily.*

podgy /pɒdʒi/ ADJ [BRIT] → see pudgy

po|dia|trist /pədaɪətrɪst/ (podiatrists) N-COUNT A **podiatrist** is a person whose job is to treat and care for people's feet. **Podiatrist** is a more modern term for chiropodist.

po|dia|try /pədaɪətri/ N-UNCOUNT **Podiatry** is the professional care and treatment of people's feet.

po|dium /poʊdiəm/ (podiums) **1** N-COUNT A **podium** is a small platform on which someone stands in order to give a lecture or conduct an orchestra. ❑ *Unsteadily he mounted the podium, adjusted the microphone, coughed, and went completely blank.* **2** → See feature box at **Olympic Games**

poem ✦✧✧ /poʊəm/ (poems) N-COUNT A **poem** is a piece of writing in which the words are chosen for their beauty and sound and are carefully arranged, often in short lines that rhyme. ❑ *...a book of love poems.*

═══ SYNONYMS ═══
poem
NOUN
verse: *...a slim volume of verse.*
rhyme: *He was teaching Helen a little rhyme.*
sonnet: *We read one of Shakespeare's sonnets.*
lyrics: *...Kurt Weill's Broadway opera with lyrics by Langston Hughes.*

poet ✦✧✧ /poʊɪt/ (poets) N-COUNT A **poet** is a person who writes poems. ❑ *He was a painter and poet.*

po|et|ess /poʊɪtɪs/ (poetesses) N-COUNT A **poetess** is a female poet. Most female poets prefer to be called poets. [OLD-FASHIONED]

po|et|ic /poʊetɪk/ **1** ADJ Something that is **poetic** is very beautiful and expresses emotions in a sensitive or moving way. ❑ *Nikolai Demidenko gave an exciting yet poetic performance.* **2** ADJ **Poetic** means relating to poetry. ❑ *...Keats' famous poetic lines.*

po|eti|cal /poʊetɪkəl/ ADJ **Poetical** means the same as **poetic**. ❑ *...a work of real merit and genuine poetical feeling.*

po|et|ic jus|tice N-UNCOUNT If you describe something bad that happens to someone as **poetic justice**, you mean that it is exactly what they deserve because of the things that they have done.

po|et|ic li|cense N-UNCOUNT If someone such as a writer or movie director uses **poetic license**, they break the usual rules of language or style, or they change the facts, in order to create a particular effect. ❑ *It was time, she thought, to resort to a little poetic license.*

poet lau|reate /poʊɪt lɒriɪt/ (poet laureates or poets laureate) N-COUNT [usu the N] The **poet laureate** is the official poet of a country or a state who is usually appointed for a fixed period.

po|et|ry ✦✧✧ /poʊɪtri/ **1** N-UNCOUNT **Poems**, considered as a form of literature, are referred to as **poetry**. ❑ *...Russian poetry.* **2** N-UNCOUNT You can describe something very beautiful as **poetry**. ❑ *His music is purer poetry than a poem in words.*

═══ SYNONYMS ═══
poetry
NOUN **1**
verse: *...a slim volume of verse.*
rhyme: *The plays are in rhyme.*

pog|rom /pɒɡrʌm, poʊɡrɒm/ (pogroms) N-COUNT A **pogrom** is organized, official violence against a group of people for racial or religious reasons.

poign|an|cy /pɔɪnjənsi/ N-UNCOUNT **Poignancy** is the quality that something has when it affects you deeply and makes you feel very sad. ❑ *The film contains moments of almost unbearable poignancy.*

poign|ant /pɔɪnjənt/ ADJ Something that is **poignant** affects you deeply and makes you feel sadness or regret. ❑ *...a poignant combination of beautiful surroundings and tragic history.* ❑ *...a poignant love story.*

poin|set|tia /pɔɪnsetiə/ (poinsettias) N-COUNT A **poinsettia** is a plant with groups of bright red, white, or pink leaves that grows in Central and South America. Poinsettias are very popular at Christmas.

┌─────── POINT ───────┐
│ ① NOUN USES   │
│ ② VERB USES   │
│ ③ PHRASES   │
└─────────────────────┘

① **point** ✦✦✦ /pɔɪnt/ (points) **1** N-COUNT You use **point** to refer to something that someone has said or written. ❑ *We disagree with every point she makes.* ❑ *The following account will clearly illustrate this point.* **2** N-SING If you say that someone **has a point**, or if you **take** their **point**, you mean that you accept that what they have said is important and should be considered. ❑ *"If he'd already killed once, surely he'd have killed Sarah?" She had a point there.* **3** N-SING **The point** of what you are saying or discussing is the most important part that provides a reason or explanation for the rest. ❑ *"Did I ask you to talk to me?"—"That's not the point."* **4** N-SING If you ask what the **point** of something is, or say that there is **no point** in it, you are indicating that a particular action has no purpose or would not be useful. ❑ *What was the point of thinking about him?* **5** N-COUNT A **point** is a detail, aspect, or quality of something or someone. ❑ *Many of the points in the report are correct.* ❑ *The most interesting point about the village was its religion.* **6** N-COUNT A **point** is a particular place or position where something happens. ❑ *I'm sure there's another point we could meet at, but not there.* **7** N-SING You use **point** to refer to a particular time, or to a particular stage in the development of something. ❑ *We're all going to die at some point.* ❑ *It got to the point where he had to leave.* **8** N-COUNT The **point** of something such as a pin, needle, or knife is the thin, sharp end of it. ❑ *Put the tomatoes into a bowl and stab each one with the point of a knife.* **9** In spoken English, you use **point** to refer to the dot or mark in a decimal number that separates the whole numbers from the fractions. ❑ *This is FM stereo one oh three point seven.* **10** N-COUNT In some sports, competitions, and games, a **point** is one of the single marks that are added together to give the total score. ❑ *Chamberlain scored 50 or more points four times in the season.* **11** N-COUNT The **points of the compass** are directions such as North, South, East, and West. ❑ *Sightseers arrived from all points of the compass.* **12** N-PLURAL On a railroad track, the **points** are the levers and rails at a place where two tracks join or separate. The points enable a train to move from one track to another. [BRIT]

┌─────────────────────────────┐
│ in AM, use **switches**   │
└─────────────────────────────┘

13 → see also **breaking point, focal point, point of sale, point of view, sticking point, vantage point**

> **SYNONYMS**
>
> **point**
> NOUN
> ① ▪
> **message:** *I think they got the message that this is wrong.*
> **subject:** *It was I who first raised the subject of plastic surgery.*
> **question:** *But the whole question of aid is a tricky, political one.*
> ① ▪
> **purpose:** *The purpose of the occasion was to raise money for medical supplies.*
> **aim:** *...a research program that has largely failed to achieve its principal aims.*
> **goal:** *The goal is to raise as much money as possible.*
> **objective:** *His objective was to play golf and win.*
> VERB ② ▪
> **aim:** *He was aiming the rifle at Wade.*
> **level:** *They leveled guns at one another.*
> **direct:** *He directed the tiny beam of light at the roof.*

② **point** ◆◆◆ /pɔɪnt/ (points, pointing, pointed) ▪ V-I If you **point at** a person or thing, you hold out your finger toward them in order to make someone notice them. ❏ *I pointed at the boy sitting nearest me.* ❏ *He pointed at me with the stem of his pipe.* ▪ V-T If you **point** something **at** someone, you aim the tip or end of it toward them. ❏ *David pointed his finger at Mary.* ▪ V-I If something **points** to a place or **points** in a particular direction, it shows where that place is or it faces in that direction. ❏ *An arrow pointed to the toilets.* ❏ *He controlled the car until it was pointing forward again.* ▪ V-I If something **points to** a particular situation, it suggests that the situation exists or is likely to occur. ❏ *Earlier reports pointed to students working harder, more continuously, and with enthusiasm.* ▪ V-I If you **point to** something that has happened or that is happening, you are using it as proof that a particular situation exists. ❏ *George Fodor points to other weaknesses in the campaign.* ▪ → see also **pointed**

③ **point** ◆◆◆ /pɔɪnt/
→ Please look at meanings ▪ to ▪ to see if the expression you are looking for is shown under another headword.
▪ PHRASE If you say that something is **beside the point**, you mean that it is not relevant to the subject that you are discussing. ❏ *Brian didn't like it, but that was beside the point.* ▪ PHRASE When someone **comes to the point** or **gets to the point**, they start talking about the thing that is most important to them. ❏ *He came to the point at once. "You did a splendid job on this case."* ▪ PHRASE If you **make** your **point** or **prove** your **point**, you prove that something is true, either by arguing about it or by your actions or behavior. ❏ *I think you've made your point, dear.* ❏ *Dr. David McCleland studied one-hundred people, aged eighteen to sixty, to prove the point.* ▪ PHRASE If you **make a point of** doing something, you do it in a very deliberate or obvious way. ❏ *She made a point of spending as much time as possible away from Oklahoma.* ▪ PHRASE If you are **on the point of** doing something, you are about to do it. ❏ *He was on the point of saying something when the phone rang.* ▪ PHRASE Something that is **to the point** is relevant to the subject that you are discussing, or expressed neatly without wasting words or time. ❏ *The description which he had been given was brief and to the point.* ▪ PHRASE If you say that something is true **up to a point**, you mean that it is partly but not completely true. ❏ *"Was she good?"—"Mmm. Up to a point."* ▪ PHRASE If a person or something they say is **on point**, it is relevant to what is being discussed. [mainly AM] ❏ *This legislation could not be more on point.* ❏ *I welcome the discussion, but they need to be polite and on point.* ▪ PHRASE If someone or something is **on point**, they are extremely good. [mainly AM] ❏ *Their live vocals were on point and highly impressive.* ❏ *The cooking is as clever and on point as it always is.* ▪ **in point of fact** → see **fact** ▪ **to point the finger at someone** → see **finger** ▪ **a sore point** → see **sore** ▪ → See feature box at **debate**

▶ **point out** ▪ PHRASAL VERB If you **point out** an object or place, you make people look at it or show them where it is. ❏ *They kept standing up to take pictures and point things out to each other.* ▪ PHRASAL VERB If you **point out** a fact or mistake, you tell someone about it or draw their attention to it. ❏ *I should point out that these estimates cover just the hospital expenditures.*

point-and-click ADJ **Point-and-click** refers to the way a computer mouse can be used to do things quickly and easily on a computer. [COMPUTING] ❏ *...a simple point-and-click interface.*

point-blank ▪ ADV [ADV after v] If you say something **point-blank**, you say it very directly or rudely, without explaining or apologizing. ❏ *The army apparently refused point-blank to do what was required of them.* • ADJ [ADJ n] **Point-blank** is also an adjective. ❏ *...a point-blank refusal.* ▪ ADV [ADV after v] If someone or something is shot **point-blank**, they are shot when the gun is touching them or extremely close to them. ❏ *He put a gun through the open window of the car and fired point-blank at Bernadette.* • ADJ [ADJ n] **Point-blank** is also an adjective. ❏ *He had been shot at point-blank range in the back of the head.*

point|ed /pɔɪntɪd/ ▪ ADJ Something that is **pointed** has a point at one end. ❏ *...a pointed roof.* ▪ ADJ **Pointed** comments or behavior express criticism in a clear and direct way. ❏ *I couldn't help notice the pointed remarks slung in my direction.* • **point|ed|ly** ADV ❏ *They were pointedly absent from the news conference.*

point|er /pɔɪntər/ (pointers) ▪ N-COUNT A **pointer** is a piece of advice or information that helps you to understand a situation or to find a way of making progress. ❏ *I hope at least my daughter was able to offer you some useful pointers.* ▪ N-COUNT A **pointer** is a long stick that is used to point at something such as a large chart or diagram when explaining something to people. ❏ *She tapped on the world map with her pointer.* ▪ N-COUNT The **pointer** on a measuring instrument is the long, thin piece of metal that points to the numbers. ❏ *A series of levers joined to a pointer shows pressure on a dial.*

point|ing /pɔɪntɪŋ/ ▪ N-UNCOUNT **Pointing** is a way of filling in the gaps between the bricks or stones on the outside of a building so that the surface becomes sealed. ❏ *He did the pointing in the stonework himself.* ▪ N-UNCOUNT **Pointing** is the cement between the bricks or stones in a wall.

point|less /pɔɪntlɪs/ ADJ If you say that something is **pointless**, you are criticizing it because it has no sense or purpose. [DISAPPROVAL] ❏ *Violence is always pointless.* ❏ *Without an audience the performance is pointless.* • **point|less|ly** ADV ❏ *Chemicals were pointlessly poisoning the soil.*

point man (point men) N-COUNT The **point man** for a particular activity or on a particular issue is in a leading or important position. [AM] ❏ *The point man for Denver's new airport says there's no way it'll go under.*

point of or|der (points of order) N-COUNT [usu sing] In a formal debate, a **point of order** is an official complaint that someone makes because the rules about how the debate is meant to be organized have been broken. [FORMAL] ❏ *Is there any more debate on the point of order?*

point of ref|er|ence (points of reference) N-COUNT A **point of reference** is something that you use to help you understand a situation or communicate with someone. ❏ *The point of reference for semantic knowledge is the world.*

point of sale (points of sale) also **point-of-sale** ▪ N-COUNT The **point of sale** is the place in a store where a product is passed from the seller to the customer. The abbreviation **POS** is also used. [BUSINESS] ❏ *...information on consumer behavior at the point of sale.* ▪ N-UNCOUNT [usu N n] **Point-of-sale** is used to describe things that occur or are located or used at the place where you buy something. The abbreviation **POS** is also used. [BUSINESS] ❏ *Introduction of electronic point-of-sale systems is improving efficiency.*

point of view ◆◇◇ (points of view) ▪ N-COUNT You can refer to the opinions or attitudes that you have about something as your **point of view**. ❏ *Thanks for your point of view, John.* ▪ N-COUNT If you consider something from a particular **point of view**, you are using one aspect of a situation in order to judge that situation. ❏ *Do you think that, from the point of view of results, this exercise was worth the cost?*

pointy /pɔɪnti/ (pointier, pointiest) ADJ [usu ADJ n] Something that is **pointy** has a point at one end. [INFORMAL] ❏ *...a pointy little beard.*

poise /pɔɪz/ N-UNCOUNT If someone has **poise**, they are calm, dignified, and self-controlled. ❏ *What amazed him even more than her appearance was her poise.*

poised /pɔɪzd/ ▪ ADJ If a part of your body is **poised**, it is completely still but ready to move at any moment. ❏ *He studied the keyboard carefully, one finger poised.* ▪ ADJ [v-link ADJ] If someone is **poised** to do something, they are ready to take action at any moment. ❏ *U.S. forces are poised for a massive air, land, and sea* assault. **3** ADJ If you are **poised**, you are calm, dignified, and self-controlled. ❏ *She was self-assured, poised, almost self-satisfied.*

poi|son /pɔɪzᵊn/ (**poisons, poisoning, poisoned**) **1** N-MASS **Poison** is a substance that harms or kills people or animals if they swallow it or absorb it. ❏ *Poison from the fish causes paralysis, swelling, and nausea.* **2** V-T If someone **poisons** another person, they kill the person or make them ill by giving them poison. ❏ *The rumors that she had poisoned him could never be proved.* • **poi|son|ing** N-UNCOUNT ❏ *She was sentenced to twenty years' imprisonment for poisoning and attempted murder.* **3** V-T If you **are poisoned** by a substance, it makes you very ill and sometimes kills you. ❏ *Employees were taken to the hospital yesterday after being poisoned by fumes.* • **poi|son|ing** N-UNCOUNT ❏ *...acute alcohol poisoning.* **4** V-T If someone **poisons** a food, drink, or weapon, they add poison to it so that it can be used to kill someone. ❏ *If I was your wife I would poison your coffee.* **5** V-T To **poison** water, air, or land means to damage it with harmful substances such as chemicals. ❏ *...the textile and fiber industries that taint the air, poison the water, and use vast amounts of natural resources.* ❏ *The land has been completely poisoned by chemicals.* **6** V-T Something that **poisons** a good situation or relationship spoils it or destroys it. ❏ *The whole atmosphere has really been poisoned.*

poi|son|er /pɔɪzənər/ (**poisoners**) N-COUNT A **poisoner** is someone who has killed or harmed another person by using poison. ❏ *Soon they were dead, victims of a mysterious poisoner.*

poi|son gas N-UNCOUNT **Poison gas** is a gas that is poisonous and is usually used to kill people in war or to execute criminals.

poi|son ivy N-UNCOUNT **Poison ivy** is a wild plant that grows in North America and that causes a rash or skin problems if you touch it.

poi|son oak N-UNCOUNT **Poison oak** is a plant, similar to poison ivy, that causes a rash or skin problems if you touch it. [AM] ❏ *We walked through poison oak and got scratched by thorns.*

poi|son|ous /pɔɪzənəs/ **1** ADJ Something that is **poisonous** will kill you or make you ill if you swallow or absorb it. **2** ADJ All parts of the yew tree are poisonous, including the berries. **2** ADJ An animal that is **poisonous** produces a poison that will kill you or make you ill if the animal bites you. ❏ *There are hundreds of poisonous spiders and snakes.* **3** ADJ If you describe something as **poisonous**, you mean that it is extremely unpleasant and likely to spoil or destroy a good relationship or situation. ❏ *...poisonous comments.* ❏ *...lying awake half the night tormented by poisonous suspicions.*

poison-pen let|ter (**poison-pen letters**) N-COUNT A **poison-pen letter** is an unpleasant unsigned letter that is sent in order to upset someone or to cause trouble.

poi|son pill (**poison pills**) N-COUNT A **poison pill** refers to what some companies do to reduce their value in order to prevent themselves being taken over by another company. [BUSINESS] ❏ *Some believe this level of compensation is essentially a poison pill to put off any rival bidders.*

poke /poʊk/ (**pokes, poking, poked**) **1** V-T If you **poke** someone or something, you quickly push them with your finger or with a sharp object. ❏ *Lindy poked him in the ribs.* • N-COUNT **Poke** is also a noun. ❏ *John smiled at them and gave Richard a playful poke.* **2** V-T If you **poke** one thing **into** another, you push the first thing into the second thing. ❏ *He poked his finger into the hole.* **3** V-I If something **pokes out of** or **through** another thing, you can see part of it appearing from behind or underneath the other thing. ❏ *He saw the dog's twitching nose poke out of the basket.* **4** V-I/V-T If you **poke** your head **through** an opening or if it **pokes** through an opening, you push it through, often so that you can see something more easily. ❏ *Julie tapped on my door and poked her head in.* **5 to poke fun at** → see **fun 6 to poke your nose into something** → see **nose**

pok|er /poʊkər/ (**pokers**) **1** N-UNCOUNT **Poker** is a card game that people usually play in order to win money. ❏ *Lon and I play in the same weekly poker game.* **2** N-COUNT A **poker** is a metal bar that you use to move coal or wood in a stove or fireplace in order to make it burn better. ❏ *Niigata stirred the wood with a poker, and put another log on.*

pok|er face (**poker faces**) N-COUNT A **poker face** is an expression on your face that shows none of your feelings. [INFORMAL] ❏ *In business a poker face can be very useful.* ❏ *She managed to keep a poker face.*

poker-faced ADJ If you are **poker-faced**, you have a calm expression on your face that shows none of your thoughts or feelings. [INFORMAL] ❏ *His expressions varied from poker-faced to blank.* ❏ *The officer listened, poker-faced.*

poky /poʊki/ (**pokier, pokiest**)

The spelling **pokey** is also used, especially for meanings **2** and **3**.

1 ADJ If you say that someone is **poky**, you are criticizing them for moving or reacting very slowly. [AM, INFORMAL, DISAPPROVAL] ❏ *"Move!" she cried. "Don't be so darn poky!"* **2** ADJ A room or house that is **poky** is uncomfortably small. [INFORMAL, DISAPPROVAL] ❏ *...pokey little offices.* **3** N-SING [usu the N] If someone is in **the poky**, they are in prison. [mainly AM, INFORMAL, OLD-FASHIONED]

po|lar /poʊlər/ **1** ADJ [ADJ n] **Polar** means near the North or South Pole. ❏ *...the rigors of life in the polar regions.* ❏ *There was a period of excessive warmth which melted some of the polar ice.* **2** ADJ [ADJ n] **Polar** is used to describe things that are completely opposite in character, quality, or type. [FORMAL] ❏ *The nomads' lifestyle was the polar opposite of collectivization.*

po|lar bear (**polar bears**) N-COUNT A **polar bear** is a large white bear found near the North Pole.

po|lar|ity /poʊlæriti/ (**polarities**) N-VAR If there is a **polarity** between two people or things, they are completely different from each other in some way. [FORMAL] ❏ *...the polarities of good and evil.*

po|lar|ize /poʊləraɪz/ (**polarizes, polarizing, polarized**)

in BRIT, also use **polarise**

V-T/V-I If something **polarizes** people or if something **polarizes**, two separate groups are formed with opposite opinions or positions. ❏ *Missile deployment did much to further polarize opinion.* ❏ *As the car rental industry polarizes, business will go to the bigger companies.* • **po|lari|za|tion** /poʊlərɪzeɪʃᵊn/ N-UNCOUNT ❏ *...the increasing polarization between rich and poor.*

Po|lar|oid /poʊləroɪd/ (**Polaroids**) **1** ADJ [ADJ n] A **Polaroid** camera is a small film camera that can take, develop, and print a photograph in a few seconds. [TRADEMARK] **2** N-COUNT A **Polaroid** is a photograph taken with a Polaroid camera. **3** ADJ [ADJ n] **Polaroid** sunglasses have been treated with a special substance in order to make the sun seem less bright.

pole ♦◇◇ /poʊl/ (**poles**) **1** N-COUNT A **pole** is a long thin piece of wood or metal, used especially for supporting things. ❏ *The truck crashed into a telegraph pole.* **2** N-COUNT The Earth's **poles** are the two opposite ends of its axis, its most northern and southern points. ❏ *For six months of the year, there is hardly any light at the poles.* **3** N-COUNT The two **poles** of a magnet are the two ends of the magnet where the magnetic force is strongest. ❏ *The important fact is that the two poles of the magnet work in opposite ways.* **4** N-COUNT The two **poles** of a range of qualities, opinions, or beliefs are the completely opposite qualities, opinions, or beliefs at either end of the range. ❏ *The two politicians represent opposite poles of the political spectrum.* **5** PHRASE If you say that two people or things **are poles apart**, you mean that they have completely different beliefs, opinions, or qualities. [EMPHASIS]

Pole /poʊl/ (**Poles**) N-COUNT A **Pole** is a Polish citizen, or a person of Polish origin.

pole|cat /poʊlkæt/ (**polecats**) N-COUNT A **polecat** is a small, thin, fierce wild animal. Polecats can release a very unpleasant smell.

pole danc|ing also **pole dancing** **1** N-UNCOUNT **Pole dancing** is a type of entertainment in a bar or club in which a woman who is wearing very few clothes dances around a pole in a sexy way. • **pole danc|er** (**pole dancers**) N-COUNT ❏ *She has been auditioning for a job as a pole dancer.* **2** N-UNCOUNT **Pole dancing** is a form of exercise which involves dancing around a pole. • **pole danc|er** (**pole dancers**) N-COUNT ❏ *The mum-of-two is a keen pole dancer, as it apparently helps her keep in shape.*

po|lem|ic /pəlɛmɪk/ (**polemics**) N-VAR A **polemic** is a very strong written or spoken attack on, or defense of, a particular belief or opinion. ❏ *...a polemic against the danger of secret societies.*

po|lemi|cal /pəlɛmɪkᵊl/ ADJ **Polemical** means arguing very strongly for or against a belief or opinion. ❏ *Daniels is at his best when he's cool and direct, rather than combative and polemical.* ❏ *...Kramer's biting polemical novel.*

po|lemi|cist /pəlɛmɪsɪst/ (polemicists) N-COUNT A **polemicist** is someone who is skilled at arguing very strongly for or against a belief or opinion. [FORMAL]

pole po|si|tion (pole positions) N-UNCOUNT [also N in pl] When a racing car is in **pole position**, it is in front of the other cars at the start of a race.

pole vault N-SING [the N] The **pole vault** is a track and field event in which athletes jump over a high bar, using a long flexible pole to help lift themselves up.

pole vault|er (pole vaulters) N-COUNT A **pole vaulter** is an athlete who performs the pole vault.

po|lice ◆◆◆ /pəlis/ (polices, policing, policed) **1** N-SING [usu with plural verb] The **police** are the official organization that is responsible for making sure that people obey the law. ☐ *The police are also looking for a second car.* ☐ *Police say they have arrested twenty people following the disturbances.* **2** N-PLURAL **Police** are men and women who are members of the official organization that is responsible for making sure that people obey the law. ☐ *More than one hundred police have ringed the area.* **3** V-T If the police or military forces **police** an area or event, they make sure that law and order is preserved in that area or at that event. ☐ *...the tiny U.N. observer force whose job it is to police the border.* **4** V-T If a person or group in authority **polices** a law or an area of public life, they make sure that what is done is fair and legal. ☐ *...the self-regulatory body that polices the investment management business.* **5** → see also **secret police**

SYNONYMS

police
VERB
3
control: *...measures to control illegal mining.*
patrol: *Prison officers continued to patrol the grounds within the jail.*
guard: *...the heavily-guarded courtroom.*
4
monitor: *Officials had not been allowed to monitor the voting.*
oversee: *...the agreement to set up a commission to oversee the peace process.*
supervise: *University instructors have refused to supervise students' examinations.*

po|lice de|part|ment (police departments) N-COUNT-COLL A **police department** is an official organization which is responsible for making sure that people obey the law. [AM] ☐ *...the Los Angeles Police Department.*

po|lice dog (police dogs) N-COUNT A **police dog** is a working dog that is owned by the police.

po|lice force (police forces) N-COUNT A **police force** is the police organization in a particular country or area. ☐ *...the Wichita police force.*

police|man ◆◇◇ /pəlismən/ (policemen) N-COUNT A **policeman** is a man who is a member of the police force.

po|lice of|fic|er ◆◇◇ (police officers) N-COUNT A **police officer** is a member of the police force. ☐ *...a meeting of senior police officers.*

po|lice state (police states) N-COUNT A **police state** is a country in which the government controls people's freedom by means of the police, especially secret police. [DISAPPROVAL]

po|lice sta|tion (police stations) N-COUNT A **police station** is the local office of a police force in a particular area. ☐ *Two police officers arrested him and took him to Gettysburg police station.*

police|woman /pəliswʊmən/ (policewomen) N-COUNT A **policewoman** is a woman who is a member of the police force.

poli|cy ◆◆◆ /pɒlɪsi/ (policies) **1** N-VAR A **policy** is a set of ideas or plans that is used as a basis for making decisions, especially in politics, economics, or business. ☐ *...plans that include changes in foreign policy and economic reforms.* **2** N-COUNT An official organization's **policy** on a particular issue or toward a country is their attitude and actions regarding that issue or country. ☐ *...the organization's future policy toward South Africa.* ☐ *...the government's policy on repatriation.* **3** N-COUNT An insurance **policy** is a document that shows the agreement that you have made with an insurance company. [BUSINESS] ☐ *You are advised to read the small print of homeowner and car insurance policies.*

COLLOCATIONS

policy
NOUN
1
noun + **policy**: energy, immigration, privacy
adjective + **policy**: economic, fiscal, foreign, monetary
verb + **policy**: change, develop, influence; tighten
2
noun + **policy**: government
verb + **policy**: adopt, implement, pursue, support
3
verb + **policy**: take out; renew

SYNONYMS

policy
NOUN **1**
procedure: *The White House said there would be no change in procedure.*
plan: *...a detailed plan of action for restructuring the group.*
protocol: *...minor breaches of protocol.*

policy|holder /pɒlɪsihoʊldər/ (policyholders) N-COUNT A **policyholder** is a person who has an insurance policy with an insurance company. [BUSINESS] ☐ *The first 10 percent of legal fees will be paid by the policyholder.*

policy|maker /pɒlɪsimeɪkər/ (policymakers) also **policy-maker** N-COUNT [usu pl] In politics, **policymakers** are people who are involved in making policies and policy decisions. ☐ *...top economic policymakers.*

policy|making /pɒlɪsimeɪkɪŋ/ N-UNCOUNT [oft N n] **Policymaking** is the making of policies. ☐ *He will play a key background role in government policymaking.*

po|lio /poʊlioʊ/ N-UNCOUNT **Polio** is a serious infectious disease that often makes people unable to use their legs. [MEDICAL] ☐ *Gladys was crippled by polio at the age of 3.*

po|lio|my|eli|tis /poʊlioʊmaɪəlaɪtɪs/ N-UNCOUNT **Poliomyelitis** is the same as **polio**. [MEDICAL]

pol|ish /pɒlɪʃ/ (polishes, polishing, polished) **1** N-MASS **Polish** is a substance that you put on the surface of an object in order to clean it, protect it, and make it shine. ☐ *The still air smelled faintly of furniture polish.* **2** V-T If you **polish** something, you put polish on it or rub it with a cloth to make it shine. ☐ *Each morning he shaved and polished his shoes.* • N-SING **Polish** is also a noun. ☐ *He gave his counter a polish with a soft duster.* • **pol|ished** ADJ ☐ *...a highly polished floor.* **3** V-T If you say that a performance or piece of work has **polish**, you mean that it is of a very high standard. [APPROVAL] ☐ *The opera lacks the polish of his later work.* **4** V-T If you **polish** your technique, performance, or skill at doing something, you work on improving it. ☐ *They just need to polish their technique.* • PHRASAL VERB **Polish up** means the same as **polish**. ☐ *Polish up your writing skills on a one-week professional course.* **5** → see also **polished** **6** → See feature box at **housework**

Po|lish /poʊlɪʃ/ **1** ADJ **Polish** means belonging or relating to Poland, or to its people, language, or culture. **2** N-UNCOUNT **Polish** is the language spoken in Poland.

pol|ished /pɒlɪʃt/ **1** ADJ Someone who is **polished** shows confidence and knows how to behave socially. [APPROVAL] ☐ *He is polished, charming, articulate, and an excellent negotiator.* **2** ADJ If you describe a performance, ability, or skill as **polished**, you mean that it is of a very high standard. [APPROVAL] ☐ *...a very polished performance.* **3** → see also **polish**

Pol|it|bu|ro /pɒlɪtbyʊəroʊ, poʊlit-/ (Politburos) N-COUNT [usu the N] In communist countries the **Politburo** is the chief committee that decides on government policy and makes decisions.

po|lite /pəlaɪt/ (politer, politest) **1** ADJ Someone who is **polite** has good manners and behaves in a way that is socially correct and not rude to other people. ☐ *Everyone around him was trying to be polite, but you could tell they were all bored.* ☐ *Gonzales, a quiet and very polite young man, made a favorable impression.* • **po|lite|ly** ADV ☐ *"Your home is beautiful," I said politely.* • **po|lite|ness** N-UNCOUNT ☐ *She listened to him, but only out of politeness.* **2** → See feature box on next page

VOCABULARY IN CONTEXT

Being polite and impolite

Has **politeness** gone out of fashion?

Today, the idea of **impeccable manners** seems a little archaic. Current **etiquette** is certainly more relaxed than it was in the relatively recent past. Behavior which was **frowned on** before is barely remarked upon today. This pertains to **common courtesy** and quite basic **social norms**, like combing your hair in the street or having your elbows on a dining table. Does anyone *really* care about these **unwritten rules** any more?

However, two aspects of modern life have dramatically increased instances of **uncivilized** behavior. The first is road rage. It's not unusual for impatient drivers to overreact and **disrespect** other motorists with **offensive** language. The second is speaking loudly on a cellphone in public. Many consider it **discourteous** and the **height of rudeness** to subject others to private conversations they have no wish to overhear.

What sort of **impolite** behavior do you find particularly **obnoxious**?

poli|tic /pɒlɪtɪk/ **1** ADJ If it seems **politic** to do a particular thing, that seems to be the most sensible thing to do in the circumstances. [FORMAL] ❑ *Many towns often found it politic to change their allegiance.* **2** → see also **politics**, **body politic**

po|liti|cal ♦♦♦ /pəlɪtɪkəl/ **1** ADJ **Political** means relating to the way power is achieved and used in a country or society. ❑ *All other political parties there have been completely banned.* ❑ *The government is facing another political crisis.* • **po|liti|cal|ly** /pəlɪtɪkli/ ADV ❑ *They do not believe the killings were politically motivated.* **2** ADJ Someone who is **political** is interested or involved in politics and holds strong beliefs about it. ❑ *Oh I'm not political, I take no interest in politics.*

SYNONYMS

political
ADJ **1**
governmental: *...a governmental agency for providing financial aid to developing countries.*
state: *...reform of the state social-security system.*
parliamentary: *He used his influence to make sure she was not selected as a parliamentary candidate.*

po|liti|cal ac|tion com|mit|tee (political action committees) N-COUNT A **political action committee** is an organization which campaigns for particular political policies, and that gives money to political parties or candidates who support those policies. The abbreviation **PAC** is also used. [AM] ❑ *...a political action committee that supports gun control.*

po|liti|cal asy|lum N-UNCOUNT **Political asylum** is the right to live in a foreign country and is given by the government of that country to people who have to leave their own country for political reasons. ❑ *...a university teacher who is seeking political asylum in California.*

po|liti|cal cor|rect|ness N-UNCOUNT **Political correctness** is the attitude or policy of being extremely careful not to offend or upset any group of people in society who have a disadvantage, or who have been treated differently because of their sex, gender, race, or disability.

po|liti|cal econo|my N-UNCOUNT **Political economy** is the study of the way in which a government influences or organizes a nation's wealth.

po|liti|cal in|cor|rect|ness N-UNCOUNT **Political incorrectness** is the attitude or policy shown by someone who does not care if they offend or upset any group of people in society who have a disadvantage, or who have been treated differently because of their sex, gender, race, or disability. ❑ *...allegations of political incorrectness.*

po|liti|cal|ly cor|rect ADJ If you say that someone is **politically correct**, you mean that they are extremely careful not to offend or upset any group of people in society who have a disadvantage, or who have been treated differently because of their sex, race, or disability. The abbreviation **PC** is also used. ❑ *His views are far from politically correct.* • N-PLURAL [the N] **The politically correct** are people who are politically correct. ❑ *...the hypocrisy of the politically correct.*

po|liti|cal|ly in|cor|rect ADJ If you say that someone is **politically incorrect**, you mean that they do not care if they offend or upset other people in society who have a disadvantage, or who have been treated differently because of their sex, gender, race, or disability. ❑ *Gershwin's lyrics would today probably be deemed politically incorrect.* • N-PLURAL [the N] **The politically incorrect** are people who are politically incorrect.

po|liti|cal pris|on|er (political prisoners) N-COUNT A **political prisoner** is someone who has been imprisoned for criticizing or disagreeing with their own government.

po|liti|cal sci|ence N-UNCOUNT **Political science** is the study of the ways in which political power is acquired and used in a country.

po|liti|cal sci|en|tist (political scientists) N-COUNT A **political scientist** is someone who studies, writes, or lectures about political science.

poli|ti|cian ♦♦◊ /pɒlɪtɪʃən/ (politicians) N-COUNT A **politician** is a person whose job is in politics, especially a member of the government. ❑ *They have arrested a number of leading opposition politicians.*

SYNONYMS

politician
NOUN
statesman: *Hamilton is a great statesman and political thinker.*
legislator: *...an attempt to get U.S. legislators to change the system.*

po|liti|cize /pəlɪtɪsaɪz/ (politicizes, politicizing, politicized)
in BRIT, also use **politicise**
V-T If you **politicize** someone or something, you make them more interested in politics or more involved with politics. ❑ *...ideas that might politicize the working classes and cause them to question the status quo.* ❑ *Some feminists had attempted to politicize personal life.* • **po|liti|cized** ADJ ❑ *The data that's being used to fault American education is highly politicized.* • **po|liti|ci|za|tion** /pəlɪtɪsaɪzeɪʃən/ N-UNCOUNT ❑ *There has been increasing politicization of the civil service.*

poli|tick|ing /pɒlɪtɪkɪŋ/ N-UNCOUNT If you describe someone's political activity as **politicking**, you think that they are engaged in it to gain votes or personal advantage for themselves. [DISAPPROVAL] ❑ *The politicking in Seattle is extremely intense.*

po|liti|co /pəlɪtɪkoʊ/ (politicos) N-COUNT You can describe a politician as a **politico**, especially if you do not like them or approve of what they do. [DISAPPROVAL]

politico- /pəlɪtɪkoʊ-/ COMB IN ADJ [ADJ n] **Politico-** is added to adjectives to form other adjectives that describe something as being both political and the other thing that is mentioned. ❑ *...the capitalist politico-economic system.*

poli|tics ♦♦◊ /pɒlɪtɪks/ **1** N-PLURAL **Politics** are the actions or activities concerned with achieving and using power in a country or society. The verb that follows **politics** may be either

polity

singular or plural. ❑ *Many people think Nixon transformed American politics.* ❑ *He quickly involved himself in local politics.* **2** N-PLURAL Your **politics** are your beliefs about how a country ought to be governed. ❑ *My politics are well to the left of center.* **3** N-UNCOUNT **Politics** is the study of the ways in which countries are governed. ❑ *He began studying politics and medieval history.* **4** N-PLURAL **Politics** can be used to talk about the ways that power is shared in an organization and the ways it is affected by personal relationships between people who work together. The verb that follows **politics** may be either singular or plural. ❑ *You need to understand how office politics influence the working environment.*

VOCABULARY IN CONTEXT

Politics

In the U.S. in the nineteenth century, women could not **cast a vote**. However, as more women began to work outside the home, organized campaigns for women's **suffrage** (right to vote) started to appear. The first women's rights **convention** was in 1848 in Seneca Falls, New York.

Women in the U.K. were also **rallying** for their rights. The movement in the U.K. had two wings, the suffragists and the suffragettes. The suffragists believed in using peaceful **tactics**, such as **petitions** and **lobbying** MPs. The suffragettes were more **radical**, and their methods were far more **militant**. They felt it was necessary to break the law, and many were sent to prison.

It is hard to be sure which approach was more effective, as the outbreak of World War I meant that both sides **suspended** the struggle. When the war was over, women's contribution to the war effort was so clear that they were immediately given the vote.

pol|ity /pɒlɪti/ (polities) N-COUNT A **polity** is an organized society, such as a nation, city, or church, together with its government and administration. [FORMAL] ❑ *...the role of religious belief in a democratic polity.*

pol|ka /pɒlkə/ (polkas) N-COUNT A **polka** is a fast lively dance from central Europe.

pol|ka dots

The spelling **polka-dot** is also used, especially as a modifier. The word **polka** is pronounced /pəʊkə/ when it is part of this compound.

N-PLURAL [oft N n] **Polka dots** are small spots printed on a piece of cloth. ❑ *...a yellow bikini with polka dots.* ❑ *...a tight-fitting polka-dot blouse.*

poll ♦♦◇ /pəʊl/ (polls, polling, polled) **1** N-COUNT A **poll** is a survey in which people are asked their opinions about something, usually in order to find out how popular something is or what people intend to do in the future. ❑ *Polls show that the European treaty has gained support in Denmark.* ❑ *We are doing a weekly poll on the president, and clearly his popularity has declined.* **2** → see also **opinion poll** **3** V-T [usu passive] If you **are polled** on something, you are asked what you think about it as part of a survey. ❑ *More than 18,000 people were polled.*

❑ *Audiences were going to be polled on which of three pieces of contemporary music they liked best.* **4** N-PLURAL **The polls** means an election for a country's government, or the place where people go to vote in an election. ❑ *Incumbent officeholders are difficult to defeat at the polls.* ❑ *Voters are due to go to the polls on Sunday to elect a new president.* **5** V-T If a political party or a candidate **polls** a particular number or percentage of votes, they get that number or percentage of votes in an election. ❑ *The result showed he had polled enough votes to force a second ballot.* **6** → see also **polling**

SYNONYMS

poll
NOUN
1
survey: *According to the survey, world trade overall has also slackened.*
4
election: *...the first fully free elections for more than fifty years.*
referendum: *Estonia said it too planned to hold a referendum on independence.*
vote: *Why do you think we should have a vote on that?*
ballot: *The result of the ballot will not be known for two weeks.*
VERB **3**
ballot: *The union said they will ballot members on whether to strike.*
survey: *Only 18 percent of those surveyed opposed the idea.*

---

pol|len /pɒlən/ (pollens) N-MASS **Pollen** is a fine powder produced by flowers. It fertilizes other flowers of the same species so that they produce seeds.

pol|len count (pollen counts) N-COUNT The **pollen count** is a measure of how much pollen is in the air at a particular place and time. Information about the pollen count is given to help people who have an allergy to pollen. ❑ *Avoid trips to the country while the pollen count is high.*

pol|li|nate /pɒlɪneɪt/ (pollinates, pollinating, pollinated) **1** V-T To **pollinate** a plant or tree means to fertilize it with pollen. This is often done by insects. ❑ *Many of the indigenous insects are needed to pollinate the local plants.* • **pol|li|na|tion** /pɒlɪneɪʃən/ N-UNCOUNT ❑ *Without sufficient pollination, the growth of the corn is stunted.* **2** → See feature box at **endanger**

pol|li|na|tor /pɒlɪneɪtər/ (pollinators) N-COUNT A **pollinator** is something that pollinates plants, especially a type of insect. [TECHNICAL]

poll|ing /pəʊlɪŋ/ N-UNCOUNT **Polling** is the act of voting in an election. ❑ *There has been a busy start to polling in today's local elections.*

poll|ing booth (polling booths) **1** N-COUNT [usu pl] **Polling booths** are the places where people go to vote in an election. ❑ *...detectives watching the polling booths on election day.* **2** N-COUNT A **polling booth** is one of the partly enclosed areas in a polling place, where people can vote in private. ❑ *When you are there, in the polling booth, nobody can see who you are voting for.*

poll|ing day N-UNCOUNT **Polling day** is the day on which people vote in an election. [mainly BRIT]

in AM, usually use **election day**

poll|ing place (polling places) N-COUNT A **polling place** is a place where people go to vote in an election. It is often a school or other public building. [AM]

poll|ing sta|tion (polling stations) N-COUNT A **polling station** is the same as a **polling place**. [BRIT]

poll|ster /pəʊlstər/ (pollsters) N-COUNT A **pollster** is a person or organization that asks large numbers of people questions to find out their opinions on particular subjects.

pol|lu|tant /pəluːtənt/ (pollutants) **1** N-VAR **Pollutants** are substances that pollute the environment, especially gases from vehicles and poisonous chemicals produced as waste by industrial processes. ❑ *Industrial pollutants are responsible for a sizable proportion of all cancers.* **2** → See feature box at **global warming**

pol|lute /pəluːt/ (pollutes, polluting, polluted) V-T To **pollute** water, air, or land means to make it dirty and dangerous to live in or to use, especially with poisonous chemicals or sewage. ❑ *Heavy industry pollutes our rivers with noxious chemicals.* ● **pol|lut|ed** ADJ ❑ *The police have warned the city's inhabitants not to bathe in the polluted river.*

pol|lut|er /pəlutər/ (**polluters**) N-COUNT A **polluter** is someone or something that pollutes the environment.

pol|lu|tion ✦✧ /pəluʃⁿn/ ◼ N-UNCOUNT **Pollution** is the process of polluting water, air, or land, especially with poisonous chemicals. ❑ *The fine was for the company's pollution of the air near its plants.* ◼ N-UNCOUNT **Pollution** is poisonous or dirty substances that are polluting the water, air, or land somewhere. ❑ *The level of pollution in the river was falling.*

SYNONYMS

pollution
NOUN ◼
contamination: *The contamination of the sea around Capri may be just the beginning.*
waste: *Up to 10 million tons of toxic waste are produced every year in the U.K.*
impurity: *The air in the factory is filtered to remove impurities.*

---

polo /poʊloʊ/ N-UNCOUNT **Polo** is a game played between two teams of players. The players ride horses and use wooden hammers with long handles to hit a ball.

polo neck (**polo necks**) also **polo-neck** N-COUNT A **polo neck** or a **polo neck sweater** is a sweater with a high neck which folds over. [BRIT]

in AM, use **turtleneck**

polo shirt (**polo shirts**) N-COUNT A **polo shirt** is a soft short-sleeved knit shirt with a collar that you put on over your head.

pol|ter|geist /poʊltərgaɪst/ (**poltergeists**) N-COUNT A **poltergeist** is a ghost or supernatural force that is believed to move furniture or throw objects around.

PREFIX

poly-
forms nouns and adjectives that have many as part of their meaning. *For example, **polygamy** is the custom in some societies of being married to more than one person at the same time.*

---

poly|es|ter /pɒliɛstər/ (**polyesters**) N-MASS **Polyester** is a type of synthetic cloth used especially to make clothes. ❑ *...a green polyester shirt.*

poly|ethyl|ene /pɒliɛθɪlin/ N-UNCOUNT **Polyethylene** is a type of plastic made into thin sheets or bags and used especially to keep food fresh or to keep things dry. [mainly AM]

in BRIT, usually use **polythene**

po|lyga|mous /pəlɪgəməs/ ADJ In a **polygamous** society, people can be legally married to more than one person at the same time. A **polygamous** person is married to more than one person. ❑ *Less than 1 percent of the men in any Muslim country are polygamous.*

po|lyga|my /pəlɪgəmi/ N-UNCOUNT **Polygamy** is the custom in some societies in which someone can be legally married to more than one person at the same time.

poly|glot /pɒliglɒt/ (**polyglots**) ◼ ADJ [usu ADJ n] **Polyglot** is used to describe something such as a book or society in which several different languages are used. [FORMAL] ❑ *Chicago's polyglot population.* ◼ N-COUNT A **polyglot** is a person who speaks or understands many languages.

poly|graph /pɒlɪgræf/ (**polygraphs**) N-COUNT A **polygraph** or a **polygraph test** is a test used by the police to try to find out whether someone is telling the truth. ❑ *Hill's lawyers announced she had taken and passed a polygraph test.*

poly|mer /pɒlɪmər/ (**polymers**) N-COUNT A **polymer** is a chemical compound with large molecules made of many smaller molecules of the same kind. Some polymers exist naturally and others are produced in laboratories and factories.

pol|yp /pɒlɪp/ (**polyps**) ◼ N-COUNT A **polyp** is a small unhealthy growth on a surface inside your body. ◼ N-COUNT A **polyp** is a small animal that lives in the sea. It has a hollow body like a tube and long parts called tentacles around its mouth.

poly|pro|pyl|ene /pɒliproʊpɪlin/ N-UNCOUNT **Polypropylene** is a strong, flexible artificial material that is used to make things such as rope, carpet, and pipes.

poly|tech|nic /pɒlitɛknɪk/ (**polytechnics**) N-VAR [oft in names] A **polytechnic** is the name for a school, college, or university that specializes in courses in science and technology.

poly|thene /pɒlɪθin/ N-UNCOUNT **Polythene** is the same as **polyethylene**. [mainly BRIT]

poly|un|satu|rate /pɒliʌnsætʃʊrɪt/ (**polyunsaturates**) N-COUNT [usu pl] **Polyunsaturates** are types of fats, mainly vegetable fats, that are used to make cooking oil and margarine. They are thought to be less harmful to your body than other fats.

poly|un|satu|rat|ed /pɒliʌnsætʃəreɪtɪd/ ADJ **Polyunsaturated** oils and margarines are made mainly from vegetable fats and are considered healthier than those made from animal fats. ● *Use polyunsaturated spread instead of butter.*

poly|urethane /pɒliyʊərəθeɪn/ (**polyurethanes**) N-MASS **Polyurethane** is a plastic material used especially to make paint or substances that prevent water or heat from passing through. ❑ *...polyurethane varnish.*

pom|egran|ate /pɒmɪgrænɪt/ (**pomegranates**) N-VAR A **pomegranate** is a round fruit with a thick reddish skin. It contains a lot of small seeds with juicy flesh around them.

pom|mel /pʌmᵊl, pɒm-/ (**pommels**) N-COUNT A **pommel** is the part of a saddle that rises up at the front, or a knob that is fixed there.

pom|mel horse (**pommel horses**) N-COUNT A **pommel horse** is a tall piece of gymnastic equipment for jumping over.

in BRIT, also use **horse, vaulting horse**

pomp /pɒmp/ N-UNCOUNT **Pomp** is the use of a lot of ceremony, fine clothes, and decorations, especially on a special occasion. ❑ *I hate all this pomp and ceremony.*

pom-pom (**pom-poms**) also **pompom** N-COUNT A **pom-pom** is a ball of threads or paper strips that is used to decorate things such as hats or furniture. Cheerleaders wave large pom-poms at sporting events.

pom|pos|ity /pɒmpɒsɪti/ N-UNCOUNT **Pomposity** means speaking or behaving in a very serious manner that shows you think you are more important than you really are. [DISAPPROVAL] ❑ *Einstein was a scientist who hated pomposity and disliked being called a genius.*

pomp|ous /pɒmpəs/ ◼ ADJ If you describe someone as **pompous**, you mean that they behave or speak in a very serious way because they think they are more important than they really are. [DISAPPROVAL] ❑ *He was somewhat pompous and had a high opinion of his own capabilities.* ● **pomp|ous|ly** ADV ❑ *Robin told me firmly and pompously that he had an important business appointment.* ◼ ADJ A **pompous** building or ceremony is very grand and elaborate. ❑ *The service was grand without being pompous.*

pon|cho /pɒntʃoʊ/ (**ponchos**) N-COUNT A **poncho** is a piece of clothing that consists of a long piece of material or plastic with a hole cut in the middle through which you put your head. Some ponchos have a hood.

pond /pɒnd/ (**ponds**) ◼ N-COUNT A **pond** is a small area of water that is smaller than a lake. Ponds are often made artificially. ❑ *She chose a bench beside the duck pond and sat down.* ◼ N-SING People sometimes refer to the Atlantic Ocean as **the pond**. [mainly JOURNALISM] ❑ *Tourist numbers from across the pond have dropped dramatically.*

pon|der /pɒndər/ (**ponders, pondering, pondered**) V-T/V-I If you **ponder** something, you think about it carefully. ❑ *I found myself constantly pondering the question: "How could anyone do these things?"* ❑ *He pondered over the difficulties involved.*

pon|der|ous /pɒndərəs/ ADJ **Ponderous** writing or speech is very serious, uses more words than necessary, and is dull. [DISAPPROVAL] ❑ *He had a dense, ponderous style.*

pon|tiff /pɒntɪf/ (**pontiffs**) N-COUNT [usu the N] The **Pontiff** is the Pope. [FORMAL] ❑ *The Pontiff celebrated mass in Mexico City.*

pon|tifi|cate (**pontificates, pontificating, pontificated**)

The verb is pronounced /pɒntɪfɪkeɪt/. The noun is pronounced /pɒntɪfɪkɪt/.

1 V-I If someone **pontificates** about something, they state their opinions as if they are the only correct ones and nobody could possibly oppose them. [FORMAL] ❑ *Politicians like to pontificate about falling standards.* **2** N-COUNT The **pontificate** of a pope is the period of time during which he is pope. ❑ *Pope Formosus died after a pontificate of four and a half years.*

pon|toon /ppntu:n/ (**pontoons**) N-COUNT A **pontoon** is a floating platform, often one used to support a bridge. ❑ *...a pontoon bridge.*

pony /pouni/ (**ponies**) N-COUNT A **pony** is a small or young horse.

pony|tail /pouniteɪl/ (**ponytails**) N-COUNT A **ponytail** is a hairstyle in which someone's hair is tied up at the back of the head and hangs down like a tail. ❑ *Her long, fine hair was swept back in a ponytail.*

poo /pu:/ (**poos**) N-VAR **Poo** is a child's word for feces. [INFORMAL]

pooch /pu:tʃ/ (**pooches**) N-COUNT A **pooch** is a dog. [INFORMAL]

poo|dle /pu:dəl/ (**poodles**) N-COUNT A **poodle** is a type of dog with thick curly hair.

poof /pʊf, pu:f/ EXCLAM Some people say **poof** to indicate that something happened very suddenly. ❑ *They approach, embrace, and poof! they disappear in a blinding flash of light.*

pooh-pooh /pu: pu:/ (**pooh-poohs, pooh-poohing, pooh-poohed**) V-T If someone **pooh-poohs** an idea or suggestion, they say or imply that it is foolish, impractical, or unnecessary. ❑ *In the past he has pooh-poohed suggestions that he might succeed Isaacs.*

pool ♦♢♢ /pu:l/ (**pools, pooling, pooled**) **1** N-COUNT A **pool** is the same as a **swimming pool**. ❑ *...a heated indoor pool.* **2** N-COUNT A **pool** is a fairly small area of still water. ❑ *The pool had dried up and was full of bracken and reeds.* **3** N-COUNT A **pool of** liquid or light is a small area of it on the ground or on a surface. ❑ *She was found lying in a pool of blood.* ❑ *It was raining quietly and steadily and there were little pools of water on the gravel drive.* **4** N-COUNT A **pool** of people, money, or things is a quantity or number of them that is available for an organization or group to use. ❑ *The available pool of healthy manpower was not as large as military officials had expected.* **5** → see also **carpool** **6** V-T If a group of people or organizations **pool** their money, knowledge, or equipment, they share it or put it together so that it can be used for a particular purpose. ❑ *We pooled ideas and information.*

COLLOCATIONS

pool
NOUN
1
noun + **pool**: hydrotherapy, plunge; hotel, rooftop; infinity
adjective + **pool**: heated; indoor, outdoor
5
noun + **pool**: gene; bonus, talent

---

pool hall (**pool halls**) N-COUNT A **pool hall** is a building where you can pay to play pool. ❑ *...an upscale pool hall in Boston.*

poop /pu:p/ (**poops, pooping, pooped**) **1** N-COUNT The **poop** of an old-fashioned sailing ship is the raised structure at the back end of it. ❑ *...the poop deck.* **2** V-I To **poop** means to get rid of feces from your body. [INFORMAL] ❑ *Ted, did you poop in your pants?* • N-UNCOUNT **Poop** is also a noun. ❑ *...piles of dog poop.*

pooped /pu:pt/ ADJ [v-link ADJ] If you are **pooped**, you are very tired. [AM, INFORMAL]

poor ♦♦♢ /pʊər/ (**poorer, poorest**) **1** ADJ Someone who is **poor** has very little money and few possessions. ❑ *The reason our schools cannot afford better teachers is because people here are poor.* • N-PLURAL The **poor** are people who are poor. ❑ *Interest rates are high and the poor can't afford bank charges.* **2** ADJ The people in a **poor** country or area have very little money and few possessions. ❑ *Many countries in the developing world are as poor as they have ever been.* **3** ADJ [ADJ n] You use **poor** to express your sympathy for someone. [FEELINGS] ❑ *I feel sorry for that poor child.* ❑ *It was way too much for the poor guy to overcome.* **4** ADJ If you describe something as **poor**, you mean that it is of a low quality or standard or that it is in bad condition. ❑ *...the poor state of the economy.* ❑ *The gap between the best and poorest childcare provision has widened.* • **poor|ly** ADV ❑ *Some are living in poorly built dormitories, even in tents.* **5** ADJ If you describe an amount, rate, or number as **poor**, you mean that it is less than expected or less than is considered reasonable. ❑ *...poor wages and working conditions.* • **poor|ly** ADV ❑ *During the first week, the evening meetings were poorly attended.* **6** ADJ You use **poor** to describe someone who is not very skillful in a particular activity. ❑ *He was a poor actor.* • **poor|ly** ADV [ADV after v] ❑ *Cheetahs breed very poorly in captivity.* **7** ADJ [v-link ADJ in n] If something is **poor in** a particular quality or substance, it contains very little of the quality or substance. ❑ *Fats and sugar are very rich in energy but poor in vitamins and minerals.*

poor|ly /pʊərli/ (**poorlier, poorliest**) ADJ If someone is **poorly**, they are ill. [mainly BRIT, INFORMAL]

poor re|la|tion (**poor relations**) N-COUNT [usu N of n] If you describe one thing as a **poor relation** of another, you mean that it is similar to or part of the other thing, but is considered to be inferior to it. ❑ *Watercolor still seems somehow to be the poor relation of oil painting.*

pop ♦♢♢ /pɒp/ (**pops, popping, popped**) **1** N-UNCOUNT **Pop** is modern music that usually has a strong rhythm and uses electronic equipment. ❑ *...the perfect combination of Caribbean rhythms, European pop, and American soul.* ❑ *...a life-size poster of a pop star.* **2** N-UNCOUNT You can refer to carbonated drinks such as cola as **pop**. [BRIT, INFORMAL] ❑ *...a can of pop.* **3** N-COUNT; SOUND **Pop** is used to represent a short sharp sound such as the sound made by bursting a balloon or by pulling a cork out of a bottle. ❑ *Each corn kernel will make a loud pop when cooked.* **4** V-I If something **pops**, it makes a short sharp sound. ❑ *He untwisted the wire off the champagne bottle, and the cork popped and shot to the ceiling.* **5** V-I If your eyes **pop**, you look very surprised or excited when you see something. [INFORMAL] ❑ *My eyes popped at the sight of the rich variety of food on show.* **6** V-T If you **pop** something somewhere, you put it there quickly. [INFORMAL] ❑ *Marianne got a couple of mugs from the cupboard and popped a teabag into each of them.* **7** N-FAMILY Some people call their father **pop**. [mainly AM, INFORMAL] ❑ *I looked at Pop and he had big tears in his eyes.* **8 to pop the question** → see **question**
▸ **pop up** PHRASAL VERB If someone or something **pops up**, they appear in a place or situation unexpectedly. [INFORMAL] ❑ *She was startled when Lisa popped up at the door all smiles.*

POP /pi: oʊ pi:/ (**POPs**) N-COUNT **POP** is something that proves that you have paid for something. **POP** is an abbreviation for 'proof of purchase.'

pop. /pɒp/ **pop.** is an abbreviation for **population**. It is used before a number when indicating the total population of a city or country. ❑ *Somalia, pop. 7.9 million, income per head about $2 a week.*

pop art N-UNCOUNT **Pop art** is a style of modern art that began in the 1950s. It uses bright colors and takes a lot of its techniques and subject matter from everyday, modern life.

pop|corn /pɒpkɔːrn/ N-UNCOUNT **Popcorn** is a snack that consists of grains of corn that have been heated until they have burst and become large and light.

pope /poʊp/ (**popes**) also **Pope** N-COUNT [usu the N; N-TITLE] The **Pope** is the head of the Roman Catholic Church. ❑ *The highlight of the pope's visit will be his message to the people.*

pop|lar /pɒplər/ (**poplars**) N-VAR A **poplar** is a type of tree with leaves that move a lot in the wind.

pop|lin /pɒplɪn/ N-UNCOUNT **Poplin** is a type of cotton material used to make clothes.

pop|over /pɒpoʊvər/ (**popovers**) N-COUNT A **popover** is a light, hollow muffin. [mainly AM] ❑ *...blueberry popovers with cinnamon ice-cream.*

pop|pa|dom /pɒpədɒm/ (**poppadoms**) N-COUNT A **poppadom** is a very thin circular crisp bread made from a mixture of flour and water that is fried in oil. Poppadoms are usually eaten with Indian food.

pop|py /pɒpi/ (**poppies**) N-COUNT A **poppy** is a plant with a large, delicate flower, usually red in color. The drug opium is obtained from one type of poppy. ❑ *...a field of poppies.*

Pop|si|cle /pɒpsɪkəl/ (**Popsicles**) N-COUNT A **Popsicle** is a piece of flavored ice on a stick. [AM, TRADEMARK]

in BRIT, use **ice lolly**

popu|lace /pɒpyələs/ N-UNCOUNT The **populace** of a country is its people. [FORMAL] □ ...*a large proportion of the populace.*

popu|lar ♦♦◊ /pɒpyələr/ **1** ADJ Something that is **popular** is enjoyed or liked by a lot of people. □ *Chocolate sauce is always popular with youngsters.* • **popu|lar|ity** /pɒpyəlærɪti/ N-UNCOUNT □ ...*the growing popularity of Australian wines among consumers.* **2** ADJ Someone who is **popular** is liked by most people, or by most people in a particular group. □ *He remained the most popular politician in Arkansas.* • **popu|lar|ity** N-UNCOUNT □ *It is his popularity with ordinary people that sets him apart.* **3** ADJ [ADJ n] **Popular** newspapers, television programs, or forms of art are aimed at ordinary people and not at experts or intellectuals. □ *Once again the popular press in Britain has been rife with stories about their marriage.* □ ...*one of the classics of modern popular music.* **4** ADJ **Popular** ideas, feelings, or attitudes are approved of or held by most people. □ *Contrary to popular belief, the oil companies can't control the price of crude.* □ *The military government has been unable to win popular support.* • **popu|lar|ity** N-UNCOUNT □ *Over time, though, Watson's views gained in popularity.* **5** ADJ [ADJ n] **Popular** is used to describe political activities that involve the ordinary people of a country, and not just members of political parties. □ *The late president Ferdinand Marcos was overthrown by a popular uprising in 1986.* **6** → See feature box at **book**

popu|lar|ize /pɒpyələraɪz/ (**popularizes**, **popularizing**, **popularized**)

in BRIT, also use **popularise**

V-T To **popularize** something means to make a lot of people interested in it and able to enjoy it. □ *Irving Brokaw, who had studied figure skating in Europe, returned to the U.S. and popularized the new sport.* • **popu|lari|za|tion** /pɒpyələrɪzeɪʃ°n/ N-UNCOUNT □ ...*the popularization of sports through television.*

popu|lar|ly /pɒpyələrli/ **1** ADV [ADV with -ed] If something or someone is **popularly** known as something, most people call them that, although it is not their official name or title. □ ...*the Mesozoic era, more popularly known as the age of dinosaurs.* □ ...*an infection popularly called mad cow disease.* **2** ADV [ADV -ed] If something is **popularly** believed or supposed to be the case, most people believe or suppose it to be the case, although it may not be true. □ *Schizophrenia is not a "split mind" as is popularly believed.* **3** ADV [ADV -ed] A **popularly elected** leader or government has been elected by a majority of the people in a country. □ *Walesa was Poland's first popularly elected president.*

popu|late /pɒpyəleɪt/ (**populates**, **populating**, **populated**) **1** V-T If an area **is populated** by certain people or animals, those people or animals live there, often in large numbers. □ *Before all this the island was populated by native American Arawaks.* • **popu|lat|ed** ADJ [adv ADJ] □ *The southeast is the most densely populated area.* **2** V-T To **populate** an area means to cause people to live there. □ *Successive regimes annexed the region and populated it with lowland people.*

popu|la|tion ♦♦◊ /pɒpyəleɪʃ°n/ (**populations**) **1** N-COUNT The **population** of a country or area is all the people who live in it. □ *The country now has a population of about 110 million.* □ ...*the annual rate of population growth.* **2** N-COUNT If you refer to a particular type of **population** in a country or area, you are referring to all the people or animals of that type there. [FORMAL] □ ...*75.6 percent of the male population over sixteen.* □ ...*areas with a large Black population.*

COLLOCATIONS

population
NOUN

1
adjective + **population**: general, local, total
verb + **population**: control, feed, support

2
noun + **population**: bee, elephant, fish; civilian, immigrant, prison, student
adjective + **population**: adult, Black, indigenous, male; aging, declining, growing, working; Jewish, Muslim

VOCABULARY IN CONTEXT

Population

At the time when humans first started to **settle** and cultivate the land, about 8,000 BC, the population of the world was around 5 million. It took until 1800, nearly another 10,000 years, for that number to slowly **swell** to a billion. However, the **boom** caused by the industrial revolution meant that world population **doubled** in just 130 years, reaching three billion by 1959, **escalating** to four billion in 1974 and five billion in 1987. **Current figures** stand at more than 7.5 billion and are **projected** to continue to **expand**, though at a slightly slower **rate** than previously.

The birth rate has, in fact, **declined** somewhat from a high of 139 million **annually** in the late 1980s, but greater **life expectancy** means that the **global** population is expected to reach between 8.3 and 10.9 billion by 2050.

pop|ulism /pɒpyəlɪzəm/ N-UNCOUNT **Populism** refers to political activities or ideas that claim to promote the interests and opinions of ordinary people. [FORMAL] □ ...*a wave of populism.*

popu|list /pɒpyəlɪst/ (**populists**) ADJ [usu ADJ n] If you describe a politician or an artist as **populist**, you mean that they claim to care about the interests and opinions of ordinary people rather than those of a small group. [FORMAL] □ ...*Jose Sarney, the current populist president.* • N-COUNT A **populist** is someone who expresses populist views.

popu|lous /pɒpyələs/ ADJ [usu ADJ n] A **populous** country or area has a lot of people living in it. [FORMAL] □ *Indonesia is the fourth most populous country in the world.*

pop-up **1** ADJ [ADJ n] A **pop-up** book, usually a children's book, has pictures that stand up when you open the pages. **2** ADJ [ADJ n] On a computer screen, a **pop-up** menu or advertisement is a small window containing a menu or advertisement that appears on the screen when you perform particular operations. [COMPUTING] □ ...*a program for stopping pop-up ads.* • N-COUNT **Pop-up** is also a noun. □ ...*like unwanted pop-ups on a computer screen.* **3** ADJ [ADJ n] A **pop-up** store, restaurant, or gallery opens only for a short time and is intended to be temporary. □ *There's a pop-up gallery where the cafeteria used to be.* • N-COUNT **Pop-up** is also a noun. □ *The chain has eight pop-ups in the Houston area.*

porce|lain /pɔrsəlɪn, pɔrslɪn/ N-UNCOUNT **Porcelain** is a hard, shiny substance made by heating clay. It is used to make delicate cups, plates, and ornaments. □ *There were lilies everywhere in tall white porcelain vases.*

porch /pɔrtʃ/ (**porches**) **1** N-COUNT A **porch** is a sheltered area at the entrance to a building. It has a roof and sometimes has walls. □ *She huddled inside the porch as she rang the bell.* **2** N-COUNT A **porch** is a raised platform built along the outside wall of a house and often covered with a roof. [AM] □ *He was standing on the porch, waving as we drove away.*

in BRIT, usually use **veranda**

3 → See feature box at **house**

por|cu|pine /pɔrkyəpaɪn/ (**porcupines**) N-COUNT A **porcupine** is an animal with many long, thin, sharp spikes on its back that stick out as protection when it is attacked.

pore /pɔr/ (pores, poring, pored) **1** N-COUNT Your **pores** are the tiny holes in your skin. ❑ *The size of your pores is determined by the amount of oil they produce.* **2** V-I If you **pore over** or **through** information, you look at it and study it very carefully. ❑ *We spent hours poring over travel brochures.*

pork /pɔrk/ N-UNCOUNT **Pork** is meat from a pig, usually fresh and not smoked or salted. ❑ *...fried pork chops.*

pork bar|rel also **pork-barrel** N-SING [usu N n] If you say that someone is using **pork barrel** politics, you mean that they are spending a lot of government money on a local project in order to win the votes of the people who live in that area. [mainly AM, DISAPPROVAL] ❑ *Pork-barrel politicians hand out rents to win votes and influence people.*

porn /pɔrn/ N-UNCOUNT **Porn** is the same as **pornography**. [INFORMAL] ❑ *...a porn cinema.*

por|no /pɔrnoʊ/ ADJ **Porno** is the same as **pornographic**. [INFORMAL] ❑ *...porno mags.*

por|nog|ra|pher /pɔrnɒgrəfər/ (pornographers) N-COUNT A **pornographer** is a person who produces or sells pornography. [DISAPPROVAL]

por|no|graph|ic /pɔrnəgræfɪk/ ADJ **Pornographic** movies, DVDs, and magazines are designed to cause sexual excitement by showing or describing sexual acts. [DISAPPROVAL] ❑ *I found out he'd been watching pornographic videos.*

por|nog|ra|phy /pɔrnɒgrəfi/ N-UNCOUNT **Pornography** refers to books, magazines, and movies that are designed to cause sexual excitement by showing naked people or referring to sexual acts. [DISAPPROVAL] ❑ *The country's leading newspaper has called for a new campaign against child pornography.*

po|ros|ity /pɔrɒsɪti/ N-UNCOUNT **Porosity** is the quality of being porous. [FORMAL] ❑ *...the porosity of the coal.*

po|rous /pɔrəs/ ADJ Something that is **porous** has many small holes in it that water and air can pass through. ❑ *The local limestone is so porous that all the rainwater immediately sinks below ground.*

por|poise /pɔrpəs/ (porpoises) **1** N-COUNT A **porpoise** is a sea animal that looks like a dolphin. Porpoises usually swim in groups. **2** → See feature box at **animal**

por|ridge /pɔrɪdʒ/ N-UNCOUNT **Porridge** is a thick sticky food made from oats cooked in water or milk and eaten hot, especially for breakfast. [mainly BRIT]

in AM, usually use **oatmeal**

port ♦◊◊ /pɔrt/ (ports) **1** N-COUNT A **port** is a town by the sea or on a river that has a harbor. ❑ *...the Mediterranean port of Marseilles.* **2** N-COUNT A **port** is a harbor area where ships load and unload goods or passengers. ❑ *...the bridges that link the port area to the rest of the city.* **3** N-COUNT A **port** on a computer is a place where you can attach another piece of equipment such as a printer. [COMPUTING] ❑ *The devices, attached to a PC through standard ports, print bar codes onto envelopes.* **4** N-COUNT In sailing, the **port** side of a ship is the left side when you are on it and facing toward the front. [TECHNICAL] ❑ *Her official number is carved on the port side of the forecabin.* • N-UNCOUNT **Port** is also a noun. ❑ *USS Ogden turned to port.* **5** N-UNCOUNT **Port** is a type of strong, sweet red wine. ❑ *He asked for a glass of port after dinner.* **6** → See also color supplement

port|able /pɔrtəbᵊl/ (portables) **1** ADJ A **portable** machine or device is designed to be easily carried or moved. ❑ *There was a little portable television switched on behind the bar.* **2** N-COUNT A **portable** is something such as a television, radio, or computer that can be easily carried or moved. ❑ *We bought a portable for the bedroom.* **3** → See feature box at **house**

por|tage /pɔrtɪdʒ/ (portages, portaging, portaged) V-T/V-I If people in a boat such as a canoe **portage** somewhere, they carry the boat overland until they can return it to another stretch of water. [AM] ❑ *When we reached the river, we decided to portage to the campsite.* ❑ *There were too few men left to portage the boats.* • N-COUNT **Portage** is also a noun ❑ *The day began with a portage of two hundred yards.*

por|tal /pɔrtᵊl/ (portals) N-COUNT On the internet, a **portal** is a website that consists of links to other sites. [COMPUTING] ❑ *The site acts as a portal for thousands of online dealers.*

port|cul|lis /pɔrtkʌlɪs/ (portcullises) N-COUNT A **portcullis** is a strong gate above an entrance to a castle and used to be lowered to the ground in order to keep out enemies.

por|tend /pɔrtɛnd/ (portends, portending, portended) V-T If something **portends** an event or occurrence, it indicates that it is likely to happen in the future. [FORMAL] ❑ *The change did not portend a basic improvement in social conditions.*

por|tent /pɔrtɛnt/ (portents) N-COUNT [oft N of n] A **portent** is something that indicates what is likely to happen in the future. [FORMAL] ❑ *The savage civil war there could be a portent of what's to come in the rest of the region.*

por|ten|tous /pɔrtɛntəs/ **1** ADJ If someone's way of speaking, writing, or behaving is **portentous**, they speak, write, or behave more seriously than necessary because they want to impress other people. [FORMAL, DISAPPROVAL] ❑ *There was nothing portentous or solemn about him. He was bubbling with humor.* ❑ *...portentous prose.* • **por|ten|tous|ly** ADV [usu ADV with v] ❑ *"The difference is," he said portentously, "you are Anglo-Saxons, we are Latins".* **2** ADJ Something that is **portentous** is important in indicating or affecting future events. [FORMAL] ❑ *In social politics, too, the city's contribution to 20th century thought and culture was no less portentous.*

por|ter /pɔrtər/ (porters) **1** N-COUNT A **porter** is a person whose job is to carry things, for example, people's luggage at a train station or in a hotel. ❑ *Our taxi pulled up at Old Delhi station and a porter sprinted to the door.* **2** N-COUNT In a hospital, a **porter** is someone whose job is to move patients from place to place. [BRIT]

in AM, use **orderly**

3 N-COUNT A **porter** is a person whose job is to be in charge of the entrance of a building such as a hotel. [BRIT]

in AM, use **doorman**

port|fo|lio /pɔrtfoʊliou/ (portfolios) **1** N-COUNT A **portfolio** is a set of pictures by someone, photographs of their work, or examples of their writing, which they use when entering competitions or applying for work. ❑ *After dinner that evening, Edith showed them a portfolio of her own political cartoons.* **2** N-COUNT In finance, a **portfolio** is the combination of investments that a particular person or company owns. [BUSINESS] ❑ *...Roger Early, a portfolio manager at Federated Investors Corp.* **3** N-COUNT In politics, a **portfolio** is a high-ranking official's responsibility for a particular area of a government's activities. ❑ *A government inquiry recommended that he never again hold the defense portfolio.* **4** N-COUNT A company's **portfolio** of products or designs is their range of products or designs. [BUSINESS] ❑ *The company has continued to invest heavily in a strong portfolio of products.* **5** N-COUNT A **portfolio** is a flat case, especially one made of leather, that is used for carrying documents such as drawings and maps.

port|hole /pɔrthoʊl/ (portholes) **1** N-COUNT A **porthole** is a small round window in the side of a ship or aircraft. **2** → See also color supplement

por|ti|co /pɔrtɪkoʊ/ (porticoes or porticos) N-COUNT A **portico** is a large covered area at the entrance to a building, with pillars supporting the roof. [FORMAL]

por|tion /pɔrʃᵊn/ (portions) **1** N-COUNT A **portion of** something is a part of it. ❑ *Damage was confined to a small portion of the castle.* ❑ *I have spent a considerable portion of my life here.* **2** N-COUNT A **portion** is the amount of food that is given to one person at a meal. ❑ *Desserts can be substituted by a portion of fresh fruit.* ❑ *The portions were generous.*

port|ly /pɔrtli/ (portlier, portliest) ADJ A **portly** person is rather fat. [FORMAL]

port of call (ports of call) **1** N-COUNT A **port of call** is a place where a ship stops. ❑ *Their first port of call will be Cape Town.* **2** N-COUNT A **port of call** is any place where you stop for a short time when you are visiting several places, stores, or people. [INFORMAL] ❑ *The local tourist office should be your first port of call in any town.*

por|trait ♦◊◊ /pɔrtrɪt, -treɪt/ (portraits) **1** N-COUNT A **portrait** is a painting, drawing, or photograph of a particular person. ❑ *...badly painted family portraits.* **2** N-COUNT [usu N of n] A **portrait** of a person, place, or thing is a verbal description of them. ❑ *...this gripping, funny portrait of Jewish life in 1950s Hoboken.* **3** → See feature box at **fine art**

por|trait|ist /pɔrtrɪtɪst, -treɪtɪst/ (portraitists) N-COUNT A **portraitist** is an artist who paints or draws people's portraits. [FORMAL]

por|trai|ture /pɔ:rtrɪtʃər, -tʃʊər/ N-UNCOUNT **Portraiture** is the art of painting or drawing portraits. [FORMAL]

por|tray /pɔ:rtreɪ/ (portrays, portraying, portrayed) **1** V-T When an actor **portrays** someone, he or she plays that person in a play or movie. ❏ *In 1975 he portrayed the king in a Los Angeles revival of "Camelot."* **2** V-T When a writer or artist **portrays** something, he or she writes a description or produces a painting of it. ❏ *The film portrays a culture of young people who live in lower Manhattan.* **3** V-T If a movie, book, or television program **portrays** someone in a certain way, it represents them in that way. ❏ *...complaints about the way women are portrayed in ads.*

por|tray|al /pɔ:rtreɪəl/ (portrayals) **1** N-COUNT An actor's **portrayal** of a character in a play or movie is the way that he or she plays the character. ❏ *Mr. Ying is well-known for his portrayal of a prison guard in the film "The Last Emperor."* **2** N-COUNT An artist's **portrayal** of something is a drawing, painting, or photograph of it. ❏ *...a moving portrayal of St. John the Evangelist by Simone Martini.* **3** N-COUNT The **portrayal** of something in a book or movie is the act of describing it or showing it. ❏ *...an accurate portrayal of family life.* **4** N-COUNT The **portrayal** of something in a book, movie, or program is the way that it is made to appear. ❏ *The media persists in its portrayal of us as muggers and gangsters.*

Por|tu|guese /pɔ:rtʃugi:z/ **1** ADJ Something that is **Portuguese** belongs or relates to Portugal, or its people, language, or culture. **2** N-PLURAL [the N] **The Portuguese** are the people of Portugal. **3** N-UNCOUNT **Portuguese** is the language spoken in Portugal, Brazil, Angola, and Mozambique.

POS /pi ou ɛs/ N-UNCOUNT The **POS** is the place in a store where a product is passed from the seller to the customer. **POS** is an abbreviation for **point of sale**. [BUSINESS] ❏ *...a POS system that doubles as an inventory and sales control system.*

pos. pos. is the written abbreviation for **positive**.

pose ♦♢♢ /poʊz/ (poses, posing, posed) **1** V-T If something **poses** a problem or a danger, it is the cause of that problem or danger. ❏ *This could pose a threat to jobs in the coal industry.* **2** V-T If you **pose** a question, you ask it. If you **pose** an issue that needs considering, you mention the issue. [FORMAL] ❏ *When I finally posed the question, "Why?" he merely shrugged.* **3** V-I If you **pose as** someone, you pretend to be that person in order to deceive people. ❏ *The team posed as drug dealers to trap the ringleaders.* **4** V-I If you **pose for** a photograph or painting, you stay in a particular position so that someone can photograph you or paint you. ❏ *Before going into their meeting the six foreign ministers posed for photographs.* **5** N-COUNT A **pose** is a particular way that you stand, sit, or lie, for example, when you are being photographed or painted. ❏ *We have had several preliminary sittings in various poses.*

pos|er /poʊzər/ (posers) N-COUNT A **poser** is the same as a **poseur**. [DISAPPROVAL]

po|seur /poʊzɜr/ (poseurs) N-COUNT You can describe someone as a **poseur** when you think that they behave in an insincere or exaggerated way because they want to make a particular impression on other people. [DISAPPROVAL] ❏ *I am sometimes accused of being a poseur.*

posh /pɒʃ/ (posher, poshest) **1** ADJ If you describe something as **posh**, you mean that it is elegant, fashionable, and expensive. [INFORMAL] ❏ *Celebrating a promotion, I took her to a posh hotel for a cocktail.* **2** ADJ If you describe a person as **posh**, you mean that they belong to or behave as if they belong to the upper classes. [mainly BRIT, INFORMAL] ❏ *I wouldn't have thought she had such posh friends.*

pos|it /pɒzɪt/ (posits, positing, posited) V-T If you **posit** something, you suggest or assume it as the basis for an argument or calculation. [FORMAL] ❏ *Several writers have posited the idea of a universal consciousness.* ❏ *Callahan posits that chemical elements radiate electromagnetic signals.*

po|si|tion ♦♦♦ /pəzɪʃən/ (positions, positioning, positioned) **1** N-COUNT The **position** of someone or something is the place where they are in relation to other things. ❏ *The ship was identified, and its name and position were reported to the Coast Guard.* **2** N-COUNT When someone or something is in a particular **position**, they are sitting, lying, or arranged in that way. ❏ *It is crucial that the upper back and neck are held in an erect position to give support for the head.* ❏ *Mr. Dambar had raised himself to a sitting position.* **3** V-T If you **position** something somewhere, you put it there carefully, so that it is in the right place or position. ❏ *Position the cursor where you want the new margins to begin.* **4** N-COUNT Your **position** in society is the role and the importance that you have in it. ❏ *Adjustment to their changing role in society can be difficult for some retired people.* **5** N-COUNT A **position** in a company or organization is a job. [FORMAL] ❏ *He left a career in teaching to take up a position with the NEH.* **6** N-COUNT Your **position** in a race or competition is how well you did in relation to the other competitors or how well you are doing. ❏ *By the ninth hour the car was running in eighth position.* **7** N-COUNT You can describe your situation at a particular time by saying that you are in a particular **position**. ❏ *He's going to be in a very difficult position if things go badly for him.* ❏ *Companies should be made to reveal more about their financial position.* **8** N-COUNT Your **position** on a particular matter is your attitude toward it or your opinion of it. [FORMAL] ❏ *He could be depended on to take a moderate position on most of the key issues.* **9** N-SING If you are **in a position** to do something, you are able to do it. If you are **in no position** to do something, you are unable to do it. ❏ *I am not in a position to comment.* **10** PHRASE If someone or something is **in position**, they are in their correct or usual place or arrangement. ❏ *28,000 U.S. troops are moving into position.*

SYNONYMS

position
NOUN **1**
location: *She knew the exact location of The Eagle's headquarters.*
place: *The best place to catch fish on a canal is close to a lock.*
site: *They are similar in size and shape to the crucibles found at the Egyptian site.*
whereabouts: *Once he knew his father's name, finding his whereabouts proved surprisingly easy.*

po|si|tion pa|per (position papers) N-COUNT A **position paper** is a detailed report that usually explains or recommends a particular course of action.

posi|tive ♦♦♢ /pɒzɪtɪv/ **1** ADJ If you are **positive** about things, you are hopeful and confident, and think of the good aspects of a situation rather than the bad ones. ❏ *Be positive about your future and get on with living a normal life.* ❏ *Her husband became much more positive and was soon back in full-time employment.* • **posi|tive|ly** ADV [ADV after v] ❏ *You really must try to start thinking positively.* **2** ADJ A **positive** fact, situation, or experience is pleasant and helpful to you in some way. ❏ *The parting from his sister had a positive effect on John.* • N-SING [the N] **The positive** in a situation is the good and pleasant aspects of it. ❏ *He prefers to focus on the positive.* **3** ADJ If you make a **positive** decision or take **positive** action, you do something definite in order to deal with a task or problem. ❏ *There are positive changes that should be implemented in the rearing of animals.* **4** ADJ A **positive** response to something indicates agreement, approval, or encouragement. ❏ *There's been a positive response to the U.N. Secretary-General's recent peace efforts.* • **posi|tive|ly** ADV [ADV after v] ❏ *He responded positively and accepted the fee of $1,000 I had offered.* **5** ADJ [v-link ADJ] If you are **positive** about something, you are completely sure about it. ❏ *"Judith's never late. You sure she said eight?" "Positive."* **6** ADJ [ADJ n] **Positive** evidence gives definite proof of the truth or identity of something. ❏ *There was no positive evidence that any birth defects had arisen as a result of Vitamin A intake.* • **posi|tive|ly** ADV [ADV with v] ❏ *He has positively identified the body as that of his wife.* **7** ADJ If a medical or scientific test is **positive**, it shows that something has happened or is present. ❏ *If the test is positive, a course of antibiotics may be prescribed.* **8** HIV **positive** → see HIV **9** ADJ [ADJ n] A **positive** number is greater than zero. ❏ *It's really a simple numbers game with negative and positive numbers.* **10** ADJ If something has a **positive** electrical charge, it has the same charge as a proton and the opposite charge to a neutron. [TECHNICAL]

posi|tive dis|crimi|na|tion N-UNCOUNT **Positive discrimination** means making sure that people such as women, members of smaller racial groups, and people with disabilities get a fair share of the opportunities available. [BRIT]

in AM, use **affirmative action**

posi|tive|ly /pɒzɪtɪvli/ ■ ADV [ADV adj-superl] You use **positively** to emphasize that you really mean what you are saying. [EMPHASIS] ❑ *This is positively the last chance for the industry to establish such a system.* ■ ADV You use **positively** to emphasize that something really is the case, although it may sound surprising or extreme. [EMPHASIS] ❑ *Mike's changed since he came back – he seems positively cheerful.*

posi|tiv|ism /pɒzɪtɪvɪzəm/ N-UNCOUNT **Positivism** is a philosophy that accepts only things that can be seen or proved. • **posi|tiv|ist** (**positivists**) N-COUNT [usu N n] ❑ *By far the most popular idea is the positivist one that we should keep only the facts.*

pos|se /pɒsi/ (**posses**) ■ N-COUNT [N of n] A **posse** of people is a group of people with the same job or purpose. [INFORMAL] ❑ *...a posse of reporters.* ■ N-COUNT In former times, a **posse** was a group of men who were brought together by the local law officer to help him chase and capture a criminal.

pos|sess /pəzɛs/ (**possesses, possessing, possessed**) V-T [no passive] If you **possess** something, you have it or own it. ❑ *He was then arrested and charged with possessing an offensive weapon.*

pos|sessed /pəzɛst/ ■ ADJ [v-link ADJ] If someone is described as being **possessed** by an evil spirit, it is believed that their mind and body are controlled by an evil spirit. ❑ *She even claimed the couple's daughter was possessed by the devil.* ■ → see also **possess**

pos|ses|sion /pəzɛʃən/ (**possessions**) ■ N-UNCOUNT If you are in **possession** of something, you have it, because you have obtained it or because it belongs to you. [FORMAL] ❑ *Those documents are now in the possession of the Washington Post.* ❑ *He was also charged with illegal possession of firearms.* ■ N-COUNT Your **possessions** are the things that you own or have with you at a particular time. ❑ *People had lost their homes and all their possessions.*

pos|ses|sive /pəzɛsɪv/ ■ ADJ Someone who is **possessive** about another person wants all that person's love and attention. ❑ *Danny could be very jealous and possessive about me.* • **pos|ses|sive|ness** N-UNCOUNT ❑ *I've ruined every relationship with my possessiveness.* ■ ADJ Someone who is **possessive** about things that they own does not like other people to use them. ❑ *People were very possessive about their coupons.* ■ ADJ [ADJ n] In grammar, a **possessive determiner** or **possessive adjective** is a word such as 'my' or 'her' that shows who or what something belongs to or is connected with. The **possessive** form of a name or noun has **'s** added to it, as in 'Jenny's' or 'cat's.'

pos|ses|sive pro|noun (**possessive pronouns**) N-COUNT A **possessive pronoun** is a pronoun such as 'mine,' 'yours,' or 'theirs' which is used to refer to the thing of a particular kind that belongs to someone, as in 'Can I borrow your pen? I've lost mine.'

pos|ses|sor /pəzɛsər/ (**possessors**) N-COUNT [usu N of n] The **possessor** of something is the person who has it. [FORMAL] ❑ *Ms. Nova is the proud possessor of a truly incredible voice.*

pos|sibil|ity ♦♦◇ /pɒsɪbɪlɪti/ (**possibilities**) ■ N-COUNT If you say there is a **possibility** that something is the case or that something will happen, you mean that it might be the case or it might happen. ❑ *We were not in the least worried about the possibility that candy could rot the teeth.* ■ N-COUNT A **possibility** is one of several different things that could be done. ❑ *There were several possibilities open to each manufacturer.*

╭─── **COLLOCATIONS** ───╮
possibility
NOUN
■
adjective + **possibility**: distinct, real, realistic, strong
verb + **possibility**: consider, investigate, raise; face; dismiss, exclude, ignore
■
adjective + **possibility**: infinite, limitless
possibility + be + adjective: endless
verb + **possibility**: discuss, explore

pos|sible ♦♦♦ /pɒsɪbəl/ (**possibles**) ■ ADJ If it is **possible** to do something, it can be done. ❑ *If it is possible to find out where your brother is, we will.* ❑ *Everything is possible if we want it enough.* ■ ADJ A **possible** event is one that might happen. ❑ *He referred the matter to the attorney general for possible action against several newspapers.* ❑ *One possible solution, if all else fails, is to take legal action.* ■ ADJ [v-link ADJ] If you say that it is **possible** that something is true or correct, you mean that although you do not know whether it is true or correct, you accept that it might be. [VAGUENESS] ❑ *It is possible that there's an explanation for all this.* ■ ADJ [as adv/pron as ADJ] If you do something **as soon as possible**, you do it as soon as you can. If you get **as much as possible** of something, you get as much of it as you can. ❑ *Please make your decision as soon as possible.* ❑ *Mrs. Pollard decided to learn as much as possible about the country before going there.* ■ ADJ You use **possible** with superlative adjectives to emphasize that something has more or less of a quality than anything else of its kind. [EMPHASIS] ❑ *They have joined the job market at the worst possible time.* ❑ *We expressed in the clearest possible way our disappointment, hurt, and anger.* ■ ADJ [ADJ n] If you describe someone as, for example, a **possible** governor, you mean that they could be elected as governor. ❑ *Government sources are now openly speculating about a possible successor for Dr. Lawrence.* • N-COUNT **Possible** is also a noun. ❑ *Kennedy was tipped as a presidential possible.* ■ N-SING **The possible** is everything that can be done in a situation. ❑ *He is a Democrat with the skill, nerve, and ingenuity to push the limits of the possible.*

pos|sibly ♦♦◇ /pɒsɪbli/ ■ ADV You use **possibly** to indicate that you are not sure whether something is true or might happen. [VAGUENESS] ❑ *Exercise will not only lower blood pressure but possibly protect against heart attacks.* ❑ *They were casually dressed, possibly students.* ■ ADV [ADV before v] You use **possibly** to emphasize that you are surprised, puzzled, or shocked by something that you have seen or heard. [EMPHASIS] ❑ *It was the most unexpected piece of news one could possibly imagine.* ■ ADV [ADV before v] You use **possibly** to emphasize that someone has tried their hardest to do something, or has done it as well as they can. [EMPHASIS] ❑ *They've done everything they can possibly think of.* ■ ADV [with brd-neg, ADV before v] You use **possibly** to emphasize that something definitely cannot happen or definitely cannot be done. [EMPHASIS] ❑ *No, I really can't possibly answer that!*

╭─── **SYNONYMS** ───╮
possibly
ADV ■
maybe: *I do think about having children, maybe when I'm 40.*
perhaps: *Perhaps, in time, the message will get through.*
conceivably: *The mission could conceivably be accomplished within a week.*

pos|sum /pɒsəm/ (**possums**) N-COUNT A **possum** is the same as an **opossum**. [mainly AM, INFORMAL]

╭─── **POST** ───╮
① LETTERS, PARCELS, AND INFORMATION
② JOBS AND PLACES
③ POLES

① **post** ♦♦◇ /poʊst/ (**posts, posting, posted**) ■ V-T If you **post** notices, signs, or other pieces of information somewhere, you attach them to a wall or board so that everyone can see them. ❑ *Officials began posting warning notices.* • PHRASAL VERB **Post up** means the same as **post** ①. ❑ *He has posted a sign up that says "No Fishing."* ■ V-T If you **post** information on the internet, you make the information available to other people on the Internet. [COMPUTING] ❑ *A consultation paper has been posted on the internet inviting input from users.* ■ PHRASE If you **keep someone posted**, you keep giving them the latest information about a situation that they are interested in. ❑ *Keep me posted on your progress.* ■ N-UNCOUNT You can use **post** to refer to letters and packages that are delivered to you. [mainly BRIT]

┌─────────────────────────────┐
│ in AM, usually use **mail** │
└─────────────────────────────┘

■ V-T If you **post** a letter or package, you send it to someone by putting it in a mailbox or by taking it to a post office. [mainly BRIT]

┌─────────────────────────────┐
│ in AM, usually use **mail** │
└─────────────────────────────┘

② **post** ♦♦◇ /poʊst/ (**posts, posting, posted**) ■ N-COUNT A **post** in a company or organization is a job or official position in it, usually one that involves responsibility. [FORMAL] ☐ *She had earlier resigned her post as President Menem's assistant.* **2** V-T [usu passive] If you **are posted** somewhere, you are sent there by the organization that you work for and usually work there for several years. ☐ *After training she was posted to Biloxi.* **3** V-T If a soldier, guard, or other person **is posted** somewhere, they are told to stand there, in order to supervise an activity or guard a place. ☐ *Police have now been posted outside all temples.* ☐ *They had to post a signalman at the entrance to the tunnel.* **4** → see also **posting**

③ **post** /poʊst/ (**posts**) **1** N-COUNT A **post** is a strong upright pole made of wood or metal that is dug into the ground. ☐ *The device is fixed to a post.* **2** N-COUNT A **post** is the same as a **goalpost**. ☐ *Jenkins missed a penalty, hitting the post in the thirteenth minute.* **3** N-SING On a horse-racing track, **the post** is a pole that marks the finishing point.

PREFIX

post-
forms words that refer to something that takes place after a particular date, period, or event. For example, *a postscript to a letter is extra information that you write at the end, after you have signed it.*

post|age /poʊstɪdʒ/ N-UNCOUNT **Postage** is the money that you pay for sending letters and packages by mail. ☐ *All prices include postage and handling.*

post|age stamp (**postage stamps**) N-COUNT A **postage stamp** is a small piece of sticky paper that you buy from the post office and stick on an envelope or package before you mail it. [FORMAL]

post|al /poʊstəl/ **1** ADJ [ADJ n] **Postal** is used to describe things or people connected with the public service of carrying letters and packages from one place to another. ☐ *Compensation for lost or damaged mail will be handled by the postal service.* **2** ADJ [ADJ n] **Postal** is used to describe activities that involve sending things by mail. ☐ *...free postal delivery.*

post|al or|der (**postal orders**) N-COUNT A **postal order** is a piece of paper representing a sum of money which you can buy at a post office and send to someone as a way of sending them money by mail. [BRIT]

in AM, use **money order**

post|box /poʊstbɒks/ (**postboxes**) also **post box** N-COUNT A **postbox** is a metal box in a public place, where you put letters and small parcels to be collected. They are then sorted and delivered. Compare **letterbox**. [BRIT]

in AM, use **mailbox**

post|card /poʊstkɑrd/ (**postcards**) also **post card** N-COUNT A **postcard** is a thin card, often with a picture on one side, which you can write on and mail to people without using an envelope.

post|code /poʊstkoʊd/ (**postcodes**) also **post code** N-COUNT A **postcode** is a short sequence of numbers and letters at the end of an address. [BRIT]

in AM, use **zip code**

post|dated /poʊstdeɪtɪd/ ADJ On a **postdated** check, the date is a later one than the date when the check was actually written. You write a postdated check to allow a period of time before the money is taken from your account.

post|doc /poʊstdɒk/ (**postdocs**) also **post-doc** N-COUNT A **postdoc** is a postdoctoral student. [INFORMAL] ☐ *This is a problem not infrequently encountered by postdocs.*

post|doc|tor|al /poʊstdɒktərəl/ also **post-doctoral** ADJ [ADJ n] A **postdoctoral** student has completed his or her doctorate and is doing further study or research. ☐ *Most postdoctoral work is funded by the research councils.*

post|er /poʊstər/ (**posters**) N-COUNT A **poster** is a large notice or picture that you stick on a wall or board, often in order to advertise something. ☐ *I had seen the poster for the jazz festival in Monterey.*

post|er child (**poster children**) also **poster boy, poster girl** N-COUNT If someone is a **poster child** for a particular cause, characteristic, or activity, they are seen as a very good or typical example of it. [mainly AM] ☐ *Zidane has become the poster child for a whole generation of French-born youths of North African extraction.*

poste res|tante /poʊst rɛstɑnt/ N-UNCOUNT **Poste restante** is a service operated by post offices by which letters and packages that are sent to you are kept at a particular post office until you collect them. [BRIT]

in AM, use **general delivery**

pos|teri|or /pɒstɪəriər/ (**posteriors**) **1** N-COUNT Someone's buttocks can be referred to as their **posterior**. [mainly HUMOROUS] **2** ADJ [ADJ n] **Posterior** describes something that is situated at the back of something else. [MEDICAL] ☐ *...the posterior leg muscles.*

pos|ter|ity /pɒstɛrɪti/ N-UNCOUNT You can refer to everyone who will be alive in the future as **posterity**. [FORMAL] ☐ *Speak clearly into the mike because we're recording this for posterity.*

post-feminist (**post-feminists**) **1** ADJ **Post-feminist** people and attitudes accept some of the ideas of feminism, but reject others. ☐ *...the post-feminist age.* **2** N-COUNT A **post-feminist** is someone who accepts some of the ideas of feminism, but rejects others. ☐ *...a generation of affluent post-feminists.* • **post-feminism** N-UNCOUNT ☐ *Post-feminism does not actually exist because we are still in the phase of pre-feminism.*

post|grad /poʊstgræd/ (**postgrads**) **1** N-COUNT A **postgrad** is the same as a **postgraduate**. [BRIT, INFORMAL]

in AM, use **grad student**

2 ADJ **Postgrad** means **postgraduate**. [BRIT, INFORMAL]

post|gradu|ate /poʊstgrædʒuɪt/ (**postgraduates**) also **post-graduate** **1** ADJ [ADJ n] **Postgraduate** study or research is done by a student who has a bachelor's degree and is studying or doing research at a more advanced level. **2** N-COUNT A **postgraduate** or a **postgraduate student** is a student with a first degree from a university who is studying or doing research at a more advanced level. [BRIT]

in AM, use **graduate student**

post-haste also **post haste** ADV [ADV after v] If you go somewhere or do something **post-haste**, you go there or do it as quickly as you can. [FORMAL] ☐ *The pilot wisely decided to return to Fresno post-haste.*

post|hu|mous /pɒstʃəməs/ ADJ [usu ADJ n] **Posthumous** is used to describe something that happens after a person's death but relates to something they did before they died. ☐ *...the posthumous publication of his first novel.* • **post|hu|mous|ly** ADV [ADV with v] ☐ *He was buried with full military honors and posthumously awarded a Purple Heart.*

post|in|dus|tri|al /poʊstɪndʌstriəl/ also **post-industrial** ADJ [ADJ n] **Postindustrial** is used to describe many western societies whose economies are no longer based on heavy industry.

post|ing /poʊstɪŋ/ (**postings**) **1** N-COUNT If a member of an armed force gets a **posting** to a particular place, they are sent to live and work there for a period. ☐ *...awaiting his posting to a field ambulance corps in early 1941.* **2** N-COUNT A **posting** is a message that is placed on the internet, for example, on a newsgroup or website, for everyone to read. [COMPUTING] ☐ *Postings on the internet can be accessed from anywhere in the world.* **3** N-COUNT If you get a **posting** to a different town or country, your employers send you to work there, usually for several years. [mainly BRIT]

in AM, usually use **assignment**

Post-it (**Post-its**) N-COUNT **Post-its** or **Post-it** notes are small pieces of paper that are sticky on one side. You write a note on the other side and stick the paper onto a surface. [TRADEMARK] ☐ *...stacks of CDs marked with yellow Post-its, one of which says "Lulu."*

post|man /poʊstmən/ (**postmen**) N-COUNT A **postman** is a man whose job is to collect and deliver letters and packages that are sent by mail. [mainly BRIT]

in AM, usually use **mail carrier**

post|mark /poʊstmɑrk/ (**postmarks**) N-COUNT A **postmark** is a mark that is printed on letters and packages. It shows the time and place at which something was mailed. ❑ *All the letters bore an Abilene postmark.*

post|marked /poʊstmɑrkt/ ADJ [usu v-link ADJ] If a letter is **postmarked**, it has a printed mark on the envelope showing when and where the letter was mailed. ❑ *The envelope was postmarked Helsinki.*

post|master /poʊstmæstər/ (postmasters) N-COUNT A **postmaster** is the person in charge of a local post office. [FORMAL]

post|mod|ern /poʊstmɒdərn/ ADJ [usu ADJ n] **Postmodern** is used to describe something or someone that is influenced by postmodernism. ❑ *...postmodern architecture.*

post|mod|ern|ism /poʊstmɒdərnɪzəm/ N-UNCOUNT **Postmodernism** is a late twentieth-century approach in art, architecture, and literature that typically mixes styles, ideas, and references to modern society, often in an ironic way.

post|mod|ern|ist /poʊstmɒdərnɪst/ (postmodernists) N-COUNT A **postmodernist** is a writer, artist, or architect who is influenced by postmodernism. • ADJ [usu ADJ n] **Postmodernist** is also an adjective. ❑ *...the postmodernist suspicion of grand ideological narratives.*

post|mor|tem /poʊstmɔrtəm/ (postmortems) **1** N-COUNT A **postmortem** is a medical examination of a dead person's body in order to find out how they died. ❑ *A postmortem was carried out to establish the cause of death.* **2** N-COUNT A **postmortem** is an examination of something that has recently happened, especially something that has failed or gone wrong. ❑ *The postmortem on the presidential campaign is under way.*

post|na|tal /poʊstneɪtəl/ ADJ [ADJ n] **Postnatal** means happening after and relating to the birth of a baby. ❑ *...postnatal depression.*

post of|fice (post offices) **1** N-COUNT A **post office** is a building where you can buy stamps, mail letters and packages, and use other services provided by the national postal service. ❑ *She rushed to get to the post office before it closed.* **2** N-SING The **Post Office** is sometimes used to refer to the U.S. Postal Service, which operates post offices. ❑ *The Post Office has confirmed that up to fifteen thousand jobs could be lost.*

post of|fice box (post office boxes) N-COUNT A **post office box** is a numbered box in a post office where a person's mail is kept for them until they come to collect it. The abbreviation **PO Box** is often used.

post|op|era|tive /poʊstɒpərətɪv/ ADJ [ADJ n] **Postoperative** means occurring after and relating to a medical operation. ❑ *...postoperative pain.*

post|partum de|pres|sion /poʊstpɑrtəm dɪprɛʃən/ N-UNCOUNT **Postpartum depression** is a mental state involving feelings of anxiety and sudden mood swings, which some women experience after they have given birth. [mainly AM] ❑ *After my birth, Mom had severe postpartum depression.*

in BRIT, usually use **postnatal depression**

post|pone /poʊstpoʊn, poʊspoʊn/ (postpones, postponing, postponed) V-T If you **postpone** an event, you delay it or arrange for it to take place at a later time than was originally planned. ❑ *He decided to postpone the expedition until the following day.*

post|pone|ment /poʊstpoʊnmənt, poʊspoʊn-/ (postponements) N-VAR The **postponement** of an event is the act of delaying it or arranging for it to take place at a later time than originally planned. ❑ *The postponement was due to a dispute over where the talks should be held.*

post-prandial /poʊst prændiəl/ also **postprandial** ADJ [ADJ n] You use **post-prandial** to refer to things you do or have after a meal. [FORMAL] ❑ *...a post-prandial nap.* ❑ *...a post-prandial cigar.*

post|pro|duc|tion /poʊstprədʌkʃən/ N-UNCOUNT [oft N n] In movies and television, **postproduction** is the work such as editing that takes place after the movie or show has been filmed. ❑ *The film's postproduction will be completed early next year.* ❑ *...a film postproduction company.*

post|script /poʊstskrɪpt/ (postscripts) **1** N-COUNT A **postscript** is something written at the end of a letter after you have signed your name. You usually write 'P.S.' in front of it. ❑ *A brief, handwritten postscript lay beneath his signature.* **2** N-COUNT A **postscript** is an addition to a finished story, account, or statement, that gives further information. ❑ *Let me add a postscript to this section on diet.*

post-traumatic stress dis|or|der N-UNCOUNT **Post-traumatic stress disorder** is a mental illness that can develop after someone has been involved in a very bad experience such as a war. The abbreviation **PTSD** is sometimes used. [MEDICAL]

post-truth ADJ [ADJ n] A **post-truth** situation is one in which people are less influenced by factual information than by their emotions or by beliefs they already hold. ❑ *We live in a world of post-truth politics.*

pos|tu|late /pɒstʃəleɪt/ (postulates, postulating, postulated) V-T If you **postulate** something, you suggest it as the basis for a theory, argument, or calculation, or assume that it is the basis. [FORMAL] ❑ *He dismissed arguments postulating differing standards for human rights in different cultures and regions.*

pos|tur|al /pɒstʃərəl/ ADJ [ADJ n] **Postural** means relating to the way a person stands or sits. [FORMAL] ❑ *Children can develop bad postural habits from quite an early age.*

pos|ture /pɒstʃər/ (postures, posturing, postured) **1** N-VAR Your **posture** is the position in which you stand or sit. ❑ *You can make your stomach look flatter instantly by improving your posture.* ❑ *Exercise, fresh air, and good posture are all helpful.* **2** N-COUNT A **posture** is an attitude that you have toward something. [FORMAL] ❑ *The military machine is ready to change its defensive posture to one prepared for action.* **3** V-I [usu cont] You can say that someone **is posturing** when you disapprove of their behavior because you think they are trying to give a particular impression in order to deceive people. [FORMAL, DISAPPROVAL] ❑ *She says the president may just be posturing.*

post|war /poʊstwɔr/ ADJ **Postwar** is used to describe things that happened, existed, or were made in the period immediately after a war, especially World War II, 1939-45. ❑ *Anesthetics and bottle feeding were popular in the early postwar years.*

posy /poʊzi/ (posies) N-COUNT [oft N of n] A **posy** is a flower or a small bunch of flowers. ❑ *There was a very small posy of flowers at my aunt's flat.*

pot ✦✧✧ /pɒt/ (pots, potting, potted) **1** N-COUNT A **pot** is a deep round container used for cooking stews, soups, and other food. ❑ *...metal cooking pots.* **2** N-COUNT You can use **pot** to refer to the pot and its contents, or to the contents only. ❑ *He was stirring a pot of soup.* **3** N-COUNT A **pot** of coffee or tea is an amount of it contained in a pot. ❑ *He spilt a pot of coffee.* • N-COUNT You can use **pot** to refer to a coffeepot or teapot. ❑ *There's tea in the pot.* **4** N-UNCOUNT **Pot** is sometimes used to refer to the drug marijuana or the cannabis plant. [INFORMAL] ❑ *I started smoking pot when I was about eleven.* **5** N-SING [the N] In a card game, the **pot** is the money from all the players which the winner of the game will take as a prize. **6** V-T If you **pot** a young plant, or part of a plant, you put it into a container filled with soil, so it can grow there. ❑ *Pot the cuttings individually.* • **pot|ted** ADJ [ADJ n] ❑ *...potted plants.* **7** → see also **melting pot**

po|table /poʊtəbəl/ ADJ [usu ADJ n] **Potable** water is clean and safe for drinking. [mainly AM]

pot|ash /pɒtæʃ/ N-UNCOUNT **Potash** is a white powder obtained from the ashes of burned wood and is sometimes used as a fertilizer.

po|tas|sium /pətæsiəm/ N-UNCOUNT **Potassium** is a soft silvery-white chemical element that occurs mainly in compounds. These compounds are used in making such things as glass, soap, and fertilizers.

po|ta|to ✦✧✧ /pəteɪtoʊ/ (potatoes) **1** N-VAR **Potatoes** are round vegetables with brown or red skins and white insides. They grow under the ground. **2** PHRASE You can refer to a difficult subject that people disagree on as a **hot potato**. ❑ *...a political hot potato such as abortion.*

po|ta|to chip (potato chips) **1** N-COUNT **Potato chips** are very thin slices of potato that have been fried until they are hard, dry, and crisp, and are eaten cold as a snack. [AM]

in BRIT, use **crisps**

2 N-COUNT **Potato chips** are long, thin pieces of potato fried in oil or fat and eaten hot, usually with a meal. [BRIT]

in AM, use **French fries**

pot|bellied /pɒtbɛlid/ ADJ Someone who is **potbellied** has a potbelly.

pot-bellied pig (pot-bellied pigs) also **potbellied pig** N-COUNT A **pot-bellied pig** is a small, dark-colored pig, originally from Vietnam, that is sometimes kept as a pet.

pot|belly /pɒtbɛli/ (potbellies) N-COUNT Someone who has a **potbelly** has a round, fat stomach that sticks out, usually because they eat or drink too much.

pot|boiler /pɒtbɔɪlər/ (potboilers) N-COUNT If you describe a book or movie as a **potboiler**, you mean that it has been created in order to earn money quickly and is of poor quality. [DISAPPROVAL] ❑ *All he wants to do is write a potboiler and get rich.*

po|ten|cy /poʊtⁿnsi/ **1** N-UNCOUNT **Potency** is the power and influence that a person, action, or idea has to affect or change people's lives, feelings, or beliefs. ❑ *All their songs have a lingering potency.* **2** N-UNCOUNT The **potency** of a drug, poison, or other chemical is its strength. ❑ *Sunscreen can lose its potency if left over winter in the bathroom cabinet.*

po|tent /poʊtⁿnt/ ADJ Something that is **potent** is very effective and powerful. ❑ *Their most potent weapon was the Exocet missile.*

po|ten|tate /poʊtⁿnteɪt/ (potentates) N-COUNT A **potentate** is a ruler who has complete power over their people. [FORMAL]

po|ten|tial ◆◇ /pətɛnʃⁿl/ **1** ADJ [ADJ n] You use **potential** to say that someone or something is capable of developing into the particular kind of person or thing mentioned. ❑ *The company has identified 60 potential customers.* ❑ *We are aware of the potential problems and have taken every precaution.* • **po|ten|tial|ly** ADV [ADV with cl/group] ❑ *Clearly this is a potentially dangerous situation.* **2** N-UNCOUNT If you say that someone or something has **potential**, you mean that they have the necessary abilities or qualities to become successful or useful in the future. ❑ *The boy has great potential.* ❑ *The school strives to treat students as individuals and to help each one to achieve their full potential.* **3** N-UNCOUNT If you say that someone or something has **potential** for doing a particular thing, you mean that it is possible they may do it. If there is **the potential for** something, it may happen. ❑ *John seemed as horrified as I about his potential for violence.* ❑ *The meeting has the potential to be a watershed event.*

SYNONYMS

potential
ADJ **1**
possible: *Her family is discussing a possible move to America.*
future: *Meanwhile, the domestic debate on the country's future role in Europe rages on.*
likely: *Experts say a 'yes' vote is still the likely outcome.*
NOUN **2**
ability: *Her drama teacher spotted her ability.*
capacity: *Our capacity for giving care, love, and attention is limited.*
capability: *They have the capability to destroy the enemy in days rather than weeks.*

---

po|ten|ti|al|ity /pətɛnʃiælɪti/ (potentialities) N-VAR If something has **potentialities** or **potentiality**, it is capable of being used or developed in particular ways. [FORMAL] ❑ *All of these are useful breeds whose potentiality has not been realized.*

pot|head /pɒthɛd/ (potheads) also **pot-head** N-COUNT If you call someone a **pothead**, you disapprove of the fact that they spend a lot of time smoking marijuana. [mainly AM, INFORMAL, DISAPPROVAL] ❑ *...a long-haired hippy pothead.*

pot|hole /pɒthoʊl/ (potholes) **1** N-COUNT A **pothole** is a large hole in the surface of a road, caused by traffic and bad weather. **2** N-COUNT A **pothole** is a deep hole in the ground. Potholes often lead to underground caves and tunnels.

pot|holed /pɒthoʊld/ ADJ [usu ADJ n] A **potholed** road has a lot of potholes in it.

pot|hol|ing /pɒthoʊlɪŋ/ N-UNCOUNT **Potholing** is the leisure activity of going into underground caves and tunnels. [BRIT]

in AM, use **spelunking**

po|tion /poʊʃⁿn/ (potions) N-COUNT A **potion** is a drink that contains medicine, poison, or something that is supposed to have magic powers. ❑ *...a magic potion that will make Siegfried forget Brünnhilde and fall in love with Gutrune.*

pot|luck /pɒtlʌk/ (potlucks) N-COUNT [oft N n] A **potluck** is a meal that consists of food brought by the people who come to the meal, or a meal that consists of whatever food happens to be available without special preparation. [AM] ❑ *The event will kick off with a potluck.* ❑ *If they drop by, I'll make a potluck supper.*

pot|pour|ri /poʊpʊri/ (potpourris) **1** N-MASS **Potpourri** is a mixture of dried petals and leaves from different flowers. Potpourri is used to make rooms smell pleasant. **2** N-SING [usu N of n] A **potpourri of** things is a collection of various items that were not originally intended to form a group. ❑ *...a potpourri of architectural styles from all over the world.*

pot roast (pot roasts) N-VAR A **pot roast** is a piece of meat that is cooked very slowly with a small amount of liquid in a covered pot.

pot|shot /pɒtʃɒt/ (potshots) **1** N-COUNT To take a **potshot** at someone or something means to shoot at them without taking the time to aim carefully. [INFORMAL] **2** N-COUNT A **potshot** is a criticism of someone that may be unexpected and unfair. [INFORMAL] ❑ *...Republicans taking potshots at the president.*

pot|ted /pɒtɪd/ → see pot 6

pot|ter's wheel (potter's wheels) N-COUNT A **potter's wheel** is a piece of equipment with a flat disk that spins around, on which a potter puts soft clay in order to shape it into a pot.

pot|tery /pɒtəri/ (potteries) **1** N-UNCOUNT You can use **pottery** to refer to pots, dishes, and other objects made from clay and then baked in an oven until they are hard. ❑ *...a fine range of pottery.* **2** N-UNCOUNT You can use **pottery** to refer to the hard clay that some pots, dishes, and other objects are made of. ❑ *Some bowls were made of pottery and wood.* **3** N-UNCOUNT **Pottery** is the craft or activity of making objects out of clay. ❑ *He became interested in sculpting and pottery.* **4** N-COUNT A **pottery** is a factory or other place where pottery is made. ❑ *...the many galleries and potteries which sell pieces by local artists.*

pot|ting shed (potting sheds) N-COUNT A **potting shed** is a small building where plants and seeds are grown in pots until they are ready to be planted outside.

pot|ting soil (potting soils) N-MASS **Potting soil** is soil that is specially prepared to help plants to grow, especially in containers. [AM] ❑ *Pot the new plant immediately in good potting soil.*

pot|ty /pɒti/ (potties) N-COUNT A **potty** is a deep bowl that a small child uses instead of a toilet.

pot|ty trained also **potty-trained** ADJ **Potty trained** means the same as **toilet trained**.

pot|ty train|ing also **potty-training** N-UNCOUNT **Potty training** is the same as **toilet training**.

pouch /paʊtʃ/ (pouches) **1** N-COUNT A **pouch** is a flexible container like a small bag. ❑ *Joe Bob took out his pipe and dug it into a pouch of tobacco.* **2** N-COUNT The **pouch** of an animal such as a kangaroo or a koala is the pocket of skin on its stomach in which its baby grows. ❑ *...a kangaroo, with a baby in its pouch.*

poul|tice /poʊltɪs/ (poultices) N-COUNT A **poultice** is a piece of cloth with a soft, often hot, substance such as clay or a mixture of herbs on it. It is put over a painful or swollen part of someone's body in order to reduce the pain or swelling.

poul|try /poʊltri/ N-PLURAL You can refer to chickens, ducks, and other birds that are kept for their eggs and meat as **poultry**. ❑ *...a poultry farm.* • N-UNCOUNT Meat from these birds is also referred to as **poultry**. ❑ *The menu features roast meats and poultry.*

pounce /paʊns/ (pounces, pouncing, pounced) **1** V-I If someone **pounces** on you, they come up toward you suddenly and take hold of you. ❑ *He pounced on the photographer, beat him up, and smashed his camera.* **2** V-I If someone **pounces** on something such as a mistake, they quickly draw attention to it, usually in order to gain an advantage for themselves or to prove that they are right. ❑ *The Democrats were ready to pounce on any Republican failings or mistakes.* **3** V-I When an animal or bird **pounces** on something, it jumps on it and holds it, in order to kill it. ❑ *...like a tiger pouncing on its prey.*

pound ♦♦♦ /paʊnd/ (pounds, pounding, pounded) **1** N-COUNT A **pound** is a unit of weight used mainly in the U.S., Britain, and other countries where English is spoken. One pound is equal to around 0.454 kilograms. A **pound of** something is a quantity of it that weighs one pound. ❑ *Her weight was under ninety pounds.* ❑ *...a pound of cheese.* **2** N-COUNT The **pound** is the unit of money which is used in Britain. It is represented by the symbol £. One British pound is divided into a hundred pence. Some other countries, for example, Egypt, also have a unit of money called a **pound**. ❑ *...multi-million-pound profits.* **3** N-SING The **pound** is used to refer to the British currency system, and sometimes to the currency systems of other countries that use pounds. ❑ *The pound is expected to continue to increase against most other currencies.* **4** N-COUNT A **pound** is a place where dogs and cats found wandering in the street are taken and kept until they are claimed by their owners. ❑ *...cages at the local pound.* **5** N-COUNT A **pound** is a place where cars that have been parked illegally are taken by the police and kept until they have been claimed by their owners. ❑ *The car remained in the police pound for a month.* **6** V-T/V-I If you **pound** something or **pound on** it, you hit it with great force, usually loudly and repeatedly. ❑ *He pounded the table with his fist.* ❑ *Somebody began pounding on the front door.* **7** V-T If you **pound** something, you crush it into a paste or a powder or into very small pieces. ❑ *She pounded the corn kernels.* **8** V-I If your heart **is pounding**, it is beating with an unusually strong and fast rhythm, usually because you are afraid. ❑ *I'm sweating, my heart is pounding. I can't breathe.*

pound cake (pound cakes) N-VAR A **pound cake** is a very rich cake, originally made using a pound of butter, a pound of sugar, and a pound of flour. [AM] ❑ *...a piece of pound cake.*

-pounder /-paʊndər/ (-pounders) **1** COMB IN N-COUNT **-pounder** can be added to numbers to form nouns that refer to animals or fish that weigh a particular number of pounds. ❑ *My fish average 2 lb 8 oz and I've had two eight-pounders.* **2** COMB IN N-COUNT **-pounder** can be added to numbers to form nouns that refer to guns that fire shells weighing a particular number of pounds. ❑ *The guns were twelve-pounders.*

pound|ing /paʊndɪŋ/ (poundings) **1** N-COUNT [usu sing, usu supp N] If someone or something takes a **pounding**, they are severely injured or damaged. [INFORMAL] ❑ *Sarajevo took one of its worst poundings in weeks.* **2** → see also **pound**

pour ♦♦◊ /pɔr/ (pours, pouring, poured) **1** V-T If you **pour** a liquid or other substance, you make it flow steadily out of a container by holding the container at an angle. ❑ *Pour a pool of sauce on two plates and arrange the meat neatly.* ❑ *Don poured a generous measure of scotch into a fresh glass.* **2** V-T If you **pour** someone a drink, you put some of the drink in a cup or glass so that they can drink it. ❑ *He got up and poured himself another drink.* ❑ *She asked Tillie to pour her a cup of coffee.* **3** V-I When a liquid or other substance **pours** somewhere, for example, through a hole, it flows quickly and in large quantities. ❑ *Blood was pouring from his broken nose.* ❑ *Tears poured down both our faces.* **4** V-I [ins cont] When it rains very heavily, you can say that **it is pouring**. ❑ *It was still pouring outside.* ❑ *The rain was pouring down.* **5** V-I If people **pour** into or out of a place, they go there quickly and in large numbers. ❑ *Any day now, the Northern forces may pour across the new border.* ❑ *At six p.m. large groups poured from the numerous offices.* **6** V-I If something such as information **pours** into a place, a lot of it is obtained or given. ❑ *Martin, 78, died yesterday. Tributes poured in from around the globe.* **7 to pour cold water on something** → see **water**
▶ **pour out 1** PHRASAL VERB If you **pour out** a drink, you put some of it in a cup or glass. ❑ *Larry was pouring out four glasses of champagne.* **2** PHRASAL VERB If you **pour out** your thoughts, feelings, or experiences, you tell someone all about them. ❑ *I poured my thoughts out on paper in an attempt to rationalize my feelings.*

pout /paʊt/ (pouts, pouting, pouted) V-I If someone **pouts**, they stick out their lips, usually in order to show that they are annoyed or to make themselves sexually attractive. ❑ *Like one of the kids, he whined and pouted when he did not get what he wanted.* • N-COUNT **Pout** is also a noun. ❑ *She shot me a reproachful pout.*

pov|er|ty ♦♦◊ /pɒvərti/ **1** N-UNCOUNT **Poverty** is the state of being extremely poor. ❑ *According to World Bank figures, 41 percent of Brazilians live in absolute poverty.* **2** N-SING [also no det, N of n] You can use **poverty** to refer to any situation in which there is not enough of something or its quality is poor. [FORMAL] ❑ *...a poverty of ideas.*

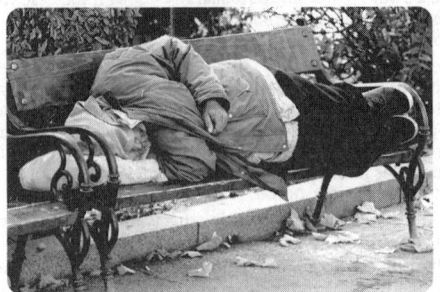

VOCABULARY IN CONTEXT

Poverty

You don't have to be living on the streets to be **homeless**. You may be **couch surfing** or living in a **shelter** or as a **squatter**. Even if you're not actually on the street, you are still **vulnerable**. Homeless people are 17 times more likely to be attacked, and **malnutrition** and poor physical health are also common. On average, a homeless person's life expectancy is just 47.

Poor **mental health** is both a cause and a result of homelessness. Other causes include getting into **debt** (meaning that the person is likely to be **evicted** from their **housing**) and escaping an **abusive** relationship.

pov|er|ty line N-SING [the N] If someone is on **the poverty line**, they have just enough income to buy the things they need in order to live. ❑ *Thirteen percent of the population live below the poverty line.*

poverty-stricken ADJ [usu ADJ n] **Poverty-stricken** people or places are extremely poor. ❑ *...a teacher of poverty-stricken kids.*

pov|er|ty trap (poverty traps) N-COUNT If someone is in a **poverty trap**, they are very poor but cannot improve their income because the money they get from the government decreases as the money they earn increases.

POW /pi oʊ dʌbᵊlyu/ (POWs) N-COUNT A **POW** is the same as a **prisoner of war**.

pow|der /paʊdər/ (powders, powdering, powdered) **1** N-MASS **Powder** consists of many tiny particles of a solid substance. ❑ *Put a small amount of the powder into a container and mix with water.* ❑ *...cocoa powder.* **2** V-T If you **powder** your face or some other part of your body, you put face powder or talcum powder on it. ❑ *She powdered her face and applied her lipstick and rouge.*

pow|der blue also **powder-blue** COLOR Something that is **powder blue** is a pale grayish-blue color.

pow|dered /paʊdərd/ ADJ A **powdered** substance is one that is in the form of a powder although it can come in a different form. ❑ *There are only two boxes of powdered milk left.*

pow|der keg (powder kegs) N-COUNT If you describe a situation or a place as a **powder keg**, you mean that it could easily become very dangerous. ❑ *Unless these questions are solved, the region will remain a powder keg.*

pow|der room (powder rooms) N-COUNT A **powder room** is a large, clean toilet for women in a public building such as a hotel. [OLD-FASHIONED]

pow|dery /paʊdəri/ **1** ADJ Something that is **powdery** looks or feels like powder. ❑ *A couple of inches of dry, powdery snow had fallen.* **2** → See feature box at **snow**

pow|er ♦♦♦ /paʊər/ (powers, powering, powered) **1** N-UNCOUNT If someone has **power**, they have a lot of control over people and activities. ❑ *In a democracy, power must be divided.* **2** N-UNCOUNT Your **power** to do something is your ability to do it. ❑ *Human societies have the power to solve the problems confronting them.* ❑ *Fathers have the power to dominate children and young people.* **3** N-UNCOUNT If it is **in** or **within** your **power** to do something, you are able to do it or you have the resources to deal with it. ❑ *Your debt situation is only temporary, and it is within your power to resolve it.* **4** N-UNCOUNT [also N in pl] If someone in authority has the **power** to do something, they have the legal right to do it. ❑ *The police have the power of arrest.* **5** N-UNCOUNT If people take **power** or come to **power**, they take charge of a country's affairs. If a group of people are **in power**, they are in charge of a country's affairs. ❑ *Idi Amin came into power several years later.* ❑ *He first assumed power in 1970.* **6** N-COUNT You can use **power** to refer to a country that is very rich or important, or has strong military forces. ❑ *....the emergence of the new major economic power, Japan.* **7** N-UNCOUNT The **power** of something is the ability that it has to move or affect things. ❑ *The vehicle had better power, better tires, and better brakes.* **8** N-UNCOUNT **Power** is energy, especially electricity, that is obtained in large quantities from a fuel source and used to operate lights, heating, and machinery. ❑ *Nuclear power is cleaner than coal.* ❑ *Power has been restored to most parts that were hit last night by high winds.* **9** V-T The device or fuel that **powers** a machine provides the energy that the machine needs in order to work. ❑ *The "flywheel" battery, it is said, could power an electric car for 600 miles on a single charge.* **10** ADJ [ADJ n] **Power** tools are operated by electricity. ❑ *...large power tools, such as chainsaws.*

▶ **power up** PHRASAL VERB When you **power up** something such as a computer or a machine, you connect it to a power supply and switch it on. ❑ *Simply power up your laptop and continue work.*

pow|er base (power bases) N-COUNT [oft with poss] The **power base** of a politician or other leader is the area or the group of people from which they get most support, and that enables him or her to become powerful. ❑ *Milan was Mr. Craxi's home town and his power base.*

power|boat /paʊərboʊt/ (powerboats) N-COUNT A **powerboat** is a very fast, powerful motorboat.

pow|er bro|ker (power brokers) N-COUNT A **power broker** is someone who has a lot of influence, especially in politics, and uses it to help other people gain power. ❑ *Jackson had been a major power broker in the presidential elections.*

pow|er cut (power cuts) N-COUNT A **power cut** is a period of time when the electricity supply to a particular building or area is stopped, sometimes deliberately. [mainly BRIT]

in AM, usually use **outage**

pow|er fail|ure (power failures) N-VAR A **power failure** is a period of time when the electricity supply to a particular building or area is interrupted, for example, because of damage to the cables.

pow|er|ful ♦♦◇ /paʊərfəl/ **1** ADJ A **powerful** person or organization is able to control or influence people and events. ❑ *You're a powerful man – people will listen to you.* ❑ *...Russia and India, two large, powerful countries.* **2** ADJ You say that someone's body is **powerful** when it is physically strong. ❑ *Hans feared his powerful muscles.* • **pow|er|ful|ly** ADV [ADV with v] ❑ *He is described as a strong, powerfully-built man of 60.* **3** ADJ A **powerful** machine or substance is effective because it is very strong. ❑ *The more powerful the car the more difficult it is to handle.* ❑ *...powerful computer systems.* • **pow|er|ful|ly** ADV [ADV adj] ❑ *Crack is a much cheaper, smokable form of cocaine which is powerfully addictive.* **4** ADJ A **powerful** smell is very strong. ❑ *There was a powerful smell of stale beer.* • **pow|er|ful|ly** ADV [ADV after v] ❑ *The air smelled powerfully of dry dust.* **5** ADJ A **powerful** voice is loud and can be heard from a long way away. ❑ *At that moment Mrs. Jones's powerful voice interrupted them, announcing a visitor.* **6** ADJ You describe a piece of writing, speech, or work of art as **powerful** when it has a strong effect on people's feelings or beliefs. ❑ *...a powerful 11-part drama about a corrupt city leader.* • **pow|er|ful|ly** ADV ❑ *It's a play – painful, funny, and powerfully acted.*

── SYNONYMS ──

powerful
ADJ
1
influential: *It helps to have influential friends.*
dominant: *She was a dominant figure in the French film industry.*
commanding: *Right now, you're in a more commanding position than you have been for ages.*
3
strong: *I'm not strong enough to carry him.*
mighty: *...a land marked with vast lakes and mighty rivers.*
vigorous: *Sir Robert was a strong and vigorous politician.*
sturdy: *She was a short, sturdy woman in her early sixties.*

pow|er game (power games) N-COUNT [oft adj N] You can refer to a situation in which different people or groups are competing for power as a **power game**, especially if you disapprove of the methods they are using in order to try to win power. ❑ *...the dangerous power games in the Kremlin following Stalin's death.*

power|house /paʊərhaʊs/ (powerhouses) N-COUNT A **powerhouse** is a person, country, or organization that has a lot of power or influence. ❑ *Nigeria is the most populous African country and an economic powerhouse for the continent.*

pow|er|less /paʊərlɪs/ **1** ADJ Someone who is **powerless** is unable to control or influence events. ❑ *If you don't have money, you're powerless.* • **pow|er|less|ness** N-UNCOUNT ❑ *If we can't bring our problems under control, feelings of powerlessness and despair often ensue.* **2** ADJ [ADJ to-inf] If you are **powerless** to do something, you are completely unable to do it. ❑ *People are being murdered every day and I am powerless to stop it.*

pow|er line (power lines) N-COUNT A **power line** is a cable, especially above ground, along which electricity is passed to an area or building.

pow|er of at|tor|ney N-UNCOUNT **Power of attorney** is a legal document that allows you to appoint someone such as a lawyer to act on your behalf in specified matters.

pow|er plant (power plants) N-COUNT A **power plant** is the same as a **power station**.

pow|er play (power plays) **1** N-COUNT A **power play** is an attempt to gain an advantage by showing that you are more powerful than another person or organization, for example, in a business relationship or negotiation. ❑ *Their politics consisted of unstable power plays between rival groups.* **2** N-UNCOUNT In a game of ice hockey, **power play** is a period of time when one team has more players because one or more of the other team is in the penalty box.

pow|er point (power points) N-COUNT A **power point** is a place in a wall where you can connect electrical equipment to the electricity supply. [BRIT]

in AM, use **outlet**

power-sharing also **power sharing** N-UNCOUNT **Power-sharing** is a political arrangement in which different or opposing groups all take part in government together. ❑ *They agreed a power-sharing arrangement, but it collapsed after five months.*

pow|er sta|tion (power stations) N-COUNT A **power station** is a place where electricity is produced.

pow|er steer|ing N-UNCOUNT In a vehicle, **power steering** is a system for steering that uses power from the engine so that it is easier for the driver to steer the vehicle.

pow|er walk|ing also **power-walking** N-UNCOUNT **Power walking** is the activity of walking very fast, as a means of keeping fit. ❑ *Do some power walking for about twenty minutes a day.*

pow|wow /paʊwaʊ/ (powwows) N-COUNT People sometimes refer to a meeting or discussion as a **powwow**. [INFORMAL] ❑ *Every year my father would call a family powwow to discuss where we were going on vacation.*

pox /pɒks/ → see **chickenpox**, **smallpox**

pp. ♦◇◇ **pp.** is the plural of 'p.' and means 'pages.' [WRITTEN] ❑ *See chapter 6, pp. 137-41.*

PPE /piː piː iː/ N-UNCOUNT **PPE** is equipment such as gloves, masks, and gowns worn by people who are at risk of injury or infection. **PPE** is an abbreviation for 'personal protective equipment.' ▢ *Workers require guidance regarding what PPE can be removed, and how, for a break.*

PPO /pi̱ pi o̱ʊ/ (**PPOs**) N-COUNT [oft N n] A **PPO** is an organization whose members receive medical care at a greatly reduced cost only if they use doctors and hospitals which belong to the organization. [AM] ▢ *...a statewide PPO plan that allows members throughout California to travel to Mexico for care.*

PPV /pi̱ pi vi̱/ N-UNCOUNT **PPV** is an abbreviation for pay-per-view.

PR /pi̱ ɑːr/ N-UNCOUNT **PR** is an abbreviation for **public relations**. [BUSINESS] ▢ *It will be good PR.*

prac|ti|cable /præ̱ktɪkəbəl/ ADJ If a task, plan, or idea is **practicable**, people are able to carry it out. [FORMAL] ▢ *It is not practicable to offer her the original job back.*

prac|ti|cal ◆◇◇ /præ̱ktɪkəl/ **1** ADJ The **practical** aspects of something involve real situations and events, rather than just ideas and theories. ▢ *...practical suggestions on how to increase the fiber in your daily diet.* **2** ADJ You describe people as **practical** when they make sensible decisions and deal effectively with problems. [APPROVAL] ▢ *You were always so practical, Maria.* ▢ *How could she be so practical when he'd just told her something so shattering?* **3** ADJ **Practical** ideas and methods are likely to be effective or successful in a real situation. ▢ *Although the causes of cancer are being uncovered, we do not yet have any practical way to prevent it.* **4** ADJ You can describe clothes and things in your house as **practical** when they are suitable for a particular purpose rather than just being fashionable or attractive. ▢ *...lightweight, practical clothes.*

prac|ti|cal|ity /præ̱ktɪkæ̱lɪti/ (**practicalities**) N-VAR The **practicalities** of a situation are the practical aspects of it, as opposed to its theoretical aspects. ▢ *Decisions about your children should be based on the practicalities of everyday life.*

prac|ti|cal joke (**practical jokes**) N-COUNT A **practical joke** is a trick that is intended to embarrass someone or make them look ridiculous.

prac|ti|cal|ly /præ̱ktɪkli/ **1** ADV [ADV with group/cl] **Practically** means almost, but not completely or exactly. ▢ *He'd known the old man practically all his life.* **2** ADV [ADV adj/-ed] You use **practically** to describe something that involves real actions or events rather than ideas or theories. ▢ *The course is more practically based than the master's degree.*

prac|tice ◆◆◆ /præ̱ktɪs/ (**practices, practicing, practiced**) **1** N-COUNT You can refer to something that people do regularly as a **practice**. ▢ *Some firms have reached agreements to cut workers' pay below the level set in their contract, a practice that is illegal in Germany.* **2** N-VAR **Practice** means doing something regularly in order to be able to do it better. A **practice** is one of these periods of doing something. ▢ *She was taking all three of her daughters to basketball practice every day.* ▢ *...the hard practice necessary to develop from a learner to an accomplished musician.* **3** N-UNCOUNT The work done by doctors and lawyers is referred to as the **practice** of medicine and law. People's religious activities are referred to as the **practice** of a religion. ▢ *...maintaining or improving his skills in the practice of internal medicine.* ▢ *I eventually realized I had to change my attitude toward medical practice.* **4** N-COUNT A doctor's or lawyer's **practice** is his or her business, often shared with other doctors or lawyers. ▢ *The new doctor's practice was miles away from where I lived.* **5** PHRASE What happens **in practice** is what actually happens, in contrast to what is supposed to happen. ▢ *...the difference between foreign policy as presented to the public and foreign policy in actual practice.* **6** PHRASE If you **put** a belief or method **into practice**, you behave or act in accordance with it. ▢ *Now that he is back, the mayor has another chance to put his new ideas into practice.* **7** V-T/V-I If you **practice**, or **practice** something, you keep doing it regularly in order to be able to do it better. ▢ *She practiced the piano in the grade school basement.*

in BRIT, use **practise**

8 → see also **practiced** **9** V-T When people **practice** something such as a custom, craft, or religion, they take part in the activities associated with it. ▢ *Her parents had yearned to be free to practice their religion.* ▢ *He was brought up in a family that practiced traditional Judaism.*

in BRIT, use **practise**

● **prac|tic|ing** ADJ [ADJ n] ▢ *And he was more or less a practicing Muslim throughout his life.* **10** V-T [usu passive] If something cruel is regularly done to people, you can say that it **is practiced on** them. ▢ *Female circumcision is practiced on 2 million girls a year.*

in BRIT, use **practise**

11 V-T/V-I Someone who **practices** medicine or law works as a doctor or a lawyer. ▢ *He doesn't practice medicine for the money.* ▢ *...the obligations of my license to practice as a lawyer.*

in BRIT, use **practise**

12 → See feature box at **farming**

---COLLOCATIONS---

practice
NOUN
1
noun + **practice**: accounting, business, management, work
adjective + **practice**: common, normal, standard; questionable, unfair
practice + be + adjective: widespread
verb + **practice**: adopt, develop; end, stop
4
noun + **practice**: law
adjective + **practice**: architectural, dental, legal, medical; private

---SYNONYMS---

practice
NOUN **1**
custom: *The custom of lighting the flame goes back centuries.*
way: *Direct confrontation was not his way.*
tradition: *...the rich traditions of Afro-Cuban music and dance.*
habit: *He has an endearing habit of licking his lips when he's nervous.*

prac|ticed /præ̱ktɪst/

in BRIT, use **practised**

ADJ Someone who is **practiced** at doing something is good at it because they have had experience and have developed their skill at it. ▢ *She worked for years as a bookkeeper, so she's practiced at budgeting.*

prac|ti|tion|er /præktɪ̱ʃənər/ (**practitioners**) N-COUNT Doctors are sometimes referred to as **practitioners** or **medical practitioners**. [FORMAL]

prag|mat|ic /prægmæ̱tɪk/ ADJ A **pragmatic** way of dealing with something is based on practical considerations, rather than theoretical ones. A **pragmatic** person deals with things in a practical way. ▢ *Robin took a pragmatic look at her situation.*
● **prag|mati|cal|ly** /prægmæ̱tɪkli/ ADV ▢ *"I can't ever see us doing anything else," stated Brian pragmatically.*

prag|mat|ics /prægmæ̱tɪks/ N-SING **Pragmatics** is the branch of linguistics that deals with the meanings and effects that come from the use of language in particular situations.

prag|ma|tism /præ̱gmətɪzəm/ N-UNCOUNT **Pragmatism** means thinking of or dealing with problems in a practical way, rather than by using theory or abstract principles. [FORMAL] ▢ *She had a reputation for clear thinking and pragmatism.*
● **prag|ma|tist** (**pragmatists**) N-COUNT ▢ *He is a political pragmatist, not an idealist.*

prai|rie /pre̱əri/ (**prairies**) N-VAR A **prairie** is a large area of flat, grassy land in North America. Prairies have very few trees.

prai|rie dog (**prairie dogs**) N-COUNT A **prairie dog** is a type of small furry animal that lives underground in the prairies and some mountains of North America.

praise ◆◇◇ /pre̱ɪz/ (**praises, praising, praised**) **1** V-T If you **praise** someone or something, you express approval for their achievements or qualities. ▢ *The American president praised Turkey for its courage.* ▢ *Many others praised Sanford for taking a strong stand.* **2** N-UNCOUNT **Praise** is what you say or write about someone when you are praising them. ▢ *All the guests are full of praise for the staff and service they received.* ▢ *I have nothing but praise for the police.*

praise|worthy /ˈpreɪzwɜrði/ ADJ If you say that something is **praiseworthy**, you mean that you approve of it and it deserves to be praised. [FORMAL, APPROVAL] ☐ ...*the government's praiseworthy efforts to improve efficiency in health and education.*

pra|line /ˈprɑlin, ˈpreɪ-/ N-UNCOUNT **Praline** is a sweet substance made from nuts cooked in boiling sugar. It is used in desserts and as a filling for chocolates.

pram /præm/ (**prams**) N-COUNT A **pram** is the same as a **baby carriage**. [BRIT]

prance /præns/ (**prances, prancing, pranced**) ◼ V-I If someone **prances** around, they walk or move around with exaggerated movements, usually because they want people to look at them and admire them. [DISAPPROVAL] ☐ *He was horrified at the thought of having to prance about on a stage in tights.* ◼ V-I When a horse **prances**, it moves with quick, high steps. ☐ *Their horses pranced and whinnied.* ☐ ...*as the carriage horses pranced through the bustling thoroughfares.* ☐ ...*a prancing light-footed mare named Princess.*

prank /præŋk/ (**pranks**) N-COUNT A **prank** is a childish trick. [OLD-FASHIONED] ☐ *Their pranks are amusing at times.*

prank|ster /ˈpræŋkstər/ (**pranksters**) N-COUNT A **prankster** is someone who plays tricks and practical jokes on people.

prat|fall /ˈprætfɔl/ (**pratfalls**) ◼ N-COUNT If someone takes a **pratfall**, they make an embarrassing mistake. [mainly AM] ☐ *They're waiting for the poor little rich girl to take a pratfall.* ◼ N-COUNT A **pratfall** is a fall onto your behind. [mainly AM]

prat|tle /ˈprætəl/ (**prattles, prattling, prattled**) V-I If you say that someone **prattles on** about something, you are criticizing them because they are talking a lot without saying anything important. [INFORMAL, DISAPPROVAL] ☐ *Lou prattled on about various trivialities till I wanted to scream.* ☐ *She prattled on as she drove out to the highway.* ☐ *Archie, shut up. You're prattling.* ● N-UNCOUNT **Prattle** is also a noun. ☐ *What a bore it was to listen to the woman's prattle!*

pray /preɪ/ (**prays, praying, prayed**) ◼ V-I When people **pray**, they speak to God in order to give thanks or to ask for help. ☐ *He spent his time in prison praying and studying.* ☐ *Now all we have to do is help ourselves and pray to God.* ◼ V-T [usu cont] When someone is hoping very much that something will happen, you can say that they **are praying** that it will happen. ☐ *I'm just praying that somebody in Congress will do something before it's too late.*

prayer /prɛər/ (**prayers**) ◼ N-UNCOUNT **Prayer** is the activity of speaking to God. ☐ *They had joined a religious order and dedicated their lives to prayer and good works.* ◼ N-COUNT A **prayer** is the words a person says when they speak to God. ☐ *They should take a little time and say a prayer for the people on both sides.* ◼ N-COUNT You can refer to a strong hope that you have as your **prayer**. ☐ *This drug could be the answer to our prayers.* ◼ N-PLURAL A short religious service at which people gather to pray can be referred to as **prayers**. ☐ *He promised that the boy would be back at school in time for evening prayers.*

prayer book (**prayer books**) N-COUNT A **prayer book** is a book that contains the prayers used in church or at home.

prayer meet|ing (**prayer meetings**) N-COUNT A **prayer meeting** is a religious meeting where people say prayers to God.

PREFIX

pre-
forms words that refer to something that takes place before a particular date, period, or event. For example, **prehistoric** people and things existed at a time before information was written down.

preach /pritʃ/ (**preaches, preaching, preached**) ◼ V-T/V-I When a member of the clergy **preaches** a sermon, he or she gives a talk on a religious or moral subject during a religious service. ☐ *At High Mass the priest preached a sermon on the devil.* ☐ *The bishop preached to a crowd of several hundred local people.* ◼ V-T/V-I When people **preach** a belief or a course of action, they try to persuade other people to accept the belief or to take the course of action. ☐ *He said he was trying to preach peace and tolerance to his people.* ☐ *Health experts are now preaching that even a little exercise is far better than none at all.* ◼ V-I If someone gives you advice in a very serious, boring way, you can say that they **are preaching at** you. [DISAPPROVAL] ☐ *"Don't preach at me," he shouted.* ◼ PHRASE If you say that someone **is preaching to the choir**, you mean that they are presenting an argument or opinion to people who already agree with it. ☐ *Most of these seminars were preaching to the choir so there was little debate to be had.*

preach|er /ˈpritʃər/ (**preachers**) N-COUNT A **preacher** is a person, usually a member of the clergy, who preaches sermons as part of a church service.

pre|am|ble /ˈpriæmbəl/ (**preambles**) N-VAR A **preamble** is an introduction that comes before something you say or write. ☐ *The controversy has arisen over the text of the preamble to the unification treaty.*

pre|ar|range /priəˈreɪndʒ/ (**prearranges, prearranging, prearranged**) V-T If you **prearrange** something, you plan or arrange it before the time when it actually happens. ☐ *When you prearrange your funeral, you can pick your own flowers and music.*

pre|ar|ranged /priəˈreɪndʒd/ ADJ [ADJ n] You use **prearranged** to indicate that something has been planned or arranged before the time when it actually happens. ☐ *Work has to be done on schedule and in a prearranged sequence.*

pre|cari|ous /prɪˈkɛəriəs/ ◼ ADJ If your situation is **precarious**, you are not in complete control of events and might fail in what you are doing at any moment. ☐ *Our financial situation had become precarious.* ● **pre|cari|ous|ly** ADV ☐ *We lived precariously. I suppose I wanted to squeeze as much pleasure from each day as I possibly could.* ◼ ADJ Something that is **precarious** is not securely held in place and seems likely to fall or collapse at any moment. ☐ *They looked really comical as they crawled up precarious ladders.* ● **pre|cari|ous|ly** ADV ☐ *One of my grocery bags was still precariously perched on the car bumper.*

pre|cau|tion /prɪˈkɔʃən/ (**precautions**) N-COUNT A **precaution** is an action that is intended to prevent something dangerous or unpleasant from happening. ☐ *Could he not, just as a precaution, move to a place of safety?*

pre|cau|tion|ary /prɪˈkɔʃəneri/ ADJ [usu ADJ n] **Precautionary** actions are taken in order to prevent something dangerous or unpleasant from happening. [FORMAL] ☐ *The local administration says the curfew is a precautionary measure.*

pre|cede /prɪˈsid/ (**precedes, preceding, preceded**) ◼ V-T If one event or period of time **precedes** another, it happens before it. [FORMAL] ☐ *Intensive negotiations between the main parties preceded the vote.* ☐ *The earthquake was preceded by a loud roar and lasted 20 seconds.* ◼ V-T If you **precede** someone somewhere, you go in front of them. [FORMAL] ☐ *He gestured to Alice to precede them from the room.* ◼ V-T A sentence, paragraph, or chapter that **precedes** another one comes just before it. ☐ *Look at the information that precedes the paragraph in question.*

prec|edence /ˈprɛsɪdəns/ N-UNCOUNT If one thing takes **precedence** over another, it is regarded as more important than the other thing. ☐ *Have as much fun as possible at college, but don't let it take precedence over work.*

prec|edent /ˈprɛsɪdənt/ (**precedents**) N-VAR If there is a **precedent** for an action or event, it has happened before, and this can be regarded as an argument for doing it again. [FORMAL] ☐ *The trial could set an important precedent for dealing with similar cases.*

pre|cept /ˈprisɛpt/ (**precepts**) N-COUNT A **precept** is a general rule that helps you to decide how you should behave in particular circumstances. [FORMAL] ☐ ...*an electoral process based on the central precept that all people are born equal.*

pre|cinct /ˈprisɪŋkt/ (**precincts**) N-COUNT A **precinct** is a part of a city or town that has its own police force. [AM] ☐ *The shooting occurred in the 34th Precinct.*

pre|cious /ˈprɛʃəs/ ◼ ADJ If you say that something such as a resource is **precious**, you mean that it is valuable and should not be wasted or used badly. ☐ *After four months in foreign parts, every hour at home was precious.* ☐ *A family break allows you to spend precious time together.* ◼ ADJ **Precious** objects and materials are worth a lot of money because they are rare. ☐ ...*jewelry and precious objects belonging to her mother.* ◼ ADJ If something **is precious** to you, you regard it as important and do not want to lose it. ☐ *Her family's support is particularly precious to Josie.*

pre|cious met|al (**precious metals**) N-VAR A **precious metal** is a valuable metal such as gold or silver.

pre|cious stone (**precious stones**) N-COUNT A **precious stone** is a valuable stone, such as a diamond or a ruby, that is used for making jewelry.

preci|pice /prɛsɪpɪs/ (precipices) **1** N-COUNT A **precipice** is a very steep cliff on a mountain. **2** N-COUNT If you say that someone is on the edge of a **precipice**, you mean that they are in a dangerous situation in which they are extremely close to disaster or failure. ☐ *The king now stands on the brink of a political precipice.*

pre|cipi|tate (precipitates, precipitating, precipitated)

The verb is pronounced /prɪsɪpɪteɪt/. The adjective is pronounced /prɪsɪpɪtɪt/.

1 V-T If something **precipitates** an event or situation, usually a bad one, it causes it to happen suddenly or sooner than normal. [FORMAL] ☐ *The killings in Vilnius have precipitated the worst crisis yet.* **2** ADJ A **precipitate** action or decision happens or is made more quickly or suddenly than most people think is sensible. [FORMAL] ☐ *I don't think we should make precipitate decisions.*

pre|cipi|ta|tion /prɪsɪpɪteɪʃən/ **1** N-UNCOUNT **Precipitation** is rain, snow, or hail. [TECHNICAL] **2** N-UNCOUNT **Precipitation** is a process in a chemical reaction that causes solid particles to become separated from a liquid. [TECHNICAL] **3** → See also color supplement

pre|cipi|tous /prɪsɪpɪtəs/ **1** ADJ [usu ADJ n] A **precipitous** slope or drop is very steep and often dangerous. ☐ *The town is perched on the edge of a steep, precipitous cliff.* • **pre|cipi|tous|ly** ADV ☐ *The ground beyond the road fell away precipitously.* **2** ADJ [usu ADJ n] A **precipitous** change is sudden and unpleasant. ☐ *The stock market's precipitous drop frightened foreign investors.* • **pre|cipi|tous|ly** ADV ☐ *The company has seen its profits fall precipitously over the past few years.* **3** ADJ [usu ADJ n] A **precipitous** action happens very quickly and often without being planned. ☐ *...a precipitous decision.* • **pre|cipi|tous|ly** ADV ☐ *They've got to act precipitously to make the deals.*

pré|cis /preɪsiː/

The form **précis** is both the singular and the plural form. It is pronounced /preɪsiːz/ when it is the plural.

N-COUNT [oft N of n] A **précis** is a short written or spoken account of something, that gives the important points but not the details. [FORMAL]

pre|cise /prɪsaɪs/ **1** ADJ [ADJ n] You use **precise** to emphasize that you are referring to an exact thing, rather than something vague. [EMPHASIS] ☐ *I can remember the precise moment when my daughter came to see me and her new baby brother in the hospital.* ☐ *The precise location of the wreck was discovered in 1988.* **2** ADJ Something that is **precise** is exact and accurate in all its details. ☐ *They speak very precise English.*

pre|cise|ly ✦✧✧ /prɪsaɪsli/ **1** ADV **Precisely** means accurately and exactly. ☐ *Nobody knows precisely how many people are still living in the camp.* ☐ *The first bell rang at precisely 10:29 a.m.* **2** ADV [ADV with cl/group] You can use **precisely** to emphasize that a reason or fact is the only important one there is, or that it is obvious. [EMPHASIS] ☐ *Children come to zoos precisely to see captive animals.* **3** ADV [as reply] You can say '**precisely**' to confirm in an emphatic way that what someone has just said is true. [EMPHASIS] ☐ *"All I did was write the truth."—"Precisely! Now everyone knows."*

SYNONYMS

precisely
ADV **1**
exactly: *Agnew's car pulled into the driveway at exactly five o'clock.*
accurately: *The test can accurately predict what a bigger explosion would do.*
strictly: *Actually, that is not strictly true.*

---

pre|ci|sion /prɪsɪʒən/ N-UNCOUNT If you do something with **precision**, you do it exactly as it should be done. ☐ *The choir sang with precision.*

pre|clude /prɪkluːd/ (precludes, precluding, precluded) **1** V-T If something **precludes** an event or action, it prevents the event or action from happening. [FORMAL] ☐ *At 84, John feels his age precludes too much travel.* **2** V-T If something **precludes** you **from** doing something or going somewhere, it prevents you from doing it or going there. [FORMAL] ☐ *A constitutional amendment precludes any president from serving more than two terms.*

pre|co|cious /prɪkoʊʃəs/ ADJ A **precocious** child is very clever, mature, or good at something, often in a way that you usually only expect to find in an adult. ☐ *Margaret was always a precocious child.* ☐ *She burst on to the world tennis scene as a precocious 14-year-old.*

pre|coc|ity /prɪkɒsɪti/ N-UNCOUNT **Precocity** is the quality of being precocious. [FORMAL]

pre|con|ceived /priːkənsiːvd/ ADJ [ADJ n] If you have **preconceived** ideas about something, you have already formed an opinion about it before you have enough information or experience. ☐ *We all start with preconceived notions of what we want from life.*

pre|con|cep|tion /priːkənsɛpʃən/ (preconceptions) N-COUNT Your **preconceptions** about something are beliefs formed about it before you have enough information or experience. ☐ *Did you have any preconceptions about the sort of people who did computing?*

pre|con|di|tion /priːkəndɪʃən/ (preconditions) N-COUNT If one thing is a **precondition** for another, it must happen or be done before the second thing can happen or exist. [FORMAL] ☐ *They have demanded the release of three prisoners as a precondition for any negotiation.*

pre|cooked /priːkʊkt/ ADJ [usu ADJ n] **Precooked** food has been prepared and cooked in advance so that it only needs to be heated quickly before you eat it.

pre|cur|sor /prɪkɜːrsər/ (precursors) N-COUNT A **precursor** of something is a similar thing that happened or existed before it, often something that led to the existence or development of that thing. ☐ *He said that the deal should not be seen as a precursor to a merger.*

pre|date /priːdeɪt/ (predates, predating, predated) V-T If you say that one thing **predated** another, you mean that the first thing happened or existed some time before the second thing. ☐ *His troubles predated the recession.*

preda|tor /prɛdətər/ (predators) **1** N-COUNT A **predator** is an animal that kills and eats other animals. ☐ *With no natural predators on the island, the herd increased rapidly.* **2** N-COUNT People sometimes refer to predatory people or organizations as **predators**. ☐ *Rumors of a takeover are probably far-fetched, but the company is worried about predators.*

preda|tory /prɛdətɔːri/ **1** ADJ **Predatory** animals live by killing other animals for food. ☐ *...predatory birds like the eagle.* **2** ADJ **Predatory** people or organizations are eager to gain something out of someone else's weakness or suffering. ☐ *People will not set up new businesses while they are frightened by the predatory behavior of the banks.*

preda|tory pric|ing N-UNCOUNT If a company practices **predatory pricing**, it charges a much lower price for its products or services than its competitors in order to force them out of the market. [BUSINESS] ☐ *Predatory pricing by large supermarkets was threatening the livelihood of smaller stores.*

pre|de|cease /priːdɪsiːs/ (predeceases, predeceasing, predeceased) V-T If one person **predeceases** another, they die before them. [FORMAL] ☐ *His wife of 63 years, Mary, predeceased him by 11 months.*

pre|de|ces|sor /prɛdɪsɛsər/ (predecessors) **1** N-COUNT Your **predecessor** is the person who had your job before you. ☐ *He maintained that he learned everything he knew from his predecessor.* **2** N-COUNT The **predecessor** of an object or machine is the object or machine that came before it in a sequence or process of development. ☐ *Although the car is some 2 inches shorter than its predecessor, its trunk is 20 percent larger.*

pre|des|ti|na|tion /priːdɛstɪneɪʃən, priːdes-/ N-UNCOUNT If you believe in **predestination**, you believe that people have no control over events because everything has already been decided by a power such as God or fate.

pre|des|tined /priːdɛstɪnd/ ADJ If you say that something was **predestined**, you mean that it could not have been prevented or changed because it had already been decided by a power such as God or fate. ☐ *His was not a political career predestined from birth.*

pre|de|ter|mined /priːdɪtɜːrmɪnd/ ADJ If you say that something is **predetermined**, you mean that its form or nature was decided by previous events or by people rather than by chance. ❑ *The prince's destiny was predetermined from the moment of his birth.* ❑ *The capsules can be made to release the pesticides at a predetermined time.*

pre|de|ter|min|er /prɪdɪtɜːrmɪnər/ (**predeterminers**) N-COUNT In grammar, a **predeterminer** is a word that is used before a determiner, but is still part of the noun group. For example, 'all' in 'all the time' and 'both' in 'both our children' are predeterminers.

pre|dica|ment /prɪdɪkəmənt/ (**predicaments**) N-COUNT If you are in a **predicament**, you are in an unpleasant situation that is difficult to get out of. ❑ *Hank explained our predicament.*

predi|cate (**predicates, predicating, predicated**)

The noun is pronounced /prɛdɪkɪt/. The verb is pronounced /prɛdɪkeɪt/.

■ N-COUNT In some systems of grammar, the **predicate** of a clause is the part of it that is not the subject. For example, in 'I decided what to do,' 'decided what to do' is the predicate. ■ V-T [usu passive] If you say that one situation **is predicated on** another, you mean that the first situation can be true or real only if the second one is true or real. [FORMAL] ❑ *Financial success is usually predicated on having money or being able to obtain it.*

pre|dict ✦✦✧ /prɪdɪkt/ (**predicts, predicting, predicted**) V-T If you **predict** an event, you say that it will happen. ❑ *The latest opinion polls are predicting a very close contest.* ❑ *He predicted that my hair would grow back "in no time."*

pre|dict|able /prɪdɪktəbəl/ ADJ If you say that an event is **predictable**, you mean that it is obvious in advance that it will happen. ❑ *This was a predictable reaction, given the bitter hostility between the two countries.* • **pre|dict|ably** ADV ❑ *His article is, predictably, a scathing attack on capitalism.* • **pre|dict|abil|ity** /prɪdɪktəbɪlɪti/ N-UNCOUNT ❑ *Your mother values the predictability of your Sunday calls.*

pre|dic|tion /prɪdɪkʃən/ (**predictions**) N-VAR If you make a **prediction** about something, you say what you think will happen. ❑ *He was unwilling to make a prediction for the coming year.* ❑ *Weather prediction has never been a perfect science.*

pre|dic|tive /prɪdɪktɪv/ ■ ADJ [usu ADJ n] You use **predictive** to describe something such as a test, science, or theory that is concerned with determining what will happen in the future. [FORMAL] ❑ *...the predictive branch of economics.* ■ ADJ GRADED; ADJ [usu ADJ n] If you have **predictive** text on your phone or computer, the word you might need is predicted from the first few letters you type. ❑ *If I am not careful with predictive text, my signature comes out as Alien Template.*

pre|dic|tor /prɪdɪktər/ (**predictors**) N-COUNT [with supp, usu N of n] You can refer to something that helps you predict something that will happen in the future as a **predictor** of that thing. ❑ *Opinion polls are an unreliable predictor of election outcomes.*

pre|di|lec|tion /prɛdəlɛkʃən, priːd-/ (**predilections**) N-COUNT [oft N for n/-ing] If you have a **predilection** for something, you have a strong liking for it. [FORMAL] ❑ *...his predilection for fast cars and fast horses.*

pre|dis|pose /priːdɪspoʊz/ (**predisposes, predisposing, predisposed**) ■ V-T If something **predisposes** you to think or behave in a particular way, it makes it likely that you will think or behave in that way. [FORMAL] ❑ *They take pains to hire people whose personalities predispose them to serve customers well.* • **pre|dis|posed** ADJ [v-link ADJ] ❑ *...people who are predisposed to violent crime.* ■ V-T If something **predisposes** you to a disease or illness, it makes it likely that you will suffer from that disease or illness. [FORMAL] ❑ *...a gene that predisposes people to alcoholism.* • **pre|dis|posed** ADJ [v-link ADJ] ❑ *Some people are genetically predisposed to diabetes.*

pre|dis|po|si|tion /priːdɪspəzɪʃən/ (**predispositions**) ■ N-COUNT If you have a **predisposition** to behave in a particular way, you tend to behave like that because of the kind of person you are or the attitudes you have. [FORMAL] ❑ *There is a thin dividing line between educating the public and creating a predisposition to panic.* ■ N-COUNT If you have a **predisposition** to a disease or illness, it is likely that you will suffer from that disease or illness. [FORMAL] ❑ *...a genetic predisposition to lung cancer.*

pre|domi|nance /prɪdɒmɪnəns/ ■ N-SING [usu N of n] If there is a **predominance** of one type of person or thing, there are many more of that type than of any other type. [FORMAL] ❑ *...the predominance of women in the industry.* ■ N-UNCOUNT [usu with supp] If someone or something has **predominance**, they have the most power or importance among a group of people or things. [FORMAL] ❑ *Eventually even their economic predominance was to suffer.*

pre|domi|nant /prɪdɒmɪnənt/ ADJ If something is **predominant**, it is more important or noticeable than anything else in a set of people or things. ❑ *Mandy's predominant emotion was confusion.*

pre|domi|nant|ly /prɪdɒmɪnəntli/ ADV You use **predominantly** to indicate which feature or quality is most noticeable in a situation. ❑ *The landscape has remained predominantly rural in appearance.*

pre|domi|nate /prɪdɒmɪneɪt/ (**predominates, predominating, predominated**) ■ V-I If one type of person or thing **predominates** in a group, there is more of that type of person or thing in the group than of any other. [FORMAL] ❑ *In older age groups women predominate because men tend to die younger.* ■ V-I When a feature or quality **predominates**, it is the most important or noticeable one in a situation. [FORMAL] ❑ *She wants to create a society where secular principles predominate.*

pre|domi|nate|ly /prɪdɒmɪnətli/ ADV **Predominately** means the same as **predominantly**. ❑ *...a predominately White, middle-class suburb.*

pre|emi|nent /priːɛmɪnənt/ also **pre-eminent** ADJ If someone or something is **preeminent** in a group, they are more important, powerful, or capable than other people or things in the group. [FORMAL] ❑ *...some of the preeminent names in baseball.* • **pre|emi|nence** /priːɛmɪnəns/ N-UNCOUNT ❑ *Europe was poised to reassert its traditional preeminence in Western art.*

pre|emi|nent|ly /priːɛmɪnəntli/ also **pre-eminently** ADV **Preeminently** means to a very great extent. ❑ *Theodore Roosevelt was preeminently a realist in foreign relations.*

pre|empt /priːɛmpt/ (**preempts, preempting, preempted**) also **pre-empt** V-T If you **preempt** an action, you prevent it from happening by doing something that makes it unnecessary or impossible. ❑ *The law would preempt stronger local rules.* ❑ *..."the survival of the fittest," a slogan that virtually preempted all debate.*

pre|emp|tive /priːɛmptɪv/ also **pre-emptive** ADJ A **preemptive** attack or strike is intended to weaken or damage an enemy or opponent, for example, by destroying their weapons before they can do any harm. ❑ *A preemptive strike against a sovereign nation raises moral and legal issues.*

preen /priːn/ (**preens, preening, preened**) ■ V-T If someone **preens** themselves, they spend a lot of time making themselves look neat and attractive; used especially if you want to show that you disapprove of this behavior or that you find it ridiculous and amusing. [DISAPPROVAL] ❑ *50% of men under 35 spend at least 20 minutes preening themselves every morning in the bathroom.* ❑ *Bill preened his beard.* ■ V-T/V-I If someone **preens**, they think in a pleased way about how attractive, clever, or good at something they are. [DISAPPROVAL] ❑ *She stood preening in their midst, delighted with the attention.* ❑ *He preened himself on the praise he had received.* ❑ *a preening prize fighter about to enter a ring.* ■ V-T When birds **preen** their feathers, they clean them and arrange them neatly using their beaks. ❑ *Rare birds preen themselves right in front of your camera.*

pre-existing also **preexisting** ADJ [ADJ n] A **pre-existing** situation or thing exists already or existed before something else. ❑ *...the pre-existing tensions between the two countries.* ❑ *...people who have been infected in the course of their treatment for a pre-existing illness.*

pre|fab /priːfæb/ (**prefabs**) ■ N-COUNT A **prefab** is a house built with parts made in a factory and then quickly put together at the place where the house was built. ■ ADJ [ADJ n] A **prefab** building or structure is one made from parts that were made in a factory and then quickly put together at the place where the structure was built.

pre|fab|ri|cat|ed /priːfæbrɪkeɪtɪd/ ADJ **Prefabricated** buildings are built with parts made in a factory so that they can be easily carried and put together.

pref|ace /prɛfɪs/ (prefaces, prefacing, prefaced) **1** N-COUNT A **preface** is an introduction at the beginning of a book that explains what the book is about or why it was written. ❑ ...*the preface to Kelman's novel.* **2** V-T If you **preface** an action or speech with something else, you do or say this other thing first. ❑ *I will preface what I am going to say with a few lines from Shakespeare.*

pre|fect /prifɛkt/ (prefects) **1** N-COUNT In some countries, a **prefect** is the head of the local government administration or of a local government department. ❑ ...*the police prefect for the district of Mehedinti.* **2** N-COUNT In some schools, especially in Britain, a **prefect** is an older student who does special duties and helps the teachers to look after the younger students.

pre|fec|ture /prifɛktʃər/ (prefectures) N-COUNT [oft in names] In some countries, administrative areas are called **prefectures**. ❑ *He was born in Yamagata prefecture, north of Tokyo.*

pre|fer ✦✧◇ /prifɜr/ (prefers, preferring, preferred) V-T [no cont] If you **prefer** someone or something, you like that person or thing better than another, and so you are more likely to choose them if there is a choice. ❑ *Does he prefer a particular sort of music?* ❑ *I became a teacher because I preferred books and people to politics.* ❑ *I prefer to think of peace not war.* ❑ *I would prefer him to be with us next season.*

pref|er|able /prɛfərəbəl, prɛfrə-, prɪfɜrə-/ ADJ If you say that one thing is **preferable** to another, you mean that it is more desirable or suitable. ❑ *A big earthquake a long way off is preferable to a smaller one nearby.* ❑ *Prevention of a problem is always preferable to trying to cure it.* • **pref|er|ably** /prɛfərəbli, prɛfrə-, prɪfɜrə-/ ADV ❑ *Do something creative or take exercise, preferably in the fresh air.*

pref|er|ence /prɛfərəns/ (preferences) **1** N-VAR If you have a **preference** for something, you would like to have or do that thing rather than something else. ❑ *It upset her when people revealed a preference for her sister.* **2** N-UNCOUNT If you **give preference** to someone with a particular qualification or feature, you choose them rather than someone else. ❑ *The Pentagon has said it will give preference to companies with which it can do business electronically.*

pref|er|ence shares N-PLURAL **Preference shares** are the same as **preferred stock**. Compare **ordinary shares**. [BRIT, BUSINESS]

pref|er|en|tial /prɛfərɛnʃəl/ ADJ If you get **preferential** treatment, you are treated better than other people and therefore have an advantage over them. ❑ *Firstborn sons received preferential treatment.*

pre|fer|ment /prifɜrmənt/ (preferments) N-VAR **Preferment** is the act of being given a better and more important job in an organization. [FORMAL] ❑ *He had no hopes of future preferment.*

pre|ferred stock N-UNCOUNT **Preferred stock** is the shares in a company that are owned by people who have the right to receive part of the company's profits before the holders of common stock. They also have the right to have their capital repaid if the company fails and has to close. Compare **common stock**. [AM, BUSINESS]

in BRIT, use **preference shares**

pre|fig|ure /prifɪgyər/ (prefigures, prefiguring, prefigured) V-T If one thing **prefigures** another, it is a first indication that suggests or determines that the second thing will happen. [FORMAL] ❑ *The wall through Berlin was finally ruptured, prefiguring the reunification of Germany.*

pre|fix /prifɪks/ (prefixes) **1** N-COUNT A **prefix** is a letter or group of letters, for example, 'un-' or 'multi-,' that is added to the beginning of a word in order to form a different word. For example, the prefix 'un-' is added to 'happy' to form 'unhappy.' Compare **affix** and **suffix**. **2** N-COUNT A **prefix** is one or more numbers or letters added to the beginning of a code number to indicate, for example, what area something belongs to. ❑ *To telephone from the U.S. use the prefix 011 33 before the numbers given here.*

pre|fixed /prifɪkst/ V-T PASSIVE A word or code number that **is prefixed** by one or more letters or numbers has them as its prefix. ❑ *Sulphur-containing compounds are often prefixed by the term "thio."*

pre|game /prigeɪm/ (pregames, pregaming, pregamed) **1** ADJ [ADJ n] **Pregame** activities take place before a sports game. ❑ *The Braves are planning to send a bald eagle in flight as part of the pregame ceremonies for the night game.* **2** VERB If someone **pregames**, they drink a lot of alcohol before they go out for a social occasion. [INFORMAL] ❑ *They meet at one of their houses to pregame before going on to a night club.*

preg|nan|cy ✦◇◇ /prɛgnənsi/ (pregnancies) **1** N-VAR **Pregnancy** is the condition of being pregnant or the period of time during which a female is pregnant. ❑ *It would be wiser to cut out all alcohol during pregnancy.* **2** → See feature box at **birth**

━━━ COLLOCATIONS ━━━
pregnancy
NOUN **1**
adjective + **pregnancy**: healthy, normal, successful; difficult, ectopic, high-risk; teenage, unplanned, unwanted
verb + **pregnancy**: confirm, continue; avoid, prevent; end, terminate

preg|nan|cy test (pregnancy tests) N-COUNT A **pregnancy test** is a medical test that women have to find out if they are pregnant.

preg|nant ✦◇◇ /prɛgnənt/ **1** ADJ If a woman or female animal is **pregnant**, she has a baby or babies developing in her body. ❑ *Lena got pregnant and married.* **2** ADJ [ADJ n, v-link ADJ with n] A **pregnant** silence or moment has a special meaning that is not obvious but that people are aware of. ❑ *There was a long, pregnant silence, which Mrs. Madrigal punctuated by reaching for the check.* **3** → See feature box at **birth**

pre|heat /prihit/ (preheats, preheating, preheated) V-T If you **preheat** an oven, you switch it on and allow it to reach a certain temperature before you put food inside it. ❑ *Preheat the oven to 400 degrees.*

pre|his|tor|ic /prihɪstɔrɪk/ ADJ **Prehistoric** people and things existed at a time before information was written down. ❑ ...*the famous prehistoric cave paintings of Lascaux.*

pre|his|to|ry /prihɪstəri, -tri/ N-UNCOUNT **Prehistory** is the time in history before any information was written down.

pre|in|dus|tri|al /priɪndʌstriəl/

in BRIT, use **pre-industrial**

ADJ [ADJ n] **Preindustrial** refers to the time before machines were introduced to produce goods on a large scale. ❑ ...*the transition from preindustrial to industrial society.*

pre|judge /pridʒʌdʒ/ (prejudges, prejudging, prejudged) V-T If you **prejudge** a situation, you form an opinion about it before you know all the facts. [FORMAL] ❑ *They tried to prejudge the commission's findings.*

preju|dice /prɛdʒədɪs/ (prejudices, prejudicing, prejudiced) **1** N-VAR **Prejudice** is an unreasonable dislike of a particular group of people or things, or a preference for one group of people or things over another. ❑ *There was a deep-rooted prejudice long before the two countries went to war.* ❑ *There is widespread prejudice against workers over 45.* **2** V-T If you **prejudice** someone or something, you influence them so that they are unfair in some way. ❑ *I think your upbringing has prejudiced you.* ❑ *The report was held back for fear of prejudicing his trial.* **3** V-T If someone **prejudices** another person's situation, they do something that makes it worse than it should be. [FORMAL] ❑ *Her study was not in any way intended to prejudice the future development of the college.*

preju|diced /prɛdʒədɪst/ ADJ A person who is **prejudiced** against someone from a different racial group has an unreasonable dislike of them. ❑ *Many people in this country are racially prejudiced.*

preju|di|cial /prɛdʒədɪʃəl/ ADJ If an action or situation is **prejudicial** to someone or something, it is harmful to them. [FORMAL] ❑ *You could face up to eight years in jail for spreading rumors considered prejudicial to security.*

prel|ate /prɛlɪt/ (prelates) N-COUNT A **prelate** is a member of the clergy holding a high rank such as a bishop or an archbishop.

pre|limi|nary /prɪlɪmɪnɛri/ (preliminaries) **1** ADJ **Preliminary** activities or discussions take place at the beginning of an event, often as a form of preparation. ❑ *Preliminary results show the Republican Party with 11 percent of the vote.* **2** N-COUNT A

preliminary is something that you do at the beginning of an activity, often as a form of preparation. ❑ *You all know why I am here. So I won't waste time on preliminaries.*

prel|ude /prɛlyud, preɪlud/ (**preludes**) N-COUNT You can describe an event as a **prelude** to another event or activity when it happens before it and acts as an introduction to it. ❑ *For him, reading was a necessary prelude to sleep.*

pre|mari|tal /primæritᵊl/ ADJ [ADJ n] **Premarital** means happening at some time before someone gets married. ❑ *I rejected the teaching that premarital sex was immoral.*

prema|ture /priməʧʊər/ **1** ADJ Something that is **premature** happens earlier than usual or earlier than people expect. ❑ *Accidents are still the number one cause of premature death for Americans.* ❑ *His career was brought to a premature end by a succession of knee injuries.* • **prema|ture|ly** ADV ❑ *The war and the years in the harsh mountains had prematurely aged him.* **2** ADJ You can say that something is **premature** when it happens too early and is therefore inappropriate. ❑ *It now seems their optimism was premature.* • **prema|ture|ly** ADV ❑ *He was careful not to celebrate prematurely.* **3** ADJ A **premature** baby is one that was born before the date when it was expected to be born. ❑ *Even very young premature babies respond to their mother's presence.* • **prema|ture|ly** ADV [ADV after v] ❑ *Danny was born prematurely, weighing only 3lb 3oz.* **4** → See feature box at **birth**

pre|med /primɛd/ also **pre-med** ADJ [usu ADJ n] A **premed** student is a student who is taking courses that are required in order for the student to study at medical school. [mainly AM, INFORMAL] ❑ *Tim is a premed student at MSU.* ❑ *...a sophomore in a pre-med program.*

pre|medi|tat|ed /primɛdɪteɪtɪd/ ADJ A **premeditated** crime is planned or thought about before it is done. ❑ *In a case of premeditated murder a life sentence is mandatory.*

pre|medi|ta|tion /primɛdɪteɪʃᵊn/ N-UNCOUNT **Premeditation** is thinking about something or planning it before you actually do it. [FORMAL] ❑ *The judge finally concluded there was insufficient evidence of premeditation.*

pre|men|stru|al /primɛnstruəl/ ADJ [ADJ n] **Premenstrual** is used to refer to the time immediately before menstruation and a woman's behavior and feelings at this time. ❑ *...premenstrual symptoms.*

pre|men|stru|al syn|drome N-UNCOUNT **Premenstrual syndrome** is used to refer to the problems, including strain and tiredness, that many women experience before menstruation. The abbreviation **PMS** is often used. ❑ *About 70% of women suffer from premenstrual syndrome.*

prem|ier♦◇◇ /prɪmɪər/ (**premiers**) **1** N-COUNT The leader of the government of a country is sometimes referred to as the country's **premier**. ❑ *...the former Australian premier Malcolm Turnbull.* **2** ADJ [ADJ n] **Premier** is used to describe something that is considered to be the best or most important thing of a particular type. ❑ *...the country's premier opera company.*

premi|ere /prɪmɪər, prɪmyɛər/ (**premieres, premiering, premiered**) **1** N-COUNT The **premiere** of a new play or movie is the first public performance of it. ❑ *Four astronauts visited for last week's premiere of the movie Space Station.* **2** V-T/V-I When a movie or show **premieres** or **is premiered**, it is shown to an audience for the first time. ❑ *The documentary premiered at the Jerusalem Film Festival.*

prem|ier|ship /prɪmɪərʃɪp/ N-SING The **premiership** of a leader of a government is the period of time during which they are the leader. ❑ *...the final years of Margaret Thatcher's premiership.*

prem|ise /prɛmɪs/ (**premises**) **1** N-PLURAL The **premises** of a business or an institution are all the buildings and land that it occupies in one place. ❑ *There is a kitchen on the premises.* **2** N-COUNT A **premise** is something that you suppose is true and that you use as a basis for developing an idea. [FORMAL] ❑ *The premise is that schools will work harder to improve if they must compete.*

prem|ised /prɛmɪst/ V-T PASSIVE If a theory or attitude **is premised on** an idea or belief, that idea or belief has been used as the basis for it. [FORMAL] ❑ *All our activities are premised on the basis of "Quality with Equality."*

prem|iss /prɛmɪs/ [BRIT] → see **premise 2**

pre|mium♦◇◇ /primiəm/ (**premiums**) **1** N-COUNT A **premium** is a sum of money that you pay regularly to an insurance company for an insurance policy. ❑ *It is too early to say whether insurance premiums will be affected.* **2** N-COUNT A **premium** is a sum of money that you have to pay for something in addition to the normal cost. ❑ *Even if customers want "solutions," most are not willing to pay a premium for them.* **3** ADJ [ADJ n] **Premium** products are of a higher than usual quality and are often expensive. ❑ *At the premium end of the market, business is booming.* **4** PHRASE If something is **at a premium**, it is wanted or needed, but is difficult to get or achieve. ❑ *If space is at a premium, choose adaptable furniture that won't fill the room.* **5** PHRASE If you buy or sell something **at a premium**, you buy or sell it at a higher price than usual, for example, because it is in short supply. ❑ *He eventually sold the shares back to the bank at a premium.*

premo|ni|tion /primənɪʃᵊn, prɛm-/ (**premonitions**) N-COUNT If you have a **premonition**, you have a feeling that something is going to happen, often something unpleasant. ❑ *He had an unshakable premonition that he would die.*

pre|na|tal /prineɪtᵊl/ ADJ **Prenatal** is used to describe things relating to the medical care of women during pregnancy. ❑ *I'd met her briefly in a prenatal class.*

pre|nup /prinʌp/ (**prenups**) also **pre-nup** N-COUNT A **prenup** is the same as a **prenuptial agreement**. [mainly AM, INFORMAL] ❑ *Paul insists there's no prenup between him and Heather Mills.*

pre|nup|tial agree|ment /prinʌpʃᵊl əgrimənt, -nʌptʃᵊl/ (**prenuptial agreements**) also **pre-nuptial agreement** N-COUNT A **prenuptial agreement** is a written contract made between a man and a woman before they marry, in which they state how their assets such as property and money should be divided if they get divorced. ❑ *My wife and I were married in 1996 and we signed a prenuptial agreement.*

pre|oc|cu|pa|tion /priɒkyəpeɪʃᵊn/ (**preoccupations**) **1** N-COUNT If you have a **preoccupation with** something or someone, you keep thinking about them because they are important to you. ❑ *Karouzos's poetry shows a profound preoccupation with the Orthodox Church.* **2** N-UNCOUNT **Preoccupation** is a state of mind in which you think about something so much that you do not consider other things to be important. ❑ *The arrest of Senator Pinochet has created a climate of preoccupation among our citizens.*

pre|oc|cu|pied /priɒkyəpaɪd/ ADJ If you are **preoccupied**, you are thinking a lot about something or someone, and so you hardly notice other things. ❑ *Tom Banbury was preoccupied with the missing Shepherd child and did not want to devote time to the new murder.*

pre|oc|cu|py /priɒkyəpaɪ/ (**preoccupies, preoccupying, preoccupied**) V-T If something **is preoccupying** you, you are thinking about it a lot. ❑ *Crime and the fear of crime preoccupy the community.*

pre|or|dained /priɔrdeɪnd/ ADJ If you say that something is **preordained**, you mean that you believe it is happening in the way that has been decided by a power such as God or fate. [FORMAL] ❑ *...the belief that our actions are the unfolding of a preordained destiny.*

pre-owned ADJ [usu ADJ n] Something that is **pre-owned** has been owned by someone else and is now for sale. ❑ *...an exciting opportunity to view hundreds of pre-owned vehicles in one location.*

prep /prɛp/ (**preps, prepping, prepped**) V-T If you **prep** something, you prepare it. [mainly AM, INFORMAL] ❑ *After prepping the boat, they sailed it down to Carloforte.*

pre|pack|aged /pripækɪdʒd/ ADJ **Prepackaged** foods have been prepared in advance and put in plastic or cardboard containers to be sold.

pre|packed /pripækt/ ADJ **Prepacked** goods are packed or wrapped before they are sent to the store where they are sold.

pre|paid /pripeɪd/ ADJ **Prepaid** items are paid for in advance, before the time when you would normally pay for them. ❑ *...prepaid funerals.*

prepa|ra|tion♦◇◇ /prɛpəreɪʃᵊn/ (**preparations**) **1** N-UNCOUNT **Preparation** is the process of getting something ready for use or for a particular purpose, or making arrangements for something. ❑ *Rub the surface of the wood in preparation for the* varnish. ❑ *Few things distracted the pastor from the preparation of his weekly sermons.* **2** N-PLURAL **Preparations** are all the arrangements that are made for a future event. ❑ *The United States is making preparations for a large-scale airlift of 1,200 American citizens.* **3** N-COUNT A **preparation** is a mixture that has been prepared for use as food, medicine, or a cosmetic. ❑ *...anti-aging creams and sensitive-skin preparations.*

SYNONYMS

preparation
NOUN **1**
groundwork: *Yesterday's meeting was to lay the groundwork for the task ahead.*
development: *What are your plans for the development of your company?*
readiness: *Security tightened in the capital in readiness for the President's arrival.*

---

pre|para|tory /prɪpærətɔri, prɛpərə-/ ADJ **Preparatory** actions are done before doing something else as a form of preparation or as an introduction. ❑ *At least a year's preparatory work will be necessary before building can start.*

pre|pare ✦✧✧ /prɪpɛər/ (**prepares, preparing, prepared**) **1** V-T If you **prepare** something, you make it ready for something that is going to happen. ❑ *Two technicians were preparing a recording of last week's program.* ❑ *On average each report requires 1,000 hours to prepare.* **2** V-T/V-I If you **prepare** for an event or action that will happen soon, you get yourself ready for it or make the necessary arrangements. ❑ *The party leadership is using management consultants to help prepare for the next election.* ❑ *He had to go back to his hotel and prepare to catch a train for New York.* **3** V-T When you **prepare** food, you get it ready to be eaten, for example, by cooking it. ❑ *She made her way to the kitchen, hoping to find someone preparing dinner.*

SYNONYMS

prepare
VERB
1
get ready: *Tomorrow, he would tell his pilot to get the aircraft ready.*
equip: *Owners of restaurants would have to equip them to admit people with disabilities.*
draw up: *They agreed to draw up a formal agreement.*
put together: *We got to work on putting the book together.*
2
train: *The U.S. was ready to train its troops to participate.*
groom: *George was already being groomed for the top job.*
prime: *Arnold primed her for her duties.*

---

pre|pared ✦✧✧ /prɪpɛərd/ **1** ADJ [v-link ADJ to-inf] If you are **prepared** to do something, you are willing to do it if necessary. ❑ *Are you prepared to take industrial action?* **2** ADJ [v-link ADJ for n] If you are **prepared for** something that you think is going to happen, you are ready for it. ❑ *Police are prepared for large numbers of demonstrators.* **3** ADJ [ADJ n] You can describe something as **prepared** when it has been done or made beforehand, so that it is ready when it is needed. ❑ *He ended his prepared statement by thanking the police.*

pre|par|ed|ness /prɪpɛərɪdnɪs/ N-UNCOUNT **Preparedness** is the state of being ready for something to happen, especially for war or a disaster. [FORMAL] ❑ *The situation in the capital forced them to maintain military preparedness.*

pre-pay (**pre-pays, pre-paying, pre-paid**) also **prepay** V-T/V-I If you **pre-pay** something or **pre-pay** for it, you pay for it before you receive it or use it. ❑ *Also, pre-paying funeral expenses can avoid the effects of inflation.* ❑ *...electricity customers who pre-pay for their energy.*

pre|pon|der|ance /prɪpɒndərəns/ N-SING [usu N of n] If there is a **preponderance of** one type of person or thing in a group, there is more of that type than of any other. ❑ *...a preponderance of bright, middle-class children in one group.* ❑ *...New York City, with its preponderance of places to eat.*

prepo|si|tion /prɛpəzɪʃən/ (**prepositions**) N-COUNT A **preposition** is a word such as 'by,' 'for,' 'into,' or 'with' that usually has a noun group as its object. ❑ *There is nothing in the rules of grammar to suggest that ending a sentence with a preposition is wrong.*

prepo|si|tion|al phrase /prɛpəzɪʃənəl freɪz/ (**prepositional phrases**) N-COUNT A **prepositional phrase** is a structure consisting of a preposition and its object. Examples are 'on the table' and 'by the sea.'

pre|pos|ter|ous /prɪpɒstərəs, -trəs/ ADJ If you describe something as **preposterous**, you mean that it is extremely unreasonable and foolish. [DISAPPROVAL] ❑ *The whole idea was preposterous.* • **pre|pos|ter|ous|ly** ADV ❑ *Some prices are preposterously high.*

prep|py /prɛpi/ (**preppies, preppier, preppiest**) **1** N-COUNT **Preppies** are young people who have often been to an expensive private school and who are conventional and conservative in their attitudes, behavior, and style of dress. [mainly AM] **2** ADJ If you describe someone or their clothes, attitudes, or behavior as **preppy**, you mean that they are like a preppy. [mainly AM] ❑ *I couldn't believe how straight-looking he was, how preppy.* ❑ *...a preppy collar and tie.*

pre|pran|di|al /priprændiəl/ ADJ [ADJ n] You use **preprandial** to refer to things you do or have before a meal. [FORMAL] ❑ *...preprandial drinks.*

prep school /prɛp skul/ (**prep schools**) **1** N-VAR In the United States, a **prep school** is a private school for students who intend to go to college after they leave. ❑ *...an exclusive prep school in Washington.* **2** N-VAR In Britain, a **prep school** is a private school where children are educated until the age of 11 or 13.

pre|pu|bes|cent /pripyubɛsənt/ ADJ [usu ADJ n] **Prepubescent** means relating to the time just before someone's body becomes physically mature. [FORMAL] ❑ *...prepubescent boys and girls.*

pre|quel /prikwəl/ (**prequels**) N-COUNT [oft N to n] A **prequel** is a movie, book, or television series that is made about an earlier stage of a story or a character's life when the later part of it has already been made into a successful movie, book, or television series. ❑ *..."Fire Walk With Me," David Lynch's prequel to the TV series "Twin Peaks."*

Pre-Raphaelite /pri ræfiəlaɪt/ (**Pre-Raphaelites**) **1** N-COUNT The **Pre-Raphaelites** were a group of British painters in the nineteenth century who painted mainly scenes from medieval history and old stories. **2** ADJ [ADJ n] **Pre-Raphaelite** art was created by the Pre-Raphaelites. **3** ADJ If you say that a woman looks **Pre-Raphaelite**, you mean that she looks like a character in a Pre-Raphaelite painting, for example, because she has long wavy hair.

pre|rec|ord|ed /prirɪkɔrdɪd/ ADJ Something that is **prerecorded** has been recorded in advance so that it can be broadcast or played later. ❑ *...a prerecorded radio speech.*

pre|requi|site /prirɛkwɪzɪt/ (**prerequisites**) N-COUNT If one thing is a **prerequisite** for another, it must happen or exist before the other thing is possible. ❑ *Good self-esteem is a prerequisite for a happy life.*

pre|roga|tive /prɪrɒgətɪv/ (**prerogatives**) N-COUNT If something is the **prerogative** of a particular person or group, it is a privilege or a power that only they have. [FORMAL] ❑ *It is your prerogative to stop seeing that particular therapist and find another one.*

pres|age /prɛsɪdʒ/ (**presages, presaging, presaged**) V-T If something **presages** a situation or event, it is considered to be a warning or sign of what is about to happen. [FORMAL] ❑ *...the dawn's loud chorus that seemed to presage a bright hot summer's day.*

Pres|by|ter|ian /prɛzbɪtɪəriən/ (**Presbyterians**) **1** ADJ **Presbyterian** means belonging or relating to a Protestant church that is governed by a body of official people all of equal rank. ❑ *...a Presbyterian minister.* **2** N-COUNT A **Presbyterian** is a member of the Presbyterian church.

pres|by|tery /prɛzbɪtəri/ (**presbyteries**) N-COUNT A **presbytery** is the house in which a Roman Catholic priest lives.

pre|school (**preschools**)

Pronounced /priskul/ for meaning 1, and /priskul/ for meaning 2.

1 ADJ [ADJ n] **Preschool** is used to describe things relating to the care and education of children before they reach the age when they have to go to school. [WRITTEN] ❑ *Looking after*

preschooler *preschool children is very tiring.* ☐ *The report emphasized the value of a preschool education.* ◼ N-VAR A **preschool** is a school for children between the ages of 2 and 5 or 6. [AM] ☐ *The state should move toward the goal of preschool for all 3- and 4-year-olds.*

pre|school|er /prisku:lər/ (**preschoolers**) also **pre-schooler** N-COUNT [usu pl] Children who are no longer babies but are not yet old enough to go to school are sometimes referred to as **preschoolers**. [WRITTEN]

pres|ci|ent /prɛʃənt, prɛʃiənt/ ADJ If you say that someone or something was **prescient**, you mean that they were able to know or predict what was going to happen in the future. [FORMAL] ☐ *...an eerily prescient comedy about a populist multimillionaire political candidate.* • **pres|ci|ence** N-UNCOUNT ☐ *Over the years he's demonstrated a certain prescience in foreign affairs.*

pre|scribe /priskraib/ (**prescribes, prescribing, prescribed**) ◼ V-T If a doctor **prescribes** medicine or treatment for you, he or she tells you what medicine or treatment to have. ☐ *The physician examines the patient then diagnoses the disease and prescribes medication.* ☐ *She took twice the prescribed dose of sleeping tablets.* ◼ V-T If a person or set of laws or rules **prescribes** an action or duty, they state that it must be carried out. [FORMAL] ☐ *...article II of the constitution, which prescribes the method of electing a president.* ◼ → See feature box at **medicine**

pre|scrip|tion /priskrip∫ən/ (**prescriptions**) ◼ N-COUNT A **prescription** is the piece of paper on which your doctor writes an order for medicine and which you give to a pharmacist to get the medicine. ☐ *The new drug will not require a physician's prescription.* ◼ N-COUNT A **prescription** is a medicine that a doctor has told you to take. ☐ *I'm not sleeping even with the prescription Ackerman gave me.* • PHRASE If a medicine is available **by** or **on prescription**, you can only get it from a pharmacist if a doctor gives you a prescription for it. ◼ N-COUNT A **prescription** is a proposal or a plan that gives ideas about how to solve a problem or improve a situation. ☐ *...the economic prescriptions of Ireland's two main political parties.*

pre|scrip|tion drug (**prescription drugs**) N-COUNT A **prescription drug** is a medicine that you can buy only if you have a doctor's prescription for it. ☐ *...the high cost of prescription drugs.*

pre|scrip|tive /priskriptiv/ ADJ A **prescriptive** approach to something involves telling people what they should do, rather than simply giving suggestions or describing what is done. [FORMAL] ☐ *...prescriptive attitudes to language on the part of teachers.* ☐ *The psychologists insist, however, that they are not being prescriptive.*

pre|sea|son /prisi:zən/ also **pre-season** ADJ [ADJ n] **Preseason** activities take place before the start of a sports season. ☐ *...a preseason game against Phoenix.*

pres|ence ◆◇ /prɛzəns/ (**presences**) ◼ N-SING Someone's **presence** in a place is the fact that they are there. ☐ *They argued that his presence in the town could only stir up trouble.* ◼ N-UNCOUNT If you say that someone has **presence**, you mean that they impress people by their appearance and manner. [APPROVAL] ☐ *They do not seem to have the vast, authoritative presence of those great men.* ◼ N-COUNT A **presence** is a person or creature that you cannot see, but that you are aware of. [LITERARY] ☐ *She started to be affected by the ghostly presence she could feel in the house.* ◼ N-SING If a country has a military **presence** in another country, it has some of its armed forces there. ☐ *The US military presence in the region has steadily increased in recent months.* ◼ N-UNCOUNT If you refer to the **presence** of a substance in another thing, you mean that it is in that thing. ☐ *The somewhat acid flavor is caused by the presence of lactic acid.* ◼ PHRASE If you are **in** someone's **presence**, you are in the same place as that person, and are close enough to them to be seen or heard. ☐ *The talks took place in the presence of a diplomatic observer.*

PRESENT
① EXISTING OR HAPPENING NOW
② BEING SOMEWHERE
③ GIFT
④ VERB USES
---

① **pres|ent** ◆◆◇ /prɛzənt/ ◼ ADJ [ADJ n] You use **present** to describe things and people that exist now, rather than those that existed in the past or those that may exist in the future. ☐ *He has brought much of the present crisis on himself.* ☐ *...the government's present economic difficulties.* ◼ N-SING The **present** is the period of time that we are in now and the things that are happening now. ☐ *...his struggle to reconcile the past with the present.* ☐ *...continuing right up to the present.* ◼ PHRASE A situation that exists **at present** exists now, although it may change. ☐ *There is no way at present of predicting which individuals will develop the disease.* ◼ PHRASE The **present day** is the period of history that we are in now. ☐ *...Western European art from the period of Giotto to the present day.* ◼ PHRASE Something that exists or will be done **for the present** exists now or will continue for a while, although the situation may change later. ☐ *The cabinet had expressed the view that sanctions should remain in place for the present.*

② **pres|ent** ◆◆◇ /prɛzənt/ ◼ ADJ [v-link ADJ] If someone is **present at** an event, they are there. ☐ *The president was not present at the meeting.* ☐ *Nearly 85 percent of men are present at the birth of their children.* ◼ ADJ [v-link ADJ] If something, especially a substance or disease, is **present in** something else, it exists within that thing. ☐ *This special form of vitamin D is naturally present in breast milk.*

③ **pres|ent** /prɛzənt/ (**presents**) N-COUNT A **present** is something that you give to someone, for example, at Christmas or when you visit them. ☐ *The carpet was a wedding present from Jack's parents.* ☐ *She bought a birthday present for her mother.*

④ **pre|sent** ◆◆◇ /prizɛnt/ (**presents, presenting, presented**) ◼ V-T If you **present** someone **with** something such as a prize or document, or if you **present** it to them, you formally give it to them. ☐ *The mayor presented him with a gold medal at an official city reception.* ☐ *Betty will present the prizes to the winners.* • **pres|en|ta|tion** /prizɛntei∫ən/ N-UNCOUNT ☐ *Then came the presentation of the awards by the First Lady.* ◼ V-T If something **presents** a difficulty, challenge, or opportunity, it causes it or provides it. ☐ *This presents a problem for many financial consumers.* ☐ *The future is going to be one that presents many challenges.* ◼ V-T If an opportunity or problem **presents** itself, it occurs, often when you do not expect it. ☐ *Their colleagues insulted them whenever the opportunity presented itself.* ◼ V-T When you **present** information, you give it to people in a formal way. ☐ *We spend the time collating and presenting the information in a variety of chart forms.* ☐ *We presented three options to the unions for discussion.* • **pres|en|ta|tion** (**presentations**) N-VAR ☐ *...in his first presentation of the theory to the Berlin Academy.* ☐ *...a fair presentation of the facts to a jury.* ◼ V-T If you **present** someone or something in a particular way, you describe them in that way. ☐ *The government has presented these changes as major reforms.* ◼ V-T The way you **present yourself** is the way you speak and act when meeting new people. ☐ *...all those tricks which would help him to present himself in a more confident way in public.* ◼ V-T If someone or something **presents** a particular appearance or image, that is how they appear or try to appear. ☐ *The small group of onlookers presented a pathetic sight.* ☐ *Cohen was making an effort to present a kinder, gentler image.* ◼ V-T If you **present yourself** somewhere, you officially arrive there, for example, for an appointment. ☐ *Get word to him right away that he's to present himself at City Hall by tomorrow afternoon.* ◼ V-T If someone **presents** a program on television or radio, they introduce each item in it. [mainly BRIT]

in AM, usually use **host**

◼ V-T When someone **presents** something such as a production of a play or an exhibition, they organize it. ☐ *They threatened to close any theater presenting a play with gay characters.* ◼ V-T If you **present** someone **to** someone else, often an important person, you formally introduce them. ☐ *Fox stepped forward, welcomed him in Malay, and presented him to Jack.*

pre|sent|able /prizɛntəbəl/ ADJ If you say that someone looks **presentable**, you mean that they look fairly neat or attractive. ☐ *She managed to make herself presentable in time for work.* ☐ *...wearing his most presentable suit.*

pres|en|ta|tion /prizɛntei∫ən/ (**presentations**) ◼ N-UNCOUNT **Presentation** is the appearance of something, that someone has worked to create. ☐ *We serve traditional French food cooked in a lighter way, keeping the presentation simple.* **2** N-COUNT A **presentation** is a formal event at which someone is given a prize or award. ☐ *...after receiving his award at a presentation in Kansas City yesterday.* **3** N-COUNT When someone gives a **presentation**, they give a formal talk, often in order to sell something or get support for a proposal. ☐ *A co-worker gave a presentation on a project we worked on a long time ago.* **4** → see also **present** ④

pres|ent-day ADJ [ADJ n] **Present-day** things, situations, and people exist at the time in history we are now in. ☐ *Even by present-day standards these were large aircraft.* ☐ *...a huge area of northern India, stretching from present-day Afghanistan to Bengal.*

pre|sent|er /prɪzɛntər/ (**presenters**) N-COUNT A radio or television **presenter** is a person who introduces the items in a particular program. [mainly BRIT]

in AM, usually use **host**

pre|sen|ti|ment /prɪzɛntɪmənt/ (**presentiments**) N-COUNT [usu N that, N of n] A **presentiment** is a feeling that a particular event, for example, someone's death, will soon take place. [FORMAL] ☐ *I had a presentiment that he represented a danger to me.* ☐ *He had a presentiment of disaster.*

pres|ent|ly /prɛzəntli/ **1** ADV If you say that something is **presently** happening, you mean that it is happening now. ☐ *She is presently developing a number of projects.* ☐ *The island is presently uninhabited.* **2** ADV [ADV with cl] You use **presently** to indicate that something happened a short time after the time or event that you have just mentioned. [WRITTEN] ☐ *He was shown to a small office. Presently, a young woman in a white coat came in.*

pres|ent par|ti|ci|ple (**present participles**) N-COUNT In grammar, the **present participle** of a verb is the form that ends in '-ing.' Present participles are used to form continuous tenses, as in 'She was wearing a neat blue suit.' They are often nouns, as in 'I hate cooking' and 'Cooking can be fun.' Many of them can be used like an adjective in front of a noun, as in 'their smiling faces.'

pres|ent per|fect ADJ [ADJ n] In grammar, the **present perfect** tenses of a verb are the ones used to talk about things that happened before the time you are speaking or writing but are relevant to the present situation, or things that began in the past and are still happening. The simple present perfect tense uses 'have' or 'has' and the past participle of the verb, as in 'They have decided what to do.'

pres|er|va|tion|ist /prɛzərveɪʃənɪst/ (**preservationists**) N-COUNT A **preservationist** is someone who takes action to preserve something such as old buildings or an area of countryside.

pre|serva|tive /prɪzɜrvətɪv/ (**preservatives**) N-MASS A **preservative** is a chemical that prevents things from decaying. Some preservatives are added to food, and others are used to treat wood or metal. ☐ *Nitrates are used as preservatives in food processing.*

pre|serve ♦◇◇ /prɪzɜrv/ (**preserves, preserving, preserved**) **1** V-T If you **preserve** a situation or condition, you make sure that it remains as it is, and does not change or end. ☐ *We will do everything to preserve peace.* • **pres|er|va|tion** /prɛzərveɪʃən/ N-UNCOUNT ☐ *...the preservation of the status quo.* **2** V-T If you **preserve** something, you take action to save it or protect it from damage or decay. ☐ *We need to preserve the forest.* • **pres|er|va|tion** N-UNCOUNT ☐ *...the preservation of buildings of architectural or historic interest.* **3** V-T If you **preserve** food, you treat it in order to prevent it from decaying so that you can store it for a long time. ☐ *I like to make puree, using only enough sugar to preserve the plums.* **4** N-PLURAL **Preserves** are foods made by cooking fruit with a large amount of sugar so that they can be stored for a long time. ☐ *She decided to make peach preserves for Christmas gifts.* **5** N-COUNT If you say that a job or activity is the **preserve of** a particular person or group of people, you mean that they are the only ones who take part in it. ☐ *The making and conduct of foreign policy is largely the preserve of the president.*

SYNONYMS

preserve
VERB
1
maintain: *...the emergency powers to try to maintain law and order.*
retain: *The interior of the shop still retains a nineteenth-century atmosphere.*
sustain: *He has sustained his fierce social conscience from young adulthood through old age.*
keep up: *There will be a major incentive among TV channels to keep standards up.*
2
maintain: *The house costs a fortune to maintain.*
protect: *So, what can women do to protect themselves from heart disease?*
safeguard: *They will press for international action to safeguard the ozone layer.*
conserve: *...a big increase in U.S. aid to help developing countries conserve their forests.*

---

pre|set /priːsɛt/ (**presets, presetting**)

The form **preset** is used in the present tense and is the past tense and past participle.

V-T [usu passive] If a piece of equipment **is preset**, its controls have been set in advance of the time you want it to work. ☐ *...a computerized timer that can be preset.*

pre|side /prɪzaɪd/ (**presides, presiding, presided**) V-I If you **preside over** a meeting or an event, you are in charge. ☐ *The PM returned to Downing Street to preside over a meeting of his inner cabinet.*

presi|den|cy ♦◇◇ /prɛzɪdənsi/ (**presidencies**) N-COUNT The **presidency** of a country or organization is the position of being the president or the period of time during which someone is president. ☐ *He is a candidate for the presidency of the organization.*

presi|dent ♦♦♦ /prɛzɪdənt/ (**presidents**) **1** N-TITLE; N-COUNT [oft the N; N-VOC] The **president** of a country that has no king or queen is the person who is the head of state of that country. ☐ *...President Mubarak.* **2** N-COUNT The **president** of an organization is the person who has the highest position in it. ☐ *...Alexandre de Merode, the president of the medical commission.*

SYNONYMS

president
NOUN **2**
chairman: *I had done business with the company's chairman.*
managing director: *She is managing director of a construction company.*
CEO: *They have replaced their CEO.*

---

president-elect N-SING The **president-elect** is the person who has been elected as the president of an organization or country, but who has not yet taken office. ☐ *...one of the president-elect's best proposals during the campaign.*

presi|den|tial ♦♦◇ /prɛzɪdɛnʃəl/ ADJ [ADJ n] **Presidential** activities or things relate or belong to a president. ☐ *...campaigning for Peru's presidential election.*

Presi|dents' Day N-UNCOUNT In the United States, **Presidents' Day** is a public holiday held in commemoration of the birthdays of George Washington and Abraham Lincoln. It is the third Monday in February. ☐ *Today is Presidents' Day, a federal holiday.*

press ♦♦♦ /prɛs/ (**presses, pressing, pressed**) **1** V-T If you **press** something somewhere, you push it firmly against something else. ☐ *He pressed his back against the door.* **2** V-T If you **press** a button or switch, you push it with your finger in order to make a machine or device work. ☐ *Drago pressed a button and the door closed.* • N-COUNT **Press** is also a noun. ☐ *...a TV which rises from a table at the press of a button.* **3** V-T/V-I If you **press** something or **press down on** it, you push hard against it with your foot or hand. ☐ *The engine stalled. He pressed the accelerator hard.* **4** V-I If you **press for** something, you try hard to persuade someone to give it to you or to agree to it. ☐ *Police might now press for changes in the law.* **5** V-T If you **press** someone, you try hard to persuade them to do something. ☐ *Trade unions* are pressing him to stand firm. ❏ Mr. Kurtz seems certain to be pressed for further details. **6** V-T If someone **presses** their claim, demand, or point, they state it in a very forceful way. ❏ The protest campaign has used mass strikes and demonstrations to press its demands. **7** V-T If you **press** something **on** someone, you give it to them and insist that they take it. ❏ All I had was money, which I pressed on her reluctant mother. **8** V-T If you **press** clothes, you iron them in order to get rid of the creases. ❏ Vera pressed his shirt. ❏ There's a couple of dresses to be pressed. **9** N-SING-COLL [the N] Newspapers are referred to as **the press**. ❏ ...interviews in the local and foreign press. ❏ ...freedom of the press. **10** N-SING-COLL Journalists and reporters are referred to as **the press**. ❏ Christie looked relaxed and calm as she faced the press afterwards. **11** N-COUNT A **press** or a **printing press** is a machine used for printing things such as books and newspapers. **12** → see also **pressed**, **pressing** **13** PHRASE If someone or something **gets bad press**, they are criticized, especially in the newspapers, on television, or on radio. If they **get good press**, they are praised. ❏ ...the bad press that successful women can get in this country. **14** PHRASE If you **press charges** against someone, you make an official accusation against them that has to be decided in a court of law. ❏ I could have pressed charges against him. **15** PHRASE When a newspaper or magazine **goes to press**, it starts being printed. ❏ We check prices at the time of going to press.

SYNONYMS

press
VERB **1**
push: He put both hands flat on the door and pushed as hard as he could.
squeeze: He squeezed her arm reassuringly.

VOCABULARY IN CONTEXT

Press and media

The **circulation** of newspapers has been in decline for some time. In the United States recently, overall **readership** fell by seven percent from one year to the next, and **distribution** of **weekend editions** fell by four percent. In the U.K., sales of **national daily** newspapers fell by half a million in one year alone. It's not that people have lost interest in the news, it's that **print media** is increasingly giving way to online platforms. Looking around passenger cars of most trains not long ago, commuters would be engrossed in **broadsheets** or **tabloids**. Today, the same passengers can be seen scrolling through news **features** on their smartphones or tablets. In fact, social media has now become the main **news source** for many, and it's not unusual for **reports** by **the press** to be replaced by **citizen journalism**. Whether you trust this type of reporting or question its reliability, it has put serious pressure on traditional **media outlets**.

press agen|cy (press agencies) N-COUNT A **press agency** is an organization, sometimes government owned, that gathers news and supplies it to journalists from all over the world.

press agent (press agents) N-COUNT [oft with poss] A **press agent** is a person who is employed by a famous person to give information about that person to the press.

press box (press boxes) N-COUNT [usu the N in sing] The **press box** at a sports stadium or arena is a room or area reserved for reporters to watch sports events.

press con|fer|ence (press conferences) N-COUNT A **press conference** is a meeting held by a famous or important person in which they answer reporters' questions. ❏ She gave her reaction to his release at a press conference.

press corps (press corps) N-COUNT-COLL [usu the N] The **press corps** is a group of journalists and reporters who are all working in a particular place, for different news organizations. ❏ David McNeil is traveling with the White House press corps.

pressed /prɛst/ **1** ADJ [v-link ADJ] If you say that you are **pressed for** time or **pressed for** money, you mean that you do not have enough time or money at the moment. ❏ Are you pressed for time? If not, I suggest we have lunch. **2** → see also **hard-pressed**

press|er /prɛsər/ (pressers) N-COUNT A **presser** is a meeting held by someone such as a politician or sportsperson in which they answer journalists' questions. [INFORMAL] ❏ 'The heavyweight business is back in business,' he said at the post-fight presser. ❏ Andrew explained at the presser that we of the press were too stupid to understand the complexities of his job.

press gal|lery (press galleries) N-COUNT [usu the N in sing] The **press gallery** is the area in a legislature, parliament, or council reserved for journalists who report on its activities.

press-gang (press-gangs, press-ganging, press-ganged) **1** V-T [usu passive] If you **are press-ganged into** doing something, you are made or persuaded to do it, even though you do not really want to. ❏ I was press-ganged into working in that business. ❏ She was a volunteer, she hadn't had to be press-ganged. **2** V-T [usu passive] If people **are press-ganged**, they are captured and forced to join the army or navy. [OLD-FASHIONED] ❏ They left their villages to evade being press-ganged into the army. ❏ The government denies that the women were press-ganged. **3** N-COUNT In former times, a **press-gang** was a group of men who used to capture boys and men and force them to join the navy.

press|ing /prɛsɪŋ/ **1** ADJ A **pressing** problem, need, or issue has to be dealt with immediately. ❏ It is one of the most pressing problems facing this country. **2** → see also **press**

press of|fic|er (press officers) N-COUNT A **press officer** is a person who is employed by an organization to give information about that organization to the press. ❏ ...the press officer of the Bavarian Government.

press re|lease (press releases) N-COUNT A **press release** is a written statement about a matter of public interest that is given to the press by an organization concerned with the matter. ❏ The next day, Fox issued a press release saying the show had sold out in 24 hours.

press|room /prɛsrum/ (pressrooms) N-COUNT A **pressroom** is a room for journalists and reporters at a special event.

press sec|re|tary (press secretaries) N-COUNT A government's or political leader's **press secretary** is someone who is employed by them to give information to the press. ❏ The press secretary told reporters that a majority of one would be a sufficient mandate.

press stud (press studs) N-COUNT A **press stud** is the same as a snap fastener. [BRIT]

press-up (press-ups) N-COUNT **Press-ups** are the same as push-ups. [BRIT]

pres|sure ♦♦♦ /prɛʃər/ (pressures, pressuring, pressured) **1** N-UNCOUNT **Pressure** is force that you produce when you press hard on something. ❏ She kicked at the door with her foot, and the pressure was enough to open it. ❏ The pressure of his fingers had relaxed. **2** N-UNCOUNT [also N in pl] The **pressure** in a place or container is the force produced by the quantity of gas or liquid in that place or container. ❏ The window in the cockpit had blown in and the pressure dropped dramatically. **3** N-UNCOUNT [also N in pl] If there is **pressure** on a person, someone is trying to persuade or force them to do something. ❏ He may have put pressure on her to agree. ❏ A lot of dot-coms were under pressure from their investors. **4** N-UNCOUNT [also N in pl] If you are experiencing **pressure**, you feel that you must do a lot of tasks or make a lot of decisions in very little time, or that people expect a lot from you. ◻ *Can you work under pressure?* ◻ *Even if I had the talent to play tennis I couldn't stand the pressure.* ◊ V-T If you **pressure** someone to do something, you try forcefully to persuade them to do it. ◻ *He will never pressure you to get married.* ◻ *The Senate should not be pressured into making hasty decisions.* • **pres|sured** ADJ ◻ *You're likely to feel anxious and pressured.* ◊ → see also **blood pressure** ◊ → See feature box at **success**

pres|sure cook|er (pressure cookers) N-COUNT A **pressure cooker** is a large metal container with a lid that fits tightly, in which you can cook food quickly using steam at high pressure.

pres|sure group (pressure groups) N-COUNT A **pressure group** is an organized group of people who are trying to persuade a government or other authority to do something, for example, to change a law. ◻ *...the environmental pressure group Greenpeace.*

pres|sur|ize /prɛʃəraɪz/ (pressurizes, pressurizing, pressurized)

in BRIT, also use **pressurise**

◊ VERB If you **are pressurized into** doing something, you are forcefully persuaded to do it. ◻ *Do not be pressurized into making your decision immediately.* ◻ *He thought she was trying to pressurize him.* ◊ → see also **pressurized**

pres|sur|ized /prɛʃəraɪzd/

in BRIT, also use **pressurised**

ADJ In a **pressurized** container or area, the pressure inside is different from the pressure outside. ◻ *Certain types of foods are also dispensed in pressurized canisters.*

pres|tige /prɛstiːʒ, -stiːdʒ/ ◊ N-UNCOUNT If a person, a country, or an organization has **prestige**, they are admired and respected because of the position they hold or the things they have achieved. ◻ *...efforts to build up the prestige of the United Nations.* ◻ *It was his responsibility for foreign affairs that gained him international prestige.* ◊ ADJ [ADJ n] **Prestige** is used to describe products, places, or activities that people admire because they are associated with being rich or having a high social position. ◻ *...such prestige cars as Cadillac, Mercedes, Porsche, and Jaguar.*

pres|tig|ious /prɛstɪdʒəs, -stiːdʒəs/ ADJ A **prestigious** institution, job, or activity is respected and admired by people. ◻ *It's one of the best equipped and most prestigious schools in the country.*

pre|sum|ably ✦✧✧ /prɪzuːməbli/ ADV If you say that something is **presumably** the case, you mean that you think it is very likely to be the case, although you are not certain. [VAGUENESS] ◻ *The spear is presumably the murder weapon.*

pre|sume /prɪzuːm/ (presumes, presuming, presumed) ◊ V-T If you **presume** that something is the case, you think that it is the case, although you are not certain. ◻ *I presume you're here on business.* ◻ *"Had he been home all week?"—"I presume so."* ◊ V-T If you say that someone **presumes** to do something, you mean that they do it even though they have no right to do it. [FORMAL] ◻ *They're resentful that outsiders presume to meddle in their affairs.* ◊ V-T If an idea, theory, or plan **presumes** certain facts, it regards them as true so that they can be used as a basis for further ideas and theories. [FORMAL] ◻ *The legal definition of "know" often presumes mental control.*

pre|sump|tion /prɪzʌmpʃən/ (presumptions) N-COUNT A **presumption** is something that is accepted as true but is not certain to be true. ◻ *...the presumption that a defendant is innocent until proved guilty.*

pre|sump|tu|ous /prɪzʌmptʃuəs/ ADJ If you describe someone or their behavior as **presumptuous**, you disapprove of them because they are doing something that they have no right or authority to do. [DISAPPROVAL] ◻ *It would be presumptuous to judge what the outcome will be.*

pre|sup|pose /priːsəpoʊz/ (presupposes, presupposing, presupposed) V-T If one thing **presupposes** another, the first thing cannot be true or exist unless the second thing is true or exists. ◻ *All your arguments presuppose that he's a rational, intelligent man.* ◻ *The end of an era presupposes the start of another.*

pre|sup|po|si|tion /priːsʌpəzɪʃən/ (presuppositions) N-COUNT A **presupposition** is something that you assume to be true, especially something that you must assume is true in order to continue with what you are saying or thinking. [FORMAL] ◻ *...the presupposition that human life must be sustained for as long as possible.*

pre|tax /priːtæks/ also **pre-tax** ADJ [ADJ n] **Pretax** profits or losses are the total profits or losses made by a company before tax has been taken away. [BUSINESS] ◻ *They announced a fall in pretax profits.* • ADV [ADV after v] **Pretax** is also an adverb. ◻ *Last year it made $2.5 million pretax.*

pre|teen /priːtiːn/ (preteens) N-COUNT [oft N n] A **preteen** is a child aged between nine and thirteen. ◻ *Some preteens are able to handle a good deal of responsibility.* ◻ *...preteen children.*

pre|tence /priːtɛns, prɪtɛns/ [BRIT] → see **pretense**

pre|tend /prɪtɛnd/ (pretends, pretending, pretended) ◊ V-T If you **pretend** that something is the case, you act in a way that is intended to make people believe that it is the case, although in fact it is not. ◻ *I pretend that things are really okay when they're not.* ◻ *Sometimes the boy pretended to be asleep.* ◊ V-T If children or adults **pretend** that they are doing something, they imagine that they are doing it, for example, as part of a game. ◻ *She can sunbathe and pretend she's in Cancun.* ◊ V-T [with neg] If you do not **pretend** that something is the case, you do not claim that it is the case. ◻ *We do not pretend that the past six years have been without problems for us.*

pre|tend|er /prɪtɛndər/ (pretenders) N-COUNT [usu N to n, adj N] A **pretender** to a position is someone who claims the right to that position, and whose claim is disputed by others. ◻ *...the Comte de Paris, pretender to the French throne.*

pre|tense /priːtɛns, prɪtɛns/ (pretenses)

in BRIT, use **pretence**

◊ N-VAR A **pretense** is an action or way of behaving that is intended to make people believe something that is not true. ◻ *He goes to the library and makes a pretense of reading some Thoreau.* ◻ *On the eighth day of questioning, she dropped the pretense that she was Japanese.* ◊ PHRASE If you do something under **false pretenses**, you do it when people do not know the truth about you and your intentions. ◻ *This interview was conducted under false pretenses.*

pre|ten|sion /prɪtɛnʃən/ (pretensions) ◊ N-VAR If you say that someone has **pretensions**, you disapprove of them because they claim or pretend that they are more important than they really are. [DISAPPROVAL] ◻ *Her wide-eyed innocence soon exposes the pretensions of the art world.* ◊ N-PLURAL If someone has **pretensions to** something, they claim to be or do that thing. ◻ *The city has unrealistic pretensions to world-class status.*

pre|ten|tious /prɪtɛnʃəs/ ADJ If you say that someone or something is **pretentious**, you mean that they try to seem important or significant, but you do not think that they are. [DISAPPROVAL] ◻ *His response was full of pretentious nonsense.*

pre|ter|natu|ral /priːtərnætʃrəl/ ADJ [ADJ n] **Preternatural** abilities, qualities, or events are very unusual in a way that might make you think that unknown forces are involved. [FORMAL] ◻ *Their parents had an almost preternatural ability to understand what was going on in their children's minds.* • **pre|ter|natu|ral|ly** ADV [ADV adj] ◻ *It was suddenly preternaturally quiet.*

pre|text /priːtɛkst/ (pretexts) N-COUNT A **pretext** is a reason that you pretend has caused you to do something. ◻ *They wanted a pretext for subduing the region by force.*

pret|ti|fy /prɪtɪfaɪ/ (prettifies, prettifying, prettified) V-T To **prettify** something, especially something that is ugly, means to try to make it appear more attractive. [DISAPPROVAL] ◻ *...just a clever effort to prettify animal slaughter.* ◻ *It presented an intolerably prettified view of the countryside.*

pret|ty ✦✦✧ /prɪti/ (prettier, prettiest) ◊ ADJ If you describe someone as **pretty**, you mean that they are attractive. ◻ *She's a very charming and very pretty girl.* • **pret|ti|ly** /prɪtɪli/ ADV ◻ *She smiled again, prettily.* ◊ ADJ A place or a thing that is **pretty** is attractive and pleasant, in a charming but not particularly unusual way. ◻ *...a very pretty little town.* • **pret|ti|ly** ADV ◻ *The living-room was prettily decorated.* ◊ ADV [ADV adj/adv]

You can use **pretty** before an adjective or adverb to slightly lessen its force. [INFORMAL] ❏ *I had a pretty good idea what she was going to do.*

▬▬ SYNONYMS ▬▬

pretty
ADJ **1**
attractive: *He's a very attractive man.*
beautiful: *She was a very beautiful woman.*
lovely: *You all look really lovely.*

pret|zel /prɛtsəl/ (**pretzels**) N-COUNT A **pretzel** is a small, crisp, shiny cracker with salt on the outside. Pretzels are usually shaped like knots or sticks.

pre|vail /prɪveɪl/ (**prevails, prevailing, prevailed**) **1** V-I If a proposal, principle, or opinion **prevails**, it gains influence or is accepted, often after a struggle or argument. ❏ *We hoped that common sense would prevail.* ❏ *Rick still believes that justice will prevail.* **2** V-I If a situation, attitude, or custom **prevails** in a particular place at a particular time, it is normal or most common in that place at that time. ❏ *A similar situation prevails in Canada.* ❏ *...the confusion which had prevailed at the time of the revolution.* **3** V-I If one side in a battle, contest, or dispute **prevails**, it wins. ❏ *He appears to have the votes he needs to prevail.*

pre|vail|ing /prɪveɪlɪŋ/ ADJ [ADJ n] The **prevailing** wind in an area is the type of wind that blows over that area most of the time. ❏ *The direction of the prevailing winds should be taken into account.*

preva|lent /prɛvələnt/ ADJ A condition, practice, or belief that is **prevalent** is common. ❏ *This condition is more prevalent in women than in men.* ❏ *Smoking is becoming increasingly prevalent among younger people.* ● **preva|lence** N-UNCOUNT ❏ *the prevalence of cocaine abuse in the 1980s.*

pre|vari|cate /prɪværɪkeɪt/ (**prevaricates, prevaricating, prevaricated**) V-I If you **prevaricate**, you avoid giving a direct answer or making a firm decision. ❏ *She saw no reason to prevaricate.* ● **pre|vari|ca|tion** /prɪværɪkeɪʃən/ (**prevarications**) N-UNCOUNT [also N in pl] ❏ *After months of prevarication, the political decision had at last been made.*

pre|vent /prɪvɛnt/ (**prevents, preventing, prevented**) **1** V-T To **prevent** something means to ensure that it does not happen. ❏ *These methods prevent pregnancy.* ❏ *Further treatment will prevent cancer from developing.* ● **pre|ven|tion** N-UNCOUNT ❏ *...the prevention of heart disease.* **2** V-T To **prevent** someone **from** doing something means to make it impossible for them to do it. ❏ *He said this would prevent companies from creating new jobs.* ❏ *Its nationals may be prevented from leaving the country.*

pre|vent|able /prɪvɛntəbəl/ ADJ **Preventable** diseases, illnesses, or deaths could be stopped from occurring. ❏ *Forty thousand children a day die from preventable diseases.*

pre|ven|ta|tive /prɪvɛntətɪv/ ADJ **Preventative** means the same as **preventive**.

pre|ven|tive /prɪvɛntɪv/ ADJ **Preventive** actions are intended to help prevent things such as disease or crime. ❏ *Too much is spent on curative medicine and too little on preventive medicine.*

pre|view /priːvjuː/ (**previews**) N-COUNT A **preview** is an opportunity to see something such as a movie, exhibition, or invention before it is open or available to the public. ❏ *He had gone to see the preview of a play.*

pre|vi|ous /priːviəs/ **1** ADJ [ADJ n] A **previous** event or thing is one that happened or existed before the one that you are talking about. ❏ *She has a teenage daughter from a previous marriage.* **2** ADJ [det ADJ] You refer to the period of time or the thing immediately before the one that you are talking about as the **previous** one. ❏ *It was a surprisingly dry day after the rain of the previous week.*

pre|vi|ous|ly /priːviəsli/ **1** ADV **Previously** means at some time before the period that you are talking about. ❏ *Guyana's railways were previously owned by private companies.* ❏ *The contract was awarded to a previously unknown company.* **2** ADV [n ADV] You can use **previously** to say how much earlier one event was than another event. ❏ *He had first entered the House 12 years previously.*

▬▬ SYNONYMS ▬▬

previously
ADV **1**
before: *The war had ended only a month or so before.*
once: *The culture minister once ran a theater.*
formerly: *He had formerly been in the Navy.*

pre|war /priːwɔːr/ also **pre-war** ADJ **Prewar** is used to describe things that happened, existed, or were made in the period immediately before a war, especially World War II, 1939-45. ❏ *...Poland's prewar leader.*

prey /preɪ/ (**preys, preying, preyed**) **1** N-UNCOUNT-COLL A creature's **prey** are the creatures that it hunts and eats in order to live. ❏ *Electric rays stun their prey with huge electrical discharges.* **2** V-I A creature that **preys on** other creatures lives by catching and eating them. ❏ *The effect was to disrupt the food chain, starving many animals and those that preyed on them.* **3** N-UNCOUNT You can refer to the people who someone tries to harm or trick as their **prey**. ❏ *Police officers lie in wait for the gangs who stalk their prey at night.* **4** V-I If someone **preys on** other people, especially people who are unable to protect themselves, they take advantage of them or harm them in some way. [DISAPPROVAL] ❏ *Pam had never learned that there were men who preyed on young runaways.* **5** V-I If something **preys on** your mind, you cannot stop thinking and worrying about it. ❏ *It was a misunderstanding and it preyed on his conscience.*

price ✦✧✧ /praɪs/ (**prices, pricing, priced**) **1** N-COUNT The **price** of something is the amount of money that you have to pay in order to buy it. ❏ *...a sharp increase in the price of gas.* ❏ *They expected house prices to rise.* **2** N-SING The **price** that you pay for something that you want is an unpleasant thing that you have to do or suffer in order to get it. ❏ *Slovenia will have to pay a high price for independence.* ❏ *There may be a price to pay for such relentless activity, perhaps ill health or even divorce.* **3** V-T If something **is priced at** a particular amount, the price is set at that amount. ❏ *The bond is currently priced at $900.* ❏ *Analysts predict that the company will price the new line at less than half the cost of comparable mainframes.* ● **pric|ing** N-UNCOUNT ❏ *It's hard to maintain competitive pricing.* **4** → see also **retail price index**, **selling price 5** PHRASE If you want something **at any price**, you are determined to get it, even if unpleasant things happen as a result. ❏ *If they wanted a deal at any price, they would have to face the consequences.* **6** PHRASE If you can buy something that you want **at a price**, it is for sale, but it is extremely expensive. ❏ *Most goods are available, but at a price.* **7** PHRASE If you get something that you want **at a price**, you get it but something unpleasant happens as a result. ❏ *Fame comes at a price.* **8 to price yourself out of the market** → see **market**

price|less /praɪsləs/ **1** ADJ If you say that something is **priceless**, you are emphasizing that it is worth a very large amount of money, or that it is very important to you although it has little financial value. [EMPHASIS] ❏ *They are priceless, unique and irreplaceable.* ❏ *Did Mom throw away your priceless Dungeons and Dragons magazine?* **2** ADJ If you say that something is **priceless**, you approve of it because it is extremely useful. [APPROVAL] ❏ *They are a priceless record of a brief period in Colorado history.*

price point (**price points**) N-COUNT The **price point** of a product is the price that it sells for. [BUSINESS] ❏ *No price point exists for the machine yet.* ❏ *The big companies dominate the lower price points.*

price tag (**price tags**) **1** N-COUNT If something has a **price tag** of a particular amount, that is the amount that you must pay in order to buy it. [WRITTEN] ❏ *The monorail can be completed at the price tag of $1.7 billion.* **2** N-COUNT In a store, the **price tag** on an article for sale is a small piece of card or paper attached to the article with the price written on it.

price war (**price wars**) N-COUNT If competing companies are involved in a **price war**, they each try to gain an advantage by lowering their prices as much as possible in order to sell more of their products and damage their competitors financially. [BUSINESS] ❏ *Their loss was partly due to a vicious price war between manufacturers that has cut margins to the bone.*

pricey /praɪsi/ (**pricier, priciest**) also **pricy** ADJ If you say that something is **pricey**, you mean that it is expensive. [INFORMAL] ❏ *Medical insurance is very pricey.*

prick /prɪk/ (pricks, pricking, pricked) **1** V-T If you **prick** something or **prick** holes in it, you make small holes in it with a sharp object such as a pin. ▢ *Prick the potatoes and rub the skins with salt.* **2** V-T If something sharp **pricks** you or if you **prick** yourself with something sharp, it sticks into you or presses your skin and causes you pain. ▢ *She had just pricked her finger with the needle.* **3** N-COUNT A **prick** is a small, sharp pain that you get when something pricks you. ▢ *At the same time she felt a prick on her neck.* **4** N-COUNT If you call someone a **prick**, you are insulting them because you think they are mean and spiteful or stupid, or you do not like them. [INFORMAL, OFFENSIVE, DISAPPROVAL] **5** N-COUNT [poss N] A man's **prick** is his penis. [INFORMAL, VULGAR]

prick|le /prɪkᵊl/ (prickles, prickling, prickled) **1** V-I If your skin **prickles**, it feels as if a lot of small sharp points are being stuck into it, either because of something touching it or because you feel a strong emotion. ▢ *He paused, feeling his scalp prickling under his hat.* • N-COUNT **Prickle** is also a noun. ▢ *I felt a prickle of disquiet.* **2** N-COUNT [usu pl] **Prickles** are small sharp points that stick out from leaves or from the stalks of plants. ▢ *...an erect stem covered at the base with a few prickles.*

prick|ly /prɪkli/ (pricklier, prickliest) **1** ADJ Something that is **prickly** feels rough and uncomfortable, as if it has a lot of prickles. ▢ *The bunk mattress was hard, the blankets prickly and slightly damp.* **2** ADJ Someone who is **prickly** loses their temper or gets upset very easily. ▢ *You know how prickly she is.* **3** ADJ A **prickly** issue or subject is one that is rather complicated and difficult to discuss or resolve. ▢ *The issue is likely to prove a prickly one.*

prick|ly heat N-UNCOUNT **Prickly heat** is a condition caused by very hot weather, in which your skin becomes hot, uncomfortable, and covered with tiny bumps.

prick|ly pear (prickly pears) N-COUNT A **prickly pear** is a kind of cactus that has round fruit with prickles on it. The fruit, which you can eat, is also called a **prickly pear**.

pricy /praɪsi/ → see **pricey**

pride ✦◇◇ /praɪd/ (prides, priding, prided) **1** N-UNCOUNT **Pride** is a feeling of satisfaction that you have because you or people close to you have done something good or possess something good. ▢ *...the sense of pride in a job well done.* ▢ *We take pride in offering you the highest standards.* **2** N-UNCOUNT **Pride** is a sense of the respect that other people have for you, and that you have for yourself. ▢ *Davis had to salvage his pride.* **3** N-UNCOUNT Someone's **pride** is the feeling that they have that they are better or more important than other people. [DISAPPROVAL] ▢ *His pride may still be his downfall.* **4** V-T If you **pride** yourself **on** a quality or skill that you have, you are very proud of it. ▢ *Suarez prides himself on being able to organize his own life.*

priest ✦◇◇ /priːst/ (priests) **1** N-COUNT A **priest** is a member of the Christian clergy in the Catholic, Anglican, or Orthodox church. ▢ *He had trained to be a Catholic priest.* **2** N-COUNT In many non-Christian religions a **priest** is someone who has particular duties and responsibilities in a place where people worship. ▢ *...a New Age priest or priestess.*

priest|ess /priːstɪs/ (priestesses) N-COUNT A **priestess** is a woman in a non-Christian religion who has particular duties and responsibilities in a place where people worship. ▢ *...the priestess of the temple.*

priest|hood /priːsthʊd/ **1** N-UNCOUNT **Priesthood** is the position of being a priest or the period of time during which someone is a priest. ▢ *...the early rites of priesthood.* **2** N-SING The **priesthood** is all the members of the Christian clergy, especially in a particular church. ▢ *He dropped out of the priesthood.*

priest|ly /priːstli/ ADJ [usu ADJ n] **Priestly** is used to describe things that belong or relate to a priest. ▢ *Priestly robes hang on the walls.* ▢ *...his priestly duties.*

prig /prɪg/ (prigs) N-COUNT If you call someone a **prig**, you disapprove of them because they behave in a very moral way and disapprove of other people's behavior as though they are superior. [DISAPPROVAL]

prig|gish /prɪgɪʃ/ ADJ If you describe someone as **priggish**, you think that they are a prig. [DISAPPROVAL]

prim /prɪm/ ADJ If you describe someone as **prim**, you disapprove of them because they behave too correctly and are too easily shocked by anything vulgar. [DISAPPROVAL] ▢ *We tend to imagine that the Victorians were very prim and proper.* • **prim|ly** ADV [ADV with v] ▢ *We sat primly at either end of a long bench.*

pri|ma|cy /praɪməsi/ N-UNCOUNT [oft N of n] The **primacy** of something is the fact that it is the most important or most powerful thing in a particular situation. [FORMAL] ▢ *The political idea at the heart of this is the primacy of the individual.*

pri|ma don|na /priːmə dɒnə/ (prima donnas) **1** N-COUNT A **prima donna** is the main female singer in an opera. ▢ *Her career began as prima donna with the Royal Carl Rosa Opera Company.* **2** N-COUNT If you describe someone as a **prima donna**, you disapprove of them because they think they can behave badly or get what they want because they have a particular talent. [DISAPPROVAL] ▢ *Nobody who comes to this club is allowed to behave like a prima donna.*

pri|mae|val /praɪmiːvᵊl/ [BRIT] → see **primeval**

pri|ma fa|cie /praɪmə feɪʃi/ ADJ [usu ADJ n] **Prima facie** is used to describe something that appears to be true when you first consider it. [FORMAL] ▢ *There was a prima facie case that a contempt of court had been committed.*

pri|mal /praɪmᵊl/ ADJ **Primal** is used to describe something that relates to the origins of things or that is very basic. [FORMAL] ▢ *Jealousy is a primal emotion.*

pri|mari|ly /praɪmerɪli/ ADV You use **primarily** to say what is mainly true in a particular situation. ▢ *...a book aimed primarily at high-energy physicists.* ▢ *Public order is primarily an urban problem.*

pri|ma|ry ✦◇◇ /praɪmeri, -məri/ (primaries) **1** ADJ [ADJ n] You use **primary** to describe something that is very important. [FORMAL] ▢ *That's the primary reason the company's share price has held up so well.* ▢ *His misunderstanding of language was the primary cause of his other problems.* **2** ADJ [ADJ n] **Primary** education is the first few years of formal education for children. ▢ *The content of primary education should be the same for everyone.* ▢ *Ninety-nine percent of primary pupils now have hands-on experience of computers.* **3** ADJ [ADJ n] **Primary** is used to describe something that occurs first. ▢ *It is not the primary tumor that kills, but secondary growths elsewhere in the body.* **4** N-COUNT A **primary** or a **primary election** is an election in an American state in which people vote for someone to become a candidate for a political office. Compare **general election**. ▢ *...the 1968 New Hampshire primary.*

> **SYNONYMS**
>
> **primary**
> ADJ **1**
> **chief:** *Financial stress is well established as a chief reason for divorce.*
> **main:** *My main concern now is to protect the children.*
> **principal:** *The principal reason for changing my mind is my health.*
> **leading:** *Britain's future as a leading industrial nation depends on investment.*

pri|ma|ry care N-UNCOUNT **Primary care** refers to those parts of the health care system, such as family practitioners and hospital emergency rooms, that deal with people who are in need of nonspecialized medical care. ▢ *...the crucial roles of primary care and of preventive work.*

pri|ma|ry col|or (primary colors)

> in BRIT, use **primary colour**

N-COUNT [usu pl] **Primary colors** are basic colors that can be mixed together to produce other colors. They are usually considered to be red, yellow, blue, and sometimes green. ▢ *It comes in bright primary colors that kids will love.*

pri|ma|ry school (primary schools) N-VAR A **primary school** is a school for children in the first four or five years of their education. [mainly BRIT]

> in AM, usually use **elementary school**

pri|mate /praɪmeɪt/ (primates)

> The pronunciation /praɪmɪt/ is also used for meaning **2**.

1 N-COUNT A **primate** is a member of the group of mammals that includes humans, monkeys, and apes. ▢ *The woolly spider monkey is the largest primate in the Americas.* **2** N-COUNT

The **Primate** of a particular country or region is the most important priest in that country or region. ◻ ...the Roman Catholic Primate of All Ireland.

prime ♦♦◊ /praɪm/ (**primes, priming, primed**) **1** ADJ [ADJ n] You use **prime** to describe something that is most important in a situation. ◻ Political stability, meanwhile, will be a prime concern. ◻ It could be a prime target for guerrilla attack. **2** ADJ [ADJ n] You use **prime** to describe something that is of the best possible quality. ◻ The location of these beaches makes them prime sites for development. **3** ADJ [ADJ n] You use **prime** to describe an example of a particular kind of thing that is absolutely typical. ◻ The prime example is Smith's, once the undisputed king of online retailers. **4** N-UNCOUNT If someone or something is in their **prime**, they are at the stage in their existence when they are at their strongest, most active, or most successful. ◻ Maybe I'm just coming into my prime now. ◻ We've had a series of athletes trying to come back well past their prime. **5** V-T If you **prime** someone to do something, you prepare them to do it, for example, by giving them information about it beforehand. ◻ Claire wished she'd primed Sarah beforehand. ◻ Marianne had not known until Arnold primed her for her duties that she was to be the sole female. **6** V-T If someone **primes** a bomb or a gun, they prepare it so that it is ready to explode or fire. ◻ He was priming the bomb to go off in an hour's time. ◻ He kept a primed shotgun in his office.

prime me|rid|ian N-SING [the N] The **prime meridian** is the line of longitude, corresponding to zero degrees and passing through Greenwich, England, from which all the other lines of longitude are calculated. [TECHNICAL]

prime min|is|ter ♦♦♦ (**prime ministers**) N-COUNT; N-TITLE The leader of the government in some countries is called the **prime minister**. ◻ ...the former prime minister of Pakistan, Miss Benazir Bhutto.

prime mov|er (**prime movers**) N-COUNT [usu N behind/in n] The **prime mover** behind a plan, idea, or situation is someone who has an important influence in starting it. ◻ He was the prime mover behind the coup.

prime num|ber (**prime numbers**) N-COUNT In mathematics, a **prime number** is a whole number greater than 1 that cannot be divided exactly by any whole number except itself and the number 1, such as 17.

pri|mer /ˈpraɪmər/ (**primers**) **1** N-MASS **Primer** is a type of paint that is put onto wood in order to prepare it for the main layer of paint. **2** N-COUNT A **primer** is a book containing basic facts about a subject, which is used by someone who is beginning to study that subject. **3** N-COUNT A **primer** is a book, written in very simple language, that teaches children how to read. ◻ ...the language used in reading primers. **4** N-COUNT A **primer** is a small explosive device that is used to set off a larger explosion. ◻ The potentially lethal device was made from a length of hose packed with gunpowder, primers, and shrapnel.

prime rate (**prime rates**) N-COUNT A bank's **prime rate** is the lowest rate of interest that it charges at a particular time and that is offered only to certain customers. [BUSINESS] ◻ At least one bank cut its prime rate today.

prime time also **primetime** N-UNCOUNT **Prime time** television or radio programs are broadcast when the greatest number of people are watching television or listening to the radio, usually in the evenings. ◻ ...a prime-time television show.

pri|meval /praɪˈmiːvəl/

in BRIT, also use **primaeval**

1 ADJ [usu ADJ n] You use **primeval** to describe things that belong to a very early period in the history of the world. [FORMAL] ◻ ...the dense primeval forests that once covered inland Virginia. **2** ADJ [usu ADJ n] You use **primeval** to describe feelings and emotions that are basic and not the result of thought. ◻ ...a primeval urge to hit out at that which causes him pain.

primi|tive /ˈprɪmɪtɪv/ **1** ADJ **Primitive** means belonging to a society in which people live in a very simple way, usually without industries or a writing system. ◻ ...studies of primitive societies. **2** ADJ **Primitive** means belonging to a very early period in the development of an animal or plant. ◻ ...primitive whales. ◻ Primitive humans needed to be able to react like this to escape from dangerous animals. **3** ADJ If you describe something as **primitive**, you mean that it is very simple in style or very old-fashioned. ◻ The conditions are primitive by any standards.

pri|mor|dial /praɪˈmɔːrdiəl/ ADJ You use **primordial** to describe things that belong to a very early time in the history of the world. [FORMAL] ◻ Twenty million years ago, Idaho was populated by dense primordial forest.

prim|rose /ˈprɪmroʊz/ (**primroses**) N-VAR A **primrose** is a wild plant that has pale yellow flowers in the spring.

primu|la /ˈprɪmjələ/ (**primulas**) N-VAR A **primula** is a plant that has brightly colored flowers in the spring.

prince ♦♦◊ /prɪns/ (**princes**) **1** N-TITLE; N-COUNT A **prince** is a male member of a royal family, especially the son of the king or queen of a country. ◻ ...Prince Edward and other royal guests. **2** N-TITLE; N-COUNT A **prince** is the male royal ruler of a small country or state. ◻ He was speaking without the prince's authority.

Prince Charm|ing N-SING [also no det] A **Prince Charming** is a man who seems to be a perfect lover or boyfriend, because he is attractive, kind, and considerate. [APPROVAL] ◻ To begin with he was Prince Charming.

prince|ly /ˈprɪnsli/ **1** ADJ GRADED; ADJ [usu ADJ n] A **princely** sum of money is a large sum of money. ◻ It'll cost them the princely sum of seventy-five dollars. **2** ADJ [usu ADJ n] **Princely** means belonging to a prince or suitable for a prince. ◻ It was the embodiment of princely magnificence.

prin|cess ♦♦◊ /ˈprɪnsɪs, -sɛs/ (**princesses**) N-TITLE; N-COUNT A **princess** is a female member of a royal family, usually the daughter of a king or queen or the wife of a prince. ◻ Princess Anne topped the guest list.

prin|ci|pal ♦♦◊ /ˈprɪnsɪpəl/ (**principals**) **1** ADJ [ADJ n] **Principal** means first in order of importance. ◻ The principal reason for my change of mind is this. ◻ ...the country's principal source of foreign exchange earnings. **2** N-COUNT The **principal** of a school is the person in charge of the school or college. ◻ ...the principal of Dartmouth High School. **3** N-COUNT [usu sing] The **principal** of a loan is the original amount of the loan, on which you pay interest. [BUSINESS]

SYNONYMS

principal
ADJ **1**
main: My main concern now is to protect the children.
leading: Britain's future as a leading industrial nation depends on investment.
chief: Financial stress is well established as a chief reason for divorce.
primary: That's the primary reason the company's share price has held up so well.

prin|ci|pal|ity /ˌprɪnsɪˈpælɪti/ (**principalities**) N-COUNT A **principality** is a country that is ruled by a prince. ◻ ...the tiny principality of Liechtenstein.

prin|ci|pal|ly /ˈprɪnsɪpli/ ADV [ADV with cl/group] **Principally** means more than anything else. ◻ This is principally because the major export markets are slowing.

prin|ci|ple ♦♦◊ /ˈprɪnsɪpəl/ (**principles**) **1** N-VAR A **principle** is a general belief about the way you should behave, which influences your behavior. ◻ Buck never allowed himself to be bullied into doing anything that went against his principles. ◻ It's not just a matter of principle. **2** N-COUNT The **principles** of a particular theory or philosophy are its basic rules or laws. ◻ ...a violation of the basic principles of Marxism. **3** N-COUNT Scientific **principles** are general scientific laws which explain how something happens or works. ◻ These people lack all understanding of scientific principles. **4** PHRASE If you agree with something **in principle**, you agree in general terms to the idea of it, although you do not yet know the details or know if it will be possible. ◻ I agree with it in principle but I doubt if it will happen in practice. **5** PHRASE If something is possible **in principle**, there is no known reason why it should not happen, even though it has not happened before. ◻ Even assuming this to be in principle possible, it will not be achieved soon. **6** PHRASE If you refuse to do something **on principle**, you refuse to do it because of a particular belief that you have. ◻ He would vote against it on principle.

COLLOCATIONS

principle
NOUN

1
adjective + **principle**: basic, moral, sound
verb + **principle**: follow; abandon

2
adjective + **principle**: biblical, founding, fundamental, guiding; democratic, liberal, socialist
verb + **principle**: apply, follow, uphold; abandon, violate

prin|ci|pled /prɪnsɪpᵊld/ ADJ If you describe someone as **principled**, you approve of them because they have strong moral principles. [APPROVAL] ❑ *She was a strong, principled woman.*

print ♦♦◊ /prɪnt/ (prints, printing, printed) **1** V-T If someone **prints** something such as a book or newspaper, they produce it in large quantities using a machine. ❑ *He started to print his own posters to distribute abroad.* ❑ *Our brochure is printed on environmentally-friendly paper.* • PHRASAL VERB In American English, **print up** means the same as **print**. ❑ *Community workers here are printing up pamphlets for peace demonstrations.* • **print|ing** N-UNCOUNT [oft N n] ❑ *His brother ran a printing and publishing company.* **2** V-T If a newspaper or magazine **prints** a piece of writing, it includes it or publishes it. ❑ *We can only print letters which are accompanied by the writer's name and address.* **3** V-T If numbers, letters, or designs **are printed** on a surface, they are put on it in ink or dye using a machine. You can also say that a surface **is printed** with numbers, letters, or designs. ❑ *...the number printed on the receipt.* ❑ *The company has for some time printed its phone number on its products.* **4** N-COUNT A **print** is a piece of clothing or material with a pattern printed on it. You can also refer to the pattern itself as a **print**. ❑ *Her mother wore one of her dark summer prints.* ❑ *In this living room we've mixed glorious floral prints.* **5** V-T When you **print** a photograph, you produce it from a negative. ❑ *Printing a black-and-white negative on to color paper produces a similar monochrome effect.* **6** N-COUNT A **print** is a photograph from a film that has been developed. ❑ *...black and white prints of Margaret and Jean as children.* **7** N-COUNT A **print** is one of a number of copies of a particular picture. It can be either a photograph, something such as a painting, or a picture made by an artist who puts ink on a prepared surface and presses it against paper. ❑ *...12 original copper plates engraved by William Hogarth for his famous series of prints.* **8** N-UNCOUNT **Print** is used to refer to letters and numbers as they appear on the pages of a book, newspaper, or printed document. ❑ *...columns of tiny print.* **9** N-SING [ADJ n] The **print** media consists of newspapers and magazines, but not television or radio. ❑ *I have been convinced that the print media are more accurate and more reliable than television.* **10** V-T If you **print** words, you write in letters that are not joined together. ❑ *Print your name and address on a postcard and send it to us.* **11** N-COUNT You can refer to a mark left by someone's foot or hand as a **print**. ❑ *He crawled from print to print, sniffing at the earth, following the scent left in the tracks.* **12** N-COUNT You can refer to oily marks left by someone's fingers as their **prints**. ❑ *Fresh prints of both girls were found in the house.* **13** → see also **printing** **14** PHRASE If you appear **in print**, or get **into print**, what you say or write is published in a book, newspaper, or magazine. ❑ *Many of these poets appeared in print only long after their deaths.* **15** PHRASE The **small print** or the **fine print** of something such as an advertisement or a contract consists of the technical details and legal conditions, which are often printed in much smaller letters than the rest of the text. ❑ *I'm looking at the small print; I don't want to sign anything that I shouldn't sign.* **16** → See feature box at **press**

▶ **print out** **1** PHRASAL VERB If a computer or a machine attached to a computer **prints** something **out**, it produces a copy of it on paper. ❑ *You measure yourself, enter measurements and the computer will print out the pattern.* **2** → see also **printout**

COLLOCATIONS

print
NOUN

3
noun + **print**: animal, leopard, paisley, zebra
adjective + **print**: floral, geometric

11
noun + **print**: hand, palm, shoe; hoof, paw

print|able /prɪntəbᵊl/ ADJ [usu with brd-neg] If you say that someone's words or remarks are not **printable**, you mean that they are likely to offend people, and are therefore not suitable to be repeated in writing or speech. [JOURNALISM] ❑ *His teammates opened hotel windows, shouting "Jump!" and somewhat less printable banter.*

print|ed cir|cuit board (printed circuit boards) N-COUNT A **printed circuit board** is an electronic circuit in which some of the parts and connections consist of thin metal lines and shapes on a thin board. [TECHNICAL]

print|ed word N-SING [the N] The **printed word** is the same as the **written word**.

print|er /prɪntər/ (printers) **1** N-COUNT A **printer** is a machine that can be connected to a computer in order to make copies on paper of documents or other information held by the computer. **2** → see also **laser printer** **3** N-COUNT A **printer** is a person or company whose job is printing things such as books. ❑ *The manuscript had already been sent off to the printer.*

print|ing /prɪntɪŋ/ (printings) **1** N-COUNT If copies of a book are printed and published on a number of different occasions, you can refer to each of these occasions as a **printing**. ❑ *"Cloud Street" is already in its third printing.* **2** → see also **print**

print|ing press (printing presses) N-COUNT A **printing press** is a machine used for printing, especially one that can print books, newspapers, or documents in large numbers.

print|mak|ing /prɪntmeɪkɪŋ/ N-UNCOUNT **Printmaking** is an artistic technique that consists of making a series of pictures from an original, or from a specially prepared surface.

print|out /prɪntaʊt/ (printouts) also **print-out** N-COUNT A **printout** is a piece of paper on which information from a computer or similar device has been printed. ❑ *...a computer printout of various financial projections.*

print run (print runs) N-COUNT In publishing, a **print run** of something such as a book or a newspaper is the number of copies of it that are printed and published at one time. ❑ *It was launched last year in paperback with an initial print run of 7,000 copies.*

print shop (print shops) N-COUNT A **print shop** is a small business that prints and copies things such as documents and cards for customers.

pri|or ♦◊◊ /praɪər/ **1** ADJ [ADJ n] You use **prior** to indicate that something has already happened, or must happen, before another event takes place. ❑ *He claimed he had no prior knowledge of the protest.* ❑ *The Constitution requires the president to seek the prior approval of Congress for military action.* **2** ADJ [ADJ n] A **prior** claim or duty is more important than other claims or duties and needs to be dealt with first. ❑ *The firm I wanted to use had prior commitments.* **3** PHRASE If something happens **prior to** a particular time or event, it happens before that time or event. [FORMAL] ❑ *A death prior to 65 is considered to be a premature death.*

SYNONYMS

prior
ADJ **1**
previous: *He has no previous convictions.*
former: *The unemployed executives include former sales managers, directors, and accountants.*
preceding: *Industrial orders had already fallen in the preceding months.*

pri|or|ess /praɪərɪs/ (prioresses) N-COUNT; N-TITLE A **prioress** is a nun who is in charge of a convent.

pri|ori|tize /praɪɒrɪtaɪz/ (prioritizes, prioritizing, prioritized)

in BRIT, also use **prioritise**

1 V-T If you **prioritize** something, you treat it as more important than other things. ❑ *Prioritize your own wants rather than constantly thinking about others.* **2** V-T If you **prioritize** the tasks that you have to do, you decide which are the most important and do them first. ❑ *Make lists of what to do and prioritize your tasks.*

pri|or|ity ♦◊◊ /praɪɒrɪti/ (priorities) **1** N-COUNT If something is a **priority**, it is the most important thing you have to do or deal with, or must be done or dealt with before everything else you have to do. ❑ *Being a parent is her first priority.* ❑ *The* government's priority is to build more power plants. **2** PHRASE If you **give priority** to something or someone, you treat them as more important than anything or anyone else. ❑ *Women are more likely to give priority to child care and education policies.* **3** PHRASE If something **takes priority** or **has priority** over other things, it is regarded as being more important than them and is dealt with first. ❑ *The fight against inflation took priority over measures to combat the deepening recession.*

pri|ory /praɪəri/ (**priories**) N-COUNT A **priory** is a place where a small group of monks live and work together.

prise /praɪz/ [mainly BRIT] → see **prize 5**

prism /prɪzəm/ (**prisms**) N-COUNT A **prism** is a block of clear glass or plastic that separates the light passing through it into different colors.

pris|on ♦♦◇ /prɪzᵊn/ (**prisons**) N-VAR A **prison** is a building where criminals are kept as punishment. ❑ *The prison's inmates are being kept in their cells.*

SYNONYMS

prison
NOUN
jail: *Three prisoners escaped from a jail.*
penitentiary: *She works at the local penitentiary.*
confinement: *He had been held in solitary confinement for four months.*
dungeon: *They were thrown in a dungeon.*

VOCABULARY IN CONTEXT

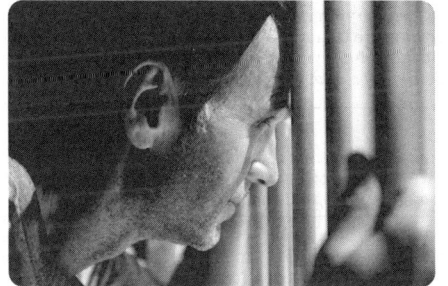

Prison

Is Bastoy prison in Norway the nicest **penal institution** in the world? Built on an island, Bastoy is more like a village community than a prison. The **inmates** all have to work hard, but they are also allowed free time to go fishing or to swim in the sea. Is it just for **white-collar criminals**? No, many of the prisoners have **committed** serious crimes. Every type of **offender**, even those in maximum security prisons, can transfer once they have five years or less of their sentence left to **serve**.

It may seem strange to give prisoners so much **liberty**, but the Norwegian government is very clear that prison is not just a **deterrent** and a punishment, but also a way of encouraging **rehabilitation**. And it does seem to work. Whereas around 40% of people **released** from state prisons in the U.S. reoffend within three years, in Norway the rate is closer to 20%, and even lower for those released from Bastoy.

pris|on camp (**prison camps**) **1** N-COUNT A **prison camp** is a guarded camp where prisoners of war or political prisoners are kept. ❑ *He was shot down over Denmark and spent three years in a prison camp.* **2** N-COUNT A **prison camp** is a prison where the prisoners are not considered dangerous and are allowed to work outside the prison. [AM]

pris|on|er ♦♦◇ /prɪzənər/ (**prisoners**) **1** N-COUNT A **prisoner** is a person who is kept in a prison as a punishment for a crime that they have committed. ❑ *The committee is concerned about the* large number of prisoners sharing cells. **2** N-COUNT [also hold/take n n] A **prisoner** is a person who has been captured by an enemy, for example, in war. ❑ *...wartime hostages and concentration-camp prisoners.*

SYNONYMS

prisoner
NOUN **2**
captive: *He described the difficulties of surviving for four months as a captive.*
hostage: *It is hopeful that two hostages will be freed in the next few days.*
detainee: *They agreed to release all the detainees.*

pris|on|er of con|science (**prisoners of conscience**) N-COUNT **Prisoners of conscience** are people who have been put into prison for their political or social beliefs or for breaking the law while protesting against a political or social system.

pris|on|er of war (**prisoners of war**) N-COUNT **Prisoners of war** are soldiers who have been captured by their enemy during a war and kept as prisoners until the end of the war.

pris|sy /prɪsi/ (**prissier, prissiest**) ADJ If you say that someone is **prissy**, you are critical of them because they are very easily shocked by anything vulgar or bad. [INFORMAL, DISAPPROVAL] ❑ *I grew to dislike the people from my background – they were uptight and prissy.*

pris|tine /prɪstin, prɪstin/ ADJ **Pristine** things are extremely clean or new. [FORMAL] ❑ *Now the house is in pristine condition.*

pri|va|cy /praɪvəsi/ N-UNCOUNT If you have **privacy**, you are in a place or situation that allows you to do things without other people seeing you or disturbing you. ❑ *He resented the publication of this book, which he saw as an embarrassing invasion of his privacy.* ❑ *Thatched pavilions provide shady retreats for relaxing and reading in privacy.*

pri|vate ♦♦◇ /praɪvɪt/ (**privates**) **1** ADJ **Private** companies, industries, and services are owned or controlled by individuals or stockholders, rather than by the government or an official organization. [BUSINESS] ❑ *...a joint venture with private industry.* ❑ *They sent their children to private schools.* ● **pri|vate|ly** ADV [ADV with v] ❑ *No other European country had so much state ownership and so few privately owned businesses.* **2** ADJ [ADJ n] **Private** individuals are acting only for themselves, and are not representing any group, company, or organization. ❑ *Private individuals with money to lend are more difficult to find than traditional lenders.* ❑ *The king was on a private visit to enable him to pray at the tombs of his ancestors.* **3** ADJ Your **private** things belong only to you, or may only be used by you. ❑ *They want more state control over private property.* **4** ADJ **Private** places or gatherings may be attended only by a particular group of people, rather than by the general public. ❑ *673 private golf clubs took part in a recent study.* ❑ *The door is marked "Private."* **5** ADJ **Private** meetings, discussions, and other activities involve only a small number of people, and very little information about them is given to other people. ❑ *Don't bug private conversations, and don't buy papers that reprint them.* ● **pri|vate|ly** ADV ❑ *Few senior figures have issued any public statements but privately the resignation's been welcomed.* **6** ADJ Your **private** life is that part of your life that is concerned with your personal relationships and activities, rather than with your work or business. ❑ *I've always kept my private and professional life separate.* **7** ADJ Your **private** thoughts or feelings are ones that you do not talk about to other people. ❑ *We all felt as if we were intruding on his private grief.* ● **pri|vate|ly** ADV ❑ *Privately, she worries about whether she's really good enough.* **8** ADJ If you describe a place as **private**, or as somewhere where you can be **private**, you mean that it is a quiet place and you can be alone there without being disturbed. ❑ *It was the only reasonably private place they could find.* **9** ADJ If you describe someone as a **private** person, you mean that they are very quiet by nature and do not reveal their thoughts and feelings to other people. ❑ *Gould was an intensely private individual.* **10** N-COUNT; N-TITLE A **private** is a soldier of the lowest rank in an army or the marines. ❑ *He was a private in the U.S. Army.* **11** → see also **privately** **12** PHRASE If you do something **in private**, you do it without other people being present, often because it is something that you want to keep secret. ❑ *Some of what we're talking about might better be discussed in private.*

pri|vate de|tec|tive (private detectives) N-COUNT A **private detective** is someone who you can pay to find missing people or do other kinds of investigation for you.

pri|vate en|ter|prise N-UNCOUNT **Private enterprise** is industry and business that is owned by individuals or stockholders, and not by the government or an official organization. [BUSINESS] ❑ ...the encouragement of private enterprise.

pri|vate eye (private eyes) N-COUNT You can refer to a private detective as a **private eye**, especially when he or she is a character in a movie or story. [INFORMAL]

pri|vate in|ves|ti|ga|tor (private investigators) N-COUNT A **private investigator** is the same as a **private detective**.

pri|vate|ly /praɪvɪtli/ ◼ ADV [ADV after v] If you buy or sell something **privately**, you buy it from or sell it to another person directly, rather than in a store or through a business. ❑ The whole process makes buying a car privately as painless as buying from a garage. ◼ → see also **private**

privately held corporation (privately held corporations) N-COUNT A **privately held corporation** is a company whose shares cannot be bought by the general public. [AM]

pri|vate parts N-PLURAL [usu poss N] Your **private parts** are your genitals. [INFORMAL]

pri|vate school (private schools) N-VAR A **private school** is a school that is not supported financially by the government and that parents have to pay for their children to go to. ❑ ...an exclusive private school.

pri|vate sec|tor N-SING The **private sector** is the part of a country's economy that consists of industries and commercial companies that are not owned or controlled by the government. [BUSINESS] ❑ ...small firms in the private sector.

pri|va|tion /praɪveɪʃ³n/ (privations) N-UNCOUNT [also N in pl] If you suffer **privation** or **privations**, you have to live without many of the things that are thought to be necessary in life, such as food, clothing, or housing. [FORMAL] ❑ They endured five years of privation during World War II. ❑ The privations of monastery life were evident in his appearance.

pri|vat|ize ◆◇◇ /praɪvətaɪz/ (privatizes, privatizing, privatized)

in BRIT, also use **privatise**

V-T If a company, industry, or service that is owned by the state **is privatized**, the government sells it and makes it a private company. [BUSINESS] ❑ Many state-owned companies were privatized. ❑ ...a move to privatize prisons. ● **pri|vati|za|tion** /praɪvətɪzeɪʃ³n/ (privatizations) N-VAR ❑ ...the privatization of government services.

priv|et /prɪvɪt/ N-UNCOUNT **Privet** is a type of bush with small leaves that stay green all year round. It is often grown in gardens to form hedges. ❑ The garden was enclosed by a privet hedge.

privi|lege /prɪvɪlɪdʒ, prɪvlɪdʒ/ (privileges) ◼ N-COUNT A **privilege** is a special right or advantage that only one person or group has. ❑ The Russian Federation has issued a decree abolishing special privileges for government officials. ◼ N-UNCOUNT If you talk about **privilege**, you are talking about the power and advantage that only a small group of people have, usually because of their wealth or their connections with powerful people. ❑ He was the son of privilege and wealth, and it showed. ◼ N-SING You can use **privilege** in expressions such as **be a privilege** or **have the privilege** when you want to show your appreciation of someone or something, or to show your respect. ❑ It must be a privilege to know such a man.

privi|leged /prɪvɪlɪdʒd, prɪvlɪdʒd/ ◼ ADJ Someone who is **privileged** has an advantage or opportunity that most other people do not have, often because of their wealth or connections with powerful people. ❑ They were, by and large, a very wealthy, privileged elite. ● N-PLURAL **The privileged** are people who are privileged. ❑ They are only interested in preserving the power of the privileged and the well off. ◼ ADJ **Privileged** information is known by only a small group of people, who are not legally required to give it to anyone else. ❑ The data is privileged information, not to be shared with the general public.

privy /prɪvi/ ADJ [v-link ADJ to n] If you are **privy to** something secret, you have been allowed to know about it. [FORMAL] ❑ Only three people, including a police officer, will be privy to the facts.

prize ◆◇◇ /praɪz/ (prizes, prizing, prized) ◼ N-COUNT A **prize** is money or something valuable that is given to someone who has the best results in a competition or game, or as a reward for doing good work. ❑ You must claim your prize by telephoning our claims line. ❑ He was awarded the Nobel Prize for Physics in 1985. ◼ ADJ [ADJ n] You use **prize** to describe things that are of such good quality that they win prizes or deserve to win prizes. ❑ ...a prize bull. ◼ N-COUNT You can refer to someone or something as a **prize** when people consider them to be of great value or importance. ❑ My mum says there could be no greater prize. ◼ V-T [usu passive] Something that **is prized** is wanted and admired because it is considered to be very valuable or very good quality. ❑ Military figures made out of lead are prized by collectors. ◼ V-T If you **prize** something open or **prize** it away from a surface, you force it to open or force it to come away from the surface. [mainly BRIT]

in AM, usually use **pry**

prize|fight /praɪzfaɪt/ (prizefights) N-COUNT A **prizefight** is a boxing match where the boxers are paid to fight, especially one that is not official.

prize|fight|er /praɪzfaɪtər/ (prizefighters) N-COUNT A **prizefighter** is a boxer who fights to win money.

pro /proʊ/ (pros) ◼ N-COUNT A **pro** is a professional. [INFORMAL] ❑ In the professional theater, there is a tremendous need to prove that you're a pro. ◼ ADJ [ADJ n] A **pro** player is a professional athlete. You can also use **pro** to refer to sports that are played by professional athletes. [AM] ❑ ...a former college and pro basketball player. ◼ PREP If you are **pro** a particular course of action or belief, you agree with it or support it. ❑ The majority of Americans have always been very pro business, pro competition, pro free market. ◼ PHRASE The **pros and cons** of something are its advantages and disadvantages, which you consider carefully so that you can make a sensible decision. ❑ Motherhood has both its pros and cons.

PREFIX

pro-
forms adjectives that refer to people who strongly support a particular person or thing. For example, if you are **pro-democracy**, you support democracy.

pro|ac|tive /proʊæktɪv/ ADJ **Proactive** actions are intended to cause changes, rather than just reacting to change. ❑ In order to survive the competition a company should be proactive not reactive.

pro-am (pro-ams) also **pro am** N-COUNT [oft N n] A **pro-am** is a sports competition in which professional and amateur players compete together. ❑ ...a sponsored pro-am golf tournament.

prob|abil|is|tic /prɒbəbɪlɪstɪk/ ADJ [usu ADJ n] **Probabilistic** actions, methods, or arguments are based on the idea that you cannot be certain about results or future events but you can judge whether or not they are likely, and act on the basis of this judgment. [FORMAL] ❑ ...probabilistic exposure to risk.

prob|abil|ity /prɒbəbɪlɪti/ (probabilities) ◼ N-VAR The **probability** of something happening is how likely it is to happen, sometimes expressed as a fraction or a percentage. ❑ Without a transfusion, the victim's probability of dying was 100%. ❑ The probabilities of crime or victimization are higher with some situations than with others. ◼ N-VAR You say that there is a **probability** that something will happen when it is likely to happen. [VAGUENESS] ❑ If you've owned property for several years, the probability is that values have increased. ❑ Formal talks are still said to be a possibility, not a probability. ◼ PHRASE If you say that something will happen **in all probability**, you mean that you think it is very likely to happen. [VAGUENESS] ❑ The party had better get used to the fact that in all probability, it is going to lose.

prob|able /prɒbəb³l/ ◼ ADJ If you say that something is **probable**, you mean that it is likely to be true or likely to happen. [VAGUENESS] ❑ It is probable that the medication will suppress the symptom without treating the condition. ◼ ADJ [ADJ n] You can use **probable** to describe a role or function that someone or something is likely to have. ❑ ...their probable presidential candidate.

prob|ably ◆◆◆ /prɒbəbli/ ◼ ADV [ADV with cl/group] If you say that something is **probably** the case, you think that it is likely

probate

to be the case, although you are not sure. [VAGUENESS] ❏ *The White House probably won't make this plan public until July.* ❏ *Van Gogh is probably the best-known painter in the world.* **2** ADV [ADV with cl/group] You can use **probably** when you want to make your opinion sound less forceful or definite, so that you do not offend people. [VAGUENESS] ❏ *What would he think of their story? He'd probably think she and Lenny were both crazy!*

SYNONYMS

probably
ADV **1**
likely: *Profits will most likely have risen by about $25 million.*
doubtless: *She took off her shoes, doubtless because her feet hurt.*
presumably: *The spear is presumably the murder weapon.*

---

pro|bate /proʊbeɪt/ N-UNCOUNT [oft N n] **Probate** is the act or process of officially proving a dead person's will to be valid. ❏ *Probate cases can go on for two years or more.*

pro|ba|tion /proʊbeɪʃən/ **1** N-UNCOUNT **Probation** is a period of time during which a person who has committed a crime has to obey the law and be supervised by a probation officer, rather than being sent to prison. ❏ *A young woman admitted three theft charges and was put on probation for two years.* **2** N-UNCOUNT **Probation** is a period of time during which someone is judging your character and ability while you work, in order to see if you are suitable for that type of work. ❏ *Employee appointment to the council will be subject to a term of probation of 6 months.*

pro|ba|tion|ary /proʊbeɪʃəneri/ ADJ [ADJ n] A **probationary** period is a period after someone starts a job, during which their employer can decide whether the person is suitable and should be allowed to continue. [BUSINESS] ❏ *Teachers should have a probationary period of two years.*

pro|ba|tion|er /proʊbeɪʃənər/ (probationers) **1** N-COUNT A **probationer** is someone who has been found guilty of committing a crime but is on probation rather than in prison. **2** N-COUNT A **probationer** is someone who is still being trained to do a job and is on trial. ❏ *...a probationer police officer.*

pro|ba|tion of|fic|er (probation officers) N-COUNT A **probation officer** is a person whose job is to supervise and help people who have committed crimes and been put on probation.

probe /proʊb/ (probes, probing, probed) **1** V-I If you **probe** into something, you ask questions or try to discover facts about it. ❏ *The more they probed into his background, the more inflamed their suspicions would become.* ❏ *For three years, I have probed for understanding.* • N-COUNT **Probe** is also a noun. ❏ *...a federal grand-jury probe into corruption within the FDA.* **2** V-I If a doctor or dentist **probes**, he or she uses a long instrument to examine part of a patient's body. ❏ *The surgeon would pick up his instruments, probe, repair, and stitch up again.* ❏ *Dr. Amid probed around the sensitive area.* **3** N-COUNT A **probe** is a long thin instrument that doctors and dentists use to examine parts of the body. ❏ *...a fiber-optic probe.* **4** V-T If you **probe** a place, you search it in order to find someone or something that you are looking for. ❏ *A flashlight beam probed the underbrush only yards away from their hiding place.*

pro|bity /proʊbɪti/ N-UNCOUNT **Probity** is a high standard of correct moral behavior. [FORMAL] ❏ *He asserted his innocence and his financial probity.*

prob|lem ✦✦✦ /prɒbləm/ (problems) **1** N-COUNT A **problem** is a situation that is unsatisfactory and causes difficulties for people. ❏ *...the economic problems of the inner city.* ❏ *I do not have a simple solution to the drug problem.* **2** N-COUNT A **problem** is a puzzle that requires logical thought or mathematics to solve it. ❏ *With mathematical problems, you can save time by approximating.*

USAGE

problem
Don't use 'problem' with **why** when you are explaining the reason something happened. Don't say, for example, '~~The problem why he couldn't come is that he is ill.~~' Say 'The **reason** why he couldn't come is that he is ill.' *That is the reason why I find her books boring.*

---

process

prob|lem|at|ic /prɒbləmætɪk/ ADJ Something that is **problematic** involves problems and difficulties. ❏ *Some places are more problematic than others for solo travelers.*

prob|lem|ati|cal /prɒbləmætɪkəl/ ADJ **Problematical** means the same as **problematic**. [FORMAL]

pro|cedur|al /prəsidʒərəl/ ADJ **Procedural** means involving a formal procedure. [FORMAL] ❏ *A Spanish judge rejected the suit on procedural grounds.*

pro|cedure ✦✦ /prəsidʒər/ (procedures) N-VAR A **procedure** is a way of doing something, especially the usual or correct way. ❏ *A biopsy is usually a minor surgical procedure.* ❏ *Police insist that Michael did not follow the correct procedure in applying for a visa.*

SYNONYMS

procedure
NOUN
method: *...new teaching methods.*
process: *They decided to spread the building process over three years.*
system: *The present system of funding for higher education is unsatisfactory.*
routine: *He checked up on you as a matter of routine.*

---

pro|ceed ✦✦ (proceeds, proceeding, proceeded)

The verb is pronounced /prəsid/. The plural noun in meaning **4** is pronounced /proʊsidz/.

1 V-T If you **proceed** to do something, you do it, often after doing something else first. ❏ *He proceeded to tell me of my birth.* **2** V-I If you **proceed with** a course of action, you continue with it. [FORMAL] ❏ *The group proceeded with a march they knew would lead to bloodshed.* **3** V-I If an activity, process, or event **proceeds**, it goes on and does not stop. ❏ *The ideas were not new. Their development had proceeded steadily since the war.* **4** N-PLURAL The **proceeds** of an event or activity are the money that has been obtained from it. ❏ *The proceeds of the concert went to charity.*

SYNONYMS

proceed
VERB **2**
continue: *There is no reason why you should not continue with any sport or activity you already enjoy.*
go on: *I'm all right here. Go on with your work.*
carry on: *'Do you mind if I ask a few questions please?'—'Carry on.'*

---

pro|ceed|ing /prəsidɪŋ/ (proceedings) **1** N-COUNT Legal **proceedings** are legal action taken against someone. [FORMAL] ❏ *...criminal proceedings against the former prime minister.* **2** N-COUNT The **proceedings** are an organized series of events that take place in a particular place. [FORMAL] ❏ *The proceedings of the inquiry will take place in private.* **3** N-PLURAL You can refer to a written record of the discussions at a meeting or conference as the **proceedings**. ❏ *The DOT is to publish the conference proceedings.*

pro|cess ✦✦✦ /prɒsɛs/ (processes, processing, processed) **1** N-COUNT A **process** is a series of actions which are carried out in order to achieve a particular result. ❏ *There was total agreement to start the peace process as soon as possible.* ❏ *They decided to spread the building process over three years.* **2** N-COUNT A **process** is a series of things that happen naturally and result in a biological or chemical change. ❏ *It occurs in elderly men, apparently as part of the aging process.* **3** V-T When raw materials or foods **are processed**, they are prepared in factories before they are used or sold. ❏ *...fish which are processed by the best methods: from freezing to canning and smoking.* ❏ *The material will be processed into plastic pellets.* • N-COUNT **Process** is also a noun. ❏ *...the cost of reengineering the production process.* • **pro|cess|ing** N-UNCOUNT [usu with supp] ❏ *America sent cotton to England for processing.* **4** V-T When people **process** information, they put it through a system or into a computer in order to deal with it. ❏ *facilities to process the data, and the right to publish the results.* • **pro|cess|ing** N-UNCOUNT ❏ *...data processing.* **5** → see also **word processing** **6** V-T [usu passive] When people **are processed** by officials, their case is dealt with in stages and they pass from one stage of the process to the next. ❏ *Patients took more than two hours to be processed through the department.* **7** PHRASE If you are **in the process of** doing something, you have started to do it and are still doing it. ☐ *The administration is in the process of drawing up a peace plan.* ◧ PHRASE If you are doing something and you do something else **in the process**, you do the second thing as part of doing the first thing. ☐ *You have to let us struggle for ourselves, even if we must die in the process.*

SYNONYMS

process
NOUN ◧
procedure: *A biopsy is usually a minor, surgical procedure.*
system: *The present system of funding for higher education is unsatisfactory.*
routine: *He checked up on you as a matter of routine.*

---

pro|cessed cheese (processed cheeses) N-MASS **Processed cheese** is cheese that has been specially made so that it can be sold and stored in large quantities. It is sometimes sold in the form of single wrapped slices.

pro|ces|sion /prəsɛʃ³n/ (processions) N-COUNT A **procession** is a group of people who are walking, riding, or driving in a line as part of a public event. ☐ *...a funeral procession.*

pro|ces|sion|al /prəsɛʃən³l/ ADJ [ADJ n] **Processional** means used for or taking part in a ceremonial procession. ☐ *...the processional route.*

pro|ces|sor /prɒsɛsər/ (processors) ◧ N-COUNT A **processor** is the part of a computer that interprets commands and performs the processes the user has requested. [COMPUTING] ◨ → see also **food processor, word processor** ◩ N-COUNT A **processor** is someone or something which carries out a process. ☐ *The frozen-food industry could be supplied entirely by growers and processors outside the country.*

pro-choice also **prochoice** ADJ Someone who is **pro-choice** thinks that women have a right to choose whether or not to continue their pregnancy and give birth or to have an abortion if they do not want the child. ☐ *...the pro-choice movement.* ☐ *Most of the electorate is pro-choice.*

pro|claim /proʊkleɪm/ (proclaims, proclaiming, proclaimed) ◧ V-T If people **proclaim** something, they formally make it known to the public. ☐ *The new government in Venezuela set up its own army and proclaimed its independence.* ☐ *Britain proudly proclaims that it is a nation of animal lovers.* ◨ V-T If you **proclaim** something, you state it in an emphatic way. ☐ *"I think we have been heard today," he proclaimed.*

proc|la|ma|tion /prɒkləmeɪʃ³n/ (proclamations) N-COUNT A **proclamation** is a public announcement about something important, often about something of national importance. ☐ *The proclamation of independence was broadcast over the radio.*

pro|cliv|ity /proʊklɪvɪti/ (proclivities) N-COUNT A **proclivity** is a tendency to behave in a particular way or to like a particular thing, often a bad way or thing. ☐ *He was indulging his own sexual proclivities.* ☐ *...a proclivity to daydream.*

pro|cras|ti|nate /proʊkræstɪneɪt/ (procrastinates, procrastinating, procrastinated) V-I If you **procrastinate**, you keep leaving things you should do until later, often because you do not want to do them. [FORMAL] ☐ *Most often we procrastinate when faced with something we do not want to do.* • **pro|cras|ti|na|tion** /proʊkræstɪneɪʃ³n, prə-/ N-UNCOUNT ☐ *He hates delay and procrastination in all its forms.*

pro|cre|ate /proʊkrieɪt/ (procreates, procreating, procreated) V-I When animals or people **procreate**, they produce young or babies. [FORMAL] ☐ *Many people feel a biological need to procreate.* • **pro|crea|tion** /proʊkrieɪʃ³n/ N-UNCOUNT ☐ *Early marriage and procreation are no longer discouraged there.*

procu|ra|tor /prɒkyʊreɪtər/ (procurators) N-COUNT A **procurator** is an administrative official with legal powers, especially in the former Soviet Union, the Roman Catholic Church, or the ancient Roman Empire.

pro|cure /prəkyʊər/ (procures, procuring, procured) V-T If you **procure** something, especially something that is difficult to get, you obtain it. [FORMAL] ☐ *It remained very difficult to procure food, fuel, and other daily necessities.*

pro|cure|ment /prəkyʊərmənt/ N-UNCOUNT **Procurement** is the act of obtaining something such as supplies for an army or other organization. [FORMAL] ☐ *Russia was cutting procurement of new weapons "by about 80 percent," he said.*

prod /prɒd/ (prods, prodding, prodded) ◧ V-T If you **prod** someone or something, you give them a quick push with your finger or with a pointed object. ☐ *He prodded Murray with the shotgun.* ☐ *Prod the windowsills to check for signs of rot.* • N-COUNT **Prod** is also a noun. ☐ *He gave the donkey a mighty prod in the backside.* ◨ V-T If you **prod** someone **into** doing something, you remind or persuade them to do it. ☐ *The question is intended to prod students into examining the concept of freedom.*

prodi|gal /prɒdɪg³l/ (prodigals) ◧ ADJ [usu ADJ n] You can describe someone as a **prodigal** son or daughter if they leave their family or friends, often after a period of behaving badly, and then return at a later time as a better person. [LITERARY] • N-COUNT **Prodigal** is also a noun. ☐ *The prodigal had returned.* ◨ ADJ [usu ADJ n] Someone who behaves in a **prodigal** way spends a lot of money carelessly without thinking about what will happen when they have none left. ☐ *Prodigal habits die hard.*

pro|di|gious /prədɪdʒəs/ ADJ Something that is **prodigious** is very large or impressive. [LITERARY] ☐ *This business generates cash in prodigious amounts.* • **pro|di|gious|ly** ADV ☐ *She ate prodigiously.*

prodi|gy /prɒdɪdʒi/ (prodigies) N-COUNT A **prodigy** is someone young who has a great natural ability for something such as music, mathematics, or sports. ☐ *The Russian tennis prodigy is well on the way to becoming the youngest world champion of all time.*

pro|duce ♦♦♦ (produces, producing, produced)

> The verb is pronounced /prədu͟ːs/. The noun is pronounced /prɒdu͟ːs/ or /proʊdu͟ːs/.

◧ V-T To **produce** something means to cause it to happen. ☐ *The drug is known to produce side-effects in women.* ◨ V-T If you **produce** something, you make or create it. ☐ *The company produced circuitry for communications systems.* ◩ V-T When things or people **produce** something, it comes from them or slowly forms from them, especially as the result of a biological or chemical process. ☐ *These plants are then pollinated and allowed to mature and produce seed.* ◪ V-T If you **produce** evidence or an argument, you show it or explain it to people in order to make them agree with you. ☐ *They challenged him to produce evidence to support his allegations.* ◫ V-T If you **produce** an object from somewhere, you show it or bring it out so that it can be seen. ☐ *To rent a car you must produce a passport and a current driver's license.* ◬ V-T If someone **produces** something such as a movie, a magazine, or a CD, they organize it and decide how it should be done. ☐ *He has produced his own sports magazine.* ◭ N-UNCOUNT **Produce** is fruit and vegetables that are grown in large quantities to be sold. ☐ *We manage to get most of our produce in farmers' markets.* ◮ → See feature box at **farming**

COLLOCATIONS

produce
NOUN ◭
noun + **produce:** farm, garden
adjective + **produce:** agricultural, dairy; fresh, local, organic, seasonal
verb + **produce:** buy, grow, import, sell

SYNONYMS

produce
VERB
◧
cause: *Attempts to limit family size among some minorities are likely to cause problems.*
lead to: *He warned yesterday that a pay raise for teachers would lead to job cuts.*
result in: *Fifty percent of car accidents result in head injuries.*
bring about: *The only way they can bring about political change is by putting pressure on the country.*
◨
make: *She made her own bread.*
create: *We set business free to create more jobs in Britain.*
manufacture: *They manufacture the class of plastics known as thermoplastic materials.*
build: *Workers at the plant build the F-16 jet fighter.*
construct: *The boxes should be constructed from rough-sawn timber.*

pro|duc|er /prədusər/ (**producers**) **1** N-COUNT A **producer** is a person whose job is to produce plays, movies, programs, or CDs. ❑ ...a freelance film producer. **2** N-COUNT A **producer** of a food or material is a company or country that grows or manufactures a large amount of it. ❑ ...Saudi Arabia, the world's leading oil producer.

SYNONYMS

producer
NOUN **2**
manufacturer: ...the world's largest doll manufacturer.
creator: I have always believed that a garden dies with its creator.
maker: ...Japan's two largest car makers.
builder: The builders have finished the roof.

prod|uct /prɒdʌkt/ (**products**) **1** N-COUNT A **product** is something that is produced and sold in large quantities, often as a result of a manufacturing process. ❑ Try to get the best product at the lowest price. **2** N-COUNT If you say that someone or something is a **product of** a situation or process, you mean that the situation or process has had a significant effect in making them what they are. ❑ We are all products of our time. **3** → See feature box at **farming**, **recycle**

COLLOCATIONS

product
NOUN **1**
noun + **product**: beauty, cleaning, consumer, dairy; savings
adjective + **product**: innovative, new; financial; finished
verb + **product**: develop, manufacture, sell; buy, use

SYNONYMS

product
NOUN **1**
goods: Money can be exchanged for goods or services.
produce: We manage to get most of our produce in Britain.
merchandise: There is a lot of merchandise associated with the movie.
commodity: The government increased prices on several basic commodities, like bread and meat.

pro|duc|tion /prədʌkʃən/ (**productions**) **1** N-UNCOUNT **Production** is the process of manufacturing or growing something in large quantities. ❑ That model won't go into production before late 2007. **2** N-UNCOUNT **Production** is the amount of goods manufactured or grown by a company or country. ❑ We needed to increase the volume of production. **3** N-UNCOUNT The **production of** something is its creation as the result of a natural process. ❑ These proteins stimulate the production of blood cells. **4** N-UNCOUNT **Production** is the process of organizing and preparing a play, movie, program, or CD, in order to present it to the public. ❑ She is head of the production company. **5** N-COUNT A **production** is a play, opera, or other show that is performed in a theater. ❑ ...a critically acclaimed production of Othello. **6** PHRASE When you can do something **on production of** or **on the production of** documents, you need to show someone those documents in order to be able to do that thing. ❑ Entry to the show is free to members on production of their membership cards. **7** → See feature box at **theater**

COLLOCATIONS

production
NOUN
1
noun + **production**: food, gas, oil
adjective + **production**: agricultural, domestic, industrial; full, mass
verb + **production**: encourage; cease, halt
2
verb + **production**: boost, increase, maintain; cut
5
noun + **production**: stage, theater
adjective + **production**: musical, theatrical; acclaimed, lavish
verb + **production**: direct

SYNONYMS

production
NOUN
1
manufacture: ...celebrating 90 years of car manufacture.
construction: ...companies who have long experience in the construction of those types of equipment.
assembly: For the rest of the day, he worked on the assembly of an explosive device.
2
output: Government statistics show the largest drop in industrial output for ten years.
yield: Polluted water lessens crop yields.
productivity: The third-quarter results reflect continued improvements in productivity.

pro|duc|tion line (**production lines**) N-COUNT A **production line** is an arrangement of machines in a factory where the products pass from machine to machine until they are finished. ❑ Honda added a production line this year, hoping to boost domestic sales.

pro|duc|tive /prədʌktɪv/ **1** ADJ Someone or something that is **productive** produces or does a lot for the amount of resources used. ❑ Training makes workers highly productive. ❑ More productive farmers have been able to provide cheaper food. **2** ADJ If you say that a relationship between people is **productive**, you mean that a lot of good or useful things happen as a result of it. ❑ He was hopeful that the next round of talks would also be productive.

prod|uc|tiv|ity /prɒdʌktɪvɪti/ N-UNCOUNT **Productivity** is the rate at which goods are produced. ❑ The third-quarter results reflect continued improvements in productivity.

prod|uct line (**product lines**) N-COUNT A **product line** is a group of related products produced by one manufacturer, for example, products that are intended to be used for similar purposes or to be sold in similar types of stores. [BUSINESS] ❑ ...the company's most successful product lines.

prod|uct place|ment (**product placements**) N-VAR **Product placement** is a form of advertising in which a company has its product placed where it can be clearly seen during a movie or television program. [BUSINESS] ❑ It was the first movie to feature onscreen product placement for its own merchandise.

Prof. /prɒf/ (**Profs**) also **prof. 1** N-TITLE **Prof.** is a written abbreviation for **Professor**. ❑ ...Prof. Irving Fisher of Yale University. **2** N-COUNT People sometimes refer to a professor as a **prof**. [INFORMAL] ❑ Write a note to my prof and tell him why I missed an exam this morning.

pro|fane /prəfeɪn, proʊ-/ (**profanes, profaning, profaned**) **1** ADJ **Profane** behavior shows disrespect for a religion or religious things. [FORMAL] ❑ ...profane language. **2** ADJ Something that is **profane** is concerned with everyday life rather than religion and spiritual things. ❑ The cardinal said that churches should not be used for profane or secular purposes. **3** V-T If someone **profanes** a religious belief or institution, they treat it with disrespect. [FORMAL] ❑ They have profaned the long upheld traditions of the church.

pro|fan|ity /prəfænɪti, proʊ-/ (**profanities**) **1** N-UNCOUNT **Profanity** is an act that shows disrespect for a religion or religious beliefs. [FORMAL] ❑ To desecrate a holy spring is considered profanity. **2** N-COUNT [usu pl] **Profanities** are swear words. [FORMAL]

pro|fess /prəfɛs/ (**professes, professing, professed**) **1** V-T If you **profess** to do or have something, you claim that you do it or have it, often when you do not. [FORMAL] ❑ She professed to hate her nickname. ❑ Why do organizations profess that they care? **2** V-T If you **profess** a feeling, opinion, or belief, you express it. [FORMAL] ❑ He professed to be content with the arrangement. ❑ Miller professed himself dissatisfied with Broadway theater.

pro|fes|sion /prəfɛʃən/ (**professions**) **1** N-COUNT [also by N] A **profession** is a type of job that requires advanced education or training. ❑ Harper was a teacher by profession. **2** N-COUNT-COLL You can use **profession** to refer to all the people who have the same profession. ❑ The attitude of the medical profession is very much more liberal now. **3** → See feature box at **work**

pro|fes|sion|al /prəfɛʃən°l/ (professionals) **1** ADJ [ADJ n] **Professional** means relating to a person's work, especially work that requires special training. ◻ *His professional career started at Colgate University.* • **pro|fes|sion|al|ly** ADV ◻ *...a professionally-qualified architect.* **2** ADJ [ADJ n] **Professional** people have jobs that require advanced education or training. ◻ *...highly qualified professional people like doctors and engineers.* • N-COUNT **Professional** is also a noun. ◻ *My father wanted me to become a professional and have more stability.* **3** ADJ You use **professional** to describe people who do a particular thing to earn money rather than as a hobby. ◻ *This has been my worst time for injuries since I started as a professional player.* • N-COUNT **Professional** is also a noun. ◻ *He had been a professional since March 1985.* • **pro|fes|sion|al|ly** ADV [ADV after v] ◻ *By age 16 he was playing professionally with bands in Greenwich Village.* **4** ADJ [ADJ n] **Professional** sports are played for money rather than as a hobby. ◻ *...an art student who had played professional football for a short time.* **5** ADJ If you say something that someone does or produces is **professional**, you approve of it because you think that it is of a very high standard. [APPROVAL] ◻ *They run it with a truly professional but personal touch.* • N-COUNT **Professional** is also a noun. ◻ *...a dedicated professional who worked harmoniously with the cast and crew.* • **pro|fes|sion|al|ly** ADV [ADV with v] ◻ *These tickets have been produced very professionally.*

SYNONYMS

professional
ADJ **2**
qualified: *Demand has far outstripped supply of qualified teachers.*
skilled: *New industries demanded skilled labor not available locally.*
white-collar: *White-collar workers now work longer hours.*

---

pro|fes|sion|al foul (professional fouls) N-COUNT In soccer, if a player commits a **professional foul**, they deliberately do something against the rules in order to prevent another player from scoring a goal.

pro|fes|sion|al|ism /prəfɛʃən°lɪzəm/ N-UNCOUNT **Professionalism** in a job is a combination of skill and high standards. [APPROVAL] ◻ *American companies pride themselves on their professionalism.*

pro|fes|sion|al|ize /prəfɛʃən°laɪz/ (professionalizes, professionalizing, professionalized)

in BRIT, also use **professionalise**

V-T To **professionalize** an organization, an institution, or an activity means to make it more professional, for example, by paying the people who are involved in it. ◻ *Foster parents will be paid salaries to professionalize their role.* • **pro|fes|sion|ali|za|tion** /prəfɛʃən°lɪzeɪʃ°n/ N-UNCOUNT [oft N of n] ◻ *The professionalization of politics is a major source of our ills.*

pro|fes|sor /prəfɛsər/ (professors) **1** N-COUNT; N-TITLE; N-VOC A **professor** in an American or Canadian university or college is a teacher of the highest rank. ◻ *...a professor of economics at George Washington University.* **2** N-TITLE; N-COUNT; N-VOC A **professor** in a British university is the most senior teacher in a department who has been appointed to the position due to their academic achievements. ◻ *...Professor Cameron.*

pro|fes|so|rial /prɒfɪsɔːriəl/ **1** ADJ If you describe someone as **professorial**, you mean that they look or behave like a professor. ◻ *His manner is not so much regal as professorial.* ◻ *I raised my voice to a professorial tone.* **2** ADJ [ADJ n] **Professorial** means relating to the work of a professor. ◻ *He went on to earn a prominent professorial position.*

pro|fes|sor|ship /prəfɛsərʃɪp/ (professorships) N-COUNT A **professorship** is the post of professor in a university or college. ◻ *He has accepted a research professorship at Stanford University.*

prof|fer /prɒfər/ (proffers, proffering, proffered) **1** V-T If you **proffer** something to someone, you hold it toward them so that they can take it or touch it. [FORMAL] ◻ *He rose and proffered a silver box full of cigarettes.* **2** V-T If you **proffer** something such as advice to someone, you offer it to them. [FORMAL] ◻ *The army has not yet proffered an explanation of how and why the accident happened.*

pro|fi|cien|cy /prəfɪʃ°nsi/ N-UNCOUNT If you show **proficiency** in something, you show ability or skill at it. ◻ *Evidence of basic proficiency in English is part of the admissions requirement.*

pro|fi|cient /prəfɪʃ°nt/ ADJ If you are **proficient** in something, you can do it well. ◻ *A great number of Egyptians are proficient in foreign languages.*

pro|file /proʊfaɪl/ (profiles) **1** N-COUNT Your **profile** is the outline of your face as it is seen when someone is looking at you from the side. ◻ *His handsome profile was turned away from us.* **2** N-UNCOUNT If you see someone **in profile**, you see them from the side. ◻ *This picture shows the girl in profile.* **3** N-COUNT A **profile** of someone is a short article or program in which their life and character are described. ◻ *A Washington newspaper published comparative profiles of the candidates.* **4** N-COUNT [oft N of n] If the police make a **profile** of someone they are looking for, they write a description of the sort of person they are looking for. ◻ *...the FBI profile of the anthrax killer.* • **pro|fil|ing** /proʊfaɪlɪŋ/ N-UNCOUNT [usu with supp] ◻ *...a former FBI agent who pioneered psychological profiling in the 1970s.* ◻ *DNA profiling would now be added to the struggle against vandalism.* **5** PHRASE If someone has a **high profile**, people notice them and what they do. If you keep a **low profile**, you avoid doing things that will make people notice you. ◻ *...a move that would give Egypt a much higher profile in the upcoming peace talks.* **6** → see also **high-profile**

SYNONYMS

profile
NOUN **1**
outline: *He could see only the hazy outline of the goalposts.*
form: *...the form of the body.*
silhouette: *The dark silhouette of the castle ruins stood out boldly against the fading light.*

---

prof|it /prɒfɪt/ (profits, profiting, profited) **1** N-VAR A **profit** is an amount of money that you gain when you are paid more for something than it cost you to make, get, or do it. ◻ *The bank made pre-tax profits of $6.5 million.* ◻ *You can improve your chances of profit by sensible planning.* **2** V-I If you **profit** from something, you earn a profit from it. ◻ *No one was profiting inordinately from the war effort.* ◻ *He has profited by selling his holdings to other investors.* **3** V-T/V-I If you **profit** from something, or it **profits** you, you gain some advantage or benefit from it. [FORMAL] ◻ *Jennifer wasn't yet totally convinced that she'd profit from a more relaxed lifestyle.* ◻ *So far the French alliance had profited the rebels little.* **4** → See feature box at **business**

prof|it|able /prɒfɪtəb°l/ **1** ADJ A **profitable** organization or practice makes a profit. ◻ *Drug manufacturing is the most profitable business in the U.S.* • **prof|it|ably** /prɒfɪtəbli/ ADV [ADV with v] ◻ *The 28 French stores are trading profitably.* • **prof|it|abil|ity** /prɒfɪtəbɪlɪti/ N-UNCOUNT ◻ *Changes were made in operating methods in an effort to increase profitability.* **2** ADJ Something that is **profitable** results in some benefit for you. ◻ *...close collaboration with industry which leads to a profitable exchange of personnel and ideas.* • **prof|it|ably** ADV [ADV with v] ◻ *In fact he could scarcely have spent his time more profitably.*

prof|it|eer /prɒfɪtɪər/ (profiteers) N-COUNT [usu pl] If you describe someone as a **profiteer**, you are critical of them because they make large profits by charging high prices for goods that are hard to get. [DISAPPROVAL] ◻ *...a new social class composed largely of war profiteers and gangsters.*

prof|it|eer|ing /prɒfɪtɪərɪŋ/ N-UNCOUNT **Profiteering** involves making large profits by charging high prices for goods that are hard to get. [BUSINESS, DISAPPROVAL] ◻ *There's been a wave of profiteering and corruption.*

profit-making **1** ADJ A **profit-making** business or organization makes a profit. [BUSINESS] ◻ *He wants to set up a profit-making company, owned mostly by the university.* **2** → see also **nonprofit**

prof|it mar|gin (profit margins) **1** N-COUNT A **profit margin** is the difference between the selling price of a product and the cost of producing and marketing it. [BUSINESS] ◻ *The group had a net profit margin of 30% last year.* **2** → See feature box at **business**

profit-sharing N-UNCOUNT **Profit-sharing** is a system by which all the people who work in a company have a share in its profits. [BUSINESS] ◻ *...the bank's profit-sharing plan.*

profit-taking N-UNCOUNT **Profit-taking** is the selling of stocks and shares at a profit after their value has risen or just

profligacy /prɒflɪɡəsi/ N-UNCOUNT **Profligacy** is the spending of too much money or the using of too much of something. [FORMAL] ❑ ...the continuing profligacy of certain states.

profligate /prɒflɪɡɪt/ ADJ Someone who is **profligate** spends too much money or uses too much of something. [FORMAL] ❑ ...the most profligate consumer of energy in the world.

pro forma /proʊ fɔːmə/ ADJ [usu ADJ n] In banking, a company's **pro forma** balance or earnings are their expected balance or earnings. [BUSINESS]

profound /prəfaʊnd/ (profounder, profoundest) **1** ADJ You use **profound** to emphasize that something is very great or intense. [EMPHASIS] ❑ ...discoveries which had a profound effect on many areas of medicine. ❑ ...profound disagreement. • **profoundly** ADV ❑ This has profoundly affected my life. **2** ADJ A **profound** idea, work, or person shows great intellectual depth and understanding. ❑ This is a book full of profound, original, and challenging insights.

profundity /prəfʌndɪti/ (profundities) **1** N-UNCOUNT **Profundity** is great intellectual depth and understanding. ❑ The profundity of this book is achieved with breathtaking lightness. **2** N-UNCOUNT [usu N of n] If you refer to the **profundity** of a feeling, experience, or change, you mean that it is deep, powerful, or serious. ❑ ...the profundity of the structural problems besetting the country. **3** N-COUNT A **profundity** is a remark that shows great intellectual depth and understanding. ❑ His work is full of profundities and asides concerning the human condition.

profuse /prəfjuːs/ **1** ADJ **Profuse** sweating, bleeding, or vomiting is sweating, bleeding, or vomiting large amounts. ❑ ...a remedy that produces profuse sweating. • **profusely** ADV [ADV after v] ❑ He was bleeding profusely. **2** ADJ If you offer **profuse** apologies or thanks, you apologize or thank someone a lot. ❑ Then the police officer recognized me, breaking into profuse apologies. • **profusely** ADV [ADV after v] ❑ They were very grateful and thanked me profusely.

profusion /prəfjuːʒ°n/ N-SING-COLL If there is a **profusion** of something or if it occurs **in profusion**, there is a very large quantity or variety of it. [FORMAL] ❑ ...a delightful river with a profusion of wild flowers along its banks.

progenitor /proʊdʒɛnɪtər/ (progenitors) **1** N-COUNT [usu with poss] A **progenitor** of someone is a direct ancestor of theirs. [FORMAL] ❑ He was also a progenitor of seven presidents of Nicaragua. **2** N-COUNT [usu with poss] The **progenitor** of an idea or invention is the person who first thought of it. [FORMAL] ❑ ...Clive Sinclair, the progenitor of the C5 electric car.

progeny /prɒdʒəni/ N-PLURAL [usu with poss] You can refer to a person's children or to an animal's young as their **progeny**. [FORMAL] ❑ ...the freed slaves and their progeny.

progesterone /proʊdʒɛstəroʊn/ N-UNCOUNT **Progesterone** is a hormone that is produced in the ovaries of women and female animals and helps prepare the body for pregnancy. ❑ The drugs block the action of progesterone.

prognosis /prɒɡnoʊsɪs/ (prognoses /prɒɡnoʊsiːz/) N-COUNT A **prognosis** is an estimate of the future of someone or something, especially about whether a patient will recover from an illness. [FORMAL] ❑ The doctor's prognosis was that Laurence might walk within 12 months.

prognostication /prɒɡnɒstɪkeɪʃ°n/ (prognostications) N-VAR A **prognostication** is a statement about what you think will happen in the future. [FORMAL] ❑ The country is currently obsessed with gloomy prognostications about its future.

program ✦✦◇ /proʊɡræm, -ɡrəm/ (programs, programming, programmed)

in BRIT, use **programme**

1 N-COUNT A **program** of actions or events is a series of actions or events that are planned to be done. ❑ The nation's largest training and education program for adults. **2** N-COUNT A television or radio **program** is something that is broadcast on television or radio. ❑ ...a network television program. **3** N-COUNT A theater or concert **program** is a small book or sheet of paper that gives information about the play or concert you are attending. ❑ When you go to concerts, it's helpful to read the program. **4** V-T When you **program** a machine or system, you set its controls so that it will work in a particular way. ❑ Parents can program the machine not to turn on at certain times. **5** N-COUNT A **program** is a set of instructions that a computer follows in order to perform a particular task. [COMPUTING] ❑ The chances of an error occurring in a computer program increase with the size of the program. **6** V-T When you **program** a computer, you give it a set of instructions to make it able to perform a particular task. [COMPUTING] ❑ He programmed his computer to compare the 1,431 possible combinations of pairs in this population. ❑ ...45 million people, about half of whom can program their own computers. • **programming** N-UNCOUNT ❑ ...programming skills.

programmable /proʊɡræməb°l, proʊɡræm-/ ADJ A **programmable** machine can be programmed, so that, for example, it will switch on and off automatically or do things in a particular order. ❑ Most CD-players are programmable.

programmatic /proʊɡrəmætɪk/ ADJ **Programmatic** ideas or policies follow a particular program. ❑ He gave up on programmatic politics and turned his back on public life.

programme /proʊɡræm/ [mainly BRIT] → see **program**

programmer /proʊɡræmər/ (programmers) N-COUNT A computer **programmer** is a person whose job involves writing programs for computers. [COMPUTING]

program note (program notes) N-COUNT A **program note** is an article written in a program for a concert that gives information about the composer, performance or production.

progress ✦✦◇ (progresses, progressing, progressed)

The noun is pronounced /prɒɡrɛs/. The verb is pronounced /prəɡrɛs/.

1 N-UNCOUNT **Progress** is the process of gradually improving or getting nearer to achieving or completing something. ❑ The medical community continues to make progress in the fight against cancer. **2** N-SING The **progress** of a situation or action is the way in which it develops. ❑ The president is reported to have been delighted with the progress of the first day's talks. **3** V-I To **progress** means to move over a period of time to a stronger, more advanced, or more desirable state. ❑ He will visit once every two weeks to see how his new employees are progressing. **4** V-I If events **progress**, they continue to happen gradually over a period of time. ❑ As the evening progressed, sadness turned to rage. **5** V-T If you **progress** something, you cause it to develop. [BRIT, FORMAL] **6** PHRASE If something is **in progress**, it has started and is still continuing. ❑ The game was already in progress when we took our seats.

COLLOCATIONS

progress
NOUN
1
adjective + **progress**: good, real, significant, steady; rapid, slow, swift; technological
verb + **progress**: achieve, make
2
verb + **progress**: assess, follow, monitor, review
VERB **4**
noun + **progress**: day, evening; game, season, war, work

---

progression /prəɡrɛʃ°n/ (progressions) N-COUNT A **progression** is a gradual development from one state to another. ❑ Both drugs slow the progression of HIV, but neither cures the disease.

progressive /prəɡrɛsɪv/ (progressives) **1** ADJ Someone who is **progressive** or has **progressive** ideas has modern ideas about how things should be done, rather than traditional ones. ❑ ...a progressive businessman who had voted for Roosevelt in 1932 and 1936. ❑ Willan was able to introduce the progressive changes he had already introduced. • N-COUNT A **progressive** is someone who is progressive. ❑ The Republicans were deeply split between progressives and conservatives. **2** ADJ A **progressive** change happens gradually over a period of time. ❑ One prominent symptom of the disease is progressive loss of memory. • **progressively** ADV ❑ Her symptoms became progressively worse.

prohibit /proʊhɪbɪt/ (prohibits, prohibiting, prohibited) V-T If a law or someone in authority **prohibits** something, they forbid it or make it illegal. [FORMAL] ❑ ...a law that prohibits tobacco advertising in newspapers and magazines. ❑ Fishing is *prohibited.* • **pro|hi|bi|tion** N-UNCOUNT ❏ *...a prohibition of the use of internet connections for personal purposes.*

pro|hi|bi|tion /proʊɪbɪʃ³n/ **(prohibitions)** **1** N-COUNT A **prohibition** is a law or rule forbidding something. ❏ *...a prohibition on discrimination.* **2** → see also **prohibit**

Pro|hi|bi|tion N-UNCOUNT **Prohibition** was the law that prevented the manufacture, sale, and transporting of alcoholic drinks in the United States between 1919 and 1933. **Prohibition** also refers to the period when this law existed.

pro|hibi|tive /proʊhɪbɪtɪv/ ADJ If the cost of something is **prohibitive**, it is so high that many people cannot afford it. [FORMAL] ❏ *The cost of private treatment can be prohibitive.* • **pro|hibi|tive|ly** ADV [ADV adj] ❏ *Meat and butter were prohibitively expensive.*

proj|ect ✦✦◇ **(projects, projecting, projected)**

The noun is pronounced /prɒdʒɛkt/. The verb is pronounced /prədʒɛkt/.

1 N-COUNT A **project** is a task that requires a lot of time and effort. ❏ *Money will also go into local development projects in Vietnam.* ❏ *...an international science project.* **2** N-COUNT A **project** is a detailed study of a subject by a student. ❏ *Students complete projects for a personal tutor, working at home at their own pace.* **3** V-T If something **is projected**, it is planned or expected. ❏ *13% of Americans are over 65; this number is projected to reach 22% by the year 2030.* ❏ *The government had been projecting a 5% consumer price increase for the year.* **4** V-T If you **project** someone or something in a particular way, you try to make people see them in that way. If you **project** a particular feeling or quality, you show it in your behavior. ❏ *Bradley projects a natural warmth and sincerity.* ❏ *He just hasn't been able to project himself as the strong leader.* **5** V-T If you **project** a film or picture onto a screen or wall, you make it appear there. ❏ *The team tried projecting the maps with two different projectors onto the same screen.* **6** V-I If something **projects**, it sticks out above or beyond a surface or edge. [FORMAL] ❏ *...a narrow ledge that projected out from the bank of the river.* **7** → See feature box at **population**

─── SYNONYMS ───

project
NOUN **1**
task: *She used the day to catch up with administrative tasks.*
scheme: *...schemes to help combat unemployment.*
plan: *...a detailed plan of action for restructuring the group.*
venture: *...his latest writing venture.*

pro|jec|tile /prədʒɛkt³l, -taɪl/ **(projectiles)** N-COUNT A **projectile** is an object that is fired from a gun or other weapon. [FORMAL]

pro|jec|tion /prədʒɛkʃ³n/ **(projections)** **1** N-COUNT A **projection** is an estimate of a future amount. ❏ *...the company's projection of 11 million visitors for the first year.* **2** N-UNCOUNT The **projection** of a film or picture is the act of projecting it onto a screen or wall. ❏ *They took me into a projection room to see a picture.*

pro|jec|tion|ist /prədʒɛkʃ³nɪst/ **(projectionists)** N-COUNT A **projectionist** is someone whose job is to work a projector at a movie theater.

proj|ect man|ag|er (project managers) N-COUNT A **project manager** is someone who organizes and oversees the work of all the people involved in a project. ❏ *She works as a project manager for an insurance company.*

pro|jec|tor /prədʒɛktər/ **(projectors)** **1** N-COUNT A **projector** is a machine that projects films or slides onto a screen or wall. ❏ *...a slide projector.* **2** → see also **overhead projector**

pro|lapse /proʊlæps/ **(prolapses, prolapsing, prolapsed)**

The verb is also pronounced /prəlæps/.

1 N-VAR A **prolapse** is when one of the organs in the body moves down from its normal position. [MEDICAL] **2** V-I If an organ in someone's body **prolapses**, it moves down from its normal position. [MEDICAL] ❏ *Sometimes the original abortion was done so badly that the uterus prolapsed.*

pro|letar|ian /proʊlɪtɛəriən/ **(proletarians)** **1** ADJ **Proletarian** means relating to the proletariat. ❏ *...a proletarian revolution.* **2** N-COUNT A **proletarian** is a member of the proletariat.

pro|letari|at /proʊlɪtɛəriət/ N-SING-COLL [*the* N] **The proletariat** refers to workers without high status, especially industrial workers. ❏ *...a struggle between the bourgeoisie and the proletariat.*

pro-life ADJ [usu ADJ n] Someone who is **pro-life** thinks that women do not have a right to choose whether or not to continue their pregnancy and give birth to a child and that abortion is wrong in most or all circumstances. ❏ *...the pro-life movement.*

pro|lif|er|ate /prəlɪfəreɪt/ **(proliferates, proliferating, proliferated)** V-I If things **proliferate**, they increase in number very quickly. [FORMAL] ❏ *Computerized databases are proliferating fast.* • **pro|lif|era|tion** /prəlɪfəreɪʃ³n/ N-UNCOUNT ❏ *...the proliferation of nuclear weapons.*

pro|lif|ic /prəlɪfɪk/ **1** ADJ A **prolific** writer, artist, or composer produces a large number of works. ❏ *She is a prolific writer of novels and short stories.* **2** ADJ An animal, person, or plant that is **prolific** produces a large number of babies, young plants, or fruit. ❏ *They are prolific breeders, with many hens laying up to six eggs.*

pro|logue /proʊlɒɡ/ **(prologues)** also **prolog** N-COUNT A **prologue** is a speech or section of text that introduces a play or book. ❏ *The prologue to the novel is written in the form of a newspaper account.*

pro|long /prəlɒŋ/ **(prolongs, prolonging, prolonged)** V-T To **prolong** something means to make it last longer. ❏ *Mr. Chesler said foreign military aid was prolonging the war.*

pro|longed /prəlɒŋd/ ADJ A **prolonged** event or situation continues for a long time, or for longer than expected. ❏ *...a prolonged period of low interest rates.*

prom /prɒm/ **(proms)** N-COUNT A **prom** is a formal dance at a school or college that is usually held at the end of the academic year. [AM] ❏ *I didn't want to go to the prom with Craig.*

prom|enade /prɒmənɛɪd, -nɑd/ **(promenades, promenading, promenaded)** **1** N-COUNT In a seaside town, the **promenade** is the road by the sea where people go for a walk. **2** N-COUNT A **promenade** is an area that is used for walking, for example, a wide road or a deck on a ship. [mainly AM] **3** N-COUNT A **promenade** is a formal dance. [AM]

promi|nence /prɒmɪnəns/ N-UNCOUNT If someone or something is in a position of **prominence**, they are well-known and important. ❏ *He came to prominence during the World Cup.* ❏ *Crime prevention had to be given more prominence.*

promi|nent ✦◇◇ /prɒmɪnənt/ **1** ADJ Someone who is **prominent** is important and well-known. ❏ *...the children of very prominent or successful parents.* **2** ADJ Something that is **prominent** is very noticeable or is an important part of something else. ❏ *Here the window plays a prominent part in the design.* • **promi|nent|ly** ADV [ADV with v] ❏ *Trade will figure prominently in the second day of talks in Washington.*

─── SYNONYMS ───

prominent
ADJ **1**
famous: *...England's most famous landscape artist, John Constable.*
leading: *...a leading member of Bristol's Sikh community.*
top: *So you want to be a top model.*

pro|mis|cu|ous /prəmɪskyuəs/ ADJ Someone who is **promiscuous** has sex with many different people. [DISAPPROVAL] ❏ *She is perceived as vain, spoiled, and promiscuous.* • **promis|cu|ity** /prɒmɪskyuɪti/ N-UNCOUNT ❏ *He has recently urged more tolerance of sexual promiscuity.*

prom|ise ✦✦◇ /prɒmɪs/ **(promises, promising, promised)** **1** V-T/V-I If you **promise** that you will do something, you say to someone that you will definitely do it. ❏ *The post office has promised to resume first class mail delivery to the area on Friday.* ❏ *He had promised that the rich and privileged would no longer get preferential treatment.* ❏ *Promise me you will not waste your time.* ❏ *I'll call you back, I promise.* **2** V-T If you **promise** someone something, you tell them that you will definitely give it to them or make sure that they have it. ❏ *In 1920 the great powers promised them an independent state.* **3** N-COUNT A **promise** is a statement that you make to a person in which you say that you will definitely do something or give them something.

❑ *If you make a promise, you should keep it.* ◆ V-T If a situation or event **promises** to have a particular quality or to be a particular thing, it shows signs that it will have that quality or be that thing. ❑ *While it will be fun, the seminar also promises to be most instructive.* ◆ N-UNCOUNT If someone or something shows **promise**, they seem likely to be very good or successful. ❑ *The boy first showed promise as an athlete in grade school.*

COLLOCATIONS

promise
NOUN
◆
noun + **promise**: campaign, election, manifesto
adjective + **promise**: broken, empty, false, vague
verb + **promise**: fulfill, honor, keep; break
◆
adjective + **promise**: early, great
verb + **promise**: show
VERB ◆
promise + noun: aid, help, support; action, change; investigation, review

---

prom|ised land (promised lands) N-COUNT [usu sing] If you refer to a place or a state as a **promised land**, you mean that people desire it and expect to find happiness or success there. ❑ *...the promised land of near-zero inflation.*

prom|is|ing /prɒmɪsɪŋ/ ADJ Someone or something that is **promising** seems likely to be very good or successful. ❑ *A school has honored one of its brightest and most promising former students.*

prom|is|ing|ly /prɒmɪsɪŋli/ ADV If something or someone starts **promisingly**, they begin well but often fail in the end. ❑ *The show starts promisingly enough.*

prom|is|sory note /prɒmɪsəri noʊt/ (promissory notes) N-COUNT A **promissory note** is a written, dated promise to pay a specific sum of money to a particular person. [mainly AM, BUSINESS] ❑ *...a $36.4 million, five-year promissory note.*

pro|mo /proʊmoʊ/ (promos) N-COUNT [oft N N] A **promo** is something such as a short video film that promotes a product. [INFORMAL, JOURNALISM] ❑ *He races his cars, and rents them out for film, TV, and promo videos.*

prom|on|tory /prɒməntɔri/ (promontories) N-COUNT A **promontory** is a cliff that stretches out into the sea.

pro|mote ◆◇ /prəmoʊt/ (promotes, promoting, promoted) ◆ V-T If people **promote** something, they help or encourage it to happen, increase, or spread. ❑ *You don't have to sacrifice environmental protection to promote economic growth.* • **pro|mo|tion** N-UNCOUNT ❑ *The government has pledged to give the promotion of democracy higher priority.* ◆ V-T If a firm **promotes** a product, it tries to increase the sales or popularity of that product. ❑ *...a tour to promote his second solo album.* ◆ V-T [usu passive] If someone **is promoted**, they are given a more important job or rank in the organization that they work for. ❑ *I was promoted to editor and then editorial director.*

SYNONYMS

promote
VERB
◆
encourage: *Slow music encourages supermarket shoppers to browse longer and spend more.*
support: *He pressed the party to support a total ban on imported coal.*
back: *The Prime Minister is backed by the civic movement, Public Against Violence.*
◆
advertise: *The players can advertise baked beans, but not rugby boots.*
publicize: *The author appeared on television to publicize her latest book.*
push: *Ministers will push the case for opening the plant.*

---

pro|mot|er /prəmoʊtər/ (promoters) ◆ N-COUNT A **promoter** is a person who helps organize and finance an event, especially a sports event. ❑ *...one of the top boxing promoters in Las Vegas.* ◆ N-COUNT The **promoter of** a cause or idea tries to make it become popular. ❑ *Aaron Copland was always the most energetic promoter of American music.*

pro|mo|tion ◆◇ /prəmoʊʃən/ (promotions) ◆ N-VAR If you are given **promotion** or **a promotion** in your job, you are given a more important job or rank in the organization that you work for. ❑ *Consider changing jobs or trying for promotion.* ◆ N-VAR A **promotion** is an attempt to make a product or event popular or successful, especially by advertising. [BUSINESS] ❑ *Advertising and promotion are what American business does best.* ◆ → see also **promote** ◆ → See feature box at **work**

pro|mo|tion|al /prəmoʊʃənəl/ ADJ **Promotional** material, events, or ideas are designed to increase the sales of a product or service. ❑ *"Jeans," according to one company's promotional material, "are designed and made to be worn hard."*

prompt ◆◇ /prɒmpt/ (prompts, prompting, prompted) ◆ V-T To **prompt** someone to do something means to make them decide to do it. ❑ *Japan's recession has prompted consumers to cut back on buying cars.* ◆ V-T If you **prompt** someone when they stop speaking, you encourage or help them to continue. If you **prompt** an actor, you tell them what their next line is when they have forgotten what comes next. ❑ *"You wouldn't have wanted to bring those people to justice anyway, would you?" Brand prompted him.* ◆ ADJ A **prompt** action is done without any delay. ❑ *It is not too late, but prompt action is needed.* ◆ ADJ [v-link ADJ] If you are **prompt** to do something, you do it without delay or you are not late. ❑ *You have been so prompt in carrying out all these commissions.*

SYNONYMS

prompt
VERB ◆
inspire: *These herbs will inspire you to try out all sorts of exotic-flavored dishes!*
stimulate: *I was stimulated to examine my deepest thoughts.*
spur: *His friend's plight had spurred him into taking part.*
provoke: *His election success has provoked a shocked reaction.*
ADJ ◆
immediate: *These tragic incidents have had an immediate effect.*
quick: *Officials played down any hope for a quick end to the bloodshed.*
rapid: *This signals a rapid change of heart by the government.*
swift: *The police were swift to act.*

---

prompt|ing /prɒmptɪŋ/ (promptings) N-UNCOUNT [also N in pl] If you respond to **prompting**, you do what someone encourages or reminds you to do. ❑ *The New York team needed little prompting from their coach Bill Parcells.*

prompt|ly /prɒmptli/ ◆ ADV [ADV with v] If you do something **promptly**, you do it immediately. ❑ *Sister Francesca entered the chapel, took her seat, and promptly fell asleep.* ◆ ADV If you do something **promptly** at a particular time, you do it at exactly that time. ❑ *Promptly at a quarter past seven, we left the hotel.*

prom|ul|gate /prɒməlgeɪt/ (promulgates, promulgating, promulgated) ◆ V-T If people **promulgate** a new law or a new idea, they make it widely known. [FORMAL] ❑ *The shipping industry promulgated a voluntary code.* ◆ V-T [usu passive] If a new law **is promulgated** by a government or national leader, it is publicly approved or made official. [FORMAL] ❑ *A new constitution was promulgated last month.* • **prom|ul|ga|tion** /prɒməlgeɪʃən/ N-UNCOUNT ❑ *...the promulgation of the constitution.*

prone /proʊn/ ◆ ADJ [v-link ADJ] To be **prone to** something, usually something bad, means to have a tendency to be affected by it or to do it. ❑ *For all her experience as a television reporter, she was still prone to camera nerves.* • COMB IN ADJ **-prone** combines with nouns to make adjectives that describe people who are frequently affected by something bad. ❑ *...the most injury-prone rider on the circuit.* ◆ ADJ [ADJ after v, ADJ n] If you are lying **prone**, you are lying on your front. [FORMAL] ❑ *Bob slid from his chair and lay prone on the floor.*

prong /prɒŋ/ (prongs) ◆ N-COUNT [usu pl] The **prongs** of something such as a fork are the long, thin pointed parts. ◆ N-COUNT The **prongs** of something such as a policy or plan are the separate parts of it. ❑ *The stockholder rights movement has two prongs.* ❑ *The second prong of the strategy is the provision of basic social services for the poor.*

-pronged /-prɒŋd/ COMB IN ADJ [ADJ n] A two-**pronged** or three-**pronged** attack, plan, or approach has two or three parts. ❑ ...*a two-pronged attack on the recession.*

pro|nomi|nal /proʊnɒmɪnəl/ ADJ **Pronominal** means relating to pronouns or like a pronoun. [TECHNICAL] ❑ ...*a pronominal use.*

pro|noun /proʊnaʊn/ (pronouns) N-COUNT A **pronoun** is a word that you use to refer to someone or something when you do not need to use a noun, often because the person or thing has been mentioned earlier. Examples are 'it,' 'she,' 'something,' and 'myself.'

pro|nounce /prənaʊns/ (pronounces, pronouncing, pronounced) **1** V-T To **pronounce** a word means to say it using particular sounds. ❑ *Have I pronounced your name correctly?* **2** V-T If you **pronounce** something to be true, you state that it is the case. [FORMAL] ❑ *A specialist has now pronounced him fully fit.*

pro|nounced /prənaʊnst/ ADJ Something that is **pronounced** is very noticeable. ❑ *Most of the art exhibitions have a pronounced Appalachian theme.*

pro|nounce|ment /prənaʊnsmənt/ (pronouncements) N-COUNT **Pronouncements** are public or official statements on an important subject. ❑ ...*the president's latest pronouncements about the protection of minorities.*

pron|to /prɒntoʊ/ ADV [ADV after v] If you say that something must be done **pronto**, you mean that it must be done quickly and at once. [INFORMAL] ❑ *Get down to the post office pronto!*

pro|nun|cia|tion /prənʌnsieɪʃən/ (pronunciations) N-VAR The **pronunciation** of a word or language is the way it is pronounced. ❑ *She gave the word its French pronunciation.*

proof ◆◇◇ /pruːf/ (proofs) **1** N-VAR **Proof** is a fact, argument, or piece of evidence showing that something is definitely true or definitely exists. ❑ *This is not necessarily proof that he is wrong.* ❑ *You have to have proof of residence in the state of Texas, such as a Texas ID card.* **2** ADJ [amount ADJ] **Proof** is used after a number of degrees or a percentage, when indicating the strength of a strong alcoholic drink such as whiskey. ❑ ...*a glass of Wild Turkey bourbon: 101 proof.*

-proof /-pruːf/ (-proofs, -proofing, -proofed) **1** COMB IN ADJ **-proof** combines with nouns and verbs to form adjectives indicating that something cannot be damaged or badly affected by the thing or action mentioned. ❑ ...*a bomb-proof aircraft.* ❑ *In a large microwave-proof dish, melt butter for 20 seconds.* **2** COMB IN VERB **-proof** combines with nouns to form verbs that refer to protecting something against being damaged or badly affected by the thing mentioned. ❑ *They recommended that the viaduct be replaced rather than quake-proofed.* **3** → see also **bulletproof, waterproof**

proof|read /pruːfriːd/ (proofreads, proofreading, proofread) V-T/V-I When someone **proofreads** something such as a book or an article, they read it before it is published in order to find and mark mistakes that need to be corrected. ❑ *I didn't even have the chance to proofread my own report.* • **proof|reader** /pruːfriːdər/ (proofreaders) N-COUNT ❑ ...*a proofreader on the Montreal Gazette.*

prop /prɒp/ (props, propping, propped) **1** V-T If you **prop** an object **on** or **against** something, you support it by putting something underneath it or by resting it somewhere. ❑ *He rocked back in the chair and propped his feet on the desk.* • PHRASAL VERB **Prop up** means the same as **prop**. ❑ *Sam slouched back and propped his elbows up on the bench behind him.* **2** N-COUNT A **prop** is a stick or other object that you use to support something. ❑ *Using the table as a prop, he dragged himself to his feet.* **3** N-COUNT To be a **prop** for a system, institution, or person means to be the main thing that keeps them strong or helps them survive. ❑ *The army is one of the main props of the government.* **4** N-COUNT The **props** in a play or movie are all the objects or pieces of furniture that are used in it. ❑ ...*the backdrop and props for a stage show.* **5** → See feature box at **theater**
▶ **prop up** **1** PHRASAL VERB To **prop up** something means to support it or help it to survive. ❑ *Investments in the U.S. money market have propped up the American dollar.* **2** → see **prop** 1

propa|gan|da /prɒpəgændə/ N-UNCOUNT **Propaganda** is information, often inaccurate information, that a political organization publishes or broadcasts in order to influence people. [DISAPPROVAL] ❑ *The party adopted an aggressive propaganda campaign against its rivals.*

propa|gan|dist /prɒpəgændɪst/ (propagandists) N-COUNT A **propagandist** is a person who tries to persuade people to support a particular idea or group, often by giving inaccurate information. [DISAPPROVAL] ❑ *He was also a brilliant propagandist for free trade.*

propa|gan|dize /prɒpəgændaɪz/ (propagandizes, propagandizing, propagandized)

in BRIT, also use **propagandise**

V-T/V-I If you say that a group of people **propagandize**, you think that they are dishonestly trying to persuade other people to share their views. [DISAPPROVAL] ❑ *You can propagandize just by calling attention to something.* ❑ ...*attempts to propagandize the public.*

propa|gate /prɒpəgeɪt/ (propagates, propagating, propagated) **1** V-T If people **propagate** an idea or piece of information, they spread it and try to make people believe it or support it. [FORMAL] ❑ *They propagated political doctrines that promised to tear apart the fabric of society.* • **propa|ga|tion** /prɒpəgeɪʃən/ N-UNCOUNT ❑ *The two governments could work together toward the propagation of these ideas.* **2** V-T If you **propagate** plants, you grow more of them from the original ones. [TECHNICAL] ❑ *The easiest way to propagate a vine is to take hardwood cuttings.*

pro|pane /proʊpeɪn/ N-UNCOUNT [oft N n] **Propane** is a gas that is used for cooking and heating. ❑ ...*a propane gas cylinder.*

pro|pel /prəpɛl/ (propels, propelling, propelled) V-T To **propel** something in a particular direction means to cause it to move in that direction. ❑ *The tiny rocket is attached to the spacecraft and is designed to propel it toward Mars.* • COMB IN ADJ **-propelled** combines with nouns to form adjectives that indicate how something, especially a weapon, is propelled. ❑ ...*rocket-propelled grenades.*

pro|pel|lant /prəpɛlənt/ (propellants) **1** N-MASS **Propellant** is a substance that causes something to move forward. ❑ ...*a propellant for nuclear rockets.* **2** N-MASS **Propellant** is a gas that is used in spray cans to force the contents out of the can when you press the button. ❑ *By 1978, the use of CFCs in aerosol propellants was banned.*

pro|pel|ler /prəpɛlər/ (propellers) **1** N-COUNT A **propeller** is a device with blades attached to a boat or aircraft. The engine makes the propeller spin around and causes the boat or aircraft to move. ❑ ...*a fixed three-bladed propeller.* **2** → See also color supplement

pro|pen|sity /prəpɛnsɪti/ (propensities) N-COUNT A **propensity** to do something or a **propensity** for something is a natural tendency to behave in a particular way. [FORMAL] ❑ *Mr. Bint has a propensity to put off decisions to the last minute.*

prop|er ◆◇◇ /prɒpər/ **1** ADJ [ADJ n] You use **proper** to describe things that you consider to be real and satisfactory rather than inadequate in some way. ❑ *Two out of five people lack a proper job.* **2** ADJ [ADJ n] The **proper** thing is the one that is correct or most suitable. ❑ *The Supreme Court will ensure that the proper procedures have been followed.* **3** ADJ If you say that a way of behaving is **proper**, you mean that it is considered socially acceptable and right. ❑ *In those days it was not thought entirely proper for a woman to be on the stage.* **4** ADJ [n ADJ] You can add **proper** after a word to indicate that you are referring to the central and most important part of a place, event, or object and want to distinguish it from other things that are not regarded as being important or central to it. ❑ *A distinction must be made between archaeology proper and science-based archaeology.*

prop|er|ly ◆◇◇ /prɒpərli/ **1** ADV If something is done **properly**, it is done in a correct and satisfactory way. ❑ *You're too thin. You're not eating properly.* **2** ADV [ADV after v] If someone behaves **properly**, they behave in a way that is considered acceptable and not rude. ❑ *He's a spoiled brat and it's about time he learned to behave properly.*

prop|er noun (proper nouns) N-COUNT A **proper noun** is the name of a particular person, place, organization, or thing. Proper nouns begin with a capital letter. Examples are 'Peggy,' 'Tucson,' and 'the United Nations.' Compare **common noun**.

prop|er|tied /prɒpərtid/ ADJ [usu ADJ n] **Propertied** people own land or property. [FORMAL] ❑ ...*the propertied classes.*

prop|er|ty /prɒpəti/ (**properties**) **1** N-UNCOUNT Someone's **property** is all the things that belong to them or something that belongs to them. [FORMAL] ▫ *A spokesman said that personal property and jewellery had been stolen.* **2** N-VAR A **property** is a building and the land belonging to it. [FORMAL] ▫ *Cecil inherited a family property near Stamford.* **3** N-COUNT The **properties** of a substance or object are the ways in which it behaves in particular conditions. ▫ *A radio signal has both electrical and magnetic properties.*

SYNONYMS

property
NOUN **1**
possessions: *She had stashed away her possessions.*
assets: *By the end of 2017, the group had assets of 3.5 billion pesos.*
belongings: *I collected my belongings and left.*

prop|er|ty tax (**property taxes**) N-VAR A **property tax** is a tax that you pay on property you own. [mainly AM] ▫ *We've got the highest property taxes in the United States.* ▫ *...the abolition of property tax.*

proph|ecy /prɒfɪsi/ (**prophecies**) N-VAR A **prophecy** is a statement in which someone says they strongly believe that a particular thing will happen. ▫ *Will the teacher's prophecy be fulfilled?*

proph|esy /prɒfɪsaɪ/ (**prophesies, prophesying, prophesied**) V-T If you **prophesy** that something will happen, you say that you strongly believe that it will happen. ▫ *He prophesied that within five years his opponent would either be dead or in prison.*

proph|et /prɒfɪt/ (**prophets**) N-COUNT A **prophet** is a person who is believed to be chosen by God to say the things that God wants to tell people. ▫ *...the sacred name of the Holy Prophet of Islam.*

pro|phet|ic /prəfetɪk/ ADJ If something was **prophetic**, it described or suggested something that did actually happen later. ▫ *This ominous warning soon proved prophetic.*

prophy|lac|tic /proʊfɪlæktɪk, prɒf-/ (**prophylactics**) **1** ADJ [usu ADJ n] **Prophylactic** means concerned with preventing disease. [MEDICAL] ▫ *Vaccination and other prophylactic measures can be carried out.* **2** N-COUNT A **prophylactic** is a substance or device used for preventing disease. [MEDICAL] ▫ *The region began to use quinine successfully as a prophylactic.* **3** N-COUNT A **prophylactic** is a condom. [FORMAL]

pro|pi|ti|ate /prəpɪʃieɪt/ (**propitiates, propitiating, propitiated**) V-T If you **propitiate** someone, you stop them from being angry or impatient by doing something to please them. [FORMAL] ▫ *I've never gone out of my way to propitiate people.* ▫ *These ancient ceremonies propitiate the spirits of the waters.*

pro|pi|tious /prəpɪʃəs/ ADJ If something is **propitious**, it is likely to lead to success. [FORMAL] ▫ *They should wait for the most propitious moment between now and the next election.* ▫ *The omens for the game are still not propitious.*

pro|po|nent /prəpoʊnənt/ (**proponents**) N-COUNT If you are a **proponent** of a particular idea or course of action, you actively support it. [FORMAL] ▫ *Halsey was identified as a leading proponent of the values of progressive education.*

pro|por|tion /prəpɔːrʃən/ (**proportions**) **1** N-COUNT A **proportion of** a group or an amount is a part of it. [FORMAL] ▫ *A large proportion of the dolphins in that area will eventually die.* **2** N-COUNT The **proportion** of one kind of person or thing in a group is the number of people or things of that kind compared to the total number of people or things in the group. ▫ *The proportion of women in the profession had risen to 17.3%.* **3** N-COUNT The **proportion** of one amount to another is the relationship between the size of the two amounts. ▫ *Women's bodies tend to have a higher proportion of fat to water.* **4** N-PLURAL If you refer to the **proportions** of something, you are referring to its size, usually when this is extremely large. [WRITTEN] ▫ *In the tropics plants grow to huge proportions.* **5** PHRASE If one thing increases or decreases **in proportion to** another thing, it increases or decreases to the same degree as that thing. ▫ *The pressure in the cylinders would go up in proportion to the boiler pressure.* **6** PHRASE If something is small or large **in proportion to** something else, it is small or large when compared with that thing. ▫ *Children tend to have relatively larger heads than adults in proportion to the rest of their body.* **7** PHRASE If you say that something is **out of all proportion to** something else, you think that it is far greater or more serious than it should be. ▫ *The punishment was out of all proportion to the crime.*

SYNONYMS

proportion
NOUN **1**
part: *Mom and Rob were able to walk part of the way together.*
share: *Sara also pays a share of the gas, electricity, and phone bills.*
segment: *...the third segment of his journey.*

pro|por|tion|al /prəpɔːrʃənəl/ ADJ If one amount is **proportional to** another, the two amounts increase and decrease at the same rate so there is always the same relationship between them. [FORMAL] ▫ *Loss of weight is directly proportional to the rate at which the disease is progressing.*

pro|por|tion|al|ity /prəpɔːrʃənælɪti/ N-UNCOUNT The principle of **proportionality** is the idea that an action should not be more severe than is necessary, especially in a war or when punishing someone for a crime. [FORMAL] ▫ *Nuclear weapons seem to violate the just war principle of proportionality.* ▫ *He said there was a need for proportionality in sentencing.*

pro|por|tion|al rep|re|sen|ta|tion N-UNCOUNT **Proportional representation** is a system of voting in which each political party is represented in a legislature or parliament in proportion to the number of people who vote for it in an election.

pro|por|tion|ate /prəpɔːrʃənɪt/ ADJ **Proportionate** means the same as **proportional**. ▫ *Republics will have voting rights proportionate to the size of their economies.* • **pro|por|tion|ate|ly** ADV ▫ *We have increased the number of teachers but the size of the classes hasn't changed proportionately.*

-proportioned /-prəpɔːrʃənd/ COMB IN ADJ **-proportioned** is added to adverbs to form adjectives that indicate that the size and shape of the different parts of something or someone are pleasing or useful. ▫ *The cabin has high ceilings and well-proportioned rooms.*

pro|po|sal /prəpoʊzəl/ (**proposals**) **1** N-COUNT A **proposal** is a plan or an idea, often a formal or written one, which is suggested for people to think about and decide upon. ▫ *The president is to put forward new proposals for resolving the country's constitutional crisis.* ▫ *...the governor's proposal to restrict cigarette sales.* **2** N-COUNT A **proposal** is the act of asking someone to marry you. ▫ *After a three-weekend courtship, Pam accepted Randy's proposal of marriage.*

COLLOCATIONS

proposal
NOUN **1**
verb + **proposal**: accept, approve, reject; put forward, submit; consider
adjective + **proposal**: controversial; concrete, detailed; draft, formal
noun + **proposal**: reform

SYNONYMS

proposal
NOUN **1**
suggestion: *I have lots of suggestions for the park's future.*
plan: *The three leaders had worked out a peace plan.*
scheme: *...schemes to help combat unemployment*
proposition: *I want to make you a proposition.*

pro|pose /prəpoʊz/ (**proposes, proposing, proposed**) **1** V-T If you **propose** something such as a plan or an idea, you suggest it for people to think about and decide upon. ▫ *Hamilton proposed a change in the traditional debating format.* **2** V-T If you **propose** to do something, you intend to do it. ▫ *It's still far from clear what action the government proposes to take over the affair.* **3** V-T If you **propose** a motion for debate, or a candidate for election, you begin the debate or the election procedure by formally stating your support for that motion or candidate. ▫ *He has proposed a resolution limiting the role of U.S. troops.* **4** V-T/V-I If you **propose to** someone, or **propose marriage** to them, you ask them to marry you. ▫ *He proposed to his girlfriend over a public-address system.*

propo|si|tion /prɒpəzɪʃ⁰n/ (propositions) **1** N-COUNT If you describe something such as a task or an activity as, for example, a difficult **proposition** or an attractive **proposition**, you mean that it is difficult or pleasant to do. ❏ *Making easy money has always been an attractive proposition.* **2** N-COUNT A **proposition** is a statement or an idea that people can consider or discuss to decide whether it is true. [FORMAL] ❏ *The proposition that democracies do not fight each other is based on a tiny historical sample.* **3** N-COUNT A **proposition** is a question or statement about an issue of public policy that appears on a voting paper so that people can vote for or against it. ❏ *Vote Yes on Proposition 136, but No on Propositions 129, 133, and 134.* **4** N-COUNT A **proposition** is an offer or a suggestion that someone makes to you, usually concerning some work or business that you might be able to do together. ❏ *You came to see me at my office the other day with a business proposition.*

pro|pound /prəpaʊnd/ (propounds, propounding, propounded) V-T If someone **propounds** an idea or point of view they have, they suggest it for people to consider. [FORMAL] ❏ *Zoologist Eugene Morton has propounded a general theory of the vocal sounds that animals make.*

pro|pri|etary /prəpraɪətəri/ ADJ [ADJ n] **Proprietary** substances or products are sold under a brand name. [FORMAL] ❏ *...some proprietary brands of dog food.*

pro|pri|eties /prəpraɪɪtiz/ N-PLURAL [usu the N] The **proprieties** are the standards of social behavior that most people consider socially or morally acceptable. [OLD-FASHIONED] ❏ *Jack was careful to observe the proprieties, treating her with exaggerated respect.*

pro|pri|etor /prəpraɪətər/ (proprietors) N-COUNT The **proprietor** of a hotel, store, newspaper, or other business is the person who owns it. [FORMAL] ❏ *...the proprietor of a local restaurant.*

pro|pri|etorial /prəpraɪətɔːriəl/ ADJ If your behavior is **proprietorial**, you are behaving in a proud way because you are, or feel like you are, the owner of something. [FORMAL] ❏ *The longer I live alone the more proprietorial I become about my home.*

pro|pri|etress /prəpraɪətrɪs/ (proprietresses) N-COUNT The **proprietress** of a hotel, store, or business is the woman who owns it. [FORMAL, OLD-FASHIONED] ❏ *The proprietress was alone in the bar.*

pro|pri|ety /prəpraɪɪti/ N-UNCOUNT **Propriety** is the quality of being socially or morally acceptable. [FORMAL] ❏ *Their sense of social propriety is eroded.*

pro|pul|sion /prəpʌlʃ⁰n/ N-UNCOUNT [oft n N, N n] **Propulsion** is the power that moves something, especially a vehicle, in a forward direction. [FORMAL] ❏ *...the submarine's propulsion system.*

pro ra|ta /proʊ reɪtə/ ADV [ADV after v] If something is distributed **pro rata**, it is distributed in proportion to the amount or size of something. [FORMAL] ❏ *All part-timers should be paid the same, pro rata, as full-timers doing the same job.* • ADJ [ADJ n] **Pro-rata** is also an adjective. ❏ *They are paid their salaries and are entitled to fringe benefits on a pro-rata basis.*

pro|rate /proʊreɪt/ (prorates, prorating, prorated) also **pro-rate** V-T [usu passive] If a cost **is prorated**, it is divided or assessed in a proportional way. [mainly AM] ❏ *If weather and/or sea conditions cause your trip to return early, the boat fare will be prorated.*

pro|sa|ic /proʊzeɪɪk/ ADJ Something that is **prosaic** is dull and uninteresting. [FORMAL] ❏ *His instructor offered a more prosaic explanation for the surge in interest.*

pro|scenium /proʊsiːniəm, prə-/ (prosceniums) N-COUNT [usu sing] A **proscenium** or a **proscenium arch** is an arch in a theater that separates the stage from the audience.

pro|scribe /proʊskraɪb/ (proscribes, proscribing, proscribed) V-T [usu passive] If something **is proscribed** by people in authority, the existence or the use of that thing is forbidden. [FORMAL] ❏ *In some cultures surgery is proscribed.* ❏ *They are proscribed by federal law from owning guns.*

pro|scrip|tion /proʊskrɪpʃ⁰n/ (proscriptions) N-VAR The **proscription** of something is the official forbidding of its existence or use. [FORMAL] ❏ *...the proscription against any religious service.* ❏ *...the proscription of his records.*

prose /proʊz/ N-UNCOUNT **Prose** is ordinary written language, in contrast to poetry. ❏ *Shute's prose is stark and chillingly unsentimental.*

pros|ecute /prɒsɪkyuːt/ (prosecutes, prosecuting, prosecuted) **1** V-T/V-I If the authorities **prosecute** someone, they charge them with a crime and put them on trial. ❏ *The police have decided not to prosecute because the evidence is not strong enough.* ❏ *Photographs taken by roadside cameras will soon be enough to prosecute drivers for speeding.* **2** V-T When a lawyer **prosecutes** a case, he or she tries to prove that the person who is on trial is guilty. ❏ *The attorney who will prosecute the case says he cannot reveal how much money is involved.* **3** → See feature box at **legal**

pros|ecu|tion ♦◊◊ /prɒsɪkyuːʃ⁰n/ (prosecutions) **1** N-VAR **Prosecution** is the action of charging someone with a crime and putting them on trial. ❏ *Yesterday the head of government called for the prosecution of those responsible for the deaths.* **2** N-SING The lawyers who try to prove that a person on trial is guilty are called **the prosecution**. ❏ *The star witness for the prosecution took the stand.*

pros|ecu|tor /prɒsɪkyuːtər/ (prosecutors) N-COUNT In some countries, a **prosecutor** is a lawyer or official who brings charges against someone or tries to prove in a trial that they are guilty.

pros|elyt|ize /prɒsɪlɪtaɪz/ (proselytizes, proselytizing, proselytized)

> in BRIT, also use **proselytise**

V-T/V-I If you **proselytize**, you try to persuade someone to share your beliefs, especially religious or political beliefs. [FORMAL] ❏ *I assured him we didn't come here to proselytize.* ❏ *Christians were arrested for trying to convert people, to proselytise them.*

pros|pect ♦◊◊ /prɒspekt/ (prospects, prospecting, prospected) **1** N-VAR If there is some **prospect** of something happening, there is a possibility that it will happen. ❏ *Unfortunately, there is little prospect of seeing these big questions answered.* ❏ *The prospects for peace in the country's eight-year civil war are becoming brighter.* **2** N-SING A particular **prospect** is something that you expect or know is going to happen. ❏ *There was a mixed reaction to the prospect of having new neighbors.* **3** N-PLURAL Someone's **prospects** are their chances of being successful, especially in their career. ❏ *I chose to work abroad to improve my career prospects.* **4** V-I When people **prospect for** oil, gold, or some other valuable substance, they look for it in the ground or under the sea. ❏ *He had prospected for minerals everywhere from the Gobi Desert to the Transvaal.*

pro|spec|tive /prəspektɪv/ **1** ADJ [ADJ n] You use **prospective** to describe someone who wants to be the thing mentioned or who is likely to be the thing mentioned. ❏ *The story should act as a warning to other prospective buyers.* **2** ADJ [ADJ n] You use **prospective** to describe something that is likely to happen soon. ❏ *The terms of the prospective deal are most clearly spelled out in BusinessWeek.*

pro|spec|tus /prəspektəs/ (prospectuses) **1** N-COUNT A **prospectus** is a detailed document produced by a company, college, or school, which gives details about it. ❏ *...a prospectus for a new issue of stock.* **2** → See feature box at **university**

pros|per /prɒspər/ (prospers, prospering, prospered) V-I If people or businesses **prosper**, they are successful and do well. [FORMAL] ❏ *His business continued to prosper.*

pros|per|ity /prɒsperɪti/ N-UNCOUNT **Prosperity** is a condition in which a person or community is doing well financially. ❏ *...a new era of peace and prosperity.*

pros|per|ous /prɒspərəs/ ADJ **Prosperous** people, places, and economies are rich and successful. [FORMAL] ❏ *...the youngest son of a relatively prosperous family.*

pros|tate /prɒsteɪt/ (prostates) N-COUNT The **prostate** or the **prostate gland** is an organ in the body of male mammals situated at the neck of the bladder that produces a liquid which forms part of semen.

pros|the|sis /prɒsθiːsɪs/ (prostheses) N-COUNT A **prosthesis** is an artificial body part that is used to replace a natural part. [MEDICAL]

pros|thet|ic /prɒsθetɪk/ ADJ [ADJ n] **Prosthetic** parts of the body are artificial ones used to replace natural ones. [MEDICAL] ❏ *He has undergone 25 operations and wears a prosthetic leg.*

pros|ti|tute /prɒstɪtuːt/ (prostitutes) N-COUNT A **prostitute** is who has sex in exchange for money. ☐ *He admitted last week he paid for sex with a prostitute.*

pros|ti|tu|tion /prɒstɪtuːʃən/ N-UNCOUNT **Prostitution** means having sex with people in exchange for money. ☐ *She eventually drifted into prostitution.*

pros|trate /prɒstreɪt/ (prostrates, prostrating, prostrated) **1** V-T If you **prostrate** yourself, you lie down flat on the ground, on your front, usually to show respect for God or a person in authority. ☐ *They prostrated themselves before their king.* **2** ADJ [ADJ after v] If you are lying **prostrate**, you are lying flat on the ground, on your front. ☐ *Percy was lying prostrate, his arms outstretched and his eyes closed.* **3** ADJ [oft ADJ with n] If someone is **prostrate**, they are so distressed or affected by a very bad experience that they are unable to do anything at all. [FORMAL] ☐ *I was prostrate with grief.*

pro|tago|nist /proʊtægənɪst/ (protagonists) **1** N-COUNT Someone who is a **protagonist of** an idea or movement is a supporter of it. [FORMAL] ☐ *...the main protagonists of their countries' integration into the world market.* **2** N-COUNT A **protagonist** in a play, novel, or real event is one of the main people in it. [FORMAL] ☐ *...the protagonist of J. D. Salinger's novel "The Catcher in the Rye."*

pro|tean /proʊtiən/ ADJ [usu ADJ n] If you describe someone or something as **protean**, you mean that they have the ability to continually change their nature, appearance, or behavior. [FORMAL] ☐ *He is a protean stylist who can move from blues to ballads and grand symphony.*

pro|tect ✦✦◇ /prətɛkt/ (protects, protecting, protected) **1** V-T To **protect** someone or something means to prevent them from being harmed or damaged. ☐ *So, what can women do to protect themselves from heart disease?* ☐ *A long thin wool coat and a purple headscarf protected her against the wind.* **2** V-T If an insurance policy **protects** you against an event such as death, injury, fire, or theft, the insurance company will give you or your family money if that event happens. ☐ *Many manufacturers have policies to protect themselves against blackmailers.*

> **SYNONYMS**
> **protect**
> VERB **1**
> **defend:** *They would have killed him if he had not defended himself.*
> **shield:** *He shielded his head from the sun with an old sack.*
> **shelter:** *...a wooden house, sheltered by a low, pointed roof.*
> **safeguard:** *They will press for international action to safeguard the ozone layer.*

pro|tect|ed /prətɛktɪd/ ADJ **Protected** is used to describe animals, plants, and areas of land that the law does not allow to be destroyed, harmed, or damaged. ☐ *...a protected zone of national forest.*

pro|tec|tion ✦✦◇ /prətɛkʃən/ (protections) **1** N-VAR To give or be **protection** against something unpleasant means to prevent people or things from being harmed or damaged by it. ☐ *Such a diet is widely believed to offer protection against a number of cancers.* ☐ *It is clear that the primary duty of parents is to provide protection for our children.* **2** N-UNCOUNT [oft N against n] If an insurance policy gives you **protection** against an event such as death, injury, fire, or theft, the insurance company will give you or your family money if that event happens. ☐ *Insurance can be purchased to provide protection against such risks.* **3** N-UNCOUNT If a government has a policy of **protection**, it helps its own industries by putting a tax on imported goods or by restricting imports in some other way. [BUSINESS] ☐ *Over the same period trade protection has increased in the rich countries.*

> **COLLOCATIONS**
> **protection**
> NOUN
> **1**
> noun + **protection:** consumer, data, payment; fire, sun; child
> adjective + **protection:** environmental, legal; adequate, effective; coastal
> verb + **protection:** afford, give, offer, provide; need, seek; enjoy
> **2**
> noun + **protection:** bankruptcy, income

> **SYNONYMS**
> **protection**
> NOUN **1**
> **defense:** *The immune system is our main defense against disease.*
> **safeguard:** *Many people took second jobs as a safeguard against unemployment.*
> **security:** *Strict security measures are in force in the capital.*
> **shield:** *He used his left hand as a shield against the reflecting sunlight.*

pro|tec|tion|ism /prətɛkʃənɪzəm/ N-UNCOUNT **Protectionism** is the policy some countries have of helping their own industries by putting a large tax on imported goods or by restricting imports in some other way. [BUSINESS] ☐ *The aim of the current round of talks is to promote free trade and to avert the threat of increasing protectionism.*

pro|tec|tion|ist /prətɛkʃənɪst/ (protectionists) **1** N-COUNT A **protectionist** is someone who agrees with and supports protectionism. [BUSINESS] ☐ *Trade frictions between the two countries had been caused by trade protectionists.* **2** ADJ **Protectionist** policies, measures, and laws are meant to stop or reduce imports. [BUSINESS] ☐ *The administration may be moving away from free trade and toward more protectionist policies.*

pro|tec|tive /prətɛktɪv/ **1** ADJ **Protective** means designed or intended to protect something or someone from harm. ☐ *Protective gloves reduce the absorption of chemicals through the skin.* **2** ADJ If someone is **protective** toward you, they look after you and show a strong desire to keep you safe. ☐ *He is very protective toward his mother.*

pro|tec|tive cus|to|dy N-UNCOUNT If a witness in a court case is being held in **protective custody**, they are being kept in prison in order to prevent them from being harmed. ☐ *They might be doing me a good turn if they took me into protective custody.*

pro|tec|tor /prətɛktər/ (protectors) **1** N-COUNT If you refer to someone as your **protector**, you mean that they protect you from being harmed. ☐ *Many mothers see their son as a potential protector and provider.* **2** N-COUNT A **protector** is a device that protects someone or something from physical harm. ☐ *He was the only National League umpire to wear an outside chest protector.*

pro|tec|tor|ate /prətɛktərɪt/ (protectorates) N-COUNT A **protectorate** is a country that is controlled and protected by a more powerful country. ☐ *In 1914 the country became a British protectorate.*

pro|té|gé /proʊtɪʒeɪ, -ʒeɪ/ (protégés)

> The spelling **protégée** is often used when referring to a woman.

N-COUNT The **protégé** of an older and more experienced person is a young person who is helped and guided by them over a period of time. ☐ *Kelley, a former lawyer and protégé of Steven Bochco.*

pro|tein ✦◇◇ /proʊtiːn/ (proteins) **1** N-MASS **Protein** is a substance found in food and drink such as meat, eggs, and milk. You need protein in order to grow and be healthy. ☐ *Fish was a major source of protein for the working man.* **2** → See feature box at **nutrition**

pro tem /proʊ tɛm/ ADV [n ADV] If someone has a particular position or job **pro tem**, they have it temporarily. [FORMAL] ☐ *...the president pro tem of the California State Senate.*

pro|test ✦✦◇ (protests, protesting, protested)

> The verb is usually pronounced /prətɛst/. The noun, and sometimes the verb, is pronounced /proʊtɛst/.

1 V-T/V-I If you **protest** something or **protest against** something, you say or show publicly that you object to it. ☐ *They were protesting soaring prices.* **2** N-VAR A **protest** is the act of saying or showing publicly that you object to something. ☐ *The opposition now seems too weak to stage any serious protests against the government.* ☐ *The Mexican president canceled a trip to Texas in protest at the state's execution of a Mexican national.* **3** V-T If you **protest that** something is the case, you insist that it is the case, when other people think that it may not be. ☐ *When we tried to protest that Mo was beaten up they didn't believe us.* ☐ *"I never said any of that to her," he protested.*

Protestant

> **SYNONYMS**
>
> **protest**
> VERB **1**
> **object:** 'Hey, I don't know what you're talking about,' Russo objected.
> **demonstrate:** 30,000 angry farmers demonstrated against possible cuts in subsidies.
> **complain:** 'I do everything you ask of me,' he complained.
> NOUN **2**
> **complaint:** People have been reluctant to make formal complaints to the police.
> **demonstration:** Riot police broke up a demonstration by students.
> **outcry:** The killing caused an international outcry.

Prot|es|tant /prɒtɪstənt/ (**Protestants**) **1** N-COUNT A **Protestant** is a Christian who belongs to the branch of the Christian church that separated from the Catholic church in the sixteenth century. **2** ADJ **Protestant** means relating to Protestants or their churches. ❏ Most Protestant churches now have some women ministers.

Prot|es|tant|ism /prɒtɪstəntɪzəm/ N-UNCOUNT **Protestantism** is the set of Christian beliefs that are held by Protestants. ❏ ...the spread of Protestantism.

pro|tes|ta|tion /prɒtɪsteɪʃən, proʊtɛ-/ (**protestations**) N-COUNT [oft N of n] A **protestation** is a strong declaration that something is true or not true. [FORMAL] ❏ Despite his constant protestations of devotion and love, her doubts persisted.

pro|test|er /prətɛstər/ (**protesters**) also **protestor** N-COUNT **Protesters** are people who protest publicly about an issue. ❏ The protesters say the government is corrupt and inefficient.

pro|test vote (**protest votes**) N-COUNT In an election, a **protest vote** is a vote against the party you usually support in order to show disapproval of something they are doing or planning to do.

> **PREFIX**
>
> **proto-**
> is used to form adjectives and nouns that indicate that something is in the early stages of its development. For example, a **prototype** is a machine or device which is not yet ready to be made in large numbers.

proto|col /proʊtəkɒl/ (**protocols**) **1** N-VAR **Protocol** is a system of rules about the correct way to act in formal situations. ❏ He has become a stickler for the finer observances of Washington protocol. **2** N-COUNT A **protocol** is a set of rules for exchanging information between computers. [COMPUTING] ❏ ...a computer protocol which could communicate across different languages. **3** N-COUNT A **protocol** is a written record of a treaty or agreement that has been made by two or more countries. [FORMAL] ❏ ...the Montreal Protocol to phase out use and production of CFCs. **4** N-COUNT A **protocol** is a plan for a course of medical treatment, or a plan for a scientific experiment. [AM, FORMAL] ❏ ...the detoxification protocol.

pro|ton /proʊtɒn/ (**protons**) N-COUNT A **proton** is an atomic particle that has a positive electrical charge. [TECHNICAL]

proto|type /proʊtətaɪp/ (**prototypes**) N-COUNT A **prototype** is a new type of machine or device that is not yet ready to be made in large numbers and sold. ❏ Chris Retzler has built a prototype of a machine called the wave rotor.

proto|typi|cal /proʊtətɪpɪkəl/ ADJ [usu ADJ n] **Prototypical** is used to indicate that someone or something is a very typical example of a type of person or thing. [FORMAL] ❏ Park Ridge is the prototypical American suburb. ❏ ...a prototypical socialist.

proto|zoan /proʊtəzoʊən/ (**protozoa** or **protozoans**) N-COUNT [usu pl] **Protozoa** are very small organisms that often live inside larger animals. [TECHNICAL]

pro|tract|ed /proʊtræktɪd/ ADJ Something, usually something unpleasant, that is **protracted** lasts a long time, especially longer than usual or longer than you hoped. [FORMAL] ❏ However, after protracted negotiations Ogden got the deal he wanted. ❏ ...a protracted civil war.

pro|trac|tor /proʊtræktər/ (**protractors**) N-COUNT A **protractor** is a flat, semicircular piece of plastic or metal that is used for measuring angles.

provide

pro|trude /proʊtruːd/ (**protrudes, protruding, protruded**) V-I If something **protrudes** from somewhere, it sticks out. [FORMAL] ❏ ...a huge round mass of smooth rock protruding from the water.

pro|tru|sion /proʊtruːʒən/ (**protrusions**) N-COUNT A **protrusion** is something that sticks out from something. [FORMAL] ❏ He grabbed at a protrusion of rock with his right hand.

pro|tu|ber|ance /proʊtuːbərəns/ (**protuberances**) N-COUNT A **protuberance** is a rounded part that sticks out from the surface of something. [FORMAL] ❏ ...a protuberance on the upper jawbone.

pro|tu|ber|ant /proʊtuːbərənt/ ADJ [usu ADJ n] **Protuberant** eyes, lips, noses, or teeth stick out more than usual from the face. [FORMAL]

proud ♦◇◇ /praʊd/ (**prouder, proudest**) **1** ADJ If you feel **proud**, you feel pleased about something good that you possess or have done, or about something good that a person close to you has done. ❏ I felt proud of his efforts. ❏ They are proud that she is doing well at school. ● **proud|ly** ADV [ADV with v] ❏ "That's the first part finished," he said proudly. **2** ADJ [ADJ n] Your **proudest** moments or achievements are the ones that you are most proud of. ❏ This must have been one of the proudest moments of his busy and hard-working life. **3** ADJ Someone who is **proud** has respect for themselves and does not want to lose the respect that other people have for them. ❏ He was too proud to ask his family for help and support. **4** ADJ Someone who is **proud** feels that they are better or more important than other people. [DISAPPROVAL] ❏ She was said to be proud and arrogant.

prove ♦♦◇ /pruːv/ (**proves, proving, proved, proven**)

> The forms **proved** and **proven** can both be used as a past participle.

1 V-LINK If something **proves** to be true or to have a particular quality, it becomes clear after a period of time that it is true or has that quality. ❏ We have been accused of exaggerating before, but unfortunately all our reports proved to be true. ❏ In the past this process of transition has often proven difficult. **2** V-T If you **prove** that something is true, you show by means of argument or evidence that it is definitely true. ❏ You brought this charge. You prove it! ❏ The results prove that regulation of the salmon farming industry is inadequate. ❏ That made me hopping mad and determined to prove him wrong. **3** V-T If you **prove** yourself to have a certain good quality, you show by your actions that you have it. ❏ Margie proved herself to be a good mother. ❏ As a composer he proved himself adept at large dramatic forms.

prov|en /pruːvən/ **Proven** is a past participle of **prove**. **Proven** is the usual form of the past participle when you are using it as an adjective.

prov|enance /prɒvɪnəns/ (**provenances**) N-VAR [usu with poss] The **provenance** of something is the place that it comes from or that it originally came from. [FORMAL] ❏ Kato was fully aware of the provenance of these treasures.

prov|erb /prɒvɜːrb/ (**proverbs**) N-COUNT A **proverb** is a short sentence that people often quote, because it gives advice or tells you something about life. ❏ An old Arab proverb says, "The enemy of my enemy is my friend."

pro|ver|bial /prəvɜːrbiəl/ ADJ [ADJ n] You use **proverbial** to show that you know the way you are describing something is one that is often used or is part of a popular saying. ❏ The limousine sped off down the road in the proverbial cloud of dust.

pro|vide ♦♦♦ /prəvaɪd/ (**provides, providing, provided**) **1** V-T If you **provide** something that someone needs or wants, or if you **provide** them with it, you give it to them or make it available to them. ❏ I'll be glad to provide a copy of this. ❏ They would not provide any details. ❏ They provided him with a car and driver. **2** V-T If a law or agreement **provides** that something will happen, it states that it will happen. [FORMAL] ❏ The treaty provides that, by the end of the century, the United States must have removed its bases. **3** → see also **provided**, **providing**

▶ **provide for** **1** PHRASAL VERB If you **provide for** someone, you support them financially and make sure that they have the things that they need. ❏ Elaine wouldn't let him provide for her. **2** PHRASAL VERB If you **provide for** something that might happen or that might need to be done, you make arrangements to deal with it. ❏ Jim had provided for just such an emergency.

pro|vid|ed /prəvaɪdɪd/ CONJ If you say that something will happen **provided** or **provided that** something else happens, you mean that the first thing will happen only if the second thing also happens. ❑ *The other banks are going to be very eager to help, provided that they see that he has a specific plan.*

provi|dence /prɒvɪdəns/ N-UNCOUNT **Providence** is God, or a force that is believed by some people to arrange the things that happen to us. [LITERARY] ❑ *These people regard his death as an act of providence.*

provi|den|tial /prɒvɪdenʃəl/ ADJ A **providential** event is lucky because it happens at exactly the right time. [FORMAL] ❑ *He explained the yellow fever epidemic as a providential act to discourage urban growth.* ❑ *The pistols were loaded so our escape is indeed providential.* • **provi|den|tial|ly** ADV ❑ *Providentially, he had earlier made friends with a Russian Colonel.*

pro|vid|ing /prəvaɪdɪŋ/ CONJ If you say that something will happen **providing** or **providing that** something else happens, you mean that the first thing will happen only if the second thing also happens. ❑ *I do believe in people being able to do what they want to do, providing they're not hurting someone else.*

prov|ince ✦✧✧ /prɒvɪns/ (**provinces**) **1** N-COUNT A **province** is a large section of a country that has its own administration. ❑ *...the Algarve, Portugal's southernmost province.* **2** N-PLURAL The **provinces** are all the parts of a country except the part where the capital is situated. ❑ *The government plans to transfer some 30,000 government jobs from Paris to the provinces.* **3** N-SING If you say that a subject or activity is a particular person's **province**, you mean that this person has a special interest in it, a special knowledge of it, or a special responsibility for it. ❑ *Tattooing is not just the province of sailors.*

pro|vin|cial /prəvɪnʃəl/ **1** ADJ [ADJ n] **Provincial** means connected with the parts of a country away from the capital city. ❑ *...the Quebec and Ontario provincial police.* **2** ADJ If you describe someone or something as **provincial**, you disapprove of them because you think that they are old-fashioned and boring. [DISAPPROVAL] ❑ *He decided to revamp the company's provincial image.*

pro|vin|cial|ism /prəvɪnʃəlɪzəm/ N-UNCOUNT **Provincialism** is the holding of old-fashioned attitudes and opinions, which some people think is typical of people in areas away from the capital city or any large city of a country. [DISAPPROVAL] ❑ *Wright grew frustrated with American provincialism.*

prov|ing ground (**proving grounds**) N-COUNT If you describe a place as a **proving ground**, you mean that new things or ideas are tried out or tested there. ❑ *New York is a proving ground today for the Democratic presidential candidates.*

pro|vi|sion ✦✦✧ /prəvɪʒən/ (**provisions**) **1** N-UNCOUNT [also a N] The **provision** of something is the act of giving it or making it available to people who need or want it. ❑ *The department is responsible for the provision of residential care services.* **2** N-VAR If you make **provision for** something that might happen or that might need to be done, you make arrangements to deal with it. ❑ *Mr. Kurtz asked if it had ever occurred to her to make provision for her retirement.* **3** N-UNCOUNT [also N in pl, N for n] If you make **provision for** someone, you support them financially and make sure that they have the things that they need. ❑ *Special provision should be made for children.* **4** N-COUNT A **provision** in a law or an agreement is an arrangement which is included in it. ❑ *He backed a provision that would allow judges to delay granting a divorce decree in some cases.*

pro|vi|sion|al /prəvɪʒənəl/ ADJ You use **provisional** to describe something that has been arranged or appointed for the present, but may be changed in the future. ❑ *...the possibility of setting up a provisional coalition government.* ❑ *These times are provisional and subject to confirmation.* • **pro|vi|sion|al|ly** ADV [ADV with v] ❑ *The U.S. and Japan provisionally agreed to add new chartered flights to serve their major cities.*

pro|vi|so /prəvaɪzoʊ/ (**provisos**) N-COUNT [oft N that] A **proviso** is a condition in an agreement. You agree to do something if this condition is fulfilled. ❑ *I told Norman I would invest in his venture as long as he agreed to one proviso.*

pro|vo|ca|teur /prəvɒkətɜr, -tuər/ (**provocateurs**) → see **agent provocateur**

provo|ca|tion /prɒvəkeɪʃən/ (**provocations**) N-VAR If you describe a person's action as **provocation** or a **provocation**, you mean that it is a reason for someone else to react angrily, violently, or emotionally. ❑ *He denies murder on the grounds of provocation.*

pro|voca|tive /prəvɒkətɪv/ **1** ADJ If you describe something as **provocative**, you mean that it is intended to make people react angrily or argue against it. ❑ *He has made a string of outspoken and sometimes provocative speeches in recent years.* **2** ADJ If you describe someone's clothing or behavior as **provocative**, you mean that it is intended to make someone feel sexual desire. ❑ *...provocative black lace.*

pro|voke ✦✧✧ /prəvoʊk/ (**provokes, provoking, provoked**) **1** V-T If you **provoke** someone, you deliberately annoy them and try to make them behave aggressively. ❑ *He started shouting at me but I didn't do anything to provoke him.* **2** V-T If something **provokes** a reaction, it causes it. ❑ *His election success has provoked a shocked reaction.*

━━━ **COLLOCATIONS** ━━━

provoke
VERB **2**
provoke + noun: controversy, debate, reaction, response; backlash, outcry, protest; anger, fury, outrage

━━━ **SYNONYMS** ━━━

provoke
VERB
1
anger: *The decision to allow more offshore oil drilling angered some Californians.*
annoy: *Try making a note of the things which annoy you.*
irritate: *Perhaps they were irritated by the sound of crying.*
infuriate: *Jimmy's presence had infuriated Hugh.*
2
rouse: *He did more to rouse the crowd there than anybody else.*
cause: *This was a genuine mistake, but it did cause me some worry.*
incite: *They pleaded guilty to possessing material likely to incite racial hatred.*

pro|vo|lo|ne /proʊvəloʊni/ also **provolone cheese** N-UNCOUNT **Provolone** is a type of cream-colored, smoked cheese, originally made in Italy. ❑ *...a slice of provolone.*

prov|ost /proʊvoʊst/ (**provosts**) **1** N-COUNT In some colleges and universities in the United States, a **provost** is an official who deals with matters such as the faculty and the courses of study. **2** N-COUNT In the Roman Catholic and Anglican Churches, a **provost** is the person who is in charge of the administration of a cathedral.

prow /praʊ/ (**prows**) N-COUNT The **prow** of a ship or boat is the front part of it.

prow|ess /praʊɪs/ N-UNCOUNT Someone's **prowess** is their great skill at doing something. [FORMAL] ❑ *He's always bragging about his prowess as a hunter.*

prowl /praʊl/ (**prowls, prowling, prowled**) V-I If an animal or a person **prowls** around, they move around quietly, for example, when they are hunting. ❑ *He prowled around the room, not sure what he was looking for or even why he was there.*

prowl|er /praʊlər/ (**prowlers**) N-COUNT A **prowler** is someone who secretly follows people or hides near their houses, especially at night, in order to steal something, frighten them, or perhaps harm them.

prox|im|ity /prɒksɪmɪti/ N-UNCOUNT **Proximity** to a place or person is nearness to that place or person. [FORMAL] ❑ *Part of the attraction is Darwin's proximity to Asia.* ❑ *He became aware of the proximity of the Afghans.*

proxy /prɒksi/ N-UNCOUNT If you do something **by proxy**, you arrange for someone else to do it for you. ❑ *Those not attending the meeting may vote by proxy.*

Pro|zac /proʊzæk/ N-UNCOUNT **Prozac** is a drug that is used to treat people who have depression. [TRADEMARK]

prude /pruːd/ (**prudes**) N-COUNT If you call someone a **prude**, you mean that they are too easily shocked by things relating to sex. [DISAPPROVAL] ❑ *Caroline was very much a prude. She wouldn't let me see her naked.*

pru|dence /pruːdəns/ N-UNCOUNT **Prudence** is care and good sense that someone shows when making a decision or taking

pru|dent /pruːdᵊnt/ ADJ Someone who is **prudent** is sensible and careful. ❏ *It is clearly prudent to take all precautions.* • **pru|dent|ly** ADV ❏ *I believe it is essential that we act prudently.*

prud|ery /pruːdəri/ N-UNCOUNT **Prudery** is prudish behavior or attitudes. [DISAPPROVAL]

prud|ish /pruːdɪʃ/ ADJ If you describe someone as **prudish**, you mean that they are too easily shocked by things relating to sex. [DISAPPROVAL] ❏ *I'm not prudish but I think these photographs are obscene.* • **prud|ish|ness** N-UNCOUNT ❏ *Older people will have grown up in a time of greater sexual prudishness.*

prune /pruːn/ (prunes, pruning, pruned) ◼ N-COUNT A **prune** is a dried plum. ◼ V-T/V-I When you **prune**, or **prune** a tree or bush, you cut off some of the branches so that it will grow better the next year. ❏ *You have to prune a bush if you want fruit.* • PHRASAL VERB **Prune back** means the same as **prune**. ❏ *Apples, pears, and cherries can be pruned back when they've lost their leaves.* ◼ V-T If you **prune** something, you cut out all the parts that you do not need. ❏ *Companies are cutting investment and pruning their product ranges.* • PHRASAL VERB **Prune back** means the same as **prune**. ❏ *The company has pruned back its workforce by 20,000 since 2003.*

prun|ing shears ◼ N-PLURAL **Pruning shears** are a gardening tool that look like a pair of strong, heavy scissors. Pruning shears are used for cutting the stems of plants. [AM]

> in BRIT, use **secateurs**

◼ → See also color supplement

pru|ri|ence /prʊəriəns/ N-UNCOUNT **Prurience** is a strong interest in sexual matters. [FORMAL, DISAPPROVAL] ❏ *Nobody ever lost money by overestimating the public's prurience.*

pru|ri|ent /prʊəriənt/ ADJ [usu ADJ n] If you describe someone as **prurient**, you mean that they show too much interest in sexual matters. [FORMAL, DISAPPROVAL] ❏ *We read the gossip written about them with prurient interest.*

pry /praɪ/ (pries, prying, pried) ◼ V-I If someone **pries**, they try to find out about someone else's private affairs, or look at their personal possessions. ❏ *We do not want people prying into our affairs.* ❏ *Imelda might think she was praying.* ◼ V-T If you **pry** something **open** or **pry** it away from a surface, you force it open or away from a surface. ❏ *They pried open a sticky can of blue paint.* ❏ *They pried the bars apart to free the dog.*

PS /piː es/ also **P.S.** You write **PS** to introduce something that you add at the end of a letter after you have signed it. ❏ *P.S. Please show your friends this letter and the enclosed leaflet.*

psalm /sɑːm/ (psalms) N-COUNT The **Psalms** are the 150 songs, poems, and prayers that together form the Book of Psalms in the Bible. ❏ *He recited a verse of the twenty-third psalm.*

pse|pholo|gist /səfɒlədʒɪst/ (psephologists) N-COUNT A **psephologist** studies how people vote in elections.

> **PREFIX**
>
> **pseudo-**
> forms nouns and adjectives that refer to something that is not really what it seems or claims to be. For example, a *pseudoscience* is something that claims to be a science, but is not.

pseudo|nym /suːdənɪm/ (pseudonyms) N-COUNT A **pseudonym** is a name that someone, usually a writer, uses instead of his or her real name. ❏ *Both plays were published under the pseudonym of Philip Dayre.*

pso|ria|sis /səraɪəsɪs/ N-UNCOUNT **Psoriasis** is a disease that causes dry red patches on the skin.

psst /pst/ **Psst** is a sound that someone makes when they want to attract another person's attention secretly or quietly. ❏ *"Psst! Come over here!" the youth hissed furtively.*

psych /saɪk/ (psychs, psyching, psyched) also **psyche**
▸ **psych out** PHRASAL VERB If you **psych out** your opponent in a contest, you try to make them feel less confident by behaving in a very confident or aggressive way. [INFORMAL] ❏ *They are like heavyweight boxers, trying to psych each other out and build themselves up.*

▸ **psych up** PHRASAL VERB If you **psych** yourself **up** before a contest or a difficult task, you prepare yourself for it mentally, especially by telling yourself that you can win or succeed. [INFORMAL] ❏ *After work, it is hard to psych yourself up for an hour at the gym.* ❏ *Before the game everyone gets psyched up and starts shouting.*

psy|che /saɪki/ (psyches) N-COUNT In psychology, your **psyche** is your mind and your deepest feelings and attitudes. [TECHNICAL] ❏ *His exploration of the myth brings insight into the American psyche.*

psychedelia /saɪkədiːliə/ N-UNCOUNT **Psychedelia** refers to psychedelic objects, clothes, and music.

psychedel|ic /saɪkədelɪk/ ◼ ADJ **Psychedelic** means relating to drugs such as LSD that have a strong effect on your mind, often making you see things that are not there. ❏ *...his first real, full-blown psychedelic experience.* ◼ ADJ **Psychedelic** art has bright colors and strange patterns. ❏ *...psychedelic patterns.*

psy|chi|at|ric /saɪkiætrɪk/ ◼ ADJ [ADJ n] **Psychiatric** means relating to psychiatry. ❏ *We finally insisted that he seek psychiatric help.* ◼ ADJ [ADJ n] **Psychiatric** means involving mental illness. ❏ *About 4% of the prison population have chronic psychiatric illnesses.*

psy|chia|trist /saɪkaɪətrɪst/ (psychiatrists) N-COUNT A **psychiatrist** is a doctor who treats people who are mentally ill.

psy|chia|try /saɪkaɪətri/ N-UNCOUNT **Psychiatry** is the branch of medicine concerned with the treatment of mental illness.

psy|chic /saɪkɪk/ (psychics) ◼ ADJ If you believe that someone is **psychic** or has **psychic** powers, you believe that they have strange mental powers, such as being able to read the minds of other people or to see into the future. ❏ *The woman helped police by using her psychic powers.* • N-COUNT A **psychic** is someone who seems to be psychic. ❏ *...her latest role as a psychic who can foretell the future.* ◼ ADJ **Psychic** means relating to ghosts and the spirits of the dead. ❏ *He declared his total disbelief in psychic phenomena.*

psy|chi|cal /saɪkɪkᵊl/ ADJ **Psychical** means relating to ghosts and the spirits of the dead. [FORMAL]

psy|cho /saɪkoʊ/ (psychos) N-COUNT A **psycho** is someone who has serious mental problems and who may act in a violent way without feeling sorry for what they have done. [INFORMAL] ❏ *Some psycho picked her up, and killed her.*

> **PREFIX**
>
> **psycho-**
> is added to words in order to form other words that describe or refer to things connected with the mind or with mental processes. For example, a *psychoanalyst* is someone whose job is to talk to people in order to help them to understand their behavior or mental problems.

psycho|ac|tive /saɪkoʊæktɪv/ ADJ **Psychoactive** drugs are drugs that affect your mind.

psycho|analy|sis /saɪkoʊənælɪsɪs/ N-UNCOUNT **Psychoanalysis** is the treatment of someone who has mental problems by asking them about their feelings and their past in order to try to discover what may be causing their condition.

psycho|ana|lyst /saɪkoʊænᵊlɪst/ (psychoanalysts) N-COUNT A **psychoanalyst** is someone who treats people who have mental problems using psychoanalysis.

psycho|ana|lyt|ic /saɪkoʊænᵊlɪtɪk/ ADJ [ADJ n] **Psychoanalytic** means relating to psychoanalysis. ❏ *...psychoanalytic therapy.*

psycho|ana|lyze /saɪkoʊænᵊlaɪz/ (psychoanalyzes, psychoanalyzing, psychoanalyzed)

> in BRIT, also use **psychoanalyse**

V-T When a psychotherapist or psychiatrist **psychoanalyzes** someone who has mental problems, he or she examines or treats them using psychoanalysis. ❏ *He was still psychoanalyzing four patients a day.*

psycho|bab|ble /saɪkoʊbæbᵊl/ N-UNCOUNT If you refer to language about people's feelings or behavior as **psychobabble**, you mean that it is very complicated and perhaps meaningless. [DISAPPROVAL] ❏ *Beneath the sentimental psychobabble, there's a likable movie trying to get out.*

psycho|dra|ma /saɪkoʊdrɑːmə/ (**psychodramas**) N-VAR **Psychodrama** is a type of psychotherapy in which people express their problems by acting them out in front of other people.

psycho|ki|ne|sis /saɪkoʊkɪniːsɪs/ N-UNCOUNT **Psychokinesis** is the ability, which some people believe exists, to move objects using the power of your mind.

psycho|logi|cal ✦✧ /saɪkəlɒdʒɪkᵊl/ **1** ADJ **Psychological** means concerned with a person's mind and thoughts. ◻ *John received constant physical and psychological abuse from his father.* • **psycho|logi|cal|ly** /saɪkəlɒdʒɪkli/ ADV ◻ *It was very important psychologically for us to succeed.* **2** ADJ [ADJ n] **Psychological** means relating to psychology. ◻ *...psychological testing.*

SYNONYMS

psychological
ADJ **1**
mental: *...the mental development of children.*
emotional: *Victims are left with emotional problems that can last for life.*
imaginary: *He seems to suffer from imaginary illnesses.*

---

psycho|logi|cal war|fare N-UNCOUNT **Psychological warfare** consists of attempts to make your enemy lose confidence, give up hope, or feel afraid, so that you can win.

psy|cholo|gist /saɪkɒlədʒɪst/ (**psychologists**) N-COUNT A **psychologist** is a person who studies the human mind and tries to explain why people behave in the way that they do.

psy|chol|ogy /saɪkɒlədʒi/ **1** N-UNCOUNT **Psychology** is the scientific study of the human mind and the reasons for people's behavior. ◻ *...Professor of Psychology at Haverford College.* **2** N-UNCOUNT The **psychology** of a person is the kind of mind that they have, which makes them think or behave in the way that they do. ◻ *...a fascination with the psychology of murderers.*

psycho|met|ric /saɪkəmɛtrɪk/ ADJ [ADJ n] **Psychometric** tests are designed to test a person's mental state, personality, and thought processes.

psycho|path /saɪkəpæθ/ (**psychopaths**) N-COUNT A **psychopath** is someone who has serious mental problems and who may act in a violent way without feeling sorry for what they have done. ◻ *She was abducted by a dangerous psychopath.*

psycho|path|ic /saɪkəpæθɪk/ ADJ Someone who is **psychopathic** is a psychopath. ◻ *...a report labeling him psychopathic.* ◻ *...a psychopathic killer.*

psy|cho|sis /saɪkoʊsɪs/ (**psychoses**) N-VAR **Psychosis** is mental illness of a severe kind that can make people lose contact with reality. [MEDICAL] ◻ *He may have some kind of neurosis or psychosis later in life.*

psycho|so|mat|ic /saɪkoʊsəmætɪk, -soʊ-/ ADJ If someone has a **psychosomatic** illness, their symptoms are caused by worry or unhappiness rather than by a physical problem. ◻ *Doctors refused to treat her, claiming that her problems were all psychosomatic.*

psycho|thera|pist /saɪkoʊθɛrəpɪst/ (**psychotherapists**) N-COUNT A **psychotherapist** is a person who treats people who are mentally ill using psychotherapy.

psycho|thera|py /saɪkoʊθɛrəpi/ N-UNCOUNT **Psychotherapy** is the use of psychological methods in treating people who are mentally ill, rather than using physical methods such as drugs or surgery. ◻ *For milder depressions, certain forms of psychotherapy do work well.*

psy|chot|ic /saɪkɒtɪk/ ADJ Someone who is **psychotic** has a type of severe mental illness. [MEDICAL] ◻ *The man, who police believe is psychotic, is thought to be responsible for eight attacks.*

psycho|trop|ic /saɪkoʊtrɒpɪk/ ADJ **Psychotropic** drugs are drugs that affect your mind.

pt (**pts**) also **pt.**

The plural in meaning **1** is either **pt** or **pts**.

1 **pt** is a written abbreviation for **pint**. ◻ *Add ½ pt tomato sauce.* **2** **pt** is the written abbreviation for **point**. ◻ *Here's how it works – 3 pts for a correct result, 1 pt for the correct winning team.*

Pt. also **Pt** (**Pt.s**) N-COUNT [N num] **Pt.** is a written abbreviation for **Part**. ◻ *Stevie Wonder earned his first Number One hit with "Fingertips, Pt. 2."*

PTA /piː tiː eɪ/ (**PTAs**) N-COUNT A **PTA** is a school association run by some of the parents and teachers to discuss matters that affect the children and to organize events to raise money. **PTA** is an abbreviation for **parent-teacher association**.

PTO /piː tiː oʊ/ also **P.T.O.** **PTO** is a written abbreviation for 'please turn over.' You write it at the bottom of a page to indicate that there is more writing on the other side.

PTSD /piː tiː ɛs diː/ N-UNCOUNT **PTSD** is an abbreviation for **post-traumatic stress disorder**.

pub ✦✧ /pʌb/ (**pubs**) N-COUNT A **pub** is a building where people can have drinks, especially alcoholic drinks, and talk to their friends. Many pubs also serve food. [mainly BRIT] ◻ *He was in the pub until closing time.*

pu|ber|ty /pyuːbərti/ N-UNCOUNT **Puberty** is the stage in someone's life when their body starts to become physically mature. ◻ *Moesha had reached the age of puberty.*

pu|bes|cent /pyuːbɛsᵊnt/ ADJ A **pubescent** girl or boy has reached the stage in their life when their body is becoming physically like an adult's. [FORMAL]

pu|bic /pyuːbɪk/ ADJ [ADJ n] **Pubic** means relating to the area just above a person's genitals. ◻ *...pubic hair.*

pub|lic ✦✦✦ /pʌblɪk/ **1** N-SING-COLL You can refer to people in general, or to all the people in a particular country or community, as **the public**. ◻ *The park is now open to the public.* ◻ *Pure alcohol is not for sale to the general public.* **2** N-SING-COLL You can refer to a set of people in a country who share a common interest, activity, or characteristic as a particular kind of **public**. ◻ *Market research showed that 93% of the viewing public wanted a hit movie channel.* **3** ADJ [ADJ n] **Public** means relating to all the people in a country or community. ◻ *The president is attempting to drum up public support for his economic program.* **4** ADJ [ADJ n] **Public** means relating to the government or state, or things that are done for the people by the state. ◻ *The social services account for a substantial part of public spending.* • **pub|lic|ly** ADV [ADV -ed] ◻ *...publicly funded legal services.* **5** ADJ [ADJ n] **Public** buildings and services are provided for everyone to use. ◻ *...the New York Public Library.* ◻ *The new museum must be accessible by public transportation.* **6** ADJ A **public** place is one where people can go about freely and where you can easily be seen and heard. ◻ *...the heavily congested public areas of international airports.* **7** ADJ [ADJ n] If someone is a **public figure** or in **public life**, many people know who they are because they are often mentioned in newspapers and on television. ◻ *He hit out at public figures who commit adultery.* **8** ADJ [ADJ n] **Public** is used to describe statements, actions, and events that are made or done in such a way that any member of the public can see them or be aware of them. ◻ *...a public inquiry into the most grievous breakdown in security our nation has ever known.* ◻ *The comments were the governor's first detailed public statement on the subject.* • **pub|lic|ly** ADV ◻ *He never spoke publicly about the affair.* **9** ADJ [v-link ADJ] If a fact is made **public** or becomes **public**, it becomes known to everyone rather than being kept secret. ◻ *The facts could cause embarrassment if they ever became public.* **10** PHRASE If a company **goes public**, it starts selling its shares on the stock exchange. [BUSINESS] ◻ *The company went public at $21 per share.* **11** PHRASE If you say or do something **in public**, you say or do it when a group of people are present. ◻ *I probably won't be performing in public much.* **12** → See feature box at **commute**, **research**

COLLOCATIONS

public
NOUN **1**
adjective + **public**: general, wider; gullible, skeptical
verb + **public**: convince, reassure, urge, warn; educate, entertain, inform, mislead; protect, serve

---

SYNONYMS

public
NOUN **1**
people: *Millions of people have lost their homes.*
society: *This reflects attitudes and values prevailing in society.*
population: *The country now has a population of about 110 million.*

---

pub|lic ad|dress sys|tem (**public address systems**) N-COUNT A **public address system** is a set of equipment which allows someone's voice, or music, to be heard throughout a large building or area. The abbreviation **PA** is also used.

pub|lic as|sis|tance N-UNCOUNT [oft *on* N] In the United States, **public assistance** is money that is paid by the government to people who are poor, unemployed, or sick. ◻ *More than 70 percent of its citizens are on public assistance.*

pub|li|ca|tion ✦◇◇ /pʌblɪkeɪʃⁿn/ (**publications**) **1** N-UNCOUNT The **publication** of a book or magazine is the act of printing it and sending it to stores to be sold. ◻ *The guide is being translated into several languages for publication near Christmas.* **2** N-COUNT A **publication** is a book or magazine that has been published. ◻ *They have started legal proceedings against two publications which spoke of an affair.* **3** N-UNCOUNT The **publication of** something such as information is the act of making it known to the public, for example, by informing journalists or by publishing a government document. ◻ *A spokesman said: "We have no comment regarding the publication of these photographs."*

pub|lic com|pa|ny (**public companies**) N-COUNT A **public company** is a company whose shares can be bought by the general public. [BUSINESS]

pub|lic de|fend|er (**public defenders**) N-COUNT A **public defender** is a lawyer who is employed by a city or county to represent people who are accused of crimes but cannot afford to pay for a lawyer themselves. [AM]

pub|lic do|main N-SING [usu *in the* N] If information is **in the public domain**, it is not secret and can be used or discussed by anyone. ◻ *It is outrageous that the figures are not in the public domain.*

pub|lic hous|ing N-UNCOUNT **Public housing** is apartments or houses that are rented to poor people, usually at a low cost, by the government. [mainly AM] ◻ *...the construction of more public housing.*

pub|li|cist /pʌblɪsɪst/ (**publicists**) N-COUNT A **publicist** is a person whose job involves getting publicity for people, events, or things such as movies or books. ◻ *...Larry Kaplan, a publicist for "Cold Mountain."*

pub|lic|ity ✦◇◇ /pʌblɪsɪti/ **1** N-UNCOUNT **Publicity** is information or actions that are intended to attract the public's attention to someone or something. ◻ *Much advance publicity was given to the talks.* ◻ *...government publicity campaigns.* **2** N-UNCOUNT When the news media and the public show a lot of interest in something, you can say that it is receiving **publicity**. ◻ *The case has generated enormous publicity in Brazil.*

pub|li|cize /pʌblɪsaɪz/ (**publicizes, publicizing, publicized**)

in BRIT, also use **publicise**

V-T If you **publicize** a fact or event, you make it widely known to the public. ◻ *The author appeared on television to publicize her latest book.* ◻ *He never publicized his plans.*

pub|lic lim|it|ed com|pa|ny (**public limited companies**) N-COUNT A **public limited company** is the same as a **public company**. The abbreviation **plc** is used after such companies' names. [BRIT, BUSINESS]

pub|lic nui|sance (**public nuisances**) N-COUNT [usu sing] If something or someone is, or causes, a **public nuisance**, they break the law by harming or annoying members of the public. [LEGAL]

pub|lic of|fice N-UNCOUNT Someone who is in **public office** is in a job that they have been elected to do by the public. ◻ *...during the 13 years he was in public office in Tennessee.* ◻ *He is unfit to hold public office.*

pub|lic opin|ion N-UNCOUNT **Public opinion** is the opinion or attitude of the public regarding a particular matter. ◻ *He mobilized public opinion all over the world against hydrogen-bomb tests.*

pub|lic prop|er|ty **1** N-UNCOUNT **Public property** is land and other assets that belong to the general public and not to a private owner. ◻ *...vandals who wrecked public property.* **2** N-UNCOUNT If you describe a person or thing as **public property**, you mean that information about them is known and discussed by everyone. ◻ *She complained that intimate aspects of her personal life had been made public property.*

pub|lic pros|e|cu|tor (**public prosecutors**) N-COUNT A **public prosecutor** is [an] official who puts people on trial on behalf of the govern[ment an]d people of a particular country.

pub|lic re|la|tions **1** N-UNCOUNT **Public relations** is the part of an organization's work that is concerned with obtaining the public's approval for what it does. The abbreviation **PR** is often used. [BUSINESS] ◻ *The move was good public relations.* **2** N-PLURAL You can refer to the opinion that the public has of an organization as **public relations**. ◻ *Limiting casualties is important for public relations.*

pub|lic school (**public schools**) **1** N-VAR In the United States, Australia, and many other countries, a **public school** is a school that is supported financially by the government and usually provides free education. ◻ *...Milwaukee's public school system.* **2** N-VAR In England and Wales, a **public school** is a private school that provides secondary education that parents have to pay for. The students often live at the school during the school term. ◻ *He was headmaster of a public school in the West of England.*

pub|lic sec|tor N-SING The **public sector** is the part of a country's economy which is controlled or supported financially by the government. [BUSINESS] ◻ *...Carlos Menem's policy of reducing the public sector and opening up the economy to free-market forces.*

pub|lic serv|ant (**public servants**) N-COUNT A **public servant** is a person who is appointed or elected to a public office, for example, working for a local or state government.

pub|lic ser|vice (**public services**) **1** N-COUNT A **public service** is something such as health care, transportation, or the removal of waste, which is organized by the government or an official body in order to benefit all the people in a particular society or community. ◻ *The money is used by local authorities to pay for public services.* **2** N-UNCOUNT [oft N n] You use **public service** to refer to activities and jobs that are provided or paid for by a government, especially through the civil service. ◻ *...a distinguished career in public service.* **3** N-UNCOUNT **Public service** activities and types of work are concerned with helping people and providing them with what they need, rather than making a profit. ◻ *...the notion of public service and obligation which has been under such attack.*

public-spirited ADJ A **public-spirited** person tries to help the community that they belong to. ◻ *Thanks to a group of public-spirited citizens, the Krippendorf garden has been preserved.*

pub|lic tele|vi|sion also **public TV** N-UNCOUNT **Public television** is television that is funded by the government, businesses, and viewers, rather than by advertising. [AM] ◻ *...the kind of program you only find on public television.*

pub|lic trans|por|ta|tion **1** N-UNCOUNT **Public transportation** is a system for taking people from one place to another, for example, using buses or trains. [AM] ◻ *And there isn't good public transportation from inner city Detroit to those suburban malls.*

in BRIT, use **public transport**

2 → See feature box at **commute**

pub|lic util|ity (**public utilities**) N-COUNT **Public utilities** are services that are regulated by the government or state, such as the supply of electricity, gas, or water. ◻ *Officials said water supplies and other public utilities in the capital were badly affected.*

pub|lic works N-PLURAL **Public works** are buildings, roads, and other projects that are built by the government or state for the public.

pub|lish ✦◇◇ /pʌblɪʃ/ (**publishes, publishing, published**) **1** V-T When a company **publishes** a book or magazine, it prints copies of it, which are sent to stores to be sold. ◻ *They publish reference books.* **2** V-T When the people in charge of a newspaper or magazine **publish** a piece of writing or a photograph, they print it in their newspaper or magazine. ◻ *Medical journals that year were starting to publish articles about Chronic Fatigue Syndrome.* **3** V-T If someone **publishes** a book or an article that they have written, they arrange to have it published. ◻ *Walker has published four books of her verse.* **4** V-T If you **publish** information or an opinion, you make it known to the public by having it printed in a newspaper, magazine, or official document. ◻ *The demonstrators called on the government to publish a list of registered voters.*

pub|lish|er ✦◇◇ /pʌblɪʃər/ (**publishers**) N-COUNT A **publisher** is a person or a company that publishes books, newspapers, or magazines. ☐ *The publishers planned to produce the journal on a weekly basis.*

pub|lish|ing /pʌblɪʃɪŋ/ N-UNCOUNT **Publishing** is the profession of publishing books. ☐ *I had a very high-powered job in publishing.*

pub|lish|ing house (publishing houses) N-COUNT A **publishing house** is a company that publishes books.

puce /pyus/ COLOR Something that is **puce** is a dark purple color.

puck /pʌk/ (pucks) N-COUNT In the game of ice hockey, the **puck** is the small rubber disk that is used instead of a ball.

puck|er /pʌkər/ (puckers, puckering, puckered) V-T/V-I When a part of your face **puckers** or when you **pucker** it, it becomes tight or stretched, often because you are trying not to cry or are going to kiss someone. ☐ *Toby's face puckered.* ☐ *She puckered her lips into a rosebud and kissed him on the nose.* • **puck|ered** ADJ ☐ *...puckered lips.* ☐ *...a long puckered scar.*

puck|ish /pʌkɪʃ/ ADJ [usu ADJ n] If you describe someone as **puckish**, you mean that they play tricks on people or tease them. [OLD-FASHIONED, WRITTEN] ☐ *He had a puckish sense of humor.*

pud|ding /pʊdɪŋ/ (puddings) N-VAR A **pudding** is a cooked sweet food made from ingredients such as milk, sugar, flour, and eggs, and is served either hot or cold. ☐ *...a banana vanilla pudding.*

pud|dle /pʌdᵊl/ (puddles) N-COUNT A **puddle** is a small, shallow pool of liquid that has spread on the ground. ☐ *The road was shiny with puddles, but the rain was at an end.*

pudgy /pʌdʒi/ (pudgier, pudgiest) ADJ If you describe someone as **pudgy**, you mean that they are rather fat in an unattractive way. [AM] ☐ *He put a pudgy arm around Harry's shoulder.*

in BRIT, usually use **podgy**

pueb|lo /pwɛbloʊ/ (pueblos) N-COUNT A **pueblo** is a village, especially in the southwestern United States. [AM] ☐ *There are several dozen Indian pueblos near Santa Fe.*

pu|er|ile /pyuərᵊl, -aɪl/ ADJ If you describe someone or something as **puerile**, you mean that they are silly and childish. [DISAPPROVAL] ☐ *Concert organizers branded the group's actions as puerile.* ☐ *...puerile, schoolboy humor.*

puff /pʌf/ (puffs, puffing, puffed) **1** V-I If someone **puffs** on or at a cigarette, cigar, or pipe, they smoke it. ☐ *He lit a cigar and puffed on it twice.* • N-COUNT **Puff** is also a noun. ☐ *I took a puff on the cigarette and started coughing.* **2** V-T/V-I If you **puff** smoke or moisture from your mouth or if it **puffs** from your mouth, you breathe it out. ☐ *Richard lit another cigarette and puffed smoke toward the ceiling.* • PHRASAL VERB **Puff out** means the same as **puff**. ☐ *He drew heavily on his cigarette and puffed out a cloud of smoke.* **3** V-T If an engine, chimney, or stove **puffs** smoke or steam, clouds of smoke or steam come out of it. ☐ *As I completed my 26th lap the Porsche puffed blue smoke.* **4** N-COUNT A **puff of** something such as air or smoke is a small amount of it that is blown out from somewhere. ☐ *Wind caught the sudden puff of dust and blew it inland.* **5** V-I [usu cont] If you **are puffing**, you are breathing loudly and quickly with your mouth open because you are out of breath after a lot of physical effort. ☐ *I know nothing about boxing, but I could see he was unfit, because he was puffing.*

puff|ball /pʌfbɔl/ (puffballs) N-COUNT A **puffball** is a round fungus that bursts when it is ripe and sends a cloud of spores into the air.

puffed /pʌft/ **1** ADJ [v-link ADJ] If a part of your body is **puffed** or **puffed up**, it is swollen because of an injury or because you are unwell. ☐ *His face was a little puffed.* **2** ADJ [v-link ADJ] If you are **puffed** or **puffed out**, you are breathing with difficulty because you have been using a lot of energy. [INFORMAL] ☐ *Do you get puffed out running up and down the stairs?*

puffed up **1** ADJ [oft ADJ with n] If you describe someone as **puffed up**, you disapprove of them because they are very proud of themselves and think that they are very important. [DISAPPROVAL] ☐ *He was too puffed up with his own importance, too blinded by vanity to accept their verdict on him.* **2** → see also **puffed**

puf|fin /pʌfɪn/ (puffins) N-COUNT A **puffin** is a black and white seabird with a large, brightly-colored beak.

puff pas|try N-UNCOUNT **Puff pastry** is a type of very light pastry that consists of a lot of thin layers.

puffy /pʌfi/ (puffier, puffiest) ADJ If a part of someone's body, especially their face, is **puffy**, it has a round, swollen appearance. ☐ *Her cheeks were puffy with crying.* ☐ *...dark-ringed puffy eyes.* • **puffi|ness** N-UNCOUNT ☐ *He noticed some slight puffiness beneath her eyes.*

pug /pʌg/ (pugs) N-COUNT A **pug** is a small, fat, short-haired dog with a flat face.

pu|gi|list /pyudʒɪlɪst/ (pugilists) N-COUNT A **pugilist** is a boxer. [OLD-FASHIONED]

pug|na|cious /pʌgneɪʃəs/ ADJ Someone who is **pugnacious** is always ready to argue or start a fight. [FORMAL] ☐ *The president was in a pugnacious mood when he spoke to journalists about the rebellion.*

pug|nac|ity /pʌgnæsɪti/ N-UNCOUNT **Pugnacity** is the quality of being pugnacious. [FORMAL] ☐ *He is legendary for his fearlessness and pugnacity.*

puke /pyuk/ (pukes, puking, puked) **1** V-I When someone **pukes**, they vomit. [INFORMAL] ☐ *They got drunk and puked out the window.* • PHRASAL VERB **Puke up** means the same as **puke**. ☐ *He peered at me like I'd just puked up on his jeans.* ☐ *I figured, why eat when I was going to puke it up again?* **2** N-UNCOUNT **Puke** is the same as **vomit**. [INFORMAL] ☐ *He was fully clothed and covered in puke.*

Pu|lit|zer Prize /pʊlɪtsər praɪz/ (Pulitzer Prizes) N-COUNT A **Pulitzer Prize** is one of a series of prizes awarded each year in the United States for outstanding achievement in the fields of journalism, literature, and music. ☐ *Last year he won the Pulitzer Prize for Poetry.*

pull /pʊl/ (pulls, pulling, pulled)
→ Please look at meanings **10** to **13** to see if the expression you are looking for is shown under another headword.

1 V-T/V-I When you **pull** something, you hold it firmly and use force in order to move it toward you or away from its previous position. ☐ *They have pulled out patients' teeth unnecessarily.* ☐ *Erica was solemn, pulling at her blonde curls.* ☐ *I helped pull him out of the water.* ☐ *Someone pulled her hair.* • N-COUNT **Pull** is also a noun. ☐ *The feather must be removed with a straight, firm pull.* **2** V-T When you **pull** an object from a bag, pocket, or cabinet, you put your hand in and bring the object out. ☐ *Jack pulled the slip of paper from his shirt pocket.* **3** V-T When a vehicle, animal, or person **pulls** a cart or piece of machinery, they are attached to it or hold it, so that it moves along behind them when they move forward. ☐ *He pulls a rickshaw, probably the oldest form of human taxi service.* **4** V-T If you **pull yourself** or **pull** a part of your body in a particular direction, you move your body or a part of your body with effort or force. ☐ *Hughes pulled himself slowly to his feet.* ☐ *He pulled his arms out of the sleeves.* **5** V-I When a driver or vehicle **pulls to** a stop or a halt, the vehicle stops. ☐ *He pulled to a stop behind a pickup truck.* **6** V-I In a race or contest, if you **pull ahead of** or **pull away from** an opponent, you gradually increase the amount by which you are ahead of them. ☐ *He pulled away, extending his lead to 15 seconds.* **7** V-T If you **pull** something **apart**, you break or divide it into small pieces, often in order to put them back together again in a different way. ☐ *If I wanted to improve the car significantly I would have to pull it apart and start again.* **8** V-T To **pull** crowds, viewers, or voters means to attract them. [INFORMAL] ☐ *The organizers have to employ performers to pull a crowd.* • PHRASAL VERB **Pull in** means the same as **pull**. ☐ *They provided a far better news service and pulled in many more viewers.* **9** N-COUNT A **pull** is a strong physical force that causes things to move in a particular direction. ☐ *...the pull of gravity.* **10** to **pull a face** → see **face** ① **11** to **pull someone's leg** → see **leg** **12** to **pull strings** → see **string** **13** to **pull your weight** → see **weight** **14** → See feature box at **storm**

▶ **pull away 1** PHRASAL VERB When a vehicle or driver **pulls away**, the vehicle starts moving forward. ☐ *I stood in the driveway and watched him back out and pull away.* **2** PHRASAL VERB If you **pull away from** someone that you have had close links with, you deliberately become less close to them. ☐ *Other daughters, faced with their mother's emotional hunger, pull away.*

▶ **pull back 1** PHRASAL VERB If someone **pulls back** from an action, they decide not to do it or continue with it, because it could have bad consequences. ☐ *They will plead with him to pull back from confrontation.* **2** PHRASAL VERB If troops **pull back** or if

their leader **pulls** them **back**, they go some or all of the way back to their own territory. ❏ *They were asked to pull back from their artillery positions around the city.*
▶ **pull down** PHRASAL VERB To **pull down** a building or statue means to deliberately destroy it. ❏ *They'd pulled the registrar's office down which then left an open space.*
▶ **pull in** **1** PHRASAL VERB When a vehicle or driver **pulls in** somewhere, the vehicle stops there. ❏ *He pulled in at the side of the road.* **2** → see **pull 8**
▶ **pull into** PHRASAL VERB When a vehicle or driver **pulls into** a place, the vehicle moves into the place and stops there. ❏ *He pulled into the driveway in front of her garage.*
▶ **pull off** **1** PHRASAL VERB If you **pull off** something very difficult, you succeed in achieving it. ❏ *The National League for Democracy pulled off a landslide victory.* **2** PHRASAL VERB If a vehicle or driver **pulls off** the road, the vehicle stops by the side of the road. ❏ *I pulled off the road at a scenic overlook.*
▶ **pull out** **1** PHRASAL VERB When a vehicle or driver **pulls out**, the vehicle moves out into the road or nearer the center of the road. ❏ *She pulled out into the street.* **2** PHRASAL VERB If you **pull out of** an agreement, a contest, or an organization, you withdraw from it. ❏ *The World Bank should pull out of the project.* ❏ *France was going to pull out of NATO.* **3** PHRASAL VERB If troops **pull out of** a place or if their leader **pulls** them **out**, they leave it. ❏ *The militia in Lebanon has agreed to pull out of Beirut.* ❏ *Economic sanctions will be lifted once two-thirds of their forces have pulled out.* **4** PHRASAL VERB If you **pull out of** a bad situation or if someone **pulls** you **out**, you begin to recover from it. ❏ *I pulled out of the depression very quickly with treatment.* ❏ *Sterling has been hit by the economy's failure to pull out of recession.*
▶ **pull over** **1** PHRASAL VERB When a vehicle or driver **pulls over**, or when a police officer **pulls** them **over**, the vehicle moves closer to the side of the road and stops there. ❏ *He noticed a man behind him in a blue Ford gesticulating to pull over.* **2** → see also **pullover**
▶ **pull through** PHRASAL VERB If someone with a serious illness or someone in a very difficult situation **pulls through**, they recover. ❏ *Everyone was very concerned whether he would pull through or not.* ❏ *It is only our determination to fight that has pulled us through.*
▶ **pull together** **1** PHRASAL VERB If people **pull together**, they help each other or work together in order to deal with a difficult situation. ❏ *The nation was urged to pull together to avoid a slide into complete chaos.* **2** PHRASAL VERB If you are upset or depressed and someone tells you to **pull** yourself **together**, they are telling you to control your feelings and behave calmly again. ❏ *Pull yourself together, you stupid woman!*
▶ **pull up** **1** PHRASAL VERB When a vehicle or driver **pulls up**, the vehicle slows down and stops. ❏ *The cab pulled up and the driver jumped out.* **2** PHRASAL VERB If you **pull up** a chair, you move it closer to something or someone and sit on it. ❏ *He pulled up a chair behind her and put his chin on her shoulder.*

▬▬▬▬▬ SYNONYMS ▬▬▬▬▬

pull
VERB **1**
haul: *A crane was used to haul the car out of the stream.*
drag: *He got up and dragged his chair towards the table.*
tow: *He had been using the vehicle to tow his work trailer.*
tug: *A little boy came running up and tugged at his sleeve excitedly.*

pull|ed pork N-UNCOUNT **Pulled pork** is pork meat that has been cooked for a long time until it is very soft, then torn into small strips.
pul|ley /pʊli/ (**pulleys**) N-COUNT A **pulley** is a device consisting of a wheel over which a rope or chain is pulled in order to lift heavy objects.
Pull|man /pʊlmən/ (**Pullmans**) **1** N-COUNT [oft N n] A **Pullman** is a type of train that is extremely comfortable and luxurious. You can also refer to a **Pullman train**. **2** N-COUNT [oft N n] A **Pullman** or a **Pullman car** on a train is a car that provides beds for passengers to sleep in. [AM]

in BRIT, use **sleeping car**

pull-out (**pull-outs**) **1** N-COUNT [usu N n] In a newspaper or magazine, a **pull-out** is a section that you can remove easily and keep. ❏ *...an eight-page pull-out supplement.* **2** N-SING [oft N from/of n] When there is a **pull-out** of armed forces from a place, troops that have occupied an area of land withdraw from it. ❏ *...a pull-out from the occupied territories.*
pull|over /pʊloʊvər/ (**pullovers**) N-COUNT A **pullover** is a piece of clothing that covers the upper part of your body and your arms. You put it on by pulling it over your head.
pul|mo|nary /pʌlməneri/ ADJ [ADJ n] **Pulmonary** means relating to your lungs. [MEDICAL] ❏ *...respiratory and pulmonary disease.*
pulp /pʌlp/ (**pulps, pulping, pulped**) **1** N-SING If an object is pressed into a **pulp**, it is crushed or beaten until it is soft, smooth, and wet. ❏ *The olives are crushed to a pulp by stone rollers.* **2** N-SING In fruit or vegetables, **the pulp** is the soft part inside the skin. ❏ *Make maximum use of the whole fruit, including the pulp which is high in fiber.* **3** N-UNCOUNT **Wood pulp** is material made from crushed wood. It is used to make paper. **4** ADJ [ADJ n] People refer to stories or novels as **pulp** fiction when they consider them to be of poor quality and intentionally shocking or sensational. ❏ *...lurid '50s pulp novels.* **5** V-T [usu passive] If vegetables or fruit **are pulped**, they are crushed into a smooth, wet paste. ❏ *Onions can be boiled and pulped to a puree.* **6** V-T [usu passive] If paper, books, or documents **are pulped**, they are destroyed. ❏ *The first edition had to be pulped because it contained inaccuracies.* **7** PHRASE If someone **is beaten to a pulp**, they are hit repeatedly until they are very badly injured. ❏ *I tried to talk myself out of a fight and got beaten to a pulp instead by three other boys.*
pul|pit /pʊlpɪt, pʌl-/ (**pulpits**) N-COUNT A **pulpit** is a small raised platform with a rail or barrier around it in a church, where a member of the clergy stands to speak. ❏ *The time came for the sermon and he ascended the pulpit steps.*
pulpy /pʌlpi/ ADJ Something that is **pulpy** is soft, smooth, and wet, often because it has been crushed or beaten. ❏ *The chutney should be a thick, pulpy consistency.*
pul|sar /pʌlsɑr/ (**pulsars**) N-COUNT A **pulsar** is a star that spins very fast and cannot be seen but produces regular radio signals.
pul|sate /pʌlseɪt/ (**pulsates, pulsating, pulsated**) V-I If something **pulsates**, it beats, moves in and out, or shakes with strong, regular movements. ❏ *The Pole Star appears to be changing from a star that pulsates.*
pulse /pʌls/ (**pulses, pulsing, pulsed**) **1** N-COUNT Your **pulse** is the regular beating of blood through your body, which you can feel when you touch particular parts of your body, especially your wrist. ❏ *Mahoney's pulse was racing, and he felt confused.* **2** N-COUNT In music, a **pulse** is a regular beat, often produced by a drum. ❏ *...the repetitive pulse of the music.* **3** N-COUNT A **pulse** of electrical current, light, or sound is a temporary increase in its level. ❏ *The switch works by passing a pulse of current between the tip and the surface.* **4** N-SING If you refer to **the pulse of** a group in society, you mean the ideas, opinions, or feelings they have at a particular time. ❏ *The White House insists that the president is in touch with the pulse of the Black community.* **5** V-I If something **pulses**, it moves, appears, or makes a sound with a strong regular rhythm. ❏ *His temples pulsed a little, threatening a headache.* **6** N-PLURAL Some seeds that can be cooked and eaten are called **pulses**, for example, peas, beans, and lentils. [mainly BRIT]

in AM, usually use **legumes**

pul|ver|ize /pʌlvəraɪz/ (**pulverizes, pulverizing, pulverized**)

in BRIT, also use **pulverise**

1 V-T To **pulverize** something means to do great damage to it or to destroy it completely. ❏ *The tsunami pulverized everything in its path.* **2** V-T If someone **pulverizes** an opponent in an election or competition, they thoroughly defeat them. [INFORMAL] ❏ *He is set to pulverize his two opponents in the race for the presidency.* **3** V-T If you **pulverize** something, you make it into a powder by crushing it. ❏ *Using a mortar and pestle, pulverize the bran to a coarse powder.* ❏ *The fries are made from pellets of pulverized potatoes.*
puma /pumə/ (**pumas**) N-COUNT A **puma** is a wild animal that is a member of the cat family. Pumas have brownish-gray fur and live in mountain regions of North and South America.
pum|ice /pʌmɪs/ **1** N-UNCOUNT **Pumice** is a kind of gray stone from a volcano and is very light in weight. It can be rubbed

over surfaces that you want to clean or make smoother, especially your skin. **2** → See also color supplement

pum|ice stone (pumice stones) **1** N-COUNT A **pumice stone** is a piece of pumice that you rub over your skin in order to clean it or make it smoother. **2** N-UNCOUNT **Pumice stone** is the same as **pumice**.

pum|mel /p_ʌ_m³l/ (pummels, pummeling or pummelling, pummeled or pummelled) V-T If you **pummel** someone or something, you hit them many times using your fists. ❏ *He trapped Chuck in a corner and pummeled him ferociously for thirty seconds.*

pump ♦◇◇ /p_ʌ_mp/ (pumps, pumping, pumped) **1** N-COUNT A **pump** is a machine or device that is used to force a liquid or gas to flow in a particular direction. ❏ *...pumps that circulate the fuel around in the engine.* ❏ *There was no water in the building, just a pump in the courtyard.* **2** V-T To **pump** a liquid or gas in a particular direction means to force it to flow in that direction using a pump. ❏ *It's not enough to get rid of raw sewage by pumping it out to sea.* ❏ *The money raised will be used to dig bore holes to pump water into the dried-up lake.* **3** N-COUNT A fuel or gas **pump** is a machine with a tube attached to it that you use to fill a car with gasoline. ❏ *The average price for all grades of gas at the pump was $3.49 a gallon.* **4** V-T [usu passive] If someone **has** their stomach **pumped**, doctors remove the contents of their stomach, for example, because they have swallowed poison or drugs. ❏ *One woman was rushed to the emergency room to have her stomach pumped.* **5** N-COUNT **Pumps** are women's shoes that do not cover the top part of the foot and are usually made of plain leather. [mainly AM]

in BRIT, usually use **court shoes**

6 → See also color supplement
▶ **pump out** PHRASAL VERB To **pump out** something means to produce or supply it continually and in large amounts. ❏ *Japanese companies have been pumping out plenty of innovative products.*
▶ **pump up** PHRASAL VERB If you **pump up** something such as a tire, you fill it with air using a pump. ❏ *Pump all the tires up.*

pum|per|nick|el /p_ʌ_mpərnɪk³l/ N-UNCOUNT **Pumpernickel** is a dark brown, heavy bread made with whole grains.

pump|kin /p_ʌ_mpkɪn/ (pumpkins) N-VAR A **pumpkin** is a large, round, orange vegetable with a thick skin. ❏ *Quarter the pumpkin and remove the seeds.*

pun /p_ʌ_n/ (puns) **1** N-COUNT A **pun** is a clever and amusing use of a word or phrase with two meanings, or of words with the same sound but different meanings. For example, if someone says 'The peasants are revolting,' this is a pun because it can be interpreted as meaning either that the peasants are fighting against authority, or that they are disgusting. ❏ *He spoke of a hatchet job, which may be a pun on some senator's name.* **2** → See feature box at **humor**

punch ♦◇◇ /p_ʌ_ntʃ/ (punches, punching, punched) **1** V-T If you **punch** someone or something, you hit them hard with your fist. ❏ *After punching him on the chin she wound up hitting him over the head.* • N-COUNT **Punch** is also a noun. ❏ *He was hurting Johansson with body punches in the fourth round.* • PHRASAL VERB **Punch out** means the same as **punch**. ❏ *"I almost lost my job today."—"What happened?"—"Oh, I punched out this guy."* **2** V-T If you **punch** something such as the buttons on a keyboard, you touch them in order to store information on a machine such as a computer or to give the machine a command to do something. ❏ *Mrs. Baylor strode to the elevator and punched the button.* **3** V-T If you **punch** holes in something, you make holes in it by pushing or pressing it with something sharp. ❏ *I took a ballpoint pen and punched a hole in the carton.* **4** N-COUNT A **punch** is a tool that you use for making holes in something. ❏ *Make two holes with a hole punch.* **5** N-UNCOUNT If you say that something has **punch**, you mean that it has force or effectiveness. ❏ *My nervousness made me deliver the vital points of my address without sufficient punch.* **6** N-MASS **Punch** is a drink made from wine, spirits, or fruit juice, mixed with things such as sugar and spices. ❏ *...a bowl of punch.*
▶ **punch in** **1** PHRASAL VERB If you **punch in** a number on a machine or **punch** numbers **into** it, you push the machine's buttons or keys in order to give it a command to do something. ❏ *You can bank by phone in the U.S., punching in account numbers on the phone.* **2** PHRASAL VERB When you **punch in** at work, you arrive there and put a special card into a device to show what time you arrived. ❏ *He would get up and get ready for work, eat, and punch in at 6 p.m.*

Punch and Judy show /p_ʌ_ntʃ ən dʒuːdi ʃoʊ/ (**Punch and Judy shows**) N-COUNT A **Punch and Judy show** is a puppet show for children. Punch and his wife Judy, the two main characters, are always fighting.

punch bowl (punch bowls) N-COUNT A **punch bowl** is a large bowl in which drinks, especially punch, are mixed and served.

punch-drunk also **punch drunk** **1** ADJ [usu ADJ n] A **punch-drunk** boxer shows signs of brain damage, for example, by being unsteady and unable to think clearly, after being hit too often on the head. **2** ADJ [usu v-link ADJ] If you say that someone is **punch-drunk**, you mean that they are very tired or confused, for example, because they have been working too hard. ❏ *He was punch-drunk with fatigue and depressed by the rain.*

punch|ing bag (punching bags) N-COUNT A **punching bag** is a heavy leather bag, filled with a firm material, that hangs on a rope. Punching bags are used by boxers and other athletes for exercise and training. [AM]

in BRIT, use **punchbag, punch bag**

punch|line /p_ʌ_ntʃlaɪn/ (punchlines) also **punch line, punch-line** **1** N-COUNT The **punchline** of a joke or funny story is its last sentence or phrase, which makes it funny. **2** → See feature box at **humor**

punchy /p_ʌ_ntʃi/ (punchier, punchiest) ADJ If you describe something as **punchy**, you mean that it expresses its meaning in a forceful or effective way. ❏ *A good way to sound confident is to use short punchy sentences.*

punc|tili|ous /p_ʌ_ŋktɪliəs/ ADJ Someone who is **punctilious** is very careful to behave correctly. [FORMAL] ❏ *He was punctilious about being ready and waiting in the entrance hall exactly on time.* ❏ *He was a punctilious young man.* • **punc|tili|ous|ly** ADV ❏ *Given the circumstances, his behavior to Laura had been punctiliously correct.*

punc|tu|al /p_ʌ_ŋktʃuəl/ ADJ If you are **punctual**, you do something or arrive somewhere at the right time and are not late. ❏ *He's always very punctual. I'll see if he's here yet.* • **punc|tu|al|ly** ADV ❏ *My guest arrived punctually.*

punc|tu|ate /p_ʌ_ŋktʃueɪt/ (punctuates, punctuating, punctuated) V-T [usu passive] If an activity or situation **is punctuated** by particular things, it is interrupted by them at intervals. [WRITTEN] ❏ *The game was punctuated by a series of injuries.*

punc|tua|tion /p_ʌ_ŋktʃueɪʃ³n/ N-UNCOUNT **Punctuation** is the use of symbols such as periods, commas, or question marks to divide written words into sentences and clauses. ❏ *He was known for his poor grammar and punctuation.* **2** N-UNCOUNT **Punctuation** is the symbols that you use to divide written words into sentences and clauses. ❏ *Jessica had rapidly scanned the lines, none of which boasted a capital letter or any punctuation.*

punc|tua|tion mark (punctuation marks) N-COUNT A **punctuation mark** is a symbol such as a period, comma, or question mark that you use to divide written words into sentences and clauses.

punc|ture /p_ʌ_ŋktʃər/ (punctures, puncturing, punctured) **1** N-COUNT A **puncture** is a small hole in a car tire or bicycle tire that has been made by a sharp object. ❏ *Somebody helped me to mend the puncture.* **2** N-COUNT A **puncture** is a small hole in someone's skin that has been made by or with a sharp object. ❏ *An instrument called a trocar makes a puncture in the abdominal wall.* **3** V-T If a sharp object **punctures** something, it makes a hole in it. ❏ *The bullet punctured the skull.* **4** V-T/V-I If a car tire or bicycle tire **punctures** or if something **punctures** it, a hole is made in the tire. ❏ *His bike's rear tire punctured.*

pun|dit /p_ʌ_ndɪt/ (pundits) N-COUNT A **pundit** is a person who knows a lot about a subject and is often asked to give information or opinions about it to the public. ❏ *...a well-known political pundit.*

pun|gent /p_ʌ_ndʒ³nt/ ADJ Something that is **pungent** has a strong, sharp smell or taste which is often so strong that it is unpleasant. ☐ *The more herbs you use, the more pungent the sauce will be.*

pun|ish /pʌnɪʃ/ (punishes, punishing, punished) **1** V-T To **punish** someone means to make them suffer in some way because they have done something wrong. ☐ *I don't believe that George ever had to punish the children.* ☐ *According to present law, the authorities can only punish smugglers with small fines.* **2** V-T To **punish** a crime means to punish anyone who commits that crime. ☐ *...federal laws to punish crimes such as murder and assault.*

pun|ish|able /pʌnɪʃəbəl/ ADJ [usu v-link ADJ by/with n] If a crime is **punishable** in a particular way, anyone who commits it is punished in that way. ☐ *Treason in this country is still punishable by death.*

pun|ish|ing /pʌnɪʃɪŋ/ ADJ A **punishing** schedule, activity, or experience requires a lot of physical effort and makes you very tired or weak. ☐ *He claimed his punishing work schedule had made him resort to taking the drug.*

pun|ish|ment /pʌnɪʃmənt/ (punishments) **1** N-UNCOUNT **Punishment** is the act of punishing someone or of being punished. ☐ *...a group that campaigns against the physical punishment of children.* **2** N-VAR A **punishment** is a particular way of punishing someone. ☐ *The government is proposing tougher punishments for officials convicted of corruption.* **3** N-UNCOUNT You can use **punishment** to refer to severe physical treatment of any kind. ☐ *Don't expect these boots to take the punishment that gardening will give them.* **4** → see also **capital punishment**, **corporal punishment**

pu|ni|tive /pyunɪtɪv/ ADJ **Punitive** actions are intended to punish people. [FORMAL] ☐ *...a punitive bombing raid.*

Pun|ja|bi /pʌndʒɑbi/ (Punjabis) **1** ADJ [usu ADJ n] **Punjabi** means belonging or relating to the Punjab region of India or Pakistan, its people, or its language. **2** N-COUNT A **Punjabi** is a person who comes from the Punjab. **3** N-UNCOUNT **Punjabi** is the language spoken by people who live in the Punjab.

punk /pʌŋk/ (punks) **1** N-UNCOUNT **Punk** or **punk rock** is rock music that is played in a fast, loud, and aggressive way and is often a protest against conventional attitudes and behavior. Punk rock was particularly popular in the late 1970s. ☐ *I was never really into punk.* **2** N-COUNT A **punk** or a **punk rocker** is a young person who likes punk music and dresses in a very noticeable and unconventional way, for example, by having brightly colored hair and wearing metal chains. ☐ *In the 1970s, punks wore safety pins through their cheeks.*

punt /pʌnt/ (punts, punting, punted) N-COUNT In football and rugby, a **punt** is a kick where you drop the ball and then kick it before it reaches the ground, so that it goes a long way. ☐ *He caught a punt and scored the winning touchdown, with a minute left to play.* ☐ *...a 66-yard punt return.* • V-T/V-I **Punt** is also a verb. ☐ *The referee told him to punt or kick the ball off the ground.* ☐ *The Redskins punted. Dallas then marched 79 yards to seal the victory.*

punt|er /pʌntər/ (punters) **1** N-COUNT People sometimes refer to their customers or clients as **punters**. [BRIT, INFORMAL] **2** N-COUNT In football and rugby, a **punter** is someone who kicks the ball by punting it.

puny /pyuni/ (punier, puniest) ADJ Someone or something that is **puny** is very small or weak. ☐ *...a puny youth.*

pup /pʌp/ (pups) **1** N-COUNT A **pup** is a young dog. ☐ *I'll get you an Alsatian pup for Christmas.* **2** N-COUNT The young of some other animals, for example, seals, are called **pups**. ☐ *Two thousand gray seal pups are born there every fall.*

pupa /pyupə/ (pupae /pyupi/) N-COUNT A **pupa** is an insect that is in the stage of development between a larva and a fully grown adult. It has a protective covering and does not move. [TECHNICAL] ☐ *The pupae remain dormant in the soil until they emerge as adult moths in the winter.*

pu|pil ♦◇◇ /pyupɪl/ (pupils) **1** N-COUNT A **pupil** of a painter, musician, or other expert is someone who studies under that expert and learns his or her skills. ☐ *After his education, Goldschmidt became a pupil of the composer Franz Schreker.* **2** N-COUNT The **pupils** of a school are the children who go to it. ☐ *...schools with over 1,000 pupils.* **3** N-COUNT The **pupils** of your eyes are the small, round, black holes in the center of them. ☐ *The sick man's pupils were dilated.* **4** → See also color supplement

---

COLLOCATIONS

pupil
NOUN **2**
adjective + **pupil**: able, bright, gifted; former, past, prospective; disruptive, unruly
verb + **pupil**: admit, exclude, expel, suspend; encourage, motivate, prepare, teach

SYNONYMS

pupil
NOUN **2**
student: *Warren's eldest son is an art student, at St Martin's.*
scholar: *The library attracts thousands of scholars and researchers.*
schoolchild: *Last year, I had an audience of schoolchildren, and they laughed at everything.*
learner: *...a new aid for younger children or slow learners.*

---

pup|pet /pʌpɪt/ (puppets) **1** N-COUNT A **puppet** is a doll that you can move, either by pulling strings that are attached to it or by putting your hand inside its body and moving your fingers. **2** N-COUNT You can refer to a person or country as a **puppet** when you mean that their actions are controlled by a more powerful person or government, even though they may appear to be independent. [DISAPPROVAL] ☐ *When the invasion occurred he seized power and ruled the country as a puppet of the occupiers.*

pup|pet|eer /pʌpɪtɪər/ (puppeteers) N-COUNT A **puppeteer** is a person who gives shows using puppets.

pup|py /pʌpi/ (puppies) N-COUNT A **puppy** is a young dog. ☐ *One Sunday he began trying to teach the two puppies to walk on a leash.*

pur|chase ♦◇◇ /pɜrtʃɪs/ (purchases, purchasing, purchased) **1** V-T When you **purchase** something, you buy it. [FORMAL] ☐ *He purchased a ticket and went up on the top deck.* • **pur|chas|er** (purchasers) N-COUNT ☐ *The broker will get 5% if he finds a purchaser.* **2** N-UNCOUNT The **purchase of** something is the act of buying it. [FORMAL] ☐ *When contemplating the purchase of a computer there are quite a few factors that a buyer must consider.* **3** N-COUNT A **purchase** is something that you buy. [FORMAL] ☐ *She opened the tie box and looked at her purchase. It was silk, with maroon stripes.*

pur|chase price (purchase prices) N-COUNT The **purchase price** of something that is being sold, especially a house or apartment, is the price you have to pay for it. ☐ *The purchase price includes all the furniture.*

pur|chas|ing pow|er **1** N-UNCOUNT The **purchasing power** of a currency is the amount of goods or services that you can buy with it. [BUSINESS] ☐ *The real purchasing power of the rouble has plummeted.* **2** N-UNCOUNT The **purchasing power** of a person or group of people is the amount of goods or services that they can afford to buy. [BUSINESS] ☐ *Wage rates must be maintained in order to maintain the purchasing power of the consumer.*

pur|dah /pɜrdə/ N-UNCOUNT **Purdah** is a custom practiced in some Muslim and Hindu societies, in which women either remain in a special part of the house or cover their faces and bodies to avoid being seen by men who are not related to them. If a woman is **in purdah**, she lives according to this custom.

pure ♦◇◇ /pyʊər/ (purer, purest) **1** ADJ A **pure** substance is not mixed with anything else. ☐ *...a carton of pure orange juice.* **2** ADJ Something that is **pure** is clean and does not contain any harmful substances. ☐ *In remote regions, the air is pure and the crops are free of poisonous insecticides.* • **pu|rity** /pyʊərɪti/ N-UNCOUNT [with poss] ☐ *They worried about the purity of tap water.* **3** ADJ If you describe something such as a color, a sound, or a type of light as **pure**, you mean that it is very clear and represents a perfect example of its type. ☐ *She was dressed in pure white clothes.* • **pu|rity** N-UNCOUNT ☐ *The soaring purity of her voice conjured up the frozen bleakness of the Far North.* **4** ADJ [ADJ n] **Pure** science or **pure** research is concerned only with theory and not with how this theory can be used in practical ways. ☐ *Physics isn't just about pure science with no immediate applications.* **5** ADJ **Pure** means complete and total. [EMPHASIS] ☐ *The old man turned to give her a look of pure surprise.*

pure|bred /pyʊərbrɛd/ also **pure-bred** ADJ [ADJ n] A **purebred** animal is one whose parents and ancestors all belong to the same breed. ☐ *...purebred Arab horses.*

pu|ree /pyʊreɪ, -ri/ (purees, pureeing, pureed) also **purée**
1 N-VAR **Puree** is food that has been crushed or beaten so that it forms a thick, smooth liquid. ❑ *...a can of tomato puree.* **2** V-T If you **puree** food, you make it into a puree. ❑ *In a blender, puree the fruit with the orange juice.*

pure|ly /pyʊərli/ ADV [ADV with cl/group] You use **purely** to emphasize that the thing you are mentioning is the most important feature or that it is the only thing which should be considered. [EMPHASIS] ❑ *It is a racing machine, designed purely for speed.*

pur|ga|tive /pɜrgətɪv/ (purgatives) **1** N-COUNT A **purgative** is a medicine that causes you to get rid of unwanted waste from your body. [FORMAL] **2** ADJ [ADJ n] A **purgative** substance acts as a purgative. [FORMAL] ❑ *...purgative oils.* ❑ *...a purgative tea.*

pur|ga|tory /pɜrgətɔri/ **1** N-PROPER **Purgatory** is the place where Roman Catholics believe the spirits of dead people are sent to suffer for their sins before they go to heaven. ❑ *Prayers were said for souls in purgatory.* **2** N-UNCOUNT You can describe a very unpleasant experience as **purgatory**. ❑ *Every step of the last three miles was purgatory.* ❑ *...five years of economic purgatory.*

purge /pɜrdʒ/ (purges, purging, purged) **1** V-T To **purge** an organization of its unacceptable members means to remove them from it. You can also talk about **purging** people from an organization. ❑ *The leadership voted to purge the party of "hostile and antipary elements."* ❑ *He recently purged the armed forces, sending hundreds of officers into retirement.* • N-COUNT **Purge** is also a noun. ❑ *The army have called for a more thorough purge of people associated with the late president.* **2** V-T If you **purge** something **of** undesirable things, you get rid of them. ❑ *He closed his eyes and lay still, trying to purge his mind of anxiety.*

pu|ri|fi|er /pyʊərɪfaɪər/ (purifiers) N-COUNT [oft n n] A **purifier** is a device or a substance that is used to purify something such as water, air, or blood. ❑ *...air purifiers.*

pu|ri|fy /pyʊərɪfaɪ/ (purifies, purifying, purified) V-T If you **purify** a substance, you make it pure by removing any harmful, dirty, or inferior substances from it. ❑ *I take wheat and yeast tablets daily to purify the blood.* • **pu|ri|fi|ca|tion** /pyʊərɪfɪkeɪʃⁿn/ N-UNCOUNT ❑ *...a water purification plant.*

pur|ist /pyʊərɪst/ (purists) **1** N-COUNT A **purist** is a person who wants something to be totally correct or unchanged, especially something they know a lot about. ❑ *The new edition of the dictionary carries 7,000 additions to the language, which purists say is under threat.* **2** ADJ **Purist** attitudes are the kind of attitudes that purists have. ❑ *...a peculiarly purist argument.*

pu|ri|tan /pyʊərɪtⁿn/ (puritans) **1** N-COUNT You describe someone as a **puritan** when they live according to strict moral or religious principles, especially when they disapprove of physical pleasures. [DISAPPROVAL] ❑ *Bykov had forgotten that Malinin was something of a puritan.* **2** ADJ **Puritan** attitudes are based on strict moral or religious principles and often involve disapproval of physical pleasures. [DISAPPROVAL] ❑ *Paul was someone who certainly had a puritan streak in him.*

Pu|ri|tan (Puritans) N-COUNT The **Puritans** were a group of English Protestants in the sixteenth and seventeenth centuries who lived in a very strict and religious way.

pu|ri|tani|cal /pyʊərɪtænɪkⁿl/ ADJ If you describe someone as **puritanical**, you mean that they have very strict moral principles, and often try to make other people behave in a more moral way. [DISAPPROVAL] ❑ *He has a puritanical attitude toward sex.*

pu|ri|tan|ism /pyʊərɪtⁿnɪzəm/ N-UNCOUNT **Puritanism** is behavior or beliefs that are based on strict moral or religious principles, especially the principle that people should avoid physical pleasures. [DISAPPROVAL] ❑ *...Southern Baptist puritanism.*

Pu|ri|tan|ism N-UNCOUNT **Puritanism** is the set of beliefs that were held by the Puritans. ❑ *Out of Puritanism came the intense work ethic.*

pu|rity /pyʊərɪtɪ/ → see **pure**

pur|loin /pɜrlɔɪn/ (purloins, purloining, purloined) V-T If someone **purloins** something, they steal it or borrow it without asking permission. [FORMAL] ❑ *Each side purloins the other's private letters.*

pur|ple ♦◇ /pɜrpⁿl/ (purples) COLOR Something that is **purple** is of a reddish-blue color. ❑ *She wore purple and green silk.*

Pur|ple Heart (Purple Hearts) N-COUNT The **Purple Heart** is a medal that is given to members of the U.S. armed forces who have been wounded during battle.

pur|plish /pɜrplɪʃ/ ADJ **Purplish** means slightly purple in color.

pur|port /pərpɔrt/ (purports, purporting, purported) V-T If you say that someone or something **purports** to do or be a particular thing, you mean that they claim to do or be that thing, although you may not always believe that claim. [FORMAL] ❑ *...a book that purports to tell the whole truth.*

pur|port|ed|ly /pərpɔrtɪdli/ ADV If you say that something has **purportedly** been done, you mean that you think that it has been done but you cannot be sure. [FORMAL] ❑ *...documents that were purportedly smuggled out of the country.*

pur|pose ♦♦◇ /pɜrpəs/ (purposes) **1** N-COUNT The **purpose** of something is the reason for which it is made or done. ❑ *The purpose of the occasion was to raise money for medical supplies.* ❑ *...the use of nuclear energy for military purposes.* **2** N-COUNT Your **purpose** is the thing that you want to achieve. ❑ *They might well be prepared to do you harm in order to achieve their purpose.* **3** N-UNCOUNT **Purpose** is the feeling of having a definite aim and of being determined to achieve it. ❑ *The teachers are enthusiastic and have a sense of purpose.* **4** PHRASE If you do something **on purpose**, you do it intentionally. ❑ *Was it an accident or did David do it on purpose?*

▬▬▬▬▬▬▬ COLLOCATIONS ▬▬▬▬▬▬▬

purpose
NOUN **1**
verb + **purpose**: fulfill, serve; defeat
adjective + **purpose**: sole, specific; express, intended, stated; commercial, educational, medicinal, recreational, scientific; practical, useful; main, primary

▬▬▬▬▬▬▬ SYNONYMS ▬▬▬▬▬▬▬

purpose
NOUN
1
reason: *The exact locations are being kept secret for reasons of security.*
point: *What was the point of thinking about him?*
function: *The main function of the merchant banks is to raise capital for industry.*
2
aim: *The aim of the festival is to increase awareness of Hindu culture and traditions.*
goal: *The goal is to raise as much money as possible.*
objective: *Our main objective was the recovery of the child, safe and well.*

purpose-built ADJ A **purpose-built** building has been specially designed and built for a particular use. [mainly BRIT]

in AM, usually use **custom-built**

pur|pose|ful /pɜrpəsfəl/ ADJ If someone is **purposeful**, they show that they have a definite aim and a strong desire to achieve it. ❑ *She had a purposeful air, and it became evident that this was not a casual visit.* • **pur|pose|ful|ly** ADV ❑ *He strode purposefully toward the barn.*

pur|pose|less /pɜrpəslɪs/ ADJ If an action is **purposeless**, it does not seem to have a sensible purpose. ❑ *Time may also be wasted in purposeless meetings.* ❑ *Surely my existence cannot be so purposeless?*

pur|pose|ly /pɜrpəsli/ ADV If you do something **purposely**, you do it intentionally. [FORMAL] ❑ *They are purposely withholding information.*

purr /pɜr/ (purrs, purring, purred) **1** V-I When a cat **purrs**, it makes a low vibrating sound with its throat because it is contented. ❑ *The kitten had settled comfortably in her arms and was purring enthusiastically.* **2** V-I When the engine of a machine such as a car **purrs**, it is working and making a quiet, continuous, vibrating sound. ❑ *Both boats purred out of the cave mouth and into open water.* • N-SING **Purr** is also a noun. ❑ *Carmela heard the purr of a motorcycle coming up the drive.*
3 → See feature box at **sound**

purse /pɜrs/ (purses, pursing, pursed) **1** N-COUNT A **purse** is a small bag or a handbag that women carry. [AM] ▫ *She looked at me and then reached in her purse for cigarettes.*

in BRIT, use **bag**

2 N-COUNT A **purse** is a very small bag that people, especially women, keep their money in. [mainly BRIT]

in AM, usually use **wallet**

3 N-SING **Purse** is used to refer to the total amount of money that a country, family, or group has. ▫ *The money could simply go into the public purse, helping to lower taxes.* **4** V-T If you **purse** your **lips**, you move them into a small, rounded shape, usually because you disapprove of something or when you are thinking. ▫ *She pursed her lips in disapproval.*

purs|er /pɜrsər/ (pursers) N-COUNT On a ship, the **purser** is an officer who deals with the accounts and official papers. On a passenger ship, the purser is also responsible for the welfare of the passengers.

purse strings N-PLURAL [the N] If you say that someone holds or controls **the purse strings**, you mean that they control the way that money is spent in a particular family, group, or country. ▫ *Women control the purse strings of most families.*

pur|su|ance /pərsuəns/ N-UNCOUNT [usu in N of n] If you do something in **pursuance of** a particular activity, you do it as part of carrying out that activity. [FORMAL] ▫ *...expenses used by a salesperson in pursuance of selling activities.*

pur|su|ant /pərsuənt/ PREP-PHRASE If someone does something **pursuant to** a law or regulation, they obey that law or regulation. [FORMAL] ▫ *He should continue to act pursuant to the United Nations Security Council resolutions.*

pur|sue ◆◇◇ /pərsu/ (pursues, pursuing, pursued) **1** V-T If you **pursue** an activity, interest, or plan, you carry it out or follow it. [FORMAL] ▫ *He said Japan would continue to pursue the policies laid down at the London summit.* **2** V-T If you **pursue** a particular aim or result, you make efforts to achieve it, often over a long period of time. [FORMAL] ▫ *He will pursue a trade policy that protects American workers.* **3** V-T If you **pursue** a particular topic, you try to find out more about it by asking questions. [FORMAL] ▫ *If your original request is denied, don't be afraid to pursue the matter.* **4** V-T If you **pursue** a person, vehicle, or animal, you follow them, usually in order to catch them. [FORMAL] ▫ *She pursued the man who had stolen a woman's bag.*

SYNONYMS

pursue
VERB
1
engage in: *I have never engaged in the drug trade.*
practice: *Acupuncture was practiced in China as long ago as the third millennium BC.*
follow: *'Do you follow any particular religion?'—'Yes, we're all Hindus.'*
4
follow: *I think we're being followed.*
chase: *She chased the thief for 100 yards.*
hunt: *Detectives have been hunting him for seven months.*
run after: *Neighboring store owners ran after the man and caught him.*

pur|su|er /pərsuər/ (pursuers) N-COUNT Your **pursuers** are the people who are chasing or searching for you. [FORMAL] ▫ *They had shaken off their pursuers.*

pur|suit /pərsut/ (pursuits) **1** N-UNCOUNT Your **pursuit** of something is your attempts at achieving it. If you do something **in pursuit of** a particular result, you do it in order to achieve that result. ▫ *...a young man whose relentless pursuit of excellence is conducted with single-minded determination.* **2** N-UNCOUNT The **pursuit of** an activity, interest, or plan consists of all the things that you do when you are carrying it out. ▫ *The vigorous pursuit of policies is no guarantee of success.* **3** N-UNCOUNT Someone who is **in pursuit of** a person, vehicle, or animal is chasing them. ▫ *...a police officer who drove a patrol car at more than 120 mph in pursuit of a motorcycle.* **4** N-COUNT Your **pursuits** are your activities, usually activities that you enjoy when you are not working. ▫ *They both love outdoor pursuits.* **5** → See feature box at **leisure**

pur|vey /pərveɪ/ (purveys, purveying, purveyed) **1** V-T If you **purvey** something such as information, you tell it to people. [FORMAL] ▫ *...one who would, for a hefty fee, purvey strategic advice to private corporations.* **2** V-T If someone **purveys** goods or services, they provide them. [FORMAL] ▫ *They have two restaurants that purvey dumplings and chicken noodle soup.*

pur|vey|or /pərveɪər/ (purveyors) N-COUNT A **purveyor of** goods or services is a person or company that provides them. [FORMAL] ▫ *...purveyors of gourmet foods.*

pur|view /pɜrvyu/ N-SING [usu N of n] The **purview of** something such as an organization or activity is the range of things it deals with. [FORMAL] ▫ *That, however, was beyond the purview of the court; it was a diplomatic matter.*

pus /pʌs/ N-UNCOUNT **Pus** is a thick yellowish liquid that forms in wounds when they are infected.

push ◆◆◇ /pʊʃ/ (pushes, pushing, pushed) **1** V-T/V-I When you **push** something, you use force to make it move away from you or away from its previous position. ▫ *The woman pushed back her chair and stood up.* ▫ *They pushed him into the car.* ▫ *...a pregnant woman pushing a stroller.* • N-COUNT **Push** is also a noun. ▫ *He gave me a sharp push.* **2** V-T/V-I If you **push through** things that are blocking your way or **push** your **way through** them, you use force in order to move past them. ▫ *I pushed through the crowds and on to the escalator.* ▫ *Dix pushed forward carrying a glass.* **3** V-I If an army **pushes into** a country or area that it is attacking or invading, it moves further into it. ▫ *One detachment pushed into the eastern suburbs toward the airfield.* • N-COUNT **Push** is also a noun. ▫ *All that was needed was one final push, and the enemy would be vanquished once and for all.* **4** V-T To **push** a value or amount **up** or **down** means to cause it to increase or decrease. ▫ *Any shortage could push up grain prices.* ▫ *The government had done everything it could to push down inflation.* **5** V-T If someone or something **pushes** an idea or project in a particular direction, they cause it to develop or progress in a particular way. ▫ *China would use its influence to help push forward the peace process.* **6** V-T If you **push** someone to do something or **push** them **into** doing it, you encourage or force them to do it. ▫ *She thanks her parents for keeping her in school and pushing her to study.* ▫ *Jason did not push her into stealing the money.* • N-COUNT **Push** is also a noun. ▫ *We need a push to take the first step.* **7** V-I If you **push for** something, you try very hard to achieve it or to persuade someone to do it. ▫ *Doctors are pushing for a ban on all cigarette advertising.* • N-COUNT **Push** is also a noun. ▫ *In its push for economic growth it has ignored projects that would improve living standards.* **8** V-T If someone **pushes** an idea, a point, or a product, they try in a forceful way to convince people to accept it or buy it. ▫ *The commissioners will push the case for opening the plant.* **9** V-T When someone **pushes** drugs, they sell them illegally. [INFORMAL] ▫ *You would be on welfare with your kids pushing drugs to pay the rent.* **10** → see also **pushed** **11** if push comes to shove → see **shove**

▶ **push ahead** also **push forward** PHRASAL VERB If you **push ahead** or **push forward** with something, you make progress with it. ▫ *The government intends to push ahead with its reform program.*

▶ **push back** PHRASAL VERB If you **push back** against something, such as a change or criticism, you refuse to accept it or try to prevent it. ▫ *Teachers who feel they have been criticized are starting to push back.*

▶ **push on** PHRASAL VERB When you **push on**, you continue with a trip or task. ▫ *Although the journey was a long and lonely one, Tumalo pushed on.*

▶ **push over** PHRASAL VERB If you **push** someone or something **over**, you push them so that they fall onto the ground. ▫ *We have had trouble with people damaging hedges, uprooting trees and pushing over walls.*

▶ **push through** PHRASAL VERB If someone **pushes through** a law, they succeed in getting it accepted although some people oppose it. ▫ *The Democratic majority pushed through a law permitting the sale of arms.*

push|back /pʊʃbæk/ N-UNCOUNT **Pushback** is a negative response to a change or a plan, often a refusal to accept it. ▫ *There's been a lot of pushback from conservatives on this issue.*

push|button /pʊʃbʌtən/ also **push button** ADJ [ADJ n] A **pushbutton** machine or process is controlled by means of buttons or switches. ▫ *...pushbutton phones.*

push|cart /pʊʃkɑrt/ (**pushcarts**) N-COUNT A **pushcart** is a cart from which fruit or other goods are sold in the street. [AM]

in BRIT, use **barrow**

push|chair /pʊʃtʃɛər/ (**pushchairs**) N-COUNT A **pushchair** is a small chair on wheels, in which a baby or small child can sit and be wheeled around. [BRIT]

in AM, use **stroller**

pushed /pʊʃt/ ADJ [v-link ADJ] If you are **pushed for** something such as time or money, you do not have enough of it. [BRIT, INFORMAL] ❑ *He's going to be a bit pushed for money.*

in AM, use **pressed for**

push|er /pʊʃər/ (**pushers**) N-COUNT A **pusher** is a person who sells illegal drugs. [INFORMAL] ❑ *His father accused him of acting as a carrier for some drug pushers.*

push|ing /pʊʃɪŋ/ PREP If you say that someone is **pushing** a particular age, you mean that they are nearly that age. [INFORMAL] ❑ *Pushing 40, he was an aging rock star.*

push|over /pʊʃoʊvər/ (**pushovers**) ◼ N-COUNT You say that someone is a **pushover** when you find it easy to persuade them to do what you want. [INFORMAL] ❑ *He is a tough negotiator. We did not expect to find him a pushover and he has not been one.* ◻ N-COUNT [usu sing] You say that something is a **pushover** when it is easy to do or easy to get. [INFORMAL] ❑ *You might think Hungarian a pushover to learn. It is not.*

push-up (**push-ups**) N-COUNT **Push-ups** are exercises to strengthen your arms and chest muscles. They are done by lying with your face toward the floor and pushing with your hands to raise your body until your arms are straight. ❑ *He did push-ups after games.*

pushy /pʊʃi/ (**pushier**, **pushiest**) ADJ If you describe someone as **pushy**, you mean that they try in a forceful way to get things done as they would like or to increase their status or influence. [INFORMAL, DISAPPROVAL] ❑ *She was a confident and pushy young woman.*

pu|sil|lani|mous /pyuːsɪlænɪməs/ ADJ If you say that someone is **pusillanimous**, you mean that they are timid or afraid. [FORMAL, DISAPPROVAL] ❑ *The authorities have been too pusillanimous in merely condemning the violence.*

puss /pʊs/ N-VOC People sometimes call a cat by saying '**Puss**.'

pussy /pʊsi/ (**pussies**) ◼ N-COUNT **Pussy** is a child's word for a cat. ◻ N-COUNT Some people use **pussy** to refer to a woman's genitals. [INFORMAL, VERY RUDE]

pussy|cat /pʊsikæt/ (**pussycats**) ◼ N-COUNT Children or people talking to children often refer to a cat as a **pussycat**. ◻ N-COUNT If you describe someone as a **pussycat**, you think that they are kind and gentle.

pussy|foot /pʊsifʊt/ (**pussyfoots**, **pussyfooting**, **pussyfooted**) V-I If you say that someone is **pussyfooting** around, you are criticizing them for behaving in a too cautious way because they are not sure what to do and are afraid to commit themselves. [DISAPPROVAL] ❑ *Why don't they stop pussyfooting around and say what they really mean?*

pus|tule /pʌstʃuːl/ (**pustules**) N-COUNT A **pustule** is a small infected swelling on the skin. [MEDICAL]

put ♦♦♦ /pʊt/ (**puts**, **putting**)

The form **put** is used in the present tense and is the past tense and past participle.

Put is used in a large number of expressions that are explained under other words in this dictionary. For example, the expression **to put someone in the picture** is explained at **picture**.

◼ V-T When you **put** something in a particular place or position, you move it into that place or position. ❑ *Leaphorn put the photograph on the desk.* ❑ *She hesitated, then put her hand on Grace's arm.* ◻ V-T If you **put** someone somewhere, you cause them to go there and to stay there for a period of time. ❑ *Rather than put him in the hospital, she had been caring for him at home.* ◾ V-T To **put** someone or something in a particular state or situation means to cause them to be in that state or situation. ❑ *This is going to put them out of business.* ❑ *He was putting himself at risk.* ◿ V-T To **put** something **on** people or things means to cause them to have it, or to cause them to be affected by it. ❑ *He didn't put any pressure on her.* ❑ *Be aware of the terrible strain it can put on a child when you expect the best grades.* ▣ V-T If you **put** your trust, faith, or confidence **in** someone or something, you trust them or have faith or confidence in them. ❑ *He had decided long ago that he would put his trust in socialism when the time came.* ▤ V-T If you **put** time, strength, or energy **into** an activity, you use it in doing that activity. ❑ *We're not saying that activists should put all their effort and time into party politics.* ▦ V-T If you **put** money **into** a business or project, you invest money in it. ❑ *Investors should consider putting some money into an annuity.* ▨ V-T When you **put** an idea or remark in a particular way, you express it in that way. You can use expressions like **to put it simply** and **to put it bluntly** before saying something when you want to explain how you are going to express it. ❑ *I had already met Pete a couple of times through – how should I put it – friends in low places.* ❑ *He admitted the security forces might have made some mistakes, as he put it.* ▩ V-T When you **put a question** to someone, you ask them the question. ❑ *Is this fair? Well, I put that question today to the mayor.* ◉ V-T If you **put** a case, opinion, or proposal, you explain it and list the reasons why you support or believe it. ❑ *He always put his point of view with clarity and with courage.* ❑ *He put the case to the Saudi foreign minister.* ◈ V-T If you **put** something **at** a particular value or **in** a particular category, you consider that it has that value or that it belongs in that category. ❑ *I would put her age at about 50 or so.* ❑ *All the more technically advanced countries put a high value on science.* ◌ V-T If you **put** written information somewhere, you write, type, or print it there. ❑ *Mary's family was so pleased that they put an announcement in the local paper to thank them.* ❑ *I think what I put in that book is now pretty much the agenda for this country.* ◍ PHRASE If you **put it to** someone that something is true, you suggest that it is true, especially when you think that they will be unwilling to admit this. ❑ *But I put it to you that they're useless.* ◎ PHRASE If you say that something is bigger or better than several other things **put together**, you mean that it is bigger or has more good qualities than all of those other things if they are added together. ❑ *Mary ate more than the rest of us put together.* ◐ → See feature box at **review**

▶ **put across** also **put over** PHRASAL VERB When you **put** something **across** or **put** it **over**, you succeed in describing or explaining it to someone. ❑ *He has taken out a half-page advertisement in his local paper to put his point across.*

▶ **put aside** PHRASAL VERB If you **put** something **aside**, you keep it to be dealt with or used at a later time. ❑ *Encourage children to put aside some of their allowance to buy Christmas presents.*

▶ **put away** PHRASAL VERB If you **put** something **away**, you put it into the place where it is normally kept when it is not being used, for example, in a drawer. ❑ *She finished putting the milk away and turned around.* ❑ *"Yes, Mom," replied Cheryl as she slowly put away her doll.*

▶ **put back** PHRASAL VERB To **put** something **back** means to delay it or arrange for it to happen later than you previously planned. ❑ *There are always new projects which seem to put the reunion back further.*

▶ **put down** ◼ PHRASAL VERB If you **put** something **down** somewhere, you write or type it there. ❑ *Never put anything down on paper which might be used in evidence against you at a later date.* ❑ *The journalists simply put down what they thought they heard.* ◻ PHRASAL VERB If you **put down** some money, you pay part of the price of something, and will pay the rest later. ❑ *He bought an investment property for $100,000 and put down $20,000.* ◾ PHRASAL VERB When soldiers, police, or the government **put down** a riot or rebellion, they stop it by using force. ❑ *Soldiers went in to put down a rebellion.* ◿ PHRASAL VERB If someone **puts** you **down**, they treat you in an unpleasant way by criticizing you in front of other people or making you appear foolish. ❑ *I know that I do put people down occasionally.* ❑ *Racist jokes often come from wanting to put down other kinds of people we feel threatened by.* ▣ → see also **put-down** ▤ PHRASAL VERB When an animal **is put down**, it is killed because it is dangerous or very ill. ❑ *The judge ordered their dog Samson to be put down immediately.*

▶ **put down to** PHRASAL VERB If you **put** something **down to** a particular thing, you believe that it is caused by that thing. ❑ *You may be a skeptic and put it down to life's inequalities.*

▶ **put forward** PHRASAL VERB If you **put forward** a plan, proposal, or name, you suggest that it should be considered for a particular purpose or job. ❑ *He has put forward new peace proposals.*

▶ **put in** ◼ PHRASAL VERB If you **put in** an amount of time or effort doing something, you spend that time or effort doing it. ❑ *Wade was going to be paid a salary, instead of by the hour, whether he put in forty hours or not.* ❑ *They've put in time and effort to keep the strike going.* ◼ PHRASAL VERB If you **put in** a request or **put in for** something, you formally request or apply for that thing. ❑ *I also put in a request for some overtime.* ◼ PHRASAL VERB If you **put in** a remark, you interrupt someone or add to what they have said with the remark. ❑ *"He was a lawyer before that," Mary Ann put in.*

▶ **put off** ◼ PHRASAL VERB If you **put** something **off**, you delay doing it. ❑ *Women who put off having a baby often make the best mothers.* ◼ PHRASAL VERB If you **put** someone **off**, you make them wait for something that they want. ❑ *The old priest tried to put them off, saying that the hour was late.* ◼ PHRASAL VERB If something **puts** you **off** something, it makes you dislike it, or decide not to do or have it. ❑ *The high divorce figures don't seem to be putting people off marriage.* ❑ *His personal habits put them off.* ◼ PHRASAL VERB If someone or something **puts** you **off**, they take your attention from what you are trying to do and make it more difficult for you to do it. ❑ *She asked me to be serious – said it put her off if I laughed.*

▶ **put on** ◼ PHRASAL VERB When you **put on** clothing or makeup, you place it on your body in order to wear it. ❑ *She put on her coat and went out.* ❑ *Maximo put on a pair of glasses.* ◼ PHRASAL VERB When people **put on** a show, exhibition, or service, they perform it or organize it. ❑ *The band is hoping to put on a show before the end of the year.* ◼ PHRASAL VERB If someone **puts on** weight, they become heavier. ❑ *I can eat what I want but I never put on weight.* ◼ PHRASAL VERB If you **put on** a piece of equipment or a device, you make it start working, for example, by pressing a switch or turning a knob. ❑ *I put the radio on.* ◼ PHRASAL VERB If you **put** a record, tape, or CD **on**, you place it in a record, tape, or CD player and listen to it. ❑ *She poured them drinks, and put a record on loud.*

▶ **put out** ◼ PHRASAL VERB If you **put out** an announcement or story, you make it known to a lot of people. ❑ *No one put out a press release aimed at the public.* ◼ PHRASAL VERB If you **put out** a fire, candle, or cigarette, you make it stop burning. ❑ *Firefighters tried to free the injured and put out the blaze.* ◼ PHRASAL VERB If you **put out** an electric light, you make it stop shining by pressing a switch. ❑ *He crossed to the nightstand and put out the light.* ◼ PHRASAL VERB If you **put out** things that will be needed, you place them somewhere ready to be used. ❑ *Paula had put out her luggage for the bus.* ◼ PHRASAL VERB If you **put out** your **hand**, you move it forward, away from your body. ❑ *He put out his hand to Alfred.* ◼ PHRASAL VERB If you **put** someone **out**, you cause them trouble because they have to do something for you. ❑ *It is a very sociable diet to follow because you don't have to put anyone out.*

▶ **put over** → see **put across**

▶ **put through** ◼ PHRASAL VERB When someone **puts through** someone who is making a telephone call, they make the connection that allows the telephone call to take place. ❑ *The operator will put you through.* ◼ PHRASAL VERB If someone **puts** you **through** an unpleasant experience, they make you experience it. ❑ *She wouldn't want to put them through the ordeal of a huge ceremony.*

▶ **put together** ◼ PHRASAL VERB If you **put** something **together**, you join its different parts to each other so that it can be used. ❑ *He took it apart brick by brick, and put it back together again.* ◼ PHRASAL VERB If you **put together** a group of people or things, you form them into a team or collection. ❑ *It will be able to put together a governing coalition.* ◼ PHRASAL VERB If you **put together** an agreement, plan, or product, you design and create it. ❑ *We wouldn't have time to put together an agreement.* ❑ *Reports speak of Berlin putting together an aid package for Moscow.* ◼ → see also **put 14**

▶ **put up** ◼ PHRASAL VERB If people **put up** a wall, building, tent, or other structure, they construct it so that it is upright. ❑ *Protesters have been putting up barricades across a number of major intersections.* ◼ PHRASAL VERB If you **put up** a poster or notice, you attach it to a wall or board. ❑ *They're putting new street signs up.* ◼ PHRASAL VERB To **put up** resistance to something means to resist it. ❑ *In the end the Kurds surrendered without putting up any resistance.* ❑ *He'd put up a real fight to keep you there.* ◼ PHRASAL VERB If you **put up** money for something, you provide the money that is needed to pay for it. ❑ *The state agreed to put up $69,000 to start his company.* ◼ PHRASAL VERB To **put up** the price of something means to cause it to increase. ❑ *Their friends suggested they should put up their prices.* ◼ PHRASAL VERB If a person or hotel **puts** you **up** or if you **put up** somewhere, you stay there for one or more nights. ❑ *I wanted to know if she could put me up for a few days.* ❑ *Hundreds of commuters had to be put up in hotel rooms.* ◼ PHRASAL VERB If a political party **puts up** a candidate in an election or if the candidate **puts up**, the candidate takes part in the election. ❑ *Barnes put up a candidate of his own for this post.*

▶ **put up with** PHRASAL VERB If you **put up with** something, you tolerate or accept it, even though you find it unpleasant or unsatisfactory. ❑ *They had put up with behavior from their son which they would not have tolerated from anyone else.*

pu|ta|tive /pyu:tətɪv/ ADJ [ADJ n] If you describe someone or something as **putative**, you mean that they are generally thought to be the thing mentioned. [FORMAL, LEGAL] ❑ *...a putative father.*

put-down (put-downs) also **putdown** N-COUNT A **put-down** is something that you say or do to criticize someone or make them appear foolish. [INFORMAL] ❑ *I see the term as a put-down of women.*

put out ADJ [v-link ADJ] If you feel **put out**, you feel annoyed or upset. ❑ *I did not blame him for feeling put out.*

pu|tre|fac|tion /pyu:trɪfækʃ°n/ N-UNCOUNT **Putrefaction** is the process of decay. [FORMAL] ❑ *...the lingering stench of putrefaction.*

pu|tre|fy /pyu:trɪfaɪ/ (putrefies, putrefying, putrefied) V-I When something **putrefies**, it decays and produces a very unpleasant smell. [FORMAL] ❑ *The meat in all of the open flasks putrefied.* ❑ *...putrefying corpses.*

pu|trid /pyu:trɪd/ ADJ Something that is **putrid** has decayed and smells very unpleasant. [FORMAL] ❑ *...a foul, putrid stench.*

putsch /pʊtʃ/ (putsches) N-COUNT A **putsch** is a sudden attempt to get rid of a government by force.

putt /pʌt/ (putts, putting, putted) ◼ N-COUNT A **putt** is a stroke in golf that you make when the ball has reached the green in an attempt to get the ball in the hole. ❑ *...a 5-foot putt.* ◼ V-T/V-I In golf, when you **putt**, or **putt** the ball, you hit a putt. ❑ *Turner, however, putted superbly, twice holing from 40 feet.*

putt|er /pʌtər/ (putters, puttering, puttered) ◼ N-COUNT A **putter** is a club used for hitting a golf ball a short distance once it is on the green. ◼ V-I If you **putter** around, you do unimportant but enjoyable things, without hurrying. [AM] ❑ *I started puttering around outside, not knowing what I was doing.* ❑ *She liked to putter in the kitchen.*

in BRIT, use **potter**

putt|ing green /pʌtɪŋ gri:n/ (putting greens) N-COUNT A **putting green** is a very small golf course on which the grass is kept very short and on which there are no obstacles.

put|ty /pʌti/ N-UNCOUNT **Putty** is a stiff paste used to secure sheets of glass into window frames.

put-upon also **put upon** ADJ If you are **put-upon**, you are treated badly by someone who takes advantage of your willingness to help them. [INFORMAL] ❑ *Volunteers from all walks of life are feeling put upon.*

puz|zle /pʌz°l/ (puzzles) ◼ V-T If something **puzzles** you, you do not understand it and feel confused. ❑ *My sister puzzles me and causes me anxiety.* ● **puz|zling** ADJ ❑ *His letter poses a number of puzzling questions.* ◼ V-I If you **puzzle over** something, you try hard to think of the answer to it or the explanation for it. ❑ *In rehearsing Shakespeare, I puzzle over the complexities of his verse and prose.* ◼ N-COUNT [oft supp N] A **puzzle** is a question, game, or toy that you have to think about carefully in order to answer it correctly or put it together properly. ❑ *...a word puzzle.* ◼ → see also **crossword, jigsaw** ◼ N-SING [a N] You can describe a person or thing that is hard to understand as **a puzzle**. ❑ *The rise in accidents remains a puzzle.*

puz|zled /pʌz°ld/ ADJ Someone who is **puzzled** is confused because they do not understand something. ❑ *Critics remain puzzled by the election results.*

puz|zle|ment /pʌzᵊlmənt/ N-UNCOUNT Puzzlement is the confusion that you feel when you do not understand something. ❏ *He frowned in puzzlement.*

PVC /pi vi si/ N-UNCOUNT PVC is a plastic material that is used for many purposes, for example, to make clothing or shoes or to cover chairs. PVC is an abbreviation for 'polyvinyl chloride.'

Pvt. N-TITLE Pvt. is used before a person's name as a written abbreviation for the military title **Private**. [AM] ❏ *...Pvt. Carlton McCarthy of the Richmond Howitzers.*

in BRIT, use **Pte**

pyg|my /pɪgmi/ (pygmies) also **pigmy** ◼ ADJ [ADJ n] Pygmy means belonging to a species of animal that is the smallest of a group of related species. ❏ *Reaching a maximum height of 56cm the pygmy goat is essentially a pet.* ◼ N-COUNT A **pygmy** is a member of a group of very short people who live in Africa or southeast Asia. ❏ *...the pygmy tribes of Papua New Guinea.*

py|ja|mas /pɪdʒɑməz/ [mainly BRIT] → see **pajamas**

py|lon /paɪlɒn/ (pylons) N-COUNT Pylons are very tall metal structures which hold electric cables high above the ground so that electricity can be transmitted over long distances. ❏ *...electricity pylons.*

pyra|mid /pɪrəmɪd/ (pyramids) ◼ N-COUNT Pyramids are ancient stone buildings with four triangular sloping sides. The most famous pyramids are those built in ancient Egypt to contain the bodies of their kings and queens. ❏ *We set off to see the Pyramids and Sphinx.* ◼ N-COUNT A **pyramid** is a shape, object, or pile of things with a flat base and sloping triangular sides that meet at a point. ❏ *On a plate in front of him was piled a pyramid of flat white crackers.* ◼ N-COUNT You can describe something as a **pyramid** when it is organized so that there are fewer people at each level as you go toward the top. ❏ *The legal world can be seen as a pyramid: the most desirable work is at the very top.*

py|rami|dal /pɪræmɪdᵊl/ ADJ Something that is **pyramidal** is shaped like a pyramid. [FORMAL] ❏ *...a black pyramidal tent.*

pyra|mid scheme N-UNCOUNT A Pyramid scheme is a method of selling in which one person buys a supply of a particular product directly from the manufacturer and then sells it to a number of other people at an increased price. These people sell it on to others in a similar way, but eventually the final buyers are only able to sell the product for less than they paid for it. [BUSINESS] ❏ *The pyramid scheme was marketed through a home page on the World Wide Web.*

pyre /paɪər/ (pyres) N-COUNT A pyre is a high pile of wood built outdoors on which people burn a dead body or other things in a ceremony.

Py|rex /paɪərɛks/ N-UNCOUNT [oft N n] Pyrex is a type of strong glass that is used for making bowls and dishes that do not break when you cook things in them. [TRADEMARK]

pyro|ma|ni|ac /paɪəroʊmeɪniæk/ (pyromaniacs) N-COUNT A **pyromaniac** is a person who has an uncontrollable desire to start fires.

pyro|tech|nics /paɪroʊtɛknɪks/ ◼ N-UNCOUNT Pyrotechnics is the making or displaying of fireworks. ❏ *The festival will feature pyrotechnics, live music, and sculptures.* ◼ N-PLURAL Impressive and exciting displays of skill are sometimes referred to as **pyrotechnics**. ❏ *...the soaring pyrotechnics of the singer's voice.*

Pyr|rhic vic|to|ry /pɪrɪk vɪktəri/ (Pyrrhic victories) also **pyrrhic victory** N-COUNT If you describe a victory as a **Pyrrhic victory**, you mean that although someone has won or gained something, they have also lost something that was worth even more.

py|thon /paɪθɒn, -θən/ (pythons) N-COUNT A python is a large snake that kills animals by squeezing them with its body.

Qq

Q also **q** /kyu/ (**Q's, q's**) N-VAR **Q** is the seventeenth letter of the English alphabet.

Q & A /kyu ən eɪ/ also **Q and A** N-UNCOUNT **Q & A** is a situation in which a person or group of people asks questions and another person or group of people answers them. **Q & A** is short for 'question and answer.'

QR code /kyu ɑr koʊd/ (**QR codes**) N-COUNT A **QR code** is a pattern of black and white squares that can be read by a smart phone, allowing the phone user to get more information about something. **QR code** is an abbreviation for 'Quick Response code.' ❏ *The ad includes a QR code.*

qt. qt. is a written abbreviation for **quart**.

Q-tip /kyu tɪp/ (**Q-tips**) N-COUNT A **Q-tip** is a small stick with a ball of absorbent cotton at each end, which people use, for example, for applying make-up. [AM, TRADEMARK] ❏ *She had cleaned under her fingernails, twirled the wax out of her ears with a Q-tip.*

> in BRIT, use **cotton bud**

quack /kwæk/ (**quacks, quacking, quacked**) **1** V-I When a duck **quacks**, it makes the noise that ducks typically make. ❏ *There were ducks quacking on the lawn.* • N-COUNT; SOUND **Quack** is also a noun. ❏ *Suddenly he heard a quack.* **2** N-COUNT [oft N n] If you call someone a **quack** or a **quack doctor**, you mean that they claim to be skilled in medicine but are not. [DISAPPROVAL] ❏ *I went everywhere for treatment, tried all sorts of quacks.* **3** ADJ [ADJ n] **Quack remedies** or **quack cures** are medical treatments that you think are unlikely to work because they are not scientific. [DISAPPROVAL]

quack|ery /kwækəri/ N-UNCOUNT If you refer to a form of medical treatment as **quackery**, you think that it is unlikely to work because it is not scientific. [DISAPPROVAL] ❏ *To some people, herbal medicine is quackery.*

quad /kwɒd/ (**quads**) **1** N-COUNT [usu pl] **Quads** are the same as **quadruplets**. ❏ *...a 34-year-old mother of quads.* **2** N-PLURAL The **quads** are the muscles that run down the front of the thigh and wrap around the knee. [INFORMAL] ❏ *To stretch the quads, you work the hamstrings.* **3** N-COUNT [usu the N] A **quad** is the same as a **quadrangle**. [INFORMAL] ❏ *His rooms were on the left-hand side of the quad.*

quad bike (**quad bikes**) N-COUNT A **quad bike** is a kind of motorbike with four large wheels that people ride for fun or in races.

quad|ran|gle /kwɒdræŋɡəl/ (**quadrangles**) N-COUNT [oft the N] A **quadrangle** is an open square area with buildings around it, especially in a college or school.

quad|rant /kwɒdrənt/ (**quadrants**) N-COUNT A **quadrant** is one of four equal parts into which a circle or other shape has been divided. ❏ *A symbol appears in the left upper quadrant of the screen.*

quad|ren|ni|al /kwɒdrɛniəl/ ADJ [ADJ n] A **quadrennial** event occurs once every four years. ❏ *...the quadrennial global festival of the World Cup.*

quad|rille /kwɒdrɪl/ (**quadrilles**) N-COUNT A **quadrille** is a type of old-fashioned dance for four or more couples.

quad|ri|plegic /kwɒdrɪplidʒɪk/ (**quadriplegics**) N-COUNT A **quadriplegic** is a person who is permanently unable to use their arms and legs. • ADJ **Quadriplegic** is also an adjective. ❏ *He is now quadriplegic and uses a wheelchair.*

quad|ru|ped /kwɒdrəped/ (**quadrupeds**) N-COUNT A **quadruped** is any animal with four legs. [FORMAL]

quad|ru|ple /kwɒdrʌpəl, -drup³l, kwɒdrup³l/ (**quadruples, quadrupling, quadrupled**) **1** V-T/V-I If someone **quadruples** an amount or if it **quadruples**, it becomes four times bigger. ❏ *China seeks to quadruple its income in twenty years.* **2** PREDET [PREDET det n] If one amount is **quadruple** another amount, it is four times bigger. ❏ *Fifty-nine percent of its residents have attended graduate school – quadruple the national average.* **3** ADJ [ADJ n] You use **quadruple** to indicate that something has four parts or happens four times. ❏ *The quadruple murder has replaced property prices as the sole topic of interest.*

quad|ru|plet /kwɒdrʌplɪt, -drup³lɪt, kwɒdruplɪt/ (**quadruplets**) N-COUNT [usu pl] **Quadruplets** are four children who are born to the same mother at the same time.

quaff /kwɒf/ (**quaffs, quaffing, quaffed**) V-T If you **quaff** an alcoholic drink, you drink a lot of it in a short time. [OLD-FASHIONED] ❏ *He's quaffed many a glass of vintage champagne in his time.*

quag|mire /kwægmaɪər/ (**quagmires**) **1** N-COUNT A **quagmire** is a difficult, complicated, or unpleasant situation which is not easy to avoid or escape from. ❏ *His people had fallen further and further into a quagmire of confusion.* **2** N-COUNT [usu sing] A **quagmire** is a soft, wet area of land which your feet sink into if you try to walk across it. ❏ *Rain had turned the grass into a quagmire.*

quail /kweɪl/ (**quails** or **quail, quails, quailing, quailed**) **1** N-COUNT A **quail** is a type of bird that lives on the ground and is often shot and eaten. **2** V-I If someone or something makes you **quail**, they make you feel very afraid, often so that you hesitate. [LITERARY] ❏ *The very words make many of us quail.* ❏ *He told Naomi she was becoming just like Maya. Naomi quailed at the thought.*

quaint /kweɪnt/ (**quainter, quaintest**) ADJ Something that is **quaint** is attractive because it is old-fashioned. ❏ *...a small, quaint town with narrow streets and traditional half-timbered houses.*

quake /kweɪk/ (**quakes, quaking, quaked**) **1** N-COUNT A **quake** is the same as an **earthquake**. [INFORMAL] ❏ *The quake destroyed mud buildings in many remote villages.* **2** V-I If you **quake**, you shake, usually because you are very afraid. ❏ *I just stood there quaking with fear.* **3** PHRASE If you **are quaking in** your **boots** or **quaking in** your **shoes**, you feel very nervous or afraid, and may be feeling slightly weak as a result. ❏ *If you stand up straight, you'll give an impression of self-confidence, even if you're quaking in your boots.*

Quak|er /kweɪkər/ (**Quakers**) N-COUNT A **Quaker** is a person who belongs to a Christian group called the Society of Friends.

quali|fi|ca|tion /kwɒlɪfɪkeɪʃən/ (**qualifications**) **1** N-COUNT Your **qualifications** are the official documents or titles you have that show your level of education and training. ❏ *"Do you have any qualifications?"—"Yes, I'm certified to teach high school."* **2** N-UNCOUNT **Qualification** is the act of passing the examinations you need to work in a particular profession. ❏ *She has met the minimum educational requirements for qualification.* **3** N-COUNT The **qualifications** you need for an activity or task are the qualities and skills that you need to be able to do it. ❏ *Responsibility and reliability are necessary qualifications, as well as a friendly and outgoing personality.* **4** N-VAR A **qualification** is a detail or explanation that you add to a statement to make it less strong or less general. ❏ *The empirical evidence considered here is subject to many qualifications.* **5** N-COUNT Your **qualifications** are the examinations you have passed. [BRIT] ❏ *Lucy Thomson, 16, wants to study theater but needs more qualifications.*

quali|fied ✦◊◊ /kwɒlɪfaɪd/ **1** ADJ Someone who is **qualified** has a certificate, license, diploma or degree in order to work in a particular profession. ❏ *Demand has far outstripped supply of qualified teachers.* ❏ *Are you qualified for this job?* **2** ADJ [ADJ n] If you give someone or something **qualified** support or approval, your support or approval is not total because you have some doubts. ❑ *The government has in the past given qualified support to the idea of tightening the legislation.* **3** PHRASE If you describe something as a **qualified success**, you mean that it is only partly successful. ❑ *Even as a humanitarian mission it has been only a qualified success.*

SYNONYMS

qualified
ADJ **1**
trained: *Mr Koutab is an American-trained lawyer.*
competent: *Most adults do not feel competent to deal with a medical emergency involving a child.*
experienced: *It's a team packed with experienced and mature professionals.*

quali|fi|er /kwɒlɪfaɪər/ (**qualifiers**) **1** N-COUNT A **qualifier** is an early round or match in some competitions. The players or teams who are successful are able to continue to the next round or to the main competition. ❑ *Crew Stadium hosted the U.S.-Mexico qualifier.* **2** → see also **qualify**

quali|fy ♦♦◇ /kwɒlɪfaɪ/ (**qualifies, qualifying, qualified**) **1** V-I If you **qualify** in a competition, you are successful in one part of it and go on to the next stage. ❑ *We qualified for the final by beating Stanford on Tuesday.* • **quali|fi|er** (**qualifiers**) N-COUNT ❑ *Kenya's Robert Kibe was the fastest qualifier for the 800 meters final.* **2** V-T/V-I To **qualify** as something or to **be qualified** as something means to have all the features that are needed to be that thing. ❑ *13 percent of American households qualify as poor, says Mr. Mishel.* **3** V-T If you **qualify** a statement, you make it less strong or less general by adding a detail or explanation to it. ❑ *I would qualify that by putting it into context.* ❑ *Boyd qualified his opinion, noting that the evidence could be interpreted in other ways.* **4** V-T/V-I If you **qualify** for something or if something **qualifies** you for it, you have the right to do it or have it. ❑ *To qualify for maternity leave you must have worked for the same employer for two years.* ❑ *The basic course does not qualify you to practice as a therapist.* **5** V-I When someone **qualifies**, they receive the certificate, license, diploma, or degree that they need to be able to work in a particular profession. ❑ *But when I'd qualified and started teaching it was a different story.* **6** → see also **qualified**

quali|ta|tive /kwɒlɪteɪtɪv/ ADJ **Qualitative** means relating to the nature or standard of something, rather than to its quantity. [FORMAL] ❑ *There are qualitative differences in the way children of different ages and adults think.*

qual|ity ♦♦◇ /kwɒlɪti/ (**qualities**) **1** N-UNCOUNT The **quality** of something is how good or bad it is. ❑ *Everyone can greatly improve the quality of life.* ❑ *Other services vary dramatically in quality.* **2** N-UNCOUNT Something of **quality** is of a high standard. ❑ *...a college of quality.* **3** N-COUNT Someone's **qualities** are the good characteristics that they have which are part of their nature. ❑ *Sometimes you wonder where your kids get their good qualities.* **4** N-COUNT You can describe a particular characteristic of a person or thing as a **quality**. ❑ *...a childlike quality.*

COLLOCATIONS

quality
NOUN **1**
noun + **quality**: air, picture, sound, water
adjective + **quality**: excellent, fine, high, top; poor
verb + **quality**: affect, assess; improve

SYNONYMS

quality
NOUN
1
standard: *The standard of professional tennis has never been lower.*
condition: *I received several compliments on the condition of my skin.*
caliber: *I was impressed by the high caliber of the researchers and analysts.*
4
characteristic: *Genes determine the characteristics of every living thing.*
feature: *The spacious gardens are a special feature of this property.*
attribute: *He has every attribute you could want and could play for any team.*

VOCABULARY IN CONTEXT

Personal qualities

You probably think you know which personal qualities are desirable and which are less so. For example, **pessimism** and **cynicism** can seem like negative traits. But, if you think about it, it can sometimes be useful to have considered what might go wrong so you can prepare for it. Moreover, the **cynic** isn't prone to being overly **idealistic**, and so takes a more critical stance, adding in a sometimes much-needed dose of **realism**. We think of **determined** people as being more likely to be successful, but when it comes to **stubbornness**, we have less sympathy. However, even stubbornness can be a positive quality in small measures – if it means sticking with an idea that seems crazy to other people. Perhaps your idea is too ahead of its time for others to understand, like Steve Jobs' confidence that personal computing was the future of computers. Some of the more negative aspects of these characteristics can be offset by traits such as being **empathetic** and **supportive** of others. As long as you can listen and think of others as well as yourself, how much harm can you do?

qual|ity con|trol N-UNCOUNT **Quality control** is the activity of checking that goods or services are of an acceptable standard. [BUSINESS] ❑ *The message is you need better quality control.*

qual|ity of life N-SING [the/poss N] Someone's **quality of life** is the extent to which their life is comfortable or satisfying. ❑ *"Would you go back to England?"—"Never, the quality of life is so much better here."* ❑ *A vibrant and growing economy does not improve everyone's quality of life.*

qual|ity time N-UNCOUNT If people spend **quality time** together, they spend a period of time relaxing or doing things that they both enjoy, and not worrying about work or other responsibilities. [APPROVAL] ❑ *Today I can spend quality time with my family for a change.*

qualm /kwɑm/ (**qualms**) N-COUNT If you have no **qualms** about doing something, you are not worried that it may be wrong in some way. ❑ *I have no qualms about recommending the same approach to other doctors.*

quan|da|ry /kwɒndəri, -dri/ (**quandaries**) N-COUNT [usu sing] If you are in a **quandary**, you have to make a decision but cannot decide what to do. ❑ *The government appears to be in a quandary about what to do with so many people.*

quan|ti|fi|able /kwɒntɪfaɪəb^əl/ ADJ Something that is **quantifiable** can be measured or counted in a scientific way. ❑ *A clearly quantifiable measure of quality is not necessary.*

quan|ti|fi|er /kwɒntɪfaɪər/ (**quantifiers**) N-COUNT In grammar, a **quantifier** is a word or phrase such as 'plenty of' or 'a lot' which you use to refer to a quantity of something without being precise. It is often followed by 'of,' as in 'a lot of money.'

quan|ti|fy /kwɒntɪfaɪ/ (**quantifies, quantifying, quantified**) V-T [usu with brd-neg] If you try to **quantify** something, you try to calculate how much of it there is. ❑ *It is difficult to quantify an exact figure as firms are reluctant to declare their losses.*

quan|ti|ta|tive /kwɒntɪteɪtɪv/ ADJ **Quantitative** means relating to different sizes or amounts of things. [FORMAL] ☐ *...the advantages of quantitative and qualitative research.*

quan|ti|ta|tive eas|ing N-UNCOUNT **Quantitative easing** is the practice of increasing the supply of money in order to encourage activity in an economy. ☐ *The bank has continued to hold interest rates and announced no change to its quantitative easing program.*

quan|tity ♦♦◊ /kwɒntɪti/ (quantities) **1** N-VAR A **quantity** is an amount. ☐ *...a small quantity of water.* **2** N-UNCOUNT Things that are produced or available in **quantity** are produced or available in large amounts. ☐ *After some initial problems, acetone was successfully produced in quantity.* **3** N-UNCOUNT You can use **quantity** to refer to the amount of something that there is, especially when you want to contrast it with its quality. ☐ *...the less discerning drinker who prefers quantity to quality.* **4** PHRASE If you say that someone or something is an **unknown quantity**, you mean that not much is known about what they are like or how they will behave. ☐ *She had known Max for some years now, but he was still pretty much an unknown quantity.*

── SYNONYMS ──
quantity
NOUN **1**
amount: *He needs that amount of money to survive.*
number: *Quite a considerable number of interviews are going on.*
size: *...a stockpile, second in size only to that of the US.*

quan|tum /kwɒntəm/ **1** ADJ [ADJ n] In physics, **quantum** theory and **quantum** mechanics are concerned with the behavior of atomic particles. ☐ *Both quantum mechanics and chaos theory suggest a world constantly in flux.* **2** ADJ [ADJ n] A **quantum leap** or **quantum jump** in something is a very great and sudden increase in its size, amount, or quality. ☐ *A vaccine which can halt this suffering represents a quantum leap in healthcare in this country.*

quar|an|tine /kwɒrəntin/ (quarantines, quarantining, quarantined) **1** N-UNCOUNT If a person or animal is in **quarantine**, they are being kept separate from other people or animals for a set period of time, usually because they have or may have a disease that could spread. ☐ *She was sent home and put in quarantine.* **2** V-T [usu passive] If people or animals **are quarantined**, they are stopped from having contact with other people or animals. If a place **is quarantined**, people and animals are prevented from entering or leaving it. ☐ *Dogs have to be quarantined for six months before they'll let them in.* ☐ *1.5 million people were told to quarantine for 12 weeks.*

quark /kwɔrk/ (quarks) N-COUNT In physics, a **quark** is one of the basic units of matter.

quar|rel /kwɔrəl/ (quarrels, quarreling or quarrelling, quarreled or quarrelled) **1** N-COUNT A **quarrel** is an angry argument between two or more friends or family members. ☐ *I had a terrible quarrel with my other brothers.* **2** V-RECIP When two or more people **quarrel**, they have an angry argument. ☐ *At one point we quarreled, over something silly.* **3** N-SING If you say that you have no **quarrel** with someone or something, you mean that you do not disagree with them. ☐ *We have no quarrel with the people of Spain or of any other country.* **4** N-COUNT **Quarrels** between countries or groups of people are disagreements, which may be diplomatic or include fighting. [JOURNALISM] ☐ *New Zealand's quarrel with France over the Rainbow Warrior incident was formally ended.*

quar|rel|some /kwɔrəlsəm/ ADJ [usu ADJ n] A **quarrelsome** person often gets involved in arguments. ☐ *Benedict had been a wild boy and a quarrelsome young man.*

quar|ry /kwɔri/ (quarries, quarrying, quarried) **1** N-COUNT A **quarry** is an area that is dug out from a piece of land or the side of a mountain in order to get stone or minerals. ☐ *...an old limestone quarry.* **2** V-T When stone or minerals **are quarried** or when an area **is quarried** for them, they are removed from the area by digging, drilling, or using explosives. ☐ *The large limestone caves are also quarried for cement.*

quart /kwɔrt/ (quarts) N-COUNT A **quart** is a unit of volume that is equal to two pints. There are four quarts in a gallon. The abbreviation **qt.** is also used. ☐ *Pick up a quart of milk and a loaf of bread.*

quar|ter ♦♦◊ /kwɔrtər/ (quarters, quartering, quartered) **1** FRACTION A **quarter** is one of four equal parts of something. ☐ *A quarter of the residents are over 55 years old.* ☐ *Prices have fallen by a quarter since January.* • PREDET **Quarter** is also a predeterminer. ☐ *The largest asteroid is Ceres, which is about a quarter the size of the moon.* • ADJ [ADJ n] **Quarter** is also an adjective. ☐ *...the past quarter century.* **2** N-COUNT A **quarter** is an American or Canadian coin that is worth 25 cents. ☐ *I dropped a quarter into the slot of the pay phone.* **3** N-COUNT A **quarter** is a fixed period of three months. Companies often divide their financial year into four quarters. ☐ *The group said results for the third quarter are due on October 29.* **4** N-UNCOUNT [also a N] When you are telling the time, you use **quarter** to talk about the fifteen minutes before or after an hour. For example, 8:15 is **quarter after** eight or **quarter** past eight and 8:45 is a **quarter** of or a **quarter** to nine. ☐ *It was a quarter to six.* **5** V-T If you **quarter** something such as a fruit or a vegetable, you cut it into four roughly equal parts. ☐ *Chop the mushrooms and quarter the tomatoes.* **6** V-T [usu passive] If the number or size of something **is quartered**, it is reduced to about a quarter of its previous number or size. ☐ *The doses I suggested for adults could be halved or quartered.* **7** N-COUNT A particular **quarter** of a town is a part of the town where a particular group of people traditionally live or work. ☐ *We wandered through the Chinese quarter.* **8** PHRASE If you do something **at close quarters**, you do it very near to a particular person or thing. ☐ *You can watch aircraft take off or land at close quarters.* **9** → See feature box at **town**

quarter|back ♦♦◊ /kwɔrtərbæk/ (quarterbacks) N-COUNT In football, a **quarterback** is the player on the attacking team who begins each play and who decides which play to use. [AM]

quarter|final /kwɔrtərfaɪnᵊl/ (quarterfinals)

in BRIT, use **quarter-final**

N-COUNT A **quarterfinal** is one of the four matches in a competition which decides which four players or teams will compete in the semifinal. ☐ *The very least I'm looking for at the Open is to reach the quarterfinals.*

quarter|final|ist /kwɔrtərfaɪnᵊlɪst/ (quarterfinalists)

in BRIT, use **quarter-finalist**

N-COUNT A **quarterfinalist** is a person or team that is competing in a quarterfinal.

quar|ter|ly /kwɔrtərli/ (quarterlies) **1** ADJ A **quarterly** event happens four times a year, at intervals of three months. ☐ *...the latest Bank of Japan quarterly survey of 5,000 companies.* • ADV [ADV after v] **Quarterly** is also an adverb. ☐ *It makes no difference whether dividends are paid quarterly or annually.* **2** N-COUNT A **quarterly** is a magazine that is published four times a year, at intervals of three months. ☐ *The quarterly had been a forum for sound academic debate.*

quar|ter note (quarter notes) N-COUNT A **quarter note** is a musical note that has a time value equal to two eighth notes. [AM]

in BRIT, use **crotchet**

Quar|ter Pound|er (Quarter Pounders) N-COUNT A **Quarter Pounder** is a hamburger that weighs four ounces before it is cooked. Four ounces is a quarter of a pound. [TRADEMARK]

quar|tet /kwɔrtɛt/ (quartets) **1** N-COUNT-COLL A **quartet** is a group of four people who play musical instruments or sing together. ☐ *...a string quartet.* **2** N-COUNT A **quartet** is a piece of music for four instruments or four singers. ☐ *The String Quartet No. 1 is an early work, composed in California in 1941.*

quartz /kwɔrts/ **1** N-UNCOUNT **Quartz** is a mineral in the form of a hard, shiny crystal. It is used in making electronic equipment and very accurate watches and clocks. ☐ *...a quartz crystal.* **2** → See also color supplement

qua|sar /kweɪzɑr/ (quasars) N-COUNT A **quasar** is an object far away in space that produces bright light and radio waves.

quash /kwɒʃ/ (quashes, quashing, quashed) **1** V-T If a court or someone in authority **quashes** a decision or judgment, they officially reject it. ☐ *The Appeal Court has quashed the convictions of all eleven people.* **2** V-T If someone **quashes** rumors, they say or do something to demonstrate that the rumors are not true. ☐ *Graham attempted to quash* rumors of growing discontent in the dressing room. ◼ V-T To **quash** a rebellion or protest means to stop it, often in a violent way. ❑ *Troops were displaying an obvious reluctance to get involved in quashing demonstrations.*

quasi- /kwe͟ɪzaɪ-, kwɑ͟ːzi-/ COMB IN ADJ **Quasi-** is used to form adjectives and nouns that describe something as being in many ways like something else, without actually being that thing. ❑ *At the time, medicine was still a primitive quasi-science.*

qua|ver /kwe͟ɪvər/ (**quavers**, **quavering**, **quavered**) ◼ V-I If someone's voice **quavers**, it sounds unsteady, usually because they are nervous or uncertain. ❑ *Her voice quavered and she fell silent.* • N-COUNT **Quaver** is also a noun. ❑ *There was a quaver in Lena's voice.* ◼ N-COUNT A **quaver** is a musical note that is half as long as a quarter note. [mainly BRIT]

in AM, use **eighth note**

quay /ki͟ː/ (**quays**) N-COUNT A **quay** is a long platform beside the sea or a river where boats can be tied up and loaded or unloaded. ❑ *Jack and Stephen were waiting for them on the quay.*

quay|side /ki͟ːsaɪd/ (**quaysides**) N-COUNT [oft N n] A **quayside** is the same as a **quay**. ❑ *A large group had gathered on the quayside to see them off.*

quea|sy /kwi͟ːzi/ (**queasier**, **queasiest**) ADJ If you feel **queasy** or if you have a **queasy** stomach, you feel sick, as if you are going to throw up. [INFORMAL] ❑ *He was very prone to seasickness and already felt queasy.* • **quea|si|ness** N-UNCOUNT ❑ *The food did nothing to stifle her queasiness.*

queen ♦♦◇ /kwi͟ːn/ (**queens**) ◼ N-TITLE; N-COUNT A **queen** is a woman who rules a country as its monarch. ❑ *...Queen Victoria.* ◼ N-TITLE; N-COUNT A **queen** is a woman who is married to a king. ❑ *The king and queen had fled.* ◼ N-COUNT If you refer to a woman as the **queen** of a particular activity, you mean that she is well-known for being very good at it. ❑ *...the queen of crime writing.* ◼ N-COUNT In chess, the **queen** is the most powerful piece. It can be moved in any direction. ❑ *Chris will either have to take his queen's knight and lose his own knight, or he'll lose a rook.* ◼ N-COUNT A **queen** is a playing card with a picture of a queen on it. ❑ *...the queen of spades.* ◼ N-COUNT A **queen** or a **queen bee** is a large female bee which can lay eggs. ❑ *Glass hives offer a close-up view of the bees at work, with the queen bee in each hive marked by a white dot.* ◼ N-COUNT A **queen** is a gay man who dresses and behaves in a feminine way. [INFORMAL]

queen|ly /kwi͟ːnli/ ADJ [usu ADJ n] You use **queenly** to describe a woman's appearance or behavior if she looks very dignified or behaves as if she is very important. ❑ *She was a queenly, organizing type.*

Queen Moth|er N-PROPER [the N] **The Queen Mother** is the mother of a ruling king or queen.

queen-size also **queen-sized** ADJ [ADJ n] A **queen-size** bed is larger than a double bed, but smaller than a king-size bed.

queer /kwi͟ər/ (**queerer**, **queerest**, **queers**) ◼ ADJ Something that is **queer** is strange. [OLD-FASHIONED] ❑ *If you ask me, there's something kind of queer going on.* ◼ N-COUNT A **queer** is someone whose sexual orientation or gender identity is not heterosexual. This use can sometimes cause offense. [INFORMAL] • ADJ **Queer** is also an adjective. ❑ *...America's first queer country music star.* ❑ *...contemporary queer culture.*

quell /kwe͟l/ (**quells**, **quelling**, **quelled**) ◼ V-T To **quell** opposition or violent behavior means to stop it. ❑ *Troops eventually quelled the unrest.* ◼ V-T If you **quell** an unpleasant feeling such as fear or anger, you stop yourself or other people from having that feeling. ❑ *The government is trying to quell fears of a looming oil crisis.*

quench /kwe͟ntʃ/ (**quenches**, **quenching**, **quenched**) V-T If someone who is thirsty **quenches** their thirst, they lose their thirst by having a drink. ❑ *He stopped to quench his thirst at a stream.*

queru|lous /kwe͟rələs, kwe͟rjə-/ ADJ Someone who is **querulous** often complains about things. [FORMAL, DISAPPROVAL] ❑ *A querulous male voice said, "Look, are you going to order, or what?"*

que|ry /kwi͟əri/ (**queries**, **querying**, **queried**) ◼ N-COUNT A **query** is a question, especially one that you ask an organization, publication, or expert. ❑ *If you have any queries about this insurance, please contact our call center.* ◼ V-T If you **query** something, you check it by asking about it because you are not sure if it is correct. ❑ *It's got a number you can call to query*

your bill. ◼ V-T To **query** means to ask a question. ❑ *"Is there something else?" Ray queried as Helen stopped speaking.*

quest /kwe͟st/ (**quests**, **questing**, **quested**) ◼ N-COUNT A **quest** is a long and difficult search for something. [LITERARY or HUMOROUS] ❑ *My quest for a better bank continues.* ❑ *...the quest for the Holy Grail.* • PHRASE If you go **in quest of** something, you try to find or obtain it. ◼ V-I [usu cont] If you **are questing** for something, you are searching for it. [LITERARY] ❑ *He had been questing for religious belief from an early age.* ❑ *...his questing mind and boundless enthusiasm.*

ques|tion ♦♦♦ /kwe͟stʃən/ (**questions**, **questioning**, **questioned**) ◼ N-COUNT A **question** is something that you say or write in order to ask a person about something. ❑ *They asked a lot of questions about China.* ◼ V-T If you **question** someone, you ask them a lot of questions about something. ❑ *This led the therapist to question Jim about his parents and their marriage.* • **ques|tion|ing** N-UNCOUNT ❑ *The police have detained thirty-two people for questioning.* ◼ V-T If you **question** something, you have or express doubts about whether it is true, reasonable, or worthwhile. ❑ *It never occurs to them to question the doctor's decisions.* ◼ N-SING If you say that there is some **question** about something, you mean that there is doubt or uncertainty about it. If something is **in question** or has been called **into question**, doubt or uncertainty has been expressed about it. ❑ *There's no question about their success.* ❑ *Her political future is in question.* ❑ *My integrity has been called into question by people who have never spoken to me.* ◼ N-COUNT A **question** is a problem, matter, or point which needs to be considered. ❑ *But the whole question of aid is a tricky political one.* ◼ N-COUNT The **questions** on an examination are the problems that test your knowledge or ability. ❑ *That question did come up on the test.* ◼ → see also **questioning** ◼ PHRASE The person, thing, or time **in question** is one which you have just been talking about or which is relevant. ❑ *Add up all the income you've received over the period in question.* ◼ PHRASE If you say that something is **out of the question**, you are emphasizing that it is completely impossible or unacceptable. [EMPHASIS] ❑ *For homeless people, private medical care is simply out of the question.* ◼ PHRASE If you **pop the question**, you ask someone to marry you. [INFORMAL] ❑ *Stuart got serious quickly and popped the question six months later.* ◼ PHRASE If you say **there is no question of** something happening, you are emphasizing that it is not going to happen. [EMPHASIS] ❑ *There was no question of my blaming Janet.*

ques|tion|able /kwe͟stʃənəbəl/ ADJ If you say that something is **questionable**, you mean that it is not completely honest, reasonable, or acceptable. [FORMAL] ❑ *He has been dogged by allegations of questionable business practices.*

ques|tion|er /kwe͟stʃənər/ (**questioners**) N-COUNT A **questioner** is a person who is asking a question. ❑ *He agreed with the questioner.*

ques|tion|ing /kwe͟stʃənɪŋ/ ◼ ADJ [ADJ n] If someone has a **questioning** expression on their face, they look as if they want to know the answer to a question. [WRITTEN] ❑ *He raised a questioning eyebrow.* ◼ → see also **question**

ques|tion mark (**question marks**) ◼ N-COUNT A **question mark** is the punctuation mark ? which is used in writing at the end of a question. ❑ *Who invented the question mark?* ◼ N-COUNT If there is doubt or uncertainty about something, you can say that there is a **question mark** over it. ❑ *There are bound to be question marks over his future.*

ques|tion|naire /kwe͟stʃəne͟ər/ (**questionnaires**) N-COUNT A **questionnaire** is a written list of questions which are answered by a lot of people in order to provide information for a report or a survey. ❑ *Teachers will be asked to fill in a questionnaire.*

ques|tion tag (**question tags**) N-COUNT In grammar, a **question tag** is a very short clause at the end of a statement which changes the statement into a question. For example, in 'She said half price, didn't she?,' the words 'didn't she' are a question tag.

queue /kyu͟ː/ (**queues**, **queuing**, **queued**)

Queueing can also be used as the continuous form.

◼ N-COUNT A **queue** is a list of computer tasks which will be done in order. [COMPUTING] ❑ *Your print job has already been sent from your PC to the network print queue.* ◼ V-T To **queue** a number of computer tasks means to arrange them to be done in order.

quibble · quietude

[COMPUTING] **3** N-COUNT A **queue** is a line of people or vehicles that are waiting for something. [mainly BRIT]

> in AM, usually use **line**

4 N-COUNT If you say there is a **queue** of people who want to do or have something, you mean that a lot of people are waiting for an opportunity to do it or have it. [mainly BRIT]

> in AM, usually use **line**

5 V-I When people **queue**, they stand in a line waiting for something. [mainly BRIT] • PHRASAL VERB **Queue up** means the same as **queue**.

> in AM, usually use **stand in line**

quib|ble /kwɪbᵊl/ (quibbles, quibbling, quibbled) **1** V-RECIP When people **quibble** over a small matter, they argue about it even though it is not important. ❑ *Lawmakers spent the day quibbling over the final wording of the resolution.* **2** N-COUNT A **quibble** is a small and unimportant complaint about something. ❑ *These are minor quibbles.*

quiche /kiːʃ/ (quiches) N-VAR A **quiche** is a pie crust filled with eggs, typically mixed with cream, cheese, and vegetables, baked and served as a main course.

quick ◆◆◆ /kwɪk/ (quicker, quickest) **1** ADJ Someone or something that is **quick** moves or does things with great speed. ❑ *You'll have to be quick. The flight leaves in about three hours.* • **quick|ly** ADV [ADV with v] ❑ *Cussane worked quickly and methodically.* • **quick|ness** N-UNCOUNT ❑ *...the natural quickness of his mind.* **2** ADV [ADV after v] **Quicker** is sometimes used to mean 'at a greater speed,' and **quickest** to mean 'at the greatest speed.' **Quick** is sometimes used to mean 'with great speed.' Some people consider this to be non-standard. [INFORMAL] ❑ *Warm the sugar slightly first to make it dissolve quicker.* **3** ADJ Something that is **quick** takes or lasts only a short time. ❑ *He took one last quick look around the room.* • **quick|ly** ADV [ADV with v] ❑ *You can get in shape quite quickly and easily.* **4** ADJ **Quick** means happening without delay or with very little delay. ❑ *Officials played down any hope for a quick end to the bloodshed.* • **quick|ly** ADV [ADV with v] ❑ *We need to get it back as quickly as possible.* **5** ADV [ADV after v] **Quick** is sometimes used to mean 'with very little delay.' [INFORMAL] ❑ *I got away as quick as I could.* **6** ADJ [v-link ADJ] If you are **quick** to do something, you do not hesitate to do it. ❑ *Mark says the ideas are Katie's own, and is quick to praise her talent.* **7** ADJ [ADJ n] If someone has a **quick** temper, they are easily made angry. ❑ *He readily admitted to the interviewer that he had a quick temper, with a tendency toward violence.* **8 quick as a flash** → see **flash**

SYNONYMS

quick
ADJ **1**
fast: *Brindley was known as a very, very fast driver.*
rapid: *...the country's rapid economic growth in the 1980's.*
speedy: *We wish Maria a speedy recovery.*
swift: *The police were swift to act.*

---

quick- /kwɪk-/ COMB IN ADJ **quick-** is added to words, especially present participles, to form adjectives which indicate that a person or thing does something quickly. ❑ *He was saved by quick-thinking neighbors.* ❑ *...quick-drying paint.*

quick|en /kwɪkən/ (quickens, quickening, quickened) V-T/V-I If something **quickens** or if you **quicken** it, it becomes faster or moves at a greater speed. ❑ *Ann's pulse quickened in alarm.*

quick|fire /kwɪkfaɪər/ also **quick-fire** ADJ [ADJ n] **Quickfire** speech or action is very fast with no pauses in it. ❑ *...that talent for quickfire response.*

quick fix (quick fixes) N-COUNT If you refer to a **quick fix** to a problem, you mean a way of solving a problem that is easy but temporary or inadequate. [DISAPPROVAL] ❑ *Any tax measures enacted now as a quick fix would only be reversed in a few years when the economy picks up.*

quickie /kwɪki/ (quickies) N-COUNT [oft N n] A **quickie** is something that only takes a very short time. [INFORMAL] ❑ *...a quickie divorce.*

quick|sand /kwɪksænd/ (quicksands) **1** N-UNCOUNT [also N in pl] **Quicksand** is deep, wet sand that you sink into if you try to walk on it. ❑ *The sandbank was uncertain, like quicksand under his feet.* **2** N-UNCOUNT [also N in pl] You can refer to a situation as **quicksand** when you want to suggest that it is dangerous or difficult to escape from, or does not provide a strong basis for what you are doing. ❑ *The research seemed founded on quicksand.*

quick|silver /kwɪksɪlvər/ **1** N-UNCOUNT **Quicksilver** is the same as **mercury**. [OLD-FASHIONED] **2** ADJ [ADJ n] **Quicksilver** movements or changes are very fast and unpredictable. ❑ *...her quicksilver changes of mood.*

quick study (quick studies) N-COUNT [usu sing] If you describe someone as a **quick study**, you mean that they are able to learn or memorize things very quickly. [AM] ❑ *But she's a quick study. She sees a thing once and remembers it.*

quick-tempered ADJ Someone who is **quick-tempered** gets angry easily, often without having a good reason.

quick-witted ADJ Someone who is **quick-witted** is intelligent and good at thinking quickly.

quid pro quo (quid pro quos) N-COUNT A **quid pro quo** is a gift or advantage that is given to someone in return for something that they have done. [FORMAL] ❑ *They share a great deal of information on a quid pro quo basis.*

qui|es|cent /kwaɪɛsᵊnt/ ADJ Someone or something that is **quiescent** is quiet and inactive. [LITERARY] ❑ *...a society which was politically quiescent and above all deferential.* • **qui|es|cence** N-UNCOUNT ❑ *...a long period of quiescence.*

qui|et ◆◆◆ /kwaɪət/ (quieter, quietest, quiets, quieting, quieted) **1** ADJ Someone or something that is **quiet** makes only a small amount of noise. ❑ *Tania kept the children reasonably quiet and contented.* • **qui|et|ly** ADV [ADV with v] ❑ *"This is goodbye, isn't it?" she said quietly.* • **qui|et|ness** N-UNCOUNT ❑ *...the smoothness and quietness of the flight.* **2** ADJ If a place is **quiet**, there is very little noise there. ❑ *She was received in a small, quiet office.* • **qui|et|ness** N-UNCOUNT ❑ *I miss the quietness of the countryside.* **3** ADJ If a place, situation, or time is **quiet**, there is no excitement, activity, or trouble. ❑ *...a quiet rural backwater.* • **qui|et|ly** ADV [ADV with v] ❑ *His most prized time, though, will be spent quietly on his farm.* • **qui|et|ness** N-UNCOUNT ❑ *He stretched, taking pleasure in the quietness of the morning hour.* **4** N-UNCOUNT **Quiet** is silence. ❑ *He called for quiet and announced that the next song was in our honor.* **5** ADJ [v-link ADJ] If you are **quiet**, you are not saying anything. ❑ *I told them to be quiet and go to sleep.* • **qui|et|ly** ADV [ADV with v] ❑ *Amy stood quietly in the doorway watching him.* **6** ADJ A **quiet** person behaves in a calm way and is not easily made angry or upset. ❑ *He's a nice quiet man.* **7** V-T/V-I If someone or something **quiets** or if you **quiet** them, they become less noisy, less active, or silent. [mainly AM] ❑ *The wind dropped and the sea quieted.*

> in BRIT, usually use **quieten**

8 V-T To **quiet** fears or complaints means to persuade people that there is no good reason for them. [mainly AM] ❑ *Supporters of the constitution had to quiet fears that aristocrats plotted to steal the fruits of the revolution.*

> in BRIT, usually use **quieten**

9 PHRASE If you **keep quiet about** something or **keep** something **quiet**, you do not say anything about it. ❑ *I told her to keep quiet about it.* **10** PHRASE If something is done **on the quiet**, it is done secretly or in such a way that people do not notice it. ❑ *She'd promised to give him driving lessons, on the quiet, when no one could see.*

SYNONYMS

quiet
ADJ
1
low: *Her voice was so low he had to strain to catch it.*
soft: *When he woke up again, he could hear soft music.*
faint: *She became aware of the soft, faint sounds of water dripping.*
inaudible: *His voice was almost inaudible.*
2
peaceful: *...a peaceful, Georgian house in the heart of Dorset.*
silent: *The room was silent, except for John's crunching.*
still: *In the room, it was very still.*

---

qui|et|en /kwaɪətᵊn/ [BRIT] → see **quiet** 7, 8

qui|etude /kwaɪɪtuːd/ N-UNCOUNT **Quietude** is quietness and calm. [FORMAL]

quill /kwɪl/ (quills) **1** N-COUNT A **quill** is a pen made from a bird's feather. ❑ *She dipped a quill in ink, then began to write.* **2** N-COUNT A bird's **quills** are large, stiff feathers on its wings and tail. **3** N-COUNT The **quills** of a porcupine are the long sharp points on its body.

quilt /kwɪlt/ (quilts, quilting, quilted) **1** N-COUNT A **quilt** is a bed cover made by sewing layers of cloth together, usually with different colors sewn together to make a design. ❑ *...an old patchwork quilt.* **2** N-COUNT A **quilt** is the same as a **comforter**. [mainly BRIT] **3** V-T/V-I If you **quilt**, or if you **quilt** a piece of fabric, you make a quilt. ❑ *Maggie knows how to quilt.* ❑ *Quilting a bed cover can be laborious.*

quilt|ed /kwɪltɪd/ ADJ Something that is **quilted** consists of two layers of fabric with a layer of thick material between them, often decorated with lines of stitching which form a pattern. ❑ *...a quilted bedspread.*

quilt|ing /kwɪltɪŋ/ N-UNCOUNT **Quilting** is the activity of making a quilt. ❑ *The best material to use for quilting is 100% lightweight cotton.* ❑ *She does a lot of quilting.*

quince /kwɪns/ (quinces) N-VAR A **quince** is a hard yellow fruit. Quinces are used for making jelly or jam.

qui|nine /kwaɪnaɪn/ N-UNCOUNT **Quinine** is a drug that is used to treat fevers such as malaria.

quinoa /kɪnwɑː/ N-UNCOUNT **Quinoa** is the small round seeds of a South American plant, eaten as a grain and popular as a health food.

quin|tes|sence /kwɪntɛsəns/ **1** N-UNCOUNT [usu the N of n] The **quintessence** of something is the most perfect or typical example of it. [FORMAL] ❑ *He was the quintessence of all that Eva most deeply loathed.* **2** N-UNCOUNT [usu the N of n] The **quintessence** of something is the aspect of it which seems to represent its central nature. [FORMAL] ❑ *...an old stone cottage, the quintessence of rural England.*

quin|tes|sen|tial /kwɪntɪsɛnʃəl/ **1** ADJ [usu ADJ n] **Quintessential** means representing a perfect or typical example of something. [FORMAL] ❑ *Everybody thinks of him as the quintessential New Yorker.* ● **quin|tes|sen|tial|ly** ADV ❑ *It is a familiar, and quintessentially Japanese, ritual.* **2** ADJ [usu ADJ n] **Quintessential** means representing the central nature of something. [FORMAL] ❑ *...the quintessential charm of his songs.*

quin|tet /kwɪntɛt/ (quintets) **1** N-COUNT A **quintet** is a group of five singers or musicians singing or playing together. **2** N-COUNT A **quintet** is a piece of music written for five instruments or five singers.

quin|tu|plet /kwɪntʌplɪt, -tuplɪt, kwɪntʊplɪt/ (quintuplets) N-COUNT [usu pl] **Quintuplets** are five children who are born to the same mother at the same time. ❑ *And then she gave birth to quintuplets.*

quip /kwɪp/ (quips) **1** N-COUNT A **quip** is a remark that is intended as be amusing or clever. [WRITTEN] ❑ *The commentators make endless quips about the players' appearance.* **2** → See feature box at **humor**

quirk /kwɜːrk/ (quirks) **1** N-COUNT A **quirk** is something unusual or interesting that happens by chance. ❑ *By a tantalizing quirk of fate, the pair have been drawn to meet in the first round of the championship.* **2** N-COUNT A **quirk** is a habit or aspect of a person's character which is odd or unusual. ❑ *Brown was always fascinated by the quirks and foibles of people in everyday situations.*

quirky /kwɜːrki/ (quirkier, quirkiest) ADJ Something or someone that is **quirky** is odd or unpredictable in their appearance, character, or behavior. ❑ *We've developed a reputation for being quirky and original.* ● **quirki|ness** N-UNCOUNT ❑ *You will probably notice an element of quirkiness in his behavior.*

quit /kwɪt/ (quits, quitting)

The form **quit** is used in the present tense and is the past tense and past participle.

1 V-T/V-I If you **quit**, or **quit** your job, you choose to leave it. [INFORMAL] ❑ *He quit his job as an office boy.* **2** V-T If you **quit** an activity or **quit** doing something, you stop doing it. [mainly AM] ❑ *A nicotine spray can help smokers quit the habit.* ❑ *Quit acting like you didn't know.* ❑ *Quit it! That hurts!* **3** V-T If you **quit** a place, you leave it completely and do not go back to it. ❑ *Science fiction writers have long dreamed that humans might one day quit the earth to colonize other planets.* **4** PHRASE If you say that you are going to **call it quits**, you mean that you have decided to stop doing something or being involved in something. ❑ *They raised $630,000 through listener donations, and then called it quits.*

┌─── SYNONYMS ───┐

quit
VERB **1**
step down/aside: *Many would prefer him to step aside in favor of a younger man.*
resign: *A hospital administrator has resigned over claims he lied to get the job.*
leave: *I am leaving to concentrate on writing fiction.*

quite ♦♦♦ /kwaɪt/ **1** ADV You use **quite** to indicate that something is the case to a fairly great extent. **Quite** is less emphatic than 'very' and 'extremely.' [VAGUENESS] ❑ *I felt quite bitter about it at the time.* ❑ *Well, actually it requires quite a bit of work and research.* **2** ADV You use **quite** to emphasize what you are saying. [EMPHASIS] ❑ *It is quite clear that we were firing in self defense.* ❑ *My position is quite different.* **3** ADV You use **quite** after a negative to make what you are saying weaker or less definite. [VAGUENESS] ❑ *Something here is not quite right.* **4** PREDET [PREDET a n] You use **quite** in front of a noun group to emphasize that a person or thing is very impressive or unusual. [APPROVAL] ❑ *"Oh, he's quite a character," Sean replied.* **5** ADV [ADV as reply] You can say **quite** to express your agreement with someone. [mainly BRIT, SPOKEN, FORMULAE] ❑ *"It's your choice isn't it."—"Quite."*

┌─── SYNONYMS ───┐

quite
ADV **1**
rather: *I grew up in rather unusual circumstances.*
fairly: *Both ships are fairly new.*
somewhat: *He concluded that Oswald was somewhat odd.*
reasonably: *I can dance reasonably well.*

┌─── USAGE ───┐

quite
You can use **quite** in front of **a**, followed by an adjective and a noun. Don't say, for example, 'She was a quite pretty girl.' She was *quite a pretty girl.*

quit|ter /kwɪtər/ (quitters) N-COUNT [usu with brd-neg] If you say that someone is not a **quitter**, you mean that they continue doing something even though it is very difficult. ❑ *He won't resign because he's not a quitter.*

quiv|er /kwɪvər/ (quivers, quivering, quivered) **1** V-I If something **quivers**, it shakes with very small movements. ❑ *Her bottom lip quivered and big tears rolled down her cheeks.* **2** V-I If you say that someone or their voice **is quivering** with an emotion such as rage or excitement, you mean that they are strongly affected by this emotion and show it in their appearance or voice. ❑ *Cooper arrived, quivering with rage.* ● N-COUNT **Quiver** is also a noun. ❑ *I recognized it instantly and felt a quiver of panic.*

quix|ot|ic /kwɪksɒtɪk/ ADJ If you describe someone's ideas or plans as **quixotic**, you mean that they are imaginative or hopeful but unrealistic. [FORMAL] ❑ *He has always lived his life by a hopelessly quixotic code of honor.*

quiz /kwɪz/ (quizzes, quizzing, quizzed) **1** N-COUNT A **quiz** is a test, game, or competition in which someone tests your knowledge by asking you questions. ❑ *We'll have a quiz at the end of class.* **2** V-T If you **are quizzed** by someone about something, they ask you questions about it. ❑ *He was quizzed about his income, debts and eligibility for financial aid.*

quiz|master /kwɪzmæstər/ (quizmasters) N-COUNT A **quizmaster** is the person who asks the questions in a game or quiz on television or the radio. [mainly BRIT]

in AM, usually use **emcee**

quiz|zi|cal /kwɪzɪkəl/ ADJ [usu ADJ n] If you give someone a **quizzical** look or smile, you look at them in a way that shows that you are surprised or amused by their behavior. ❑ *He gave Robin a mildly quizzical glance.* ● **quiz|zi|cal|ly** ADV ❑ *She looked at him quizzically.*

quo /kwoʊ/ → see **quid pro quo**, **status quo**

quoits /kwɔɪts/ N-UNCOUNT **Quoits** is a game which is played by throwing rings over a small post. Quoits is usually played on board ships.

Quon|set hut /kwɒnsɪt hʌt/ (**Quonset huts**) N-COUNT A **Quonset hut** is a military hut made of metal. The walls and roof form the shape of a semicircle. [AM]

in BRIT, use **Nissen hut**

quor|um /kwɔːrəm/ N-SING A **quorum** is the minimum number of people that a committee needs in order to carry out its business officially. When a meeting has a quorum, there are at least that number of people present. ❑ ...*enough deputies to make a quorum.*

quo|ta /kwoʊtə/ (**quotas**) ■ N-COUNT A **quota** is the limited number or quantity of something which is officially allowed. ❑ *The quota of four tickets per person had been reduced to two.* ■ N-COUNT A **quota** is a fixed maximum or minimum proportion of people from a particular group who are allowed to do something, such as come and live in a country or work for the government. ❑ *The bill would force employers to adopt a quota system when recruiting workers.* ■ N-COUNT Someone's **quota** of something is their expected or deserved share of it. ❑ *They have the usual quota of human weaknesses, no doubt.*

quot|able /kwoʊtəbəl/ ADJ **Quotable** comments are written or spoken comments that people think are interesting and worth quoting. ❑ ...*one of his more quotable sayings.*

quo|ta|tion /kwoʊteɪʃən/ (**quotations**) ■ N-COUNT A **quotation** is a sentence or phrase taken from a book, poem, speech, or play, which is repeated by someone else. ❑ *He illustrated his argument with quotations from Martin Luther King Jr.* ■ N-COUNT When someone gives you a **quotation**, they tell you how much they will charge to do a particular piece of work. ❑ *Get several written quotations and check exactly what's included in the cost.*

quo|ta|tion mark (**quotation marks**) N-COUNT **Quotation marks** are punctuation marks that are used in writing to show where speech or a quotation begins and ends. They are usually written or printed as "...". ❑ *Make sure you have quotation marks at both the beginning and the end of quotes.*

quote ♦♦◊ /kwoʊt/ (**quotes, quoting, quoted**) ■ V-T/V-I If you **quote** someone as saying something, you repeat what they have written or said. ❑ *He quoted Mr. Polay as saying that peace negotiations were already underway.* ❑ *I gave the letter to the local press and they quoted from it.* ■ N-COUNT A **quote** from a book, poem, play, or speech is a passage or phrase from it. ❑ *The paper starts its editorial comment with a quote from an unnamed member of the House.* ■ V-T If you **quote** something such as a law or a fact, you state it because it supports what you are saying. ❑ *The Congresswoman quoted statistics saying that the standard of living of the poorest people had fallen.* ■ V-T If someone **quotes** a price for doing something, they say how much money they would charge you for a service they are offering or a for a job that you want them to do. ❑ *A travel agent quoted her $260 for a flight from Boston to New Jersey.* ■ N-COUNT A **quote** for a piece of work is the price that someone says they will charge you to do the work. ❑ *Always get a written quote for any repairs needed.* ■ V-T PASSIVE If a company's shares, a substance, or a currency **is quoted** at a particular price, that is its current market price. [BUSINESS] ❑ *In early trading in Hong Kong yesterday, gold was quoted at $368.20 an ounce.* ■ N-PLURAL **Quotes** are the same as **quotation marks.** [INFORMAL] ❑ *The word "remembered" is in quotes.*

---- COLLOCATIONS ----

quote
NOUN
■
adjective + **quote**: famous, favorite, inspirational, memorable; direct; scandalous
■
noun + **quote**: insurance, price, renewal
adjective + **quote**: written; cheap, competitive, free
VERB ■
noun + **quote**: newspaper, report
quote + noun: official, source
quote + adverb: anonymously, approvingly; extensively, frequently, publicly, widely; accurately, directly, verbatim

---- SYNONYMS ----

quote
VERB ■
repeat: *I trust you not to repeat that to anyone else.*
recite: *They recited poetry to one another.*
reproduce: *I will not try to reproduce the police officer's English.*
cite: *She cites a favorite poem by George Herbert.*
NOUN ■
quotation: *He illustrated his argument with quotations from Pasternak.*
excerpt: *...an excerpt from Tchaikovsky's Nutcracker.*
extract: *Read this extract from an information booklet about the work of an airline cabin crew.*
citation: *The article included several citations from government documents.*

quoth /kwoʊθ/ V-T **Quoth** means 'said.' **Quoth** comes before the subject of the verb. [HUMOROUS or OLD-FASHIONED] ❑ *"I blame the judges," quoth he.*

quo|tid|ian /kwoʊtɪdiən/ ADJ [ADJ n] **Quotidian** activities or experiences are basic, everyday activities or experiences. [FORMAL] ❑ *I had hopes of escaping my quotidian world.*

quo|tient /kwoʊʃənt/ (**quotients**) N-COUNT [usu sing, usu n N, N of n] **Quotient** is used when indicating the presence or degree of a characteristic in someone or something. ❑ *Being rich doesn't actually increase your happiness quotient.* ❑ *The island has a high quotient of new age therapists.*

Quran /kɔːrɑːn, -ræn, kʊ-/ also **Koran, Qur'an** N-PROPER The **Quran** is the holy book on which the religion of Islam is based. ❑ *Still a devout Muslim, Lindh reads the Quran and prays every day.*

Quran|ic /kɔːrænɪk, kʊ-/ also **Koranic, Qur'anic** ADJ [ADJ n] **Quranic** is used to describe something which belongs or relates to the Quran.

QWER|TY /kwɜːrti/ also **Qwerty, qwerty** ADJ [ADJ n] A **QWERTY** keyboard on a typewriter or computer is the standard English language keyboard, on which the top line of keys begins with the letters q, w, e, r, t, and y. ❑ *You can enter text on the QWERTY keyboard or simply write on the screen.*

Rr

R also **r** /ɑr/ (**R's**, **r's**) N-VAR **R** is the eighteenth letter of the English alphabet.

rab|bi /ræbaɪ/ (**rabbis**) N-COUNT; N-TITLE A **rabbi** is a Jewish religious leader, usually one who is in charge of a synagogue, one who is qualified to teach Judaism, or one who is an expert on Jewish law.

rab|bini|cal /ræbɪnɪkəl/ also **rabbinic** /ræbɪnɪk/ ADJ **Rabbinical** or **rabbinic** refers to the teachings of Jewish religious teachers and leaders. ❑ ...early rabbinic scholars.

rab|bit /ræbɪt/ (**rabbits**) N-COUNT A **rabbit** is a small, furry animal with long ears. Rabbits are sometimes kept as pets, or live wild in holes in the ground.

rab|ble /ræbəl/ N-SING A **rabble** is a crowd of noisy people who seem likely to cause trouble. ❑ He seems to attract a rabble of supporters more loyal to the man than to the cause.

rabble-rouser (**rabble-rousers**) N-COUNT A **rabble-rouser** is a speaker who can persuade a group of people to behave violently or aggressively, often for the speaker's own political advantage. [DISAPPROVAL]

rabble-rousing N-UNCOUNT **Rabble-rousing** is encouragement that a person gives to a group of people to behave violently or aggressively, often for that person's own political advantage. [DISAPPROVAL] ❑ Critics have accused him of rabble-rousing.

rab|id /ræbɪd/ **1** ADJ [usu ADJ n] You can use **rabid** to describe someone who has very strong and unreasonable opinions or beliefs about a subject, especially in politics. [DISAPPROVAL] ❑ The party has distanced itself from the more rabid nationalist groups in the country. ● **rab|id|ly** ADV [ADV adj, ADV -ed] ❑ Mead calls the group "rabidly right-wing." **2** ADJ [usu ADJ n] A **rabid** dog or other animal has the disease rabies.

ra|bies /reɪbiz/ N-UNCOUNT **Rabies** is a serious disease that causes people and animals to go mad and die.

rac|coon /rækun/ (**raccoons** or **raccoon**) also **racoon** N-COUNT A **raccoon** is a small animal that has dark-colored fur with white stripes on its face and on its long tail. Raccoons live in forests in North and Central America.

race ♦♦♦ /reɪs/ (**races**, **racing**, **raced**) **1** N-COUNT A **race** is a competition to see who is the fastest, for example in running, swimming, or driving. ❑ The women's race was won by the only American in the field, Patti Sue Plummer. **2** V-T/V-I If you **race**, you take part in a race. ❑ In the 10 years I raced in Europe, 30 drivers were killed. ❑ We raced them to the summit. **3** N-PLURAL **The races** are a series of horse races that are held in a particular place on a particular day. People go to watch and to bet on which horse will win. ❑ The high point of this trip was a day at the races. **4** N-COUNT A **race** is a situation in which people or organizations compete with each other for power or control. ❑ The race for the White House begins in earnest today. **5** → see also **rat race** **6** N-VAR A **race** is one of the major groups which human beings can be divided into according to their physical features, such as the color of their skin. ❑ The college welcomes students of all races, faiths, and nationalities. **7** → see also **human race**, **race relations** **8** V-T If you **race** somewhere, you go there as quickly as possible. ❑ He raced across town to the State House building. **9** V-I If something **races** toward a particular state or position, it moves very fast toward that state or position. ❑ Do they realize we are racing toward complete economic collapse? **10** V-T If you **race** a vehicle or animal, you prepare it for races and make it take part in races. ❑ He still raced sports cars as often as he could. **11** V-I If your mind **races**, or if thoughts **race** through your mind, you think very fast about something, especially when you are in a difficult or dangerous situation. ❑ I made sure I sounded calm but my mind was racing. **12** V-I If your heart **races**, it beats very quickly because you are excited or afraid. ❑ Her heart raced uncontrollably. **13** → see also **racing** **14** PHRASE You describe a situation as a **race against time** when you have to work very fast in order to do something before a particular time, or before another thing happens. ❑ A spokesperson said the rescue operation was a race against time.

> **SYNONYMS**
>
> **race**
> NOUN **4**
> **competition:** the competition to get into the university has been extremely tough.
> **contest:** Few contests in the recent history of British boxing have been as thrilling.
> **quest:** My quest for a better bank continues.
> VERB **8**
> **dash:** She dashed in from the garden.
> **speed:** Trains speed through the Channel Tunnel at 186mph.
> **fly:** I flew downstairs.
> **tear:** The door flew open, and Miranda tore into the room.

race|course /reɪskɔrs/ (**racecourses**) N-COUNT A **racecourse** is a track on which horses race. [mainly BRIT]

> in AM, usually use **racetrack**

race|horse /reɪshɔrs/ (**racehorses**) N-COUNT A **racehorse** is a horse that is trained to run in races.

rac|er /reɪsər/ (**racers**) **1** N-COUNT A **racer** is a person or animal that takes part in races. ❑ Tim Powell is a former champion powerboat racer. **2** N-COUNT A **racer** is a vehicle such as a car or bicycle that is designed to be used in races and therefore travels fast. ❑ ...everything from small boats to ocean racers.

race re|la|tions N-PLURAL **Race relations** are the ways in which people of different races living together in the same community behave toward one another. ❑ ...a breakdown in race relations.

race riot (**race riots**) N-COUNT [usu pl] **Race riots** are violent fights between people of different races living in the same community.

race|track /reɪstræk/ (**racetracks**) also **race track** **1** N-COUNT A **racetrack** is a track on which horses race. [AM] ❑ ...the Breeders' Cup, run Oct. 26 at Arlington racetrack near Chicago.

> in BRIT, use **racecourse**

2 N-COUNT A **racetrack** is a track for races, for example car or bicycle races. ❑ ...the sound of cars roaring around a racetrack.

race|way /reɪsweɪ/ (**raceways**) N-IN-NAMES A **raceway** is a racetrack. ❑ ...the garage area of Pocono Raceway.

ra|cial ♦◊◊ /reɪʃəl/ ADJ **Racial** describes things relating to people's race. ❑ ...the protection of national and racial minorities. ● **ra|cial|ly** ADV ❑ We are both children of racially mixed marriages.

> **SYNONYMS**
>
> **racial**
> ADJ
> **ethnic:** ...a survey of Britain's ethnic minorities.
> **national:** ...the national characteristics and history of the country.

ra|cial|ism /reɪʃəlɪzəm/ N-UNCOUNT **Racialism** means the same as **racism**. [mainly BRIT]

ra|cial pro|fil|ing N-UNCOUNT **Racial profiling** is government or police activity that involves using people's racial and cultural characteristics to identify people to investigate. □ ...controversies involving racial profiling and corruption.

rac|ing ✦✧ /reɪsɪŋ/ N-UNCOUNT **Racing** refers to races between animals, especially horses, or between vehicles. □ Four horse racing tracks operate in Pennsylvania.

rac|ism /reɪsɪzəm/ N-UNCOUNT **Racism** is the belief that people of some races are inferior to others, and the behavior which is the result of this belief. □ ...a campaign to combat racism.

rac|ist /reɪsɪst/ (**racists**) ADJ If you describe people, things, or behavior as **racist**, you mean that they are influenced by the belief that some people are inferior because they belong to a particular race. [DISAPPROVAL] □ You have to acknowledge that we live in a racist society. • N-COUNT A **racist** is someone who is racist. □ I have made it clear that the organization will not tolerate racists in its ranks.

rack /ræk/ (**racks, racking, racked**)

The spelling **wrack** is also used for meanings **2** and **3**.

1 N-COUNT A **rack** is a frame or shelf, usually with bars or hooks, that is used for holding things or for hanging things on. □ A luggage rack is a sensible option. **2** V-T [usu passive] If someone **is racked** by something such as illness or anxiety, it causes them great suffering or pain. □ His already infirm body was racked by high fever. **3** PHRASE If you **rack** your **brains**, you try very hard to think of something. □ She began to rack her brains to remember what had happened at the nursing home.

▶ **rack up** PHRASAL VERB [no passive] If a business **racks up** profits, losses, or sales, it makes a lot of them. If a sportsman, sportswoman, or team **racks up** wins, they win a lot of games or races. □ Lower rates mean that firms are more likely to rack up profits in the coming months.

rack|et /rækɪt/ (**rackets**)

The spelling **racquet** is also used for meaning **3**.

1 N-SING A **racket** is a loud, unpleasant noise. □ He makes such a racket I'm afraid he disturbs the neighbors. **2** N-COUNT You can refer to an illegal activity used to make money as a **racket**. [INFORMAL] □ I'm sure he'll admit he was in the drug racket in the end. **3** N-COUNT A **racket** is an oval-shaped bat with strings across it. Rackets are used in tennis, squash, and badminton. □ Tennis rackets and balls are provided. **4** → See also color supplement

rack|et|eer /rækɪtɪər/ (**racketeers**) N-COUNT A **racketeer** is someone who makes money from illegal activities such as threatening people or selling worthless, immoral, or illegal goods or services.

rack|et|eer|ing /rækɪtɪərɪŋ/ N-UNCOUNT **Racketeering** is making money from illegal activities such as threatening people or selling worthless, immoral, or illegal goods or services. □ Edwards was indicted on racketeering charges but never convicted.

rack|ing /rækɪŋ/ **1** ADJ [ADJ n] A **racking** pain or emotion is a distressing one that you feel very strongly. □ She was now shaking with long, racking sobs. **2** → see also **nerve-racking**

rac|on|teur /rækɒntɜr/ (**raconteurs**) N-COUNT A **raconteur** is someone who can tell stories in an interesting or amusing way. □ He spoke eight languages and was a noted raconteur.

ra|coon /rækun/ → see **raccoon**

rac|quet /rækɪt/ → see **racket**

rac|quet|ball /rækɪtbɔl/ N-UNCOUNT **Racquetball** is a game which is similar to squash but which uses a different ball, racket, and court size. □ ...a health club with racquetball courts.

racy /reɪsi/ (**racier, raciest**) ADJ **Racy** writing or behavior is lively, amusing, and slightly shocking. □ He listened to David Bright's racy stories about life in the navy.

ra|dar /reɪdɑr/ (**radars**) N-VAR **Radar** is a way of discovering the position or speed of objects such as aircraft or ships when they cannot be seen, by using radio signals. □ ...a ship's radar screen.

ra|dial /reɪdiəl/ ADJ [usu ADJ n] **Radial** refers to the pattern that you get when straight lines are drawn from the center of a circle to a number of points round the edge. □ The white marble floors were inlaid in a radial pattern of brass.

ra|di|ance /reɪdiəns/ **1** N-UNCOUNT [also a N] **Radiance** is great happiness which shows in someone's face and makes them look very attractive. □ She has great vigor and radiance. **2** N-UNCOUNT [also a N] **Radiance** is a glowing light shining from something. □ The dim bulb of the bedside lamp cast a soft radiance over his face.

ra|di|ant /reɪdiənt/ **1** ADJ Someone who is **radiant** is so happy that their happiness shows in their face. □ On her wedding day the bride looked truly radiant. **2** ADJ Something that is **radiant** glows brightly. □ The evening sun warms the old red brick wall to a radiant glow.

ra|di|ate /reɪdieɪt/ (**radiates, radiating, radiated**) **1** V-I If things **radiate** out from a place, they form a pattern that is like lines drawn from the center of a circle to various points on its edge. □ Many kinds of woodland can be seen on the various walks which radiate from the Heritage Center. **2** V-T/V-I If you **radiate** an emotion or quality or if it **radiates** from you, people can see it very clearly in your face and in your behavior. □ She radiates happiness and health. **3** V-T If something **radiates** heat or light, heat or light comes from it. □ The metal plate behind my head radiated heat.

ra|dia|tion /reɪdieɪʃən/ **1** N-UNCOUNT **Radiation** consists of very small particles of a radioactive substance. Large amounts of radiation can cause illness and death. □ They suffer from health problems and fear the long term effects of radiation. **2** N-UNCOUNT **Radiation** is energy, especially heat, that comes from a particular source. □ The $617 million satellite will study energy radiation from the most violent stars in the universe.

ra|dia|tion sick|ness N-UNCOUNT **Radiation sickness** is an illness that people get when they are exposed to too much radiation.

ra|dia|tor /reɪdieɪtər/ (**radiators**) **1** N-COUNT A **radiator** is a hollow metal device, usually connected by pipes to a central heating system, that is used to heat a room. **2** N-COUNT The **radiator** in a car is the part of the engine that is filled with water in order to cool the engine.

radi|cal ✦✧ /rædɪkəl/ (**radicals**) **1** ADJ **Radical** changes and differences are very important and great in degree. □ The country needs a period of calm without more surges of radical change. • **radi|cal|ly** /rædɪkli/ ADV □ ...two large groups of people with radically different beliefs and cultures. **2** ADJ **Radical** people believe that there should be great changes in society and try to bring about these changes. □ ...threats by left-wing radical groups to disrupt the proceedings. • N-COUNT A **radical** is someone who has radical views. □ Vanessa and I had been student radicals together at Berkeley from 1965 to 1967. **3** → See feature box at **politics**

SYNONYMS

radical
ADJ **1**
extreme: The scheme has been condemned as extreme.
sweeping: The new government has started to make sweeping changes in the economy.
far-reaching: The economy is in danger of collapse unless far-reaching reforms are implemented.

---

radi|cal|ism /rædɪkəlɪzəm/ N-UNCOUNT **Radicalism** is radical beliefs, ideas, or behavior. □ Jones himself was a curious mixture of radicalism and conservatism.

radi|cal|ize /rædɪkəlaɪz/ (**radicalizes, radicalizing, radicalized**)

in BRIT, also use **radicalise**

V-T/V-I If something **radicalizes** a process, situation, or person, it makes them more radical. □ He says the opposition will radicalize its demands if these conditions aren't met. □ ...women radicalized by feminism. □ The trial was a radicalizing experience for her. • **radi|cali|za|tion** /rædɪkəlaɪzeɪʃən/ N-UNCOUNT [oft N of n] □ ...the radicalization of the conservative right.

ra|dic|chio /rɑdikioʊ, rə-/ N-UNCOUNT **Radicchio** is a vegetable with purple and white leaves that is usually eaten raw in salads.

ra|dii /reɪdiaɪ/ **Radii** is the plural of **radius**.

ra|dio /reɪdioʊ/ (radios, radioing, radioed) **1** N-UNCOUNT **Radio** is the broadcasting of programs for the public to listen to, by sending out signals from a transmitter. ❑ *The last 12 months have been difficult ones for local radio.* **2** N-SING You can refer to the programs broadcast by radio stations as **the radio**. ❑ *A lot of people listen to the radio in the mornings.* **3** N-COUNT A **radio** is the piece of equipment that you use in order to listen to radio programs. ❑ *He sat down in the armchair and turned on the radio.* **4** N-UNCOUNT **Radio** is a system of sending sound over a distance by transmitting electrical signals. ❑ *They are in twice daily radio contact with the rebel leader.* **5** N-COUNT A **radio** is a piece of equipment that is used for sending and receiving messages. ❑ *The judge praised the courage of the young police officer, who managed to raise the alarm on his radio.* **6** V-T/V-I If you **radio** someone, you send a message to them by radio. ❑ *The officer radioed for advice.*

radio|ac|tive /reɪdioʊæktɪv/ ADJ Something that is **radioactive** contains a substance that produces energy in the form of powerful and harmful rays. ❑ *The government has been storing radioactive waste at Fernald for 50 years.* • **radio|ac|tiv|ity** /reɪdioʊæktɪvɪti/ N-UNCOUNT ❑ *...the storage and disposal of solid waste that is contaminated with low levels of radioactivity.*

ra|dio as|trono|my N-UNCOUNT **Radio astronomy** is a branch of science in which radio telescopes are used to receive and analyze radio waves from space.

radio|car|bon /reɪdioʊkɑrbən/ N-UNCOUNT [usu N n] **Radiocarbon** is a type of carbon that is radioactive, and which therefore breaks up slowly at a regular rate. Its presence in an object can be measured in order to find out how old the object is. ❑ *The most frequently used method is radiocarbon dating.*

radio-controlled ADJ [usu ADJ n] A **radio-controlled** device works by receiving radio signals which operate it. ❑ *...radio-controlled model planes.*

ra|di|og|ra|pher /reɪdiɒɡrəfər/ (radiographers) N-COUNT A **radiographer** is a person who is trained to take X-rays.

ra|di|og|ra|phy /reɪdiɒɡrəfi/ N-UNCOUNT **Radiography** is the process of taking X-rays.

radio|logi|cal /reɪdiəlɒdʒɪkəl/ **1** ADJ [ADJ n] **Radiological** means relating to radiology. ❑ *...patients subjected to extensive radiological examinations.* **2** ADJ [ADJ n] **Radiological** means relating to radioactive materials. ❑ *...the National Radiological Protection Board's guidelines for storing nuclear waste.*

ra|di|olo|gist /reɪdiɒlədʒɪst/ (radiologists) N-COUNT A **radiologist** is a doctor who is trained in radiology.

ra|di|ol|ogy /reɪdiɒlədʒi/ N-UNCOUNT **Radiology** is the branch of medical science that uses X-rays and radioactive substances to treat diseases.

ra|dio tele|scope (radio telescopes) N-COUNT A **radio telescope** is an instrument that receives radio waves from space and finds the position of stars and other objects in space.

radio|thera|pist /reɪdioʊθerəpɪst/ (radiotherapists) N-COUNT A **radiotherapist** is a person who treats diseases such as cancer by using radiation.

radio|thera|py /reɪdioʊθerəpi/ N-UNCOUNT **Radiotherapy** is the treatment of diseases such as cancer by using radiation.

rad|ish /rædɪʃ/ (radishes) N-VAR **Radishes** are small red or white vegetables that are the roots of a plant. They are eaten raw in salads.

ra|dium /reɪdiəm/ N-UNCOUNT **Radium** is a radioactive element which is used in the treatment of cancer.

ra|dius /reɪdiəs/ (radii /reɪdiaɪ/) **1** N-SING The **radius** around a particular point is the distance from it in any direction. ❑ *Nick has searched for work in a ten-mile radius around his home.* **2** N-COUNT The **radius** of a circle is the distance from its center to its outside edge. ❑ *He indicated a semicircle with a radius of about thirty miles.*

ra|don /reɪdɒn/ N-UNCOUNT **Radon** is a radioactive element in the form of a gas.

raf|fia /ræfiə/ N-UNCOUNT [oft N n] **Raffia** is a fiber made from palm leaves. It is used to make mats and baskets.

raff|ish /ræfɪʃ/ ADJ [usu ADJ n] **Raffish** people and places are not very respectable but are attractive and stylish in spite of this. [WRITTEN] ❑ *He was handsome in a raffish kind of way.*

raf|fle /ræfəl/ (raffles, raffling, raffled) **1** N-COUNT A **raffle** is a competition in which you buy tickets with numbers on them. Afterward some numbers are chosen, and if your ticket has one of these numbers on it, you win a prize. ❑ *Any more raffle tickets? Twenty-five cents each or five for a dollar.* **2** V-T If someone **raffles** something, they give it as a prize in a raffle. ❑ *During each show we will be raffling a fabulous prize.*

raft /ræft/ (rafts) **1** N-COUNT A **raft** is a floating platform made from large pieces of wood or other materials tied together. ❑ *...a river trip on bamboo rafts through dense rainforest.* **2** N-COUNT A **raft** is a small rubber or plastic boat that you blow air into to make it float. ❑ *The crew spent two days and nights in their raft.* **3** → See also color supplement

raft|er /ræftər/ (rafters) N-COUNT **Rafters** are the sloping pieces of wood that support a roof. ❑ *From the rafters of the thatched roofs hung strings of dried onions and garlic.*

raft|ing /ræftɪŋ/ N-UNCOUNT **Rafting** is the sport of traveling down a river on a raft. ❑ *...water sports such as boating, fishing, and rafting.*

rag /ræɡ/ (rags, ragging, ragged) **1** N-VAR A **rag** is a piece of old cloth which you can use to clean or wipe things. ❑ *He was wiping his hands on an oily rag.* **2** N-PLURAL **Rags** are old torn clothes. ❑ *There were men, women, and small children, some dressed in rags.* **3** N-COUNT People refer to a newspaper as a **rag** when they have a poor opinion of it. [INFORMAL, DISAPPROVAL] ❑ *"This man Tom works for a local rag," he said.* **4** V-T If someone **rags** you, they tease you in a friendly way. [INFORMAL] ❑ *"They always rag me about my car," he says.*
▶ **rag on** PHRASAL VERB If you **rag on** someone, you speak angrily to them because they have done something wrong. [AM, INFORMAL] ❑ *Ma, quit ragging on Ruthie.*

raga /rɑɡə/ (ragas) N-COUNT A **raga** is a piece of Indian music based on a traditional scale or pattern of notes that is also called a **raga**.

raga|muf|fin /ræɡəmʌfɪn/ (ragamuffins) N-COUNT A **ragamuffin** is someone, especially a child, who is dirty and has torn clothes. [OLD-FASHIONED] ❑ *They looked like little ragamuffins.*

rag|bag /ræɡbæɡ/ also **rag-bag** N-SING [usu N of n] A **ragbag** of things is a group of things which do not have much in common with each other, but which are being considered together. ❑ *He had taken a ragbag bunch of men and turned them into a fighting force.*

rag doll (rag dolls) N-COUNT A **rag doll** is a soft doll made of cloth.

rage /reɪdʒ/ (rages, raging, raged) **1** N-VAR **Rage** is strong anger that is difficult to control. ❑ *He was red-cheeked with rage.* **2** V-I You say that something powerful or unpleasant **rages** when it continues with great force or violence. ❑ *Train service was halted as the fire raged for more than four hours.* **3** V-I If you **rage about** something, you speak or think very angrily about it ❑ *Monroe was on the phone, raging about her mistreatment by the brothers.* ❑ *Inside, Frannie was raging.* **4** N-UNCOUNT You can refer to the strong anger that someone feels in a particular situation as a particular **rage**, especially when this results in violent or aggressive behavior. ❑ *Cabin crews are reporting up to nine cases of air rage a week.* **5** → see also **raging**, **road rage**

rag|ga /ræɡə/ N-UNCOUNT **Ragga** is a style of pop music similar to rap music which began in the West Indies.

rag|ged /ræɡɪd/ **1** ADJ Someone who is **ragged** looks messy and is wearing clothes that are old and torn. ❑ *The five survivors eventually reached safety, ragged, half-starved, and exhausted.* **2** ADJ **Ragged** clothes are old and torn. ❑ *...an elderly, bearded man in ragged clothes.* **3** ADJ You can say that something is **ragged** when it is rough or uneven. ❑ *O'Brien formed the men into a ragged line.*

rag|gedy /ræɡɪdi/ ADJ People and things that are **raggedy** are dirty and messy. **Raggedy** clothes are old and torn. [INFORMAL] ❑ *...an old man in a raggedy topcoat.*

rag|ing /reɪdʒɪŋ/ **1** ADJ [ADJ n] **Raging** water moves very forcefully and violently. ❑ *The field trip involved crossing a raging torrent.* **2** ADJ [ADJ n] **Raging** fire is very hot and fierce. ❑ *As he came closer he saw a gigantic wall of raging flame before him.* **3** ADJ [ADJ n] **Raging** is used to describe things, especially bad things, that are very intense. ❑ *If raging inflation returns, then interest rates will shoot up.* **4** → see also **rage**

ra|gout /ræɡuː/ (ragouts) N-VAR A **ragout** is a strongly flavored stew of meat or vegetables or both.

rag rug (rag rugs) N-COUNT A **rag rug** is a small carpet made of old pieces of cloth stitched or woven together.

rag|tag /rǽɡtæɡ/ ADJ [ADJ n] If you want to say that a group of people or an organization is badly organized and not very respectable, you can describe it as a **ragtag** group or organization. [INFORMAL] ❑ *We started out with a little ragtag team of 30 people.*

rag|time /rǽɡtaɪm/ N-UNCOUNT **Ragtime** is a kind of jazz piano music that was invented in the United States in the early 1900s.

rag trade N-SING [the N] The **rag trade** is the business and industry of making and selling clothes, especially women's clothes. [INFORMAL] ❑ *The rag trade is extremely competitive, and one needs plenty of contacts in order to survive.*

rag|weed /rǽɡwiːd/ N-UNCOUNT **Ragweed** is a plant, found mainly in North America, that produces large amounts of pollen, which causes hay fever. ❑ *...an allergic reaction to a particular type of ragweed.*

rah-rah /rɑːrɑː/ ADJ [ADJ n] **Rah-rah** speech or behavior is enthusiastic and is intended to encourage someone such as a sports player or team. [mainly AM, INFORMAL] ❑ *He stepped up to the microphone and swung into his rah-rah speech.*

raid ✦◇◇ /reɪd/ (raids, raiding, raided) **1** V-T When soldiers **raid** a place, they make a sudden armed attack against it, with the aim of causing damage rather than occupying any of the enemy's land. ❑ *The guerrillas raided banks and destroyed a police barracks and an electricity substation.* • N-COUNT **Raid** is also a noun. ❑ *The rebels attempted a surprise raid on a military camp.* **2** → see also **air raid** **3** V-T If the police **raid** a building, they enter it suddenly and by force in order to look for dangerous criminals or for evidence of something illegal, such as drugs or weapons. ❑ *Police raided their headquarters and other offices.* • N-COUNT **Raid** is also a noun. ❑ *They were arrested early this morning after a raid on a house by thirty armed police.*

raid|er /reɪdər/ → see **corporate raider**

rail ✦◇◇ /reɪl/ (rails) **1** N-COUNT A **rail** is a horizontal bar attached to posts or around the edge of something as a fence or support. ❑ *They had to walk across an emergency footbridge, holding onto a rope that served as a rail.* **2** N-COUNT A **rail** is a horizontal bar that you hang things on. ❑ *This pair of curtains will fit a rail up to 7 ft 6 in wide.* **3** N-COUNT **Rails** are the steel bars which trains run on. ❑ *The train left the rails but somehow forced its way back onto the line.* **4** N-UNCOUNT If you travel or send something by **rail**, you travel or send it on a train. ❑ *The president traveled by rail to his home town.* **5** PHRASE If something is **back on the rails**, it is beginning to be successful again after a period when it almost failed. [mainly BRIT, JOURNALISM]

in AM, use **back on track**

6 PHRASE If someone **goes off the rails**, they start to behave in a way that other people think is unacceptable or very strange, for example, they start taking drugs or breaking the law. [mainly BRIT] ❑ *They've got to do something about these children because clearly they've gone off the rails.*

rail|ing /reɪlɪŋ/ (railings) N-COUNT A fence made from metal bars is called a **railing** or **railings**. ❑ *He walked out on to the balcony where he rested his arms on the railing.*

rail|road /reɪlroʊd/ (railroads, railroading, railroaded) **1** N-COUNT A **railroad** is a route between two places along which trains travel on steel rails. [AM] ❑ *...railroad tracks that led to nowhere.*

in BRIT, use **railway**

2 N-COUNT A **railroad** is a company or organization that operates railroad routes. [AM] ❑ *The Chicago and Northwestern Railroad wouldn't go along with that arrangement and said it would shut down completely.*

in BRIT, use **railway**

3 V-T If you **railroad** someone into doing something, you make them do it although they do not really want to, by hurrying them and putting pressure on them. ❑ *He more or less railroaded the rest of Europe into recognizing the new "independent" states.*

rail|road cross|ing (railroad crossings) N-COUNT A **railroad crossing** is a place where a railroad track crosses a road at the same level. [AM] ❑ *...a day after his van was hit by a freight train at a railroad crossing.*

in BRIT, use **level crossing**

rail|way ✦◇◇ /reɪlweɪ/ (railways) **1** N-COUNT A **railway** is the system and network of tracks that trains travel on. [mainly AM] **2** N-COUNT A **railway** is a route between two places along which trains travel on steel rails. [mainly BRIT]

in AM, usually use **railroad**

3 N-COUNT A **railway** is a company or organization that operates railroad routes. [BRIT]

in AM, use **railroad**

rail|way|man /reɪlweɪmən/ (railwaymen) N-COUNT **Railwaymen** are men who work for the railroad. [BRIT]

in AM, use **rail worker**

rai|ment /reɪmənt/ (raiments) N-COUNT [also N in pl] **Raiment** is clothing. [LITERARY] ❑ *I want nothing but raiment and daily bread.*

rain ✦◇◇ /reɪn/ (rains, raining, rained) **1** N-UNCOUNT [also the N] **Rain** is water that falls from the clouds in small drops. ❑ *I hope you didn't get soaked standing out in the rain.* **2** N-PLURAL In countries where rain only falls in certain seasons, this rain is referred to as **the rains**. ❑ *...the spring, when the rains came.* **3** V-I When rain falls, you can say that **it is raining**. ❑ *It was raining hard, and she didn't have an umbrella.* **4** V-T/V-I If someone **rains** blows, kicks, or bombs **on** a person or place, the person or place is attacked by many blows, kicks, or bombs. You can also say that blows, kicks, or bombs **rain on** a person or place. ❑ *The opponents were raining blows on each other long after the bell had gone.* • PHRASAL VERB **Rain down** means the same as **rain**. ❑ *Fighter aircraft rained down high explosives.* **5** → See feature box at **hot**

┌─── COLLOCATIONS ───┐
rain
NOUN **1**
noun + **rain**: monsoon
adjective + **rain**: driving, heavy, pouring, torrential; light
verb + **rain**: brave
└──────────────────┘

rain|bow /reɪnboʊ/ (rainbows) N-COUNT A **rainbow** is an arch of different colors that you can sometimes see in the sky when it is raining. ❑ *...silk and satin in every shade of the rainbow.*

rain check PHRASE If you say you will take a **rain check** on an offer or suggestion, you mean that you do not want to accept it now, but you might accept it at another time. ❑ *I was planning to ask you in for a brandy, but if you want to take a rain check, that's fine.*

rain|coat /reɪnkoʊt/ (raincoats) N-COUNT A **raincoat** is a waterproof coat.

rain|drop /reɪndrɒp/ (raindrops) N-COUNT A **raindrop** is a single drop of rain.

rain|fall /reɪnfɔːl/ **1** N-UNCOUNT **Rainfall** is the amount of rain that falls in a place during a particular period. ❑ *There have been four years of below average rainfall.* **2** → See feature box at **weather**

rain for|est (rain forests) also **rainforest** **1** N-VAR A **rain forest** is a thick forest of tall trees which is found mainly in tropical areas where there is a lot of rain. ❑ *...the destruction of the Amazon rain forest.* **2** → See feature box at **deforest, ecosystem**

rain|storm /reɪnstɔːm/ (rainstorms) N-COUNT A **rainstorm** is a fall of very heavy rain. ❑ *The cars collided during a heavy rainstorm.*

rain-swept also **rainswept** ADJ [ADJ n] A **rain-swept** place is a place where it is raining heavily. ❑ *He looked up and down the rain-swept street.*

rain|water /reɪnwɔːtər/ N-UNCOUNT **Rainwater** is water that has fallen as rain.

rainy /reɪni/ (rainier, rainiest) ADJ During a **rainy** day, season, or period it rains a lot. ❑ *The rainy season in the Andes normally starts in December.*

raise ✦✦✦ /reɪz/ (raises, raising, raised)

→ Please look at meanings **15** to **16** to see if the expression you are looking for is shown under another headword.

1 V-T If you **raise** something, you move it so that it is in a higher position. ❑ *He raised his hand to wave.* ❑ *Milton raised the glass to his lips.* **2** V-T If you **raise** a flag, you display it by moving it up a pole or into a high place where it can be seen. ❑ *They had raised the white flag in surrender.* **3** V-T If you **raise** yourself, you lift your body so that you are standing up straight, or so that you are no longer lying flat. ❑ *He raised himself into a sitting position.* **4** V-T If you **raise** the rate or level of something, you increase it. ❑ *The Federal Reserve Board is expected to raise interest rates.* **5** V-T To **raise** the standard of something means to improve it. ❑ *...a new drive to raise standards of literacy in New York's schools.* **6** V-T If you **raise** your voice, you speak more loudly, usually because you are angry. ❑ *Don't you raise your voice to me!* **7** N-COUNT A **raise** is an increase in your wages or salary. [AM] ❑ *Within two months Kelly got a raise.*

> in BRIT, use **rise**

8 V-T If you **raise** money for a charity or an institution, you ask people for money which you collect on its behalf. ❑ *...events held to raise money for flood victims.* **9** V-T If a person or company **raises** money that they need, they manage to get it, for example by selling their property or by borrowing. ❑ *They raised the money to buy the house and two hundred acres of land.* **10** V-T If an event **raises** a particular emotion or question, it makes people feel the emotion or consider the question. ❑ *The agreement has raised hopes that the war may end soon.* **11** V-T If you **raise** a subject, an objection, or a question, you mention it or bring it to someone's attention. ❑ *He had been consulted and had raised no objections.* **12** V-T Someone who **raises** a child takes care of it until it is grown up. ❑ *My mother was an amazing woman. She raised four of us kids virtually singlehandedly.* **13** V-T If someone **raises** a particular type of animal or crop, they breed that type of animal or grow that type of crop. ❑ *He raises 2,000 acres of wheat and hay.* **14 to raise the alarm** → see **alarm** **15 to raise your eyebrows** → see **eyebrow** **16 to raise a finger** → see **finger** **17** → See feature box at **family**

SYNONYMS

raise
VERB
1
lift: *She lifted the last of her drink to her lips.*
elevate: *Jack elevated the gun at the sky.*
4
increase: *The company has increased the price of its cars.*
elevate: *Emotional stress can elevate blood pressure.*
inflate: *The promotion of a big release can inflate a film's final cost.*
augment: *While searching for a way to augment the family income, she began making dolls.*

---

rai|sin /reɪzᵊn/ (**raisins**) N-COUNT **Raisins** are dried grapes. ❑ *...homemade oatmeal with brown sugar and raisins.*

rai|son d'etre /reɪzoʊn detrə, reɪzɔn/ also **raison d'être** N-SING [usu with poss] A person's or organization's **raison d'etre** is the most important reason for them existing in the way that they do. ❑ *...a debate about the raison d'etre of the armed forces.*

Raj /rɑːdʒ/ N-SING [the N] The British **Raj** was the period of British rule in India which ended in 1947. ❑ *...Indian living conditions under the Raj.*

rake /reɪk/ (**rakes, raking, raked**) **1** N-COUNT A **rake** is a garden tool consisting of a row of metal or wooden teeth attached to a long handle. You can use a rake to make the earth smooth and level before you put plants in, or to gather leaves together. **2** V-T If you **rake** a surface, you move a rake across it in order to make it smooth and level. ❑ *Rake the soil, press the seed into it, then cover it lightly.* **3** V-T If you **rake** leaves or ashes, you move them somewhere using a rake or a similar tool. ❑ *I watched the men rake leaves into heaps.* **4** → See also color supplement

▶ **rake in** PHRASAL VERB If you say that someone **is raking in** money, you mean that they are making a lot of money very easily, more easily than you think they should. [INFORMAL] ❑ *The privatization allowed companies to rake in huge profits.*

raked /reɪkt/ ADJ [ADJ n] A **raked** stage or other surface is sloping, for example so that all the audience can see more clearly. ❑ *The action takes place on a steeply raked stage.*

rake-off (**rake-offs**) N-COUNT If someone who has helped to arrange a business deal takes or gets a **rake-off**, they illegally or unfairly take a share of the profits. [INFORMAL] ❑ *Hall takes a rake-off, often amounting to tens of thousands of dollars on most project deals.*

rak|ish /reɪkɪʃ/ ADJ [usu ADJ n] A **rakish** person or appearance is stylish in a confident, bold way. ❑ *...a soft-brimmed hat which he wore at a rakish angle.* • **rak|ish|ly** ADV ❑ *...a hat cocked rakishly over one eye.*

ral|ly ✦✧✧ /ræli/ (**rallies, rallying, rallied**) **1** N-COUNT A **rally** is a large public meeting that is held in order to show support for something such as a political party. ❑ *About three thousand people held a rally to mark international human rights day.* **2** V-T/V-I When people **rally** to something or when something **rallies** them, they unite to support it. ❑ *Her cabinet colleagues have continued to rally to her support.* **3** V-I When someone or something **rallies**, they begin to recover or improve after having been weak. ❑ *He rallied enough to thank his doctors.* • N-COUNT **Rally** is also a noun. ❑ *After a brief rally the shares returned to $2.15.* **4** N-COUNT A **rally** in tennis, badminton, or squash is a continuous series of shots that the players exchange without stopping. ❑ *...a long rally.* **5** N-COUNT A **rally** is a competition in which vehicles are driven over public roads. ❑ *Carlos Sainz of Spain has won the New Zealand Motor Rally.* **6** → See feature box at **politics**

▶ **rally around** PHRASAL VERB When people **rally around**, they work as a group in order to support someone or something at a difficult time. ❑ *So many people have rallied around to help the family.*

ral|ly|ing cry (**rallying cries**) N-COUNT A **rallying cry** or **rallying call** is something such as a word or phrase, an event, or a belief which encourages people to unite and to act in support of a particular group or idea. ❑ *...an issue that is fast becoming a rallying cry for many Democrats: national health care.*

ral|ly|ing point (**rallying points**) N-COUNT A **rallying point** is a place, event, or person that people are attracted to as a symbol of a political group or ideal. ❑ *Students used the death of political activists as a rallying point for antigovernment protests.*

ram /ræm/ (**rams, ramming, rammed**) **1** V-T If a vehicle **rams** something such as another vehicle, it crashes into it with a lot of force, usually deliberately. ❑ *The thieves fled, ramming the police officer's car.* **2** V-T If you **ram** something somewhere, you push it there with great force. ❑ *He rammed the key into the lock and kicked the front door open.* **3** N-COUNT A **ram** is an adult male sheep. **4** PHRASE If something **rams home** a message or a point, it makes it clear in a way that is very forceful and that people are likely to listen to. ❑ *The report by the chairman will ram this point home.* **5 to ram something down someone's throat** → see **throat**

RAM /ræm/ **1** N-UNCOUNT **RAM** is the part of a computer in which information is stored while you are using it. **RAM** is an abbreviation for 'Random Access Memory'. [COMPUTING] ❑ *...a PC with 512 MB RAM.* **2** → See feature box at **computer**

Rama|dan /ræmədæn/ N-UNCOUNT **Ramadan** is the ninth month of the Muslim year, when Muslims do not eat between the rising and setting of the sun. During Ramadan, Muslims celebrate the fact that it was in this month that God first revealed the words of the Koran to Mohammed.

ram|ble /ræmbᵊl/ (**rambles, rambling, rambled**) **1** N-COUNT A **ramble** is a long walk in the countryside. ❑ *...an hour's ramble through the woods.* **2** V-I If you **ramble**, you go on a long walk in the countryside. ❑ *...freedom to ramble across the rolling hills.* **3** V-I If you say that a person **rambles** in their speech or writing, you mean they do not make much sense because they keep going off the subject in a confused way. ❑ *Sometimes she spoke sensibly; sometimes she rambled.*

ram|bling /ræmblɪŋ/ **1** ADJ [usu ADJ n] A **rambling** building is big and old with an irregular shape. ❑ *...that rambling house and its bizarre contents.* **2** ADJ [usu ADJ n] If you describe a speech or piece of writing as **rambling**, you are criticizing it for being too long and very confused. [DISAPPROVAL] ❑ *His actions were accompanied by a rambling monologue.* **3** → See feature box at **leisure**

ram|blings /ræmblɪŋz/ N-PLURAL [usu with poss] If you describe a speech or piece of writing as someone's **ramblings**, you are saying that it is meaningless because the person who said or wrote it was very confused or insane. [DISAPPROVAL] ❑ *The official dismissed the speech as the ramblings of a desperate man.*

ram|bunc|tious /ræmbʌŋkʃəs/ ADJ [usu ADJ n] A rambunctious person is energetic in a cheerful, noisy way. [mainly AM] ❑ *...a very rambunctious and energetic class.*

in BRIT, usually use **rumbustious**

ram|ekin /ræmɪkɪn/ (ramekins) N-COUNT A ramekin or a ramekin dish is a small dish in which food for one person can be baked in the oven.

rami|fi|ca|tion /ræmɪfɪkeɪʃ°n/ (ramifications) N-COUNT The ramifications of a decision, plan, or event are all its consequences and effects, especially ones that are not obvious at first. ❑ *The book analyzes the social and political ramifications of AIDS for the gay community.*

ramp /ræmp/ (ramps) N-COUNT A ramp is a sloping surface between two places that are at different levels. ❑ *Lillian was coming down the ramp from the museum.*

ram|page (rampages, rampaging, rampaged)

Pronounced /ræmpeɪdʒ/ for meaning 1, and /ræmpeɪdʒ/ for meaning 2.

1 V-I When people or animals rampage through a place, they rush around there in a wild or violent way, causing damage or destruction. ❑ *Hundreds of youths rampaged through the town, smashing store windows and overturning cars.* **2** PHRASE If people go **on a rampage**, they rush around in a wild or violent way, causing damage or destruction. ❑ *The prisoners went on a rampage destroying everything in their way.*

ram|pant /ræmpənt/ ADJ If you describe something bad, such as a crime or disease, as rampant, you mean that it is very common and is increasing in an uncontrolled way. ❑ *Inflation is rampant and industry in decline.*

ram|part /ræmpɑrt/ (ramparts) N-COUNT [usu pl] The ramparts of a castle or city are the earth walls, often with stone walls on them, that were built to protect it. ❑ *...a walk along the ramparts of the Old City.*

ram|rod /ræmrɒd/ (ramrods) **1** N-COUNT A ramrod is a long, thin rod which can be used for pushing something into a narrow tube. Ramrods were used, for example, for forcing an explosive substance down the barrel of an old-fashioned gun, or for cleaning the barrel of a gun. **2** PHRASE If someone sits or stands **like a ramrod** or **straight as a ramrod**, they have a very straight back and appear rather stiff and formal. ❑ *...a woman with iron gray hair, high cheekbones, and a figure like a ramrod.* **3** ADJ [ADJ n] If someone has a ramrod back or way of standing, they have a very straight back and hold themselves in a rather stiff and formal way. ❑ *I don't have the ramrod posture I had when I was in the navy.* • ADV [ADV adj] Ramrod is also an adverb. ❑ *At 75, she's still ramrod straight.*

ram|shack|le /ræmʃækəl/ **1** ADJ A ramshackle building is badly made or in bad condition, and looks as if it is likely to fall down. ❑ *They entered the shop, which was a curious ramshackle building.* **2** ADJ A ramshackle system, union, or collection of things has been put together without much thought and is not likely to work very well. ❑ *They joined with a ramshackle alliance of other rebels.*

ran /ræn/ Ran is the past tense of **run**.

ranch /ræntʃ/ (ranches) N-COUNT A ranch is a large farm used for raising animals, especially cattle, horses, or sheep. ❑ *He lives on a cattle ranch in Texas.*

ranch|er /ræntʃər/ (ranchers) N-COUNT A rancher is someone who owns or manages a large farm, especially one used for raising cattle, horses, or sheep. ❑ *...a cattle rancher.*

ranch house (ranch houses) **1** N-COUNT A ranch house is a single-story house, usually with a low roof and an open-plan interior. [AM] ❑ *...residential streets full of treeless lawns and one-story ranch houses.* **2** N-COUNT A ranch house is the main house on a ranch.

ranch|ing /ræntʃɪŋ/ N-UNCOUNT Ranching is the activity of running a large farm, especially one used for raising cattle, horses, or sheep.

ran|cid /rænsɪd/ ADJ If butter, bacon, or other oily foods are rancid, they have gone bad and taste old and unpleasant. ❑ *Butter is perishable and can go rancid.*

ran|cor /ræŋkər/

in BRIT, use **rancour**

N-UNCOUNT Rancor is a feeling of bitterness and anger. [FORMAL]

ran|cor|ous /ræŋkərəs/ ADJ A rancorous argument or person is full of bitterness and anger. [FORMAL] ❑ *The deal ended after a series of rancorous disputes.*

ran|cour /ræŋkər/ [BRIT] → see rancor

rand /rænd/ (rands or rand) N-COUNT [usu num N] The rand is the unit of currency used in South Africa. ❑ *...12 million rand.* • N-SING [the N] The rand is also used to refer to the South African currency system. ❑ *The rand slumped by 22% against the dollar.*

R&B /ɑr ən bi/ N-UNCOUNT [oft N n] R&B is a style of popular music developed in the 1940s from blues music, but using electrically amplified instruments. R&B is an abbreviation for rhythm and blues.

R & D /ɑr ən di/ also **R and D** N-UNCOUNT R & D refers to the research and development work or department within a large company or organization. R & D is an abbreviation for 'Research and Development.' ❑ *Businesses need to train their workers better, and spend more on R & D.*

ran|dom /rændəm/ **1** ADJ A random sample or method is one in which all the people or things involved have an equal chance of being chosen. ❑ *The survey used a random sample of two thousand people across the Midwest.* • **ran|dom|ly** ADV [ADV with v] ❑ *...interviews with a randomly selected sample of 30 girls aged between 13 and 18.* **2** ADJ If you describe events as random, you mean that they do not seem to follow a definite plan or pattern. ❑ *...random violence against innocent victims.* • **ran|dom|ly** ADV [ADV with v] ❑ *...drinks and magazines left scattered randomly around.* **3** PHRASE If you choose people or things **at random**, you do not use any particular method, so they all have an equal chance of being chosen. ❑ *We received several answers, and we picked one at random.* **4** PHRASE If something happens **at random**, it happens without a definite plan or pattern. ❑ *Three African-Americans were killed by shots fired at random from a minibus.*

ran|dom|ize /rændəmaɪz/ (randomizes, randomizing, randomized)

in BRIT, also use **randomise**

V-T If you randomize the events or people in scientific experiments or academic research, you use a method that gives them all an equal chance of happening or being chosen. [TECHNICAL] ❑ *The wheel is designed with obstacles in the ball's path to randomize its movement.* ❑ *Properly randomized studies are only now being completed.*

R & R /ɑr ən ɑr/ also **R and R** **1** N-UNCOUNT R & R refers to time that you spend relaxing, when you are not working. R & R is an abbreviation for 'rest and recreation.' [mainly AM] ❑ *Winter spas are now the best choice for serious R & R.* **2** N-UNCOUNT R & R refers to time that members of the armed forces spend relaxing, away from their usual duties. R & R is an abbreviation for 'rest and recuperation.' [AM] ❑ *Twenty-five years ago Pattaya was a sleepy fishing village. Then it was discovered by American soldiers on R & R from Vietnam.*

rang /ræŋ/ Rang is the past tense of **ring**.

range ♦♦◊ /reɪndʒ/ (ranges, ranging, ranged) **1** N-COUNT A range of things is a number of different things of the same general kind. ❑ *A wide range of colors and patterns are available.* **2** N-COUNT A range is the complete group that is included between two points on a scale of measurement or quality. ❑ *The average age range is between 35 and 55.* **3** N-COUNT The range of something is the maximum area in which it can reach things or detect things. ❑ *The 120mm mortar has a range of 18,000 yards.* **4** V-I If things range between two points or range from one point to another, they vary within these points on a scale of measurement or quality. ❑ *They range in price from $3 to $15.* ❑ *...offering merchandise ranging from the everyday to the esoteric.* **5** N-COUNT A range of mountains or hills is a line of them. ❑ *...the massive mountain ranges to the north.* **6** N-COUNT A rifle range or a shooting range is a place where people can practice shooting at targets. ❑ *It reminds me of my days on the rifle range* preparing for duty in Vietnam. ▧ N-COUNT A **range** is a large area of open land, especially land in the United States, where cattle are kept. ❑ *He grazed his cattle on the open range.* ▧ N-COUNT A **range** or **kitchen range** is a large metal device for cooking food using gas or electricity. A range consists of a broiler, an oven, and some gas or electric burners. [AM]

in BRIT, usually use **cooker**

▧ → see also **free-range** ▧ PHRASE If something is **in range** or **within range**, it is near enough to be reached or detected. If it is **out of range**, it is too far away to be reached or detected. ❑ *Cars are driven through the mess, splashing everyone within range.* ▧ PHRASE If you see or hit something **at close range** or **from close range**, you are very close to it when you see it or hit it. If you do something **at a range of** half a mile, for example, you are half a mile away from it when you do it. ❑ *He was shot in the head at close range.* ▧ → See feature box at **water**

range find|er (range finders) also **rangefinder** N-COUNT A **range finder** is an instrument, usually part of a camera or a piece of military equipment, that measures the distance between things that are far away from each other.

rang|er /ˈreɪndʒər/ (rangers) N-COUNT A **ranger** is a person whose job is to take care of a forest or large park. ❑ *Bill Justice is a park ranger at the Carlsbad Caverns National Park.*

rangy /ˈreɪndʒi/ ADJ [usu ADJ n] If you describe a person or animal as **rangy**, you mean that they have long, thin, powerful legs. [WRITTEN] ❑ *...a tall, rangy, redheaded girl.*

rank ◆◇◇ /ræŋk/ (ranks, ranking, ranked) ▧ N-VAR Someone's **rank** is the position or grade that they have in an organization. ❑ *He eventually rose to the rank of captain.* ▧ N-VAR Someone's **rank** is the social class, especially the high social class, that they belong to. [FORMAL] ❑ *He must be treated as a hostage of high rank, not as a common prisoner.* ▧ V-T/V-I If an official organization **ranks** someone or something 1st, 5th, or 50th, for example, they calculate that the person or thing has that position on a scale. You can also say that someone or something **ranks** 1st, 5th, or 50th, for example. ❑ *The report ranks the U.S. 20th out of 22 advanced nations.* ❑ *...the only Canadian woman to be ranked in the top 50 of the women's world rankings.* ▧ V-T/V-I If you say that someone or something **ranks** high or low on a scale, you are saying how good or important you think they are. ❑ *His prices rank high among those of other contemporary photographers.* ❑ *Investors ranked South Korea high among Asian nations.* ❑ *St. Petersburg's night life ranks as more exciting than the capital's.* ▧ N-PLURAL The **ranks** of a group or organization are the people who belong to it. ❑ *There were some misgivings within the ranks of the media too.* ▧ N-PLURAL The **ranks** are the ordinary members of an organization, especially of the armed forces. ❑ *Most store managers have worked their way up through the ranks.* ▧ N-COUNT A **rank** of people or things is a row of them. ❑ *Ranks of police in riot gear stood nervously by.* ▧ N-COUNT A taxi **rank** is a place on a city street where taxis park when they are available. [mainly BRIT]

in AM, use **stand**

▧ PHRASE If you say that a member of a group or organization **breaks ranks**, you mean that they disobey the instructions of their group or organization. ❑ *The country appears unlikely to break ranks with other members of the European Union.* ▧ PHRASE If you say that the members of a group **close ranks**, you mean that they are supporting each other only because their group is being criticized. ❑ *Institutions tend to close ranks when a member has been accused of misconduct.*

rank and file N-SING The **rank and file** are the ordinary members of an organization or the ordinary workers in a company, as opposed to its leaders or managers. [JOURNALISM] ❑ *There was widespread support for him among the rank and file.*

-ranked /ræŋkt/ COMB IN ADJ [ADJ n] **-ranked** is added to words, usually numbers like 'first,' 'second,' and 'third,' to form adjectives which indicate what position someone or something has in a list or scale. ❑ *The world's second-ranked team were 26-25 down at the halfway point.* ❑ *...the world's ten highest-ranked players.*

rank|ing ◆◇◇ /ˈræŋkɪŋ/ (rankings) ▧ N-PLURAL [the N] In many sports, the list of the best players made by an official organization is called **the rankings**. ❑ *...the 25 leading teams in the world rankings.* ▧ N-COUNT [usu with poss] Someone's **ranking** is their position in an official list of the best players of a sport. ❑ *Agassi was playing well above his world ranking of 12.* ▧ ADJ [ADJ n] The **ranking** member of a group, usually a political group, is the most senior person in it. [AM] ❑ *...the ranking Republican on the senate intelligence committee.*

-ranking /ˈræŋkɪŋ/ COMB IN ADJ [ADJ n] **-ranking** is used to form adjectives which indicate what rank someone has in an organization. ❑ *...a colonel on trial with three lower-ranking officers.*

ran|kle /ˈræŋkəl/ (rankles, rankling, rankled) V-T/V-I If an event or situation **rankles**, it makes you feel angry or bitter afterward, because you think it was unfair or wrong. ❑ *They paid him only $10 for it and it really rankled.* ❑ *Their refusal to sell the country arms in 1937 still rankled with him.* ❑ *The only thing that rankles me is what she says about Ireland.*

ran|sack /ˈrænsæk/ (ransacks, ransacking, ransacked) V-T If people **ransack** a building, they damage things in it or make it very messy, often because they are looking for something in a quick and careless way. ❑ *Demonstrators ransacked and burned the house where he was staying.*

ran|som /ˈrænsəm/ (ransoms, ransoming, ransomed) ▧ N-VAR A **ransom** is the money that has to be paid to someone so that they will set free a person they have kidnapped. ❑ *Her kidnapper successfully extorted a $250,000 ransom for her release.* ▧ V-T If you **ransom** someone who has been kidnapped, you pay the money to set them free. ❑ *The same system was used for ransoming or exchanging captives.* ▧ PHRASE If a kidnapper is **holding** a person **for ransom**, they keep that person prisoner until they are given what they want. ❑ *He is charged with kidnaping a businessman last year and holding him for ransom.* ▧ → See feature box at **history**

ran|som|ware /ˈrænsəmwɛər/ N-UNCOUNT **Ransomware** is illegal computer software that stops a computer from working or prevents the computer user from getting information until they have paid some money. [COMPUTING] ❑ *You need to protect your computer from ransomware.*

rant /rænt/ (rants, ranting, ranted) ▧ V-T/V-I If you say that someone **rants**, you mean that they talk loudly or angrily, and exaggerate or say foolish things. ❑ *As the boss began to rant, I stood up and went out.* ❑ *Even their three dogs got bored and fell asleep as he ranted on.* ❑ *"Let's get it over and done with," he ranted.* • N-COUNT **Rant** is also a noun. ❑ *Part I is a rant against organized religion.* • **rant|ing** (rantings) N-VAR ❑ *He had been listening to Goldstone's rantings all night.*

rap /ræp/ (raps, rapping, rapped) ▧ N-UNCOUNT **Rap** is a type of music in which the words are not sung but are spoken in a rapid, rhythmic way. ❑ *Her favorite music was by Run DMC, a rap group.* ▧ V-I Someone who **raps** performs rap music. ❑ *They rap about life in the inner city.* ▧ N-COUNT A **rap** is a piece of music performed in rap style, or the words that are used in it. ❑ *Every member contributes to the rap, singing either solo or as part of a rap chorus.* ▧ V-T/V-I If you **rap** on something or **rap** it, you hit it with a series of quick blows. ❑ *Mary Ann turned and rapped on Charlie's door.* ❑ *...rapping the glass with the knuckles of his right hand.* • N-COUNT **Rap** is also a noun. ❑ *There was a sharp rap on the door.* ▧ N-UNCOUNT A **rap** is a statement in a court of law that someone has committed a particular crime, or the punishment for committing it. [AM, INFORMAL] ❑ *With that old man dead, you're up against a murder rap.* ▧ N-COUNT A **rap** is an act of criticizing or blaming someone or something. [JOURNALISM] ❑ *Bad corks get the rap for as much as 15 percent of tainted wine.* ▧ V-T If you **rap** someone for something, you criticize or blame them for it. [JOURNALISM] ❑ *Water industry chiefs were rapped yesterday for failing their customers.* ▧ PHRASE If someone in authority **raps** your **knuckles** or **raps** you **on the knuckles**, they criticize you or blame you for doing something they think is wrong. [JOURNALISM] ❑ *I joined the workers on strike and was rapped on the knuckles.* ▧ PHRASE If you say that someone has gotten **a bum rap**, you mean that they have been treated unfairly or punished unfairly. [mainly AM, INFORMAL] ❑ *She's gotten kind of a bum rap, you know. She's not at all the person she's perceived to be.* ▧ PHRASE If you **take the rap**, you are blamed or punished for something, especially something that is not your fault or of which other people are equally guilty.

[INFORMAL] ❑ *When the client was murdered, his wife took the rap, but did she really do it?* ⓫ PHRASE If you **beat the rap**, you avoid being blamed for something wrong that you have done. [INFORMAL] ❑ *...an attorney who boasts he can beat any rap, for a $5,000 fee.*

ra|pa|cious /rəpeɪʃəs/ ADJ [usu ADJ n] If you describe a person or their behavior as **rapacious**, you disapprove of their greedy or selfish behavior. [FORMAL, DISAPPROVAL] ❑ *...a rapacious exploitation policy.*

ra|pac|ity /rəpæsɪti/ N-UNCOUNT [oft with poss] **Rapacity** is very greedy or selfish behavior. [FORMAL, DISAPPROVAL] ❑ *He argued that the overcrowded cities were the product of a system based on "selfishness and "rapacity."*

rape ♦⟨⟩ /reɪp/ (**rapes, raping, raped**) ❶ V-T If someone **is raped**, they are forced to have sex, usually by violence or threats of violence. ❑ *A young woman was brutally raped in her own home.* ❷ N-VAR **Rape** is the crime of forcing someone to have sex. ❑ *Almost 90 percent of all rapes and violent assaults went unreported.* ❸ N-COUNT **Rape** is a plant with yellow flowers which is grown as a crop. Its seeds are crushed to make cooking oil.

rap|id ♦♦⟨⟩ /ræpɪd/ ❶ ADJ A **rapid** change is one that happens very quickly. ❑ *...the country's rapid economic growth in the 1980s.* ● **rap|id|ly** ADV ❑ *...countries with rapidly growing populations.* ❑ *Try to rip it apart as rapidly as possible.* ● **ra|pid|ity** /rəpɪdɪti/ N-UNCOUNT ❑ *...the rapidity with which the weather can change.* ❷ ADJ A **rapid** movement is one that is very fast. ❑ *He walked at a rapid pace along Charles Street.* ● **rap|id|ly** ADV [ADV with v] ❑ *He was moving rapidly around the room.* ● **ra|pid|ity** N-UNCOUNT ❑ *The water rushed through the holes with great rapidity.*

rapid-fire ❶ ADJ [ADJ n] A **rapid-fire** gun is one that shoots a lot of bullets very quickly, one after the other. ❑ *In the back of the truck was a 12.7 millimeter rapid-fire machine gun.* ❷ ADJ [ADJ n] A **rapid-fire** conversation or speech is one in which people talk or reply very quickly. ❑ *Joe listened to their sophisticated, rapid-fire conversation.* ❸ ADJ [ADJ n] A **rapid-fire** economic activity or development is one that takes place very quickly. [mainly AM, JOURNALISM] ❑ *...the rapid-fire buying and selling of stocks.*

rap|ids /ræpɪdz/ N-PLURAL **Rapids** are a section of a river where the water moves very fast, often over rocks. ❑ *His canoe was there, on the river below the rapids.*

rap|id tran|sit ADJ [ADJ n] A **rapid transit** system is a transportation system in a city which allows people to travel quickly, using trains that run underground or above the streets. ❑ *Two rapid transit trains collided early this morning in Boston.*

ra|pi|er /reɪpiər/ (**rapiers**) ❶ N-COUNT A **rapier** is a very thin sword with a long, sharp point. ❷ ADJ [ADJ n] If you say that someone has a **rapier** wit, you mean that they are very intelligent and quick at making clever comments or jokes in a conversation. ❑ *Julie Burchill is famous for her rapier wit.*

rap|ist /reɪpɪst/ (**rapists**) N-COUNT A **rapist** is a person who has raped someone. ❑ *The convicted murderer and rapist is scheduled to be executed next Friday.*

rap|pel /ræpel, rə-/ (**rappels, rappelling, rappelled**) V-I To **rappel** down a cliff or rock face means to slide down it in a controlled way using a rope, with your feet against the cliff or rock. [AM] ❑ *They learned to rappel down a cliff.*

in BRIT, use **abseil**

rap|per /ræpər/ (**rappers**) N-COUNT A **rapper** is a person who performs rap music. ❑ *The charts have been dominated by rappers in recent months.*

rap|port /ræpɔr/ N-SING [also no det, oft N with/between n] If two people or groups have a **rapport**, they have a good relationship in which they are able to understand each other's ideas or feelings very well. ❑ *The success depends on good rapport between interviewer and interviewee.*

rap|por|teur /ræpɔrtɜr/ (**rapporteurs**) N-COUNT [usu with supp] A **rapporteur** is a person who is officially appointed by an organization to investigate a problem or attend a meeting and to report on it. [FORMAL] ❑ *...the United Nations special rapporteur on torture.*

rap|proche|ment /ræproʊʃmɒn, ræproʊʃmɒn/ N-SING [also no det, oft N with/between n] A **rapprochement** is an increase in friendliness between two countries, groups, or people, especially after a period of unfriendliness. [FORMAL] ❑ *There have been growing signs of a rapprochement with Vietnam.* ❑ *...the process of political rapprochement between the two former foes.*

rap sheet (**rap sheets**) N-COUNT A **rap sheet** is a legal document which records someone's arrests and crimes. [AM] ❑ *His rap sheet includes a recent conviction for stabbing a record executive.*

rapt /ræpt/ ADJ [usu ADJ n] If someone watches or listens with **rapt** attention, they are extremely interested or fascinated. [LITERARY] ❑ *I noticed that everyone was watching me with rapt attention.* ● **rapt|ly** ADV [ADV with v] ❑ *...listening raptly to stories about fascinating people.*

rap|tor /ræptər/ (**raptors**) N-COUNT **Raptors** are birds of prey, such as eagles and hawks. [TECHNICAL]

rap|ture /ræptʃər/ N-UNCOUNT **Rapture** is a feeling of extreme happiness or pleasure. [LITERARY] ❑ *The film was shown to gasps of rapture at the Democratic Convention.* ❑ *His speech was received with rapture by his supporters.*

rap|tures /ræptʃərz/ PHRASE If you are **in raptures** or go **into raptures** about something, you are extremely impressed by it and enthusiastic about it. [mainly BRIT, WRITTEN] ❑ *They will be in raptures over the French countryside.*

rap|tur|ous /ræptʃərəs/ ADJ A **rapturous** feeling or reaction is one of extreme happiness or enthusiasm. [JOURNALISM] ❑ *The students gave him a rapturous welcome.*

rare ♦♦⟨⟩ /rɛər/ (**rarer, rarest**) ❶ ADJ Something that is **rare** is not common and is therefore interesting or valuable. ❑ *...the black-necked crane, one of the rarest species in the world.* ❷ ADJ An event or situation that is **rare** does not occur very often. ❑ *...on those rare occasions when he did eat alone.* ❸ ADJ [ADJ n] You use **rare** to emphasize an extremely good or remarkable quality. [EMPHASIS] ❑ *Ferris has a rare ability to record her observations on paper.* ❹ ADJ Meat that is **rare** is cooked very lightly so that the inside is still red. ❑ *Thick tuna steaks are eaten rare, like beef.*

SYNONYMS

rare
ADJ ❶
unusual: *To be appreciated as a parent is quite unusual.*
uncommon: *A 15-year lifespan is not uncommon for a dog.*
exceptional: *...if the courts hold that this case is exceptional.*

---

rar|efied /rɛərɪfaɪd/ ❶ ADJ [usu ADJ n] If you talk about the **rarefied** atmosphere of a place or institution, you are expressing your disapproval of it, because it has a special social or academic status that makes it very different from ordinary life. [DISAPPROVAL] ❑ *It is important for the state's future administrators to get out of the rarefied air of the capital.* ❷ ADJ **Rarefied** air is air that does not contain much oxygen, for example in mountain areas. ❑ *...living at very high altitudes where the atmosphere is rarefied.*

rare|ly ♦⟨⟩ /rɛərli/ ADV If something **rarely** happens, it does not happen very often. ❑ *They battled against other Indian tribes, but rarely fought with the Whites.*

SYNONYMS

rarely
ADV
seldom: *They seldom speak.*
hardly: *Hardly a day goes by without a visit from someone.*
infrequently: *The bridge is used infrequently.*

---

rar|ing /rɛərɪŋ/ ❶ PHRASE If you say that you **are raring to go**, you mean that you are very eager to start doing something. ❑ *After a good night's sleep, Paul said he was raring to go.* ❷ ADJ [v-link ADJ] If you are **raring** to do something or are **raring** for it, you are very eager to do it or very eager that it should happen. ❑ *He is raring to charge into the fray and lay down the law.* ❑ *Baker suggested the administration wasn't raring for a fight.*

rar|ity /rɛərɪti/ (**rarities**) ❶ N-COUNT If someone or something is a **rarity**, they are interesting or valuable because they are so unusual. [JOURNALISM] ❑ *Sontag has always been that rarity, a glamorous intellectual.* ❷ N-UNCOUNT The **rarity** of something is the fact that it is very uncommon. ❑ *It was a real prize due to its rarity and good condition.*

ras|cal /ræskəl/ (rascals) **1** N-COUNT If you call a man a **rascal**, you mean that he behaves badly and is rude or dishonest. [OLD-FASHIONED] ❑ *What's that old rascal been telling you?* • **ras|cal|ly** ADJ [usu ADJ n] ❑ *They stumble across a ghost town inhabited by a rascally gold prospector.* **2** N-COUNT If you call a child a **rascal**, you mean that they behave badly. [HUMOROUS] ❑ *He's a little rascal - but he's still great fun.*

rash /ræʃ/ (rashes) **1** ADJ If someone is **rash** or does **rash** things, they act without thinking carefully first, and therefore make mistakes or behave foolishly. ❑ *It would be rash to rely on such evidence.* • **rash|ly** ADV ❑ *I made a lot of money, but I rashly gave most of it away.* **2** N-COUNT A **rash** is an area of red spots that appears on your skin when you are ill or have a bad reaction to something that you have eaten or touched. ❑ *He may break out in a rash when he eats these nuts.* **3** N-SING If you talk about a **rash of** events or things, you mean a large number of unpleasant events or undesirable things, which have happened or appeared within a short period of time. ❑ *...one of the few major airlines left untouched by the industry's rash of takeovers.* **4** → See feature box at **illness**

rash|er /ræʃər/ (rashers) N-COUNT A **rasher** of bacon is a slice of bacon. [BRIT]

in AM, use **slice**

rasp /ræsp/ (rasps, rasping, rasped) **1** V-T/V-I If someone **rasps**, their voice or breathing is harsh and unpleasant to listen to. ❑ *"Where did you put it?" he rasped.* • N-SING **Rasp** is also a noun. ❑ *He was still laughing when he heard the rasp of Rennie's voice.* **2** V-T/V-I If something **rasps** or if you **rasp** it, it makes a harsh, unpleasant sound as it rubs against something hard or rough. ❑ *The key rasped in the lock and the door swung open.* ❑ *Frank rasped a hand across his chin.* • N-SING **Rasp** is also a noun. ❑ *...the rasp of something being drawn across the sand.*

rasp|berry /ræzbəri/ (raspberries) N-COUNT **Raspberries** are small, soft, red fruit that grow on bushes.

raspy /ræspi/ ADJ If someone has a **raspy** voice, they make rough sounds as if they have a sore throat or have difficulty in breathing. [LITERARY] ❑ *Both men sang in a deep, raspy tone.*

Ras|ta /ræstə/ (Rastas) **1** N-COUNT A **Rasta** is the same as a **Rastafarian**. [INFORMAL] ❑ *The CD was called Rastas Never Die.* **2** ADJ [ADJ n] **Rasta** means the same as **Rastafarian**. [INFORMAL] ❑ *...Rasta singer Pablo Moses.*

Ras|ta|far|ian /ræstəfɛəriən/ (Rastafarians) **1** N-COUNT A **Rastafarian** is a member of a Jamaican religious group which considers Haile Selassie, the former Emperor of Ethiopia, to be God. Rastafarians often have long hair which they wear in a hairstyle called dreadlocks. ❑ *He was one of the few thousand committed Rastafarians in South Africa.* **2** ADJ [ADJ n] **Rastafarian** is used to describe Rastafarians and their beliefs and lifestyle. ❑ *...Rastafarian poet Benjamin Zephaniah.*

rat /ræt/ (rats, ratting, ratted) **1** N-COUNT A **rat** is an animal which has a long tail and looks just like a large mouse. ❑ *This was demonstrated in a laboratory experiment with rats.* **2** N-COUNT If you call someone a **rat**, you mean that you are angry with them or dislike them, often because they have cheated you or betrayed you. [INFORMAL, DISAPPROVAL] ❑ *What did you do with the gun you took from that little rat Turner?* **3** V-I If someone **rats on** you, they tell someone in authority about things that you have done, especially bad things. [INFORMAL] ❑ *They were accused of encouraging children to rat on their parents.* **4** V-I If someone **rats on** an agreement, they do not do what they said they would do. [INFORMAL] ❑ *She claims he ratted on their divorce settlement.* **5** PHRASE If you **smell a rat**, you begin to suspect or realize that something is wrong in a particular situation, for example that someone is trying to deceive you or harm you. ❑ *If I don't send a picture, he will smell a rat.*

ra|ta /rɑːtə/ → see **pro rata**

rat-a-tat N-SING; SOUND You use **rat-a-tat** to represent a series of sharp, repeated sounds, such as the sound of someone knocking at a door. ❑ *...the rat-a-tat at the door.*

ra|ta|touille /rætətuːi/ N-UNCOUNT [also a N] **Ratatouille** is a cooked dish made with vegetables such as tomatoes, onions, eggplant, zucchini, and peppers.

ratch|et /rætʃɪt/ (ratchets, ratcheting, ratcheted) **1** N-COUNT In a tool or machine, a **ratchet** is a wheel or bar with sloping teeth, which can move only in one direction, because a piece of metal stops the teeth from moving backward. ❑ *The chair has a ratchet below it to adjust the height.* **2** V-T/V-I If a tool or machine **ratchets** or if you **ratchet** it, it makes a clicking noise as it operates, because it has a ratchet in it. ❑ *The rod bent double, the reel shrieked and ratcheted.* ❑ *She took up a sheet and ratcheted it into the typewriter.*
▸ **ratchet down** PHRASAL VERB If something **ratchets down** or **is ratcheted down**, it decreases by a fixed amount or degree, and seems unlikely to increase again. [mainly JOURNALISM] ❑ *We're trying to ratchet down the administrative costs.*
▸ **ratchet up** PHRASAL VERB If something **ratchets up** or **is ratcheted up**, it increases by a fixed amount or degree, and seems unlikely to decrease again. [JOURNALISM] ❑ *...an attempt to ratchet up the pressure.* ❑ *He fears inflation will ratchet up as the year ends.*

rate ◆◆◆ /reɪt/ (rates, rating, rated) **1** N-COUNT The **rate** at which something happens is the speed with which it happens. ❑ *The rate at which hair grows can be agonizingly slow.* **2** N-COUNT The **rate** at which something happens is the number of times it happens over a period of time. ❑ *New diet books appear at a rate of nearly one a week.* **3** N-COUNT A **rate** is the amount of money that is charged for goods or services. ❑ *A special weekend rate is available from mid-November.* **4** → see also **exchange rate** **5** N-COUNT The **rate** of taxation or interest is the amount of tax or interest that needs to be paid. It is expressed as a percentage of the amount that is earned, gained as profit, or borrowed. [BUSINESS] ❑ *The government insisted that it would not be panicked into interest rate cuts.* **6** V-T/V-I [no cont] If you **rate** someone or something as good or bad, you consider them to be good or bad. You can also say that someone or something **rates** as good or bad. ❑ *Of all the men in the survey, they rate themselves the least fun-loving and the most responsible.* ❑ *Most rated it a hit.* ❑ *We rate him as one of the best.* **7** V-T PASSIVE [no cont] If someone or something **is rated** at a particular position or rank, they are calculated or considered to be in that position on a list. ❑ *He is generally rated the country's No. 3 industrialist.* **8** V-T [no cont] If you say that someone or something **rates** a particular reaction, you mean that this is the reaction you consider to be appropriate. ❑ *This is so extraordinary, it rates a medal and a phone call from the president.* **9** → see also **rating** **10** PHRASE You use **at any rate** to indicate that what you have just said might be incorrect or unclear in some way, and that you are now being more precise. ❑ *His friends liked her - well, most of them at any rate.* **11** PHRASE If you say that **at this rate** something bad or extreme will happen, you mean that it will happen if things continue to develop as they have been doing. ❑ *At this rate they'd be lucky to get home before eight-thirty or nine.* **12** → See feature box at **global warming**, **population**

SYNONYMS

rate
NOUN **1**
speed: *In the late 1850s, the speed of technological change quickened.*
pace: *Many people were not satisfied with the pace of change.*
tempo: *...the slow tempo of change in an overwhelmingly rural country.*

---

rate cap (rate caps) N-COUNT A **rate cap** is a limit placed by the government on the amount of interest that banks or credit card companies can charge their customers. [AM]

rate of ex|change (rates of exchange) N-COUNT A **rate of exchange** is the same as an **exchange rate**. ❑ *...four thousand dinars - about four hundred dollars at the official rate of exchange.*

rate of re|turn (rates of return) N-COUNT The **rate of return** on an investment is the amount of profit it makes, often shown as a percentage of the original investment. [BUSINESS] ❑ *High rates of return can be earned on these investments.*

ra|ther ◆◆◆ /rɑːðər/ **1** PHRASE You use **rather than** when you are contrasting two things or situations. **Rather than** introduces the thing or situation that is not true or that you do not want. ❑ *The problem was psychological rather than*

ratification 1060 **rave**

physiological. • CONJ **Rather** is also a conjunction. ☐ *She made students think for themselves, rather than telling them what to think.* **2** ADV [ADV with cl/group] You use **rather** when you are correcting something that you have just said, especially when you are describing a particular situation after saying what it is not. ☐ *Twenty million years ago, Idaho was not the arid place it is now. Rather, it was warm and damp, populated by dense primordial forest.* **3** PHRASE If you say that you **would rather** do something or you'**d rather** do it, you mean that you would prefer to do it. If you say that you **would rather not** do something, you mean that you do not want to do it. ☐ *If it's all the same to you, I'd rather work at home.* ☐ *Kids would rather play than study.* **4** ADV You use **rather** to indicate that something is true to a fairly great extent, especially when you are talking about something unpleasant or undesirable. ☐ *I grew up in a rather unusual circumstances.* ☐ *I'm afraid it's a rather long story.* **5** ADV [ADV before v] You use **rather** before verbs that introduce your thoughts and feelings, in order to express your opinion politely, especially when a different opinion has been expressed. [mainly BRIT, POLITENESS] ☐ *I rather think he was telling the truth.*

rati|fi|ca|tion /ˌrætɪfɪˈkeɪʃᵊn/ (ratifications) N-VAR The **ratification** of a treaty or written agreement is the process of ratifying it. ☐ *We welcome this development and we look forward to early ratification of the treaty by China.*

rati|fy /ˈrætɪfaɪ/ (ratifies, ratifying, ratified) V-T When national leaders or organizations **ratify** a treaty or written agreement, they make it official by giving their formal approval to it, usually by signing it or voting for it. ☐ *The parliaments of Australia and Indonesia have yet to ratify the treaty.*

rat|ing ✦◇◇ /ˈreɪtɪŋ/ (ratings) **1** N-COUNT A **rating** of something is a score or measurement of how good or popular it is. ☐ *New public opinion polls show the president's approval rating at its lowest point since he took office.* **2** → see also **credit rating** **3** N-PLURAL The **ratings** are the statistics published each week which show how popular each television program is. ☐ *CBS's ratings again showed huge improvement over the previous year.*

─── COLLOCATIONS ───

rating
NOUN
1
noun + **rating**: approval, popularity, satisfaction; player, poll, safety, star
adjective + **rating**: average, high, low, top; overall
verb + **rating**: achieve, earn, receive; give
3
noun + **ratings**: audience, TV
adjective + **ratings**: dismal, poor; good, solid
verb + **ratings**: boost

ra|tio /ˈreɪʃoʊ, -ʃioʊ/ (ratios) N-COUNT A **ratio** is a relationship between two things when it is expressed in numbers or amounts. For example, if there are ten boys and thirty girls in a room, the ratio of boys to girls is 1:3, or one to three. ☐ *The adult to child ratio is one to six.*

ra|tion /ˈræʃᵊn/ (rations, rationing, rationed) **1** N-COUNT When there is not enough of something, your **ration** of it is the amount that you are allowed to have. ☐ *The meat ration was down to one pound per person per week.* **2** V-T When something **is rationed** by a person or government, you are only allowed to have a limited amount of it, usually because there is not enough of it. ☐ *Staples such as bread, rice, and tea are already being rationed.* ☐ *The City Council of Moscow has decided that it will begin rationing bread, butter, and meat.* **3** N-PLURAL **Rations** are the food that is given to people who do not have enough food or to soldiers. ☐ *Aid officials said that the first emergency food rations of wheat and oil were handed out here last month.* **4** N-COUNT Your **ration** of something is the amount of it that you normally have. ☐ *...after consuming his ration of junk food and two cigarettes.* **5** → see also **rationing**

ra|tion|al /ˈræʃᵊnᵊl/ **1** ADJ **Rational** decisions and thoughts are based on reason rather than on emotion. ☐ *He's asking you to look at both sides of the case and come to a rational decision.* • **ra|tion|al|ly** ADV ☐ *It can be very hard to think rationally when you're feeling so vulnerable and alone.* • **ra|tion|al|ity** /ˌræʃᵊnˈælɪti/

N-UNCOUNT ☐ *We live in an era of rationality.* **2** ADJ A **rational** person is someone who is sensible and is able to make decisions based on intelligent thinking rather than on emotion. ☐ *Did he come across as a sane, rational person?*

ra|tion|ale /ˌræʃᵊˈnæl, -ˈnɑːl/ (rationales) N-COUNT The **rationale** for a course of action, practice, or belief is the set of reasons on which it is based. [FORMAL] ☐ *However, the rationale for such initiatives is not, of course, solely economic.*

ra|tion|al|ism /ˈræʃᵊnᵊlɪzᵊm/ N-UNCOUNT **Rationalism** is the belief that your life should be based on reason and logic, rather than emotions or religious beliefs. ☐ *Coleridge was to spend the next thirty years attacking rationalism.*

ra|tion|al|ist /ˈræʃᵊnᵊlɪst/ (rationalists) **1** ADJ If you describe someone as **rationalist**, you mean that their beliefs are based on reason and logic rather than emotion or religion. ☐ *White was both visionary and rationalist.* **2** N-COUNT If you describe someone as a **rationalist**, you mean that they base their life on rationalist beliefs. ☐ *...the rationalists and scientists of the nineteenth century.*

ra|tion|al|ize /ˈræʃᵊnᵊlaɪz/ (rationalizes, rationalizing, rationalized)

in BRIT, also use **rationalise**

V-T If you try to **rationalize** attitudes or actions that are difficult to accept, you think of reasons to justify or explain them. ☐ *He further rationalized his activity by convincing himself that he was actually promoting peace.*

ra|tion|ing /ˈræʃᵊnɪŋ/ N-UNCOUNT **Rationing** is the system of limiting the amount of food, water, gasoline, or other necessary substances that each person is allowed to have or buy when there is not enough of them. ☐ *The municipal authorities here are preparing for food rationing.*

rat race N-SING If you talk about getting out of **the rat race**, you mean leaving a job or way of life in which people compete aggressively with each other to be successful. ☐ *I had to get out of the rat race and take a look at the real world again.*

rat|tan /ræˈtæn, rə-/ N-UNCOUNT [usu N n] **Rattan** furniture is made from the woven strips of stems of a plant which grows in Southeast Asia. ☐ *...a light, airy room set with cloth-covered tables and rattan chairs.*

rat|tle /ˈrætᵊl/ (rattles, rattling, rattled) **1** V-T/V-I When something **rattles** or when you **rattle** it, it makes short, sharp, knocking sounds because it is being shaken or it keeps hitting against something hard. ☐ *She slams the kitchen door so hard I hear dishes rattle.* • **Rattle** is also a noun. ☐ *There was a rattle of rifle fire.* **2** N-COUNT A **rattle** is a baby's toy with small, loose objects inside which make a noise when the baby shakes it. **3** V-T If something or someone **rattles** you, they make you nervous. ☐ *Officials are not normally rattled by any reporter's question.* • **rat|tled** ADJ ☐ *He swore in Spanish, an indication that he was rattled.*

rat|tler /ˈrætlər/ (rattlers) N-COUNT A **rattler** is the same as a **rattlesnake**. [AM, INFORMAL]

rattle|snake /ˈrætᵊlsneɪk/ (rattlesnakes) N-COUNT A **rattlesnake** is a poisonous American snake which can make a rattling noise with its tail.

rat|ty /ˈræti/ (rattier, rattiest) ADJ **Ratty** clothes and objects are torn or in bad condition, especially because they are old. [AM] ☐ *...an old, ratty suitcase.*

rau|cous /ˈrɔːkəs/ ADJ A **raucous** sound is loud, harsh, and rather unpleasant. ☐ *They heard a bottle being smashed, then more raucous laughter.* • **rau|cous|ly** ADV ☐ *They laughed together raucously.*

raun|chy /ˈrɔːntʃi/ (raunchier, raunchiest) ADJ Someone or something that is **raunchy** is sexually exciting. [INFORMAL] ☐ *...her raunchy new movie.*

rav|age /ˈrævɪdʒ/ (ravages, ravaging, ravaged) V-T [usu passive] A town, country, or economy that **has been ravaged** is one that has been damaged so much that it is almost completely destroyed. ☐ *The country has been ravaged by civil war.*

rav|ages /ˈrævɪdʒɪz/ N-PLURAL The **ravages** of time, war, or the weather are the damaging effects that they have. ☐ *...the ravages of two world wars.*

rave /reɪv/ (raves, raving, raved) **1** V-T/V-I If someone **raves**, they talk in an excited and uncontrolled way. ☐ *She cried and* raved for weeks, and people did not know what to do. ◻ "What is wrong with you, acting like that," she raved. **2** V-T/V-I If you **rave** about something, you speak or write about it with great enthusiasm. ◻ Rachel raved about the new foods she ate while she was there. ◻ "I'd no idea Milan was so wonderful," he raved. **3** N-COUNT A **rave** is a big event at which young people dance to electronic music in a large building or in the open air. Raves are often associated with illegal drugs. ◻ ...an all-night rave. **4** → see also **raving**

ravel /rævəl/ (**ravels, raveling** or **ravelling, raveled** or **ravelled**) V-T/V-I If something such as a rope or wire **ravels**, or if you **ravel** it, it becomes tangled or twisted together. ◻ I felt her hand in my hair, fingers toying with the locks at my neck, raveling them up, tugging.

ra|ven /reɪvən/ (**ravens**) N-COUNT A **raven** is a bird with shiny black feathers and a deep harsh call.

rav|en|ous /rævənəs/ ADJ If you are **ravenous**, you are extremely hungry. ◻ Amy realized that she had eaten nothing since leaving home that morning, and she was ravenous. • **rav|en|ous|ly** ADV ◻ She began to eat ravenously.

rav|er /reɪvər/ (**ravers**) N-COUNT A **raver** is a young person who has a busy social life and goes to a lot of parties, raves, or nightclubs. [INFORMAL]

rave re|view (**rave reviews**) N-COUNT [usu pl] When journalists write **rave reviews**, they praise something such as a play or book in a very enthusiastic way. ◻ The play received rave reviews.

ra|vine /rəvin/ (**ravines**) N-COUNT A **ravine** is a very deep, narrow valley with steep sides. ◻ The bus overturned and fell into a ravine.

rav|ing /reɪvɪŋ/ **1** ADJ You use **raving** to describe someone who you think is completely mad. [INFORMAL] ◻ Malcolm looked at her as if she were a raving lunatic. • ADV [ADV adj] **Raving** is also an adverb. ◻ I'm afraid Paul has gone raving mad. **2** → see also **rave**

rav|ings /reɪvɪŋz/ N-PLURAL [usu the N of n] If you describe what someone says or writes as their **ravings**, you mean that it makes no sense because they are mad or very ill. ◻ Haig and Robertson saw it as the desperate ravings of a mad politician.

ra|vio|li /rævioʊli/ (**raviolis**) N-MASS **Ravioli** is a type of pasta that is shaped into small squares, filled with ground meat or cheese and served in a sauce.

rav|ish /rævɪʃ/ (**ravishes, ravishing, ravished**) V-T [usu passive] To **ravish** someone means to rape them. [LITERARY] ◻ She'll never know how close she came to being dragged off and ravished.

rav|ish|ing /rævɪʃɪŋ/ ADJ If you describe someone or something as **ravishing**, you mean that they are very beautiful. [LITERARY] ◻ She looked ravishing.

raw ♦◊◊ /rɔ/ (**rawer, rawest**) **1** ADJ **Raw** materials or substances are in their natural state before being processed or used in manufacturing. ◻ We import raw materials and energy and export mainly industrial products. **2** ADJ **Raw** food is food that is eaten uncooked, that has not yet been cooked, or that has not been cooked enough. ◻ ...a popular dish made of raw fish. **3** ADJ If a part of your body is **raw**, it is red and painful, perhaps because the skin has come off or has been burned. ◻ ...the drag of the rope against the raw flesh of my shoulders. **4** ADJ **Raw** emotions are strong basic feelings or responses which are not weakened by other influences. ◻ Her grief was still raw and he did not know how to help her. **5** ADJ If you describe something as **raw**, you mean that it is simple, powerful, and real. ◻ ...the raw power of instinct. **6** ADJ **Raw** data is facts or information that has not yet been sorted, analyzed, or prepared for use. ◻ Analyses were conducted on the raw data. **7** ADJ If you describe someone in a new job as **raw**, or as a **raw** recruit, you mean that they lack experience in that job. ◻ ...replacing experienced men with raw recruits. **8** ADJ **Raw** weather feels unpleasantly cold. ◻ ...a raw December morning. **9** ADJ [ADJ n] **Raw** sewage is sewage that has not been treated to make it cleaner. ◻ ...contamination of drinking water by raw sewage. **10** PHRASE If you say that you are getting **a raw deal**, you mean that you are being treated unfairly. [INFORMAL] ◻ I think women have a raw deal. **11** → See feature box at **recycle**

SYNONYMS
raw ADJ **1**
unrefined: Unrefined carbohydrates include brown rice and other grains.
natural: We only use natural ingredients.
crude: ...8.5 million tons of crude steel.

raw|hide /rɔhaɪd/ N-UNCOUNT [usu N n] **Rawhide** is leather that comes from cattle, and has not been treated or tanned. [AM] ◻ At his belt he carried a rawhide whip.

ray ♦◊◊ /reɪ/ (**rays**) **1** N-COUNT **Rays** of light are narrow beams of light. ◻ The sun's rays can penetrate water up to 10 feet. **2** → see also **X-ray** **3** N-COUNT A **ray** of hope, comfort, or other positive quality is a small amount of it that you welcome because it makes a bad situation seem less bad. ◻ They could provide a ray of hope amid the general economic gloom. **4** → See also color supplement

ray|on /reɪɒn/ N-UNCOUNT [oft N n] **Rayon** is a smooth, artificial fabric that is made from cellulose. ◻ ...the old woman's rayon dress.

raze /reɪz/ (**razes, razing, razed**) **1** V-T [usu passive] If buildings, villages, or towns are **razed** to the ground, they are completely destroyed. ◻ Dozens of villages have been razed. ◻ Cities such as Berlin and Dresden were virtually razed to the ground. **2** → See feature box at **disaster**

ra|zor /reɪzər/ (**razors**) N-COUNT A **razor** is a tool that people use for shaving. ◻ ...a plastic disposable razor.

ra|zor blade (**razor blades**) N-COUNT A **razor blade** is a small, flat piece of metal with a very sharp edge which is put into a razor and used for shaving.

razor-sharp 1 ADJ [usu ADJ n] A cutting tool that is **razor-sharp** is extremely sharp. ◻ ...a razor-sharp butcher's knife. **2** ADJ If you describe someone or someone's mind as **razor-sharp**, you mean that they have a very accurate and clear understanding of things. ◻ ...his razor-sharp intelligence.

razor-thin ADJ A **razor-thin** majority or profit is a very small one. [mainly AM] ◻ There is a razor-thin Democratic majority of one seat in the Senate. ◻ ...the consumer retail arena, where profits are razor-thin.

ra|zor wire N-UNCOUNT **Razor wire** is strong wire with sharp blades sticking out of it. In wars or civil conflict it is sometimes used to prevent people from entering or leaving buildings or areas of land. ◻ ...plans to use razor wire to seal off hostels for migrant workers.

razz /ræz/ (**razzes, razzing, razzed**) V-T To **razz** someone means to tease them, especially in an unkind way. [mainly AM, INFORMAL] ◻ Molly razzed me about my rotten sense of direction.

razz|a|ma|tazz /ræzəmətæz/ N-UNCOUNT **Razzamatazz** is the same as **razzmatazz**. [mainly BRIT]

razzle-dazzle /ræzəldæzəl/ N-UNCOUNT [oft N n] **Razzle-dazzle** is the same as **razzmatazz**. ◻ ...a razzle-dazzle marketing man.

razz|ma|tazz /ræzmətæz/ N-UNCOUNT **Razzmatazz** is a noisy and showy display. ◻ ...the color and razzmatazz of a U.S. election.

RC ♦◊◊ /ɑr si/ also **R.C.** ADJ **RC** is an abbreviation for **Roman Catholic**. ◻ ...St. Mary's RC Cathedral.

Rd. also **Rd** **Rd.** is a written abbreviation for **road**. It is used especially in addresses and on maps or signs. ◻ Chicago Botanic Garden, Lake Cook Rd., Glencoe.

-rd **-rd** is added to numbers that end in 3, except those ending in 13, in order to form ordinal numbers such as 3rd or 33rd. 3rd is pronounced 'third.' ◻ ...September 3rd, 1990. ◻ ...the 33rd Boston Marathon. ◻ Canada's 123rd birthday.

RDA /ɑr di eɪ/ (**RDAs**) N-COUNT [usu singular] The **RDA** of a particular vitamin or mineral is the amount that people need each day to stay healthy. **RDA** is an abbreviation for 'recommended daily allowance.'

re /ri/ PREP You use **re** in documents such as business letters, e-mails, faxes and memos to introduce a subject or item which you are going to discuss or refer to in detail. ◻ Dear Mrs. Cox, Re: Homeowners Insurance. We note from our files that we have not yet received your renewal instructions.

PREFIX

re- forms verbs and nouns that refer to an action or process being repeated. *For example, if you **reread** something, you read it again.*

R.E. /ɑr i/ N-UNCOUNT **R.E.** is a school subject in which children learn about religion and other social matters. **R.E.** is an abbreviation for 'religious education.' [BRIT]

-'re /ər/ **-'re** is the usual spoken form of 'are.' It is added to the end of the pronoun or noun which is the subject of the verb. For example, 'they are' can be shortened to 'they're.'

reach ✦✦✦ /ritʃ/ (**reaches**, **reaching**, **reached**) **1** V-T When someone or something **reaches** a place, they arrive there. ◻ *He did not stop until he reached the door.* **2** V-T If someone or something has **reached** a certain stage, level, or amount, they are at that stage, level, or amount. ◻ *The process of political change in South Africa has reached the stage where it is irreversible.* **3** V-I If you **reach** somewhere, you move your arm and hand to take or touch something. ◻ *Judy reached into her handbag and handed me a small, printed leaflet.* **4** V-T If you can **reach** something, you are able to touch it by stretching out your arm or leg. ◻ *Can you reach your toes with your fingertips?* **5** V-T If you try to **reach** someone, you try to contact them, usually by telephone. ◻ *Has the doctor told you how to reach him or her in emergencies?* **6** V-T/V-I If something **reaches** a place, point, or level, it extends as far as that place, point, or level. ◻ *...a nightshirt that reached to his knees.* **7** V-T When people **reach** an agreement or a decision, they succeed in achieving it. ◻ *A meeting of agriculture ministers has so far failed to reach agreement over farm subsidies.* **8** N-UNCOUNT Someone's or something's **reach** is the distance or limit to which they can stretch, extend, or travel. ◻ *Isabelle placed a wine cup on the table within his reach.* **9** N-UNCOUNT If a place or thing is within **reach**, it is possible to have it or get to it. If it is out of **reach**, it is not possible to have it or get to it. ◻ *It is located within reach of many important Norman towns, including Bayeux.*

SYNONYMS

reach
VERB
1
arrive at: *The Princess Royal arrived at Gatwick this morning from Jamaica.*
get to: *Generally, I get to work at 9:30 am.*
end up: *The result was that the box ended up at the bottom of the canal.*
2
attain: *...attaining a state of calmness and confidence.*
amount to: *Consumer spending on sports-related items amounted to $9.75 billion.*
get to: *We haven't got to the stage of a full-scale military conflict.*
rise to: *Pre-tax profits rose to $1.8 million.*

reaches /ritʃiz/ **1** N-PLURAL [usu the adj N of n] The upper, middle, or lower **reaches** of a river are parts of a river. The upper **reaches** are nearer to the river's source and the lower **reaches** are nearer to the sea into which it flows. ◻ *This year water levels in the middle and lower reaches of the Yangtze are unusually high.* **2** N-PLURAL [usu the adj N of n] You can refer to the distant or outer parts of a place or area as the far, farthest, or outer **reaches**. [FORMAL] ◻ *...the outer reaches of the solar system.* **3** N-PLURAL [usu the adj N of n] You can refer to the higher or lower levels of an organization as its upper or lower **reaches**. [FORMAL] ◻ *...the upper reaches of the legal profession.*

re|act ✦✧✧ /riækt/ (**reacts**, **reacting**, **reacted**) **1** V-I When you **react** to something that has happened to you, you behave in a particular way because of it. ◻ *They reacted violently to the news.* **2** V-I If you **react against** someone's way of behaving, you deliberately behave in a different way because you do not like the way they behave. ◻ *My father never saved money and perhaps I reacted against that.* **3** V-I If you **react** to a substance such as a drug, or to something you have touched, you are affected unpleasantly or made ill by it. ◻ *Someone allergic to milk is likely to react to cheese.* **4** V-RECIP When one chemical substance **reacts** with another, or when two chemical substances **react**, they combine chemically to form another substance. ◻ *Calcium reacts with water but less violently than sodium and potassium do.*

SYNONYMS

react
VERB **1**
respond: *The army responded with gunfire and tear gas.*
answer: *He answered her smile with one of his own.*

re|ac|tion ✦✦✧ /riækʃən/ (**reactions**) **1** N-VAR Your **reaction** to something that has happened or something that you have experienced is what you feel, say, or do because of it. ◻ *Reaction to the visit is mixed.* **2** N-COUNT A **reaction against** something is a way of behaving or doing something that is deliberately different from what has been done before. ◻ *All new fashion starts out as a reaction against existing convention.* **3** N-SING [also no det, N against n] If there is a **reaction against** something, it becomes unpopular. ◻ *Premature moves in this respect might well provoke a reaction against the reform.* **4** N-PLURAL Your **reactions** are your ability to move quickly in response to something, for example when you are in danger. ◻ *The sport requires very fast reactions.* **5** N-UNCOUNT **Reaction** is the belief that the political or social system of your country should not change. [DISAPPROVAL] ◻ *Thus, he aided reaction and thwarted progress.* **6** N-COUNT A chemical **reaction** is a process in which two substances combine together chemically to form another substance. ◻ *Ozone is produced by the reaction between oxygen and ultraviolet light.* **7** N-COUNT If you have a **reaction** to a substance such as a drug, or to something you have touched, you are affected unpleasantly or made ill by it. ◻ *Every year, 5,000 people have life-threatening reactions to anesthetics.* **8** → See feature box at **illness**

SYNONYMS

reaction
NOUN **1**
response: *The meeting was called in response to a request from Venezuela.*
answer: *In answer to speculation that she wouldn't finish the race, she boldly declared her intention of winning it.*

re|ac|tion|ary /riækʃəneri/ (**reactionaries**) ADJ A **reactionary** person or group tries to prevent changes in the political or social system of their country. [DISAPPROVAL] ◻ *It became clear to everyone that the chairman was too reactionary, too blinkered.* • N-COUNT A **reactionary** is someone with reactionary views. ◻ *Critics viewed him as a reactionary, even a monarchist.*

re|ac|ti|vate /riæktɪveɪt/ (**reactivates**, **reactivating**, **reactivated**) V-T If people **reactivate** a system or organization, they make it work again after a period in which it has not been working. ◻ *...a series of economic reforms to reactivate the economy.*

re|ac|tive /riæktɪv/ **1** ADJ Something that is **reactive** is able to react chemically with a lot of different substances. ◻ *Ozone is a highly reactive form of oxygen gas.* **2** ADJ [usu v-link ADJ] If someone is **reactive**, they behave in response to what happens to them, rather than deciding in advance how they want to behave. ◻ *I want our organization to be less reactive and more proactive.*

re|ac|tor /riæktər/ (**reactors**) N-COUNT A **reactor** is the same as a **nuclear reactor**.

read ✦✦✦ (**reads**, **reading**)

The form **read** is pronounced /rid/ when it is the present tense, and /rɛd/ when it is the past tense and past participle.

1 V-T/V-I When you **read** something such as a book or article, you look at and understand the words that are written there. ◻ *Have you read this book?* ◻ *I read about it in the paper.* ◻ *She spends her days reading and watching television.* • N-SING **Read** is also a noun. ◻ *I settled down to have a good read.* **2** V-T/V-I When you **read** a piece of writing to someone, you say the words aloud. ◻ *Jay reads poetry so beautifully.* ◻ *I like it when she reads to us.* **3** V-T/V-I People who can **read** have the ability to look at and understand written words. ◻ *He couldn't read or write.* ◻ *The kid can read words, but did miserably on the test.* **4** V-T If you can **read**

music, you have the ability to look at and understand the symbols that are used in written music to represent musical sounds. ❏ *Later on I learned how to read music.* **5** V-T When a computer **reads** a file or a document, it takes information from a disk or tape. [COMPUTING] ❏ *How can I read an Excel file on a computer that only has Word installed?* **6** V-T [no cont] You can use **read** when saying what is written on something or in something. For example, if a notice **reads** 'Entrance,' the word 'Entrance' is written on it. ❏ *The sign on the bus read "Private: Not In Service."* **7** V-I If you refer to how a piece of writing **reads**, you are referring to its style. ❏ *The book reads like a ballad.* **8** N-COUNT [adj N] If you say that a book or magazine is a good **read**, you mean that it is very enjoyable to read. ❏ *Ben Okri's latest novel is a good read.* **9** V-T If something **is read** in a particular way, it is understood or interpreted in that way. ❏ *The play is being widely read as an allegory of imperialist conquest.* **10** V-T If you **read** someone's mind or thoughts, you know exactly what they are thinking without them telling you. ❏ *From behind her, as if he could read her thoughts, Benny said, "You're free to go any time you like, Madame."* **11** V-T If you can **read** someone or you can **read** their gestures, you can understand what they are thinking or feeling by the way they behave or the things they say. ❏ *If you have to work as part of a team, you must learn to read people.* **12** V-T When you **read** a measuring device, you look at it to see what the figure or measurement on it is. ❏ *It is essential that you are able to read a thermometer.* **13** V-T If a measuring device **reads** a particular amount, it shows that amount. ❏ *The thermometer read 105 degrees Fahrenheit.* **14** → see also **reading**

▶ **read into** PHRASAL VERB If you **read** a meaning **into** something, you think it is there although it may not actually be there. ❏ *It is dangerous to read too much into one year's figures.*

▶ **read out** PHRASAL VERB If you **read out** a piece of writing, you say it aloud. ❏ *He's obliged to take his turn at reading out the announcements.*

▶ **read up on** PHRASAL VERB If you **read up on** a subject, you read a lot about it so that you become informed about it. ❏ *I've read up on the dangers of all these drugs.*

SYNONYMS

read
VERB **1**
scan: *She scanned the advertisement pages of the newspapers.*
pore over: *We spent hours poring over travel brochures.*
skim: *She skimmed the pages quickly, then read them again more carefully.*
glance at/through: *I never even glanced at the political page of a daily paper.*

---

read|able /rídəbəl/ **1** ADJ If you say that a book or article is readable, you mean that it is enjoyable and easy to read. ❏ *This is a well researched and very readable book.* **2** ADJ A piece of writing that is **readable** is written or printed clearly and can be read easily. ❏ *My secretary worked long hours translating my almost illegible writing into a typewritten and readable script.*

read|er ♦♦◊ /rídər/ (**readers**) **1** N-COUNT The **readers** of a newspaper, magazine, or book are the people who read it. ❏ *These texts give the reader an insight into the Chinese mind.* ❏ *The paper's success is simple: we give our readers what they want.* **2** N-COUNT A **reader** is a person who reads, especially one who reads for pleasure. ❏ *Thanks to that job I became an avid reader.*

read|er|ship /rídərʃɪp/ (**readerships**) **1** N-COUNT The **readership** of a book, newspaper, or magazine is the number or type of people who read it. ❏ *Its readership has grown to over 15,000 subscribers.* **2** → See feature box at **press**

read|ily /rédɪli/ **1** ADV [ADV with v] If you do something **readily**, you do it in a way which shows that you are very willing to do it. ❏ *I asked her if she would allow me to interview her, and she readily agreed.* **2** ADV You also use **readily** to say that something can be done or obtained quickly and easily. For example, if you say that something can be readily understood, you mean that people can understand it quickly and easily. ❏ *The components are readily available in hardware stores.*

readi|ness /rédɪnɪs/ **1** N-UNCOUNT If someone is very willing to do something, you can talk about their **readiness** to do it. ❏ *…their readiness to co-operate with the new U.S. envoy.* **2** N-UNCOUNT If you do something in **readiness** for a future event, you do it so that you are prepared for that event. ❏ *Security tightened in the capital in readiness for the president's arrival.*

read|ing ♦◊◊ /rídɪŋ/ (**readings**) **1** N-UNCOUNT **Reading** is the activity of reading books. ❏ *I have always loved reading.* **2** N-COUNT A **reading** is an event at which poetry or extracts from books are read to an audience. ❏ *…a poetry reading.* **3** N-COUNT Your **reading** of a word, text, or situation is the way in which you understand or interpret it. ❏ *My reading of her character makes me feel that she was too responsible a person to do those things.* **4** N-COUNT The **reading** on a measuring device is the figure or measurement that it shows. ❏ *The gauge must be giving a faulty reading.*

read|ing glasses N-PLURAL [also *a pair of* N] **Reading glasses** are glasses that are worn by people, for example when they are reading, because they cannot see things close to them very well.

read|ing lamp (**reading lamps**) N-COUNT A **reading lamp** is a small lamp that you keep on a desk or table. You can move part of it in order to direct the light to where you need it for reading.

read|ing room (**reading rooms**) N-COUNT A **reading room** is a quiet room in a library or museum where you can read and study.

re|adjust /riədʒʌ́st/ (**readjusts, readjusting, readjusted**) **1** V-I When you **readjust** to a new situation, usually one you have been in before, you adapt to it. ❏ *I can understand why astronauts find it difficult to readjust to life on earth.* **2** V-T If you **readjust** the level of something, your attitude to something, or the way you do something, you change it to make it more effective or appropriate. ❏ *In the end you have to readjust your expectations.* **3** V-T If you **readjust** something such as a piece of clothing or a mechanical device, you correct or alter its position or setting. ❏ *Readjust your watch. You are now on Moscow time.*

re|adjust|ment /riədʒʌ́stmənt/ (**readjustments**) N-VAR **Readjustment** is the process of adapting to a new situation, usually one that you have been in before. ❏ *The next few weeks will be a period of readjustment, and will probably not be easy.*

read|out /rídaʊt/ (**readouts**) N-COUNT If an electronic measuring device gives you a **readout**, it displays information about the level of something such as a speed, height, or sound. ❏ *The system provides a digital readout of the vehicle's speed.*

ready ♦♦◊ /rédi/ (**readier, readiest, readies, readying, readied**) **1** ADJ [v-link ADJ] If someone is **ready**, they are properly prepared for something. If something is **ready**, it has been properly prepared and is now able to be used. ❏ *It took her a long time to get ready for church.* ❏ *Are you ready to board, Mr. Daly?* **2** ADJ [v-link ADJ] If you are **ready** for something or **ready** to do something, you have enough experience to do it or you are old enough and sensible enough to do it. ❏ *She says she's not ready for marriage.* **3** ADJ [v-link ADJ to-inf] If you are **ready** to do something, you are willing to do it. ❏ *They were ready to die for their beliefs.* **4** ADJ [v-link ADJ *for* n] If you are **ready for** something, you need it or want it. ❏ *I don't know about you, but I'm ready for bed.* **5** ADJ [v-link ADJ to-inf] To be **ready** to do something means to be about to do it or likely to do it. ❏ *She looked ready to cry.* **6** ADJ [ADJ n] You use **ready** to describe things that are able to be used very quickly and easily. ❏ *I didn't have a ready answer for this dilemma.* **7** V-T When you **ready** something, you prepare it for a particular purpose. [FORMAL] ❏ *John's soldiers were readying themselves for the final assault.*

ready-made **1** ADJ If something that you buy is **ready-made**, you can use it immediately, because the work you would normally have to do has already been done. ❏ *We rely quite a bit on ready made meals – they are so convenient.* **2** ADJ **Ready-made** means extremely convenient or useful for a particular purpose. ❏ *Those wishing to study urban development have a ready-made example on their doorstep.*

ready-to-wear ADJ [ADJ n] **Ready-to-wear** clothes are made in standard sizes so that they fit most people, rather than being made specially for a particular person. ❏ *In 1978 he launched his first major ready-to-wear collection for the Target stores.*

re|affirm /riəfɜrm/ (reaffirms, reaffirming, reaffirmed) V-T If you **reaffirm** something, you state it again clearly and firmly. [FORMAL] ❑ *He reaffirmed his commitment to the country's economic reform program.*

re|agent /rieɪdʒənt/ (reagents) N-COUNT A **reagent** is a substance that is used to cause a chemical reaction. Reagents are often used in order to indicate the presence of another substance. [TECHNICAL]

real ♦♦♦ /riːl/ **1** ADJ Something that is **real** actually exists and is not imagined, invented, or theoretical. ❑ *No, it wasn't a dream. It was real.* **2** ADJ If something is **real** to someone, they experience it as though it really exists or happens, even though it does not. ❑ *Whitechild's life becomes increasingly real to the reader.* **3** ADJ A material or object that is **real** is natural or functioning, and not artificial or an imitation. ❑ *...the smell of real leather.* **4** ADJ [ADJ n] You can use **real** to describe someone or something that has all the characteristics or qualities that such a person or thing typically has. ❑ *...his first real girlfriend.* **5** ADJ [ADJ n] You can use **real** to describe something that is the true or original thing of its kind, in contrast to one that someone wants you to believe is true. ❑ *This was the real reason for her call.* **6** ADJ [ADJ n] You can use **real** to describe something that is the most important or typical part of a thing. ❑ *When he talks, he only gives glimpses of his real self.* **7** ADJ You can use **real** when you are talking about a situation or feeling to emphasize that it exists and is important or serious. [EMPHASIS] ❑ *Global warming is a real problem.* ❑ *The prospect of civil war is very real.* **8** ADJ [ADJ n] You can use **real** to emphasize a quality that is genuine and sincere. [EMPHASIS] ❑ *You've been drifting from job to job without any real commitment.* **9** ADJ [ADJ n] You can use **real** before nouns to emphasize your description of something or someone. [mainly SPOKEN, EMPHASIS] ❑ *"You must think I'm a real idiot."* **10** ADJ [ADJ n] The **real** cost or value of something is its cost or value after other amounts have been added or subtracted and when factors such as the level of inflation have been considered. ❑ *...the real cost of borrowing.* • PHRASE You can also talk about the cost or value of something **in real terms**. ❑ *In real terms the cost of driving is cheaper than a decade ago.* **11** ADV [ADV adj/adv] You can use **real** to emphasize an adjective or adverb. [AM, INFORMAL, EMPHASIS] ❑ *He is finding prison life "real tough."* **12** PHRASE If you say that someone does something **for real**, you mean that they actually do it and do not just pretend to do it. [INFORMAL] ❑ *I have gone to premieres in my dreams but I never thought I'd do it for real.*

real es|tate ♦♦◊ **1** N-UNCOUNT **Real estate** is property in the form of land and buildings, rather than personal possessions. [mainly AM] ❑ *By investing in real estate, he was one of the richest men in the United States.* **2** N-UNCOUNT **Real estate** businesses or **real estate** agents sell houses, buildings, and land. [AM] ❑ *...the real estate agent who sold you your house.*

in BRIT, use **estate agency**

re|align /riəlaɪn/ (realigns, realigning, realigned) V-T If you **realign** your ideas, policies, or plans, you organize them in a different way in order to take account of new circumstances. ❑ *Following the plant shutdown, New Hampshire Yankee realigned senior management at the plant.*

re|align|ment /riəlaɪnmənt/ (realignments) N-VAR [usu N of n] If a company, economy, or system goes through a **realignment**, it is organized or arranged in a new way. ❑ *...a realignment of the existing political structure.*

re|al|ism /riəlɪzəm/ **1** N-UNCOUNT When people show **realism** in their behavior, they recognize and accept the true nature of a situation and try to deal with it in a practical way. [APPROVAL] ❑ *It was time now to show more political realism.* **2** N-UNCOUNT If things and people are presented with **realism** in paintings, stories, or movies, they are presented in a way that is like real life. [APPROVAL] ❑ *Greene's stories had an edge of realism that made it easy to forget they were fiction.* **3** → See feature box at **quality**

re|al|ist /riəlɪst/ (realists) **1** N-COUNT A **realist** is someone who recognizes and accepts the true nature of a situation and tries to deal with it in a practical way. [APPROVAL] ❑ *I see myself not as a cynic but as a realist.* **2** ADJ [ADJ n] A **realist** painter or writer is one who represents things and people in a way that is like real life. ❑ *...perhaps the foremost realist painter of our time.*

re|al|is|tic /riəlɪstɪk/ **1** ADJ If you are **realistic** about a situation, you recognize and accept its true nature and try to deal with it in a practical way. ❑ *Police have to be realistic about violent crime.* • **re|al|is|ti|cal|ly** ADV ❑ *As an adult, you can assess the situation realistically.* **2** ADJ Something such as a goal or target that is **realistic** is one that you can sensibly expect to achieve. ❑ *A more realistic figure is 11 million.* **3** ADJ You say that a painting, story, or movie is **realistic** when the people and things in it are like people and things in real life. ❑ *...extraordinarily realistic paintings of Indians.* • **re|al|is|ti|cal|ly** ADV ❑ *The film starts off realistically and then develops into a ridiculous fantasy.*

re|al|is|ti|cal|ly /riəlɪstɪkli/ **1** ADV [ADV with cl] You use **realistically** when you want to emphasize that what you are saying is true, even though you would prefer it not to be true. [EMPHASIS] ❑ *Realistically, there is never one right answer.* **2** → see also **realistic**

re|al|ity ♦♦◊ /riæliti/ (realities) **1** N-UNCOUNT You use **reality** to refer to real things or the real nature of things rather than imagined, invented, or theoretical ideas. ❑ *Fiction and reality were increasingly blurred.* **2** → see also **virtual reality** **3** N-COUNT The **reality** of a situation is the truth about it, especially when it is unpleasant or difficult to deal with. ❑ *...the harsh reality of top international competition.* **4** N-SING You say that something has become a **reality** when it actually exists or is actually happening. ❑ *...the whole procedure that made this book become a reality.* **5** PHRASE You can use **in reality** to introduce a statement about the real nature of something, when it contrasts with something incorrect that has just been described. ❑ *He came across as streetwise, but in reality he was not.*

> **COLLOCATIONS**
>
> **reality**
> NOUN **3**
> adjective + **reality**: grim, harsh, sad, stark
> verb + **reality**: accept, confront, face, recognize; expose, reflect

re|al|ity check (reality checks) N-COUNT [usu sing] If you say that something is a **reality check** for someone, you mean that it makes them recognize the truth about a situation, especially about the difficulties involved in something they want to achieve. ❑ *Dylan thinks fans who idolize him need a reality check.*

re|al|ity show (reality shows) N-COUNT A **reality show** is a type of television program that aims to show how ordinary people behave in everyday life, or in situations, often created by the program makers, which are intended to represent everyday life. ❑ *...NBC's new reality show, "The Restaurant."*

re|al|ity TV N-UNCOUNT **Reality TV** is a type of television programming that aims to show how ordinary people behave in everyday life, or in situations, often created by the program makers, which are intended to represent everyday life. ❑ *"Storm Warning" is really just typical voyeuristic reality TV.*

re|al|iz|able /riəlaɪzəbəl/

in BRIT, also use **realisable**

1 ADJ If your hopes or aims are **realizable**, there is a possibility that the things that you want to happen will happen. [FORMAL] ❑ *...the reasonless assumption that one's dreams and desires were realizable.* **2** ADJ **Realizable** wealth is money that can be easily obtained by selling something. [FORMAL] ❑ *In many cases this realizable wealth is not realized during the lifetime of the home owner.*

re|al|ize ♦♦◊ /riəlaɪz/ (realizes, realizing, realized)

in BRIT, also use **realise**

1 V-T/V-I If you **realize** that something is true, you become aware of that fact or understand it. ❑ *As soon as we realized something was wrong, we moved the children away.* ❑ *People don't realize how serious this recession has actually been.* • **re|ali|za|tion** /riəlɪzeɪʃən/ (realizations) N-VAR ❑ *There is now a growing realization that things cannot go on like this for much longer.* **2** V-T [usu passive] If your hopes, desires, or fears **are realized**, the things that you hope for, desire, or fear actually happen.

❑ *All his worst fears were realized.* • **re|ali|za|tion** N-UNCOUNT ❑ *In Kravis's venomous tone he recognized the realization of his worst fears.* **3** V-T When someone **realizes** a design or an idea, they make or organize something based on that design or idea. [FORMAL] ❑ *I knew the technique that I would have to create in order to realize that structure.* **4** V-T If someone or something **realizes** their potential, they do everything they are capable of doing, because they have been given the opportunity to do so. ❑ *The support systems to enable women to realize their potential at work are seriously inadequate.* **5** V-T If something **realizes** a particular amount of money when it is sold, that amount of money is paid for it. [FORMAL] ❑ *A selection of correspondence from P.G. Wodehouse realized 2,000 dollars.* • **re|ali|za|tion** N-VAR ❑ *...a total cash realization of about $23 million.*

> **SYNONYMS**
>
> **realize**
> VERB **1**
> **understand:** *They are too young to understand what is going on.*
> **appreciate:** *He appreciates that co-operation with the media is part of his professional duties.*
> **grasp:** *He instantly grasped that Stephen was talking about his wife.*

real life N-UNCOUNT If something happens in **real life**, it actually happens and is not just in a story or in someone's imagination. ❑ *In real life, the underdog doesn't always win the day.* • ADJ [ADJ n] **Real life** is also an adjective. ❑ *...a real-life horror story.*

re|allo|cate /riˈæləkeɪt/ (**reallocates, reallocating, reallocated**) V-T When organizations **reallocate** money or resources, they decide to change the way they spend the money or use the resources. ❑ *...a cost-cutting program to reallocate people and resources within the company.*

re|al|ly ♦♦♦ /ˈriːli/ **1** ADV You can use **really** to emphasize a statement. [SPOKEN, EMPHASIS] ❑ *I'm very sorry. I really am.* **2** ADV [ADV adj/adv] You can use **really** to emphasize an adjective or adverb. [EMPHASIS] ❑ *It was really good.* **3** ADV You use **really** when you are discussing the real facts about something, in contrast to the ones someone wants you to believe. ❑ *My father didn't really love her.* **4** ADV [ADV before v] People use **really** in questions and negative statements when they want you to answer 'no.' [EMPHASIS] ❑ *Do you really think he would be that stupid?* **5** ADV [ADV before v] If you refer to a time when something **really** begins to happen, you are emphasizing that it starts to happen at that time to a much greater extent and much more seriously than before. [EMPHASIS] ❑ *That's when the pressure really started.* **6** ADV People sometimes use **really** to slightly reduce the force of a negative statement. [SPOKEN, VAGUENESS] ❑ *I'm not really surprised.* **7** CONVENTION You can say **really** to express surprise or disbelief at what someone has said. [SPOKEN, FEELINGS] ❑ *"We discovered it was totally the wrong decision."—"Really?"*

> **SYNONYMS**
>
> **really**
> ADV **2**
> **extremely:** *Three of them are working extremely well.*
> **very:** *I'm very sorry.*
> **particularly:** *Progress has been particularly disappointing.*
> **incredibly:** *Their father was incredibly good-looking.*

realm /relm/ (**realms**) **1** N-COUNT You can use **realm** to refer to any area of activity, interest, or thought. [FORMAL] ❑ *...the realm of politics.* **2** N-COUNT A **realm** is a country that has a king or queen. [FORMAL] ❑ *Defense of the realm is crucial.*

real prop|er|ty N-UNCOUNT **Real property** is property in the form of land and buildings, rather than personal possessions. [AM] ❑ *...the owner or tenant of a piece of real property.*

real time N-UNCOUNT [oft *in* N] If something is done in **real time**, there is no noticeable delay between the action and its effect or consequence. ❑ *...umpires, who have to make every decision in real time.*

real-time ADJ [ADJ n] **Real-time** processing is a type of computer programming or data processing in which the information received is processed by the computer almost immediately. [COMPUTING] ❑ *...real-time language translations.*

Real|tor /ˈriːəltər, -tɔːr/ (**Realtors**) also **realtor** N-COUNT A **Realtor** is a person whose job is to sell houses, buildings, and land, and who is a member of the National Association of Realtors. [AM, TRADEMARK] ❑ *When the Realtor showed us this house, we knew we wanted it right away.*

> in BRIT, use **estate agent**

re|al|ty /ˈriːəlti/ N-UNCOUNT [usu N n] **Realty** is property in the form of land and buildings, rather than personal possessions. [AM] ❑ *Our realty agent says the sales contract is valid.*

real world N-SING If you talk about the **real world**, you are referring to the world and life in general, in contrast with a particular person's own life, experience, and ideas, which may seem untypical and unrealistic. ❑ *When they eventually leave the school they will be totally ill-equipped to deal with the real world.*

ream /riːm/ (**reams**) N-COUNT [usu pl, usu N *of* n] If you say that there are **reams** of paper or **reams** of writing, you mean that there are large amounts of it. [INFORMAL] ❑ *Their specific task is to sort through the reams of information and try to determine what it means.*

reap /riːp/ (**reaps, reaping, reaped**) V-T If you **reap** the benefits or the rewards of something, you enjoy the good things that happen as a result of it. ❑ *You'll soon begin to reap the benefits of being fitter.*

reap|er /ˈriːpər/ (**reapers**) **1** N-COUNT A **reaper** is a machine used to cut and gather crops. **2** → see also **Grim Reaper**

re|appear /riːəˈpɪər/ (**reappears, reappearing, reappeared**) V-I When people or things **reappear**, they return again after they have been away or out of sight for some time. ❑ *Thirty seconds later she reappeared and beckoned them forward.*

re|appear|ance /riːəˈpɪərəns/ (**reappearances**) N-COUNT The **reappearance** of someone or something is their return after they have been away or out of sight for some time. ❑ *His sudden reappearance must have been a shock.*

re|apprais|al /riːəˈpreɪzəl/ (**reappraisals**) N-VAR If there is a **reappraisal** of something such as an idea or plan, people think about the idea carefully and decide whether they want to change it. [FORMAL] ❑ *The state's worst prison riot will force a fundamental reappraisal of prison policy.*

re|appraise /riːəˈpreɪz/ (**reappraises, reappraising, reappraised**) V-T If you **reappraise** something such as an idea or a plan, you think carefully about it and decide whether it needs to be changed. [FORMAL] ❑ *It did not persuade them to abandon the war but it did force them to reappraise their strategy.*

rear ♦⬦⬦ /rɪər/ (**rears, rearing, reared**) **1** N-SING The **rear** of something such as a building or vehicle is the back part of it. ❑ *He settled back in the rear of the taxi.* • ADJ [ADJ n] **Rear** is also an adjective. ❑ *Manufacturers have been obliged to fit rear seat belts in all new cars.* **2** N-SING If you are at the **rear** of a moving line of people, you are the last person in it. [FORMAL] ❑ *Musicians played at the front and rear of the procession.* **3** N-COUNT Your **rear** is the part of your body that you sit on. [INFORMAL] ❑ *He plans to have a dragon tattooed on his rear.* **4** V-T If you **rear** children, you take care of them until they are old enough to take care of themselves. ❑ *She reared sixteen children, six her own and ten her husband's.* **5** V-T If you **rear** a young animal, you keep and take care of it until it is old enough to be used for work or food, or until it can look after itself. ❑ *She spends a lot of time rearing animals.* **6** V-I When a horse **rears**, it moves the front part of its body upward, so that its front legs are high in the air and it is standing on its back legs. ❑ *The horse reared and threw off its rider.* **7** PHRASE If a person or vehicle is **bringing up the rear**, they are the last person or vehicle in a moving line of them. ❑ *...police motorcyclists bringing up the rear of the procession.*

rear ad|mi|ral (**rear admirals**) N-TITLE; N-COUNT **Rear admiral** is a rank in the navy. It is the rank below vice admiral. ❑ *...Rear Admiral Douglas Carter, commander of the USS America.*

rear end (**rear ends**) **1** N-COUNT The **rear end** of a vehicle is the back part of it. ❑ *...the rear end of a black car.* **2** N-COUNT Your **rear end** is the part of your body that you sit on. [INFORMAL] ❑ *I had a few bruises on my rear end.*

rear-end (rear-ends, rear-ending, rear-ended) V-T If a driver or vehicle **rear-ends** the vehicle in front, they crash into the back of it. [INFORMAL] ▢ *A few days earlier somebody had rear-ended him.*

rear|guard /rɪ͡ərgɑrd/ also **rear guard** ◼ N-SING [the N] In a battle, **the rearguard** is a group of soldiers who protect the back part of an army, especially when the army is leaving the battle. ◼ PHRASE If someone is **fighting a rearguard action** or **mounting a rearguard action**, they are trying very hard to prevent something from happening, even though it is probably too late for them to succeed. [JOURNALISM] ▢ *Mr. Lin looks increasingly like someone fighting a rearguard action to keep their job.*

re|arm /riɑrm/ (rearms, rearming, rearmed) V-T/V-I If a country **rearms** or **is rearmed**, it starts to build up a new stock of military weapons. ▢ *They neglected to rearm in time and left the country exposed to disaster.* ▢ *...NATO's decision to rearm West Germany.*

re|arma|ment /riɑrməmənt/ N-UNCOUNT **Rearmament** is the process of building up a new stock of military weapons.

re|arrange /ri͡əreɪndʒ/ (rearranges, rearranging, rearranged) ◼ V-T If you **rearrange** things, you change the way in which they are organized or ordered. ▢ *When she returned, she found Malcolm had rearranged all her furniture.* ◼ V-T If you **rearrange** a meeting or an appointment, you arrange for it to take place at a different time from that originally intended. ▢ *You may cancel or rearrange the appointment.*

re|arrange|ment /ri͡əreɪndʒmənt/ (rearrangements) N-VAR A **rearrangement** is a change in the way that something is arranged or organized. ▢ *...a rearrangement of the job structure.*

rear|view mir|ror /rɪ͡ərvyu mɪrər/ (rearview mirrors) N-COUNT Inside a car, the **rearview mirror** is the mirror that enables you to see the traffic behind when you are driving.

rear|ward /rɪ͡ərwərd/ ADV [ADV with v] If something moves or faces **rearward**, it moves or faces backward. ▢ *...a rearward facing infant carrier.* ▢ *The center of pressure moves rearward and the airplane becomes unbalanced.* • ADJ [ADJ n] **Rearward** is also an adjective. ▢ *...the rearward window.*

rea|son ✦✦✦ /ri͡zᵊn/ (reasons, reasoning, reasoned) ◼ N-COUNT The **reason** for something is a fact or situation which explains why it happens or what causes it to happen. ▢ *There is a reason for every important thing that happens.* ◼ N-UNCOUNT If you say that you have **reason** to believe something or to have a particular emotion, you mean that you have evidence for your belief or there is a definite cause of your feeling. ▢ *They had reason to believe there could be trouble.* ◼ N-UNCOUNT The ability that people have to think and to make sensible judgments can be referred to as **reason**. ▢ *...a conflict between emotion and reason.* ◼ V-T If you **reason** that something is true, you decide that it is true after thinking carefully about all the facts. ▢ *I reasoned that changing my diet would lower my cholesterol level.* ◼ → see also **reasoned**, **reasoning** ◼ PHRASE If one thing happens **by reason of** another, it happens because of it. [FORMAL] ▢ *The boss retains enormous influence by reason of his position.* ◼ PHRASE If you try to make someone **listen to reason**, you try to persuade them to listen to sensible arguments and be influenced by them. ▢ *The company's top executives had refused to listen to reason.* ◼ PHRASE If you say that something happened or was done **for no reason**, **for no good reason**, or **for no reason at all**, you mean that there was no obvious reason why it happened or was done. ▢ *The guards, he said, would punch them for no reason.* ◼ PHRASE If you say that you will do anything **within reason**, you mean that you will do anything that is fair or reasonable and not too extreme. ▢ *I will take any job that comes along, within reason.* ◼ see reason → see see ② ◼ **it stands to reason** → see stand ①

▶ **reason with** PHRASAL VERB If you try to **reason with** someone, you try to persuade them to do or accept something by using sensible arguments. ▢ *He's impossible. I can't reason with him.*

rea|son|able ✦◇◇ /ri͡zənəbᵊl/ ◼ ADJ If you think that someone is fair and sensible, you can say that they are **reasonable**. ▢ *He's a reasonable sort of person.* • **rea|son|ably** /ri͡zənəbli/ ADV ▢ *"I'm sorry, Andrew," she said reasonably.* • **rea|son|able|ness** N-UNCOUNT ▢ *"I can understand how you feel," Dan said with great reasonableness.* ◼ ADJ If you say that a decision or action is **reasonable**, you mean that it is fair and sensible. ▢ *...a perfectly reasonable decision.* ◼ ADJ If you say that an expectation or explanation is **reasonable**, you mean that there are good reasons why it may be correct. ▢ *It seems reasonable to expect rapid urban growth.* • **rea|son|ably** ADV [ADV with v] ▢ *You can reasonably expect your goods to arrive within six to eight weeks.* ◼ ADJ If you say that the price of something is **reasonable**, you mean that it is fair and not too high. ▢ *You get a good meal for a reasonable price.* • **rea|son|ably** ADV [ADV with v] ▢ *...reasonably priced accommodations.* ◼ ADJ You can use **reasonable** to describe something that is fairly good, but not very good. ▢ *The boy answered him in reasonable French.* • **rea|son|ably** ADV [ADV adj/adv] ▢ *I can dance reasonably well.* ◼ ADJ A **reasonable** amount of something is a fairly large amount of it. ▢ *They will need a reasonable amount of desk area and good light.* • **rea|son|ably** ADV [ADV adj/adv] ▢ *From now on events moved reasonably quickly.*

SYNONYMS

reasonable
ADJ
◼
sensible: *Oh come on, let's be sensible about this.*
reasoned: *This is an issue which produces little reasoned argument.*
rational: *He's asking you to look at both sides of the case and come to a rational decision.*
◼
fair: *It didn't seem fair to leave out her father.*
just: *Was Pollard's life sentence just, or was it too severe?*
acceptable: *The air pollution exceeds most acceptable levels by 10 times or more.*

---

rea|soned /ri͡zᵊnd/ ADJ A **reasoned** discussion or argument is based on sensible reasons, rather than on an appeal to people's emotions. [APPROVAL] ▢ *Their opinions are not based on reasoned argument.*

rea|son|ing /ri͡zᵊnɪŋ/ (reasonings) N-VAR **Reasoning** is the process by which you reach a conclusion after thinking about all the facts. ▢ *...the reasoning behind the decision.*

re|as|sem|ble /ri͡əsɛmbᵊl/ (reassembles, reassembling, reassembled) ◼ V-T If you **reassemble** something, you put it back together after it has been taken apart. ▢ *We will now try to reassemble pieces of the wreckage.* ◼ V-T/V-I If a group of people **reassembles** or if you **reassemble** them, they gather together again in a group. ▢ *We'll reassemble in the parking lot in thirty minutes.* ▢ *Coach Lucas reassembled his team in September.*

re|as|sert /ri͡əsɜrt/ (reasserts, reasserting, reasserted) ◼ V-T If you **reassert** your control or authority, you make it clear that you are still in a position of power, or you strengthen the power that you had. ▢ *...the government's continuing effort to reassert its control in the region.* ◼ V-T If something such as an idea or habit **reasserts** itself, it becomes noticeable again. ▢ *His sense of humor was beginning to reassert itself.*

re|as|sess /ri͡əsɛs/ (reassesses, reassessing, reassessed) ◼ V-T If you **reassess** something, you think about it and decide whether you need to change your opinion about it. ▢ *I will reassess the situation when I get home.* ◼ → See feature box at **research**

re|as|sess|ment /ri͡əsɛsmənt/ (reassessments) N-VAR If you make a **reassessment** of something, you think about it and decide whether you need to change your opinion about it. ▢ *There's a total reassessment of what people want out of life.*

re|assur|ance /ri͡əʃʊərəns/ (reassurances) ◼ N-UNCOUNT If someone needs **reassurance**, they are very worried and need someone to help them stop worrying by saying kind or helpful things. ▢ *She needed reassurance that she belonged somewhere.* ◼ N-COUNT **Reassurances** are things that you say to help people stop worrying about something. ▢ *...reassurances that pesticides are not harmful.*

re|assure /ri͡əʃʊər/ (reassures, reassuring, reassured) V-T If you **reassure** someone, you say or do things to make them stop worrying about something. ▢ *I tried to reassure her, "Don't worry about it. We won't let it happen again."*

re|assured /ri͡əʃʊərd/ ADJ If you feel **reassured**, you feel less worried about something, usually because you have received help or advice. ▢ *I feel much more reassured when I've had a physical exam.*

re|assur|ing /riəʃʊərɪŋ/ ADJ If you find someone's words or actions **reassuring**, they make you feel less worried about something. ◻ *It was reassuring to hear John's familiar voice.* • **re|assur|ing|ly** ADV ◻ *"It's okay now," he said reassuringly.*

re|awak|en /riəweɪkən/ (**reawakens, reawakening, reawakened**) V-T If something **reawakens** an issue, or an interest or feeling that you used to have, it makes you think about it or feel it again. ◻ *The president's stand is bound to reawaken the painful debate about abortion.* • **re|awak|en|ing** N-UNCOUNT ◻ *...a reawakening of interest in stained glass.*

re|bate /riːbeɪt/ (**rebates**) N-COUNT A **rebate** is an amount of money which is returned to you after you have paid for goods or services or after you have paid tax or rent. ◻ *Citicorp will guarantee its credit card customers a rebate on a number of products.*

re|bel ♦♦◇ (**rebels, rebelling, rebelled**)

The noun is pronounced /rɛbəl/. The verb is pronounced /rɪbɛl/.

1 N-COUNT **Rebels** are people who are fighting against their own country's army in order to change the political system there. ◻ *...fighting between rebels and government forces.* **2** N-COUNT Politicians who oppose some of their own party's policies can be referred to as **rebels**. ◻ *The rebels want another 1% cut in interest rates.* **3** V-I If politicians **rebel** against one of their own party's policies, they show that they oppose it. ◻ *Voters rebelled against high property taxes.* **4** N-COUNT You can say that someone is a **rebel** if you think that they behave differently from other people and have rejected the values of society or of their parents. ◻ *She had been a rebel at school.* **5** V-I When someone **rebels**, they start to behave differently from other people and reject the values of society or of their parents. ◻ *The child who rebels is unlikely to be overlooked.*

> **SYNONYMS**
>
> **rebel**
> NOUN **1**
> **revolutionary:** *The revolutionaries laid down their arms, and their leaders went into voluntary exile.*
> **insurgent:** *By early yesterday, the insurgents had taken control of the country's main military air base.*
> VERB **5**
> **revolt:** *In 1375 the townspeople revolted.*
> **rise:** *The National Convention has promised armed support to any people who wish to rise against armed oppression.*
> **dissent:** *Just one of the 10 members dissented.*
> **disobey:** *They were threatened with punishment if they disobeyed.*

re|bel|lion /rɪbɛljən/ (**rebellions**) **1** N-VAR A **rebellion** is a violent organized action by a large group of people who are trying to change their country's political system. ◻ *The government soon put down the rebellion.* **2** N-VAR A situation in which people show their opposition to the way things have been done in the past can be referred to as a **rebellion**. ◻ *Women are waging a quiet rebellion against the traditional roles their mothers have played.*

re|bel|lious /rɪbɛljəs/ **1** ADJ If you think someone behaves in an unacceptable way and does not do what they are told, you can say they are **rebellious**. ◻ *...a rebellious teenager.* • **re|bel|lious|ness** N-UNCOUNT ◻ *...the normal rebelliousness of youth.* **2** ADJ [ADJ n] A **rebellious** group of people is a group involved in taking violent action against the rulers of their own country, usually in order to change the system of government there. ◻ *The rebellious officers, having seized the radio station, broadcast the news of the overthrow of the monarchy.*

re|birth /riːbɜːθ/ N-UNCOUNT You can refer to a change that leads to a new period of growth and improvement in something as its **rebirth**. ◻ *...the rebirth of democracy in Latin America.*

re|boot /riːbuːt/ (**reboots, rebooting, rebooted**) V-T/V-I If you **reboot** a computer, or if you **reboot**, you shut it down and start it again. [COMPUTING] ◻ *Once you've installed it and rebooted your PC, you'll find two new icons in the Control Panel.* ◻ *Click on OK, then reboot.* • N-COUNT **Reboot** is also a noun. ◻ *Minutes are lost waiting for a reboot.*

re|born /riːbɔːn/ V-T PASSIVE If you say that someone or something **has been reborn**, you mean that they have become active again after a period of being inactive. ◻ *The country was being reborn as a great power.*

re|bound /rɪbaʊnd/ (**rebounds, rebounding, rebounded**) **1** V-I If something **rebounds** from a solid surface, it bounces or springs back from it. ◻ *His shot in the 21st minute of the game rebounded from a post.* **2** V-I If an action or situation **rebounds** on you, it has an unpleasant effect on you, especially when this effect was intended for someone else. ◻ *Mia realized her trick had rebounded on her.*

re|brand /riːbrænd/ (**rebrands, rebranding, rebranded**) V-T To **rebrand** a product or organization means to present it to the public in a new way, for example by changing its name or appearance. [BUSINESS] ◻ *There are plans to rebrand many Texas stores.*

re|brand|ing /riːbrændɪŋ/ N-UNCOUNT **Rebranding** is the process of giving a product or an organization a new image, in order to make it more attractive or successful. [BUSINESS] ◻ *A complete rebranding of the school is expected within two years.*

re|buff /rɪbʌf/ (**rebuffs, rebuffing, rebuffed**) V-T If you **rebuff** someone or **rebuff** a suggestion that they make, you refuse to do what they suggest. ◻ *His proposals have already been rebuffed by the governor.* • N-VAR **Rebuff** is also a noun. ◻ *The results of the poll dealt a humiliating rebuff to Mr. Jones.*

re|build /riːbɪld/ (**rebuilds, rebuilding, rebuilt**) **1** V-T When people **rebuild** something such as a building or a city, they build it again after it has been damaged or destroyed. ◻ *They say they will stay to rebuild their homes rather than retreat to refugee camps.* ◻ *The old south grandstand must be rebuilt.* **2** V-T When people **rebuild** something such as an institution, a system, or an aspect of their lives, they take action to bring it back to its previous condition. ◻ *The president's message was that everyone would have to work hard together to rebuild the economy.*

re|buke /rɪbjuːk/ (**rebukes, rebuking, rebuked**) V-T If you **rebuke** someone, you speak severely to them because they have said or done something that you do not approve of. [FORMAL] ◻ *The president rebuked the House and Senate for not passing those bills within 100 days.* • N-VAR **Rebuke** is also a noun. ◻ *His statements drew a stinging rebuke from the chairman.*

re|but /rɪbʌt/ (**rebuts, rebutting, rebutted**) V-T If you **rebut** a charge or criticism that is made against you, you give reasons why it is untrue or unacceptable. [FORMAL] ◻ *He spent most of his speech rebutting criticisms of his foreign policy.*

re|but|tal /rɪbʌtəl/ (**rebuttals**) N-COUNT [oft N of/to n] If you make a **rebuttal** of a charge or accusation that has been made against you, you make a statement that gives reasons why the accusation is untrue. [FORMAL] ◻ *He is conducting a point-by-point rebuttal of charges from former colleagues.*

re|cal|ci|trant /rɪkælsɪtrənt/ ADJ [usu ADJ n] If you describe someone or something as **recalcitrant**, you mean that they are unwilling to obey orders or are difficult to deal with. [FORMAL] ◻ *The danger is that recalcitrant local authorities will reject their responsibilities.* • **re|cal|ci|trance** /rɪkælsɪtrəns/ N-UNCOUNT ◻ *...the government's recalcitrance over introducing even the smallest political reform.*

re|call ♦♦◇ (**recalls, recalling, recalled**)

The verb is pronounced /rɪkɔːl/. The noun is pronounced /riːkɔːl/.

1 V-T/V-I When you **recall** something, you remember it and tell others about it. ◻ *Henderson recalled that he first met Pollard during a business trip to Washington.* ◻ *His mother later recalled: "He used to stay up until two o'clock in the morning playing these war games."* ◻ *"What was his name?"—"I don't recall."* **2** N-UNCOUNT **Recall** is the ability to remember something that has happened in the past or the act of remembering it. ◻ *He had a good memory, and total recall of her spoken words.* **3** V-T If you are **recalled** to your home, country, or the place where you work, you are ordered to return there. ◻ *The U. S. envoy was recalled to Washington.* • N-SING **Recall** is also a noun. ◻ *The recall of the ambassador is a public signal of America's concern.* **4** V-T If a company **recalls** a product, it asks the stores or the people who have bought that product to return it because there is something wrong with it. ◻ *The company said it was recalling one of its drugs and had stopped selling two others.* • N-COUNT **Recall** is also a noun. ◻ *...a recall of the laptops due to defective supply parts.*

> **SYNONYMS**
>
> **recall**
> VERB ①
> **remember:** *I certainly don't remember talking to you at all.*
> **recollect:** *His efforts, the Duke recollected many years later, were distinctly half-hearted.*

re|cant /rɪkænt/ (recants, recanting, recanted) V-T/V-I If you **recant**, you say publicly that you no longer hold a set of beliefs that you had in the past. [FORMAL] ❑ *White House officials ordered Williams to recant.* ❑ *...a man who had refused after torture to recant his heresy.*

re|cap /rikæp/ (recaps, recapping, recapped) V-T/V-I You can say that you are going to **recap** when you want to draw people's attention to the fact that you are going to repeat the main points of an explanation, argument, or description, as a summary of it. ❑ *To recap briefly, the agreement was rejected 10 days ago.* ❑ *Can you recap the points included in the proposal?* • N-SING **Recap** is also a noun. ❑ *Each report starts with a recap of how we did versus our projections.*

re|capi|tal|ize /rikæpɪtəlaɪz/ (recapitalizes, recapitalizing, recapitalized) V-T/V-I If a company **recapitalizes**, it changes the way it manages its financial affairs, for example by borrowing money or reissuing shares. [AM, BUSINESS] ❑ *Mr. Warnock resigned as the company abandoned a plan to recapitalize.* ❑ *He plans to recapitalize the insurance fund.* • **re|capi|tali|za|tion** /rikæpɪtəlɪzeɪʃən/ (recapitalizations) N-COUNT ❑ *A substantial thrust of the effort of management is to explore a recapitalization of the company.*

re|ca|pitu|late /rikəpɪtʃəleɪt/ (recapitulates, recapitulating, recapitulated) V-T/V-I You can say that you are going to **recapitulate** the main points of an explanation, argument, or description when you want to draw attention to the fact that you are going to repeat the most important points as a summary. ❑ *Let's just recapitulate the essential points.* ❑ *It will be put up for sale under the terms already communicated to you, which, to recapitulate, call for a very minimum of publicity.* • **re|ca|pitu|la|tion** /rikəpɪtʃəleɪʃən/ N-SING ❑ *Chapter nine provides a valuable recapitulation of the material already presented.*

re|cap|ture /rikæptʃər/ (recaptures, recapturing, recaptured) ① V-T When soldiers **recapture** an area of land or a place, they gain control of it again from an opposing army who had taken it from them. ❑ *They said the bodies were found when rebels recaptured the area.* • N-SING **Recapture** is also a noun. ❑ *...an offensive to be launched for the recapture of the city.* ② V-T When people **recapture** something that they have lost to a competitor, they get it back again. ❑ *I believe that he would be the best possibility to recapture the center vote in the upcoming election.* ③ V-T To **recapture** a person or animal that has escaped from somewhere means to catch them again. ❑ *Police have recaptured Alan Lewis, who escaped from a jail cell in Boston.* • N-SING **Recapture** is also a noun. ❑ *...the recapture of a renegade police chief in Panama.*

re|cast /rikæst/ (recasts, recasting)

> The form **recast** is used in the present tense and is the past tense and past participle.

① V-T If you **recast** something, you change it by organizing it in a different way. ❑ *The shake-up aims to recast IBM as a federation of flexible and competing subsidiaries.* • **re|cast|ing** N-SING [N of n] ❑ *...the recasting of the political map of Europe.* ② V-T To **recast** an actor's role means to give the role to another actor. ❑ *Stoppard had to recast four of the principal roles.*

recd. In written English, **recd.** can be used as an abbreviation for **received**.

re|cede /rɪsiːd/ (recedes, receding, receded) ① V-I If something **recedes** from you, it moves away. ❑ *Luke's footsteps receded into the night.* ❑ *As she receded he waved goodbye.* ② V-I When something such as a quality, problem, or illness **recedes**, it becomes weaker, smaller, or less intense. ❑ *Just as I started to think that I was never going to get well, the illness began to recede.* ③ V-I If someone's hair starts to **recede**, it no longer grows on the front of their head. ❑ *...a youngish man with dark hair just beginning to recede.* ④ → See feature box at **appearance**

re|ceipt /rɪsiːt/ (receipts) ① N-COUNT A **receipt** is a piece of paper that you get from someone as proof that they have received money or goods from you. ❑ *I wrote her a receipt for the money.* ② N-PLURAL **Receipts** are the amount of money received during a particular period, for example by a store or theater. ❑ *He was tallying the day's receipts.* ③ N-UNCOUNT The **receipt** of something is the act of receiving it. [FORMAL] ❑ *Goods should be supplied within 28 days after the receipt of your order.* ④ PHRASE If you are **in receipt of** something, you have received it or you receive it regularly. [FORMAL] ❑ *We are taking action, having been in receipt of a letter from him.*

re|ceive ♦♦♦ /rɪsiːv/ (receives, receiving, received) ① V-T When you **receive** something, you get it after someone gives it to you or sends it to you. ❑ *They will receive their awards at a ceremony in Stockholm.* ② V-T You can use **receive** to say that certain kinds of things happen to someone. For example if they are injured, you can say that they **received** an injury. ❑ *He received more of the blame than anyone when the plan failed to work.* ③ V-T When you **receive** a visitor or a guest, you greet them. ❑ *The following evening the hotel was again receiving guests.* ④ V-T [usu passive] If you say that something **is received** in a particular way, you mean that people react to it in that way. ❑ *The resolution had been received with great disappointment within the PLO.* ⑤ V-T When a radio or television **receives** signals that are being transmitted, it picks them up and converts them into sound or pictures. ❑ *The reception was a little faint but clear enough for him to receive the signal.* ⑥ PHRASE If you **are on the receiving end** or **at the receiving end** of something unpleasant, you are the person that it happens to. ❑ *You saw hate in their eyes and you were on the receiving end of that hate.*

> **SYNONYMS**
>
> **receive**
> VERB ①
> **collect:** *She had just collected her pension from the post office.*
> **obtain:** *Evans was trying to obtain a false passport.*
> **acquire:** *I recently acquired some wood from a holly tree.*

re|ceived /rɪsiːvd/ ADJ [ADJ n] The **received** opinion about something or the **received** way of doing something is generally accepted by people as being correct. [FORMAL] ❑ *He was among the first to question the received wisdom of the time.*

Re|ceived Pro|nun|cia|tion N-UNCOUNT **Received Pronunciation** is a standard way of pronouncing British English when it is taught as a foreign language. The abbreviation **RP** is usually used.

re|ceiv|er /rɪsiːvər/ (receivers) ① N-COUNT A telephone's **receiver** is the part that you hold near to your ear and speak into. ❑ *She picked up the receiver and started to dial.* ② N-COUNT A **receiver** is the part of a radio or television that picks up signals and converts them into sound or pictures. ❑ *Auto-tuning VHF receivers are now common in cars.* ③ N-COUNT [usu the N] The **receiver** is someone who is appointed by a court of law to manage the affairs of a business, usually when it is facing financial failure. [BUSINESS] ❑ *...the receivers handling his bankruptcy case.* ④ → See feature box at **telephone**

re|ceiv|er|ship /rɪsiːvərʃɪp/ (receiverships) N-VAR If a company goes into **receivership**, it faces financial failure and the administration of its business is handled by the receiver. [BUSINESS] ❑ *The company has now gone into receivership with debts of several million.*

re|cent ♦♦♢ /riːsənt/ ADJ A **recent** event or period of time happened only a short while ago. ❑ *In the most recent attack, one man was shot dead and two others were wounded.*

re|cent|ly ♦♦♢ /riːsəntli/ ADV If you have done something **recently** or if something happened **recently**, it happened only a short time ago. ❑ *The bank recently opened a branch in Miami.*

> **SYNONYMS**
>
> **recently**
> ADV
> **newly:** *She was young at the time, and newly married.*
> **lately:** *Dad's health hasn't been too good lately.*
> **just:** *I've just bought a new house.*

re|cep|ta|cle /rɪsɛptɪkəl/ (receptacles) N-COUNT A **receptacle** is an object that you use to put or keep things in. [FORMAL]

re|cep|tion /rɪsɛpʃªn/ (receptions) **1** N-COUNT A **reception** is a formal party which is given to welcome someone or to celebrate a special event. ❑ *At the reception they served smoked salmon.* **2** N-SING [the N, oft N n, also at N] **Reception** in a hotel is the desk or office that books rooms for people and answers their questions. ❑ *Have him bring a car around to reception.* **3** N-SING [the N, oft N n, also at N] **Reception** in an office or hospital is the place where people's appointments and questions are dealt with. ❑ *Wait at reception for me.* **4** N-COUNT If someone or something has a particular kind of **reception**, that is the way that people react to them. ❑ *Mr. Mandela was given a warm reception in Washington.* **5** N-UNCOUNT If you get good **reception** from your radio or television, the sound or picture is clear because the signal is strong. If the **reception** is poor, the sound or picture is unclear because the signal is weak. ❑ *...poor radio reception.*

re|cep|tion|ist /rɪsɛpʃªnɪst/ (receptionists) **1** N-COUNT In an office or hospital, the **receptionist** is the person whose job is to answer the telephone, arrange appointments, and deal with people when they first arrive. **2** N-COUNT In a hotel, the **receptionist** is the person whose job is to reserve rooms for people and answer their questions.

re|cep|tive /rɪsɛptɪv/ **1** ADJ Someone who is **receptive** to new ideas or suggestions is prepared to consider them or accept them. ❑ *The voters had seemed receptive to his ideas.* **2** ADJ [v-link ADJ to n] If someone who is ill is **receptive** to treatment, they start to get better when they are given treatment. ❑ *For those patients who are not receptive to treatment, the chance for improvement is small.*

re|cep|tor /rɪsɛptər/ (receptors) N-COUNT **Receptors** are nerve endings in your body which react to changes and stimuli and make your body respond in a particular way. [TECHNICAL] ❑ *...the information receptors in our brain.*

re|cess /rises, risɛs/ (recesses, recessing, recessed) **1** N-COUNT [also in/from N] A **recess** is a break between the periods of work of an official body such as a committee, a court of law, or a government. ❑ *The conference broke for a recess, but the 10-minute break stretched to two hours.* **2** N-VAR In a school, **recess** is the period of time between classes when the children are allowed to play. [AM] ❑ *She decides to visit the school library during recess.* ❑ *...the children's first morning recess.* **3** V-I When formal meetings or court cases **recess**, they stop temporarily. [FORMAL] ❑ *The hearings have now recessed for dinner.* **4** N-COUNT In a room, a **recess** is part of a wall which is built further back than the rest of the wall. Recesses are often used as a place to put furniture such as shelves. ❑ *...a discreet recess next to a fireplace.* **5** N-COUNT The **recesses** of something or somewhere are the parts of it that are hard to see because light does not reach them or they are hidden from view. ❑ *He emerged from the dark recesses of the garage.* **6** N-COUNT If you refer to the **recesses** of someone's mind or soul, you are referring to thoughts or feelings they have which are hidden or difficult to describe. ❑ *There was something in the darker recesses of his unconscious that was troubling him.*

re|cessed /risɛst/ ADJ If something such as a door or window is **recessed**, it is set into the wall that surrounds it. ❑ *...a wide passage, lit from one side by recessed windows.*

re|ces|sion /rɪsɛʃªn/ (recessions) **1** N-VAR A **recession** is a period when the economy of a country is doing badly, for example because industry is producing less and more people are becoming unemployed. ❑ *The oil price increases sent Europe into deep recession.* **2** → See feature box at **banking**

COLLOCATIONS

recession
NOUN
adjective + **recession**: deep, economic, global; deepening, looming, prolonged
verb + **recession**: avoid, beat, survive, weather

SYNONYMS

recession
NOUN
depression: *He never forgot the hardships he witnessed during the Great Depression of the 1930s.*
slump: *...the slump of the early 1980s.*
downturn: *They predicted a severe economic downturn.*

re|ces|sion|al /rɪsɛʃªnªl/ **1** N-SING The **recessional** is a religious song which is sung at the end of a church service. **2** ADJ [ADJ n] **Recessional** means related to an economic recession. ❑ *Many home sellers remain stuck in a recessional rut.*

re|ces|sion|ary /rɪsɛʃªnɛri/ ADJ [ADJ n] **Recessionary** means relating to an economic recession or having the effect of creating a recession. ❑ *Reduced interest rates would help ease recessionary pressures in the economy.*

re|ces|sive /rɪsɛsɪv/ ADJ [usu ADJ n] A **recessive** gene produces a particular characteristic only if a person has two of these genes, one from each parent. [TECHNICAL] ❑ *Sickle-cell anemia is passed on through a recessive gene.*

re|charge /ritʃɑrdʒ/ (recharges, recharging, recharged) **1** V-T If you **recharge** a battery, you put an electrical charge back into the battery by connecting it to a machine that draws power from another source of electricity. ❑ *The device can recharge a battery in about 25 minutes.* **2** PHRASE If you **recharge** your **batteries**, you take a break from activities which are tiring or difficult in order to relax and feel better when you return to these activities. ❑ *He wanted to recharge his batteries and come back feeling fresh and positive.*

re|charge|able /ritʃɑrdʒəbªl/ ADJ [usu ADJ n] **Rechargeable** batteries can be recharged and used again. Some electrical products are described as **rechargeable** when they contain rechargeable batteries. ❑ *It derives all its power from rechargeable batteries.* ❑ *...a rechargeable drill.*

re|cher|ché /rəʃɛərʃeɪ/ ADJ If you describe something as **recherché**, you mean that it is very sophisticated or is associated with people who like things that are unusual and of a very high quality. [FORMAL] ❑ *Only extra-virgin olive oil will do on recherché dinner tables.*

re|cidi|vist /rɪsɪdɪvɪst/ (recidivists) N-COUNT A **recidivist** is someone who has committed crimes in the past and has begun to commit crimes again, for example after a period in prison. [FORMAL] ❑ *Six prisoners are still at large along with four dangerous recidivists.* ● **re|cidi|vism** /rɪsɪdɪvɪzəm/ N-UNCOUNT ❑ *Their basic criticism was that prisons do not reduce the crime rate, they cause recidivism.*

reci|pe /rɛsɪpi/ (recipes) **1** N-COUNT A **recipe** is a list of ingredients and a set of instructions that tell you how to cook something. ❑ *...a traditional recipe for buttermilk biscuits.* **2** N-SING If you say that something is **a recipe for** a particular situation, you mean that it is likely to result in that situation. ❑ *Large-scale inflation is a recipe for disaster.*

re|cipi|ent /rɪsɪpiənt/ (recipients) N-COUNT The **recipient** of something is the person who receives it. [FORMAL] ❑ *...the largest recipient of U.S. foreign aid.*

re|cip|ro|cal /rɪsɪprəkªl/ ADJ A **reciprocal** action or agreement involves two people or groups who do the same thing to each other or agree to help each another in a similar way. [FORMAL] ❑ *They expected a reciprocal gesture before more hostages could be freed.*

re|cip|ro|cate /rɪsɪprəkeɪt/ (reciprocates, reciprocating, reciprocated) V-T/V-I If your feelings or actions toward someone **are reciprocated**, the other person feels or behaves in the same way toward you as you have felt or behaved toward them. ❑ *I would like to think the way I treat people is reciprocated.* ❑ *He needs these people to fulfill his ambitions and reciprocates by bringing out the best in each of them.*

reci|proc|ity /rɛsɪprɒsɪti/ N-UNCOUNT **Reciprocity** is the exchange of something between people or groups of people when each person or group gives or allows something to the other. [FORMAL] ❑ *They said they would press for reciprocity with Greece in the issuing of visas.*

re|cit|al /rɪsaɪtªl/ (recitals) N-COUNT A **recital** is a performance of music or poetry, usually given by one person. ❑ *...a solo recital by the harpsichordist Maggie Cole.*

reci|ta|tion /rɛsɪteɪʃªn/ (recitations) **1** N-VAR When someone does a **recitation**, they say aloud a piece of poetry or other writing that they have learned. ❑ *The transmission began with a recitation from the Koran.* **2** → See feature box at **university**

re|cite /rɪsaɪt/ (recites, reciting, recited) **1** V-T When someone **recites** a poem or other piece of writing, they say it aloud after they have learned it. ❑ *They recited poetry to one* another. **2** V-T If you **recite** something such as a list, you say it aloud. ◻ *All he could do was recite a list of government failings.*

reck|less /rɛklɪs/ ADJ If you say that someone is **reckless**, you mean that they act in a way which shows that they do not care about danger or the effect their behavior will have on other people. ◻ *He is charged with reckless driving.* • **reck|less|ly** ADV ◻ *He was leaning recklessly out of the open window.* • **reck|less|ness** N-UNCOUNT ◻ *He felt a surge of recklessness.*

reck|on ♦⬦ /rɛkən/ (reckons, reckoning, reckoned) **1** V-T If you **reckon** that something is true, you think that it is true. [INFORMAL] ◻ *Toni reckoned that it must be about three o'clock.* **2** V-T [usu passive] If something **is reckoned** to be a particular figure, it is calculated to be roughly that amount. ◻ *The market is reckoned to be worth $1.4 bn in the U.S. alone.*
▸ **reckon with** **1** PHRASAL VERB [with brd-neg] If you say that you had not **reckoned with** something, you mean that you had not expected it and so were not prepared for it. ◻ *Gary had not reckoned with the strength of Sally's feelings for him.* **2** PHRASE If you say that there is someone or something **to be reckoned with**, you mean that they must be dealt with and it will be difficult. ◻ *This act was a signal to his victim's friends that he was someone to be reckoned with.*

SYNONYMS

reckon
VERB **1**
think: *Nora thought he was seventeen years old.*
believe: *Experts believe that the coming drought will be extensive.*
assume: *If the package is wrapped well, we assume the contents are also wonderful.*
suppose: *It had been supposed that, by then, Peter would be married.*

---

reck|on|ing /rɛkənɪŋ/ (reckonings) N-VAR Someone's **reckoning** is a calculation they make about something, especially a calculation which is not very exact. ◻ *By my reckoning we were seven or eight miles from the campground.*

re|claim /rɪkleɪm/ (reclaims, reclaiming, reclaimed) **1** V-T If you **reclaim** something that you have lost or that has been taken away from you, you succeed in getting it back. ◻ *In 1986, they got the right to reclaim South African citizenship.* **2** V-T If you **reclaim** an amount of money, for example tax that you have paid, you claim it back. ◻ *The good news for the industry was that investors don't seem to be in any hurry to reclaim their money.* **3** V-T When people **reclaim** land, they make it suitable for a purpose such as farming or building, for example by draining it or by building a barrier against the sea. ◻ *The Netherlands has been reclaiming farmland from water.* **4** V-T [usu passive] If a piece of land that was used for farming or building **is reclaimed** by a desert, forest, or the sea, it turns back into desert, forest, or sea. ◻ *The diamond towns are gradually being reclaimed by the desert.*

rec|la|ma|tion /rɛkləmeɪʃən/ N-UNCOUNT **Reclamation** is the process of changing land that is unsuitable for farming or building into land that can be used. ◻ *...centuries of seawall construction and the reclamation of dry land from the marshes.*

re|cline /rɪklaɪn/ (reclines, reclining, reclined) **1** V-I If you **recline** on something, you sit or lie on it with the upper part of your body supported at an angle. ◻ *She proceeded to recline on a chaise longue.* **2** V-T/V-I When a seat **reclines** or when you **recline** it, you lower the back so that it is more comfortable to sit in. ◻ *Air France first-class seats recline almost like beds.* ◻ *Ramesh had reclined his seat and was lying back smoking.*

re|clin|er /rɪklaɪnər/ (recliners) **1** N-COUNT A **recliner** is a type of armchair with a back which can be adjusted to slope at different angles. **2** → See also color supplement

re|cluse /rɪkluːs, rɛkluːs/ (recluses) N-COUNT A **recluse** is a person who lives alone and deliberately avoids other people. ◻ *His widow became a virtual recluse for the remainder of her life.*

re|clu|sive /rɪkluːsɪv/ ADJ A **reclusive** person or animal lives alone and deliberately avoids the company of others. ◻ *All that neighbors knew about the reclusive man was that he had lived in the building for about 20 years.*

rec|og|ni|tion ♦⬦ /rɛkəgnɪʃən/ **1** N-UNCOUNT **Recognition** is the act of recognizing someone or identifying something when you see it. ◻ *He searched for a sign of recognition on her face, but there was none.* **2** N-UNCOUNT **Recognition** of something is an understanding and acceptance of it. ◻ *Recognition of the importance of career development is increasing.* **3** N-UNCOUNT When a government gives diplomatic **recognition** to another country, they officially accept that its status is valid. ◻ *His government did not receive full recognition by the United States until July.* **4** N-UNCOUNT When a person receives **recognition** for the things that they have done, people acknowledge the value or skill of their work. ◻ *At last, her father's work has received popular recognition.* **5** PHRASE If something is done **in recognition of** someone's achievements, it is done as a way of showing official appreciation of them. ◻ *...a small plaque in recognition of her contribution to the university.* **6** → See feature box at **working**

COLLOCATIONS

recognition
NOUN
1
noun + **recognition**: fingerprint, name, speech, voice; brand, pattern
verb + **recognition**: aid
4
adjective + **recognition**: belated, international
verb + **recognition**: achieve, gain, receive, win; deserve, crave, seek

---

SYNONYMS

recognition
NOUN **2**
acceptance: *There was a general acceptance that the defense budget would shrink.*
acknowledgment: *This is an acknowledgment that the president has lost all hope of keeping the country together.*
admission: *She wanted some admission of guilt from her father.*

---

rec|og|niz|able /rɛkəgnaɪzəbəl/

in BRIT, also use **recognisable**

ADJ If something can be easily recognized or identified, you can say that it is easily **recognizable**. ◻ *The vault was opened and the body found to be well preserved, his features easily recognizable.*

re|cog|ni|zance /rɪkɒgnɪzəns/ N-UNCOUNT In law, if someone who is due to stand trial is released on their own **recognizance**, they promise to return to the court at a particular time. [AM] ◻ *Emery was released on his own recognizance and will make a court appearance next week.*

rec|og|nize ♦⬦ /rɛkəgnaɪz/ (recognizes, recognizing, recognized)

in BRIT, also use **recognise**

1 V-T [no cont] If you **recognize** someone or something, you know who that person is or what that thing is. ◻ *The receptionist recognized him at once.* **2** V-T [no cont] If someone says that they **recognize** something, they acknowledge that it exists or that it is true. ◻ *I recognize my own shortcomings.* **3** V-T If people or organizations **recognize** something as valid, they officially accept it or approve of it. ◻ *Many doctors recognize homeopathy as a legitimate form of medicine.* ◻ *France is on the point of recognizing the independence of the Baltic States.* **4** V-T When people **recognize** the work that someone has done, they show their appreciation of it, often by giving that person an award of some kind. ◻ *The army recognized him as an outstandingly able engineer.*

re|coil (recoils, recoiling, recoiled)

The verb is pronounced /rɪkɔɪl/. The noun is pronounced /riːkɔɪl/.

1 V-I If something makes you **recoil**, you move your body quickly away from it because it frightens, offends, or hurts you. ◻ *For a moment I thought he was going to kiss me. I recoiled in horror.* • N-UNCOUNT **Recoil** is also a noun. ◻ *...his small body jerking in recoil from the volume of his shouting.* **2** V-I If you **recoil** from doing something or **recoil** at the idea of something, you refuse to do it or accept it because you dislike it so much. ◻ *People used to recoil from the idea of getting into debt.*

rec|ol|lect /rɛkəlɛkt/ (recollects, recollecting, recollected)
v-T If you **recollect** something, you remember it. ☐ *Ramona spoke with warmth when she recollected the doctor who used to be at the community hospital.*

rec|ol|lec|tion /rɛkəlɛkʃən/ (recollections) N-VAR If you have a **recollection** of something, you remember it. ☐ *Pat has vivid recollections of the trip, and remembers some of the frightening aspects I had forgotten.*

re|com|mence /rikəmɛns/ (recommences, recommencing, recommenced) v-T/v-I If you **recommence** something or if it **recommences**, it begins again after having stopped. [WRITTEN] ☐ *He recommenced work on his novel.* ☐ *His course at Howard University will not recommence until next year.*

rec|om|mend ✦✧ /rɛkəmɛnd/ (recommends, recommending, recommended) ■ v-T If someone **recommends** a person or thing to you, they suggest that you would find that person or thing good or useful. ☐ *I just spent a vacation there and would recommend it to anyone.* ☐ *"You're a good worker," he told him. "I'll recommend you for a promotion."* • **rec|om|mend|ed** ADJ ☐ *Though ten years old, this book is highly recommended.* ■ v-T If you **recommend** that something is done, you suggest that it should be done. ☐ *The judge recommended that he serve 20 years in prison.* ☐ *We strongly recommend reporting the incident to the police.* ■ v-T If something or someone has a particular quality to **recommend** them, that quality makes them attractive or gives them an advantage over similar things or people. ☐ *La Cucina restaurant has much to recommend it.*

USAGE

recommend
Don't say that you 'recommend someone' an action. Don't say, for example, 'I recommend you a visit to Paris.' Say 'I **recommend a visit** to Paris,' 'I **recommend visiting** Paris,' or 'I **recommend that you visit** Paris.' *We recommend that you pay in advance.*

SYNONYMS

recommend
VERB ■
advocate: *MrWilliams is a conservative who advocates fewer government controls on business.*
suggest: *I suggest you ask him some specific questions about his past.*
propose: *Britain is about to propose changes to some institutions.*
advise: *I would strongly advise against it.*

---

rec|om|men|da|tion ✦✧ /rɛkəmɛndeɪʃən/ (recommendations) ■ N-VAR The **recommendations** of a person or a committee are their suggestions or advice on what is the best thing to do. ☐ *The committee's recommendations are unlikely to be made public.* ■ N-VAR A **recommendation** of something is the suggestion that someone should have or use it because it is good. ☐ *The best way of finding a lawyer is through personal recommendation.*

SYNONYMS

recommendation
NOUN ■
advice: *Take my advice and stay away from him!*
proposal: *The President is to put forward new proposals for resolving the country's constitutional crisis.*
suggestion: *I have lots of suggestions for the park's future.*

---

rec|om|pense /rɛkəmpɛns/ (recompenses, recompensing, recompensed) ■ N-UNCOUNT If you are given something, usually money, in **recompense**, you are given it as a reward or because you have suffered. [FORMAL] ☐ *He demands no financial recompense for his troubles.* ■ v-T If you **recompense** someone for their efforts or their loss, you give them something, usually money, as a payment or reward. [FORMAL] ☐ *If they succeed in court, they will be fully recompensed for their loss.*

rec|on|cile /rɛkənsaɪl/ (reconciles, reconciling, reconciled) ■ v-T If you **reconcile** two beliefs, facts, or demands that seem to be opposed or completely different, you find a way in which they can both be true or both be successful. ☐ *It's difficult to reconcile the demands of my job and the desire to be a good father.* ■ V-RECIP-PASSIVE If you **are reconciled** with someone, you become friendly with them again after a quarrel or disagreement. ☐ *He never believed he and Susan would be reconciled.* ■ v-T If you **reconcile** two people, you make them become friends again after a quarrel or disagreement. ☐ *...my attempt to reconcile him with Toby.* ■ v-T If you **reconcile** yourself to an unpleasant situation, you accept it, although it does not make you happy to do so. ☐ *She had reconciled herself to never seeing him again.* • **rec|on|ciled** ADJ [v-link ADJ to n/-ing] ☐ *She felt, if not grateful for her own situation, at least a little more reconciled to it.*

rec|on|cilia|tion /rɛkənsɪlieɪʃən/ (reconciliations) ■ N-VAR **Reconciliation** between two people or countries who have quarreled is the process of their becoming friends again. A **reconciliation** is an instance of this. ☐ *...an appeal for reconciliation between Catholics and Protestants.* ■ N-SING The **reconciliation** of two beliefs, facts, or demands that seem to be opposed is the process of finding a way in which they can both be true or both be successful. ☐ *...the ideal of democracy based upon a reconciliation of the values of equality and liberty.*

re|con|dite /rɛkəndaɪt, rikɒn-/ ADJ [usu ADJ n] **Recondite** areas of knowledge or learning are difficult to understand, and not many people know about them. [FORMAL] ☐ *Her poems are modishly experimental in style and recondite in subject matter.*

re|con|di|tion /rikəndɪʃən/ (reconditions, reconditioning, reconditioned) v-T To **recondition** a machine or piece of equipment means to repair or replace all the parts that are damaged or broken. ☐ *He made contact with someone with an idea for reconditioning laser copiers.* ☐ *They sell used and reconditioned motorcycle parts.*

re|con|fig|ure /rikənfɪgyər/ (reconfigures, reconfiguring, reconfigured) v-T If you **reconfigure** a system, device, or computer application, you rearrange its elements or settings. [COMPUTING] ☐ *It should be simple to reconfigure the mail servers.*

re|con|firm /rikənfɜrm/ (reconfirms, reconfirming, reconfirmed) v-T **Reconfirm** means the same as **confirm**.

re|con|nais|sance /rɪkɒnɪsəns/ N-UNCOUNT **Reconnaissance** is the activity of obtaining military information about a place by sending soldiers or planes there, or by the use of satellites. ☐ *The helicopter was returning from a reconnaissance mission.*

re|con|nect /rikənɛkt/ (reconnects, reconnecting, reconnected) v-T If a company **reconnects** your electricity, water, gas, or telephone after it has been stopped, they provide you with it once again. ☐ *They charge a $75.00 fee for reconnecting cutoff customers.*

rec|on|noi|ter /rɛkənɔɪtər/ (reconnoiters, reconnoitering, reconnoitered) also **reconnoitre** v-T/v-I To **reconnoiter** an area means to obtain information about its geographical features or about the size and position of an army there. ☐ *He reconnoitered the Gulf of Saint Lawrence, traveling up the magnificent river as far as modern Montreal.* ☐ *I left a sergeant in command and rode forward to reconnoiter.*

re|con|quer /rikɒnkər/ (reconquers, reconquering, reconquered) v-T If an army **reconquers** a country or territory after having lost it, they win control over it again. ☐ *A crusade left Europe in an attempt to reconquer the Holy City.*

re|con|sid|er /rikənsɪdər/ (reconsiders, reconsidering, reconsidered) v-T/v-I If you **reconsider** a decision or opinion, you think about it and try to decide whether it should be changed. ☐ *We want you to reconsider your decision to resign from the board.* ☐ *If at the end of two years you still feel the same, we will reconsider.*

re|con|sti|tute /rikɒnstɪtut/ (reconstitutes, reconstituting, reconstituted) ■ v-T [usu passive] If an organization or state **is reconstituted**, it is formed again in a different way. ☐ *Slowly Jewish communities were reconstituted and Jewish life began anew.* ■ v-T To **reconstitute** dried food means to add water to it so that it can be eaten. ☐ *To reconstitute dried tomatoes, simmer in plain water until they are tender.* ☐ *Try eating reconstituted dried prunes, figs, or apricots.*

re|con|struct /rikənstrʌkt/ (reconstructs, reconstructing, reconstructed) ■ v-T If you **reconstruct** something that has been destroyed or badly damaged, you build it and make it work again. ◻ *The government must reconstruct the shattered economy.* **2** V-T To **reconstruct** a system or policy means to change it so that it works in a different way. ◻ *She actually wanted to reconstruct the state and transform society.* **3** V-T If you **reconstruct** an event that happened in the past, you try to get a complete understanding of it by combining a lot of small pieces of information. ◻ *He began to reconstruct the events of December 21, 1988, when flight 103 disappeared.*

re|con|struc|tion /ri:kənstrʌkʃ°n/ (**reconstructions**)
1 N-UNCOUNT **Reconstruction** is the process of making a country normal again after a war, for example by making the country stronger and by replacing buildings that have been damaged. ◻ *...America's part in the postwar reconstruction of Germany.* ◻ *...the Reconstruction period immediately following the Civil War.* **2** N-UNCOUNT The **reconstruction** of a building, structure, or road is the activity of building it again, because it has been damaged. ◻ *Work began on the reconstruction of the road.* **3** N-COUNT The **reconstruction** of a crime or event is when people try to understand or show exactly what happened, often by acting it out. ◻ *Mrs. Kerr was too upset to take part in a reconstruction of her ordeal.*

re|con|struc|tive /ri:kənstrʌktɪv/ ADJ [ADJ n] **Reconstructive** surgery or treatment involves rebuilding a part of someone's body because it has been badly damaged, or because the person wants to change its shape. ◻ *I needed reconstructive surgery to give me a new nose.*

re|con|vene /ri:kənvi:n/ (**reconvenes, reconvening, reconvened**) V-T/V-I If a legislature, court, or conference **reconvenes** or if someone **reconvenes** it, it meets again after a break. ◻ *The conference might reconvene after its opening session.*

rec|ord ♦♦♦ (**records, recording, recorded**)

> The noun is pronounced /rɛkərd/. The verb is pronounced /rɪkɔ:rd/.

1 N-COUNT If you keep a **record** of something, you keep a written account or photographs of it so that it can be referred to later. ◻ *Keep a record of all the payments.* ◻ *There's no record of any marriage or children.* **2** V-T If you **record** a piece of information or an event, you write it down, photograph it, or put it into a computer so that in the future people can refer to it. ◻ *Her letters record the domestic and social details of diplomatic life in China.* **3** V-T If you **record** something such as a speech or performance, you put it on tape or film so that it can be heard or seen again later. ◻ *There is nothing to stop viewers from recording the films at home.* **4** V-T If a musician or performer **records** a piece of music or a television or radio show, they perform it so that it can be put onto CD, tape, or film. ◻ *It took the musicians two and a half days to record their soundtrack for the film.* **5** N-COUNT A **record** is a round, flat piece of black plastic on which sound, especially music, is stored, and which can be played on a record player. You can also refer to the music stored on this piece of plastic as a **record**. ◻ *This is one of my favorite records.* **6** V-T If a dial or other measuring device **records** a certain measurement or value, it shows that measurement or value. ◻ *The test records the electrical activity of the brain.* **7** N-COUNT A **record** is the best result that has ever been achieved in a particular sport or activity, for example the fastest time, the farthest distance, or the greatest number of victories. ◻ *Roger Kingdom set the world record of 12.92 seconds.* **8** ADJ [ADJ n] You use **record** to say that something is higher, lower, better, or worse than has ever been achieved before. ◻ *Profits were at record levels.* **9** N-COUNT Someone's **record** is the facts that are known about their achievements or character. ◻ *His record reveals a tough streak.* **10** N-COUNT If someone has a criminal **record**, it is officially known that they have committed crimes in the past. ◻ *...a heroin addict with a criminal record going back 15 years.* **11** → see also **recording, track record** **12** PHRASE If you say that what you are going to say next is **for the record**, you mean that you are saying it publicly and officially and that you want it to be written down and remembered. ◻ *We're willing to state for the record that it has enormous value.* **13** PHRASE If you give some information **for the record**, you give it in case people might find it useful at a later time, although it is not a very important part of what you are talking about. ◻ *For the record, most Moscow girls leave school at about 18.* **14** PHRASE If something that you say is **off the record**, you do not intend it to be considered as official, or published with your name attached to it. ◻ *May I speak off the record?* **15** PHRASE If you are **on record** as saying something, you have said it publicly and officially and it has been written down. ◻ *The president is on record as saying that the increase in unemployment is "a price worth paying" to keep inflation down.* **16** PHRASE If you keep information **on record**, you write it down or store it in a computer so that it can be used later. ◻ *The practice is to keep on record any analysis of samples.* **17** → See feature box at **Olympic Games, research**

rec|ord break|er (**record breakers**) N-COUNT A **record breaker** is someone or something that beats the previous best result in a sport or other activity. ◻ *The movie became a box-office record breaker.*

record-breaking ADJ [ADJ n] A **record-breaking** success, result, or performance is one that beats the previous best success, result, or performance. ◻ *Woods won record-breaking performance of the year for winning four majors in a row.*

rec|ord|ed de|liv|ery [BRIT] → see **certified mail**

re|cord|er /rɪkɔ:rdər/ (**recorders**) **1** N-COUNT You can refer to a cassette recorder, a tape recorder, or a video recorder as a **recorder**. ◻ *Rodney put the recorder on the desk top and pushed the play button.* **2** → see also **tape recorder, video recorder** **3** N-VAR A **recorder** is a wooden or plastic musical instrument in the shape of a pipe. You play the recorder by blowing into the top of it and covering and uncovering the holes with your fingers. **4** N-COUNT A **recorder** is a machine or instrument that keeps a record of something, for example in an experiment or on a vehicle. ◻ *Data recorders also pinpoint mechanical faults rapidly, reducing repair times.*

rec|ord hold|er (**record holders**) N-COUNT [usu the N] The **record holder** in a particular sport or activity is the person or team that holds the record for doing it fastest or best. ◻ *...the Olympic record holder for the 200-meter backstroke.*

re|cord|ing ♦◇◇ /rɪkɔ:rdɪŋ/ (**recordings**) **1** N-COUNT A **recording** of something is a record, CD, tape, or video of it. ◻ *...a video recording of a police interview.* **2** N-UNCOUNT **Recording** is the process of making records, CDs, tapes, or videos. ◻ *...the recording industry.*

rec|ord play|er (**record players**) N-COUNT A **record player** is a machine on which you can play a record in order to listen to the music or other sounds on it. ◻ *His parents had no record player or television.*

re|count (**recounts, recounting, recounted**)

> The verb is pronounced /rɪkaʊnt/. The noun is pronounced /ri:kaʊnt/.

1 V-T If you **recount** a story or event, you tell or describe it to people. [FORMAL] ◻ *He then recounted the story of the interview for his first job.* **2** N-COUNT A **recount** is a second count of votes in an election when the result is very close. ◻ *She wanted a recount. She couldn't believe that I got more votes than she did.*

re|coup /rɪku:p/ (**recoups, recouping, recouped**) V-T If you **recoup** a sum of money that you have spent or lost, you get it back. ◻ *Insurance companies are trying to recoup their losses by increasing premiums.*

re|course /rɪkɔ:rs/ N-UNCOUNT If you achieve something without **recourse** to a particular course of action, you succeed without carrying out that action. To have **recourse** to a particular course of action means to have to do that action in order to achieve something. [FORMAL] ◻ *It enabled its members to settle their differences without recourse to war.*

re|cov|er ♦◇◇ /rɪkʌvər/ (**recovers, recovering, recovered**) **1** V-I When you **recover** from an illness or an injury, you become well again. ◻ *He is recovering from a knee injury.* **2** V-I If you **recover** from an unhappy or unpleasant experience, you stop being upset by it. ◻ *...a tragedy from which he never fully recovered.* **3** V-I If something **recovers** from a period of weakness or difficulty, it improves or gets stronger again. ◻ *He recovered from a 4–2 deficit to reach the quarter-finals.* **4** V-T If you **recover** something that has been lost or stolen, you find it or get it back. ◻ *Police raided five houses in Brooklyn and recovered* stolen goods. **5** V-T If you **recover** a mental or physical state, it comes back again. For example, if you **recover** consciousness, you become conscious again. ❑ *She had a severe attack of asthma and it took an hour to recover her breath.* **6** V-T If you **recover** money that you have spent, invested, or lent to someone, you get the same amount back. ❑ *Legal action is being taken to recover the money.*

re|cov|er|able /rɪkʌvərəbəl/ ADJ If something is **recoverable**, it is possible for you to get it back. ❑ *If you decide not to buy, the money you have spent on the survey is not recoverable.*

re|cov|ery ♦◇◇ /rɪkʌvəri/ (**recoveries**) **1** N-VAR If a sick person makes a **recovery**, he or she becomes well again. ❑ *He made a remarkable recovery from a shin injury.* **2** N-VAR When there is a **recovery** in a country's economy, it improves. ❑ *Interest-rate cuts have failed to bring about economic recovery.* **3** N-UNCOUNT You talk about the **recovery** of something when you get it back after it has been lost or stolen. ❑ *A substantial reward is being offered for the recovery of a painting by Turner.* **4** N-UNCOUNT You talk about the **recovery** of someone's physical or mental state when they return to this state. ❑ *...the abrupt loss and recovery of consciousness.* **5** PHRASE If someone is **in recovery**, they are being given a course of treatment to help them recover from something such as a drug habit or mental illness. ❑ *...Carole, a compulsive pot smoker and alcoholic in recovery.*

COLLOCATIONS

recovery
NOUN
1
adjective + **recovery**: full, remarkable, speedy, slow
2
adjective + **recovery**: economic, global, strong, sustained
noun + **recovery**: market

re|cov|ery room (**recovery rooms**) N-COUNT A **recovery room** is a room in a hospital where patients are placed after they have had an operation under anesthesia, so that they can be monitored while they recover. ❑ *He was monitored in the recovery room for approximately 30 minutes following the anesthesia.*

re|cre|ate /riːkrieɪt/ (**recreates, recreating, recreated**) V-T If you **recreate** something, you succeed in making it exist or seem to exist in a different time or place from its original time or place. ❑ *I am trying to recreate family life far from home.*

rec|rea|tion (**recreations**)

Pronounced /rɛkrieɪʃən/ for meaning 1. Pronounced /riːkrieɪʃən/ and hyphenated re|crea|tion for meaning 2.

1 N-VAR **Recreation** consists of things that you do in your spare time to relax. ❑ *Saturday afternoon is for recreation and outings.* **2** N-COUNT A **recreation** of something is the process of making it exist or seem to exist again in a different time or place. ❑ *They are planning to build a faithful recreation of the original frontier town.*

rec|rea|tion|al /rɛkrieɪʃənəl/ **1** ADJ **Recreational** means relating to things people do in their spare time to relax. ❑ *...parks and other recreational facilities.* **2** → See feature box at **leisure**

rec|rea|tion|al drug (**recreational drugs**) N-COUNT **Recreational drugs** are illegal drugs such as cannabis or cocaine that some people take occasionally for enjoyment, especially when they are spending time socially with other people. ❑ *Society largely turns a blind eye to recreational drug use.*

rec|rea|tion|al ve|hi|cle (**recreational vehicles**) N-COUNT A **recreational vehicle** is a large vehicle that you can live in. The abbreviation **RV** is also used. [mainly AM]

re|crimi|na|tion /rɪkrɪmɪneɪʃən/ (**recriminations**) N-UNCOUNT [also N in pl] **Recriminations** are accusations that two people or groups make about each other. ❑ *The bitter arguments and recriminations have finally ended the relationship.*

rec room /rɛk rum/ (**rec rooms**) N-COUNT A **rec room** is a room in a house that is used for relaxation and entertainment. [AM] ❑ *Down in the rec room I lay on my side under the pool table.*

re|cruit ♦◇◇ /rɪkruːt/ (**recruits, recruiting, recruited**) **1** V-T If you **recruit** people for an organization, you select them and persuade them to join it or work for it. ❑ *The police are trying to recruit more Black and Hispanic officers.* ❑ *She set up her stand to recruit students to the Anarchist Association.* ● **re|cruit|ing** N-UNCOUNT ❑ *A bomb exploded at an army recruiting office.* **2** N-COUNT A **recruit** is a person who has recently joined an organization or an army. ❑ *...a new recruit to the LA Police Department.*

re|cruit|ment /rɪkruːtmənt/ N-UNCOUNT The **recruitment** of workers, soldiers, or members is the act or process of selecting them for an organization or army and persuading them to join. ❑ *...the examination system for the recruitment of civil servants.*

rec|tal /rɛktəl/ ADJ [ADJ n] **Rectal** means relating to the rectum. [MEDICAL] ❑ *...rectal cancer.*

rec|tan|gle /rɛktæŋɡəl/ (**rectangles**) N-COUNT A **rectangle** is a four-sided shape whose corners are all ninety-degree angles. Each side of a rectangle is the same length as the one opposite to it.

rec|tan|gu|lar /rɛktæŋɡyələr/ **1** ADJ Something that is **rectangular** is shaped like a rectangle. ❑ *...a rectangular table.* **2** → See feature box at **football**

rec|ti|fi|ca|tion /rɛktɪfɪkeɪʃən/ N-UNCOUNT The **rectification** of something that is wrong is the act of changing it to make it correct or satisfactory. ❑ *...the rectification of an injustice.*

rec|ti|fy /rɛktɪfaɪ/ (**rectifies, rectifying, rectified**) V-T If you **rectify** something that is wrong, you change it so that it becomes correct or satisfactory. ❑ *Only an act of Congress could rectify the situation.*

rec|ti|tude /rɛktɪtuːd/ N-UNCOUNT **Rectitude** is a quality or attitude that is shown by people who behave honestly and morally according to accepted standards. [FORMAL] ❑ *...people of the utmost moral rectitude.*

rec|tor /rɛktər/ (**rectors**) N-COUNT A **rector** is a priest in the Episcopal Church who is in charge of a particular area.

rec|tory /rɛktəri/ (**rectories**) N-COUNT A **rectory** is a house in which a rector or priest lives.

rec|tum /rɛktəm/ (**rectums**) N-COUNT Someone's **rectum** is the bottom end of the tube down which waste food passes out of their body. [MEDICAL]

re|cum|bent /rɪkʌmbənt/ ADJ [usu ADJ n] A **recumbent** figure or person is lying down. [FORMAL] ❑ *He looked down at the recumbent figure.*

re|cu|per|ate /rɪkuːpəreɪt/ (**recuperates, recuperating, recuperated**) V-I When you **recuperate**, you recover your health or strength after you have been ill or injured. ❑ *I went away to the country to recuperate.* ● **re|cu|pera|tion** /rɪkuːpəreɪʃən/ N-UNCOUNT ❑ *Leonard was very pleased with his powers of recuperation.*

re|cu|pera|tive /rɪkuːpərətɪv/ ADJ [usu ADJ n] Something that is **recuperative** helps you to recover your health and strength after an illness or injury. ❑ *Human beings have great recuperative powers.*

re|cur /rɪkɜːr/ (**recurs, recurring, recurred**) V-I If something **recurs**, it happens more than once. ❑ *...a theme that was to recur frequently in his work.*

re|cur|rence /rɪkɜːrəns/ (**recurrences**) N-VAR If there is a **recurrence** of something, it happens again. ❑ *Police are out in force to prevent a recurrence of the violence.*

re|cur|rent /rɪkɜːrənt/ ADJ A **recurrent** event or feeling happens or is experienced more than once. ❑ *Race is a recurrent theme in the work.*

re|cuse /rɪkyuːz/ (**recuses, recusing, recused**) V-T If someone such as a judge **recuses** himself or herself from a legal case, they state that they will not be involved in making decisions about the case, for example because they consider themselves to be biased. ❑ *If her husband became governor, Judge Rendell would have to recuse herself from cases involving the state.*

re|cy|clable /riːsaɪkləbəl/ ADJ **Recyclable** waste or materials can be processed and used again. ❑ *...a separate bin for recyclable waste products.*

re|cy|cle /riːsaɪkəl/ (**recycles, recycling, recycled**) V-T If you **recycle** things that have already been used, such as bottles or sheets of paper, you process them so that they can be used again. ❑ *The objective would be to recycle 98 percent of domestic waste.* • **re|cy|cling** N-UNCOUNT ❑ *...a recycling plan.*

VOCABULARY IN CONTEXT

Recycling

You have probably heard of 'the three Rs': **reduce**, **reuse**, and **recycle**. Nowadays, most people are aware of the **environmental impact** of **waste**, and its effect on **sustainability**. However, many people don't realize that of the three Rs, recycling has the least **benefit** for the environment. To recycle, we need to use **energy** to **convert waste products** back into usable materials. By reducing **consumption** of these products in the first place, or looking for **biodegradable** alternatives, however, we can actually reduce **energy consumption**. Reusing objects such as **plastic bags**, **glass jars**, or **metal food cans** rather than throwing them away doesn't lead to much reduction of energy use, as people often use the packaging for a different purpose. As such, the same amount of energy is still used to **manufacture** packaging for the original products. However, the energy used to convert the objects back into their **raw material** is saved. So try to reduce. If you can't reduce, then reuse, and if you can't reuse, recycle.

red ✦✦✦ /rɛd/ (**reds**, **redder**, **reddest**) **1** COLOR Something that is **red** is the color of blood or fire. ❑ *...a bunch of red roses.* **2** ADJ If you say that someone's face is **red**, you mean that it is redder than its normal color, because they are embarrassed, angry, or out of breath. ❑ *With a bright red face I was forced to admit that I had no real idea.* **3** ADJ You describe someone's hair as **red** when it is between red and brown in color. ❑ *...a girl with red hair.* **4** N-MASS You can refer to red wine as **red**. ❑ *The spicy flavors in these dishes call for reds rather than whites.* **5** ADJ If a U.S. state is described as **red**, it means that the majority of its residents vote for the Republican Party in elections, especially in the presidential elections. ❑ *...policies that could guarantee her enough support in red states to win the White House in 2008.* **6** PHRASE If a person or company is **in the red** or if their bank account is **in the red**, they have spent more money than they have in their account and therefore they owe money to the bank. ❑ *The theater is $500,000 in the red.* **7** PHRASE If you **see red**, you suddenly become very angry. ❑ *I didn't mean to break his nose. I just saw red.* **8** → See feature box at **body language**

red alert (**red alerts**) N-VAR If a hospital, a police force, or a military force is on **red alert**, they have been warned that there may be an emergency, so they should be ready to deal with it. ❑ *All the St. Louis hospitals are on red alert.*

red-blooded ADJ [ADJ n] If someone is described as **red-blooded**, they are considered to be strong and healthy and have a strong interest in sex. [INFORMAL] ❑ *...a red-blooded action man.*

red cab|bage (**red cabbages**) N-VAR A **red cabbage** is a cabbage with dark red leaves.

red card (**red cards**) N-COUNT In soccer, if a player is shown the **red card**, the referee holds up a red card to indicate that the player must leave the field for breaking the rules. ❑ *He was shown a red card for a rough tackle.*

red car|pet (**red carpets**) N-COUNT [usu sing] The **red carpet** is special treatment given to an important or honored guest, for example the laying of a strip of red carpet for them to walk on. ❑ *We'll give her some VIP treatment and roll out the red carpet.*

Red Cres|cent N-PROPER [*the* N] **The Red Crescent** is an organization in Muslim countries that helps people who are suffering, for example as a result of war, floods, or disease.

Red Cross N-PROPER [*the* N] **The Red Cross** is an international organization that helps people who are suffering, for example as a result of war, floods, or disease.

red|den /rɛdᵊn/ (**reddens**, **reddening**, **reddened**) V-I If someone **reddens** or their face **reddens**, their face turns pink or red, often because they are embarrassed or angry. [WRITTEN] ❑ *He was working himself up to a fury, his face reddening.*

red|dish /rɛdɪʃ/ ADJ **Reddish** means slightly red in color. ❑ *He had reddish brown hair.*

re|deco|rate /ridɛkəreɪt/ (**redecorates**, **redecorating**, **redecorated**) V-T/V-I If you **redecorate** a room or a building, you paint or wallpaper the walls or change the furniture, carpet, or curtains. ❑ *Americans redecorate their houses and offices every few years.* ❑ *Our children have left home, and we now want to redecorate.* • **re|deco|ra|tion** /ridɛkəreɪʃᵊn/ N-UNCOUNT ❑ *The house is in desperate need of redecoration.*

re|deem /rɪdim/ (**redeems**, **redeeming**, **redeemed**) **1** V-T If you **redeem** yourself or your reputation, you do something that makes people have a good opinion of you again after you have behaved or performed badly. ❑ *He realized the mistake he had made and wanted to redeem himself.* **2** V-T When something **redeems** an unpleasant thing or situation, it prevents it from being completely bad. ❑ *Work is the way that people seek to redeem their lives from futility.* **3** V-T If you **redeem** a debt or money that you have promised to someone, you pay money that you owe or that you promised to pay. [FORMAL] ❑ *The amount required to redeem the mortgage was $358,587.* **4** V-T In religions such as Christianity, to **redeem** someone means to save them by freeing them from sin and evil. ❑ *...a new female spiritual force to redeem the world.*

re|deem|able /rɪdiməbᵊl/ ADJ If something is **redeemable**, it can be exchanged for a particular sum of money or for goods worth a particular sum. ❑ *Their full catalog costs $5, redeemable against a first order.*

Re|deem|er /rɪdimər/ N-PROPER [*the* N] In the Christian religion, **the Redeemer** is Jesus Christ.

re|de|fine /ridɪfaɪn/ (**redefines**, **redefining**, **redefined**) V-T If you **redefine** something, you cause people to consider it in a new way. ❑ *Feminists have redefined the role of women.*

re|defi|ni|tion /ridɛfɪnɪʃᵊn/ N-UNCOUNT The **redefinition** of something is the act or process of causing people to consider it in a new way. ❑ *...the redefinition of the role of the intellectual.*

re|demp|tion /rɪdɛmpʃᵊn/ (**redemptions**) **1** N-VAR **Redemption** is the act of redeeming something or of being redeemed by something. [FORMAL] ❑ *He craves redemption for his sins.* ❑ *...redemption of the loan.* **2** PHRASE If you say that someone or something is **beyond redemption**, you mean that they are so bad it is unlikely that anything can be done to improve them. ❑ *No man is beyond redemption.*

re|demp|tive /rɪdɛmptɪv/ ADJ [usu ADJ n] In Christianity, a **redemptive** act or quality is something that leads to freedom from the consequences of sin and evil. ❑ *...the redemptive power of love.*

re|deploy /ridɪplɔɪ/ (**redeploys**, **redeploying**, **redeployed**) **1** V-T/V-I If forces or troops **are redeployed** or if they **redeploy**, they go to new positions so that they are ready for action. ❑ *We were forced to redeploy our forces.* ❑ *U.S. troops are redeploying to positions held earlier.* **2** V-T If resources or workers **are redeployed**, they are used for a different purpose or task. ❑ *Some of the workers there will be redeployed to other sites.* ❑ *It would give us an opportunity to redeploy our resources.*

re|deploy|ment /ridɪplɔɪmənt/ (**redeployments**) N-VAR The **redeployment** of forces, troops, workers, or resources involves putting them in a different place from where they were before, or using them for a different task or purpose. ❑ *...a redeployment of troops in the border areas.*

re|design /ˌriːdɪzaɪn/ (redesigns, redesigning, redesigned) V-T If a building, vehicle, or system **is redesigned**, it is rebuilt according to a new design in order to improve it. ❑ *The hotel has recently been redesigned and redecorated.* ❑ *We need to redesign the school system so that it produces a well-educated population.*

re|devel|op /ˌriːdɪvɛləp/ (redevelops, redeveloping, redeveloped) V-T When an area **is redeveloped**, existing buildings and roads are removed and new ones are built in their place. ❑ *Birmingham is now going to be redeveloped again.*

re|devel|op|ment /ˌriːdɪvɛləpmənt/ N-UNCOUNT When **redevelopment** takes place, the buildings in one area of a town are knocked down and new ones are built in their place. ❑ *The group's intention is to clear the site for redevelopment.*

red-eye (red-eyes) also **redeye** ▊ N-COUNT A **red-eye** or a **red-eye flight** is a plane trip during the night. [INFORMAL] ❑ *She was running to catch a red-eye to New York.* ▋ N-UNCOUNT [usu N n] In photography, **redeye** is the unwanted effect that you sometimes get in photographs of people or animals where their eyes appear red because of the reflection of a camera flash or other light. ❑ *The camera incorporates a redeye reduction facility.*

red-faced ADJ A **red-faced** person has a face that looks red, often because they are embarrassed or angry. ❑ *A red-faced Mr. Jones was led away by police.*

red flag (red flags) ▊ N-COUNT A **red flag** is a flag that is red in color and is used as a symbol to represent communism and socialism or to indicate danger or as a sign that you should stop. ❑ *Then the rain came and the red flag went up to signal a halt.* ▋ N-COUNT If you refer to something as a **red flag**, you mean that it acts as a danger signal. ❑ *The abnormal bleeding is your body's own red flag of danger.*

red-handed PHRASE If someone **is caught red-handed**, they are caught while they are in the act of doing something wrong. ❑ *My boyfriend and I robbed a store and were caught red-handed.*

red|head /rɛdhɛd/ (redheads) N-COUNT A **redhead** is person, especially a woman, whose hair is a color that is between red and brown.

red|headed /rɛdhɛdɪd/ ADJ [usu ADJ n] A **redheaded** person is a person whose hair is between red and brown in color.

red her|ring (red herrings) N-COUNT If you say that something is a **red herring**, you mean that it is not important and it takes your attention away from the main subject or problem you are considering. ❑ *As Dr. Smith left he said that the inquiry was something of a red herring.*

red-hot ▊ ADJ **Red-hot** metal or rock has been heated to such a high temperature that it has turned red. ❑ *...red-hot iron.* ▋ ADJ A **red-hot** object is too hot to be touched safely. ❑ *In the main rooms red-hot radiators were left exposed.* ▍ ADJ **Red-hot** is used to describe a person or thing that is very popular, especially someone who is very good at what they do or something that is new and exciting. [JOURNALISM] ❑ *Some traders are already stacking the red-hot book on their shelves.*

re|di|rect /ˌriːdɪrɛkt, -daɪ-/ (redirects, redirecting, redirected) ▊ V-T If you **redirect** your energy, resources, or ability, you begin doing something different or trying to achieve something different. ❑ *Controls were used to redistribute or redirect resources.* ▋ V-T If you **redirect** someone or something, you change their course or destination. ❑ *She redirected them to the men's department.*

re|dis|cov|er /ˌriːdɪskʌvər/ (rediscovers, rediscovering, rediscovered) V-T If you **rediscover** something good or valuable that you had forgotten or lost, you become aware of it again or find it again. ❑ *...a one-time rebel who had rediscovered his faith.*

re|dis|cov|ery /ˌriːdɪskʌvəri/ (rediscoveries) N-VAR [N of n] The **rediscovery** of something good that you had forgotten or lost is the fact or process of becoming aware of it again or finding it again. ❑ *The best part of his expedition had been the rediscovery of his natural passion for making things.*

re|dis|trib|ute /ˌriːdɪstrɪbjuːt/ (redistributes, redistributing, redistributed) V-T If something such as money or property **is redistributed**, it is shared among people or organizations in a different way from the way that it was previously shared. ❑ *Wealth was redistributed more equitably among society.*

• **re|dis|tri|bu|tion** /ˌriːdɪstrɪbjuːʃən/ N-UNCOUNT ❑ *One of government's primary duties is the redistribution of income, so that the better off can help the worse off out of poverty.*

re|dis|trict|ing /ˌriːdɪstrɪktɪŋ/ N-UNCOUNT **Redistricting** is the division of an area into new administrative or election districts. [AM] ❑ *Following statewide redistricting last fall, Black representation in both the House and Senate doubled.*

red-letter day (red-letter days) N-COUNT A **red-letter day** is a day that you will always remember because something good happened to you on that day.

red light (red lights) ▊ N-COUNT A **red light** is a traffic signal that shines red to indicate that drivers must stop. ▋ ADJ [ADJ n] The **red-light** district of a city is the area where prostitutes work.

red meat (red meats) N-MASS **Red meat** is meat such as beef or lamb, which is dark brown in color after it has been cooked.

red|neck /rɛdnɛk/ (rednecks) N-COUNT If someone describes a White person, especially a lower-class American from the countryside, as a **redneck**, they disapprove of that person because they think he or she is uneducated and has strong, unreasonable opinions. [mainly AM, INFORMAL, DISAPPROVAL] ❑ *A large Texas redneck was shouting obscenities at Ali.*

red|ness /rɛdnɪs/ N-UNCOUNT **Redness** is the quality of being red. ❑ *Slowly the redness left Sophie's face.*

redo /riːduː/ (redoes, redoing, redid, redone) V-T If you **redo** a piece of work, you do it again in order to improve it or change it. ❑ *They had redone their calculations.*

redo|lent /rɛdələnt/ ADJ [v-link ADJ] If something is **redolent** of something else, it has features that make you think of that other thing. [LITERARY] ❑ *...percussion instruments, redolent of East Asian cultures.*

re|dou|ble /riːdʌbəl/ (redoubles, redoubling, redoubled) V T/V-I If you **redouble** your efforts, you try much harder to achieve something. If something **redoubles**, it increases in volume or intensity. ❑ *The campaign has redoubled its efforts to win the backing of women.* ❑ *The applause redoubled.*

re|doubt /rɪdaʊt/ (redoubts) N-COUNT A **redoubt** is a place or situation in which someone feels safe because they know that nobody can attack them or spoil their peace. [LITERARY] ❑ *...the last redoubt of hippy culture.*

re|doubt|able /rɪdaʊtəbəl/ ADJ [usu ADJ n] If you describe someone as **redoubtable**, you respect them because they have a very strong character, even though you are slightly afraid of them. ❑ *He is a redoubtable fighter.*

re|dound /rɪdaʊnd/ (redounds, redounding, redounded) V-I If an action or situation **redounds** to your benefit or advantage, it gives people a good impression of you or brings you something that can improve your situation. ❑ *The success in the Middle East redounds to his benefit.*

red pep|per (red peppers) ▊ N-VAR **Red peppers** are peppers which are sweet-tasting and can be used in cooking or eaten raw in salads. ▋ N-MASS **Red pepper** is a hot tasting spicy powder made from the flesh and seeds of small, dried, red peppers. It is used for flavoring food.

re|draft /riːdræft/ (redrafts, redrafting, redrafted) V-T If you **redraft** something you have written, you write it again in order to improve it or change it. ❑ *The speech had already been redrafted 22 times.*

re|draw /riːdrɔː/ (redraws, redrawing, redrew, redrawn) ▊ V-T If people in a position of authority **redraw** the boundaries or borders of a country or region, they change the borders so that the country or region covers a slightly different area than before. ❑ *They have redrawn the country's boundaries along ethnic lines.* ▋ V-T If people **redraw** something, for example an arrangement or plan, they change it because circumstances have changed. ❑ *With both countries experiencing economic revolutions, it might be time to redraw the traditional relationship.*

re|dress /rɪdrɛs/ (redresses, redressing, redressed)

The noun is also pronounced /riːdrɛs/ in American English.

▊ V-T If you **redress** something such as a wrong or a complaint, you do something to correct it or to improve things for the person who has been badly treated. [FORMAL] ❑ *More and more victims turn to litigation to redress wrongs done to them.* ▋ V-T If you **redress** the balance or the imbalance between two things that have become unfair or unequal, you make them fair and equal again. [FORMAL] ❑ *So we're trying to*

red tape — **reenter**

redress the balance and to give teachers a sense that both spoken and written language are equally important. **3** N-UNCOUNT **Redress** is money that someone pays you because they have caused you harm or loss. [FORMAL] ◻ *They are continuing their legal battle to seek some redress from the government.*

red tape N-UNCOUNT You refer to official rules and procedures as **red tape** when they seem unnecessary and cause delay. [DISAPPROVAL] ◻ *The little money that was available was tied up in bureaucratic red tape.*

re|duce /rɪdjuːs/ (reduces, reducing, reduced) **1** V-T If you **reduce** something, you make it smaller in size or amount, or less in degree. ◻ *It reduces the risks of heart disease.* **2** V-T [usu passive] If someone **is reduced** to a weaker or inferior state, they become weaker or inferior as a result of something that happens to them. ◻ *They were reduced to extreme poverty.* **3** V-T [usu passive] If you say that someone **is reduced** to doing something, you mean that they have to do it, although it is unpleasant or embarrassing. ◻ *He was reduced to begging for a living.* **4** V-T [usu passive] If something is changed to a different or less complicated form, you can say that it **is reduced** to that form. ◻ *All the buildings in the town have been reduced to rubble.* **5** V-T/V-I If you **reduce** liquid when you are cooking, or if it **reduces**, it is boiled in order to make it less in quantity and thicker. ◻ *Boil the liquid in a small saucepan to reduce it by half.* **6** PHRASE If someone or something **reduces** you **to tears**, they make you feel so unhappy that you cry. ◻ *The attentions of the media reduced her to tears.* **7** → See feature box at **recycle**

COLLOCATIONS

reduce
VERB **1**
reduce + noun: amount, cost, level, rate; crime, debt, deficit; chance, risk
reduce + adverb: drastically, sharply, significantly, substantially

---

re|duc|ible /rɪdjuːsɪbəl/ ADJ [v-link ADJ to n, usu with brd-neg] If you say that an idea, problem, or situation is not **reducible** to something simple, you mean that it is complicated and cannot be described in a simple way. [FORMAL] ◻ *The structure of the universe may not be reducible to a problem in physics.*

re|duc|tion /rɪdʌkʃən/ (reductions) **1** N-COUNT When there is a **reduction** in something, it is made smaller. ◻ *...a future reduction in interest rates.* **2** N-UNCOUNT **Reduction** is the act of making something smaller in size or amount, or less in degree. ◻ *...a new strategic arms reduction agreement.*

SYNONYMS

reduction
NOUN **1**
decrease: *...a decrease in the number of young people out of work.*
cut: *The economy needs an immediate 2 percent cut in interest rates.*
lowering: *...a package of social measures which included the lowering of the retirement age.*

---

re|duc|tion|ist /rɪdʌkʃənɪst/ ADJ [usu ADJ n] **Reductionist** describes a way of analyzing problems and things by dividing them into simpler parts. ◻ *...reductionist science.*

re|duc|tive /rɪdʌktɪv/ ADJ [usu ADJ n] If you describe something such as a theory or a work of art as **reductive**, you disapprove of it because it reduces complex things to simple elements. [FORMAL, DISAPPROVAL] ◻ *...a cynical, reductive interpretation.*

re|dun|dan|cy /rɪdʌndənsi/ (redundancies) **1** N-UNCOUNT **Redundancy** means being made redundant. [BUSINESS] ◻ *Thousands of bank employees are facing redundancy as their employers cut costs.* **2** N-COUNT When there are **redundancies**, an organization tells some of its employees to leave because their jobs are no longer necessary or because the organization can no longer afford to pay them. [BRIT, BUSINESS]

in AM, use **dismissals**

re|dun|dant /rɪdʌndənt/ **1** ADJ Something that is **redundant** is unnecessary, for example, because it is no longer needed or because its job is being done by something else. ◻ *Changes in* technology may mean that once-valued skills are now redundant. **2** ADJ If you are made **redundant**, your employer tells you to leave because your job is no longer necessary or because your employer cannot afford to keep paying you. [BRIT, BUSINESS]

in AM, use **be dismissed**

re|dux /riːdʌks/ ADJ [ADJ n, n ADJ] If a work of art is **redux**, it is presented in a new way. ◻ *She first hit our screens in Besson's brilliantly preposterous Pygmalion redux.*

red|wood /rɛdwʊd/ (redwoods) N-COUNT A **redwood** is an extremely tall tree that grows in California. • N-UNCOUNT **Redwood** is the wood from this tree.

reed /riːd/ (reeds) **1** N-COUNT **Reeds** are tall plants that grow in large groups in shallow water or on ground that is always wet and soft. They have strong, hollow stems that can be used for making things such as mats or baskets. **2** N-COUNT A **reed** is a small piece of cane or metal inserted into the mouthpiece of a woodwind instrument. The reed vibrates when you blow through it and makes a sound.

re|edu|cate /riːɛdʒʊkeɪt/ (reeducates, reeducating, reeducated) also **re-educate** V-T If an organization such as a government tries to **reeducate** a group of people, they try to make them adopt new attitudes, beliefs, or types of behavior. ◻ *We are having to reeducate the public very quickly about something they have always taken for granted.* • **re|edu|ca|tion** /riːɛdʒʊkeɪʃən/ N-UNCOUNT ◻ *...a program of punishment and reeducation of political dissidents.*

reedy /riːdi/ **1** ADJ [usu ADJ n] If you say that someone has a **reedy** voice, you think their voice is unpleasant because it is high and unclear. ◻ *The big man had a high-pitched reedy voice.* **2** → See feature box at **water**

reef /riːf/ (reefs) N-COUNT A **reef** is a long line of rocks or sand, the top of which is just above or just below the surface of the sea. ◻ *An unspoiled coral reef encloses the bay.*

reef|er /riːfər/ (reefers) N-COUNT A **reefer** is a cigarette containing marijuana. [INFORMAL, OLD-FASHIONED]

reek /riːk/ (reeks, reeking, reeked) **1** V-I To **reek** of something, usually something unpleasant, means to smell very strongly of it. ◻ *Your breath reeks of stale cigar smoke.* • N-SING **Reek** is also a noun. ◻ *He smelled the reek of whiskey.* **2** V-I If you say that something **reeks** of unpleasant ideas, feelings, or practices, you disapprove of it because it gives a strong impression that it involves those ideas, feelings, or practices. [DISAPPROVAL] ◻ *The whole thing reeks of hypocrisy.*

reel /riːl/ (reels, reeling, reeled) **1** N-COUNT A **reel** is a cylindrical object around which you wrap something such as movie film, magnetic tape, or fishing line. ◻ *...a 30-meter reel of cable.* **2** V-I If someone **reels**, they move about in an unsteady way as if they are going to fall. ◻ *He was reeling a little. He must be very drunk.* **3** V-I [usu cont] If you are **reeling** from a shock, you are feeling extremely surprised or upset because of it. ◻ *I'm still reeling from the shock of hearing about it.* **4** V-I If you say that your brain or your mind **is reeling**, you mean that you are very confused because you have too many things to think about. ◻ *His mind reeled at the question.*

▶ **reel off** PHRASAL VERB If you **reel off** information, you repeat it from memory quickly and easily. ◻ *She reeled off the titles of a dozen or so of the novels.*

re|elect /riːɪlɛkt/ (reelects, reelecting, reelected) also **re-elect** V-T When someone such as a politician or an official who has been elected **is reelected**, they win another election and are therefore able to continue in their position as, for example, president, or an official in an organization. ◻ *He needs 51 percent to be reelected.* ◻ *James Rhodes was reelected governor of Ohio.* • **re|elec|tion** /riːɪlɛkʃən/ N-UNCOUNT ◻ *He is heavily favored to win reelection.*

re|en|act /riːɪnækt/ (reenacts, reenacting, reenacted) also **re-enact** V-T If you **reenact** a scene or incident, you repeat the actions that occurred in the scene or incident. ◻ *After enjoying the story the children reenacted it.*

re|en|act|ment /riːɪnæktmənt/ (reenactments) also **re-enactment** N-COUNT [usu N of n] When a **reenactment** of a scene or incident takes place, people reenact it.

re|en|ter /riːɛntər/ (reenters, reentering, reentered)

in BRIT, sometimes in AM, use **re-enter**

reentry /ri‿ɛntri/ also **re-entry** ▮ N-UNCOUNT [also a N] V-T If you **reenter** a place, organization, or area of activity that you have left, you return to it. ❑ *Ten minutes later he reentered the hotel.* **Reentry** is the act of returning to a place, organization, or area of activity that you have left. ❑ *...the successful reentry into the Japanese auto market of U.S.-manufactured autos.* ▮ N-UNCOUNT [also a N] **Reentry** is used to refer to the moment when a spacecraft comes back into the Earth's atmosphere after being in space. ❑ *The station would burn up on reentry into the Earth's atmosphere.* ▮ → See feature box at **travel**

re|eval|u|ate /ri‿ɪvælyueɪt/ (**reevaluates, reevaluating, reevaluated**) V-T If you **reevaluate** something or someone, you consider them again in order to reassess your opinion of them, for example, about how good or bad they are. ❑ *This may be the time to reevaluate the whole issue.* ❑ *Williams will be reevaluated on a weekly basis, with surgery a possible option.* • **re|eval|u|ation** /ri‿ɪvælyueɪʃən/ N-VAR ❑ *It's time for a rest, and a reevaluation of your life.* ❑ *...a period of reevaluation.*

re|ex|am|ine /ri‿ɪgzæmɪn/ (**reexamines, reexamining, reexamined**) also **re-examine** V-T If a person or group of people **reexamines** their ideas, beliefs, or attitudes, they think about them carefully because they are no longer sure if they are correct. ❑ *The marriage will cause Drew to reexamine his life.* • **re|ex|ami|na|tion** /ri‿ɪgzæmɪneɪʃən/ (**reexaminations**) N-VAR ❑ *The issue has led to a reexamination of censorship rules.*

ref /rɛf/ (**refs**) ▮ **Ref.** is an abbreviation for **reference**. It is written in front of a code at the top of business letters and documents. The code refers to a file where all the letters and documents about the same matter are kept. [BUSINESS] ❑ *Our Ref: JAH/JW.* ▮ N-COUNT The **ref** in a sports game, such as football, soccer, or boxing, is the same as the **referee**. [INFORMAL] ❑ *The ref said it was a fumble.*

re|fec|tory /rɪfɛktəri/ (**refectories**) N-COUNT A **refectory** is a large room in a monastery or other institution, where meals are served and eaten.

re|fer ♦♢♢ /rɪfɜr/ (**refers, referring, referred**) ▮ V-I If you **refer** to a particular subject or person, you talk about them or mention them. ❑ *In his speech, he referred to a recent trip to Canada.* ▮ V-I If you **refer** to someone or something as a particular thing, you use a particular word, expression, or name to mention or describe them. ❑ *Marcia had referred to him as a dear friend.* ▮ V-I If a word **refers** to a particular thing, situation, or idea, it describes it in some way. ❑ *The term electronics refers to electrically induced action.* ▮ V-T [usu passive] If a person who is ill **is referred** to a hospital or a specialist, they are sent there by a doctor in order to be treated. ❑ *She was referred to the hospital by a neighborhood clinic.* ▮ V-T If you **refer** a task or a problem to a person or an organization, you formally tell them about it, so that they can deal with it. ❑ *He could refer the matter to the high court.* ▮ V-T If you **refer** someone to a person or organization, you send them there for the help they need. ❑ *Now and then I referred a client to him.* ▮ V-I If you **refer** to a book or other source of information, you look at it in order to find something out. ❑ *He referred briefly to his notebook.* ▮ V-T If you **refer** someone to a source of information, you tell them the place where they will find the information they need or that you think will interest them. ❑ *Mr. Bryan also referred me to a book by the American journalist Anthony Scaduto.*

┌─────────── SYNONYMS ───────────┐
refer
VERB ▮
mention: *She did not mention her mother's absence.*
allude to: *She also alluded to her rival's past marital troubles.*
bring up: *Why are you bringing it up now?*
touch on: *The film touches on these issues, but only superficially.*
└────────────────────────────────┘

ref|eree /rɛfəri/ (**referees, refereeing, refereed**) ▮ N-COUNT The **referee** is the official who controls a sports event such as a football game or a boxing match. ▮ V-T/V-I When someone **referees** a sports event or contest, they act as referee. ❑ *Vautrot has refereed in two World Cups.* ▮ N-COUNT A **referee** is a person who gives you a reference, for example when you are applying for a job. [BRIT]

in AM, use **reference**

▮ → See feature box at **football**

ref|er|ence ♦♢♢ /rɛfərəns, rɛfrəns/ (**references**) ▮ N-VAR **Reference** to someone or something is the act of talking about them or mentioning them. A **reference** is a particular example of this. ❑ *He made no reference to any agreement.* ▮ N-UNCOUNT **Reference** is the act of consulting someone or something in order to get information or advice. ❑ *Please keep this sheet in a safe place for reference.* ▮ ADJ [ADJ n] **Reference** books are ones that you look at when you need specific information or facts about a subject. ❑ *...a useful reference work for teachers.* ▮ N-COUNT A **reference** is a word, phrase, or idea which comes from something such as a book, poem, or play and which you use when making a point about something. ❑ *...a reference from the Koran.* ▮ N-COUNT A **reference** is something such as a number or a name that tells you where you can obtain the information you want. ❑ *Make a note of the reference number shown on the form.* ▮ N-COUNT A **reference** is a letter that is written by someone who knows you and which describes your character and abilities. When you apply for a job, an employer might ask for **references**. ❑ *The firm offered to give her a reference.* ▮ N-COUNT A **reference** is a person who gives you a reference, for example when you are applying for a job. [mainly AM] ❑ *The official at the American embassy asked me for two references.*

in BRIT, usually use **referee**

▮ PHRASE You use **with reference to** or **in reference to** in order to indicate what something relates to. ❑ *I am writing with reference to your article on salaries for scientists.* ▮ → see also **cross-reference** ▮ → See feature box at **research**

┌─────────── SYNONYMS ───────────┐
reference
NOUN
▮
allusion: *The title is perhaps an allusion to AIDS.*
comment: *There's been no comment so far from police about the allegations.*
mention: *The statement made no mention of government casualties.*
▮
testimonial: *She could hardly expect her employer to provide her with testimonials to her character and ability.*
recommendation: *The best way of finding a lawyer is through personal recommendation.*
endorsement: *This is a powerful endorsement for his softer style of government.*
└────────────────────────────────┘

ref|er|ence li|brary (**reference libraries**) N-COUNT A **reference library** is a library that contains books which you can look at in the library itself but which you cannot borrow.

ref|er|en|dum ♦♢♢ /rɛfərɛndəm/ (**referendums** or **referenda** /rɛfərɛndə/) N-COUNT If a country holds a **referendum** on a particular policy, they ask the people to vote on the policy and show whether or not they agree with it. ❑ *Estonia said today it too plans to hold a referendum on independence.*

re|fer|ral /rɪfɜrəl/ (**referrals**) N-VAR **Referral** is the act of officially sending someone to a person or authority that is qualified to deal with them. A **referral** is an instance of this. ❑ *Legal Aid can often provide referral to other types of agencies.*

re|fill (**refills, refilling, refilled**)

The verb is pronounced /rifɪl/. The noun is pronounced /rifɪl/.

▮ V-T If you **refill** something, you fill it again after it has been emptied. ❑ *I refilled our wine glasses.* • N-COUNT **Refill** is also a noun. [INFORMAL] ❑ *Max held out his cup for a refill.* ▮ N-COUNT A **refill** of a particular product is a quantity of that product sold in a cheaper container than the one it is usually sold in. You use a refill to fill the more permanent container when it is empty. ❑ *Refill packs are cheaper and lighter.*

re|fi|nance /rifənæns, rifaɪnæns/ (**refinances, refinancing, refinanced**) V-T/V-I If a person or a company **refinances** a debt or if they **refinance**, they borrow money in order to pay the debt. [BUSINESS] ❑ *A loan was arranged to refinance existing debt.*

re|fine /rɪfaɪn/ (**refines, refining, refined**) ▮ V-T [usu passive] When a substance **is refined**, it is made pure by having all other substances removed from it. ❑ *Oil is refined*

refined to remove naturally occurring impurities. • **re|fin|ing** N-UNCOUNT ❏ ...*oil refining.* **2** V-T [usu passive] If something such as a process, theory, or machine **is refined**, it is improved by having small changes made to it. ❏ *Surgical techniques are constantly being refined.*

re|fined /rɪfaɪnd/ **1** ADJ A **refined** substance has been made pure by having other substances removed from it. ❏ ...*refined sugar.* **2** ADJ If you say that someone is **refined**, you mean that they are very polite and have good manners and good taste. ❏ ...*refined and well-dressed ladies.* **3** ADJ If you describe a machine or a process as **refined**, you mean that it has been carefully developed and is therefore very efficient or elegant. ❏ *This technique is becoming more refined and more acceptable all the time.*

re|fine|ment /rɪfaɪnmənt/ (**refinements**) **1** N-VAR **Refinements** are small changes or additions that you make to something in order to improve it. **Refinement** is the process of making refinements. ❏ *Older cars inevitably lack the latest safety refinements.* **2** N-UNCOUNT **Refinement** is politeness and good manners.

re|fin|er /rɪfaɪnər/ (**refiners**) N-COUNT **Refiners** are people or organizations that refine substances such as oil or sugar in order to sell them.

re|fin|ery /rɪfaɪnəri/ (**refineries**) N-COUNT A **refinery** is a factory where a substance such as oil or sugar is refined. ❏ ...*an oil refinery.*

re|fit (**refits, refitting, refitted**)

> The verb is pronounced /riːfɪt/. The noun is pronounced /riːfɪt/.

V-T [usu passive] When a ship **is refitted**, it is repaired or is given new parts, equipment, or furniture. ❏ *During the war, navy ships were refitted here.* • N-COUNT **Refit** is also a noun. ❏ *The ship finished an extensive refit last year.*

re|flate /riːfleɪt/ (**reflates, reflating, reflated**) V-T If a government tries to **reflate** its country's economy, it increases the amount of money that is available in order to encourage more economic activity. [BUSINESS] ❏ *The administration may try to reflate the economy next year.* • **re|fla|tion** /riːfleɪʃən/ N-UNCOUNT ❏ *They're talking about reflation and price controls.*

re|flect ♦♦◊ /rɪflɛkt/ (**reflects, reflecting, reflected**) **1** V-T If something **reflects** an attitude or situation, it shows that the attitude or situation exists or it shows what it is like. ❏ *A newspaper report seems to reflect the view of most members of Congress.* **2** V-T/V-I When light, heat, or other rays **reflect** off a surface or when a surface **reflects** them, they are sent back from the surface and do not pass through it. ❏ *The sun reflected off the snow-covered mountains.* **3** V-T [usu passive] When something **is reflected** in a mirror or in water, you can see its image in the mirror or in the water. ❏ *His image was reflected many times in the mirror.* **4** V-I When you **reflect** on something, you think deeply about it. ❏ *We should all give ourselves time to reflect.* **5** V-T You can use **reflect** to indicate that a particular thought occurs to someone. ❏ *Things were very much changed since before the war, he reflected.* **6** V-I If an action or situation **reflects** in a particular way on someone or something, it gives people a good or bad impression of them. ❏ *The affair hardly reflected well on the president.*

SYNONYMS

reflect
VERB
1
show: *These figures show an increase of over one million in unemployment.*
reveal: *A survey of the British diet has revealed that a growing number of people are overweight.*
express: *The anxiety of the separation often expresses itself as anger towards the child.*
4
consider: *Consider how much you can afford to pay for a course, and what your upper limit is.*
contemplate: *As he lay in his hospital bed that night, he cried as he contemplated his future.*
deliberate: *She deliberated over the decision for a long time before she made up her mind.*

---

re|flec|tion /rɪflɛkʃən/ (**reflections**) **1** N-COUNT A **reflection** is an image that you can see in a mirror or in glass or water. ❏ *Meg stared at her reflection in the bedroom mirror.* **2** N-UNCOUNT **Reflection** is the process by which light and heat are sent back from a surface and do not pass through it. ❏ ...*the reflection of a beam of light off a mirror.* **3** N-COUNT If you say that something is a **reflection** of a particular person's attitude or of a situation, you mean that it is caused by that attitude or situation and therefore reveals something about it. ❏ *Inhibition in adulthood seems to be a reflection of a person's experiences as a child.* **4** N-SING If something is a **reflection** or a **sad reflection** on a person or thing, it gives a bad impression of them. ❏ *Infection with head lice is no reflection on personal hygiene.* **5** N-UNCOUNT [also N in pl] **Reflection** is careful thought about a particular subject. Your **reflections** are your thoughts about a particular subject. ❏ *After days of reflection she decided to write back.* • PHRASE If someone admits or accepts something **on reflection**, they admit or accept it after having thought carefully about it. ❏ *While the news at first shocked me, on reflection it made perfect sense.*

re|flec|tive /rɪflɛktɪv/ **1** ADJ If you are **reflective**, you are thinking deeply about something. [WRITTEN] ❏ *I walked on in a reflective mood to the car, thinking about the poor honeymooners.* **2** ADJ [v-link ADJ of n] If something is **reflective** of a particular situation or attitude, it is typical of that situation or attitude, or is a consequence of it. ❏ *The German government's support of the U.S. is not entirely reflective of German public opinion.* **3** ADJ A **reflective** surface or material sends back light or heat. [FORMAL] ❏ *Avoid using pans with a shiny, reflective base as the heat will be reflected back.*

re|flec|tor /rɪflɛktər/ (**reflectors**) **1** N-COUNT A **reflector** is a small piece of specially patterned glass or plastic which is fitted to the back of a bicycle or car or to a post beside the road, and which glows when light shines on it. **2** N-COUNT A **reflector** is a type of telescope which uses a mirror that is shaped like a ball.

re|flex /riːflɛks/ (**reflexes**) **1** N-COUNT A **reflex** or a **reflex action** is something that you do automatically and without thinking, as a habit or as a reaction to something. ❏ *Walt fumbled in his pocket, a reflex from his smoking days.* **2** N-COUNT A **reflex** or a **reflex action** is a normal, uncontrollable reaction of your body to something that you feel, see, or experience. ❏ ...*tests for reflexes, like tapping the knee or the heel with a rubber hammer.* **3** N-PLURAL Your **reflexes** are your ability to react quickly with your body when something unexpected happens, for example when you are involved in sports or when you are driving a car. ❏ *It takes great skill, cool nerves, and the reflexes of an athlete.*

re|flex|ive /rɪflɛksɪv/ ADJ [usu ADJ n] A **reflexive** reaction or movement occurs immediately in response to something that happens. [FORMAL] ❏ *The program tries to make children more rational, less reflexive consumers.* • **re|flex|ive|ly** ADV [usu ADV with v] ❏ *He felt his head jerk reflexively.*

re|flex|ive pro|noun (**reflexive pronouns**) N-COUNT A **reflexive pronoun** is a pronoun such as 'myself' which refers back to the subject of a sentence or clause. For example, in the sentence 'She made herself a cup of coffee,' the reflexive pronoun 'herself' refers back to 'she.'

re|flex|ive verb (**reflexive verbs**) N-COUNT A **reflexive verb** is a transitive verb whose subject and object always refer to the same person or thing, so the object is always a reflexive pronoun. An example is 'to enjoy yourself,' as in 'Did you enjoy yourself?'

re|flex|ol|ogy /riːflɛksɒlədʒi/ N-UNCOUNT **Reflexology** is the practice of massaging particular areas of the body, especially the feet, in the belief that it can heal particular organs. • **re|flex|olo|gist** (**reflexologists**) N-COUNT ❏ *A reflexologist can often tell what is wrong with his client by the condition of parts of the feet.*

re|for|est /riːfɒrɪst/ (**reforests, reforesting, reforested**) V-T To **reforest** an area where there used to be a forest means to plant trees over it. ❏ *He decided to do something about reforesting man-made wastes of western Australia.*

re|for|esta|tion /riːfɒrɪsteɪʃən/ N-UNCOUNT **Reforestation** of an area where there used to be a forest is planting trees over it. ❏ ...*the reforestation of the Apennine Mountains.*

re|form /rɪfɔrm/ (reforms, reforming, reformed) **1** N-VAR Reform consists of changes and improvements to a law, social system, or institution. A **reform** is an instance of such a change or improvement. ❑ *The party embarked on a program of economic reform.* **2** V-T If someone **reforms** something such as a law, social system, or institution, they change or improve it. ❑ *...his plans to reform the country's economy.* **3** V-T/V-I When someone **reforms** or when something **reforms** them, they stop doing things that society does not approve of, such as breaking the law or drinking too much alcohol. ❑ *When his court case was coming up, James promised to reform.* • **re|formed** ADJ ❑ *...a reformed alcoholic.*

SYNONYMS

reform
NOUN **1**
improvement: *...the dramatic improvements in organ transplantation in recent years.*
amendment: *...a constitutional amendment.*
correction: *...legislation to require the correction of factual errors.*
VERB **2**
improve: *He improved their house.*
better: *He had dedicated his life to bettering the lives of the oppressed people of South Africa.*
correct: *He may need surgery to correct the problem.*

---

re-form (re-forms, re-forming, re-formed) V-T/V-I When an organization, group, or shape **re-forms**, or when someone **re-forms** it, it is created again after a period during which it did not exist or existed in a different form. ❑ *The council voted to disband and re-form as a confederation.* ❑ *The singer re-formed his band.*

ref|or|ma|tion /rɛfərmeɪʃən/ **1** N-UNCOUNT The **reformation** of something is the act or process of changing and improving it. ❑ *He devoted his energies to the reformation of science.* **2** N-PROPER [the N] **The Reformation** is the movement to reform the Catholic Church in the sixteenth century, which led to the Protestant Church being set up. ❑ *...a famous statue of the Virgin which was destroyed during the Reformation.*

re|form|er /rɪfɔrmər/ (reformers) N-COUNT A **reformer** is someone who tries to change and improve something such as a law or a social system. ❑ *How could he be a reformer and a defender of established interests at the same time?*

re|form|ism /rɪfɔrmɪzəm/ N-UNCOUNT **Reformism** is the belief that a system or law should be reformed.

re|form|ist /rɪfɔrmɪst/ (reformists) ADJ **Reformist** groups or policies are trying to reform a system or law. ❑ *...a strong supporter of reformist policies.* • N-COUNT A **reformist** is someone with reformist views.

re|form school (reform schools) N-VAR A **reform school** is a kind of prison for young criminals, who are not old enough to be sent to ordinary prisons. ❑ *...a reform school for delinquent adolescent girls.* ❑ *...his narrow escape from being sent to reform school.*

re|fract /rɪfrækt/ (refracts, refracting, refracted) V-T/V-I When a ray of light or a sound wave **refracts** or **is refracted**, the path it follows bends at a particular point, for example when it enters water or glass. ❑ *As we age, the lenses of the eyes thicken, and thus refract light differently.* ❑ *...surfaces that cause the light to reflect and refract.* • **re|frac|tion** /rɪfrækʃən/ N-UNCOUNT ❑ *...the refraction of the light on the dancing waves.*

re|frac|tory /rɪfræktəri/ ADJ [usu ADJ n] **Refractory** people are difficult to deal with or control, usually because they are unwilling to obey orders. [FORMAL] ❑ *...refractory priests who refused to side with the king.*

re|frain /rɪfreɪn/ (refrains, refraining, refrained) **1** V-I If you **refrain** from doing something, you deliberately do not do it. ❑ *Mrs. Hardie refrained from making any comment.* **2** N-COUNT A **refrain** is a short, simple part of a song, which is repeated many times. ❑ *...a refrain from an old song.* **3** N-COUNT A **refrain** is a comment or saying that people often repeat. ❑ *Rosa's constant refrain is that she doesn't have a life.*

re|fresh /rɪfrɛʃ/ (refreshes, refreshing, refreshed) **1** V-T If something **refreshes** you when you are hot, tired, or thirsty, it makes you feel cooler or more energetic. ❑ *The lotion cools and refreshes the skin.* • **re|freshed** ADJ ❑ *He awoke feeling completely refreshed.* **2** V-T If you **refresh** something old or dull, you make it as good as it was when it was new. ❑ *Many view these meetings as an occasion to share ideas and refresh friendship.* **3** V-T If someone **refreshes** your memory, they tell you something that you had forgotten. ❑ *He walked on the opposite side of the street to refresh his memory of the building.* **4** V-T If you **refresh** a web page, you click a button in order to get the most recent version of the page. [COMPUTING] ❑ *I've refreshed the page a few times and still see no comments.*

re|fresh|er course (refresher courses) N-COUNT A **refresher course** is a training course in which people improve their knowledge or skills and learn about new developments that are related to the job that they do.

re|fresh|ing /rɪfrɛʃɪŋ/ **1** ADJ You say that something is **refreshing** when it is pleasantly different from what you are used to. ❑ *It's refreshing to hear somebody speaking common sense.* • **re|fresh|ing|ly** ADV ❑ *He was refreshingly honest.* **2** ADJ A **refreshing** bath or drink makes you feel energetic or cool again after you have been tired or hot. ❑ *Herbs have been used for centuries to make refreshing drinks.*

re|fresh|ment /rɪfrɛʃmənt/ (refreshments) **1** N-PLURAL **Refreshments** are drinks and small amounts of food that are provided, for example, during a meeting or a trip. ❑ *Lunch and refreshments will be provided.* **2** N-UNCOUNT You can refer to food and drink as **refreshment**. [FORMAL] ❑ *May I offer you some refreshment?*

re|fried beans /rɪfraɪd binz/ N-PLURAL **Refried beans** are beans that have been boiled and crushed before being fried. They are used especially in Mexican cooking.

re|frig|er|ate /rɪfrɪdʒəreɪt/ (refrigerates, refrigerating, refrigerated) V-T If you **refrigerate** food, you make it cold by putting it in a refrigerator, usually in order to preserve it. ❑ *Refrigerate the dough overnight.*

re|frig|era|tor /rɪfrɪdʒəreɪtər/ (refrigerators) N-COUNT A **refrigerator** is a large container which is kept cool inside, usually by electricity, so that the food and drink in it stays fresh.

re|fu|el /rifyuəl/ (refuels, refueling or refuelling, refueled or refuelled) V-T/V-I When an aircraft or other vehicle **refuels** or when someone **refuels** it, it is filled with more fuel so that it can continue its journey. ❑ *His plane stopped in Hawaii to refuel.* • **re|fu|el|ing** N-UNCOUNT ❑ *...nighttime refueling of vehicles.*

ref|uge /rɛfyudʒ/ (refuges) **1** N-UNCOUNT If you take **refuge** somewhere, you try to protect yourself from physical harm by going there. ❑ *They took refuge in a bomb shelter.* **2** N-COUNT A **refuge** is a place where you go for safety and protection, for example from violence or from bad weather. ❑ *...a refuge for women who had experienced domestic abuse.* **3** N-UNCOUNT If you take **refuge** in a particular way of behaving or thinking, you try to protect yourself from unhappiness or unpleasantness by behaving or thinking in that way. ❑ *All too often, they get bored and seek refuge in drink and drugs.*

refu|gee /rɛfyudʒi/ (refugees) N-COUNT **Refugees** are people who have been forced to leave their homes or their country, either because there is a war there, because of their political or religious beliefs, or because of natural disaster. ❑ *A political refugee from Cameroon has moved into our neighborhood.*

re|fund (refunds, refunding, refunded)

> The noun is pronounced /rifʌnd/. The verb is pronounced /rɪfʌnd/.

1 N-COUNT A **refund** is a sum of money that is returned to you, for example because you have paid too much or because you have returned goods to a store. ❑ *Face it – you'll just have to take those cowboy boots back and ask for a refund.* **2** V-T If someone **refunds** your money, they return it to you, for example because you have paid too much or because you have returned goods to a store. ❑ *We guarantee to refund your money if you're not delighted with your purchase.*

re|fund|able /rɪfʌndəbəl/ ADJ A **refundable** payment will be paid back to you in certain circumstances. ❑ *A refundable deposit is payable on arrival.*

re|fur|bish /rifɜrbɪʃ/ (refurbishes, refurbishing, refurbished) V-T To **refurbish** a building or room means to clean it and decorate it and make it more attractive or better equipped. ❑ *We have spent money on refurbishing the offices.*

re|fur|bish|ment /rɪfɜrbɪʃmənt/ (refurbishments) N-UNCOUNT [also N in pl] The **refurbishment** of something is the act or process of cleaning it, decorating it, and providing it with new equipment or facilities.

re|fus|al /rɪfyuzəl/ (refusals) **1** N-VAR Someone's **refusal** to do something is the fact of them showing or saying that they will not do it, allow it, or accept it. ▫ *Her country suffered through her refusal to accept change.* **2** PHRASE If someone has **first refusal** on something that is being sold or offered, they have the right to decide whether or not to buy it or take it before it is offered to anyone else. ▫ *A tenant may have a right of first refusal if a property is offered for sale.*

re|fuse ♦♢♢ (refuses, refusing, refused)

The verb is pronounced /rɪfyuz/. The noun is pronounced /rɛfyus/ and is hyphenated ref|use.

1 V-T/V-I If you **refuse** to do something, you deliberately do not do it, or you say firmly that you will not do it. ▫ *He refused to comment after the trial.* ▫ *I could hardly refuse, could I?* **2** V-T If someone **refuses** you something, they do not give it to you or do not allow you to have it. ▫ *The United States has refused him a visa.* **3** V-T If you **refuse** something that is offered to you, you do not accept it. ▫ *The patient has the right to refuse treatment.* **4** N-UNCOUNT **Refuse** consists of the trash and all the things that are not wanted in a house, store, or factory, and that are regularly thrown away; used mainly in official language. ▫ *The town made a weekly collection of refuse.*

SYNONYMS

refuse
VERB **1**
decline: *The band declined to comment on the story.*
demur: *The doctor demurred, but Piercey was insistent.*
reject: *Seventeen publishers rejected the manuscript before Jenks saw its potential.*
turn down: *I thanked him for the offer but turned it down.*

---

ref|use col|lec|tor (refuse collectors) N-COUNT A **refuse collector** is a person whose job is to take people's garbage away.

refu|ta|tion /rɛfyuteɪʃən/ (refutations) N-VAR A **refutation** of an argument, accusation, or theory is something that proves it is wrong or untrue. [FORMAL] ▫ *He prepared a complete refutation of the Republicans' most serious charges.*

re|fute /rɪfyut/ (refutes, refuting, refuted) **1** V-T If you **refute** an argument, accusation, or theory, you prove that it is wrong or untrue. [FORMAL] ▫ *It was the kind of rumor that it is impossible to refute.* **2** V-T If you **refute** an argument or accusation, you say that it is not true. [FORMAL] ▫ *Isabelle is quick to refute any suggestion of intellectual snobbery.*

re|gain /rɪgeɪn/ (regains, regaining, regained) V-T If you **regain** something that you have lost, you get it back again. ▫ *Troops have regained control of the city.*

re|gal /rigəl/ ADJ If you describe something as **regal**, you mean that it is suitable for a king or queen, because it is very impressive or beautiful. ▫ *He sat with such regal dignity.*

re|gale /rɪgeɪl/ (regales, regaling, regaled) V-T If someone **regales** you with stories or jokes, they tell you a lot of them, whether you want to hear them or not. ▫ *He was constantly regaled with tales of woe.*

re|ga|lia /rɪgeɪlyə, -geɪliə/ N-UNCOUNT **Regalia** consists of all the traditional clothes and items that someone such as a king or a judge wears and carries on official occasions. ▫ *...officials in full regalia.*

re|gard ♦♦♢ /rɪgɑrd/ (regards, regarding, regarded) **1** V-T If you **regard** someone or something as being a particular thing or as having a particular quality, you believe that they are that thing or have that quality. ▫ *He was regarded as the most successful president of modern times.* **2** V-T If you **regard** something or someone with a feeling such as dislike or respect, you have that feeling about them. ▫ *He regarded drug dealers with loathing.* **3** N-UNCOUNT If you have **regard** for someone or something, you respect them and care about them. If you hold someone in high **regard**, you have a lot of respect for them. ▫ *I have a very high regard for him and what he has achieved.* **4** N-PLURAL **Regards** are greetings. You use **regards** in expressions such as **best regards** and **with kind regards** as a way of expressing friendly feelings toward someone, especially in a letter. [FORMULAE] ▫ *Give my regards to your family.* **5** PHRASE You can use **as regards** to indicate the subject that is being talked or written about. ▫ *As regards the war, Haig believed in victory at any price.* **6** PHRASE You can use **with regard to** or **in regard to** to indicate the subject that is being talked or written about. ▫ *The department is reviewing its policy with regard to immunization.*

SYNONYMS

regard
VERB **1**
consider: *I consider activities such as jogging and weightlifting to be unnatural.*
judge: *I judged it to be one of the worst programs ever screened.*
deem: *French and German were deemed essential.*
view: *Sectors in the economy can be viewed in a variety of ways.*
NOUN **3**
respect: *I have tremendous respect for Dean.*
esteem: *Their public esteem has never been lower.*
admiration: *I have always had the greatest admiration for him.*

---

re|gard|ing /rɪgɑrdɪŋ/ PREP You can use **regarding** to indicate the subject that is being talked or written about. ▫ *He refused to divulge any information regarding the man's whereabouts.*

re|gard|less /rɪgɑrdlɪs/ **1** PHRASE If something happens **regardless of** something else, it is not affected or influenced at all by that other thing. ▫ *It takes in anybody regardless of religion, color, or creed.* **2** ADV [ADV after v] If you say that someone did something **regardless**, you mean that they did it even though there were problems or factors that could have stopped them, or perhaps should have stopped them. ▫ *Despite her recent surgery she has been carrying on regardless.*

re|gat|ta /rɪgætə, -gɑtə/ (regattas) N-COUNT [oft in names] A **regatta** is a sports event consisting of races between yachts or other boats.

re|gen|cy /ridʒənsi/ (regencies)

The spelling **Regency** is usually used for meaning **1**.

1 ADJ [usu ADJ n] **Regency** is used to refer to the period in Britain at the beginning of the nineteenth century, and to the style of architecture, literature, and furniture that was popular at the time. ▫ *...a huge, six-bedroom Regency house.* **2** N-COUNT A **regency** is a period of time when a country is governed by a regent, because the king or queen is unable to rule.

re|gen|er|ate /rɪdʒɛnəreɪt/ (regenerates, regenerating, regenerated) **1** V-T To **regenerate** something means to develop and improve it to make it more active, successful, or important, especially after a period when it has been getting worse. ▫ *The government will continue to try to regenerate inner-city areas.* • **re|gen|era|tion** /rɪdʒɛnəreɪʃən/ N-UNCOUNT ▫ *...the physical and economic regeneration of the area.* **2** V-T/V-I If organs or tissues **regenerate** or if something **regenerates** them, they heal and grow again after they have been damaged. ▫ *Nerve cells have limited ability to regenerate if destroyed.* • **re|gen|era|tion** N-UNCOUNT ▫ *Vitamin B assists in red-blood-cell regeneration.*

re|gen|era|tive /rɪdʒɛnərətɪv, -əreɪtɪv/ ADJ [usu ADJ n] **Regenerative** powers or processes cause something to heal or become active again after it has been damaged or inactive. ▫ *...the regenerative power of nature.*

re|gent /ridʒənt/ (regents) N-COUNT A **regent** is a person who rules a country when the king or queen is unable to rule, for example because they are too young or too ill.

reg|gae /rɛgeɪ/ N-UNCOUNT **Reggae** is a kind of West Indian popular music with a very strong beat. ▫ *Many people will remember Bob Marley for giving them their first taste of reggae music.*

regi|cide /rɛdʒɪsaɪd/ (regicides) **1** N-UNCOUNT **Regicide** is the act of killing a king. ▫ *He had become czar through regicide.* **2** N-COUNT A **regicide** is a person who kills a king. ▫ *Some of the regicides were sentenced to death.*

re|gime ♦♢♢ /rəʒim, reɪ-/ (regimes) **1** N-COUNT If you refer to a government or system of running a country as a **regime**, you are critical of it because you think it is not democratic and uses unacceptable methods. [DISAPPROVAL] ❏ ...the collapse of the Fascist regime at the end of the war. ◼2 N-COUNT A **regime** is the way that something such as an institution, company, or economy is run, especially when it involves tough or severe action. ❏ The authorities moved him to the less rigid regime of an open prison. ◼3 N-COUNT A **regime** is a set of rules about food, exercise, or beauty that some people follow in order to stay healthy or attractive. ❏ He has a new fitness regime to strengthen his back.

─────── SYNONYMS ───────

regime
NOUN ◼1
government: ...democratic governments in countries like Britain and the U.S.
administration: O'Leary served in federal energy posts in both the Ford and Carter administrations.
leadership: He is expected to hold talks with both the Croatian and Slovenian leaderships.

regi|men /rɛdʒɪmən/ (regimens) N-COUNT A **regimen** is a set of rules about food and exercise that some people follow in order to stay healthy. ❏ Whatever regimen has been prescribed should be rigorously followed.

regi|ment /rɛdʒɪmənt/ (regiments) ◼1 N-COUNT A **regiment** is a large group of soldiers that is commanded by a colonel. ◼2 N-COUNT A **regiment of** people is a large number of them. ❏ ...robust food, good enough to satisfy a regiment of hungry customers.

regi|men|tal /rɛdʒɪmɛntəl/ ADJ [ADJ n] **Regimental** means belonging to a particular regiment. ❏ Mills was regimental colonel.

regi|men|ta|tion /rɛdʒɪmɛnteɪʃən/ N-UNCOUNT **Regimentation** is very strict control over the way a group of people behave or the way something is done. ❏ Democracy is incompatible with excessive, bureaucratic regimentation of social life.

regi|ment|ed /rɛdʒɪmɛntɪd/ ADJ Something that is **regimented** is very strictly controlled. ❏ ...the regimented atmosphere of the orphanage.

re|gion ✦✦◇ /riːdʒən/ (regions) ◼1 N-COUNT A **region** is a large area of land that is different from other areas of land, for example because it is one of the different parts of a country with its own customs and characteristics, or because it has a particular geographical feature. ❏ ...Barcelona, capital of the autonomous region of Catalonia. ◼2 N-COUNT You can refer to a part of your body as a **region**. ❏ ...the pelvic region. ◼3 PHRASE You say **in the region of** to indicate that an amount that you are stating is approximate. [VAGUENESS] ❏ The plan will cost in the region of six million dollars. ◼4 → See feature box at **disaster, global warming**

─────── COLLOCATIONS ───────

region
NOUN ◼1
noun + **region**: border, mountain, wine
adjective + **region**: eastern, northern, southern, western; central, coastal, mountainous, remote; autonomous, tribal
verb + **region**: explore, visit; affect, destabilize

re|gion|al ✦✦◇ /riːdʒənəl/ ADJ **Regional** is used to describe things which relate to a particular area of a country or of the world. ❏ The Garden's menu is based on Hawaiian regional cuisine.

─────── SYNONYMS ───────

regional
ADJ
local: We'd better check the scores in the local paper.
provincial: ...in Rasht, the provincial capital of Gilan province.
district: ...the district health authority.

re|gion|al|ism /riːdʒənəlɪzəm/ N-UNCOUNT **Regionalism** is a strong feeling of pride or loyalty that people in a region have for that region, often including a desire to govern themselves. ❏ A grassroots regionalism appears to be emerging.

reg|is|ter ✦✦◇ /rɛdʒɪstər/ (registers, registering, registered) ◼1 N-COUNT A **register** is an official list or record of people or things. ❏ ...registers of births, deaths, and marriages. ◼2 V-T/V-I If you **register** to do something, you put your name on an official list, in order to be able to do that thing or to receive a service. ❏ Have you come to register at the school? ❏ Thousands lined up to register to vote. ◼3 V-T If you **register** something, such as the name of a person who has just died or information about something you own, you have these facts recorded on an official list. ❏ In order to register a car in Japan, the owner must have somewhere to park it. ◼4 V-T/V-I When something **registers** on a scale or measuring instrument, it shows on the scale or instrument. ❏ It will only register on sophisticated X-ray equipment. ❏ The earthquake registered 5.7 on the Richter scale. ◼5 V-T If you **register** your feelings or opinions about something, you do something that makes them clear to other people. ❏ Voters wish to register their dissatisfaction with the ruling party. ◼6 V-I If a feeling **registers** on someone's face, their expression shows clearly that they have that feeling. ❏ Surprise again registered on Rodney's face. ◼7 V-T/V-I If a piece of information does not **register** or if you do not **register** it, you do not really pay attention to it, and so you do not remember it or react to it. ❏ It wasn't that she couldn't hear me, it was just that what I said sometimes didn't register in her brain. ◼8 → see also **cash register**

─────── SYNONYMS ───────

register
NOUN ◼1
list: There were six names on the list.
roll: ...the electoral roll.
catalogue: ...the world's biggest seed catalogue.
VERB ◼2
enlist: He enlisted as a private in the Mexican War.
sign up: He signed up as a steward with P&O Lines.
enrol: She enrolled in a local Women Into Management course.

reg|is|tered /rɛdʒɪstərd/ ADJ [usu ADJ n] A **registered** letter or package is sent by a special postal service, for which you pay extra money for insurance in case it gets lost. ❏ He asked his mother to send it by registered mail.

reg|is|tered nurse (registered nurses) N-COUNT A **registered nurse** is someone who is qualified to work as a nurse. [AM, AUSTRALIAN]

reg|is|trar /rɛdʒɪstrɑːr/ (registrars) N-COUNT A **registrar** is an administrative official in a college or university who is responsible for student records.

reg|is|tra|tion /rɛdʒɪstreɪʃən/ N-UNCOUNT The **registration** of something such as a person's name or the details of an event is the recording of it in an official list. ❏ They have campaigned strongly for compulsory registration of dogs. ❏ With the high voter registration, many will be voting for the first time.

reg|is|tra|tion num|ber [BRIT] → see **license number**

reg|is|try /rɛdʒɪstri/ (registries) N-COUNT A **registry** is a collection of all the official records relating to something, or the place where they are kept. ❏ There is no international registry of stolen art.

re|gress /rɪgrɛs/ (regresses, regressing, regressed) V-I When people or things **regress**, they return to an earlier and less advanced stage of development. [FORMAL] ❏ If your child regresses to babyish behavior, all you know for certain is that the child is under stress. • **re|gres|sion** /rɪgrɛʃən/ (regressions) N-VAR ❏ Calderdale accepts that this can cause regression in a student's learning process.

re|gres|sive /rɪgrɛsɪv/ ADJ **Regressive** behavior, activities, or processes involve a return to an earlier and less advanced stage of development. [FORMAL] ❏ ...some of the symptoms of regressive behaviors: thumb sucking, bed wetting, having problems sleeping.

re|gret ✦◇◇ /rɪgrɛt/ (regrets, regretting, regretted) ◼1 V-T If you **regret** something that you have done, you wish that you had not done it. ❏ I simply gave in to him, and I've regretted it ever since. ❏ Ellis seemed to be regretting that he had asked the question. ◼2 N-VAR **Regret** is a feeling of sadness or disappointment, which is caused by something that has happened or something that you have done or not done. ❏ Larry said he had no regrets about retiring. ◼3 V-T You can say that you **regret** something as a polite way of saying that you are sorry about it. You use expressions such as **I regret to say** or **I regret to**

inform you to show that you are sorry about something. [POLITENESS] ☐ "I very much regret the injuries he sustained," he said. ☐ I regret that the United States has added its voice to such protests.

re|gret|ful /rɪgrɛtfəl/ ADJ [oft ADJ about n, ADJ that] If you are **regretful**, you show that you regret something. ☐ Mr. Griffin gave a regretful smile. ● **re|gret|ful|ly** ADV ☐ He shook his head regretfully.

re|gret|table /rɪgrɛtəbəl/ ADJ You describe something as **regrettable** when you think that it is bad and that it should not happen or have happened. [FORMAL, FEELINGS] ☐ The army said it had started an investigation into what it described as a regrettable incident. ● **re|gret|tably** ADV ☐ Regrettably we could find no sign of the men and the search was terminated.

re|group /riːgruːp/ (regroups, regrouping, regrouped) V-T/V-I When people, especially soldiers, **regroup**, or when someone **regroups** them, they form an organized group again, in order to continue fighting. ☐ Now the rebel army has regrouped and reorganized.

regu|lar ✦✦✧ /rɛgyələr/ (regulars) **1** ADJ **Regular** events have equal amounts of time between them, so that they happen, for example, at the same time each day or each week. ☐ Get regular exercise. ☐ We're going to be meeting there on a regular basis. ● **regu|lar|ly** ADV [ADV with v] ☐ He also writes regularly for "International Management" magazine. ● **regu|lar|ity** N-UNCOUNT ☐ The overdraft arrangements had been generous because of the regularity of the half-yearly payments. **2** ADJ **Regular** events happen often. ☐ Although it may look unpleasant, this condition is harmless and usually clears up with regular shampooing. ● **regu|lar|ly** ADV [ADV with v] ☐ Fox, badger, and weasel are regularly seen here. ● **regu|lar|ity** N-UNCOUNT ☐ Closures and job losses are again being announced with monotonous regularity. **3** ADJ [ADJ n] If you are, for example, a **regular** customer at a store or a **regular** visitor to a place, you go there often. ☐ She has become a regular visitor to Houghton Hall. **4** N-COUNT The **regulars** at a place or on a team are the people who often go to the place or are often on the team. ☐ Regulars at his local bar have set up a fund to help out. **5** ADJ [det ADJ n] You use **regular** when referring to the thing, person, time, or place that is usually used by someone. For example, someone's **regular** place is the place where they usually sit. ☐ The man shook his hand and then sat at his regular table near the windows. **6** ADJ A **regular** rhythm consists of a series of sounds or movements with equal periods of time between them. ☐ ...a very regular beat. ● **regu|lar|ly** ADV [ADV with v] ☐ Remember to breathe regularly. ● **regu|lar|ity** N-UNCOUNT ☐ Experimenters have succeeded in controlling the rate and regularity of the heartbeat. **7** ADJ [ADJ n] **Regular** is used to mean 'normal'. [mainly AM] ☐ The product looks and burns like a regular cigarette. **8** ADJ [ADJ n] In some restaurants, a **regular** drink or quantity of food is of medium size. [mainly AM] ☐ ...a cheeseburger and regular fries. **9** ADJ A **regular** pattern or arrangement consists of a series of things with equal spaces between them. ☐ The village was laid out in regular patterns. **10** ADJ If something has a **regular** shape, both halves are the same and it has straight edges or a smooth outline. ☐ ...some regular geometrical shape. ● **regu|lar|ity** N-UNCOUNT ☐ ...the chessboard regularity of their fields. **11** ADJ In grammar, a **regular** verb, noun, or adjective inflects in the same way as most verbs, nouns, or adjectives in the language.

regu|lar|ity /rɛgyəlærɪti/ (regularities) **1** N-COUNT A **regularity** is the fact that the same thing always happens in the same circumstances. [FORMAL] ☐ Children seek out regularities and rules in acquiring language. **2** → see also regular

regu|lar|ize /rɛgyələraɪz/ (regularizes, regularizing, regularized)

in BRIT, also use **regularise**

V-T If someone **regularizes** a situation or system, they make it officially acceptable or put it under a system of rules. [FORMAL] ☐ Cohabiting couples would regularize their unions, they said.

regu|late /rɛgyəleɪt/ (regulates, regulating, regulated) V-T To **regulate** an activity or process means to control it, especially by means of rules. ☐ Under such a plan, the government would regulate competition among insurance companies so that everyone gets care at lower cost.

regu|la|tion ✦✧✧ /rɛgyəleɪʃən/ (regulations) **1** N-COUNT **Regulations** are rules made by a government or other authority in order to control the way something is done or the way people behave. ☐ The European Union has proposed new regulations to control the hours worked by its employees. **2** N-UNCOUNT **Regulation** is the controlling of an activity or process, usually by means of rules. ☐ Some in the market now want government regulation in order to reduce costs.

───── **COLLOCATIONS** ─────

regulation
NOUN **1**
noun + **regulation**: banking, building, safety, workplace
adjective + **regulation**: financial, statutory; strict, stringent, tough
verb + **regulation**: enforce, impose, tighten; breach, contravene, violate; comply with, meet

regu|la|tor ✦✧✧ /rɛgyəleɪtər/ (regulators) N-COUNT A **regulator** is a person or organization appointed by a government to regulate an area of activity such as banking or industry. ☐ An independent regulator will be appointed to ensure fair competition. ● **regu|la|tory** /rɛgyələtɔri/ ADJ [ADJ n] ☐ ...the U.S.'s financial regulatory system.

re|gur|gi|tate /rɪgɜːrdʒɪteɪt/ (regurgitates, regurgitating, regurgitated) **1** V-T If you say that someone is **regurgitating** ideas or facts, you mean that they are repeating them without understanding them properly. [DISAPPROVAL] ☐ You can get sick to death of a friend regurgitating her partner's opinions. **2** V-T If a person or animal **regurgitates** food, they bring it back up from their stomach before it has been digested. [FORMAL] ☐ Sometimes he regurgitates the food we give him because he cannot swallow.

re|hab /riːhæb/ (rehabs, rehabbing, rehabbed) **1** N-UNCOUNT **Rehab** is the process of helping someone to lead a normal life again after they have been ill, or when they have had a drug or alcohol problem. **Rehab** is short for **rehabilitation**. [INFORMAL] ☐ ...a hospital rehab program. **2** V-T If you **rehab** an old building, you repair and improve it and get it back into good condition. [AM, INFORMAL] ☐ People are improving and rehabbing homes throughout the city.

re|ha|bili|tate /riːhəbɪlɪteɪt/ (rehabilitates, rehabilitating, rehabilitated) **1** V-T To **rehabilitate** someone who has been ill or in prison means to help them to live a normal life again. To **rehabilitate** someone who has a drug or alcohol problem means to help them stop using drugs or alcohol. ☐ Considerable efforts have been made to rehabilitate patients who have suffered in this way. ● **re|ha|bili|ta|tion** /riːhəbɪlɪteɪʃən/ N-UNCOUNT ☐ A number of other techniques are now being used by psychologists in the rehabilitation of young offenders. **2** → See feature box at **prison**

re|hash (rehashes, rehashing, rehashed)

The noun is pronounced /riːhæʃ/. The verb is pronounced /riːhæʃ/.

1 N-COUNT [usu sing, N of n] If you describe something as a **rehash**, you are criticizing it because it repeats old ideas, facts, or themes, though some things have been changed to make it appear new. [DISAPPROVAL] ☐ The critic found the play "a feeble rehash of familiar Miller themes." **2** V-T If you say that someone **rehashes** old ideas, facts, or accusations, you disapprove of the fact that they present them in a slightly different way so that they seem new or original. [DISAPPROVAL] ☐ They've taken some of the best parts out of the best things and rehashed them.

re|hears|al /rɪhɜːrsəl/ (rehearsals) **1** N-VAR A **rehearsal** of a play, dance, or piece of music is a practice of it in preparation for a performance. ☐ The band was scheduled to begin rehearsals for a concert tour. **2** → see also **dress rehearsal** **3** N-COUNT You can describe an event or object that is a preparation for a more important event or object as a **rehearsal for** it. ☐ Daydreams may seem to be rehearsals for real-life situations, but we know they are not. **4** → See feature box at **theater**

re|hearse /rɪhɜːrs/ (rehearses, rehearsing, rehearsed) **1** V-T/V-I When people **rehearse** a play, dance, or piece of music, they practice it in order to prepare for a performance. ☐ In his version, a group of actors are rehearsing a play about Joan of Arc. ☐ Tens of thousands of people have been rehearsing for the opening ceremony in the new stadium. **2** V-T If you **rehearse** something that you are going to say or do, you silently practice it by imagining that you are saying or doing it. ❑ *Anticipate any tough questions and rehearse your answers.*

re|house /riːhaʊz/ **(rehouses, rehousing, rehoused)** V-T If someone **is rehoused**, their local government or other authority provides them with a different house to live in. [BRIT]

reign /reɪn/ **(reigns, reigning, reigned)** **1** V-I If you say, for example, that silence **reigns** in a place or confusion **reigns** in a situation, you mean that the place is silent or the situation is confused. [WRITTEN] ❑ *Last night confusion reigned about how the debate, which continues today, would end.* **2** V-I When a king or queen **reigns**, he or she rules a country. ❑ *...Henry II, who reigned from 1154 to 1189.* • N-COUNT **Reign** is also a noun. ❑ *...Queen Victoria's reign.* **3** → See feature box at **history**

reign|ing /ˈreɪnɪŋ/ ADJ [ADJ n] The **reigning** champion is the most recent winner of a contest or competition at the time you are talking about. ❑ *...the reigning world champion.*

Reilly /ˈraɪli/ → see Riley

re|im|burse /riːɪmbɜːrs/ **(reimburses, reimbursing, reimbursed)** V-T If you **reimburse** someone for something, you pay them back the money that they have spent or lost because of it. [FORMAL] ❑ *I'll be happy to reimburse you for any expenses you've had.*

re|im|burse|ment /riːɪmbɜːrsmənt/ **(reimbursements)** N-VAR If you receive **reimbursement** for money that you have spent, you get your money back, for example because the money should have been paid by someone else. [FORMAL] ❑ *She is demanding reimbursement for medical and other expenses.*

rein /reɪn/ **(reins, reining, reined)** **1** N-PLURAL **Reins** are the thin leather straps attached around a horse's neck which are used to control the horse. ❑ *Cord held the reins while the stallion tugged and snorted.* **2** N-PLURAL Journalists sometimes use the expression **the reins** or **the reins of power** to refer to the control of a country or organization. ❑ *He was determined to see the party keep a hold on the reins of power.* **3** PHRASE If you **give free rein** to someone or something, you give them a lot of freedom to do what they want. ❑ *The government continued to believe it should give free rein to the private sector in transportation.* **4** PHRASE If you **keep a tight rein on** someone or something, you control them firmly. ❑ *The company has kept a tight rein on costs.* ❑ *Her parents kept her on a tight rein with their narrow and inflexible views.*

▸ **rein back** PHRASAL VERB To **rein back** something such as spending means to control it strictly. ❑ *He promised that between now and the end of the year the government would try to rein back inflation.*

▸ **rein in** PHRASAL VERB To **rein in** something means to control it. ❑ *Many people have begun looking for long-term ways to rein in spending.*

re|incar|nate /riːɪnkɑːrneɪt/ **(reincarnates, reincarnating, reincarnated)** V-T [usu passive] If people believe that they will **be reincarnated** when they die, they believe that their spirit will be born again and will live in the body of another person or animal. ❑ *...their belief that human souls were reincarnated in the bodies of turtles.*

re|incar|na|tion /riːɪnkɑːrneɪʃən/ **(reincarnations)** **1** N-UNCOUNT If you believe in reincarnation, you believe that you will be reincarnated after you die. ❑ *Many different kinds of people believe in reincarnation.* **2** N-COUNT A **reincarnation** is a person or animal whose body is believed to contain the spirit of a dead person. ❑ *Another little girl, believed to be the reincarnation of her grandmother, was obsessed with sewing.*

rein|deer /ˈreɪndɪər/ **(reindeer)**

Reindeer is both the singular and the plural form.

N-COUNT A **reindeer** is a deer with large horns called antlers that lives in northern areas of Europe, Asia, and America ❑ *...a herd of reindeer.*

re|inforce /riːɪnfɔːrs/ **(reinforces, reinforcing, reinforced)** **1** V-T If something **reinforces** a feeling, situation, or process, it makes it stronger or more intense. ❑ *I hope this will reinforce Indonesian determination to deal with this kind of threat.* **2** V-T If something **reinforces** an idea or point of view, it provides more evidence or support for it. ❑ *The delegation hopes to reinforce the idea that human rights are not purely internal matters.* **3** V-T To **reinforce** an object means to make it stronger or harder. ❑ *Eventually, they had to reinforce the walls with exterior beams.* **4** V-T To **reinforce** an army or a police force means to make it stronger by increasing its size or providing it with more weapons. To **reinforce** a position or place means to make it stronger by sending more soldiers or weapons. ❑ *Both sides have been reinforcing their positions after yesterday's fierce fighting.*

re|inforced con|crete N-UNCOUNT **Reinforced concrete** is concrete that is made with pieces of metal inside it to make it stronger.

re|inforce|ment /riːɪnfɔːrsmənt/ **(reinforcements)** **1** N-PLURAL **Reinforcements** are soldiers or police officers who are sent to join an army or group of police in order to make it stronger. ❑ *Mr. Vlok promised new measures to protect residents, including the dispatch of police and troop reinforcements.* **2** N-VAR The **reinforcement** of something is the process of making it stronger. ❑ *I am sure that this meeting will contribute to the reinforcement of peace and security all over the world.*

re|install /riːɪnstɔːl/ **(reinstalls, reinstalling, reinstalled)** V-T If you **reinstall** something such as software on your computer, you set it up again, usually because you have been having problems with it. ❑ *It will be best to wipe the system and reinstall everything.*

re|instate /riːɪnsteɪt/ **(reinstates, reinstating, reinstated)** **1** V-T If you **reinstate** someone, you give them back a job or position that had been taken away from them. ❑ *The governor is said to have agreed to reinstate five senior workers who were dismissed.* **2** V-T To **reinstate** a law, facility, or practice means to start having it again. ❑ *She says the public response was a factor in the decision to reinstate the grant.*

re|instate|ment /riːɪnsteɪtmənt/ **1** N-UNCOUNT **Reinstatement** is the act of giving someone back a job or position that has been taken away from them. ❑ *Parents campaigned in vain for her reinstatement.* **2** N-UNCOUNT The **reinstatement** of a law, facility, or practice is the act of causing it to exist again. ❑ *He welcomed the reinstatement of the 10 percent bank base rate.*

re|invent /riːɪnvɛnt/ **(reinvents, reinventing, reinvented)** **1** V-T To **reinvent** something means to change it so that it seems different and new. ❑ *They have tried to reinvent their retail stores.* ❑ *He was determined to reinvent himself as a poet and writer.* • **re|inven|tion** /riːɪnvɛnʃən/ N-UNCOUNT ❑ *...a reinvention of the styles of the 1940s.* **2** PHRASE If someone is trying to **reinvent the wheel**, they are trying to do something that has already been done successfully. ❑ *Some of these ideas are worth pursuing, but there is no need to reinvent the wheel.*

re|is|sue /riːɪʃuː/ **(reissues, reissuing, reissued)** **1** N-COUNT A **reissue** is a book, CD, or movie that has not been available for some time but is now published or produced again. ❑ *...this welcome reissue of a 1955 Ingmar Bergman classic.* **2** V-T [usu passive] If something such as a book, CD, or movie **is reissued** after it has not been available for some time, it is published or produced again. ❑ *Her novels have just been reissued with eye-catching new covers.*

re|it|er|ate /riːɪtəreɪt/ **(reiterates, reiterating, reiterated)** V-T If you **reiterate** something, you say it again, usually in order to emphasize it. [FORMAL, JOURNALISM] ❑ *He reiterated his opposition to the creation of a central bank.*

re|ject ✦✦◇ **(rejects, rejecting, rejected)**

The verb is pronounced /rɪdʒɛkt/. The noun is pronounced /riːdʒɛkt/.

1 V-T If you **reject** something such as a proposal, a request, or an offer, you do not accept it or you do not agree to it. ❑ *The government is expected to reject the idea of state subsidy for a new high-speed railroad.* • **re|jec|tion** /rɪdʒɛkʃən/ **(rejections)** N-VAR ❑ *The rejection of such initiatives by no means indicates that voters are unconcerned about the environment.* **2** V-T If you **reject** a belief or a political system, you refuse to believe in it or to live by its rules. ❑ *...the children of Eastern European immigrants who had rejected their parents' political and religious beliefs.* • **re|jec|tion** N-VAR ❑ *His rejection of our values is far more complete than that of D. H. Lawrence.* **3** V-T If someone **is rejected** for a job or course of

rejig

study, it is not offered to them. ▫ *One of my most able students was rejected by another university.* • **re|jec|tion** N-COUNT ▫ *Be prepared for lots of rejections before you land a job.* **4** V-T If someone **rejects** another person who expects affection from them, they are cold and unfriendly toward them. ▫ *...people who had been rejected by their lovers.* • **re|jec|tion** N-VAR ▫ *These feelings of rejection and hurt remain.* **5** V-T If a person's body **rejects** something such as a new heart that has been transplanted into it, it tries to attack and destroy it. ▫ *It was feared his body was rejecting a kidney he received in a transplant four years ago.* • **re|jec|tion** N-VAR ▫ *...a special drug which stops rejection of transplanted organs.* **6** N-COUNT A **reject** is a product that has not been accepted for use or sale, because there is something wrong with it. ▫ *The check shirt is a reject - too small.*

re|jig /rɪdʒɪg/ → see rejigger

re|jig|ger /rɪdʒɪgər/ (**rejiggers, rejiggering, rejiggered**) V-T If someone **rejiggers** an organization or a piece of work, they arrange or organize it in a different way, in order to improve it. [AM] ▫ *The government is rejiggering some tax assessment methods.*

in BRIT, use **rejig**

re|joice /rɪdʒɔɪs/ (**rejoices, rejoicing, rejoiced**) V-T/V-I If you **rejoice**, you are very pleased about something and you show it in your behavior. ▫ *Garbo plays the queen, rejoicing in the love she has found with Antonio.* ▫ *Party activists in New Hampshire rejoiced that the presidential campaign had finally started.* • **re|joic|ing** N-UNCOUNT ▫ *There was general rejoicing at the news.*

re|join /rɪdʒɔɪn/ (**rejoins, rejoining, rejoined**) **1** V-T If you **rejoin** a group, club, or organization, you become a member of it again after not being a member for a period of time. ▫ *The prime minister of Fiji has said Fiji is in no hurry to rejoin the Commonwealth.* **2** V-T If you **rejoin** someone, you go back to them after a short time away from them. ▫ *Mimi and her family went off to Tunisia to rejoin her father.* **3** V-T If you **rejoin** a route, you go back to it after traveling along a different route for a time. ▫ *At Bridge Street go left to rejoin the river.*

re|join|der /rɪdʒɔɪndər/ (**rejoinders**) N-COUNT A **rejoinder** is a reply, especially a quick, witty, or critical one, to a question or remark. [FORMAL]

re|ju|venate /rɪdʒuːvəneɪt/ (**rejuvenates, rejuvenating, rejuvenated**) **1** V-T If something **rejuvenates** you, it makes you feel or look young again. ▫ *Shelley was advised that the Italian climate would rejuvenate him.* **2** V-T If you **rejuvenate** an organization or system, you make it more lively and more efficient, for example by introducing new ideas. ▫ *The government pushed through plans to rejuvenate the inner cities.*

re|kin|dle /riːkɪndəl/ (**rekindles, rekindling, rekindled**) **1** V-T If something **rekindles** an interest, feeling, or thought that you used to have, it makes you think about it or feel it again. ▫ *Ben Brantley's article on Sir Ian McKellen rekindled many memories.* **2** V-T If something **rekindles** an unpleasant situation, it makes the unpleasant situation happen again. ▫ *There are fears that the series could rekindle animosity between the two countries.*

re|lapse /rɪlæps/ (**relapses, relapsing, relapsed**)

The noun can be pronounced /rɪlæps/ or /riːlæps/.

1 V-I If you say that someone **relapses into** a way of behaving that is undesirable, you mean that they start to behave in that way again. ▫ *"I wish I did," said Phil Jordan, relapsing into his usual gloom.* • N-COUNT **Relapse** is also a noun. ▫ *...a relapse into the nationalism of the nineteenth century.* **2** V-I If a sick person **relapses**, their health suddenly gets worse after it had been improving. ▫ *In 90 percent of cases the patient will relapse within six months.* • N-VAR **Relapse** is also a noun. ▫ *The treatment is usually given to women with a high risk of relapse after surgery.*

re|lat|able /rɪleɪtəbəl/ ADJ GRADED; ADJ If someone or something is **relatable**, you feel an emotional connection with them. ▫ *The characters are well drawn and relatable.* ▫ *Her story is relatable to anyone who has ever felt out of place and far from home.*

re|late /rɪleɪt/ (**relates, relating, related**) **1** V-I If something **relates to** a particular subject, it concerns that subject. ▫ *Other recommendations relate to the details of how such data is stored.* **2** V-RECIP The way that two things **relate**, or the way that one thing **relates** to another, is the sort of connection that exists between them. ▫ *I don't think he understood the dynamics of how the police and the city administration relate.* ▫ *Trainees should be invited to relate new ideas to their past experiences.* **3** V-RECIP If you can **relate** to someone, you can understand how they feel or behave so that you are able to communicate with them or deal with them easily. ▫ *He is unable to relate to other people.*

SYNONYMS

relate
VERB **1**
concern: *The bulk of the book concerns Sandy's two middle-aged children.*
refer to: *The term electronics refers to electrically-induced action.*
pertain to: *I would much rather that you asked Mrs Zuckerman any questions pertaining to herself.*

---

re|lat|ed /rɪleɪtɪd/ **1** ADJ If two or more things are **related**, there is a connection between them. ▫ *The philosophical problems of chance and of free will are closely related.* **2** ADJ [v-link ADJ] People who are **related** belong to the same family. ▫ *The children, although not related to us by blood, had become as dear to us as our own.* **3** ADJ If you say that different types of things, such as languages, are **related**, you mean that they developed from the same language. ▫ *He recognized that Sanskrit, the language of India, was related very closely to Latin, Greek, and the Germanic and Celtic languages.*

SYNONYMS

related
ADJ **1**
associated: *Listening is a skill associated with good management.*
linked: *Liver cancer is linked to the Hepatitis B virus.*
connected: *They are not connected with our company.*

-related /-rɪleɪtɪd/ COMB IN ADJ **-related** combines with nouns to form adjectives with the meaning 'connected with the thing referred to by the noun.' ▫ *More than 50 arrests were made, mostly for drug-related offenses.*

re|la|tion /rɪleɪʃən/ (**relations**) **1** N-COUNT **Relations** between people, groups, or countries are contacts between them and the way in which they behave toward each other. ▫ *Greece has established full diplomatic relations with Israel.* **2** → see also **industrial relations, public relations, race relations** **3** N-COUNT If you talk about the **relation** of one thing to another, you are talking about the ways in which they are connected. ▫ *It is a question of the relation of ethics to economics.* **4** N-COUNT Your **relations** are the members of your family. ▫ *...visits to friends and relations.* **5** PHRASE You can talk about something **in relation to** something else when you want to compare the size, condition, or position of the two things. ▫ *The money he'd been ordered to pay was minimal in relation to his salary.* **6** PHRASE If something is said or done **in relation to** a subject, it is said or done in connection with that subject. ▫ *...a question that has been asked many times in relation to Irish affairs.*

SYNONYMS

relation
NOUN
3
link: *...the link between smoking and lung cancer.*
similarity: *She is also 25 and a native of Birmingham, but the similarity ends there.*
connection: *He has denied any connection to the bombing.*
4
relative: *Get a relative to look after the children.*
family: *Her family came to Los Angeles at the turn of the century.*

---

re|la|tion|ship /rɪleɪʃənʃɪp/ (**relationships**) **1** N-COUNT The **relationship** between two people or groups is the way in which they feel and behave toward each other. ▫ *...the friendly relationship between France and Britain.* **2** N-COUNT A **relationship** is a close connection between two people, especially one involving romantic or sexual feelings. ▫ *We had been together for two years, but both of us felt the relationship wasn't really going anywhere.* **3** N-COUNT The **relationship** between two things is the way in which they are connected. ▫ *A number of small-scale studies have already indicated that there is a relationship between diet and cancer.* **4** → See feature box on next page

SYNONYMS

relationship
NOUN
2
affair: *She was having an affair with someone at work.*
romance: *...a summer romance.*
fling: *She claims she had a brief fling with him 30 years ago.*
liaison: *She embarked on a series of liaisons with society figures.*
3
connection: *The police say he had no connection with the security forces.*
bond: *The experience created a very special bond between us.*
association: *The association between the two companies stretches back thirty years.*

VOCABULARY IN CONTEXT

Relationships

The nature of our relationships and the priority we place on them change over our lifetimes. In early childhood, we have a **wide circle** of friends, based mostly on who lives nearby and is fun to play with. As teenagers, we might have an **inner circle** of best friends, but an enormous list of 'friends' on social media. **Arguing with** a friend at this age can be devastating, though it's likely to be only temporary. But once friends start **drifting apart** because of work or study, we often replace them with more **intimate** and **romantic** relationships. Typically, at the beginning of the relationship, a couple will be **inseparable**, though they still find time for their friends. But often, if a couple begin **cohabiting** or start a family, even the most **close-knit** friendships can be reduced to occasional catch-ups over coffee.

rela|tive ✦◇◇ /rɛlətɪv/ (**relatives**) **1** N-COUNT Your **relatives** are the members of your family. ❑ *Get a relative to look after the children.* **2** ADJ [ADJ n] You use **relative** to say that something is true to a certain degree, especially when compared with other things of the same kind. ❑ *The fighting resumed after a period of relative calm.* **3** ADJ [ADJ n] You use **relative** when you are comparing the quality or size of two things. ❑ *They chatted about the relative merits of London and Paris as places to live.* **4** PHRASE **Relative to** something means with reference to it or in comparison with it. ❑ *Japanese interest rates rose relative to America's.* **5** ADJ If you say that something is **relative**, you mean that it needs to be considered and judged in relation to other things. ❑ *Fitness is relative; one must always ask "Fit for what?"* **6** N-COUNT If one animal, plant, language, or invention is a **relative** of another, they have both developed from the same type of animal, plant, language, or invention. ❑ *The pheasant is a close relative of the guinea hen.*

SYNONYMS

relative
NOUN **1**
relation: *...visits to friends and relations.*
kin: *She has gone to live with her husband's kin.*
family: *Her family came to Los Angeles at the turn of the century.*

rela|tive clause (**relative clauses**) N-COUNT In grammar, a **relative clause** is a subordinate clause which specifies or gives information about a person or thing. Relative clauses come after a noun or pronoun and, in English, often begin with a relative pronoun such as 'who,' 'which,' or 'that.'

rela|tive|ly ✦◇◇ /rɛlətɪvli/ ADV [ADV adj/adv] **Relatively** means to a certain degree, especially when compared with other things of the same kind. ❑ *The sums needed are relatively small.*

SYNONYMS

relatively
ADV
comparatively: *...a comparatively small nation.*
rather: *I grew up in rather unusual circumstances.*
somewhat: *He concluded that Oswald was somewhat abnormal.*

rela|tive pro|noun (**relative pronouns**) N-COUNT A **relative pronoun** is a word such as 'who,' 'that,' or 'which' that is used to introduce a relative clause. 'Whose,' 'when,' 'where,' and 'why' are generally called **relative pronouns**, though they are actually adverbs.

rela|tiv|ism /rɛlətɪvɪzəm/ N-UNCOUNT **Relativism** is the belief that the truth is not always the same but varies according to circumstances. ❑ *Traditionalists may howl, but in today's world, cultural relativism rules.*

rela|tiv|ist /rɛlətɪvɪst/ ADJ A **relativist** position or argument is one according to which the truth is not always the same, but varies according to circumstances.

rela|tiv|ity /rɛlətɪvɪti/ N-UNCOUNT The theory of **relativity** is Einstein's theory concerning space, time, and motion. [TECHNICAL]

re|launch /riːlɔːntʃ/ (**relaunches, relaunching, relaunched**) V-T To **relaunch** something such as a company, a product, or a program means to start it again or to produce it in a different way. ❑ *He is hoping to relaunch his film career with a remake of the 1971 British thriller.* • N-COUNT /riːlɔːntʃ/ **Relaunch** is also a noun. ❑ *Relaunches are often simply a way of boosting sales.*

re|lax ✦◇◇ /rɪlæks/ (**relaxes, relaxing, relaxed**) **1** V-T/V-I If you **relax** or if something **relaxes** you, you feel more calm and less worried or tense. ❑ *I ought to relax and stop worrying about it.* **2** V-T/V-I When a part of your body **relaxes**, or when you **relax** it, it becomes less stiff or firm. ❑ *Massage is used to relax muscles, relieve stress and improve the circulation.* **3** V-T If you **relax** your grip or hold on something, you hold it less tightly than before. ❑ *He gradually relaxed his grip on the arms of the chair.* **4** V-T/V-I If you **relax** a rule or your control over something, or if it **relaxes**, it becomes less firm or strong. ❑ *Rules governing student conduct have relaxed somewhat in recent years.* **5** → see also **relaxed**, **relaxing** **6** → See feature box at **commute**

re|laxa|tion /riːlækseɪʃən/ **1** N-UNCOUNT **Relaxation** is a way of spending time in which you rest and feel comfortable. ❑ *You should be able to find the odd moment for relaxation.* **2** N-UNCOUNT If there is **relaxation** of a rule or control, it is made less firm or strong. ❑ *The relaxation of travel restrictions means they are free to travel and work.*

re|laxed /rɪlækst/ **1** ADJ If you are **relaxed**, you are calm and not worried or tense. ❑ *As soon as I had made the final decision, I felt a lot more relaxed.* **2** ADJ If a place or situation is **relaxed**, it is calm and peaceful. ❑ *The atmosphere at lunch was relaxed.*

re|lax|ing /rɪlæksɪŋ/ ADJ Something that is **relaxing** is pleasant and helps you to relax. ❑ *I find cooking very relaxing.*

re|lay (**relays, relaying, relayed**)

The noun is pronounced /riːleɪ/. The verb is pronounced /rɪleɪ/.

1 N-COUNT A **relay** or a **relay race** is a race between two or more teams, for example teams of runners or swimmers. Each member of the team runs or swims one section of the race. ❑ *Britain's prospects of beating the United States in the relay looked poor.* **2** V-T To **relay** television or radio signals means to send them or broadcast them. ❑ *The satellite will be used mainly to relay television programs.* **3** V-T If you **relay** something that has been said to you, you repeat it to another person. [FORMAL] ❑ *She relayed the message, then frowned.*

re|lease ✦✦✦ /rɪliːs/ (**releases, releasing, released**) **1** V-T [usu passive] If a person or animal **is released** from somewhere

where they have been locked up or cared for, they are set free or allowed to go. ❑ *He was released from custody the next day.* **2** N-COUNT [with supp] When someone is released, you refer to their **release**. ❑ *He called for the immediate release of all political prisoners.* **3** V-T If someone or something **releases** you from a duty, task, or feeling, they free you from it. [FORMAL] ❑ *Divorce releases both the husband and wife from all marital obligations to each other.* • N-UNCOUNT [also a N, oft N *from* n] **Release** is also a noun. ❑ *Our therapeutic style offers release from stored tensions, traumas, and grief.* **4** V-T To **release** feelings or abilities means to allow them to be expressed. ❑ *Becoming your own person releases your creativity.* • N-UNCOUNT **Release** is also a noun. ❑ *She felt the sudden sweet release of her own tears.* **5** V-T If someone in authority **releases** something such as a document or information, they make it available. ❑ *They're not releasing any more details yet.* • N-COUNT **Release** is also a noun. ❑ *Action had been taken to speed up the release of checks.* **6** V-T If you **release** someone or something, you stop holding them. [FORMAL] ❑ *He stopped and faced her, releasing her wrist.* **7** V-T If something **releases** gas, heat, or a substance, it causes it to leave its container or the substance that it was part of and enter the surrounding atmosphere or area. ❑ *...a weapon that releases toxic nerve gas.* • N-COUNT **Release** is also a noun. ❑ *Under the agreement, releases of cancer-causing chemicals will be cut by about 80 percent.* **8** V-T When an entertainer or company **releases** a new CD, DVD, or movie, it becomes available so that people can buy it or see it. ❑ *He is releasing an album of love songs.* **9** N-COUNT A new **release** is a new CD, DVD, or movie that has just become available for people to buy or see. ❑ *Of the new releases that are out there now, which do you think are really good?* **10** → see also **press release** **11** → See feature box at **prison**

─── SYNONYMS ───
release
VERB **1**
free: *They are set to free more prisoners.*
set free: *Most of the prisoners were set free.*
let out: *I'd better go and let the dog out.*
liberate: *The government is devising a plan to liberate prisoners held in detention camps.*

rel|egate /rɛlɪgeɪt/ (**relegates, relegating, relegated**) V-T If you **relegate** someone or something to a less important position, you give them this position. ❑ *Might it not be better to relegate the king to a purely ceremonial function?*

re|lent /rɪlɛnt/ (**relents, relenting, relented**) V-I If you **relent**, you allow someone to do something that you had previously refused to allow them to do. ❑ *Finally his mother relented and gave permission for her youngest son to marry.*

re|lent|less /rɪlɛntlɪs/ **1** ADJ Something bad that is **relentless** never stops or never becomes less intense. ❑ *The pressure now was relentless.* • **re|lent|less|ly** ADV ❑ *The sun is beating down relentlessly.* **2** ADJ Someone who is **relentless** is determined to do something and refuses to give up, even if what they are doing is unpleasant or cruel. ❑ *Relentless in his pursuit of quality, his technical ability was remarkable.* • **re|lent|less|ly** ADV ❑ *She always questioned me relentlessly.*

rel|evance /rɛləvəns/ N-UNCOUNT Something's **relevance** to a situation or person is its importance or significance in that situation or to that person. ❑ *Politicians' private lives have no relevance to their public roles.*

rel|evant /rɛləvənt/ ADJ Something that is **relevant** to a situation or person is important or significant in that situation or to that person. ❑ *Is conventional politics still relevant to people's lives?*

re|li|able ♦◇◇ /rɪlaɪəbəl/ **1** ADJ People or things that are **reliable** can be trusted to work well or to behave in the way that you want them to. ❑ *She was efficient and reliable.* • **re|li|ably** /rɪlaɪəbli/ ADV ❑ *It's been working reliably for years.* • **re|li|abil|ity** /rɪlaɪəbɪlɪti/ N-UNCOUNT ❑ *He's not at all worried about his car's reliability.* **2** ADJ Information that is **reliable** or that is from a **reliable** source is very likely to be correct. ❑ *There is no reliable information about civilian casualties.* • **re|li|ably** ADV ❑ *Sonia, we are reliably informed, loves her family very much.* • **re|li|abil|ity** N-UNCOUNT ❑ *Both questioned the reliability of recent opinion polls.*

─── SYNONYMS ───
reliable
ADJ **1**
trustworthy: *He is a trustworthy and level-headed leader.*
dependable: *He was a good friend, a dependable companion.*
staunch: *He's a staunch supporter of controls on government spending.*

re|li|ance /rɪlaɪəns/ N-UNCOUNT A person's or thing's **reliance** on something is the fact that they need it and often cannot live or work without it. ❑ *...the country's increasing reliance on foreign aid.*

re|li|ant /rɪlaɪənt/ ADJ [v-link ADJ *on/upon* n] A person or thing that is **reliant** on something needs it and often cannot live or work without it. ❑ *These people are not wholly reliant on Western charity.*

rel|ic /rɛlɪk/ (**relics**) **1** N-COUNT If you refer to something or someone as a **relic** of an earlier period, you mean that they belonged to that period but have survived into the present. ❑ *This legislation is a relic of an era in European history that has passed.* **2** N-COUNT A **relic** is something which was made or used a long time ago and which is kept for its historical significance. ❑ *...a museum of war relics.*

re|lief ♦♦◇ /rɪli:f/ (**reliefs**) **1** N-UNCOUNT [also a N] If you feel a sense of **relief**, you feel happy because something unpleasant has not happened or is no longer happening. ❑ *I breathed a sigh of relief.* **2** N-UNCOUNT If something provides **relief** from pain or distress, it stops the pain or distress. ❑ *...a self-help program which can give lasting relief from the torment of hay fever.* **3** N-UNCOUNT **Relief** is money, food, or clothing that is provided for people who are very poor, or who have been affected by war or a natural disaster. ❑ *Relief agencies are stepping up efforts to provide food, shelter, and agricultural equipment.* **4** N-COUNT A **relief** worker is someone who does your work when you go home, or who is employed to do it instead of you when you are sick. ❑ *No relief drivers were available.* **5** → See feature box at **hot**

─── COLLOCATIONS ───
relief
NOUN
1
adjective + **relief**: blessed, great, huge, welcome; palpable
relief + be + adjective: short-lived
verb + **relief**: bring, offer, provide; express, feel; seek
3
noun + **relief**: disaster, emergency, famine, flood
adjective + **relief**: humanitarian
verb + **relief**: provide

re|lief map (**relief maps**) N-COUNT [usu N *of* n] A **relief map** is a map that shows the height of the land, usually by means of contours. ❑ *...a relief map of the Himalayas.*

re|lieve /rɪli:v/ (**relieves, relieving, relieved**) **1** V-T If something **relieves** an unpleasant feeling or situation, it makes it less unpleasant or causes it to disappear completely. ❑ *Drugs can relieve much of the pain.* **2** V-T If someone or something **relieves** you of an unpleasant feeling or difficult task, they take it from you. ❑ *A part-time bookkeeper will relieve you of the burden of chasing unpaid invoices.* **3** V-T If you **relieve** someone, you take their place and continue to do the job or duty that they have been doing. ❑ *At seven o'clock the night nurse came in to relieve her.* **4** V-T [usu passive] If someone **is relieved** of their duties or **is relieved** of their post, they are told that they are no longer required to continue in their job. [FORMAL] ❑ *The officer involved was relieved of his duties because he had violated strict guidelines.*

re|lieved /rɪli:vd/ ADJ If you are **relieved**, you feel happy because something unpleasant has not happened or is no longer happening. ❑ *We are all relieved to be back home.*

re|li|gion ♦♦◇ /rɪlɪdʒən/ (**religions**) **1** N-UNCOUNT **Religion** is belief in a god or gods and the activities that are connected with this belief, such as praying or worshiping in a building such as a church or temple. ❑ *...his understanding of Indian philosophy and religion.* **2** N-COUNT A **religion** is a particular system of belief in a god or gods and the activities that are connected with this system. ❑ *...the Christian religion.*

SYNONYMS

religion
NOUN **1**
belief: He refuses to compete on Sundays because of his religious beliefs.
faith: England shifted officially from a Catholic to a Protestant faith in the 16th century.
creed: The center is open to all, no matter what race or creed.

re|ligi|os|ity /rɪlɪdʒɪɒsɪti/ N-UNCOUNT [usu with supp] If you refer to a person's **religiosity**, you are referring to the fact that they are religious in a way that seems exaggerated and insincere. [FORMAL] ☐ ...their hypocritical religiosity.

re|li|gious ♦♦♢ /rɪlɪdʒəs/ **1** ADJ [ADJ n] You use **religious** to describe things that are connected with religion or with one particular religion. ☐ Religious groups are now able to meet quite openly. **2** ADJ Someone who is **religious** has a strong belief in a god or gods. ☐ They are both very religious and felt it was a gift from God.

re|li|gious|ly /rɪlɪdʒəsli/ **1** ADV [ADV with v] If you do something **religiously**, you do it very regularly because you feel you have to. ☐ Do these exercises religiously every day. **2** → see also **religious**

re|lin|quish /rɪlɪŋkwɪʃ/ (relinquishes, relinquishing, relinquished) V-T If you **relinquish** something such as power or control, you give it up. [FORMAL] ☐ He does not intend to relinquish power.

reli|quary /rɛlɪkwɛri/ (reliquaries) N-COUNT A **reliquary** is a container where religious objects connected with a saint are kept.

rel|ish /rɛlɪʃ/ (relishes, relishing, relished) V-T If you **relish** something, you get a lot of enjoyment from it. ☐ I relish the challenge of doing jobs that others turn down. • N-UNCOUNT Relish is also a noun. ☐ The three men ate with relish.

re|live /riːlɪv/ (relives, reliving, relived) V-T If you **relive** something that has happened to you in the past, you remember it and imagine that you are experiencing it again. ☐ There is no point in reliving the past.

re|load /riːloʊd/ (reloads, reloading, reloaded) V-T/V-I If someone **reloads** a gun, they load it again by putting in more bullets or explosive. If you **reload** a container, you fill it again. ☐ She reloaded the gun as quickly as she could. ☐ He reloaded and nodded to the gamekeeper.

re|lo|cate /riːloʊkeɪt/ (relocates, relocating, relocated) V-T/V-I If people or businesses **relocate** or if someone **relocates** them, they move to a different place. ☐ If the company was to relocate, most employees would move. • **re|lo|ca|tion** /riːloʊkeɪʃən/ (relocations) N-UNCOUNT ☐ The company says the cost of relocation will be negligible.

re|lo|ca|tion ex|penses N-PLURAL **Relocation expenses** are a sum of money that a company pays to someone who moves to a new area in order to work for the company. The money is to help them pay for moving their belongings. [BUSINESS] ☐ Relocation expenses were paid to encourage senior staff to move to the region.

re|luc|tant ♦♢♢ /rɪlʌktənt/ ADJ If you are **reluctant** to do something, you are unwilling to do it and hesitate before doing it, or do it slowly and without enthusiasm. ☐ Mr. Spero was reluctant to ask for help • **re|luc|tant|ly** ADV [ADV with v] ☐ We have reluctantly agreed to let him go. • **re|luc|tance** N-UNCOUNT ☐ Committee members have shown extreme reluctance to explain their position to the media.

SYNONYMS

reluctant
ADJ
unwilling: Initially, the government was unwilling to accept the defeat.
grudging: He even earned his opponents' grudging respect.
hesitant: She was hesitant about coming forward with her story.

rely ♦♢♢ /rɪlaɪ/ (relies, relying, relied) **1** V-I If you **rely** on someone or something, you need them and depend on them in order to live or work properly. ☐ They relied heavily on the advice of their professional advisers. **2** V-I If you can **rely** on someone to work well or to behave as you want them to, you can trust them to do this. ☐ I know I can rely on you to sort it out. **3** → See feature box at **electricity**

REM /rɛm/ ADJ [ADJ n] **REM** sleep is a period of sleep that is very deep, during which your eyes and muscles make many small movements. It is the period during which most of your dreams occur. **REM** is an abbreviation for 'rapid eye movement.'

re|main ♦♦♦ /rɪmeɪn/ (remains, remaining, remained) **1** V-LINK If someone or something **remains** in a particular state or condition, they stay in that state or condition and do not change. ☐ The three men remained silent. ☐ The government remained in control. **2** V-I If you **remain** in a place, you stay there and do not move away. ☐ They have asked the residents to remain in their homes. **3** V-I You can say that something **remains** when it still exists. ☐ The wider problem remains. **4** V-LINK If something **remains** to be done, it has not yet been done and still needs to be done. ☐ Major questions remain to be answered about his work. **5** N-PLURAL The **remains** of something are the parts of it that are left after most of it has been taken away or destroyed. ☐ They were cleaning up the remains of their picnic. **6** N-PLURAL The **remains** of a person or animal are the parts of their body that are left after they have died, sometimes after they have been dead for a long time. ☐ The unrecognizable remains of a man had been found. **7** → see also **remaining**

SYNONYMS

remain
VERB
1
continue: He insisted that the conflict would continue.
endure: Somehow, the language endures and continues to survive.
persist: Contact your doctor if the cough persists.
go on: The population failed to understand the necessity for the war to go on.
2
stay: 'Stay here,' Trish said.
stay put: Nigel says for the moment he is very happy to stay put in Lyon.
wait: Angus got out of the car to wait.

re|main|der /rɪmeɪndər/ QUANT [QUANT of def-n] The **remainder** of a group are the things or people that still remain after the other things or people have gone or have been dealt with. ☐ He gulped down the remainder of his coffee. • PRON **Remainder** is also a pronoun. ☐ Only 5.9 percent of the area is now covered in trees. Most of the remainder is farmland.

re|main|ing ♦♢♢ /rɪmeɪnɪŋ/ **1** ADJ [ADJ n] The **remaining** things or people out of a group are the things or people that still exist, are still present, or have not yet been dealt with. ☐ The three parties will meet next month to work out remaining differences. **2** → see also **remain**

re|make (remakes, remaking, remade)

The noun is pronounced /riːmeɪk/. The verb is pronounced /riːmeɪk/.

1 N-COUNT A **remake** is a movie that has the same story, and often the same title, as a movie that was made earlier. ☐ ...a 1953 remake of the thirties musical "Roberta." **2** V-T [usu passive] If a movie **is remade**, a new movie is made that has the same story, and often the same title, as a movie that was made earlier. ☐ Originally released in 1957, the film was remade as "The Magnificent Seven." **3** V-T If you have something **remade**, you ask someone to make it again, especially in a way that is better than before. ☐ He had all the window frames in the room remade.

re|mand /rɪmænd/ (remands, remanding, remanded) **1** V-T [usu passive] If a person who is accused of a crime **is remanded** in custody, they are kept in prison until their trial begins. If a person **is remanded** on bail, they are told to return to the court at a later date, when their trial will take place. ☐ Carter was remanded in custody for seven days. **2** N-UNCOUNT **Remand** is used to refer to the process of remanding someone in custody or on bail, or to the period of time until their trial begins. ☐ The remand hearing is often over in three minutes.

re|mark ♦♦♢ /rɪmɑrk/ (remarks, remarking, remarked) **1** V-T/V-I If you **remark** that something is the case, you say that it is the case. ☐ I remarked that I would go shopping that afternoon. ☐ On several occasions she had remarked on the boy's

remarkable improvement. **2** N-COUNT If you make a **remark** about something, you say something about it. ❑ *She has made outspoken remarks about the legalization of marijuana.*

SYNONYMS

remark
NOUN **2**
comment: *She made her comments at a news conference in Amsterdam.*
observation: *'Is that a criticism,' I said, 'or just an observation?'*
statement: *'Things are moving ahead.'– I found that statement vague and unclear.*

---

re|mark|able ✦◇◇ /rɪmɑ̱rkəbəl/ ADJ Someone or something that is **remarkable** is unusual or special in a way that makes people notice them and be surprised or impressed. ❑ *He was a remarkable man.* ● **re|mark|ably** /rɪmɑ̱rkəbli/ ADV ❑ *Herbal remedies are remarkably successful in treating eczema.*

re|mar|riage /rɪmæ̱rɪdʒ/ (remarriages) N-VAR **Remarriage** is the act of remarrying. ❑ *The question of divorce and remarriage in church remains highly contentious.*

re|mar|ry /rɪmæ̱ri/ (remarries, remarrying, remarried) V-T/V-I If someone **remarries**, they marry again after they have obtained a divorce from their previous husband or wife, or after their previous husband or wife has died. ❑ *Her mother had never remarried.* ❑ *When that marriage was dissolved he remarried his first wife.*

re|mas|ter /rimæ̱stər/ (remasters, remastering, remastered) V-T If a movie or musical recording **is remastered**, a new recording is made of the old version, using modern technology to improve the quality. ❑ *A special remastered version of Casablanca is being released.*

re|match /ri̱mætʃ/ (rematches) **1** N-COUNT A **rematch** is a second game that is played between two people or teams, for example because their first match was a draw or because there was a dispute about some aspect of it. ❑ *Duff said he would be demanding a rematch.* **2** N-COUNT A **rematch** is a second game or contest between two people or teams who have already faced each other. [mainly AM] ❑ *Stanford will face UCLA in a rematch.*

in BRIT, usually use **return match**

3 → See feature box at **competition**

re|medial /rɪmi̱diəl/ **1** ADJ **Remedial** action is intended to correct something that has been done wrong or that has not been successful. [FORMAL] ❑ *Some authorities are now having to take remedial action.* **2** ADJ **Remedial** education is intended to improve a person's ability to read, write, or do mathematics, especially when they find these things difficult. ❑ *...children who required remedial education.*

rem|edy /re̱mədi/ (remedies, remedying, remedied) **1** N-COUNT A **remedy** is a successful way of dealing with a problem. ❑ *The remedy lies in the hands of the government.* **2** N-COUNT A **remedy** is something that is intended to cure you when you are ill or in pain. ❑ *There are many different kinds of natural remedies to help overcome winter infections.* **3** V-T If you **remedy** something that is wrong or harmful, you correct it or improve it. ❑ *A great deal has been done internally to remedy the situation.*

re|mem|ber ✦✦✦ /rɪme̱mbər/ (remembers, remembering, remembered) **1** V-T/V-I If you **remember** people or events from the past, you still have an idea of them in your mind and you are able to think about them. ❑ *You wouldn't remember me. I was in another group.* ❑ *I remembered that we had made the last of the coffee the day before.* ❑ *What a day that was, do you remember?* **2** V-T If you **remember** that something is the case, you become aware of it again after a time when you did not think about it. ❑ *She remembered that she was going to the club that evening.* **3** V-T/V-I [usu with brd-neg] If you cannot **remember** something, you are not able to bring it back into your mind when you make an effort to do so. ❑ *If you can't remember your number, write it in code in an appointment book.* ❑ *I can't remember what I said.* ❑ *Don't tell me you can't remember.* **4** V-T If you **remember** to do something, you do it when you intend to. ❑ *Please remember to enclose a stamped self-addressed envelope when writing.* **5** V-T You tell someone to **remember** that something is the case when you want to emphasize its importance. It may be something that they already know about or a new piece of information. [EMPHASIS] ❑ *It is important to remember that each person reacts differently.*

re|mem|brance /rɪme̱mbrəns/ N-UNCOUNT If you do something in **remembrance** of a dead person, you do it as a way of showing that you want to remember them and that you respect them. [FORMAL] ❑ *They wore black in remembrance of those who had died.*

re|mind ✦◇◇ /rɪma̱ɪnd/ (reminds, reminding, reminded) **1** V-T If someone **reminds** you of a fact or event that you already know about, they say something which makes you think about it. ❑ *So she simply welcomed Tim and reminded him of the last time they had met.* **2** V-T You use **remind** in expressions such as **Let me remind you that** and **May I remind you that** to introduce a piece of information that you want to emphasize. It may be something that the hearer already knows about or a new piece of information. Sometimes these expressions can sound unfriendly. [SPOKEN, EMPHASIS] ❑ *"Let me remind you," said Marianne, "that Milwaukee is also my home town."* **3** V-T If someone **reminds** you to do a particular thing, they say something which makes you remember to do it. ❑ *Can you remind me to buy a bottle of wine?* **4** V-T If you say that someone or something **reminds** you **of** another person or thing, you mean that they are similar to the other person or thing and that they make you think about them. ❑ *She reminds me of the wife of the pilot who used to work for you.*

re|mind|er /rɪma̱ɪndər/ (reminders) **1** N-COUNT Something that serves as a **reminder** of another thing makes you think about the other thing. ❑ *The last thing you'd want is a constant reminder of a bad experience.* **2** N-COUNT A **reminder** is a letter or note that is sent to tell you that you have not done something such as pay a bill or return library books. ❑ *...the final reminder for the gas bill.*

remi|nisce /re̱mɪnɪ̱s/ (reminisces, reminiscing, reminisced) V-I If you **reminisce** about something from your past, you write or talk about it, often with pleasure. [FORMAL] ❑ *I don't like reminiscing because it makes me feel old.*

remi|nis|cence /re̱mɪnɪ̱səns/ (reminiscences) N-VAR Someone's **reminiscences** are things that they remember from the past, and which they talk or write about. **Reminiscence** is the process of remembering these things and talking or writing about them. [FORMAL] ❑ *Here I am boring you with my reminiscences.*

remi|nis|cent /re̱mɪnɪ̱sənt/ ADJ [v-link ADJ of n] If you say that one thing is **reminiscent of** another, you mean that it reminds you of it. [FORMAL] ❑ *We drank from wax-coated paper cups reminiscent of a visit to the dentist.*

re|miss /rɪmɪ̱s/ ADJ [v-link ADJ] If someone is **remiss**, they are careless about doing things that ought to be done. [FORMAL] ❑ *I would be remiss if I did not do something about it.*

re|mis|sion /rɪmɪ̱ʃən/ (remissions) N-VAR If someone who has had a serious disease such as cancer is in **remission** or if the disease is in **remission**, the disease has been controlled so that they are not as ill as they were. ❑ *Brain scans have confirmed that the disease is in remission.*

re|mit /rɪmɪ̱t/ (remits, remitting, remitted) V-T If you **remit** money to someone, you send it to them. [FORMAL] ❑ *Many immigrants regularly remit money to their families.*

re|mit|tance /rɪmɪ̱təns/ (remittances) N-VAR A **remittance** is a sum of money that you send to someone. [FORMAL] ❑ *Please enclose your remittance, making checks payable to Valley Technology Services.*

re|mix (remixes, remixing, remixed)

The noun is pronounced /ri̱mɪks/. The verb is pronounced /rimɪ̱ks/.

1 N-COUNT A **remix** is a new version of a piece of music which has been created by putting together the individual instrumental and vocal parts in a different way. ❑ *Their new album features remixes of some of their previous hits.* **2** V-T To **remix** a piece of music means to make a new version of it by putting together the individual instrumental and vocal parts in a different way. ❑ *The band is remixing some tracks.*

rem|nant /re̱mnənt/ (remnants) N-COUNT The **remnants** of something are small parts of it that are left over when the main part has disappeared or has been used or destroyed. ❑ *Beneath the present church were remnants of Roman flooring.*

re|mod|el /rɪmɒdəl/ (**remodels, remodeling** or **remodelling, remodeled** or **remodelled**) V-T To **remodel** something such as a building or a room means to give it a different form or shape. ❑ *Workmen were hired to remodel and enlarge the farm buildings.*

re|mold /rɪmoʊld/ (**remolds, remolding, remolded**) V-T To **remold** something such as an idea or an economy means to change it so that it has a new structure or is based on new principles. ❑ *...our ability to continue or to remold a life shattered by a severe loss.*

re|mon|strate /rɪmɒnstreɪt/ (**remonstrates, remonstrating, remonstrated**) V-I If you **remonstrate with** someone, you protest to them about something that you do not approve of or agree with, and you try to get it changed or stopped. [FORMAL] ❑ *He remonstrated with the referee.* ❑ *Stewart expected him to remonstrate, and was surprised at his acceptance of defeat.*

re|morse /rɪmɔrs/ N-UNCOUNT **Remorse** is a strong feeling of sadness and regret about something wrong that you have done. ❑ *He was full of remorse and asked Beatrice what he could do to make amends.*

re|morse|ful /rɪmɔrsfəl/ ADJ If you are **remorseful**, you feel very guilty and sorry about something wrong that you have done. ❑ *He was genuinely remorseful.* • **re|morse|ful|ly** ADV [ADV with v] ❑ *"My poor wife!" he said, remorsefully.*

re|morse|less /rɪmɔrsləs/ **1** ADJ If you describe something, especially something unpleasant, as **remorseless**, you mean that it goes on for a long time and cannot be stopped. ❑ *...the remorseless pressure of recession and financial constraint.* • **re|morse|less|ly** ADV [usu ADV with v] ❑ *There have been record bankruptcies and remorselessly rising unemployment.* **2** ADJ Someone who is **remorseless** is prepared to be cruel to other people and feels no pity for them. ❑ *...the capacity for quick, remorseless violence.* • **re|morse|less|ly** ADV [ADV with v] ❑ *They remorselessly beat up anyone they suspected of supporting the opposition.*

re|mote ✦✧✧ /rɪmoʊt/ (**remoter, remotest, remotes**) **1** ADJ **Remote** areas are far away from cities and places where most people live, and are therefore difficult to get to. ❑ *Landslides have cut off many villages in remote areas.* **2** ADJ The **remote** past or **remote** future is a time that is many years distant from the present. ❑ *Slabs of rock had slipped sideways in the remote past and formed this hole.* **3** ADJ If something is **remote** from a particular subject or area of experience, it is not relevant to it because it is very different. ❑ *This government depends on the wishes of a few who are remote from the people.* **4** ADJ If you say that there is a **remote** possibility or chance that something will happen, you are emphasizing that there is only a very small chance that it will happen. [EMPHASIS] ❑ *I use sunscreen whenever there is even a remote possibility that I will be in the sun.* **5** ADJ If you describe someone as **remote**, you mean that they behave as if they do not want to be friendly or closely involved with other people. ❑ *She looked so beautiful, and at the same time so remote.* **6** N-COUNT A **remote** is the same as a **remote control**. ❑ *He flipped through the channels with the remote.*

SYNONYMS

remote
ADJ **1**
distant: *...the war in that distant land.*
isolated: *Many of the refugee villages are in isolated areas.*
out-of-the-way: *...an out-of-the-way spot.*

---

re|mote ac|cess N-UNCOUNT **Remote access** is a system that allows you to gain access to a particular computer or network using a separate computer. [COMPUTING] ❑ *The diploma course would offer remote access to course materials via the Internet's world wide web.*

re|mote con|trol (**remote controls**) **1** N-UNCOUNT **Remote control** is a system of controlling a machine or a vehicle from a distance by using radio or electronic signals. ❑ *The bomb was detonated by remote control.* **2** N-COUNT The **remote control** for a piece of electrical equipment such as a television is the device that you use to control the equipment from a distance, by pressing the buttons on it. ❑ *Richard picked up the remote control and turned on the television.* **3** → See also color supplement

re|mote-con|trolled ADJ [usu ADJ n] A **remote-controlled** machine or device is controlled from a distance by the use of radio or electronic signals. ❑ *...a remote-controlled bomb.*

re|mote|ly /rɪmoʊtli/ **1** ADV You use **remotely** with a negative statement to emphasize the statement. [EMPHASIS] ❑ *We had never seen anything remotely like it before.* **2** ADV [ADV -ed] If someone or something is **remotely** placed or situated, they are a long way from other people or places. ❑ *...the remotely situated, five bedroom house.* **3** ADV [ADV -ed] If something is controlled **remotely**, it is controlled from a distance using a computer or other device. ❑ *The missions were flown remotely using drones.*

re|mote sens|ing N-UNCOUNT [oft N n] **Remote sensing** is the gathering of information about something by observing it from space or from the air.

re|mould /rɪmoʊld/ [BRIT] → see **remold**

re|mount /rɪmaʊnt/ (**remounts, remounting, remounted**) V-T/V-I When you **remount** a bicycle or horse, you get back on it after you have gotten off it or fallen off it. ❑ *He was told to remount his horse and ride back to Lexington.* ❑ *The pony scrambled up and waited for the rider, who remounted and carried on.*

re|mov|able /rɪmuvəbəl/ ADJ [usu ADJ n] A **removable** part of something is a part that can easily be moved from its place or position. ❑ *...a cake pan with a removable base.*

re|mov|al /rɪmuvəl/ (**removals**) **1** N-UNCOUNT The **removal** of something is the act of removing it. ❑ *What they expected to be the removal of a small lump turned out to be major surgery.* **2** N-VAR **Removal** is the process of transporting furniture or equipment from one building to another. [BRIT]

in AM, use **moving**

re|mov|al man (**removal men**) N-COUNT **Removal men** are men whose job is to move furniture or equipment from one building to another. [BRIT]

in AM, use **movers**

re|move ✦✦✧ /rɪmuv/ (**removes, removing, removed**) **1** V-T If you **remove** something from a place, you take it away. [WRITTEN] ❑ *As soon as the cake is done, remove it from the oven.* **2** V-T If you **remove** clothing, you take it off. [WRITTEN] ❑ *He removed his jacket.* **3** V-T If you **remove** a stain from something, you make the stain disappear by treating it with a chemical or by washing it. ❑ *This treatment removes the most stubborn stains.* **4** V-T If people **remove** someone from power or from something such as a committee, they stop them from being in power or being a member of the committee. ❑ *The student senate voted to remove Fuller from office.* **5** V-T If you **remove** an obstacle, a restriction, or a problem, you get rid of it. ❑ *The agreement removes the last serious obstacle to the signing of the arms treaty.*

re|moved /rɪmuvd/ ADJ [v-link adv ADJ from n] If you say that an idea or situation is far **removed from** something, you mean that it is very different from it. ❑ *Central office was too far removed from operating decisions at the department level.*

re|mov|er /rɪmuvər/ (**removers**) N-MASS [usu supp N] **Remover** is a substance that you use for removing an unwanted stain, mark, or coating from a surface. ❑ *We got some paint remover and scrubbed it off.*

re|mu|ner|ate /rɪmyunəreɪt/ (**remunerates, remunerating, remunerated**) V-T [usu passive] If you are **remunerated** for work that you do, you are paid for it. [FORMAL] ❑ *You will be remunerated and so will your staff.*

re|mu|nera|tion /rɪmyunəreɪʃən/ (**remunerations**) **1** N-VAR Someone's **remuneration** is the amount of money that they are paid for the work that they do. [FORMAL] ❑ *...the continuing marked increases in the remuneration of the company's directors.* **2** → See feature box at **working**

re|mu|nera|tive /rɪmyunərətɪv, -əreɪtɪv/ ADJ [usu ADJ n] **Remunerative** work is work that you are paid for. [FORMAL] ❑ *A doctor advised her to seek remunerative employment.*

re|nais|sance /rɛnɪsɑns/ **1** N-PROPER The **Renaissance** was the period in Europe, especially Italy, in the 14th, 15th, and 16th centuries, when there was a new interest in art, literature, science, and learning. ❑ *...the Renaissance masterpieces in London's galleries.* **2** N-SING If something experiences a **renaissance**, it becomes popular or successful again after a time when people were not interested in it. ☐ *Popular art is experiencing a renaissance.*

Re|nais|sance man (Renaissance men) N-COUNT If you describe a man as a **Renaissance man**, you mean that he has a wide range of abilities and interests, especially in the arts and sciences. [APPROVAL]

Re|nais|sance wom|an (Renaissance women) N-COUNT If you describe a woman as a **Renaissance woman**, you mean that she has a wide range of abilities and interests, especially in the arts and sciences. [APPROVAL]

re|nal /riːnəl/ ADJ [ADJ n] **Renal** describes things that concern or are related to the kidneys. [MEDICAL] ☐ *He collapsed from acute renal failure.*

re|name /riːneɪm/ (renames, renaming, renamed) V-T If you **rename** something, you change its name to a new name. ☐ *Tel Aviv's Kings Square was renamed Yitzhak Rabin Square.*

rend /rɛnd/ (rends, rending, rent) **1** V-T/V-I To **rend** something means to tear it. [LITERARY] ☐ *...pain that rends the heart.* ☐ *...a twisted urge to rend and tear.* **2** V-T If a loud sound **rends** the air, it is sudden and violent. [LITERARY] ☐ *He bellows, rends the air with anguish.* **3** → see also **heartrending**

ren|der /rɛndər/ (renders, rendering, rendered) V-T You can use **render** with an adjective that describes a particular state to say that someone or something is changed into that state. For example, if someone or something makes a thing harmless, you can say that they **render** it harmless. ☐ *It contained so many errors as to render it worthless.*

ren|der|ing /rɛndərɪŋ/ (renderings) **1** N-COUNT [usu N of n] A **rendering** of a play, poem, or piece of music is a performance of it. ☐ *...a rendering of Verdi's Requiem by the Chicago Symphony Orchestra.* **2** N-COUNT [usu N of n] A **rendering** of an expression or piece of writing or speech is a translation of it. ☐ *This phrase may well have been a rendering of a popular Arabic expression.*

ren|dez|vous /rɒndeɪvuː/ (rendezvousing, rendezvoused)

The form **rendezvous** is pronounced /rɒndeɪvuːz/ when it is the plural of the noun or the third person singular of the verb.

1 N-COUNT A **rendezvous** is a meeting, often a secret one, that you have arranged with someone for a particular time and place. ☐ *I had almost decided to keep my rendezvous with Tony.* **2** N-COUNT A **rendezvous** is the place where you have arranged to meet someone, often secretly. ☐ *Their rendezvous would be the Plaza Hotel.* **3** V-RECIP If you **rendezvous** with someone or if the two of you **rendezvous**, you meet them at a time and place that you have arranged. ☐ *The plan was to rendezvous with him on Sunday afternoon.*

ren|di|tion /rɛndɪʃən/ (renditions) N-COUNT [usu N of n] A **rendition** of a play, poem, or piece of music is a performance of it. ☐ *The musicians burst into a rousing rendition of "Paddy Casey's Reel."*

ren|egade /rɛnɪɡeɪd/ (renegades) N-COUNT A **renegade** is a person who abandons the religious, political, or philosophical beliefs that he or she used to have, and accepts opposing or different beliefs. ☐ *He has shown himself to be a renegade without respect for the rule of law.*

re|nege /rɪnɪɡ/ (reneges, reneging, reneged) V-I If someone **reneges** on a promise or an agreement, they do not do what they have promised or agreed to do. ☐ *He reneged on a promise to leave his wife.*

re|new ♦◇◇ /rɪnuː/ (renews, renewing, renewed) **1** V-T If you **renew** an activity, you begin it again. ☐ *He renewed his attack on government policy toward Europe.* **2** V-RECIP If you **renew** a relationship with someone, you start it again after you have not seen them or have not been friendly with them for some time. ☐ *When the two men met again after the war they renewed their friendship.* **3** V-T When you **renew** something such as a license or a contract, you extend the period of time for which it is valid. ☐ *Larry's landlord threatened not to renew his lease.* **4** V-T [usu passive] You can say that something **is renewed** when it grows again or is replaced after it has been destroyed or lost. ☐ *Nature's repair process is slow and steady, with cells being constantly renewed.*

re|new|able /rɪnuːəbəl/ **1** ADJ **Renewable** resources are natural ones such as wind, water, and sunlight which are always available. ☐ *...renewable energy sources.* **2** ADJ If a contract or agreement is **renewable**, it can be extended when it reaches the end of a fixed period of time. ☐ *A formal contract is signed which is renewable annually.*

re|new|al /rɪnuːəl/ (renewals) **1** N-SING If there is a **renewal** of an activity or a situation, it starts again. ☐ *They will discuss the possible renewal of diplomatic relations.* **2** N-VAR The **renewal** of a document such as a license or a contract is an official increase in the period of time for which it remains valid. ☐ *His contract came up for renewal.* **3** N-UNCOUNT **Renewal** of something lost, dead, or destroyed is the process of it growing again or being replaced. ☐ *...a political lobbyist concentrating on urban renewal and regeneration.*

re|nounce /rɪnaʊns/ (renounces, renouncing, renounced) V-T If you **renounce** a belief or a way of behaving, you decide and declare publicly that you no longer have that belief or will no longer behave in that way. ☐ *After a period of imprisonment she renounced terrorism.*

reno|vate /rɛnəveɪt/ (renovates, renovating, renovated) V-T If someone **renovates** an old building, they repair and improve it and get it back into good condition. ☐ *The couple spent thousands renovating the house.* • **reno|va|tion** /rɛnəveɪʃən/ (renovations) N-VAR ☐ *...a property which will need extensive renovation.*

re|nown /rɪnaʊn/ N-UNCOUNT A person of **renown** is well known, usually because they do or have done something good. ☐ *She used to be a singer of some renown.*

re|nowned /rɪnaʊnd/ ADJ A person or place that is **renowned** for something, usually something good, is well known because of it. ☐ *The area is renowned for its Romanesque churches.*

rent ♦◇◇ /rɛnt/ (rents, renting, rented) **1** V-T If you **rent** something, you regularly pay its owner a sum of money in order to be able to have it and use it yourself. ☐ *She rents a house with three other girls.* **2** V-T If you **rent** something to someone, you let them have it and use it in exchange for a sum of money which they pay you regularly. ☐ *She rented rooms to university students.* • PHRASAL VERB **Rent out** means the same as **rent**. ☐ *Last summer Brian Williams rented out his house and went camping.* **3** N-VAR **Rent** is the amount of money that you pay regularly to use a house, apartment, or piece of land. ☐ *She worked to pay the rent while I went to college.* **4** PHRASE If something is **for rent**, it is available for you to use in exchange for a sum of money. [mainly AM] ☐ *Helmets will be available for rent at all Vail Resort ski areas.*

in BRIT, usually use **for hire**

rent|al /rɛntəl/ (rentals) **1** N-UNCOUNT [also N in pl] The **rental** of something such as a car or piece of equipment is the activity or process of renting it. ☐ *We can arrange car rental from Chicago's O'Hare Airport.* **2** N-COUNT The **rental** is the amount of money that you pay when you rent something such as a car, property, or piece of equipment. ☐ *It has been let at an annual rental of $393,000.* **3** ADJ [ADJ n] You use **rental** to describe things that are connected with the renting out of goods, properties, and services. ☐ *A friend drove her to Atlanta, where she picked up a rental car.*

rent-free ADJ [usu ADJ n] If you have a **rent-free** house or office, you do not have to pay anything to use it. ☐ *He was given a new rent-free apartment.* • ADV [ADV after v] **Rent-free** is also an adverb. ☐ *They told James he could no longer live rent-free.*

re|nun|cia|tion /rɪnʌnsieɪʃən/ (renunciations) **1** N-UNCOUNT [also N in pl] The **renunciation** of a belief or a way of behaving is the public declaration that you reject it and have decided to stop having that belief or behaving in that way. ☐ *The talks were dependent on a renunciation of terrorism.* **2** N-UNCOUNT The **renunciation** of a claim, title, or privilege is the act of officially giving it up. ☐ *...the renunciation of territory in the Mediterranean.* **3** N-UNCOUNT **Renunciation** is the act of not allowing yourself certain pleasures for moral or religious reasons. ☐ *Gandhi exemplified the virtues of renunciation, asceticism, and restraint.*

re|of|fend /riːəfɛnd/ (reoffends, reoffending, reoffended) VERB [no cont] If a criminal **reoffends**, they commit more crime after having been punished for a previous crime. [FORMAL] ❑ *On average, 60 percent of these prisoners will reoffend within 2 years of release.*

re|open /riˈoʊpən/ (reopens, reopening, reopened) **1** V-T/V-I If you **reopen** a public building such as a factory, airport, or school, or if it **reopens**, it opens and starts working again after it has been closed for some time. ❑ *Iran reopened its embassy in London.* ❑ *The restaurant will reopen in November.* **2** V-T If police or the courts **reopen** a legal case, they investigate it again because it has never been solved or because there was something wrong in the way it was investigated before. ❑ *There was a call today to reopen the investigation into the bombing.* **3** V-T/V-I If people or countries **reopen** talks or negotiations or if talks or negotiations **reopen**, they begin again after they have stopped for some time. ❑ *But now high-level delegations will reopen talks that broke up earlier this year.* ❑ *...the possibility of reopening negotiations with the government.* ❑ *Middle East peace talks reopen in Washington on Wednesday.* **4** V-RECIP If people or countries **reopen** ties or relations, they start being friendly again after a time when they were not friendly. ❑ *He reopened ties with Moscow earlier this year.* ❑ *Britain and Argentina reopened diplomatic relations.* **5** V-T If something **reopens** a question or debate, it makes the question or debate relevant again and causes people to start discussing it again. ❑ *His results are likely to reopen the debate on race and education.* **6** V-T/V-I If a country **reopens** a border or route, or if it **reopens**, it becomes possible to cross or travel along it again after it has been closed. ❑ *Jordan reopened its border with Iraq.* ❑ *The important Beijing-Shanghai route has reopened.*

re|or|gan|ize /riˈɔːrɡənaɪz/ (reorganizes, reorganizing, reorganized)

in BRIT, also use **reorganise**

V-T/V-I To **reorganize** something means to change the way in which it is organized, arranged, or done. ❑ *It is the mother who is expected to reorganize her busy schedule.* ❑ *Four thousand troops have been reorganized into a fighting force.* ● **re|or|gani|za|tion** /riˌɔːrɡənɪˈzeɪʃən/ (reorganizations) N-VAR ❑ *...the reorganization of the legal system.*

rep /rɛp/ (reps) **1** N-COUNT A **rep** is a person whose job is to sell a company's products or services, especially by traveling around and visiting other companies. **Rep** is short for **representative**. ❑ *I'd been working as a sales rep for a photographic company.* **2** N-COUNT A **rep** is a person who acts as a representative for a group of people, usually a group of people who work together. ❑ *Contact the health and safety rep at your union.*

Rep. [AM] Rep. is a written abbreviation for **Representative**. ❑ *...Rep. Barbara Boxer.*

re|paid /riˈpeɪd/ **Repaid** is the past tense and past participle of **repay**.

re|pair ✦✧✧ /rɪˈpɛər/ (repairs, repairing, repaired) **1** V-T If you **repair** something that has been damaged or is not working properly, you fix it. ❑ *Goldsmith has repaired the roof to ensure the house is windproof.* ● **re|pair|er** (repairers) N-COUNT ❑ *...services provided by builders, plumbers, and TV repairers.* **2** V-T If you **repair** a relationship or someone's reputation after it has been damaged, you do something to improve it. ❑ *The administration continued to try to repair the damage caused by the secretary's interview.* **3** N-VAR A **repair** is something that you do to mend a machine, building, piece of clothing, or other thing that has been damaged or is not working properly. ❑ *Many people don't know how to make repairs on their cars.*

SYNONYMS

repair
VERB **1**
mend: *They took a long time to mend the roof.*
fix: *If something is broken, we get it fixed.*
restore: *...the beautifully-restored old town square.*

---

re|pair|man /rɪˈpɛərmæn/ (repairmen) N-COUNT [usu supp N] A **repairman** is a man who mends broken machines such as televisions and phones. ❑ *...a cheerful telephone repairman.*

re|pair|woman /rɪˈpɛərwʊmən/ (repairwomen) N-COUNT A **repairwoman** is a woman who mends broken machines such as televisions and phones. ❑ *Her mother was a San Leandro telephone repairwoman.*

repa|ra|tion /ˌrɛpəˈreɪʃən/ (reparations) **1** N-UNCOUNT [also N in pl] **Reparations** are sums of money that are paid after a war by the defeated country for the damage and injuries it caused in other countries. ❑ *Israel accepted billions of dollars in war reparations.* **2** N-UNCOUNT **Reparation** is help or payment that someone gives you for damage, loss, or suffering that they have caused you. ❑ *There is a clear demand among victims for some sort of reparation from offenders.*

rep|ar|tee /ˌrɛpɑːrˈtiː, -ˈteɪ, ˌrɛpɑːr-/ N-UNCOUNT **Repartee** is conversation that consists of quick, witty comments and replies. ❑ *She was good at repartee.*

re|past /rɪˈpæst/ (repasts) N-COUNT A **repast** is a meal. [LITERARY]

re|pat|ri|ate /riˈpeɪtrieɪt/ (repatriates, repatriating, repatriated) **1** V-T If a country **repatriates** someone, it sends them back to their home country. ❑ *It was not the policy of the government to repatriate genuine refugees.* ● **re|pat|ria|tion** /riˌpeɪtriˈeɪʃən/ (repatriations) N-VAR ❑ *They began the forced repatriation of Vietnamese boat people.* **2** V-T If someone **repatriates** money that is invested in another country, they change their investments so that the money is invested in their own country.

re|pay /rɪˈpeɪ/ (repays, repaying, repaid) **1** V-T If you **repay** a loan or a debt, you pay back the money that you owe to the person who you borrowed or took it from. ❑ *He advanced funds of his own to his company, which was unable to repay him.* **2** V-T If you **repay** a favor that someone did for you, you do something for them in return. ❑ *It was very kind. I don't know how I can ever repay you.*

re|pay|able /rɪˈpeɪəbəl/ ADJ A loan that is **repayable** within a certain period of time must be paid back within that time. [mainly BRIT]

in AM, usually use **payable**

re|pay|ment /rɪˈpeɪmənt/ (repayments) **1** N-COUNT **Repayments** are amounts of money which you pay at regular intervals to a person or organization in order to repay a debt. [mainly BRIT]

in AM, usually use **payment**

2 N-UNCOUNT The **repayment** of money is the act or process of paying it back to the person you owe it to. ❑ *He failed to meet last Friday's deadline for repayment of a $114 million loan.* **3** → See feature box at **finance**

re|peal /rɪˈpiːl/ (repeals, repealing, repealed) V-T If the government **repeals** a law, it officially ends it, so that it is no longer valid. ❑ *The government has just repealed the law segregating public facilities.* ● N-UNCOUNT **Repeal** is also a noun. ❑ *Next year will be the 60th anniversary of the repeal of Prohibition.*

re|peat ✦✦✧ /rɪˈpiːt/ (repeats, repeating, repeated) **1** V-T If you **repeat** something, you say or write it again. You can say **I repeat** to show that you feel strongly about what you are repeating. ❑ *He repeated that he had been misquoted.* ❑ *She repeated her call yesterday for an investigation into the incident.* **2** V-T If you **repeat** something that someone else has said or written, you say or write the same thing, or tell it to another person. ❑ *She had an irritating habit of repeating everything I said to her.* ❑ *I trust you not to repeat that to anyone else.* **3** V-T If you **repeat** yourself, you say something which you have said before, usually by mistake. ❑ *He spoke well to begin with, but then started rambling and repeating himself.* **4** V-T/V-I If you **repeat** an action, you do it again. ❑ *The next day I repeated the procedure.* ❑ *Move the leg up and down several times and rotate the foot. Repeat on the right leg.* **5** V-T If an event or series of events **repeats** itself, it happens again. ❑ *The UN will have to work hard to stop history from repeating itself.* **6** N-COUNT If there is a **repeat** of an event, usually an undesirable event, it happens again. ❑ *There were fears that there might be a repeat of last year's campaign of strikes.* **7** ADJ [ADJ n] If a company gets **repeat** business or **repeat** customers, people who have bought their goods or services before buy them again. [BUSINESS] ❑ *Nearly 60% of our bookings come from repeat business and personal recommendation.* **8** N-COUNT A **repeat** is a television or radio program that has been broadcast before. ❑ *There's nothing except sports and repeats on TV.*

SYNONYMS

repeat
VERB **1**
reiterate: *He reiterated his opposition to the creation of a central bank.*
restate: *He continued throughout to restate his opposition to violence.*
recapitulate: *Let's just recapitulate the essential points.*

re|peat|ed /rɪpiːtɪd/ ADJ [ADJ n] **Repeated** actions or events are ones that happen many times. ❑ *Mr. Lawssi apparently did not return the money, despite repeated reminders.*

re|peat|ed|ly /rɪpiːtɪdli/ ADV [ADV with v] If you do something **repeatedly**, you do it many times. ❑ *Both men have repeatedly denied the allegations.*

re|peat of|fend|er (repeat offenders) N-COUNT A **repeat offender** is someone who commits the same sort of crime more than once.

re|pel /rɪpɛl/ (repels, repelling, repelled) **1** V-T When an army **repels** an attack, they successfully fight and drive back soldiers from another army who have attacked them. [FORMAL] ❑ *They have fifty thousand troops along the border ready to repel any attack.* **2** V-T [no cont] If something **repels** you, you find it horrible and disgusting. ❑ *...a violent excitement that frightened and repelled her.* ● **re|pelled** ADJ ❑ *She was very striking but in some way I felt repelled.* **3** V-RECIP When a magnetic pole **repels** another magnetic pole, it gives out a force that pushes the other pole away. You can also say that two magnetic poles **repel** each other or that they **repel.** [TECHNICAL]

re|pel|lant /rɪpɛlənt/ → see repellent

re|pel|lent /rɪpɛlənt/ (repellents) also **repellant 1** ADJ If you think that something is horrible and disgusting you can say that it is **repellent.** [FORMAL] ❑ *...a very large, very repellent toad.* **2** N-MASS Insect **repellent** is a product containing chemicals that you spray into the air or on your body in order to keep insects away. ❑ *...mosquito repellent.*

re|pent /rɪpɛnt/ (repents, repenting, repented) V-I If you **repent**, you show or say that you are sorry for something wrong you have done. ❑ *Those who refuse to repent, he said, will be punished.*

re|pent|ance /rɪpɛntəns/ N-UNCOUNT If you show **repentance** for something wrong that you have done, you make it clear that you are sorry for doing it. ❑ *They showed no repentance during their trial.*

re|pent|ant /rɪpɛntənt/ ADJ Someone who is **repentant** shows or says that they are sorry for something wrong they have done. ❑ *He was feeling guilty and depressed, repentant and scared.*

re|per|cus|sion /riːpərkʌʃən/ (repercussions) N-COUNT [usu pl] If an action or event has **repercussions**, it causes unpleasant things to happen some time after the original action or event. [FORMAL] ❑ *It was an effort which was to have painful repercussions.*

rep|er|toire /rɛpərtwɑːr/ (repertoires) N-COUNT A performer's **repertoire** is all the plays or pieces of music that he or she has learned and can perform. ❑ *Meredith D'Ambrosio has thousands of songs in her repertoire.*

rep|er|tory /rɛpərtɔːri/ N-UNCOUNT [usu N n] A **repertory** company is a group of actors and actresses who perform a small number of plays for just a few weeks at a time. They work in a **repertory** theater. ❑ *...a well-known repertory company in Boston.*

rep|eti|tion /rɛpɪtɪʃən/ (repetitions) **1** N-VAR If there is a **repetition** of an event, usually an undesirable event, it happens again. ❑ *Today the city government has taken measures to prevent a repetition of last year's confrontation.* **2** N-VAR **Repetition** means using the same words again. ❑ *He could also have cut out much of the repetition and thus saved many pages.*

rep|eti|tious /rɛpɪtɪʃəs/ ADJ Something that is **repetitious** involves actions or elements that are repeated many times and is therefore boring. [DISAPPROVAL] ❑ *The manifesto is long-winded, repetitious and often ambiguous or poorly drafted.*

re|peti|tive /rɪpɛtɪtɪv/ **1** ADJ Something that is **repetitive** involves actions or elements that are repeated many times and is therefore boring. [DISAPPROVAL] ❑ *...factory workers who do repetitive jobs.* **2** ADJ **Repetitive** movements or sounds are repeated many times. ❑ *This technique is particularly successful where problems occur as the result of repetitive movements.*

re|peti|tive strain in|ju|ry N-UNCOUNT **Repetitive strain injury** is the same as RSI. ❑ *...computer users suffering from repetitive strain injury.*

re|phrase /riːfreɪz/ (rephrases, rephrasing, rephrased) V-T If you **rephrase** a question or statement, you ask it or say it again in a different way. ❑ *Again, the executive rephrased the question.*

re|place ♦♦◇ /rɪpleɪs/ (replaces, replacing, replaced) **1** V-T If one thing or person **replaces** another, the first is used or acts instead of the second. ❑ *One species of tree replaces another as a forest ages.* ❑ *...the lawyer who replaced Robert as chairman of the company.* **2** V-T If you **replace** one thing or person with another, you put something or someone else in their place to do their job. ❑ *I clean out all the grease and replace it with oil so it works better in very low temperatures.* **3** V-T If you **replace** something that is broken, damaged, or lost, you get a new one to use instead. ❑ *The shower that we put in a few years back has broken and we cannot afford to replace it.* **4** V-T If you **replace** something, you put it back where it was before. ❑ *Replace the caps on the bottles.*

re|place|able /rɪpleɪsəbəl/ **1** ADJ If something is **replaceable**, you can throw it away when it is finished and put a new one in its place. ❑ *...replaceable butane gas cartridges.* **2** ADJ [usu v-link ADJ] If you say that someone is **replaceable**, you mean that they are not so important that someone else could not take their place. ❑ *He would see I was not so easily replaceable.*

re|place|ment ♦◇◇ /rɪpleɪsmənt/ (replacements) **1** N-UNCOUNT [with supp] If you refer to the **replacement** of one thing by another, you mean that the second thing takes the place of the first. ❑ *...the replacement of damaged or lost books.* **2** N-COUNT Someone who takes someone else's place in an organization, government, or team can be referred to as their **replacement.** ❑ *Taylor has nominated Adams as his replacement.*

SYNONYMS

replacement
NOUN **1**
substitution: *In my experience, a straight substitution of carob for chocolate doesn't work.*
renewal: *...urban renewal and regeneration.*

re|place|ment value N-SING The **replacement value** of something that you own is the amount of money it would cost you to replace it if it was stolen or damaged.

re|play (replays, replaying, replayed)

The verb is pronounced /riːpleɪ/. The noun is pronounced /riːpleɪ/.

1 V-T [usu passive] If a game or match between two sports teams **is replayed**, the two teams play it again, because neither team won the first time, or because the game was stopped because of bad weather. ❑ *The game had to be replayed at the end of the season.* ● N-COUNT You can refer to a game that is replayed as a **replay.** ❑ *If there has to be a replay we are confident of victory.* **2** V-T If you **replay** something that you have recorded on film or tape, you play it again in order to watch it or listen to it. ❑ *He stopped the machine and replayed the message.* ● N-COUNT **Replay** is also a noun. ❑ *I watched a slow-motion videotape replay of his fall.* **3** V-T If you **replay** an event in your mind, you think about it again and again. ❑ *She spends her nights lying in bed, replaying the fire in her mind.*

re|plen|ish /rɪplɛnɪʃ/ (replenishes, replenishing, replenished) V-T If you **replenish** something, you make it full or complete again. [FORMAL] ❑ *Three hundred thousand tons of cereals are needed to replenish stocks.*

re|plen|ish|ment /rɪplɛnɪʃmənt/ N-UNCOUNT [usu with supp] **Replenishment** is the process by which something is made full or complete again. [FORMAL] ❑ *There is a concern about replenishment of the population.*

re|plete /rɪpliːt/ **1** ADJ [v-link ADJ with n] To be **replete with** something means to be full of it. [FORMAL] ❑ *The harbor was replete with boats.* **2** ADJ [usu v-link ADJ] If you are **replete**, you are pleasantly full of food and drink. [FORMAL] ❑ *Replete, guests can then retire to the modern conservatory for coffee.*

rep|li|ca /rɛplɪkə/ (replicas) N-COUNT A **replica** of something such as a statue, building, or weapon is an accurate copy of it. ❑ ...a human-sized replica of the Statue of Liberty.

rep|li|cate /rɛplɪkeɪt/ (replicates, replicating, replicated) V-T If you **replicate** someone's experiment, work, or research, you do it yourself in exactly the same way. [FORMAL] ❑ He invited her to his laboratory to see if she could replicate the experiment.

re|ply ✦✧ /rɪplaɪ/ (replies, replying, replied) **1** V-T/V-I When you **reply** to something that someone has said or written to you, you say or write an answer to them. ❑ "That's a nice dress," said Michael. "Thanks," she replied solemnly. ❑ He replied that this was absolutely impossible. ❑ He never replied to the letters. **2** N-COUNT [oft N to/from n, also in N] A **reply** is something that you say or write when you answer someone or answer a letter or advertisement. ❑ I called out a challenge, but there was no reply. ❑ He said in reply that the question was unfair. **3** V-I If you **reply** to something such as an attack with violence or with another action, you do something in response. ❑ During a number of violent incidents farmers threw eggs and empty bottles at police, who replied with tear gas.

---- COLLOCATIONS ----

reply
VERB **1**
reply + adverb: calmly, coolly, curtly, tersely; individually, personally
NOUN **2**
adjective + reply: immediate, instant, prompt, succinct; genuine, personal, standard; written
verb + reply: receive; send

---

re|port ✦✦✦ /rɪpɔːrt/ (reports, reporting, reported) **1** V-T If you **report** something that has happened, you tell people about it. ❑ I reported the theft to the police. ❑ The officials also reported that two more ships were apparently heading for Malta. ❑ "He seems to be all right now," reported a relieved Taylor. ❑ She reported him missing the next day. **2** V-I If you **report** on an event or subject, you tell people about it, because it is your job or duty to do so. ❑ Many journalists based outside of Sudan have been refused visas to enter the country to report on political affairs. **3** N-COUNT A **report** is a news article or broadcast which gives information about something that has just happened. ❑ According to a report in the newspaper, he still has control over the remaining shares. **4** N-COUNT A **report** is an official document which a group of people issue after investigating a situation or event. ❑ The education committee will today publish its report on the supply of teachers for the next decade. **5** N-COUNT If you give someone a **report** on something, you tell them what has been happening. ❑ She came back to give us a progress report on how the project is going. **6** N-COUNT If you say that there are **reports** that something has happened, you mean that some people say it has happened but you have no direct evidence of it. [VAGUENESS] ❑ There are unconfirmed reports that two people have been shot in the neighboring town of Springfield. **7** V-T If someone **reports** you to a person in authority, they tell that person about something wrong that you have done. ❑ His ex-wife reported him to police a few days later. **8** V-I If you **report** to a person or place, you go to that person or place and say that you are ready to start work or say that you are present. ❑ Mr. Ashwell has to surrender his passport and report to the police every five days. **9** V-I [no cont] If you say that one employee **reports** to another, you mean that the first employee is told what to do by the second and is responsible to them. [FORMAL] ❑ He reported to a section chief, who reported to a division chief, and so on up the line. **10** → see also **report card**, **reporting** **11** → See feature box at **press**, **research**

re|port|age /rɪpɔːrtɪdʒ, rɛpɔːrtɑːʒ/ N-UNCOUNT **Reportage** is the reporting of news and other events of general interest for newspapers, television, and radio. [FORMAL] ❑ ...the magazine's acclaimed mix of reportage and fashion.

re|port card (report cards) **1** N-COUNT A **report card** is an official written account of how well or how badly a student has done during the term or year that has just finished. [AM] ❑ The only time I got their attention was when I brought home straight A's on my report card.

in BRIT, use **report**

2 N-COUNT A **report card** is a report on how well a person, organization, or country has been doing recently. [AM]

JOURNALISM] ❑ The president today issued his final report card on the state of the economy.

re|port|ed clause (reported clauses) N-COUNT A **reported clause** is a subordinate clause that indicates what someone said or thought. For example, in 'She said that she was hungry,' 'she was hungry' is a reported clause.

re|port|ed|ly /rɪpɔːrtɪdli/ ADV If you say that something is **reportedly** true, you mean that someone has said that it is true, but you have no direct evidence of it. [FORMAL, VAGUENESS] ❑ More than two hundred people have reportedly been killed in the past week's fighting.

re|port|ed ques|tion (reported questions) N-COUNT A **reported question** is a question which is reported using a clause beginning with a word such as 'why' or 'whether,' as in 'I asked her why she'd done it.'

re|port|ed speech N-UNCOUNT **Reported speech** is speech which tells you what someone said, but does not use the person's actual words: for example, 'They said you didn't like it,' 'I asked her what her plans were,' and 'Citizens complained about the smoke.'

re|port|er ✦✧ /rɪpɔːrtər/ (reporters) N-COUNT A **reporter** is someone who writes news articles or who broadcasts news reports. ❑ ...a TV reporter.

---- COLLOCATIONS ----

reporter
NOUN
noun + reporter: news, newspaper, television; crime, sports, war
adjective + reporter: financial, foreign, local, political; intrepid, investigative, roving, undercover; freelance
verb + reporter: brief, tell; assign

---

re|port|ing ✦✧ /rɪpɔːrtɪŋ/ N-UNCOUNT **Reporting** is the presenting of news in newspapers, on radio, and on television. ❑ This newspaper has achieved a reputation for honest and impartial political reporting.

re|port|ing clause (reporting clauses) N-COUNT A **reporting clause** is the same as a **reported clause**.

re|port struc|ture (report structures) N-COUNT A **report structure** is a structure containing a reporting clause and a reported clause or a quote.

re|pose /rɪpoʊz/ N-UNCOUNT **Repose** is a state in which you are resting and feeling calm. [LITERARY] ❑ He had a still, almost blank face in repose.

re|po|si|tion /riːpəzɪʃən/ (repositions, repositioning, repositioned) **1** V-T To **reposition** an object means to move it to another place or to change its position. ❑ It is not possible to reposition the rug without damaging it. **2** V-T To **reposition** something such as a product or service means to try to interest more or different people in it, for example by changing certain things about it or the way it is marketed. ❑ The sell-off is aimed at repositioning the company as a publisher of business information. ❑ The company needs to reposition itself to boost its sales and reputation.

re|posi|tory /rɪpɒzɪtɔːri/ (repositories) N-COUNT A **repository** is a place where something is kept safely. [FORMAL] ❑ A church in Moscow became a repository for police files.

re|pos|sess /riːpəzɛs/ (repossesses, repossessing, repossessed) V-T [usu passive] If your car or house is **repossessed**, the people who supplied it take it back because they are still owed money for it. ❑ His car was repossessed by the company.

re|pos|ses|sion /riːpəzɛʃən/ (repossessions) N-VAR The **repossession** of someone's house or car is the act of repossessing it. ❑ ...the problem of home repossessions.

re|pot /riːpɒt/ (repots, repotting, repotted) V-T If you **repot** a plant, you take it out of its pot and put it in a larger one. ❑ As your plants flourish, you'll need to repot them in bigger pots.

rep|re|hen|sible /rɛprɪhɛnsɪbəl/ ADJ [usu v-link ADJ] If you think that a type of behavior or an idea is very bad and morally wrong, you can say that it is **reprehensible**. [FORMAL] ❑ Mr. Cramer said the violence by anti-government protestors was reprehensible.

rep|re|sent ✦✦✦ /rɛprɪzɛnt/ (represents, representing, represented) **1** V-T If someone such as a lawyer or a politician represents a person, a group of people, or a place, they act on behalf of that person, group, or place. ❑ ...*the politicians we elect to represent us.* ❑ *...Richard Bolling, a Democrat who represented Missouri in Congress.* **2** V-T If you **represent** a person or group at an official event, you go there on their behalf. ❑ *The general secretary may represent the president at official ceremonies.* **3** V-T If you **represent** your country or city in a competition or sports event, you take part in it on behalf of the country or city where you live. ❑ *My only aim is to represent the United States at the Olympics.* **4** V-T PASSIVE If a group of people or things **is well represented** in a particular activity or in a particular place, a lot of them can be found there. ❑ *Women are starting to be represented in the area of TV drama.* **5** V-T [no cont] If a sign or symbol **represents** something, it is accepted as meaning that thing. ❑ *...a black dot in the middle of the circle is supposed to represent the source of the radiation.* **6** V-T [no cont, no passive] To **represent** an idea or quality means to be a symbol or an expression of that idea or quality. ❑ *New York represents everything that's great about America.* **7** V-T If you **represent** a person or thing as a particular thing, you describe them as being that thing. ❑ *The popular press tends to represent him as an environmental guru.*

SYNONYMS

represent
VERB
2
stand in: *I had to stand in for her on Tuesday when she didn't show up.*
substitute: *He was substituting for the injured William Wales.*
7
exemplify: *The room's style exemplifies Conran's ideal of 'beauty and practicality.'*
embody: *Jack Kennedy embodied all the hopes of the 1960s.*
symbolize: *...the post-war world order symbolized by the United Nations.*
epitomize: *...the sleek lobby that epitomized the hotel's glossy decor.*

rep|re|sen|ta|tion /rɛprɪzɛnteɪʃən/ (**representations**) **1** N-UNCOUNT If a group or person has **representation** in a legislature or on a committee, someone in the legislature or on the committee supports them and makes decisions on their behalf. ❑ *Puerto Ricans are U.S. citizens but they have no representation in Congress.* **2** → see also **proportional representation** **3** N-COUNT You can describe a picture, model, or statue of a person or thing as a **representation** of them. [FORMAL] ❑ *...a lifelike representation of Christ.*

rep|re|sen|ta|tion|al /rɛprɪzɛnteɪʃənəl/ ADJ In a **representational** painting, the artist attempts to show things as they really are. [FORMAL] ❑ *His painting went through both representational and abstract periods.*

rep|re|sen|ta|tive ♦◊ /rɛprɪzɛntətɪv/ (**representatives**) **1** N-COUNT A **representative** is a person who has been chosen to act or make decisions on behalf of another person or a group of people. ❑ *...labor union representatives.* **2** N-COUNT A **representative** is a person whose job is to sell a company's products or services, especially by traveling around and visiting other companies. [FORMAL] ❑ *She had a stressful job as a sales representative.* **3** N-COUNT In the United States, a **representative** is a member of the House of Representatives, the less powerful of the two parts of Congress. ❑ *...a Republican representative from Wyoming.* **4** ADJ [ADJ n] A **representative** group consists of a small number of people who have been chosen to make decisions on behalf of a larger group. ❑ *The new head of state should be chosen by an 87-member representative council.* **5** ADJ Someone who is typical of the group to which they belong can be described as **representative**. ❑ *He was in no way representative of dog trainers in general.* **6** → see also **House of Representatives**

SYNONYMS

representative
NOUN **1**
delegate: *She was elected as their delegate.*
agent: *You are buying direct, rather than through an agent.*
deputy: *...Jack Lang, France's minister for culture, and his deputy, Catherine Tasca.*
proxy: *Price differences are used as a proxy for differences in quality.*

re|press /rɪprɛs/ (**represses, repressing, repressed**) **1** V-T If you **repress** a feeling, you make a deliberate effort not to show or have this feeling. ❑ *It is anger that is repressed that leads to violence and loss of control.* **2** V-T If you **repress** a smile, sigh, or moan, you try hard not to smile, sigh, or moan. ❑ *He repressed a smile.* **3** V-T If a section of society **is repressed**, their freedom is restricted by the people who have authority over them. [DISAPPROVAL] ❑ *...a UN resolution banning him from repressing his people.*

re|pressed /rɪprɛst/ ADJ A **repressed** person does not allow themselves to have natural feelings and desires, especially sexual ones. ❑ *Some have charged that the Puritans were sexually repressed.*

re|pres|sion /rɪprɛʃən/ (**repressions**) **1** N-VAR **Repression** is the use of force to restrict and control a society or other group of people. [DISAPPROVAL] ❑ *...a society conditioned by violence and repression.* **2** N-UNCOUNT **Repression** of feelings, especially sexual ones, is a person's unwillingness to allow themselves to have natural feelings and desires. ❑ *Much of the anger he's felt during his life has stemmed from the repression of his feelings about men.*

re|pres|sive /rɪprɛsɪv/ ADJ A **repressive** government is one that restricts people's freedom and controls them by using force. [DISAPPROVAL] ❑ *The military regime in power was unpopular and repressive.*

re|prieve /rɪpriv/ (**reprieves, reprieving, reprieved**) **1** V-T [no cont] If someone who has been sentenced in a court **is reprieved**, their punishment is officially delayed or canceled. ❑ *Fourteen people, waiting to be hanged for the murder of a former prime minister, have been reprieved.* • N-VAR **Reprieve** is also a noun. ❑ *A man awaiting death by lethal injection has been saved by a last-minute reprieve.* **2** N-COUNT A **reprieve** is a delay before a very unpleasant or difficult situation which may or may not take place. ❑ *It looked as though the college would have to shut, but this week it was given a reprieve.*

rep|ri|mand /rɛprɪmænd/ (**reprimands, reprimanding, reprimanded**) V-T If someone **is reprimanded**, they are spoken to angrily or seriously for doing something wrong, usually by a person in authority. [FORMAL] ❑ *He was reprimanded by a teacher for talking in the corridor.* • N-VAR **Reprimand** is also a noun. ❑ *He has been fined five thousand dollars and given a severe reprimand.*

re|print (**reprints, reprinting, reprinted**)

The verb is pronounced /rɪprɪnt/. The noun is pronounced /riprɪnt/.

1 V-T [usu passive] If a book **is reprinted**, further copies of it are printed when all the other ones have been sold. ❑ *It remained an exceptionally rare book until it was reprinted in 1918.* **2** N-COUNT A **reprint** is a process in which new copies of a book or article are printed because all the other ones have been sold. ❑ *Demand picked up and a reprint was required last November.* **3** N-COUNT A **reprint** is a new copy of a book or article, printed because all the other ones have been sold or because minor changes have been made to the original. ❑ *...a reprint of a 1962 novel.*

re|pris|al /rɪpraɪzəl/ (**reprisals**) N-VAR If you do something to a person in **reprisal**, you hurt or punish them because they have done something violent or unpleasant to you. ❑ *There were fears that some of the Western hostages might be killed in reprisal.*

re|prise /rɪpriz/ (**reprises**) N-COUNT In music, if there is a **reprise**, an earlier section of music is repeated.

re|proach /rɪproʊtʃ/ (**reproaches, reproaching, reproached**) **1** V-T If you **reproach** someone, you say or show that you are disappointed, upset, or angry because they have done something wrong. ❑ *She is quick to reproach anyone who doesn't live up to her own high standards.* **2** N-VAR If you look at or speak to someone with **reproach**, you show or say that you are disappointed, upset, or angry because they have done something wrong. ❑ *He looked at her with reproach.* **3** V-T If you **reproach** yourself, you think with regret about something you have done wrong. ❑ *You've no reason to reproach yourself, no reason to feel shame.*

re|proach|ful /rɪproʊtʃfəl/ ADJ **Reproachful** expressions or remarks show that you are disappointed, upset, or angry because someone has done something wrong. ❑ *She gave Isabelle a reproachful look.* • **re|proach|ful|ly** ADV [ADV after v] ❑ *Luke's mother stopped smiling and looked reproachfully at him.*

rep|ro|bate /rɛprəbeɪt/ (reprobates) N-COUNT If you describe someone as a **reprobate**, you mean that they behave in a way that is not respectable or morally correct. [OLD-FASHIONED, DISAPPROVAL] ❑ ...a drunken reprobate.

re|pro|duce /riːprədjuːs/ (reproduces, reproducing, reproduced) **1** V-T If you try to **reproduce** something, you try to copy it. ❑ The effect has proved hard to reproduce. **2** V-T If you **reproduce** a picture, speech, or piece of writing, you make a photograph or printed copy of it. ❑ We are grateful to you for permission to reproduce this article. **3** V-T If you **reproduce** an action or an achievement, you repeat it. ❑ If we can reproduce the form we have shown in the last couple of months we will be successful. **4** V-T/V-I When people, animals, or plants **reproduce**, they produce young. ❑ ...a society where women are defined by their ability to reproduce. ❑ We are reproducing ourselves at such a rate that our numbers threaten the ecology of the planet. ● **re|pro|duc|tion** /riːprədʌkʃən/ N-UNCOUNT ❑ Treatments using assisted reproduction techniques jumped 30 percent.

re|pro|duc|tion /riːprədʌkʃən/ (reproductions) **1** N-COUNT A **reproduction** is a copy of something such as a piece of furniture or a work of art. ❑ ...a reproduction of a popular religious painting. **2** → see also **reproduce**

re|pro|duc|tion num|ber (reproduction numbers) N-COUNT The **reproduction number** of an infectious disease is a measure of how many people will catch it from a single infected person. The abbreviation 'R number' is also used. ❑ At its height, the Spanish flu had a reproduction number of 2.0, meaning that each person with the disease infected two others.

re|pro|duc|tive /riːprədʌktɪv/ **1** ADJ **Reproductive** processes and organs are concerned with the reproduction of living things. ❑ ...the female reproductive system. **2** → See feature box at **body**

re|proof /rɪpruːf/ (reproofs) N-VAR If you say or do something in **reproof**, you say or do it to show that you disapprove of what someone has done or said. [FORMAL] ❑ She raised her eyebrows in reproof. ❑ ...a reproof that she responded to right away.

re|prove /rɪpruːv/ (reproves, reproving, reproved) V-T If you **reprove** someone, you speak angrily or seriously to them because they have behaved in a wrong or foolish way. [FORMAL] ❑ "There's no call for talk like that," Mrs. Evans reproved him. ❑ Women were reproved if they did not wear hats in church.

re|prov|ing /rɪpruːvɪŋ/ ADJ [usu ADJ n] If you give someone a **reproving** look or speak in a **reproving** voice, you show or say that you think they have behaved in a wrong or foolish way. [FORMAL] ❑ "Flatterer," she said giving him a mock reproving look. ● **reprov|ing|ly** ADV ❑ "I'm trying to sleep," he lied, speaking reprovingly.

rep|tile /rɛptaɪl, -tɪl/ (reptiles) N-COUNT **Reptiles** are a group of cold-blooded animals which lay eggs and have skins covered with small, hard plates called scales. Snakes, lizards, and crocodiles are reptiles.

rep|til|ian /rɛptɪliən/ **1** ADJ [usu ADJ n] A **reptilian** creature is a reptile. ❑ ...a prehistoric jungle occupied by reptilian creatures. **2** ADJ You can also use the word **reptilian** to describe something that is characteristic of a reptile or that is like a reptile. ❑ The chick is ugly and almost reptilian in its appearance.

re|pub|lic ✦✧ /rɪpʌblɪk/ (republics) N-COUNT A **republic** is a country where power is held by the people or the representatives that they elect. Republics have presidents who are elected, rather than kings or queens. ❑ In 1918, Austria became a republic. ❑ ...the Baltic republics.

re|pub|li|can ✦✧ /rɪpʌblɪkən/ (republicans) **1** ADJ **Republican** means relating to a republic. In **republican** systems of government, power is held by the people or the representatives that they elect. ❑ ...the nations that had adopted the republican form of government. **2** ADJ If someone is **Republican**, they belong to or support the Republican Party. ❑ Lower taxes made Republican voters happier with their party. ● N-COUNT A **Republican** is someone who supports or belongs to the Republican Party. ❑ What made you decide to become a Republican, as opposed to a Democrat?

re|pub|li|can|ism /rɪpʌblɪkənɪzəm/ **1** N-UNCOUNT **Republicanism** is the belief that the best system of government is a republic. **2** N-UNCOUNT **Republicanism** is support for or membership of the Republican Party in the United States.

Re|pub|li|can Par|ty N-PROPER The **Republican Party** is one of the two main political parties in the United States. It is more right-wing or conservative than the Democratic Party.

re|pu|di|ate /rɪpjuːdieɪt/ (repudiates, repudiating, repudiated) V-T If you **repudiate** something or someone, you show that you strongly disagree with them and do not want to be connected with them in any way. [FORMAL or WRITTEN] ❑ Leaders urged people to turn out in large numbers to repudiate the violence. ● **re|pu|dia|tion** /rɪpjuːdieɪʃən/ (repudiations) N-VAR ❑ He believes his public repudiation of the conference decision will enhance his standing as a leader.

re|pug|nant /rɪpʌgnənt/ ADJ [oft ADJ to n] If you think that something is horrible and disgusting, you can say that it is **repugnant**. [FORMAL] ❑ Everything about the affair was repugnant to her. ● **re|pug|nance** N-UNCOUNT ❑ She felt a deep sense of shame and repugnance.

re|pulse /rɪpʌls/ (repulses, repulsing, repulsed) **1** V-T [usu passive] If you **are repulsed** by something, you think that it is horrible and disgusting and you want to avoid it. ❑ Evil has charisma. Though people are repulsed by it, they also are drawn to its power. **2** V-T If an army or other group **repulses** a group of people, they drive it back using force. ❑ The armed forces were prepared to repulse any attacks.

re|pul|sion /rɪpʌlʃən/ N-UNCOUNT **Repulsion** is an extremely strong feeling of disgust. ❑ She gave a dramatic shudder of repulsion.

re|pul|sive /rɪpʌlsɪv/ ADJ If you describe something or someone as **repulsive**, you mean that they are horrible and disgusting and you want to avoid them. ❑ ...repulsive, fat, white slugs.

re|pur|pose /riːpɜːrpəs/ (repurposes, repurposing, repurposed) VERB If you **repurpose** something, you use it for a different purpose from that for which it was originally used. ❑ They repurposed maps as decorations. ❑ She lives in a repurposed garage.

repu|table /rɛpjətəbəl/ ADJ A **reputable** company or person is reliable and can be trusted. ❑ You are well advised to buy your car through a reputable dealer.

repu|ta|tion ✦✧ /rɛpjəteɪʃən/ (reputations) **1** N-COUNT To have a **reputation** for something means to be known or remembered for it. ❑ She has a reputation for being a very depressing writer. **2** N-COUNT Something's or someone's **reputation** is the opinion that people have about how good they are. If they have a good reputation, people think they are good. ❑ This college has a good academic reputation. **3** PHRASE If you know someone **by reputation**, you have never met them but you have heard of their reputation. ❑ She was by reputation a good organizer.

re|pute /rɪpjuːt/ **1** PHRASE [n PHR] A person or thing **of repute** or of high repute is respected and known to be good. [FORMAL] ❑ He was a writer of repute. **2** N-UNCOUNT [usu with supp] A person's or organization's **repute** is their reputation, especially when this is good. [FORMAL] ❑ Under his leadership, the U.N.'s repute has risen immeasurably.

re|put|ed /rɪpjuːtɪd/ V-T PASSIVE If you say that something **is reputed to be** true, you mean that people say it is true, but you do not know if it is definitely true. [FORMAL, VAGUENESS] ❑ He was reputed to be a fine cook. ● **re|put|ed|ly** /rɪpjuːtɪdli/ ADV ❑ He reputedly earns two million dollars a year.

re|quest ✦✧ /rɪkwɛst/ (requests, requesting, requested) **1** V-T If you **request** something, you ask for it politely or formally. [FORMAL] ❑ Mr. Dennis said he had requested access to a telephone. **2** V-T If you **request** someone to do something, you politely or formally ask them to do it. [FORMAL] ❑ Students are requested to park at the rear of the building. **3** N-COUNT If you make a **request**, you politely or formally ask someone to do something. ❑ France had agreed to his request for political asylum. **4** PHRASE If you do something **at** someone's **request**, you do it because they have asked you to. ❑ The evacuation is being organized at the request of the United Nations Secretary General. **5** PHRASE If something is given or done **on request**, it is given or done whenever you ask for it. ❑ Details are available on request.

COLLOCATIONS

request
VERB **1**
request + *noun*: access, anonymity, information, permission; hearing, meeting
request + *adverb*: formally, specifically; politely, respectfully
NOUN **3**
noun + **request**: extradition, interview, transfer
adjective + **request**: formal, official, polite, special; repeated, written
verb + **request**: make, submit; deny, decline, refuse, reject; consider, grant, receive

SYNONYMS

request
VERB **1**
ask for: *I decided to go to the next house and ask for food.*
appeal for: *The United Nations has appealed for help from the international community.*
demand: *Mr Byers last night demanded an immediate explanation from the Education Secretary.*
NOUN **3**
appeal: *Romania's government issued a last-minute appeal to him to call off his trip.*
demand: *There have been demands for services from tenants up there.*
call: *There have been calls for a new kind of security arrangement.*
plea: *Mr Nicholas made his emotional plea for help in solving the killing.*

requi|em /rɛkwiɛm/ (**requiems**) **1** N-COUNT A **requiem** or a **requiem mass** is a Catholic church service in memory of someone who has recently died. **2** N-COUNT [oft in names] A **requiem** is a piece of music for singers and musicians that can be performed either as part of a requiem mass or as part of a concert. ❑ *...a performance of Verdi's Requiem.*

re|quire ✦✧✧ /rɪkwaɪər/ (**requires, requiring, required**) **1** V-T If you **require** something or if something **is required**, you need it or it is necessary. [FORMAL] ❑ *If you require further information, you should consult the registrar.* ❑ *This isn't the kind of crisis that requires us to drop everything else.* **2** V-T If a law or rule **requires** you to do something, you have to do it. [FORMAL] ❑ *The rules also require employers to provide safety training.* ❑ *At least 35 manufacturers have flouted a law requiring prompt reporting of such malfunctions.*

SYNONYMS

require
VERB **1**
need: *He desperately needed money.*
depend on: *He depended on his writing for his income.*
necessitate: *Frank was carrying out fuel-system tests which necessitated turning the booster pumps off.*

re|quire|ment ✦✧✧ /rɪkwaɪərmənt/ (**requirements**) **1** N-COUNT A **requirement** is a quality or qualification that you must have in order to be allowed to do something or to be suitable for something. ❑ *Its products met all legal requirements.* **2** N-COUNT Your **requirements** are the things that you need. [FORMAL] ❑ *Variations of this program can be arranged to suit your requirements.* **3** → See feature box at **review**

SYNONYMS

requirement
NOUN **1**
necessity: *There is agreement on the necessity of reforms.*
need: *There's no need for you to stay.*

requi|site /rɛkwɪzɪt/ (**requisites**) **1** ADJ You can use **requisite** to indicate that something is necessary for a particular purpose. [FORMAL] ❑ *She filled in the requisite paperwork.* **2** N-COUNT A **requisite** is something that is necessary for a particular purpose. [FORMAL] ❑ *An understanding of accounting techniques is a requisite for the work of the analysts.*

requi|si|tion /rɛkwɪzɪʃən/ (**requisitions, requisitioning, requisitioned**) **1** V-T If people in authority **requisition** a vehicle, building, or food, they formally demand it and take it for official use. [FORMAL] ❑ *Authorities requisitioned hotel rooms to lodge more than 3,000 stranded vacationers.* **2** N-COUNT A **requisition** is a written document which allows a person or organization to obtain goods. ❑ *...a requisition for a replacement photocopier.*

re|route /riːruːt, riːraʊt/ (**reroutes, rerouting, rerouted**) V-T If vehicles or planes **are rerouted**, they are directed along a different route because the usual route cannot be used. ❑ *Trains on Chicago's subway system also had to be rerouted because of the storms.* ❑ *They rerouted the planes to La Guardia airport.*

re|run (**reruns, rerunning, reran**)

> The form **rerun** is used in the present tense and is also the past participle of the verb. The noun is pronounced /riːrʌn/. The verb is pronounced /riːrʌn/.

1 N-SING [N of n] If you say that something is a **rerun of** a particular event or experience, you mean that what happens now is very similar to what happened in the past. ❑ *Leaders are eager to prevent a rerun of the diplomatic disaster of 1991.* **2** V-T If someone **reruns** a process or event, they do it or organize it again. ❑ *...the opportunity to edit the input text and rerun the software.* ● N-COUNT **Rerun** is also a noun. ❑ *In the rerun he failed to make the final at all, finishing sixth.* **3** V-T [usu passive] If an election **is rerun**, it is organized again, for example because the correct procedures were not followed or because no candidate got a large enough majority. ❑ *The parties are divided on whether the election should be rerun.* ● N-COUNT [oft N of n] **Rerun** is also a noun. ❑ *The opposition has demanded a re-run of parliamentary elections held yesterday.* **4** V-T To **rerun** a movie, play, or television program means to show it or put it on again. ❑ *...the first time in TV history that a network paid to rerun a cable series.* **5** N-COUNT A **rerun** is a movie, play, or television program that is shown or put on again. ❑ *I just watched the rerun of Pride and Prejudice.*

re|sale /riːseɪl/ N-UNCOUNT The **resale** price of something that you own is the amount of money that you would get if you sold it. ❑ *...a well-maintained used car with a good resale value.*

re|sat /riːsæt/ **Resat** is the past tense and past participle of **resit**.

re|sched|ule /riːskɛdʒuːl, -dʒuəl/ (**reschedules, rescheduling, rescheduled**) **1** V-T If someone **reschedules** an event, they change the time at which it is supposed to happen. ❑ *Since I'll be away, I'd like to reschedule the meeting.* **2** V-T To **reschedule** a debt means to arrange for the person, organization, or country that owes money to pay it back over a longer period because they are in financial difficulty. ❑ *...companies that have gone bust or had to reschedule their debts.*

re|scind /rɪsɪnd/ (**rescinds, rescinding, rescinded**) V-T If a government or a group of people in power **rescind** a law or agreement, they officially withdraw it and state that it is no longer valid. [FORMAL] ❑ *The governor does not have the authority to rescind the ruling.*

res|cue ✦✧✧ /rɛskjuː/ (**rescues, rescuing, rescued**) **1** V-T If you **rescue** someone, you get them out of a dangerous or unpleasant situation. ❑ *Helicopters rescued nearly 20 people from the roof of the burning building.* ● **res|cu|er** (**rescuers**) N-COUNT ❑ *It took rescuers 90 minutes to reach the trapped men.* **2** N-UNCOUNT **Rescue** is help which gets someone out of a dangerous or unpleasant situation. ❑ *A big rescue operation has been launched for a trawler missing in the North Atlantic.* **3** N-COUNT A **rescue** is an attempt to save someone from a dangerous or unpleasant situation. ❑ *A major air-sea rescue is under way.* **4** PHRASE If you **go to** someone's **rescue** or **come to** their **rescue**, you help them when they are in danger or difficulty. ❑ *The 23-year-old's screams alerted a passerby who went to her rescue.*

re|search ✦✦✦ /rɪsɜːrtʃ, riːsɜːrtʃ/ (**researches, researching, researched**) **1** N-UNCOUNT [also N in pl] **Research** is work that involves studying something and trying to discover facts about it. ❑ *Expenditure on weapons research and development accounts for nearly $100 billion.* **2** V-T If you **research** something, you try to discover facts about it. ❑ *She spent two years in South Florida researching and filming her documentary.* ● **re|search|er** (**researchers**) N-COUNT ❑ *He chose to join the company as a market researcher.* **3** → See feature box on next page

SYNONYMS

research

NOUN **1**
study: ...*the use of maps and visual evidence in the study of local history.*
investigation: *He ordered an investigation into the affair.*
analysis: *The report is a result of careful analysis of the data.*
experimentation: ...*the ethical aspects of animal experimentation.*

VERB **2**
investigate: *Police are still investigating how the accident happened.*
study: *I know that you've been studying chimpanzees for thirty years now.*
examine: *Forensic scientists are examining what police believe to have been the bombers' car.*
experiment: *In 1857, Mendel started experimenting with peas in his monastery garden.*

VOCABULARY IN CONTEXT

Research

In order to carry out effective research, you should start from an appropriate, **valid** research question, or **hypothesis**. The next step is to list possible **sources of information**. The internet is an obvious choice, of course, but for research to be thorough, other sources such as **reference books, academic journals, public records, indexes, databases,** and **historical documents** should also be consulted. At this stage, it may be a good idea to **revisit** your hypothesis and **reassess** the **scope** of your project. Once you have **settled on** an area to work on, you should plan your research carefully. You may need to include **active research,** such as **surveys, interviews,** or **experiments,** in order to form valid **conclusions**. Finally, once you are sure you have investigated every possible source, you can begin to draw conclusions and **write up a report** to present your **findings**.

re|search fel|low (research fellows) N-COUNT A **research fellow** is a member of an academic institution whose job is to do research.

re|sell /riːsɛl/ (resells, reselling, resold) V-T/V-I If you **resell** something that you have bought, you sell it again. ❏ *Storekeepers buy them in bulk and resell them for $150 each.* ❏ *It makes sense to buy at dealer prices so you can maximize your profits if you resell.*

re|sem|blance /rɪzɛmbləns/ (resemblances) N-VAR If there is a **resemblance** between two people or things, they are similar to each other. ❏ *There was a remarkable resemblance between him and Pete.*

re|sem|ble /rɪzɛmbəl/ (resembles, resembling, resembled) V-T [no cont] If one thing or person **resembles** another, they are similar to each other. ❏ *Some of the commercially produced venison resembles beef in flavor.*

re|sent /rɪzɛnt/ (resents, resenting, resented) V-T If you **resent** someone or something, you feel bitter and angry about them. ❏ *She resents her mother for being so tough on her.*

re|sent|ful /rɪzɛntfəl/ ADJ If you are **resentful**, you feel resentment. ❏ *At first I felt very resentful and angry about losing my job.*

re|sent|ment /rɪzɛntmənt/ (resentments) N-UNCOUNT [also N in pl] **Resentment** is bitterness and anger that someone feels about something. ❏ *She expressed resentment at being interviewed by a social worker.*

res|er|va|tion /rɛzərveɪʃən/ (reservations) **1** N-VAR If you have **reservations** about something, you are not sure that it is entirely good or right. ❏ *I told him my main reservation about his film was the ending.* **2** N-COUNT If you make a **reservation**, you arrange for something such as a table in a restaurant or a room in a hotel to be kept for you. ❏ *He went to the desk to inquire and make a reservation.* **3** N-COUNT A **reservation** is an area of land that is kept separate for a particular group of people to live in. ❏ *Seventeen thousand Indians live in Arizona on a reservation.*

re|serve ♦♦◇ /rɪzɜːrv/ (reserves, reserving, reserved) **1** V-T [usu passive] If something **is reserved** for a particular person or purpose, it is kept specially for that person or purpose. ❏ *A double room with a balcony overlooking the sea had been reserved for him.* **2** V-T If you **reserve** something such as a table, ticket, or magazine, you arrange for it to be kept specially for you, rather than sold or given to someone else. ❏ *I'll reserve a table for five.* **3** N-COUNT A **reserve** is a supply of something that is available for use when it is needed. ❏ *The Persian Gulf has 65 percent of the world's oil reserves.* **4** N-COUNT A nature **reserve** is an area of land where the animals, birds, and plants are officially protected. [mainly BRIT]

in AM, use **preserve**

5 N-UNCOUNT If someone shows **reserve**, they keep their feelings hidden. ❏ *I hope that you'll overcome your reserve and let me know.* **6** PHRASE If you have something **in reserve**, you have it available for use when it is needed. ❏ *He poked around the top of his cabinet for the bottle of whiskey that he kept in reserve.* **7** to reserve judgment → see **judgment** **8** to reserve the right → see **right** ③

re|served /rɪzɜːrvd/ **1** ADJ Someone who is **reserved** keeps their feelings hidden. ❏ *He was unemotional, quiet, and reserved.* **2** ADJ A table in a restaurant or a seat in a theater that is **reserved** is being kept for someone rather than given or sold to anyone else. ❏ *Seats, or sometimes entire tables, were reserved.* **3** → See feature box at **personality**

re|serv|ist /rɪzɜːrvɪst/ (reservists) N-COUNT **Reservists** are soldiers who are not serving in the regular army of a country, but who can be called to serve whenever they are needed.

res|er|voir /rɛzərvwɑːr/ (reservoirs) **1** N-COUNT A **reservoir** is a lake that is used for storing water before it is supplied to people. **2** N-COUNT A **reservoir** of something is a large quantity of it that is available for use when needed. ❏ *...the huge oil reservoir beneath the Kuwaiti desert.*

re|set /riːsɛt/ (resets, resetting)

The form **reset** is used in the present tense and is the past tense and past participle.

V-T If you **reset** a machine or device, you adjust or set it, so that it is ready to work again or ready to perform a particular function. ❏ *She was careful to reset the alarm before she left the office.*

re|set|tle /riːsɛtəl/ (resettles, resettling, resettled) V-T/V-I If people **are resettled** by a government or organization, or if people **resettle**, they move to a different place to live because they are no longer able or allowed to stay in the area where they used to live. ❏ *The refugees were put in camps in Italy before being resettled.* ❏ *In 1990, 200,000 Soviet Jews resettled on Israeli territory.*

re|set|tle|ment /riːsɛtəlmənt/ N-UNCOUNT [oft N of n] **Resettlement** is the process of moving people to a different place to live, because they are no longer allowed to stay in the area where they used to live. ❏ *Only refugees are eligible for resettlement abroad.*

re|shape /riːʃeɪp/ (reshapes, reshaping, reshaped) V-T To **reshape** something means to change its structure or organization. ❏ *If they succeed, then they will have reshaped the political and economic map of the world.* • **re|shap|ing** N-SING [also no det, usu N of n] ❑ *This thesis led to a radical reshaping of Democratic policies.*

re|shuf|fle /riʃʌfᵊl/ (**reshuffles, reshuffling, reshuffled**) V-T When a political leader **reshuffles** the ministers in a government, he or she changes their jobs so that some of the ministers change their responsibilities. [mainly BRIT] ❑ *The prime minister told reporters this morning that he plans to reshuffle his entire cabinet.* • N-COUNT [usu sing, with supp] **Reshuffle** is also a noun. ❑ *He has carried out a partial cabinet reshuffle.*

re|side /rɪzaɪd/ (**resides, residing, resided**) **1** V-I If someone **resides** somewhere, they live there or are staying there. [FORMAL] ❑ *Margaret resides with her invalid mother in a Seattle suburb.* **2** V-I [no cont] If a quality **resides** in something, the thing has that quality. [FORMAL] ❑ *Happiness does not reside in strength or money.*

resi|dence /rɛzɪdəns/ (**residences**) **1** N-COUNT A **residence** is a house where people live. [FORMAL] ❑ *The house is currently run as a country inn, but could easily convert back into a private residence.* **2** N-UNCOUNT Your place of **residence** is the place where you live. [FORMAL] ❑ *There were significant differences among women based on age, place of residence, and educational levels.* **3** N-UNCOUNT Someone's **residence** in a particular place is the fact that they live there or that they are officially allowed to live there. ❑ *They had entered the country and had applied for permanent residence.* **4** → see also **residence hall** **5** PHRASE If someone is **in residence** in a particular place, they are living there. ❑ *The king and queen of Jordan are in residence.*

resi|dence hall (**residence halls**) **1** N-COUNT **Residence halls** are buildings with rooms or apartments, usually built by universities or colleges, in which students live during the school year. [AM] ❑ *A freshman adviser lives in each residence hall.*

in BRIT, use **hall of residence**

2 → See feature box at **university**

resi|den|cy /rɛzɪdənsi/ (**residencies**) **1** N-UNCOUNT Someone's **residency** in a particular place, especially in a country, is the fact that they live there or that they are officially allowed to live there. ❑ *He applied for Canadian residency.* **2** N-COUNT A doctor's **residency** is the period of specialized training in a hospital that he or she receives after completing an internship. [AM] ❑ *He completed his pediatric residency at Stanford University Hospital.*

resi|dent /rɛzɪdənt/ (**residents**) **1** N-COUNT The **residents** of a house or area are the people who live there. ❑ *The archbishop called on the government to build more low cost homes for local residents.* **2** ADJ [v-link ADJ] Someone who is **resident** in a country or a town lives there. ❑ *He moved to the United States in 1990 to live with his son, who had been resident in Baltimore since 1967.* **3** N-COUNT A **resident** or a **resident** doctor is a doctor who is receiving a period of specialized training in a hospital after completing his or her internship. [AM] ❑ *Many resident doctors complain that they are assigned too many duties that are usually not performed by physicians.*

SYNONYMS

resident
NOUN **1**
inhabitant: *...the inhabitants of Glasgow.*
citizen: *...American citizens.*
native: *Dr Aubin is a native of St Blaise.*
householder: *Millions of householders are eligible to claim council tax benefit.*

resi|dent al|ien (**resident aliens**) N-COUNT A **resident alien** is a person who was born in one country but has moved to another country and has official permission to live there. ❑ *Both left school in the fourth grade in Mexico and are resident aliens in the United States.*

resi|den|tial /rɛzɪdɛnʃᵊl/ **1** ADJ A **residential** area contains houses rather than offices or factories. ❑ *...a posh residential area 20 minutes from the White House.* **2** ADJ A **residential** institution is one where people live while they are studying there or being cared for there. ❑ *Training involves a two-year residential course.*

resi|dents' as|so|cia|tion (**residents' associations**) N-COUNT A **residents' association** is an organization of people who live in a particular area. Residents' associations have meetings and take action to make the area more pleasant to live in.

re|sid|ual /rɪzɪdʒuəl/ ADJ **Residual** is used to describe what remains of something when most of it has gone. ❑ *...residual radiation from nuclear weapons testing.*

resi|due /rɛzɪdu, -dyu/ (**residues**) N-COUNT A **residue** of something is a small amount that remains after most of it has gone. ❑ *Always using the same shampoo means that a residue can build up on the hair.*

re|sign /rɪzaɪn/ (**resigns, resigning, resigned**) **1** V-T/V-I If you **resign** from a job or position, you formally announce that you are leaving it. ❑ *A hospital administrator has resigned over claims he lied to get the job.* ❑ *Mr Robb resigned his position last month.* **2** V-T If you **resign** yourself to an unpleasant situation or fact, you accept it because you realize that you cannot change it. ❑ *Pat and I resigned ourselves to yet another summer without a boat.* **3** → see also **resigned**

res|ig|na|tion /rɛzɪgneɪʃᵊn/ (**resignations**) **1** N-VAR Your **resignation** is a formal statement of your intention to leave a job or position. ❑ *Bob Morgan has offered his resignation and it has been accepted.* **2** N-UNCOUNT **Resignation** is the acceptance of an unpleasant situation or fact because you realize that you cannot change it. ❑ *He sighed with profound resignation.*

re|signed /rɪzaɪnd/ ADJ If you are **resigned** to an unpleasant situation or fact, you accept it without complaining because you realize that you cannot change it. ❑ *He is resigned to the noise, the mess, the constant upheaval.*

re|sili|ent /rɪzɪlyənt/ **1** ADJ Something that is **resilient** is strong and not easily damaged by being hit, stretched, or squeezed. ❑ *...an armchair of some resilient plastic material.* • **re|sili|ence** N-UNCOUNT [also a N] ❑ *Do you feel that your muscles do not have the strength and resilience that they should have?* **2** ADJ People and things that are **resilient** are able to recover easily and quickly from unpleasant or damaging events. ❑ *When the U.S. stock market collapsed in October 1987, the Japanese stock market was the most resilient.* • **re|sili|ence** N-UNCOUNT [also a N] ❑ *...the resilience of human beings to fight after they've been attacked.*

res|in /rɛzɪn/ (**resins**) **1** N-MASS **Resin** is a sticky substance that is produced by some trees. ❑ *...a tropical tree that is bled regularly for its resin.* **2** N-MASS **Resin** is a substance that is produced chemically and used to make plastics. ❑ *The plastic resin is used in a wide range of products, including electrical wire insulation.*

res|in|ous /rɛzɪnəs/ ADJ Something that is **resinous** is like resin or contains resin. ❑ *Propolis is a hard resinous substance made by bees from the juices of plants.*

re|sist /rɪzɪst/ (**resists, resisting, resisted**) **1** V-T If you **resist** something such as a change, you refuse to accept it and try to prevent it. ❑ *They resisted our attempts to modernize the distribution of books.* **2** V-T/V-I If you **resist** someone or **resist** an attack by them, you fight back against them. ❑ *The man was shot outside his house as he tried to resist arrest.* ❑ *When she attempted to cut his nails he resisted.* **3** V-T [oft with neg] If you **resist** doing something, or **resist** the temptation to do it, you stop yourself from doing it although you would like to do it. ❑ *Congress should resist the temptation to try quick economic fixes.* **4** V-T If someone or something **resists** damage of some kind, they are not damaged. ❑ *...bodies trained and toughened to resist the cold.*

re|sist|ance /rɪzɪstəns/ (**resistances**) **1** N-UNCOUNT **Resistance** to something such as a change or a new idea is a refusal to accept it. ❑ *The U.S. wants big cuts in European agricultural export subsidies, but this is meeting resistance.* **2** N-UNCOUNT **Resistance** to an attack consists of fighting back against the people who have attacked you. ❑ *A CBS correspondent in Colombo says the troops are encountering stiff resistance.* **3** N-UNCOUNT The **resistance** of your body to germs or diseases is its power to remain unharmed or unaffected by them. ❑ *This disease is surprisingly difficult to catch, as most people have a natural resistance to it.* **4** N-UNCOUNT Wind or air **resistance** is a force which slows down a moving object or vehicle. ❑ *The design of the bicycle reduces the effects of wind resistance and drag.* **5** N-VAR In electrical engineering or physics, **resistance** is the ability of a substance or an electrical circuit to stop the flow of an electrical current through it. ❑ *The salt reduces the electrical resistance of the water.*

resistant 1099 **resource**

SYNONYMS

resistance
NOUN **1**
hostility: *There is hostility among traditionalists regarding this method of teaching history.*
opposition: *Much of the opposition to this plan has come from the media.*
aversion: *Many people have a natural and emotional aversion to insects.*

re|sist|ant /rɪzɪstənt/ **1** ADJ Someone who is **resistant** to something is opposed to it and wants to prevent it. ◻ *Some people are very resistant to the idea of exercise.* **2** ADJ If something is **resistant** to a particular thing, it is not harmed by it. ◻ *...how to improve plants to make them more resistant to disease.*

-resistant /-rɪzɪstənt/ COMB IN ADJ **-resistant** is added to nouns to form adjectives that describe something as not being harmed or affected by the thing mentioned. ◻ *Children's suncare products are normally water-resistant.*

re|sis|tor /rɪzɪstər/ (**resistors**) N-COUNT A **resistor** is a device that is designed to increase the ability of an electric circuit to stop the flow of an electric current through it. [TECHNICAL]

re|sit (**resits, resitting, resat**)

The verb is pronounced /riːsɪt/. The noun is pronounced /riːsɪt/.

V-T/V-I If someone **resits** a test or examination, they take it again, usually because they failed the first time. [BRIT]

in AM, use **retake**

• N-COUNT **Resit** is also a noun. ◻ *He failed his exams and didn't bother about the resits.*

re|skill /riːskɪl/ (**reskills, reskilling, reskilled**) V-T/V-I If you **reskill**, or if someone **reskills** you, you learn new skills, so that you can do a different job or do your old job in a different way. [BRIT, BUSINESS]

in AM, use **retrain**

re|sold /riːsoʊld/ **Resold** is the past tense and past participle of **resell**.

reso|lute /rɛzəluːt/ ADJ If you describe someone as **resolute**, you approve of them because they are very determined not to change their mind or not to give up a course of action. [FORMAL] ◻ *Voters perceive him as a decisive and resolute international leader.* • **reso|lute|ly** ADV ◻ *He resolutely refused to speak English unless forced to.*

reso|lu|tion ♦◇◇ /rɛzəluːʃən/ (**resolutions**) **1** N-COUNT A **resolution** is a formal decision made at a meeting by means of a vote. ◻ *He replied that the UN had passed two major resolutions calling for a complete withdrawal.* **2** N-COUNT If you make a **resolution**, you decide to try very hard to do something. ◻ *They made a resolution to lose all the weight gained during the Christmas holidays.* **3** N-UNCOUNT **Resolution** is determination to do something or not do something. ◻ *"I think I'll try a hypnotist," I said with sudden resolution.* **4** N-SING The **resolution** of a problem or difficulty is the final solving of it. [FORMAL] ◻ *...the successful resolution of a dispute involving UN inspectors in Baghdad.*

SYNONYMS

resolution
NOUN **1**
decision: *The moment of decision cannot be delayed.*
ruling: *Goodwin tried to have the court ruling overturned.*
judgment: *The industry was awaiting a judgment from the European Court.*
decree: *He issued a decree ordering all unofficial armed groups in the country to disband.*

re|solve ♦◇◇ /rɪzɒlv/ (**resolves, resolving, resolved**) **1** V-T To **resolve** a problem, argument, or difficulty means to find a solution to it. [FORMAL] ◻ *We must find a way to resolve these problems before it's too late.* **2** V-T If you **resolve** to do something, you make a firm decision to do it. [FORMAL] ◻ *She resolved to report the matter to the hospital's nursing supervisor.* **3** N-VAR **Resolve** is determination to do what you have decided to do. [FORMAL] ◻ *So you're saying this will strengthen the American public's resolve to go to war if necessary?*

SYNONYMS

resolve
VERB
1
work out: *People involved in it think it's a nightmare, but I'm sure it will work itself out.*
solve: *Their domestic reforms did nothing to solve the problem of unemployment.*
clear up: *During dinner, the confusion was cleared up: they had mistaken me for Kenny.*
2
decide: *She decided to take a course.*
determine: *The final wording had not yet been determined.*
settle: *They agreed to try to settle their dispute by negotiation.*
make up your mind: *Once he made up his mind to do something, there was no stopping him.*

re|solved /rɪzɒlvd/ ADJ [v-link ADJ to-inf] If you are **resolved** to do something, you are determined to do it. [FORMAL] ◻ *Most people with property to lose were resolved to defend it.*

reso|nance /rɛzənəns/ (**resonances**) **1** N-VAR If something has a **resonance** for someone, it has a special meaning or is particularly important to them. ◻ *The ideas of order, security, family, religion and country had the same resonance for them as for Michael.* **2** N-UNCOUNT If a sound has **resonance**, it is deep, clear, and strong. ◻ *His voice had lost its resonance; it was tense and strained.*

reso|nant /rɛzənənt/ ADJ A sound that is **resonant** is deep and strong. ◻ *His voice sounded oddly resonant in the empty room.*

reso|nate /rɛzəneɪt/ (**resonates, resonating, resonated**) **1** V-I If something **resonates**, it vibrates and produces a deep, strong sound. ◻ *The bass guitar began to thump so loudly that it resonated in my head.* **2** V-I You say that something **resonates** when it has a special meaning or when it is particularly important to someone. ◻ *What are the issues resonating with voters?*

re|sort ♦◇◇ /rɪzɔːrt/ (**resorts, resorting, resorted**) **1** V-I If you **resort** to a course of action that you do not really approve of, you adopt it because you cannot see any other way of achieving what you want. ◻ *Students who resort to plagiarism lose marks or they get disqualified from writing exams.* **2** N-UNCOUNT If you achieve something without **resort** to a particular course of action, you succeed without carrying out that action. To have **resort** to a particular course of action means to have to do that action in order to achieve something. ◻ *Congress has a responsibility to ensure that all peaceful options are exhausted before resort to war.* **3** PHRASE If you do something **as a last resort**, you do it because you can find no other way of getting out of a difficult situation or of solving a problem. ◻ *Nuclear weapons should be used only as a last resort.* **4** N-COUNT A **resort** is a place where a lot of people spend their vacation. ◻ *The ski resorts are expanding to meet the growing number of skiers that come here.* **5** → See feature box at **tourism**

COLLOCATIONS

resort
NOUN **4**
noun + **resort**: beach, golf, tourist, vacation
adjective + **resort**: all-inclusive, coastal, five-star, popular

re|sound /rɪzaʊnd/ (**resounds, resounding, resounded**) **1** V-I When a noise **resounds**, it is heard very loudly and clearly. [LITERARY] ◻ *A roar of approval resounded through the legislature.* **2** V-I If a place **resounds** with or to particular noises, it is filled with them. [LITERARY] ◻ *The whole place resounded with music.* ◻ *Kabul resounded to the crack of Kalashnikov fire and a flood of artillery.*

re|sound|ing /rɪzaʊndɪŋ/ **1** ADJ A **resounding** sound is loud and clear. ◻ *There was a resounding slap as Andrew struck him violently across the face.* **2** ADJ You can refer to a very great success as a **resounding** success. [EMPHASIS] ◻ *The good weather helped to make the occasion a resounding success.*

re|source ♦◇◇ /riːsɔːrs/ (**resources**) **1** N-COUNT The **resources** of an organization or person are the materials, money, and other things that they have and can use in order to function properly. ◻ *Some families don't have the resources to feed themselves adequately.* **2** N-COUNT A country's **resources** are the things

resourceful — **resplendent**

that it has and can use to increase its wealth, such as coal, oil, or land. ❑ ...*resources like coal, tungsten, oil, and copper.* ❸ → See feature box at **disaster**

COLLOCATIONS

resource
NOUN
❶
noun + **resource**: cash; police
adjective + **resource**: educational, financial, online; limited, precious, valuable
verb + **resource**: allocate, devote, divert, provide; lack, stretch
❷
noun + **resource**: energy, gas, mineral, oil
adjective + **resource**: natural, renewable; dwindling, finite, scarce
verb + **resource**: use, waste; conserve

SYNONYMS

resource
NOUN ❶
supply: *The brain requires a constant supply of oxygen.*
materials: *We have plenty of raw materials.*
fund: *He is possessed of an extraordinary fund of energy.*

---

re|source|ful /rɪsɔrsfəl/ ADJ Someone who is **resourceful** is good at finding ways of dealing with problems. ❑ *He was amazingly inventive and resourceful, and played a major role in my career.* • **re|source|ful|ness** N-UNCOUNT ❑ *Because of his adventures, he is a person of far greater experience and resourcefulness.*

re|spect ✦✦◇ /rɪspɛkt/ (respects, respecting, respected) ❶ V-T If you **respect** someone, you have a good opinion of their character or ideas. ❑ *I want him to respect me as a career woman.* ❷ N-UNCOUNT If you have **respect** for someone, you have a good opinion of them. ❑ *I have tremendous respect for Dean.* ❸ → see also **self-respect** ❹ V-T If you **respect** someone's wishes, rights, or customs, you avoid doing things that they would dislike or regard as wrong. ❑ *Finally, trying to respect her wishes, I said I'd leave.* ❺ N-UNCOUNT If you show **respect** for someone's wishes, rights, or customs, you avoid doing anything they would dislike or regard as wrong. ❑ *They will campaign for respect for aboriginal rights and customs.* ❻ V-T If you **respect** a law or moral principle, you agree not to break it. ❑ *It is about time tour operators respected the law and their own code of conduct.* • N-UNCOUNT **Respect** is also a noun. ❑ ...*respect for the law and the rejection of the use of violence.* ❼ PHRASE You can say **with all due respect** when you are politely disagreeing with someone or criticizing them. [POLITENESS] ❑ *With all due respect, I hardly think that's the point.* ❽ PHRASE If you **pay** your **respects** to someone, you go to see them or speak to them. You usually do this to be polite, and not necessarily because you want to do it. [FORMAL] ❑ *Carl had asked him to visit the hospital and to pay his respects to Francis.* ❾ PHRASE You use expressions like **in this respect** and **in many respects** to indicate that what you are saying applies to the feature you have just mentioned or to many features of something. ❑ *Within the Department of Justice are several drug-fighting agencies. The lead agency in this respect is the DEA.* ❿ PHRASE You use **with respect to** to say what something relates to. [FORMAL] ❑ *Parents often have little choice with respect to the way their child is medically treated.* ⓫ → see also **respected**

COLLOCATIONS

respect
VERB
❶
respect + adverb: greatly, highly
❹
respect + noun: privacy, right, view, wish
❻
respect + noun: law
NOUN
❷
adjective + **respect**: mutual; grudging, healthy, utmost
verb + **respect**: command, deserve, earn, gain; lose
❺
verb + **respect**: promote, show, teach

SYNONYMS

respect
VERB ❶
honor: *Those conservative people who most honor their monarch see no reason for any apology.*
admire: *He admired the way she had coped with life.*
esteem: *I greatly esteem your message in the midst of our hard struggle.*
look up to: *You're a popular girl, Grace, and a lot of the younger ones look up to you.*
NOUN ❷
regard: *I have a very high regard for him and what he has achieved.*
esteem: *Their public esteem has never been lower.*
admiration: *I have always had the greatest admiration for him.*

---

re|spect|able /rɪspɛktəbəl/ ❶ ADJ Someone or something that is **respectable** is approved of by society and considered to be morally correct. ❑ *He came from a perfectly respectable family.* • **re|spect|abil|ity** /rɪspɛktəbɪlɪti/ N-UNCOUNT ❑ *If she left, she would lose the respectability she had as a local business owner.* ❷ ADJ You can say that something is **respectable** when you mean that it is good enough or acceptable. ❑ ...*investments that offer respectable and highly attractive rates of return.* ❸ → See feature box at **urban**

re|spect|ed /rɪspɛktɪd/ ADJ Someone or something that is **respected** is admired and considered important by many people. ❑ *He is highly respected for his novels and plays as well as his translations of American novels.*

re|spect|er /rɪspɛktər/ (respecters) ❶ N-COUNT [usu N of n] If you say that someone is a **respecter** of something such as a belief or idea, you mean that they behave in a way which shows that they have a high opinion of it. ❑ *Ford was a respecter of proprieties and liked to see things done properly.* ❷ PHRASE [v-link PHR] If you say that someone or something is **no respecter of** a rule or tradition, you mean that the rule or tradition is not important to them. ❑ *Accidents and sudden illnesses are no respecters of age.*

re|spect|ful /rɪspɛktfəl/ ADJ If you are **respectful**, you show respect for someone. ❑ *The children in our family are always respectful to their elders.* • **re|spect|ful|ly** ADV ❑ *"You are an artist,"* she said respectfully.

re|spec|tive /rɪspɛktɪv/ ADJ [ADJ n] **Respective** means relating or belonging separately to the individual people you have just mentioned. ❑ *Steve and I were at very different stages in our respective careers.*

re|spec|tive|ly /rɪspɛktɪvli/ ADV [ADV with cl/group] **Respectively** means in the same order as the items that you have just mentioned. ❑ *Their sons were three and six respectively.*

res|pi|ra|tion /rɛspɪreɪʃən/ ❶ N-UNCOUNT Your **respiration** is your breathing. [MEDICAL] ❑ *His respiration grew fainter throughout the day.* ❷ → see also **artificial respiration**

res|pi|ra|tor /rɛspɪreɪtər/ (respirators) ❶ N-COUNT A **respirator** is a device that allows people to breathe when they cannot breathe naturally, for example because they are ill or have been injured. ❑ *She was so ill that she was put on a respirator.* ❷ N-COUNT A **respirator** is a device you wear over your mouth and nose in order to breathe when you are surrounded by smoke or poisonous gas. ❑ *It's smart to use a respirator if you're working with paint.*

res|pira|tory /rɛspərətɔri/ ❶ ADJ [ADJ n] **Respiratory** means relating to breathing. [MEDICAL] ❑ ...*people with severe respiratory problems.* ❷ → See also color supplement

res|pite /rɛspɪt/ ❶ N-SING [also no det, oft N from n] A **respite** is a short period of rest from something unpleasant. [FORMAL] ❑ *It was some weeks now since they'd had any respite from shellfire.* ❷ N-SING [also no det] A **respite** is a short delay before a very unpleasant or difficult situation which may or may not take place. [FORMAL] ❑ *Devaluation would only give the economy a brief respite.*

res|pite care N-UNCOUNT **Respite care** is short-term care that is provided for very old or very sick people so that the person who usually cares for them can have a break. [mainly BRIT] ❑ ...*respite care for their very ill child for short periods.*

re|splend|ent /rɪsplɛndənt/ ADJ [oft ADJ in n] If you describe someone or something as **resplendent**, you mean that their

respond appearance is very impressive and expensive-looking. [FORMAL] ❑ *Bessie, resplendent in royal blue velvet, was hovering beside the table.*

re|spond ♦♦◊ /rɪspɒnd/ (responds, responding, responded) **1** V-T/V-I When you **respond** to something that is done or said, you react to it by doing or saying something yourself. ❑ *They are likely to respond positively to the president's request for aid.* ❑ *The army responded with gunfire and tear gas.* ❑ *"I have no idea," she responded.* **2** V-I When you **respond** to a need, crisis, or challenge, you take the necessary or appropriate action. ❑ *This modest group size allows our teachers to respond to the needs of each student.* **3** V-I If a patient or their injury or illness **is responding** to treatment, the treatment is working and they are getting better. ❑ *I'm pleased to say that he is now doing well and responding to treatment.*

SYNONYMS

respond
VERB **1**
answer: *I knew Ben was lying when he answered me.*
reply: *Grace was too terrified to reply.*
retort: *'Was he afraid?' he was asked. 'Afraid of what?' he retorted.*

re|spond|ent /rɪspɒndənt/ (respondents) N-COUNT [usu pl] A **respondent** is a person who replies to something such as a survey or set of questions. ❑ *Sixty percent of the respondents said they disapproved of the president's performance.*

re|sponse ♦♦◊ /rɪspɒns/ (responses) N-COUNT [oft N to/from n, also in N] Your **response** to an event or to something that is said is your reply or reaction to it. ❑ *There has been no response to his remarks from the government.*

COLLOCATIONS

response
NOUN
adjective + **response**: direct, immediate, overwhelming, swift; angry, emotional, lukewarm, positive; appropriate, immune, initial, official
verb + **response**: draw, elicit, prompt, provoke; require

SYNONYMS

response
NOUN
answer: *I don't quite know what to say in answer to your question.*
reply: *He said in reply that the question was unfair.*
retort: *His sharp retort clearly made an impact.*

re|sponse time (response times) **1** N-COUNT The **response time** of an emergency service such as the police or the fire department is the length of time it takes them to arrive at an incident such as a crime or a fire after it has been reported to them. ❑ *Kyle says the average 911 response time is about 9.2 minutes.* **2** N-COUNT **Response time** is the time taken for a computer to do something after you have given an instruction. [COMPUTING] ❑ *The only flaw is the slightly slow response times when you press the buttons.*

re|spon|sibil|ity ♦♦◊ /rɪspɒnsɪbɪlɪti/ (responsibilities) **1** N-UNCOUNT If you have **responsibility** for something or someone, or if they are your **responsibility**, it is your job or duty to deal with them and to make decisions relating to them. ❑ *Each manager had responsibility for just under 600 properties.* **2** N-UNCOUNT If you accept **responsibility** for something that has happened, you agree that you were to blame for it or you caused it. ❑ *No one admitted responsibility for the attacks.* **3** N PLURAL Your **responsibilities** are the duties that you have because of your job or position. ❑ *I am told that he handled his responsibilities as a counselor in a highly intelligent and caring fashion.* **4** N-UNCOUNT If someone is given **responsibility**, they are given the right or opportunity to make important decisions or to take action without having to get permission from anyone else. ❑ *She would have loved to have a better-paying job with more responsibility.* **5** N-SING If you think that you have a **responsibility** to do something, you feel that you ought to do it because it is morally right to do it. ❑ *The court feels it has a responsibility to ensure that customers are not misled.* **6** N-SING If you think that you have a **responsibility** to someone, you feel that it is your duty to take action that will protect their interests. ❑ *She had decided that as a doctor she had a responsibility to her fellow creatures.*

COLLOCATIONS

responsibility
NOUN
1
adjective + **responsibility**: individual, overall, personal, sole; corporate, fiscal, legal; full, total
verb + **responsibility**: assume, bear, shoulder, take; have, share
2
verb + **responsibility**: accept, admit, claim; deny

SYNONYMS

responsibility
NOUN **1**
obligation: *When teachers assign homework, students usually feel an obligation to do it.*
duty: *My duty is to look after the animals.*
liability: *They have admitted liability but dispute the amount of his claim.*

re|spon|sible ♦♦◊ /rɪspɒnsɪbəl/ **1** ADJ [v-link ADJ] If someone or something is **responsible** for a particular event or situation, they are the cause of it or they can be blamed for it. ❑ *He still felt responsible for her death.* **2** ADJ [v-link ADJ] If you are **responsible** for something, it is your job or duty to deal with it and make decisions relating to it. ❑ *...the cabinet member responsible for the environment.* **3** ADJ [v-link ADJ to n] If you are **responsible to** a person or group, they have authority over you and you have to report to them about what you do. ❑ *I'm responsible to my board of directors.* **4** ADJ **Responsible** people behave properly and sensibly, without needing to be supervised. ❑ *He feels that the media should be more responsible in what they report.* • **re|spon|sibly** ADV [ADV with V] ❑ *He urged everyone to act responsibly.* **5** ADJ [ADJ n] **Responsible** jobs involve making important decisions or carrying out important tasks. ❑ *You are too young for such a responsible position.*

re|spon|sive /rɪspɒnsɪv/ **1** ADJ A **responsive** person is quick to react to people or events and to show emotions such as pleasure and affection. ❑ *Harriet was an easy, responsive little girl.* • **re|spon|sive|ness** N-UNCOUNT ❑ *This condition decreases sexual desire and responsiveness.* **2** ADJ If someone or something is **responsive**, they react quickly and favorably. ❑ *With an election coming soon, your representative should be very responsive to your request.* • **re|spon|sive|ness** N-UNCOUNT ❑ *Such responsiveness to public pressure is extraordinary.*

REST
① QUANTIFIER USES
② VERB AND NOUN USES

① **rest** ♦♦◊ /rɛst/ **1** QUANT [QUANT of def-n] **The rest** is used to refer to all the parts of something or all the things in a group that remain or that you have not already mentioned. ❑ *It was an experience I will treasure for the rest of my life.* • PRON **Rest** is also a pronoun. ❑ *The first payment was made yesterday, and the rest will be paid next month.* **2** PHRASE You can add **and the rest** or **all the rest of it** to the end of a statement or list when you want to refer in a vague way to other things that are associated with the ones you have already mentioned. [SPOKEN, VAGUENESS] ❑ *...a man with nice clothes, an SUV, and the rest.*

② **rest** ♦♦◊ /rɛst/ (rests, resting, rested)
→ Please look at meanings **14** and **15** to see if the expression you are looking for is shown under another headword.
1 V-T/V-I If you **rest** or if you **rest** your body, you do not do anything active for a time. ❑ *He's tired and exhausted, and has been advised to rest for two weeks.* **2** N-VAR If you get some **rest** or have a **rest**, you do not do anything active for a time. ❑ *"You're worn out, Laura," he said. "Go home and get some rest."* **3** V-I If something such as a theory or someone's success **rests** on a particular thing, it depends on that thing. [FORMAL] ❑ *Such a view rests on a number of incorrect assumptions.* **4** V-I If authority, a responsibility, or a decision **rests** with you, you have that authority or responsibility, or you are the one who will make that decision. [FORMAL] ❑ *The final decision rested with the president.* **5** V-T If you **rest** something somewhere, you put it there so that its weight is supported. ❑ *He rested his arms on the back of*

the chair. ◻ V-T/V-I If something **is resting** somewhere, or if you **are resting** it there, it is in a position where its weight is supported. ◻ *His head was resting on her shoulder.* ◻ V-I If you **rest** on or against someone or something, you lean on them so that they support the weight of your body. ◻ *He rested on his pickax for a while.* ◻ N-COUNT A **rest** is an object that is used to support something, especially your head, arms, or feet. ◻ *When you are sitting, keep your elbow on the arm rest.* ◻ V-I If your eyes **rest** on a particular person or object, you look directly at them, rather than somewhere else. [WRITTEN] ◻ *As she spoke, her eyes rested on her husband's face.* ◻ → see also **rested** ◻ PHRASE When an object that has been moving **comes to rest**, it finally stops. [FORMAL] ◻ *The plane had plowed a path through a patch of forest before coming to rest in a field.* ◻ PHRASE If someone refuses to **let** a subject **rest**, they refuse to stop talking about it, especially after they have been talking about it for a long time. ◻ *I am not prepared to let this matter rest.* ◻ PHRASE To **put someone's mind at rest** or **set** their **mind at rest** means to tell them something that stops them from worrying. ◻ *A brain scan last Friday finally set his mind at rest.* ◻ **rest assured** → see **assured** ◻ **to rest on your laurels** → see **laurel**

COLLOCATIONS
---

rest
NOUN ② ◻
adjective + **rest**: adequate, complete, short, well-earned
verb + **rest**: deserve, enjoy

SYNONYMS
---

rest
VERB ② ◻
relax: *For the first time since his arrival, he relaxed slightly.*
sleep: *I've not been able to sleep for the last few nights.*
lie down: *Why don't you go upstairs and lie down for a bit?*

rest area (rest areas) N-COUNT A **rest area** is a place beside a highway where you can buy gas and other things, use a toilet or have a meal. [mainly AM] ◻ *...a freeway rest area in Texas Canyon.*

in BRIT, use **services**

re|start /riːstɑːrt/ (restarts, restarting, restarted) V-T/V-I If you **restart** something that has been interrupted or stopped, or if it **restarts**, it starts to happen or function again. ◻ *The commissioners agreed to restart talks as soon as possible.* ◻ *The trial will restart today with a new jury.* • N-COUNT /riːstɑːrt/ **Restart** is also a noun. ◻ *After a goalless first half, Australia took the lead within a minute of the restart.*

re|state /riːsteɪt/ (restates, restating, restated) V-T If you **restate** something, you say it again in words or writing, usually in a slightly different way. [FORMAL] ◻ *He continued throughout to restate his opposition to violence.*

re|state|ment /riːsteɪtmənt/ (restatements) ◻ N-COUNT [usu N of n] A **restatement** of something that has been said or written is another statement that repeats it, usually in a slightly different form. [FORMAL] ◻ *I hope this book is not yet another restatement of the prevailing wisdom.* ◻ N-COUNT A company's **restatement** of its earnings or financial results is the act of officially restating them, for example because they have changed. ◻ *The amounts of cash involved are too small to require a restatement of earnings.*

res|tau|rant ✦✦◇ /rɛstərənt, -tərɑnt, -trɑnt/ (restaurants) N-COUNT A **restaurant** is a place where you can eat a meal and pay for it. In restaurants, your food is usually served to you at your table by a waiter or waitress. ◻ *They ate in an Italian restaurant in Forth Street.*

COLLOCATIONS
---

restaurant
NOUN
noun + **restaurant**: fast food, fish, pizza, seafood; hotel, staff, theater
adjective + **restaurant**: fine, gourmet, posh; Chinese, Indian, Italian, Japanese
restaurant + be + adjective: open; closed
verb + **restaurant**: open, own, run

res|tau|rant car [BRIT] → see **dining car**

res|tau|ra|teur /rɛstərətɜːr/ (restaurateurs) N-COUNT A **restaurateur** is a person who owns and manages a restaurant. [FORMAL]

rest|ed /rɛstɪd/ ADJ [v-link ADJ] If you feel **rested**, you feel more energetic because you have just had a rest. ◻ *He looked tanned and well rested after his vacation.*

rest|ful /rɛstfəl/ ADJ Something that is **restful** helps you to feel calm and relaxed. ◻ *Adjust the lighting so it is soft and restful.*

rest home (rest homes) N-COUNT A **rest home** is a place where old people live and are cared for when they cannot take care of themselves.

rest|ing place (resting places) ◻ N-COUNT A **resting place** is a place where you can stay and rest, usually for a short period of time. ◻ *The area was an important resting place for many types of migrant birds.* ◻ N-COUNT [usu with poss] You can refer to the place where a dead person is buried as their **resting place** or their final **resting place**. ◻ *The hill is supposed to be the resting place of the legendary King Lud.*

res|ti|tu|tion /rɛstɪtjuːʃən/ N-UNCOUNT **Restitution** is the act of giving back to a person something that was lost or stolen, or of paying them money for the loss. [FORMAL] ◻ *The victims are demanding full restitution.*

res|tive /rɛstɪv/ ADJ If you are **restive**, you are impatient, bored, or dissatisfied. [FORMAL] ◻ *The audience grew restive.* • **res|tive|ness** N-UNCOUNT ◻ *There were signs of restiveness among the younger members.*

rest|less /rɛstlɪs/ ◻ ADJ If you are **restless**, you are bored, impatient, or dissatisfied, and you want to do something else. ◻ *By 2012, she was restless and needed a new impetus for her talent.* • **rest|less|ness** N-UNCOUNT ◻ *From the audience came increasing sounds of restlessness.* ◻ ADJ If someone is **restless**, they keep moving around because they find it difficult to keep still. ◻ *My father seemed very restless and excited.* • **rest|less|ness** N-UNCOUNT ◻ *Karen complained of hyperactivity and restlessness.* • **rest|less|ly** ADV ◻ *He paced up and down restlessly, trying to put his thoughts in order.*

re|stock /riːstɒk/ (restocks, restocking, restocked) V-T/V-I If you **restock** something such as a shelf, refrigerator, or store, you fill it with food or other goods to replace what you have used or sold. ◻ *I have to restock the freezer.* ◻ *Manufacturers are testing a system that tracks products leaving the shelves and alerts employees to restock.*

Res|to|ra|tion ✦◇◇ /rɛstəreɪʃən/ ◻ N-PROPER [the N] **The Restoration** was the event in 1660 when Charles the Second became king of England, Scotland, and Ireland after a period when there had been no king or queen. ◻ ADJ [ADJ n] **Restoration** is used to refer to the style of drama and architecture that was popular during and just after the rule of Charles the Second. ◻ *...a Restoration comedy.* ◻ → see **restore**

re|stora|tive /rɪstɔːrətɪv/ (restoratives) ◻ ADJ Something that is **restorative** makes you feel healthier, stronger, or more cheerful after you have been feeling tired, weak, or miserable. ◻ *She opened the door to her bedroom, thinking how restorative a hot bath would feel tonight.* ◻ N-COUNT If you describe something as a **restorative**, you mean that it makes you feel healthier, stronger, or more cheerful after you have been feeling tired, weak, or miserable. ◻ *Seven days off could be a wonderful restorative.*

re|store ✦◇◇ /rɪstɔːr/ (restores, restoring, restored) ◻ V-T To **restore** a situation or practice means to cause it to exist again. ◻ *The army has recently been brought in to restore order.* • **res|to|ra|tion** /rɛstəreɪʃən/ N-UNCOUNT ◻ *His visit is expected to lead to the restoration of diplomatic relations.* ◻ V-T To **restore** someone or something to a previous condition or place means to cause them to be in that condition or place once again. ◻ *We will restore her to health but it may take time.* • **res|to|ra|tion** N-UNCOUNT ◻ *I owe the restoration of my hearing to this remarkable new technique.* ◻ V-T When someone **restores** something such as an old building, painting, or piece of furniture, they repair and clean it, so that it looks like it did when it was new. ◻ *...experts who specialize in examining and restoring ancient parchments.* • **res|to|ra|tion** (restorations) N-VAR ◻ *I specialized in the restoration of old houses.* • **re|stored** /rɪstɔːrd/ ADJ ◻ *The restored building helps people understand the historic significance of our neighborhood.* ◻ V-T [usu passive] If something that was lost or stolen **is restored** to its owner, it is returned to them. [FORMAL] ❑ *The following day their horses and goods were restored to them.*

re|stor|er /rɪstɔ:rər/ (**restorers**) N-COUNT [oft n N] A **restorer** is someone whose job it is to repair old buildings, paintings, or furniture so that they look like they did when they were new. ❑ *...an antique restorer.*

re|strain /rɪstreɪn/ (**restrains, restraining, restrained**) **1** V-T If you **restrain** someone, you stop them from doing what they intended or wanted to do, usually by using your physical strength. ❑ *Wally gripped my arm, partly to restrain me and partly to reassure me.* **2** V-T If you **restrain** an emotion or you **restrain** yourself from doing something, you prevent yourself from showing that emotion or doing what you wanted or intended to do. ❑ *She was unable to restrain her desperate anger.* **3** V-T To **restrain** something that is growing or increasing means to prevent it from getting too large. ❑ *The radical 500-day plan was very clear on how it intended to try to restrain inflation.*

re|strained /rɪstreɪnd/ **1** ADJ Someone who is **restrained** is very calm and unemotional. ❑ *Under the circumstances, he felt he'd been very restrained.* **2** ADJ If you describe someone's clothes or the decorations in a house as **restrained**, you mean that you like them because they are simple and not too brightly colored. [APPROVAL] ❑ *Her black suit was restrained and expensive.*

re|strain|ing or|der (**restraining orders**) N-COUNT A **restraining order** is an order by a court of law that someone should stop doing something until a court decides whether they are legally allowed to continue doing it. [mainly AM, LEGAL] ❑ *His estranged wife had taken out a restraining order against him.*

re|straint /rɪstreɪnt/ (**restraints**) **1** N-VAR **Restraints** are rules or conditions that limit or restrict someone or something. ❑ *The president is calling for spending restraints in some areas.* **2** N-UNCOUNT **Restraint** is calm, controlled, and unemotional behavior. ❑ *They behaved with more restraint than I'd expected.*

re|strict /rɪstrɪkt/ (**restricts, restricting, restricted**) **1** V-T If you **restrict** something, you put a limit on it in order to reduce it or prevent it from becoming too great. ❑ *There is talk of raising the admission requirements to restrict the number of students on campus.* ● **re|stric|tion** /rɪstrɪkʃən/ N-UNCOUNT ❑ *Since the costs of science were rising faster than inflation, some restriction on funding was necessary.* **2** V-T To **restrict** the movement or actions of someone or something means to prevent them from moving or acting freely. ❑ *The government imprisoned dissidents, forbade travel, and restricted the press.* ● **re|stric|tion** N-UNCOUNT ❑ *...the justification for this restriction of individual liberty.* **3** V-T If you **restrict** someone or their activities to one thing, they can only do, have, or deal with that thing. If you **restrict** them to one place, they cannot go anywhere else. ❑ *For the first two weeks, patients are restricted to the grounds.* **4** V-T If you **restrict** something to a particular group, only that group can do it or have it. If you **restrict** something to a particular place, it is allowed only in that place. ❑ *Trustees had decided to restrict university entry to about 30 percent of applicants.*

re|strict|ed /rɪstrɪktɪd/ **1** ADJ Something that is **restricted** is quite small or limited. ❑ *...the monotony of a heavily restricted diet.* **2** ADJ [v-link ADJ to n] If something is **restricted** to a particular group, only members of that group have it. If it is **restricted** to a particular place, it exists only in that place. ❑ *Discipline problems are by no means restricted to children in families dependent on benefits.* **3** ADJ A **restricted** area is one that only people with special permission can enter. ❑ *...a highly restricted area close to the old naval airfield.*

re|stric|tion ♦◇◇ /rɪstrɪkʃən/ (**restrictions**) **1** N-COUNT A **restriction** is an official rule that limits what you can do or that limits the amount or size of something. ❑ *...the lifting of restrictions on political parties and the news media.* **2** N-COUNT You can refer to anything that limits what you can do as a **restriction**. ❑ *His parents are trying to make up to him for the restrictions of urban living.* **3** → see also **restrict**

SYNONYMS

restriction
NOUN **1**
curb: *He called for much stricter curbs on immigration.*
limit: *There is no limit to how much fresh fruit you can eat in a day.*
control: *Critics question whether price controls would do any good.*
constraint: *Water shortages in the area will be the main constraint on development.*

re|stric|tive /rɪstrɪktɪv/ ADJ Something that is **restrictive** prevents people from doing what they want to do, or from moving freely. ❑ *The state will adopt a more restrictive policy on arms sales.*

rest|room /rɛstrum, -rʊm/ (**restrooms**) also **rest room** N-COUNT In a restaurant, theater, or other public place, a **restroom** is a room with a toilet for customers to use. [AM]

in BRIT, usually use **toilet**

re|struc|ture /ri:strʌktʃər/ (**restructures, restructuring, restructured**) V-T To **restructure** an organization or system means to change the way it is organized, usually in order to make it work more effectively. ❑ *The president called on educators and politicians to help him restructure American education.* ● **re|struc|tur|ing** (**restructurings**) N-VAR ❑ *The company is to lay off 1,520 workers as part of a restructuring.*

rest stop (**rest stops**) **1** N-COUNT On a long trip by road, a **rest stop** is a short period when you stop and leave your vehicle, for example to eat or go to the bathroom. **2** N-COUNT A **rest stop** is a place beside a highway where you can buy gas and other things, or have a meal. [mainly AM]

in BRIT, use **services**

re|sult ♦♦♦ /rɪzʌlt/ (**results, resulting, resulted**) **1** N-COUNT A **result** is something that happens or exists because of something else that has happened. ❑ *Compensation is available for people who have developed asthma as a direct result of their work.* **2** V-I If something **results** in a particular situation or event, it causes that situation or event to happen. ❑ *Fifty percent of road accidents result in head injuries.* **3** V-I If something **results** from a particular event or action, it is caused by that event or action. ❑ *Many hair problems result from what you eat.* **4** N-COUNT A **result** is the situation that exists at the end of a contest. ❑ *The final election results will be announced on Friday.* **5** N-COUNT A **result** is the number that you get when you do a calculation. ❑ *They found their computers producing different results from exactly the same calculation.* **6** N-COUNT Your **results** are the marks or grades that you get for examinations you have taken. [mainly BRIT]

in AM, usually use **scores**

re|sult|ant /rɪzʌltənt/ ADJ [ADJ n] **Resultant** means caused by the event just mentioned. [FORMAL] ❑ *At least a quarter of a million people have died in the fighting and the resultant famines.*

re|sume ♦◇◇ /rɪzu:m/ (**resumes, resuming, resumed**) **1** V-T/V-I If you **resume** an activity or if it **resumes**, it begins again. [FORMAL] ❑ *After the war he resumed his duties at Wellesley College.* ● **re|sump|tion** /rɪzʌmpʃən/ N-UNCOUNT ❑ *It is premature to speculate about the resumption of negotiations.* **2** V-T If you **resume** your seat or position, you return to the seat or position you were in before you moved. [FORMAL] ❑ *"I changed my mind," Blanche said, resuming her seat.*

SYNONYMS

resume
VERB **1**
continue: *I went up to my room to continue with my packing.*
restart: *The trial will restart today with a new jury.*
carry on: *Rachael Carr intends to carry on teaching.*

ré|su|mé /rɛzʊmeɪ/ (**résumés**) also **resumé, resume** **1** N-COUNT Your **résumé** is a brief account of your personal details, your education, and the jobs you have had. You are often asked to send a résumé when you are applying for a job. [mainly AM]

in BRIT, usually use **curriculum vitae**

2 N-COUNT [oft N of n/wh] A **résumé** is a short account, either spoken or written, of something that has happened or that someone has said or written. ❑ *I will leave with you a résumé of his most recent speech.*

re|sur|face /ri:sɜ:rfɪs/ (**resurfaces, resurfacing, resurfaced**) **1** V-I If something such as an idea or problem **resurfaces**, it becomes important or noticeable again. ❑ *These ideas resurfaced again in the American civil rights movement.* **2** V-I If someone who has not been seen for a long time **resurfaces**, they suddenly appear again. [INFORMAL] ❑ *It is likely that they would go into hiding for a few weeks, and resurface when the publicity died down.* **3** V-I If someone or something that has been under water

resurfaces, they come back to the surface of the water again. ☐ *George struggled wildly, going under and resurfacing at regular intervals.* ◳ V-T To **resurface** something such as a road means to put a new surface on it. ☐ *Meanwhile the race is on to resurface the road before next Wednesday.*

re|sur|gence /rɪsɜːrdʒəns/ N-SING [also no det, oft N *of* n] If there is a **resurgence** of an attitude or activity, it reappears and grows. [FORMAL] ☐ *Police say drugs traffickers are behind the resurgence of violence.*

re|sur|gent /rɪsɜːrdʒənt/ ADJ [usu ADJ n] You use **resurgent** to say that something is becoming stronger and more popular after a period when it has been weak and unimportant. [FORMAL] ☐ *...the threat from the resurgent nationalist movement.*

res|ur|rect /rɛzərɛkt/ (resurrects, resurrecting, resurrected) V-T If you **resurrect** something, you cause it to exist again after it had disappeared or ended. ☐ *Attempts to resurrect the ceasefire have already failed once.* • **res|ur|rec|tion** /rɛzərɛkʃən/ N-UNCOUNT ☐ *This is a resurrection of an old story from the mid-70s.*

Res|ur|rec|tion /rɛzərɛkʃən/ N-PROPER [the N] In Christian belief, **the Resurrection** is the event in which Jesus Christ came back to life after he had been killed.

re|sus|ci|tate /rɪsʌsɪteɪt/ (resuscitates, resuscitating, resuscitated) ◳ V-T If you **resuscitate** someone who has stopped breathing, you cause them to start breathing again. ☐ *A police officer and then a paramedic tried to resuscitate her.* • **re|sus|ci|ta|tion** /rɪsʌsɪteɪʃən/ N-UNCOUNT ☐ *They must even now be rushing her to the hospital for resuscitation and treatment.* ◲ V-T If you **resuscitate** something, you cause it to become active or successful again. ☐ *He has submitted a bid to resuscitate the weekly magazine, which closed in April with losses of $1 million a year.* • **re|sus|ci|ta|tion** N-UNCOUNT ☐ *The economy needs vigorous resuscitation.*

re|tail ✦◇◇ /riːteɪl/ (retails, retailing, retailed) ◳ N-UNCOUNT **Retail** is the activity of selling products direct to the public, usually in small quantities. Compare **wholesale**. [BUSINESS] ☐ *Retail stores usually count on the Christmas season to make up to half of their annual profits.* ◲ ADV [ADV after v] If something is sold **retail**, it is sold in ordinary stores direct to the public. [BUSINESS] ☐ *We sell wholesale to several chains that sell retail to the public.* ◳ V-I If an item in a store **retails** at or for a particular price, it is for sale at that price. [BUSINESS] ☐ *It originally retailed at $23.50.* ◴ → see also **retailing**

re|tail|er /riːteɪlər/ (retailers) N-COUNT A **retailer** is a person or business that sells goods to the public. [BUSINESS] ☐ *Furniture and carpet retailers are among those reporting the sharpest annual decline in sales.*

re|tail|ing /riːteɪlɪŋ/ N-UNCOUNT **Retailing** is the activity of selling products direct to the public, usually in small quantities. Compare **wholesaling**. [BUSINESS] ☐ *She spent fourteen years in retailing.*

re|tail park (retail parks) N-COUNT A **retail park** is a large, specially built area, usually at the edge of a town or city, where there are a lot of large stores and sometimes other facilities such as movie theaters and restaurants. [BRIT]

in AM, use **shopping mall**

re|tail price in|dex N-PROPER The **retail price index** is a list of the prices of typical goods which shows how much the cost of living changes from one month to the next. [BRIT, BUSINESS]

re|tail ther|apy N-UNCOUNT **Retail therapy** is the activity of shopping for clothes and other things in order to make yourself feel happier. [HUMOROUS] ☐ *There's nothing better than a bit of retail therapy.*

re|tain ✦◇◇ /rɪteɪn/ (retains, retaining, retained) ◳ V-T To **retain** something means to continue to have that thing. [FORMAL] ☐ *The interior of the shop still retains a nineteenth-century atmosphere.* ◲ → See feature box at **study**

SYNONYMS

retain
VERB ◳
keep: *'I like this dress,' she said. 'Keep it. You can have it,' said Daphne.*
reserve: *A double room with a balcony overlooking the sea had been reserved for him.*
preserve: *We will do everything to preserve peace.*
maintain: *Push yourself to make friends and to maintain the friendships.*

---

re|tain|er /rɪteɪnər/ (retainers) N-COUNT A **retainer** is a fee that you pay to someone in order to make sure that they will be available to do work for you if you need them to. ☐ *I'll need a five-hundred-dollar retainer.*

re|tain|ing wall (retaining walls) N-COUNT A **retaining wall** is a wall that is built to prevent the earth behind it from moving.

re|take (retakes, retaking, retook, retaken)

The verb is pronounced /riːteɪk/. The noun is pronounced /riːteɪk/.

◳ V-T If a military force **retakes** a place or building which it has lost in a war or battle, it captures it again. ☐ *Residents were moved 30 miles away as the rebels retook the town.* ◲ N-COUNT If during the making of a movie there is a **retake** of a particular scene, that scene is filmed again because it needs to be changed or improved. ☐ *The director was dissatisfied with the actor's response even after several retakes.* ◳ V-T If you **retake** a course or an examination, you take it again because you failed it the first time. [mainly AM] ☐ *Those who fail can retake the exam in 60 days.*

in BRIT, usually use **resit**

re|tali|ate /rɪtælieɪt/ (retaliates, retaliating, retaliated) V-I If you **retaliate** when someone harms or annoys you, you do something which harms or annoys them in return. ☐ *I was sorely tempted to retaliate.* ☐ *The company would retaliate against employees who joined a union.* • **re|talia|tion** /rɪtælieɪʃən/ N-UNCOUNT ☐ *Police said they believed the attack was in retaliation for the death of the drug trafficker.*

re|talia|tory /rɪtæliətɔːri/ ADJ [usu ADJ n] If you take **retaliatory** action, you try to harm or annoy someone who has harmed or annoyed you. [FORMAL] ☐ *There's been talk of a retaliatory blockade to prevent supplies from getting through.*

re|tard (retards, retarding, retarded)

The verb is pronounced /rɪtɑːrd/. The noun is pronounced /riːtɑːrd/.

◳ V-T If something **retards** a process, or the development of something, it makes it happen more slowly. [FORMAL] ☐ *Continuing violence will retard negotiations over the country's future.* ◲ N-COUNT If you describe someone as a **retard**, you mean that they have not developed normally, either mentally or socially. [INFORMAL, OFFENSIVE, DISAPPROVAL]

re|tar|da|tion /riːtɑːrdeɪʃən/ N-UNCOUNT [usu supp N] **Retardation** is the process of making something happen or develop more slowly, or the fact of being less well developed than other people or things of the same kind. [FORMAL] ☐ *...other parents whose children had mental retardation.*

re|tard|ed /rɪtɑːrdɪd/ ADJ Someone who is **retarded** is much less advanced mentally than most people of their age. [OLD-FASHIONED, OFFENSIVE] ☐ *...a special school for mentally retarded children.*

retch /rɛtʃ/ (retches, retching, retched) V-I If you **retch**, your stomach moves as if you are vomiting. ☐ *The smell made me retch.*

retd. **retd.** is a written abbreviation for **retired**. It is used after someone's name to indicate that they have retired from the army, navy, or air force. ☐ *...Commander J. R. Simpson, RN (retd.).*

re|tell /riːtɛl/ (retells, retelling, retold) V-T If you **retell** a story, you write it, tell it, or present it again, often in a different way from its original form. ☐ *Lucilla often asks her sisters to retell the story.*

re|ten|tion /rɪtɛnʃən/ N-UNCOUNT The **retention** of something is the keeping of it. [FORMAL] ☐ *The Citizens' Forum supported special powers for Quebec but also argued for the retention of a strong central government.*

re|ten|tive /rɪtɛntɪv/ ADJ [usu ADJ n] If you have a **retentive** memory, you are able to remember things very well. ☐ *Luke had an amazingly retentive memory.*

re|think (rethinks, rethinking, rethought) ◳ V-T If you **rethink** something such as a problem, a plan, or a policy, you think about it again and change it. ☐ *Both major political parties are having to rethink their policies.* ◲ N-SING If you have a **rethink** of a problem, a plan, or a policy, you think about it again and change it. [JOURNALISM] ❑ *There must be a rethink of government policy toward this vulnerable group.*

> The verb is pronounced /riθɪŋk/. The noun is pronounced /ˈriːθɪŋk/.

re|thought /riθɔːt/ Rethought is the past tense and past participle of **rethink**.

reti|cent /ˈrɛtɪsənt/ ADJ Someone who is **reticent** does not tell people about things. ❑ *She is so reticent about her achievements.* • **reti|cence** N-UNCOUNT ❑ *Pearl didn't mind his reticence; in fact she liked it.*

reti|na /ˈrɛtɪnə/ (retinas) **1** N-COUNT Your **retina** is the area at the back of your eye. It receives the image that you see and then sends the image to your brain. ❑ *Bruno had to have eye surgery on a torn retina two years ago.* **2** → See feature box at **eyesight**; See also color supplement

reti|nal /ˈrɛtɪnəl/ ADJ [ADJ n] **Retinal** means relating to a person's retina. [TECHNICAL] ❑ *...retinal cancer.*

reti|nue /ˈrɛtɪnuː, -ˈnjuː/ (retinues) N-COUNT An important person's **retinue** is the group of servants, friends, or assistants who go with them and take care of their needs. ❑ *Mind trainers are now part of a tennis star's retinue.*

re|tire ✧✧ /rɪˈtaɪər/ (retires, retiring, retired) **1** V-I When older people **retire**, they leave their job and usually stop working completely. ❑ *At the age when most people retire, he is ready to face a new career.* **2** V-I When an athlete **retires** from their sport, they stop playing in competitions. When they **retire** from a race or a game, they stop competing in it. ❑ *I have decided to retire from Formula One racing at the end of the season.* **3** V-I When a jury in a court of law **retires**, the members of it leave the court in order to decide whether someone is guilty or innocent. ❑ *The jury will retire to consider its verdict today.* **4** → see also **retired** **5** → See feature box at **work**

re|tired /rɪˈtaɪərd/ **1** ADJ A **retired** person is an older person who has left his or her job and has usually stopped working completely. ❑ *...a seventy-three-year-old retired teacher from Florida.* **2** → see also **retire**

re|tiree /rɪtaɪəˈriː/ (retirees) N-COUNT A **retiree** is a retired person. [mainly AM] ❑ *...retirees who have completely different expectations of what later life might bring.*

re|tire|ment ✧✧✧ /rɪˈtaɪərmənt/ (retirements) **1** N-VAR **Retirement** is the time when a worker retires. ❑ *The proportion of the population who are over retirement age has grown tremendously in the past few years.* **2** N-UNCOUNT A person's **retirement** is the period in their life after they have retired. ❑ *"Growing Older" considered the needs of the elderly for financial support during retirement.*

re|tire|ment fund (retirement funds) N-COUNT A **retirement fund** is a special fund which people pay money into so that, when they retire from their job, they will receive money regularly as a pension. [mainly AM]

re|tire|ment home (retirement homes) **1** N-COUNT A **retirement home** is the same as a **rest home**. **2** N-COUNT A **retirement home** is a house or apartment that is part of a housing development built for retired persons.

re|tire|ment plan (retirement plans) N-COUNT A **retirement plan** is a savings plan in which part of the money that you earn is invested in the plan for you to use when you retire. [AM, BUSINESS] ❑ *I started putting money into my retirement plan at work when I was 26.*

re|tir|ing /rɪˈtaɪərɪŋ/ **1** ADJ Someone who is **retiring** is shy and avoids meeting other people. ❑ *I'm still that shy, retiring little girl who was afraid to ask for candy in the store.* **2** → see also **retire**

re|told /riːˈtoʊld/ **Retold** is the past tense and past participle of **retell**.

re|took /riːˈtʊk/ **Retook** is the past tense of **retake**.

re|tool /riːˈtuːl/ (retools, retooling, retooled) V-T/V-I If the machines in a factory or the items of equipment used by a firm **are retooled**, they are replaced or changed so that they can do new tasks. ❑ *Each time the product changes, the machines have to be retooled.* ❑ *His company will have to retool for a new line of products.* • **re|tool|ing** N-UNCOUNT ❑ *Retooling, or recasting new toy molds, is a slow and expensive process.*

re|tort /rɪˈtɔːrt/ (retorts, retorting, retorted) V-T To **retort** means to reply angrily to someone. [WRITTEN] ❑ *"You can't smoke in here," Shaw said.—"Don't worry, it's not tobacco," he retorted.* • N-COUNT **Retort** is also a noun. ❑ *His sharp retort clearly made an impact.*

re|touch /riːˈtʌtʃ/ (retouches, retouching, retouched) V-T If someone **retouches** something such as a picture or a photograph, they improve it, for example by painting over parts of it. ❑ *He said the photographs had been retouched.* ❑ *She retouched her makeup.*

re|trace /rɪˈtreɪs/ (retraces, retracing, retraced) V-T If you **retrace** your steps or **retrace** your way, you return to the place you started from by going back along the same route. ❑ *He retraced his steps to the spot where he'd left the case.*

re|tract /rɪˈtrækt/ (retracts, retracting, retracted) **1** V-T/V-I If you **retract** something that you have said or written, you say that you did not mean it. [FORMAL] ❑ *Mr. Smith hurriedly sought to retract the statement, but it had just been broadcast on national radio.* ❑ *He's hoping that if he makes me feel guilty, I'll retract.* • **re|trac|tion** /rɪˈtrækʃən/ (retractions) N-COUNT ❑ *Miss Pearce said she expected an unqualified retraction of his comments within twenty-four hours.* **2** V-T/V-I When a part of a machine or a part of a person's body **retracts** or **is retracted**, it moves inward or becomes shorter. [FORMAL] ❑ *Torn muscles retract and lose strength, structure, and tightness.*

re|tract|able /rɪˈtræktəbəl/ ADJ [usu ADJ n] A **retractable** part of a machine or a building can be moved inward or backward. ❑ *A 20,000-seat arena with a retractable roof is planned.*

re|train /riːˈtreɪn/ (retrains, retraining, retrained) V-T/V-I If you **retrain**, or if someone **retrains** you, you learn new skills, especially in order to get a new job. ❑ *Look at what you can do to retrain for a job that will make you happier.* • **re|train|ing** N-UNCOUNT ❑ *measures such as the retraining of the workforce at their place of work.*

re|tread /ˈriːtrɛd/ (retreads) **1** N-COUNT [usu sing, oft N of n] If you describe something such as a book, movie, or song as a **retread**, you mean that it contains ideas or elements that have been used before, and that it is not very interesting or original. [DISAPPROVAL] ❑ *His last book, "Needful Things," was a retread of tired material.* **2** N-COUNT A **retread** is an old tire which has been given a new surface or tread and can be used again.

re|treat ✧✧ /rɪˈtriːt/ (retreats, retreating, retreated) **1** V-I If you **retreat**, you move away from something or someone. ❑ *"I've already got a job," I said quickly, and retreated from the room.* **2** V-I When an army **retreats**, it moves away from enemy forces in order to avoid fighting them. ❑ *The French, suddenly outnumbered, were forced to retreat.* • N-VAR **Retreat** is also a noun. ❑ *In June 1942, the British 8th Army was in full retreat.* **3** V-I If you **retreat** from something such as a plan or a way of life, you give it up, usually in order to do something safer or less extreme. ❑ *She retreated from public life.* • N-VAR **Retreat** is also a noun. ❑ *The president's remarks appear to signal that there will be no retreat from his position.* **4** N-COUNT A **retreat** is a quiet, isolated place that you go to in order to rest or to do things in private. ❑ *He spent yesterday hidden away in his country retreat.*

re|trench /rɪˈtrɛntʃ/ (retrenches, retrenching, retrenched) V-I If a person or organization **retrenches**, they spend less money. [FORMAL] ❑ *Shortly afterwards, cuts in defense spending forced the aerospace industry to retrench.*

re|trench|ment /rɪˈtrɛntʃmənt/ (retrenchments) N-VAR **Retrenchment** means spending less money. [FORMAL] ❑ *Defense planners predict an extended period of retrenchment.*

re|tri|al /ˈriːtraɪəl/ (retrials) N-COUNT [usu sing] A **retrial** is a second trial of someone for the same offense. ❑ *Judge Hill said the jury's task was "beyond the realms of possibility" and ordered a retrial.*

ret|ri|bu|tion /ˌrɛtrɪˈbjuːʃən/ N-UNCOUNT **Retribution** is punishment for a crime, especially punishment that is carried out by someone other than the official authorities. [FORMAL] ❑ *He didn't want any further involvement for fear of retribution.*

re|triev|al /rɪˈtriːvəl/ **1** N-UNCOUNT The **retrieval** of information from a computer is the process of getting it back. ❑ *...electronic storage and retrieval systems.* **2** N-UNCOUNT The **retrieval** of something is the process of getting it back

re|trieve /rɪtriːv/ (retrieves, retrieving, retrieved) **1** V-T If you **retrieve** something, you get it back from the place where you left it. ❏ *The men were trying to retrieve weapons left when the army abandoned the island.* **2** V-T If you manage to **retrieve** a situation, you succeed in bringing it back into a more acceptable state. ❏ *He, the one man who could retrieve that situation, might receive the call.* **3** V-T To **retrieve** information from a computer or from your memory means to get it back. ❏ *Computers can instantly retrieve millions of information bits.*

re|triev|er /rɪtriːvər/ (retrievers) N-COUNT A **retriever** is a kind of dog. Retrievers are traditionally used to bring back birds and animals that their owners have shot.

ret|ro /rɛtroʊ/ ADJ **Retro** clothes, music, and objects are based on the styles of the past. [JOURNALISM] ❏ *...clothing stores where original versions of many of today's retro looks can be found for a fraction of the price.*

PREFIX
retro-
is used to form adjectives and nouns which indicate that something goes back or goes backward. *For example, a* **retrogressive** *step returns a situation to a state that is worse than the current one.*

retro|ac|tive /rɛtroʊæktɪv/ ADJ If a decision or action is **retroactive**, it is intended to take effect from a date in the past. [FORMAL] ❏ *There are few precedents for this sort of retroactive legislation.* • **retro|ac|tive|ly** ADV [ADV with v] ❏ *It isn't yet clear whether the new law can actually be applied retroactively.*

retro|fit /rɛtroʊfɪt/ (retrofits, retrofitting, retrofitted) V-T To **retrofit** a machine or a building means to put new parts or new equipment in it after it has been in use for some time, especially to improve its safety or make it work better. ❏ *Much of this business involves retrofitting existing planes.* • N-COUNT [also N n] **Retrofit** is also a noun. ❏ *A retrofit may involve putting in new door jambs.*

retro|grade /rɛtroʊɡreɪd/ ADJ [usu ADJ n] A **retrograde** action is one that you think makes a situation worse rather than better. [FORMAL] ❏ *This is, as far as we're concerned, a real retrograde step for human rights.*

retro|gres|sion /rɛtroʊɡrɛʃən/ N-UNCOUNT [also a N] **Retrogression** means moving back to an earlier and less efficient stage of development. [FORMAL] ❏ *There has been a retrogression in the field of human rights since 1975.*

retro|gres|sive /rɛtroʊɡrɛsɪv/ ADJ If you describe an action or idea as **retrogressive**, you disapprove of it because it returns to old ideas or beliefs and does not take advantage of recent progress. [FORMAL, DISAPPROVAL] ❏ *...the retrogressive policies of the national parties.*

retro|spect /rɛtroʊspɛkt/ PHRASE When you consider something **in retrospect**, you think about it afterward, and often have a different opinion about it from the one that you had at the time. ❏ *In retrospect, I wish that I had thought about alternative courses of action.*

retro|spec|tive /rɛtroʊspɛktɪv/ (retrospectives) **1** N-COUNT A **retrospective** is an exhibition or showing of work done by an artist over many years, rather than his or her most recent work. ❏ *...a retrospective of the films of Judy Garland.* **2** ADJ **Retrospective** feelings or opinions concern things that happened in the past. ❏ *Afterwards, retrospective fear of the responsibility would make her feel almost faint.* • **retro|spec|tive|ly** ADV ❏ *Retrospectively, it seems as if they probably were negligent.* **3** ADJ **Retrospective** laws or legal actions take effect from a date before the date when they are officially approved. [mainly BRIT]

in AM, use **retroactive**

re|tune /riːtuːn/ (retunes, retuning, retuned) V-T/V-I To **retune** a piece of equipment such as a radio, television, or video means to adjust it so that it receives a different channel, or so that it receives the same channel on a different frequency. ❏ *...this means that listeners in cars should not have to retune as they drive across the country.* ❏ *...plans to retune VCRs to allow viewers to receive the signal.*

re|turn ♦♦♦ /rɪtɜːrn/ (returns, returning, returned) **1** V-I When you **return** to a place, you go back there after you have been away. ❏ *There are unconfirmed reports that Aziz will return to Moscow within hours.* **2** N-SING Your **return** is your arrival back at a place where you had been before. ❏ *Kenny explained the reason for his sudden return to Dallas.* **3** V-T If you **return** something that you have borrowed or taken, you give it back or put it back. ❏ *I enjoyed the book and said so when I returned it.* • N-SING **Return** is also a noun. ❏ *The main demand of the Indians is for the return of one-and-a-half-million acres of forest to their communities.* **4** V-T If you **return** something somewhere, you put it back where it was. ❏ *He returned the notebook to his jacket.* **5** V-T If you **return** someone's action, you do the same thing to them as they have just done to you. If you **return** someone's feelings, you feel the same way toward them as they feel toward you. ❏ *Back at the station the chief inspector returned the call.* **6** V-I If a feeling or situation **returns**, it comes back or happens again after a period when it was not present. ❏ *Official reports in Algeria suggest that calm is returning to the country.* • N-SING **Return** is also a noun. ❏ *It was like the return of his youth.* **7** V-I If you **return** to a state that you were in before, you start being in that state again. ❏ *Life has improved and returned to normal.* • N-SING **Return** is also a noun. ❏ *He made an uneventful return to mental health.* **8** V-I If you **return** to a subject that you have mentioned before, you begin talking about it again. ❏ *The power of the church is one theme all these writers return to.* **9** V-I If you **return** to an activity that you were doing before, you start doing it again. ❏ *At that stage he will be 52, young enough to return to politics if he wishes to do so.* • N-SING **Return** is also a noun. ❏ *He has not ruled out the shock possibility of a return to football.* **10** V-T When a judge or jury **returns** a verdict, they announce whether they think the person on trial is guilty or not. ❏ *They returned a verdict of not guilty.* **11** ADJ A **return** ticket is a ticket for a trip from one place to another and then back again. [mainly BRIT]

in AM, usually use **round trip**

12 ADJ [ADJ n] The **return** trip is the part of a trip that takes you back to where you started from. ❏ *Buy an extra ticket for the return trip.* **13** N-COUNT The **return** on an investment is the profit that you get from it. [BUSINESS] ❏ *Profits have picked up this year but the return on capital remains tiny.* **14** PHRASE If you do something **in return** for what someone else has done for you, you do it because they did that thing for you. ❏ *You pay regular premiums and in return the insurance company will pay out a lump sum.* **15 to return fire** → see **fire** ②

SYNONYMS
return
VERB
1
go back: *I went back to bed.*
retreat: *The young nurse made a face at the supervisor's retreating figure.*
turn back: *They were nearly forced to turn back.*
3
put back: *Put it back in the freezer.*
replace: *Replace the caps on the bottles.*
restore: *We expect to restore the power supply within two hours.*
give back: *I gave the textbook back to him.*

re|turn|able /rɪtɜːrnəbəl/ **1** ADJ [usu ADJ n] **Returnable** containers are intended to be taken back to the place they came from so that they can be used again. ❏ *All beverages must be sold in returnable containers.* **2** ADJ [usu ADJ n] If something such as a sum of money or a document is **returnable**, it will eventually be given back to the person who provided it. ❏ *Landlords can charge a returnable deposit.*

re|turn|ee /rɪtɜːrniː/ (returnees) N-COUNT [usu pl] A **returnee** is a person who returns to the country where they were born, usually after they have been away for a long time. ❏ *The number of returnees could go as high as half a million.*

re|turn match [BRIT] → see **rematch**

re|turn vis|it (return visits) N-COUNT If you make a **return visit**, you visit someone who has already visited you, or you go back to a place where you have already been once. ❑ *He made a nostalgic return visit to Hawaii.*

re|tweet /ri:twi:t/ (**retweets, retweeting, retweeted**) V-T If you **retweet** something, you copy another user's comment on the Twitter website for your own followers to read. ❑ *His comments were immediately retweeted by hundreds of people.*

re|uni|fi|ca|tion /ri:ju:nɪfɪkeɪʃ°n/ N-UNCOUNT [with supp] The **reunification** of a country or city that has been divided into two or more parts for some time is the joining of it together again. ❑ *...the reunification of East and West Beirut in 1991.*

re|union /ri:ju:niən/ (**reunions**) ◼ N-COUNT A **reunion** is a party attended by members of the same family, school, or other group who have not seen each other for a long time. ❑ *The association holds an annual reunion.* ◼ N-VAR A **reunion** is a meeting between people who have been separated for some time. ❑ *The children weren't allowed to see her for nearly a week. It was a very emotional reunion.*

re|unite /ri:ju:naɪt/ (**reunites, reuniting, reunited**) ◼ V-T If people **are reunited**, or if they **reunite**, they meet each other again after they have been separated for some time. ❑ *She and her youngest son were finally allowed to be reunited with their family.* ◼ V-T/V-I If a divided organization or country **is reunited**, or if it **reunites**, it becomes one united organization or country again. ❑ *As of this evening, Germany is reunited. In Berlin they're celebrating.* ❑ *His first job will be to reunite the army.*

re|us|able /ri:ju:zəb°l/ ADJ Things that are **reusable** can be used more than once. ❑ *Store refrigerated food in reusable containers rather than in plastic wrap or aluminum foil.*

re|use (**reuses, reusing, reused**)

The verb is pronounced /ri:ju:z/. The noun is pronounced /ri:ju:s/.

◼ V-T When you **reuse** something, you use it again instead of throwing it away. ❑ *Try where possible to reuse paper.* • N-UNCOUNT **Reuse** is also a noun. ❑ *Copper, brass, and aluminium are separated and remelted for reuse.* ◼ → See feature box at **recycle**

rev /rɛv/ (**revs, revving, revved**) ◼ V-T/V-I When the engine of a vehicle **revs**, or when you **rev** it, the engine speed is increased as the accelerator is pressed. ❑ *The engine started, revved, and the car jerked away down the hill.* ❑ *The old bus was revving its engine, ready to start the journey back towards Mexico City.* • PHRASAL VERB **Rev up** means the same as **rev**. ❑ *...drivers revving up their engines.* ❑ *...the sound of a car revving up.* ◼ N-PLURAL If you talk about the **revs** of an engine, you are referring to its speed, which is measured in revolutions per minute. ❑ *The engine delivers instant acceleration whatever the revs.*

Rev. also **Rev** **Rev.** is a written abbreviation for **Reverend**. ❑ *...the Rev. John Roberts.*

re|value /ri:vælju:/ (**revalues, revaluing, revalued**) ◼ V-T When a country **revalues** its currency, it increases the currency's value so that it can buy more foreign currency than before. ❑ *Countries enjoying surpluses will be under no pressure to revalue their currencies.* ◼ V-T To **revalue** something means to increase the amount that you calculate it is worth so that its value stays roughly the same in comparison with other things, even if there is inflation. ❑ *It is now usual to revalue property assets on a more regular basis.*

re|vamp /ri:væmp/ (**revamps, revamping, revamped**) V-T If someone **revamps** something, they make changes to it in order to try and improve it. ❑ *All the country's political parties have accepted that it is time to revamp the system.* • N-SING **Revamp** is also a noun. ❑ *The revamp includes replacing the old navy uniform with a crisp blue and white cotton outfit.*

The verb is pronounced /ri:væmp/. The noun is pronounced /ri:væmp/.

Revd [BRIT] **Revd** is a written abbreviation for **Reverend**.

in AM, use **Rev.**

re|veal ✦✦◇ /rɪvi:l/ (**reveals, revealing, revealed**) ◼ V-T To **reveal** something means to make people aware of it. ❑ *She has refused to reveal the whereabouts of her daughter.* ❑ *A survey of the American diet has revealed that a growing number of people are overweight.* ◼ V-T If you **reveal** something that has been out of sight, you uncover it so that people can see it. ❑ *In the principal room, a gray carpet was removed to reveal the original pine floor.*

═══ SYNONYMS ═══

reveal
VERB
◼
disclose: *Neither side would disclose details of the transaction.*
impart: *I am about to impart knowledge to you that you will never forget.*
divulge: *Officials refuse to divulge details of the negotiations.*
let on: *She never let on that anything was wrong.*
◼
show: *These figures show an increase of over one million in unemployment.*
display: *It was unlike Gordon to display his feelings.*
exhibit: *The economy continued to exhibit signs of decline in September.*

re|veal|ing /rɪvi:lɪŋ/ ADJ A **revealing** statement, account, or action tells you something that you did not know, especially about the person doing it or making it. ❑ *...a revealing interview.*

re|veille /rɛvəli/ N-UNCOUNT **Reveille** is the time when soldiers have to get up in the morning. ❑ *Many crew members were up before reveille.*

rev|el /rɛv°l/ (**revels, reveling** or **revelling, reveled** or **revelled**) V-I If you **revel** in a situation or experience, you enjoy it very much. ❑ *Annie was smiling and laughing, clearly reveling in the attention.*

rev|ela|tion /rɛvəleɪʃ°n/ (**revelations**) ◼ N-COUNT A **revelation** is a surprising or interesting fact that is made known to people. ❑ *...the seemingly everlasting revelations about his private life.* ◼ N-VAR The **revelation** of something is the act of making it known. ❑ *...following the revelation of his affair with a former secretary.* ◼ N-SING If you say that something you experienced was a **revelation**, you are saying that it was very surprising or very good. ❑ *Degas's work had been a revelation to her.*

rev|ela|tory /rɛvələtɔri/ ADJ A **revelatory** account or statement tells you a lot that you did not know. ❑ *...Barbara Stoney's revelatory account of the author's life.*

rev|el|er /rɛvələr/ (**revelers**) also **reveller** N-COUNT [usu pl] **Revelers** are people who are enjoying themselves in a noisy way, often while they are drunk. [LITERARY] ❑ *...a crowd of Fourth of July revelers.*

rev|el|ry /rɛv°lri/ (**revelries**) N-UNCOUNT [also N in pl] **Revelry** is people enjoying themselves in a noisy way, often while they are drunk. [LITERARY] ❑ *...New Year revelries.*

re|venge /rɪvɛndʒ/ (**revenges, revenging, revenged**) ◼ N-UNCOUNT **Revenge** involves hurting or punishing someone who has hurt or harmed you. ❑ *The prisoners took revenge on their captors, eventually overcoming them.* ◼ V-T If you **revenge** yourself on someone who has hurt you, you hurt them in return. [WRITTEN] ❑ *The paper accused her of trying to revenge herself on her former lover.*

rev|enue ✦◇◇ /rɛvənju:/ (**revenues**) ◼ N-UNCOUNT [also N in pl] **Revenue** is money that a company, organization, or government receives from people. [BUSINESS] ❑ *...a boom year at the movies, with record advertising revenue and high ticket sales.* ◼ → see also **Internal Revenue Service** ◼ → See feature box at **business**

═══ SYNONYMS ═══

revenue
NOUN ◼
income: *Over a third of their income comes from comedy videos.*
profit: *The bank made pre-tax profits of $3.5 million.*
proceeds: *The proceeds from the concert will go towards famine relief.*

rev|enue stream (**revenue streams**) N-COUNT A company's **revenue stream** is the amount of money that it receives from selling a particular product or service. [BUSINESS] ❑ *The events business, she said, was crucial to the group in that it provides a constant revenue stream.*

re|verb /ri:vɜrb, rɪvɜrb/ N-UNCOUNT **Reverb** is a shaking or echoing effect that is added to a sound, often by an electronic device. ❑ *The unit includes built-in digital effects like reverb.*

re|ver|ber|ate /rɪvɜrbəreɪt/ (**reverberates, reverberating, reverberated**) ◼ V-I When a loud sound **reverberates** through a place, it echoes through it. ❑ *Day in and day out, the flat crack of*

re|ver|ber|a|tion /rɪvɜrbəreɪʃən/ (**reverberations**) **1** N-COUNT [usu pl] **Reverberations** are serious effects that follow a sudden, dramatic event. ❑ *In the end, the attempt failed, but the reverberations still can be felt today.* **2** N-VAR A **reverberation** is the shaking and echoing effect that you hear after a loud sound has been made. ❑ *Jason heard the reverberation of the slammed door.*

re|vere /rɪvɪər/ (**reveres, revering, revered**) V-T If you **revere** someone or something, you respect and admire them greatly. [FORMAL] ❑ *The Chinese revered corn as a gift from heaven.* ● **re|vered** ADJ ❑ *...some of the country's most revered institutions.*

rev|er|ence /rɛvərəns/ N-UNCOUNT **Reverence** for someone or something is a feeling of great respect for them. [FORMAL] ❑ *We stand together now in mutual support and in reverence for the dead.*

Rev|er|end /rɛvərənd/ N-TITLE **Reverend** is a title used before the name or rank of an officially appointed Christian religious leader. The abbreviation **Rev.** is also used. ❑ *The service was led by the Reverend Jim Simons.*

rev|er|ent /rɛvərənt/ ADJ If you describe someone's behavior as **reverent**, you mean that they are showing great respect for a person or thing. ❑ *...the reverent hush of a rapt audience.* ● **rev|er|ent|ly** ADV [usu ADV after v] ❑ *He got up and took the book out almost reverently.*

rev|er|en|tial /rɛvərɛnʃəl/ ADJ Something that is **reverential** has the qualities of respect and admiration. [FORMAL] ❑ *They approach their work with an almost reverential air.* ● **rev|er|en|tial|ly** ADV [ADV with v] ❑ *He reverentially returned the novel to a glass-fronted bookcase.*

rev|erie /rɛvəri/ (**reveries**) N-COUNT A **reverie** is a state of imagining or thinking about pleasant things, as if you are dreaming. [FORMAL] ❑ *The announcer's voice brought Holden out of his reverie.*

re|ver|sal /rɪvɜrsəl/ (**reversals**) **1** N-COUNT A **reversal** of a process, policy, or trend is a complete change in it. ❑ *The paper says the move represents a complete reversal of previous U.S. policy.* **2** N-COUNT When there is a role **reversal** or a **reversal of** roles, two people or groups exchange their positions or functions. ❑ *When children end up taking care of their parents, it is a strange role reversal indeed.*

re|verse ◆◇◇ /rɪvɜrs/ (**reverses, reversing, reversed**) **1** V-T When someone or something **reverses** a decision, policy, or trend, they change it to the opposite decision, policy, or trend. ❑ *They have made it clear they will not reverse the decision to increase prices.* **2** V-T If you **reverse** the order of a set of things, you arrange them in the opposite order, so that the first thing comes last. ❑ *Because the normal word order is reversed in passive sentences, they are sometimes hard to follow.* **3** V-T If you **reverse** the positions or functions of two things, you change them so that each thing has the position or function that the other one had. ❑ *He reversed the position of the two stamps.* **4** V-T/V-I When a car **reverses** or when you **reverse** it, the car is driven backward. [mainly BRIT]

in AM, usually use **back up**

5 N-UNCOUNT If your car is in **reverse**, you have changed gears so that you can drive it backward. ❑ *He lurched the car in reverse along the ruts to the access road.* **6** ADJ **Reverse** means opposite from what you expect or to what has just been described. ❑ *The wrong attitude will have exactly the reverse effect.* **7** N-SING If you say that one thing is **the reverse** of another, you are emphasizing that the first thing is the complete opposite of the second thing. ❑ *He was not at all jolly. Quite the reverse.* **8** N-SING The **reverse** or the **reverse** side of a flat object which has two sides is the less important or the other side. ❑ *A chart on the reverse of this letter highlights your savings.* **9** PHRASE If something happens **in reverse** or goes **into reverse**, things happen in the opposite way from what usually happens or from what has been happening. ❑ *Amis tells the story in reverse, from the moment the man dies.* **10** PHRASE If you **reverse the charges** when you make a telephone call, the person who you are phoning pays the cost of the call and not you. [mainly BRIT]

in AM, usually use **call collect**

SYNONYMS

reverse
VERB **1**
cancel: *The Navy has decided to cancel its contract for the A-12 Stealth attack plane.*
overturn: *His nine-month sentence was overturned by Appeals Court judge Justice Watkins.*
undo: *If Michael won, he would undo everything I have fought for.*
rescind: *Trade Union leaders have demanded the government rescind the price rise.*

re|verse dis|cri|mi|na|tion N-UNCOUNT **Reverse discrimination** is the policy of deliberately giving jobs and other opportunities to members of less advantaged groups, such as ethnic minorities or women, instead of to those who traditionally have more power and more advantages, such as White people or men. ❑ *...a policy of reverse discrimination in favor of children from poor backgrounds.*

re|verse en|gi|neer|ing N-UNCOUNT **Reverse engineering** is a process in which a product or system is analyzed in order to see how it works, so that a similar version of the product or system can be produced more cheaply. [BUSINESS] ❑ *Xerox set about a process of reverse engineering. It pulled the machines apart and investigated the Japanese factories to find out how they could pull off such feats.*

re|verse gear (**reverse gears**) N-VAR The **reverse gear** of a vehicle is the gear which you use in order to make the vehicle go backward.

re|verse psy|chol|ogy N-UNCOUNT If you use **reverse psychology** on someone, you try to get them to do something by saying or doing the opposite of what they expect. ❑ *But how about a little reverse psychology? Playing hard-to-get is known to be more effective than begging.*

re|verse video N-UNCOUNT **Reverse video** is the process of reversing the colors of normal characters and background on a computer screen, in order to highlight the display. [COMPUTING]

re|vers|ible /rɪvɜrsɪbəl/ **1** ADJ If a process or an action is **reversible**, its effects can be reversed so that the original situation returns. ❑ *Heart disease is reversible in some cases, according to a study published last summer.* **2** ADJ **Reversible** clothes or materials have been made so that either side can be worn or shown as the outside. ❑ *...a reversible vest.*

re|vers|ing light [BRIT] → see **backup light**

re|ver|sion /rɪvɜrʒən/ (**reversions**) **1** N-SING [also no det, N to n] A **reversion** to a previous state, system, or kind of behavior is a change back to it. ❑ *This looks like a reversion to Mexico's previous solidarity with the global left.* **2** N-VAR [oft the N of n to n] The **reversion** of land or property to a person, family, or country is the return to them of the ownership or control of the land or property. [LEGAL]

re|vert /rɪvɜrt/ (**reverts, reverting, reverted**) **1** V-I When people or things **revert** to a previous state, system, or type of behavior, they go back to it. ❑ *Jackson said her boss became increasingly depressed and reverted to smoking heavily.* **2** V-I When someone **reverts** to a previous topic, they start talking or thinking about it again. [WRITTEN] ❑ *In the car she reverted to the subject uppermost in her mind. "You know, I really believe what Grandma told you."* **3** V-I If property, rights, or money **revert** to someone, they become that person's again after someone else has had them for a period of time. [LEGAL] ❑ *When the lease ends, the property reverts to the owner.*

re|view ◆◆◇ /rɪvyu/ (**reviews, reviewing, reviewed**) **1** N-COUNT [oft N of n, also prep N] A **review** of a situation or system is its formal examination by people in authority. This is usually done in order to see whether it can be improved or corrected. ❑ *The president ordered a review of U.S. economic aid to Jordan.* **2** V-T If you **review** a situation or system, you consider it carefully to see what is wrong with it or how it could be improved. ❑ *The president reviewed the situation with his cabinet yesterday.* **3** N-COUNT A **review** is a report in the media in which someone gives their opinion of something such as a new book or movie. ❑ *We've never had a good review in the music press.* **4** V-T If someone **reviews** something such as a new book or movie, they write a report or give a talk on television or radio

review board in which they express their opinion of it. ☐ *Richard Coles reviews all the latest movie releases.* **5** V-T/V-I When you **review** for an examination, you read things again and make notes in order to be prepared for the examination. [AM] ☐ *Reviewing for exams gives you a chance to bring together all the individual parts of the course.* ☐ *Review all the notes you need to cover for each course.* • N-COUNT **Review** is also a noun. ☐ *If you have to cover 12 chapters in American history, begin by planning on three two-hour reviews with four chapters per session.*

in BRIT, use **revise**

6 → See feature box at **learning**

VOCABULARY IN CONTEXT

Won't be back!

If you want delicious food served by **courteous** staff, do not go to this restaurant. I booked a table for a family celebration recently, and almost everything there was **appalling**. Once seated, we realized our table **left a lot to be desired**. It was too small, and was in an extremely noisy spot. Not wishing to **grumble**, we resolved to **put up with** it. To say that the menu had serious **limitations** would be an **understatement**. The seafood section was **inadequate**, and vegetarian options were non-existent. I suggested we leave, but my parents didn't want a **fuss**. The server who took our order was **brusque**. My appetizer was overly salted, which I felt was **unacceptable**, so I sent it back. Two of our main courses were **unsatisfactory**; one was cold, and the other had overcooked meat. It gives me no pleasure to **find fault** with a local business, but this restaurant simply does not **satisfy basic requirements**.

re|view board (review boards) N-COUNT A **review board** is a group of people in authority who examine a situation or system to see if it should be improved, corrected, or changed.

re|view|er /rɪvyuər/ (reviewers) N-COUNT A **reviewer** is a person who reviews new books, movies, television programs, CDs, plays, or concerts. ☐ *...the reviewer for Atlantic Monthly.*

re|view|ing stand (reviewing stands) N-COUNT A **reviewing stand** is a special raised platform from which military and political leaders watch military parades.

re|vile /rɪvaɪl/ (reviles, reviling, reviled) V-T If someone or something is **reviled**, people hate them intensely or show their hatred of them. [FORMAL] ☐ *He was just as feared and reviled as his tyrannical parents.* ☐ *What right had the crowd to revile the players for something they could not help?* • **re|viled** ADJ ☐ *He is probably the most reviled man in contemporary theater.*

re|vise /rɪvaɪz/ (revises, revising, revised) **1** V-T If you **revise** the way you think about something, you adjust your thoughts, usually in order to make them better or more suited to how things are. ☐ *With time he came to revise his opinion of the profession.* **2** V-T If you **revise** a price, amount, or estimate, you change it to make it more fair, realistic, or accurate. ☐ *They realized that some of their prices were higher than their competitors' and revised prices accordingly.* **3** V-T When you **revise** an article, a book, a law, or a piece of music, you change

it in order to improve it, make it more modern, or make it more suitable for a particular purpose. ☐ *Three editors handled the work of revising the articles for publication.* **4** V-I When you **revise** for an examination, you read things again and make notes in order to be prepared for the examination. [BRIT]

in AM, use **review**

re|vi|sion /rɪvɪʒ³n/ (revisions) **1** N-VAR To make a **revision** of something that is written or something that has been decided means to make changes to it in order to improve it, make it more modern, or make it more suitable for a particular purpose. ☐ *The phase of writing that is actually most important is revision.* **2** N-UNCOUNT When people who are studying do **revision**, they read things again and make notes in order to prepare for an examination. [BRIT]

in AM, use **review**

3 → See feature box at **study**

re|vi|sion|ism /rɪvɪʒ³nɪzəm/ N-UNCOUNT **Revisionism** is a theory of socialism that is more moderate than normal Marxist theory, and is therefore considered unacceptable by most Marxists. [FORMAL, DISAPPROVAL] ☐ *The reforms come after decades of hostility to revisionism.*

re|vi|sion|ist /rɪvɪʒ³nɪst/ (revisionists) **1** ADJ If you describe a person or their views as **revisionist**, you mean that they reject traditionally held beliefs about a particular historical event or events. [FORMAL] ☐ *...the revisionist interpretation of the French Revolution.* • N-COUNT A **revisionist** is a person who has revisionist views. [FORMAL] ☐ *The reputation of the navigator is under assault from historical revisionists.* **2** ADJ If a socialist describes another socialist's actions or opinions as **revisionist**, they mean that they are unacceptable because they are more moderate than normal Marxist theory allows. [FORMAL, DISAPPROVAL] ☐ *This revisionist thesis departs even further from Marxist assertions.* • N-COUNT A **revisionist** is a person who has revisionist views. [FORMAL] ☐ *...ferocious infighting between Stalinist hardliners and revisionists.*

re|vis|it /riːvɪzɪt/ (revisits, revisiting, revisited) **1** V-T If you **revisit** a place, you return there for a visit after you have been away for a long time, often after the place has changed a lot. ☐ *In the summer, when we returned to Canada, we revisited this lake at dawn.* **2** V-T If you **revisit** a subject or topic, you discuss it again or consider it again. ☐ *The committee agreed to revisit the issue at their next meeting.* **3** → See feature box at **research**

re|vi|tal|ize /riːvaɪt³laɪz/ (revitalizes, revitalizing, revitalized)

in BRIT, also use **revitalise**

V-T To **revitalize** something that has lost its activity or its health means to make it active or healthy again. ☐ *This hair conditioner is excellent for revitalizing dry, lifeless hair.*

re|viv|al /rɪvaɪv³l/ (revivals) **1** N-COUNT When there is a **revival** of something, it becomes active or popular again. ☐ *This return to realism has produced a revival of interest in a number of artists.* **2** N-COUNT A **revival** is a new production of a play, an opera, or a ballet. ☐ *...John Clement's revival of Chekhov's "The Seagull."* **3** N-UNCOUNT A **revival** meeting is a public religious event that is intended to make people more interested in Christianity. ☐ *He toured the country organizing revival meetings.*

re|viv|al|ism /rɪvaɪvəlɪzəm/ N-UNCOUNT [usu adj N] **Revivalism** is a movement whose aim is to make a religion more popular and more influential. ☐ *...a time of intense religious revivalism.*

re|viv|al|ist /rɪvaɪvəlɪst/ (revivalists) ADJ [ADJ n] **Revivalist** people or activities are involved in trying to make a particular religion more popular and more influential. ☐ *...the Hindu revivalist party.* • N-COUNT **Revivalist** is also a noun. ☐ *Booth was a revivalist intent on his Christian vocation.*

re|vive /rɪvaɪv/ (revives, reviving, revived) **1** V-T/V-I When something such as the economy, a business, a trend, or a feeling **is revived** or when it **revives**, it becomes active, popular, or successful again. ☐ *...an attempt to revive the economy.* **2** V-T When someone **revives** a play, opera, or ballet, they present a new production of it. ☐ *His plays continue to be revived both here and abroad.* **3** V-T/V-I If you **revive** someone who has fainted or if they **revive**, they become conscious again. ☐ *She and a neighbor tried in vain to revive him.*

re|vivi|fy /rɪvɪvɪfaɪ/ (revivifies, revivifying, revivified) V-T To revivify a situation, event, or activity means to make it more active, lively, or efficient. [FORMAL] ❑ *They've revivified rhythm and blues singing by giving it dance beats.*

re|voke /rɪvoʊk/ (revokes, revoking, revoked) V-T When people in authority **revoke** something such as a license, a law, or an agreement, they cancel it. [FORMAL] ❑ *The government revoked her husband's license to operate migrant labor crews.*

re|volt /rɪvoʊlt/ (revolts, revolting, revolted) **1** N-VAR A **revolt** is an illegal and often violent attempt by a group of people to change their country's political system. ❑ *It was undeniably a revolt by ordinary people against their leaders.* **2** V-I When people **revolt**, they make an illegal and often violent attempt to change their country's political system. ❑ *In 1375 the townspeople revolted.* **3** N-VAR A **revolt** by a person or group against someone or something is a refusal to accept the authority of that person or thing. ❑ *Conservative Republicans had led the revolt against the budget package.* **4** V-I When people **revolt** against someone or something, they reject the authority of that person or reject that thing. ❑ *In 1978 California taxpayers revolted against higher taxes.*

re|volt|ing /rɪvoʊltɪŋ/ ADJ If you say that something or someone is **revolting**, you mean you think they are horrible and disgusting. ❑ *The smell in the cell was revolting.*

revo|lu|tion ✦✧ /rɛvəluːʃᵊn/ (revolutions) **1** N-COUNT A **revolution** is a successful attempt by a large group of people to change the political system of their country by force. ❑ *The period since the revolution has been one of political turmoil.* **2** N-COUNT A **revolution** in a particular area of human activity is an important change in that area. ❑ *The nineteenth century witnessed a revolution in ship design and propulsion.*

> **SYNONYMS**
> **revolution**
> NOUN **1**
> **revolt**: *It was undeniably a revolt by ordinary people against their leaders.*
> **uprising**: *...a popular uprising against the authoritarian government.*
> **coup**: *...a military coup.*
> **rebellion**: *The British soon put down the rebellion.*

revo|lu|tion|ary ✦✧ /rɛvəluːʃəneri/ (revolutionaries) **1** ADJ **Revolutionary** activities, organizations, or people have the aim of causing a political revolution. ❑ *Do you know anything about the revolutionary movement?* **2** N-COUNT A **revolutionary** is a person who tries to cause a revolution or who takes an active part in one. ❑ *The revolutionaries laid down their arms and their leaders went into voluntary exile.* **3** ADJ **Revolutionary** ideas and developments involve great changes in the way that something is done or made. ❑ *Invented in 1951, the rotary engine is a revolutionary concept in internal combustion.*

> **SYNONYMS**
> **revolutionary**
> ADJ
> **1**
> **radical**: *...threats by left-wing radical groups to disrupt the proceedings.*
> **extremist**: *...a marked rise in extremist violence.*
> **subversive**: *This courageous and subversive movie has attracted widespread critical support.*
> **3**
> **innovative**: *He was one of the most creative and innovative engineers of his generation.*
> **novel**: *It will also be used to test novel ideas for data handling and workflow.*
> **radical**: *The country needs a period of calm without more surges of radical change.*

revo|lu|tion|ize /rɛvəluːʃənaɪz/ (revolutionizes, revolutionizing, revolutionized)

> in BRIT, also use **revolutionise**

V-T When something **revolutionizes** an activity, it causes great changes in the way that it is done. ❑ *Over the past forty years plastics have revolutionised the way we live.*

re|volve /rɪvɒlv/ (revolves, revolving, revolved) **1** V-I If you say that one thing **revolves** around another thing, you mean that the second thing is the main feature or focus of the first thing. ❑ *Since childhood, her life has revolved around tennis.* **2** V-I If a discussion or conversation **revolves** around a particular topic, it is mainly about that topic. ❑ *The debate revolves around specific accounting techniques.* **3** V-I If one object **revolves** around another object, the first object turns in a circle around the second object. ❑ *The satellite revolves around the earth every hundred minutes.* **4** V-T/V-I When something **revolves** or when you **revolve** it, it moves or turns in a circle around a central point or line. ❑ *Overhead, the fan revolved slowly.*

re|volv|er /rɪvɒlvər/ (revolvers) N-COUNT A **revolver** is a kind of hand gun. Its bullets are kept in a revolving cylinder in the gun.

re|volv|ing door (revolving doors) **1** N-COUNT [usu pl] Some large buildings have **revolving doors** instead of an ordinary door. They consist of four glass doors which turn together in a circle around a vertical post. ❑ *As he went through the revolving doors he felt his courage deserting him.* **2** N-COUNT [usu sing] When you talk about a **revolving door**, you mean a situation in which the employees or owners of an organization keep changing. [DISAPPROVAL] ❑ *They have accepted an offer from another firm with a busy revolving door.*

re|vue /rɪvjuː/ (revues) N-COUNT A **revue** is a theatrical performance consisting of songs, dances, and jokes about recent events.

re|vul|sion /rɪvʌlʃᵊn/ N-UNCOUNT Someone's **revulsion** at something is the strong feeling of disgust or disapproval they have toward it. ❑ *...their revulsion at the act of desecration.*

revved up ADJ [v-link ADJ] If someone is **revved up**, they are prepared for an important or exciting activity. [INFORMAL] ❑ *My people come to work and I get them all revved up.*

re|ward ✦✧ /rɪwɔːrd/ (rewards, rewarding, rewarded) **1** N-COUNT A **reward** is something that you are given, for example because you have behaved well, worked hard, or provided a service to the community. ❑ *A bonus of up to five percent can be added to a student's final exam score as a reward for good spelling, punctuation, and grammar.* **2** N-COUNT A **reward** is a sum of money offered to anyone who can give information about lost or stolen property, a missing person, or someone who is wanted by the police. ❑ *The firm last night offered a $10,000 reward for information leading to the conviction of the killer.* **3** V-T If you do something and **are rewarded** with a particular benefit, you receive that benefit as a result of doing that thing. ❑ *Make the extra effort to impress the buyer and you will be rewarded with a quicker sale at a better price.* **4** N-COUNT The **rewards** of something are the benefits that you receive as a result of doing or having that thing. ❑ *The company is just starting to reap the rewards of long-term investments.* **5** VERB If you say that something **rewards** your attention or effort, you mean that it is worth spending time or effort on it. [FORMAL] ❑ *It is a difficult book to read, but it richly rewards the effort.*

> **COLLOCATIONS**
> **reward**
> NOUN
> **2**
> adjective + **reward**: generous
> verb + **reward**: offer, pay
> **4**
> adjective + **reward**: immense, just, rich; financial
> verb + **reward**: reap
> VERB **3**
> **reward** + adverb: amply, handsomely, richly; financially
> **reward** + noun: effort, loyalty, patience, persistence

> **SYNONYMS**
> **reward**
> NOUN **1**
> **honor**: *He was showered with honors – among them an Oscar.*
> **prize**: *You can only claim your prize by calling our claims number.*
> **bonus**: *...a special bonus payment.*

re|ward|ing /rɪwɔːrdɪŋ/ ADJ An experience or action that is **rewarding** gives you satisfaction or brings you benefits. ❑ *...a career that she found stimulating and rewarding.*

re|wind /riwaɪnd/ (rewinds, rewinding, rewound) V-T/V-I When the tape in a video **rewinds** or when you **rewind** it, the tape goes backward so that you can play it again. Compare **fast forward**. ❑ *He rewound the video and turned up the volume.*

re|wire /riwaɪər/ (rewires, rewiring, rewired) V-T If someone **rewires** a building or an electrical appliance, a new system of electrical wiring is put into it. ❑ *Their first job was to rewire the whole house and install a new furnace.* ❑ *I have had to spend a lot of money having my house rewired.* • **re|wir|ing** N-UNCOUNT *The rewiring of the apartment ran very smoothly.*

re|word /riwɜrd/ (rewords, rewording, reworded) V-T When you **reword** something that is spoken or written, you try to express it in a way that is more accurate, more acceptable, or more easily understood. ❑ *All right, I'll reword my question.*

re|work /riwɜrk/ (reworks, reworking, reworked) V-T If you **rework** something such as an idea or a piece of writing, you reorganize it and make changes to it in order to improve it or bring it up to date. ❑ *See if you can rework your schedule and come up with practical ways to reduce the number of hours you're on call.*

re|wound /riwaʊnd/ **Rewound** is the past tense and past participle of **rewind**.

re|write /riraɪt/ (rewrites, rewriting, rewrote, rewritten) **1** V-T If someone **rewrites** a piece of writing such as a book, an article, or a law, they write it in a different way in order to improve it. ❑ *Following this critique, students rewrite their papers and submit them for final evaluation.* **2** V-T If you accuse someone such as a government of **rewriting** history, you are criticizing them for selecting and presenting particular historical events in a way that suits their own purposes. [DISAPPROVAL] ❑ *We have always been an independent people, no matter how they rewrite history.*

RFD /ɑr ɛf di/ [AM] **RFD** is a mail service in rural areas. **RFD** is an abbreviation of 'rural free delivery.' ❑ *Barbara Lally, RFD 5, Mountain Road, Goffstown, NH 03045.*

rhap|sod|ic /ræpsɒdɪk/ ADJ Language and feelings that are **rhapsodic** are very powerful and full of delight in something. [FORMAL] ❑ *...a rhapsodic letter about the birth of her first baby.*

rhap|so|dize /ræpsədaɪz/ (rhapsodizes, rhapsodizing, rhapsodized)

in BRIT, also use **rhapsodise**

V-I If you **rhapsodize** about someone or something, you express great delight or enthusiasm about them. [FORMAL] ❑ *The critics rhapsodized over her performance in "Autumn Sonata."*

rhap|so|dy /ræpsədi/ (rhapsodies) N-COUNT [oft in names] A **rhapsody** is a piece of music that has an irregular form and is full of feeling. ❑ *...George Gershwin's Rhapsody In Blue.*

rhe|sus fac|tor /risəs fæktər/ N-SING The **rhesus factor** is something that is in the blood of most people. If someone's blood contains this factor, they are rhesus positive. If it does not, they are rhesus negative.

rheto|ric /rɛtərɪk/ **1** N-UNCOUNT If you refer to speech or writing as **rhetoric**, you disapprove of it because it is intended to convince and impress people but may not be sincere or honest. [DISAPPROVAL] ❑ *The change is largely cosmetic, a matter of acceptable political rhetoric rather than social reality.* **2** N-UNCOUNT **Rhetoric** is the skill or art of using language effectively. [FORMAL] ❑ *...the noble institutions of political life, such as political rhetoric, public office, and public service.*

rhe|tori|cal /rɪtɒrɪkəl/ **1** ADJ A **rhetorical** question is one that is asked in order to make a statement rather than to get an answer. ❑ *He grimaced slightly, obviously expecting no answer to his rhetorical question.* • **rhe|tori|cal|ly** /rɪtɒrɪkli/ ADV [ADV with v] ❑ *"Do these kids know how lucky they are?" Jackson asked rhetorically.* **2** ADJ **Rhetorical** language is intended to be grand and impressive. [FORMAL] ❑ *These arguments may have been used as a rhetorical device to argue for a perpetuation of a United Nations role.* • **rhe|tori|cal|ly** ADV *Suddenly, the narrator speaks in his most rhetorically elevated mode.*

rhe|tori|cian /rɛtərɪʃən/ (rhetoricians) N-COUNT A **rhetorician** is a person who is good at public speaking or who is trained in the art of rhetoric. ❑ *...an able and fiercely contentious rhetorician.*

rheu|mat|ic /rumætɪk/ ADJ [ADJ n] **Rheumatic** is used to describe conditions and pains that are related to rheumatism. **Rheumatic** joints are swollen and painful because they are affected by rheumatism. ❑ *...new treatments for a range of rheumatic diseases.*

rheu|mat|ic fe|ver N-UNCOUNT **Rheumatic fever** is a disease which causes fever, and swelling and pain in your joints.

rheu|ma|tism /rumətɪzəm/ N-UNCOUNT **Rheumatism** is an illness that makes your joints or muscles stiff and painful. Older people, especially, suffer from rheumatism.

rheu|ma|toid ar|thri|tis /rumətɔɪd ɑrθraɪtɪs/ N-UNCOUNT **Rheumatoid arthritis** is a long-lasting disease that causes your joints, for example your hands or knees, to swell up and become painful.

rheu|ma|tol|ogy /rumətɒlədʒi/ N-UNCOUNT **Rheumatology** is the area of medicine that is concerned with rheumatism, arthritis, and related diseases. • **rheu|ma|tolo|gist** (rheumatologists) N-COUNT ❑ *He was a consultant rheumatologist at the local hospital.*

rheumy /rumi/ ADJ [usu ADJ n] If someone has **rheumy** eyes, their eyes are red and watery, usually because they are very ill or old. [LITERARY]

Rh fac|tor /ɑr eɪtʃ fæktər/ N-UNCOUNT The **Rh factor** is the same as the **rhesus factor**.

rhine|stone /raɪnstoʊn/ (rhinestones) N-COUNT [oft N n] **Rhinestones** are shiny, glass jewels that are used in cheap jewelry and to decorate clothes.

rhi|ni|tis /raɪnaɪtɪs/ N-UNCOUNT If you have **rhinitis** or allergic **rhinitis**, your nose is very sore and liquid keeps coming out of it. [MEDICAL]

rhi|no /raɪnoʊ/ (rhinos) **1** N-COUNT A **rhino** is the same as a **rhinoceros**. [INFORMAL] **2** → See feature box at **animal**

rhi|noc|er|os /raɪnɒsərəs/ (rhinoceroses) N-COUNT A **rhinoceros** is a large Asian or African animal with thick, gray skin and a horn, or two horns, on its nose.

---WORD HISTORY---

rhinoceros

Rhinoceros came into English via Latin from Greek *rhinokerōs*, from *rhino-*, meaning 'of the nose,' and *keras*, meaning 'horn.'

---

rhi|zome /raɪzoʊm/ (rhizomes) N-COUNT **Rhizomes** are the horizontal stems from which some plants, such as irises, grow. Rhizomes are found on or just under the surface of the earth.

rho|do|den|dron /roʊdədɛndrən/ (rhododendrons) N-VAR A **rhododendron** is a large bush with large flowers which are usually pink, red, or purple.

rhom|bus /rɒmbəs/ (rhombuses) N-COUNT A **rhombus** is a geometric shape which has four equal sides but is not a square. [TECHNICAL]

rhu|barb /rubɑrb/ N-UNCOUNT **Rhubarb** is a plant with large leaves and long red stems. You can cook the stems with sugar to make jam or pie.

rhyme /raɪm/ (rhymes, rhyming, rhymed) **1** V-RECIP If one word **rhymes** with another or if two words **rhyme**, they have a very similar sound. Words that rhyme with each other are often used in poems. ❑ *June always rhymes with moon in old love songs.* ❑ *...the sort of people who give their children names that rhyme: Donnie, Ronnie, Connie.* **2** V-I If a poem or song **rhymes**, the lines end with words that have very similar sounds. ❑ *In his efforts to make it rhyme, he seems to have chosen the first word that came into his head.* **3** N-COUNT A **rhyme** is a word which rhymes with another word, or a set of lines which rhyme. ❑ *The one rhyme for passion is fashion.* **4** N-COUNT A **rhyme** is a short poem which has rhyming words at the ends of its lines. ❑ *He was teaching Helen a little rhyme.* **5** N-UNCOUNT **Rhyme** is the use of rhyming words as a technique in poetry. If something is written **in rhyme**, it is written as a poem in which the lines rhyme. ❑ *The plays are in rhyme.*

rhym|ing slang N-UNCOUNT **Rhyming slang** is a spoken, informal kind of language used in Britain and Australia in which you do not use the normal word for something, but say a word or phrase that rhymes with it instead. In Cockney rhyming slang, for example, people say 'apples and pears' to mean 'stairs'.

rhythm ♦⬦⬦ /rɪðəm/ (rhythms) **1** N-VAR A **rhythm** is a regular series of sounds or movements. ❑ *His music of that period fused the rhythms of jazz with classical forms.* **2** N-COUNT A **rhythm** is a regular pattern of changes, for example changes in your body, in the seasons, or in the tides. ❑ *Begin to listen to your own body rhythms.* **3** → See feature box at **music**

rhythm and blues N-UNCOUNT **Rhythm and blues** is a style of popular music developed in the 1940s from blues music, but using electrically amplified instruments. The abbreviation **R&B** is also used.

rhyth|mic /rɪðmɪk/ also **rhythmical** /rɪðmɪkəl/ ADJ A **rhythmic** movement or sound is repeated at regular intervals, forming a regular pattern or beat. ❑ *Good breathing is slow, rhythmic and deep.* ● **rhyth|mi|cal|ly** /rɪðmɪkli/ ADV [ADV after v] ❑ *She stood, swaying her hips, moving rhythmically.*

rhythm meth|od N-SING [usu the N] The **rhythm method** is a practice in which a couple try to prevent pregnancy by having sex only at times when the woman is not likely to become pregnant.

rhythm sec|tion N-SING The **rhythm section** of a band is the musicians whose main job is to supply the rhythm. It usually consists of bass and drums, and sometimes keyboard instruments.

rib /rɪb/ (ribs) **1** N-COUNT Your **ribs** are the 12 pairs of curved bones that surround your chest. ❑ *Her heart was thumping against her ribs.* **2** N-COUNT A **rib** of meat such as beef or pork is a piece that has been cut to include one of the animal's ribs. ❑ *...a rib of beef.* ❑ *...pork ribs.* **3** → See feature box at **body**; See also color supplement

rib|ald /rɪbəld/ ADJ [usu ADJ n] A **ribald** remark or sense of humor is rather vulgar and refers to sex in a humorous way. ❑ *...her ribald comments about a fellow guest's body language.*

ribbed /rɪbd/ ADJ [usu ADJ n] A **ribbed** surface, material, or garment has a raised pattern of parallel lines on it. ❑ *...ribbed cashmere sweaters.*

rib|bing /rɪbɪŋ/ **1** N-UNCOUNT **Ribbing** is friendly teasing. [INFORMAL] ❑ *I got quite a lot of ribbing from my teammates.* **2** N-UNCOUNT **Ribbing** is a method of knitting that makes a raised pattern of parallel lines. You use ribbing, for example, around the edge of sweaters so that the material can stretch without losing its shape.

rib|bon /rɪbən/ (ribbons) **1** N-VAR A **ribbon** is a long, narrow piece of cloth that you use for tying things together or as a decoration. ❑ *She had tied back her hair with a peach satin ribbon.* **2** N-COUNT A typewriter or printer **ribbon** is a long, narrow piece of cloth containing ink and is used in a typewriter or printer.

rib cage (rib cages) N-COUNT Your **rib cage** is the structure of ribs in your chest. It protects your lungs and other organs.

ri|bo|fla|vin /raɪboʊfleɪvɪn/ N-UNCOUNT **Riboflavin** is a vitamin that occurs in green vegetables, milk, fish, eggs, liver, and kidneys.

rice ♦⬦⬦ /raɪs/ (rices) N-MASS **Rice** consists of white or brown grains taken from a cereal plant. You cook rice and usually eat it with meat or vegetables. ❑ *...a meal consisting of chicken, rice, and vegetables.*

rice pa|per N-UNCOUNT **Rice paper** is very thin paper made from rice plants. It is used in cooking.

rice pud|ding (rice puddings) N-VAR **Rice pudding** is a dessert made from rice, milk, and sugar.

rich ♦♦⬦ /rɪtʃ/ (richer, richest, riches) **1** ADJ A **rich** person has a lot of money or valuable possessions. ❑ *You're going to be a very rich man.* ● N-PLURAL **The rich** are rich people. ❑ *This is a system in which the rich are taken care of and the poor are left to suffer.* **2** N-PLURAL **Riches** are valuable possessions or large amounts of money. ❑ *An Olympic gold medal can lead to untold riches for an athlete.* **3** ADJ A **rich** country has a strong economy and produces a lot of wealth, so many people who live there have a high standard of living. ❑ *There is hunger in many parts of the world, even in rich countries.* **4** N-PLURAL If you talk about the Earth's **riches**, you are referring to things that exist naturally in large quantities and that are useful and valuable, for example minerals, wood, and oil. ❑ *...Russia's vast natural riches.* **5** ADJ [v-link ADJ in n, ADJ n] If you say that something is **rich in** a useful or valuable substance or is a **rich source** of it, it contains a lot of it. ❑ *Liver and kidneys are particularly rich in vitamin A.* **6** ADJ **Rich** food contains a lot of fat or oil. ❑ *Additional cream would make it too rich.* ● **rich|ness** N-UNCOUNT ❑ *A squeeze of fresh lime juice cuts the richness of the avocado.* **7** ADJ **Rich** soil contains large amounts of substances that make it good for growing crops or flowers. ❑ *Farmers grow rice in the rich soil.* **8** ADJ A **rich** deposit of a mineral or other substance is a large amount of it. ❑ *...the country's rich deposits of the metal lithium.* ● **rich|ness** N-UNCOUNT ❑ *...the richness of Tibet's mineral deposits.* **9** ADJ [ADJ n] If you say that something is a **rich** vein or source of something such as humor, ideas, or information, you mean that it can provide a lot of that thing. ❑ *The director discovered a rich vein of sentimentality.* **10** ADJ **Rich** smells are strong and very pleasant. **Rich** colors and sounds are deep and very pleasant. ❑ *...a rich and luxuriously perfumed bath essence.* ● **rich|ness** N-UNCOUNT ❑ *His musicals were infused with richness of color and visual detail.* **11** ADJ A **rich** life or history is one that is interesting because it is full of different events and activities. ❑ *A rich and varied cultural life is essential for this couple.* ● **rich|ness** N-UNCOUNT ❑ *It all adds to the richness of human life.* **12** ADJ A **rich** collection or mixture contains a wide and interesting variety of different things. ❑ *Visitors can view a rich and colorful array of aquatic plants and animals.* ● **rich|ness** N-UNCOUNT ❑ *...a huge country, containing a richness of culture and diversity of landscape.*

SYNONYMS

rich
ADJ **1**
affluent: *Cigarette smoking used to be commoner among affluent people.*
prosperous: *...the youngest son of a relatively prosperous British family.*
wealthy: *...a wealthy international businessman.*
well-off: *My grandparents were quite well-off.*
well-to-do: *...two well-educated girls from well-to-do homes.*

-rich /-rɪtʃ/ COMB IN ADJ [usu ADJ n] **-rich** combines with the names of useful or valuable substances to form adjectives that describe something as containing a lot of a particular substance. ❑ *...Angola's northern oil-rich coastline.*

rich|ly /rɪtʃli/ **1** ADV If something is **richly** colored, flavored, or perfumed, it has a pleasantly strong color, flavor, or perfume. ❑ *...Renaissance masterpieces, so richly colored and lustrous.* **2** ADV If something is **richly** decorated, patterned, or furnished, it has a lot of elaborate and beautiful decoration, patterns, or furniture. ❑ *Coffee steamed in the richly decorated silver pot.* **3** ADV If you say that someone **richly** deserves an award, success, or victory, you approve of what they have done and feel very strongly that they deserve it. [FEELINGS] ❑ *He achieved the success he so richly deserved.* **4** ADV If you are **richly** rewarded for doing something, you get something very valuable or pleasant in return for doing it. ❑ *It is a difficult book to read, but it richly rewards the effort.*

Richter scale /rɪktər skeɪl/ N-SING [the N] **The Richter scale** is a scale which is used for measuring how severe an earthquake is. ❑ *An earthquake measuring 6.1 on the Richter Scale struck California yesterday.*

rick /rɪk/ (ricks, ricking, ricked) **1** N-COUNT A **rick** is a large pile of dried grass or straw that is built in a regular shape and kept in a field until it is needed. **2** V-T If you **rick** your neck, you hurt it by pulling or twisting it in an unusual way. [BRIT]

in AM, use **wrench**

rick|ets /rɪkɪts/ N-UNCOUNT **Rickets** is a disease that children can get when their food does not contain enough Vitamin D. It makes their bones soft and causes their liver and spleen to become too large.

rick|ety /rɪkɪti/ ADJ A **rickety** structure or piece of furniture is not very strong or well made, and seems likely to collapse or break. ❑ *Mona climbed the rickety wooden stairs.*

rick|shaw /rɪkʃɔː/ (rickshaws) N-COUNT A **rickshaw** is a simple vehicle originally used in Asia for carrying passengers. Some rickshaws are pulled by someone walking, running or cycling in front.

rico|chet /rɪkəʃeɪ/ (ricochets, ricocheting, ricocheted) V-I When a bullet **ricochets**, it hits a surface and bounces away

ricotta

from it. ❑ *The bullets ricocheted off the hood and windshield.* • N-COUNT **Ricochet** is also a noun. ❑ *He was wounded in the shoulder by a ricochet.*

ri|cot|ta /rɪkɒtə/ also **ricotta cheese** N-UNCOUNT **Ricotta** is a soft, white, unsalted cheese made from sheep's milk. ❑ *...ravioli made with cottage cheese instead of ricotta.*

rid ♦◇◇ /rɪd/ (rids, ridding)

> The form **rid** is used in the present tense and is the past tense and past participle of the verb.

1 PHRASE When you **get rid of** something that you do not want or do not like, you take action so that you no longer have it or suffer from it. ❑ *The owner needs to get rid of the car for financial reasons.* **2** PHRASE If you **get rid of** someone who is causing problems for you or who you do not like, you do something to prevent them from affecting you anymore, for example by making them leave. ❑ *He believed that his manager wanted to get rid of him for personal reasons.* **3** V-T If you **rid** a place or person **of** something undesirable or unwanted, you succeed in removing it completely from that place or person. ❑ *The proposals are an attempt to rid the country of political corruption.* **4** V-T If you **rid** yourself **of** something you do not want, you take action so that you no longer have it or are no longer affected by it. ❑ *Why couldn't he ever rid himself of those thoughts, those worries?* **5** ADJ [v-link ADJ **of** n] If you **are rid of** someone or something that you did not want or that caused problems for you, they are no longer with you or causing problems for you. ❑ *The family had sought a way to be rid of her and the problems she had caused them.*

rid|dance /rɪdəns/ PHRASE [oft PHR *to* n] You say '**good riddance**' to indicate that you are pleased that someone has left or that something has gone. [FEELINGS] ❑ *He's gone back to Cleveland in a huff, and good riddance.*

rid|den /rɪdən/ **Ridden** is the past participle of **ride**.

-ridden /-rɪdən/ COMB IN ADJ **-ridden** combines with nouns to form adjectives that describe something as having a lot of a particular undesirable thing or quality, or suffering very much because of it. ❑ *...debt-ridden local authorities.*

rid|dle /rɪdəl/ (riddles, riddling, riddled) **1** N-COUNT A **riddle** is a puzzle or joke in which you ask a question that seems to be nonsense but which has a clever or amusing answer. ❑ *All comers to the Sphinx were asked a riddle, and failure to solve it meant death.* **2** N-COUNT You can describe something as a **riddle** if people have been trying to understand or explain it but have not been able to. ❑ *Scientists claimed yesterday to have solved the riddle of the birth of the universe.* **3** V-T If someone **riddles** something **with** bullets or bullet holes, they fire a lot of bullets into it. ❑ *Unknown attackers riddled two homes with gunfire.*

rid|dled /rɪdəld/ **1** ADJ If something is **riddled with** bullets or bullet holes, it is full of bullet holes. ❑ *The bodies of four people were found riddled with bullets.* **2** ADJ [v-link ADJ **with** n] If something is **riddled with** undesirable qualities or features, it is full of them. ❑ *They were the principal shareholders in a bank riddled with corruption.*

-riddled /-rɪdəld/ COMB IN ADJ [usu ADJ n] **-riddled** combines with nouns to form adjectives that describe something as being full of a particular undesirable thing or quality. ❑ *She pushed the bullet-riddled door open.* ❑ *It is a dangerous, crime-riddled, filthy city.*

ride ♦♦◇ /raɪd/ (rides, riding, rode, ridden) **1** V-T/V-I When you **ride** a horse, you sit on it and control its movements. ❑ *I saw a girl riding a horse.* ❑ *Can you ride?* **2** V-T/V-I When you **ride** a bicycle or a motorcycle, you sit on it, control it, and travel along on it. ❑ *Riding a bike is great exercise.* ❑ *Two men riding on motorcycles opened fire on him.* **3** V-I When you **ride** in a vehicle such as a car, you travel in it. ❑ *He prefers traveling on the subway to riding in a limousine.* **4** N-COUNT A **ride** is a trip on a horse or bicycle, or in a vehicle. ❑ *She took some friends for a ride in the family car.* **5** N-COUNT In an amusement park, a **ride** is a large machine that people ride on for fun. ❑ *...roller coasters or other thrill rides at amusement parks.* **6** V-I [oft cont] If you say that one thing **is riding on** another, you mean that the first thing depends on the second thing. ❑ *Billions of dollars are riding on the outcome of the election.* **7** → see also **riding** **8** PHRASE If

rifle range

you say that someone faces **a rough ride**, you mean that things are going to be difficult for them because people will criticize them a lot or treat them badly. [INFORMAL] ❑ *The president could face a rough ride unless the plan works.* **9** PHRASE If you describe something as **a free ride**, you mean that things are going to be very easy and that people will take advantage of this. [INFORMAL] ❑ *I've had an opponent every time. I've never had a free ride. I've had to fight.* **10** PHRASE If you say that someone **has been taken for a ride**, you mean that they have been deceived or cheated. [INFORMAL] ❑ *You got taken for a ride. Why did you give him five thousand dollars?* **11** PHRASE [PHR n] If someone **rides herd on** other people or their actions, they supervise them or watch them closely. [AM] ❑ *...state efforts to ride herd on the oil companies.* ❑ *...Hank, who often stayed late riding herd on the day-to-day business of the magazine.* **12** PHRASE Someone who **rides the rails** travels by train, especially over a long period of time and without buying a ticket. [AM] ❑ *Jacob decides to ride the rails and look for work in the city.*

▶ **ride out** PHRASAL VERB If someone **rides out** a storm or a crisis, they manage to survive a difficult period without suffering serious harm. ❑ *The Republicans think they can ride out the political storm.*

rid|er ♦◇◇ /raɪdər/ (riders) N-COUNT A **rider** is someone who rides a horse, a bicycle, or a motorcycle as a hobby or job. You can also refer to someone who is riding a horse, a bicycle, or a motorcycle as a rider. ❑ *She is a very good and experienced rider.*

ridge /rɪdʒ/ (ridges) **1** N-COUNT A **ridge** is a long, narrow piece of raised land. ❑ *...a high road along a mountain ridge.* **2** N-COUNT A **ridge** is a raised line on a flat surface. ❑ *...the bony ridge of the eye socket.*

ridged /rɪdʒd/ ADJ [usu ADJ n] A **ridged** surface has raised lines on it. ❑ *...boots with thick, ridged soles for walking.*

ridi|cule /rɪdɪkjuːl/ (ridicules, ridiculing, ridiculed) **1** V-T If you **ridicule** someone or **ridicule** their ideas or beliefs, you make fun of them in an unkind way. ❑ *I admired her all the more for allowing them to ridicule her and never striking back.* **2** N-UNCOUNT If someone or something is an object of **ridicule** or is held up to **ridicule**, someone makes fun of them in an unkind way. ❑ *As a heavy child, she became the object of ridicule from classmates.*

ri|dicu|lous /rɪdɪkjələs/ ADJ If you say that something or someone is **ridiculous**, you mean that they are very foolish. ❑ *It is ridiculous to suggest we are having a romance.*

ri|dicu|lous|ly /rɪdɪkjələsli/ ADV You use **ridiculously** to emphasize the fact that you think something is unreasonable or very surprising. [EMPHASIS] ❑ *Dana bought rolls of silk that seemed ridiculously cheap.*

rid|ing /raɪdɪŋ/ N-UNCOUNT **Riding** is the activity or sport of riding horses. ❑ *The next morning we went riding again.*

rife /raɪf/ ADJ [v-link ADJ] If you say that something, usually something bad, is **rife in** a place or that the place is **rife** with it, you mean that it is very common. ❑ *Speculation is rife that he will be fired.*

riff /rɪf/ (riffs) **1** N-COUNT In jazz and rock music, a **riff** is a short, repeated tune. **2** N-COUNT A **riff** is a short piece of speech or writing that develops a particular theme or idea. ❑ *Rowe does a very clever riff on the nature of prejudice.*

rif|fle /rɪfəl/ (riffles, riffling, riffled) V-T/V-I If you **riffle** through the pages of a book or **riffle** them, you turn them over quickly, without reading everything that is on them. ❑ *I riffled through the pages until I reached the index.*

riff|raff /rɪfræf/ N-UNCOUNT If you refer to a group of people as **riffraff**, you disapprove of them because you think they are not respectable. [DISAPPROVAL]

ri|fle /raɪfəl/ (rifles, rifling, rifled) **1** N-COUNT A **rifle** is a gun with a long barrel. ❑ *They shot him at point blank range with an automatic rifle.* **2** V-T/V-I If you **rifle** through things or **rifle** them, you make a quick search among them in order to find something or steal something. ❑ *I discovered my husband rifling through the filing cabinet.*

rifle|man /raɪfəlmən/ (riflemen) N-COUNT A **rifleman** is a man, especially a soldier, who is skilled in the use of a rifle.

ri|fle range (rifle ranges) N-COUNT A **rifle range** is a place where you can practice shooting with a rifle.

rifle|woman /ˈraɪfəlwʊmən/ (**riflewomen**) N-COUNT A **riflewoman** is a woman, especially a soldier, who is skilled in the use of a rifle.

rift /rɪft/ (**rifts**) **1** N-COUNT A **rift** between people or countries is a serious quarrel or disagreement that stops them from having a good relationship. ☐ *The interview reflected a growing rift between the president and Congress.* **2** N-COUNT A **rift** is a split that appears in something solid, especially in the ground. ☐ *The earth convulsed uncontrollably, a rift opened suddenly and, with a horrid sucking sound, swallowed the entire pool.*

rig /rɪɡ/ (**rigs, rigging, rigged**) **1** V-T If someone **rigs** an election, a job appointment, or a game, they dishonestly arrange it to get the result they want or to give someone an unfair advantage. ☐ *She accused her opponents of rigging the vote.* **2** N-COUNT A **rig** is a large structure that is used for looking for oil or gas and for taking it out of the ground or the sea bed. ☐ *...a supply vessel for oil rigs in the Gulf of Mexico.* **3** N-COUNT A **rig** is a truck that is made in two or more sections which are jointed together by metal bars, so that the vehicle can turn more easily. [AM] ☐ *An inspection of his rig showed that three of the brakes were faulty.*

rig|ging /ˈrɪɡɪŋ/ **1** N-UNCOUNT [usu supp N] Vote or ballot **rigging** is the act of dishonestly organizing an election to get a particular result. ☐ *She was accused of corruption, of vote rigging on a massive scale.* **2** N-UNCOUNT On a ship, the **rigging** is the ropes which support the ship's masts and sails. ☐ *...the howling of the wind in the rigging.*

RIGHT

① CORRECT, APPROPRIATE, OR ACCEPTABLE
② DIRECTION AND POLITICAL GROUPINGS
③ ENTITLEMENT
④ DISCOURSE USES
⑤ USED FOR EMPHASIS

---

① **right** ♦♦♦ /raɪt/ (**rights, righting, righted**)
→ Please look at meanings **15** and **16** to see if the expression you are looking for is shown under another headword.

1 ADJ If something is **right**, it is correct and agrees with the facts. ☐ *That's absolutely right.* ☐ *Clocks never told the right time.* • ADV [ADV after v] **Right** is also an adverb. ☐ *He guessed right about some things.* **2** ADJ If you do something in the **right** way or in the **right** place, you do it as or where it should be done or was planned to be done. ☐ *Walking, done in the right way, is a form of aerobic exercise.* ☐ *They have computerized systems to ensure delivery of the right pizza to the right place.* • ADV [ADV after v] **Right** is also an adverb. ☐ *To make sure I did everything right, I bought a fat instruction book.* **3** ADJ If you say that someone is seen in all the **right** places or knows all the **right** people, you mean that they go to places that are socially acceptable or know people who are socially acceptable. ☐ *He was always to be seen in the right places.* **4** ADJ If someone is **right** about something, they are correct in what they say or think about it. ☐ *Ron has been right about the result of every general election but one.* **5** ADJ If something such as a choice, action, or decision is the **right** one, it is the best or most suitable one. ☐ *She'd made the right choice in leaving New York.* **6** ADJ [v-link ADJ, with brd-neg] If something is not **right**, there is something unsatisfactory about the situation or thing that you are talking about. ☐ *Ratatouille doesn't taste right with any other oil.* **7** ADJ [v-link ADJ] If you think that someone was **right** to do something, you think that there were good moral reasons why they did it. ☐ *You were right to do what you did, under the circumstances.* • **right|ly** ADV [ADV before v] ☐ *Education, quite rightly, is currently at the forefront of the political agenda.* **8** ADJ [v-link ADJ, oft with brd-neg] **Right** is used to refer to activities or actions that are considered to be morally good and acceptable. ☐ *It's not right, leaving her like this.* • N-UNCOUNT **Right** is also a noun. ☐ *At least he knew right from wrong.* • **right|ness** N-UNCOUNT ☐ *Many people have very strong opinions about the rightness or wrongness of abortion.* **9** V-T If you **right** something or if it **rights** itself, it returns to its normal or correct state, after being in an undesirable state. ☐ *They recognize the urgency of righting the economy.* **10** V-T If you **right** a wrong, you do something to make up for a mistake or something bad that you did in the past. ☐ *We've made progress in righting the wrongs of the past.* **11** V-T If you **right** something that has fallen or rolled over, or if it **rights** itself, it returns to its normal upright position. ☐ *He righted the yacht and continued the race.* **12** ADJ [ADJ n] The **right** side of a material is the side that is intended to be seen and that faces outward when it is made into something. ☐ *Trim off excess fabric and turn the right side out.* **13** PHRASE If you say that things **are going right**, you mean that your life or a situation is developing as you intended or expected and you are pleased with it. ☐ *I can't think of anything in my life that's going right.* **14** PHRASE If you **put** something **right**, you correct something that was wrong or that was causing problems. ☐ *We've discovered what went wrong and are going to put it right.* **15 heart in the right place** → see **heart** ② **16 it serves you right** → see **serve**

② **right** ♦♦♦ /raɪt/

The spelling **Right** is also used for meaning **3**.

1 N-SING The **right** is one of two opposite directions, sides, or positions. If you are facing north and you turn to the right, you will be facing east. In the word 'to,' the 'o' is to the right of the 't.' ☐ *Ahead of you on the right will be a lovely garden.* • ADV [ADV after v] **Right** is also an adverb. ☐ *Turn right into the street.* **2** ADJ [ADJ n] Your **right** arm, leg, or ear, for example, is the one which is on the right side of your body. Your **right** shoe or glove is the one which is intended to be worn on your right foot or hand. ☐ *She shattered her right leg in a fall.* **3** N-SING-COLL You can refer to people who support the political ideals of capitalism and conservatism as **the right**. They are often contrasted with **the left**, who support the political ideals of socialism. ☐ *The Republican Right despise him.*

③ **right** ♦♦♦ /raɪt/ (**rights**) **1** N-PLURAL Your **rights** are what you are morally or legally entitled to do or to have. ☐ *They don't know their rights.* **2** N-SING If you have a **right** to do or to have something, you are morally or legally entitled to do it or to have it. ☐ *...a woman's right to choose.* **3** N-PLURAL If someone has **the rights** to a story or book, they are legally allowed to publish it or reproduce it in another form, and nobody else can do so without their permission. ☐ *An agent bought the rights to his life.* **4** PHRASE If something is not the case but you think that it should be, you can say that **by rights** it should be the case. ☐ *She did work which by rights should be done by someone else.* **5** PHRASE If someone is a successful or respected person **in** their **own right**, they are successful or respected because of their own efforts and talents rather than those of the people they are closely connected with. ☐ *Although now a success in her own right, she knows the difficulties of living in the shadow of her famous older sister.* **6** PHRASE If you say that you **reserve the right** to do something, you mean that you will do it if you feel that it is necessary. ☐ *He reserved the right to change his mind.* **7** PHRASE If you say that someone is **within** their **rights** to do something, you mean that they are morally or legally entitled to do it. ☐ *You were quite within your rights to refuse to cooperate with him.*

④ **right** ♦♦♦ /raɪt/ **1** ADV [ADV cl] You use **right** in order to attract someone's attention or to indicate that you have dealt with one thing so you can go on to another. [SPOKEN] ☐ *Right, I'll be back in a minute.* **2** CONVENTION You can use **right** to check whether what you have just said is correct. [SPOKEN] ☐ *They have a small plane, right?* **3** ADV [ADV as reply] You can say '**right**' to show that you are listening to what someone is saying and that you accept it or understand it. [SPOKEN] ☐ *"It was probably much harder for older people. Don't you think?"—"Right."* **4** → see also **all right**

⑤ **right** ♦♦♦ /raɪt/ **1** ADV [ADV adv/prep] You can use **right** to emphasize the precise place, position, or time of something. [EMPHASIS] ☐ *The back of a car appeared right in front of him.* **2** ADV [ADV prep/adv] You can use **right** to emphasize how far something moves or extends or how long it continues. [EMPHASIS] ☐ *...the highway that runs through the neutral zone right to the army positions.* **3** ADV [ADV adv/prep] You can use **right** to emphasize that an action or state is complete. [EMPHASIS] ☐ *The candle had burned right down.* **4** ADV [ADV prep/adv] If you say that something happened **right** after a particular time or event or **right** before it, you mean that it happened immediately after or before it. [EMPHASIS] ☐ *All of a sudden,* right after the summer, Mother gets married. **5** ADV [ADV adj] If you say **I'll be right there** or **I'll be right back**, you mean that you will get to a place or get back to it in a very short time. [EMPHASIS] ❏ *I'm going to get some water. I'll be right back.* **6** PHRASE If you do something **right away**, you do it immediately. [INFORMAL, EMPHASIS] ❏ *He wants to see you right away.* **7** PHRASE You can use **right now** to emphasize that you are referring to the present moment. [INFORMAL, EMPHASIS] ❏ *Right now I'm feeling very excited.* **8** → See feature box at **history**

right an|gle (right angles) **1** N-COUNT A **right angle** is an angle of ninety degrees. A square has four right angles. **2** PHRASE If two things are **at right angles**, they are situated so that they form an angle of 90° where they touch each other. You can also say that one thing is **at right angles** to another. ❏ *...two lasers at right angles.*

right-angled 1 ADJ [ADJ n] A **right-angled** bend is a sharp bend that turns through approximately ninety degrees. **2** ADJ [ADJ n] A **right-angled** triangle has one angle that is a right angle. [BRIT]

in AM, use **right triangle**

right-click (right-clicks, right-clicking, right-clicked) V-I To **right-click** or to **right-click** on something means to press the right-hand button on a computer mouse. [COMPUTING] ❏ *All you have to do is right-click on the desktop and select New Folder.*

right|eous /ˈraɪtʃəs/ ADJ If you think that someone behaves or lives in a way that is morally good, you can say that they are **righteous**. People sometimes use **righteous** to express their disapproval when they think someone is only behaving in this way so that others will admire or support them. [FORMAL] ❏ *Aren't you afraid of being seen as a righteous crusader?*

right|ful /ˈraɪtfəl/ ADJ [ADJ n] If you say that someone or something has been returned to its **rightful** place or position, they have returned to the place or position that you think they should have. ❏ *We have restored Hamill to his rightful place as editor.* • **right|ful|ly** ADV [ADV group] ❏ *Jealousy is the feeling that someone else has something that rightfully belongs to you.*

right-hand ADJ [ADJ n] If something is on the **right-hand** side of something, it is positioned on the right of it. ❏ *...a church on the right-hand side of the road.*

right-hand drive ADJ [usu ADJ n] A **right-hand drive** vehicle has its steering wheel on the right side. It is designed to be driven in countries such as Britain, Japan, and Australia, where people drive on the left side of the road.

right-handed ADJ Someone who is **right-handed** uses their right hand rather than their left hand for activities such as writing and sports, and for picking things up. • ADV [ADV after v] **Right-handed** is also an adverb. ❏ *I batted left-handed and bowled right-handed.*

right-hander (right-handers) N-COUNT You can describe someone as a **right-hander** if they use their right hand rather than their left hand for activities such as writing and sports and for picking things up.

right-hand man (right-hand men) N-COUNT Someone's **right-hand man** is the man who acts as their chief assistant and helps and supports them a lot in their work. ❏ *He is Rupert Murdoch's right-hand man at News International.*

right-hand wom|an (right-hand women) N-COUNT [usu poss n] Someone's **right-hand woman** is the woman who acts as their chief assistant and helps and supports them a lot in their work. ❏ *He was bowled over by her audacity and she soon became his right-hand woman.*

right|ist /ˈraɪtɪst/ (rightists) **1** N-COUNT If someone is described as a **rightist**, they are politically conservative and traditional. Rightists support the ideals of capitalism. **2** ADJ [usu ADJ n] If someone has **rightist** views or takes part in **rightist** activities, they are politically conservative and traditional and support the ideas of capitalism.

right-justify (right-justifies, right-justifying, right-justified) V-T If printed text is **right-justified**, each line finishes at the same distance from the right-hand edge of the page or column. ❏ *Click this option to right-justify the selected text.*

right-minded ADJ [usu ADJ n] If you think that someone's opinions or beliefs are sensible and you agree with them, you can describe them as a **right-minded** person. [APPROVAL] ❏ *He is an able, right-minded, and religious man.*

right-of-center

in BRIT, use **right-of-centre**

ADJ [usu ADJ n] You can describe a person or political party as **right-of-center** if they have political views which are closer to capitalism and conservatism than to socialism but which are not very extreme. ❏ *...the right-of-center candidate.*

right of way (rights of way) **1** N-COUNT A **right of way** is a strip of land that is used for a road, railroad line, or power line. [AM] **2** N-UNCOUNT When someone who is driving or walking along a road has **right of way** or the **right of way**, they have the right to continue along a particular road or path, and other people must stop for them. **3** N-COUNT A **right of way** is a public path across private land.

right on ✦◇◇ **1** ADJ If you describe something as **right on**, you mean that it is extremely good. ❏ *The film's comic moments are well-timed, and as the party animal Stuart, Baldwin is right on.* **2** CONVENTION You say **right on** to encourage someone or to emphasize that you agree with them.

right-thinking ADJ [usu ADJ n] If you think that someone's opinions or beliefs are sensible and you agree with them, you can describe them as a **right-thinking** person. [APPROVAL] ❏ *Every right-thinking American would be proud of them.*

right to life N-SING [oft N n] When people talk about an unborn baby's **right to life**, they mean that a baby has the right to be born, even if it has a severe disability or if its mother does not want it. ❏ *...the right to life campaign.*

right tri|an|gle (right triangles) N-COUNT A **right triangle** has one angle that is a right angle. [AM]

in BRIT, use **right-angled triangle**

right|ward /ˈraɪtwərd/ also **rightwards** ADJ [ADJ n] If there is a **rightward** trend in the politics of a person or party, their views become more right-wing. ❏ *The result reflects a modest rightward shift in opinion.* • ADV [ADV after v] **Rightward** is also an adverb. ❏ *He continued to urge the Republican Party to tilt rightward.*

right-wing ✦◇◇

The spelling **right wing** is also used for meaning **2**.

1 ADJ A **right-wing** person or group has conservative or capitalist views. ❏ *...a right-wing government.* **2** N-SING The **right wing** of a political party consists of the members who have the most conservative or the most capitalist views. ❏ *...the right wing of the Republican Party.*

╔══════ SYNONYMS ══════╗

right-wing
ADJ **1**
conservative: *...counties whose citizens invariably support the most conservative candidate in any election.*
traditionalist: *I hold firmly traditionalist views.*
reactionary: *Many people have taken a more reactionary approach.*

right-winger (right-wingers) N-COUNT If you think someone has views which are more right-wing than most other members of their party, you can say they are a **right-winger**. ❏ *It would appear that some hard-line right wingers are gaining power.*

rig|id /ˈrɪdʒɪd/ **1** ADJ Laws, rules, or systems that are **rigid** cannot be changed or varied, and are therefore considered to be rather severe. [DISAPPROVAL] ❏ *Several colleges in our study have rigid rules about student conduct.* • **ri|gid|ity** /rɪˈdʒɪdɪti/ N-UNCOUNT ❏ *...the rigidity of government policy.* • **rig|id|ly** ADV [ADV with v] ❏ *The caste system was so rigidly enforced that non-Hindus were not even allowed inside a Hindu house.* **2** ADJ If you disapprove of someone because you think they are not willing to change their way of thinking or behaving, you can describe them as **rigid**. [DISAPPROVAL] ❏ *She was a fairly rigid person who had strong religious views.* **3** ADJ A **rigid** substance or object is stiff and does not bend, stretch, or twist easily. ❏ *...rigid plastic containers.* • **ri|gid|ity** N-UNCOUNT ❏ *...the strength and rigidity of glass.*

rig|ma|role /ˈrɪɡməroʊl/ (rigmaroles) N-COUNT [usu sing] You can describe a long and complicated process as a **rigmarole**. [DISAPPROVAL] ❏ *Then the whole rigmarole starts over again.*

ri|gor /rɪgər/ (rigors)

[in BRIT, use **rigour**]

1 N-PLURAL If you refer to the **rigors** of an activity or job, you mean the difficult, demanding, or unpleasant things that are associated with it. ❑ *They're accustomed to the rigors of army life.* **2** N-UNCOUNT If something is done with **rigor**, it is done in a strict, thorough way. ❑ *The prince had performed his social duties with professional rigor.*

ri|gor mor|tis /rɪgər mɔrtɪs/ N-UNCOUNT In a dead body, when **rigor mortis** sets in, the joints and muscles become very stiff.

rig|or|ous /rɪgərəs/ **1** ADJ A test, system, or procedure that is **rigorous** is very thorough and strict. ❑ *The selection process is based on rigorous tests of competence and experience.* • **rig|or|ous|ly** ADV ❑ *...rigorously conducted research.* **2** ADJ If someone is **rigorous** in the way that they do something, they are very careful and thorough. ❑ *He is rigorous in his control of expenditure.*

rig|our /rɪgər/ [mainly BRIT] → see **rigor**

rile /raɪl/ (riles, riling, riled) V-T If something **riles** you, it makes you angry. ❑ *Cancellations and late departures rarely rile him.* • **riled** ADJ ❑ *He saw that I was riled.*

Riley /raɪli/ PHRASE [usu v PHR] If you say that someone is living **the life of Riley**, you mean that they have a very easy and comfortable life with few worries.

rim /rɪm/ (rims) **1** N-COUNT The **rim** of a container such as a cup or glass is the edge that goes all the way around the top. ❑ *She looked at him over the rim of her glass.* **2** N-COUNT The **rim** of a circular object is its outside edge. ❑ *...a round mirror with white metal rim.* **3** → See also color supplement

rim|less /rɪmlɪs/ ADJ [usu ADJ n] **Rimless** glasses are glasses which have no frame around the lenses or which have a frame only along the top of the lenses.

rimmed /rɪmd/ **1** ADJ [usu v-link ADJ with n] If something is **rimmed** with a substance or color, it has that substance or color around its border. ❑ *The plates and glassware were rimmed with gold.* **2** → see also **rim**, **-rimmed**

-rimmed /-rɪmd/ **1** COMB IN ADJ **-rimmed** combines with nouns to form adjectives that describe something as having a border or frame made of a particular substance. ❑ *...horn-rimmed glasses.* **2** → see also **rim**, **rimmed**

rind /raɪnd/ (rinds) **1** N-VAR The **rind** of a fruit such as a lemon or orange is its thick outer skin. ❑ *...grated lemon rind.* **2** N-VAR The **rind** of cheese or bacon is the hard outer edge which you do not usually eat. ❑ *...a cream cheese with a soft rind.*

RING
① TELEPHONING OR MAKING A SOUND
② SHAPES AND GROUPS
---

① **ring** ♦♦◊ /rɪŋ/ (rings, ringing, rang, rung)

→ Please look at meaning **9** to see if the expression you are looking for is shown under another headword.

1 V-I When a telephone **rings**, it makes a sound to let you know that someone is phoning you. ❑ *As soon as he got home, the phone rang.* • N-COUNT **Ring** is also a noun. ❑ *After at least eight rings, someone answered the phone.* • **ring|ing** N-UNCOUNT ❑ *She was jolted out of her sleep by the ringing of the telephone.* **2** V-T/V-I When you **ring** someone, you telephone them. [mainly BRIT]

[in AM, usually use **call**]

• PHRASAL VERB **Ring up** means the same as **ring**. **3** V-T/V-I When you **ring** a bell or when a bell **rings**, it makes a sound. ❑ *He heard the school bell ring.* • N-COUNT **Ring** is also a noun. ❑ *There was a ring of the bell.* • **ring|ing** N-UNCOUNT ❑ *...the ringing of church bells.* **4** V-I If you say that a place **is ringing** with sound, usually pleasant sound, you mean that the place is completely filled with that sound. [LITERARY] ❑ *The whole place was ringing with music.* **5** N-SING You can use **ring** to describe a quality that something such as a statement, discussion, or argument seems to have. For example, if an argument **has a familiar ring**, it seems familiar. ❑ *His proud boast of leading "the party of low taxation" has a hollow ring.* **6** PHRASE If you **give someone a ring**, you phone them. [mainly BRIT, INFORMAL] ❑ *We'll give him a ring as soon as we get back.*

[in AM, usually use **call**]

7 PHRASE If a statement **rings true**, it seems to be true or genuine. If it **rings hollow**, it does not seem to be true or genuine. ❑ *Joanna's denial rang true.* **8** → see also **ringing** **9 to ring a bell** → see **bell**

▶ **ring around** [BRIT] → see **ring round**
▶ **ring back** PHRASAL VERB [no passive] If you **ring** someone **back**, you phone them either because they phoned you earlier and you were not there or because you did not finish an earlier telephone conversation. [BRIT]

[in AM, use **call back**]

▶ **ring in** PHRASAL VERB If you **ring in**, you phone a place, such as the place where you work. [BRIT]

[in AM, use **call in**]

▶ **ring off** PHRASAL VERB When you **ring off**, you put down the receiver at the end of a telephone call. [BRIT]

[in AM, use **hang up**]

▶ **ring round** PHRASAL VERB If you **ring round** or **ring around**, you phone several people, usually when you are trying to organize something or to find some information. [BRIT]

[in AM, use **call around**]

▶ **ring up** **1** → see **ring** ① **2 2** PHRASAL VERB If a store clerk **rings up** a sale on a cash register, he or she presses the keys in order to record the amount that is being spent. ❑ *She was ringing up her sale on an ancient cash register.* **3** PHRASAL VERB If a company **rings up** an amount of money, usually a large amount of money, it makes that amount of money in sales or profits. ❑ *The advertising agency rang up 1.4 billion dollars in yearly sales.*

② **ring** ♦◊◊ /rɪŋ/ (rings, ringing, ringed) **1** N-COUNT A **ring** is a small circle of metal or other substance that you wear on your finger as jewelry. ❑ *...a gold wedding ring.* **2** N-COUNT An object or substance that is in the shape of a circle can be described as a **ring**. ❑ *Frank took a large ring of keys from his pocket.* **3** N-COUNT A group of people or things arranged in a circle can be described as a **ring**. ❑ *They then formed a ring around the square.* **4** N-COUNT At a boxing or wrestling match or a circus, the **ring** is the place where the contest or performance takes place. It consists of an enclosed space with seats around it. ❑ *He will never again be allowed inside a boxing ring.* **5** N-COUNT You can refer to an organized group of people who are involved in an illegal activity as a **ring**. ❑ *Police are investigating the suspected drug ring at the school.* **6** N-COUNT [BRIT] → see **burner** **7** V-T [usu passive] If a building or place **is ringed** with or by something, it is surrounded by it. ❑ *The areas are sealed off and ringed by troops.*

ring bind|er (ring binders) N-COUNT A **ring binder** is a file with hard covers, which you can insert pages into. The pages are held in by metal rings on a bar attached to the inside of the file.

ring|er /rɪŋər/ (ringers) PHRASE [usu v-link PHR for n] If you say that one person is **a ringer** or **a dead ringer** for another, you mean that they look exactly like each other. [INFORMAL]

ring fin|ger (ring fingers) N-COUNT Your **ring finger** is the third finger of your left or right hand, without counting your thumb. In some countries, people wear a ring on this finger to show that they are engaged or married.

ring|ing /rɪŋɪŋ/ **1** ADJ [ADJ n] A **ringing** sound is loud and can be heard very clearly. ❑ *He hit the metal steps with a ringing crash.* **2** ADJ [ADJ n] A **ringing** statement or declaration is one that is made forcefully and is intended to make a powerful impression. ❑ *...the party's 14th congress, which gave a ringing endorsement to capitalist-style economic reforms.*

ring|leader /rɪŋlidər/ (ringleaders) N-COUNT The **ringleaders** in a quarrel, disturbance, or illegal activity are the people who started it and who cause most of the trouble. [DISAPPROVAL] ❑ *The soldiers were well informed about the ringleaders of the protest.*

ring|let /rɪŋlɪt/ (ringlets) N-COUNT [usu pl] **Ringlets** are long curls of hair that hang down.

ring|master /rɪŋmæstər/ (ringmasters) N-COUNT A circus **ringmaster** is the person who introduces the performers and the animals.

ring-pull (ring-pulls) N-COUNT A **ring-pull** is a metal strip that you pull off the top of a can of drink in order to open it. [BRIT]

in AM, use **tab**

ring road (ring roads) also **ringroad** N-COUNT A **ring road** is a road that goes around the edge of a city or town so that traffic does not have to go through the center. [mainly BRIT]

in AM, usually use **beltway**

ring|side /rɪŋsaɪd/ ◼ N-SING The **ringside** is the area around the edge of a circus ring, boxing ring, or show jumping ring. ◻ *Most of the top trainers were at the ringside.* ◼ ADJ [ADJ n] If you have a **ringside** seat or a **ringside** view, you are close to an event and can see it clearly. ◻ *I had a ringside seat for the whole performance.*

ring tone (ring tones) N-COUNT The **ring tone** is the sound made by a phone, especially a cellphone, when it rings. ◻ *They offer 70 hours' standby time, 2hr. 50min. talk time, and 15 ring tones.*

ring|worm /rɪŋwɜːrm/ N-UNCOUNT **Ringworm** is a skin disease caused by a fungus. It produces itchy, red patches on a person's or animal's skin, especially on their head and between their legs and toes. [MEDICAL]

rink /rɪŋk/ (rinks) N-COUNT A **rink** is a large area covered with ice where people go to ice-skate, or a large area of concrete where people go to roller-skate. ◻ *The other skaters were ordered off the rink.*

rinky-dink /rɪŋkɪdɪŋk/ ADJ [usu ADJ n] **Rinky-dink** things are small or unimportant. [AM, INFORMAL] ◻ *I moved to this rinky-dink little place in Massachusetts.*

rinse /rɪns/ (rinses, rinsing, rinsed) ◼ V-T When you **rinse** something, you wash it in clean water in order to remove dirt or soap from it. ◻ *It's important to rinse the rice to remove the starch.* • N-COUNT **Rinse** is also a noun. ◻ *Clean skin means plenty of lather followed by a rinse with water.* ◼ V-T If you **rinse** your mouth, you wash it by filling your mouth with water or with a liquid that kills germs, then spitting it out. ◻ *Use a toothbrush on your tongue as well, and rinse your mouth frequently.* • PHRASAL VERB **Rinse out** means the same as **rinse**. ◻ *After her meal she invariably rinsed out her mouth.* • N-MASS **Rinse** is also a noun. ◻ *...mouth rinses with fluoride.* ◼ → See feature box at **housework**

riot ◆◇◇ /raɪət/ (riots, rioting, rioted) ◼ N-COUNT When there is a **riot**, a crowd of people behave violently in a public place, for example they fight, throw stones, or damage buildings and vehicles. ◻ *Twelve inmates have been killed during a riot at the prison.* ◼ V-I If people **riot**, they behave violently in a public place. ◻ *Last year 600 inmates rioted, starting fires and building barricades.* • **ri|ot|er** (rioters) N-COUNT ◻ *The militia dispersed the rioters.* • **ri|ot|ing** N-UNCOUNT ◻ *At least fifteen people are now known to have died in three days of rioting.* ◼ N-SING If you say that there is **a riot of** something pleasant such as color, you mean that there is a large amount of various types of it. [APPROVAL] ◻ *It would be a riot of color, of poppies and irises and flowers of every kind.* ◼ PHRASE If **someone** in authority **reads** you **the riot act**, they tell you that you will be punished unless you start behaving properly. ◻ *I'm glad you read the riot act to Billy. He's still a kid and still needs to be told what to do.* ◼ PHRASE If people **run riot**, they behave in a wild and uncontrolled manner. ◻ *Rampaging prisoners ran riot through the jail.* ◼ PHRASE If something such as your imagination **runs riot**, it is not limited or controlled, and produces ideas that are new or exciting, rather than sensible. ◻ *She dressed strictly for comfort and economy, but let her imagination run riot with costume jewelry.*

SYNONYMS

riot
NOUN ◼
disturbance: *During the disturbance which followed, three people were hurt.*
disorder: *He called on the authorities to stop the disorder in the city.*
commotion: *He heard a commotion outside.*

---

riot gear N-UNCOUNT **Riot gear** is the special clothing and equipment worn by police officers or soldiers when they have to deal with a riot.

ri|ot|ous /raɪətəs/ ◼ ADJ [usu ADJ n] If you say that someone has a **riotous** lifestyle, you mean that they frequently behave in an excessive and uncontrolled way, for example by eating or drinking too much. [FORMAL] ◻ *...aristocrats who wasted their inheritances in riotous living.* ◼ ADJ [usu ADJ n] You can describe someone's behavior or an event as **riotous** when it is noisy and lively in a rather wild way. ◻ *The dinner was often a riotous affair enlivened by superbly witty speeches.* • **ri|ot|ous|ly** ADV [ADV adj/-ed] ◻ *...a slapstick affair which I found riotously amusing.*

riot po|lice N-SING-COLL The **riot police** is the section of the police force that is trained to deal with people who cause trouble in public places. ◻ *After about 10 minutes the riot police arrived.*

riot shield (riot shields) N-COUNT [usu pl] **Riot shields** are pieces of equipment made of transparent plastic which are used by the police to protect themselves against angry crowds.

rip /rɪp/ (rips, ripping, ripped) ◼ V-T/V-I When something **rips** or when you **rip** it, you tear it forcefully with your hands or with a tool such as a knife. ◻ *I felt the banner rip as we were pushed in opposite directions.* ◼ N-COUNT A **rip** is a long cut or split in something made of cloth or paper. ◻ *Looking at the rip in her new dress, she flew into a rage.* ◼ V-T If you **rip** something away, you remove it quickly and forcefully. ◻ *He ripped away a wire that led to the alarm button.* ◼ V-I If something **rips** into someone or something or **rips** through them, it enters that person or thing so quickly and forcefully that it often goes completely through them. ◻ *A volley of bullets ripped into the facing wall.* ◼ PHRASE If you **let it rip**, you do something forcefully and without trying to control yourself. [INFORMAL] ◻ *Turn the guitars up full and let it rip.*

▶ **rip off** ◼ PHRASAL VERB If someone **rips** you **off**, they cheat you by charging you too much money for something or by selling you something that is broken or damaged. [INFORMAL] ◻ *The bigger, more reputable online casinos are not going to rip you off.* ◼ → see also **rip-off**

▶ **rip up** PHRASAL VERB If you **rip** something **up**, you tear it into small pieces. ◻ *If we wrote, I think he would rip up the letter.*

R.I.P. /ɑːr aɪ piː/ CONVENTION **R.I.P.** is written on gravestones and expresses the hope that the person buried there may rest in peace. **R.I.P.** is an abbreviation for 'rest in peace' or for the Latin 'requiescat in pace.'

rip|cord /rɪpkɔːrd/ (ripcords) also **rip cord** N-COUNT A **ripcord** is the cord that you pull to open a parachute.

ripe /raɪp/ (riper, ripest) ◼ ADJ **Ripe** fruit or grain is fully grown and ready to eat. ◻ *Always choose firm, but ripe fruit.* ◼ ADJ [v-link ADJ for n/-ing] If a situation is **ripe for** a particular development or event, you mean that development or event is likely to happen soon. ◻ *A hospital consultant said conditions were ripe for an outbreak of cholera and typhoid.* ◼ PHRASE If someone lives to a **ripe old age**, they live until they are very old. ◻ *He lived to the ripe old age of 95.*

rip|en /raɪpən/ (ripens, ripening, ripened) V-T/V-I When crops **ripen** or when the sun **ripens** them, they become ripe. ◻ *I'm waiting for the apples to ripen.*

rip-off (rip-offs) N-COUNT If you say that something that you bought was a **rip-off**, you mean that you were charged too much money or that it was of very poor quality. [INFORMAL] ◻ *The service charge is a rip-off, but I'm willing to pay if I'm guaranteed a seat.*

ri|poste /rɪpoʊst/ (ripostes, riposting, riposted) ◼ N-COUNT A **riposte** is a quick, clever reply to something that someone has said. [WRITTEN] ◻ *Laura glanced at Grace, expecting a clever riposte.* ◼ V-T If you **riposte**, you make a quick, clever response to something someone has said. [WRITTEN] ◻ *"It's tough at the top," he said. "It's tougher at the bottom," riposted the billionaire.* ◼ N-COUNT [oft N to n] You can refer to an action as a **riposte** to something when it is in response to that thing. [JOURNALISM] ◻ *The operation is being seen as a swift riposte to the killing of a senior army commander.*

rip|ple /rɪpəl/ (ripples, rippling, rippled) ◼ N-COUNT **Ripples** are little waves on the surface of water caused by the wind or by something moving in or on the water. ◻ *Gleaming ripples cut* the lake's surface. **2** V-T/V-I When the surface of an area of water **ripples** or when something **ripples** it, a number of little waves appear on it. ❏ *You throw a pebble in a pool and it ripples.* **3** V-I If something such as a feeling **ripples** over someone's body, it moves across it or through it. [LITERARY] ❏ *A chill shiver rippled over his skin.* **4** N-COUNT If an event causes **ripples**, its effects gradually spread, causing several other events to happen one after the other. ❏ *If Brazil defaults on its foreign debt, it will cause ripples throughout the world.*

rip|ple ef|fect (ripple effects) N-COUNT If an event or action has a **ripple effect**, it causes several other events to happen one after the other. ❏ *Ships could be diverted to other ports and that would have a serious ripple effect through the local economy.*

rip-roaring ADJ [ADJ n] If you describe something as **rip-roaring**, you mean that it is very exciting and full of energy. [INFORMAL] ❏ *...a rip-roaring movie with a great array of special effects.*

rip|tide /rɪptaɪd/ (riptides) N-COUNT A **riptide** is an area of sea where two different currents meet or where the water is extremely deep. Riptides make the water very rough and dangerous.

rise ♦♦♦ /raɪz/ (rises, rising, rose, risen)
→ Please look at meanings **18** and **19** to see if the expression you are looking for is shown under another headword.
1 V-I If something **rises**, it moves upward. ❏ *Wilson's ice-cold eyes watched the smoke rise from his cigarette.* • PHRASAL VERB **Rise up** means the same as **rise**. ❏ *Spray rose up from the surface of the water.* **2** V-I When you **rise**, you stand up. [FORMAL] ❏ *Luther rose slowly from the chair.* • PHRASAL VERB **Rise up** means the same as **rise**. ❏ *The only thing I wanted was to rise up from the table and leave this house.* **3** V-I When you **rise**, you get out of bed. [FORMAL] ❏ *Tony had risen early and gone to the cottage to work.* **4** V-I When the sun or moon **rises**, it appears in the sky. ❏ *He wanted to be over the line of the ridge before the sun had risen.* **5** V-I You can say that something **rises** when it appears as a large, tall shape. [LITERARY] ❏ *The building rose before him, tall and stately.* • PHRASAL VERB **Rise up** means the same as **rise**. ❏ *The White Mountains rose up before me.* **6** V-I If the level of something such as the water in a river **rises**, it becomes higher. ❏ *The waters continue to rise as more than 1,000 people are evacuated.* **7** V-I If land **rises**, it slopes upward. ❏ *He looked up the slope of land that rose from the house.* **8** V-I If an amount **rises**, it increases. ❏ *Interest rates rise from 4% to 5%.* ❏ *Real estate prices rose by 7.8% from a year ago.* ❏ *Exports rose 23%.* **9** N-COUNT A **rise** in the amount of something is an increase in it. ❏ *...the prospect of another rise in interest rates.* **10** N-SING The **rise of** a movement or activity is an increase in its popularity or influence. ❏ *The rise of racism is a serious concern.* **11** N-COUNT A **rise** is an increase in your wages or your salary. [BRIT]

in AM, use **raise**

12 V-I If the wind **rises**, it becomes stronger. ❏ *The wind was still rising, approaching a force nine gale.* **13** V-I If a sound **rises** or if someone's voice **rises**, it becomes louder or higher. ❏ *"Bernard?" Her voice rose hysterically.* **14** V-I When the people in a country **rise**, they try to defeat the government or army that is controlling them. ❏ *This lawlessness gave the army the excuse to rise against the Republican Government.* • PHRASAL VERB **Rise up** means the same as **rise**. ❏ *He warned that if the government moved against him the people would rise up.* **15** V-I If someone **rises** to a higher position or status, they become more important, successful, or powerful. ❏ *She is a strong woman who has risen to the top of a deeply sexist organization.* • PHRASAL VERB **Rise up** means the same as **rise**. ❏ *I started with Hoover 26 years ago in sales and rose up through the ranks.* **16** N-SING The **rise of** someone is the process by which they become more important, successful, or powerful. ❏ *Haig's rise was fueled by an all-consuming sense of patriotic duty.* **17** PHRASE If something **gives rise to** an event or situation, it causes that event or situation to happen. ❏ *Low levels of choline in the body can give rise to high blood pressure.* **18 to rise to the challenge** → see **challenge** **19 to rise to the occasion** → see **occasion**
▶ **rise above** PHRASAL VERB If you **rise above** a difficulty or problem, you manage not to let it affect you. ❏ *It tells the story of an aspiring young man's attempt to rise above the squalor of the street.*
▶ **rise up** → see **rise** 1, 2, 5, 14, 15

ris|en /rɪzᵊn/ **Risen** is the past participle of **rise**.

ris|er /raɪzər/ (risers) **1** N-COUNT [supp N] An early **riser** is someone who likes to get up early in the morning. A late **riser** is someone who likes to get up late. ❏ *He was an early riser and he would be at the breakfast table at seven.* **2** N-COUNT A **riser** is the flat vertical part of a step or a stair. [TECHNICAL]

ris|ible /rɪzɪbᵊl/ ADJ If you describe something as **risible**, you mean that it is ridiculous and does not deserve to be taken seriously. [FORMAL, DISAPPROVAL]

ris|ing star (rising stars) N-COUNT A **rising star** in a particular sport, art, or area of business is someone who is starting to do very well and who people think will soon be very successful. [JOURNALISM] ❏ *Anna is a rising star in the world of modeling.*

risk ♦♦◊ /rɪsk/ (risks, risking, risked) **1** N-VAR If there is a **risk** of something unpleasant, there is a possibility that it will happen. ❏ *There is a small risk of brain damage from the procedure.* **2** N-COUNT If something that you do is a **risk**, it might have unpleasant or undesirable results. ❏ *You're taking a big risk showing this to Kravis.* **3** N-COUNT If you say that something or someone is a **risk**, you mean they are likely to cause harm. ❏ *It's being obese that constitutes a health risk.* **4** N-COUNT If you are considered a good **risk**, a bank or store thinks that it is safe to lend you money or let you have goods without paying for them at the time. ❏ *Before providing the cash, they will have to decide whether you are a good or bad risk.* **5** V-T If you **risk** something unpleasant, you do something which might result in that thing happening or affecting you. ❏ *Those who fail to register risk severe penalties.* **6** V-T If you **risk** doing something, you do it, even though you know that it might have undesirable consequences. ❏ *The skipper was not willing to risk taking his ship through the straits until he could see where he was going.* **7** V-T If you **risk** your life or something else important, you behave in a way that might result in it being lost or harmed. ❏ *She risked her own life to help a disabled woman.* **8** PHRASE To be **at risk** means to be in a situation where something unpleasant might happen. ❏ *Up to 25,000 jobs are still at risk.* **9** PHRASE If you do something **at the risk of** something unpleasant happening, you do it even though you know that the unpleasant thing might happen as a result. ❏ *At the risk of being repetitive, I will say again that statistics are only a guide.* **10** PHRASE If you tell someone that they are doing something **at** their **own risk**, you are warning them that, if they are harmed, it will be their own responsibility. ❏ *Those who wish to come here will do so at their own risk.* **11** PHRASE If you **run the risk** of doing or experiencing something undesirable, you do something knowing that the undesirable thing might happen as a result. ❏ *The officers had run the risk of being dismissed.*

─────────── SYNONYMS ───────────
risk
NOUN
1
danger: *If there is a danger of famine, we should help.*
chance: *Do you think they have a chance of beating Australia?*
threat: *Some people see ambitious colleagues as a threat to their position.*
2
gamble: *Yesterday, he named his cabinet and took a big gamble in the process.*
chance: *From then on, they were taking no chances.*
venture: *...his latest writing venture.*

risk man|age|ment N-UNCOUNT **Risk management** is the skill or job of deciding what the risks are in a particular situation and taking action to prevent or reduce them. ❏ *Good risk management and higher sales can both boost profits.*

risk-taking N-UNCOUNT **Risk-taking** means taking actions which might have unpleasant or undesirable results. ❏ *...a more entrepreneurial climate, with positive encouragement of risk-taking and innovation.*

risky /rɪski/ (riskier, riskiest) ADJ If an activity or action is **risky**, it is dangerous or likely to fail. ❏ *Investing in airlines is a very risky business.*

ri|sot|to /rɪzɒtoʊ/ (risottos) N-VAR **Risotto** is an Italian dish consisting of rice cooked with ingredients such as tomatoes, meat, or fish.

ris|qué /rɪskeɪ/ ADJ If you describe something as **risqué**, you mean that it is slightly vulgar because it refers to sex. ❑ *The risqué headlines don't necessarily reflect a new sexual libertinism.*

Rita|lin /rɪtªlɪn/ N-UNCOUNT **Ritalin** is a drug that is used especially in the treatment of attention deficit disorder and attention deficit hyperactivity disorder. [TRADEMARK]

rite /raɪt/ (rites) N-COUNT A **rite** is a traditional ceremony that is carried out by a particular group or within a particular society. ❑ *Most traditional societies have transition rites at puberty.*

ritu|al /rɪtʃuəl/ (rituals) ▪ N-VAR A **ritual** is a religious service or other ceremony which involves a series of actions performed in a fixed order. ❑ *This is the most ancient, and holiest of the Shinto rituals.* ▪ ADJ [ADJ n] **Ritual** activities happen as part of a ritual or tradition. ❑ *...fasting and ritual dancing.* ▪ N-VAR A **ritual** is a way of behaving or a series of actions that people regularly carry out in a particular situation, because it is their custom to do so. ❑ *The whole culture revolves around the ritual of eating.* ▪ ADJ [ADJ n] You can describe something as a **ritual** action when it is done in exactly the same way whenever a particular situation occurs. ❑ *I realized that here the conventions required me to make the ritual noises.*

ritu|al|is|tic /rɪtʃuəlɪstɪk/ ▪ ADJ [usu ADJ n] **Ritualistic** actions or behavior follow a similar pattern every time they are used. ❑ *Each evening she bursts into her apartment with a ritualistic shout of "Honey I'm home!"* ▪ ADJ [usu ADJ n] **Ritualistic** acts are the fixed patterns of behavior that form part of a religious service or ceremony. ❑ *...the meditative and ritualistic practices of Buddhism.*

ritu|al|ized /rɪtʃuəlaɪzd/

in BRIT, also use **ritualised**

ADJ [usu ADJ n] **Ritualized** acts are carried out in a fixed, structured way rather than being natural. ❑ *...highly ritualized courtship displays.*

ritzy /rɪtsi/ (ritzier, ritziest) ADJ If you describe something as **ritzy**, you mean that it is fashionable or expensive. [INFORMAL] ❑ *Palm Springs has ritzy restaurants and glitzy nightlife.*

ri|val ✦✧✧ /raɪvªl/ (rivals, rivaling, rivaled)

in BRIT, use **rivalling, rivalled**

▪ N-COUNT Your **rival** is a person, business, or organization who you are competing or fighting against in the same area or for the same things. ❑ *The world champion finished more than two seconds ahead of his nearest rival.* ▪ N-COUNT If you say that someone or something has no **rivals** or is without **rival**, you mean that it is best of its type. ❑ *The area is famous for its wonderfully fragrant wine which has no rivals in the Rhone.* ▪ V-T If you say that one thing **rivals** another, you mean that they are both of the same standard or quality. ❑ *Cassette recorders cannot rival the sound quality of CDs.* ▪ → See feature box at **competition**

COLLOCATIONS

rival
NOUN ▪
noun + **rival**: leadership; love
adjective + **rival**: arch, bitter, fierce, great; chief, close, main, nearest; local, old, political, traditional
verb + **rival**: beat, crush, defeat, undercut; face

ri|val|ry /raɪvªlri/ (rivalries) N-VAR **Rivalry** is competition or fighting between people, businesses, or organizations who are in the same area or want the same things. ❑ *The rivalry between the Inkatha and the ANC has resulted in violence in the Black townships.*

riv|en /rɪvªn/ ADJ [usu v-link ADJ by/with n] If a country or organization is **riven** by conflict, it is damaged or destroyed by violent disagreements. ❑ *The four provinces are riven by deep family and tribal conflicts.*

riv|er ✦✦✧ /rɪvər/ (rivers) ▪ N-COUNT A **river** is a large amount of fresh water flowing continuously in a long line across the land. ❑ *...a chemical plant on the banks of the river.* ▪ → See feature box at **water**

river|bank /rɪvərbæŋk/ (riverbanks) also **river-bank** N-COUNT A **riverbank** is the land along the edge of a river.

riv|er ba|sin (river basins) N-COUNT A **river basin** is the area of land from which all the water flows into a particular river.

river|bed /rɪvərbɛd/ (riverbeds) also **river-bed** N-COUNT A **riverbed** is the ground which a river flows over.

river|boat /rɪvərboʊt/ (riverboats) N-COUNT [also by N] A **riverboat** is a large boat that carries passengers along a river.

river|front /rɪvərfrʌnt/ N-SING [the N, N n] The **riverfront** is an area of land next to a river with buildings such as houses, stores, or restaurants on it.

river|side /rɪvərsaɪd/ N-SING The **riverside** is the area of land by the banks of a river. ❑ *They walked back along the riverside.*

riv|et /rɪvɪt/ (rivets, riveting, riveted) V-T If you **are riveted** by something, it fascinates you and holds your interest completely. ❑ *As a child I remember being riveted by my grandfather's appearance.* ❑ *He was riveted to the John Wayne movie.*

riv|et|ing /rɪvɪtɪŋ/ ADJ If you describe something as **riveting**, you mean that it is extremely interesting and exciting, and that it holds your attention completely. ❑ *...Jeffrey Wolf's riveting new novel.*

rivu|let /rɪvyəlɪt/ (rivulets) N-COUNT A **rivulet** is a small stream. [FORMAL]

RN /ɑːr ɛn/ also **R.N.** **RN** is an abbreviation for **registered nurse**. [AM] ❑ *...a pediatric nurse, Kathleen McAdam RN.*

RNA /ɑːr ɛn eɪ/ N-UNCOUNT **RNA** is an acid in the chromosomes of the cells of living things which plays an important part in passing information about protein structure between different cells. **RNA** is an abbreviation for 'ribonucleic acid.' [TECHNICAL]

R num|ber (R numbers) N-COUNT **R number** is an abbreviation for **reproduction number**.

roach /roʊtʃ/ (roaches) N-COUNT A **roach** is the same as a **cockroach**. [mainly AM] ❑ *He found his brother in a seedy, roach-infested apartment*

road ✦✦✦ /roʊd/ (roads) ▪ N-COUNT A **road** is a long piece of hard ground that is built between two places so that people can drive or ride easily from one place to the other. ❑ *There was very little traffic on the roads.* ❑ *We just go straight up the Boston Post Road.* ▪ N-COUNT The **road** to a particular result is the means of achieving it or the process of achieving it. ❑ *We are bound to see some ups and downs along the road to recovery.* ▪ PHRASE If you say that someone is **on the road** to something, you mean that they are likely to achieve it. ❑ *The government took another step on the road to political reform.* ▪ **the end of the road** → see **end** ① ▪ → See feature box at **drive**

road|block /roʊdblɒk/ (roadblocks) N-COUNT When the police or the army put a **roadblock** across a road, they stop all the traffic going through, for example because they are looking for a criminal. ❑ *The city police set up roadblocks to check passing vehicles.*

road hog (road hogs) N-COUNT If you describe someone as a **road hog**, you mean that they drive too fast or in a way which is dangerous to other people. [INFORMAL, DISAPPROVAL]

road|house /roʊdhaʊs/ (roadhouses) N-COUNT A **roadhouse** is a bar or restaurant on a road outside a city.

road|ie /roʊdi/ (roadies) N-COUNT A **roadie** is a person who transports and sets up equipment for a band.

road|kill /roʊdkɪl/ also **road kill** N-UNCOUNT **Roadkill** is the remains of an animal or animals that have been killed on the road by cars or other vehicles. ❑ *I don't feel good about seeing roadkill.*

road man|ag|er (road managers) N-COUNT [oft poss N] The **road manager** of someone such as a singer or athlete is the person who organizes their travel and other arrangements during a tour.

road map (road maps) also **roadmap** ▪ N-COUNT A **road map** is a map which shows the roads in a particular area in detail. ▪ N-COUNT A **road map** of something is a detailed account of it, often intended to help people use or understand it. ❑ *The idea was to create a comprehensive road map of the Web.* ▪ N-COUNT [usu N to/for n] When politicians or journalists speak about a **road map** to or for peace or democracy, they mean a set of general principles that can be used as a basis for achieving peace or democracy. ❑ *He raised doubts about the American road map to a peace settlement.*

road rage N-UNCOUNT **Road rage** is anger or violent behavior caused by someone else's bad driving or the stress of being in heavy traffic. ◻ *Two women were being hunted by police after a road rage attack on a male motorist.*

road|runner /roʊdrʌnər/ (**roadrunners**) N-COUNT A **roadrunner** is a bird with a long tail, found mainly in the southwestern United States, that is able to run very quickly. ◻ *Roadrunners are frequently seen sprinting through the inn's grounds.*

road show (**road shows**) also **roadshow** **1** N-COUNT A **road show** is a show presented by traveling actors. [AM] **2** N-COUNT A **road show** is a group of people who travel around a country, for example as part of an advertising or political campaign. [mainly AM] ◻ *The Democratic presidential ticket plans another road show, this time through the industrial Midwest.* **3** N-COUNT [usu supp N] A **road show** is a traveling show organized by a radio station, magazine, or company. ◻ *...a road show that promotes Washington wines.*

road|side /roʊdsaɪd/ (**roadsides**) N-COUNT The **roadside** is the area at the edge of a road. ◻ *Bob was forced to leave the car at the roadside and run for help.*

road|ster /roʊdstər/ (**roadsters**) **1** N-COUNT A **roadster** is a car with no roof and only two seats. [OLD-FASHIONED] **2** → See also color supplement

road test (**road tests, road testing, road tested**) also **road-test** **1** V-T If you **road test** a car or other vehicle, for example, after it has been repaired, you drive it on roads in order to make sure that it is working properly. ◻ *While road testing the car, a mechanic injures another motorist and is sued for $50,000.* • N-COUNT **Road test** is also a noun ◻ *...during a recent road test of the Fiesta LX 5-door.* **2** N-COUNT A **road test** is a driving test that you must pass in order to get a driver's license. [AM] ◻ *When I went for my road test, I got utterly confused and flunked.* **3** V-T If someone **road tests** a new product, they use it in order to make sure that it works properly. ◻ *Catherine Young road tests affordable waterproof jackets.* • N-COUNT **Road test** is also a noun. ◻ *The new format is great but the show needs more road tests.*

road|way /roʊdweɪ/ (**roadways**) N-COUNT [oft the N in sing] The **roadway** is the part of a road that is used by traffic. ◻ *Marks in the roadway seem to indicate that he skidded taking a sharp turn.*

road|work /roʊdwɜrk/ N-UNCOUNT **Roadwork** is repairs or other work being done on a road. ◻ *The traffic was stationary due to three sets of roadwork in less than a mile.*

road|worthy /roʊdwɜrði/ ADJ A vehicle that is **roadworthy** is in good enough condition to be used on the roads. ◻ *...his 1927 Dodge, which he purchased new and is still roadworthy today.*

roam /roʊm/ (**roams, roaming, roamed**) V-T/V-I If you **roam** an area or **roam around** it, you wander or travel around it without having a particular purpose. ◻ *Barefoot children roamed the streets.* ◻ *I spent a couple of years roaming around the countryside.*

roam|ing /roʊmɪŋ/ N-UNCOUNT **Roaming** refers to the service provided by a cellphone company which makes it possible for you to use your cellphone when you travel. ◻ *Ignorance of roaming call charges is common.*

roan /roʊn/ (**roans**) N-COUNT A **roan** is a horse that is brown or black with some white hairs.

roar /rɔr/ (**roars, roaring, roared**) **1** V-I If something, usually a vehicle, **roars** somewhere, it goes there very fast, making a loud noise. [WRITTEN] ◻ *A police car roared past.* **2** V-I If something **roars**, it makes a very loud noise. [WRITTEN] ◻ *The engine roared, and the vehicle leapt forward.* • N-COUNT **Roar** is also a noun. ◻ *...the roar of traffic.* **3** V-I If someone **roars** with laughter, they laugh in a very noisy way. ◻ *Max threw back his head and roared with laughter.* • N-COUNT **Roar** is also a noun. ◻ *There were roars of laughter as he stood up.* **4** V-T/V-I If someone **roars**, they shout something in a very loud voice. [WRITTEN] ◻ *"I'll kill you for that," he roared.* ◻ *During the playing of the national anthem the crowd roared and whistled.* • N-COUNT **Roar** is also a noun. ◻ *There was a roar of approval.* **5** V-I When a lion **roars**, it makes the loud sound that lions typically make. ◻ *The lion roared once, and sprang.* • N-COUNT **Roar** is also a noun. ◻ *...the roar of lions in the distance.* **6** → See feature box at **onomatopoeia**

roar|ing /rɔrɪŋ/ **1** ADJ [ADJ n] A **roaring** fire has large flames and sends out a lot of heat. ◻ *...nighttime beach parties, with a roaring fire.* **2** ADJ [ADJ n] If something is a **roaring** success, it is extremely successful. ◻ *The government's first effort to privatize a company has been a roaring success.* **3** → see also **roar**

roast /roʊst/ (**roasts, roasting, roasted**) **1** V-T When you **roast** meat or other food, you cook it by dry heat in an oven or over a fire. ◻ *I personally would rather roast a chicken whole.* **2** ADJ [ADJ n] **Roast** meat has been cooked by roasting. ◻ *They serve the most delicious roast beef.* **3** N-COUNT A **roast** is a piece of meat that is cooked by roasting. ◻ *Come into the kitchen. I've got to put the roast in.*

rob /rɒb/ (**robs, robbing, robbed**) **1** V-T If someone **is robbed**, they have money or property stolen from them. ◻ *Mrs. Yacoub was robbed of her designer watch at her Westchester home.* **2** V-T If someone or something **is robbed** of something that they deserve, have, or need, it is taken away from them. ◻ *When Miles Davis died jazz was robbed of its most distinctive voice.*

rob|ber /rɒbər/ (**robbers**) N-COUNT A **robber** is someone who steals money or property from a bank, store, or vehicle, often by using force or threats. ◻ *Armed robbers broke into a jeweler's through a hole in the wall.*

rob|ber bar|on (**robber barons**) N-COUNT If you refer to someone as a **robber baron**, you mean that they have made a very large amount of money and have been prepared to act illegally or in an immoral way in order to do so.

rob|bery /rɒbəri/ (**robberies**) **1** N-VAR **Robbery** is the crime of stealing money or property from a bank, store, or vehicle, often by using force or threats. ◻ *The gang members committed dozens of armed robberies over the past year.* **2** → See feature box at **crime**

robe /roʊb/ (**robes**) **1** N-COUNT A **robe** is a loose piece of clothing that covers all of your body and reaches the ground. You can describe someone as wearing a **robe** or as wearing **robes**. [FORMAL] ◻ *Pope John Paul II knelt in his white robes before the simple altar.* **2** N-COUNT A **robe** is a piece of clothing, usually made of toweling, which people wear in the house, especially when they have just gotten up or taken a bath. ◻ *Kyle put on a robe and went down to the kitchen.*

-robed /-roʊbd/ COMB IN ADJ [ADJ n] **-robed** combines with the names of colors to indicate that someone is wearing robes of a particular color. ◻ *...a brown-robed monk.*

rob|in /rɒbɪn/ (**robins**) **1** N-COUNT A **robin** is a fairly large brown bird found in North America that has a reddish brown breast. **2** N-COUNT A **robin** is a small brown bird found in Europe that has an orangey red neck and breast. European robins are smaller then North American ones, and are a completely different species of bird. **3** → see also **round-robin**

ro|bot /roʊbət, -bɒt/ (**robots**) N-COUNT A **robot** is a machine that is programmed to move and perform certain tasks automatically. ◻ *...very lightweight robots that we could send to the moon for planetary exploration.*

ro|bot|ic /roʊbɒtɪk/ ADJ [ADJ n] **Robotic** equipment can perform certain tasks automatically. ◻ *Astronaut Pierre Thuot tried to latch the 15-foot robotic arm onto the satellite.*

ro|bot|ics /roʊbɒtɪks/ N-UNCOUNT **Robotics** is the science of designing and building robots. [TECHNICAL]

ro|bust /roʊbʌst, roʊbʌst/ **1** ADJ Someone or something that is **robust** is very strong or healthy. ◻ *He was always the robust one, physically strong and mentally sharp.* **2** ADJ **Robust** views or opinions are strongly held and forcefully expressed. ◻ *The Secretary of State has made a robust defense of the agreement.*

rock ✦✧ /rɒk/ (**rocks, rocking, rocked**) **1** N-UNCOUNT **Rock** is the hard substance which the earth is made of. ◻ *The hills above the valley are bare rock.* **2** N-COUNT A **rock** is a large piece of rock that sticks up out of the ground or the sea, or that has broken away from a mountain or a cliff. ◻ *She sat cross-legged on the rock.* **3** N-COUNT A **rock** is a piece of rock that is small enough for you to pick up. ◻ *She bent down, picked up a rock, and threw it into the trees.* **4** V-T/V-I When something **rocks** or when you **rock** it, it moves slowly and regularly backward and forward or from side to side. ◻ *His body rocked from side to side with the train.* **5** V-T/V-I If an explosion or an earthquake **rocks** a building or an area, it causes the building or area to shake. [JOURNALISM] ◻ *Three people were injured yesterday when an explosion rocked the factory.* ◻ *In Taipei buildings rocked back and forth.* **6** V-T If an event or a piece of news **rocks** a group or society, it shocks them or makes them feel less secure. [JOURNALISM] ◻ *His death rocked the fashion business.* **7** N-UNCOUNT **Rock** is loud music with a strong beat that is usually played and sung by a

rockabilly

small group of people using instruments such as electric guitars and drums. ❑ ...*a rock concert*. ❽ → See also color supplement

---
SYNONYMS

rock
VERB ❹
sway: *The people swayed back and forth with arms linked.*
pitch: *The movement took him by surprise, and he pitched forward.*
swing: *The sail of the little boat swung crazily from one side to the other.*

---

rocka|bil|ly /rɒkəbɪli/ N-UNCOUNT **Rockabilly** is a kind of fast rock music which developed in the southern United States in the 1950s.

rock and roll also **rock'n'roll** N-UNCOUNT **Rock and roll** is a kind of popular music developed in the 1950s which has a strong beat and is played on electrical instruments. ❑ ...*Elvis Presley – the King of Rock and Roll.*

rock bot|tom also **rock-bottom** ❶ N-UNCOUNT If something has reached **rock bottom**, it is at such a low level that it cannot go any lower. ❑ *Morale in the armed forces was at rock bottom.* ❷ ADJ A **rock-bottom** price or level is a very low one, mainly in advertisements. [APPROVAL] ❑ *What they do offer is a good product at a rock-bottom price.*

rock candy N-UNCOUNT **Rock candy** is a hard candy that is made of crystallized sugar. [AM]

rock climb|er (rock climbers) N-COUNT A **rock climber** is a person whose hobby or sport is climbing cliffs or large rocks.

rock climb|ing N-UNCOUNT **Rock climbing** is the activity of climbing cliffs or large rocks, as a hobby or sport.

rock|er /rɒkər/ (rockers) ❶ N-COUNT A **rocker** is a chair that is built on two curved pieces of wood so that you can rock yourself backward and forward while you are sitting in it. [mainly AM]

| in BRIT, usually use **rocking chair** |

❷ N-COUNT A **rocker** is someone who performs rock music. ❑ ...*American rockers Guns 'N' Roses.*

rock|ery /rɒkəri/ [mainly BRIT] → see **rock garden**

rock|et ♦◇◇ /rɒkɪt/ (rockets, rocketing, rocketed) ❶ N-COUNT A **rocket** is a space vehicle that is shaped like a long tube. ❑ ...*the Apollo 12 rocket that took astronauts to the moon.* ❷ N-COUNT A **rocket** is a missile containing explosives that is powered by gas. ❑ *There has been a renewed rocket attack on the capital.* ❸ N-COUNT A **rocket** is a firework that quickly goes high into the air and then explodes. ❹ V-I If things such as prices or social problems **rocket**, they increase very quickly and suddenly. [JOURNALISM] ❑ *Fresh food is so scarce that prices have rocketed.* ❺ V-I If something such as a vehicle **rockets** somewhere, it moves there very quickly. ❑ *A train rocketed by, shaking the walls of the row houses.* ❻ N-UNCOUNT **Rocket** is the same as **arugula**. [BRIT]

rock|et launch|er (rocket launchers) N-COUNT A **rocket launcher** is a device that can be carried by soldiers and used for firing rockets.

rock|et sci|ence N-UNCOUNT If you say that something is not **rocket science**, you mean that you do not have to be intelligent in order to do it. ❑ *Interviewing politicians may not be rocket science, but it does matter.*

rock|et sci|en|tist (rocket scientists) N-COUNT [with brd-neg] If you say that it does not take a **rocket scientist** to do something, you mean that you do not have to be intelligent to do it. ❑ *It doesn't take a rocket scientist to figure it out.*

rock gar|den (rock gardens) N-COUNT A **rock garden** is a garden which consists of rocks with small plants growing among them.

rock-hard also **rock hard** ADJ Something that is **rock-hard** is extremely hard. ❑ *During the dry season the land is rock hard.*

rock|ing chair (rocking chairs) ❶ N-COUNT A **rocking chair** is a chair that is built on two curved pieces of wood so that you can rock yourself backward and forward when you are sitting in it. ❷ → See also color supplement

rock|ing horse (rocking horses) N-COUNT A **rocking horse** is a toy horse which a child can sit on and which can be made to rock backward and forward.

rock|like /rɒklaɪk/ ADJ [usu ADJ n] Something that is **rocklike** is very strong or firm, and is unlikely to change. ❑ ...*his rocklike integrity.*

rock'n'roll /rɒkənroʊl/ → see **rock and roll**

rock pool (rock pools) N-COUNT A **rock pool** is a small pool between rocks on the edge of the sea.

rock salt N-UNCOUNT **Rock salt** is salt that is formed in the ground. It is obtained by mining.

rock-solid also **rock solid** ❶ ADJ Something that is **rock-solid** is extremely hard. ❑ *Freeze it only until firm but not rock solid.* ❷ ADJ If you describe someone or something as **rock-solid**, you approve of them because they are extremely reliable or unlikely to change. [APPROVAL] ❑ *Mayhew is a man of rock-solid integrity.*

rock steady also **rock-steady** ADJ Something that is **rock steady** is very firm and does not shake or move about. ❑ *He reached for a cigarette and lit it, fingers rock steady.*

rocky /rɒki/ (rockier, rockiest) ❶ ADJ A **rocky** place is covered with rocks or consists of large areas of rock and has nothing growing on it. ❑ *The paths are often very rocky so strong boots are advisable.* ❷ ADJ A **rocky** situation or relationship is unstable and full of difficulties. ❑ *They had gone through some rocky times together when Ann was first married.*

ro|co|co /rəkoʊkoʊ/ N-UNCOUNT [oft N n] **Rococo** is a decorative style that was popular in Europe in the eighteenth century. Rococo buildings, furniture, and works of art often include complicated curly decoration.

rod /rɒd/ (rods) N-COUNT A **rod** is a long, thin, metal or wooden bar. ❑ ...*a 15-foot thick roof that was reinforced with steel rods.*

rode /roʊd/ **Rode** is the past tense of **ride**.

ro|dent /roʊdənt/ (rodents) N-COUNT **Rodents** are small mammals which have sharp front teeth. Rats, mice, and squirrels are rodents.

ro|deo /roʊdioʊ, roʊdeɪoʊ/ (rodeos) N-COUNT A **rodeo** is a public entertainment event in which cowboys show different skills, including riding wild horses and catching cattle with ropes.

roe /roʊ/ (roes) N-VAR [oft supp N] **Roe** is the eggs or sperm of a fish, which is eaten as food. ❑ ...*cod's roe.*

roe deer (roe deer) N-COUNT A **roe deer** is a small deer which lives in woods in Europe and Asia.

rogue /roʊg/ (rogues) ❶ N-COUNT A **rogue** is someone who behaves in a dishonest or criminal way. ❑ *Mr. Ward wasn't a rogue at all.* ❷ N-COUNT If someone behaves in a way that you do not approve of but you still like them, you can refer to them as a **rogue**. [FEELINGS] ❑ ...*Falstaff, the lovable rogue.* ❸ ADJ [ADJ n] A **rogue** element is someone or something that behaves differently from others of its kind, often causing damage. ❑ *Computer systems throughout the country are being affected by a series of mysterious rogue programs, known as viruses.*

rogues' gal|lery ❶ N-SING [oft N of n] A **rogues' gallery** is a collection of photographs of criminals that is kept by the police and used when they want to identify someone. [JOURNALISM] ❑ ...*a rogues' gallery of juvenile crime gangs.* ❷ N-SING [oft N of n] You can refer to a group of people or things that you consider undesirable as a **rogues' gallery**. [JOURNALISM, DISAPPROVAL] ❑ *He and others in the rogues' gallery of international terrorists may be running out of time.*

rogue state (rogue states) N-COUNT When politicians or journalists talk about a **rogue state**, they mean a country that they regard as a threat to their own country's security, for example, because it supports terrorism. [JOURNALISM, DISAPPROVAL] ❑ ...*possible missile attacks from rogue states and terrorists.*

rogue trad|er (rogue traders) N-COUNT A **rogue trader** is an employee of a financial institution who carries out business without the knowledge or approval of his or her bosses. [BUSINESS, DISAPPROVAL] ❑ ...*the unauthorized dealings by rogue trader Nick Leeson which brought down the bank*

ro|guish /roʊgɪʃ/ ADJ If someone has a **roguish** expression or manner, they look as though they are about to behave badly. ❑ *She was a mature lady with dyed red hair and a roguish grin.*

Ro|hyp|nol /roʊhɪpnɒl/ N-UNCOUNT **Rohypnol** is a powerful drug that makes a person unconscious. It is sometimes used by rapists to drug their victims. [TRADEMARK]

roil /rɔɪl/ (roils, roiling, roiled) **1** V-I If water **roils**, it is rough and disturbed. [mainly AM] ☐ *The water roiled to his left as he climbed carefully at the edge of the waterfall.* **2** V-T Something that **roils** a state or situation makes it disturbed and confused. ☐ *Times of national turmoil generally roil a country's financial markets.*

role ♦♦♦ /roʊl/ (roles) **1** N-COUNT If you have a **role** in a situation or in society, you have a particular position and function in it. ☐ *Until now scientists had very little clear evidence about the drug's role in preventing more serious effects of infection.* **2** N-COUNT A **role** is one of the characters that an actor or singer can play in a movie, play, or opera. ☐ *She has just landed the lead role in their latest production.*

role mod|el (role models) N-COUNT A **role model** is someone you admire and try to imitate. ☐ *Five out of the ten top role models for teenagers are Black.*

role-play (role-plays, role-playing, role-played) also **role play** **1** N-VAR **Role-play** is the act of imitating the character and behavior of someone who is different from yourself, for example as a training exercise. ☐ *We have to communicate with each other through role-play.* **2** V-T/V-I If people **role-play**, they do a role-play. ☐ *Role-play the interview with a friend beforehand.* • **role-play|ing** N-UNCOUNT ☐ *We did a lot of role-playing.*

role re|ver|sal (role reversals) N-VAR **Role reversal** is a situation in which two people have chosen or been forced to exchange their duties and responsibilities, so that each is now doing what the other used to do. ☐ *...men who have undertaken the most extreme role reversal and become house husbands.*

roll ♦♦◇ /roʊl/ (rolls, rolling, rolled) **1** V-T/V-I When something **rolls** or when you **roll** it, it moves along a surface, turning over many times. ☐ *The ball rolled into the net.* **2** V-I If you **roll** somewhere, you move on a surface while lying down, turning your body over and over, so that you are sometimes on your back, sometimes on your side, and sometimes on your front. ☐ *When I was a little kid I rolled down a hill and broke my leg.* **3** V-I When vehicles **roll** along, they move along slowly. ☐ *The truck quietly rolled forward and demolished all the old wooden fencing.* **4** V-I If a machine **rolls**, it is operating. ☐ *He slipped and fell on the step as the cameras rolled.* **5** V-I If drops of liquid **roll** down a surface, they move quickly down it. ☐ *She looked at Ginny and tears rolled down her cheeks.* **6** V-T If you **roll** something flexible into a cylinder or a ball, you form it into a cylinder or a ball by wrapping it several times around itself or by shaping it between your hands. ☐ *He took off his sweater, rolled it into a pillow, and lay down on the grass.* • PHRASAL VERB **Roll up** means the same as **roll**. ☐ *Stein rolled up the paper bag with the money inside.* **7** N-COUNT A **roll** of paper, plastic, cloth, or wire is a long piece of it that has been wrapped many times around itself or around a tube. ☐ *The photographers had already shot a dozen rolls of film.* **8** V-T If you **roll up** something such as a car window or a blind, you cause it to move upward by turning a handle. If you **roll** it down, you cause it to move downward by turning a handle. ☐ *In mid-afternoon, shopkeepers began to roll down their shutters.* **9** V-T/V-I If you **roll** your eyes or if your eyes **roll**, they move around and upward. People sometimes roll their eyes when they are frightened, bored, or annoyed. [WRITTEN] ☐ *People may roll their eyes and talk about overprotective parents.* **10** N-COUNT A **roll** is a small piece of bread that is round or long and is made to be eaten by one person. Rolls can be eaten plain, with butter, or with a filling. ☐ *He sipped at his coffee and spread butter and marmalade on a roll.* **11** N-COUNT A **roll** of drums is a long, low, fairly loud sound made by drums. ☐ *As the town clock struck two, they heard the roll of drums.* **12** N-COUNT A **roll** is an official list of people's names. ☐ *Pro-democracy activists say a new electoral roll should be drawn up.* **13** → see also **rolling, rock and roll 14** PHRASE If something is several things **rolled into one**, it combines the main features or qualities of those things. ☐ *This is our kitchen, living room, and dining room all rolled into one.* **15 heads will roll** → see **head** ③ **16** → See feature box at **body language**

▶ **roll back** PHRASAL VERB To **roll back** prices, taxes, or benefits means to reduce them. [mainly AM] ☐ *One provision of the law was to roll back taxes to the 1975 level.*

▶ **roll in** PHRASAL VERB If something such as money **is rolling in**, it is appearing or being received in large quantities. [INFORMAL] ☐ *Don't forget, I have always kept the money rolling in.*

▶ **roll out** PHRASAL VERB If a company **rolls out** a new product or service, or if the product or service **rolls out**, it is made available to the public. ☐ *On Thursday Microsoft rolls out its new operating system.* ☐ *Northern Telecom says its products will roll out over 18 months beginning early next year.*

▶ **roll over 1** PHRASAL VERB If you are lying down and you **roll over**, you turn your body so that a different part of you is facing upward. ☐ *I rolled over and went back to sleep.* **2** PHRASAL VERB If a moving vehicle such as a car **rolls over**, it turns over many times, usually because it has crashed. ☐ *Those kinds of vehicles are more likely to roll over than passenger cars.* **3** PHRASAL VERB If you say that someone **rolls over**, you mean that they stop resisting someone and do what the other person wants them to do. ☐ *That's why most people and organizations just roll over and give up when they're challenged or attacked by the I.R.S.* **4** PHRASAL VERB If you **roll over** a loan or other financial arrangement, you extend it, for example by adding it to another loan. [BUSINESS] ☐ *There seems to be no way to spread out the tax or roll over the cash into another pension plan.* **5** → see also **rollover 6** PHRASAL VERB In lotteries and similar games, if a jackpot **rolls over**, it is not won by anyone and the money is added to the prize money for the next lottery. ☐ *If the jackpot isn't won this week it will roll over again to next week.* **7** → see also **rollover**

▶ **roll up 1** PHRASAL VERB If you **roll up** your sleeves or pant legs, you fold the ends back several times, making them shorter. ☐ *The jacket was too big for him so he rolled up the cuffs.* **2** PHRASAL VERB If people **roll up** somewhere, they arrive there, especially in a car and often late. [INFORMAL] ☐ *They eventually rolled up two hours late.* **3** → see also **roll 6**

roll|back /roʊlbæk/ (rollbacks) N-COUNT [usu with supp] A **rollback** is a reduction in price or some other change that makes something like it was before. [mainly AM] ☐ *Silber says the tax rollback would decimate basic services for the needy.*

roll call (roll calls) **1** N-VAR If you take a **roll call**, you check which of the members of a group are present by reading their names out. ☐ *We had to stand in the snow every morning for roll call.* **2** N-SING [N of n] A **roll call** of a particular type of people or things is a list of them. [JOURNALISM] ☐ *Her list of students read like a roll call of the great and good.*

rolled-up 1 ADJ [ADJ n] **Rolled-up** objects have been folded or wrapped into a cylindrical shape. ☐ *...a rolled-up newspaper.* **2** ADJ [ADJ n] **Rolled-up** sleeves or pant legs have been made shorter by being folded over at the lower edge. ☐ *...an open-necked shirt, with rolled-up sleeves.*

roll|er /roʊlər/ (rollers) **1** N-COUNT A **roller** is a cylinder that turns around in a machine or device. **2** N-COUNT **Rollers** are hollow tubes that you roll your hair round in order to make it curly. ☐ *She gets up every morning and puts her hair in rollers.*

Roll|er|blade /roʊlərbleɪd/ (Rollerblades) N-COUNT **Rollerblades** are a type of in-line skate. [TRADEMARK] • **roll|er|blad|ing** N-UNCOUNT ☐ *Rollerblading is great for all ages.*

roll|er coast|er (roller coasters) **1** N-COUNT A **roller coaster** is a small railroad at an amusement park that goes up and down steep slopes fast and that people ride on for pleasure or excitement. ☐ *It's great to go on the roller coaster five times and not be sick.* **2** N-COUNT If you say that someone or something is on a **roller coaster**, you mean that they go through many sudden or extreme changes in a short time. [JOURNALISM] ☐ *I've been on an emotional roller coaster since I've been here.*

roll|er skate (roller skates, roller-skates, roller-skating, roller-skated) **1** N-COUNT **Roller skates** are shoes with four small wheels on the bottom. ☐ *A boy of about ten came up on roller skates.* **2** V-I If you **roller-skate**, you move over a flat surface wearing roller skates. ☐ *On the day of the accident, my son Gary was roller-skating outside our house.*

rol|lick|ing /rɒlɪkɪŋ/ ADJ [ADJ n] A **rollicking** occasion is cheerful and usually noisy. A **rollicking** book or movie is entertaining and enjoyable, and not very serious. ☐ *The diaries are a rollicking read.* • ADV [ADV adj] **Rollicking** is also an adverb. ☐ *I'm having a rollicking good time.*

roll|ing /roʊlɪŋ/ ADJ [ADJ n] **Rolling** hills are small hills with gentle slopes that extend a long way into the distance. ☐ *...the rolling countryside of southwestern France.*

roll|ing mill (rolling mills) N-COUNT A **rolling mill** is a machine or factory in which metal is rolled into sheets or bars.

roll|ing pin (rolling pins) N-COUNT A **rolling pin** is a cylinder that you roll backward and forward over uncooked pastry in order to make the pastry flat.

roll|ing stock N-UNCOUNT **Rolling stock** is all the engines and cars that are used on a railroad. ❑ *Many stations needed repairs or rebuilding and there was a shortage of rolling stock.*

roll-neck [mainly BRIT] → see **turtleneck**

roll of hon|our [BRIT] → see **honor roll**

roll-on (roll-ons) N-COUNT [oft N n] A **roll-on** is a deodorant or cosmetic that you apply to your body using a container with a ball which turns around in the neck of the container. ❑ *I use unperfumed, roll-on deodorant.*

roll|over /ro͟ʊloʊvər/ (rollovers) **1** N-COUNT [usu singular] In finance, a **rollover** is when a loan or other financial arrangement is extended, or when an investment is taken out of one fund or bank and put into another one of the same kind. **2** N-COUNT [usu singular] In a lottery draw, a **rollover** is a prize that includes the prize money from the previous draw, because nobody won it. [BRIT]

roll-top desk (roll-top desks) also **rolltop desk** N-COUNT A **roll-top desk** is a desk with a wooden cover that can be pulled down over the writing surface when the desk is not being used.

roll-up (roll-ups) N-COUNT A **roll-up** is a cigarette that someone makes for themselves, using tobacco and cigarette papers.

roly-poly /ro͟ʊli po͟ʊli/ ADJ [ADJ n] **Roly-poly** people are pleasantly fat and round. [INFORMAL] ❑ *...a short, roly-poly man with laughing eyes.*

ROM /rɒm/ **1** N-UNCOUNT **ROM** is the permanent part of a computer's memory. The information stored there can be read but not changed. **ROM** is an abbreviation for 'read-only memory.' [COMPUTING] ❑ *It's got 256 megabytes of ROM and 512 megabytes of RAM.* **2** → see also **CD-ROM**

ro|maine /roʊme͟ɪn/ also **romaine lettuce** N-UNCOUNT **Romaine** is a type of lettuce with a long narrow head and crisp leaves. [AM] ❑ *...a salad of romaine and honeydew melon.*

Ro|man ✦✧✧ /ro͟ʊmən/ (Romans) **1** ADJ **Roman** means related to or connected with ancient Rome and its empire. ❑ *...the fall of the Roman Empire.* ● N-COUNT A **Roman** was a citizen of ancient Rome or its empire. ❑ *When they conquered Britain, the Romans brought this custom with them.* **2** ADJ **Roman** means related to or connected with modern Rome. ❑ *...a Roman hotel room.* ● N-COUNT A **Roman** is someone who lives in or comes from Rome. ❑ *...soccer-mad Romans.*

Ro|man al|pha|bet N-SING [the N] The **Roman alphabet** is the alphabet that was used by the Romans in ancient times and that is used for writing most western European languages, including English.

Ro|man Catho|lic (Roman Catholics) **1** ADJ The **Roman Catholic** Church is the same as the **Catholic** Church. ❑ *...a Roman Catholic priest.* **2** N-COUNT A **Roman Catholic** is the same as a **Catholic**. ❑ *Like her, Maria was a Roman Catholic.*

Ro|man Ca|tholi|cism N-UNCOUNT **Roman Catholicism** is the same as **Catholicism**.

ro|mance /roʊmæ͟ns, ro͟ʊmæns/ (romances) **1** N-COUNT A **romance** is a relationship between two people who are in love with each other but who are not married to each other. ❑ *After a whirlwind romance the couple announced their engagement in July.* **2** N-UNCOUNT **Romance** refers to the actions and feelings of people who are in love, especially behavior that is very caring or affectionate. ❑ *He still finds time for romance by cooking candlelit dinners for his girlfriend.* **3** N-UNCOUNT You can refer to the pleasure and excitement of doing something new or exciting as **romance**. ❑ *We want to recreate the romance and excitement that used to be part of rail journeys.* **4** N-COUNT A **romance** is a novel or movie about a love affair. ❑ *Their taste in fiction was for chunky historical romances.*

Ro|man|esque /ro͟ʊmənɛ͟sk/ ADJ [usu ADJ n] **Romanesque** architecture is the style that was common in western Europe around the eleventh century. It is characterized by rounded arches and thick pillars.

Ro|ma|nian /roʊme͟ɪniən/ (Romanians) also **Rumanian** **1** ADJ [usu ADJ n] **Romanian** means belonging or relating to Romania, or to its people, language, or culture. **2** N-COUNT A **Romanian** is a Romanian citizen, or a person of Romanian origin. **3** N-UNCOUNT **Romanian** is the language spoken in Romania.

Ro|man nu|mer|al /ro͟ʊmən nu͟ːmərəl/ (Roman numerals) N-COUNT [usu pl] **Roman numerals** are the letters used by the ancient Romans to represent numbers, for example I, IV, VIII, and XL, which represent 1, 4, 8, and 40. Roman numerals are still sometimes used today.

ro|man|tic ✦✧✧ /roʊmæ͟ntɪk/ (romantics) **1** ADJ Someone who is **romantic** or does **romantic** things says and does things that make their wife, husband, girlfriend, or boyfriend feel special and loved. ❑ *When we're together, all he talks about is business. I wish he were more romantic.* **2** ADJ [ADJ n] **Romantic** means connected with sexual love. ❑ *He was not interested in a romantic relationship with Ingrid.* ● **ro|man|ti|cal|ly** ADV ❑ *We are not romantically involved.* **3** ADJ [ADJ n] A **romantic** play, movie, or story describes or represents a love affair. ❑ *It is a lovely romantic comedy, well worth seeing.* **4** ADJ If you say that someone has a **romantic** view or idea of something, you are critical of them because their view of it is unrealistic and they think that thing is better or more exciting than it really is. [DISAPPROVAL] ❑ *He has a romantic view of rural society.* ● N-COUNT A **romantic** is a person who has romantic views. ❑ *You're a hopeless romantic.* **5** ADJ Something that is **romantic** is beautiful in a way that strongly affects your feelings. ❑ *It is considered one of the most romantic restaurants in the city.* ● **ro|man|ti|cal|ly** ADV ❑ *...the romantically named, but very muddy, Cave of the Wild Horses.* **6** → See feature box at **relationship**

ro|man|ti|cism /roʊmæ͟ntɪsɪzəm/ **1** N-UNCOUNT **Romanticism** is attitudes, ideals, and feelings which are romantic rather than realistic. ❑ *Her determined romanticism was worrying me.* **2** N-UNCOUNT **Romanticism** is the artistic movement of the eighteenth and nineteenth centuries which was concerned with the expression of the individual's feelings and emotions.

ro|man|ti|cize /roʊmæ͟ntɪsaɪz/ (romanticizes, romanticizing, romanticized)

in BRIT, also use **romanticise**

V-T If you **romanticize** someone or something, you think or talk about them in a way which is not at all realistic and which makes them seem better than they really are. ❑ *He romanticized the past as he became disillusioned with his present.* ● **ro|man|ti|cized** ADJ ❑ *Mr. Lane's film takes a highly romanticized view of life on the streets.*

Roma|ny /ro͟ʊməni/ (Romanies) **1** N-COUNT A **Romany** is a member of a race of people who travel from place to place, usually living in trailers, rather than living in one place. **2** ADJ [usu ADJ n] **Romany** means related or connected to the Romany people. ❑ *...the Romany community.*

Romeo /ro͟ʊmioʊ/ (Romeos) N-COUNT You can describe a man as a **Romeo** if you want to indicate that he is very much in love with someone, or that he frequently has sexual relationships with different people. [HUMOROUS, INFORMAL, JOURNALISM] ❑ *...one of Hollywood's most notorious Romeos.*

romp /rɒmp/ (romps, romping, romped) **1** V-I Journalists use **romp** in expressions like **romp home**, **romp in**, or **romp to victory**, to say that a person or horse has won a race or competition very easily. ❑ *Mr. Foster romped home with 141 votes.* **2** V-I When children or animals **romp**, they play noisily and happily. ❑ *Dogs and little children romped happily in the garden.*

roof ✦✧✧ /ru͟ːf/ (roofs)

The plural can be pronounced /ru͟ːfs/ or /ru͟ːvz/.

1 N-COUNT The **roof** of a building is the covering on top of it that protects the people and things inside from the weather. ❑ *...a small stone cottage with a red slate roof.* **2** N-COUNT The **roof** of a car or other vehicle is the top part of it, which protects passengers or goods from the weather. ❑ *The car rolled onto its roof, trapping him.* **3** N-COUNT The **roof** of your mouth is the highest part of the inside of your mouth. ❑ *She clicked her tongue against the roof of her mouth.* **4** PHRASE If the level of something such as the price of a product or the rate of inflation **goes through the roof**, it suddenly increases very rapidly indeed. [INFORMAL] ❑ *Prices for Korean art have gone through the roof.* **5** PHRASE If you **hit the roof** or **go through the roof**, you become very angry, and usually show your anger by shouting at someone. [INFORMAL] ❑ *Sergeant Long will hit the roof when I tell him you've gone off.* **6** PHRASE If a number of things or people are **under one roof** or **under the same roof**, they are in the same building. ☐ *The firms intend to open either together under one roof or alongside each other in shopping malls.*

roofed /ruːft, ruːvd/ ADJ A **roofed** building or area is covered by a roof. ☐ *...a roofed corridor.* ☐ *...a peasant hut roofed with branches.*

-roofed /-ruːft, -ruːvd/ COMB IN ADJ [usu ADJ n] **-roofed** combines with adjectives and nouns to form adjectives that describe what kind of roof a building has. ☐ *...a huge flat-roofed concrete and glass building.*

roof|er /ruːfər/ (**roofers**) N-COUNT A **roofer** is a person whose job is to put roofs on buildings and to repair damaged roofs.

roof gar|den (**roof gardens**) N-COUNT A **roof garden** is a garden on the flat roof of a building.

roof|ing /ruːfɪŋ/ ◼ N-UNCOUNT [oft N n] **Roofing** is material used for making or covering roofs. ☐ *A gust of wind pried loose a section of sheet-metal roofing.* ◼ N-UNCOUNT [oft N n] **Roofing** is the work of putting new roofs on houses. ☐ *...a roofing company.*

roof|less /ruːflɪs/ ADJ A **roofless** building has no roof, usually because the building has been damaged or has not been used for a long time.

roof rack (**roof racks**) also **roof-rack** N-COUNT A **roof rack** is a metal frame that is fixed on top of a car and used for carrying large objects. [mainly BRIT]

in AM, usually use **luggage rack**

roof|top /ruːftɒp/ (**rooftops**) ◼ N-COUNT A **rooftop** is the outside part of the roof of a building. ☐ *Below us you could glimpse the rooftops of a few small villages.* ◼ PHRASE [PHR after v] If you shout something **from the rooftops**, you say it or announce it in a very public way. ☐ *When we have something definite to say, we will shout it from the rooftops.*

rook /rʊk/ (**rooks**) ◼ N-COUNT A **rook** is a large, black bird. Rooks are members of the crow family. ◼ N-COUNT In chess, a **rook** is one of the chess pieces that stand in the corners of the board at the beginning of a game. Rooks can move forward, backward, or sideways, but not diagonally.

rookie /rʊki/ (**rookies**) ◼ N-COUNT A **rookie** is someone who has just started doing a job and does not have much experience, especially someone who has just joined the army or police force. [mainly AM, INFORMAL] ☐ *I don't want to have another rookie to train.* ◼ N-COUNT A **rookie** is a person who has been competing in a professional sport for less than a year. [AM] ☐ *...the oldest rookie on the European Tour.*

room ✦✦✦ /ruːm/ (**rooms, rooming, roomed**) ◼ N-COUNT A **room** is one of the separate sections or parts of the inside of a building. Rooms have their own walls, ceilings, floors, and doors, and are usually used for particular activities. You can refer to all the people who are in a room as **the room**. ☐ *A minute later he excused himself and left the room.* ☐ *The largest conference room could seat 5,000 people.* ◼ N-COUNT If you talk about your **room**, you are referring to the room that you alone use, especially your bedroom at home or your office at work. ☐ *If you're running upstairs, go to my room and bring down my sweater, please.* ◼ N-COUNT A **room** is a bedroom in a hotel. ☐ *Toni reserved a room in a hotel not far from Arzfeld.* ◼ V-I If you **room** with someone, you share a rented room, apartment, or house with them, for example when you are a student. [AM] ☐ *I had roomed with him in New Haven when we were both at Yale Law School.* ◼ N-UNCOUNT If there is **room** somewhere, there is enough empty space there for people or things to be fitted in, or for people to move freely or do what they want to. ☐ *There is usually room to accommodate up to 80 visitors.* ◼ N-UNCOUNT If there is **room** for a particular kind of behavior or action, people are able to behave in that way or to take that action. ☐ *The intensity of the work left little room for personal grief or anxiety.* ◼ → see also **chat room, dining room, drawing room, emergency room, living room, restroom**

-room /-ruːm/ COMB IN ADJ [usu ADJ n] **-room** combines with numbers to form adjectives which tell you how many rooms a house or apartment contains. ☐ *They found a little two-room apartment to rent.*

room and board N-UNCOUNT If you are provided with **room and board**, you are provided with food and a place to sleep, especially as part of the conditions of a job or a course. ☐ *Participants receive free room and board while they are in the academy.*

room|ful /ruːmfʊl/ (**roomfuls**) N-COUNT [usu N of n] A **roomful** of things or people is a room that is full of them. You can also refer to the amount or number of things or people that a room can contain as a **roomful**. ☐ *It was like a teacher disciplining a roomful of second graders.*

roomie /ruːmi/ (**roomies**) N-COUNT A person's **roomie** is their roommate. [AM, INFORMAL] ☐ *...the husband of her old college roomie.*

room|ing house (**rooming houses**) N-COUNT A **rooming house** is a building that is divided into small apartments or single rooms which people rent to live in. [AM]

room|mate /ruːmmeɪt/ (**roommates**) N-COUNT Your **roommate** is the person you share a room, apartment, or house with, for example when you are in college. [AM] ☐ *Derek and I are close; we were roommates for two years.*

room ser|vice N-UNCOUNT **Room service** is a service in a hotel by which meals or drinks are provided for guests in their rooms. ☐ *The hotel did not normally provide room service.*

roomy /ruːmi/ (**roomier, roomiest**) ADJ If you describe a place as **roomy**, you mean that you like it because it is large inside and you can move around freely and comfortably. [APPROVAL] ☐ *The car is roomy and a good choice for anyone who needs to carry equipment.*

roost /ruːst/ (**roosts, roosting, roosted**) ◼ N-COUNT A **roost** is a place where birds or bats rest or sleep. ☐ *Something disturbed the bird on its roost.* ◼ V-I When birds or bats **roost** somewhere, they rest or sleep there. ☐ *The peacocks roost in nearby shrubs.* ◼ PHRASE If bad or wrong things that someone has done in the past **have come home to roost**, or if their chickens **have come home to roost**, they are now experiencing the unpleasant effects of these actions. ☐ *Appeasement has come home to roost.* ◼ PHRASE If you say that someone **rules the roost** in a particular place, you mean that they have control and authority over the people there. [INFORMAL] ☐ *Today the country's nationalists rule the roost and hand out the jobs.*

roost|er /ruːstər/ (**roosters**) N-COUNT A **rooster** is an adult male chicken. [AM]

in BRIT, use **cock**

root ✦◇◇ /ruːt/ (**roots, rooting, rooted**) ◼ N-COUNT The **roots** of a plant are the parts of it that grow under the ground. ☐ *...the twisted roots of an apple tree.* ◼ V-T/V-I If you **root** a plant or cutting or if it **roots**, roots form on the bottom of its stem and it starts to grow. ☐ *Most plants will root in about six to eight weeks.* ◼ ADJ [ADJ n] **Root** vegetables or **root** crops are grown for their roots, which are large and can be eaten. ☐ *...root crops such as carrots and potatoes.* ◼ N-COUNT The **root** of a hair or tooth is the part of it that is underneath the skin. ☐ *...decay around the roots of teeth.* ◼ N-PLURAL You can refer to the place or culture that a person or their family comes from as their **roots**. ☐ *I am proud of my Brazilian roots.* ◼ N-COUNT You can refer to the cause of a problem or of an unpleasant situation as the **root** of it or the **roots** of it. ☐ *We got to the root of the problem.* ◼ V-I If you **root** through or in something, you search for something by moving other things around. ☐ *She rooted through the bag, found what she wanted, and headed toward the door.* ◼ → see also **grassroots, rooted, square root** ◼ PHRASE If someone **puts down roots**, they make a place their home, for example by taking part in activities there or by making a lot of friends there. ☐ *When they got to Montana, they put down roots and built a life.* ◼ PHRASE If an idea, belief, or custom **takes root**, it becomes established among a group of people. ☐ *Time would be needed for democracy to take root.*

▶ **root out** ◼ PHRASAL VERB If you **root out** a person, you find them and force them from the place they are in, usually in order to punish them. ☐ *The generals have to root out traitors.* ◼ PHRASAL VERB If you **root out** a problem or an unpleasant situation, you find out who or what is the cause of it and put an end to it. ☐ *There would be a major drive to root out corruption.*

SYNONYMS

root
NOUN ◼
source: *This gave me a clue as to the source of the problem.*
cause: *The causes are a complex blend of local and national tensions.*
germ: *The germ of an idea took root in Rosemary's mind.*

root beer (root beers) N-UNCOUNT **Root beer** is a carbonated nonalcoholic drink flavored with the roots of various plants and herbs. • N-COUNT A glass, can, or bottle of root beer can be referred to as a **root beer**. ❑ *Kevin buys a root beer.*

root|ed /rutɪd/ **1** ADJ [v-link ADJ in n] If you say that one thing is **rooted in** another, you mean that it is strongly influenced by it or has developed from it. ❑ *The crisis is rooted in deep rivalries between the two groups.* **2** ADJ If someone has deeply **rooted** opinions or feelings, they believe or feel something extremely strongly and are unlikely to change. ❑ *Racism is a deeply rooted prejudice which has existed for thousands of years.* **3** PHRASE If you are **rooted to the spot**, you are unable to move because you are very frightened or shocked. ❑ *We just stopped there, rooted to the spot.*

root|less /rutlɪs/ ADJ [usu ADJ n] If someone has no permanent home or job and is not settled in any community, you can describe them as **rootless**. ❑ *These rootless young people have nowhere else to go.*

rope /roup/ (ropes, roping, roped) **1** N-VAR A **rope** is a thick cord or wire that is made by twisting together several thinner cords or wires. Ropes are used for jobs such as pulling cars, tying up boats, or tying things together. ❑ *He tied the rope around his waist.* **2** V-T If you **rope** one thing to another, you tie the two things together with a rope. ❑ *I roped myself to the chimney.* **3** PHRASE If you **give** someone **enough rope to hang** themselves, you give them the freedom to do a job in their own way because you hope that their attempts will fail and that they will look foolish. ❑ *The king has merely given the politicians enough rope to hang themselves.* **4** PHRASE If you are **learning the ropes**, you are learning how a particular job or task is done. [INFORMAL] ❑ *He tried hiring more salesmen to push his radio products, but they took too much time to learn the ropes.* **5** PHRASE If you **know the ropes**, you know how a particular job or task should be done. [INFORMAL] ❑ *The moment she got to know the ropes, there was no stopping her.* **6** PHRASE If you **show** someone **the ropes**, you show them how to do a particular job or task. [INFORMAL] ❑ *We had a patrol out on the border, breaking in some young soldiers, showing them the ropes.*
▶ **rope in** PHRASAL VERB If you say that you **were roped in** to do a particular task, you mean that someone persuaded you to help them do that task. [INFORMAL] ❑ *Visitors were roped in for potato picking and harvesting.*

rope lad|der (rope ladders) N-COUNT A **rope ladder** is a ladder made of two long ropes connected by short pieces of rope, wood, or metal.

ro|sary /rouzəri/ (rosaries) N-COUNT A **rosary** is a string of beads that members of certain religions, especially Catholics, use for counting prayers. A series of prayers counted in this way is also called a **rosary**.

rose ✦✧✧ /rouz/ (roses) **1** Rose is the past tense of rise. **2** N-COUNT A **rose** is a flower, often with a pleasant smell, which grows on a bush with stems that have sharp points called thorns on them. ❑ *She bent to pick a red rose.* **3** N-COUNT A **rose** is a bush that roses grow on. ❑ *Prune rambling roses when the flowers have faded.* **4** COLOR Something that is **rose** is reddish pink in color. [LITERARY] ❑ *...the rose and violet hues of a twilight sky.* **5** PHRASE If you say that a situation is not a **bed of roses**, you mean that it is not as pleasant as it seems, and that there are some unpleasant aspects to it. ❑ *We all knew that life was unlikely to be a bed of roses back in Nebraska.*

rosé /rouzeɪ/ (rosés) N-MASS **Rosé** is wine that is pink in color. ❑ *The vast majority of wines produced in this area are reds or rosés.*

rose|bud /rouzbʌd/ (rosebuds) N-COUNT A **rosebud** is a young rose whose petals have not yet opened out fully.

rose-colored

in BRIT, use **rose-coloured**

PHRASE [usu PHR after v] If you look at a person or situation through **rose-colored glasses** or **rose-tinted glasses**, you see only their good points and therefore your view of them is unrealistic. ❑ *Optimists really do seem to look at the world through rose-colored glasses.*

rose|hip /rouzhɪp/ (rosehips) N-COUNT A **rosehip** is a bright red or orange fruit that grows on some kinds of rose bushes.

rose|mary /rouzmɛəri/ N-UNCOUNT **Rosemary** is a herb used in cooking. It comes from an evergreen plant with small, narrow leaves. The plant is also called **rosemary**.

rose-tinted → see rose-colored

ro|sette /rouzɛt/ (rosettes) N-COUNT A **rosette** is a large, circular decoration made from colored ribbons which is given as a prize in a competition, or is worn to show support for a political party or sports team. ❑ *Marjorie stood on the porch with a big yellow rosette tied around the post.*

rose|water /rouzwɔtər/ N-UNCOUNT **Rosewater** is a liquid which is made from roses and which has a pleasant smell. It is used as a perfume and in cooking.

rose win|dow (rose windows) N-COUNT A **rose window** is a large, round, stained glass window in a church.

rose|wood /rouzwʊd/ N-UNCOUNT **Rosewood** is a hard dark-colored wood that is used for making furniture. Rosewood comes from a species of tropical tree. ❑ *...a heavy rosewood desk.*

ros|ter /rɒstər/ (rosters) **1** N-COUNT A **roster** is a list which gives details of the order in which different people have to do a particular job. ❑ *The next day he put himself first on the new roster for domestic chores.* **2** N-COUNT A **roster** is a list, especially of the people who work for a particular organization or are available to do a particular job. It can also be a list of the athletes who are available for a particular team. [mainly AM] ❑ *The Amateur Softball Association's roster of umpires has declined to 57,000.*

ros|trum /rɒstrəm/ (rostrums or rostra /rɒstrə/) N-COUNT A **rostrum** is a raised platform on which someone stands when they are speaking to an audience, receiving a prize, or conducting an orchestra. ❑ *As he stood on the winner's rostrum, he sang the words of the national anthem.*

rosy /rouzi/ (rosier, rosiest) **1** ADJ If you say that someone has a **rosy** face, you mean that they have pink cheeks and look very healthy. ❑ *Bethan's round, rosy face seemed hardly to have aged at all.* **2** ADJ If you say that a situation looks **rosy** or that the picture looks **rosy**, you mean that the situation seems likely to be good or successful. ❑ *The job prospects for those graduating in engineering are far less rosy now than they used to be.*

rot /rɒt/ (rots, rotting, rotted) **1** V-T/V-I When food, wood, or another substance **rots**, or when something **rots** it, it becomes softer and is gradually destroyed. ❑ *If we don't unload it soon, the grain will start rotting in the silos.* **2** N-UNCOUNT If there is **rot** in something, especially something that is made of wood, parts of it have decayed and fallen apart. ❑ *Investigations had revealed extensive rot in the beams under the ground floor.* **3** N-SING You can use **the rot** to refer to the way something gradually gets worse. For example, if you are talking about the time when **the rot** set in, you are talking about the time when a situation began to get steadily worse and worse. ❑ *In many schools, the rot is beginning to set in. Standards are falling all the time.* **4** V-I If you say that someone is being left to **rot** in a particular place, especially in a prison, you mean that they are being left there and their physical and mental condition is being allowed to get worse and worse. ❑ *Most governments simply leave the long-term jobless to rot.*

ro|ta|ry /routəri/ **1** ADJ [ADJ n] **Rotary** means turning or able to turn around a fixed point. ❑ *...turning linear into rotary motion.* **2** ADJ [ADJ n] **Rotary** is used in the names of some machines that have parts that turn around a fixed point. ❑ *...a rotary engine.* **3** → See feature box at telephone

ro|tate /routeɪt/ (rotates, rotating, rotated) **1** V-T/V-I When something **rotates** or when you **rotate** it, it turns with a circular movement. ❑ *The earth rotates around the sun.* **2** V-T/V-I If people or things **rotate**, or if someone **rotates** them, they take turns to do a particular job or serve a particular purpose. ❑ *The members of the club can rotate and one person can do all the preparation for the evening.*

ro|ta|tion /routeɪʃən/ (rotations) **1** N-VAR **Rotation** is circular movement. A **rotation** is the movement of something through one complete circle. ❑ *...the daily rotation of the earth upon its axis.* **2** N-UNCOUNT The **rotation** of a group of things or people is the fact of them taking turns to do a particular job or serve a particular purpose. If people do something **in rotation**, they take turns to do it. ❑ *He grew a different crop on the same field five years in a row, what researchers call crop rotation.*

ROTC /ɑr ou ti si/ N-PROPER [usu the N] The **ROTC** is a military organization that trains people to become officers in the armed forces, so that they are ready to join a military operation if they are needed. **ROTC** is an abbreviation for 'Reserve Officers Training Corps.' ◻ ...the Army ROTC program at Fresno State University.

rote /roʊt/ ▮ N-UNCOUNT [N n, by N] **Rote** learning or learning **by rote** is learning things by repeating them without thinking about them or trying to understand them. ◻ He is very skeptical about the value of rote learning. ▯ → See feature box at **study**

rot|gut /rɒtgʌt/ N-UNCOUNT If you refer to an alcoholic drink such as whiskey or gin as **rotgut**, you mean that it is of very poor quality. [INFORMAL, DISAPPROVAL] ◻ Doesn't he ever get tired of drinking the same rotgut?

ro|tor /roʊtər/ (rotors) N-COUNT The **rotors** or **rotor blades** of a helicopter are the four long, flat, thin pieces of metal on top of it which go around and lift it off the ground.

rot|ten /rɒtᵊn/ ▮ ADJ If food, wood, or another substance is **rotten**, it has decayed and can no longer be used. ◻ The smell outside this building is overwhelming – like rotten eggs. ▯ ADJ If you describe something as **rotten**, you think it is very unpleasant or of very poor quality. [INFORMAL] ◻ I personally think it's a rotten idea. ▮ ADJ If you feel **rotten**, you feel bad, either because you are ill or because you are sorry about something. [INFORMAL] ◻ I had rheumatic fever and spent that year feeling rotten.

rot|ten ap|ple (rotten apples) N-COUNT You can use **rotten apple** to talk about a person who is dishonest and therefore causes a lot of problems for the group or organization they belong to. ◻ Police corruption is not just a few rotten apples.

Rott|wei|ler /rɒtwaɪlər/ (Rottweilers) also **rottweiler** N-COUNT A **Rottweiler** is a large black and brown breed of dog which is often used as a guard dog.

ro|tund /roʊtʌnd/ ADJ If someone is **rotund**, they are round and fat. [FORMAL] ◻ A rotund, smiling, red-faced gentleman appeared.

ro|tun|da /roʊtʌndə/ (rotundas) N-COUNT A **rotunda** is a round building or room, especially one with a round, bowl-shaped roof.

rou|ble /ruːbᵊl/ → see **ruble**

rouge /ruːʒ/ (rouges, rouging, rouged) ▮ N-UNCOUNT **Rouge** is a red powder or cream which you can put on your cheeks in order to give them more color. [OLD-FASHIONED] ▯ V-T If someone **rouges** their cheeks or lips, they put red powder or cream on them to give them more color. ◻ Florentine women rouged their earlobes. ◻ She had curly black hair and rouged cheeks.

rough ✦✧ /rʌf/ (rougher, roughest) ▮ ADJ If a surface is **rough**, it is uneven and not smooth. ◻ His hands were rough and callused, from years of karate practice. ● **rough|ness** N-UNCOUNT ◻ She rested her cheek against the roughness of his jacket. ▯ ADJ You say that people or their actions are **rough** when they use too much force and not enough care or gentleness. ◻ Football's a rough game at the best of times. ● **rough|ly** ADV ◻ They roughly pushed her forward. ● **rough|ness** N-UNCOUNT ◻ He regretted his roughness. ▮ ADJ A **rough** area, city, school, or other place is unpleasant and dangerous because there is a lot of violence or crime there. ◻ It was quite a rough part of our town. ▮ ADJ If you say that someone has had a **rough** time, you mean that they have had some difficult or unpleasant experiences. ◻ Many people have a rough time in our society. ▮ ADJ A **rough** calculation or guess is approximately correct, but not exact. ◻ We were only able to make a rough estimate of how much fuel would be required. ● **rough|ly** ADV [ADV with cl/group] ◻ Gambling and tourism pay roughly half the entire state budget. ▮ ADJ If you give someone a **rough** idea, description, or drawing of something, you indicate only the most important features, without much detail. ◻ I've got a rough idea of what he looks like. ● **rough|ly** ADV ◻ He knew roughly what was about to be said. ▮ ADJ You can say that something is **rough** when it is not neat and well made. ◻ The bench had a rough wooden table in front of it. ● **rough|ly** ADV [ADV with v] ◻ Roughly chop the tomatoes and add them to the casserole. ▮ ADJ If the sea or the weather at sea is **rough**, the weather is windy or stormy and there are very big waves. ◻ A fishing vessel and a cargo ship collided in rough seas. ▮ PHRASE If you have to **rough it**, you have to live without the possessions and comforts that you normally have. [INFORMAL] ◻ There is a campsite but, if you prefer not to rough it, the Lake Hotel is nearby.

▶ **rough up** PHRASAL VERB If someone **roughs** you **up**, they attack you and hit or beat you. [INFORMAL] ◻ They threw him in a cell and roughed him up a bit. ◻ He was fired from his job after roughing up a colleague.

---SYNONYMS---

rough
ADJ
▮
uneven: He staggered on the uneven surface of the pavement.
rugged: ...rugged, mountainous terrain.
jagged: ...jagged, black cliffs.
bumpy: ...bumpy, cobbled streets.
coarse: ...a jacket made of very coarse cloth.
▯
brutal: He took an anguished breath. He had to be brutal and say it.
harsh: ...the cold, harsh cruelty of her husband.
▮
vague: ...vague information.
crude: Birthplace data are only the crudest indicator of actual migration paths.
approximate: The approximate cost varies from around $150 to $250.
ballpark: I can't give you anything more than just a ballpark figure.

---

rough|age /rʌfɪdʒ/ N-UNCOUNT **Roughage** consists of the tough parts of vegetables and grains that help you to digest your food and help your bowels to work properly.

rough-and-ready ▮ ADJ A **rough-and-ready** solution or method is one that is rather simple and not very exact because it has been thought of or done in a hurry. ◻ Here is a rough-and-ready measurement. ▯ ADJ A **rough-and-ready** person is not very polite or gentle. ◻ ...rough-and-ready soldiers.

rough-and-tum|ble ▮ N-UNCOUNT [oft the N of n] You can use **rough-and-tumble** to refer to a situation in which the people involved try hard to get what they want, and do not worry about upsetting or harming others, and you think this is acceptable and normal. ◻ ...the rough-and-tumble of political combat. ▯ N-UNCOUNT **Rough-and-tumble** is physical playing that involves noisy and slightly violent behavior. ◻ He enjoys rough-and-tumble play.

rough|en /rʌfᵊn/ (roughens, roughening, roughened) V-T [usu passive] If something has **been roughened**, its surface has become less smooth. ◻ ...complexions that have been roughened by long periods in the hot sun.

rough-hewn ADJ [usu ADJ n] **Rough-hewn** wood or stone has been cut into a shape but has not yet been smoothed or finished off. ◻ It is a rough-hewn carving of a cat's head.

rough|neck /rʌfnɛk/ (roughnecks) ▮ N-COUNT If you describe someone as a **roughneck**, you disapprove of them because you think they are not gentle or polite, and can be violent. [INFORMAL, DISAPPROVAL] ▯ N-COUNT A **roughneck** is someone who operates an oil well. [mainly AM, INFORMAL]

rough|shod /rʌfʃɒd/ PHRASE If you say that someone **is riding roughshod over** a person or their views, you disapprove of them because they are using their power or authority to do what they want, completely ignoring that person's wishes. [DISAPPROVAL] ◻ These laws allow the security forces to continue to ride roughshod over the human rights of the people.

rou|lette /ruːlɛt/ N-UNCOUNT **Roulette** is a gambling game in which a ball is dropped onto a wheel with numbered holes in it while the wheel is spinning around. The players bet on which hole the ball will be in when the wheel stops spinning. ◻ I had been playing roulette at the casino.

---ROUND---
① PHRASE
② NOUN USE
③ ADJECTIVE USES
④ VERB USES

---

① **round** ✦✦✧ /raʊnd/

Round is used mainly in British English. See **around**.

PHRASE If something happens **all year round**, it happens throughout the year. ◻ Many of these plants are evergreen, so you can enjoy them all year round.

② **round** ♦♦◇ /raʊnd/ (rounds) **1** N-COUNT A **round** of events is a series of related events, especially one which comes after or before a similar series of events. ❑ *It was agreed that another round of preliminary talks would be held in Beijing.* **2** N-COUNT In sports, a **round** is a series of games in a competition. The winners of these games go on to play in the next round, and so on, until only one player or team is left. ❑ *...in the third round of the Ryder Cup.* **3** N-COUNT In a boxing or wrestling match, a **round** is one of the periods during which the boxers or wrestlers fight. ❑ *He was declared the victor in the 11th round.* **4** N-COUNT A **round** of golf is one game, usually including 18 holes. ❑ *...two rounds of golf.* **5** N-COUNT If you do your **rounds** or your **round**, you make a series of visits to different places or people, for example as part of your job. ❑ *The doctors still did their morning rounds.* **6** N-COUNT If you buy a **round** of drinks, you buy a drink for each member of the group of people that you are with. ❑ *They sat on the clubhouse terrace, downing a round of drinks.* **7** N-COUNT A **round** of ammunition is the bullet or bullets released when a gun is fired. ❑ *...firing 1,650 rounds of ammunition during a period of ten minutes.* **8** N-COUNT If there is a **round** of applause, everyone claps their hands to welcome someone or to show that they have enjoyed something. ❑ *Sue got a sympathetic round of applause.* **9** PHRASE If you **make the rounds** or **do the rounds**, you visit a series of different places. ❑ *After school, I had picked up Nick and Ted and made the rounds of the dry cleaner and the food stores.*

③ **round** /raʊnd/ (rounder, roundest) **1** ADJ Something that is **round** is shaped like a circle or ball. ❑ *She had small feet and hands and a flat, round face.* **2** ADJ [ADJ n] A **round** number is a multiple of 10, 100, 1,000, and so on. Round numbers are used instead of precise ones to give the general idea of a quantity or proportion. ❑ *I asked how much silver could be bought for a million dollars, which seemed a suitably round number.*

④ **round** /raʊnd/ (rounds, rounding, rounded) **1** V-T If you **round** a place or obstacle, you move in a curve past the edge or corner of it. ❑ *The house disappeared from sight as we rounded a corner.* **2** V-T If you **round** an amount up or down, or if you **round** it off, you change it to the nearest whole number or nearest multiple of 10, 100, 1000, and so on. ❑ *We needed to do decimals to round up and round down numbers.* ❑ *The fraction was then multiplied by 100 and rounded to the nearest half or whole number.* **3** → see also **rounded**
▶ **round up 1** PHRASAL VERB If the police or army **round up** a number of people, they arrest or capture them. ❑ *The police rounded up a number of suspects.* **2** PHRASAL VERB If you **round up** animals or things, you gather them together. ❑ *He had sought work as a cowboy, rounding up cattle.* **3** → see also **round** ④ 2, **roundup**

round|about /ˈraʊndəbaʊt/ (roundabouts) **1** ADJ If you go somewhere by a **roundabout** route, you do not go there by the shortest and quickest route. ❑ *He left today on a roundabout route for Jordan and is also due soon in Egypt.* **2** ADJ If you do or say something in a **roundabout** way, you do not do or say it in a simple, clear, and direct way. ❑ *We made a little fuss in a roundabout way.* **3** N-COUNT A **roundabout** is a circular structure in the road at a place where several roads meet. You drive around it until you come to the road that you want. [BRIT]

in AM, use **traffic circle, rotary**

4 N-COUNT A **roundabout** at an amusement park is a large, circular mechanical device with seats, often in the shape of animals or cars, on which children sit and go around and around. [BRIT]

in AM, use **merry-go-round**

5 N-COUNT A **roundabout** in a park or school play area is a circular platform that children sit or stand on. People push the platform to make it spin around. [BRIT]

in AM, use **merry-go-round**

round|ed /ˈraʊndɪd/ **1** ADJ Something that is **rounded** is curved in shape, without any points or sharp edges. ❑ *...a low, rounded hill.* **2** ADJ You describe something or someone as **rounded** when you are expressing approval of them because they have a personality which is fully developed in all aspects. [APPROVAL] ❑ *...his carefully organized narrative, full of rounded, believable, and interesting characters.*

roun|del /ˈraʊndəl/ (roundels) N-COUNT A **roundel** is a circular design, for example one painted on a military aircraft.

round|ly /ˈraʊndli/ ADV [usu ADV before v] If you are **roundly** condemned or criticized, you are condemned or criticized forcefully or by many people. If you are **roundly** defeated, you are defeated completely. ❑ *Political leaders have roundly condemned the shooting.*

round-robin (round-robins) also **round robin** N-COUNT [usu N n] A **round-robin** is a sports competition in which each player or team plays against every other player or team. ❑ *They beat Canada 4-1 in their last round-robin match at Nagoya in Japan.*

round-shouldered ADJ If someone is **round-shouldered**, they bend forward when they sit or stand, and their shoulders are curved rather than straight. [DISAPPROVAL] ❑ *Cissie was round-shouldered and dumpy.*

round ta|ble (round tables) also **round-table, roundtable** N-COUNT [usu N n] A **round table** discussion is a meeting where experts gather together in order to discuss a particular topic. ❑ *...a round-table conference of the leading heart specialists of America.*

round-the-clock → see **clock**

round trip (round trips) **1** N-COUNT If you make a **round trip**, you travel to a place and then back again. ❑ *The train operates the 2,400-mile round trip once a week.* **2** ADJ [ADJ n] A **round-trip** ticket is a ticket for a train, bus, or plane that allows you to travel to a particular place and then back again. [AM]
❑ *Mexicana Airlines has announced cheaper round-trip tickets between Los Angeles and cities it serves in Mexico.*

in BRIT, use **return**

round|up /ˈraʊndʌp/ (roundups) N-COUNT In journalism, especially television or radio, a **roundup** of news is a summary of the main events that have happened. ❑ *First, we have this roundup of the day's news.*

round|worm /ˈraʊndwɜːrm/ (roundworms) N-VAR A **roundworm** is a very small worm that lives in the intestines of people, pigs, and other animals.

rouse /raʊz/ (rouses, rousing, roused) **1** V-T/V-I If someone **rouses** you when you are sleeping or if you **rouse**, you wake up. [LITERARY] ❑ *Hilton roused him at eight-thirty by rapping on the door.* **2** V-T If you **rouse** yourself, you stop being inactive and start doing something. ❑ *She seemed to be unable to rouse herself to do anything.* **3** V-T If something or someone **rouses** you, they make you very emotional or excited. ❑ *He did more to rouse the crowd there than anybody else.* • **rous|ing** ADJ ❑ *...a rousing speech to the convention in support of the president.* **4** V-T If something **rouses** a feeling in you, it causes you to have that feeling. ❑ *It roused a feeling of rebellion in him.*

roust /raʊst/ (rousts, rousting, rousted) V-T If you **roust** someone, you disturb, upset, or hit them, or make them move from their place. [AM] ❑ *Relax, kid, we're not about to roust you. We just want some information.* ❑ *Bruce had gone to bed, but they rousted him out.*

roust|about /ˈraʊstəbaʊt/ (roustabouts) N-COUNT A **roustabout** is a unskilled worker, especially one who works in a port or at an oil well. [AM]

rout /raʊt/ (routs, routing, routed) V-T If an army, sports team, or other group **routs** its opponents, it defeats them completely and easily. ❑ *...the Battle of Hastings at which the Norman army routed the English opposition.* • N-COUNT **Rout** is also a noun. ❑ *One after another the Italian bases in the desert fell as the retreat turned into a rout.*

route ♦♦◇ /ruːt, raʊt/ (routes, routing, routed) **1** N-COUNT A **route** is a way from one place to another. ❑ *...the most direct route to the center of town.* **2** N-COUNT A bus, air, or shipping **route** is the way between two places along which buses, planes, or ships travel regularly. ❑ *...the main shipping routes to Japan.* **3** N-IN-NAMES In the United States, **Route** is used in front of a number in the names of main roads between major cities. ❑ *From San Francisco take the freeway to the Broadway-Webster exit on Route 580.* **4** N-COUNT Your **route** is the series of visits you make to different people or places, as part of your job. [mainly AM] ❑ *He began cracking open big blue tins of butter cookies and feeding the dogs on his route.*

in BRIT, usually use **round**

route map

5 N-COUNT You can refer to a way of achieving something as a **route**. ◻ *Researchers are trying to get at the same information through an indirect route.* **6** V-T [usu passive] If vehicles, goods, or passengers **are routed** in a particular direction, they are made to travel in that direction. ◻ *Trains are taking a lot of freight that used to be routed via trucks.* **7** PHRASE **En route** to a place means on the way to that place. **En route** is sometimes spelled **on route** in nonstandard English. ◻ *They have arrived in London en route to the United States.* **8** PHRASE Journalists sometimes use **en route** when they are mentioning an event that happened as part of a longer process or before another event. ◻ *The German set three tournament records and equaled two others en route to grabbing golf's richest prize.*

route map (route maps) N-COUNT A **route map** is a map that shows the main roads in a particular area or the main routes used by buses, trains, and other forms of transportation in a particular area.

rout|er /rutər/ (routers) **1** N-COUNT On a computer or network of computers, a **router** is a piece of equipment which allows access to other computers or networks, for example the internet. **2** N-COUNT A **router** is an electric tool that is used for making grooves or hollows in material such as wood.

rou|tine ♦◇◇ /rutin/ (routines) **1** N-VAR A **routine** is the usual series of things that you do at a particular time. A **routine** is also the practice of regularly doing things in a fixed order. ◻ *The players had to change their daily routine and lifestyle.* **2** ADJ You use **routine** to describe activities that are done as a normal part of a job or process. ◻ *...a series of routine medical tests including X-rays and blood tests.* **3** ADJ A **routine** situation, action, or event is one which seems completely ordinary, rather than interesting, exciting, or different. [DISAPPROVAL] ◻ *So many days are routine and uninteresting, especially in winter.* **4** N-VAR You use **routine** to refer to a way of life that is uninteresting and ordinary, or hardly ever changes. [DISAPPROVAL] ◻ *...the mundane routine of her life.* **5** N-COUNT A **routine** is a computer program, or part of a program, that performs a specific function. [COMPUTING] ◻ *...an installation routine.* **6** N-COUNT A **routine** is a short sequence of jokes, remarks, actions, or movements that forms part of a longer performance. ◻ *...an athletic dance routine.*

rou|tine|ly /rutinli/ **1** ADV If something is **routinely** done, it is done as a normal part of a job or process. ◻ *Vitamin K is routinely given in the first week of life to prevent bleeding.* **2** ADV [ADV with v] If something happens **routinely**, it happens repeatedly and is not surprising, unnatural, or new. ◻ *Any outside criticism is routinely dismissed as interference.*

rou|tin|ize /rutinaɪz/ (routinizes, routinizing, routinized)

in BRIT, also use **routinise**

V-T If you **routinize** a way of doing something, you make it a normal part of a job or process. ◻ *Parents who routinize child care are minimizing expense and maximizing their control.*

rove /roʊv/ (roves, roving, roved) **1** V-T/V-I If someone **roves** around an area or **roves** an area, they wander around it. [LITERARY] ◻ *...roving around the town in the dead of night and seeing something peculiar.* ◻ *She became a photographer, roving the world with her camera in her hand.* **2** → see also **roving**

rov|ing /roʊvɪŋ/ ADJ [ADJ n] You use **roving** to describe a person who travels around, rather than staying in a fixed place. ◻ *He is to join NBC to cover the competition in Barcelona next month as a roving reporter.*

ROW
① ARRANGEMENT OR SEQUENCE
② MAKING A BOAT MOVE

---

① **row** ♦◇◇ /roʊ/ (rows) **1** N-COUNT A **row** of things or people is a number of them arranged in a line. ◻ *...a row of pretty little cottages.* **2** N-IN-NAMES **Row** is sometimes used in the names of streets. ◻ *...the house at 236 Larch Row.* **3** → see also **death row** **4** PHRASE If something happens several times **in a row**, it happens that number of times without a break. If something happens several days **in a row**, it happens on each of those days. ◻ *They have won five championships in a row.*

② **row** /roʊ/ (rows, rowing, rowed) **1** V-T/V-I When you **row**, you sit in a boat and make it move through the water by using oars. If you **row** someone somewhere, you take them there in a boat, using oars. ◻ *He rowed as quickly as he could to the shore.* ◻ *The boatman refused to row him back.* • N-COUNT **Row** is also a noun. ◻ *I took Daniel for a row.* **2** → see also **rowing**

ro|wan /roʊən, raʊən/ (rowans) N-VAR A **rowan** or a **rowan tree** is a tree with a silvery trunk that has red berries in the fall. • N-UNCOUNT **Rowan** is the wood of this tree.

row|boat /roʊboʊt/ (rowboats) **1** N-COUNT A **rowboat** is a small boat that you move through the water by using oars. [AM]

in BRIT, use **rowing boat**

2 → See also color supplement

row|dy /raʊdi/ (rowdier, rowdiest) ADJ When people are **rowdy**, they are noisy, rough, and likely to cause trouble. ◻ *He has complained to the police about rowdy neighbors.*

row|er /roʊər/ (rowers) N-COUNT A **rower** is a person who rows a boat, especially as a sport. ◻ *...the first rower ever to win golds at four Olympic Games.*

row house (row houses) N-COUNT A **row house** is one of a row of similar houses that are joined together by both of their side walls. [AM] ◻ *...a city block of row houses.*

in BRIT, use **terraced house**

row|ing /roʊɪŋ/ N-UNCOUNT **Rowing** is a sport in which people or teams race against each other in boats with oars. ◻ *...competitions in rowing, swimming, and water skiing.*

row|ing boat [BRIT] → see **rowboat**

row|ing ma|chine (rowing machines) N-COUNT A **rowing machine** is an exercise machine with moving parts which you move as if you were rowing a rowboat.

row|lock /rɒlək, roʊlɒk/ [BRIT] → see **oarlock**

roy|al ♦♦◇ /rɔɪəl/ (royals) **1** ADJ **Royal** is used to indicate that something is connected with a king, queen, or emperor, or their family. A **royal** person is a king, queen, or emperor, or a member of their family. ◻ *...an invitation to a royal garden party.* **2** ADJ [ADJ n] **Royal** is used in the names of institutions or organizations that are officially appointed or supported by a member of a royal family. ◻ *...the Royal Academy of Music.* **3** N-COUNT Members of the royal family are sometimes referred to as **royals**. [INFORMAL] ◻ *The royals have always been patrons of charities pulling in large donations.*

roy|al blue COLOR Something that is **royal blue** is deep blue in color.

roy|al fami|ly (royal families) N-COUNT The **royal family** of a country is the king, queen, or emperor, and all the members of their family.

Roy|al High|ness (Royal Highnesses) N-VOC [poss N; PRON: poss PRON] Expressions such as **Your Royal Highness** and **Their Royal Highnesses** are used to address or refer to members of royal families who are not kings or queens. [POLITENESS]

roy|al|ist /rɔɪəlɪst/ (royalists) N-COUNT A **royalist** is someone who supports their country's royal family or who believes that their country should have a king or queen. ◻ *He was hated by the royalists and mistrusted by the communists.*

roy|al jel|ly N-UNCOUNT **Royal jelly** is a substance that bees make in order to feed young bees and queen bees.

roy|al|ly /rɔɪəli/ ADV If you say that something is done **royally**, you are emphasizing that it is done in an impressive or grand way, or that it is very great in degree. [EMPHASIS] ◻ *They were royally received in every aspect.*

roy|al|ty /rɔɪəlti/ (royalties) **1** N-UNCOUNT The members of royal families are sometimes referred to as **royalty**. ◻ *Royalty and government leaders from all around the world are gathering in Japan.* **2** N-PLURAL **Royalties** are payments made to authors and musicians when their work is sold or performed. They usually receive a fixed percentage of the profits from these sales or performances. ◻ *I lived on about $5,000 a year from the royalties on my book.* **3** N-COUNT Payments made to someone whose invention, idea, or property is used by a commercial company can be referred to as **royalties**. ◻ *The royalties enabled the inventor to re-establish himself in business.*

RP /ɑr pi/ **RP** is a standard way of pronouncing British English when it is taught as a foreign language. **RP** is an abbreviation for **Received Pronunciation**.

rpm /ɑr pi ɛm/ also **r.p.m. rpm** is used to indicate the speed of something by saying how many times per minute it will go around in a circle. **rpm** is an abbreviation for 'revolutions per minute.' ☐ *Both engines were running at 2,500 rpm.*

RR also **R. R.** ◼ **RR** is a written abbreviation for **rural route**. [AM] ☐ *William Farr Day, RR 1, Box 64, West Lebanon, IN 47991.* ◻ **RR** is a written abbreviation for **railroad**. [AM]

RSI /ɑr ɛs aɪ/ N-UNCOUNT People who suffer from **RSI** have pain in their hands and arms as a result of repeating similar movements over a long period of time, usually as part of their job. **RSI** is an abbreviation for **repetitive strain injury**. ☐ *The women developed painful RSI because of poor working conditions.*

RSS /ɑr ɛs ɛs/ N-UNCOUNT **RSS** is a way of allowing internet users to receive the most recent news from particular websites as soon as it is published. ☐ *RSS allows the delivery of news headlines directly to subscribers' PCs, cellphones or iPods, almost the instant they are published.* ☐ *...an RSS (news) feed.*

RSVP /ɑr ɛs vi pi/ also **R.S.V.P. RSVP** is an abbreviation for 'répondez s'il vous plaît,' which means 'please reply.' It is written on the bottom of a card inviting you to a party or special occasion. [FORMAL]

Rte. Rte. is used in front of a number in the names of main roads between major cities. **Rte.** is a written abbreviation for **route**. ☐ *Winterthur is on Rte. 52 in Delaware.*

rub /rʌb/ (**rubs, rubbing, rubbed**) ◼ V-T/V-I If you **rub** a part of your body or if you **rub** at it, you move your hand or fingers backward and forward over it while pressing firmly. ☐ *He rubbed his arms and stiff legs.* ◻ V-T/V-I If you **rub** against a surface or **rub** a part of your body against a surface, you move it backward and forward while pressing it against the surface. ☐ *A cat was rubbing against my leg.* ◼ V-T/V-I If you **rub** an object or a surface or you **rub** at it, you move a cloth backward and forward over it in order to clean or dry it. ☐ *She took off her glasses and rubbed them hard.* ◼ V-T If you **rub** a substance into a surface or **rub** something such as dirt from a surface, you spread it over the surface or remove it from the surface using your hand or something such as a cloth. ☐ *He rubbed oil into my back.* ◼ V-T/V-I If you **rub** two things together or if they **rub** together, they move backward and forward, pressing against each other. ☐ *He rubbed his hands together a few times.* ◼ V-I If something you are wearing or holding **rubs**, it makes you sore because it keeps moving backward and forward against your skin. ☐ *It should be comfortable against the skin without rubbing, chafing, or cutting into anything.* ◼ N-COUNT A massage can be referred to as a **rub**. ☐ *She sometimes asks if I want a back rub.* ◼ PHRASE If you **rub shoulders with** famous people, you meet them and talk to them. You can also say that you **rub elbows with** someone. ☐ *He regularly rubbed shoulders with the likes of Elizabeth Taylor and Kylie Minogue.* ◼ PHRASE If you **rub** someone **the wrong way**, you offend or annoy them without intending to. [INFORMAL] ☐ *What are you going to get out of him if you rub him the wrong way?* ◼ **to rub someone's nose in it** → see **nose**

▶ **rub down** ◼ PHRASAL VERB If you **rub down** a rough surface, you make it smooth by rubbing it with something such as sandpaper. ☐ *They were settling to their work, rubbing down the woodwork with sandpaper.* ◻ → See feature box at **DIY**

▶ **rub out** PHRASAL VERB If you **rub out** something that you have written on paper or a board, you remove it using an eraser. [BRIT]

in AM, use **erase**

rub|ber /rʌbər/ (**rubbers**) ◼ N-UNCOUNT **Rubber** is a strong, waterproof, elastic substance made from the juice of a tropical tree or produced chemically. It is used for making tires, boots, and other products. ☐ *...the smell of burning rubber.* ◻ N-COUNT A **rubber** is a condom. [AM, INFORMAL] ◼ N-COUNT A **rubber** is a small piece of rubber or other material that is used to remove mistakes that you have made while writing, or drawing. [BRIT]

in AM, use **eraser**

rub|ber band (**rubber bands**) N-COUNT A **rubber band** is a thin circle of very elastic rubber. You put it around things such as papers in order to keep them together.

rub|ber boot (**rubber boots**) ◼ N-COUNT [usu pl] **Rubber boots** are boots made of rubber that you wear to keep your feet dry. [AM]

in BRIT, use **wellington**

◻ → See also color supplement

rub|ber bul|let (**rubber bullets**) N-COUNT A **rubber bullet** is a bullet made of a metal ball coated with rubber. It is intended to injure people rather than kill them, and is used by police or soldiers to control crowds during a riot. ☐ *Rubber bullets were used to break up the demonstration.*

rubber|neck /rʌbərnɛk/ (**rubbernecks, rubbernecking, rubbernecked**) V-I If someone is **rubbernecking**, they are staring at someone or something, especially in a rude or silly way. [INFORMAL, DISAPPROVAL] ☐ *The accident was caused by people slowing down to rubberneck.* • **rubber|necker** (**rubberneckers**) N-COUNT ☐ *Phil planted tall trees outside his home to block rubberneckers.*

rub|ber plant (**rubber plants**) N-COUNT A **rubber plant** is a type of plant with shiny leaves. It grows naturally in Asia but is also grown as a houseplant in other parts of the world.

rub|ber stamp (**rubber stamps, rubber stamping, rubber stamped**) also **rubber-stamp** ◼ N-COUNT A **rubber stamp** is a small device with a name, date, or symbol on it. You press it onto an ink pad and then on to a document in order to show that the document has been officially dealt with. ☐ *In post offices, virtually every document that's passed across the counter is stamped with a rubber stamp.* ◻ V-T When someone in authority **rubber-stamps** a decision, plan, or law, they agree to it without thinking about it much. ☐ *The board's job is to rubber-stamp his decisions.*

rub|bery /rʌbəri/ ◼ ADJ Something that is **rubbery** looks or feels soft or elastic like rubber. ☐ *The mask is left on for about 15 minutes while it sets to a rubbery texture.* ◻ ADJ Food such as meat that is **rubbery** is difficult to chew.

rub|bing /rʌbɪŋ/ (**rubbings**) ◼ N-COUNT [oft n N] A **rubbing** is a picture that you make by putting a piece of paper over a carved surface and then rubbing wax or chalk over it. ☐ *...a brass rubbing.* ◻ → see also **rub**

rub|bing al|co|hol N-UNCOUNT **Rubbing alcohol** is a liquid which is used to clean wounds or surgical instruments. [AM]

in BRIT, use **surgical spirit**

rub|bish /rʌbɪʃ/ (**rubbishes, rubbishing, rubbished**) ◼ N-UNCOUNT **Rubbish** consists of unwanted things or waste material such as used paper, empty cans and bottles, and waste food. [mainly BRIT]

in AM, usually use **garbage**

◻ N-UNCOUNT If you think that something is of very poor quality, you can say that it is **rubbish**. [mainly BRIT, INFORMAL] ◼ V-T If you **rubbish** a person, their ideas or their work, you say they are of little value. [BRIT, INFORMAL]

in AM, use **trash**

rub|bishy /rʌbɪʃi/ ADJ [usu ADJ n] If you describe something as **rubbishy**, you think it is of very poor quality. [mainly BRIT, INFORMAL] ☐ *...some old rubbishy cop movie.*

rub|ble /rʌbəl/ ◼ N-UNCOUNT When a building is destroyed, the pieces of brick, stone, or other materials that remain are referred to as **rubble**. ☐ *Thousands of bodies are still buried under the rubble.* ◻ N-UNCOUNT **Rubble** is used to refer to the small pieces of bricks and stones that are used as a bottom layer on which to build roads, paths, or houses. ☐ *Brick rubble is useful as the base for paths and patios.*

rub|down /rʌbdaʊn/ (**rubdowns**) N-COUNT If you give someone a **rubdown**, you dry them or massage them with something such as a towel or cloth. ☐ *He found a towel and gave his body a vigorous rubdown.*

rube /rub/ (**rubes**) N-COUNT If you refer to someone as a **rube**, you consider them stupid and uneducated because they come from the countryside. [AM, INFORMAL, DISAPPROVAL] ☐ *He's no rube. He's a very smart guy.*

ru|bel|la /rubɛlə/ N-UNCOUNT **Rubella** is a disease. The symptoms are a cough, a sore throat, and red spots on your skin. [MEDICAL]

Ru|bi|con /ruːbɪkɒn/ PHRASE If you say that someone **has crossed the Rubicon**, you mean that they have reached a point where they cannot change a decision or course of action. [JOURNALISM] ❑ *He's crossed the Rubicon with regard to the use of military force as an option.*

ru|ble /ruːbəl/ (**rubles**) N-COUNT [usu num N] The **ruble** is the unit of money of Russia and Belarus.

ru|bric /ruːbrɪk/ (**rubrics**) **1** N-COUNT A **rubric** is a title or heading under which something operates or is studied. [FORMAL] ❑ *The aid comes under the rubric of technical cooperation between governments.* **2** N-COUNT A **rubric** is a set of rules or instructions, for example the rules at the beginning of an examination paper. [FORMAL] ❑ *When the final information is sent to teachers, examples of answers are sent along as part of the rubric.*

ruby /ruːbi/ (**rubies**) **1** N-COUNT A **ruby** is a dark red jewel. ❑ *...a ruby and diamond ring.* **2** COLOR Something that is **ruby** is dark red in color. ❑ *...a glass of ruby-red Cabernet Sauvignon.* **3** → See also color supplement

ruched /ruːʃt/ ADJ **Ruched** curtains or garments are gathered so that they hang in soft folds.

ruck /rʌk/ (**rucks**) N-COUNT In the sport of rugby, a **ruck** is a situation where a group of players struggle for possession of the ball.

ruck|sack /rʌksæk/ (**rucksacks**) **1** N-COUNT A **rucksack** is a bag with straps that go over your shoulders, so that you can carry things on your back, for example when you are walking or climbing. [BRIT]

> in AM, usually use **backpack**

2 → See also color supplement

ruck|us /rʌkəs/ N-SING If someone or something causes a **ruckus**, they cause a great deal of noise, argument, or confusion. [AM, INFORMAL] ❑ *This caused such a ruckus all over Japan that they had to change their minds.*

rud|der /rʌdər/ (**rudders**) **1** N-COUNT A **rudder** is a device for steering a boat. It consists of a vertical piece of wood or metal at the back of the boat. **2** N-COUNT An airplane's **rudder** is a vertical piece of metal at the back which is used to make the plane turn to the right or to the left. **3** → See also color supplement

rud|der|less /rʌdərlɪs/ ADJ A country or a person that is **rudderless** does not have a clear aim or a strong leader to follow. ❑ *The country was politically rudderless for almost three months.*

rud|dy /rʌdi/ (**ruddier, ruddiest**) ADJ If you describe someone's face as **ruddy**, you mean that their face is a reddish color, usually because they are healthy or have been working hard, or because they are angry or embarrassed. ❑ *He had a naturally ruddy complexion, even more flushed now from dancing.*

rude /ruːd/ (**ruder, rudest**) **1** ADJ When people are **rude**, they act in an impolite way toward other people or say impolite things about them. ❑ *He's rude to her friends and obviously jealous.* • **rude|ly** ADV ❑ *I could not understand why she felt compelled to behave so rudely to a friend.* • **rude|ness** N-UNCOUNT ❑ *Mother is annoyed at Caleb's rudeness, but I can forgive it.* **2** ADJ **Rude** is used to describe words and behavior that are likely to embarrass or offend people, because they relate to sex or to body functions. ❑ *Fred keeps cracking rude jokes with the guests.* **3** ADJ [ADJ n] If someone receives a **rude** shock, something unpleasant happens unexpectedly. ❑ *It will come as a rude shock when their salary or income-tax refund cannot be cashed.* • **rude|ly** ADV [ADV with v] ❑ *People were rudely awakened by a siren just outside their window.* **4 rude awakening** → see **awakening** **5** → See feature box at **polite**

ru|di|men|ta|ry /ruːdɪmɛntəri, -tri/ **1** ADJ **Rudimentary** things are very basic or simple and are therefore unsatisfactory. [FORMAL] ❑ *The earth surface of the courtyard extended into a kind of rudimentary kitchen.* **2** ADJ **Rudimentary** knowledge includes only the simplest and most basic facts. [FORMAL] ❑ *He had only a rudimentary knowledge of French.*

ru|di|ments /ruːdɪmənts/ N-PLURAL [usu the N of n] When you learn the **rudiments** of something, you learn the simplest or most essential things about it. ❑ *She helped to build a house, learning the rudiments of bricklaying as she went along.*

rue /ruː/ (**rues, ruing, rued**) **1** V-T If you **rue** something that you have done, you are sorry that you did it, because it has had unpleasant results. [LITERARY] ❑ *Tavare was probably ruing his decision.* **2** PHRASE If you **rue the day** that you did something, you are sorry that you did it, because it has had unpleasant results. [LITERARY] ❑ *You'll live to rue the day you said that to me, my girl.*

rue|ful /ruːfəl/ ADJ If someone is **rueful**, they feel or express regret or sorrow in a quiet and gentle way. [LITERARY] ❑ *He shook his head and gave me a rueful smile.* • **rue|ful|ly** ADV [usu ADV with v] ❑ *He grinned at her ruefully.*

ruff /rʌf/ (**ruffs**) **1** N-COUNT A **ruff** is a stiff strip of cloth or other material with many small folds in it, which some people wore around their neck in former times. ❑ *...an Elizabethan ruff.* **2** N-COUNT A **ruff** is a thick band of feathers or fur around the neck of a bird or animal.

ruf|fian /rʌfiən/ (**ruffians**) N-COUNT A **ruffian** is someone who behaves violently and is involved in crime. [OLD-FASHIONED] ❑ *...gangs of ruffians who lurk about intent on troublemaking.*

ruf|fle /rʌfəl/ (**ruffles, ruffling, ruffled**) **1** V-T If you **ruffle** someone's hair, you move your hand backward and forward through it as a way of showing your affection toward them. ❑ *"Don't let that get you down," he said, ruffling Ben's dark curls.* **2** V-T When the wind **ruffles** something such as the surface of the sea, it causes it to move gently in a wavelike motion. [LITERARY] ❑ *The evening breeze ruffled the pond.* **3** V-T If something **ruffles** someone, it causes them to panic and lose their confidence or to become angry or upset. ❑ *I could tell that my refusal to allow him to ruffle me infuriated him.* **4** V-T/V-I If a bird **ruffles** its feathers or if its feathers **ruffle**, they stand out on its body, for example when it is cleaning itself or when it is frightened. ❑ *Tame birds, when approached, will stretch out their necks and ruffle their neck feathering.* **5** N-COUNT **Ruffles** are folds of cloth at the neck or the ends of the arms of a piece of clothing, or are sometimes sewn on things as a decoration. ❑ *...a white blouse with ruffles at the neck and cuffs.* **6** PHRASE To **ruffle** someone's **feathers** means to cause them to become very angry, nervous, or upset. ❑ *His direct, often abrasive approach will doubtless ruffle a few feathers.*

ruf|fled /rʌfəld/ ADJ Something that is **ruffled** is no longer smooth or neat. ❑ *Her short hair was oddly ruffled and then flattened around her head.*

rug /rʌg/ (**rugs**) **1** N-COUNT A **rug** is a piece of thick material that you put on a floor. It is like a carpet but covers a smaller area. ❑ *A Persian rug covered the hardwood floors.* **2** N-COUNT A **rug** is a small blanket which you use to cover your shoulders or your knees to keep them warm. [mainly BRIT] ❑ *The woman was seated in her chair at the window, a rug over her knees.* **3** PHRASE If someone **pulls the rug from under** a person or thing or **pulls the rug from under** someone's **feet**, they stop giving their help or support. ❑ *If the banks opt to pull the rug from under the ill-fated project, it will go into liquidation.* **4 to sweep something under the rug** → see **sweep**

rug|by ♦◇◇ /rʌgbi/ N-UNCOUNT **Rugby** or **rugby football** is a game played by two teams using an oval ball. Players try to score points by carrying the ball to their opponents' end of the field, or by kicking it over a bar fixed between two posts.

rug|ged /rʌgɪd/ **1** ADJ A **rugged** area of land is uneven and covered with rocks, with few trees or plants. [LITERARY] ❑ *We left the rough track and bumped our way over a rugged mountainous terrain.* **2** ADJ If you describe a man as **rugged**, you mean that he has strong, masculine features. [LITERARY, APPROVAL] ❑ *A look of pure disbelief crossed Shankly's rugged face.* **3** ADJ If you describe someone's character as **rugged**, you mean that they are strong and determined, and have the ability to cope with difficult situations. [APPROVAL] ❑ *Rugged individualism forged America's frontier society.* **4** ADJ A **rugged** piece of equipment is strong and is designed to last a long time, even if it is treated roughly. ❑ *The camera combines rugged reliability with unequalled optical performance and speed.*

ruin ♦◇◇ /ruːɪn/ (**ruins, ruining, ruined**) **1** V-T To **ruin** something means to severely harm, damage, or spoil it. ❑ *My wife was ruining her health through worry.* **2** V-T To **ruin** someone means to cause them to no longer have any money. ❑ *She accused him of ruining her financially with his taste for the high*

ruination ... **ruminative**

life. **3** N-UNCOUNT **Ruin** is the state of no longer having any money. ▫ *The farmers say recent inflation has driven them to the brink of ruin.* **4** N-UNCOUNT **Ruin** is the state of being severely damaged or spoiled, or the process of reaching this state. ▫ *The vineyards were falling into ruin.* **5** N-PLURAL **The ruins of** something are the parts of it that remain after it has been severely damaged or weakened. ▫ *The new Turkish republic he helped to build emerged from the ruins of a great empire.* **6** N-COUNT The **ruins** of a building are the parts of it that remain after the rest has fallen down or been destroyed. ▫ *One dead child was found in the ruins almost two hours after the explosion.* **7** → see also **ruined** **8** PHRASE If something is **in ruins**, it is completely spoiled. ▫ *Its heavily subsidized economy is in ruins.* **9** PHRASE If a building or place is **in ruins**, most of it has been destroyed and only parts of it remain. ▫ *The abbey was in ruins.*

SYNONYMS

ruin
VERB **1**
harm: *...a warning that the product may harm the environment.*
damage: *He maliciously damaged a car with a baseball bat.*
destroy: *The building was completely destroyed in the explosion.*
spoil: *Peaceful summer evenings can be spoiled by mosquitoes.*

---

ru|ina|tion /ruːɪneɪʃən/ N-UNCOUNT [oft *the* N *of* n] The **ruination** of someone or something is the act of ruining them or the process of being ruined. [FORMAL] ▫ *Money was the ruination of him.*

ruined /ruːɪnd/ ADJ [ADJ n] A **ruined** building or place has been very badly damaged or has gradually fallen down because no one has taken care of it. ▫ *...a ruined church.*

ru|in|ous /ruːɪnəs/ **1** ADJ [usu ADJ n] If you describe the cost of something as **ruinous**, you mean that it costs far more money than you can afford or than is reasonable. ▫ *Many Americans will still fear the potentially ruinous costs of their legal system.* • **ru|in|ous|ly** ADV [ADV adj] ▫ *...a ruinously expensive court case.* **2** ADJ [usu ADJ n] A **ruinous** process or course of action is one that is likely to lead to ruin. ▫ *The economy of the state is experiencing the ruinous effects of the conflict.* • **ru|in|ous|ly** ADV [usu ADV -ed] ▫ *...cities ruinously choked by uncontrolled traffic.*

rule ♦♦♦ /ruːl/ (rules, ruling, ruled) **1** N-COUNT **Rules** are instructions that tell you what you are allowed to do and what you are not allowed to do. ▫ *...a thirty-two-page pamphlet explaining the rules of basketball.* **2** N-COUNT A **rule** is a statement telling people what they should do in order to achieve success or a benefit of some kind. ▫ *An important rule is to drink plenty of water during any flight.* **3** N-COUNT The **rules** of something such as a language or a science are statements that describe the way that things usually happen in a particular situation. ▫ *...according to the rules of quantum theory.* **4** N-SING If something is **the rule**, it is the normal state of affairs. ▫ *However, for many Americans today, weekend work has unfortunately become the rule rather than the exception.* **5** V-T/V-I The person or group that **rules** a country controls its affairs. ▫ *For four centuries, he says, foreigners have ruled Angola.* ▫ *He ruled for eight months.* • N-UNCOUNT **Rule** is also a noun. ▫ *...demands for an end to one-party rule.* **6** V-T If something **rules** your life, it influences or restricts your actions in a way that is not good for you. ▫ *Scientists have always been aware of how fear can rule our lives and make us ill.* **7** V-T/V-I When someone in authority **rules** that something is true or should happen, they state that they have officially decided that it is true or should happen. [FORMAL] ▫ *The court ruled that laws passed by the assembly remained valid.* ▫ *The Israeli court has not yet ruled on the case.* **8** V-T If you **rule** a straight line, you draw it using something that has a straight edge. ▫ *...a ruled grid of horizontal and vertical lines.* **9** → see also **golden rule, ground rule, ruling** **10** PHRASE If you say that something happens **as a rule**, you mean that it usually happens. ▫ *As a rule, however, such attacks have been aimed at causing damage rather than taking life.* **11** PHRASE If someone in authority **bends the rules** or **stretches the rules**, they do something even though it is against the rules. ▫ *There happens to be a particular urgency in this case, and it would help if you could bend the rules.* **12** PHRASE A **rule of thumb** is a rule or principle that you follow which is not based on exact calculations, but rather on experience. ▫ *A good rule of thumb is that a broker must generate sales of ten times his salary if his employer is to make a profit.* **13** → See feature box at **drive, polite**

▶ **rule out** **1** PHRASAL VERB If you **rule out** a course of action, an idea, or a solution, you decide that it is impossible or unsuitable. ▫ *The Treasury Department has ruled out using a weak dollar as the main solution for the country's trade problems.* **2** PHRASAL VERB If something **rules out** a situation, it prevents it from happening or from being possible. ▫ *A serious car accident ruled out a permanent future for him in farming.*

rule book (rule books) **1** N-COUNT A **rule book** is a book containing the official rules for a particular game, job, or organization. ▫ *...one of the most serious offenses mentioned in the party rule book.* **2** N-COUNT [*the* N] If you say that someone is doing something by **the rule book**, you mean that they are doing it in the normal, accepted way. ▫ *This was not the time to take risks; he knew he should play it by the rule book.*

rule of law N-SING [usu *the* N] The **rule of law** refers to a situation in which the people in a society obey its laws and enable it to function properly. [FORMAL] ▫ *I am confident that we can restore peace, stability, and respect for the rule of law.*

rul|er /ruːlər/ (rulers) **1** N-COUNT The **ruler** of a country is the person who rules the country. ▫ *The former military ruler of Lesotho has been placed under house arrest.* **2** N-COUNT A **ruler** is a long, flat piece of wood, metal, or plastic with straight edges marked in or inches or centimeters. Rulers are used to measure things and to draw straight lines. ▫ *...a twelve-inch ruler.* **3** → See feature box at **history**

rul|ing ♦◇◇ /ruːlɪŋ/ (rulings) **1** ADJ [ADJ n] The **ruling** group of people in a country or organization is the group that controls its affairs. ▫ *...the Mexican voters' growing dissatisfaction with the ruling party.* **2** N-COUNT A **ruling** is an official decision made by a judge or court. ▫ *He tried to have the court ruling overturned.* **3** ADJ [ADJ n] Someone's **ruling** passion or emotion is the feeling they have most strongly, which influences their actions. ▫ *Even my love of literary fame, my ruling passion, never soured my temper.*

COLLOCATIONS

ruling
NOUN **2**
noun + **ruling**: court, landmark, trade, tribunal
adjective + **ruling**: favorable, preliminary
verb + **ruling**: issue, uphold; appeal, challenge, overturn

---

rum /rʌm/ (rums) N-MASS **Rum** is an alcoholic drink made from sugar. ▫ *...a bottle of rum.*

Ru|ma|nian /ruːmeɪniən/ → see **Romanian**

rum|ba /rʌmbə, rʊm-, ruːm-/ (rumbas) N-COUNT [oft *the* N] The **rumba** is a popular dance that comes from Cuba, or the music that the dance is performed to.

rum|ble /rʌmbəl/ (rumbles, rumbling, rumbled) **1** N-COUNT A **rumble** is a low, continuous noise. ▫ *The silence of the night was punctuated by the distant rumble of traffic.* **2** V-I If a vehicle **rumbles** somewhere, it moves slowly forward while making a low, continuous noise. ▫ *A bus rumbled along the road.* **3** V-I If something **rumbles**, it makes a low, continuous noise. ▫ *The sky, swollen like a black bladder, rumbled and crackled.* **4** V-I If your stomach **rumbles**, it makes a vibrating noise, usually because you are hungry. ▫ *Her stomach rumbled. She hadn't eaten any breakfast.*

rum|bling /rʌmblɪŋ/ (rumblings) **1** N-COUNT A **rumbling** is a low, continuous noise. ▫ *...the rumbling of an empty stomach.* **2** N-COUNT **Rumblings** are signs that a bad situation is developing or that people are becoming annoyed or unhappy. ▫ *Even Baldwin had become aware that there were rumblings of discontent within the ranks.*

ru|mi|nate /ruːmɪneɪt/ (ruminates, ruminating, ruminated) **1** V-I If you **ruminate** on something, you think about it very carefully. [FORMAL] ▫ *He ruminated on the terrible wastefulness that typified American life.* **2** V-I When animals **ruminate**, they bring food back from their stomach into their mouth and chew it again. [TECHNICAL]

ru|mi|na|tion /ruːmɪneɪʃən/ (ruminations) N-COUNT [oft with poss] Your **ruminations** are your careful thoughts about something. [FORMAL] ▫ *Many of Vasari's ruminations on the subject are not always to be believed.*

ru|mi|na|tive /ruːmɪneɪtɪv/ ADJ If you are **ruminative**, you are thinking very deeply and carefully about something. [FORMAL] ▫ *He was uncharacteristically depressed and ruminative.*

• **ru|mi|na|tive|ly** ADV [ADV with v] ❏ *He smiles and swirls the ice ruminatively around his almost empty glass.*

rum|mage /rʌmɪdʒ/ (**rummages, rummaging, rummaged**) V-I If you **rummage** through something, you search for something you want by moving things around in a careless or hurried way. ❏ *They rummage through piles of secondhand clothes for something that fits.* • N-SING **Rummage** is also a noun. ❏ *A brief rummage will provide several pairs of gloves.* • PHRASAL VERB **Rummage around** means the same as **rummage**. ❏ *I opened the fridge and rummaged around.*

rum|mage sale (**rummage sales**) N-COUNT A **rummage sale** is a sale of cheap used goods that is usually held to raise money for charity. [AM]

in BRIT, use **jumble sale**

rum|my /rʌmi/ N-UNCOUNT **Rummy** is a card game in which players try to collect cards of the same value or cards in a sequence in the same suit.

ru|mor ✦✧✧ /ruːmər/ (**rumors**)

in BRIT, use **rumour**

1 N-VAR A **rumor** is a story or piece of information that may or may not be true, but that people are talking about. ❏ *U.S. officials are discounting rumors of a coup.* **2** → See feature box at **truth**

ru|mored /ruːmərd/

in BRIT, use **rumoured**

V-T PASSIVE If something **is rumored** to be the case, people are suggesting that it is the case, but they do not know for certain. ❏ *The company is rumored to be a takeover target.*

ru|mor mill (**rumor mills**)

in BRIT, use **rumour mill**

N-COUNT [oft the N] You can refer to the people in a particular place or profession who spread rumors as the **rumor mill**. [mainly JOURNALISM] ❏ *The Hollywood rumor mill is already buzzing about a marriage between Paramount Studios and Caps Cities.*

rumor|monger /ruːmərmʌŋɡər/ (**rumormongers**)

in BRIT, use **rumour-monger**

N-COUNT If you call someone a **rumormonger**, you disapprove of the fact that they spread rumors. [DISAPPROVAL]

rump /rʌmp/ (**rumps**) **1** N-COUNT An animal's **rump** is its rear end. ❏ *The cows' rumps were marked with their owner's initials and a number.* **2** N-UNCOUNT **Rump** or **rump steak** is meat cut from the rear end of a cow. ❏ *...a pound of rump.* **3** N-SING The **rump** of a group, organization, or country consists of the members who remain in it after the rest have left. [mainly BRIT] ❏ *The rump of the party does in fact still have considerable assets.*

rum|ple /rʌmpəl/ (**rumples, rumpling, rumpled**) V-T If you **rumple** someone's hair, you move your hand backward and forward through it as your way of showing affection to them. ❏ *I leaned forward to rumple his hair, but he jerked out of the way.*

rum|pled /rʌmpəld/ ADJ **Rumpled** means creased or messy. ❏ *I hurried to the tent and grabbed a few clean, if rumpled, clothes.*

rum|pus /rʌmpəs/ (**rumpuses**) N-COUNT If someone or something causes a **rumpus**, they cause a lot of noise or argument. ❏ *He had actually left the company a year before the rumpus started.*

RUN

① VERB USES
② NOUN USES
③ PHRASES
④ PHRASAL VERBS

---

① **run** ✦✦✦ /rʌn/ (**runs, running, ran**)

The form **run** is used in the present tense and is also the past participle of the verb.

1 V-T/V-I When you **run**, you move more quickly than when you walk, for example because you are in a hurry to get somewhere, or for exercise. ❏ *I excused myself and ran back to the telephone.* ❏ *He ran the last block to the White House with two cases of gear.* **2** V-T/V-I When someone **runs** in a race, they run in competition with other people. ❏ *...when I was running in the New York Marathon.* ❏ *He ran a tremendous race.* **3** V-T/V-I When a horse **runs** in a race or when its owner **runs** it, it competes in a race. ❏ *He was overruled by the owner who insisted on Cool Ground running in the Gold Cup.* **4** V-I If you say that something long, such as a road, **runs** in a particular direction, you are describing its course or position. You can also say that something **runs** the length or width of something else. ❏ *...the sun-dappled trail which ran through the beech woods.* **5** V-T If you **run** a wire or tube somewhere, you attach it or pull it from, to, or across a particular place. ❏ *Our host ran a long extension cord out from the house and set up a screen and a projector.* **6** V-T If you **run** your hand or an object through something, you move your hand or the object through it. ❏ *He laughed and ran his fingers through his hair.* **7** V-T If you **run** something through a machine, process, or series of tests, you make it go through the machine, process, or tests. ❏ *They have gathered the best statistics they can find and run them through their own computers.* **8** V-I If someone **runs** for office in an election, they take part as a candidate. ❏ *It was only last February that he announced he would run for president.* ❏ *It is no easy job to run against Ohio's Democratic senator.* **9** V-T If you **run** something such as a business or an activity, you are in charge of it or you organize it. ❏ *His stepfather ran a prosperous paint business.* ❏ *...a well-run, profitable organization.* **10** V-I [usu cont] If you talk about how a system, an organization, or someone's life **is running**, you are saying how well it is operating or progressing. ❏ *Officials in charge of the camps say the system is now running extremely smoothly.* **11** V-T/V-I If you **run** an experiment, computer program, or other process, or start it **running**, you start it and let it continue. ❏ *He ran a lot of tests and it turned out I had an infection called mycoplasma.* **12** V-T/V-I [usu cont] When a machine **is running** or when you **are running** it, it is switched on and is working. ❏ *We told him to wait out front with the engine running.* **13** V-I A machine or equipment that **runs** on or off a particular source of energy functions using that source of energy. ❏ *The buses run on diesel.* **14** V-I When you say that vehicles such as trains and buses **run** from one place to another, you mean that they regularly travel along that route. ❏ *A shuttle bus runs frequently between the inn and the country club.* **15** V-T If you **run** someone somewhere in a car, you drive them there. [INFORMAL] ❏ *Could you run me up to Baltimore?* **16** V-I If you **run** over or down to a place that is quite near, you drive there. [INFORMAL] ❏ *I'll run over to Short Mountain and check on Mrs. Adams.* **17** V-I If a liquid **runs** in a particular direction, it flows in that direction. ❏ *Tears were running down her cheeks.* **18** V-T If you **run** water, or if you **run** a faucet or a bath, you cause water to flow from a faucet. ❏ *She went to the sink and ran water into her empty glass.* **19** V-I [only cont] If a faucet or a bath **is running**, water is coming out of a faucet. ❏ *The kitchen sink had been stopped up and the faucet left running, so water spilled over onto the floor.* **20** V-I [usu cont] If your nose **is running**, liquid is flowing out of it, usually because you have a cold. ❏ *Timothy was crying, mostly from exhaustion, and his nose was running.* **21** V-I [usu cont] If a surface **is running** with a liquid, that liquid is flowing down it. ❏ *After an hour he realized he was completely running with sweat.* **22** V-T/V-I When you **run** a cassette or videotape or when it **runs**, it moves through the machine as the machine operates. ❏ *Leaphorn pushed the play button again, ran the tape, pushed stop, pushed rewind.* **23** V-I If the dye in some cloth or the ink on some paper **runs**, it comes off or spreads when the cloth or paper gets wet. ❏ *The ink had run on the wet paper.* **24** V-I If a feeling **runs** through your body or a thought **runs** through your mind, you experience it or think it quickly. ❏ *She felt a surge of excitement run through her.* **25** V-I If a feeling or noise **runs** through a group of people, it spreads among them. ❏ *A buzz of excitement ran through the crowd.* **26** V-I If a theme or feature **runs** through something such as someone's actions or writing, it is present in all of it. ❏ *Another thread running through this series is the role of doctors in the treatment of mental illness.* **27** V-T/V-I When newspapers or magazines **run** a particular item or story or if it **runs**, it is published or printed. ❏ *The New Orleans Times-Picayune ran a series of four scathing editorials entitled "The Choice of Our Lives."* **28** V-I If an amount **is running** at a particular level, it is at that level. ❏ *Today's figures show inflation running at 10.9 percent.* **29** V-I If a play, event, or legal contract **runs** for a particular period of time, it lasts for that period of time. ❏ *It pleased critics but ran for only three months on Broadway.*

run

□ *The contract was to run from 1992 to 2020.* **30** V-I [usu cont] If someone or something **is running** late, they have taken more time than had been planned. If they **are running** on time or ahead of time, they have taken the time planned or less than the time planned. □ *Tell her I'll call her back later, I'm running late again.* **31** V-T If you **are running** a temperature or a fever, you have a high temperature because you are ill. □ *The little girl is running a fever and she needs help.* **32** → see also **running**

② **run** ♦♦♦ /rʌn/ (runs) **1** N-COUNT A **run** is a time when you move somewhere on foot more quickly than when you walk, usually for exercise. □ *After a six-mile run, Jackie returns home for a substantial breakfast.* **2** N-SING [N for n] A **run for** office is an attempt to be elected to office. [mainly AM] □ *He was already preparing his run for the presidency.*

> in BRIT, usually use **bid**

3 N-COUNT A **run** is a trip somewhere. □ *...doing the morning school run.* **4** N-COUNT A **run** of a play or television program is the period of time during which performances are given or programmes are shown. □ *The show will transfer to Broadway on October 9, after a month's run in Philadelphia.* **5** N-SING A **run** of successes or failures is a series of successes or failures. □ *The team is haunted by a run of low scores.* **6** N-COUNT A **run** of a product is the amount that a company or factory decides to produce at one time. □ *Wayne plans to increase the print run to 1,000.* **7** N-COUNT In baseball or cricket, a **run** is a score of one, which is made by players running between marked places on the field after hitting the ball. □ *The Padres scored four runs off Terry Adams in the last 2 innings.* **8** N-SING If someone gives you **the run of** a place, they give you permission to go where you like in it and use it as you wish. □ *He had the run of the house and the pool.* **9** N-SING If there is a **run on** something, a lot of people want to buy it or get it at the same time. □ *A run on the dollar has killed off hopes of a rate cut.* **10** N-COUNT A **run** is a hole or torn part in someone's stocking or pantyhose, where some of the vertical threads have broken, leaving only the horizontal threads. □ *I had a run in my stocking.* **11** N-COUNT A ski **run** or bobsled **run** is a course or route that has been designed for skiing or for riding in a bobsled. □ *...an avalanche on Colorado's highest ski run.*

③ **run** ♦♦♦ /rʌn/ (runs, running, ran)

> The form **run** is used in the present tense and is also the past participle of the verb.

→ Please look at meanings **12** to **16** to see if the expression you are looking for is shown under another headword.

1 PHRASE If you **run** someone **a close second**, or **run a close second**, you almost beat them in a race or competition. □ *While "Nightly" has led in the ratings all season, "World News Tonight" is running a close second.* **2** PHRASE If a river or well **runs dry**, it no longer has any water in it. If an oil well **runs dry**, it no longer produces any oil. □ *Streams had run dry for the first time in memory.* **3** PHRASE If a source of information or money **runs dry**, no more information or money can be obtained from it. □ *Three days into production, the kitty had run dry.* **4** PHRASE If a characteristic **runs in** someone's **family**, it often occurs in members of that family, in different generations. □ *The insanity which ran in his family haunted him.* **5** PHRASE If you **make a run for it** or if you **run for it**, you run away in order to escape from someone or something. □ *A helicopter hovered overhead as one of the gang made a run for it.* **6** PHRASE If people's feelings **are running high**, they are very angry, concerned, or excited. □ *Feelings there have been running high in the wake of last week's killing.* **7** PHRASE If you talk about what will happen **in the long run**, you are saying what you think will happen over a long period of time in the future. If you talk about what will happen **in the short run**, you are saying what you think will happen in the near future. □ *Sometimes expensive drugs or other treatments can be economical in the long run.* **8** PHRASE If you say that someone could **give** someone else **a run for** their **money**, you mean you think they are almost as good as the other person. □ *...a youngster who even now could give her a run for her money.* **9** PHRASE If someone is **on the run**, they are trying to escape or hide from someone such as the police or an enemy. □ *Fifteen-year-old Danny is on the run from a juvenile detention center.* **10** PHRASE If someone is **on the run**, they are being severely defeated in a contest or competition. □ *I knew I had him on the run.* **11** PHRASE If you **are running short** of something or **running low** on something, you do not have much of it left. If a supply of something **is running short** or **running low**, there is not much of it left. □ *Government forces are running short of ammunition and fuel.* **12 to run deep** → see **deep** **13 to run an errand** → see **errand** **14 to run the gauntlet** → see **gauntlet** **15 to run riot** → see **riot** **16 to run a risk** → see **risk**

④ **run** ♦♦♦ /rʌn/ (runs, running, ran)

> The form **run** is used in the present tense and is also the past participle of the verb.

▶ **run across** PHRASAL VERB If you **run across** someone or something, you meet them or find them unexpectedly. □ *We ran across some old friends in the village.*

▶ **run around** PHRASAL VERB If you **run around**, you go to a lot of places and do a lot of things, often in a rushed or disorganized way. □ *We had been running around cleaning up.* □ *Jessica was running around with the camera snapping pictures.* □ *I will not have you running around the countryside without my authority.*

▶ **run away** **1** PHRASAL VERB If you **run away** from a place, you leave it because you are unhappy there. □ *I ran away from home when I was sixteen.* □ *After his beating, Colin ran away and hasn't been heard of since.* **2** PHRASAL VERB If you **run away** with someone, you secretly go away with them in order to live with them or marry them. □ *She ran away with a man called McTavish last year.* **3** PHRASAL VERB If you **run away** from something unpleasant or new, you try to avoid dealing with it or thinking about it. □ *They run away from the problem, hoping it will disappear of its own accord.* **4** → see also **runaway**

▶ **run away with** PHRASAL VERB If you let your imagination or your emotions **run away with** you, you fail to control them and cannot think sensibly. □ *You're letting your imagination run away with you.*

▶ **run by** PHRASAL VERB If you **run** something **by** someone, you tell them about it or mention it, to see if they think it is a good idea, or can understand it. □ *I'm definitely interested, but I'll have to run it by Larry Estes.*

▶ **run down** **1** PHRASAL VERB If you **run** people or things **down**, you criticize them strongly. □ *I'm always running myself down.* **2** PHRASAL VERB If a vehicle or its driver **runs** someone **down**, the vehicle hits them and injures them. □ *He claimed that the motorcycle driver was trying to run him down.* **3** PHRASAL VERB If a machine or device **runs down**, it gradually loses power or works more slowly. □ *The batteries are running down.* **4** PHRASAL VERB If people **run down** an industry or an organization, they deliberately reduce its size or the amount of work that it does. □ *The government is cynically running down Sweden's welfare system.* **5** PHRASAL VERB If someone **runs down** an amount of something, they reduce it or allow it to decrease. □ *But the survey also revealed firms were running down stocks instead of making new products.* **6** → see also **run-down**

▶ **run into** **1** PHRASAL VERB If you **run into** problems or difficulties, you unexpectedly begin to experience them. □ *Wang agreed to sell IBM Systems last year after it ran into financial problems.* **2** PHRASAL VERB If you **run into** someone, you meet them unexpectedly. □ *He ran into Krettner in the corridor a few minutes later.* **3** PHRASAL VERB If a vehicle or its driver **runs into** something, it accidentally hits it. □ *The driver failed to negotiate a bend and ran into a tree.* **4** PHRASAL VERB You use **run into** when indicating that the cost or amount of something is very great. □ *He said companies should face punitive civil penalties running into millions of dollars.*

▶ **run off** **1** PHRASAL VERB If you **run off** with someone, you secretly go away with them in order to live with them or marry them. □ *The last thing I'm going to do is run off with somebody's husband.* **2** PHRASAL VERB If you **run off** copies of a piece of writing, you produce them using a machine. □ *If you want to run off a copy sometime today, you're welcome to.* **3** PHRASE [v inflects] If you say that someone **is running off at the mouth**, you are criticizing them for talking too much. [DISAPPROVAL] □ *That was when she really started running off at the mouth. I'll bet she hasn't shut up yet.*

▶ **run out** **1** PHRASAL VERB If you **run out** of something, you have no more of it left. □ *They have run out of ideas.* □ *We're running out of time.* **2** PHRASAL VERB If something **runs out**, it becomes used up so that there is no more left. □ *Conditions* are getting worse and supplies are running out. **3** PHRASAL VERB When a legal document **runs out**, it stops being valid. ❑ *When the lease ran out the family moved to Cleveland.* **4 to run out of steam** → see **steam**

▶ **run over** PHRASAL VERB If a vehicle or its driver **runs** a person or animal **over**, it knocks them down or drives over them. ❑ *You can always run him over and make it look like an accident.*

▶ **run through** **1** PHRASAL VERB If you **run through** a list of items, you read or mention all the items quickly. ❑ *I ran through the options with him.* **2** PHRASAL VERB If you **run through** a performance or a series of actions, you practice it. ❑ *Doug stood still while I ran through the handover procedure.*

▶ **run up** **1** PHRASAL VERB If someone **runs up** bills or debts, they acquire them by buying a lot of things or borrowing money. ❑ *She managed to run up a credit card debt of $60,000.* **2** → see also **run-up**

▶ **run up against** PHRASAL VERB If you **run up against** problems, you suddenly begin to experience them. ❑ *I ran up against the problem of getting taken seriously long before I became a writer.*

run|about /rʌnəbaʊt/ (**runabouts**) **1** N-COUNT A **runabout** is a small car with an open top. **2** N-COUNT A **runabout** is a small, light boat with a motor. [AM]

run|around /rʌnəraʊnd/ PHRASE If someone **gives** you **the runaround**, they deliberately do not give you all the information or help that you want, and send you to another person or place to get it. [INFORMAL]

run|away /rʌnəweɪ/ (**runaways**) **1** ADJ [ADJ n] You use **runaway** to describe a situation in which something increases or develops very quickly and cannot be controlled. ❑ *Our June sale was a runaway success.* **2** N-COUNT A **runaway** is someone, especially a child, who leaves home without telling anyone or without permission. ❑ *...a teenage runaway.* **3** ADJ [ADJ n] A **runaway** vehicle or animal is moving forward quickly, and its driver or rider has lost control of it. ❑ *The runaway car careered into a bench, hitting an elderly couple.*

run-down

The spelling **rundown** is also used. The adjective is pronounced /rʌndaʊn/. The noun is pronounced /rʌndaʊn/.

1 ADJ If someone is **run-down**, they are tired or slightly ill. [INFORMAL] ❑ *When the 23-year-old started to feel run-down last December, it never occurred to her that she could have tuberculosis.* **2** ADJ A **run-down** building or area is in very poor condition. ❑ *They have put substantial funds into rebuilding one of the most run-down areas.* **3** ADJ A **run-down** place of business is not as active as it used to be or does not have many customers. ❑ *...a run-down slate quarry.* **4** N-SING If you give someone a **rundown** of a group of things or a **rundown** on something, you give them details about it. [INFORMAL] ❑ *Here's a rundown of the options.* **5** → See feature box at **town**

rune /ruːn/ (**runes**) N-COUNT **Runes** are letters from an alphabet that was used by people in Northern Europe in former times. They were carved on wood or stone and were believed to have magical powers.

rung /rʌŋ/ (**rungs**) **1 Rung** is the past participle of **ring**. **2** N-COUNT The **rungs** on a ladder are the wooden or metal bars that form the steps. ❑ *I swung myself onto the ladder and felt for the next rung.* **3** N-COUNT If you reach a particular **rung** in your career, in an organization, or in a process, you reach that level in it. ❑ *I first worked with him in 1971 when we were both on the lowest rung of our careers.*

run-in (**run-ins**) N-COUNT A **run-in** is an argument or quarrel with someone. [INFORMAL] ❑ *I had a monumental run-in with him a couple of years ago.*

run|ner ✦◇◇ /rʌnər/ (**runners**) **1** N-COUNT A **runner** is a person who runs, especially for sport or pleasure. ❑ *...a marathon runner.* **2** N-COUNT The **runners** in a horse race are the horses taking part. ❑ *There are 18 runners in the top race of the day.* **3** N-COUNT A drug **runner** or gun **runner** is someone who illegally takes drugs or guns into a country. ❑ *...a gang of evil gun runners.* **4** N-COUNT Someone who is a **runner** for a particular person or company is employed to take messages, collect money, or do other small tasks for them. ❑ *...a bookie's runner.* **5** N-COUNT **Runners** are thin strips of wood or metal underneath something which help it to move smoothly. ❑ *...the runners of his sled.*

runner-up (**runners-up**) N-COUNT A **runner-up** is someone who has finished in second place in a race or competition. ❑ *The ten runners-up will receive a case of wine.*

run|ning ✦◇◇ /rʌnɪŋ/ **1** N-UNCOUNT **Running** is the activity of moving fast on foot, especially as a sport. ❑ *We chose to do cross-country running.* **2** N-SING The **running** of something such as a business is the managing or organizing of it. ❑ *...the committee in charge of the day-to-day running of the party.* **3** ADJ [ADJ n] You use **running** to describe things that continue or keep occurring over a period of time. ❑ *He also began a running feud with his closest competitor.* **4** ADJ [ADJ n] A **running** total is a total which changes because numbers keep being added to it as something progresses. ❑ *He kept a running tally of who had called him, who had visited, who had sent flowers.* **5** ADV [N ADV] You can use **running** when indicating that something keeps happening. For example, if something has happened every day for three days, you can say that it has happened for the third day **running** or for three days **running**. ❑ *He said drought had led to severe crop failure for the second year running.* **6** ADJ [ADJ n] **Running** water is water that is flowing rather than standing still. ❑ *The forest was filled with the sound of running water.* **7** ADJ [ADJ n] If a house has **running** water, water is supplied to the house through pipes and faucets. ❑ *...a house without electricity or running water in a tiny African village.* **8** PHRASE If someone is **in the running** for something, they have a good chance of winning or obtaining it. If they are **out of the running** for something, they have no chance of winning or obtaining it. ❑ *Until this week he appeared to have ruled himself out of the running because of his age.* **9** PHRASE If something such as a system or place is **up and running**, it is operating normally. ❑ *We're trying to get the medical facilities up and running again.*

-running /-rʌnɪŋ/ COMB IN N-UNCOUNT **-running** combines with nouns to form nouns which refer to the illegal importing of drugs or guns. ❑ *...a serviceman suspected of drug-running.*

run|ning bat|tle (**running battles**) N-COUNT When two groups of people fight a **running battle**, they keep attacking each other in various parts of a place, or in various ways. ❑ *They fought running battles in the narrow streets with police.*

run|ning com|men|tary (**running commentaries**) N-COUNT If someone provides a **running commentary** on an event, they give a continuous description of it while it is taking place. ❑ *I would accompany the pictures with a running commentary, instead of music.*

run|ning costs N-PLURAL The **running costs** of a business are the amount of money that is regularly spent on things such as salaries, heating, lighting, and rent. [BRIT, BUSINESS]

in AM, use **overhead**

run|ning mate (**running mates**) N-COUNT In an election campaign, a candidate's **running mate** is the person that they have chosen to help them in the election. If the candidate wins, the running mate will become the second most important person after the winner. [mainly AM] ❑ *...Clinton's selection of Al Gore as his running mate.*

run|ning or|der N-SING [usu the N] The **running order** of the items in a broadcast, concert, or show is the order in which the items will come. ❑ *We had reversed the running order.*

run|ning time (**running times**) N-COUNT The **running time** of something such as a movie, video, or CD is the time it takes to play from start to finish.

run|ny /rʌni/ (**runnier**, **runniest**) **1** ADJ Something that is **runny** is more liquid than usual or than was intended. ❑ *Warm the honey until it becomes runny.* **2** ADJ If someone has a **runny** nose or **runny** eyes, liquid is flowing from their nose or eyes. ❑ *Symptoms are streaming eyes, a runny nose, headache, and a cough.*

run|off /rʌnɒf/ (**runoffs**) N-COUNT [usu sing, oft N between pl-n] A **runoff** is an extra vote or contest which is held in order to decide the winner of an election or competition, because no one has yet clearly won. ❑ *There will be a runoff between these two candidates on December 9th.*

run-of-the-mill ADJ [usu ADJ n] A **run-of-the-mill** person or thing is very ordinary, with no special or interesting features. [DISAPPROVAL] ❏ *I was just a very average run-of-the-mill kind of student.*

runt /rʌnt/ (runts) N-COUNT [oft N of n] The **runt** of a group of animals born to the same mother at the same time is the smallest and weakest of them. ❏ *Animals reject the runt of the litter.*

run-through (run-throughs) N-COUNT A **run-through** for a show or event is a practice for it. ❏ *Charles and Eddie are getting ready for their final run-through before the evening's recording.*

run time (run times) N-COUNT **Run time** is the time during which a computer program is running. [COMPUTING] ❏ *With run time for most applications lasting days or weeks, the queue fills up quickly.*

run-up (run-ups) N-SING The **run-up** to an event is the period of time just before it. [mainly BRIT] ❏ *The company believes the products will sell well in the run-up to Christmas.*

run|way /rʌnweɪ/ (runways) N-COUNT At an airport, the **runway** is the long strip of ground with a hard surface which an airplane takes off from or lands on. ❏ *The plane started taxiing down the runway.*

ru|pee /rupi/ (rupees) N-COUNT A **rupee** is a unit of money that is used in India, Pakistan, and some other countries. ❏ *He earns 20 rupees a day.*

rup|ture /rʌptʃər/ (ruptures, rupturing, ruptured) **1** N-COUNT A **rupture** is a severe injury in which an internal part of your body tears or bursts open, especially the part between the bowels and the abdomen. ❏ *He died of an abdominal infection caused by a rupture of his stomach.* **2** V-T/V-I If a person or animal **ruptures** a part of their body or if it **ruptures**, it tears or bursts open. ❏ *His stomach might rupture from all the acid.* ❏ *While playing badminton, I ruptured my Achilles tendon.* **3** V-T If you **rupture** yourself, you rupture a part of your body, usually because you have lifted something heavy. ❏ *He ruptured himself playing football.* **4** V-T/V-I If an object **ruptures** or if something **ruptures** it, it bursts open. ❏ *Certain gasoline tanks in trucks can rupture and burn in a collision.* **5** N-COUNT If there is a **rupture** between people, relations between them get much worse or end completely. ❏ *The incidents have not yet caused a major rupture in the political ties between countries.* **6** V-T If someone or something **ruptures** relations between people, they damage them, causing them to become worse or to end. ❏ *Brutal clashes between squatters and police yesterday ruptured the city's governing coalition.*

ru|ral ♦◇◇ /rʊərəl/ **1** ADJ **Rural** places are far away from large towns or cities. ❏ *These plants have a tendency to grow in the more rural areas.* **2** ADJ [ADJ n] **Rural** means having features which are typical of areas that are far away from large towns or cities. ❏ *...the old rural way of life.*

> **SYNONYMS**
> **rural**
> ADJ **1**
> **rustic:** *...the rustic charm of a country lifestyle.*
> **agricultural:** *...agricultural land.*
> **country:** *I was a simple country boy from Norfolk.*
> **pastoral:** *the pastoral beauty of a park.*

ru|ral route (rural routes) N-COUNT A **rural route** is a mail delivery route in an area away from any large towns or cities. The abbreviation **RR** is also used. [AM] ❏ *Use the P.O. box, rural route or box number for destinations without street addresses.*

ruse /ruz, rus/ (ruses) N-COUNT A **ruse** is an action or plan which is intended to deceive someone. [FORMAL] ❏ *It is now clear that this was a ruse to divide them.*

rush ♦◇◇ /rʌʃ/ (rushes, rushing, rushed) **1** V-T/V-I If you **rush** somewhere, you go there quickly. ❏ *A schoolgirl rushed into a burning apartment to save a man's life.* ❏ *I've got to rush. Got a meeting in a few minutes.* ❏ *I rushed to get the 7:00 a.m. train.* **2** V-T If people **rush** to do something, they do it as soon as they can, because they are very eager to do it. ❏ *Russian banks rushed to buy as many dollars as they could.* **3** N-SING A **rush** is a situation in which you need to go somewhere or do something very quickly. ❏ *The men left in a rush.* **4** N-SING If there is a **rush** for something, many people suddenly try to get it or do it. ❏ *Record stores are expecting a huge rush for the single.* **5** N-SING The **rush** is a period of time when many people go somewhere or do something. ❏ *The store's opening coincided with the Christmas rush.* **6** V-T/V-I If you **rush** something, you do it in a hurry, often too quickly and without much care. ❏ *You can't rush a search.* ❏ *Instead of rushing at life, I wanted something more meaningful.* • **rushed** ADJ ❏ *The report had all the hallmarks of a rushed job.* **7** V-T If you **rush** someone or something to a place, you take them there quickly. ❏ *They had rushed him to a hospital for a lifesaving operation.* **8** V-T/V-I If you **rush** into something or **are rushed** into it, you do it without thinking about it for long enough. ❏ *He will not rush into any decisions.* ❏ *They had rushed in without adequate appreciation of the task.* • **rushed** ADJ ❏ *At no time did I feel rushed or under pressure.* **9** V-T/V-I If you **rush** something or someone, or **rush** at them, you move quickly and forcefully at them, often in order to attack them. ❏ *They rushed the entrance and forced their way in.* ❏ *Reporters rushed at him and he ran back inside.* **10** V-I If air or liquid **rushes** somewhere, it flows there suddenly and quickly. ❏ *Water rushes out of huge tunnels.* • N-COUNT **Rush** is also a noun. ❏ *A rush of air on my face woke me.* **11** N-COUNT If you experience a **rush** of a feeling, you suddenly experience it very strongly. ❏ *A rush of pure affection swept over him.*

> **SYNONYMS**
> **rush**
> VERB **1**
> **hurry:** *Claire hurried along the road.*
> **race:** *He raced across town to the State House building.*
> **dash:** *Suddenly, she dashed down to the cellar.*
> **bolt:** *I made an excuse and bolted for the exit.*

> **COLLOCATIONS**
> **rush**
> NOUN
> **4**
> adjective + **rush**: last-minute; frantic, mad
> **5**
> noun + **rush**: evening, morning
> **rush** + noun: hour
> verb + **rush**: avoid, beat

rush hour (rush hours) **1** N-COUNT [also at/during N] The **rush hour** is one of the periods of the day when most people are traveling to or from work. ❏ *During the evening rush hour it was often solid with vehicles.* **2** → See feature box at **commute**

rusk /rʌsk/ (rusks) N-VAR **Rusks** are hard, dry biscuits that are given to babies and young children. [mainly BRIT]

rus|set /rʌsɪt/ (russets) COLOR **Russet** is used to describe things that are reddish brown in color. ❏ *...a russet apple.*

Rus|sian /rʌʃən/ (Russians) **1** ADJ **Russian** means belonging or relating to Russia, or to its people, language, or culture. ❏ *the Russian parliament.* **2** N-COUNT A **Russian** is a Russian citizen, or a person of Russian origin. ❏ *Three-quarters of Russians live in cities.* **3** N-UNCOUNT **Russian** is the language spoken in Russia.

Rus|sian doll (Russian dolls) N-COUNT A **Russian doll** is a hollow wooden doll that is made in two halves. Inside it are a series of similar wooden dolls, each smaller than the last, placed one inside the other.

Rus|sian dress|ing N-UNCOUNT **Russian dressing** is a salad dressing made from mayonnaise mixed with chili sauce and chopped pickles or peppers. [AM] ❏ *...smoked salmon on rye with Russian dressing.*

Rus|sian rou|lette **1** N-UNCOUNT If you say that someone is playing **Russian roulette**, or that what they are doing is like playing **Russian roulette**, you mean that what they are doing is very dangerous because it involves unpredictable risks. ❏ *This is like playing Russian roulette with your finances.* **2** N-UNCOUNT If someone plays **Russian roulette**, they fire a gun with only one bullet at their head without knowing whether it will shoot them.

rust /rʌst/ (rusts, rusting, rusted) **1** N-UNCOUNT **Rust** is a brown substance that forms on iron or steel, for example when it comes into contact with water. ❏ *...a decaying tractor, red with rust.* **2** V-I When a metal object **rusts**, it becomes covered in rust and often loses its strength. ❏ *Copper nails are better than iron nails because the iron rusts.* **3** COLOR **Rust** is sometimes used to describe things that are reddish brown in color. ❏ *...rust and gold leaves from the maples.*

Rust Belt also **rust belt** N-SING [the N] In the United States and some other countries, **the Rust Belt** is a region which used to have a lot of manufacturing industry, but whose economy is now in difficulty. ❏ *...in the rust belt of the Midwest.*

rus|tic /rʌstɪk/ ADJ You can use **rustic** to describe things or people that you approve of because they are simple or unsophisticated in a way that is typical of the countryside. [APPROVAL] ❏ *...the rustic charm of a country lifestyle.*

rus|tic|ity /rʌstɪsɪti/ N-UNCOUNT You can refer to the simple, peaceful character of life in the countryside as **rusticity**. [WRITTEN, APPROVAL] ❏ *It pleases me to think of young Tyndale growing up here in deep rusticity.*

rus|tle /rʌsᵊl/ (rustles, rustling, rustled) V-T/V-I When something thin and dry **rustles** or when you **rustle** it, it makes soft sounds as it moves. ❏ *The leaves rustled in the wind.* ❏ *She rustled her papers impatiently.* • N-COUNT **Rustle** is also a noun. ❏ *She sat perfectly still, without even a rustle of her frilled petticoats.* • **rus|tling** (rustlings) N-VAR ❏ *We were all terrified by a rustling sound coming from beneath one of the seats.*
▸ **rustle up** PHRASAL VERB If you **rustle up** something to eat or drink, you make or prepare it quickly, with very little planning. ❏ *Let's see if somebody can rustle up a cup of coffee.*

rus|tler /rʌslər/ (rustlers) N-COUNT [usu pl, oft n N] **Rustlers** are people who steal farm animals, especially cattle, horses, and sheep. [mainly AM] ❏ *...the old Wyoming Trail once used by cattle rustlers and outlaws.*

rus|tling /rʌslɪŋ/ ◼ N-UNCOUNT [usu n N] **Rustling** is the activity of stealing farm animals, especially cattle. [mainly AM] ❏ *...cattle rustling and horse stealing.* ◼ → see also **rustle**

rusty /rʌsti/ (rustier, rustiest) ◼ ADJ A **rusty** metal object such as a car or a machine is covered with rust, which is a brown substance that forms on iron or steel when it comes into contact with water. ❏ *...a rusty iron gate.* ◼ ADJ If a skill that you have or your knowledge of something is **rusty**, it is not as good as it used to be, because you have not used it for a long time. ❏ *You may be a little rusty, but past experience and teaching skills won't have been lost.*

rut /rʌt/ (ruts) ◼ N-COUNT If you say that someone is in a **rut**, you disapprove of the fact that they have become fixed in their way of thinking and doing things, and find it difficult to change. You can also say that someone's life or career is in a **rut**. [DISAPPROVAL] ❏ *I don't like being in a rut – I like to keep moving on.* ◼ N-COUNT A **rut** is a deep, narrow mark made in the ground by the wheels of a vehicle. ❏ *Our driver slowed up as we approached the ruts in the road.*

ru|ta|ba|ga /ruːtəbeɪgə/ (rutabagas) N-VAR A **rutabaga** is a round, yellow root vegetable with a brown or purple skin. [AM]

in BRIT, use **swede**

ruth|less /ruːθlɪs/ ◼ ADJ If you say that someone is **ruthless**, you mean that you disapprove of them because they are very harsh or cruel, and will do anything that is necessary to achieve what they want. [DISAPPROVAL] ❏ *The president was ruthless in dealing with any hint of internal political dissent.*
• **ruth|less|ly** ADV [ADV with v] ❏ *The party has ruthlessly crushed any sign of organized opposition.* • **ruth|less|ness** N-UNCOUNT ❏ *...a powerful political figure with a reputation for ruthlessness.* ◼ ADJ A **ruthless** action or activity is done forcefully and thoroughly, without much concern for its effects on other people. ❏ *Her lawyers have been ruthless in thrashing out a divorce settlement.*
• **ruth|less|ly** ADV ❏ *Gloria showed signs of turning into the ruthlessly efficient woman her father wanted her to be.* • **ruth|less|ness** N-UNCOUNT ❏ *...a woman with a brain and business acumen and a certain healthy ruthlessness.*

rut|ted /rʌtɪd/ ◼ ADJ [oft adv ADJ] A **rutted** road or track is very uneven because it has long, deep, narrow marks in it made by the wheels of vehicles. ❏ *...an uncomfortable ride along deeply rutted roads.* ◼ → see also **rut**

rut|ting /rʌtɪŋ/ ◼ ADJ **Rutting** male animals such as deer are in a period of sexual excitement and activity. ❏ *...jokes about bitches in heat and rutting stags.* • N-UNCOUNT [oft N n] **Rutting** is also a noun. ❏ *During the rutting season the big boars have the most terrible mating battles.* ◼ → see also **rut**

RV /ɑːr viː/ (RVs) N-COUNT An **RV** is a van that is equipped with such things as beds and cooking equipment, so that people can live in it, usually while they are on vacation. **RV** is an abbreviation for **recreational vehicle**. [mainly AM] ❏ *...a group of RVs pulled over on the side of the highway.*

in BRIT, usually use **camper**

Rx /ɑːr ɛks/ (Rxs) ◼ N-COUNT An **Rx** is a doctor's prescription. [AM] ❏ *...an Rx for a mild painkiller.* ◼ N-COUNT An **Rx** is a solution to a problem. [AM] ❏ *Rx sought for overtaxed parks.*

rye /raɪ/ ◼ N-UNCOUNT **Rye** is a cereal grown in cold countries. Its grains can be used to make flour, bread, or other foods. ❏ *One of the first crops that I grew when we came here was rye.*
◼ N-UNCOUNT **Rye** is bread made from rye. [AM] ❏ *I was eating ham and Swiss cheese on rye.*

rye bread N-UNCOUNT **Rye bread** is brown bread made with rye flour. ❏ *...two slices of rye bread.*

rye grass also **ryegrass** N-UNCOUNT **Rye grass** is a type of grass that is grown for animals such as cows to eat.

Ss

S also s /ɛs/ (S's, s's) N-VAR S is the nineteenth letter of the English alphabet.

SUFFIX

-s
1 is added to a verb to form the third person singular, present tense. *For example, in 'he never **thinks** about it,' the letter **s** at the end of the word '**thinks**' shows that the verb agrees with the third person pronoun '**he**.'*
2 is also added to a noun to form a plural. *For example, in 'her beloved **cats**,' the letter **s** at the end of the word '**cats**' shows that there is more than one cat.*

-'s

Pronounced /-s/ after the consonant sounds /p, t, k, f/ or /θ/, and /-ɪz/ after the consonant sounds /s, z, ʃ, ʒ, tʃ/ or /dʒ/. After other sounds -'s is pronounced /-z/. A final -s' is pronounced in the same way as a final -s.

1 -'s is added to nouns to form possessives. However, with plural nouns ending in -s and sometimes with names ending in -s you form the possessive by adding -'. ❑ *...the chairman's son.* ❑ *...women's rights.* ❑ *...a boys' boarding-school.* ❑ *...Charles' car.* **2** -'s is the usual spoken form of 'is'. It is added to the end of the pronoun or noun which is the subject of the verb. For example, 'he is' and 'she is' can be shortened to 'he's' and 'she's.' **3** -'s is the usual spoken form of 'has,' especially where 'has' is an auxiliary verb. It is added to the end of the pronoun or noun which is the subject of the verb. For example, 'It has gone' can be shortened to 'It's gone.' **4** -'s is sometimes added to numbers, letters, and abbreviations to form plurals, although many people think you should just add -s. ❑ *...bands from the 1990's.* ❑ *...p's and q's.*

Sab|bath /sæbəθ/ N-PROPER The **Sabbath** is the day of the week when members of some religious groups do not work. The Jewish Sabbath is on Saturday and the Christian Sabbath is on Sunday. ❑ *...a deeply religious man who will not discuss politics on the Sabbath.*

sab|bati|cal /səbætɪkəl/ (sabbaticals) N-COUNT [also on N] A **sabbatical** is a period of time during which someone such as a university teacher can leave their ordinary work and travel or study. ❑ *He took a year's sabbatical from teaching to write a book.*

sa|ber /seɪbər/ (sabers)
in BRIT, use **sabre**

N-COUNT A **saber** is a heavy sword with a curved blade that was used in the past by soldiers on horseback.

saber-rattling
in BRIT, use **sabre-rattling**

N-UNCOUNT If you describe a threat, especially a threat of military action, as **saber-rattling**, you do not believe that the threat will actually be carried out. ❑ *It is too early to say whether the threats are mere saber-rattling.*

sa|ble /seɪbəl/ (sables) N-COUNT A **sable** is a small, furry animal with valued fur. • N-UNCOUNT [oft N of N] **Sable** is the fur of a sable. ❑ *...a full-length sable coat.*

sabo|tage /sæbətɑːʒ/ (sabotages, sabotaging, sabotaged)
1 V-T [usu passive] If a machine, railroad line, or bridge **is sabotaged**, it is deliberately damaged or destroyed, for example, in a war or as a protest. ❑ *The main pipeline supplying water was sabotaged by rebels.* • N-UNCOUNT **Sabotage** is also a noun. ❑ *The bombing was a spectacular act of sabotage.* **2** V-T If someone **sabotages** a plan or a meeting, they deliberately prevent it from being successful. ❑ *He accused the opposition of doing everything they could to sabotage the election.*

sabo|teur /sæbətɜr/ (saboteurs) N-COUNT A **saboteur** is a person who deliberately damages or destroys things such as machines, railroad lines, and bridges in order to weaken an enemy or to make a protest. ❑ *The saboteurs had planned to bomb buses and offices.*

sa|bre /seɪbər/ [BRIT] → see saber

sac /sæk/ (sacs) N-COUNT A **sac** is a small part of an animal's body, shaped like a little bag. It contains air, liquid, or some other substance. ❑ *The lungs consist of millions of tiny air sacs.*

sac|cha|rin /sækərɪn/ also **saccharine** N-UNCOUNT **Saccharin** is a very sweet chemical substance that some people use instead of sugar, especially when they are trying to lose weight.

sac|cha|rine /sækərɪn, -əraɪn, -ərɪn/ ADJ [usu ADJ n] You describe something as **saccharine** when you find it unpleasantly sweet and sentimental. [DISAPPROVAL] ❑ *...a saccharine sequel to the Peter Pan story.*

sa|chet /sæʃeɪ/ (sachets) N-COUNT A **sachet** is a small, soft bag containing a perfumed powder or other substance placed in drawers to give clothing a pleasant smell. [AM] ❑ *...a lilac sachet.*

sack ♦◇◇ /sæk/ (sacks, sacking, sacked) **1** N-COUNT A **sack** is a large bag made of thick paper or rough material. Sacks are used to carry or store things such as food or groceries. ❑ *...a sack of potatoes.* **2** V-T If your employers **sack** you, they tell you that you can no longer work for them because you have done something that they did not like or because your work was not good enough. [mainly BRIT, INFORMAL]

in AM, usually use **fire**

• N-SING **Sack** is also a noun.

sack|cloth /sækklɒθ/ **1** N-UNCOUNT **Sackcloth** is rough woven material that is used to make sacks. ❑ *He kept the club wrapped in sackcloth.* **2** N-UNCOUNT If you talk about **sackcloth** or **sackcloth and ashes** you are referring to an exaggerated attempt by someone to show that they are sorry for doing something wrong.

sack|ful /sækfʊl/ (sackfuls) N-COUNT [oft N of n] A **sackful** is the amount of something that a sack contains or could contain. ❑ *...a sackful of presents.*

sack|ing /sækɪŋ/ (sackings) **1** N-UNCOUNT **Sacking** is rough woven material that is used to make sacks. ❑ *...a piece of sacking.* **2** N-COUNT A **sacking** is when an employer tells a worker to leave their job. [mainly BRIT, INFORMAL]

in AM, usually use **firing**

sac|ra|ment /sækrəmənt/ (sacraments) **1** N-COUNT A **sacrament** is a Christian religious ceremony such as communion, baptism, or marriage. ❑ *...the holy sacrament of baptism.* **2** N-SING [the N] In the Roman Catholic church, **the Sacrament** is the holy bread eaten at the Eucharist. In the Anglican church, **the Sacrament** is the holy bread and wine taken at Holy Communion.

sac|ra|men|tal /sækrəməntəl/ **1** ADJ Something that is **sacramental** is connected with a Christian religious ceremony. ❑ *...the sacramental wine.* **2** ADJ **Sacramental** is used to describe something that is considered holy or religious. ❑ *...her view that music is a sacramental art.*

sa|cred /seɪkrɪd/ **1** ADJ Something that is **sacred** is believed to be holy and to have a special connection with God. ❑ *The owl is sacred for many Native American people.* **2** ADJ [ADJ n] Something connected with religion or used in religious ceremonies is described as **sacred**. ❑ *...sacred art.* **3** ADJ You can describe something as **sacred** when it is regarded as too important to be changed or interfered with. ❑ *My memories are sacred.*

sa|cred cow (sacred cows) N-COUNT If you describe a belief, custom, or institution as a **sacred cow**, you disapprove of people treating it with too much respect and being afraid to criticize or question it. [DISAPPROVAL] ❑ *Public schools are often viewed as infallible sacred cows.*

sac|ri|fice ✦✧✧ /sækrɪfaɪs/ (sacrifices, sacrificing, sacrificed) **1** V-T To **sacrifice** an animal or person means to kill them in a special religious ceremony as an offering to a god. ❑ *The priest sacrificed a chicken.* • N-COUNT **Sacrifice** is also a noun. ❑ *...animal sacrifices to the gods.* **2** V-T If you **sacrifice** something that is valuable or important, you give it up, usually to obtain something else for yourself or for other people. ❑ *They sacrificed family life to their careers.* ❑ *Kitty Aldridge has sacrificed all for her first film.* • N-VAR **Sacrifice** is also a noun. ❑ *She made many sacrifices to get Anita a good education.*

sac|ri|fi|cial /sækrɪfɪʃᵊl/ ADJ [ADJ n] **Sacrificial** means connected with or used in a sacrifice. ❑ *...the sacrificial altar.*

sac|ri|fi|cial lamb (sacrificial lambs) N-COUNT If you refer to someone as a **sacrificial lamb**, you mean that they have been blamed unfairly for something they did not do, usually in order to protect another more powerful person or group. ❑ *He was a sacrificial lamb to a system that destroyed him.*

sac|ri|lege /sækrɪlɪdʒ/ **1** N-UNCOUNT [also a N] **Sacrilege** is behavior that shows great disrespect for a holy place or object. ❑ *Stealing from a place of worship was regarded as sacrilege.* **2** N-UNCOUNT [also a N] You can use **sacrilege** to refer to disrespect that is shown for someone who is widely admired or for a belief that is widely accepted. ❑ *It is a sacrilege to offend democracy.*

sac|ri|legious /sækrɪlɪdʒəs, -lɪdʒəs/ ADJ If someone's behavior or actions are **sacrilegious**, they show great disrespect toward something holy or toward something that people think should be respected. ❑ *A number of churches were looted and sacrilegious acts committed.*

sac|ris|ty /sækrɪsti/ (sacristies) N-COUNT A **sacristy** is the room in a church where the priest or minister changes into their official clothes and where holy objects are kept.

sac|ro|sanct /sækroʊsæŋkt/ ADJ [usu v-link ADJ] If you describe something as **sacrosanct**, you consider it to be special and are unwilling to see it criticized or changed. ❑ *Freedom of the press is sacrosanct.*

sad ✦✦✧ /sæd/ (sadder, saddest) **1** ADJ If you are **sad**, you feel unhappy, usually because something has happened that you do not like. ❑ *The relationship had been important to me and its loss left me feeling sad and empty.* ❑ *I'm sad that Julie's marriage is on the verge of splitting up.* • **sad|ly** ADV ❑ *...a gallant man who will be sadly missed by all his comrades.* • **sad|ness** N-UNCOUNT ❑ *It is with a mixture of sadness and joy that I say farewell.* **2** ADJ **Sad** stories and **sad** news make you feel sad. ❑ *...a desperately humorous, impossibly sad novel.* **3** ADJ A **sad** event or situation is unfortunate or undesirable. ❑ *It's a sad truth that children are the biggest victims of passive smoking.* • **sad|ly** ADV ❑ *Sadly, bamboo plants die after flowering.* **4** ADJ If you describe someone as **sad**, you do not have any respect for them and think their behavior or ideas are ridiculous. [INFORMAL, DISAPPROVAL] ❑ *...sad old bikers and youngsters who think that Jim Morrison is God.*

SAD /sæd/ N-UNCOUNT **SAD** is an abbreviation for **seasonal affective disorder**.

sad|den /sædᵊn/ (saddens, saddening, saddened) V-T [no cont] If something **saddens** you, it makes you feel sad. ❑ *The cruelty in the world saddens me incredibly.* • **sad|dened** ADJ [v-link ADJ] ❑ *He was disappointed and saddened that legal argument had stopped the trial.*

sad|dle /sædᵊl/ (saddles, saddling, saddled) **1** N-COUNT A **saddle** is a leather seat that you put on the back of an animal so that you can ride the animal. **2** V-T If you **saddle** a horse, you put a saddle on it so that you can ride it. ❑ *Why don't we saddle a couple of horses and go for a ride?* • PHRASAL VERB **Saddle up** means the same as **saddle**. ❑ *I want to be gone from here as soon as we can saddle up.* **3** N-COUNT A **saddle** is a seat on a bicycle or motorcycle. **4** → See also color supplement

saddle|bag /sædᵊlbæg/ (saddlebags) **1** N-COUNT A **saddlebag** is a bag fastened to the saddle of a bicycle or motorcycle, or the saddle of a horse. **2** → See also color supplement

sad|dler /sædlər/ (saddlers) N-COUNT A **saddler** is a person who makes, repairs, and sells saddles and other equipment for riding horses.

sad|dlery /sædləri/ N-UNCOUNT Saddles and other leather goods made by a saddler can be referred to as **saddlery**.

sad|ism /seɪdɪzəm, sæd-/ N-UNCOUNT **Sadism** is a type of behavior in which a person obtains pleasure from hurting other people and making them suffer physically or mentally. ❑ *Psychoanalysts tend to regard both sadism and masochism as arising from childhood deprivation.* • **sad|ist** /seɪdɪst, sæd-/ (sadists) N-COUNT ❑ *The man was a sadist who tortured animals and people.*

sa|dis|tic /sədɪstɪk/ ADJ A **sadistic** person obtains pleasure from hurting other people and making them suffer physically or mentally. ❑ *The prisoners rioted against mistreatment by sadistic guards.*

sado|maso|chism /seɪdoʊmæsəkɪzəm/ also **sado-masochism** N-UNCOUNT **Sadomasochism** is the enjoyment of hurting people and being hurt. ❑ *...the sadomasochism of the Marquis de Sade.* • **sado|maso|chist** (sadomasochists) N-COUNT ❑ *...an island resort where sadomasochists can act out their sexual fantasies.*

sado|maso|chis|tic /seɪdoʊmæsəkɪstɪk/ also **sado-masochistic** ADJ [usu ADJ n] Something that is **sadomasochistic** is connected with the practice of sadomasochism. ❑ *...a sadomasochistic relationship.*

s.a.e. /ɛs eɪ iː/ (s.a.e.s) N-COUNT An **s.a.e.** is the same as an **SASE**. [BRIT]

sa|fa|ri /səfɑri/ (safaris) N-COUNT [also on N] A **safari** is a trip to observe or hunt wild animals, especially in East Africa. ❑ *He'd like to go on safari to photograph snakes and tigers.*

sa|fa|ri park (safari parks) N-COUNT A **safari park** is a large enclosed area of land where wild animals, such as lions and elephants, live freely. People can pay to drive through the park and look at the animals.

sa|fa|ri suit (safari suits) N-COUNT A **safari suit** is a casual suit made from a light-colored material such as linen or cotton. Safari suits are usually worn in hot weather.

safe ✦✦✧ /seɪf/ (safer, safest, safes) **1** ADJ Something that is **safe** does not cause physical harm or danger. ❑ *Officials arrived to assess whether it is safe to bring emergency food supplies into the city.* ❑ *Most foods that we eat are safe for birds.* **2** ADJ [v-link ADJ] If a person or thing is **safe** from something, they cannot be harmed or damaged by it. ❑ *They are safe from the violence that threatened them.* **3** ADJ [v-link ADJ] If you are **safe**, you have not been harmed, or you are not in danger of being harmed. ❑ *Where is Sophy? Is she safe?* • **safe|ly** ADV [ADV with v] ❑ *All 140 guests were brought out of the building safely by firemen.* **4** ADJ A **safe** place is one where it is unlikely that any harm, damage, or unpleasant things will happen to the people or things that are there. ❑ *The continuing tension has prompted more than half the inhabitants of the refugee camp to flee to safer areas.* • **safe|ly** ADV [ADV after v] ❑ *The banker keeps the money tucked safely under his bed.* **5** ADJ [ADJ n] If people or things have a **safe** trip, they reach their destination without harm, damage, or unpleasant things happening to them. ❑ *I told him good night, come back any time, and have a safe trip home.* • **safe|ly** ADV ❑ *The space shuttle returned safely today from a 10-day mission.* **6** ADJ [ADJ n] If you are at a **safe** distance from something or someone, you are far enough away from them to avoid any danger, harm, or unpleasant effects. ❑ *I shall conceal myself at a safe distance from the battlefield.* **7** ADJ If something you have or expect to obtain is **safe**, you cannot lose it or be prevented from having it. ❑ *We as consumers need to feel confident that our jobs are safe before we will spend spare cash.* **8** ADJ A **safe** course of action is one in which there is very little risk of loss or failure. ❑ *Electricity shares are still a safe investment.* • **safe|ly** ADV ❑ *We reveal only as much information as we can safely risk at a given time.* **9** ADJ If it is **safe** to say or assume something, you can say it with very little risk of being wrong. ☐ *I think it is safe to say that very few students expend the effort to do quality work in school.* ● **safe|ly** ADV [ADV before v] ☐ *I think you can safely say she will not be appearing in another of my films.* **10** N-COUNT A **safe** is a strong metal cabinet with special locks, in which you keep money, jewelry, or other valuable things. ☐ *The files are now in a safe to which only he has the key.* **11** → see also **safely 12** PHRASE If you say that a person or thing is **in safe hands**, or is **safe** in someone's **hands**, you mean that they are being taken care of by a reliable person and will not be harmed. ☐ *I had a huge responsibility to ensure these packets remained in safe hands.* **13** PHRASE If you **play safe** or **play it safe**, you do not take any risks. ☐ *If you want to play safe, cut down on the amount of salt you eat.* **14** PHRASE If you say you are doing something **to be on the safe side**, you mean that you are doing it in case something undesirable happens, even though this may be unnecessary. ☐ *You might still want to go for an X-ray, however, just to be on the safe side.* **15** PHRASE If you say '**it's better to be safe than sorry**,' you are advising someone to take action in order to avoid possible unpleasant consequences later, even if this seems unnecessary. ☐ *Don't be afraid to have this checked by a doctor – better safe than sorry!* **16** PHRASE You say that someone is **safe and sound** when they are still alive or unharmed after being in danger. ☐ *All I'm hoping for is that wherever Trevor is he will come home safe and sound.* **17** → See feature box at **drive**

USAGE

safe
When **safe** is used to describe people, it is never used in front of a noun. Don't say, for example, 'the safe children.' You can say that you are **safe from** something or someone to mean that you cannot be harmed by them. *They want to keep their families safe from crime.*

safe area (safe areas) N-COUNT If part of a country that is involved in a war is declared to be a **safe area**, neutral forces will try to keep peace there so that it is safe for people. ☐ *The UN declared it a safe area.*

safe con|duct also **safe-conduct** N-UNCOUNT [also a N] If you are given **safe conduct**, the authorities officially allow you to travel somewhere, guaranteeing that you will not be arrested or harmed while doing so. ☐ *Her family was given safe conduct to the US when civil war broke out.*

safe de|pos|it box (safe deposit boxes) N-COUNT A **safe deposit box** is a small box, usually kept in a special room in a bank, in which you can store valuable objects.

safe|guard /seɪfgɑːd/ (safeguards, safeguarding, safeguarded) **1** V-T To **safeguard** something or someone means to protect them from being harmed, lost, or badly treated. [FORMAL] ☐ *They will press for international action to safeguard the ozone layer.* **2** N-COUNT A **safeguard** is a law, rule, or measure intended to prevent someone or something from being harmed. ☐ *As an additional safeguard against weeds we can always use an underlay of heavy duty polyethylene.*

safe ha|ven (safe havens) **1** N-COUNT If part of a country is declared a **safe haven**, people who need to escape from a dangerous situation such as a war can go there and be protected. ☐ *Countries overwhelmed by the human tide of refugees want safe havens set up at once.* **2** N-UNCOUNT If a country provides **safe haven** for people from another country who have been in danger, it allows them to stay there under its official protection. [AM] ☐ *Some Democrats support granting the Haitians temporary safe haven in the U.S.* **3** N-COUNT A **safe haven** is a place, a situation, or an activity which provides people with an opportunity to escape from things that they find unpleasant or worrying. ☐ *...the idea of the family as a safe haven from the brutal outside world.*

safe house (safe houses) also **safe-house** N-COUNT You can refer to a building as a **safe house** when it is used as a place where someone can stay and be protected. Safe houses are often used by spies, criminals, and the police. ☐ *...a farm which operates as a safe house for criminals on the run.*

safe|keep|ing /seɪfkiːpɪŋ/ N-UNCOUNT [usu for N] If something is given to you for **safekeeping**, it is given to you so that you will make sure that it is not harmed or stolen. ☐ *Hampton had been given the bills for safekeeping by a business partner.*

safe|ly /seɪfli/ **1** ADV If something is done **safely**, it is done in a way that makes it unlikely that anyone will be harmed. ☐ *The waste is safely locked away until it is no longer radioactive.* ☐ *"Drive safely," he said and waved goodbye.* **2** ADV You also use **safely** to say that there is no risk of a situation being changed. ☐ *Once events are safely in the past, this idea seems to become less alarming.* **3** → see also **safe**

safe pas|sage N-UNCOUNT [also a N, oft N for/to n] If someone is given **safe passage**, they are allowed to go somewhere safely, without being attacked or arrested. ☐ *They were unwilling, or unable, to guarantee safe passage from the city to the aircraft.*

safe sex also **safer sex** N-UNCOUNT **Safe sex** is sexual activity in which people protect themselves against the risk of sexually transmitted diseases, usually by using condoms. ☐ *You must practice safe sex and know your partner well.*

safe|ty ♦♦◇ /seɪfti/ **1** N-UNCOUNT **Safety** is the state of being safe from harm or danger. ☐ *The report goes on to make a number of recommendations to improve safety on aircraft.* **2** N-UNCOUNT If you reach **safety**, you reach a place where you are safe from danger. ☐ *He stumbled through smoke and fumes to pull her to safety.* ☐ *People scurried for safety as the firing started.* **3** N-SING If you are concerned about the **safety** of something, you are concerned that it might be harmful or dangerous. ☐ *Consumers are showing growing concern about the safety of the food they buy.* **4** N-SING If you are concerned for someone's **safety**, you are concerned that they might be in danger. ☐ *There is grave concern for the safety of witnesses.* **5** ADJ [ADJ n] **Safety** features or measures are intended to make something less dangerous. ☐ *The built-in safety device compensates for a fall in water pressure.* **6** → See feature box at **drive**

safe|ty belt (safety belts) also **safety-belt** N-COUNT A **safety belt** is a strap attached to a seat in a car or airplane. You fasten it around your body and it stops you from being thrown forward if there is an accident. ☐ *Please return to your seats and fasten your safety belts.*

safe|ty catch (safety catches) N-COUNT The **safety catch** on a gun is a device that stops you firing the gun accidentally. ☐ *Eddie slipped the safety catch on his automatic back into place.*

safe|ty glass N-UNCOUNT **Safety glass** is very strong glass that does not break into sharp pieces if it is hit.

safe|ty net (safety nets) **1** N-COUNT A **safety net** is something that you can rely on to help you if you get into a difficult situation. ☐ *Welfare is the only real safety net for low-income workers.* **2** N-COUNT In a circus, a **safety net** is a large net that is placed below performers on a high wire or trapeze in order to catch them and prevent them being injured if they fall off.

safe|ty of|fic|er (safety officers) N-COUNT The **safety officer** in a company or an organization is the person who is responsible for the safety of the people who work or visit there. ☐ *Organizers had consulted widely with police and safety officers to ensure tight security.*

safe|ty pin (safety pins) N-COUNT A **safety pin** is a bent metal pin used for fastening things together. The point of the pin has a cover so that when the pin is closed it cannot hurt anyone. ☐ *...trousers which were held together with safety pins.*

safe|ty valve (safety valves) **1** N-COUNT A **safety valve** is a device which allows liquids or gases to escape from a machine when the pressure inside it becomes too great. ☐ *Residents heard an enormous bang as a safety valve on the boiler failed.* **2** N-COUNT A **safety valve** is something that allows you to release strong feelings without hurting yourself or others. ☐ *Crying is a natural safety valve.*

safe|ty zone (safety zones) also **safety island** N-COUNT A **safety zone** is a place in the middle of a road crossing where you can wait before you cross the other half of the road. [AM]

saf|fron /sæfrən/ **1** N-UNCOUNT **Saffron** is a yellowish-orange powder obtained from a flower and used to give flavor and coloring to some foods. ☐ *...saffron rice.* **2** COLOR **Saffron** is a yellowish-orange color. ☐ *...a Buddhist in saffron robes.*

sag /sæg/ (sags, sagging, sagged) V-I When something **sags**, it hangs down loosely or sinks downward in the middle. ☐ *The shirt's cuffs won't sag and lose their shape after washing.*

saga /sɑːgə/ (sagas) **1** N-COUNT A **saga** is a long story, account, or sequence of events. ☐ *...a 600 page saga about 18th* century slavery. **2** N-COUNT A **saga** is a long story composed in medieval times in Norway or Iceland. ❏ ...*a Nordic saga of giants and trolls.*

sa|ga|cious /səgeɪʃəs/ ADJ A **sagacious** person is intelligent and has the ability to make good decisions. [FORMAL] ❏ ...*a sagacious leader.*

sa|gac|ity /səgæsɪti/ N-UNCOUNT **Sagacity** is the quality of being sagacious. [FORMAL] ❏ ...*a man of great sagacity and immense experience.*

sage /seɪdʒ/ N-UNCOUNT **Sage** is a herb used in cooking.

sag|gy /sægi/ (**saggier, saggiest**) ADJ If you describe something as **saggy**, you mean that it has become less firm over a period of time and become unattractive. ❏ *Is the mattress lumpy and saggy?*

Sag|it|ta|rius /sædʒɪteəriəs/ **1** N-UNCOUNT **Sagittarius** is one of the twelve signs of the zodiac. Its symbol is a creature that is half horse, half man, shooting an arrow. People who are born approximately between the 22nd of November and the 21st of December come under this sign. **2** N-SING [*a* N] A **Sagittarius** is a person whose sign of the zodiac is Sagittarius.

sago /seɪgoʊ/ N-UNCOUNT **Sago** is a white substance obtained from the trunk of some palm trees. Sago is used for making sweet puddings.

sa|hib /sɑɪb, -ɪb, -hɪb/ (**sahibs**) N-TITLE; N-COUNT **Sahib** is a term used by some people in India to address or to refer to a man in a position of authority. Sahib was used especially for government officials in the period of British rule. [POLITENESS]

said /sɛd/ **Said** is the past tense and past participle of **say**.

sail ✦◇◇ /seɪl/ (**sails, sailing, sailed**) **1** N-COUNT **Sails** are large pieces of material attached to the mast of a ship. The wind blows against the sails and pushes the ship along. ❏ *The white sails billow with the breezes they catch.* **2** V-I You say a ship **sails** when it moves over the sea. ❏ *The trawler had sailed from the port of Zeebrugge.* **3** V-T/V-I If you **sail** a boat or if a boat **sails**, it moves across water using its sails. ❏ *His crew's job is to sail the boat.* ❏ *I'd buy a big boat and sail around the world.* **4** → see also **sailing 5** PHRASE When a ship **sets sail**, it leaves a port. ❏ *He loaded his vessel with another cargo and set sail.* **6** → See feature box at **boat**
▸ **sail through** PHRASAL VERB If someone or something **sails through** a difficult situation or experience, they deal with it easily and successfully. ❏ *While she sailed through her exams, he struggled.*

sail|boat /seɪlboʊt/ (**sailboats**) N-COUNT A **sailboat** is a boat with sails. [mainly AM]

in BRIT, use **sailing boat**

sail|cloth /seɪlklɔθ/ **1** N-UNCOUNT **Sailcloth** is a strong heavy cloth that is used for making things such as sails or tents. ❏ *The mainsails are hand-cut and sewn from real sailcloth.* **2** N-UNCOUNT **Sailcloth** is a light canvas material that is used for making clothes. ❏ ...*red sailcloth trousers.*

sail|ing /seɪlɪŋ/ (**sailings**) **1** N-UNCOUNT **Sailing** is the activity or sport of sailing boats. ❏ *There was swimming and sailing down on the lake.* **2** N-COUNT **Sailings** are trips made by a ship carrying passengers. ❏ *Ferry companies are providing extra sailings from Calais.* **3** PHRASE If you say that a task was not all **plain sailing**, you mean that it was not very easy. ❏ *Pregnancy wasn't all plain sailing and once again there were problems.*

sail|ing boat (**sailing boats**) also **sailing-boat** N-COUNT A **sailing boat** is the same as a **sailboat**. [BRIT]

sail|ing ship (**sailing ships**) **1** N-COUNT A **sailing ship** is a large ship with sails, especially of the kind that were used to carry passengers or cargo. ❏ *American clippers were the ultimate sailing ships.* **2** → See also color supplement

sail|or /seɪlər/ (**sailors**) N-COUNT A **sailor** is someone who works on a ship or sails a boat. ❏ ...*sailors, marines and Coast Guard personnel.*

saint ✦◇◇ /seɪnt/ (**saints**) **1** N-COUNT; N-TITLE A **saint** is someone who has died and been officially recognized and honored by the Christian church because his or her life was a perfect example of the way Christians should live. ❏ *Every parish was named after a saint.* **2** N-COUNT If you refer to a living person as a **saint**, you mean that they are extremely kind, patient, and unselfish. [APPROVAL] ❏ *My girlfriend Geraldine is a saint to put up with me.*

saint|hood /seɪnthʊd/ N-UNCOUNT [usu supp N] **Sainthood** is the state of being a saint. ❏ *His elevation to sainthood is entirely justified.*

saint|ly /seɪntli/ (**saintlier, saintliest**) ADJ A **saintly** person behaves in a very good or very holy way. [APPROVAL] ❏ *She has been saintly in her self-restraint.*

sake ✦◇◇ /seɪk/ (**sakes**) **1** PHRASE If you do something **for the sake of** something, you do it for that purpose or in order to achieve that result. You can also say that you do it **for** something's **sake**. ❏ *Let's assume for the sake of argument that we manage to build a satisfactory database.* ❏ *For the sake of historical accuracy, please permit us to state the true facts.* **2** PHRASE If you do something **for** its **own sake**, you do it because you want to, or because you enjoy it, and not for any other reason. You can also talk about, for example, **art for art's sake** or **sport for sport's sake**. ❏ *Economic change for its own sake did not appeal to him.* **3** PHRASE When you do something **for** someone's **sake**, you do it in order to help them or make them happy. ❏ *I trust you to do a good job for Stan's sake.* **4** PHRASE Some people use expressions such as **for God's sake, for heaven's sake, for goodness' sake**, or **for Pete's sake** in order to express annoyance or impatience, or to add force to a question or request. The expressions 'for God's sake' and 'for Christ's sake' could cause offense. [INFORMAL, FEELINGS] ❏ *For goodness' sake, why didn't you call me?*

saké /sɑki, -keɪ/ also **sake** N-UNCOUNT **Saké** is a Japanese alcoholic drink that is made from rice.

sa|laam /səlɑm/ (**salaams, salaaming, salaamed**) **1** V-I When someone **salaams**, they bow with their right hand on their forehead. This is used as a formal and respectful way of greeting someone in India and Muslim countries. ❏ *He looked from one to the other of them, then salaamed and left.* **2** CONVENTION Some Muslims greet people by saying 'Salaam.'

sal|able /seɪləbəl/ → see **saleable**

sa|la|cious /səleɪʃəs/ ADJ [usu ADJ n] If you describe something such as a book or joke as **salacious**, you think that it deals with sexual matters in an unnecessarily detailed way. ❏ *The newspapers once again filled their columns with salacious details.*

sal|ad /sæləd/ (**salads**) N-VAR A **salad** is a mixture of cold foods such as lettuce, tomatoes, or cold cooked potatoes, cut up and mixed with a dressing. It is often served with other food as part of a meal. ❏ ...*a salad of tomato, onion and cucumber.*

sal|ad bowl (**salad bowls**) N-COUNT A **salad bowl** is a large bowl from which salad is served at a meal.

sal|ad dress|ing (**salad dressings**) N-MASS **Salad dressing** is a mixture of oil, vinegar, herbs, and other flavorings, which you pour over a salad. ❏ ...*low-calorie salad dressings.*

sala|man|der /sæləmændər/ (**salamanders**) N-COUNT A **salamander** is an animal that looks rather like a lizard, and that can live both on land and in water.

sa|la|mi /səlɑmi/ (**salamis**) N-VAR **Salami** is a type of strong-flavored sausage. It is usually thinly sliced and eaten cold.

sala|ried /sælərid/ ADJ **Salaried** people receive a salary from their job. [BUSINESS] ❏ ...*salaried employees.*

sala|ry ✦◇◇ /sæləri/ (**salaries**) N-VAR A **salary** is the money that someone earns each month or year from their employer. [BUSINESS] ❏ *The lawyer was paid a huge salary.*

COLLOCATIONS

salary
NOUN
noun + **salary**: base; executive, graduate
adjective + **salary**: annual, average, basic, monthly; final, starting; competitive, decent, six-figure, top
verb + **salary**: draw, earn, receive; increase, negotiate, pay

---

SYNONYMS

salary
NOUN
pay: ...*their complaints about their pay and conditions.*
income: *Many families with low incomes will be unable to afford to buy their own home.*
wage: *His wages have gone up.*
earnings: *Average weekly earnings rose by 1.5% in July.*

sale /seɪl/ (sales) **1** N-SING The **sale** of goods is the act of selling them for money. ❑ *Efforts were made to limit the sale of alcohol.* ❑ *...a proposed arms sale to Saudi Arabia.* **2** N-PLURAL The **sales** of a product are the quantity of it that is sold. ❑ *The newspaper has sales of 1.72 million.* ❑ *...the huge Christmas sales of computer games.* **3** N-PLURAL The part of a company that deals with **sales** deals with selling the company's products. ❑ *Until 2013 he worked in sales and marketing.* **4** N-COUNT A **sale** is an occasion when a store sells things at less than their normal price. ❑ *...a pair of jeans bought half-price in a sale.* **5** N-COUNT A **sale** is an event when goods are sold to the person who offers the highest price. ❑ *The Old Master was bought by dealers at the Christie's sale.* **6** PHRASE If something is **for sale**, it is being offered to people to buy. ❑ *The yacht is for sale at a price of 1.7 million dollars.* **7** PHRASE If products in a store are **on sale**, they can be bought for less than their normal price. ❑ *A good shopper doesn't just buy things because they're on sale.* **8** PHRASE Products that are **on sale** can be bought. ❑ *English textbooks and dictionaries are on sale everywhere.* ❑ *Tickets go on sale this week.* **9** PHRASE If a property or company is **up for sale**, its owner is trying to sell it. ❑ *The mansion has been put up for sale.*

sale|able /ˈseɪləbəl/ also **salable** ADJ Something that is **saleable** is easy to sell to people. ❑ *The Salvation Army shops depend on regular supplies of saleable items.*

sales|clerk /ˈseɪlzklɜrk/ (salesclerks) also **sales clerk** N-COUNT A **salesclerk** is a person who works in a store selling things to customers and helping them to find what they want. [AM]

in BRIT, use **shop assistant**

sales force (sales forces) also **salesforce** N-COUNT A company's **sales force** is all the people that work for that company selling its products. [BUSINESS] ❑ *His sales force is signing up schools at the rate of 25 a day.*

sales|girl /ˈseɪlzgɜrl/ (salesgirls) N-COUNT A **salesgirl** is a young woman who sells things, especially in a store. Many women prefer to be called a 'saleswoman' or a 'salesperson' rather than a 'salesgirl.' [OLD-FASHIONED]

sales|man /ˈseɪlzmən/ (salesmen) N-COUNT A **salesman** is a man whose job is to sell things, especially directly to stores or other businesses on behalf of a company. ❑ *...an insurance salesman.*

sales|man|ship /ˈseɪlzmənʃɪp/ N-UNCOUNT **Salesmanship** is the skill of persuading people to buy things. ❑ *I was captured by her brilliant salesmanship.*

sales|person /ˈseɪlzpɜrsən/ (salespeople or salespersons) N-COUNT A **salesperson** is a person who sells things, either in a store or directly to customers on behalf of a company. [BUSINESS] ❑ *They will usually send a salesperson out to measure your bathroom.*

sales pitch (sales pitches) N-COUNT A salesperson's **sales pitch** is what they say in order to persuade someone to buy something from them. ❑ *His sales pitch was smooth and convincing.*

sales|room /ˈseɪlzrum/ (salesrooms) N-COUNT A **salesroom** is a place where things are sold by auction. [AM]

in BRIT, use **saleroom**

sales slip (sales slips) N-COUNT A **sales slip** is a piece of paper that you are given when you buy something in a store, which shows when you bought it and how much you paid. [AM]

sales tax (sales taxes) N-VAR The **sales tax** on things that you buy is the percentage of money that you pay to the local or state government. [BUSINESS] ❑ *The state's unpopular sales tax on snacks has ended.*

sales|wom|an /ˈseɪlzwʊmən/ (saleswomen) N-COUNT A **saleswoman** is a woman who sells things, either in a store or directly to customers on behalf of a company. [BUSINESS] ❑ *...an insurance saleswoman.*

sali|ent /ˈseɪliənt, ˈseɪlyənt/ **1** ADJ The **salient** points or facts of a situation are the most important ones. [FORMAL] ❑ *He read the salient facts quickly.* **2** → See feature box at **debate**

sali|nate /ˈsælɪneɪt/ (salinates, salinating, salinated) VERB To **salinate** something means to add salt to it. ❑ *The seahorse was reintroduced to salinated water gradually to avoid shocking it.*

sali|na|tion /ˌsælɪˈneɪʃən/ N-UNCOUNT **Salination** is a process in which salt is added to something. ❑ *...the salination of fresh water supplies.*

sa|line /ˈseɪlɪn/ **1** ADJ [usu ADJ n] A **saline** substance or liquid contains salt. ❑ *...a saline solution.* **2** → See feature box at **experiment**

sa|li|va /səˈlaɪvə/ N-UNCOUNT **Saliva** is the watery liquid that forms in your mouth and helps you to chew and digest food. ❑ *He noticed a lot of saliva settling in his mouth.*

sali|vary gland /ˈsælɪveri glænd/ (salivary glands) N-COUNT [usu pl] Your **salivary glands** are the glands that produce saliva in your mouth.

sali|vate /ˈsælɪveɪt/ (salivates, salivating, salivated) V-I When people or animals **salivate**, they produce a lot of saliva in their mouth, often as a result of seeing or smelling food. ❑ *Any dog will salivate when presented with food.*

sal|low /ˈsæloʊ/ ADJ If a person has **sallow** skin, their skin, especially on their face, is a pale yellowish color and looks unhealthy. ❑ *She had lank hair and sallow skin.*

sal|ly /ˈsæli/ (sallies, sallying, sallied) **1** N-COUNT **Sallies** are clever and amusing remarks. [LITERARY] ❑ *He had thus far succeeded in fending off my conversational sallies.* **2** V-I If someone **sallies** forth or **sallies** somewhere, they go out into a rather difficult, dangerous, or unpleasant situation in a brave or confident way. [LITERARY] ❑ *...worrying about her when she sallies forth on her first date.* ❑ *Tamara would sally out on bitterly cold nights.* • N-COUNT **Sally** is also a noun. ❑ *...their first sallies outside the student world.*

salm|on /ˈsæmən/ (salmon)

Salmon is both the singular and the plural form.

N-COUNT A **salmon** is a large silver-colored fish. • N-UNCOUNT **Salmon** is the orangey-pink flesh of this fish which is eaten as food. It is often smoked and eaten raw. ❑ *He gave them a splendid lunch of smoked salmon.*

sal|mo|nel|la /ˌsælməˈnelə/ N-UNCOUNT **Salmonella** is a disease caused by bacteria in food. You can also refer to the bacteria itself as **salmonella**. ❑ *He was suffering from salmonella poisoning.*

salm|on pink COLOR Something that is **salmon pink** or **salmon** is the orangey-pink color of a salmon's flesh.

sa|lon /səˈlɒn/ (salons) N-COUNT A **salon** is a place where people have their hair cut or colored, or have beauty treatments. ❑ *...a new hair salon.*

sa|loon /səˈlun/ (saloons) N-COUNT A **saloon** is a place where alcoholic drinks are sold and drunk. [AM, OLD-FASHIONED] ❑ *In the saloon, he drank whiskey and let his eyes become accustomed to the dimness.*

sal|sa /ˈsɑlsə/ (salsas) **1** N-MASS **Salsa** is a hot, spicy sauce made from onions and tomatoes, usually eaten with Mexican or Spanish food. **2** N-UNCOUNT **Salsa** is a type of dance music especially popular in Latin America. ❑ *A band played salsa, and the crowd danced wildly.*

salt /sɔlt/ (salts, salting, salted) **1** N-UNCOUNT **Salt** is a strong-tasting substance, in the form of white powder or crystals, which is used to improve the flavor of food or to preserve it. Salt occurs naturally in sea water. ❑ *Season lightly with salt and pepper.* **2** V-T When you **salt** food, you add salt to it. ❑ *Salt the stock to your taste and leave it simmering very gently.* • **salt|ed** ADJ ❑ *Put a pan of salted water on to boil.* **3** N-COUNT **Salts** are substances that are formed when an acid reacts with an alkali. ❑ *The rock is rich in mineral salts.* **4** PHRASE If you **take** something **with a grain of salt**, you do not believe that it is completely accurate or true. ❑ *You have to take these findings with a grain of salt because respondents tend to give the answers they feel they should.* **5** PHRASE If you say, for example, that any doctor **worth** his or her **salt** would do something, you mean that any doctor who was good at his or her job or who deserved respect would do it. ❑ *No golf teacher worth his salt would ever recommend that you grip the club tightly.* **6** → See feature box at **experiment**

salt|ed cara|mel (salted caramels) N-VAR **Salted caramel** is a soft sweet food made from heated sugar and butter or cream, with salt added as a flavoring. ❑ *He makes shortbread* topped with salted caramel. ☐ ...chocolate soufflé with salted caramel sauce. ☐ ...a box of salted caramels.

salt|ine /sɔltin/ (saltines) N-COUNT A **saltine** is a thin square cracker with salt baked into its surface. [AM]

salt marsh (salt marshes) N-VAR A **salt marsh** is an area of flat, wet ground which is sometimes covered by salt water or contains areas of salt water.

salt shak|er (salt shakers) N-COUNT A **salt shaker** is a small container for salt, with a hole or holes in the top for shaking salt onto food. [mainly AM]

in BRIT, usually use **salt cellar**

salt|water /sɔltwɔtər/ also **salt water** ◼ N-UNCOUNT **Saltwater** is water, especially from the ocean, which has salt in it. ◪ ADJ [ADJ n] **Saltwater** fish live in water which is salty. **Saltwater** lakes contain salty water. ☐ ...useful information for owners of saltwater fish.

salty /sɔlti/ (saltier, saltiest) ◼ ADJ Something that is **salty** contains salt or tastes of salt. ☐ ...salty foods such as ham and bacon. ◪ ADJ If someone is **salty** about something, they feel bitter or resentful about it. [INFORMAL]

sa|lu|bri|ous /səlubriəs/ ◼ ADJ A place that is **salubrious** is pleasant and healthy. [FORMAL] ☐ ...the salubrious climate of the north. ◪ ADJ Something that is described as **salubrious** is respectable or socially desirable. [FORMAL] ☐ ...the city's less salubrious quarters.

salu|tary /sælyəteri/ ADJ [usu ADJ n] A **salutary** experience is good for you, even though it may seem difficult or unpleasant at first. [FORMAL] ☐ It was a salutary experience to be in the minority.

salu|ta|tion /sælyəteɪʃən/ (salutations) N-COUNT [also in/of N] **Salutation** or a **salutation** is a greeting to someone. [FORMAL] ☐ Jackson nodded a salutation. ☐ The old man moved away, raising his hand in salutation.

sa|lute /səlut/ (salutes, saluting, saluted) ◼ V-T/V-I If you **salute** someone, you greet them or show your respect with a formal sign. Soldiers usually salute officers by raising their right hand so that their fingers touch their forehead. ☐ One of the company stepped out and saluted the General. • N-COUNT [also in N] **Salute** is also a noun. ☐ He gave his salute and left. ◪ V-T To **salute** a person or their achievements means to publicly show or state your admiration for them. ☐ I salute the governor for the leadership role that he is taking.

sal|vage /sælvɪdʒ/ (salvages, salvaging, salvaged) ◼ V-T [usu passive] If something **is salvaged**, someone manages to save it, for example, from a ship that has sunk, or from a building that has been damaged. ☐ The team's first task was to decide what equipment could be salvaged. ◪ N-UNCOUNT **Salvage** is the act of salvaging things from somewhere such as a damaged ship or building. ☐ The salvage operation went on. ◾ N-UNCOUNT The **salvage** from somewhere such as a damaged ship or building is the things that are saved from it. ☐ They climbed up on the rock with their salvage. ◱ V-T If you manage to **salvage** a difficult situation, you manage to get something useful from it so that it is not a complete failure. ☐ Officials tried to salvage the situation. ◲ V-T If you **salvage** something such as your pride or your reputation, you manage to keep it even though it seems likely you will lose it, or you get it back after losing it. ☐ We definitely wanted to salvage some pride for American tennis.

sal|va|tion /sælveɪʃən/ ◼ N-UNCOUNT In Christianity, **salvation** is the fact that Christ has saved a person from evil. ☐ The church's message of salvation has changed the lives of many. ◪ N-UNCOUNT The **salvation** of someone or something is the act of saving them from harm, destruction, or an unpleasant situation. ☐ ...those whose marriages are beyond salvation. ◾ N-SING If someone or something is your **salvation**, they are responsible for saving you from harm, destruction, or an unpleasant situation. ☐ The country's salvation lies in forcing through democratic reforms.

Sal|va|tion Army N-PROPER [the N, N n] The **Salvation Army** is a Christian organization that aims to spread Christianity and care for the poor. Its members wear military-style uniforms. ☐ ...a Salvation Army hostel.

salve /sæv/ (salves, salving, salved) ◼ V-T If you do something to **salve** your conscience, you do it in order to feel less guilty. [FORMAL] ☐ I give myself treats and justify them to salve my conscience. ◪ N-MASS **Salve** is an oily substance that is put on sore skin or a wound to help it heal. ☐ ...a soothing salve for sore, dry lips.

sal|ver /sælvər/ (salvers) N-COUNT A **salver** is a flat object, usually made of silver, on which things are carried. ☐ ...silver salvers laden with flutes of champagne.

sal|vo /sælvoʊ/ (salvoes) ◼ N-COUNT A **salvo** is the firing of several guns or missiles at the same time in a battle or ceremony. ☐ They were to fire a salvo of blanks, after the national anthem. ◪ N-COUNT [with supp] A **salvo** of angry words is a lot of them spoken or written at about the same time. ☐ His testimony, however, was only one in a salvo of new attacks.

Sa|mari|tan /səmærɪtən/ (Samaritans) N-COUNT You refer to someone as a **Samaritan** if they help you when you are in difficulty. ☐ A good Samaritan offered us a room in his house.

sam|ba /sæmbə, sɑm-/ (sambas) N-COUNT A **samba** is a lively Brazilian dance.

same ♦♦♦ /seɪm/ ◼ ADJ If two or more things, actions, or qualities are **the same**, or if one is **the same** as another, they are very like each other in some way. ☐ The houses were all the same – square, close to the street, needing paint. ☐ People with the same experience in the job should be paid the same. ◪ PHRASE If something is happening **the same as** something else, the two things are happening in a way that is similar or exactly the same. ☐ I mean, it's a relationship, the same as a marriage is a relationship. ◾ ADJ You use **same** to indicate that you are referring to only one place, time, or thing, and not to different ones. ☐ Bernard works at the same institution as Arlette. ☐ It's impossible to get everybody together at the same time. ◱ ADJ [the ADJ] Something that is still **the same** has not changed in any way. ☐ Taking ingredients from the same source means the beers stay the same. ◲ PRON [the PRON] You use **the same** to refer to something that has previously been mentioned or suggested. ☐ We made the decision which was right for us. Other parents must do the same. ☐ In the United States small bookstores survive quite well. The same applies to small publishers. • ADJ [the ADJ] **Same** is also an adjective. ☐ He's so effective. I admire Ginny for pretty much the same reason. ◶ CONVENTION You say 'same here' in order to suggest that you feel the same way about something as the person who has just spoken to you, or that you have done the same thing. [INFORMAL, SPOKEN, FORMULAE] ☐ "Nice to meet you," said Michael. "Same here," said Mary Ann. ◷ CONVENTION You say 'same to you' in response to someone who wishes you well with something. [INFORMAL, SPOKEN, FORMULAE] ☐ "Have a nice Easter."—"And the same to you Bridie." ◸ PHRASE You say 'same again' when you want to order another drink of the same kind as the one you have just had. [INFORMAL, SPOKEN] ☐ Give Roger another pint, Imogen, and I'll have the same again. ◹ PHRASE You can say **all the same** or **just the same** to introduce a statement which indicates that a situation or your opinion has not changed, in spite of what has happened or what has just been said. ☐ I arranged to pay him the dollars when he got there, a purely private arrangement. All the same, it was illegal. ◐ PHRASE If you say '**It's all the same to me**,' you mean that you do not care which of several things happens or is chosen. [mainly SPOKEN] ☐ Whether I've got a mustache or not it's all the same to me. ⓫ **at the same time** → see **time** ③

USAGE

same
Don't use 'like' after **the same**. Don't say, for example, 'He was not the same like the other boys.' Say 'He was not like the other boys.' You can put a noun between **the same** and **as**. You can say, for example, 'She goes to **the same** school **as** her sister.' Her dress was **the same** color **as** her eyes.

same|ness /seɪmnɪs/ N-UNCOUNT [usu with supp] The **sameness** of something is its lack of variety. ☐ He grew bored by the sameness of the speeches.

same-sex ◼ ADJ [usu ADJ n] **Same-sex** people are the same sex as each other, or the same sex as a particular person. ☐ ...women's same-sex friends. ◪ ADJ [usu ADJ n] **Same-sex** marriage is marriage between two people of the same sex. ☐ Same-sex marriage has been legal in Canada since 2005.

Sami /sæmi/ (Sami) N-COUNT A **Sami** is a member of a people living mainly in northern Scandinavia. ☐ The Sami have strong views on environmental matters.

sa|miz|dat /sɑmɪzdɑt, sæmɪzdæt/ N-UNCOUNT [usu N n] Samizdat referred to a system in the former USSR and Eastern Europe by which books and magazines forbidden by the state were illegally printed by groups who opposed the state. [FORMAL] ❑ ...a publisher specializing in samizdat literature.

sa|mo|sa /səmoʊsə/ (**samosas**) N-COUNT A **samosa** is an Indian food consisting of vegetables, spices, and sometimes meat, wrapped in pastry and fried.

samo|var /sæməvɑr/ (**samovars**) N-COUNT A **samovar** is a large decorated container for heating water, traditionally used in Russia for making tea.

sam|ple ✦◇◇ /sæmpᵊl/ (**samples, sampling, sampled**) **1** N-COUNT A **sample** of a substance or product is a small quantity of it that shows you what it is like. ❑ You'll receive samples of paint, curtains and upholstery. ❑ We're giving away 2,000 free samples. **2** N-COUNT A **sample** of a substance is a small amount of it that is examined and analyzed scientifically. ❑ They took samples of my blood. **3** N-COUNT A **sample** of people or things is a number of them chosen out of a larger group and then used in tests or used to provide information about the whole group. ❑ We based our analysis on a random sample of more than 200 males. **4** V-T If you **sample** food or drink, you taste a small amount of it in order to find out if you like it. ❑ We sampled a selection of different bottled waters. **5** V-T If you **sample** a place or situation, you experience it for a short time in order to find out about it. ❑ ...the chance to sample a different way of life.

COLLOCATIONS
sample
NOUN
2
noun + **sample**: blood, DNA, saliva, urine; soil
verb + **sample**: collect, obtain, take; analyze, test; provide
3
adjective + **sample**: random, representative, small, statistical
verb + **sample**: analyze, interview, study

SYNONYMS
sample
NOUN **1**
specimen: Job applicants have to submit a specimen of handwriting.
example: The plaque illustrated in Figure 1 is an example of his work at this time.
model: ...a working scale model of the whole Bay Area.

sam|pler /sæmplər/ (**samplers**) **1** N-COUNT A **sampler** is a piece of cloth with words and patterns sewn on it, which is intended to show the skill of the person who made it. **2** N-COUNT A **sampler** is a piece of equipment that is used for copying a piece of music and using it to make a new piece of music.

samu|rai /sæmʊraɪ/ (**samurai**) N-COUNT In former times, a samurai was a member of a powerful class of fighters in Japan.

sana|to|rium /sænətɔriəm/ (**sanatoriums** or **sanatoria** /sænətɔriə/) also **sanitarium** N-COUNT A **sanatorium** is an institution that provides medical treatment and rest, often in a healthy climate, for people who have been ill for a long time.

sanc|ti|fy /sæŋktɪfaɪ/ (**sanctifies, sanctifying, sanctified**) V-T [usu passive] If something **is sanctified** by a priest or other holy person, the priest or holy person officially approves of it, or declares it to be holy. ❑ She is trying to make amends for her marriage not being sanctified.

sanc|ti|mo|ni|ous /sæŋktɪmoʊniəs/ ADJ If you say that someone is **sanctimonious**, you disapprove of them because you think that they are trying to appear morally better than other people. [DISAPPROVAL] ❑ He writes smug, sanctimonious rubbish.

sanc|tion ✦◇◇ /sæŋkʃᵊn/ (**sanctions, sanctioning, sanctioned**) **1** V-T If someone in authority **sanctions** an action or practice, they officially approve of it and allow it to be done. ❑ He may now be ready to sanction the use of force. • N-UNCOUNT **Sanction** is also a noun. ❑ ...a newspaper run by citizens without the sanction of the government. **2** N-PLURAL **Sanctions** are measures taken by countries to restrict trade and official contact with a country that has broken international law. ❑ The continued abuse of human rights has now led the United States to impose sanctions against the regime.

SYNONYMS
sanction
VERB **1**
permit: He can let the court's decision stand and permit the execution.
allow: Smoking will not be allowed.
back: The Prime Minister is backed by the civic movement, Public Against Violence.
support: The Vice President insisted that he supported the hard-working people of New York.
NOUN **2**
ban: The General also lifted a ban on political parties.
restriction: The relaxation of travel restrictions means they are free to travel and work.
boycott: Opposition leaders had called for a boycott of the vote.
embargo: He has called on the government to lift its trade embargo.

sanc|tity /sæŋktɪti/ N-UNCOUNT If you talk about the **sanctity** of something, you mean that it is very important and must be treated with respect. ❑ ...the sanctity of human life.

sanc|tu|ary /sæŋktʃueri/ (**sanctuaries**) **1** N-COUNT A **sanctuary** is a place where people who are in danger from other people can go to be safe. ❑ His church became a sanctuary for thousands of people who fled the civil war. **2** N-UNCOUNT **Sanctuary** is the safety provided in a sanctuary. ❑ Some of them have sought sanctuary in the church. **3** N-COUNT A **sanctuary** is a place where birds or animals are protected and allowed to live freely. ❑ ...a bird sanctuary.

sanc|tum /sæŋktəm/ (**sanctums**) **1** N-COUNT [usu sing] If you refer to someone's inner **sanctum**, you mean a room which is private and sometimes secret, where they can be quiet and alone. ❑ His bedroom's his inner sanctum. **2** N-COUNT A **sanctum** is the holiest place inside a holy building such as a temple or mosque.

sand ✦◇◇ /sænd/ (**sands, sanding, sanded**) **1** N-UNCOUNT **Sand** is a substance that looks like powder, and consists of extremely small pieces of stone. Some deserts and many beaches are made up of sand. ❑ They all walked barefoot across the damp sand to the water's edge. **2** N-PLURAL **Sands** are a large area of sand, for example, a beach. ❑ ...miles of golden sands. **3** V-T If you **sand** a wood or metal surface, you rub sandpaper over it in order to make it smooth or clean. ❑ Sand the surface softly and carefully. • PHRASAL VERB **Sand down** means the same as **sand**. ❑ I was going to sand down the chairs and repaint them.

san|dal /sændᵊl/ (**sandals**) **1** N-COUNT **Sandals** are light shoes that you wear in warm weather, which have straps instead of a solid part over the top of your foot. ❑ ...a pair of old sandals. **2** → See also color supplement

sandal|wood /sændᵊlwʊd/ **1** N-UNCOUNT **Sandalwood** is the sweet-smelling wood of a tree that is found in South Asia and Australia. It is also the name of the tree itself. **2** N-UNCOUNT **Sandalwood** is the oil extracted from the wood of the tree. It is used to make perfume.

sand|bag /sændbæg/ (**sandbags, sandbagging, sandbagged**) **1** N-COUNT A **sandbag** is a cloth bag filled with sand. Sandbags are usually used to build walls for protection against floods or explosions. **2** V-T To **sandbag** something means to protect or strengthen it using sandbags. ❑ They sandbagged their homes to keep out floods.

sand|bank /sændbæŋk/ (**sandbanks**) N-COUNT A **sandbank** is a bank of sand below the surface of the sea or a river. ❑ The ship hit a sandbank.

sand|bar /sændbɑr/ (**sandbars**) N-COUNT A **sandbar** is a sandbank which is found especially at the mouth of a river or harbor.

sand|box /sændbɒks/ (**sandboxes**) N-COUNT A **sandbox** is a shallow hole or box in the ground with sand in it where children can play. [AM]

in BRIT, use **sandpit**

sand cas|tle (sand castles) N-COUNT A **sand castle** is a pile of sand, usually shaped like a castle, which children make when they are playing on the beach.

sand dune (sand dunes) N-COUNT [usu pl] A **sand dune** is a hill of sand near the sea or in a sand desert.

sand|er /sændər/ (sanders) **1** N-COUNT A **sander** is a machine for making wood or metal surfaces smoother. **2** → See also color supplement

S & L /ɛs ən ɛl/ (S & Ls) N-COUNT **S & L** is an abbreviation for savings and loan. [BUSINESS]

S & M /ɛs ən ɛm/ N-UNCOUNT **S & M** is an abbreviation for sadomasochism.

sand|paper /sændpeɪpər/ **1** N-UNCOUNT **Sandpaper** is strong paper that has a coating of sand on it. It is used for rubbing wood or metal surfaces to make them smoother. ❑ ...*a piece of sandpaper.* **2** → See feature box at DIY; See also color supplement

sand|pit /sændpɪt/ (sandpits) also **sand-pit** N-COUNT A **sandpit** is the same as a **sandbox**. [BRIT]

sand|stone /sændstoʊn/ (sandstones) **1** N-MASS **Sandstone** is a type of rock which contains a lot of sand. It is often used for building houses and walls. ❑ ...*the reddish sandstone walls.* **2** → See also color supplement

sand|storm /sændstɔrm/ (sandstorms) N-COUNT A **sandstorm** is a strong wind in a desert area, which carries sand through the air.

sand trap (sand traps) N-COUNT On a golf course, a **sand trap** is a hollow area filled with sand, which is put there as an obstacle that players must try to avoid. [mainly AM]

in BRIT, usually use **bunker**

sand|wich /sænwɪtʃ, sænd-/ (sandwiches, sandwiching, sandwiched) **1** N-COUNT A **sandwich** usually consists of two slices of bread with a layer of food such as cheese or meat between them. ❑ ...*a ham sandwich.* **2** V-T If you **sandwich** two things together with something else, you put that other thing between them. If you **sandwich** one thing between two other things, you put it between them. ❑ *Carefully split the sponge ring, then sandwich the two halves together with whipped cream.*

WORD HISTORY

sandwich
This popular snack takes its name from John Montagu, the 4th Earl of Sandwich in the 18th century. A keen card player, he used to ask for beef served between two slices of bread, the idea being that he wouldn't get grease on the cards from his hands. His fellow players then began asking for 'the same as Sandwich,' which gradually became, simply 'a sandwich.'

sand|wiched /sænwɪtʃt, sænd-/ **1** ADJ [v-link ADJ between pl-n] If something is **sandwiched between** two other things, it is in a narrow space between them. ❑ *It was a small store sandwiched between a coffee shop on one side and a bakery on the other.* **2** → see also **sandwich**

sandy /sændi/ (sandier, sandiest) ADJ A **sandy** area is covered with sand. ❑ ...*long, sandy beaches.*

sane /seɪn/ (saner, sanest) **1** ADJ Someone who is **sane** is able to think and behave normally and reasonably, and is not mentally ill. ❑ *He seemed perfectly sane.* **2** ADJ If you refer to a **sane** person, action, or system, you mean one that you think is reasonable and sensible. ❑ *No sane person wishes to see conflict or casualties.*

sang /sæŋ/ **Sang** is the past tense of **sing**.

sang-froid /spŋ frwɑ/ also **sangfroid** N-UNCOUNT A person's **sang-froid** is their ability to remain calm in a dangerous or difficult situation. [FORMAL] ❑ *He behaves throughout with a certain sang-froid.*

san|gria /sæŋgriə/ N-UNCOUNT **Sangria** is a Spanish drink made of red wine, orange or lemon juice, soda, and brandy.

san|guine /sæŋgwɪn/ ADJ If you are **sanguine** about something, you are cheerful and confident that things will happen in the way you want them to. ❑ *He's remarkably sanguine about the problems involved.*

sani|ta|rium /sænɪtɛəriəm/ (sanitariums) → see **sanatorium**

sani|tary /sænɪteri/ **1** ADJ [ADJ n] **Sanitary** means concerned with keeping things clean and healthy, especially by providing a sewage system and a clean water supply. ❑ *Sanitary conditions are appalling.* **2** ADJ If you say that a place is not **sanitary**, you mean that it is not very clean. ❑ *It's not the most sanitary place one could swim.*

sani|tary nap|kin (sanitary napkins) N-COUNT A **sanitary napkin** is a pad of thick soft material which women wear to absorb the blood during their periods. [AM]

in BRIT, use **sanitary towel**

sani|tary pro|tec|tion N-UNCOUNT **Sanitary protection** is sanitary towels or tampons.

sani|tary tow|el (sanitary towels) N-COUNT A **sanitary towel** is the same as a **sanitary napkin**. [BRIT]

sani|ta|tion /sænɪteɪʃn/ N-UNCOUNT **Sanitation** is the process of keeping places clean and healthy, especially by providing a sewage system and a clean water supply. ❑ ...*the hazards of contaminated water and poor sanitation.*

sani|tize /sænɪtaɪz/ (sanitizes, sanitizing, sanitized)

in BRIT, also use **sanitise**

V-T To **sanitize** an activity or a situation that is unpleasant or unacceptable means to describe it in a way that makes it seem more pleasant or more acceptable. ❑ ...*crime writers who sanitize violence and make it respectable.*

sani|tizer /sænɪtaɪzər/ (sanitizers) **1** N-MASS **Sanitizer** is a product for cleaning something so that there are no germs or bacteria on it. ❑ *The sanitizer was sold to clean humidifiers.* **2** → see also **hand sanitizer**

san|ity /sænɪti/ N-UNCOUNT A person's **sanity** is their ability to think and behave normally and reasonably. ❑ *He and his wife finally had to move from their apartment just to preserve their sanity.*

sank /sæŋk/ **Sank** is the past tense of **sink**.

sans /sænz/ PREP If someone or something is **sans** another thing, they lack the other thing. [INFORMAL] ❑ *She would not be happy with people seeing her sans makeup.*

San|skrit /sænskrɪt/ N-UNCOUNT **Sanskrit** is an ancient language which used to be spoken in India and is now used only in religious writings and ceremonies.

Santa Claus /sæntə klɔz/ N-PROPER **Santa Claus** or **Santa** is an imaginary old man with a long white beard and a red coat. Traditionally, young children in many countries are told that he brings their Christmas presents.

sap /sæp/ (saps, sapping, sapped) **1** V-T If something **saps** your strength or confidence, it gradually weakens or destroys it. ❑ *I was afraid the sickness had sapped my strength.* **2** N-UNCOUNT **Sap** is the watery liquid in plants and trees. ❑ *The leaves, bark and sap are also common ingredients of local herbal remedies.*

sa|pi|ens /seɪpiənz, -ɛnz/ → see **homo sapiens**

sap|ling /sæplɪŋ/ (saplings) N-COUNT A **sapling** is a young tree.

sap|phire /sæfaɪər/ (sapphires) **1** N-VAR A **sapphire** is a precious stone which is blue in color. ❑ ...*a sapphire engagement ring.* **2** COLOR Something that is **sapphire** is bright blue in color. [LITERARY] ❑ ...*white snow and sapphire skies.* **3** → See also color supplement

sap|py /sæpi/ (sappier, sappiest) **1** ADJ **Sappy** stems or leaves contain a lot of liquid. **2** ADJ If you describe someone or something as **sappy**, you think they are foolish. [AM, INFORMAL, DISAPPROVAL] ❑ *I wrote this sappy love song.*

Sa|ran wrap /səræn ræp/ N-UNCOUNT **Saran wrap** is a thin, clear, stretchy plastic which you use to cover food to keep it fresh. [AM, TRADEMARK]

in BRIT, use **clingfilm**

sar|casm /sɑrkæzəm/ N-UNCOUNT **Sarcasm** is speech or writing which actually means the opposite of what it seems to say. Sarcasm is usually intended to mock or insult someone. ❑ *Sarcasm and demeaning remarks have no place in parenting.*

sar|cas|tic /sɑrkæstɪk/ ADJ Someone who is **sarcastic** says or does the opposite of what they really mean in order to mock or insult someone. ❑ *She poked fun at people's shortcomings with*

sarcoma 1145 **satisfaction**

sarcastic remarks. • **sar|cas|ti|cal|ly** /sɑrkæstɪkli/ ADV ❏ "What a surprise!" Caroline murmured sarcastically.

sar|co|ma /sɑrkoʊmə/ (sarcomas) N-VAR Sarcoma is one of the two main forms of cancer. It affects tissues such as muscle and bone.

sar|copha|gus /sɑrkɒfəgəs/ (sarcophaguses or sarcophagi /sɑrkɒfəgaɪ/) N-COUNT A **sarcophagus** is a large decorative container in which a dead body was placed in ancient times. ❏ ...an Egyptian sarcophagus.

sar|dine /sɑrdin/ (sardines) N-COUNT **Sardines** are a kind of small sea fish, often eaten as food. ❏ They opened a can of sardines.

sar|don|ic /sɑrdɒnɪk/ ADJ If you describe someone as **sardonic**, you mean their attitude to people or things is humorous but rather critical. ❏ He was a big, sardonic man, who intimidated even the most self-confident students.

sarge /sɑrdʒ/ N-VOC; N-SING [the N] A sergeant is sometimes addressed as **sarge** or referred to as **the sarge**. [INFORMAL] ❏ "Good luck, sarge," he said.

sari /sɑri/ (saris) N-COUNT A **sari** is a piece of clothing worn especially by Indian women. It consists of a long piece of thin material that is wrapped around the body.

sar|in /sɑrɪn/ N-UNCOUNT **Sarin** is an extremely poisonous gas that is used in chemical weapons.

sa|rong /sərɒŋ/ (sarongs) N-COUNT A **sarong** is a piece of clothing that is worn especially by Malaysian men and women. It consists of a long piece of cloth wrapped around the waist or body.

SARS /sɑrz/ N-UNCOUNT **SARS** is a serious disease which affects your ability to breathe. **SARS** is an abbreviation for 'severe acute respiratory syndrome.'

sar|to|rial /sɑrtɔriəl/ ADJ [ADJ n] **Sartorial** means relating to clothes and to the way they are made or worn. [FORMAL] ❏ ...Sebastian's sartorial elegance.

SASE /ɛs eɪ ɛs i/ (SASEs) N-SING An **SASE** is an envelope on which you have stuck a stamp and written your own name and address. You send it to a person or organization so that they can reply to you in it. **SASE** is an abbreviation for 'self-addressed stamped envelope.' [AM]

in BRIT, use **s.a.e.**

sash /sæʃ/ (sashes) N-COUNT A **sash** is a long piece of cloth which people wear around their waist or over one shoulder, especially with formal or official clothes. ❏ She wore a white dress with a thin blue sash.

sash|ay /sæʃeɪ/ (sashays, sashaying, sashayed) V-I If someone **sashays**, they walk in a graceful but rather noticeable way. ❏ The models sashayed down the catwalk.

sash win|dow (sash windows) N-COUNT A **sash window** is a window which consists of two frames placed one above the other. The window can be opened by sliding one frame over the other.

sass /sæs/ (sasses, sassing, sassed) ◼ N-UNCOUNT **Sass** is disrespectful talk. [AM, INFORMAL, DISAPPROVAL] ❏ It's straight home we're going, and I want no sass from you. ◼ V-T If someone **sasses** you, they speak to you in a disrespectful way. [AM, INFORMAL, DISAPPROVAL] ❏ The girl sassed the teacher all day.

sas|sa|fras /sæsəfræs/ (sassafras) ◼ N-UNCOUNT **Sassafras** is a herb which is produced from the dried roots of the sassafras tree. ◼ N-COUNT [oft N n] A **sassafras** or a **sassafras tree** is a tree, found mainly in North America, the roots of which are used to make the herb sassafras.

sas|sy /sæsi/ (sassier, sassiest) ADJ If an older person describes a younger person as **sassy**, they mean that they are disrespectful in a lively, confident way. [AM, INFORMAL] ❏ Are you that sassy with your parents?

sat /sæt/ **Sat** is the past tense and past participle of sit.

SAT /ɛs eɪ ti/ (SATs) N-PROPER The **SAT** is a set of examinations which are usually taken by students who wish to enter a college or university. [AM] ❏ The average SAT score among their freshman class was 1,200.

Sat. Sat. is a written abbreviation for Saturday.

Satan /seɪtən/ N-PROPER In the Christian religion, **Satan** is the Devil, a powerful evil being who is the chief opponent of God.

sa|tan|ic /sətænɪk, seɪ-/ ADJ Something that is **satanic** is considered to be caused by or influenced by Satan. ❏ ...satanic cults.

Sa|tan|ism /seɪtənɪzəm/ also **satanism** N-UNCOUNT **Satanism** is worship of Satan. ❏ ...black magic and satanism. • **Sa|tan|ist** /seɪtənɪst/ (Satanists) N-COUNT ❏ ...a Satanist accused of fire attacks on churches.

sa|tay /sɑteɪ/ N-UNCOUNT **Satay** is pieces of meat cooked on thin sticks and served with a peanut sauce. ❏ ...chicken satay.

satch|el /sætʃəl/ (satchels) ◼ N-COUNT A **satchel** is a bag with a long strap that schoolchildren use for carrying books. [OLD-FASHIONED] ◼ → See also color supplement

sat|ed /seɪtɪd/ ADJ [v-link ADJ] If you are **sated** with something, you have had more of it than you can enjoy at one time. [FORMAL] ❏ ...children happily sated with ice cream.

sat|el|lite ✦◇ /sætəlaɪt/ (satellites) ◼ N-COUNT [also by N] A **satellite** is an object which has been sent into space in order to collect information or to be part of a communications system. Satellites move continually around the earth or around another planet. ❏ The rocket launched two communications satellites. ◼ ADJ [ADJ n] **Satellite** television is broadcast using a satellite. ❏ They have four satellite channels. ◼ N-COUNT A **satellite** is a natural object in space that moves around a planet or star. ❏ ...the satellites of Jupiter. ◼ N-COUNT You can refer to a country, area, or organization as a **satellite** when it is controlled by or depends on a larger and more powerful one. ❏ Some companies are outfitting their satellite offices with wireless LANs.

sat|el|lite dish (satellite dishes) N-COUNT A **satellite dish** is a piece of equipment which people have on their house in order to receive satellite television.

sa|ti|ate /seɪʃieɪt/ (satiates, satiating, satiated) V-T If something such as food or pleasure **satiates** you, you have all that you need or all that you want of it, often so much that you become tired of it. [FORMAL] ❏ The dinner was enough to satiate the gourmets.

sat|in /sætən/ (satins) ◼ N-MASS **Satin** is a smooth, shiny kind of cloth, usually made from silk. ❏ ...a peach satin ribbon. ◼ ADJ [ADJ n] If something such as a paint, wax, or cosmetic gives something a **satin** finish, it reflects light to some extent but is not very shiny. ❏ The final stage of waxing left it with a satin sheen.

satin|wood /sætənwʊd/ N-UNCOUNT **Satinwood** is a smooth hard wood which comes from an East Indian tree and is used to make furniture.

sat|ire /sætaɪər/ (satires) ◼ N-UNCOUNT **Satire** is the use of humor or exaggeration in order to show how foolish or wicked some people's behavior or ideas are. ❏ The commercial side of the Christmas season is an easy target for satire. ◼ N-COUNT A **satire** is a play, movie, or novel in which humor or exaggeration is used to criticize something. ❏ ...a sharp satire on the American political process.

sa|tir|ic /sətɪrɪk/ ADJ **Satiric** means the same as satirical. ❏ ...Ibsen's satiric attack on bourgeois convention.

sa|tiri|cal /sətɪrɪkəl/ ADJ A **satirical** drawing, piece of writing, or comedy show is one in which humor or exaggeration is used to criticize something. ❏ ...a satirical novel about New York life in the late 80s.

sati|rist /sætɪrɪst/ (satirists) N-COUNT A **satirist** is someone who writes or uses satire. ❏ He built a reputation in the 1970s as a social satirist.

sati|rize /sætɪraɪz/ (satirizes, satirizing, satirized)

in BRIT, also use **satirise**

V-T If you **satirize** a person or group of people, you use satire to criticize them or make fun of them in a play, movie, or novel. ❏ The newspaper came out weekly. It satirized political leaders.

sat|is|fac|tion /sætɪsfækʃən/ ◼ N-UNCOUNT **Satisfaction** is the pleasure that you feel when you do something or get something that you wanted or needed to do or get. ❏ She felt a small glow of satisfaction. ❏ Both sides expressed satisfaction with the progress so far. ◼ N-UNCOUNT If you get **satisfaction** from someone, you get money or an apology from them because you have been treated badly. ❏ If you can't get any satisfaction, complain to the park owner. ◼ PHRASE If you do something **to**

someone's **satisfaction**, they are happy with the way that you have done it. ☐ *She never could seem to do anything right or to his satisfaction.*

sat|is|fac|tory /sætɪsfæktəri/ ADJ Something that is **satisfactory** is acceptable to you or fulfills a particular need or purpose. ☐ *I never got a satisfactory answer.*

sat|is|fied ♦⬦ /sætɪsfaɪd/ **1** ADJ If you are **satisfied** with something, you are happy because you have gotten what you wanted or needed. ☐ *We are not satisfied with these results.* **2** ADJ [v-link ADJ] If you are **satisfied** that something is true or has been done properly, you are convinced about this after checking it. ☐ *People must be satisfied that the treatment is safe.*

sat|is|fy /sætɪsfaɪ/ (**satisfies, satisfying, satisfied**) **1** V-T If someone or something **satisfies** you, they give you enough of what you want or need to make you pleased or contented. ☐ *The pace of change has not been quick enough to satisfy everyone.* **2** V-T To **satisfy** someone that something is true or has been done properly means to convince them by giving them more information or by showing them what has been done. ☐ *He has to satisfy the environmental lobby that real progress will be made to cut emissions.* **3** V-T If you **satisfy** the requirements for something, you are good enough or have the right qualities to fulfill these requirements. ☐ *The executive committee recommends that the procedures should satisfy certain basic requirements.* **4** → See feature box at **review**

sat|is|fy|ing /sætɪsfaɪɪŋ/ ADJ Something that is **satisfying** makes you feel happy, especially because you feel you have achieved something. ☐ *I found wood carving satisfying.*

sat|nav /sætnæv/ N-UNCOUNT **Satnav** is a system that uses information from satellites to find the best way of getting to a place. It is often found in cars. **Satnav** is an abbreviation for 'satellite navigation.' ☐ *We didn't have satnav, so the traditional map and compass took over.*

sat|su|ma /sætsumə/ (**satsumas**) N-COUNT A **satsuma** is a fruit that looks like a small orange.

satu|rate /sætʃəreɪt/ (**saturates, saturating, saturated**) **1** V-T If people or things **saturate** a place or object, they fill it completely so that no more can be added. ☐ *In the last days before the vote, both sides are saturating the airwaves.* **2** V-T If someone or something **is saturated**, they become extremely wet. ☐ *If the filter has been saturated with motor oil, it should be discarded and replaced.*

satu|rat|ed /sætʃəreɪtɪd/ ADJ [usu ADJ n] **Saturated** fats are types of fat that are found in some foods, especially meat, eggs, and things such as butter and cheese. They are believed to cause heart disease and some other illnesses if eaten too often. ☐ *...foods rich in cholesterol and saturated fats.*

satu|ra|tion /sætʃəreɪʃən/ **1** N-UNCOUNT **Saturation** is the process or state that occurs when a place or thing is filled completely with people or things, so that no more can be added. ☐ *Japanese car makers have been equally blind to the saturation of their markets at home and abroad.* **2** ADJ [ADJ n] **Saturation** is used to describe a campaign or other activity that is carried out very thoroughly, so that nothing is missed. ☐ *The concept of saturation marketing makes perfect sense.*

Sat|ur|day ♦♦♦ /sætərdeɪ, -di/ (**Saturdays**) N-VAR **Saturday** is the day after Friday and before Sunday. ☐ *He called her on Saturday morning at the studio.* ☐ *Every Saturday dad made a beautiful pea and ham soup.*

sat|ur|nine /sætɜrnaɪn/ ADJ [usu ADJ n] Someone who is **saturnine** is serious and unfriendly. [LITERARY] ☐ *He had a rather forbidding, saturnine manner.*

sa|tyr /seɪtər, sæt-/ (**satyrs**) N-COUNT In classical mythology a **satyr** is a creature that is half man and half goat.

sauce ♦⬦ /sɔs/ (**sauces**) N-MASS A **sauce** is a thick liquid which is served with other food. ☐ *...pasta cooked in a sauce of garlic, tomatoes, and cheese.*

sauce|pan /sɔspæn/ (**saucepans**) N-COUNT A **saucepan** is a deep metal cooking pot, usually with a long handle and a lid. ☐ *Place the potatoes and turnips in a large saucepan, cover with cold water and bring to the boil.*

sau|cer /sɔsər/ (**saucers**) N-COUNT A **saucer** is a small curved plate on which you stand a cup. ☐ *Rae's coffee cup clattered against the saucer as she picked it up.*

saucy /sɔsi/ (**saucier, sauciest**) ADJ Someone or something that is **saucy** refers to sex in a light-hearted, amusing way. ☐ *...a saucy joke.*

Sau|di /saudi/ (**Saudis**) **1** ADJ [usu ADJ n] **Saudi** or **Saudi Arabian** means belonging or relating to Saudi Arabia or to its people, language, or culture. ☐ *Saudi officials have dismissed such reports as rumors.* **2** N-COUNT The **Saudis** or **Saudi Arabians** are the people who come from Saudi Arabia.

sau|er|kraut /sauərkraut/ N-UNCOUNT **Sauerkraut** is cabbage which has been cut into thin strips and pickled.

sau|na /sɔnə/ (**saunas**) **1** N-COUNT If you have a **sauna**, you sit or lie in a room that is so hot that it makes you sweat. People have saunas in order to relax and to clean their skin thoroughly. ☐ *Every month I have a sauna.* **2** N-COUNT A **sauna** is a room or building where you can have a sauna. ☐ *The hotel has a sauna, solarium and heated indoor swimming pool.*

saun|ter /sɔntər/ (**saunters, sauntering, sauntered**) V-I If you **saunter** somewhere, you walk there in a slow, casual way. ☐ *We watched our fellow students saunter into the building.*

sau|sage /sɔsɪdʒ/ (**sausages**) N-VAR A **sausage** consists of minced meat, usually pork, mixed with other ingredients, and is contained in a tube made of skin or a similar material. ☐ *...sausages and fries.*

sau|té /soʊteɪ/ (**sautés, sautéing, sautéed**) V-T When you **sauté** food, you fry it quickly in hot oil or butter. ☐ *Sauté the chicken until golden brown.*

sav|age /sævɪdʒ/ (**savages, savaging, savaged**) **1** ADJ Someone or something that is **savage** is extremely cruel, violent, and uncontrolled. ☐ *This was a savage attack on a defenseless young girl.* ☐ *...the savage wave of violence that swept the country in November.* • **sav|age|ly** ADV ☐ *He was savagely beaten.* **2** N-COUNT If you refer to people as **savages**, you dislike them because you think that they do not have an advanced society and are violent. [DISAPPROVAL] ☐ *...their conviction that the area was a frozen desert peopled with uncouth savages.* **3** V-T [usu passive] If someone **is savaged** by a dog or other animal, the animal attacks them violently. ☐ *The animal then turned on him and he was savaged to death.*

sav|age|ry /sævɪdʒri/ N-UNCOUNT **Savagery** is extremely cruel and violent behavior. ☐ *...the sheer savagery of war.*

sa|van|nah /səvænə/ (**savannahs**) also **savanna** **1** N-VAR A **savannah** is a large area of flat, grassy land, usually in Africa. **2** → See feature box at **ecosystem**

sa|vant /sævənt/ (**savants**) N-COUNT A **savant** is a person of great learning or natural ability. [FORMAL] ☐ *...the opinion of savants on the composition of the lunar surface.*

save ♦♦⬦ /seɪv/ (**saves, saving, saved**) **1** V-T If you **save** someone or something, you help them to avoid harm or to escape from a dangerous or unpleasant situation. ☐ *...an austerity program designed to save the country's failing economy.* ☐ *The meeting is an attempt to mobilize nations to save children from death by disease and malnutrition.* **2** V-T/V-I If you **save**, you gradually collect money by spending less than you get, usually in order to buy something that you want. ☐ *The majority of people intend to save, but find that by the end of the month there is nothing left.* ☐ *Tim and Barbara are now saving for a house in the suburbs.* ☐ *I was trying to save money to go to college.* • PHRASAL VERB **Save up** means the same as **save**. ☐ *Julie wanted to put some of her money aside for holidays or save up for something special.* **3** V-T/V-I If you **save** something such as time or money, you prevent the loss or waste of it. ☐ *It saves time in the kitchen to have things you use a lot within reach.* ☐ *I'll try to save him the expense of a flight from Perth.* ☐ *A new filter can save on energy bills.* **4** V-T If you **save** something, you keep it because it will be needed later. ☐ *Drain the beans thoroughly and save the stock for soup.* **5** V-T If someone or something **saves** you from an unpleasant action or experience, they change the situation so that you do not have to do it or experience it. ☐ *The scanner will reduce the need for exploratory operations which will save risk and pain for patients.* ☐ *She was hoping that something might save her from having to make a decision.* **6** V-T/V-I If you **save** data in a computer, you give the computer an instruction to store the data on a tape or disk. [COMPUTING] ☐ *Try to get into the habit of saving your work regularly.* ☐ *Save frequently when you are creating graphics.* **7** V-T/V-I If a goalkeeper **saves**, or **saves** a shot, they succeed in preventing the ball

from going into the goal. ❏ *He saved one shot when the ball hit him on the head.* • N-COUNT **Save** is also a noun. ❏ *The goalie made some great saves.* ◨ **to save the day** → see **day** ◨ **to save face** → see **face** ①
▶ **save up** → see **save** 2

SYNONYMS

save
VERB ◨
rescue: *He had rescued her from a horrible life.*
recover: *Police raided five houses in south-east London and recovered stolen goods.*
extricate: *...extricate the survivors.*

sav|er /seɪvər/ (**savers**) N-COUNT A **saver** is a person who regularly saves money, especially by paying it into a bank account. ❏ *Low interest rates are bad news for savers, who have seen their income halved over the last year.*

-saver /-seɪvər/ (**-savers**) COMB IN N-COUNT **-saver** combines with words such as 'time' and 'energy' to indicate that something prevents the thing mentioned from being wasted. ❏ *These zip-top bags are great space-savers if storage is limited.*

sav|ing ♦♢♢ /seɪvɪŋ/ (**savings**) ◨ N-COUNT A **saving** is a reduction in the amount of time or money that is used or needed. ❏ *You can enjoy a year's membership for just $28 – a saving of $7 off the regular rate.* ◪ N-PLURAL Your **savings** are the money that you have saved, especially in a bank or a building society. ❏ *Her savings were in the First National Bank.*

sav|ing grace (**saving graces**) N-COUNT [with supp] A **saving grace** is a good quality or feature in a person or thing that prevents them from being completely bad or worthless. ❏ *Aging's one saving grace is you worry less about what people think.*

sav|ings and loan (**savings and loans**) N-COUNT A **savings and loan** association is a business where people save money to earn interest, and which lends money to savers to buy houses. [mainly AM, BUSINESS]

sav|ior /seɪvyər/ (**saviors**)
in BRIT, use **saviour**
N-COUNT A **savior** is a person who saves someone or something from danger, ruin, or defeat. ❏ *...the savior of his country.*

savoir-faire /sævwɑr fɛər/ N-UNCOUNT **Savoir-faire** is the confidence and ability to do the appropriate thing in a social situation. [FORMAL] ❏ *He was full of jocularity and savoir-faire.*

sa|vor /seɪvər/ (**savors, savoring, savored**)
in BRIT, use **savour**
◨ V-T If you **savor** an experience, you enjoy it as much as you can. ❏ *She savored her newfound freedom.* ◪ V-T If you **savor** food or drink, you eat or drink it slowly in order to taste its full flavor and to enjoy it properly. ❏ *Just relax, eat slowly and savor the full flavor of your food.*

sa|vory /seɪvəri/
in BRIT, use **savoury**
ADJ **Savory** food has a salty or spicy flavor rather than a sweet one. ❏ *...all sorts of sweet and savory breads.*

sav|vy /sævi/ ◨ N-UNCOUNT [oft supp N] If you describe someone as having **savvy**, you think that they have a good understanding and practical knowledge of something. [INFORMAL] ❏ *He is known for his political savvy and strong management skills.* ◪ ADJ If you describe someone as **savvy**, you think that they show a lot of practical knowledge. [INFORMAL] ❏ *She was a pretty savvy woman.*

saw /sɔ/ (**saws, sawing, sawed, sawed** or **sawn**) ◨ **Saw** is the past tense of **see**. ◪ N-COUNT A **saw** is a tool for cutting wood, which has a blade with sharp teeth along one edge. Some saws are pushed backward and forward by hand, and others are powered by electricity. ◧ V-T/V-I If you **saw** something, you cut it with a saw. ❏ *He escaped by sawing through the bars of his cell.* ◨ → See also color supplement

saw|dust /sɔdʌst/ N-UNCOUNT **Sawdust** is dust and very small pieces of wood which are produced when you saw wood. ❏ *...a layer of sawdust.*

sawed-off shot|gun (**sawed-off shotguns**) N-COUNT A **sawed-off shotgun** is a shotgun on which the barrel has been cut short. Guns like this are often used by criminals because they can be easily hidden. [AM] ❏ *A sailor carrying a sawed-off shotgun was arrested in Los Angeles.*

in BRIT, use **sawn-off shotgun**

saw|mill /sɔmɪl/ (**sawmills**) N-COUNT A **sawmill** is a factory in which wood from trees is sawn into long flat pieces.

sawn /sɔn/ **Sawn** is the past participle of **saw**. [mainly BRIT]

sawn-off shot|gun (**sawn-off shotguns**) N-COUNT A **sawn-off shotgun** is the same as a **sawed-off shotgun**. [mainly BRIT]

sax /sæks/ (**saxes**) N-COUNT A **sax** is the same as a **saxophone**. [INFORMAL]

Sax|on /sæksən/ (**Saxons**) ◨ N-COUNT In former times, **Saxons** were members of a West Germanic tribe. Some members of this tribe settled in Britain and were known as **Anglo-Saxons**. ◪ ADJ Something that is **Saxon** is related to or characteristic of the ancient Saxons, the Anglo-Saxons, or their descendants. ❏ *...a seventh-century Saxon church.*

saxo|phone /sæksəfoʊn/ (**saxophones**) N-VAR A **saxophone** is a musical instrument in the shape of a curved metal tube with a narrower part that you blow into and keys that you press.

sax|opho|nist /sæksəfoʊnɪst/ (**saxophonists**) N-COUNT A **saxophonist** is someone who plays the saxophone.

SAY
① VERB AND NOUN USES
② PHRASES AND CONVENTIONS

① **say** ♦♦♦ /seɪ/ (**says** /sɛz/, **saying, said** /sɛd/) ◨ V-T When you **say** something, you speak words. ❏ *"I'm sorry," he said.* ❏ *She said they were very impressed.* ❏ *Forty-one people are said to have been seriously hurt.* ❏ *I packed and said goodbye to Charlie.* ◪ V-T You use **say** in expressions such as **I would just like to say** to introduce what you are actually saying, or to indicate that you are expressing an opinion or admitting a fact. If you state that you **can't say** something or you **wouldn't say** something, you are indicating in a polite or indirect way that it is not the case. ❏ *I would just like to say that this is the most hypocritical thing I have ever heard in my life.* ❏ *I must say that rather shocked me, too.* ◧ V-T You can mention the contents of a piece of writing by mentioning what it **says** or what someone **says** in it. ❏ *The report says there is widespread and routine torture of political prisoners in the country.* ❏ *You can't have one without the other, as the song says.* ◨ V-T If you **say** something to yourself, you think it. ❏ *Perhaps I'm still dreaming, I said to myself.* ◩ N-SING [usu a N, also more/some N] If you have a **say** in something, you have the right to give your opinion and influence decisions relating to it. ❏ *You can get married at sixteen, and yet you haven't got a say in the running of the country.* ◪ V-T You indicate the information given by something such as a clock, dial, or map by mentioning what it **says**. ❏ *The clock said four minutes past eleven when we set off.* ◧ V-T If something **says** something about a person, situation, or thing, it gives important information about them. ❏ *I think that says a lot about how well Safin is playing.* ◨ V-T If something **says** a lot for a person or thing, it shows that this person or thing is very good or has a lot of good qualities. ❏ *The fact that a nearly 50-year-old camera could still be functioning says a lot for the workmanship at that time.* ◩ V-T You use **say** in expressions such as **I'll say that for them** and **you can say this for them** after or before you mention a good quality that someone has, usually when you think they do not have many good qualities. ❏ *He's usually well-dressed, I'll say that for him.* ◐ V-T [only imper] You can use **say** when you want to discuss something that might possibly happen or be true. ❏ *Say you were buying a new car, would your discussion begin and end with the monthly payment?* ◑ PHRASE You can use **say** or **let's say** when you mention something as an example. ❏ *To see the problem here more clearly, let's look at a different biological system, say, an acorn.*

USAGE

say
Don't put a word such as 'me' or 'her' directly after **say**. For example, don't say '~~The woman said me that Tom had left.~~' Say 'The woman **said** that Tom had left.' *She **said** (that) they were very pleased.*

say /seɪ/ (says /sɛz/, saying, said /sɛd/) **1** PHRASE If you say that something **says it all**, you mean that it shows you very clearly the truth about a situation or someone's feelings. ◻ *This is my third visit in a week, which says it all.* **2** CONVENTION You can use '**You don't say**' to express surprise at what someone has told you. People often use this expression to indicate that in fact they are not surprised. [FEELINGS] ◻ *"I'm a writer."—"You don't say. What kind of book are you writing?"* **3** PHRASE If you say there is a lot **to be said for** something, you mean you think it has a lot of good qualities or aspects. ◻ *There's a lot to be said for being based in the country.* **4** PHRASE If someone asks **what** you **have to say for** yourself, they are asking what excuse you have for what you have done. ◻ *"Well," she said eventually, "what have you to say for yourself?"* **5** PHRASE If something **goes without saying**, it is obvious. ◻ *It goes without saying that if someone has lung problems they should not smoke.* **6** PHRASE When one of the people or groups involved in a discussion **has** their **say**, they give their opinion. ◻ *Voters were finally having their say today.* **7** CONVENTION You use '**I wouldn't say no**' to indicate that you would like something, especially something that has just been offered to you. [INFORMAL, FORMULAE] ◻ *I wouldn't say no to a drink.* **8** PHRASE You use **that is to say** or **that's to say** to indicate that you are about to express the same idea more clearly or precisely. [FORMAL] ◻ *That would mean voting no, that is to say, using the veto.* **9** CONVENTION You can use '**You can say that again**' to express strong agreement with what someone has just said. [INFORMAL, EMPHASIS] ◻ *"You are in enough trouble already."—"You can say that again," sighed Richard.* **10** → See feature box at **debate**

say|ing /ˈseɪɪŋ/ (sayings) N-COUNT A **saying** is a sentence that people often say and that gives advice or information about human life and experience. ◻ *We also realize the truth of that old saying: Charity begins at home.*

say-so N-SING [oft with poss] If you do something on someone's **say-so**, they tell you to do it or they give you permission to do it. [INFORMAL] ◻ *Directors call the shots and nothing happens on set without their say-so.*

scab /skæb/ (scabs) N-COUNT A **scab** is a hard, dry covering that forms over the surface of a wound. ◻ *The area can be very painful until scabs form after about ten days.*

scab|bard /ˈskæbərd/ (scabbards) N-COUNT A **scabbard** is a container for a sword and can hang from a belt.

scab|by /ˈskæbi/ (scabbier, scabbiest) ADJ If a person, an animal, or a part of their body is **scabby**, it has scabs on it. ◻ *He had short trousers and scabby knees.*

sca|bies /ˈskeɪbiz/ N-UNCOUNT **Scabies** is a very infectious skin disease caused by very small creatures and makes you want to scratch a lot.

sca|brous /ˈskæbrəs/ ADJ If you describe something as **scabrous**, you mean that it deals with sex or describes sex in a shocking way. [LITERARY, DISAPPROVAL] ◻ *...the scabrous lower reaches of the film business.*

scads /skædz/ QUANT If you refer to **scads** of people or things, you are emphasizing that there are a lot of them. [AM, INFORMAL, EMPHASIS] ◻ *...scads of vegetarian dishes.* ◻ *The Voyager workload is divided among 157 scientists and scads of graduate students.*

in BRIT, use **loads**, **heaps**

scaf|fold /ˈskæfəld, -oʊld/ (scaffolds) **1** N-COUNT A **scaffold** was a raised platform on which criminals were hanged or had their heads cut off. ◻ *Ascending the shaky ladder to the scaffold, More addressed the executioner.* **2** N-COUNT A **scaffold** is a temporary raised platform on which workers stand to paint, repair, or build high parts of a building. ◻ *They were standing on top of a giant scaffold.*

scaf|fold|ing /ˈskæfəldɪŋ/ N-UNCOUNT **Scaffolding** consists of poles and boards made into a temporary framework that is used by workers when they are painting, repairing, or building high parts of a building, usually outside. ◻ *Workers have erected scaffolding around the base of the tower below the roadway.*

scald /skɔld/ (scalds, scalding, scalded) **1** V-T If you **scald** yourself, you burn yourself with very hot liquid or steam. ◻ *A patient jumped into a bath being prepared by a member of staff and scalded herself.* **2** N-COUNT A **scald** is a burn caused by very hot liquid or steam. ◻ *Scalds, burns and poisoning can all be life-threatening.*

scald|ing /ˈskɔldɪŋ/ ADJ **Scalding** or **scalding hot** liquids are extremely hot. ◻ *I tried to sip the tea but it was scalding.* ◻ *...scalding hot water.*

scale /skeɪl/ (scales, scaling, scaled) **1** N-SING If you refer to the **scale** of something, you are referring to its size or extent, especially when it is very big. ◻ *However, he underestimates the scale of the problem.* ◻ *The break-down of law and order could result in killing on a massive scale.* **2** → see also **full-scale**, **large-scale**, **small-scale** **3** N-COUNT A **scale** is a set of levels or numbers which are used in a particular system of measuring things or are used when comparing things. ◻ *...an earthquake measuring 5.5 on the Richter scale.* ◻ *The patient rates the therapies on a scale of zero to ten.* **4** → see also **timescale** **5** N-COUNT A pay **scale** or **scale** of fees is a list that shows how much someone should be paid, depending, for example, on their age or what work they do. ◻ *...those on the high end of the pay scale.* **6** N-COUNT The **scale** of a map, plan, or model is the relationship between the size of something in the map, plan, or model and its size in the real world. ◻ *The map, on a scale of 1:10,000, shows over 5,000 individual paths.* **7** → see also **full-scale**, **large-scale** **8** ADJ [ADJ n] A **scale** model or **scale** replica of a building or object is a model of it which is smaller than the real thing but has all the same parts and features. ◻ *Franklin made his mother an intricately detailed scale model of the house.* **9** N-COUNT In music, a **scale** is a fixed sequence of musical notes, each one higher than the next, which begins at a particular note. ◻ *...the scale of C major.* **10** N-COUNT The **scales** of a fish or reptile are the small, flat pieces of hard skin that cover its body. ◻ *Remove any excess scales from the fish skin.* **11** N-COUNT [usu pl] A **scale** is a piece of equipment used for weighing things, for example, for weighing amounts of food that you need in order to make a particular meal. ◻ *...a pair of kitchen scales.* ◻ *...a bathroom scale.* **12** V-T If you **scale** something such as a mountain or a wall, you climb up it or over it. [WRITTEN] ◻ *...the first British woman to scale the world's highest mountain.* **13** PHRASE If something is **out of scale** with the things near it, it is too big or too small in relation to them. ◻ *The tiny church was out of scale with the new banks and offices around it.* **14** PHRASE If the different parts of a map, drawing, or model are **to scale**, they are the right size in relation to each other. ◻ *...a miniature garden, with little pagodas and bridges all to scale.* **15** → See also color supplement

▶ **scale down** PHRASAL VERB If you **scale down** something, you make it smaller in size, amount, or extent than it used to be. ◻ *One factory has had to scale down its workforce from six hundred to only six.*

▶ **scale up** PHRASAL VERB If you **scale up** something, you make it greater in size, amount, or extent than it used to be. ◻ *...a major push to scale up treatment programs for people in poor countries.*

SYNONYMS

scale
NOUN **1**
degree: *Politicians have used television with varying degrees of success.*
size: *He knows the size of the task.*
extent: *The full extent of the losses was disclosed yesterday.*
magnitude: *No one seems to realize the magnitude of this problem.*

---

scal|lion /ˈskælyən/ (scallions) N-COUNT A **scallion** is a small onion with long green leaves. [AM]

in BRIT, use **spring onion**

scal|lop /ˈskɒləp, ˈskæl-/ (scallops) N-COUNT [usu pl] **Scallops** are large shellfish with two flat fan-shaped shells. Scallops can be eaten.

scal|loped /ˈskɒləpt, ˈskæl-/ ADJ [usu ADJ n] **Scalloped** objects are decorated with a series of small curves along the edges. ◻ *The quilt has pretty, scalloped edges and intricate quilting.*

scal|ly|wag /ˈskæliwæg/ (scallywags) N-COUNT If you call someone a **scallywag**, you mean that they behave badly but you like them, so you find it difficult to be really angry with them. [INFORMAL, OLD-FASHIONED] ◻ *It's his idea of a joke, I suppose, the scallywag.*

scalp /skælp/ (scalps, scalping, scalped) **1** N-COUNT Your **scalp** is the skin under the hair on your head. ◻ *He smoothed his hair back over his scalp.* **2** V-T If someone **scalps** tickets, they

scalpel

sell them outside a sports stadium or theater, usually for more than their original value. [AM] ❏ *He was trying to pick up some cash scalping tickets.*

in BRIT, use **tout**

scal|pel /skǽlpəl/ (**scalpels**) N-COUNT A **scalpel** is a knife with a short, thin, sharp blade. Scalpels are used by surgeons during operations.

scalp|er /skǽlpər/ (**scalpers**) N-COUNT A **scalper** is someone who sells tickets outside a sports stadium or theater, usually for more than their original value. [AM] ❏ *Another scalper said he'd charge $1,000 for a $125 ticket.*

in BRIT, use **tout**

scaly /skéɪli/ (**scalier, scaliest**) **1** ADJ [usu adj n] A **scaly** animal has small pieces of hard skin covering its body. ❏ *The brown rat has prominent ears and a long scaly tail.* **2** ADJ If someone's skin is **scaly**, it has dry areas and small pieces of it come off. ❏ *If your skin becomes red, sore or very scaly, consult your doctor.*

scam /skǽm/ (**scams, scamming, scammed**) **1** V-T If someone **scams** a person or organization, they deceive them in order to get something valuable from them, especially money. [INFORMAL] ❏ *When I told them they were being scammed, they couldn't believe it.* ❏ *Ryan's campaign fund allegedly scammed the state out of a million dollars.* ❏ *...a prisoner who scammed his way out of court.* **2** N-COUNT A **scam** is an illegal trick, usually with the purpose of getting money from people or avoiding paying tax. [INFORMAL] ❏ *They believed they were participating in an insurance scam, not a murder.* **3** → See feature box at **crime**

scamp /skǽmp/ (**scamps**) N-COUNT If you call a child a **scamp**, you mean that they are naughty or disrespectful but you like them, so you find it difficult to be angry with them. [INFORMAL] ❏ *Have some respect for me, you scamp!*

scamp|er /skǽmpər/ (**scampers, scampering, scampered**) V-I When people or small animals **scamper** somewhere, they move there quickly with small, light steps. ❏ *Children scampered off the yellow school bus and into the playground.*

scam|pi /skǽmpi/ N-PLURAL **Scampi** are large shrimps.

scan /skǽn/ (**scans, scanning, scanned**) **1** V-T/V-I When you **scan** written material, you look through it quickly in order to find important or interesting information. ❏ *She scanned the advertisement pages of the newspapers.* • N-SING **Scan** is also a noun. ❏ *I just had a quick scan through your book again.* **2** V-T/V-I [no passive] When you **scan** a place or group of people, you look at it carefully, usually because you are looking for something or someone. ❏ *The officer scanned the room.* ❏ *She was nervous and kept scanning the crowd for Paul.* **3** V-T If people **scan** something such as luggage, they examine it using a machine that can show or find things inside it that cannot be seen from the outside. ❏ *Their approach is to scan every checked-in bag with a bomb detector.* **4** V-T If a computer disk **is scanned**, a program on the computer checks the disk to make sure that it does not contain a virus. [COMPUTING] ❏ *Not all ISPs are equipped to scan for viruses.* **5** V-T [usu passive] If a picture or document **is scanned** into a computer, a machine passes a beam of light over it to make a copy of it in the computer. [COMPUTING] ❏ *The entire paper contents of all libraries will eventually be scanned into computers.* **6** V-I If a radar or sonar machine **scans** an area, it examines or searches it by sending radar or sonar beams over it. ❏ *The ship's radar scanned the sea ahead.* **7** N-COUNT A **scan** is a medical test in which a machine sends a beam of X-rays over a part of your body in order to check that it is healthy. ❏ *A brain scan revealed the blood clot.*

scan|dal ✦◇◇ /skǽndəl/ (**scandals**) **1** N-COUNT A **scandal** is a situation or event that is thought to be shocking and immoral and that everyone knows about. ❏ *...a financial scandal.* **2** N-UNCOUNT **Scandal** is talk about the shocking and immoral aspects of someone's behavior or something that has happened. ❏ *He loved gossip and scandal.*

━━━ COLLOCATIONS ━━━

scandal
NOUN **1**
noun + **scandal**: accounting, corruption, drug, sex
adjective + **scandal**: corporate, financial, political, public
verb + **scandal**: expose, uncover, investigate; cause

---

scarce

scan|dal|ize /skǽndəlaɪz/ (**scandalizes, scandalizing, scandalized**)

in BRIT, also use **scandalise**

V-T If something **scandalizes** people, they are shocked or offended by it. ❏ *She scandalized her family by falling in love with a married man.*

scan|dal|ous /skǽndələs/ **1** ADJ **Scandalous** behavior or activity is considered immoral and shocking. ❏ *They would be sacked for criminal or scandalous behavior.* • **scan|dal|ous|ly** ADV [ADV with v] ❏ *He asked only that Ingrid stop behaving so scandalously.* **2** ADJ **Scandalous** stories or remarks are concerned with the immoral and shocking aspects of someone's behavior or something that has happened. ❏ *Newspaper columns were full of scandalous tales.*

scan|dal sheet (**scandal sheets**) N-COUNT You can refer to newspapers and magazines which print mainly stories about sex and crime as **scandal sheets**. [AM] ❏ *What if someone sells the story to the scandal sheets?*

in BRIT, use **gutter press**

Scan|di|na|vian /skǽndɪnéɪviən/ (**Scandinavians**) **1** ADJ **Scandinavian** means belonging or relating to a group of northern European countries that includes Denmark, Norway, and Sweden, or to the people, languages, or culture of those countries. ❏ *The Baltic republics have called on the Scandinavian countries for help.* **2** N-COUNT **Scandinavians** are people from Scandinavian countries.

scan|ner /skǽnər/ (**scanners**) **1** N-COUNT A **scanner** is a machine which is used to examine, identify, or record things, for example by using a beam of light, sound, or X-rays. ❏ *...brain scanners.* **2** N-COUNT A **scanner** is a piece of computer equipment that you use for copying a picture or document into a computer. [COMPUTING] ❏ *...a color printer and scanner.*

scant /skǽnt/ ADJ You use **scant** to indicate that there is very little of something or not as much of something as there should be. ❏ *She began to berate the police for paying scant attention to the theft from her car.*

scanty /skǽnti/ (**scantier, scantiest**) **1** ADJ You describe something as **scanty** when there is less of it than you think there should be. ❏ *So far, what scanty evidence we have points to two suspects.* **2** ADJ If someone is wearing **scanty** clothing, he or she is wearing clothes which are sexually revealing. ❏ *...a model in scanty clothing.* • **scanti|ly** ADV [ADV -ed/adj] ❏ *...a troupe of scantily-clad dancers.*

scape|goat /skéɪpgoʊt/ (**scapegoats, scapegoating, scapegoated**) **1** N-COUNT If you say that someone is made a **scapegoat** for something bad that has happened, you mean that people blame them and may punish them for it although it may not be their fault. ❏ *I don't think I deserve to be made the scapegoat for a couple of bad results.* **2** V-T To **scapegoat** someone means to blame them publicly for something bad that has happened, even though it was not their fault. ❏ *...a climate where ethnic minorities are continually scapegoated for the lack of jobs and housing problems.*

scapu|la /skǽpyələ/ (**scapulae** /skǽpyəli/) N-COUNT Your **scapula** is your shoulder blade. [MEDICAL]

scar /skɑr/ (**scars, scarring, scarred**) **1** N-COUNT A **scar** is a mark on the skin which is left after a wound has healed. ❏ *He had a scar on his forehead.* **2** V-T [usu passive] If your skin **is scarred**, it is badly marked as a result of a wound. ❏ *He was scarred for life during a fight.* **3** V-T [usu passive] If a surface **is scarred**, it is damaged and there are ugly marks on it. ❏ *The arena was scarred by deep muddy ruts.* **4** N-COUNT If an unpleasant or emotional experience leaves a **scar** on someone, it has a permanent effect on their mind. ❏ *The early years of fear and hostility left a deep scar on the young boy.* **5** V-T If an unpleasant physical or emotional experience **scars** you, it has a permanent effect on your mind. ❏ *This is something that's going to scar him forever.*

scarce /skɛərs/ (**scarcer, scarcest**) **1** ADJ If something is **scarce**, there is not enough of it. ❏ *Food was scarce and expensive.* ❏ *Jobs are becoming increasingly scarce.* **2** PHRASE If you **make yourself scarce**, you quickly leave the place you are in, usually in order to avoid a difficult or embarrassing situation.

scarce|ly /skeəsli/ **1** ADV You use **scarcely** to emphasize that something is only just true or only just the case. [EMPHASIS] ☐ *He could scarcely breathe.* ☐ *I scarcely knew him.* **2** ADV You can use **scarcely** to say that something is not true or is not the case, in a humorous or critical way. ☐ *It can scarcely be coincidence.* **3** ADV [ADV before v] If you say **scarcely** had one thing happened when something else happened, you mean that the first event was followed immediately by the second. ☐ *Scarcely had the votes been counted, when the telephone rang.*

scar|city /skeəsɪti/ (**scarcities**) N-VAR If there is a **scarcity** of something, there is not enough of it for the people who need it or want it. [FORMAL] ☐ *...an ever increasing scarcity of water.*

scare /skeər/ (**scares, scaring, scared**) **1** V-T If something **scares** you, it frightens or worries you. ☐ *You're scaring me.* ☐ *The prospect of failure scares me rigid.* • PHRASE If you want to emphasize that something scares you a lot, you can say that it **scares the hell out of** you or **scares the life out of** you. [INFORMAL, EMPHASIS] **2** N-SING If a sudden unpleasant experience gives you a **scare**, it frightens you. ☐ *Don't you realize what a scare you've given us all?* **3** N-COUNT A **scare** is a situation in which many people are afraid or worried because they think something dangerous is happening which will affect them all. ☐ *The news set off a continent-wide health scare.* **4** N-COUNT A bomb **scare** or a security **scare** is a situation in which there is believed to be a bomb in a place. ☐ *Despite many recent bomb scares, no one has yet been hurt.* **5** → see also **scared**
▶ **scare away** → see **scare off**
▶ **scare off** **1** PHRASAL VERB If you **scare off** or **scare away** a person or animal, you frighten them so that they go away. ☐ *...an alarm to scare off an attacker.* **2** PHRASAL VERB If you **scare** someone **off**, you accidentally make them unwilling to become involved with you. ☐ *I don't think that revealing your past to your boyfriend scared him off.*

scare|crow /skeərkroʊ/ (**scarecrows**) N-COUNT A **scarecrow** is an object in the shape of a person, which is put in a field where crops are growing, in order to frighten birds away.

scared /skeərd/ **1** ADJ If you are **scared** of someone or something, you are frightened of them. ☐ *I'm certainly not scared of him.* ☐ *I was too scared to move.* **2** ADJ If you are **scared** that something unpleasant might happen, you are nervous and worried because you think that it might happen. ☐ *I was scared that I might be sick.*

scare|monger|ing /skeərmʌŋgərɪŋ, -mɒŋ-/ N-UNCOUNT If one person or group accuses another person or group of **scaremongering**, they accuse them of deliberately spreading worrying stories to try and frighten people. ☐ *The government yesterday accused the organization of scaremongering.*

scare sto|ry (**scare stories**) N-COUNT A **scare story** is something that is said or written to make people feel frightened and think that a situation is much more unpleasant or dangerous than it really is. ☐ *He described talk of sackings as scare stories.*

scarf /skɑrf/ (**scarfs** or **scarves**) N-COUNT A **scarf** is a piece of cloth that you wear around your neck or head, usually to keep yourself warm. ☐ *He reached up to loosen the scarf around his neck.*

scar|let /skɑrlɪt/ (**scarlets**) COLOR Something that is **scarlet** is bright red. ☐ *...her scarlet lipstick.*

scar|let fe|ver N-UNCOUNT **Scarlet fever** is an infectious disease which gives you a painful throat, a high temperature, and red spots on your skin.

-scarred /-skɑrd/ **1** COMB IN ADJ [ADJ n] **-scarred** is used after nouns such as 'bullet' and 'fire' to form adjectives which indicate that something has been damaged or marked by the thing mentioned. ☐ *...a bullet-scarred bus.* ☐ *...a lightning-scarred tree.* **2** COMB IN ADJ [usu ADJ n] **-scarred** is used after nouns such as 'battle' or 'drug' to form adjectives which indicate that the thing mentioned has had a permanent effect on someone's mind. ☐ *...battle-scarred soldiers.* **3** → see also **scar**

scarves /skɑrvz/ **Scarves** is a plural of **scarf**.

scary /skeəri/ (**scarier, scariest**) ADJ Something that is **scary** is rather frightening. [INFORMAL] ☐ *I think prison is going to be a scary thing for Harry.* ☐ *There's something very scary about him.* [INFORMAL] ☐ *It probably would be a good idea if you made yourself scarce.* **3** → See feature box at **deforest**

scat /skæt/ N-UNCOUNT **Scat** is a type of jazz singing in which the singer sings sounds rather than complete words.

scath|ing /skeɪðɪŋ/ ADJ If you say that someone is being **scathing** about something, you mean that they are being very critical of it. ☐ *Republican senators were scathing in their criticism of today's hearing.*

scato|logi|cal /skætəlɒdʒɪkəl/ ADJ [usu ADJ n] If you describe something as **scatological**, you mean that it deliberately refers to or represents feces in some way. [FORMAL] ☐ *...scatological anecdotes.*

scat|ter /skætər/ (**scatters, scattering, scattered**) **1** V-T If you **scatter** things over an area, you throw or drop them so that they spread all over the area. ☐ *She tore the rose apart and scattered the petals over the grave.* ☐ *They've been scattering toys everywhere.* **2** V-T/V-I If a group of people **scatter** or if you **scatter** them, they suddenly separate and move in different directions. ☐ *After dinner, everyone scattered.* **3** → see also **scattered, scattering**

scat|ter|brained /skætərbreɪnd/ also **scatter-brained** ADJ If you describe someone as **scatterbrained**, you mean that they often forget things and are unable to organize their thoughts properly.

scat|ter cush|ion (**scatter cushions**) N-COUNT [usu pl] **Scatter cushions** are small cushions for use on sofas and chairs.

scat|tered /skætərd/ **1** ADJ [ADJ n] **Scattered** things are spread over an area in an untidy or irregular way. ☐ *He picked up the scattered toys.* ☐ *Tomorrow there will be a few scattered showers.* **2** ADJ [v-link ADJ with n] If something is **scattered with** a lot of small things, they are spread all over it. ☐ *Every surface is scattered with photographs.*

scat|ter|ing /skætərɪŋ/ (**scatterings**) N-COUNT A **scattering** of things or people is a small number of them spread over an area. ☐ *...the scattering of houses east of the village.*

scatter|shot /skætərʃɒt/ ADJ [usu ADJ n] A **scattershot** approach or method involves doing something to a lot of things or people in a disorganized way, rather than focusing on particular things or people. ☐ *The report condemns America's scattershot approach to training workers.*

scav|enge /skævɪndʒ/ (**scavenges, scavenging, scavenged**) V-T/V-I If people or animals **scavenge** for things, they collect them by searching among waste or unwanted objects. ☐ *Many are orphans, their parents killed as they scavenged for food.* ☐ *Children scavenge through garbage.* • **scav|en|ger** (**scavengers**) N-COUNT ☐ *...scavengers such as rats.*

scav|en|ger hunt (**scavenger hunts**) N-COUNT A **scavenger hunt** is a game, usually played outdoors, in which the players must collect various objects from a list of things they have been given. ☐ *On scavenger hunts I would always ask Mrs. Martin for empty coffee cans.*

sce|nario /sɪneəriəʊ/ (**scenarios**) N-COUNT If you talk about a likely or possible **scenario**, you are talking about the way in which a situation may develop. ☐ *The conflict degenerating into civil war is everybody's nightmare scenario.*

scene ◆◇◇ /siːn/ (**scenes**) **1** N-COUNT A **scene** in a play, movie, or book is part of it in which a series of events happen in the same place. ☐ *...the opening scene of "A Christmas Carol."* ☐ *...Act I, scene 1.* **2** N-COUNT You refer to a place as a **scene** when you are describing its appearance and indicating what impression it makes on you. ☐ *It's a scene of complete devastation.* ☐ *Thick black smoke billowed over the scene.* **3** N-COUNT You can describe an event that you see, or that is broadcast or shown in a picture, as a **scene** of a particular kind. ☐ *There were emotional scenes as the refugees enjoyed their first breath of freedom.* ☐ *Television broadcasters were warned to exercise caution over depicting scenes of violence.* **4** N-COUNT The **scene** of an event is the place where it happened. ☐ *The area has been the scene of fierce fighting for three months.* ☐ *...traces left at the scene of a crime.* **5** N-SING You can refer to an area of activity as a particular type of **scene**. ☐ *Sandman's experimentation has made him something of a cult figure on the local music scene.* **6** N-COUNT If you make a **scene**, you embarrass people by publicly showing your anger about something. ☐ *I'm sorry I made such a scene.* **7** PHRASE If something is done **behind the scenes**, it is done secretly

scenery — schism

rather than publicly. ❑ *But behind the scenes Mr. Cain will be working quietly to try to get a deal done.* **8** PHRASE If you refer to what happens **behind the scenes**, you are referring to what happens during the making of a movie, play, or radio or television program. ❑ *It's an exciting opportunity to learn what goes on behind the scenes.* **9** PHRASE If you have **a change of scene**, you go somewhere different after being in a particular place for a long time. ❑ *What you need is a change of scene. Why not go on a cruise?* **10** PHRASE Something that **sets the scene for** a particular event creates the conditions in which the event is likely to happen. ❑ *An improving economy helped set the scene for his re-election.* **11** PHRASE When a person or thing appears **on the scene**, they come into being or become involved in something. When they disappear **from the scene**, they are no longer there or are no longer involved. ❑ *He could react jealously when and if another child comes on the scene.*

COLLOCATIONS

scene
NOUN
1
noun + **scene**: action, fight, love, sex; crowd, street
adjective + **scene**: dramatic, explicit, funny, graphic
verb + **scene**: film, rehearse, shoot; delete
3
adjective + **scene**: chaotic, horrific, ugly; angry, emotional, violent
verb + **scene**: depict, describe
5
noun + **scene**: art, dance, music, party
adjective + **scene**: international, literary, political, social
verb + **scene**: dominate

scen|ery /sˈiːnəri/ **1** N-UNCOUNT The **scenery** in a country area is the land, water, or plants that you can see around you. ❑ *...the island's spectacular scenery.* **2** N-UNCOUNT In a theater, the **scenery** consists of the structures and painted backgrounds that show where the action in the play takes place. ❑ *Instead of stagehands, the actors will move the scenery right in front of the audience.* **3** PHRASE If you have **a change of scenery**, you go somewhere different after being in a particular place for a long time. ❑ *A change of scenery might do you good.*

sce|nic /sˈiːnɪk/ **1** ADJ A **scenic** place has attractive scenery. ❑ *This is an extremely scenic part of America.* **2** ADJ A **scenic** route goes through attractive scenery and has nice views. ❑ *It was even marked on the map as a scenic route.*

scent /sɛnt/ (**scents, scenting, scented**) **1** N-COUNT The **scent** of something is the pleasant smell that it has. ❑ *Flowers are chosen for their scent as well as their look.* **2** V-T If something **scents** a place or thing, it makes it smell pleasant. ❑ *Jasmine flowers scent the air.* **3** N-MASS **Scent** is a liquid which women put on their necks and wrists to make themselves smell nice. ❑ *She dabbed herself with scent.* **4** N-VAR The **scent** of a person or animal is the smell that they leave and that other people sometimes follow looking for them. ❑ *A police dog picked up the murderer's scent.* **5** V-T [no cont] When an animal **scents** something, it becomes aware of it by smelling it. ❑ *...dogs which scent the hidden birds.*

scent|ed /sˈɛntɪd/ ADJ **Scented** things have a pleasant smell, either naturally or because perfume has been added to them. ❑ *The white flowers are pleasantly scented.*

scep|ter /sˈɛptər/ (**scepters**)

in BRIT, use **sceptre**

N-COUNT A **scepter** is an ornamental rod that a king or queen carries on ceremonial occasions or as a symbol of his or her power.

scep|tic /sˈkɛptɪk/ [mainly BRIT] → see **skeptic**
scep|ti|cal /sˈkɛptɪkəl/ [mainly BRIT] → see **skeptical**
scep|ti|cism /sˈkɛptɪsɪzəm/ [mainly BRIT] → see **skepticism**
scep|tre /sˈɛptər/ [mainly BRIT] → see **scepter**

sched|ule ♦♦◊ /sˈkɛdʒuːl, -ʊl/ (**schedules, scheduling, scheduled**) **1** N-COUNT A **schedule** is a plan that gives a list of events or tasks and the times at which each one should happen or be done. ❑ *He has been forced to adjust his schedule.* **2** N-UNCOUNT You can use **schedule** to refer to the time or way something is planned to be done. For example, if something is completed **on schedule**, it is completed at the time planned. ❑ *The jet arrived in Johannesburg two minutes ahead of schedule.* ❑ *Everything went according to schedule.* **3** V-T [usu passive] If something **is scheduled** to happen at a particular time, arrangements are made for it to happen at that time. ❑ *The space shuttle had been scheduled to blast off at 04:38.* ❑ *A presidential election was scheduled for last December.* **4** N-COUNT A **schedule** is a written list of things, for example, a list of prices, details, or conditions. ❑ *Ticket plans and a pricing schedule will not be released until later this year.* **5** N-COUNT A **schedule** is a list of all the times when trains, boats, buses, or aircraft are supposed to arrive at or leave a particular place. [mainly AM] ❑ *...a bus schedule.*

in BRIT, usually use **timetable**

6 N-COUNT In a school or college, a **schedule** is a diagram that shows the times in the week at which particular subjects are taught. [AM] ❑ *He began college with a schedule that included biology, calculus and political science.*

in BRIT, usually use **timetable**

7 → See feature box at **study**

SYNONYMS

schedule
NOUN **1**
plan: *...a detailed plan of action for restructuring the group.*
program: *The program of sell-offs has been implemented by the new chief executive.*
agenda: *Please find attached the agenda for tomorrow's meeting.*
timetable: *The timetable was hopelessly optimistic.*

sche|ma /sˈkiːmə/ (**schemas** or **schemata** /sˈkiːmətə, skɪmətə, -mætə/) N-COUNT A **schema** is an outline of a plan or theory. [FORMAL] ❑ *...a definite position in the schema of the economic process.*

sche|mat|ic /skɪmˈætɪk/ ADJ [usu ADJ n] A **schematic** diagram or picture shows something in a simple way. ❑ *This is represented in the schematic diagram below.*

scheme ♦♦◊ /skˈiːm/ (**schemes, scheming, schemed**) **1** N-COUNT A **scheme** is someone's plan for achieving something, especially something that will bring them some benefit. ❑ *...a quick money-making scheme to get us through the summer.* ❑ *They would first have to work out some scheme for getting the treasure out.* **2** V-T/V-I [oft cont] If you say that people **are scheming**, you mean that they are making secret plans in order to gain something for themselves. [DISAPPROVAL] ❑ *Everyone's always scheming and plotting.* ❑ *The bride's family were scheming to prevent a wedding.* **3** N-COUNT A **scheme** is a plan or arrangement involving many people which is made by a government or other organization. [BRIT] ❑ *...a private pension scheme.*

in AM, use **plan**

4 PHRASE When people talk about **the scheme of things** or **the grand scheme of things**, they are referring to the way that everything in the world seems to be organized. ❑ *We realize that we are infinitely small within the scheme of things.*

SYNONYMS

scheme
NOUN **1**
plan: *...a detailed plan of action for restructuring the group.*
program: *The program of sell-offs has been implemented by the new chief executive.*
strategy: *What should our marketing strategy have achieved?*
system: *...a flexible and relatively efficient filing system.*

schem|er /sˈkiːmər/ (**schemers**) N-COUNT If you refer to someone as a **schemer**, you mean that they make secret plans in order to get some benefit for themselves. [DISAPPROVAL] ❑ *...office schemers who think of nothing but their own advancement.*

scher|zo /skˈɛərtsoʊ/ (**scherzos**) N-COUNT A **scherzo** is a short, lively piece of classical music which is usually part of a longer piece of music.

schism /sˈkɪzəm, sˈɪz-/ (**schisms**) N-VAR When there is a **schism**, a group or organization divides into two groups as a result of differences in thinking and beliefs. [FORMAL] ❑ *The church seems to be on the brink of schism.*

schiz|oid /skɪtsɔɪd/ **1** ADJ If you describe someone as **schizoid**, you mean that they seem to have very different opinions and purposes at different times. [OFFENSIVE, DISAPPROVAL] ❑ *...a rather schizoid fellow.* **2** ADJ Someone who is **schizoid** has schizophrenia. ❑ *...a schizoid personality.*

schizo|phre|nia /skɪtsəfriniə/ N-UNCOUNT **Schizophrenia** is a serious mental illness. People who have it are unable to relate their thoughts and feelings to what is happening around them and often withdraw from society.

schizo|phren|ic /skɪtsəfrɛnɪk/ (**schizophrenics**) N-COUNT A **schizophrenic** is a person who has schizophrenia. ❑ *He was diagnosed as a paranoid schizophrenic.* • ADJ **Schizophrenic** is also an adjective. ❑ *...a schizophrenic patient.*

schlep /ʃlɛp/ (**schleps, schlepping, schlepped**) also **schlepp** **1** V-T/V-I If you **schlep** somewhere, or if you **schlep** something or someone to a place, you go there or take the thing or person there with a lot of difficulty or effort. [mainly AM, INFORMAL] ❑ *You no longer have to schlep to New York to see the most celebrated show on Broadway.* ❑ *Schlepping your own bags and equipment is exhausting.* **2** N-COUNT [usu sing] A **schlep** is a long or difficult journey. [mainly AM, INFORMAL] ❑ *Then it was back in the truck for a 150-mile schlep up the coast to Malibu.* **3** N-COUNT If you describe someone as a **schlep**, you mean that they are stupid or clumsy. [AM, INFORMAL, DISAPPROVAL]

schlock /ʃlɒk/ N-UNCOUNT If you refer to movies, pop songs, or books as **schlock**, you mean that they have no artistic or social value. [INFORMAL, DISAPPROVAL] ❑ *...a showman with a good eye for marketable schlock.*

schmaltz /ʃmɑlts/ N-UNCOUNT If you describe a song, movie, or book as **schmaltz**, you do not like it because it is too sentimental. [DISAPPROVAL]

schmaltzy /ʃmɑltsi/ (**schmaltzier, schmaltziest**) ADJ If you describe songs, movies, or books as **schmaltzy**, you do not like them because they are too sentimental. [DISAPPROVAL]

schmooze /ʃmuz/ (**schmoozes, schmoozing, schmoozed**) V-I If you **schmooze**, you talk casually and socially with someone. [mainly AM, INFORMAL] ❑ *...those coffee houses where you can schmooze for hours.*

schmuck /ʃmʌk/ (**schmucks**) N-COUNT If you call someone a **schmuck**, you mean that they are stupid or you do not like them. [AM, INFORMAL, DISAPPROVAL] ❑ *I played like a schmuck. I am a schmuck. That's how I feel right now.*

schnapps /ʃnɒps, ʃnæps/ N-UNCOUNT **Schnapps** is a strong alcoholic drink made from potatoes. • N-SING A **schnapps** is a glass of schnapps.

schol|ar /skɒlər/ (**scholars**) N-COUNT A **scholar** is a person who studies an academic subject and knows a lot about it. [FORMAL] ❑ *The library attracts thousands of scholars and researchers.*

schol|ar|ly /skɒlərli/ **1** ADJ A **scholarly** person spends a lot of time studying and knows a lot about academic subjects. ❑ *He was an intellectual, scholarly man.* **2** ADJ A **scholarly** book or article contains a lot of academic information and is intended for academic readers. ❑ *...the more scholarly academic journals.* **3** ADJ **Scholarly** matters and activities involve people who do academic research. ❑ *This has been the subject of intense scholarly debate.*

schol|ar|ship /skɒlərʃɪp/ (**scholarships**) **1** N-COUNT If you get a **scholarship** to a school or university, your studies are paid for by the school or university or by some other organization. ❑ *He got a scholarship to the Pratt Institute of Art.* **2** N-UNCOUNT **Scholarship** is serious academic study and the knowledge that is obtained from it. ❑ *I want to take advantage of your lifetime of scholarship.*

scho|las|tic /skəlæstɪk/ ADJ [ADJ n] Your **scholastic** achievement or ability is your academic achievement or ability while you are at school. [FORMAL] ❑ *...the values which encouraged her scholastic achievement.*

school ◆◆◆ /skul/ (**schools, schooling, schooled**) **1** N-VAR A **school** is a place where children are educated. You usually refer to this place as **school** when you are talking about the time that children spend there and the activities that they do there. ❑ *...a boy who was in my class at school.* ❑ *Even the good students say homework is what they most dislike about school.* ❑ *...a school built in the Sixties.* **2** N-COUNT-COLL A **school** is the students or staff at a school. ❑ *Deirdre, the whole school's going to hate you.* **3** N-COUNT; N-IN-NAMES A privately-run place where a particular skill or subject is taught can be referred to as a **school**. ❑ *...a riding school.* **4** N-VAR; N-IN-NAMES A university, college, or university department specializing in a particular type of subject can be referred to as a **school**. ❑ *...a lecturer in the school of veterinary medicine at the University of Pennsylvania.* **5** N-UNCOUNT **School** is used to refer to college. [AM] ❑ *Jack eventually graduated from school, got married, and got his first real job.* **6** N-COUNT-COLL [usu with supp] A particular **school** of writers, artists, or thinkers is a group of them whose work, opinions, or theories are similar. ❑ *...the Chicago school of economists.* **7** V-T If you **school** someone in something, you train or educate them to have a certain skill, type of behavior, or way of thinking. [WRITTEN] ❑ *Many mothers schooled their daughters in the myth of female inferiority.* **8** → see also **schooling, boarding school, grade school, graduate school, grammar school, high school, nursery school, prep school, primary school, private school, public school, state school**

school age also **school-age** N-UNCOUNT [oft prep n] When a child reaches **school age**, he or she is old enough to go to school. ❑ *Most of them have young children below school age.* • ADJ [usu ADJ n] **School-age** is also an adjective. ❑ *...families with school-age children.*

school|bag /skulbæg/ (**schoolbags**) also **school bag** N-COUNT A **schoolbag** is a bag that children use to carry books and other things to and from school.

school board (**school boards**) N-COUNT-COLL A **school board** is a committee in charge of education in a particular city or area, or in a particular school, especially in the United States. [AM] ❑ *Colonel Richard Nelson served on the school board until this year.*

school book (**school books**) also **schoolbook** N-COUNT [usu pl] **School books** are books giving information about a particular subject, which children use at school.

school|boy /skulbɔɪ/ (**schoolboys**) N-COUNT A **schoolboy** is a boy who goes to school. ❑ *...a group of ten-year-old schoolboys.*

school bus (**school buses**) N-COUNT A **school bus** is a special bus which takes children to and from school.

school|child /skultʃaɪld/ (**schoolchildren**) N-COUNT **Schoolchildren** are children who go to school. ❑ *Last year I had an audience of schoolchildren and they laughed at everything.*

school|days /skuldeɪz/ also **school days** N-PLURAL Your **schooldays** are the period of your life when you were at school. ❑ *He was happily married to a girl he had known since his schooldays.*

school dis|trict (**school districts**) N-COUNT A **school district** is an area which includes all the schools that are situated within that area and are governed by a particular authority. [AM] ❑ *...the San Francisco school district, one of the largest in the state.*

schooled /skuld/ **1** ADJ [v-link ADJ] If you are **schooled** in something, you have learned about it as the result of training or experience. [WRITTEN] ❑ *They were both well schooled in the ways of the Army.* **2** → see also **school**

school friend (**school friends**) also **schoolfriend** N-COUNT A **school friend** is a friend of yours who is at the same school as you, or who used to be at the same school when you were children. ❑ *I spent the evening with an old school friend.*

school|girl /skulgɜrl/ (**schoolgirls**) N-COUNT A **schoolgirl** is a girl who goes to school. ❑ *...half a dozen giggling schoolgirls.*

school|house /skulhaʊs/ (**schoolhouses**) N-COUNT A **schoolhouse** is a small building used as a school. [AM] ❑ *McCreary lives in a converted schoolhouse outside Charlottesville.*

school|ing /skulɪŋ/ N-UNCOUNT **Schooling** is education that children receive at school. ❑ *His formal schooling continued erratically until he reached the age of eleven.*

school kid (**school kids**) also **schoolkid** N-COUNT [usu pl] **School kids** are schoolchildren. [INFORMAL]

school lunch (**school lunches**) N-VAR **School lunches** are midday meals provided for children at a school. ❑ *School lunches are getting healthier, but they still have a long way to go.*

school|master /skuːlmæstər/ (**schoolmasters**) N-COUNT A **schoolmaster** is a man who teaches children in a school. [OLD-FASHIONED]

school|mate /skuːlmeɪt/ (**schoolmates**) N-COUNT [oft with poss] A **schoolmate** is a child who goes to the same school as you, especially one who is your friend. [mainly BRIT] ❑ *He started the magazine with a schoolmate.*

school|mistress /skuːlmɪstrɪs/ (**schoolmistresses**) N-COUNT A **schoolmistress** is a female teacher in a school. [OLD-FASHIONED]

school|room /skuːlrum/ (**schoolrooms**) N-COUNT A **schoolroom** is a classroom, especially the only classroom in a small school.

school|teacher /skuːltiːtʃər/ (**schoolteachers**) N-COUNT A **schoolteacher** is a teacher in a school.

school|work /skuːlwɜːrk/ N-UNCOUNT **Schoolwork** is the work that a child does at school or is given at school to do at home. ❑ *My mother would help me with my schoolwork.*

school|yard /skuːljɑːrd/ (**schoolyards**) also **school yard** N-COUNT [usu the N in sing] The **schoolyard** is the large open area with a hard surface just outside a school building, where the schoolchildren can play and do other activities. ❑ *...the sound of the kids in the schoolyard.*

schoon|er /skuːnər/ (**schooners**) ◼ N-COUNT A **schooner** is a medium-sized sailing ship. ◼ N-COUNT A **schooner** is a tall glass for beer. [AM]

schtick /ʃtɪk/ (**schticks**) also **shtick** N-VAR An entertainer's **schtick** is a series of funny or entertaining things that they say or do. [mainly AM, INFORMAL]

schwa /ʃwɑː/ (**schwas**) N-VAR In the study of language, **schwa** is the name of the neutral vowel sound represented by the symbol ə in this dictionary.

sci|ati|ca /saɪætɪkə/ N-UNCOUNT **Sciatica** is a severe pain in the nerve in your legs or the lower part of your back. [MEDICAL]

sci|ence ✦✧ /saɪəns/ (**sciences**) ◼ N-UNCOUNT **Science** is the study of the nature and behavior of natural things and the knowledge that we obtain about them. ❑ *The best discoveries in science are very simple.* ◼ N-COUNT A **science** is a particular branch of science such as physics, chemistry, or biology. ❑ *Physics is the best example of a science which has developed strong, abstract theories.* ◼ N-COUNT A **science** is the study of some aspect of human behavior, for example, sociology or anthropology. ❑ *...the modern science of psychology.* ◼ → see also **social science**

sci|ence fic|tion N-UNCOUNT **Science fiction** consists of stories in books, magazines, and movies about events that take place in the future or in other parts of the universe.

sci|en|tif|ic ✦✧ /saɪəntɪfɪk/ ◼ ADJ **Scientific** is used to describe things that relate to science or to a particular science. ❑ *Scientific research is widely claimed to be the source of the high standard of living in the U.S.* ❑ *...the use of animals in scientific experiments.* • **sci|en|tifi|cal|ly** /saɪəntɪfɪkli/ ADV ❑ *...scientifically advanced countries.* ◼ ADJ If you do something in a **scientific** way, you do it carefully and thoroughly, using experiments or tests ❑ *It's not a scientific way to test their opinions.* • **sci|en|tifi|cal|ly** ADV ❑ *Efforts are being made to research it scientifically.*

sci|en|tist ✦✧ /saɪəntɪst/ (**scientists**) N-COUNT A **scientist** is someone who has studied science and whose job is to teach or do research in science. ❑ *Scientists say they've already collected more data than had been expected.*

sci-fi /saɪ faɪ/ N-UNCOUNT **Sci-fi** is short for **science fiction**. [INFORMAL] ❑ *...a two-and-a-half hour sci-fi film.*

scimi|tar /sɪmɪtər/ (**scimitars**) N-COUNT A **scimitar** is a sword with a curved blade that was used in former times in some Eastern countries.

scin|til|la /sɪntɪlə/ QUANT [with brd-neg, QUANT of n-uncount] If you say that there is **not a scintilla** of evidence, hope, or doubt about something, you are emphasizing that there is none at all. [LITERARY, EMPHASIS] ❑ *He says there is "not a scintilla of evidence" to link him to any controversy.*

scin|til|lat|ing /sɪntəleɪtɪŋ/ ADJ [usu ADJ n] A **scintillating** conversation or performance is very lively and interesting. ❑ *You can hardly expect scintillating conversation from a kid that age.*

sci|on /saɪən/ (**scions**) N-COUNT [usu N of n] A **scion** of a rich or famous family is one of its younger or more recent members. [LITERARY] ❑ *Nabokov was the scion of an aristocratic family.*

scis|sors /sɪzərz/ N-PLURAL [also a pair of N] **Scissors** are a small cutting tool with two sharp blades that are screwed together. You use scissors for cutting things such as paper and cloth. ❑ *He told me to get some scissors.*

scle|ro|sis /sklərəʊsɪs/ ◼ N-UNCOUNT **Sclerosis** is a medical condition in which a part inside your body becomes hard. [MEDICAL] ◼ → see also **multiple sclerosis**

scoff /skɒf/ (**scoffs, scoffing, scoffed**) V-I If you **scoff** at something, you speak about it in a way that shows you think it is ridiculous or inadequate. ❑ *At first I scoffed at the notion.*

scoff|law /skɒflɔː/ (**scofflaws**) N-COUNT If you refer to someone as a **scofflaw**, you mean that they refuse to obey the law, for example, by failing to pay their debts or by ignoring minor legal regulations. [AM, DISAPPROVAL] ❑ *We want unsafe trucks off the road and scofflaws brought to justice.*

scold /skoʊld/ (**scolds, scolding, scolded**) V-T If you **scold** someone, you speak angrily to them because they have done something wrong. [FORMAL] ❑ *If he finds out, he'll scold me.* ❑ *Later she scolded her daughter for having talked to her father like that.*

sconce /skɒns/ (**sconces**) N-COUNT A **sconce** is a decorated object that holds candles or an electric light, and that is attached to the wall of a room.

scone /skoʊn, skɒn/ (**scones**) N-COUNT A **scone** is a small cake made from flour and fat, usually eaten with butter.

scoop /skuːp/ (**scoops, scooping, scooped**) ◼ V-T If you **scoop** something from a container, you remove it with something such as a spoon. ❑ *...the sound of a spoon scooping dog food out of a can.* ◼ N-COUNT A **scoop** is an object like a spoon which is used for picking up a quantity of a food such as ice cream or an ingredient such as flour. ❑ *...a small ice-cream scoop.* ◼ N-COUNT You can use **scoop** to refer to an exciting news story which is reported in one newspaper or on one television program before it appears anywhere else. ❑ *...one of the biggest scoops in the history of newspapers.* ◼ V-T If you **scoop** a person or thing somewhere, you put your hands or arms under or around them and quickly move them there. ❑ *Michael knelt next to her and scooped her into his arms.*

▶ **scoop up** PHRASAL VERB If you **scoop** something **up**, you put your hands or arms under it and lift it in a quick movement. ❑ *Use both hands to scoop up the leaves.*

scoot /skuːt/ (**scoots, scooting, scooted**) V-I If you **scoot** somewhere, you go there very quickly. [INFORMAL] ❑ *Sam said, "I'm going to hide," and scooted up the stairs.*

scoot|er /skuːtər/ (**scooters**) ◼ N-COUNT A **scooter** is a small light motorcycle which has a low seat. ◼ N-COUNT A **scooter** is a type of child's bicycle which has two wheels joined by a wooden board and a handle on a long pole attached to the front wheel. The child stands on the board with one foot, and uses the other foot to move forward. ◼ → See also color supplement

scope /skoʊp/ ◼ N-UNCOUNT If there is **scope** for a particular kind of behavior or activity, people have the opportunity to behave in this way or do that activity. ❑ *He believed in giving his staff scope for initiative.* ◼ N-SING The **scope** of an activity, topic, or piece of work is the whole area which it deals with or includes. ❑ *Mr. Dobson promised to widen the organization's scope of activity.* ◼ → See feature box at **research**

scorch /skɔːrtʃ/ (**scorches, scorching, scorched**) ◼ V-T To **scorch** something means to burn it slightly. ❑ *The bomb scorched the side of the building.* • **scorched** ADJ ❑ *...scorched black earth.* ◼ V-T/V-I If something **scorches** or **is scorched**, it becomes marked or changes color because it is affected by too much heat or by a chemical. ❑ *The leaves are inclined to scorch in hot sunshine.*

scorched earth N-UNCOUNT [usu N n] A **scorched earth** policy is the deliberate burning, destruction, and removal by an army of everything that would be useful to an enemy coming into the area. ❑ *He employed a scorched-earth policy, destroying villages and burning crops.*

scorch|ing /skɔːrtʃɪŋ/ ADJ **Scorching** or **scorching hot** weather or temperatures are very hot indeed. [INFORMAL, EMPHASIS] ❑ *That race was run in scorching weather.*

score /skɔr/ (scores, scoring, scored)

In meaning **9**, the plural form is **score**.

1 V-T/V-I In a sport or game, if a player **scores** a goal or a point, they gain a goal or point. ☐ *Patten scored his second touchdown of the game.* ☐ *He scored late in the third quarter to cut the gap to 10 points.* **2** V-T/V-I If you **score** a particular number or amount, for example, as a mark in a test, you achieve that number or amount. ☐ *Kelly had scored an average of 147 on three separate IQ tests.* ☐ *Congress scores low in public opinion polls.* **3** N-COUNT Someone's **score** in a game or test is a number, for example, a number of points or runs, which shows what they have achieved or what level they have reached. ☐ *The U.S. Open golf tournament was won by Ben Hogan, with a score of 287.* ☐ *He won this year's title with a score of 9.687.* **4** N-COUNT The **score** in a game is the result of it or the current situation, as indicated by the number of goals, runs, or points obtained by the two teams or players. ☐ *4-1 was the final score.* ☐ *They beat the Giants by a score of 7 to 3.* **5** V-T If you score a success, a victory, or a hit, you are successful in what you are doing. [WRITTEN] ☐ *His abiding passion was ocean racing, at which he scored many successes.* **6** N-COUNT The **score** of a movie, play, or similar production is the music which is written or used for it. ☐ *The dance is accompanied by an original score by Henry Torgue.* **7** N-COUNT The **score** of a piece of music is the written version of it. ☐ *He recognizes enough notation to be able to follow a score.* **8** QUANT [QUANT of pl-n] If you refer to **scores of** things or people, you are emphasizing that there are very many of them. [WRITTEN, EMPHASIS] ☐ *Campaigners lit scores of bonfires in ceremonies to mark the anniversary.* **9** NUM A **score** is twenty or approximately twenty. [WRITTEN] ☐ *A score of countries may be either producing or planning to obtain chemical weapons.* **10** V-T If you **score** a surface with something sharp, you cut a line or number of lines in it. ☐ *Lightly score the surface of the steaks with a sharp cook's knife.* **11** PHRASE If you **keep score** of the number of things that are happening in a certain situation, you count them and record them. ☐ *You can keep score of your baby's movements before birth by recording them on a kick chart.* **12** PHRASE If you **know the score**, you know what the real facts of a situation are and how they affect you, even though you may not like them. [SPOKEN] ☐ *I don't feel sorry for Carl. He knew the score, he knew what he had to do and couldn't do it.* **13** PHRASE You can use **on that score** or **on this score** to refer to something that has just been mentioned, especially an area of difficulty or concern. ☐ *I became pregnant easily. At least I've had no problems on that score.* **14** PHRASE If you **settle a score** or **settle an old score** with someone, you take revenge on them for something they have done in the past. ☐ *The groups had historic scores to settle with each other.*

score|board /skɔrbɔrd/ (scoreboards) N-COUNT A **scoreboard** is a large board, for example, at a sports arena or stadium, which shows the score in a game or competition. ☐ *The figures flash up on the scoreboard.*

score|card /skɔrkɑrd/ (scorecards) **1** N-COUNT A **scorecard** is a printed card that tells you who is taking part in a game or competition, and on which officials, players, or people watching can record each player's score. **2** N-COUNT [with supp] A **scorecard** is a system or procedure that is used for checking or testing something. [AM] ☐ *This commission would keep environmental scorecards on UN member nations.*

score|less /skɔrlɪs/ ADJ In baseball, soccer, and some other sports, a **scoreless** game or part of a game is one in which neither team has scored any goals or points. [JOURNALISM] ☐ *Norway had held Holland to a scoreless draw in Rotterdam.*

scor|er /skɔrər/ (scorers) **1** N-COUNT In football, hockey, and many other sports and games, a **scorer** is a player who scores a goal, runs, or points. ☐ *...David Hirst, the scorer of 11 goals this season.* **2** N-COUNT A **scorer** is an official who writes down the score of a game or competition as it is being played.

scorn /skɔrn/ (scorns, scorning, scorned) **1** N-UNCOUNT If you treat someone or something with **scorn**, you show contempt for them. ☐ *Researchers greeted the proposal with scorn.* **2** V-T If you **scorn** someone or something, you feel or show contempt for them. ☐ *Several leading officers have quite openly scorned the peace talks.* **3** V-T If you **scorn** something, you refuse to have it or accept it because you think it is not good enough or suitable for you. ☐ *...people who scorned traditional methods.*

scorn|ful /skɔrnfəl/ ADJ If you are **scornful** of someone or something, you show contempt for them. ☐ *He is deeply scornful of politicians.*

Scor|pio /skɔrpioʊ/ (Scorpios) **1** N-UNCOUNT **Scorpio** is one of the twelve signs of the zodiac. Its symbol is a scorpion. People who are born approximately between the 23rd of October and the 21st of November come under this sign. **2** N-COUNT A **Scorpio** is a person whose sign of the zodiac is Scorpio.

scor|pi|on /skɔrpiən/ (scorpions) N-COUNT A **scorpion** is a small creature which looks rather like a large insect. Scorpions have a long curved tail, and some of them are poisonous.

Scot /skɒt/ (Scots) **1** N-COUNT A **Scot** is a person of Scottish origin. **2** N-UNCOUNT **Scots** is a dialect of the English language that is spoken in Scotland. ☐ *There are things you can express in Scots that you can't say in English.* **3** ADJ [usu ADJ n] **Scots** means the same as **Scottish**. ☐ *...his guttural Scots accent.*

scotch /skɒtʃ/ (scotches, scotching, scotched) V-T If you **scotch** a rumor, plan, or idea, you put an end to it before it can develop any further. ☐ *They have scotched rumors that they are planning a special show.*

Scotch /skɒtʃ/ (Scotches) N-MASS **Scotch** or **Scotch whisky** is whiskey made in Scotland. ☐ *...a bottle of Scotch.* • N-COUNT A **Scotch** is a glass of Scotch. ☐ *He poured himself a Scotch.*

Scotch-Irish ADJ If someone, especially an American, is **Scotch-Irish**, they are descended from both Scottish and Irish people, especially from Scottish people who had settled in Northern Ireland. [mainly AM] • N-PLURAL [usu the N] **Scotch-Irish** is also a noun. ☐ *...Virginia's Great Valley, where the Scotch-Irish had settled in the eighteenth century.*

Scotch tape N-UNCOUNT **Scotch tape** is a clear sticky tape that is sold in rolls and that you use to stick paper or card together or onto a wall. [AM, TRADEMARK] ☐ *A small sign was attached to the wall with peeling Scotch tape.*

in BRIT, use **Sellotape**

scot-free /skɒt friː/ ADV [ADV after v] If you say that someone got away **scot-free**, you are emphasizing that they escaped punishment for something that you believe they should have been punished for. [EMPHASIS] ☐ *Others who were guilty were being allowed to get off scot-free.*

Scots|man /skɒtsmən/ (Scotsmen) N-COUNT A **Scotsman** is a man of Scottish origin.

Scots|woman /skɒtswʊmən/ (Scotswomen) N-COUNT A **Scotswoman** is a woman of Scottish origin.

Scot|tish /skɒtɪʃ/ ADJ Something that is **Scottish** belongs or relates to Scotland, its people, or its language.

scoun|drel /skaʊndrəl/ (scoundrels) N-COUNT If you refer to a man as a **scoundrel**, you mean that he behaves very badly toward other people, especially by cheating them or deceiving them. [OLD-FASHIONED, DISAPPROVAL] ☐ *He is a lying scoundrel!*

scour /skaʊər/ (scours, scouring, scoured) **1** V-T If you **scour** something such as a place or a book, you make a thorough search of it to try to find what you are looking for. ☐ *Rescue crews had scoured an area of 30 square miles.* **2** V-T If you **scour** something such as a sink, floor, or pan, you clean its surface by rubbing it hard with something rough. ☐ *He decided to scour the sink.*

scourge /skɜrdʒ/ (scourges, scourging, scourged) **1** N-COUNT [oft N of n] A **scourge** is something that causes a lot of trouble or suffering to a group of people. ☐ *...the best chance in 20 years to end the scourge of terrorism.* **2** V-T If something **scourges** a place or group of people, it causes great pain and suffering to people. ☐ *Economic anarchy scourged the post-war world.*

scout /skaʊt/ (scouts, scouting, scouted) **1** N-COUNT A **scout** is someone who is sent to an area of countryside to find out the position of an enemy army. ☐ *They set off, two men out in front as scouts, two behind in case of any attack from the rear.* **2** V-T/V-I If you **scout** somewhere for something, you go through that area searching for it. ☐ *I wouldn't have time to scout the area for junk.* ☐ *A team of four was sent to scout a nuclear test site.*

Scout (Scouts) **1** N-COUNT A **Scout** is a member of the Boy Scouts or Girl Scouts. ☐ *...a party of seven Scouts and three leaders on a camping trip.* **2** N-PROPER-COLL [the N] **The Scouts** is the same as the **Boy Scouts** or the **Girl Scouts**.

scout|master /skaʊtmæstər/ (scoutmasters) N-COUNT A scoutmaster is a man who is in charge of a troop of Scouts.

scowl /skaʊl/ (scowls, scowling, scowled) V-I When someone scowls, an angry or hostile expression appears on their face. ▫ He scowled, and slammed the door behind him. • N-COUNT Scowl is also a noun. ▫ Chris met the remark with a scowl.

scrab|ble /skræbəl/ (scrabbles, scrabbling, scrabbled) **1** V-T/V-I If you scrabble for something, especially something that you cannot see, you move your hands or your feet about quickly and hurriedly in order to find it. ▫ He grabbed his jacket and scrabbled in his desk drawer for some loose change. ▫ I hung there, scrabbling with my feet to find a foothold. • PHRASAL VERB Scrabble around or scrabble about means the same as scrabble. ▫ Alberg scrabbled around for pen and paper. ▫ Gleb scrabbled about in the hay, pulled out a book and opened it. **2** V-T/V-I If you say that someone is scrabbling to do something, you mean that they are having difficulty because they are in too much of a hurry, or because the task is almost impossible. ▫ The banks are now desperately scrabbling to recover their costs. ▫ The opportunity had gone. His mind scrabbled for alternatives. • PHRASAL VERB Scrabble around means the same as scrabble. ▫ You get a six-month contract, and then you have to scrabble around for the next job.

Scrab|ble /skræbəl/ N-UNCOUNT Scrabble is a board game in which players score points by forming words from a set of tiles with letters of the alphabet on them. [TRADEMARK] ▫ In the living room below, my parents were playing Scrabble.

scrag|gly /skrægli/ (scragglier, scraggliest) ADJ Scraggly hair or plants are thin and grow in a messy way. [mainly AM] ▫ ...a scraggly mustache.

scrag|gy /skrægi/ (scraggier, scraggiest) ADJ If you describe a person or animal as scraggy, you mean that they look unattractive because they are so thin. [DISAPPROVAL] ▫ ...his scraggy neck. ▫ ...a flock of scraggy sheep.

scram|ble /skræmbəl/ (scrambles, scrambling, scrambled) **1** V-I If you scramble over rocks or up a hill, you move quickly over them or up it using your hands to help you. ▫ Tourists were scrambling over the rocks looking for the perfect camera angle. **2** V-I If you scramble to a different place or position, you move there in a hurried, awkward way. ▫ Ann threw back the covers and scrambled out of bed. **3** V-T/V-I If a number of people scramble for something, they compete energetically with each other for it. ▫ More than three million fans are expected to scramble for tickets. • N-COUNT Scramble is also a noun. ▫ ...the scramble for jobs. **4** V-T If you scramble eggs, you break them, mix them together and then cook them in butter. ▫ Make the toast and scramble the eggs. • **scram|bled** ADJ ▫ ...scrambled eggs and bacon. **5** V-T If a device scrambles a radio or telephone message, it interferes with the sound so that the message can only be understood by someone with special equipment. ▫ The system lets you encrypt or scramble the data that's sent between machines.

scram|bler /skræmblər/ (scramblers) N-COUNT A scrambler is an electronic device which alters the sound of a radio or telephone message so that it can only be understood by someone who has special equipment.

scrap /skræp/ (scraps, scrapping, scrapped) **1** N-COUNT A scrap of something is a very small piece or amount of it. ▫ A crumpled scrap of paper was found in her handbag. **2** N-PLURAL Scraps are pieces of unwanted food which are thrown away or given to animals. ▫ ...the scraps from the Sunday dinner table. **3** V-T If you scrap something, you get rid of it or cancel it. [JOURNALISM] ▫ A strike last month forced the government to backtrack on fully scrapping fuel subsidies. **4** ADJ [ADJ n] Scrap metal or paper is no longer wanted for its original purpose, but may have some other use. ▫ There's always tons of scrap paper in Dad's office. **5** N-UNCOUNT Scrap is metal from old or damaged machinery or cars. ▫ Thousands of tanks, artillery pieces and armored vehicles will be cut up for scrap. **6** N-UNCOUNT You can refer to a fight or a quarrel as a scrap, especially if it is not very serious. [INFORMAL] ▫ He had suffered a mild concussion in a scrap for a loose ball. • V-I Scrap is also a verb. ▫ Our guys scrapped and competed and went right to the wire.

scrap|book /skræpbʊk/ (scrapbooks) N-COUNT A scrapbook is a book with empty pages on which you can stick things such as pictures or newspaper articles in order to keep them. ▫ ...a large scrapbook of press clippings and photographs.

scrape /skreɪp/ (scrapes, scraping, scraped) **1** V-T If you scrape something from a surface, you remove it, especially by pulling a sharp object over the surface. ▫ She went around the car scraping the frost off the windows. **2** V-T/V-I If something scrapes against something else, it rubs against it, making a noise or causing slight damage. ▫ The only sound is that of knives and forks scraping against china. ▫ The car hurtled past us, scraping the wall and screeching to a halt. **3** V-T If you scrape a part of your body, you accidentally rub it against something hard and rough, and damage it slightly. ▫ She stumbled and fell, scraping her palms and knees.
▶ **scrape through** PHRASAL VERB If you scrape through an examination, you just succeed in passing it. If you scrape through a competition or a vote, you just succeed in winning it. ▫ He was a poor student, barely scraping through his final year.
▶ **scrape together** PHRASAL VERB If you scrape together an amount of money or a number of things, you succeed in obtaining it with difficulty. ▫ They only just managed to scrape the money together.

scrap|er /skreɪpər/ (scrapers) N-COUNT A scraper is a tool that has a small handle and a metal or plastic blade and can be used for scraping a particular surface clean.

scrap|heap /skræphiːp/ also **scrap heap** **1** N-SING If you say that someone has been thrown on the scrapheap, you mean that they have been forced to leave their job by an uncaring employer and are unlikely to get other work. ▫ Thousands of miners have been thrown on the scrapheap with no jobs and no prospects. **2** N-SING If things such as machines or weapons are thrown on the scrapheap, they are thrown away because they are no longer needed. ▫ Thousands of Europe's tanks and guns are going to the scrap heap.

scrap|ings /skreɪpɪŋz/ N-PLURAL Scrapings are small amounts or pieces that have been scraped off something. ▫ There might be scrapings under his fingernails.

scrap|py /skræpi/ (scrappier, scrappiest) ADJ [usu ADJ n] If you describe something as scrappy, you disapprove of it because it seems to be badly planned or messy. [DISAPPROVAL] ▫ The final chapter is no more than a scrappy addition.

scrap|yard /skræpjɑːrd/ (scrapyards) also **scrap yard** N-COUNT A scrapyard is a place where old machines such as cars or ships are destroyed and where useful parts are saved. [BRIT]

in AM, use **junkyard**

scratch /skrætʃ/ (scratches, scratching, scratched) **1** V-T If you scratch yourself, you rub your fingernails against your skin because it is itching. ▫ He scratched himself under his arm. ▫ The old man lifted his cardigan to scratch his side. **2** V-T If a sharp object scratches someone or something, it makes small shallow cuts on their skin or surface. ▫ The branches tore at my jacket and scratched my hands and face. **3** N-COUNT Scratches on someone or something are small shallow cuts. ▫ The seven-year-old was found crying with scratches on his face and neck. **4** PHRASE If you do something from scratch, you do it without making use of anything that has been done before. ▫ Building a home from scratch can be both exciting and challenging. **5** PHRASE If you say that someone is scratching their head, you mean that they are thinking hard and trying to solve a problem or puzzle. ▫ The Institute spends a lot of time scratching its head about how to boost American productivity.

scratch card (scratch cards) also **scratchcard** N-COUNT A scratch card is a card with hidden words or symbols on it. You scratch the surface off to reveal the words or symbols and find out if you have won a prize.

scratch file (scratch files) N-COUNT A scratch file is a temporary computer file which you use as a work area or as a store while a program is operating. [COMPUTING]

scratch pad (scratch pads) N-COUNT A scratch pad is a temporary storage memory in a computer. [COMPUTING]

scratch pa|per N-UNCOUNT Scratch paper is paper that is used for quick notes, drafts, or sketches. [AM] ▫ The notes were always on scratch paper or the back of an envelope, nothing fancy. ▫ ...a piece of scratch paper.

scratchy /skrætʃi/ (scratchier, scratchiest) **1** ADJ Scratchy sounds are thin and harsh. ▫ Listening to the scratchy recording, I recognized Walt Whitman immediately. **2** ADJ Scratchy clothes or

scrawl /skrɔl/ (scrawls, scrawling, scrawled) **1** V-T If you **scrawl** something, you write it in a careless and messy way. ☐ *He scrawled a hasty note to his wife.* ☐ *Someone had scrawled "Scum" on his car.* **2** N-VAR You can refer to writing that looks careless and messy as a **scrawl**. ☐ *The letter was handwritten, in a hasty, barely decipherable scrawl.*

scrawny /skrɔni/ (scrawnier, scrawniest) ADJ If you describe a person or animal as **scrawny**, you mean that they look unattractive because they are so thin. [DISAPPROVAL] ☐ *...a scrawny woman with dyed black hair.*

scream ✦✧✧ /skrim/ (screams, screaming, screamed) **1** V-I When someone **screams**, they make a very loud, high-pitched cry, for example, because they are in pain or are very frightened. ☐ *Women were screaming; some of the houses nearest the bridge were on fire.* • N-COUNT **Scream** is also a noun. ☐ *Hilda let out a scream.* **2** V-T If you **scream** something, you shout it in a loud, high-pitched voice. ☐ *"Brigid!" she screamed. "Get up!"*

COLLOCATIONS

scream
NOUN **1**
adjective + **scream**: blood-curdling, guttural, high-pitched, piercing; muffled
VERB **2**
noun + **scream**: audience, crowd, fans; baby
scream + adverb: loudly, hysterically

---

scream|ing|ly /skrimiŋli/ ADV [ADV adj] If you say that something is, for example, **screamingly** funny or **screamingly** boring, you mean that it is extremely funny or extremely boring. [EMPHASIS] ☐ *...a screamingly funny joke.*

scree /skri/ (screes) N-VAR **Scree** is a mass of loose stones on the side of a mountain. ☐ *Occasionally scree fell in a shower of dust.*

screech /skritʃ/ (screeches, screeching, screeched) **1** V-I If a vehicle **screeches** somewhere or if its tires **screech**, its tires make an unpleasant high-pitched noise on the road. ☐ *A black Mercedes screeched to a halt beside the helicopter.* **2** V-T When you **screech** something, you shout it in a loud, unpleasant, high-pitched voice. ☐ *"Get me some water, Jeremy!" I screeched.* • N-COUNT **Screech** is also a noun. ☐ *The figure gave a screech.* **3** V-I When a bird, animal, or thing **screeches**, it makes a loud, unpleasant, high-pitched noise. ☐ *A macaw screeched at him from its perch.* • N-COUNT **Screech** is also a noun. ☐ *He heard the screech of brakes.*

screen ✦✦✧ /skrin/ (screens, screening, screened) **1** N-COUNT A **screen** is a flat vertical surface on which pictures or words are shown. Television sets and computers have screens, and movies are shown on a screen in movie theaters. **2** → see also **widescreen** **3** N-SING [the N, also on/off N] You can refer to movies or television as **the screen**. ☐ *Many viewers have strong opinions about violence on the screen.* **4** V-T When a movie or a television program **is screened**, it is shown in the movie theater or broadcast on television. ☐ *The series is likely to be screened in January.* • **screen|ing** (screenings) N-COUNT ☐ *The film-makers will be present at the screenings to introduce their works.* **5** N-COUNT A **screen** is a vertical panel which can be moved around. It is used to keep cold air away from part of a room, or to create a smaller area within a room. ☐ *They put a screen in front of me so I couldn't see what was going on.* **6** V-T [usu passive] If something **is screened** by another thing, it is behind it and hidden by it. ☐ *Most of the road behind the hotel was screened by an apartment block.* **7** V-I To **screen** for a disease means to examine people to make sure that they do not have it. ☐ *...a quick saliva test that would screen for people at risk of tooth decay.* • **screen|ing** N-VAR ☐ *Our country has an enviable record on breast screening for cancer.* **8** V-T When an organization **screens** people who apply to join it, it investigates them to make sure that they are not likely to cause problems. ☐ *They will screen all their candidates.* **9** V-T To **screen** people or luggage means to check them using special equipment to make sure they are not carrying a weapon or a bomb. ☐ *The airline had not been searching unaccompanied baggage by hand, but only screening it on X-ray machines.* **10** → See feature box at **medicine**; See also color supplement

---

SYNONYMS

screen
VERB **4**
broadcast: *The concert will be broadcast live on television and radio.*
show: *The BBC World Service Television news showed the same film clip.*
air: *Tonight, PBS will air a documentary called 'Democracy In Action.'*
televise: *The Grand Prix will be televised by the BBC.*

---

screen door (screen doors) N-COUNT A **screen door** is a door made of fine netting which is on the outside of the main door of a house. It is used to keep insects out when the main door is open.

screen es|tate N-UNCOUNT **Screen estate** is the amount of space available on the screen of a computer or phone. ☐ *The new phone will appeal to those who want bigger screen estate.*

screen grab (screen grabs) N-COUNT A **screen grab** is an image that you create by capturing and copying part or all of a television or computer display at a particular moment. ☐ *Her manager had taken screen grabs of the tweets before they were deleted.*

screen name (screen names) N-COUNT Someone's **screen name** is a name that they use when communicating with other people on the internet. [COMPUTING] ☐ *...someone with the screen name of nirvanakcf.*

screen|play /skrinpleɪ/ (screenplays) N-COUNT A **screenplay** is the words to be spoken in a movie, and instructions about what will be seen in it.

screen|saver /skrinseɪvər/ (screensavers) also **screen saver** N-COUNT A **screensaver** is a moving picture which appears or is put on a computer screen when the computer is not used for a while. [COMPUTING]

screen|shot /skrinʃɒt/ (screenshots) N-COUNT A **screenshot** is an image that you create by copying part of all of the display on a computer screen at a particular moment. [COMPUTING]

screen test (screen tests) N-COUNT When a movie studio gives an actor a **screen test**, they film a short scene in order to test how good he or she would be in movies.

screen|writer /skrinraɪtər/ (screenwriters) N-COUNT A **screenwriter** is a person who writes screenplays.

screen|writing /skrinraɪtɪŋ/ N-UNCOUNT **Screenwriting** is the process of writing screenplays.

screw /skru/ (screws, screwing, screwed) **1** N-COUNT A **screw** is a metal object similar to a nail, with a raised spiral line around it. You turn a screw using a screwdriver so that it goes through two things, for example, two pieces of wood, and fastens them together. ☐ *Each bracket is fixed to the wall with just three screws.* **2** V-T/V-I If you **screw** something somewhere or if it **screws** somewhere, you fix it in place by means of a screw or screws. ☐ *I had screwed the shelf on the wall myself.* ☐ *Screw down any loose floorboards.* **3** ADJ [ADJ n] A **screw** lid or fitting is one that has a raised spiral line on the inside or outside of it, so that it can be fixed in place by twisting. ☐ *...an ordinary jam jar with a screw lid.* **4** V-T/V-I If you **screw** something somewhere or if it **screws** somewhere, you fix it in place by twisting it around and around. ☐ *"Yes, I know that," Kelly said, screwing the silencer onto the pistol.* ☐ *Screw down the lid fairly tightly.* **5** V-T If you **screw** something such as a piece of paper **into** a ball, you squeeze it or twist it tightly so that it is in the shape of a ball. ☐ *He screwed the paper into a ball and tossed it into the fire.* **6** V-T If you **screw** your face or your eyes **into** a particular expression, you tighten the muscles of your face to form that expression, for example, because you are in pain or because the light is too bright. ☐ *He screwed his face into an expression of mock pain.* **7** V-RECIP If someone **screws** someone else or if two people **screw**, they have sex together. [INFORMAL, VULGAR] ☐ *"Are you screwing her?" she said.* **8** V-T [only imper] Some people use **screw** in expressions such as **screw you** or **screw that** to show that they are not concerned about someone or something or that they feel contempt for them. [INFORMAL, VULGAR, FEELINGS] ☐ *Something inside me snapped. "Well, screw you then!"* **9** V-T If someone **screws** something, especially money, **out of** you, they get it from you by putting pressure on you.

[INFORMAL] ❑ *After decades of rich nations screwing money out of poor nations, it's about time some went the other way.* **10** → See also color supplement

▶ **screw up** **1** PHRASAL VERB If you **screw up** your eyes or your face, you tighten your eye or face muscles, for example, because you are in pain or because the light is too bright. ❑ *She had screwed up her eyes, as if she found the sunshine too bright.* ❑ *Close your eyes and screw them up tight.* **2** PHRASAL VERB If you **screw up** a piece of paper, you squeeze it tightly so that it becomes very creased and no longer flat, usually when you are throwing it away. ❑ *He would start writing to his family and would screw the letter up in frustration.* **3** PHRASAL VERB To **screw** something **up**, or to **screw up**, means to cause something to fail or be spoiled. [INFORMAL] ❑ *You can't open the window because it screws up the air conditioning.* ❑ *Get out. Haven't you screwed things up enough already, you idiot!*

screw|ball /skrˈuːbɔːl/ (**screwballs**) **1** ADJ [ADJ n] **Screwball** comedy is silly and eccentric in an amusing and harmless way. [INFORMAL] ❑ *...a remake of a '50s classic screwball comedy.* **2** N-COUNT If you say that someone is a **screwball**, you mean that they do strange or crazy things. [INFORMAL, DISAPPROVAL]

screw|driver /skrˈuːdraɪvər/ (**screwdrivers**) **1** N-COUNT A **screwdriver** is a tool that is used for turning screws. It consists of a metal rod with a flat or cross-shaped end that fits into the top of the screw. **2** → See feature box at **DIY**; See also color supplement

screwed up ADJ If you say that someone is **screwed up**, you mean that they are very confused or worried, or that they have psychological problems. [INFORMAL] ❑ *He was really screwed up with his emotional problems.*

screw-top ADJ [ADJ n] A **screw-top** bottle or jar has a lid that is secured by being twisted on.

scrib|ble /skrˈɪbəl/ (**scribbles, scribbling, scribbled**) **1** V-T/V-I If you **scribble** something, you write it quickly and roughly. ❑ *She scribbled a note to tell Mom she'd gone out.* **2** V-I To **scribble** means to make meaningless marks or rough drawings using a pencil or pen. ❑ *When Caroline was five she scribbled on a wall.* **3** N-VAR **Scribble** is something that has been written or drawn quickly and roughly. ❑ *I'm sorry what I wrote was such a scribble.*

scrib|bler /skrˈɪblər/ (**scribblers**) N-COUNT [usu pl] People sometimes refer to writers as **scribblers** when they think they are not very good writers. [mainly JOURNALISM, DISAPPROVAL]

scribe /skrˈaɪb/ (**scribes**) N-COUNT In the days before printing was common, a **scribe** was a person who wrote copies of things such as letters or documents.

scrim|mage /skrˈɪmɪdʒ/ (**scrimmages**) **1** N-UNCOUNT In football, **scrimmage** is the action during a single period of play. ❑ *Bloom scored two touchdowns Saturday in a scrimmage.* **2** N-COUNT In sports such as football and hockey, a **scrimmage** is a session of practice that consists of an actual game. ❑ *...the first full scrimmage in Flyers training camp.*

scrimp /skrˈɪmp/ (**scrimps, scrimping, scrimped**) V-I If you **scrimp** on things, you live cheaply and spend as little money as possible. ❑ *Scrimping on safety measures can be a false economy.*

scrip /skrˈɪp/ (**scrips**) N-COUNT A **scrip** is a certificate which shows that an investor owns part of a share or stock. [BUSINESS] ❑ *The cash or scrip would be offered as part of a pro rata return of capital to shareholders.*

script ✦◇◇ /skrˈɪpt/ (**scripts, scripting, scripted**) **1** N-COUNT The **script** of a play, movie, or television program is the written version of it. ❑ *Jenny's writing a film script.* **2** V-T The person who **scripts** a movie or a radio or television play writes it. ❑ *...James Cameron, who scripted and directed both films.* **3** N-VAR [usu adj n] You can refer to a particular system of writing as a particular **script**. ❑ *...a text in the Malay language but written in Arabic script.* **4** N-VAR **Script** is handwriting in which the letters are joined together. ❑ *When you're writing in script, there are four letters of the alphabet that you can't complete in one stroke.*

script|ed /skrˈɪptɪd/ ADJ [usu ADJ n] A **scripted** speech has been written in advance, although the speaker may pretend that it is spoken without preparation. ❑ *He had prepared scripted answers.*

scrip|tur|al /skrˈɪptʃərəl/ ADJ [ADJ n] **Scriptural** is used to describe things that are written in or based on the Christian Bible. ❑ *...scriptural accounts of the process of salvation.*

scrip|ture /skrˈɪptʃər/ (**scriptures**) N-VAR **Scripture** or **the scriptures** refers to writings that are regarded as holy in a particular religion, for example, the Bible in Christianity. ❑ *...a quote from scripture.*

script|writer /skrˈɪptraɪtər/ (**scriptwriters**) N-COUNT A **scriptwriter** is a person who writes scripts for movies or for radio or television programs.

scroll /skrˈoʊl/ (**scrolls, scrolling, scrolled**) **1** N-COUNT A **scroll** is a long roll of paper or a similar material with writing on it. ❑ *Ancient scrolls were found in caves by the Dead Sea.* **2** N-COUNT A **scroll** is a painted or carved decoration made to look like a scroll. ❑ *...a handsome suite of chairs incised with Grecian scrolls.* **3** V-I If you **scroll** through text on a computer screen, you move the text up or down to find the information that you need. [COMPUTING] ❑ *I scrolled down to find "United States of America."* **4** → See feature box at **email**

scroll bar (**scroll bars**) N-COUNT On a computer screen, a **scroll bar** is a long thin box along one edge of a window, which you click on with the mouse to move the text up, down, or across the window. [COMPUTING]

Scrooge /skrˈuːdʒ/ (**Scrooges**) N-VAR If you call someone a **Scrooge**, you disapprove of them because they are very mean and hate spending money. [DISAPPROVAL] ❑ *What a bunch of Scrooges.*

scro|tum /skrˈoʊtəm/ (**scrotums**) N-COUNT A man's **scrotum** is the bag of skin that contains his testicles.

scrounge /skrˈaʊndʒ/ (**scrounges, scrounging, scrounged**) V-T/V-I If you say that someone **scrounges** something such as food or money, you disapprove of them because they get it by asking for it, rather than by buying it or earning it. [INFORMAL, DISAPPROVAL] ❑ *We managed to scrounge every piece of gear you requested.*

scrub /skrˈʌb/ (**scrubs, scrubbing, scrubbed**) **1** V-T If you **scrub** something, you rub it hard in order to clean it, using a stiff brush and water. ❑ *Surgeons began to scrub their hands and arms with soap and water before operating.* • N-SING **Scrub** is also a noun. ❑ *The walls needed a good scrub.* **2** V-T If you **scrub** dirt or stains off something, you remove them by rubbing hard. ❑ *I started to scrub off the dirt.* **3** N-UNCOUNT **Scrub** consists of low trees and bushes, especially in an area that has very little rain. ❑ *There is an area of scrub and woodland beside the railroad.* **4** N-PLURAL **Scrubs** are the protective clothes that surgeons and other hospital staff wear in operating rooms. [mainly AM, INFORMAL] ❑ *...a man wearing blue hospital scrubs.* **5** → See feature box at **housework**

scrub|by /skrˈʌbi/ ADJ [usu ADJ n] **Scrubby** land is rough and dry and covered with scrub. ❑ *...the hot, scrubby hills of western Eritrea.*

scrub|land /skrˈʌblænd/ (**scrublands**) N-VAR **Scrubland** is an area of land covered with low trees and bushes. ❑ *Thousands of acres of forests and scrubland have been burnt.*

scruff /skrˈʌf/ PHRASE [V n PHR] If someone takes an animal or person **by the scruff of the neck**, they take hold of the back of the neck or collar suddenly and roughly. ❑ *He picked the dog up by the scruff of the neck.*

scruffy /skrˈʌfi/ (**scruffier, scruffiest**) ADJ Someone or something that is **scruffy** is dirty and messy. ❑ *...a young man, pale, scruffy and unshaven.*

scrum /skrˈʌm/ (**scrums**) N-COUNT In rugby, a **scrum** is a tight group formed by players from both sides pushing against each other with their heads down in an attempt to get the ball.

scrum|mage /skrˈʌmɪdʒ/ (**scrummages**) N-COUNT In rugby, a **scrummage** is the same as a **scrum**.

scrump|tious /skrˈʌmpʃəs/ ADJ If you describe food as **scrumptious**, you mean that it tastes extremely good. [INFORMAL] ❑ *...a scrumptious apple pie.*

scrunch /skrˈʌntʃ/ (**scrunches, scrunching, scrunched**)
▶ **scrunch up** PHRASAL VERB If you **scrunch** something **up**, you squeeze it or bend it so that it is no longer in its natural shape and is often crushed. ❑ *She scrunched up three pages of notes and threw them in the bin.*

scrunchie /skrˈʌntʃi/ (**scrunchies**) N-COUNT A **scrunchie** is a rubber band that is covered with material and is used to tie back someone's hair, for example in a ponytail.

scru|ple /skruːpəl/ (scruples) N-VAR Scruples are moral principles or beliefs that make you unwilling to do something that seems wrong. ❑ ...a man with no moral scruples.

scru|pu|lous /skruːpjələs/ ■ ADJ Someone who is **scrupulous** takes great care to do what is fair, honest, or morally right. [APPROVAL] ❑ You're being very scrupulous, but to what end? ❑ I have been scrupulous about telling them the dangers. ■ ADJ **Scrupulous** means thorough, exact, and careful about details. ❑ Both readers commend Knutson for his scrupulous attention to detail.

scru|ti|nize /skruːtənaɪz/ (scrutinizes, scrutinizing, scrutinized)

in BRIT, also use **scrutinise**

V-T If you **scrutinize** something, you examine it very carefully, often to find out some information from it or about it. ❑ Her purpose was to scrutinize his features to see if he was an honest man.

scru|ti|ny /skruːtəni/ N-UNCOUNT If a person or thing is under **scrutiny**, they are being studied or observed very carefully. ❑ His private life came under media scrutiny.

scu|ba dive /skuːbə daɪv/ (scuba dives, scuba diving, scuba dived) VERB If you **scuba dive**, you swim underwater using special breathing equipment. The equipment consists of cylinders of air which you carry on your back and which are connected to your mouth by rubber tubes. ❑ I signed up to learn how to scuba dive. • **scu|ba div|ing** N-UNCOUNT ❑ Snorkeling and scuba diving have grown in popularity in recent years.

scud /skʌd/ (scuds, scudding, scudded) V-I If clouds **scud** along, they move quickly and smoothly through the sky. [LITERARY] ❑ ...heavy, rain-laden clouds scudding across from the south-west.

scuff /skʌf/ (scuffs, scuffing, scuffed) ■ V-T/V-I If you **scuff** something or if it **scuffs**, you mark the surface by scraping it against other things or by scraping other things against it. ❑ Constant wheelchair use will scuff almost any floor surface. ❑ Molded plastic is almost indestructible, but scuffs easily. • **scuffed** ADJ ❑ ...scuffed brown shoes. ■ V-T If you **scuff** your feet, you pull them along the ground as you walk. ❑ Polly, bewildered and embarrassed, dropped her head and scuffed her feet.

scuf|fle /skʌfəl/ (scuffles, scuffling, scuffled) ■ N-COUNT A **scuffle** is a short, disorganized fight or struggle. ❑ Violent scuffles broke out between rival groups demonstrating for and against independence. ■ V-RECIP If people **scuffle**, they fight for a short time in a disorganized way. ❑ Police scuffled with some of the protesters.

scuf|fling /skʌflɪŋ/ ADJ [ADJ n] A **scuffling** noise is a noise made by a person or animal moving about, usually one that you cannot see. ❑ There was a scuffling noise in the background, which turned out to be mice.

scuff mark (scuff marks) N-COUNT [usu pl] **Scuff marks** are marks made on a smooth surface when something is rubbed against it. ❑ Scuff marks from shoes are difficult to remove.

scull /skʌl/ (sculls) ■ N-COUNT [usu pl] **Sculls** are small oars which are held by one person and used to move a boat through water. ■ N-COUNT A **scull** is a small light racing boat which is rowed with two sculls.

sculpt /skʌlpt/ (sculpts, sculpting, sculpted) ■ V-T/V-I When an artist **sculpts**, or **sculpts** something, they carve or shape it out of a material such as stone or clay. ❑ An artist sculpted a full-size replica of her head. ■ V-T If something **is sculpted**, it is made into a particular shape. ❑ More familiar landscapes have been sculpted by surface erosion.

sculp|tor /skʌlptər/ (sculptors) N-COUNT A **sculptor** is someone who creates sculptures.

sculp|tur|al /skʌlptʃərəl/ ADJ [usu ADJ n] **Sculptural** means relating to sculpture. ❑ He enjoyed working with clay as a sculptural form.

sculp|ture /skʌlptʃər/ (sculptures) ■ N-VAR A **sculpture** is a work of art that is produced by carving or shaping stone, wood, clay, or other materials. ❑ ...stone sculptures of figures and animals. ■ N-UNCOUNT **Sculpture** is the art of creating sculptures. ❑ Both studied sculpture. ■ → See feature box at **fine art**

sculp|tured /skʌlptʃərd/ ADJ **Sculptured** objects have been carved or shaped from something. ❑ ...a beautifully sculptured bronze horse.

scum /skʌm/ ■ N-PLURAL If you refer to people as **scum**, you are expressing your feelings of dislike and disgust for them. [INFORMAL, DISAPPROVAL] ❑ She never would have even spoken to scum like him when Mom was alive. ■ N-UNCOUNT **Scum** is a layer of a dirty or unpleasant-looking substance on the surface of a liquid. ❑ ...scum marks around the bath.

scum|bag /skʌmbæg/ (scumbags) N-COUNT If you refer to someone as a **scumbag**, you are expressing your feelings of dislike and disgust for them. [INFORMAL, DISAPPROVAL]

scur|ril|ous /skɜrɪləs/ ADJ [usu ADJ n] **Scurrilous** accusations or stories are untrue and unfair, and are likely to damage the reputation of the person that they relate to. ❑ Scurrilous and untrue stories were being invented.

scur|ry /skɜri/ (scurries, scurrying, scurried) V-I When people or small animals **scurry** somewhere, they move there quickly and hurriedly, especially because they are frightened. [WRITTEN] ❑ The attack began, sending residents scurrying for cover.

scur|vy /skɜrvi/ N-UNCOUNT **Scurvy** is a disease that is caused by a lack of vitamin C.

scut|tle /skʌtəl/ (scuttles, scuttling, scuttled) ■ V-I When people or small animals **scuttle** somewhere, they move there with short quick steps. ❑ Two very small children scuttled away in front of them. ■ V-T To **scuttle** a plan or a proposal means to make it fail or cause it to stop. ❑ Such threats could scuttle the peace conference.

scuttle|butt /skʌtəlbʌt/ N-UNCOUNT **Scuttlebutt** is rumors or gossip. [AM, INFORMAL] ❑ Besides, he has no proof that the allegations are true; Washington is full of scuttlebutt.

scuz|zy /skʌzi/ (scuzzier, scuzziest) ADJ Something that is **scuzzy** is dirty or disgusting. [INFORMAL] ❑ ...a scuzzy drug district in New York.

scythe /saɪð/ (scythes, scything, scythed) ■ N-COUNT A **scythe** is a tool with a long curved blade at right angles to a long handle. It is used to cut long grass or grain. ■ V-T If you **scythe** grass or grain, you cut it with a scythe. ❑ Two men were attempting to scythe the long grass.

SE SE is a written abbreviation for **southeast**.

sea ✦✧ /siː/ (seas) ■ N-SING [the N, also by N] The **sea** is the salty water that covers about three-quarters of the Earth's surface. ❑ Most of the kids have never seen the sea. ■ N-PLURAL You use **seas** when you are describing the sea at a particular time or in a particular area. [LITERARY] ❑ He drowned after 30 minutes in the rough seas. ■ N-COUNT; N-IN-NAMES A **sea** is a large area of salty water that is part of an ocean or is surrounded by land. ❑ ...the North Sea. ■ PHRASE **At sea** means on or under the sea, far away from land. ❑ The boats remain at sea for an average of ten days at a time. ■ PHRASE If you go or look out **to sea**, you go or look across the sea. ❑ ...fishermen who go to sea for two weeks at a time. ■ → See feature box at **boat**, **water**

COLLOCATIONS

sea
■
adjective + **sea**: calm, rough; azure, blue, turquoise; deep, open
sea + be+ adjective: calm, cold, warm; choppy
verb + **sea**: cross, sail
■
adjective + **sea**: high, tropical; choppy, heavy, rough, stormy; calm

---

sea air N-UNCOUNT The **sea air** is the air at the seaside, which is regarded as being good for people's health. ❑ I took a deep breath of the fresh sea air.

sea|bed /siːbed/ also **sea bed** N-SING The **seabed** is the ground under the sea. ❑ The wreck was raised from the seabed in June 2000.

sea|bird /siːbɜrd/ (seabirds) also **sea bird** N-COUNT **Seabirds** are birds that live near the sea and get their food from it. ❑ The island is covered with seabirds.

sea|board /siːbɔrd/ (seaboards) N-COUNT [usu the N in sing] The **seaboard** is the part of a country that is next to the sea; used especially of the east coast of North America. ❑ ...the Eastern seaboard of the U.S.

sea|borne /siːbɔrn/ ADJ [ADJ n] **Seaborne** actions or events take place on the sea in ships. ❑ ...a seaborne invasion.

sea breeze (sea breezes) N-COUNT A **sea breeze** is a light wind blowing from the sea toward the land.

sea cap|tain (sea captains) N-COUNT A **sea captain** is a person in command of a ship, usually a ship that carries goods for trade.

sea change (sea changes) N-COUNT A **sea change** in someone's attitudes or behavior is a complete change. ❑ *A sea change has taken place in young people's attitudes to their parents.*

sea dog (sea dogs) also **seadog** N-COUNT A **sea dog** is a sailor who has spent many years at sea. [OLD-FASHIONED]

sea|farer /sίːfeǝrǝr/ (seafarers) N-COUNT [usu pl] **Seafarers** are people who work on ships or people who travel regularly on the sea. [WRITTEN] ❑ *The Estonians have always been seafarers.*

sea|faring /sίːfeǝrɪŋ/ ADJ [ADJ n] **Seafaring** means working as a sailor or traveling regularly on the sea. ❑ *The Lebanese were a seafaring people.*

sea|floor /sίːflɔr/ N-SING The **seafloor** is the ground under the sea.

sea|food /sίːfuːd/ N-UNCOUNT **Seafood** is shellfish such as lobsters, mussels, and crabs, and sometimes other sea creatures that you can eat. ❑ *...a seafood restaurant.*

sea|front /sίːfrʌnt/ (seafronts) N-COUNT The **seafront** is the part of a seaside town that is nearest to the sea. It usually consists of a road with buildings that face the sea. ❑ *They decided to meet on the seafront.*

sea|going /sίːgoʊɪŋ/ also **sea-going** ADJ [ADJ n] **Seagoing** boats and ships are designed for traveling on the sea, rather than on lakes, rivers, or canals.

sea|grass /sίːgræs/ (seagrasses) also **sea grass** N-VAR [oft N n] **Seagrass** is a plant that grows in shallow salt water and is used especially to make mats and floor coverings. ❑ *...the biggest mangrove and seagrass areas in the region.* ❑ *Like seaweed, sea grasses are very susceptible to human pollution.* ❑ *The floor is covered in seagrass matting.*

sea-green also **sea green** COLOR Something that is **sea-green** is a bluish-green color like the color of the sea. ❑ *...her sea-green eyes.*

sea|gull /sίːgʌl/ (seagulls) N-COUNT A **seagull** is a common kind of bird with white or gray feathers.

sea|horse /sίːhɔrs/ (seahorses) also **sea horse** N-COUNT A **seahorse** is a type of small fish which appears to swim in a vertical position and whose head looks a little like the head of a horse.

SEAL
① CLOSING
② ANIMAL
---

① **seal** ✦◇◇ /sίːl/ (seals, sealing, sealed) ◼ V-T When you **seal** an envelope, you close it by folding part of it over and sticking it down, so that it cannot be opened without being torn. ❑ *He sealed the envelope and put on a stamp.* ❑ *Write your letter and seal it in a blank envelope.* ◼ V-T If you **seal** a container or an opening, you cover it with something in order to prevent air, liquid, or other material from getting in or out. If you **seal** something **in** a container, you put it inside and then close the container tightly. ❑ *She filled the containers, sealed them with a cork, and stuck on labels.* ❑ *A woman picks them up and seals them in plastic bags.* ◼ N-COUNT The **seal** on a container or opening is the part where it has been sealed. ❑ *When assembling the pie, wet the edges where the two crusts join, to form a seal.* ◼ N-COUNT [oft N n] A **seal** is a device or a piece of material, for example, in a machine, which closes an opening tightly so that air, liquid, or other substances cannot get in or out. ❑ *Check seals on fridges and freezers regularly.* ◼ N-COUNT [oft N on n] A **seal** is something such as a piece of sticky paper or wax that is fixed to a container or door and must be broken before the container or door can be opened. ❑ *The seal on the box broke when it fell from its hiding-place.* ◼ N-COUNT A **seal** is a special mark or design, for example, on a document, representing someone or something. It may be used to show that something is genuine or officially approved. ❑ *...a supply of note paper bearing the presidential seal.* ◼ V-T If someone in authority **seals** an area, they stop people entering or passing through it, for example, by placing barriers in the way. ❑ *The soldiers were deployed to help paramilitary police seal the border.* • PHRASAL VERB **Seal off** means the same as **seal** ①. ❑ *Police and troops sealed off the area after the attack.* ◼ V-T To **seal** something means to make it definite or confirm how it is going to be. [WRITTEN] ❑ *McLaren are close to sealing a deal with Renault.* ❑ *A general election will be held which will seal his destiny one way or the other.*

▶ **seal off** ◼ PHRASAL VERB If one object or area **is sealed off** from another, there is a physical barrier between them, so that nothing can pass between them. ❑ *Windows are usually sealed off.* ◼ → see **seal** ① 7

COLLOCATIONS

seal
NOUN ① ◼
adjective + **seal**: airtight, waterproof; faulty
verb + **seal**: break, form
VERB ① ◼
seal + noun: deal, fate, victory, win
---

② **seal** /sίːl/ (seals) ◼ N-COUNT A **seal** is a large animal with a rounded body and flat legs called flippers. Seals eat fish and live in and near the sea, usually in cold parts of the world. ◼ → See feature box at **ocean**

sea lane (sea lanes) N-COUNT [usu pl] **Sea lanes** are particular routes which ships regularly use in order to cross a sea or ocean.

seal|ant /sίːlǝnt/ (sealants) N-MASS A **sealant** is a substance that is used to seal holes, cracks, or gaps.

seal|er /sίːlǝr/ (sealers) N-MASS A **sealer** is the same as a **sealant**.

sea lev|el also **sea-level** N-UNCOUNT **Sea level** is the average level of the sea with respect to the land. The height of mountains or other areas is calculated in relation to **sea level**. ❑ *The stadium was 5,000 feet above sea level.* ❑ *The whole place is at sea level.*

seal|ing wax N-UNCOUNT **Sealing wax** is a hard, usually red, substance that melts quickly and is used for putting seals on documents or letters.

sea lion (sea lions) also **sea-lion** N-COUNT A **sea lion** is a type of large seal.

seal|skin /sίːlskɪn/ N-UNCOUNT [oft N n] **Sealskin** is the fur of a seal, used to make coats and other clothing. ❑ *...waterproof sealskin boots.*

seam /sίːm/ (seams) ◼ N-COUNT A **seam** is a line of stitches which joins two pieces of cloth together. ❑ *The skirt ripped along a seam.* ◼ N-COUNT A **seam** of coal is a long, narrow layer of it underneath the ground. ❑ *The average coal seam here is three feet thick.* ◼ PHRASE If something **is coming apart at the seams** or **is falling apart at the seams**, it is no longer working properly and may soon stop working completely. ❑ *Our university system is in danger of falling apart at the seams.* ◼ PHRASE If a place is very full, you can say that it **is bursting at the seams**. ❑ *The hotels of Warsaw, Prague and Budapest were bursting at the seams.*

sea|man /sίːmǝn/ (seamen) N-COUNT A **seaman** is a sailor, especially one who is not an officer. ❑ *The men emigrate to work as seamen.*

sea|man|ship /sίːmǝnʃɪp/ N-UNCOUNT **Seamanship** is skill in managing a boat and controlling its movement through the sea. ❑ *...the art of seamanship and navigation.*

seam|less /sίːmlǝs/ ADJ You use **seamless** to describe something that has no breaks or gaps in it or which continues without stopping. ❑ *It was a seamless procession of wonderful electronic music.* • **seam|less|ly** ADV [ADV with v] ❑ *It's a class move, allowing new and old to blend seamlessly.*

seam|stress /sίːmstrɪs/ (seamstresses) ◼ N-COUNT A **seamstress** is a woman who sews and makes clothes as her job. [OLD-FASHIONED] ◼ → See feature box at **sewing**

seamy /sίːmi/ (seamier, seamiest) ADJ [usu ADJ n] If you describe something as **seamy**, you mean that it involves unpleasant aspects of life such as crime, prostitution, or violence. ❑ *...Hamburg's seamy St Pauli's district.*

se|ance /seɪɑːns/ (seances) also **séance** N-COUNT A **seance** is a meeting in which people try to make contact with people who have died.

sea|plane /síːpleɪn/ (seaplanes) N-COUNT A **seaplane** is a type of airplane that can take off from or land on water.

sea|port /síːpɔːrt/ (seaports) N-COUNT A **seaport** is a town with a large harbor that is used by ships. ❑ ...the Baltic seaport of Rostock.

sea pow|er (sea powers) **1** N-UNCOUNT **Sea power** is the size and strength of a country's navy. ❑ The transformation of American sea power began in 1940. **2** N-COUNT A **sea power** is a country that has a large navy.

sear /sɪər/ (sears, searing, seared) **1** V-T To **sear** something means to burn its surface with a sudden intense heat. ❑ Grass fires have seared the land near the farming village of Basekhai. **2** V-T If something **sears** a part of your body, it causes a painful burning feeling there. [LITERARY] ❑ I distinctly felt the heat start to sear my throat. **3** → see also **searing**

search ♦♦◊ /sɜːrtʃ/ (searches, searching, searched) **1** V-I If you **search** for something or someone, you look carefully for them. ❑ The Turkish security forces have started searching for the missing men. ❑ They searched for a spot where they could sit on the floor. **2** V-T/V-I If you **search** a place, you look carefully for something or someone there. ❑ Armed troops searched the hospital yesterday. ❑ She searched her desk for the necessary information. ❑ Relief workers are still searching through collapsed buildings. **3** N-COUNT A **search** is an attempt to find something or someone by looking for them carefully. ❑ There was no chance of him being found alive and the search was abandoned. **4** V-T If a police officer or someone else in authority **searches** you, they look carefully to see whether you have something hidden on you. ❑ The man took her suitcase from her and then searched her. **5** V-I If you **search** for information on a computer, you give the computer an instruction to find that information. [COMPUTING] ❑ You can use a directory service to search for people on the Internet. • N-COUNT **Search** is also a noun. ❑ He was doing this story while he was doing a computer search of local news articles. **6** → see also **searching** **7** PHRASE If you go **in search of** something or someone, you try to find them. ❑ Miserable, and unexpectedly lonely, she went in search of Jean-Paul. **8** CONVENTION You say '**search me**' when someone asks you a question and you want to emphasize that you do not know the answer. [INFORMAL, EMPHASIS] ❑ "So why did he get interested all of a sudden?"—"Search me."

search and res|cue also **search-and-rescue** N-UNCOUNT [usu N N] **Search and rescue** operations involve looking for people who are lost or in danger, for example, after a war or a natural disaster, and bringing them back safely. ❑ An alpine search and rescue team found Lancaster the day after he disappeared.

search en|gine (search engines) N-COUNT A **search engine** is a computer program that searches for documents containing a particular word or words on the internet. [COMPUTING]

search|er /sɜːrtʃər/ (searchers) **1** N-COUNT [usu pl] **Searchers** are people who are looking for someone or something that is missing. ❑ Searchers have found three mountain climbers missing since Saturday. **2** N-COUNT [oft N after/for n] A **searcher** is someone who is trying to find something such as the truth or the answer to a problem. ❑ He's not a real searcher after truth.

search|ing /sɜːrtʃɪŋ/ ADJ A **searching** question or look is intended to discover the truth about something. ❑ They asked her some searching questions on moral philosophy and logic.

search|light /sɜːrtʃlaɪt/ (searchlights) N-COUNT A **searchlight** is a large powerful light that can be turned to shine a long way in any direction. ❑ Helicopters threw searchlights over the meadows and the lake.

search par|ty (search parties) N-COUNT A **search party** is an organized group of people who are searching for someone who is missing.

search war|rant (search warrants) N-COUNT A **search warrant** is a special document that gives the police permission to search a house or other building. ❑ Officers armed with a search warrant entered the apartment.

sear|ing /sɪərɪŋ/ **1** ADJ [ADJ n] **Searing** is used to indicate that something such as pain or heat is very intense. ❑ She woke to feel a searing pain in her feet. **2** ADJ [ADJ n] A **searing** speech or piece of writing is very critical. ❑ There's a searing column in today's paper about the president's decision.

sea|scape /síːskeɪp/ (seascapes) N-COUNT A **seascape** is a painting or photograph of a scene at sea.

sea|shell /síːʃɛl/ (seashells) N-COUNT [usu pl] **Seashells** are the empty shells of small sea creatures.

sea|shore /síːʃɔːr/ (seashores) N-COUNT The **seashore** is the part of a coast where the land slopes down into the sea. ❑ She takes her inspiration from shells and stones she finds on the seashore.

sea|sick /síːsɪk/ **1** ADJ If someone is **seasick** when they are traveling in a boat, they vomit or feel sick because of the way the boat is moving. ❑ It was quite rough at times, and she was seasick. • **sea|sick|ness** N-UNCOUNT ❑ He was very prone to seasickness and already felt queasy. **2** → See feature box at **boat**

sea|side /síːsaɪd/ N-SING You can refer to an area that is close to the sea, especially one where people go for their vacation, as the **seaside**. ❑ I went to spend a few days at the seaside.

sea|son ♦♦♦ /síːzən/ (seasons, seasoning, seasoned) **1** N-COUNT The **seasons** are the main periods into which a year can be divided and which each have their own typical weather conditions. ❑ Fall is my favorite season. ❑ ...the only region of Brazil where all four seasons are clearly defined. **2** N-COUNT You can use **season** to refer to the period during each year when a particular activity or event takes place. For example, the planting **season** is the period when a particular plant or crop is planted. ❑ ...birds arriving for the breeding season. **3** N-COUNT [n N, also in/out of N] You can use **season** to refer to the period when a particular fruit, vegetable, or other food is ready for eating and is widely available. ❑ The plum season is about to begin. **4** N-COUNT You can use **season** to refer to a fixed period during each year when a particular sport is played or when a particular activity is allowed. ❑ ...the baseball season. ❑ Deer hunting season is only a couple of weeks long. **5** N-COUNT A **season** is a period in which a play or show, or a series of plays or shows, is performed in one place. ❑ ...a season of three new plays. **6** N-COUNT A **season** of movies is several of them shown as a series because they are connected in some way. ❑ ...a brief season of films in which Artaud appeared. **7** N-COUNT [usu sing, usu supp N, also in/out of N] The vacation **season** is the time when most people take their vacation. ❑ ...the peak vacation season. **8** V-T If you **season** food with salt, pepper, or spices, you add them to it in order to improve its flavor. ❑ Season the meat with salt and pepper. **9** → see also **seasoned**, **seasoning** **10** PHRASE If a female animal is **in season**, she is in a state where she is ready to have sex. ❑ There are a few ideas around on how to treat fillies and mares in season. **11** → See feature box at **tourism**

SYNONYMS

season
NOUN **2**
period: This crisis might last for a long period of time.
time: It was a time of terrible uncertainty.
spell: There has been a long spell of dry weather.

sea|son|al /síːzənəl/ ADJ [ADJ n] A **seasonal** factor, event, or change occurs during one particular time of the year. ❑ The figures aren't adjusted for seasonal variations. • **sea|son|al|ly** ADV ❑ The seasonally adjusted unemployment figures show a rise of twelve hundred.

sea|son|al af|fec|tive dis|or|der N-UNCOUNT **Seasonal affective disorder** is a feeling of tiredness and sadness that some people have during the fall and winter when there is very little sunshine. The abbreviation **SAD** is often used.

sea|soned /síːzənd/ ADJ You can use **seasoned** to describe a person who has had a lot of experience of something. For example, a **seasoned** traveler is a person who has traveled a lot. ❑ The author is a seasoned academic.

sea|son|ing /síːzənɪŋ/ (seasonings) N-MASS **Seasoning** is salt, pepper, or other spices that are added to food to improve its flavor. ❑ Mix the meat with the onion, carrot, and some seasoning.

sea|son tick|et (season tickets) N-COUNT A **season ticket** is a ticket that you can use repeatedly during a certain period, without having to pay each time. You can buy **season tickets** for things such as buses, trains, regular sports events, or theater performances. ❑ We went to renew our monthly season ticket.

seat ♦♦◊ /siːt/ (seats, seating, seated) **1** N-COUNT A **seat** is an object that you can sit on, for example, a chair. ❑ Stephen returned to his seat. **2** N-COUNT The **seat** of a chair is the part that you sit on. ❑ The stool had a torn, red plastic seat.

seat belt   1161   **secondary**

3 V-T If you **seat** yourself somewhere, you sit down. [WRITTEN] ❑ *He waved toward a chair, and seated himself at the desk.* **4** V-T A building or vehicle that **seats** a particular number of people has enough seats for that number. ❑ *The theater seats 570.* **5** N-SING [usu the N of n] The **seat** of a piece of clothing is the part that covers your bottom. ❑ *Then he got up, brushed off the seat of his jeans, and headed slowly down the slope.* **6** N-COUNT When someone is elected to a legislature you can say that they, or their party, have won a **seat**. ❑ *Independent candidates won the majority of seats on the local council.* **7** N-COUNT If someone has a **seat** on the board of a company or on a committee, they are a member of it. ❑ *He has been unsuccessful in his attempt to win a seat on the board of the company.* **8** N-COUNT The **seat** of an organization, a wealthy family, or an activity is its base. ❑ *Gunfire broke out early this morning around the seat of government in Lagos.* **9** → see also **deep-seated** **10** PHRASE If you **take a back seat**, you allow other people to have all the power and to make all the decisions. ❑ *You need to take a back seat and think about both past and future.* **11** PHRASE If you **take a seat**, you sit down. [FORMAL] ❑ *"Take a seat," he said in a bored tone.*

seat belt (seat belts) also **seatbelt** N-COUNT A **seat belt** is a strap attached to a seat in a car or an aircraft. You fasten it across your body in order to prevent yourself being thrown out of the seat if there is a sudden movement or stop. ❑ *The fact I was wearing a seat belt saved my life.*

-seater /-siːtər/ (-seaters) COMB IN ADJ; N-COUNT **-seater** combines with numbers to form adjectives and nouns which indicate how many people something such as a car has seats for. ❑ *...a three-seater sofa.* ❑ *The plane is an eight-seater with twin propellers.*

seat|ing /siːtɪŋ/ **1** N-UNCOUNT You can refer to the seats in a place as the **seating**. ❑ *The stadium has been filled with seating for over eighty thousand spectators.* **2** N-UNCOUNT The **seating** at a public place or a formal occasion is the arrangement of where people will sit. ❑ *She made a mental note to check the seating arrangements before the guests filed into the dining-room.*

seat of learn|ing (seats of learning) N-COUNT People sometimes refer to a university or a similar institution as a **seat of learning**. [WRITTEN] ❑ *...one department of that great seat of learning.*

sea tur|tle (sea turtles) N-COUNT A **sea turtle** is a large reptile which has a thick shell covering its body and which lives in the sea most of the time. [AM]

in BRIT, use **turtle**

sea ur|chin (sea urchins) N-COUNT A **sea urchin** is a small round sea creature that has a hard shell covered with sharp points.

sea wall (sea walls) N-COUNT A **sea wall** is a wall built along the edge of the sea to stop the sea flowing over the land or destroying it. ❑ *Cherbourg had a splendid harbor enclosed by a long sea wall.*

sea|ward /siːwərd/

The form **seawards** can also be used for meaning **1**.

1 ADV [ADV after v] Something that moves or faces **seaward** or **seawards** moves or faces in the direction of the sea or further out to sea. ❑ *A barge was about a hundred yards away, waiting to return seaward.* ❑ *It faced seawards to the north.* **2** ADJ [ʊsu ADJ n] The **seaward** side of something faces in the direction of the sea or further out to sea. ❑ *The houses on the seaward side of the road were all in ruins.*

sea wa|ter also **seawater** N-UNCOUNT **Sea water** is salt water from the sea.

sea|weed /siːwiːd/ (seaweeds) N-MASS **Seaweed** is a plant that grows in the sea. There are many kinds of seaweed. ❑ *...seaweed washed up on a beach.*

sea|worthy /siːwɜːrði/ ADJ A ship or boat which is **seaworthy** is fit to travel at sea. ❑ *The ship was completely seaworthy.*
• **sea|worthiness** N-UNCOUNT ❑ *It didn't reach required standards of safety and seaworthiness.*

se|bum /siːbəm/ N-UNCOUNT **Sebum** is an oily substance produced by glands in your skin.

sec /sek/ (secs) N-COUNT If you ask someone to wait a **sec**, you are asking them to wait for a very short time. [INFORMAL] ❑ *Can you just hang on a sec?*

SEC /es iː siː/ N-PROPER [the N] In the United States, the **SEC** is a government agency that regulates the buying and selling of securities. **SEC** is an abbreviation for 'Securities and Exchange Commission.' ❑ *The SEC has filed fraud charges and is launching an investigation.*

sec. /sek/ (secs) **Sec.** is a written abbreviation for **second** ① or **seconds**. ❑ *The first woman to finish was Grete Waitz of Norway, with a time of 2 hrs, 29 min., 30 sec.*

seca|teurs /sekətɜːrz/ N-PLURAL **Secateurs** are the same as **pruning shears**. [BRIT]

se|cede /sɪsiːd/ (secedes, seceding, seceded) V-I If a region or group **secedes** from the country or larger group to which it belongs, it formally becomes a separate country or stops being a member of the larger group. ❑ *Singapore seceded from the Federation of Malaysia and became an independent sovereign state.* ❑ *The region decided to secede.*

se|ces|sion /sɪseʃən/ N-UNCOUNT The **secession** of a region or group from the country or larger group to which it belongs is the action of formally becoming separate. ❑ *...secession from the Union.*

se|ces|sion|ist /sɪseʃənɪst/ (secessionists) N-COUNT [usu pl] **Secessionists** are people who want their region or group to become separate from the country or larger group to which it belongs. ❑ *...Lithuanian secessionists.*

se|clud|ed /sɪkluːdɪd/ ADJ A **secluded** place is quiet and private. ❑ *We were tucked away in a secluded corner of the room.*

se|clu|sion /sɪkluːʒən/ N-UNCOUNT If you are living in **seclusion**, you are in a quiet place away from other people. ❑ *She lived in seclusion with her husband on their farm in Panama.*

SECOND
① PART OF A MINUTE
② COMING AFTER SOMETHING ELSE

---

① **sec|ond** ✦✦✦ /sekənd/ (seconds) N-COUNT A **second** is one of the sixty parts that a minute is divided into. People often say 'a second' or 'seconds' when they simply mean a very short time. ❑ *For a few seconds nobody said anything.* ❑ *It only takes forty seconds.*

② **sec|ond** ✦✦✦ /sekənd/ (seconds, seconding, seconded)
→ Please look at meanings **12** and **13** to see if the expression you are looking for is shown under another headword.

1 ORD The **second** item in a series is the one that you count as number two. ❑ *...the second day of his visit to Delhi.* ❑ *...their second child.* ❑ *...the Second World War.* **2** ORD [ORD adj-superl] **Second** is used before superlative adjectives to indicate that there is only one thing better or larger than the thing you are referring to. ❑ *The party is still the second strongest in Italy.* **3** ADV [ADV cl] You say **second** when you want to make a second point or give a second reason for something. ❑ *First, the weapons should be intended for use only in retaliation after a nuclear attack. Second, the possession of the weapons must be a temporary expedient.* **4** N-PLURAL If you have **seconds**, you have a second helping of food. [INFORMAL] ❑ *There's seconds if you want them.* **5** N-COUNT **Seconds** are goods that are sold cheaply in stores because they have slight faults. ❑ *These are not seconds, or unbranded goods, but first-quality products.* **6** V-T If you **second** a proposal in a meeting or debate, you formally express your agreement with it so that it can then be discussed or voted on. ❑ *She seconded the motion.* **7** V-T If you **second** what someone has said, you say that you agree with them or say the same thing yourself. ❑ *The UN secretary-general seconded the appeal for peace.* **8** PHRASE If you experience something **at second hand**, you are told about it by other people rather than experiencing it yourself. ❑ *Most of them, after all, had not been at the battle and had only heard of the massacre at second hand.* **9** → see also **secondhand** **10** PHRASE If you say that something is **second to none**, you are emphasizing that it is very good indeed or the best that there is. [EMPHASIS] ❑ *Our scientific research is second to none.* **11** PHRASE If you say that something is **second only to** something else, you mean that only that thing is better or greater than it. ❑ *As a major health risk hepatitis is second only to tobacco.* **12 second nature** → see **nature** **13 in the second place** → see **place** ③

sec|ond|ary /sekənderi/ **1** ADJ If you describe something as **secondary**, you mean that it is less important than something else. ◻ *The street erupted in a huge explosion, with secondary explosions in the adjoining buildings.* ◻ *They argue that human rights considerations are now of only secondary importance.* ◻ ADJ **Secondary** diseases or infections happen as a result of another disease or infection that has already happened. ◻ *These patients had been operated on for the primary cancer but there was evidence of secondary tumors.* ◻ ADJ **Secondary** education is given to students between the ages of 11 or 12 and 17 or 18. ◻ *Examinations are taken after about five years of secondary education.*

sec|ond|ary school (secondary schools) N-VAR A **secondary school** is a school for students between the ages of 11 or 12 and 17 or 18. ◻ *She taught history at a secondary school.*

sec|ond best also **second-best** ◻ ADJ **Second best** is used to describe something that is not as good as the best thing of its kind but is better than all the other things of that kind. ◻ *He put on his second best suit.* ◻ ADJ You can use **second best** to describe something that you have to accept even though you would have preferred something else. ◻ *...a messy, second-best solution.* • N-SING **Second best** is also a noun. ◻ *Oatmeal is a good second best.*

sec|ond cham|ber N-SING The **second chamber** is one of the two groups that a legislature is divided into. In the United States, the second chamber can be either the Senate or the House of Representatives.

sec|ond child|hood N-SING If you say that an old person is in their **second childhood**, you mean that their mind is becoming weaker and that their behavior is similar to that of a young child.

second-class also **second class** ◻ ADJ [ADJ n] If someone treats you as a **second-class** citizen, they treat you as if you are less valuable and less important than other people. ◻ *Too many airlines treat our children as second-class citizens.* ◻ ADJ If you describe something as **second-class**, you mean that it is of poor quality. ◻ *I am not prepared to see children in some parts of this country having to settle for a second-class education.* ◻ ADJ [ADJ n] The **second-class** accommodations on a train or ship are the ordinary accommodations, which are cheaper and less comfortable than the first-class accommodations. ◻ *He sat in the corner of a second-class compartment.* ◻ *Seven second-class passengers prepared to disembark.* • ADV [ADV after v] **Second class** is also an adverb. ◻ *I recently travelled second class from Pisa to Ventimiglia.* • N-UNCOUNT **Second-class** is second-class accommodations on a train or ship. ◻ *"Is there any chance of a compartment to myself?"—"Not in second class."* ◻ ADJ [ADJ n] **Second-class** postage is a slower and cheaper type of postage. [BRIT]

sec|ond com|ing N-SING [the N] When Christians refer to the **second coming**, they mean the expected return to earth of Jesus Christ.

sec|ond cous|in (second cousins) N-COUNT Your **second cousins** are the children of your parents' first cousins. Compare **first cousin**.

second-degree ◻ ADJ [ADJ n] **Second-degree** is used to describe crimes that are considered to be less serious than first-degree crimes. ◻ *The judge reduced the charge to second-degree murder.* ◻ ADJ [ADJ n] A **second-degree** burn is more severe than a first-degree burn but less severe than a third-degree burn. ◻ *James Bell suffered second-degree burns in an explosion.*

second-guess (second-guesses, second-guessing, second-guessed) V-T If you try to **second-guess** something, you try to guess in advance what someone will do or what will happen. ◻ *Editors and contributors are trying to second-guess the future.*

second|hand /sɛkəndhænd/ also **second-hand** ◻ ADJ **Secondhand** things are not new and have been owned by someone else. ◻ *They could afford a secondhand car, she thought.* • ADV [ADV after v] **Secondhand** is also an adverb. ◻ *Household appliances were bought secondhand and are outdated.* ◻ ADJ [ADJ n] A **secondhand** store sells secondhand goods. ◻ *...lovingly restored old pieces bought from a secondhand store.* ◻ ADJ **Secondhand** stories, information, or opinions are those you learn about from other people rather than directly or from your own experience. ◻ *He urged the committee to discount any secondhand knowledge or hearsay.* • ADV [ADV after v] **Secondhand** is also an adverb. ◻ *I only heard about it secondhand.* ◻ **at second hand** → see **second** ②

second|hand smoke also **second-hand smoke** N-UNCOUNT **Secondhand smoke** is tobacco smoke that people breathe in because other people around them are smoking. [mainly AM] ◻ *...the first definitive evidence that secondhand smoke causes lung cancer.*

second-in-command also **second in command** N-SING A **second-in-command** is someone who is next in rank to the leader of a group, and who has authority to give orders when the leader is not there. ◻ *He was posted to Hong Kong as second-in-command of C Squadron.*

sec|ond lan|guage (second languages) N-COUNT Someone's **second language** is a language which is not their native language but which they use at work or at school. ◻ *Lucy teaches English as a second language.*

sec|ond lieu|ten|ant (second lieutenants) N-COUNT A **second lieutenant** is an officer in the army, air force, or marines who ranks directly below a first lieutenant. [AM]

sec|ond|ly /sɛkəndli/ ADV You say **secondly** when you want to make a second point or give a second reason for something. ◻ *It makes you look firstly at how you're treated and secondly how you treat everybody else.*

sec|ond name (second names) N-COUNT Someone's **second name** is their family name, or the name that comes after their first name and before their family name.

sec|ond opin|ion (second opinions) N-COUNT If you get a **second opinion**, you ask another qualified person for their opinion about something such as your health. ◻ *I would like to see a specialist for a second opinion on my doctor's diagnosis.*

sec|ond per|son N-SING [the N] A statement in the **second person** is a statement about the person or people you are talking to. The subject of a statement like this is 'you.'

second-rate ADJ If you describe something as **second-rate**, you mean that it is of poor quality. ◻ *...second-rate restaurants.*

sec|ond sight N-UNCOUNT If you say that someone has **second sight**, you mean that they seem to have the ability to know or see things that are going to happen in the future, or are happening in a different place.

sec|ond string also **second-string** N-SING [oft N n] If you describe a person or thing as someone's **second string**, you mean that they are only used if another person or thing is not available. ◻ *...a second string team.*

sec|ond thought (second thoughts) ◻ N-SING If you do something without **a second thought**, you do it without thinking about it carefully, usually because you do not have enough time or you do not care very much. ◻ *This murderous lunatic could kill them both without a second thought.* ◻ N-PLURAL If you have **second thoughts** about a decision that you have made, you begin to doubt whether it was the best thing to do. ◻ *I had never had second thoughts about my decision to leave the company.* ◻ PHRASE You can say **on second thoughts** or **on second thought** when you suddenly change your mind about something that you are saying or something that you have decided to do. ◻ *"Wait there!" Kathryn rose. "No, on second thought, follow me."*

sec|ond wind N-SING When you get your **second wind**, you become able to continue doing something difficult or energetic after you have been tired or out of breath. ◻ *Finding a second wind, he rode away from his pursuers.*

Sec|ond World War N-PROPER [the N] The **Second World War** is the major war that was fought between 1939 and 1945.

se|cre|cy /siːkrəsi/ N-UNCOUNT **Secrecy** is the act of keeping something secret, or the state of being kept secret. ◻ *The government has thrown a blanket of secrecy over the details.*

se|cret ✦✧ /siːkrɪt/ (secrets) ◻ ADJ If something is **secret**, it is known about by only a small number of people, and is not told or shown to anyone else. ◻ *Soldiers have been training at a secret location.* • **se|cret|ly** ADV ◻ *This feature enables you to secretly read emails that are sent or received on an iPad.* ◻ → see also **top secret** ◻ N-COUNT A **secret** is a fact that is known by only a small number of people, and is not told to anyone else. ◻ *I think he enjoyed keeping our love a secret.* ◻ N-SING If you say that a particular way of doing things is **the secret** of achieving something, you mean that it is the best or only way to achieve it. ◻ *The secret of success is honesty and fair dealing.* ◻ N-COUNT Something's **secrets** are the things about it which have never been fully explained. ❑ *We have an opportunity now to really unlock the secrets of the universe.* ◊ PHRASE If you do something **in secret**, you do it without anyone else knowing. ❑ *Dan found out that I had been meeting my ex-boyfriend in secret.* ◊ PHRASE If you say that someone can **keep a secret**, you mean that they can be trusted not to tell other people a secret that you have told them. ❑ *Tom was utterly indiscreet, and could never keep a secret.* ◊ PHRASE If you **make no secret** of something, you tell others about it openly and clearly. ❑ *His wife made no secret of her hatred for the formal occasions.*

COLLOCATIONS

secret
NOUN
◊
noun + **secret**: family, state
adjective + **secret**: guilty, shameful, terrible; innermost, intimate; official
verb + **secret**: guard, harbor, hide, keep; betray, discover, reveal, share
◊
adjective + **secret**: dark, hidden
verb + **secret**: learn, uncover, unlock

se|cret agent (secret agents) N-COUNT A **secret agent** is a person who is employed by a government to find out the secrets of other governments.

sec|re|tar|ial /sɛkrɪtɛəriəl/ ADJ [ADJ n] **Secretarial** work is the work done by a secretary in an office. ❑ *I was doing temporary secretarial work.*

sec|re|tari|at /sɛkrɪtɛəriət/ (secretariats) N-COUNT A **secretariat** is a department that is responsible for the administration of an international political organization. ❑ *...the UN secretariat.*

sec|re|tary ♦♦♦ /sɛkrɪtɛri/ (secretaries) ◊ N-COUNT A **secretary** is a person who is employed to do office work, such as typing letters, answering phone calls, and arranging meetings. ◊ N-COUNT The **secretary** of a company is the person who has the legal duty of keeping the company's records. ◊ N-COUNT; N-TITLE **Secretary** is used in the titles of high officials who are in charge of main government departments. ❑ *...a former Venezuelan foreign secretary.*

secretary-general ♦◊◊ (secretaries-general) also **Secretary General** N-COUNT The **secretary-general** of an international political organization is the person in charge of its administration. ❑ *...the United Nations Secretary-General.*

Sec|re|tary of State ♦◊◊ (Secretaries of State) N-COUNT In the United States, **the Secretary of State** is the head of the government department which deals with foreign affairs.

se|crete /sɪkriːt/ (secretes, secreting, secreted) ◊ V-T If part of a plant, animal, or human **secretes** a liquid, it produces it. ❑ *The sweat glands secrete water.* ◊ V-T If you **secrete** something somewhere, you hide it there so that nobody will find it. [LITERARY] ❑ *She secreted the gun in the kitchen cabinet.*

se|cre|tion /sɪkriːʃən/ (secretions) ◊ N-UNCOUNT **Secretion** is the process by which certain liquid substances are produced by parts of plants or from the bodies of people or animals. ❑ *...the secretion of adrenaline.* ◊ N-PLURAL **Secretions** are liquid substances produced by parts of plants or bodies. ❑ *...gastric secretions.*

se|cre|tive /sɪkrətɪv, sɪkriːt-/ ADJ If you are **secretive**, you like to have secrets and to keep your knowledge, feelings, or intentions hidden. ❑ *Billionaires are usually fairly secretive about the exact amount that they're worth.*

se|cret po|lice N-UNCOUNT [also the N] The **secret police** is a police force in some countries that works secretly and deals with political crimes committed against the government. ❑ *...former members of the secret police.*

se|cret ser|vice (secret services) ◊ N-COUNT A country's **secret service** is a secret government department whose job is to find out enemy secrets and to prevent its own government's secrets from being discovered. ❑ *...French secret service agents.* ◊ N-COUNT The **Secret Service** is the government department in the United States which protects the president, the vice president, and their families. [AM] ❑ *He finished his career as head of the Secret Service team assigned to the President.*

se|cret weap|on (secret weapons) N-COUNT Someone's **secret weapon** is a thing or person which they believe will help them achieve something and which other people do not know about. ❑ *Discipline was the new coach's secret weapon.*

sect /sɛkt/ (sects) N-COUNT A **sect** is a group of people that has separated from a larger group and has a particular set of religious or political beliefs.

sec|tar|ian /sɛktɛəriən/ ADJ **Sectarian** means resulting from the differences between different religions. ❑ *He was the fifth person to be killed in sectarian violence last week.* ❑ *The police said the murder was sectarian.*

sec|tari|an|ism /sɛktɛəriənɪzəm/ N-UNCOUNT **Sectarianism** is strong support for the religious or political group you belong to, and often involves conflict with other groups. ❑ *...political rivalry and sectarianism within our movement.*

sec|tion ♦♦◊ /sɛkʃən/ (sections, sectioning, sectioned) ◊ N-COUNT A **section** of something is one of the parts into which it is divided or from which it is formed. ❑ *He said it was wrong to single out any section of society for AIDS testing.* ❑ *...the Georgetown section of Washington, D.C.* ◊ → see also **cross-section** ◊ V-T [usu passive] If something **is sectioned**, it is divided into sections. ❑ *It holds vegetables in place while they are being peeled or sectioned.* ◊ N-COUNT A **section** is a diagram of something such as a building or a part of the body. It shows how the object would appear to you if it were cut from top to bottom and looked at from the side. ❑ *For some buildings a vertical section is more informative than a plan.*

sec|tion|al /sɛkʃənəl/ ADJ [ADJ n] **Sectional** interests are those of a particular group within a community or country. ❑ *Voters elected him to represent them, rather than narrow sectional interests.*

sec|tor ♦♦◊ /sɛktər/ (sectors) ◊ N-COUNT A particular **sector** of a country's economy is the part connected with that specified type of industry. ❑ *...the nation's manufacturing sector.* ◊ → see also **public sector**, **private sector** ◊ N-COUNT A **sector** of a large group is a smaller group which is part of it. ❑ *Workers who went to the Gulf came from the poorest sectors of Pakistani society.* ◊ N-COUNT A **sector** is an area of a city or country which is controlled by a military force. ❑ *Officers were going to retake sectors of the city.*

sec|tor|al /sɛktərəl/ ADJ [ADJ n] **Sectoral** means relating to the various economic sectors of a society or to a particular economic sector. [TECHNICAL] ❑ *...sectoral differences within social classes.*

secu|lar /sɛkyələr/ ADJ You use **secular** to describe things that have no connection with religion. ❑ *He spoke about preserving the country as a secular state.*

secu|lar|ism /sɛkyələrɪzəm/ N-UNCOUNT **Secularism** is a system of social organization and education where religion is not allowed to play a part in civil affairs. • **secu|lar|ist** (secularists) N-COUNT ❑ *The country is being torn to pieces by conflict between fundamentalists and secularists.*

secu|lar|ized /sɛkyələraɪzd/

in BRIT, also use **secularised**

ADJ **Secularized** societies are no longer under the control or influence of religion. ❑ *He had no great sympathy for the secularized West.*

se|cure ♦♦◊ /sɪkyʊər/ (secures, securing, secured) ◊ V-T If you **secure** something that you want or need, you obtain it, often after a lot of effort. [FORMAL] ❑ *Federal leaders continued their efforts to secure a ceasefire.* ◊ V-T If you **secure** a place, you make it safe from harm or attack. [FORMAL] ❑ *Staff withdrew from the main part of the prison but secured the perimeter.* ◊ ADJ A **secure** place is tightly locked or well protected, so that people cannot enter it or leave it. ❑ *We'll make sure our home is as secure as possible from now on.* • **se|cure|ly** ADV ❑ *He locked the heavy door securely and kept the key in his pocket.* ◊ V-T If you **secure** an object, you fasten it firmly to another object. ❑ *He helped her close the cases up, and then he secured the canvas straps as tight as they would go.* ◊ ADJ If an object is **secure**, it is fixed firmly in position. ❑ *Check that joints are secure and the wood is sound.* • **se|cure|ly** ADV [ADV with v] ❑ *Ensure that the frame is securely fixed to the ground with* bolts. **6** ADJ If you describe something such as a job as **secure**, it is certain not to change or end. ☐ ...*demands for secure wages and employment.* ☐ *Many people long for a more predictable and secure future.* **7** ADJ A **secure** base or foundation is strong and reliable. ☐ *He was determined to give his family a secure and solid base.* **8** ADJ If you feel **secure**, you feel safe and happy and are not worried about life. ☐ *She felt secure and protected when she was with her.* **9** V-T [usu passive] If a loan **is secured**, the person who lends the money may take property such as a house from the person who borrows the money if they fail to repay it. [BUSINESS] ☐ *The loan is secured against your home.*

SYNONYMS

secure
VERB
1
obtain: *Evans was trying to obtain a false passport and other documents.*
get: *I got a job at the sawmill.*
acquire: *I recently acquired some wood from a holly tree.*
4
attach: *We attach labels to things before we file them away.*
stick: *Don't forget to clip the token and stick it on your card.*
fix: *The cupboard is fixed on the wall.*
fasten: *There were no instructions on how to fasten the carrying strap to the box.*

---

se|cure unit (secure units) N-COUNT A **secure unit** is a building or part of a building where dangerous prisoners or violent psychiatric patients are kept. ☐ ...*the secure unit at Cane Hill hospital.*

se|cu|ri|ty ◆◆◆ /sɪkjʊərɪti/ (securities) **1** N-UNCOUNT **Security** refers to all the measures that are taken to protect a place, or to ensure that only people with permission enter it or leave it. ☐ *They are now under a great deal of pressure to tighten their airport security.* ☐ *Strict security measures are in force in the capital.* **2** N-UNCOUNT A feeling of **security** is a feeling of being safe and free from worry. ☐ *He loves the security of a happy home life.* ☐ *If an alarm gives you that feeling of security, then it's worth carrying.* • PHRASE If something gives you **a false sense of security**, it makes you believe that you are safe when you are not. **3** N-UNCOUNT If something is **security** for a loan, you promise to give that thing to the person who lends you money, if you fail to pay the money back. [BUSINESS] ☐ *The central bank will provide special loans, and the banks will pledge the land as security.* **4** N-PLURAL **Securities** are stocks, shares, bonds, or other certificates that you buy in order to earn regular interest from them or to sell them later for a profit. [BUSINESS] ☐ *National banks can package their own mortgages and underwrite them as securities.* **5** → see also **Social Security 6** → See feature box at **work**

COLLOCATIONS

security
NOUN **1**
noun + **security**: airport, border, state
adjective + **security**: national, maximum, top; lax, tight
verb + **security**: guarantee, improve, tighten

---

se|cu|ri|ty blan|ket (security blankets) **1** N-COUNT If you refer to something as a **security blanket**, you mean that it provides someone with a feeling of safety and comfort when they are in a situation that worries them or makes them feel nervous. ☐ *Alan sings with shy intensity, hiding behind the security blanket of his guitar.* **2** N-COUNT A baby's **security blanket** is a piece of cloth or clothing which the baby holds and chews in order to feel comforted.

se|cu|ri|ty cam|era (security cameras) N-COUNT A **security camera** is a video camera that records people's activities in order to detect and prevent crime.

Se|cu|ri|ty Coun|cil ◆◇◇ N-PROPER **The Security Council** is the committee which governs the United Nations. It has permanent representatives from the United States, Russia, China, France, and the United Kingdom, and temporary representatives from some other countries.

se|cu|ri|ty guard (security guards) N-COUNT A **security guard** is someone whose job is to protect a building or to collect and deliver large amounts of money.

se|cu|ri|ty risk (security risks) N-COUNT If you describe someone as a **security risk**, you mean that they may be a threat to the safety of a country or organization. ☐ *Individuals considered a security risk will have to report to immigration authorities within 30 days.*

se|dan /sɪdæn/ (sedans) N-COUNT A **sedan** is a car with seats for four or more people, a fixed roof, and a trunk that is separate from the part of the car that you sit in. [AM]

in BRIT, use **saloon**

se|dan chair (sedan chairs) N-COUNT A **sedan chair** is an enclosed chair for one person carried on two poles by two men, one in front and one behind. Sedan chairs were used in the 17th and 18th centuries.

se|date /sɪdeɪt/ (sedates, sedating, sedated) **1** ADJ If you describe someone or something as **sedate**, you mean that they are quiet and rather dignified, though perhaps a bit dull. ☐ *She took them to visit her sedate, elderly cousins.* ☐ *Her life was sedate, almost mundane.* **2** ADJ If you move along at a **sedate** pace, you move slowly, in a controlled way. ☐ *We set off again at a more sedate pace.* **3** V-T If someone **is sedated**, they are given a drug to calm them or to make them sleep. ☐ *The patient is sedated with intravenous use of sedative drugs.*

se|da|tion /sɪdeɪʃən/ N-UNCOUNT If someone is under **sedation**, they have been given medicine or drugs in order to calm them or make them sleep. ☐ *His mother was under sedation after the boy's body was brought back from Germany.*

seda|tive /sɛdətɪv/ (sedatives) N-COUNT A **sedative** is a medicine or drug that calms you or makes you sleep. ☐ *They use opium as a sedative, rather than as a narcotic.*

sed|en|tary /sɛdəntɛri/ ADJ Someone who has a **sedentary** lifestyle or job sits down a lot of the time and does not do much exercise. ☐ *Obesity and a sedentary lifestyle have been linked with an increased risk of heart disease.*

sedge /sɛdʒ/ (sedges) N-MASS **Sedge** is a plant that looks like grass and grows in wet ground.

sedi|ment /sɛdɪmənt/ (sediments) N-VAR **Sediment** is solid material that settles at the bottom of a liquid, especially earth and pieces of rock that have been carried along and then left somewhere by water, ice, or wind. ☐ *Many organisms that die in the sea are soon buried by sediment.*

sedi|men|tary /sɛdɪmɛntəri/ ADJ [ADJ n] **Sedimentary** rocks are formed from sediment left by water, ice, or wind.

se|di|tion /sɪdɪʃən/ N-UNCOUNT **Sedition** is speech, writing, or behavior intended to encourage people to fight against or oppose the government. ☐ *Government officials charged him with sedition.*

se|di|tious /sɪdɪʃəs/ ADJ [usu ADJ n] A **seditious** act, speech, or piece of writing encourages people to fight against or oppose the government. ☐ *He fell under suspicion for distributing seditious pamphlets.*

se|duce /sɪdus/ (seduces, seducing, seduced) **1** V-T If something **seduces** you, it is so attractive that it makes you do something that you would not otherwise do. ☐ *The view of lake and plunging cliffs seduces visitors.* • **se|duc|tion** /sɪdʌkʃən/ (seductions) N-VAR ☐ ...*the seduction of words.* **2** V-T If someone **seduces** another person, they use their charm to persuade that person to have sex with them. ☐ *She has set out to seduce Stephen.* • **se|duc|tion** N-VAR ☐ *Her methods of seduction are subtle.*

se|duc|er /sɪdusər/ (seducers) N-COUNT A **seducer** is someone who seduces someone else. ☐ *He has a bad reputation as a seducer of both men and women.*

se|duc|tive /sɪdʌktɪv/ **1** ADJ Something that is **seductive** is very attractive or makes you want to do something that you would not otherwise do. ☐ *It's a seductive argument.* • **se|duc|tive|ly** ADV ☐ ...*his seductively simple assertion.* **2** ADJ A person who is **seductive** is very attractive sexually. ☐ ...*a seductive woman.* • **se|duc|tive|ly** ADV ☐ ...*looking seductively over her shoulder.*

se|duc|tress /sɪdʌktrɪs/ (seductresses) N-COUNT A **seductress** is a woman who seduces someone. ☐ *She was typecast as a self-confident seductress.*

SEE
① VERB USES
② EXPRESSIONS, PHRASES AND CONVENTIONS
③ PHRASAL VERBS

① **see** ♦♦♦ /siː/ (sees, seeing, saw, seen) **1** V-T/V-I [no cont] When you **see** something, you notice it using your eyes. ❏ *You can't see colors at night.* ❏ *She can see, hear, touch, smell, and taste.* **2** V-T If you **see** someone, you visit them or meet them. ❏ *I saw him yesterday.* ❏ *Mick wants to see you in his office right away.* **3** V-T [no cont] If you **see** an entertainment such as a play, movie, concert, or sports game, you watch it. ❏ *I haven't been to see a movie in 10 years.* **4** V-T/V-I [no cont] If you **see** that something is true or exists, you realize by observing it that it is true or exists. ❏ *I could see she was lonely.* ❏ *...a lot of people saw what was happening but did nothing about it.* ❏ *My taste has changed a bit over the years as you can see.* **5** V-T [no cont, no passive] If you **see** what someone means or **see** why something happened, you understand what they mean or understand why it happened. ❏ *Oh, I see what you're saying.* ❏ *I really don't see any reason for changing it.* **6** V-T If you **see** someone or something as a certain thing, you have the opinion that they are that thing. ❏ *She saw him as a visionary, but her father saw him as a man who couldn't make a living.* ❏ *Others saw it as a betrayal.* ❏ *As I see it, Steve has three choices open to him.* **7** V-T [no cont, no passive] If you **see** a particular quality in someone, you believe they have that quality. If you ask what someone **sees** in a particular person or thing, you want to know what they find attractive about that person or thing. ❏ *Frankly, I don't know what Paul sees in her.* **8** V-T [no cont] If you **see** something happening in the future, you imagine it, or predict that it will happen. ❏ *A good idea, but can you see Taylor trying it?* **9** V-T [no passive] If a period of time or a person **sees** a particular change or event, it takes place during that period of time or while that person is alive. ❏ *Yesterday saw the resignation of the chief financial officer.* ❏ *He had worked with the general for three years and was sorry to see him go.* **10** V-T If you **see** that something is done or if you **see** to it that it is done, you make sure that it is done. ❏ *See that you take care of him.* **11** V-T If you **see** someone to a particular place, you accompany them to make sure that they get there safely, or to show politeness. ❏ *He didn't offer to see her to her car.* **12** V-T If you **see** a lot of someone, you often meet each other or visit each other. ❏ *We used to see quite a lot of his wife, Carolyn.* **13** V-T If you **are seeing** someone, you spend time with them socially, and are having a romantic or sexual relationship. ❏ *My husband was still seeing her and he was having an affair with her.* **14** V-T [only imper] **See** is used in books to indicate to readers that they should look at another part of the book, or at another book, because more information is given there. ❏ *Surveys consistently find that men report feeling safe on the street after dark. See, for example, Hindelang and Garofalo (1978, p.127).*

USAGE
see
If you are talking about the present, you usually use **can see**. Don't say 'I see the sea.' Also, don't use **see** in progressive forms. Don't say 'I am seeing the sea.' Say 'I can see the sea.' *I could see someone approaching in the distance.*

② **see** ♦♦♦ /siː/ (sees, seeing, saw, seen)
→ Please look at meanings **12** – **19** to see if the expression you are looking for is shown under another headword.

1 V-T You can use **see** in expressions to do with finding out information. For example, if you say 'I'll see what's happening,' you mean that you intend to find out what is happening. ❏ *Let me just see what the next song is.* ❏ *Every time we asked our mother, she said, "Well, see what your father says."* **2** V-T You can use **see** in expressions in which you promise to try and help someone. For example, if you say 'I'll see if I can do it,' you mean that you will try to do the thing concerned. ❏ *I'll see if I can call her for you.* **3** V-T Some writers use **see** in expressions such as **we saw** and **as we have seen** to refer to something that has already been explained or described. ❏ *We saw in Chapter 16 how annual cash budgets are produced.* ❏ *Laws are often not clear, as we saw in Chapter 1.* **4** PHRASE You can use **seeing that** or **seeing as** to introduce a reason for what you are saying. [INFORMAL, SPOKEN] ❏ *Seeing as Mr. Moreton is a doctor, I assume he is reasonably intelligent.* **5** CONVENTION You can say 'I see' to indicate that you understand what someone is telling you. [SPOKEN, FORMULAE] ❏ *"He came home in my car."—"I see."* **6** CONVENTION People say 'I'll see' or 'We'll see' to indicate that they do not intend to make a decision immediately, and will decide later. ❏ *We'll see. It's a possibility.* **7** CONVENTION People say 'let me see' or 'let's see' when they are trying to remember something, or are trying to find something. ❏ *Let's see, they're six – no, make that five hours ahead of us.* **8** PHRASE If you try to make someone **see sense** or **see reason**, you try to make them realize that they are wrong or are being stupid. ❏ *He was hopeful that by sitting together they could both see sense and live as good neighbors.* **9** CONVENTION You can say '**you see**' when you are explaining something to someone, to encourage them to listen and understand. [SPOKEN] ❏ *Well, you see, you shouldn't really feel that way about it.* **10** CONVENTION '**See you**,' '**be seeing you**,' and '**see you later**' are ways of saying goodbye to someone when you expect to meet them again soon. [INFORMAL, SPOKEN, FORMULAE] ❏ *"Talk to you later."—"All right. See you, love."* **11** CONVENTION You can say '**You'll see**' to someone if they do not agree with you about what you think will happen in the future, and you believe that you will be proved right. ❏ *The thrill wears off after a few years of marriage. You'll see.* **12 to have seen better days** → see **day** **13 to be seen dead** → see **dead** **14 as far as the eye can see** → see **eye** ① **15 to see eye to eye** → see **eye** ① **16 as far as I can see** → see **far** ② **17 to see fit** → see **fit** ① **18 to see red** → see **red** **19 wait and see** → see **wait**

③ **see** ♦♦♦ /siː/ (sees, seeing, saw, seen)
▶ **see about** PHRASAL VERB When you **see about** something, you arrange for it to be done or provided. ❏ *Tony announced it was time to see about lunch.*
▶ **see off** PHRASAL VERB When you **see** someone **off**, you go with them to the station, airport, or port that they are leaving from, and say goodbye to them there. ❏ *Ben had planned a steak dinner for himself after seeing Jackie off on her plane.*
▶ **see out** PHRASAL VERB If you **see out** a period of time, you continue to do what you are doing until that period of time is over. ❏ *The lease runs for 21 years, and they are committed to seeing out that time.*
▶ **see through 1** PHRASAL VERB If you **see through** someone or their behavior, you realize what their intentions are, even though they are trying to hide them. ❏ *I saw through your little ruse from the start.* **2** → see also **see-through**
▶ **see to** PHRASAL VERB If you **see to** something that needs attention, you deal with it. ❏ *While Franklin saw to the luggage, Sara took Eleanor home.*

seed ♦♦◊ /siːd/ (seeds, seeding, seeded) **1** N-VAR A **seed** is the small, hard part of a plant from which a new plant grows. ❏ *I sow the seed in pots of soil-based compost.* **2** V-T If you **seed** a piece of land, you plant seeds in it. ❏ *Men mowed the wide lawns and seeded them.* ❏ *The primroses should begin to seed themselves down the steep hillside.* **3** N-PLURAL You can refer to the **seeds** of something when you want to talk about the beginning of a feeling or process that gradually develops and becomes stronger or more important. [LITERARY] ❏ *He raised questions meant to plant seeds of doubts in the minds of jurors.* **4** N-COUNT In sports such as tennis or badminton, a **seed** is a player who has been ranked according to his or her ability. ❏ *Roger Federer, Wimbledon's top seed and the world No.1.* **5** V-T [usu passive] When a player or a team **is seeded** in a sports competition, they are ranked according to their ability. ❏ *The Longhorns have won a national title and are seeded first overall.* ❏ *He is seeded second, behind Brad Beven.* **6** PHRASE If vegetable plants **go to seed**, they produce flowers and seeds as well as leaves ❏ *...plants that had long since flowered, gone to seed, and died.* **7** PHRASE If you say that someone or something **has gone to seed**, you mean that they have become much less attractive, healthy, or efficient. ❏ *He says the economy has gone to seed.* ❏ *...a retired cop who has gone to seed.*

seed|bed /siːdbɛd/ (seedbeds) also **seed-bed 1** N-COUNT A **seedbed** is an area of ground, usually with specially prepared earth, where young plants are grown from seed. **2** N-COUNT [oft N for/of n] You can refer to a place or a situation as a **seedbed** when it seems likely that a particular type of thing or person will develop in that place or situation. ❏ *TV is using radio as a seedbed for ideas.*

seed capi|tal N-UNCOUNT **Seed capital** is an amount of money that a new company needs to pay for the costs of producing a business plan so that they can raise further capital to develop the company. [BUSINESS] ❑ *I am negotiating with financiers to raise seed capital for my latest venture.*

seed|less /siːdləs/ ADJ A **seedless** fruit has no seeds in it. ❑ *...seedless grapes.*

seed|ling /siːdlɪŋ/ (**seedlings**) N-COUNT A **seedling** is a young plant that has been grown from a seed.

seed mon|ey N-UNCOUNT **Seed money** is money that is given to someone to help them start a new business or project. [BUSINESS] ❑ *The government will give seed money to the project.*

seedy /siːdi/ (**seedier, seediest**) ADJ If you describe a person or place as **seedy**, you disapprove of them because they look dirty and messy, or they have a bad reputation. [DISAPPROVAL] ❑ *Frank ran errands for a seedy local villain.* ❑ *We were staying in a seedy hotel close to the red light district.*

See|ing Eye dog (**Seeing Eye dogs**) also **Seeing-Eye dog** N-COUNT A **Seeing Eye dog** is a dog that has been trained to lead a blind person. [AM, TRADEMARK]

in BRIT, use **guide dog**

seek ✦✧✧ /siːk/ (**seeks, seeking, sought**) **1** V-T If you **seek** something such as a job or a place to live, you try to find one. [FORMAL] ❑ *They have had to seek work as laborers.* ❑ *Four people who sought refuge in the Italian embassy have left voluntarily.* **2** V-T When someone **seeks** something, they try to obtain it. [FORMAL] ❑ *The prosecutors have warned they will seek the death penalty.* **3** V-T If you **seek** someone's help or advice, you contact them in order to ask for it. [FORMAL] ❑ *Always seek professional legal advice before entering into any agreement.* ❑ *On important issues, they seek a second opinion.* **4** V-T If you **seek** to do something, you try to do it. [FORMAL] ❑ *He also denied that he would seek to annex the country.* ▶ **seek out** PHRASAL VERB If you **seek out** someone or something or **seek** them **out**, you keep looking for them until you find them. ❑ *Now is the time for local companies to seek out business opportunities in Europe.*

---SYNONYMS---

seek
VERB **1**
look: *I had gone to Maine looking for a place to work.*
search: *They searched for a spot where they could sit on the floor.*
hunt: *A forensic team was hunting for clues.*

---

seek|er /siːkər/ (**seekers**) **1** N-COUNT A **seeker** is someone who is looking for or trying to get something. ❑ *I am a seeker after truth.* **2** → see also **asylum seeker**

seem ✦✦✦ /siːm/ (**seems, seeming, seemed**) **1** V-LINK [no cont] You use **seem** to say that someone or something gives the impression of having a particular quality, or of happening in the way you describe. ❑ *The explosions seemed quite close by.* ❑ *To everyone who knew them, they seemed an ideal couple.* ❑ *The calming effect seemed to last for about ten minutes.* ❑ *It seems that the attack was carefully planned.* ❑ *It seemed as if she'd been gone forever.* **2** V-LINK [no cont] You use **seem** when you are describing your own feelings or thoughts, or describing something that has happened to you, in order to make your statement less forceful. [VAGUENESS] ❑ *I seem to have lost all my self-confidence.* ❑ *I seem to remember giving you very precise instructions.* **3** PHRASE If you say that you **cannot seem** or **could not seem** to do something, you mean that you have tried to do it and were unable to. ❑ *No matter how hard I try I cannot seem to catch up on all the bills.*

---SYNONYMS---

seem
VERB **1**
appear: *The aircraft appears to have crashed near Katmandu.*
look: *They look like stars to the naked eye.*
come across: *When sober, he can come across as an extremely pleasant young man.*

---

seem|ing /siːmɪŋ/ ADJ [ADJ n] **Seeming** means appearing to be the case, but not necessarily the case. For example, if you talk about someone's **seeming** ability to do something, you mean that they appear to be able to do it, but you are not certain. [FORMAL, VAGUENESS] ❑ *Wall Street analysts have been highly critical of the company's seeming inability to control costs.*

seem|ing|ly /siːmɪŋli/ **1** ADV [ADV adj/adv] If something is **seemingly** the case, you mean that it appears to be the case, even though it may not really be so. ❑ *A seemingly endless line of trucks waits in vain to load up.* **2** ADV You use **seemingly** when you want to say that something seems to be true. [VAGUENESS] ❑ *He has moved to Spain, seemingly to enjoy a slower style of life.*

seem|ly /siːmli/ ADJ **Seemly** behavior or dress is appropriate in the particular circumstances. [OLD-FASHIONED] ❑ *Self-assertion was not thought seemly in a woman.*

seen /siːn/ **Seen** is the past participle of **see**.

seep /siːp/ (**seeps, seeping, seeped**) **1** V-I If something such as liquid or gas **seeps** somewhere, it flows slowly and in small amounts into a place where it should not go. ❑ *Radioactive water had seeped into underground reservoirs.* ❑ *The gas is seeping out of the rocks.* • N-COUNT **Seep** is also a noun. ❑ *...an oil seep.* **2** V-I If something such as information or an emotion **seeps** into or out of a place, it enters or leaves it gradually. ❑ *Many of us thrive on competition, but it can seep into areas of our lives where we do not want it.*

seep|age /siːpɪdʒ/ N-UNCOUNT **Seepage** is the slow flow of a liquid through something. ❑ *Chemical seepage has caused untold damage.*

seer /sɪər/ (**seers**) N-COUNT A **seer** is a person who tells people what will happen in the future. [LITERARY] ❑ *...the writings of the 16th century French seer, Nostradamus.*

see|saw /siːsɔː/ (**seesaws**) also **see-saw** N-COUNT A **seesaw** is a long board which is balanced in the middle. To play on it, a child sits on each end, and when one end goes up, the other goes down. ❑ *There was a sandpit, a seesaw and a swing in the playground.*

seethe /siːð/ (**seethes, seething, seethed**) V-I When you **are seething**, you are very angry about something but do not express your feelings about it. ❑ *She took it calmly at first but under the surface was seething.* ❑ *She put a hand on her hip, grinning derisively, while I seethed with rage.*

see-through ADJ **See-through** clothes are made of thin cloth, so that you can see a person's body or underwear through them. ❑ *She was wearing a white, see-through blouse, a red bra showing beneath.*

seg|ment ✦✧✧ /sɛgmənt/ (**segments**) **1** N-COUNT A **segment** of something is one part of it, considered separately from the rest. ❑ *...the poorer segments of society.* **2** N-COUNT A **segment** of fruit such as an orange or grapefruit is one of the sections into which it is easily divided. ❑ *Peel all the fruit except the lime and separate into segments.* **3** N-COUNT A **segment** of a circle is one of the two parts into which it is divided when you draw a straight line through it. ❑ *The other children stood around the circle, one in each segment.*

---SYNONYMS---

segment
NOUN **1**
section: *...a geological section of a rock.*
part: *It was a very severe accident, and he lost part of his foot.*
piece: *...a piece of cake.*

---

seg|men|ta|tion /sɛgmənteɪʃən/ N-UNCOUNT **Segmentation** is the dividing of something into parts which are loosely connected. [TECHNICAL]

seg|ment|ed /sɛgmɛntɪd, sɛgmənt-/ ADJ [ADJ n] **Segmented** means divided into parts that are loosely connected to each other. ❑ *...segmented oranges.*

seg|re|gate /sɛgrɪgeɪt/ (**segregates, segregating, segregated**) V-T To **segregate** two groups of people or things means to keep them physically apart from each other. ❑ *A large detachment of police was used to segregate the two rival camps of protesters.*

seg|re|gat|ed /sɛgrɪgeɪtɪd/ ADJ **Segregated** buildings or areas are kept for the use of only one group of people who are the same race, sex, or religion, and no other group is allowed to use them. ❑ *...racially segregated schools.*

seg|re|ga|tion /sɛgrɪgeɪʃən/ N-UNCOUNT **Segregation** is the official practice of keeping people apart, usually people of different sexes, races, or religions. ❑ *The Supreme Court unanimously ruled that racial segregation in schools was unconstitutional.*

seg|re|ga|tion|ist /sɛgrɪgeɪʃənɪst/ (**segregationists**) N-COUNT [oft N n] A **segregationist** is someone who thinks people of

segue /sɛgweɪ/ (segues, segueing, segued) V-I If something such as a piece of music or conversation **segues into** another piece of music or conversation, it changes into it or is followed by it without a break. ❑ *The piece segues into his solo with the strings.* • N-COUNT [usu sing] Segue is also a noun. ❑ *...a neat segue into an arrangement of "Eleanor Rigby."*

seis|mic /saɪzmɪk/ **1** ADJ [ADJ n] Seismic means caused by or relating to an earthquake. ❑ *Earthquakes produce two types of seismic waves.* **2** ADJ [usu ADJ n] A **seismic** shift or change is a very sudden or dramatic change. ❑ *I have never seen such a seismic shift in public opinion in such a short period of time.*

seis|mo|graph /saɪzməgræf/ (seismographs) N-COUNT A seismograph is an instrument for recording and measuring the strength of earthquakes.

seis|mol|ogy /saɪzmɒlədʒi/ N-UNCOUNT Seismology is the scientific study of earthquakes. • **seis|mo|logi|cal** /saɪzməlɒdʒɪkəl/ ADJ [usu ADJ n] ❑ *...the Seismological Society of America.* • **seis|molo|gist (seismologists)** N-COUNT ❑ *Peter Ward is a seismologist with the U.S. Geological Survey.*

seize ♦◇◇ /siːz/ (seizes, seizing, seized) **1** V-T If you **seize** something, you take hold of it quickly, firmly, and forcefully. ❑ *"Leigh," he said seizing my arm to hold me back.* **2** V-T When a group of people **seize** a place or **seize** control of it, they take control of it quickly and suddenly, using force. ❑ *Troops have seized the airport and railroad terminals.* **3** V-T If a government or other authority **seize** someone's property, they take it from them, often by force. ❑ *Police were reported to have seized all copies of this morning's edition of the newspaper.* **4** V-T When someone **is seized**, they are arrested or captured. ❑ *Two military observers were seized by enemy troops yesterday.* **5** V-T When you **seize** an opportunity, you take advantage of it and do something that you want to do. ❑ *During the riots hundreds of people seized the opportunity to steal property.*
▶ **seize on** PHRASAL VERB If you **seize on** something or **seize upon** it, you show great interest in it, often because it is useful to you. ❑ *Newspapers seized on the results as proof that global warming wasn't really happening.*
▶ **seize up 1** PHRASAL VERB If a part of your body **seizes up**, it suddenly stops working, because you have strained it or because you are getting old. ❑ *After two days' exertions, it's the arms and hands that seize up, not the legs.* **2** PHRASAL VERB If something such as an engine **seizes up**, it stops working, because it has not been properly cared for. ❑ *She put diesel fuel, instead of gasoline, into the tank causing the motor to seize up.*

SYNONYMS

seize
VERB **1**
grab: *I managed to grab her sleeve.*
grasp: *He grasped both my hands.*
snatch: *Mick snatched the cards from Archie's hand.*

---

sei|zure /siːʒər/ (seizures) **1** N-COUNT If someone has a **seizure**, they have a sudden violent attack of an illness, especially one that affects their heart or brain. ❑ *...a mild cardiac seizure.* **2** N-COUNT If there is a **seizure** of power or a **seizure** of an area of land, a group of people suddenly take control of the place, using force. ❑ *...the seizure of territory through force.* **3** N-COUNT When an organization such as the police or customs makes a **seizure** of illegal goods, they find them and take them away. ❑ *Police have made one of the biggest seizures of heroin there's ever been.*

sel|dom /sɛldəm/ ADV If something **seldom** happens, it happens only occasionally. ❑ *They seldom speak.* ❑ *I've seldom felt so happy.*

se|lect ♦◇◇ /sɪlɛkt/ (selects, selecting, selected) **1** V-T If you **select** something, you choose it from a number of things of the same kind. ❑ *Voters are selecting candidates for both U.S. Senate seats and for 52 congressional seats.* ❑ *With a difficult tee shot, select a club which will keep you short of the trouble.* **2** V-T If you **select** a file or a piece of text on a computer screen, you click on it so that it is marked in a different color, usually in order for you to give the computer an instruction relating to that file or piece of text. [COMPUTING] ❑ *I selected a file and pressed the delete key.* **3** ADJ [ADJ n] A **select** group is a small group of some of the best people or things of their kind. ❑ *...a select group of French cheeses.* **4** ADJ If you describe something as **select**, you mean it has many desirable features, but is available only to people who have a lot of money or who belong to a high social class. ❑ *The famous designer is throwing a very lavish and very select party.*

SYNONYMS

select
VERB **1**
choose: *They will be able to choose their own leaders in democratic elections.*
pick: *I had deliberately picked a city with a tropical climate.*
opt for: *Depending on your circumstances, you may wish to opt for one method or the other.*

---

se|lect com|mit|tee (select committees) N-COUNT A **select committee** is a committee of members of a legislature which is set up to investigate and report on a particular matter.

se|lec|tion ♦◇◇ /sɪlɛkʃən/ (selections) **1** N-UNCOUNT Selection is the act of selecting one or more people or things from a group. ❑ *...Darwin's principles of natural selection.* ❑ *Dr. Sullivan's selection to head the Department of Health was greeted with satisfaction.* **2** N-COUNT A **selection** of people or things is a set of them that have been selected from a larger group. ❑ *...this selection of popular songs.* **3** N-COUNT The **selection** of goods in a store is the particular range of goods that it has available and from which you can choose what you want. ❑ *It offers the widest selection of antiques of every description in a one day market.* **4** N-COUNT In computing, a **selection** is an area of the screen that you have highlighted, for example because you want to copy it to another file. [COMPUTING]

SYNONYMS

selection
NOUN **1**
choice: *It's available in a choice of colors.*
pick: *We had the pick of suits from the shop.*
option: *What other options do you have?*
preference: *Parents can express a preference for the school their child attends.*

---

se|lec|tive /sɪlɛktɪv/ **1** ADJ [ADJ n] A **selective** process applies only to a few things or people. ❑ *Selective breeding may result in a greyhound running faster and seeing better than a wolf.* • **se|lec|tive|ly** ADV ❑ *Within the project, trees are selectively cut on a 25-year rotation.* **2** ADJ When someone is **selective**, they choose things carefully, for example, the things that they buy or do. ❑ *Sales still happen, but buyers are more selective.* • **se|lec|tive|ly** ADV [ADV with v] ❑ *...people on small incomes who wanted to shop selectively.* **3** ADJ If you say that someone has a **selective** memory, you disapprove of the fact that they remember certain facts about something and deliberately forget others, often because it is convenient for them to do so. [DISAPPROVAL] ❑ *We seem to have a selective memory for the best bits of the past.* • **se|lec|tive|ly** ADV [ADV with v] ❑ *...a tendency to remember only the pleasurable effects of the drug and selectively forget all the adverse effects.*

se|lec|tive ser|vice N-UNCOUNT In the United States, **selective service** is a system of selecting and ordering young people to serve in the armed forces for a limited period of time.

self ♦◇◇ /sɛlf/ (selves) **1** N-COUNT Your **self** is your basic personality or nature, especially considered in terms of what you are really like as a person. ❑ *You're looking more like your usual self.* **2** N-COUNT A person's **self** is the essential part of their nature which makes them different from everyone and everything else. ❑ *I want to explore and get in touch with my inner self.* ❑ *The face is the true self visible to others.*

self- /sɛlf-/ **1** COMB IN ADJ; N **Self-** is used to form words which indicate that you do something to yourself or by yourself. ❑ *He is a self-proclaimed Anglophile.* ❑ *...self-destructive behavior.* **2** COMB IN ADJ; N **Self-** is used to form words which describe something such as a device that does something automatically by itself. ❑ *...a self-loading pistol.*

self-absorbed ADJ Someone who is **self-absorbed** thinks so much about things concerning themselves that they do not notice other people or the things around them.

self-addressed ADJ [usu ADJ n] A **self-addressed** envelope is an envelope which you have written your address on and which you send to someone in another envelope so that they can send something back to you. ❑ *Please enclose a stamped self-addressed envelope.*

self-adhesive ADJ Something that is **self-adhesive** is covered on one side with a sticky substance like glue, so that it will stick to surfaces. ❑ *...self-adhesive labels.*

self-aggrandizement

in BRIT, also use **self-aggrandisement**

N-UNCOUNT If you say that someone is guilty of **self-aggrandizement**, you mean that they do certain things in order to make themselves more powerful, wealthy, or important. [DISAPPROVAL] ❑ *He was interested in service, not self-aggrandizement.*

self-appointed ADJ [usu ADJ n] A **self-appointed** leader or ruler has taken the position of leader or ruler without anyone else asking them or choosing them to have it. ❑ *...the new self-appointed leaders of the movement.*

self-assembly ADJ [usu ADJ n] **Self-assembly** is used to refer to furniture and other products that you buy in parts and that you have to put together yourself. ❑ *...a range of self-assembly bedroom furniture.*

self-assertion N-UNCOUNT **Self-assertion** is confidence that you have in speaking firmly about your opinions and demanding the rights that you believe you should have. ❑ *...her silence and lack of self-assertion.*

self-assertive ADJ Someone who is **self-assertive** acts in a confident way, speaking firmly about their opinions and demanding the rights that they believe they should have. ❑ *If you want good relationships, you must have the confidence to be self-assertive when required.*

self-assurance N-UNCOUNT Someone who has **self-assurance** shows confidence in the things that they say and do because they are sure of their abilities.

self-assured ADJ Someone who is **self-assured** shows confidence in what they say and do because they are sure of their own abilities. ❑ *He's a self-assured, confident negotiator.*

self-aware ADJ [usu v-link ADJ] Someone who is **self-aware** knows and judges their own character well. ❑ *Going back to college has increased my confidence and I feel much more self-aware.*
• **self-awareness** N-UNCOUNT ❑ *It is assumed that you are interested in achieving greater self-awareness.*

self-belief N-UNCOUNT **Self-belief** is confidence in your own abilities or judgment.

self-care N-UNCOUNT **Self-care** is when a person looks after their own emotional wellbeing. ❑ *Practicing self-care tends to reduce stress and allow you to think more fully.*

self-centered

in BRIT, use **self-centred**

ADJ Someone who is **self-centered** is only concerned with their own wants and needs and never thinks about other people. [DISAPPROVAL] ❑ *It's very self-centered to think that people are talking about you.*

self-confessed ADJ [ADJ n] If you describe someone as a **self-confessed** murderer or a **self-confessed** romantic, for example, you mean that they admit openly that they are a murderer or a romantic. ❑ *The self-confessed drug addict was arrested 13 months ago.*

self-confidence N-UNCOUNT If you have **self-confidence**, you behave confidently because you feel sure of your abilities or value. ❑ *With the end of my love affair, I lost all the self-confidence I once had.*

self-confident ADJ Someone who is **self-confident** behaves confidently because they feel sure of their abilities or value. ❑ *She'd blossomed into a self-confident young woman.*

self-congratulation N-UNCOUNT If someone keeps emphasizing how well they have done or how good they are, you can refer to their behavior as **self-congratulation**. [DISAPPROVAL] ❑ *This is not a matter for self-congratulation.*

self-congratulatory ADJ If you describe someone or their behavior as **self-congratulatory**, you mean that they keep emphasizing how well they have done or how good they are. [DISAPPROVAL] ❑ *Officials were self-congratulatory about how well the day had gone.*

self-conscious ADJ Someone who is **self-conscious** is easily embarrassed and nervous because they feel that everyone is looking at them and judging them. ❑ *I felt a bit self-conscious in my bikini.*

self-contained ◨ ADJ You can describe someone or something as **self-contained** when they are complete and separate and do not need help or resources from outside. ❑ *He seems completely self-contained and he doesn't miss you when you're not there.* ◩ ADJ **Self-contained** accommodations such as an apartment have all their own facilities, so that a person living there does not have to share rooms such as a kitchen or bathroom with other people. ❑ *Her family lives in a self-contained three-bedroom suite in the back of the main house.*

self-contradictory ADJ If you say or write something that is **self-contradictory**, you make two statements which cannot both be true. ❑ *He is notorious for making unexpected, often self-contradictory, comments.*

self-control N-UNCOUNT **Self-control** is the ability to not show your feelings or not do the things that your feelings make you want to do. ❑ *His self-control, reserve and aloofness were almost inhuman.*

self-controlled ADJ Someone who is **self-controlled** is able to not show their feelings or not do the things that their feelings make them want to do. ❑ *My father, who had always been very self-controlled, became bad-tempered.*

self-deception N-UNCOUNT **Self-deception** involves allowing yourself to believe something about yourself that is not true, because the truth is more unpleasant. ❑ *Human beings have an infinite capacity for self-deception.*

self-declared ADJ [ADJ n] **Self-declared** means the same as **self-proclaimed**. ❑ *...the self-declared interim president.* ❑ *He is a self-declared populist.*

self-defeating ADJ A plan or action that is **self-defeating** is likely to cause problems or difficulties instead of producing useful results. ❑ *Dishonesty is ultimately self-defeating.*

self-defense

in BRIT, use **self-defence**

◨ N-UNCOUNT **Self-defense** is the use of force to protect yourself against someone who is attacking you. ❑ *The women acted in self-defense after years of abuse.* ◩ N-UNCOUNT **Self-defense** is the action of protecting yourself against something bad. ❑ *Tai Chi is an ancient form of self-defense.*

self-delusion N-UNCOUNT **Self-delusion** is the state of having a false idea about yourself or the situation you are in. ❑ *...the grandiose self-delusion of the addict.*

self-denial N-UNCOUNT **Self-denial** is the habit of refusing to do or have things that you would like, either because you cannot afford them, or because you believe it is morally good for you not to do them or have them. ❑ *Should motherhood necessarily mean sacrifice and self-denial?*

self-denying ADJ Someone who is **self-denying** refuses to do or have things that they would like, either because they cannot afford them, or because they believe it is morally good for them not to do them or have them. ❑ *They believed that good parents should be self-sacrificing and self-denying.*

self-deprecating ADJ [usu ADJ n] If you describe someone's behavior as **self-deprecating**, you mean that they criticize themselves or represent themselves as foolish in a light-hearted way. ❑ *Sharon tells the story of that night with self-deprecating humor.*

self-destruct (self-destructs, self-destructing, self-destructed) V-I If someone **self-destructs**, they do something that seriously damages their chances of success. ❑ *They're going to be famous, but unless something happens, they're going to self-destruct.*

self-destructive ADJ **Self-destructive** behavior is harmful to the person who behaves in that way. ❑ *He had a reckless, self-destructive streak.*

self-determination N-UNCOUNT **Self-determination** is the right of a country to be independent, instead of being controlled by a foreign country, and to choose its own form of government. ❑ ...Lithuania's right to self-determination.

self-discipline N-UNCOUNT **Self-discipline** is the ability to control yourself and to make yourself work hard or behave in a particular way without needing anyone else to tell you what to do. ❑ Exercising at home alone requires a tremendous amount of self-discipline.

self-disciplined ADJ Someone who is **self-disciplined** has the ability to control themselves and to make themselves work hard or behave in a particular way without needing anyone else to tell them what to do. ❑ Most religions teach you to be truthful and self-disciplined.

self-doubt N-UNCOUNT **Self-doubt** is a lack of confidence in yourself and your abilities.

self-educated ADJ People who are **self-educated** have acquired knowledge or a skill by themselves, rather than being taught it by someone else such as a teacher at school. ❑ ...a self-educated man from a working class background.

self-effacement N-UNCOUNT Someone's **self-effacement** is their unwillingness to talk about themselves or draw attention to themselves. ❑ He was modest to the point of self-effacement.

self-effacing ADJ Someone who is **self-effacing** does not like talking about themselves or drawing attention to themselves. ❑ As women we tend to be self-effacing and make light of what we have achieved.

self-employed ADJ If you are **self-employed**, you organize your own work and taxes and are paid by people for a service you provide, rather than being paid a regular salary by a person or a firm. [BUSINESS] ❑ There are no paid holidays or sick leave if you are self-employed. • N-PLURAL **The self-employed** are people who are self-employed. ❑ We want more support for the self-employed.

self-esteem N-UNCOUNT Your **self-esteem** is how you feel about yourself. For example, if you have low **self-esteem**, you do not like yourself, you do not think that you are a valuable person, and therefore you do not behave confidently. ❑ Poor self-esteem is at the center of many of the difficulties we experience in our relationships.

self-evident ADJ A fact or situation that is **self-evident** is so obvious that there is no need for proof or explanation. ❑ It is self-evident that we will never have enough resources to meet the demand.

self-examination ◼ N-UNCOUNT [also a N] **Self-examination** is thought that you give to your own character and actions, for example, in order to judge whether you have been behaving in a way that is acceptable to your own set of values. ❑ The events in Los Angeles have sparked a new national self-examination. ◻ N-UNCOUNT **Self-examination** is the act of examining your own body to check whether or not you have any signs of a particular disease or illness. ❑ Breast self-examination is invaluable for detecting cancer in its very early stages.

self-explanatory ADJ Something that is **self-explanatory** is clear and easy to understand without needing any extra information or explanation. ❑ I hope the graphs on the following pages are self-explanatory.

self-expression N-UNCOUNT **Self-expression** is the expression of your personality, feelings, or opinions, for example, through an artistic activity such as drawing or dancing. ❑ Clothes are a fundamental form of self-expression.

self-fulfilling ADJ If you describe a statement or belief about the future as **self-fulfilling**, you mean that what is said or believed comes true because people expect it to come true. ❑ Fear of failure can become a self-fulfilling prophecy.

self-governing ADJ A **self-governing** region or organization is governed or run by its own people rather than by the people of another region or organization. ❑ ...a self-governing province.

self-government N-UNCOUNT **Self-government** is government of a country or region by its own people rather than by others.

self-harm (self-harms, self-harming, self-harmed) VERB If you **self-harm**, you deliberately hurt yourself, for example by cutting yourself, because of mental illness. ❑ Her parents discovered that she had been self-harming.

self-help N-UNCOUNT **Self-help** consists of people providing support and help for each other in an informal way, rather than relying on the government, authorities, or other official organizations. ❑ She set up a self-help group for parents with overweight children.

selfie /sɛlfi/ (selfies) N-COUNT A **selfie** is a photograph that you take of yourself, especially using a smart phone. [INFORMAL] ❑ He took a selfie in front of the Taj Mahal.

selfie stick (selfie sticks) N-COUNT A **selfie stick** is a long device with a holder for your phone at one end and a button at the other that you can press to take a photograph of yourself. [INFORMAL] ❑ The square is full of tourists with selfie sticks.

self-image (self-images) N-COUNT Your **self-image** is the set of ideas you have about your own qualities and abilities. ❑ Children who have a positive self-image are less likely to present behavior and discipline problems.

self-important ADJ If you say that someone is **self-important**, you disapprove of them because they behave as if they are more important than they really are. [DISAPPROVAL] ❑ He was self-important, vain and ignorant. • **self-importance** N-UNCOUNT ❑ Many visitors complained of his bad manners and self-importance.

self-imposed ADJ A **self-imposed** restriction, task, or situation is one that you have deliberately created or accepted for yourself. ❑ He returned home after eleven years of self-imposed exile.

self-indulgence (self-indulgences) N-VAR **Self-indulgence** is the act of allowing yourself to have or do the things that you enjoy very much. ❑ He prayed to be saved from self-indulgence.

self-indulgent ADJ If you say that someone is **self-indulgent**, you mean that they allow themselves to have or do the things that they enjoy very much. ❑ Why give publicity to this self-indulgent, adolescent oaf?

self-inflicted ADJ A **self-inflicted** wound or injury is one that you do to yourself deliberately. ❑ He is being treated for a self-inflicted gunshot wound.

self-interest N-UNCOUNT If you accuse someone of **self-interest**, you disapprove of them because they always want to do what is best for themselves rather than for anyone else. [DISAPPROVAL] ❑ Their current protests are motivated purely by self-interest.

self-interested ADJ If you describe someone as **self-interested**, you disapprove of them because they always want to do what is best for themselves rather than for other people. [DISAPPROVAL] ❑ Narrowly self-interested behavior is ultimately self-defeating.

self|ish /sɛlfɪʃ/ ADJ If you say that someone is **selfish**, you mean that he or she cares only about himself or herself, and not about other people. [DISAPPROVAL] ❑ I think I've been very selfish. I've been mainly concerned with myself. • **self|ish|ly** ADV ❑ Someone has selfishly emptied the cookie jar. • **self|ish|ness** N-UNCOUNT ❑ The arrogance and selfishness of different interest groups never ceases to amaze me.

self-isolate (self-isolates, self-isolating, self-isolated) VERB If someone who has or may have an infectious disease **self-isolates**, they stay at home and do not see any other people. ❑ Anyone who has a fever or is ill will be ordered to self-isolate and be tested for the disease. • **self-isolation** N-UNCOUNT ❑ She decided to go into self-isolation.

self-knowledge N-UNCOUNT **Self-knowledge** is knowledge that you have about your own character and nature. ❑ The more self-knowledge we have, the more control we can exert over our feelings and behavior.

self|less /sɛlflɪs/ ADJ If you say that someone is **selfless**, you approve of them because they care about other people more than themselves. [APPROVAL] ❑ She was a wonderful companion and her generosity to me was entirely selfless.

self-loathing N-UNCOUNT If someone feels **self-loathing**, they feel great dislike and disgust for themselves.

self-made ADJ [usu ADJ n] **Self-made** is used to describe people who have become successful and rich through their own efforts, especially if they started life without money, education, or high social status. ❑ He is a self-made man. ❑ ...a self-made millionaire.

self-obsessed ADJ If you describe someone as **self-obsessed**, you are criticizing them for spending too much time thinking about themselves or their own problems. [DISAPPROVAL]

self-parody (**self-parodies**) N-VAR **Self-parody** is a way of performing or behaving in which you exaggerate and make fun of the way you normally perform or behave. ❏ *By the end of his life, his vocals often descended close to self-parody*

self-pity N-UNCOUNT **Self-pity** is a feeling of unhappiness that you have about yourself and your problems, especially when this is unnecessary or greatly exaggerated. [DISAPPROVAL] ❏ *I was unable to shake off my self-pity.*

self-pitying ADJ Someone who is **self-pitying** is full of self-pity. [DISAPPROVAL] ❏ *At the risk of sounding self-pitying, I'd say it has been harder on me than it has on Joanne.*

self-portrait (**self-portraits**) N-COUNT A **self-portrait** is a drawing, painting, or written description that you do of yourself.

self-possessed ADJ Someone who is **self-possessed** is calm and confident and in control of their emotions. ❏ *She is clearly the most articulate and self-possessed member of her family.*

self-possession N-UNCOUNT **Self-possession** is the quality of being self-possessed. ❏ *She found her customary self-possession had deserted her.*

self-preservation N-UNCOUNT **Self-preservation** is the action of keeping yourself safe or alive in a dangerous situation, often without thinking about what you are doing. ❏ *The police have the same human urge for self-preservation as the rest of us.*

self-proclaimed ◼ ADJ [ADJ n] **Self-proclaimed** is used to show that someone has given themselves a particular title or status rather than being given it by other people. ❏ *...a self-proclaimed expert.* ❏ *He is president of his own self-proclaimed republic.* ◼ ADJ [ADJ n] **Self-proclaimed** is used to show that someone says themselves that they are a type of person which most people would be embarrassed or ashamed to be. ❏ *She's a self-proclaimed survival expert.*

self-promotion N-UNCOUNT If you accuse someone of **self-promotion**, you disapprove of them because they are trying to make themselves seem more important than they actually are. [DISAPPROVAL] ❏ *His ruthless ambition and drive for self-promotion have not made him popular among his co-workers.*

self-raising flour N-UNCOUNT **Self-raising flour** is the same as **self-rising flour**. [BRIT]

self-referential /sɛlfrɛfərɛnʃ°l/ ADJ If you describe something such as a book or film as **self-referential**, you mean that it is concerned with things such as its own composition or with other similar books or films. ❏ *...self-referential novels about writer's block.*

self-regulation N-UNCOUNT **Self-regulation** is the controlling of a process or activity by the people or organizations that are involved in it rather than by an outside organization such as the government. ❏ *Competition between companies is too fierce for self-regulation to work.*

self-regulatory also **self-regulating** ADJ [usu ADJ n] **Self-regulatory** systems, organizations, or activities are controlled by the people involved in them, rather than by outside organizations or rules. ❏ *For a self-regulatory system to work, the consent of all those involved is required.*

self-reliance N-UNCOUNT **Self-reliance** is the ability to do things and make decisions by yourself, without needing other people to help you. ❏ *People learned self-reliance because they had to.*

self-reliant ADJ If you are **self-reliant**, you are able to do things and make decisions by yourself, without needing other people to help you. ❏ *She is intelligent and self-reliant, able to work well on her own.*

self-respect N-UNCOUNT **Self-respect** is a feeling of confidence and pride in your own ability and worth. ❏ *They have lost not only their jobs, but their homes, their self-respect and even their reason for living.*

self-respecting ADJ [ADJ n] You can use **self-respecting** with a noun describing a particular type of person to indicate that something is typical of, or necessary for, that type of person. ❏ *He died as any self-respecting gangster should—in a hail of bullets.*

self-restraint N-UNCOUNT If you show **self-restraint**, you do not do something even though you would like to do it, because you think it would be better not to.

self-righteous ADJ If you describe someone as **self-righteous**, you disapprove of them because they are convinced that they are right in their beliefs, attitudes, and behavior and that other people are wrong. [DISAPPROVAL] ❏ *He is critical of the monks, whom he considers narrow-minded and self-righteous.*
● **self-righteousness** N-UNCOUNT ❏ *Her aggressiveness and self-righteousness caused prickles of anger at the back of his neck.*

self-rising flour N-UNCOUNT **Self-rising flour** is flour that makes cakes rise when they are cooked because it has chemicals added to it. [AM]

in BRIT, use **self-raising flour**

self-rule N-UNCOUNT **Self-rule** is the same as **self-government**. ❏ *The agreement gives the territory limited self-rule.*

self-sacrifice N-UNCOUNT **Self-sacrifice** is the giving up of what you want so that other people can have what they need or want. ❏ *I thanked my parents for all their self-sacrifice on my behalf.*

self-sacrificing ADJ Someone who is **self-sacrificing** gives up what they want so that other people can have what they need or want. ❏ *He was a generous self-sacrificing man.*

self-same also **selfsame** ADJ [ADJ n] You use **self-same** when you want to emphasize that the person or thing mentioned is exactly the same as the one mentioned previously. [EMPHASIS] ❏ *You find yourself worshipped by the self-same people who beat you up at school.*

self-satisfaction N-UNCOUNT **Self-satisfaction** is the feeling you have when you are self-satisfied. [DISAPPROVAL] ❏ *He tried hard not to smile in smug self-satisfaction.*

self-satisfied ADJ If you describe someone as **self-satisfied**, you mean that they are too pleased with themselves about their achievements or their situation and they think that nothing better is possible. [DISAPPROVAL] ❏ *She handed the cigar back to Jason with a self-satisfied smile.*

self-seeking ADJ If you describe someone as **self-seeking**, you disapprove of them because they are interested only in doing things which give them an advantage over other people. [DISAPPROVAL] ❏ *He said that democracy would open the way for self-seeking politicians to abuse the situation.*

self-service ADJ A **self-service** store, restaurant, or garage is one where you get things for yourself rather than being served by another person. ❏ *...a self-service cafeteria with a wide choice.*

self-serving ADJ If you describe someone as **self-serving**, you are critical of them because they are only interested in what they can get for themselves. [DISAPPROVAL] ❏ *...corrupt, self-serving politicians.*

self-standing ◼ ADJ An object or structure that is **self-standing** is not supported by other objects or structures. ❏ *...self-standing plastic cases.* ◼ ADJ A company or organization that is **self-standing** is independent of other companies or organizations. [BUSINESS] ❏ *Five separate companies, all operating as self-standing units, are now one.*

self-study N-UNCOUNT **Self-study** is study that you do on your own, without a teacher. ❏ *Individuals can enrol on self-study courses in the university's language institute.*

self-styled ADJ [ADJ n] If you describe someone as a **self-styled** leader or expert, you disapprove of them because they claim to be a leader or expert but they do not actually have the right to call themselves this. [DISAPPROVAL] ❏ *Two of those arrested are said to be self-styled area commanders.*

self-sufficiency /sɛlf səfɪʃ°nsi/ N-UNCOUNT **Self-sufficiency** is the state of being self-sufficient.

self-sufficient ◼ ADJ If a country or group is **self-sufficient**, it is able to produce or make everything that it needs. ❏ *This enabled the country to become self-sufficient in sugar.* ◼ ADJ Someone who is **self-sufficient** is able to live happily without anyone else. ❏ *Although she had various boyfriends, Madeleine was, and remains, fiercely self-sufficient.*

self-supporting ADJ **Self-supporting** is used to describe organizations, programs, and people who earn enough money to not need financial help from anyone else. ❑ *The income from visitors makes the museum self-supporting.*

self-sustaining ADJ A **self-sustaining** process or system is able to continue by itself without anyone or anything else becoming involved. ❑ *Asia's emerging economies will be on a self-sustaining cycle of growth.*

self-taught ADJ If you are **self-taught**, you have learned a skill by yourself rather than being taught it by someone else such as a teacher at school. ❑ *...a self-taught musician.*

self-will N-UNCOUNT Someone's **self-will** is their determination to do what they want without caring what other people think. ❑ *She had a little core of self-will.*

self-willed ADJ Someone who is **self-willed** is determined to do the things that they want to do and will not take advice from other people. ❑ *He was very independent and self-willed.*

self-worth N-UNCOUNT **Self-worth** is the feeling that you have good qualities and have achieved good things. ❑ *Try not to link your sense of self-worth to the opinions of others.*

sell ♦♦♦ /sɛl/ (sells, selling, sold) **1** V-T/V-I If you **sell** something that you own, you let someone have it in return for money. ❑ *Catlin sold the paintings to Philadelphia industrialist Joseph Harrison.* ❑ *The directors sold the business for $14.8 million.* ❑ *When is the best time to sell?* **2** V-T If a store **sells** a particular thing, it is available for people to buy there. ❑ *It sells everything from hair ribbons to oriental rugs.* **3** V-I If something **sells** for a particular price, that price is paid for it. ❑ *Unmodernized property can sell for up to 40 percent of its modernized market value.* **4** V-I If something **sells**, it is bought by the public, usually in fairly large quantities. ❑ *Even if this album doesn't sell and the critics don't like it, we wouldn't ever change.* **5** V-T/V-I Something that **sells** a product makes people want to buy the product. ❑ *It is only the sensational that sells news magazines.* ❑ *...the maxim that safety doesn't sell.* **6** V-T If you **sell** someone an idea or proposal, or **sell** someone **on** an idea, you convince them that it is a good one. ❑ *She tried to sell me the idea of buying my own paper shredder.* ❑ *She is hoping she can sell the idea to clients.* **7** PHRASE If someone **sells** their **body**, they have sex for money. ❑ *85 percent said they would rather not sell their bodies for a living.* **8** PHRASE If you talk about someone **selling** their **soul** in order to get something, you are criticizing them for abandoning their principles. [DISAPPROVAL] ❑ *...a man who would sell his soul for political viability.*
▸ **sell off** **1** PHRASAL VERB If you **sell** something **off**, you sell it because you need the money. ❑ *The company is selling off some sites and concentrating on cutting debts.* **2** → see also **sell-off**
▸ **sell on** PHRASAL VERB If you buy something and then **sell** it **on**, you sell it to someone else soon after buying it, usually in order to make a profit. ❑ *Mr. Farrier bought cars at auctions and sold them on.*
▸ **sell out** **1** PHRASAL VERB If a store **sells out** of something, it sells all its stocks of it, so that there is no longer any left for people to buy. ❑ *Hardware stores have sold out of water pumps and tarpaulins.* **2** PHRASAL VERB If a performance, sports event, or other entertainment **sells out**, all the tickets for it are sold. ❑ *Football games often sell out well in advance.* **3** PHRASAL VERB When things **sell out**, all of them that are available are sold. ❑ *Sleeping bags sold out almost immediately.* **4** PHRASAL VERB If you accuse someone of **selling out**, you disapprove of the fact that they do something which used to be against their principles, or give in to an opposing group. [DISAPPROVAL] ❑ *You don't have to sell out and work for some corporation.* **5** PHRASAL VERB If you **sell out**, you sell everything you have, such as your house or your business, because you need the money. ❑ *I'll have a going out of business sale. I'll sell out and move out of here.* **6** → see also **sell-out**, **sold out**

sell-by date (sell-by dates) N-COUNT The **sell-by date** on a food container is the date by which the food should be sold or eaten before it starts to decay. ❑ *...a piece of cheese four weeks past its sell-by date.*

sell|er /sɛlər/ (sellers) **1** N-COUNT A **seller** of a type of thing is a person or company that sells that type of thing. ❑ *...a flower seller.* **2** N-COUNT In a business deal, the **seller** is the person who is selling something to someone else. ❑ *In theory, the buyer could ask the seller to have a test carried out.* **3** N-COUNT If you describe a product as, for example, a big **seller**, you mean that large numbers of it are being sold. ❑ *The gift store's biggest seller is a photo of Elvis Presley.* **4** → see also **bestseller**

sell|er's mar|ket N-SING When there is a **seller's market** for a particular product, there are fewer of the products for sale than people who want to buy them, so buyers have little choice and prices go up. [BUSINESS] ❑ *It's a seller's market, and no one is forced to discount to remain competitive.*

sell|ing point (selling points) N-COUNT A **selling point** is a desirable quality or feature that something has which makes it likely that people will want to buy it. [BUSINESS] ❑ *A garden is one of the biggest selling points with house-hunters.*

sell|ing price (selling prices) N-COUNT The **selling price** of something is the price for which it is sold. [BUSINESS] ❑ *Palm said the average selling price of its devices was $183.*

sell-off (sell-offs) also **selloff** N-COUNT The **sell-off** of something, for example, an industry owned by the state or a company's shares, is the selling of it. [BUSINESS] ❑ *The privatization of the electricity industry was the biggest sell-off of them all.*

Sel|lo|tape /sɛləteɪp/ N-UNCOUNT **Sellotape** is a clear sticky tape that you use to stick paper or card together or onto a wall. [BRIT, TRADEMARK]

in AM, use **Scotch tape**

sell-out (sell-outs) also **sellout** **1** N-COUNT If a play, sports event, or other entertainment is a **sell-out**, all the tickets for it are sold. ❑ *Their concert there was a sell-out.* **2** N-COUNT If you describe someone's behavior as a **sell-out**, you disapprove of the fact that they have done something which used to be against their principles, or given in to an opposing group. [DISAPPROVAL] ❑ *For some, his decision to become a Socialist candidate at Sunday's election was simply a sell out.*

sell-through (sell-throughs) N-COUNT A **sell-through** is the amount or percentage of something that is sold relative to the total quantity available to buy in a store.

selt|zer /sɛltsər/ (seltzers) also **seltzer water** N-MASS **Seltzer** is carbonated water with a lot of minerals in it that is considered healthy to drink. [AM] ❑ *...drinks made of wine and seltzer or soda water.* ❑ *...a glass of seltzer water.*

selves /sɛlvz/ **Selves** is the plural of **self**.

se|man|tic /sɪmæntɪk/ ADJ [usu ADJ n] **Semantic** is used to describe things that deal with the meanings of words and sentences. ❑ *He did not want to enter into a semantic debate.*

se|man|tics /sɪmæntɪks/

The form **semantic** is used as a modifier.

N-UNCOUNT **Semantics** is the branch of linguistics that deals with the meanings of words and sentences.

sema|phore /sɛməfɔr/ N-UNCOUNT **Semaphore** is a system of sending messages by using two flags. You hold a flag in each hand and move your arms to various positions representing different letters of the alphabet.

sem|blance /sɛmbləns/ N-UNCOUNT If there is a **semblance of** a particular condition or quality, it appears to exist, even though this may be a false impression. [FORMAL] ❑ *At least a semblance of normality has been restored to parts of the country.*

se|men /simən/ N-UNCOUNT **Semen** is the liquid containing sperm that is produced by the sex organs of men and male animals.

se|mes|ter /sɪmɛstər/ (semesters) N-COUNT In colleges and universities in some countries, a **semester** is one of the two main periods into which the year is divided. ❑ *...February 22nd when most of their students begin their spring semester.*

semi /sɛmi, sɛmaɪ/ (semis) **1** N-COUNT In a sports competition, the **semis** are the semifinals. [INFORMAL] ❑ *He reached the semis after beating Nadal in the quarterfinal.* **2** N-COUNT A **semi** is the same as a **tractor-trailer**. [AM]

PREFIX

semi-
forms nouns and adjectives that refer to people and things that are partly, but not completely, in a particular state. *For example, if you are semiconscious, you are partly, but not completely, conscious.*

semi|an|nual /sɛmiænyuəl, sɛmaɪ-/ ADJ [usu ADJ n] A **semiannual** event happens twice a year. [AM] ❑ ...*the semiannual meeting of the International Monetary Fund.*

in BRIT, usually use **biannual**

semi|breve /sɛmibriv, -brɛv, sɛmaɪ-/ (**semibreves**) N-COUNT A **semibreve** is the same as a **whole note**. [BRIT]

semi|cir|cle /sɛmisɜrkᵊl, sɛmaɪ-/ (**semicircles**) also **semi-circle** N-COUNT A **semicircle** is one half of a circle, or something having the shape of half a circle. ❑ *They sit cross-legged in a semicircle and share stories.*

semi|cir|cu|lar /sɛmisɜrkyʊlər, sɛmaɪ-/ ADJ Something that is **semicircular** has the shape of half a circle. ❑ ...*a semicircular amphitheater.*

semi|co|lon /sɛmikoʊlən/ (**semicolons**) N-COUNT A **semicolon** is the punctuation mark ; which is used in writing to separate different parts of a sentence or list or to indicate a pause.

semi|con|duc|tor /sɛmikəndʌktər, sɛmaɪ-/ (**semiconductors**) N-COUNT A **semiconductor** is a substance used in electronics whose ability to conduct electricity increases with greater heat.

semi-detached /sɛmidɪtætʃt, sɛmaɪ-/ also **semidetached** ADJ A **semi-detached** house is a house that is joined to another house on one side by a shared wall. [mainly BRIT]

in AM, usually use **duplex**

• N-SING **Semi-detached** is also a noun.

semi|fi|nal /sɛmifaɪnᵊl, sɛmaɪ-/ (**semifinals**) N-COUNT A **semifinal** is one of the two games or races in a competition that are held to decide who will compete in the final. ❑ *We want to go into the semifinal, no matter who the rival is.*
• N-PLURAL The **semifinals** is the round of a competition in which these two games or races are held. ❑ *Team USA reached the semifinals by defeating New Zealand in the second round.*

semi|fi|nal|ist /sɛmifaɪnəlɪst, sɛmaɪ-/ (**semifinalists**) N-COUNT A **semifinalist** is a player, athlete, or team that is competing in a semi-final.

semi|nal /sɛmɪnᵊl/ ADJ **Seminal** is used to describe things such as books, works, events, and experiences that have a great influence in a particular field. [FORMAL] ❑ ...*author of the seminal book "Animal Liberation."*

semi|nar /sɛmɪnɑr/ (**seminars**) ❶ N-COUNT A **seminar** is a meeting where a group of people discuss a problem or topic. ❑ ...*a series of half-day seminars to help businesspeople get the best value from investing in information technology.* ❷ N-COUNT A **seminar** is a class at a college or university in which the teacher and a small group of students discuss a topic. ❑ *Students are asked to prepare material in advance of each weekly seminar.* ❸ → See feature box at **university**

semi|nar|ian /sɛmɪnɛəriən/ (**seminarians**) N-COUNT A **seminarian** is a student at a seminary.

semi|nary /sɛmɪnɛri/ (**seminaries**) N-COUNT A **seminary** is a college where priests, ministers, or rabbis are trained.

se|mi|ot|ics /simiɒtɪks, sɛmi-/ N-UNCOUNT **Semiotics** is the academic study of the relationship of language and other signs to their meanings.

semi|pre|cious /sɛmiprɛʃəs, sɛmaɪ-/ ADJ [usu ADJ n] **Semiprecious** stones are stones such as turquoises and amethysts that are used in jewelry but are less valuable than precious stones such as diamonds and rubies.

semi|pro|fes|sion|al /sɛmiprəfɛʃənᵊl, sɛmaɪ-/ ADJ **Semiprofessional** athletes, musicians, and singers receive some money for playing their sport or for performing but they also have another job as well. ❑ ...*a semiprofessional country musician.*

semi|skilled /sɛmiskɪld, sɛmaɪ-/ ADJ A **semiskilled** worker has some training and skills, but not enough to do specialized work. [BUSINESS]

semi-skimmed milk N-UNCOUNT **Semi-skimmed milk** or **semi-skimmed** is the same as **two-percent milk**. [BRIT]

Se|mit|ic /sɪmɪtɪk/ ❶ ADJ [usu ADJ n] **Semitic** languages are a group of languages that include Arabic and Hebrew. ❷ ADJ [usu ADJ n] **Semitic** people belong to one of the groups of people who speak a Semitic language. ❑ ...*the Semitic races.* ❸ ADJ [usu ADJ n] **Semitic** is sometimes used to mean Jewish. ❹ → see also **anti-Semitic**

semi|tone /sɛmitoʊn, sɛmaɪ-/ (**semitones**) N-COUNT In Western music, a **semitone** is the smallest interval between two musical notes. Two semitones are equal to one tone.

semi|trail|er /sɛmitreɪlər, sɛmaɪ-/ (**semitrailers**) also **semi-trailer** N-COUNT A **semitrailer** is the long rear section of a truck that can bend when it turns. [AM]

semi|tropi|cal /sɛmitrɒpɪkᵊl, sɛmaɪ-/ also **semi-tropical** ❶ ADJ [usu ADJ n] **Semitropical** places have warm, wet air. ❑ ...*a semitropical island.* ❷ ADJ [usu ADJ n] **Semitropical** plants and trees grow in places where the air is warm and wet. ❑ *The inn has a garden of semi-tropical vegetation.*

semo|li|na /sɛməlinə/ N-UNCOUNT **Semolina** consists of small, hard grains of wheat that are used for making sweet puddings with milk and for making pasta.

Sen|ate ♦♦◊ /sɛnɪt/ (**Senates**) ❶ N-PROPER-COLL The **Senate** is the smaller and more important of the two parts of the legislature in some U.S. states and in some countries, for example, the United States and Australia. ❑ *The Senate is expected to pass the bill shortly.* ❷ N-PROPER-COLL The **Senate** is the governing council at some universities. ❑ *By the time I was vice chancellor, the Senate had become a much larger and a much more democratic body.*

sena|tor ♦♦◊ /sɛnɪtər/ (**senators**) N-COUNT; N-TITLE A **senator** is a member of a political Senate, for example, in the United States or Australia. ❑ ...*Texas' first Black senator.*

sena|to|rial /sɛnɪtɔriəl/ ADJ [ADJ n] **Senatorial** means belonging to or relating to a Senate. [FORMAL] ❑ *He has senatorial experience in defense and foreign policy.*

send ♦♦♦ /sɛnd/ (**sends, sending, sent**) ❶ V-T When you **send** someone something, you arrange for it to be taken and delivered to them, for example, by mail. ❑ *Myra Cunningham sent me a note thanking me for dinner.* ❑ *I sent a copy to the school principal.* ❷ V-T If you **send** someone somewhere, you tell them to go there. ❑ *Inspector Banbury came up to see her, but she sent him away.* ❑ ...*the government's decision to send troops to the region.* ❑ *I suggested that he rest, and sent him for an X-ray.* ❸ V-T If you **send** someone to an institution such as a school or a prison, you arrange for them to stay there for a period of time. ❑ *It's his parents' choice to send him to a boarding school, rather than a convenient day school.* ❹ V-T To **send** a signal means to cause it to go to a place by means of radio waves or electricity. ❑ *The transmitters will send a signal automatically to a local base station.* ❺ V-T If something **sends** things or people in a particular direction, it causes them to move in that direction. ❑ *The explosion sent shrapnel flying through the sides of cars on the crowded highway.* ❑ *A left hook sent him reeling.* ❻ V-T To **send** someone or something into a particular state means to cause them to go into or be in that state. ❑ *My attempt to fix it sent Lawrence into fits of laughter.* ❑ ...*before civil war and famine sent the country plunging into anarchy.* ❼ **to send someone packing** → see **pack**
▶ **send away for** → see **send for 2**
▶ **send for** ❶ PHRASAL VERB If you **send for** someone, you send them a message asking them to come and see you. ❑ *I've sent for the doctor.* ❷ PHRASAL VERB If you **send for** something, or **send away for** it, or **send off for** it, you write and ask for it to be sent to you. ❑ *Send for your free catalog today.*
▶ **send in** ❶ PHRASAL VERB If you **send in** something such as a competition entry or a letter applying for a job, you mail it to the organization concerned. ❑ *Applicants are asked to send in a résumé and a cover letter.* ❷ PHRASAL VERB When a government **sends in** troops or police officers, it orders them to deal with a crisis or problem somewhere. ❑ *He has asked the government to send in troops to end the fighting.*
▶ **send off** ❶ PHRASAL VERB When you **send off** a letter or package, you send it somewhere by mail. ❑ *He sent off copies to various people for them to read and make comments.* ❷ PHRASAL VERB If a soccer player **is sent off**, the referee makes them leave the field during a game, as a punishment for seriously breaking the rules. [mainly BRIT]

in AM, use **eject**

▶ **send off for** → see **send for 2**

▶ **send out** **1** PHRASAL VERB If you **send out** things such as letters or bills, you send them to a large number of people at the same time. ❑ *She had sent out well over four hundred invitations that afternoon.* **2** PHRASAL VERB To **send out** a signal, sound, light, or heat means to produce it. ❑ *The crew did not send out any distress signals.*

▶ **send out for** PHRASAL VERB If you **send out for** food, for example, pizza or sandwiches, you phone and ask for it to be delivered to you. ❑ *Let's send out for a pizza.*

send|er /sɛndər/ (**senders**) N-COUNT The **sender** of a letter, package, or radio message is the person who sent it. ❑ *The sender of the best letter every week will win a check for $50.*

send-off (**send-offs**) also **sendoff** N-COUNT [usu adj N] If a group of people give someone who is going away a **send-off**, they come together to say goodbye to them. [INFORMAL] ❑ *All the people in the buildings came to give me a rousing send-off.*

send-up (**send-ups**) N-COUNT [usu sing, oft N of n] A **send-up** is a piece of writing or acting in which someone or something is imitated in an amusing way that makes them appear foolish. [INFORMAL] ❑ *...his classic send-up of sixties rock, "Get Crazy."*

Sen|ega|lese /sɛnɪɡəliz/ (**Senegalese**) **1** ADJ **Senegalese** means belonging or relating to Senegal, or to its people or culture. ❑ *...the Senegalese navy.* **2** N-COUNT A **Senegalese** is a Senegalese citizen, or a person of Senegalese origin.

se|nile /sinaɪl/ ADJ If old people become **senile**, they become confused, can no longer remember things, and are unable to take care of themselves. • **se|nil|ity** /sɪnɪlɪti/ N-UNCOUNT ❑ *The old man was forced to resign after showing unmistakable signs of senility.*

se|nile de|men|tia N-UNCOUNT Senile dementia is a mental illness that affects some old people and that causes them to become confused and to forget things. ❑ *She is suffering from senile dementia.*

sen|ior ♦♦◇ /sinyər/ (**seniors**) **1** ADJ [ADJ n] The **senior** people in an organization or profession have the highest and most important jobs. ❑ *...senior officials in the Israeli government.* ❑ *...the company's senior management.* **2** ADJ If someone is **senior** to you in an organization or profession, they have a higher and more important job than you or they are considered to be superior to you because they have worked there for longer and have more experience. ❑ *The position had to be filled by an officer senior to Haig.* • N-PLURAL Your **seniors** are the people who are senior to you. ❑ *He was described by his seniors as a model officer.* **3** N-SING **Senior** is used when indicating how much older one person is than another. For example, if someone is ten years your **senior**, they are ten years older than you. ❑ *She became involved with a married man many years her senior.* **4** N-COUNT **Seniors** are students in a high school, university, or college who are in their fourth year of study. [AM] ❑ *...the number of high school seniors who go on to college.* **5** N-COUNT A **senior** is the same as a **senior citizen**. ❑ *Tickets at the gate are $10, $7 for seniors (age 55 and up).* **6** ADJ [ADJ n] If you take part in a sport at **senior** level, you take part in competitions with adults and people who have reached a high degree of achievement in that sport. ❑ *This will be his fifth international championship and his third at senior level.*

SYNONYMS

senior
ADJ **2**
superior: *...negotiations between the mutineers and their superior officers.*
better: *The train's average speed was no better than that of our bicycles.*
---

sen|ior citi|zen (**senior citizens**) N-COUNT A **senior citizen** is an older person who has retired or receives social security benefits. ❑ *...services for senior citizens.*

sen|ior high school (**senior highs schools**) also **senior high** N-VAR; N-IN-NAMES A **senior high school** or a **senior high** is a school for students between the ages of 14 or 15 and 17 or 18. [AM] ❑ *...children in senior high school.* ❑ *The dropout rate in the District's senior high schools last year was 12.3 percent.* ❑ *...Mount Pearl Senior High.*

sen|ior|ity /sinjɔrɪti/ N-UNCOUNT A person's **seniority** in an organization is the importance and power that they have compared with others, or the fact that they have worked there for a long time. ❑ *He has said he will fire editorial employees without regard to seniority.*

sen|ior mo|ment (**senior moments**) N-COUNT If an elderly person forgets something or makes a mistake and you refer to this as a **senior moment**, you mean that the person forgot the thing or made the mistake because they are old and their mental abilities are declining. [mainly AM, INFORMAL] ❑ *He is 69 in February and sometimes has a senior moment, when the flow of words dries up.*

Se|nor /sɛnyɔr/ (**Senors**) also **Señor** **1** N-TITLE; N-VOC You use **Senor** when you are speaking to or referring to a Spanish-speaking man. ❑ *...the opposition challenge to Senor Chavez.* ❑ *This is not helpful, Señor.* **2** N-COUNT A **senor** is a Spanish-speaking man. ❑ *From the airport: Don't be tempted by the helpful senors at arrivals, take an authorized taxi.*

Se|no|ra /sɛnyɔrə/ (**Senoras**) also **Señora** **1** N-TITLE; N-VOC You use **Senora** when you are speaking to or referring to a married Spanish-speaking woman. ❑ *...our charming hostess, Senora de Aldasoro.* ❑ *"I am sorry, Señora," Doctor Perez said gently.* **2** N-COUNT A **senora** is a Spanish-speaking woman who is married. ❑ *The senora brought him coffee in the courtyard.*

Se|no|ri|ta /sɛnyɔritə/ (**Senoritas**) also **Señorita** **1** N-TITLE; N-VOC You use **Senorita** when you are speaking to or referring to a young, unmarried Spanish-speaking woman. ❑ *Senorita Zorreguieta is a Roman Catholic.* ❑ *Where do you want to go, Señorita?* **2** N-COUNT A **senorita** is a Spanish-speaking woman who is young and unmarried. ❑ *The Spanish senorita was snapped on the red carpet at the awards ceremony.*

sen|sa|tion /sɛnseɪʃən/ (**sensations**) **1** N-COUNT A **sensation** is a physical feeling. ❑ *Floating can be a very pleasant sensation.* **2** N-UNCOUNT **Sensation** is your ability to feel things physically, especially through your sense of touch. ❑ *The pain was so bad that she lost all sensation.* **3** N-COUNT You can use **sensation** to refer to the general feeling or impression caused by a particular experience. ❑ *It's a funny sensation to know someone's talking about you in a language you don't understand.* **4** N-COUNT If a person, event, or situation is a **sensation**, it causes great excitement or interest. ❑ *...the film that turned her into an overnight sensation.* **5** N-SING If a person, event, or situation causes **a sensation**, they cause great interest or excitement. ❑ *She was just 14 when she caused a sensation at the Montreal Olympics.*

sen|sa|tion|al /sɛnseɪʃənəl/ **1** ADJ A **sensational** result, event, or situation is so remarkable that it causes great excitement and interest. ❑ *The world champions suffered a sensational defeat.* • **sen|sa|tion|al|ly** ADV ❑ *The rape trial was sensationally halted yesterday.* **2** ADJ You can describe stories or reports as **sensational** if you disapprove of them because they present facts in a way that is intended to cause feelings of shock, anger, or excitement. [DISAPPROVAL] ❑ *...sensational tabloid newspaper reports.* **3** ADJ You can describe something as **sensational** when you think that it is extremely good. ❑ *Her voice is sensational.* • **sen|sa|tion|al|ly** ADV ❑ *...sensationally good food.*

sen|sa|tion|al|ism /sɛnseɪʃənəlɪzəm/ N-UNCOUNT **Sensationalism** is the presenting of facts or stories in a way that is intended to produce strong feelings of shock, anger, or excitement. [DISAPPROVAL] ❑ *The report criticizes the newspaper for sensationalism.*

sen|sa|tion|al|ist /sɛnseɪʃənəlɪst/ ADJ **Sensationalist** news reports and television and radio programs present the facts in a way that makes them seem worse or more shocking than they really are. [DISAPPROVAL] ❑ *...sensationalist headlines.*

sen|sa|tion|al|ize /sɛnseɪʃənəlaɪz/ (**sensationalizes, sensationalizing, sensationalized**)

in BRIT, also use **sensationalise**

V-T If someone **sensationalizes** a situation or event, they make it seem worse or more shocking than it really is. [DISAPPROVAL] ❑ *Local news organizations are being criticized for sensationalizing the story.*

sense ♦♦♦ /sɛns/ (**senses, sensing, sensed**) **1** N-COUNT Your **senses** are the physical abilities of sight, smell, hearing, touch, and taste. ❑ *She stared at him again, unable to believe the evidence of her senses.* **2** V-T If you **sense** something, you become

senseless

aware of it or you realize it, although it is not very obvious. ❑ *She probably sensed that I wasn't telling her the whole story.* ❑ *He looks about him, sensing danger.* **3** N-SING If you have a **sense** that something is the case, you think that it is the case, although you may not have firm, clear evidence for this belief. ❑ *Suddenly you got this sense that people were drawing themselves away from each other.* **4** N-SING If you have a **sense of** guilt or relief, for example, you feel guilty or relieved. ❑ *When your child is struggling for life, you feel this overwhelming sense of guilt.* **5** N-SING If you have a **sense of** something such as duty or justice, you are aware of it and believe it is important. ❑ *My sense of justice was offended.* ❑ *We must keep a sense of proportion about all this.* **6** N-SING [N *of* n, also n N] Someone who has a **sense** of timing or style has a natural ability with regard to timing or style. You can also say that someone has a bad **sense** of timing or style. ❑ *He has an impeccable sense of timing.* ❑ *Her dress sense is appalling.* **7** → see also **sense of humor** **8** N-UNCOUNT **Sense** is the ability to make good judgments and to behave sensibly. ❑ *...when he was younger and had a bit more sense.* ❑ *When that doesn't work they sometimes have the sense to seek help.* **9** → see also **common sense** **10** N-SING If you say that there is no **sense** or little **sense** in doing something, you mean that it is not a sensible thing to do because nothing useful would be gained by doing it. ❑ *There's no sense in pretending this doesn't happen.* **11** N-COUNT A **sense** of a word or expression is one of its possible meanings. ❑ *...a noun which has two senses.* **12** PHRASE **Sense** is used in several expressions to indicate how true your statement is. For example, if you say that something is true **in a sense**, you mean that it is partly true, or true in one way. If you say that something is true **in a** general **sense**, you mean that it is true in a general way. ❑ *In a sense, both were right.* ❑ *Though his background was modest, it was in no sense deprived.* **13** PHRASE If something **makes sense**, you can understand it. ❑ *He was sitting there saying, "Yes, the figures make sense."* **14** PHRASE When you **make sense of** something, you succeed in understanding it. ❑ *Provided you didn't try to make sense of it, it sounded beautiful.* **15** PHRASE If a course of action **makes sense**, it seems sensible. ❑ *It makes sense to look after yourself.* ❑ *The project should be re-appraised to see whether it made sound economic sense.* **16** PHRASE If you say that someone **has come to** their **senses** or **has been brought to** their **senses**, you mean that they have stopped being foolish and are being sensible again. ❑ *Eventually the world will come to its senses and get rid of them.* **17** PHRASE If you say that someone **talks sense**, you mean that what they say is sensible. ❑ *When he speaks, he talks sense.* **18** PHRASE If you **have a sense that** something is true or **get a sense that** something is true, you think that it is true. [mainly SPOKEN] ❑ *Do you have the sense that you are loved by the public?* **19** see sense → see see ②

sense|less /sɛnslɪs/ **1** ADJ If you describe an action as **senseless**, you think it is wrong because it has no purpose and produces no benefit. ❑ *...people whose lives have been destroyed by acts of senseless violence.* **2** ADJ If someone is **senseless**, they are unconscious. ❑ *They were knocked to the ground, beaten senseless and robbed of their wallets.*

sense of di|rec|tion **1** N-SING Your **sense of direction** is your ability to know roughly where you are, or which way to go, even when you are in an unfamiliar place. ❑ *He had a poor sense of direction and soon got lost.* **2** N-SING If you say that someone has a **sense of direction**, you mean that they seem to have clear ideas about what they want to do or achieve. [APPROVAL] ❑ *The country now had a sense of direction again.*

sense of hu|mor

in BRIT, use **sense of humour**

1 N-SING Someone who has a **sense of humor** often finds things amusing, rather than being serious all the time. ❑ *She seems to have a good sense of humor.* **2** → See feature box at **humor**

sense of oc|ca|sion N-SING If there is a **sense of occasion** when a planned event takes place, people feel that something special and important is happening. ❑ *There is a great sense of occasion and a terrific standard of musicianship.*

sense or|gan (sense organs) N-COUNT [usu pl] Your **sense organs** are the parts of your body, for example, your eyes and your ears, which enable you to be aware of things around you. [FORMAL]

sensuous

sen|sibil|ity /sɛnsɪbɪlɪti/ (sensibilities) **1** N-UNCOUNT **Sensibility** is the ability to experience deep feelings. ❑ *Everything he writes demonstrates the depth of his sensibility.* **2** N-VAR Someone's **sensibility** is their tendency to be influenced or offended by things. ❑ *He was unable to control his sensibility.*

sen|sible ◆◇◇ /sɛnsɪbəl/ **1** ADJ **Sensible** actions or decisions are good because they are based on reasons rather than emotions. ❑ *It might be sensible to get a lawyer.* ❑ *The sensible thing is to leave them alone.* ● **sen|sibly** /sɛnsɪbli/ ADV ❑ *He sensibly decided to lie low for a while.* **2** ADJ **Sensible** people behave in a sensible way. ❑ *She was a sensible girl and did not panic.* ❑ *Oh come on, let's be sensible about this.* **3** ADJ **Sensible** shoes or clothes are practical and strong rather than fashionable and attractive. ❑ *Wear loose clothing and sensible footwear.* ● **sen|sibly** ADV ❑ *They were not sensibly dressed.*

sen|si|tive ◆◇◇ /sɛnsɪtɪv/ **1** ADJ If you are **sensitive** to other people's needs, problems, or feelings, you show understanding and awareness of them. [APPROVAL] ❑ *The classroom teacher must be sensitive to a child's needs.* ● **sen|si|tive|ly** ADV ❑ *The abuse of women needs to be treated seriously and sensitively.* ● **sen|si|tiv|ity** /sɛnsɪtɪvɪti/ N-UNCOUNT [oft N *for* n] ❑ *A good relationship involves concern and sensitivity for each other's feelings.* **2** ADJ If you are **sensitive** about something, you are easily worried and offended when people talk about it. ❑ *Young people are very sensitive about their appearance.* ● **sen|si|tiv|ity** (sensitivities) N-VAR ❑ *...people who suffer extreme sensitivity about what others think.* **3** ADJ A **sensitive** subject or issue needs to be dealt with carefully because it is likely to cause disagreement or make people angry or upset. ❑ *Employment is a very sensitive issue.* ● **sen|si|tiv|ity** N-UNCOUNT [oft N *of* n] ❑ *Due to the obvious sensitivity of the issue he would not divulge any details.* **4** ADJ **Sensitive** documents or reports contain information that needs to be kept secret and dealt with carefully. ❑ *He instructed staff to shred sensitive documents.* **5** ADJ Something that is **sensitive** to a physical force, substance, or treatment is easily affected by it and often harmed by it. ❑ *...a chemical which is sensitive to light.* ● **sen|si|tiv|ity** N-UNCOUNT ❑ *...the sensitivity of cells damaged by chemotherapy.* **6** ADJ A **sensitive** piece of scientific equipment is capable of measuring or recording very small changes. ❑ *...an extremely sensitive microscope.* ● **sen|si|tiv|ity** N-UNCOUNT ❑ *...the sensitivity of the detector.*

sen|si|tize /sɛnsɪtaɪz/ (sensitizes, sensitizing, sensitized)

in BRIT, also use **sensitise**

1 V-T If you **sensitize** people to a particular problem or situation, you make them aware of it. [FORMAL] ❑ *It seems important to sensitize people to the fact that depression is more than the blues.* ❑ *How many judges in our male-dominated courts are sensitized to the particular issues faced by many women?* **2** V-T [usu passive] If a substance **is sensitized** to something such as light or touch, it is made sensitive to it. ❑ *Skin is easily irritated, chapped, chafed, and sensitized.* ❑ *...sensitized nerve endings.*

sen|sor /sɛnsər/ (sensors) N-COUNT A **sensor** is an instrument which reacts to certain physical conditions or impressions such as heat or light, and which is used to provide information. ❑ *The latest Japanese vacuum cleaners contain sensors that detect the amount of dust and type of floor.*

sen|so|ry /sɛnsəri/ ADJ [ADJ n] **Sensory** means relating to the physical senses. [FORMAL] ❑ *Almost all sensory information from the trunk and limbs passes through the spinal cord.*

sen|sual /sɛnʃuəl/ **1** ADJ Someone or something that is **sensual** shows or suggests a great liking for physical pleasures, especially sexual pleasures. ❑ *He was a very sensual person.* ❑ *...the sensual curve of her lips.* ● **sen|su|al|ity** /sɛnʃuælɪti/ N-UNCOUNT ❑ *...her sensuality and youth.* **2** ADJ Something that is **sensual** gives pleasure to your physical senses rather than to your mind. ❑ *It was an opera, very glamorous and very sensual.* ● **sen|su|al|ity** N-UNCOUNT ❑ *These perfumes have warmth and sensuality.*

sen|su|ous /sɛnʃuəs/ **1** ADJ Something that is **sensuous** gives pleasure to the mind or body through the senses. ❑ *The film is ravishing to look at and boasts a sensuous musical score.* ● **sen|su|ous|ly** ADV ❑ *She lay in the deep bath for a long time, enjoying its sensuously perfumed water.* **2** ADJ Someone or something that is **sensuous** shows or suggests a great liking for sexual pleasure. ❑ *The silky material had a sensuous feel to it.* ❑ *...wide sensuous lips.* • **sen|su|ous|ly** ADV ❑ *The nose was straight, the mouth sensuously wide and full.*

sent /sɛnt/ Sent is the past tense and past participle of **send**.

sen|tence ♦♦♢ /sɛntəns/ (**sentences, sentencing, sentenced**) **1** N-COUNT A **sentence** is a group of words which, when they are written down, begin with a capital letter and end with a period, question mark, or exclamation mark. Most sentences contain a subject and a verb. ❑ *Here we have several sentences incorrectly joined by commas.* **2** N-VAR In a law court, a **sentence** is the punishment that a person receives after they have been found guilty of a crime. ❑ *They are already serving prison sentences for their part in the assassination.* ❑ *He was given a four-year sentence.* ❑ *The court is expected to pass sentence later today.* **3** → see also **death sentence** **4** V-T When a judge **sentences** someone, he or she states in court what their punishment will be. ❑ *A military court sentenced him to death in his absence.* ❑ *She was sentenced to nine years in prison.* **5** → See feature box at **legal**

SYNONYMS

sentence
NOUN **2**
punishment: *The usual punishment is a fine.*
verdict: *Three judges will deliver their verdict in October.*
judgment: *The Court is expected to give its judgment within the next ten days.*
VERB **4**
convict: *There was insufficient evidence to convict him.*
condemn: *He was condemned to life imprisonment.*
penalize: *Use of the car is penalized by increasing the fees of parking lots.*

---

sen|tence ad|verb (**sentence adverbs**) N-COUNT Adverbs such as 'fortunately' and 'perhaps' which apply to the whole clause, rather than to part of it, are sometimes called **sentence adverbs**.

sen|ti|ent /sɛnʃənt/ ADJ [usu ADJ n] A **sentient** being is capable of experiencing things through its senses. [FORMAL]

sen|ti|ment /sɛntɪmənt/ (**sentiments**) **1** N-VAR A **sentiment** that people have is an attitude which is based on their thoughts and feelings. ❑ *Public sentiment rapidly turned anti-American.* ❑ *He's found growing sentiment for military action.* **2** N-COUNT A **sentiment** is an idea or feeling that someone expresses in words. ❑ *I agree with those sentiments.* **3** N-UNCOUNT **Sentiment** is feelings such as pity or love, especially for things in the past, and may be considered exaggerated and foolish. ❑ *Laura kept that letter out of sentiment.*

sen|ti|men|tal /sɛntɪmɛntəl/ **1** ADJ Someone or something that is **sentimental** feels or shows pity or love, sometimes to an extent that is considered exaggerated and foolish. ❑ *I'm trying not to be sentimental about the past.* • **sen|ti|men|tal|ly** ADV ❑ *Childhood had less freedom and joy than we sentimentally attribute to it.* • **sen|ti|men|tal|ity** /sɛntɪmɛntælɪti/ N-UNCOUNT ❑ *In this book there is no sentimentality.* **2** ADJ **Sentimental** means relating to or involving feelings such as pity or love, especially for things in the past. ❑ *Our paintings and photographs are of sentimental value only.*

sen|ti|men|tal|ist /sɛntɪmɛntəlɪst/ (**sentimentalists**) N-COUNT If you describe someone as a **sentimentalist**, you believe that they are sentimental about things.

sen|ti|men|tal|ize /sɛntɪmɛntəlaɪz/ (**sentimentalizes, sentimentalizing, sentimentalized**)

in BRIT, also use **sentimentalise**

V-T/V-I If you **sentimentalize** something, you make it seem sentimental or think about it in a sentimental way. ❑ *He seems either to fear women or to sentimentalize them.* ❑ *He's the kind of filmmaker who doesn't hesitate to over-sentimentalize.* ❑ *...Rupert Brooke's sentimentalized glorification of war.*

sen|ti|nel /sɛntɪnəl/ (**sentinels**) N-COUNT A **sentinel** is a sentry. [LITERARY, OLD-FASHIONED]

sen|try /sɛntri/ (**sentries**) N-COUNT A **sentry** is a soldier who guards a camp or a building. ❑ *The sentry would not let her enter.*

sen|try box (**sentry boxes**) N-COUNT A **sentry box** is a narrow shelter with an open front in which a sentry can stand while on duty.

Sep. Sep. is a written abbreviation for **September**. The more usual abbreviation is **Sept.** ❑ *...Friday Sep. 21, 1990.*

sepa|rable /sɛpərəbəl/ ADJ If things are **separable**, they can be separated from each other. ❑ *Character is not separable from physical form but is governed by it.*

sepa|rate ♦♦♢ (**separates, separating, separated**)

The adjective and noun are pronounced /sɛpərɪt/. The verb is pronounced /sɛpəreɪt/.

1 ADJ If one thing is **separate** from another, there is a barrier, space, or division between them, so that they are clearly two things. ❑ *They are now making plans to form their own separate party.* ❑ *Business bank accounts were kept separate from personal ones.* **2** ADJ If you refer to **separate** things, you mean several different things, rather than just one thing. ❑ *Use separate chopping boards for raw meats, cooked meats, vegetables and salads.* ❑ *Men and women have separate exercise rooms.* **3** V-RECIP If you **separate** people or things that are together, or if they **separate**, they move apart. ❑ *Police moved in to separate the two groups.* ❑ *The pans were held in both hands and swirled around to separate gold particles from the dirt.* ❑ *The front end of the car separated from the rest of the vehicle.* **4** V-RECIP If you **separate** people or things that have been connected, or if one **separates** from another, the connection between them is ended. ❑ *They want to separate teaching from research.* ❑ *It's very possible that we may see a movement to separate the two parts of the country.* **5** V-RECIP If a couple who are married or living together **separate**, they decide to live apart. ❑ *Her parents separated when she was very young.* **6** V-T An object, obstacle, distance, or period of time which **separates** two people, groups, or things exists between them. ❑ *...the white-railed fence that separated the yard from the paddock.* ❑ *They had undoubtedly made progress in the six years that separated the two periods.* **7** V-T If you **separate** one idea or fact from another, you clearly see or show the difference between them. ❑ *It is difficult to separate legend from truth.* ❑ *...learning how to separate real problems from imaginary illnesses.* • PHRASAL VERB **Separate out** means the same as **separate**. ❑ *How can one ever separate out the act from the attitudes that surround it?* **8** V-T A quality or factor that **separates** one thing from another is the reason why the two things are different from each other. ❑ *The single most important factor that separates ordinary photographs from good photographs is the lighting.* **9** V-T If a particular number of points **separate** two teams or competitors, one of them is winning or has won by that number of points. ❑ *In the end only three points separated the two teams.* **10** V-T/V-I If you **separate** a group of people or things into smaller elements, or if a group **separates**, it is divided into smaller elements. ❑ *The police wanted to separate them into smaller groups.* ❑ *Let's separate into smaller groups.* • PHRASAL VERB **Separate out** means the same as **separate**. ❑ *If prepared many hours ahead, the mixture may separate out.* **11** N-PLURAL **Separates** are clothes such as skirts, pants, and shirts which cover just the top half or the bottom half of your body. ❑ *She wears coordinated separates instead of a suit.* **12** → see also **separated** **13** PHRASE When two or more people who have been together for some time go their **separate ways**, they go to different places or end their relationship. ❑ *Sue was 27 when she and her husband decided to go their separate ways.*

▶ **separate out** **1** PHRASAL VERB If you **separate out** something from the other things it is with, you take it out. ❑ *The ability to separate out reusable elements from other waste is crucial.* **2** → see also **separate 7, 10**

sepa|rat|ed /sɛpəreɪtɪd/ **1** ADJ [v-link ADJ] Someone who is **separated** from their wife or husband lives apart from them, but is not divorced. ❑ *Some single parents are either divorced or separated.* **2** ADJ If you are **separated** from someone, for example, your family, you are not able to be with them. ❑ *The idea of being separated from him, even for a few hours, was torture.*

sepa|rate|ly /sɛpərɪtli/ ADV If people or things are dealt with **separately** or do something **separately**, they are dealt with or do something at different times or places, rather than together. ❑ *Cook each vegetable separately until just tender.*

sepa|ra|tion /sɛpəreɪʃən/ (**separations**) **1** N-VAR [oft N of/ from/between n] The **separation** of two or more things or groups is the fact that they are separate or become separate, and are not linked. ❑ *He believes in the separation of Church and State.* ❷ N-VAR During a **separation**, people who usually live together are not together. ❑ *She wondered if Harry had been unfaithful to her during this long separation.* ❸ N-VAR If a couple who are married or living together have a **separation**, they decide to live apart. ❑ *They agreed to a trial separation.*

sepa|ra|tism /sɛpərətɪzəm/ N-UNCOUNT **Separatism** is the beliefs and activities of separatists. ❑ *...a doctrine of racial separatism.*

sepa|ra|tist /sɛpərətɪst/ (separatists) ❶ ADJ [ADJ n] **Separatist** organizations and activities within a country involve members of a group of people who want to establish their own separate government or are trying to do so. ❑ *Spanish police say they have arrested ten people suspected of being members of the Basque separatist movement.* ❷ N-COUNT **Separatists** are people who want their own separate government or are involved in separatist activities. ❑ *The army has come under attack by separatists.*

se|pia /sipiə/ COLOR Something that is **sepia** is deep brown in color, like the color of very old photographs. ❑ *The walls are hung with sepia photographs of old school heroes.*

Sept. Sept. is a written abbreviation for **September**. ❑ *I've booked it for Thurs. Sept. 8th.*

Sep|tem|ber ✦✦✦ /sɛptɛmbər/ (Septembers) N-VAR **September** is the ninth month of the year in the Western calendar. ❑ *Her son, Jerome, was born in September.* ❑ *We didn't make the original September 30 release date.*

sep|tic /sɛptɪk/ ADJ If a wound or a part of your body becomes **septic**, it becomes infected. ❑ *A flake of plaster from the ceiling fell into his eye, which became septic.*

sep|ti|ce|mia /sɛptɪsimiə/

in BRIT, use **septicaemia**

N-UNCOUNT **Septicemia** is the same as **blood poisoning**. [MEDICAL]

sep|tic tank (septic tanks) N-COUNT A **septic tank** is an underground tank where feces, urine, and other waste matter is made harmless using bacteria.

sep|tua|genar|ian /sɛptʃuədʒɪnɛəriən/ (septuagenarians) N-COUNT [oft N n] A **septuagenarian** is a person between 70 and 79 years old. [FORMAL] ❑ *She was a very active septuagenarian.*

sep|ul|cher /sɛpəlkər/ (sepulchers)

in BRIT, use **sepulchre**

N-COUNT A **sepulcher** is a building or room in which a dead person is buried. [LITERARY]

se|pul|chral /sɪpʌlkrəl/ ❶ ADJ Something that is **sepulchral** is serious or sad and somewhat frightening. [LITERARY] ❑ *"He's gone," Rory whispered in sepulchral tones.* ❷ ADJ A **sepulchral** place is dark, quiet, and empty. [LITERARY] ❑ *He made his way along the sepulchral corridors.*

se|quel /sikwəl/ (sequels) N-COUNT A book or movie which is a **sequel** to an earlier one continues the story of the earlier one. ❑ *She is currently writing a sequel to Daphne du Maurier's "Rebecca."*

se|quence /sikwəns/ (sequences) ❶ N-COUNT A **sequence** of events or things is a number of events or things that come one after another in a particular order. ❑ *...the sequence of events which led to the murder.* ❷ N-COUNT A particular **sequence** is a particular order in which things happen or are arranged. ❑ *...the color sequence yellow, orange, purple, blue, green and white.*

se|quenc|er /sikwənsər/ (sequencers) N-COUNT A **sequencer** is an electronic instrument that can be used for recording and storing sounds so that they can be replayed as part of a new piece of music.

se|quenc|ing /sikwənsɪŋ/ N-UNCOUNT [supp N] Gene **sequencing** or DNA **sequencing** involves identifying the order in which the elements making up a particular gene are combined. ❑ *...the U.S. government's own gene sequencing program.*

se|quen|tial /sɪkwɛnʃəl/ ADJ [usu ADJ n] Something that is **sequential** follows a fixed order. [FORMAL] ❑ *...the sequential story of the universe.* • **se|quen|tial|ly** ADV [ADV after v] ❑ *The pages are numbered sequentially.*

se|ques|ter /sɪkwɛstər/ (sequesters, sequestering, sequestered) ❶ V-T **Sequester** means the same as **sequestrate**. [LEGAL] ❑ *Everything he owned was sequestered.* ❷ V-T If someone **is sequestered** somewhere, they are isolated from other people. [FORMAL] ❑ *This jury is expected to be sequestered for at least two months.*

se|ques|tered /sɪkwɛstərd/ ADJ A **sequestered** place is quiet and far away from busy places. [LITERARY]

se|ques|trate /sikwɛstreɪt/ (sequestrates, sequestrating, sequestrated) V-T [usu passive] When property **is sequestrated**, it is taken officially from someone who has debts, usually after a decision in a court of law. If the debts are paid off, the property is returned to its owner. [LEGAL] ❑ *He tried to prevent union money from being sequestrated by the courts.* • **se|ques|tra|tion** /sikwɛstreɪʃən/ N-UNCOUNT ❑ *...the sequestration of large areas of land.*

se|quin /sikwɪn/ (sequins) N-COUNT **Sequins** are small, shiny disks that are sewn on clothes to decorate them. ❑ *The frocks were covered in sequins, thousands of them.*

se|quined /sikwɪnd/ also **sequinned** ADJ [usu ADJ n] A **sequined** piece of clothing is decorated or covered with sequins. ❑ *...a strapless sequined evening gown.*

se|quoia /sɪkwɔɪə/ (sequoias) N-COUNT A **sequoia** is a very tall tree which grows in California. There are several different types of sequoia. ❑ *...a grove of majestic sequoias.*

ser|aph /sɛrəf/ (seraphim /sɛrəfɪm/ or seraphs) N-COUNT In the Bible, a **seraph** is a kind of angel.

Serbo-Croat /sɜrboʊ kroʊæt/ N-UNCOUNT **Serbo-Croat** is one of the languages spoken in the former Yugoslavia.

ser|enade /sɛrɪneɪd/ (serenades, serenading, serenaded) ❶ V-T If one person **serenades** another, they sing or play a piece of music for them. Traditionally men did this outside the window of the woman they loved. ❑ *In the interval a blond boy dressed in white serenaded the company on the flute.* • N-COUNT **Serenade** is also a noun. ❑ *Placido Domingo sang his serenade of love.* ❷ N-COUNT [oft in names] In classical music, a **serenade** is a piece in several parts written for a small orchestra. ❑ *...Vaughan Williams's Serenade to Music.*

ser|en|di|tous /sɛrɪndɪpɪtəs/ ADJ A **serendipitous** event is one that is not planned but has a good result. [LITERARY] ❑ *...a serendipitous discovery.*

ser|en|dip|ity /sɛrɪndɪpɪti/ N-UNCOUNT **Serendipity** is the luck some people have in finding or creating interesting or valuable things by chance. [LITERARY] ❑ *Some of the best effects in my garden have been the result of serendipity.*

se|rene /sɪrin/ ADJ Someone or something that is **serene** is calm and quiet. ❑ *She looked as calm and serene as she always did.* ❑ *He didn't speak much, he just smiled with that serene smile of his.* • **se|rene|ly** ADV ❑ *We sailed serenely down the river.* ❑ *She carried on serenely sipping her gin and tonic.* • **se|ren|ity** /sɪrɛnɪti/ N-UNCOUNT ❑ *I had a wonderful feeling of peace and serenity when I saw my husband.*

serf /sɜrf/ (serfs) N-COUNT In former times, **serfs** were a class of people who had to work on a particular person's land and could not leave without that person's permission.

serf|dom /sɜrfdəm/ ❶ N-UNCOUNT The system of **serfdom** was the social and economic system by which the owners of land had serfs. ❷ N-UNCOUNT If someone was in a state of **serfdom**, they were a serf.

serge /sɜrdʒ/ N-UNCOUNT **Serge** is a type of strong woolen cloth used to make clothes such as skirts, coats, and pants. ❑ *He wore a blue serge suit.*

ser|geant /sɑrdʒənt/ (sergeants) ❶ N-COUNT; N-TITLE; N-VOC A **sergeant** is a noncommissioned officer of middle rank in the army, marines, or air force. ❑ *A sergeant with a detail of four men came into view.* ❷ N-COUNT; N-TITLE; N-VOC A **sergeant** is an officer with the rank immediately below a captain. ❑ *A police sergeant patrolling the area spotted flames at the store.*

ser|geant ma|jor (sergeant majors) also sergeant-major N-COUNT; N-TITLE; N-VOC A **sergeant major** is a noncommissioned army or marine officer of the highest rank.

se|rial /sɪəriəl/ (serials) ❶ N-COUNT A **serial** is a story which is broadcast on television or radio or is published in a magazine or newspaper in a number of parts over a period of time. ❑ *...one of television's most popular serials.* ❷ ADJ [ADJ n] **Serial** killings or attacks are a series of killings or attacks committed by the same person. This person is known as a **serial** killer or attacker. ❑ *...serial murders.*

se|ri|ali|za|tion /sɪəriəlaɪzeɪʃᵊn/ (serializations)

in BRIT, also use **serialisation**

1 N-UNCOUNT **Serialization** is the act of serializing a book. ❑ *It was first written for serialization in a magazine.* **2** N-COUNT A **serialization** is a story, originally written as a book, which is being published or broadcast in a number of parts. ❑ *...the serialization of Jane Austen's Pride and Prejudice.*

se|ri|al|ize /sɪəriəlaɪz/ (serializes, serializing, serialized)

in BRIT, also use **serialise**

V-T [usu passive] If a book **is serialized**, it is broadcast on the radio or television or is published in a magazine or newspaper in a number of parts over a period of time. ❑ *Attention was first drawn to the book when a condensed version was serialized in The New Yorker.*

se|rial num|ber (serial numbers) **1** N-COUNT The **serial number** of an object is a number on that object which identifies it. ❑ *...the gun's serial number.* ❑ *...your bike's serial number.* **2** N-COUNT The **serial number** of a member of the United States military forces is a number which identifies them. ❑ *He could never ever give any responses to his captor other than name, rank, serial number and date of birth.*

se|rial port (serial ports) N-COUNT A **serial port** on a computer is a place where you can connect the computer to a device such as a modem or a mouse. [COMPUTING]

se|ries ♦♦◊ /sɪəriz/ (series)

Series is both the singular and the plural form.

1 N-COUNT A **series** of things or events is a number of them that come one after the other. ❑ *...a series of meetings with students and political leaders.* **2** N-COUNT A radio or television **series** is a set of programs of a particular kind which have the same title. ❑ *...Captain Kirk's chair from the TV series "Star Trek."*

se|ri|ous ♦♦♦ /sɪəriəs/ **1** ADJ **Serious** problems or situations are very bad and cause people to be worried or afraid. ❑ *Crime is an increasingly serious problem in Russian society.* ❑ *The government still face very serious difficulties.* • **se|ri|ous|ly** ADV ❑ *If this ban was to come in it would seriously damage my business.* • **se|ri|ous|ness** N-UNCOUNT [oft N of n] ❑ *...the seriousness of the crisis.* **2** ADJ **Serious** matters are important and deserve careful and thoughtful consideration. ❑ *I regard this as a serious matter.* ❑ *Don't laugh, boy. This is serious.* **3** ADJ When important matters are dealt with in a **serious** way, they are given careful and thoughtful consideration. ❑ *My parents never really faced up to my drug use in any serious way.* ❑ *It was a question which deserved serious consideration.* • **se|ri|ous|ly** ADV [ADV with v] ❑ *The management will have to think seriously about their positions.* **4** ADJ [ADJ n] **Serious** music or literature requires concentration to understand or appreciate it. ❑ *...serious classical music.* **5** ADJ If someone is **serious** about something, they are sincere about what they are saying, doing, or intending to do. ❑ *You really are serious about this, aren't you?* • **se|ri|ous|ly** ADV ❑ *Are you seriously jealous of Erica?* • **se|ri|ous|ness** N-UNCOUNT [oft N of n] ❑ *In all seriousness, there is nothing else I can do.* **6** ADJ **Serious** people are thoughtful and quiet, and do not laugh very often. ❑ *He's quite a serious person.* • **se|ri|ous|ly** ADV [ADV with v] ❑ *They spoke to me very seriously but politely.*

se|ri|ous|ly ♦◊◊ /sɪəriəsli/ **1** ADV [ADV with cl] You use **seriously** to indicate that you are not joking and that you really mean what you say. ❑ *Seriously, I only smoke in the evenings.* **2** CONVENTION You say **'seriously'** when you are surprised by what someone has said, as a way of asking them if they really mean it. [SPOKEN, FEELINGS] ❑ *"I tried to chat him up at the general store." He laughed. "Seriously?"* **3** → see also **serious 4** PHRASE If you **take** someone or something **seriously**, you believe that they are important and deserve attention. ❑ *It's hard to take them seriously in their garish purple uniforms.*

ser|mon /sɜrmən/ (sermons) N-COUNT A **sermon** is a talk on a religious or moral subject that is given by a member of the clergy as part of a church service. ❑ *Cardinal Murphy will deliver the sermon on Sunday.*

sero|to|nin /sɛrətoʊnɪn/ N-UNCOUNT **Serotonin** is a chemical produced naturally in your brain that affects the way you feel, for example, making you feel happier, calmer, or less hungry.

ser|pent /sɜrpənt/ (serpents) N-COUNT A **serpent** is a snake. [LITERARY] ❑ *...the serpent in the Garden of Eden.*

ser|pen|tine /sɜrpəntaɪn/ ADJ Something that is **serpentine** is curving and winding in shape, like a snake when it moves. [LITERARY] ❑ *...serpentine woodland pathways.*

ser|rat|ed /sɛreɪtɪd, səreɪ-/ ADJ [usu ADJ n] A **serrated** object such as a knife or blade has a row of V-shaped points along the edge. ❑ *Bread knives should have a serrated edge.*

ser|ried /sɛrid/ ADJ [ADJ n] **Serried** things or people are closely crowded together in rows. [LITERARY] ❑ *...serried rows of law books and law reports.* ❑ *...the serried ranks of fans.*

se|rum /sɪərəm/ (serums) **1** N-VAR A **serum** is a liquid that is injected into someone's blood to protect them against a poison or disease. ❑ *...painful injections of anti-cancer serum.* **2** N-UNCOUNT **Serum** is the watery, pale yellow part of blood. ❑ *The strip, which accepts blood, serum or plasma, is inserted into the analyzer.*

serv|ant ♦◊◊ /sɜrvᵊnt/ (servants) **1** N-COUNT A **servant** is someone who is employed to work at another person's home, for example, as a cleaner or a gardener. ❑ *...a large Victorian family with several servants.* **2** N-COUNT You can use **servant** to refer to someone or something that provides a service for people or can be used by them. ❑ *Like any other public servants, police must respond to public demand.* **3** → see also **civil servant**

serve ♦♦◊ /sɜrv/ (serves, serving, served) **1** V-T If you **serve** your country, an organization, or a person, you do useful work for them. ❑ *It is unfair to soldiers who have served their country well for many years.* **2** V-I If you **serve** in a particular place or as a particular official, you perform official duties, especially in the armed forces, as a civil servant, or as a politician. ❑ *During the second world war he served with 92nd Airborne.* ❑ *They have both served on the school board.* **3** V-T/V-I If something **serves** as a particular thing or **serves** a particular purpose, it performs a particular function, which is often not its intended function. ❑ *She ushered me into the front room, which served as her office.* ❑ *I really do not think that an inquiry would serve any useful purpose.* **4** V-T If something **serves** people or an area, it provides them with something that they need. ❑ *This could mean the closure of thousands of small businesses which serve the community.* ❑ *...improvements in the public water-supply system serving the Nairobi area.* **5** V-T Something that **serves** someone's interests benefits them. ❑ *The economy should be organized to serve the interests of all the people.* **6** V-T/V-I When you **serve** food and drinks, you give people food and drinks. ❑ *Serve it with French bread.* ❑ *Serve the cakes warm.* ❑ *Refrigerate until ready to serve.* • PHRASAL VERB **Serve up** means the same as **serve**. ❑ *After all, it is no use serving up TV dinners if the kids won't eat them.* **7** V-T [no cont] **Serve** is used to indicate how much food a recipe produces. For example, a recipe that **serves** six provides enough food for six people. ❑ *Garnish with fresh herbs. Serves 4.* **8** V-T/V-I Someone who **serves** customers in a store or a bar helps them and provides them with what they want to buy. ❑ *They wouldn't serve me in any bars because I looked too young.* **9** V-T When the police or other officials **serve** someone with a legal order or **serve** an order on them, they give or send the legal order to them. [LEGAL] ❑ *Immigration officers tried to serve her with a deportation order.* **10** V-T If you **serve** something such as a prison sentence or an apprenticeship, you spend a period of time doing it. ❑ *...Leo, who is currently serving a life sentence for murder.* **11** V-T/V-I When you **serve** in games such as tennis and badminton, you throw up the ball or shuttlecock and hit it to start play. ❑ *He served 17 double faults.* • N-COUNT **Serve** is also a noun. ❑ *His second serve clipped the net.* **12** N-COUNT When you describe someone's **serve**, you are indicating how well or how fast they serve a ball or shuttlecock. ❑ *His powerful serve was too much for the defending champion.* **13** → see also **serving 14** PHRASE If you say **it serves** someone **right** when something unpleasant happens to them, you mean that it is their own fault and you have no sympathy for them. [FEELINGS] ❑ *Serves her right for being so stubborn.* **15** → See feature box at **prison**

▶ **serve up** → see serve 6

serv|er /sɜrvər/ (servers) **1** N-COUNT In computing, a **server** is part of a computer network which does a particular task, such as storing or processing information, for all or part of the network. [COMPUTING] **2** N-COUNT A **server** is a person

service

who works in a restaurant, serving people with food and drink. [AM] ❏ *A server came by balancing a tray of wineglasses.* **8** N-COUNT In tennis and badminton, the **server** is the player whose turn it is to hit the ball or shuttlecock to start play. ❏ *...the fastest server in tennis.*

SERVICE
① NOUN AND ADJECTIVE USES
② VERB USES
③ PHRASES

① **ser|vice** ✦✦✦ /sɜrvɪs/ (**services**) **1** N-COUNT A **service** is something that the public needs, such as transportation, communications facilities, hospitals, or energy supplies, which is provided in a planned and organized way by the government or an official body. ❏ *The postal service has been trying to cut costs.* ❏ *We have started a campaign for better nursery and school services.* **2** N-COUNT You can sometimes refer to an organization or private company as a particular **service** when it provides something for the public or acts on behalf of the government. ❏ *The Agriculture Department has ultimate control over the Forest Service.* **3** N-COUNT If an organization or company provides a particular **service**, they can do a particular job or a type of work for you. ❏ *The kitchen maintains a twenty-four hour service and can be contacted via reception.* **4** N-PLURAL **Services** are activities such as tourism, banking, and selling things which are part of a country's economy, but are not concerned with producing or manufacturing goods. ❏ *Mining rose by 9.1%, manufacturing by 9.4% and services by 4.3%.* **5** N-UNCOUNT The level or standard of **service** provided by an organization or company is the amount or quality of the work it can do for you. ❏ *Taking risks is the only way employees can provide effective and efficient customer service.* **6** N-COUNT A bus or train **service** is a route or regular trip that is part of a transportation system. ❏ *The local bus service is well run and extensive.* **7** N-PLURAL Your **services** are the things that you do or the skills that you use in your job, which other people find useful and are usually willing to pay you for. ❏ *I have obtained the services of a top photographer to take our pictures.* **8** N-UNCOUNT [also N in pl, oft N to n] If you refer to someone's **service** or **services** to a particular organization or activity, you mean that they have done a lot of work for it or spent a lot of their time on it. ❏ *You've given a lifetime of service to athletics.* ❏ *Most employees had long service with the company and were familiar with our products.* **9** N-COUNT The **Services** are the army, the navy, the air force and the marines. ❏ *Some of the money could be spent on persuading key specialists to stay in the Services.* **10** N-UNCOUNT **Service** is the work done by people or equipment in the army, navy, or air force, for example, during a war. ❏ *Units are being called up today for service in the Gulf.* **11** N-UNCOUNT When you receive **service** in a restaurant, hotel, or store, an employee asks you what you want or gives you what you have ordered. ❏ *Service was attentive and the meal proceeded at a leisurely pace.* **12** N-COUNT [also no det] A **service** is a religious ceremony that takes place in a church or synagogue. ❏ *After the hour-long service, his body was taken to a cemetery in the south of the city.* **13** N-COUNT [also no det] If a vehicle or machine has a **service**, it is examined, adjusted, and cleaned so that it will keep working efficiently and safely. ❏ *The car needs a service.* **14** N-COUNT A dinner **service** or a tea **service** is a complete set of plates, cups, saucers, and other pieces of china. ❏ *...a 60-piece dinner service.* **15** N-COUNT In tennis, badminton, and some other sports, when it is your **service**, it is your turn to serve. ❏ *She conceded just three points on her service during the first set.* **16** ADJ [ADJ n] **Service** is used to describe the parts of a building or structure that are used by the staff who clean, repair, or take care of it, and are not usually used by the public. ❏ *I went out through the kitchen and down the service elevator.* **17** → see also **civil service, community service, emergency services, in-service, public service, room service**

② **ser|vice** /sɜrvɪs/ (**services, servicing, serviced**) **1** V-T If you have a vehicle or machine **serviced**, you arrange for someone to examine, adjust, and clean it so that it will keep working efficiently and safely. ❏ *I had my car serviced at the local garage.* **2** V-T If someone or something **services** an organization, a project, or a group of people, they provide it with the things that it needs in order to function properly or effectively. ❏ *There are now 400 staff at headquarters, servicing our regional and overseas work.*

③ **ser|vice** /sɜrvɪs/ **1** PHRASE If you **do** someone **a service**, you do something that helps or benefits them. ❏ *You are doing me a great service, and I'm very grateful to you.* **2** PHRASE If a piece of equipment or type of vehicle is **in service**, it is being used or is able to be used. If it is **out of service**, it is not being used, usually because it is not working properly. ❏ *Cuts in funding have meant that equipment has been kept in service long after it should have been replaced.* ❏ *In 1882, the city's first electric tram cars went into service.*

VOCABULARY IN CONTEXT

Service encounters

The type of service encounter you have when you are making a reservation, using an ATM, joining a gym, or purchasing goods can determine whether you use that service again. In fact, it's safe to say that reliable **customer service** is essential for the success of a business. When the quality of a service encounter is **substandard**, customers usually communicate their issue to the **service provider** over the phone, over the internet, or in person. This might happen if, for example, a member of staff is inefficient or **incompetent**, or if a product is faulty while still **under warranty**. In this **interaction**, how a business or **vendor** resolves the situation and improves the **customer experience** is key. Meeting **consumer** expectations and maintaining positive **customer relations** are very high priorities for businesses to run successfully and to ensure ongoing **customer satisfaction** and **loyalty**.

ser|vice|able /sɜrvɪsəbəl/ ADJ If you describe something as **serviceable**, you mean that it is good enough to be used and to perform its function. ❏ *His Arabic was not as good as his English, but serviceable enough.*

ser|vice charge (**service charges**) N-COUNT A **service charge** is an amount that is added to your bill in a restaurant to pay for the work of the person who comes and serves you. ❏ *Most restaurants add a 10 percent service charge to the bill.*

ser|vice in|dus|try (**service industries**) N-COUNT A **service industry** is an industry such as banking or insurance that provides a service but does not produce anything. ❏ *Seventy-two percent of people now work in service industries.*

ser|vice|man /sɜrvɪsmən/ (**servicemen**) N-COUNT A **serviceman** is a man who is in the army, navy, air force, or marines. ❏ *He was an American serviceman based in Vietnam during the war.*

ser|vice pro|vid|er (**service providers**) **1** N-COUNT A **service provider** is a company that provides a service, especially an internet service. [COMPUTING] **2** → See feature box at **service**

ser|vice sta|tion (**service stations**) N-COUNT A **service station** is a place that sells things for vehicles such as gas, oil, and spare parts. Service stations often sell food, drinks, and other products.

ser|vice|woman /sɜrvɪswʊmən/ (**servicewomen**) N-COUNT A **servicewoman** is a woman who is in the army, navy, air force, or marines.

ser|vi|ette /sɜrviɛt/ (**serviettes**) N-COUNT A **serviette** is the same as a **napkin**. [BRIT]

ser|vile /sɜrvᵊl, -vaɪl/ ADJ If you say that someone is **servile**, you disapprove of them because they are too eager to obey someone or do things for them. [FORMAL, DISAPPROVAL] ❑ *He was subservient and servile.* • **ser|vil|ity** /sɜrvɪlɪti/ N-UNCOUNT ❑ *She's a curious mixture of stubbornness and servility.*

serv|ing /sɜrvɪŋ/ (servings) **1** N-COUNT A **serving** is an amount of food that is given to one person at a meal. ❑ *Quantities will vary according to how many servings of soup you want to prepare.* **2** ADJ [ADJ n] A **serving** spoon or dish is used for giving out food at a meal. ❑ *Pile the potatoes into a warm serving dish.*

ser|vi|tude /sɜrvɪtud/ N-UNCOUNT **Servitude** is the condition of being enslaved or of being completely under the control of someone else. ❑ *...a life of servitude.*

sesa|me /sɛsəmi/ N-UNCOUNT [usu N n] **Sesame** is a plant grown for its seeds and oil, which are used in cooking. ❑ *...sesame seeds.*

ses|sion ◆◇◇ /sɛʃᵊn/ (sessions) **1** N-COUNT [also in N] A **session** is a meeting of a court, legislature, or other official group. ❑ *After two late night sessions, the Security Council has failed to reach agreement.* ❑ *The Arab League is meeting in emergency session today.* **2** N-COUNT [also in N] A **session** is a period during which the meetings of a court, legislature, or other official group are regularly held. ❑ *From September until December, Congress remained in session.* **3** N-COUNT A **session** of a particular activity is a period of that activity. ❑ *The two leaders emerged for a photo session.*

---- COLLOCATIONS ----

session
NOUN **3**
noun + **session**: coaching, gym, practice, training; counseling, therapy; bonding, drinking, recording
verb + **session**: attend, run

---- SET ----

① NOUN USES
② VERB AND ADJECTIVE USES

① **set** ◆◆◆ /sɛt/ (sets) **1** N-COUNT A **set** of things is a number of things that belong together or that are thought of as a group. ❑ *There must be one set of laws for the whole of the country.* ❑ *The mattress and base are normally bought as a set.* ❑ *...a chess set.* **2** N-COUNT In tennis, a **set** is one of the groups of six or more games that form part of a match. ❑ *She was leading 5–1 in the first set.* **3** N-COUNT In mathematics, a **set** is a group of mathematical quantities that have some characteristic in common. ❑ *...the field of set theory.* **4** N-COUNT [also on/off N] The **set** for a play, movie, or television show is the furniture and scenery that is on the stage when the play is being performed or in the studio where filming takes place. ❑ *From the first moment he got on the set, he wanted to be a director too.* ❑ *He achieved fame for his stage sets for the Folies Bergeres.* **5** N-COUNT A **set** is an appliance that receives television or radio signals. For example, a television set is a television. ❑ *Children spend so much time in front of the television set.* **6** → See feature box at **theater**

② **set** ◆◆◆ /sɛt/ (sets, setting)

The form **set** is used in the present tense and is the past tense and past participle of the verb.

→ Please look at meanings **22**–**28** to see if the expression you are looking for is shown under another headword.

1 V-T If you **set** something somewhere, you put it there, especially in a careful or deliberate way. ❑ *He took the case out of her hand and set it on the floor.* **2** ADJ [v-link ADJ prep/adv] If something is **set** in a particular place or position, it is in that place or position. ❑ *The castle is set in 25 acres of beautiful grounds.* **3** ADJ [v-link ADJ prep/adv] If something is **set** into a surface, it is fixed there and does not stick out. ❑ *The man unlocked a gate set in a high wall and let me through.* **4** V-T You can use **set** to say that a person or thing causes another person or thing to be in a particular condition or situation. For example, to **set** someone free means to cause them to be free, and to **set** something going means to cause it to start working. ❑ *Set the kitchen timer going.* ❑ *Dozens of people have been injured and many vehicles set on fire.* **5** V-T When you **set** a clock or control, you adjust it to a particular point or level. ❑ *Set the volume as high as possible.* **6** V-T If you **set** a date, price, goal, or level, you decide what it will be. ❑ *The conference chairman has set a deadline of noon tomorrow.* ❑ *A date will be set for a future meeting.* **7** V-T If you **set** a certain value on something, you think it has that value. ❑ *She sets a high value on autonomy.* **8** V-T If you **set** something such as a record, an example, or a precedent, you do something that people will want to copy or try to achieve. ❑ *Legal experts said her case would not set a precedent because it was an out-of-court settlement.* **9** V-T If someone **sets** you a task or aim or if you **set** yourself a task or aim, you need to succeed in doing it. ❑ *I have to plan my academic work very rigidly and set myself clear objectives.* **10** ADJ You use **set** to describe something which is fixed and cannot be changed. ❑ *A set period of fasting is supposed to bring us closer to godliness.* **11** ADJ [ADJ n] A **set** book must be studied by students taking a particular course. [BRIT]

in AM, use **required**

12 ADJ [v-link ADJ prep/adv] If a play, movie, or story is **set** in a particular place or period of time, the events in it take place in that place or period. ❑ *The play is set in a small Midwestern town.* **13** ADJ [v-link ADJ to-inf] If you are **set** to do something, you are ready to do it or are likely to do it. If something is **set** to happen, it is about to happen or likely to happen. ❑ *She was set to become one of the greatest players of all time.* **14** ADJ [v-link ADJ on/against n/-ing] If you are **set on** something, you are strongly determined to do or have it. If you are **set against** something, you are strongly determined not to do or have it. ❑ *She was set on going to an all-girls school.* **15** V-I When something such as jelly, melted plastic, or cement sets, it becomes firm or hard. ❑ *You can add ingredients to these desserts as they begin to set.* **16** V-I When the sun **sets**, it goes below the horizon. ❑ *They watched the sun set behind the distant dales.* **17** V-T To **set** a trap means to prepare it to catch someone or something. ❑ *He seemed to think I was setting some sort of trap for him.* **18** V-T When someone **sets** the table, they prepare it for a meal by putting plates and flatware on it. ❑ *One would shop and cook, another would set the table and another would wash up.* **19** V-T If someone **sets** a poem or a piece of writing to music, they write music for the words to be sung to. ❑ *He has attracted much interest by setting ancient religious texts to music.* **20** → see also **setting** **21** PHRASE If someone **sets the scene** or **sets the stage** for an event to take place, they make preparations so that it can take place. ❑ *The Democratic convention has set the scene for a ferocious election campaign this fall.* **22** to set fire to something → see fire ① **23** to set foot somewhere → see foot ① **24** to set your heart on something → see heart ② **25** to set sail → see sail **26** to set to work → see work ② **27** → See feature box at **legal**, **theater**

▶ **set aside** **1** PHRASAL VERB If you **set** something **aside** for a special use or purpose, you keep it available for that use or purpose. ❑ *Some doctors advise setting aside time each day for meditation.* **2** PHRASAL VERB If you **set aside** a belief, principle, or feeling, you decide that you will not be influenced by it. ❑ *He urged the participants to set aside minor differences for the sake of achieving peace.*

▶ **set back** **1** PHRASAL VERB If something **sets** you **back** or **sets back** a project or plan, it causes a delay. ❑ *It has set us back in so many respects that I'm not sure how long it will take for us to catch up.* **2** PHRASAL VERB If something **sets** you **back** a certain amount of money, it costs you that much money. [INFORMAL] ❑ *A bottle of imported beer will set you back $7.* **3** → see also **setback**

▶ **set down** **1** PHRASAL VERB If a committee or organization **sets down** rules for doing something, it decides what they should be and officially records them. ❑ *I like to make suggestions rather than setting down laws and forcing people to follow them.* **2** PHRASAL VERB If you **set down** your thoughts or experiences, you write them all down. ❑ *Old Walter is setting down his memories of village life.*

▶ **set in** PHRASAL VERB If something unpleasant **sets in**, it begins and seems likely to continue or develop. ❑ *Winter is setting in and the population is facing food and fuel shortages.*

▶ **set off** **1** PHRASAL VERB When you **set off**, you start a journey. ❑ *Nichols set off for his remote farmhouse in Connecticut.* ❑ *The president's envoy set off on another diplomatic trip.* **2** PHRASAL VERB If something **sets off** something such as an alarm or a bomb, it makes it start working so that, for example, the alarm rings or the bomb explodes. ❑ *Any escape, once it's detected, sets off the alarm.* ❑ *Someone set off a fire extinguisher.* **3** PHRASAL VERB If something **sets off** an event or a series of events, it causes it to start happening. ❑ *The arrival of the charity van set off a minor riot as villagers scrambled for a share of the aid.*

▶ **set out** ◼ PHRASAL VERB When you **set out**, you start a journey. ❑ *When setting out on a long walk, always wear suitable boots.* ◼ PHRASAL VERB If you **set out** to do something, you start trying to do it. ❑ *He has achieved what he set out to do three years ago.* ◼ PHRASAL VERB If you **set** things **out**, you arrange or display them somewhere. ❑ *Set out the cakes attractively, using lacy doilies.* ◼ PHRASAL VERB If you **set out** a number of facts, beliefs, or arguments, you explain them in writing or speech in a clear, organized way. ❑ *He has written a letter to The Times setting out his views.*

▶ **set up** ◼ PHRASAL VERB If you **set** something **up**, you create or arrange it. ❑ *The two sides agreed to set up a commission to investigate claims.* ❑ *...an organization which sets up meetings about potential solutions for homelessness.* • **set|ting up** N-UNCOUNT ❑ *The government announced the setting up of a special fund.* ◼ PHRASAL VERB If you **set up** a temporary structure, you place it or build it somewhere. ❑ *They took to the streets, setting up roadblocks of burning tires.* ◼ PHRASAL VERB If you **set up** a device or piece of machinery, you do the things that are necessary for it to be able to start working. ❑ *Setting up the camera can be tricky.* ◼ PHRASAL VERB If you **set up** somewhere or **set** yourself **up** somewhere, you establish yourself in a new business or new area. ❑ *The mayor's plan offers incentives to firms setting up in lower Manhattan.* ❑ *He worked as a dance instructor in London before setting himself up in Bucharest.* ❑ *Grandfather set them up in a printing business.* ◼ PHRASAL VERB If you **set up** house or home or **set up** shop, you buy a house or business of your own and start living or working there. ❑ *They married, and set up home in Atlanta.* ◼ PHRASAL VERB If you **are set up** by someone, they make it seem that you have done something wrong when you have not. [INFORMAL] ❑ *He claimed yesterday that he had been set up after drugs were discovered at his home.* ◼ → see also **setup**

set|back /sɛtbæk/ (**setbacks**) N-COUNT [oft N for/in/to n] A **setback** is an event that delays your progress or reverses some of the progress that you have made. ❑ *The move represents a setback for the Middle East peace process.*

set piece (**set pieces**) ◼ N-COUNT [oft N n] A **set piece** is an occasion such as a battle or a move in a game of soccer that is planned and carried out in an ordered way. ❑ *Guerrillas avoid fighting set-piece battles.* ◼ N-COUNT A **set piece** is a part of a movie, novel, or piece of music which has a strong dramatic effect and which is often not an essential part of the main story. ❑ *...the film's martial arts set pieces.*

sett /sɛt/ (**setts**) N-COUNT A **sett** is the place where a badger lives.

set|tee /sɛti/ (**settees**) N-COUNT A **settee** is a long comfortable seat with a back and arms, which two or more people can sit on.

set|ter /sɛtər/ (**setters**) N-COUNT A **setter** is a long-haired dog that can be trained to show hunters where birds and animals are.

set|ting /sɛtɪŋ/ (**settings**) ◼ N-COUNT A particular **setting** is a particular place or type of surroundings where something is or takes place. ❑ *Rome is the perfect setting for romance.* ◼ N-COUNT A **setting** is one of the positions to which the controls of a device such as a stove or heater can be adjusted. ❑ *You can boil the fish fillets on a high setting.*

set|tle ♦♦◊ /sɛtəl/ (**settles, settling, settled**) ◼ V-T If people **settle** an argument or problem, or if something **settles** it, they solve it, for example, by making a decision about who is right or about what to do. ❑ *They agreed to try to settle their dispute by negotiation.* ◼ V-T/V-I If people **settle** a legal dispute or if they **settle**, they agree to end the dispute without going to a court of law, for example, by paying some money or by apologizing. ❑ *In an attempt to settle the case, Molken has agreed to pay restitution.* ❑ *She got much less than she would have done if she had settled out of court.* ◼ V-T/V-I If you **settle** a bill or debt, you pay the amount that you owe. ❑ *I settled the bill for my coffee and his two glasses of wine.* ❑ *She has now settled with her landlord.* ◼ V-T [usu passive] If something **is settled**, it has all been decided and arranged. ❑ *As far as we're concerned, the matter is settled.* ◼ V-T/V-I When people **settle** a place or in a place, or when a government **settles** them there, they start living there permanently. ❑ *Refugees settling in a new country suffer from a number of problems.* ❑ *He visited Paris and eventually settled there.* ◼ V-T/V-I If you **settle** yourself somewhere or **settle** somewhere, you sit down or make yourself comfortable. ❑ *Albert settled himself on the sofa.* ◼ V-T/V-I If something **settles** or if you **settle** it, it sinks slowly down and becomes still. ❑ *A black dust settled on the walls.* ❑ *Once its impurities had settled, the oil could be graded.* ◼ V-I If your eyes **settle** on or upon something, you stop looking around and look at that thing for some time. ❑ *The man let his eyes settle upon Blume's face.* ◼ V-I When birds or insects **settle on** something, they land on it from above. ❑ *Moths flew in front of it, eventually settling on the rough painted metal.* ◼ → see also **settled** ◼ **when the dust settles** → see **dust** ◼ **to settle a score** → see **score** ◼ → See feature box at **population, research**

▶ **settle down** ◼ PHRASAL VERB When someone **settles down**, they start living a quiet life in one place, especially when they get married or buy a house. ❑ *One day I'll want to settle down and have a family.* ◼ PHRASAL VERB If a situation or a person that has been going through a lot of problems or changes **settles down**, they become calm. ❑ *It'd be fun, after the situation in Europe settles down, to take a trip to France.* ◼ PHRASAL VERB If you **settle down** to do something or to something, you prepare to do it and concentrate on it. ❑ *He got his coffee, came back and settled down to listen.* ◼ PHRASAL VERB If you **settle down** for the night, you get ready to lie down and sleep. ❑ *They put up their tents and settled down for the night.*

▶ **settle for** PHRASAL VERB If you **settle for** something, you choose or accept it, especially when it is not what you really want but there is nothing else available. ❑ *Virginia was a perfectionist. She was just not prepared to settle for anything mediocre.*

▶ **settle in** PHRASAL VERB If you **settle in**, you become used to living in a new place, doing a new job, or going to a new school. ❑ *I enjoyed school enormously once I'd settled in.*

▶ **settle on** PHRASAL VERB If you **settle on** a particular thing, you choose it after considering other possible choices. ❑ *I finally settled on a Mercedes. It's the ideal car for me.*

▶ **settle up** PHRASAL VERB When you **settle up**, you pay a bill or a debt. ❑ *I'll have to settle up what I owe for the phone.*

set|tled /sɛtəld/ ◼ ADJ If you have a **settled** way of life, you stay in one place, in one job, or with one person, rather than moving around or changing. ❑ *He decided to lead a more settled life with his partner.* ◼ ADJ A **settled** situation or system stays the same all the time. ❑ *There has been a period of settled weather.*

set|tle|ment ♦♦◊ /sɛtəlmənt/ (**settlements**) ◼ N-COUNT A **settlement** is an official agreement between two sides who were involved in a conflict or argument. ❑ *Our objective must be to secure a peace settlement.* ◼ N-COUNT A **settlement** is an agreement to end a disagreement or dispute without going to a court of law, for example, by offering someone money. ❑ *She accepted an out-of-court settlement of $40,000.* ◼ N-UNCOUNT The **settlement** of a debt is the act of paying back money that you owe. ❑ *...ways to delay the settlement of debts.* ◼ N-COUNT A **settlement** is a place where people have come to live and have built homes. ❑ *The village is a settlement of just fifty houses.*

COLLOCATIONS

settlement
NOUN
◼
noun + **settlement**: dispute, divorce, pay, peace
adjective + **settlement**: amicable; political
verb + **settlement**: achieve, announce, reach, secure; negotiate, propose
◼
noun + **settlement**: cash; lawsuit, libel
adjective + **settlement**: confidential, out-of-court
verb + **settlement**: accept, agree, negotiate

set|tler /sɛtlər, sɛtəl-/ (**settlers**) N-COUNT **Settlers** are people who go to live in a new country. ❑ *The first German village in southwestern Siberia was founded a century ago by settlers from the Volga region.*

set-to (**set-tos**) N-COUNT A **set-to** is a dispute or fight. [INFORMAL] ❑ *This was the subject of a major set-to between Smith and his record company.*

set-top box (**set-top boxes**) N-COUNT A **set-top box** is a piece of equipment that rests on top of your television and receives digital television signals.

set|up ♦♦◊ /sɛtʌp/ (**setups**) also **set-up** ◼ N-COUNT A particular **setup** is a particular system or way of organizing something. [INFORMAL] ❑ *It appears to be an idyllic domestic setup.* ◼ N-COUNT If you describe a situation as a **setup**, you mean that people have planned it in order to deceive you or to make it look as if you have done something wrong. [INFORMAL] ❑ He was asked to pick somebody up and bring them to a party, not realizing it was a setup. ❸ N-SING The **setup** of computer hardware or software is the process of installing it and making it ready to use. [COMPUTING] ❑ The worst part of the setup is the poor instruction manual.

sev|en ✦✦✦ /sɛvᵊn/ (sevens) NUM **Seven** is the number 7. ❑ Sarah and Ella have been friends for seven years.

sev|en|teen ✦✦✦ /sɛvᵊntiːn/ (seventeens) NUM **Seventeen** is the number 17. ❑ Jenny is seventeen years old.

sev|en|teenth ✦✦◇ /sɛvᵊntiːnθ/ ORD The **seventeenth** item in a series is the one that you count as number seventeen. ❑ She gave birth to Annabel just after her seventeenth birthday.

sev|enth ✦✦◇ /sɛvᵊnθ/ (sevenths) ❶ ORD The **seventh** item in a series is the one that you count as number seven. ❑ I was the seventh child in the family. ❷ FRACTION A **seventh** is one of seven equal parts of something. ❑ A million people died, a seventh of the population.

Sev|enth Day Ad|vent|ist /sɛvᵊnθ deɪ ædvɛntɪst/ (Seventh Day Adventists) ❶ ADJ [ADJ n] **Seventh Day Adventist** churches are churches that hold services on Saturday and that believe that Jesus Christ will return very soon. ❷ N-COUNT A **Seventh Day Adventist** is a member of the Seventh Day Adventist church.

sev|enth heav|en N-UNCOUNT [in n] If you say that you are **in seventh heaven**, you mean that you are in a state of complete happiness. [INFORMAL]

sev|en|ti|eth ✦✦◇ /sɛvᵊntiəθ/ (seventieths) ❶ ORD The **seventieth** item in a series is the one that you count as number seventy. ❑ ...the seventieth anniversary of the discovery of Tutankhamun's tomb. ❷ FRACTION A **seventieth** is one of seventy equal parts of something.

sev|en|ty ✦✦✦ /sɛvᵊnti/ (seventies) ❶ NUM **Seventy** is the number 70. ❑ Seventy people were killed. ❷ N-PLURAL When you talk about the **seventies**, you are referring to numbers between 70 and 79. For example, if you are **in your seventies**, you are aged between 70 and 79. If the temperature is **in the seventies**, it is between 70 and 79. ❑ I thought it was a long way to go for two people in their seventies, but Sylvia loved the idea. ❸ N-PLURAL The **seventies** is the decade between 1970 and 1979. ❑ In the late Seventies, things had to be new, modern, revolutionary.

sev|er /sɛvər/ (severs, severing, severed) ❶ V-T To **sever** something means to cut completely through it or to cut it completely off. [FORMAL] ❑ Richardson severed his right foot in a motorcycle accident. ❷ V-T If you **sever** a relationship or connection that you have with someone, you end it suddenly and completely. [FORMAL] ❑ She severed her ties with her homeland.

sev|er|al ✦✦✦ /sɛvrəl/ DET **Several** is used to refer to a number of people or things that is not large but is greater than two. ❑ I had lived two doors away from this family for several years. ❑ Several blue plastic boxes under the window were filled with CDs. ● QUANT [QUANT of pl-n] **Several** is also a quantifier. ❑ The building was picketed by demonstrators, several of whom were well-known actors. ● PRON **Several** is also a pronoun. ❑ No one drug will suit or work for everyone and sometimes several may have to be tried.

SYNONYMS

several
DET
some: He went to fetch some books.
a few: I gave a dinner party for a few close friends.
a handful: One spring morning, a handful of potential investors assembled in Quincy.

sev|er|ance /sɛvrəns, -ərəns/ ADJ [ADJ n] **Severance** pay is a sum of money that a company gives to its employees when it has to stop employing them. [BUSINESS] ❑ We were offered 13 weeks' severance pay.

se|vere ✦✦◇ /sɪvɪər/ (severer, severest) ❶ ADJ You use **severe** to indicate that something bad or undesirable is great or intense. ❑ ...a business with severe cash flow problems. ❑ Shortages of professional staff are very severe in some places. ● **se|vere|ly** ADV ❑ The UN wants to send food aid to 10 countries in Africa severely affected by the drought. ❑ An aircraft overshot the runway and was severely damaged. ● **se|ver|ity** /sɪvɛrɪti/ N-UNCOUNT [usu with supp] ❑ Several drugs are used to lessen the severity of the symptoms. ❷ ADJ **Severe** punishments or criticisms are very strong or harsh. ❑ This was a dreadful crime and a severe sentence is necessary. ● **se|vere|ly** ADV [ADV with v] ❑ ...a campaign to try to change the law to punish dangerous drivers more severely. ● **se|ver|ity** N-UNCOUNT [usu with supp] ❑ He was sickened by the severity of the sentence.

SYNONYMS

severe
ADJ
❶
serious: The government still face very serious difficulties.
critical: Its day-to-day finances are in a critical state.
terrible: Tens of thousands of people suffered terrible injuries.
grave: I have grave doubts that the documents tell the whole story.
❷
strict: My parents were very strict.
harsh: ...the cold, harsh cruelty of her husband.
cruel: ...struggling to survive in a cruel world with which they cannot cope.

sew /soʊ/ (sews, sewing, sewed, sewn) V-T/V-I When you **sew** something such as clothes, you make them or repair them by joining pieces of cloth together by passing thread through them with a needle. ❑ She sewed the dresses on the sewing machine. ❑ Anyone can sew on a button, including you.

sew|age /suːɪdʒ/ N-UNCOUNT **Sewage** is waste matter such as feces or dirty water from homes and factories, which flows away through sewers. ❑ ...treatment of raw sewage.

sew|er /suːər/ (sewers) N-COUNT A **sewer** is a large underground channel that carries waste matter and rain water away, usually to a place where it is treated and made harmless. ❑ ...the city's sewer system.

sew|er|age /suːərɪdʒ/ N-UNCOUNT [usu N n] **Sewerage** is the system by which waste matter is carried away in sewers and made harmless. ❑ ...without access to any services such as water or sewerage.

sew|ing /soʊɪŋ/ ❶ N-UNCOUNT **Sewing** is the activity of making or mending clothes or other things using a needle and thread.

VOCABULARY IN CONTEXT

Sewing and textiles

Not many of us regularly visit our **tailor** to **be measured** for a new **garment**, do we? At most, we might leave something with a local **seamstress** for minor alterations, getting sleeves shortened or jeans **hemmed**. If you had to, you could probably sew a button onto a shirt yourself, but the skill of **mending** anything more complicated is mainly reserved for the **dressmaker**. At one time, **needlework** was a popular hobby for women. You would find them in Jane Austen novels sitting with their **embroidery** frames, **stitching** delicately. Modernity, of course, changed our relationship with sewing and **textiles**. Trade in **cotton** and **silk** isn't what it once was. Today's **synthetic fabrics** are cheaper and more practical. Industrialization brought clothing factories and great machines that could **spin** and **weave** in a fraction of the time. Nevertheless, thanks to sewing shows on reality TV, dressmaking as a hobby is enjoying a resurgence.

❏ Her mother had always done all the sewing. **2** N-UNCOUNT **Sewing** is clothes or other things that are being sewn. ❏ *We all got out our own sewing and sat in front of the log fire.*

sew|ing ma|chine (sewing machines) N-COUNT A **sewing machine** is a machine that you use for sewing.

sewn /soʊn/ **Sewn** is the past participle of **sew**.

sex ✦✧ /sɛks/ (sexes, sexing, sexed) **1** N-COUNT The two **sexes** are the two groups, male and female, into which people and animals are divided according to the function they have in producing young. ❏ *...a movie star who appeals to all ages and both sexes.* **2** → see also **opposite sex 3** N-COUNT The **sex** of a person or animal is their characteristic of being either male or female. ❏ *She continually failed to gain promotion because of her sex.* ❏ *The new technique has been used to identify the sex of fetuses.* **4** N-UNCOUNT **Sex** is the physical activity between people that involves the sexual organs. ❏ *He was very open in his attitudes about sex.* ❏ *The entire film revolves around drugs, sex and violence.* **5** PHRASE If two people **have sex**, they perform the act of sex. ❏ *Have you ever thought about having sex with someone other than your husband?*

▸ **sex up** PHRASAL VERB To **sex** something **up** means to make it seem more attractive or interesting than it actually is. [INFORMAL] ❏ *Nintendo is sexing up its U.S. advertising to launch the new handheld device.*

sex aid (sex aids) N-COUNT A **sex aid** is an object or piece of equipment that is designed to make sex easier or more enjoyable.

sex ap|peal N-UNCOUNT Someone's **sex appeal** is their sexual attractiveness. ❏ *She still has the energy and sex appeal of a woman less than half her age.*

sex edu|ca|tion N-UNCOUNT **Sex education** is education in schools on the subject of sexual activity and sexual relationships.

sex god|dess (sex goddesses) N-COUNT If you refer to a woman, especially a movie star, as a **sex goddess**, you mean that many people consider her to be sexually attractive. [JOURNALISM] ❏ *Raquel Welch was at the height of her popularity as a sex goddess.*

sex|ism /sɛksɪzəm/ N-UNCOUNT **Sexism** is the belief that the members of one sex, usually women, are less intelligent or less capable than those of the other sex and need not be treated equally. It is also the behavior which is the result of this belief. ❏ *Groups like ours are committed to eradicating homophobia, racism and sexism.*

sex|ist /sɛksɪst/ (sexists) ADJ If you describe people or their behavior as **sexist**, you mean that they are influenced by the belief that the members of one sex, usually women, are less intelligent or less capable than those of the other sex and need not be treated equally. [DISAPPROVAL] ❏ *Old-fashioned sexist attitudes are still common.* • N-COUNT A **sexist** is someone with sexist views or behavior. ❏ *It's got nothing to do with sexism. You know I'm not a sexist.*

sex|less /sɛkslɪs/ ADJ If you describe a person as **sexless**, you mean that they have no sexual feelings or that they are not sexually active. A **sexless** relationship does not involve sex. ❏ *We had been in a sexless relationship for four years.*

sex life (sex lives) N-COUNT [oft with poss] If you refer to someone's **sex life**, you are referring to their sexual relationships and sexual activity.

sex ob|ject (sex objects) N-COUNT If someone is described as a **sex object**, he or she is considered only in terms of their physical attractiveness and not their character or abilities. ❏ *He cared for her as a whole person rather than just a sex object.*

sex of|fend|er (sex offenders) N-COUNT A **sex offender** is a person who has been found guilty of a sexual crime such as rape or sexual assault. ❏ *Schwartz must register as a sex offender in New York.*

sex|olo|gist /sɛksɒlədʒɪst/ (sexologists) N-COUNT A **sexologist** is a person who studies sexual relationships. ❏ *...Alfred Kinsey, the pioneering sexologist.*

sex|pot /sɛkspɒt/ (sexpots) N-COUNT If you describe someone as a **sexpot**, you mean that they are sexually very attractive. [INFORMAL, OLD-FASHIONED]

sex shop (sex shops) N-COUNT A **sex shop** is a store that sells products that are associated with sex, for example, magazines, films, and special clothing or equipment.

sex sym|bol (sex symbols) N-COUNT A **sex symbol** is a famous person, especially an actor or a singer, who is considered by many people to be sexually attractive. ❏ *...Hollywood sex symbols of the Forties.*

sex|tant /sɛkstənt/ (sextants) N-COUNT A **sextant** is an instrument used for measuring angles, for example between the sun and the horizon, so that the position of a ship or airplane can be calculated.

sex|tet /sɛkstɛt/ (sextets) **1** N-COUNT A **sextet** is a group of six musicians or singers who play or sing together. ❏ *...the Paul Rogers Sextet.* **2** N-COUNT A **sextet** is a piece of music written for six performers.

sext|ing /sɛkstɪŋ/ N-UNCOUNT **Sexting** is the activity of using a smart phone to send text messages that are about sex or to send sexual photographs. ❏ *He was expelled from school for sexting.*

sex toy (sex toys) N-COUNT A **sex toy** is an object that can be used to give sexual pleasure.

sex|ual ✦✧ /sɛkʃuəl/ **1** ADJ **Sexual** feelings or activities are connected with the act of sex or with people's desire for sex. ❏ *This was the first sexual relationship I'd had.* • **sex|ual|ly** ADV ❏ *...sexually transmitted diseases.* **2** ADJ **Sexual** means relating to the differences between male and female people. ❏ *Women's groups denounced sexual discrimination.* • **sex|ual|ly** ADV [ADV with v] ❏ *If you're sexually harassed, you ought to do something about it.* **3** ADJ **Sexual** means relating to whether a person is for example, heterosexual, homosexual, or bisexual. ❏ *...couples of all sexual persuasions.* **4** ADJ **Sexual** means relating to the biological process by which people and animals produce young. ❏ *Girls generally reach sexual maturity two years earlier than boys.* • **sex|ual|ly** ADV ❏ *The first organisms that reproduced sexually were free-floating plankton.*

sex|ual abuse N-UNCOUNT If a child or other person suffers **sexual abuse**, someone forces them to take part in sexual activity. ❏ *...victims of sexual abuse.*

sex|ual har|ass|ment N-UNCOUNT **Sexual harassment** is repeated and unwelcome sexual comments, looks, or physical contact at work. ❏ *Sexual harassment of women workers by their bosses is believed to be widespread.*

sex|ual inter|course N-UNCOUNT **Sexual intercourse** is the physical act of sex between two people. [FORMAL] ❏ *I have never had sexual intercourse with her and that is the truth.*

sexu|al|ity /sɛkʃuælɪti/ **1** N-UNCOUNT A person's **sexuality** is their sexual feelings. ❏ *...the growing discussion of women's sexuality.* **2** N-UNCOUNT You can refer to a person's **sexuality** when you are talking about whether they are sexually attracted to people of the same sex or a different sex. ❏ *He believes he has been discriminated against because of his sexuality.*

sex|ual|ize /sɛkʃuəlaɪz/ (sexualizes, sexualizing, sexualized)

in BRIT, also use **sexualise**

V-T To **sexualize** something or someone means to make them sexual or consider them in a sexual way. ❏ *Sales have been suspended as the tourism authorities say they sexualize the country's image.* ❏ *... sexualized images.*

sex|ual ori|en|ta|tion (sexual orientations) N-VAR [oft poss N] Someone's **sexual orientation** is whether they are sexually attracted to people of the same sex, people of the opposite sex, or both.

sex|ual pref|er|ence (sexual preferences) N-VAR [oft poss N] Someone's **sexual preference** is the same as their **sexual orientation**.

sex work|er (sex workers) N-COUNT A **sex worker** is someone who takes part in sexual activity for money.

sexy /sɛksi/ (sexier, sexiest) ADJ You can describe people and things as **sexy** if you think they are sexually exciting or sexually attractive. ❏ *She was one of the sexiest women I had seen.*

SF /ɛs ɛf/ N-UNCOUNT [usu N n] **SF** is the same as **science fiction**. ❏ *Her books were hugely popular with SF fans all over the world.*

sfx **Sfx** is a written abbreviation for **special effects**.

SGML /ɛs dʒi ɛm gl/ N-UNCOUNT **SGML** is a computer language for creating files using a system of codes. **SGML** is an abbreviation for 'standard generalized mark-up language.'

Sgt.

in BRIT, use **Sgt**

N-TITLE **Sgt.** is the written abbreviation for **Sergeant** when it is used as a title. ❑ *...Sgt. Johnston.*

sh /ʃ/ → see shh

shab|by /ʃæbi/ (shabbier, shabbiest) ADJ **Shabby** things or places look old and in bad condition. ❑ *His clothes were old and shabby.*

Shab|by Chic N-UNCOUNT **Shabby Chic** is a style of decorating the inside of a house in which the furniture and fabric look slightly used or old in a way that is attractive. [TRADEMARK] ❑ *Her apartment is the ultimate in Shabby Chic.*

shack /ʃæk/ (shacks, shacking, shacked) N-COUNT A **shack** is a simple hut built from tin, wood, or other materials.
▶ **shack up** PHRASAL VERB If someone **has shacked up with** someone else or two people **have shacked up** together, they have started living together as lovers. [INFORMAL] ❑ *...the deserters who had shacked up with local women.* ❑ *Young people are afraid to get married, so they shack up.*

shack|le /ʃækəl/ (shackles, shackling, shackled) **1** V-T [usu passive] If you **are shackled** by something, it prevents you from doing what you want to do. [FORMAL] ❑ *The labor unions are shackled by the law.* ❑ *...people who find themselves shackled to a high-stress job.* **2** N-PLURAL [with supp] If you throw off the **shackles** of something, you reject it or free yourself from it because it was preventing you from doing what you wanted to do. [LITERARY] ❑ *...a country ready to throw off the shackles of its colonial past.* **3** N-PLURAL **Shackles** are two metal rings joined by a chain which are fastened around someone's wrists or ankles in order to prevent them from moving or escaping. ❑ *He unbolted the shackles on Billy's hands.* **4** V-T To **shackle** someone means to put shackles on them. ❑ *...the chains that were shackling his legs.*

shade ♦◇◇ /ʃeɪd/ (shades, shading, shaded) **1** N-COUNT A **shade** of a particular color is one of its different forms. For example, emerald green and olive green are shades of green. ❑ *In the mornings the sky appeared a heavy shade of mottled gray.* ❑ *The walls were painted in two shades of green.* **2** N-UNCOUNT **Shade** is an area of darkness next to or under an object such as a tree, where sunlight does not reach. ❑ *Temperatures in the shade can reach forty-eight degrees Celsius at this time of year.* ❑ *Alexis walked up the coast, and resumed his reading in the shade of an overhanging cliff.* **3** V-T If you say that a place or person **is shaded** by objects such as trees, you mean that the place or person cannot be reached, harmed, or bothered by strong sunlight because those objects are in the way. ❑ *...a health resort whose beaches are shaded by palm trees.* **4** V-T If you **shade** your eyes, you put your hand or an object partly in front of your face in order to prevent a bright light from shining into your eyes. ❑ *You can't look directly into it; you've got to shade your eyes or close them altogether.* **5** N-UNCOUNT **Shade** is darkness or shadows as they are shown in a picture. ❑ *...Rembrandt's skillful use of light and shade to create the atmosphere of movement.* **6** N-COUNT The **shades** of something abstract are its many, slightly different forms. ❑ *...the capacity to convey subtle shades of meaning.* **7** N-COUNT A **shade** is a piece of stiff cloth or heavy paper that you can pull down over a window as a covering. [AM] ❑ *Nancy left the shades down and the lights off.*

in BRIT, use **blind**

shad|ed /ʃeɪdɪd/ ADJ A **shaded** area on something such as a map is one that is colored darker than the surrounding areas, so that it can be distinguished from them.

-shaded /-ʃeɪdɪd/ COMB IN ADJ **-shaded** combines with nouns to form adjectives which indicate that sunlight is prevented from reaching a certain place by the thing mentioned. ❑ *...a winding, tree-shaded driveway.*

shad|ing /ʃeɪdɪŋ/ **1** N-UNCOUNT **Shading** is material such as nets or dark paint that provide shade, especially for plants. ❑ *The conservatory will get very hot in summer unless shading is used.* **2** → see also **shade**

shad|ow ♦◇◇ /ʃædoʊ/ (shadows, shadowing, shadowed) **1** N-COUNT A **shadow** is a dark shape on a surface that is made when something stands between a light and the surface. ❑ *An oak tree cast its shadow over a tiny round pool.* ❑ *Nothing would grow in the shadow of the gray wall.* **2** N-UNCOUNT **Shadow** is darkness in a place caused by something preventing light from reaching it. ❑ *Most of the lake was in shadow.* **3** V-T If something **shadows** a thing or place, it covers it with a shadow. ❑ *The hood shadowed her face.* **4** V-T If someone **shadows** you, they follow you very closely wherever you go. ❑ *The president is constantly shadowed by bodyguards.* **5** ADJ [ADJ n] A British Member of Parliament who is a member of the **shadow** cabinet or who is a **shadow** cabinet minister belongs to the main opposition party and takes a special interest in matters which are the responsibility of a particular government minister. ❑ *...the shadow chancellor.* • N-COUNT **Shadow** is also a noun. ❑ *Clarke swung at his shadow the accusation that he was "a tabloid politician."* **6** PHRASE If you say that something is true without **a shadow of a doubt** or without **a shadow of doubt**, you are emphasizing that there is no doubt at all that it is true. [EMPHASIS] ❑ *It was without a shadow of a doubt the best we've played.* **7** PHRASE If you live **in the shadow of** someone or **in their shadow**, their achievements and abilities are so great that you are not noticed or valued. ❑ *He has always lived in the shadow of his brother.*

shad|ow box|ing 1 N-UNCOUNT **Shadow boxing** is a form of physical exercise or training in which you move your hands and feet as if you are boxing someone. **2** N-UNCOUNT If you describe what two people or groups are doing as **shadow boxing**, you mean that they seem to be taking action against each other but in fact are not serious about the dispute. ❑ *...the tedious shadow boxing that we normally see between bosses and workers.*

shad|owy /ʃædoʊi/ **1** ADJ A **shadowy** place is dark or full of shadows. ❑ *I watched him from a shadowy corner.* **2** ADJ [ADJ n] A **shadowy** figure or shape is someone or something that you can hardly see because they are in a dark place. ❑ *...a tall, shadowy figure silhouetted against the pale wall.* **3** ADJ You describe activities and people as **shadowy** when very little is known about them. ❑ *...the shadowy world of spies.*

shady /ʃeɪdi/ (shadier, shadiest) **1** ADJ You can describe a place as **shady** when you like the fact that it is sheltered from bright sunlight, for example, by trees or buildings. ❑ *After flowering, place the pot in a shady spot in the garden.* **2** ADJ You can describe activities as **shady** when you think that they might be dishonest or illegal. You can also use **shady** to describe people who are involved in such activities. [DISAPPROVAL] ❑ *In the 1980s, the company was notorious for shady deals.*

shaft /ʃæft/ (shafts) **1** N-COUNT A **shaft** is a long vertical passage, for example, for an elevator. ❑ *The fire began in an elevator shaft and spread to the roof.* **2** N-COUNT In a machine, a **shaft** is a rod that turns around continually in order to transfer movement in the machine. ❑ *...a drive shaft.* **3** N-COUNT A **shaft** is a long thin piece of wood or metal that forms part of a spear, ax, golf club, or other object. ❑ *...golf clubs with steel shafts.* **4** N-COUNT A **shaft** of light is a beam of light, for example, sunlight shining through an opening. ❑ *A brilliant shaft of sunlight burst through the doorway.*

shag|gy /ʃægi/ (shaggier, shaggiest) ADJ **Shaggy** hair or fur is long and messy. ❑ *Tim, who still has longish, shaggy hair, used to turn up at official dinners in jeans and T-shirt.*

Shah /ʃɑ/ (Shahs) N-PROPER [the N] In former times, **the Shah** of Iran was its ruler.

shaikh /ʃeɪk/ → see sheikh

shake ♦◆◇ /ʃeɪk/ (shakes, shaking, shook, shaken) **1** V-T If you **shake** something, you hold it and move it quickly backward and forward or up and down. You can also **shake** a person, for example, because you are angry with them or because you want them to wake up. ❑ *The nurse took the thermometer, shook it, and put it under my armpit.* • N-COUNT **Shake** is also a noun. ❑ *She picked up the bag of salad and gave it a shake.* **2** V-T If you **shake** yourself or your body, you make a lot of quick, small, repeated movements without moving from the place where you are. ❑ *As soon as he got inside, the dog shook himself.* • N-COUNT **Shake** is also a noun. ❑ *Take some slow, deep breaths and give your body a bit*

of a shake. **3** V-T If you **shake** your head, you turn it from side to side in order to say 'no' or to show disbelief or sadness. ❑ *"Anything else?" Chris asked. Kathryn shook her head wearily.* • N-COUNT **Shake** is also a noun. ❑ *"The elm trees are all dying," said Palmer, with a sad shake of his head.* **4** V-I If you **are shaking**, or a part of your body **is shaking**, you are making quick, small movements that you cannot control, for example, because you are cold or afraid. ❑ *He roared with laughter, shaking in his chair.* ❑ *My hand shook so much that I could hardly hold the microphone.* **5** V-T If you **shake** your fist or an object such as a stick at someone, you wave it in the air in front of them because you are angry with them. ❑ *The colonel rushed up to Earle and shook his gun at him.* **6** V-T/V-I If a force **shakes** something, or if something **shakes**, it moves from side to side or up and down with quick, small, but sometimes violent movements. ❑ *...an explosion that shook buildings several kilometers away.* **7** V-T To **shake** something into a certain place or state means to bring it into that place or state by moving it quickly up and down or from side to side. ❑ *She shook some pepper onto her sandwich.* **8** V-I If your voice **is shaking**, you cannot control it properly and it sounds very unsteady, for example, because you are nervous or angry. ❑ *His voice shaking with rage, he asked how the committee could keep such a report from the public.* **9** V-T If an event or a piece of news **shakes** you, or **shakes** your confidence, it makes you feel upset and unable to think calmly. ❑ *There was no doubt that the news of Tandy's escape had shaken them all.* **10** V-T If an event **shakes** a group of people or their beliefs, it causes great uncertainty and makes them question their beliefs. ❑ *The five years she spent as a news correspondent in Moscow were five years that shook the world.* **11** PHRASE If you **shake** someone's **hand** or **shake** someone **by the hand**, you shake hands with them. ❑ *I said congratulations and walked over to him and shook his hand.* **12** PHRASE If you **shake hands** with someone, you take their right hand in your own for a few moments, often moving it up and down slightly, when you are saying hello or goodbye to them, congratulating them, or agreeing on something. You can also say that two people **shake hands**. ❑ *He nodded greetings to Mary Ann and Michael and shook hands with Burke.* **13** → See feature box at **body language**
▶ **shake down** **1** PHRASAL VERB If someone **shakes** you **down**, they use threats or search you physically in order to obtain something from you. [AM] ❑ *He accused the lawyer of shaking him down.* ❑ *...crooks who had tried to shake down other hotels.* **2** → see also **shakedown**
▶ **shake off** **1** PHRASAL VERB If you **shake off** something that you do not want such as an illness or a bad habit, you manage to recover from it or get rid of it. ❑ *Businessmen are frantically trying to shake off the bad habits learned under six decades of a protected economy.* **2** PHRASAL VERB If you **shake off** someone who is following you, you manage to get away from them, for example, by running faster than them. ❑ *Although I could pass him I could not shake him off.*
▶ **shake out** PHRASAL VERB If you wonder how something will **shake out**, you wonder how it will develop and what the outcome will be. [AM] ❑ *We don't know how this situation will shake out.*
▶ **shake up** **1** PHRASAL VERB If someone **shakes up** something such as an organization, an institution, or a profession, they make major changes to it. ❑ *The government wanted to accelerate the reform of the institutions, to find new ways of shaking up the country.* **2** → see also **shakeup**

shake|down /ʃeɪkdaʊn/ (**shakedowns**) **1** N-COUNT If an organization or system is given a **shakedown**, it is thoroughly reorganized in order to make it more efficient. **2** N-COUNT A **shakedown** is an illegal or deceitful attempt to get money from someone, for example by swindling or blackmailing them. [AM, INFORMAL] ❑ *Janie's lawyers say his lawsuits are just a shakedown.* **3** N-COUNT A **shakedown** of a boat, plane, or car is its final test before it starts to be used.

shak|en /ʃeɪkən/ Shaken is the past participle of **shake**.

shake|out /ʃeɪkaʊt/ (**shakeouts**)

in BRIT, use **shake-out**

N-COUNT [usu sing] A **shakeout** is a major set of changes in a system or an organization which results in a large number of companies closing or a large number of people losing their jobs. [JOURNALISM] ❑ *This should be the year of a big shakeout in Italian banking.*

Shak|er /ʃeɪkər/ (**Shakers**) **1** N-COUNT A **Shaker** is a member of an American religious group whose members live in communities and have a very simple life. **2** ADJ [ADJ n] **Shaker** furniture is usually made of wood and has a very simple design.

shake|up /ʃeɪkʌp/ (**shakeups**)

in BRIT, use **shake-up**

N-COUNT A **shakeup** is a major set of changes in an organization or a system. [JOURNALISM] ❑ *Community leaders say a complete departmental shakeup is needed.*

shaky /ʃeɪki/ (**shakier**, **shakiest**) **1** ADJ If you describe a situation as **shaky**, you mean that it is weak or unstable, and seems unlikely to last long or be successful. ❑ *A shaky ceasefire is holding after three days of fighting between rival groups.* **2** ADJ If your body or your voice is **shaky**, you cannot control it properly and it shakes, for example, because you are ill or nervous. ❑ *We have all had a shaky hand and a dry mouth before speaking in public.*

shale /ʃeɪl/ (**shales**) **1** N-MASS **Shale** is smooth, soft rock that breaks easily into thin layers. **2** → See also color supplement

shale gas N-UNCOUNT **Shale gas** is a natural gas that is removed from rock by forcing liquid and sand into the rock. ❑ *This area has huge deposits of shale gas.*

shall ♦♦◊ /ʃəl, STRONG ʃæl/

Shall is a modal verb. It is used with the base form of a verb.

1 MODAL You use **shall** with 'I' and 'we' in questions in order to make offers or suggestions, or to ask for advice. ❑ *Shall I get the keys?* ❑ *Well, shall we go?* ❑ *Let's have a nice little stroll, shall we?* **2** MODAL You use **shall**, usually with 'I' and 'we,' when you are referring to something that you intend to do, or when you are referring to something that you are sure will happen to you in the future. [FORMAL] ❑ *We shall be landing in Paris in sixteen minutes, exactly on time.* ❑ *I shall know more next month, I hope.* **3** MODAL You use **shall** with 'I' or 'we' during a speech or piece of writing to say what you are going to discuss or explain later. [FORMAL] ❑ *In Chapter 3, I shall describe some of the documentation that I gathered.* **4** MODAL You use **shall** to indicate that something must happen, usually because of a rule or law. You use **shall not** to indicate that something must not happen. ❑ *The president shall hold office for five years.* **5** MODAL You use **shall**, usually with 'you,' when you are telling someone that they will be able to do or have something they want. ❑ *Very well, if you want to go, go you shall.*

shal|lot /ʃəlɒt/ (**shallots**) N-VAR **Shallots** are small, round vegetables that are similar to onions. They have a strong taste and are used for flavoring other food.

shal|low /ʃæloʊ/ (**shallower**, **shallowest**) **1** ADJ A **shallow** container, hole, or area of water measures only a short distance from the top to the bottom. ❑ *Put the milk in a shallow dish.* **2** ADJ If you describe a person, piece of work, or idea as **shallow**, you disapprove of them because they do not show or involve any serious or careful thought. [DISAPPROVAL] ❑ *I think he is shallow, vain and untrustworthy.* **3** ADJ If your breathing is **shallow**, you take only a very small amount of air into your lungs at each breath. ❑ *She began to hear her own taut, shallow breathing.*

shal|lows /ʃæloʊz/ N-PLURAL [the N] **The shallows** are the shallow part of an area of water. ❑ *At dusk more fish come into the shallows.*

shalt /ʃəlt, STRONG ʃælt/ MODAL **Shalt** is an old-fashioned form of **shall**. ❑ *Thou shalt not kill.*

sham /ʃæm/ (**shams**) N-COUNT Something that is a **sham** is not real or is not really what it seems to be. [DISAPPROVAL] ❑ *The government's promises were exposed as a hollow sham.*

sham|an /ʃeɪmən/ (**shamans**) **1** N-COUNT A **shaman** is a priest or priestess in shamanism. **2** N-COUNT Among some Native American peoples, a **shaman** is a person who is believed to have powers to heal sick people or to remove evil spirits from them.

sham|an|ism /ʃeɪmənɪzəm/ N-UNCOUNT **Shamanism** is a religion which is based on the belief that the world is controlled by good and evil spirits, and that these spirits can be directed by people with special powers.

sham|ble /ʃæmbᵊl/ (shambles, shambling, shambled) VERB If you **shamble** somewhere, you walk clumsily, pulling your feet along the ground. [LITERARY] ☐ *The conductor shambled to the next car.* ☐ *...his tall, shambling figure.*

sham|bles /ʃæmbᵊlz/ N-SING If a place, event, or situation is a **shambles** or is **in a shambles**, everything is in disorder. ☐ *The ship's interior was an utter shambles.*

shame ◆◇◇ /ʃeɪm/ (shames, shaming, shamed) **1** N-UNCOUNT **Shame** is an uncomfortable feeling that you get when you have done something wrong or embarrassing, or when someone close to you has. ☐ *She felt a deep sense of shame.* ☐ *Her father and her brothers would die of shame.* **2** N-UNCOUNT If someone brings **shame** on you, they make other people lose their respect for you. ☐ *I don't want to bring shame on the family name.* **3** V-T If something **shames** you, it causes you to feel shame. ☐ *Her son's affair had humiliated and shamed her.* **4** V-T If you **shame** someone into doing something, you force them to do it by making them feel ashamed not to. ☐ *He would not let neighbors shame him into silence.* **5** N-SING If you say that something is a **shame**, you are expressing your regret about it and indicating that you wish it had happened differently. [FEELINGS] ☐ *It's a crying shame that police have to put up with these mindless attacks.* **6** CONVENTION You can use **shame** in expressions such as **shame on you** and **shame on them** to indicate that someone ought to feel shame for something they have said or done. [FEELINGS] ☐ *He tried to deny it. Shame on him!* **7** PHRASE If someone **puts** you **to shame**, they make you feel ashamed because they do something much better than you do. ☐ *His playing really put me to shame.*

shame|faced /ʃeɪmfeɪst/ ADJ If you are **shamefaced**, you feel embarrassed because you have done something that you know you should not have done. [FORMAL] ☐ *There was a long silence, and my father looked shamefaced.*

shame|ful /ʃeɪmfəl/ ADJ If you describe a person's action or attitude as **shameful**, you think that it is so bad that the person ought to be ashamed. [DISAPPROVAL] ☐ *...the most shameful episode in U.S. naval history.* • **shame|ful|ly** ADV ☐ *At times they have been shamefully neglected.*

shame|less /ʃeɪmlɪs/ ADJ If you describe someone as **shameless**, you mean that they should be ashamed of their behavior, which is unacceptable to other people. [DISAPPROVAL] ☐ *...a shameless attempt to stifle democratic debate.* • **shame|less|ly** ADV ☐ *...a shamelessly lazy week-long trip.*

sham|poo /ʃæmpuː/ (shampoos, shampooing, shampooed) **1** N-MASS **Shampoo** is a soapy liquid that you use for washing your hair. ☐ *...a bottle of shampoo.* **2** V-T When you **shampoo** your hair, you wash it using shampoo. ☐ *Shampoo your hair and dry it.*

━━━ **WORD HISTORY** ━━━
shampoo
A **shampoo** was originally a massage rather than a wash. The word 'shampoo' comes from the Hindi verb *chāmpnā*, meaning 'press,' 'knead,' or 'massage.'

sham|rock /ʃæmrɒk/ (shamrocks) N-COUNT A **shamrock** is a small plant with three round leaves on each stem. The shamrock is the national symbol of Ireland.

shank /ʃæŋk/ (shanks) **1** N-COUNT The **shank** of an object is the long, thin, straight part of the object. ☐ *These hooks are sharp with long shanks.* **2** N-COUNT [usu pl] **Shanks** are the lower parts of the legs; used especially with reference to meat. ☐ *Turn the shanks and baste them once or twice as they cook.*

shan't /ʃænt/ **Shan't** is the usual spoken form of 'shall not.'

shan|ty /ʃænti/ (shanties) **1** N-COUNT A **shanty** is a small rough hut which poor people live in, built from tin, cardboard, or other materials that are not very strong. **2** N-COUNT A **shanty** is a song which sailors used to sing while they were doing work on a ship.

shanty|town /ʃæntitaʊn/ (shantytowns) also **shanty town** N-COUNT A **shantytown** is a collection of rough huts which poor people live in, usually in or near a large city.

shape ◆◇◇ /ʃeɪp/ (shapes, shaping, shaped) **1** N-COUNT [oft N of n, also in n] The **shape** of an object, a person, or an area is the appearance of their outside edges or surfaces, for example, whether they are round, square, curved, or fat. ☐ *Each mirror is made to order and can be designed to almost any shape or size.* ☐ *...little pens in the shape of baseball bats.* ☐ *...sofas and chairs of contrasting shapes and colors.* **2** N-COUNT You can refer to something that you can see as a **shape** if you cannot see it clearly, or if its outline is the clearest or most striking aspect of it. ☐ *The great gray shape of a tank rolled out of the village.* **3** N-COUNT A **shape** is a space enclosed by an outline, for example, a circle, a square, or a triangle. ☐ *Imagine a sort of a kidney shape.* **4** N-SING The **shape** of something that is planned or organized is its structure and character. ☐ *The last two weeks have seen a lot of talk about the future shape of Europe.* **5** V-T Someone or something that **shapes** a situation or an activity has a very great influence on the way it develops. ☐ *Like it or not, our families shape our lives and make us what we are.* **6** V-T If you **shape** an object, you give it a particular shape, using your hands or a tool. ☐ *Cut the dough in half and shape each half into a loaf.* **7** → see also **shaped** **8** PHRASE If you say, for example, that you will not accept something **in any shape or form**, or **in any way, shape, or form**, you are emphasizing that you will not accept it in any circumstances. [EMPHASIS] ☐ *I don't condone violence in any shape or form.* **9** PHRASE If someone or something is **in shape**, or **in good shape**, they are in a good state of health or in a good condition. If they are **in bad shape**, they are in a bad state of health or in a bad condition. ☐ *...the Fatburner Diet Book, a comprehensive guide to getting in shape.* ☐ *He was still in better shape than many young men.* **10** PHRASE If you **lick**, **knock**, or **whip** someone or something **into shape**, you use whatever methods are necessary to change or improve them so that they are in the condition that you want them to be in. ☐ *You'll have four months in which to lick the recruits into shape.* **11** PHRASE If something is **out of shape**, it is no longer in its proper or original shape, for example, because it has been damaged or wrongly handled. ☐ *Once most wires are bent out of shape, they don't return to the original position.* **12** PHRASE If you are **out of shape**, you are unhealthy and unable to do a lot of physical activity without getting tired. ☐ *I weighed 245 pounds and was out of shape.* **13** PHRASE When something **takes shape**, it develops or starts to appear in such a way that it becomes fairly clear what its final form will be. ☐ *In 1912 women's events were added, and the modern Olympic program began to take shape.*
▸ **shape up 1** PHRASAL VERB If something is **shaping up**, it is starting to develop or seems likely to happen. ☐ *There are also indications that a major tank battle may be shaping up for tonight.* ☐ *The accident is already shaping up as a significant environmental disaster.* **2** PHRASAL VERB If you ask how someone or something **is shaping up**, you want to know how well they are doing in a particular situation or activity. ☐ *I did have a few worries about how Hugh and I would shape up as parents.* **3** PHRASAL VERB If you tell someone to **shape up**, you are telling them to start behaving in a sensible and responsible way. ☐ *They were given a year to shape up or risk losing their scholarships.*

shaped ◆◇◇ /ʃeɪpt/ ADJ [v-link ADJ] Something that is **shaped** like a particular object or in a particular way has the shape of that object or a shape of that type. ☐ *A new perfume from Russia came in a bottle shaped like a diamond.*

-shaped /-ʃeɪpt/ COMB IN ADJ **-shaped** combines with nouns to form adjectives that describe the shape of an object. ☐ *...large, heart-shaped leaves.* ☐ *...an L-shaped couch.*

shape|less /ʃeɪplɪs/ ADJ [usu ADJ n] Something that is **shapeless** does not have a distinct or attractive shape. ☐ *Aunt Mary wore shapeless black dresses.*

shape|ly /ʃeɪpli/ (shapelier, shapeliest) ADJ [usu ADJ n] If you describe a woman as **shapely**, you mean that she has an attractively curvy body. [APPROVAL] ☐ *...their shapely legs.*

shard /ʃɑːrd/ (shards) N-COUNT [oft N of n] **Shards** are pieces of broken glass, pottery, or metal. ☐ *Eyewitnesses spoke of rocks and shards of glass flying in the air.*

share ◆◆◆ /ʃɛər/ (shares, sharing, shared) **1** N-COUNT A company's **shares** are the many equal parts into which its ownership is divided. Shares can be bought by people as an investment. [BUSINESS] ☐ *People in China are eager to buy shares in*

new businesses. ◻ V-RECIP If you **share** something with another person, you both have it, use it, or occupy it. You can also say that two people **share** something. ◻ *...the small income he had shared with his brother from his father's estate.* ◻ *Two Americans will share this year's Nobel Prize for Medicine.* ◻ V-RECIP If you **share** a task, duty, or responsibility with someone, you each carry out or accept part of it. You can also say that two people **share** something. ◻ *You can find out whether they are prepared to share the cost of the flowers with you.* ◻ V-RECIP If you **share** an experience with someone, you have the same experience, often because you are with them at the time. You can also say that two people **share** something. ◻ *Yes, I want to share my life with you.* ◻ V-T [no cont] If you **share** someone's opinion, you agree with them. ◻ *The forum's members share his view that business can be a positive force for change in developing countries.* ◻ V-RECIP [no cont] If one person or thing **shares** a quality or characteristic with another, they have the same quality or characteristic. You can also say that two people or things **share** something. ◻ *La Repubblica and El Pais are politically independent newspapers which share similar characteristics.* ◻ V-T/V-I If you **share** something that you have with someone, you give some of it to them or let them use it. ◻ *He shared his food with the family.* ◻ *Scientists now have to compete for funding, and do not share information among themselves.* ◻ *I wanted everybody to share.* ◻ V-T If you **share** something personal such as a thought or a piece of news with someone, you tell them about it. ◻ *It can be beneficial to share your feelings with someone you trust.* ◻ V-T If you **share** something such as a message, photograph, or link, you post it on social media so that other people can see it. ◻ *With your smartphone you can take great pictures and share them instantly.* ◻ *Social media platforms are always encouraging us to share.* ◻ N-COUNT If something is divided or distributed among a number of different people or things, each of them has, or is responsible for, a **share** of it. ◻ *Sara also pays a share of the gas, electricity and phone bills.* ◻ N-COUNT If you have or do your **share** of something, you have or do an amount that seems reasonable to you, or to other people. ◻ *Women must receive their fair share of training for well-paying jobs.* ◻ → see also **lion's share**, **market share**, **power-sharing** ◻ → See feature box at **banking**
▶ **share out** PHRASAL VERB If you **share out** an amount of something, you give each person in a group an equal or fair part of it.

share capi|tal N-UNCOUNT A company's **share capital** is the money that shareholders invest in order to start or expand the business. [BUSINESS] ◻ *The bank has a share capital of almost 100 million dollars.*

share|crop|per /ʃɛərkrɒpər/ (**sharecroppers**) N-COUNT A **sharecropper** is a farmer who pays the rent for their land with some of the crops they produce.

share|holder /ʃɛərhoʊldər/ (**shareholders**) N-COUNT A **shareholder** is a person who owns shares in a company. [BUSINESS] ◻ *...a shareholders' meeting.*

share|holding /ʃɛərhoʊldɪŋ/ (**shareholdings**) N-COUNT If you have a **shareholding** in a company, you own some of its shares. [BUSINESS] ◻ *She will retain her very significant shareholding in the company.*

share in|dex (**share indices** or **share indexes**) N-COUNT A **share index** is a number that indicates the state of a stock market. It is based on the combined share prices of a set of companies. [BUSINESS] ◻ *The share index was up 16.4 points to 1,599.6.*

share is|sue (**share issues**) N-COUNT When there is a **share issue**, shares in a company are made available for people to buy. [BUSINESS] ◻ *The deal will be financed by a share issue that will raise $128.9 million.*

share op|tion (**share options**) N-COUNT A **share option** is the same as a **stock option**. [BRIT, BUSINESS]

share-out (**share-outs**) N-COUNT [usu sing] If there is a **share-out** of something, several people are given equal or fair parts of it. ◻ *...the share-out of seats in the transitional government.*

share shop (**share shops**) N-COUNT A **share shop** is a store or internet website where members of the public can buy shares in companies. [BUSINESS]

share|ware /ʃɛərwɛər/ N-UNCOUNT **Shareware** is computer software that you can try before deciding whether or not to buy the legal right to use it. [COMPUTING] ◻ *...a shareware program.*

shark /ʃɑrk/ (**shark**)

The plural can also be **sharks**.

N-VAR A **shark** is a very large fish. Some sharks have very sharp teeth and may attack people.

sharp /ʃɑrp/ (**sharps**, **sharper**, **sharpest**) ◻ ADJ A **sharp** point or edge is very thin and can cut through things very easily. A **sharp** knife, tool, or other object has a point or edge of this kind. ◻ *With a sharp knife, make diagonal slashes in the chicken breast.* ◻ ADJ You can describe a shape or an object as **sharp** if part of it or one end of it comes to a point or forms an angle. ◻ *His nose was thin and sharp.* ◻ ADJ A **sharp** bend or turn is one that changes direction suddenly. ◻ *I was approaching a fairly sharp bend that swept downhill to the left.* • ADV [ADV adv] **Sharp** is also an adverb. ◻ *Do not cross the bridge but turn sharp left to go down on to the towpath.* • **sharp|ly** ADV [ADV after v] ◻ *Room number nine was at the far end of the corridor where it turned sharply to the right.* ◻ ADJ If you describe someone as **sharp**, you are praising them because they are quick to notice, hear, understand, or react to things. [APPROVAL] ◻ *He is very sharp, a quick thinker and swift with repartee.* ◻ ADJ If someone says something in a **sharp** way, they say it suddenly and rather firmly or angrily, for example, because they are warning or criticizing you. ◻ *"Don't contradict your mother," was Charles's sharp reprimand.* • **sharp|ly** ADV ◻ *"You've known," she said sharply, "and you didn't tell me?"* ◻ ADJ A **sharp** change, movement, or feeling occurs suddenly, and is great in amount, force, or degree. ◻ *There's been a sharp rise in the rate of inflation.* ◻ *Tennis requires a lot of short sharp movements.* • **sharp|ly** ADV ◻ *Unemployment has risen sharply in recent years.* ◻ ADJ A **sharp** difference, image, or sound is very easy to see, hear, or distinguish. ◻ *Many people make a sharp distinction between humans and other animals.* ◻ *All the footmarks are quite sharp and clear.* • **sharp|ly** ADV ◻ *Opinions on this are sharply divided.* • **sharp|ness** N-UNCOUNT ◻ *The telescope shows us our Universe with wonderful sharpness and clarity.* ◻ ADJ A **sharp** taste or smell is rather strong or bitter, but is often also clear and fresh. ◻ *The apple tasted just as I remembered – sharp, sour, yet sweet.* ◻ ADV [n ADV] **Sharp** is used after stating a particular time to show that something happens at exactly the time stated. ◻ *She planned to unlock the store at 8:00 sharp this morning.* ◻ N-COUNT **Sharp** is used after a letter representing a musical note to show that the note should be played or sung half a tone higher. **Sharp** is often represented by the symbol ♯. ◻ *A solitary viola plucks a lonely, soft F sharp.*

sharp|en /ʃɑrpən/ (**sharpens**, **sharpening**, **sharpened**) ◻ V-T/V-I If your senses, understanding, or skills **sharpen** or **are sharpened**, you become better at noticing things, thinking, or doing something. ◻ *Her gaze sharpened, as if she had seen something unusual.* ◻ *He will need to sharpen his diplomatic skills in order to work with Congress.* ◻ V-T If you **sharpen** an object, you make its edge very thin or you make its end pointed. ◻ *He started to sharpen his knife.*

sharp|en|er /ʃɑrpənər/ (**sharpeners**) N-COUNT A **sharpener** is a tool or machine used for sharpening pencils or knives. ◻ *...a pencil sharpener.*

sharp-eyed ADJ [usu ADJ n] A **sharp-eyed** person is good at noticing and observing things. ◻ *A sharp-eyed store clerk spotted the fake.*

sharp|shooter /ʃɑrpʃutər/ (**sharpshooters**) N-COUNT A **sharpshooter** is a person who can fire a gun very accurately. [AM]

sharp tongue (**sharp tongues**) N-COUNT If you say that someone has a **sharp tongue**, you are critical of the fact that they say things which are unkind though often clever. [DISAPPROVAL] ◻ *Despite her sharp tongue, she inspires loyalty from her friends.*

sharp-tongued ADJ [usu ADJ n] If you describe someone as **sharp-tongued**, you are being critical of them for speaking in a way which is unkind though often clever. [DISAPPROVAL] ◻ *Julia was a very tough, sharp-tongued woman.*

shat /ʃæt/ **Shat** is the past tense and past participle of **shit**.

shat|ter /ʃætər/ (**shatters**, **shattering**, **shattered**) ◻ V-T/V-I If something **shatters** or **is shattered**, it breaks into a lot of small pieces. ◻ *...safety glass that won't shatter if it's broken.* ◻ *The car shattered into a thousand burning pieces in a 200 mph crash.* • **shat|ter|ing** N-UNCOUNT ◻ *...the shattering of glass.* ◻ V-T If something **shatters** your dreams, hopes, or beliefs, it

shattered completely destroys them. ❑ *A failure would shatter the hopes of many people.* ❸ V-T If someone **is shattered** by an event, it shocks and upsets them very much. ❑ *He had been shattered by his son's death.* ❹ → see also **shattered, shattering**

shat|tered /ʃætərd/ ADJ If you are **shattered** by something, you are extremely shocked and upset about it. ❑ *It is desperately sad news and I am absolutely shattered to hear it.*

shat|ter|ing /ʃætərɪŋ/ ❶ ADJ Something that is **shattering** shocks and upsets you very much. ❑ *The experience of their daughter's death had been absolutely shattering.* ❷ → see also **shatter, earth-shattering**

shave /ʃeɪv/ (shaves, shaving, shaved) ❶ V-T/V-I When you **shave**, you remove the hair from your face using a razor or shaver so that your face is smooth. ❑ *He took a bath and shaved before dinner.* ❑ *He had shaved his face until it was smooth.* • N-COUNT **Shave** is also a noun. ❑ *He never seemed to need a shave.* • **shav|ing** N-UNCOUNT ❑ *...a range of shaving products.* ❷ V-T If you **shave off** part of a piece of wood or other material, you cut very thin pieces from it. ❑ *I set the log on the ground and shaved off the bark.* ❸ V-T If you **shave** a small amount off something such as a record, cost, or price, you reduce it by that amount. ❑ *She's already shaved four seconds off the national record for the mile.* ❹ → see also **shaving** ❺ PHRASE If you describe a situation as a **close shave**, you mean that there was nearly an accident or a disaster but it was avoided. ❑ *I can't quite believe the close shaves I've had just recently.*

> **USAGE**
> **shave**
> **Shave** is not usually a reflexive verb. Don't say 'He had a bath and shaved himself.' Say 'He had a bath and **shaved**.'

shav|en /ʃeɪvən/ ❶ ADJ If a part of someone's body is **shaven**, it has been shaved. ❑ *...a small boy with a shaven head.* ❷ → see also **clean-shaven**

shav|er /ʃeɪvər/ (shavers) N-COUNT A **shaver** is an electric device, used for shaving hair from the face and body. ❑ *...men's electric shavers.*

shav|ing /ʃeɪvɪŋ/ (shavings) ❶ N-COUNT **Shavings** are small very thin pieces of wood or other material which have been cut from a larger piece. ❑ *The floor was covered with shavings from his wood carvings.* ❷ → see also **shave**

shav|ing cream (shaving creams) also **shaving foam** N-MASS **Shaving cream** is a soft soapy substance which you put on your skin before you shave. ❑ *...a can of shaving cream.*

shawl /ʃɔl/ (shawls) N-COUNT A **shawl** is a large piece of woolen cloth which a woman wears over her shoulders or head, or which is wrapped around a baby to keep it warm.

she ♦♦♦ /ʃi, STRONG ʃiː/

> **She** is a third person singular pronoun. **She** is used as the subject of a verb.

❶ PRON-SING You use **she** to refer to a woman, girl, or female animal who has already been mentioned or whose identity is clear. ❑ *When Ann arrived home that night, she found Brian in the house watching TV.* ❑ *She was seventeen and she had no education or employment.* ❷ PRON-SING Some writers may use **she** to refer to a person who is not identified as either male or female. Many people prefer to use 'he or she' or 'they' as an alternative to 'she'. ❑ *The student may show signs of feeling the strain of responsibility and she may give up.* ❸ PRON-SING **She** is sometimes used to refer to a country or nation. ❑ *The country needs new leadership if she is to play a role in future development.* ❹ PRON-SING Some people use **she** to refer to a car or machine. People who sail often use **she** to refer to a ship or boat. Some people think it is better to refer to these things as 'it.' ❑ *The Seaflower was being repaired, but soon she was fit to sail again.*

s/he PRON Some writers use **s/he** instead of either 'he' or 'she' when they are referring to someone who has not been identified. By using **s/he**, the writer does not need to say whether the person is male or female. ❑ *Talk to your doctor and see if s/he knows of any local groups.*

sheaf /ʃiːf/ (sheaves) ❶ N-COUNT [usu N of n] A **sheaf** of papers is a number of them held or fastened together. ❑ *He took out a sheaf of papers and leafed through them.* ❷ N-COUNT A **sheaf** of corn or wheat is a number of corn or wheat plants that have been cut down and tied together.

shear /ʃɪər/ (shears, shearing, sheared, sheared or shorn) ❶ V-T To **shear** a sheep means to cut its wool off. ❑ *Competitors have six minutes to shear four sheep.* • **shear|ing** N-UNCOUNT ❑ *...a display of sheep shearing.* ❷ N-PLURAL A pair of **shears** is a garden tool like a very large pair of scissors. Shears are used especially for cutting hedges. ❑ *Trim the shrubs with shears.* ❸ → See also color supplement

sheath /ʃiːθ/ (sheaths) N-COUNT A **sheath** is a covering for the blade of a knife.

sheathe /ʃiːð/ (sheathes, sheathing, sheathed) ❶ V-T [usu passive] If something **is sheathed** in a material or other covering, it is closely covered with it. [LITERARY] ❑ *His long legs were sheathed in leather pants.* ❑ *...the new edition of the magazine, sheathed in a plastic bag.* ❷ V-T When someone **sheathes** a knife, they put it in its sheath. [LITERARY] ❑ *He sheathed the knife and strapped it to his shin.*

sheaves /ʃiːvz/ **Sheaves** is the plural of **sheaf**.

she|bang /ʃɪbæŋ/ PHRASE **The whole shebang** is the whole situation or business that you are describing. [INFORMAL]

shed ♦♢♢ /ʃɛd/ (sheds, shedding)

> The form **shed** is used in the present tense and is the past tense and past participle of the verb.

❶ N-COUNT A **shed** is a small building that is used for storing things such as garden tools. ❑ *...a garden shed.* ❷ N-COUNT A **shed** is a large shelter or building, for example, at a train station, port, or factory. ❑ *...a vast factory shed.* ❸ V-T When a tree **sheds** its leaves, its leaves fall off in the autumn. When an animal **sheds** hair or skin, some of its hair or skin drops off. ❑ *Some of the trees were already beginning to shed their leaves.* ❹ V-T To **shed** something means to get rid of it. [FORMAL] ❑ *The firm is to shed 700 jobs.* ❺ V-T If you **shed** tears, you cry. ❑ *They will shed a few tears at their daughter's wedding.* ❻ V-T To **shed** blood means to kill people in a violent way. If someone **sheds** their blood, they are killed in a violent way, usually when they are fighting in a war. [FORMAL] ❑ *...young warriors, eager to shed blood.* ❼ **to shed light on something** → see **light** ①

she'd /ʃɪd, ʃiːd/ ❶ **She'd** is the usual spoken form of 'she had,' especially when 'had' is an auxiliary verb. ❑ *She'd been to clubs all over the world.* ❷ **She'd** is a spoken form of 'she would.' ❑ *She'd do anything for a bit of money.*

sheen /ʃiːn/ N-SING If something has a **sheen**, it has a smooth and gentle brightness on its surface. ❑ *The carpet had a silvery sheen to it.*

sheep /ʃiːp/ (sheep)

> **Sheep** is both the singular and the plural form.

N-COUNT A **sheep** is a farm animal which is covered with thick curly hair called wool. Sheep are kept for their wool or for their meat. ❑ *...grassland on which a flock of sheep were grazing.*

sheep|dog /ʃiːpdɒɡ/ (sheepdogs) N-COUNT A **sheepdog** is a breed of dog. Some sheepdogs are used for controlling sheep.

sheep|ish /ʃiːpɪʃ/ ADJ If you look **sheepish**, you look slightly embarrassed because you feel foolish or you have done something silly. ❑ *I asked him why. He looked a little sheepish when he answered.* • **sheep|ish|ly** ADV ❑ *He grinned sheepishly.*

sheep|skin /ʃiːpskɪn/ (sheepskins) N-VAR [oft N n] **Sheepskin** is the skin of a sheep with the wool still attached to it, used especially for making coats and rugs. ❑ *...a sheepskin coat.*

sheer /ʃɪər/ (sheerer, sheerest) ❶ ADJ [ADJ n] You can use **sheer** to emphasize that a state or situation is complete and does not involve or is not mixed with anything else. [EMPHASIS] ❑ *His music is sheer delight.* ❑ *Sheer chance quite often plays an important part in sparking off an idea.* ❷ ADJ A **sheer** cliff or drop is extremely steep or completely vertical. ❑ *There was a sheer drop just outside my window.* ❸ ADJ **Sheer** material is very thin, light, and delicate. ❑ *...sheer black tights.*

sheet ♦♢♢ /ʃiːt/ (sheets) ❶ N-COUNT A **sheet** is a large rectangular piece of cotton or other cloth that you sleep on or cover yourself with in a bed. ❑ *Once a week, a maid changes the sheets.* ❷ N-COUNT A **sheet** of paper is a rectangular piece of paper. ❑ *...a sheet of newspaper.* ❸ N-COUNT You can use **sheet**

to refer to a piece of paper which gives information about something. ◻ ...information sheets on each country in the world. **4** N-COUNT A **sheet** of glass, metal, or wood is a large, flat, thin piece of it. ◻ ...a cracked sheet of glass. ◻ Overhead cranes were lifting giant sheets of steel. **5** N-COUNT A **sheet** of something is a thin wide layer of it over the surface of something else. ◻ ...a sheet of ice. **6** → see also **balance sheet, broadsheet, fact sheet, spreadsheet, worksheet**

sheet|ing /ʃiːtɪŋ/ N-UNCOUNT [oft n N] **Sheeting** is metal, plastic, or other material that is made in the form of sheets. ◻ They put plastic sheeting on the insides of our windows.

sheet met|al N-UNCOUNT **Sheet metal** is metal which has been made into thin sheets.

sheet mu|sic N-UNCOUNT **Sheet music** is music that is printed on sheets of paper without a hard cover. ◻ ...a copy of the sheet music to "Happy Days."

sheikh /ʃiːk, ʃeɪk/ (sheikhs) N-TITLE; N-COUNT A **sheikh** is a male Arab chief or ruler. ◻ ...Sheikh Khalifa.

sheikh|dom /ʃiːkdəm, ʃeɪk-/ (sheikhdoms) also **sheikdom** N-COUNT A **sheikhdom** is a country or region that is ruled by a sheikh.

shelf /ʃɛlf/ (shelves) **1** N-COUNT A **shelf** is a flat piece of wood, metal, or glass which is attached to a wall or to the sides of a cabinet. Shelves are used for keeping things on. ◻ He took a book from the shelf. **2** PHRASE If you buy something **off the shelf**, you buy something that is not specially made for you. ◻ Lower-priced jewelry will be sold off the shelf by this fall.

shelf life (shelf lives) N-COUNT [usu sing] The **shelf life** of a product, especially food, is the length of time that it can be kept in a store or at home before it becomes too old to sell or use. ◻ The meat is chemically treated to extend shelf life.

shell ✦✧✧ /ʃɛl/ (shells, shelling, shelled) **1** N-COUNT The **shell** of a nut or egg is the hard covering which surrounds it. ◻ They cracked the nuts and removed their shells. • N-UNCOUNT **Shell** is the substance that a shell is made of. ◻ ...beads made from ostrich egg shell. **2** N-COUNT The **shell** of an animal such as a tortoise, snail, or crab is the hard protective covering that it has around its body or on its back. ◻ ...the spiral form of a snail shell. **3** N-COUNT **Shells** are hard objects found on beaches. They are usually pink, white, or brown and are the coverings which used to surround small sea creatures. ◻ I collect shells and interesting seaside items. **4** V-T If you **shell** nuts, peas, shrimp, or other food, you remove their natural outer covering. ◻ She shelled and ate a few nuts. **5** N-COUNT If someone comes out of their **shell**, they become more friendly and interested in other people and less quiet, shy, and reserved. ◻ Her normally shy son had come out of his shell. **6** N-COUNT The **shell** of a building, boat, car, or other structure is the outside frame of it. ◻ ...the shells of burned buildings. **7** N-COUNT A **shell** is a weapon consisting of a metal container filled with explosives that can be fired from a large gun over long distances. ◻ Tanks fired shells at the house. **8** V-T To **shell** a place means to fire explosive shells at it. ◻ The rebels shelled the densely-populated suburbs near the port. • **shell|ing** (shellings) N-VAR ◻ Out on the streets, the shelling continued.

▶ **shell out** PHRASAL VERB If you **shell out** for something, you spend a lot of money on it. [INFORMAL] ◻ You won't have to shell out a fortune for it. ◻ ...an insurance policy which saves you from having to shell out for repairs.

she'll /ʃiːl, ʃɪl/ **She'll** is the usual spoken form of 'she will.' ◻ Sharon was a wonderful lady and I know she'll be greatly missed.

shel|lac /ʃəlæk/ N-UNCOUNT **Shellac** is a kind of natural varnish which you paint on to wood to give it a shiny surface.

shell com|pa|ny (shell companies) **1** N-COUNT A **shell company** is a company that another company takes over in order to use its name to gain an advantage. [BUSINESS] ◻ The U.S. shell company was set up to mount a bid for Kingston Communications. **2** N-COUNT A **shell company** is a company which does not conduct legitimate business but which has been officially registered, so that it can be used for fraud. [BUSINESS]

shell|fire /ʃɛlfaɪr/ N-UNCOUNT **Shellfire** is the firing of large military guns. ◻ The radio said other parts of the capital also came under shellfire.

shell|fish /ʃɛlfɪʃ/ (shellfish)

Shellfish is both the singular and the plural form.

N-VAR **Shellfish** are small creatures that live in the sea and have a shell. ◻ Fish and shellfish are the specialties.

shell pro|gram (shell programs) N-COUNT A **shell program** is a basic computer program that provides a framework within which the user can develop the program to suit their own needs. [COMPUTING]

shell shock also **shell-shock** N-UNCOUNT **Shell shock** is the confused or nervous mental condition of people who have been under fire in a war. ◻ The men were suffering from shell shock.

shell-shocked also **shell shocked 1** ADJ If you say that someone is **shell-shocked**, you mean that they are very shocked, usually because something bad has happened. [INFORMAL] ◻ We were shell-shocked when Toronto took the lead. ◻ ...shell-shocked investors. **2** ADJ If someone is **shell-shocked**, they have a confused or nervous mental condition as a result of a shocking experience such as being in a war or an accident. ◻ ...a shell-shocked war veteran.

shel|ter ✦✧✧ /ʃɛltər/ (shelters, sheltering, sheltered) **1** N-COUNT A **shelter** is a small building or covered place which is made to protect people from bad weather or danger. ◻ The city's bomb shelters were being prepared for possible air raids. **2** N-UNCOUNT If a place provides **shelter**, it provides you with a place to stay or live, especially when you need protection from bad weather or danger. ◻ The number of families seeking shelter rose by 17 percent. ◻ Although horses do not generally mind the cold, shelter from rain and wind is important. **3** N-COUNT A **shelter** is a building where homeless people can sleep and get food. ◻ ...a shelter for homeless women. **4** V-I If you **shelter** in a place, you stay there and are protected from bad weather or danger. ◻ ...a man sheltering in a doorway. **5** V-T [usu passive] If a place or thing **is sheltered** by something, it is protected by that thing from wind and rain. ◻ ...a wooden house, sheltered by a low pointed roof. **6** V-T If you **shelter** someone, usually someone who is being hunted by police or other people, you provide them with a place to stay or live. ◻ A neighbor sheltered the boy for seven days. **7** → See feature box at **poverty, storm**

shel|tered /ʃɛltərd/ **1** ADJ A **sheltered** place is protected from wind and rain. ◻ ...a shallow-sloping beach next to a sheltered bay. **2** ADJ If you say that someone has led a **sheltered** life, you mean that they have been protected from difficult or unpleasant experiences. ◻ Perhaps I've just led a really sheltered life. **3** ADJ [ADJ n] **Sheltered** accommodations or work is designed for people who are old or who have a disability. It allows them to be independent but also allows them to get help when they need it. ◻ Call the family service agencies to find out if they sponsor this kind of sheltered housing. **4** → see also **shelter**

shelve /ʃɛlv/ (shelves, shelving, shelved) **1** V-T If someone **shelves** a plan or project, they decide not to continue with it, either for a while or permanently. ◻ King County has shelved plans to build a driving range. **2** **Shelves** is the plural of **shelf**.

shelv|ing /ʃɛlvɪŋ/ N-UNCOUNT **Shelving** is a set of shelves, or material which is used for making shelves. ◻ ...the shelving on the long, windowless wall.

she|nani|gans /ʃɪnænɪɡənz/ N-PLURAL You can use **shenanigans** to refer to slightly dishonest or immoral behavior, especially when you think it is amusing or interesting. [INFORMAL] ◻ ...the private shenanigans of public figures.

shep|herd /ʃɛpərd/ (shepherds, shepherding, shepherded) **1** N-COUNT A **shepherd** is a person whose job is to look after sheep. **2** V-T [usu passive] If you **are shepherded** somewhere, someone takes you there to make sure that you arrive at the right place safely. ◻ She was shepherded by her guards up the rear ramp of the aircraft.

shep|herd|ess /ʃɛpərdɪs/ (shepherdesses) N-COUNT A **shepherdess** is a woman whose job is to take care of sheep.

sher|bet /ʃɜrbɪt/ (sherbets) N-VAR **Sherbet** is like ice cream but made with fruit juice, sugar, and water. [AM] ◻ ...lemon sherbet.

in BRIT, use **sorbet**

sher|iff /ʃerɪf/ (sheriffs) N-COUNT; N-TITLE In the United States, a **sheriff** is a person who is elected to make sure that the law is obeyed in a particular county. ❏ ...*the local sheriff.*

sher|ry /ʃeri/ (sherries) N-MASS **Sherry** is a type of strong wine that is made in southwestern Spain. It is usually drunk before a meal. ❏ *I poured us a glass of sherry.*

she's /ʃiz, ʃɪz/ **1** **She's** is the usual spoken form of 'she is.' ❏ *She's an exceptionally good cook.* **2** **She's** is a spoken form of 'she has,' especially when 'has' is an auxiliary verb. ❏ *She's been married for seven years and has two daughters.*

shh /ʃ/ also **sh** CONVENTION You can say **'Shh!'** to tell someone to be quiet. [INFORMAL, SPOKEN] ❏ *Shh, don't wake Danny.*

shi|at|su /ʃiɑtsu/ N-UNCOUNT **Shiatsu** is a form of massage that is used to treat illness and reduce pain.

shib|bo|leth /ʃɪbəlɪθ, -lɛθ/ (shibboleths) N-COUNT If you describe an idea or belief as a **shibboleth**, you mean that it is thought important by a group of people but may be old-fashioned or wrong. [FORMAL] ❏ *It is time to go beyond the shibboleth that conventional forces cannot deter.*

shield /ʃild/ (shields, shielding, shielded) **1** N-COUNT Something or someone which is a **shield** against a particular danger or risk provides protection from it. ❏ *He used his left hand as a shield against the reflecting sunlight.* **2** V-T If something or someone **shields** you **from** a danger or risk, they protect you from it. ❏ *He shielded his head from the sun with an old sack.* **3** V-T If you **shield** your eyes, you put your hand above your eyes to protect them from direct sunlight. ❏ *He squinted and shielded his eyes.* **4** N-COUNT A **shield** is a large piece of metal or leather which soldiers used to carry to protect their bodies while they were fighting. ❏ *He clanged his sword three times on his shield.* **5** N-COUNT A **shield** is a sports prize or badge that is shaped like a shield.

shift ✦✧✧ /ʃɪft/ (shifts, shifting, shifted) **1** V-T/V-I If you **shift** something or if it **shifts**, it moves slightly. ❏ *He stopped, shifting his cane to his left hand.* ❏ *He shifted from foot to foot.* **2** V-T/V-I If someone's opinion, a situation, or a policy **shifts** or is **shifted**, it changes slightly. ❏ *Attitudes to mental illness have shifted in recent years.* • N-COUNT [usu N prep] **Shift** is also a noun. ❏ *...a shift in government policy.* **3** V-T If someone **shifts** the responsibility or blame for something onto you, they unfairly make you responsible or make people blame you for it, instead of them. [DISAPPROVAL] ❏ *It was a vain attempt to shift the responsibility for the murder to somebody else.* **4** V-T If you **shift** gears in a car, you put the car into a different gear. [AM] ❏ *He shifts gears and pulls away slowly.*

in BRIT, use **change**

5 N-COUNT If a group of factory workers, nurses, or other people work **shifts**, they work for a set period before being replaced by another group, so that there is always a group working. Each of these set periods is called a **shift**. You can also use **shift** to refer to a group of workers who work together on a particular shift. ❏ *His father worked shifts in a steel mill.* **6** → See feature box at **working**

SYNONYMS

shift
VERB
1
move: *She moved the sheaf of papers into position.*
budge: *The window refused to budge.*
2
change: *In the union office, the mood gradually changed from resignation to rage.*
alter: *They have never altered their programs by a single day.*
revise: *He soon came to revise his opinion of the profession.*

---

shift|ing /ʃɪftɪŋ/ **1** ADJ [ADJ n] **Shifting** is used to describe something which is made up of parts that are continuously moving and changing position in relation to other parts. ❏ *The Croatian town of Ilok is a classic case of shifting populations.* **2** → see also **shift**

shift|less /ʃɪftlɪs/ ADJ If you describe someone as **shiftless**, you mean that they are lazy and have no desire to achieve anything. [DISAPPROVAL] ❏ *...a shiftless person*

shifty /ʃɪfti/ (shiftier, shiftiest) ADJ Someone who looks **shifty** gives the impression of being dishonest. [INFORMAL, DISAPPROVAL] ❏ *He had a shifty face and previous convictions.*

shih-tzu /ʃɪtsu/ (shih-tzus) also **Shih Tzu** N-COUNT A shih-tzu is a breed of small dog with short legs and long silky hair.

Shi|ite /ʃiaɪt/ (Shiites) also **Shi'ite** **1** N-COUNT **Shiites** are members of a branch of the Islamic religion which regards Mohammed's cousin Ali and his successors, rather than Mohammed himself, as the final authority on religious matters. ❏ *...the Shiites in southern Iraq.* **2** ADJ **Shiite** means relating to Shiites and their religious beliefs or practices. ❏ *...Shiite Muslims.* ❏ *Iraq's population is roughly half Shi'ite.*

shill /ʃɪl/ (shills) N-COUNT [oft N for n] If you refer to someone as a **shill**, you mean that they are paid to sell something or to participate in an activity in order to persuade others to buy or participate. [AM, INFORMAL, DISAPPROVAL] ❏ *He is tarnishing his reputation by being a shill for the tobacco industry.*

shilly-shally /ʃɪli ʃæli/ (shilly-shallies, shilly-shallying, shilly-shallied) V-I [usu cont] If you say that someone **is shilly-shallying**, you disapprove of the fact that they are hesitating when they should make a decision. [INFORMAL, DISAPPROVAL] ❏ *It's time for Brooke to stop shilly-shallying.*

shim|mer /ʃɪmər/ (shimmers, shimmering, shimmered) V-I If something **shimmers**, it shines with a faint, unsteady light or has an unclear, unsteady appearance. ❏ *The lights shimmered on the water.* • N-SING **Shimmer** is also a noun. ❏ *...a shimmer of starlight.*

shim|my /ʃɪmi/ (shimmies, shimmying, shimmied) V-I If you **shimmy**, you dance or move in a way that involves shaking your hips and shoulders from side to side. ❏ *Dancers shimmied in the streets.*

shin /ʃɪn/ (shins) N-COUNT Your **shins** are the front parts of your legs between your knees and your ankles. ❏ *She punched him on the nose and kicked him in the shins.*

shin|dig /ʃɪndɪg/ (shindigs) N-COUNT A **shindig** is a large, noisy, enjoyable party. [INFORMAL]

shine /ʃaɪn/ (shines, shining, shined or shone) **1** V-I When the sun or a light **shines**, it gives out bright light. ❏ *It is a mild morning and the sun is shining.* **2** V-T If you **shine** a flashlight or other light somewhere, you point it there, so that you can see something when it is dark. ❏ *One of the men shone a torch in his face.* ❏ *The man walked slowly toward her, shining the flashlight.* **3** V-I Something that **shines** is very bright and clear because it is reflecting light. ❏ *Her blue eyes shone and caught the light.* ❏ *...a pair of patent leather shoes that shone like mirrors.* **4** N-SING Something that has a **shine** is bright and clear because it is reflecting light. ❏ *This gel gives a beautiful shine to the hair.* **5** V-I Someone who **shines** at a skill or activity does it extremely well. ❏ *Did you shine at school?* **6** → see also **shining**

shin|gle /ʃɪŋg²l/ (shingles) **1** N-UNCOUNT **Shingle** is a mass of small rough pieces of stone on the shore of a sea or a river. ❏ *...a beach of sand and shingle.* **2** N-UNCOUNT **Shingles** is a disease in which painful red spots spread in bands over a person's body or face. **3** N-COUNT [usu pl] **Shingles** are thin pieces of wood or other material which are fixed in rows to cover a roof or wall. ❏ *The roofs had shingles missing.* **4** N-COUNT A **shingle** is a small sign that is hung outside a building, such as the place where a doctor or lawyer works. [AM] **5** PHRASE [v and n inflect] If you **hang out your shingle** or **hang out a shingle**, you start your own business. [AM] ❏ *She hung out her shingle under the name Designs by Pamela.* ❏ *The industry isn't regulated, so anybody can hang out a shingle.*

shin guard (shin guards) N-COUNT A **shin guard** is a thick piece of material that you wear inside your socks to protect the lower part of your leg when you are playing a game such as soccer.

shin|ing /ʃaɪnɪŋ/ **1** ADJ A **shining** achievement or quality is a very good one which should be greatly admired. ❏ *She is a shining example to us all.* **2** → see also **shine**

shin pad (shin pads) N-COUNT A **shin pad** is a thick piece of material that you wear inside your socks to protect the lower part of your leg when you are playing a game such as football or soccer.

Shin|to /ʃɪntoʊ/ N-UNCOUNT **Shinto** is the traditional religion of Japan.

shiny /ʃaɪni/ (**shinier, shiniest**) ADJ Shiny things are bright and reflect light. ❑ *Her blonde hair was shiny and clean.*

ship ✦✦◇ /ʃɪp/ (**ships, shipping, shipped**) **1** N-COUNT [also *by* N] A **ship** is a large boat which carries passengers or cargo. ❑ *Within ninety minutes the ship was ready for departure.* ❑ *We went by ship over to America.* **2** V-T [usu passive] If people, supplies, or goods **are shipped** somewhere, they are sent there on a ship or by some other means of transportation. ❑ *We'll ship your order to the address we print on your checks.* ❑ *Food is being shipped to drought-stricken Southern Africa.* **3** → see also **shipping** **4** → See also color supplement

ship|board /ʃɪpbɔrd/ ADJ [ADJ n] **Shipboard** means taking place on a ship. ❑ *Here's one shipboard romance that won't last the duration of the cruise.*

ship|builder /ʃɪpbɪldər/ (**shipbuilders**) N-COUNT A **shipbuilder** is a company or a person that builds ships.

ship|building /ʃɪpbɪldɪŋ/ N-UNCOUNT **Shipbuilding** is the industry of building ships.

ship|load /ʃɪploʊd/ (**shiploads**) N-COUNT [usu *n of* n] A **shipload** of people or goods is as many people or goods as a ship can carry. ❑ *...a shipload of refugees.*

ship|mate /ʃɪpmeɪt/ (**shipmates**) N-COUNT [oft poss N] Sailors who work together on the same ship are **shipmates**. ❑ *His shipmates stayed at their stations.*

ship|ment /ʃɪpmənt/ (**shipments**) **1** N-COUNT A **shipment** is an amount of a particular kind of cargo that is sent to another country on a ship, train, airplane, or other vehicle. ❑ *After that, food shipments to the port could begin in a matter of weeks.* **2** N-UNCOUNT The **shipment** of a cargo or goods somewhere is the sending of it there by ship, train, airplane, or some other vehicle. ❑ *Bananas are packed before being transported to the docks for shipment overseas.*

ship|owner /ʃɪpoʊnər/ (**shipowners**) N-COUNT A **shipowner** is someone who owns a ship or ships or who has shares in a shipping company.

ship|per /ʃɪpər/ (**shippers**) N-COUNT [usu pl] **Shippers** are people or companies who ship cargo as a business.

ship|ping /ʃɪpɪŋ/ **1** N-UNCOUNT [usu with supp] **Shipping** is the transportation of cargo or goods as a business, especially on ships. ❑ *...the international shipping industry.* ❑ *...a coupon for free shipping of your catalog order.* **2** N-UNCOUNT You can refer to the amount of money that you pay to a company to transport cargo or goods as **shipping**. ❑ *It is $39.95 plus $3 shipping.*

ship|shape /ʃɪpʃeɪp/ ADJ [usu v-link ADJ] If something is **shipshape**, it looks neat and in good condition. ❑ *The house only needs an occasional coat of paint to keep it shipshape.*

ship|wreck /ʃɪprɛk/ (**shipwrecks, shipwrecked**) **1** N-VAR If there is a **shipwreck**, a ship is destroyed in an accident at sea. ❑ *He was drowned in a shipwreck off the coast of Spain.* **2** N-COUNT A **shipwreck** is a ship which has been destroyed in an accident at sea. ❑ *More than 1,000 shipwrecks litter the coral reef ringing the islands.* **3** V-T PASSIVE If someone **is shipwrecked**, their ship is destroyed in an accident at sea but they survive and manage to reach land. ❑ *He was shipwrecked after visiting the island.*

ship|wright /ʃɪpraɪt/ (**shipwrights**) N-COUNT A **shipwright** is a person who builds or repairs ships as a job.

ship|yard /ʃɪpyɑrd/ (**shipyards**) N-COUNT A **shipyard** is a place where ships are built and repaired. ❑ *The Queen Mary 2 is currently docked at the shipyard.*

shirk /ʃɜrk/ (**shirks, shirking, shirked**) V-T/V-I If someone **shirks** their responsibility or duty, they do not do what they have a responsibility to do. ❑ *He said the city had shirked its responsibility by not overseeing construction.* ❑ *The government will not shirk from considering the need for further action.*

shirt ✦◇◇ /ʃɜrt/ (**shirts**) **1** N-COUNT A **shirt** is a piece of clothing that you wear on the upper part of your body. Shirts have a collar, sleeves, and buttons down the front. **2** → see also **sweatshirt, T-shirt**

-shirted /-ʃɜrtɪd/ COMB IN ADJ **-shirted** is used to form adjectives which indicate what color or type of shirt someone is wearing. ❑ *...white-shirted men.*

shirt|sleeve /ʃɜrtsliv/ (**shirtsleeves**) N-COUNT [usu pl] **Shirtsleeves** are the sleeves of a shirt. If someone is **in shirtsleeves** or **in** their **shirtsleeves**, they are wearing a shirt but not a jacket. ❑ *He rolled up his shirtsleeves.*

shirt|tail /ʃɜrtteɪl/ (**shirttails**) also **shirt-tail** N-COUNT **Shirttails** are the long parts of a shirt below the waist. ❑ *He wore sandals and old jeans and his shirttails weren't tucked in.*

shit /ʃɪt/ (**shits, shitting, shat**) **1** N-UNCOUNT Some people use **shit** to refer to solid waste matter from the body of a human being or animal. [INFORMAL, VULGAR] ❑ *...a pile of dog shit.* **2** V-I To **shit** means to get rid of solid waste matter from the body. [INFORMAL, VULGAR] ❑ *...his memories of the yellow dog shitting on the stairs.* **3** N-SING To have a **shit** means to get rid of solid waste matter from the body. [INFORMAL, VULGAR] ❑ *Before dying he confesses that he hasn't taken a shit in weeks.* **4** N-UNCOUNT People sometimes refer to things that they do not like as **shit**. [INFORMAL, VULGAR, DISAPPROVAL] ❑ *This is a load of shit.*

shit|less /ʃɪtlɪs/ ADV [adj ADV] If someone says that they are scared **shitless** or bored **shitless**, they are emphasizing that they are extremely scared or bored. [INFORMAL, VULGAR, EMPHASIS]

shit show (**shit shows**) N-COUNT If someone describes a situation as a **shit show**, they think that it is extremely badly organized. [INFORMAL, VULGAR, DISAPPROVAL]

shit|ty /ʃɪti/ (**shittier, shittiest**) ADJ If someone describes something as **shitty**, they do not like it or they think that it is of poor quality. [INFORMAL, VULGAR, DISAPPROVAL]

shiv|er /ʃɪvər/ (**shivers, shivering, shivered**) V-I When you **shiver**, your body shakes slightly because you are cold or frightened. ❑ *He shivered in the cold.* • N-COUNT **Shiver** is also a noun. ❑ *The emptiness here sent shivers down my spine.*

shiv|ery /ʃɪvəri/ ADJ If you are **shivery**, you cannot stop shivering because you feel cold, frightened, or ill. ❑ *She felt shivery and a little sick.*

shoal /ʃoʊl/ (**shoals**) N-COUNT A **shoal** of fish is a large group of them swimming together. ❑ *Among them swam shoals of fish.*

shock ✦✦◇ /ʃɒk/ (**shocks, shocking, shocked**) **1** N-COUNT If you have a **shock**, something suddenly happens which is unpleasant, upsetting, or very surprising. ❑ *The extent of the violence came as a shock.* ❑ *He has never recovered from the shock of your brother's death.* **2** N-UNCOUNT **Shock** is a person's emotional and physical condition when something very frightening or upsetting has happened to them. ❑ *The little boy was speechless with shock.* **3** N-UNCOUNT If someone is in **shock**, they are suffering from a serious physical condition in which their blood is not flowing around their body properly, for example, because they have had a bad injury. ❑ *He was found beaten and in shock.* **4** V-T If something **shocks** you, it makes you feel very upset, because it involves death or suffering and because you had not expected it. ❑ *After forty years in the police force nothing much shocks me.* • **shocked** ADJ ❑ *This was a nasty attack and the woman is still very shocked.* **5** V-T/V-I If someone or something **shocks** you, it upsets or offends you because you think it is vulgar or morally wrong. ❑ *You can't shock me.* ❑ *They were easily shocked in those days.* ❑ *...the desire to shock* • **shocked** ADJ ❑ *Don't look so shocked.* **6** N-VAR A **shock** is the force of something suddenly hitting or pulling something else. ❑ *Steel barriers can bend and absorb the shock.* **7** N-COUNT A **shock** is the same as an **electric shock**. **8** → see also **electric shock**

━━━ COLLOCATIONS ━━━
shock
NOUN **1**
adjective + **shock**: complete, nasty, sudden, terrible
verb + **shock**: spring; receive, suffer

shock ab|sorb|er (**shock absorbers**) N-COUNT A **shock absorber** is a device fitted near the wheels of a car or other vehicle to reduce the effects of traveling over uneven ground. ❑ *...a pair of rear shock absorbers.*

shock|er /ʃɒkər/ (**shockers**) N-COUNT A **shocker** is something such as a story, a piece of news, or a movie that shocks people or that is intended to shock them. [INFORMAL] ❑ *Marsha Hunt's second novel, "Free," is a shocker.*

shock|ing /ʃɒkɪŋ/ **1** ADJ You can say that something is **shocking** if you think that it is very bad. [INFORMAL] ❑ *The media coverage was shocking.* • **shock|ing|ly** ADV [ADV adj/adv]

❏ *His memory was becoming shockingly bad.* ▊2 ADJ You can say that something is **shocking** if you think that it is morally wrong. ❏ *It is shocking that nothing was said.* • **shock|ing|ly** ADV ❏ *Shockingly, this useless and dangerous surgery did not end until the 1930s.* ▊3 → see also **shock**

shock|ing pink COLOR Something that is **shocking pink** is very bright pink. ❏ *...a shocking pink T-shirt.*

shock jock (shock jocks) N-COUNT A **shock jock** is a radio disc jockey who deliberately uses language or expresses opinions that many people find offensive. [INFORMAL]

shock tac|tic (shock tactics) N-COUNT [usu pl] **Shock tactics** are a way of trying to influence people's attitudes to a particular matter by shocking them. ❏ *We must use shock tactics if we are to stop AIDS becoming another accepted disease.*

shock thera|py ▊1 N-UNCOUNT You can refer to the use of extreme policies or actions to solve a particular problem quickly as **shock therapy**. ❏ *...Prague's policy of economic shock therapy.* ▊2 N-UNCOUNT **Shock therapy** is a way of treating mentally ill patients by passing an electric current through their brain.

shock treat|ment (shock treatments) N-UNCOUNT [also N in pl] **Shock treatment** is the same as **shock therapy**.

shock troops N-PLURAL **Shock troops** are soldiers who are specially trained to carry out a quick attack.

shock wave (shock waves) also **shockwave** ▊1 N-COUNT A **shock wave** is an area of very high pressure moving through the air, earth, or water. It is caused by an explosion or an earthquake, or by an object traveling faster than sound. ❏ *The shock waves yesterday were felt from Las Vegas to San Diego.* ▊2 N-COUNT A **shock wave** is the effect of something surprising, such as a piece of unpleasant news, that causes strong reactions when it spreads through a place. ❏ *The crime sent shock waves throughout the country.*

shod /ʃɒd/ ▊1 ADJ [v-link ADJ] You can use **shod** when you are describing the kind of shoes that a person is wearing. [FORMAL] ❏ *He has demonstrated a strong preference for being shod in running shoes.* ▊2 **Shod** is the past participle of **shoe**.

shod|dy /ʃɒdi/ (shoddier, shoddiest) ADJ **Shoddy** work or a **shoddy** product has been done or made carelessly or badly. ❏ *I'm normally quick to complain about shoddy service.* • **shod|di|ly** ADV ❏ *These products are shoddily produced.*

shoe ✦✧ /ʃuː/ (shoes, shoeing, shoed or shod) ▊1 N-COUNT **Shoes** are objects which you wear on your feet. They cover most of your foot and you wear them over socks or stockings. ❏ *...a pair of shoes.* ❏ *Low-heeled comfortable shoes are best.* ▊2 N-COUNT A **shoe** is the same as a **horseshoe**. ▊3 V-T When a blacksmith **shoes** a horse, they attach horseshoes onto the horse's feet. ❏ *Blacksmiths spent most of their time repairing tools and shoeing horses.* ▊4 PHRASE If you **fill** someone's **shoes** or **step into** their **shoes**, you take their place by doing the job they were doing. ❏ *No one has been able to fill his shoes.* ▊5 PHRASE If you talk about being **in** someone's **shoes**, you talk about what you would do or how you would feel if you were in their situation. ❏ *I wouldn't want to be in his shoes.*

shoe|horn /ʃuːhɔːrn/ (shoehorns, shoehorning, shoehorned) ▊1 N-COUNT A **shoehorn** is a piece of metal or plastic with a slight curve that you put in the back of your shoe so that your heel will go into the shoe easily. ▊2 V-T If you **shoehorn** something into a tight place, you manage to get it in there even though it is difficult. ❏ *Their cars are shoehorned into tiny spaces.* ❏ *I was shoehorning myself into my skin-tight ball gown.*

shoe|lace /ʃuːleɪs/ (shoelaces) N-COUNT [usu pl] **Shoelaces** are long, narrow pieces of material like pieces of string that you use to fasten your shoes. ❏ *He began to tie his shoelaces.*

shoe|maker /ʃuːmeɪkər/ (shoemakers) N-COUNT A **shoemaker** is a person whose job is making shoes and boots.

shoe|string /ʃuːstrɪŋ/ ▊1 ADJ [ADJ n] A **shoestring** budget is one where you have very little money to spend. ❏ *The movie was made on a shoestring budget.* ▊2 PHRASE If you do something or make something **on a shoestring**, you do it using very little money. ❏ *The theater will be run on a shoestring.* ▊3 → See feature box at **tourism**

shone /ʃoʊn/ **Shone** is a past tense and past participle of **shine**.

shoo /ʃuː/ (shoos, shooing, shooed) ▊1 V-T If you **shoo** an animal or a person away, you make them go away by waving your hands or arms at them. ❏ *You'd better shoo him away.* ❏ *I shooed him out of the room.* ▊2 EXCLAM You say '**shoo!**' to an animal when you want it to go away. ❏ *Shoo, bird, shoo.*

shoo-in (shoo-ins) N-COUNT A **shoo-in** is a person or thing that seems sure to succeed. [mainly AM, INFORMAL] ❏ *Ms. Hayes is still no shoo-in for the November election.*

shook /ʃʊk/ **Shook** is the past tense of **shake**.

shoot ✦✦✧ /ʃuːt/ (shoots, shooting, shot) ▊1 V-T If someone **shoots** a person or an animal, they kill them or injure them by firing a bullet or arrow at them. ❏ *The police had orders to shoot anyone who attacked them.* ❏ *The man was shot dead by the police during a raid on his house.* ▊2 V-I To **shoot** means to fire a bullet from a weapon such as a gun. ❏ *He taunted armed officers by pointing to his head, as if inviting them to shoot.* ❏ *The police came around the corner and they started shooting at us.* ▊3 V-I If someone or something **shoots** in a particular direction, they move in that direction quickly and suddenly. ❏ *They had almost reached the boat when a figure shot past them.* ▊4 V-T/V-I If you **shoot** something somewhere or if it **shoots** somewhere, it moves there quickly and suddenly. ❏ *Masters shot a hand across the table and gripped his wrist.* ❏ *As soon as she got close, the old woman's hand shot out.* ▊5 V-T If you **shoot** a look at someone, you look at them quickly and briefly, often in a way that expresses your feelings. ❏ *Mary Ann shot him a rueful look.* ▊6 V-I If someone **shoots** to fame, they become famous or successful very quickly. ❏ *She shot to fame a few years ago with her extraordinary first novel.* ▊7 V-T When people **shoot** a movie or **shoot** photographs, they make a movie or take photographs using a camera. ❏ *He'd love to shoot his film in Cuba.* • N-COUNT **Shoot** is also a noun. ❏ *...a barn presently being used for a video shoot.* ▊8 N-COUNT **Shoots** are plants that are beginning to grow, or new parts growing from a plant or tree. ❏ *Prune established plants annually as new shoots appear.* ▊9 V-I In sports such as soccer or basketball, when someone **shoots**, they try to score by kicking or throwing the ball toward the goal or hoop. ❏ *Spencer scuttled away from Singh to shoot wide when he should have scored.* ▊10 → see also **shooting**, **shot** ▊11 **to shoot from the hip** → see **hip**

▶ **shoot down** ▊1 PHRASAL VERB If someone **shoots down** an airplane, a helicopter, or a missile, they make it fall to the ground by hitting it with a bullet or missile. ❏ *They claimed to have shot down one incoming missile.* ▊2 PHRASAL VERB If one person **shoots down** another, they shoot them with a gun. ❏ *He was prepared to suppress rebellion by shooting down protesters.*

▶ **shoot up** PHRASAL VERB If something **shoots up**, it grows or increases very quickly. ❏ *Sales shot up by 9% last month.*

shoot-em-up (shoot-em-ups) N-COUNT A **shoot-em-up** is a story, movie, or computer game that involves shooting and killing characters. [INFORMAL]

shoot|er /ʃuːtər/ (shooters) ▊1 N-COUNT A **shooter** is a person who shoots a gun. ❏ *An eyewitness identified him as the shooter.* ▊2 N-COUNT A **shooter** is a gun. [INFORMAL]

shoot|ing /ʃuːtɪŋ/ (shootings) ▊1 N-COUNT A **shooting** is an occasion where someone is killed or injured by being shot with a gun. ❏ *Two more bodies were found nearby after the shooting.* ▊2 N-UNCOUNT **Shooting** is hunting animals with a gun as a leisure activity. ❏ *Grouse shooting begins in August.* ▊3 N-UNCOUNT The **shooting** of a movie is the act of filming it. ❏ *Ingrid was busy learning her lines for the next day's shooting.* ▊4 N-UNCOUNT In sports such as basketball and soccer, a player's **shooting** is their ability to score points or goals. ❏ *When asked whether the injury affected his shooting, Iverson said: "Not at all."*

shoot|ing gal|lery (shooting galleries) N-COUNT A **shooting gallery** is a place where people use rifles to shoot at targets, especially in order to win prizes.

shoot|ing star (shooting stars) N-COUNT A **shooting star** is a piece of rock or metal that burns very brightly when it enters the Earth's atmosphere from space, and is seen from earth as a bright star traveling very fast across the sky.

shoot|ing war (shooting wars) N-COUNT When two countries in conflict engage in a **shooting war**, they fight each other with weapons rather than opposing each other by diplomatic or other means. [JOURNALISM]

shoot-out (shoot-outs) **1** N-COUNT A **shoot-out** is a fight in which people shoot at each other with guns. ▫ *Three IRA men were killed in the shoot-out.* **2** N-COUNT In games such as soccer, a **shoot-out** or a **penalty shoot-out** is a way of deciding the result of a game that has ended in a draw. Players from each team try to score a goal in turn until one player fails to score and their team loses the game. ▫ *The Danes won that UEFA tie in a shoot-out.*

shop ◆◆◇ /ʃɒp/ (shops, shopping, shopped) **1** N-COUNT A **shop** is a small store that sells one type of merchandise. ▫ *...a gift shop.* ▫ *He and his wife run their own antiques shop.* **2** N-COUNT A **shop** is a building or part of a building where things are sold. [mainly BRIT]

in AM, usually use **store**

3 V-I When you **shop**, you go to stores or shops and buy things. ▫ *He always shopped at the co-op.* ▫ *...some advice that's worth bearing in mind when shopping for a new carpet.* • **shop|per** (**shoppers**) N-COUNT ▫ *...crowds of Christmas shoppers.* **4** N-COUNT You can refer to a place where a particular service is offered as a particular type of **shop**. ▫ *...the barber shop where Rodney sometimes had his hair cut.* ▫ *...betting shops.* **5** → see also **shopping**, **coffee shop** **6** PHRASE If you say that people **are talking shop**, you mean that they are talking about their work, and this is boring for other people who do not do the same work. ▫ *Although I get on well with my colleagues, if you hang around together all the time you just end up talking shop.*
▶ **shop around** PHRASAL VERB If you **shop around**, you go to different stores or companies in order to compare the prices and quality of goods or services before you decide to buy them. ▫ *Prices may vary so it's well worth shopping around before you buy.*

shopa|hol|ic /ʃɒpəhɒlɪk/ (shopaholics) N-COUNT A **shopaholic** is someone who greatly enjoys going shopping and buying things, or who cannot stop themselves from doing this. [INFORMAL]

shop as|sis|tant (shop assistants) N-COUNT A **shop assistant** is a person who works in a store selling things to customers. [mainly BRIT]

in AM, usually use **salesclerk**

shop floor also **shop-floor**, **shopfloor** N-SING The **shop floor** is used to refer to all the ordinary workers in a factory or the area where they work, especially in contrast to the people who are in charge. ▫ *Cost must be controlled, not just on the shop floor but in the boardroom too.*

shop front (shop fronts) also **shopfront** N-COUNT A **shop front** is the same as a **storefront**. [mainly BRIT]

shop|keep|er /ʃɒpkiːpər/ (shopkeepers) N-COUNT A **shopkeeper** is a person who owns or manages a shop.

shop|lift /ʃɒplɪft/ (shoplifts, shoplifting, shoplifted) V-T/V-I If someone **shoplifts**, they steal goods from a store by hiding them in a bag or in their clothes. ▫ *He openly shoplifted from a supermarket.* • **shop|lift|er** (**shoplifters**) N-COUNT ▫ *A persistent shoplifter has been banned from every store in town.*

shop|lift|ing /ʃɒplɪftɪŋ/ N-UNCOUNT **Shoplifting** is stealing from a store by hiding things in a bag or in your clothes. ▫ *The grocer accused her of shoplifting and demanded to look in her bag.*

shop|ping ◆◇◇ /ʃɒpɪŋ/ **1** N-UNCOUNT When you do the **shopping**, you go to the stores or shops and buy things. ▫ *I'll do the shopping this afternoon.* **2** N-UNCOUNT Your **shopping** is the things that you have bought from stores, especially food. [mainly BRIT]

in AM, usually use **groceries**

shop|ping cart (shopping carts) N-COUNT A **shopping cart** is a large metal basket on wheels which is provided by stores such as supermarkets for customers to use while they are in the store. [AM]

in BRIT, use **shopping trolley**

shop|ping cen|ter (shopping centers)

in BRIT, use **shopping centre**

N-COUNT A **shopping center** is a specially built area containing a lot of different stores. ▫ *They met in the parking lot at the new shopping center.*

shop|ping chan|nel (shopping channels) N-COUNT A **shopping channel** is a television channel that broadcasts programs showing products that you can buy over the phone or online.

shop|ping list (shopping lists) N-COUNT A **shopping list** is a list of the things that you want to buy when you go shopping, which you write on a piece of paper.

shop|ping mall (shopping malls) N-COUNT A **shopping mall** is a specially built covered area containing stores and restaurants which people can walk between, and where cars are not allowed.

shop|ping trol|ley (shopping trolleys) N-COUNT A **shopping trolley** is the same as a **shopping cart**. [BRIT]

shop stew|ard (shop stewards) N-COUNT A **shop steward** is a labor union member who is elected by the other members in a factory or office to speak for them at official meetings.

shore ◆◇◇ /ʃɔːr/ (shores, shoring, shored) N-COUNT [also prep n] The **shores** or the **shore** of a sea, lake, or wide river is the land along the edge of it. Someone who is **on shore** is on the land rather than on a ship. ▫ *They walked down to the shore.* ▫ *...elephants living on the shores of Lake Kariba.*
▶ **shore up** PHRASAL VERB If you **shore up** something that is weak or about to fail, you do something in order to strengthen it or support it. ▫ *The democracies of the West may find it hard to shore up their defenses.*

shore|line /ʃɔːrlaɪn/ (shorelines) N-COUNT A **shoreline** is the edge of a sea, lake, or wide river. ▫ *...the rocks along the shoreline.*

shorn /ʃɔːrn/ **Shorn** is the past participle of **shear**.

SHORT
① ADJECTIVE AND ADVERB USES
② NOUN USES
---

① **short** ◆◆◆ /ʃɔːrt/ (shorter, shortest)
→ Please look at meanings **16** – **20** to see if the expression you are looking for is shown under another headword.

1 ADJ If something is **short** or lasts for a **short** time, it does not last very long. ▫ *The announcement was made a short time ago.* ▫ *Kemp gave a short laugh.* **2** ADJ A **short** speech, letter, or book does not have many words or pages in it. ▫ *They were performing a short extract from Shakespeare's Two Gentlemen of Verona.* **3** ADJ Someone who is **short** is not as tall as most people are. ▫ *I'm tall and thin and he's short and fat.* ▫ *...a short, elderly woman with gray hair.* **4** ADJ Something that is **short** measures only a small amount from one end to the other. ▫ *The restaurant is only a short distance away.* ▫ *A short flight of steps led to a grand doorway.* **5** ADJ [v-link ADJ] If you are **short of** something or if it is **short**, you do not have enough of it. If you are running **short of** something or if it is running **short**, you do not have much of it left. ▫ *Her father's illness left the family short of money.* ▫ *Government forces are running short of ammunition and fuel.* **6** ADJ [v-link ADJ of n] If someone or something is or stops **short of** a place, they have not quite reached it. If they are or fall **short of** an amount, they have not quite achieved it. ▫ *He stopped a hundred yards short of the building.* **7** PHRASE **Short of** a particular thing means except for that thing or without actually doing that thing. ▫ *Short of gagging the children, there was not much she could do about the noise.* **8** ADV [ADV after v] If something is cut **short** or stops **short**, it is stopped before people expect it to or before it has finished. ▫ *His glittering career was cut short by a heart attack.* **9** ADJ [v-link ADJ for n] If a name or abbreviation is **short for** another name, it is the short version of that name. ▫ *Her friend Kes (short for Kesewa) was in tears.* **10** ADJ If you have a **short** temper, you get angry very easily. ▫ *...an awkward, self-conscious woman with a short temper.* **11** ADJ [v-link ADJ] If you are **short with** someone, you speak briefly and rather rudely to them, because you are impatient or angry. ▫ *She seemed nervous or tense, and she was definitely short with me.* **12** PHRASE If a person or thing is called something **for short**, that is the short version of their name. ▫ *Opposite me was a woman called Jasminder (Jazzy for short).* **13** PHRASE You use **in short** when you have been giving a lot of details and you want to give a conclusion or summary. ▫ *Try tennis, badminton or windsurfing. In short, anything challenging.* **14** PHRASE If someone or something **is short on** a particular good quality, they do not have as much of it as you think they should have. [DISAPPROVAL] ❑ *The proposals were short on detail.* **🗓 PHRASE** If someone **stops short of** doing something, they come close to doing it but do not actually do it. ❑ *He stopped short of explicitly criticizing the government.* **🗓 short of breath** → see **breath** **🗓 on short notice** → see **notice** **🗓 to draw the short straw** → see **straw** **🗓 in short supply** → see **supply** **🗓 in the short term** → see **term**

② **short** /ʃɔrt/ (**shorts**) **1 N-PLURAL** [also *a pair of* N] **Shorts** are pants with very short legs that people wear in hot weather or for taking part in sports. ❑ *...two women in bright cotton shorts and tee shirts.* **2 N-PLURAL** [also *a pair of* N] **Shorts** are men's underpants with short legs. [mainly AM] **3 N-COUNT** A **short** is a short film, especially one that is shown before the main film at the cinema.

short|age ♦◊◊ /ʃɔrtɪdʒ/ (**shortages**) **N-VAR** If there is a **shortage** of something, there is not enough of it. ❑ *A shortage of funds is preventing the UN from monitoring relief.* ❑ *Thre is no shortage of suggestions.*

COLLOCATIONS

shortage
NOUN
noun + **shortage**: food, housing, staff, water; skill
adjective + **shortage**: acute, chronic, critical, severe; global, nationwide, widespread, worldwide
verb + **shortage**: address, experience, face; ease, overcome; cause, create

---

SYNONYMS

shortage
NOUN
deficiency: *They did blood tests on him for signs of a vitamin deficiency.*
lack: *Despite his lack of experience, he got the job.*
shortfall: *The government has refused to make up a $30,000 shortfall in funding.*
scarcity: *...an ever-increasing scarcity of water.*
want: *...a want of manners and charm.*

---

short|bread /ʃɔrtbrɛd/ (**shortbreads**) **N-VAR Shortbread** is a kind of cookie made from flour, sugar, and butter.

short|cake /ʃɔrtkeɪk/ **N-UNCOUNT Shortcake** is a cake or dessert which consists of a crisp cake with layers of fruit and cream. [mainly AM] ❑ *...desserts like strawberry shortcake.*

short-change (**short-changes**, **short-changing**, **short-changed**) **1 V-T** If someone **short-changes** you, they do not give you enough change after you have bought something from them. ❑ *The cashier made a mistake and short-changed him.* **2 V-T** [usu passive] If you **are short-changed**, you are treated unfairly or dishonestly, often because you are given less of something than you deserve. ❑ *Women are in fact still being short-changed in the press.*

short-circuit (**short-circuits**, **short-circuiting**, **short-circuited**) **1 V-T/V-I** If an electrical device **short-circuits** or if someone or something **short-circuits** it, a wrong connection or damaged wire causes electricity to travel along the wrong route and damage the device. ❑ *Carbon dust and oil build up in large motors and cause them to short-circuit.* ❑ *Once inside they short-circuited the electronic security.* • **N-COUNT Short-circuit** is also a noun. ❑ *The fire was started by an electrical short-circuit.* **2 V-T** If someone or something **short-circuits** a process or system, they avoid long or difficult parts of it and use a quicker, more direct method to achieve their aim. ❑ *The approach was intended to short-circuit normal complaints procedures.*

short|coming /ʃɔrtkʌmɪŋ/ (**shortcomings**) **N-COUNT** Someone's or something's **shortcomings** are the faults or weaknesses which they have. ❑ *Marriages usually break down as a result of the shortcomings of both partners.*

short|cut /ʃɔrtkʌt/ (**shortcuts**) **1 N-COUNT** A **shortcut** is a quicker way of getting somewhere than the usual route. ❑ *I tried to take a shortcut and got lost.* **2 N-COUNT** A **shortcut** is a method of achieving something more quickly or more easily than if you use the usual methods. ❑ *Fame can be a shortcut to love and money.* **3 N-COUNT** On a computer, a **shortcut** is an icon on the desktop that allows you to go immediately to a program or document. [COMPUTING] ❑ *There are any number of ways to move or copy icons or create shortcuts in Windows.* **4 N-COUNT** On a computer, a **shortcut** is a keystroke or a combination of keystrokes that allows you to give commands without using the mouse. [COMPUTING] ❑ *There is a handy keyboard shortcut to save you having to scroll up to the top of the screen.*

short|en /ʃɔrt²n/ (**shortens**, **shortening**, **shortened**) **1 V-T/V-I** If you **shorten** an event or the length of time that something lasts, or it it **shortens**, it does not last as long as it would otherwise do or as it used to do. ❑ *Smoking can shorten your life.* ❑ *The trading day is shortened in observance of the Labor Day holiday.* **2 V-T/V-I** If you **shorten** an object or if it **shortens**, it becomes smaller in length. ❑ *Her father paid $5,000 for an operation to shorten her nose.* **3 V-T** If you **shorten** a name or other word, you change it by removing some of the letters. ❑ *Originally called Lili, she eventually shortened her name to Lee.*

short|en|ing /ʃɔrtnɪŋ/ (**shortenings**) **N-MASS Shortening** is cooking fat that you use with flour in order to make pastry or dough. [mainly AM]

short|fall /ʃɔrtfɔl/ (**shortfalls**) **N-COUNT** If there is a **shortfall** in something, there is less of it than you need. ❑ *The government has refused to make up a $30,000 shortfall in funding.*

short|hand /ʃɔrthænd/ **1 N-UNCOUNT Shorthand** is a quick way of writing and uses signs to represent words or syllables. Shorthand is sometimes used by secretaries and journalists to write down what someone is saying. ❑ *Ben took notes in shorthand.* **2 N-UNCOUNT** [also *a* N] You can use **shorthand** to mean a quick or simple way of referring to something. ❑ *Laslett uses the shorthand of "second age" for the group of younger people who are creating families.*

short-handed also **shorthanded** ADJ [usu v-link ADJ] If a company, organization, or group is **short-handed**, it does not have enough people to work on a particular job or for a particular purpose. ❑ *We're actually a bit short-handed at the moment.*

short-haul ADJ [ADJ n] **Short-haul** is used to describe things that involve transporting passengers or goods over short distances. Compare **long-haul**. ❑ *...short-haul flights, for example Chicago to Philadelphia.*

short|ish /ʃɔrtɪʃ/ ADJ [usu ADJ n] **Shortish** means fairly short. ❑ *...a shortish man, with graying hair.*

short|list /ʃɔrtlɪst/ (**shortlists**, **shortlisting**, **shortlisted**) also **short list** **1 N-COUNT** If someone is on a **shortlist**, for example, for a job or a prize, they are one of a small group of people who have been chosen from a larger group. The successful person is then chosen from the small group. ❑ *If you've been asked for an interview you are probably on a shortlist of no more than six.* **2 V-T** [usu passive] If someone or something **is shortlisted** for a job or a prize, they are put on a shortlist. ❑ *He was shortlisted for the Nobel Prize for literature several times.*

short-lived ADJ Something that is **short-lived** does not last very long. ❑ *Any hope that the speech would end the war was short-lived.*

short|ly ♦◊◊ /ʃɔrtli/ ADV If something happens **shortly** after or before something else, it happens not long after or before it. If something is going to happen **shortly**, it is going to happen soon. ❑ *Their trial will shortly begin.* ❑ *Shortly after moving into her apartment, she found a job.*

short mes|sage sys|tem (**short message systems**) also **short message service** **N-COUNT** A **short message system** is a way of sending short written messages from one cellphone to another. The abbreviation **SMS** is also used.

short-order ADJ [ADJ n] A **short-order** cook is a person who is employed in a small restaurant such as a diner to cook food that is easily and quickly prepared. [AM] ❑ *They employed short-order cooks to make the burgers.*

short-range ADJ [ADJ n] **Short-range** weapons or missiles are designed to be fired across short distances.

short|sighted /ʃɔrtsaɪtɪd/ also **short-sighted** **1 ADJ** If someone is **shortsighted** about something, or if their ideas are **shortsighted**, they do not make proper or careful judgments about the future. ❑ *Environmentalists fear that this is a shortsighted approach to the problem of global warming.* **2 ADJ** If you are **short-sighted**, you cannot see things properly when they are far away, because there is something wrong with your eyes. [mainly BRIT]

in AM, usually use **nearsighted**

short-staffed ADJ A company or place that is **short-staffed** does not have enough people working there. ❑ *The hospital is desperately short-staffed.*

short|stop /ʃɔrtstɒp/ (**shortstops**) N-COUNT In baseball, a **shortstop** is a player who tries to stop balls that go between second and third base.

short sto|ry (**short stories**) N-COUNT A **short story** is a written story about imaginary events that is only a few pages long. ❑ *He published a collection of short stories.*

short-tempered ◼ ADJ Someone who is **short-tempered** gets angry very quickly. ❑ *I'm a bit short-tempered sometimes.* ◼ → See feature box at **emotion**

short-term ♦♢◊ ◼ ADJ **Short-term** is used to describe things that will last for a short time, or things that will have an effect soon rather than in the distant future. ❑ *Investors weren't concerned about short-term profits over the next few years.* ❑ *The company has 90 staff, almost all on short-term contracts.* ◼ N-SING When you talk about what happens in **the short term**, you are talking about what happens over a short time rather than in the distant future.

short|wave /ʃɔrtweɪv/ also **short-wave** N-UNCOUNT [oft N n] **Shortwave** is a range of short radio wavelengths used for broadcasting. ❑ *I use the shortwave radio to get the latest war news.*

shot ♦♦◊ /ʃɒt/ (**shots**) ◼ **Shot** is the past tense and past participle of **shoot**. ◼ N-COUNT A **shot** is an act of firing a gun. ❑ *He had murdered Perceval at point blank range with a single shot.* ◼ N-COUNT Someone who is a good **shot** can shoot well. Someone who is a bad **shot** cannot shoot well. ❑ *He was not a particularly good shot because of his eyesight.* ◼ N-COUNT In sports such as soccer, golf, or tennis, a **shot** is an act of kicking, hitting, or throwing the ball, especially in an attempt to score a point. ❑ *He had only one shot at goal.* ◼ N-COUNT A **shot** is a photograph or a particular sequence of pictures in a movie. ❑ *I decided to try for a more natural shot of a fox peering from the bushes.* ◼ N-COUNT If you have a **shot** at something, you attempt to do it. [INFORMAL] ❑ *The heavyweight champion will be given a shot at the world title.* ◼ N-COUNT A **shot** of a drug is an injection of it. ❑ *He administered a shot of Nembutal.* ◼ N-COUNT A **shot** of a strong alcoholic drink is a small glass of it. ❑ *...a shot of vodka.* ◼ PHRASE If you **give** something your **best shot**, you do it as well as you possibly can. [INFORMAL] ❑ *I don't expect to win. But I am going to give it my best shot.* ◼ PHRASE The person who **calls the shots** is in a position to tell others what to do. ❑ *The directors call the shots and nothing happens without their say-so.* ◼ PHRASE If you do something **like a shot**, you do it without any delay or hesitation. [INFORMAL] ❑ *I heard the key turn in the front door and I was out of bed like a shot.* ◼ PHRASE If you describe something as a **long shot**, you mean that it is unlikely to succeed, but is worth trying. ❑ *The deal was a long shot, but Bagley had little to lose.* ◼ PHRASE People sometimes use the expression **by a long shot** to emphasize the opinion they are giving. [EMPHASIS] ❑ *The missile-reduction treaty makes sweeping cuts, but the arms race isn't over by a long shot.*

shot|gun /ʃɒtɡʌn/ (**shotguns**) N-COUNT A **shotgun** is a gun used for shooting birds and animals which fires a lot of small metal balls at one time.

shot|gun wed|ding (**shotgun weddings**) ◼ N-COUNT A **shotgun wedding** is a wedding that has to take place quickly, often because the woman is pregnant. ◼ N-COUNT A **shotgun wedding** is a merger between two companies which takes place in a hurry because one or both of the companies is having difficulties. [BUSINESS]

shot put N-SING [usu the N] In track and field, the **shot put** is a competition in which people throw a heavy metal ball as far as possible. • **shot put|ter** (**shot putters**) N-COUNT ❑ *...Canadian shot-putter Georgette Reed.*

should ♦♦◊ /ʃəd, STRONG ʃʊd/

Should is a modal verb. It is used with the base form of a verb.

◼ MODAL You use **should** when you are saying what would be the right thing to do or the right state for something to be in. ❑ *I should exercise more.* ❑ *He's never going to be able to forget it. And I don't think he should.* ❑ *Should our children be taught to swim at school?* ◼ MODAL You use **should** to give someone an order to do something, or to report an official order. ❑ *18-year-olds are sent reminders that they should register to vote.* ◼ MODAL If you say that something **should have** happened, you mean that it did not happen, but that you wish it had. If you say that something **should not have** happened, you mean that it did happen, but that you wish it had not. ❑ *I should have gone this morning but I was feeling a bit ill.* ❑ *You should have written to the area manager again.* ◼ MODAL You use **should** when you are saying that something is probably the case or will probably happen in the way you are describing. If you say that something **should have** happened by a particular time, you mean that it will probably have happened by that time. ❑ *You should have no problem with reading this language.* ❑ *The doctor said it will take six weeks and I should be fine by then.* ◼ MODAL You use **should** in questions when you are asking someone for advice, permission, or information. ❑ *Should I take out a loan?* ❑ *What should I do?* ◼ MODAL You say '**I should**,' usually with the expression 'if I were you,' when you are giving someone advice by telling them what you would do if you were in their position. [mainly BRIT, FORMAL] ❑ *I should look out if I were you!* ◼ MODAL You use **should** in conditional clauses when you are talking about things that might happen. [FORMAL] ❑ *If you should be fired, your health and pension benefits will not be automatically cut off.* ◼ MODAL You use **should** in 'that' clauses after certain verbs, nouns, and adjectives when you are talking about a future event or situation. ❑ *He raised his glass and indicated that I should do the same.* ❑ *I insisted that we should have a look at every car.* ◼ MODAL You use **should** in expressions such as **I should think** and **I should imagine** to indicate that you think something is true but you are not sure. [VAGUENESS] ❑ *I should think it's going to rain soon.* ◼ MODAL You use **should** in expressions such as **You should have seen us** and **You should have heard her** to emphasize how funny, shocking, or impressive something that you experienced was. [SPOKEN, EMPHASIS] ❑ *You should have heard him last night!*

shoul|der ♦♦◊ /ʃoʊldər/ (**shoulders, shouldering, shouldered**) ◼ N-COUNT Your **shoulders** are between your neck and the tops of your arms. ❑ *She led him to an armchair, with her arm round his shoulder.* ◼ N-PLURAL When you talk about someone's problems or responsibilities, you can say that they carry them on their **shoulders**. ❑ *No one suspected the anguish he carried on his shoulders.* ◼ V-T If you **shoulder** the responsibility or the blame for something, you accept it. ❑ *He has had to shoulder the responsibility of his father's mistakes.* ◼ V-T/V-I If you **shoulder** someone aside or if you **shoulder** your way somewhere, you push past people roughly using your shoulder. ❑ *The policemen rushed past him, shouldering him aside.* ❑ *She could do nothing to stop him as he shouldered his way into the house.* ◼ N-VAR A **shoulder** is a cut of meat from the upper part of the front leg of an animal. ❑ *...shoulder of lamb.* ◼ N-COUNT On a busy road such as a freeway, the **shoulder** is the area at the side of the road where vehicles are allowed to stop in an emergency. [AM]

in BRIT, use **hard shoulder**

◼ PHRASE If someone offers you **a shoulder to cry on** or is **a shoulder to cry on**, they listen sympathetically as you talk about your troubles. ❑ *Mrs. Barrantes longs to be at her daughter's side to offer her a shoulder to cry on.* ◼ PHRASE If you say that someone or something stands **head and shoulders** above other people or things, you mean that they are a lot better than them. ❑ *The two candidates stood head and shoulders above the rest.* ◼ PHRASE If two or more people stand **shoulder to shoulder**, they are next to each other, with their shoulders touching. ❑ *They fell into step, walking shoulder to shoulder with their heads bent against the rain.* ◼ PHRASE If people work or stand **shoulder to shoulder**, they work together in order to achieve something, or support each other. ❑ *They could fight shoulder-to-shoulder against a common enemy.* ◼ **to rub shoulders** with → see **rub**

shoul|der bag (**shoulder bags**) ◼ N-COUNT A **shoulder bag** is a bag that has a long strap so that it can be carried on a person's shoulder. ◼ → See also color supplement

shoul|der blade (**shoulder blades**) N-COUNT Your **shoulder blades** are the two large, flat, triangular bones that you have in the upper part of your back, below your shoulders.

shoulder-high ADJ [usu ADJ n] A **shoulder-high** object is as high as your shoulders. ❑ *...a shoulder-high hedge.* • ADV [ADV

shoulder-length ADJ [usu ADJ n] **Shoulder-length** hair is long enough to reach your shoulders.

shoul|der pad (shoulder pads) N-COUNT **Shoulder pads** are small pads that are put inside the shoulders of a jacket, coat, or other article of clothing in order to raise them.

shoul|der strap (shoulder straps) ◼ N-COUNT The **shoulder straps** on a piece of clothing such as a dress are two narrow straps that go over the shoulders. ◼ N-COUNT A **shoulder strap** on a bag is a long strap that you put over your shoulder to carry the bag.

shouldn't /ʃʊdᵊnt/ **Shouldn't** is the usual spoken form of 'should not.'

should've /ʃʊdəv/ **Should've** is the usual spoken form of 'should have,' when 'have' is an auxiliary verb.

shout ◆◇◇ /ʃaʊt/ (shouts, shouting, shouted) ◼ V-T/V-I If you **shout**, you say something very loudly, usually because you want people a long distance away to hear you or because you are angry. ❑ He had to shout to make himself heard above the wind. ❑ "She's alive!" he shouted triumphantly. ❑ Andrew rushed out of the house, shouting for help. • N-COUNT **Shout** is also a noun. ❑ The decision was greeted with shouts of protest from the crowd. ◼ → See feature box at **debate**
▶ **shout out** PHRASAL VERB If you **shout** something **out**, you say it very loudly so that people can hear you clearly. ❑ They shouted out the names of those detained. ❑ I shouted out "I'm OK!"

shout|ing match (shouting matches) N-COUNT [oft N with/ between n] A **shouting match** is an angry quarrel in which people shout at each other. ❑ We had a real shouting match with each other.

shout|out /ʃaʊtaʊt/ (shoutouts) also **shout-out** N-COUNT A **shoutout** is a short, public greeting, or an expression of thanks, or praise to a named person, especially on a broadcast or a recording. [INFORMAL] ❑ I just want to give a shoutout to my friends Bill and Jack. ❑ Each show even included a timely shout-out to the late Johnny Cash.

shove /ʃʌv/ (shoves, shoving, shoved) ◼ V-T/V-I If you **shove** someone or something, you push them with a quick, violent movement. ❑ He shoved her out of the way. ❑ He's the one who shoved me. • N-COUNT **Shove** is also a noun. ❑ She gave Gracie a shove toward the house. ◼ V-T If you **shove** something somewhere, you push it there quickly and carelessly. ❑ We shoved a copy of the newsletter beneath their door. ◼ PHRASE If you talk about what you think will happen if **push comes to shove**, you are talking about what you think will happen if a situation becomes very bad or difficult. [INFORMAL] ❑ If push comes to shove, if you should lose your case in the court, what will you do?

shov|el /ʃʌvᵊl/ (shovels, shoveling or shovelling, shoveled or shovelled) ◼ N-COUNT A **shovel** is a tool with a long handle that is used for lifting and moving earth, coal, or snow. ❑ ...a coal shovel. ◼ V-T If you **shovel** earth, coal, or snow, you lift and move it with a shovel. ❑ He has to get out and shovel snow. ◼ V-T If you **shovel** something somewhere, you push a lot of it quickly into that place. ❑ There was silence, except for Randall, who was obliviously shoveling food into his mouth. ◼ → See also color supplement

---
SHOW

① VERB USES
② NOUN AND ADJECTIVE USES
③ PHRASAL VERBS

---

① **show** ◆◆◆ /ʃoʊ/ (shows, showing, showed, shown)
→ Please look at meanings ◼ and ◼ to see if the expression you are looking for is shown under another headword.

◼ V-T If something **shows** that a state of affairs exists, it gives information that proves it or makes it clear to people. ❑ Research shows that young people still look to parents as their main source for health information. ❑ These figures show an increase of over one million in unemployment. ◼ V-T If a picture, chart, movie, or piece of writing **shows** something, it represents it or gives information about it. ❑ Figure 4.1 shows the respiratory system. ❑ The cushions, shown left, measure 20 x 12 inches and cost $39.95. ❑ Much of the film shows the painter simply going about his task. ◼ V-T If you **show** someone something, you give it to them, take them to it, or point to it, so that they can see it or know what you are referring to. ❑ Cut out this article and show it to your boss. ❑ He showed me the apartment he shares with Esther. ◼ V-T If you **show** someone to a room or seat, you lead them there. ❑ It was very good of you to come. Let me show you to my study. ❑ Milton was shown into the office. ◼ V-T If you **show** someone how to do something, you do it yourself so that they can watch you and learn how to do it. ❑ Claire showed us how to make a chocolate cake. ❑ There are seasoned professionals who can teach you and show you what to do. ◼ V-T/V-I If something **shows** or if you **show** it, it is visible or noticeable. ❑ When he smiled he showed a row of strong white teeth. ❑ Faint glimmers of daylight were showing through the trees. ◼ V-T/V-I If you **show** a particular attitude, quality, or feeling, or if it **shows**, you behave in a way that makes this attitude, quality, or feeling clear to other people. ❑ She showed no interest in her children. ❑ Ferguson was unhappy and it showed. ❑ You show me respect. ◼ V-T If something **shows** a quality or characteristic or if that quality or characteristic **shows** itself, it can be noticed or observed. ❑ The story shows a strong narrative gift and a vivid eye for detail. ❑ Her popularity clearly shows no sign of waning. ◼ V-T If a company **shows** a profit or a loss, its accounts indicate that it has made a profit or a loss. ❑ It is the only one of the three companies expected to show a profit for the quarter. ◼ V-I If a person you are expecting to meet does not **show**, they do not arrive at the place where you expect to meet them. [mainly AM] ❑ There was always a chance he wouldn't show. • PHRASAL VERB **Show up** means the same as **show** ①. ❑ We waited until five o'clock, but he did not show up. ◼ V-T/V-I If someone **shows** a film or television program, it is broadcast or appears on television or in the movie theater. ❑ The TV news showed the same film clip. ❑ The movie is now showing at theaters around the country. ◼ V-T To **show** things such as works of art means to put them in an exhibition where they can be seen by the public. ❑ 50 dealers will show oils, watercolors, drawings and prints from 1900 to 1992. ◼ PHRASE If you **have** something **to show for** your efforts, you have achieved something as a result of what you have done. ❑ I'm nearly 31 and it's about time I had something to show for my time in my job. ◼ PHRASE If you say **it just goes to show** or **it just shows** that something is the case, you mean that what you have just said or experienced demonstrates that it is the case. ❑ I forgot all about the ring. Which just goes to show that getting good grades in school doesn't mean you're clever. ◼ **to show someone the door** → see **door** ◼ **to show your face** → see **face** ①

② **show** ◆◆◆ /ʃoʊ/ (shows) ◼ N-COUNT [usu a N of n] A **show** of a feeling or quality is an attempt by someone to make it clear that they have that feeling or quality. ❑ Miners gathered in the center of Bucharest in a show of support for the government. ◼ N-UNCOUNT If you say that something is for **show**, you mean that it has no real purpose and is done just to give a good impression. ❑ The change in government is more for show than for real. ◼ N-COUNT A television or radio **show** is a program on television or radio. ❑ I had my own TV show. ❑ ...a popular talk show on a Cuban radio station. ◼ N-COUNT A **show** in a theater is an entertainment or concert, especially one that includes different items such as music, dancing, and comedy. ❑ How about going shopping and seeing a show? ◼ N-COUNT [also on N] A **show** is a public exhibition of things, such as works of art, fashionable clothes, or things that have been entered in a competition. ❑ Currently, the show is in Boston. ❑ It plans about 30 such fashion shows this fall in department stores.

③ **show** ◆◆◆ /ʃoʊ/ (shows, showing, showed, shown)
▶ **show off** ◼ PHRASAL VERB If you say that someone is **showing off**, you are criticizing them for trying to impress people by showing in a very obvious way what they can do or what they own. [DISAPPROVAL] ❑ All right, there's no need to show off. ◼ PHRASAL VERB If you **show off** something that you have, you show it to a lot of people or make it obvious that you have it, because you are proud of it. ❑ Naomi was showing off her engagement ring. ◼ → see also **show-off**
▶ **show up** ◼ PHRASAL VERB If something **shows up** or if something **shows** it **up**, it can be clearly seen or noticed. ❑ You may have some strange disease that may not show up for 10 or 15 years. ❑ The orange color shows up well against most backgrounds.

show and tell

2 PHRASAL VERB If someone or something **shows** you **up**, they make you feel embarrassed or ashamed of them. ❏ *He wanted to teach her a lesson for showing him up in front of Leonov.* **3** → see **show** ① 10

show and tell also **show-and-tell** N-UNCOUNT **Show and tell** is a school activity in which children present an object to their class and talk about it. [AM] ❏ *She can bring her puppy to school for show-and-tell.*

show|biz /ʃoʊbɪz/ N-UNCOUNT **Showbiz** is the same as **show business**. [INFORMAL]

show busi|ness N-UNCOUNT **Show business** is the entertainment industry of movies, theater, and television. ❏ *He started his career in show business by playing the saxophone and singing.*

show|case /ʃoʊkeɪs/ (showcases, showcasing, showcased) **1** N-COUNT A **showcase** is a glass container with valuable objects inside it, for example, at an exhibition or in a museum. **2** N-COUNT [with supp] You use **showcase** to refer to a situation or setting in which something is displayed or presented to its best advantage. ❏ *The festival remains a valuable showcase for new talent.* **3** V-T [usu passive] If something **is showcased**, it is displayed or presented to its best advantage. [JOURNALISM] ❏ *Restored films are being showcased this month at a festival in Paris.*

show|down /ʃoʊdaʊn/ (showdowns) N-COUNT A **showdown** is a big argument or conflict which is intended to settle a dispute that has lasted for a long time. ❏ *They may be pushing the president toward a final showdown with his party.*

show|er /ʃaʊər/ (showers, showering, showered) **1** N-COUNT A **shower** is a device for washing yourself. It consists of a pipe which ends in a flat cover with a lot of holes in it so that water comes out in a spray. ❏ *She heard him turn on the shower.* **2** N-COUNT A **shower** is a small enclosed area containing a shower. ❏ *Do you sing in the shower?* **3** N-COUNT The **showers** or the **shower** in a place such as a gym is the area containing showers. ❏ *The showers are a mess.* **4** N-COUNT If you take a **shower**, you wash yourself by standing under a spray of water from a shower. ❏ *I think I'll take a shower before dinner.* **5** V-I If you **shower**, you wash yourself by standing under a spray of water from a shower. ❏ *There wasn't time to shower or change clothes.* **6** N-COUNT A **shower** is a short period of rain, especially light rain. ❏ *There'll be bright or sunny spells and scattered showers this afternoon.* **7** N-COUNT You can refer to a lot of things that are falling as a **shower** of them. ❏ *Showers of sparks flew in all directions.* **8** V-T [usu passive] If you **are showered with** a lot of small objects or pieces, they are scattered over you. ❏ *They were showered with rice in the traditional manner.* **9** N-COUNT A **shower** is a party or celebration at which the guests bring gifts. [mainly AM] ❏ *...a baby shower.*

show|er gel (shower gels) N-VAR **Shower gel** is a type of liquid soap designed for use in the shower.

show|ery /ʃaʊəri/ ADJ If the weather is **showery**, there are showers of rain but it does not rain all the time.

show|girl /ʃoʊɡɜrl/ (showgirls) N-COUNT A **showgirl** is a young woman who sings and dances as part of a group in a musical show.

show|ground /ʃoʊɡraʊnd/ (showgrounds) N-COUNT A **showground** is a large area of land where events such as fairs or horseback competitions are held.

show jump|er (show jumpers) N-COUNT A **show jumper** is a person who takes part in the sport of show jumping. ❏ *I loved horses as a child and was a junior show jumper.*

show jump|ing also **showjumping** N-UNCOUNT **Show jumping** is a sport in which horses are ridden in competitions to demonstrate their skill in jumping over fences and walls.

show|man /ʃoʊmən/ (showmen) N-COUNT A **showman** is a man who is very entertaining and dramatic in the way that he performs, or the way that he presents things.

show|man|ship /ʃoʊmənʃɪp/ N-UNCOUNT **Showmanship** is a person's skill at performing or presenting things in an entertaining and dramatic way.

shown /ʃoʊn/ **Shown** is the past participle of **show**.

show-off (show-offs) also **showoff** N-COUNT If you say that someone is a **show-off**, you are criticizing them for trying to impress people by showing in a very obvious way what they can do or what they own. [INFORMAL, DISAPPROVAL] ❏ *Many jet ski riders are big show-offs who stick around populated areas so everyone can see their turns and maneuvers.*

show|piece /ʃoʊpiːs/ (showpieces) also **show-piece** N-COUNT A **showpiece** is something that is admired because it is the best thing of its type, especially something that is intended to be impressive. ❏ *The factory was to be a showpiece of Western investment in the East.*

show|room /ʃoʊruːm/ (showrooms) N-COUNT A **showroom** is a store in which goods are displayed for sale, especially goods such as cars or electrical or gas appliances. ❏ *...a car showroom.*

show|stopper /ʃoʊstɒpər/ (showstoppers) also **show-stopper** N-COUNT If something is a **showstopper**, it is very impressive. [INFORMAL, APPROVAL] ❏ *Her natural creativity and artistic talent make her home a real showstopper.*

show-stopping also **showstopping** ADJ [ADJ n] A **show-stopping** performance or product is very impressive. [INFORMAL, APPROVAL]

show|time /ʃoʊtaɪm/ N-UNCOUNT **Showtime** is the time when a particular stage or television show starts. ❏ *It's close to showtime now, so you retire into the dressing room.*

show tri|al (show trials) N-COUNT People describe a trial as a **show trial** if they believe that the trial is unfair and is held for political reasons rather than in order to find out the truth. [DISAPPROVAL] ❏ *...the show trials of political dissidents.*

show|woman /ʃoʊwʊmən/ (showwomen) N-COUNT A **showwoman** is a woman who is very entertaining and dramatic in the way that she performs, or the way that she presents things.

showy /ʃoʊi/ (showier, showiest) ADJ Something that is **showy** is very noticeable because it is large, colorful, or bright. ❏ *Since he was color blind, he favored large, showy flowers.*

shrank /ʃræŋk/ **Shrank** is the past tense of **shrink**.

shrap|nel /ʃræpnəl/ N-UNCOUNT **Shrapnel** consists of small pieces of metal which are scattered from exploding bombs and shells. ❏ *He was hit by shrapnel from a grenade.*

shred /ʃrɛd/ (shreds, shredding, shredded) **1** V-T If you **shred** something such as food or paper, you cut it or tear it into very small, narrow pieces. ❏ *They may be shredding documents.* **2** N-COUNT If you cut or tear food or paper into **shreds**, you cut or tear it into small, narrow pieces. ❏ *Cut the cabbage into fine long shreds.* **3** N-COUNT If there is not a **shred** of something, there is not even a small amount of it. ❏ *He said there was not a shred of evidence to support such remarks.* ❏ *There is not a shred of truth in the story.*

shred|der /ʃrɛdər/ (shredders) N-COUNT A **shredder** is a machine for shredding things such as documents, food, or parts of bushes or trees that have been cut off. ❏ *...a document shredder.*

shrew /ʃruː/ (shrews) N-COUNT A **shrew** is a small brown animal like a mouse with a long pointed nose.

shrewd /ʃruːd/ (shrewder, shrewdest) ADJ A **shrewd** person is able to understand and judge a situation quickly and to use this understanding to their own advantage. ❏ *She's a shrewd businesswoman.*

shriek /ʃriːk/ (shrieks, shrieking, shrieked) V-I When someone **shrieks**, they make a short, very loud cry, for example, because they are suddenly surprised, are in pain, or are laughing. ❏ *She shrieked and leapt from the bed.* • N-COUNT **Shriek** is also a noun. ❏ *Sue let out a terrific shriek and leapt out of the way.*

shrift /ʃrɪft/ PHRASE [PHR after v] If someone or something gets **short shrift**, they are paid very little attention. ❏ *The idea has been given short shrift by philosophers.*

shrill /ʃrɪl/ (shriller, shrillest) ADJ A **shrill** sound is high-pitched and unpleasant. ❏ *Shrill cries and startled oaths flew up around us as pandemonium broke out.* ❏ *...the shrill whistle of the engine.*

shrimp /ʃrɪmp/ (shrimp)

> The plural can also be **shrimps**.

N-COUNT **Shrimps** are small shellfish with long tails and many legs. ❏ *Add the shrimp and cook for 30 seconds.*

shrimp cock|tail (shrimp cocktails) N-VAR A **shrimp cocktail** is a dish that consists of shrimp and a sauce. It is usually eaten at the beginning of a meal. [mainly AM]

in BRIT, use **prawn cocktail**

shrine /ʃraɪn/ (shrines) **1** N-COUNT A **shrine** is a place of worship which is associated with a particular holy person or object. □ ...the holy shrine of Mecca. **2** N-COUNT A **shrine** is a place that people visit and treat with respect because it is connected with a dead person or with dead people that they want to remember. □ The monument has been turned into a shrine to the dead and the missing.

shrink /ʃrɪŋk/ (shrinks, shrinking, shrank, shrunk) **1** V-I If cloth or clothing **shrinks**, it becomes smaller in size, usually as a result of being washed. □ People were short in those days – or else those military uniforms all shrank in the wash! **2** V-T/V-I If something **shrinks** or something else **shrinks** it, it becomes smaller. □ The vast forests of West Africa have shrunk. **3** V-I If you **shrink away from** someone or something, you move away from them because you are frightened, shocked, or disgusted by them. □ One child shrinks away from me when I try to talk to him. **4** V-I [usu with neg] If you do not **shrink from** a task or duty, you do it even though it is unpleasant or dangerous. □ He is decisive and won't shrink from a fight. **5** N-COUNT A **shrink** is a psychiatrist. [INFORMAL] □ I've seen a shrink already. **6 no shrinking violet** → see violet

shrink|age /ʃrɪŋkɪdʒ/ N-UNCOUNT **Shrinkage** is a decrease in the size or amount of something. □ Allow for some shrinkage in both length and width.

shrink-wrapped ADJ [usu ADJ n] A **shrink-wrapped** product is sold in a tight covering of thin plastic. □ ...a shrink-wrapped package.

shriv|el /ʃrɪvᵊl/ (shrivels, shriveling or shrivelling, shriveled or shrivelled) V-T/V-I When something **shrivels** or when something **shrivels** it, it becomes dryer and smaller, often with lines in its surface, as a result of losing the water it contains. □ The plant shrivels and dies. ● PHRASAL VERB **Shrivel up** means the same as **shrivel**. □ The leaves started to shrivel up. ● **shriv|eled** ADJ □ ...a shriveled chestnut.

shroud /ʃraʊd/ (shrouds, shrouding, shrouded) **1** N-COUNT A **shroud** is a cloth which is used for wrapping a dead body. □ ...the burial shroud. **2** V-T If something **has been shrouded in** mystery or secrecy, very little information about it has been made available. □ For years the teaching of acting has been shrouded in mystery. **3** V-T If darkness, fog, or smoke **shrouds** an area, it covers it so that it is difficult to see. □ Mist shrouded the hilltops.

Shrove Tues|day /ʃroʊv tuzdeɪ/ N-UNCOUNT **Shrove Tuesday** is the Tuesday before Ash Wednesday.

shrub /ʃrʌb/ (shrubs) N-COUNT **Shrubs** are plants that have several woody stems. □ ...flowering shrubs.

shrub|bery /ʃrʌbəri/ N-UNCOUNT You can refer to a lot of shrubs or to shrubs in general as **shrubbery**.

shrub|by /ʃrʌbi/ (shrubbier, shrubbiest) ADJ [usu ADJ n] A **shrubby** plant is like a shrub. □ ...a shrubby tree.

shrug /ʃrʌg/ (shrugs, shrugging, shrugged) V-T/V-I If you **shrug**, you raise your shoulders to show that you are not interested in something or that you do not know or care about something. □ I shrugged, as if to say, "Why not?" ● N-COUNT **Shrug** is also a noun. □ "I suppose so," said Anna with a shrug.
▶ **shrug off** PHRASAL VERB If you **shrug** something **off**, you ignore it or treat it as if it is not really important or serious. □ He shrugged off the criticism.

shrunk /ʃrʌŋk/ **Shrunk** is the past participle of **shrink**.

shrunk|en /ʃrʌŋkən/ ADJ Someone or something that is **shrunken** has become smaller than they used to be. □ She now looked small, shrunken and pathetic.

shtick /ʃtɪk/ → see schtick

shuck /ʃʌk/ (shucks, shucking, shucked) **1** N-COUNT The **shuck** of something is its outer covering, for example, the leaves around an ear of corn, or the shell of a shellfish. [AM] □ ...corn shucks. **2** V-T If you **shuck** something such as corn or shellfish, you remove it from its outer covering. [AM] □ On a good day, each employee will shuck 3,500 oysters. **3** V-T If you **shuck** something that you are wearing, you take it off. [AM, INFORMAL] □ He shucked his coat and set to work. **4** EXCLAM **Shucks** is an exclamation that is used to express embarrassment, disappointment, or annoyance. [AM, INFORMAL, FEELINGS] □ Terry actually says "Oh, shucks!" when complimented on her singing.

shud|der /ʃʌdər/ (shudders, shuddering, shuddered) **1** V-I If you **shudder**, you shake with fear, horror, or disgust, or because you are cold. □ Lloyd had urged her to eat caviar. She had shuddered at the thought. ● N-COUNT [usu sing] **Shudder** is also a noun. □ She gave a violent shudder. **2** V-I If something such as a machine or vehicle **shudders**, it shakes suddenly and violently. □ The train began to pull out of the station – then suddenly shuddered to a halt. **3** N-COUNT If something sends **a shudder** or **shudders** through a group of people, it makes them worried or afraid. □ The next crisis sent a shudder of fear through the UN community.

shuf|fle /ʃʌfᵊl/ (shuffles, shuffling, shuffled) **1** V-I If you **shuffle** somewhere, you walk there without lifting your feet properly off the ground. □ Moira shuffled across the kitchen. ● N-SING **Shuffle** is also a noun. □ She noticed her own proud walk had become a shuffle. **2** V-T/V-I If you **shuffle** around, you move your feet about while standing or you move your bottom about while sitting, often because you feel uncomfortable or embarrassed. □ He shuffles around in his chair. **3** V-T If you **shuffle** playing cards, you mix them up before you begin a game. □ There are various ways of shuffling and dealing the cards.

shun /ʃʌn/ (shuns, shunning, shunned) V-T If you **shun** someone or something, you deliberately avoid them or keep away from them. □ From that time forward everybody shunned him.

shunt /ʃʌnt/ (shunts, shunting, shunted) V-T [usu passive] If a person or thing **is shunted** somewhere, they are moved or sent there, usually because someone finds them inconvenient. [DISAPPROVAL] □ He has spent most of his life being shunted between his mother, father and various foster families.

shush /ʃʌʃ/ (shushes, shushing, shushed) **1** CONVENTION You say **shush** when you are telling someone to be quiet. □ Shush! Here he comes. I'll talk to you later. **2** V-T If you **shush** someone, you tell them to be quiet by saying 'shush' or 'sh,' or by indicating in some other way that you want them to be quiet. □ Frannie shushed her with a forefinger to the lips.

shut ♦◊◊ /ʃʌt/ (shuts, shutting)

The form **shut** is used in the present tense and is the past tense and past participle.

1 V-T/V-I If you **shut** something such as a door or if it **shuts**, it moves so that it fills a hole or a space. □ Just make sure you shut the gate. ● ADJ [v-link ADJ] **Shut** is also an adjective. □ They have warned residents to stay inside and keep their doors and windows shut. **2** V-T If you **shut** your eyes, you lower your eyelids so that you cannot see anything. □ Lucy shut her eyes so she wouldn't see it happen. ● ADJ [v-link ADJ] **Shut** is also an adjective. □ His eyes were shut and he seemed to have fallen asleep. **3** V-T/V-I If your mouth **shuts** or if you **shut** your mouth, you place your lips firmly together. □ Daniel's mouth opened, and then shut again. ● ADJ [v-link ADJ] **Shut** is also an adjective. □ She was silent for a moment, lips tight shut, eyes distant. **4** V-T/V-I When a store, bar, or other public building **shuts** or when someone **shuts** it, it is closed and you cannot use it until it is open again. □ There is a tendency to shut museums or shops at a moment's notice. □ Stores usually shut from noon-3pm, and stay open late. ● ADJ [v-link ADJ] **Shut** is also an adjective. □ Make sure you have food to tide you over when the local shop may be shut. **5** PHRASE If someone tells you to **keep** your **mouth shut** about something, they are telling you not to let anyone else know about it. □ I don't have to tell you how important it is for you to keep your mouth shut about all this. **6** PHRASE If you **keep** your **mouth shut**, you do not express your opinions about something, even though you would like to. □ If she had kept her mouth shut she would still have her job now.
▶ **shut down 1** PHRASAL VERB If a factory or business **shuts down** or if someone **shuts** it **down**, work there stops or it is no longer in business. □ Smaller contractors had been forced to shut down. □ It is required by law to shut down banks which it regards as chronically short of capital. **2** → see also shutdown
▶ **shut in 1** PHRASAL VERB If you **shut** someone or something **in** a room, you close the door so that they cannot leave it. □ The door enables us to shut the birds in the shelter in bad weather. **2** → see also shut-in

▶ **shut off** ◼ PHRASAL VERB If you **shut off** something such as an engine or an electrical item, you turn it off to stop it from working. ◻ *They pulled over and shut off the engine.* ◼ PHRASAL VERB If you **shut** yourself **off**, you avoid seeing other people, usually because you are feeling depressed. ◻ *Billy tends to keep things to himself more and shut himself off.* ◼ PHRASAL VERB If an official organization **shuts off** the supply of something, they no longer send it to the people they supplied in the past. ◻ *The State Water Project has shut off all supplies to farmers.*
▶ **shut out** ◼ PHRASAL VERB If you **shut** something or someone **out**, you prevent them from getting into a place, for example, by closing the doors. ◻ *"I shut him out of the bedroom," says Maureen.* ◼ PHRASAL VERB If you **shut out** a thought or a feeling, you prevent yourself from thinking or feeling it. ◻ *I shut out the memory which was too painful to dwell on.* ◼ PHRASAL VERB If you **shut** someone **out** of something, you prevent them from having anything to do with it. ◻ *She is very reclusive, to the point of shutting me out of her life.* ◼ PHRASAL VERB In sports such as football and hockey, if one team **shuts out** the team they are playing against, they win and prevent the opposing team from scoring. ◻ *Harvard shut out Yale, 14-0.* ◼ → see also **shutout**
▶ **shut up** PHRASAL VERB If someone **shuts up** or if someone **shuts** them **up**, they stop talking. You can say '**shut up**' as an impolite way to tell a person to stop talking. ◻ *Just shut up, will you?*

SYNONYMS

shut
VERB ◼
close: *If you are cold, close the window.*
secure: *The shed was secured by a hasp and staple fastener.*
fasten: *...the dress, which fastens with a long back zipper.*
lock: *Are you sure you locked the front door?*

shut|down /ʃʌtdaʊn/ (shutdowns) N-COUNT A **shutdown** is the closing of a factory, store, or other business, either for a short time or forever. ◻ *The shutdown is the latest in a series of painful budget measures.*

shut|eye /ʃʌtaɪ/ also **shut-eye** N-UNCOUNT **Shuteye** is sleep. [INFORMAL] ◻ *Go home and get some shuteye.*

shut-in (shut-ins) N-COUNT A **shut-in** is someone who is ill for a long time, and has to stay in bed or at home. [AM] ◻ *...Meals on Wheels or similar programs that bring outside life to shut-ins.*

shut|out /ʃʌtaʊt/ (shutouts) also **shut-out** N-COUNT In sports such as football and hockey, a **shutout** is a game or part of a game in which one of the teams wins and prevents the opposing team from scoring. ◻ *It was the Mariners' 10th shutout.*

shut|ter /ʃʌtər/ (shutters) ◼ N-COUNT **Shutters** are wooden or metal covers fitted on the outside of a window. They can be opened to let in the light, or closed to keep out the sun or the cold. ◻ *She opened the shutters and gazed out over village roofs.* ◼ N-COUNT The **shutter** in a camera is the part which opens to allow light through the lens when a photograph is taken. ◻ *There are a few things you should check before pressing the shutter release.* ◼ → See feature box at **house**

shut|tered /ʃʌtərd/ ◼ ADJ A **shuttered** window, room, or building has its shutters closed. ◻ *I opened a shuttered window.* ◼ ADJ [ADJ n] A **shuttered** window, room, or building has shutters fitted to it. ◻ *...green-shuttered colonial villas.*

shut|tle /ʃʌtəl/ (shuttles, shuttling, shuttled) ◼ N-COUNT A **shuttle** is the same as a **space shuttle**. ◼ N-COUNT A **shuttle** is a plane, bus, or train which makes frequent trips between two places. ◻ *There is a free 24-hour shuttle between the airport terminals.* ◼ V-T/V-I If someone or something **shuttles** or **is shuttled** from one place to another place, they frequently go from one place to the other. ◻ *He and colleagues have shuttled back and forth between the three capitals.* ◼ → See feature box at **travel**

shuttle|cock /ʃʌtəlkɒk/ (shuttlecocks) N-COUNT A **shuttlecock** is the small object that you hit over the net in a game of badminton. It has a rounded end with real or artificial feathers attached to it.

shut|tle di|plo|ma|cy N-UNCOUNT **Shuttle diplomacy** is the movement of diplomats between countries whose leaders refuse to talk directly to each other, in order to try to settle the argument between them. ◻ *UN mediators are conducting shuttle diplomacy between the two sides.*

shy /ʃaɪ/ (shyer, shyest, shies, shying, shied) ◼ ADJ A **shy** person is nervous and uncomfortable in the company of other people. ◻ *She was a shy, quiet girl.* ◻ *She was a shy and retiring person off-stage.* • **shy|ly** ADV ◻ *The children smiled shyly.* • **shy|ness** N-UNCOUNT ◻ *Eventually he overcame his shyness.* ◼ ADJ If you are **shy** about or **shy** of doing something, you are unwilling to do it because you are afraid of what might happen. ◻ *They feel shy about showing their feelings.*
▶ **shy away from** PHRASAL VERB If you **shy away from** doing something, you avoid doing it, often because you are afraid or not confident enough. ◻ *We frequently shy away from making decisions.*

-shy /-ʃaɪ/ COMB IN ADJ **-shy** is added to nouns to form adjectives which indicate that someone does not like a particular thing, and tries to avoid it. For example, someone who is camera-shy does not like having their photograph taken. ◻ *...camera-shy red deer.*

shy|ster /ʃaɪstər/ (shysters) N-COUNT If you refer to someone, especially a lawyer or politician, as a **shyster**, you mean that they are dishonest and immoral. [mainly AM, INFORMAL, DISAPPROVAL]

Sia|mese cat /saɪəmiːz kæt/ (Siamese cats) N-COUNT A **Siamese cat** is a type of cat with short cream and brown fur, blue eyes, dark ears, and a dark tail.

Sia|mese twin /saɪəmiːz twɪn/ (Siamese twins) N-COUNT **Siamese twins** are twins who are born with their bodies joined. [OLD-FASHIONED]

sibi|lant /sɪbɪlənt/ ADJ [usu ADJ n] **Sibilant** sounds are soft 's' sounds. [FORMAL] ◻ *A sibilant murmuring pervaded the room.*

sib|ling /sɪblɪŋ/ (siblings) ◼ N-COUNT Your **siblings** are your brothers and sisters. [FORMAL] ◻ *His siblings are in their twenties.* ◼ → See feature box at **family**

sic /sɪk/ (sics, sicking or siccing, sicked or sicced) ◼ V-T If someone **sics** animals or people such as police or lawyers on you, they cause the animals or people to attack you or pursue you. [AM] ◻ *On one occasion, he threatened to sic his dogs on a reporter.* ◻ *"So Dick gets to sic the FBI on you," Frank grumbled.* ◼ You write **sic** in brackets after a word or expression when you want to indicate to the reader that although the word looks odd or wrong, you intended to write it like that or the original writer wrote it like that. ◻ *How many more day [sic] till the end of term?*

Si|cil|ian /sɪsɪliən/ (Sicilians) ◼ ADJ **Sicilian** means belonging or relating to Sicily, or to its people or culture. ◼ N-COUNT A **Sicilian** is a Sicilian citizen, or a person of Sicilian origin.

sick ♦♢♢ /sɪk/ (sicker, sickest) ◼ ADJ If you are **sick**, you are ill. **Sick** usually means physically ill, but it can sometimes be used to mean mentally ill. ◻ *He's very sick. He needs medication.* ◻ *She found herself with two small children, a sick husband, and no money.* • N-PLURAL The **sick** are people who are sick. ◻ *There were no doctors to treat the sick.* ◼ ADJ [v-link ADJ] If you are **sick**, the food that you have eaten comes up from your stomach and out of your mouth. If you feel **sick**, you feel as if you are going to be sick. ◻ *She got up and was sick in the sink.* ◻ *The very thought of food made him feel sick.* ◼ ADJ [v-link ADJ of n/-ing] If you say that you are **sick of** something or **sick and tired of** it, you are emphasizing that you are very annoyed by it and want it to stop. [INFORMAL, EMPHASIS] ◻ *I am sick and tired of hearing all these people moaning.* ◼ ADJ If you describe something such as a joke or story as **sick**, you mean that it deals with death or suffering in an unpleasantly humorous way. [DISAPPROVAL] ◻ *...a sick joke about a cat.* ◼ ADJ You can describe something as **sick** when you think it is excellent. [INFORMAL] ◻ *Those new sneakers are sick.* ◼ PHRASE If you say that something or someone **makes** you **sick**, you mean that they make you feel angry or disgusted. [INFORMAL] ◻ *It makes me sick that this wasn't disclosed.* ◼ PHRASE [usu v-link PHR] If you are **out sick**, you are not at work because you are sick. ◻ *That afternoon she was fired from her job as a nurse, because she'd been out sick so much.* ◼ PHRASE If you say that you are **worried sick**, you are emphasizing that you are extremely worried. [INFORMAL, EMPHASIS] ◻ *He was worried sick about what our mothers would say.* ◼ → See feature box at **illness**

sick bay (sick bays) also **sickbay** N-COUNT [also prep N] A **sick bay** is an area, especially on a ship or navy base, where medical treatment is given and where beds are provided for people who are ill. ❑ *Neumann lay down on the cot in sick bay.*

sick|bed /sɪkbed/ (sickbeds) N-COUNT [usu poss N] Your **sickbed** is the bed that you are lying in while you are ill. ❑ *Michael left his sickbed to entertain his house guests.*

sick build|ing syn|drome N-UNCOUNT Sick building syndrome is a group of conditions, including headaches, sore eyes, and tiredness, which people who work in offices may experience because the air there is not healthy to breathe.

sick|en /sɪkən/ (sickens, sickening, sickened) V-T If something **sickens** you, it makes you feel disgusted. ❑ *The notion that art should be controlled by intellectuals sickened him.*

sick|en|ing /sɪkənɪŋ/ ADJ You describe something as **sickening** when it gives you feelings of horror or disgust, or makes you feel sick. ❑ *...the sickening rise in the number of suicide bombings.*

sick|le /sɪkəl/ (sickles) N-COUNT A **sickle** is a tool that is used for cutting grass and grain crops. It has a short handle and a long curved blade.

sick leave N-UNCOUNT **Sick leave** is the time that a person spends away from work because of illness or injury. [BUSINESS] ❑ *I have been on sick leave for seven months with depression.*

sickle-cell anemia

in BRIT, use **sickle-cell anaemia**

N-UNCOUNT **Sickle-cell anemia** is an inherited illness in which the red blood cells become curved, causing a number of health problems.

sick|ly /sɪkli/ (sicklier, sickliest) **1** ADJ A **sickly** person or animal is weak, unhealthy, and often ill. ❑ *He had been a sickly child.* **2** ADJ A **sickly** smell or taste is unpleasant and makes you feel slightly sick, often because it is extremely sweet. ❑ *...the sickly smell of rum.*

sick|ness /sɪknɪs/ (sicknesses) **1** N-UNCOUNT **Sickness** is the state of being ill or unhealthy. ❑ *In fifty-two years of working he had one week of sickness.* **2** N-UNCOUNT **Sickness** is the uncomfortable feeling that you are going to vomit. ❑ *After a while, the sickness gradually passed and she struggled to the mirror.* **3** N-VAR A **sickness** is a particular illness. ❑ *More than 930 local people are registered as suffering from radiation sickness.*

sick pay N-UNCOUNT When you are ill and unable to work, **sick pay** is the money that you get from your employer instead of your normal wages. [BUSINESS] ❑ *They are not eligible for sick pay.*

sick|room /sɪkrum/ (sickrooms) N-COUNT A **sickroom** is a room in which a sick person is lying in bed. ❑ *Close friends were allowed into the sickroom.*

SIDE

① A SURFACE, POSITION, OR PLACE
② ONE ASPECT OR ONE POINT OF VIEW
③ PHRASES

---

① **side** ♦♦♦ /saɪd/ (sides) **1** N-COUNT The **side** of something is a position to the left or right of it, rather than in front of it, behind it, or on it. ❑ *On one side of the main entrance there's a red plaque.* ❑ *...a photograph with Joe and Ken on each side of me.* ❑ *...the nations on either side of the Pacific.* **2** N-COUNT The **side** of an object, building, or vehicle is any of its flat surfaces which is not considered to be its front, its back, its top, or its bottom. ❑ *We put a notice on the side of the box.* ❑ *A carton of milk lay on its side.* **3** N-COUNT The **sides** of a hollow or a container are its inside vertical surfaces. ❑ *The rough rock walls were like the sides of a deep canal.* ❑ *Line the base of the dish with greaseproof paper and lightly grease the sides.* **4** N-COUNT The **sides** of an area or surface are its edges. ❑ *Park on the side of the road.* ❑ *...a small beach on the north side of the peninsula.* **5** N-COUNT The two **sides** of an area, surface, or object are its two halves. ❑ *She turned over on her stomach on the other side of the bed.* ❑ *The major center for language is in the left side of the brain.* **6** N-COUNT The two **sides** of a road are its two halves on which traffic travels in opposite directions. ❑ *It had gone on to the wrong side of the road and hit a car coming in the other direction.* **7** N-COUNT If you talk about the other **side** of a town, a country, or the world, you mean a part of the town, the country, or the world that is very far from where you are. ❑ *He lives the other side of town.* ❑ *He saw the ship that was to transport them to the other side of the world.* **8** N-COUNT Your **sides** are the parts of your body between your front and your back, from under your arms to your hips. ❑ *His arms were limp at his sides.* **9** N-COUNT If someone is **by** your **side** or **at** your **side**, they stay near you and give you comfort or support. ❑ *He was constantly at his wife's side.* ❑ *He calls me 20 times a day and needs me by his side in the evening.* **10** N-COUNT The two **sides** of something flat, for example, a piece of paper, are its two flat surfaces. You can also refer to one side of a piece of paper filled with writing as one **side** of writing. ❑ *The new copiers only copy onto one side of the paper.* ❑ *Fry the chops until brown on both sides.* **11** N-COUNT One **side** of a tape or record is what you can hear or record if you play the tape or record from beginning to end without turning it over. ❑ *We want to hear side A.* **12** ADJ [ADJ n] **Side** is used to describe things that are not the main or most important ones of their kind. ❑ *She slipped in and out of the theater by a side door.*

② **side** ♦♦♦ /saɪd/ (sides, siding, sided) **1** N-COUNT The different **sides** in a war, argument, or negotiation are the groups of people who are opposing each other. ❑ *Both sides appealed for a new ceasefire.* ❑ *Any solution must be acceptable to all sides.* **2** N-COUNT The different **sides** of an argument or deal are the different points of view or positions involved in it. ❑ *His words drew sharp reactions from people on both sides of the issue.* **3** V-I If one person or country **sides** with another, they support them in an argument or a war. If people or countries **side** against another person or country, they support each other against them. ❑ *There has been much speculation that they might be siding with the rebels.* **4** N-COUNT In sports, a **side** is a team. [BRIT] **5** N-COUNT A particular **side** of something such as a situation or someone's character is one aspect of it. ❑ *He is in charge of the civilian side of the UN mission.* **6** N-COUNT The **mother's side** and the **father's side** of your family are your mother's relatives and your father's relatives. ❑ *So was your father's side more well off?*

③ **side** ♦♦♦ /saɪd/ (sides)
→ Please look at meanings **11** – **14** to see if the expression you are looking for is shown under another headword.
1 PHRASE If two people or things are **side by side**, they are next to each other. ❑ *We sat side by side on two wicker seats.* **2** PHRASE If people work or live **side by side**, they work or live closely together in a friendly way. ❑ *...areas where different nationalities have lived side by side for centuries.* **3** PHRASE If something moves **from side to side**, it moves repeatedly to the left and to the right. ❑ *She was shaking her head from side to side.* **4** PHRASE If you are **on** someone's **side**, you are supporting them in an argument or a war. ❑ *He has the Democrats on his side.* **5** PHRASE If something is **on** your **side** or if you have it **on** your **side**, it helps you when you are trying to achieve something. ❑ *The weather is rather on our side.* **6** PHRASE If you say that something is **on the** small **side**, you are saying politely that you think it is slightly too small. If you say that someone is **on the** young **side**, you are saying politely that you think they are slightly too young. [POLITENESS] ❑ *He's quiet and a bit on the shy side.* **7** PHRASE If someone does something **on the side**, they do it in addition to their main work. ❑ *...ways of making a little bit of money on the side.* **8** PHRASE If you **put** something **to one side** or **put** it **on one side**, you temporarily ignore it in order to concentrate on something else. ❑ *He can now concentrate on a project he'd originally put to one side.* **9** PHRASE If you **take** someone **to one side** or **draw** them **to one side**, you speak to them privately, usually in order to give them advice or a warning. ❑ *He took Sabrina to one side and told her about the safe.* **10** PHRASE If you **take sides** or **take** someone's **side** in an argument or war, you support one of the sides against the other. ❑ *We cannot take sides in a civil war.* **11 the other side of the coin** → see **coin 12 to err on the side of something** → see **err 13 to be on the safe side** → see **safe 14 someone's side of the story** → see **story**

side|arm /sˈaɪdɑːm/ (sidearms) N-COUNT [usu pl] **Sidearms** are weapons, usually small guns, that you can wear on a belt. ❏ *Two guards with sidearms patrolled the wall.*

side|bar /sˈaɪdbɑː/ (sidebars) N-COUNT A **sidebar** is a short article that is placed beside a longer one in a newspaper or on a website, and provides other relevant information.

side|board /sˈaɪdbɔːd/ (sideboards) N-COUNT A **sideboard** is a long cupboard which is about the same height as a table. Sideboards are usually kept in dining rooms to put plates and glasses in.

side|burns /sˈaɪdbɜːnz/ N-PLURAL If a man has **sideburns**, he has a strip of hair growing down the side of each cheek. ❏ *...a young man with long sideburns.*

side|car /sˈaɪdkɑː/ (sidecars) N-COUNT A **sidecar** is a kind of box with wheels which you can attach to the side of a motorcycle so that you can carry a passenger in it.

-sided /-sˈaɪdɪd/ ◼ COMB IN ADJ [usu ADJ n] **-sided** combines with numbers or adjectives to describe how many sides something has, or what kind of sides something has. ❏ *...a three-sided pyramid.* ❏ *We drove up a steep-sided valley.*
◼ → see also **one-sided**

side dish (side dishes) N-COUNT A **side dish** is a portion of food served at the same time as the main dish. ❏ *These mushrooms would make a delicious side dish.*

side-effect (side-effects) also **side effect** ◼ N-COUNT The **side-effects** of a drug are the effects, usually bad ones, that the drug has on you in addition to its function of curing illness or pain. ❏ *Side-effects include nausea, tiredness, and dizziness.* ◼ N-COUNT A **side-effect** of a situation is something unplanned and usually unpleasant that happens in addition to the main effects of that situation. ❏ *One side effect of modern life is stress.* ◼ → See feature box at **medicine**

side is|sue (side issues) N-COUNT A **side issue** is an issue or subject that is not considered to be as important as the main one. ❏ *I must forget these side issues and remember my mission.*

side|kick /sˈaɪdkɪk/ (sidekicks) N-COUNT [oft poss N] Someone's **sidekick** is a person who accompanies them and helps them, and who you believe to be less intelligent or less important than the other person. [INFORMAL] ❏ *His sons, brother and nephews were his armed sidekicks.*

side|light /sˈaɪdlaɪt/ (sidelights) ◼ N-COUNT The **sidelights** on a vehicle are lights on its sides. [AM] ◼ N-COUNT The **sidelights** on a vehicle are the small lights at the front that help other drivers to notice the vehicle and to judge its width. [BRIT]

in AM, use **parking lights**

◼ N-COUNT [oft N on n] A **sidelight** on a particular situation is a piece of information about that situation which is interesting but which is not particularly important. ❏ *The book is full of amusing sidelights on his family background.*

side|line /sˈaɪdlaɪn/ (sidelines, sidelining, sidelined)
◼ N-COUNT A **sideline** is something that you do in addition to your main job in order to earn extra money. ❏ *It was quite a lucrative sideline.* ◼ N-PLURAL The **sidelines** are the lines marking the long sides of the playing area, for example, on a football field or tennis court. ◼ N-PLURAL If you are on **the sidelines** in a situation, you do not influence events at all, either because you have chosen not to be involved, or because other people have not involved you. ❏ *France no longer wants to be left on the sidelines when critical decisions are made.* ◼ V-T [usu passive] If someone or something **is sidelined**, they are made to seem unimportant and not included in what people are doing. ❏ *For months he had been under pressure to resign and was about to be sidelined anyway.*

side|long /sˈaɪdlɒŋ/ ADJ [ADJ n] If you give someone a **sidelong** look, you look at them out of the corner of your eyes. ❏ *She gave him a quick sidelong glance.*

side-on ADJ A **side-on** collision or view is a collision or view from the side of an object. ❏ *...steel beams built into the doors for protection against a side-on crash.*

side or|der (side orders) N-COUNT A **side order** is an amount of a food that you order in a restaurant to be served at the same time as the main dish. ❏ *...a side order of potato salad.*

side road (side roads) N-COUNT A **side road** is a road which leads off a busier, more important road.

side|saddle /sˈaɪdsædᵊl/ ADV [ADV after v] When you ride a horse **sidesaddle**, you sit on a special saddle with both your legs on one side rather than one leg on each side of the horse. ❏ *Naomi was given a pony and taught to ride sidesaddle.*

side sal|ad (side salads) N-COUNT A **side salad** is a bowl of salad for one person which is served with a main meal.

side|show /sˈaɪdʃoʊ/ (sideshows) ◼ N-COUNT [oft N to n] A **sideshow** is a less important or less significant event or situation related to a larger, more important one that is happening at the same time. ❏ *In the end, the meeting was a sideshow to a political storm that broke Thursday.* ◼ N-COUNT At a circus or fair, a **sideshow** is a performance that you watch or a game of skill that you play, that is provided in addition to the main entertainment.

side-splitting ◼ ADJ Something that is **side-splitting** is very funny and makes you laugh a lot. [INFORMAL] ❏ *...a side-splitting joke.* ◼ → See feature box at **humor**

side|step /sˈaɪdstɛp/ (sidesteps, sidestepping, sidestepped) also **side-step** V-T If you **sidestep** a problem, you avoid discussing it or dealing with it. ❏ *Rarely, if ever, does he sidestep a question.*

side street (side streets) N-COUNT A **side street** is a quiet, often narrow street which leads off a busier street.

side|swipe /sˈaɪdswaɪp/ (sideswipes) N-COUNT [usu N at n] If you take a **sideswipe** at someone, you make an unexpected critical remark about them while you are talking about something else. ❏ *Despite the increasingly hostile sideswipes at him, the CEO is secure in his post.*

side|track /sˈaɪdtræk/ (sidetracks, sidetracking, sidetracked) also **side-track** V-T If you **are sidetracked** by something, it makes you forget what you intended to do or say, and start instead doing or talking about a different thing. ❏ *He'd managed to avoid being sidetracked by Schneider's problems.* ❏ *The leadership moved to sidetrack the proposal.* ❏ *They have a tendency to try to sidetrack you from your task.*

side-view mir|ror (side-view mirrors) ◼ N-COUNT The **side-view mirrors** on a car are the mirrors on each side of the car on the outside. [AM]

in BRIT, use **wing mirror**

◼ → See also color supplement

side|walk /sˈaɪdwɔːk/ (sidewalks) ◼ N-COUNT A **sidewalk** is a path with a hard surface by the side of a road. [AM] ❏ *Two men and a woman were walking briskly down the sidewalk toward him.*

in BRIT, use **pavement**

◼ → See feature box at **drive**

side|ways /sˈaɪdweɪz/ ◼ ADV [ADV after v] **Sideways** means from or toward the side of something or someone. ❏ *Piercey glanced sideways at her.* ❏ *The ladder blew sideways.* • ADJ [ADJ n] **Sideways** is also an adjective. ❏ *Alfred shot him a sideways glance.* ◼ ADV [ADV after v] If you are moved **sideways** at work, you move to another job at the same level as your old job. ❏ *He would be moved sideways, rather than demoted.* • ADJ [ADJ n] **Sideways** is also an adjective. ❏ *...her recent sideways move.*

sid|ing /sˈaɪdɪŋ/ (sidings) ◼ N-UNCOUNT **Siding** is a wooden, plastic, or metal covering on the outside walls of a building. [AM] ◼ N-COUNT A **siding** is a short railroad track beside the main tracks, where engines and cars are left when they are not being used.

si|dle /sˈaɪdᵊl/ (sidles, sidling, sidled) V-I If you **sidle** somewhere, you walk there in a quiet or cautious way, as if you do not want anyone to notice you. ❏ *A young man sidled up to me and said, "May I help you?"*

SIDS /sˈɪdz/ N-UNCOUNT **SIDS** is used to talk about the sudden death of a baby while it is asleep, when it had not previously been ill. **SIDS** is an abbreviation for 'sudden infant death syndrome.'

siè|cle → see **fin de siècle**

siege /sˈiːdʒ/ (sieges) ◼ N-COUNT [also under N] A **siege** is a military or police operation in which soldiers or police surround a place in order to force the people there to come out or give up control of the place. ❏ *We must do everything possible to lift the siege.* ◼ PHRASE If police, soldiers, or journalists **lay siege** to a place, they surround it in order to force the people there to come out or give up control of the place. ❑ *The rebels laid siege to the governor's residence.* **3** → See feature box at **conflict**

siege men|tal|ity N-SING [also no det] If a group of people have a **siege mentality**, they think that other people are constantly trying to harm or defeat them, and so they care only about protecting themselves. ❑ *Police officers had a siege mentality that isolated them from the people they served.*

si|er|ra /siɛrə/ (**sierras**) N-COUNT; N-IN-NAMES A **sierra** is a range of mountains with jagged peaks. [AM] ❑ *...the remote sierras of the south.* ❑ *...a bustling commercial center in the Sierra Madre.*

si|es|ta /siɛstə/ (**siestas**) N-COUNT A **siesta** is a short sleep or rest which you have in the early afternoon, especially in hot countries. ❑ *They have a siesta during the hottest part of the day.*

sieve /sɪv/ (**sieves, sieving, sieved**) **1** N-COUNT A **sieve** is a tool used for separating solids from liquids or larger pieces of something from smaller pieces. It consists of a metal or plastic ring with a wire or plastic net underneath, which the liquid or smaller pieces pass through. ❑ *Press the raspberries through a fine sieve to form a puree.* **2** V-T When you **sieve** a substance, you put it through a sieve. ❑ *Cream the margarine in a small bowl, then sieve the powdered sugar into it.* **3** → See feature box at **household**

sift /sɪft/ (**sifts, sifting, sifted**) **1** V-T If you **sift** a powder such as flour or sand, you put it through a sieve in order to remove large pieces or lumps. ❑ *Sift the flour and baking powder into a medium-sized mixing bowl.* **2** V-T/V-I If you **sift** through something such as evidence, you examine it thoroughly. ❑ *Police officers have continued to sift through the wreckage following yesterday's bomb attack.*

sigh ♦◇◇ /saɪ/ (**sighs, sighing, sighed**) **1** V-I When you **sigh**, you let out a deep breath, as a way of expressing feelings such as disappointment, tiredness, or pleasure. ❑ *Michael sighed wearily.* ❑ *Roberta sighed with relief.* • N-COUNT **Sigh** is also a noun. ❑ *She kicked off her shoes with a sigh.* **2** PHRASE If people breathe or heave a **sigh of relief**, they feel happy that something unpleasant has not happened or is no longer happening. ❑ *With monetary mayhem now retreating into memory, European countries can breathe a collective sigh of relief.*

COLLOCATIONS

sigh
NOUN **1**
adjective + **sigh**: audible, deep, long, weary; collective
verb + **sigh**: breathe, emit, heave; hear
VERB **1**
sigh + adverb: audibly, deeply, heavily, loudly; inwardly, wearily, wistfully

---

sight ♦♦◇ /saɪt/ (**sights, sighting, sighted**) **1** N-UNCOUNT Someone's **sight** is their ability to see. ❑ *My sight is failing, and I can't see to read any more.* **2** N-SING The **sight of** something is the act of seeing it or an occasion on which you see it. ❑ *I faint at the sight of blood.* **3** N-COUNT A **sight** is something that you see. ❑ *The practice of hanging clothes across the street is a common sight in many parts of the city.* **4** V-T If you **sight** someone or something, you suddenly see them, often briefly. ❑ *The security forces sighted a group of young men that had crossed the border.* **5** N-PLURAL The **sights** are the places that are interesting to see and that are often visited by tourists. ❑ *We'd toured the sights of Paris.* **6** → see also **sighting** **7** PHRASE If you **catch sight of** someone, you suddenly see them, often briefly. ❑ *Then he caught sight of her small black velvet hat in the crowd.* **8** PHRASE If you say that something seems to have certain characteristics **at first sight**, you mean that it appears to have the features you describe when you first see it but later it is found to be different. ❑ *The theory is not as simple as you might think at first sight.* **9** PHRASE If something **is in sight** or **within sight**, you can see it. If it is **out of sight**, you cannot see it. ❑ *The sandy beach was in sight.* ❑ *The Atlantic coast is within sight of the hotel.* **10** PHRASE If a result or a decision is **in sight** or **within sight**, it is likely to happen within a short time. ❑ *An agreement on many aspects of trade policy was in sight.* **11** PHRASE If you **lose sight of** an important aspect of something, you no longer pay attention to it because you are worrying about less important things. ❑ *In some cases, U.S. industry has lost sight of customer needs in designing products.* **12** PHRASE If someone is ordered to do something **on sight**, they have to do it without delay, as soon as a person or thing is seen. ❑ *Troops shot anyone suspicious on sight.* **13** PHRASE If you **set** your **sights on** something, you decide that you want it and try hard to get it. ❑ *They have set their sights on the world record.* **14** PHRASE If you **have** something **in** your **sights**, you are trying hard to achieve it, and you have a good chance of success. If you **have** someone **in** your **sights**, you are determined to catch, defeat, or overcome them. ❑ *The Giants' slugger also has fourth place in his sights, needing 13 homers to move past Frank Robinson's 586.* ❑ *Is this knowledge of yours the reason the murderer now has you in his sights?*

COLLOCATIONS

sight
NOUN **3**
adjective + **sight**: familiar; depressing, sad, sorry; welcome; common, rare; awesome, spectacular

---
SYNONYMS

sight
NOUN
1
vision: *It causes blindness or serious loss of vision.*
eyesight: *He suffered from poor eyesight and could no longer read properly.*
2
view: *He stood up to get a better view of the blackboard.*
sighting: *...the sighting of a rare sea bird at Lundy island.*
glimpse: *They had waited 24 hours to catch a glimpse of their heroine.*

---

sight|ed /saɪtɪd/ **1** ADJ [ADJ n] **Sighted** people have the ability to see. This word is usually used to contrast people who can see with people who are blind. ❑ *Blind children tend to be more passive in this area of motor development than sighted children.* **2** → see also **clear-sighted, farsighted, long-sighted, nearsighted, shortsighted**

sight|ing /saɪtɪŋ/ (**sightings**) N-COUNT A **sighting** of something, especially something unusual or unexpected is an occasion on which it is seen. ❑ *...the sighting of a rare sea bird at Lundy island.*

sight|less /saɪtlɪs/ ADJ Someone who is **sightless** is blind. [LITERARY] ❑ *He wiped a tear from his sightless eyes.*

sight-read (**sight-reads, sight-reading**)

The form **sight-read** is used in the present tense, where it is pronounced /saɪt riːd/, and is the past tense and past participle, pronounced /saɪt rɛd/.

V-I Someone who can **sight-read** can play or sing music from a printed sheet the first time they see it, without practicing it beforehand. ❑ *Symphony musicians cannot necessarily sight-read.*

sight|see|ing /saɪtsiːɪŋ/ N-UNCOUNT If you go **sightseeing** or do some **sightseeing**, you travel around visiting the interesting places that tourists usually visit. ❑ *...a day's sightseeing in Venice.*

sight|seer /saɪtsiːər/ (**sightseers**) N-COUNT A **sightseer** is someone who is traveling around visiting the interesting places that tourists usually visit. ❑ *...busloads of sightseers.*

sign ♦♦♦ /saɪn/ (**signs, signing, signed**) **1** N-COUNT A **sign** is a mark or shape that always has a particular meaning, for example, in mathematics or music. ❑ *Equations are generally written with an equal sign.* **2** N-COUNT A **sign** is a movement of your arms, hands, or head which is intended to have a particular meaning. ❑ *They gave Lavalle the thumbs-up sign.* **3** V-T If you **sign**, you communicate with someone using sign language. If a program or performance **is signed**, someone uses sign language so that deaf people can understand it. ❑ *All programs will be either "signed" or subtitled.* **4** N-COUNT A **sign** is a piece of wood, metal, or plastic with words or pictures on it. Signs give you information about something, or give you a warning or an instruction. ❑ *...a sign saying that the highway was closed because of snow.* **5** N-VAR If there is a **sign** of something, there is something which shows that it exists or is happening. ❑ *They are prepared to hand back a hundred prisoners of war a day as a sign of good will.* ❑ *His face and movements rarely betrayed a sign of nerves.* **6** V-T When you **sign** a document, you write your name on it, usually at the end or in a special space. You do this to indicate that you have written the document, that you agree with what is written, or that you were present as a witness. ❑ *World leaders are expected to sign a treaty pledging to increase environmental protection.* **7** V-T/V-I If an organization **signs** someone or if someone **signs** for an organization, they sign a contract agreeing to work for that organization for a specified period of time. ❑ *They signed a new quarterback* **8** N-COUNT In astrology, a **sign** or a **sign** of the zodiac is one of the twelve areas into which the heavens are divided. ❑ *The new moon takes place in your opposite sign of Libra on the 15th.* **9** → see also **signing** **10** PHRASE If you say that there is **no sign of** someone, you mean that they have not yet arrived, although you are expecting them to come. ❑ *The train was on time, but there was no sign of my Finnish friend.* **11** → See feature box at **learning**

▶ **sign for** PHRASAL VERB If you **sign for** something, you officially state that you have received it, by signing a form or book. ❑ *When the letter carrier delivers your order, check the carton before signing for it.*

▶ **sign in** PHRASAL VERB If you **sign in**, you officially indicate that you have arrived at a hotel or club by signing a book or form. ❑ *I signed in and crunched across the gravel to my room.*

▶ **sign over** PHRASAL VERB If you **sign** something **over**, you sign documents that give someone else property, possessions, or rights that were previously yours. ❑ *Two years ago, he signed over his art collection to the New York Metropolitan Museum of Art.*

▶ **sign up** PHRASAL VERB If you **sign up** for an organization or if an organization **signs** you **up**, you sign a contract officially agreeing to do a job or course of study. ❑ *He signed up as a flight attendant with Korean Air.*

sign|age /sáɪnɪdʒ/ N-UNCOUNT **Signage** is signs, especially road signs and advertising signs, considered collectively. ❑ *They don't allow signage around the stadium.*

sig|nal ✦✧✧ /sɪgnəl/ (**signals, signaling** or **signalling, signaled** or **signalled**) **1** N-COUNT A **signal** is a gesture, sound, or action which is intended to give a particular message to the person who sees or hears it. ❑ *They fired three distress signals.* ❑ *As soon as it was dark, Mrs. Evans gave the signal.* **2** V-T/V-I If you **signal** to someone, you make a gesture or sound in order to send them a particular message. ❑ *Mandy started after him, signaling to Jesse to follow.* ❑ *She signaled to Ted that she was moving forward.* **3** N-COUNT If an event or action is a **signal** of something, it suggests that this thing exists or is going to happen. ❑ *Kurdish leaders saw the visit as an important signal of support.* **4** V-T If someone or something **signals** an event, they suggest that the event is happening or likely to happen. ❑ *He seemed to be signaling important shifts in U.S. government policy.* **5** N-COUNT A **signal** is a piece of equipment beside a railroad, which indicates to train drivers whether they should stop the train or not. ❑ *A signal failure contributed to the crash.* **6** N-COUNT A **signal** is a series of radio waves, light waves, or changes in electrical current which may carry information. ❑ *...high-frequency radio signals.* **7** → See feature box at **drive**

sig|nal box (**signal boxes**) N-COUNT A **signal box** is a small building near a railroad, which contains the switches used to control the signals.

signal|man /sɪgnəlmən/ (**signalmen**) N-COUNT A **signalman** is a man whose job is to control the signals on a particular section of a railroad.

signal|woman /sɪgnəlwʊmən/ (**signalwomen**) N-COUNT A **signalwoman** is a woman whose job is to control the signals on a particular section of a railroad.

sig|na|tory /sɪgnətɔri/ (**signatories**) N-COUNT The **signatories** of an official document are the people, organizations, or countries that have signed it. [FORMAL] ❑ *Both countries are signatories to the Nuclear Non-Proliferation Treaty.*

sig|na|ture /sɪgnətʃər, -tʃʊər/ (**signatures**) N-COUNT Your **signature** is your name, written in your own characteristic way, often at the end of a document to indicate that you wrote the document or that you agree with what it says. ❑ *I was writing my signature at the bottom of the page.*

sig|na|ture tune (**signature tunes**) N-COUNT A **signature tune** is the same as a **theme song**. [mainly BRIT]

sign|board /sáɪnbɔrd/ (**signboards**) N-COUNT A **signboard** is a piece of wood which has been painted with pictures or words and which gives some information about a particular place, product, or event. ❑ *The signboard outside the factory read 'baby milk plant.'*

sign|er /sáɪnər/ (**signers**) **1** N-COUNT A **signer** is someone who communicates to deaf people using sign language. ❑ *We provide signers for deaf people and readers for blind people.* **2** N-COUNT The **signer** of a document such as a contract is the person who has signed it. [AM] ❑ *You understand that any authorized signer on your checking account can access your credit line.* ❑ *...one of the signers of the treaty.*

sig|net ring /sɪgnɪt rɪŋ/ (**signet rings**) N-COUNT A **signet ring** is a ring which has a flat oval or circular section at the front with a pattern or letters carved into it.

sig|nifi|cance /sɪgnɪfɪkəns/ N-UNCOUNT The **significance** of something is the importance that it has, usually because it will have an effect on a situation or shows something about a situation. ❑ *Ideas about the social significance of religion have changed over time.*

sig|nifi|cant ✦✧✧ /sɪgnɪfɪkənt/ **1** ADJ A **significant** amount or effect is large enough to be important or affect a situation to a noticeable degree. ❑ *A small, but significant number of 11-year-olds are illiterate.* • **sig|nifi|cant|ly** ADV ❑ *The number of Senators now supporting him had increased significantly.* **2** ADJ A **significant** fact, event, or thing is one that is important or shows something. ❑ *I think it was significant that he never knew his own father.* • **sig|nifi|cant|ly** ADV ❑ *Significantly, the company recently opened a huge store in Atlanta.*

SYNONYMS

significant
ADJ **1**
important: *This project is every bit as important to me as it is to you.*
marked: *There has been a marked increase in crimes against property.*
notable: *The proposed new structure is notable not only for its height, but also for its shape.*
considerable: *To be without Pearce would be a considerable blow.*

sig|nifi|cant oth|er (**significant others**) N-COUNT If you refer to your **significant other**, you are referring to your wife, husband, or the person you are having a romantic relationship with.

sig|ni|fy /sɪgnɪfaɪ/ (**signifies, signifying, signified**) **1** V-T If an event, a sign, or a symbol **signifies** something, it is a sign of that thing or represents that thing. ❑ *These were not the only changes that signified the end of boyhood.* **2** V-T If you **signify** something, you make a sign or gesture in order to communicate a particular meaning. ❑ *Two jurors signified their dissent.*

sign|ing /sáɪnɪŋ/ (**signings**) **1** N-UNCOUNT The **signing of** a document is the act of writing your name to indicate that you agree with what it says or to say that you have been present to witness other people writing their signature. ❑ *Spain's top priority is the signing of the treaty.* **2** N-COUNT [usu with supp] A **signing** is someone who has recently signed a contract agreeing to play for a sports team or work for a record company. ❑ *...the salary paid to the club's latest signing.* **3** N-UNCOUNT The **signing of** a player by a sports team or a group by a record company is the act of drawing up a legal document setting out the length and terms of the association between them. ❑ *The ranks of professional tennis swelled with the signing of Bobby Riggs.* **4** N-UNCOUNT **Signing** is the use of sign language to communicate with someone who is deaf. ❑ *The two deaf actors converse solely in signing.*

sign lan|guage (**sign languages**) N-VAR **Sign language** is movements of your hands and arms used to communicate. There are several official systems of sign language, used, for example, by deaf people. Movements are also sometimes invented by people when they want to communicate with someone who does not speak the same language. ❑ *Her son used sign language to tell her what happened.*

sign|post /sáɪnpoʊst/ (**signposts**) N-COUNT A **signpost** is a sign where roads meet that tells you which direction to go in to reach a particular place or different places. ❑ *Turn off at the signpost for the East 71st Street exit.*

sign|post|ed /sáɪnpoʊstɪd/ ADJ A place or route that is **signposted** has signposts beside the road to show the way. ❑ *The entrance is well signposted and is in Marbury Road.*

Sikh /siːk/ (Sikhs) N-COUNT A **Sikh** is a person who follows the Indian religion of Sikhism. ❑ *For traditional Sikhs, the external appearance is sacred.* ❑ *...a Sikh temple.*

Sikh|ism /siːkɪzəm/ N-UNCOUNT **Sikhism** is an Indian religion which separated from Hinduism in the sixteenth century and which teaches that there is only one God.

si|lage /saɪlɪdʒ/ N-UNCOUNT **Silage** is food for cattle that is made by cutting a crop such as grass or corn when it is green and then keeping it covered.

si|lence ✦✧ /saɪləns/ (silences, silencing, silenced) **1** N-VAR If there is **silence**, nobody is speaking. ❑ *They stood in silence.* ❑ *He never lets those long silences develop during dinner.* **2** N-UNCOUNT Someone's **silence** about something is their failure or refusal to speak to other people about it. ❑ *The district court ruled that Popper's silence in court today should be entered as a plea of not guilty.* • PHRASE If someone **breaks** their **silence** about something, they talk about something that they have not talked about before or for a long time. **3** V-T If someone **silences** you, they stop you from expressing opinions that they do not agree with. ❑ *Like other tyrants, he tried to silence anyone who spoke out against him.*

SYNONYMS

silence
NOUN **1**
quiet: *Jeremy wants some peace and quiet before his big match.*
peace: *One more question and I'll leave you in peace.*
hush: *A hush suddenly fell over the crowd.*
calm: *...the rural calm of Grand Rapids, Michigan.*

COLLOCATIONS

silence
NOUN
1
adjective + **silence**: awkward, embarrassed, stunned, uncomfortable; long, two-minute; stony, sullen
verb + **silence**: maintain, observe; break, interrupt
2
adjective + **silence**: deathly, eerie
verb + **silence**: shatter

---

si|lenc|er /saɪlənsər/ (silencers) **1** N-COUNT A **silencer** is a device that is fitted onto a gun to make it very quiet when it is fired. ❑ *...a pistol that was equipped with a silencer.* **2** N-COUNT A **silencer** is a device on a car exhaust that makes it quieter. [BRIT]

in AM, use **muffler**

si|lent ✦✧ /saɪlənt/ **1** ADJ [v-link ADJ] Someone who is **silent** is not speaking. ❑ *Trish was silent because she was reluctant to put her thoughts into words.* ❑ *He spoke no English and was completely silent during the visit.* • **si|lent|ly** ADV [ADV with v] ❑ *She and Ned sat silently for a moment, absorbing the peace of the lake.* **2** ADJ A place that is **silent** is completely quiet, with no sound at all. Something that is **silent** makes no sound at all. ❑ *The room was silent except for the TV.* • **si|lent|ly** ADV [ADV with v] ❑ *Strange shadows moved silently in the almost permanent darkness.* **3** ADJ [ADJ n] A **silent** movie has pictures usually accompanied by music but does not have the actors' voices or any other sounds. ❑ *...one of the famous silent films of Charlie Chaplin.* **4** PHRASE If you **give** someone **the silent treatment**, you do not speak to them for a period of time because you are annoyed at something they have done. ❑ *He fully expected his mother to give him the silent treatment.*

si|lent ma|jor|ity N-SING-COLL If you believe that, in society or in a particular group, the opinions of most people are very different from the opinions that are most often heard in public, you can refer to these people as the **silent majority**. ❑ *The silent majority of supportive parents and teachers should make their views known.*

si|lent part|ner (silent partners) N-COUNT A **silent partner** is a person who provides some of the capital for a business but who does not take an active part in managing the business. [AM, BUSINESS] ❑ *...firms run by his friends in which he was a silent partner.*

in BRIT, use **sleeping partner**

si|lent treat|ment N-SING If you give someone the **silent treatment**, you refuse to speak to them because you are annoyed with them or disapprove of something that they have done. ❑ *Even parents giving each other the silent treatment can disrupt children's sleep, says the report.*

sil|hou|ette /sɪluɛt/ (silhouettes) **1** N-COUNT A **silhouette** is the solid dark shape that you see when someone or something has a bright light or pale background behind them. ❑ *The dark silhouette of the castle ruins stood out boldly against the fading light.* **2** N-COUNT The **silhouette** of something is the outline that it has, which often helps you to recognize it. ❑ *...the distinctive silhouette of the Manhattan skyline.*

sil|hou|ett|ed /sɪluɛtɪd/ ADJ [usu v-link ADJ against n] If someone or something is **silhouetted** against a background, you can see their silhouette. ❑ *Silhouetted against the sun stood the figure of a man.*

sili|ca /sɪlɪkə/ N-UNCOUNT **Silica** is silicon dioxide, a compound of silicon which is found in sand, quartz, and flint, and which is used to make glass.

sili|cate /sɪlɪkɪt/ (silicates) N-MASS A **silicate** is a compound of silica which does not dissolve. There are many different kinds of silicate. ❑ *...large amounts of aluminum silicate.*

sili|con /sɪlɪkən/ N-UNCOUNT **Silicon** is an element that is found in sand and in minerals such as quartz and granite. Silicon is used to make parts of computers and other electronic equipment. ❑ *The new chip will be made from a piece of silicon about the size of a postage stamp.*

sili|con chip (silicon chips) N-COUNT A **silicon chip** is a very small piece of silicon inside a computer. It has electronic circuits on it and can hold large quantities of information or perform mathematical or logical operations. ❑ *Today's silicon chip-based computers can't come close.*

sili|cone /sɪlɪkoʊn/ N-UNCOUNT **Silicone** is a tough artificial substance made from silicon, which is used to make polishes, and also used in cosmetic surgery and plastic surgery. ❑ *...women who suffered health problems from silicone breast implants that leak.*

silk /sɪlk/ (silks) **1** N-MASS **Silk** is a substance which is made into smooth fine cloth and sewing thread. You can also refer to this cloth or thread as **silk**. ❑ *They continued to get their silks from China.* ❑ *Pauline wore a silk dress with a strand of pearls.* **2** → See feature box at **sewing**

silk|en /sɪlkən/ **1** ADJ [usu ADJ n] **Silken** is used to describe things that are very pleasantly smooth and soft. [LITERARY] ❑ *...her long silken hair.* **2** ADJ [ADJ n] A **silken** garment, fabric, or rope is made of silk or a material that looks like silk. [LITERARY] ❑ *...silken cushions.*

silk-screen also **silkscreen** ADJ [ADJ n] **Silk-screen** printing is a method of printing patterns onto cloth by forcing paint or dyes through silk or similar material. ❑ *...silk-screen prints.*

silk|worm /sɪlkwɜːrm/ (silkworms) N-COUNT A **silkworm** is the young form of a Chinese moth and it produces silk.

silky /sɪlki/ (silkier, silkiest) ADJ If something has a **silky** texture, it is smooth, soft, and shiny, like silk. ❑ *...dresses in seductively silky fabrics.*

sill /sɪl/ (sills) N-COUNT A **sill** is a shelf along the bottom edge of a window, either inside or outside a building. ❑ *Whitlock was perched on the sill of the room's only window.*

sil|ly /sɪli/ (sillier, silliest) ADJ If you say that someone or something is **silly**, you mean that they are foolish, childish, or ridiculous. ❑ *My best friend tells me that I am silly to be upset about this.* ❑ *I thought it would be silly to be too rude at that stage.*

silo /saɪloʊ/ (silos) **1** N-COUNT A **silo** is a tall, round, metal tower on a farm, in which grass, grain, or some other substance is stored. ❑ *Before silos were invented, cows gave less milk during winter because they had no green grass to eat.* ❑ *...a grain silo.* **2** N-COUNT A **silo** is a specially built place underground where a nuclear missile is kept. ❑ *...underground nuclear missile silos.*

silt /sɪlt/ N-UNCOUNT **Silt** is fine sand, soil, or mud which is carried along by a river. ❑ *The lake was almost solid with silt and vegetation.*

sil|ver ✦✧ /sɪlvər/ **1** N-UNCOUNT **Silver** is a valuable pale gray metal that is used for making jewelry and ornaments. ❑ *...a hand-crafted brooch made from silver.* ❑ *...amber earrings set in silver.* **2** N-UNCOUNT **Silver** consists of coins that are made from silver or that look like silver. ❑ ...*the basement where $150,000 in silver was buried.* **3** N-UNCOUNT [also the N] You can use **silver** to refer to all the things in a house that are made of silver, especially the flatware and dishes. ❑ *He beat the rugs and polished the silver.* **4** COLOR **Silver** is used to describe things that are shiny and pale gray in color. ❑ *He had thick silver hair which needed cutting.* **5** → See also color supplement

sil|ver birch (silver birches or silver birch) N-COUNT A **silver birch** is a tree with a grayish-white trunk and branches.

sil|ver dol|lar (silver dollars) N-COUNT A **silver dollar** is an American coin, worth one dollar, that is made of silver.

sil|vered /sɪlvərd/ ADJ [usu ADJ n] You can describe something as **silvered** when it has become silver in color. [LITERARY] ❑ *He had a magnificent head of silvered hair.*

sil|ver ju|bi|lee (silver jubilees) N-COUNT A **silver jubilee** is the 25th anniversary of an important event such as a person becoming king or queen, or an organization being started.

sil|ver lin|ing **1** PHRASE If you say that **every cloud has a silver lining**, you mean that every sad or unpleasant situation has a positive side to it. ❑ *As they say, every cloud has a silver lining. We have drawn lessons from the decisions taken.* **2** N-SING If you talk about a **silver lining**, you are talking about something positive that comes out of a sad or unpleasant situation. ❑ *The fall in inflation is the silver lining of the prolonged recession.*

sil|ver med|al (silver medals) N-COUNT If you win a **silver medal**, you come second in a competition, especially a sports contest, and are given a medal made of silver as a prize. ❑ *Gillingham won the silver medal in the 200 meters at Seoul.*

sil|ver plate N-UNCOUNT [oft N n] **Silver plate** is metal that has been coated with a thin layer of silver. ❑ ...*silver-plate flatware.*

silver-plated ADJ Something that is **silver-plated** is covered with a very thin layer of silver. ❑ ...*silver-plated cutlery.*

sil|ver screen N-SING [the N] People sometimes refer to the movies that are shown in theaters as **the silver screen**. ❑ *Marlon Brando, Steve McQueen, and James Dean are now legends of the silver screen.*

silver|smith /sɪlvərsmɪθ/ (silversmiths) N-COUNT A **silversmith** is a person who makes things out of silver.

silver-tongued ADJ [usu ADJ n] A **silver-tongued** person is very skillful at persuading people to believe what they say or to do what they want them to do. ❑ ...*a silver-tongued lawyer.*

silver|ware /sɪlvərwɛər/ N-UNCOUNT You can use **silverware** to refer to all the things in a house that are made of silver, especially the flatware and dishes. ❑ *There was a serving spoon missing when Nina put the silverware back in its box.*

sil|ver wed|ding (silver weddings) N-COUNT [usu poss N] A married couple's **silver wedding** or **silver wedding anniversary** is the 25th anniversary of their wedding. ❑ *He and Helen celebrated their silver wedding last year.*

sil|very /sɪlvəri/ ADJ **Silvery** things look like silver or are the color of silver. ❑ *My father is a small, intense man with silvery hair.*

sim /sɪm/ (sims) N-COUNT A **sim** is a computer game that simulates an activity such as playing a sport or flying an aircraft. [COMPUTING]

SIM card /sɪm kɑrd/ (SIM cards) N-COUNT A **SIM card** is a microchip in a cell phone that connects it to a particular phone network. **SIM** is an abbreviation for 'Subscriber Identity Module.'

sim|ian /sɪmiən/ **1** ADJ [usu ADJ n] If someone has a **simian** face, they look a little like a monkey. [FORMAL] ❑ *Ada had a wrinkled, simian face.* **2** ADJ [usu ADJ n] **Simian** is used to describe things relating to monkeys or apes. [TECHNICAL] ❑ ...*a simian virus.*

simi|lar ✦✦✧ /sɪmɪlər/ ADJ If one thing is **similar to** another, or if two things are **similar**, they have features that are the same. ❑ ...*a savory cake with a texture similar to that of carrot cake.* ❑ *The accident was similar to one that happened in 1973.*

SYNONYMS

similar
ADJ
comparable: *In other comparable countries, real wages increased much more rapidly.*
alike: *We looked very alike.*

simi|lar|ity /sɪmɪlærɪti/ (similarities) **1** N-UNCOUNT If there is a **similarity** between two or more things, they are similar to each other. ❑ ...*the astonishing similarity between my brother and my first-born son.* ❑ *There was a very basic similarity in our philosophy.* **2** N-COUNT **Similarities** are features that things have which make them similar to each other. ❑ *There were significant similarities between mother and son.*

simi|lar|ly /sɪmɪlərli/ **1** ADV You use **similarly** to say that something is similar to something else. ❑ *Most of the men who now gathered around him again were similarly dressed.* **2** ADV [ADV with cl] You use **similarly** when mentioning a fact or situation that is similar to the one you have just mentioned. ❑ *Same-sex marriages are not recognized. Similarly, civil unions are not legal.*

simi|le /sɪmɪli/ (similes) N-COUNT A **simile** is an expression which describes a person or thing as being similar to someone or something else. For example, the sentences 'She runs like a deer' and 'He's as white as a sheet' contain similes.

sim|mer /sɪmər/ (simmers, simmering, simmered) **1** V-T/V-I When you **simmer** food or when it **simmers**, you cook it by keeping it at boiling point or just below boiling point. ❑ *Make an infusion by boiling and simmering the rhubarb and camomile together.* • N-SING **Simmer** is also a noun. ❑ *Combine the stock, whole onion and peppercorns in a pan and bring to a simmer.* **2** V-I If a conflict or a quarrel **simmers**, it does not actually happen for a period of time, but eventually builds up to the point where it does. ❑ ...*bitter divisions that have simmered for more than half a century.* **3** → See feature box at **cooking**

sim|per /sɪmpər/ (simpers, simpering, simpered) V-I When someone **simpers**, they smile in a rather silly way. ❑ *The maid lowered her chin and simpered.* • N-COUNT **Simper** is also a noun. ❑ *Thank you doctor, he said with a simper.*

sim|ple ✦✦✧ /sɪmp°l/ (simpler, simplest) **1** ADJ If you describe something as **simple**, you mean that it is not complicated, and is therefore easy to understand. ❑ ...*simple pictures and diagrams.* ❑ ...*pages of simple advice on filling in your tax form.* • **simp|ly** ADV [ADV with v] ❑ *When applying for a visa extension state simply and clearly the reasons why you need an extension.* **2** ADJ If you describe people or things as **simple**, you mean that they have all the basic or necessary things they require, but nothing extra. ❑ *He ate a simple dinner of rice and beans.* ❑ ...*the simple pleasures of childhood.* • **simp|ly** ADV [ADV after v] ❑ *The living room is furnished simply with white wicker furniture and blue-and-white fabrics.* **3** ADJ If a problem is **simple** or if its solution is **simple**, the problem can be solved easily. ❑ *Some puzzles look difficult but are actually quite simple.* **4** ADJ A **simple** task is easy to do. ❑ *The job itself had been simple enough.* • **simp|ly** ADV [ADV after v] ❑ *We can do things that were not possible before, and they can be done simply.* **5** ADJ [ADJ n] You use **simple** to emphasize that the thing you are referring to is the only important or relevant reason for something. [EMPHASIS] ❑ *His refusal to talk was simple stubbornness.* **6** ADJ In grammar, **simple** tenses are ones which are formed without an auxiliary verb 'be,' for example, 'I dressed and went for a walk' and 'This tastes nice.' **Simple** verb groups are used especially to refer to completed actions, regular actions, and situations. Compare **continuous**. **7** → see also **simply**

SYNONYMS

simple
ADJ **1**
uncomplicated: ...*good, fresh British cooking with its uncomplicated, direct flavors.*
clear: *The book is clear, readable, and adequately illustrated.*
plain: *It was a plain, gray stone house.*
straightforward: ...*simple, straightforward language.*

sim|ple in|ter|est N-UNCOUNT **Simple interest** is interest that is calculated on an original sum of money and not also on interest which has previously been added to the sum. Compare **compound interest**. [BUSINESS] ❑ ...*an investment that pays only simple interest.*

simple-minded ADJ If you describe someone as **simple-minded**, you believe that they interpret things in a way that is too simple and do not understand how complicated things are. [DISAPPROVAL] ❑ *They were all simple-minded romantics.*

sim|ple|ton /sɪmpəltən/ (simpletons) N-COUNT If you call someone a **simpleton**, you think they are easily deceived or not very intelligent. [DISAPPROVAL] ❑ *"But Ian's such a simpleton,"* she laughed.

sim|plic|ity /sɪmplɪsɪti/ N-UNCOUNT The **simplicity** of something is the fact that it is not complicated and can be understood or done easily. ❑ *The apparent simplicity of his plot is deceptive.*

sim|pli|fi|ca|tion /sɪmplɪfɪkeɪʃ°n/ (simplifications) **1** N-COUNT You can use **simplification** to refer to the thing that is produced when you make something simpler or when you reduce it to its basic elements. ❑ *Like any such diagram, it is a simplification.* **2** N-UNCOUNT **Simplification** is the act or process of making something simpler. ❑ *Everyone favors the simplification of court procedures.*

sim|pli|fy /sɪmplɪfaɪ/ (simplifies, simplifying, simplified) V-T If you **simplify** something, you make it easier to understand or you remove the things which make it complex. ❑ *Our aim is to simplify the complex social security system.*

sim|plis|tic /sɪmplɪstɪk/ ADJ A **simplistic** view or interpretation of something makes it seem much simpler than it really is. ❑ *He has a simplistic view of the treatment of eczema.*

simp|ly /sɪmpli/ **1** ADV You use **simply** to emphasize that something consists of only one thing, happens for only one reason, or is done in only one way. [EMPHASIS] ❑ *The table is simply a chipboard circle on a base.* ❑ *Most of the damage that's occurred was simply because of fallen trees.* **2** ADV You use **simply** to emphasize what you are saying. [EMPHASIS] ❑ *This sort of increase simply cannot be justified.* **3** → see also **simple**

SYNONYMS

simply
ADV **1**
just: *It's just a suggestion.*
merely: *Michael is now merely a good friend.*
purely: *It is a racing machine, designed purely for speed.*
only: *At the moment, it is only a theory.*

---

simu|late /sɪmyəleɪt/ (simulates, simulating, simulated) **1** V-T If you **simulate** an action or a feeling, you pretend that you are doing it or feeling it. ❑ *They rolled about on the Gilligan Road, simulating a bloodthirsty fight.* **2** V-T If you **simulate** a set of conditions, you create them artificially, for example, in order to conduct an experiment. ❑ *The scientist developed one model to simulate a full year of the globe's climate.*

simu|la|tion /sɪmyəleɪʃ°n/ (simulations) N-VAR **Simulation** is the process of simulating something or the result of simulating it. ❑ *Training includes realistic simulation of casualty procedures.*

simu|la|tor /sɪmyəleɪtər/ (simulators) N-COUNT A **simulator** is a device which artificially creates the effect of being in conditions of some kind. Simulators are used in training people such as pilots or astronauts. ❑ *...pilots practicing a difficult landing in a flight simulator.*

sim|ul|cast /sɪməlkæst/ (simulcasts, simulcasting)

The form **simulcast** is used in the present tense and is the past tense and past participle of the verb.

1 N-COUNT [oft N of n] A **simulcast** is a program which is broadcast at the same time on radio and television, or on more than one channel. ❑ *...tonight's simulcast of Verdi's Aida.* **2** V-T To **simulcast** a program means to broadcast it at the same time on radio and television, or on more than one channel. ❑ *The show will be simulcast on NBC, Fox and a number of cable networks.*

sim|ul|ta|neous /saɪməltenɪəs/ ADJ Things which are **simultaneous** happen or exist at the same time. ❑ *...the simultaneous release of the book and the CD.* • **sim|ul|ta|neous|ly** ADV ❑ *The two guns fired almost simultaneously.*

sin /sɪn/ (sins, sinning, sinned) **1** N-VAR **Sin** or a **sin** is an action or type of behavior which is believed to break the laws of God. ❑ *I believe that sex outside marriage is a sin.* **2** V-I If you **sin**, you do something that is believed to break the laws of God. ❑ *The Spanish Inquisition charged him with sinning against God and man.* • **sin|ner** /sɪnər/ (sinners) N-COUNT ❑ *I was shown that I am a sinner, that I needed to repent of my sins.* **3** N-COUNT A **sin** is any action or behavior that people disapprove of or consider morally wrong. ❑ *...the sin of arrogant hard-heartedness.*

sin-bin also **sin bin** N-SING In the sport of ice hockey, if a player is sent to the **sin-bin**, they are ordered to leave the playing area for a short period of time because they have done something that is against the rules.

since ♦♦♦ /sɪns/ **1** PREP You use **since** when you are mentioning a time or event in the past and indicating that a situation has continued from then until now. ❑ *He's been in exile in India since 1959.* ❑ *She had a sort of breakdown some years ago, and since then she has been very shy.* • ADV [ADV with v] **Since** is also an adverb. ❑ *They worked together in the 1960s, and have kept in contact ever since.* • CONJ **Since** is also a conjunction. ❑ *I've earned my own living since I was seven, doing all kinds of jobs.* **2** PREP You use **since** to mention a time or event in the past when you are describing an event or situation that has happened after that time. ❑ *The percentage increase in reported crime this year is the highest since the war.* • CONJ **Since** is also a conjunction. ❑ *So much has changed in the sport since I was a teenager.* ❑ *Since I have become a mother, the sound of children's voices has lost its charm.* **3** ADV [ADV with v] When you are talking about an event or situation in the past, you use **since** to indicate that another event happened at some point later in time. ❑ *About six thousand people were arrested, several hundred of whom have since been released.* **4** CONJ You use **since** to introduce reasons or explanations. ❑ *I'm forever on a diet, since I put on weight easily.*

sin|cere /sɪnsɪər/ ADJ If you say that someone is **sincere**, you approve of them because they really mean the things they say. You can also describe someone's behavior and beliefs as **sincere**. [APPROVAL] ❑ *He's sincere in his views.* • **sin|cer|ity** /sɪnsɛrɪti/ N-UNCOUNT ❑ *I was impressed with his deep sincerity.*

sin|cere|ly /sɪnsɪərli/ **1** ADV If you say or feel something **sincerely**, you really mean or feel it, and are not pretending. ❑ *"Congratulations," he said sincerely.* ❑ *...sincerely held religious beliefs.* **2** CONVENTION People write '**Sincerely yours**' or '**Sincerely**' before their signature at the end of a formal letter when they have addressed it to someone by name. People sometimes write '**Yours sincerely**' instead. ❑ *Sincerely yours, Robbie Weinz.*

si|necure /saɪnɪkyʊər, sɪn-/ (sinecures) N-COUNT A **sinecure** is a job for which you receive payment but which does not involve much work or responsibility. ❑ *She found him an exalted sinecure as a Fellow of the Library of Congress.*

sine qua non /saɪni kweɪ nɑn, sɪneɪ kwɑ noʊn/ N-SING [a N] A **sine qua non** is something that is essential if you want to achieve a particular thing. [FORMAL] ❑ *Successful agricultural reform is also a sine qua non of Mexico's modernization.*

sin|ew /sɪnyu/ (sinews) N-COUNT A **sinew** is a cord in your body that connects a muscle to a bone. ❑ *...the sinews of the neck.*

sin|ewy /sɪnyui/ ADJ Someone who is **sinewy** has a lean body with strong muscles. ❑ *...a short, sinewy young man.*

sin|ful /sɪnfəl/ ADJ If you describe someone or something as **sinful**, you mean that they are wicked or immoral. ❑ *"I am a sinful man, Magda," he said quietly.* ❑ *This is a sinful world.* • **sin|ful|ness** N-UNCOUNT ❑ *...the sinfulness of apartheid.*

sing ♦♦♦ /sɪŋ/ (sings, singing, sang, sung) **1** V-T/V-I When you **sing**, you make musical sounds with your voice, usually producing words that fit a tune. ❑ *I can't sing* ❑ *I sing about love most of the time.* ❑ *They were all singing the same song.* **2** → see also **singing** **3** → See feature box at **music**
▶ **sing along** PHRASAL VERB If you **sing along** with a piece of music, you sing it while you are listening to someone else perform it. ❑ *We listen to children's shows on the radio, and Janey can sing along with all the tunes.* ❑ *Would-be Elvis Presleys can sing along to "Jailhouse Rock," "Love me Tender," and "Blue Suede Shoes."*

sing. **Sing.** is a written abbreviation for **singular**.

sing|along /sɪnəlɔŋ/ (singalongs) also **sing-along** N-COUNT A **singalong** is an occasion when a group of people sing songs together for pleasure. ❑ *How about a nice sing-along around the piano?*

Sin|ga|po|rean /sɪŋɡəpɔriən/ (Singaporeans) **1** ADJ **Singaporean** means belonging or relating to Singapore, or to its people or culture. **2** N-COUNT A **Singaporean** is a citizen of Singapore or a person of Singaporean origin.

singe /sɪndʒ/ (singes, singeing, singed) V-T/V-I If you singe something or if it singes, it burns very slightly and changes color but does not catch fire. ❑ *The fire had begun to singe the bottoms of his pants.* ❑ *Toast the dried chiles in a hot pan until they start to singe.*

sing|er ✧✧ /sɪŋər/ (singers) N-COUNT A **singer** is a person who sings, especially as a job. ❑ *My mother was a singer in a dance band.*

singer-songwriter (singer-songwriters) N-COUNT A **singer-songwriter** is someone who writes and performs their own songs, especially popular songs. ❑ *Twenty years ago singer-songwriter John Prine released his first album.*

sing|ing /sɪŋɪŋ/ N-UNCOUNT **Singing** is the activity of making musical sounds with your voice. ❑ *...a people's carnival, with singing and dancing in the streets.* ❑ *...the singing of a traditional hymn.*

sin|gle ✧✧✧ /sɪŋɡəl/ (singles, singling, singled) **1** ADJ [ADJ n] You use **single** to emphasize that you are referring to one thing, and no more than one thing. [EMPHASIS] ❑ *A single shot rang out.* ❑ *Over six hundred people were wounded in a single day.* **2** ADJ [det ADJ] You use **single** to indicate that you are considering something on its own and separately from other things like it. [EMPHASIS] ❑ *Every single house in town had been damaged.* **3** ADJ Someone who is **single** is not married. You can also use **single** to describe someone who does not have a girlfriend or boyfriend. ❑ *Is it difficult being a single mother?* **4** ADJ A **single** room is a room intended for one person to stay or live in. ❑ *Each guest has her own single room, or shares, on request, a double room.* • N-COUNT **Single** is also a noun. ❑ *It's $65 for a single, $98 for a double and $120 for an entire suite.* **5** ADJ [ADJ n] A **single** bed is wide enough for one person to sleep in. ❑ *...his bedroom with its single bed.* **6** ADJ A **single** ticket is a ticket for a trip from one place to another but not back again. [BRIT] • N-COUNT **Single** is also a noun.

in AM, use **one-way**

7 N-COUNT A **single** is a small record which has one song on each side. A **single** is also a CD which has a few short songs on it. You can also refer to the main song on a record or CD as a **single**. ❑ *The winners will pocket a cash sum and get a chance to release their debut CD single.* **8** N-UNCOUNT **Singles** is a game of tennis or badminton in which one player plays another. The plural **singles** can be used to refer to one or more of these matches. ❑ *Lleyton Hewitt won the men's singles.* **9** → see also **single-** **10** → see file
▸ **single out** PHRASAL VERB If you **single** someone **out** from a group, you choose them and give them special attention or treatment. ❑ *The gunman had singled Debilly out and waited for him.* ❑ *His immediate superior has singled him out for a special mention.*

---SYNONYMS---

single
ADJ **1**
sole: *Their sole aim is to destabilize the government.*
solitary: *...the occasional, solitary figure making a study of wildflowers.*
lone: *He was shot by a lone gunman.*

---

single- /sɪŋɡəl-/ COMB IN ADJ **single-** is used to form words which describe something that has one part or feature, rather than having two or more of them. ❑ *The single-engine plane landed in western Arizona.*

single-breasted ADJ A **single-breasted** coat, jacket, or suit fastens in the center of the chest and has only one row of buttons.

sin|gle cream N-UNCOUNT **Single cream** is the same as **light cream**. [BRIT]

single-handed also **single-handedly** ADV [ADV after v] If you do something **single-handed**, you do it on your own, without help from anyone else. ❑ *I brought up my seven children single-handed.*

single-minded ADJ Someone who is **single-minded** has only one aim or purpose and is determined to achieve it. ❑ *They were effective politicians, ruthless and single-minded in their pursuit of political power.*

sin|gle par|ent (single parents) **1** N-COUNT A **single parent** is someone who is bringing up a child on their own, because the other parent is not living with them. ❑ *I was bringing up my three children as a single parent.* ❑ *...single-parent families.* **2** → See feature box at **family**

sin|gles bar (singles bars) N-COUNT In North America, a **singles bar** is a bar where single people can go in order to drink and meet other single people.

single-sex ADJ [usu ADJ n] At a **single-sex** school, the students are either all boys or all girls. ❑ *Is single-sex education good for girls?*

sin|gle sup|ple|ment (single supplements) also **single person supplement** N-COUNT A **single supplement** is an additional sum of money that a hotel charges for one person to stay in a room meant for two people. ❑ *You can avoid the single supplement by agreeing to share a twin room.*

sin|gle|ton /sɪŋɡəltən/ (singletons) N-COUNT A **singleton** is someone who is neither married nor in a long-term relationship. ❑ *Bank is a 38-year-old singleton who grew up in Philadelphia.*

sin|gly /sɪŋɡli/ ADV [ADV with v] If people do something **singly**, they each do it on their own, or do it one by one. ❑ *They marched out singly or in pairs.*

sing-song also **singsong** ADJ [ADJ n] A **sing-song** voice repeatedly rises and falls in pitch. ❑ *He started to speak in a nasal sing-song voice.*

sin|gu|lar /sɪŋɡyələr/ **1** ADJ The **singular** form of a word is the form that is used when referring to one person or thing. ❑ *...the fifteen case endings of the singular form of the Finnish noun.* **2** N-SING The **singular** of a noun is the form of it that is used to refer to one person or thing. ❑ *The inhabitants of the Arctic are known as the Inuit. The singular is Inuk.*

sin|gu|lar noun (singular nouns) N-COUNT A **singular noun** is a noun such as 'standstill' or 'vicinity' that does not have a plural form and always has a determiner such as 'a' or 'the' in front of it.

sin|is|ter /sɪnɪstər/ ADJ Something that is **sinister** seems evil or harmful. ❑ *There was something sinister about him that she found disturbing.*

---WORD HISTORY---

sinister
In Latin, **sinister** means 'left' or 'on the left-hand side.' The word came to have its 'evil or harmful' meaning because the left side was considered unlucky.

---

sink ✧✧✧ /sɪŋk/ (sinks, sinking, sank, sunk) **1** N-COUNT A **sink** is a large fixed container in a kitchen or bathroom, with faucets to supply water. In the kitchen, it is used for washing dishes, and in the bathroom, it is used to wash your hands and face. ❑ *The sink was full of dirty dishes.* ❑ *The bathroom is furnished with 2 toilets, 2 showers, and 2 sinks.* **2** V-T/V-I If a boat **sinks** or if someone or something **sinks** it, it disappears below the surface of a mass of water. ❑ *In a naval battle your aim is to sink the enemy's ship.* ❑ *The boat was beginning to sink fast.* **3** V-I If something **sinks**, it disappears below the surface of a mass of water. ❑ *A fresh egg will sink and an old egg will float.* **4** V-I If something **sinks**, it moves slowly downward. ❑ *Far off to the west the sun was sinking.* **5** V-I If something **sinks** to a lower level or standard, it falls to that level or standard. ❑ *Share prices would have sunk – hurting small and big investors.* ❑ *Pay increases have sunk to around seven percent.* **6** V-I If your heart or your spirits **sink**, you become depressed or lose hope. ❑ *My heart sank because I thought he was going to dump me for another girl.* **7** V-T/V-I If something sharp **sinks** or **is sunk** into something solid, it goes deeply into it. ❑ *I sank my teeth into a peppermint cream.* **8** V-T If someone **sinks** a well, mine, or other large hole, they make a deep hole in the ground, usually by digging or drilling. ❑ *...the site where Stephenson sank his first mineshaft.* **9** V-T If you **sink** money into a business or project, you spend money on it in the hope of making more money. ❑ *He has already sunk $25 million into the project.* **10** → see also **sinking**, **sunk** **11** PHRASE If you say that someone will have to **sink or swim**, you mean that they will have to succeed through their own efforts, or fail. ❑ *I think athletes sink or swim depending on how they motivate themselves.*

▶ **sink in** PHRASAL VERB When a statement or fact **sinks in**, you finally understand or realize it fully. ❑ *The implication took a while to sink in.*

sink|er /sɪŋkər/ PHRASE [PHR after v] You can use **hook, line, and sinker** to emphasize that someone is tricked or forced into a situation completely. [EMPHASIS] ❑ *We fell for it hook, line, and sinker.*

sink|ing /sɪŋkɪŋ/ **1** ADJ [ADJ n] If you have a **sinking** feeling, you suddenly become depressed or lose hope. ❑ *I began to have a sinking feeling that I was not going to get rid of her.* **2** → see also **sink**

Sino- /saɪnoʊ-/ COMB IN ADJ [ADJ n] **Sino-** is added to adjectives indicating nationality to form adjectives which describe relations between China and another country. ❑ *...Sino-Vietnamese friendship.*

sinu|ous /sɪnyuəs/ ADJ [usu ADJ n] Something that is **sinuous** moves with smooth twists and turns. [LITERARY] ❑ *...the silent, sinuous approach of a snake through the long grass.*

si|nus /saɪnəs/ (**sinuses**) N-COUNT [usu pl] Your **sinuses** are the spaces in the bone behind your nose. ❑ *I still suffer from catarrh and sinus problems.*

si|nusi|tis /saɪnəsaɪtɪs/ N-UNCOUNT If you have **sinusitis**, the layer of flesh inside your sinuses is swollen and painful, which can cause headaches and a blocked nose.

sip /sɪp/ (**sips, sipping, sipped**) **1** V-T/V-I If you **sip** a drink or **sip at** it, you drink by taking just a small amount at a time. ❑ *Jessica sipped her drink thoughtfully.* ❑ *He sipped at the glass and then put it down.* **2** N-COUNT A **sip** is a small amount of drink that you take into your mouth. ❑ *Harry took a sip of bourbon.*

si|phon /saɪfᵊn/ (**siphons, siphoning, siphoned**) also **syphon** **1** V-T If you **siphon** liquid from a container, you make it come out through a tube and down into a lower container by enabling the pressure of the air on it to push it out. ❑ *He told police someone had tried to siphon gas from his car.* • PHRASAL VERB **Siphon off** means the same as **siphon**. ❑ *Surgeons siphoned off fluid from his left lung.* **2** N-COUNT A **siphon** is a tube that you use for siphoning liquid. **3** V-T If you **siphon** money or resources from something, you cause them to be used for a purpose for which they were not intended. ❑ *He siphoned $1.2 billion from his companies to prop up his crumbling media empire.* • PHRASAL VERB **Siphon off** means the same as **siphon**. ❑ *He had siphoned off a small fortune in aid money from the United Nations.*

sir ♦♦◊ /sɜr/ (**sirs**) **1** N-VOC People sometimes say **sir** as a polite way of addressing a man whose name they do not know, or an older man. For example, a store clerk might address a male customer as **sir**. [POLITENESS] ❑ *Excuse me sir, but would you mind telling me what sort of car that is?* **2** N-TITLE **Sir** is the title used in front of the name of a knight or baronet. ❑ *She introduced me to Sir Tobias and Lady Clarke.* **3** CONVENTION You use the expression **Dear Sir** at the beginning of a formal letter or a business letter when you are writing to a man. ❑ *Dear Sir, Enclosed is a copy of my résumé for your consideration.*

sire /saɪər/ (**sires, siring, sired**) V-T When a male animal, especially a horse, **sires** a young animal, he makes a female pregnant so that she gives birth to it. [TECHNICAL] ❑ *Comet also sired the champion foal out of Spinway Harvest.*

si|ren /saɪrən/ (**sirens**) N-COUNT A **siren** is a warning device which makes a long, loud noise. Most fire engines, ambulances, and police cars have sirens. ❑ *It sounds like an air raid siren.*

╔══ **WORD HISTORY** ══╗

siren
The *Sirens* in Greek mythology were female sea spirits with beautiful voices who sang to tempt sailors to their deaths on the rocks where they lived.

sir|loin /sɜrlɔɪn/ (**sirloins**) N-VAR A **sirloin** is a piece of beef which is cut from the bottom and side parts of a cow's back. ❑ *...sirloin steaks.*

si|sal /saɪsᵊl/ N-UNCOUNT **Sisal** is the fiber from the leaves of a plant that is grown in the West Indies, South America, and Africa. **Sisal** is used to make rope, cord, and mats.

sis|sy /sɪsi/ (**sissies**) N-COUNT Some people describe a boy as a **sissy** when they disapprove of him because he does not like rough, physical activities or is afraid to do things which might be dangerous. [INFORMAL, DISAPPROVAL] ❑ *They were rough kids, and thought we were sissies.*

sis|ter ♦♦♦ /sɪstər/ (**sisters**) **1** N-COUNT [oft poss N] Your **sister** is a girl or woman who has the same parents as you. ❑ *His sister Sarah helped him.* ❑ *...Vanessa Bell, the sister of Virginia Woolf.* **2** → see also **half sister, stepsister 3** N-COUNT; N-TITLE; N-VOC **Sister** is a title given to a woman who belongs to a religious community. ❑ *Sister Francesca entered the chapel.* **4** N-COUNT You can describe a woman as your **sister** if you feel a connection with her, for example, because she belongs to the same race, religion, country, or profession. ❑ *Modern woman has been freed from many of the duties that befell her sisters in times past.* **5** ADJ [ADJ n] You can use **sister** to describe something that is of the same type or is connected in some way to another thing you have mentioned. For example, if a company has a **sister** company, they are connected. ❑ *...the International Monetary Fund and its sister organization, the World Bank.*

sis|ter city (**sister cities**) N-COUNT **Sister cities** are cities in different countries that have formally established a special relationship with each other involving, for example, cultural and sports events. [AM] ❑ *...dancers from Palo Alto's Mexican sister city, Oaxaca.* ❑ *But during those days, Harlem and Soweto were sister cities.*

sis|ter|hood /sɪstərhʊd/ N-UNCOUNT **Sisterhood** is the affection and loyalty that women feel for other women who they have something in common with. ❑ *There was a degree of solidarity and sisterhood among the women.*

sis|ter-in-law (**sisters-in-law**) N-COUNT Someone's **sister-in-law** is the sister of their husband or wife, or the woman who is married to their brother.

sis|ter|ly /sɪstərli/ ADJ [usu ADJ n] A woman's **sisterly** feelings are the feelings of love and loyalty which you expect a sister to show. ❑ *Bernadette gave him a shy, sisterly kiss.*

sit ♦♦♦ /sɪt/ (**sits, sitting, sat**) **1** V-I If you **are sitting** somewhere, for example, in a chair, your bottom is resting on the chair and the upper part of your body is upright. ❑ *Mother was sitting in her chair in the kitchen.* ❑ *They had been sitting watching television.* **2** V-I When you **sit** somewhere, you lower your body until you are sitting on something. ❑ *He set the cases against a wall and sat on them.* ❑ *Eva pulled over a chair and sat beside her husband.* • PHRASAL VERB **Sit down** means the same as **sit**. ❑ *I sat down, stunned.* **3** V-T If you **sit** someone somewhere, you tell them to sit there or put them in a sitting position. ❑ *He used to sit me on his lap.* • PHRASAL VERB To **sit** someone **down** somewhere means to sit them there. ❑ *She helped him out of the water and sat him down on the rock.* **4** V-I [no cont] If you **sit** on a committee or other official group, you are a member of it. ❑ *He was asked to sit on numerous committees.* **5** V-I When a legislature, court, or other official body **sits**, it officially carries out its work. [FORMAL] ❑ *The court sits under tight security in a former museum.* **6** PHRASE If you **sit tight**, you remain in the same place or situation and do not take any action, usually because you are waiting for something to happen. ❑ *Sit tight. I'll be right back.* **7** to **sit on the fence** → see **fence**

▶ **sit back** PHRASAL VERB If you **sit back** while something is happening, you relax and do not become involved in it. [INFORMAL] ❑ *They didn't have to do anything except sit back and enjoy life.*

▶ **sit in on** PHRASAL VERB If you **sit in on** a lesson, meeting, or discussion, you are present while it is taking place but do not take part in it. ❑ *Will they permit you to sit in on a few classes as an observer?*

▶ **sit on** PHRASAL VERB If you say that someone **is sitting on** something, you mean that they are delaying dealing with it. [INFORMAL] ❑ *He had been sitting on the document for at least two months.*

▶ **sit out** PHRASAL VERB If you **sit** something **out**, you wait for it to finish, without taking any action. ❑ *The only thing I can do is keep quiet and sit this one out.*

▶ **sit through** PHRASAL VERB If you **sit through** something such as a movie, lecture, or meeting, you stay until it is finished although you are not enjoying it. ❑ *...movies so bad you can hardly bear to sit through them.*

▶ **sit up** **1** PHRASAL VERB If you **sit up**, you move into a sitting position when you have been leaning back or lying down.

❑ Her head spins dizzily as soon as she sits up. **2** PHRASAL VERB If you **sit** someone **up**, you move them into a sitting position when they have been leaning back or lying down. ❑ *She sat him up and made him comfortable.* **3** PHRASAL VERB If you **sit up**, you do not go to bed although it is very late. ❑ *We sat up drinking and talking.* **4** → see also **sit-up**

COLLOCATIONS

sit
VERB **1**
sit + *adverb*: comfortably, idly, patiently, quietly; uneasily

---

si|tar /sɪtɑːr/ (**sitars**) N-VAR [oft *the* N] A **sitar** is an Indian musical instrument with two layers of strings, a long neck, and a round body.

sit|com /sɪtkɒm/ (**sitcoms**) N-COUNT A **sitcom** is an amusing television drama series about a set of characters. **Sitcom** is an abbreviation for **situation comedy**.

sit-down 1 ADJ [ADJ n] A **sit-down** meal is served to people sitting at tables. ❑ *A sit-down dinner was followed by a disco.* **2** ADJ [ADJ n] In a **sit-down** protest, people refuse to leave a place until they get what they want. ❑ *Teachers staged a sit-down protest in front of the president's office.*

site ♦♦◊ /saɪt/ (**sites, siting, sited**) **1** N-COUNT A **site** is a piece of ground that is used for a particular purpose or where a particular thing happens. ❑ *I was working as a foreman on a building site.* **2** N-COUNT The **site** of an important event is the place where it happened. ❑ *Scientists have described the Aral sea as the site of the worst ecological disaster on earth.* **3** N-COUNT A **site** is a piece of ground where something such as a statue or building stands or used to stand. ❑ *...the site of Moses' tomb.* **4** N-COUNT A **site** is the same as a **website**. **5** V-T [usu passive] If something is **sited** in a particular place or position, it is put there or built there. ❑ *He said chemical weapons had never been sited in Germany.* • **sit|ing** N-SING ❑ *...controls on the siting of gas storage vessels.* **6** PHRASE If someone or something is **on site**, they are in a particular area or group of buildings where people work, study, or stay. ❑ *It is cheaper to have extra building work done when the builder is on site, rather than bringing him back for a small job.* **7** PHRASE If someone or something is **off site**, they are away from a particular area or group of buildings where people work, study, or stay. ❑ *There is ample car parking off site.*

SYNONYMS

site
NOUN
1
area: *...a picnic area.*
plot: *I thought I'd buy myself a small plot of land and build a house on it.*
ground: *...a stretch of untouched ground.*
patch: *...a patch of land covered in forest.*
2
location: *The first thing he looked at was his office's location.*
place: *...Temple Mount, the place where the Temple actually stood.*
setting: *The house is in a lovely setting in the Malvern hills.*
spot: *They stayed at several of the island's top tourist spots.*

---

site map (**site maps**) N-COUNT A **site map** is a plan of a website showing what is on it and providing links to the different sections. [COMPUTING]

sit-in (**sit-ins**) N-COUNT A **sit-in** is a protest in which people go to a public place and stay there for a long time. ❑ *The campaigners held a sit-in outside the Supreme Court.*

sit|ter /sɪtər/ (**sitters**) N-COUNT A **sitter** is the same as a **babysitter**.

sit|ting /sɪtɪŋ/ (**sittings**) **1** N-COUNT A **sitting** is one of the periods when a meal is served when there is not enough space for everyone to eat at the same time. ❑ *Dinner was in two sittings.* **2** N-COUNT [usu N *of* n] A **sitting** of a legislature, court, or other official body is one of the occasions when it meets in order to carry out its work. ❑ *...the recent emergency sittings of the UN Security Council.* **3** ADJ [ADJ n] A **sitting** president or congressman is a present one, not a future or past one. ❑ *...the greatest clash in our history between a sitting president and an ex-president.* **4** → see also **sit**

sit|ting duck (**sitting ducks**) N-COUNT If you say that someone is a **sitting duck**, you mean that they are easy to attack, cheat, or take advantage of. [INFORMAL] ❑ *Nancy knew she'd be a sitting duck when she raised the trap door.*

sit|ting room (**sitting rooms**) also **sitting-room** N-COUNT A **sitting room** is a room in a house where people sit and relax. [OLD-FASHIONED]

sit|ting tar|get (**sitting targets**) N-COUNT A **sitting target** is the same as a **sitting duck**. ❑ *They know they are a sitting target for the press.*

situ|ate /sɪtʃueɪt/ (**situates, situating, situated**) V-T If you **situate** something such as an idea or fact in a particular context, you relate it to that context, especially in order to understand it better. [FORMAL] ❑ *How do we situate Christianity in the context of modern physics and psychology?*

situ|at|ed /sɪtʃueɪtɪd/ ADJ If something is **situated** in a particular place or position, it is in that place or position. ❑ *His hotel is situated in one of the loveliest places on the Loire.*

situa|tion ♦♦♦ /sɪtʃueɪʃən/ (**situations**) N-COUNT You use **situation** to refer generally to what is happening in a particular place at a particular time, or to refer to what is happening to you. ❑ *Army officers said the situation was under control.* ❑ *And now for a look at the travel situation in the rest of the country.*

situa|tion com|edy (**situation comedies**) N-VAR A **situation comedy** is an amusing television drama series about a set of characters. The abbreviation **sitcom** is also used. ❑ *...a situation comedy that was set in an acupuncture clinic.*

sit-up (**sit-ups**) also **situp** N-COUNT **Sit-ups** are exercises that you do to strengthen your stomach muscles. They involve sitting up from a lying position, usually while keeping your feet on the floor. ❑ *He does 100 sit-ups each day.*

six ♦♦♦ /sɪks/ (**sixes**) NUM **Six** is the number 6. ❑ *...a glorious career spanning more than six decades.*

six-footer (**six-footers**) N-COUNT Someone who is six feet tall can be called a **six-footer**. [INFORMAL]

six-pack (**six-packs**) **1** N-COUNT [oft N *of* n] A **six-pack** is a pack containing six bottles or cans sold together. ❑ *He picked up a six-pack of beer.* **2** N-COUNT [oft N n] If someone has a **six-pack**, their stomach muscles are very well developed. ❑ *He has a six-pack stomach and is extremely well-proportioned.*

six-shooter (**six-shooters**) N-COUNT A **six-shooter** is a small gun that holds six bullets.

six|teen ♦♦♦ /sɪkstiːn/ (**sixteens**) NUM **Sixteen** is the number 16. ❑ *...exams taken at the age of sixteen.* ❑ *He worked sixteen hours a day.*

six|teenth ♦♦◊ /sɪkstiːnθ/ ORD The **sixteenth** item in a series is the one that you count as number sixteen. ❑ *...the sixteenth century AD.*

sixth ♦♦◊ /sɪksθ/ (**sixths**) **1** ORD The **sixth** item in a series is the one that you count as number six. ❑ *...the sixth round of the World Cup.* **2** FRACTION A **sixth** is one of six equal parts of something. ❑ *The company yesterday shed a sixth of its workforce.*

sixth form (**sixth forms**) also **sixth-form** N-COUNT The **sixth form** in a British school consists of students aged 16 to 18, usually studying for A levels.

sixth sense N-SING If you say that someone has a **sixth sense**, you mean that they seem to have a natural ability to know about things before other people, or to know things that other people do not know. ❑ *The interesting thing about O'Reilly is his sixth sense for finding people who have good ideas.*

six|ti|eth ♦♦◊ /sɪkstiəθ/ (**sixtieths**) **1** ORD The **sixtieth** item in a series is the one that you count as number sixty. ❑ *He is to retire on his sixtieth birthday.* **2** FRACTION A **sixtieth** is one of sixty equal parts of something.

six|ty ♦♦♦ /sɪksti/ (**sixties**) **1** NUM **Sixty** is the number 60. ❑ *...the sunniest April for more than sixty years.* **2** N-PLURAL When you talk about the **sixties**, you are referring to numbers between 60 and 69. For example, if you are in your **sixties**, you are aged between 60 and 69. If the temperature is **in the sixties**, it is between 60 and 69 degrees. ❑ *She was in her sixties.* **3** N-PLURAL The **sixties** is the decade between 1960 and 1969. ❑ *In the sixties there were the deaths of the two Kennedy brothers and Martin Luther King.*

siz|able /saɪzəbᵊl/ also **sizeable** ADJ **Sizable** means fairly large. ❏ *Harry inherited the house and a sizable piece of land that surrounds it.*

size ✦✦◇ /saɪz/ (**sizes, sizing, sized**) **1** N-VAR The **size** of something is how big or small it is. Something's **size** is determined by comparing it to other things, counting it, or measuring it. ❏ *In 1970 the average size of a French farm was 19 hectares.* ❏ *...shelves containing books of various sizes.* **2** N-UNCOUNT The **size** of something is the fact that it is very large. ❏ *He knows the size of the task.* **3** N-COUNT A **size** is one of a series of graded measurements, especially for things such as clothes or shoes. ❏ *My sister is the same height but only a size 12.*
▸ **size up** PHRASAL VERB If you **size up** a person or situation, you carefully look at the person or think about the situation, so that you can decide how to act. [INFORMAL] ❏ *Some U.S. manufacturers have been sizing up the UK as a possible market for their clothes.*

-size /-saɪz/ also **-sized 1** COMB IN ADJ You can use **-size** or **-sized** in combination with nouns to form adjectives which indicate that something is the same size as something else. ❏ *...golfball-sized lumps of coarse black rock.* **2** COMB IN ADJ You can use **-size** or **-sized** in combination with adjectives to form adjectives which describe the size of something. ❏ *...full-size gymnasiums.* ❏ *...a medium-sized college.* **3** COMB IN ADJ You can use **-size** or **-sized** in combination with nouns to form adjectives which indicate that something is big enough or small enough to be suitable for a particular job or purpose. ❏ *...a small passport-size photograph.* ❏ *...a child-sized knife.*

size|able /saɪzəbᵊl/ [mainly BRIT] → see **sizable**

-sized /-saɪzd/ → see **-size**

siz|zle /sɪzᵊl/ (**sizzles, sizzling, sizzled**) V-I If something such as hot oil or fat **sizzles**, it makes hissing sounds. ❏ *The sausages and burgers sizzled on the barbecue.*

skate /skeɪt/ (**skates, skating, skated**) **1** N-COUNT **Skates** are ice-skates. **2** N-COUNT **Skates** are roller-skates. **3** V-I If you **skate**, you move around wearing ice-skates or roller-skates. ❏ *I actually skated, and despite some teetering I did not fall on the ice.*
• **skat|ing** N-UNCOUNT ❏ *They all went skating together in the winter.*
• **skat|er** N-COUNT ❏ *West Lake, an outdoor ice-skating rink, attracts skaters during the day and night.*

skate|board /skeɪtbɔrd/ (**skateboards**) N-COUNT A **skateboard** is a narrow board with wheels at each end, which people stand on and ride for pleasure.

skate|board|er /skeɪtbɔrdər/ (**skateboarders**) N-COUNT A **skateboarder** is someone who rides on a skateboard.

skate|board|ing /skeɪtbɔrdɪŋ/ N-UNCOUNT **Skateboarding** is the activity of riding on a skateboard. ❏ *...a skateboarding competition.*

skate|park /skeɪtpɑrk/ (**skateparks**) N-COUNT A **skatepark** is an area that is designed for people to practice skateboarding.

skat|ing rink (**skating rinks**) N-COUNT A **skating rink** is the same as a **rink**.

ske|dad|dle /skɪdædᵊl/ (**skedaddles, skedaddling, skedaddled**) V-I If you tell someone to **skedaddle**, you are telling them to run away or to leave a place quickly. [INFORMAL] ❏ *Now you children skedaddle. Go outside and play.*

skein /skeɪn/ (**skeins**) N-COUNT A **skein** is a length of thread, especially wool or silk, wound loosely around itself. ❏ *...a skein of wool.*

skel|etal /skɛlɪtᵊl/ **1** ADJ [ADJ n] **Skeletal** means relating to the bones in your body. ❏ *...the skeletal remains of seven adults.* **2** ADJ A **skeletal** person is so thin that you can see their bones through their skin. ❏ *...a hospital filled with skeletal children.*

skel|eton /skɛlɪtᵊn/ (**skeletons**) **1** N-COUNT Your **skeleton** is the framework of bones in your body. ❏ *...a human skeleton.* **2** ADJ [ADJ n] A **skeleton** staff is the smallest number of staff necessary in order to run an organization or service. ❏ *Only a skeleton staff remains to show anyone interested around the site.* **3** N-COUNT The **skeleton** of something such as a building or a plan is its basic framework. ❏ *The town of Rudbar had ceased to exist, with only skeletons of buildings remaining.* **4** → See also color supplement

skel|eton key (**skeleton keys**) N-COUNT A **skeleton key** is a key which has been specially made so that it will open many different locks.

skep|tic /skɛptɪk/ (**skeptics**)
in BRIT, use **sceptic**
N-COUNT A **skeptic** is a person who has doubts about things that other people believe. ❏ *He is a skeptic who tries to keep an open mind.*

skep|ti|cal /skɛptɪkᵊl/
in BRIT, use **sceptical**
ADJ If you are **skeptical** about something, you have doubts about it. ❏ *Others here are more skeptical about the chances for justice being done.*

skep|ti|cism /skɛptɪsɪzəm/
in BRIT, use **scepticism**
N-UNCOUNT **Skepticism** is great doubt about whether something is true or useful. ❏ *A survey reflects business skepticism about the strength of the economic recovery.*

sketch /skɛtʃ/ (**sketches, sketching, sketched**) **1** N-COUNT A **sketch** is a drawing that is done quickly without a lot of details. Artists often use sketches as a preparation for a more detailed painting or drawing. ❏ *...a sketch of a soldier by Orpen.* **2** V-T/V-I If you **sketch** something, you make a quick, rough drawing of it. ❏ *Clare and David Astor are sketching a view of far Spanish hills.* **3** N-COUNT A **sketch** of a situation, person, or incident is a brief description of it without many details. ❏ *...thumbnail sketches of heads of state and political figures.* **4** V-T If you **sketch** a situation or incident, you give a short description of it, including only the most important facts. ❏ *Cross sketched the story briefly, telling the facts just as they had happened.* • PHRASAL VERB **Sketch out** means the same as **sketch**. ❏ *He sketched out plans to give consumers more affordable choices.* **5** N-COUNT A **sketch** is a short humorous piece of acting, usually forming part of a comedy show. ❏ *...a five-minute sketch about a folk singer.* **6** → See feature box at **fine art**

sketch|book /skɛtʃbʊk/ (**sketchbooks**) N-COUNT A **sketchbook** is a book of plain paper for drawing on.

sketch|pad /skɛtʃpæd/ (**sketchpads**) N-COUNT A **sketchpad** is the same as a **sketchbook**.

sketchy /skɛtʃi/ (**sketchier, sketchiest**) ADJ **Sketchy** information about something does not include many details and is therefore incomplete or inadequate. ❏ *Details of what actually happened are still sketchy.*

skew /skyu/ (**skews, skewing, skewed**) V-T If something **is skewed**, it is changed or affected to some extent by a new or unusual factor, and so is not correct or normal. ❏ *The arithmetic of nuclear running costs has been skewed by the fall in the cost of other fuels.*

skew|er /skyuər/ (**skewers**) **1** N-COUNT A **skewer** is a long pin made of wood or metal that is used to hold pieces of food together during cooking. **2** → See also color supplement

ski ✦◇ /ski/ (**skis, skiing, skied**) **1** N-COUNT **Skis** are long, flat, narrow pieces of wood, metal, or plastic that are fastened to boots so that you can move easily on snow or water. ❏ *...a pair of skis.* **2** V-I When people **ski**, they move over snow or water on skis. ❏ *They surf, ski and ride.* • **ski|er** /skiər/ (**skiers**) N-COUNT ❏ *He is an enthusiastic skier.* • **ski|ing** N-UNCOUNT ❏ *My hobbies were skiing and scuba diving.* **3** ADJ [ADJ n] You use **ski** to refer to things that are concerned with skiing. ❏ *...the Swiss ski resort of Klosters.* ❏ *...a private ski instructor.*

skid /skɪd/ (**skids, skidding, skidded**) **1** V-I If a vehicle **skids**, it slides sideways or forward while moving, for example, when you are trying to stop it suddenly on a wet road. ❏ *The car pulled up too fast and skidded on the dusty shoulder of the road.* • N-COUNT **Skid** is also a noun. ❏ *I slammed the brakes on and went into a skid.* **2** → See feature box at **accident**

skid row /skɪd roʊ/ also **Skid Row** N-UNCOUNT [oft N n] You can refer to the poorest part of town, where drunks and homeless people live, as **skid row**. [mainly AM] ❏ *He became a skid row type of drunkard.*

skiff /skɪf/ (**skiffs**) N-COUNT A **skiff** is a small, light rowboat or sailboat, which usually has room for only one person.

skif|fle /skɪfᵊl/ N-UNCOUNT **Skiffle** is a type of music, popular in the 1950s, played by a small group using household objects as well as guitars and drums.

ski jump (ski jumps) N-COUNT A **ski jump** is a specially-built steep slope covered in snow whose lower end curves upward. People ski down it and go into the air at the end.

skil|ful /skɪlfəl/ [mainly BRIT] → see skillful

ski lift (ski lifts) also **ski-lift** N-COUNT A **ski lift** is a machine for taking people to the top of a slope so that they can ski down it. It consists of a series of seats hanging down from a moving wire.

skill ♦♦♦ /skɪl/ (skills) **1** N-COUNT A **skill** is a type of work or activity which requires special training and knowledge. ❏ *Most of us will know someone who is always learning new skills, or studying new fields.* **2** N-UNCOUNT **Skill** is the knowledge and ability that enables you to do something well. ❏ *The cut of a diamond depends on the skill of its craftsman.*

skilled /skɪld/ **1** ADJ Someone who is **skilled** has the knowledge and ability to do something well. ❏ *Few doctors are actually trained, and not all are skilled, in helping their patients make choices.* **2** ADJ **Skilled** work can only be done by people who have had some training. ❏ *New industries demanded skilled labor not available locally.*

skil|let /skɪlɪt/ (skillets) N-COUNT A **skillet** is a shallow iron pan which is used for frying.

skill|ful /skɪlfəl/

in BRIT, use **skilful**

ADJ Someone who is **skillful** at something does it very well. ❏ *He actually is quite a skillful campaigner.* ● **skill|ful|ly** ADV [ADV with v] ❏ *The city's rulers skillfully played both powers off against each other.*

skim /skɪm/ (skims, skimming, skimmed) **1** V-T If you **skim** something from the surface of a liquid, you remove it. ❏ *Rough seas today prevented specially equipped ships from skimming oil off the water's surface.* **2** V-T/V-I If something **skims** a surface, it moves quickly along just above it. ❏ *...seagulls skimming the waves.* **3** V-T/V-I If you **skim** a piece of writing, you read through it quickly. ❏ *He skimmed the pages quickly, then read them again more carefully.*

▶ **skim off** PHRASAL VERB If someone **skims off** the best part of something, or money which belongs to other people, they take it for themselves. ❏ *The regime was able to skim off about $10 billion in illegal revenue.* ❏ *She admitted she skimmed cash off the top of the fees she collected.*

skimmed milk [BRIT] → see skim milk

skim milk

in BRIT, sometimes in AM, use **skimmed milk**

N-UNCOUNT **Skim milk** is milk from which the cream has been removed.

skimp /skɪmp/ (skimps, skimping, skimped) V-I If you **skimp on** something, you use less time, money, or material for it than you really need, so that the result is not good enough. ❏ *Many families must skimp on their food and other necessities just to meet the monthly rent.*

skimpy /skɪmpi/ (skimpier, skimpiest) ADJ Something that is **skimpy** is too small in size or quantity. ❏ *...skimpy underwear.*

skin ♦♦♦ /skɪn/ (skins, skinning, skinned) **1** N-VAR Your **skin** is the natural covering of your body. ❏ *His skin is clear and smooth.* ❏ *There are three major types of skin cancer.* **2** N-VAR An animal **skin** is skin which has been removed from a dead animal. Skins are used to make things such as coats and rugs. ❏ *That was real crocodile skin.* **3** N-VAR The **skin** of a fruit or vegetable is its outer layer or covering. ❏ *The outer skin of the orange is called the "zest."* **4** N-SING If a **skin** forms on the surface of a liquid, a thin, fairly solid layer forms on it. ❏ *Stir the custard occasionally to prevent a skin forming.* **5** N-COUNT In computing, a **skin** is a set of colors, fonts, and background images that can be used to change how a computer, phone screen or app looks. [COMPUTING] ❏ *The new skins will be available for download soon.* **6** V-T If you **skin** a dead animal, you remove its skin. ❏ *...with the expertise of a chef skinning a rabbit.*

skin care also **skincare** N-UNCOUNT [oft N n] **Skin care** involves keeping your skin clean, healthy-looking, and attractive. ❏ *...a unique range of natural skincare products.*

skin deep also **skin-deep** ADJ [usu v-link ADJ] Something that is only **skin deep** is not a major or important feature of something, although it may appear to be. ❏ *Beauty is only skin deep.*

skin|flint /skɪnflɪnt/ (skinflints) N-COUNT If you describe someone as a **skinflint**, you are saying that they are a mean person who hates spending money. [DISAPPROVAL]

skin|head /skɪnhɛd/ (skinheads) N-COUNT A **skinhead** is a young person whose hair is shaved or cut very short. Skinheads are usually regarded as violent and aggressive.

skin|less /skɪnlɪs/ ADJ [usu ADJ n] **Skinless** meat has had its skin removed. ❏ *...skinless chicken breast fillets.*

-skinned /-skɪnd/ COMB IN ADJ **-skinned** is used after adjectives such as 'dark' and 'clear' to form adjectives that indicate what kind of skin someone has. ❏ *She was clear-skinned and looked very healthy.* ❏ *He was smooth-skinned and quite handsome.*

skin|ny /skɪni/ (skinnier, skinniest) ADJ A **skinny** person is extremely thin, often in a way that you find unattractive. [INFORMAL] ❏ *He was quite a skinny little boy.*

skinny-dip (skinny-dips, skinny-dipping, skinny-dipped) also **skinny dip** V-I If you **skinny-dip**, you go swimming with no clothes on. [INFORMAL] ❏ *They used to take off their clothes and go skinny dipping in the creek.*

skin tag (skin tags) N-COUNT A **skin tag** is a small growth attached loosely to the skin, especially on the face or neck, or under the arms. ❏ *For years I had a skin tag on my eyelid.*

skin-tight also **skintight** ADJ [usu ADJ n] **Skin-tight** clothes fit very tightly so that they show the shape of your body. ❏ *...the guy with the slicked down hair and skin-tight jeans.*

skip /skɪp/ (skips, skipping, skipped) **1** V-I If you **skip** along, you move almost as if you are dancing, with a series of little jumps from one foot to the other. ❏ *They saw the man with a little girl skipping along behind him.* ❏ *We went skipping down the street arm in arm.* ● N-COUNT **Skip** is also a noun. ❏ *The boxer gave a little skip as he came out of his corner.* **2** V-T When someone **skips rope**, they jump up and down over a rope which they or two other people are holding at each end and turning around and around. ❏ *They skip rope and play catch, waiting for the bell.* ● **skip|ping** N-UNCOUNT ❏ *We did rope skipping and things like that.* **3** V-T If you **skip** something that you usually do or something that most people do, you decide not to do it. ❏ *It is important not to skip meals.* **4** V-T/V-I If you **skip** or **skip over** a part of something you are reading or a story you are telling, you miss it out or pass over it quickly and move on to something else. ❏ *You might want to skip the exercises in this chapter.* **5** V-I If you **skip** from one subject or activity to another, you move quickly from one to the other, although there is no obvious connection between them. ❏ *She kept up a continuous chatter, skipping from one subject to the next.* **6** N-COUNT A **skip** is a large, open, metal container which is used to hold and take away large unwanted items and trash. [BRIT]

in AM, use **Dumpster**

skip|per /skɪpər/ (skippers) N-COUNT; N-VOC You can use **skipper** to refer to the captain of a ship or boat. ❏ *...the skipper of an English fishing boat.*

skip rope (skip ropes)

in BRIT, use **skipping rope**

N-COUNT A **skip rope** is a piece of rope, usually with handles at each end. You exercise or play with it by turning it around and around and jumping over it.

skir|mish /skɜrmɪʃ/ (skirmishes, skirmishing, skirmished) **1** N-COUNT A **skirmish** is a minor battle. ❏ *Border skirmishes between India and Pakistan were common.* **2** V-RECIP If people **skirmish**, they fight. ❏ *They were skirmishing close to the minefield now.* **3** → See feature box at **conflict**

skirt /skɜrt/ (skirts, skirting, skirted) **1** N-COUNT A **skirt** is a piece of clothing that fastens at the waist and hangs down around the legs. **2** V-T Something that **skirts** an area is situated around the edge of it. ❏ *We raced across a large field that skirted the slope of a hill.* **3** V-T/V-I If you **skirt** a problem or question, you avoid dealing with it. ❏ *He skirted the hardest issues, concentrating on areas of possible agreement.*

skirt|ing board (skirting boards) N-VAR **Skirting board** or **skirting** is a narrow length of wood which goes along the

ski slope

bottom of a wall in a room and makes a border between the walls and the floor. [BRIT]

in AM, use **baseboard**

ski slope (ski slopes) N-COUNT A **ski slope** is a sloping surface which you can ski down, either on a snow-covered mountain or on a specially made structure.

skit /skɪt/ (skits) N-COUNT A **skit** is a short performance in which the actors make fun of people, events, and types of literature by imitating them. ❏ ...*clever skits on popular songs.*

skit|ter /skɪtər/ (skitters, skittering, skittered) V-I If something **skitters**, it moves about very lightly and quickly. ❏ *The rats skittered around them in the drains and under the floorboards.*

skit|tish /skɪtɪʃ/ **1** ADJ If you describe a person or animal as **skittish**, you mean they are easily made frightened or excited. ❏ *The declining dollar gave heart to skittish investors.* **2** ADJ Someone who is **skittish** does not concentrate on anything or take life very seriously. ❏ ...*his relentlessly skittish sense of humor.*

skiv|vies /skɪviz/ N-PLURAL **Skivvies** are men's underwear. [AM, INFORMAL] ❏ *He was wearing only his skivvies.*

skul|dug|gery /skʌldʌgəri/ N-UNCOUNT **Skulduggery** is behavior in which someone acts in a dishonest way in order to achieve their aim. [WRITTEN] ❏ ...*accusations of political skulduggery.*

skulk /skʌlk/ (skulks, skulking, skulked) V-I If you **skulk** somewhere, you hide or move around quietly because you do not want to be seen. ❏ *You, meanwhile, will be skulking in the safety of the car.*

skull /skʌl/ (skulls) **1** N-COUNT Your **skull** is the bony part of your head which encloses your brain. ❏ *Her husband was later treated for a fractured skull.* **2** → See feature box at **body**; See also color supplement

skull and cross|bones N-SING A **skull and crossbones** is a picture of a human skull above a pair of crossed bones which warns of death or danger. It used to appear on the flags of pirate ships and is now sometimes found on containers holding poisonous substances. ❏ *Skull and crossbones stickers on the drums aroused the suspicion of the customs officers.*

skull|cap /skʌlkæp/ (skullcaps) also **skull cap** N-COUNT A **skullcap** is a small, close-fitting cap.

skunk /skʌŋk/ (skunks) **1** N-COUNT A **skunk** is a small, black and white animal which releases an unpleasant smelling liquid if it is frightened or attacked. Skunks live in North America. **2** N-UNCOUNT **Skunk** is a type of powerful, strong-smelling marijuana. [INFORMAL]

sky ✦◇◇ /skaɪ/ (skies) **1** N-VAR The **sky** is the space around the earth which you can see when you stand outside and look upward. ❏ *The sun is already high in the sky.* ❏ ...*warm sunshine and clear blue skies.* **2** → See feature box at **hot, weather**

sky-blue COLOR Something that is **sky-blue** is a very pale blue in color. ❏ *Her silk shirt dress was sky-blue, the color of her eyes.*

sky|cap /skaɪkæp/ (skycaps) N-COUNT A **skycap** is a porter at an airport. [AM] ❏ *Skycaps handle hundreds of bags each day.*

sky|div|er /skaɪdaɪvər/ (skydivers) also **sky diver** N-COUNT A **skydiver** is someone who goes skydiving.

sky|div|ing /skaɪdaɪvɪŋ/ N-UNCOUNT **Skydiving** is the sport of jumping out of an airplane and falling freely through the air before opening your parachute.

sky-high ADJ If you say that prices or confidence are **sky-high**, you are emphasizing that they are at a very high level. [EMPHASIS] ❏ *Christie said: "My confidence is sky high."* ❏ ...*the effect of falling house prices and sky-high interest rates.* • ADV [ADV after v] Sky high is also an adverb. ❏ *Their prestige went sky high.*

sky|lark /skaɪlɑrk/ (skylarks) N-COUNT A **skylark** is a small brown bird that sings while flying high above the ground.

sky|light /skaɪlaɪt/ (skylights) **1** N-COUNT A **skylight** is a window in a roof. **2** → See feature box at **house**

sky|line /skaɪlaɪn/ (skylines) N-COUNT The **skyline** is the line or shape that is formed where the sky meets buildings or the land. ❏ *The village church dominates the skyline.*

sky mar|shal (sky marshals) N-COUNT A **sky marshal** is an armed security guard who travels on passenger flights. [mainly AM]

Skype /skaɪp/ (Skypes, Skyping, Skyped) N-UNCOUNT **Skype** is a computer program that you can use to make voice calls or video calls on the internet. [TRADEMARK] ❏ *Catch up with your American cousins or chat to your friend on her travels around India, on Skype.* • VERB **Skype** is also a verb. ❏ *I Skyped Emma while she was in LA.* ❏ *My parents and I Skype with my sister, who is living in the UK.* ❏ *Since then, we've Skyped and emailed loads.*

sky|rocket /skaɪrɒkɪt/ (skyrockets, skyrocketing, skyrocketed) V-I If prices or amounts **skyrocket**, they suddenly increase by a very large amount. ❏ *Production has dropped while prices and unemployment have skyrocketed.* ❏ ...*the skyrocketing costs of health care.*

sky|scrap|er /skaɪskreɪpər/ (skyscrapers) N-COUNT A **skyscraper** is a very tall building in a city.

sky|ward /skaɪwərd/ also **skywards** ADV [ADV after v] If you look **skyward** or **skywards**, you look up toward the sky. [LITERARY] ❏ *He pointed skywards.*

slab /slæb/ (slabs) N-COUNT [with supp] A **slab** of something is a thick, flat piece of it. ❏ ...*slabs of stone.*

slack /slæk/ (slacker, slackest, slacks, slacking, slacked) **1** ADJ Something that is **slack** is loose and not firmly stretched or tightly in position. ❏ *The boy's jaw went slack.* **2** ADJ A **slack** period is one in which there is not much work or activity. ❏ *The workload can be evened out, instead of the shop having busy times and slack periods.* **3** ADJ Someone who is **slack** in their work does not do it properly. [DISAPPROVAL] ❏ *Many publishers have simply become far too slack.* **4** V-I [only cont] If someone is **slacking**, they are not working as hard as they should. [DISAPPROVAL] ❏ *He had never let a foreman see him slacking.*
• PHRASAL VERB **Slack off** means the same as **slack**. ❏ *If someone slacks off, Bill comes down hard.*

slack|en /slækən/ (slackens, slackening, slackened) **1** V-T/V-I If something **slackens** or if you **slacken** it, it becomes slower, less active, or less intense. ❏ *Inflationary pressures continued to slacken last month.* **2** V-T/V-I If your grip or a part of your body **slackens** or if you **slacken** your grip, it becomes looser or more relaxed. ❏ *Her grip slackened on Arnold's arm.*

slack|er /slækər/ (slackers) N-COUNT If you describe someone as a **slacker**, you mean that they are lazy and do less work than they should. [DISAPPROVAL] ❏ *He's not a slacker, he's the best worker they've got.*

slack-jawed ADJ If you say that someone is **slack-jawed**, you mean that their mouth is hanging open, often because they are surprised. ❏ *He just gazed at me slack-jawed.*

slacks /slæks/ N-PLURAL [also a pair of N] **Slacks** are casual pants. [OLD-FASHIONED] ❏ *She was wearing black slacks and a white sweater.*

slag heap /slæg hip/ (slag heaps) also **slagheap** N-COUNT A **slag heap** is a hill made from waste material, such as rock and mud, left over from mining.

slain /sleɪn/ **Slain** is the past participle of **slay**.

slake /sleɪk/ (slakes, slaking, slaked) V-T If you **slake** your thirst, you drink something that stops you from being thirsty. [WRITTEN]

sla|lom /slɑləm/ (slaloms) N-COUNT A **slalom** is a race on skis or in canoes in which the competitors have to avoid a series of obstacles in a very twisting and difficult course.

slam /slæm/ (slams, slamming, slammed) **1** V-T/V-I If you **slam** a door or window or if it **slams**, it shuts noisily and with great force. ❏ *She slammed the door and locked it behind her.* ❏ *I was relieved to hear the front door slam.* **2** V-T If you **slam** something down, you put it there quickly and with great force. ❏ *She listened in a mixture of shock and anger before slamming the phone down.* **3** V-T To **slam** someone or something means to criticize them very severely. [JOURNALISM] ❏ *The famed filmmaker slammed the claims as "an outrageous lie."* **4** V-T/V-I If one thing **slams** into or against another, it crashes into it with great force. ❏ *The plane slammed into the building after losing an engine shortly after take-off.* **5** → See feature box at **accident**

slam dunk (slam dunks) also **slam-dunk** **1** N-COUNT [usu sing: v-link a N] If you say that something is a **slam dunk**, you mean that a success or victory will be easily achieved. [INFORMAL] ❏ *So it's an easy decision. It's a slam dunk.* **2** N-COUNT In basketball, a **slam dunk** is a shot in which a player jumps up and forces the ball through the basket. ❑ ...*a series of spectacular slam dunks.*

slam|mer /slǽmər/ N-SING [*the* N] **The slammer** is prison. [INFORMAL]

slan|der /slǽndər/ (**slanders, slandering, slandered**) **1** N-VAR **Slander** is an untrue spoken statement about someone which is intended to damage their reputation. Compare **libel**. ❑ *Dr. Bach is now suing the company for slander.* **2** V-T To **slander** someone means to say untrue things about them in order to damage their reputation. ❑ *He accused me of slandering him and trying to undermine his position.* **3** → See feature box at **truth**

slan|der|ous /slǽndərəs/ ADJ A spoken statement that is **slanderous** is untrue and intended to damage the reputation of the person that it refers to. ❑ *Herr Kohler wanted an explanation for what he described as "slanderous" remarks.*

slang /slǽŋ/ N-UNCOUNT **Slang** consists of words, expressions, and meanings that are informal and are used by people who know each other very well or who have the same interests. ❑ *Archie liked to think he kept up with current slang.*

slangy /slǽŋi/ ADJ [usu ADJ n] **Slangy** speech or writing has a lot of slang in it. ❑ *The play was full of slangy dialogue.*

slant /slǽnt/ (**slants, slanting, slanted**) **1** V-I Something that **slants** is sloping, rather than horizontal or vertical. ❑ *The morning sun slanted through the glass roof.* **2** N-SING If something is on a **slant**, it is in a slanting position. ❑ *...long pockets cut on the slant.* **3** V-T [usu passive] If information or a system **is slanted**, it is made to show favor toward a particular group or opinion. ❑ *The program was deliberately slanted to make the home team look good.* **4** N-SING A particular **slant** on a subject is a particular way of thinking about it, especially one that is unfair. ❑ *The political slant at Focus can be described as center-right.*

slap /slǽp/ (**slaps, slapping, slapped**) **1** V-T If you **slap** someone, you hit them with the palm of your hand. ❑ *He would push or slap them once in a while.* ❑ *I slapped him hard across the face.* • N-COUNT **Slap** is also a noun. ❑ *He reached forward and gave her a slap.* **2** V-T If you **slap** something onto a surface, you put it there quickly, roughly, or carelessly. ❑ *He emptied his drink and slapped the money on the bar.* **3** V-T If journalists say that the authorities **slap** something such as a tax or a ban **on** something, they think it is unreasonable or put on without careful thought. [INFORMAL, DISAPPROVAL] ❑ *The government slapped a ban on the export of unprocessed logs.* **4** → See feature box at **onomatopoeia**

slap bang also **slap-bang** ADV **Slap bang** is the same as **smack dab**. [mainly BRIT, INFORMAL]

slap|dash /slǽpdæʃ/ also **slap-dash** ADJ If you describe someone as **slapdash**, you mean that they do things carelessly without much thinking or planning. [DISAPPROVAL] ❑ *Malcolm's work methods appear amazingly slapdash.*

slap-happy ADJ If you describe someone as **slap-happy**, you believe they are irresponsible and careless. ❑ *...a slap-happy kind of cook.*

slap|stick /slǽpstɪk/ **1** N-UNCOUNT [oft N n] **Slapstick** is a simple type of comedy in which the actors behave in a rough and foolish way. ❑ *...slapstick comedy.* **2** → See feature box at **humor**

slash /slǽʃ/ (**slashes, slashing, slashed**) **1** V-T If you **slash** something, you make a long, deep cut in it. ❑ *He came within two minutes of bleeding to death after slashing his wrists.* • N-COUNT **Slash** is also a noun. ❑ *Make deep slashes in the meat and push in the spice paste.* **2** V-I If you **slash** at a person or thing, you quickly hit at them with something such as a knife. ❑ *He slashed at her, aiming carefully.* **3** V-T To **slash** something such as costs or jobs means to reduce them by a large amount. [JOURNALISM] ❑ *Car makers could be forced to slash prices.* **4** N-COUNT You say **slash** to refer to a sloping line that separates letters, words, or numbers. For example, if you are giving the number 340/2/K you say 'Three four zero, slash two, slash K.' [SPOKEN]

slash and burn also **slash-and-burn** N-UNCOUNT [usu N n] **Slash and burn** is a method of farming that involves clearing land by destroying and burning all the trees and plants on it, farming there for a short time, and then moving on to clear a new piece of land. ❑ *Traditional slash and burn farming methods have exhausted the soil.*

slat /slǽt/ (**slats**) N-COUNT [usu pl] **Slats** are narrow pieces of wood, metal, or plastic, usually with spaces between them, that are part of things such as Venetian blinds or cabinet doors.

slate /sleɪt/ (**slates, slating, slated**) **1** N-UNCOUNT **Slate** is a dark gray rock that can be easily split into thin layers. Slate is often used for covering roofs. ❑ *...a stone-built cottage, with a traditional slate roof.* **2** N-COUNT A **slate** is one of the small flat pieces of slate that are used for covering roofs. ❑ *Thieves had stolen the slates from the roof.* **3** V-T PASSIVE If something **is slated** to happen, it is planned to happen at a particular time or on a particular occasion. [mainly AM] ❑ *Bromfield was slated to become U.S. Secretary of Agriculture.* **4** PHRASE If you start with **a clean slate**, you do not take account of previous mistakes or failures and make a fresh start. ❑ *The proposal is to pay everything you owe, so that you can start with a clean slate.* **5** → See also color supplement

slath|er /slǽðər/ (**slathers, slathering, slathered**) V-T If you **slather** something with a substance, or **slather** a substance onto something, you put the substance on in a thick layer. ❑ *If your skin is dry, you have to slather on moisturizer to soften it.* ❑ *...pieces of toast slathered with butter and jam.*

slat|ted /slǽtɪd/ ADJ Something that is **slatted** is made with slats. ❑ *...slatted window blinds.*

slaugh|ter /slɔ́tər/ (**slaughters, slaughtering, slaughtered**) **1** V-T [usu passive] If large numbers of people or animals **are slaughtered**, they are killed in a way that is cruel or unnecessary. ❑ *Thirty-four people were slaughtered while lining up to cast their votes.* • N-UNCOUNT **Slaughter** is also a noun. ❑ *This was only a small part of a war where the slaughter of civilians was commonplace.* **2** V-T To **slaughter** animals such as cows and sheep means to kill them for their meat. ❑ *Lack of chicken feed means that chicken farms are having to slaughter their stock.* • N-UNCOUNT **Slaughter** is also a noun. ❑ *More than 491,000 sheep were exported for slaughter last year.*

slaughter|house /slɔ́tərhaʊs/ (**slaughterhouses**) N-COUNT A **slaughterhouse** is a place where animals are killed for their meat.

Slav /slɑ́v/ (**Slavs**) N-COUNT A **Slav** is a member of any of the peoples of Eastern Europe who speak a Slavonic language.

slave /sleɪv/ (**slaves, slaving, slaved**) **1** N-COUNT A **slave** is someone who is the property of another person and has to work for that person. ❑ *The state of Liberia was formed a century and a half ago by freed slaves from the United States.* **2** N-COUNT You can describe someone as a **slave** when they are completely under the control of another person or of a powerful influence. ❑ *She may no longer be a slave to the studio system, but she still has a duty to her fans.* **3** V-I If you say that a person **is slaving** over something or **is slaving** for someone, you mean that they are working very hard. ❑ *When you're busy all day the last thing you want to do is spend hours slaving over a hot stove.* • PHRASAL VERB **Slave away** means the same as **slave**. ❑ *He stares at the hundreds of workers slaving away in the intense sun.*

slave la|bor

in BRIT, use **slave labour**

1 N-UNCOUNT **Slave labor** refers to slaves or to work done by slaves. ❑ *The children were used as slave labor in gold mines in the jungle.* **2** N-UNCOUNT If people work very hard for long hours for very little money, you can refer to it as **slave labor**. [DISAPPROVAL] ❑ *He's been forced into slave labor at burger bars to earn a bit of cash.*

slav|er /slǽvər/ (**slavers, slavering, slavered**) V-I If an animal **slavers**, liquid comes from its mouth, for example, because it is about to attack and eat something. ❑ *Mad guard dogs slavered at the end of their chains.* ❑ *...the wolf's slavering jaws.*

slav|ery /sleɪvəri, sleɪvri/ N-UNCOUNT **Slavery** is the system by which people are owned by other people as slaves. ❑ *My people have survived 400 years of slavery.*

slave trade N-SING [*the* N] **The slave trade** is the buying and selling of slaves, especially Black Africans, from the 16th to the 19th centuries. ❑ *...profits from the slave trade.*

Slav|ic /slǽvɪk, slɑ́v-/ ADJ Something that is **Slavic** belongs or relates to Slavs. ❑ *...Americans of Slavic descent.*

slav|ish /sleɪvɪʃ/ ADJ You use **slavish** to describe things that copy or imitate something exactly, without any attempt to be original. [DISAPPROVAL] ❏ *She herself insists she is no slavish follower of fashion.* • **slav|ish|ly** ADV ❏ *Most have slavishly copied the design of IBM's big mainframe machines.*

Sla|von|ic /sləvɒnɪk/ ADJ Something that is **Slavonic** relates to East European languages such as Russian, Czech, and Serbo-Croat, or to the people who speak them. ❏ *The Ukrainians speak a Slavonic language.*

slaw /slɔː/ N-UNCOUNT **Slaw** is a salad of chopped raw cabbage, carrots, and other vegetables in mayonnaise. [mainly AM]

in BRIT, usually use **coleslaw**

slay /sleɪ/ (**slays, slaying, slew** or **slayed, slain**) **1** V-T If someone **slays** an animal, they kill it in a violent way. [FORMAL] ❏ *...the hill where St. George slew the dragon.* **2** V-T PASSIVE If someone **has been slain**, they have been murdered. [mainly AM] ❏ *Two Australian tourists were slain.*

slay|ing /sleɪɪŋ/ (**slayings**) N-COUNT [usu with supp] A **slaying** is a murder. [mainly AM] ❏ *...a trail of motiveless slayings.*

in BRIT, usually use **killing**

sleaze /sliːz/ N-UNCOUNT You use **sleaze** to describe activities that you consider immoral, dishonest, or not respectable, especially in politics, business, journalism, or entertainment. [INFORMAL, DISAPPROVAL] ❏ *She claimed that an atmosphere of sleaze and corruption now surrounded the government.*

slea|zy /sliːzi/ (**sleazier, sleaziest**) **1** ADJ If you describe a place as **sleazy**, you dislike it because it looks dirty and badly cared for, and not respectable. [INFORMAL, DISAPPROVAL] ❏ *...sleazy bars.* **2** ADJ If you describe something or someone as **sleazy**, you disapprove of them because you think they are not respectable and are rather disgusting. [INFORMAL, DISAPPROVAL] ❏ *The accusations are making the government's conduct appear increasingly sleazy.*

sled /slɛd/ (**sleds, sledding, sledded**)

in BRIT, use **sledge**

1 N-COUNT A **sled** is an object used for traveling over snow. It consists of a framework which slides on two strips of wood or metal. [AM] ❏ *I saw her pulling three children through the snow on a sled.* **2** V-I If you **sled** or go **sledding**, you ride on a sled. [AM] ❏ *We got home and went sledding on the small hill in our back yard.*

sledge /slɛdʒ/ (**sledges, sledging, sledged**) **1** N-COUNT A **sledge** is the same as a **sled**. [BRIT] **2** V-I If you **sledge** or go **sledging**, you ride on a sledge. [BRIT]

sledge|hammer /slɛdʒhæmər/ (**sledgehammers**) also **sledge-hammer** N-COUNT A **sledgehammer** is a large, heavy hammer with a long handle, used for breaking up rocks and concrete.

sleek /sliːk/ (**sleeker, sleekest**) **1** ADJ **Sleek** hair or fur is smooth and shiny and looks healthy. ❏ *...sleek black hair.* **2** ADJ If you describe someone as **sleek**, you mean that they look rich and stylish. ❏ *He is as sleek and elegant as any other millionaire businessman.* **3** ADJ **Sleek** vehicles, furniture, or other objects look smooth, shiny, and expensive. ❏ *...a sleek white BMW.*

sleep ♦♦♢ /sliːp/ (**sleeps, sleeping, slept**) **1** N-UNCOUNT **Sleep** is the natural state of rest in which your eyes are closed, your body is inactive, and your mind does not think. ❏ *They were exhausted from lack of sleep.* ❏ *Be quiet and go to sleep.* **2** V-I When you **sleep**, you rest with your eyes closed and your mind and body inactive. ❏ *During the drive, the baby slept.* ❏ *I've not been able to sleep for the last few nights.* **3** N-COUNT A **sleep** is a period of sleeping. ❏ *I think he may be ready for a sleep soon.* **4** V-T [no cont, no passive] If a building or room **sleeps** a particular number of people, it has beds for that number of people. ❏ *The villa sleeps 10.* **5** → see also **sleeping** **6** PHRASE If you cannot **get to sleep**, you are unable to sleep. ❏ *I can't get to sleep with all that singing.* **7** PHRASE If you say that you didn't **lose** any **sleep** over something, you mean that you did not worry about it at all. ❏ *I didn't lose too much sleep over that investigation.* **8** PHRASE If you are trying to make a decision and you say that you will **sleep on it**, you mean that you will delay making a decision on it until the following day, so you have time to think about it. ❏ *I need more time to sleep on it. It's a big decision and I want to make the right one.* **9** PHRASE If a sick or injured animal **is put to sleep**, it is killed by a vet in a way that does not cause it pain. ❏ *I'm going take the dog down to the vet's and have her put to sleep.*

▶ **sleep around** PHRASAL VERB If you say that someone **sleeps around**, you disapprove of them because they have sex with a lot of different people. [INFORMAL, DISAPPROVAL] ❏ *I don't sleep around.*

▶ **sleep in** PHRASAL VERB If you **sleep in**, you stay asleep in the morning for longer than you usually do. ❏ *Yesterday, few players turned up because most slept in.*

▶ **sleep off** PHRASAL VERB If you **sleep off** the effects of too much traveling, drink, or food, you recover from it by sleeping. ❏ *It's a good idea to spend the first night of your vacation sleeping off the jet lag.*

▶ **sleep over** PHRASAL VERB If someone, especially a child, **sleeps over** in a place such as a friend's home, they stay there for one night. ❏ *She said his friends could sleep over.*

▶ **sleep together** PHRASAL VERB If two people **are sleeping together**, they are having a sexual relationship, but are not usually married to each other. ❏ *I'm pretty sure they slept together before they were married.*

▶ **sleep with** PHRASAL VERB If you **sleep with** someone, you have sex with them. ❏ *One character is sleeping with a married man.*

sleep|er /sliːpər/ (**sleepers**) N-COUNT You can use **sleeper** to indicate how well someone sleeps. For example, if someone is a light **sleeper**, they are easily woken up. ❏ *I'm a very light sleeper and I can hardly get any sleep at all.*

sleep|ing /sliːpɪŋ/ **1** ADJ [ADJ n] You use **sleeping** to describe places where people sleep or things concerned with where people sleep. ❏ *On the top floor we have sleeping quarters for women and children.* **2** → see also **sleep**

USAGE

sleeping or asleep?
Don't use **asleep** in front of a noun. Don't, for example, talk about an '*asleep child*.' Instead, you can say a '*sleeping child*.'

sleep|ing bag (**sleeping bags**) N-COUNT A **sleeping bag** is a large, deep bag with a warm lining, used for sleeping in, especially when you are camping.

sleep|ing car (**sleeping cars**) N-COUNT A **sleeping car** is a car on a train containing beds for passengers to sleep in at night.

sleep|ing gi|ant (**sleeping giants**) N-COUNT If you refer to someone or something as a **sleeping giant**, you mean that they are powerful but they have not yet shown the full extent of their power. [JOURNALISM] ❏ *The trust, which has 2.3 million members, has been characterized as a sleeping giant of the environment movement.*

sleep|ing part|ner (**sleeping partners**) N-COUNT A **sleeping partner** is the same as a **silent partner**. [BRIT, BUSINESS]

sleep|ing pill (**sleeping pills**) N-COUNT A **sleeping pill** is a pill that you can take to help you sleep.

sleep|ing sick|ness N-UNCOUNT **Sleeping sickness** is a serious tropical disease which causes great tiredness and often leads to death.

sleep|ing tab|let (**sleeping tablets**) N-COUNT A **sleeping tablet** is the same as a **sleeping pill**.

sleep|less /sliːplɪs/ **1** ADJ A **sleepless** night is one during which you do not sleep. ❏ *I have sleepless nights worrying about her.* **2** ADJ Someone who is **sleepless** is unable to sleep. ❏ *A sleepless baby can seem to bring little reward.*

sleep|over /sliːpoʊvər/ (**sleepovers**) also **sleep-over** N-COUNT A **sleepover** is an occasion when someone, especially a child, sleeps for one night in a place such as a friend's home. ❏ *Emily couldn't ask a friend for a sleepover until she cleaned her room.*

sleep|walk /sliːpwɔːk/ (**sleepwalks, sleepwalking, sleepwalked**) V-I If someone **is sleepwalking**, they are walking around while they are asleep. ❏ *He once sleepwalked to the middle of the road outside his home at 1 a.m.*

sleepy /sliːpi/ (**sleepier, sleepiest**) **1** ADJ If you are **sleepy**, you are very tired and are almost asleep. ❏ *I was beginning to feel amazingly sleepy.* • **sleepi|ly** ADV [ADV with v] ❏ *Joanna sat up,*

sleet blinking sleepily. **2** ADJ A **sleepy** place is quiet and does not have much activity or excitement. ❏ *Valence is a sleepy little town just south of Lyon.*

sleet /sliːt/ **1** N-UNCOUNT **Sleet** is rain that is partly frozen. ❏ *...blinding snow, driving sleet and wind.* **2** → See feature box at **hot**

sleeve /sliːv/ (**sleeves**) **1** N-COUNT The **sleeves** of a coat, shirt, or other item of clothing are the parts that cover your arms. ❏ *His sleeves were rolled up to his elbows.* **2** N-COUNT A record **sleeve** is the stiff cover in which a record is kept. [mainly BRIT] ❏ *...an album sleeve.* **3** PHRASE If you have something **up** your **sleeve**, you have an idea or plan which you have not told anyone about. You can also say that someone has **an ace, card,** or **trick up** their **sleeve**. ❏ *He wondered what tricks Shearson had up his sleeve.*

-sleeved /-sliːvd/ COMB IN ADJ [usu ADJ n] **-sleeved** is added to adjectives such as 'long' and 'short' to form adjectives which indicate that an item of clothing has long or short sleeves. ❏ *...a short-sleeved blue shirt.*

sleeve|less /sliːvlɪs/ ADJ [usu ADJ n] A **sleeveless** dress, top, or other item of clothing has no sleeves. ❏ *She wore a sleeveless silk dress.*

sleeve note (**sleeve notes**) N-COUNT [usu pl] **Sleeve notes** are the same as **liner notes**. [BRIT]

sleigh /sleɪ/ (**sleighs**) N-COUNT A **sleigh** is a vehicle which can slide over snow. Sleighs are usually pulled by horses.

sleight of hand /slaɪt əv hænd/ (**sleights of hand**) N-VAR **Sleight of hand** is the deceiving of someone in a skillful way. ❏ *He accused Mr. MacGregor of "sleight of hand."*

slen|der /slɛndər/ **1** ADJ A **slender** person is attractively thin and graceful. [WRITTEN, APPROVAL] ❏ *She was slender, with delicate wrists and ankles.* ❏ *...a tall, slender figure in a straw hat.* **2** ADJ You can use **slender** to describe a situation which exists but only to a very small degree. [WRITTEN] ❏ *The United States held a slender lead.* **3** → See feature box at **appearance**

slept /slɛpt/ **Slept** is the past tense and past participle of **sleep**.

sleuth /sluːθ/ (**sleuths**) N-COUNT A **sleuth** is a detective. [OLD-FASHIONED]

sleuth|ing /sluːθɪŋ/ N-UNCOUNT **Sleuthing** is the investigation of a crime or mystery by someone who is not a police officer. [LITERARY] ❏ *I did a little sleuthing to see if I could find any footprints.*

slew /sluː/ (**slews, slewing, slewed**) **1 Slew** is the past tense of **slay**. **2** V-T/V-I If a vehicle **slews** or **is slewed** across a road, it slides across it. ❏ *The bus slewed sideways.* ❏ *He slewed the car against the side of the building.* **3** N-COUNT A **slew** of things is a large number of them. [mainly AM] ❏ *There have been a whole slew of shooting incidents.*

slice ♦◇◇ /slaɪs/ (**slices, slicing, sliced**) **1** N-COUNT A **slice** of bread, meat, fruit, or other food is a thin piece that has been cut from a larger piece. ❏ *Try to eat at least four slices of bread a day.* **2** V-T If you **slice** bread, meat, fruit, or other food, you cut it into thin pieces. ❏ *Helen sliced the cake.* • PHRASAL VERB **Slice up** means the same as **slice**. ❏ *I sliced up an onion.* **3** N-COUNT You can use **slice** to refer to a part of a situation or activity. ❏ *Fiction takes up a large slice of the publishing market.* **4 a slice of the action** → see **action**

SYNONYMS

slice
VERB **2**
cut: *Theo was cutting himself a piece of the pink cake.*
carve: *Carve the beef into slices.*
chop: *Chop the onions very finely.*

sliced /slaɪst/ ADJ [usu ADJ n] **Sliced** bread has been cut into slices before being wrapped and sold. ❏ *...a sliced white loaf.*

slick /slɪk/ (**slicker, slickest, slicks**) **1** ADJ A **slick** performance, production, or advertisement is skillful and impressive. ❏ *There's a big difference between an amateur video and a slick Hollywood production.* **2** ADJ A **slick** action is done quickly and smoothly, and without any obvious effort. ❏ *They were outplayed by the Colombians' slick passing and decisive finishing.* **3** ADJ A **slick** person speaks easily in a way that is likely to convince people, but is not sincere. [DISAPPROVAL] ❏ *Don't be fooled by slick politicians.* **4** N-COUNT A **slick** is the same as an **oil slick**. ❏ *Experts are trying to devise ways to clean up the huge slick.*

slick|er /slɪkər/ (**slickers**) **1** N-COUNT A **slicker** is a long, loose waterproof coat. [AM]

in BRIT, use **oilskins**

2 → see also **slick**

slide ♦◇◇ /slaɪd/ (**slides, sliding, slid**) **1** V-T/V-I When something **slides** somewhere or when you **slide** it there, it moves there smoothly over or against something. ❏ *She slid the door open.* ❏ *I slid the wallet into his pocket.* **2** V-I If you **slide** somewhere, you move there smoothly and quietly. ❏ *He slid into the driver's seat.* **3** V-I To **slide into** a particular mood, attitude, or situation means to gradually start to have that mood, attitude, or situation often without intending to. ❏ *She had slid into a depression.* **4** V-T/V-I If currencies or prices **slide**, they gradually become worse or lower in value. [JOURNALISM] ❏ *The dollar continued to slide.* • N-COUNT **Slide** is also a noun. ❏ *...the dangerous slide in oil prices.* **5** N-COUNT A **slide** is a small piece of photographic film which you project onto a screen so that you can see the picture. ❏ *...a slide show.* **6** N-COUNT A **slide** is a piece of glass on which you put something that you want to examine through a microscope. ❏ *...a drop of blood on a slide.* **7** N-COUNT A **slide** is a piece of playground equipment that has a steep slope for children to go down for fun. ❏ *...two young children playing on a slide.*

SYNONYMS

slide
VERB **1**
slip: *He had slipped on an icy sidewalk.*
glide: *Waiters glide between tightly-packed tables, bearing trays of pasta.*
slither: *Robert lost his footing and slithered down the bank.*

slide rule (**slide rules**) N-COUNT A **slide rule** is an instrument that you use for calculating numbers. It looks like a ruler and has a middle part that slides backward and forward.

slid|ing door (**sliding doors**) N-COUNT **Sliding doors** are doors which slide in tracks rather than swinging on hinges.

slid|ing scale (**sliding scales**) N-COUNT Payments such as wages or taxes that are calculated on a **sliding scale** are higher or lower depending on various different factors. ❏ *Many practitioners have a sliding scale of fees.*

slight ♦◇◇ /slaɪt/ (**slighter, slightest, slights, slighting, slighted**) **1** ADJ Something that is **slight** is very small in degree or quantity. ❏ *Doctors say he has made a slight improvement.* ❏ *He's not the slightest bit worried.* **2** ADJ A **slight** person has a fairly thin and delicate looking body. ❏ *She is smaller and slighter than Christie.* • **slight|ly** ADV [ADV -ed] ❏ *...a slightly built man.* **3** V-T [usu passive] If you **are slighted**, someone does or says something that insults you by treating you as if your views or feelings are not important. ❏ *They felt slighted by not being adequately consulted.* • N-COUNT **Slight** is also a noun. ❏ *It's difficult to persuade my husband that it isn't a slight on him that I enjoy my evening class.* **4** PHRASE You use **in the slightest** to emphasize a negative statement. [EMPHASIS] ❏ *That doesn't interest me in the slightest.*

SYNONYMS

slight
ADJ **1**
minor: *Western officials say it's a minor problem, and should be quickly overcome.*
insignificant: *In 1949, Bonn was a small, insignificant city.*
negligible: *The pay that the soldiers received was negligible.*
meager: *The bank's staff were already angered by a meager 3.1% pay raise.*
VERB **3**
snub: *He snubbed her in public and made her feel like an idiot.*
insult: *I did not mean to insult you.*
ignore: *She said her husband ignored her.*

slight|ly ♦♦◇ /slaɪtli/ ADV **Slightly** means to some degree but not to a very large degree. ❏ *His family then moved to a slightly larger house.* ❏ *Each person learns in a slightly different way.*

slim

> **SYNONYMS**
>
> **slightly**
> ADV
> **rather:** *I grew up in rather unusual circumstances.*
> **somewhat:** *He concluded that Oswald was somewhat odd.*
> **quite:** *I felt quite bitter about it at the time.*
> **fairly:** *Both ships are fairly new.*

slim ♦♦◊ /slɪm/ (**slimmer, slimmest, slims, slimming, slimmed**) **1** ADJ A **slim** person has an attractively thin and well-shaped body. [APPROVAL] ❑ *The young woman was tall and slim.* **2** ADJ A **slim** book, wallet, or other object is thinner than usual. ❑ *The slim booklets describe a range of services and facilities.* **3** ADJ A **slim** chance or possibility is a very small one. ❑ *There's still a slim chance that he may become president.* **4** V-T If an organization **slims** its products or workers, it reduces the number of them that it has. [BUSINESS] ❑ *The company recently slimmed its product line.*
▸ **slim down** **1** PHRASAL VERB If you **slim down**, you lose weight and become thinner. ❑ *People will lose weight when they slim down with a friend.* **2** PHRASAL VERB If a company or other organization **slims down** or **is slimmed down**, it employs fewer people, in order to save money or become more efficient. [BUSINESS] ❑ *Many firms have had little choice but to slim down.*

> **SYNONYMS**
>
> **slim**
> ADJ **1**
> **thin:** *He was a tall, thin man with gray hair.*
> **slender:** *She was slender, with delicate wrists and ankles.*
> **slight:** *She is smaller and slighter than Christie.*
> **lean:** *Like most athletes, she was lean and muscular.*

slime /slaɪm/ N-UNCOUNT **Slime** is a thick, wet substance which covers a surface or comes from the bodies of animals such as snails. ❑ *He swam down and retrieved his glasses from the muck and slime at the bottom of the pond.*

slim|line /slɪmlaɪn/ ADJ [usu ADJ n] **Slimline** objects are thinner or narrower than normal ones. ❑ *The slimline diary fits easily into a handbag.*

slimy /slaɪmi/ (**slimier, slimiest**) ADJ **Slimy** substances are thick, wet, and unpleasant. **Slimy** objects are covered in a slimy substance. ❑ *His feet slipped in the slimy mud.*

sling /slɪŋ/ (**slings, slinging, slung**) **1** V-T If you **sling** something somewhere, you throw it there carelessly. ❑ *He lost it completely and started slinging chairs, a television, books, and pictures around his flat.* **2** V-T If you **sling** something over your shoulder or over something such as a chair, you hang it there loosely. ❑ *She slung her coat over her desk chair.* ❑ *He had a small green backpack slung over one shoulder.* **3** V-T [usu passive] If a rope, blanket, or other object **is slung** between two points, someone has hung it loosely between them. ❑ *...two long poles with a blanket slung between them.* **4** N-COUNT A **sling** is an object made of ropes, straps, or cloth that is used for carrying things. ❑ *They used slings of rope to lower us from one set of arms to another.* **5** N-COUNT A **sling** is a piece of cloth which supports someone's broken or injured arm and is tied around their neck. ❑ *She was back at work with her arm in a sling.*

sling|shot /slɪŋʃɒt/ (**slingshots**) N-COUNT A **slingshot** is a device for shooting small stones. It is made of a Y-shaped stick with a piece of elastic tied between the two top posts. [AM]

> in BRIT, use **catapult**

slink /slɪŋk/ (**slinks, slinking, slunk**) V-I If you **slink** somewhere, you move there quietly because you do not want to be seen. ❑ *He decided that he couldn't just slink away, so he went and sat next to his wife.*

slinky /slɪŋki/ (**slinkier, slinkiest**) ADJ [usu ADJ n] **Slinky** clothes fit very closely to a woman's body in a way that makes her look sexually attractive. ❑ *She's wearing a slinky black mini-skirt.*

slip ♦♦◊ /slɪp/ (**slips, slipping, slipped**) **1** V-I If you **slip**, you accidentally slide and lose your balance. ❑ *He had slipped on an icy pavement.* **2** V-I If something **slips**, it slides out of place or out of your hand. ❑ *His glasses had slipped.* **3** V-I If you **slip** somewhere, you go there quickly and quietly. ❑ *Amy slipped downstairs and out of the house.* **4** V-T If you **slip** something somewhere, you put it there quickly in a way that does not attract attention. ❑ *I slipped a note under Louise's door.* ❑ *He found a coin in his pocket and slipped it into her hand.* **5** V-T If you **slip** something to someone, you give it to them secretly. ❑ *Robert had slipped her a note in school.* **6** V-I To **slip into** a particular state or situation means to pass gradually into it, in a way that is hardly noticed. ❑ *It amazed him how easily one could slip into a routine.* **7** V-T/V-I If something **slips** to a lower level or standard, it falls to that level or standard. ❑ *Shares slipped to $1.17.* ❑ *In June, producer prices slipped 0.1% from May.* • N-SING **Slip** is also a noun. ❑ *...a slip in consumer confidence.* **8** V-T/V-I If you **slip** into or out of clothes or shoes, you put them on or take them off quickly and easily. ❑ *She slipped out of the jacket and tossed it on the couch.* **9** N-COUNT A **slip** is a small or unimportant mistake. ❑ *We must be well prepared, there must be no slips.* **10** N-COUNT A **slip** of paper is a small piece of paper. ❑ *...little slips of paper he had torn from a notebook.* ❑ *I put her name on the slip.* **11** N-COUNT A **slip** is a thin piece of clothing that can be worn under a dress or skirt. **12** PHRASE If you **let slip** information, you accidentally tell it to someone, when you wanted to keep it secret. ❑ *I bet he let slip that I'd gone to America.* **13** PHRASE If something **slips** your **mind**, you forget about it. ❑ *The reason for my visit had obviously slipped his mind.*
▸ **slip up** PHRASAL VERB If you **slip up**, you make a small or unimportant mistake. ❑ *There were occasions when we slipped up.*

slip|cover /slɪpkʌvər/ (**slipcovers**) also **slip cover** N-COUNT A **slipcover** is a piece of cloth that fits over a chair or sofa and can easily be removed. [mainly AM] ❑ *...the slipcovers on the dining room chairs.*

slip-on (**slip-ons**) ADJ [ADJ n] **Slip-on** shoes have nothing fastening them. ❑ *...slip-on boat shoes.* • N-COUNT **Slip-on** is also a noun. ❑ *He removed his brown slip-ons.*

slip|page /slɪpɪdʒ/ (**slippages**) N-VAR **Slippage** is a failure to maintain a steady position or rate of progress, so that a particular target or standard is not achieved. ❑ *...a substantial slippage in the value of sterling.*

slipped disk (**slipped disks**) N-COUNT If you have a **slipped disk**, you have a bad back because one of the disks in your spine has moved out of its proper position. [AM]

> in BRIT, use **slipped disc**

slip|per /slɪpər/ (**slippers**) **1** N-COUNT **Slippers** are loose, soft shoes that you wear at home. ❑ *...a pair of old slippers.* **2** → See also color supplement

slip|pery /slɪpəri/ (**slipperier, slipperiest**) **1** ADJ Something that is **slippery** is smooth, wet, or oily and is therefore difficult to walk on or to hold. ❑ *The tiled floor was wet and slippery.* **2** ADJ You can describe someone as **slippery** if you think that they are dishonest in a clever way and cannot be trusted. [DISAPPROVAL] ❑ *He is a slippery customer, and should be carefully watched.* **3** PHRASE If someone is on a **slippery slope**, they are involved in a course of action that is difficult to stop and that will eventually lead to failure or trouble. ❑ *The company started down the slippery slope of believing that they knew better than the customer.* **4** → See feature box at **snow**

slip road (**slip roads**) N-COUNT A **slip road** is a road which cars use to drive on and off a highway. [BRIT]

> in AM, use **entrance ramp**

slip|shod /slɪpʃɒd/ ADJ [usu ADJ n] If something is **slipshod**, it has been done in a careless way. ❑ *The hotel had always been run in a slipshod way.*

slip|stream /slɪpstriːm/ (**slipstreams**) N-COUNT [usu the N] The **slipstream** of a fast-moving object such as a car, plane, or boat is the flow of air directly behind it. ❑ *He left a host of other riders trailing in his slipstream.*

slip-up (**slip-ups**) N-COUNT A **slip-up** is a small or unimportant mistake. [INFORMAL] ❑ *There's been a slip-up somewhere.*

slip|way /slɪpweɪ/ (**slipways**) N-COUNT A **slipway** is a large platform that slopes down into the sea, from which boats are put into the water.

slit /slɪt/ (**slits, slitting**)

> The form **slit** is used in the present tense and is the past tense and past participle.

1 V-T If you **slit** something, you make a long narrow cut in it. ❑ *They say somebody slit her throat.* ❑ *He began to slit open each envelope.* **2** N-COUNT A **slit** is a long narrow cut. ❑ *Make a slit in* the stem about half an inch long. **3** N-COUNT A **slit** is a long narrow opening in something. ◻ *She watched them through a slit in the curtains.*

slith|er /slɪðər/ (**slithers**, **slithering**, **slithered**) **1** V-I If you **slither** somewhere, you slide along in an uneven way. ◻ *Robert lost his footing and slithered down the bank.* **2** V-I If an animal such as a snake **slithers**, it moves along in a curving way. ◻ *The snake slithered into the water.*

slith|ery /slɪðəri/ ADJ Something that is **slithery** is wet or smooth, and so slides easily over things or is easy to slip on. ◻ *...slithery rice noodles.*

sliv|er /slɪvər/ (**slivers**) N-COUNT A **sliver** of something is a small thin piece or amount of it. ◻ *Not a sliver of glass remains where the windows were.*

slob /slɒb/ (**slobs**) N-COUNT If you call someone a **slob**, you mean that they are very lazy and messy. [INFORMAL, DISAPPROVAL] ◻ *My boyfriend used to call me a fat slob.*

slob|ber /slɒbər/ (**slobbers**, **slobbering**, **slobbered**) V-I If a person or an animal **slobbers**, they let liquid fall from their mouth. ◻ *...slobbering on his eternal cigarette end.*

sloe /sloʊ/ (**sloes**) N-VAR A **sloe** is a small, sour fruit that has a dark purple skin. It is often used to flavor gin.

slog /slɒg/ (**slogs**, **slogging**, **slogged**) **1** V-T/V-I If you **slog** through something, you work hard and steadily through it. [INFORMAL] ◻ *They secure their degrees by slogging through an intensive 11-month course.* • PHRASAL VERB **Slog away** means the same as **slog**. ◻ *Edward slogged away, always learning.* **2** N-SING [also no det] If you describe a task as a **slog**, you mean that it is tiring and requires a lot of effort. [INFORMAL] ◻ *There is little to show for the two years of hard slog.*

slo|gan /sloʊgən/ (**slogans**) N-COUNT A **slogan** is a short phrase that is easy to remember. Slogans are used in advertisements and by political parties and other organizations who want people to remember what they are saying or selling. ◻ *They could campaign on the slogan "We'll take less of your money."*

WORD HISTORY

slogan
Slogan comes from Gaelic *sluaghghairm*, which means 'war cry.'

---

slo|gan|eer|ing /sloʊgənɪərɪŋ/ N-UNCOUNT **Sloganeering** is the use of slogans by people such as politicians or advertising agencies. ◻ *...the sloganeering of the marketing department.*

sloop /sluːp/ (**sloops**) N-COUNT A **sloop** is a small sailing boat with one mast.

slop /slɒp/ (**slops**, **slopping**, **slopped**) V-T/V-I If liquid **slops** from a container or if you **slop** liquid somewhere, it comes out over the edge of the container, usually accidentally. ◻ *A little cognac slopped over the edge of the glass.*

slope /sloʊp/ (**slopes**, **sloping**, **sloped**) **1** N-COUNT A **slope** is the side of a mountain, hill, or valley. ◻ *Saint-Christo is perched on a mountain slope.* **2** N-COUNT A **slope** is a surface that is at an angle, so that one end is higher than the other. ◻ *The street must have been on a slope.* **3** V-I If a surface **slopes**, it is at an angle, so that one end is higher than the other. ◻ *The bank sloped down sharply to the river.* • **slop|ing** ADJ ◻ *...a brick building, with a sloping roof.* **4** V-I If something **slopes**, it leans to the right or to the left rather than being upright. ◻ *The writing sloped backwards.* **5** N-COUNT The **slope** of something is the angle at which it slopes. ◻ *The slope increases as you go up the curve.* **6 slippery slope** → see **slippery**

slop|py /slɒpi/ (**sloppier**, **sloppiest**) ADJ If you describe someone's work or activities as **sloppy**, you mean they have been done in a careless and lazy way. [DISAPPROVAL] ◻ *He has little patience for sloppy work from colleagues.*

slop|py joe /slɒpi dʒoʊ/ (**sloppy joes**) N-COUNT A **sloppy joe** is a sandwich consisting of a bun filled with sauce and cooked meat. [INFORMAL]

slosh /slɒʃ/ (**sloshes**, **sloshing**, **sloshed**) **1** V-T/V-I If a liquid **sloshes** around or if you **slosh** it around, it moves around in different directions. ◻ *The water sloshed around the bridge.* ◻ *He took a mouthful of the cheap wine and sloshed it around his mouth.* ◻ *The champagne sloshed and spilt.* **2** V-I If you **slosh** through mud or water, you walk through it in an energetic way, so that the mud or water makes sounds as you walk. ◻ *The two girls joined arms and sloshed through the mud together.*

sloshed /slɒʃt/ ADJ [v-link ADJ] If someone is **sloshed**, they have drunk too much alcohol. [INFORMAL] ◻ *Everyone else was getting sloshed.*

slot /slɒt/ (**slots**, **slotting**, **slotted**) **1** N-COUNT A **slot** is a narrow opening in a machine or container, for example, a hole that you put coins in to make a machine work. ◻ *He dropped a coin into the slot and dialed.* **2** V-T/V-I If you **slot** something into something else, or if it **slots** into it, you put it into a space where it fits. ◻ *He was slotting a CD into a CD player.* ◻ *The car seat belt slotted into place easily.* **3** N-COUNT A **slot** in a schedule or program is a place in it where an activity can take place. ◻ *Visitors can book a time slot a week or more in advance.*

sloth /slɒθ/ (**sloths**) **1** N-UNCOUNT **Sloth** is laziness, especially with regard to work. [FORMAL] ◻ *He admitted a lack of motivation and a feeling of sloth.* **2** N-COUNT A **sloth** is an animal from Central and South America. Sloths live in trees and move very slowly.

sloth|ful /slɒθfəl/ ADJ Someone who is **slothful** is lazy and unwilling to make an effort to work. [FORMAL] ◻ *He was not slothful: he had been busy all night.*

slot ma|chine (**slot machines**) N-COUNT A **slot machine** is a machine from which you can get food or cigarettes or on which you can gamble. You make it work by putting coins into a slot.

slot|ted spoon (**slotted spoons**) N-COUNT A **slotted spoon** is a large plastic or metal spoon with holes in it. It is used to take food out of a liquid.

slouch /slaʊtʃ/ (**slouches**, **slouching**, **slouched**) V-I If someone **slouches**, they sit or stand with their shoulders and head bent so they look lazy and unattractive. ◻ *Try not to slouch when you are sitting down.*

slough /slʌf/ (**sloughs**, **sloughing**, **sloughed**) V-T When a plant **sloughs** its leaves, or an animal such as a snake **sloughs** its skin, the leaves or skin come off naturally. ◻ *All reptiles have to slough their skin to grow.* • PHRASAL VERB **Slough off** means the same as **slough**. ◻ *Our bodies slough off dead cells.*

slov|en|ly /slʌvənli/ ADJ [usu ADJ n] **Slovenly** people are careless, messy, or inefficient. [DISAPPROVAL] ◻ *Lisa was irritated by the slovenly attitude of her boyfriend Sean.*

slow ♦♦◊ /sloʊ/ (**slower**, **slowest**, **slows**, **slowing**, **slowed**) **1** ADJ Something that is **slow** moves, happens, or is done without much speed. ◻ *The traffic is heavy and slow.* ◻ *Electric whisks should be used on a slow speed.* • **slow|ly** ADV [ADV with v] ◻ *He spoke slowly and deliberately.* • **slow|ness** N-UNCOUNT ◻ *She lowered the glass with calculated slowness.* **2** ADV [ADV after v] In informal English, **slower** is used to mean 'at a slower speed' and **slowest** is used to mean 'at the slowest speed.' In nonstandard English, **slow** is used to mean 'with little speed.' ◻ *I began to walk slower and slower.* **3** ADJ Something that is **slow** takes a long time. ◻ *The distribution of passports has been a slow process.* • **slow|ly** ADV [ADV with v] ◻ *My resentment of her slowly began to fade.* • **slow|ness** N-UNCOUNT ◻ *...the slowness of political and economic progress.* **4** ADJ [v-link ADJ] If someone is **slow** to do something, they do it after a delay. ◻ *The world community has been slow to respond to the crisis.* **5** V-T/V-I If something **slows** or if you **slow** it, it starts to move or happen more slowly. ◻ *The rate of bombing has slowed considerably.* ◻ *She slowed the car and began driving up a narrow road.* **6** ADJ Someone who is **slow** is not very clever and takes a long time to understand things. ◻ *He got hit on the head and he's been a bit slow since.* **7** ADJ If you describe a situation, place, or activity as **slow**, you mean that it is not very exciting. ◻ *Don't be faint-hearted when things seem a bit slow or boring.* **8** ADJ If a clock or watch is **slow**, it shows a time that is earlier than the correct time. ◻ *The clock is about two and a half minutes slow.* **9 slowly but surely** → see **surely**

▶ **slow down 1** PHRASAL VERB If something **slows down** or if something **slows** it **down**, it starts to move or happen more slowly. ◻ *The bus slowed down for the next stop.* ◻ *There is no cure for the disease, although drugs can slow down its rate of development.* **2** PHRASAL VERB If someone **slows down** or if something **slows** them **down**, they become less active. ◻ *You will need to slow down for a while.* **3** → see also **slowdown**

▶ **slow up** PHRASAL VERB **Slow up** means the same as **slow down** 1. ❑ *Sales are slowing up.*

SYNONYMS

slow
ADJ **3**
protracted: *The struggle would be bitter and protracted.*
lengthy: *...the lengthy process of filling out passport application forms.*
long drawn-out: *...a long, drawn-out, election campaign.*

COLLOCATIONS

slow
VERB **5**
slow + noun: economy, growth, progress, recovery; decline, pace, rate, spread; process, traffic
noun + **slow**: economy, growth, inflation, recovery; decline, pace, rate; activity, metabolism, traffic
slow + adverb: dramatically, markedly, sharply, significantly

---

slow- /sloʊ-/ COMB IN ADJ **slow-** is used to form words which describe something that happens slowly. ❑ *He was stuck in a line of slow-moving traffic.* ❑ *...a slow-burning fuse.*

slow burn ◼ N-SING If something is a **slow burn**, or if it happens on a **slow burn**, it develops slowly. ❑ *This death had been a slow burn.* ❑ *Because it worked on a slow burn before becoming a hit around the country, many people missed out on seeing the early episodes.* ❑ *This is a slow-burn romance.* ◼ PHRASE If someone **does a slow burn**, their angry feelings grow slowly but steadily. ❑ *It was the sort of thing that might make anyone do a slow burn.*

slow|down /sloʊdaʊn/ (**slowdowns**) ◼ N-COUNT A **slowdown** is a reduction in speed or activity. ❑ *There has been a sharp slowdown in economic growth.* ◼ N-COUNT A **slowdown** is a protest in which workers deliberately work slowly and cause problems for their employers. [AM, BUSINESS] ❑ *It's impossible to assess how many officers are participating in the slowdown.*

in BRIT, use **go-slow**

slow lane (**slow lanes**) ◼ N-COUNT [usu sing, usu the N] On a highway, the **slow lane** is the lane for vehicles which are moving more slowly than the other vehicles. ◼ N-SING [usu the N] If you say that a person, country, or company is in the **slow lane**, you mean that they are not progressing as fast as other people, countries, or companies in a particular area of activity. ❑ *She quit her job in favor of life in the slow lane.*

slow mo|tion also **slow-motion** N-UNCOUNT When film or television pictures are shown in **slow motion**, they are shown much more slowly than normal. ❑ *It seemed almost as if he were falling in slow motion.*

slow|poke /sloʊpoʊk/ (**slowpokes**) N-COUNT If you call someone a **slowpoke**, you are criticizing the fact that they do something slowly. [AM, INFORMAL] ❑ *"Come on, slowpoke," said Frank, pushing up the pace still more.*

in BRIT, use **slowcoach**

slow-witted ADJ Someone who is **slow-witted** is slow to understand things.

sludge /slʌdʒ/ (**sludges**) N-VAR **Sludge** is thick mud, sewage, or industrial waste. ❑ *More than a million gallons of sludge has seeped into the water.*

slug /slʌɡ/ (**slugs**) ◼ N-COUNT A **slug** is a small slow-moving creature with a long soft body and no legs, like a snail without a shell. ◼ N-COUNT If you take a **slug** of an alcoholic drink, you take a large mouthful of it. [INFORMAL] ❑ *Edgar took a slug of his drink.*

slug|ger /slʌɡər/ (**sluggers**) N-COUNT In sports such as baseball and tennis, a **slugger** is a person who hits the ball very hard. In boxing, a **slugger** is a person who hits his opponent very hard but without a great deal of skill. [mainly AM, INFORMAL] ❑ *...the great New York Yankee slugger Babe Ruth.* ❑ *They've changed me from a slugger into a boxer.*

slug|gish /slʌɡɪʃ/ ADJ You can describe something as **sluggish** if it moves, works, or reacts much slower than you would like or is normal. ❑ *The economy remains sluggish.* ❑ *Circulation is much more sluggish in the feet than in the hands.*

sluice /sluːs/ (**sluices, sluicing, sluiced**) ◼ N-COUNT A **sluice** is a passage that carries a current of water and has a barrier, called a sluice gate, which can be opened and closed to control the flow of water. ◼ V-T If you **sluice** something or **sluice** it down or out, you wash it with a stream of water. ❑ *He sluiced the bath and filled it.*

slum /slʌm/ (**slums**) ◼ N-COUNT A **slum** is an area of a city where living conditions are very bad and where the houses are in bad condition. ❑ *...a slum area of St. Louis.* ◼ → See feature box at **urban**

slum|ber /slʌmbər/ (**slumbers, slumbering, slumbered**) N-VAR **Slumber** is sleep. [LITERARY] ❑ *He had fallen into exhausted slumber.* • V-I **Slumber** is also a verb. ❑ *The older three girls are still slumbering peacefully.*

slum|ber par|ty (**slumber parties**) N-COUNT A **slumber party** is an occasion when a group of young friends spend the night together at the home of one of the group. [mainly AM] ❑ *I'm having a slumber party for my birthday.*

slump /slʌmp/ (**slumps, slumping, slumped**) ◼ V-I If something such as the value of something **slumps**, it falls suddenly and by a large amount. ❑ *Net profits slumped by 41%.* • N-COUNT **Slump** is also a noun. ❑ *The council's land is now worth much less than originally hoped because of a slump in property prices.* ◼ N-COUNT A **slump** is a time when many people in a country are unemployed and poor. ❑ *...the slump of the early 1980s.* ◼ V-T/V-I If you **slump** somewhere, you fall or sit down there heavily, for example, because you are very tired or you feel ill. ❑ *She slumped into a chair.*

slung /slʌŋ/ **Slung** is the past tense and past participle of **sling**.

slunk /slʌŋk/ **Slunk** is the past tense and past participle of **slink**.

slur /slɜːr/ (**slurs, slurring, slurred**) ◼ N-COUNT A **slur** is an insulting remark which could damage someone's reputation. ❑ *This is yet another slur on the integrity of the police.* ◼ V-T/V-I If someone **slurs** their speech or if their speech **slurs**, they do not pronounce each word clearly, because they are drunk, ill, or sleepy. ❑ *He repeated himself and slurred his words more than usual.*

slurp /slɜːrp/ (**slurps, slurping, slurped**) ◼ V-T/V-I If you **slurp** a liquid, you drink it noisily. ❑ *He blew on his soup before slurping it off the spoon.* ◼ N-COUNT A **slurp** is a noise that you make with your mouth when you drink noisily, or a mouthful of liquid that you drink noisily. ❑ *He takes a slurp from a cup of black coffee.*

slur|ry /slɜːri/ (**slurries**) N-VAR **Slurry** is a watery mixture of something such as mud, animal waste, or dust. ❑ *...farm slurry and industrial waste.*

slush /slʌʃ/ N-UNCOUNT **Slush** is snow that has begun to melt and is therefore very wet and dirty. ❑ *Front-drive cars work better in the snow and slush.*

slush fund (**slush funds**) N-COUNT A **slush fund** is a sum of money collected to pay for an illegal activity, especially in politics or business. ❑ *He's accused of misusing $17.5 million from a secret government slush fund.*

slushy /slʌʃi/ (**slushier, slushiest**) ◼ ADJ **Slushy** ground is covered in dirty, wet snow. ❑ *Here and there a drift across the road was wet and slushy.* ◼ ADJ If you describe a story or idea as **slushy**, you mean you dislike it because it is extremely romantic and sentimental. [DISAPPROVAL]

slut /slʌt/ (**sluts**) N-COUNT **Slut** is an offensive word for a woman who has a lot of sexual partners. [OFFENSIVE, DISAPPROVAL]

sly /slaɪ/ (**slyer** or **slier, slyest** or **sliest**) ◼ ADJ A **sly** look, expression, or remark shows that you know something that other people do not know or that was meant to be a secret. ❑ *His lips were spread in a sly smile.* • **sly|ly** ADV ❑ *Anna grinned slyly.* ◼ ADJ If you describe someone as **sly**, you disapprove of them because they keep their feelings or intentions hidden and are clever at deceiving people. [DISAPPROVAL] ❑ *She is devious and sly and manipulative.*

smack /smæk/ (**smacks, smacking, smacked**) ◼ V-T If you **smack** someone, you hit them with your hand. ❑ *She smacked me on the side of the head.* • N-COUNT **Smack** is also a noun.

❏ *Sometimes he just doesn't listen and I end up shouting at him or giving him a smack.* **2** V-T If you **smack** something somewhere, you put it or throw it there so that it makes a loud, sharp noise. ❏ *He smacked his hands down on his knees.* **3** V-I If one thing **smacks of** another thing that you consider bad, it reminds you of it or is like it. ❏ *The engineers' union was unhappy with the motion, saying it smacked of racism.* **4** ADV [ADV prep] Something that is **smack** in a particular place is exactly in that place. [INFORMAL] ❏ *In part that's because industry is smack in the middle of the city.* **5** N-UNCOUNT **Smack** is heroin. [INFORMAL] ❏ *...a smack addict.* **6** PHRASE If you **smack** your **lips**, you open and close your mouth noisily, especially before or after eating, to show that you are eager to eat or enjoyed eating. ❏ *"I really want some dessert," Keaton says, smacking his lips.*

smack dab ADV [ADV prep] **Smack dab** is used in expressions such as 'smack dab in the middle' of somewhere to mean exactly in that place. [mainly AM, INFORMAL] ❏ *...an old brick building smack dab in the middle of downtown.*

in BRIT, also use **slap bang**

small ✦✦✦ /smɔːl/ (**smaller**, **smallest**) **1** ADJ A **small** person, thing, or amount of something is not large in physical size. ❏ *She is small for her age.* ❏ *Stick them on using a small amount of glue.* **2** ADJ A **small** group or quantity consists of only a few people or things. ❏ *A small group of students meets regularly to learn Japanese.* **3** ADJ A **small** child is a very young child. ❏ *I have a wife and two small children.* **4** ADJ You use **small** to describe something that is not significant or great in degree. ❏ *It's quite easy to make quite small changes to the way that you work.* ❏ *No detail was too small to escape her attention.* **5** ADJ **Small** businesses or companies employ a small number of people and do business with a small number of clients. ❏ *...shops, restaurants and other small businesses.* **6** ADJ [v-link ADJ] If someone makes you look or feel **small**, they make you look or feel stupid or ashamed. ❏ *This may just be another of her schemes to make me look small.* **7** N-SING **The small of** your back is the bottom part of your back that curves in slightly. ❏ *Place your hands on the small of your back and breathe in.* **8** **the small hours** → see **hour** **9** **small wonder** → see **wonder**

small ad (**small ads**) N-COUNT The **small ads** are the same as the classifieds. [BRIT]

small arms N-PLURAL **Small arms** are guns that are light and easy to carry. ❏ *The two sides exchanged small arms fire for about three hours.*

small change N-UNCOUNT **Small change** is coins of low value. ❏ *She was counting out a dollar, mostly in small change, into my hand.*

small claims court (**small claims courts**) also **small-claims court** N-VAR **Small claims court** is a local law court which settles disputes between people that involve relatively small amounts of money. ❏ *...the Los Angeles mother who took a caregiver to small claims court over a $70 phone bill.* ❏ *The 27-year-old was taken to a small claims court.*

small fry (**small fry**) N-UNCOUNT [also N in pl] **Small fry** is used to refer to someone or something that is considered to be unimportant. ❏ *This small fry was soon mixing with top executives from major corporations.*

small hours N-PLURAL [usu in the N, oft N of n] If something happens in the **small hours**, it happens soon after midnight, in the very early morning. ❏ *They were arrested in the small hours of Saturday morning.*

small|ish /smɔːlɪʃ/ ADJ Something that is **smallish** is fairly small. ❏ *Some smallish firms may close.*

small-minded ADJ If you say that someone is **small-minded**, you are critical of them because they have fixed opinions and are unwilling to change them or to think about more general subjects. [DISAPPROVAL] ❏ *...their small-minded preoccupation with making money.*

small po|ta|toes N-UNCOUNT If you say that something is **small potatoes**, you mean that it is unimportant in comparison with something else. [mainly AM, INFORMAL] ❏ *Our monumental worries are often small potatoes in the larger scheme of life.*

small|pox /smɔːlpɒks/ N-UNCOUNT **Smallpox** is a serious infectious disease that causes spots which leave deep marks on the skin.

small print N-UNCOUNT The **small print** of a contract or agreement is the part of it that is written in very small print. You refer to it as the **small print** especially when you think that it might include unfavorable conditions which someone might not notice or understand. ❏ *Read the small print in your contract to find out exactly what you are insured for.*

small-scale ADJ A **small-scale** activity or organization is small in size and limited in extent. ❏ *...the small-scale production of farmhouse cheeses in Vermont.*

small screen N-SING [usu the N] When people talk about **the small screen**, they are referring to television, in contrast to movies that are made for the movie theater. ❏ *Now he is also to become a star of the small screen.*

small talk N-UNCOUNT **Small talk** is polite conversation about unimportant things that people make at social occasions. ❏ *Smiling for the cameras, the two men strained to make small talk.*

small-time ADJ If you refer to workers or businesses as **small-time**, you think they are not very important because their work is limited in extent or not very successful. ❏ *...small time drug dealers.*

small town

in BRIT, also use **smalltown**

ADJ [usu ADJ n] **Small town** is used when referring to small places, usually in the United States, where people are friendly, honest, and polite, or to the people there. **Small town** is also sometimes used to suggest that someone has old-fashioned ideas. [mainly AM] ❏ *...an idealized small-town America of neat, middle-class homes.*

smart ✦✦◇ /smɑːrt/ (**smarter**, **smartest**, **smarts**, **smarting**, **smarted**) **1** ADJ You can describe someone who is clever or intelligent as **smart**. ❏ *He thinks he's smarter than Sarah is.* **2** ADJ **Smart** people and things are pleasantly neat and clean in appearance. [mainly BRIT] ❏ *He was smart and well groomed but not good looking.* ❏ *I was dressed in a smart navy blue suit.* • **smart|ly** ADV [ADV with v] ❏ *He dressed very smartly, which was important in those days.* **3** ADJ A **smart** place or event is connected with wealthy and fashionable people. [mainly BRIT] ❏ *...smart dinner parties.* **4** V-I If a part of your body or a wound **smarts**, you feel a sharp stinging pain in it. ❏ *My eyes smarted from the smoke.* **5** V-I [usu cont] If you are **smarting** from something such as criticism or failure, you feel upset about it. [JOURNALISM] ❏ *It appeared that her opponent was smarting from successive defeats.* **6** **the smart money** → see **money**

smart aleck (**smart alecks**) also **smart alec** N-COUNT [oft N n] If you describe someone as a **smart aleck**, you dislike the fact that they think they are very clever and always have an answer for everything. [INFORMAL, DISAPPROVAL] ❏ *...a fortyish smart-aleck TV reporter.*

smart ass (**smart asses**) also **smart-ass** N-COUNT [oft N n] If you describe someone as a **smart ass**, you dislike the fact that they think they are very clever and like to show everyone this. [INFORMAL, VULGAR, DISAPPROVAL] ❏ *...smart-ass comments.*

smart card (**smart cards**) N-COUNT A **smart card** is a plastic card which looks like a credit card and can store and process computer data. ❏ *We encourage the use of smart cards for online payments.*

smart drug (**smart drugs**) N-COUNT [usu pl] **Smart drugs** are drugs which some people think can improve your memory and intelligence.

smart|en /smɑːrtən/ (**smartens**, **smartening**, **smartened**)
▶ **smarten up** PHRASAL VERB If you **smarten** yourself or a place **up**, you make yourself or the place look neater and tidier. ❏ *...a 10-year program to smarten up the city.* ❏ *She had wisely smartened herself up.*

smart growth N-UNCOUNT [oft N n] People such as architects and environmentalists use **smart growth** to refer to the construction of new buildings and roads within a town or city so that they are close to people's workplaces and mass transit systems and so that open spaces are not built on. ❏ *The Environmental Defense Fund has gotten $800,000 in federal grants to promote smart growth.* ❏ *...New Jersey's smart-growth policy.*

smart phone (**smart phones**) **1** N-COUNT A **smart phone** is a type of cellphone that can perform many of the operations that a computer does, such as accessing the internet. **2** → See feature box at **technology, telephone**

smarts /smɑrts/ **1** N-PLURAL [poss/the N] You can use **smarts** to mean the skill and intelligence that people need in order to be successful in difficult situations. [AM, INFORMAL] ❑ *I didn't even think he had the smarts to do something like that.* ❑ *Nobody doubts his physical ability or his smarts.* **2** → see also **street smarts**

smart speak|er (smart speakers) N-COUNT A **smart speaker** is a wireless electronic device that can respond to spoken commands, for example by giving information or playing music. ❑ *He instructed the smart speaker to play some jazz.*

smart|watch /smɑrtwɒtʃ/ (smartwatches) N-COUNT A **smartwatch** is a wireless electronic device that can respond to spoken commands, for example by giving information or playing music. ❑ *The smartwatch is just one example of wearable tech.*

smash ✦◇ /smæʃ/ (smashes, smashing, smashed) **1** V-T/V-I If you **smash** something or if it **smashes**, it breaks into many pieces, for example, when it is hit or dropped. ❑ *Someone smashed a bottle.* ❑ *A crowd of youths started smashing windows.* **2** V-T/V-I If you **smash** through a wall, gate, or door, you get through it by hitting and breaking it. ❑ *The demonstrators used trucks to smash through embassy gates.* **3** V-T/V-I If something **smashes** or **is smashed** against something solid, it moves very fast and with great force against it. ❑ *The bottle smashed against a wall.* **4** V-T To **smash** a political group or system means to deliberately destroy it. [INFORMAL] ❑ *Their attempts to clean up politics and smash the power of party machines failed.*
▶ **smash up** **1** PHRASAL VERB If you **smash** something **up**, you completely destroy it by hitting it and breaking it into many pieces. ❑ *She took revenge on her ex boyfriend by smashing up his home.* **2** PHRASAL VERB If you **smash up** your car, you damage it by crashing it into something. ❑ *All you told me was that he'd smashed up yet another car.*

smash-and-grab (smash-and-grabs) also **smash and grab** N-COUNT [oft N n] A **smash-and-grab** is a robbery in which a person breaks a store window, takes the things that are on display there, and runs away with them. ❑ *...a smash and grab raid.*

smashed /smæʃt/ ADJ [usu v-link ADJ] Someone who is **smashed** is extremely drunk. [INFORMAL]

smash hit (smash hits) N-COUNT A **smash hit** or a **smash** is a very popular show, play, or song. ❑ *The show was a smash hit.*

smat|ter|ing /smætərɪŋ/ N-SING [usu a N of n] A **smattering** of something is a very small amount of it. ❑ *I had acquired a smattering of Greek.*

smear /smɪər/ (smears, smearing, smeared) **1** V-T If you **smear** a surface with an oily or sticky substance or **smear** the substance onto the surface, you spread a layer of the substance over the surface. ❑ *My sister smeared herself with suntan oil and slept by the swimming pool.* **2** N-COUNT A **smear** is a dirty or oily mark. ❑ *There was a smear of gravy on his chin.* **3** V-T To **smear** someone means to spread unpleasant and untrue rumors or accusations about them in order to damage their reputation. [JOURNALISM] ❑ *They planned to smear him by publishing information about his private life.* **4** N-COUNT A **smear** is an unpleasant and untrue rumor or accusation that is intended to damage someone's reputation. [JOURNALISM] ❑ *He puts all the accusations down to a smear campaign by his political opponents.* **5** N-COUNT A **smear** or a **smear test** is a medical test in which a few cells are taken from a woman's cervix and examined to see if any cancer cells are present. [BRIT]

in AM, use **Pap smear**

smeared /smɪərd/ ADJ If something is **smeared**, it has dirty or oily marks on it. ❑ *The other child's face was smeared with dirt.*

smell ✦◇◇ /smɛl/ (smells, smelling, smelled) **1** N-COUNT The **smell** of something is a quality it has which you become aware of when you breathe in through your nose. ❑ *...the smell of freshly baked bread.* ❑ *...horrible smells.* **2** N-UNCOUNT Your sense of **smell** is the ability that your nose has to detect things. ❑ *...people who lose their sense of smell.* **3** V-LINK If something **smells** a particular way, it has a quality which you become aware of through your nose. ❑ *The room smelled of lemons.* ❑ *It smells delicious.* **4** V-I If you say that something **smells**,

you mean that it smells unpleasant. ❑ *Ma threw that out. She said it smelled.* **5** V-T If you **smell** something, you become aware of it when you breathe in through your nose. ❑ *As soon as we opened the front door we could smell the gas.* **6** V-T If you **smell** something, you put your nose near it and breathe in, so that you can discover its smell. ❑ *I took a fresh rose out of the vase on our table, and smelled it.* **7** **to smell a rat** → see **rat**

-smelling /-smɛlɪŋ/ COMB IN ADJ **-smelling** combines with adjectives to form adjectives which indicate how something smells. ❑ *...sweet-smelling dried flowers.* ❑ *The city is covered by a foul-smelling cloud of smoke.*

smell|ing salts N-PLURAL A bottle of **smelling salts** contains a chemical with a strong smell which is used to help someone recover after they have fainted.

smelly /smɛli/ (smellier, smelliest) ADJ Something that is **smelly** has an unpleasant smell. ❑ *He had extremely smelly feet.*

smid|gen /smɪdʒɪn/ (smidgens) also **smidgeon, smidgin** N-COUNT [oft N of n] A **smidgen** is a small amount of something. [INFORMAL] ❑ *...a smidgen of tobacco.* ❑ *...a smidgen of luck.*

smile ✦◆◇ /smaɪl/ (smiles, smiling, smiled) **1** V-I When you **smile**, the corners of your mouth curve up and you sometimes show your teeth. People smile when they are pleased or amused, or when they are being friendly. ❑ *When he saw me, he smiled and waved.* ❑ *He rubbed the back of his neck and smiled ruefully at me.* **2** N-COUNT A **smile** is the expression that you have on your face when you smile. ❑ *She gave a wry smile.* ❑ *"There are some sandwiches if you're hungry," she said with a smile.*

───── SYNONYMS ─────
smile
VERB **1**
grin: *He grins, delighted at the memory.*
beam: *Frances beamed at her friend with undisguised admiration.*
smirk: *Two men looked at me, nudged each other, and smirked.*

smi|ley /smaɪli/ (smileys, smilier, smiliest) **1** ADJ [usu ADJ n] A **smiley** person smiles a lot or is smiling. [INFORMAL] ❑ *Two smiley babies are waiting for their lunch.* **2** N-COUNT A **smiley** or a **smiley face** is a symbol used in email to show how someone is feeling. :-) is a smiley showing happiness. [COMPUTING]

smil|ing|ly /smaɪlɪŋli/ ADV [ADV with v] If someone does something **smilingly**, they smile as they do it. [WRITTEN] ❑ *He opened the gate and smilingly welcomed the travelers home.*

smirk /smɜrk/ (smirks, smirking, smirked) V-I If you **smirk**, you smile in an unpleasant way, often because you believe that you have gained an advantage over someone else or know something that they do not know. ❑ *Two men standing nearby looked at me, nudged each other and smirked.*

smite /smaɪt/ (smites, smiting, smote, smitten) **1** V-T To **smite** something means to hit it hard. [LITERARY] ❑ *The heroic leader charged into battle, ready to smite the enemy.* **2** → see also **smitten**

smith|er|eens /smɪðəriːnz/ N-PLURAL [usu to n] If something is blown or smashed to **smithereens**, it breaks into very small pieces. ❑ *She dropped the vase and smashed it to smithereens.*

smithy /smɪθi, smɪði/ (smithies) N-COUNT A **smithy** is a place where a blacksmith works.

smit|ten /smɪt(ə)n/ **1** ADJ If you are **smitten**, you find someone so attractive that you are or seem to be in love with them. ❑ *They were totally smitten with each other.* **2** **Smitten** is the past participle of **smite**.

SMO /ɛs ɛm oʊ/ N-UNCOUNT **SMO** is short for **social media optimization**.

smock /smɒk/ (smocks) **1** N-COUNT A **smock** is a loose garment, like a long blouse, usually worn by women. ❑ *She was wearing wool slacks and a paisley smock.* **2** N-COUNT A **smock** is a loose garment worn by people such as artists to protect their clothing.

smocked /smɒkt/ ADJ A **smocked** dress or top is decorated with smocking. ❑ *She was pretty and young, in a loose smocked sundress.*

smock|ing /smɒkɪŋ/ N-UNCOUNT **Smocking** is a decoration on tops and dresses which is made by gathering the material into folds using small stitches.

smog /smɒg/ (smogs) N-VAR Smog is a mixture of fog and smoke which occurs in some busy industrial cities. ❑ *Cars cause pollution, both smog and acid rain.*

smog|gy /smɒgi/ (smoggier, smoggiest) ADJ A smoggy city or town is badly affected by smog. ❑ *...the smoggy sprawl of L.A.*

smoke ✦✧ /smoʊk/ (smokes, smoking, smoked)
1 N-UNCOUNT Smoke consists of gas and small bits of solid material that are sent into the air when something burns. ❑ *A cloud of black smoke blew over the city.* **2** V-I If something is smoking, smoke is coming from it. ❑ *The chimney was smoking fiercely.* **3** V-T/V-I When someone smokes a cigarette, cigar, or pipe, they suck the smoke from it into their mouth and blow it out again. If you smoke, you regularly smoke cigarettes, cigars, or a pipe. ❑ *He was sitting alone, smoking a big cigar.* ❑ *It's not easy to quit smoking.* • N-SING Smoke is also a noun. ❑ *Someone came out for a smoke.* **4** V-T [usu passive] If fish or meat is smoked, it is hung over burning wood so that the smoke preserves it and gives it a special flavor. ❑ *...the grid where the fish were being smoked.* **5** → see also smoking **6** PHRASE If someone says where there's smoke there's fire, they mean that there are rumors or signs that something is true so it must be at least partly true. ❑ *A lot of the stuff in the story is not true, but I have to say that where there's smoke there's fire.* **7** PHRASE If something goes up in smoke, it is destroyed by fire. ❑ *The crew were able to put out the fire after only 25 acres had gone up in smoke.* **8** PHRASE If something that is very important to you goes up in smoke, it fails or ends without anything being achieved. ❑ *I was afraid you'd say no, and my dream would go up in smoke.*

smoke alarm (smoke alarms) also **smoke detector** N-COUNT A smoke alarm or a smoke detector is a device fixed to the ceiling of a room which makes a loud noise if there is smoke in the air, to warn people.

smoke bomb (smoke bombs) N-COUNT A smoke bomb is a bomb that produces clouds of smoke when it explodes.

smoked /smoʊkt/ **1** ADJ Smoked glass has been darkened by being treated with smoke. ❑ *...a white van with smoked glass windows.* **2** → see also smoke

smoke de|tec|tor (smoke detectors) N-COUNT A smoke detector is the same as a smoke alarm.

smoked salm|on N-UNCOUNT Smoked salmon is the flesh of a salmon which is smoked and eaten raw.

smoke-filled room (smoke-filled rooms) N-COUNT If you talk about a decision being made in a smoke-filled room, you mean that it is made by a small group of people in a private meeting, rather than in a more democratic or open way. [DISAPPROVAL] ❑ *...long discussions in smoke-filled rooms.*

smoke|less /smoʊklɪs/ ADJ Smokeless fuel burns without producing smoke.

smok|er /smoʊkər/ (smokers) **1** N-COUNT A smoker is a person who smokes cigarettes, cigars, or a pipe. ❑ *...a 64-year-old former smoker.* **2** N-COUNT On a train, a smoker is a car in which you are allowed to smoke.

smoke|screen /smoʊkskrin/ (smokescreens) also **smoke screen** N-COUNT If something that you do or say is a smokescreen, it is intended to hide the truth about your activities or intentions. ❑ *He was accused of putting up a smokescreen to hide poor standards in schools.*

smoke sig|nal (smoke signals) N-COUNT [usu pl] If someone such as a politician or businessperson sends out smoke signals, they give an indication of their views and intentions. This indication is often not clear and needs to be worked out. ❑ *The smoke signals from the bank suggest further cuts are coming.*

smoke|stack /smoʊkstæk/ (smokestacks) N-COUNT A smokestack is a very tall chimney that carries smoke away from a factory.

smoke|stack in|dus|try (smokestack industries) N-COUNT A smokestack industry is a traditional industry such as heavy engineering or manufacturing, rather than a modern industry such as electronics. ❑ *There has been a shift from smokestack industries into high-tech ones.*

smok|ing ✦✧ /smoʊkɪŋ/ **1** N-UNCOUNT Smoking is the act or habit of smoking cigarettes, cigars, or a pipe. ❑ *Smoking is now banned in many places of work.* **2** ADJ [ADJ n] A smoking area is intended for people who want to smoke. ❑ *California no longer allows smoking areas in restaurants.* **3** → see also smoke

smok|ing gun (smoking guns) N-COUNT [usu sing] A smoking gun is a piece of evidence that proves that something is true or that someone is responsible for a crime. [mainly AM] ❑ *The search for other kinds of evidence tying him to trafficking has not produced a smoking gun.*

smoky /smoʊki/ (smokier, smokiest) also **smokey** **1** ADJ A place that is smoky has a lot of smoke in the air. ❑ *His main problem was the extremely smoky atmosphere at work.* **2** ADJ [ADJ n, ADJ color] You can use smoky to describe something that looks like smoke, for example, because it is slightly blue or gray or because it is not clear. ❑ *At the center of the dial is a piece of smoky glass.* **3** ADJ Something that has a smoky flavor tastes as if it has been smoked. ❑ *The fish had just the right amount of smoky flavor for my taste.*

smol|der /smoʊldər/ (smolders, smoldering, smoldered)

in BRIT, use **smoulder**

1 V-I If something smolders, it burns slowly, producing smoke but not flames. ❑ *The wreckage was still smoldering several hours after the crash.* **2** V-I If a feeling such as anger or hatred smolders inside you, you continue to feel it but do not show it. ❑ *...the guilt that had so long smoldered in her heart.* **3** V-I If you say that someone smolders, you mean that they are sexually attractive, usually in a mysterious or very intense way. ❑ *He was good-looking, with dark eyes which could smolder with just the right intimation of passion.*

smooch /smuːtʃ/ (smooches, smooching, smooched) V-RECIP If two people smooch, they kiss and hold each other closely. People sometimes smooch while they are dancing. ❑ *I smooched with him on the dance floor.* ❑ *The customers smooch and chat.*

smooth ✦✧ /smuːð/ (smoother, smoothest, smooths, smoothing, smoothed) **1** ADJ A smooth surface has no roughness, lumps, or holes. ❑ *...a rich cream that keeps skin soft and smooth.* ❑ *...a smooth surface such as glass.* **2** ADJ A smooth liquid or mixture has been mixed well so that it has no lumps. ❑ *Continue whisking until the mixture looks smooth and creamy.* **3** ADJ If you describe a drink such as wine, whiskey, or coffee as smooth, you mean that it is not bitter and is pleasant to drink. ❑ *This makes the whiskeys much smoother.* **4** ADJ A smooth line or movement has no sudden breaks or changes in direction or speed. ❑ *This exercise is done in one smooth motion.* • **smooth|ly** ADV [ADV with v] ❑ *Make sure that you execute all movements smoothly and without jerking.* **5** ADJ A smooth ride, flight, or sea crossing is very comfortable because there are no unpleasant movements. ❑ *The active suspension system gives the car a very smooth ride.* **6** ADJ You use smooth to describe something that is going well and is free of problems or trouble. ❑ *Political hopes for a swift and smooth transition to democracy have been dashed.* • **smooth|ly** ADV [ADV with v] ❑ *So far, talks at GM have gone smoothly.* **7** ADJ If you describe a man as smooth, you mean that he is extremely smart, confident, and polite, often in a way that you find rather unpleasant. ❑ *He was an older man, with a reputation as being rather smooth.* **8** V-T If you smooth something, you move your hands over its surface to make it smooth and flat. ❑ *She stood up and smoothed down her frock.* **9** → See feature box at snow

▶ **smooth out** PHRASAL VERB If you smooth out a problem or difficulty, you solve it, especially by talking to the people concerned. ❑ *Baker was smoothing out differences with European allies.*

▶ **smooth over** PHRASAL VERB If you smooth over a problem or difficulty, you make it less serious and easier to deal with, especially by talking to the people concerned. ❑ *...an attempt to smooth over the violent splits that have occurred.* ❑ *The president is trying to smooth things over.*

smoothie /smuːði/ (smoothies) **1** N-COUNT If you describe a someone as a smoothie, you mean that they are extremely smart, confident, and polite, often in a way that you find rather unpleasant. [INFORMAL] **2** N-COUNT A smoothie is a thick drink made from fruit crushed in a machine, sometimes with yogurt or ice cream added. ❑ *He ordered waffles and a fruit smoothie from a waiter.*

smooth-talking ADJ A smooth-talking person talks very confidently in a way that is likely to persuade people, but may not be sincere or honest. ❑ *...the smooth-talking conman who has wrecked their lives.*

smor|gas|bord /smɔrgəsbɔrd/ **1** N-SING [also no det] **Smorgasbord** is a meal with a variety of hot and cold savory dishes, from which people serve themselves. **2** N-SING [usu N of n] A **smorgasbord** of things is a number of different things that are combined together as a whole. [JOURNALISM] ☐ ...a smorgasbord of paintings and sculpture.

smote /smoʊt/ **Smote** is the past tense of **smite**.

smoth|er /smʌðər/ (smothers, smothering, smothered) **1** V-T If you **smother** a fire, you cover it with something in order to put it out. ☐ The girl's parents were also burned as they tried to smother the flames. **2** V-T To **smother** someone means to kill them by covering their face with something so that they cannot breathe. ☐ He tried to smother me with a pillow. **3** V-T Things that **smother** something cover it completely. ☐ Once the shrubs begin to smother the little plants, we have to move them. **4** V-T If you **smother** someone, you show your love for them too much and protect them too much. ☐ She loved her own children, almost smothering them with love. **5** V-T If you **smother** an emotion or a reaction, you control it so that people do not notice it. ☐ She tried to smother her anger and help them resolve their conflicts.

smoul|der /smoʊldər/ [mainly BRIT] → see **smolder**

SMS /ɛs ɛm ɛs/ N-UNCOUNT **SMS** is a way of sending short written messages from one cellphone to another. **SMS** is an abbreviation for **short message system** or **short message system**.

smudge /smʌdʒ/ (smudges, smudging, smudged) **1** N-COUNT A **smudge** is a dirty mark. ☐ There was a dark smudge on his forehead. **2** V-T If you **smudge** a substance such as ink, paint, or make-up that has been put on a surface, you make it less neat by touching or rubbing it. ☐ She rubbed her eyes, smudging her make-up. **3** V-T If you **smudge** a surface, you make it dirty by touching it and leaving a substance on it. ☐ She kissed me, careful not to smudge me with her fresh lipstick.

smudgy /smʌdʒi/ (smudgier, smudgiest) ADJ If something is **smudgy**, its outline is unclear. ☐ The hand-writing is smudgy. ☐ ...smudgy photos.

smug /smʌg/ (smugger, smuggest) ADJ If you say that someone is **smug**, you are criticizing the fact they seem very pleased with how good, clever, or lucky they are. [DISAPPROVAL] ☐ Thomas and his wife looked at each other in smug satisfaction.

smug|gle /smʌgəl/ (smuggles, smuggling, smuggled) V-T If someone **smuggles** things or people into a place or out of it, they take them there illegally or secretly. ☐ My message is "If you try to smuggle drugs you are stupid." ☐ Police have foiled an attempt to smuggle a bomb into Belfast airport. • **smug|gling** N-UNCOUNT ☐ An air hostess was arrested and charged with drug smuggling.

smug|gler /smʌglər/ (smugglers) N-COUNT **Smugglers** are people who take things or people into or out of a country illegally. ☐ ...drug smugglers.

smut /smʌt/ (smuts) **1** N-UNCOUNT If you refer to words or pictures that are related to sex as **smut**, you disapprove of them because you think they are rude and unpleasant and have been said or published just to shock or excite people. [DISAPPROVAL] ☐ ...schoolboy smut. **2** N-UNCOUNT [also N in pl] **Smut** or **smuts** is dirt such as soot which makes a dirty mark on something.

smut|ty /smʌti/ (smuttier, smuttiest) ADJ [usu ADJ n] If you describe something such as a joke, book, or movie as **smutty**, you disapprove of it because it shows naked people or refers to sex in a vulgar or unpleasant way. [DISAPPROVAL] ☐ ...smutty jokes.

snack /snæk/ (snacks, snacking, snacked) **1** N-COUNT A **snack** is a simple meal that is quick to cook and to eat. ☐ Lunch was a snack in the fields. **2** N-COUNT A **snack** is something such as a chocolate bar that you eat between meals. ☐ Do you eat sweets, cakes or sugary snacks? **3** V-I If you **snack**, you eat snacks between meals. ☐ Instead of snacking on crisps and chocolate, nibble on celery or carrot.

snack|able /snækəbəl/ ADJ **Snackable** food can be eaten in small quantities between meals, as a snack. ☐ They sell snackable small cans of salmon and tuna.

snack bar (snack bars) N-COUNT A **snack bar** is a place where you can buy drinks and simple meals such as sandwiches.

snaf|fle /snæfəl/ (snaffles) N-COUNT A **snaffle** is an object consisting of two short joined bars of metal that is put in a horse's mouth and attached to the straps that the rider uses to control the horse.

sna|fu /snæfuː/ (snafus) N-COUNT [usu adj N] If you describe a situation as a **snafu**, you mean that it is disorderly or disorganized and that it is usually like this. [AM, INFORMAL, DISAPPROVAL] ☐ Her internship was cut short because of a technical snafu. ☐ It may be the judge's fault. It may be a lawyer's fault. It may be a procedural snafu.

snag /snæg/ (snags, snagging, snagged) **1** N-COUNT A **snag** is a small problem or disadvantage. ☐ A police clampdown on car thieves hit a snag when villains stole one of their cars. **2** V-T/V-I If you **snag** part of your clothing on a sharp or rough object or if it **snags**, it gets caught on the object and tears. ☐ She snagged a heel on a root and tumbled to the ground. ☐ Brambles snagged his suit.

snail /sneɪl/ (snails) **1** N-COUNT A **snail** is a small animal with a long, soft body, no legs, and a spiral-shaped shell. Snails move very slowly. **2** PHRASE If you say that someone does something **at a snail's pace**, you are emphasizing that they are doing it very slowly, usually when you think it would be better if they did it much more quickly. [EMPHASIS] ☐ The train was moving now at a snail's pace.

snail mail N-UNCOUNT Some computer users refer to the postal system as **snail mail**, because it is very slow in comparison with email.

snake /sneɪk/ (snakes, snaking, snaked) **1** N-COUNT A **snake** is a long, thin reptile without legs. **2** V-I Something that **snakes** in a particular direction goes in that direction in a line with a lot of bends. [LITERARY] ☐ The road snaked through forested mountains.

snake|bite /sneɪkbaɪt/ (snakebites) also **snake bite** N-VAR A **snakebite** is the bite of a snake, especially a poisonous one.

snake charm|er (snake charmers) N-COUNT A **snake charmer** is a person who entertains people by controlling the behavior of a snake, for example, by playing music and causing the snake to rise out of a basket and drop back in again.

snake oil N-UNCOUNT **Snake oil** is used to refer to any substance that is claimed to be a medical remedy but which in fact has no healing properties. [DISAPPROVAL] ☐ Traditional and folk remedies are often labeled as snake oil and witches' potions. ☐ ...these modern-day snake oil salesmen.

snake|skin /sneɪkskɪn/ N-UNCOUNT [oft N n] **Snakeskin** is the skin of snakes used to make shoes and clothes.

snap /snæp/ (snaps, snapping, snapped) **1** V-T/V-I If something **snaps** or if you **snap** it, it breaks suddenly, usually with a sharp cracking noise. ☐ He shifted his weight and a twig snapped. ☐ The brake pedal had just snapped off. • N-SING **Snap** is also a noun. ☐ Every minute or so I could hear a snap, a crack and a crash as another tree went down. **2** V-T/V-I If you **snap** something into a particular position, or if it **snaps** into that position, it moves quickly into that position, with a sharp sound. ☐ He snapped the notebook shut. ☐ He snapped the cap on his ballpoint. • N-SING **Snap** is also a noun. ☐ He shut the book with a snap and stood up. **3** V-T If you **snap** your fingers, you make a sharp sound by moving your middle finger quickly across your thumb, for example, in order to accompany music or to order someone to do something. ☐ She had millions of listeners snapping their fingers to her first single. ☐ He snapped his fingers, and Wilson produced a sheet of paper. • N-SING [N of n] **Snap** is also a noun. ☐ I could obtain with the snap of my fingers anything I chose. **4** V-T/V-I If someone **snaps** at you, they speak to you in a sharp, unfriendly way. ☐ "Of course I don't know her," Roger snapped. **5** V-I If someone **snaps**, or if something **snaps** inside them, they suddenly stop being calm and become very angry because the situation has become too tense or too difficult for them. ☐ He finally snapped when she prevented their children from visiting him one weekend. **6** V-I If an animal such as a dog **snaps** at you, it opens and shuts its jaws quickly near you, as if it were going to bite you. ☐ His teeth clicked as he snapped at my ankle. **7** ADJ [ADJ n] A **snap** decision or action is one that is taken suddenly, often without careful thought. ☐ I think this is too important for a snap decision. **8** N-COUNT A **snap** is the same as a **snap fastener**. [AM] **9** N-COUNT A **snap** is a photograph. [INFORMAL] ☐ ...a snap my mother took last year.

▶ **snap up** PHRASAL VERB If you **snap** something **up**, you buy it quickly because it is cheap or is just what you want. ❑ ...*a millionaire ready to snap them up at the premium price of $200 a gallon.*

snap|dragon /snæpdrægən/ (**snapdragons**) N-COUNT A **snapdragon** is a common garden plant with small colorful flowers that can open and shut like a mouth.

snap fas|ten|er (**snap fasteners**) N-COUNT A **snap fastener** is a small metal object used to fasten clothes, made up of two parts which can be pressed together. [AM]

in BRIT, use **press stud, popper**

snap|per /snæpər/ (**snappers** or **snapper**) N-COUNT A **snapper** is a fish that has sharp teeth and lives in warm seas. • N-UNCOUNT **Snapper** is this fish eaten as food.

snap|pish /snæpɪʃ/ ADJ [usu v-link ADJ] If someone is **snappish**, they speak to people in a sharp, unfriendly manner. ❑ *"That is beautiful, Tony," Momma said, no longer sounding at all snappish.* • **snap|pish|ly** ADV ❑ *"I'm not pregnant," she said snappishly.*

snap|py /snæpi/ (**snappier, snappiest**) ❶ ADJ [usu ADJ n] If someone has a **snappy** style of speaking, they speak in a quick, clever, brief, and often funny way. ❑ *Each film gets a snappy two-line summary.* ❷ ADJ [ADJ n] If someone is a **snappy** dresser or if they wear **snappy** clothes, they wear attractive, stylish clothes. ❑ *She has already made a name for herself as a snappy dresser.*

snap|shot /snæpʃɒt/ (**snapshots**) ❶ N-COUNT A **snapshot** is a photograph that is taken quickly and casually. ❑ *Let me take a snapshot of you guys, so friends back home can see you.* ❷ N-COUNT [usu sing, usu N of n] If something provides you with a **snapshot** of a place or situation, it gives you a brief idea of what that place or situation is like. ❑ *The interviews present a remarkable snapshot of Britain in these dark days of recession.*

snare /snɛər/ (**snares, snaring, snared**) ❶ N-COUNT A **snare** is a trap for catching birds or small animals. It consists of a loop of wire or rope which pulls tight around the animal. ❑ *I felt like an animal caught in a snare.* ❷ N-COUNT If you describe a situation as a **snare**, you mean that it is a trap from which it is difficult to escape. [FORMAL] ❑ *Given data which are free from bias there are further snares to avoid in statistical work.* ❸ V-T If someone **snares** an animal, they catch it using a snare. ❑ *He'd snared a rabbit earlier in the day.*

snare drum (**snare drums**) N-COUNT A **snare drum** is a small drum used in orchestras and bands. Snare drums are usually played with wooden sticks, and make a continuous sound.

snark /snɑrk/ (**snarks, snarking, snarked**) ❶ VERB If someone **snarks**, they criticize another person in an unkind way. [INFORMAL] ❑ *Politicians snarked that he didn't know what he was talking about.* ❷ *It's a wonderful idea that shouldn't be snarked or sneered at in any way.* ❷ N-UNCOUNT **Snark** is unkind criticism of someone or something. [AM, INFORMAL] ❑ *Of the many funny writers in this newspaper, none regularly uses snark.*

snarl /snɑrl/ (**snarls, snarling, snarled**) V-I When an animal **snarls**, it makes a fierce, rough sound in its throat while showing its teeth. ❑ *He raced ahead up into the bush, barking and snarling.* • N-COUNT **Snarl** is also a noun. ❑ *With a snarl, the second dog made a dive for his heel.*

snatch /snætʃ/ (**snatches, snatching, snatched**) ❶ V-T/V-I If you **snatch** something or **snatch** at something, you take it or pull it away quickly. ❑ *Mick snatched the cards from Archie's hand.* ❑ *He snatched up the telephone.* ❷ V-T [usu passive] If something **is snatched** from you, it is stolen, usually using force. If a person **is snatched**, they are taken away by force. ❑ *If your bag is snatched, let it go.* ❸ V-T If you **snatch** an opportunity, you take it quickly. If you **snatch** something to eat or a rest, you have it quickly in between doing other things. ❑ *I snatched a glance at the mirror.* ❹ V-T If you **snatch** victory in a competition, you defeat your opponent by a small amount or just before the end of the contest. ❑ *The American came from behind to snatch victory by a mere eight seconds.* ❺ N-COUNT A **snatch** of a conversation or a song is a very small piece of it. ❑ *I heard snatches of the conversation.*

snaz|zy /snæzi/ (**snazzier, snazziest**) ADJ [usu ADJ n] Something that is **snazzy** is stylish and attractive, often in a rather bright or noticeable way. [INFORMAL] ❑ ...*a snazzy new Porsche.*

sneak /snik/ (**sneaks, sneaking, sneaked** or **snuck**)

The form **snuck** is informal.

❶ V-I If you **sneak** somewhere, you go there very quietly on foot, trying to avoid being seen or heard. ❑ *Sometimes he would sneak out of his house late at night to be with me.* ❷ V-T If you **sneak** something somewhere, you take it there secretly. ❑ *He smuggled papers out each day, photocopied them, and snuck them back.* ❸ V-T If you **sneak** a look at someone or something, you secretly have a quick look at them. ❑ *You sneak a look at your watch to see how long you've got to wait.*

sneak|er /snikər/ (**sneakers**) ❶ N-COUNT [usu pl] **Sneakers** are casual shoes with rubber soles that people wear often for running or other sports. [mainly AM] ❑ ...*a new pair of sneakers.*

in BRIT, usually use **trainer**

❷ → See also color supplement

sneak|ing /snikɪŋ/ ADJ [ADJ n] A **sneaking** feeling is a slight or vague feeling, especially one that you are unwilling to accept. ❑ *I have a sneaking suspicion that they are going to succeed.*

sneak pre|view (**sneak previews**) N-COUNT [oft N of n] A **sneak preview** of something is an unofficial opportunity to have a look at it before it is officially published or shown to the public.

sneaky /sniki/ (**sneakier, sneakiest**) ADJ If you describe someone as **sneaky**, you disapprove of them because they do things secretly rather than openly. [INFORMAL, DISAPPROVAL] ❑ *It is a sneaky and underhand way of doing business.*

sneer /snɪər/ (**sneers, sneering, sneered**) V-T/V-I If you **sneer** at someone or something, you express your contempt for them by the expression on your face or by what you say. ❑ *Most critics have sneered at the movie, calling it dull and cheaply made.* ❑ *"I don't need any help from you," he sneered.* • N-COUNT **Sneer** is also a noun. ❑ *Canete's mouth twisted in a contemptuous sneer.*

sneer|ing|ly /snɪərɪŋli/ ADV To refer **sneeringly** to someone or something means to refer to them in a way that shows your contempt for them. [WRITTEN] ❑ *They were sneeringly dismissive.*

sneeze /sniz/ (**sneezes, sneezing, sneezed**) ❶ V-I When you **sneeze**, you suddenly take in your breath and then blow it down your nose noisily without being able to stop yourself, for example, because you have a cold. ❑ *What exactly happens when we sneeze?* • N-COUNT **Sneeze** is also a noun. ❑ *Coughs and sneezes spread infections.* ❷ PHRASE If you say that something is **not to be sneezed at**, you mean that it is worth having. [INFORMAL] ❑ *The money's not to be sneezed at.*

snick|er /snɪkər/ (**snickers, snickering, snickered**) V-I If you **snicker**, you laugh quietly in a disrespectful way, for example, at something rude or embarrassing. ❑ *We all snickered at Mrs. Swenson.* • N-COUNT **Snicker** is also a noun. ❑ ...*a chorus of jeers and snickers.*

snide /snaɪd/ ADJ [usu ADJ n] A **snide** comment or remark is one which criticizes someone in an unkind and often indirect way. ❑ *He made a snide comment about her taste in wine.*

sniff /snɪf/ (**sniffs, sniffing, sniffed**) ❶ V-I When you **sniff**, you breathe in air through your nose hard enough to make a sound, for example, when you are trying not to cry, or in order to show disapproval. ❑ *She wiped her face and sniffed loudly.* ❑ *Then he sniffed. There was a smell of burning.* • N-COUNT **Sniff** is also a noun. ❑ *At last the sobs ceased, to be replaced by sniffs.* ❷ V-T/V-I If you **sniff** something or **sniff at** it, you smell it by sniffing. ❑ *Suddenly, he stopped and sniffed the air.* ❸ V-T You can use **sniff** to indicate that someone says something in a way that shows their disapproval or contempt. ❑ *"Tourists!" she sniffed.* ❹ V-T/V-I [usu passive, usu with brd-neg] If you say that something is **not to be sniffed at**, you think it is very good or worth having. If someone **sniffs at** something, they do not think it is good enough, or they express their contempt for it. ❑ *The salary was not to be sniffed at either.* ❺ V-T If someone **sniffs** a substance such as glue, they deliberately breathe in the substance or the gases from it as a drug. ❑ *He felt light-headed, as if he'd sniffed glue.*

▶ **sniff out** ❶ PHRASAL VERB If you **sniff out** something, you discover it after some searching. [INFORMAL] ❑ ...*journalists who are trained to sniff out scandal.* ❷ PHRASAL VERB When a dog used by a group such as the police **sniffs out** hidden explosives or drugs, it finds them using its sense of smell. ❑ ...*a police dog trained to sniff out explosives.*

sniff|er dog (sniffer dogs) N-COUNT A **sniffer dog** is a dog used by the police or army to find explosives or drugs by their smell.

snif|fle /snɪfᵊl/ (sniffles, sniffling, sniffled) **1** V-I If you **sniffle**, you keep sniffing, usually because you are crying or have a cold. ❑ *"Please don't yell at me." She began to sniffle.* **2** N-COUNT [also the N in pl] A **sniffle** is a slight cold. You can also say that someone has **the sniffles**. [INFORMAL]

snif|fy /snɪfi/ (sniffier, sniffiest) ADJ GRADED; ADJ Someone who is **sniffy** about something does not think it is of high quality, perhaps unfairly. ❑ *Some people are a bit sniffy about television.* ❑ *...sniffy art critics.* • **sniffi|ly** /snɪfɪli/ ADV GRADED [usu ADV with v] ❑ *The broadcast media sniffily affects to distance itself from the press.*

snif|ter /snɪftər/ (snifters) N-COUNT A **snifter** is a bowl-shaped glass used for drinking brandy. [AM]

snig|ger /snɪgər/ (sniggers, sniggering, sniggered) V-I If someone **sniggers**, they laugh quietly in a disrespectful way, for example at something rude or unkind. ❑ *Suddenly, three schoolkids sitting near me started sniggering.* • N-COUNT **Snigger** is also a noun. ❑ *...trying to suppress a snigger.*

snip /snɪp/ (snips, snipping, snipped) V-T/V-I If you **snip** something, or if you **snip at** or **through** something, you cut it quickly using sharp scissors. ❑ *He has now begun to snip away at the piece of paper.*

snipe /snaɪp/ (snipes, sniping, sniped) **1** V-I If someone **snipes** at you, they criticize you. ❑ *The media were still sniping at the president's adviser yesterday.* **2** V-I To **snipe** at someone means to shoot at them from a hidden position. ❑ *Gunmen have repeatedly sniped at U.S. Army positions.*

snip|er /snaɪpər/ (snipers) N-COUNT A **sniper** is someone who shoots at people from a hidden position. ❑ *...a sniper attack.*

snip|pet /snɪpɪt/ (snippets) N-COUNT A **snippet** of something is a small piece of it. ❑ *...snippets of popular classical music.*

snip|py /snɪpi/ (snippier, snippiest) ADJ A **snippy** person is often bad-tempered and speaks rudely to people. [AM, INFORMAL, DISAPPROVAL] ❑ *It is your job to correct them gracefully and not to be snippy about it.* ❑ *...Muriel's snippy, prudish father.*

snitch /snɪtʃ/ (snitches, snitching, snitched) **1** V-I To **snitch** on a person means to tell someone in authority that the person has done something bad or wrong. [INFORMAL] ❑ *She felt like a fifth-grader who had snitched on a classmate.* **2** N-COUNT A **snitch** is a person who snitches on other people. [INFORMAL]

sniv|el /snɪvᵊl/ (snivels, sniveling or snivelling, sniveled or snivelled) V-I If someone **is sniveling**, they are crying or sniffing in a way that irritates you. ❑ *Billy started to snivel. His mother smacked his hand.*

snob /snɒb/ (snobs) N-COUNT If you call someone a **snob**, you disapprove of them because they behave as if they are superior to other people because of their intelligence, taste, or social status. [DISAPPROVAL] ❑ *She was an intellectual snob.*

snob|bery /snɒbəri/ N-UNCOUNT **Snobbery** is the attitude of a snob. ❑ *There has often been an element of snobbery in golf.*

snob|bish /snɒbɪʃ/ ADJ If you describe someone as **snobbish**, you disapprove of them because they are too proud of their social status, intelligence, or taste. [DISAPPROVAL] ❑ *They had a snobbish dislike for their intellectual and social inferiors.*

snob|by /snɒbi/ (snobbier, snobbiest) ADJ **Snobby** means the same as **snobbish**.

snook|er /snʊkər/ N-UNCOUNT **Snooker** is a game involving balls on a large table. The players use a long stick to hit a white ball, and score points by knocking colored balls into the pockets at the sides of the table. ❑ *...a game of snooker.*

snoop /snup/ (snoops, snooping, snooped) **1** V-I If someone **snoops** around a place, they secretly look around it in order to find out things. ❑ *Ricardo was the one she'd seen snooping around Kim's hotel room.* • N-COUNT **Snoop** is also a noun. ❑ *The second house that Grossman had a snoop around contained "strong simple furniture."* • **snoop|er** (snoopers) N-COUNT ❑ *Even if the information is intercepted by a snooper, it is impossible for them to decipher it.* **2** V-I If someone **snoops on** a person, they watch them secretly in order to find out things about their life. ❑ *Governments have been known to snoop on and harass innocent citizens in the past.*

snooty /snuti/ (snootier, snootiest) ADJ If you say that someone is **snooty**, you disapprove of them because they behave as if they are superior to other people. [DISAPPROVAL] ❑ *...snooty intellectuals.*

snooze /snuz/ (snoozes, snoozing, snoozed) **1** N-COUNT A **snooze** is a short, light sleep, especially during the day. [INFORMAL] ❑ *I lay down on the bed with my shoes off to have a snooze.* **2** V-I If you **snooze**, you sleep lightly for a short period of time. [INFORMAL] ❑ *Mark snoozed in front of the television.*

snore /snɔr/ (snores, snoring, snored) V-I When someone who is asleep **snores**, they make a loud noise each time they breathe. ❑ *His mouth was open, and he was snoring.* • N-COUNT **Snore** is also a noun. ❑ *Uncle Arthur, after a loud snore, woke suddenly.*

snor|kel /snɔrkᵊl/ (snorkels, snorkeling, snorkeled) **1** N-COUNT A **snorkel** is a tube through which a person swimming just under the surface of the sea can breathe. **2** V-I When someone **snorkels**, they swim under water using a snorkel. ❑ *Swim off the side of the ship and snorkel in some of the clearest waters imaginable.*

snort /snɔrt/ (snorts, snorting, snorted) **1** V-I When people or animals **snort**, they breathe air noisily out through their noses. People sometimes snort in order to express disapproval or amusement. ❑ *Harrell snorted with laughter.* • N-COUNT **Snort** is also a noun. ❑ *...snorts of laughter.* **2** V-T To **snort** a drug such as cocaine means to breathe it in quickly through your nose. ❑ *He died of cardiac arrest after snorting cocaine at a party.*

snot /snɒt/ N-UNCOUNT **Snot** is the thick liquid that is produced inside your nose. [INFORMAL, VULGAR]

snot|ty /snɒti/ (snottier, snottiest) **1** ADJ [ADJ n] Something that is **snotty** produces or is covered in snot. [INFORMAL, VULGAR] ❑ *He suffered from a snotty nose, runny eyes and a slight cough.* **2** ADJ If you describe someone as **snotty**, you disapprove of them because they have a very proud and superior attitude to other people. [INFORMAL, DISAPPROVAL] ❑ *...snotty college kids.*

snout /snaʊt/ (snouts) N-COUNT The **snout** of an animal such as a pig is its long nose. ❑ *Two alligators rest their snouts on the water's surface.*

snow ♦◊◊ /snoʊ/ (snows, snowing, snowed) **1** N-UNCOUNT **Snow** consists of a lot of soft white pieces of frozen water that fall from the sky in cold weather. ❑ *Six inches of snow blocked roads.* **2** V-I When **it snows**, snow falls from the sky. ❑ *It had been snowing all night.* **3** → See feature box at **hot**

VOCABULARY IN CONTEXT

Snow

If you aren't a skier, you probably don't realize just how many different types of snow there are, or the impact of different **textures**. Freshly fallen snow is dry and **powdery**, making the ski slopes **smooth** and fairly easy to negotiate, at least for more experienced skiers. It is easier to control your speed because it is not as **slippery** as it is when ice starts to form on it after a few days without snow.

However, if the snow begins to melt, the surface can become **lumpy** and **uneven**. **Mushy**, **soggy** snow can stick to the bottom of skis, slowing you down. **Sticky** snow is great for making snowmen, but terrible for skiing.

snow|ball /snoʊbɔl/ (snowballs, snowballing, snowballed) **1** N-COUNT A **snowball** is a ball of snow. Children often throw snowballs at each other. **2** V-I If something such as a project or campaign **snowballs**, it rapidly increases and grows. ❑ *From those early days the business has snowballed.*

snow|board /snoʊbɔrd/ (snowboards) N-COUNT A **snowboard** is a narrow board that you stand on in order to slide quickly down snowy slopes as a sport or for fun.

snow|board|ing /snoʊbɔrdɪŋ/ N-UNCOUNT **Snowboarding** is the sport or activity of traveling down snowy slopes using a snowboard. ❑ *New snowboarding facilities should attract more people.*

snow|bound /snoʊbaʊnd/ ADJ If people or vehicles are **snowbound**, they cannot go anywhere because of heavy snow. ❑ *The farm became snowbound.*

snow|capped /snoʊkæpt/ ADJ [ADJ n] A **snowcapped** mountain is covered with snow at the top. [LITERARY] ❑ *...the snowcapped Himalayan peaks.*

snow-covered ADJ [usu ADJ n] **Snow-covered** places and things are covered over with snow. ❑ *...a Swiss chalet set in the snow-covered hills.*

snow|drift /snoʊdrɪft/ (snowdrifts) N-COUNT A **snowdrift** is a deep pile of snow formed by the wind.

snow|drop /snoʊdrɒp/ (snowdrops) N-COUNT A **snowdrop** is a small white flower which appears in the early spring.

snowed in ADJ If you are **snowed in**, you cannot go anywhere because of heavy snow. ❑ *We may all be snowed in here together for days.*

snowed un|der ADJ [v-link ADJ] If you say that you are **snowed under**, you are emphasizing that you have a lot of work or other things to deal with. [INFORMAL, EMPHASIS] ❑ *Ed was snowed under with fan mail when he was doing his television show.*

snow|fall /snoʊfɔl/ (snowfalls) **1** N-UNCOUNT The **snowfall** in an area or country is the amount of snow that falls there during a particular period. ❑ *The total rain and snowfall amounted to 5 inches.* **2** N-COUNT A **snowfall** is a fall of snow.

snow|field /snoʊfild/ (snowfields) N-COUNT A **snowfield** is a large area which is always covered in snow.

snow|flake /snoʊfleɪk/ (snowflakes) N-COUNT A **snowflake** is one of the soft, white pieces of frozen water that fall as snow.

snow|man /snoʊmæn/ (snowmen) N-COUNT A **snowman** is a large shape which is made out of snow, especially by children, and is supposed to look like a person.

snow|mobile /snoʊməbil/ (snowmobiles) N-COUNT A **snowmobile** is a small vehicle built to move across snow and ice.

snow pea (snow peas) N-COUNT [usu pl] **Snow peas** are a type of pea whose pods are eaten as well as the peas inside them. [AM, AUSTRALIAN]

in BRIT, use **mangetout**

snow|plow /snoʊplaʊ/ (snowplows)

in BRIT, use **snowplough**

N-COUNT A **snowplow** is a vehicle which is used to push snow off roads or railroad tracks.

snow|shoe /snoʊʃu/ (snowshoes) N-COUNT [usu pl] **Snowshoes** are large oval frames which you fasten to your feet so that you can walk on deep snow.

snow|storm /snoʊstɔrm/ (snowstorms) N-COUNT A **snowstorm** is a very heavy fall of snow, usually when there is also a strong wind blowing at the same time.

snow-white ADJ Something that is **snow-white** is of a bright white color. ❑ *His hair was snow-white like an old man's.*

snowy /snoʊi/ (snowier, snowiest) ADJ A **snowy** place is covered in snow. A **snowy** day is a day when a lot of snow has fallen. ❑ *...the snowy peaks of the Bighorn Mountains.*

Snr [BRIT] → see **Sr.**

snub /snʌb/ (snubs, snubbing, snubbed) **1** V-T If you **snub** someone, you deliberately insult them by ignoring them or by behaving or speaking rudely toward them. ❑ *He snubbed her in public and made her feel an idiot.* **2** N-COUNT If you snub someone, your behavior or your remarks can be referred to as a **snub**. ❑ *Ryan took it as a snub.*

snuck /snʌk/ **Snuck** is a past tense and past participle of **sneak**. [INFORMAL]

snuff /snʌf/ (snuffs, snuffing, snuffed) N-UNCOUNT **Snuff** is powdered tobacco which people take by breathing it in quickly through their nose. ❑ *...the old man's habit of taking snuff.*
▶ **snuff out** PHRASAL VERB To **snuff out** something such as a disagreement means to stop it, usually in a forceful or sudden way. ❑ *Every time a new flicker of resistance appeared, the government snuffed it out.*

snuf|fle /snʌfəl/ (snuffles, snuffling, snuffled) V-I If a person or an animal **snuffles**, they breathe in noisily through their nose, for example because they have a cold. ❑ *She snuffled and wiped her nose on the back of her hand.*

snug /snʌg/ (snugger, snuggest) **1** ADJ If you feel **snug** or are in a **snug** place, you are very warm and comfortable, especially because you are protected from cold weather. ❑ *They lay snug and warm amid the blankets and watched their sister hard at work.* **2** ADJ Something such as a piece of clothing that is **snug** fits very closely or tightly. ❑ *...a snug black T-shirt and skin-tight black jeans.* ● **snug|ly** ADV GRADED [ADV with v] ❑ *The jeans fit snugly.*

snug|gle /snʌgəl/ (snuggles, snuggling, snuggled) V-I If you **snuggle** somewhere, you settle yourself into a warm, comfortable position, especially by moving closer to another person. ❑ *Jane snuggled up against his shoulder.*

so ♦♦♦ /soʊ/

Usually pronounced /soʊ/ for meanings 1, 6, 7, 8, 15 and 16.

1 ADV [ADV after v] You use **so** to refer back to something that has just been mentioned. ❑ *"Do you think that made much of a difference to the family?"—"I think so."* ❑ *If you can't play straight, then say so.* **2** ADV [ADV cl] You use **so** when you are saying that something which has just been said about one person or thing is also true of another one. ❑ *I enjoy Ann's company and so does Martin.* ❑ *They had a wonderful time and so did I.* **3** CONJ You use the structures **as...so** and **just as...so** when you want to indicate that two events or situations are similar in some way. ❑ *As computer systems become even more sophisticated, so too do the methods of those who exploit the technology.* ❑ *Just as John has changed, so has his wife.* **4** ADV [v-link ADV] If you say that a state of affairs **is so**, you mean that it is the way it has been described. ❑ *In those days English dances as well as songs were taught at school, but that seems no longer to be so.* ❑ *It is strange to think that he held strong views on many things, but it must have been so.* **5** ADV [ADV after v] You can use **so** with actions and gestures to show a person how to do something, or to indicate the size, height, or length of something. ❑ *Clasp the chain like so.* **6** CONJ You use **so** and **so that** to introduce the result of the situation you have just mentioned. ❑ *I am not an emotional type and so cannot bring myself to tell him I love him.* ❑ *People are living longer than ever before, so even people who are 65 or 70 have a surprising amount of time left.* **7** CONJ You use **so**, **so that**, and **so as** to introduce the reason for doing the thing that you have just mentioned. ❑ *Come to my suite so I can tell you all about this wonderful play I saw in Boston.* ❑ *He took her arm and hurried her upstairs so that they wouldn't be overheard.* **8** ADV [ADV cl] You can use **so** in conversations to introduce a new topic, or to introduce a question or comment about something that has been said. ❑ *So how was your day?* ❑ *So you're a runner, huh?* ❑ *So as for your question, Miles, the answer still has to be no.* **9** ADV [ADV cl] You can use **so** in conversations to show that you are accepting what someone has just said. ❑ *"It makes me feel, well, important."—"And so you are."* ❑ *"You can't possibly use this word."—"So I won't."* **10** CONVENTION You say '**So?**' and '**So what?**' to indicate that you think that something that someone has said is unimportant. [INFORMAL] ❑ *"My name's Bruno."—"So?"* **11** ADV [ADV adj/adv] You can use **so** in front of adjectives and adverbs to emphasize the quality that they are describing. [EMPHASIS] ❑ *He was surprised they had married – they had seemed so different.* **12** ADV You can use **so...that** and **so...as** to emphasize the degree of something by mentioning the result or consequence of it. [EMPHASIS] ❑ *The tears were streaming so fast she could not see.* ❑ *He's not so stupid as to listen to rumors.* **13** → see also **insofar as** **14** PHRASE You use **and so on** or **and so forth** at the end of a list to indicate that there are other items that you could also

soak mention. ❏ ...the government's policies on such important issues as health, education, tax, and so on. **15** PHRASE You use **so much** and **so many** when you are saying that there is a definite limit to something but you are not saying what this limit is. ❏ There is only so much time in the day for answering letters. ❏ There is only so much fuel in the tank and if you burn it up too quickly you are in trouble. **16** PHRASE You use the structures **not...so much** and **not so much...as** to say that something is one kind of thing rather than another kind. ❏ I did not really object to Will's behavior so much as his personality. **17** PHRASE You use **or so** when you are giving an approximate amount. [VAGUENESS] ❏ Though rates are heading down, they still offer real returns of 8% or so. **18 so much the better** → see **better** ① **19 so far so good** → see **far** ② **20 so long** → see **long** ③ **21 so much so** → see **much** **22 every so often** → see **often** **23 so there** → see **there**

soak /soʊk/ (**soaks, soaking, soaked**) **1** V-T/V-I If you **soak** something or leave it to **soak**, you put it into a liquid and leave it there. ❏ Soak the beans for 2 hours. **2** V-T If a liquid **soaks** something or if you **soak** something with a liquid, the liquid makes the thing very wet. ❏ The water had soaked his jacket and shirt. **3** V-I If a liquid **soaks** through something, it passes through it. ❏ There was so much blood it had soaked through my boxer shorts. **4** V-I If someone **soaks**, they spend a long time in a hot bath, because they enjoy it. ❏ What I need is to soak in a hot tub. • N-COUNT **Soak** is also a noun. ❏ I was having a long soak in the bath. **5** → see also **soaked, soaking**

▶ **soak up** **1** PHRASAL VERB If a soft or dry material **soaks up** a liquid, the liquid goes into the substance. ❏ The cells will promptly start to soak up moisture. **2** PHRASAL VERB If you **soak up** the atmosphere in a place that you are visiting, you observe or get involved in the way of life there, because you enjoy it or are interested in it. [INFORMAL] ❏ Keaton comes here once or twice a year to soak up the atmosphere. **3** PHRASAL VERB If something **soaks up** something such as money or other resources, it uses a great deal of money or other resources. ❏ Defence soaks up 40 percent of the budget.

soaked /soʊkt/ ADJ If someone or something gets **soaked** or **soaked through**, water or some other liquid makes them extremely wet. ❏ I have to check my tent - it got soaked last night in the storm. ❏ We got soaked to the skin.

-soaked /-soʊkt/ COMB IN ADJ [usu ADJ n] **-soaked** combines with nouns such as 'rain' and 'blood' to form adjectives which describe someone or something that is extremely wet or extremely damp because of the thing mentioned. ❏ He trudged through the rain-soaked woods. ❏ ...blood-soaked clothes.

soaking /soʊkɪŋ/ ADJ If something is **soaking** or **soaking wet**, it is very wet. ❏ My face and raincoat were soaking wet.

so-and-so (**so-and-sos**) PRON-SING You use **so-and-so** instead of a word, expression, or name when you are talking generally rather than giving a specific example of a particular thing. [INFORMAL] ❏ It would be a case of "just do so-and-so and here's your cash."

soap /soʊp/ (**soaps**) **1** N-MASS **Soap** is a substance that you use with water for washing yourself or sometimes for washing clothes. ❏ ...a bar of lavender soap. ❏ ...a large box of soap powder. **2** N-COUNT A **soap** is the same as a **soap opera**. [INFORMAL]

soapbox /soʊpbɒks/ (**soapboxes**) **1** N-COUNT A **soapbox** is a small temporary platform on which a person stands when he or she is making a speech outdoors. ❏ One of them climbed aboard a soapbox and began informing the locals why gay people should be allowed in the military. **2** N-COUNT If you say that someone is on their **soapbox**, you mean that they are speaking or writing about something they have strong feelings about. ❏ We were interested in pushing forward certain issues and getting up on our soapbox about them.

soap opera (**soap operas**) N-COUNT A **soap opera** is a popular television drama series about the daily lives and problems of a group of people who live in a particular place.

soapy /soʊpi/ (**soapier, soapiest**) ADJ [usu ADJ n] Something that is **soapy** is full of soap or covered with soap. ❏ Wash your hands thoroughly with hot soapy water before handling any food.

soar /sɔr/ (**soars, soaring, soared**) **1** V-I If the amount, value, level, or volume of something **soars**, it quickly increases by a great deal. [JOURNALISM] ❏ Insurance claims are expected to soar. ❏ Shares soared on the New York stock exchange. **2** V-I If something such as a bird **soars** into the air, it goes quickly up into the air. [LITERARY] ❏ If you're lucky, a splendid golden eagle may soar into view.

sob /sɒb/ (**sobs, sobbing, sobbed**) **1** V-I When someone **sobs**, they cry in a noisy way, breathing in short breaths. ❏ She began to sob again, burying her face in the pillow. • **sobbing** N-UNCOUNT ❏ The room was silent except for her sobbing. **2** N-COUNT A **sob** is one of the noises that you make when you are crying. ❏ Her sobs grew louder.

sober /soʊbər/ (**sobers, sobering, sobered**) **1** ADJ When you are **sober**, you are not drunk. ❏ He'd been drunk when I arrived. Now he was sober. **2** ADJ A **sober** person is serious and thoughtful. ❏ We are now far more sober and realistic. ❏ It was a room filled with sad, sober faces. • **soberly** ADV ❏ "There's a new development," he said soberly. **3** ADJ **Sober** colors and clothes are plain and rather dull. ❏ He dresses in sober gray suits. • **soberly** ADV [ADV with v] ❏ She saw Ellis, soberly dressed in a well-cut dark suit. **4** → see also **sobering**

▶ **sober up** PHRASAL VERB If someone **sobers up**, or if something **sobers** them **up**, they become sober after being drunk. ❏ He was left to sober up in a police cell.

sobering /soʊbərɪŋ/ ADJ You say that something is a **sobering** thought or has a **sobering** effect when a situation seems serious and makes you become serious and thoughtful. ❏ It is a sobering thought that in the 17th century she could have been burned as a witch.

sobriety /səbraɪɪti/ **1** N-UNCOUNT **Sobriety** is the state of being sober rather than drunk. [FORMAL] **2** N-UNCOUNT **Sobriety** is serious and thoughtful behavior. [FORMAL] ❏ ...the values society depends upon, such as honesty, sobriety and trust.

sobriquet /soʊbrɪkeɪ/ (**sobriquets**) also **soubriquet** N-COUNT [usu sing] A **sobriquet** is a humorous name that people give someone or something. [WRITTEN] ❏ From his staff he earned the sobriquet "Mumbles."

sob story (**sob stories**) N-COUNT You describe what someone tells you about their own or someone else's difficulties as a **sob story** when you think that they have told you about it in order to get your sympathy. ❏ Any sob story moved Jarvis to generosity.

Soc. Soc. is the written abbreviation for **Society**.

so-called ♦♢♢ also **so called** **1** ADJ [ADJ n] You use **so-called** to indicate that you think a word or expression used to describe someone or something is in fact wrong. ❏ These are the facts that explode their so-called economic miracle. **2** ADJ [ADJ n] You use **so-called** to indicate that something is generally referred to by the name that you are about to use. ❏ ...a summit of the world's seven leading market economies, the so-called G-7.

soccer ♦♢♢ /spkər/ **1** N-UNCOUNT **Soccer** is a game played by two teams of eleven players using a round ball. Players kick the ball to each other and try to score goals by kicking the ball into a large net. Outside the United States, this game is also referred to as **football**. ❏ ...a soccer match. **2** → See feature box at **football**

soccer player (**soccer players**) N-COUNT A **soccer player** is a person who plays soccer, especially as a profession. [AM]

in BRIT, use **footballer**

sociable /soʊʃəbᵊl/ ADJ **Sociable** people are friendly and enjoy talking to other people. ❏ She was, and remained, extremely sociable, enjoying dancing, golf, tennis, skating, and bicycling.

social ♦♦♦ /soʊʃᵊl/ **1** ADJ [ADJ n] **Social** means relating to society or to the way society is organized. ❏ ...the worst effects of unemployment, low pay, and other social problems. ❏ ...long-term social change. ❏ ...changing social attitudes. • **socially** ADV [ADV adj/-ed] ❏ Let's face it - drinking is still seen as a socially acceptable habit. **2** ADJ [ADJ n] **Social** means relating to the status or rank that someone has in society. ❏ Higher education is unequally distributed across social classes. • **socially** ADV ❏ For socially ambitious couples this is a problem. **3** ADJ [ADJ n] **Social** means relating to leisure activities that involve meeting other people. ❏ We ought to organize more social events.

• **so|cial|ly** ADV ❑ *We have known each other socially for a long time.* **4** → See feature box at **polite, socialize**

so|cial climb|er (social climbers) N-COUNT You describe someone as a **social climber** when they try to get accepted into a higher social class by becoming friendly with people who belong to that class. [DISAPPROVAL] ❑ *That Rob was a snob and a social climber could not be denied.*

so|cial climb|ing N-UNCOUNT You describe someone's behavior as **social climbing** when they try to get accepted into a higher social class by becoming friendly with people who belong to that class. [DISAPPROVAL] ❑ *All that vulgar social climbing!* • ADJ [ADJ n] **Social-climbing** is also an adjective. ❑ *...Leroy's ambitious social-climbing wife.*

so|cial club (social clubs) N-COUNT A **social club** is a club where members go in order to meet each other and enjoy leisure activities.

so|cial de|moc|ra|cy (social democracies) **1** N-UNCOUNT **Social democracy** is a political system according to which social justice and equality can be achieved within the framework of a market economy. ❑ *...western-style social democracy.* **2** N-COUNT A **social democracy** is a country where there is social democracy.

so|cial demo|crat|ic ADJ [ADJ n] A **social democratic** party is a political party whose principles are based on social democracy. ❑ *...relations with the social democratic governments in Europe.*

so|cial dis|tanc|ing N-UNCOUNT **Social distancing** is a set of measures aimed at stopping the spread of an infectious disease, based on staying away from other people as much as possible. It includes things like working from home, only going out to buy food and other essentials, and avoiding contact with other people. ❑ *The social distancing guidelines have been updated.*

so|cial en|gi|neer|ing N-UNCOUNT **Social engineering** is the use of planned measures, for example, measures that affect people's social or economic position, in order to create a desirable society. [DISAPPROVAL] ❑ *Education is not social engineering, it is about preserving and passing on knowledge.*

so|cial ex|clu|sion N-UNCOUNT **Social exclusion** is the act of making certain groups of people within a society feel isolated and unimportant. [DISAPPROVAL] ❑ *...projects aimed at tackling unemployment and social exclusion.*

so|cial gam|ing N-UNCOUNT **Social gaming** is the activity of playing online games with other members of the same online group. ❑ *The company plans to move into the social gaming market.*

so|cial in|clu|sion N-UNCOUNT **Social inclusion** is the act of making all groups of people within a society feel valued and important. [APPROVAL] ❑ *This will cost money, but if social inclusion is to succeed, it must be spent.*

so|cial|ism /ˈsoʊʃəlɪzəm/ N-UNCOUNT **Socialism** is a set of political principles whose general aim is to create a system in which everyone has an equal opportunity to benefit from a country's wealth. Under socialism, the country's main industries are usually owned by the state.

so|cial|ist ✦◇◇ /ˈsoʊʃəlɪst/ (socialists) **1** ADJ **Socialist** means based on socialism or relating to socialism. ❑ *...members of the ruling Socialist Party.* **2** N-COUNT A **socialist** is a person who believes in socialism or who is a member of a socialist party. ❑ *The electorate voted out the socialists.*

─── SYNONYMS ───

socialist
ADJ **1**
left-wing: *They said they would not be voting for him because he was too left-wing.*
communist: *...a communist party.*
Marxist: *...Marxist ideology.*

so|cial|is|tic /ˌsoʊʃəˈlɪstɪk/ ADJ If you describe a policy or organization as **socialistic**, you mean that it has some of the features of socialism. [DISAPPROVAL] ❑ *The Republicans denounced it as socialistic.*

so|cial|ite /ˈsoʊʃəlaɪt/ (socialites) N-COUNT A **socialite** is a person who attends many fashionable upper-class social events and who is well known because of this. [JOURNALISM]

so|ciali|za|tion /ˌsoʊʃəlɪˈzeɪʃən/
in BRIT, also use **socialisation**

1 N-UNCOUNT **Socialization** is the process by which people, especially children, are made to behave in a way which is acceptable in their culture or society. [TECHNICAL] ❑ *Female socialization still emphasizes getting along with others.* **2** N-UNCOUNT **Socialization** is the process by which something is made to operate on socialist principles. [TECHNICAL]

so|cial|ize /ˈsoʊʃəlaɪz/ (socializes, socializing, socialized)
in BRIT, also use **socialise**

V-I If you **socialize**, you meet other people socially, for example at parties. ❑ *...an open meeting, where members socialized and welcomed any new members.*

┌─── VOCABULARY IN CONTEXT ───┐

Socializing

It seems that the tradition of **dining out** and enjoying the **nightlife** is not as popular as it once was. This is according to a recent survey which indicates that adults in the U.K. and the U.S. are now **socializing** differently in the evenings and on the weekends. It showed that in the last five years, there has been close to a 25 percent increase in the number of people **entertaining at home** instead of going out to meet friends. For some, cost savings are the main motivation. After all, **dropping by** friends' homes or **inviting people over** is far cheaper than paying retail prices. For others, a **get-together** at home offers better opportunities for **mingling** and **interacting** meaningfully with pals than the noise and bright lights of downtown **social gatherings**. Many favor easy **banter** around the dining-room table in the comfort of their own home.

so|cial life (social lives) N-COUNT Your **social life** involves spending time with your friends, for example at parties or in bars.

so|cial|ly dis|tance (socially distances, socially distancing, socially distanced) VERB If you **socially distance**, you practice social distancing measures. ❑ *Consider other people and socially distance while out walking.*

so|cial me|dia N-UNCOUNT [with sing or pl verb] **Social media** refers to websites and computer programs that make communication possible with the use of computers or smart phones. ❑ *Politicians are increasingly using social media to get their message across.*

so|cial me|dia op|ti|mi|za|tion N-UNCOUNT **Social media optimization** is the process of ensuring that material posted on the internet is seen by as many people as possible on social media.

so|cial net|work|ing N-UNCOUNT **Social networking** is the activity of using a particular website to contact other people and share information. ❑ *Social networking is part of everyday life, both for consumer and business-to-business applications.* ❑ *...a social networking site.*

so|cial or|der (social orders) N-VAR The **social order** in a place is the way that society is organized there. ❑ *...the threat to social order posed by right-wing extremists.*

so|cial sci|ence (social sciences) **1** N-UNCOUNT **Social science** is the scientific study of society. ❏ *The research methods of social science generate two kinds of data.* **2** N-COUNT The **social sciences** are the various types of social science, for example sociology and politics. ❏ *...a degree in a social science.*

so|cial sci|en|tist (social scientists) N-COUNT A **social scientist** is a person who studies or teaches social science.

So|cial Se|cu|rity N-UNCOUNT **Social Security** is a system by which workers and employers in the U.S. have to pay money to the government, which gives money to people who are retired, who have a disability, or who cannot work. ❏ *My mother never worked, so she's not eligible for Social Security.* ❏ *Future retirees are expected to get smaller Social Security benefits than promised.*

So|cial Se|cu|rity num|ber (Social Security numbers) N-COUNT A **Social Security number** is a nine digit number that is given to U.S. citizens and to people living in the U.S. You need it to get a job, collect Social Security benefits and receive some government services. ❏ *Questions such as date of birth and Social Security number are straightforward.*

so|cial ser|vices N-PLURAL **Social services** in a district are the services provided by the local authority or government to help people who have serious family problems or financial problems. ❏ *Schools and social services are also struggling to absorb the influx.*

so|cial stud|ies N-UNCOUNT **Social studies** is a subject that is taught in schools, and includes history, geography, sociology, and politics.

so|cial work N-UNCOUNT **Social work** is work which involves giving help and advice to people with serious family problems or financial problems.

so|cial work|er (social workers) N-COUNT A **social worker** is a person whose job is to do social work.

so|ci|etal /səsaɪɪtᵊl/ ADJ [ADJ n] **Societal** means relating to society or to the way society is organized. [FORMAL] ❏ *...the societal changes that have taken place over the last two decades.* ❏ *...societal norms.*

so|ci|ety ♦♦♦ /səsaɪɪti/ (societies) **1** N-UNCOUNT **Society** is people in general, thought of as a large organized group. ❏ *This reflects attitudes and values prevailing in society.* **2** N-VAR A **society** is the people who live in a country or region, their organizations, and their way of life. ❏ *We live in a capitalist society.* **3** N-COUNT A **society** is an organization for people who have the same interest or aim. ❏ *...the Atlanta Horticultural Society.* **4** N-UNCOUNT **Society** is the rich, fashionable people in a particular place who meet on social occasions. ❏ *The couple quickly became a fixture in society.*

---PREFIX---

socio- is used to form adjectives and nouns which describe or refer to things relating to or involving social factors. For example, someone's *socioeconomic* background relates to the social aspects of the family or culture they come from.

---

so|cio|eco|nom|ic /sousiouɛkənɒmɪk, -ikə-/ ADJ [ADJ n] **Socioeconomic** circumstances or developments involve a combination of social and economic factors. ❏ *The age, education, and socioeconomic status of these young mothers led to less satisfactory child care.*

so|ci|ol|ogy /sousiɒlədʒi/ N-UNCOUNT **Sociology** is the study of society or of the way society is organized. • **so|cio|logi|cal** /sousiəlɒdʒɪkᵊl/ ADJ ❏ *Psychological and sociological studies were emphasizing the importance of the family.* • **so|ci|olo|gist** (sociologists) N-COUNT ❏ *By the 1950s some sociologists were confident that they had identified the key characteristics of capitalist society.*

so|cio|path /sousiəpæθ/ (sociopaths) N-COUNT A **sociopath** is the same as a **psychopath**.

so|cio|po|liti|cal /sousioupəlɪtɪkᵊl/ ADJ [ADJ n] **Sociopolitical** systems and problems involve a combination of social and political factors. ❏ *...contemporary sociopolitical issues such as ecology, human rights, and nuclear arms.*

sock /sɒk/ (socks, socking, socked) **1** N-COUNT **Socks** are pieces of clothing which cover your foot and ankle and are worn inside shoes. ❏ *...a pair of knee-high socks.* **2** V-T If you **sock** someone or something, you hit them hard. [INFORMAL] ❏ *Once, after a boy made a comment, she socked him.* **3** V-T If someone **is socked** with something bad, it happens to them. ❏ *Phil got socked with a bill for nearly $1,000.*

sock|et /sɒkɪt/ (sockets) **1** N-COUNT A **socket** is a device on a piece of electrical equipment into which you can put a bulb or plug. ❏ *On the stairway to the basement, he took the light bulb out of the socket.* **2** N-COUNT A **socket** is a device or point in a wall where you can connect electrical equipment to the power supply. [mainly BRIT]

in AM, usually use **outlet**

3 N-COUNT You can refer to any hollow part or opening in a structure which another part fits into as a **socket**. ❏ *Rotate the shoulders in their sockets five times.*

soda /soudə/ (sodas) **1** N-MASS **Soda** is a sweet carbonated drink. [AM] ❏ *...a glass of diet soda.* • N-COUNT A **soda** is a bottle of soda. ❏ *They had liquor for the adults and sodas for the children.* **2** N-UNCOUNT **Soda** is the same as **soda water**. **3** → see also **baking soda**, **club soda**

soda crack|er (soda crackers) N-COUNT A **soda cracker** is a thin, square, salty cracker. [AM]

soda foun|tain (soda fountains) N-COUNT A **soda fountain** is a counter in a drugstore or café, where snacks and nonalcoholic drinks are prepared and sold. [AM]

soda pop (soda pops) N-UNCOUNT **Soda pop** is a sweet carbonated drink. [AM] ❏ *Beer and soda pop are served before the bus departs.* • N-COUNT A **soda pop** is a bottle or a glass of soda pop. ❏ *He bought me a soda pop.*

soda si|phon (soda siphons) also **soda syphon** N-COUNT A **soda siphon** is a special bottle for putting soda water in a drink.

soda wa|ter also **soda-water** (soda waters) N-MASS **Soda water** is carbonated water and is often used for mixing with alcoholic drinks and fruit juice.

sod|den /sɒdᵊn/ ADJ Something that is **sodden** is extremely wet. ❏ *We stripped off our sodden clothes.*

-sodden /-sɒdᵊn/ **1** COMB IN ADJ [usu ADJ n] **-sodden** combines with words such as 'rain' to form adjectives which describe someone or something that has become extremely wet as a result of the thing that is mentioned. ❏ *We hung up our rain-sodden coats in the porch.* **2** COMB IN ADJ [usu ADJ n] **-sodden** combines with the names of alcoholic drinks to form adjectives which describe someone who has drunk too much alcohol and is in a bad state as a result. ❏ *Both of them are gin-sodden; both weep.*

so|dium /soudiəm/ N-UNCOUNT **Sodium** is a silvery white chemical element which combines with other chemicals. Salt is a sodium compound. ❏ *The fish or seafood is heavily salted with pure sodium chloride.*

so|dium bi|car|bo|nate N-UNCOUNT **Sodium bicarbonate** is a white powder which is used in baking to make cakes rise, and also as a medicine for your stomach.

sodo|my /sɒdəmi/ N-UNCOUNT **Sodomy** is anal sexual intercourse.

sofa /soufə/ (sofas) N-COUNT A **sofa** is a long, comfortable seat with a back and usually with arms, which two or three people can sit on.

sofa bed (sofa beds) also **sofa-bed** **1** N-COUNT A **sofa bed** is a type of sofa whose seat folds out so that it can also be used as a bed. **2** → See also color supplement

soft ♦♦♢ /sɒft/ (softer, softest) **1** ADJ Something that is **soft** is pleasant to touch, and not rough or hard. ❏ *Regular use of a body lotion will keep the skin soft and supple.* ❏ *When it's dry, brush the hair using a soft, nylon baby brush.* • **soft|ness** N-UNCOUNT ❏ *The sea air robbed her hair of its softness.* **2** ADJ Something that is **soft** changes shape or bends easily when you press it. ❏ *She lay down on the soft, comfortable bed.* ❏ *Add enough milk to form a soft dough.* **3** ADJ Something that has a **soft** appearance has smooth curves rather than sharp or distinct edges. ❏ *This is a smart, yet soft and feminine look.* • **soft|ly** ADV [ADV with v] ❏ *She wore a softly tailored suit.* **4** ADJ Something that is **soft** is very gentle and has no force. For example, a **soft** sound or voice is quiet and not harsh. A **soft** light or color is pleasant to look at because it is not bright. ❏ *There was a soft tapping on my door.* ● **soft|ly** ADV [ADV with v] ❏ *She crossed the softly lit room.* **5** ADJ If you are **soft** on someone, you do not treat them as strictly or severely as you should. [DISAPPROVAL] ❏ *The president says the measure is soft and weak on criminals.* **6** ADJ If you say that someone has a **soft** heart, you mean that they are sensitive and sympathetic toward other people. [APPROVAL] ❏ *Her rather tough and worldly exterior hides a very soft and sensitive heart.* **7** ADJ You use **soft** to describe a way of life that is easy and involves very little work. ❏ *...a soft life and easy living.* **8** ADJ **Soft** water does not contain much of the mineral calcium and so makes bubbles easily when you use soap. ❏ *...an area where the water is very soft.* **9** ADJ [ADJ n] **Soft** drugs are drugs, such as cannabis, which are illegal but which many people do not consider to be strong or harmful. [mainly BRIT]

in AM, use **recreational**

SYNONYMS
soft
ADJ
1
silky: *Claire smoothed Katy's silky hair.*
velvety: *The grass grew thick and velvety.*
smooth: *...a rich cream that keeps skin smooth.*
2
pliable: *As your baby grows bigger, his bones become less pliable.*
flexible: *...brushes with long, flexible bristles.*
spongy: *The earth was spongy from rain.*

soft|back /sɒftbæk/ (**softbacks**) N-COUNT [also *in* N] A **softback** is the same as a **softcover**. [BRIT]

soft|ball /sɒftbɔːl/ (**softballs**) **1** N-UNCOUNT **Softball** is a game similar to baseball, but played with a larger, softer ball. Compare **baseball**. **2** N-COUNT A **softball** is the ball used in the game of softball.

soft-boiled ADJ A **soft-boiled** egg is one that has been boiled for only a few minutes, so that the yellow part is still liquid.

soft-core also **softcore** ADJ [ADJ n] **Soft-core** pornography shows or describes sex, but in an indirect way. Compare **hard core**.

soft|cover /sɒftkʌvər/ (**softcovers**) N-COUNT [also N n, *in* N] A **softcover** is a book with a thin cardboard, paper, or plastic cover. Compare **hardcover**. [AM] ❏ *...this set of 6 softcover books.*

in BRIT, use **softback**

soft drink (**soft drinks**) N-COUNT A **soft drink** is a cold, nonalcoholic drink such as lemonade or fruit juice, or a carbonated drink.

sof|ten /sɒfᵊn/ (**softens**, **softening**, **softened**) **1** V-T/V-I If you **soften** something or if it **softens**, it becomes less hard, stiff, or firm. ❏ *Soften the butter mixture in a small saucepan.* **2** V-T If one thing **softens** the damaging effect of another thing, it makes the effect less severe. ❏ *There were also pledges to soften the impact of the subsidy cuts on the poorer regions.* **3** V-T/V-I If you **soften** your position, if your position **softens**, or if you **soften**, you become more sympathetic and less hostile or critical. ❏ *The letter shows no sign that the Germans have softened their position.* ❏ *His party's policy has softened a lot in recent years.* **4** V-T/V-I If your voice or expression **softens** or if you **soften** it, it becomes much more gentle and friendly. ❏ *All at once, Mick's serious expression softened into a grin.* **5** V-T If you **soften** something such as light, a color, or a sound, you make it less bright or harsh. ❏ *We wanted to soften the light without destroying the overall effect of space.* **6** V-T Something that **softens** your skin makes it very smooth and pleasant to touch. ❏ *...products designed to moisturize and soften the skin.*

sof|ten|er /sɒfənər/ (**softeners**) **1** N-COUNT A water **softener** is a device or substance which removes certain minerals, for example calcium, from water, so that it makes bubbles easily when you use soap to wash things. **2** N-MASS A fabric **softener** is a chemical substance that you add to water when you wash clothes in order to make the clothes feel softer.

soft fo|cus N-UNCOUNT If something in a photograph or film is in **soft focus**, it has been made slightly unclear to give it a more romantic impression. ❏ *In the background, in soft focus, we see his smiling wife.*

soft fur|nish|ings N-PLURAL **Soft furnishings** are the same as **soft goods**. [BRIT]

soft goods N-PLURAL **Soft goods** are things that are made of cloth, such as cushions, curtains, and furniture covers. [AM]

in BRIT, use **soft furnishings**

soft-hearted ADJ Someone who is **soft-hearted** has a very sympathetic and kind nature.

softie /sɒfti/ (**softies**) also **softy** N-COUNT If you describe someone as a **softie**, you mean that they are very emotional or that they can easily be made to feel sympathy toward other people. [INFORMAL] ❏ *He's just a big softie.*

soft land|ing (**soft landings**) N-COUNT In economics, a **soft landing** is a situation in which the economy stops growing but this does not produce a recession. ❏ *...the belief that the economy is on course for a so-called soft landing.*

soft loan (**soft loans**) N-COUNT A **soft loan** is a loan with a very low interest rate. Soft loans are usually made to developing countries or to businesses in developing countries. [BUSINESS]

soft-pedal (**soft-pedals**, **soft-pedaling** or **soft-pedalling**, **soft-pedaled** or **soft-pedalled**) V-T If you **soft-pedal** something, you deliberately reduce the amount of activity or pressure that you have been using to get something done or seen. ❏ *He refused to soft-pedal an investigation into the scandal.*

soft porn N-UNCOUNT **Soft porn** is pornography that shows or describes sex, but not very violent or unpleasant sex, or not in a very detailed way. [INFORMAL]

soft sell also **soft-sell** N-SING A **soft sell** is a method of selling or advertising that involves persuading people in a gentle way rather than putting a lot of pressure on people to buy things. [BUSINESS] ❏ *I think more customers probably prefer a soft sell.*

soft shoul|der (**soft shoulders**) N-COUNT [usu *the* N *in sing*] On a busy road, the **soft shoulder** is an unpaved area at the side of the road where vehicles are allowed to stop in an emergency. [AM]

in BRIT, use **verge**

soft skills N-PLURAL **Soft skills** are interpersonal skills such as the ability to communicate well with other people and to work on a team.

soft-soap (**soft-soaps**, **soft-soaping**, **soft-soaped**) V-T If you **soft-soap** someone, you flatter them or tell them what you think they want to hear in order to try and persuade them to do something. ❏ *The administration is not soft-soaping the voters here.*

soft-spoken ADJ Someone who is **soft-spoken** has a quiet, gentle voice. ❏ *He was a gentle, soft-spoken, intelligent man.*

soft|ware ♦◇◇ /sɒftweər/ **1** N-UNCOUNT Computer programs are referred to as **software**. Compare **hardware**. [COMPUTING] ❏ *...the people who write the software for big computer projects.* **2** → See feature box at **email**

COLLOCATIONS
software
NOUN
verb + **software**: download, install, load; develop; update
adjective + **software**: antivirus; malicious; proprietary; sophisticated
noun + **software**: computer; gaming; open-source

soft|wood /sɒftwʊd/ (**softwoods**) N-MASS **Softwood** is the wood from trees such as pines, that grow quickly and can be cut easily.

softy /sɒfti/ [mainly BRIT] → see **softie**

sog|gy /sɒgi/ (**soggier**, **soggiest**) **1** ADJ Something that is **soggy** is unpleasantly wet. ❏ *...soggy cheese sandwiches.* **2** → See feature box at **snow**

soi|gnée /swɑnjeɪ/

The spelling **soigné** is also used when referring to a man.

ADJ If you describe a person as **soignée**, you mean that they are very elegant. [FORMAL] ❏ *She looked very soignée in black.*

soil /sɔɪl/ (soils) **1** N-MASS **Soil** is the substance on the surface of the earth in which plants grow. ❑ *We have the most fertile soil in the Midwest.* **2** → See feature box at **garden**

soi|ree /swɑreɪ/ (soirees) also **soirée** N-COUNT A **soiree** is a social gathering held in the evening. [FORMAL]

so|journ /sɒdʒɜːrn/ (sojourns) N-COUNT A **sojourn** is a short stay in a place that is not your home. [LITERARY]

sol|ace /sɒlɪs/ N-UNCOUNT **Solace** is a feeling of comfort that makes you feel less sad. [FORMAL] ❑ *I found solace in writing when my father died three years ago.*

so|lar /soʊlər/ **1** ADJ **Solar** is used to describe things relating to the sun. ❑ *A total solar eclipse is due to take place some time tomorrow.* **2** ADJ **Solar** power is obtained from the sun's light and heat. ❑ *...the financial savings from solar energy.*

so|lar cell (solar cells) N-COUNT A **solar cell** is a device that produces electricity from the sun's rays.

so|lar col|lec|tor (solar collectors) N-COUNT A **solar collector** is a device that collects heat from the sun and converts it into electricity. ❑ *Large homes should have solar collectors in their designs.*

so|lar|ium /səlɛəriəm, soʊ-/ (solariums) **1** N-COUNT A **solarium** is a room with glass walls that let in a lot of sunlight. **2** N-COUNT A **solarium** is a place equipped with special lamps, where you can go to get an artificial suntan.

so|lar plex|us /soʊlər plɛksəs/ N-SING [the N, N with poss] Your **solar plexus** is the part of your stomach, below your ribs, where it is painful if you are hit hard.

so|lar sys|tem (solar systems) **1** N-COUNT The **solar system** is the sun and all the planets that go around it. ❑ *Saturn is the second biggest planet in the solar system.* **2** → See feature box at **space**

sold /soʊld/ **Sold** is the past tense and past participle of **sell**.

sol|der /sɒdər/ (solders, soldering, soldered) **1** V-T If you **solder** two pieces of metal together, you join them by melting a small piece of soft metal and putting it between them so that it holds them together after it has cooled. ❑ *Fewer workers are needed to solder circuit boards.* **2** N-UNCOUNT **Solder** is the soft metal used for soldering.

sol|der|ing iron (soldering irons) N-COUNT A **soldering iron** is a tool used to solder things together.

sol|dier /soʊldʒər/ (soldiers) N-COUNT A **soldier** is a member of an army, especially a person who is not an officer.

COLLOCATIONS

soldier
NOUN
noun + **soldier**: rebel; toy
adjective + **soldier**: dead, injured, wounded; brave, loyal
verb + **soldier**: injure, kill, shoot, wound; capture

---

sol|dier|ly /soʊldʒərli/ ADJ [usu ADJ n] If you act in a **soldierly** way, you behave like a good or brave soldier. [FORMAL] ❑ *There was a great deal of soldierly good fellowship.*

sol|diery /soʊldʒəri/ N-UNCOUNT **Soldiery** is a group or body of soldiers. [LITERARY] ❑ *...the distant shouts and songs of the drunken soldiery.*

sold out **1** ADJ [v-link ADJ] If a performance, sports event, or other entertainment is **sold out**, all the tickets for it have been sold. ❑ *The premiere on Monday is sold out.* **2** ADJ [v-link ADJ] If a store is **sold out** of something, it has sold all of it that it had. ❑ *The stores are sometimes sold out of certain groceries.* **3** → see also **sell out**

sole /soʊl/ (soles) **1** ADJ [ADJ n] The **sole** thing or person of a particular type is the only one of that type. ❑ *Their sole aim is to destabilize the Indian government.* **2** ADJ [ADJ n] If you have **sole** charge or ownership of something, you are the only person in charge of it or who owns it. ❑ *Many women are left as the sole providers in families after their husband has died.* **3** N-COUNT The **sole** of your foot or of a shoe or sock is the underneath surface of it. ❑ *...shoes with rubber soles.* **4** → See feature box at **body**

-soled /-soʊld/ COMB IN ADJ [usu ADJ n] **-soled** combines with adjectives and nouns to form adjectives which describe shoes with a particular kind of sole. ❑ *The boy was wearing rubber-soled shoes.*

sole|ly /soʊlli/ ADV If something involves **solely** one thing or one person, it involves only this thing or this one person and no others. ❑ *Too often we make decisions based solely upon what we see in the magazines.*

sol|emn /sɒləm/ **1** ADJ Someone or something that is **solemn** is very serious rather than cheerful or humorous. ❑ *His solemn little face broke into smiles.* • **so|lem|nity** /səlɛmnɪti/ N-UNCOUNT ❑ *The setting for this morning's signing ceremony matched the solemnity of the occasion.* **2** ADJ A **solemn** promise or agreement is one that you make in a very formal, sincere way. ❑ *She made a solemn promise to him when they became engaged that she would give up cigarettes for good.*

sole pro|pri|etor (sole proprietors) N-COUNT The **sole proprietor** of a business is the owner of the business, when it is owned by only one person. [BUSINESS] ❑ *...a law firm of which he was the sole proprietor.*

sole trad|er (sole traders) N-COUNT A **sole trader** is a person who owns their own business and does not have a partner or any shareholders. [BRIT, BUSINESS]

in AM, use **sole proprietor**

so|lic|it /səlɪsɪt/ (solicits, soliciting, solicited) **1** V-T If you **solicit** money, help, support, or an opinion from someone, you ask them for it. [FORMAL] ❑ *He's already solicited their support on health care reform.* **2** V-I When prostitutes **solicit**, they offer to have sex with people in return for money. ❑ *Prostitutes were forbidden to solicit on public roads and in public places.* • **so|lic|it|ing** N-UNCOUNT ❑ *Girls could get very heavy sentences for soliciting – nine months or more.*

so|lici|ta|tion /səlɪsɪteɪʃən/ (solicitations) N-VAR **Solicitation** is the act of asking someone for money, help, support, or an opinion. [mainly AM] ❑ *Republican leaders are making open solicitation of the Italian-American vote.*

so|lici|tor /səlɪsɪtər/ (solicitors) N-COUNT In the United States, a **solicitor** is the chief lawyer in a government or city department.

So|lici|tor Gen|er|al also solicitor-general N-SING; N-TITLE The **Solicitor General** in the United States, or in one of the states, is the second most important legal officer, next in rank below an Attorney General.

so|lici|tous /səlɪsɪtəs/ ADJ [oft ADJ of n] A person who is **solicitous** shows anxious concern for someone or something. [FORMAL] ❑ *He was so solicitous of his guests.* • **so|lici|tous|ly** ADV ❑ *He took her hand in greeting and asked solicitously how everything was.*

so|lici|tude /səlɪsɪtuːd/ N-UNCOUNT **Solicitude** is anxious concern for someone. [FORMAL] ❑ *He is full of tender solicitude towards my sister.*

sol|id /sɒlɪd/ (solids) **1** ADJ A **solid** substance or object stays the same shape whether it is in a container or not. ❑ *...the potential of greatly reducing our solid waste problem.* **2** N-COUNT A **solid** is a substance that stays the same shape whether it is in a container or not. ❑ *Solids turn to liquids at certain temperatures.* **3** ADJ A substance that is **solid** is very hard or firm. ❑ *The snow had melted, but the lake was still frozen solid.* **4** ADJ A **solid** object or mass does not have a space inside it, or holes or gaps in it. ❑ *...a tunnel carved through 50 ft of solid rock.* ❑ *The train station was packed solid with people.* **5** ADJ [ADJ n] If an object is made of **solid** gold or **solid** wood, for example, it is made of gold or wood all the way through, rather than just on the outside. ❑ *The faucets appeared to be made of solid gold.* ❑ *...solid wood doors.* **6** ADJ A structure that is **solid** is strong and is not likely to collapse or fall over. ❑ *Banks are built to look solid to reassure their customers.* • **sol|id|ly** ADV [ADV with v] ❑ *Their house, which was solidly built, resisted the main shock.* • **so|lid|ity** /səlɪdɪti/ N-UNCOUNT ❑ *...the solidity of walls and floors.* **7** ADJ If you describe someone as **solid**, you mean that they are very reliable and respectable. [APPROVAL] ❑ *Someone who is solid and stable can also be quite boring.* • **sol|id|ly** ADV ❑ *Graham is so solidly consistent.* • **so|lid|ity** N-UNCOUNT ❑ *He had the proverbial solidity of the English.* **8** ADJ **Solid** evidence or information is reliable because it is based on facts. ❑ *We don't have good solid information on where the people are.* **9** ADJ You use **solid** to describe something such as advice or a piece of work which is useful and reliable. ❑ *The organization provides churches with solid advice on a wide range of subjects.* • **sol|id|ly** ADV [ADV with v] ❑ *She's played solidly throughout the spring.* **10** ADJ You use **solid** to describe something such as the basis for a policy or support for an organization when it is strong, because it has been developed carefully and slowly. ◻ ...a Democratic nominee with solid support within the party and broad appeal beyond. • **sol|id|ly** ADV ◻ The Los Alamos district is solidly Republican. • **sol|id|ity** N-UNCOUNT ◻ ...doubts over the solidity of European backing for the American approach. **11** ADJ [ADJ n, -ed ADJ] If you do something for a **solid** period of time, you do it without any pause or interruption throughout that time. ◻ We had worked together for two solid years. • **sol|id|ly** ADV [ADV with v] ◻ People who had worked solidly since Christmas enjoyed the chance of a Friday off.

---- SYNONYMS ----
solid
ADJ **4**
firm: Fruit should be firm and in excellent condition.
hard: He shuffled his feet on the hard, wooden floor.
compact: He looked physically very powerful, athletic in a compact way.
dense: ...a small, dense star.
----

soli|dar|ity /sɒlɪdæ̱rɪti/ N-UNCOUNT If a group of people show **solidarity**, they show support for each other or for another group, especially in political or international affairs. ◻ Supporters want to march tomorrow to show solidarity with their leaders.

so|lidi|fy /səlɪ̱dɪfaɪ/ (solidifies, solidifying, solidified) **1** V-T/V-I When a liquid **solidifies** or **is solidified**, it changes into a solid. ◻ The thicker lava would have taken two weeks to solidify. ◻ The Energy Department plans to solidify the deadly waste in a high-tech billion-dollar factory. **2** V-T/V-I If something such as a position or opinion **solidifies**, or if something **solidifies** it, it becomes firmer and more definite and unlikely to change. ◻ Her attitudes solidified through privilege and habit. ◻ ...his attempt to solidify his position as chairman.

solid-state ADJ [ADJ n] **Solid-state** electronic equipment is made using transistors or silicon chips, instead of valves or other mechanical parts. [TECHNICAL]

so|lilo|quy /səlɪ̱ləkwi/ (soliloquies) N-COUNT A **soliloquy** is a speech in a play in which an actor speaks to himself or herself and to the audience, rather than to another actor.

soli|taire /sɒlɪtɛ͟ər/ (solitaires) **1** N-UNCOUNT **Solitaire** is a card game for only one player. It is often played on a computer. [mainly AM] **2** N-COUNT A **solitaire** is a diamond or other jewel that is set on its own in a ring or other piece of jewelry.

soli|tary /sɒlɪtri/ **1** ADJ A person or animal that is **solitary** spends a lot of time alone. ◻ Paul was a shy, pleasant, solitary man. **2** ADJ [ADJ n] A **solitary** activity is one that you do alone. ◻ His evenings were spent in solitary drinking. **3** ADJ [ADJ n] A **solitary** person or object is alone, with no others near them. ◻ You could see the occasional solitary figure making a study of wildflowers or grasses.

soli|tary con|fine|ment N-UNCOUNT [usu in N] A prisoner who is in **solitary confinement** is being kept alone away from all other prisoners, usually as a punishment. ◻ Last night he was being held in solitary confinement in Douglas jail.

soli|tude /sɒlɪtud/ N-UNCOUNT **Solitude** is the state of being alone, especially when this is peaceful and pleasant. ◻ He enjoyed his moments of solitude before the pressures of the day began in earnest.

solo /so͟ʊloʊ/ (solos) **1** ADJ You use **solo** to indicate that someone does something alone rather than with other people. ◻ He had just completed his final solo album. ◻ ...Daniel Amokachi's spectacular solo goal. • ADV [ADV after v] **Solo** is also an adverb. ◻ Charles Lindbergh became the very first person to fly solo across the Atlantic. **2** N-COUNT A **solo** is a piece of music or a dance performed by one person. ◻ The original version featured a guitar solo.

so|lo|ist /so͟ʊloʊɪst/ (soloists) N-COUNT A **soloist** is a musician or dancer who performs a solo. ◻ ...the relationship between soloist and orchestra.

sol|stice /sɒ̱lstɪs, soʊl-/ (solstices) N-COUNT The **summer solstice** is the day of the year with the most hours of daylight, and the **winter solstice** is the day of the year with the fewest hours of daylight.

sol|uble /sɒ̱lyəbəl/ **1** ADJ A substance that is **soluble** will dissolve in a liquid. ◻ Uranium is soluble in sea water. **2** COMB IN ADJ If something is **water-soluble** or **fat-soluble**, it will dissolve in water or in fat. ◻ The red dye on the leather is water-soluble.

so|lu|tion ♦♦♢ /səlu͟ːʃən/ (solutions) **1** N-COUNT A **solution** to a problem or difficult situation is a way of dealing with it so that the difficulty is removed. ◻ Although he has sought to find a peaceful solution, he is facing pressure to use greater military force. **2** N-COUNT The **solution** to a puzzle is the answer to it. ◻ We invited readers who completed the puzzle to send in their solutions. **3** N-COUNT [also in N] A **solution** is a liquid in which a solid substance has been dissolved. ◻ ...a warm solution of liquid detergent. **4** → See feature box at **experiment**

---- COLLOCATIONS ----
solution
NOUN **1**
adjective + **solution**: ideal, obvious, possible, simple; long-term, peaceful, practical
verb + **solution**: find, need, seek; offer, propose, provide
----

---- SYNONYMS ----
solution
NOUN **1**
resolution: ...in order to find a peaceful resolution to the crisis.
answer: Prison is not the answer for most young offenders.
key: The key to success is to be ready from the start.
----

solve ♦♢♢ /sɒ̱lv/ (solves, solving, solved) V-T If you **solve** a problem or a question, you find a solution or an answer to it. ◻ Their domestic reforms did nothing to solve the problem of unemployment.

sol|ven|cy /sɒ̱lvənsi/ N-UNCOUNT A person's or organization's **solvency** is their ability to pay their debts. [BUSINESS] ◻ ...unsound investments that could threaten the company's solvency.

sol|vent /sɒ̱lvənt/ (solvents) **1** ADJ If a person or a company is **solvent**, they have enough money to pay all their debts. [BUSINESS] ◻ They're going to have to show that the company is now solvent. **2** N-MASS A **solvent** is a liquid that can dissolve other substances. ◻ ...a small amount of cleaning solvent.

som|ber /sɒ̱mbər/

in BRIT, use **sombre**

1 ADJ If someone is **somber**, they are serious or sad. ◻ Spencer cried as she described the somber mood of her co-workers. **2** ADJ **Somber** colors and places are dark and dull. ◻ His room is somber and dark.

som|brero /sɒmbre͟əroʊ/ (sombreros) N-COUNT A **sombrero** is a hat with a very wide brim which is worn especially in Mexico.

some ♦♦♦ /səm, STRONG sʌm/ **1** DET You use **some** to refer to a quantity of something or to a number of people or things, when you are not stating the quantity or number precisely. ◻ Robin opened some champagne. ◻ He went to fetch some books. • PRON **Some** is also a pronoun. ◻ This year all the apples are all red. My niece and nephew are going out this morning with step-ladders to pick some. **2** DET You use **some** to emphasize that a quantity or number is fairly large. For example, if an activity takes **some** time, it takes quite a lot of time. [EMPHASIS] ◻ I have discussed this topic in some detail. ◻ He remained silent for some time. **3** DET You use **some** to emphasize that a quantity or number is fairly small. For example, if something happens to **some** extent, it happens a little. [EMPHASIS] ◻ "Isn't there some chance that William might lead a normal life?" asked Jill. ◻ All mothers share to some extent in the tension of a wedding. **4** QUANT If you refer to **some of** the people or things in a group, you mean a few of them but not all of them. If you refer to **some of** a particular thing, you mean a part of it but not all of it. ◻ Some of the people already in work will lose their jobs. ◻ Remove the cover and spoon some of the sauce into a bowl. • PRON **Some** is also a pronoun. ◻ When the chicken is cooked I'll freeze some. **5** DET If you refer to **some** person or thing, you are referring to that person or thing but in a vague way, without stating precisely which person or thing you mean. [VAGUENESS] ◻ If you are worried about some aspect of your child's health, call us. **6** ADV [ADV num] You can use **some** in front of a number to indicate that it is approximate. [VAGUENESS] ❏ *I have kept birds for some 30 years.* **7** ADV [ADV after v] **Some** is used to mean to a small extent or degree. [AM] ❏ *If Susanne is off somewhere, I'll kill time by looking around some.* **8** DET You can use **some** in front of a noun in order to express your approval or disapproval of the person or thing you are mentioning. [INFORMAL, FEELINGS] ❏ *"Some party!"—"Yep. One hell of a party."*

USAGE
some
Don't use 'some' in negative sentences. Use **any**. You can use **any** in front of a plural or uncountable noun. For example, don't say 'We made this without some help.' Say 'We made this without **any** help.' *I don't have **any** plans for the upcoming holidays.*

some|body ✦✧ /sʌmbɑdi, -bʌdi/ PRON-INDEF **Somebody** means the same as **someone**.

some|day /sʌmdeɪ/ ADV **Someday** means at a date in the future that is unknown or that has not yet been decided. ❏ *Someday I'll be a pilot.*

some|how ✦✧ /sʌmhaʊ/ **1** ADV You use **somehow** to say that you do not know or cannot say how something was done or will be done. ❏ *We'll manage somehow, you and me. I know we will.* ❏ *Somehow Karin managed to cope with the demands of her career.* **2 somehow or other** → see **other**

some|one ✦✧ /sʌmwʌn/

> The form **somebody** is also used.

1 PRON-INDEF You use **someone** or **somebody** to refer to a person without saying exactly who you mean. ❏ *Her father was shot by someone trying to rob his small retail store.* ❏ *I need someone to help me.* **2** PRON-INDEF If you say that a person is **someone** or **somebody** in a particular kind of work or in a particular place, you mean that they are considered to be important in that kind of work or in that place. ❏ *"Before she came around," she says, "I was somebody in this town."*

USAGE
someone
You don't usually use 'someone' or 'somebody' as part of the object of a negative sentence. Don't say, for example, 'I don't know someone who lives in York.' You say 'I don't know **anyone** who lives in York.' *There wasn't **anyone** there.*

some|place /sʌmpleɪs/ ADV [ADV after v] **Someplace** means the same as **somewhere**. [AM] ❏ *Maybe if we could go someplace together, just you and I.*

som|er|sault /sʌmərsɔlt/ (**somersaults, somersaulting, somersaulted**) **1** N-COUNT If someone or something does a **somersault**, they turn over completely in the air. ❏ *Trained dogs did somersaults on a man's shoulders.* **2** V-I If someone or something **somersaults**, they perform one or more somersaults. ❏ *His boat hit a wave and somersaulted.*

some|thing ✦✦✦ /sʌmθɪŋ/ **1** PRON-INDEF You use **something** to refer to a thing, situation, event, or idea, without saying exactly what it is. ❏ *He realized right away that there was something wrong.* ❏ *There was something vaguely familiar about him.* ❏ *"You said there was something you wanted to ask me," he said politely.* **2** PRON-INDEF [PRON prep] You can use **something** to say that the description or amount that you are giving is not exact. ❏ *Clive made a noise, something like a grunt.* ❏ *Their membership seems to have risen to something over 10,000.* **3** PRON-INDEF If you say that a person or thing is **something** or is really **something**, you mean that you are very impressed by them. [INFORMAL] ❏ *You're really something.* **4** PRON-INDEF You can use **something** in expressions like '**that's something**' when you think that a situation is not very good but is better than it might have been. ❏ *Well, at least he was in town. That was something.* **5** PRON-INDEF [PRON of n] If you say that a thing is **something of** a disappointment, you mean that it is quite disappointing. If you say that a person is **something of** an artist, you mean that they are quite good at art. ❏ *The city proved to be something of a disappointment.* **6** PRON-INDEF [PRON in n] If you say that there is **something in** an idea or suggestion, you mean that it is quite good and should be considered seriously. ❏ *Could there be something in what he said?* **7** PRON-INDEF You use **something** in expressions such as '**or something**' and '**or something like**

that' to indicate that you are referring to something similar to what you have just mentioned but you are not being exact. [VAGUENESS] ❏ *This guy, his name was Briarly or Beardly or something.* **8 something like** → see **like** ③

USAGE
something
Don't use 'something' in negative sentences. Instead, use **anything**. *He never seemed to do **anything** at all.*

-something /-sʌmθɪŋ/ (**-somethings**) COMB IN ADJ **-something** is combined with numbers such as twenty and thirty to form adjectives which indicate an approximate amount, especially someone's age. For example, if you say that someone is **thirty-something**, you mean they are between thirty and forty years old.

some|time /sʌmtaɪm/ ADV You use **sometime** to refer to a time in the future or the past that is unknown or that has not yet been decided. ❏ *The sales figures won't be released until sometime next month.* ❏ *Why don't you come and see me sometime.*

some|times ✦✦✦ /sʌmtaɪmz/ ADV You use **sometimes** to say that something happens on some occasions rather than all the time. ❏ *During the summer, my skin sometimes gets greasy.* ❏ *Sometimes I think he dislikes me.*

some|what ✦✧ /sʌmwʌt, -wɒt/ ADV [ADV with cl/group] You use **somewhat** to indicate that something is the case to a limited extent or degree. [FORMAL] ❏ *He concluded that Oswald was somewhat abnormal.* ❏ *He explained somewhat unconvincingly that the company was paying for everything.*

SYNONYMS
somewhat
ADV
rather: *The reality is rather complex.*
quite: *I felt quite bitter about it at the time.*
fairly: *Both ships are fairly new.*
pretty: *Pretty soon after my arrival, I found lodgings.*

some|where ✦✧ /sʌmwɛər/ **1** ADV You use **somewhere** to refer to a place without saying exactly where you mean. ❏ *I've got a feeling I've seen him before somewhere.* ❏ *I'm not going home yet. I have to go somewhere else first.* ❏ *I needed somewhere to live.* **2** ADV [ADV prep] You use **somewhere** when giving an approximate amount, number, or time. ❏ *He is believed to be worth somewhere between seven million and ten million dollars.* ❏ *Caray is somewhere between 73 and 80 years of age.* **3** PHRASE If you say that you **are getting somewhere**, you mean that you are making progress toward achieving something. ❏ *At last they were agreeing, at last they were getting somewhere.*

USAGE
somewhere
Don't use 'somewhere' in negative sentences. Use **anywhere**. *I don't have **anywhere** to live.*

som|no|lent /sɒmnələnt/ ADJ [usu ADJ n] If you are **somnolent**, you feel sleepy. [FORMAL] ❏ *The sedative makes people very somnolent.*

son ✦✦✦ /sʌn/ (**sons**) **1** N-COUNT Someone's **son** is their male child. ❏ *He shared a pizza with his son Laurence.* ❏ *Sam is the seven-year-old son of Eric Davies.* **2** N-COUNT A man, especially a famous man, can be described as a **son** of the place he comes from. [JOURNALISM] ❏ *…New Orleans's most famous son, Louis Armstrong.* **3** N-VOC Some people use **son** as a form of address when they are showing kindness or affection to a boy or a man who is younger than them. [INFORMAL, FEELINGS] ❏ *Don't be frightened by failure, son.*

so|nar /soʊnɑr/ (**sonars**) N-VAR **Sonar** is equipment on a ship which can calculate the depth of the sea or the position of an underwater object using sound waves.

so|na|ta /sənɑtə/ (**sonatas**) N-COUNT A **sonata** is a piece of classical music written either for a single instrument, or for one instrument and a piano.

song ✦✦✦ /sɔŋ/ (**songs**) **1** N-COUNT A **song** is words and music sung together. ❏ *…a voice singing a Spanish song.* **2** N-UNCOUNT **Song** is the art of singing. ❏ *…dance, music, mime, and song.* **3** N-COUNT A bird's **song** is the pleasant, musical sounds that it makes. ☐ *It's been a long time since I heard a blackbird's song in the evening.* ◳ PHRASE If someone **bursts into song** or **breaks into song**, they start singing. ☐ *I feel as if I should break into song.*

COLLOCATIONS

song
NOUN ◳
noun + **song**: hit, love, pop, protest
adjective + **song**: catchy, favorite; classic, popular, traditional
verb + **song**: play, perform, sing; record, release, write

---

song and dance ◳ N-UNCOUNT [usu N n] A **song and dance** act is a performance in which a person or group of people sing and dance. ◳ PHRASE If you say that someone is giving someone a **song and dance** about something, you mean they are giving a long explanation about it. [AM]

song|bird /sɒŋbɜrd/ (**songbirds**) also **song bird** ◳ N-COUNT A **songbird** is a bird that produces musical sounds which are like singing. There are many different kinds of songbird. ◳ → See feature box at **sound**

song|book /sɒŋbʊk/ (**songbooks**) ◳ N-COUNT A songwriter's **songbook** is all the songs that he or she has written. You can also refer to the songs that a singer performs as their **songbook**. ☐ *When you have a songbook as powerful as hers, why not use it.* ◳ N-COUNT A **songbook** is a book containing the words and music of a lot of songs. ☐ *...a pop songbook.*

song|ster /sɒŋstər/ (**songsters**) N-COUNT Journalists sometimes refer to a popular singer, especially a male singer, as a **songster**.

song|stress /sɒŋstrɪs/ (**songstresses**) N-COUNT Journalists sometimes refer to a female popular singer as a **songstress**.

song|writer /sɒŋraɪtər/ (**songwriters**) ◳ N-COUNT A **songwriter** is someone who writes the words or the music, or both, for popular songs. ☐ *...one of rock'n'roll's greatest songwriters.* ◳ → see also **singer-songwriter**

son|ic /sɒnɪk/ ADJ [ADJ n] **Sonic** is used to describe things related to sound. [TECHNICAL] ☐ *...the sonic boom of enemy fighter-bombers.*

son-in-law (**sons-in-law**) N-COUNT Someone's **son-in-law** is the husband of their daughter.

son|net /sɒnɪt/ (**sonnets**) N-COUNT A **sonnet** is a poem that has 14 lines. Each line has 10 syllables, and the poem has a fixed pattern of rhymes.

son|ny /sʌni/ N-VOC Some people address a boy or young man as **sonny**. [INFORMAL] ☐ *Well, sonny, I'll give you a bit of advice.*

son of a bitch (**sons of bitches**) also **son-of-a-bitch** N-COUNT If someone is very angry with another person, or if they want to insult them, they sometimes call them a **son of a bitch**. [OFFENSIVE, VULGAR, DISAPPROVAL]

so|nor|ity /sənɒrɪti/ (**sonorities**) N-UNCOUNT [also N in pl] The **sonority** of a sound is its deep, rich quality. [FORMAL] ☐ *The lower strings contribute a splendid richness of sonority.*

so|no|rous /sɒnərəs, sənɔrəs/ ADJ A **sonorous** sound is deep and rich. [LITERARY] ☐ *"Doctor McKee?" the man called in an even, sonorous voice.*

soon ♦♦♦ /suːn/ (**sooner, soonest**) ◳ ADV If something is going to happen **soon**, it will happen after a short time. If something happened **soon** after a particular time or event, it happened a short time after it. ☐ *You'll be hearing from us very soon.* ☐ *This chance has come sooner than I expected.* ◳ PHRASE If you say that something happens **as soon as** something else happens, you mean that it happens immediately after the other thing. ☐ *As soon as relations improve they will be allowed to go.* ◳ PHRASE If you say that you **would just as soon** do something or you**'d just as soon** do it, you mean that you would prefer to do it. ☐ *These people could afford to retire to Florida but they'd just as soon stay put.* ☐ *I'd just as soon not have to make this public.*

soon|er /suːnər/ ◳ **Sooner** is the comparative of **soon**. ◳ PHRASE You say **the sooner the better** when you think something should be done as soon as possible. ☐ *Detective Holt said: "The kidnapper is a man we must catch and the sooner the better."* ◳ PHRASE [PHR with cl] If you say that something will happen **sooner or later**, you mean that it will happen at some time in the future, even though it might take a long time. ☐ *Sooner or later she would be caught by the police.* ◳ PHRASE If you say that **no sooner** has one thing happened **than** another thing happens, you mean that the second thing happens immediately after the first thing. ☐ *No sooner had he arrived in Rome than he was kidnapped.* ◳ PHRASE If you say that you **would sooner** do something or you**'d sooner** do it, you mean that you would prefer to do it. ☐ *Ford vowed that he would sooner burn his factory to the ground than build a single vehicle for war purposes.* ☐ *I'd sooner not talk about it.* ☐ *I'd sooner he didn't know till I've talked to Pete.* ☐ *I would sooner give up sleep than miss my evening class.*

soot /sʊt, suːt/ N-UNCOUNT **Soot** is black powder which rises in the smoke from a fire and collects usually on the inside of chimneys. ☐ *...a wall blackened by soot.*

soothe /suːð/ (**soothes, soothing, soothed**) ◳ V-T If you **soothe** someone who is angry or upset, you make them feel calmer. ☐ *He would take her in his arms and soothe her.* • **sooth|ing** ADJ ☐ *Put on some nice soothing music.* ◳ V-T Something that **soothes** a part of your body where there is pain or discomfort makes the pain or discomfort less severe. ☐ *...body lotion to soothe dry skin.* • **sooth|ing** ADJ ☐ *Cold tea is very soothing for burns.*

sooth|say|er /suːθseɪər/ (**soothsayers**) N-COUNT In former times, **soothsayers** were people who believed they could see into the future and say what was going to happen.

sooty /sʊti, suː-/ (**sootier, sootiest**) ADJ Something that is **sooty** is covered with soot. ☐ *Their uniforms are torn and sooty.*

sop /sɒp/ (**sops**) N-COUNT [oft N to n] You describe something as a **sop** to a person when they are offered something small or unimportant in order to prevent them from getting angry or causing trouble. [DISAPPROVAL] ☐ *This is an obvious sop to the large Irish-American audience.*

so|phis|ti|cate /səfɪstɪkɪt/ (**sophisticates**) N-COUNT A **sophisticate** is someone who knows about culture, fashion, and other matters that are considered socially important.

so|phis|ti|cat|ed ♦◊◊ /səfɪstɪkeɪtɪd/ ◳ ADJ A **sophisticated** machine, device, or method is more advanced or complex than others. ☐ *Honeybees use one of the most sophisticated communication systems of any insect.* ◳ ADJ Someone who is **sophisticated** is comfortable in social situations and knows about culture, fashion, and other matters that are considered socially important. ☐ *Claude was a charming, sophisticated companion.* ◳ ADJ A **sophisticated** person is intelligent and knows a lot, so that they are able to understand complicated situations. ☐ *These people are very sophisticated observers of the foreign policy scene.*

so|phis|ti|ca|tion /səfɪstɪkeɪʃən/ N-UNCOUNT The **sophistication** of people, places, machines, or methods is their quality of being sophisticated. ☐ *It would take many decades to build up the level of education and sophistication required.*

soph|ist|ries /sɒfɪstriz/ N-PLURAL **Sophistries** are clever arguments that sound convincing but are in fact false. [FORMAL] ☐ *They refuted the "sophistries of the economists."*

soph|ist|ry /sɒfɪstri/ N-UNCOUNT **Sophistry** is the practice of using clever arguments that sound convincing but are in fact false. [FORMAL] ☐ *Political selection is more dependent on sophistry and less on economic literacy.*

sopho|more /sɒfəmɔr/ (**sophomores**) N-COUNT A **sophomore** is a student in the second year of college or high school. [AM]

sopo|rif|ic /sɒpərɪfɪk/ ADJ Something that is **soporific** makes you feel sleepy. [FORMAL] ☐ *...the soporific effect of the alcohol.*

sop|ping /sɒpɪŋ/ ADJ Something that is **sopping** or **sopping wet** is extremely wet. [INFORMAL] ☐ *They came back sopping wet.*

so|pra|no /səprænoʊ, -prɑːn-/ (**sopranos**) N-COUNT A **soprano** is a woman, girl, or boy with a high singing voice. ☐ *She was the main soprano at the Bolshoi theatre.*

sor|bet /sɔrbɪt/ (**sorbets**) N-MASS **Sorbet** is a frozen dessert made with fruit juice, sugar, and water. ☐ *...a light lemon sorbet.*

sor|cer|er /sɔrsərər/ (**sorcerers**) N-COUNT In fairy tales, a **sorcerer** is a person who performs magic by using the power of evil spirits.

sor|cer|ess /sɔrsərɪs/ (**sorceresses**) N-COUNT In fairy tales, a **sorceress** is a woman who performs magic by using the power of evil spirits.

sor|cery /sɔrsəri/ N-UNCOUNT **Sorcery** is magic performed by using the power of evil spirits.

sor|did /sɔrdɪd/ **1** ADJ If you describe someone's behavior as **sordid**, you mean that it is immoral or dishonest. [DISAPPROVAL] ❏ *He sat with his head buried in his hands as his sordid double life was revealed.* **2** ADJ If you describe a place as **sordid**, you mean that it is dirty, unpleasant, or depressing. [DISAPPROVAL] ❏ *...the attic windows of their sordid little rooms.*

sore /sɔr/ (**sorer**, **sorest**, **sores**) **1** ADJ If part of your body is **sore**, it causes you pain and discomfort. ❏ *It's years since I've had a sore throat like I did last night.* **2** ADJ [v-link ADJ] If you are **sore** about something, you are angry and upset about it. [mainly AM, INFORMAL] ❏ *The result is that they are now all feeling very sore at you.* **3** N-COUNT A **sore** is a painful place on the body where the skin is infected. ❏ *Our backs and hands were covered with sores and burns from the ropes.* **4** PHRASE If something is **a sore point** with someone, it is likely to make them angry or embarrassed if you try to discuss it. ❏ *The continuing presence of troops on South Korean soil remains a very sore point with these students.*

sore|ly /sɔrli/ ADV **Sorely** is used to emphasize that a feeling such as disappointment or need is very strong. [EMPHASIS] ❏ *I for one was sorely disappointed.* ❏ *He will be sorely missed.*

sor|ghum /sɔrgəm/ N-UNCOUNT **Sorghum** is a type of grass that is grown in warm areas. Its grain can be made into flour or syrup.

so|ror|ity /sərɔriti/ (**sororities**) N-COUNT A **sorority** is a society of female university or college students.

sor|rel /sɔrəl/ N-UNCOUNT **Sorrel** is a plant whose leaves have a sharp taste and are sometimes used in salads and sauces.

sor|row /sɒroʊ/ N-UNCOUNT **Sorrow** is a feeling of deep sadness or regret. ❏ *Words cannot express my sorrow.*

sor|row|ful /sɒroʊfəl/ ADJ **Sorrowful** means very sad. [LITERARY] ❏ *His father's face looked suddenly soft and sorrowful.*

sor|rows /sɒroʊz/ **1** N-PLURAL **Sorrows** are events or situations that cause deep sadness. ❏ *...the joys and sorrows of everyday living.* **2** to drown one's sorrows → see drown

sor|ry ♦♦◇ /sɒri/ (**sorrier**, **sorriest**) **1** CONVENTION You say '**Sorry**' or '**I'm sorry**' as a way of apologizing to someone for something that you have done which has upset them or caused them difficulties, or when you bump into them accidentally. [FORMULAE] ❏ *"We're all talking at the same time."—"Yeah. Sorry."* ❏ *Sorry I took so long.* ❏ *I'm really sorry if I said anything wrong.* **2** ADJ [v-link ADJ] If you are **sorry** about a situation, you feel regret, sadness, or disappointment about it. ❏ *She was very sorry about all the trouble she'd caused.* ❏ *I'm sorry he's gone.* **3** CONVENTION You use **I'm sorry** or **sorry** as an introduction when you are telling a person something that you do not think they will want to hear, for example when you are disagreeing with them or giving them bad news. ❏ *No, I'm sorry, I can't agree with you.* ❏ *"I'm sorry," he told the real estate agent, "but we really must go now."* **4** PHRASE You use the expression **I'm sorry to say** to express regret together with disappointment or disapproval. [FEELINGS] ❏ *I've only done half of it, I'm sorry to say.* **5** CONVENTION You say '**I'm sorry**' to express your regret and sadness when you hear sad or unpleasant news. [FEELINGS] ❏ *"I'm afraid he's ill."—"I'm sorry to hear that."* **6** ADJ [v-link ADJ for n] If you feel **sorry for** someone who is unhappy or in an unpleasant situation, you feel sympathy and sadness for them. ❏ *I felt sorry for him and his colleagues – it must have been so frustrating for them.* **7** ADJ [v-link ADJ] You say that someone is feeling **sorry for** themselves when you disapprove of the fact that they keep thinking unhappily about their problems, rather than trying to be cheerful and positive. [DISAPPROVAL] ❏ *What he must not do is to sit around at home feeling sorry for himself.* **8** CONVENTION You say '**Sorry?**' when you have not heard something that someone has said and you want them to repeat it. [FORMULAE] ❏ *Once or twice I heard her muttering, but when I said, "Sorry? What did you say?" she didn't respond.* **9** CONVENTION You use **sorry** when you correct yourself and use different words to say what you have just said, especially when what you say the second time does not use the words you would normally choose to use. ❏ *Barcelona will be hoping to bring the trophy back to Spain (sorry, Catalonia) for the first time.* **10** ADJ [ADJ n] If someone or something is in a **sorry** state, they are in a bad state, mentally or physically. ❏ *The fire left Kuwait's oil industry in a sorry state.* **11** better safe than sorry → see safe

sort ♦♦♦ /sɔrt/ (**sorts**, **sorting**, **sorted**) **1** N-COUNT If you talk about a particular **sort** of something, you are talking about a class of things that have particular features in common and that belong to a larger group of related things. ❏ *What sort of school did you go to?* ❏ *There are so many different sorts of mushrooms available these days.* ❏ *A dozen trees of various sorts were planted.* **2** N-SING [with supp] You describe someone as a particular **sort** when you are describing their character. ❏ *He seemed to be just the right sort for the job.* ❏ *She was a very vigorous sort of person.* **3** V-T/V-I If you **sort** things, you separate them into different classes, groups, or places, for example so that you can do different things with them. ❏ *He sorted the materials into their folders.* ❏ *He unlatched the box and sorted through the papers.* **4** PHRASE **All sorts** of things or people means a large number of different things or people. ❏ *There are all sorts of animals, including bears, pigs, kangaroos, and penguins.* ❏ *It was used by all sorts of people.* **5** PHRASE If you describe something as a thing **of sorts** or as a thing **of a sort**, you are suggesting that the thing is of a rather poor quality or standard. ❏ *He made a living of sorts selling encyclopedias door-to-door.* **6** PHRASE You use **sort of** when you want to say that your description of something is not very accurate. [INFORMAL, VAGUENESS] ❏ *You could even order windows from a catalogue – a sort of mail order stained glass service.* **7** nothing of the sort → see nothing

▶ **sort out** **1** PHRASAL VERB If you **sort out** a group of things, you separate them into different classes, groups, or places, for example so that you can do different things with them. ❏ *Sort out all your bills, receipts, invoices, and expenses as quickly as possible and keep detailed accounts.* ❏ *Davina was sorting out scraps of material.* **2** PHRASAL VERB If you **sort out** a problem or the details of something, you do what is necessary to solve the problem or organize the details. ❏ *India and Nepal have sorted out their trade and security dispute.* **3** PHRASAL VERB If you **sort yourself out**, you organize yourself or calm yourself so that you can act effectively and reasonably. ❏ *We're in a state of complete chaos here and I need a little time to sort myself out.*

sor|tie /sɔrti/ (**sorties**) N-COUNT If a military force makes a **sortie**, it leaves its own position and goes briefly into enemy territory to make an attack. [FORMAL] ❏ *His men made a sortie to Guazatan and took a prisoner.*

SOS /ɛs oʊ ɛs/ N-SING An **SOS** is a signal which indicates to other people that you are in danger and need help quickly. ❏ *The ferry did not even have time to send out an SOS.*

so-so ADJ If you say that something is **so-so**, you mean that it is average in quality, rather than being very good or very bad. [INFORMAL] ❏ *Their lunch was only so-so.*

sot|to voce /sɒtoʊ voʊtʃeɪ/ ADV [usu ADV after v] If you say something **sotto voce**, you say it in a soft voice. [LITERARY]

sou|bri|quet /soʊbrɪkeɪ/ [mainly BRIT] → see sobriquet

souf|flé /sufleɪ/ (**soufflés**) also **souffle** N-VAR A **soufflé** is a light food made from a mixture of beaten egg whites and other ingredients that is baked in the oven. ❏ *...a superb cheese soufflé.*

sought /sɔt/ **Sought** is the past tense and past participle of **seek**.

sought-after ADJ Something that is **sought-after** is in great demand, usually because it is rare or of very good quality. ❏ *An Olympic gold medal is the most sought-after prize in world sport.*

souk /suk/ (**souks**) also **suq** N-COUNT A **souk** is an outdoor market in a Muslim country, especially in North Africa and the Middle East.

soul ♦◇◇ /soʊl/ (**souls**) **1** N-COUNT Your **soul** is the part of you that consists of your mind, character, thoughts, and feelings. Many people believe that your soul continues existing after your body is dead. ❏ *She went to pray for the soul of her late husband.* **2** N-COUNT You can refer to someone as a particular kind of **soul** when you are describing their character or condition. ❏ *He's a jolly soul.* **3** N-SING You use **soul** in negative statements like **not a soul** to mean nobody at all. ❏ *I've never harmed a soul in my life.* **4** N-UNCOUNT **Soul** is the same as **soul music**. ❏ *...American soul singer Anita Baker.*

soul-destroying ADJ Activities or situations that are **soul-destroying** make you depressed, because they are boring or because there is no hope of improvement. ❏ *Believing yourself to be in the wrong job can be soul-destroying.*

soul food N-UNCOUNT **Soul food** is used to refer to the kind of food, for example corn bread, ham, and greens, that was traditionally eaten by African-Americans in the southern United States. [mainly AM]

soul|ful /sˈoʊlfəl/ ADJ Something that is **soulful** expresses deep feelings, especially sadness or love. ❏ *...his great, soulful, brown eyes.* ❏ *...soulful music.* • **soul|ful|ly** ADV ❏ *She gazed at him soulfully.*

soul|less /sˈoʊlɪs/ ADJ If you describe a thing or person as **soulless**, you mean that they lack human qualities and the ability to feel or produce deep feelings. ❏ *...a clean and soulless hotel.* ❏ *...a gray and soulless existence.*

soul|mate /sˈoʊlmeɪt/ (soulmates) also **soul mate** N-COUNT A **soulmate** is someone with whom you share a close friendship and deep personal understanding. ❏ *Steve and I became soul mates, near-constant companions.*

soul mu|sic N-UNCOUNT **Soul music** or **soul** is a type of pop music performed mainly by African-American musicians. It developed from gospel and blues music and often expresses deep emotions.

soul-searching N-UNCOUNT **Soul-searching** is a long and careful examination of your thoughts and feelings, especially when you are trying to make a difficult moral decision or thinking about something that has gone wrong. ❏ *My year was really spent doing a lot of soul-searching and trying to find out what had gone wrong in my life.*

SOUND
① NOUN AND VERB USES
② ADJECTIVE USES

① **sound** ♦♦♦ /sˈaʊnd/ (sounds, sounding, sounded)
→ Please look at meanings 🔟 and 🕅 to see if the expression you are looking for is shown under another headword.

1 N-COUNT A **sound** is something that you hear. ❏ *Peter heard the sound of gunfire.* ❏ *Liza was so frightened she couldn't make a sound.* **2** N-UNCOUNT **Sound** is energy that travels in waves through air, water, or other substances, and can be heard. ❏ *The airplane will travel at twice the speed of sound.* **3** N-SING The **sound** on a television, radio, or CD player is what you hear coming from the machine. Its loudness can be controlled. ❏ *She went and turned the sound down.* **4** N-COUNT A singer's or band's **sound** is the distinctive quality of their music. ❏ *They have started showing a strong soul element in their sound.* **5** V-T/V-I If something such as a horn or a bell **sounds** or if you **sound** it, it makes a noise. ❏ *The buzzer sounded in Daniel's office.* **6** V-T If you **sound** a warning, you publicly give it. If you **sound** a note of caution or optimism, you say publicly that you are cautious or optimistic. ❏ *The archbishop has sounded a warning to world leaders on third world debt.* **7** V-LINK When you are describing a noise, you can talk about the way it **sounds**. ❏ *They heard what sounded like a huge explosion.* ❏ *The creaking of the hinges sounded very loud in that silence.* **8** V-LINK When you talk about the way someone **sounds**, you are describing the impression you have of them when they speak. ❏ *She sounded a bit worried.* ❏ *Murphy sounds like a child.* **9** V-LINK When you are describing your impression or opinion of something you have heard about or read about, you can talk about the way it **sounds**. ❏ *It sounds like a wonderful idea to me, does it really work?* ❏ *It sounds as if they might have made a dreadful mistake.* **10** N-SING You can describe your impression of something you have heard about or read about by talking about **the sound of** it. ❏ *Here's a new idea we liked the sound of.* ❏ *I don't like the sound of Toby Osborne.* **11** to sound the alarm → see **alarm** **12** safe and sound → see **safe**
▶ **sound out** PHRASAL VERB If you **sound** someone **out**, you question them in order to find out what their opinion is about something. ❏ *He is sounding out Middle Eastern governments on ways to resolve the conflict.*

② **sound** /sˈaʊnd/ (sounder, soundest) **1** ADJ If a structure, part of someone's body, or someone's mind is **sound**, it is in good condition or healthy. ❏ *When we bought the house, it was structurally sound.* ❏ *Although the car is basically sound, I was worried about certain areas.* **2** ADJ **Sound** advice, reasoning, or evidence is reliable and sensible. ❏ *They are trained nutritionists who can give sound advice on diets.* ❏ *Buy a policy only from an insurance company that is financially sound.* **3** ADJ If you describe someone's ideas as **sound**, you mean that you approve of them and think they are correct. [APPROVAL] ❏ *I am not sure that this is sound democratic practice.* **4** ADJ [ADJ n] If someone is in a **sound** sleep, they are sleeping very deeply. ❏ *She had woken me out of a sound sleep.* • ADV [ADV adj] **Sound** is also an adverb. ❏ *He was lying in bed, sound asleep.* **5** → see also **soundly**

VOCABULARY IN CONTEXT

Animal sounds

What's your favorite animal sound? Many people love to hear the **chirping** of **songbirds** or the **hooting** of an owl as it hunts mice at night. Horse-lovers might claim that there is no sound nicer than the **neigh** of a contented horse as it gallops around a field. Other animal sounds might be special because they are rarely heard, such as dolphin **clicks** or the song of whales as they call to each other through the oceans. The **cuckoo** sound of the eponymous bird signals the arrival of spring, which is, for many, a favorite season, and the **buzz** of honey bees may bring back memories of a vacation in tropical climes. But for me, the **purr** of a contented cat just can't be beaten. Would you agree?

sound|alike /sˈaʊndəlaɪk/ (soundalikes) also **sound-alike** N-COUNT [oft n-proper N] A **soundalike** is someone, especially a singer, whose voice resembles that of a famous person. ❏ *...an Elvis-soundalike.*

sound bar|ri|er N-SING [usu the N] If an aircraft breaks the **sound barrier**, it reaches a speed that is faster than the speed of sound.

sound|bite /sˈaʊndbaɪt/ (soundbites) also **sound bite**, **sound-bite** N-COUNT A **soundbite** is a short sentence or phrase, usually from a politician's speech, which is broadcast during a news program.

sound|card /sˈaʊndkɑrd/ (soundcards) also **sound card** N-COUNT A **soundcard** is a piece of equipment which can be put into a computer so that the computer can produce music or other sounds. [COMPUTING]

sound ef|fect (sound effects) N-COUNT [usu pl] **Sound effects** are the sounds that are created artificially to make a play more realistic, especially a radio play.

sound en|gi|neer (sound engineers) N-COUNT A **sound engineer** is a person who works in a recording studio or for a radio or television station, and whose job it is to alter and balance the levels of different sounds as they are recorded.

sound|ing /sˈaʊndɪŋ/ (soundings) **1** N-SING [the N of n] The **sounding of** a bell or a horn is the act of causing it to make a sound. ❏ *There were 15 minutes between the first air raid alert and the sounding of the all-clear signal.* **2** N-COUNT [usu pl] If you take **soundings**, you try to find out people's opinions on a subject. ❏ *She will take soundings of the people's wishes before deciding on a course of action.*

-sounding /-saʊndɪŋ/ **1** COMB IN ADJ **-sounding** combines with adjectives to indicate a quality that a word, phrase, or name seems to have. ❏ *Many literary academics simply parrot a set of impressive-sounding phrases.* ❏ *...faraway places with strange-sounding names.* **2** → see also **high-sounding**

sound|ing board (sounding boards) N-COUNT If you use someone as a **sounding board**, you discuss your ideas with them in order to get another opinion. ❑ *He needed a sounding board rather than thinking alone.*

sound|less /ˈsaʊndlɪs/ ADJ Something that is **soundless** does not make a sound. [LITERARY] ❑ *My bare feet were soundless over the carpet.* ● **sound|less|ly** ADV ❑ *Joe's lips moved soundlessly.*

sound|ly /ˈsaʊndli/ **1** ADV [ADV -ed] If someone is **soundly** defeated or beaten, they are defeated or beaten thoroughly. ❑ *Needing just a point from their match at St. Helens, they were soundly beaten, going down by 35 points to 10.* **2** ADV [ADV -ed] If a decision, opinion, or statement is **soundly** based, there are sensible or reliable reasons behind it. [APPROVAL] ❑ *Changes must be soundly based in economic reality.* **3** ADV If you sleep **soundly**, you sleep deeply and do not wake during your sleep. ❑ *How can he sleep soundly at night? He's the one responsible for all those crimes.*

sound mix|er (sound mixers) N-COUNT A **sound mixer** is the same as a **sound engineer**.

sound|proof /ˈsaʊndpruːf/ (soundproofs, soundproofing, soundproofed) **1** ADJ A **soundproof** room, door, or window is designed to prevent all sound from getting in or out. ❑ *The studio isn't soundproof.* **2** V-T If you **soundproof** a room, you line it with special materials to stop all sound from getting in or out. ❑ *We've soundproofed our home studio.*

sound stage (sound stages) also **sound-stage, soundstage** N-COUNT A **sound stage** is a stage or set which is suitable for recording sound, especially for a movie.

sound sys|tem (sound systems) N-COUNT A **sound system** is a set of equipment for playing recorded music, or for making a band's music able to be heard by everyone at a concert.

sound|track /ˈsaʊndtræk/ (soundtracks) also **sound track** N-COUNT The **soundtrack** of a movie is its sound, speech, and music. It is used especially to refer to the music. ❑ *...the soundtrack to a movie called "Judgement Night."*

sound wave (sound waves) also **soundwave** N-COUNT Sound waves are the waves of energy that we hear as sound.

soup /suːp/ (soups) N-MASS Soup is liquid food made by boiling meat, fish, or vegetables in water. ❑ *...home-made chicken soup.*

soup kitch|en (soup kitchens) also **soup-kitchen** N-COUNT A **soup kitchen** is a place where homeless people or very poor people are provided with free food.

soup plate (soup plates) N-COUNT A **soup plate** is a deep plate with a wide edge in which soup is served.

soup spoon (soup spoons) N-COUNT A **soup spoon** is a spoon used for eating soup. The bowl-like part at the end of it is round.

soupy /ˈsuːpi/ ADJ **Soupy** things are like soup or look like soup. ❑ *...swirling soupy water.*

sour /ˈsaʊər/ (sourer, sourest, sours, souring, soured) **1** ADJ Something that is **sour** has a sharp, unpleasant taste like the taste of a lemon. ❑ *The stewed apple was sour even with honey.* **2** ADJ **Sour** milk is milk that has an unpleasant taste because it is no longer fresh. ❑ *The milk had gone sour.* **3** ADJ Someone who is **sour** is bad-tempered and unfriendly. ❑ *She made a sour face in his direction.* ● **sour|ly** ADV [ADV with v] ❑ *"Leave my mother out of it," he said sourly.* **4** ADJ If a situation or relationship turns **sour** or goes **sour**, it stops being enjoyable or satisfactory. ❑ *Everything turned sour for me there.* ❑ *The American dream is beginning to turn sour.* **5** V-T/V-I If a friendship, situation, or attitude **sours** or if something **sours** it, it becomes less friendly, enjoyable, or hopeful. ❑ *If anything sours the relationship, it is likely to be real differences in their world-views.*

source ✦✧ /sɔːrs/ (sources, sourcing, sourced) **1** N-COUNT The **source** of something is the person, place, or thing which you get it from. ❑ *Over 40 percent of adults use television as their major source of information about the arts.* ❑ *Renewable sources of energy must be used.* **2** V-T In business, if a person or firm **sources** a product or a raw material, they find someone who will supply it. [BUSINESS] ❑ *Together they travel the world, sourcing clothes for the small, privately owned company.* **3** N-COUNT A **source** is a person or book that provides information for a news story or for a piece of research. ❑ *Military sources say the boat was heading south at high speed.* **4** N-COUNT The **source of** a difficulty is its cause. ❑ *This gave me a clue as to the source of the problem.* **5** N-COUNT The **source** of a river or stream is the place where it begins. ❑ *...the source of the Tiber.* **6** → See feature box at **deforest, global warming, press, research**

SYNONYMS

source
VERB **2**
obtain: *Evans was trying to obtain a false passport and other documents.*
get: *We get all our ingredients from local suppliers.*
acquire: *I recently acquired some wood from a holly tree.*
NOUN **4**
cause: *Smoking is the biggest preventable cause of death and disease.*

---

source code (source codes) N-VAR **Source code** is the original form of a computer program as it is written by a programmer. It is then converted into code that the computer can understand. [COMPUTING]

sour cream N-UNCOUNT **Sour cream** is cream that has been artificially made sour by being mixed with bacteria. It is used in cooking.

sour|dough /ˈsaʊərdoʊ/ also **sour dough, sour-dough** ADJ [ADJ n] **Sourdough** bread is made with fermented dough that has been saved from a previous baking, so that fresh yeast is not needed. ❑ *...big chunks of sourdough bread.* ❑ *...a sourdough bun.*

south ✦✦✦ /saʊθ/ also **South 1** N-UNCOUNT [also the N] The **south** is the direction which is on your right when you are looking toward the direction where the sun rises. ❑ *The town lies ten miles to the south of here.* **2** N-SING [usu the N, oft N of n] The **south** of a place, country, or region is the part which is in the south. ❑ *...vacations in the south of Mexico.* **3** ADV [ADV after v] If you go **south**, you travel toward the south. ❑ *I drove south on Highway 9.* **4** ADV [ADV of n] Something that is **south of a place** is positioned to the south of it. ❑ *They now own and operate a farm 50 miles south of Rochester.* **5** ADJ [ADJ n] The **south** edge, corner, or part of a place or country is the part which is toward the south. ❑ *...the south coast of Long Island.* **6** ADJ [ADJ n] **South** is used in the names of some countries, states, and regions in the south of a larger area. ❑ *Next week the president will visit five South American countries in six days.* **7** ADJ A **south** wind is a wind that blows from the south. ❑ *...a mild south wind.* **8** N-SING [the N] **The South** is used to refer to the poorer, less developed countries of the world. ❑ *The debate will pit the industrial North against developing countries in the South.* **9** → See also color supplement

south|bound /ˈsaʊθbaʊnd/ ADJ [usu ADJ n] **Southbound** roads or vehicles lead or are traveling toward the south. ❑ *...the southbound train from Philadelphia.* ❑ *...the southbound Pacific Coast Highway.*

south|east ✦✧ /ˌsaʊθˈiːst/ **1** N-UNCOUNT [also the N] The **southeast** is the direction which is halfway between south and east. ❑ *It shook buildings as far away as Galveston, 90 miles to the southeast.* **2** N-SING The **southeast** of a place, country, or region is the part which is in the southeast. ❑ *Record levels of rainfall fell over the southeast of the country.* **3** ADV [ADV after v] If you go **southeast**, you travel toward the southeast. ❑ *I know we have to go southeast, more or less.* **4** ADV [ADV of n] Something that is **southeast of** a place is positioned to the south-east of it. ❑ *...a vessel that is believed to have sunk 500 miles southeast of Nova Scotia.* **5** ADJ [ADJ n] The **southeast** part of a place, country, or region is the part which is toward the southeast. ❑ *...rural southeast Kansas.* ❑ *...Southeast Asia.* **6** ADJ [ADJ n] A **southeast** wind is a wind that blows from the southeast. ❑ *Thick clothes keeping the chill southeast wind from freezing his bones.* **7** → See also color supplement

south|easter|ly /ˌsaʊθˈiːstərli/ ADJ [usu ADJ n] A **southeasterly** point, area, or direction is to the southeast or toward the southeast.

south|eastern /ˌsaʊθˈiːstərn/ ADJ **Southeastern** means in or from the southeast of a region or country. ❑ *...this city on the southeastern edge of the United States.*

south|er|ly /ˈsʌðərli/ **1** ADJ A **southerly** point, area, or direction is to the south or toward the south. ❑ *We set off in a southerly direction.* **2** ADJ A **southerly** wind is a wind that blows from the south. ❑ *...a strong southerly wind.*

south|ern ♦♦◇ /sʌðərn/ also **Southern** ADJ [ADJ n] **Southern** means in or from the south of a region, state, or country. ❏ *The Everglades National Park stretches across the southern tip of Florida.*

south|ern|er /sʌðərnər/ (**southerners**) N-COUNT A **southerner** is a person who was born in or lives in the south of a country. ❏ *Bob Wilson is a southerner, from Texas.*

south|ern|most /sʌðərnmoʊst/ ADJ [usu ADJ n] The **southernmost** part of an area or the **southernmost** place is the one that is farthest toward the south. ❏ *The ancient province of Satsuma lies in the southernmost part of the Japanese island of Kyushu.* ❏ *...Aswan, Egypt's southernmost city.*

south|paw /saʊθpɔ/ (**southpaws**) N-COUNT In sports such as boxing, baseball, football, and basketball, a **southpaw** is someone who mainly uses his left hand rather than his right hand. ❏ *Claussen was the league's best southpaw last season.*

South Pole N-PROPER [the N] The **South Pole** is the place on the surface of the earth which is farthest toward the south.

south|ward /saʊθwərd/ also **southwards** ADV [ADV after v] **Southward** or **southwards** means toward the south. ❏ *They drove southward.* ● ADJ **Southward** is also an adjective. ❏ *Instead of her normal southward course towards Alexandria and home, she headed west.*

south|west ♦♦◇ /saʊθwɛst/ **1** N-UNCOUNT [also the N] The **southwest** is the direction which is halfway between south and west. ❏ *...some 500 kilometers to the southwest of Johannesburg.* **2** N-SING The **southwest** of a place, country, or region is the part which is toward the southwest. ❏ *...the southwest of France.* **3** ADV [ADV after v] If you go **southwest**, you travel toward the southwest. ❏ *We took a plane southwest across the Anatolian plateau to Cappadocia.* **4** ADV [ADV of n] Something that is **southwest of** a place is positioned to the southwest of it. ❏ *It's some 65 miles southwest of Houston.* **5** ADJ [ADJ n] The **southwest** part of a place, country, or region is the part which is toward the southwest. ❏ *...a Labor Day festival in southwest Louisiana.* **6** ADJ [ADJ n] A **southwest** wind is a wind that blows from the southwest. ❏ *Then the southwest wind began to blow.* **7** → See also color supplement

south|wester|ly /saʊθwɛstərli/ ADJ [usu ADJ n] A **southwesterly** point, area, or direction is to the southwest or toward the southwest. ❏ *...the most southwesterly tip of Florida.*

south|western /saʊθwɛstərn/ ADJ **Southwestern** means in or from the southwest of a region or country. ❏ *...remote areas in the southwestern part of the country.*

sou|venir /suvənɪər/ (**souvenirs**) N-COUNT A **souvenir** is something which you buy or keep to remind you of a vacation, place, or event. ❏ *...a souvenir of the summer of 1992.*

sou'|west|er /saʊwɛstər/ (**sou'westers**) **1** N-COUNT A **sou'wester** is a waterproof hat that is worn especially by sailors in stormy weather. It has a wide brim at the back to keep your neck dry. **2** → See also color supplement

sov|er|eign /sɒvrɪn/ (**sovereigns**) **1** ADJ A **sovereign** state or country is independent and not under the authority of any other country. ❏ *Lithuania and Armenia signed a treaty in Vilnius recognizing each other as independent sovereign states.* **2** ADJ **Sovereign** is used to describe the person or institution that has the highest power in a country. ❏ *Sovereign power will continue to lie with the Supreme People's Assembly.* **3** N-COUNT A **sovereign** is a king, queen, or other royal ruler of a country. ❏ *In March 1889, she became the first British sovereign to set foot on Spanish soil.*

sov|er|eign|ty /sɒvrɪnti/ N-UNCOUNT **Sovereignty** is the power that a country has to govern itself or another country or state. ❏ *Concern to protect national sovereignty is far from new.*

So|vi|et /soʊviət, sɒv-/ (**Soviets**) **1** ADJ [usu ADJ n] **Soviet** is used to describe something that belonged or related to the former Soviet Union. ❏ *...the former Soviet empire.* **2** N-PLURAL The **Soviets** were the people of the former Soviet Union. ❏ *In 1957, the Soviets launched Sputnik 1 into outer space.* **3** N-COUNT A **soviet** was an elected local, regional, or national council in the former Soviet Union.

SOW
① VERB USES
② NOUN USE

① **sow** /soʊ/ (**sows, sowing, sowed, sown**) **1** V-T If you **sow** seeds or **sow** an area of land with seeds, you plant the seeds in the ground. ❏ *Sow the seed in a warm place in February/March.* **2** V-T If someone **sows** an undesirable feeling or situation, they cause it to begin and develop. ❏ *He cleverly sowed doubts into the minds of his rivals.* **3** PHRASE If one thing **sows the seeds of** another, it starts the process which leads eventually to the other thing. ❏ *Rich industrialized countries have sown the seeds of global warming.*

② **sow** /saʊ/ (**sows**) N-COUNT A **sow** is an adult female pig.

sown /soʊn/ **Sown** is the past participle of **sow**.

soy /sɔɪ/ N-UNCOUNT [usu N n] **Soy** flour, butter, or other food is made from soybeans. [AM] ❏ *Most breads, if they are not wheat flour, tend to be soy flour.*

in BRIT, use **soya**

soya /sɔɪə/ **1** N-UNCOUNT **Soya** is the same as **soy**. [BRIT] **2** → See feature box at **nutrition**

soya bean (**soya beans**) N-COUNT **Soya beans** are the same as **soybeans**. [BRIT]

soy|bean /sɔɪbin/ (**soybeans**) also **soy bean** N-COUNT **Soybeans** are beans that can be eaten or used to make flour, oil, or soy sauce. [AM]

in BRIT, use **soya beans**

soy sauce

in BRIT, also use **soya sauce**

N-UNCOUNT **Soy sauce** is a dark brown liquid made from soybeans and used as a flavoring, especially in Asian cooking.

spa /spɑ/ (**spas**) **1** N-COUNT A **spa** is a place where water with minerals in it comes out of the ground. People drink the water or go in it in order to improve their health. ❏ *...Fiuggi, a spa town famous for its water.* **2** N-COUNT A health **spa** is a kind of hotel where people go to exercise and have special treatments in order to improve their health. ❏ *There's also an excellent spa with a large pool, steam room, and sauna.* **3** N-COUNT A **spa** is a type of bathtub that can send out jets of water to massage your body. ❏ *...a large bathroom with a shower and a spa.*

space ♦♦◇ /speɪs/ (**spaces, spacing, spaced**) **1** N-VAR You use **space** to refer to an area that is empty or available. The area can be any size. For example, you can refer to a large area outside as a large open **space** or to a small area between two objects as a small **space**. ❏ *...cutting down yet more trees to make space for houses.* ❏ *I had plenty of space to write and sew.* ❏ *The space underneath could be used as a storage area.* **2** N-VAR A particular kind of **space** is the area that is available for a particular activity or for putting a particular kind of thing in. ❏ *...the high cost of office space.* ❏ *You don't want your living space to look like a bedroom.* **3** N-UNCOUNT If a place gives a feeling of **space**, it gives an impression of being large and open. ❏ *Large paintings can enhance the feeling of space in small rooms.* **4** N-UNCOUNT If you give someone **space** to think about something or to develop as a person, you allow them the time and freedom to do this. ❏ *You need space to think everything over.* **5** N-UNCOUNT The amount of **space** for a topic to be discussed in a document is the number of pages available to discuss the topic. ❏ *We can't promise to publish a reply as space is limited.* **6** N-SING A **space of** time is a period of time. ❏ *They've come a long way in a short space of time.* **7** N-UNCOUNT **Space** is the area beyond the Earth's atmosphere, where the stars and planets are. ❏ *The six astronauts on board will spend ten days in space.* ❏ *...launching satellites into space.* **8** N-UNCOUNT **Space** is the whole area within which everything exists. ❏ *She felt herself transcending time and space.* **9** V-T If you **space** a series of things, you arrange them so that they are not all together but have gaps or intervals of time between them. ❏ *Women once again are having fewer children and spacing them further apart.* ● PHRASAL VERB **Space out** means the same as **space**. ❏ *He talks quite slowly and spaces his words out.* ● **spac|ing** N-UNCOUNT ❏ *Generous spacing gives healthier trees and better crops.* **10** → see also **airspace, breathing space, outer space, spacing** **11** PHRASE If you are staring **into space**, you are looking straight in front of you, without actually looking at anything in particular, for example because you are thinking or because you are feeling shocked. ▫ *He just sat in the dressing room staring into space.*

VOCABULARY IN CONTEXT

Space

For hundreds of years, humans have **gazed** at the heavens and wondered about what they saw there. Early **astronomers** observed **celestial bodies** and plotted their movements through the sky. The invention of the **telescope** by Galileo meant that astronomers could observe **planets**, **comets**, and **asteroids** in more detail. Nowadays, the Hubble telescope **orbits** the Earth in the ionosphere. The fact that its view of the **solar system** and beyond is not obscured by our atmosphere means that it can take incredibly clear and detailed pictures, helping scientists discover distant, previously unknown solar systems, **black holes**, **galaxies**, and the mysterious '**dark matter**'. Since 1957, when Laika the dog became the first living creature to travel into space, all the way up to the present day, with the **international space station** that orbits the Earth, humans have made steady progress outwards and upwards. Who knows what will be conquered next? Perhaps Mars?

space age also **space-age** ◼ N-SING [*the* N] The **space age** is the present period in the history of the world, when travel in space has become possible. ◻ ADJ [usu ADJ n] You use **space-age** to describe something that is very modern and makes you think of the technology of the space age. ▫ *...a space-age tower of steel and glass.*

space|craft /speɪskræft/ (**spacecraft**)

Spacecraft is both the singular and the plural form.

◼ N-COUNT A **spacecraft** is a rocket or other vehicle that can travel in space. ▫ *...the world's largest and most expensive unmanned spacecraft.* ◻ → See feature box at **travel**

spaced-out also **spaced out** ADJ Someone who is **spaced-out** feels as if nothing around them is real, usually because they have taken drugs or because they are very tired. [INFORMAL] ▫ *He's got this spaced-out look.*

space flight (**space flights**) N-VAR A **space flight** is a trip into space. ▫ *She made her first and only space flight last September.*

space|man /speɪsmæn/ (**spacemen**) N-COUNT A **spaceman** is a male astronaut; used mainly by children.

space probe (**space probes**) N-COUNT A **space probe** is a spacecraft with no people in it which is sent into space in order to study the planets and send information about them back to earth.

space|ship /speɪsʃɪp/ (**spaceships**) N-COUNT A **spaceship** is a spacecraft that carries people through space. ▫ *...an alien spaceship.*

space shut|tle (**space shuttles**) N-COUNT A **space shuttle** or a **shuttle** is a spacecraft that is designed to travel into space and back to earth several times.

space sta|tion (**space stations**) ◼ N-COUNT A **space station** is a place built for astronauts to live and work in, which is sent into space and then keeps going around the earth. ◻ → See feature box at **space**

space|suit /speɪssuːt/ (**spacesuits**) also **space suit** N-COUNT A **spacesuit** is a special protective suit that is worn by astronauts in space.

space|walk /speɪswɔːk/ (**spacewalks**) also **space walk** N-COUNT When an astronaut goes on a **spacewalk**, he or she leaves the spacecraft and works outside it while floating in space.

space|woman /speɪswʊmən/ (**spacewomen**) N-COUNT A **spacewoman** is a female astronaut; used mainly by children.

spacey /speɪsi/ (**spacier, spaciest**) also **spacy** ◼ ADJ You can use **spacey** to describe things, especially music, which seem strange, especially because they are very modern or like things in a dream. [INFORMAL] ▫ *...brilliant, spacey guitar sounds.* ◻ ADJ Someone who is **spacey** does not seem to be fully aware of what is happening around them, often because they have been taking drugs. ▫ *The doctors gave me all these drugs that made me really spacey.*

spac|ing /speɪsɪŋ/ ◼ N-UNCOUNT **Spacing** refers to the way that typing or printing is arranged on a page, especially in relation to the amount of space that is left between words or lines. ▫ *Single spacing is used within paragraphs, double spacing between paragraphs.* ◻ → see also **space**

spa|cious /speɪʃəs/ ADJ A **spacious** room or other place is large in size or area, so that you can move around freely in it. ▫ *The house has a spacious kitchen and dining area.*

spacy /speɪsi/ [mainly BRIT] → see **spacey**

spade /speɪd/ (**spades**) ◼ N-COUNT A **spade** is a tool used for digging, with a flat metal blade and a long handle. ▫ *...a garden spade.* ◻ N-UNCOUNT-COLL **Spades** is one of the four suits in a deck of playing cards. Each card in the suit is marked with one or more black symbols: ♠. ▫ *...the ace of spades.* • N-COUNT A **spade** is a playing card of this suit. ▫ *He would have done better to play a spade now.* ◻ → See also color supplement

spa|ghet|ti /spəgɛti/ N-UNCOUNT **Spaghetti** is a type of pasta. It looks like long pieces of string and is usually served with a sauce.

spa|ghet|ti west|ern (**spaghetti westerns**) N-COUNT A **spaghetti western** is a movie made in Europe, usually by an Italian director, about life in the American Wild West. [INFORMAL]

spake /speɪk/ **Spake** is the very old-fashioned form of the past tense of **speak**.

spam /spæm/ (**spams, spamming, spammed**) ◼ V-T In computing, to **spam** people or organizations means to send unwanted email to a large number of them, usually as advertising. [COMPUTING] ▫ *...programs that let you spam the newspapers.* • N-VAR **Spam** is also a noun. ▫ *...a small group of people fighting the spam plague.* • **spam|mer** /spæmər/ (**spammers**) N-COUNT ▫ *The real culprits are the spammers.* ◻ → See feature box at **email**

span /spæn/ (**spans, spanning, spanned**) ◼ N-COUNT A **span** is the period of time between two dates or events during which something exists, functions, or happens. ▫ *The batteries had a life span of six hours.* ◻ N-COUNT Your concentration **span** or your attention **span** is the length of time you are able to concentrate on something or be interested in it. ▫ *His ability to absorb information was astonishing, but his concentration span was short.* ◼ V-T [no passive] If something **spans** a long period of time, it lasts throughout that period of time or relates to that whole period of time. ▫ *His professional career spanned 16 years.* ◼ V-T [no passive] If something **spans** a range of things, all those things are included in it. ▫ *Bernstein's compositions spanned all aspects of music, from symphonies to musicals.* ◼ N-COUNT [usu with supp] The **span** of something that extends or is spread out sideways is the total width of it from one end to the other. ▫ *It is a very pretty butterfly, with a 2 inch wing span.* ◼ V-T A bridge or other structure that **spans** something such as a river or a valley stretches right across it. ▫ *Travelers get from one side to the other by walking across a footbridge that spans a little stream.*

span|dex /spændɛks/ also **Spandex** N-UNCOUNT **Spandex** is a type of stretch fabric that is used to make sports clothing. ▫ *...spandex bike shorts.*

span|gle /spæŋɡəl/ (**spangles**) N-COUNT [usu pl] **Spangles** are small pieces of shiny metal or plastic which are used to decorate clothing or hair. ▫ *...robes that glittered with spangles.*

span|gled /spæŋɡᵊld/ ADJ Something that is **spangled** is covered with small shiny objects. ❑ ...spangled, backless dresses.

span|gly /spæŋɡli/ ADJ **Spangly** clothes are decorated with a lot of small shiny objects. ❑ He certainly liked spangly jackets.

Span|iard /spænyərd/ (**Spaniards**) N-COUNT A **Spaniard** is a Spanish citizen, or a person of Spanish origin.

span|iel /spænyəl/ (**spaniels**) N-COUNT A **spaniel** is a type of dog with long ears that hang down.

Span|ish /spænɪʃ/ ❶ ADJ [usu ADJ n] **Spanish** means belonging or relating to Spain, or to its people, language, or culture. ❑ ...a Spanish sherry. ❑ ...the Spanish ambassador. ❷ N-UNCOUNT **Spanish** is the main language spoken in Spain, and in many countries in South and Central America. ❸ N-PLURAL [usu the n] The **Spanish** are the people who come from Spain.

spank /spæŋk/ (**spanks, spanking, spanked**) V-T If someone **spanks** a child, they punish them by hitting them on the bottom several times with their hand. ❑ When I used to do that when I was a kid, my mom would spank me.

spank|ing /spæŋkɪŋ/ (**spankings**) ❶ N-COUNT If someone gives a child a **spanking**, they punish them by hitting them on the bottom several times with their hand. ❑ Andrea gave her son a sound spanking. ❷ ADV [ADV adj] If you describe something as **spanking** new, **spanking** clean, or **spanking** white, you mean that it is very new, very clean, or very white. [INFORMAL, EMPHASIS] ❑ ...a spanking new Mercedes.

span|ner /spænər/ (**spanners**) N-COUNT A **spanner** is the same as a **wrench**. [mainly BRIT]

spar /spɑr/ (**spars, sparring, sparred**) V-RECIP If you **spar** with someone, you box using fairly gentle blows instead of hitting your opponent hard, either when you are training or when you want to test how quickly your opponent reacts. ❑ He entered the ring to spar a few one-minute rounds with an old friend.

spare ♦◇◇ /spɛər/ (**spares, sparing, spared**) ❶ ADJ You use **spare** to describe something that is the same as things that you are already using, but that you do not need yet and are keeping ready in case another one is needed. ❑ If possible keep a spare pair of glasses accessible in case your main pair is broken or lost. ❑ He could have taken a spare key. • N-COUNT **Spare** is also a noun. ❑ Give me the trunk key and I'll get the spare. ❷ ADJ You use **spare** to describe something that is not being used by anyone, and is therefore available for someone to use. ❑ They don't have a lot of spare cash. ❑ The spare bedroom is on the second floor. ❸ V-I [only to-inf] If you have something such as time, money, or space **to spare**, you have some extra time, money, or space that you have not used or that you do not need. ❑ You got here with ninety seconds to spare. ❹ V-T If you **spare** time or another resource for a particular purpose, you make it available for that purpose. ❑ She said that she could only spare 35 minutes for our meeting. ❺ V-T [usu passive] If a person or a place **is spared**, they are not harmed, even though other people or places have been. [LITERARY] ❑ We have lost everything, but thank God, our lives have been spared. ❻ V-T If you **spare** someone an unpleasant experience, you prevent them from suffering it. ❑ I wanted to spare Frances the embarrassment of discussing this subject. ❑ Prisoners are spared the indignity of wearing uniforms. ❼ → see also **sparing** ❽ PHRASE If you **spare a thought for** an unfortunate person, you make an effort to think sympathetically about them and their bad luck. ❑ Spare a thought for the nation's shopkeepers – consumer sales slid again in May.

━━━━ SYNONYMS ━━━━

spare
ADJ ❶
extra: There's an extra blanket in the bottom drawer of the cupboard.
surplus: Few people have large sums of surplus cash.
leftover: ...leftover pieces of wallpaper.

spare part (**spare parts**) N-COUNT **Spare parts** are parts that you can buy separately to replace old or broken parts in a piece of equipment. They are usually parts that are designed to be easily removed or fitted. ❑ In the future the machines will need spare parts and maintenance.

spare room (**spare rooms**) N-COUNT A **spare room** is a bedroom which is kept especially for visitors to sleep in.

spare time N-UNCOUNT Your **spare time** is the time during which you do not have to work and you can do whatever you like. ❑ In her spare time she goes hillwalking.

spare tire (**spare tires**)

in BRIT, use **spare tyre**

❶ N-COUNT A **spare tire** is a wheel with a tire on it that you keep in your car in case you get a flat tire and need to replace one of your wheels. ❷ N-COUNT If you describe someone as having a **spare tire**, you mean that they are fat around the waist. [INFORMAL]

spar|ing /spɛərɪŋ/ ADJ Someone who is **sparing** with something uses it or gives it only in very small quantities. ❑ I'm never sparing with the garlic. • **spar|ing|ly** ADV [ADV after v] ❑ Medication is used sparingly.

spark ♦◇◇ /spɑrk/ (**sparks, sparking, sparked**) ❶ N-COUNT A **spark** is a tiny bright piece of burning material that flies up from something that is burning. ❑ The fire gradually got bigger and bigger. Sparks flew off in all directions. ❷ N-COUNT A **spark** is a flash of light caused by electricity. It often makes a loud sound. ❑ He passed an electric spark through a mixture of gases. ❸ V-I If something **sparks**, sparks of fire or light come from it. ❑ The wires were sparking above me. ❹ V-T If a burning object or electricity **sparks** a fire, it causes a fire. ❑ A dropped cigarette may have sparked the fire. ❺ N-COUNT A **spark** of a quality or feeling, especially a desirable one, is a small but noticeable amount of it. ❑ His music lacked that vital spark of imagination. ❻ V-T If one thing **sparks** another, the first thing cause the second thing to start happening. ❑ My teacher organized a unit on space exploration that really sparked my interest. • PHRASAL VERB **Spark off** means the same as **spark**. ❑ That incident sparked it off. ❼ PHRASE If **sparks fly** between people, they discuss something in an excited or angry way. ❑ They are not afraid to tackle the issues or let the sparks fly when necessary.

━━━━ COLLOCATIONS ━━━━

spark
NOUN ❺
adjective + **spark**: creative, definite, vital; missing
verb + **spark**: ignite, rekindle, provide; lack
VERB ❻
spark + noun: controversy, debate, interest, speculation; fury, outrage, protest, row
noun + **spark**: claim, comment, death, incident

spar|kle /spɑrkᵊl/ (**sparkles, sparkling, sparkled**) ❶ V-I If something **sparkles**, it is clear and bright and shines with a lot of very small points of light. ❑ The jewels on her fingers sparkled. ❑ His bright eyes sparkled. • N-UNCOUNT **Sparkle** is also a noun. ❑ ...the sparkle of colored glass. ❷ N-COUNT **Sparkles** are small points of light caused by light reflecting off a clear bright surface. ❑ ...sparkles of light. ❸ V-I Someone who **sparkles** is lively, intelligent, and witty. [APPROVAL] ❑ They positively sparkle, and are so full of life. • N-UNCOUNT **Sparkle** is also a noun. ❑ There was little sparkle in their performance. • **spar|kling** ADJ ❑ He is sparkling and versatile in front of the camera. ❹ → See feature box at **light**

spar|kler /spɑrklər/ (**sparklers**) N-COUNT A **sparkler** is a small firework that you can hold as it burns. It looks like a piece of thick wire and burns with a lot of small bright sparks.

spar|kling /spɑrklɪŋ/ ❶ ADJ **Sparkling** drinks are slightly carbonated. ❑ ...a glass of sparkling wine. ❷ → see also **sparkle**

spar|kly /spɑrkli/ (**sparklier, sparkliest**) ADJ **Sparkly** things sparkle. [INFORMAL] ❑ ...a sparkly toy necklace. ❑ Her eyes were sparkly.

spark plug (**spark plugs**) N-COUNT A **spark plug** is a device in the engine of a motor vehicle, which produces electric sparks to make the gasoline burn.

spar|ring part|ner (**sparring partners**) ❶ N-COUNT A boxer's **sparring partner** is another boxer who he or she fights regularly in training. ❷ N-COUNT Your **sparring partner** is a person with whom you regularly have friendly arguments.

spar|row /spæroʊ/ (**sparrows**) N-COUNT A **sparrow** is a small brown bird that is very common in the United States and in other parts of the world.

sparse /spɑrs/ (**sparser, sparsest**) ADJ Something that is **sparse** is small in number or amount and spread out over an area. ❑ Many slopes are rock fields with sparse vegetation. ❑ He was a tubby little man in his fifties, with sparse hair. • **sparse|ly** ADV ❑ ...the sparsely populated interior region, where there are few roads.

spar|tan /spɑːrtᵊn/ ADJ A **spartan** lifestyle or existence is very simple or strict, with no luxuries. ❑ Their spartan lifestyle prohibits a fridge or a phone.

spasm /spæzəm/ (spasms) N-VAR A **spasm** is a sudden tightening of your muscles, which you cannot control. ❑ A muscular spasm in the coronary artery can cause a heart attack.

spas|mod|ic /spæzmɒdɪk/ ADJ Something that is **spasmodic** happens suddenly, for short periods of time, and at irregular intervals. ❑ He managed to stifle the spasmodic sobs of panic rising in his throat.

spas|tic /spæstɪk/ (spastics) ADJ Someone who is **spastic** is born with a disability which makes it difficult for them to control their muscles, especially in their arms and legs. Most people now refer to someone with this disability as having cerebral palsy. [OFFENSIVE] • N-COUNT A **spastic** is someone who is spastic. [OFFENSIVE]

spat /spæt/ **Spat** is a past tense and past participle of **spit**.

spate /speɪt/ (spates) N-COUNT A **spate** of things, especially unpleasant things, is a large number of them that happen or appear within a short period of time. ❑ ...the recent spate of attacks on horses.

spa|tial /speɪʃᵊl/ **1** ADJ [ADJ n] **Spatial** is used to describe things relating to areas. ❑ ...the spatial distribution of employment and population in South Africa. **2** ADJ [ADJ n] Your **spatial** ability is your ability to see and understand the relationships between shapes, spaces, and areas. ❑ His manual dexterity and fine spatial skills were wasted on routine tasks.

spat|ter /spætər/ (spatters, spattering, spattered) V-T/V-I If a liquid **spatters** a surface or you **spatter** a liquid over a surface, drops of the liquid fall on an area of the surface. ❑ He stared at the rain spattering on the glass. ❑ Gently turn the fish, being careful not to spatter any hot butter on yourself.

-spattered /-spætərd/ COMB IN ADJ **-spattered** is added to nouns to form adjectives which indicate that a liquid has spattered onto something. ❑ ...the blood-spattered body.

spatu|la /spætʃələ/ (spatulas) **1** N-COUNT A **spatula** is an object with a handle and a wide, flat blade. Spatulas are used in cooking. ❑ Spoon the batter into the prepared pan, smoothing over the top with a spatula. **2** → See also color supplement

spawn /spɔːn/ (spawns, spawning, spawned) **1** N-UNCOUNT [usu n n] **Spawn** is a soft, jelly-like substance containing the eggs of fish, or of animals such as frogs. ❑ ...her passion for collecting frog spawn. **2** V-I When fish or animals such as frogs **spawn**, they lay their eggs. ❑ ...fish species like salmon and trout which go upstream, spawn and then die. **3** V-T If something **spawns** something else, it causes it to happen or to be created. [LITERARY] ❑ Tyndall's inspired work spawned a whole new branch of science.

spay /speɪ/ (spays, spaying, spayed) V-T [usu passive] When a female animal **is spayed**, it has its ovaries removed so that it cannot become pregnant. ❑ All bitches should be spayed unless being used for breeding.

speak ♦♦♦ /spiːk/ (speaks, speaking, spoke, spoken) **1** V-I When you **speak**, you use your voice in order to say something. ❑ He tried to speak, but for once, his voice had left him. ❑ I rang the hotel and spoke to Louie. ❑ She cried when she spoke of Oliver • **spo|ken** ADJ [ADJ n] ❑ ...a marked decline in the standards of written and spoken English. **2** V-I When someone **speaks** to a group of people, they make a speech. ❑ When speaking to the seminar Mr. Franklin spoke of his experience, gained on a recent visit to Trinidad. ❑ He's determined to speak at the Democratic Convention. **3** V-I If you **speak for** a group of people, you make their views and demands known, or represent them. ❑ He said it was the job of the Church to speak for the underprivileged. ❑ I speak for all 7,000 members of our organization. **4** V-T If you **speak** a foreign language, you know the language and are able to have a conversation in it. ❑ He doesn't speak English. **5** V-I People sometimes mention something that has been written by saying what the author **speaks of**.
❑ Throughout the book he speaks of the challenges his family has faced. **6** V-RECIP [with neg] If two people **are** not **speaking**, they no longer talk to each other because they have argued. ❑ He is not speaking to his mother because of her friendship with his ex-wife. **7** V-I

[no cont] If you say that something **speaks for** itself, you mean that its meaning or quality is so obvious that it does not need explaining or pointing out. ❑ ...the figures speak for themselves – bleak prospects at home and a worsening outlook for exports. **8** PHRASE If a person or thing **is spoken for** or **has been spoken for**, someone has claimed them or asked for them, so no one else can have them. ❑ He'd probably drop some comment about his 'partner' into the conversation so that he'd think he was already spoken for. **9** PHRASE If you **speak well of** someone or **speak highly of** someone, you say good things about them. If you **speak ill of** someone, you criticize them. ❑ Both spoke highly of the president. **10** PHRASE You use **so to speak** to draw attention to the fact that you are describing or referring to something in a way that may be amusing or unusual rather than completely accurate. ❑ I ought not to tell you but I will, since you're in the family, so to speak. **11 to speak your mind** → see **mind** ① **12 to speak volumes** → see **volume**

▶ **speak out** PHRASAL VERB If you **speak out** against something or in favor of something, you say publicly that you think it is bad or good. ❑ As tempers rose, he spoke out strongly against some of the radical ideas for selling off state-owned property.

▶ **speak up** **1** PHRASAL VERB If you **speak up**, you say something, especially to defend a person or protest about something, rather than just saying nothing. ❑ Uncle Herbert never argued, never spoke up for himself. **2** PHRASAL VERB [no cont] If you ask someone to **speak up**, you are asking them to speak more loudly. ❑ I'm quite deaf – you'll have to speak up. **3** → See feature box at **speak**

COLLOCATIONS

speak
VERB
2
speak + adverb: briefly, eloquently, exclusively, movingly; directly
4
speak + noun: English, French, language
speak + adverb: fluently, well

-speak /-spiːk/ COMB IN N-UNCOUNT **-speak** is used to form nouns which refer to the kind of language used by a particular person or by people involved in a particular activity. You use **-speak** when you disapprove of this kind of language because it is difficult for other people to understand. [DISAPPROVAL] ❑ Team building, motivation, and performance feature widely in modern business-speak.

speak|easy /spiːkiːzi/ (speakeasies) N-COUNT A **speakeasy** was a place where people could buy alcoholic drinks illegally in the United States between 1920 and 1933, when alcohol was forbidden.

speak|er ♦♢♢ /spiːkər/ (speakers) **1** N-COUNT A **speaker** at a meeting, conference, or other gathering is a person who is making a speech or giving a talk. ❑ Among the speakers at the gathering was Treasury Secretary Nicholas Brady. ❑ Bruce Wyatt will be the guest speaker at next month's meeting. **2** N-COUNT A **speaker** of a particular language is a person who speaks it, especially one who speaks it as their first language. ❑ ...in the Ukraine, where a fifth of the population are Russian speakers. **3** N-PROPER; N-VOC In the legislature or parliament of many countries, the **Speaker** is the person who is in charge of meetings. ❑ ...the Speaker of the House. **4** N-COUNT A **speaker** is a person who is speaking. ❑ From a simple gesture or the speaker's tone of voice, the Japanese listener gleans the whole meaning. **5** N-COUNT A **speaker** is a piece of electrical equipment, for example part of a radio or set of equipment for playing CDs or tapes, through which sound comes out. ❑ For a good stereo effect, the speakers should not be too wide apart.

COLLOCATIONS

speaker
NOUN **1**
noun + speaker: guest, keynote
adjective + speaker: after-dinner, public; inspirational, interesting, motivational
verb + speaker: invite; feature

---

speak|er|phone /spiːkərfoʊn/ (speakerphones) N-VAR A **speakerphone** is a telephone that has a microphone and a loudspeaker, allowing you to talk to someone without putting the phone to your ear, as well as allowing other people to hear the person you are talking to. ❑ ...a 10-channel cordless speakerphone with 13-number memory. ❑ She put me on speakerphone and he heard me talking.

speak|ing ✦✧ /spiːkɪŋ/ **1** N-UNCOUNT **Speaking** is the activity of giving speeches and talks. ❑ It would also train new union members in public speaking and decision-making. **2** PHRASE You can say '**speaking as a parent**' or '**speaking as a teacher**,' for example, to indicate that the opinion you are giving is based on your experience as a parent or as a teacher. ❑ Well, speaking as a journalist I'm dismayed by the amount of pressure there is for pictures of combat. **3** PHRASE You use **speaking** in expressions such as **generally speaking** and **technically speaking** to indicate which things or which particular aspect of something you are talking about. ❑ Generally speaking there was no resistance to the idea.

VOCABULARY IN CONTEXT

Speaking

It's a given that, in order for communication to be successful, we need to understand each other. **Communication breakdown** happens when there is a **language barrier**, or when people simply can't **see eye to eye**. But it also happens when people can't *hear* each other properly. Unclear **diction** often prevents understanding, so why do people **mumble**? Why take the trouble of saying something if you know you're being **indistinct**? Natural shyness, or having a lack of confidence, is one explanation. Having a **speech impediment**, such as a **stutter**, is another. To **speak up** and **enunciate** clearly doesn't come easily to everyone. However, it seems there is now a wilful tendency to **mutter**. Recently in the U.K., the BBC received hundreds of complaints about TV dramas in which it was difficult to follow the dialogue. Viewers complained that they had to **strain to hear** the actors who **murmured** all their lines. It seems to defeat the purpose.

-speaking /-spiːkɪŋ/ COMB IN ADJ [ADJ n] **-speaking** combines with nouns referring to languages to form adjectives which indicate what language someone speaks, or what language is spoken in a particular region. ❑ Lessons with English-speaking instructors can be booked and paid for in the resort. ❑ ...in the mainly French-speaking province of Quebec.

spear /spɪər/ (spears, spearing, speared) **1** N-COUNT A **spear** is a weapon consisting of a long pole with a sharp metal point attached to the end. **2** V-T If you **spear** something, you push or throw a pointed object into it. ❑ Spear a piece of fish with a carving fork and dip it in the batter.

spear|head /spɪərhɛd/ (spearheads, spearheading, spearheaded) V-T If someone **spearheads** a campaign or an attack, they lead it. [JOURNALISM] ❑ She is spearheading a nationwide campaign against domestic violence.

spear|mint /spɪərmɪnt/ N-UNCOUNT **Spearmint** is a plant whose leaves have a strong smell and taste. It is often used for as a flavoring, especially in toothpaste and chewing gum.

spec /spɛk/ (specs) **1** N-COUNT The **spec** for something, especially a machine or vehicle, is its design and the features included in it. [INFORMAL] ❑ The standard spec includes stainless steel holding tanks. **2** N-PLURAL [also a pair of n] Someone's **specs** are their glasses. [INFORMAL] ❑ She looked great in her new specs. **3** PHRASE If you do something **on spec**, you do it hoping to get something that you want, but without being asked or without being certain to get it. [INFORMAL] ❑ When searching for a job Adrian favors networking and writing letters on spec.

spe|cial ✦✦✦ /spɛʃəl/ (specials) **1** ADJ Someone or something that is **special** is better or more important than other people or things. ❑ You're very special to me, darling. ❑ My special guest will be Jerry Seinfeld. **2** ADJ [ADJ n] **Special** means different from normal. ❑ In special cases, deductions can be made for family members. ❑ So you didn't notice anything special about him? **3** ADJ [ADJ n] You use **special** to describe someone who is officially appointed or who has a particular position specially created for them. ❑ Due to his wife's illness, he returned to the State Department as special adviser to the president. **4** ADJ [ADJ n] You use **special** to describe something that relates to one particular person, group, or place. ❑ Every anxious person will have his or her own special problems or fears. **5** N-COUNT A **special** is a product, program, or meal which is not normally available, or which is made for a particular purpose. ❑ ...complaints about the Halloween special, "Ghostwatch." ❑ Grocery stores have to offer enough specials to bring people into the store.

SYNONYMS

special
ADJ **1**
extraordinary: She is an extraordinary musician.
exceptional: ...children with exceptional ability.
out of the ordinary: The boy's knowledge was out of the ordinary.

---

spe|cial edu|ca|tion N-UNCOUNT [oft N n] **Special education** is teaching for students with mental or physical disabilities who need extra help with their studies. ❑ The school has a special education section.

spe|cial ef|fect (special effects) N-COUNT In a movie, **special effects** are unusual pictures or sounds that are created by using special techniques. ❑ ...a Hollywood horror film with special effects that are not for the nervous.

spe|cial|ism /spɛʃəlɪzəm/ (specialisms) N-VAR **Specialism** is the same as **specialization**. [BRIT]

spe|cial|ist ✦✧ /spɛʃəlɪst/ (specialists) N-COUNT A **specialist** is a person who has a particular skill or knows a lot about a particular subject. ❑ Peckham, himself a cancer specialist, is well aware of the wide variations in medical practice.

spe|cial|ity /spɛʃiælɪti/ (specialities) N-COUNT A **speciality** is the same as a **specialty**. [mainly BRIT]

spe|cial|ize ✦✧ /spɛʃəlaɪz/ (specializes, specializing, specialized)

in BRIT, also use **specialise**

V-I If you **specialize in** a thing, you know a lot about it and concentrate a great deal of your time and energy on it, especially in your work or when you are studying or training. You also use **specialize** to talk about a restaurant which concentrates on a particular type of food. ❑ ...a University professor who specializes in the history of the Russian empire. ● **spe|ciali|za|tion** /spɛʃəlaɪzeɪʃən/ (specializations) N-VAR ❑ This degree offers a major specialization in social policy alongside a course in sociology.

spe|cial|ized /spɛʃəlaɪzd/

in BRIT, also use **specialised**

1 ADJ Someone or something that is **specialized** is trained or developed for a particular purpose or area of knowledge. ❑ Cocaine addicts get specialized support from knowledgeable staff. **2** → See feature box at **deforest**

spe|cial|ly /spɛʃəli/ **1** ADV If something has been done **specially** for a particular person or purpose, it has been done only for that person or purpose. ❑ ...a soap specially designed for those with sensitive skin. ❑ Patrick needs to use specially adapted computer equipment. **2** ADV **Specially** is used to mean more than usually or more than other things. [INFORMAL] ❑ Stay in bed extra late or get up specially early.

spe|cial needs N-PLURAL [oft N n] People with **special needs** are people who need special help or care, for example because they have a disability. ❑ ...a school for children with special needs.

spe|cial of|fer (special offers) N-COUNT A **special offer** is a product, service, or program that is offered at reduced prices or rates. ◻ *Ask about special offers on our new 2-week vacations.*

spe|cial|ty /spɛʃ°lti/ (specialties) **1** N-COUNT Someone's **specialty** is a particular type of work that they do most or do best, or a subject that they know a lot about. [AM] ◻ *His specialty is international law.*

> in BRIT, use **speciality**

2 N-COUNT A **specialty** of a particular place is a special food or product that is always very good there. [AM] ◻ *...seafood, paella, and other specialties.*

> in BRIT, use **speciality**

spe|cies ♦◇◇ /spiʃiz/ (species)

> Species is both the singular and the plural form.

N-COUNT A **species** is a class of plants or animals whose members have the same main characteristics and are able to breed with each other. ◻ *Pandas are an endangered species.*

SYNONYMS

species
NOUN
breed: *Certain breeds are more dangerous than others.*
variety: *She has 12 varieties of old-fashioned roses.*
class: *...the division of the stars into six classes of brightness.*

---

spe|cif|ic ♦♦◇ /spɪsɪfɪk/ **1** ADJ [ADJ n] You use **specific** to refer to a particular exact area, problem, or subject. ◻ *Massage may help to increase blood flow to specific areas of the body.* ◻ *There are several specific problems to be dealt with.* **2** ADJ If someone is specific, they give a description that is precise and exact. You can also use **specific** to describe their description. ◻ *She declined to be more specific about the reasons for the separation.* **3** ADJ Something that is **specific** to a particular thing is connected with that thing only. ◻ *Send your résumé with a cover letter that is specific to that particular job.* • COMB IN ADJ **Specific** is also used after nouns. ◻ *Most studies of trade have been country-specific.*

SYNONYMS

specific
ADJ
1
particular: *...if there are particular things you're interested in.*
special: *It requires a very special brand of courage to fight dictators.*
2
precise: *He was not clear on the precise nature of his mission.*
exact: *I don't remember the exact words.*
explicit: *...explicit references to age in recruitment advertising.*

---

spe|cifi|cal|ly ♦◇◇ /spɪsɪfɪkli/ **1** ADV [ADV with v] You use **specifically** to emphasize that something is given special attention and considered separately from other things of the same kind. [EMPHASIS] ◻ *...the first nursing home designed specifically for people with AIDS.* ◻ *We haven't specifically targeted school children.* **2** ADV [ADV with group] You use **specifically** to add something more precise or exact to what you have already said. ◻ *Death frightens me, specifically my own death.* ◻ *...the Christian, and specifically Protestant, religion.* **3** ADV [ADV adj] You use **specifically** to indicate that something has a restricted nature, as opposed to being more general in nature. ◻ *...a specifically female audience.* **4** ADV [ADV with v] If you state or describe something **specifically**, you state or describe it precisely and clearly. ◻ *I specifically asked for this steak rare.*

SYNONYMS

specifically
ADV
1
particularly: *Keep your office space looking good, particularly your desk.*
peculiarly: *Cricket is so peculiarly English.*
uniquely: *The problem isn't uniquely American.*
2
precisely: *We don't yet know precisely how many people were involved.*
exactly: *Exactly what are you looking for?*
explicitly: *The contract states explicitly that all content remains the property of the author.*

---

speci|fi|ca|tion /spɛsɪfɪkeɪʃ°n/ (specifications) N-COUNT A **specification** is a requirement which is clearly stated, for example about the necessary features in the design of something. ◻ *I'd like to buy some land and have a house built to my specification.*

spe|cif|ics /spɪsɪfɪks/ N-PLURAL The **specifics** of a subject are the details of it that need to be considered. ◻ *Things improved when we got down to the specifics.*

speci|fy /spɛsɪfaɪ/ (specifies, specifying, specified) **1** V-T If you **specify** something, you give information about what is required or should happen in a certain situation. ◻ *They specified a spacious entrance hall.* **2** V-T If you **specify** what should happen or be done, you explain it in an exact and detailed way. ◻ *Each recipe specifies the size of egg to be used.* ◻ *A new law specified that houses must be a certain distance back from the water.*

speci|men /spɛsɪmɪn/ (specimens) **1** N-COUNT [usu with supp] A **specimen** is a single plant or animal which is an example of a particular species or type and is examined by scientists. ◻ *200,000 specimens of fungus are kept at the Komarov Botanical Institute.* **2** N-COUNT [usu with supp] A **specimen** of something is an example of it which gives an idea of what the whole of it is like. ◻ *Job applicants have to submit a specimen of handwriting.* **3** N-COUNT A **specimen** is a small quantity of someone's urine, blood, or other body fluid which is examined in a medical laboratory, in order to find out if they are ill or if they have been drinking alcohol or taking drugs. ◻ *He refused to provide a specimen.*

spe|cious /spiʃəs/ ADJ Something that is **specious** seems to exist or be true, but is not real or true. [FORMAL] ◻ *It is unlikely that the Duke was convinced by such specious arguments.*

speck /spɛk/ (specks) **1** N-COUNT [oft N of n] A **speck** is a very small stain, mark, or shape. ◻ *He has even cut himself shaving. There is a speck of blood by his ear.* **2** N-COUNT [oft N of n] A **speck** is a very small piece of a powdery substance. ◻ *Billy leaned forward and brushed a speck of dust off his shoes.*

speck|led /spɛk°ld/ ADJ [usu ADJ n] A **speckled** surface is covered with small marks, spots, or shapes. ◻ *...a large brown speckled egg.* ◻ *The sky was speckled with stars.*

specs /spɛks/ → see **spec**

spec|ta|cle /spɛktək°l/ (spectacles) **1** N-COUNT A **spectacle** is a strange or interesting sight. ◻ *It was a spectacle not to be missed.* **2** N-VAR A **spectacle** is a grand and impressive event or performance. ◻ *Ninety-four thousand people turned up for the spectacle.* **3** N-PLURAL [also *a pair of* N] Glasses are sometimes referred to as **spectacles**. [OLD-FASHIONED] ◻ *He looked at me over the tops of his spectacles.*

spec|tacu|lar ♦◇◇ /spɛktækyələr/ (spectaculars) **1** ADJ Something that is **spectacular** is very impressive or dramatic. ◻ *...spectacular views of the Sugar Loaf Mountain.* • **spec|tacu|lar|ly** ADV ◻ *My turnover increased spectacularly.* **2** N-COUNT [usu n N] A **spectacular** is a show or performance which is very grand and impressive. ◻ *...a television spectacular.*

spec|ta|tor /spɛkteɪtər/ (spectators) **1** N-COUNT A **spectator** is someone who watches something, especially a sports event. ◻ *Thirty thousand spectators watched the final game.* **2** → See feature box at **Olympic Games**

spec|ta|tor sport (spectator sports) N-COUNT A **spectator sport** is a sport that is interesting and entertaining to watch. ◻ *The most popular spectator sport is football.*

spec|ter /spɛktər/ (specters)

> in BRIT, use **spectre**

N-COUNT [usu *the* N *of* n] If you refer to the **specter** of something unpleasant, you are referring to something that you are frightened might occur. ◻ *The arrests raised the specter of revenge attacks.*

spec|tra /spɛktrə/ **Spectra** is a plural form of **spectrum**.

spec|tral /spɛktrəl/ ADJ If you describe someone or something as **spectral**, you mean that they look like a ghost. [LITERARY] ◻ *She is compelling, spectral, fascinating, an unforgettably unique performer.*

spec|trum /spɛktrəm/ (spectra or spectrums) **1** N-SING The **spectrum** is the range of different colors which is produced when light passes through a glass prism or through a drop of water. A rainbow shows the colors in the spectrum. **2** N-COUNT A **spectrum** is a range of a particular type of thing. ▫ *She'd seen his moods range across the emotional spectrum.* ▫ *Politicians across the political spectrum have denounced the act.*

spec|u|late ✦◇◇ /spɛkyəleɪt/ (**speculates, speculating, speculated**) **1** V-T/V-I If you **speculate** about something, you make guesses about its nature or identity, or about what might happen. ▫ *Critics of the project speculate about how many hospitals could be built instead.* ▫ *The doctors speculate that he died of a cerebral hemorrhage caused by a blow on the head.* • **specu|la|tion** /spɛkyəleɪʃ°n/ (**speculations**) N-VAR ▫ *The president has gone out of his way to dismiss speculation over the future of the economy.* **2** V-I If someone **speculates** financially, they buy property, stocks, or shares, in the hope of being able to sell them again at a higher price and make a profit. ▫ *The banks made too many risky loans which now can't be repaid, and they speculated in property whose value has now dropped.* **3** → See feature box at **banking**

SYNONYMS
speculate
VERB **1**
guess: *You can only guess at what mental suffering they endure.*
surmise: *There's so little to go on, we can only surmise what happened.*
imagine: *'Was he meeting someone?'—'I imagine so.'*

specu|la|tive /spɛkyəleɪtɪv, -lətɪv/ ADJ A piece of information that is **speculative** is based on guesses rather than knowledge. ▫ *The papers ran speculative stories about the mysterious disappearance of Eddie Donagan.* **2** ADJ **Speculative** is used to describe activities which involve buying goods or shares, or buildings and properties, in the hope of being able to sell them again at a higher price and make a profit. ▫ *Thousands of retirees were persuaded to mortgage their homes to invest in speculative bonds.*

specu|la|tor /spɛkyəleɪtər/ (**speculators**) N-COUNT A **speculator** is a person who speculates financially. ▫ *He sold the contracts to another speculator for a profit.*

sped /spɛd/ **Sped** is a past tense and past participle of **speed**.

speech ✦✦◇ /spitʃ/ (**speeches**) **1** N-UNCOUNT **Speech** is the ability to speak or the act of speaking. ▫ *...the development of speech in children.* ▫ *Intoxication interferes with speech and coordination.* **2** N-SING Your **speech** is the way in which you speak. ▫ *His speech became increasingly thick and nasal.* **3** N-UNCOUNT **Speech** is spoken language. ▫ *He could imitate in speech or writing most of those he admired.* **4** N-COUNT A **speech** is a formal talk which someone gives to an audience. ▫ *She is due to make a speech on the economy next week.* ▫ *He delivered his speech in French.* **5** → see also **direct speech, indirect speech 6** → See feature box at **speak**

COLLOCATIONS
speech
NOUN
2
adjective + **speech**: slurred; clear, fluent
4
noun + **speech**: acceptance, conference, keynote, victory
adjective + **speech**: impassioned, motivational, rousing; inaugural, televised
verb + **speech**: deliver, give, make

speechi|fy|ing /spitʃɪfaɪɪŋ/ N-UNCOUNT **Speechifying** is the making of speeches, especially because you want to appear important. [DISAPPROVAL] ▫ *...five tedious days of speechifying and punditing.*

speech|less /spitʃlɪs/ ADJ If you are **speechless**, you are temporarily unable to speak, usually because something has shocked you. ▫ *Alex was almost speechless with rage and despair.*

speech thera|pist (**speech therapists**) N-COUNT A **speech therapist** is a person whose job is to help people to overcome speech and language problems.

speech thera|py N-UNCOUNT **Speech therapy** is the treatment of people who have speech and language problems. ▫ *A stammering child can benefit from speech therapy.*

speech|writ|er /spitʃraɪtər/ (**speechwriters**) N-COUNT A **speechwriter** is a person who writes speeches for important people such as politicians.

speed ✦✦◇ /spid/ (**speeds, speeding, sped** or **speeded**)

The form of the past tense and past participle is **sped** in meaning **5** but **speeded** for the phrasal verb.

1 N-VAR The **speed** of something is the rate at which it moves or travels. ▫ *He drove off at high speed.* ▫ *Wind speeds reached force five.* **2** N-COUNT The **speed** of something is the rate at which it happens or is done. ▫ *In the late 1850s the speed of technological change quickened.* **3** N-UNCOUNT **Speed** is very fast movement or travel. ▫ *Speed is the essential ingredient of all athletics.* ▫ *He put on a burst of speed.* **4** N-UNCOUNT **Speed** is a very fast rate at which something happens or is done. ▫ *I was amazed at his speed of working.* **5** V-I If you **speed** somewhere, you move or travel there quickly, usually in a vehicle. ▫ *Trains will speed through the tunnel at 186 mph.* **6** V-I [usu cont] Someone who is **speeding** is driving a vehicle faster than the legal speed limit. ▫ *This man was not qualified to drive and was speeding.* • **speed|ing** N-UNCOUNT ▫ *He was fined for speeding last year.* **7** N-UNCOUNT **Speed** is an illegal drug such as amphetamine which some people take to increase their energy and excitement. [INFORMAL] **8 to pick up speed** → see **pick**
▸ **speed up 1** PHRASAL VERB When something **speeds up** or when you **speed** it **up**, it moves or travels faster. ▫ *You notice that your breathing has speeded up a bit.* **2** PHRASAL VERB When a process or activity **speeds up** or when something **speeds** it **up**, it happens at a faster rate. ▫ *Job losses are speeding up.* ▫ *I had already taken steps to speed up a solution to the problem.*

-speed /-spid/ COMB IN ADJ **-speed** is used after numbers to form adjectives that indicate that a bicycle or car has a particular number of gears. ▫ *...a 10-speed bicycle.*

speed|boat /spidboʊt/ (**speedboats**) N-COUNT A **speedboat** is a boat that can go very fast because it has a powerful engine.

speed bump (**speed bumps**) **1** N-COUNT A **speed bump** is something that stops a person or thing from progressing. ▫ *It was little more than a speed bump – a minor distraction during my day.* **2** N-COUNT A **speed bump** is a raised part in a road that is designed to make the traffic travel more slowly.

speed cam|era (**speed cameras**) N-COUNT A **speed camera** is a camera positioned at the side of a road which automatically photographs vehicles that are going faster than is allowed. The photographs can be used as evidence in a court of law.

speed da|ting N-UNCOUNT **Speed dating** is a method of introducing unattached people to potential partners by arranging for them to meet a series of people on a single occasion. ▫ *If you're a busy person, looking to meet several potential mates at the same event, speed dating could be for you.*

speed dial (**speed dials**) N-VAR **Speed dial** is a facility on a telephone that allows you to call a number by pressing a single button rather than by dialing the full number. ▫ *Who's at the top of your speed-dial list?*

speed lim|it (**speed limits**) **1** N-COUNT The **speed limit** on a road is the maximum speed at which you are legally allowed to drive. ▫ *I was fined $158 for exceeding the speed limit by 15 mph.* **2** → See feature box at **drive**

speed|om|eter /spidɒmɪtər/ (**speedometers**) **1** N-COUNT A **speedometer** is the instrument in a vehicle which shows how fast the vehicle is moving. **2** → See also color supplement

speed|way /spidweɪ/ (**speedways**) **1** N-COUNT A **speedway** is a special track for car or motorcycle racing. [AM] **2** N-UNCOUNT **Speedway** is the sport of racing motorcycles on special tracks.

speedy /spidi/ (**speedier, speediest**) ADJ A **speedy** process, event, or action happens or is done very quickly. ▫ *We wish Bill a speedy recovery.* • **speedi|ly** ADV [ADV with v] ▫ *This review is being conducted as speedily as possible.*

spell ✦◇◇ /spɛl/ (**spells, spelling, spelled** or **spelt**) **1** V-T When you **spell** a word, you write or speak each letter in the word in the correct order. ▫ *He gave his name and then helpfully spelled it.* ▫ *How do you spell "potato"?* • PHRASAL VERB **Spell out** means the same as **spell**. ▫ *If I don't know a word, I ask them to spell it out for me.* **2** V-T/V-I [no cont] Someone who can **spell** knows the correct order of letters in words. ▫ *It's worrying how many students can't really spell properly.* ▫ *He can't even spell his own name.* **3** V-T [no cont] If something **spells** a particular outcome, often an unpleasant one, it suggests that this will be the

result. ❏ *If the irrigation plan goes ahead, it could spell disaster for the birds.* **4** N-COUNT A **spell** of a particular type of weather or a particular activity is a short period of time during which this type of weather or activity occurs. ❏ *There has been a long spell of dry weather.* **5** N-COUNT A **spell** is a situation in which events are controlled by a magical power. ❏ *They say she died after a witch cast a spell on her.* **6** → see also **spelling**
▶ **spell out** **1** PHRASAL VERB If you **spell** something **out**, you explain it in detail or in a very clear way. ❏ *Spelling out the terms and conditions helps to minimize the emotional fallout.* **2** → see **spell 1**

spell|bind|ing /spɛlbaɪndɪŋ/ ADJ [usu ADJ n] A **spellbinding** image or sound is one that is so fascinating that you can think about nothing else. ❏ *Gray describes in dramatic and spellbinding detail the lives of these five ladies.*

spell|bound /spɛlbaʊnd/ ADJ If you are **spellbound** by something or someone, you are so fascinated that you cannot think about anything else. ❏ *His audience had listened like children, spellbound by his words.*

spell-check (spell-checks, spell-checking, spell-checked) also **spell check** **1** V-T If you **spell-check** something you have written on a computer, you use a special program to check whether you have made any spelling mistakes. [COMPUTING] ❏ *This model allows you to spell-check over 100,000 different words.* **2** N-COUNT If you run a **spell-check** over something you have written on a computer, you use a special program to check whether you have made any spelling mistakes. [COMPUTING]

spell-checker (spell-checkers) also **spell checker** N-COUNT A **spell-checker** is a special program on a computer which you can use to check whether something you have written contains any spelling mistakes. [COMPUTING]

spell|er /spɛlər/ (spellers) N-COUNT [adj N] If you describe someone as a good or bad **speller**, you mean that they find it easy or difficult to spell words correctly. ❏ *I am an absolutely appalling speller.*

spell|ing /spɛlɪŋ/ (spellings) **1** N-COUNT A **spelling** is the correct order of the letters in a word. ❏ *In most languages adjectives have slightly different spellings for masculine and feminine.* **2** N-UNCOUNT **Spelling** is the ability to spell words in the correct way. It is also an attempt to spell a word in the correct way. ❏ *His spelling is very bad.* **3** → see also **spell**

spell|ing bee (spelling bees) N-COUNT A **spelling bee** is a competition in which children try to spell words correctly. Anyone who makes a mistake is out and the competition continues until only one person is left.

spelt /spɛlt/ **Spelt** is a past tense and past participle form of **spell**. [mainly BRIT]

spe|lunk|er /spɪlʌŋkər/ (spelunkers) N-COUNT A **spelunker** is someone who goes into underground caves and tunnels as a leisure activity. [AM]

in BRIT, use **potholer**

spe|lunk|ing /spɪlʌŋkɪŋ/ N-UNCOUNT **Spelunking** is the leisure activity of going into underground caves and tunnels. [AM]

in BRIT, use **potholing**

spend ◆◆◆ /spɛnd/ (spends, spending, spent) **1** V-T When you **spend** money, you pay money for things that you want or need. ❏ *By the end of the vacation I had spent all my money.* ❏ *Businessmen spend enormous amounts advertising their products.* **2** V-T If you **spend** time or energy doing something, you use your time or effort doing it. ❏ *Engineers spend much time and energy developing brilliant solutions.* **3** V-T If you **spend** a period of time in a place, you stay there for a period of time. ❏ *We spent the night in a hotel.* **4** → See feature box at **leisure, time**

spend|er /spɛndər/ (spenders) N-COUNT If a person or organization is a big **spender** or a compulsive **spender**, for example, they spend a lot of money or are unable to stop themselves from spending money. ❏ *The Swiss are Europe's biggest spenders on food.*

spend|ing mon|ey N-UNCOUNT **Spending money** is money that you have or are given to spend on personal things for pleasure, especially when you are on vacation. ❏ *Jo will use her winnings as spending money on her vacation to the Costa Brava.*

spend|thrift /spɛndθrɪft/ (spendthrifts) N-COUNT If you call someone a **spendthrift**, you mean that they spend too much money. [DISAPPROVAL] • ADJ [usu ADJ n] **Spendthrift** is also an adjective. ❏ *...his father's spendthrift ways.*

spent /spɛnt/ **Spent** is the past tense and past participle of **spend**.

sperm /spɜrm/ (sperms)

Sperm can also be used as the plural form.

1 N-COUNT A **sperm** is a cell which is produced in the sex organs of a male animal and can enter a female animal's egg and fertilize it. ❏ *Conception occurs when a single sperm fuses with an egg.* **2** N-UNCOUNT **Sperm** is used to refer to the liquid that contains sperm when it is produced. ❏ *...a sperm donor.*

sper|ma|to|zo|on /spɜrmətəzoʊɒn/ (spermatozoa /spɜrmətəzoʊə/) N-COUNT A **spermatozoon** is a sperm. [TECHNICAL]

sperm bank (sperm banks) N-COUNT A **sperm bank** is a place where sperm is frozen and stored so that it can be used to help women become pregnant.

sper|mi|ci|dal /spɜrmɪsaɪdəl/ ADJ [ADJ n] A **spermicidal** cream or jelly contains spermicide.

sper|mi|cide /spɜrmɪsaɪd/ (spermicides) N-MASS **Spermicide** is a substance that kills sperm. ❏ *Although most condoms contain spermicide, there are some manufactured without.*

sperm whale (sperm whales) N-COUNT A **sperm whale** is a large whale with a large head that has a section in it which contains oil.

spew /spyu/ (spews, spewing, spewed) V-T/V-I When something **spews** out a substance or when a substance **spews** from something, the substance flows out quickly in large quantities. ❏ *The volcano spewed out more scorching volcanic ashes, gases, and rocks.*

SPF /ɛs pi ɛf/ (SPFs) N-COUNT [usu before num] **SPF** is used before a number to indicate the degree of protection from the sun's rays that is provided by a sunscreen or similar product. The higher a product's SPF, the more protection it provides. SPF is an abbreviation for 'sun protection factor.' ❏ *First, use a high-quality sunscreen of at least SPF 15 or higher.* ❏ *However, today there are some products on the market that have SPFs as high as 50.*

sphere /sfɪər/ (spheres) **1** N-COUNT A **sphere** is an object that is completely round in shape like a ball. ❏ *Because the earth spins, it is not a perfect sphere.* **2** N-COUNT A **sphere** of activity or interest is a particular area of activity or interest. ❏ *...the sphere of international politics.*

spheri|cal /sfɛrɪkəl, sfɪər-/ ADJ Something that is **spherical** is round like a ball. [FORMAL] ❏ *...purple and gold spherical earrings.*

sphinc|ter /sfɪŋktər/ (sphincters) N-COUNT A **sphincter** is a ring of muscle that surrounds an opening to the body and that can tighten to close this opening. [TECHNICAL] ❏ *...the anal sphincter.*

sphinx /sfɪŋks/ (sphinxes) also **Sphinx** N-COUNT [usu the N in sing] The **sphinx** is a large ancient statue of a creature with a human head and a lion's body that stands near the pyramids in Egypt. In mythology, sphinxes gave people puzzles to solve, and so a person who is mysterious or puzzling is sometimes referred to as a **sphinx**.

spice /spaɪs/ (spices, spicing, spiced) **1** N-MASS A **spice** is a part of a plant, or a powder made from that part, which you put in food to give it flavor. Cinnamon, ginger, and paprika are spices. ❏ *...herbs and spices.* **2** V-T If you **spice** something that you say or do, you add excitement or interest to it. ❏ *They spiced their conversations and discussions with intrigue.* • PHRASAL VERB **Spice up** means the same as **spice**. ❏ *Her publisher wants her to spice up her stories with sex.*

spiced /spaɪst/ ADJ Food that is **spiced** has had spices or other strong-tasting foods added to it. ❏ *Every dish was served heavily spiced.*

spick-and-span /spɪk ənd spæn/ also **spick and span** ADJ [usu v-link ADJ] A place that is **spick-and-span** is very clean and neat. ❏ *The apartment was spick-and-span.*

spicy /spaɪsi/ (spicier, spiciest) ADJ **Spicy** food is strongly flavored with spices. ❏ *Thai food is hot and spicy.*

spi|der /spaɪdər/ (spiders) N-COUNT A **spider** is a small creature with eight legs. Most types of spiders make structures called webs in which they catch insects for food.

spi|dery /spaɪdəri/ ADJ [usu ADJ n] If you describe something such as handwriting as **spidery**, you mean that it consists of thin, dark, pointed lines. ☐ *He saw her spidery writing on the envelope.*

spiel /spiːl, ʃpiːl/ (spiels) N-COUNT Someone's **spiel** is a well-prepared speech that they make, and that they have usually made many times before, often in order to persuade you to buy something. [INFORMAL]

spif|fy /spɪfi/ (spiffier, spiffiest) ADJ Something that is **spiffy** is stylish and attractive and often new. Someone who looks **spiffy** is smartly and attractively dressed. [AM] ☐ *Customers are offered preapproved loans for a spiffy new vehicle.* ☐ *He is looking pretty spiffy in a white tux and black bow-tie.*

spig|ot /spɪgət/ (spigots) **1** N-COUNT A **spigot** is a faucet. [AM] ☐ *...lifeguards, trash cans, a volleyball net, and a spigot to rinse the sand off your feet.* **2** N-COUNT A **spigot** is a device that controls the flow of liquid from a container, especially a cask or barrel. ☐ *He opened a Kuwaiti oil spigot and polluted the waterway.*

spike /spaɪk/ (spikes) N-COUNT A **spike** is a long piece of metal with a sharp point. ☐ *...a 15-foot wall topped with iron spikes.*

spiked /spaɪkt/ **1** ADJ [usu ADJ n] Something that is **spiked** has one or more spikes on it. ☐ *...spiked railings.* **2** ADJ [usu ADJ n] If someone has **spiked** hair, their hair is short and sticks up all over their head. **3** → see also spike

spike heels N-PLURAL [also *a pair of* n] **Spike heels** are the same as stilettos. [AM]

spiky /spaɪki/ (spikier, spikiest) ADJ Something that is **spiky** has one or more sharp points. ☐ *Her short spiky hair is damp with sweat.*

spill /spɪl/ (spills, spilling, spilled or spilt) **1** V-T/V-I If a liquid **spills** or if you **spill** it, it accidentally flows over the edge of a container. ☐ *Seventy thousand tons of oil spilled from the tanker.* ☐ *He always spilled the drinks.* **2** N-COUNT A **spill** is an amount of liquid that has spilled from a container. ☐ *She wiped a spill of milkshake off the counter.* **3** V-T/V-I If the contents of a bag, box, or other container **spill** or **are spilled**, they come out of the container onto a surface. ☐ *A number of bags had split and were spilling their contents.* **4** V-I If people or things **spill** out of a place, they come out of it in large numbers. ☐ *Tears began to spill out of the boy's eyes.*

spill|age /spɪlɪdʒ/ (spillages) N-VAR If there is a **spillage**, a substance such as oil escapes from its container. **Spillage** is also used to refer to the substance that escapes. ☐ *...an oil spillage off the coast of Texas.*

spill|over /spɪloʊvər/ (spillovers) N-COUNT [usu with supp] A **spillover** is a situation or feeling that starts in one place but then begins to happen or have an effect somewhere else. ☐ *Some jobs are quite likely to have a negative spillover into family life.*

spilt /spɪlt/ **Spilt** is a past tense and past participle form of spill. [mainly BRIT]

spin /spɪn/ (spins, spinning, spun) **1** V-T/V-I If something **spins** or if you **spin** it, it turns quickly around a central point. ☐ *The latest disks, used for small portable computers, spin 3,600 times a minute.* ☐ *He spun the wheel sharply and made a U turn in the middle of the road.* • N-VAR **Spin** is also a noun. ☐ *This driving mode allows you to move off in third gear to reduce wheel-spin in icy conditions.* **2** V-I If your head **is spinning**, you feel unsteady or confused, for example because you are drunk, ill, or excited. ☐ *My head was spinning from the wine.* **3** N-SING If someone puts a certain **spin** on an event or situation, they interpret it and try to present it in a particular way. [INFORMAL] ☐ *He interpreted the vote as support for the constitution and that is the spin his supporters are putting on the results today.* **4** N-UNCOUNT In politics, **spin** is the way in which political parties try to present everything they do in a positive way to the public and the media. ☐ *The public is sick of spin and tired of promises.* **5** N-SING If you go for a **spin** or take a car for a **spin**, you make a short trip in a car just to enjoy yourself. ☐ *Tom Wright celebrated his 99th birthday by going for a spin in his sporty Mazda.* **6** V-T When people **spin**, they make thread by twisting together pieces of a fiber such as wool or cotton using a device or machine. ☐ *Michelle will also spin a customer's wool fleece to specification at a cost of $2.25 an ounce.* **7** N-UNCOUNT In a game such as tennis or baseball, if you put **spin** on a ball, you deliberately make it spin rapidly when you hit it or throw it. ☐ *He threw it back again, putting a slight spin on the ball.* **8** → See feature box at sewing

▶ **spin off** PHRASAL VERB To **spin off** something such as a company means to create a new company that is separate from the original organization. [BUSINESS] ☐ *He rescued the company and later spun off its textile division into a separate entity.*

▶ **spin out** PHRASAL VERB If you **spin** something **out**, you make it last longer than it normally would. ☐ *My wife's lawyer was anxious to spin things out for as long as possible.*

SYNONYMS

spin
VERB **1**
revolve: *Overhead, the fan revolved slowly.*
turn: *As the wheel turned, the potter shaped the clay.*
rotate: *Take each foot in both hands and rotate it to relax the ankle.*

---

spi|na bi|fi|da /spaɪnə bɪfɪdə/ N-UNCOUNT **Spina bifida** is a condition of the spine that some people are born with. It often makes them unable to use their legs.

spin|ach /spɪnɪtʃ/ N-UNCOUNT **Spinach** is a vegetable with large, dark green leaves.

spi|nal /spaɪnᵊl/ ADJ [ADJ n] **Spinal** means relating to your spine. ☐ *...spinal fluid.*

spi|nal col|umn (spinal columns) N-COUNT Your **spinal column** is your spine.

spi|nal cord (spinal cords) N-COUNT Your **spinal cord** is a thick cord of nerves inside your spine which connects your brain to nerves in all parts of your body.

spin|dle /spɪndᵊl/ (spindles) **1** N-COUNT A **spindle** is a rod in a machine, around which another part of the machine turns. **2** N-COUNT A **spindle** is a pointed rod which you use when you are spinning wool by hand. You twist the wool with the spindle to make it into a thread.

spin|dly /spɪndli/ (spindlier, spindliest) ADJ Something that is **spindly** is long and thin and looks very weak. ☐ *I did have rather spindly legs.*

spin doc|tor (spin doctors) N-COUNT In politics, a **spin doctor** is someone who is skilled in public relations and who advises political parties on how to present their policies and actions. [INFORMAL] ☐ *...two spin doctors in the majority leader's office.*

spine /spaɪn/ (spines) **1** N-COUNT Your **spine** is the row of bones down your back. ☐ *...injuries to his spine.* **2** N-COUNT The **spine** of a book is the narrow stiff part which the pages and covers are attached to. ☐ *...a book with "Lifestyle" on the spine.* **3** N-COUNT **Spines** are also long, sharp points on an animal's body or on a plant. ☐ *An adult hedgehog can boast 7,500 spines.* **4** → See also color supplement

spine-chilling ADJ [usu ADJ n] A **spine-chilling** movie or story makes you feel very frightened.

spine|less /spaɪnlɪs/ ADJ If you say that someone is **spineless**, you mean that they are afraid to take action or oppose people when they should. [DISAPPROVAL] ☐ *...bureaucrats and spineless politicians.*

spine-tingling ADJ A **spine-tingling** movie or piece of music is enjoyable because it causes you to feel a strong emotion such as excitement or fear. ☐ *...Martin Scorsese's spine-tingling and stylish thriller.*

spin|na|ker /spɪnəkər/ (spinnakers) N-COUNT A **spinnaker** is a large, light, triangular sail that is attached to the front mast of a boat.

spin|ner /spɪnər/ (spinners) **1** N-COUNT A **spinner** is a person who makes thread by spinning. **2** N-COUNT [usu supp n] A **spinner** is a cricketer who makes the ball spin when he or she bowls it so that it changes direction when it hits the ground or the bat.

spin|ney /spɪni/ (spinneys) N-COUNT A **spinney** is the same as a copse. [BRIT]

spin|ning wheel (spinning wheels) also **spinning-wheel** N-COUNT A **spinning wheel** is a wooden machine that

spinoff

people used in their homes to make thread from wool, in former times.

spin|off /spɪnɔf/ (spinoffs) **1** N-COUNT A **spinoff** is an unexpected but useful or valuable result of an activity that was designed to achieve something else. ❑ *The company put out a report on commercial spinoffs from its research.* **2** N-COUNT A **spinoff** is a book, film, or television series that comes after and is related to a successful book, film, or television series. ❑ *The film is a spinoff from the TV series "Sabrina The Teenage Witch."*

spin|ster /spɪnstər/ (spinsters) N-COUNT A **spinster** is a woman who has never been married; used especially when talking about an old or middle-aged woman. [OLD-FASHIONED]

WORD HISTORY

spinster

A **spinster** was originally a *spinner*, that is, a person – not necessarily a woman – whose occupation was spinning. It is said that a young woman was not considered fit to be a wife until she had spun a certain amount of household linen. Hence, the word came to designate an unmarried woman.

spiny /spaɪni/ ADJ A **spiny** plant or animal is covered with long sharp points. ❑ *...a spiny lobster.* ❑ *...a spiny cactus.*

spi|ral /spaɪrəl/ (spirals, spiraling or spiralling, spiraled or spiralled) **1** N-COUNT A **spiral** is a shape which winds around and around, with each curve above or outside the previous one. ❑ *The maze is actually two interlocking spirals.* • ADJ [ADJ n] **Spiral** is also an adjective. ❑ *...a spiral staircase.* **2** V-T/V-I If something **spirals** or **is spiraled** somewhere, it grows or moves in a spiral curve. ❑ *Vines spiraled upward toward the roof.* ❑ *The aircraft began spiraling out of control.* • N-COUNT **Spiral** is also a noun. ❑ *Larks were rising in spirals from the ridge.* **3** V-I If an amount or level **spirals**, it rises quickly and at an increasing rate. ❑ *Production costs began to spiral.* ❑ *...spiraling health care costs.* • N-SING **Spiral** is also a noun. ❑ *...an inflationary spiral.* **4** V-I If an amount or level **spirals** downward, it falls quickly and at an increasing rate. ❑ *House prices will continue to spiral downwards.* • N-SING **Spiral** is also a noun. ❑ *...a spiral of debt.*

spire /spaɪər/ (spires) N-COUNT The **spire** of a building such as a church is the tall pointed structure on the top. ❑ *...a church spire poking above the trees.*

spir|it ✦✧✧ /spɪrɪt/ (spirits) **1** N-SING Your **spirit** is the part of you that is not physical and that consists of your character and feelings. ❑ *The human spirit is virtually indestructible.* **2** N-COUNT A person's **spirit** is the nonphysical part of them that is believed to remain alive after their death. ❑ *His spirit has left him and all that remains is the shell of his body.* **3** N-COUNT A **spirit** is a ghost or supernatural being. ❑ *In the Middle Ages branches were hung outside country houses as a protection against evil spirits.* **4** N-UNCOUNT **Spirit** is the courage and determination that helps people to survive in difficult times and to keep their way of life and their beliefs. ❑ *She was a very brave girl and everyone who knew her admired her spirit.* **5** N-UNCOUNT **Spirit** is the liveliness and energy that someone shows in what they do. ❑ *They played with spirit.* **6** N-SING The **spirit** in which you do something is the attitude you have when you are doing it. ❑ *Their problem can only be solved in a spirit of compromise.* **7** N-UNCOUNT A particular kind of **spirit** is the feeling of loyalty to a group that is shared by the people who belong to the group. ❑ *There is a great sense of team spirit in the squad.* **8** N-SING A particular kind of **spirit** is the set of ideas, beliefs, and aims that are held by a group of people. ❑ *...the real spirit of the anti-war movement.* **9** N-SING The **spirit of** something such as a law or an agreement is the way that it was intended to be interpreted or applied. ❑ *The requirement for work permits violates the spirit of the 1950 treaty.* **10** N-COUNT You can refer to a person as a particular kind of **spirit** if they show a certain characteristic or if they show a lot of enthusiasm in what they are doing. ❑ *I like to think of myself as a free spirit.* **11** N-PLURAL Your **spirits** are your feelings at a particular time, especially feelings of happiness or unhappiness. ❑ *At supper, everyone was in high spirits.* **12** N-PLURAL **Spirits** are strong alcoholic drinks such as whiskey and gin. ❑ *The only problem here is that they don't serve beer - only wine and spirits.*

COLLOCATIONS

spirit
NOUN
8
adjective + **spirit**: adventurous, competitive, entrepreneurial
7
noun + **spirit**: community, team
verb + **spirit**: embody, enter into, foster
11
adjective + **spirits**: good, high, low
verb + **spirits**: dampen, lift, raise

spir|it|ed /spɪrɪtɪd/ **1** ADJ A **spirited** action shows great energy and courage. ❑ *This television program provoked a spirited debate.* **2** ADJ A **spirited** person is very active, lively, and confident. ❑ *He was by nature a spirited little boy.*

-spirited /-spɪrɪtɪd/ **1** COMB IN ADJ **-spirited** combines with adjectives to describe a person's character, attitude, or behavior. For example, a **mean-spirited** person behaves in a way that is unkind to other people; a **free-spirited** person behaves freely and does as they please. ❑ *That's a mean-spirited thing for a mother to say.* ❑ *Murray was an affable, free-spirited man.* **2** → see also **high-spirited**, **public-spirited**

spir|it|less /spɪrɪtləs/ ADJ If someone is **spiritless**, they lack energy, courage, and liveliness. ❑ *They were too spiritless even to resist.*

spir|it lev|el [BRIT] → see **level 6**

spir|itu|al ✦✧✧ /spɪrɪtʃuəl/ **1** ADJ **Spiritual** means relating to people's thoughts and beliefs, rather than to their bodies and physical surroundings. ❑ *She lived entirely by spiritual values, in a world of poetry and imagination.* • **spir|itu|al|ly** ADV ❑ *Our whole program is spiritually oriented but not religious.* • **spir|itu|al|ity** /spɪrɪtʃuæliti/ N-UNCOUNT ❑ *...the peaceful spirituality of Japanese culture.* **2** ADJ **Spiritual** means relating to people's religious beliefs. ❑ *He is the spiritual leader of the world's Catholics.*

spir|itu|al|ism /spɪrɪtʃuəlɪzəm/ N-UNCOUNT **Spiritualism** is the belief that the spirits of people who are dead can communicate with people who are still alive. • **spir|itu|al|ist** (spiritualists) N-COUNT ❑ *He was a poet and an ardent spiritualist.*

spit /spɪt/ (spits, spitting, spit or spat) **1** N-UNCOUNT **Spit** is the watery liquid produced in your mouth. You usually use **spit** to refer to an amount of it that has been forced out of someone's mouth. ❑ *A trickle of spit collected at the corner of her mouth.* **2** V-I If someone **spits**, they force an amount of liquid out of their mouth, often to show hatred or contempt. ❑ *The gang thought of hitting him too, but decided just to spit.* ❑ *They spat at me and taunted me.* **3** V-T If you **spit** liquid or food somewhere, you force a small amount of it out of your mouth. ❑ *Spit out that gum and pay attention.* **4** N-COUNT A **spit** is a long rod which is pushed through a piece of meat and hung over an open fire to cook the meat. ❑ *She roasted the meat on a spit.* **5** PHRASE If you say that one person is **the spitting image of** another, you mean that they look very similar. [INFORMAL] ❑ *Nina looks the spitting image of Sissy Spacek.* **6** → See feature box at **onomatopoeia**

spite ✦✧✧ /spaɪt/ **1** PHRASE You use **in spite of** to introduce a fact which makes the rest of the statement you are making seem surprising. ❑ *He was hired in spite of the fact he had no experience.* **2** PHRASE If you do something **in spite of** yourself, you do it although you did not really intend to or expect to. ❑ *The blunt comment made Richard laugh in spite of himself.* **3** N-UNCOUNT If you do something cruel **out of spite**, you do it because you want to hurt or upset someone. ❑ *I refused her a divorce, out of spite I suppose.* **4** V-T [only to-inf] If you do something cruel to **spite** someone, you do it in order to hurt or upset them. ❑ *Pantelaras was giving his art collection away for nothing, to spite Marie and her husband.*

USAGE

in spite of
Don't use 'in spite of' as a conjunction. Don't say, for example, '~~In spite of we protested, they took him away.~~' Say '**Although** we protested, they took him away.' *Although he was late, he stopped to buy a sandwich.*

spite|ful /spaɪtfəl/ ADJ Someone who is **spiteful** does cruel things to hurt people they dislike. ▫ *He could be spiteful.* ▫ *...a stream of spiteful telephone calls.* • **spite|ful|ly** ADV [ADV with v] ▫ *We crept into our little sister's bedroom and spitefully defaced her posters.*

spit|tle /spɪtᵊl/ N-UNCOUNT **Spittle** is the watery liquid which is produced in your mouth. [OLD-FASHIONED] ▫ *Spittle oozed down his jaw.*

splash /splæʃ/ (splashes, splashing, splashed) **1** V-I If you **splash** around or **splash** about in water, you hit or disturb the water in a noisy way, causing some of it to fly up into the air. ▫ *A lot of people were in the water, swimming or simply splashing about.* ▫ *She could hear the voices of her friends as they splashed in a nearby rock pool.* **2** V-T/V-I If you **splash** a liquid somewhere or if it **splashes**, it hits someone or something and scatters in a lot of small drops. ▫ *He closed his eyes tight, and splashed the water on his face.* ▫ *A little wave, the first of many, splashed in my face.* **3** N-SING A **splash** is the sound made when something hits water or falls into it. ▫ *There was a splash and something fell clumsily into the water.* **4** N-COUNT A **splash** of a liquid is a small quantity of it that falls on something or is added to something. ▫ *Wallcoverings and floors should be able to withstand steam and splashes.* **5** N-COUNT A **splash** of color is an area of a bright color which contrasts strongly with the colors around it. ▫ *...shady walks punctuated by splashes of color.* **6** V-T If a magazine or newspaper **splashes** a story, it prints it in such a way that it is very noticeable. ▫ *The newspapers splashed the story all over their front pages.* **7** PHRASE If you **make a splash**, you become noticed or become popular because of something that you have done. ▫ *Now she's made a splash in the television show "Civil Wars."* **8** → See feature box at **onomatopoeia**

splash|down /splæʃdaʊn/ (splashdowns) N-COUNT A **splashdown** is the landing of a spacecraft in the sea after a flight.

splat /splæt/ N-SING; SOUND **Splat** is used to describe the sound of something wet hitting a surface with a lot of force. ▫ *The egg landed on my cheek with a splat.*

splat|ter /splætər/ (splatters, splattering, splattered) V-T/V-I If a thick wet substance **splatters** on something or is **splattered** on it, it drops or is thrown over it. ▫ *The rain splattered against the windows.* ▫ *"Sorry Edward," I said, splattering the cloth with jam.*

splay /spleɪ/ (splays, splaying, splayed) If things **splay** or are **splayed**, their ends are spread out away from each other. ▫ *He splayed his fingers across his face.* ▫ *His fingers splay out in a star shape.* ▫ *He was on his stomach, his legs splayed apart.*

spleen /splin/ (spleens) **1** N-COUNT Your **spleen** is an organ near your stomach that controls the quality of your blood. **2** N-UNCOUNT [usu poss N] **Spleen** is great and bitter anger. [FORMAL] ▫ *Her latest blog vents her spleen against everything she hates about society.* **3** → See feature box at **body**

splen|did /splɛndɪd/ ADJ If you say that something is **splendid**, you mean that it is very good. ▫ *The book includes a wealth of splendid photographs.* • **splen|did|ly** ADV [ADV with v] ▫ *I have heard him tell people that we get along splendidly.*

splen|dor /splɛndər/ (splendors)

in BRIT, use **splendour**

1 N-UNCOUNT The **splendor** of something is its beautiful and impressive appearance. ▫ *She gazed down upon the nighttime splendor of the city.* **2** N-PLURAL The **splendors** of a place or way of life are its beautiful and impressive features. ▫ *...such splendors as the Acropolis and the Parthenon.*

splice /splaɪs/ (splices, splicing, spliced) V-T If you **splice** two pieces of rope, film, or tape together, you join them neatly at the ends so that they make one continuous piece. ▫ *He taught me to edit and splice film.*

spliff /splɪf/ (spliffs) N-COUNT A **spliff** is a cigarette which contains hashish or marijuana. [INFORMAL]

splint /splɪnt/ (splints) N-COUNT A **splint** is a long piece of wood or metal that is fastened to a broken arm, leg, or back to keep it still.

splin|ter /splɪntər/ (splinters, splintering, splintered) **1** N-COUNT A **splinter** is a very thin, sharp piece of wood, glass, or other hard substance, which has broken off from a larger piece. ▫ *...splinters of glass.* **2** V-T/V-I If something **splinters** or is **splintered**, it breaks into thin, sharp pieces. ▫ *The ruler cracked and splintered into pieces.*

splin|ter group (splinter groups) N-COUNT A **splinter group** is a group of people who break away from a larger group and form a separate organization, usually because they no longer agree with the views of the larger group.

split ✦✧ /splɪt/ (splits, splitting)

> The form **split** is used in the present tense and is the past tense and past participle of the verb.

1 V-T/V-I If something **splits** or if you **split** it, it is divided into two or more parts. ▫ *In a severe gale the ship split in two.* ▫ *If the chicken is fairly small, you may simply split it in half.* **2** V-T/V-I If an organization **splits** or is **split**, one group of members disagree strongly with the other members, and may form a group of their own. ▫ *Yet it is feared the Republican leadership could split over the agreement.* • ADJ **Split** is also an adjective. ▫ *The Kremlin is deeply split in its approach to foreign policy.* **3** N-COUNT A **split** in an organization is a disagreement between its members. ▫ *They accused both radicals and conservatives of trying to provoke a split in the party.* **4** N-SING A **split** between two things is a division or difference between them. ▫ *...a split between what is thought and what is felt.* **5** V-T/V-I If something such as wood or a piece of clothing **splits** or is **split**, a long crack or tear appears in it. ▫ *The seat of his gray pants split.* **6** N-COUNT A **split** is a long crack or tear. ▫ *The plastic-covered seat has a few small splits around the corners.* **7** V-T If two or more people **split** something, they share it between them. ▫ *I would rather pay for a meal than watch nine friends pick over and split a bill.*

▶ **split up** **1** PHRASAL VERB If two people **split up**, or if someone or something **splits** them **up**, they end their relationship or marriage. ▫ *Research suggests that children whose parents split up are more likely to drop out of high school.* ▫ *I was beginning to think that nothing could ever split us up.* **2** PHRASAL VERB If a group of people **split up** or are **split up**, they go away in different directions. ▫ *Did the two of you split up in the woods?* ▫ *This situation has split up the family.* **3** PHRASAL VERB If you **split** something **up**, or if it **splits up**, you divide it so that it is in a number of smaller separate sections. ▫ *Any thought of splitting up the company was unthinkable, they said.* ▫ *Even though museums have begged to borrow her collection, she could never split it up.*

split ends N-PLURAL If you have **split ends**, some of your hairs are split at the ends because they are dry or damaged.

split in|fini|tive (split infinitives) N-COUNT A **split infinitive** is a structure in which an adverb is put between 'to' and the infinitive of a verb, as in 'to really experience it.' Some people think it is incorrect to use split infinitives.

split-level ADJ [usu ADJ n] A **split-level** house or room has part of the ground floor at a different level from another part, usually because the house has been built on ground that slopes.

split per|son|al|ity (split personalities) N-COUNT If you say that someone has a **split personality**, you mean that their moods can change so much that they seem to have two separate personalities.

split-screen (split-screens) **1** ADJ [usu ADJ n] **Split-screen** is used to describe the technique in making movies and television programs in which two different pieces of film are shown at the same time. ▫ *...split-screen movies.* **2** N-COUNT [oft N n] On a computer screen, a **split-screen** is a display of two different things in separate parts of the screen.

split sec|ond also split-second **1** N-SING A **split second** is an extremely short period of time. ▫ *Her gaze met Michael's for a split second.* ▫ *In law enforcement, we have to make split-second decisions.* **2** → See feature box at **brain**

split|ting /splɪtɪŋ/ ADJ [ADJ n] A **splitting** headache is a very severe and painful one.

splodge /splɒdʒ/ (splodges) N-COUNT A **splodge** is the same as a **splotch**. [BRIT]

splotch /splɒtʃ/ (splotches) N-COUNT A **splotch** is a large uneven mark or stain, especially one that has been caused by a liquid. [mainly AM]

in BRIT, usually use **splodge**

splurge /splɜrdʒ/ (splurges, splurging, splurged) **1** V-I If you **splurge on** something, you spend a lot of money, usually on things that you do not need. ❑ *We splurged on Bohemian glass for gifts, and for ourselves.* **2** → See feature box at **finance**

splut|ter /splʌtər/ (splutters, spluttering, spluttered) **1** V-T/V-I If someone **splutters**, they make short sounds and have difficulty speaking clearly, for example because they are embarrassed or angry. ❑ *"But it cannot be," he spluttered.* **2** V-I If something **splutters**, it makes a series of short, sharp sounds. ❑ *Suddenly the engine coughed, spluttered, and died.*

spoil /spɔɪl/ (spoils, spoiling, spoiled or spoilt) **1** V-T If you **spoil** something, you prevent it from being successful or satisfactory. ❑ *It's important not to let mistakes spoil your life.* **2** V-T If you **spoil** children, you give them everything they want or ask for. This is considered to have a bad effect on a child's character. ❑ *Grandparents are often tempted to spoil their grandchildren whenever they come to visit.* **3** V-T If you **spoil** yourself or **spoil** another person, you give yourself or them something nice as a treat or do something special for them. ❑ *Spoil yourself with a new perfume this summer.* **4** V-T/V-I If food **spoils** or if it **is spoiled**, it is no longer fit to be eaten. ❑ *We all know that fats spoil by becoming rancid.* **5** PHRASE If you say that someone is **spoiled for choice** or **spoilt for choice**, you mean that they have a great many things of the same type to choose from. [mainly BRIT]

spoil|age /spɔɪlɪdʒ/ N-UNCOUNT When **spoilage** occurs, something, usually food, decays or is harmed, so that it is no longer fit to be used. [TECHNICAL]

spoil|er /spɔɪlər/ (spoilers) **1** N-COUNT If you describe someone or something as a **spoiler**, you mean that they try to spoil the performance of other people or things. ❑ *I was a talentless spoiler. If I couldn't be good, why should they?* **2** N-COUNT A **spoiler** is an object which forms part of an aircraft's wings or part of the body of a car. It changes the flow of air around the vehicle, allowing an aircraft to change direction or making a car's forward movement more efficient. **3** → See also color supplement

spoil|sport /spɔɪlspɔrt/ (spoilsports) N-COUNT If you say that someone is a **spoilsport**, you mean that they are behaving in a way that ruins other people's pleasure or enjoyment. [INFORMAL, DISAPPROVAL]

spoilt /spɔɪlt/ Spoilt is a past participle and past tense of **spoil**. [BRIT]

spoke /spoʊk/ (spokes) **1** Spoke is the past tense of **speak**. **2** N-COUNT [usu pl] The **spokes** of a wheel are the bars that connect the outer ring to the center. **3** → See also color supplement

spo|ken /spoʊkən/ Spoken is the past participle of **speak**.

-spoken /-spoʊkən/ COMB IN ADJ **-spoken** combines with adverbs and adjectives to form adjectives which indicate how someone speaks. ❑ *The woman was smartly dressed and well-spoken.* ❑ *...a soft-spoken man in his early thirties.*

spo|ken word N-SING [usu the N] The **spoken word** is used to refer to language expressed in speech, for example in contrast to written texts or music. ❑ *There is a potential educational benefit in allowing pictures to tell the story, rather than the spoken word.*

spokes|man /spoʊksmən/ (spokesmen) N-COUNT A **spokesman** is a male spokesperson. ❑ *A UN spokesman said that the mission will carry 20 tons of relief supplies.*

spokes|person /spoʊkspɜrsən/ (spokespersons or spokespeople) N-COUNT A **spokesperson** is a person who speaks as the representative of a group or organization. ❑ *A spokesperson for Amnesty, Norma Johnston, describes some cases.*

spokes|woman /spoʊkswʊmən/ (spokeswomen) N-COUNT A **spokeswoman** is a female spokesperson. ❑ *A United Nations spokeswoman in New York said the request would be considered.*

sponge /spʌndʒ/ (sponges, sponging, sponged) **1** N-COUNT **Sponge** is a very light soft substance with lots of little holes in it, which can be either artificial or natural. It is used to clean things or as a soft layer. ❑ *...a sponge mattress.* **2** N-COUNT A **sponge** is a piece of sponge that you use for washing yourself or for cleaning things. ❑ *He wiped off the table with a sponge.* **3** V-T If you **sponge** something, you clean it by wiping it with a wet sponge. ❑ *Fill a bowl with water and gently sponge your face and body.* • PHRASAL VERB **Sponge down** means the same as **sponge**. ❑ *If your child's temperature rises, sponge her down gently with tepid water.* **4** V-I If you say that someone **sponges off** other people or **sponges on** them, you mean that they regularly get money from other people when they should be trying to support themselves. [INFORMAL, DISAPPROVAL] ❑ *He should just get an honest job and stop sponging off the rest of us!* **5** N-VAR A **sponge** is a light cake or pudding made from flour, eggs, sugar, and sometimes shortening. [BRIT]

in AM, use **sponge cake**

sponge cake (sponge cakes) N-VAR A **sponge cake** is a very light cake made from flour, eggs, and sugar, usually without any shortening.

spong|er /spʌndʒər/ (spongers) N-COUNT If you describe someone as a **sponger**, you mean that they sponge off other people or organizations. [INFORMAL, DISAPPROVAL]

spon|gy /spʌndʒi/ (spongier, spongiest) ADJ Something that is **spongy** is soft and can be pressed in, like a sponge. ❑ *The earth was spongy from rain.*

spon|sor ♦♦◊ /spɒnsər/ (sponsors, sponsoring, sponsored) **1** V-T If an organization or an individual **sponsors** something such as an event or someone's training, they pay some or all of the expenses connected with it, often in order to get publicity for themselves. ❑ *Dozens of companies, including Hewlett-Packard, are sponsoring the event.* **2** V-T If you **sponsor** someone who is doing something to raise money for charity, for example trying to walk a certain distance, you agree to give them a sum of money for the charity if they succeed in doing it. ❑ *Could you sponsor me for next year's marathon?* **3** V-T If you **sponsor** a proposal or suggestion, you officially put it forward and support it. ❑ *Eight senators sponsored legislation to stop the military funding.* **4** V-T When a country or an organization such as the United Nations **sponsors** negotiations between countries, it suggests holding the negotiations and organizes them. ❑ *Given the strength of pressure on both sides, the superpowers may well have difficulties sponsoring negotiations.* **5** V-T If one country accuses another of **sponsoring** attacks on it, they mean that the other country does not do anything to prevent the attacks, and may even encourage them. ❑ *We have to make the states that sponsor terrorism pay a price.* **6** V-T If a company or organization **sponsors** a television program, they pay to have a special advertisement shown at the beginning and end of the program, and at each commercial break. ❑ *The company plans to sponsor television programs as part of its marketing strategy.* **7** N-COUNT A **sponsor** is a person or organization that sponsors something or someone. ❑ *Race officials announced a handful of new sponsors on Tuesday.*

COLLOCATIONS

sponsor
VERB **1**
sponsor + noun: competition, event, exhibition; program, project, scheme
noun + sponsor: company, firm
sponsor + adverb: jointly, proudly
NOUN **7**
noun + sponsor: club, company, event
adjective + sponsor: major, main, potential, principal; corporate, official; proud
verb + sponsor: attract, find, need, seek; name, thank

---

spon|sored /spɒnsərd/ ADJ [ADJ n] A **sponsored** event is an event in which people try to do something such as walk or run a particular distance in order to raise money for charity. ❑ *The sponsored walk will raise money for AIDS care.*

spon|sor|ship /spɒnsərʃɪp/ N-UNCOUNT [also N in pl] **Sponsorship** is financial support given by a sponsor. ❑ *Campbell is one of an ever-growing number of skiers in need of sponsorship.*

spon|ta|neity /spɒntəniɪti, -neɪ-/ N-UNCOUNT **Spontaneity** is spontaneous, natural behavior. ❑ *He had the spontaneity of a child.*

spon|ta|neous /spɒnteɪniəs/ **1** ADJ **Spontaneous** acts are not planned or arranged, but are done because someone suddenly wants to do them. ◻ *Diana's house was crowded with happy people whose spontaneous outbursts of song were accompanied by lively music.* ● **spon|ta|neous|ly** ADV ◻ *Many people spontaneously stood up and cheered.* ◳ ADJ A **spontaneous** event happens because of processes within something rather than being caused by things outside it. ◻ *I had another spontaneous miscarriage at around the 16th to 18th week.* ● **spon|ta|neous|ly** ADV [ADV after v] ◻ *Usually a woman's breasts produce milk spontaneously after the birth.*

spoof /spuf/ (spoofs) N-COUNT A **spoof** is something such as an article or television program that seems to be about a serious matter but is actually a joke. ◻ *...a spoof on Hollywood life.*

spook /spuk/ (spooks, spooking, spooked) ◳ N-COUNT A **spook** is a ghost. [INFORMAL] ◳ N-COUNT A **spook** is a spy. [AM, INFORMAL] ◻ *...a U.S. intelligence spook.* ◳ V-T If people **are spooked**, something has scared them or made them nervous. [mainly AM] ◻ *But was it the wind that spooked her?* ◻ *Investors were spooked by slowing economies.* ● **spooked** ADJ [v-link ADJ] ◻ *He was so spooked that he, too, began to believe that he heard strange clicks and noises on their telephones.*

spooky /spuki/ (spookier, spookiest) ADJ A place that is **spooky** has a frightening atmosphere, and makes you feel that there are ghosts around. [INFORMAL] ◻ *The whole place has a slightly spooky atmosphere.*

spool /spul/ (spools) N-COUNT A **spool** is a round object onto which thread, tape, or film can be wound, especially before it is put into a machine. ◻ *...a hinged sewing box, complete with spools of thread.*

spoon /spun/ (spoons, spooning, spooned) ◳ N-COUNT A **spoon** is an object used for eating, stirring, and serving food. One end of it is shaped like a shallow bowl and it has a long handle. ◻ *He stirred his coffee with a spoon.* ◳ V-T If you **spoon** food into something, you put it there with a spoon. ◻ *He spooned instant coffee into two of the mugs.*

spoon|er|ism /spunərɪzəm/ (spoonerisms) N-COUNT A **spoonerism** is a mistake made by a speaker in which the first sounds of two words are switched, often with a humorous result, for example when someone says 'wrong load' instead of 'long road.'

spoon-feed (spoon-feeds, spoon-feeding, spoon-fed) ◳ V-T [usu passive] If you think that someone is being given too much help with something and is not making enough effort themselves, you can say they **are being spoon-fed**. [DISAPPROVAL] ◻ *Some students do want to be spoon-fed.* ◳ V-T [usu passive] If you say that someone **is spoon-fed** ideas or information, you mean that they are told about them and are expected to accept them without questioning them. [DISAPPROVAL] ◻ *Students across the country are routinely spoon-fed lies about their job prospects.* ◳ V-T If you **spoon-feed** a small child or a sick person, you feed them using a spoon. ◻ *It took two years for me to get better, during which time he spoon-fed me and did absolutely everything around the house.*

spoon|ful /spunful/ (spoonfuls) N-COUNT [usu N *of* n] You can refer to an amount of food resting on a spoon as a **spoonful** of food. ◻ *He took a spoonful of the stew and ate it.*

spoor /spʊər/ N-SING The **spoor** of an animal is the marks or substances that it leaves behind as it moves along, which hunters can follow.

spo|rad|ic /spərædɪk/ ADJ **Sporadic** occurrences of something happen at irregular intervals. ◻ *a year of sporadic fighting in the north of the country.* ● **spo|radi|cal|ly** ADV [ADV with v] ◻ *The distant thunder from the coast continued sporadically.*

spore /spɔr/ (spores) N-COUNT **Spores** are cells produced by bacteria and fungi which can develop into new bacteria or fungi.

spor|ran /spɒrən/ (sporrans) N-COUNT A **sporran** is a flat bag made out of leather or fur, which a Scotsman wears on a belt around his waist when he is wearing a skirt called a kilt.

sport ♦♢♢ /spɔrt/ (sports) ◳ N-VAR **Sports** are games such as football and basketball and other competitive leisure activities which need physical effort and skill. ◻ *I chose boxing because it is my favorite sport.* ◻ *She excels at sports.* ◳ → See feature box at **competition, Olympic Games**

COLLOCATIONS

sport
NOUN ◳
noun + **sport**: contact, spectator, team; motor, water, winter
adjective + **sport**: competitive, elite, extreme, professional
verb + **sport**: enjoy, play, pursue, quit; dominate, promote; watch

---

sport coat (sport coats) also **sports coat** N-COUNT A **sport coat** is a jacket. It is worn on informal occasions with pants of a different material. [AM] ◻ *He wore a sport coat, dark tie, and blue shirt.*

in BRIT, use **sports jacket**

sport|ing /spɔrtɪŋ/ ◳ ADJ [ADJ n] **Sporting** means relating to sports or used for sports. ◻ *...major sporting events, such as the U.S. Open and the World Series.* ◳ → See feature box at **Olympic Games**

sport jack|et (sport jackets) N-COUNT A **sport jacket** is the same as a **sport coat**. [AM] ◻ *...casually dressed in a green turtleneck and sport jacket.*

sports car (sports cars) ◳ N-COUNT A **sports car** is a low, fast car, usually with room for only two people. ◳ → See also color supplement

sports|cast /spɔrtskæst/ (sportscasts) N-COUNT A **sportscast** is a radio or television broadcast of a sports event. [mainly AM]

sports|caster /spɔrtskæstər/ (sportscasters) N-COUNT A **sportscaster** is a radio or television broadcaster who describes or comments on sports events. [mainly AM]

sports jack|et (sports jackets) N-COUNT A **sports jacket** is the same as a **sport coat**. [BRIT]

sports|man /spɔrtsmən/ (sportsmen) N-COUNT A **sportsman** is a man who takes part in sports.

sports|man|ship /spɔrtsmənʃɪp/ N-UNCOUNT **Sportsmanship** is behavior and attitudes that show respect for the rules of a game and for the other players.

sports|wear /spɔrtswɛər/ N-UNCOUNT **Sportswear** is the special clothing worn for playing sports or for informal leisure activities.

sports|woman /spɔrtswʊmən/ (sportswomen) N-COUNT A **sportswoman** is a woman who takes part in sports.

sports writ|er (sports writers) also **sportswriter** N-COUNT A **sports writer** is a journalist who writes about sport.

sport util|ity ve|hi|cle (sport utility vehicles) also **sports utility vehicle** ◳ N-COUNT A **sport utility vehicle** is a powerful vehicle with four-wheel drive that can be driven over rough ground. The abbreviation **SUV** is often used. ◳ → See also color supplement

sporty /spɔrti/ (sportier, sportiest) ◳ ADJ You can describe a car as **sporty** when it performs like a racing car but can be driven on normal roads. ◻ *The steering and braking are exactly what you want from a sporty car.* ◳ ADJ Someone who is **sporty** likes playing sports. ◻ *I'm an outdoor, sporty type and don't want to sit behind a desk all day.*

spot ♦♦♢ /spɒt/ (spots, spotting, spotted) ◳ N-COUNT **Spots** are small, round, colored areas on a surface. ◻ *The leaves have yellow areas on the top and underneath are powdery orange spots.* ◳ N-COUNT **Spots** on a person's skin are small lumps or marks.

in AM, usually use **pimples**

◳ N-COUNT You can refer to a particular place as a **spot**. ◻ *They stayed at several of the island's top tourist spots.* ◳ N-COUNT A **spot** in a television or radio show is a part of it that is regularly reserved for a particular performer or type of entertainment. ◻ *Unsuccessful at screen writing, he got a spot on a CNN show.* ◳ V-T If you **spot** something or someone, you notice them. ◻ *Vicenzo failed to spot the error.* ◳ N-COUNT A **spot** of a liquid is a small amount of it. [mainly BRIT] ◻ *Spots of rain had begun to fall.* ◳ PHRASE If you do something **on the spot**, you do it immediately. ◻ *James was called to see the producer and got the job on the spot.* ◳ **rooted to the spot** → see **rooted**

spot check (spot checks) also **spot-check** N-COUNT [oft N *on* n] If someone carries out a **spot check**, they examine one thing from a group in order to make sure that it is satisfactory.

spot|less /spɒtlɪs/ ADJ Something that is **spotless** is completely clean. ❑ *Each morning cleaners make sure everything is spotless.* • **spot|less|ly** ADV [ADV adj] ❑ *The house had huge, spotlessly clean rooms.*

spot|light /spɒtlaɪt/ (spotlights, spotlighting, spotlighted) **1** N-COUNT A **spotlight** is a powerful light, for example in a theater, which can be directed so that it lights up a small area. **2** V-T If something **spotlights** a particular problem or situation, it makes people notice it and think about it. ❑ *The budget crisis also spotlighted a weakening economy.* **3** PHRASE Someone or something that is **in the spotlight** is getting a great deal of public attention. ❑ *Webb is back in the spotlight.* **4** → See feature box at **personality**

spot|lit /spɒtlɪt/ ADJ Something that is **spotlit** is brightly lit up by one or more spotlights. ❑ *She caught a clear view upwards of the spotlit temple.*

spot|ted /spɒtɪd/ **1** ADJ [oft ADJ with n] Something that is **spotted** has a pattern of spots on it. ❑ *...hand-painted spotted cups and saucers in green and blue.* ❑ *His cheeks were spotted with blackheads.* **2** → see also **spot**

spot|ty /spɒti/ (spottier, spottiest) **1** ADJ Something that is **spotty** does not stay the same but is sometimes good and sometimes bad. [AM] ❑ *He quit in 1981 – had a spotty political career.* ❑ *His attendance record was spotty.* **2** ADJ Someone who is **spotty** has spots on their face. ❑ *He's no longer that spotty 16-year-old we last met.*

spous|al /spaʊzəl/ ADJ [ADJ n] **Spousal** rights and duties are ones which you gain if you are married. [AM, FORMAL]

spouse /spaʊs/ (spouses) N-COUNT Someone's **spouse** is the person they are married to. ❑ *You, or your spouse, must be at least 60 to participate.*

spout /spaʊt/ (spouts, spouting, spouted) **1** V-T/V-I If something **spouts** liquid or fire, or if liquid or fire **spout** out of something, it comes out very quickly with a lot of force. ❑ *He replaced the boiler when the last one began to spout flames.* ❑ *The main square has a fountain that spouts water 40 feet into the air.* **2** V-T If you say that a person **spouts** something, you disapprove of them because they say something which you do not agree with or which you think they do not honestly feel. [DISAPPROVAL] ❑ *My mother would go red in the face and spout bitter recriminations.* **3** N-COUNT A **spout** is a long, hollow part of a container through which liquids can be poured out easily. ❑ *She lifted the kettle a little and tilted its spout over the tea-pot.*

sprain /spreɪn/ (sprains, spraining, sprained) **1** V-T If you **sprain** a joint such as your ankle or wrist, you accidentally damage it by twisting it or bending it violently. ❑ *He fell and sprained his ankle.* **2** N-COUNT A **sprain** is the injury caused by spraining a joint. ❑ *Rubin suffered a right ankle sprain when she rolled over on her ankle.*

sprang /spræŋ/ **Sprang** is the past tense of **spring**.

sprat /spræt/ (sprats) N-COUNT **Sprats** are very small European sea fish which can be eaten.

sprawl /sprɔːl/ (sprawls, sprawling, sprawled) **1** V-I If you **sprawl** somewhere, you sit or lie down with your legs and arms spread out in a careless way. ❑ *She sprawled on the couch, watching TV.* • PHRASAL VERB **Sprawl out** means the same as **sprawl**. ❑ *He would take two aspirin and sprawl out on his bed.* **2** V-I If you say that a place **sprawls**, you mean that it covers a large area of land. ❑ *The State Recreation Area sprawls over 900 acres on the southern tip of Key Biscayne.* **3** N-UNCOUNT You can use **sprawl** to refer to an area where a city has grown outward in an uncontrolled way. ❑ *The whole urban sprawl of Ankara contains over 2.6 million people.*

sprawled /sprɔːld/ ADJ [v-link ADJ] If you are **sprawled** somewhere, you are sitting or lying with your legs and arms spread out in a careless way. ❑ *People are sprawled on makeshift beds in the cafeteria.*

spray ✦◇◇ /spreɪ/ (sprays, spraying, sprayed) **1** N-VAR **Spray** is a lot of small drops of water which are being thrown into the air. ❑ *The moon was casting a rainbow through the spray from the waterfall.* **2** N-MASS A **spray** is a liquid kept under pressure in a can or other container, which you can force out in very small drops. ❑ *...hair spray.* **3** V-T/V-I If you **spray** a liquid somewhere or if it **sprays** somewhere, drops of the liquid cover a place or shower someone. ❑ *A sprayer hooked to a tractor can spray five gallons onto ten acres.* ❑ *Inmates threw bricks at prison officers who were spraying them with a hose.* **4** V-T/V-I If a lot of small things **spray** somewhere or if something **sprays** them, they are scattered somewhere with a lot of force. ❑ *A shower of mustard seeds sprayed into the air and fell into the grass.* ❑ *The intensity of the blaze shattered windows, spraying glass on the streets below.* **5** V-T If someone **sprays** bullets somewhere, they fire a lot of bullets at a group of people or things. ❑ *He ran to the top of the building, spraying bullets into shoppers below.* **6** V-T [usu passive] If something **is sprayed**, it is painted using paint kept under pressure in a container. ❑ *The bare metal was sprayed with several coats of primer.* **7** V-T/V-I When someone **sprays** against insects, they cover plants or crops with a chemical which prevents insects from feeding on them. ❑ *He doesn't spray against pests or diseases.* ❑ *Confine the use of insecticides to the evening and do not spray plants that are in flower.* **8** N-COUNT A **spray** is a piece of equipment for spraying water or another liquid, especially over growing plants. ❑ *Farmers can use the spray to kill weeds without harming the soy crop.*

SYNONYMS

spray
VERB **3**
squirt: *Norman cut open his pie and squirted tomato sauce into it.*
splash: *He closed his eyes tight and splashed the water on his face.*
sprinkle: *At the festival, candles are blessed and sprinkled with holy water.*

---

spray can (spray cans) also **spray-can** N-COUNT A **spray can** is a small metal container containing liquid such as paint under pressure so that it can be sprayed.

spray|er /spreɪər/ (sprayers) N-COUNT A **sprayer** is a piece of equipment used for spraying liquid somewhere.

spray gun (spray guns) also **spray-gun** N-COUNT A **spray gun** is a piece of equipment which you use to spray paint under pressure onto a surface.

spray paint (spray paints, spray painting, spray painted) also **spray-paint** **1** N-MASS **Spray paint** is paint bought in a special can which you spray on a surface by pressing a button on the top of the can. ❑ *The walls have been horribly vandalized with spray paint.* **2** V-T If you **spray paint** a surface, you paint it using spray paint. If you **spray paint** something on a surface, you paint it on that surface using spray paint. ❑ *The youths are taught how to spray paint cars and mend fences.* ❑ *He spray-painted his name on the wall.*

spread ✦◆◇ /spred/ (spreads, spreading, spread) **1** V-T If you **spread** something somewhere, you open it out or arrange it over a place or surface, so that all of it can be seen or used easily. ❑ *She spread a towel on the sand and lay on it.* • PHRASAL VERB **Spread out** means the same as **spread**. ❑ *He extracted several glossy prints and spread them out on a low coffee table.* **2** V-T If you **spread** your arms, hands, fingers, or legs, you stretch them out until they are far apart. ❑ *Sitting on the floor, spread your legs as far as they will go without overstretching.* • PHRASAL VERB **Spread out** means the same as **spread**. ❑ *David made a gesture, spreading out his hands as if he were showing that he had no explanation to make.* **3** V-T If you **spread** a substance on a surface or **spread** the surface with the substance, you put a thin layer of the substance over the surface. ❑ *Spread the mixture in the cake pan and bake for 30 minutes.* **4** V-T/V-I If something **is spread** by people, it gradually reaches or affects a larger and larger area or more and more people. ❑ *The industrial revolution, which started a couple of hundred years ago in Europe, is now spreading across the world.* ❑ *...the sense of fear spreading in residential neighborhoods.* • N-SING **Spread** is also a noun. ❑ *The greatest hope for reform is the gradual spread of information.* **5** V-T/V-I If something such as a liquid, gas, or smoke **spreads** or **is spread**, it moves outward in all directions so that it covers a larger area. ❑ *Fire spread rapidly after a chemical truck exploded.* ❑ *A dark red stain was spreading across his shirt.* • N-SING **Spread** is also a noun. ❑ *The situation was complicated by the spread of a serious forest fire.* **6** V-T If you **spread** something **over** a period of time, it takes place regularly or continuously over that period, rather than happening at one time. ❑ *There seems to be little difference whether you eat all your calorie allowance at once, or spread it over the day.* **7** V-T If you **spread** something such as wealth or work, you distribute it evenly or equally. ❑ *...policies*

that spread the state's wealth more evenly. • N-SING **Spread** is also a noun. ❑ *There are easier ways to encourage the even spread of wealth.* ❽ N-SING A **spread** of ideas, interests, or other things is a wide variety of them. ❑ *A topic-based approach can be hard to assess in schools with a typical spread of ability.* ❾ N-COUNT A **spread** is two pages of a book, magazine, or newspaper that are opposite each other when you open it at a particular place. ❑ *There was a double-page spread of a dinner for 46 people.* ❿ N-SING **Spread** is used to refer to the difference between the price that a seller wants someone to pay for a particular stock or share and the price that the buyer is willing to pay. [BUSINESS] ❑ *Market makers earn their livings from the spread between buying and selling prices.* ⓫ **to spread your wings** → see **wing**
▸ **spread out** ❶ PHRASAL VERB If people, animals, or vehicles **spread out**, they move apart from each other. ❑ *Felix watched his men move like soldiers, spreading out into two teams.* ❷ PHRASAL VERB If something such as a city or forest **spreads out**, it gets larger and gradually begins to cover a larger area. ❑ *Cities such as Tokyo are spreading out.* ❸ → see **spread** 1, 2

SYNONYMS

spread
VERB
❶
open out: *...oval tables which open out to become circular.*
extend: *... a table which extends to accommodate extra guests.*
stretch: *Ease the pastry into the corners of the pan, making sure you don't stretch it.*
unfold: *The bird's wings unfold to an impressive six-foot span.*
❸
coat: *Coat the fish with seasoned flour.*
smear: *Smear a little olive oil over the inside of the salad bowl.*
smooth: *She smoothed the lotion across his shoulder blades.*
plaster: *She plastered herself from head to toe in high-factor sunscreen.*

spread bet|ting N-UNCOUNT **Spread betting** is a form of gambling that involves predicting a range of possible scores or outcomes rather than one particular score or outcome.

spread|eagled /sprɛdiɡəld/ also **spread-eagled** ADJ [usu v-link ADJ] Someone who is **spreadeagled** is lying with their arms and legs spread out. ❑ *They lay spreadeagled on the floor.*

spread out ADJ If people or things are **spread out**, they are a long way apart. ❑ *The Kurds are spread out across five nations.*

spread|sheet /sprɛdʃiːt/ (**spreadsheets**) N-COUNT A **spreadsheet** is a computer program that is used for displaying and dealing with numbers. Spreadsheets are used mainly for financial planning. [COMPUTING]

spree /spriː/ (**sprees**) N-COUNT If you spend a period of time doing something in an excessive way, you can say that you are going on a particular kind of **spree**. ❑ *Some people went on a spending spree in December to beat the new tax.*

sprig /sprɪɡ/ (**sprigs**) N-COUNT [usu N of n] A **sprig** is a small stem with leaves on it which has been picked from a bush or plant, especially so that it can be used in cooking or as a decoration.

sprigged /sprɪɡd/ ADJ [usu ADJ n] **Sprigged** material or paper has a pattern of small leaves or flowers on it. ❑ *...a sprigged cotton dress.*

spright|ly /spraɪtli/ (**sprightlier, sprightliest**) ADJ [usu ADJ n] A **sprightly** person, especially an old person, is lively and active. ❑ *...the sprightly 85-year-old president.*

spring ✦◇ /sprɪŋ/ (**springs, springing, sprang, sprung**) ❶ N-VAR **Spring** is the season between winter and summer when the weather becomes warmer and plants start to grow again. ❑ *They are planning to move house next spring.* ❷ N-COUNT A **spring** is a spiral of wire which returns to its original shape after it is pressed or pulled. ❑ *Unfortunately, as a standard mattress wears, the springs soften and so do not support your spine.* ❸ N-COUNT A **spring** is a place where water comes up through the ground. It is also the water that comes from that place. ❑ *To the north are the hot springs.* ❹ V-I When a person or animal **springs**, they jump upward or forward suddenly or quickly. ❑ *He sprang to his feet, grabbing his keys off the coffee table.* ❑ *The lion roared once and sprang.* ❺ V-I If something **springs** in a particular direction, it moves suddenly and quickly. ❑ *Sadly when the lid of the trunk sprang open, it was empty.* ❻ V-I If one thing **springs from** another thing, it is the result of it. ❑ *Ethiopia's art springs from its early Christian as well as its Muslim heritage.* ❼ V-T If you **spring** some news or a surprise on someone, you tell them something that they did not expect to hear, without warning them. ❑ *McLaren sprang a new idea on him.* ❽ **to spring to mind** → see **mind** ①
▸ **spring up** PHRASAL VERB If something **springs up**, it suddenly appears or begins to exist. ❑ *New theaters and arts centers sprang up all over the country.*

spring|board /sprɪŋbɔːd/ (**springboards**) ❶ N-COUNT If something is a **springboard** for something else, it makes it possible for that thing to happen or start. ❑ *Infrastructure is the springboard for growth and development.* ❷ N-COUNT A **springboard** is a flexible board from which you jump into a swimming pool or onto a piece of gymnastic equipment.

spring chick|en (**spring chickens**) PHRASE [usu v-link PHR] If you say that someone is **no spring chicken**, you are saying that they are not young. [HUMOROUS] ❑ *At 85, he is no spring chicken, but he is busier than ever.*

spring-clean (**spring-cleans, spring-cleaning, spring-cleaned**) VERB When you **spring-clean** a house, you thoroughly clean everything in it. ❑ *It's almost as easy to give your rooms a new coat of paint as to spring-clean them.* • N-SING **Spring-clean** is also a noun. ❑ *It needs a thorough spring clean.* • **spring-cleaning** N-SING *The rooms inside were undergoing a spring-cleaning.*

spring-cleaning N-SING **Spring-cleaning** is the process of thoroughly cleaning a place, especially your home. You can also say that you give a place a **spring-cleaning**. ❑ *The rooms inside were undergoing a spring-cleaning.*

spring on|ion (**spring onions**) N-VAR **Spring onions** are the same as **scallions**. [BRIT]

spring roll (**spring rolls**) N-COUNT A **spring roll** is a Chinese food consisting of a small roll of thin pastry filled with vegetables and sometimes meat, and then fried.

spring tide (**spring tides**) N-COUNT A **spring tide** is an unusually high tide that happens at the time of a new moon or a full moon.

spring|time /sprɪŋtaɪm/ N-UNCOUNT **Springtime** is the period of time during which spring lasts.

springy /sprɪŋi/ (**springier, springiest**) ADJ If something is **springy**, it returns quickly to its original shape after you press it. ❑ *Steam for about 12 minutes until the cake is springy to touch in the center.*

sprin|kle /sprɪŋkəl/ (**sprinkles, sprinkling, sprinkled**) ❶ V-T If you **sprinkle** a thing with something such as a liquid or powder, you scatter the liquid or powder over it. ❑ *Sprinkle the meat with salt and place in the pan.* ❑ *At the festival, candles are blessed and sprinkled with holy water.* ❷ V-T If something **is sprinkled** with particular things, it has a few of them throughout it and they are far apart from each other. ❑ *Unfortunately, the text is sprinkled with errors.*

sprin|kler /sprɪŋklər/ (**sprinklers**) N-COUNT A **sprinkler** is a device used to spray water. Sprinklers are used to water plants or grass, or to put out fires in buildings.

sprin|kling /sprɪŋklɪŋ/ N-SING [usu N of n] A **sprinkling** of something is a small quantity or amount of it, especially if it is spread over a large area. ❑ *...a light sprinkling of snow.*

sprint /sprɪnt/ (**sprints, sprinting, sprinted**) ❶ N-SING The **sprint** is a short, fast running race. ❑ *Rob Harmeling won the sprint in Bordeaux.* ❷ N-COUNT A **sprint** is a short race in which the competitors run, drive, ride, or swim very fast. ❑ *Lewis will compete in both sprints in Stuttgart.* ❸ N-SING A **sprint** is a fast run that someone does, either at the end of a race or because they are in a hurry. ❑ *Gilles Delion, of France, won the Tour of Lombardy in a sprint finish at Monza yesterday.* ❹ V-I If you **sprint**, you run or ride as fast as you can over a short distance. ❑ *Sergeant Horne sprinted to the car.*

sprint|er /sprɪntər/ (**sprinters**) N-COUNT A **sprinter** is a person who takes part in short, fast races.

sprite /spraɪt/ (**sprites**) N-COUNT In fairy tales and legends, a **sprite** is a small, magic creature which lives near water.

sprit|zer /sprɪtsər, ʃprɪt-/ (spritzers) N-COUNT A **spritzer** is a drink consisting of white wine and soda water.

sprock|et /sprɒkɪt/ (sprockets) N-COUNT A **sprocket** is a wheel with teeth around the outer edge that fit into the holes in a chain or a length of film or tape in order to move it around.

sprout /spraʊt/ (sprouts, sprouting, sprouted) **1** V-I When plants, vegetables, or seeds **sprout,** they produce new shoots or leaves. ❑ *It only takes a few days for beans to sprout.* **2** V-I When leaves, shoots, or plants **sprout** somewhere, they grow there. ❑ *Leaf-shoots were beginning to sprout on the hawthorn.* **3** V-T/V-I [no passive] If something such as hair **sprouts** from a person or animal, or if they **sprout** it, it grows on them. ❑ *She is very old now, with little, round, wire-rimmed glasses and whiskers sprouting from her chin.* **4** N-COUNT [usu pl] **Sprouts** are vegetables that look like tiny cabbages. They are also called **brussels sprouts.**

spruce /spruːs/ (spruces, sprucing, spruced)

Spruce is both the singular and the plural form.

1 N-VAR A **spruce** is a kind of evergreen tree. ❑ *Trees such as spruce, pine, and oak have been planted.* ❑ *...a young blue spruce.* **2** ADJ Someone who is **spruce** is very neat and clean in appearance. ❑ *Chris was looking spruce in his stiff-collared black shirt and new short hair cut.*
▶ **spruce up** PHRASAL VERB If something **is spruced up,** its appearance is improved. If someone **is spruced up,** they have made themselves look very smart. ❑ *Many buildings have been spruced up.*

sprung /sprʌŋ/ **Sprung** is the past participle of **spring.**

spry /spraɪ/ (sprier or spryer, spriest or spryest) ADJ [usu v-link ADJ] Someone, especially an old person, who is **spry,** is lively and active. ❑ *The old gentleman was as spry as ever.*

spud /spʌd/ (spuds) N-COUNT [usu pl] **Spuds** are potatoes. [INFORMAL]

spun /spʌn/ **Spun** is the past tense and past participle of **spin.**

spunk /spʌŋk/ N-UNCOUNT **Spunk** is courage. [INFORMAL, APPROVAL] ❑ *I admired her independence and her spunk.*

spunky /spʌŋki/ (spunkier, spunkiest) ADJ A **spunky** person shows courage. [INFORMAL, APPROVAL] ❑ *She's so spunky and spirited.*

spur ◆◇◇ /spɜr/ (spurs, spurring, spurred) **1** V-T If one thing **spurs** you to do another, it encourages you to do it. ❑ *It's the money that spurs these fishermen to risk a long ocean journey in their flimsy boats.* • PHRASAL VERB **Spur on** means the same as **spur.** ❑ *Their attitude, rather than reining him back, only seemed to spur Philip on.* **2** V-T If something **spurs** a change or event, it makes it happen faster or sooner. [JOURNALISM] ❑ *The administration may put more emphasis on spurring economic growth.* **3** N-COUNT Something that acts as a **spur** to something else encourages a person or organization to do that thing or makes it happen more quickly. ❑ *...a belief in competition as a spur to efficiency.* **4** PHRASE If you do something **on the spur of the moment,** you do it suddenly, without planning it beforehand. ❑ *They admitted they had taken a vehicle on the spur of the moment.*

spu|ri|ous /spyʊəriəs/ **1** ADJ Something that is **spurious** seems to be genuine, but is false. [DISAPPROVAL] ❑ *He was arrested in 1979 on spurious corruption charges.* **2** ADJ A **spurious** argument or way of reasoning is incorrect, and so the conclusion is probably incorrect. [DISAPPROVAL] ❑ *...a spurious framework for analysis.*

spurn /spɜrn/ (spurns, spurning, spurned) V-T If you **spurn** someone or something, you reject them. ❑ *He spurned the advice of management consultants.*

spurt /spɜrt/ (spurts, spurting, spurted) **1** V-T/V-I When liquid or fire **spurts** from somewhere, it comes out quickly in a thin, powerful stream. ❑ *He hit her on the head, causing her to spurt blood.* ❑ *I saw flames spurt from the roof.* • PHRASAL VERB **Spurt out** means the same as **spurt.** ❑ *When the washing machine spurts out water at least we can mop it up.* **2** N-COUNT A **spurt** of liquid is a stream of it which comes out of something very forcefully. ❑ *A spurt of diesel came from one valve and none from the other.* **3** N-COUNT A **spurt** of activity, effort, or emotion is a sudden, brief period of intense activity, effort, or emotion. ❑ *The average boy of 14 years old is only beginning his adolescent growth spurt.* **4** V-I If someone or something **spurts** somewhere, they suddenly increase their speed for a short while in order to get there. ❑ *The back wheels spun and the van spurted up the last few feet.* **5** PHRASE If something happens **in spurts,** there are periods of activity followed by periods in which it does not happen. ❑ *The deals came in spurts: three in 1977, none in 1978, three more in 1979.*

sput|ter /spʌtər/ (sputters, sputtering, sputtered) **1** V-I If something such as an engine or a flame **sputters,** it works or burns in an uneven way and makes a series of soft popping sounds. ❑ *The truck sputtered and stopped.* ❑ *The flame sputters out.* **2** → See feature box at **onomatopoeia**

spu|tum /spyuːtəm/ N-UNCOUNT **Sputum** is the wet substance which is coughed up from someone's lungs. [MEDICAL]

spy /spaɪ/ (spies, spying, spied) **1** N-COUNT A **spy** is a person whose job is to find out secret information about another country or organization. ❑ *He was jailed for five years as an alleged spy.* **2** ADJ [ADJ n] A **spy** satellite or **spy** plane obtains secret information about another country by taking photographs from the sky. ❑ *...pictures from unmanned spy planes operated by the U.S. military.* **3** V-I Someone who **spies** for a country or organization tries to find out secret information about another country or organization. ❑ *The agent spied for East Germany for more than twenty years.* ❑ *East and West are still spying on one another.* • **spy|ing** N-UNCOUNT ❑ *...a ten-year sentence for spying.* **4** V-T If you **spy on** someone, you watch them secretly. ❑ *That day he spied on her while pretending to work on the shrubs.*

spy|cam /spaɪkæm/ (spycams) N-COUNT A **spycam** is a hidden camera used to film people without them knowing. ❑ *They had fitted a spycam in his office.*

spy|master /spaɪmæstər/ (spymasters) N-COUNT A **spymaster** is a spy who is in charge of a group of spies.

spy|ware /spaɪwɛər/ N-UNCOUNT **Spyware** is computer software that secretly records information about which websites you visit. [COMPUTING] ❑ *The publishers promise not to use spyware to grab your personal information.*

sq. sq. is used as a written abbreviation for **square** when you are giving the measurement of an area. ❑ *The building provides about 25,500 sq. ft. of air-conditioned offices.*

squab|ble /skwɒbəl/ (squabbles, squabbling, squabbled) V-RECIP When people **squabble,** they quarrel about something that is not really important. ❑ *Mother is devoted to Dad although they squabble all the time.* ❑ *The children were squabbling over the remote-control for the television.* • **squab|bling** N-UNCOUNT ❑ *In recent months its government has been paralyzed by political squabbling.* • N-COUNT **Squabble** is also a noun. ❑ *There have been minor squabbles about phone bills.*

squad ◆◇◇ /skwɒd/ (squads) **1** N-COUNT A **squad** is a section of a police force that is responsible for dealing with a particular type of crime. ❑ *The building was evacuated and the bomb squad called.* **2** N-COUNT A **squad** is a group of players from which a sports team will be chosen. ❑ *The American squad has pulled out of the four-day basketball tournament.*

squad car (squad cars) N-COUNT A **squad car** is a car used by the police. [AM]

in BRIT, usually use **patrol car, police car**

squad|ron /skwɒdrən/ (squadrons) N-COUNT-COLL A **squadron** is a section of one of the armed forces, especially the air force. ❑ *A squadron of F-15 fighters is on its way home.*

squal|id /skwɒlɪd/ ADJ A **squalid** place is dirty, untidy, and in bad condition. ❑ *The early industrial cities were squalid and unhealthy places.*

squall /skwɔl/ (squalls, squalling, squalled) **1** N-COUNT A **squall** is a sudden strong wind which often causes a brief, violent rainstorm or snowstorm. ❑ *The boat was hit by a squall north of the island.* **2** V-I If a person or animal **squalls,** they make a loud unpleasant noise like the noise made by a crying baby. ❑ *There was an infant squalling in the back of the church.* ❑ *...squalling guitars.*

squal|ly /skwɔli/ ADJ [usu ADJ n] In **squally** weather, there are sudden strong winds which often cause brief, violent storms. ❑ *The competitors had to contend with squally weather conditions.*

squal|or /skwɒlər/ N-UNCOUNT You can refer to very dirty, unpleasant conditions as **squalor**. ❏ *He was out of work and living in squalor.*

squan|der /skwɒndər/ (**squanders, squandering, squandered**) V-T If you **squander** money, resources, or opportunities, you waste them. ❏ *Hobbs didn't squander his money on flashy cars or other vices.*

square ✦✧ /skweər/ (**squares, squaring, squared**) **1** N-COUNT A **square** is a shape with four sides that are all the same length and four corners that are all right angles. ❏ *Serve the cake warm or at room temperature, cut in squares.* ❏ *There was a calendar on the wall, with large squares around the dates.* **2** N-COUNT; N-IN-NAMES In a town or city, a **square** is a flat, open place, often in the shape of a square. ❏ *The house is located in one of the city's prettiest squares.* **3** ADJ Something that is **square** has a shape the same as a square or similar to a square. ❏ *Round tables seat more people in the same space as a square table.* **4** ADJ [ADJ n] **Square** is used before units of length when referring to the area of something. For example, if something is three feet long and two feet wide, its area is six square feet. ❏ *The new complex will provide 10 million square feet of office space.* **5** ADJ [amount ADJ] **Square** is used after units of length when you are giving the length of each side of something that is square in shape. ❏ *...a linen cushion cover, 45 cm. square.* **6** V-T To **square** a number means to multiply it by itself. For example, 3 **squared** is 3 x 3, or 9. 3 **squared** is usually written as 3^2. ❏ *Take the time in seconds, square it, and multiply by 5.12.* **7** N-COUNT The **square** of a number is the number produced when you multiply that number by itself. For example, the square of 3 is 9. ❏ *...the square of the speed of light, an exceedingly large number.* **8** V-T/V-I If you **square** two different ideas or actions **with** each other or if they **square with** each other, they fit or match each other. ❏ *That explanation squares with the facts, doesn't it?* **9** V-T If you **square** something **with** someone, you ask their permission or check with them that what you are doing is acceptable to them. ❏ *I squared it with Dan, who said it was all right so long as I was back next Monday morning.* **10** → see also **squarely** **11** PHRASE If you are **back to square one**, you have to start dealing with something from the beginning again because the way you were dealing with it has failed. ❏ *If your complaint is not upheld, you may feel you are back to square one.* **12** **fair and square** → see **fair**

squared /skweərd/ **1** ADJ Something that is **squared** has the shape of a square, or has a pattern of squares on it. ❏ *...buttons in rectangular and squared shapes.* **2** → see also **square**

square dance (**square dances**) **1** N-COUNT A **square dance** is a traditional dance in which sets of four couples dance together, forming a square at the beginning of the dance. **2** N-COUNT A **square dance** is a social event where people dance square dances.

square|ly /skweərli/ **1** ADV [ADV with v] **Squarely** means directly or in the middle, rather than indirectly or at an angle. ❏ *I kept the gun aimed squarely at his eyes.* **2** ADV [ADV with v] If something such as blame or responsibility lies **squarely** with someone, they are definitely the person responsible. ❏ *The president put the blame squarely on his opponent.*

square meal (**square meals**) N-COUNT A **square meal** is a meal which is big enough to satisfy you. ❏ *They haven't had a square meal for four or five days.*

square root (**square roots**) N-COUNT The **square root** of a number is another number which produces the first number when it is multiplied by itself. For example, the square root of 16 is 4.

squash /skwɒʃ/ (**squashes, squashing, squashed**) **1** V-T If someone or something **is squashed**, they are pressed or crushed with such force that they become injured or lose their shape. ❏ *Robert was lucky to escape with just a broken foot after being squashed against a fence by a car.* ❏ *Whole neighborhoods have been squashed flat by shelling.* **2** ADJ [v-link ADJ into n] If people or things are **squashed into** a place, they are put or pushed into a place where there is not enough room for them to be. ❏ *There were 2,000 people squashed into her recent show.* **3** V-T If you **squash** something that is causing you trouble, you put a stop to it, often by force. ❏ *The troops would stay in position to squash the first murmur of trouble.* **4** N-VAR A **squash** is one of a family of vegetables that have thick skin and soft or firm flesh inside. **5** N-UNCOUNT **Squash** is a game in which two players hit a small rubber ball against the walls of a court using rackets. ❏ *I also play squash.* **6** N-SING If you say that getting a number of people into a small space is **a squash**, you mean that it is only just possible for them all to get into it. [BRIT, INFORMAL]

in AM, use **squeeze**

squashy /skwɒʃi/ (**squashier, squashiest**) ADJ [usu ADJ n] **Squashy** things are soft and able to be squashed easily. ❏ *...deep, squashy sofas.*

squat /skwɒt/ (**squats, squatting, squatted**) **1** V-I If you **squat**, you lower yourself toward the ground, balancing on your feet with your legs bent. ❏ *We squatted beside the pool and watched the diver sink slowly down.* • PHRASAL VERB **Squat down** means the same as **squat**. ❏ *Albert squatted down and examined it.* • N-SING **Squat** is also a noun. ❏ *He bent to a squat and gathered the puppies on his lap.* **2** ADJ If you describe someone or something as **squat**, you mean that they are short and thick, usually in an unattractive way. ❏ *Eddie was a short squat fellow in his forties with thinning hair.* **3** V-I People who **squat** occupy an unused building or unused land without having a legal right to do so. ❏ *You can't simply wander around squatting on other people's property.*

squat|ter /skwɒtər/ (**squatters**) **1** N-COUNT A **squatter** is someone who lives in an unused building without having a legal right to do so and without paying any rent or any property tax. ❏ *...another violent clash as police evicted squatters from empty buildings.* **2** → See feature box at **poverty, urban**

squaw /skwɔː/ (**squaws**) N-COUNT In the past, people sometimes referred to a Native American woman as a **squaw**. [OFFENSIVE]

squawk /skwɔːk/ (**squawks, squawking, squawked**) **1** V-I When a bird **squawks**, it makes a loud, harsh noise. ❏ *I threw pebbles at the hens, and that made them jump and squawk.* • N-COUNT **Squawk** is also a noun. ❏ *A mallard suddenly took wing, rising steeply into the air with an angry squawk.* **2** V-T/V-I If a person **squawks**, they complain loudly, often in a high-pitched, harsh tone. [INFORMAL] ❏ *Mr. Arbor squawked that the deal was a double-cross.*

squeak /skwiːk/ (**squeaks, squeaking, squeaked**) V-I If something or someone **squeaks**, they make a short, high-pitched sound. ❏ *My boots squeaked a little as I walked.* ❏ *The door squeaked open.* • N-COUNT **Squeak** is also a noun. ❏ *He gave an outraged squeak.*

squeaky /skwiːki/ (**squeakier, squeakiest**) ADJ Something that is **squeaky** makes high-pitched sounds. ❏ *...squeaky floorboards.* ❏ *He had a squeaky voice.*

squeaky clean also **squeaky-clean** ADJ If you say that someone is **squeaky clean**, you mean that they live a very moral life and have never done anything wrong. [INFORMAL] ❏ *Maybe this guy isn't so squeaky clean after all.*

squeal /skwiːl/ (**squeals, squealing, squealed**) V-I If someone or something **squeals**, they make a long, high-pitched sound. ❏ *Jennifer squealed with delight and hugged me.* • N-COUNT **Squeal** is also a noun. ❏ *At that moment there was a squeal of brakes and the angry blowing of a car horn.*

squeam|ish /skwiːmɪʃ/ ADJ If you are **squeamish**, you are easily upset by unpleasant sights or situations. ❏ *I'm terribly squeamish. I can't bear gory films.*

squeeze ✦✧ /skwiːz/ (**squeezes, squeezing, squeezed**) **1** V-T If you **squeeze** something, you press it firmly, usually with your hands. ❏ *He squeezed her arm reassuringly.* • N-COUNT **Squeeze** is also a noun. ❏ *I liked her way of reassuring you with a squeeze of the hand.* **2** V-T If you **squeeze** a liquid or a soft substance out of an object, you get the liquid or substance out by pressing the object. ❏ *Joe put the plug in the sink and squeezed some detergent over the dishes.* **3** V-T/V-I If you **squeeze** a person or thing somewhere or if they **squeeze** there, they manage to get through or into a small space. ❏ *They lowered him gradually into the cockpit. Somehow they squeezed him in the tight space, and strapped him in.* **4** N-SING If you say that getting a number of people into a small space is **a squeeze**, you mean that it is only just possible for them all to get into it. [INFORMAL] ❏ *It was a squeeze in the car with five of them.*

squelch

> **SYNONYMS**
>
> **squeeze**
> VERB ❶
> **press:** *They pressed the silver knife into the cake.*
> **squash:** *She made clay models and squashed them flat again.*
> **crush:** *Andrew crushed his empty can.*
> **pinch:** *She pinched his arm as hard as she could.*

squelch /skwɛltʃ/ (squelches, squelching, squelched) ❶ V-T If you **squelch** something, you stop it from developing or succeeding. ❑ *The company increased its stake in the business, squelching rumors of a takeover bid.* ❷ V-I To **squelch** means to make a wet, sucking sound, like the sound you make when you are walking on wet, muddy ground. ❑ *He squelched across the turf.*

squid /skwɪd/ (squids)

> Squid can also be used as the plural form.

N-COUNT A **squid** is a sea creature with a long soft body and many soft arms called tentacles. • N-UNCOUNT **Squid** is pieces of this creature eaten as food. ❑ *Add the prawns and squid and cook for 2 minutes.*

squig|gle /skwɪgᵊl/ (squiggles) N-COUNT A **squiggle** is a line that bends and curls in an irregular way.

squig|gly /skwɪgli/ ADJ **Squiggly** lines are lines that bend and curl in an irregular way. ❑ *He drew three squiggly lines.*

squint /skwɪnt/ (squints, squinting, squinted) ❶ V-I If you **squint** at something, you look at it with your eyes partly closed. ❑ *The girl squinted at the photograph.* ❑ *The bright sunlight made me squint.* ❷ N-COUNT If someone has a **squint**, their eyes look in different directions from each other. ❑ *...a pimple-faced man with a squint.* ❸ → See feature box at **eyesight**

squirm /skwɜrm/ (squirms, squirming, squirmed) ❶ V-I If you **squirm**, you move your body from side to side, usually because you are nervous or uncomfortable. ❑ *He had squirmed and wriggled and screeched when his father had washed his face.* ❑ *He gave a feeble shrug and tried to squirm free.* ❷ V-I If you **squirm**, you are very embarrassed or ashamed. ❑ *Mentioning religion is a sure way to make him squirm.*

squir|rel /skwɜrəl/ (squirrels) N-COUNT A **squirrel** is a small animal with a long furry tail. Squirrels live mainly in trees.

squirt /skwɜrt/ (squirts, squirting, squirted) ❶ V-T/V-I If you **squirt** a liquid somewhere or if it **squirts** somewhere, the liquid comes out of a narrow opening in a thin fast stream. ❑ *Norman cut open his pie and squirted tomato sauce into it.* • N-COUNT **Squirt** is also a noun. ❑ *It just needs a little squirt of oil.* ❷ V-T If you **squirt** something **with** a liquid, you squirt the liquid at it. ❑ *They squirted each other with soapy water.*

squishy /skwɪʃi/ (squishier, squishiest) ADJ Something that is squishy is soft and easy to squash. ❑ *...squishy pink leather chairs.*

Sr. Sr. is a written abbreviation for **Senior**, and is written after a man's name. It is used in order to distinguish a man from his son when they both have the same name. ❑ *...Donald Cunningham, Sr.*

SS /ɛs ɛs/ SS is used in the names of some ships. SS is an abbreviation for **steamship**. ❑ *...seven-day cruises to Alaska aboard the SS Rotterdam.*

SSI /ɛs ɛs aɪ/ N-UNCOUNT SSI is money that is paid by the government to elderly and disabled people with limited income or assets. SSI is an abbreviation for 'Supplemental Security Income.' [AM] ❑ *Blind and disabled people are eligible for SSI even under age 65.*

St.

> The form SS is used as the plural for meaning ❷.

❶ St. is a written abbreviation for **Street**. ❑ *...116 Princess St.* ❷ St. is a written abbreviation for **Saint**. ❑ *...St. Thomas.*

> **SUFFIX**
>
> **-st**
> is added to numbers written in figures and ending in 1 – but not 11 – in order to form ordinal numbers. *For example, 'August 1st' is day number 1 in the month of August.*

stab /stæb/ (stabs, stabbing, stabbed) ❶ V-T If someone **stabs** you, they push a knife or sharp object into your body. ❑ *Somebody stabbed him in the stomach.* ❑ *Dean tried to stab him with a screwdriver.* ❷ V-T/V-I If you **stab** something or **stab at** it, you push at it with your finger or with something pointed that you are holding. ❑ *Bess stabbed a slice of cucumber.* ❑ *Goldstone flipped through the pages and stabbed his thumb at the paragraph he was looking for.* ❸ N-SING If you have **a stab at** something, you try to do it. [INFORMAL] ❑ *Several tennis stars have had a stab at acting.* ❹ N-SING You can refer to a sudden, usually unpleasant feeling as **a stab of** something. [LITERARY] ❑ *...a stab of pain just above his eye.* ❺ PHRASE If you say that someone **has stabbed you in the back**, you mean that they have done something very harmful to you when you thought that you could trust them. You can refer to an action of this kind as **a stab in the back**. ❑ *She felt betrayed, as though her daughter had stabbed her in the back.*

stab|bing /stæbɪŋ/ (stabbings) ❶ N-COUNT A **stabbing** is an incident in which someone stabs someone else with a knife. ❑ *...the victim of a stabbing.* ❷ ADJ [ADJ n] A **stabbing** pain is a sudden sharp pain. ❑ *He was struck by a stabbing pain in his midriff.*

sta|bil|ity /stəbɪlɪti/ → see **stable**

sta|bi|lize /steɪbɪlaɪz/ (stabilizes, stabilizing, stabilized)

> in BRIT, also use **stabilise**

V-T/V-I If something **stabilizes**, or **is stabilized**, it becomes stable. ❑ *Although her illness is serious, her condition is beginning to stabilize.* • **sta|bi|li|za|tion** /steɪbɪlɪzeɪʃᵊn/ N-UNCOUNT ❑ *...the stabilization of property prices.*

sta|bi|liz|er /steɪbɪlaɪzər/ (stabilizers)

> in BRIT, also use **stabiliser**

N-COUNT A **stabilizer** is a device, mechanism, or chemical that makes something stable.

sta|ble ✦✦◇ /steɪbᵊl/ (stabler, stablest, stables) ❶ ADJ If something is **stable**, it is not likely to change or come to an end suddenly. ❑ *The price of oil should remain stable for the rest of the year.* • **sta|bil|ity** /stəbɪlɪti/ N-UNCOUNT ❑ *It was a time of political stability and progress.* ❷ ADJ If someone has a **stable** personality, they are calm and reasonable and their mood does not change suddenly. ❑ *Their characters are fully formed and they are both very stable children.* ❸ ADJ You can describe someone who is seriously ill as **stable** when their condition has stopped getting worse. ❑ *The injured man was in a stable condition.* ❹ ADJ Chemical substances are described as **stable** when they tend to remain in the same chemical or atomic state. [TECHNICAL] ❑ *The less stable compounds were converted into a compound called Delta-A THC.* ❺ ADJ If an object is **stable**, it is firmly fixed in position and is not likely to move or fall. ❑ *This structure must be stable.* ❻ N-COUNT A **stable** or **stables** is a building in which horses are kept. ❼ N-COUNT A **stable** or **stables** is an organization that breeds and trains horses for racing. ❑ *Miss Curling won on two horses from Mick Trickey's stable.*

> **SYNONYMS**
>
> **stable**
> ADJ
> ❶
> **secure:** *...trade union demands for secure wages and employment.*
> **lasting:** *We are well on our way to a lasting peace.*
> **strong:** *He felt he had a relationship strong enough to talk frankly to Sarah.*
> **sound:** *When we bought the house, it was structurally sound.*
> ❷
> **well-balanced:** *...a fun-loving, well-balanced individual.*
> **sensible:** *She was a sensible girl and did not panic.*
> **reasonable:** *He's a reasonable sort of fellow.*
> ADJ ❺
> **solid:** *Banks are built to look solid to reassure their customers.*
> **firm:** *If you have to climb up, use a firm platform or a sturdy ladder.*
> **secure:** *Shelves are only as secure as their fixings.*

sta|ble boy (stable boys) N-COUNT A **stable boy** is a young man who works in a stable taking care of the horses.

stable|mate /steɪbᵊlmeɪt/ (stablemates) N-COUNT [usu poss N] **Stablemates** are racehorses that come from the same

stab wound (stab wounds) N-COUNT A **stab wound** is a wound that someone has when they have been stabbed with a knife.

stac|ca|to /stəkɑtoʊ/ ADJ [usu ADJ n] A **staccato** noise consists of a series of short, sharp, separate sounds. ❑ *He spoke in Arabic, a short staccato burst.*

stack /stæk/ (stacks, stacking, stacked) ◼ N-COUNT A **stack** of things is a pile of them. ❑ *There were stacks of books on the bedside table and floor.* ◼ V-T If you **stack** a number of things, you arrange them in neat piles. ❑ *Mrs. Cathiard was stacking the clean bottles in crates.* • PHRASAL VERB **Stack up** means the same as **stack**. ❑ *He ordered them to stack up pillows behind his back.* ◼ N-PLURAL If you say that someone has **stacks of** something, you mean that they have a lot of it. [INFORMAL] ❑ *If the job's that good, you'll have stacks of money.* ◼ PHRASE If you say that **the odds are stacked against** someone, or that particular factors **are stacked against** them, you mean that they are unlikely to succeed in what they want to do because the conditions are not favorable. ❑ *The odds are stacked against civilians getting a fair trial.*

stacked /stækt/ ADJ If a place or surface is **stacked with** objects, it is filled with piles of them. ❑ *Shops in Ho Chi Minh City are stacked with goods.*

sta|dium ✦◇◇ /steɪdiəm/ (stadiums or stadia /steɪdiə/) N-COUNT; N-IN-NAMES A **stadium** is a large sports field with rows of seats all around it. ❑ *...a baseball stadium.*

staff ✦✦✦ /stæf/ (staffs, staffing, staffed) ◼ N-COUNT-COLL The **staff** of an organization are the people who work for it. ❑ *The staff were very good.* ❑ *The outpatient program has a staff of six people.* ❑ *...staff members.* ◼ → see also **Chief of Staff** ◼ N-PLURAL People who are part of a particular staff are often referred to as **staff**. ❑ *10 staff were allocated to the task.* ◼ V-T [usu passive] If an organization **is staffed** by particular people, they are the people who work for it. ❑ *They are staffed by volunteers.*
• **staffed** ADJ [adv ADJ] ❑ *The house allocated to them was pleasant and spacious, and well staffed.*

---SYNONYMS---

staff
NOUN ◼
workers: *...office workers.*
employees: *They are all employees of Fuji Bank.*
personnel: *There has been very little turnover of personnel in higher education.*
workforce: *...a country where half the workforce is unemployed.*

---

staff|er /stæfər/ (staffers) N-COUNT [usu n n] A **staffer** is a member of a staff, especially in political organizations or in journalism. [mainly AM] ❑ *The president invited 3,500 guests, mostly White House staffers and their families.*

staff|ing /stæfɪŋ/ N-UNCOUNT **Staffing** refers to the number of workers employed to work in a particular organization or building. [BUSINESS] ❑ *Staffing levels in prisons are too low.*

staff of|fic|er (staff officers) N-COUNT In the army and air force, a **staff officer** is an officer who works for a commander or in the headquarters.

staff ser|geant (staff sergeants) also **Staff Sergeant** N-COUNT; N-TITLE A **staff sergeant** is someone who ranks just above sergeant in the United States army, marines, or air force. ❑ *His father is a staff sergeant in the army.* ❑ *...Staff Sergeant Robert Daily.*

stag /stæg/ (stags) N-COUNT A **stag** is an adult male deer belonging to one of the larger species of deer. Stags usually have large branch-like horns called antlers.

stage ✦✦✦ /steɪdʒ/ (stages, staging, staged) ◼ N-COUNT A **stage** of an activity, process, or period is one part of it. ❑ *The way children talk about or express their feelings depends on their age and stage of development.* ◼ N-COUNT [also on N] In a theater, the **stage** is an area where actors or other entertainers perform. ❑ *The road crew needed more than 24 hours to move and rebuild the stage after a concert.* ◼ V-T If someone **stages** a play or other show, they organize and present a performance of it. ❑ *Maya Angelou first staged the play "And I Still Rise" in the late 1970s.* ◼ V-T If you **stage** an event or ceremony, you organize it and usually take part in it. ❑ *Russian workers have staged a number of strikes in protest at the republic's declaration of independence.* ◼ N-SING You can refer to a particular area of activity as a particular **stage**, especially when you are talking about politics. ❑ *He was finally forced off the political stage last year by the deterioration of his physical condition.* ◼ **to set the stage** → see **set** ② ◼ → See feature box at **theater**

stage|coach /steɪdʒkoʊtʃ/ (stagecoaches) N-COUNT [also by N] **Stagecoaches** were large carriages pulled by horses which carried passengers and mail.

stage|craft /steɪdʒkræft/ N-UNCOUNT **Stagecraft** is skill in writing or producing or directing plays in the theater.

stage di|rec|tion (stage directions) N-COUNT **Stage directions** are the notes in the text of a play which say what the actors should do.

stage door (stage doors) N-COUNT [usu the N in sing] The **stage door** of a theater is the entrance used by actors and actresses and by employees of the theater.

stage fright ◼ N-UNCOUNT **Stage fright** is a feeling of fear or nervousness that some people have just before they appear in front of an audience. ◼ → See feature box at **theater**

stage|hand /steɪdʒhænd/ (stagehands) also **stage hand** ◼ N-COUNT A **stagehand** is a person whose job is to move the scenery and equipment on the stage in a theater. ◼ → See feature box at **theater**

stage left ADV **Stage left** is the left side of the stage for an actor who is standing facing the audience. ❑ *He entered stage left.*

stage-manage (stage-manages, stage-managing, stage-managed) V-T If someone **stage-manages** an event, they carefully organize and control it, rather than letting it happen in a natural way. [DISAPPROVAL] ❑ *The party hired her to stage-manage their convention.*

stage man|ag|er (stage managers) N-COUNT At a theater, a **stage manager** is the person who is responsible for the scenery and lights and for the way that actors or other performers move around and use the stage during a performance.

stage name (stage names) N-COUNT A **stage name** is a name that an actor or entertainer uses instead of his or her real name when they work. ❑ *Under the stage name of Beverly Brooks, Patricia had small parts in several movies.*

stage right ADV **Stage right** is the right side of the stage for an actor who is standing facing the audience.

stage-struck also **stagestruck** ADJ Someone who is **stage-struck** is fascinated by the theater and wants to become an actor.

stage whis|per (stage whispers) also **stage-whisper** N-COUNT If someone says something in a **stage whisper**, they say it as if they are speaking privately to one person, although it is actually loud enough to be heard by other people.

stag|fla|tion /stæɡfleɪʃən/ N-UNCOUNT If an economy is suffering from **stagflation**, inflation is high but there is no increase in the demand for goods or in the number of people who have jobs. [BUSINESS] ❑ *Many of the industrialized economies would be pushed into a cycle of stagflation.*

stag|ger /stæɡər/ (staggers, staggering, staggered) ◼ V-I If you **stagger**, you walk very unsteadily, for example because you are ill or drunk. ❑ *He lost his balance, staggered back against the rail and toppled over.* ◼ V-T If something **staggers** you, it surprises you very much. ❑ *The whole thing staggers me.*
• **staggered** ADJ [v-link ADJ] ❑ *I was simply staggered by the heat of the Argentinian high-summer.* ◼ V-T To **stagger** things such as people's vacations or hours of work means to arrange them so that they do not all happen at the same time. ❑ *During the past few years the university has staggered the summer vacation periods for students.*

stag|ger|ing /stæɡərɪŋ/ ADJ Something that is **staggering** is very surprising. ❑ *...a staggering $900 million in short- and long-term debt.*

stag|nant /stæɡnənt/ ◼ ADJ If something such as a business or society is **stagnant**, there is little activity or change.

stagnate [DISAPPROVAL] ❏ *He is seeking advice on how to revive the stagnant economy.* ❷ ADJ **Stagnant** water is not flowing, and therefore often smells unpleasant and is dirty. ❏ *...a stagnant pond.*

stag|nate /stægneɪt/ (**stagnates**, **stagnating**, **stagnated**) V-I If something such as a business or society **stagnates**, it stops changing or progressing. [DISAPPROVAL] ❏ *Industrial production is stagnating.* • **stag|na|tion** /stægneɪʃən/ N-UNCOUNT ❏ *...the stagnation of the steel industry.*

stag night (**stag nights**) N-COUNT A **stag night** is the same as a **stag party**. [BRIT]

stag par|ty (**stag parties**) N-COUNT A **stag party** is a party for a man who is getting married very soon, to which usually only men are invited.

staid /steɪd/ ADJ If you say that someone or something is **staid**, you mean that they are serious, dull, and rather old-fashioned. ❏ *...a staid seaside resort.*

stain /steɪn/ (**stains**, **staining**, **stained**) ❶ N-COUNT A **stain** is a mark on something that is difficult to remove. ❏ *Remove stains by soaking in a mild solution of bleach.* ❷ V-T If a liquid **stains** something, the thing becomes colored or marked by the liquid. ❏ *Some foods can stain the teeth, as of course can smoking.* • **stained** ADJ ❏ *His clothing was stained with mud.* • **-stained** COMB IN ADJ ❏ *...ink-stained fingers.* ❸ → See feature box at **housework**

stained glass also **stained-glass** N-UNCOUNT **Stained glass** consists of pieces of glass of different colors which are fitted together to make decorative windows or other objects. ❏ *...the stained glass window in St. John's Cathedral.*

stain|less steel /steɪnlɪs stil/ N-UNCOUNT **Stainless steel** is a metal made from steel and chromium which does not rust. ❏ *...a stainless steel sink.*

stair /stɛər/ (**stairs**) N-PLURAL **Stairs** are a set of steps inside a building which go from one floor to another. ❏ *Nancy began to climb the stairs.* ❏ *We walked up a flight of stairs.*

stair|case /stɛərkeɪs/ (**staircases**) ❶ N-COUNT A **staircase** is a set of stairs inside a building. ❏ *They walked down the staircase together.* ❷ → See feature box at **house**

stair|lift /stɛərlɪft/ also **stair lift** (**stairlifts**) N-COUNT A **stairlift** is a device that is attached to a staircase in a house in order to allow an elderly or sick person to go upstairs.

stair|way /stɛərweɪ/ (**stairways**) N-COUNT A **stairway** is a staircase or a flight of steps, inside or outside a building. ❏ *...the stairway leading to the top floor.*

stair|well /stɛərwɛl/ (**stairwells**) N-COUNT The **stairwell** is the part of a building that contains the staircase.

stake ◆◇◇ /steɪk/ (**stakes**, **staking**, **staked**) ❶ PHRASE If something is **at stake**, it is being risked and might be lost or damaged if you are not successful. ❏ *The tension was naturally high for a game with so much at stake.* ❷ N-PLURAL The **stakes** involved in a contest or a risky action are the things that can be gained or lost. ❏ *The game was usually played for high stakes between two large groups.* ❸ V-T If you **stake** something such as your money or your reputation on the result of something, you risk your money or reputation on it. ❏ *He has staked his political future on an election victory.* ❹ N-COUNT If you have a **stake in** something such as a business, it matters to you, for example because you own part of it or because its success or failure will affect you. ❏ *He was eager to return to a more entrepreneurial role in which he had a big financial stake in his own efforts.* ❺ N-PLURAL You can use **stakes** to refer to something that is like a contest. For example, you can refer to the choosing of a leader as **the leadership stakes**. ❏ *We are lagging behind in the childcare stakes.* ❻ N-COUNT A **stake** is a pointed wooden post which is pushed into the ground, for example in order to support a young tree. ❏ *His arms were tied to wooden stakes to hold him flat.* ❼ PHRASE If you **stake a claim**, you say that something is yours or that you have a right to it. ❏ *Jane is determined to stake her claim as an actress.*

COLLOCATIONS

stake
NOUN ❹
noun + **stake**: equity, majority, minority
adjective + **stake**: high, large, significant; controlling
verb + **stake**: acquire, buy, take; sell; hold, own, retain

---

stake|hold|er /steɪkhoʊldər/ (**stakeholders**) N-COUNT **Stakeholders** are people who have an interest in a company's or organization's affairs. [BUSINESS] ❏ *...the Delaware River Port Authority, a major stakeholder in Penn's Landing.*

stake|out /steɪkaʊt/ (**stakeouts**) N-COUNT If police officers are on a **stakeout**, they are secretly watching a building for evidence of criminal activity.

stal|ac|tite /stəlæktaɪt/ (**stalactites**) N-COUNT A **stalactite** is a long piece of rock which hangs down from the roof of a cave. Stalactites are formed by the slow dropping of water containing the mineral lime.

stal|ag|mite /stəlægmaɪt/ (**stalagmites**) N-COUNT A **stalagmite** is a long piece of rock which sticks up from the floor of a cave. Stalagmites are formed by the slow dropping of water containing the mineral lime.

stale /steɪl/ (**staler**, **stalest**) ❶ ADJ **Stale** food is no longer fresh or good to eat. ❏ *Their daily diet consisted of a lump of stale bread, a bowl of rice, and stale water.* ❷ ADJ **Stale** air or smells are unpleasant because they are no longer fresh. ❏ *...the smell of stale sweat.* ❸ ADJ If you say that a place, an activity, or an idea is **stale**, you mean that it has become boring because it is always the same. [DISAPPROVAL] ❏ *Her relationship with Mark has become stale.*

stale|mate /steɪlmeɪt/ (**stalemates**) ❶ N-VAR **Stalemate** is a situation in which neither side in an argument or contest can win or in which no progress is possible. ❏ *The proportional representation system was widely blamed for two inconclusive election results and a year of political stalemate.* ❷ → See feature box at **conflict**

stalk /stɔk/ (**stalks**, **stalking**, **stalked**) ❶ N-COUNT The **stalk** of a flower, leaf, or fruit is the thin part that joins it to the plant or tree. ❏ *A single pale blue flower grows up from each joint on a long stalk.* ❷ V-T If you **stalk** a person or a wild animal, you follow them quietly in order to kill them, catch them, or observe them carefully. ❏ *He stalks his victims like a hunter after a deer.* ❸ V-T If someone **stalks** someone else, especially a famous person or a person they used to have a relationship with, they keep following them or contacting them in an annoying and frightening way. ❏ *Even after their divorce he continued to stalk and threaten her.*

stalk|er /stɔkər/ (**stalkers**) N-COUNT A **stalker** is someone who keeps following or contacting someone else, especially a famous person or a person they used to have a relationship with, in an annoying and frightening way. ❏ *She had been followed and then trapped by a stalker.*

stalk|ing horse (**stalking horses**) ❶ N-COUNT If you describe something as a **stalking horse**, you mean that it is being used to obtain a temporary advantage so that someone can get what they really want. [DISAPPROVAL] ❏ *I think the development is a stalking horse for exploitation of the surrounding countryside.* ❷ N-COUNT [oft N n] In politics, a **stalking horse** is someone who runs against a leader in order to see how strong the opposition is. The stalking horse then withdraws in favor of a stronger challenger. ❏ *The possibility of another stalking horse challenge this fall cannot be ruled out.*

stall /stɔl/ (**stalls**, **stalling**, **stalled**) ❶ V-T/V-I If a process **stalls**, or if someone or something **stalls** it, the process stops but may continue at a later time. ❏ *The Social Democratic Party has vowed to try to stall the bill until the current session ends.* ❏ *...but the peace process stalled.* ❷ V-I If you **stall**, you try to avoid doing something until later. ❏ *Thomas had spent all week stalling over his decision.* ❸ V-T If you **stall** someone, you prevent them from doing something until a later time. ❏ *The store manager stalled the man until the police arrived.* ❹ V-T/V-I If a vehicle **stalls** or if you accidentally **stall** it, the engine stops suddenly. ❏ *The engine stalled.* ❺ N-COUNT A **stall** is a large table on which you put goods that you want to sell, or information that you want to give people. ❏ *...market stalls selling local fruits.* ❻ N-PLURAL The **stalls** in a theater or concert hall are the seats on the ground floor directly in front of the stage. [mainly BRIT]

in AM, use **orchestra**

❼ N-COUNT A **stall** is a small enclosed area in a room which is used for a particular purpose, for example a shower. [AM] ❏ *She went into the shower stall, turned on the water, and grabbed the soap.*

in BRIT, usually use **cubicle**

stal|lion /stælyən/ (stallions) N-COUNT A **stallion** is a male horse, especially one kept for breeding.

stal|wart /stɔlwərt/ (stalwarts) N-COUNT A **stalwart** is a loyal worker or supporter of an organization, especially a political party. ◻ *His free-trade policies aroused suspicion among party stalwarts.*

sta|men /steɪmɛn/ (stamens) **1** N-COUNT The **stamens** of a flower are the small, delicate stalks which grow at the flower's center and produce pollen. [TECHNICAL] **2** → See also color supplement

stami|na /stæmɪnə/ N-UNCOUNT **Stamina** is the physical or mental energy needed to do a tiring activity for a long time. ◻ *You have to have a lot of stamina to be a top-class dancer.*

stam|mer /stæmər/ (stammers, stammering, stammered) **1** V-T/V-I If you **stammer**, you speak with difficulty, hesitating and repeating words or sounds. ◻ *Five percent of children stammer at some point.* ◻ *"Forgive me," I stammered.* • **stam|mer|ing** N-UNCOUNT ◻ *Of all speech impediments stammering is probably the most embarrassing.* **2** N-SING Someone who has a **stammer** tends to stammer when they speak. ◻ *A speech therapist cured his stammer.*

stamp ✦✧✧ /stæmp/ (stamps, stamping, stamped) **1** N-COUNT A **stamp** or a **postage stamp** is a small piece of paper which you stick on an envelope or package before you mail it to pay for the cost of the postage. ◻ *...a book of stamps.* ◻ *As of February 3rd, the price of a first class stamp will go up to 29 cents.* **2** N-COUNT A **stamp** is a small block of wood or metal which has a pattern or a group of letters on one side. You press it onto a pad of ink and then onto a piece of paper in order to produce a mark on the paper. The mark that that produces is also called a **stamp**. ◻ *...a date stamp and an ink pad.* **3** V-T If you **stamp** a mark or word on an object, you press the mark or word onto the object using a stamp or other device. ◻ *Car manufacturers stamp a vehicle identification number at several places on new cars to help track down stolen vehicles.* **4** V-T/V-I If you **stamp** or **stamp** your foot, you lift your foot and put it down very hard on the ground, for example because you are angry or because your feet are cold. ◻ *Often he teased me till my temper went and I stamped and screamed, feeling furiously helpless.* ◻ *His foot stamped down on the accelerator.* • N-COUNT **Stamp** is also a noun. ◻ *...hearing the creak of a door and the stamp of cold feet.* **5** V-I If you **stamp** somewhere, you walk there putting your feet down very hard on the ground because you are angry. ◻ *"I'm going before things get any worse!" he shouted as he stamped out of the bedroom.* **6** V-I If you **stamp on** something, you put your foot down on it very hard. ◻ *He received the original ban last week after stamping on the referee's foot during the final.* **7** N-SING If something bears the **stamp** of a particular quality or person, it clearly has that quality or was done by that person. ◻ *Most of us want to make our home a familiar place and put the stamp of our personality on its walls.* **8** → see also **rubber stamp**

▶ **stamp out** PHRASAL VERB If you **stamp** something **out**, you put an end to it. ◻ *Dr. Muffett stressed that he was opposed to bullying in schools and that action would be taken to stamp it out.*

stamp col|lect|ing N-UNCOUNT **Stamp collecting** is the hobby of building up a collection of stamps.

stamped /stæmpt/ ADJ [usu ADJ n] A **stamped** envelope or package has a stamp stuck on it.

stamped ad|dressed en|velope (stamped addressed envelopes) N-COUNT A **stamped addressed envelope** is the same as an **SASE**. [BRIT]

stam|pede /stæmpiːd/ (stampedes, stampeding, stampeded) **1** N-COUNT If there is a **stampede**, a group of people or animals run in a wild, uncontrolled way. ◻ *There was a stampede for the exit.* **2** V-T/V-I If a group of animals or people **stampede** or if something or someone **stampedes** them, they run in a wild, uncontrolled way. ◻ *The crowd stampeded and many were crushed or trampled underfoot.* ◻ *...a herd of stampeding cattle.* **3** N-COUNT If a lot of people all do the same thing at the same time, you can describe it as a **stampede**. ◻ *...a stampede of consumers rushing to buy merchandise at bargain prices.*

stamp|ing ground (stamping grounds) N-COUNT [usu with poss] A **stamping ground** is the same as a **stomping ground**.

stance /stæns/ (stances) **1** N-COUNT Your **stance** on a particular matter is your attitude to it. ◻ *Congress had agreed to reconsider its stance on the armed struggle.* **2** N-COUNT Your **stance** is the way that you are standing. [FORMAL] ◻ *Take a comfortably wide stance and flex your knees a little.*

stan|chion /stæntʃ°n/ (stanchions) N-COUNT A **stanchion** is a pole or bar that stands upright and is used as a support. [FORMAL]

STAND
① VERB USES AND PHRASES
② NOUN USES
③ PHRASAL VERBS

---

① **stand** ✦✦✦ /stænd/ (stands, standing, stood)

→ Please look at meanings **21** – **23** to see if the expression you are looking for is shown under another headword.

1 V-I When you **are standing**, your body is upright, your legs are straight, and your weight is supported by your feet. ◻ *She was standing beside my bed staring down at me.* ◻ *They told me to stand still and not to turn round.* • PHRASAL VERB **Stand up** means the same as **stand** ①. ◻ *We waited, standing up, for an hour.* **2** V-I When someone who is sitting **stands**, they change their position so that they are upright and on their feet. ◻ *Becker stood and shook hands with Ben.* • PHRASAL VERB **Stand up** means the same as **stand** ①. ◻ *When I walked in, they all stood up and started clapping.* **3** V-I If you **stand aside** or **stand back**, you move a short distance sideways or backward, so that you are standing in a different place. ◻ *I stood aside to let her pass me.* **4** V-I If something such as a building or a piece of furniture **stands** somewhere, it is in that position, and is upright. [WRITTEN] ◻ *The house stands alone on top of a small hill.* **5** V-I You can say that a building **is standing** when it remains after other buildings around it have fallen down or been destroyed. ◻ *The palace, which was damaged by bombs in World War II, still stood.* **6** V-T If you **stand** something somewhere, you put it there in an upright position. ◻ *Stand the plant in the open in a sunny, sheltered place.* **7** V-I If you leave food or a mixture of something to **stand**, you leave it without disturbing it for some time. ◻ *The salad improves if made in advance and left to stand.* **8** V-I If you ask someone where or how they **stand** on a particular issue, you are asking them what their attitude or view is. ◻ *The amendment will force senators to show where they stand on the issue of sexual harassment.* **9** V-I If you do not know where you **stand** with someone, you do not know exactly what their attitude to you is. ◻ *No one knows where they stand with him; he is utterly unpredictable.* **10** V-LINK You can use **stand** instead of 'be' when you are describing the present state or condition of something or someone. ◻ *The alliance stands ready to do what is necessary.* **11** V-I If a decision, law, or offer **stands**, it still exists and has not been changed or canceled. ◻ *Although exceptions could be made, the rule still stands.* **12** V-I If something that can be measured **stands at** a particular level, it is at that level. ◻ *The inflation rate now stands at 3.6 percent.* **13** V-T If something can **stand** a situation or a test, it is good enough or strong enough to experience it without being damaged, harmed, or shown to be inadequate. ◻ *These are the first machines that can stand the wear and tear of continuously crushing glass.* **14** V-T If you cannot **stand** something, you cannot bear it or tolerate it. ◻ *I can't stand any more. I'm going to run away.* ◻ *Stoddart can stand any amount of personal criticism.* **15** V-T If you cannot **stand** someone or something, you dislike them very strongly. [INFORMAL] ◻ *I can't stand that man and his arrogance.* **16** V-T If you **stand to gain** something, you are likely to gain it. If you **stand to lose** something, you are likely to lose it. ◻ *The management group would stand to gain millions of dollars if the company were sold.* **17** V-I If you **stand** in an election, you are a candidate in it. [BRIT]

in AM, use **run**

18 → see also **standing** **19** PHRASE If you say it **stands to reason** that something is true or likely to happen, you mean that it is obvious. ◻ *It stands to reason that if you are considerate and friendly to people you will get a lot more back.* **20** PHRASE If you **stand in the way of** something or **stand in** a person's **way**, you prevent that thing from happening or prevent that person from doing something. ◻ *The administration would not stand in the way of such a proposal.* **21** to **stand a chance** → see **chance** **22** to **stand firm** → see **firm** **23** to **stand on your own two**

feet → see foot ①   24 to stand your ground → see ground ③
25 to stand someone in good stead → see stead   26 to stand trial → see trial

② **stand** ♦♦♦ /stænd/ (stands) **1** N-COUNT If you take or make a **stand**, you do something or say something in order to make it clear what your attitude to a particular thing is. ❏ *It's very important to me to make a stand against the consensus that our youth are a lost cause.* **2** N-COUNT A **stand** is a small store or stall, outdoors or in a large public building. ❏ *He ran a newspaper stand outside the American Express office.* **3** N-PLURAL The **stands** at a sports stadium or arena are a large structure where people sit or stand to watch what is happening. ❏ *The people in the stands at Candlestick Park are standing and cheering with all their might.* • N-COUNT In British English, **stand** is used with the same meaning. ❏ *I was sitting in the stand for the first game.* **4** N-COUNT A **stand** is an object or piece of furniture that is designed for supporting or holding a particular kind of thing. ❏ *The teapot came with a stand to catch the drips.* **5** N-COUNT A **stand** is an area where taxis or buses can wait to pick up passengers. ❏ *Luckily there was a taxi stand nearby.* **6** N-SING In a law court, **the stand** is the place where a witness sits to answer questions. ❏ *When the father took the stand today, he contradicted his son's testimony.*

③ **stand** ♦♦♦ /stænd/ (stands, standing, stood)
▶ **stand aside** [BRIT] → see **stand down**
▶ **stand back** PHRASAL VERB If you **stand back** and think about a situation, you think about it as if you were not involved in it. ❏ *Stand back and look objectively at the problem.*
▶ **stand by** **1** PHRASAL VERB If you **are standing by**, you are ready and waiting to provide help or to take action. ❏ *British and American warships are standing by to evacuate their citizens if necessary.* **2** → see also **standby** **3** PHRASAL VERB If you **stand by** and let something bad happen, you do not do anything to stop it. [DISAPPROVAL] ❏ *The Secretary of Defense has said that he would not stand by and let democracy be undermined.* **4** PHRASAL VERB If you **stand by** someone, you continue to give them support, especially when they are in trouble. [APPROVAL] ❏ *I wouldn't break the law for a friend, but I would stand by her if she did.* **5** PHRASAL VERB If you **stand by** an earlier decision, promise, or statement, you continue to support it or keep it. ❏ *The decision has been made and I have got to stand by it.*
▶ **stand down** PHRASAL VERB If someone **stands down**, they resign from an important job or position, often in order to let someone else take their place. ❏ *Four days later, the despised leader finally stood down, just 17 days after taking office.*
▶ **stand for** **1** PHRASAL VERB If you say that a letter **stands for** a particular word, you mean that it is an abbreviation for that word. ❏ *AIDS stands for Acquired Immune Deficiency Syndrome.* **2** PHRASAL VERB The ideas or attitudes that someone or something **stands for** are the ones that they support or represent. ❏ *The party is trying to give the impression that it alone stands for democracy.* **3** PHRASAL VERB [with neg] If you will **not stand for** something, you will not allow it to happen or continue. ❏ *It's outrageous, and we won't stand for it any more.*
▶ **stand in** **1** PHRASAL VERB If you **stand in** for someone, you take their place or do their job, because they are sick or away. ❏ *I had to stand in for her on Tuesday when she didn't show up.* **2** → see also **stand-in**
▶ **stand out** **1** PHRASAL VERB If something **stands out**, it is very noticeable. ❏ *Every tree, wall and fence stood out against dazzling white fields.* **2** PHRASAL VERB If something **stands out** from a surface, it rises up from it. ❏ *His tendons stood out like rope beneath his skin.*
▶ **stand up** **1** → see **stand** ① 1, **stand** ① 2 **2** PHRASAL VERB If something such as a claim or a piece of evidence **stands up**, it is accepted as true or satisfactory after being carefully examined. ❏ *He made wild accusations that did not stand up.* **3** PHRASAL VERB If a boyfriend or girlfriend **stands you up**, they fail to keep an arrangement to meet you. [INFORMAL] ❏ *We were to have had dinner together yesterday evening, but he stood me up.*
▶ **stand up for** PHRASAL VERB If you **stand up for** someone or something, you defend them and make your feelings or opinions very clear. [APPROVAL] ❏ *They stood up for what they believed to be right.*
▶ **stand up to** **1** PHRASAL VERB If something **stands you up to** bad conditions, it is not damaged or harmed by them. ❏ *Is this building going to stand up to the strongest gales?* **2** PHRASAL VERB If you **stand up to** someone, especially someone more powerful than you are, you defend yourself against their attacks or demands. ❏ *He hit me, so I hit him back–the first time in my life I'd stood up to him.*

stand-alone **1** ADJ [ADJ n] A **stand-alone** business or organization is independent and does not receive financial support from another organization. [BUSINESS] ❏ *They plan to relaunch it as a stand-alone company.* **2** ADJ [ADJ n] A **stand-alone** computer is one that can operate on its own and does not have to be part of a network. [COMPUTING] ❏ *...an operating system that can work on networks and stand-alone machines.*

stand|ard ♦♦◇ /stændərd/ (standards) **1** N-COUNT A **standard** is a level of quality or achievement, especially a level that is thought to be acceptable. ❏ *The standard of professional cricket has never been lower.* **2** N-COUNT A **standard** is something that you use in order to judge the quality of something else. ❏ *...systems that were by later standards absurdly primitive.* **3** N-PLURAL **Standards** are moral principles which affect people's attitudes and behavior. ❏ *My father has always had high moral standards.* **4** ADJ You use **standard** to describe things which are usual and normal. ❏ *It was standard practice for untrained clerks to advise in serious cases such as murder.* **5** ADJ [ADJ n] A **standard** work or text on a particular subject is one that is widely read and often recommended. ❏ *At twenty he translated Euler's standard work on algebra into English.* **6** → See feature box at **working**

╔══════════ SYNONYMS ══════════╗
standard
NOUN
1
level: *The exercises are marked according to their level of difficulty.*
grade: *...a good grade of plywood.*
quality: *...high-quality paper and plywood.*
caliber: *I was impressed by the high caliber of the researchers and analysts.*
3
principle: *...moral principles.*
ideal: *The party has drifted too far from its socialist ideals.*
moral: *...Western ideas and morals.*
ADJ **4**
usual: *She's smiling her usual friendly smile.*
normal: *The two countries resumed normal diplomatic relations.*
customary: *The king carried himself with his customary elegance.*
typical: *He is everyone's image of a typical cop.*

standard-bearer (standard-bearers) also **standard bearer** N-COUNT [usu with supp] If you describe someone as the **standard-bearer** of a group, you mean that they act as the leader or public representative of a group of people who have the same aims or interests. ❏ *He was a standard-bearer for the causes of African-Americans.*

stand|ard|ize /stændərdaɪz/ (standardizes, standardizing, standardized)

in BRIT, also use **standardise**

V-T To **standardize** things means to change them so that they all have the same features. ❏ *There is a drive both to standardize components and to reduce the number of models.* • **stand|ardi|za|tion** /stændərdɪzeɪʃən/ N-UNCOUNT ❏ *...the standardization of working hours.*

stand|ard lamp (standard lamps) N-COUNT A **standard lamp** is the same as a **floor lamp**. [BRIT]

stand|ard of liv|ing (standards of living) **1** N-COUNT Your **standard of living** is the level of comfort and wealth which you have. ❏ *We'll continue to fight for a decent standard of living for our members.* **2** → See feature box at **leisure**

stand|ard time N-UNCOUNT **Standard time** is the official local time of a region or country. ❏ *Tonight the nation switches from daylight-saving time to standard time.*

stand|by /stændbaɪ/ (standbys) also **stand-by** **1** N-COUNT A **standby** is something or someone that is always ready to be used if they are needed. ❏ *Canned varieties of beans and peas are a good standby.* **2** PHRASE If someone or something is **on standby**, they are ready to be used if they are needed. ❏ *Five* ambulances are on standby at the port. ◼ ADJ [ADJ N] A **standby** ticket for something such as the theater or a plane trip is a cheap ticket that you buy just before the performance starts or the plane takes off, if there are still some seats left. ◻ *He bought a standby ticket to New York at 5:30 a.m. the following morning and flew to JFK airport six hours later.* • ADV [ADV after v] **Standby** is also an adverb. ◻ *Magda was going to fly standby.*

stand-in (stand-ins) N-COUNT A **stand-in** is a person who takes someone else's place or does someone else's job for a while, for example because the other person is sick or away. ◻ *He was a stand-in for my regular doctor.*

stand|ing /stǽndɪŋ/ (standings) ◼ N-UNCOUNT Someone's **standing** is their reputation or status. ◻ *...an artist of international standing.* ◻ *He has improved his country's standing abroad.* ◼ N-COUNT A party's or person's **standing** is their popularity. ◻ *But, as the opinion poll shows, the party's standing with the people at large has never been so low.* ◼ ADJ [ADJ N] You use **standing** to describe something which is permanently in existence. ◻ *Israel has a relatively small standing army and its strength is based on its reserves.* ◼ → see also **long-standing**

stand|ing joke (standing jokes) N-COUNT [usu sing] If something is a **standing joke** among a group of people, they often make jokes about it. ◻ *Her precision became a standing joke with colleagues.*

stand|ing ova|tion (standing ovations) N-COUNT If a speaker or performer gets a **standing ovation** when they have finished speaking or performing, the audience stands up to clap in order to show its admiration or support.

stand|ing room ◼ N-UNCOUNT **Standing room** is space in a room or bus, where people can stand when all the seats have been occupied. ◻ *The place quickly fills up so it's soon standing room only.* ◼ → See feature box at **commute**

stand|off /stǽndɒf/ (standoffs) N-COUNT A **standoff** is a situation in which neither of two opposing groups or forces will make a move until the other one does something, so nothing can happen until one of them gives way. ◻ *There is no sign of an end to the standoff between Mohawk Indians and the Quebec provincial police.*

stand|offish /stændɒ́fɪʃ/ ADJ If you say that someone is **standoffish**, you mean that they behave in a formal and rather unfriendly way. [DISAPPROVAL] ◻ *He can be quite standoffish and rude, even to his friends.*

stand|out /stǽndaʊt/ (standouts) N-COUNT [oft N n] Journalists use **standout** to refer to a person or thing that is much better than the other people or things involved in something. [AM, AUSTRALIAN] ◻ *In the earlier rounds, Ferguson and Dickinson were the standouts.*

stand|pipe /stǽndpaɪp/ (standpipes) N-COUNT A **standpipe** is a vertical pipe that is connected to a water supply and stands in a street or other public place.

stand|point /stǽndpɔɪnt/ (standpoints) N-COUNT From a particular **standpoint** means looking at an event, situation, or idea in a particular way. ◻ *He believes that from a military standpoint, the situation is under control.*

stand|still /stǽndstɪl/ N-SING If movement or activity comes to or is brought to a **standstill**, it stops completely. ◻ *Abruptly the group ahead of us came to a standstill.*

stand-up also **standup** (stand-ups) ◼ ADJ [ADJ N] A **stand-up** comic or comedian stands alone in front of an audience and tells jokes. ◻ *He does all kinds of accents, he can do jokes – he could be a stand-up comic.* ◼ N-UNCOUNT **Stand-up** is stand-up comedy. ◻ *...likability, professionalism and the kind of nerve you need to do stand-up.* ◼ N-COUNT A **stand-up** is a stand-up comedian. ◻ *...one of the worst stand-ups alive.* ◼ → See feature box at **humor**

stank /stǽŋk/ **Stank** is the past tense of **stink**.

Stanley knife (Stanley knives) N-COUNT A **Stanley knife** is a very sharp knife that is used to cut materials such as carpet and paper. It consists of a small blade fixed in the end of a handle. [mainly BRIT, TRADEMARK]

in AM, usually use **razor knife**

stan|za /stǽnzə/ (stanzas) N-COUNT A **stanza** is one of the parts into which a poem is divided. [TECHNICAL]

sta|ple /stéɪpəl/ (staples, stapling, stapled) ◼ ADJ [ADJ N] A **staple** food, product, or activity is one that is basic and important in people's everyday lives. ◻ *Rice is the staple food of more than half the world's population.* ◻ *The Chinese also eat a type of pasta as part of their staple diet.* • N-COUNT **Staple** is also a noun. ◻ *Fish is a staple in the diet of many Africans.* ◼ N-COUNT A **staple** is something that forms an important part of something else. ◻ *Political reporting has become a staple of American journalism.* ◼ N-COUNT **Staples** are small pieces of bent wire that are used mainly for holding sheets of paper together firmly. You put the staples into the paper using a device called a stapler. ◼ V-T If you **staple** something, you fasten it to something else or fix it in place using staples. ◻ *Staple some sheets of paper together into a book.*

sta|ple gun (staple guns) N-COUNT A **staple gun** is a small machine used for forcing staples into wood or brick.

sta|pler /stéɪplər/ (staplers) N-COUNT A **stapler** is a device used for putting staples into sheets of paper.

star ✦✦✦ /stɑ́r/ (stars, starring, starred) ◼ N-COUNT A **star** is a large ball of burning gas in space. Stars appear to us as small points of light in the sky on clear nights. ◻ *The nights were pure with cold air and lit with stars.* ◼ N-COUNT You can refer to a shape or an object as a **star** when it has four, five, or more points sticking out of it in a regular pattern. ◻ *Children at school receive colored stars for work well done.* ◼ N-COUNT You can say how many **stars** something such as a hotel or restaurant has as a way of talking about its quality, which is often indicated by a number of star-shaped symbols. The more stars something has, the better it is. ◻ *...five-star hotels.* ◼ N-COUNT Famous actors, musicians, and sports players are often referred to as **stars**. ◻ *...star of the TV series Scrubs.* ◻ *McCarthy is now one of Hollywood's top comedy stars.* ◼ V-I If an actor or actress **stars in** a play or movie, he or she has one of the most important parts in it. ◻ *The previous year Adolphson had starred in a play in which Ingrid had been an extra.* ◼ V-T If a play or movie **stars** a famous actor or actress, he or she has one of the most important parts in it. ◻ *...a Hollywood movie, "The Secret of Santa Vittoria," directed by Stanley Kramer and starring Anthony Quinn.* ◼ N-PLURAL Predictions about people's lives which are based on astrology and appear regularly in a newspaper or magazine are sometimes referred to as the **stars**. ◻ *There was nothing in my stars to say I'd have travel problems!*

star|board /stɑ́rbərd, -bɔrd/ ADJ The **starboard** side of a ship or an aircraft is the right side when you are on it and facing toward the front. [TECHNICAL] ◻ *He detected a ship moving down the starboard side of the submarine.* • N-UNCOUNT **Starboard** is also a noun. ◻ *I could see the fishing boat to starboard.*

star|burst /stɑ́rbɜrst/ (starbursts) N-COUNT A **starburst** is a bright light with rays coming from it, or a patch of bright color with points extending from it. [LITERARY] ◻ *...a starburst of multi-colored smoke.*

starch /stɑ́rtʃ/ (starches) ◼ N-MASS **Starch** is a substance that is found in foods such as bread, potatoes, pasta, and rice and gives you energy. ◻ *She reorganized her eating so that she was taking more fruit and vegetables and less starch, salt, and fat.* ◼ N-UNCOUNT **Starch** is a substance that is used for making cloth stiffer, especially cotton and linen. ◻ *He never puts enough starch in my shirts.*

starched /stɑ́rtʃt/ ADJ [usu ADJ n] A **starched** garment or piece of cloth has been made stiffer using starch. ◻ *...a starched white shirt.* ◻ *...starched napkins.*

starchy /stɑ́rtʃi/ (starchier, starchiest) ADJ **Starchy** foods contain a lot of starch. ◻ *...starchy and sticky glutinous rices.*

star-crossed ADJ [usu ADJ n] If someone is **star-crossed**, they keep having bad luck. [LITERARY] ◻ *...star-crossed lovers parted by war and conflict.*

star|dom /stɑ́rdəm/ N-UNCOUNT **Stardom** is the state of being very famous, usually as an actor, musician, or athlete. ◻ *In 1929 she shot to stardom on Broadway in a Noel Coward play.*

stare ✦✧✧ /stɛ́ər/ (stares, staring, stared) ◼ V-I If you **stare** at someone or something, you look at them for a long time. ◻ *Tamara stared at him in disbelief, shaking her head.* ◻ *Ben continued to stare out the window.* • N-COUNT **Stare** is also a noun. ◻ *Hlasek gave him a long, cold stare.* ◼ PHRASE If a situation or the answer to a problem **is staring** you **in the face**, it is very obvious, although you may not be immediately aware of it. [INFORMAL] ◻ *Then the answer hit me. It had been staring me in the face ever since Lullington.* ◼ → See feature box at **look**

COLLOCATIONS

stare
NOUN **1**
adjective + **stare**: blank, glassy, unblinking, unwavering; disapproving, icy, stony; curious, incredulous, wide-eyed
verb + **stare**: draw; meet; return
VERB **1**
stare + adverb: blankly, vacantly; fixedly, intently; dreamily, longingly

star|fish /stɑrfɪʃ/ (**starfish**) N-COUNT A **starfish** is a flat, star-shaped creature, usually with five arms, that lives in the sea.

star|gaz|er /stɑrgeɪzər/ (**stargazers**) N-COUNT A **stargazer** is someone who studies the stars as an astronomer or astrologer. [INFORMAL]

star|gaz|ing /stɑrgeɪzɪŋ/ N-UNCOUNT **Stargazing** is the activity of studying the stars as an astronomer or astrologer. [INFORMAL]

stark /stɑrk/ (**starker, starkest**) **1** ADJ **Stark** choices or statements are harsh and unpleasant. ❏ *Companies face a stark choice if they want to stay competitive.* • **stark|ly** ADV ❏ *That issue is presented starkly and brutally by Bob Graham and David Cairns.* **2** ADJ If two things are in **stark** contrast to one another, they are very different from each other in a way that is very obvious. ❏ *...secret cooperation between London and Washington that was in stark contrast to official policy.* • **stark|ly** ADV ❏ *Angus's child-like paintings contrast starkly with his adult subject matter in these portraits.* **3** ADJ Something that is **stark** is very plain in appearance. ❏ *...the stark white, characterless fireplace in the drawing room.* • **stark|ly** ADV ❏ *The room was starkly furnished.*

stark na|ked ADJ Someone who is **stark naked** is completely naked. [EMPHASIS] ❏ *All contestants competed stark naked.*

star|let /stɑrlət/ (**starlets**) N-COUNT A **starlet** is a young actress who is expected to become a movie star in the future. [JOURNALISM]

star|light /stɑrlaɪt/ N-UNCOUNT **Starlight** is the light that comes from the stars at night.

star|ling /stɑrlɪŋ/ (**starlings**) N-COUNT A **starling** is a very common bird with greenish black feathers covered in pale spots which is found in North America and Europe. Starlings often fly around in large groups.

star|lit /stɑrlɪt/ ADJ [ADJ n] **Starlit** means made lighter or brighter by the stars. ❏ *...a clear starlit sky.* ❏ *...this cold, starlit night.*

Star of David /stɑr əv deɪvɪd/ (**Stars of David**) N-COUNT The **Star of David** is a six-pointed star that is a symbol of Judaism and the state of Israel. ❏ *Sarah wears a small gold Star of David around her neck.*

star|ry /stɑri/ ADJ [ADJ n] A **starry** night or sky is one in which a lot of stars are visible. ❏ *She stared up at the starry sky.*

starry-eyed ADJ If you say that someone is **starry-eyed**, you mean that they have such a positive or hopeful view of a situation that they do not see what it is really like. ❏ *I'm not starry-eyed about Europe.* ❏ *...a starry-eyed young couple.*

Stars and Stripes N-PROPER [the N] The **Stars and Stripes** is a name for the national flag of the United States of America.

star|ship /stɑrʃɪp/ (**starships**) N-COUNT A **starship** is a large spacecraft that can travel outside our solar system. [AM] ❏ *He finds himself on a starship populated by escaping political prisoners from various alien cultures.*

star sign (**star signs**) N-COUNT Your **star sign** is the sign of the zodiac under which you were born. ❏ *'What star sign are you?'—'Gemini.'*

star|struck /stɑrstrʌk/ ADJ If you describe someone as **starstruck**, you mean that they are very interested in and impressed by famous performers, or that they want to be a performer themselves. ❏ *...a starstruck teenager who auditions for a TV dance show.*

star-studded ADJ [ADJ n] A **star-studded** show, event, or cast is one that includes a large number of famous performers. [JOURNALISM] ❏ *...a star-studded production of Hamlet.*

start ✦✦✦ /stɑrt/ (**starts, starting, started**) **1** V-T If you **start** to do something, you do something that you were not doing before and you continue doing it. ❏ *John then unlocked the front door and I started to follow him up the stairs.* ❏ *It was 1956 when Susanna started the work on the garden.* • N-COUNT **Start** is also a noun. ❏ *After several starts, she read the report properly.* **2** V-T/V-I When something **starts**, or if someone **starts** it, it takes place from a particular time. ❏ *The fire is thought to have started in an upstairs room.* ❏ *All of the passengers started the day with a swim.* • N-SING **Start** is also a noun. ❏ *...1918, four years after the start of the Great War.* **3** V-I If you **start by** doing something, or if you **start with** something, you do that thing first in a series of actions. ❏ *I started by asking how many day-care centers were located in the United States.* **4** V-I You use **start** to say what someone's first job was. For example, if their first job was that of a factory worker, you can say that they **started as** a factory worker. ❏ *Betty started as a shipping clerk at the clothes factory.* • PHRASAL VERB **Start off** means the same as **start**. ❏ *Mr. Dambar had started off as an assistant to Mrs. Spear's husband.* **5** V-T When someone **starts** something such as a new business, they create it or cause it to begin. ❏ *George Granger has started a health center and I know he's looking for qualified staff.* • PHRASAL VERB **Start up** means the same as **start**. ❏ *The cost of starting up a day-care center for children ranges from $150,000 to $300,000.* **6** → see also **startup** **7** V-T/V-I If you **start** an engine, car, or machine, or if it **starts**, it begins to work. ❏ *He started the car, which hummed smoothly.* • PHRASAL VERB **Start up** means the same as **start**. ❏ *He waited until they went inside the building before starting up the car and driving off.* ❏ *Put the key in the ignition and turn it to start the car up.* **8** V-I If you **start**, your body suddenly moves slightly as a result of surprise or fear. ❏ *She put the bottle on the coffee table beside him, banging it down hard. He started at the sound, his concentration broken.* • N-COUNT **Start** is also a noun. ❏ *Sylvia woke with a start.* **9** → see also **false start, head start** **10** PHRASE **You use for a start** or to **start with** to introduce the first of a number of things or reasons that you want to mention or could mention. ❏ *You must get her name and address, and that can be a problem for a start.* **11** PHRASE **To start with** means at the very first stage of an event or process. ❏ *To start with, the pressure on her was very heavy, but it's eased off a bit now.* **12 to get off to a flying start** → see **flying**

▶ **start off 1** PHRASAL VERB If you **start off** by doing something, you do it as the first part of an activity. ❏ *She started off by accusing him of blackmail but he more or less ignored her.* **2** PHRASAL VERB To **start** someone **off** means to cause them to begin doing something. ❏ *Her mother started her off acting in children's theater.* **3** PHRASAL VERB To **start** something **off** means to cause it to begin. ❏ *He became more aware of the things that started that tension off.* **4** → see **start 4**

▶ **start on** PHRASAL VERB If you **start on** something that needs to be done, you start dealing with it. ❏ *Before you start on these chapters, clear your head.*

▶ **start out 1** PHRASAL VERB If someone or something **starts out as** a particular thing, they are that thing at the beginning although they change later. ❏ *Daly was a fast-talking Irish-American who had started out as a salesman.* **2** PHRASAL VERB If you **start out by** doing something, you do it at the beginning of an activity. ❏ *I'm careful to start out by saying clearly what I want.*

▶ **start over** PHRASAL VERB If you **start over** or **start** something **over**, you begin something again from the beginning. [mainly AM] ❏ *...moving the kids to some other schools, closing them down and starting over with a new staff.*

in BRIT, use **start again**

▶ **start up** → see **start 5, 7**

SYNONYMS

start
VERB **1**
begin: *He stood up and began to move around the room.*
proceed: *He proceeded to tell me of my birth.*
embark on: *He's embarking on a new career as a writer.*
launch: *The police have launched an investigation into the incident.*

start|er /stɑrtər/ (**starters**) N-COUNT A **starter** is a small quantity of food that is served as the first course of a meal. [mainly BRIT]

in AM, usually use **appetizer**

start|er home (starter homes) N-COUNT A **starter home** is a small, new house which is cheap enough for people who are buying their first home to afford.

start|ing block (starting blocks) N-COUNT [usu pl] **Starting blocks** are blocks which runners put their feet against to help them move quickly forward at the start of a race.

start|ing point (starting points) also **starting-point** ◼ N-COUNT Something that is a **starting point** for a discussion or process can be used to begin it or act as a basis for it. ❑ *These proposals represent a realistic starting point for negotiation.* ◼ N-COUNT When you make a journey, your **starting point** is the place from which you start. ❑ *They had already walked a couple of miles or more from their starting point.*

star|tle /stɑːrtᵊl/ (startles, startling, startled) V-T If something sudden and unexpected **startles** you, it surprises and frightens you slightly. ❑ *The telephone startled him.* • **star|tled** ADJ ❑ *Martha gave her a startled look.*

star|tling /stɑːrtlɪŋ/ ADJ Something that is **startling** is so different, unexpected, or remarkable that people react to it with surprise. ❑ *Sometimes the results may be rather startling.*

start|up /stɑːrtʌp/ (startups) ◼ ADJ [ADJ n] The **startup** costs of something such as a new business or new product are the costs of starting to run or produce it. [BUSINESS] ❑ *That is enough to pay the startup costs for fourteen research projects.* ◼ ADJ [ADJ n] A **startup** company is a small business that has recently been started by someone. [BUSINESS] ❑ *Thousands and thousands of startup firms have poured into the computer market.* • N-COUNT **Startup** is also a noun. ❑ *For now the only bright spots in the labor market are small businesses and high-tech startups.* ◼ → See feature box at **business**

star|va|tion /stɑːrveɪʃᵊn/ N-UNCOUNT **Starvation** is extreme suffering or death, caused by lack of food. ❑ *Over three hundred people have died of starvation since the beginning of the year.*

starve /stɑːrv/ (starves, starving, starved) ◼ V-I If people **starve**, they suffer greatly from lack of food, which sometimes leads to their death. ❑ *A number of the prisoners we saw are starving.* ❑ *In the 1930s, millions starved to death or were deported.* ◼ V-T To **starve** someone means not to give them any food. ❑ *He said the only alternative was to starve the people, and he said this could not be allowed to happen.* ◼ V-T If a person or thing **is starved** of something that they need, they are suffering because they are not getting enough of it. ❑ *The electricity industry is not the only one to have been starved of investment.*

starv|ing /stɑːrvɪŋ/ ADJ [v-link ADJ] If you say that you are **starving**, you mean that you are very hungry. [INFORMAL] ❑ *Apart from anything else I was starving.*

stash /stæʃ/ (stashes, stashing, stashed) ◼ V-T If you **stash** something valuable in a secret place, you store it there to keep it safe. [INFORMAL] ❑ *We went for the bottle of whiskey that we had stashed behind the bookcase.* ◼ N-COUNT A **stash** of something valuable is a secret store of it. [INFORMAL] ❑ *A large stash of drugs had been found aboard the yacht.*

sta|sis /steɪsɪs/ N-UNCOUNT **Stasis** is a state in which something remains the same, and does not change or develop. [FORMAL] ❑ *Rock 'n' roll had entered a period of stasis.*

state ✦✦✦ /steɪt/ (states, stating, stated) ◼ N-COUNT You can refer to countries as **states**, particularly when you are discussing politics. ❑ *Mexico is a secular state and does not have diplomatic relations with the Vatican.* ◼ N-COUNT Some large countries such as the U.S. are divided into smaller areas called **states**. ❑ *Leaders of the Southern states are meeting in Louisville.* ◼ N-PROPER The U.S. is sometimes referred to as **the States**. [INFORMAL] ❑ *She bought it last year in the States.* ◼ N-SING You can refer to the government of a country as **the state**. ❑ *The state does not collect enough revenue to cover its expenditure.* ◼ ADJ [ADJ n] **State** industries or organizations are financed and organized by the government rather than private companies. ❑ *...reform of the state social-security system.* ◼ → see **state school** ◼ ADJ [ADJ n] A **state** occasion is a formal one involving the head of a country. ❑ *The president of the Czech Republic is in Washington on a state visit.* ◼ N-COUNT When you talk about the **state** of someone or something, you are referring to the condition they are in or what they are like at a particular time. ❑ *For the first few months after Daniel died, I was in a state of clinical depression.* ◼ V-T If you **state** something, you say or write it in a formal or definite way. ❑ *Clearly state your address and telephone number.* ❑ *The police report stated that he was arrested for allegedly assaulting his wife.* ◼ → see also **head of state, welfare state** ◼ PHRASE If you say that someone **is not in a fit state** to do something, you mean that they are too upset or ill to do it. ❑ *When you left our place, you weren't in a fit state to drive.* ◼ PHRASE If you are **in a state** or if you get **into a state**, you are very upset or nervous about something. ❑ *I was in a terrible state because nobody could understand why I had this illness.* ◼ PHRASE If the dead body of an important person **lies in state**, it is publicly displayed for a few days before it is buried. ❑ *...the 30,000 people who filed past the cardinal's body while it lay in state last week.*

SYNONYMS

state
NOUN
◼
country: *...that disputed boundary between the two countries.*
nation: *The Arab nations agreed to meet in Baghdad.*
kingdom: *The kingdom's power declined.*
◼
region: *...a remote, mountainous region.*
province: *...the Algarve, Portugal's southernmost province.*
district: *...the home of the governor of the district.*
VERB ◼
say: *Did he say where he was going?*
report: *'He seems to be all right now,' reported a relieved Taylor.*
declare: *He declared his intention to become the best golfer in the world.*
express: *He expressed grave concern at American attitudes.*

---

state at|tor|ney (state attorneys) N-COUNT A **state attorney** is the same as a **state's attorney**.

State De|part|ment ✦◇◇ N-PROPER In the United States, **the State Department** is the government department that is concerned with foreign affairs. ❑ *Officials at the State Department say the issue is urgent.*

state|hood /steɪthʊd/ N-UNCOUNT **Statehood** is the condition of being an independent state or nation.

state|house /steɪthaʊs/ (statehouses) N-COUNT In the United States, a **statehouse** is where the governor of a state has his or her offices, and where the state legislature meets.

state|less /steɪtlɪs/ ADJ A person who is **stateless** is not a citizen of any country and therefore has no nationality. ❑ *If I went back I'd be a stateless person.*

state|let /steɪtlɪt/ (statelets) N-COUNT A **statelet** is a small independent state, especially one that until recently was part of a larger country. [JOURNALISM]

state line (state lines) N-COUNT A **state line** is a border between two states within a country. [AM] ❑ *Then they crossed the state line into Mississippi.*

state|ly /steɪtli/ (statelier, stateliest) ADJ Something or someone that is **stately** is impressive and graceful or dignified. ❑ *Instead of moving at his usual stately pace, he was almost running.*

state|ment ✦✦◇ /steɪtmənt/ (statements) ◼ N-COUNT A **statement** is something that you say or write which gives information in a formal or definite way. ❑ *Andrew now disowns that statement, saying he was depressed when he made it.* ◼ N-COUNT A **statement** is an official or formal announcement that is issued on a particular occasion. ❑ *The statement by the military denied any involvement in last night's attack.* ◼ N-COUNT You can refer to the official account of events which a suspect or a witness gives to the police as a **statement**. ❑ *The 350-page report was based on statements from witnesses to the events.* ◼ N-COUNT If you describe an action or thing as a **statement**, you mean that it clearly expresses a particular opinion or idea that you have. ❑ *The following recipe is a statement of another kind – food is fun!* ◼ N-COUNT A printed document showing how much money has been paid into and taken out of a bank or investment account is called a **statement**. ❑ *...the address at the top of your monthly statement.*

COLLOCATIONS

statement
NOUN

1
adjective + **statement**: clear, simple; bold, sweeping; opening
statement + be + adjective: false, true

2
noun + **statement**: government, policy, press
adjective + **statement**: formal, official, political, public; brief, joint
verb + **statement**: make, issue, publish, release; read; withdraw

state of af|fairs N-SING If you refer to a particular **state of affairs**, you mean the general situation and circumstances connected with someone or something. ☐ *Some say this state of affairs just can't last.*

state of emer|gen|cy (states of emergency) N-COUNT If a government or other authority declares a **state of emergency** in an area, it introduces special measures such as increased powers for the police or army, usually because of civil disorder or because of a natural disaster such as an earthquake. ☐ *The State Governor declared a state of emergency the morning after the earthquake.*

state of mind (states of mind) N-COUNT Your **state of mind** is your mood or mental state at a particular time. ☐ *I want you to get into a whole new state of mind.*

state of siege N-SING A **state of siege** is a situation in which a government or other authority puts restrictions on the movement of people into or out of a country, city, or building. ☐ *Under the state of siege, the police could arrest suspects without charges or warrants.*

state-of-the-art ADJ If you describe something as **state-of-the-art**, you mean that it is the best available because it has been made using the most modern techniques and technology. ☐ *...the production of state-of-the-art military equipment.*

State of the Un|ion N-UNCOUNT [N n] A **State of the Union** speech or address is a speech, given once a year, in which the president of the United States talks about the current political issues that affect the country as a whole and about his plans for the year ahead. [AM] ☐ *In his State of the Union message, the president talked about campaign reform.*

state|room /stˈeɪtrʊm/ (staterooms) **1** N-COUNT On a passenger ship, a **stateroom** is a private room, especially one that is large and comfortable. [OLD-FASHIONED] **2** N-COUNT In a palace or other impressive building, a **stateroom** is a large room for use on formal occasions.

state's at|tor|ney (state's attorneys) also **state attorney** N-COUNT A **state's attorney** is a lawyer who prepares cases on behalf of the state and represents the state in court. [AM] ☐ *...James O'Malley, the state's attorney for Cook County.*

state school (state schools) **1** N-COUNT In the United States, a **state school** is a college or university that is part of the public education system provided by the state government. ☐ *At all 14 state schools, tuition and fees are going up this fall by an average of about 10 percent.* **2** N-COUNT In Britain, a **state school** is a school that is controlled and funded by the government or a local authority, and which children can attend without having to pay. [BRIT]

state's evi|dence PHRASE If someone who is accused of a crime **turns state's evidence**, they agree to give evidence in a law court against another person such as a former accomplice, usually in exchange for a reduced sentence for themselves. [AM] ☐ *Defendants who had turned state's evidence were also pardoned.*

state|side /stˈeɪtsaɪd/ also **Stateside** ADJ **Stateside** means in, from, or to the United States. [INFORMAL] ☐ *The band is currently planning a series of stateside gigs.* • ADV [ADV after v] **Stateside** is also an adverb. ☐ *His debut album was hugely successful Stateside.*

states|man /stˈeɪtsmən/ (statesmen) N-COUNT A **statesman** is an important and experienced male politician, especially one who is widely known and respected. ☐ *Hamilton is a great statesman and political thinker.*

states|man|like /stˈeɪtsmənlaɪk/ ADJ If you describe someone, especially a political leader, as **statesmanlike**, you approve of them because they give the impression of being very able and experienced. [APPROVAL] ☐ *He was widely respected as a wise and statesmanlike governor.*

states|man|ship /stˈeɪtsmənʃɪp/ N-UNCOUNT **Statesmanship** is the skill and activities of a statesman. ☐ *He praised the two leaders warmly for their statesmanship.*

states|woman /stˈeɪtswʊmən/ (stateswomen) N-COUNT A **stateswoman** is an important and experienced female politician, especially one who is widely known and respected. ☐ *She was also a scholar, a brilliant stateswoman and a voracious art collector.*

state troop|er (state troopers) N-COUNT In the U.S., a **state trooper** is a member of the police force in one of the states. [AM] ☐ *State troopers said the truck driver was going too fast when he lost control.*

state uni|ver|sity (state universities) N-COUNT A **state university** is the same as a **state school**. [AM] ☐ *He was a professor at the local state university.*

state|wide /stˈeɪtwaɪd/ ADJ [usu ADJ n] **Statewide** means across or throughout the whole of one of the states of the United States. ☐ *These voters often determine the outcome of statewide elections.* • ADV [ADV after v] **Statewide** is also an adverb. ☐ *In the weeks since flooding began, 16 people have died statewide.*

stat|ic /stˈætɪk/ **1** ADJ Something that is **static** does not move or change. ☐ *The number of young people obtaining qualifications has remained static or decreased.* **2** N-UNCOUNT **Static** or **static electricity** is electricity which can be caused by things rubbing against each other and which collects on things such as your body or metal objects. ☐ *When the weather turns cold and dry, my clothes develop a static problem.* **3** N-UNCOUNT If there is **static** on the radio or television, you hear a series of loud noises which spoils the sound. ☐ *After only a minute an authoritative voice came through the static on the radio.* **4** → See feature box at **electricity**

sta|tion ✦✦◇ /stˈeɪʃən/ (stations, stationing, stationed) **1** N-COUNT A **station** or a train **station** is a building by a railroad track where trains stop so that people can get on or off. ☐ *Ingrid went with him to the train station to see him off.* **2** N-COUNT A bus **station** is a building, usually in a town or city, where buses stop, usually for a while, so that people can get on or off. ☐ *I walked the two miles back to the bus station and bought a ticket home.* **3** N-COUNT If you talk about a particular radio or television **station**, you are referring to the company that broadcasts programs. ☐ *...an independent local radio station.* **4** V-T PASSIVE If soldiers or officials **are stationed** in a place, they are sent there to do a job or to work for a period of time. ☐ *Reports from the capital, Lome, say troops are stationed on the streets.* **5** → see **gas station**, **police station**, **power station**, **service station**, **space station**

sta|tion|ary /stˈeɪʃəneri/ ADJ Something that is **stationary** is not moving. ☐ *Stationary cars in traffic jams cause a great deal of pollution.*

sta|tion|er /stˈeɪʃənər/ (stationers) N-COUNT A **stationer** is a person who sells paper, envelopes, pens, and other equipment used for writing.

sta|tion|ery /stˈeɪʃəneri/ N-UNCOUNT **Stationery** is paper, envelopes, and other materials or equipment used for writing. ☐ *...envelopes and other office stationery.*

sta|tion house (station houses) N-COUNT A **station house** is a police station or a fire station, or a building that is attached to a police station or a fire station. [AM] ☐ *They were taken in a police van to the 60th Precinct station house for the lineup.* ☐ *Both the station house and the fire truck were destroyed.*

station|master /stˈeɪʃənmæstər/ (stationmasters) also **station master** N-COUNT A **stationmaster** is the official who is in charge of a train station.

sta|tion wag|on (station wagons) **1** N-COUNT A **station wagon** is a car with a long body, a door at the rear, and space behind the back seats. [AM]

in BRIT, use **estate car**

2 → See also color supplement

stat|ist /stéɪtɪst/ ADJ [usu ADJ n] When a country has **statist** policies, the state has a lot of control over the economy. ❑ ...*statist economic controls*.

sta|tis|tic ♦◇◇ /stətɪ́stɪk/ (**statistics**) **1** N-COUNT **Statistics** are facts which are obtained from analyzing information expressed in numbers, for example information about the number of times that something happens. ❑ *Official statistics show real wages declining by 24%.* **2** N-UNCOUNT **Statistics** is a branch of mathematics concerned with the study of information that is expressed in numbers. ❑ ...*a professor of mathematical statistics*.

sta|tis|ti|cal /stətɪ́stɪk°l/ ADJ **Statistical** means relating to the use of statistics. ❑ *The report contains a great deal of statistical information*. ● **sta|tis|ti|cal|ly** /stətɪ́stɪkli/ ADV ❑ *The results are not statistically significant*.

stat|is|ti|cian /stætɪstɪ́ʃ°n/ (**statisticians**) N-COUNT A **statistician** is a person who studies statistics or who works using statistics.

stats /stǽts/ **1** N-PLURAL **Stats** are facts which are obtained from analyzing information expressed in numbers. **Stats** is an abbreviation for **statistics**. [INFORMAL] ❑ ...*a fall in April's retail sales stats*. **2** N-UNCOUNT **Stats** is a branch of mathematics concerned with the study of information that is expressed in numbers. **Stats** is an abbreviation for **statistics**. [INFORMAL]

statu|ary /stǽtʃueri/ N-UNCOUNT If you talk about the **statuary** in a place, you are referring to all the statues and sculpture there. [FORMAL]

statue /stǽtʃu/ (**statues**) N-COUNT A **statue** is a large sculpture of a person or an animal, made of stone or metal. ❑ ...*a bronze statue of an Arabian horse*.

statu|esque /stætʃuésk/ ADJ [usu ADJ n] A **statuesque** woman is big and tall, and stands straight. [WRITTEN] ❑ *She was a statuesque brunette*.

statu|ette /stætʃuét/ (**statuettes**) N-COUNT A **statuette** is a very small sculpture of a person or an animal which is often displayed on a shelf or stand.

stat|ure /stǽtʃər/ **1** N-UNCOUNT Someone's **stature** is their height. ❑ *It's more than his physical stature that makes him remarkable*. ❑ *Mother was of very small stature, barely five feet tall*. **2** N-UNCOUNT The **stature** of a person is the importance and reputation that they have. ❑ *Who can deny his stature as the world's greatest cellist?*

sta|tus ♦◇◇ /stéɪtəs, stǽt-/ **1** N-UNCOUNT Your **status** is your social or professional position. ❑ *Status was very important to him*. ❑ ...*women and men of wealth and status*. **2** N-UNCOUNT **Status** is the importance and respect that someone has among the public or a particular group. ❑ *Nurses are undervalued, and they never enjoy the same status as doctors*. **3** N-UNCOUNT The **status** of something is the importance that people give it. ❑ *Those things that can be assessed by external tests are being given unduly high status*. **4** N-UNCOUNT A particular **status** is an official description that says what category a person, organization, or place belongs to, and gives them particular rights or advantages. ❑ *The Snoqualmie tribe regained its status as a federally recognized tribe*. **5** N-UNCOUNT The **status** of something is its state of affairs at a particular time. ❑ *The council unanimously directed city staff to prepare a status report on the project*.

sta|tus quo /stéɪtəs kwóʊ, stǽt-/ N-SING The **status quo** is the state of affairs that exists at a particular time, especially in contrast to a different possible state of affairs. ❑ *By 492 votes to 391, the federation voted to maintain the status quo*.

sta|tus sym|bol (**status symbols**) N-COUNT A **status symbol** is something that a person has or owns that shows they have money or importance in society.

stat|ute /stǽtʃut/ (**statutes**) N-VAR A **statute** is a rule or law which has been made by a government or other organization and formally written down. ❑ *The new statute covers the care for, raising, and protection of children*.

stat|ute book (**statute books**) N-COUNT [the/poss N] The **statute book** is a record of all the laws made by the government. ❑ *The bill could reach the statute book by the summer*.

stat|ute of limi|ta|tions (**statutes of limitations**) N-COUNT [oft the N on n] If there is a **statute of limitations** on a legal case such as a crime, people can no longer be accused after a certain period of time has passed. ❑ *The statute of limitations on crimes other than homicide is five years, so Reyes cannot be prosecuted for the attack*.

statu|tory /stǽtʃutɔri/ ADJ **Statutory** means relating to rules or laws which have been formally written down. [FORMAL] ❑ *The FCC has no statutory authority to regulate the Internet*.

statu|tory rape N-UNCOUNT **Statutory rape** is the crime committed by an adult when they have sex with someone who is under the age when they can legally agree to have sex.

staunch /stɔ́ntʃ/ (**stauncher, staunchest**) ADJ A **staunch** supporter or believer is very loyal to a person, organization, or set of beliefs, and supports them strongly. ❑ *He's a staunch supporter of controls on government spending*. ● **staunch|ly** ADV ❑ *He was staunchly opposed to a public confession*.

stave /stéɪv/ (**staves, staving, staved**) **1** N-COUNT A **stave** is a strong stick, especially one that is used as a weapon. ❑ *Many of the men had armed themselves with staves and pieces of iron*. **2** N-COUNT A **stave** is the five lines that music is written on. [mainly BRIT]

in AM, use **staff**

▶ **stave off** PHRASAL VERB If you **stave off** something bad, or if you **stave** it **off**, you succeed in stopping it from happening for a while. ❑ ...*a cost-saving plan intended to stave off bankruptcy*. ❑ *We'll never be able to stop beach erosion, we can only stave it off*.

stay ♦♦♦ /stéɪ/ (**stays, staying, stayed**) **1** V-I If you **stay** where you are, you continue to be there and do not leave. ❑ *"Stay here," Trish said. "I'll bring the car down the drive to take you back."* **2** V-I If you **stay** in a town, or hotel, or at someone's house, you live there for a short time. ❑ *Gordon stayed at The Park Hotel, Milan*. ❑ *Can't you stay a few more days?* ● N-COUNT **Stay** is also a noun. ❑ *An experienced Indian guide is provided during your stay*. **3** V-LINK If someone or something **stays** in a particular state or situation, they continue to be in it. ❑ *The Republican candidate said he would "work like crazy to stay ahead."* ❑ ...*community care networks that offer classes on how to stay healthy*. **4** V-I If you **stay** away from a place, you do not go there. ❑ *Management also stayed away from work during the strike*. **5** PHRASE If you **stay put**, you remain somewhere. ❑ *He was forced by his condition to stay put and remain out of politics*. **6** PHRASE If you **stay the night** in a place, you sleep there for one night. ❑ *They had invited me to come to supper and stay the night*. **7** → See feature box at **tourism**

▶ **stay in** PHRASAL VERB If you **stay in** during the evening, you remain at home and do not go out. ❑ *If I stay in, my boyfriend cooks a wonderful lasagne or chicken or steak*.

▶ **stay on** PHRASAL VERB If you **stay on** somewhere, you remain there after other people have left or after the time when you were going to leave. ❑ *He had managed to arrange to stay on in Adelaide*.

▶ **stay out** **1** PHRASAL VERB If you **stay out** at night, you remain away from home, especially when you are expected to be there. ❑ *That was the first time Elliot stayed out all night*. **2** PHRASAL VERB If you **stay out of** something, you do not get involved in it. ❑ *In the past, the UN has stayed out of the internal affairs of countries unless invited in*.

▶ **stay up** PHRASAL VERB If you **stay up**, you remain out of bed at a time when most people have gone to bed or at a time when you are normally in bed yourself. ❑ *I used to stay up late with my mom and watch movies*.

stay-at-home (**stay-at-homes**) N-COUNT [usu N n] If you describe someone as a **stay-at-home**, you mean that they stay at home rather than going out to work or traveling. ❑ *I was a stay-at-home mom until my husband lost his job*.

stay|ca|tion /steɪkéɪʃ°n/ (**staycations**) N-COUNT A **staycation** is a vacation that you spend in your own home or nearby. [INFORMAL] ❑ *Yes, this is the year to have a staycation: a vacation in your own country*.

stay|ing pow|er also **staying-power** N-UNCOUNT If you have **staying power**, you have the strength or determination to keep going until you reach the end of what you are doing. ❑ *Someone who lacks staying power and persistence is unlikely to make a good researcher*.

stay of ex|ecu|tion (stays of execution) N-COUNT If you are given a **stay of execution**, you are legally allowed to delay obeying an order of a court of law. [LEGAL]

STD /ɛs ti di/ (STDs) N-COUNT [usu N n] **STD** is an abbreviation for 'sexually transmitted disease.' [MEDICAL] ❑ ...an STD clinic.

stead /stɛd/ PHRASE If you say that something will **stand** someone **in good stead**, you mean that it will be very useful to them in the future. ❑ These two games here will stand them in good stead for the future.

stead|fast /stɛdfæst/ ADJ If someone is **steadfast** in something that they are doing, they are convinced that what they are doing is right and they refuse to change it or to give up. ❑ He remained steadfast in his belief that he had done the right thing.

steady ✦◇◇ /stɛdi/ (steadier, steadiest, steadies, steadying, steadied) **1** ADJ A **steady** situation continues or develops gradually without any interruptions and is not likely to change quickly. ❑ Despite the steady progress of building work, the campaign against it is still going strong. ❑ The improvement in standards has been steady and persistent, but has attracted little comment from educationalists. • **steadi|ly** /stɛdɪli/ ADV [ADV with v] ❑ Relax as much as possible and keep breathing steadily. **2** ADJ If an object is **steady**, it is firm and does not shake or move around. ❑ Get as close to the subject as you can and hold the camera steady. **3** ADJ If you look at someone or speak to them in a **steady** way, you look or speak in a calm, controlled way. ❑ "Well, go on," said Camilla, her voice fairly steady. • **steadi|ly** ADV [ADV after v] ❑ He moved back a little and stared steadily at Elaine. **4** ADJ If you describe a person as **steady**, you mean that they are sensible and reliable. ❑ He was firm and steady unlike other men she knew. **5** V-T/V-I If you **steady** something or if it **steadies**, it stops shaking or moving around. ❑ Two men were on the bridge-deck, steadying a ladder. **6** V-T If you **steady** yourself, you control your voice or expression, so that people will think that you are calm and not nervous. ❑ Somehow she steadied herself and murmured, "Have you got a cigarette?"

steak /steɪk/ (steaks) **1** N-VAR A **steak** is a large flat piece of beef without much fat on it. You cook it by grilling or frying it. ❑ ...a steak sizzling on the grill. **2** N-COUNT A fish **steak** is a large piece of fish that contains few bones. ❑ ...fresh salmon steaks.

steak|house /steɪkhaʊs/ (steakhouses) also **steak house** N-COUNT A **steakhouse** is a restaurant that serves mainly steaks.

steal ✦◇◇ /stil/ (steals, stealing, stole, stolen) **1** V-T/V-I If you **steal** something from someone, you take it away from them without their permission and without intending to return it. ❑ He was accused of stealing a small boy's bicycle. ❑ People who are drug addicts come in and steal. • **sto|len** ADJ ❑ We have now found the stolen car. **2** V-T If you **steal** someone else's ideas, you pretend that they are your own. ❑ A writer is suing the director for allegedly stealing his film idea.

stealth /stɛlθ/ N-UNCOUNT [oft by N] If you use **stealth** when you do something, you do it quietly and carefully so that no one will notice what you are doing. ❑ Health policy is being changed by stealth without consultation. ❑ Both sides advanced by stealth.

stealthy /stɛlθi/ (stealthier, stealthiest) ADJ **Stealthy** actions or movements are performed quietly and carefully, so that no one will notice what you are doing. ❑ I would creep in and with stealthy footsteps explore the second floor. • **stealthi|ly** /stɛlθɪli/ ADV [ADV with v] ❑ Slowly and stealthily, someone was creeping up the stairs.

steam ✦◇◇ /stim/ (steams, steaming, steamed) **1** N-UNCOUNT **Steam** is the hot mist that forms when water boils. **Steam** vehicles and machines are operated using steam as a means of power. ❑ In an electric power plant the heat converts water into high-pressure steam. **2** V-I If something **steams**, it gives off steam. ❑ ...restaurants where coffee pots steamed on their burners. **3** V-T/V-I If you **steam** food or if it **steams**, you cook it in steam rather than in water. ❑ Steam the carrots until they are just beginning to be tender. ❑ Leave the vegetables to steam over the rice for the 20 minutes cooking time. **4** PHRASE If something such as a plan or a project goes **full steam ahead**, it progresses quickly. ❑ The administration was determined to go full steam ahead with its reform program. **5** PHRASE If you **run out of steam**, you stop doing something because you have no more energy or enthusiasm left. [INFORMAL] ❑ I decided to paint the bathroom ceiling but ran out of steam halfway through.
▶ **steam up** PHRASAL VERB When a window, mirror, or pair of glasses **steams up**, it becomes covered with steam or mist. ❑ ...the irritation of living with lenses that steam up when you come in from the cold.

steam|boat /stimboʊt/ (steamboats) **1** N-COUNT A **steamboat** is a boat or ship that has an engine powered by steam. **2** → See also color supplement

steam|er /stimər/ (steamers) **1** N-COUNT A **steamer** is a ship that has an engine powered by steam. **2** N-COUNT A **steamer** is a special container used for steaming food such as vegetables and fish.

steam iron (steam irons) N-COUNT A **steam iron** is an electric iron that produces steam from water that you put into it. The steam makes it easier to get the creases out of your clothes.

steam|roller /stimroʊlər/ (steamrollers, steamrollering, steamrollered) **1** N-COUNT A **steamroller** is a large, heavy vehicle with wide, solid metal wheels, which is used to make the surface of a road flat. In the past steamrollers were powered by steam. **2** V-T If you **steamroller** someone who disagrees with you or opposes you, you defeat them or you force them to do what you want by using your power or by putting a lot of pressure on them. ❑ They could simply steamroller all opposition.

steam|ship /stimʃɪp/ (steamships) N-COUNT A **steamship** is a ship that has an engine powered by steam.

steamy /stimi/ (steamier, steamiest) **1** ADJ **Steamy** means involving exciting sex. [INFORMAL] ❑ He'd had a steamy affair with an office colleague. **2** ADJ A **steamy** place has hot, wet air. ❑ ...a steamy cafe.

steed /stid/ (steeds) N-COUNT A **steed** is a large, strong horse used for riding. [LITERARY]

steel ✦◇◇ /stil/ (steels, steeling, steeled) **1** N-MASS **Steel** is a very strong metal which is made mainly from iron. **Steel** is used for making many things, for example bridges, buildings, vehicles, and flatware. ❑ ...steel pipes. ❑ ...the iron and steel industry. **2** → see also **stainless steel** **3** V-T If you **steel** yourself, you prepare to deal with something unpleasant. ❑ Those involved are steeling themselves for the coming battle.

steel band (steel bands) N-COUNT A **steel band** is a band of people who play music on special metal drums. Steel bands started in the West Indies.

steel|maker /stilmeɪkər/ (steelmakers) N-COUNT A **steelmaker** is a company that makes steel.

steel wool N-UNCOUNT **Steel wool** is a mass of fine steel threads twisted together into a small ball and used for cleaning hard surfaces or removing paint.

steel|worker /stilwɜrkər/ (steelworkers) also **steel worker** N-COUNT A **steelworker** is a person who works in a factory where steel is made.

steel|works /stilwɜrks/ (steelworks) N-COUNT A **steelworks** is a factory where steel is made.

steely /stili/ (steelier, steeliest) ADJ **Steely** is used to emphasize that a person is strong and determined. [EMPHASIS] ❑ Clad in their black sweatsuits, the Maryland players had a steely determination.

steep /stip/ (steeper, steepest) **1** ADJ A **steep** slope rises at a very sharp angle and is difficult to go up. ❑ San Francisco is built on 40 hills and some are very steep. • **steep|ly** ADV [ADV with v] ❑ The road climbs steeply, with good views of Orvieto through the trees. ❑ ...steeply terraced valleys. **2** ADJ A **steep** increase or decrease in something is a very big increase or decrease. ❑ Consumers are rebelling at steep price increases. • **steep|ly** ADV [ADV with v] ❑ Unemployment is rising steeply. **3** ADJ If you say that the price of something is **steep**, you mean that it is expensive. [INFORMAL] ❑ The annual premium can be a little steep, but will be well worth it if your dog is injured.

steeped /stipt/ ADJ [v-link ADJ in n] If a place or person is **steeped in** a quality or characteristic, they are surrounded by it or deeply influenced by it. ❑ The castle is steeped in history and legend.

steep|en /stiːpən/ (steepens, steepening, steepened) V-I If a slope or an angle **steepens**, it becomes steeper. [LITERARY] ❑ *The road steepened and then leveled out suddenly.*

stee|ple /stiːpəl/ (steeples) N-COUNT A **steeple** is a tall pointed structure on top of the tower of a church.

steeple|chase /stiːpəltʃeɪs/ (steeplechases) **1** N-COUNT A **steeplechase** is a long horse race in which the horses have to jump over obstacles such as hedges and water jumps. ❑ *In the steeplechase, if you hit a fence, you went down, not the fence.* **2** N-COUNT A **steeplechase** is a 3,000 meter race around a track, during which people jump over obstacles and water jumps.

steer /stɪər/ (steers, steering, steered) **1** V-T When you **steer** a car, boat, or plane, you control it so that it goes in the direction that you want. ❑ *What is it like to steer a ship this size?* **2** V-T If you **steer** people toward a particular course of action or attitude, you try to lead them gently in that direction. ❑ *The new government is seen as one that will steer the country in the right direction.* **3** V-T If you **steer** someone in a particular direction, you guide them there. ❑ *Nick steered them into the nearest seats.* **4** PHRASE If you **steer clear** of someone or something, you deliberately avoid them. ❑ *I think a lot of people, women in particular, steer clear of these sensitive issues.*

steer|ing /stɪərɪŋ/ **1** N-UNCOUNT The **steering** in a car or other vehicle is the mechanical parts of it which make it possible to steer. **2** ADJ [ADJ n] A **steering** committee or a **steering** group is a group of people that organizes the early stages of a project, and makes sure it progresses in a satisfactory way. ❑ *There will be an economic steering committee with representatives of each of the republics.*

steer|ing col|umn (steering columns) N-COUNT In a car or other vehicle, the **steering column** is the rod to which the steering wheel is attached.

steer|ing wheel (steering wheels) **1** N-COUNT In a car or other vehicle, the **steering wheel** is the wheel which the driver holds when he or she is driving. **2** → See also color supplement

stel|lar /stɛlər/ **1** ADJ [ADJ n] **Stellar** is used to describe anything connected with stars. ❑ *A stellar wind streams outward from the star.* **2** ADJ [usu ADJ n] A **stellar** person or thing is considered to be very good. ❑ *The French companies are registering stellar profits.*

stem ✦✧✧ /stɛm/ (stems, stemming, stemmed) **1** V-I If a condition or problem **stems from** something, it was caused originally by that thing. ❑ *All my problems stem from a feeling of inadequacy.* **2** V-T If you **stem** something, you stop it spreading, increasing, or continuing. [FORMAL] ❑ *Austria has sent three army battalions to its border with Hungary to stem the flow of illegal immigrants.* **3** N-COUNT The **stem** of a plant is the thin, upright part on which the flowers and leaves grow. ❑ *He stooped down, cut the stem for her with his knife and handed her the flower.* **4** → See also color supplement

---
COLLOCATIONS

stem
VERB
1
noun + **stem**: dispute, problem
stem + *adverb*: directly, largely, partly
2
stem + *noun*: flood, flow, spread, tide; loss, violence

SYNONYMS

stem
VERB **1**
originate: *All carbohydrates originate from plants.*
derive: *Anna's strength is derived from her parents and her sisters.*
arise: *...an overwhelming sense of guilt arising from my actions.*
flow: *Undesirable consequences flow from these misconceptions.*

---

stem cell (stem cells) N-COUNT A **stem cell** is a type of cell that can produce other cells which are able to develop into any kind of cell in the body. ❑ *Stem cell research is supported by many doctors.*

-stemmed /-stɛmd/ COMB IN ADJ [usu ADJ n] **-stemmed** is added to adjectives to form adjectives which indicate what the stem of something is like. ❑ *...an enormous bouquet of long-stemmed roses.*

stench /stɛntʃ/ (stenches) N-COUNT A **stench** is a strong and very unpleasant smell. ❑ *The stench of burning rubber was overpowering.*

sten|cil /stɛnsəl/ (stencils, stenciling or stencilling, stenciled or stencilled) **1** N-COUNT A **stencil** is a piece of paper, plastic, or metal which has a design cut out of it. You place the stencil on a surface and paint it so that paint goes through the holes and leaves a design on the surface. **2** V-T If you **stencil** a design or if you **stencil** a surface with a design, you put a design on a surface using a stencil. ❑ *He then stenciled the ceiling with a moon and stars motif.*

ste|nog|ra|pher /stənɒɡrəfər/ (stenographers) N-COUNT A **stenographer** is a person who types and writes shorthand, usually in an office. [AM]

> in BRIT, use **shorthand typist**

sten|to|rian /stɛntɔːriən/ ADJ [usu ADJ n] A **stentorian** voice is very loud and strong. [FORMAL] ❑ *He bellowed in a stentorian voice.*

step ✦✦✦ /stɛp/ (steps, stepping, stepped) **1** N-COUNT If you take a **step**, you lift your foot and put it down in a different place, for example when you are walking. ❑ *I took a step toward him.* ❑ *She walked on a few steps.* **2** V-I If you **step** on something or **step** in a particular direction, you put your foot on the thing or move your foot in that direction. ❑ *This was the moment when Neil Armstrong became the first man to step on the Moon.* ❑ *She accidentally stepped on his foot on a crowded commuter train.* **3** N-COUNT **Steps** are a series of surfaces at increasing or decreasing heights, on which you put your feet in order to walk up or down to a different level. ❑ *This little room was along a passage and down some steps.* **4** N-COUNT A **step** is a raised flat surface in front of a door. ❑ *A little girl was sitting on the step of the end house.* **5** → see also **doorstep** **6** N-COUNT A **step** is one of a series of actions that you take in order to achieve something. ❑ *He greeted the agreement as the first step toward peace.* **7** N-COUNT A **step** in a process is one of a series of stages. ❑ *The next step is to put the theory into practice.* **8** N-COUNT The **steps** of a dance are the sequences of foot movements which make it up. ❑ *She was a better dancer than Gordon. At least she knew the steps.* **9** N-SING Someone's **step** is the way they walk. ❑ *He quickened his step.* **10** PHRASE If you stay **one step ahead of** someone or something, you manage to achieve more than they do or avoid competition or danger from them. ❑ *Successful travel is partly a matter of keeping one step ahead of the crowd.* **11** PHRASE If people who are walking or dancing are **in step**, they are moving their feet forward at exactly the same time as each other. If they are **out of step**, their feet are moving forward at different times. ❑ *They were almost the same height and they moved perfectly in step.* **12** PHRASE If people are **in step** with each other, their ideas or opinions are the same. If they are **out of step** with each other, their ideas or opinions are different. ❑ *Moscow is anxious to stay in step with Washington.* **13** PHRASE If you do something **step by step**, you do it by progressing gradually from one stage to the next. ❑ *I am not rushing things and I'm taking it step by step.* **14** PHRASE If someone tells you to **watch** your **step**, they are warning you to be careful about how you behave or what you say so that you do not get into trouble. ❑ *He said I'd come to a bad end, if I didn't watch my step.*

▶ **step aside** → see **step down**

▶ **step back** PHRASAL VERB If you **step back** and think about a situation, you think about it as if you were not involved in it. ❑ *I stepped back and analysed the situation.*

▶ **step down** also **step aside** PHRASAL VERB If someone **steps down** or **steps aside**, they resign from an important job or position, often in order to let someone else take their place. ❑ *The judge said that if his wife was called as a witness, he would step down as trial judge.*

▶ **step in** PHRASAL VERB If you **step in**, you get involved in a difficult situation because you think you can or should help with it. ❑ *If no agreement was reached, the army would step in.*

▶ **step up** PHRASAL VERB If you **step up** something, you increase it or increase its intensity. ❑ *He urged donors to step up their efforts to send aid to Somalia.*

SYNONYMS

step
NOUN **1**
pace: Take three paces forwards.
stride: He walked with long strides.
footstep: I heard footsteps outside.
VERB **2**
walk: She turned and walked away.
tread: She trod casually, enjoying the touch of the damp grass on her feet.
pace: He found John pacing around the apartment, unable to sleep.
stride: He turned abruptly and strode off down the corridor.

step|brother /stɛpbrʌðər/ (**stepbrothers**) also **step-brother** N-COUNT Someone's **stepbrother** is the son of their stepfather or stepmother.

step change (**step changes**) N-COUNT [usu sing, usu N in n] A **step change** is a sudden or major change in the way that something happens or the way that someone behaves. [mainly BRIT]

in AM, usually use **sea change**

step|child /stɛptʃaɪld/ (**stepchildren**) also **step-child**
1 N-COUNT [oft poss N] Someone's **stepchild** is a child that was born to their husband or wife during a previous relationship. **2** → See feature box at **family**

step|dad /stɛpdæd/ (**stepdads**) N-COUNT [oft poss N] Someone's **stepdad** is a man who is not their biological father, but is married to their parent. ❑ I went to live with my dad because I didn't get on with my stepdad.

step|daughter /stɛpdɔtər/ (**stepdaughters**) also **step-daughter** N-COUNT Someone's **stepdaughter** is a daughter that was born to their husband or wife during a previous relationship.

step|family /stɛpfæmɪli, -fæmli/ (**stepfamilies**) N-COUNT A **stepfamily** is a family that consists of a married couple and one or more children from a previous marriage or relationship. ❑ Stepfamilies are becoming more and more common.

step|father /stɛpfɑðər/ (**stepfathers**) also **step-father** N-COUNT Someone's **stepfather** is a man who is not their biological father, but is married to their parent.

step|ladder /stɛplædər/ (**stepladders**) **1** N-COUNT A **stepladder** is a portable ladder that is made of two sloping parts that are hinged together at the top so that it will stand up on its own. **2** → See feature box at **DIY**

step|mom /stɛpmɒm/ (**stepmoms**) N-COUNT [oft poss N] Someone's **stepmom** is a woman who is not their biological mother, but is married to their parent. [AM, INFORMAL] ❑ She's become both a wife and a stepmom.

in BRIT, use **stepmum**

step|mother /stɛpmʌðər/ (**stepmothers**) also **step-mother** N-COUNT Someone's **stepmother** is a woman who is not their biological mother, but is married to their parent.

step|mum /stɛpmʌm/ (**stepmums**) N-COUNT [oft poss N] Someone's **stepmum** is a woman who is not their biological mother, but is married to their parent. [BRIT, INFORMAL] ❑ My dad and my stepmum were very supportive.

in AM, use **stepmom**

step|parent /stɛppɛərənt, -pær-/ (**stepparents**) also **step-parent** N-COUNT [oft poss N] Someone's **stepparent** is their stepmother or stepfather.

steppe /stɛp/ (**steppes**) N-UNCOUNT [also N in pl] **Steppes** are large areas of flat grassy land where there are no trees, especially the area that stretches from Eastern Europe across the south of the former Soviet Union to Siberia.

step|ping stone (**stepping stones**) also **stepping-stone**, **steppingstone** **1** N-COUNT You can describe a job or event as a **stepping stone** when it helps you to make progress, especially in your career. ❑ It is just another stepping stone to bigger and better things. **2** N-COUNT **Stepping stones** are a line of large stones which you can walk on in order to cross a shallow stream or river.

step|sister /stɛpsɪstər/ (**stepsisters**) also **step-sister** N-COUNT Someone's **stepsister** is the daughter of their stepfather or stepmother.

step|son /stɛpsʌn/ (**stepsons**) also **step-son** N-COUNT Someone's **stepson** is a son born to their husband or wife during a previous relationship.

ste|reo /stɛriou, stɪər-/ (**stereos**) **1** ADJ **Stereo** is used to describe a sound system in which the sound is played through two speakers. Compare **mono**. ❑ ...loudspeakers that give all-around stereo sound. **2** N-COUNT A **stereo** is a CD player with two speakers.

ste|reo|type /stɛriətaɪp, stɪər-/ (**stereotypes, stereotyping, stereotyped**) **1** N-COUNT A **stereotype** is a fixed general image or set of characteristics that a lot of people believe represent a particular type of person or thing. ❑ There's always been a stereotype about successful businessmen. **2** V-T [usu passive] If someone **is stereotyped** as something, people form a fixed general idea or image of them, so that it is assumed that they will behave in a particular way. ❑ He was stereotyped by some as a renegade.

ste|reo|typi|cal /stɛriətɪpɪkəl, stɪər-/ ADJ A **stereotypical** idea of a type of person or thing is a fixed general idea that a lot of people have about it, that may be false in many cases. ❑ These are men whose masculinity does not conform to stereotypical images of the unfeeling male.

ster|ile /stɛrəl/ **1** ADJ Something that is **sterile** is completely clean and free from germs. ❑ He always made sure that any cuts were protected by sterile dressings. • **ste|ril|ity** /stərɪlɪti/ N-UNCOUNT ❑ ...the antiseptic sterility of the hospital. **2** ADJ A person or animal that is **sterile** is unable to have or produce babies. ❑ George was sterile. • **ste|ril|ity** N-UNCOUNT ❑ This disease causes sterility in both males and females.

steri|lize /stɛrɪlaɪz/ (**sterilizes, sterilizing, sterilized**)

in BRIT, also use **sterilise**

1 V-T If you **sterilize** a thing or a place, you make it completely clean and free from germs. ❑ Sulfur is also used to sterilize equipment. • **steri|li|za|tion** /stɛrɪlɪzeɪʃən/ N-UNCOUNT ❑ ...the pasteurization and sterilization of milk. **2** V-T [usu passive] If a person or an animal **is sterilized**, they have a medical operation that makes it impossible for them to have or produce babies. ❑ My wife was sterilized after the birth of her fourth child. • **steri|li|za|tion** (**sterilizations**) N-VAR ❑ In some cases, a sterilization is performed through the vaginal wall.

ster|ling ✦✧✧ /stɜrlɪŋ/ **1** ADJ **Sterling** means very good in quality; used to describe someone's work or character. [FORMAL, APPROVAL] ❑ Those are sterling qualities to be admired in anyone. **2** N-UNCOUNT **Sterling** is the money system of Great Britain. ❑ The stamps had to be paid for in sterling.

stern /stɜrn/ (**sterner, sternest**) **1** ADJ **Stern** words or actions are very severe. ❑ Mr. Monroe issued a stern warning to those who persist in violence. • **stern|ly** ADV ❑ "We will take the necessary steps," she said sternly. **2** ADJ Someone who is **stern** is very serious and strict. ❑ Her father was stern and hard to please. **3** → See also color supplement

ster|num /stɜrnəm/ (**sternums**) N-COUNT Your **sternum** is the long flat bone which goes from your throat to the bottom of your ribs and to which your ribs are attached. [MEDICAL]

ster|oid /stɪərɔɪd, stɛr-/ (**steroids**) N-COUNT A **steroid** is a type of chemical substance found in your body. Steroids can be artificially introduced into the bodies of athletes to improve their strength.

stetho|scope /stɛθəskoʊp/ (**stethoscopes**) **1** N-COUNT A **stethoscope** is an instrument that a doctor uses to listen to your heart and breathing. It consists of a small disk that is placed on your body, connected to a hollow tube with two pieces that the doctor puts in his or her ears. **2** → See also color supplement

Stet|son /stɛtsən/ (**Stetsons**) N-COUNT A **Stetson** is a type of hat with a wide brim that is traditionally worn by cowboys. [TRADEMARK]

ste|via /stiviə/ N-UNCOUNT **Stevia** is a substance taken from a plant, which is used to make food taste sweet without adding any calories. ❑ We sweeten our cookies with stevia.

stew /stu/ (stews, stewing, stewed) **1** N-VAR A **stew** is a meal which you make by cooking meat and vegetables in liquid at a low temperature. ▫ *She served him a bowl of beef stew.* **2** V-T When you **stew** meat, vegetables, or fruit, you cook them slowly in liquid in a covered pot. ▫ *Stew the apple and blackberries to make a thick pulp.*

stew|ard /stuərd/ (stewards) **1** N-COUNT A **steward** is someone who works on a ship, plane, or train, taking care of passengers and serving meals to them. **2** N-COUNT A **steward** is someone who helps to organize a race, march, or other public event. ▫ *The steward at the march stood his ground while the rest of the marchers decided to run.*

stew|ard|ess /stuərdɪs/ (stewardesses) N-COUNT A **stewardess** is a woman who works on a ship, plane, or train, taking care of passengers and serving meals to them. [OLD-FASHIONED]

stew|ard|ship /stuərdʃɪp/ N-UNCOUNT [usu N of n] **Stewardship** is the responsibility of taking care of property. [FORMAL]

stew|ing steak N-UNCOUNT **Stewing steak** is the same as **stew meat**. [BRIT]

stew meat N-UNCOUNT **Stew meat** is beef which is suitable for cooking slowly in a stew. [AM]

in BRIT, use **stewing steak**

STICK
① NOUN USES
② VERB USES
---

① **stick** ♦◊◊ /stɪk/ (sticks) **1** N-COUNT A **stick** is a thin branch which has fallen off a tree. ▫ *...people carrying bundles of dried sticks to sell for firewood.* **2** N-COUNT A **stick** is a long thin piece of wood which is used for a particular purpose. ▫ *...lollipop sticks.* ▫ *...drum sticks.* **3** N-COUNT Some long thin objects that are used in sports are called **sticks**. ▫ *...lacrosse sticks.* ▫ *...hockey sticks.* **4** N-COUNT A **stick** of something is a long thin piece of it. ▫ *...a stick of celery.* **5** N-COUNT A **stick** is a long thin piece of wood which is used for supporting someone's weight or for hitting people or animals. [BRIT]

in AM, use **cane**

6 PHRASE If someone **gets the wrong end of the stick** or **gets hold of the wrong end of the stick**, they do not understand something correctly and get the wrong idea about it. [INFORMAL] ▫ *I think someone has got the wrong end of the stick. They should have established the facts before speaking out.* **7** → See also color supplement

② **stick** ♦♦◊ /stɪk/ (sticks, sticking, stuck) **1** V-T If you **stick** something somewhere, you put it there in a rather casual way. [INFORMAL] ▫ *He folded the papers and stuck them in his desk drawer.* **2** V-T/V-I If you **stick** a pointed object in something, or if it **sticks** in something, it goes into it or through it by making a cut or hole. ▫ *They sent in loads of nurses and stuck a needle in my back.* **3** V-I If something **is sticking out** from a surface or object, it extends up or away from it. If something **is sticking into** a surface or object, it is partly in it. ▫ *They lay where they had fallen from the crane, sticking out of the water.* **4** V-T If you **stick** one thing to another, you attach it using glue, Scotch tape, or another sticky substance. ▫ *Don't forget to clip the token and stick it on your card.* **5** V-I If one thing **sticks** to another, it becomes attached to it and is difficult to remove. ▫ *The soil sticks to the blade and blocks the plough.* ▫ *Peel away the waxed paper if it has stuck to the bottom of the cake.* **6** V-I If something **sticks in** your mind, you remember it for a long time. ▫ *The incident stuck in my mind because it was the first example I had seen of racism in that country.* **7** V-I If something which can usually be moved **sticks**, it becomes fixed in one position. ▫ *The needle on the dial went right around to fifty feet, which was as far as it could go, and there it stuck.* **8** → see also **stuck**

▶ **stick around** PHRASAL VERB If you **stick around**, you stay where you are, often because you are waiting for something. [INFORMAL] ▫ *Stick around a while and see what develops.*

▶ **stick by 1** PHRASAL VERB If you **stick by** someone, you continue to give them help or support. ▫ *...friends who stuck by me during the difficult times.* **2** PHRASAL VERB If you **stick by** a promise, agreement, decision, or principle, you do what you said you would do, or do not change your mind. ▫ *But I made my decision then and stuck by it.*

▶ **stick out 1** PHRASAL VERB If you **stick out** part of your body, you extend it away from your body. ▫ *She made a face and stuck out her tongue at him.* **2 to stick your neck out** → see **neck** **3** PHRASAL VERB If something **sticks out**, it is very noticeable because it is unusual. ▫ *What had Cutter done to make him stick out from the crowd?* **4** PHRASE If someone in an unpleasant or difficult situation **sticks it out**, they do not leave or give up. ▫ *I really didn't like New York, but I wanted to stick it out a little bit longer.*

▶ **stick to 1** PHRASAL VERB If you **stick to** something or someone when you are traveling, you stay close to them. ▫ *Let's stick to the road we know.* **2** PHRASAL VERB If you **stick to** something, you continue doing, using, saying, or talking about it, rather than changing to something else. ▫ *Perhaps he should have stuck to writing.* **3** PHRASAL VERB If you **stick to** a promise, agreement, decision, or principle, you do what you said you would do, or do not change your mind. ▫ *Immigrant support groups are waiting to see if he sticks to his word.* **4 to stick to your guns** → see **gun**

▶ **stick together** PHRASAL VERB If people **stick together**, they stay with each other and support each other. ▫ *If we all stick together, we ought to be okay.*

▶ **stick up for** PHRASAL VERB If you **stick up for** a person or a principle, you support or defend them forcefully. ▫ *You would think my own father would stick up for me once in a while.*

▶ **stick with 1** PHRASAL VERB If you **stick with** something, you do not change to something else. ▫ *If you're in a job that keeps you busy, stick with it.* **2** PHRASAL VERB If you **stick with** someone, you stay close to them. ▫ *Tugging the woman's arm, she pulled her to her side saying: "You just stick with me, dear."*

stick|er /stɪkər/ (stickers) N-COUNT A **sticker** is a small piece of paper or plastic, with writing or a picture on one side, that you can stick onto a surface. ▫ *...a bumper sticker that said, Flowers Make Life Lovelier.*

stick|er price (sticker prices) N-COUNT The **sticker price** of an item, especially a car, is the price at which it is advertised. [AM] ▫ *This model carries a sticker price of nearly $27,000.*

stick|er shock N-UNCOUNT **Sticker shock** is the shock you feel when you find out how expensive something is. [AM] ▫ *Get over the sticker shock and invest in good kitchen knives.*

stick fig|ure (stick figures) N-COUNT A **stick figure** is a simple drawing of a person that uses straight lines to show the arms and legs. ▫ *Claire drew a stick figure on a sheet of paper.*

stick|ing point (sticking points) N-COUNT A **sticking point** in a discussion or series of negotiations is a point on which the people involved cannot agree and which may delay or stop the talks. A **sticking point** is also one aspect of a problem which you have trouble dealing with. ▫ *The main sticking point was the question of taxes.*

stick in|sect [mainly BRIT] → see **walking stick 2**

stick-in-the-mud (stick-in-the-muds) N-COUNT If you describe someone as a **stick-in-the-mud**, you disapprove of them because they do not like doing anything that is new or fun. [INFORMAL, DISAPPROVAL]

stickle|back /stɪkəlbæk/ (sticklebacks) N-COUNT A **stickleback** is a small fish which has sharp points along its back.

stick|ler /stɪklər/ (sticklers) N-COUNT [usu N for n] If you are a **stickler** for something, you always demand or require it. ▫ *Lucy was a stickler for perfection, and everything had to be exactly right.*

stick-on ADJ [ADJ n] **Stick-on** labels, shapes, and objects have a sticky material on one side so that they will stick to things.

stick shift (stick shifts) N-COUNT A **stick shift** is the lever that you use to change gear in a car or other vehicle. [mainly AM] ▫ *I'm having trouble with this stick shift because I'm left-handed.*

in BRIT, usually use **gear lever**

sticky /stɪki/ (stickier, stickiest) **1** ADJ A **sticky** substance is soft, or thick and liquid, and can stick to other things. **Sticky** things are covered with a sticky substance. ▫ *...sticky toffee.* ▫ *If the dough is sticky, add more flour.* **2** ADJ **Sticky** weather is unpleasantly hot and damp. ▫ *four desperately hot, sticky days in the middle of August.* **3** ADJ A **sticky** situation involves

sticky tape N-UNCOUNT Sticky tape is the same as Scotch tape. [BRIT]

problems or is embarrassing. [INFORMAL] ◻ Inevitably the transition will yield some sticky moments. **4** → See feature box at **snow**

stiff /stɪf/ (stiffer, stiffest) **1** ADJ Something that is **stiff** is firm or does not bend easily. ◻ The furniture was stiff, uncomfortable, too delicate, and too neat. ◻ His gaberdine trousers were brand new and stiff. • **stiff|ly** ADV ◻ Moira sat stiffly upright in her straight-backed chair. **2** ADJ Something such as a door or drawer that is **stiff** does not move as easily as it should. ◻ There have been problems with doors being too stiff to open. **3** ADJ If you are **stiff**, your muscles or joints hurt when you move, because of illness or because of too much exercise. ◻ The mud bath is particularly recommended for relieving tension and stiff muscles. • **stiff|ly** ADV ◻ He climbed stiffly from the Volkswagen. **4** ADJ Stiff behavior is rather formal and not very friendly or relaxed. ◻ They always seemed a little awkward with each other, a bit stiff and formal. • **stiff|ly** ADV ◻ "Why don't you borrow your sister's car?" said Cassandra stiffly. **5** ADJ **Stiff** can be used to mean difficult or severe. ◻ She faces stiff competition in the Best Actress category. **6** ADV [adj ADV] If you are bored **stiff**, worried **stiff**, or scared **stiff**, you are extremely bored, worried, or scared. [INFORMAL, EMPHASIS] ◻ Anna tried to look interested. Actually, she was bored stiff. • ADJ [v n ADJ] **Stiff** is also an adjective. ◻ Even if he bores you stiff, it is good manners not to let him know it.

stiff|en /stɪfən/ (stiffens, stiffening, stiffened) **1** V-I If you **stiffen**, you stop moving and stand or sit with muscles that are suddenly tense, for example because you feel afraid or angry. ◻ Ada stiffened at the sound of his voice. **2** V-I If your muscles or joints **stiffen**, or if something **stiffens** them, they become difficult to bend or move. ◻ The blood supply to the skin is reduced when muscles stiffen. • PHRASAL VERB **Stiffen up** means the same as **stiffen**. ◻ These clothes restrict your freedom of movement and stiffen up the whole body. **3** V-T [usu passive] If something such as cloth **is stiffened**, it is made firm so that it does not bend easily. ◻ This special paper was actually thin, soft Sugiwara paper that had been stiffened with a kind of paste.

stiff-necked also **stiffnecked** ADJ If you say that someone is **stiff-necked**, you mean that they are proud and unwilling to do what other people want. [DISAPPROVAL]

sti|fle /staɪfəl/ (stifles, stifling, stifled) **1** V-T If someone **stifles** something you consider to be a good thing, they prevent it from continuing. [DISAPPROVAL] ◻ Regulations on children stifled creativity. **2** V-T If you **stifle** a yawn or laugh, you prevent yourself from yawning or laughing. ◻ She makes no attempt to stifle a yawn. **3** V-T If you **stifle** your natural feelings or behavior, you prevent yourself from having those feelings or behaving in that way. ◻ It is best to stifle curiosity and leave birds' nests alone.

sti|fling /staɪflɪŋ/ **1** ADJ **Stifling** heat is so intense that it makes you feel uncomfortable. You can also use **stifling** to describe a place that is extremely hot. ◻ The stifling heat of the little room was beginning to make me nauseous. **2** ADJ If a situation is **stifling**, it makes you feel uncomfortable because you cannot do what you want. ◻ Life at home with her parents and two sisters was stifling. **3** → see also **stifle** **4** → See feature box at **hot**

stig|ma /stɪɡmə/ (stigmas) **1** N-VAR If something has a **stigma** attached to it, people think it is something to be ashamed of. ◻ There is still a stigma attached to cancer. **2** → See also color supplement

stig|ma|ta /stɪɡmɑːtə/ N-PLURAL **Stigmata** are marks that appear on a person's body in the same places where Christ was wounded when he was nailed to the cross. Some Christians believe that these marks are a sign of holiness.

stig|ma|tize /stɪɡmətaɪz/ (stigmatizes, stigmatizing, stigmatized)

in BRIT, also use **stigmatise**

V-T If someone or something **is stigmatized**, they are unfairly regarded by many people as being bad or having something to be ashamed of. ◻ Children in single-parent families must not be stigmatized.

stile /staɪl/ (stiles) N-COUNT A **stile** is an entrance to a field or path consisting of a step on either side of a fence or wall to help people climb over it.

sti|let|to /stɪlɛtoʊ/ (stilettos) **1** N-COUNT **Stilettos** are women's shoes that have high, very narrow heels. ◻ Off came her sneakers and on went a pair of stilettos. **2** → See also color supplement

---
STILL

① ADVERB USES
② NOT MOVING OR MAKING A NOISE
③ EQUIPMENT
---

① **still** ♦♦♦ /stɪl/ **1** ADV If a situation that used to exist **still** exists, it has continued and exists now. ◻ I still dream of home. ◻ Brian's toe is still badly swollen and he cannot put his shoe. **2** ADV [ADV before v] If something that has not yet happened could **still** happen, it is possible that it will happen. If something that has not yet happened is **still** to happen, it will happen at a later time. ◻ Big money could still be made if the crisis keeps oil prices high. ◻ We could still make it, but we won't get there till three. **3** ADV [be ADV n] If you say that there **is still** an amount of something left, you are emphasizing that there is that amount left. ◻ There are still some outstanding problems. **4** ADV [ADV before v] You use **still** to emphasize that something remains the case or is true in spite of what you have just said. ◻ I'm average for my height. But I still feel I'm fatter than I should be. **5** ADV [ADV with cl] You use **still** to indicate that a problem or difficulty is not really worth worrying about. ◻ Their luck had simply run out. Still, never fear. **6** ADV [ADV n/adv] You use **still** in expressions such as **still further**, **still another**, and **still more** to show that you find the number or quantity of things you are referring to surprising or excessive. [EMPHASIS] ◻ We look forward to strengthening still further our already close co-operation with the police. **7** ADV [ADV with compar] You use **still** with comparatives to indicate that something has even more of a quality than something else. [EMPHASIS] ◻ Formula One motor car racing is supposed to be dangerous. "Indycar" racing is supposed to be more dangerous still.

② **still** ♦♦♦ /stɪl/ (stiller, stillest, stills) **1** ADJ [ADJ after v] If you stay **still**, you stay in the same position and do not move. ◻ David had been dancing about like a child, but suddenly he stood still and looked at Brad. **2** ADJ If air or water is **still**, it is not moving. ◻ The night air was very still. **3** ADJ If a place is **still**, it is quiet and shows no sign of activity. ◻ In the room it was very still. • **still|ness** N-UNCOUNT ◻ Four deafening explosions shattered the stillness of the night air. **4** ADJ Drinks that are **still** do not contain any bubbles of carbon dioxide. ◻ ...a glass of still water. **5** N-COUNT A **still** is a photograph taken from a movie which is used for publicity purposes. ◻ ...stills from the James Bond movie series.

SYNONYMS

still
ADJ ② **1**
stationary: Stationary cars in traffic jams cause a great deal of pollution.
motionless: Her hands were motionless.
inert: He covered the inert body with a blanket.
static: Both your pictures are of static subjects.
---

③ **still** /stɪl/ (stills) N-COUNT A **still** is a piece of equipment used to make strong alcoholic drinks by a process called distilling.

still|birth /stɪlbɜːrθ/ (stillbirths) N-VAR A **stillbirth** is the birth of a dead baby.

still|born /stɪlbɔːrn/ ADJ A **stillborn** baby is dead when it is born. ◻ It was a miracle that she survived the birth of her stillborn baby.

still life (still lifes) N-VAR A **still life** is a painting or drawing of an arrangement of objects such as flowers or fruit. **Still life** refers to this type of painting or drawing. ◻ ...a still life by one of France's finest artists.

stilt /stɪlt/ (stilts) **1** N-COUNT [usu pl, oft on N] **Stilts** are long upright pieces of wood or metal on which some buildings are built, especially where the ground is wet or very soft. ◻ They inhabit reed huts built on stilts above the water. **2** N-COUNT **Stilts** are two long pieces of wood with pieces for the feet fixed high up on the sides so that people can stand on them and walk high above the ground.

stilt|ed /stɪltɪd/ ADJ If someone speaks in a **stilted** way, they speak in a formal or unnatural way, for example because they are not relaxed. ◻ We made polite, stilted conversation.

stimu|lant /stɪmyələnt/ (stimulants) N-COUNT A **stimulant** is a drug that makes your body work faster, often increasing your heart rate and making you less likely to sleep. ❑ *It is not a good idea to fight fatigue by taking stimulants.*

stimu|late ♦◇◇ /stɪmyəleɪt/ (stimulates, stimulating, stimulated) **1** V-T To **stimulate** something means to encourage it to begin or develop further. ❑ *America's priority is rightly to stimulate its economy.* • **stimu|la|tion** /stɪmyəleɪʃ°n/ N-UNCOUNT ❑ *...an economy in need of stimulation.* **2** V-T [usu passive] If you are **stimulated** by something, it makes you feel full of ideas and enthusiasm. ❑ *Bill was stimulated by the challenge.* • **stimu|lat|ing** ADJ ❑ *It is a complex yet stimulating book.* • **stimu|la|tion** N-UNCOUNT ❑ *Many enjoy the mental stimulation of a challenging job.* **3** V-T If something **stimulates** a part of a person's body, it causes it to move or start working. ❑ *Exercise stimulates the digestive and excretory systems.* • **stimu|lat|ing** ADJ ❑ *...the stimulating effect of adrenaline.* • **stimu|la|tion** N-UNCOUNT [usu with supp] ❑ *...physical stimulation.*

stimu|la|tive /stɪmyələtɪv/ ADJ If a government policy has a **stimulative** effect on the economy, it encourages the economy to grow. ❑ *It is possible that a tax cut might have some stimulative effect.*

stimu|lus /stɪmyələs/ (stimuli /stɪmyəlaɪ/) N-VAR A **stimulus** is something that encourages activity in people or things. ❑ *Interest rates could fall soon and be a stimulus to the U.S. economy.*

sting /stɪŋ/ (stings, stinging, stung) **1** V-T/V-I If a plant, animal, or insect **stings** you, a sharp part of it, usually covered with poison, touches or is pushed into your skin so that you feel a sharp pain. ❑ *The nettles stung their legs.* **2** N-COUNT The **sting** of an insect or animal is the part that stings you. ❑ *Remove the bee sting with tweezers.* **3** N-COUNT If you feel a **sting**, you feel a sharp pain in your skin or other part of your body. ❑ *This won't hurt – you will just feel a little sting.* **4** V-T/V-I If a part of your body **stings**, or if a substance **stings** it, you feel a sharp pain there. ❑ *His cheeks were stinging from the icy wind.* **5** V-T [no cont] If someone's remarks **sting** you, they make you feel hurt and annoyed. ❑ *Some of the criticism has stung him.*

sting|ray /stɪŋreɪ/ (stingrays) N-COUNT A **stingray** is a type of large flat fish with a long tail which it can use as a weapon.

stin|gy /stɪndʒi/ (stingier, stingiest) ADJ If you describe someone as **stingy**, you are criticizing them for being unwilling to spend money. [INFORMAL, DISAPPROVAL] ❑ *The West is stingy with aid.*

stink /stɪŋk/ (stinks, stinking, stank, stunk) **1** V-I To **stink** means to smell very bad. ❑ *We all stank and nobody minded.* ❑ *The place stinks of fried onions.* • N-SING **Stink** is also a noun. ❑ *He was aware of the stink of stale beer on his breath.* **2** V-I If you say that something **stinks**, you mean that you disapprove of it because it involves ideas, feelings, or practices that you do not like. [INFORMAL, DISAPPROVAL] ❑ *I think their methods stink.* **3** N-SING If someone makes **a stink** about something they are angry about, they show their anger in order to make people take notice. [INFORMAL] ❑ *The family's making a hell of a stink.*

stink|er /stɪŋkər/ (stinkers) N-COUNT If you describe someone or something as a **stinker**, you mean that you think they are very unpleasant or bad. [INFORMAL, DISAPPROVAL] ❑ *I think he's an absolute stinker to do that to her.*

stink|ing /stɪŋkɪŋ/ **1** ADJ [ADJ n] You use **stinking** to describe something that is unpleasant or bad. [INFORMAL] ❑ *I had a stinking cold.* **2** → see also **stink**

stinky /stɪŋki/ (stinkier, stinkiest) ADJ [usu ADJ n] If something is **stinky**, it smells extremely unpleasant. ❑ *...sweaty, stinky socks.*

stint /stɪnt/ (stints) N-COUNT A **stint** is a period of time which you spend doing a particular job or activity or working in a particular place. ❑ *He is returning to this country after a five-year stint in Hong Kong.*

sti|pend /staɪpɛnd/ (stipends) **1** N-COUNT A **stipend** is a sum of money that is paid to a student or volunteer for their living expenses. [mainly AM] **2** N-COUNT A **stipend** is a sum of money that is paid regularly to someone, for example a member of the clergy, for their services or to cover their living expenses.

sti|pen|di|ary /staɪpɛndieri/ ADJ [ADJ n] A **stipendiary** magistrate or member of the clergy receives a stipend.

stip|pled /stɪp°ld/ ADJ A surface that is **stippled** is covered with tiny spots. ❑ *The room remains simple with bare, stippled green walls.*

stipu|late /stɪpyəleɪt/ (stipulates, stipulating, stipulated) V-T If you **stipulate** a condition or **stipulate** that something must be done, you say clearly that it must be done. ❑ *She could have stipulated that she would pay when she collected the computer.* • **stipu|la|tion** /stɪpyəleɪʃ°n/ (stipulations) N-COUNT ❑ *Clifford's only stipulation is that his clients obey his advice.*

stir ♦◇◇ /stɜr/ (stirs, stirring, stirred) **1** V-T If you **stir** a liquid or other substance, you move it around or mix it in a container using something such as a spoon. ❑ *Stir the soup for a few seconds.* ❑ *There was Mrs. Bellingham, stirring sugar into her tea.* **2** V-I If you **stir**, you move slightly, for example because you are uncomfortable or beginning to wake up. [WRITTEN] ❑ *Eileen shook him, and he started to stir.* **3** V-I [usu with brd-neg] If you do not **stir** from a place, you do not move from it. [WRITTEN] ❑ *She had not stirred from the house that evening.* **4** V-T/V-I If something **stirs** or if the wind **stirs** it, it moves gently in the wind. [WRITTEN] ❑ *Palm trees stir in the soft Pacific breeze.* **5** V-T/V-I If a particular memory, feeling, or mood **stirs** or **is stirred** in you, you begin to think about it or feel it. [WRITTEN] ❑ *Then a memory stirs in you and you start feeling anxious.* ❑ *Amy remembered the anger he had stirred in her.* **6** N-SING If an event causes a **stir**, it causes great excitement, shock, or anger among people. ❑ *His movie has caused a stir.* **7** → see also **stirring**
▶ **stir up** **1** PHRASAL VERB If something **stirs up** dust or **stirs up** mud in water, it causes it to rise up and move around. ❑ *They saw first a cloud of dust and then the car that was stirring it up.* **2** PHRASAL VERB If you **stir up** a particular mood or situation, usually a bad one, you cause it. [DISAPPROVAL] ❑ *As usual, Harriet is trying to stir up trouble.*

SYNONYMS

stir
VERB **1**
mix: *Mix the ingredients together slowly.*
blend: *Blend the ingredients until you have a smooth cream.*
whisk: *In a separate bowl, whisk together the remaining sugar and the yolks.*
beat: *Beat the eggs and sugar until they start to thicken.*

COLLOCATIONS

stir
VERB
1
stir + adverb: constantly, continuously, well; gently, occasionally
6
stir + noun: anger, controversy, emotion, unrest; imagination, memory, soul

---

stir-fry (stir-fries, stir-frying, stir-fried) **1** V-T If you **stir-fry** vegetables, meat, or fish, you cook small pieces of them quickly by stirring them in a small quantity of very hot oil. This method is often used in Chinese cookery. ❑ *Stir-fry the vegetables until crisp.* ❑ *...stir-fried vegetables.* **2** N-COUNT A **stir-fry** is a Chinese dish consisting of small pieces of vegetables, meat, or fish which have been stir-fried. ❑ *Serve the stir-fry with "instant" noodles.* **3** ADJ [ADJ n] **Stir-fry** vegetables, meat, or fish or **stir-fry** dishes are cooked by the stir-fry method.

stir|ring /stɜrɪŋ/ (stirrings) **1** ADJ A **stirring** event, performance, or account of something makes people very excited or enthusiastic. ❑ *The president made a stirring speech.* **2** N-COUNT [usu N of n] A **stirring** of a feeling or thought is the beginning of one. ❑ *I feel a stirring of curiosity.*

stir|rup /stɜrəp, stɪr-/ (stirrups) **1** N-COUNT **Stirrups** are the two metal loops which are attached to a horse's saddle by long pieces of leather. You place your feet in the stirrups when riding a horse. **2** N-COUNT The **stirrup** is the innermost bone of the three small bones in the ear of mammals. **3** → See also color supplement

stitch /stɪtʃ/ (stitches, stitching, stitched) **1** V-T/V-I If you **stitch** cloth, you use a needle and thread to join two pieces together or to make a decoration. ❑ *Fold the fabric and stitch the* two layers together. ☐ *We stitched incessantly.* **2** N-COUNT **Stitches** are the short pieces of thread that have been sewn in a piece of cloth. ☐ *...a row of straight stitches.* **3** N-COUNT In knitting and crochet, a **stitch** is a loop made by one turn of wool around a knitting needle or crochet hook. ☐ *Her mother counted the stitches on her knitting needles.* **4** N-COUNT If you sew or knit something in a particular **stitch**, you sew or knit in a way that produces a particular pattern. ☐ *The design can be worked in cross stitch.* **5** V-T When doctors **stitch** a wound, they use a special needle and thread to sew the skin together. ☐ *Jill washed and stitched the wound.* **6** N-COUNT A **stitch** is a piece of thread that has been used to sew the skin of a wound together. ☐ *He had six stitches in a head wound.* **7** N-SING A **stitch** is a sharp pain in your side, usually caused by running or laughing a lot. ☐ *One of them was laughing so much he got a stitch.* **8** → See feature box at **sewing**

stitch|ing /stɪtʃɪŋ/ N-UNCOUNT **Stitching** is a row of stitches that have been sewn in a piece of cloth. ☐ *The stitching had begun to fray at the edges.*

stoat /stoʊt/ (stoats) N-COUNT A **stoat** is a small, thin, wild animal that has brown fur. Some stoats that live in northern Europe have fur that turns white in winter.

stock ✦✧ /stɒk/ (stocks, stocking, stocked) **1** N-COUNT **Stocks** are shares in the ownership of a company, or investments on which a fixed amount of interest will be paid. [BUSINESS] ☐ *...the buying and selling of stocks and shares.* **2** N-UNCOUNT A company's **stock** is the amount of money which the company has through selling shares. [BUSINESS] ☐ *Two years later, when the company went public, their stock was valued at $38 million.* **3** V-T [no cont] If a store **stocks** particular products, it keeps a supply of them to sell. ☐ *The store stocks everything from cigarettes to recycled paper.* **4** N-COUNT A store's **stock** is the total amount of goods which it has available to sell. ☐ *When a nearby store burned down, our stock was ruined by smoke.* **5** V-T If you **stock** something such as a cupboard, shelf, or room, you fill it with food or other things. ☐ *I worked stocking shelves in a grocery store.* ☐ *Some families stocked their cellars with food and water.* • PHRASAL VERB **Stock up** means the same as **stock**. ☐ *I had to stock the boat up with food.* **6** N-COUNT If you have a **stock** of things, you have a supply of them stored in a place ready to be used. ☐ *It is a good idea to keep a stock of healthy snacks at hand.* **7** ADJ [ADJ n] A **stock** answer, expression, or way of doing something is one that is very commonly used, especially because people cannot be bothered to think of something new. ☐ *My boss had a stock response – "If it ain't broke, don't fix it!"* **8** N-MASS **Stock** is a liquid, usually made by boiling meat, bones, or vegetables in water, that is used to give flavor to soups and sauces. ☐ *Finally, add the beef stock.* **9** → see also **stocking** **10** PHRASE If goods are **in stock**, a store has them available to sell. If they are **out of stock**, it does not. ☐ *Check that your size is in stock.* **11** PHRASE If you **take stock**, you pause to think about all the aspects of a situation or event before deciding what to do next. ☐ *It was time to take stock of the situation.* **12** **lock, stock, and barrel** → see **barrel**
▶ **stock up** **1** → see **stock 5** **2** PHRASAL VERB If you **stock up** on something, you buy a lot of it, in case you cannot get it later. ☐ *The authorities have urged people to stock up on fuel.*

stock|ade /stɒkeɪd/ (stockades) N-COUNT A **stockade** is a wall of large wooden posts built around an area to keep out enemies or wild animals. ☐ *...the inner stockade.*

stock|broker /stɒkbroʊkər/ (stockbrokers) N-COUNT A **stockbroker** is a person whose job is to buy and sell stocks and shares for people who want to invest money. [BUSINESS]

stock|broking /stɒkbroʊkɪŋ/ N-UNCOUNT **Stockbroking** is the professional activity of buying and selling stocks and shares for clients. [BUSINESS] ☐ *His stockbroking firm was hit by the 1987 crash.*

stock car (stock cars) **1** N-COUNT A **stock car** is a car which has had changes made to it so that it is suitable for races in which the cars often crash into each other. ☐ *He acted as grand marshal of a stock car race.* **2** → See also color supplement

stock con|trol N-UNCOUNT **Stock control** is the activity of making sure that a company always has exactly the right amount of goods available to sell. [BUSINESS] ☐ *Better stock control helped them reduced their expenses.*

stock cube (stock cubes) N-COUNT A **stock cube** is the same as a **bouillon cube**. [BRIT]

stock ex|change ✦✧ (stock exchanges) N-COUNT A **stock exchange** is a place where people buy and sell stocks and shares. The **stock exchange** is also the trading activity that goes on there and the trading organization itself. [BUSINESS] ☐ *The shortage of good stock has kept some investors away from the stock exchange.*

stock|holder /stɒkhoʊldər/ (stockholders) N-COUNT A **stockholder** is a person who owns shares in a company. [AM, BUSINESS] ☐ *He was a stockholder in a hotel corporation.*

in BRIT, use **shareholder**

stock|ing /stɒkɪŋ/ (stockings) N-COUNT **Stockings** are items of women's clothing which fit closely over the feet and legs. Stockings are usually made of nylon and are held in place by garters. ☐ *...a pair of nylon stockings.*

stock|inged /stɒkɪŋd/ ADJ [ADJ n] If someone is in their **stockinged** feet, they are wearing socks, tights, or stockings, but no shoes. [LITERARY] ☐ *He tip-toed to the door in his stockinged feet.*

stock|ing fill|er (stocking fillers) also **stocking-filler** N-COUNT A **stocking filler** is the same as a **stocking stuffer**. [mainly BRIT]

stock|ing stuff|er (stocking stuffers) N-COUNT A **stocking stuffer** is a small present that is suitable for putting in a Christmas stocking. [AM]

in BRIT, use **stocking filler**

stock-in-trade also **stock in trade** N-SING [with poss] If you say that something is someone's **stock-in-trade**, you mean that it is a usual part of their behavior or work. ☐ *Patriotism is every politician's stock-in-trade.*

stock mar|ket ✦✧ (stock markets) **1** N-COUNT The **stock market** consists of the general activity of buying stocks and shares, and the people and institutions that organize it. [BUSINESS] ☐ *He's been studying and playing the stock market since he was 14.* **2** → See feature box at **banking**

stock op|tion (stock options) N-COUNT A **stock option** is an opportunity for the employees of a company to buy shares at a special price. [AM, BUSINESS] ☐ *He made a huge profit from the sale of shares purchased in January under the company's stock option program.*

in BRIT, use **share option**

stock|pile /stɒkpaɪl/ (stockpiles, stockpiling, stockpiled) **1** V-T If people **stockpile** things such as food or weapons, they store large quantities of them for future use. ☐ *People are stockpiling food for the coming winter.* **2** N-COUNT A **stockpile** of things is a large quantity of them that have been stored for future use. ☐ *The two leaders also approved treaties to cut stockpiles of chemical weapons.*

stock|room /stɒkrʊm/ (stockrooms) N-COUNT A **stockroom** is a room, especially in a store or a factory, where a stock of goods is kept.

stock-still ADJ [ADJ after v] If someone stands or sits **stock-still**, they do not move at all. ☐ *The lieutenant stopped and stood stock-still.*

stock|taking /stɒkteɪkɪŋ/ N-UNCOUNT **Stocktaking** is the same as doing an **inventory**. [mainly BRIT, BUSINESS]

stocky /stɒki/ (stockier, stockiest) ADJ A **stocky** person has a body that is broad, solid, and often short. ☐ *...a short stocky man in his forties.*

stodgy /stɒdʒi/ (stodgier, stodgiest) **1** ADJ [usu ADJ n] If someone or something is **stodgy**, they are dull, unimaginative, and commonplace. ☐ *The company hasn't been able to shake off its image as stodgy and old-fashioned.* **2** ADJ [usu ADJ n] **Stodgy** food is very solid and heavy. It makes you feel very full, and is difficult to digest. [mainly BRIT]

sto|gie /stoʊgi/ (stogies) N-COUNT A **stogie** is a long thin cigar. [AM]

sto|ic /stoʊɪk/ (stoics) **1** ADJ **Stoic** means the same as **stoical**. [FORMAL, APPROVAL] ☐ *The kids of Kobe try to be as stoic as their parents in this tragic situation.* **2** N-COUNT If you say that someone is a **stoic**, you approve of them because they do not complain or show they are upset in bad situations. [FORMAL, APPROVAL]

stoi|cal /stóʊɪkəl/ ADJ If you say that someone behaves in a **stoical** way, you approve of them because they do not complain or show they are upset in bad situations. [FORMAL, APPROVAL] ❑ *She never ceased to admire the stoical courage of those soldiers.* • **stoi|cal|ly** ADV [usu ADV with v] ❑ *She put up with it all stoically.*

stoi|cism /stóʊɪsɪzəm/ N-UNCOUNT **Stoicism** is stoical behavior. [FORMAL, APPROVAL] ❑ *They bore their plight with stoicism and fortitude.*

stoke /stoʊk/ (stokes, stoking, stoked) **1** V-T If you **stoke** a fire, you add coal or wood to it to keep it burning. ❑ *She was stoking the stove with sticks of maple.* • PHRASAL VERB **Stoke up** means the same as **stoke**. ❑ *He stoked up the fire in the hearth.* **2** V-T If you **stoke** something such as a feeling, you cause it to be felt more strongly. ❑ *These demands are helping to stoke fears of civil war.* • PHRASAL VERB **Stoke up** means the same as **stoke**. ❑ *He has sent his proposals in the hope of stoking up interest for the idea.*

stoked /stoʊkt/ ADJ If you are **stoked** about something, you are very excited about it. [AM, INFORMAL] ❑ *"I can't wait to get there," she said. "I am so stoked about this trip."* ❑ *The kids were happy, the crowds were stoked.*

stok|er /stóʊkər/ (stokers) N-COUNT In former times a **stoker** was a person whose job was to stoke fires, especially on a ship or a steam train.

stole /stoʊl/ **Stole** is the past tense of **steal**.

sto|len /stóʊlən/ **Stolen** is the past participle of **steal**.

stol|id /stɒlɪd/ ADJ [usu ADJ n] If you describe someone as **stolid**, you mean that they do not show much emotion or are not very exciting or interesting. ❑ *He glanced furtively at the stolid faces of the two detectives.*

stom|ach /stʌmək/ (stomachs, stomaching, stomached) **1** N-COUNT Your **stomach** is the organ inside your body where food is digested before it moves into the intestines. ❑ *He had an upset stomach.* **2** N-COUNT You can refer to the front part of your body below your waist as your **stomach**. ❑ *The children lay down on their stomachs.* **3** N-COUNT If the front part of your body below your waist feels uncomfortable because you are feeling worried or frightened, you can refer to it as your **stomach**. ❑ *His stomach was in knots.* **4** N-COUNT If you say that someone has a strong **stomach**, you mean that they are not disgusted by things that disgust most other people. ❑ *Surgery often demands actual physical strength, as well as the possession of a strong stomach.* **5** V-T [with brd-neg] If you cannot **stomach** something, you cannot accept it because you dislike it or disapprove of it. ❑ *I could never stomach the cruelty involved in the wounding of animals.* **6** PHRASE If you do something **on an empty stomach**, you do it without having eaten. ❑ *Avoid drinking on an empty stomach.* **7** → See feature box at **body, illness**; See also color supplement

---
COLLOCATIONS

stomach
NOUN
1
adjective + **stomach**: bloated, distended; empty; queasy, upset; cast-iron
stomach + verb: growl, rumble
verb + **stomach**: upset
2
adjective + **stomach**: flat; bloated, distended, swollen
3
stomach + verb: churn, flip, lurch

---

stom|ach ache (stomach aches) also **stomachache** N-VAR If you have a **stomach ache**, you have a pain in your stomach.

stomach-churning ADJ If you describe something as **stomach-churning**, you mean that it is so unpleasant that it makes you feel physically sick. ❑ *The stench from rotting food is stomach-churning.*

stom|ach sta|pling N-UNCOUNT **Stomach stapling** is an operation in which part of the stomach is removed in order to help a person to eat less and lose weight. [MEDICAL] ❑ *The most popular method of surgical weight loss is the stomach stapling operation.*

stomp /stɒmp/ (stomps, stomping, stomped) V-I If you **stomp** somewhere, you walk there with very heavy steps, often because you are angry. ❑ *He turned his back on them and stomped off up the hill.*

stomp|ing ground (stomping grounds) N-COUNT Someone's **stomping ground** is a place where they like to go often.

stone /stoʊn/ (stones, stoning, stoned) **1** N-MASS **Stone** is a hard solid substance found in the ground and often used for building houses. ❑ *He could not tell whether the floor was wood or stone.* ❑ *People often don't appreciate that marble is a natural stone.* **2** N-COUNT A **stone** is a small piece of rock that is found on the ground. ❑ *He removed a stone from his shoe.* **3** N-COUNT A **stone** is a large piece of stone put somewhere in memory of a person or event, or as a religious symbol. ❑ *The monument consists of a circle of gigantic stones.* **4** N-UNCOUNT **Stone** is used in expressions such as **set in stone** and **tablets of stone** to suggest that an idea or rule is firm and fixed, and cannot be changed. ❑ *He is merely throwing the idea forward for discussion, it is not cast in stone.* **5** N-COUNT You can refer to a jewel as a **stone**. ❑ *...a diamond ring with three stones.* **6** N-COUNT A **stone** is a small hard ball of minerals and other substances which sometimes forms in a person's kidneys or gallbladder. ❑ *He had kidney stones.* **7** N-COUNT The **stone** in a plum, cherry, or other fruit is the large hard seed in the middle of it. [mainly BRIT]

in AM, usually use **pit**

8 V-T If people **stone** someone or something, they throw stones at them. ❑ *Youths burned cars and stoned police.* **9** → see also **stepping stone, stoned**

Stone Age N-PROPER [the N] **The Stone Age** is a very early period of human history, when people used tools and weapons made of stone, not metal.

stone-cold **1** ADJ If something that should be warm is **stone-cold**, it is very cold. ❑ *Hillsden took a sip of tea, but it was stone cold.* **2** PHRASE If someone is **stone-cold sober**, they are not drunk at all. [INFORMAL]

stoned /stoʊnd/ ADJ If someone is **stoned**, their mind is greatly affected by a drug such as marijuana. [INFORMAL] ❑ *Half of them were so stoned they couldn't even see.*

stone dead also **stone-dead** ADJ If something such as an idea or emotion is **stone-dead**, it has been completely destroyed. [EMPHASIS] ❑ *By the end of 1930, the silent picture was stone dead.*

stone deaf also **stone-deaf** ADJ [usu v-link ADJ] Someone who is **stone deaf** cannot hear at all.

stone-ground also **stoneground** ADJ [usu ADJ n] **Stone-ground** flour or bread is made from grain that has been crushed between two large, heavy pieces of stone.

stone|mason /stóʊnmeɪsən/ (stonemasons) N-COUNT A **stonemason** is a person who is skilled at cutting and preparing stone so that it can be used for walls and buildings.

stone|wall /stóʊnwɔːl/ (stonewalls, stonewalling, stonewalled) V-T/V-I If you say that someone **stonewalls**, you disapprove of them because they delay giving a clear answer or making a clear decision, often because there is something that they want to hide or avoid doing. [DISAPPROVAL] ❑ *The administration is just stonewalling in an attempt to hide their political embarrassment.* • **stone|wall|ing** N-UNCOUNT ❑ *After 18 days of stonewalling, he at last came out and faced the issue.*

stone|ware /stóʊnwɛər/ N-UNCOUNT [oft N n] **Stoneware** is hard clay pottery which is baked at a high temperature. ❑ *...hand-painted blue-and-white stoneware.*

stone-washed also **stonewashed** ADJ **Stone-washed** jeans are jeans which have been specially washed with small pieces of stone so that when you buy them they are fairly pale and soft.

stone|work /stóʊnwɜːrk/ N-UNCOUNT **Stonework** consists of objects or parts of a building that are made of stone. ❑ *...the crumbling stonework of the derelict church.*

stony /stóʊni/ (stonier, stoniest) **1** ADJ **Stony** ground is rough and contains a lot of stones. ❑ *The steep, stony ground is well drained.* **2** ADJ A **stony** expression or attitude does not show any sympathy or friendliness. ❑ *She gave me the stoniest look I ever got.*

stood /stʊd/ **Stood** is the past tense and past participle of **stand**.

stooge /stuːdʒ/ (stooges) N-COUNT [usu with supp] If you refer to someone as a **stooge**, you are criticizing them

stool /stuːl/ (stools) **1** N-COUNT A **stool** is a seat with legs but no support for your arms or back. ❏ *O'Brien sat on a bar stool and leaned his elbows on the counter.* **2** → See also color supplement

stoop /stuːp/ (stoops, stooping, stooped) **1** V-I If you **stoop**, you stand or walk with your shoulders bent forward. ❏ *She was taller than he was and stooped slightly.* • N-SING **Stoop** is also a noun. ❏ *He was a tall, thin fellow with a slight stoop.* **2** V-I If you **stoop**, you bend your body forward and downward. ❏ *He stooped to pick up the carrier bag of groceries.* ❏ *Two men in shirt sleeves stooped over the car.* **3** V-I If you say that a person **stoops** to doing something, you are criticizing them because they do something wrong or immoral that they would not normally do. [DISAPPROVAL] ❏ *He had not, until recently, stooped to personal abuse.*

stop ♦♦♦ /stɒp/ (stops, stopping, stopped) **1** V-T/V-I If you have been doing something and then you **stop** doing it, you no longer do it. ❏ *Stop throwing those stones!* ❏ *Does either of the parties want to stop the fighting?* ❏ *She stopped in mid-sentence.* **2** V-T If you **stop** something from happening, or you **stop** something happening, you prevent it from happening or prevent it from continuing. ❏ *He proposed a new diplomatic initiative to try to stop the war.* ❏ *He would do what he must to stop her from destroying him.* **3** V-I If an activity or process **stops**, it is no longer happening. ❏ *The rain had stopped and a star or two was visible over the mountains.* ❏ *The system overheated and filming had to stop.* **4** V T/V-I If something such as machine **stops** or is **stopped**, it is no longer moving or working. ❏ *The clock stopped at 11:59 Saturday night.* ❏ *Arnold stopped the engine and got out of the car.* **5** V-T/V-I When a moving person or vehicle **stops** or is **stopped**, they no longer move and they remain in the same place. ❏ *The car failed to stop at an army checkpoint.* ❏ *He stopped and let her catch up with him.* **6** N-SING If something that is moving comes **to a stop** or is brought **to a stop**, it slows down and no longer moves. ❏ *People often wrongly open doors before the train has come to a stop.* **7** V-T/V-I If someone does not **stop** to think or to explain, they continue with what they are doing without taking any time to think about or explain it. ❏ *She doesn't stop to think about what she's saying.* ❏ *There is something rather strange about all this if one stops to consider it.* **8** V-I If you say that a quality or state **stops** somewhere, you mean that it exists or is true up to that point, but no further. ❏ *The cafe owner has put up the required "no smoking" signs, but thinks his responsibility stops there.* **9** N-COUNT A **stop** is a place where buses or trains regularly stop so that people can get on and off. ❏ *The closest subway stop is Houston Street.* **10** V-I If you **stop** somewhere on a journey, you stay there for a short while. ❏ *He insisted we stop at a small restaurant just outside of Atlanta.* **11** N-COUNT A **stop** is a time or place at which you stop during a journey. ❏ *The last stop in Mr. Robinson's lengthy tour was Paris.* **12** PHRASE If you say that someone will **stop at nothing** to get something, you are emphasizing that they are willing to do things that are extreme, wrong, or dangerous in order to get it. [EMPHASIS] ❏ *Their motive is money, and they will stop at nothing to get it.* **13** PHRASE If you **put a stop to** something that you do not like or approve of, you prevent it from happening or continuing. ❏ *His daughter should have stood up and put a stop to all these rumours.* **14** PHRASE If you say that someone does not **know when to stop**, you mean that they do not control their own behavior very well and so they often annoy or upset other people. ❏ *Like many politicians before him, Mr. Bentley did not know when to stop.* **15 to stop dead** → see **dead 16 to stop short of** → see **short** ① **17 to stop someone in their tracks** → see **track**

▸ **stop by** also **stop in** PHRASAL VERB If you **stop by** somewhere, you make a short visit to a person or place. [INFORMAL] ❏ *Perhaps I'll stop by the hospital.*

▸ **stop off** PHRASAL VERB If you **stop off** somewhere, you stop for a short time in the middle of a trip. ❏ *The president stopped off in Poland on his way to Munich for the economic summit.*

stop|cock /stɒpkɒk/ (stopcocks) N-COUNT A **stopcock** is a faucet on a pipe, which you turn in order to allow something to pass through the pipe or to stop it from passing through.

stop|gap /stɒpgæp/ (stopgaps) N-COUNT [oft N n] A **stopgap** is something that serves a purpose for a short time, but is replaced as soon as possible. ❏ *The job was just a stopgap between leaving college and going abroad.*

stop-go also **stop-and-go** ADJ [usu ADJ n] **Stop-go** is used to describe processes in which there are periods of inactivity between periods of activity. ❏ *...stop-go economic cycles.* ❏ *...in-town stop-and-go driving.*

stop|light /stɒplaɪt/ (stoplights) also **stop light** N-COUNT A **stoplight** is a set of colored lights which controls the flow of traffic on a road. [AM] ❏ *Holly waited at a stoplight, impatient for the signal to change.*

in BRIT, use **traffic light**

stop|over /stɒpoʊvər/ (stopovers) N-COUNT A **stopover** is a short stay in a place in between parts of a trip. ❏ *The Sunday flights will make a stopover in Paris.*

stop|page /stɒpɪdʒ/ (stoppages) **1** N-COUNT When there is a **stoppage**, people stop working because of a disagreement with their employers. [BUSINESS] ❏ *Mineworkers in the Ukraine have voted for a one-day stoppage next month.* **2** N-COUNT A **stoppage** is the same as **time out**. [mainly BRIT]

stop|page time N-UNCOUNT In soccer and some other sports, **stoppage time** is the period of time that is added to the end of a game because play was stopped during the game as a result of, for example, injuries to players. [mainly BRIT] ❏ *...a spectacular goal in stoppage time.*

stop|per /stɒpər/ (stoppers) **1** N-COUNT A **stopper** is a piece of glass, plastic, or cork that fits into the top of a bottle or jar to close it. ❏ *...a bottle of colorless liquid sealed with a cork stopper.* **2** → see also **showstopper**

stop|watch /stɒpwɒtʃ/ (stopwatches) also **stop-watch** **1** N-COUNT A **stopwatch** is a watch with buttons which you press at the beginning and end of an event, so that you can measure exactly how long it takes. **2** → See also color supplement

stor|age /stɔːrɪdʒ/ **1** N-UNCOUNT If you refer to the **storage** of something, you mean that it is kept in a special place until it is needed. ❏ *...the storage of toxic waste.* ❏ *Some of the space will at first be used for storage.* **2** → See feature box at **house**

store ♦♦◊ /stɔːr/ (stores, storing, stored) **1** N-COUNT A **store** is a building or part of a building where things are sold. ❏ *They are selling them for $10 apiece at a few stores in Texas and Oklahoma.* ❏ *...grocery stores.* **2** V-T When you **store** things, you put them in a container or other place and leave them there until they are needed. ❏ *Store the cookies in an airtight tin.* • PHRASAL VERB **Store away** means the same as **store**. ❏ *He simply stored the tapes away.* **3** V-T When you **store** information, you keep it in your memory, in a file, or in a computer. ❏ *Where in the brain do we store information about colors?* **4** N-COUNT A **store** of things is a supply of them that you keep somewhere until you need them. ❏ *I handed over my secret store of chocolate.* **5** N-COUNT A **store** is a place where things are kept while they are not being used. ❏ *...a store for spent fuel from submarines.* **6** → see also **department store 7** PHRASE If something is **in store** for you, it is going to happen at some time in the future. ❏ *Surprises were also in store for me.*

▸ **store away** → see **store 2**

▸ **store up** PHRASAL VERB If you **store** something **up**, you keep it until you think that the time is right to use it. ❏ *Investors were storing up a lot of cash in anticipation of disaster.*

store-bought ADJ **Store-bought** products are sold in stores, rather than being made at home. ❏ *Many of these sauces can be served with store-bought pasta.*

store brand (store brands) N-COUNT **Store brands** are products which have the trademark or label of the store which sells them, especially a supermarket chain. [AM] ❏ *Are store brands always cheaper?* ❏ *...a half-gallon of store-brand ice cream.*

store|card /stɔːrkɑːrd/ (storecards) also **store card** N-COUNT A **storecard** is a plastic card that you use to buy goods on credit from a particular store or group of stores. [mainly BRIT]

in AM, usually use **charge card**

store de|tec|tive (store detectives) N-COUNT A **store detective** is someone who is employed by a store to walk around the store looking for people who are secretly stealing goods.

store|front /stɔrfrʌnt/ (storefronts) **1** N-COUNT A **storefront** is the outside part of a store which faces the street, including the door and windows. [mainly AM]

> in BRIT, usually use **shop front**

2 N-COUNT [oft N n] A **storefront** is a small store or office that opens onto the street and is part of a row of stores or offices. [AM] ❑ ...*a tiny storefront office on the Main Street.*

store|house /stɔrhaʊs/ (storehouses) N-COUNT A **storehouse** is a building in which things, usually food, are stored.

store|keeper /stɔrkipər/ (storekeepers) N-COUNT A **storekeeper** is a shopkeeper. [mainly AM]

store|room /stɔrum/ (storerooms) N-COUNT A **storeroom** is a room in which you keep things until they are needed. ❑ ...*a storeroom filled with massive old furniture covered with dust.*

sto|rey /stɔri/ [mainly BRIT] → see **story**

-storey /-stɔri/ [mainly BRIT] → see **-story**

-storeyed /-stɔrid/ [mainly BRIT] → see **-storied**

-storied /-stɔrid/

> in BRIT, use **-storeyed**

COMB IN ADJ **-storied** means the same as **-story**. ❑ *We arrived at a multistoried gray building.*

stork /stɔrk/ (storks) N-COUNT A **stork** is a large bird with a long beak and long legs, which lives near water.

VOCABULARY IN CONTEXT

Storms and wind

Windy weather can be a lot of fun. On a **blustery** day, you can fly a kite or go windsurfing. A cool, fresh **breeze** can seem heaven-sent on a hot day. But the wind can be dangerous during a **gale**, and it is always good to know what to do in an emergency. If you are **on foot** during **high winds** or a **hurricane**, your best option is to take cover and wait for the wind to **die down**. Be careful, however, about where you choose to **shelter** from the wind: trees and power lines may get **blown down**. If you are driving, the best advice would be to slow down or even **pull over** and wait for the wind to die down if you can. If you choose to continue driving, keep both your hands on the steering wheel so that you have more control over the vehicle in case of strong **gusts**. Finally, maintain a safe distance from large vehicles such as trucks or buses.

storm ♦◇◇ /stɔrm/ (storms, storming, stormed) **1** N-COUNT A **storm** is very bad weather, with heavy rain, strong winds, and often thunder and lightning. ❑ ...*the violent storms which whipped the East Coast.* **2** N-COUNT If something causes a **storm**, it causes an angry or excited reaction from a large number of people. ❑ *The photos caused a storm when they were first published.* **3** N-COUNT A **storm** of applause or other noise is a sudden loud amount of it made by an audience or other group of people in reaction to something. ❑ *His speech was greeted with a storm of applause.* **4** V-I If you **storm** into or out of a place, you enter or leave it quickly and noisily, because you are angry. ❑ *After a bit of an argument, he stormed out.* **5** V-T If a place that is being defended **is stormed**, a group of people attack it, usually in order to get inside it. ❑ *Government buildings have been stormed and looted.* • **storm|ing** N-UNCOUNT ❑ ...*the storming of the Bastille.* **6** PHRASE If someone or something **takes** a place **by storm**, they are extremely successful. ❑ *Kenya's long distance runners have taken the athletics world by storm.*

storm cloud (storm clouds) also **stormcloud** **1** N-COUNT [usu pl] **Storm clouds** are the dark clouds which are seen before a storm. **2** N-COUNT [usu pl] You can use **storm clouds** to refer to a sign that something very unpleasant is going to happen. [FORMAL] ❑ *Over the past three weeks, the storm clouds have gathered again over the government.*

storm|trooper /stɔrmtrupər/ (stormtroopers) also **storm trooper** N-COUNT **Stormtroopers** were members of a private Nazi army who were well-known for being violent.

stormy /stɔrmi/ (stormier, stormiest) **1** ADJ If there is **stormy** weather, there are strong winds and heavy rain. ❑ *It had been a night of stormy weather, with torrential rain and high winds.* **2** ADJ **Stormy** seas have very large strong waves because there are strong winds. ❑ *They make the treacherous journey across stormy seas.* **3** ADJ If you describe a situation as **stormy**, you mean it involves a lot of angry argument or criticism. ❑ *The letter was read at a stormy meeting.*

sto|ry ♦♦♦ /stɔri/ (stories) **1** N-COUNT A **story** is a description of imaginary people and events, which is written or told in order to entertain. ❑ *The second story in the book is titled "The Scholar."* ❑ *I shall tell you a story about four little rabbits.* **2** N-COUNT A **story** is a description of an event or something that happened to someone, especially a spoken description of it. ❑ *The parents all shared interesting stories about their children.* **3** N-COUNT The **story** of something is a description of all the important things that have happened to it since it began. ❑ ...*the story of the women's movement.* **4** N-COUNT If someone invents a **story**, they give a false explanation or account of something. ❑ *He invented some story about a cousin.* **5** N-COUNT A news **story** is a piece of news in a newspaper or in a news broadcast. ❑ *Those are some of the top stories in the news.* ❑ *They'll do anything for a story.* **6** N-COUNT A **story** of a building is one of its different levels, which is situated above or below other levels. ❑ ...*long brick buildings, two stories high.*

> in BRIT, use **storey**

7 PHRASE You use **a different story** to refer to a situation, usually a bad one, which exists in one set of circumstances when you have mentioned that it does not exist in another set of circumstances. ❑ *Where Marcella lives, the rents are fairly cheap, but a little further north it's a different story.* **8** PHRASE If you say **it's the same old story** or **it's the old story**, you mean that something unpleasant or undesirable seems to happen again and again. ❑ *It's the same old story. They want one person to do three people's jobs.* **9** PHRASE If you say that something is **only part of the story** or is **not the whole story**, you mean that the explanation or information given is not enough for a situation to be fully understood. ❑ *This may be true but it is only part of the story.* **10** PHRASE If someone tells you their **side of the story**, they tell you why they behaved in a particular way and why they think they were right, when other people think that person behaved wrongly. ❑ *He had already made up his mind before even hearing her side of the story.*

-story /-stɔri/

> in BRIT, use **-storey**

1 COMB IN ADJ **-story** is used after numbers to form adjectives that indicate that a building has a particular number of floors or levels. ❑ ...*a second-story apartment.* **2** → see also **multistory**

story|board /stɔribɔrd/ (storyboards) N-COUNT A **storyboard** is a set of pictures which show what will happen in something such as a movie or advertisement that is being planned.

story|book /stɔribʊk/ (storybooks) N-COUNT A **storybook** is a book of stories for children.

story|line /stɔrilaɪn/ (storylines) N-COUNT The **storyline** of a book, movie, or play is its story and the way in which it develops. ❑ *The surprise twists in the storyline are the film's greatest strength.*

story|teller /stɔritɛlər/ (storytellers) also **story-teller** N-COUNT A **storyteller** is someone who tells or writes stories. ❑ *He was the one who first set down the stories of the Celtic storytellers.*

story|telling /stɔ̱ɪritelɪŋ/ N-UNCOUNT **Storytelling** is the activity of telling or writing stories. ❑ *The programme is 90 minutes of dynamic Indian folk dance, live music, and storytelling.*

stout /sta͟ʊt/ (stouter, stoutest) **1** ADJ A **stout** person is rather fat. ❑ *He was a tall, stout man with gray hair.* **2** ADJ **Stout** shoes, branches, or other objects are thick and strong. ❑ *I hope you've both got stout shoes.*

stove /sto͟ʊv/ (stoves) **1** N-COUNT A **stove** is a piece of equipment which provides heat, either for cooking or for heating a room. ❑ *She put the kettle on the gas stove.* **2** → See feature box at **cooking**

stow /sto͟ʊ/ (stows, stowing, stowed) V-T If you **stow** something somewhere, you carefully put it there until it is needed. ❑ *Luke stowed his camera bags into the trunk.*

stow|age /sto͟ʊɪdʒ/ N-UNCOUNT **Stowage** is the space that is available for stowing things on a ship or airplane. ❑ *Stowage is provided in lined lockers beneath the berths.*

stow|away /sto͟ʊəweɪ/ (stowaways) N-COUNT A **stowaway** is a person who hides in a ship, airplane, or other vehicle in order to make a journey secretly or without paying. ❑ *The crew discovered the stowaway about two days into their voyage.*

strad|dle /stræ̱dəl/ (straddles, straddling, straddled) **1** V-T If you **straddle** something, you put or have one leg on either side of it. ❑ *He looked at her with a grin and sat down, straddling the chair.* **2** V-T If something **straddles** a river, road, border, or other place, it stretches across it or exists on both sides of it. ❑ *A small wooden bridge straddled the dike.* **3** V-T Someone or something that **straddles** different periods, groups, or fields of activity exists in, belongs to, or takes elements from them all. ❑ *He straddles two cultures, having been brought up in the United States and later converted to Islam.*

strafe /stre͟ɪf/ (strafes, strafing, strafed) V-T To **strafe** an enemy means to attack them with a lot of bombs or bullets from a low-flying aircraft. ❑ *It seemed that the plane was going to swoop down and strafe the town, so we dived for cover.*

strag|gle /stræ̱gəl/ (straggles, straggling, straggled) **1** V-I If people **straggle** somewhere, they move there slowly, in small groups with large, irregular gaps between them. ❑ *They came straggling up the cliff road.* **2** V-I If a small quantity of things **straggle** over an area, they cover it in an uneven or messy way. ❑ *Her gray hair straggled in wisps about her face.* ❑ *They were beyond the last straggling suburbs now.*

strag|gler /stræ̱glər/ (stragglers) N-COUNT [usu pl] The **stragglers** are the people in a group who are moving more slowly or making less progress than the others. ❑ *There were two stragglers twenty yards back.*

strag|gly /stræ̱gli/ (stragglier, straggliest) ADJ **Straggly** hair or a **straggly** plant is thin and grows or spreads out messily in different directions. ❑ *Her long fair hair was knotted and straggly.*

straight ✦✦✦ /stre͟ɪt/ (straighter, straightest, straights) **1** ADJ A **straight** line or edge continues in the same direction and does not bend or curve. ❑ *Keep the boat in a straight line.* ❑ *His teeth were perfectly straight.* • ADV [ADV after v] **Straight** is also an adverb. ❑ *Stand straight and stretch the left hand to the right foot.* **2** ADJ **Straight** hair has no curls or waves in it. ❑ *Grace had long straight dark hair which she wore in a bun.* **3** ADV [ADV prep/adv] You use **straight** to indicate that the way from one place to another is very direct, with no changes of direction. ❑ *...squirting the medicine straight to the back of the child's throat.* ❑ *He finished his conversation and stood up, looking straight at me.* **4** ADV [ADV prep/adv] If you go **straight** to a place, you go there immediately. ❑ *As always, we went straight to the experts for advice.* **5** ADJ [ADJ n] If you give someone a **straight** answer, you answer them clearly and honestly. ❑ *What a shifty arguer he is, refusing ever to give a straight answer to a straight question.* • ADV [ADV after v] **Straight** is also an adverb. ❑ *I lost my temper and told him straight that I hadn't been looking for any job.* **6** ADJ [ADJ n] **Straight** means following one after the other, with no gaps or intervals. ❑ *They'd won 12 straight games before they lost.* • ADV [n ADV] **Straight** is also an adverb. ❑ *He called from Washington, having been there for 31 hours straight.* **7** ADJ [ADJ n] A **straight** choice or a **straight** fight involves only two people or things. ❑ *It's a straight choice between low-paid jobs and no jobs.* **8** ADJ If you describe someone as **straight**, you mean that they are normal and conventional, for example in their opinions and in the way they live. ❑ *Dorothy was described as a very straight woman, a very strict Christian who was married to her job.* **9** ADJ If you describe someone as **straight**, you mean that they are heterosexual. [INFORMAL] ❑ *His sexual orientation was a lot more gay than straight.* • N-COUNT **Straight** is also a noun. ❑ *...a standard of sexual conduct that applies equally to gays and straights.* **10** PHRASE If you **get** something **straight**, you make sure that you understand it properly or that someone else does. [SPOKEN] ❑ *You need to get your facts straight.* **11** **to keep a straight face** → see **face** ①

straight ar|row (straight arrows) N-COUNT [oft N n] A **straight arrow** is someone who is very traditional, honest, and moral. [mainly AM] ❑ *...a well-scrubbed, straight-arrow group of young people.*

straight away also **straightaway** ADV [ADV with v] If you do something **straight away**, you do it immediately and without delay. ❑ *I should go and see a doctor straight away.*

straight|en /stre͟ɪtən/ (straightens, straightening, straightened) **1** V-T If you **straighten** something, you make it neat or put it in its proper position. ❑ *She sipped her coffee and straightened a picture on the wall.* • PHRASAL VERB **Straighten up** means the same as **straighten**. ❑ *This is my job, to straighten up, to file things.* **2** V-I If you are standing in a relaxed or slightly bent position and then you **straighten**, you make your back or body straight and upright. ❑ *The three men straightened and stood waiting.* • PHRASAL VERB **Straighten up** means the same as **straighten**. ❑ *He straightened up and slipped his hands in his pockets.* **3** V-T/V-I If you **straighten** something, or it **straightens**, it becomes straight. ❑ *Straighten both legs until they are fully extended.* • PHRASAL VERB **Straighten out** means the same as **straighten**. ❑ *No one would dream of straightening out the church's knobbly spire.*

▶ **straighten out 1** PHRASAL VERB If you **straighten out** a confused situation, you succeed in getting it organized and cleaned up. ❑ *He would make an appointment with him to straighten out a couple of things.* **2** → see **straighten** 3

▶ **straighten up** → see **straighten** 1, 2

straight-faced ADJ A **straight-faced** person appears not to be amused in a funny situation. ❑ *...a straight-faced, humorless character.* ❑ *"Whatever gives you that idea?" she replied straight-faced.*

straight|forward /stre͟ɪtfɔ̱ːrwərd/ **1** ADJ If you describe something as **straightforward**, you approve of it because it is easy to do or understand. [APPROVAL] ❑ *Disposable diapers are fairly straightforward to put on.* ❑ *The question seemed straightforward enough.* **2** ADJ If you describe a person or their behavior as **straightforward**, you approve of them because they are honest and direct, and do not try to hide their feelings. [APPROVAL] ❑ *She is very blunt, very straightforward, and very honest.*

straight-laced [mainly BRIT] → see **strait-laced**

strain ✦◆◇ /stre͟ɪn/ (strains, straining, strained) **1** N-VAR If **strain** is put on an organization or system, it has to do more than it is able to do. ❑ *The prison service is already under considerable strain.* **2** V-T If you **strain** something, you make it do more than it is able to do. ❑ *The volume of scheduled flights is straining the air traffic control system.* **3** N-UNCOUNT [also N in pl] **Strain** is a state of worry and tension caused by a difficult situation. ❑ *She was tired and under great strain.* **4** N-SING If you say that a situation is **a strain**, you mean that it makes you worried and tense. ❑ *I sometimes find it a strain to be responsible for the mortgage.* **5** N-UNCOUNT **Strain** is a force that pushes, pulls, or stretches something in a way that may damage it. ❑ *Place your hands under your buttocks to take some of the strain off your back.* **6** N-VAR **Strain** is an injury to a muscle in your body, caused by using the muscle too much or twisting it. ❑ *Avoid muscle strain by warming up with slow jogging.* **7** V-T If you **strain** a muscle, you injure it by using it too much or twisting it. ❑ *He strained his back during a practice session.* **8** V-T If you **strain** to do something, you make a great effort to do it when it is difficult to do. ❑ *I had to strain to hear.* **9** V-T When you **strain** food, you separate the liquid part of it from the solid parts. ❑ *Strain the stock and put it back into the pan.* **10** N-COUNT A **strain** of a germ, plant, or other organism is a particular type of it. ❑ *Every year new strains of influenza develop.* **11** → See feature box at **speak**

strained /stre͟ɪnd/ **1** ADJ If someone's appearance, voice, or behavior is **strained**, they seem worried and nervous. ❑ *She looked a little pale and strained.* **2** ADJ If relations between people are **strained**, those people do not like or trust each other. ❑ *...a period of strained relations between the mayor and his deputy.*

strain|er /streɪnər/ (strainers) N-COUNT A **strainer** is an object with holes which you pour a liquid through in order to separate the liquid from the solids in it. □ *Pour the broth through a strainer.* □ *...a tea strainer.*

strait /streɪt/ (straits) **1** N-COUNT; N-IN-NAMES You can refer to a narrow strip of sea which joins two large areas of sea as a **strait** or the **straits**. □ *An estimated 1,600 vessels pass through the strait annually.* **2** N-PLURAL [adj N] If someone is in dire or desperate **straits**, they are in a very difficult situation, usually because they do not have much money. □ *The company's closure has left many small businessmen in desperate financial straits.*

strait|ened /streɪtᵊnd/ ADJ [usu ADJ n] If someone is living in **straitened** circumstances, they do not have as much money as they used to, and are finding it very hard to buy or pay for everything that they need. [FORMAL] □ *His father died when he was ten, leaving the family in straitened circumstances.*

strait|jacket /streɪtdʒækɪt/ (straitjackets) **1** N-COUNT A **straitjacket** is a special jacket used to tie the arms of a violent person tightly around their body. □ *Occasionally his behavior became so uncontrollable that he had to be placed in a straitjacket.* **2** N-COUNT If you describe an idea or a situation as a **straitjacket**, you mean that it is very limited and restricting. □ *...the ideological straitjacket of religious fundamentalism.*

strait-laced also **straight-laced**, **straitlaced** ADJ If you describe someone as **strait-laced**, you disapprove of them because they have very strict views about what kind of behavior is moral or acceptable. [DISAPPROVAL] □ *He was criticized for being boring, strait-laced and narrow-minded.*

strand /strænd/ (strands, stranding, stranded) **1** N-COUNT A **strand** of something such as hair, wire, or thread is a single thin piece of it. □ *She tried to blow a gray strand of hair from her eyes.* **2** V-T If you **are stranded**, you are prevented from leaving a place, for example because of bad weather. □ *The climbers had been stranded by a storm.*

strange ♦♦◇ /streɪndʒ/ (stranger, strangest) **1** ADJ Something that is **strange** is unusual or unexpected, and makes you feel slightly nervous or afraid. □ *Then a strange thing happened.* □ *There was something strange about the flickering blue light.* • **strange|ly** ADV □ *She noticed he was acting strangely.* • **strange|ness** N-UNCOUNT □ *...the breathy strangeness of the music.* **2** ADJ [ADJ n] A **strange** place is one that you have never been to before. A **strange** person is someone that you have never met before. □ *I ended up alone in a strange city.* **3** → see also **stranger**

strange|ly /streɪndʒli/ **1** ADV [ADV with cl] You use **strangely** to emphasize that what you are saying is surprising. [EMPHASIS] □ *Strangely, they hadn't invited her to join them.* **2** → see also **strange**

stran|ger /streɪndʒər/ (strangers) **1** N-COUNT A **stranger** is someone you have never met before. □ *Telling a complete stranger about your life is difficult.* **2** N-PLURAL If two people are **strangers**, they do not know each other. □ *The women knew nothing of the dead girl. They were strangers.* **3** N-COUNT If you are a **stranger** to something, you have had no experience of it or do not understand it. □ *He is no stranger to controversy.* **4** → see also **strange**

stran|gle /stræŋɡᵊl/ (strangles, strangling, strangled) **1** V-T To **strangle** someone means to kill them by squeezing their throat tightly so that they cannot breathe. □ *He tried to strangle a border policeman and steal his gun.* **2** V-T To **strangle** something means to prevent it from succeeding or developing. □ *The country's economic plight is strangling its scientific institutions.*

stran|gled /stræŋɡᵊld/ ADJ [ADJ n] A **strangled** voice or cry sounds unclear because the throat muscles of the person speaking or crying are tight. [LITERARY] □ *In a strangled voice he said, "This place is going to be unthinkable without you."*

strangle|hold /stræŋɡᵊlhoʊld/ N-SING To have a **stranglehold** on something means to have control over it and prevent it from being free or from developing. □ *These companies are determined to keep a stranglehold on the banana industry.*

stran|gu|la|tion /stræŋɡyəleɪʃᵊn/ N-UNCOUNT **Strangulation** is the act of killing someone by squeezing their throat tightly so that they cannot breathe. □ *He is charged with the strangulation of two students.*

strap /stræp/ (straps, strapping, strapped) **1** N-COUNT A **strap** is a narrow piece of leather, cloth, or other material. Straps are used to carry things, fasten things together, or to hold a piece of clothing in place. □ *Nancy gripped the strap of her beach bag.* □ *She pulled the strap of her nightgown onto her shoulder.* **2** V-T If you **strap** something somewhere, you fasten it there with a strap. □ *She strapped the baby seat into the car.*

strap|less /stræplɪs/ ADJ [usu ADJ n] A **strapless** dress or bra does not have the usual narrow bands of material over the shoulders. □ *...a black, strapless evening dress.*

strapped /stræpt/ **1** ADJ [oft ADJ for n, adv ADJ] If someone is **strapped** for money, they do not have enough money to buy or pay for the things they want or need. □ *My husband and I are really strapped for cash.* **2** → see also **cash-strapped**

strap|ping /stræpɪŋ/ ADJ [usu ADJ n] If you describe someone as **strapping**, you mean that they are tall and strong, and look healthy. [APPROVAL] □ *He was a bricklayer – a big, strapping fellow.*

strap|py /stræpi/ **1** ADJ A **strappy** dress or top has thin shoulder straps. **2** ADJ **Strappy** shoes have thin straps over the feet. □ *...strappy sandals.*

stra|ta /streɪtə, strætə/ **Strata** is the plural of **stratum**.

strata|gem /strætədʒəm/ (stratagems) N-COUNT A **stratagem** is a plan that is intended to achieve a particular effect, often by deceiving people. [FORMAL] □ *Trade discounts may be used as a competitive stratagem to secure customer loyalty.*

stra|tegic ♦◇◇ /strətidʒɪk/ **1** ADJ **Strategic** means relating to the most important, general aspects of something such as a military operation or political policy, especially when these are decided in advance. □ *...the new strategic thinking which NATO leaders produced at the recent London summit.* • **stra|tegi|cal|ly** /strətidʒɪkli/ ADV □ *...strategically important roads, bridges and buildings.* **2** ADJ **Strategic** weapons are very powerful missiles that can be fired only after a decision to use them has been made by a political leader. □ *...strategic nuclear weapons.* **3** ADJ If you put something in a **strategic** position, you place it cleverly in a position where it will be most useful or have the most effect. □ *...the marble benches Eve had placed at strategic points throughout the gardens, where the views were spectacular.* • **stra|tegi|cal|ly** ADV □ *We had kept its presence hidden with a strategically placed chair.*

SYNONYMS

strategic
ADJ **1**
tactical: *The security forces had made a tactical withdrawal from the area.*
calculated: *The President took a calculated, political risk in throwing his full support behind the rebels.*
deliberate: *It has a deliberate policy to introduce world art to Britain.*

strat|egist /strætədʒɪst/ (strategists) N-COUNT A **strategist** is someone who is skilled in planning the best way to gain an advantage or to achieve success, especially in war. □ *Military strategists had devised a plan that guaranteed a series of stunning victories.*

strat|egy ♦♦◇ /strætədʒi/ (strategies) **1** N-VAR A **strategy** is a general plan or set of plans intended to achieve something, especially over a long period. □ *The energy secretary will present the strategy tomorrow afternoon.* **2** N-UNCOUNT **Strategy** is the art of planning the best way to gain an advantage or achieve success, especially in war. □ *I've just been explaining the basic principles of strategy to my generals.* **3** → See feature box at **study**

COLLOCATIONS

strategy
NOUN **1**
noun + **strategy**: business, growth, investment, marketing
adjective + **strategy**: clear, coherent, effective, long-term; high-risk, risky; corporate, economic, global, military
verb + **strategy**: adopt, devise, implement, pursue

SYNONYMS

strategy
NOUN **2**
policy: *...the government's policy on repatriation.*
procedure: *The White House said there would be no change in procedure.*

strati|fi|ca|tion /strætɪfɪkeɪʃ³n/ N-UNCOUNT **Stratification** is the division of something, especially society, into different classes or layers. [FORMAL] ❑ *She was concerned about the stratification of American society.*

strati|fied /strætɪfaɪd/ ADJ A **stratified** society is one that is divided into different classes or social layers. [FORMAL] ❑ *...a highly stratified, unequal and class-divided society.*

strato|sphere /strætəsfɪər/ ❶ N-SING [the N] **The stratosphere** is the layer of the Earth's atmosphere which lies between 7 and 31 miles above the earth. ❷ N-SING [the N] If you say that someone or something climbs or is sent into **the stratosphere**, you mean that they reach a very high level. [JOURNALISM] ❑ *This was enough to launch their careers into the stratosphere.*

strato|spher|ic /strætəsfɪrɪk, -fɛrɪk/ ADJ [ADJ n] **Stratospheric** means found in or related to the stratosphere. ❑ *...stratospheric ozone.*

stra|tum /streɪtəm, stræt-/ (**strata**) ❶ N-COUNT [usu with supp] A **stratum** of society is a group of people in it who are similar in their education, income, or social status. [FORMAL] ❑ *It was an enormous task that affected every stratum of society.* ❷ N-COUNT [usu pl] **Strata** are different layers of rock. [TECHNICAL] ❑ *Contained within the rock strata is evidence that the region was intensely dry 15,000 years ago.*

stra|tus /streɪtəs/ (**strati** /streɪtaɪ/) N-VAR **Stratus** is a type of thick gray cloud that forms at low altitudes. [TECHNICAL]

straw /strɔ/ (**straws**) ❶ N-UNCOUNT **Straw** consists of the dried, yellowish stalks from crops such as wheat or barley. ❑ *The barn was full of bales of straw.* ❑ *I stumbled through mud to a yard strewn with straw.* ❷ N-COUNT A **straw** is a thin tube of paper or plastic, which you use to suck a drink into your mouth. ❑ *...a bottle of lemonade with a straw in it.* ❸ PHRASE If you **are clutching at straws** or **grasping at straws**, you are trying unusual or extreme ideas or methods because other ideas or methods have failed. ❑ *...a badly thought-out plan from an administration clutching at straws.* ❹ PHRASE If an event is **the last straw** or **the straw that broke the camel's back**, it is the latest in a series of unpleasant or undesirable events, and makes you feel that you cannot tolerate a situation any longer. ❑ *For him the Church's decision to allow the ordination of women had been the last straw.* ❺ PHRASE If you draw **the short straw**, you are chosen from a number of people to perform a job or duty that you will not enjoy. ❑ *...if a few of your guests have drawn the short straw and agreed to drive others home after your summer barbecue.*

straw|berry /strɔberi/ (**strawberries**) N-COUNT A **strawberry** is a small red fruit which is soft and juicy and has tiny yellow seeds on its skin. ❑ *...strawberries and cream.*

straw|berry blonde (**strawberry blondes**) also **strawberry blond** ❶ ADJ **Strawberry blonde** hair is reddish blonde. ❷ N-COUNT A **strawberry blonde** is a person who has strawberry blonde hair.

straw-colored ADJ [usu ADJ n] If you describe something, especially hair, as **straw-colored**, you mean that it is pale yellow.

straw poll (**straw polls**) N-COUNT A **straw poll** is the unofficial questioning of a group of people to find out their opinion about something. ❑ *A straw poll conducted at the end of the meeting found most people agreed with Mr. Forth.*

stray /streɪ/ (**strays, straying, strayed**) ❶ V-I If someone **strays** somewhere, they wander away from where they are supposed to be. ❑ *Tourists often get lost and stray into dangerous areas.* ❷ ADJ [ADJ n] A **stray** dog or cat has wandered away from its owner's home. ❑ *A stray dog came up to him.* • N-COUNT **Stray** is also a noun. ❑ *The dog was a stray which had been adopted.* ❸ V-I If your mind or your eyes **stray**, you do not concentrate on or look at one particular subject, but start thinking about or looking at other things. ❑ *Even with the simplest cases I find my mind straying.* ❹ ADJ [ADJ n] You use **stray** to describe something that exists separated from other similar things. ❑ *An 8-year-old boy was killed by a stray bullet.*

streak /strik/ (**streaks, streaking, streaked**) ❶ N-COUNT A **streak** is a long stripe or mark on a surface which contrasts with the surface because it is a different color. ❑ *There are these dark streaks on the surface of the moon.* ❷ V-T If something **streaks** a surface, it makes long stripes or marks on the surface. ❑ *Rain had begun to streak the windowpanes.* ❸ N-COUNT [usu sing, with supp] If someone has a **streak** of a particular type of behavior, they sometimes behave in that way. ❑ *We're both alike – there is a streak of madness in us both.* ❹ V-I If something or someone **streaks** somewhere, they move there very quickly. ❑ *A meteorite streaked across the sky.* ❺ N-COUNT A winning **streak** or a lucky **streak** is a continuous series of successes, for example in gambling or sports. A losing **streak** or an unlucky **streak** is a series of failures or losses. ❑ *The casinos had better watch out since I'm obviously on a lucky streak!*

streak|er /strikər/ (**streakers**) N-COUNT A **streaker** is someone who runs quickly through a public place wearing no clothes, as a joke.

streaky /striki/ (**streakier, streakiest**) ADJ Something that is **streaky** is marked with long stripes that are a different color to the rest of it. ❑ *She has streaky fair hair and blue eyes.* ❑ *...the empty house with its streaky windows.*

stream ✦◇◇ /strim/ (**streams, streaming, streamed**) ❶ N-COUNT A **stream** is a small narrow river. ❑ *There was a small stream at the end of the garden.* ❷ N-COUNT A **stream** of smoke, air, or liquid is a narrow moving mass of it. ❑ *He breathed out a stream of cigarette smoke.* ❸ N-COUNT A **stream** of vehicles or people is a long moving line of them. ❑ *There was a stream of traffic behind him.* ❹ N-COUNT A **stream** of things is a large number of them occurring one after another. ❑ *The discovery triggered a stream of readers' letters.* ❑ *...a never-ending stream of jokes.* ❺ V-I If a liquid **streams** somewhere, it flows or comes out in large amounts. ❑ *Tears streamed down their faces.* ❻ V-I [usu cont] If your eyes **are streaming**, liquid is coming from them, for example because you have a cold. You can also say that your nose **is streaming**. ❑ *Her eyes were streaming now from the wind.* ❼ V-I If people or vehicles **stream** somewhere, they move there quickly and in large numbers. ❑ *Refugees have been streaming into Travnik for months.* ❽ V-I When light **streams** into or out of a place, it shines strongly into or out of it. ❑ *Sunlight was streaming into the courtyard.* ❾ PHRASE If something starts as a new factory or a new system comes **on stream** or is brought **on stream**, it begins to operate or becomes available. ❑ *As new mines come on stream, Chile's share of world copper output will increase sharply.*

COLLOCATIONS

stream
NOUN
❶
noun + **stream**: mountain
adjective + **stream**: shallow, small; freshwater, tidal
verb + **stream**: cross
❹
adjective + **stream**: constant, continuous, endless, never-ending
VERB ❺
noun + **stream**: blood, tears, water
stream + adverb: down

---

stream|er /strimər/ (**streamers**) N-COUNT **Streamers** are long rolls of colored paper used for decorating rooms at parties.

stream|ing /strimɪŋ/ ❶ N-UNCOUNT [usu N n] **Streaming** is a method of transmitting data from the internet directly to a user's computer screen without the need to download it. [COMPUTING] ❑ *...web sites that feature streaming media.* ❷ → see also **stream**

stream|ing ser|vice N-COUNT A **streaming service** is a service that allows you to play movies and TV programs on your TV, cellphone, or computer directly from the internet, without needing to download them. [COMPUTING] ❑ *Television networks are under increasing pressure from a range of streaming services.*

stream|line /strimlaɪn/ (**streamlines, streamlining, streamlined**) V-T To **streamline** an organization or process means to make it more efficient by removing unnecessary parts of it. ❑ *They're making efforts to streamline their normally cumbersome bureaucracy.*

stream|lined /strimlaɪnd/ ADJ A **streamlined** vehicle, animal, or object has a shape that allows it to move quickly or efficiently through air or water. ❑ *...these beautifully streamlined and efficient cars.*

stream of con|scious|ness (streams of consciousness) also **stream-of-consciousness** N-VAR [oft N n] If you describe what someone writes or says as a **stream of consciousness**, you mean that it expresses their thoughts as they occur, rather than in a structured way. [FORMAL] ❑ *The novel is an intensely lyrical stream-of-consciousness about an Indian woman who leaves her family home to be married.*

street ✦✦✦ /strit/ (streets) **1** N-COUNT; N-IN-NAMES A **street** is a road in a city, town, or village, usually with houses along it. ❑ *He lived at 66 Bingfield Street.* **2** N-COUNT You can use **street** or **streets** when talking about activities that happen out of doors in a city or town rather than inside a building. ❑ *Changing money on the street is illegal – always use a bank.* ❑ *Their aim is to raise a million dollars to get the homeless off the streets.* **3** → see also **Downing Street**, **Main Street**, **Wall Street**

street|car /strítkɑr/ (streetcars) N-COUNT A **streetcar** is an electric vehicle for carrying people which travels on rails in the streets of a city or town. [AM]

in BRIT, use **tram**

street child (street children) N-COUNT [usu pl] **Street children** are homeless children who live outdoors in a city and live by begging or stealing.

street cred also **street-cred** N-UNCOUNT If someone says that you have **street cred**, they mean that ordinary young people would approve of you and consider you to be part of their culture, usually because you share their sense of fashion or their views. [INFORMAL, APPROVAL] ❑ *Having children was the quickest way to lose your street cred.*

street cred|ibil|ity N-UNCOUNT **Street credibility** is the same as **street cred**.

street crime N-UNCOUNT **Street crime** refers to crime such as vandalism, car theft, and mugging that are usually committed outdoors.

street food N-UNCOUNT **Street food** is food that is cooked and sold in the street or in other public places and is intended to be eaten immediately. ❑ *Wonton is one of the most popular soups in street food stalls throughout southern China.*

street|lamp /strítlæmp/ (streetlamps) also **street-lamp** N-COUNT A **streetlamp** is the same as a **streetlight**. ❑ *He paused under a streetlamp and looked across at the cafe.*

street|light /strítlaɪt/ (streetlights) also **street light** N-COUNT A **streetlight** is a tall post with a light at the top, which stands by the side of a road to light it up, usually in a city. ❑ *As the day darkened the streetlights came on.*

street map (street maps) N-COUNT A **street map** is a map of a city or town, showing the positions and names of all the streets.

street par|ty (street parties) N-COUNT A **street party** is the same as a **block party**. [BRIT]

street peo|ple N-PLURAL **Street people** are homeless people who live outdoors in a city or town.

street smart also **street-smart** ADJ Someone who is **street smart** knows how to deal with difficult or dangerous situations, especially in big cities. [mainly AM, INFORMAL] ❑ *He is street smart and is not afraid of this neighborhood.*

street smarts N-PLURAL You can use **street smarts** to refer to the skills and intelligence people need to be successful in difficult situations, especially in a city. [AM, INFORMAL] ❑ *The boys learned their street smarts early.*

street value N-SING [usu N of amount] The **street value** of a drug is the price that is paid for it when it is sold illegally to drug users. [JOURNALISM] ❑ *...cocaine with a street value of two million dollars.*

street|walker /strítwɔkər/ (streetwalkers) N-COUNT A **streetwalker** is a prostitute who stands or walks in the streets in order to get customers. [OLD-FASHIONED]

street|wise /strítwaɪz/ ADJ Someone who is **streetwise** knows how to deal with difficult or dangerous situations in big cities. [INFORMAL] ❑ *They are two streetwise and sassy girls from Queens.*

strength ✦✦ /strɛŋkθ, strɛŋθ/ (strengths) **1** N-UNCOUNT Your **strength** is the physical energy that you have, which gives you the ability to perform various actions, such as lifting or moving things. ❑ *She has always been encouraged to swim to build up the strength of her muscles.* ❑ *He threw it forward with all his strength.* **2** N-UNCOUNT [also a N] Someone's **strength** in a difficult situation is their confidence or courage. ❑ *Something gave me the strength to overcome the difficulty.* ❑ *He copes incredibly well. His strength is an inspiration to me in my life.* **3** N-UNCOUNT [also N in pl] The **strength** of an object or material is its ability to be treated roughly, or to carry heavy weights, without being damaged or destroyed. ❑ *He checked the strength of the cables.* **4** N-UNCOUNT [also N in pl] The **strength** of a person, organization, or country is the power or influence that they have. ❑ *America values its economic leadership, and the political and military strength that goes with it.* ❑ *The alliance, in its first show of strength, drew a hundred thousand-strong crowd to a rally.* **5** N-UNCOUNT If you refer to the **strength** of a feeling, opinion, or belief, you are talking about how deeply it is felt or believed by people, or how much they are influenced by it. ❑ *He was surprised at the strength of his own feeling.* **6** N-VAR Someone's **strengths** are the qualities and abilities that they have which are an advantage to them, or which make them successful. ❑ *Take into account your own strengths and weaknesses.* ❑ *Tact was never Mr. Moore's strength.* **7** N-UNCOUNT If you refer to the **strength** of a currency, economy, or industry, you mean that its value or success is steady or increasing. ❑ *...the long-term competitive strength of the economy.* **8** N-UNCOUNT [also N in pl] The **strength** of a group of people is the total number of people in it. ❑ *...elite forces, comprising about one-tenth of the strength of the army.* **9** N-UNCOUNT [also N in pl] The **strength** of a wind, current, or other force is its power or speed. ❑ *Its oscillation depends on the strength of the gravitational field.* **10** N-UNCOUNT [also N in pl] The **strength** of a drink, chemical, or drug is the amount of the particular substance in it that gives it its particular effect. ❑ *It is very alcoholic, sometimes near the strength of port.* **11** PHRASE If a person or organization **goes from strength to strength**, they become more and more successful or confident. ❑ *A decade later, the company has gone from strength to strength.* **12** PHRASE If a team or army is at **full strength**, all the members that it needs or usually has are present. ❑ *He needed more time to bring U.S. forces there up to full strength.* **13** PHRASE If one thing is done **on the strength of** another, it is done because of the influence of that other thing. ❑ *He was elected to power on the strength of his charisma.*

strength|en ✦✧ /strɛŋθən/ (strengthens, strengthening, strengthened) **1** V-T If something **strengthens** a person or group or if they **strengthen** their position, they become more powerful and secure, or more likely to succeed. ❑ *Giving the president the authority to go to war would strengthen his hand for peace.* **2** V-T If something **strengthens** a case or argument, it supports it by providing more reasons or evidence for it. ❑ *He does not seem to be familiar with research which might have strengthened his own arguments.* **3** V-T/V-I If a currency, economy, or industry **strengthens**, or if something **strengthens** it, it increases in value or becomes more successful. ❑ *The dollar strengthened against most other currencies.* **4** V-T If something **strengthens** you or **strengthens** your resolve or character, it makes you more confident and determined. ❑ *Any experience can teach and strengthen you, but particularly the more difficult ones.* ❑ *This merely strengthens our resolve to win the pennant.* **5** V-T/V-I If something **strengthens** a relationship or link, or if it **strengthens**, it makes it closer and more likely to last for a long time. ❑ *It will draw you closer together, and it will strengthen the bond of your relationship.* **6** V-T/V-I If something **strengthens** an impression, feeling, or belief, or if it **strengthens**, it becomes greater or affects more people. ❑ *His speech strengthens the impression he is the main power in the organization.* ❑ *Every day of sunshine strengthens the feelings of optimism.* **7** V-T If something **strengthens** your body or a part of your body, it makes it healthier, often in such a way that you can move or carry heavier things. ❑ *Cycling is good exercise. It strengthens all the muscles of the body.* **8** V-T If something **strengthens** an object or structure, it makes it able to be treated roughly or able to support heavy weights, without being damaged or destroyed. ❑ *The builders will have to strengthen the existing joists with additional timber.*

strenu|ous /strɛ́njuəs/ ADJ A **strenuous** activity or action involves a lot of energy or effort. ❑ *Avoid strenuous exercise in the evening.* ❑ *Strenuous efforts had been made to improve conditions in* the jail. • **strenu|ous|ly** ADV GRADED [ADV with v] ❑ *Exercising too much or too strenuously is just as bad as not doing it at all.* ❑ *The company concerned has strenuously denied the accusations.*

strep /strɛp/ also **strep throat** N-UNCOUNT **Strep** or **strep throat** is an illness that is caused by bacteria and which gives you a fever and a very sore throat. [AM] ❑ *Nicola got her prescription for strep.* ❑ *I have strep throat.*

stress ♦♦◊ /strɛs/ (**stresses, stressing, stressed**) **1** V-T If you **stress** a point in a discussion, you put extra emphasis on it because you think it is important. ❑ *The spokesman stressed that the measures did not amount to an overall ban.* ❑ *They have stressed the need for co-operation between all the groups.* • N-VAR **Stress** is also a noun. ❑ *Japanese car makers are laying ever more stress on overseas sales.* **2** N-VAR If you feel under **stress**, you feel worried and tense because of difficulties in your life. ❑ *Katy could think clearly when not under stress.* **3** V-T If you **stress** a word or part of a word when you say it, you put emphasis on it so that it sounds slightly louder. ❑ *She stresses the syllables as though teaching a child.* • N-VAR **Stress** is also a noun. ❑ *...the misplaced stress on the first syllable of this last word.*

stressed /strɛst/ ADJ If you are **stressed**, you feel tense and anxious because of difficulties in your life. ❑ *Work out what situations or people make you feel stressed and avoid them.*

stressed out **1** ADJ If someone is **stressed out**, they are very tense and anxious because of difficulties in their lives. [INFORMAL] ❑ *I can't imagine sitting in traffic, getting stressed out.* **2** → See feature box at **commute**

stress frac|ture (**stress fractures**) N-COUNT A **stress fracture** is a slight break in a bone that is usually caused by using a part of your body too much, for example, as a result of exercise or sport. ❑ *I had a stress fracture in my left shin.*

stress|ful /strɛsfəl/ ADJ If a situation or experience is **stressful**, it causes the person involved to feel stress. ❑ *I think I've got one of the most stressful jobs there is.*

stretch ♦◊◊ /strɛtʃ/ (**stretches, stretching, stretched**) **1** V-I [no cont] Something that **stretches** over an area or distance covers or exists in the whole of that area or distance. ❑ *The procession stretched for several miles.* **2** N-COUNT A **stretch** of road, water, or land is a length or area of it. ❑ *It's a very dangerous stretch of road.* **3** V-T/V-I When you **stretch**, you put your arms or legs out straight and tighten your muscles. ❑ *He yawned and stretched.* ❑ *Try stretching your legs and pulling your toes upwards.* • N-COUNT **Stretch** is also a noun. ❑ *At the end of a workout spend time cooling down with some slow stretches.* **4** N-COUNT A **stretch** of time is a period of time. ❑ *...after an 18-month stretch in the army.* **5** V-I If something **stretches** from one time to another, it begins at the first time and ends at the second, which is longer than expected. ❑ *...a working day that stretches from seven in the morning to eight at night.* **6** V-I If a group of things **stretch** from one type of thing to another, the group includes a wide range of things. ❑ *...a trading empire, with interests that stretched from chemicals to sugar.* **7** V-T/V-I When something soft or elastic **stretches** or **is stretched**, it becomes longer or bigger as well as thinner, usually because it is pulled. ❑ *The cables are designed not to stretch.* **8** V-T/V-I If you **stretch** an amount of something or if it **stretches**, you make it last longer than it usually would by being careful and not wasting any of it. ❑ *They're used to stretching their budgets.* **9** V-T If something **stretches** your money or resources, it uses them up so you have hardly enough for your needs. ❑ *The drought there is stretching resources.* **10** V-T If you say that a job or task **stretches** you, you mean that you like it because it makes you work hard and use all your energy and skills so that you do not become bored or achieve less than you should. [APPROVAL] ❑ *I'm trying to move on and stretch myself with something different.* **11** PHRASE If you say that something is not true or possible **by any stretch of the imagination**, you are emphasizing that it is completely untrue or absolutely impossible. [EMPHASIS] ❑ *Her husband was not a womanizer by any stretch of the imagination.*
▶ **stretch out** **1** PHRASAL VERB If you **stretch out** or **stretch** yourself out, you lie with your legs and body in a straight line. ❑ *The bathtub was too small to stretch out in.* **2** PHRASAL VERB If you **stretch out** a part of your body, you hold it out straight. ❑ *He was about to stretch out his hand to grab me.*

stretch|er /strɛtʃər/ (**stretchers, stretchered**) **1** N-COUNT A **stretcher** is a long piece of canvas with a pole along each side, which is used to carry an injured or sick person. ❑ *The two ambulance attendants quickly put Plover on a stretcher and got him into the ambulance.* **2** V-T PASSIVE If someone **is stretchered** somewhere, they are carried there on a stretcher. ❑ *I was close by as Lester was stretchered into the ambulance.*

stretch limo (**stretch limos**) N-COUNT A **stretch limo** is a very long and luxurious car in which a rich, famous, or important person is driven somewhere.

stretch marks N-PLURAL **Stretch marks** are lines or marks on someone's skin caused by the skin stretching after the person's weight has changed rapidly. Women who have had children often have stretch marks.

stretchy /strɛtʃi/ (**stretchier, stretchiest**) ADJ **Stretchy** material is slightly elastic and stretches easily.

strew /struː/ (**strews, strewing, strewed, strewn**) **1** V-T To **strew** things somewhere, or to **strew** a place with things, means to scatter them there. ❑ *The racoons knock over the trash cans in search of food, and strew the contents all over the ground.* ❑ *An elderly woman was strewing the floor with chalk so that the dancing shoes would not slip.* ❑ *By the end, bodies were strewn all round the building.* **2** → See feature box at **housework**

strewn /struːn/ ADJ [v-link ADJ with n] If a place is **strewn with** things, they are lying scattered there. ❑ *The front room was strewn with books and clothes.* • COMB IN ADJ **Strewn** is also a combining form. ❑ *...a litter-strewn street.*

strick|en /strɪkən/ **1** **Stricken** is the past participle of some meanings of **strike**. **2** ADJ If a person or place is **stricken** by something such as an unpleasant feeling, an illness, or a natural disaster, they are severely affected by it. ❑ *...a family stricken by genetically inherited cancer.* • COMB IN ADJ **Stricken** is also a combining form. ❑ *...a leukemia-stricken child.*

strict ♦◊◊ /strɪkt/ (**stricter, strictest**) **1** ADJ A **strict** rule or order is very clear and precise or severe and must always be obeyed completely. ❑ *The officials had issued strict instructions that we were not to get out of the jeep.* ❑ *French privacy laws are very strict.* • **strict|ly** ADV [ADV with v] ❑ *The acceptance of new members is strictly controlled.* **2** ADJ If a parent or other person in authority is **strict**, they regard many actions as unacceptable and do not allow them. ❑ *My parents were very strict.* • **strict|ly** ADV ❑ *My own mother was brought up very strictly and correctly.* **3** ADJ [ADJ n] If you talk about the **strict** meaning of something, you mean the precise meaning of it. ❑ *It's not quite peace in the strictest sense of the word, rather the absence of war.* • **strict|ly** ADV [ADV adj] ❑ *Actually, that is not strictly true.* **4** ADJ [ADJ n] You use **strict** to describe someone who never does things that are against their beliefs. ❑ *Millions of Americans are now strict vegetarians.*

strict|ly /strɪktli/ ADV [ADV group] You use **strictly** to emphasize that something is of one particular type, or intended for one particular thing or person, rather than any other. [EMPHASIS] ❑ *He seemed fond of her in a strictly professional way.*

stric|ture /strɪktʃər/ (**strictures**) **1** N-COUNT [usu pl, oft N on/ against n] You can use **strictures** to refer to severe criticism or disapproval of something. [FORMAL] ❑ *...Mencken's strictures on the 1920s, with its self-righteous prohibition on alcohol and unconventional ideas.* **2** N-COUNT [usu pl, usu with supp] You can refer to things that limit what you can do as **strictures** of a particular kind. [mainly FORMAL] ❑ *Your goals are hindered by financial strictures.*

stride /straɪd/ (**strides, striding, strode**) **1** V-I If you **stride** somewhere, you walk there with quick, long steps. ❑ *They were joined by a newcomer who came striding across a field.* **2** N-COUNT A **stride** is a long step which you take when you are walking or running. ❑ *With every stride, runners hit the ground with up to five times their body-weight.* **3** N-COUNT If you make **strides** in something that you are doing, you make rapid progress in it. ❑ *The country has made enormous strides politically but not economically.* **4** PHRASE If you **get into** your **stride** or **hit** your **stride**, you start to do something easily and confidently, after being slow and uncertain. ❑ *The campaign is just getting into its stride.* **5** PHRASE If you **take** a problem or difficulty **in stride**, you deal with it calmly and easily. ❑ *He took the ridiculous accusation in stride.*

stri|den|cy /ˈstraɪdənsi/ N-UNCOUNT **Stridency** is the quality of being strident. ❑ *Many voters were alarmed by the president's new stridency.*

stri|dent /ˈstraɪdənt/ ADJ If you use **strident** to describe someone or the way they express themselves, you mean that they make their feelings or opinions known in a very strong way that perhaps makes people uncomfortable. [DISAPPROVAL] ❑ *She was increasingly seen as a strident feminist.*

strife /straɪf/ N-UNCOUNT **Strife** is strong disagreement or fighting. [FORMAL] ❑ *Money is a major cause of strife in many marriages.*

STRIKE

① NOUN USES
② VERB USES AND PHRASES
③ PHRASAL VERBS

---

① **strike** ♦♦◊ /straɪk/ (**strikes**) **1** N-COUNT [also on N] When there is a **strike**, workers stop doing their work for a period of time, usually in order to try to get better pay or conditions for themselves. [BUSINESS] ❑ *Air traffic controllers have begun a three-day strike in a dispute over pay.* ❑ *Staff at the hospital went on strike in protest at the incidents.* **2** N-COUNT A military **strike** is a military attack, especially an air attack. ❑ *...a punitive air strike.* **3** → see also **hunger strike**

SYNONYMS

strike
NOUN ① **1**
walkout: *They organized a walkout.*
mutiny: *They were shot yesterday after being convicted of mutiny and high treason.*

② **strike** ♦♦◊ /straɪk/ (**strikes, striking, struck, stricken**)

> The form **struck** is the past tense and past participle. The form **stricken** can also be used as the past participle for meanings **5** and **13**.

→ Please look at meanings **18** and **20** to see if the expression you are looking for is shown under another headword.

1 V-I When workers **strike**, they go on strike. [BUSINESS] ❑ *...their recognition of the workers' right to strike.* ❑ *They shouldn't be striking for more money.* • **strik|er** (**strikers**) N-COUNT ❑ *The strikers want higher wages, which state governments say they can't afford.* **2** V-T If you **strike** someone or something, you deliberately hit them. [FORMAL] ❑ *She took two quick steps forward and struck him across the mouth.* ❑ *It is impossible to say who struck the fatal blow.* **3** V-T If something that is falling or moving **strikes** something, it hits it. [FORMAL] ❑ *His head struck the bottom when he dived into the 6 ft end of the pool.* ❑ *One 16-inch shell struck the control tower.* **4** V-T/V-I If you **strike** one thing against another, or if one thing **strikes** against another, the first thing hits the second thing. [FORMAL] ❑ *Wilde fell and struck his head on the stone floor.* **5** V-T/V-I If something such as an illness or disaster **strikes**, it suddenly happens. ❑ *Fed officials continued to insist that the dollar would soon return to stability but disaster struck.* ❑ *A moderate earthquake struck the northeastern United States early on Saturday.* **6** V-I To **strike** means to attack someone or something quickly and violently. ❑ *He was the only cabinet member out of the country when the terrorists struck.* **7** V-T [no cont] If an idea or thought **strikes** you, it suddenly comes into your mind. ❑ *A thought struck her. Was she jealous of her mother, then?* **8** V-T If something **strikes** you as being a particular thing, it gives you the impression of being that thing. ❑ *He struck me as a very serious but friendly person.* **9** V-T If you **are struck** by something, you think it is very impressive, noticeable, or interesting. ❑ *She was struck by his simple, spellbinding eloquence.* **10** V-RECIP If you **strike** a deal or a bargain with someone, you come to an agreement with them. ❑ *They struck a deal with their paper supplier, getting two years of newsprint on credit.* ❑ *The two struck a deal in which Rendell took half of what a manager would.* **11** V-T If you **strike** a balance, you do something that is halfway between two extremes. ❑ *At times like that you have to strike a balance between sleep and homework.* **12** V-T If you **strike** a pose or attitude, you put yourself in a particular position, for example when someone is taking your photograph. ❑ *She struck a pose, one hand on her hip and the other waving an imaginary cigarette.* **13** V-T If something **strikes** fear into people, it makes them very frightened or anxious. [LITERARY] ❑ *If there is a single subject guaranteed to strike fear in the hearts of parents, it is drugs.* **14** V-T/V-I When a clock **strikes**, its bells make a sound to indicate what the time is. ❑ *The clock struck nine.* **15** V-T If you **strike** words from a document or an official record, you remove them. [FORMAL] ❑ *Strike that from the minutes.* • PHRASAL VERB **Strike out** means the same as **strike** ② **15**. ❑ *The censor struck out the next two lines.* **16** V-T When you **strike** a match, you make it produce a flame by moving it quickly against something rough. ❑ *Robina struck a match and held it to the crumpled newspaper in the grate.* **17** V-T If someone **strikes** oil or gold, they discover it in the ground as a result of mining or drilling. ❑ *Oil industry sources say that Marathon Oil Company has struck oil in Syria.* **18** → see also **stricken, striking 19** to **strike a chord** → see **chord 20** to **strike home** → see **home** ①

SYNONYMS

strike
VERB ② **2**
hit: *She hit him hard across his left arm.*
smack: *She smacked me on the side of the head.*
thump: *He thumped my shoulder affectionately, nearly knocking me over.*
slap: *I slapped him hard across the face.*

③ **strike** ♦♦◊ /straɪk/ (**strikes, striking, struck, stricken**)
▶ **strike down** PHRASAL VERB If someone **is struck down**, especially by an illness, they are killed or severely harmed. [WRITTEN] ❑ *Frank had been struck down by a massive heart attack.*
▶ **strike out** **1** PHRASAL VERB In baseball, if a batter **strikes out**, they fail three times to hit the ball and end their turn. If a pitcher **strikes out**, they throw three balls that the batter fails to hit, and end the batter's turn. ❑ *Trachsel has struck Bonds out on seven occasions.* ❑ *The third baseman struck out four times.* ❑ *The Marlin pitcher struck out the first batter he faced.* **2** PHRASAL VERB If you **strike out**, you begin to do something different, often because you want to become more independent. ❑ *She wanted me to strike out on my own, buy a business.* **3** PHRASAL VERB If you **strike out** at someone, you hit, attack, or speak angrily to them. ❑ *He seemed always ready to strike out at anyone and for any cause.* **4** → see also **strike** ② **15**
▶ **strike up** PHRASAL VERB When you **strike up** a conversation or friendship with someone, you begin one. [WRITTEN] ❑ *I trailed her into Penney's and struck up a conversation.*

strike|breaker /ˈstraɪkbreɪkər/ (**strike breakers**) N-COUNT A **strikebreaker** is a person who continues to work during a strike, or someone who takes over the work of a person who is on strike.

strik|er /ˈstraɪkər/ (**strikers**) **1** N-COUNT In soccer and some other team sports, a **striker** is a player who mainly attacks and scores goals, rather than defends. ❑ *...and the striker scored his sixth goal of the season.* **2** → see also **strike** ② **1**

strik|ing ♦♦◊ /ˈstraɪkɪŋ/ **1** ADJ Something that is **striking** is very noticeable or unusual. ❑ *The most striking feature of those statistics is the high proportion of suicides.* ❑ *He bears a striking resemblance to Lenin.* • **strik|ing|ly** ADV ❑ *In one respect, however, the men really were strikingly similar.* ❑ *...a strikingly handsome man.* **2** ADJ Someone who is **striking** is very attractive, in a noticeable way. ❑ *She was a striking woman with long blonde hair.*

string ♦♦◊ /strɪŋ/ (**strings, stringing, strung**) **1** N-VAR **String** is thin rope made of twisted threads, used for tying things together or tying up packages. ❑ *He held out a small bag tied with string.* **2** N-COUNT A **string** of things is a number of them on a piece of string, thread, or wire. ❑ *She wore a string of pearls around her neck.* **3** N-COUNT A **string** of places or objects is a number of them that form a line. ❑ *The landscape is broken only by a string of villages.* **4** N-COUNT A **string** of similar events is a series of them that happen one after the other. ❑ *The incident was the latest in a string of attacks.* **5** N-COUNT The **strings** on a musical instrument such as a violin or guitar are the thin pieces of wire or nylon stretched across it that make sounds when the instrument is played. ❑ *He went off to change a guitar string.* **6** N-PLURAL The **strings** are the section of an orchestra which consists of stringed instruments played with a bow. ❑ *The strings provided a melodic background to the passages played by the soloist.* **7** PHRASE If something is offered to you with **no strings attached** or with **no strings**, it is offered without any

special conditions. ❑ *Aid should be given to developing countries with no strings attached.* **8** PHRASE If you **pull strings**, you use your influence with other people in order to get something done, often unfairly. ❑ *Tony is sure he can pull a few strings and get you in.*
▶ **string together** PHRASAL VERB If you **string** things **together**, you form something from them by adding them to each other, one at a time. ❑ *As speech develops, the child starts to string more words together.*

string bean (string beans) N-COUNT [usu pl] **String beans** are the same as **green beans**. [AM]

stringed in|stru|ment (stringed instruments) N-COUNT A **stringed instrument** is a musical instrument that has strings, such as a violin or a guitar.

strin|gen|cy /strɪndʒənsi/ N-UNCOUNT [supp N] Financial **stringency** is a situation in which a government or person does not have much money or is trying not to spend much. [FORMAL] ❑ *In times of financial stringency it is clear that public expenditure has to be closely scrutinized.*

strin|gent /strɪndʒənt/ ADJ **Stringent** laws, rules, or conditions are very severe or are strictly controlled. [FORMAL] ❑ *He announced that there would be more stringent controls on the possession of weapons.*

string|er /strɪŋər/ (stringers) N-COUNT A **stringer** is a journalist who is employed part-time by a newspaper or news service in order to report on a particular area. [JOURNALISM] ❑ *He picked up extra money as a local stringer for the New York Herald.*

string quar|tet (string quartets) **1** N-COUNT A **string quartet** is a group of four musicians who play stringed instruments together. The instruments are two violins, a viola, and a cello. ❑ *...a recital by the Borodin String Quartet.* **2** N-COUNT A **string quartet** is a piece of music played on two violins, a viola, and a cello. ❑ *...Dvorak's String Quartet Opus 34.*

stringy /strɪŋi/ (stringier, stringiest) ADJ **Stringy** food contains long, thin pieces that are difficult or unpleasant to eat. ❑ *The meat was stringy.*

strip ♦♢♢ /strɪp/ (strips, stripping, stripped) **1** N-COUNT A **strip** of something such as paper, cloth, or food is a long, narrow piece of it. ❑ *...a new kind of manufactured wood made by pressing strips of wood together and baking them.* ❑ *The simplest rag-rugs are made with strips of fabric braided together.* **2** N-COUNT A **strip** of land or water is a long narrow area of it. ❑ *The coastal cities of Liguria sit on narrow strips of land lying under steep mountains.* **3** N-COUNT A **strip** is a long street in a city or town, where there are a lot of stores, restaurants, and hotels. [AM] ❑ *...Goff's Charcoal Hamburgers on Lover's Lane, a busy commercial strip in North Dallas.* **4** V-I If you **strip**, you take off your clothes. ❑ *They stripped completely, and lay and turned in the damp grass.*
• PHRASAL VERB **Strip off** means the same as **strip**. ❑ *The children were brazenly stripping off and leaping into the sea.* **5** V-T [usu passive] If someone **is stripped**, their clothes are taken off by another person, for example in order to search for hidden or illegal things. ❑ *One prisoner claimed he'd been dragged to a cell, stripped, and beaten.* **6** V-T To **strip** something means to remove everything that covers it. ❑ *After Mike left for work I stripped the beds and vacuumed the carpets.* **7** V-T If you **strip** an engine or a piece of equipment, you take it to pieces so that it can be cleaned or repaired. ❑ *Volvo's three-man team stripped the car and treated it to a restoration.* • PHRASAL VERB **Strip down** means the same as **strip**. ❑ *In five years I had to strip the water pump down four times.* **8** V-T To **strip** someone of their property, rights, or titles means to take those things away from them. ❑ *The soldiers have stripped the civilians of their passports, and every other type of document.* **9** N-COUNT In a newspaper or magazine, a **strip** is a series of drawings which tell a story. The words spoken by the characters are often written on the drawings. ❑ *...the Doonesbury strip.*
▶ **strip away** PHRASAL VERB To **strip away** something, especially something that hides the true nature of a thing, means to remove it completely. ❑ *Altman strips away the pretense and mythology to expose the film industry as a business like any other.*
▶ **strip off** **1** PHRASAL VERB If you **strip off** your clothes, you take them off. ❑ *He stripped off his wet clothes and stepped into the shower.* **2** → see also **strip 4**

strip car|toon (strip cartoons) N-COUNT A **strip cartoon** is the same as a **comic strip**. [BRIT]

strip club (strip clubs) N-COUNT A **strip club** is a club which people go to in order to see striptease.

stripe /straɪp/ (stripes) N-COUNT A **stripe** is a long line which is a different color from the areas next to it. ❑ *She wore a bright green jogging suit with a white stripe down the sides.*

striped /straɪpt/ ADJ Something that is **striped** has stripes on it. ❑ *...a bottle green and maroon striped tie.*

strip|ey /straɪpi/ [BRIT] → see **stripy**

strip joint (strip joints) N-COUNT A **strip joint** is the same as a **strip club**. [INFORMAL]

strip|ling /strɪplɪŋ/ (striplings) N-COUNT People sometimes refer to a young man as a **stripling** when they want to say in a slightly humorous way that although he is no longer a boy, he is not yet really a man. [OLD-FASHIONED] ❑ *...a stripling of 20.*

strip mall (strip malls) N-COUNT A **strip mall** is a shopping area consisting of one or more long buildings. [AM] ❑ *...a parking lot outside a strip mall.*

strip mine (strip mines) N-COUNT A **strip mine** is a mine in which the coal, metal, or mineral is near the surface, and so underground passages are not needed. [AM]

in BRIT, use **opencast mine**

strip min|ing also strip-mining N-UNCOUNT **Strip mining** is a method of mining that is used when a mineral is near the surface and underground passages are not needed. [AM]

in BRIT, use **opencast mining**

strip|per /strɪpər/ (strippers) N-COUNT A **stripper** is a person who earns money by stripping their clothes off. ❑ *She worked as a stripper and did some acting.*

strip-search (strip-searches, strip searching, strip-searched) also **strip search** V-T [usu passive] If a person **is strip-searched**, someone such as a police officer makes them take off all their clothes and searches them, usually to see if they are carrying drugs or weapons. Compare **body-search**. ❑ *All 23 of them were strip-searched for drugs.*

strip|tease /strɪptiz/ (stripteases) also **strip-tease** N-VAR **Striptease** is a form of entertainment in which someone slowly takes off their clothes in a sexually exciting way, usually while music is played.

stripy /straɪpi/ also **stripey** ADJ [usu ADJ n] Something that is **stripy** has stripes on it. [INFORMAL] ❑ *He was wearing a stripy shirt and baggy blue trousers.*

strive /straɪv/ (strives, striving)

The past tense is either **strove** or **strived**, and the past participle is either **striven** or **strived**.

V-T/V-I If you **strive** to do something or **strive** for something, you make a great effort to do it or get it. ❑ *He strives hard to keep himself very fit.*

strobe /stroʊb/ (strobes) N-COUNT A **strobe** or a **strobe light** is a very bright light which flashes on and off very quickly.

strode /stroʊd/ **Strode** is the past tense and past participle of **stride**.

stroke ♦♢♢ /stroʊk/ (strokes, stroking, stroked) **1** V-T If you **stroke** someone or something, you move your hand slowly and gently over them. ❑ *Carla, curled up on the sofa, was smoking a cigarette and stroking her cat.* **2** N-COUNT If someone has a **stroke**, a blood vessel in their brain bursts or becomes blocked, which may kill them or make them unable to move one side of their body. ❑ *He had a minor stroke in 1987, which left him partly paralyzed.* **3** N-COUNT The **strokes** of a pen or brush are the movements or marks that you make with it when you are writing or painting. ❑ *Fill in gaps by using short, upward strokes of the pencil.* **4** N-COUNT When you are swimming or rowing, your **strokes** are the repeated movements that you make with your arms or the oars. ❑ *I turned and swam a few strokes further out to sea.* **5** N-COUNT A swimming **stroke** is a particular style or method of swimming. ❑ *She spent hours practicing the breast stroke.* **6** N-COUNT The **strokes** of a clock are the sounds that indicate each hour. ❑ *On the stroke of 12, fireworks suddenly exploded into the night.* **7** N-COUNT In sports such as tennis, baseball, golf, and cricket, a **stroke** is the action of hitting the ball. ❑ *Compton was sending the ball here, there, and everywhere with each stroke.* **8** N-SING A **stroke of** luck or good fortune is something lucky

stroll that happens. □ *It didn't rain, which turned out to be a stroke of luck.* **9** N-SING **A stroke of** genius or inspiration is a very good idea that someone suddenly has. □ *At the time, his appointment seemed a stroke of genius.* **10** PHRASE If someone does not **do a stroke** of work, they are very lazy and do no work at all. [INFORMAL, EMPHASIS] □ *I never did a stroke of work in college.*

---SYNONYMS---
stroke
VERB **1**
rub: *He rubbed his arms and stiff legs.*
pet: *I petted and smoothed her hair.*
pat: *'Don't you worry,' she said patting me on the knee.*
---

stroll /stroʊl/ (**strolls, strolling, strolled**) V-I If you **stroll** somewhere, you walk there in a slow, relaxed way. □ *He collected some orange juice from the refrigerator and, glass in hand, strolled to the kitchen window.* • N-COUNT **Stroll** is also a noun. □ *After dinner, I took a stroll round the city.*

strol|ler /stroʊlər/ (**strollers**) N-COUNT A **stroller** is a small chair on wheels, in which a baby or small child can sit and be wheeled around. [AM]
• in BRIT, use **pushchair**

strong ♦♦♦ /strɔŋ/ (**stronger** /strɔŋɡər/, **strongest** /strɔŋɡɪst/) **1** ADJ Someone who is **strong** is healthy with good muscles and can move or carry heavy things, or do hard physical work. □ *I'm not strong enough to carry him.* **2** ADJ Someone who is **strong** is confident and determined, and is not easily influenced or worried by other people. □ *He is sharp and manipulative with a strong personality.* □ *It's up to managers to be strong and do what they believe is right.* **3** ADJ **Strong** objects or materials are not easily broken and can support a lot of weight or resist a lot of strain. □ *The vacuum flask has a strong casing, which won't crack or chip.* □ *Glue the mirror in with a strong adhesive.* • **strong|ly** ADV [ADV -ed] □ *The fence was very strongly built, with very large posts.* **4** ADJ A **strong** wind, current, or other force has a lot of power or speed, and can cause heavy things to move. □ *Strong winds and torrential rain combined to make conditions terrible for golfers in the Scottish Open.* □ *A fairly strong current seemed to be moving the whole boat.* • **strong|ly** ADV [ADV with v] □ *The metal is strongly attracted to the surface.* **5** ADJ A **strong** impression or influence has a great effect on someone. □ *We're glad if our music makes a strong impression, even if it's a negative one.* □ *There will be a strong incentive to enter into a process of negotiation.* • **strong|ly** ADV [ADV with v] □ *He is strongly influenced by Spanish painters such as Goya and El Greco.* **6** ADJ If you have **strong** opinions on something or express them using **strong** words, you have extreme or very definite opinions which you are willing to express or defend. □ *She is known to hold strong views on Cuba.* □ *I am a strong supporter of the president.* • **strong|ly** ADV □ *Obviously you feel very strongly about this.* □ *Republicans in the House were strongly opposed to lifting the ban.* **7** ADJ If someone in authority takes **strong** action, they act firmly and severely. □ *The American public deserves strong action from Congress.* **8** ADJ If there is a **strong** case or argument for something, it is supported by a lot of evidence. □ *The testimony presented offered a strong case for acquitting her on grounds of self-defense.* • **strong|ly** ADV □ *He argues strongly for retention of NATO as a guarantee of peace.* **9** ADJ If there is a **strong** possibility or chance that something is true or will happen, it is very likely to be true or to happen. □ *There is a strong possibility that the cat contracted the condition by eating contaminated pet food.* **10** ADJ [ADJ n] Your **strong** points are your best qualities or talents, or the things you are good at. □ *Discretion is not Jeremy's strong point.* □ *Exports may be the only strong point in the economy over the next six to 12 months.* **11** ADJ A **strong** competitor, candidate, or team is good or likely to succeed. □ *She was a strong contender for the Olympic team.* **12** ADJ If a relationship or link is **strong**, it is close and likely to last for a long time. □ *He felt he had a relationship strong enough to talk frankly to Sarah.* □ *This has tested our marriage, and we have come through it stronger than ever.* **13** ADJ A **strong** currency, economy, or industry has a high value or is very successful. □ *The U.S. dollar continued its strong performance in Tokyo today.* **14** ADJ If something is a **strong** element or part of something else, it is an important or large part of it. □ *We are especially encouraged by the strong representation, this year, of women in information technology disciplines.* **15** ADJ [num ADJ] You can use **strong** when you are saying how many people there are in a

group. For example, if a group is twenty **strong**, there are twenty people in it. □ *The regime indicated that it would establish its own army, 400,000 strong.* **16** ADJ A **strong** drink, chemical, or drug contains a lot of the particular substance which makes it effective. □ *Strong coffee or tea late at night may cause sleeplessness.* **17** ADJ A **strong** color, flavor, smell, sound, or light is intense and easily noticed. □ *As she went past there was a gust of strong perfume.* • **strong|ly** ADV [ADV with v] □ *He leaned over her, smelling strongly of sweat.* **18** ADJ If someone has a **strong** accent, they speak in a distinctive way that shows very clearly what country or region they come from. □ *"Good, Mr. Ryle," he said in English with a strong French accent.* **19** PHRASE If someone or something is still **going strong**, they are still alive, in good condition, or popular after a long time. [INFORMAL] □ *The old machinery was still going strong.*

strong-arm ADJ [ADJ n] If you refer to someone's behavior as **strong-arm** tactics or methods, you disapprove of it because it consists of using threats or force in order to achieve something. [DISAPPROVAL] □ *The government was willing to use strong-arm tactics to get its way.*

strong|hold /strɔŋhoʊld/ (**strongholds**) N-COUNT If you say that a place or region is a **stronghold** of a particular attitude or belief, you mean that most people there share this attitude or belief. □ *The city is a stronghold for environmental activists.*

strong|man /strɔŋmæn/ (**strongmen**) **1** N-COUNT A **strongman** is a man who performs acts that require an enormous amount of strength. □ *She was entertained by dancers and acrobats and circus strongmen.* **2** N-COUNT If you refer to a male political leader as a **strongman**, you mean that he has great power and control over his country, although his methods may sometimes be violent or morally wrong. [JOURNALISM] □ *He was a military strongman who ruled the country after a coup.*

strong-minded ADJ If you describe someone as **strong-minded**, you approve of them because they have their own firm attitudes and opinions, and are not easily influenced by other people. [APPROVAL] □ *She is a strong-minded, independent woman.*

strong-willed ADJ Someone who is **strong-willed** has a lot of determination and always tries to do what they want, even though other people may advise them not to. □ *He is a very determined and strong-willed person.*

strong|woman /strɔŋwʊmən/ (**strongwomen**) N-COUNT A **strongwoman** is a woman who performs acts that require an enormous amount of strength. □ *The show includes a trapeze act, a human cannonball, and a strongwoman who can lift five men.*

strove /stroʊv/ **Strove** is a past tense of **strive**.

struck /strʌk/ **Struck** is a past tense and past participle of **strike**.

struc|tur|al /strʌktʃərəl/ ADJ **Structural** means relating to or affecting the structure of something. □ *The explosion caused little structural damage to the office towers themselves.* • **struc|tur|al|ly** ADV □ *When we bought the house, it was structurally sound, but I decided to redecorate throughout.*

struc|tur|al en|gi|neer (**structural engineers**) N-COUNT A **structural engineer** is an engineer who works on large structures such as roads, bridges, and large buildings.

struc|tur|al|ism /strʌktʃərəlɪzəm/ N-UNCOUNT **Structuralism** is a method of interpreting and analyzing such things as language, literature, and society, which focuses on contrasting ideas or elements of structure and attempts to show how they relate to the whole structure. [TECHNICAL]

struc|tur|al|ist /strʌktʃərəlɪst/ (**structuralists**) **1** N-COUNT A **structuralist** is someone whose work is based on structuralism. **2** ADJ [ADJ n] **Structuralist** is used to refer to people and things that are connected with structuralism. □ *There are two main structuralist techniques incorporated into critical social research.*

struc|ture ♦♦◊ /strʌktʃər/ (**structures, structuring, structured**) **1** N-VAR The **structure** of something is the way in which it is made, built, or organized. □ *The typical family structure of Freud's patients involved two parents and two children.* **2** N-COUNT A **structure** is something that consists of parts connected together in an ordered way. □ *The feet are highly specialized structures made up of 26 small delicate bones.* **3** N-COUNT

struggle

A **structure** is something that has been built. ❑ *About half of those funds has gone to repair public roads, structures, and bridges.* ◼ V-T If you **structure** something, you arrange it in a careful, organized pattern or system. ❑ *By structuring the course this way, we're forced to produce something the companies think is valuable.* ◼ → See feature box at **fashion**

strug|gle ✦✧✧ /strʌgᵊl/ (**struggles, struggling, struggled**) ◼ V-T/V-I If you **struggle** to do something, you try hard to do it, even though other people or things may be making it difficult for you to succeed. ❑ *They had to struggle against all kinds of adversity.* ◼ N-VAR A **struggle** is a long and difficult attempt to achieve something such as freedom or political rights. ❑ *Life became a struggle for survival.* ❑ *...a young boy's struggle to support his poverty-stricken family.* ◼ V-I If you **struggle** when you are being held, you twist, kick, and move violently in order to get free. ❑ *I struggled, but he was a tall man, well built.* ◼ V-RECIP If two people **struggle** with each other, they fight. ❑ *She screamed at him to "stop it" as they struggled on the ground.* • N-COUNT **Struggle** is also a noun. ❑ *He died in a struggle with prison officers less than two months after coming to Britain.* ◼ V-T/V-I If you **struggle** to move yourself or to move a heavy object, you try to do it, but it is difficult. ❑ *I could see the young boy struggling to free himself.* ◼ V-T/V-I [only cont] If a person or organization **is struggling**, they are likely to fail in what they are doing, even though they might be trying very hard. ❑ *The company is struggling to find buyers for its new product.* ❑ *One in five young adults was struggling with everyday mathematics.* ◼ N-SING An action or activity that is **a struggle** is very difficult to do. ❑ *Losing weight was a terrible struggle.* ◼ → See feature box at **challenge**

SYNONYMS

struggle
VERB ◼
strive: *He strives hard to keep himself very fit.*
strain: *I had to strain to hear.*
battle: *He was battling against the wind and rain.*
endeavor: *They are endeavoring to protect trade union rights.*
NOUN ◼
effort: *With effort, she contained her irritation.*
battle: *...the eternal battle between good and evil in the world.*
strain: *I sometimes find it a strain to be responsible for the mortgage.*

---

strum /strʌm/ (**strums, strumming, strummed**) V-T If you **strum** a stringed instrument such as a guitar, you play it by moving your fingers backward and forward across the strings. ❑ *In the corner, one youth sat alone, softly strumming a guitar.*

strung /strʌŋ/ **Strung** is the past tense and past participle of **string**.

strung out ◼ ADJ If things are **strung out** somewhere, they are spread out in a line. ❑ *Buildings were strung out on the north side of the river.* ◼ ADJ [v-link ADJ] If someone is **strung out** on drugs, they are heavily affected by drugs. [INFORMAL] ❑ *He was permanently strung out on heroin.*

strut /strʌt/ (**struts, strutting, strutted**) ◼ V-I Someone who **struts** walks in a proud way, with their head held high and their chest out, as if they are very important. [DISAPPROVAL] ❑ *He struts around town like he owns the place.* ◼ N-COUNT A **strut** is a piece of wood or metal which holds the weight of other pieces in a building or other structure. ❑ *...the struts of a suspension bridge.*

strych|nine /strɪknaɪn, -nɪn, -nin/ N-UNCOUNT **Strychnine** is a very poisonous drug which is sometimes used in very small amounts as a medicine.

stub /stʌb/ (**stubs, stubbing, stubbed**) ◼ N-COUNT The **stub** of a cigarette or a pencil is the last short piece of it which remains when the rest has been used. ❑ *He pulled the stub of a pencil from behind his ear.* ◼ N-COUNT A ticket **stub** is the part that you keep when you go in to watch a performance. ❑ *Fans who still have their ticket stubs should contact the box office by July 3.* ◼ N-COUNT A check **stub** is the small part that you keep as a record of what you have paid. ❑ *I have every check stub we've written since 1959.* ◼ V-T If you **stub** your toe, you hurt it by accidentally kicking something. ❑ *I stubbed my toes against a table leg.*
▶ **stub out** PHRASAL VERB When someone **stubs out** a cigarette, they put it out by pressing it against something

student body

hard. ❑ *Signs across the entrances warn all visitors to stub out their cigarettes.*

stub|ble /stʌbᵊl/ ◼ N-UNCOUNT **Stubble** is the short stalks which are left standing in fields after corn or wheat has been cut. ❑ *The stubble was burning in the fields.* ◼ N-UNCOUNT The very short hairs on someone's skin when they have not shaved recently, especially the hairs on a man's face, are referred to as **stubble**. ❑ *His face was covered with the stubble of several nights.*

stub|bly /stʌbli/ (**stubblier, stubbliest**) ADJ [usu ADJ n] **Stubbly** skin has not been shaved recently. ❑ *...a stubbly chin.*

stub|born /stʌbərn/ ◼ ADJ Someone who is **stubborn** or who behaves in a **stubborn** way is determined to do what they want and is very unwilling to change their mind. ❑ *He is a stubborn character used to getting his own way.* • **stub|born|ly** ADV ❑ *He stubbornly refused to tell her how he had come to be in such a state.* • **stub|born|ness** N-UNCOUNT ❑ *I couldn't tell if his refusal to talk was simple stubbornness.* ◼ ADJ A **stubborn** stain or problem is difficult to remove or to deal with. ❑ *This treatment removes the most stubborn stains.* • **stub|born|ly** ADV ❑ *Some interest rates have remained stubbornly high.* ◼ → See feature box at **quality**

stub|by /stʌbi/ (**stubbier, stubbiest**) ADJ An object that is **stubby** is shorter and thicker than usual. ❑ *He pointed a stubby finger at a wooden chair opposite him.*

stuc|co /stʌkoʊ/ N-UNCOUNT [oft N n] **Stucco** is a type of plaster used for covering walls and decorating ceilings.

stuck /stʌk/ ◼ **Stuck** is the past tense and past participle of **stick**. ◼ ADJ [v-link ADJ] If something is **stuck** in a particular position, it is fixed tightly in this position and is unable to move. ❑ *He said his car had gotten stuck in the snow.* ◼ ADJ [v-link ADJ prep/adv] If you are **stuck** in a place, you want to get away from it, but are unable to. ❑ *I was stuck at home with flu.* ◼ ADJ [v-link ADJ prep/adv] If you are **stuck** in a boring or unpleasant situation, you are unable to change it or get away from it. ❑ *I don't want to get stuck in another job like that.* ◼ ADJ [v-link ADJ prep/adv] If something is **stuck** at a particular level or stage, it is not progressing or changing. ❑ *I think the economy is stuck on a plateau of slow growth.* ❑ *U.S. unemployment figures for March showed the jobless rate stuck at 7 percent.* ◼ ADJ [v-link ADJ with n] If you are **stuck with** something that you do not want, you cannot get rid of it. ❑ *Many people are now stuck with expensive fixed-rate mortgages.* ◼ ADJ [v-link ADJ] If you get **stuck** when you are trying to do something, you are unable to continue doing it because it is too difficult. ❑ *They will be there to help if you get stuck.* ◼ → See feature box at **commute**

stuck-up ADJ If you say that someone is **stuck-up**, you mean that they are very proud and unfriendly because they think they are very important. [INFORMAL, DISAPPROVAL] ❑ *He was a famous actor, but he wasn't a bit stuck-up.*

stud /stʌd/ (**studs**) ◼ N-COUNT **Studs** are small pieces of metal which are attached to a surface for decoration. ❑ *You see studs on lots of front doors.* ◼ N-COUNT **Studs** are small round objects attached to the bottom of boots, especially sports boots, so that the person wearing them does not slip. [BRIT]

in AM, use **cleats**

◼ N-UNCOUNT Horses or other animals that are kept for **stud** are kept to be used for breeding. ❑ *He was voted horse of the year and then was retired to stud.*

stud book (**stud books**) also **studbook** N-COUNT A **stud book** is a written record of the breeding of a particular horse, especially a racehorse.

stud|ded /stʌdɪd/ ADJ Something that is **studded** is decorated with studs or things that look like studs. ❑ *...studded leather jackets.*

stu|dent ✦✦✦ /stud²nt/ (**students**) ◼ N-COUNT A **student** is a person who is studying at an elementary school, secondary school, college, or university. ❑ *Warren's eldest son is an art student.* ◼ → see also **graduate student** ◼ N-COUNT Someone who is a **student of** a particular subject is interested in the subject and spends time learning about it. ❑ *...a passionate student of history and an expert on nineteenth century prime ministers.* ◼ → See feature box at **university**

stu|dent body (**student bodies**) N-COUNT [usu sing] A **student body** is all the students of a particular college or university, considered as a group. ▫ *We take seriously the concerns of the student body and recognise our failure.* ▫ *City College of New York has one of the most diversified student bodies in the nation.*

stu|dent coun|cil (student councils) N-VAR A **student council** is an organization of students within a school that represents the interests of the students who study there. [mainly AM] ▫ *...Jim Blaschek, student council president at Sandburg High School.*

stu|dent loan (student loans) **1** N-COUNT A **student loan** is a government loan that is available to students at a college or university in order to help them pay their expenses. ▫ *...the government's $12 billion student loan program.* **2** → See feature box at **university**

stu|dent un|ion (student unions) N-COUNT [oft the N, oft in names] The **student union** is the building at a college or university which usually has food services, a bookstore, meeting places for leisure activities, and offices for the student government.

stud farm (stud farms) N-COUNT A **stud farm** is a place where horses are bred.

stud|ied /stʌdid/ **1** ADJ [ADJ n] A **studied** action is deliberate or planned. ▫ *We both have an interesting 10 days coming up, said the Chief Executive with studied understatement.* **2** → see also **study**

stu|dio ♦♦◇ /studiou/ (studios) **1** N-COUNT A **studio** is a room where a painter, photographer, or designer works. ▫ *She was in her studio again, painting onto a large canvas.* **2** N-COUNT A **studio** is a room where radio or television programs are recorded, CDs are produced, or movies are made. ▫ *She's much happier performing live than in a recording studio.* **3** N-COUNT You can also refer to film-making or recording companies as **studios**. ▫ *She wrote to Paramount Studios and asked if they would audition her.* **4** N-COUNT A **studio** or a **studio** apartment is a small apartment with one room for living and sleeping in, a kitchen, and a bathroom. ▫ *Home for a couple of years was a studio apartment.*

stu|dio audi|ence (studio audiences) N-COUNT-COLL A **studio audience** is a group of people who are in a television or radio studio watching while a program is being made, so that their clapping, laughter, or questions are recorded on the program.

stu|di|ous /studiəs/ ADJ Someone who is **studious** spends a lot of time reading and studying books. ▫ *I was a very quiet, studious little girl.*

stu|di|ous|ly /studiəsli/ ADV If you do something **studiously**, you do it carefully and deliberately. ▫ *When I looked at Clive, he studiously avoided my eyes.*

study ♦♦◇ /stʌdi/ (studies, studying, studied) **1** V-T/V-I If you **study**, you spend time learning about a particular subject or subjects. ▫ *...a relaxed and happy atmosphere that will allow you to study to your full potential.* ▫ *He studied History and Economics.* **2** N-UNCOUNT [also N in pl] **Study** is the activity of studying. ▫ *...the use of maps and visual evidence in the study of local history.* **3** N-COUNT A **study** of a subject is a piece of research on it. ▫ *Recent studies suggest that as many as 5 in 1,000 new mothers are likely to have this problem.* **4** N-PLURAL You can refer to educational subjects or courses that contain several elements as **studies** of a particular kind. ▫ *...a center for Islamic studies.* **5** V-T If you **study** something, you look at it or watch it very carefully, in order to find something out. ▫ *Debbie studied her friend's face for a moment.* **6** V-T If you **study** something, you consider it or observe it carefully in order to be able to understand it fully. ▫ *I know that you've been studying chimpanzees for thirty years now.* **7** N-COUNT A **study** is a room in a house which is used for reading, writing, and studying. ▫ *That evening we sat together in his study.* **8** → see also **case study**

SYNONYMS
study
VERB **1**
learn: *Their children were going to learn English.*
cram: *She was cramming for her Economics exam.*
review: *I have to review for math.*
NOUN **3**
investigation: *He ordered an investigation into the affair.*
analysis: *We did an analysis of the way that government money has been spent in the past.*

VOCABULARY IN CONTEXT

Studying and learning

Learning by rote has fallen out of favor because it doesn't guarantee that students have truly understood a **concept**. What experts call **active learning** is now more popular because it engages students with meaningful activities that encourage them to think hard about the **subject matter**. When it comes to **revision**, cultivating particular **study strategies** can dramatically improve our ability to **retain** information. It requires some **discipline**, but so does anything that is worth doing. Simple steps like setting a study **schedule**, or finding a quiet space conducive to **concentration** and focus, make a significant difference. Developing a systematic approach to identifying the key points is both a time-saving **device** and an invaluable study skill. So is effective note-taking. Successful learners know how to **distil** the main points, and this enables them to remember content more easily. Getting into a routine and applying proven **study techniques** will help them to achieve the learning outcomes they want.

study hall (study halls) N-VAR A **study hall** is a room where students can study during free time between classes, or a period of time during which such study takes place. [AM] ▫ *Children are hard at work in the study hall.* ▫ *She'd go to the library during ninth period, when she had study hall.*

stuff ♦♦◇ /stʌf/ (stuffs, stuffing, stuffed) **1** N-UNCOUNT [usu with supp] You can use **stuff** to refer to things such as a substance, a collection of things, events, or ideas, or the contents of something in a general way without mentioning the thing itself by name. [INFORMAL] ▫ *I'd like some coffee, and I don't object to the powdered stuff if it's all you've got.* ▫ *He pointed to a duffle bag. "That's my stuff."* **2** V-T If you **stuff** something somewhere, you push it there quickly and roughly. ▫ *I stuffed my hands in my pockets.* **3** V-T If you **stuff** a container or space with something, you fill it with something or with a quantity of things until it is full. ▫ *He grabbed my purse, opened it and stuffed it full, then gave it back to me.* **4** V-T If you **stuff** yourself, you eat a lot of food. [INFORMAL] ▫ *I could stuff myself with ten chocolate bars and half an hour later eat a big meal.* **5** V-T If you **stuff** a bird such as a chicken or a vegetable such as a pepper, you put a mixture of food inside it before cooking it. ▫ *Will you stuff the turkey and shove it in the oven for me?* **6** V-T [usu passive] If a dead animal **is stuffed**, it is filled with a substance so that it can be preserved and displayed. ▫ *...his collections of stamps and books and stuffed birds.* **7** PHRASE If you say that someone **knows their stuff**, you mean that they are good at doing something because they know a lot about it. [INFORMAL, APPROVAL] ▫ *These guys know their stuff after seven years of war.*

stuffed ani|mal (stuffed animals) N-COUNT **Stuffed animals** are toys that are made of cloth filled with a soft material and which look like animals. [AM]

in BRIT, use **soft toy**

stuffed shirt (stuffed shirts) N-COUNT If you describe someone, especially someone with an important position, as a **stuffed shirt**, you mean that they are extremely formal

stuffed toy and old-fashioned. [INFORMAL, DISAPPROVAL] ❑ *In a pinstriped suit he instantly looked like a stuffed shirt.*

stuffed toy (stuffed toys) N-COUNT A **stuffed toy** is the same as a **stuffed animal**. [AM]

in BRIT, use **soft toy**

stuff|ing /stʌfɪŋ/ (stuffings) **1** N-MASS **Stuffing** is a mixture of food that is put inside a bird such as a chicken, or a vegetable such as a pepper, before it is cooked. ❑ *Chestnuts can be used at Christmastime, as a stuffing for turkey, guinea fowl, or chicken.* **2** N-UNCOUNT **Stuffing** is material that is used to fill things such as cushions or toys in order to make them firm or solid. ❑ *...a rag doll with all the stuffing coming out.*

stuffy /stʌfi/ (stuffier, stuffiest) ADJ If it is **stuffy** in a place, it is unpleasantly warm and there is not enough fresh air. ❑ *It was hot and stuffy in the classroom even though two of the windows at the back had been opened.*

stul|ti|fy /stʌltɪfaɪ/ (stultifies, stultifying, stultified) V-T If something **stultifies** you, or if it **stultifies** your energy or ambition, it makes you feel empty or dull in your mind, because it is so boring. [FORMAL] ❑ *...a uniformed guard stultified with boredom.* ❑ *We must fight low expectations because they stultify ambition.* ● **stul|ti|fy|ing** ADJ ❑ *...the stultifying routines of life at home.*

stum|ble /stʌmbəl/ (stumbles, stumbling, stumbled) V-I If you **stumble**, you put your foot down awkwardly while you are walking or running and nearly fall over. ❑ *He stumbled and almost fell.* ● N-COUNT **Stumble** is also a noun. ❑ *I make it into the darkness with only one stumble.*

▶ **stumble across** also **stumble on** PHRASAL VERB If you **stumble across** something or **stumble on** it, you find it or discover it unexpectedly. ❑ *I stumbled across an extremely simple but very exact method for understanding where my money went.*

stum|bling block (stumbling blocks) N-COUNT A **stumbling block** is a problem which stops you from achieving something. ❑ *The major stumbling block in the talks has been money.*

stump /stʌmp/ (stumps, stumping, stumped) **1** N-COUNT A **stump** is a small part of something that remains when the rest of it has been removed or broken off. ❑ *If you have a tree stump, check it for fungus.* **2** V-T If you **are stumped** by a question or problem, you cannot think of any solution or answer to it. ❑ *John Diamond is stumped by an unexpected question.* **3** V-I If politicians **stump** for a candidate, they travel around making campaign speeches before an election. [AM] ❑ *Since September, the president has stumped for Republicans in 23 states.*

stumpy /stʌmpi/ (stumpier, stumpiest) ADJ **Stumpy** things are short and thick. ❑ *Does this dress make my legs look too stumpy?*

stun /stʌn/ (stuns, stunning, stunned) **1** V-T [usu passive] If you **are stunned** by something, you are extremely shocked or surprised by it and are therefore unable to speak or do anything. ❑ *He's stunned by today's resignation of his longtime ally.* ● **stunned** ADJ ❑ *When they told me she was missing I was totally stunned.* **2** V-T If something such as a blow on the head **stuns** you, it makes you unconscious or confused and unsteady. ❑ *Sam stood his ground and got a blow that stunned him.* **3** → see also **stunning**

stung /stʌŋ/ **Stung** is the past tense and past participle of **sting**.

stun gun (stun guns) N-COUNT A **stun gun** is a device that can immobilize a person or animal for a short time without causing them serious injury.

stunk /stʌŋk/ **Stunk** is the past participle of **stink**.

stun|ner /stʌnər/ (stunners) N-COUNT A **stunner** is an extremely attractive person. [INFORMAL]

stun|ning /stʌnɪŋ/ **1** ADJ A **stunning** person or thing is extremely beautiful or impressive. ❑ *A stunning display of fireworks lit up the sky.* **2** ADJ A **stunning** event is extremely unusual or unexpected. ❑ *He resigned last night after a stunning defeat in Sunday's vote.*

stunt /stʌnt/ (stunts, stunting, stunted) **1** N-COUNT A **stunt** is something interesting that is done in order to attract attention and get publicity for the person or company responsible for it. ❑ *In a bold promotional stunt for the movie, he smashed his car into a passing truck.* **2** N-COUNT A **stunt** is a dangerous and exciting piece of action in a movie.

❑ *She insisted on living dangerously for her new film by performing her own stunts.* **3** V-T If something **stunts** the growth or development of a person or thing, it prevents it from growing or developing as much as it should. ❑ *The heart condition had stunted his growth a bit.* ● **stunt|ed** ADJ ❑ *Damage may result in stunted growth and sometimes death of the plant.*

stunt|man /stʌntmæn/ (stuntmen) N-COUNT A **stuntman** is a man whose job is to do dangerous things, either for publicity, or in a movie instead of an actor so that the actor does not risk being injured.

stunt|woman /stʌntwʊmən/ (stuntwomen) N-COUNT A **stuntwoman** is a woman whose job is to do dangerous things, either for publicity, or in a movie instead of an actor so that the actor does not risk being injured.

stu|pefy /stupɪfaɪ/ (stupefies, stupefying, stupefied) V-T If something **stupefies** you, it shocks or surprises you so much that you cannot think properly for a while. [FORMAL] ❑ *...a violent slap on the side of the head, which stunned and stupefied him.*

stu|pen|dous /stupɛndəs/ ADJ [usu ADJ n] Something that is **stupendous** is surprisingly impressive or large. ❑ *He was a man of stupendous stamina and energy.* ❑ *This stupendous novel keeps you gripped to the end.*

stu|pid ✦✦◇ /stupɪd/ (stupider, stupidest) **1** ADJ If you say that someone or something is **stupid**, you mean that they show a lack of good judgment or intelligence and they are not at all sensible. ❑ *I'll never do anything so stupid again.* ❑ *I made a stupid mistake.* ● **stu|pid|ly** ADV ❑ *We had stupidly been looking at the wrong column of figures.* ● **stu|pid|ity** /stupɪdɪti/ (stupidities) N-VAR ❑ *I stared at him, astonished by his stupidity.* **2** ADJ You say that something is **stupid** to indicate that you do not like it or that it annoys you. [DISAPPROVAL] ❑ *I wouldn't call it art. It's just stupid and tasteless.*

stu|por /stupər/ (stupors) N-COUNT [usu sing, oft in/into a n] Someone who is in a **stupor** is almost unconscious and is unable to act or think normally, especially as a result of drink or drugs. ❑ *He fell back onto the sofa in a drunken stupor.*

stur|dy /stɜrdi/ (sturdier, sturdiest) ADJ Someone or something that is **sturdy** looks strong and is unlikely to be easily injured or damaged. ❑ *She was a short, sturdy woman in her early sixties.* ● **stur|di|ly** ADV ❑ *It was a good table too, sturdily constructed of elm.*

stur|geon /stɜrdʒən/ (sturgeon) N-VAR A **sturgeon** is a large fish which lives in northern parts of the world. Sturgeon are usually caught for their eggs, which are known as caviar.

stut|ter /stʌtər/ (stutters, stuttering, stuttered) **1** N-COUNT [usu sing] If someone has a **stutter**, they find it difficult to say the first sound of a word, and so they often hesitate or repeat it two or three times. ❑ *He spoke with a pronounced stutter.* **2** V-I If someone **stutters**, they have difficulty speaking because they find it hard to say the first sound of a word. ❑ *I was trembling so hard, I thought I would stutter when I spoke.* ● **stut|ter|ing** N-UNCOUNT ❑ *He had to stop talking because if he'd kept on, the stuttering would have started.* **3** → See feature box at **speak**

sty /staɪ/ (sties) N-COUNT A **sty** is the same as a **pigsty**.

stye /staɪ/ (styes) also **sty** N-COUNT If you have a **stye**, your eyelid is red and swollen because part of it is infected.

style ✦✦◇ /staɪl/ (styles, styling, styled) **1** N-COUNT The **style** of something is the general way in which it is done or presented, which often shows the attitudes of the people involved. ❑ *Our children's different needs and learning styles created many problems.* ❑ *Belmont Park is a broad sweeping track which will suit the European style of running.* **2** N-UNCOUNT If people or places have **style**, they are fashionable and elegant. ❑ *Boston, you have to admit, has style.* ❑ *Both love doing things in style.* **3** N-VAR The **style** of a product is its design. ❑ *His 50 years of experience have given him strong convictions about style.* **4** N-COUNT In the arts, a particular **style** is characteristic of a particular period or group of people. ❑ *...six scenes in the style of a classical Greek tragedy.* ❑ *...a mixture of musical styles.* **5** V-T [usu passive] If something such as a piece of clothing, a vehicle, or someone's hair **is styled** in a particular way, it is designed or shaped in that way. ❑ *His thick blond hair had just been styled before his trip.* **6** → see also **self-styled** **7** → See feature box at **fashion**

-style /-staɪl/ **1** COMB IN ADJ [usu adj n] **-style** combines with nouns and adjectives to form adjectives which describe the style or characteristics of something. ☐ ...*the development of a Western-style political system.* ☐ ...*a hearty country-style dinner.* **2** COMB IN ADV [ADV after v] **-style** combines with adjectives and nouns to form adverbs which describe how something is done. ☐ *Guests have been asked to dress 1920s-style.*

styl|ing /sta<u>ɪ</u>lɪŋ/ **1** N-UNCOUNT [oft supp N] The **styling** of an object is the design and appearance of it. ☐ *The car neatly blends classic styling into a smooth modern package.* **2** N-UNCOUNT [oft N n] The **styling** of someone's hair is the way in which it is cut and arranged. ☐ ...*shampoos and styling products.* **3** → see also **style**

styl|ised /sta<u>ɪ</u>laɪzd/ [BRIT] → see **stylized**

styl|ish /sta<u>ɪ</u>lɪʃ/ ADJ Someone or something that is **stylish** is elegant and fashionable. ☐ ...*a very attractive and very stylish woman of 27.* • **styl|ish|ly** ADV ☐ ...*stylishly dressed middle aged women and men*

styl|ist /sta<u>ɪ</u>lɪst/ (**stylists**) **1** N-COUNT A **stylist** is a person whose job is to cut and arrange people's hair. ☐ *Choose a stylist recommended by someone whose hair you like.* **2** N-COUNT A **stylist** is someone whose job is to create the style of something such as an advertisement or the image of people such as pop singers. ☐ *She is now a writer and fashion stylist.*

sty|lis|tic /sta<u>ɪ</u>lɪstɪk/ ADJ **Stylistic** describes things relating to the methods and techniques used in creating a piece of writing, music, or art. ☐ *There are some stylistic elements in the statue that just don't make sense.*

styl|ized /sta<u>ɪ</u>laɪzd/

in BRIT, also use **stylised**

ADJ Something that is **stylized** is shown or done in a way that is not natural in order to create an artistic effect. ☐ *Some of it has to do with recent stage musicals, which have been very, very stylized.*

sty|lus /sta<u>ɪ</u>ləs/ (**styluses**) **1** N-COUNT The **stylus** on a record player is the small needle that picks up the sound signals on the records. **2** N-COUNT A **stylus** is a device like a pen with which you can input written text or drawing directly into a computer. [COMPUTING] ☐ *It has a stylus-operated on-screen keyboard that takes great skill to master.*

sty|mie /sta<u>ɪ</u>mi/ (**stymies, stymieing, stymied**) V-T [usu passive] If you **are stymied** by something, you find it very difficult to take action or to continue what you are doing. [INFORMAL] ☐ *Companies have been stymied by the length of time it takes to reach an agreement.*

Styro|foam /sta<u>ɪ</u>rəfoʊm/ N-UNCOUNT **Styrofoam** is a very light, plastic substance, used especially to make containers. [AM, TRADEMARK]

in BRIT, use **polystyrene**

suave /swɑ<u>ː</u>v/ (**suaver, suavest**) ADJ Someone who is **suave** is charming, polite, and elegant, but may be insincere. ☐ *He is a suave, cool, and cultured man.*

sub /sʌ<u>b</u>/ (**subs**) **1** N-COUNT A **sub** is a long soft bread roll filled with a combination of things such as meat, cheese, eggs, and salad. **2** N-COUNT A **sub** is the same as a **substitute teacher**. [AM] **3** N-COUNT In team games such as football, a **sub** is a player who is brought into a game to replace another player. [INFORMAL] ☐ *We had a few injuries and had to use youth team kids as subs.* **4** N-COUNT A **sub** is the same as a **submarine**. [INFORMAL]

PREFIX

sub-
forms nouns that refer to things that are part of a larger thing. *For example, a subculture is the culture of a group of people within a society.*

sub|atom|ic /sʌ<u>b</u>ətɒmɪk/ ADJ [ADJ n] A **subatomic** particle is a particle which is part of an atom, for example an electron, a proton, or a neutron. [TECHNICAL]

sub|com|mit|tee /sʌ<u>b</u>kəmɪti/ (**subcommittees**) also **sub-committee** N-COUNT-COLL A **subcommittee** is a small committee made up of members of a larger committee.

sub|com|pact /sʌ<u>b</u>kɒmpækt/ (**subcompacts**) ADJ [ADJ n] A **subcompact** car is a very small car. [AM] ☐ ...*a subcompact Hyundai Excel.* • N-COUNT **Subcompact** is also a noun ☐ ...*a subcompact made in Japan by Suzuki.*

sub|con|scious /sʌ<u>b</u>kɒnʃəs/ **1** N-SING Your **subconscious** is the part of your mind that can influence you or affect your behavior even though you are not aware of it. ☐ ...*the hidden power of the subconscious.* **2** ADJ A **subconscious** feeling or action exists in or is influenced by your subconscious. ☐ *He caught her arm in a subconscious attempt to detain her.* • **sub|con|scious|ly** ADV ☐ *Subconsciously I had known that I would not be in personal danger.*

sub|con|ti|nent /sʌ<u>b</u>kɒntɪnənt/ (**subcontinents**) also **sub-continent** N-COUNT [usu sing] A **subcontinent** is part of a larger continent, made up of a number of countries that form a large mass of land. **The subcontinent** is often used to refer to the area that contains India, Pakistan, and Bangladesh.

sub|con|tract /sʌ<u>b</u>kəntrækt/ (**subcontracts, subcontracting, subcontracted**) V-T If one company **subcontracts** part of its work to another company, it pays the other company to do part of the work that it has been employed to do. [BUSINESS] ☐ *The company is subcontracting production of most of the parts.*

sub|con|trac|tor /sʌ<u>b</u>kɒntræktər/ (**subcontractors**) N-COUNT A **subcontractor** is a person or company that has a contract to do part of a job which another company is responsible for. [BUSINESS] ☐ *The company was considered as a possible subcontractor to build the airplane.*

sub|cul|ture /sʌ<u>b</u>kʌltʃər/ (**subcultures**) N-COUNT A **subculture** is the ideas, art, and way of life of a group of people within a society, which are different from the ideas, art, and way of life of the rest of the society. ☐ ...*the latest American subculture.*

sub|cu|ta|neous /sʌ<u>b</u>kyuteɪniəs/ ADJ [ADJ n] **Subcutaneous** is used to indicate that something is situated, used, or put under your skin. ☐ ...*subcutaneous fat.*

sub|di|vide /sʌ<u>b</u>dɪvaɪd/ (**subdivides, subdividing, subdivided**) V-T [usu passive] If something **is subdivided**, it is divided into several smaller areas, parts, or groups. ☐ *The verbs were subdivided into transitive and intransitive categories.*

sub|di|vi|sion /sʌ<u>b</u>dɪvɪʒən/ (**subdivisions**) **1** N-COUNT A **subdivision** is an area, part, or section of something which is itself a part of something larger. ☐ *Months are a conventional subdivision of the year.* **2** N-COUNT A **subdivision** is an area of land for building houses on. [AM] ☐ *Rammick lives high on a ridge in a 400-home subdivision.*

sub|due /səbdu<u>ː</u>/ (**subdues, subduing, subdued**) **1** V-T If soldiers or the police **subdue** a group of people, they defeat them or bring them under control by using force. ☐ *Senior government officials admit they have not been able to subdue the rebels.* **2** V-T To **subdue** feelings means to make them less strong. ☐ *He forced himself to subdue and overcome his fears.*

sub|dued /səbdu<u>ː</u>d/ **1** ADJ Someone who is **subdued** is very quiet, often because they are sad or worried about something. ☐ *He faced the press, initially, in a somewhat subdued mood.* **2** ADJ **Subdued** lights or colors are not very bright. ☐ *The lighting was subdued.*

sub-editor (**sub-editors**) N-COUNT A **sub-editor** is the same as a **copy editor**. [BRIT]

sub|group /sʌ<u>b</u>gruːp/ (**subgroups**) N-COUNT A **subgroup** is a group that is part of a larger group. ☐ *The Action Group worked by dividing its tasks among a large number of subgroups.*

sub|head|ing /sʌ<u>b</u>hɛdɪŋ/ (**subheadings**) N-COUNT **Subheadings** are titles that divide part of a piece of writing into shorter sections.

sub|hu|man /sʌ<u>b</u>hyuːmən/ ADJ If you describe someone or their situation as **subhuman**, you mean that they behave or live in a much worse way than human beings normally do. ☐ *The dictatorship treated women as subhuman.*

sub|ject ♦♦◊ (**subjects, subjecting, subjected**)

The noun and adjective are pronounced /sʌ<u>b</u>dʒɪkt/. The verb is pronounced /səbdʒɛ<u>k</u>t/.

1 N-COUNT The **subject** of something such as a conversation, letter, or book is the thing that is being discussed or written about. ☐ *It was I who first raised the subject of plastic surgery.* ☐ ...*the president's own views on the subject.* **2** N-COUNT Someone or something that is the **subject of** criticism, study, or an investigation is being criticized, studied, or investigated. ☐ *Over the past few years, some of the positions Mr. Meredith has adopted have made him the subject of criticism.* **3** N-COUNT A **subject**

is an area of knowledge or study, especially one that you study in school, or college. ❑ *Surprisingly, math was voted their favorite subject.* **4** N-COUNT In an experiment or piece of research, the **subject** is the person or animal that is being tested or studied. [FORMAL] ❑ *"White noise" was played through the subject's ears through headphones.* **5** N-COUNT An artist's **subjects** are the people, animals, or objects that he or she paints, models, or photographs. ❑ *Sailboats and fish are popular subjects for local artists.* **6** N-COUNT In grammar, the **subject** of a clause is the noun group that refers to the person or thing that is doing the action expressed by the verb. For example, in 'My cat keeps catching birds,' 'my cat' is the subject. **7** ADJ [v-link ADJ to n] To be **subject** to something means to be affected by it or to be likely to be affected by it. ❑ *Prices may be subject to alteration.* **8** ADJ [v-link ADJ to n] If someone is **subject to** a particular set of rules or laws, they have to obey those rules or laws. ❑ *The tribunal is unique because Mr. Jones is not subject to the normal police discipline code.* **9** V-T If you **subject** someone to something unpleasant, you make them experience it. ❑ *They subjected me to endless threats to sabotage my business.* **10** N-COUNT The people who live in or belong to a particular country, usually one ruled by a monarch, are the **subjects** of that monarch or country. ❑ *His subjects regarded him as a great and wise monarch.* **11** PHRASE When someone involved in a conversation **changes the subject**, they start talking about something else, often because the previous subject was embarrassing. ❑ *He tried to change the subject, but she wasn't to be put off.* **12** PHRASE If an event will take place **subject to** a condition, it will take place only if that thing happens. ❑ *They denied a report that Egypt had agreed to a summit, subject to certain conditions.*

COLLOCATIONS

subject
NOUN
1
adjective + **subject**: controversial, difficult, sensitive, taboo
verb + **subject**: address, broach, discuss, raise
3
noun + **subject**: degree; art, science
adjective + **subject**: academic, compulsory, core, vocational; favorite, specialist
verb + **subject**: research, study, teach

SYNONYMS

subject
NOUN **1**
topic: *The main topic for discussion is political union.*
question: *But the whole question of aid is a tricky political one.*
issue: *Is it right for the Church to express a view on political issues?*
matter: *It was clear that she wanted to discuss some private matter.*

---

sub|jec|tion /səbdʒɛkʃᵊn/ N-UNCOUNT **Subjection** to someone involves being completely controlled by them. ❑ *...their complete subjection to their captors.* ❑ *...the worst forms of economic subjection and drudgery.*

sub|jec|tive /səbdʒɛktɪv/ ADJ Something that is **subjective** is based on personal opinions and feelings rather than on facts. ❑ *We know that taste in art is a subjective matter.* • **sub|jec|tive|ly** ADV ❑ *Our preliminary results suggest that people do subjectively find the speech clearer.* • **sub|jec|tiv|ity** /sʌbdʒɛktɪvɪti/ N-UNCOUNT ❑ *They accused her of flippancy and subjectivity in her reporting of events in their country.*

sub|ject mat|ter **1** N-UNCOUNT The **subject matter** of something such as a book, lecture, movie, or painting is the thing that is being written about, discussed, or shown. ❑ *Then, attitudes changed and artists were given greater freedom in their choice of subject matter.* **2** → See feature box at **study**

sub ju|di|ce /sʌb dʒudɪsi/ also **sub-judice** ADJ [usu v-link ADJ] When something is **sub judice**, it is the subject of a trial in a court of law. [LEGAL] ❑ *He declined further comment on the grounds that the case was sub judice.*

sub|ju|gate /sʌbdʒəgeɪt/ (**subjugates**, **subjugating**, **subjugated**) **1** V-T If someone **subjugates** a group of people, they take complete control of them, especially by defeating them in a war. [FORMAL] ❑ *Their costly and futile attempt to subjugate the Afghans lasted just 10 years.* • **sub|ju|ga|tion** /sʌbdʒəgeɪʃᵊn/ N-UNCOUNT [usu N of n] ❑ *...the brutal subjugation of native tribes.* **2** V-T [usu passive] If your wishes or desires are **subjugated** to something, they are treated as less important than that thing. [FORMAL] ❑ *She was no longer willing to see her own needs subjugated to his ambitions.*

sub|junc|tive /səbdʒʌŋktɪv/ N-SING [the N] In English, a clause expressing a wish or suggestion can be put in the **subjunctive**, or in the **subjunctive** mood, by using the base form of a verb or 'were.' Examples are 'She asked that they be removed' and 'I wish I were somewhere else.' These structures are formal. [TECHNICAL]

sub|let /sʌblɛt/ (**sublets**, **subletting**)

The form **sublet** is used in the present tense and is the past tense and past participle of the verb.

V-T If you **sublet** a building or part of a building, you allow someone to use it and you take rent from them, although you are not the owner and pay rent for it yourself. ❑ *The company rented the building, occupied part and sublet the rest.*

sub|li|mate /sʌblɪmeɪt/ (**sublimates**, **sublimating**, **sublimated**) V-T If you **sublimate** a strong desire or feeling, you express it in a way that is socially acceptable. [FORMAL] ❑ *He could try to sublimate the problem by writing, in detail, about it.*

sub|lime /səblaɪm/ ADJ If you describe something as **sublime**, you mean that it has a wonderful quality that affects you deeply. [LITERARY, APPROVAL] ❑ *Sublime music floats on a scented summer breeze to the spot where you lie.* • N-SING You can refer to sublime things as **the sublime**. ❑ *She elevated every rare small success to the sublime.* • PHRASE If you describe something as going **from the sublime to the ridiculous**, you mean that it involves a change from something very good or serious to something silly or unimportant.

sub|limi|nal /sʌblɪmɪnᵊl/ ADJ **Subliminal** influences or messages affect your mind without you being aware of it. ❑ *Color has a profound, though often subliminal, influence on our senses and moods.*

sub|ma|chine gun /sʌbməʃin gʌn/ (**submachine guns**) also **sub-machine gun** N-COUNT A **submachine gun** is a light portable type of machine gun.

sub|ma|rine /sʌbmərin/ (**submarines**) **1** N-COUNT A **submarine** is a type of ship that can travel both above and below the surface of the sea. The abbreviation **sub** is also used. ❑ *...a nuclear submarine.* **2** → See also color supplement

sub|ma|rin|er /sʌbmərinər, sʌbmærənər/ (**submariners**) N-COUNT A **submariner** is a sailor or other person who goes in a submarine.

sub|merge /səbmɜrdʒ/ (**submerges**, **submerging**, **submerged**) V-T/V-I If something **submerges** or if you **submerge** it, it goes below the surface of some water or another liquid. ❑ *Hippos are unable to submerge in the few remaining water holes.*

sub|merged /səbmɜrdʒd/ ADJ If something is **submerged**, it is below the surface of some water. ❑ *My right toe struck against a submerged rock.*

sub|mers|ible /səbmɜrsɪbᵊl/ ADJ If something is **submersible**, it can go or operate under water. ❑ *a submersible pump.*

sub|mis|sion /səbmɪʃᵊn/ N-UNCOUNT **Submission** is a state in which people can no longer do what they want to do because they have been brought under the control of someone else. ❑ *The army intends to take the city or simply starve it into submission.*

sub|mis|sive /səbmɪsɪv/ ADJ If you are **submissive**, you obey someone without arguing. ❑ *Some doctors want their patients to be submissive.* • **sub|mis|sive|ly** ADV ❑ *The troops submissively laid down their weapons.*

sub|mit /səbmɪt/ (**submits**, **submitting**, **submitted**) **1** V-I If you **submit** to something, you unwillingly allow something to be done to you, or you do what someone wants, for example because you are not powerful enough to resist. ❑ *In desperation, Mrs. Jones submitted to an operation on her right knee to relieve the pain.* **2** V-T If you **submit** a proposal, report, or request to someone, you formally send it to them so that they can consider it or decide about it. ❑ *They submitted their reports to the chancellor yesterday.*

sub|nor|mal /sʌbnɔ̱rm³l/ ADJ If someone is **subnormal**, they have less ability or intelligence than a normal person of their age. [OLD-FASHIONED] ❑ ...*educationally subnormal children*.

sub|or|di|nate (**subordinates**, **subordinating**, **subordinated**)

The noun and adjective are pronounced /sʌbɔ̱rd³nɪt/. The verb is pronounced /səbɔ̱rd³neɪt/.

1 N-COUNT If someone is your **subordinate**, they have a less important position than you in the organization that you both work for. ❑ *Haig tended not to seek guidance from subordinates.* **2** ADJ Someone who is **subordinate** to you has a less important position than you and has to obey you. ❑ *Sixty of his subordinate officers followed his example.* **3** ADJ Something that is **subordinate** to something else is less important than the other thing. ❑ *It was an art in which words were subordinate to images.* **4** V-T If you **subordinate** something to another thing, you regard it or treat it as less important than the other thing. ❑ *He was both willing and able to subordinate all else to this aim.* • **sub|or|di|na|tion** /səbɔ̱rd³neɪʃ³n/ N-UNCOUNT ❑ ...*the social subordination of women.*

sub|or|di|nate clause (**subordinate clauses**) N-COUNT A **subordinate clause** is a clause in a sentence which adds to or completes the information given in the main clause. It cannot usually stand alone as a sentence. Compare **main clause**. [TECHNICAL]

sub|or|di|nat|ing con|junc|tion (**subordinating conjunctions**) N-COUNT A **subordinating conjunction** is a word such as 'although,' 'because,' or 'when' which begins a subordinate clause. Compare **coordinating conjunction**. [TECHNICAL]

sub|plot /sʌ̱bplɒt/ (**subplots**) N-COUNT The **subplot** in a play, movie, or novel is a story that is separate from and less important than the main story. ❑ ...*a fascinating subplot to the main drama.*

sub|poe|na /səpiːnə/ (**subpoenas**, **subpoenaing**, **subpoenaed**) **1** N-COUNT A **subpoena** is a legal document telling someone that they must attend a court of law and give evidence as a witness. ❑ *He has been served with a subpoena to answer the charges in court.* **2** V-T If someone **subpoenas** a person, they give them a legal document telling them to attend a court of law and give evidence. If someone **subpoenas** a piece of evidence, the evidence must be produced in a court of law. ❑ *Select committees have the power to subpoena witnesses.*

sub|prime /sʌ̱bpraɪm/ **1** ADJ A **subprime** loan is a loan that is made to a borrower who has been unable to pay back loans in the past, usually with a high interest rate. ❑ *Billions of dollars worth of subprime loans were issued in the US.* **2** → See feature box at **banking**

sub|scribe /səbskraɪb/ (**subscribes**, **subscribing**, **subscribed**) **1** V-I If you **subscribe to** an opinion or belief, you are one of a number of people who have this opinion or belief. ❑ *I've personally never subscribed to the view that either sex is superior to the other.* **2** V-I If you **subscribe to** a magazine or a newspaper, you pay to receive copies of it regularly. ❑ *My main reason for subscribing to New Scientist is to keep abreast of advances in science.* **3** V-I If you **subscribe to** an online newsgroup or service, you send a message saying that you wish to receive it or belong to it. [COMPUTING] ❑ *Usenet is a collection of discussion groups, known as newsgroups, to which anybody can subscribe.* **4** V-I If you **subscribe** for shares in a company, you apply to buy shares in that company. [BUSINESS] ❑ *Employees subscribed for far more shares than were available.*

sub|scrib|er /səbskraɪbər/ (**subscribers**) **1** N-COUNT A magazine's or a newspaper's **subscribers** are the people who pay to receive copies of it regularly. ❑ *I have been a subscriber to Newsweek for many years.* **2** N-COUNT **Subscribers** to a website or internet channel are people who agree to receive information regularly from it. ❑ *He has over a million subscribers to his YouTube channel.* **3** N-COUNT **Subscribers** to a service are the people who pay to receive the service. ❑ *China had almost 15 million subscribers to satellite and cable television.*

sub|scrip|tion /səbskrɪpʃ³n/ (**subscriptions**) **1** N-COUNT A **subscription** is an amount of money that you pay regularly in order to belong to an organization, to help a charity or campaign, or to receive copies of a magazine or newspaper. ❑ *You can become a member by paying the yearly subscription.*

2 ADJ [ADJ n] **Subscription** television is television that you can watch only if you pay a subscription. A **subscription** channel is a channel that you can watch only if you pay a subscription. ❑ *Live sport is increasingly in the hands of subscription channels.*

sub|sec|tion /sʌ̱bsɛkʃ³n/ (**subsections**) N-COUNT [also N num] A **subsection** of a text or a document such as a law is one of the smaller parts into which its main parts are divided.

sub|se|quent ♦◇◇ /sʌ̱bsɪkwənt/ ADJ [ADJ n] You use **subsequent** to describe something that happened or existed after the time or event that has just been referred to. [FORMAL] ❑ ...*the increase of population in subsequent years.* • **sub|se|quent|ly** ADV ❑ *He subsequently worked on Boeing's 747, 767 and 737 jetliner programs.*

> **SYNONYMS**
>
> **subsequent**
> ADJ
> **following:** *We went to dinner the following Monday evening.*
> **next:** *I got up early the next morning.*
> **ensuing:** *The ensuing argument had been bitter.*
> **later:** *At a later news conference, he said differences should not be dramatized.*

sub|ser|vi|ent /səbsɜ̱rviənt/ **1** ADJ If you are **subservient**, you do whatever someone wants you to do. ❑ *Her willingness to be subservient to her children isolated her.* • **sub|ser|vi|ence** /səbsɜ̱rviəns/ N-UNCOUNT ❑ ...*an austere regime stressing obedience and subservience to authority.* **2** ADJ [v-link ADJ to n] If you treat one thing as **subservient to** another, you treat it as less important than the other thing. ❑ *The woman's needs are seen as subservient to the group interest.*

sub|set /sʌ̱bsɛt/ (**subsets**) N-COUNT [oft N of n] A **subset** of a group of things is a smaller number of things that belong together within that group. ❑ ...*subsets of the population such as men, women, ethnic groups, etc.*

sub|side /səbsaɪd/ (**subsides**, **subsiding**, **subsided**) **1** V-I If a feeling or noise **subsides**, it becomes less strong or loud. ❑ *The pain had subsided during the night.* **2** V-I If fighting **subsides**, it becomes less intense or general. ❑ *Violence has subsided following two days of riots.* **3** V-I If the ground or a building **is subsiding**, it is very slowly sinking to a lower level. ❑ *Does that mean the whole house is subsiding?* **4** V-I If a level of water, especially flood water, **subsides**, it goes down. ❑ *Local officials say the flood waters have subsided.*

sub|sid|ence /səbsaɪd³ns, sʌ̱bsɪd³ns/ N-UNCOUNT When there is **subsidence** in a place, the ground there sinks to a lower level.

sub|sidi|ary /səbsɪ̱diɛri/ (**subsidiaries**) **1** N-COUNT A **subsidiary** or a **subsidiary** company is a company which is part of a larger and more important company. [BUSINESS] ❑ *WM Financial Services is a subsidiary of Washington Mutual.* **2** ADJ If something is **subsidiary**, it is less important than something else with which it is connected. ❑ *The marketing department has always played a subsidiary role to the sales department.*

sub|si|dize /sʌ̱bsɪdaɪz/ (**subsidizes**, **subsidizing**, **subsidized**)

in BRIT, also use **subsidise**

V-T If a government or other authority **subsidizes** something, they pay part of the cost of it. ❑ *Around the world, governments have subsidized the housing of middle- and upper-income groups.* • **sub|si|dized** ADJ ❑ ...*heavily subsidized prices for housing, bread, and meat.*

sub|si|dy ♦◇◇ /sʌ̱bsɪdi/ (**subsidies**) N-COUNT A **subsidy** is money that is paid by a government or other authority in order to help an industry or business, or to pay for a public service. ❑ *European farmers are planning a massive demonstration against farm subsidy cuts.*

> **SYNONYMS**
>
> **subsidy**
> NOUN
> **aid:** *They have already pledged billions of dollars in aid.*
> **support:** ...*the government's proposal to cut agricultural support by only about 15%.*
> **grant:** *They'd gotten a special grant to encourage research.*
> **contribution:** *This list ranked companies that make charitable contributions of a half million dollars or more.*

sub|sist /səbsɪst/ (subsists, subsisting, subsisted) V-I If people **subsist**, they are just able to obtain the food or money that they need in order to stay alive. [FORMAL] ☐ *The prisoners subsisted on one mug of the worst quality porridge three times a day.*

sub|sist|ence /səbsɪstəns/ **1** N-UNCOUNT **Subsistence** is the condition of just having enough food or money to stay alive. ☐ *...below the subsistence level.* **2** ADJ [ADJ n] In **subsistence** farming or **subsistence** agriculture, farmers produce food to eat themselves rather than to sell. ☐ *Many Namibians are subsistence farmers who live in the arid borderlands.*

sub|soil /sʌbsɔɪl/ N-UNCOUNT [also a N] The **subsoil** is a layer of earth that is just below the surface soil but above hard rock. ☐ *...the chalk subsoil on the site.*

sub|son|ic /sʌbsɒnɪk/ ADJ [ADJ n] **Subsonic** speeds or airplanes are very fast but slower than the speed of sound. ☐ *This is 20,000 feet higher than most subsonic airliners.*

sub|spe|cies /sʌbspiːʃiːz/ (subspecies) also **sub-species** N-COUNT [oft N of n] A **subspecies** of a plant or animal is one of the types that a particular species is divided into. ☐ *Several other subspecies of gull are found in the region.*

sub|stance ♦◇◇ /sʌbstəns/ (substances) **1** N-COUNT A **substance** is a solid, powder, liquid, or gas with particular properties. ☐ *There's no regulation of these diet pills to make sure they don't include toxic substances.* **2** N-UNCOUNT **Substance** is the quality of being important or significant. [FORMAL] ☐ *It's questionable whether anything of substance has been achieved.* **3** N-SING The **substance of** what someone says or writes is the main thing that they are trying to say. ☐ *The substance of his discussions doesn't really matter.* **4** N-UNCOUNT If you say that something has no **substance**, you mean that it is not true. [FORMAL] ☐ *There is no substance in any of these allegations.*

sub|stance abuse N-UNCOUNT **Substance abuse** is the use of illegal drugs. ☐ *...job-related accidents caused by substance abuse.*

sub|stand|ard /sʌbstændərd/ **1** ADJ A **substandard** service or product is unacceptable because it is below a required standard. ☐ *Residents in general are poor and undereducated, and live in substandard housing.* **2** → See feature box at **service**

sub|stan|tial ♦◇◇ /səbstænʃəl/ ADJ **Substantial** means large in amount or degree. [FORMAL] ☐ *A substantial number of mothers with young children are deterred from undertaking paid work because they lack access to childcare.*

SYNONYMS

substantial
ADJ
large: *The gang finally fled with a large amount of cash and jewelry.*
significant: *...foods that offer a significant amount of protein.*
considerable: *To be without Pearce would be a considerable blow*
ample: *The design of the ground floor created ample space for a good-sized kitchen.*

---

sub|stan|tial|ly /səbstænʃəli/ ADV If something changes **substantially** or is **substantially** different, it changes a lot or is very different. [FORMAL] ☐ *The percentage of girls in engineering has increased substantially.*

sub|stan|ti|ate /səbstænʃieɪt/ (substantiates, substantiating, substantiated) V-T To **substantiate** a statement or a story means to supply evidence which proves that it is true. [FORMAL] ☐ *There is little scientific evidence to substantiate the claims.*

sub|stan|tive /sʌbstəntɪv/ ADJ **Substantive** negotiations or issues deal with the most important and central aspects of a subject. [FORMAL] ☐ *They plan to meet again in Rome very soon to begin substantive negotiations.*

sub|sta|tion /sʌbsteɪʃən/ (substations) N-COUNT A **substation** is a place where high-voltage electricity from power plants is converted to lower-voltage electricity for homes or factories.

sub|sti|tute ♦◇◇ /sʌbstɪtuːt/ (substitutes, substituting, substituted) **1** V-T/V-I If you **substitute** one thing for another, or if one thing **substitutes** for another, it takes the place or performs the function of the other thing. ☐ *They were substituting violence for dialogue.* ☐ *He was substituting for the injured William Wales.* ● **sub|sti|tu|tion** /sʌbstɪtuːʃən/ (substitutions) N-VAR ☐ *In my experience a straight substitution of carob for chocolate doesn't work.* **2** N-COUNT A **substitute** is something that you have or use instead of something else. ☐ *She is seeking a substitute for the very person whose departure made her cry.* **3** N-COUNT If you say that one thing is no **substitute** for another, you mean that it does not have certain desirable features that the other thing has, and is therefore unsatisfactory. If you say that there is no **substitute** for something, you mean that it is the only thing which is really satisfactory. ☐ *The printed word is no substitute for personal discussion with a great thinker.* **4** N-COUNT In team games such as football, a **substitute** is a player who is brought into a game to replace another player. ☐ *Jefferson entered as a substitute in the 60th minute.*

sub|sti|tute teach|er (substitute teachers) N-COUNT A **substitute teacher** is a teacher whose job is to take the place of other teachers at different schools when they are unable to be there. [AM]

in BRIT, use **supply teacher**

sub|stra|tum /sʌbstreɪtəm, -strætəm/ (substrata) N-COUNT [with supp, usu N of n] A **substratum** of something is a layer that lies under the surface of another layer, or a feature that is less obvious than other features. [FORMAL] ☐ *...its deep substratum of chalk.*

sub|sume /səbsuːm/ (subsumes, subsuming, subsumed) V-T If something **is subsumed** within a larger group or class, it is included within it, rather than being considered as something separate. [FORMAL] ☐ *After that the two alliances might be subsumed into a new European security system.* ☐ *With unification, East Germany was subsumed by capitalist West Germany.*

sub|ter|fuge /sʌbtərfjuːdʒ/ (subterfuges) N-VAR **Subterfuge** is a trick or a dishonest way of getting what you want. ☐ *Most people can see right through that type of subterfuge.*

sub|ter|ra|nean /sʌbtəreɪniən/ ADJ A **subterranean** river or tunnel is under the ground. [FORMAL] ☐ *The city has 9 miles of such subterranean passages.*

sub|text /sʌbtekst/ (subtexts) N-VAR [usu with supp] The **subtext** is the implied message or subject of something that is said or written. ☐ *Europe's divisions are the subtext of a new movie thriller called "Zentropa."*

sub|ti|tle /sʌbtaɪtəl/ (subtitles, subtitling, subtitled) **1** N-COUNT The **subtitle** of a piece of writing is a second title which is often longer and explains more than the main title. ☐ *"Kathleen" was, as its 1892 subtitle asserted, "An Irish Drama."* **2** N-PLURAL **Subtitles** are a printed translation of the words of a foreign film that are shown at the bottom of the picture. ☐ *The dialogue is in Spanish, with English subtitles.* **3** V-T If you say how a book or play **is subtitled**, you say what its subtitle is. ☐ *"Lorna Doone" is subtitled "a Romance of Exmoor."*

sub|ti|tled /sʌbtaɪtəld/ ADJ If a foreign film is **subtitled**, a printed translation of the words is shown at the bottom of the picture. ☐ *Much of the film is subtitled.*

sub|tle /sʌtəl/ (subtler, subtlest) **1** ADJ Something that is **subtle** is not immediately obvious or noticeable. ☐ *...the slow and subtle changes that take place in all living things.* ● **sub|tly** ADV ☐ *The truth is subtly different.* **2** ADJ A **subtle** person cleverly uses indirect methods to achieve something. ☐ *I even began to exploit him in subtle ways.* ● **sub|tly** ADV [ADV with v] ☐ *Nathan is subtly trying to turn her against Barry.* **3** ADJ **Subtle** smells, tastes, sounds, or colors are pleasantly complex and delicate. ☐ *...subtle shades of brown.* ● **sub|tly** ADV ☐ *...a white sofa teamed with subtly colored rugs.*

sub|tle|ty /sʌtəlti/ (subtleties) **1** N-COUNT **Subtleties** are very small details or differences which are not obvious. ☐ *His fascination with the subtleties of human behavior makes him a good storyteller.* **2** N-UNCOUNT **Subtlety** is the quality of being not immediately obvious or noticeable, and therefore difficult to describe. ☐ *African dance is vigorous, but full of subtlety, requiring great strength and control.* **3** N-UNCOUNT **Subtlety** is the ability to notice and recognize things which are not obvious, especially small differences between things. ☐ *She analyzes herself with great subtlety.* **4** N-UNCOUNT **Subtlety** is the ability to use indirect methods to achieve something, rather than doing something that is obvious. ☐ *They had obviously been hoping to approach the topic with more subtlety.*

sub|to|tal /sʌbtoʊtᵊl/ (**subtotals**) N-COUNT A **subtotal** is a figure that is the result of adding some numbers together but is not the final total. ❑ ...the subtotals for each category of investments.

sub|tract /səbtrækt/ (**subtracts, subtracting, subtracted**) V-T If you **subtract** one number from another, you do a calculation in which you take it away from the other number. For example, if you subtract 3 from 5, you get 2. ❑ Mandy subtracted the date of birth from the date of death. • **sub|trac|tion** /səbtrækʃᵊn/ (**subtractions**) N-VAR ❑ She's ready to learn simple addition and subtraction.

sub|tropi|cal /sʌbtrɒpɪkᵊl/ ADJ **Subtropical** places have a climate that is warm and wet, and are often near tropical regions. ❑ ...the subtropical region of the Chapare.

sub|urb /sʌbɜrb/ (**suburbs**) **1** N-COUNT A **suburb** of a city or large town is a smaller area which is part of the city or large town but is outside its center. ❑ Anna was born in 1923 in a suburb of Philadelphia. **2** N-PLURAL If you live in the **suburbs**, you live in an area of houses outside the center of a city or large town. ❑ His family lived in the suburbs.

sub|ur|ban /səbɜrbən/ ADJ [ADJ n] **Suburban** means relating to a suburb. ❑ ...a comfortable suburban home.

sub|ur|bia /səbɜrbiə/ N-UNCOUNT Journalists often use **suburbia** to refer to the suburbs of cities and large towns considered as a whole. ❑ ...summer mornings in leafy suburbia.

sub|ver|sion /səbvɜrʒᵊn/ N-UNCOUNT **Subversion** is the attempt to weaken or destroy a political system or a government. ❑ He was arrested on charges of subversion for organizing the demonstration.

sub|ver|sive /səbvɜrsɪv/ (**subversives**) **1** ADJ Something that is **subversive** is intended to weaken or destroy a political system or government. ❑ The play was promptly banned as subversive and possibly treasonous. **2** N-COUNT **Subversives** are people who attempt to weaken or destroy a political system or government. ❑ Agents regularly rounded up suspected subversives.

sub|vert /səbvɜrt/ (**subverts, subverting, subverted**) V-T To **subvert** something means to destroy its power and influence. [FORMAL] ❑ ...an alleged plot to subvert the state.

sub|way /sʌbweɪ/ (**subways**) **1** N-COUNT [oft N n, also by N] A **subway** is an underground railroad. [mainly AM] ❑ I don't ride the subway late at night.

in BRIT, use **underground**

2 N-COUNT A **subway** is the same as an **underpass**. [BRIT]

sub|zero /sʌbzɪəroʊ/ ADJ **Subzero** temperatures are below 0° Fahrenheit. ❑ ...passengers stranded in subzero temperatures.

suc|ceed ♦♦◇ /səksid/ (**succeeds, succeeding, succeeded**) **1** V-I If you **succeed** in doing something, you manage to do it. ❑ We have already succeeded in working out ground rules with the Department of Defense. **2** V-I If something **succeeds**, it works in a satisfactory way or has the result that is intended. ❑ The talks can succeed if both sides are flexible and serious. **3** V-I Someone who **succeeds** gains a high position in what they do, for example in business or politics. ❑ ...the skills and qualities needed to succeed in small and medium-sized businesses. **4** V-T If you **succeed** another person, you are the next person to have their job or position. ❑ She is almost certain to succeed him as chairperson on January 1. **5** V-T [usu passive] If one thing is **succeeded** by another thing, the other thing happens or comes after it. ❑ The presentation was succeeded by a roundtable discussion. **6** → See feature box at **success**

suc|cess ♦♦◇ /səksɛs/ (**successes**) **1** N-UNCOUNT **Success** is the achievement of something that you have been trying to do. ❑ It's important for the success of any diet that you vary your meals. **2** N-UNCOUNT **Success** is the achievement of a high position in a particular field, for example in business or politics. ❑ We all believed that work was the key to success. **3** N-UNCOUNT The **success** of something is the fact that it works in a satisfactory way or has the result that is intended. ❑ We were amazed by the play's success. **4** N-COUNT Someone or something that is a **success** achieves a high position, makes a lot of money, or is admired a great deal. ❑ We hope it will be a commercial success.

COLLOCATIONS

success
NOUN
1
verb + **success**: achieve, enjoy, ensure; judge, measure
4
adjective + **success**: commercial, instant, runaway; huge, notable, phenomenal

---

VOCABULARY IN CONTEXT

Success and failure

In the 19th century, Thomas Edison famously invented the light bulb, but it was a **breakthrough** only after he had tried hundreds of experiments that failed. Edison didn't **give up**, and today we have the electric light. Wanting to **accomplish** an **aim** is natural. And of course it's normal to feel proud of our **achievements**. It's a good feeling when we meet our goals, and it's **empowering** to **surmount obstacles**, to **persist**, to succeed! The 'never give up' philosophy is seen as one that is character-building; however, it's possible that too much emphasis is placed on **success**. The **pressure to succeed** can be intense, and can lead to anxiety and unhappiness. **Failure** has so many **negative connotations** that some people cannot **cope** with it, and that's not healthy. Every time we fail – and we all do – we can learn something from it. Just think of Thomas Edison and the light bulb.

---

suc|cess|ful ♦♦◇ /səksɛsfəl/ **1** ADJ Something that is **successful** achieves what it was intended to achieve. Someone who is **successful** achieves what they intended to achieve. ❑ How successful will this new treatment be? ❑ I am looking forward to a long and successful partnership with him. • **suc|cess|ful|ly** ADV [ADV with v] ❑ The doctors have successfully concluded preliminary tests. **2** ADJ Something that is **successful** is popular or makes a lot of money. ❑ ...the hugely successful movie that brought Robert Redford an Oscar for his directing. **3** ADJ Someone who is **successful** achieves a high position in what they do, for example in business or politics. ❑ Women do not have to imitate men to be successful.

suc|ces|sion /səksɛʃᵊn/ **1** N-SING [oft N of n, also in N] A **succession** of things of the same kind is a number of them that exist or happen one after the other. ❑ Adams took a succession of jobs which have stood him in good stead. **2** N-UNCOUNT **Succession** is the act or right of being the next person to have an important job or position. ❑ She is now seventh in line of succession to the throne.

suc|ces|sive /səksɛsɪv/ ADJ **Successive** means happening or existing one after another without a break. ❑ Jackson was the winner for a second successive year.

suc|ces|sor /səksɛsər/ (**successors**) N-COUNT Someone's **successor** is the person who takes their job after they have left. ❑ He set out several principles that he hopes will guide his successors.

suc|cess sto|ry (**success stories**) N-COUNT Someone or something that is a **success story** is very successful, often

succinct /səksɪŋkt/ ADJ Something that is **succinct** expresses facts or ideas clearly and in few words. [APPROVAL] ◻ *The book gives an admirably succinct account of the technology and its history.* • **suc|cinct|ly** ADV ◻ *He succinctly summed up his manifesto as "Work hard, train hard and play hard."*

suc|cor /sʌkər/ (succors, succoring, succored)

> in BRIT, use **succour**

1 N-UNCOUNT **Succor** is help given to people who are suffering or in difficulties. [FORMAL] ◻ *...a commitment to give succor to populations involved in the conflict.* **2** V-T If you **succor** someone who is suffering or in difficulties, you help them. [FORMAL] ◻ *Helicopters fly in appalling weather to succor shipwrecked mariners.*

suc|cu|lent /sʌkyələnt/ ADJ **Succulent** food, especially meat or vegetables, is juicy and good to eat. [APPROVAL] ◻ *Cook pieces of succulent chicken with ample garlic and a little sherry.*

suc|cumb /səkʌm/ (succumbs, succumbing, succumbed) V-I If you **succumb to** temptation or pressure, you do something that you want to do, or that other people want you to do, although you feel it might be wrong. [FORMAL] ◻ *Don't succumb to the temptation to have just one cigarette.*

such ♦♦♦ /sʌtʃ/

> When **such** is used as a predeterminer, it is followed by 'a' and a count noun in the singular. When it is used as a determiner, it is followed by a count noun in the plural or by an uncountable noun.

1 DET You use **such** to refer back to the thing or person that you have just mentioned, or a thing or person like the one that you have just mentioned. You use **such as** and **such...as** to introduce a reference to the person or thing that has just been mentioned. ◻ *There have been previous attempts at coups. We regard such methods as entirely unacceptable.* • PREDET [PREDET *a* n] **Such** is also a predeterminer. ◻ *If your request is for information about a child, please contact the registrar to find out how to make such a request.* ◻ *She has told us that when she goes back to stay with her family, they make her pay rent. We could not believe such a thing.* • PRON **Such** is also a pronoun used before **be**. ◻ *We are scared because we are being watched – such is the atmosphere in Pristina and other cities in Kosovo.* **2** DET You use **such...as** or **such as** to link something or someone with a clause in which you give a description of the kind of thing or person that you mean. ◻ *...incentive payments for such activities as planting hardwood trees.* ◻ *Children do not use inflections such as are used in mature adult speech.* **3** DET You use **such...as** or **such as** to introduce one or more examples of the kind of thing or person that you have just mentioned. ◻ *...such careers as teaching, nursing, hairdressing and catering.* ◻ *...serious offenses, such as assault on a police officer.* **4** DET You use **such** before noun groups to emphasize the extent of something or to emphasize that something is remarkable. [EMPHASIS] ◻ *I think most of us don't want to read what's in the newspaper anyway in such detail.* ◻ *One will never be able to understand why these political issues can acquire such force.* • PREDET [PREDET *a* n] **Such** is also a predeterminer. ◻ *It was such a pleasant surprise.* **5** PREDET [PREDET *a* n that] You use **such...that** or **such that** in order to emphasize the degree of something by mentioning the result or consequence of it. [EMPHASIS] ◻ *This is something where you can earn such a lot of money that there is not any risk that you will lose it.* ◻ *Though Vivaldi had earned a great deal in his lifetime, his extravagance was such that he died in poverty.* • DET **Such** is also a determiner. ◻ *She looked at him in such distress that he had to look away.* **6** DET You use **such...that** or **such that** in order to say what the result or consequence of something that you have just mentioned is. ◻ *The operation has uncovered such backstreet dealing in stolen property that police might now press for changes in the law.* ◻ *Their cost structure is such that they just can't compete with the low-cost carriers.* • PREDET [PREDET *a* n that/*as* to] **Such** is also a predeterminer. ◻ *He could put an idea in such a way that Alan would believe it was his own.* **7** PHRASE You use **such and such** to refer to a thing or person when you do not want to be exact or precise. [SPOKEN, VAGUENESS] ◻ *I said, "Well, what time'll I get to Baltimore?" and he said such and such a time but I missed my connection.* **8** PHRASE You use **as such** with a negative to indicate that a word or expression is not a very accurate description of the actual situation. ◻ *I am not a learner as such – I used to ride a bike years ago.* **9** PHRASE You use **as such** after a noun to indicate that you are considering that thing on its own, separately from other things or factors. ◻ *Mr. Simon said he was not against taxes as such, "but I do object when taxation is justified on spurious or dishonest grounds," he says.* **10** **no such thing** → see **thing** ②

such|like /sʌtʃlaɪk/ PRON You use **suchlike** to refer to other things that are like the ones you have already mentioned. ◻ *...objets d'art, gold, silver, and ivory assortments, ceramics, and suchlike.* • DET **Suchlike** is also a determiner. ◻ *The prices of polymers and suchlike materials will decrease.*

suck /sʌk/ (sucks, sucking, sucked) **1** V-T/V-I If you **suck** something, you hold it in your mouth and pull at it with the muscles in your cheeks and tongue, for example in order to get liquid out of it. ◻ *They waited in silence and sucked their sweets.* ◻ *He sucked on his cigarette.* **2** V-T If something **sucks** a liquid, gas, or object in a particular direction, it draws it there with a powerful force. ◻ *The pollution-control team is at the scene and is due to start sucking up oil any time now.* **3** V-T PASSIVE If you **are sucked** into a bad situation, you are unable to prevent yourself from becoming involved in it. ◻ *...the extent to which they have been sucked into the cycle of violence.*

suck|er /sʌkər/ (suckers, suckering, suckered) **1** N-COUNT; N-VOC If you call someone a **sucker**, you mean that it is very easy to cheat them. [INFORMAL, DISAPPROVAL] ◻ *But that is what the suckers want so you give it them.* **2** N-COUNT [N *for* n] If you describe someone as a **sucker for** something, you mean that they find it very difficult to resist it. [INFORMAL] ◻ *I'm such a sucker for romance.* **3** V-T If you **sucker** a person into doing something, you deceive them, usually so that they do something that is against their own interests. [mainly AM] ◻ *If you tell those folks the truth, they won't vote for you. But if you sucker them, they'll vote for you twice over.* ◻ *It is becoming harder for the authorities to sucker healthy banks into taking over smaller ones.* **4** N-COUNT The **suckers** on some animals and insects are the parts on the outside of their body which they use in order to stick to a surface. **5** N-COUNT A **sucker** is a small device used for attaching things to surfaces. It consists of a cup-shaped piece of rubber that sticks to a surface when it is pressed flat. ◻ *...sucker pads.*

suck|le /sʌkəl/ (suckles, suckling, suckled) **1** V-T When a mother **suckles** her baby, she feeds it by letting it suck milk from her breast. [OLD-FASHIONED] ◻ *A young woman suckling a baby is one of life's most natural and delightful scenes.* **2** V-I When a baby **suckles**, it sucks milk from its mother's breast. [FORMAL] ◻ *As the baby suckles, a further supply of milk is generated.*

su|crose /sukroʊs/ N-UNCOUNT **Sucrose** is a common type of sugar. [TECHNICAL]

suc|tion /sʌkʃən/ (suctions, suctioning, suctioned) **1** N-UNCOUNT **Suction** is the process by which liquids, gases, or other substances are drawn out of somewhere. ◻ *Dust bags act as a filter and suction will be reduced if they are too full.* **2** V-T It a doctor or nurse **suctions** a liquid, they remove it by using a machine which sucks it away. ◻ *Michael was showing the nurse how to suction his saliva.* **3** N-UNCOUNT [oft N n] **Suction** is the process by which two surfaces stick together when the air between them is removed. ◻ *...their pneumatic robot which uses air to move and sticks to surfaces by suction.*

Su|da|nese /sudəniːz/ (Sudanese) **1** ADJ **Sudanese** means belonging or relating to Sudan, or to its people or culture. **2** N-PLURAL The **Sudanese** are the people of Sudan.

sud|den ♦◇◇ /sʌdən/ **1** ADJ **Sudden** means happening quickly and unexpectedly. ◻ *He had been deeply affected by the sudden death of his father-in-law.* ◻ *It was all very sudden.* • **sud|den|ness** N-UNCOUNT ◻ *The enemy seemed stunned by the suddenness of the attack.* **2** PHRASE If something happens **all of a sudden**, it happens quickly and unexpectedly. ◻ *All of a sudden she didn't look sleepy any more.*

SYNONYMS

sudden
ADJ **1**
hasty: *They have airplane tickets in case they need to make a hasty escape.*
rapid: *...the rapid decline in the birth rate in Western Europe.*
abrupt: *His abrupt departure is bound to raise questions.*

sud|den death N-UNCOUNT [oft N N] **Sudden death** is a way of quickly deciding the winner of something such as a basketball game or a golf tournament when there are equal scores at the time when it would normally end. In a **sudden-death** situation, the first team to score or the first golfer to win a hole is the winner.

sud|den|ly ♦♦◇ /sʌdᵊnli/ ADV If something happens **suddenly**, it happens quickly and unexpectedly. ❑ *Suddenly, she looked ten years older.* ❑ *Her expression suddenly altered.*

su|do|ku /sudouku/ (**sudokus**) N-VAR **Sudoku** is a type of puzzle in which certain numbers must be arranged within a grid. The aim is to avoid repeating any number in the same row or column.

suds /sʌdz/ N-PLURAL **Suds** are the bubbles that are produced when a substance such as soap is mixed with water. ❑ *He had soap suds in his ears.*

sue /su/ (**sues, suing, sued**) V-T/V-I If you **sue** someone, you start a legal case against them, usually in order to claim money from them because they have harmed you in some way. ❑ *Mr. Warren sued for libel over the remarks.* ❑ *The company could be sued for damages.*

suede /sweɪd/ N-UNCOUNT **Suede** is leather with a soft, slightly rough surface. ❑ *Albert wore a brown suede jacket and jeans.*

suet /suɪt/ N-UNCOUNT [oft N N] **Suet** is hard animal fat that is used in cooking.

suf|fer ♦♦◇ /sʌfər/ (**suffers, suffering, suffered**) ■ V-T/V-I If you **suffer** pain, you feel it in your body or in your mind. ❑ *Within a few days she had become seriously ill, suffering great pain and discomfort.* ❑ *He suffered terribly the last few days.* ■ V-I If you **suffer from** an illness or from some other bad condition, you are badly affected by it. ❑ *He was eventually diagnosed as suffering from terminal cancer.* ■ V-T If you **suffer** something bad, you are in a situation in which something painful, harmful, or very unpleasant happens to you. ❑ *The peace process has suffered a serious blow now.* ■ V-I If you **suffer**, you are badly affected by an event or situation. ❑ *There are few who have not suffered.* ■ V-I If something **suffers**, it becomes worse because it has not been given enough attention or is in a bad situation. ❑ *I'm not surprised that your studies are suffering.*

> **SYNONYMS**
>
> **suffer**
> VERB ■
> **undergo:** *He underwent an agonizing 48-hour wait for the results of tests.*
> **go through:** *He was going through a very difficult time.*
> **endure:** *The company endured heavy financial losses.*

suf|fer|ance /sʌfrəns/ N-UNCOUNT [usu on N] If you are allowed to do something on **sufferance**, you can do it, although you know that the person who gave you permission would prefer that you did not do it. ❑ *His party held office on sufferance.*

suf|fer|er /sʌfərər/ (**sufferers**) N-COUNT [oft N from/of N, N N] A **sufferer** from an illness or some other bad condition is a person who is affected by the illness or condition. ❑ *Frequently sufferers of this kind of allergy are also sufferers of asthma.* ❑ *...hay-fever sufferers.*

suf|fer|ing /sʌfərɪŋ/ (**sufferings**) ■ N-UNCOUNT [also N in pl] **Suffering** is serious pain which someone feels in their body or their mind. ❑ *They began to recover slowly from their nightmare of pain and suffering.* ❑ *It has caused terrible suffering to animals.* ■ → see also **long-suffering**

suf|fice /səfaɪs/ (**suffices, sufficing, sufficed**) ■ V-I [no cont] If you say that something will **suffice**, you mean it will be enough to achieve a purpose or to fulfill a need. [FORMAL] ❑ *A cover letter should never exceed one page; often a far shorter letter will suffice.* ■ PHRASE **Suffice it to say** or **suffice to say** is used at the beginning of a statement to indicate that what you are saying is obvious, or that you will only give a short explanation. ❑ *Suffice it to say that afterwards we never met again.*

suf|fi|cien|cy /səfɪʃᵊnsi/ ■ N-UNCOUNT [also a N, oft N of n] **Sufficiency** of something is enough of that thing to achieve a purpose or to fulfill a need. [FORMAL] ❑ *There's a sufficiency of drama in these lives to sustain your interest.* ■ → see also **self-sufficiency**

suf|fi|cient ♦◇◇ /səfɪʃᵊnt/ ADJ If something is **sufficient** for a particular purpose, there is enough of it for the purpose. ❑ *One yard of fabric is sufficient to cover the exterior of an 18-in.-diameter hatbox.* ❑ *Lighting levels should be sufficient for photography without flash.* ● **suf|fi|cient|ly** ADV ❑ *She recovered sufficiently to accompany Chou on his tour of Africa in 1964.*

> **SYNONYMS**
>
> **sufficient**
> ADJ
> **adequate:** *The old methods weren't adequate to meet current needs.*
> **enough:** *They had enough cash for a one-way ticket.*
> **ample:** *There'll be ample opportunity to relax, swim, and soak up some sun.*

suf|fix /sʌfɪks/ (**suffixes**) N-COUNT A **suffix** is a letter or group of letters, for example '-ly' or '-ness,' which is added to the end of a word in order to form a different word, often of a different word class. For example, the suffix '-ly' is added to 'quick' to form 'quickly.' Compare **affix** and **prefix**.

suf|fo|cate /sʌfəkeɪt/ (**suffocates, suffocating, suffocated**) ■ V-T/V-I If someone **suffocates** or **is suffocated**, they die because there is no air for them to breathe. ❑ *He either suffocated, or froze to death.* ● **suf|fo|ca|tion** /sʌfəkeɪʃᵊn/ N-UNCOUNT ❑ *Many of the victims died of suffocation.* ■ V-T/V-I If you say that you **are suffocating** or that something **is suffocating** you, you mean that you feel very uncomfortable because there is not enough fresh air and it is difficult to breathe. ❑ *That's better. I was suffocating in that cell of a room.*

suf|frage /sʌfrɪdʒ/ ■ N-UNCOUNT **Suffrage** is the right of people to vote for a government or national leader. [FORMAL] ❑ *...the women's suffrage movement.* ■ → See feature box at **politics**

suf|fra|gette /sʌfrədʒɛt/ (**suffragettes**) N-COUNT In the early twentieth century in the United States, a **suffragette** was a woman who was involved in the campaign for women to have the right to vote. ❑ *She was a suffragette and a birth control pioneer.*

suf|fra|gist /sʌfrədʒɪst/ (**suffragists**) N-COUNT A **suffragist** is a person who is in favor of women having the right to vote, especially in societies where women are not allowed to vote. [mainly AM]

suf|fuse /səfyuz/ (**suffuses, suffusing, suffused**) ■ V-T If something, especially a color or feeling, **suffuses** a person or thing, it gradually spreads over or through them. [LITERARY] ❑ *A dull red flush suffused Selby's face.* ■ V-T If something such as a book, movie, or piece of music **is suffused** with a quality, it is full of that quality. [FORMAL] ❑ *This book is suffused with Shaw's characteristic wry Irish humor.*

Sufi /sufi/ (**Sufis**) N-COUNT [oft N N] A **Sufi** is a member of a very spiritual group of Muslims. ❑ *...the teachings of the Sufi mystics.*

sug|ar ♦◇◇ /ʃʊgər/ (**sugars**) ■ N-UNCOUNT **Sugar** is a sweet substance that is used to make food and drinks sweet. It is usually in the form of small white or brown crystals. ❑ *...bags of sugar.* ■ N-COUNT If someone has one **sugar** in their tea or coffee, they have one small spoon of sugar or one sugar lump in it. ❑ *How many sugars do you take?* ■ N-COUNT **Sugars** are substances that occur naturally in food. When you eat them, the body converts them into energy. ❑ *Plants produce sugars and starch to provide themselves with energy.*

sug|ar beet (**sugar beets**) N-VAR **Sugar beet** is a crop with a large round root. It is grown for the sugar which can be obtained from this root.

sug|ar bowl (**sugar bowls**) N-COUNT A **sugar bowl** is a small bowl in which sugar is kept.

sug|ar cane also **sugarcane** N-UNCOUNT **Sugar cane** is a tall tropical plant. It is grown for the sugar that can be obtained from its thick stems.

sugar-coated ■ ADJ [usu ADJ n] **Sugar-coated** food is covered with a sweet substance made of sugar. ❑ *Some sugar-coated cereals are 50% sugar.* ■ ADJ [usu ADJ n] If you describe something such as a story as **sugar-coated**, you disapprove of it because it appears to be pleasant or attractive but in fact describes something very unpleasant. [DISAPPROVAL] ❑ *...a sugar-coated view of a boy's introduction to sex.*

sug|ar dad|dy (sugar daddies) also **sugar-daddy** N-COUNT [usu poss N] A woman's **sugar daddy** is a rich older man who gives her money and presents in return for her company, affection, and usually a sexual relationship. [INFORMAL] ❑ *He was viewed as her sugar daddy.*

sug|ared al|mond (sugared almonds) N-COUNT [usu pl] **Sugared almonds** are nuts which have been covered with a hard sweet coating.

sug|ar lump (sugar lumps) also **sugar-lump** N-COUNT **Sugar lumps** are small cubes of sugar. You put them in cups of tea and coffee.

sug|ar rush (sugar rushes) N-COUNT If you get a **sugar rush**, you suddenly feel excited or full of energy after having eaten food with a lot of sugar in it. ❑ *Some kids get a sugar rush when they eat candy.*

sug|ary /ʃʊgəri/ ADJ [usu ADJ n] **Sugary** food or drink contains a lot of sugar. ❑ *Sugary canned drinks rot your teeth.* ❑ *...sugary tea.*

sug|gest ✦✦✦ /səgdʒɛst/ (suggests, suggesting, suggested) **1** V-T If you **suggest** something, you put forward a plan or idea for someone to think about. ❑ *He suggested a link between class size and test results of seven-year-olds.* ❑ *I suggest you ask him some specific questions about his past.* ❑ *No one has suggested how this might occur.* **2** V-T If you **suggest** the name of a person or place, you recommend them to someone. ❑ *Could you suggest someone to advise me how to do this?* **3** V-T If you **suggest** that something is the case, you say something which you believe is the case. ❑ *I'm not suggesting that is what is happening.* ❑ *It is wrong to suggest that there are easy alternatives.* **4** V-T If one thing **suggests** another, it implies it or makes you think that it might be the case. ❑ *Earlier reports suggested that a meeting would take place on Sunday.*

USAGE

suggest
Don't use the name of a person directly after **suggest**. If you want to say who the suggestion is for, use **to**. Don't say, for example 'John suggested me the idea.' Say 'John suggested the idea **to me**.'

---

sug|gest|ible /səgdʒɛstɪbəl/ ADJ Someone who is **suggestible** can be easily influenced by other people. ❑ *...highly suggestible and compliant individuals.*

sug|ges|tion ✦◇◇ /səgdʒɛstʃən/ (suggestions) **1** N-COUNT If you make a **suggestion**, you put forward an idea or plan for someone to think about. ❑ *The dietitian was helpful, making suggestions as to how I could improve my diet.* ❑ *Perhaps he'd followed her suggestion of a stroll to the river.* **2** N-COUNT A **suggestion** is something that a person says which implies that something is the case. ❑ *We reject any suggestion that the law needs amending.* **3** N-SING If there is no **suggestion** that something is the case, there is no reason to think that it is the case. ❑ *There is no suggestion whatsoever that the two sides are any closer to agreeing.*

sug|ges|tive /səgdʒɛstɪv/ **1** ADJ [v-link ADJ of n] Something that is **suggestive of** something else is quite like it or may be a sign of it. ❑ *The fingers were gnarled, lumpy, with long, curving nails suggestive of animal claws.* **2** ADJ **Suggestive** remarks or looks cause people to think about sex, often in a way that makes them feel uncomfortable. ❑ *...another former employee who claims Thomas made suggestive remarks to her.*

sui|cid|al /suːɪsaɪdəl/ ADJ People who are **suicidal** want to kill themselves. ❑ *I was suicidal and just couldn't stop crying.*

sui|cide ✦◇◇ /suːɪsaɪd/ (suicides) N-VAR People who commit **suicide** deliberately kill themselves because they do not want to continue living. ❑ *She tried to commit suicide on several occasions.* ❑ *...a case of attempted suicide.*

COLLOCATIONS

suicide
NOUN
noun + **suicide**: copycat; mass
adjective + **suicide**: apparent, suspected; assisted
verb + **suicide**: attempt, commit, contemplate, consider; prevent

---

sui|cide bomb|er (suicide bombers) N-COUNT A **suicide bomber** is a terrorist who carries out a bomb attack, knowing that he or she will be killed in the explosion. ❑ *The blast was caused by a suicide bomber.*

sui|cide note (suicide notes) N-COUNT A **suicide note** is a note written by someone who intends to kill themselves saying that this is what they are going to do and sometimes explaining why.

sui|cide pact (suicide pacts) N-COUNT A **suicide pact** is an arrangement that two or more people make to kill themselves at the same time and usually in the same place. ❑ *Police refused to say if the couple died in a suicide pact.*

sui|cide vest (suicide vests) N-COUNT A **suicide vest** is a jacket with explosives attached to it, worn by a terrorist in order to carry out a bomb attack, knowing that he or she will be killed in the explosion. ❑ *A bomber wearing a suicide vest walked up to a group of police officers.*

sui gen|eris /suːi dʒɛnərɪs/ ADJ If you describe a person or thing as **sui generis**, you mean that there is no one else or nothing else of the same kind and so you cannot make judgments about them based on other things. [FORMAL] ❑ *Japanese politics are sui generis.*

suit ✦✦◇ /suːt/ (suits, suiting, suited) **1** N-COUNT A man's **suit** consists of a jacket, pants, and sometimes a vest, all made from the same fabric. ❑ *...a dark pin-striped business suit.* **2** N-COUNT A woman's **suit** consists of a jacket and skirt or trousers, made from the same fabric. ❑ *I was wearing my tweed suit.* **3** N-COUNT A particular type of **suit** is a piece of clothing that you wear for a particular activity. ❑ *The six survivors only lived through their ordeal because of the special rubber suits they were wearing.* **4** V-T [no cont] If something **suits** you, it is convenient for you or is the best thing for you in the circumstances. ❑ *They will only release information if it suits them.* **5** V-T [no cont] If something **suits** you, you like it. ❑ *I don't think a sedentary life would altogether suit me.* **6** V-T [no cont] If a piece of clothing or a particular style or color **suits** you, it makes you look attractive. ❑ *Green suits you.* **7** V-T If you **suit** yourself, you do something just because you want to do it, without bothering to consider other people. ❑ *People have tended to suit themselves, not paying much heed to the reformers.* **8** N-COUNT In a court of law, a **suit** is a case in which someone tries to get a legal decision against a person or company, often so that the person or company will have to pay them money for having done something wrong to them. ❑ *Up to 2,000 former employees have filed personal injury suits against the company.* • N-UNCOUNT You can also say that someone files or brings **suit** against another person. ❑ *One insurance company has already filed suit against the city of Chicago.* **9** → see also **pantsuit** **10** PHRASE If people **follow suit**, they do the same thing that someone else has just done. ❑ *Efforts to persuade the remainder to follow suit have continued.* **11** → See feature box at **fashion**

suit|able ✦◇◇ /suːtəbəl/ ADJ Someone or something that is **suitable** for a particular purpose or occasion is right or acceptable for it. ❑ *Employers usually decide within five minutes whether someone is suitable for the job.* • **suit|abil|ity** /suːtəbɪlɪti/ N-UNCOUNT ❑ *...information on the suitability of a product for use in the home.*

suit|ably /suːtəbli/ ADV [ADV adj/-ed] You use **suitably** to indicate that someone or something has the right qualities or things for a particular activity, purpose, or situation. ❑ *There are problems in recruiting suitably qualified scientific officers for our laboratories.*

suit|case /suːtkeɪs/ (suitcases) **1** N-COUNT A **suitcase** is a box or bag with a handle and a hard frame in which you carry your clothes when you are traveling. ❑ *It did not take Andrew long to pack a suitcase.* **2** → See also color supplement

suite /swiːt/ (suites) **1** N-COUNT A **suite** is a set of rooms in a hotel or other building. ❑ *They had a fabulous time during their week in a suite at the Paris Hilton.* **2** N-COUNT A **suite** is a set of matching furniture. ❑ *...a three-piece suite.* **3** N-COUNT A bathroom **suite** is a matching bathtub, sink, and toilet. ❑ *...the horrible pink suite in the bathroom.*

suit|ed /suːtɪd/ ADJ [v-link ADJ] If something is well **suited** to a particular purpose, it is right or appropriate for that purpose. If someone is well **suited** to a particular job, they are right or appropriate for that job. ❑ *The area is well suited to road cycling as well as off-road riding.*

suit|ing /sˈuːtɪŋ/ (**suitings**) N-MASS **Suiting** is cloth from which pants, jackets, skirts, and men's suits are made.

suit|or /sˈuːtər/ (**suitors**) ◼ N-COUNT A person's **suitor** is someone who wants to marry them. [OLD-FASHIONED] ❑ *My mother had a suitor who adored her.* ◼ N-COUNT A **suitor** is a company or organization that wants to buy another company. [BUSINESS] ❑ *The company was making little progress in trying to find a suitor.*

sul|fate /sˈʌlfeɪt/ (**sulfates**)

in BRIT, use **sulphate**

N-MASS [oft n N, N of n] A **sulfate** is a salt of sulfuric acid.

sul|fide /sˈʌlfaɪd/ (**sulfides**)

in BRIT, use **sulphide**

N-MASS [oft n N] A **sulfide** is a compound of sulfur with some other chemical elements. ❑ *...hydrogen sulfide.*

sul|fur /sˈʌlfər/

in BRIT, use **sulphur**

N-UNCOUNT **sulfur** is a yellow chemical which has a strong smell. ❑ *Burning sulfur creates poisonous fumes.*

sul|fu|ric acid /sʌlfjˈʊərɪk æsɪd/

in BRIT, use **sulphuric acid**

N-UNCOUNT **Sulfuric acid** is a colorless, oily, and very powerful acid.

sul|fur|ous /sˈʌlfərəs/

in BRIT, use **sulphurous**

ADJ [usu ADJ n] **Sulfurous** air or places contain sulfur or smell of sulfur. ❑ *...sulfurous volcanic gases.* ❑ *...a sulfurous spring.*

sulk /sˈʌlk/ (**sulks, sulking, sulked**) V-I If you **sulk**, you are silent and bad-tempered for a while because you are annoyed about something. ❑ *He turned his back and sulked.* • N-COUNT **Sulk** is also a noun. ❑ *He went off in a sulk.*

sulky /sˈʌlki/ (**sulkier, sulkiest**) ADJ Someone who is **sulky** is sulking or is unwilling to enjoy themselves. ❑ *I was quite sulky, so I didn't take part in much.* ❑ *...a sulky adolescent.*

sul|len /sˈʌlən/ ADJ Someone who is **sullen** is bad-tempered and does not speak much. ❑ *The offenders lapsed into a sullen silence.*

sul|ly /sˈʌli/ (**sullies, sullying, sullied**) ◼ V-T If something is **sullied** by something else, it is damaged so that it is no longer pure or of such high value. [FORMAL] ❑ *Its image has been sullied by $9 billion in improper accounting.* ❑ *She claimed they were sullying her good name.* ◼ V-T If someone **sullies** something, they make it dirty. [FORMAL] ❑ *I felt loath to sully the gleaming brass knocker by handling it.*

sul|phate /sˈʌlfeɪt/ [mainly BRIT] → see **sulfate**
sul|phide /sˈʌlfaɪd/ [mainly BRIT] → see **sulfide**
sul|phur /sˈʌlfər/ [mainly BRIT] → see **sulfur**
sul|phu|ric acid /sʌlfjˈʊərɪk æsɪd/ [mainly BRIT] → see **sulfuric acid**
sul|phur|ous /sˈʌlfərəs/ [mainly BRIT] → see **sulfurous**

sul|tan /sˈʌltən/ (**sultans**) N-TITLE; N-COUNT A **sultan** is a ruler in some Muslim countries. ❑ *...during the reign of Sultan Abdul Hamid.*

sul|try /sˈʌltri/ (**sultrier, sultriest**) ◼ ADJ **Sultry** weather is hot and damp. [WRITTEN] ❑ *The climax came one sultry August evening.* ◼ ADJ Someone who is **sultry** is attractive in a way that suggests hidden passion. [WRITTEN] ❑ *...a dark-haired sultry woman.*

sum ✦✧✧ /sˈʌm/ (**sums, summing, summed**) ◼ N-COUNT A **sum** of money is an amount of money. ❑ *Large sums of money were lost.* ◼ N-SING In mathematics, **the sum of** two or more numbers is the number that is obtained when they are added together. ❑ *The sum of all the angles of a triangle is 180 degrees.* ◼ N-SING **The sum of** something is all of it. You often use **sum** in this way to indicate that you are disappointed because the extent of something is rather small, or because it is not very good. ❑ *To date, the sum of my gardening experience had been futile* efforts to rid the flower beds of grass. ◼ N-COUNT A **sum** is a simple calculation in arithmetic. [BRIT] ◼ → see also **lump sum**

▶ **sum up** ◼ PHRASAL VERB If you **sum** something **up**, you describe it as briefly as possible. ❑ *One voter in Brasilia summed up the mood – "Politicians have lost credibility," he complained.* ◼ PHRASAL VERB If something **sums** a person or situation **up**, it represents their most typical characteristics. ❑ *"I love my wife, my horse and my dog," he said, and that summed him up.* ◼ PHRASAL VERB If you **sum up** after a speech or at the end of a piece of writing, you briefly state the main points again. When a judge **sums up** after a trial, he or she reminds the jury of the evidence and the main arguments of the case they have heard. ❑ *When the judge summed up, it was clear he wanted a guilty verdict.*

COLLOCATIONS

sum
NOUN ◼

adjective + **sum**: princely, substantial, tiny, vast; fixed, six-figure, undisclosed
verb + **sum**: invest, pay, spend; borrow, owe; raise, receive

SYNONYMS

sum
NOUN
◼
amount: *He needs that amount of money to survive.*
quantity: *...a small quantity of water.*
volume: *Senior officials will be discussing how the volume of sales might be reduced.*
◼
total: *The companies have a total of 1,776 employees.*
aggregate: *...society viewed as an aggregate of individuals.*
tally: *The final tally was 817 votes for her and 731 for Mr Lee.*

sum|ma cum lau|de /sˈʊmɑ kʊm lˈaʊdeɪ/ ADV If a college student graduates **summa cum laude**, they receive the highest honor that is possible. [AM] ❑ *Jeremy Heyl graduated summa cum laude with a degree in Astrophysics.* • ADJ [ADJ n] **Summa cum laude** is also an adjective. ❑ *...a summa cum laude graduate of Princeton.*

sum|ma|rize /sˈʌməraɪz/ (**summarizes, summarizing, summarized**)

in BRIT, also use **summarise**

V-T/V-I If you **summarize** something, you give a summary of it. ❑ *Table 3.1 summarizes the information given above.* ❑ *Basically, the article can be summarized in three sentences.*

sum|mary /sˈʌməri/ (**summaries**) ◼ N-COUNT A **summary** of something is a short account of it, which gives the main points but not the details. ❑ *What follows is a brief summary of the process.* • PHRASE You use **in summary** to indicate that what you are about to say is a summary of what has just been said. ❑ *In summary, it is my opinion that this complete treatment process was very successful.* ◼ ADJ [ADJ n] **Summary** actions are done without delay, often when something else should have been done first or done instead. [FORMAL] ❑ *It says torture and summary execution are common.*

sum|ma|tion /sʌmˈeɪʃən/ (**summations**) N-COUNT [usu sing, oft N of n] A **summation** is a summary of what someone has said or done. [FORMAL] ❑ *Her introduction is a model of fairness, a lively summation of Irish history.*

sum|mer ✦✦◇ /sˈʌmər/ (**summers**) N-VAR **Summer** is the season between spring and fall. In the summer the weather is usually warm or hot. ❑ *I escaped the heatwave in Washington earlier this summer and flew to Maine.* ❑ *It was a perfect summer's day.*

sum|mer camp (**summer camps**) N-COUNT A **summer camp** is a place in the country where parents can pay to send their children during the school summer vacation. The children staying there can take part in many outdoor and social activities.

sum|mer house (**summer houses**) ◼ N-COUNT Someone's **summer house** is a house in the country or by the sea where they spend the summer. ❑ *He visited relatives at their summer house on the river.* ◼ N-COUNT A **summer house** is a small building in a garden. It contains seats, and people can sit there in the summer.

sum|mer school (summer schools) **1** N-VAR **Summer school** is a summer term at a school, college, or university, for example for students who need extra teaching or who want to take extra courses. [mainly AM] **2** N-VAR A **summer school** is an educational course on a particular subject that is run during the summer. The students usually stay at the place where the summer school is being held. [mainly BRIT] ❏ ...*a summer school for young professional singers.*

sum|mer squash (summer squashes) N-COUNT A **summer squash** is a type of squash that is used after being picked rather than being stored for the winter. ❏ *The markets offer everything from golden summer squashes to brilliant sunflowers.*

sum|mer|time /sʌmərtaɪm/ N-UNCOUNT [also *the* N] **Summertime** is the period of time during which the summer lasts. ❏ *It's a very beautiful place in the summertime.*

sum|mery /sʌməri/ ADJ Something that is **summery** is suitable for summer or characteristic of summer. ❏ ...*light summery fruit salads.*

summing-up (summings-up) also **summing up** N-COUNT In a trial, the judge's **summing-up** is the speech the judge makes at the end of the trial to remind the jury of the evidence and the main arguments of the case they have heard. ❏ *There was pandemonium in court as the judge gave his summing-up.*

sum|mit ♦♢♢ /sʌmɪt/ (summits) **1** N-COUNT A **summit** is a meeting at which the leaders of two or more countries discuss important matters. ❏ ...*next week's Washington summit.* **2** N-COUNT The **summit** of a mountain is the top of it. ❏ ...*the first man to reach the summit of Mount Everest.*

sum|mon /sʌmən/ (summons, summoning, summoned) **1** V-T If you **summon** someone, you order them to come to you. [FORMAL] ❏ *Howe summoned a doctor and hurried over.* ❏ *Suddenly we were summoned to the interview room.* **2** V-T If you **summon** a quality, you make a great effort to have it. For example, if you **summon** the courage or strength to do something, you make a great effort to be brave or strong, so that you will be able to do it. ❏ *It took her a full month to summon the courage to tell her mother.* • PHRASAL VERB **Summon up** means the same as **summon**. ❏ *Painfully shy, he finally summoned up courage to ask her to a game.*

sum|mons /sʌmənz/ (summonses) **1** N-COUNT A **summons** is an order to come and see someone. ❏ *I received a summons to the Warden's office.* **2** N-COUNT A **summons** is an official order to appear in court. ❏ *She had received a summons to appear in court.*

sumo /sumoʊ/ N-UNCOUNT [oft N n] **Sumo** is the Japanese style of wrestling. ❏ ...*a sumo wrestler.*

sump /sʌmp/ (sumps) **1** N-COUNT A **sump** is a low-lying open area where waste water gathers. **2** N-COUNT A **sump** is a deep cave which is often filled with water. **3** N-COUNT The **sump** is the place under an engine which holds the engine oil. [mainly BRIT]

in AM, use **oil pan**

sump|tu|ous /sʌmptʃuəs/ ADJ Something that is **sumptuous** is grand and obviously very expensive. ❏ ...*a sumptuous feast.*

sum to|tal N-SING [usu *the* N *of* n] The **sum total** of a number of things is all the things added or considered together. You often use this expression to indicate that you are disappointed because the total amount is rather small. ❏ *That small room contained the sum total of the family's possessions.*

sun ♦♦♢ /sʌn/ **1** N-SING The **sun** is the ball of fire in the sky that the Earth goes around, and that gives us heat and light. ❏ *The sun was now high in the southern sky.* ❏ *The sun came out, briefly.* **2** N-UNCOUNT You refer to the light and heat that reach us from the sun as the **sun**. ❏ *Dena took them into the courtyard to sit in the sun.* **3** → See also color supplement

Sun. **Sun.** is a written abbreviation for **Sunday**. ❏ *The museum is open Mon.-Sun.*

sun-baked ADJ [ADJ n] **Sun-baked** land or earth has been made hard and dry by the sun shining on it. ❏ ...*a dry, sun-baked lawn.*

sun|bathe /sʌnbeɪð/ (sunbathes, sunbathing, sunbathed) V-I When people **sunbathe**, they sit or lie in a place where the sun shines on them, so that their skin becomes browner. ❏ *Franklin swam and sunbathed at the pool every morning.* • **sun|bath|ing** N-UNCOUNT ❏ *Nearby there is a stretch of white sand beach perfect for sunbathing.*

sun|beam /sʌnbim/ (sunbeams) N-COUNT A **sunbeam** is a ray of sunlight. ❏ *A sunbeam slants through the west window.*

sun|bed /sʌnbɛd/ (sunbeds) N-COUNT A **sunbed** is a piece of equipment with ultraviolet lights. You lie on it to make your skin browner.

sun|belt /sʌnbɛlt/ N-SING [usu *the* N] The warmer, sunnier parts of a country or continent, especially the southern United States, are sometimes referred to as the **sunbelt**. ❏ *During the last recession, migration to the sunbelt accelerated.*

sun|block /sʌnblɒk/ (sunblocks) N-MASS **Sunblock** is a cream which you put on your skin to protect it completely from the sun.

sun|burn /sʌnbɜrn/ (sunburns) N-VAR If someone has **sunburn**, their skin is bright pink and sore because they have spent too much time in hot sunshine. ❏ *The risk and severity of sunburn depend on the body's natural skin color.*

sun|burned /sʌnbɜrnd/ also **sunburnt** ADJ Someone who is **sunburned** has sore bright pink skin because they have spent too much time in hot sunshine. ❏ *A badly sunburned face or back is extremely painful.*

sun|burst /sʌnbɜrst/ (sunbursts) N-COUNT A **sunburst** is a pattern or design that resembles the sun with rays coming from it. ❏ ...*a bronze sunburst pendant.*

sun|dae /sʌndeɪ, -di/ (sundaes) N-COUNT [usu n N] A **sundae** is a tall glass of ice cream with whipped cream and nuts or fruit on top. ❏ ...*a chocolate sundae.*

Sun|day ♦♦♢ /sʌndeɪ, -di/ (Sundays) N-VAR **Sunday** is the day after Saturday and before Monday. ❏ *I thought we might go for a drive on Sunday.*

Sun|day best N-SING [POSS N] If you are in your **Sunday best**, you are wearing your best clothes, which you only wear for special occasions.

Sun|day school (Sunday schools) N-VAR **Sunday school** is a class organized by a church that some children go to on Sundays in order to learn about Christianity. ❏ ...*a Sunday School teacher.*

sun|der /sʌndər/ (sunders, sundering, sundered) V-T [usu passive] If people or things **are sundered**, they are separated or split by something. [LITERARY] ❏ *The city is being sundered by racial tension.* ❏ *Police moved in to separate the two groups, already sundered by distrust.*

sun|dial /sʌndaɪəl/ (sundials) **1** N-COUNT A **sundial** is a device used for telling the time when the sun is shining. The shadow of an upright rod falls onto a flat surface that is marked with the hours, and points to the correct hour. **2** → See also color supplement

sun|down /sʌndaʊn/ N-UNCOUNT **Sundown** is the time when the sun sets. [mainly AM] ❏ *The fighting broke out about two hours after sundown.*

sun-drenched also **sundrenched** ADJ [ADJ n] **Sun-drenched** places have a lot of hot sunshine. ❏ *He sat on the terrace of his sun-drenched villa in the South of France.*

sun|dries /sʌndriz/ N-PLURAL When someone is making a list of things, items that are not important enough to be listed separately are sometimes referred to together as **sundries**. [FORMAL] ❏ *The inn gift shop stocks quality Indian crafts and sundries.*

sun|dry /sʌndri/ **1** ADJ [ADJ n] If someone refers to **sundry** people or things, they are referring to several people or things that are all different from each other. [FORMAL] ❏ *Scientists, business people, and sundry others gathered on Monday for the official opening.* **2** PHRASE **All and sundry** means everyone. ❏ *I made tea for all and sundry at the office.*

sun|flower /sʌnflaʊər/ (sunflowers) N-COUNT A **sunflower** is a very tall plant with large yellow flowers. Oil from sunflower seeds is used in cooking and to make margarine.

sung /sʌŋ/ **Sung** is the past participle of **sing**.

sun|glasses /sʌnglæsɪz/ N-PLURAL [also *a pair of* N] **Sunglasses** are glasses with dark lenses which you wear to protect your eyes from bright sunlight. ❏ *She slipped on a pair of sunglasses.*

sun hat (sun hats) also **sunhat** N-COUNT A **sun hat** is a wide-brimmed hat that protects your head from the sun.

sunk /sʌŋk/ Sunk is the past participle of **sink**.

sunk|en /sʌŋkən/ **1** ADJ [ADJ n] **Sunken** ships have sunk to the bottom of a sea, ocean, or lake. ❑ *The sunken sail boat was a glimmer of white on the bottom.* **2** ADJ [ADJ n] **Sunken** gardens, roads, or other features are below the level of their surrounding area. ❑ *Steps lead down to the sunken garden.* **3** ADJ **Sunken** eyes, cheeks, or other parts of the body curve inward and make you look thin and unwell. ❑ *Her eyes were sunken and black-ringed.*

sun lamp (sun lamps) also **sunlamp** N-COUNT A **sun lamp** is a lamp that produces ultraviolet light. People use sun lamps to make their skin browner.

sun|less /sʌnlɪs/ **1** ADJ On **sunless** days, the sun does not shine. ❑ *The day dawned sunless and with a low cloud base.* **2** ADJ [ADJ n] **Sunless** places are not lit by the sun. ❑ *Carmen stayed behind in the dark, sunless room.*

sun|light /sʌnlaɪt/ N-UNCOUNT **Sunlight** is the light that comes from the sun during the day. ❑ *I saw her sitting at a window table, bathed in sunlight.*

sun|lit /sʌnlɪt/ ADJ [ADJ n] **Sunlit** places are brightly lit by the sun. ❑ *Her house has two big sunlit rooms with floor-to-ceiling windows.*

Sun|ni /suni/ (**Sunnis**) **1** N-UNCOUNT **Sunni** is the main branch of Islam. ❑ *The Ottoman empire was a Sunni state.* **2** N-COUNT A **Sunni** is a Muslim who follows the Sunni branch of Islam.

sun|ny /sʌni/ (**sunnier, sunniest**) **1** ADJ When it is **sunny**, the sun is shining brightly. ❑ *The weather was surprisingly warm and sunny.* **2** ADJ **Sunny** places are brightly lit by the sun. ❑ *Most roses like a sunny position in a fairly fertile soil.*

sun|rise /sʌnraɪz/ (**sunrises**) **1** N-UNCOUNT **Sunrise** is the time in the morning when the sun first appears in the sky. ❑ *The rain began before sunrise.* **2** N-COUNT A **sunrise** is the colors and light that you see in the eastern part of the sky when the sun first appears. ❑ *There was a spectacular sunrise yesterday.*

sun|roof /sʌnruːf/ (**sunroofs**) N-COUNT A **sunroof** is a panel in the roof of a car that opens to let sunshine and air enter the car. ❑ *...extras like a sunroof, a CD player, or chrome wheels.*

sun|screen /sʌnskriːn/ (**sunscreens**) N-MASS A **sunscreen** is a cream that protects your skin from the sun's rays, especially in hot weather. ❑ *Use a sunscreen suitable for your skin type.*

sun|set /sʌnsɛt/ (**sunsets**) **1** N-UNCOUNT **Sunset** is the time in the evening when the sun disappears out of sight from the sky. ❑ *The dance ends at sunset.* **2** N-COUNT A **sunset** is the colors and light that you see in the western part of the sky when the sun disappears in the evening. ❑ *There was a red sunset over Paris.*

sun|shine /sʌnʃaɪn/ N-UNCOUNT **Sunshine** is the light and heat that comes from the sun. ❑ *In the marina yachts sparkle in the sunshine.* ❑ *She was sitting outside a cafe in bright sunshine.*

sun|spot /sʌnspɒt/ (**sunspots**) N-COUNT **Sunspots** are dark cool patches that appear on the surface of the sun and last for about a week.

sun|stroke /sʌnstroʊk/ N-UNCOUNT **Sunstroke** is an illness caused by spending too much time in hot sunshine. ❑ *I was suffering from acute sunstroke, starvation and exhaustion.*

sun|tan /sʌntæn/ (**suntans**) **1** N-COUNT If you have a **suntan**, the sun has turned your skin an attractive brown color. ❑ *They want to go to the Bahamas and get a suntan.* **2** ADJ [ADJ n] **Suntan** lotion, oil, or cream protects your skin from the sun. ❑ *She playfully rubs suntan lotion on his neck.*

sun|tanned /sʌntænd/ ADJ Someone who is **suntanned** has an attractive brown color from being in the sun. ❑ *He is always suntanned and incredibly fit.*

sun|up /sʌnʌp/ N-UNCOUNT **Sunup** is the time of day when the sun rises. [AM] ❑ *We worked from sunup to sunset.*

in BRIT, use **sunrise**

sup /sʌp/ (**sups, supping, supped**) **1** V-T If you **sup** something, you drink it, especially in small amounts. [LITERARY, OLD-FASHIONED] ❑ *We supped mulled wine.* **2** V-I If you **sup**, you eat dinner in the evening. [LITERARY, OLD-FASHIONED] ❑ *He had been invited to sup with a colleague and his wife.*

su|per ✦◇◇ /suːpər/ **1** ADV [ADV adj] **Super** is used before adjectives to indicate that something has a lot of a quality. ❑ *I'm going to Greece in the summer so I've got to be super slim.* **2** ADJ [ADJ n] **Super** is used before nouns to indicate that something is larger, better, or more advanced than similar things. ❑ *Winners of each regional will advance to the super regionals.* **3** ADJ Some people use **super** to mean very nice or very good. [INFORMAL, OLD-FASHIONED] ❑ *We had a super time.* ❑ *That's a super idea.*

PREFIX

super-
forms nouns and adjectives that refer to people and things that are larger, better, or more advanced than others. *For example, a superfit athlete is extremely fit.*

super|an|nu|at|ed /suːpərænjueɪtɪd/ ADJ [usu ADJ n] If you describe something as **superannuated**, you mean that it is old and no longer used for its original purpose. [FORMAL] ❑ *...the superannuated idealism of the Sixties.*

super|an|nua|tion /suːpərænjueɪʃən/ N-UNCOUNT **Superannuation** is the same as a **retirement fund**. [mainly BRIT, BUSINESS]

su|perb ✦◇◇ /suːpɜːrb/ **1** ADJ If something is **superb**, its quality is very good indeed. ❑ *There is a superb 18-hole golf course 6 miles away.* • **su|perb|ly** ADV ❑ *The orchestra played superbly.* **2** ADJ If you say that someone has **superb** confidence, control, or skill, you mean that they have very great confidence, control, or skill. ❑ *With superb skill he managed to make a perfect landing.* • **su|perb|ly** ADV ❑ *...his superbly disciplined opponent.*

SYNONYMS

superb
ADJ **1**
excellent: *The recording quality is excellent.*
wonderful: *I've always thought she was a wonderful singer.*
marvellous: *He certainly is a marvellous actor.*

Su|per Bowl (**Super Bowls**) also **Superbowl** N-COUNT [usu sing] The **Super Bowl** is a football game that is held each year in the United States between the two best professional football teams. [AM] ❑ *The Giants won the Super Bowl in 1987.* ❑ *Joe Montana won four Superbowls with the 49ers.*

su|per|bug /suːpərbʌg/ (**superbugs**) N-COUNT Journalists refer to a type of bacteria as a **superbug** when it is very difficult to deal with because it cannot be killed by antibiotics.

super|charged /suːpərtʃɑːrdʒd/ ADJ If a car engine is **supercharged**, it has more air than normal forced into it so that the gasoline burns more quickly and the car has more power.

super|cili|ous /suːpərsɪliəs/ ADJ If you say that someone is **supercilious**, you disapprove of them because they behave in a way that shows they think they are better than other people. [DISAPPROVAL] ❑ *His manner is supercilious and arrogant.*

super|com|mit|tee /suːpərkəmɪti/ (**supercommittees**) N-COUNT A **supercommittee** is a committee which has members from two or more organizations or political groups.

super|com|put|er /suːpərkəmpjuːtər/ (**supercomputers**) N-COUNT A **supercomputer** is a powerful computer that can process large amounts of data very quickly.

super|con|duc|tiv|ity /suːpərkɒndʌktɪvɪti/ N-UNCOUNT **Superconductivity** is the ability of certain metals to allow electricity to pass through them without any resistance at very low temperatures. [TECHNICAL]

super|con|duc|tor /suːpərkəndʌktər/ (**superconductors**) N-COUNT A **superconductor** is a metal that allows electricity to pass through it without resistance at very low temperatures. [TECHNICAL]

super|ego /suːpərigoʊ/ (**superegos**) N-COUNT Your **superego** is the part of your mind which makes you aware of what is right and wrong, and which causes you to feel guilty when you have done something wrong. [TECHNICAL]

super|fi|cial /suːpərfɪʃəl/ **1** ADJ If you describe someone as **superficial**, you disapprove of them because they do not think deeply, and have little understanding of anything serious or important. [DISAPPROVAL] ❑ *This guy is a superficial yuppie with no* intellect whatsoever. **2** ADJ If you describe something such as an action, feeling, or relationship as **superficial**, you mean that it includes only the simplest and most obvious aspects of that thing, and not those aspects which require more effort to deal with or understand. ☐ *Their arguments do not withstand the most superficial scrutiny.* **3** ADJ **Superficial** is used to describe the appearance of something or the impression that it gives, especially if its real nature is very different. ☐ *Despite these superficial resemblances, this is a darker work than her earlier novels.* **4** ADJ **Superficial** injuries are not very serious, and affect only the surface of the body. You can also describe damage to an object as **superficial**. ☐ *The 69-year-old clergyman escaped with superficial wounds.*

super|flu|ity /sup̱əfluɪti/ (**superfluities**) N-COUNT [usu N of n] If there is a **superfluity of** something, there is more of it than is needed. [FORMAL] ☐ *The city has a superfluity of five-star hotels.*

super|flu|ous /supɜ̱ːfluəs/ ADJ Something that is **superfluous** is unnecessary or is no longer needed. ☐ *My presence at the afternoon's proceedings was superfluous.*

super|food /sup̱əfuːd/ (**superfoods**) N-COUNT A **superfood** is a food that contains many vitamins and other substances that are considered to be very good for your health. ☐ *The article recommends eating more superfoods, such as pomegranates and broccoli.*

super|group /sup̱əgruːp/ (**supergroups**) N-COUNT A **supergroup** is a pop group that has become very popular and famous. ☐ *He played in the supergroup Raisins in the Sun.*

super|heat|ed /sup̱əhiːtɪd/ ADJ If a liquid is **superheated**, it has been heated to a temperature that is higher than its boiling point without being allowed to boil. [TECHNICAL]

super|he|ro /sup̱əhɪərəʊ/ (**superheroes**) N-COUNT A **superhero** is a character in a cartoon or movie who has special powers and fights against evil. ☐ *...superheroes like Batman and Superman.*

super|high|way /sup̱əhaɪweɪ/ (**superhighways**) **1** N-COUNT A **superhighway** is a large, fast highway or freeway with several lanes. [AM] ☐ *He took off for the city on the eight-lane superhighway.* **2** N-COUNT The information **superhighway** is the network of computer links that enables computer users all over the world to communicate with each other. [COMPUTING] ☐ *...a superhighway using digital and fiber optic technology to provide new telecommunications links.*

super|hu|man /sup̱əhjuːmən/ ADJ [usu ADJ n] If you describe a quality that someone has as **superhuman**, you mean that it seems to be much greater than that of ordinary people. ☐ *Officers were terrified of his superhuman strength.*

super|im|pose /sup̱ərɪmpoʊz/ (**superimposes, superimposing, superimposed**) **1** V-T [usu passive] If one image is **superimposed** on another, it is put on top of it so that you can see the second image through it. ☐ *The image of a seemingly tiny dancer was superimposed on the image of the table.* **2** V-T [usu passive] If features or characteristics from one situation **are superimposed** onto or on another, they are transferred onto or used in the second situation, though they may not fit. ☐ *Patterns of public administration and government are superimposed on traditional societies.*

super|in|tend /sup̱ərɪnte̱nd, suprɪn-/ (**superintends, superintending, superintended**) V-T If you **superintend** something, you have responsibility for ensuring that it is carried out properly. [FORMAL] ☐ *Meese was to superintend the administration's entire domestic policy.*

super|in|ten|dent /sup̱ərɪnte̱ndənt, suprɪn-/ (**superintendents**) **1** N-COUNT A **superintendent** is a person who is responsible for a particular thing or the work done in a particular department. ☐ *He became superintendent of the bank's East African branches.* **2** N-COUNT A **superintendent** is a person whose job is to take care of a large building such as a school or an apartment building and deal with small repairs to it. [AM] ☐ *The superintendent, a bundle of keys hanging from his belt, was standing at the door.*

in BRIT, use **caretaker**

3 N-COUNT; N-TITLE A **superintendent** is the head of a police department. [BRIT]

su|pe|ri|or ♦◇ /sup̱ɪəriər/ (**superiors**) **1** ADJ If one thing or person is **superior to** another, the first is better than the second. ☐ *We have a relationship infinitely superior to those of many of our friends.* • **su|pe|ri|or|ity** N-UNCOUNT ☐ *They demonstrated the technical superiority of the process over traditional methodologies.* **2** ADJ If you describe something as **superior**, you mean that it is good, and better than other things of the same kind. ☐ *A few years ago it was virtually impossible to find superior quality coffee in local shops.* **3** ADJ A **superior** person or thing is more important than another person or thing in the same organization or system. ☐ *...negotiations between the mutineers and their superior officers.* **4** N-COUNT Your **superior** in an organization that you work for is a person who has a higher rank than you. ☐ *Other army units are completely surrounded and cut-off from communication with their superiors.* **5** ADJ If you describe someone as **superior**, you disapprove of them because they behave as if they are better, more important, or more intelligent than other people. [DISAPPROVAL] ☐ *Finch gave a superior smile.* • **su|pe|ri|or|ity** N-UNCOUNT ☐ *...a false sense of his superiority over mere journalists.* **6** ADJ If one group of people has **superior** numbers to another group, the first has more people than the second, and therefore has an advantage over it. [FORMAL] ☐ *The demonstrators fled when they saw the authorities' superior numbers.*

SYNONYMS

superior
ADJ **2**
first-rate: *People who used his service knew they were dealing with a first-rate professional.*
exclusive: *He is already a member of Britain's most exclusive club.*
exceptional: *Her translation is exceptional in its poetic quality.*
world-class: *He was determined to become a world-class player.*
outstanding: *He was outstanding at tennis and golf.*

su|pe|ri|or court (**superior courts**) also **Superior Court** N-VAR A **superior court** is a law court that deals with serious or important cases. [mainly AM] ☐ *The suit is being heard in Superior Court in San Francisco.* ☐ *...a jury trial in a Superior Court of the District of Columbia.* ☐ *...a Los Angeles Superior Court judge.*

su|pe|ri|or|ity /sup̱ɪəriɒ̱rɪti/ **1** N-UNCOUNT If one side in a war or conflict has **superiority**, it has an advantage over its enemy, for example because it has more soldiers or better equipment. [FORMAL] ☐ *We have air superiority.* **2** → see also **superior**

super|la|tive /supɜ̱ːlətɪv/ (**superlatives**) **1** ADJ If you describe something as **superlative**, you mean that it is extremely good. ☐ *Some superlative wines are made in this region.* **2** N-COUNT If someone uses **superlatives** to describe something, they use adjectives and expressions which indicate that it is extremely good. ☐ *...a spectacle which has critics world-wide reaching for superlatives.* **3** ADJ [ADJ n] In grammar, the **superlative** form of an adjective or adverb is the form that indicates that something has more of a quality than anything else in a group. For example, 'biggest' is the superlative form of 'big'. Compare **comparative**. • N-COUNT **Superlative** is also a noun. ☐ *...his tendency toward superlatives and exaggeration.*

super|man /sup̱əmæn/ (**supermen**) N-COUNT A **superman** is a man who has very great physical or mental abilities. ☐ *He nurtured the idea that he was a superman, who single-handedly could resolve the country's economic crisis.*

super|mar|ket /sup̱əmɑːkɪt/ (**supermarkets**) N-COUNT A **supermarket** is a large store which sells all kinds of food and some household goods. ☐ *Most of us do our food shopping in the supermarket.*

super|mod|el /sup̱əmɒdəl/ (**supermodels**) N-COUNT A **supermodel** is a very famous fashion model.

super|natu|ral /sup̱ənæ̱tʃərəl, -nætʃrəl/ ADJ **Supernatural** creatures, forces, and events are believed by some people to exist or happen, although they are impossible according to scientific laws. ☐ *The Nakani were evil spirits who looked like humans and possessed supernatural powers.* • N-SING **The supernatural** is things that are supernatural. ☐ *He writes short stories with a touch of the supernatural.*

super|no|va /sup̱ənoʊvə/ (**supernovas** or **supernovae** /sup̱ənoʊviː/) N-COUNT A **supernova** is an exploding star. ☐ *At least one supernova occurs per decade in our galaxy.*

super|pow|er /supərpauər/ (**superpowers**) N-COUNT A **superpower** is a very powerful and influential country, usually one that is rich and has nuclear weapons. ❏ *The United States could claim to be both a military and an economic superpower.*

super|sede /supərsid/ (**supersedes, superseding, superseded**) V-T [usu passive] If something **is superseded** by something newer, it is replaced because it has become old-fashioned or unacceptable. ❏ *Hand tools are relics of the past that have now been superseded by the machine.*

super|size /supərsaɪz/ (**supersizes, supersizing, supersized**) **1** ADJ **Supersize** or **supersized** things are very large. ❏ *A supersize portion of fries contains 600 calories.* ❏ *...a supersized mug of coffee.* **2** V-T If a fast-food restaurant **supersizes** a portion of food, it offers the customer a larger portion. ❏ *Fast-food restaurants encourage people to supersize their orders.*

super|son|ic /supərsɒnɪk/ ADJ [ADJ n] **Supersonic** aircraft travel faster than the speed of sound. ❏ *There was a huge bang; it sounded like a supersonic jet.*

super|spread|er /supərsprɛdər/ (**superspreaders**) N-COUNT A **superspreader** is someone who passes an infectious disease on to a very large number of people. ❏ *Scientists are increasingly interested in another type of superspreader: people who pass on infections while remaining healthy themselves.*

super|star /supərstɑr/ (**superstars**) N-COUNT A **superstar** is a very famous entertainer or athlete. [INFORMAL] ❏ *He was more than a basketball superstar, he was a celebrity.*

super|state /supərsteɪt/ (**superstates**) N-COUNT A **superstate** is a group of several countries that are very closely linked politically. ❏ *...a European superstate.*

super|sti|tion /supərstɪʃən/ (**superstitions**) N-VAR **Superstition** is belief in things that are not real or possible, for example magic. ❏ *Fortune-telling is a very much debased art surrounded by superstition.*

super|sti|tious /supərstɪʃəs/ **1** ADJ People who are **superstitious** believe in things that are not real or possible, for example magic. ❏ *Jean was extremely superstitious and believed the color green brought bad luck.* **2** ADJ [ADJ n] **Superstitious** fears or beliefs are irrational and not based on fact. ❏ *A wave of superstitious fear spread among the townspeople.*

super|store /supərstɔr/ (**superstores**) N-COUNT **Superstores** are very large supermarkets or stores selling household goods and equipment. Superstores are usually built outside cities and away from other stores. ❏ *...a Do-It-Yourself superstore.*

super|struc|ture /supərstrʌktʃər/ (**superstructures**) N-COUNT [usu sing] The **superstructure** of a ship is the part of it that is above its main deck. ❏ *We might try to clear up some of the cabins in the superstructure.*

super|tank|er /supərtæŋkər/ (**supertankers**) **1** N-COUNT A **supertanker** is an extremely large ship that is used for transporting oil. **2** → See also color supplement

super|ti|tle /supərtaɪtəl/ (**supertitles**) N-COUNT [usu pl] At an opera or play that is being performed in a foreign language, **supertitles** are a translation or summary of the words, which appear on a screen above the stage. [AM]

in BRIT, use **surtitle**

super|vise /supərvaɪz/ (**supervises, supervising, supervised**) V-T If you **supervise** an activity or a person, you make sure that the activity is done correctly or that the person is doing a task or behaving correctly. ❏ *A team was sent to supervise the elections in Nicaragua.*

super|vi|sion /supərvɪʒən/ N-UNCOUNT **Supervision** is the supervising of people, activities, or places. ❏ *A toddler requires close supervision and firm control at all times.*

super|vi|sor /supərvaɪzər/ (**supervisors**) N-COUNT A **supervisor** is a person who supervises activities or people, especially workers or students. ❏ *...a full-time job as a supervisor at a factory.*

super|vi|sory /supərvaɪzəri/ ADJ [ADJ n] **Supervisory** means involved in supervising people, activities, or places. ❏ *Most supervisory boards meet only twice a year.* ❏ *...staff with a minor supervisory role.*

super|woman /supərwʊmən/ (**superwomen**) N-VAR **Superwoman** is used to refer to a type of ideal woman who is able to do many things in her life successfully at the same time. ❏ *Superwoman exists only in the minds of journalists and Hollywood producers.*

su|pine /supaɪn/ ADJ If you are **supine**, you are lying flat on your back. [FORMAL] ❏ *...bedridden persons confined to the supine position.* • ADV [ADV after v] **Supine** is also an adverb. ❏ *I lay supine on the poolside grass.*

sup|per /sʌpər/ (**suppers**) **1** N-VAR Some people refer to the main meal eaten in the early part of the evening as **supper**. ❏ *Some guests like to dress for supper.* **2** N-VAR **Supper** is a simple meal eaten just before you go to bed at night. ❏ *She gives the children their supper, then puts them to bed.*

sup|per club (**supper clubs**) N-COUNT A **supper club** is a small expensive nightclub.

sup|per|time /sʌpərtaɪm/ N-UNCOUNT **Suppertime** is the period of the day when people have their supper. It can be in the early part of the evening or just before they go to bed at night. ❏ *They'll be back by suppertime.*

sup|plant /səplænt/ (**supplants, supplanting, supplanted**) V-T If a person or thing **is supplanted**, another person or thing takes their place. [FORMAL] ❏ *He may be supplanted by a younger man.* ❏ *By the 1930s the wristwatch had almost completely supplanted the pocket watch.*

sup|ple /sʌpəl/ (**suppler, supplest**) **1** ADJ A **supple** object or material bends or changes shape easily without cracking or breaking. ❏ *The leather is supple and sturdy enough to last for years.* **2** ADJ A **supple** person can move and bend their body very easily. ❏ *Paul was incredibly supple and strong.*

sup|plement /sʌplɪmənt/ (**supplements, supplementing, supplemented**) **1** V-T If you **supplement** something, you add something to it in order to improve it. ❏ *...people doing extra jobs outside their regular jobs to supplement their incomes.* • N-COUNT **Supplement** is also a noun. ❏ *Business sponsorship must be a supplement to, not a substitute for, public funding.* **2** N-COUNT A **supplement** is a pill that you take or a special kind of food that you eat in order to improve your health. ❏ *...a multiple vitamin and mineral supplement.* **3** N-COUNT A **supplement** is a separate part of a magazine or newspaper, often dealing with a particular topic. ❏ *...a special supplement to a monthly financial magazine.* **4** N-COUNT A **supplement** to a book is an additional section, written some time after the main text and published either at the end of the book or separately. ❏ *...the supplement to the Encyclopedia Britannica.* **5** N-COUNT A **supplement** is an extra amount of money that you pay in order to obtain special facilities or services, for example when you are traveling or staying at a hotel. ❏ *If you are traveling alone, the single room supplement is $25 a night.*

sup|plemen|tal /sʌplɪmɛntəl/ ADJ [ADJ n] **Supplemental** means the same as **supplementary**. [mainly AM, FORMAL] ❏ *You'll probably be able to buy supplemental insurance at an extra cost.*

sup|plemen|ta|ry /sʌplɪmɛntəri, -tri/ ADJ **Supplementary** things are added to something in order to improve it. ❏ *...the question of whether or not we need to take supplementary vitamins.*

sup|plemen|ta|tion /sʌplɪməntɛɪʃən/ N-UNCOUNT **Supplementation** is the use of pills or special types of food in order to improve your health. [MEDICAL] ❏ *The product provided inadequate vitamin and mineral supplementation.*

sup|pli|cant /sʌplɪkənt/ (**supplicants**) N-COUNT A **supplicant** is a person who prays to God or respectfully asks an important person to help them or to give them something that they want very much. [FORMAL] ❏ *He flung himself down in the flat submissive posture of a mere supplicant.*

sup|pli|ca|tion /sʌplɪkeɪʃən/ (**supplications**) N-VAR A **supplication** is a prayer to God or a respectful request to someone in authority for help. [FORMAL] ❏ *He raised his arms in a gesture of supplication.*

sup|plied /səplaɪd/ **1** ADJ [v-link ADJ with n] If you say that a place or person is well **supplied with** particular things, you mean that they have a large number of them. ❏ *The area is abundantly supplied with excellent family-run hotels.* **2** → see also **supply**

sup|pli|er /səplaɪər/ (**suppliers**) N-COUNT A **supplier** is a person, company, or organization that sells or supplies something such as goods or equipment to customers. [BUSINESS] ❏ *...one of the country's biggest food suppliers.*

sup|ply ♦♦◊ /səplaɪ/ (supplies, supplying, supplied) **1** V-T If you **supply** someone with something that they want or need, you give them a quantity of it. ❏ ...*an agreement not to produce or supply chemical weapons.* ❏ ...*a pipeline which will supply the major Greek cities with Russian natural gas.* **2** N-PLURAL You can use **supplies** to refer to food, equipment, and other essential things that people need, especially when these are provided in large quantities. ❏ *What happens when food and gasoline supplies run low?* **3** N-VAR A **supply** of something is an amount of it which someone has or which is available for them to use. ❏ *The brain requires a constant supply of oxygen.* **4** N-UNCOUNT **Supply** is the quantity of goods and services that can be made available for people to buy. [BUSINESS] ❏ *Prices change according to supply and demand.* **5** PHRASE If something is **in short supply**, there is very little of it available and it is difficult to find or obtain. ❏ *Food is in short supply all over the country.* **6** → See feature box at **global warming**

SYNONYMS
supply
VERB **1**
provide: *The government was not in a position to provide them with food.*
equip: *They did not possess the modern guns to equip the army properly.*
furnish: *They'll be able to furnish you with the rest of the details.*

sup|ply chain (supply chains) N-COUNT A **supply chain** is the entire process of making and selling commercial goods, including every stage from the supply of materials and the manufacture of the goods through to their distribution and sale. ❏ ...*companies looking for a shortened supply chain and increased efficiency.*

sup|ply line (supply lines) N-COUNT A **supply line** is a route along which goods and equipment are transported to an army during a war. ❏ *Soldiers get training setting up supply lines and building roads.*

sup|ply teach|er (supply teachers) N-COUNT A **supply teacher** is the same as a **substitute teacher**. [BRIT]

sup|port ♦♦♦ /səpɔrt/ (supports, supporting, supported) **1** V-T If you **support** someone or their ideas or aims, you agree with them, and perhaps help them because you want them to succeed. ❏ *The vice president insisted that he supported the hard-working people of New York.* • N-UNCOUNT **Support** is also a noun. ❏ *The president gave his full support to the reforms.* **2** N-UNCOUNT If you give **support** to someone during a difficult or unhappy time, you are kind to them and help them. ❏ *It was hard to come to terms with her death after all the support she gave to me and the family.* **3** N-UNCOUNT Financial **support** is money provided to enable an organization to continue. ❏ *State agencies continue to cut budgets and support to a number of organizations.* **4** V-T If you **support** someone, you provide them with money or the things they need. ❏ *I have children to support, money to be earned, and a home to be maintained.* **5** V-T If a fact **supports** a statement or a theory, it helps to show that it is true or correct. ❏ *The Freudian theory about daughters falling in love with their father has little evidence to support it.* • N-UNCOUNT **Support** is also a noun. ❏ *The two largest powers in any system must always be major rivals. History offers some support for this view.* **6** V-T If something **supports** an object, it is underneath the object and holding it up. ❏ ...*the thick wooden posts that supported the ceiling.* **7** N-COUNT A **support** is a bar or other object that supports something. ❏ *Each slab was nailed to two straight wooden supports.* **8** V-T If you **support** yourself, you prevent yourself from falling by holding onto something or by leaning on something. ❏ *He supported himself by means of a nearby post.* • N-UNCOUNT **Support** is also a noun. ❏ *Alice, very pale, was leaning against him as if for support.* **9** V-T If you **support** a sports team, you always want them to win and perhaps go regularly to their games. ❏ *Tim, 17, supports the Knicks.*

USAGE
support
Don't use 'support' to say that someone accepts pain or an unpleasant situation. Say that they **bear** it or **put up with** it. If you do not like something at all, don't say that you 'can't support' it. Say that you **can't bear** it or **can't stand** it. *He can't bear the pain.*

COLLOCATIONS
support
NOUN
1
adjective + **support**: full, overwhelming, strong, widespread; public
verb + **support**: express, give, lend, show; enjoy, gain, rally, win
2
noun + **support**: community
adjective + **support**: emotional, moral; invaluable
verb + **support**: offer, provide; receive
3
noun + **support**: government, income
adjective + **support**: financial, generous
verb + **support**: provide, receive; need, seek

SYNONYMS
support
VERB **1**
back: *The Prime Minister is backed by the civic movement, Public Against Violence.*
champion: *He passionately championed the poor.*
encourage: *When things aren't going well, he encourages me, telling me not to give up.*
defend: *Matt defended all of Clarence's decisions, right or wrong.*
stand up for: *Don't be afraid to stand up for yourself.*
NOUN
2
help: *Thanks very much for your help.*
backing: *Mr Bach set up his own consulting business with the backing of his old boss.*
assistance: *She can still come downstairs with assistance, but she's very weak.*
encouragement: *I also had friends who gave me a great deal of encouragement.*
3
aid: ...*regular flights carrying humanitarian aid to Cambodia.*
help: *Thanks very much for your help.*
benefits: *The very poorest parents are not employed, they are living on benefits.*
relief: ...*famine relief.*
VERB **4**
provide for: *Elaine wouldn't let him provide for her.*
fund: *The airport is being privately funded by a construction group.*
keep: *She could just about afford to keep her five kids.*
finance: *The fund has been used largely to finance the construction of federal prisons.*

sup|port|er ♦♦ /səpɔrtər/ (supporters) N-COUNT **Supporters** are people who support someone or something, for example a political leader or a sports team. ❏ *Attacks against opposition supporters are continuing at levels higher than before the election.*

SYNONYMS
supporter
NOUN
follower: ...*the Democratic Party's most loyal followers.*
fan: *As a boy he was a Manchester United fan.*
advocate: *He was a strong advocate of free market policies and a multi-party system.*
champion: *He received acclaim as a champion of the oppressed.*
defender: ...*the most ardent defenders of conventional family values.*

sup|port group (support groups) N-COUNT [oft with supp] A **support group** is an organization run by and for people who have a particular problem or medical condition. ❏ *She attended a cancer support group at her local hospital.*

sup|port|ing /səpɔrtɪŋ/ **1** ADJ [ADJ n] In a movie or play, a **supporting** actor or actress is one who has an important part, but not the most important part. ❏ ...*the winner of the best supporting actress award.* **2** → see also **support**

sup|port|ive /səpɔrtɪv/ **1** ADJ If you are **supportive**, you are kind and helpful to someone at a difficult or unhappy time in their life. ❏ *They were always supportive of each other.* **2** → See feature box at **quality**

sup|pose ♦♦◇ /səpoʊz/ (supposes, supposing, supposed) **1** V-T You can use **suppose** or **supposing** before mentioning a possible situation or action. You usually then go on to consider the effects that this situation or action might have. ☐ *Suppose someone gave you an egg and asked you to describe exactly what was inside.* **2** V-T If you **suppose** that something is true, you believe that it is probably true, because of other things that you know. ☐ *The policy is perfectly clear and I see no reason to suppose that it isn't working.* ☐ *I knew very well that the problem was more complex than he supposed.* **3** PHRASE You can say '**I suppose**' when you want to express slight uncertainty. [SPOKEN, VAGUENESS] ☐ *I suppose I'd better do some homework.* ☐ *"Is that the right way up?"—"Yeah. I suppose so."* **4** PHRASE You can say '**I suppose**' or '**I don't suppose**' before describing someone's probable thoughts or attitude, when you are impatient or slightly angry with them. [SPOKEN, FEELINGS] ☐ *I suppose you think you're funny.* **5** PHRASE You can say '**I don't suppose**' as a way of introducing a polite request. [SPOKEN, POLITENESS] ☐ *I don't suppose you could tell me where James Street is, could you?* **6** PHRASE You can use '**do you suppose**' to introduce a question when you want someone to give their opinion about something, although you know that they are unlikely to have any more knowledge or information about it than you. [SPOKEN] ☐ *Do you suppose he was telling the truth?*

> **SYNONYMS**
>
> **suppose**
> VERB **2**
> **imagine:** *I imagine you're referring to Jean-Paul Sartre.*
> **assume:** *If the package is wrapped well, we assume the contents are also wonderful.*
> **presume:** *Dido's told you the whole sad story, I presume?*

sup|posed ♦♦◇

Pronounced /səpoʊzd/ or /səpoʊst/ for meanings **1** to **4**, and /səpoʊzɪd/ for meaning **5**.

1 PHRASE If you say that something **is supposed to** happen, you mean that it is planned or expected. Sometimes this use suggests that the thing does not really happen in this way. ☐ *He produced a hand-written list of nine men he was supposed to kill.* **2** PHRASE If something **was supposed to** happen, it was planned or intended to happen, but did not in fact happen. ☐ *He was supposed to go back to Bergen on the last bus, but of course the accident prevented him.* **3** PHRASE If you say that something **is supposed to** be true, you mean that people say it is true but you do not know for certain that it is true. ☐ *"The Whipping Block" has never been published, but it's supposed to be a really good poem.* **4** PHRASE You can use '**be supposed to**' to express annoyance at someone's ideas, or because something is not happening in the right way. [FEELINGS] ☐ *You're supposed to be my friend!* **5** ADJ [ADJ n] You can use **supposed** to suggest that something that people talk about or believe in may not in fact exist, happen, or be as it is described. ☐ *Not all developing countries are willing to accept the supposed benefits of free trade.*
● **sup|pos|ed|ly** /səpoʊzɪdli/ ADV ☐ *He was more of a victim that any of the people he supposedly offended.*

sup|po|si|tion /sʌpəzɪʃən/ (suppositions) **1** N-COUNT [oft N that] A **supposition** is an idea or statement which someone believes or assumes to be true, although they may have no evidence for it. [FORMAL] ☐ *There's a popular supposition that we're publicly funded but the bulk of our money comes from competitive contracts.* **2** N-UNCOUNT You can describe someone's ideas or statements as **supposition** if you disapprove of the fact that they have no evidence to support them. [DISAPPROVAL] ☐ *The report has been rejected by the authorities, who said much of it was based on supposition or inaccuracy.*

sup|posi|tory /səpɒzɪtəri/ (suppositories) N-COUNT A **suppository** is a solid block of medicine that is put into the rectum, where it gradually dissolves.

sup|press /səprɛs/ (suppresses, suppressing, suppressed) **1** V-T If someone in authority **suppresses** an activity, they prevent it from continuing, by using force or making it illegal. ☐ *...drug traffickers, who continue to flourish despite international attempts to suppress them.* ● **sup|pres|sion** /səprɛʃən/ N-UNCOUNT ☐ *...people who were imprisoned after the violent suppression of the pro-democracy movement protests.* **2** V-T If a natural function or reaction of your body **is suppressed**, it is stopped, for example by drugs or illness. ☐ *The reproduction and growth of the cancerous cells can be suppressed by bombarding them with radiation.* ● **sup|pres|sion** N-UNCOUNT ☐ *Eye problems can indicate an unhealthy lifestyle with subsequent suppression of the immune system.* **3** V-T If you **suppress** your feelings or reactions, you do not express them, even though you might want to. ☐ *Liz thought of Barry and suppressed a smile.* ● **sup|pres|sion** N-UNCOUNT ☐ *A mother's suppression of her own feelings can cause problems.* **4** V-T If someone **suppresses** a piece of information, they prevent other people from learning it. ☐ *At no time did they try to persuade me to suppress the information.* ● **sup|pres|sion** N-UNCOUNT ☐ *The inspectors found no evidence which supported any allegation of suppression of official documents.* **5** V-T If someone or something **suppresses** a process or activity, they stop it continuing or developing. ☐ *The government is suppressing inflation by increasing interest rates.*

sup|pres|sant /səprɛsənt/ (suppressants) N-COUNT [n N] A **suppressant** is a drug which is used to stop one of the natural functions of the body. [MEDICAL] ☐ *...the brief period in his life when he took an appetite suppressant.*

sup|pres|sor /səprɛsər/ ADJ [ADJ n] **Suppressor** cells or genes are ones that prevent a cancer from developing or spreading. [MEDICAL]

supra|na|tion|al /suːprənæʃənəl/ ADJ [ADJ n] A **supranational** organization or authority involves or relates to more than one country. ☐ *...NATO and other Western supranational institutions.*

su|prema|cist /suːprɛməsɪst/ (supremacists) N-COUNT [oft N n] A **supremacist** is someone who believes that one group of people should be more powerful and have more influence than another group. ☐ *...a White supremacist group.*

su|prema|cy /suːprɛməsi/ **1** N-UNCOUNT If one group of people has **supremacy** over another group, they have more political or military power than the other group. ☐ *The conservative old guard had re-established its political supremacy.* **2** N-UNCOUNT If someone or something has **supremacy** over another person or thing, they are better. ☐ *In the Grand Slam final, she retained overall supremacy.*

su|preme ♦♦◇ /suːpriːm/ **1** ADJ [ADJ n] **Supreme** is used in the title of a person or an official group to indicate that they are at the highest level in a particular organization or system. ☐ *MacArthur was Supreme Commander for the allied powers in the Pacific.* ☐ *...the Supreme Court.* **2** ADJ You use **supreme** to emphasize that a quality or thing is very great. [EMPHASIS] ☐ *Her approval was of supreme importance.* ● **su|preme|ly** ADV [ADV adj/adv] ☐ *She does her job supremely well.*

Supt. Supt. is a written abbreviation for **superintendent**. ☐ *...School Supt. Linda Cowen.*

in BRIT, use **Supt**

sur|charge /sɜːrtʃɑːrdʒ/ (surcharges) N-COUNT A **surcharge** is an extra payment of money in addition to the usual payment for something. It is added for a specific reason, for example by a company because costs have risen or by a government as a tax. ☐ *The government introduced a 15% surcharge on imports.*

sure ♦♦♦ /ʃʊər/ (surer, surest) **1** ADJ [v-link ADJ] If you are **sure** that something is true, you are certain that it is true. If you are not **sure** about something, you do not know for certain what the true situation is. ☐ *He'd never been in a class before and he was not even sure that he should have been teaching.* ☐ *The president has never been sure which direction he wanted to go in on this issue.* **2** ADJ [v-link ADJ of -ing/n] If someone is **sure of** getting something, they will definitely get it or they think they will definitely get it. ☐ *A lot of people think that it's better to pay for their education so that they can be sure of getting quality.* **3** PHRASE If you say that something **is sure to** happen, you are emphasizing your belief that it will happen. [EMPHASIS] ☐ *With over 80 beaches to choose from, you are sure to find a place to lay your towel.* **4** ADJ [ADJ n] **Sure** is used to emphasize that something such as a sign or ability is reliable or accurate. [EMPHASIS] ☐ *Sharpe's leg and shoulder began to ache, a sure sign of rain.* **5** ADJ [v-link ADJ] If you tell someone to **be sure** to do something, you mean that they must not forget to do it. [EMPHASIS] ☐ *Be sure to read about how mozzarella is made, on page 65.* **6** CONVENTION **Sure** is an informal way of saying 'yes' or 'all right.' [FORMULAE]

❑ "Do you know where she lives?"—"Sure." **7** ADV [ADV before v] You can use **sure** in order to emphasize what you are saying. [INFORMAL, EMPHASIS] ❑ "Has the whole world just gone crazy?"—"Sure looks that way, doesn't it?" **8** PHRASE You say **sure enough**, especially when telling a story, to confirm that something was really true or was actually happening. ❑ We found the apple pie pudding too good to resist. Sure enough, it was delicious. **9** PHRASE If you say that something is **for sure** or that you know it **for sure**, you mean that it is definitely true. ❑ One thing's for sure, Manilow's vocal style hasn't changed much over the years. **10** PHRASE If you **make sure** that something is done, you take action so that it is done. ❑ Make sure that you follow the instructions carefully. **11** PHRASE If you **make sure** that something is the way that you want or expect it to be, you check that it is that way. ❑ He looked in the bathroom to make sure that he was alone. **12** PHRASE If you are **sure of yourself**, you are very confident about your own abilities or opinions. ❑ I'd never seen him like this, so sure of himself, so in command.

SYNONYMS

sure
ADJ **1**
certain: It wasn't a balloon–I'm certain of that.
positive: 'She's never late. You sure she said eight?'—'Positive.'
definite: Mary is very definite about this.
convinced: He was convinced that I was part of the problem.

sure|fire /ʃʊərfaɪər/ also **sure-fire** ADJ [ADJ n] A **surefire** thing is something that is certain to succeed or win. [INFORMAL] ❑ These products are promoted as surefire cures for various diseases.

sure-footed also **surefooted** **1** ADJ A person or animal that is **sure-footed** can move easily over steep or uneven ground without falling. ❑ My horse is small but wiry and sure-footed. **2** ADJ If someone is **sure-footed**, they are confident in what they are doing. ❑ ...his image as a sure-footed leader.

sure|ly ✦◇◇ /ʃʊərli/ **1** ADV [ADV with cl/group] You use **surely** to emphasize that you think something should be true, and you would be surprised if it was not true. [EMPHASIS] ❑ You're an intelligent woman, surely you realize by now that I'm helping you? ❑ You surely haven't forgotten Dr. Walters? **2** ADV If something will **surely** happen or is **surely** the case, it will definitely happen or is definitely the case. [FORMAL] ❑ He knew that under the surgeon's knife he would surely die. **3** PHRASE If you say that something is happening **slowly but surely**, you mean that it is happening gradually but it is definitely happening. ❑ Slowly but surely she started to fall in love with him.

sure|ty /ʃʊərɪti/ (**sureties**) N-VAR A **surety** is money or something valuable which you give to someone to show that you will do what you have promised. ❑ The insurance company will take warehouse stocks or treasury bonds as surety.

surf /sɜrf/ (**surfs, surfing, surfed**) **1** N-UNCOUNT **Surf** is the mass of white bubbles that is formed by waves as they fall upon the shore. ❑ ...surf rolling onto white sand beaches. **2** V-I If you **surf**, you ride on big waves in the sea on a special board. ❑ I'm going to buy a surfboard and learn to surf. • **surf|er** (**surfers**) N-COUNT ❑ ...this small fishing village, which continues to attract painters and surfers. **3** V-T If you **surf** the internet, you spend time finding and looking at things on the internet. [COMPUTING] ❑ No one knows how many people currently surf the Net. • **surf|er** N-COUNT ❑ Net surfers can use their credit cards to pay for anything from toys to train tickets.

sur|face ✦✦◇ /sɜrfɪs/ (**surfaces, surfacing, surfaced**) **1** N-COUNT The **surface** of something is the flat top part of it or the outside of it. ❑ Ozone forms a protective layer between 12 and 30 miles above the Earth's surface. ❑ ...tiny little waves on the surface of the water. **2** N-COUNT A work **surface** is a flat area, for example the top of a table, desk, or kitchen counter, on which you can work. ❑ It can simply be left on the work surface. **3** N-SING When you refer to the **surface** of a situation, you are talking about what can be seen easily rather than what is hidden or not immediately obvious. ❑ Back home, things appear, on the surface, simpler. **4** V-I If someone or something under water **surfaces**, they come up to the surface of the water. ❑ He surfaced, gasping for air. **5** V-I When something such as a piece of news, a feeling, or a problem **surfaces**, it becomes known or becomes obvious. ❑ The paper says the evidence, when it surfaces, is certain to cause uproar.

SYNONYMS

surface
NOUN **1**
exterior: In one ad, the viewer scarcely sees the car's exterior.
outside: ...the outside of the building.
face: ...the north face of the Eiger.
covering: Sawdust was used as a hygienic floor covering.

sur|face mail N-UNCOUNT **Surface mail** is the system of sending letters and packages by road, rail, or sea, not by air. ❑ Goods may be sent by surface mail or airmail.

surface-to-air ADJ [ADJ n] **Surface-to-air** missiles are fired from the ground or a boat and aimed at aircraft or at other missiles.

surface-to-surface ADJ [ADJ n] **Surface-to-surface** missiles are fired from the ground or a boat and aimed at targets on the ground or at other boats. ❑ The surface-to-surface missiles were fired from the west of the capital.

surf|board /sɜrfbɔrd/ (**surfboards**) N-COUNT A **surfboard** is a long narrow board that is used for surfing. ❑ He borrowed a friend's surfboard and paddled out into the ocean at sunset.

sur|feit /sɜrfɪt/ N-SING [usu N of n] A **surfeit** of something is an amount which is too large. [FORMAL] ❑ Rationing had put an end to a surfeit of biscuits long ago.

surf|ing /sɜrfɪŋ/ **1** N-UNCOUNT **Surfing** is the sport of riding on the top of a wave while standing or lying on a special board. ❑ ...every type of watersport from jetskiing and surfing to sailing and fishing. **2** N-UNCOUNT **Surfing** is the activity of looking at different sites on the internet, especially when you are not looking for anything in particular. [COMPUTING] ❑ The simple fact is that, for most people, surfing is too expensive to do on a regular basis.

surge /sɜrdʒ/ (**surges, surging, surged**) **1** N-COUNT A **surge** is a sudden large increase in something that has previously been steady, or has only increased or developed slowly. ❑ Specialists see various reasons for the recent surge in inflation. **2** V-I If something **surges**, it increases suddenly and greatly, after being steady or developing only slowly. ❑ The Freedom Party's electoral support surged from just under 10 percent to nearly 17 percent. **3** V-I If a crowd of people **surge** forward, they suddenly move forward together. ❑ The photographers and cameramen surged forward. **4** N-COUNT A **surge** is a sudden powerful movement of a physical force such as wind or water. ❑ The whole car shuddered with an almost frightening surge of power. **5** V-I If a physical force such as water or electricity **surges** through something, it moves through it suddenly and powerfully. ❑ Thousands of volts surged through his car after he careered into a lamp post, ripping out live wires.

sur|geon /sɜrdʒən/ (**surgeons**) N-COUNT A **surgeon** is a doctor who is specially trained to perform surgery. ❑ ...a heart surgeon.

sur|geon gen|er|al (**surgeons general**) also **Surgeon General** N-COUNT [oft the N] In the United States, the **surgeon general** is the head of the public health service. [AM] ❑ The current surgeon general, Antonia Novello, will continue in the job until June.

surge pric|ing N-UNCOUNT **Surge pricing** is the practice of increasing the price of goods or services when there is the greatest demand for them. ❑ The company is working on making its controversial surge pricing more transparent.

sur|gery ✦◇◇ /sɜrdʒəri/ (**surgeries**) **1** N-UNCOUNT **Surgery** is medical treatment in which someone's body is cut open so that a doctor can repair, remove, or replace a diseased or damaged part. ❑ His father has just recovered from heart surgery. **2** → see also **cosmetic surgery, plastic surgery 3** N-COUNT A **surgery** is the area in a hospital with operating rooms where surgeons operate on their patients. [AM]

> in BRIT, use **theatre**

4 N-COUNT A **surgery** is the room or house where a doctor or dentist works. [BRIT]

> in AM, use **doctor's office**

5 N-COUNT A doctor's **surgery** is the period of time each day when a doctor sees patients at his or her surgery. [BRIT]

> in AM, use **office hours**

sur|gi|cal /sɜ́rdʒɪkəl/ **1** ADJ [ADJ n] **Surgical** equipment and clothing is used in surgery. ☐ ...an array of surgical instruments. **2** ADJ [ADJ n] **Surgical** treatment involves surgery. ☐ A biopsy is usually a minor surgical procedure. • **sur|gi|cal|ly** ADV [ADV with v] ☐ In very severe cases, bunions may be surgically removed.

sur|gi|cal spir|it N-UNCOUNT **Surgical spirit** is a liquid which is used to clean wounds or surgical instruments. It consists mainly of alcohol. [BRIT]

in AM, use **rubbing alcohol**

sur|ly /sɜ́rli/ (surlier, surliest) ADJ Someone who is **surly** behaves in a rude bad-tempered way. [WRITTEN] ☐ He became surly and rude toward me.

sur|mise /sərmάɪz/ (surmises, surmising, surmised) **1** V-T If you **surmise** that something is true, you guess it from the available evidence, although you do not know for certain. [FORMAL] ☐ There's so little to go on, we can only surmise what happened. **2** N-VAR If you say that a particular conclusion is **surmise**, you mean that it is a guess based on the available evidence and you do not know for certain that it is true. [FORMAL] ☐ It is mere surmise that Bosch had Brant's poem in mind when doing this painting.

sur|mount /sərmάʊnt/ (surmounts, surmounting, surmounted) **1** V-T If you **surmount** a problem or difficulty, you deal successfully with it. ☐ I realized I had to surmount the language barrier. **2** → See feature box at **success**

sur|name /sɜ́rneɪm/ (surnames) N-COUNT Your **surname** is the name that you share with other members of your family. In English-speaking countries and many other countries it is your last name. ☐ She'd never known his surname, only his first name.

sur|pass /sərpǽs/ (surpasses, surpassing, surpassed) **1** V-T If one person or thing **surpasses** another, the first is better than, or has more of a particular quality than, the second. ☐ He was determined to surpass the achievements of his older brothers. **2** V-T If something **surpasses** expectations, it is much better than it was expected to be. ☐ Conrad Black gave an excellent party that surpassed expectations.

sur|plice /sɜ́rplɪs/ (surplices) N-COUNT A **surplice** is a loose white knee-length garment which is worn over a longer garment by priests and members of the choir in some churches. ☐ The priest and choir in their lace surplices led the service.

sur|plus ✦◇◇ /sɜ́rplʌs, -pləs/ (surpluses) **1** N-VAR If there is a **surplus** of something, there is more than is needed. ☐ ...countries where there is a surplus of labor. **2** ADJ **Surplus** is used to describe something that is extra or that is more than is needed. ☐ Few people have large sums of surplus cash. ☐ I sell my surplus birds to a local pet shop. **3** N-COUNT If a country has a trade **surplus**, it exports more than it imports. ☐ Japan's annual trade surplus is in the region of 100 billion dollars. **4** N-COUNT If a government has a budget **surplus**, it has spent less than it received in taxes. ☐ When will an Australian federal government next return a budget surplus?

sur|prise ✦◇◇ /sərprάɪz/ (surprises, surprising, surprised) **1** N-COUNT A **surprise** is an unexpected event, fact, or piece of news. ☐ I have a surprise for you: We are moving to Switzerland! ☐ It may come as a surprise to some that a normal, healthy child is born with many skills. • ADJ [ADJ n] **Surprise** is also an adjective. ☐ Baxter arrived here this afternoon, on a surprise visit. **2** N-UNCOUNT **Surprise** is the feeling that you have when something unexpected happens. ☐ The Pentagon has expressed surprise at these allegations. ☐ "You mean he's going to vote against her?" Scobie asked in surprise. **3** V-T If something **surprises** you, it gives you a feeling of surprise. ☐ We'll solve the case ourselves and surprise everyone. ☐ It surprised me that a driver of Alain's experience should make those mistakes. **4** V-T If you **surprise** someone, you give them, tell them, or do something pleasant that they are not expecting. ☐ Surprise a new neighbor with one of your favorite home-made dishes. **5** N-COUNT If you describe someone or something as a **surprise**, you mean that they are very good or pleasant although you were not expecting this. ☐ ...Senga MacFie, one of the surprises of the World Championships three months ago. **6** V-T If you **surprise** someone, you attack, capture, or find them when they are not expecting it. ☐ U.S. troops surprised eight enemy fighters in a cave complex. **7** → see also **surprised, surprising** **8** PHRASE If something **takes** you **by surprise**, it happens when you are not expecting it or when you are not prepared for it. ☐ His question took his two companions by surprise.

---COLLOCATIONS---

surprise
NOUN
1
adjective + **surprise**: nasty, unpleasant, unwelcome; pleasant, wonderful; complete
verb + **surprise**: deliver, pull, spring
2
verb + **surprise**: express, feign, register

sur|prised ✦◇◇ /sərprάɪzd/ **1** ADJ If you are **surprised** at something, you have a feeling of surprise, because it is unexpected or unusual. ☐ This lady was genuinely surprised at what happened to her pet. **2** → see also **surprise**

---SYNONYMS---

surprised
ADJ
amazed: I was amazed to learn she was still writing her stories.
astonished: They were astonished to find the driver was a six-year-old boy.
startled: Martha gave her a startled look.

sur|pris|ing ✦◇◇ /sərprάɪzɪŋ/ **1** ADJ Something that is **surprising** is unexpected or unusual and makes you feel surprised. ☐ It is not surprising that children learn to read at different rates. • **sur|pris|ing|ly** ADV ☐ The party did surprisingly well in the South. **2** → see also **surprise**

---SYNONYMS---

surprising
ADJ
amazing: It's amazing what we can remember with a little prompting.
astonishing: ...an astonishing display of physical strength.
incredible: It seemed incredible that people would play football during a war.

sur|re|al /səríəl/ ADJ If you describe something as **surreal**, you mean that the elements in it are combined in a strange way that you would not normally expect, like in a dream. ☐ "Performance" is one of the most surreal movies ever made.

sur|re|al|ism /səríəlɪzəm/ N-UNCOUNT **Surrealism** is a style in art and literature in which ideas, images, and objects are combined in a strange way, like in a dream.

sur|re|al|ist /səríəlɪst/ (surrealists) **1** ADJ **Surrealist** means related to or in the style of surrealism. ☐ Dali's shoe hat was undoubtedly the most surrealist idea he ever worked on with Schiaparelli. **2** N-COUNT A **surrealist** is an artist or writer whose work is based on the ideas of surrealism.

sur|re|al|is|tic /səriəlɪ́stɪk/ **1** ADJ **Surrealistic** means the same as **surreal**. ☐ ...the surrealistic way the movie plays with time. **2** ADJ [ADJ n] **Surrealistic** means related to or in the style of surrealism. ☐ ...Man Ray's surrealistic study of a woman's face.

sur|ren|der ✦◇◇ /sərέndər/ (surrenders, surrendering, surrendered) **1** V-I If you **surrender**, you stop fighting or resisting someone and agree that you have been beaten. ☐ General Martin Bonnet called on the rebels to surrender. • N-VAR **Surrender** is also a noun. ☐ ...the government's apparent surrender to demands made by the religious militants. **2** V-T If you **surrender** something you would rather keep, you give it up or let someone else have it, for example after a struggle. ☐ Nadja had to fill out forms surrendering all rights to her property. • N-UNCOUNT **Surrender** is also a noun. ☐ ...the sixteen-day deadline for the surrender of weapons and ammunition. **3** V-T If you **surrender** something such as a ticket or your passport, you give it to someone in authority when they ask you to. [FORMAL] ☐ They have been ordered to surrender their passports. **4** → See feature box at **conflict**

sur|ren|der val|ue (surrender values) N-COUNT The **surrender value** of a life insurance policy is the amount of money you receive if you decide that you no longer wish to continue with the policy. [BUSINESS] ☐ An ordinary life policy may have a cash surrender value of $50,000.

sur|rep|ti|tious /sɜːrəptɪ́ʃəs/ ADJ A **surreptitious** action is done secretly. ☐ He made a surreptitious entrance to the club through

surrogacy ... *the little door in the brick wall.* • **sur|rep|ti|tious|ly** ADV [ADV with v] ☐ *Surreptitiously Mark looked at his watch.*

sur|ro|ga|cy /sɜrəgəsi/ N-UNCOUNT **Surrogacy** is an arrangement by which a woman gives birth to a baby on behalf of someone who is physically unable to have babies themselves, and then gives the baby to that person. ☐ *In this country it is illegal to pay for surrogacy.*

sur|ro|gate /sɜrəgeɪt, -gɪt/ (**surrogates**) ADJ [ADJ n] You use **surrogate** to describe a person or thing that is given a particular role because the person or thing that should have the role is not available. ☐ *Martin had become his surrogate son.* • N-COUNT **Surrogate** is also a noun. ☐ *Arms control should not be made into a surrogate for peace.*

sur|ro|gate moth|er (**surrogate mothers**) N-COUNT A **surrogate mother** is a woman who has agreed to give birth to a baby on behalf of someone else.

sur|round ♦♦◇ /səraʊnd/ (**surrounds, surrounding, surrounded**) ◻ V-T/V-I If a person or thing **is surrounded** by something, that thing is situated all around them. ☐ *The small churchyard was surrounded by a rusted wrought-iron fence.* ☐ *The shell surrounding the egg has many important functions.* ☐ *...Chicago and the surrounding area.* ◻ V-T If you **are surrounded** by soldiers or police, they spread out so that they are in positions all the way around you. ☐ *When the car stopped in the town square it was surrounded by soldiers and militiamen.* ◻ V-T The circumstances, feelings, or ideas which **surround** something are those that are closely associated with it. ☐ *The decision had been agreed in principle before today's meeting, but some controversy surrounded it.* ◻ V-T If you **surround** yourself **with** certain people or things, you make sure that you have a lot of them near you all the time. ☐ *He had made it his business to surround himself with a hand-picked group of bright young officers.*

sur|round|ings /səraʊndɪŋz/ N-PLURAL When you are describing the place where you are at the moment, or the place where you live, you can refer to it as your **surroundings**. ☐ *Schumacher adapted effortlessly to his new surroundings.*

sur|tax /sɜrtæks/ N-UNCOUNT **Surtax** is an additional tax on incomes higher than the level at which ordinary tax is paid. [BUSINESS] ☐ *...a 10% surtax for Americans earning more than $250,000 a year.*

sur|ti|tle /sɜrtaɪtəl/ (**surtitles**) N-COUNT [usu pl] **Surtitles** are the same as **supertitles**. [BRIT]

sur|veil|lance /sərveɪləns/ N-UNCOUNT **Surveillance** is the careful watching of someone, especially by an organization such as the police or the army. ☐ *He was arrested after being kept under constant surveillance.* ☐ *Police swooped on the home after a two-week surveillance operation.*

sur|vey ♦♦◇ (**surveys, surveying, surveyed**)

The noun is pronounced /sɜrveɪ/. The verb is pronounced /sərveɪ/, and can also be pronounced /sɜrveɪ/ in meanings 2 and 5.

◻ N-COUNT If you carry out a **survey**, you try to find out detailed information about a lot of different people or things, usually by asking people a series of questions. ☐ *The council conducted a survey of the uses to which farm buildings are put.* ◻ V-T If you **survey** a number of people, companies, or organizations, you try to find out information about their opinions or behavior, usually by asking them a series of questions. ☐ *Business Development Advisers surveyed 211 companies for the report.* ◻ V-T If you **survey** something, you look at or consider the whole of it carefully. ☐ *He pushed himself to his feet and surveyed the room.* ◻ N-COUNT If someone carries out a **survey** of an area of land, they examine it and measure it, usually in order to make a map of it. ☐ *...the organizer of the geological survey of India.* ◻ V-T If someone **surveys** an area of land, they examine it and measure it, usually in order to make a map of it. ☐ *The city council commissioned geological experts earlier this year to survey the cliffs.* ◻ N-COUNT A **survey** is a careful examination of the condition and structure of a house, usually carried out in order to give information to a person who wants to buy it. [mainly BRIT] ◻ V-T If someone **surveys** a house, they examine it carefully and report on its structure, usually in order to give advice to a person who is thinking of buying it. [mainly BRIT] ◻ → See feature box at **research**

COLLOCATIONS

survey
NOUN ◻
noun + **survey**: consumer, employee, household; opinion; crime
adjective + **survey**: comprehensive, detailed; national, nationwide, online; annual, recent
verb + **survey**: carry out, conduct, undertake; commission; publish, release

---

sur|vey|or /sərveɪər/ (**surveyors**) ◻ N-COUNT A **surveyor** is a person whose job is to survey land. ☐ *...the surveyor's maps of the Queen Alexandra Range.* ◻ N-COUNT A **surveyor** is a person whose job is to survey buildings. [BRIT]

in AM, use **structural engineer**

sur|viv|al ♦◇◇ /sərvaɪvəl/ ◻ N-UNCOUNT If you refer to the **survival** of something or someone, you mean that they manage to continue or exist in spite of difficult circumstances. ☐ *...companies which have been struggling for survival in the advancing recession.* ◻ N-UNCOUNT If you refer to the **survival** of a person or living thing, you mean that they live through a dangerous situation in which it was possible that they might die. ☐ *If cancers are spotted early there's a high chance of survival.*

sur|vive ♦♦◇ /sərvaɪv/ (**survives, surviving, survived**)
◻ V-T/V-I If a person or living thing **survives** in a dangerous situation such as an accident or an illness, they do not die. ☐ *...the sequence of events that left the eight pupils battling to survive in icy seas for over four hours.* ☐ *Those organisms that are most suited to the environment will be those that will survive.* ☐ *He had survived heart bypass surgery.* ◻ V-T/V-I If you **survive** in difficult circumstances, you manage to live or continue in spite of them and do not let them affect you very much. ☐ *On my first day here I thought, "Ooh, how will I survive?"* ☐ *...people who are struggling to survive without jobs.* ◻ V-T/V-I If something **survives**, it continues to exist even after being in a dangerous situation or existing for a long time. ☐ *When the market economy is introduced, many factories will not survive.* ☐ *No one survived the crash.* ◻ V-T If you **survive** someone, you continue to live after they have died. ☐ *Most women will survive their spouses.*

SYNONYMS

survive
VERB ◻
pull through: *Everyone was very concerned whether he would pull through or not.*
live: *He's got a terrible disease and will not live long.*
last: *The marriage had lasted for less than two years.*

---

sur|vi|vor /sərvaɪvər/ (**survivors**) ◻ N-COUNT A **survivor** of a disaster, accident, or illness is someone who continues to live afterward in spite of coming close to death. ☐ *Officials said there were no survivors of the plane crash.* ◻ N-COUNT A **survivor** of a very unpleasant experience is a person who has had such an experience, and who is still affected by it. ☐ *This book is written with survivors of child sexual abuse in mind.* ◻ N-COUNT A person's **survivors** are the members of their family who continue to live after they have died. [AM] ☐ *The compensation bill offers the miners or their survivors as much as $100,000 apiece.*

sus|cep|tibil|ity /səseptɪbɪlɪti/ (**susceptibilities**) ◻ N-VAR If you have a **susceptibility** to something unpleasant, you are likely to be affected by it. ☐ *...his increased susceptibility to infections.* ◻ N-PLURAL A person's **susceptibilities** are feelings which can be easily hurt. [FORMAL] ☐ *I am well aware that in saying this I shall outrage a few susceptibilities.*

sus|cep|tible /səseptɪbəl/ ◻ ADJ [v-link ADJ to n] If you are **susceptible** to something or someone, you are very likely to be influenced by them. ☐ *Young people are often seen as being the most susceptible to advertisements.* ☐ *James was extremely susceptible to flattery.* ◻ ADJ If you are **susceptible** to a disease or injury, you are very likely to be affected by it. ☐ *Walking with weights makes the shoulders very susceptible to injury.*

su|shi /suʃi/ N-UNCOUNT **Sushi** is a Japanese dish of rice with sweetened vinegar, often served with raw fish.

sus|pect ♦♦◇ (**suspects, suspecting, suspected**)

The verb is pronounced /səspekt/. The noun and adjective are pronounced /sʌspekt/.

suspend

1 V-T You use **suspect** when you are stating something that you believe is probably true, in order to make it sound less strong or direct. [VAGUENESS] ☐ *I suspect they were right.* ☐ *The above complaints are, I suspect, just the tip of the iceberg.* **2** V-T If you **suspect** that something dishonest or unpleasant has been done, you believe that it has probably been done. If you **suspect** someone of doing an action of this kind, you believe that they probably did it. ☐ *He suspected that the woman staying in the flat above was using heroin.* ☐ *It was perfectly all right, he said, because the police had not suspected him of anything.* **3** N-COUNT A **suspect** is a person who the police or authorities think may be guilty of a crime. ☐ *Police have arrested a suspect in a series of killings and sexual assaults in the city.* **4** ADJ **Suspect** things or people are ones that you think may be dangerous or may be less good or genuine than they appear. ☐ *Delegates evacuated the building when a suspect package was found.*

COLLOCATIONS

suspect
NOUN **3**
noun + **suspect**: murder, terror, terrorist
adjective + **suspect**: key, likely, prime, usual
verb + **suspect**: arrest, charge, detain, hold; describe, identify

sus|pend ♦◇◇ /səspɛ́nd/ (**suspends**, **suspending**, **suspended**) **1** V-T If you **suspend** something, you delay it or stop it from happening for a while or until a decision is made about it. ☐ *The union suspended strike action this week.* **2** V-T If someone **is suspended**, they are prevented from holding a particular job or position for a fixed length of time or until a decision is made about them. ☐ *Julie was suspended from her job shortly after the incident.* **3** V-T [usu passive] If something **is suspended** from a high place, it is hanging from that place. ☐ *...instruments that are suspended on cables.* **4** → See feature box at **politics**

SYNONYMS

suspend
VERB **1**
postpone: *He decided to postpone the expedition until the following day.*
delay: *For sentimental reasons, I wanted to delay my departure until June.*
put off: *They put off having a baby until they were in their late 30s.*
defer: *Customers often defer payment for as long as possible.*

sus|pend|ed ani|ma|tion **1** N-UNCOUNT **Suspended animation** is a state in which an animal is unconscious, with its body functioning very slowly, for example so that the animal can survive the winter. **2** N-UNCOUNT If you describe someone as being in a state of **suspended animation**, you mean that they have become inactive and are doing nothing. ☐ *She lay in a state of suspended animation, waiting for dawn, when she would rise.*

sus|pend|ed sen|tence (**suspended sentences**) N-COUNT If a criminal is given a **suspended sentence**, they are given a prison sentence which they have to serve if they commit another crime within a specified period of time. ☐ *John was given a four-month suspended sentence.*

sus|pend|er belt (**suspender belts**) N-COUNT A **suspender belt** is the same as a **garter belt**. [BRIT]

sus|pend|ers /səspɛ́ndərz/ **1** N-PLURAL [also *a pair of* N] **Suspenders** are a pair of straps that go over someone's shoulders and are fastened to their pants at the front and back to prevent the pants from falling down. [AM] ☐ *He also wore a pair of suspenders.*

in BRIT, use **braces**

2 [BRIT] → see **garter 1**

sus|pense /səspɛ́ns/ **1** N-UNCOUNT **Suspense** is a state of excitement or anxiety about something that is going to happen very soon, for example about some news that you are waiting to hear. ☐ *The suspense over the two remaining hostages ended last night when the police discovered the bullet ridden bodies.* **2** PHRASE If you **keep** or **leave** someone **in suspense**, you deliberately delay telling them something that they are very eager to know about. ☐ *Keppler kept all his men in suspense until that morning before announcing which two would be going.*

sus|pense|ful /səspɛ́nsfəl/ ADJ [usu ADJ n] A **suspenseful** story makes you feel excited or anxious about what is going to happen in the story next. ☐ *...a suspenseful and sinister tale.*

sustain

sus|pen|sion /səspɛ́nʃən/ (**suspensions**) **1** N-UNCOUNT The **suspension** of something is the act of delaying or stopping it for a while or until a decision is made about it. ☐ *There's been a temporary suspension of flights out of LA.* **2** N-VAR Someone's **suspension** is their removal from a job or position for a period of time or until a decision is made about them. ☐ *The minister warned that any civil servant not at his desk faced immediate suspension.* **3** N-VAR A vehicle's **suspension** consists of the springs and other devices attached to the wheels, which give a smooth ride over uneven ground. ☐ *...the only small car with independent front suspension.*

sus|pen|sion bridge (**suspension bridges**) N-COUNT A **suspension bridge** is a type of bridge that is supported from above by cables.

sus|pi|cion ♦◇◇ /səspɪ́ʃən/ (**suspicions**) **1** N-VAR **Suspicion** or a **suspicion** is a belief or feeling that someone has committed a crime or done something wrong. ☐ *There was a suspicion that this runner attempted to avoid the procedures for drug testing.* ☐ *The police said their suspicions were aroused because Mr. Owens had other marks on his body.* **2** N-VAR If there is **suspicion** of someone or something, people do not trust them or consider them to be reliable. ☐ *This tendency in his thought is deepened by his suspicion of all Utopian political programs.* **3** N-COUNT A **suspicion** is a feeling that something is probably true or is likely to happen. ☐ *I have a sneaking suspicion that they are going to succeed.*

sus|pi|cious /səspɪ́ʃəs/ **1** ADJ If you are **suspicious** of someone or something, you do not trust them, and are careful when dealing with them. ☐ *He was rightly suspicious of meeting me until I reassured him I was not writing about him.* ● **sus|pi|cious|ly** ADV [ADV after v] ☐ *"What is it you want me to do?" Adams asked suspiciously.* **2** ADJ If you are **suspicious** of someone or something, you believe that they are probably involved in a crime or some dishonest activity. ☐ *Two officers on patrol became suspicious of two men in a car.* **3** ADJ If you describe someone or something as **suspicious**, you mean that there is some aspect of them which makes you think that they are involved in a crime or a dishonest activity. ☐ *He reported that two suspicious-looking characters had approached Callendar.* ● **sus|pi|cious|ly** ADV ☐ *They'll question them as to whether anyone was seen acting suspiciously in the area over the last few days.*

sus|pi|cious|ly /səspɪ́ʃəsli/ **1** ADV [ADV prep] If you say that one thing looks or sounds **suspiciously** like another thing, you mean that it probably is that thing, or something very similar to it, although it may be intended to seem different. ☐ *The tan-colored dog looks suspiciously like a pit bull terrier.* **2** ADV [ADV adj/adv] You can use **suspiciously** when you are describing something that you think is slightly strange or not as it should be. ☐ *He lives alone in a suspiciously tidy apartment.* **3** → see also **suspicious**

sus|tain ♦◇◇ /səstéɪn/ (**sustains**, **sustaining**, **sustained**) **1** V-T If you **sustain** something, you continue it or maintain it for a period of time. ☐ *He has sustained his fierce social conscience from young adulthood through old age.* ☐ *Recovery can't be sustained unless more jobs are created.* **2** V-T If you **sustain** something such as a defeat, loss, or injury, it happens to you. [FORMAL] ☐ *Every aircraft in there has sustained some damage.* **3** V-T If something **sustains** you, it supports you by giving you help, strength, or encouragement. [FORMAL] ☐ *The cash dividends they get from the cash crop would sustain them during the lean season.*

SYNONYMS

sustain
VERB
1
maintain: *Push yourself to make friends and to maintain the friendships.*
continue: *Outside the building, people continue their vigil, huddling around bonfires.*
keep up: *I was so hungry all the time that I could not keep the diet up for longer than a month.*
prolong: *The actual action of the drug can be prolonged significantly.*
2
suffer: *The peace process has suffered a serious blow now.*
undergo: *He underwent an agonizing 48-hour wait for the results of tests.*
experience: *British business is now experiencing a severe recession.*

sus|tain|able /səstˈeɪnəbəl/ **1** ADJ You use **sustainable** to describe the use of natural resources when this use is kept at a steady level that is not likely to damage the environment. ❑ ...the management, conservation and sustainable development of forests. • **sus|tain|abil|ity** /səstˌeɪnəbˈɪlɪti/ N-UNCOUNT ❑ ...the issue of long-term environmental sustainability. • **sus|tain|ably** ADV [ADV with v] ❑ It wants timber to come, where possible, from sustainably managed sources. **2** ADJ A **sustainable** plan, method, or system is designed to continue at the same rate or level of activity without any problems. ❑ The creation of an efficient and sustainable transport system is critical. • **sus|tain|abil|ity** N-UNCOUNT ❑ ...unease about the sustainability of the American economic recovery. **3** → See feature box at **recycle**

sus|te|nance /sˈʌstɪnəns/ N-UNCOUNT **Sustenance** is food or drink which a person, animal, or plant needs to remain alive and healthy. [FORMAL] ❑ The state provided a basic quantity of food for daily sustenance, but little else.

su|ture /sˈuːtʃər/ (sutures) N-COUNT A **suture** is a stitch made to join together the open parts of a wound, especially one made after a patient has been operated on. [MEDICAL]

SUV /ˌɛs juː vˈiː/ (SUVs) N-COUNT An **SUV** is a powerful vehicle with four-wheel drive that can be driven over rough terrain. SUV is an abbreviation for **sport utility vehicle**.

svelte /svˈɛlt, sfˈɛlt/ ADJ Someone who is **svelte** is slim and looks attractive and elegant. [APPROVAL]

SW SW is a written abbreviation for **southwest**. ❑ ...L'Enfant Plaza SW, Washington, D.C.

swab /swˈɒb/ (swabs) N-COUNT A **swab** is a small piece of cotton used by a doctor or nurse for cleaning a wound or putting a substance on it. ❑ "Okay," he replied and winced as she dabbed the cotton swab over the gash.

swad|dle /swˈɒdəl/ (swaddles, swaddling, swaddled) V-T If you **swaddle** a baby, you wrap cloth around it in order to keep it warm or to prevent it from moving. [OLD-FASHIONED] ❑ Swaddle your newborn baby so that she feels secure. ❑ ...a baby swaddled in silk brocade.

swag /swˈæɡ/ (swags) **1** N-UNCOUNT **Swag** is stolen goods, or money obtained illegally. [INFORMAL, OLD-FASHIONED] **2** N-COUNT A **swag** is a piece of material that is put above a window and hangs down in a decorative way.

swag|ger /swˈæɡər/ (swaggers, swaggering, swaggered) V-I If you **swagger**, you walk in a very proud, confident way, holding your body upright and swinging your hips. ❑ A broad shouldered man wearing a dinner jacket swaggered confidently up to the bar. • N-SING **Swagger** is also a noun. ❑ He walked with something of a swagger.

swain /swˈeɪn/ (swains) N-COUNT A **swain** is a young man who is in love. [OLD-FASHIONED]

swal|low /swˈɒloʊ/ (swallows, swallowing, swallowed) **1** V-T/V-I If you **swallow** something, you cause it to go from your mouth down into your stomach. ❑ You are asked to swallow a capsule containing vitamin B. ❑ Polly took a bite of the apple, chewed, and swallowed. • N-COUNT **Swallow** is also a noun. ❑ Jan lifted her glass and took a quick swallow. **2** V-I If you **swallow**, you make a movement in your throat as if you are swallowing something, often because you are nervous or frightened. ❑ Nancy swallowed hard and shook her head. **3** V-T If someone **swallows** a story or a statement, they believe it completely. ❑ They cast doubt on his words when it suited their case, but swallowed them whole when it did not. **4** N-COUNT A **swallow** is a kind of small bird with pointed wings and a forked tail. **5 a bitter pill to swallow** → see **pill**
▶ **swallow up 1** PHRASAL VERB If one thing **is swallowed up** by another, it becomes part of the first thing and no longer has a separate identity of its own. ❑ During the 1980s monster publishing houses started to swallow up smaller companies. **2** PHRASAL VERB If something **swallows up** money or resources, it uses them entirely while giving very little in return. ❑ A seven-day TV ad campaign could swallow up the best part of $100,000.

swam /swˈæm/ **Swam** is the past tense of **swim**.

swamp /swˈɒmp/ (swamps, swamping, swamped) **1** N-VAR A **swamp** is an area of very wet land with wild plants growing in it. ❑ I spent one whole night by a swamp behind the road listening to frogs. **2** V-T If something **swamps** a place or object, it fills it with water. ❑ Their electronic navigation failed and a rogue wave swamped the boat. **3** V-T [usu passive] If you **are swamped** by things or people, you have more of them than you can deal with. ❑ He is swamped with work.

swamp|land /swˈɒmplænd/ (swamplands) N-VAR **Swampland** is an area of land that is always very wet.

swampy /swˈɒmpi/ (swampier, swampiest) ADJ A **swampy** area of land is always very wet.

swan /swˈɒn/ (swans) N-COUNT A **swan** is a large bird with a very long neck. Swans live on rivers and lakes and are usually white.

swanky /swˈæŋki/ (swankier, swankiest) ADJ [usu ADJ n] If you describe something as **swanky**, you mean that it is fashionable and expensive. [INFORMAL] ❑ ...one of the swanky hotels that line the Pacific shore at Acapulco.

swan song also **swan-song** N-SING Someone's **swan song** is the last time that they do something for which they are famous, for example the last time that an actor gives a performance in the theater. ❑ I competed in the winter Olympics, which was my swan song.

swap /swˈɒp/ (swaps, swapping, swapped)

in BRIT, also use **swop**

1 V-RECIP If you **swap** something with someone, you give it to them and receive a different thing in exchange. ❑ Next week they will swap places and will repeat the switch weekly. ❑ I know a sculptor who swaps her pieces for drawings by a well-known artist. • N-COUNT **Swap** is also a noun. ❑ Over the long term, a swap of some kind is clearly in the public interest. **2** V-T If you **swap** one thing for another, you remove the first thing and replace it with the second, or you stop doing the first thing and start doing the second. ❑ Despite the heat, he'd swapped his overalls for a suit and tie. ❑ He has swapped his hectic rock star's lifestyle for that of a country gentleman.

swarm /swˈɔːrm/ (swarms, swarming, swarmed) **1** N-COUNT-COLL A **swarm** of bees or other insects is a large group of them flying together. ❑ ...a swarm of locusts. **2** V-I When bees or other insects **swarm**, they move or fly in a large group. ❑ A dark cloud of bees comes swarming out of the hive. **3** V-I When people **swarm** somewhere, they move there quickly in a large group. ❑ People swarmed to the stores, buying up everything in sight. **4** N-COUNT-COLL A **swarm** of people is a large group of them moving about quickly. ❑ A swarm of people encircled the hotel. **5** V-I [usu cont] If a place **is swarming** with people, it is full of people moving about in a busy way. ❑ Within minutes the area was swarming with officers who began searching a nearby wood.

swarthy /swˈɔːrði/ (swarthier, swarthiest) ADJ A **swarthy** person has a dark face. ❑ He had a broad swarthy face.

swash|buck|ling /swˈɒʃbʌklɪŋ/ ADJ If you describe someone or something as **swashbuckling**, you mean that they are connected with adventure and excitement. ❑ ...a swashbuckling adventure story.

swas|ti|ka /swˈɒstɪkə/ (swastikas) N-COUNT A **swastika** is a symbol in the shape of a cross with each arm bent over at right angles. It is used in India as a good luck sign, but it was also used by the Nazis in Germany as their official symbol.

swat /swˈɒt/ (swats, swatting, swatted) V-T If you **swat** something such as an insect, you hit it with a quick, swinging movement, using your hand or a flat object. ❑ Hundreds of flies buzz around us, and the workman keeps swatting them.

swathe /swˈeɪð/ (swathes, swathing, swathed)

The noun is also spelled **swath**.

1 N-COUNT [usu N of n] A **swathe** of land is a long strip of land. ❑ Year by year great swathes of this small nation's countryside disappear. **2** N-COUNT [usu N of n] A **swathe** of cloth is a long strip of cloth, especially one that is wrapped around someone or something. ❑ ...swathes of white silk. **3** V-T To **swathe** someone or something **in** cloth means to wrap them in it completely. ❑ She swathed her enormous body in thin black fabrics. ❑ His head was swathed in bandages made from a torn sheet.

SWAT team /swˈɒt tiːm/ (SWAT teams) N-COUNT A **SWAT team** is a group of police officers who have been specially trained to deal with very dangerous or violent situations. SWAT is an abbreviation for 'Special Weapons and Tactics.' [mainly AM]

sway /sweɪ/ (sways, swaying, swayed) **1** V-I When people or things **sway**, they lean or swing slowly from one side to the other. ❑ *The people swayed back and forth with arms linked.* ❑ *The whole boat swayed and tipped.* **2** V-T If you **are swayed** by someone or something, you are influenced by them. ❑ *Don't ever be swayed by fashion.* **3** PHRASE If someone or something **holds sway**, they have great power or influence over a particular place or activity. ❑ *Powerful traditional chiefs hold sway over more than 15 million people in rural areas.*

swear /swɛər/ (swears, swearing, swore, sworn) **1** V-I If someone **swears**, they use language that is considered to be vulgar or offensive, usually because they are angry. ❑ *It's wrong to swear and shout.* **2** V-T If you **swear** to do something, you promise in a serious way that you will do it. ❑ *Alan swore that he would do everything in his power to help us.* ❑ *We have sworn to fight cruelty wherever we find it.* **3** V-T/V-I If you say that you **swear** that something is true or that you can **swear** to it, you are saying very firmly that it is true. [EMPHASIS] ❑ *I swear I've told you all I know.* ❑ *I swear on all I hold dear that I had nothing to do with this.* **4** V-T [usu passive] If someone **is sworn** to secrecy or **is sworn** to silence, they promise another person that they will not reveal a secret. ❑ *She was bursting to announce the news but was sworn to secrecy.* **5** → see also **sworn**
▶ **swear by** PHRASAL VERB If you **swear by** something, you believe that it can be relied on to have a particular effect. [INFORMAL] ❑ *Many people swear by vitamin C's ability to ward off colds.*
▶ **swear in** PHRASAL VERB When someone **is sworn in**, they formally promise to fulfill the duties of a new job or appointment. ❑ *Mary Robinson was formally sworn in as Ireland's first woman president.*

swearing-in N-SING The **swearing-in** at the beginning of a trial or official appointment is the act of making formal promises to fulfill the duties it involves.

swear word (swear words) also **swearword** N-COUNT A **swear word** is a word which is considered to be vulgar or offensive. Swear words are usually used when people are angry.

sweat /swɛt/ (sweats, sweating, sweated) **1** N-UNCOUNT **Sweat** is the salty colorless liquid which comes through your skin when you are hot, sick, or afraid. ❑ *Both horse and rider were dripping with sweat within five minutes.* **2** V-I When you **sweat**, sweat comes through your skin. ❑ *Already they were sweating as the sun beat down upon them.* • **sweat|ing** N-UNCOUNT ❑ *...symptoms such as sweating, irritability, anxiety, and depression.* **3** N-COUNT If someone is in a **sweat**, they are sweating a lot. ❑ *Every morning I would break out in a sweat.* ❑ *Cool down very gradually after working up a sweat.* **4** PHRASE If someone is **in a cold sweat** or **in a sweat**, they feel frightened or embarrassed. ❑ *The very thought brought me out in a cold sweat.*

sweat|er /swɛtər/ (sweaters) N-COUNT A **sweater** is a warm knitted piece of clothing which covers the upper part of your body and your arms.

sweat|pants /swɛtpænts/ also **sweat pants** N-PLURAL **Sweatpants** are the part of a sweatsuit that covers your legs. [AM]

sweat|shirt /swɛtʃɜrt/ (sweatshirts) also **sweat shirt** N-COUNT A **sweatshirt** is a loose warm piece of casual clothing, usually made of thick stretchy cotton, which covers the upper part of your body and your arms.

sweat|shop /swɛtʃɒp/ (sweatshops) also **sweat shop** N-COUNT If you describe a small factory as a **sweatshop**, you mean that many people work there in poor conditions for low pay. [DISAPPROVAL]

sweat|suit /swɛtsut/ (sweatsuits) also **sweat suit** N-COUNT A **sweatsuit** is a loose, warm, stretchy suit consisting of long pants and a top which people wear to relax and do exercise. [AM]

sweaty /swɛti/ (sweatier, sweatiest) **1** ADJ If parts of your body or your clothes are **sweaty**, they are soaked or covered with sweat. ❑ *...sweaty hands.* **2** ADJ A **sweaty** place or activity makes you sweat because it is hot or tiring. ❑ *...a sweaty nightclub.*

swede /swid/ (swedes) N-VAR A **swede** is the same as a **rutabaga**. [BRIT]

Swede /swid/ (Swedes) N-COUNT A **Swede** is a Swedish citizen, or a person of Swedish origin.

Swe|dish /swidɪʃ/ **1** ADJ **Swedish** means belonging or relating to Sweden, or to its people, language, or culture. **2** N-UNCOUNT **Swedish** is the language spoken in Sweden.

sweep ♦◇◇ /swip/ (sweeps, sweeping, swept) **1** V-T/V-I If you **sweep** an area of floor or ground, you push dirt or garbage off it using a brush with a long handle. ❑ *The owner of the store was sweeping his floor when I walked in.* ❑ *She was in the kitchen sweeping crumbs into a dust pan.* **2** V-T If you **sweep** things off something, you push them off with a quick smooth movement of your arm. ❑ *I swept rainwater off the flat top of a gravestone.* ❑ *With a gesture of frustration, she swept the cards from the table.* **3** V-T If someone with long hair **sweeps** their hair into a particular style, they put it into that style. ❑ *...stylish ways of sweeping your hair off your face.* **4** V-T/V-I If your arm or hand **sweeps** in a particular direction, or if you **sweep** it there, it moves quickly and smoothly in that direction. ❑ *His arm swept around the room.* ❑ *Daniels swept his arm over his friend's shoulder.* • N-COUNT **Sweep** is also a noun. ❑ *With one sweep of her hand she threw back the sheets.* **5** V-T If wind, a stormy sea, or another strong force **sweeps** someone or something along, it moves them quickly along. ❑ *...landslides that buried homes and swept cars into the sea.* **6** V-T If you **are swept** somewhere, you are taken there very quickly. ❑ *The visitors were swept past various monuments.* **7** V-I If something **sweeps** from one place to another, it moves there extremely quickly. ❑ *An icy wind swept through the streets.* [WRITTEN] **8** V-T/V-I If events, ideas, or beliefs **sweep** through a place or **sweep** a place, they spread quickly through it. ❑ *A flu epidemic is sweeping through Moscow.* **9** V-T/V-I If a person or group **sweeps** an election or **sweeps** to victory, they win the election easily. ❑ *A man who's promised to make radical changes to benefit the poor has swept the election.* **10** N-COUNT If someone makes a **sweep** of a place, they search it, usually because they are looking for people who are hiding or for an illegal activity. ❑ *Two of the soldiers swiftly began making a sweep of the premises.* **11** → see also **sweeping** **12** PHRASE If someone **sweeps** something bad or wrong **under the carpet**, or if they **sweep** it **under the rug**, they try to prevent people from hearing about it. ❑ *For a long time this problem has been swept under the carpet.* **13** PHRASE If you make **a clean sweep** of something such as a series of games or tournaments, you win them all. ❑ *...the first club to make a clean sweep of all three trophies.* **14 to sweep the board** → see **board**
▶ **sweep up** PHRASAL VERB If you **sweep up** rubbish or dirt, you push it together with a brush and then remove it. ❑ *Get a broom and sweep up that glass, will you?*

SYNONYMS
---

sweep
VERB **1**
brush: *Using a small brush, he brushed away the fine sawdust.*
wipe: *I'll just wipe the table.*
vacuum: *I vacuumed the carpets today.*

COLLOCATIONS
---

sweep
NOUN **4**
adjective + **sweep**: broad, grand, majestic, panoramic; downward

sweep|er /swipər/ (sweepers) N-COUNT In soccer, a **sweeper** is a player whose position is behind the main defenders but in front of the goalkeeper.

sweep|ing /swipɪŋ/ **1** ADJ [ADJ n] A **sweeping** curve is a long wide curve. ❑ *...the long sweeping curve of Rio's Guanabara Bay.* **2** ADJ If someone makes a **sweeping** statement or generalization, they make a statement which applies to all things of a particular kind, although they have not considered all the relevant facts carefully. [DISAPPROVAL] ❑ *It is far too early to make sweeping statements about gene therapy.* **3** ADJ **Sweeping** changes are large and very important or significant. ❑ *The new government has started to make sweeping changes in the economy.* **4** → see also **sweep**

sweep|stakes /swipsteɪks/ (sweepstakes) also **sweepstake** N-COUNT A **sweepstakes** is a method of gambling in which each person pays a small amount of money and is given the name of a competitor before a race or contest. The person who has the name of the winner receives all the money. [AM]

sweet ✦✧ /swiːt/ (sweeter, sweetest, sweets) **1** ADJ Sweet food and drink contains a lot of sugar. ▫ ...a mug of sweet tea. ▫ If the sauce seems too sweet, add a dash of red wine vinegar. • **sweet|ness** N-UNCOUNT ▫ Florida oranges have a natural sweetness. **2** ADJ A **sweet** smell is a pleasant one, for example the smell of a flower. ▫ ...the sweet smell of her shampoo. **3** ADJ A **sweet** sound is pleasant, smooth, and gentle. ▫ Her voice was as soft and sweet as a young girl's. • **sweet|ly** ADV ▫ He sang much more sweetly than he has before. **4** ADJ If you describe something as **sweet**, you mean that it gives you great pleasure and satisfaction. [WRITTEN] ▫ There are few things quite as sweet as revenge. **5** ADJ If you describe someone as **sweet**, you mean that they are pleasant, kind, and gentle toward other people. ▫ He is a very kind and sweet man. • **sweet|ly** ADV ▫ I just smiled sweetly and said no. **6** ADJ If you describe a small person or thing as **sweet**, you mean that they are attractive in a simple or unsophisticated way. [INFORMAL] ▫ ...a sweet little baby girl. **7** N-PLURAL **Sweets** are foods that have a lot of sugar. [AM] ▫ To maintain her weight, she simply chooses fruits and vegetables over fats and sweets. **8** N-COUNT **Sweets** are small sweet things such as chocolates and mints. [BRIT]

in AM, use **candy**

9 N-VAR A **sweet** is the same as a **dessert**. [BRIT] **10** → see also **sweetness** **11** **a sweet tooth** → see **tooth**

sweet and sour also **sweet-and-sour** ADJ [ADJ n] **Sweet and sour** is used to describe Chinese food that contains both a sweet flavor and something sharp or sour such as lemon or vinegar.

sweet|bread /swiːtbrɛd/ (sweetbreads) N-COUNT **Sweetbreads** are meat obtained from the pancreas of a calf or a lamb.

sweet|corn /swiːtkɔːrn/ N-UNCOUNT **Sweetcorn** is a long rounded vegetable covered in small yellow seeds. It is part of the maize plant. The seeds themselves can also be referred to as **sweetcorn**.

sweet|en /swiːtən/ (sweetens, sweetening, sweetened) **1** V-T If you **sweeten** food or drink, you add sugar, honey, or another sweet substance to it. ▫ He liberally sweetened his coffee. **2** V-T If you **sweeten** something such as an offer or a business deal, you try to make someone want it more by improving it or by increasing the amount you are willing to pay. ▫ The organization has sweetened its takeover offer for the startup.

sweet|en|er /swiːtnər/ (sweeteners) **1** N-MASS **Sweetener** is an artificial substance that can be used in drinks instead of sugar. **2** N-COUNT A **sweetener** is something that you give or offer someone in order to persuade them to accept an offer or business deal. ▫ A corporation can buy back its bonds by paying investors the face value (plus a sweetener).

sweet|heart /swiːthɑːrt/ (sweethearts) **1** N-VOC You call someone **sweetheart** if you are very fond of them. ▫ Happy birthday, sweetheart. **2** N-COUNT Your **sweetheart** is your boyfriend or your girlfriend. [OLD-FASHIONED] ▫ I married Shurla, my childhood sweetheart.

sweet|ie /swiːti/ (sweeties) **1** N-VOC You can call someone **sweetie** if you are fond of them, especially if they are younger than you. [INFORMAL] **2** N-COUNT If you say that someone is a **sweetie**, you mean that they are kind and nice. [INFORMAL]

sweet|ish /swiːtɪʃ/ ADJ A **sweetish** smell or taste is fairly sweet.

sweet|ly /swiːtli/ **1** ADV [ADV with v] If an engine or machine is running **sweetly**, it is working smoothly and efficiently. ▫ He heard the car engine running sweetly beyond the open door. **2** → see also **sweet**

sweet|meat /swiːtmiːt/ (sweetmeats) N-COUNT [usu pl] **Sweetmeats** are sweet items of food, especially ones that are considered special. [OLD-FASHIONED]

sweet|ness /swiːtnəs/ **1** PHRASE If you say that a relationship or situation is not **all sweetness and light**, you mean that it is not as pleasant as it appears to be. ▫ It has not all been sweetness and light between him and the mayor. **2** → see also **sweet**

sweet noth|ings N-PLURAL If someone whispers **sweet nothings** to you, they quietly say nice, loving, and flattering things to you.

sweet pea (sweet peas) also **sweetpea** N-COUNT A **sweet pea** is a climbing plant which has delicate, sweet-smelling flowers.

sweet pep|per (sweet peppers) N-COUNT A **sweet pepper** is a hollow green, red, or yellow vegetable.

sweet po|ta|to (sweet potatoes) N-VAR **Sweet potatoes** are vegetables that look like large ordinary potatoes but taste sweet. They have pinkish-brown skins and yellow flesh.

sweet shop (sweet shops) N-COUNT A **sweet shop** is the same as a **candy store**. [BRIT]

sweet talk (sweet talks, sweet talking, sweet talked) also **sweet-talk** V-T If you **sweet talk** someone, you talk to them very nicely so that they will do what you want. ▫ She could always sweet talk Pamela into letting her stay up late. ▫ He even tried to sweet talk the police officer who arrested him.

swell /swɛl/ (swells, swelling, swelled, swollen)

The forms **swelled** and **swollen** are both used as the past participle.

1 V-T/V-I If the amount or size of something **swells** or if something **swells** it, it becomes larger than it was before. ▫ The human population swelled, at least temporarily, as migrants moved south. ▫ His bank balance has swelled by $222,000 in the last three weeks. **2** V-I If something such as a part of your body **swells**, it becomes larger and rounder than normal. ▫ Do your ankles swell at night? **3** N-COUNT A **swell** is the regular movement of waves up and down in the open sea. ▫ We bobbed gently up and down on the swell of the incoming tide. **4** → see also **swollen** **5** → See feature box at **boat, population**

swell|ing /swɛlɪŋ/ (swellings) N-VAR A **swelling** is a raised, curved shape on the surface of your body which appears as a result of an injury or an illness. ▫ His eye was partly closed, and there was a swelling over his lid.

swel|ter /swɛltər/ (swelters, sweltering, sweltered) V-I If you **swelter**, you are very uncomfortable because the weather is extremely hot. ▫ They sweltered in temperatures rising to a hundred degrees.

swel|ter|ing /swɛltərɪŋ/ ADJ If you describe the weather as **sweltering**, you mean that it is extremely hot and makes you feel uncomfortable. ▫ ...the sweltering heat of the St. Petersburg summer.

swept /swɛpt/ **Swept** is the past tense and past participle of **sweep**.

swerve /swɜːrv/ (swerves, swerving, swerved) **1** V-T/V-I If a vehicle or other moving thing **swerves** or if you **swerve** it, it suddenly changes direction, often in order to avoid hitting something. ▫ Drivers coming in the opposite direction swerved to avoid the bodies. ▫ Her car swerved off the road into a 6 ft high brick wall. • N-COUNT **Swerve** is also a noun. ▫ He swung the car to the left and that swerve saved Malone's life. **2** → See feature box at **accident**

swift /swɪft/ (swifter, swiftest, swifts) **1** ADJ A **swift** event or process happens very quickly or without delay. ▫ Our task is to challenge the U.N. to make a swift decision. • **swift|ly** ADV ▫ Wall Street reacted swiftly to yesterday's verdict. **2** ADJ Something that is **swift** moves very quickly. ▫ With a swift movement, Matthew Jerrold sat upright. • **swift|ly** ADV [ADV with v] ▫ Lenny moved swiftly and silently across the front lawn. **3** N-COUNT A **swift** is a small bird with long curved wings.

swig /swɪɡ/ (swigs, swigging, swigged) V-I If you **swig** a drink, you drink it from a bottle or cup quickly and in large amounts. ▫ I swigged down two white wines. ▫ He was still hanging around, swigging the Coke out of the can. • N-COUNT **Swig** is also a noun. ▫ Brian took a swig of his beer.

swill /swɪl/ (swills, swilling, swilled) **1** N-UNCOUNT **Swill** is a liquid mixture containing waste food that is given to pigs to eat. **2** V-T If you **swill** an alcoholic drink, you drink a lot of it. ▫ A crowd of men were standing around swilling beer. **3** V-T/V-I If a liquid **swills** around, or if you **swill** it around, it moves around the area that it is contained in. ▫ Gallons of sea water had rushed into the cabin and were now swilling about in the bilges. ▫ She swilled the whiskey around in her glass.

swim ✦✧ /swɪm/ (swims, swimming, swam, swum) **1** V-T/V-I When you **swim**, you move through water by making movements with your arms and legs. ▫ She learned to swim when she was really tiny. ▫ He was rescued only when an exhausted friend swam ashore. ▫ I swim a mile a day. • N-SING **Swim**

is also a noun. ☐ *When can we go for a swim?* **2** V-T If you **swim** a race, you take part in a swimming race. ☐ *She swam the 400 meters medley.* **3** V-T If you **swim** a stretch of water, you keep swimming until you have crossed it. ☐ *By the time we reached the other side, Maram vowed that he would never swim a river again.* **4** V-I When a fish **swims**, it moves through water by moving its body. ☐ *The barriers are lethal to fish trying to swim upstream.* **5** V-I If your head **is swimming**, you feel unsteady and slightly ill. ☐ *The musty aroma of incense made her head swim.* **6 sink or swim** → see **sink**

swim|mer /swɪmər/ (**swimmers**) N-COUNT A **swimmer** is a person who swims, especially for sport or pleasure, or a person who is swimming. ☐ *You don't have to worry about me. I'm a good swimmer.*

swim|ming /swɪmɪŋ/ N-UNCOUNT **Swimming** is the activity of moving through water by making movements with your arms and legs, especially as a sport or for pleasure. ☐ *Swimming is probably the best form of exercise you can get.*

swim|ming bath (**swimming baths**) N-COUNT A **swimming bath** is the same as a **swimming pool**. [BRIT]

swim|ming cap (**swimming caps**) N-COUNT A **swimming cap** is a rubber cap which you wear to keep your hair dry when you are swimming.

swim|ming cos|tume (**swimming costumes**) N-COUNT A **swimming costume** is the same as a **swimsuit**. [BRIT]

swim|ming|ly /swɪmɪŋli/ PHRASE If you say that something **is going swimmingly**, you mean that everything is happening in a satisfactory way, without any problems. [INFORMAL] ☐ *The work has been going swimmingly.*

swim|ming pool (**swimming pools**) N-COUNT A **swimming pool** is a large hole in the ground that has been made and filled with water so that people can swim in it.

swim|ming trunks N-PLURAL [also *a pair of* N] **Swimming trunks** are the shorts that a man wears when he goes swimming.

swim|suit /swɪmsuːt/ (**swimsuits**) N-COUNT A **swimsuit** is a piece of clothing that is worn for swimming, especially by women and girls. ☐ *...pictures of models in swimsuits.*

swim|wear /swɪmwɛər/ N-UNCOUNT **Swimwear** is the things people wear for swimming.

swin|dle /swɪndᵊl/ (**swindles, swindling, swindled**) V-T If someone **swindles** a person or an organization, they deceive them in order to get something valuable from them, especially money. ☐ *A businessman swindled investors out of millions of dollars.* • N-COUNT **Swindle** is also a noun. ☐ *He fled to Switzerland rather than face trial for a tax swindle.*

swine /swaɪn/ (**swine** or **swines**)

The form **swines** is used as the plural for meaning **1**; **swine** is used as both the singular and plural for meaning **2**.

1 N-COUNT If you call someone a **swine**, you dislike them or think that they are a bad person, usually because they have behaved unpleasantly toward you. [INFORMAL, DISAPPROVAL] **2** N-COUNT A **swine** is a pig. [OLD-FASHIONED] ☐ *...imports of live swine from Canada.*

swing ♦◇◇ /swɪŋ/ (**swings, swinging, swung**) **1** V-T/V-I If something **swings** or if you **swing** it, it moves repeatedly backward and forward or from side to side from a fixed point. ☐ *The sail of the little boat swung crazily from one side to the other.* ☐ *She was swinging a bottle of wine by its neck.* • N-COUNT **Swing** is also a noun. ☐ *...a woman in a tight red dress, walking with a slight swing to her hips.* **2** V-T/V-I If something **swings** in a particular direction or if you **swing** it in that direction, it moves in that direction with a smooth, curving movement. ☐ *The torchlight swung across the little beach and out over the water, searching.* ☐ *The canoe found the current and swung around.* • N-COUNT **Swing** is also a noun. ☐ *When he's not on the tennis court, you'll find him practicing his golf swing.* **3** V-T/V-I If a vehicle **swings** in a particular direction, or if the driver **swings** it in a particular direction, they turn suddenly in that direction. ☐ *Joanna swung back on to the main approach and headed for the airport.* **4** V-I If someone **swings** around, they turn around quickly, usually because they are surprised. ☐ *She swung around to him, spilling her tea without noticing it.* **5** V-I If you **swing** at a person or thing, you try to hit them with your arm or with something that you are

holding. ☐ *Blanche swung at her but she moved her head back and Blanche missed.* • N-COUNT **Swing** is also a noun. ☐ *I often want to take a swing at someone to relieve my feelings.* **6** N-COUNT A **swing** is a seat hanging by two ropes or chains from a metal frame or from the branch of a tree. You can sit on the seat and move forward and backward through the air. ☐ *Go to the neighborhood park. Run around, push the kids on the swings.* **7** N-COUNT A **swing** in people's opinions, attitudes, or feelings is a change in them, especially a sudden or big change. ☐ *Educational practice is liable to sudden swings and changes.* ☐ *Dieters suffer from violent mood swings.* **8** V-I If people's opinions, attitudes, or feelings **swing**, they change, especially in a sudden or extreme way. ☐ *In two years' time there is a presidential election, and the voters could swing again.* **9** PHRASE If something is **in full swing**, it is operating fully and is no longer in its early stages. ☐ *When we returned, the party was in full swing and the dance floor was crowded.* **10** PHRASE If you **get into the swing of** something, you become very involved in it and enjoy what you are doing. ☐ *Everyone understood how hard it was to get back into the swing of things after such a long absence.*

COLLOCATIONS

swing
NOUN **7**
noun + **swing**: mood
adjective + **swing**: dramatic, sharp, sudden, violent; political
verb + **swing**: experience, suffer; achieve, gain, record
VERB **8**
noun + **swing**: momentum, mood, opinion
swing + adverb: decisively, dramatically, sharply, violently; back

---

swing bridge (**swing bridges**) N-COUNT A **swing bridge** is a low bridge that can be opened either in the middle or on one side in order to let ships pass through.

swing door (**swing doors**) N-COUNT **Swing doors** are the same as **swinging doors**. [mainly BRIT]

swing|er /swɪŋər/ (**swingers**) **1** N-COUNT A **swinger** is a person who is lively and fashionable. [INFORMAL, OLD-FASHIONED] **2** N-COUNT **Swingers** are people who are married or in a long-term relationship and who like to have sex with other people's partners.

swing|ing /swɪŋɪŋ/ ADJ [usu ADJ n] If you describe something or someone as **swinging**, you mean that they are lively and fashionable. [INFORMAL, OLD-FASHIONED] ☐ *The stuffy '50s gave way to the swinging '60s.*

swing|ing door (**swinging doors**) N-COUNT [usu pl] **Swinging doors** are doors that can open both toward you and away from you. [AM]

in BRIT, use **swing door**

swing vote (**swing votes**) N-COUNT In a situation when people are about to vote, the **swing vote** is used to talk about the vote of a person or group which is difficult to predict and which will be important in deciding the result. [mainly AM, JOURNALISM] ☐ *...a Democrat who holds the swing vote on the committee.*

swing vot|er (**swing voters**) N-COUNT A **swing voter** is a person who is not a firm supporter of any political party, and whose vote in an election is difficult to predict. [AM]

in BRIT, use **floating voter**

swipe /swaɪp/ (**swipes, swiping, swiped**) **1** V-I If you **swipe** at a person or thing, you try to hit them with a stick or other object, making a swinging movement with your arm. ☐ *She swiped at Rusty as though he was a fly.* • N-COUNT **Swipe** is also a noun. ☐ *He took a swipe at Andrew that deposited him on the floor.* **2** V-T If you **swipe** something, you steal it quickly. [INFORMAL] ☐ *She was convicted of swiping more than $5,500 worth of goods from Saks Fifth Avenue.* **3** N-COUNT If you take a **swipe at** a person or an organization, you criticize them, usually in an indirect way. ☐ *They recorded a song which took a swipe at greedy property developers.* **4** V-T If you **swipe** a credit card or swipe card through a machine, you pass it through a narrow space in the machine so that the machine can read information on the card's magnetic strip. ☐ *Swipe your card through the phone, then dial.*

swipe card (swipe cards) also **swipecard** N-COUNT A **swipe card** is a plastic card with a magnetic strip on it which contains information that can be read or transferred by passing the card through a special machine. ❑ *They use a swipe card to go in and out of their offices.*

swirl /swɜrl/ (swirls, swirling, swirled) V-T/V-I If you **swirl** something liquid or flowing, or if it **swirls**, it moves around and around quickly. ❑ *She smiled, swirling the wine in her glass.* ❑ *The black water swirled around his legs, reaching almost to his knees.* • N-COUNT **Swirl** is also a noun. ❑ *...small swirls of chocolate cream.*

swish /swɪʃ/ (swishes, swishing, swished) V-T/V-I If something **swishes** or if you **swish** it, it moves quickly through the air, making a soft sound. ❑ *A car swished by steady and fast heading for the coast.* ❑ *He swished his cape around his shoulders.* • N-COUNT **Swish** is also a noun. ❑ *She turned with a swish of her skirt.*

Swiss /swɪs/ (**Swiss**) **1** ADJ **Swiss** means belonging or relating to Switzerland, or to its people or culture. **2** N-COUNT [usu pl, the N] The **Swiss** are the people of Switzerland.

Swiss cheese (Swiss cheeses) N-VAR **Swiss cheese** is hard cheese with holes in it.

swiss roll (swiss rolls) also **swiss-roll** N-VAR A **swiss roll** is a cylindrical cake made from a thin flat sponge which is covered with jam or cream on one side, then rolled up. [BRIT]

in AM, use **jelly roll**

switch ✦◇◇ /swɪtʃ/ (switches, switching, switched) **1** N-COUNT A **switch** is a small control for an electrical device which you use to turn the device on or off. ❑ *Leona put some detergent into the dishwasher, shut the door, and pressed the switch.* **2** N-PLURAL On a railroad track, the **switches** are the levers and rails at a place where two tracks join or separate. The **switches** enable a train to move from one track to another. [AM] ❑ *...a set of railroad tracks – including switches – and a model train.*

in BRIT, use **points**

3 V-T/V-I If you **switch** to something different, for example to a different system, task, or subject of conversation, you change to it from what you were doing or saying before. ❑ *Estonia is switching to a market economy.* ❑ *The law would encourage companies to switch from coal to cleaner fuels.* • N-COUNT [usu with supp] **Switch** is also a noun. ❑ *The spokesman implicitly condemned the United States policy switch.* • PHRASAL VERB **Switch over** means the same as **switch**. ❑ *Everywhere communists are tending to switch over to social democracy.* **4** V-T/V-I If you **switch** your attention from one thing to another or if your attention **switches**, you stop paying attention to the first thing and start paying attention to the second. ❑ *My mother's interest had switched to my health.* **5** V-T If you **switch** two things, you replace one with the other. ❑ *In half an hour, they'd switched the tags on every cable.*
▶ **switch off** **1** PHRASAL VERB If you **switch off** a light or other electrical device, you stop it working by operating a switch. ❑ *She switched off the coffee-machine.* **2** PHRASAL VERB If you **switch off**, you stop paying attention or stop thinking or worrying about something. [INFORMAL] ❑ *Thankfully, I've learned to switch off and let it go over my head.*
▶ **switch on** PHRASAL VERB If you **switch on** a light or other electrical device, you make it start working by operating a switch. ❑ *She emptied both their mugs and switched on the electric kettle.*

--- SYNONYMS ---

switch
VERB **3**
exchange: *We exchanged addresses and Christmas cards.*
trade: *Kids used to trade baseball cards.*
swap: *Next week, they will swap places and will repeat the switch weekly.*

switch|back /swɪtʃbæk/ (switchbacks) N-COUNT A **switchback** is a road which goes up a steep hill in a series of sharp bends, or a sharp bend in a road.

switch|blade /swɪtʃbleɪd/ (switchblades) N-COUNT A **switchblade** is a knife with a blade that is hidden in the handle and that springs out when a button is pressed.

switch|board /swɪtʃbɔrd/ (switchboards) N-COUNT A **switchboard** is a place in a large office or business where all the telephone calls are connected. ❑ *He asked to be connected to the central switchboard.*

switched-on ADJ If you describe someone as **switched-on**, you mean that they are aware of the latest developments in a particular area or activity. [INFORMAL] ❑ *I am very impressed with Brian Hanlon, who seems a switched-on sort of guy.*

switch-hitter (switch-hitters) N-COUNT In baseball, a **switch-hitter** is a player who can hit the ball well with either hand. ❑ *A switch-hitter, he has very good speed on the bases.*

swiv|el /swɪvəl/ (swivels, swiveling or swivelling, swiveled or swivelled) V-T/V-I If something **swivels** or if you **swivel** it, it turns around a central point so that it is facing in a different direction. ❑ *She swiveled her chair and stared out the window.*

swiv|el chair (swivel chairs) N-COUNT A **swivel chair** is a chair whose seat can be turned around a central point to face in a different direction without moving the legs.

swol|len /swoʊlən/ **1** **Swollen** is the past participle of **swell**. **2** ADJ If a part of your body is **swollen**, it is larger and rounder than normal, usually as a result of injury or illness. ❑ *My eyes were so swollen I could hardly see.* **3** ADJ A **swollen** river has more water in it and flows faster than normal, usually because of heavy rain. ❑ *The river, brown and swollen with rain, was running fast.*

swoon /swun/ (swoons, swooning, swooned) V-I If you **swoon**, you are strongly affected by your feelings for someone you love or admire very much. ❑ *Virtually every woman in the '20s swooned over Valentino.* ❑ *They shriek and swoon at their every word.*

swoop /swup/ (swoops, swooping, swooped) **1** V-I If police or soldiers **swoop** on a place, they go there suddenly and quickly, usually in order to arrest someone or to attack the place. [JOURNALISM] ❑ *The terror ended when armed police swooped on the car.* • N-COUNT **Swoop** is also a noun. ❑ *Police held 10 suspected illegal immigrants after a swoop on a Mexican truck.* **2** V-I When a bird or airplane **swoops**, it suddenly moves downwards through the air in a smooth curving movement. ❑ *More than 20 helicopters began swooping in low over the ocean.* **3** PHRASE If something is done **in one fell swoop**, it is done on a single occasion or by a single action. ❑ *In one fell swoop the bank wiped away the tentative benefits of this policy.*

swop /swɒp/ [BRIT] → see **swap**

sword /sɔrd/ (swords) **1** N-COUNT A **sword** is a weapon with a handle and a long sharp blade. **2** PHRASE If you **cross swords** with someone, you disagree with them and argue with them about something. ❑ *...a candidate who's crossed swords with labor by supporting the free-trade pact.* **3** PHRASE If you say that something is a **double-edged sword**, you mean that it has negative effects as well as positive effects. ❑ *A person's looks are a double-edged sword. Sometimes it works in your favor, sometimes it works against you.*

sword|fish /sɔrdfɪʃ/ (swordfish) N-VAR A **swordfish** is a large sea fish with a very long upper jaw. • N-UNCOUNT **Swordfish** is this fish eaten as food. ❑ *...grilled swordfish with a yogurt dressing.*

swords|man /sɔrdzmən/ (swordsmen) N-COUNT A **swordsman** is a man who is skilled at fighting with a sword.

swords|woman /sɔrdzwʊmən/ (swordswomen) N-COUNT A **swordswoman** is a woman who is skilled at fighting with a sword.

swore /swɔr/ **Swore** is the past tense of **swear**.

sworn /swɔrn/ **1** **Sworn** is the past participle of **swear**. **2** ADJ [ADJ n] If you make a **sworn** statement or declaration, you swear that everything that you have said in it is true. ❑ *The allegations against them were made in sworn evidence to the inquiry.* **3** ADJ [ADJ n] If two people or two groups of people are **sworn enemies**, they dislike each other very much. ❑ *It somehow seems hardly surprising that Ms. Player is now his sworn enemy.*

swum /swʌm/ **Swum** is the past participle of **swim**.

swung /swʌŋ/ **Swung** is the past tense and past participle of **swing**.

syba|rit|ic /sɪbərɪtɪk/ ADJ [usu ADJ n] Someone who has a **sybaritic** way of life spends a lot of time relaxing in a luxurious way. [FORMAL]

syca|more /sɪkəmɔr/ (sycamores) N-VAR A **sycamore** or a **sycamore tree** is a tree that has large leaves with five points.

• N-UNCOUNT **Sycamore** is the wood of this tree. ❑ *The furniture is made of sycamore, beech, and leather.*

syco|phan|cy /sɪkəfənsi/ N-UNCOUNT **Sycophancy** is the quality or action of being sycophantic. [FORMAL, DISAPPROVAL]

syco|phant /sɪkəfənt/ (**sycophants**) N-COUNT A **sycophant** is a person who behaves in a sycophantic way. [FORMAL, DISAPPROVAL] ❑ *...a dictator surrounded by sycophants, frightened to tell him what he may not like.*

syco|phan|tic /sɪkəfæntɪk/ ADJ If you describe someone as **sycophantic**, you disapprove of them because they flatter people who are more important and powerful than they are in order to gain an advantage for themselves. [DISAPPROVAL] ❑ *...his clique of sycophantic friends.*

syl|la|ble /sɪləbəl/ (**syllables**) N-COUNT A **syllable** is a part of a word that contains a single vowel sound and that is pronounced as a unit. So, for example, 'book' has one syllable, and 'reading' has two syllables. ❑ *We children called her Oma, accenting both syllables.*

syl|la|bus /sɪləbəs/ (**syllabuses**) ◼ N-COUNT A **syllabus** is an outline or summary of the subjects to be covered in a course. [mainly AM] ❑ *The course syllabus consisted mainly of novels by African-American authors, male and female.* ◼ N-COUNT You can refer to the subjects that are studied in a particular course as the **syllabus**. [mainly BRIT]

in AM, usually use **curriculum**

syl|van /sɪlvən/ ADJ [usu ADJ n] **Sylvan** is used to describe things that have an association with woods and trees. [LITERARY]

sym|bio|sis /sɪmbioʊsɪs, -baɪ-/ ◼ N-UNCOUNT **Symbiosis** is a close relationship between two organisms of different kinds which benefits both organisms. [TECHNICAL] ❑ *...the link between bacteria, symbiosis, and the evolution of plants and animals.* ◼ N-UNCOUNT **Symbiosis** is any relationship between different things, people, or groups that benefits all the things or people concerned. ❑ *...the cosy symbiosis of the traditional political parties.*

sym|bi|ot|ic /sɪmbiɒtɪk, -baɪ-/ ADJ [usu ADJ n] A **symbiotic** relationship is one in which organisms, people, or things exist together in a way that benefits them all. ❑ *...fungi that have a symbiotic relationship with the trees of these northwestern forests.*

sym|bol ✦✧✧ /sɪmbəl/ (**symbols**) ◼ N-COUNT Something that is a **symbol** of a society or an aspect of life seems to represent it because it is very typical of it. ❑ *To them, the monarchy is the special symbol of nationhood.* ◼ N-COUNT A **symbol** of something such as an idea is a shape or design that is used to represent it. ❑ *Later in this same passage Yeats resumes his argument for the Rose as an Irish symbol.* ◼ N-COUNT A **symbol** for an item in a calculation or scientific formula is a number, letter, or shape that represents that item. ❑ *What's the chemical symbol for mercury?* ◼ → see also **sex symbol**

sym|bol|ic /sɪmbɒlɪk/ ◼ ADJ If you describe an event, action, or procedure as **symbolic**, you mean that it represents an important change, although it has little practical effect. ❑ *A lot of Latin-American officials are stressing the symbolic importance of the trip.* • **sym|boli|cal|ly** /sɪmbɒlɪkli/ ADV ❑ *It was a simple enough gesture, but symbolically important.* ◼ ADJ Something that is **symbolic of** a person or thing is regarded or used as a symbol of them. ❑ *Yellow clothes are worn as symbolic of spring.* • **sym|boli|cal|ly** ADV [ADV with v] ❑ *Each circle symbolically represents the whole of humanity.* ◼ ADJ [ADJ n] **Symbolic** is used to describe things involving or relating to symbols. ❑ *...symbolic representations of landscape.*

sym|bol|ism /sɪmbəlɪzəm/ ◼ N-UNCOUNT **Symbolism** is the use of symbols in order to represent something. ❑ *The scene is so rich in symbolism that any explanation risks spoiling the effect.* ◼ N-UNCOUNT You can refer to the **symbolism** of an event or action when it seems to show something important about a situation. ❑ *The symbolism of every gesture will be of vital importance during the short state visit.*

sym|bol|ize /sɪmbəlaɪz/ (**symbolizes, symbolizing, symbolized**)

in BRIT, also use **symbolise**

V-T If one thing **symbolizes** another, it is used or regarded as a symbol of it. ❑ *The fall of the Berlin Wall symbolized the end of the Cold War between East and West.*

sym|met|ri|cal /sɪmetrɪkəl/ ADJ If something is **symmetrical**, it has two halves which are exactly the same, except that one half is the mirror image of the other. ❑ *...the neat rows of perfectly symmetrical windows.* • **sym|met|ri|cal|ly** /sɪmetrɪkli/ ADV [ADV with v] ❑ *The south garden was composed symmetrically.*

sym|me|try /sɪmɪtri/ (**symmetries**) ◼ N-VAR Something that has **symmetry** is symmetrical in shape, design, or structure. ❑ *...the incredible beauty and symmetry of a snowflake.* ◼ N-UNCOUNT **Symmetry** in a relationship or agreement is the fact of both sides giving and receiving an equal amount. ❑ *The superpowers pledged to maintain symmetry in their arms shipments.*

sym|pa|thet|ic /sɪmpəθetɪk/ ◼ ADJ If you are **sympathetic** to someone who is in a bad situation, you are kind to them and show that you understand their feelings. ❑ *She was very sympathetic to the problems of adult students.* • **sym|pa|theti|cal|ly** /sɪmpəθetɪkli/ ADV [ADV with v] ❑ *She nodded sympathetically.* ◼ ADJ If you are **sympathetic** to a proposal or action, you approve of it and are willing to support it. ❑ *Many of these early visitors were sympathetic to the Chinese socialist experiment.* • **sym|pa|theti|cal|ly** ADV [ADV with v] ❑ *After a year we will sympathetically consider an application for reinstatement.*

sym|pa|thize /sɪmpəθaɪz/ (**sympathizes, sympathizing, sympathized**)

in BRIT, also use **sympathise**

◼ V-I If you **sympathize** with someone who is in a bad situation, you show that you are sorry for them. ❑ *I must tell you how much I sympathize with you for your loss, Professor.* ◼ V-I If you **sympathize** with someone's feelings, you understand them and are not critical of them. ❑ *Some Europeans sympathize with the Americans over the issue.* ◼ V-I If you **sympathize** with a proposal or action, you approve of it and are willing to support it. ❑ *Most of the people living there sympathized with the guerrillas.*

sym|pa|thiz|er /sɪmpəθaɪzər/ (**sympathizers**)

in BRIT, also use **sympathiser**

N-COUNT The **sympathizers** of an organization or cause are the people who approve of it and support it. ❑ *She was a well-known playwright and Communist sympathizer.*

sym|pa|thy ✦✧✧ /sɪmpəθi/ (**sympathies**) ◼ N-UNCOUNT [also N in pl] If you have **sympathy** for someone who is in a bad situation, you are sorry for them, and show this in the way you behave toward them. ❑ *We expressed our sympathy for her loss.* ❑ *I have had very little help from doctors and no sympathy whatsoever.* ◼ N-UNCOUNT [also N in pl, oft N with/for n] If you have **sympathy** with someone's ideas or opinions, you agree with them. ❑ *I have some sympathy with this point of view.* ❑ *Lithuania still commands considerable international sympathy for its cause.* ◼ N-UNCOUNT If you take some action in **sympathy** with someone else, you do it in order to show that you support them. ❑ *Several hundred workers struck in sympathy with their colleagues.*

sym|phon|ic /sɪmfɒnɪk/ ADJ [usu ADJ n] **Symphonic** means relating to or like a symphony.

sym|pho|ny /sɪmfəni/ (**symphonies**) N-COUNT; N-IN-NAMES A **symphony** is a piece of music written to be played by an orchestra. Symphonies are usually made up of four separate sections called movements. ❑ *...Beethoven's Ninth Symphony.*

sym|pho|ny or|ches|tra (**symphony orchestras**) N-COUNT; N-IN-NAMES A **symphony orchestra** is a large orchestra that plays classical music.

sym|po|sium /sɪmpoʊziəm/ (**symposia** /sɪmpoʊziə/ or **symposiums**) N-COUNT A **symposium** is a conference in which experts or academics discuss a particular subject. ❑ *He had been taking part in an international symposium on population.*

symp|tom ✦✧✧ /sɪmptəm/ (**symptoms**) ◼ N-COUNT A **symptom** of an illness is something wrong with your body or mind that is a sign of the illness. ❑ *One of the most common symptoms of schizophrenia is hearing imaginary voices.* ❑ *...patients with flu symptoms.* ◼ N-COUNT A **symptom** of a bad situation is something that happens which is considered to be a sign of this situation. ❑ *Your problem with keeping boyfriends is just a*

symptomatic

symptom of a larger problem: making and keeping friends. **3** → See feature box at **illness**

SYNONYMS

symptom
NOUN **1**
sign: *Your blood would have been checked for any sign of kidney failure.*
indication: *He gave no indication that he was ready to compromise.*
signal: *The first warning signals came in March.*

---

symp|to|mat|ic /sɪmptəmætɪk/ ADJ [v-link ADJ] If something is **symptomatic** of something else, especially something bad, it is a sign of it. [FORMAL] ❑ *The city's problems are symptomatic of the crisis that is spreading throughout the country.*

syna|gogue /sɪnəgɒg/ (synagogues) N-COUNT; N-IN-NAMES A **synagogue** is a building where Jewish people meet to worship or to study their religion.

syn|apse /sɪnæps/ (synapses) **1** N-COUNT A **synapse** is one of the points in the nervous system at which a signal passes from one nerve cell to another. [TECHNICAL] **2** → See feature box at **brain**

sync /sɪŋk/ also **synch** PHRASE If two things are **out of sync**, they do not match or do not happen together as they should. If two things are **in sync**, they match or happen together as they should. [INFORMAL] ❑ *Normally, when demand and supply are out of sync, you either increase the supply, or you adjust the price mechanism.*

synch /sɪŋk/ → see **sync**

syn|chro|nize /sɪŋkrənaɪz/ (synchronizes, synchronizing, synchronized)

in BRIT, also use **synchronise**

V-RECIP If you **synchronize** two activities, processes, or movements, or if you **synchronize** one activity, process, or movement with another, you cause them to happen at the same time and speed as each other. ❑ *It was virtually impossible to synchronize our lives so as to take vacations and weekends together.* ❑ *Synchronize the score with the film action.*

syn|chro|nized swim|ming

in BRIT, also use **synchronised swimming**

N-UNCOUNT **Synchronized swimming** is a sport in which two or more people perform complicated and carefully planned movements in water in time to music.

syn|co|pat|ed /sɪŋkəpeɪtɪd/ ADJ In **syncopated** music, the weak beats in the bar are stressed instead of the strong beats. ❑ *Some spirituals are based on syncopated rhythms.*

syn|co|pa|tion /sɪŋkəpeɪʃᵊn/ (syncopations) N-VAR **Syncopation** is the quality that music has when the weak beats in a bar are stressed instead of the strong ones.

syn|di|cate (syndicates, syndicating, syndicated)

The verb is pronounced /sɪndɪkeɪt/. The noun is pronounced /sɪndɪkɪt/.

1 N-COUNT A **syndicate** is an association of people or organizations that is formed for business purposes or in order to carry out a project. ❑ *They formed a syndicate to buy the car in which they competed in the race.* ❑ *...a syndicate of 152 banks.* **2** V-T [usu passive] When newspaper articles or television programs **are syndicated**, they are sold to several different newspapers or television stations, who then publish the articles or broadcast the programs. ❑ *Today his program is syndicated to 500 stations.* **3** N-COUNT A press **syndicate** is a group of newspapers or magazines that are all owned by the same person or company.

syn|drome /sɪndroʊm/ (syndromes) N-COUNT; N-IN-NAMES A **syndrome** is a medical condition that is characterized by a particular group of signs and symptoms. ❑ *Irritable bowel syndrome seems to affect more women than men.*

syn|er|gy /sɪnərdʒi/ (synergies) N-VAR If there is **synergy** between two or more organizations or groups, they are more successful when they work together than when they work separately. [BUSINESS] ❑ *Of course, there's quite obviously a lot of synergy between the two companies.*

syringe

syn|od /sɪnɒd/ (synods) N-COUNT A **synod** is a special council of members of a Church, which meets regularly to discuss religious issues.

syno|nym /sɪnənɪm/ (synonyms) N-COUNT A **synonym** is a word or expression which means the same as another word or expression. ❑ *The term "industrial democracy" is often used as a synonym for worker participation.*

syn|ony|mous /sɪnɒnɪməs/ ADJ If you say that one thing is **synonymous** with another, you mean that the two things are very closely associated with each other so that one suggests the other or one cannot exist without the other. ❑ *Paris has always been synonymous with elegance, luxury and style.*

syn|op|sis /sɪnɒpsɪs/ (synopses /sɪnɒpsiz/) N-COUNT A **synopsis** is a summary of a longer piece of writing or work. ❑ *For each title there is a brief synopsis of the book.*

syn|tac|tic /sɪntæktɪk/ ADJ [ADJ n] **Syntactic** means relating to syntax. [TECHNICAL] ❑ *...three common syntactic devices in English.*

syn|tax /sɪntæks/ **1** N-UNCOUNT **Syntax** is the ways that words can be put together, or are put together, in order to make sentences. [TECHNICAL] ❑ *His grammar and syntax, both in oral and written expression, were much better than the average.* **2** N-UNCOUNT **Syntax** is the set of rules that describes how a computer language can be used to make programs. [COMPUTING] ❑ *Each computer language has its own syntax and vocabulary.*

synth /sɪnθ/ (synths) N-COUNT A **synth** is the same as a **synthesizer**. [INFORMAL]

syn|the|sis /sɪnθɪsɪs/ (syntheses /sɪnθɪsiz/) **1** N-COUNT A **synthesis** of different ideas or styles is a mixture or combination of these ideas or styles. [FORMAL] ❑ *His novels are a rich synthesis of Balkan history and mythology.* **2** N-VAR The **synthesis** of a substance is the production of it by means of chemical or biological reactions. [TECHNICAL] ❑ *...the genes that regulate the synthesis of these compounds.*

syn|the|size /sɪnθɪsaɪz/ (synthesizes, synthesizing, synthesized)

in BRIT, also use **synthesise**

1 V-T To **synthesize** a substance means to produce it by means of chemical or biological reactions. [TECHNICAL] ❑ *After extensive research, Albert Hoffman first succeeded in synthesizing the acid in 1938.* **2** V-T If you **synthesize** different ideas, facts, or experiences, you combine them to form a single idea or impression. [FORMAL] ❑ *The movement synthesized elements of modern art that hadn't been brought together before, such as Cubism and Surrealism.*

syn|the|sized /sɪnθɪsaɪzd/

in BRIT, also use **synthesised**

ADJ [ADJ n] **Synthesized** sounds are produced electronically using a synthesizer. ❑ *...synthesized dance music.*

syn|the|siz|er /sɪnθɪsaɪzər/ (synthesizers)

in BRIT, also use **synthesiser**

N-COUNT A **synthesizer** is an electronic machine that produces speech, music, or other sounds, usually by combining individual syllables or sounds that have been previously recorded. ❑ *Now he can only communicate through a voice synthesizer.*

syn|thet|ic /sɪnθetɪk/ **1** ADJ **Synthetic** products are made from chemicals or artificial substances rather than from natural ones. ❑ *Boots made from synthetic materials can usually be washed in a machine.* **2** → See feature box at **sewing**

syn|thet|ics /sɪnθetɪks/ N-PLURAL You can refer to synthetic clothing, fabric, or materials as **synthetics**. ❑ *Natural fabrics like silk and wool are better insulators than synthetics.*

syphi|lis /sɪfɪlɪs/ N-UNCOUNT **Syphilis** is a serious disease which is passed on through sexual intercourse.

sy|phon /saɪfᵊn/ [mainly BRIT] → see **siphon**

Syr|ian /sɪriən/ (Syrians) **1** ADJ **Syrian** means belonging or relating to Syria, or to its people or culture. **2** N-COUNT A **Syrian** is a Syrian citizen, or a person of Syrian origin.

sy|ringe /sɪrɪndʒ/ (syringes) N-COUNT A **syringe** is a small tube with a thin hollow needle at the end. Syringes are used for putting liquids into things and for taking liquids out,

syrup for example for injecting drugs or for taking blood from someone's body. ❏ *As he reached over, Azrak slid a hypodermic syringe into his left arm.*

syr|up /sɪrəp, sɜr-/ (syrups) **1** N-MASS **Syrup** is a sweet liquid made by cooking sugar with water, and sometimes with fruit juice as well. ❏ *...canned fruit with sugary syrup.* **2** N-MASS **Syrup** is a medicine in the form of a thick, sweet liquid. ❏ *...cough syrup.*

syr|upy /sɪrəpi, sɜr-/ **1** ADJ Liquid that is **syrupy** is sweet or thick like syrup. **2** ADJ If you describe something as **syrupy**, you dislike it because it is too sentimental. [DISAPPROVAL] ❏ *...this syrupy film version of Conroy's novel.*

sys|tem ✦✦✦ /sɪstəm/ (systems) **1** N-COUNT A **system** is a way of working, organizing, or doing something which follows a fixed plan or set of rules. You can use **system** to refer to an organization or institution that is organized in this way. ❏ *The present system of funding for higher education is unsatisfactory.* ❏ *...a flexible and relatively efficient filing system.* **2** N-COUNT A **system** is a set of devices powered by electricity, for example a computer or an alarm. ❏ *Viruses tend to be good at surviving when a computer system crashes.* **3** N-COUNT A **system** is a set of equipment or parts such as water pipes or electrical wiring, which is used to supply water, heat, or electricity. ❏ *...a central heating system.* **4** N-COUNT A **system** is a network of things that are linked together so that people or things can travel from one place to another or communicate. ❏ *...Australia's road and rail system.* **5** N-COUNT Your **system** is your body's organs and other parts that together perform particular functions.

❏ *He had slept for over fourteen hours, and his system seemed to have recuperated admirably.* **6** N-COUNT A **system** is a particular set of rules, especially in mathematics or science, which is used to count or measure things. ❏ *...the decimal system of metric weights and measures.* **7** N-SING People sometimes refer to the government or administration of a country as **the system**. ❏ *These feelings are likely to make people attempt to overthrow the system.* **8** → see also **ecosystem, immune system, nervous system, solar system, sound system**

sys|tem|at|ic /sɪstəmætɪk/ ADJ Something that is done in a **systematic** way is done according to a fixed plan, in a thorough and efficient way. ❏ *They went about their business in a systematic way.* • **sys|tem|ati|cal|ly** /sɪstəmætɪkli/ ADV ❏ *The army has systematically violated human rights.*

sys|tema|tize /sɪstəmətaɪz/ (systematizes, systematizing, systematized)

> in BRIT, also use **systematise**

V-T/V-I If you **systematize** things, you make them organized. [FORMAL] ❏ *You need to systematize your approach to problem solving.* • **sys|tema|ti|za|tion** /sɪstəmətaɪzeɪʃən/ N-UNCOUNT [usu N *of* n] ❏ *...a systematization of management practice.*

sys|tem|ic /sɪstemɪk/ ADJ **Systemic** means affecting the whole of something. [FORMAL] ❏ *The economy is locked in a systemic crisis.*

sys|tems ana|lyst (systems analysts) N-COUNT A **systems analyst** is someone whose job is to decide what computer equipment and software a company needs, and to provide it.

Tt

T also **t** /tiː/ (**T's, t's**) ◼ N-VAR T is the twentieth letter of the English alphabet. ◼ PHRASE You can use **to a T** or **to a tee** to mean perfectly or exactly right. For example, if something suits you **to a T**, it suits you perfectly. If you have an activity or skill **down to a T**, you have succeeded in doing it exactly right. [INFORMAL] ❏ *Everything had to be rehearsed down to a T.* ❏ *The description fits us to a tee.*

tab /tæb/ (**tabs**) ◼ N-COUNT A **tab** is a small piece of cloth or paper that is attached to something, usually with information about that thing written on it. ❏ *A clerk had slipped the wrong tab on Tony's X-ray.* ◼ N-COUNT A **tab** is the total cost of goods or services that you have to pay, or the bill or check for those goods or services. [mainly AM] ❏ *At least one estimate puts the total tab at $7 million.* ◼ PHRASE If someone **keeps tabs on** you, they make sure that they always know where you are and what you are doing, often in order to control you. [INFORMAL] ❏ *It was obvious Hill had come over to keep tabs on Johnson and make sure he didn't do anything drastic.* ◼ PHRASE If you **pick up the tab**, you pay a bill on behalf of a group of people or provide the money that is needed for something. [INFORMAL] ❏ *Pollard picked up the tab for dinner that night.*

Ta|bas|co /təbæskoʊ/ N-UNCOUNT Tabasco is a hot spicy sauce made from peppers. [TRADEMARK]

tab|by /tæbi/ (**tabbies**) N-COUNT A **tabby** or a **tabby cat** is a cat whose fur has dark stripes on a lighter background.

tab|er|nac|le /tæbərnækəl/ (**tabernacles**) ◼ N-COUNT [oft in names] A **tabernacle** is a place of worship used by certain Christian groups. ◼ N-PROPER [the N] **The Tabernacle** was a small tent which contained the most holy writings of the ancient Jews and which they took with them when they were traveling.

ta|ble ✦✧ /teɪbəl/ (**tables, tabling, tabled**) ◼ N-COUNT A **table** is a piece of furniture with a flat top that you put things on or sit at. ❏ *She was sitting at the kitchen table eating a peach.* ◼ V-T If someone **tables** a proposal or plan which has been put forward, they decide to discuss it or deal with it at a later date, rather than right away. [AM] ❏ *We will table that for later.* ◼ V-T If someone **tables** a proposal, they say formally that they want it to be discussed at a meeting. [BRIT] ❏ *They've tabled a motion criticizing the government for doing nothing about the problem.* ◼ N-COUNT [also N num] A **table** is a written set of facts and figures arranged in columns and rows. ❏ *Consult the table on page 104.* ◼ → see also **negotiating table**

SYNONYMS
table
NOUN ◼
counter: *We were sitting on stools at the counter, having coffee.*
bench: *...the laboratory bench.*
stand: *She bought a hot dog from a stand on a street corner.*

tab|leau /tæbloʊ, tæbloʊ/ (**tableaux**) ◼ N-COUNT A **tableau** is a scene, for example, from the Bible, history, or mythology, that consists of a group of people in costumes who do not speak or move. The people are sometimes on a float in a procession. ❏ *...tableaux depicting the foundation of Barcelona.* ◼ N-COUNT A **tableau** is a piece of art such as a sculpture or painting that shows a scene, especially one from the Bible, history, or mythology. ❏ *...Gaudi's luxuriant stone tableau of the Nativity on the cathedral's east face.*

table|cloth /teɪbəlklɔθ/ (**tablecloths**) N-COUNT A **tablecloth** is a cloth used to cover a table.

ta|ble danc|ing N-UNCOUNT **Table dancing** is a type of entertainment in a bar or club in which a woman who is wearing very few clothes dances in a sexy way close to a customer or group of customers.

ta|ble lamp (**table lamps**) N-COUNT A **table lamp** is a small electric lamp which stands on a table or other piece of furniture.

ta|ble man|ners N-PLURAL [usu supp N] You can use **table manners** to refer to the way you behave when you are eating a meal at a table. ❏ *He attacked the food as quickly as decent table manners allowed.*

table|spoon /teɪbəlspuːn/ (**tablespoons**) N-COUNT A **tablespoon** is a fairly large spoon used for serving food and in cooking.

table|spoon|ful /teɪbəlspuːnfʊl/ (**tablespoonfuls** or **tablespoonsful**) N-COUNT [usu N of n] You can refer to an amount of food resting on a tablespoon as a **tablespoonful** of food. ❏ *Grate a tablespoonful of fresh ginger into a pan.*

tab|let /tæblɪt/ (**tablets**) ◼ N-COUNT A **tablet** is a small solid mass of medicine which you swallow. ❏ *...half a tablet of aspirin.* ◼ N-COUNT A **tablet** is a small flat computer that you operate by touching the screen. [COMPUTING] ❏ *...a free guide to the best tablets on the market.* ◼ N-COUNT Clay **tablets** or stone **tablets** are the flat pieces of clay or stone which people used to write on before paper was invented. ◼ **tablets of stone** → see **stone**

ta|ble ten|nis also **table-tennis** ◼ N-UNCOUNT **Table tennis** is a game played inside by two or four people. The players stand at each end of a table which has a low net across the middle and hit a small light ball over the net, using small paddles. ◼ → See also color supplement

ta|ble top (**table tops**) also **tabletop** N-COUNT A **table top** is the flat surface on a table.

table|ware /teɪbəlwɛər/ N-UNCOUNT **Tableware** consists of the objects used on the table at meals, for example, plates, glasses, or flatware. [FORMAL]

ta|ble wine (**table wines**) N-MASS **Table wine** is fairly cheap wine that is served with meals.

tab|loid /tæblɔɪd/ (**tabloids**) ◼ N-COUNT A **tabloid** is a newspaper that has small pages, short articles, and a lot of photographs. Tabloids are usually considered to be less serious than other newspapers. Compare **broadsheet**. ❏ *The tabloids speculated as to whether she was having an affair, and with whom.* ◼ → See feature box at **press**

La|boo /təbuː/ (**taboos**) N-COUNT A **taboo** against a subject or activity is a social custom to avoid doing that activity or talking about that subject, because people find them embarrassing or offensive. ❏ *The topic of addiction remains something of a taboo in our family.* • ADJ **Taboo** is also an adjective. ❏ *Cancer is a taboo subject and people are frightened or embarrassed to talk openly about it.*

tabu|late /tæbjəleɪt/ (**tabulates, tabulating, tabulated**) V-T To **tabulate** information means to arrange it in columns on a page so that it can be analyzed. ❏ *Results for the test program haven't been tabulated.*

tach|om|eter /tækɒmətər/ (**tachometers**) ◼ N-COUNT A **tachometer** is an instrument in a car or an airplane which shows the speed of the engine. [mainly AM] ❏ *The tachometer registers a rather high 3,000 rpm at 70 mph.* ◼ → See also color supplement

tac|it /tæsɪt/ ADJ If you refer to someone's **tacit** agreement or approval, you mean they are agreeing to something or approving it without actually saying so, often because they are unwilling to admit to doing so. ❏ *The question was a tacit admission that a mistake had indeed been made.* ● **tac|it|ly** ADV [ADV with v] ❏ *He tacitly admitted that the government had breached regulations.*

taci|turn /tæsɪtɜrn/ ADJ A **taciturn** person does not say very much and can seem unfriendly. ❏ *A taciturn man, he replied to my questions in monosyllables.*

tack /tæk/ (tacks, tacking, tacked) **1** N-COUNT A **tack** or a **thumbtack** is a short pin with a wide head that you can push with your thumb, especially for a bulletin board. ❏ *...a box of carpet tacks.* **2** N-COUNT A **tack** is a short nail with a broad, flat head, especially one that is used for fastening carpets to the floor. ❏ *...a box of carpet tacks.* **3** → see also **thumbtack** **4** V-T If you **tack** something to a surface, you pin it there with tacks or thumbtacks. ❏ *He had tacked this note to her door.* **5** N-SING [also no det] If you change **tack** or try a different **tack**, you try a different method for dealing with a situation. ❏ *Seeing the puzzled look on his face, she tried a different tack.* **6** V-T If you **tack** pieces of material together, you sew them together with big, loose stitches in order to hold them firmly or check that they fit, before sewing them permanently. ❏ *Tack them together with a 1 cm seam.*

▶ **tack on** PHRASAL VERB If you say that something **is tacked on** to something else, you think that it is added in a hurry and in an unsatisfactory way. ❏ *The child-care bill is to be tacked on to the budget plan now being worked out in the Senate.*

tack|le ◆◇◇ /tækəl/ (tackles, tackling, tackled) **1** V-T If you **tackle** a difficult problem or task, you deal with it in a very determined or efficient way. ❏ *The first reason to tackle these problems is to save children's lives.* **2** V-T If you **tackle** someone in a game such as football or rugby, you knock them to the ground. If you **tackle** someone in soccer or hockey, you try to take the ball away from them. ❏ *Foley tackled the quarterback.* ● N-COUNT **Tackle** is also a noun. ❏ *...a tackle by fullback Brian Burrows.* **3** V-T If you **tackle** someone about a particular matter, you speak to them honestly about it, usually in order to get it changed or done. ❏ *I tackled him about how anyone could live amidst so much poverty.* **4** V-T If you **tackle** someone, you attack them and fight them. ❏ *Two security guards tackled and apprehended a man suspected of robbing 17 banks.* **5** N-UNCOUNT **Tackle** is the equipment that you need for a sport or activity, especially fishing. ❏ *...fishing tackle.*

tacky /tæki/ (tackier, tackiest) **1** ADJ If you describe something as **tacky**, you dislike it because it is cheap and badly made or vulgar. [INFORMAL, DISAPPROVAL] ❏ *...a woman in a fake leopard-skin coat and tacky red sunglasses.* **2** ADJ If something such as paint or glue is **tacky**, it is slightly sticky and not yet dry. ❏ *Test to see if the finish is tacky, and if it is, leave it to harden.*

taco /tɑkoʊ/ (tacos) N-COUNT A **taco** is a crispy corn tortilla folded in half to hold a filling such as meat, vegetables, cheese, and chili. It is a traditional Mexican food.

tact /tækt/ N-UNCOUNT **Tact** is the ability to avoid upsetting or offending people by being careful not to say or do things that would hurt their feelings. ❏ *Her tact and intuition never failed.*

tact|ful /tæktfəl/ ADJ If you describe a person or what they say as **tactful** you approve of them because they are careful not to offend or upset another person. [APPROVAL] ❏ *He had been extremely tactful in dealing with the financial question.* ● **tact|ful|ly** ADV ❏ *Alex tactfully refrained from further comment.*

tac|tic ◆◇◇ /tæktɪk/ (tactics) **1** N-COUNT **Tactics** are the methods that you choose to use in order to achieve what you want in a particular situation. ❏ *The rebels would still be able to use guerrilla tactics to make the country ungovernable.* **2** → See feature box at **politics**

SYNONYMS

tactics
NOUN **1**
approach: *We will be exploring different approaches to gathering information.*
strategy: *What should our marketing strategy have achieved?*
method: *This is the usual method of getting through the Amsterdam traffic.*

---

tac|ti|cal /tæktɪkəl/ **1** ADJ You use **tactical** to describe an action or plan which is intended to help someone achieve what they want in a particular situation. ❏ *It's not yet clear whether his resignation offer is a serious one, or whether it's simply a tactical move.* ● **tac|ti|cal|ly** ADV ❏ *The electorate is astute enough to vote tactically against the government.* **2** ADJ [ADJ n] **Tactical** weapons or forces are those which a military leader can decide for themselves to use in a battle, rather than waiting for a decision by a political leader. ❏ *They have removed all tactical nuclear missiles that could strike Europe.*

tac|ti|cian /tæktɪʃən/ (tacticians) N-COUNT [usu supp N] If you say that someone is a good **tactician**, you mean that they are skillful at choosing the best methods in order to achieve what they want. ❏ *He is an extremely astute political tactician.*

tac|tile /tæktəl, -taɪl/ **1** ADJ If you describe someone as **tactile**, you mean that they tend to touch other people a lot when talking to them. ❏ *The children are very tactile with warm, loving natures.* **2** ADJ Something such as fabric which is **tactile** is pleasant or interesting to touch. ❏ *Tweed is timeless, tactile and tough.* **3** ADJ [usu ADJ n] **Tactile** experiences or sensations are received or felt by touch. [FORMAL] ❏ *Babies who sleep with their parents receive much more tactile stimulation than babies who sleep in a crib.*

tact|less /tæktlɪs/ ADJ If you describe someone as **tactless**, you think what they say or do is likely to offend other people. ❏ *He had alienated many people with his tactless remarks.*

tad /tæd/ PHRASE [PHR adj/adv] You can use **a tad** in expressions such as **a tad big** or **a tad small** when you mean that it is slightly too big or slightly too small. [INFORMAL] ❏ *It was a tad confusing.*

tad|pole /tædpoʊl/ (tadpoles) N-COUNT **Tadpoles** are small water creatures that look like fish and grow into frogs or toads.

taf|fe|ta /tæfɪtə/ N-UNCOUNT **Taffeta** is shiny stiff material made of silk or nylon that is used mainly for making women's clothes.

taf|fy /tæfi/ N-UNCOUNT **Taffy** is a sticky candy that you chew. It is made by boiling sugar and butter together with water. [AM]

in BRIT, use **toffee**

tag /tæg/ (tags, tagging, tagged) **1** N-COUNT A **tag** is a small piece of card or cloth which is attached to an object or person and has information about the object or person on it. ❏ *Staff wore name tags and called inmates by their first names.* **2** → see also **price tag** **3** N-COUNT An electronic **tag** is a device that is firmly attached to someone or something and sets off an alarm if that person or thing moves away or is removed. ❏ *Ranchers are testing electronic tags on animals' ears to create a national cattle-tracking system.* **4** N-UNCOUNT **Tag** is a children's game where one child runs to touch or tag the others. **5** V-T If you **tag** something, you attach something to it or mark it so that it can be identified later. ❏ *Professor Orr has developed interesting ways of tagging chemical molecules using existing laboratory lasers.*

▶ **tag along** PHRASAL VERB If someone goes somewhere and you **tag along**, you go with them, especially when they have not asked you to. ❏ *I let him tag along because he had not been too well recently.*

tag line (tag lines) also **tag-line** N-COUNT The **tag line** of something such as a television commercial or a joke is the phrase that comes at the end and is meant to be amusing or easy to remember.

tai chi /taɪ tʃi/ also **Tai Chi** N-UNCOUNT **Tai chi** is a type of Chinese physical exercise in which you make slow, controlled movements.

tai|ga /taɪgə/ (taigas) **1** N-VAR **Taiga** is the coniferous forest located in the northern regions of the world. It is just south of the tundra. **2** → See feature box at **ecosystem**

tail ◆◇◇ /teɪl/ (tails, tailing, tailed) **1** N-COUNT The **tail** of an animal, bird, or fish is the part extending beyond the end of its body. ❏ *...a black dog with a long tail.* **2** N-COUNT You can use **tail** to refer to the end or back of something, especially something long and thin. ❏ *...the horizontal stabilizer bar on the plane's tail.* **3** N-PLURAL If someone is wearing **tails**, they are wearing a formal jacket which has two long pieces hanging

down at the back. ◻ ...*men in tails and women in party dresses.* **4** V-T To **tail** someone means to follow close behind them and watch where they go and what they do. [INFORMAL] ◻ *Officers had tailed the gang during a major undercover operation.* **5** ADV [ADV after v] If you toss a coin and it comes down **tails**, you can see the side of it that does not have a picture of a head on it. ◻ *"Heads or tails?"* ◻ *The captain called heads as usual — and the coin came down tails.* **6 cannot make head or tail of something** → see **head** ③ **7** → See also color supplement
▶ **tail off** PHRASAL VERB When something **tails off**, it gradually becomes less in amount or value, often before coming to an end completely. ◻ *Last year, economic growth tailed off to below four percent.*

tail|back /teɪlbæk/ (tailbacks) **1** N-COUNT In football, a **tailback** is the player furthest from the front line. The **tailback** often runs with the ball. [AM] **2** N-COUNT A **tailback** is the same as a **backup**. [BRIT]

tail|coat /teɪlkoʊt/ (tailcoats) also **tail coat** N-COUNT A **tailcoat** is a coat which is short at the front with long pieces at the back. Tailcoats were popular in the 19th century and are now worn only for very formal occasions such as weddings.

tail end also **tail-end** N-SING [usu N *of* n] The **tail end** of an event, situation, or period of time is the last part of it. ◻ *Barry had obviously come in on the tail-end of the conversation.*

tail|gate /teɪlgeɪt/ (tailgates, tailgating, tailgated) **1** N-COUNT A **tailgate** is a door at the back of a truck or car, that is hinged at the bottom so that it opens downward. **2** V-T/V-I If you **tailgate** someone, you drive very closely behind them. ◻ *Perhaps the fact that the car was tailgating him made him accelerate.* ◻ *Police pulled him over for doing 90 mph, making rapid changes and tailgating.*

tail|gate par|ty (tailgate parties) N-COUNT A **tailgate party** is a social gathering at which food is served from or near a vehicle, especially in a parking lot before a sports game. [AM, INFORMAL] ◻ *He routinely holds tailgate parties at Flyers games with 30 or 40 fans.*

tail|light /teɪllaɪt/ (taillights) N-COUNT The **taillights** on a car or other vehicle are the two red lights at the back.

tai|lor /teɪlər/ (tailors, tailoring, tailored) **1** N-COUNT A **tailor** is a person whose job is to make men's clothes. **2** V-T If you **tailor** something such as a plan or system to someone's needs, you make it suitable for a particular person or purpose by changing the details of it. ◻ *We can tailor the program to the patient's needs.* **3** → See feature box at **sewing**

tai|lored /teɪlərd/ ADJ [usu ADJ n] **Tailored** clothes are designed to fit close to the body, rather than being loose. ◻ ...*a white tailored shirt.*

tai|lor-made 1 ADJ If something is **tailor-made**, it has been specially designed for a particular person or purpose. ◻ *Each client's portfolio is tailor-made.* **2** ADJ If you say that someone or something is **tailor-made** for a particular task, purpose, or need, you are emphasizing that they are perfectly suitable for it. [EMPHASIS] ◻ *He was tailor-made, it was said, for the task ahead.* **3** ADJ **Tailor-made** clothes have been specially made to fit a particular person. ◻ *He was wearing a suit that looked tailor-made.*

tai|lor-make (tailor-makes, tailor-making, tailor-made) **1** V If someone **tailor-makes** something for you, they make or design it to suit your requirements. ◻ *The company can tailor-make your entire vacation.* **2** → see also **tailor-made**

tail|pipe /teɪlpaɪp/ (tailpipes) N-COUNT A **tailpipe** is the end pipe of a car's exhaust system. [AM] ◻ ...*a dramatic reduction in tailpipe emissions.*

tail|spin /teɪlspɪn/ **1** N-SING [a N] If something such as an industry or an economy goes into a **tailspin**, it begins to perform very badly or to fail. ◻ *The disruption of European trade during the war had thrown the economy into a tailspin.* **2** N-SING [a N] If an aircraft goes into a **tailspin**, it falls very rapidly toward the ground in a spiral movement. ◻ *The aircraft went into a tailspin before crashing.*

tail|wind /teɪlwɪnd/ (tailwinds) also **tail wind** N-COUNT A **tailwind** is a wind that is blowing from behind an airplane, boat, or other vehicle, making it move faster.

taint /teɪnt/ (taints, tainting, tainted) **1** V-T If a person or thing **is tainted** by something bad or undesirable, their status or reputation is harmed because they are associated with it. ◻ *Opposition leaders said that the elections had been tainted by corruption.* • **taint|ed** ADJ ◻ *He came out only slightly tainted by telling millions of viewers he and his wife had had marital problems.* **2** N-COUNT A **taint** is an undesirable quality which ruins the status or reputation of someone or something. ◻ *Her government never really shook off the taint of corruption.* **3** V-T If an unpleasant substance **taints** food or medicine, the food or medicine is spoiled or damaged by it. ◻ *Rancid oil will taint the flavor.*

TAKE

① USED WITH NOUNS DESCRIBING ACTIONS
② OTHER USES

---

① **take** ♦♦♦ /teɪk/ (takes, taking, took, taken)

Take is used in combination with a wide range of nouns, where the meaning of the combination is mostly given by the noun. Many of these combinations are common idiomatic expressions whose meanings can be found at the appropriate nouns. For example, the expression **take care** is explained at **care**.

1 V-T You can use **take** followed by a noun to talk about an action or event, when it would also be possible to use the verb that is related to that noun. For example, you can say '**she took a shower**' instead of 'she showered.' ◻ *She was too tired to take a shower.* ◻ *Betty took a photograph of us.* **2** V-T In ordinary spoken or written English, people use **take** with a range of nouns instead of using a more specific verb. For example, people often say '**he took control**' or '**she took a positive attitude**' instead of 'he assumed control' or 'she adopted a positive attitude.' ◻ *The Patriotic Front took power after a three-month civil war.* ◻ *I felt it was important for more women from ethnic minority groups to join and take a leading role.*

② **take** ♦♦♦ /teɪk/ (takes, taking, took, taken)
→ Please look at meanings **40** to **50** to see if the expression you are looking for is shown under another headword.

1 V-T If you **take** something, you reach out for it and hold it. ◻ *Here, let me take your coat.* ◻ *Colette took her by the shoulders and shook her.* **2** V-T If you **take** something with you when you go somewhere, you carry it or have it with you. ◻ *Mark often took his books to Bess's house to study.* ◻ *You should take your passport with you when changing money.* **3** V-T If a person, vehicle, or path **takes** someone somewhere, they transport or lead them there. ◻ *She took me to a Mexican restaurant.* **4** V-T If something such as a job or interest **takes** you to a place, it is the reason for you going there. ◻ *He was a poor student from Madras whose genius took him to Stanford.* **5** V-T If you **take** something such as your problems or your business to someone, you go to that person when you have problems you want to discuss or things you want to buy. ◻ *You need to take your problems to a trained counselor.* **6** V-T If one thing **takes** another to a particular level, condition, or state, it causes it to reach that level or condition. ◻ *A combination of talent, hard work and good looks have taken him to the top.* **7** V-T If you **take** something from a place, you remove it from there. ◻ *He took a handkerchief from his pocket and lightly wiped his mouth.* **8** V-T If you **take** something from someone who owns it, you steal it or go away with it without their permission. ◻ *He has taken my money, and I have no chance of getting it back.* **9** V-I If an army or political party **takes** something or someone, they win them from their enemy or opponent. ◻ *A Serb army unit took the town.* **10** V-T If you **take** one number or amount from another, you subtract it or deduct it. ◻ *Take off the price of the house, that's another hundred thousand.* **11** V-T [no passive, usu with brd-neg] If you cannot **take** something difficult, painful, or annoying, you cannot tolerate it without becoming upset, ill, or angry. ◻ *Don't ever ask me to look after those kids again. I just can't take it!* **12** V-T If you **take** something such as damage or loss, you suffer it, especially in war or in a battle. ◻ *They have taken heavy casualties.* **13** V-T [no passive] If something **takes** a certain amount of time, that amount of time is needed in order to do it. ◻ *Since the roads are very bad, the trip took us a long time.* ◻ *I had heard an appeal could take years.* ◻ *The sauce takes 25 minutes to prepare and cook.* ◻ *It takes 15 minutes to convert the plane into a car* by removing the wings and the tail. **14** V-T [no passive] If something **takes** a particular quality or thing, that quality or thing is needed in order to do it. ▫ *At one time, walking across the room took all her strength.* ▫ *It takes courage to say what you think.* **15** V-T If you **take** something that is given or offered to you, you agree to accept it. ▫ *When I took the job I thought I could change the system, but it's hard.* **16** V-T If you **take** a feeling such as pleasure, pride, or delight in a particular thing or activity, it gives you that feeling. ▫ *They take great pride in their heritage.* **17** V-T If you **take** a prize or medal, you win it. ▫ *The Aftershock, a children's rock band, took first prize at the event.* **18** V-T If you **take** the blame, responsibility, or credit for something, you agree to accept it. ▫ *His brother Raoul did it, but Leonel took the blame and kept his mouth shut.* **19** V-T If you **take** patients or clients, you accept them as your patients or clients. ▫ *Some universities would be forced to take more students than they wanted.* **20** V-T If you **take** a telephone call, you speak to someone who is telephoning you. ▫ *Douglas telephoned Catherine at her office. She refused to take his calls.* **21** V-T If you **take** something in a particular way, you react in the way mentioned to a situation or to someone's beliefs or behavior. ▫ *Unfortunately, no one took my opinion seriously.* **22** V-T [usu imper] You use **take** when you are discussing or explaining a particular question, in order to introduce an example or to say how the question is being considered. ▫ *There's confusion and resentment, and it's almost never expressed out in the open. Take this office, for example.* **23** V-T If you **take** someone's meaning or point, you understand and accept what they are saying. ▫ *I had made it as plain as I could so that he could not fail to take my meaning.* **24** V-T If you **take** someone for something, you believe wrongly that they are that thing. ▫ *She had taken him for a journalist.* **25** V-T If you **take** a road or route, you choose to travel along it. ▫ *From the community college take Old Mill Road to the outskirts of town.* **26** V-T If you **take** a car, train, bus, or plane, you use it to go from one place to another. ▫ *It's the other end of town so we should take the car.* **27** V-T If you **take** a subject or course at school or college, you choose to study it. ▫ *Students are allowed to take European history and American history.* **28** V-T If you **take** a test or examination, you do it in order to show your knowledge or ability. ▫ *She took her driving test yesterday.* **29** V-T If someone **takes** drugs, pills, or other medicines, they take them into their body, for example, by swallowing them. ▫ *She's been taking sleeping pills.* **30** V-T If you **take** a note or a letter, you write down something you want to remember or the words that someone says. ▫ *She sat expressionless, carefully taking notes.* **31** V-T If you **take** a measurement, you find out what it is by measuring. ▫ *By drilling, geologists can take measurements at various depths.* **32** V-T [no passive] If a place or container **takes** a particular amount or number, there is enough space for that amount or number. ▫ *The place could just about take 2,000 people.* **33** V-T If you **take** a particular size in shoes or clothes, that size fits you. ▫ *"What size do you take?"— "I take a size 7."* **34** N-SING You can use **take** to refer to the amount of money that a business such as a store or theater gets from selling its goods or tickets during a particular period. [mainly AM, BUSINESS] ▫ *It added another $11.8 million to the take, for a grand total of $43 million.*

in BRIT, usually use **takings**

35 V-T If a store, restaurant, theater, or other business **takes** a certain amount of money, they get that amount from people buying goods or services. [mainly BRIT, BUSINESS]

in AM, usually use **take in**

36 V-T If you **are taken** by someone, you are cheated or deceived by them. [INFORMAL] ▫ *They got taken by a scam artist.* **37** N-COUNT A **take** is a short piece of action which is filmed in one continuous process for a movie. ▫ *She couldn't get it right – she never knew the lines and we had to do several takes.* **38** N-SING Someone's **take** on a particular situation or fact is their attitude to it or their interpretation of it. ▫ *What's your take on the new government? Do you think it can work?* **39** CONVENTION If you say to someone '**take it or leave it**,' you are telling them that they can accept something or not accept it, but that you are not prepared to discuss any other alternatives. ▫ *A 72-hour week, 12 hours a day, six days a week, take it or leave it.* **40** PHRASE If someone **takes** an insult or attack **lying down**, they accept it without protesting. ▫ *The government is not taking such criticism lying down.* **41** PHRASE If something **takes a lot out of** you or **takes it out of** you, it requires a lot of energy or effort and makes you feel very tired and weak afterward. ▫ *He looked tired, as if the argument had taken a lot out of him.* **42** PHRASE If someone tells you to **take five** or to **take ten**, they are telling you to have a five or ten minute break from what you are doing. [mainly AM, INFORMAL] **43** PHRASE Someone who is **on the take** is receiving illegal income such as bribes. [INFORMAL] ▫ *I can also name cops who are on the take.* **44 to be taken aback** → see **aback 45 to take up arms** → see **arm** ② **46 to take the cake** → see **cake 47 to take your hat off to someone** → see **hat 48 to be taken for a ride** → see **ride 49 to take someone by surprise** → see **surprise 50 take my word for it** → see **word** ②

▶ **take after** PHRASAL VERB [no passive] If you **take after** a member of your family, you resemble them in your appearance, your behavior, or your character. ▫ *She was a smart, brave woman. You take after her.*

▶ **take apart** PHRASAL VERB If you **take** something **apart**, you separate it into the different parts that it is made of. ▫ *When the clock stopped, he took it apart, found what was wrong, and put the whole thing together again.*

▶ **take away 1** PHRASAL VERB If you **take** something **away** from someone, you remove it from them, so that they no longer possess it or have it with them. ▫ *They're going to take my citizenship away.* ▫ *"Give me the toy," he said softly, "or I'll take it away from you."* **2** PHRASAL VERB If you **take** one number or amount **away** from another, you subtract one number from the other. ▫ *Add up the bills for each month. Take this away from the income.* **3** PHRASAL VERB To **take** someone **away** means to bring them from their home to an institution such as a prison or hospital. ▫ *Two men claiming to be police officers went to the pastor's house and took him away.* **4** → see also **takeaway**

▶ **take back 1** PHRASAL VERB If you **take** something **back**, you return it to the place where you bought it or where you borrowed it from, because it is unsuitable or broken, or because you have finished with it. ▫ *If I buy something and he doesn't like it I'll take it back.* **2** PHRASAL VERB If you **take** something **back**, you admit that something that you said or thought is wrong. ▫ *Take back what you said about Jeremy!* **3** PHRASAL VERB If you **take** someone **back**, you allow them to come home again, after they have gone away because of an argument or other problem. ▫ *Why did she take him back?* **4** PHRASAL VERB If you say that something **takes** you **back**, you mean that it reminds you of a period of your past life and makes you think about it again. ▫ *I enjoyed experimenting with colors – it took me back to being five years old.*

▶ **take down 1** PHRASAL VERB If you **take** something **down**, you reach up and get it from a high place such as a shelf. ▫ *Alberto took the portrait down from the wall.* **2** PHRASAL VERB If you **take down** a structure, you remove each piece of it. ▫ *The Canadian army took down the barricades erected by the Indians.* **3** PHRASAL VERB If you **take down** a piece of information or a statement, you write it down. ▫ *We've been trying to get back to you, Tom, but we think we took your number down incorrectly.*

▶ **take in 1** PHRASAL VERB If you **take** someone **in**, you allow them to stay in your house or your country, especially when they do not have anywhere to stay or are in trouble. ▫ *He persuaded Jo to take him in.* **2** PHRASAL VERB If the police **take** someone **in**, they remove them from their home in order to question them. ▫ *The police have taken him in for questioning in connection with the murder of a girl.* **3** PHRASAL VERB If you **are taken in** by someone or something, you are deceived by them, so that you get a false impression of them. ▫ *I married in my late teens and was taken in by his charm – which soon vanished.* **4** PHRASAL VERB If you **take** something **in**, you pay attention to it and understand it when you hear it or read it. ▫ *Lesley explains possible treatments but you can tell she's not taking it in.* **5** PHRASAL VERB If you **take** something **in**, you see all of it. ▫ *The eyes behind the lenses were dark and quick-moving, taking in everything at a glance.* **6** PHRASAL VERB If people, animals, or plants **take in** air, drink, or food, they allow it to enter their body, usually by breathing or swallowing. ▫ *They will certainly need to take in plenty of liquid.* **7** PHRASAL VERB If a store, restaurant, theater, or other business **takes in** a certain amount of money, they get that amount from people buying goods or services. [mainly AM] ❏ *They plan to take in $1.6 billion.*

in BRIT, usually use **take**

▶ **take off** ◼ PHRASAL VERB When an airplane **takes off**, it leaves the ground and starts flying. ❏ *We eventually took off at 11 o'clock and arrived in Juneau at 1:30.* ◼ PHRASAL VERB If something such as a product, an activity, or someone's career **takes off**, it suddenly becomes very successful. ❏ *In 1944, he met Edith Piaf, and his career took off.* ◼ PHRASAL VERB If you **take off** or **take yourself off**, you go away, often suddenly and unexpectedly. ❏ *He took off at once and headed back to the motel.* ◼ PHRASAL VERB If you **take** a garment **off**, you remove it. ❏ *He wouldn't take his hat off.* ◼ PHRASAL VERB If you **take** time **off**, you obtain permission not to go to work for a short period of time. ❏ *Mitchel's schedule had not permitted him to take time off.*

▶ **take on** ◼ PHRASAL VERB If you **take on** a job or responsibility, especially a difficult one, you accept it. ❏ *No other organization was able or willing to take on the job.* ◼ PHRASAL VERB [no passive] If something **takes on** a new appearance or quality, it develops that appearance or quality. ❏ *Believing he had only a year to live, his writing took on a feverish intensity.* ◼ PHRASAL VERB If a vehicle such as a bus or ship **takes on** passengers, goods, or fuel, it stops in order to allow them to get on or to be loaded on. ❏ *This is a brief stop to take on passengers and water.* ◼ PHRASAL VERB If you **take** someone **on**, you employ them to do a job. ❏ *He's spoken to a publishing company. They're going to take him on.* ◼ PHRASAL VERB [no passive] If you **take** someone **on**, you fight them or compete against them, especially when they are bigger or more powerful than you are. ❏ *Democrats were reluctant to take on a president whose popularity ratings were historically high* ◼ PHRASAL VERB [no passive] If you **take** something **on** or **upon** yourself, you decide to do it without asking anyone for permission or approval. ❏ *Knox had taken it on himself to choose the wine.* ❏ *He took upon himself the responsibility of protecting her.*

▶ **take out** ◼ PHRASAL VERB If you **take** something **out**, you remove it permanently from its place. ❏ *I got an abscess so he took the tooth out.* ◼ PHRASAL VERB If you **take out** something such as a loan, a license, or an insurance policy, you obtain it by fulfilling the conditions and paying the money that is necessary. ❏ *I'll have to stop by the bank and take out a loan.* ◼ PHRASAL VERB If you **take** someone **out**, they go to something such as a restaurant or theater with you after you have invited them, and usually you pay for them. ❏ *Jessica's grandparents took her out for the day.* ❏ *Sophia took me out to lunch.*

▶ **take over** ◼ PHRASAL VERB If you **take over** a company, you get control of it, for example, by buying its shares. [BUSINESS] ❏ *I'm going to take over the company one day.* ◼ PHRASAL VERB If someone **takes over** a country or building, they get control of it by force, for example, with the help of the army. ❏ *The Belgians took over Rwanda under a League of Nations mandate.* ◼ PHRASAL VERB If you **take over** a job or role or if you **take over**, you become responsible for the job after someone else has stopped doing it. ❏ *His widow has taken over the running of his empire, including six theaters.* ❏ *In 2001, I took over from him as governing mayor.* ◼ PHRASAL VERB If one thing **takes over** from something else, it becomes more important, successful, or powerful than the other thing, and eventually replaces it. ❏ *Cars gradually took over from horses.* ◼ → see also **takeover**

▶ **take to** ◼ PHRASAL VERB If you **take to** someone or something, you like them, especially after knowing or thinking about them for only a short time. ❏ *Did the children take to him?* ◼ PHRASAL VERB If you **take to** doing something, you begin to do it as a regular habit. ❏ *They had taken to wandering through the streets arm-in-arm.*

▶ **take up** ◼ PHRASAL VERB If you **take up** an activity or a subject, you become interested in it and spend time doing it, either as a hobby or as a career. ❏ *He did not particularly want to take up a competitive sport.* ◼ PHRASAL VERB If you **take up** a question, problem, or cause, you act on it or discuss how you are going to act on it. ❏ *If you have a problem with the law, take it up with your legislators.* ❏ *She had taken up the cause of a generation of American youth.* ◼ PHRASAL VERB If you **take up** a job, you begin to work at it. ❏ *He will take up his post as the head of the civil courts at the end of next month.* ◼ PHRASAL VERB If you **take up** an offer or a challenge, you accept it. ❏ *Increasingly, more winemakers are taking up the challenge of growing Pinot Noir.* ◼ PHRASAL VERB If something **takes up** a particular amount of time, space, or effort, it uses that amount. ❏ *I know how busy you must be and naturally I wouldn't want to take up too much of your time.* ❏ *A good deal of my time is taken up with driving the children to soccer games.*

▶ **take upon** → see take on 6

take|away /ˈteɪkəweɪ/ (**takeaways**) ◼ N-COUNT A **takeaway** is a store or restaurant which sells hot cooked food that you eat somewhere else. [BRIT]

in AM, use **takeout**

◼ N-COUNT A **takeaway** is hot cooked food that you buy from a store or restaurant and eat somewhere else. [BRIT]

in AM, use **takeout**

take-home pay N-UNCOUNT Your **take-home pay** is the amount of your wages or salary that is left after income tax and other payments have been subtracted. [BUSINESS] ❏ *Her monthly take-home pay is $1,500 after taxes.*

tak|en /ˈteɪkən/ ◼ **Taken** is the past participle of **take**. ◼ ADJ [v-link ADJ] If you are **taken** with something or someone, you are very interested in them or attracted to them. [INFORMAL] ❏ *She seems very taken with the idea.*

take|off /ˈteɪkɒf/ (**takeoffs**) also **take-off** N-VAR **Takeoff** is the beginning of a flight, when an aircraft leaves the ground. ❏ *What time is takeoff?*

take|out /ˈteɪkaʊt/ (**takeouts**) ◼ N-COUNT A **takeout** is a store or restaurant which sells hot cooked food that you eat somewhere else. [AM] ❏ *...a Chinese takeout restaurant.*

in BRIT, use **takeaway**

◼ N-COUNT **Takeout** or **takeout** food is hot cooked food which you buy from a store or restaurant and eat somewhere else. [AM] ❏ *...a takeout pizza.*

in BRIT, use **takeaway**

take|over ◆◇◇ /ˈteɪkoʊvər/ (**takeovers**) ◼ N-COUNT A **takeover** is the act of gaining control of a company by buying more of its shares than anyone else. [BUSINESS] ❏ *He lost his job in a corporate takeover.* ◼ N-COUNT A **takeover** is the act of taking control of a country, political party, or movement by force. ❏ *There's been a military takeover of some kind.*

▬▬▬ SYNONYMS ▬▬▬
takeover
NOUN ◼
merger: *...the proposed merger of two Japanese banks.*
coup: *...a military coup.*

tak|er /ˈteɪkər/ (**takers**) N-COUNT [usu with brd-neg, usu pl, oft N *for* n] If there are no **takers** for something such as an investment or a challenge, nobody is willing to accept it. ❏ *Over 100 buyers or investors were approached, but there were no takers.*

-taker /-teɪkər/ (**-takers**) COMB IN N-COUNT **-taker** combines with nouns to form other nouns which refer to people who take things, for example, risks or notes. ❏ *Of these, 40% told census-takers they were Muslims.* ❏ *...the top 10 percent of test-takers.*

take-up N-UNCOUNT **Take-up** is the rate at which people apply for or buy something which is offered, for example, financial help from the government or shares in a company. [mainly BRIT]

tak|ings /ˈteɪkɪŋz/ N-PLURAL You can use **takings** to refer to the amount of money that a business such as a store or a movie theater gets from selling its goods or tickets during a particular period. [BUSINESS] ❏ *Their takings were fifteen to twenty thousand dollars a week.*

talc /tælk/ N-UNCOUNT **Talc** is the same as **talcum powder**. [INFORMAL]

tal|cum pow|der /ˈtælkəm paʊdər/ N-UNCOUNT **Talcum powder** is fine powder with a pleasant smell which people put on their bodies to keep their skin dry after washing.

tale ◆◇◇ /teɪl/ (**tales**) ◼ N-COUNT; N-IN-NAMES A **tale** is a story, often involving magic or exciting events. ❏ *...a collection of stories, poems and folk tales.* ◼ N-COUNT You can refer to an interesting, exciting, or dramatic account of a real event as a **tale**. ❏ *The media have been filled with tales of horror and loss resulting from Monday's earthquake.* ◼ → see also **fairy tale**

SYNONYMS

tale
NOUN **1**
story: *The second story in the book is titled 'The Scholar.'*
account: *He gave a detailed account of what happened on the fateful night.*
narrative: *Sloan began his narrative with the day of the murder.*
anecdote: *Pete was telling them an anecdote about their mother.*

tal|ent ✦✧ /ˈtælənt/ (talents) N-VAR **Talent** is the natural ability to do something well. □ *She is proud that both her children have a talent for music.* □ *He's got lots of talent.*

COLLOCATIONS

talent
NOUN
adjective + **talent**: exceptional, outstanding, prodigious; artistic, creative, musical, vocal; natural
verb + **talent**: develop, display; nurture, spot

tal|ent|ed /ˈtæləntɪd/ ADJ Someone who is **talented** has a natural ability to do something well. □ *Howard is a talented pianist.*

tal|ent scout (talent scouts) N-COUNT A **talent scout** is someone whose job is to find people who have talent, for example, as actors, athletes, or musicians, so that they can be offered work.

tal|ent show (talent shows) N-COUNT A **talent show**, **talent competition**, or **talent contest** is a show where ordinary people perform an act on stage, usually in order to try to win a prize for the best performance.

tal|is|man /ˈtælɪsmən, -ɪz-/ (talismans) N-COUNT A **talisman** is an object which you believe has magic powers to protect you or bring you luck.

talk ✦✦✦ /tɔːk/ (talks, talking, talked)
→ Please look at meaning **17** to see if the expression you are looking for is shown under another headword.

1 V-I When you **talk**, you use spoken language to express your thoughts, ideas, or feelings. □ *He was too distressed to talk.* □ *The boys all began to talk at once.* • N-UNCOUNT **Talk** is also a noun. □ *That's not the kind of talk one usually hears from accountants.* **2** V-RECIP If you **talk** to someone, you have a conversation with them. You can also say that two people **talk**. □ *We talked and laughed a lot.* □ *I talked to him yesterday.* □ *When she came back, they were talking about American food.* • N-COUNT **Talk** is also a noun. □ *We had a long talk about her father, Tony, who was a friend of mine.* **3** V-RECIP If you **talk** to someone, you tell them about the things that are worrying you. You can also say that two people **talk**. □ *Your first step should be to talk to a teacher or school counselor.* □ *Do call if you want to talk about it.* • N-COUNT **Talk** is also a noun. □ *I think it's time we had a talk.* **4** V-I If you **talk** on or about something, you make an informal speech telling people what you know or think about it. □ *She will talk on the issues she cares passionately about including education and nursery care.* • N-COUNT **Talk** is also a noun. □ *A guide gives a brief talk on the history of the site.* **5** N-PLURAL **Talks** are formal discussions intended to produce an agreement, usually between different countries or between employers and employees. □ *...the next round of Middle East peace talks.* **6** V-RECIP If one group of people **talks** to another, or if two groups **talk**, they have formal discussions in order to do a deal or produce an agreement. □ *We're talking to some people about opening an office in Boston.* □ *It triggered speculation that GM and Jaguar might be talking.* **7** V-RECIP When different countries or different sides in a dispute **talk**, or **talk** to each other, they discuss their differences in order to try and settle the dispute. □ *They are collecting information in preparation for the day when the two sides sit down and talk.* **8** V-I If people **are talking** about another person or **are talking**, they are discussing that person. □ *Everyone is talking about him.* □ *We'd better not be seen together. People will talk.* • N-UNCOUNT **Talk** is also a noun. □ *There has been a lot of talk about me getting married.* **9** V-I If someone **talks** when they are being held by police or soldiers, they reveal important or secret information, usually unwillingly. □ *They'll talk, they'll implicate me.* **10** V-T/V-I [no passive] If you **talk** a particular language or **talk** with a particular accent, you use that language or have that accent when you speak. □ *You don't sound like a foreigner talking English.* **11** V-T [no passive] If you **talk** something such as politics or sports, you discuss it. □ *The guests were mostly middle-aged men talking business.* **12** V-T You can use **talk** to say what you think of the ideas that someone is expressing. For example, if you say that someone is **talking sense**, you mean that you think the opinions they are expressing are sensible. □ *You must admit George, you're talking absolute nonsense.* **13** V-T [no passive] You can say that you **are talking** a particular thing to draw attention to your topic or to point out a characteristic of what you are discussing. [SPOKEN] □ *We're talking megabucks this time.* **14** N-UNCOUNT If you say that something such as an idea or threat is just **talk**, or **all talk**, you mean that it does not mean or matter much, because people are exaggerating about it or do not really intend to do anything about it. □ *Has much of this actually been tried here? Or is it just talk?* **15** PHRASE You can say **talk about** before mentioning a particular expression or situation, when you mean that something is a very striking or clear example of that expression or situation. [INFORMAL, EMPHASIS] □ *Took us quite a while to get here, didn't it? Talk about fate moving in a mysterious way!* **16** PHRASE You can use the expression **talking of** to introduce a new topic that you want to discuss, and to link it to something that has already been mentioned. □ *I'll give a prize to the best idea. Talking of good ideas, here's one to break the ice at a wedding reception.* **17 to talk shop** → see **shop** **18** → See feature box at **debate**

▶ **talk back** PHRASAL VERB If you **talk back** to someone in authority such as a parent or teacher, you answer them in a rude way. □ *How dare you talk back to me!*

▶ **talk down** **1** PHRASAL VERB To **talk down** someone who is flying an aircraft in an emergency means to give them instructions so that they can land safely. □ *The pilot began to talk him down by giving instructions over the radio.* **2** PHRASAL VERB If someone **talks down** a particular thing, they make it less interesting, valuable, or likely than it originally seemed. □ *They even blame the government for talking down the nation's fourth biggest industry.* □ *Businessmen are tired of politicians talking the economy down.*

▶ **talk into** PHRASAL VERB If you **talk** a person **into** doing something they do not want to do, especially something wrong or stupid, you persuade them to do it. □ *He talked me into marrying him. He also talked me into having a baby.*

▶ **talk out of** PHRASAL VERB If you **talk** someone **out of** doing something they want or intend to do, you persuade them not to do it. □ *My mother tried to talk me out of getting a divorce.*

▶ **talk over** PHRASAL VERB If you **talk** something **over**, you discuss it thoroughly and honestly. □ *He always talked things over with his friends.* □ *We should go somewhere quiet, and talk it over.*

▶ **talk through** **1** PHRASAL VERB If you **talk** something **through** with someone, you discuss it with them thoroughly. □ *He and I have talked through this whole tricky problem.* □ *Now her children are grown-up and she has talked through with them what happened.* **2** PHRASAL VERB If someone **talks** you **through** something that you do not know, they explain it to you carefully. □ *Now she must talk her sister through the process a step at a time.*

▶ **talk up** PHRASAL VERB If someone **talks up** a particular thing, they make it sound more interesting, valuable, or likely than it originally seemed. □ *Politicians accuse the media of talking up the possibility of a riot.* □ *He'll be talking up his plans for the economy.*

SYNONYMS

talk
VERB **1**
chat: *The women were chatting.*
chatter: *Everyone's chattering away in different languages.*
speak: *I rang the hotel and spoke to Louie.*
converse: *Luke sat directly behind the pilot and conversed with him.*
NOUN **4**
speech: *She is due to make a speech on the economy next week.*
presentation: *...a business presentation.*
seminar: *...a series of half-day seminars on the subject.*
lecture: *In his lecture, Riemann covered an enormous variety of topics.*

talka|tive /tɔ̱kətɪv/ ADJ Someone who is **talkative** talks a lot. ❑ *He suddenly became very talkative, his face slightly flushed, his eyes much brighter.*

talk|er /tɔ̱kər/ **(talkers)** N-COUNT [usu supp N] You can use **talker** to refer to someone when you are considering how much they talk, or how good they are at talking to people. ❑ *...a fluent talker.*

talkie /tɔ̱ki/ **(talkies)** N-COUNT A **talkie** is a movie made with sound, as opposed to a silent movie. [OLD-FASHIONED]

talk|ing head **(talking heads)** N-COUNT **Talking heads** are people who appear in television discussion programs and interviews to give their opinions about a topic. [JOURNALISM]

talk|ing point **(talking points)** **1** N-COUNT A **talking point** is an interesting subject for discussion or argument. ❑ *It's bound to be the main talking point during discussions between the prime minister and the president.* **2** N-PLURAL The **talking points** in a speech or presentation are short summaries of the subjects that the speaker intends to discuss. ❑ *Baker is coming to Israel with four major talking points.*

talk|ing shop **(talking shops)** N-COUNT If you say that a conference or a committee is just a **talking shop**, you disapprove of it because nothing is achieved as a result of what is discussed. [BRIT, DISAPPROVAL]

talking-to N-SING [a N] If you give someone **a talking-to**, you speak to them severely, usually about something unacceptable that they have done, in order to show them they were wrong. [INFORMAL]

talk ra|dio N-UNCOUNT **Talk radio** is radio broadcasting which consists mainly of discussions with people who call the show rather than, for example, music or drama. ❑ *The subject dominates the air waves on talk radio.* ❑ *...a talk radio show.*

talk show **(talk shows)** also **talk-show** N-COUNT A **talk show** is a television or radio show in which people talk to a host in an informal way.

tall ✦◇◇ /tɔ̱l/ **(taller, tallest)** **1** ADJ Someone or something that is **tall** has a greater height than is normal or average. ❑ *Being tall can make you feel incredibly self-confident.* **2** ADJ You use **tall** to ask or talk about the height of someone or something. ❑ *How tall are you?* **3** PHRASE If something is a **tall order**, it is very difficult. ❑ *Financing your studies may seem like a tall order, but there is plenty of help available.* **4** PHRASE If you say that someone **walks tall**, you mean that they behave in a way that shows that they have pride in themselves and in what they are doing. ❑ *They shouldn't be disappointed or let their heads fall, but walk tall.*

tal|low /tæ̱loʊ/ N-UNCOUNT **Tallow** is hard animal fat that is used for making candles and soap.

tall ship **(tall ships)** N-COUNT A **tall ship** is a sailing ship which has very tall masts and square sails.

tall tale **(tall tales)** also **tall story** N-COUNT A **tall tale** is a long and complicated story that is difficult to believe because most of the events it describes seem unlikely or impossible. ❑ *...the imaginative tall tales of sailors.*

tal|ly /tæ̱li/ **(tallies, tallying, tallied)** **1** N-COUNT A **tally** is a record of amounts or numbers which you keep changing and adding to as the activity which it affects it progresses. ❑ *They do not keep a tally of visitors to the palace, but it is very popular.* **2** V-RECIP If one number or statement **tallies** with another, they agree with each other or are exactly the same. You can also say that two numbers or statements **tally**. ❑ *Its own estimate of three hundred tallies with that of another survey.*

Tal|mud /tɑ̱lmʊd/ N-PROPER [the N] **The Talmud** is the collection of ancient texts that form the basis of Jewish religious law.

tal|on /tæ̱lən/ **(talons)** **1** N-COUNT [usu pl] The **talons** of a bird of prey are its hooked claws. **2** → See also color supplement

tama|rind /tæ̱mərɪnd/ **(tamarinds)** N-VAR A **tamarind** is a sour fruit which grows on a tropical evergreen tree and is used in cooking. You can also refer to the tree on which this fruit grows as a **tamarind**.

tama|risk /tæ̱mərɪsk/ **(tamarisks)** N-COUNT A **tamarisk** is a bush or small tree which grows mainly around the Mediterranean and in Asia, and has pink and white flowers.

tam|bou|rine /tæ̱mbərin/ **(tambourines)** N-COUNT [oft the N] A **tambourine** is a musical instrument which you shake or hit with your hand. It consists of a drum skin on a circular frame with pairs of small round pieces of metal all around the edge.

tame /te̱ɪm/ **(tames, taming, tamed, tamer, tamest)** **1** ADJ A **tame** animal or bird is one that is not afraid of humans. ❑ *They never became tame; they would run away if you approached them.* **2** ADJ If you say that something or someone is **tame**, you are criticizing them for being weak and uninteresting, rather than forceful or shocking. [DISAPPROVAL] ❑ *These ideas may seem tame today, but they were inflammatory in his time.* **3** V-T If someone **tames** a wild animal or bird, they train it not to be afraid of humans and to do what they say. ❑ *The Amazons were believed to have been the first to tame horses.*

ta|moxi|fen /təmɒ̱ksɪfɛn, -fən/ N-UNCOUNT **Tamoxifen** is a drug that is used for treating women who have breast cancer.

tamp /tæ̱mp/ **(tamps, tamping, tamped)** V-T If you **tamp** something, you press it down by tapping it several times so that it becomes flatter and more solid. ❑ *Then I tamp down the soil with the back of a rake.* ❑ *Philpott tamped a wad of tobacco into his pipe.*

tam|per /tæ̱mpər/ **(tampers, tampering, tampered)** V-I If someone **tampers with** something, they interfere with it or try to change it when they have no right to do so. ❑ *I don't want to be accused of tampering with the evidence.*

tam|pon /tæ̱mpɒn/ **(tampons)** N-COUNT A **tampon** is a tube made of cotton that a woman puts inside her vagina in order to absorb blood during menstruation.

tan /tæ̱n/ **(tans, tanning, tanned)** **1** N-SING If you have a **tan**, your skin has become darker than usual because you have been in the sun. ❑ *He is small and blond, with a permanent tan.* **2** V-T/V-I If a part of your body **tans** or if you **tan** it, your skin becomes darker than usual because you spend a lot of time in the sun. ❑ *I have very pale skin that never tans.* • **tanned** ADJ ❑ *Their skin was tanned and glowing from their weeks at the sea.*

tan|dem /tæ̱ndəm/ **(tandems)** **1** N-COUNT A **tandem** is a bicycle designed for two riders, on which one rider sits behind the other. **2** PHRASE If one thing happens or is done **in tandem** with another thing, the two things happen at the same time. ❑ *...when literature is used in tandem with textbooks.* **3** → See also color supplement

tan|doori /tændʊ̱əri/ ADJ [usu ADJ n] **Tandoori** dishes are Indian meat dishes which are cooked in a clay oven.

tang /tæ̱ŋ/ N-SING A **tang** is a strong, sharp smell or taste. ❑ *She could smell the salty tang of the sea.*

tan|gent /tæ̱ndʒənt/ **(tangents)** **1** N-COUNT A **tangent** is a line that touches the edge of a curve or circle at one point, but does not cross it. **2** PHRASE [V and N inflect] If someone **goes off on a tangent**, they start saying or doing something that is not directly connected with what they were saying or doing before. ❑ *The conversation went off on a tangent.*

tan|gen|tial /tændʒɛ̱nʃəl/ ADJ If you describe something as **tangential**, you mean that it has only a slight or indirect connection with the thing you are concerned with, and is therefore not worth considering seriously. [FORMAL] ❑ *Too much time was spent discussing tangential issues.* **2** ADJ [oft ADJ to n] If something is **tangential to** something else, it is at a tangent to it. ❑ *He closed his office on the street tangential to the courthouse square and walked the two blocks to his house..*

tan|ge|rine /tæ̱ndʒərin/ **(tangerines)** N-COUNT A **tangerine** is a small, sweet orange.

tan|gible /tæ̱ndʒɪbəl/ ADJ If something is **tangible**, it is clear enough or definite enough to be easily seen, felt, or noticed. ❑ *There should be some tangible evidence that the economy is starting to recover.*

tan|gle /tæ̱ŋgəl/ **(tangles, tangling, tangled)** **1** N-COUNT A **tangle** of something is a mass of it twisted together in a messy way. ❑ *A tangle of wires is all that remains of the computer and phone systems.* **2** V-T/V-I If something **is tangled** or **tangles**, it becomes twisted together in a messy way. ❑ *Animals get tangled in fishing nets and drown.* ❑ *Her hair tends to tangle.*

tan|go /tæ̱ŋgoʊ/ **(tangos, tangoing, tangoed)** **1** N-SING [usu the N] The **tango** is a South American dance in which two people hold each other closely, walk quickly in one direction, then walk quickly back again. **2** N-VAR A **tango** is a piece of music intended for tango dancing. ❏ *A tango was playing on the jukebox.* ❏ *The sounds of tango filled the air.* **3** V-I If you **tango**, you dance the tango. ❏ *They can rock and roll, they can tango, but they can't bop.* **4 it takes two to tango** → see **two**

tangy /tǽŋi/ (tangier, tangiest) ADJ A **tangy** flavor or smell is one that is sharp, especially a flavor like that of lemon juice or a smell like that of sea air.

tank ✦◇◇ /tǽŋk/ (tanks, tanking, tanked) **1** N-COUNT A **tank** is a large container for holding liquid or gas. ❏ *...an empty fuel tank.* ❏ *Two water tanks provide a total capacity of 400 liters.* **2** N-COUNT A **tank** is a large military vehicle that is equipped with weapons and moves along on metal tracks that are fitted over the wheels. **3** V-I If something such as a stock price or a movie **tanks**, it performs very badly, for example because it loses a lot of money. [AM, INFORMAL] ❏ *Tech stocks have tanked.* ❏ *The movie, which cost $137 million, tanked, grossing only $32 million.* ❏ *His career tanked after the show left the air.*

COLLOCATIONS

tank
NOUN
1
noun + **tank**: fuel, gas, oxygen, water; fish; storage
adjective + **tank**: empty, full
verb + **tank**: drain, empty; fill; install
2
noun + **tank**: army
verb + **tank**: deploy; destroy

---

tank|ard /tǽŋkərd/ (tankards) **1** N-COUNT A **tankard** is a large metal cup with a handle, that you can drink beer from. **2** N-COUNT A **tankard** of beer is an amount of beer contained in a tankard. ❏ *...a tankard of ale.* **3** → See also color supplement

tanked /tǽŋkt/ ADJ [usu v-link ADJ] If someone is **tanked** or **tanked up**, they are drunk. [INFORMAL]

tank|er /tǽŋkər/ (tankers) **1** N-COUNT [oft supp N, also by N] A **tanker** is a very large ship used for transporting large quantities of gas or liquid, especially oil. ❏ *A Greek oil tanker has run aground.* **2** N-COUNT [usu supp N, also by N] A **tanker** is a large truck, railroad vehicle, or aircraft used for transporting large quantities of a substance. ❏ *...aerial refueling tankers.* **3** → See also color supplement

tank top (tank tops) N-COUNT A **tank top** is a soft cotton shirt with no sleeves, collar, or buttons. [AM]

tan|ner /tǽnər/ (tanners) N-COUNT A **tanner** is someone whose job is making leather from animal skins.

tan|nin /tǽnɪn/ N-UNCOUNT **Tannin** is a yellow or brown chemical that is found in plants such as tea. It is used in the process of making leather and in dyeing.

tan|ning bed (tanning beds) N-COUNT A **tanning bed** is a piece of equipment with ultraviolet lights. You lie on it to make your skin browner. [mainly AM] ❏ *...the dangers of using tanning beds.*

Tan|noy /tǽnɔɪ/ N-SING [oft over N] A **Tannoy** is a system of loudspeakers used to make public announcements, for example, at a fair or at a sports stadium. [BRIT, TRADEMARK]

in AM, use **public address system**

tan|ta|lize /tǽntəlaɪz/ (tantalizes, tantalizing, tantalized)

in BRIT, also use **tantalise**

V-T If someone or something **tantalizes** you, they make you feel hopeful and excited about getting what you want, usually before disappointing you by not letting you have what they appeared to offer. ❏ *...the dreams of democracy that have so tantalized them.* ● **tan|ta|liz|ing** ADJ ❏ *A tantalizing aroma of fresh bread fills the air.*

tan|ta|mount /tǽntəmaʊnt/ ADJ [v-link ADJ to n/-ing] If you say that one thing is **tantamount** to another, more serious thing, you are emphasizing how bad, unacceptable, or unfortunate the first thing is by comparing it to the second thing. [FORMAL, EMPHASIS] ❏ *What Bracey is saying is tantamount to heresy.*

tan|tric /tǽntrɪk/ also **Tantric** ADJ [ADJ n] **Tantric** is used to describe practices in Buddhist and Hindu scriptures. ❏ *...tantric yoga.*

tan|trum /tǽntrəm/ (tantrums) N-COUNT If a child has a **tantrum**, they lose their temper in a noisy and uncontrolled way. If you say that an adult is throwing a **tantrum**, you are criticizing them for losing their temper and acting in a childish way. [DISAPPROVAL] ❏ *He immediately threw a tantrum, screaming and stomping up and down like a child.* ❏ *...a temper tantrum.*

Tao|ism /daʊɪzəm, taʊ-/ N-UNCOUNT **Taoism** is a Chinese religious philosophy which teaches that people should lead a simple honest life and not interfere with the course of natural events.

tap ✦◇◇ /tǽp/ (taps, tapping, tapped) **1** N-COUNT A **tap** is a device that controls the flow of a liquid or gas from a pipe or container, for example, on a sink or on a cask or barrel. [mainly BRIT]

in AM, usually use **faucet**

2 V-T/V-I If you **tap** something, you hit it with a quick light blow or a series of quick light blows. ❏ *He tapped the table nervously with his fingers.* ❏ *Grace tapped on the bedroom door and went in.* ● N-COUNT **Tap** is also a noun. ❏ *A tap on the door interrupted him and Sally Pierce came in.* **3** V-T If you **tap** your fingers or feet, you make a regular pattern of sound by hitting a surface lightly and repeatedly with them, especially while you are listening to music. ❏ *The song's so catchy it makes you bounce around the living room or tap your feet.* **4** V-T If someone **taps** your telephone, they attach a special device to the line so that they can secretly listen to your conversations. ❏ *The government passed laws allowing the police to tap telephones.* ● N-COUNT **Tap** is also a noun. ❏ *He assured us that we were not subjected to phone taps.* **5** PHRASE [usu v-link PHR] If drinks are **on tap**, they come from a tap rather than from a bottle. ❏ *Filtered water is always on tap here.* **6** → See feature box at **body language**

tap|as /tɑpɑs, -pəs/ N-PLURAL **Tapas** are small plates of food that are served with drinks or before a main meal.

tap danc|er (tap dancers) N-COUNT A **tap dancer** is a dancer who does tap dancing.

tap danc|ing also **tap-dancing, tap** N-UNCOUNT **Tap dancing** is a style of dancing in which the dancers wear special shoes with pieces of metal on the heels and toes. The shoes make loud sharp sounds as the dancers move their feet.

tape ✦◆◇ /teɪp/ (tapes, taping, taped) **1** N-UNCOUNT **Tape** is a sticky strip of plastic used for sticking things together. ❏ *...strong adhesive tape.* **2** N-UNCOUNT **Tape** is a narrow plastic strip covered with a magnetic substance. In the past, it was used to record sounds, pictures, and computer information. ❏ *The sound quality of tape dictations was sometimes poor, and therefore transcribing was often time consuming and stressful.* **3** N-COUNT A **tape** is a cassette or spool with magnetic tape wound around it. ❏ *...an old cassette tape.* **4** V-T/V-I In the past, if you **taped** music, sounds, or television pictures, you recorded them using a tape recorder or a video recorder. ❏ *She had just taped an interview.* **5** V-T If you **tape** one thing to another, you attach it using adhesive tape. ❏ *I taped the base of the feather onto the velvet.* **6** N-COUNT A **tape** is a ribbon that is stretched across the finishing line of a race. ❏ *...the finishing tape.* **7** → see also **red tape, videotape**

tape meas|ure (tape measures) **1** N-COUNT A **tape measure** is a strip of metal, plastic, or cloth which has numbers marked on it and is used for measuring. **2** → See also color supplement

ta|per /teɪpər/ (tapers, tapering, tapered) **1** V-T/V-I If something **tapers**, or if you **taper** it, it becomes gradually thinner at one end. ❏ *Unlike other trees, it doesn't taper very much. It stays fat all the way up.* ● **ta|pered** ADJ ❏ *...the elegantly tapered legs of the dressing-table.* **2** N-COUNT A **taper** is a long, thin candle or a thin wooden strip that is used for lighting fires. ❏ *Taking up a candlestick, he touched the wick to a lighted taper.*

tape re|cord|er (tape recorders) also **tape-recorder** N-COUNT A **tape recorder** is a machine used for recording and playing music, speech, or other sounds.

tap|es|try /tǽpɪstri/ (tapestries) N-VAR A **tapestry** is a large piece of heavy cloth with a picture woven into it using colored threads. ❏ *He stared in wonder at the tapestries on the walls.*

tape|worm /téɪpwɜrm/ (tapeworms) N-COUNT A **tapeworm** is a long, flat parasite which lives in the stomach and intestines of animals or people.

tapio|ca /tæpióʊkə/ N-UNCOUNT **Tapioca** is a food consisting of white grains, similar to rice, which come from the cassava plant. It is used as a thickener and as a dessert.

tap wa|ter N-UNCOUNT **Tap water** is the water that comes out of a faucet in a building such as a house or a hotel.

tar /tɑr/ **1** N-UNCOUNT **Tar** is a thick, black, sticky substance that is used especially for making roads. ❏ *The oil has hardened to tar.* **2** N-UNCOUNT **Tar** is one of the poisonous substances contained in tobacco. ❏ *...strict guidelines as to the amount of tar contained in cigarettes.*

ta|ra|ma|sa|la|ta /tǽrəməsəlɑtə/ N-UNCOUNT **Taramasalata** is a pink creamy food made from the eggs of a fish such as cod or mullet. It is usually eaten at the beginning of a meal.

ta|ran|tu|la /tərǽntʃələ/ (tarantulas) N-COUNT A **tarantula** is a very large hairy spider which has a mildly poisonous bite.

tar|dy /tɑ́rdi/ (tardier, tardiest) ADJ If someone or something is **tardy**, they do something later than expected or later than they should. ❏ *I was as tardy as ever for the afternoon appointments.* ❏ *...companies who are tardy in paying bills.* • **tar|di|ness** N-UNCOUNT ❏ *His legendary tardiness left audiences waiting for hours.*

tar|get ✦✦◇ /tɑ́rgɪt/ (targets, targeting or targetting, targeted or targetted) **1** N-COUNT A **target** is something at which someone is aiming a weapon or other object. ❏ *The village lies beside a main road, making it an easy target for bandits.* **2** N-COUNT A **target** is a result that you are trying to achieve. ❏ *She's won back her place too late to achieve her target of 20 goals this season.* **3** V-T To **target** a particular person or thing means to decide to attack or criticize them. ❏ *Republicans targeted her as vulnerable in her bid for reelection this year.* • N-COUNT [oft N of/for n] **Target** is also a noun. ❏ *In the past they have been the target of racist abuse.* **4** V-T If you **target** a particular group of people, you try to appeal to those people or affect them. ❏ *The campaign will target American insurance companies.* • N-COUNT **Target** is also a noun. ❏ *Families with young children are a prime target group for marketing strategies.* **5** PHRASE If someone or something is **on target**, they are making good progress and are likely to achieve the result that was wanted. ❏ *We were still right on target for our deadline.*

SYNONYMS

target
NOUN **2**
goal: *The goal is to raise as much money as possible.*
aim: *...a research program that has largely failed to achieve its principal aims.*
objective: *Our main objective was the recovery of the child, safe and well.*

---

tar|get mar|ket (target markets) N-COUNT A **target market** is a market in which a company is trying to sell its products or services. [BUSINESS] ❏ *We decided that we needed to change our target market from the over-45's to the 35-45's.*

tar|iff /tǽrɪf/ (tariffs) N-COUNT A **tariff** is a tax that a government collects on goods coming into a country. [BUSINESS] ❏ *America wants to eliminate tariffs on items such as electronics.*

tar|mac /tɑ́rmæk/ **1** N-UNCOUNT **Tarmac** is a material used for making road surfaces, consisting of crushed stones mixed with tar. [BRIT, TRADEMARK]

in AM, usually use **blacktop**

2 N-SING **The tarmac** is an area with a surface made of tarmac, especially the area from which planes take off at an airport. ❏ *Standing on the tarmac were two American planes.*

tar|nish /tɑ́rnɪʃ/ (tarnishes, tarnishing, tarnished) **1** V-T If you say that something **tarnishes** someone's reputation or image, you mean that it causes people to have a worse opinion of them than they would otherwise have had. ❏ *The affair could tarnish the reputation of the senator.* • **tar|nished** ADJ ❏ *He says he wants to improve the tarnished image of his country.* **2** V-T/V-I If a metal **tarnishes** or if something **tarnishes** it, it becomes stained and loses its brightness. ❏ *It never rusts or tarnishes.*

Ta|rot /tǽroʊ/ N-UNCOUNT [also the N, oft N n] The **Tarot** is a pack of cards with pictures on them that is used to predict what will happen to people in the future. **Tarot** is also used to refer to the system of predicting people's futures using these cards. ❏ *...tarot cards.*

tarp /tɑrp/ (tarps) N-COUNT A **tarp** is a sheet of heavy waterproof material that is used as a protective cover. [mainly AM]

in BRIT, usually use **tarpaulin**

tar|pau|lin /tɑrpɔ́lɪn, tɑ́rpəlɪn/ (tarpaulins) **1** N-UNCOUNT [oft N n] **Tarpaulin** is a fabric made of canvas or similar material coated with tar, wax, paint, or some other waterproof substance. ❏ *...a piece of tarpaulin.* ❏ *...tarpaulin covers.* **2** N-COUNT A **tarpaulin** is a sheet of heavy waterproof material that is used as a protective cover.

tar|ra|gon /tǽrəgɒn, -gən/ N-UNCOUNT **Tarragon** is an herb with narrow leaves which are used to add flavor to food.

tarred /tɑrd/ ADJ A **tarred** road or roof has a surface of tar.

tar|ry (tarries, tarrying, tarried)

The verb is pronounced /tǽri/. The adjective is pronounced /tɑ́ri/.

1 V-I If you **tarry** somewhere, you stay there longer than you meant to and delay leaving. [OLD-FASHIONED] ❏ *Two old boys tarried on the street corner discussing cattle.* **2** ADJ If you describe something as **tarry**, you mean that it has a lot of tar in it or is like tar. ❏ *I smelled tarry melted asphalt.* ❏ *...cups of tarry coffee.*

tart /tɑrt/ (tarts) **1** N-VAR A **tart** is a shallow pastry case with a filling of food, especially sweet food. ❏ *...apple tarts.* **2** ADJ If something such as fruit is **tart**, it has a sharp taste. ❏ *The blackberries were too tart on their own, so we stewed them gently with some apples.* **3** ADJ A **tart** remark or way of speaking is sharp and unpleasant, often in a way that is a little cruel. ❏ *The words were more tart than she had intended.* **4** N-COUNT **Tart** is an offensive word for a woman who dresses or behaves in a way that suggests she wants to have sex with a lot of different people. [INFORMAL, OFFENSIVE, DISAPPROVAL] ❏ *You look like a tart.*

tar|tan /tɑ́rtⁿn/ (tartans) N-VAR **Tartan** is a group of designs for cloth traditionally associated with Scotland. The design is made up of lines of different widths and colors crossing each other at right angles. **Tartan** is also used to refer to cloth which has this pattern. ❏ *...traditional tartan kilts.*

tar|tar /tɑ́rtər/ (tartars) **1** N-UNCOUNT **Tartar** is a hard yellowish substance that forms on your teeth and causes them to decay if it is not removed. **2** N-COUNT If you describe someone in a position of authority as a **tartar**, you mean that they are fierce, bad-tempered, and strict. [INFORMAL, mainly BRIT] ❏ *She can be quite a tartar.* **3** → see also **cream of tartar**

tar|tar sauce also **tartare sauce** N-UNCOUNT **Tartar sauce** is a thick cold sauce eaten with fish made from mayonnaise and chopped pickles.

tarty /tɑ́rti/ (tartier, tartiest) ADJ If you describe a person or their clothes as **tarty**, you are criticizing them for trying to look sexually attractive in a vulgar way. [INFORMAL, DISAPPROVAL] ❏ *That coat made her look so tarty.*

task ✦✦◇ /tæsk/ (tasks, tasking, tasked) **1** N-COUNT A **task** is an activity or piece of work which you have to do, usually as part of a larger project. ❏ *Walker had the unenviable task of breaking the bad news to Mark.* **2** V-T If you **are tasked** with doing a particular activity or piece of work, someone in authority asks you to do it. ❏ *Jen was tasked with running a charity basketball tournament.*

task|bar /tǽskbɑr/ (taskbars) also **task bar** N-COUNT The **taskbar** on a computer screen is the narrow strip of icons, usually located at the bottom of the screen, that shows you which windows are currently open and that allows you to control functions such as the Start button and the clock. Compare **toolbar**. [COMPUTING] ❏ *Rather than crowd your screen with new shortcuts, you can switch to a new desktop by clicking on the taskbar at the bottom of the screen.*

task force ◆◇◇ (**task forces**) also **taskforce** **1** N-COUNT A **task force** is a small section of an army, navy, or air force that is sent to a particular place to deal with a military crisis. ☐ *The United States is sending a naval task force to the area to evacuate American citizens.* **2** N-COUNT A **task force** is a group of people working together on a particular task. ☐ *He created a task force charged with looking at a range of issues.*

task|master /tæskmæstər/ (**taskmasters**) N-COUNT [usu adj N] If you refer to someone as a hard **taskmaster**, you mean that they expect the people they supervise to work very hard.

tas|sel /tæsəl/ (**tassels**) N-COUNT **Tassels** are bunches of short pieces of wool or other material tied together at one end and attached as decorations to something such as a piece of clothing or a lampshade.

tas|seled /tæsəld/

in BRIT, use **tasselled**

ADJ **Tasseled** means decorated with tassels. ☐ *...tasseled cushions.*

taste ◆◆◇ /teɪst/ (**tastes, tasting, tasted**) **1** N-UNCOUNT **Taste** is one of the five senses that people have. When you have food or drink in your mouth, your sense of taste makes it possible for you to recognize what it is. ☐ *...a keen sense of taste.* **2** N-COUNT The **taste** of something is the individual quality that it has when you put it in your mouth and that distinguishes it from other things. For example, something may have a sweet, bitter, sour, or salty taste. ☐ *I like the taste of wine and enjoy trying different kinds.* **3** N-SING If you have a **taste** of some food or drink, you try a small amount of it in order to see what the flavor is like. ☐ *Yves sometimes gives customers a taste of a wine before they order.* **4** V-I [no cont] If food or drink **tastes** of something, it has that particular flavor, which you notice when you eat or drink it. ☐ *I drank a cup of tea that tasted of diesel.* ☐ *It tastes like chocolate.* **5** V-T If you **taste** some food or drink, you eat or drink a small amount of it in order to try its flavor, for example, to see if you like it or not. ☐ *I tasted the wine the waiter had produced.* **6** V-T [no passive] If you can **taste** something that you are eating or drinking, you are aware of its flavor. ☐ *You can taste the green chili in the dish but it is a little sweet.* **7** N-SING If you have a **taste of** a particular way of life or activity, you have a brief experience of it. ☐ *This voyage was his first taste of freedom.* **8** V-T [no passive] If you **taste** something such as a way of life or a pleasure, you experience it for a short period of time. ☐ *Once you have tasted the outdoor life in southern California, it's hard to return to Montana in winter.* **9** N-SING If you have a **taste for** something, you have a liking or preference for it. ☐ *That gave me a taste for reading.* **10** N-UNCOUNT [also N in pl] A person's **taste** is their choice in the things that they like or buy, for example, their clothes, possessions, or music. If you say that someone has good **taste**, you mean that you approve of their choices. If you say that they have bad **taste**, you disapprove of their choices. ☐ *His taste in clothes is extremely good.* **11** PHRASE If you say that something that is said or done is **in bad taste** or **in poor taste**, you mean that it is offensive, often because it concerns death or sex and is inappropriate for the situation. If you say that something is **in good taste**, you mean that it is not offensive and that it is appropriate for the situation. ☐ *He rejects the idea that his film is in bad taste.*

taste bud (**taste buds**) also **tastebud** N-COUNT [usu pl, oft poss N] Your **taste buds** are the little points on the surface of your tongue which enable you to recognize the flavor of a food or drink.

taste|ful /teɪstfəl/ ADJ If you say that something is **tasteful**, you consider it to be attractive, elegant, and in good taste. ☐ *The decor is tasteful and restrained.* • **taste|ful|ly** ADV ☐ *...a large and tastefully decorated home.*

taste|less /teɪstlɪs/ **1** ADJ If you describe something such as furniture, clothing, or the way that a house is decorated as **tasteless**, you consider it to be vulgar and unattractive. ☐ *...a house crammed with tasteless furniture.* **2** ADJ If you describe something such as a remark or joke as **tasteless**, you mean that it is offensive. ☐ *I think that is the most vulgar and tasteless remark I have ever heard in my life.* **3** ADJ If you describe food or drink as **tasteless**, you mean that it has very little or no flavor. ☐ *The fish was mushy and tasteless.*

tast|er /teɪstər/ (**tasters**) **1** N-COUNT A **taster** is someone whose job is to taste different wines, teas, or other foods or drinks, in order to test their quality. ☐ *...a wine taster.* **2** N-COUNT [usu sing, oft N *of* n] If you refer to something as a **taster** of something greater, or of something that will come later, you mean that it gives you an idea what that thing is like, and often makes you interested in it or want more of it. ☐ *The book is essentially a taster for those unfamiliar with the subject.*

tast|ing /teɪstɪŋ/ (**tastings**) N-COUNT [usu supp N] **Tasting** is used in expressions such as **wine tasting** to refer to a social event at which people try different kinds of the specified drink or food in small amounts.

tasty /teɪsti/ (**tastier, tastiest**) ADJ If you say that food is **tasty**, you mean that it has a fairly strong and pleasant flavor which makes it good to eat. ☐ *Try this tasty dish for supper with a crispy salad.*

ta-ta /tæ tɑ/ also **ta ta** CONVENTION **Ta-ta** is used to say goodbye. [BRIT, INFORMAL or DIALECT, FORMULAE]

tat|tered /tætərd/ ADJ If something such as clothing or a book is **tattered**, it is damaged or torn, especially because it has been used a lot over a long period of time. ☐ *He fled wearing only a sarong and a tattered shirt.*

tat|ters /tætərz/ **1** N-PLURAL Clothes that are in **tatters** are badly torn in several places, so that pieces can easily come off. ☐ *His jeans were left in tatters.* **2** N-PLURAL If you say that something such as a plan or a person's state of mind is in **tatters**, you are emphasizing that it is weak, has suffered a lot of damage, and is likely to fail completely. [EMPHASIS] ☐ *The economy is in tatters.*

tat|tle /tætəl/ (**tattles, tattling, tattled**) V-I If you **tattle** on someone, you give information about them to a person in authority, especially if they have done something wrong. This word is used by and about children ☐ *...instruct our children not to tattle on one another.*

tat|too /tætu/ (**tattoos, tattooing, tattooed**) **1** N-COUNT A **tattoo** is a design that is drawn on someone's skin using needles to make little holes and filling them with colored dye. ☐ *On the back of his neck he has a tattoo of a cross.* **2** V-T If someone **tattoos** you, they give you a tattoo. ☐ *In the old days, they would paint and tattoo their bodies for ceremonies.*

tat|ty /tæti/ (**tattier, tattiest**) ADJ If you describe something as **tatty**, you think it is messy, not very clean, and looks as if it has not been cared for. ☐ *...a very tatty old bathrobe.*

taught /tɔt/ **Taught** is the past tense and past participle of **teach**.

taunt /tɔnt/ (**taunts, taunting, taunted**) V-T If someone **taunts** you, they say unkind or insulting things to you, especially about your weaknesses or failures. ☐ *A gang taunted a disabled man.* • N-COUNT **Taunt** is also a noun. ☐ *For years they suffered racist taunts.*

taupe /toʊp/ COLOR Something that is **taupe** is a pale brownish-gray color.

Tau|rus /tɔrəs/ **1** N-UNCOUNT **Taurus** is one of the twelve signs of the zodiac. Its symbol is a bull. People who are born between approximately the 20th of April and the 20th of May come under this sign. **2** N-SING [a N] A **Taurus** is a person whose sign of the zodiac is Taurus.

taut /tɔt/ (**tauter, tautest**) **1** ADJ Something that is **taut** is stretched very tight. ☐ *The clothes line is pulled taut and secured.* **2** ADJ If someone has a **taut** expression, they look very worried and tense. ☐ *Ben sat up quickly, his face taut and terrified.*

taut|en /tɔtən/ (**tautens, tautening, tautened**) V-T/V-I If a part of your body **tautens** or if you **tauten** it, it becomes stiff or firm. ☐ *Her whole body tautened violently.* ☐ *There are exercises that tauten facial muscles.*

tau|to|logi|cal /tɔtəlɒdʒɪkəl/ ADJ A **tautological** statement involves tautology.

tau|tol|ogy /tɔtɒlədʒi/ (**tautologies**) N-VAR **Tautology** is the use of different words to say the same thing twice in the same statement. 'The money should be adequate enough' is an example of tautology.

tav|ern /tævərn/ (**taverns**) N-COUNT; N-IN-NAMES A **tavern** is a bar. [OLD-FASHIONED] ☐ *Drinkers line the bar at Byrnes Tavern.*

taw|dry /tɔ́dri/ (tawdrier, tawdriest) **1** ADJ If you describe something such as clothes or decorations as **tawdry**, you mean that they are cheap and show a lack of taste. ◻ ...tawdry jewelry. **2** ADJ [usu ADJ n] If you describe something such as a story or an event as **tawdry**, you mean that it is unpleasant or immoral. ◻ ...the yawning gulf between her fantasies and the tawdry reality.

taw|ny /tɔ́ni/ COLOR **Tawny** hair, fur, or skin is a pale brown color. ◻ She had tawny hair.

tax ♦♦♦ /tǽks/ (taxes, taxing, taxed) **1** N-VAR **Tax** is an amount of money that you have to pay to the government so that it can pay for public services such as road and schools. [BUSINESS] ◻ No-one enjoys paying tax. ◻ ...a pledge not to raise taxes on people below a certain income. **2** V-T When a person or company **is taxed**, they have to pay a part of their income or profits to the government. When goods **are taxed**, a percentage of their price has to be paid to the government. [BUSINESS] ◻ Husband and wife may be taxed separately on their incomes. **3** → see also **taxing**, **income tax**

SYNONYMS

tax
NOUN **1**
duty: Import duties still average 30%.
levy: ...an annual highway levy on all drivers.
tariff: America wants to eliminate tariffs on items such as electronics.

---

tax|able /tǽksəbəl/ ADJ **Taxable** income is income on which you have to pay tax. [BUSINESS] ◻ It is worth consulting the guide to see whether your income is taxable.

tax|a|tion /tækseɪʃən/ **1** N-UNCOUNT **Taxation** is the system by which a government takes money from people and spends it on things such as education, health, and defense. [BUSINESS] ◻ ...the proposed reforms to taxation. **2** N-UNCOUNT **Taxation** is the amount of money that people have to pay in taxes. [BUSINESS] ◻ The result will be higher taxation.

tax avoid|ance **1** N-UNCOUNT **Tax avoidance** is the use of legal methods to pay the smallest possible amount of tax. **2** → see also **tax evasion**

tax break (tax breaks) N-COUNT If the government gives a **tax break** to a particular group of people or type of organization, it reduces the amount of tax they have to pay or changes the tax system in a way that benefits them. [BUSINESS] ◻ Today they'll consider tax breaks for businesses that create jobs in inner cities.

tax cred|it (tax credits) N-COUNT A **tax credit** is an amount of money on which you do not have to pay tax. [BUSINESS] ◻ The president proposed tax credits for buying environmentally-friendly cars.

tax-deductible /tǽks dɪdʌ́ktɪbəl/ ADJ If an expense is **tax-deductible**, it can be paid out of the part of your income on which you do not pay tax, so that the amount of tax you pay is reduced. [BUSINESS] ◻ The cost of private childcare should be made tax-deductible.

tax-deferred ADJ [ADJ n] If you have savings in a **tax-deferred** account, you do not have to pay tax on them until a later time. [AM] ◻ If your retirement plan includes both taxable and tax-deferred accounts, it is worth considering which funds should be placed in each.

tax eva|sion N-UNCOUNT **Tax evasion** is the crime of not paying the full amount of tax that you should pay. [BUSINESS] ◻ He was later charged with tax evasion.

tax-exempt ADJ Income or property that is **tax-exempt** is income or property that you do not have to pay tax on. ◻ About 15 percent of the township's property is tax-exempt.

tax-free ADJ **Tax-free** is used to describe income on which you do not have to pay tax. [BUSINESS] ◻ ...a tax-free investment plan.

tax ha|ven (tax havens) N-COUNT A **tax haven** is a country or place which has a low rate of tax so that people choose to live there or register companies there in order to avoid paying higher tax in their own countries. [BUSINESS] ◻ The Caribbean has become an important location for international banking because it is a tax haven.

taxi /tǽksi/ (taxis, taxiing, taxied) **1** N-COUNT [also by N] A **taxi** is a car driven by a person whose job is to take people where they want to go in return for money. ◻ The taxi drew up in front of the Riviera Club. **2** V-T/V-I When an aircraft **taxis** along the ground or when a pilot **taxis** a plane somewhere, it moves slowly along the ground. ◻ She gave permission to the plane to taxi into position and hold for takeoff.

taxi|cab /tǽksikæb/ (taxicabs) also **taxi-cab** N-COUNT A **taxicab** is the same as a **taxi**. [mainly AM]

taxi|der|mist /tǽksɪdɜrmɪst/ (taxidermists) N-COUNT A **taxidermist** is a person whose job is to prepare the skins of dead animals and birds and fill them with a special material to make them look as if they are alive.

taxi|der|my /tǽksɪdɜrmi/ N-UNCOUNT **Taxidermy** is the craft of preparing the skins of dead animals and birds and filling them with a special material to make them look as if they are alive.

tax in|cen|tive (tax incentives) N-COUNT A **tax incentive** is a government measure that is intended to encourage individuals and businesses to spend money or to save money by reducing the amount of tax that they have to pay. ◻ ...a new tax incentive to encourage the importation of manufactured products.

tax|ing /tǽksɪŋ/ ADJ A **taxing** task or problem is one that requires a lot of mental or physical effort. ◻ It's unlikely that you'll be asked to do anything too taxing.

taxi stand (taxi stands) N-COUNT A **taxi stand** is a place where taxis wait for passengers, for example, at an airport or outside a station. [mainly AM]

in BRIT, usually use **taxi rank**

tax|ono|my /tæksɒ́nəmi/ (taxonomies) N-VAR **Taxonomy** is the process of naming and classifying things such as animals and plants into groups within a larger system, according to their similarities and differences. [TECHNICAL]

tax|payer /tǽkspeɪər/ (taxpayers) N-COUNT **Taxpayers** are people who pay a percentage of their income to the government as tax. [BUSINESS] ◻ This is not going to cost the taxpayer anything. The company will bear the costs for the delay.

tax re|lief N-UNCOUNT **Tax relief** is a reduction in the amount of tax that a person or company has to pay, for example, because of expenses associated with their business or property. [BUSINESS] ◻ ...mortgage interest tax relief.

tax re|turn (tax returns) N-COUNT A **tax return** is an official form that you fill in with details about your income and personal situation, so that the tax you owe can be calculated. [BUSINESS]

tax shel|ter (tax shelters) N-COUNT A **tax shelter** is a way of arranging the finances of a business or a person so that they have to pay less tax. [BUSINESS]

tax year (tax years) N-COUNT A **tax year** is a particular period of twelve months which is used by the government as a basis for calculating taxes and for organizing its finances and accounts. [BUSINESS]

TB /tí bí/ N-UNCOUNT **TB** is an extremely serious infectious disease that affects someone's lungs and other parts of their body. **TB** is an abbreviation for **tuberculosis**.

TBA also **tba** **TBA** is sometimes written in announcements to indicate that something such as the place where something will happen or the people who will take part is not yet known and will be announced at a later date. **TBA** is an abbreviation for 'to be announced.' ◻ When a manufacturer could not supply requested information, we have shown TBA.

T-ball N-UNCOUNT **T-ball** is a game for children, similar to baseball, in which the batter hits a ball that has been placed on top of a post. [AM] ◻ ...a T-ball game.

tbc also **TBC** [BRIT] **Tbc** is sometimes written in announcements about future events to indicate that details of the event are not yet certain and will be confirmed later. **Tbc** is an abbreviation for 'to be confirmed.'

T-bone steak (T-bone steaks) N-VAR A **T-bone steak** is a thick flat piece of beef that contains a T-shaped bone.

tbsp. (tbsps) or **tbs**. In recipes, **tbsp**. is a written abbreviation for **tablespoon**.

T-cell (T-cells) N-COUNT A **T-cell** is a type of white blood cell.

TCP/IP N-UNCOUNT **TCP/IP** is a set of rules for putting data onto the internet. **TCP/IP** is a written abbreviation for

'Transmission Control Protocol/Internet Protocol.' [COMPUTING] ❏ *Securities firms have begun using Internet technologies, in particular TCP/IP, for intranets.*

tea ✦✦◇ /tiː/ (teas) **1** N-MASS **Tea** is a drink made by adding boiling water to tea leaves or tea bags. Tea usually refers to black tea from India or China. Herbal tea is made from various plants. ❏ *...a cup of tea.* ❏ *Would you like some tea?* ❏ *...chamomile tea.* **2** N-MASS The chopped dried leaves of the plant that tea is made from is referred to as **tea**. ❏ *...a box of tea.*

tea bag (tea bags) also **teabag** N-COUNT **Tea bags** are small paper bags with tea leaves in them. You pour hot water onto them to make tea.

tea break (tea breaks) N-COUNT If you have a **tea break**, you stop working and have a cup of tea or coffee. [mainly BRIT]

in AM, usually use **coffee break**

tea cad|dy (tea caddies) N-COUNT A **tea caddy** is a small tin in which you keep tea. [mainly BRIT]

teach ✦✦◇ /tiːtʃ/ (teaches, teaching, taught) **1** V-T If you **teach** someone something, you give them instructions so that they know about it or how to do it. ❏ *She taught me fractions and counting.* ❏ *George had taught him how to ride a horse.* **2** V-T To **teach** someone something means to make them think, feel, or act in a new or different way. ❏ *Their daughter's death had taught him humility.* ❏ *He taught his followers that they could all be members of the kingdom of God.* **3** V-T/V-I If you **teach** or **teach** a subject, you help students to learn about it by explaining it or showing them how to do it, usually as a job at a school or college. ❏ *Ingrid is currently teaching mathematics at the high school.* ❏ *She taught English to Japanese business people.* ❏ *She has taught for 34 years.* **4** → see also **teaching** **5 to teach someone a lesson** → see **lesson**

teach|er ✦✦◇ /tiːtʃər/ (teachers) N-COUNT A **teacher** is a person who teaches, usually at a school or similar institution. ❏ *I'm a teacher with 21 years' experience.*

SYNONYMS

teacher
NOUN
instructor: *...tuition from an approved driving instructor.*
coach: *What you need is a drama coach.*
tutor: *He is a math tutor for high school students.*
educator: *She is an educator.*

teach|er's aide (teacher's aides) N-COUNT A **teacher's aide** is a person who helps a teacher in a school classroom but who is not a qualified teacher. [AM] ❏ *She works as a teacher's aide.*

teach|ing ✦◇◇ /tiːtʃɪŋ/ (teachings) **1** N-UNCOUNT **Teaching** is the work that a teacher does in helping students to learn. ❏ *The quality of teaching in the school is excellent.* **2** N-COUNT The **teachings** of a particular person, school of thought, or religion are all the ideas and principles that they teach. ❏ *...the teachings of Jesus.*

teach|ing as|sis|tant (teaching assistants) **1** N-COUNT In the United States, a **teaching assistant** is a graduate student at a college or university who teaches some classes. ❏ *He's also a teaching assistant for a freshman urban-studies class.* **2** N-COUNT In Britain, a **teaching assistant** is a person who helps a teacher in a school classroom but who is not a qualified teacher.

in AM, use **teacher's aide**

teach|ing hos|pi|tal (teaching hospitals) N-COUNT A **teaching hospital** is a hospital that is linked with a medical school, where medical students and newly qualified doctors receive practical training.

teach|ing prac|tice N-UNCOUNT **Teaching practice** is a period that a student teacher spends teaching at a school as part of his or her training. [mainly BRIT]

in AM, usually use **student teaching**

tea cozy (tea cozies) also **tea-cozy** N-COUNT A **tea cozy** is a soft knitted or fabric cover which you put over a teapot in order to keep the tea hot.

tea|cup /tiːkʌp/ (teacups) **1** N-COUNT A **teacup** is a cup that you use for drinking tea. **2** → See also color supplement

teak /tiːk/ N-UNCOUNT **Teak** is the wood of a tall tree with very hard, light-colored wood which grows in Southeast Asia. ❏ *The door is beautifully made in solid teak.*

tea|kettle /tiːkɛtəl/ (teakettles) also **tea kettle** N-COUNT A **teakettle** is a kettle that is used for boiling water to make tea. [mainly AM]

teal /tiːl/ (teals or teal) **1** N-COUNT A **teal** is a small duck found in Europe and Asia. **2** COLOR Something that is **teal** is greenish-blue. ❏ *...a teal sofa.* ❏ *...Spanish-style buildings done in cream and teal.*

tea leaf (tea leaves) also **tea-leaf** N-COUNT [usu pl] **Tea leaves** are the small pieces of dried leaves that you use to make tea.

team ✦✦✦ /tiːm/ (teams, teaming, teamed) **1** N-COUNT-COLL A **team** is a group of people who play a particular sport or game together against other similar groups of people. ❏ *...a soccer team.* ❏ *...the swim team.* **2** N-COUNT-COLL You can refer to any group of people who work together as a **team**. ❏ *Each specialist has a team of doctors under him or her.* **3** → See feature box at **football**
▶ **team up** PHRASAL VERB If you **team up** with someone, you join them in order to work together for a particular purpose. You can also say that two people or groups **team up**. ❏ *She teamed up with her old bass player to wow them at the concert.*

SYNONYMS

team
NOUN **1**
side: *Which side are you rooting for?*
squad: *She has been named to the squad to tour Argentina.*
lineup: *He is likely to be in the starting lineup for the World Cup qualifying match.*

team|mate /tiːmmeɪt/ (teammates) also **team-mate** N-COUNT In a game or sport, your **teammates** are the other members of your team. ❏ *He was always a solid player, a hard worker, a great example to his teammates.*

team play|er (team players) N-COUNT If you refer to someone as a **team player**, you mean that they work well with other people in order to achieve things. [APPROVAL]

team spir|it N-UNCOUNT **Team spirit** is the feeling of pride and loyalty that exists among the members of a team and that makes them want their team to do well or to be the best.

team|ster /tiːmstər/ (teamsters) **1** N-COUNT A **teamster** is a person who drives a truck. [AM]

in BRIT, use **lorry driver**

2 N-COUNT A **Teamster** is a person who belongs to an American labor union, called the International Brotherhood of Teamsters. [AM]

team|work /tiːmwɜːrk/ N-UNCOUNT **Teamwork** is the ability a group of people have to work well together. ❏ *Today's complex buildings require close teamwork between the architect and the builders.*

tea par|ty (tea parties) also **tea-party** N-COUNT A **tea party** is a social gathering in the afternoon at which tea, cakes, and sandwiches are served. [OLD-FASHIONED]

Tea Par|ty N-PROPER The **Tea Party** is a right-wing political movement in the United States that wants taxes and government spending to be reduced. ❏ *The Tea Party has become an umbrella group for many different causes and angry protesters, making it hard to pin down.*

tea|pot /tiːpɒt/ (teapots) also **tea pot** **1** N-COUNT A **teapot** is a container with a lid, a handle, and a spout, used for making and serving tea. **2** PHRASE [PHR after v, v-link PHR] If you describe a situation as **a tempest in a teapot**, you think that a lot of fuss is being made about something that is not important. [AM] ❏ *For some, it may seem silly, a tempest in a teapot.*

in BRIT, use **a storm in a teacup**

TEAR
① CRYING
② DAMAGING OR MOVING

① **tear** ✦◇◇ /tɪər/ (tears) **1** N-COUNT **Tears** are the drops of salty liquid that come out of your eyes when you are crying.

❑ *Her eyes filled with tears.* ❑ *I just broke down and wept with tears of joy.* ◨ N-PLURAL You can use **tears** in expressions such as **in tears**, **burst into tears**, and **close to tears** to indicate that someone is crying or is almost crying. ❑ *He was in floods of tears on the phone.* ❑ *She burst into tears and ran from the kitchen.*

② **tear** ♦♦◊ /tɛər/ (**tears**, **tearing**, **tore**, **torn**) ◧ V-T/V-I If you **tear** paper, cloth, or another material, or if it **tears**, you pull it into two pieces or you pull it so that a hole appears in it. ❑ *I tore my coat on a nail.* • PHRASAL VERB **Tear up** means the same as **tear 1**. ❑ *She tore the letter up.* ❑ *Don't you dare tear up her ticket.* ◨ N-COUNT A **tear** in paper, cloth, or another material is a hole that has been made in it. ❑ *I peered through a tear in the van's curtains.* ◩ V-T/V-I If you **tear** one of your muscles or ligaments, or if it **tears**, you injure it by accidentally moving it in the wrong way. ❑ *He tore a muscle in his right thigh.* ❑ *If the muscle is stretched again it could even tear.* ◪ V-T To **tear** something from somewhere means to remove it roughly and violently. ❑ *She tore the windscreen wipers from his car.* ◫ V-I If a person or animal **tears at** something, they pull it violently and try to break it into pieces. ❑ *Fans fought their way past bodyguards and tore at their clothes* ◬ V-I If you **tear** somewhere, you run, drive, or move there very quickly. ❑ *The door flew open and Miranda tore into the room.* ◮ V-T PASSIVE If you say that a place **is torn** by particular events, you mean that unpleasant events which cause suffering and division among people are happening there. ❑ *...a country that has been torn by civil war and foreign invasion since its independence.* ◨ → see also **torn**, **wear and tear**

▶ **tear apart** ◧ PHRASAL VERB If something **tears** people **apart**, it causes them to argue or to leave each other. ❑ *Her pregnancy was tearing the family apart.* ◨ PHRASAL VERB If something **tears** you **apart**, it makes you feel very upset, worried, and unhappy. ❑ *Don't think it hasn't torn me apart to be away from you.*

▶ **tear away** PHRASAL VERB If you **tear** someone **away** from a place or activity, you force them to leave the place or stop doing the activity, even though they want to remain there or carry on. ❑ *He finally tore himself away from the table long enough to pour me a drink.*

▶ **tear down** PHRASAL VERB If you **tear** something **down**, you destroy it or remove it completely. ❑ *Angry protesters have torn down the statue.*

▶ **tear off** PHRASAL VERB If you **tear off** your clothes, you take them off in a rough and violent way. ❑ *Totally exhausted, he tore his clothes off and fell into bed.*

▶ **tear up** ◧ PHRASAL VERB If something such as a road, railroad, or area of land **is torn up**, it is completely removed or destroyed. ❑ *Dozens of miles of railroad track have been torn up.* ◨ → see **tear** ② 1

tear|drop /tɛərdrɒp/ (**teardrops**) N-COUNT A **teardrop** is a tear that comes from your eye when you are crying.

tear|ful /tɛərfəl/ ADJ If someone is **tearful**, their face or voice shows signs that they have been crying or that they want to cry. ❑ *She became very tearful when pressed to talk about it.*

tear gas /tɛər gæs/ N-UNCOUNT **Tear gas** is a gas that causes your eyes to sting and fill with tears so that you cannot see. It is sometimes used by the police or army to control crowds. ❑ *Police used tear gas to disperse the demonstrators.*

tear|jerker /tɛərdʒɜːrkər/ (**tearjerkers**) also **tear-jerker** N-COUNT If you refer to a play, movie, or book as a **tearjerker**, it is very sad or sentimental. [INFORMAL]

tea|room /tiːrʊm/ (**tearooms**) also **tea room** N-COUNT; N-IN-NAMES A **tearoom** is a small restaurant where tea and often food is served.

tease /tiːz/ (**teases**, **teasing**, **teased**) ◧ V-T To **tease** someone means to laugh at them or make jokes about them in order to embarrass, annoy, or upset them. ❑ *He told her how the boys had set on him, teasing him.* ❑ *He teased me mercilessly about going to Hollywood.* • N-COUNT **Tease** is also a noun. ❑ *Calling her by her real name had always been one of his teases.* ◨ N-COUNT If you refer to someone as a **tease**, you mean that they like laughing at people or making jokes about them. ❑ *My brother's such a tease.* ◩ V-T If someone **teases** their hair, they separate the individual strands from each other, for example by combing it. ❑ *Her hair was teased until it stood out and around her face.* ❑ *...two women in party dresses and teased hair.*

teas|er /tiːzər/ (**teasers**) ◧ N-COUNT A **teaser** is a difficult question, especially one in a competition. [INFORMAL] ◨ N-COUNT A **teaser** is someone who makes fun of people.

tea ser|vice (**tea services**) N-COUNT A **tea service** is a set of cups, saucers, and plates, with a milk pitcher, sugar bowl, and teapot.

tea set (**tea sets**) N-COUNT A **tea set** is the same as a **tea service**.

tea shop (**tea shops**) also **teashop** N-COUNT; N-IN-NAMES A **tea shop** is the same as a **tearoom**.

teas|ing /tiːzɪŋ/ ADJ A **teasing** expression or manner shows that the person is not completely serious about what they are saying or doing. ❑ *"But we're having such fun, aren't we?" he protested with a teasing smile.*

tea|spoon /tiːspuːn/ (**teaspoons**) N-COUNT A **teaspoon** is a small spoon used for putting sugar into tea or coffee, and in cooking. ❑ *Drop the dough onto a baking sheet with a teaspoon.*

tea|spoon|ful /tiːspuːnfʊl/ (**teaspoonfuls** or **teaspoonsful**) N-COUNT [usu N of n] You can refer to an amount of liquid or food in a teaspoon as a **teaspoonful**. ❑ *...a heaped teaspoonful of salt.*

teat /tiːt/ (**teats**) ◧ N-COUNT A **teat** is a pointed part on the body of a female animal which her babies suck in order to get milk. ◨ N-COUNT A **teat** is a piece of rubber or plastic that is shaped like a teat, especially one that is fitted to a bottle so that a baby can drink from it. [BRIT]

in AM, use **nipple**

tea tow|el (**tea towels**) N-COUNT A **tea towel** is a cloth used to dry dishes after they have been washed. [mainly BRIT]

in AM, usually use **dishtowel**

tech /tɛk/ N-UNCOUNT **Tech** is short for **technology**.

techie /tɛki/ (**techies**) N-COUNT Some people refer to someone who understands technology or works in a technological industry, especially computing, as a **techie**. [INFORMAL]

tech|ni|cal ♦◊◊ /tɛknɪkəl/ ◧ ADJ **Technical** means involving the sorts of machines, processes, and materials that are used in industry, transportation, and communications. ❑ *In order to reach this limit a number of technical problems will have to be solved.* • **tech|ni|cal|ly** /tɛknɪkli/ ADV [ADV adj] ❑ *...the largest and most technically advanced furnace company in the world.* ◨ ADJ You use **technical** to describe the practical skills and methods used to do an activity such as an art, a craft, or a sport. ❑ *Their technical ability is exceptional.* • **tech|ni|cal|ly** ADV [ADV adj] ❑ *While her voice isn't technically brilliant it has a quality which is unmistakable.* ◩ ADJ **Technical** language involves using special words to describe the details of a specialized activity. ❑ *The technical term for sunburn is erythema.* ◪ → see also **technically**

---SYNONYMS---

technical
ADJ ◧
scientific: ...*scientific instruments.*
technological: ...*an era of very rapid technological change.*

tech|ni|cal col|lege (**technical colleges**) N-VAR [oft in names] A **technical college** is a college where you can study arts and technical subjects, often as part of the qualifications and training required for a particular job.

tech|ni|cal|ity /tɛknɪkælɪti/ (**technicalities**) ◧ N-PLURAL The **technicalities** of a process or activity are the detailed methods used to do it or to carry it out. ❑ *...the technicalities of classroom teaching.* ◨ N-COUNT A **technicality** is a point, especially a legal one, that is based on a strict interpretation of the law or of a set of rules but that may seem unimportant compared to a larger issue. ❑ *The earlier verdict was overturned on a legal technicality.*

tech|ni|cal|ly /tɛknɪkli/ ◧ ADV If something is **technically** the case, it is the case according to a strict interpretation of facts, laws, or rules, but may not be important or relevant in a particular situation. ❑ *More than a third of workers said they called into the office while technically on vacation.* ◨ → see also **technical**

tech|ni|cal sup|port N-UNCOUNT **Technical support** is a repair and advice service that some companies such as computer companies provide for their customers, usually by telephone, fax, or email. ❑ *...technical support for America Online users.*

tech|ni|cian /tɛknɪʃən/ (**technicians**) ◧ N-COUNT A **technician** is someone whose job involves skilled practical

Technicolor

work with scientific equipment, for example, in a laboratory. ❑ ...a laboratory technician. **2** N-COUNT A **technician** is someone who is very good at the detailed technical aspects of an activity. ❑ ...a versatile, veteran player, a superb technician.

Tech|ni|col|or /tɛknɪkʌlər/

> The spelling **technicolour** is also used in British English for meaning **2**.

1 N-UNCOUNT **Technicolor** is a system of color photography used in making movies. [TRADEMARK] ❑ ...films in Technicolor. **2** N-UNCOUNT You can use **technicolor** to describe real or imagined scenes when you want to emphasize that they are very colorful, especially in an exaggerated way. [INFORMAL] ❑ I was seeing it all in glorious technicolor: mountains, valleys, lakes, summer sunshine. ❑ ...Technicolor dreams.

tech|nique ◆◇ /tɛknik/ (**techniques**) **1** N-COUNT A **technique** is a particular method of doing an activity, usually a method that involves practical skills. ❑ ...tests performed using a new technique. **2** N-UNCOUNT **Technique** is skill and ability in an artistic, sporting, or other practical activity that you develop through training and practice. ❑ He went off to the Amsterdam Academy to improve his technique. **3** → See feature box at **farming, study**

> **SYNONYMS**
>
> **technique**
> NOUN **1**
> **method**: ...new teaching methods.
> **way**: Freezing isn't a bad way of preserving food.
> **system**: ...a flexible and relatively efficient filing system.
> **approach**: We will be exploring different approaches to gathering information.
> **procedure**: A biopsy is usually a minor surgical procedure.

tech|no /tɛknoʊ/ N-UNCOUNT **Techno** is a form of modern electronic music with a very fast beat.

> **PREFIX**
>
> **techno-**
> is used at the beginning of words that refer to technology. For example, a **technophobe** is someone who does not like new technology.

tech|noc|ra|cy /tɛknɒkrəsi/ (**technocracies**) **1** N-COUNT-COLL A **technocracy** is a group of scientists, engineers, and other experts who have political power as well as technical knowledge. ❑ ...the power of the Brussels technocracy. **2** N-COUNT A **technocracy** is a country or society that is controlled by scientists, engineers, and other experts. ❑ ...a centralized technocracy.

tech|no|crat /tɛknəkræt/ (**technocrats**) N-COUNT A **technocrat** is a scientist, engineer, or other expert who is one of a group of similar people who have political power as well as technical knowledge.

tech|no|crat|ic /tɛknəkrætɪk/ ADJ [usu ADJ n] **Technocratic** means consisting of or influenced by technocrats. ❑ ...the current technocratic administration.

tech|no|logi|cal /tɛknəlɒdʒɪkəl/ ADJ [ADJ n] **Technological** means relating to or associated with technology. ❑ ...an era of very rapid technological change.
• **tech|no|logi|cal|ly** /tɛknəlɒdʒɪkli/ ADV ❑ ...technologically advanced aircraft.

tech|nol|ogy ◆◆ /tɛknɒlədʒi/ (**technologies**) N-VAR **Technology** refers to methods, systems, and devices which are the result of scientific knowledge being used for practical purposes. ❑ Technology is changing fast. ❑ They should be allowed to wait for cheaper technologies to be developed.

> **COLLOCATIONS**
>
> **technology**
> NOUN
> noun + **technology**: communications, computer, internet, mobile
> adjective + **technology**: advanced, cutting-edge, emerging, modern; digital, medical, nuclear, wireless; green, renewable
> verb + **technology**: develop, embrace, introduce, use

> **VOCABULARY IN CONTEXT**

Technology

Can we predict which futuristic-sounding technology will become commonplace, while some things just never take off? 3D television is a good example of technology that people have not fully embraced, and **wearable** technology has not yet had the impact some manufacturers were hoping for. **Smart phones** quickly became the norm in many countries, but will the Internet of Things have the same instant appeal? Nowadays, voice-**activated** interface devices are the ultimate **hands-free** experience compared with **touchscreens**, but voice-activated devices have been known to listen to private conversations. Not all technology fans are comfortable with devices in their homes sending their data to others but others aren't that bothered. Embeddable technology could be an even harder sell, as it means inserting a chip under the skin to hold data like passwords. Maybe the future is for the **luddites** after all.

tech|no|phobe /tɛknəfoʊb/ (**technophobes**) N-COUNT If you refer to someone as a **technophobe**, you mean that they do not like new technology, such as computers or cellphones, and are afraid to use it.

tec|ton|ic /tɛktɒnɪk/ ADJ [ADJ n] **Tectonic** means relating to the structure of the Earth's surface or crust. [TECHNICAL] ❑ ...the tectonic plates of the Pacific region.

tec|ton|ics /tɛktɒnɪks/ → see **plate tectonics**

ted|dy /tɛdi/ (**teddies**) N-COUNT A **teddy** is the same as a **teddy bear**. Children often call their teddies 'Teddy' when they are talking to them or about them.

> **WORD HISTORY**
>
> **teddy**
> **Teddy bears** are named after the American president Theodore (Teddy) Roosevelt (1859-1919), who was keen on bear hunting.

ted|dy bear (**teddy bears**) also **teddy-bear** N-COUNT A **teddy bear** is a children's toy, made from soft or furry material, which looks like a friendly bear.

te|di|ous /tidiəs/ ADJ If you describe something such as a job, task, or situation as **tedious**, you mean it is boring and frustrating. ❑ Such lists are long and tedious to read. • **te|di|ous|ly** ADV ❑ ...the most tediously boring aspects of international relations.

te|dium /tidiəm/ N-UNCOUNT [oft N of n] If you talk about the **tedium** of a job, task, or situation, you think it is boring and frustrating. ❑ She began to wonder whether she would go crazy with the tedium of the job.

tee /ti/ (**tees, teeing, teed**) **1** N-COUNT In golf, a **tee** is a small piece of wood or plastic which is used to support the ball before it is hit at the start of each hole. **2** N-COUNT On a golf course, a **tee** is one of the small flat areas of ground from which people hit the ball at the start of each hole. **3** **to a tee** → see **T**

▶ **tee off 1** PHRASAL VERB If someone or something **tees** you **off**, they make you angry or annoyed. [mainly AM, INFORMAL] ❑ Something the boy said to him teed him off. ❑ That really teed off the

teem /tiːm/ (teems, teeming, teemed) V-I [usu cont] If you say that a place **is teeming** with people or animals, you mean that it is crowded and the people and animals are moving around a lot. ❏ *For most of the year, the area is teeming with tourists.*

teen /tiːn/ (teens) **1** N-PLURAL If you are a **teen**, or you are in your **teens**, you are between thirteen and nineteen years old. Teen is informal for teenager. ❏ *Most people who smoke began smoking in their teens.* **2** ADJ [ADJ n] **Teen** is used to describe things such as movies, magazines, bands, or activities that are aimed at or are done by people who are in their teens. ❏ *...a new teen center.*

teen|age /tiːneɪdʒ/ **1** ADJ [ADJ n] **Teenage** children are aged between thirteen and nineteen years old. ❏ *She looked like any other teenage girl.* **2** ADJ [ADJ n] **Teenage** is used to describe things such as movies, magazines, bands, or activities that are aimed at or are done by teenage children. ❏ *..."Smash Hits," a teenage magazine.*

teen|aged /tiːneɪdʒd/ ADJ [ADJ n] **Teenaged** people are aged between thirteen and nineteen. ❏ *She is the mother of two teenaged daughters.*

teen|ager ✦✧✧ /tiːneɪdʒər/ (teenagers) N-COUNT A **teenager** is someone who is between thirteen and nineteen years old. ❏ *As a teenager he attended Tulse Hill Senior High School.*

tee|ny /tiːni/ (teenier, teeniest) ADJ [ADJ n] If you describe something as **teeny**, you are emphasizing that it is very small. [INFORMAL, EMPHASIS] ❏ *...little teeny bugs.*

teeny|bopper /tiːnibɒpər/ (teenyboppers) also **teeny-bopper** N-COUNT A **teenybopper** is a young teenager, usually a girl, who is very interested in pop music. [INFORMAL, OLD-FASHIONED]

tee|pee /tiːpi/ → see tepee

tee-shirt → see T-shirt

tee|ter /tiːtər/ (teeters, teetering, teetered) **1** V-I **Teeter** is used in expressions such as **teeter on the brink** and **teeter on the edge** to emphasize that something seems to be in a very unstable situation or position. [EMPHASIS] ❏ *The hotel is teetering on the brink of bankruptcy.* **2** V-I If someone or something **teeters**, they shake in an unsteady way, and seem to be about to lose their balance and fall over. ❏ *Hyde shifted his weight and felt himself teeter forward, beginning to overbalance.*

teeth /tiːθ/ **1** **Teeth** is the plural of **tooth**. **2** → See also color supplement

teeth|ing /tiːðɪŋ/ V-I [only cont] When babies **are teething**, their teeth are starting to appear through their gums, often causing them pain. ❏ *Babies often get red cheeks when they're teething.* • N-UNCOUNT **Teething** is also a noun. ❏ *Teething can be painful and make your baby irritable.*

tee|to|tal /tiːtoʊtəl/ ADJ [usu v-link ADJ] Someone who is **teetotal** does not drink alcohol. ❏ *He will not be having a celebratory drink, as he is teetotal.*

tee|to|tal|er /tiːtoʊtələr/ (teetotalers) N-COUNT A **teetotaler** is someone who does not drink alcohol.

TEFL /tɛfəl/ **1** N-UNCOUNT **TEFL** is the teaching of English to people whose first language is not English, especially people from a country where English is not spoken. TEFL is an abbreviation for 'teaching English as a foreign language.' **2** → see also **TESL**

Tef|lon /tɛflɒn/ N-UNCOUNT **Teflon** is a type of plastic which is often used to coat pans. Teflon provides a very smooth surface which food does not stick to, so the pan can be cleaned easily. [TRADEMARK]

Te|ja|no /teɪhɑːnoʊ/ (Tejanos) N-COUNT [usu N n] A **Tejano** is a person from Mexico, or a person whose family is from Mexico, who lives in Texas. [AM] ❏ *...the growing popularity of Tejano music.*

tel. tel. is a written abbreviation for **telephone number**.

tele|cast /tɛlɪkæst/ (telecasts) N-COUNT A **telecast** is a program that is broadcast on television, especially a program that is broadcast live. [AM]

old boy. • **teed off** ADJ [oft ADJ with n] [mainly AM, INFORMAL] ❏ *I bet Bernard is really teed off with me!* **2** PHRASAL VERB In golf, when you **tee off**, you hit the ball from a tee at the start of a hole. ❏ *In a few hours time most of the world's top golfers tee off in the U.S. Masters.*

tele|com|mu|ni|ca|tions /tɛlɪkəmjuːnɪkeɪʃənz/

> The form **telecommunication** is used as a modifier.

N-UNCOUNT **Telecommunications** is the technology of sending signals and messages over long distances using electronic equipment, for example, by radio and telephone. ❏ *...the telecommunications industry.*

tele|com|mut|er /tɛlɪkəmjuːtər/ (telecommuters) N-COUNT **Telecommuters** are people who work from home using equipment such as telephones, the internet, and email to contact the people they work with and their customers. [BUSINESS]

tele|com|mut|ing /tɛlɪkəmjuːtɪŋ/ N-UNCOUNT **Telecommuting** is working from home using equipment such as telephones, the internet, and email to contact people. [BUSINESS] ❏ *There is also the potential to develop telecommuting and other more flexible working practices.*

tele|con|fer|ence /tɛlɪkɒnfərəns, -frəns/ (teleconferences) N-COUNT A **teleconference** is a meeting involving people in various places around the world who use telephones or video links to communicate with each other. [BUSINESS] ❏ *Managers at their factory hold a two-hour teleconference with head office every day.* • **tele|con|fer|enc|ing** N-UNCOUNT ❏ *...teleconferencing facilities.*

tele|gen|ic /tɛlɪdʒɛnɪk/ ADJ Someone who is **telegenic** behaves confidently and looks attractive when they are on television. ❏ *The bright and telegenic Ms. Aragon is paid $90,000 a year.*

tele|gram /tɛlɪɡræm/ (telegrams) N-COUNT [also by n] A **telegram** is a message that is sent by telegraph and then printed and delivered to someone's home or office. ❏ *The president received a briefing by telegram.*

tele|graph /tɛlɪɡræf/ (telegraphs, telegraphing, telegraphed) **1** N-UNCOUNT [also the N] **Telegraph** is a system of sending messages over long distances, either by means of electricity or by radio signals. Telegraph was used more often before the invention of telephones. **2** V-T To **telegraph** someone meant to send them a message by telegraph. ❏ *Churchill telegraphed an urgent message to Wavell.* **3** V-T If someone **telegraphs** something that they are planning or intending to do, they make it obvious, either deliberately or accidentally, that they are going to do it. ❏ *The commission telegraphed its decision earlier this month by telling an official to prepare the order.*

tele|graph pole [BRIT] → see telephone pole

tele|ki|net|ic /tɛlɪkɪnɛtɪk/ ADJ If someone is thought to have **telekinetic** powers, they are believed to have the ability to move objects using the power of their mind. ❏ *...aliens with telekinetic powers.*

tele|mar|ket|er /tɛlɪmɑːrkɪtər/ (telemarketers) N-COUNT **Telemarketers** are salespeople who are employed by a company to telephone people in order to persuade them to buy the company's products or services. ❏ *They found that 18 million people a day were being called by telemarketers.*

tele|mar|ket|ing /tɛlɪmɑːrkɪtɪŋ/ N-UNCOUNT **Telemarketing** is a method of selling in which someone employed by a company telephones people to try and persuade them to buy the company's products or services. [BUSINESS] ❏ *As postal rates go up, many businesses have been turning to telemarketing as a way of contacting new customers.*

te|lem|etry /təlɛmɪtri/ N-UNCOUNT **Telemetry** is the science of using automatic equipment to make scientific measurements and transmit them by radio to a receiving station. [TECHNICAL]

tele|path|ic /tɛlɪpæθɪk/ ADJ If you believe that someone is **telepathic**, you believe that they have mental powers which cannot be explained by science, such as being able to communicate with other people's minds, and know what other people are thinking. ❏ *About half the subjects considered themselves to be telepathic.*

te|lepa|thy /təlɛpəθi/ N-UNCOUNT If you refer to **telepathy**, you mean the direct communication of thoughts and feelings between people's minds, without the need to use speech, writing, or any other normal signals. ❏ *You never tell me what you're thinking. Am I supposed to use telepathy?*

telephone

tele|phone ♦♦◊ /tɛlɪfoʊn/ (telephones, telephoning, telephoned) **1** N-UNCOUNT The **telephone** is the electrical system of communication that you use to talk directly to someone else in a different place. You use the telephone by dialing a number on a piece of equipment and speaking into it. ❑ *It's easier to reach her by telephone than by mail or email.* ❑ *I hate to think what our telephone bill is going to be.* **2** N-COUNT A **telephone** is the piece of equipment that you use when you talk to someone by telephone. ❑ *He got up and answered the telephone.* **3** V-T/V-I If you **telephone** someone, you dial their telephone number and speak to them by telephone. ❑ *I felt so badly I had to telephone Owen to say I was sorry.* ❑ *They usually telephone first to see if she's home.* **4** PHRASE If you are **on the telephone**, you are speaking to someone by telephone. ❑ *Linda remained on the telephone to the police for three hours.*

VOCABULARY IN CONTEXT

The telephone

Once upon a time the phone was a rare commodity. In 1970, fewer than 10 percent of the world's households had a telephone. A **landline** was a luxury, not a necessity. **Making a call** was something of a ritual: lifting the **receiver**; waiting for a **dial tone**; **dialing** the number on the **rotary dial**; then **getting through**, or getting a **busy signal**. **Operators** were needed to connect certain calls. **Long-distance calls** were reserved for very good or very bad news. How many people stood in their hallway, learning over the crackling **line** about a birth or death in the family? Then, as technology developed, home phones became more common. Soon we had push-button phones with **answering machines** and features like 'call waiting.' It sounds like ancient history when you consider that almost everyone today carries a **smartphone**, which they're much more likely to use for sending **text messages** than making actual calls or leaving **voice mails**.

tele|phone book (telephone books) N-COUNT The **telephone book** is a book that contains an alphabetical list of the names, addresses, and telephone numbers of the people in a particular area.

tele|phone box (telephone boxes) N-COUNT A **telephone box** is the same as a **phone booth**. [BRIT]

tele|phone di|rec|tory (telephone directories) N-COUNT A **telephone directory** is the same as a **telephone book**.

tele|phone ex|change (telephone exchanges) N-COUNT A **telephone exchange** is a building where connections are made between telephone lines.

tele|phone num|ber (telephone numbers) N-COUNT Your **telephone number** is the number that other people dial when they want to talk to you on the telephone.

tele|phone pole (telephone poles) N-COUNT A **telephone pole** is a tall wooden pole with telephone and electrical wires attached to it, connecting several different buildings to the telephone and electrical system. [AM]

in BRIT, use **telegraph pole**

tell

te|leph|o|ny /təlɛfəni/ N-UNCOUNT **Telephony** is a system of sending voice signals using electronic equipment. ❑ *These optical fibers may be used for new sorts of telephony.*

tele|photo lens /tɛlɪfoʊtoʊ lɛnz/ (telephoto lenses) N-COUNT A **telephoto lens** is a powerful camera lens which allows you to take close-up pictures of something that is far away.

Tele|prompt|er /tɛlɪprɒmptər/ (Teleprompters) also **teleprompter** N-COUNT A **Teleprompter** is a device used by people speaking on television or at a public event, which displays words for them to read. [mainly AM, TRADEMARK]

in BRIT, usually use **Autocue**

tele|sales /tɛlɪseɪlz/ N-UNCOUNT **Telesales** is the selling of a company's products or services by telephone, either by phoning possible customers or by answering calls from customers. [BUSINESS] ❑ *Many people start their careers in telesales.*

tele|scope /tɛlɪskoʊp/ (telescopes) **1** N-COUNT A **telescope** is a long instrument shaped like a tube. It has lenses inside it that make distant things seem larger and nearer when you look through it. ❑ *It's hoped that the telescope will enable scientists to see deeper into the universe than ever before.* **2** → See feature box at **space**; See also color supplement

tele|scop|ic /tɛlɪskɒpɪk/ **1** ADJ [usu ADJ n] **Telescopic** lenses and instruments are used to make things seem larger and nearer, and are usually longer than others of the same type. ❑ *...a sporting rifle fitted with a telescopic sight.* **2** ADJ [usu ADJ n] A **telescopic** object is made of cylindrical sections that fit or slide into each other, so that it can be made longer or shorter, for example, to save space when it is not being used. ❑ *...this new lightweight telescopic ladder.*

tele|van|gelist /tɛlɪvændʒəlɪst/ (televangelists) N-COUNT A **televangelist** is someone who makes regular television broadcasts to promote a particular form of Christianity and raise money for particular Christian groups or projects.

tele|vise /tɛlɪvaɪz/ (televises, televising, televised) V-T [usu passive] If an event or program **is televised**, it is broadcast so that it can be seen on television. ❑ *His comeback fight will be televised on network TV.*

tele|vi|sion ♦♦◊ /tɛlɪvɪʒ³n, -vɪʒ-/ (televisions) **1** N-COUNT A **television** or **television set** is a piece of electrical equipment consisting of a box with a glass screen on it on which you can watch programs with pictures and sounds. ❑ *She turned the television on and flicked around between news programs.* **2** N-UNCOUNT **Television** is the system of sending pictures and sounds by electrical signals over a distance so that people can receive them on a television in their home. ❑ *Toy manufacturers began promoting some of their products on television.* **3** N-UNCOUNT **Television** refers to all the programs that you can watch. ❑ *I don't have much time to watch very much television.* **4** N-UNCOUNT **Television** is the business or industry concerned with making programs and broadcasting them on television. ❑ *I'd like a job in television.*

tele|vis|ual /tɛləvɪʒuəl/ ADJ [ADJ n] **Televisual** means broadcast on or related to television. [mainly BRIT] ❑ *...a televisual masterpiece.*

tele|work|er /tɛlɪwɜrkər/ (teleworkers) N-COUNT **Teleworkers** are the same as **telecommuters**.

tele|work|ing /tɛlɪwɜrkɪŋ/ N-UNCOUNT **Teleworking** is the same as **telecommuting**.

tel|ex /tɛlɛks/ (telexes, telexing, telexed) **1** N-UNCOUNT **Telex** is an international system of sending written messages. Messages are converted into signals which are transmitted, either by electricity or by radio signals, and then printed out by a machine in another place. **2** N-COUNT A **telex** is a machine that transmits and receives telex messages. **3** N-COUNT A **telex** is a message that you send or that has been received and printed by telex. **4** V-T [v n] If you **telex** a message to someone, you send it to them by telex.

tell ♦♦♦ /tɛl/ (tells, telling, told)

→ Please look at meanings **15** and **16** to see if the expression you are looking for is shown under another headword.

1 V-T If you **tell** someone something, you give them information. ❑ *In the evening I returned to tell Phyllis I got the job.* ❑ *I called Andie to tell her how spectacular the stuff looked.*

❑ Claire had made me promise to tell her the truth. ◼ V-T If you **tell** something such as a joke, a story, or your personal experiences, you communicate it to other people using speech. ❑ His friends say he was always quick to tell a joke. ❑ He told his story to The L.A. Times and produced photographs. ◼ V-T If you **tell** someone to do something, you order or advise them to do it. ❑ He said officers told him to get out of his car and lean against it. ◼ V-T If you **tell** yourself something, you put it into words in your own mind because you need to encourage or persuade yourself about something. ❑ "Come on," she told herself. ◼ V-T [no cont, oft with brd-neg] If you can **tell** what is happening or what is true, you are able to judge correctly what is happening or what is true. ❑ It was already impossible to tell where the bullet had entered. ◼ V-T [no cont, oft with brd-neg] If you can **tell** one thing from another, you are able to recognize the difference between it and other similar things. ❑ I can't really tell the difference between their policies and ours. ❑ How do you tell one from another? ◼ V-I If you **tell**, you reveal or give away a secret. [INFORMAL] ❑ Many of the children know who they are but are not telling. ◼ V-T If facts or events **tell** you something, they reveal certain information to you through ways other than speech. ❑ The facts tell us that this is not true. ❑ I don't think the unemployment rate ever tells us much about the future. ◼ V-I If an unpleasant or tiring experience begins to **tell**, it begins to have a serious effect. ❑ It wasn't long before the strain began to tell on our relationship. ◼ → see also **telling** ◼ PHRASE You use **as far as I can tell** or **so far as I could tell** to indicate that what you are saying is based on the information you have, but that there may be things you do not know. [VAGUENESS] ❑ As far as I can tell, Jason is basically a nice guy. ◼ CONVENTION You can say '**I tell you,**' '**I can tell you,**' or '**I can't tell you**' to add emphasis to what you are saying. [INFORMAL, EMPHASIS] ❑ I tell you this, I will not rest until that day has come. ◼ CONVENTION If someone disagrees with you or refuses to do what you suggest and you are eventually proved to be right, you can say '**I told you so.**' [INFORMAL] ❑ Her parents did not approve of her decision and, if she failed, her mother would say, "I told you so." ◼ CONVENTION You use **I'll tell you what** or **I tell you what** to introduce a suggestion or a new topic of conversation. [SPOKEN] ❑ I tell you what, I'll bring the beer over to your house. ◼ **to tell the time** → see **time** ⑤ ◼ **time will tell** → see **time** ⑤

▶ **tell apart** PHRASAL VERB If you can **tell** people or things **apart**, you are able to recognize the differences between them and can therefore identify each of them. ❑ It's easy to tell my pills apart because they're all different colors.

▶ **tell off** PHRASAL VERB If you **tell** someone **off**, you speak to them angrily or seriously because they have done something wrong. ❑ He never listened to us when we told him off. ❑ I'm always being told off for being so awkward.

USAGE

tell
Don't use 'to' after **tell**. Don't say, for example 'He told me that he was sorry.' He **told** me that he was sorry.

tell|er /tɛlər/ (tellers) N-COUNT A **teller** is a someone who works in a bank and who customers pay money to or get money from. [mainly AM or SCOTTISH] ❑ Every bank pays close attention to the speed and accuracy of its tellers ❑ a bank teller.

tell|ing /tɛlɪŋ/ (tellings) ◼ N-VAR The **telling** of a story or of something that has happened is the reporting of it to other people. ❑ Juan sat quietly through the telling of this saga. ◼ ADJ If something is **telling**, it shows the true nature of a person or a situation. ❑ His treatment of women could be a telling clue to his age.
• **tell|ing|ly** ADV ❑ Most tellingly, perhaps, chimpanzees do not draw as much information from the world around them as we do.

telling-off (tellings-off) also **telling off** N-COUNT [usu sing] If you give someone a **telling-off**, you tell them that you are very angry with them about something they have done. [INFORMAL] ❑ I got a severe telling off for not phoning him.

tell|tale /tɛlteɪl/ ADJ [ADJ n] Something that is described as **telltale** gives away information, often about something bad that would otherwise not be noticed. ❑ Only occasionally did the telltale redness around his eyes betray the fatigue he was suffering.

tel|ly /tɛli/ (tellies) N-VAR A **telly** is a television. [BRIT, INFORMAL] in AM, use **TV**

te|maze|pam /təmæzɪpæm/ N-UNCOUNT **Temazepam** is a drug that is used to make people feel calmer or less anxious.

tem|blor /tɛmblɔr/ (temblors) N-COUNT A **temblor** is an earthquake. [AM] ❑ ...the 1906 temblor that struck San Francisco.

te|mer|ity /tɪmɛrɪti/ N-UNCOUNT [usu N to-inf] If you say that a person has the **temerity** to do something, you are annoyed about something they have done which you think showed a lack of respect. [DISAPPROVAL] ❑ "Difficult" patients have the temerity to challenge their doctors' decisions.

temp /tɛmp/ (temps, temping, temped) ◼ N-COUNT A **temp** is a person who is employed by an agency that sends them to work in different offices for short periods of time, for example, to replace someone who is ill or on vacation. [BUSINESS] ❑ She began working for the company as a temp. ◼ V-I [only cont] If someone **is temping**, they are working as a temp. [BUSINESS] ❑ Like so many aspiring actresses, she ended up waiting tables and temping in office jobs.

tem|per /tɛmpər/ (tempers) ◼ N-VAR If you refer to someone's **temper** or say that they have a **temper**, you mean that they become angry very easily. ❑ He had a temper and could be nasty. ❑ His short temper had become notorious. ◼ N-VAR Your **temper** is the way you are feeling at a particular time. If you are in a good **temper**, you feel cheerful. If you are in a bad **temper**, you feel angry and impatient. ❑ I was in a bad temper last night. ◼ PHRASE If someone is **in a temper** or gets **into a temper**, the way that they are behaving shows that they are feeling angry and impatient. ❑ She was still in a temper when Colin arrived. ◼ PHRASE If you **lose** your **temper**, you become so angry that you shout at someone or show in some other way that you are no longer in control of yourself. ❑ I've never seen him get mad or lose his temper.

tem|pera|ment /tɛmpərəmənt/ (temperaments) ◼ N-VAR Your **temperament** is your basic nature, especially as it is shown in the way that you react to situations or to other people. ❑ His impulsive temperament regularly got him into difficulties. ◼ N-UNCOUNT **Temperament** is the tendency to behave in an uncontrolled, bad-tempered, or unreasonable way. ❑ Some of the models were given to fits of temperament.

tem|pera|men|tal /tɛmpərəmɛntəl/ ◼ ADJ If you say that someone is **temperamental**, you are criticizing them for not being calm or quiet by nature, but having moods that change often and suddenly. [DISAPPROVAL] ❑ He is very temperamental and critical. ◼ ADJ If you describe something such as a machine or car as **temperamental**, you mean that it often does not work well. ❑ The boys couldn't start the temperamental motor.

tem|pera|men|tal|ly /tɛmpərəmɛntəli/ ADV **Temperamentally** means because of someone's basic nature or related to someone's basic nature. ❑ He is a quitter who is temperamentally unsuited to remaining a champion.

tem|per|ance /tɛmpərəns, -prəns/ ◼ N-UNCOUNT If you believe in **temperance**, you disapprove of drinking alcohol. ❑ ...a reformed alcoholic extolling the joys of temperance. ◼ N-UNCOUNT A person who shows **temperance** has a strong mind and does not eat too much or drink too much and practices moderation. [FORMAL] ❑ The age of hedonism is being ushered out by a new era of temperance.

tem|per|ate /tɛmpərət, -prət/ ◼ ADJ **Temperate** is used to describe a climate or a place which is never extremely hot or extremely cold. ❑ The Nile Valley keeps a temperate climate throughout the year. ◼ → See feature box at **ecosystem**

tem|pera|ture ♦◇◇ /tɛmprətʃər, -tʃʊər/ (temperatures) ◼ N-VAR The **temperature** of something is a measure of how hot or cold it is. ❑ Winter closes in and the temperature drops below freezing. ◼ N-UNCOUNT Your **temperature** is the temperature of your body. A normal temperature is about 98.6° Fahrenheit. ❑ His temperature continued to rise and the cough worsened until Tania finally persuaded him to see a doctor. ◼ N-COUNT You can use **temperature** to talk about the feelings and emotions that people have in particular situations. ❑ There's also been a noticeable rise in the political temperature. ◼ PHRASE If you **are running a temperature** or if you **have a temperature**, your temperature is higher than it should be. ❑ He began to run an extremely high temperature. ◼ → see also **fever** ◼ PHRASE If you **take** someone's **temperature** you use an instrument called a thermometer to measure the temperature of their body in order to see if they are ill. ❑ *He will probably take your child's temperature too.* **7** → See feature box at **illness**

COLLOCATIONS

temperature
NOUN **1**
noun + **temperature**: air, body, daytime, oven
adjective + **temperature**: ambient, average; cool, freezing, low, subzero; high, rising, scorching, soaring
verb + **temperature**: control, lower, raise; brave

---

tem|pest /tɛmpɪst/ (tempests) **1** N-COUNT A **tempest** is a very violent storm. [LITERARY] **2** N-COUNT [usu with supp] You can refer to a situation in which people are very angry or excited as a **tempest**. [LITERARY] ❑ *I hadn't foreseen the tempest my request would cause.* **3 a tempest in a teapot** → see **teapot**

tem|pes|tu|ous /tɛmpɛstʃuəs/ ADJ [usu adj n] If you describe a relationship or a situation as **tempestuous**, you mean that very strong and intense emotions, especially anger, are involved. ❑ *For years, the couple's tempestuous relationship made the headlines.*

tem|pi /tɛmpi/ **Tempi** is a plural of **tempo**.

tem|plate /tɛmplɪt/ (templates) **1** N-COUNT A **template** is a thin piece of metal or plastic which is cut into a particular shape. It is used to help you cut wood, paper, metal, or other materials accurately, or to reproduce the same shape many times. ❑ *Trace around your template and transfer the design onto a sheet of card.* **2** N-COUNT In computing, a **template** is a model of a document that you can use as a guide when creating a document of your own. [COMPUTING] ❑ *Open any of the layout templates, insert your text, make any other changes, and print.* **3** N-COUNT If one thing is a **template** for something else, the second thing is based on the first thing. ❑ *The template for Adair's novel is not somebody else's fiction, but fact.*

tem|ple ✦✧ /tɛmpəl/ (temples) **1** N-COUNT; N-IN-NAMES A **temple** is a building used for the worship of a god or gods, especially in the Buddhist, Jewish, Mormon, and Hindu religions, and in ancient Greek and Roman times. ❑ *...a small Hindu temple.* ❑ *We go to temple on Saturdays.* **2** N-COUNT Your **temples** are the flat parts on each side of the front part of your head, near your forehead. ❑ *Threads of silver ran through his beard and the hair at his temples.*

tem|po /tɛmpoʊ/ (tempos)

Tempi can also be used as the plural form.

1 N-SING The **tempo** of an event is the speed at which it happens. ❑ *...owing to the slow tempo of change in an overwhelmingly rural country.* **2** N-VAR The **tempo** of a piece of music is the speed at which it is played. ❑ *In a new recording, the Boston Philharmonic tried the original tempo.*

tem|po|ral /tɛmpərəl/ **1** ADJ [ADJ n] **Temporal** powers or matters relate to ordinary institutions and activities rather than to religious or spiritual ones. [FORMAL] ❑ *...the spiritual and temporal leader of the Tibetan people.* **2** ADJ [ADJ n] **Temporal** means relating to time. [FORMAL] ❑ *One is also able to see how specific acts are related to a temporal and spatial context.*

tem|po|rary ✦✧ /tɛmpəreri/ ADJ Something that is **temporary** lasts for only a limited time. ❑ *His job here is only temporary.* ❑ *Most adolescent problems are temporary.*
● **tem|po|rari|ly** /tɛmpərɛrɪli/ ADV ❑ *The peace agreement has at least temporarily halted the civil war.*

SYNONYMS

temporary
ADJ
impermanent: *We are reminded just how small and how impermanent we are.*
passing: *Hamnett does not believe environmental concern is a passing fad.*
transitory: *Most teenage romances are transitory.*
fleeting: *The girls caught only a fleeting glimpse of the driver.*
ephemeral: *These paintings are in some ways a reminder that earthly pleasures are ephemeral.*

---

tem|po|rize /tɛmpəraɪz/ (temporizes, temporizing, temporized)

in BRIT, also use **temporise**

V-T/V-I If you say that someone **is temporizing**, you mean that they keep doing unimportant things in order to delay something important such as making a decision or stating their real opinion. [FORMAL] ❑ *They are still temporizing in the face of what can only be described as a disaster.* ❑ *"Not exactly, sir," temporized Sloan.*

tempt /tɛmpt/ (tempts, tempting, tempted) **1** V-T Something that **tempts** you attracts you and makes you want it, even though it may be wrong or harmful. ❑ *Cars like that may tempt drivers to speed.* ❑ *It is the fresh fruit that tempts me at this time of year.* **2** V-T If you **tempt** someone, you offer them something they want in order to encourage them to do what you want them to do. ❑ *...a million dollar marketing campaign to tempt American tourists back to Britain.* ❑ *Don't let credit tempt you to buy something you can't afford.* **3** → see also **tempted**

temp|ta|tion /tɛmpteɪʃən/ (temptations) N-VAR If you feel you want to do something or have something, even though you know you really should avoid it, you can refer to this feeling as **temptation**. You can also refer to the thing you want to do or have as a **temptation**. ❑ *Will they be able to resist the temptation to buy?*

tempt|ed /tɛmptɪd/ ADJ [v-link ADJ] If you say that you are **tempted** to do something, you mean that you would like to do it. ❑ *I'm very tempted to sell my house.*

tempt|ing /tɛmptɪŋ/ ADJ If something is **tempting**, it makes you want to do it or have it. ❑ *In the end, I turned down Raoul's tempting offer of the Palm Beach trip.* ● **tempt|ing|ly** ADV ❑ *The good news is that prices are still temptingly low.*

tempt|ress /tɛmptrɪs/ (temptresses) N-COUNT If you describe a woman as a **temptress**, you mean that she uses her female charm to attract people sexually.

ten ✦✦✦ /tɛn/ (tens) NUM **Ten** is the number 10. ❑ *Over the past ten years things have changed.*

ten|able /tɛnəbəl/ ADJ If you say that an argument, point of view, or situation is **tenable**, you believe that it is reasonable and could be successfully defended against criticism. ❑ *This argument is simply not tenable.*

te|na|cious /tɪneɪʃəs/ ADJ If you are **tenacious**, you are very determined and do not give up easily. ❑ *He is regarded as a tenacious and persistent interviewer.* ● **te|na|cious|ly** ADV ❑ *In spite of his illness, he clung tenaciously to his job.*

te|nac|ity /tɪnæsɪti/ N-UNCOUNT If you have **tenacity**, you are very determined and do not give up easily. ❑ *Talent, hard work and sheer tenacity are all crucial to career success.*

ten|an|cy /tɛnənsi/ (tenancies) N-VAR **Tenancy** is the use that you have of land or property belonging to someone else, for which you pay rent. ❑ *His father took over the tenancy of the farm 40 years ago.*

ten|ant /tɛnənt/ (tenants) N-COUNT A **tenant** is someone who pays rent for the place they live in, or for land or buildings that they use. ❑ *Regulations placed clear obligations on the landlord for the benefit of the tenant.*

tench /tɛntʃ/ (tench) N-VAR **Tench** are dark green fish that live in lakes and rivers.

tend ✦✧ /tɛnd/ (tends, tending, tended) **1** V-T If something **tends** to happen, it usually happens or it often happens. ❑ *A problem for manufacturers is that lighter cars tend to be noisy.* **2** V-I If you **tend** toward a particular characteristic, you often display that characteristic. ❑ *Artistic and intellectual people tend toward left-wing views.* **3** V-T You can say that you **tend to** think something when you want to give your opinion, but do not want it to seem too forceful or definite. [VAGUENESS] ❑ *I tend to think that our Representatives by and large do a good job.*

ten|den|cy ✦✧ /tɛndənsi/ (tendencies) **1** N-COUNT A **tendency** is a worrying or unpleasant habit or action that keeps occurring. ❑ *...the government's tendency to secrecy in recent years.* **2** N-COUNT A **tendency** is a part of your character that makes you often behave in an unpleasant or worrying way. ❑ *He is spoiled, arrogant and has a tendency toward snobbery.*

tendentious

> **SYNONYMS**
>
> **tendency**
> NOUN ❷
> **inclination:** *He set out to follow his artistic inclinations.*
> **bent:** *His bent for natural history directed him towards his first job.*
> **leaning:** *Many companies are wary of their socialist leanings.*
> **penchant:** *He had a penchant for playing jokes on people.*
> **propensity:** *She hasn't reckoned on his propensity for violence.*

ten|den|tious /tɛndɛnʃəs/ ADJ Something that is **tendentious** expresses a particular opinion or point of view very strongly, especially one that many people disagree with. [FORMAL] ❏ *His analysis was rooted in a somewhat tendentious reading of French history.*

> **TENDER**
> ① ADJECTIVE USES
> ② NOUN AND VERB USES

① **ten|der** /tɛndər/ (tenderer, tenderest) ❶ ADJ Someone or something that is **tender** expresses gentle and caring feelings. ❏ *Her voice was tender, full of pity.* • **ten|der|ly** ADV [ADV with v] ❏ *Mr. White tenderly embraced his wife.* • **ten|der|ness** N-UNCOUNT ❏ *She smiled, politely rather than with tenderness.* ❷ ADJ [ADJ n] If you say that someone does something at a **tender** age, you mean that they do it when they are still young and have not had much experience. ❏ *He took up the game at the tender age of seven.* ❸ ADJ Meat or other food that is **tender** is easy to cut or chew. ❏ *Cook for a minimum of 2 hours, or until the meat is tender.* ❹ ADJ If part of your body is **tender**, it is sensitive and painful when it is touched. ❏ *My tummy felt very tender.* • **ten|der|ness** N-UNCOUNT ❏ *There is still some tenderness in her ankle.*

② **ten|der** /tɛndər/ (tenders, tendering, tendered) ❶ N-VAR A **tender** is a formal offer to supply goods or to do a particular job, and a statement of the price that you or your company will charge. If a contract is **put out to tender**, formal offers are invited. If a company **wins a tender**, their offer is accepted. [BUSINESS] ❏ *Builders will then be sent the specifications and asked to submit a tender for the work.* ❷ V-I If a company **tenders for** something, it makes a formal offer to supply goods or do a job for a particular price. [BUSINESS] ❏ *The staff are forbidden to tender for private-sector work.* ❸ → see also **legal tender** ❹ → See feature box at **cooking**

tender|foot /tɛndərfʊt/ (tenderfoots or tenderfeet) N-COUNT A **tenderfoot** is a newcomer to a place or activity, especially a newcomer to the mines or ranches of the western United States. [AM] ❏ *I may look like a tenderfoot, but I think I can follow a trail or carry a pack if necessary.*

tender-hearted ADJ If you are **tender-hearted**, you have a gentle and caring nature.

ten|der|ize /tɛndəraɪz/ (tenderizes, tenderizing, tenderized)

> in BRIT, also use **tenderise**

V-T If you **tenderize** meat, you make it softer by preparing it in a particular way. ❏ *Wine vinegar tenderizes meat.*

ten|din|itis /tɛndənaɪtɪs/ N-UNCOUNT **Tendinitis** is a medical condition in which a tendon becomes swollen and painful. [MEDICAL] ❏ *Tendinitis can usually be relieved with rest and ice massage.*

ten|don /tɛndən/ (tendons) N-COUNT A **tendon** is a strong cord in a person's or animal's body which joins a muscle to a bone. ❏ *...a torn tendon in his right shoulder.*

ten|dril /tɛndrɪl/ (tendrils) ❶ N-COUNT A **tendril** is something light and thin, for example, a piece of hair which hangs loose and is away from the main part. ❏ *Tendrils of hair strayed to the edge of her pillow.* ❷ N-COUNT [usu pl] **Tendrils** are thin stems which grow on some plants so that they can attach themselves to supports such as walls or other plants.

ten|ement /tɛnəmənt/ (tenements) ❶ N-COUNT A **tenement** is a large, old building which is divided into a number of individual apartments. ❏ *...streets of low-cost tenements.* ❷ N-COUNT A **tenement** is one of the apartments in a tenement. ❏ *He struggled to pay the rent on his $88 a month tenement.*

ten|et /tɛnɪt/ (tenets) N-COUNT The **tenets** of a theory or belief are the main principles on which it is based. [FORMAL] ❏ *Non-violence and patience are the central tenets of their faith.*

ten-gallon hat (ten-gallon hats) also **10-gallon hat**
N-COUNT A **ten-gallon hat** is a hat with a broad brim and a high crown, often worn by cowboys. [AM] ❏ *...an old man in a 10-gallon hat.*

ten|nis ✦✦◇ /tɛnɪs/ ❶ N-UNCOUNT **Tennis** is a game played by two or four players on a rectangular court. The players use an oval racket with strings across it to hit a ball over a net across the middle of the court. ❷ → See also color supplement

ten|or /tɛnər/ (tenors) ❶ N-COUNT A **tenor** is a male singer whose voice is fairly high. ❏ *...a free, open-air concert given by the Italian tenor, Luciano Pavarotti.* ❷ ADJ A **tenor** saxophone or other musical instrument has a range of notes that are of a fairly low pitch. ❏ *...one of the best tenor sax players ever.*

ten|pin bowl|ing /tɛnpɪn boʊlɪn/ also **ten-pin bowling**
N-UNCOUNT **Tenpin bowling** is a game in which you roll a heavy ball down a narrow track toward a group of wooden objects and try to knock down as many of them as possible. [mainly BRIT]

> in AM, usually use **bowling**

tense /tɛns/ (tenser, tensest, tenses, tensing) ❶ ADJ A **tense** situation or period of time is one that makes people anxious, because they do not know what is going to happen next. ❏ *This gesture of goodwill did little to improve the tense atmosphere at the talks.* ❷ ADJ If you are **tense**, you are anxious and nervous and cannot relax. ❏ *Mark, who had at first been very tense, at last relaxed.* ❸ ADJ If your body is **tense**, your muscles are tight and not relaxed. ❏ *A bath can relax tense muscles.* ❹ V-T/V-I If your muscles **tense**, if you **tense**, or if you **tense** your muscles, your muscles become tight and stiff, often because you are anxious or frightened. ❏ *Newman's stomach muscles tensed.*
• PHRASAL VERB **tense up** means the same as **tense**. ❏ *When we are under stress our bodies tend to tense up.* ❺ N-COUNT The **tense** of a verb group is its form, which usually shows whether you are referring to past, present, or future time. ❏ *It was as though Corinne was already dead: they were speaking of her in the past tense.*

ten|sile /tɛnsɪl/ ADJ [ADJ n] You use **tensile** when you are talking about the amount of stress that materials such as wire, rope, and concrete can take without breaking; a technical term in engineering. ❏ *Certain materials can be manufactured with a high tensile strength.*

ten|sion ✦◇◇ /tɛnʃən/ (tensions) ❶ N-UNCOUNT [also N in pl] **Tension** is a feeling of worry and anxiety which makes it difficult for you to relax. ❏ *Smiling and laughing has actually been shown to relieve tension and stress.* ❷ N-UNCOUNT [also N in pl] **Tension** is the feeling that is produced in a situation when people are anxious and do not trust each other, and when there is a possibility of sudden violence or conflict. ❏ *The tension between the two countries is likely to remain.* ❸ N-VAR If there is a **tension** between forces, arguments, or influences, there are differences between them that cause difficulties. ❏ *The film explored the tension between public duty and personal affections.* ❹ N-UNCOUNT The **tension** in something such as a rope or wire is the extent to which it is stretched tight. ❏ *As the cable wraps itself around the wheel, there is provision for adjusting the tension of the cable.*

> **SYNONYMS**
>
> **tension**
> NOUN
> ❶
> **friction:** *The plan is likely only to aggravate ethnic frictions.*
> **hostility:** *There is a lot of hostility between them.*
> **antagonism:** *There is still much antagonism between trade unions and the oil companies.*
> ❷
> **stress:** *Katy could think clearly when not under stress.*
> **worry:** *His last years were overshadowed by financial worry.*
> **anxiety:** *Her voice was full of anxiety.*
> **strain:** *She was tired and under great strain.*

tent /tɛnt/ (tents) N-COUNT A **tent** is a shelter made of canvas or nylon which is held up by poles and ropes, and is used mainly by people who are camping.

ten|ta|cle /tɛntəkəl/ (tentacles) ❶ N-COUNT The **tentacles** of an animal such as an octopus are the long thin parts that are used for feeling and holding things, for getting food, and for moving. **2** N-COUNT If you talk about the **tentacles** of a political, commercial, or social organization, you are referring to the power and influence that it has in the outside community. [DISAPPROVAL] ❑ *Free speech is being gradually eroded year after year by new tentacles of government control.*

ten|ta|tive /tɛntətɪv/ **1** ADJ **Tentative** agreements, plans, or arrangements are not definite or certain, but have been made as a first step. ❑ *Political leaders have reached a tentative agreement to hold a preparatory conference next month.* • **ten|ta|tive|ly** ADV [ADV with v] ❑ *The next round of talks is tentatively scheduled to begin October 21st in Washington.* **2** ADJ If someone is **tentative**, they are cautious and not very confident because they are uncertain or afraid. ❑ *My first attempts at complaining were kind of tentative.* • **ten|ta|tive|ly** ADV [ADV with v] ❑ *Perhaps, he suggested tentatively, they should send for Dr. Esteves.*

tent|ed /tɛntɪd/ **1** ADJ [usu ADJ n] A **tented** field or a **tented** camp is an area where a number of people are living in tents. **2** ADJ [usu ADJ n] A **tented** room has long pieces of material hanging down from the center of the ceiling to the walls, so that the room has the appearance of the inside of a large tent. ❑ *...a tented dining area.*

tenter|hooks /tɛntərhʊks/ PHRASE [v-link PHR] If you are **on tenterhooks**, you are very nervous and excited because you are wondering what is going to happen in a particular situation. ❑ *He was still on tenterhooks waiting for his directors' decision about the job.*

tenth ✦✧✧ /tɛnθ/ (**tenths**) **1** ORD The **tenth** item in a series is the one that you count as number ten. ❑ *...her tenth birthday.* **2** FRACTION A **tenth** is one of ten equal parts of something. ❑ *He finished three-tenths of a second behind Prost.*

tenu|ous /tɛnyuəs/ ADJ If you describe something such as a connection, a reason, or someone's position as **tenuous**, you mean that it is very uncertain or weak. ❑ *He did not speculate on the future of his tenuous career.*

ten|ure /tɛnyər/ **1** N-UNCOUNT **Tenure** is the legal right to live in a particular building or to use a particular piece of land during a fixed period of time. ❑ *Lack of security of tenure was a reason for many families becoming homeless.* **2** N-UNCOUNT **Tenure** is the period of time during which someone holds an important job. ❑ *...the challenges he faced during his tenure as chief executive officer.* **3** N-UNCOUNT If you have **tenure** in your job, you have the right to keep it until you retire.

te|pee /tipi/ (**tepees**) also **teepee** N-COUNT A **tepee** is a round tent. Tepees were first made by Native American peoples from animal skins.

tep|id /tɛpɪd/ ADJ Water or another liquid that is **tepid** is slightly warm.

te|qui|la /tɪkilə/ (**tequilas**) N-MASS **Tequila** is a strong alcoholic drink made in Mexico from the agave cactus plant.

ter|cen|te|nary /tɜrsɛntɛnəri/ N-SING [oft the N of n] A **tercentenary** is a day or a year which is exactly three hundred years after an important event such as the birth of a famous person. ❑ *...the tercentenary of Purcell's death.*

term ✦✦✦ /tɜrm/ (**terms, terming, termed**) **1** PHRASE If you talk about something **in terms of** something or **in** particular **terms**, you are specifying which aspect of it you are discussing or from what point of view you are considering it. ❑ *Our goods compete in terms of product quality, reliability and above all variety.* **2** PHRASE If you say something **in** particular **terms**, you say it using a particular type or level of language or using language which clearly shows your attitude. ❑ *The article explains in simple terms how the new tax works.* **3** N-COUNT A **term** is a word or expression with a specific meaning, especially one which is used in relation to a particular subject. ❑ *Myocardial infarction is the medical term for a heart attack.* **4** V-T If you say that something **is termed** a particular thing, you mean that that is what people call it or that is their opinion of it. ❑ *He had been termed a temporary employee.* **5** N-VAR A **term** is one of the periods of time that a school, college, or university divides the year into. ❑ *...the summer term.* **6** N-COUNT A **term** is a period of time between two elections during which a particular party or government is in power. ❑ *Nixon never completed his term of office.* **7** N-COUNT A **term** is a period of time that someone spends doing a particular job or in a particular place. ❑ *...a 12 month term of service.* **8** N-COUNT A **term** is the period for which a legal contract or insurance policy is valid. ❑ *Premiums are guaranteed throughout the term of the policy.* **9** N-UNCOUNT The **term** of a woman's pregnancy is the nine month period that it lasts. **Term** is also used to refer to the end of the nine month period. ❑ *That makes her the first TV presenter to work the full term of her pregnancy.* **10** N-PLURAL The **terms** of an agreement, treaty, or other arrangement are the conditions that must be accepted by the people involved in it. ❑ *...the terms of the Helsinki agreement.* **11** PHRASE If you **come to terms with** something difficult or unpleasant, you learn to accept and deal with it. ❑ *She had come to terms with the fact that her husband would always be crippled.* **12** PHRASE If two people or groups compete **on equal terms** or **on the same terms**, neither of them has an advantage over the other. ❑ *I had at last found a sport where I could compete on equal terms with able-bodied people.* **13** PHRASE If two people are **on good terms** or **on friendly terms**, they are friendly with each other. ❑ *Madeleine is on good terms with Sarah.* **14** PHRASE You use the expressions **in the long term**, **in the short term**, and **in the medium term** to talk about what will happen over a long period of time, over a short period of time, and over a medium period of time. ❑ *Organic fertilizers will have very positive results in the long term.* **15** PHRASE If you do something **on** your **terms**, you do it under conditions that you decide because you are in a position of power. ❑ *They will sign the union treaty only on their terms.* **16** PHRASE If you say that you **are thinking in terms of** doing a particular thing, you mean that you are considering it. ❑ *You should be thinking in terms of graduating next year.* **17 in no uncertain terms** → see **uncertain**

SYNONYMS

term
NOUN **3**
word: *The word 'ginseng' comes from a Chinese word.*
name: *They changed the name of the street.*
expression: *She spoke in a quiet voice but used remarkably coarse expressions.*
phrase: *He used a phrase I hate: 'You have to be cruel to be kind.'*
VERB **4**
call: *Everybody called each other by their surnames.*
label: *Certain estates are labeled as undesirable.*
name: *...a man named John T. Benson.*

---

ter|mi|nal /tɜrmɪnᵊl/ (**terminals**) **1** ADJ A **terminal** illness or disease causes death, often slowly, and cannot be cured. ❑ *...terminal cancer.* • **ter|mi|nal|ly** ADV [ADV adj] ❑ *The patient is terminally ill.* **2** N-COUNT [usu supp N] A **terminal** is a place where vehicles, passengers, or goods begin or end a journey. ❑ *Plans are underway for a new terminal at Dulles airport.* **3** N-COUNT A computer **terminal** is a piece of equipment consisting of a keyboard and a screen that is used for putting information into a computer or getting information from it. [COMPUTING] ❑ *Carl sits at a computer terminal 40 hours a week.* **4** N-COUNT On a piece of electrical equipment, a **terminal** is one of the points where electricity enters or leaves it. ❑ *...the positive terminal of the battery.*

ter|mi|nate /tɜrmɪneɪt/ (**terminates, terminating, terminated**) **1** V-T/V-I When you **terminate** something or when it **terminates**, it ends completely. [FORMAL] ❑ *Her next remark abruptly terminated the conversation.* • **ter|mi|na|tion** /tɜrmɪneɪʃᵊn/ N-UNCOUNT ❑ *...a dispute which led to the abrupt termination of trade.* **2** V-T To **terminate** a pregnancy means to end it. [MEDICAL] ❑ *After a lot of agonizing she decided to terminate the pregnancy.* • **ter|mi|na|tion** (**terminations**) N-VAR ❑ *You should also have a medical check-up after the termination of a pregnancy.* **3** V-I When a train or bus **terminates** somewhere, it ends its journey there. [FORMAL] ❑ *This train will terminate at Lamy.*

ter|mi|ni /tɜrmɪnaɪ/ **Termini** is the plural of **terminus**.

ter|mi|nol|ogy /tɜrmɪnɒlədʒi/ (**terminologies**) N-VAR The **terminology** of a subject is the set of special words and expressions used in connection with it. ❑ *...gastritis, which in medical terminology means an inflammation of the stomach.*

ter|mi|nus /tɜrmɪnəs/ (**termini**) N-COUNT On a bus or train route, the **terminus** is the last stop, where the bus or train turns around or starts going in the opposite direction.

ter|mite /tɜrmaɪt/ (termites) N-COUNT Termites are small insects that do a lot of damage by eating wood.

term pa|per (term papers) N-COUNT A term paper is an important essay or report which a student writes on a subject that he or she has studied during a term at a school, college, or university. [AM]

tern /tɜrn/ (terns) N-COUNT A tern is a small black and white seabird with long wings and a forked tail.

ter|race /tɛrɪs/ (terraces) **1** N-COUNT A terrace is a flat area of stone or grass next to a building where people can sit. ❑ *Some guests recline in deck chairs on the sea-facing terrace.* **2** N-COUNT Terraces are a series of flat areas built like steps on the side of a hill so that crops can be grown there. ❑ *...massive terraces of corn and millet carved into the mountainside like giant steps.*

ter|raced /tɛrɪst/ ADJ [usu ADJ n] A terraced slope or side of a hill has flat areas like steps cut into it, where crops or other plants can be grown.

ter|raced house /tɛrɪst haʊs/ (terraced houses) N-COUNT A terraced house or a terrace house is one of a row of similar houses joined together by their side walls. [BRIT]

in AM, use **row house**

ter|rac|ing /tɛrəsɪŋ/ N-UNCOUNT Terracing is a sloping piece of land that has had flat areas like steps built on it, for example, so that people can grow crops there.

terra|cotta /tɛrəkɒtə/ also **terra cotta** N-UNCOUNT Terracotta is a brownish-red clay that has been baked and is used for making things such as flower pots, small statues, and tiles. ❑ *...plants in terracotta pots.*

ter|ra fir|ma /tɛrə fɜrmə/ N-UNCOUNT If you describe the ground as terra firma, you mean that it feels safe in contrast to being in the air or at sea. ❑ *...his relief on finding himself once more on terra firma.*

ter|rain /tərɛɪn/ (terrains) N-VAR Terrain is used to refer to an area of land or a type of land when you are considering its physical features. ❑ *The terrain changed quickly from arable land to desert.*

ter|ra|pin /tɛrəpɪn/ (terrapins) N-COUNT A terrapin is a turtle which lives partly in water and partly on land.

ter|res|trial /təɹɛstriəl/ **1** ADJ [ADJ n] Terrestrial means relating to the planet Earth rather than to some other part of the universe. ❑ *...terrestrial life forms.* **2** → see also **extraterrestrial** **3** → See feature box at **ecosystem, water**

ter|ri|ble ♦♢♢ /tɛrɪbəl/ **1** ADJ A terrible experience or situation is very bad or very unpleasant. ❑ *Tens of thousands more suffered terrible injuries in the world's worst industrial disaster.* ❑ *I often have terrible nightmares.* ● **ter|ri|bly** ADV [ADV after v] ❑ *My son has suffered terribly. He has lost his best friend.* **2** ADJ If something is **terrible**, it is very bad or of very poor quality. ❑ *She admits her French is terrible.* **3** ADJ [ADJ n] You use **terrible** to emphasize the great extent or degree of something. [EMPHASIS] ❑ *I was a terrible fool, you know.* ● **ter|ri|bly** ADV ❑ *I'm terribly sorry to bother you at this hour.*

SYNONYMS

terrible
ADJ **1**
awful: *Even if the weather's awful, there's lots to do.*
appalling: *They have been living under the most appalling conditions.*
dreadful: *They told us the dreadful news.*
horrendous: *He described it as the most horrendous experience of his life.*

---

ter|ri|er /tɛriər/ (terriers) **1** N-COUNT A terrier is a small breed of dog. There are many different types of terrier. **2** → see also **bull terrier, pit bull terrier**

ter|rif|ic /təɹɪfɪk/ **1** ADJ If you describe something or someone as **terrific**, you are very pleased with them or very impressed by them. [INFORMAL] ❑ *What a terrific idea!* **2** ADJ [ADJ n] **Terrific** means very great in amount, degree, or intensity. [EMPHASIS] ❑ *All of a sudden there was a terrific bang and a flash of smoke.*

ter|ri|fy /tɛrɪfaɪ/ (terrifies, terrifying, terrified) **1** V-T If something **terrifies** you, it makes you feel extremely frightened. ❑ *Flying terrifies him.* ● **ter|ri|fied** ADJ ❑ *He was terrified of heights.* **2** → see also **terror**

ter|ri|fy|ing /tɛrɪfaɪɪŋ/ ADJ If something is **terrifying**, it makes you very frightened. ❑ *I still find it terrifying to find myself surrounded by large numbers of horses.*

ter|ri|to|rial /tɛrɪtɔriəl/ **1** ADJ **Territorial** means concerned with the ownership of a particular area of land or water. ❑ *It is the only republic which has no territorial disputes with the others.* **2** ADJ If you describe an animal or its behavior as **territorial**, you mean that it has an area which it regards as its own, and which it defends when other animals try to enter it. ❑ *Two cats or more in one house will also exhibit territorial behavior.*

Ter|ri|to|rial Army **1** N-PROPER [the N] **The Territorial Army** is a British armed force whose members are not professional soldiers but train as soldiers in their spare time. **2** → see also **National Guard**

ter|ri|to|rial wa|ters N-PLURAL [usu poss/adj N] A country's **territorial waters** are the parts of the ocean close to its coast which are recognized by international agreement to be under its control, especially with regard to fishing rights.

ter|ri|to|ry ♦♦♢ /tɛrɪtɔri/ (territories) **1** N-UNCOUNT **Territory** is land which is controlled by a particular country or ruler. ❑ *The government denies that any of its territory is under rebel control.* ❑ *...the view that the US should use military force only when our borders or US territories are attacked.* **2** N-COUNT A **territory** is a country or region that is controlled by another country. ❑ *He toured some of the disputed territories now under UN control.* **3** N-UNCOUNT [with supp] You can use **territory** to refer to an area of knowledge or experience. ❑ *Following the futuristic "The Handmaid's Tale," Margaret Atwood's seventh novel, "Cat's Eye," returned to more familiar territory.* **4 virgin territory** → see **virgin** **5** N-VAR An animal's **territory** is an area which it regards as its own and which it defends when other animals try to enter it. ❑ *The territory of a cat only remains fixed for as long as the cat dominates the area.* **6** N-UNCOUNT **Territory** is land with a particular character. ❑ *...mountainous territory.*

SYNONYMS

territory
NOUN **1**
district: *...the home of the governor of the district.*
area: *If there is an election in your area, you should go and vote.*
land: *...this land of free speech.*
region: *...a remote, mountain region.*

---

ter|ror ♦♦♢ /tɛrər/ (terrors) **1** N-UNCOUNT **Terror** is very great fear. ❑ *I shook with terror whenever I was about to fly in a plane.* **2** N-UNCOUNT **Terror** is violence or the threat of violence, especially when it is used for political reasons. ❑ *...the war on terror.* ❑ *The bomb attack on the capital could signal the start of a pre-election terror campaign.* **3** N-COUNT A **terror** is something that makes you very frightened. ❑ *As a boy, he had a real terror of facing people.*

ter|ror|ism ♦♦♢ /tɛrərɪzəm/ N-UNCOUNT **Terrorism** is the use of violence, especially murder and bombing, in order to achieve political goals or to force a government to do something. [DISAPPROVAL] ❑ *...the threat of global terrorism.*

ter|ror|ist ♦♦♢ /tɛrərɪst/ (terrorists) N-COUNT A **terrorist** is a person who uses violence, especially murder and bombing, in order to achieve political aims. [DISAPPROVAL] ❑ *One American was killed and three were wounded in terrorist attacks.*

SYNONYMS

terrorist
NOUN
freedom fighter: *He calls himself a freedom fighter.*
bomber: *Detectives hunting for the London bombers will be keen to interview him.*
revolutionary: *The revolutionaries laid down their arms, and their leaders went into voluntary exile.*
guerrilla: *The guerrillas threatened to kill their hostages.*

---

ter|ror|ize /tɛrəraɪz/ (terrorizes, terrorizing, terrorized)

in BRIT, also use **terrorise**

V-T If someone **terrorizes** you, they keep you in a state of fear by making it seem likely that they will attack you. ❑ *Bands of gunmen have hijacked food shipments and terrorized relief workers.*

ter|ry /tɛri/ also **terry cloth** N-UNCOUNT [usu N n] **Terry** or **terry cloth** is a type of fabric which has a lot of very small loops covering both sides. It is used especially for making towels. ❑ ...*a terry cloth bathrobe.*

terse /tɜrs/ (terser, tersest) ADJ A **terse** statement or comment is brief and unfriendly. ❑ *He issued a terse statement, saying he is discussing his future with colleagues before announcing his decision on Monday.* • **terse|ly** ADV [ADV with v] ❑ *"It's too late," he said tersely.*

ter|tiary /tɜrʃieri/ **1** ADJ **Tertiary** means third in order, third in importance, or at a third stage of development. [FORMAL] ❑ *He must have come to know those philosophers through secondary or tertiary sources.* **2** ADJ [ADJ n] **Tertiary education** is education at the university or college level. [mainly BRIT]

in AM, usually use **higher education**

3 → see **primary, secondary** **4** → See feature box at **university**

ter|tiary sec|tor (tertiary sectors) N-COUNT The **tertiary sector** consists of industries which provide a service, such as transportation and finance. [BUSINESS] ❑ ...*economies that are slowly increasing the proportion of their labor force in the tertiary sector.*

TESL /tɛsᵊl/ **1** N-UNCOUNT **TESL** is the teaching of English to people who live in an English-speaking country, but whose first language is not English. **TESL** is an abbreviation for 'teaching English as a second language.' **2** → see also **TEFL**

TESOL /tisɔl/ **1** N-UNCOUNT **TESOL** is the teaching of English to people whose first language is not English. **TESOL** is an abbreviation for 'teaching English to speakers of other languages.' **2** → see also **TEFL, TESL**

test ✦✦✦ /tɛst/ (tests, testing, tested)

→ Please look at meaning **13** to see if the expression you are looking for is shown under another headword.

1 V-T When you **test** something, you try it, for example, by touching it or using it for a short time, in order to find out what it is, what condition it is in, or how well it works. ❑ *Either measure the temperature with a thermometer or test the water with your wrist.* **2** N-COUNT A **test** is a deliberate action or experiment to find out how well something works. ❑ ...*the banning of nuclear tests.* **3** V-T If you **test** someone, you ask them questions or tell them to perform certain actions in order to find out how much they know about a subject or how well they are able to do something. ❑ *There was a time when each teacher spent an hour, one day a week, testing students in every subject.* **4** N-COUNT A **test** is a series of questions that you must answer or actions that you must perform in order to show how much you know about a subject or how well you are able to do something. ❑ *Out of a total of 25 students only 15 passed the test.* **5** → see also **quiz** **6** V-T If you **test** someone, you deliberately make things difficult for them in order to see how they react. ❑ *From the first day, Rudolf was testing me, seeing if I would make him tea, bring him a Coke.* **7** N-COUNT If an event or situation is a **test** of a person or thing, it reveals their qualities or effectiveness. ❑ *It is a fact that holidays are a major test of any relationship.* **8** V-T [usu passive] If you **are tested** for a particular disease or medical condition, you are examined or go through various procedures in order to find out whether you have that disease or condition. ❑ *My doctor wants me to be tested for diabetes.* **9** N-COUNT A medical **test** is an examination of a part of your body in order to check that you are healthy or to find out what is wrong with you. ❑ *If necessary, X-rays and blood tests will also be used to aid diagnosis.* ❑ ...*a pregnancy test.* **10** PHRASE If you **put** something **to the test**, you find out how useful or effective it is by using it. ❑ *The team are now putting their theory to the test.* **11** PHRASE If new circumstances or events **put** something or someone **to the test**, they put a strain on it and indicate how strong or stable it really is. ❑ *Multiple hijackings are putting air traffic controllers to the test.* **12** PHRASE If you say that something **will stand the test of time**, you mean that it is strong or effective enough to last for a very long time. ❑ *It says a lot for her cooking skills that so many of her recipes have stood the test of time.* **13 to test the waters** → see **water** **14** → See feature box at **challenge**

SYNONYMS

test
VERB **1**
check: *It's worth checking each item for obvious flaws.*
try out: *London Transport hopes to try out the system in September.*
assess: *It would be a matter of assessing whether she was well enough to travel.*
NOUN **2**
trial: *They have been treated with this drug in clinical trials.*
check: *He is being constantly monitored with regular checks of his blood pressure.*
assessment: *Heggie was sent to a psychiatric hospital for an assessment.*
experiment: ...*a proposed new law on animal experiments.*

---

tes|ta|ment /tɛstəmənt/ (testaments) **1** N-VAR If one thing is a **testament** to another, it shows that the other thing exists or is true. [FORMAL] ❑ *For him to win the game like that is a testament to his perseverance.* **2** PHRASE Someone's **last will and testament** is the most recent will that they have made, especially the last will that they make before they die. [LEGAL]

test bed (test beds) N-COUNT A **test bed** is a piece of equipment used for testing new machines.

test case (test cases) N-COUNT A **test case** is a legal case which becomes an example for deciding other similar cases. ❑ *It is considered an important test case by both advocates and opponents of gun control.*

test drive (test drives, test driving, test drove) also **test-drive** **1** V-T If you **test drive** a car or other vehicle, you drive it for a short period in order to assess its performance before deciding whether to buy it. ❑ ...*three invitations to test drive expensive cars.* • N-COUNT **Test drive** is also a noun. ❑ *Consumers are buying cars from websites without ever going for a test drive.* **2** V-T If you **test drive** a product, you try it for a short period in order to assess its qualities before deciding whether to buy it. ❑ *Kids can test drive the latest games on large-screen TVs with state-of-the-art sound.*

test|er /tɛstər/ (testers) **1** N-COUNT A **tester** is a person who has been asked to test a particular thing. **2** N-COUNT [usu n n] A **tester** is a machine or device that you use to test whether another machine or device is working correctly. ❑ *I have a battery tester in my garage.*

tes|ti|cle /tɛstɪkᵊl/ (testicles) N-COUNT A man's **testicles** are the two reproductive glands that produce sperm and are contained in the scrotum.

tes|ticu|lar /tɛstɪkyələr/ ADJ [ADJ n] **Testicular** means relating to or involving the testicles. ❑ ...*testicular cancer.*

tes|ti|fy /tɛstɪfaɪ/ (testifies, testifying, testified) V-T/V-I When someone **testifies** in a court of law, they give a statement of what they saw someone do or what they know of a situation, after having promised to tell the truth. ❑ *Several eyewitnesses testified that they saw the officers hit Miller in the face.* ❑ *Eva testified to having seen Herndon with his gun on the stairs.*

tes|ti|mo|nial /tɛstɪmoʊniəl/ (testimonials) **1** N-COUNT A **testimonial** is a written statement about a person's character and abilities, often written by their employer. ❑ *She could hardly expect her employer to provide her with testimonials to her character and ability.* **2** N-COUNT A **testimonial** is an event which is held to honor someone for their services or achievements. ❑ ...*a testimonial dinner held in New York.*

tes|ti|mo|ny /tɛstɪmoʊni/ (testimonies) **1** N-VAR In a court of law, someone's **testimony** is a formal statement that they make about what they saw someone do or what they know of a situation, after having promised to tell the truth. ❑ *His testimony was an important element of the prosecution's case.* **2** N-UNCOUNT [also a N, usu N to n] If you say that one thing is **testimony** to another, you mean that it shows clearly that the second thing has a particular quality. ❑ *The environmental movement is testimony to the widespread feelings of support for nature's importance.*

test|ing ✦◇◇ /tɛstɪŋ/ **1** ADJ A **testing** problem or situation is very difficult to deal with and shows a lot about the character of the person who is dealing with it. ❑ *The most testing time is undoubtedly in the early months of your return to work.* **2** N-UNCOUNT **Testing** is the activity of testing something or someone in order to find out information. ❑ ...*product testing and labeling.*

tes|tis /tɛstɪs/ (testes /tɛstiz/) N-COUNT [usu pl] A man's testes are his **testicles**. [MEDICAL]

tes|tos|ter|one /tɛstɒstəroʊn/ N-UNCOUNT **Testosterone** is a hormone found in men and male animals, which can also be produced artificially. It is thought to be responsible for the male sexual instinct and other male characteristics.

test pi|lot (test pilots) N-COUNT A **test pilot** is a pilot who flies aircraft of a new design in order to test their performance.

test run (test runs) N-COUNT If you give a machine or system a **test run**, you try it out to see if it will work correctly when it is actually in use.

test tube (test tubes) also **test-tube** N-COUNT A **test tube** is a small tube-shaped container made from glass. Test tubes are used in laboratories.

test-tube baby (test-tube babies) also **test tube baby** N-COUNT A **test-tube baby** is a baby that develops from an egg which has been removed from the mother's body, fertilized, and then replaced in her uterus.

tes|ty /tɛsti/ (testier, testiest) ADJ [usu v-link ADJ] If you describe someone as **testy**, you mean that they easily become impatient or angry. ◻ *Ben's getting a little testy in his old age.* ● **tes|ti|ly** ADV ◻ *He reacted testily to the suggestion he should lose weight.*

teta|nus /tɛtᵊnəs/ N-UNCOUNT **Tetanus** is a serious painful disease caused by bacteria getting into wounds. It makes your muscles, especially your jaw muscles, go stiff.

tetchy /tɛtʃi/ (tetchier, tetchiest) ADJ If you say that someone is **tetchy**, you mean they are bad-tempered and likely to get angry suddenly without an obvious reason. [mainly BRIT, INFORMAL] ◻ *You always get tetchy when you're hungry.* ◻ *He was in a particularly tetchy mood yesterday.*

teth|er /tɛðər/ (tethers, tethering, tethered) **1** PHRASE If you say that you are at **the end of** your **tether**, you mean that you are so worried, tired, and unhappy because of your problems that you feel you cannot cope. ◻ *She was jealous, humiliated, and emotionally at the end of her tether.* **2** N-COUNT A **tether** is a rope or chain which is used to tie an animal to a post or fence so that it can only move around within a small area. ◻ *...a dog that choked to death on its tether.* **3** V-T If you **tether** an animal or object to something, you attach it there with a rope or chain so that it cannot move very far. ◻ *The officer dismounted, tethering his horse to a tree.*

Teu|ton|ic /tutɒnɪk/ ADJ [usu ADJ n] **Teutonic** means typical of or relating to German people. [FORMAL] ◻ *...a masterpiece of Teutonic engineering.*

Tex-Mex /tɛksmɛks/ ADJ [usu ADJ n] You use **Tex-Mex** to describe things such as food or music that combine typical elements from Mexico and Texas. [AM, INFORMAL] ◻ *...Tex-Mex restaurants.*

text ✦✧✧ /tɛkst/ (texts, texting, texted) **1** N-SING The **text** of a book is the main part of it, rather than the introduction, pictures, or notes. ◻ *The text was informative and well written.* **2** N-UNCOUNT **Text** is any written material. ◻ *The machine can recognize handwritten characters and turn them into printed text.* **3** N-COUNT The **text** of a speech, broadcast, or recording is the written version of it. ◻ *The text of his recent speech was circulated among leading republicans.* **4** N-COUNT A **text** is a book or other piece of writing, especially one connected with science or learning. ◻ *Her text is believed to be the oldest surviving manuscript by a female physician.* **5** N-COUNT A **text** is the same as a **text message**. ◻ *The new system can send a text to a cellphone, or to another landline phone.* **6** V-T If you **text** someone, you send them a text message on a cellphone. ◻ *Mary texted me when she got home.*

SYNONYMS

text
NOUN
2
words: *Can you hear the words on the album?*
wording: *The wording is so vague that no one actually knows what it means.*
content: *The letter's contents were not disclosed.*
4
passage: *He reads a passage from Milton.*
extract: *Read this extract from an information booklet about the work of an airline cabin crew.*
excerpt: *...an excerpt from her new novel.*

text|book /tɛkstbʊk/ (textbooks) also **text book** **1** N-COUNT A **textbook** is a book containing facts about a particular subject that is used by people studying that subject. ◻ *She wrote a textbook on international law.* **2** ADJ [ADJ n] If you say that something is a **textbook** case or example, you are emphasizing that it provides a clear example of a type of situation or event. [EMPHASIS] ◻ *The house is a textbook example of medieval domestic architecture.*

text edi|tor (text editors) N-COUNT A **text editor** is a piece of computer software that helps you to create a document on a computer. [COMPUTING]

tex|tile /tɛkstaɪl/ (textiles) **1** N-COUNT **Textiles** are types of cloth or fabric, especially ones that have been woven. ◻ *...decorative textiles for the home.* **2** N-PLURAL [no det] **Textiles** are the industries concerned with the manufacture of cloth. ◻ *Another 75,000 jobs will be lost in textiles and clothing.* **3** → See feature box at **sewing**

text|ing /tɛkstɪŋ/ N-UNCOUNT **Texting** is the same as **text messaging**.

text mes|sage (text messages) **1** N-COUNT A **text message** is a message that you send using a cellphone. ◻ *She has sent text messages to her family telling them not to worry.* **2** → See feature box at **telephone**

text mes|sag|ing N-UNCOUNT **Text messaging** is the sending of written messages using a cellphone. ◻ *...the popularity of text messaging.*

tex|tu|al /tɛkstʃuəl/ ADJ [ADJ n] **Textual** means relating to written texts, especially literary texts. ◻ *...close textual analysis of Shakespeare.*

tex|ture /tɛkstʃər/ (textures) **1** N-VAR The **texture** of something is the way that it feels when you touch it, for example, how smooth or rough it is. ◻ *It is used in moisturizers to give them a wonderfully silky texture.* **2** N-VAR The **texture** of something, especially food or soil, is its structure, for example, whether it is light with lots of holes, or very heavy and solid. ◻ *Matured over 18 months, this cheese has an open, crumbly texture with a strong flavor.* **3** → See feature box at **cooking**, **snow**

tex|tured /tɛkstʃərd/ ADJ [usu ADJ n] A **textured** surface is not smooth, but has a particular texture, for example, it feels rough. ◻ *The shoe's sole had a slightly textured surface.*

TGIF /ti dʒi aɪ ɛf/ **TGIF** is used to say that you are glad the work week is almost over. **TGIF** is an abbreviation for 'Thank God it's Friday.'

SUFFIX

-th
You add -th to numbers written in figures and ending in 4, 5, 6, 7, 8, 9, 10, 11, 12, or 13 in order to form ordinal numbers. These numbers are pronounced as if they were written as words. For example, 7th is pronounced the same as 'seventh,' and 5th is pronounced the same as 'fifth.' *For example, 'May 10th' is day number 10 in the month of May.*

Thai /taɪ/ (Thais) **1** ADJ **Thai** means belonging or relating to Thailand, or to its people, language, or culture. **2** N-COUNT A **Thai** is a citizen of Thailand, or a person of Thai origin. **3** N-UNCOUNT **Thai** is the language spoken in Thailand.

tha|lido|mide /θəlɪdəmaɪd/ **1** N-UNCOUNT **Thalidomide** is a drug which used to be given to pregnant women, before it was discovered that it resulted in babies being born with arms and legs that had not developed properly. **2** ADJ [ADJ n] **Thalidomide** is used to describe someone whose arms and legs have not developed properly because their mother took thalidomide when she was pregnant. ◻ *...the special needs of thalidomide children.*

than ✦✦✦ /ðən, STRONG ðæn/ **1** PREP [compar PREP group] You use **than** after a comparative adjective or adverb in order to link two parts of a comparison. ◻ *Children learn faster than adults.* ◻ *The radio only weighs a few ounces and is smaller than a pack of cigarettes.* ● CONJ **Than** is also a conjunction. ◻ *He wished he could have helped her more than he did.* **2** PREP [more/less PREP n] You use **than** when you are stating a number, quantity, or value approximately by saying that it is above or below another number, quantity, or value. ◻ *They talked on the phone for more than an hour.* **3** CONJ You use **than** in order to link two parts of a contrast, for example, in order to state a preference. ❏ *The arrangement was more a formality than a genuine partnership of two nations.* **4** **less than** → see **less** **5** **more than** → see **more** **6** **more often than not** → see **often** **7** **other than** → see **other** **8** **rather than** → see **rather**

thank ✦✦✦ /θæŋk/ (**thanks**, **thanking**, **thanked**) **1** CONVENTION You use **thank you** or, in more informal English, **thanks** to express your gratitude when someone does something for you or gives you what you want. [FORMULAE] ❏ *Thank you very much for your call.* ❏ *Thanks for the information.* **2** CONVENTION You use **thank you** or, in more informal English, **thanks** to politely accept something that has just been offered to you. [FORMULAE] ❏ *"Would you like a cup of coffee?"—"Thank you, I'd love one."* **3** CONVENTION You use **no thank you** or, in more informal English, **no thanks** to politely refuse something that has just been offered to you. [FORMULAE] ❏ *"Would you like a cigarette?"—"No thank you."* **4** CONVENTION You use **thank you** or, in more informal English, **thanks** to politely acknowledge what someone has said to you, especially when they have answered your question or said something nice to you. [FORMULAE] ❏ *"You look very nice indeed."—"Thank you."* **5** CONVENTION You use **thank you** or **thank you very much** in order to say firmly that you do not want someone's help or to tell them that you do not like the way that they are behaving toward you. [EMPHASIS] ❏ *I can find my own way home, thank you.* **6** V-T When you **thank** someone **for** something, you express your gratitude to them for it. ❏ *I thanked them for their long and loyal service.* **7** N-PLURAL When you express your **thanks** to someone, you express your gratitude to them for something. ❏ *They accepted their certificates with words of thanks.* **8** PHRASE You say '**Thank God**', '**Thank Goodness**', or '**Thank heavens**' when you are very relieved about something. [FEELINGS] ❏ *I was wrong, thank God.* **9** PHRASE If you say that you **have** someone **to thank** for something, you mean that they caused it to happen. ❏ *I have her to thank for my life.* ❏ *You have only yourself to thank for this mess.* **10** PHRASE If you say that something happens **thanks to** a particular person or thing, you mean that they are responsible for it happening or caused it to happen. ❏ *It is thanks to this committee that many new sponsors have come forward.*

thank|ful /θæŋkfəl/ ADJ When you are **thankful**, you are very happy and relieved to have something, or that something has happened. ❏ *Most of the time I'm just thankful that I've got a job.*

thank|ful|ly /θæŋkfəli/ ADV [ADV with cl/group] You use **thankfully** in order to express approval or happiness about a statement that you are making. ❏ *Thankfully, she was not injured.*

thank|less /θæŋklɪs/ ADJ [usu ADJ n] If you describe a job or task as **thankless**, you mean that it is hard work and brings very few rewards. ❏ *Soccer referees have a thankless task.*

thanks|giving /θæŋksgɪvɪŋ/ N-UNCOUNT **Thanksgiving** is the giving of thanks to God, especially in a religious ceremony.

Thanks|giving (**Thanksgivings**) **1** N-VAR In the United States, **Thanksgiving** or **Thanksgiving Day** is a public holiday on the fourth Thursday in November. On this day, people remember the first American thanksgiving, when the first European settlers had been taught how to grow food by the Native Americans, and they celebrated the successful harvest together. ❏ *No matter where his business took him, he always managed to be home for Thanksgiving.* **2** N-VAR In Canada, **Thanksgiving** or **Thanksgiving Day** is a public holiday on the second Monday in October. On this day, people celebrate a successful harvest.

thank|you /θæŋkyu/ (**thankyous**) also **thank-you** **1** N-COUNT [oft N n] If you refer to something as a **thankyou** for what someone has done for you, you mean that it is intended as a way of thanking them. ❏ *The surprise gift is a thankyou for our help.* ❏ *...a thank-you note.* **2** → see also **thank**

THAT
① DEMONSTRATIVE USES
② CONJUNCTION AND RELATIVE PRONOUN USES
---

① **that** ✦✦✦ /ðæt/
→ Please look at meanings **19** – **21** to see if the expression you are looking for is shown under another headword.

1 PRON You use **that** to refer back to an idea or situation expressed in a previous sentence or sentences. ❏ *They said you particularly wanted to talk to me. Why was that?* ❏ *"There's a party tonight."—"Is that why you're phoning?"* • DET **That** is also a determiner. ❏ *She's away; for that reason I'm cooking tonight.* **2** DET You use **that** to refer to someone or something already mentioned. ❏ *The salespeople get between $50,000 and $60,000 a year but that amount can double with commission.* **3** DET When you have been talking about a particular period of time, you use **that** to indicate that you are still referring to the same period. You use expressions such as **that morning** or **that afternoon** to indicate that you are referring to an earlier period of the same day. ❏ *The story was published in a Sunday newspaper later that week.* **4** PRON You use **that** in expressions such as **that of** and **that which** to introduce more information about something already mentioned, instead of repeating the noun which refers to it. [FORMAL] ❏ *A recession like that of 1973-74 could put one in ten American companies into bankruptcy.* **5** PRON You use **that** in front of words or expressions which express agreement, responses, or reactions to what has just been said. ❏ *"She said she'd met you in England."—"That's true."* **6** DET You use **that** when you are referring to someone or something which is a distance away from you in position or time, especially when you indicate or point to them. When there are two or more things near you, **that** refers to the more distant one. ❏ *Look at that guy. He's got red socks.* • PRON **That** is also a pronoun. ❏ *Leo, what's that you're writing?* **7** PRON You use **that** when you are identifying someone or asking about their identity. ❏ *That's my wife you were talking to.* ❏ *"Who's that with you?"—"A friend of mine."* **8** DET You can use **that** when you expect the person you are talking to to know what or who you are referring to, without needing to identify the particular person or thing fully. [SPOKEN] ❏ *I really thought I was something when I wore that hat and my patent leather shoes.* • PRON **That** is also a pronoun. ❏ *That was a terrible case of blackmail in the paper today.* **9** ADV [with brd-neg, ADV adj/adv] If something is not **that** bad, funny, or expensive for example, it is not as bad, funny, or expensive as it might be or as has been suggested. ❏ *Not even Gary, he said, was that stupid.* **10** ADV [ADV adj/adv] You can use **that** to emphasize the degree of a feeling or quality. [INFORMAL, EMPHASIS] ❏ *I would have walked out, I was that angry.* **11** → see also **those** **12** PHRASE You use **and all that** or **and that** to refer generally to everything else which is associated with what you have just mentioned. [INFORMAL, VAGUENESS] ❏ *You got married, I'm not a cook myself but I am interested in nutrition and all that.* **13** PHRASE You use **at that** after a statement which modifies or emphasizes what you have just said. [EMPHASIS] ❏ *Success never seems to come but through hard work, often physically demanding work at that.* **14** PHRASE You use **that is** or **that is to say** to indicate that you are about to express the same idea more clearly or precisely. ❏ *I am a disappointing, though generally dutiful, student. That is, I do as I'm told.* **15** PHRASE You use **that's it** to indicate that nothing more needs to be done or that the end has been reached. ❏ *When he left the office, that was it, the workday was over.* **16** CONVENTION You use **that's it** to express agreement with or approval of what has just been said or done. [FORMULAE] ❏ *You got married, right?"—"Yeah, that's it."* **17** PHRASE You use **just like that** to emphasize that something happens or is done immediately or in a very simple way, often without much thought or discussion. [INFORMAL, EMPHASIS] ❏ *Just like that, I was in love.* **18** PHRASE You use **that's that** to say there is nothing more you can do or say about a particular matter. [SPOKEN] ❏ *"Well, if that's the way you want it," he replied, tears in his eyes, "I guess that's that."* **19** **like that** → see **like** ③ **20** **this and that** → see **this** **21** **this, that, and the other** → see **this**

② **that** ✦✦✦ /ðət, STRONG ðæt/ **1** CONJ You can use **that** after many verbs, adjectives, nouns, and expressions to introduce a clause in which you report what someone has said, or what they think or feel. ❏ *He called her up one day and said that he and his wife were coming to New York.* **2** CONJ You use **that** after 'it' and a linking verb and an adjective to comment on a situation or fact. ❏ *It's interesting that you like him.* **3** PRON-REL You use **that** to introduce a clause which gives more information to help identify the person or thing you are talking about. ❏ *...pills that will make the problem disappear.* **4** CONJ You use **that** after expressions with 'so' and 'such' in order to introduce the result or effect of something. ❏ *She became so nervous that she shook violently.*

thatch /θætʃ/ (thatches) **1** N-COUNT A **thatch** or a **thatch roof** is a roof made from straw or reeds. ❑ *They would live in a small house with a green door and a new thatch.* **2** N-UNCOUNT **Thatch** is straw or reeds used to make a roof. **3** N-SING [oft N *of* n] You can refer to someone's hair as their **thatch** of hair, especially when it is very thick and messy. ❑ *Teddy ran thick fingers through his unruly thatch of hair.*

thatched /θætʃt/ ADJ A **thatched** house or a house with a **thatched** roof has a roof made of straw or reeds. ❑ *...a 400-year-old thatched cottage.*

thatch|er /θætʃər/ (thatchers) N-COUNT A **thatcher** is a person whose job is making roofs from straw or reeds.

thatch|ing /θætʃɪŋ/ **1** N-UNCOUNT **Thatching** is straw or reeds used to make a roof. **2** N-UNCOUNT **Thatching** is the skill or activity of making roofs from straw or reeds.

that'd /ðætəd/ **That'd** is a spoken form of 'that would,' or of 'that had' when 'had' is an auxiliary verb.

that'll /ðætəl/ **That'll** is a spoken form of 'that will.'

that's /ðæts/ **That's** is a spoken form of 'that is.'

thaw /θɔ/ (thaws, thawing, thawed) **1** V-I When ice, snow, or something else that is frozen **thaws**, it melts. ❑ *It's so cold the snow doesn't get a chance to thaw.* **2** N-COUNT A **thaw** is a period of warmer weather when snow and ice melt, usually at the end of winter. ❑ *We slogged through the mud of an early spring thaw.* **3** V-T/V-I When you **thaw** frozen food or when it **thaws**, you leave it in a place where it can reach room temperature so that it is ready for use. ❑ *Always thaw pastry thoroughly.* • PHRASAL VERB **Thaw out** means the same as **thaw**. ❑ *Thaw it out completely before reheating in a saucepan.* **4** → See feature box at **hot**

the ✦✦✦

The is the definite article. It is used at the beginning of noun groups. **The** is usually pronounced /ðə/ before a consonant and /ði/ before a vowel, but pronounced /ði/ when you are emphasizing it.

1 DET You use **the** at the beginning of noun groups to refer to someone or something that you have already mentioned or identified. ❑ *Six of the 38 people were U.S. citizens.* **2** DET You use **the** at the beginning of a noun group when the first noun is followed by an 'of' phrase or a clause which identifies the person or thing. ❑ *There has been a slight increase in the consumption of meat.* **3** DET You use **the** in front of some nouns that refer to something in our general experience of the world. ❑ *It's always hard to speculate about the future.* **4** DET You use **the** in front of nouns that refer to people, things, services, or institutions that are associated with everyday life. ❑ *The doctor's on his way.* **5** DET You use **the** instead of a possessive determiner, especially when you are talking about a part of someone's body or a member of their family. ❑ *"How's the family?"—"Just fine, thank you."* **6** DET You use **the** in front of a singular noun when you want to make a general statement about things or people of that type. ❑ *An area in which the computer has made considerable strides in recent years is in playing chess.* **7** DET You use **the** with the name of a musical instrument when you are talking about someone's ability to play the instrument. ❑ *Did you play the piano as a child?* **8** DET You use **the** with nationality adjectives and nouns to talk about the people who live in a country. ❑ *The economic policies of the world's biggest nations are judged by results.* **9** DET You use **the** with words such as 'rich,' 'poor,' or 'unemployed' to refer to all people of a particular type. ❑ *Conditions for the poor in Los Angeles have not improved.* **10** DET If you want to refer to a whole family or to a married couple, you can make their surname into a plural and use **the** in front of it. ❑ *The Taylors decided that they would employ an architect to do the work.* **11** DET You use **the** in front of an adjective when you are referring to a particular thing that is described by that adjective. ❑ *He knows he's wishing for the impossible.* **12** DET You use **the** to indicate whether or not you have enough of the thing mentioned for a particular purpose. ❑ *She may not have the money to maintain or restore her property.* **13** DET You use **the** with some titles, place names, and other names. ❑ *...the Seattle Times.* ❑ *...the White House.* ❑ *...The Great Gatsby.* **14** DET You use **the** in front of numbers such as first, second, and third. ❑ *The meeting should take place on the fifth of May.* **15** DET You use **the** in front of numbers when they refer to decades. ❑ *It's sometimes hard to imagine how bad things were in the thirties.* **16** DET You use **the** in front of superlative adjectives and adverbs. ❑ *Brisk daily walks are still the best exercise for young and old alike.* **17** DET You use **the** in front of each of two comparative adjectives or adverbs when you are describing how one amount or quality changes in relation to another. ❑ *The longer the therapy goes on, the more successful it will be.* **18** DET When you express rates, prices, and measurements, you can use **the** to say how many units apply to each of the items being measured. ❑ *...cars that get more miles to the gallon.* **19** DET You use **the** to indicate that something or someone is the most famous, important, or best thing of its kind. In spoken English, you put more stress on it, and in written English, you often underline it or write it in capitals or italics. ❑ *The circus is the place to be this Saturday or Sunday.*

thea|ter ✦✦◇ /θiətər/ (theaters) also **theatre**

in BRIT, use **theatre**

1 N-COUNT; N-IN-NAMES A **theater** is a building with a stage in it, on which plays, shows, and other performances take place. ❑ *They brought her to the theater where their new musical was in production.* **2** N-SING You can refer to work in the theater such as acting or writing plays as **the theater**. ❑ *The story of her career in the theater is told in a new biography.* **3** N-COUNT A **theater** or a **movie theater** is a place where people go to watch movies for entertainment. [AM] ❑ *A movie theater and roller rink attracted customers and profit.*

in BRIT, use **cinema**

4 N-UNCOUNT **Theater** is entertainment that involves the performance of plays. ❑ *...American musical theater.*

SYNONYMS

theater
NOUN **1**
playhouse: *By 1910, the seating capacity of its playhouses and movie theaters approached two million.*
auditorium: *The Albert Hall is a huge auditorium.*
amphitheater: *We visited the amphitheater.*

VOCABULARY IN CONTEXT

Theater

If someone mentions a career in the theater, what image does it conjure for you? Do you immediately think of insufferable **thespian** types **treading the boards**, melodramatic and self-important? It's a widely held view, but a rather unfair one. Actors who are successful in **auditions** have to attend long **rehearsals** and put up with sometimes difficult **directors**. They must **learn their lines** by heart, and know the entire play intimately. Coping with **stage fright** on **opening night**, then waiting for the verdict from the **critics** is not for the faint of heart. And being in the **cast** is only one aspect of theater life. **Staging a production** takes tremendous effort. Someone has to take care of the **costumes**, for example. Then there's the **set design** and the **props**, and **stagehands** to manage them. You need a technician to do the **lighting design**. One thing is for sure: life on the stage is a labor of love.

theater|goer /θiːətərɡoʊər/ (theatergoers)

in BRIT, use **theatre-goer**

N-COUNT **Theatergoers** are people who are at the theater to see a play, or who regularly go to the theater to see plays.

the|at|ri|cal /θiætrɪkəl/ **1** ADJ [ADJ n] **Theatrical** means relating to the theater. □ ...*the most outstanding theatrical performances of the year.* • **the|at|ri|cal|ly** /θiætrɪkli/ ADV □ *Shaffer's great gift lies in his ability to animate ideas theatrically.* **2** ADJ **Theatrical** behavior is exaggerated and unnatural, and intended to create an effect. □ *In a theatrical gesture Jim clamped his hand over his eyes.* • **the|at|ri|cal|ly** ADV □ *He looked theatrically at his watch.*

thee /ðiː/ PRON [v PRON, prep PRON] **Thee** is an old-fashioned, poetic, or religious word for 'you' when you are talking to only one person. It is used as the object of a verb or preposition. □ *I miss thee, beloved father.*

theft /θɛft/ (thefts) N-VAR **Theft** is the crime of stealing. □ *Over the last decade, auto theft has increased by over 56 percent.*

their ◆◆◆ /ðɛər/

Their is the third person plural possessive determiner.

1 DET You use **their** to indicate that something belongs or relates to the group of people, animals, or things that you are talking about. □ *Janis and Kurt have announced their engagement.* **2** DET You use **their** instead of 'his or her' to indicate that something belongs or relates to a person without saying whether that person is a man or a woman. □ *Each student determines their own pace in the yoga class.*

theirs /ðɛərz/

Theirs is the third person plural possessive pronoun.

1 PRON-POSS You use **theirs** to indicate that something belongs or relates to the group of people, animals, or things that you are talking about. □ *There was a big group of a dozen people at the table next to theirs.* **2** PRON-POSS You use **theirs** instead of 'his or hers' to indicate that something belongs or relates to a person without saying whether that person is a man or a woman. □ *He would leave the trailer unlocked. If there was something inside that someone wanted, it would be theirs for the taking.*

them ◆◆◆ /ðəm, STRONG ðɛm/

Them is a third person plural pronoun. Them is used as the object of a verb or preposition.

1 PRON-PLURAL [v PRON, prep PRON] You use **them** to refer to a group of people, animals, or things. □ *The Beatles – I never get tired of listening to them.* □ *Kids these days have no one to tell them what's right and wrong.* **2** PRON-PLURAL [v PRON, prep PRON] You use **them** instead of 'his or her' to refer to a person without saying whether that person is a man or a woman. □ *It takes great courage to face your child and tell them the truth.*

the|mat|ic /θiːmætɪk/ ADJ [usu ADJ n] **Thematic** means concerned with the subject or theme of something, or with themes and topics in general. [FORMAL] □ ...*assembling this material into thematic groups.* • **the|mati|cal|ly** /θiːmætɪkli/ ADV □ ...*a thematically-linked threesome of songs.*

theme ◆◇◇ /θiːm/ (themes) **1** N-COUNT A **theme** in a piece of writing, a talk, or a discussion is an important idea or subject that runs through it. □ *The theme of the conference is renaissance Europe.* **2** N-COUNT A **theme** in an artist's work or in a work of literature is an idea in it that the artist or writer develops or repeats. □ *The novel's central theme is the ongoing conflict between men and women.* **3** N-COUNT A **theme** is a short simple tune on which a piece of music is based. □ ...*variations on themes from Mozart's The Magic Flute.* **4** N-COUNT **Theme** music or a **theme song** is a piece of music that is played at the beginning and end of a movie or of a television or radio program. □ ...*the theme from Dr. Zhivago.*

SYNONYMS

theme
NOUN **1**
subject: ...*steering the conversation around to his favorite subject.*
topic: *The main topic for discussion is political union.*
motif: *The motif of these volumes is that 'solitude is the richness of the soul, loneliness is its poverty.'*

themed /θiːmd/ ADJ [usu ADJ n] A **themed** place or event has been created so that it shows a particular historical time or way of life, or tells a well-known story. [mainly BRIT] □ ...*themed restaurants, bars, and nightclubs.*

-themed /θiːmd/ COMB IN ADJ **-Themed** can be added to adjectives and nouns to form adjectives which describe the particular theme that a place or event has. □ ...*a movie-themed amusement park.* □ ...*a Hawaiian-themed party.*

theme park (theme parks) N-COUNT A **theme park** is a large outdoor area where people pay to go to enjoy themselves. All the different activities in a theme park are usually based on a particular idea or theme.

them|self /ðəmsɛlf/ PRON [v PRON, prep PRON] **Themself** is sometimes used instead of 'himself,' 'herself,' or 'themselves' when it clearly refers to a singular subject. Some people consider this use to be incorrect. □ *No one perceived themself to be in a position to hire such a man.*

them|selves ◆◆◆ /ðəmsɛlvz/

Themselves is the third person plural reflexive pronoun.

1 PRON-REFL [v PRON, prep PRON] You use **themselves** to refer to people, animals, or things when the object of a verb or preposition refers to the same people or things as the subject of the verb. □ *They all seemed to be enjoying themselves.* **2** PRON-REFL-EMPH You use **themselves** to emphasize the people or things that you are referring to. **Themselves** is also sometimes used instead of 'them' as the object of a verb or preposition. [EMPHASIS] □ *Many people with serious health issues are themselves unhappy about the idea of community care.* **3** PRON-REFL [v PRON, prep PRON] You use **themselves** instead of 'himself or herself' to refer back to the person who is the subject of the sentence without saying whether it is a man or a woman. □ *What can a patient with emphysema do to help themselves?* **4** PRON-REFL-EMPH You use **themselves** instead of 'himself or herself' to emphasize the person you are referring to without saying whether it is a man or a woman. **Themselves** is also sometimes used as the object of a verb or preposition. [EMPHASIS] □ *Each student makes only one item themselves.* **5** → see also **ourselves**

then ◆◆◆ /ðɛn/ **1** ADV **Then** means at a particular time in the past or in the future. □ *He wanted to have a source of income after his retirement; until then, he wouldn't require additional money.* □ *Executives pledged to get the company back on track. Since then, though, shares have fallen 30 per cent.* **2** ADJ [ADJ n] **Then** is used when you refer to something which was true at a particular time in the past but is not true now. □ ...*a tour of the then new airport.* • ADV [ADV group] **Then** is also an adverb. □ *Richard Strauss, then 76 years old, suffered through the war years in silence.* **3** ADV You use **then** to say that one thing happens after another, or is after another on a list. □ *Add the oil and then the scallops to the pan, leaving a little space for the garlic.* **4** ADV [cl/group ADV] You use **then** in conversation to indicate that what you are about to say follows logically in some way from what has just been said or implied. □ *"I wasn't a very good scholar in school."—"Then why did you become a teacher?"* **5** ADV [cl/group ADV] You use **then** to signal the end of a topic or the end of a conversation. □ *"I'll talk to you on Friday anyway."—"Yep. Okay then."* **6** ADV [adv ADV] You use **then** with words like 'now,' 'well,' and 'okay,' to introduce a new topic or a new point of view. □ *Now then, I'm going to explain everything to you before we do it.* **7** ADV [ADV cl] You use **then** to introduce the second part of a sentence which begins with 'if.' The first part of the sentence describes a possible situation, and **then** introduces the result of the situation. □ *If the answer is "yes," then we need to leave now.* **8** ADV [ADV cl] You use **then** at the beginning of a sentence or after 'and' or 'but' to introduce a comment or an extra piece of information to what you have already said. □ *He sounded sincere, but then, he always did.* **9 now and then** → see **now** **10 there and then** → see **there**

thence /ðɛns/ **1** ADV **Thence** means from a particular place, especially when you are giving directions about how to get somewhere. [LITERARY, OLD-FASHIONED] □ *I ran straight up to Columbia County, then turned East, came down the Harlem Valley and thence home.* **2** ADV **Thence** is used to say that something changes from one state or condition to another. [LITERARY, OLD-FASHIONED] □ ...*the conversion of sunlight into heat and thence into electricity.*

thence|forth /ðɛnsfɔrθ/ ADV [ADV with cl] **Thenceforth** means starting from a particular time in the past that you have mentioned. [FORMAL] ❑ *My life was totally different thenceforth.*

the|oc|ra|cy /θiɒkrəsi/ (**theocracies**) N-VAR A **theocracy** is a society which is ruled by priests who represent a god.

theo|crat|ic /θiəkrætɪk/ ADJ [usu ADJ n] A **theocratic** society is ruled by priests who represent a god.

theo|lo|gian /θiəloʊdʒən, -dʒiən/ (**theologians**) N-COUNT A **theologian** is someone who studies the nature of God, religion, and religious beliefs.

the|ol|ogy /θiɒlədʒi/ N-UNCOUNT **Theology** is the study of the nature of God and of religion and religious beliefs. ❑ *...questions of theology.* ● **theo|logi|cal** /θiəlɒdʒɪkəl/ ADJ ❑ *...theological books.*

theo|rem /θiərəm/ (**theorems**) N-COUNT A **theorem** is a statement in mathematics or logic that can be proved to be true by reasoning.

theo|reti|cal /θiərɛtɪkəl/ **1** ADJ A **theoretical** study or explanation is based on or uses the ideas and abstract principles that relate to a particular subject, rather than the practical aspects or uses of it. ❑ *...theoretical physics.* **2** ADJ If you describe a situation as a **theoretical** one, you mean that although it is supposed to be true or to exist in the way stated, it may not in fact be true or exist in that way. ❑ *This is certainly a theoretical risk but in practice there is seldom a problem.*

theo|reti|cal|ly /θiərɛtɪkli/ ADV [ADV with cl/group] You use **theoretically** to say that although something is supposed to be true or to happen in the way stated, it may not in fact be true or happen in that way. ❑ *Theoretically, the price is supposed to be marked on the shelf.*

theo|reti|cian /θiərətɪʃən/ (**theoreticians**) N-COUNT A **theoretician** is the same as a **theorist**.

theo|rist /θiərɪst/ (**theorists**) N-COUNT A **theorist** is someone who develops an abstract idea or set of ideas about a particular subject in order to explain it. ❑ *...theorists unaligned with any particular doctrine.*

theo|rize /θiəraɪz/ (**theorizes, theorizing, theorized**)

in BRIT, also use **theorise**

V-T/V-I If you **theorize** that something is true or **theorize** about it, you develop an abstract idea or set of ideas about something in order to explain it. ❑ *Police are theorizing that the robbers may be posing as hitchhikers.* ❑ *By studying the way people behave, we can theorize about what is going on in their mind.* ● **theo|riz|ing** N-UNCOUNT ❑ *This was no time for theorizing.*

theo|ry ✦✧✧ /θiəri/ (**theories**) **1** N-VAR A **theory** is a formal idea or set of ideas that is intended to explain something. ❑ *Marx produced a new theory about historical change based upon conflict between competing groups.* **2** N-COUNT If you have a **theory** about something, you have your own opinion about it which you cannot prove but which you think is true. ❑ *There was a theory that he wanted to marry her.* **3** N-UNCOUNT The **theory** of a practical subject or skill is the set of rules and principles that form the basis of it. ❑ *He taught us music theory.* **4** PHRASE You use **in theory** to say that although something is supposed to be true or to happen in the way stated, it may not in fact be true or happen in that way. ❑ *Achieving these goals is relatively easy in theory, yet quite difficult in practice.*

> **COLLOCATIONS**
>
> **theory**
> NOUN **1**
> noun + **theory**: chaos, quantum, relativity; management
> adjective + **theory**: economic, evolutionary, Marxist, political; classical, linguistic, literary, scientific
> verb + **theory**: apply, develop, formulate, test; challenge, dismiss, disprove, reject; prove, support

thera|peu|tic /θɛrəpyutɪk/ ADJ If something is **therapeutic**, it helps you to relax or to feel better about things, especially about a situation that made you unhappy. ❑ *Having a garden is therapeutic.*

thera|pist /θɛrəpɪst/ (**therapists**) N-COUNT A **therapist** is a person who is skilled in a particular type of therapy, especially psychotherapy. ❑ *My therapist helped me to deal with my anger.*

thera|py ✦✧✧ /θɛrəpi/ (**therapies**) **1** N-UNCOUNT **Therapy** is the process or talking to a trained counselor about your emotional and mental problems and your relationships in order to understand and improve the way you feel and behave. ❑ *Children may need therapy to help them deal with grief and death.* ❑ *Since I've been in therapy, I've grown to be a better husband and father.* **2** N-VAR **Therapy** or a **therapy** is a treatment for a particular illness or condition. [MEDICAL] ❑ *...hormonal therapies.*

> **SYNONYMS**
>
> **therapy**
> NOUN **2**
> **remedy:** *...natural remedies to help overcome winter infections.*
> **treatment:** *Many patients are not getting the medical treatment they need.*
> **cure:** *There is still no cure for a cold.*

there ✦✦✦

Pronounced /ðər/, STRONG /ðɛr/ for meanings 1 and 2, and /ðɛər/ for meanings 3 to 19.

1 PRON [PRON be n] **There** is used as the subject of the verb 'be' to say that something exists or does not exist, or to draw attention to it. ❑ *There are temporary traffic lights now at the school.* ❑ *Are there any cookies left?* **2** PRON [PRON v n] You use **there** in front of certain verbs when you are saying that something exists, develops, or can be seen. Whether the verb is singular or plural depends on the noun which follows the verb. ❑ *There remains considerable doubt over when the road will be completed.* **3** CONVENTION **There** is used after 'hello' or 'hi' when you are greeting someone. [INFORMAL] ❑ *"Hello there," said the woman, smiling at them.—"Hi!" they chorused.* **4** ADV If something is **there**, it exists or is available. ❑ *The group of old buildings is still there today.* **5** ADV You use **there** to refer to a place which has already been mentioned. ❑ *The next day we drove 33 miles to Siena (the Villa Arceno is a great place to stay while you are there).* ❑ *"Come on over, if you want."—"How do I get there?"* **6** ADV You use **there** to indicate a place that you are pointing to or looking at, in order to draw someone's attention to it. ❑ *There it is, on the corner over there.* ❑ *There she is on the left up there.* **7** ADV [ADV cl] You use **there** in expressions such as '**there she was**' or '**there we were**' to sum up part of a story or to slow a story down for dramatic effect. [SPOKEN] ❑ *So there he was all covered in mud, and still in a good mood.* **8** ADV [ADV with be] You use **there** when speaking on the telephone to ask if someone is available to speak to you. ❑ *Hello, is Gordon there please?* **9** ADV [ADV after v] You use **there** to refer to a point that someone has made in a conversation. ❑ *I think you're right there John.* **10** ADV You use **there** to refer to a stage that has been reached in an activity or process. ❑ *We are making further investigations and will take the matter from there.* **11** ADV You use **there** to indicate that something has reached a point or level which is completely successful. ❑ *We had hoped to fill the back page with extra news; we're not quite there yet.* **12** ADV [ADV cl] You can use **there** in expressions such as **there you go** or **there we are** when accepting that an unsatisfactory situation cannot be changed. [SPOKEN] ❑ *This is a little cruel, but there you go.* **13** ADV [ADV cl] You can use **there** in expressions such as **there you go** and **there we are** when emphasizing that something proves that you were right. [SPOKEN, EMPHASIS] ❑ *You see? There you go. That's why I didn't mention it earlier. I knew you'd take it the wrong way.* **14** PHRASE Phrases such as **there you go again** are used to show anger at someone who is repeating something that has annoyed you in the past. [SPOKEN] ❑ *"There you go again, upsetting the child!" said Shirley.* **15** PHRASE You can add '**so there**' to what you are saying to show that you have won an argument, or that you will not change your mind about a decision you have made, even though the person you are talking to disagrees with you. This is usually said by children or to be funny. [INFORMAL] ❑ *I didn't that's sweet, so there.* ❑ *You see? Mom said I could - so there!* **16** PHRASE If something happens **there and then** or **then and there**, it happens immediately. ❑ *Many felt that he should have resigned there and then.* **17** CONVENTION You say '**there there**' to someone who is very upset, especially a small child, in order to comfort them. [SPOKEN] ❑ *"There, there," said Mommy. "You've been having a bad dream."* **18** CONVENTION You say '**there you are**' or '**there you go**' when you are offering something to someone. [SPOKEN, FORMULAE] ❑ *"There you go, Mr. Walters," she said, giving him his* documents. **10** PHRASE If someone **is there for** you, they help and support you, especially when you have problems. [INFORMAL] ◻ *Despite what happened in the past I want her to know I am there for her.*

USAGE

there

1 Don't use 'there is' or 'there are' with **since** to say how long ago something happened. Don't say, for example, 'There are four days since she arrived in London.' Say '**It's been** four days since she arrived in London' or 'She arrived in London four days **ago**.' *It's been three months since you were there last.*

2 Don't use 'to' in front of **there**. Don't say, for example, 'I like going to there.' Say 'I like going **there**.' *My family lives in India. I still go **there** often.*

there|abouts /ðɛərəbaʊts/ PHRASE [n/num PHR] You add **or thereabouts** after a number or date to indicate that it is approximate. ◻ *He told us that her age was forty-eight or thereabouts.*

there|after /ðɛəræftər/ ADV [ADV with cl] **Thereafter** means after the event or date mentioned. [FORMAL] ◻ *The plan will help you lose 3-4 pounds the first week, and 1-2 pounds the weeks thereafter.*

there|by /ðɛərbaɪ/ ADV [ADV with cl] You use **thereby** to introduce an important result or consequence of the event or action you have just mentioned. [FORMAL] ◻ *Our bodies can sweat, thereby losing heat by evaporation.*

there|fore ♦♦◇ /ðɛərfɔr/ ADV [ADV with cl/group] You use **therefore** to introduce a logical result or conclusion. ◻ *Muscle cells need lots of fuel and therefore burn lots of calories.*

SYNONYMS

therefore
ADV
consequently: *Relations between the two companies had, consequently, never been close.*
thus: *...women's access to the basic means of production, and thus to political power.*
so: *I was an only child, and so had no experience of large families.*
hence: *The Socialist Party was profoundly divided, and hence very weak.*

there|in /ðɛərɪn/ **1** ADV [n ADV] **Therein** means contained in the place that has been mentioned. [LITERARY] ◻ *By burning tree branches, pine needles, and pine cones, many not only warm their houses but improve the smell therein.* **2** ADV [n ADV] **Therein** means relating to something that has just been mentioned. [FORMAL] ◻ *Afternoon groups relate to the specific addictions and problems therein.*

there|of /ðɛərʌv/ ADV [n ADV] **Thereof** is used after a noun to relate that noun to a situation or thing that you have just mentioned. [FORMAL] ◻ *...his belief in God—or the lack thereof.*

there|on /ðɛərɒn/ **1** ADV [ADV after v] **Thereon** means on the object or surface just mentioned. [FORMAL] ◻ *...broad porches with Victorian ladies fanning themselves thereon.* **2** ADV [n ADV, ADV after v] **Thereon** can be used to refer back to a thing that has previously been mentioned to show that the word just used relates to that thing. [FORMAL] ◻ *You will, in addition, pay to the bank any losses, costs, expenses or legal fees (including tax thereon).*

there|upon /ðɛərəpɒn/ ADV [ADV with cl] **Thereupon** means happening immediately after something else has happened and usually as a result of it. [FORMAL] ◻ *Some months ago angry demonstrators mounted a noisy demonstration beneath his window. His neighbors thereupon insisted upon more security.*

therm /θɜrm/ (**therms**) N-COUNT [num N] A **therm** is a measurement of heat.

ther|mal /θɜrm°l/ (**thermals**) **1** ADJ [ADJ n] **Thermal** means relating to or caused by heat or by changes in temperature. ◻ *...thermal power stations.* **2** ADJ [ADJ n] **Thermal** streams or baths contain water which is naturally hot or warm. ◻ *Volcanic activity has created thermal springs and boiling mud pools.* **3** ADJ [ADJ n] **Thermal** clothes are specially designed to keep you warm in cold weather. ◻ *...thermal underwear.* ◻ *My feet were like blocks of ice despite the thermal socks.* • N-PLURAL **Thermals** are thermal clothes. ◻ *Have you got your thermals on?* **4** N-COUNT A **thermal** is a movement of rising warm air. ◻ *Birds use thermals to lift them through the air.*

ther|mal im|ag|ing N-UNCOUNT **Thermal imaging** is the use of special equipment that can detect the heat produced by people or things and use it to produce images of them. ◻ *He was found by a police helicopter using thermal imaging equipment.*

ther|mo- /θɜrmoʊ/ COMB IN ADJ **Thermo-** combines with adjectives to form adjectives that mean using or relating to heat. ◻ *...the dangers of thermonuclear war.* • COMB IN N **Thermo-** also combines to form nouns. ◻ *The body is made of mineral-reinforced thermoplastic.*

ther|mo|dy|nam|ics /θɜrmoʊdaɪnæmɪks/

The form **thermodynamic** is used as a modifier.

N-UNCOUNT **Thermodynamics** is the branch of physics that is concerned with the relationship between heat and other forms of energy.

ther|mom|eter /θərmɒmɪtər/ (**thermometers**) N-COUNT A **thermometer** is an instrument for measuring temperature. It usually consists of a narrow glass tube containing a thin column of a liquid which rises and falls as the temperature rises and falls.

ther|mo|nu|clear /θɜrmoʊnukliər/ ADJ [ADJ n] A **thermonuclear** weapon or device uses the high temperatures from a nuclear reaction in order to cause a very powerful explosion.

ther|mo|plas|tic /θɜrmoʊplæstɪk/ (**thermoplastics**) N-COUNT [usu N n] **Thermoplastics** are types of plastic which becomes soft when they are heated and hard when they cool down.

Ther|mos /θɜrməs/ (**Thermoses**) N-COUNT A **Thermos** is a container which is used to keep hot drinks hot or cold drinks cold. It has two thin shiny glass walls with no air between them. [TRADEMARK]

ther|mo|stat /θɜrməstæt/ (**thermostats**) N-COUNT A **thermostat** is a device that switches a system or motor on or off according to the temperature. Thermostats are used, for example, in central heating systems and refrigerators.

the|sau|rus /θɪsɔrəs/ (**thesauruses**) N-COUNT A **thesaurus** is a reference book in which words with similar meanings are grouped together.

these ♦♦♦

The determiner is pronounced /ðiz/. The pronoun is pronounced /ðiz/.

1 DET You use **these** at the beginning of noun groups to refer to someone or something that you have already mentioned or identified. ◻ *A committee has been formed. These people can make decisions in ten minutes which would take us months.* • PRON **These** is also a pronoun. ◻ *"I have faith in these guys," the coach said. "These are good players."* **2** DET You use **these** to introduce people or things that you are going to talk about. ◻ *Make sure that they include these features: 24/7 accessibility, and full technical support.* • PRON **These** is also a pronoun. ◻ *Take care of yourself while you are pregnant. These are some of the things you can do for yourself.* **3** DET In spoken English, people use **these** to introduce people or things into a story. ◻ *I was by myself and these guys suddenly came towards me.* **4** PRON You use **these** when you are identifying a group or asking about their identity. ◻ *These are my children.* **5** DET You use **these** to refer to people or things that are near you, especially when you touch them or point to them. ◻ *These scissors are awfully heavy.* • PRON **These** is also a pronoun. ◻ *These are the people who are helping us.* **6** DET You use **these** when you refer to something which you expect the person you are talking to to know about, or when you are checking that you are both thinking of the same person or thing. ◻ *You know these last few months when we've been expecting it to warm up a little bit?* **7** DET You use **these** in the expression **these days** to mean 'at the present time.' ◻ *These days, people appreciate a chance to relax.*

the|sis /θisɪs/ (**theses** /θisiz/) **1** N-COUNT A **thesis** is an idea or theory that is expressed as a statement and is discussed in a logical way. ◻ *This thesis does not stand up to close inspection.* **2** N-COUNT A **thesis** is a long piece of writing based on your own ideas and research that you do as part of a college degree, especially a higher degree such as a Ph.D.

thes|pian /θɛspiən/ (**thespians**) **1** N-COUNT A **thespian** is an actor or actress. [HUMOROUS or OLD-FASHIONED] **2** ADJ [ADJ n]

Thespian means relating to drama and the theater. [OLD-FASHIONED] → See feature box at **theater**

they /ðeɪ/

They is a third person plural pronoun. They is used as the subject of a verb.

1 PRON-PLURAL You use **they** to refer to a group of people, animals, or things. ▫ *Feed the dogs because they haven't eaten.* ▫ *The two men were far more alike than they would ever admit.* ▫ *People matter because of what they are, not what they have.* **2** PRON-PLURAL You use **they** instead of 'he or she' to refer to a person without saying whether that person is a man or a woman. ▫ *The teacher is not responsible for the student's success or failure. They are only there to help the student learn.* **3** PRON-PLURAL You use **they** in expressions such as 'they say' or 'they call it' to refer to people in general when you are making general statements about what people say, think, or do. [VAGUENESS] ▫ *They say there's plenty of opportunities out there, you just have to look carefully and you'll find them.*

USAGE

they
Don't use 'they' with **are** to say that a number of things exist or are in a particular place. Don't say, for example, 'They are two bottles of juice in the refrigerator.' Say 'There are two bottles of juice in the refrigerator.' **There are** always plenty of jobs to be done.

they'd /ðeɪd/ **1** **They'd** is a spoken form of 'they had,' especially when 'had' is an auxiliary verb. ▫ *They'd both lived on this road all their lives.* **2** **They'd** is a spoken form of 'they would.' ▫ *He agreed that they'd visit her after they stopped at Jan's for coffee.*

they'll /ðeɪl/ **They'll** is the usual spoken form of 'they will.' ▫ *They'll probably be here Monday and Tuesday.*

they're /ðɛər/ **They're** is the usual spoken form of 'they are.' ▫ *Some people eat when they're depressed.*

they've /ðeɪv/ **They've** is the usual spoken form of 'they have,' especially when 'have' is an auxiliary verb. ▫ *The worst thing is when you call friends and they've gone out.*

thick /θɪk/ (**thicker, thickest**) **1** ADJ Something that is **thick** has a large distance between its two opposite sides. ▫ *For breakfast I had a thick slice of bread and butter.* ▫ *He wore thick glasses.* • **thick|ly** ADV [ADV with v] ▫ *Slice the meat thickly.* **2** ADJ You can use **thick** to talk or ask about how wide or deep something is. ▫ *The folder was two inches thick.* • COMB IN ADJ [ADJ n] **Thick** is also a combining form. ▫ *His life was saved by a quarter-inch-thick bullet-proof vest.* • **thick|ness** (**thicknesses**) N-VAR ▫ *The size of the fish will determine the thickness of the steaks.* **3** ADJ If something that consists of several things is **thick**, it has a large number of them very close together. ▫ *She inherited our father's thick, wavy hair.* • **thick|ly** ADV ▫ *I rounded a bend where the trees and brush grew thickly.* **4** ADJ [v-link ADJ with n] If something is **thick with** another thing, the first thing is full of or covered with the second. ▫ *The air is thick with acrid smoke from the fires.* **5** ADJ **Thick** clothes are made from heavy cloth, so that they will keep you warm in cold weather. ▫ *In the winter she wears thick socks, boots and gloves.* **6** ADJ **Thick** smoke, fog, or cloud is difficult to see through. ▫ *The smoke was bluish-black and thick.* **7** ADJ **Thick** liquids are fairly stiff and solid and do not flow easily. ▫ *It had rained last night, so the garden was thick mud.* **8** → See feature box at **weather**

thick|en /θɪkən/ (**thickens, thickening, thickened**) **1** V-T/V-I When you **thicken** a liquid or when it **thickens**, it becomes stiffer and more solid. ▫ *Thicken the broth with the mashed potato.* **2** V-I If something **thickens**, it becomes more closely grouped together or more solid than it was before. ▫ *The dust behind us grew closer and thickened into a cloud.*

thick|en|er /θɪkənər/ (**thickeners**) N-MASS A **thickener** is a substance that is added to a liquid in order to make it stiffer and more solid. ▫ *...cornstarch, used as a thickener.* ▫ *How much thickener is used?*

thick|et /θɪkɪt/ (**thickets**) N-COUNT A **thicket** is a small group of trees or bushes which are growing closely together.

thick|set /θɪksɛt/ also **thick-set** ADJ Someone who is **thickset** is broad and heavy, with a solid-looking body. ▫ *He was of middle height, thick-set.* ▫ *...his stout, thickset figure.*

thick-skinned ADJ [usu v-link ADJ] If you say that someone is **thick-skinned**, you mean that they are not easily upset by criticism or insults. ▫ *He was thick-skinned enough to cope with her taunts.*

thief /θiːf/ (**thieves** /θiːvz/) N-COUNT A **thief** is a person who steals something from another person. ▫ *The thieves snatched the camera.*

thiev|ing /θiːvɪŋ/ **1** ADJ [ADJ n] **Thieving** means involved in stealing things or intending to steal something. ▫ *In the midst of a heated argument, Charlotte evicts her thieving houseguest from her home.* **2** N-UNCOUNT **Thieving** is the act of stealing things from people. [OLD-FASHIONED] ▫ *...an ex-con who says he's given up thieving.*

thigh /θaɪ/ (**thighs**) N-COUNT Your **thighs** are the top parts of your legs, between your knees and your hips. ▫ *The shorts are so small I can't fit my thighs into any of them.*

thim|ble /θɪmbəl/ (**thimbles**) N-COUNT A **thimble** is a small metal or plastic object which you use to protect your finger when you are sewing.

thin /θɪn/ (**thinner, thinnest, thins, thinning, thinned**) **1** ADJ Something that is **thin** is much narrower than it is long. ▫ *A thin cable carries the signal to a computer.* **2** ADJ A person or animal that is **thin** has no extra fat on their body. ▫ *He was a tall, thin man with gray hair that fell in a wild tangle to his shoulders.* **3** ADJ Something such as paper or cloth that is **thin** is flat and has only a very small distance between its two opposite surfaces. ▫ *...a small, blue-bound book printed in fine type on thin paper.* • **thin|ly** ADV [ADV with v] ▫ *Peel and thinly slice the onion.* **4** ADJ Liquids that are **thin** are weak and watery. ▫ *The soup was thin and clear, yet mysteriously rich.* **5** ADJ A crowd or audience that is **thin** does not have many people in it. ▫ *The crowd, which had been thin for the first half of the race, had now grown considerably.* • **thin|ly** ADV [ADV -ed] ▫ *The island is thinly populated.* **6** ADJ **Thin** clothes are made from light cloth and are not warm to wear. ▫ *Her gown was thin, and she shivered, partly from cold.* **7** ADJ If you describe an argument, an explanation, or evidence as **thin**, you mean that it is weak and difficult to believe. ▫ *The DA was certain she had the right man, but the evidence was thin.* • **thin|ly** ADV ▫ *Much of the speech was a thinly disguised attack on environmentalists.* **8** ADJ If someone's hair is described as **thin**, they do not have a lot of hair. ▫ *She had pale thin yellow hair she pulled back into a bun.* **9** V-T/V-I When you **thin** something or when it **thins**, it becomes less crowded because people or things have been removed from it. ▫ *It would have been better to have thinned the trees over several winters rather than all at one time.* • PHRASAL VERB **Thin out** means the same as **thin**. ▫ *NATO will continue to thin out its forces.* **10** PHRASE If someone's patience, for example, **is wearing thin**, they are beginning to become impatient or angry with someone. ▫ *War has achieved little, and public patience is wearing thin.* **11** on thin ice → see **ice** **12** thin air → see **air**

thine /ðaɪn/ PRON **Thine** is an old-fashioned, poetic, or religious word for 'yours' when you are talking to only one person. ▫ *I am Thine, O Lord, I have heard Thy voice.*

THING
① NOUN USES
② PHRASES

① **thing** /θɪŋ/ (**things**) **1** N-COUNT You can use **thing** to refer to any object, feature, or event when you cannot, need not, or do not want to refer to it more precisely. ▫ *"What's that thing in the middle of the fountain?"—"Some kind of statue, I guess."* ▫ *She was in the middle of clearing the breakfast things.* **2** N-COUNT **Thing** is used in lists and descriptions to give examples or to increase the range of what you are referring to. ▫ *They spend their money on things like rent and groceries.* **3** N-COUNT **Thing** is often used after an adjective, where it would also be possible just to use the adjective. For example, you can say **it's a different thing** instead of **it's different**. ▫ *Of course, literary isn't the same thing as intelligence.* **4** N-SING **Thing** is often used instead of the pronouns 'anything' or 'everything' in order to emphasize what you are saying. [EMPHASIS] ▫ *I haven't done a thing all day.* ▫ *It isn't going to solve a single thing.* **5** N-COUNT **Thing** is used in expressions such as **such a thing** or **a thing like that**, especially in negative statements, in order to emphasize the bad or difficult situation you are referring back to. [EMPHASIS]

❑ *I don't believe he would tell Leo such a thing.* **6** N-COUNT You can use **thing** to refer in a vague way to a situation, activity, or idea, especially when you want to suggest that it is not very important. [INFORMAL, VAGUENESS] ❑ *I'm a bit unsettled tonight. This war thing's upsetting me.* **7** N-COUNT You often use **thing** to indicate to the person you are addressing that you are about to mention something important, or something that you particularly want them to know. ❑ *One thing I am sure of was that she was scared.* **8** N-COUNT A **thing** is often used to refer back to something that has just been mentioned, either to emphasize it or to give more information about it. ❑ *Getting drunk is a thing many young people do.* **9** N-COUNT A **thing** is a physical object that is considered as having no life of its own. ❑ *It's not a thing. It's a human being!* **10** N-COUNT **Thing** is used to refer to something, especially a physical object, when you want to express contempt or anger toward it. [SPOKEN, DISAPPROVAL] ❑ *Turn that thing off!* **11** N-COUNT You can call a person or an animal a particular **thing** when you want to mention a particular quality that they have and express your feelings toward them, usually affectionate feelings. [INFORMAL] ❑ *She is such a cute little thing.* **12** N-PLURAL Your **things** are your clothes or possessions. ❑ *Sara told him to take all his things and not to return.* **13** N-PLURAL **Things** can refer to the situation or life in general and the way it is changing or affecting you. ❑ *Everyone agrees things are getting better.*

② **thing** ♦♦♦ /θɪŋ/ (things)
→ Please look at meaning **11** to see if the expression you are looking for is shown under another headword.

1 PHRASE If, for example, you **do the right thing** or **do the decent thing** in a situation, you do something which is considered correct or socially acceptable in that situation. ❑ *People want to do the right thing and buy "green."* **2** PHRASE If you do something **first thing**, you do it at the beginning of the day, before you do anything else. If you do it **last thing**, you do it at the end of the day, before you go to bed or go to sleep. ❑ *I'll go see her, first thing.* **3** PHRASE You say **it is a** good **thing to** do something to introduce a piece of advice or a comment on a situation or activity. ❑ *Can you tell me whether it is a good thing to prune an apple tree?* **4** PHRASE You can say that the first of two ideas, actions, or situations **is one thing** when you want to contrast it with a second idea, action, or situation and emphasize that the second one is much more difficult, important, or extreme. [EMPHASIS] ❑ *It was one thing to talk about leaving; it was another to physically walk out the door.* **5** PHRASE You can say **for one thing** when you are explaining a statement or answering a question, to suggest that you are not giving the whole explanation or answer, and that there are other points that you could add to it. ❑ *She was a monster. For one thing, she really enjoyed cruelty.* **6** PHRASE You can use the expression '**one thing and another**' to suggest that there are several reasons for something or several items on a list, but you are not going to explain or mention them all. [SPOKEN] ❑ *What with one thing and another, it was fairly late in the day when we got home.* **7** PHRASE If you say **it is just one of those things** you mean that you cannot explain something because it seems to happen by chance. ❑ *"I wonder why." Mr. Dambar shrugged. "It must be just one of those things, I guess."* **8** PHRASE If you say that someone **is seeing** or **hearing things**, you mean that they believe they are seeing or hearing something, but it is not really there. ❑ *Dr. Payne led Lana back into the examination room and told her she was seeing things.* **9** PHRASE You can say there **is no such thing** as something to emphasize that it does not exist or is not possible. [EMPHASIS] ❑ *There really is no such thing as a totally risk-free industry.* **10** PHRASE You say **the thing is** to introduce an explanation, comment, or statement that relates to something that has just been said. **The thing is** is often used to identify a problem relating to what has just been said. [SPOKEN] ❑ *"What does your market research consist of?"—"Well, the thing is, it depends on our target age group."* **11** **other things being equal** → see equal

thingum|my /ˈθɪŋəmi/ (thingummies) N-COUNT Thingummy is the same as **thingy**. [BRIT, INFORMAL, SPOKEN]

thingy /ˈθɪŋi/ (thingies) N-COUNT You refer to something or someone as **thingy** when you do not know or cannot be bothered to use the proper word or name for them. [INFORMAL, SPOKEN] ❑ *...the new phone thingy.* ❑ *...what's his name, Jack Thingy.*

THINK
① VERB AND NOUN USES
② PHRASES
③ PHRASAL VERBS

① **think** ♦♦♦ /θɪŋk/ (thinks, thinking, thought) **1** V-T/V-I [no cont] If you **think** that something is the case, you believe that it is the case. ❑ *I certainly think that the film will attract people into the country.* ❑ *A generation ago, it was thought that babies born this small could not survive.* ❑ *Tell me, what do you think of my theory?* **2** V-T [no cont] If you say that you **think** that something is true or will happen, you mean that you have the impression that it is true or will happen, although you are not certain of the facts. ❑ *Nora thought he was seventeen years old.* ❑ *The storm is thought to be responsible for as many as four deaths.* **3** V-T/V-I [no cont, no passive] If you **think** in a particular way, you have those general opinions or attitudes. ❑ *You were probably brought up to think like that.* ❑ *If you think as I do, vote as I do.* ❑ *I don't blame you for thinking that way.* **4** V-I When you **think** about ideas or problems, you make a mental effort to consider them. ❑ *She closed her eyes for a moment, trying to think.* ❑ *I have often thought about this problem.* • N-SING [a N] **Think** is also a noun. [mainly BRIT] ❑ *I'll have a think about that.* **5** V-T/V-I [no passive] If you **think** in a particular way, you consider things, solve problems, or make decisions in this way, for example, because of your job or your background. ❑ *To make the computer work at full capacity, the programmer has to think like the machine.* ❑ *Why do they think the way they do?* **6** V-T/V-I [no cont] If you **think** of something, it comes into your mind or you remember it. ❑ *Nobody could think of anything to say.* ❑ *I was trying to think what else we had to do.* **7** V-I If you **think of** an idea, you make a mental effort and use your imagination and intelligence to create it or develop it. ❑ *He thought of another way of making electricity.* **8** V-T [no passive] If you **are thinking** something at a particular moment, you have words or ideas in your mind without saying them out loud. ❑ *She must be sick, Tatiana thought.* ❑ *I remember thinking how lovely he looked.* **9** V-T/V-I [no cont] If you **think of** someone or something as having a particular quality or purpose, you regard them as having this quality or purpose. ❑ *We all thought of him as a father.* ❑ *He thinks of it as his home.* ❑ *I wouldn't have thought him capable of it.* **10** V-T/V-I [no cont] If you **think** a lot **of** someone or something, you admire them very much or think they are very good. ❑ *To tell the truth, I don't think much of politicians.* ❑ *Everyone in my family thought very highly of him.* **11** V-I If you **think of** someone or about someone, you show consideration for them and pay attention to their needs. ❑ *I'm only thinking of you.* **12** V-I If you **are thinking of** or **are thinking about** taking a particular course of action, you are considering it as a possible course of action. ❑ *Martin was thinking of taking legal action against Zuckerman.* **13** V-I [usu cont] You can say that you **are thinking of** a particular aspect or subject, in order to introduce an example or explain more exactly what you are talking about. ❑ *The parts of the enterprise which are scientifically the most exciting are unlikely to be militarily useful. I am thinking here of the development of new kinds of lasers.* **14** V-I [only interrog] You use **think** in questions where you are expressing your anger or shock at someone's behavior. [DISAPPROVAL] ❑ *What were you thinking of? You shouldn't steal.* **15** V-T/V-I [no cont, no passive] You use **think** when you are commenting on something which you did or experienced in the past and which now seems surprising, foolish, or shocking to you. ❑ *To think I left you alone in a strange place.* ❑ *When I think of how you've behaved and the trouble you've caused!* **16** → see also **thinking**, **thought**

SYNONYMS

think
VERB ① **2**
consider: *I consider activities such as jogging and weightlifting as unnatural.*
reckon: *He reckoned he was still fond of her.*
believe: *Experts believe that the coming drought will be extensive.*
imagine: *I imagine you're referring to Jean-Paul Sartre.*

---

② **think** ♦♦♦ /θɪŋk/ (thinks, thinking, thought)
→ Please look at meanings **8** – **11** to see if the expression you are looking for is shown under another headword.

think

☐ PHRASE You use expressions such as **come to think of it**, **when you think about it**, or **thinking about it**, when you mention something that you have suddenly remembered or realized. ☐ *He was her distant relative, as was everyone else on the island, come to think of it.* ☐ PHRASE You use '**I think**' as a way of being polite when you are explaining or suggesting to someone what you want to do, or when you are accepting or refusing an offer. [POLITENESS] ☐ *I think I'll go home and have a shower.* ☐ PHRASE You use '**I think**' in conversations or speeches to make your statements and opinions sound less forceful, rude, or direct. [VAGUENESS] ☐ *Thanks, but I think I can handle it.* ☐ PHRASE You say **just think** when you feel excited, fascinated, or shocked by something, and you want the listener to feel the same. ☐ *Just think; tomorrow we shall walk out of this place and leave it all behind us forever.* ☐ PHRASE If you **think again** about an action or decision, you consider it very carefully, often with the result that you change your mind and decide to do things differently. ☐ *It has forced politicians to think again about the wisdom of trying to evacuate refugees.* ☐ PHRASE If you **think nothing of** doing something that other people might consider difficult, strange, or wrong, you consider it to be easy or normal. ☐ *I thought nothing of betting $1,000 on a horse.* ☐ PHRASE If something happens and you **think nothing of it**, you do not pay much attention to it or think of it as strange or important, although later you realise that it is. ☐ *When she went off to see her parents for the weekend I thought nothing of it.* ☐ you can't hear yourself think → see hear ☐ to think better of it → see better ① ☐ to think big → see big ☐ to think twice → see twice

③ **think** ♦♦♦ /θɪŋk/ (thinks, thinking, thought)
▶ **think back** PHRASAL VERB If you **think back**, you make an effort to remember things that happened to you in the past. ☐ *I thought back to the time in 1995 when my son was desperately ill.*
▶ **think over** PHRASAL VERB If you **think** something **over**, you consider it carefully before making a decision. ☐ *She said she needs time to think it over.*
▶ **think through** PHRASAL VERB If you **think** a situation **through**, you consider it thoroughly, together with all its possible effects or consequences. ☐ *I didn't think through the consequences of promotion.* ☐ *The administration has not really thought through what it plans to do once the fighting stops.*
▶ **think up** PHRASAL VERB If you **think** something **up**, for example, an idea or plan, you invent it using mental effort. ☐ *Julian has been thinking up new ways of raising money.*

think|er /θɪŋkər/ (thinkers) N-COUNT A **thinker** is a person who spends a lot of time thinking deeply about important things, especially someone who is famous for thinking of new or interesting ideas. ☐ *...some of the world's greatest thinkers.*

think|ing ♦♦◊ /θɪŋkɪŋ/ ☐ N-UNCOUNT **Thinking** is the activity of using your brain by considering a problem or possibility or creating an idea. ☐ *This is a time of decisive action and quick thinking.* ☐ N-UNCOUNT The general ideas or opinions of a person or group can be referred to as their **thinking**. ☐ *There was undeniably a strong theoretical dimension to his thinking.* ☐ → see also **wishful thinking**

think piece (think pieces) N-COUNT A **think piece** is an article in a newspaper or magazine that discusses a particular subject in a serious and thoughtful way.

think-tank (think-tanks) N-COUNT-COLL A **think-tank** is a group of experts who are gathered together by an organization, especially by a government, to consider various problems and try and work out ways to solve them. ☐ *...Moscow's leading foreign policy think-tank.*

thin|ner /θɪnər/ (thinners) N-VAR **Thinner** is a liquid such as turpentine that you add to paint or varnish in order to dilute it. ☐ *...toxic solvents like paint thinners.*

thin-skinned ADJ [usu v-link ADJ] If you say that someone is **thin-skinned**, you mean that they are easily upset by criticism. [DISAPPROVAL] ☐ *Some fear he is too thin-skinned to survive a presidential campaign.*

third ♦♦◊ /θɜːrd/ (thirds) ☐ ORD The **third** item in a series is the one that you count as number three. ☐ *I sleep on the third floor.* ☐ FRACTION A **third** is one of three equal parts of something. ☐ *A third of the cost went into technology and services.* ☐ ADV You say **third** when you want to make a third point or give a third reason for something. ☐ *First, interest rates may take longer to fall than is hoped. Second, lending may fall. Third, bad loans could wipe out much of any improvement.* ☐ N-COUNT A **third** is the lowest honors degree that can be obtained from a British university. ☐ *...Ms. Hodge, who graduated in 2002 with a third in economics.*

third-class ☐ ADJ In the United States, **third-class** mail is mail consisting of advertising material such as brochures and fliers, which is cheaper to send than other types of mail. [AM] ☐ *The cost of third-class mail has gone up by 50 per cent.* ☐ ADJ [usu ADJ n] In the past, the **third-class** accommodations on a train or ship were the cheapest and least comfortable accommodations. ☐ *...third-class passengers.* ☐ ADJ [ADJ n] A **third-class** degree is the lowest honors degree that can be obtained from a British university.

third-degree ☐ ADJ [ADJ n] **Third-degree** burns are very severe, destroying tissue under the skin. ☐ *He suffered third-degree burns over 98 percent of his body.* ☐ N-SING [usu the N] If you say that someone has been given the **third degree**, you mean that they have been questioned extremely severely, sometimes with physical violence. [INFORMAL] ☐ *I'm not going to give you the third degree or anything.*

third|ly /θɜːrdli/ ADV You use **thirdly** when you want to make a third point or give a third reason for something. ☐ *First of all, there are not many of them, and secondly, they have little money and, thirdly, they're hungry.*

third par|ty (third parties) N-COUNT A **third party** is someone who is not one of the main people involved in a business agreement or legal case, but who is involved in it in a minor role. ☐ *You can instruct your bank to allow a third party to remove money from your account.*

third per|son ☐ N-SING [the N] In grammar, a statement in the **third person** is a statement about another person or thing, and not directly about yourself or about the person you are talking to. The subject of a statement like this is 'he,' 'she,' 'it,' or a name or noun. ☐ → see also **first person**, **second person**

third rail (third rails) ☐ N-COUNT The **third rail** on a railroad track is the steel bar which passes electric current to a train. ☐ N-SING [the N] If you refer to something as the **third rail** of a political situation, you mean that it would be dangerous to make changes to that thing because people feel very strongly about it. [AM] ☐ *Politicians speak of Social Security as the third rail. To touch it is to commit political suicide.*

third-rate ADJ [usu ADJ n] If you describe something as **third-rate**, you mean that it is of a very low quality or standard. ☐ *...a third-rate movie.*

Third World ♦◊◊ N-PROPER The countries of Africa, Asia, and Central and South America are sometimes referred to all together as **the Third World**, especially those parts that are poor, do not have much power, and are not considered to be highly developed. [OLD-FASHIONED] ☐ *...development in the Third World.*

thirst /θɜːrst/ (thirsts) ☐ N-VAR **Thirst** is the feeling of wanting to drink something. ☐ *Instead of tea or coffee, drink water to quench your thirst.* ☐ N-UNCOUNT **Thirst** is the condition of not having enough to drink. ☐ *They died of thirst on the voyage.*

thirsty /θɜːrsti/ (thirstier, thirstiest) ADJ If you are **thirsty**, you feel a need to drink something. ☐ *Drink whenever you feel thirsty during exercise.*

thir|teen ♦♦◊ /θɜːrtiːn/ (thirteens) NUM **Thirteen** is the number 13.

thir|teenth ♦♦◊ /θɜːrtiːnθ/ ORD The **thirteenth** item in a series is the one that you count as number thirteen. ☐ *...his thirteenth birthday.*

thir|ti|eth ♦♦◊ /θɜːrtiəθ/ ORD The **thirtieth** item in a series is the one that you count as number thirty. ☐ *...the thirtieth anniversary of my parents' wedding.*

thir|ty ♦♦♦ /θɜːrti/ (thirties) ☐ NUM **Thirty** is the number 30. ☐ N-PLURAL When you talk about the **thirties**, you are referring to numbers between 30 and 39. For example, if you are **in your thirties**, you are aged between 30 and 39. If the temperature is **in the thirties**, the temperature is between 30 and 39 degrees. ☐ *Mozart clearly enjoyed good health throughout his twenties and early thirties.* ☐ N-PLURAL **The thirties** is the decade between 1930 and 1939. ☐ *She became quite a notable director in the thirties and forties.*

this ♦♦♦

The determiner is pronounced /ðɪs/. In other cases, **this** is pronounced /ðɪs/.

1 DET You use **this** to refer back to a particular person or thing that has been mentioned or implied. ◻ *The entire portfolio is worth $160,312. Of this amount, my investment is worth only $7,748.* • PRON **This** is also a pronoun. ◻ *I don't know how bad the injury is, because I have never had one like this before.* **2** PRON You use **this** to introduce someone or something that you are going to talk about. ◻ *This is what I will do. I will telephone Anna and explain.* • DET **This** is also a determiner. ◻ *This report is from our Science Unit.* **3** PRON You use **this** to refer back to an idea or situation expressed in a previous sentence or sentences. ◻ *You feel that it's uneconomical. Why is this?* • DET **This** is also a determiner. ◻ *There have been continual demands to put an end to this situation.* **4** DET In spoken English, people use **this** to introduce a person or thing into a story. ◻ *I came here by chance and was just watching what was going on, when this girl came up to me.* **5** PRON You use **this** to refer to a person or thing that is near you, especially when you touch them or point to them. When there are two or more people or things near you, **this** refers to the nearest one. ◻ *I like this coat better than that one.* ◻ *"If you'd prefer something else I'll gladly have it changed for you."—"No, this is great."* • DET **This** is also a determiner. ◻ *This church was built by the Emperor Constantine Monomarchus in the eleventh century.* **6** PRON [PRON with *be*] You use **this** when you refer to a general situation, activity, or event which is happening or has just happened and which you feel involved in. ◻ *I thought, this is why I've traveled thousands of miles.* **7** DET You use **this** when you refer to the place you are in now or to the present time. ◻ *This country is weird.* ◻ *This place is run like a hotel ought to be run.* • PRON **This** is also a pronoun. ◻ *This is the worst place I've come across.* **8** DET You use **this** to refer to the next occurrence in the future of a particular day, month, season, or festival. ◻ *...this Sunday's 7:45 performance.* **9** ADV [ADV adj] You use **this** when you are indicating the size or shape of something with your hands. ◻ *"They'd said the wound was only about this big," and he showed me with his fingers.* **10** ADV [ADV adv] You use **this** when you are going to specify how much you know or how much you can tell someone. ◻ *I don't know if it's the best team I've ever had, but I can tell you this much, they're incredible people to be around.* **11** CONVENTION If you say **this is it**, you are agreeing with what someone else has just said. [BRIT, FORMULAE] ◻ *"You know, people conveniently forget the things they say."—"Well this is it."* **12** PRON You use **this is** in order to say who you are or what organization you are representing, when you are speaking on the telephone, radio, or television. ◻ *Hello, this is John Thompson.* **13** DET You use **this** to refer to the medium of communication that you are using at the time of speaking or writing. ◻ *What I'm going to do in this lecture is focus on something very specific.* **14** → see also **these** **15** PHRASE If you say that you are doing or talking about **this and that**, or **this, that, and the other** you mean that you are doing or talking about a variety of things that you do not want to specify. ◻ *"And what are you doing now?"—"Oh this and that."*

this|tle /ˈθɪsəl/ (thistles) N-COUNT A **thistle** is a wild plant which has leaves with sharp points and purple flowers.

thith|er /ˈðɪðər/ **1** ADV [ADV after v] **Thither** means to the place that has already been mentioned. [OLD-FASHIONED] ◻ *They have dragged themselves thither for shelter.* **2** **hither and thither** → see **hither**

tho' also **tho** **Tho'** and **tho** are informal written forms of **though**.

thong /θɔːŋ/ (thongs) **1** N-COUNT A **thong** is a long thin strip of leather, plastic, or rubber. **2** N-COUNT [usu pl] **Thongs** are open shoes which are held on your foot by a V-shaped strap that goes between your big toe and the toe next to it. [mainly AM] **3** N-COUNT A **thong** is a type of underwear, or the bottom of a bikini, that is very narrow at the back.

tho|rac|ic /θəˈræsɪk/ ADJ [ADJ n] **Thoracic** means relating to or affecting your thorax. [MEDICAL] ◻ *...diseases of the thoracic area.*

thor|ax /ˈθɔːræks/ (thoraxes or thoraces /ˈθɔːrəsiːz/) **1** N-COUNT [usu sing] Your **thorax** is the part of your body between your neck and your waist. [MEDICAL] **2** N-COUNT [usu sing] An insect's **thorax** is the central part of its body to which the legs and wings are attached. [TECHNICAL] **3** → See also color supplement

thorn /θɔːrn/ (thorns) **1** N-COUNT **Thorns** are the sharp points on some plants and trees, for example, on a rose bush. ◻ *Roses will always have thorns but with care they can be avoided.* **2** N-VAR A **thorn** or a **thorn bush** or a **thorn tree** is a bush or tree which has a lot of thorns on it. ◻ *...the shade of a thorn bush.*

thorny /ˈθɔːrni/ (thornier, thorniest) **1** ADJ A **thorny** plant or tree is covered with thorns. ◻ *...thorny hawthorn trees.* **2** ADJ If you describe a problem as **thorny**, you mean that it is very complicated and difficult to solve, and that people are often unwilling to discuss it. ◻ *...the thorny issue of immigration policy.*

thor|ough ♦◇◇ /ˈθɜːroʊ/ **1** ADJ A **thorough** action or activity is one that is done very carefully and in a detailed way so that nothing is forgotten. ◻ *We are making a thorough investigation.* ◻ *This very thorough survey goes back to 1784.* • **thor|ough|ly** ADV [ADV with v] ◻ *Food that is being offered hot must be reheated thoroughly.* • **thor|ough|ness** N-UNCOUNT ◻ *The thoroughness of the evaluation process we went through was impressive.* **2** ADJ Someone who is **thorough** is always very careful in their work, so that nothing is forgotten. ◻ *Martin would be a good judge, I thought. He was calm and thorough.* • **thor|ough|ness** N-UNCOUNT ◻ *His thoroughness and attention to detail is legendary.* **3** ADJ [det ADJ] **Thorough** is used to emphasize the large degree or extent of something. [EMPHASIS] ◻ *To me, this seemed like a thorough waste of time.* • **thor|ough|ly** ADV ◻ *I thoroughly enjoy your program.*

SYNONYMS

thorough
ADJ

1
comprehensive: *The Rough Guide to Nepal is a comprehensive guide to the region.*
full: *We should conserve oil and gas by making full use of other energy sources.*
complete: *The rebels had taken complete control.*
exhaustive: *The author's treatment of the subject is exhaustive.*

2
conscientious: *We are generally very conscientious about our work.*
painstaking: *Forensic experts carried out a painstaking search of the debris.*
meticulous: *The painting had been executed with meticulous attention to detail.*

thorough|bred /ˈθɜːroʊbred/ (thoroughbreds) **1** N-COUNT A **thoroughbred** is a horse that has parents that are of the same high quality breed. **2** N-COUNT [oft N n] A **thoroughbred** is a particular breed of racing horse. ◻ *...a thoroughbred stallion.*

thorough|fare /ˈθɜːroʊfeər/ (thoroughfares) N-COUNT [usu supp N] A **thoroughfare** is a main road in a city or town which usually has stores along it and a lot of traffic. [FORMAL] ◻ *...a busy thoroughfare.*

thorough|going /ˈθɜːroʊɡoʊɪŋ/ **1** ADJ [usu ADJ n] You use **thoroughgoing** to emphasize that someone or something is fully or completely the type of person or thing specified. [EMPHASIS] ◻ *...a thoroughgoing conservative.* ◻ *...readers who are unhappy with such thoroughgoing materialism.* **2** ADJ [usu ADJ n] If you describe a piece of work as **thoroughgoing**, you approve of it because it has been carefully and thoroughly put together. [APPROVAL] ◻ *...a thoroughgoing review of prison conditions.*

those ♦♦♦

The determiner is pronounced /ðoʊz/. The pronoun is pronounced /ðoʊz/.

1 DET You use **those** to refer to people or things which have already been mentioned. ◻ *Witnesses said that two people were killed, but those accounts could not be confirmed.* • PRON **Those** is also a pronoun. ◻ *I understand that there are a number of projects going on. Could you tell us a little bit about those?* **2** DET You use **those** when you are referring to people or things that are a distance away from you in position or time, especially when you indicate or point to them. ◻ *What are those buildings?* • PRON **Those** is also a pronoun. ◻ *I like these but not those.* ◻ *Those are nice shoes. Where'd you get them?* **3** DET You use **those** to refer to someone or something when you are going to give details or information about them. [FORMAL] ❏ *Those people who took up weapons to defend themselves are political prisoners.* ❹ PRON You use **those** to introduce more information about something already mentioned, instead of repeating the noun which refers to it. [FORMAL] ❏ *The interests he is most likely to enjoy will be those which enable him to show off himself or his talents.* ❺ PRON You use **those** to mean 'people.' ❏ *A little selfish behavior is unlikely to cause real damage to those around us.* ❻ DET You use **those** when you refer to things that you expect the person you are talking to to know about or when you are checking that you are both thinking of the same people or things. ❏ *He did buy me those daffodils a week or so ago.*

thou /ðaʊ/ ❶ PRON **Thou** is an old-fashioned, poetic, or religious word for 'you' when you are talking to only one person. It is used as the subject of a verb. ❷ → see also **holier-than-thou**

though ✦✦✦ /ðoʊ/ ❶ CONJ You use **though** to introduce a statement in a subordinate clause which contrasts with the statement in the main clause. You often use **though** to introduce a fact which you regard as less important than the fact in the main clause. ❏ *Everything I told them was correct, though I forgot a few things.* ❏ *I like him. Though he makes me angry sometimes.* ❷ CONJ You use **though** to introduce a subordinate clause which gives some information that is relevant to the main clause and weakens the force of what it is saying. ❏ *He did reply, though not immediately.* ❸ **as though** → see **as** ② ❹ **even though** → see **even** ①

thought ✦✦✦ /θɔt/ (thoughts) ❶ **Thought** is the past tense and past participle of **think**. ❷ N-COUNT A **thought** is an idea that you have in your mind. ❏ *The thought of Nick made her throat tighten.* ❏ *I've just had a thought.* ❸ N-PLURAL A person's **thoughts** are their mind, or all the ideas in their mind when they are concentrating on one particular thing. ❏ *I jumped to my feet so my thoughts wouldn't start to wander.* ❏ *Usually at this time our thoughts are on Christmas.* ❹ N-PLURAL A person's **thoughts** are their opinions on a particular subject. ❏ *Many of you have written to us to express your thoughts on the conflict.* ❺ N-UNCOUNT **Thought** is the activity of thinking, especially deeply, carefully, or logically. ❏ *Alice had been so deep in thought that she had walked past her car without even seeing it.* ❏ *He had given some thought to what she had told him.* ❻ N-COUNT A **thought** is an intention, hope, or reason for doing something. ❏ *Sarah's first thought was to run back and get Max.* ❼ N-UNCOUNT **Thought** is the group of ideas and beliefs which belongs, for example, to a particular religion, philosophy, science, or political party. ❏ *Aristotle's scientific theories dominated Western thought for fifteen hundred years.* ❽ → see also **second thought**

thought|ful /θɔtfəl/ ❶ ADJ If you are **thoughtful**, you are quiet and serious because you are thinking about something. ❏ *Nancy, who had been thoughtful for some time, suddenly spoke.* • **thought|ful|ly** ADV [ADV with v] ❏ *Daniel nodded thoughtfully.* ❷ ADJ If you describe someone as **thoughtful**, you approve of them because they remember what other people want, need, or feel, and try not to upset them. [APPROVAL] ❏ *...a thoughtful and caring man.* • **thought|ful|ly** ADV [ADV with v] ❏ *...the bottle of wine he had thoughtfully purchased for the celebrations.* ❸ ADJ If you describe something such as a book, film, or speech as **thoughtful**, you mean that it is serious and well thought out. ❏ *...a thoughtful and scholarly book.* • **thought|ful|ly** ADV [ADV with v] ❏ *...these thoughtfully designed machines.*

thought|less /θɔtlɪs/ ADJ If you describe someone as **thoughtless**, you are critical of them because they forget or ignore other people's wants, needs, or feelings. [DISAPPROVAL] ❏ *...a small minority of thoughtless and inconsiderate people.* ❏ *It was a thoughtless remark and I regretted it immediately.* • **thought|less|ly** ADV [ADV with v] ❏ *They thoughtlessly planned a picnic without him.*

thought-provoking ADJ If something such as a book or a movie is **thought-provoking**, it contains interesting ideas that make people think seriously. ❏ *This is an entertaining yet thought-provoking film.*

thou|sand ✦✦✦ /θaʊzənd/ (thousands)

The plural form is **thousand** after a number, or after a word or expression referring to a number, such as 'several' or 'a few.'

❶ NUM A **thousand** or one **thousand** is the number 1,000. ❏ *...five thousand acres.* ❷ QUANT [QUANT of pl-n] If you refer to **thousands of** things or people, you are emphasizing that there are very many of them. [EMPHASIS] ❏ *Thousands of refugees are packed into overcrowded towns and villages.* • PRON You can also use **thousands** as a pronoun. ❏ *Hundreds have been killed in the fighting and thousands made homeless.* ❸ **a thousand and one** → see **one** ③

thou|sandth /θaʊzənθ/ (thousandths) ❶ ORD The **thousandth** item in a series is the one that you count as number one thousand. ❏ *The magazine has just published its six thousandth edition.* ❷ ORD If you say that something has happened for the **thousandth** time, you are emphasizing that it has happened again and that it has already happened a large number of times. [EMPHASIS] ❏ *The phone rings for the thousandth time.* ❸ FRACTION A **thousandth** is one of a thousand equal parts of something. ❏ *...a dust particle weighing only a thousandth of a gram.*

thrall /θrɔl/ N-UNCOUNT [oft in N to n] If you say that someone is in **thrall** to a person or thing, you mean that they are completely in their power or are greatly influenced by them. [FORMAL] ❏ *He is not in thrall to the media.* ❏ *Tomorrow's children will be even more in the thrall of the silicon chip.*

thrash /θræʃ/ (thrashes, thrashing, thrashed) ❶ V-T If one player or team **thrashes** another in a game or contest, they defeat them easily or by a large score. [INFORMAL] ❏ *The Kings were thrashed by the Knicks last night.* ❷ V-T If you **thrash** someone, you hit them several times as a punishment. ❏ *"Liar!" Sarah screamed, as she thrashed the child. "You stole it."* ❸ V-T/V-I If someone **thrashes** around or **thrashes** their arms or legs around, they move in a wild or violent way, often hitting against something. You can also say that someone's arms or legs **thrash** around. ❏ *She would thrash around in her hospital bed and remove her intravenous line.* ❏ *Many of the crew died a terrible death as they thrashed about in shark-infested waters.* ❹ V-T/V-I If a person or thing **thrashes** something, or **thrashes** at something, they hit it continually in a violent or noisy way. ❏ *...a magnificent paddle-steamer on the mighty Mississippi, her huge wheel thrashing the muddy water.* ❺ → see also **thrashing**
▶ **thrash out** ❶ PHRASAL VERB If people **thrash out** something such as a plan or an agreement, they decide on it after a lot of discussion. ❏ *John and Monica have thrashed out a divorce agreement.* ❷ PHRASAL VERB If people **thrash out** a problem or a dispute, they discuss it thoroughly until they reach an agreement. ❏ *...a sincere effort by two people to thrash out differences about which they have strong feelings.*

thrash|ing /θræʃɪŋ/ (thrashings) ❶ N-COUNT If one player or team gives another one a **thrashing**, they defeat them easily or by a large score. [INFORMAL] ❏ *She dropped only eight points in the 43-minute thrashing of the former champion.* ❷ N-COUNT If someone gives someone else a **thrashing**, they hit them several times as a punishment. ❏ *If Sarah caught her, she would get a terrible thrashing.* ❸ → see also **thrash**

thread /θrɛd/ (threads, threading, threaded) ❶ N-VAR **Thread** or a **thread** is a long very thin piece of a material such as cotton, nylon, or silk, especially one that is used in sewing. ❏ *This time I'll do it right with a spool of thread.* ❷ V-T When you **thread** a needle, you put a piece of thread through the hole in the top of the needle in order to sew with it. ❏ *I sit down, thread a needle, snip off an old button.* ❸ N-COUNT The **thread** of an argument, a story, or a situation is an aspect of it that connects all the different parts together. ❏ *The thread running through many of these proposals was the theme of individual power and opportunity.* ❹ N-COUNT A **thread** of something such as liquid, light, or color is a long thin line or piece of it. ❏ *A thin, glistening thread of moisture ran along the rough concrete sill.* ❺ N-COUNT The **thread** on a screw, or on something such as a lid or a pipe, is the raised spiral line of metal or plastic around it which allows it to be fixed in place by twisting. ❏ *The screw threads will be able to get a good grip.* ❻ V-T/V-I If you **thread** your way through a group of people or things, or **thread** through it, you move through it carefully or slowly, changing direction frequently as you move. ❏ *Slowly she threaded her way back through the moving mass of bodies.* ❼ V-T If you **thread** a long thin object through something, you pass it through one or more holes or narrow spaces. ❏ *...threading the laces through the eyelets*

threadbare 1344 **thrilling**

of his shoes. ▪ V-T If you **thread** small objects such as beads onto a string or thread, you join them together by pushing the string through them. ❑ *Wipe the mushrooms clean and thread them on a string.* ▪ N-COUNT On the internet, a **thread** is a series of messages from different people about a particular subject. ❑ *I saw the post but I didn't read the thread below it.*

thread|bare /θrɛdbɛər/ ▪ ADJ **Threadbare** clothes, carpets, and other pieces of cloth look old, dull, and very thin, because they have been worn or used too much. ❑ *She sat cross-legged on a square of threadbare carpet.* ▪ ADJ If you describe an activity, an idea, or an argument as **threadbare**, you mean that it is very weak, or inadequate, or old and no longer interesting. ❑ *...the government's threadbare domestic policies.*

threat ✦✧ /θrɛt/ (threats) ▪ N-VAR A **threat** to a person or thing is a danger that something bad might happen to them. A **threat** is also the cause of this danger. ❑ *Some couples see single people as a threat to their relationships.* ▪ N-COUNT A **threat** is a statement by someone that they will hurt you in some way, especially if you do not do what they want. ❑ *He may be forced to carry out his threat to resign.* ▪ PHRASE If a person or thing is **under threat**, there is a danger that something bad might be done to them, or that they might cease to exist. ❑ *His position as leader is under threat.*

> **SYNONYMS**
>
> **threat**
> NOUN ▪
> **danger:** *...the dangers of smoking.*
> **risk:** *She was told there was a small risk of brain damage from the procedure.*
> **hazard:** *A new report suggests that chewing gum may be a health hazard.*

threat|en ✦✦ /θrɛtᵊn/ (threatens, threatening, threatened) ▪ V-T If a person **threatens** to do something bad to you, or if they **threaten** you, they say or imply that they will hurt you in some way, especially if you do not do what they want. ❑ *He said army officers had threatened to destroy the town.* ❑ *He tied her up and threatened her with a six-inch knife.* ▪ V-T If something or someone **threatens** a person or thing, they are likely to harm that person or thing. ❑ *The newcomers directly threaten the livelihood of the established workers.* ▪ V-T If something bad **threatens** to happen, it seems likely to happen. ❑ *It's threatening to rain.* ❑ *The fighting is threatening to turn into full-scale war.* ▪ → see also **threatening**

threat|ened /θrɛtᵊnd/ ▪ ADJ [v-link ADJ] If you feel **threatened**, you feel as if someone is trying to harm you. ❑ *Anger is the natural reaction we experience when we feel threatened or frustrated.* ▪ → see also **threaten**

threat|en|ing ✦✧ /θrɛtᵊnɪŋ/ ▪ ADJ You can describe someone's behavior as **threatening** when you think that they are trying to harm you. ❑ *People who engage in threatening behavior should expect to be arrested.* ▪ → see also **threaten**

three ✦✦✦ /θri/ (threes) NUM **Three** is the number 3. ❑ *We waited over three months before going back to see the specialist.*

three-dimensional ▪ ADJ A **three-dimensional** object is solid rather than flat, because it can be measured in three different directions, usually the height, length, and width. The abbreviation **3-D** can also be used. ❑ *...a three-dimensional model.* ▪ ADJ A **three-dimensional** picture, image, or movie looks as though it is deep or solid rather than flat. The abbreviation **3-D** can also be used. ❑ *The software generates both two-dimensional drawings and three-dimensional images.*

three-fourths QUANT [QUANT of n] **Three-fourths** is the same as **three-quarters**. [AM] ❑ *Three-fourths of the apartments in the ghetto had no heat.* • PRON **Three-fourths** is also a pronoun. ❑ *Three-fourths said they were worried about the possibility of another attack.*

three-piece ADJ [ADJ n] A **three-piece** suit is a set of three pieces of matching clothing, usually a jacket, vest, and pants.

three-point turn (three-point turns) N-COUNT When the driver of a vehicle does a **three-point turn**, he or she turns the vehicle by driving forward in a curve, then backward in a curve, and then forward in a curve.

three-quarter also **three quarter** ADJ [ADJ n] You can use **three-quarter** to describe something which is three fourths of the usual size or three fourths of a standard measurement. ❑ *Choose short or three-quarter sleeves for summer.* ❑ *...a session which lasted one and three-quarter hours.*

three-quarters QUANT [QUANT of n] **Three-quarters** is an amount that is three out of four equal parts of something. ❑ *Three-quarters of the students are African American.* • PRON **Three-quarters** is also a pronoun. ❑ *Applications have increased by three-quarters.* • ADV [ADV adj/-ed] **Three-quarters** is also an adverb. ❑ *We were left with an open bottle of champagne three-quarters full.*

three Rs N-PLURAL [the N] When talking about children's education, **the three Rs** are the basic skills of reading, writing, and arithmetic. ❑ *...ministers who want teachers to concentrate on the three Rs.*

three|some /θrisəm/ (threesomes) N-COUNT A **threesome** is a group of three people.

three-wheeler (three-wheelers) ▪ N-COUNT A **three-wheeler** is a bicycle or car with three wheels. ▪ → see also **tricycle**

thresh /θrɛʃ/ (threshes, threshing, threshed) V-T/V-I [usu passive] When a cereal such as barley, wheat, or rice **is threshed**, it is beaten in order to separate the grains from the rest of the plant. ❑ *The grain was still sown, cut and threshed as it was a hundred years ago.* ❑ *Machines that reap and thresh in one operation.*

thresh|old /θrɛʃhoʊld/ (thresholds) ▪ N-COUNT The **threshold** of a building or room is the floor in the doorway, or the doorway itself. ❑ *He stopped at the threshold of the bedroom.* ▪ N-COUNT A **threshold** is an amount, level, or limit on a scale. When the **threshold** is reached, something else happens or changes. ❑ *Moss has a high threshold for pain and a history of fast healing.* ▪ PHRASE If you are **on the threshold of** something exciting or new, you are about to experience it. ❑ *We are on the threshold of a new era in astronomy.*

threw /θru/ **Threw** is the past tense of **throw**.

thrice /θraɪs/ ▪ ADV Something that happens **thrice** happens three times. [OLD-FASHIONED] ❑ *They should think not twice, but thrice, before ignoring such advice.* ▪ ADV [ADV n] You can use **thrice** to indicate that something is three times the size, value, or intensity of something else. [OLD-FASHIONED] ❑ *...moving at thrice the speed of sound.*

thrift /θrɪft/ (thrifts) ▪ N-UNCOUNT **Thrift** is the quality and practice of being careful with money and not wasting things. [APPROVAL] ❑ *They were rightly praised for their thrift and enterprise.* ▪ N-COUNT A **thrift** or a **thrift institution** is a kind of savings bank. [AM, BUSINESS]

thrift shop (thrift shops) N-COUNT A **thrift shop** or **thrift store** is a store that sells used goods cheaply and gives its profits to a charity. [AM]

> in BRIT, use **charity shop**

thrifty /θrɪfti/ (thriftier, thriftiest) ADJ If you say that someone is **thrifty**, you are praising them for saving money, not buying unnecessary things, and not wasting things. [APPROVAL] ❑ *My mother taught me to be thrifty.* ❑ *...thrifty shoppers.*

thrill /θrɪl/ (thrills, thrilling, thrilled) ▪ N-COUNT If something gives you a **thrill**, it gives you a sudden feeling of great excitement, pleasure, or fear. ❑ *I can remember the thrill of not knowing what I would get on Christmas morning.* ▪ V-T/V-I If something **thrills** you, or if you **thrill** at it, it gives you a feeling of great pleasure and excitement. ❑ *The electric atmosphere both terrified and thrilled him.* ▪ → see also **thrilled**, **thrilling**

thrilled /θrɪld/ ▪ ADJ [v-link ADJ] If someone is **thrilled**, they are extremely happy and excited about something. ❑ *I was so thrilled to get a good grade from him.* ▪ → see also **thrill** ▪ → See feature box at **emotion**

thrill|er /θrɪlər/ (thrillers) N-COUNT A **thriller** is a book, movie, or play that tells an exciting fictional story about something such as criminal activities or spying. ❑ *...a tense psychological thriller.*

thrill|ing /θrɪlɪŋ/ ▪ ADJ Something that is **thrilling** is very exciting and enjoyable. ❑ *Our wildlife trips offer a thrilling encounter with wildlife in its natural state.* ▪ → see also **thrill**

thrive /θraɪv/ (thrives, thriving, thrived) **1** V-I If someone or something **thrives**, they do well and are successful, healthy, or strong. ☐ *He appears to be thriving.* ☐ *Today her company continues to thrive.* **2** V-I If you say that someone **thrives on** a particular situation, you mean that they enjoy it or that they can deal with it very well, especially when other people find it unpleasant or difficult. ☐ *Many people thrive on a stressful lifestyle.*

thro' also **thro** Thro' is sometimes used as a written abbreviation for **through** ①.

throat ◆◇◇ /θroʊt/ (throats) **1** N-COUNT Your **throat** is the back of your mouth and the top part of the tubes that go down into your stomach and your lungs. ☐ *She had a sore throat.* **2** N-COUNT Your **throat** is the front part of your neck. ☐ *His striped tie was loosened at his throat.* **3** PHRASE If you **clear your throat**, you cough once either to make it easier to speak or to attract people's attention. ☐ *Cross cleared his throat and spoke in low, polite tones.* **4** PHRASE If you **ram** something **down** someone's **throat** or **force** it **down** their **throat**, you keep mentioning a situation or idea in order to make them accept it or believe it. ☐ *I've always been close to my dad but he's never rammed his career down my throat.* **5** PHRASE If two people or groups are **at each other's throats**, they are arguing or fighting violently with each other. ☐ *The idea that we are at each other's throats couldn't be further from the truth.* **6** **a lump in your throat** → see **lump** **7** → See also color supplement

throaty /θroʊti/ (throatier, throatiest) ADJ A **throaty** voice or laugh is low and rough.

throb /θrɒb/ (throbs, throbbing, throbbed) **1** V-I If part of your body **throbs**, you feel a series of strong and usually painful beats there. ☐ *His head throbbed.* **2** V-I If something **throbs**, it vibrates and makes a steady noise. [LITERARY] ☐ *The engines throbbed.* **3** → See feature box at **illness**

throes /θroʊz/ **1** N-PLURAL [usu prep N, N of n] If someone is experiencing something bad or emotionally painful, you can say that they are in the **throes** of it, especially when it is in its final stages. [FORMAL] ☐ *...when the country was going through the final throes of civil war.* **2** PREP-PHRASE If you are **in the throes of** doing or experiencing something, especially something difficult, you are busy doing it or are deeply involved in it. [FORMAL] ☐ *The country is in the throes of a general election.* **3** → see also **death throes**

throm|bo|sis /θrɒmboʊsɪs/ (thromboses /θrɒmboʊsiːz/) **1** N-VAR **Thrombosis** is the formation of a blood clot in a person's heart or in one of their blood vessels, which can cause death. [MEDICAL] **2** → see also **coronary thrombosis**, **deep vein thrombosis**

throne /θroʊn/ (thrones) **1** N-COUNT A **throne** is a decorative chair used by a king, queen, or emperor on important official occasions. **2** N-SING You can talk about **the throne** as a way of referring to the position of being king, queen, or emperor. ☐ *...the queen's 40th anniversary on the throne.* **3** → See also color supplement

throng /θrɒŋ/ (throngs, thronging, thronged) **1** N-COUNT A **throng** is a large crowd of people. [LITERARY] ☐ *An official pushed through the throng.* **2** V-I When people **throng** somewhere, they go there in great numbers. [LITERARY] ☐ *The crowds thronged into the stadium.*

throt|tle /θrɒtəl/ (throttles, throttling, throttled) **1** V-T To **throttle** someone means to kill or injure them by squeezing their throat or tightening something around it and preventing them from breathing. ☐ *The gang tried to throttle the victim with a rope.* **2** N-COUNT The **throttle** of a motor vehicle or aircraft is the device, lever, or pedal that controls the quantity of fuel entering the engine and is used to control the vehicle's speed. ☐ *He gently opened the throttle, and the ship began to ease forward.*

THROUGH

① ADVERBS AND PREPOSITIONS: PHYSICAL MOVEMENTS AND POSITIONS
② ADVERBS AND PREPOSITIONS, ABSTRACT USES: TIMES, EXPERIENCES, CAUSES
③ ADJECTIVES

---

① **through** ◆◆◆

In addition to the uses shown here, **through** is used in phrasal verbs such as 'follow through,' 'see through,' and 'think through.'

The preposition is pronounced /θruː/. In other cases, **through** is pronounced /θru/.

1 PREP To move **through** something such as a hole, opening, or pipe means to move directly from one side or end of it to the other. ☐ *The theater was evacuated when rain poured through the roof.* ☐ *Go straight through that door under the EXIT sign.* • ADV [ADV after v] **Through** is also an adverb. ☐ *There was a hole in the wall and water was seeping through.* **2** PREP To cut **through** something means to cut it in two pieces or to make a hole in it. ☐ *Use a genuine fish knife and fork if possible as they are designed to cut through the flesh but not the bones.* • ADV **Through** is also an adverb. ☐ *Score lightly at first and then repeat, scoring deeper each time until the board is cut through.* **3** PREP To go **through** a town, area, or country means to travel across it or in it. ☐ *Go through North Carolina and into Virginia.* • ADV [ADV after v] **Through** is also an adverb. ☐ *Few know that the tribe was just passing through.* **4** PREP If you move **through** a group of things or a mass of something, it is on either side of you or all around you. ☐ *We made our way through the crowd to the river.* • ADV [ADV after v] **Through** is also an adverb. ☐ *He pushed his way through to the edge of the crowd where he waited.* **5** PREP To get **through** a barrier or obstacle means to get from one side of it to the other. ☐ *Allow twenty-five minutes to get through passport control and customs.* • ADV [ADV after v] **Through** is also an adverb. ☐ *...a maze of concrete and steel barriers, designed to prevent vehicles driving straight through.* **6** PREP If a driver goes **through** a red light, they keep driving even though they should stop. ☐ *He was killed at an intersection by a driver who went through a red light.* **7** PREP If something goes into an object and comes out of the other side, you can say that it passes **through** the object. ☐ *The ends of the net pass through a wooden bar at each end.* • ADV **Through** is also an adverb. ☐ *I bored a hole so that the bolt would pass through.* **8** PREP To go **through** a system means to move around it or to pass from one end of it to the other. ☐ *...electric currents traveling through copper wires.* • ADV [ADV after v] **Through** is also an adverb. ☐ *Food should be allowed to go through immediately with fewer restrictions.* **9** PREP If you see, hear, or feel something **through** a particular thing, that thing is between you and the thing you can see, hear, or feel. ☐ *Alice gazed pensively through the wet glass.* **10** PREP If something such as a feeling, attitude, or quality happens **through** an area, organization, or a person's body, it happens everywhere in it or affects all of it. ☐ *An atmosphere of anticipation vibrated through the crowd.*

② **through** ◆◆◆ **1** PREP If something happens or exists **through** a period of time, it happens or exists from the beginning until the end. ☐ *She kept quiet all through breakfast.* • ADV [ADV after v] **Through** is also an adverb. ☐ *We'll be working right through to the summer.* **2** PREP If something happens from a particular period of time **through** another, it starts at the first period and continues until the end of the second period. [AM] ☐ *...open Monday through Friday from 9 to 5.*

in BRIT, use **to**

3 PREP If you go **through** a particular experience or event, you experience it, and if you behave in a particular way **through** it, you behave in that way while it is happening. ☐ *Men go through a change of life emotionally just like women.* **4** PREP [n PREP n] You use **through** in expressions such as **half-way through** and **all the way through** to indicate to what extent an action or task is completed. ☐ *A thirty-nine-year-old competitor collapsed half-way through the marathon.* • ADV [n ADV] **Through** is also an adverb. ☐ *Stir the pork until it turns white all the way through.* **5** PREP If something happens because of something else, you can say that it happens **through** it. ☐ *I only succeeded through hard work.* **6** PREP You use **through** when stating the means by which a particular thing is achieved. ☐ *Those who seek to grab power through violence deserve punishment.* **7** PREP If you do something **through** someone else, they take the necessary action for you. ☐ *Do I need to go through my doctor to get an appointment?* **8** ADV [ADV after v] If something such as a proposal or idea goes **through**, it is accepted by people in authority and is made legal or official. ☐ *We're waiting for the* building permit to go through. • PREP **Through** is also a preposition. ☐ *They want to get the plan through Congress as quickly as possible.* **9** PREP If someone gets **through** an examination or a round of a competition, they succeed or win. ☐ *She was bright, learned languages quickly, and sailed through her exams.* • ADV [ADV after v] **Through** is also an adverb. ☐ *Only the top four teams go through.* **10** ADV [ADV after v] When you get **through** while making a telephone call, the call is connected and you can speak to the person you are phoning. ☐ *Telephones are down so he can't get through.* **11** PREP If you look or go **through** a lot of things, you look at them or deal with them one after the other. ☐ *Let's go through the numbers together and see if a workable deal is possible.* **12** PREP If you read **through** something, you read it from beginning to end. ☐ *She read through pages and pages of the music I had brought her.* • ADV [ADV after v] **Through** is also an adverb. ☐ *The article had been authored by Raymond Kennedy. He read it right through, looking for any scrap of information that might have passed him by.* **13** ADV [adj ADV] If you say that someone or something is wet **through**, you are emphasizing how wet they are. [EMPHASIS] ☐ *I returned to the inn cold and wet, soaked through by the drizzling rain.*

③ **through** ♦♦◇ **1** ADJ [v-link ADJ] If you are **through** with something or if it is **through**, you have finished doing it. ☐ *We're through with dinner.* ☐ *Are you through with this?* **2** ADJ [v-link ADJ] If you are **through** with someone, you do not want to have anything to do with them again. ☐ *I'm through with her; she's bad news!*

through|out ♦♦◇ /θruaʊt/ **1** PREP If you say that something happens **throughout** a particular period of time, you mean that it happens during the whole of that period. ☐ *Work began in June 2010, and continued throughout the winter season.* ☐ *Movie music can be made memorable because its themes are repeated throughout the film.* • ADV [ADV with cl] **Throughout** is also an adverb. ☐ *The first song, "Blue Moon," didn't go too badly except that everyone talked throughout.* **2** PREP If you say that something happens or exists **throughout** a place, you mean that it happens or exists in all parts of that place. ☐ *The charity, founded in 2000, now runs projects throughout the world.* • ADV [ADV with cl] **Throughout** is also an adverb. ☐ *The route is well sign-posted throughout.*

SYNONYMS
---

throughout
PREP **2**
all through: *I carried that precious book with me all through Europe.*
all over: *...the letters she received from people all over the world.*

through|put /θruput/ N-UNCOUNT The **throughput** of an organization or system is the amount of things it can do or deal with in a particular period of time. ☐ *...technologies which will allow us to get much higher throughput.*

through|way /θruweɪ/ → see **thruway**

throw ♦♦◇ /θroʊ/ (throws, throwing, threw, thrown)
→ Please look at meanings **16** to **19** to see if the expression you are looking for is shown under another headword.
1 V-T When you **throw** an object that you are holding, you move your hand or arm quickly and let go of the object, so that it moves through the air. ☐ *He spent hours throwing a tennis ball against a wall.* ☐ *The crowd began throwing stones.* • N-COUNT **Throw** is also a noun. ☐ *That was a good throw.* ☐ *A throw of the dice allows a player to move himself forward.* **2** V-T If you **throw** your body or part of your body into a particular position or place, you move it there suddenly and with a lot of force. ☐ *She threw her arms around his shoulders.* ☐ *She threatened to throw herself in front of a train.* **3** V-T If you **throw** something into a particular place or position, you put it there in a quick and careless way. ☐ *He struggled out of his bulky jacket and threw it on to the back seat.* **4** V-T To **throw** someone into a particular place or position means to force them roughly into that place or position. ☐ *He threw me to the ground.* **5** V-T If you say that someone **is thrown** into prison, you mean that they are put there by the authorities. ☐ *Those two should have been thrown in jail.* **6** V-T If a horse **throws** its rider, it makes him or her fall off, by suddenly jumping or moving violently. ☐ *The horse reared, throwing its rider and knocking down a youth standing beside it.* **7** V-T If a person or thing **is thrown** into a bad situation or state, something causes them to be in that situation or state. ☐ *Abidjan was thrown into turmoil because of a protest by taxi drivers.* **8** V-T If something **throws** light or a shadow on a surface, it causes that surface to have light or a shadow on it. ☐ *The sunlight is white and blinding, throwing hard-edged shadows on the ground.* **9** V-T If something **throws** doubt on a person or thing, it causes people to doubt or suspect them. ☐ *This new information does throw doubt on their choice.* **10** V-T [no cont] If you **throw** a look or smile at someone or something, you look or smile at them quickly and suddenly. ☐ *Emily turned and threw her a suggestive grin.* **11** V-T If you **throw** yourself, your energy, or your money into a particular job or activity, you become involved in it very actively or enthusiastically. ☐ *She threw herself into a modeling career.* **12** V-T If you **throw** a fit or a tantrum, you suddenly start to behave in an uncontrolled way. ☐ *I used to get very upset and scream and swear, throwing tantrums all over the place.* **13** V-T If something such as a remark or an experience **throws** you, it surprises you or confuses you because it is unexpected. ☐ *Her sudden change in attitude threw me.* ☐ *This new confession threw me for a loop.* **14** V-T If you **throw** a punch, you punch someone. ☐ *Everything was fine until someone threw a punch.* **15** V-T When someone **throws** a party, they organize one, usually in their own home. [INFORMAL] ☐ *Why not throw a party for your friends?* **16 to throw down the gauntlet →** see **gauntlet 17 to throw light on something →** see **light** ① **18 to throw money at something →** see **money 19 to throw in the towel →** see **towel**

▶ **throw away** also **throw out** **1** PHRASAL VERB When you **throw away** or **throw out** something that you do not want, you get rid of it, for example, by putting it in the trash. ☐ *I never throw anything away.* **2** PHRASAL VERB If you **throw away** an opportunity, advantage, or benefit, you waste it, rather than using it sensibly. ☐ *Failing to tackle the deficit would be throwing away an opportunity we haven't had for a generation.*

▶ **throw out** **1** → see **throw away 1 2** PHRASAL VERB If a judge **throws out** a case, he or she rejects it and the accused person does not have to stand trial. ☐ *The defense wants the district Judge to throw out the case.* **3** PHRASAL VERB If you **throw** someone **out**, you force them to leave a place or group. ☐ *He was thrown out of the Olympic team after testing positive for drugs.* ☐ *I wanted to kill him, but instead I just threw him out of the house.*

▶ **throw up** **1** PHRASAL VERB When someone **throws up**, they vomit. ☐ *She said she had thrown up after reading reports of the trial.* **2** PHRASAL VERB If something **throws up** dust, stones, or water, when it moves or hits the ground, it causes them to rise up into the air. ☐ *If it had hit the Earth, it would have made a crater 100 miles across and thrown up an immense cloud of dust.*

throw|away /θroʊəweɪ/ **1** ADJ [ADJ n] A **throwaway** product is intended to be used only for a short time, and then to be thrown away. ☐ *Now they are producing throwaway razors.* **2** ADJ [ADJ n] If you say that someone makes a **throwaway** remark or gesture, you mean that they make it in a casual way, although it may be important, or have some serious or humorous effect. ☐ *...a throwaway remark she later regretted.*

throw|back /θroʊbæk/ (throwbacks) N-COUNT [usu sing, oft N to n] If you say that something is a **throwback** to a former time, you mean that it is like something that existed a long time ago. ☐ *The hall is a throwback to another era with its old prints and stained glass.*

throw-in (throw-ins) N-COUNT When there is a **throw-in** in a soccer or rugby match, the ball is thrown back onto the field after it has been kicked off it.

thrown /θroʊn/ **Thrown** is the past participle of **throw**.

throw rug (throw rugs) N-COUNT A **throw rug** is a small carpet. [AM] ☐ *The cabin has a few throw rugs on the old wooden floor.*

thru **Thru** is sometimes used as a written abbreviation for **through** ①.

thrum /θrʌm/ (thrums, thrumming, thrummed) V-I When something such as a machine or engine **thrums**, it makes a low beating sound. ☐ *The air-conditioner thrummed.* • N-COUNT; SOUND **Thrum** is also a noun. ☐ *...the thrum of refrigeration motors.* ☐ *My head was going thrum thrum thrum.*

thrush /θrʌʃ/ (thrushes) **1** N-COUNT A **thrush** is a fairly small bird with a brown back and sometimes a spotted breast. There are several different kinds of **thrush**. **2** N-UNCOUNT **Thrush** is a medical condition caused by a fungus called Candida. It most often occurs in a baby's mouth or in a woman's vagina. ☐ *...a medicine that's used to prevent and treat thrush and other fungal infections.*

thrust /θrʌst/ (thrusts, thrusting, thrust) **1** V-T If you **thrust** something or someone somewhere, you push or move them there quickly with a lot of force. ▢ *They thrust him into the back of a jeep.* • N-COUNT **Thrust** is also a noun. ▢ *Two of the knife thrusts were fatal.* **2** V-T If you **thrust** your way somewhere, you move there, pushing between people or things which are in your way. ▢ *She thrust her way into the crowd.* **3** V-I If something **thrusts** up or out of something else, it sticks up or sticks out in a noticeable way. [LITERARY] ▢ *...a seedling ready to thrust up into any available light.* **4** N-UNCOUNT **Thrust** is the power or force that is required to make a vehicle move in a particular direction. ▢ *It provides the thrust that makes the craft move forward.*

thru|way /θruːweɪ/ (thruways) also **throughway** N-COUNT A **thruway** is a wide road designed so that a lot of traffic can move along it very quickly. It is usually divided along the middle, so that traffic traveling in one direction is separated from the traffic traveling in the opposite direction. [AM]

Thu. → see **Thurs.**

thud /θʌd/ (thuds, thudding, thudded) **1** N-COUNT A **thud** is a dull sound, such as that which a heavy object makes when it hits something soft. ▢ *She tripped and fell with a sickening thud.* **2** V-I If something **thuds** somewhere, it makes a dull sound, usually when it falls onto or hits something else. ▢ *She ran up the stairs, her bare feet thudding on the wood.* **3** V-I When your heart **thuds**, it beats strongly and somewhat quickly, for example, because you are very frightened or very happy. ▢ *My heart had started to thud, and my mouth was dry.*

thug /θʌg/ (thugs) N-COUNT You can refer to a violent person or criminal as a **thug**. [DISAPPROVAL] ▢ *...the cowardly thugs who mug old people.*

thug|gery /θʌgəri/ N-UNCOUNT **Thuggery** is rough, violent behavior.

thug|gish /θʌgɪʃ/ ADJ If you describe a person or their behavior as **thuggish**, you mean they behave in a violent, rough, or threatening way. [DISAPPROVAL] ▢ *The owner of the stall, a large, thuggish man, grabbed Dave by the collar.*

thumb /θʌm/ (thumbs, thumbing, thumbed) **1** N-COUNT Your hand has four fingers and one **thumb**. ▢ *She bit the tip of her left thumb, not looking at me.* **2** V-T If you **thumb** a lift or **thumb** a ride, you stand by the side of the road holding out your thumb until a driver stops and gives you a lift. ▢ *It may interest you to know that a boy answering Rory's description thumbed a ride to San Antonio.* **3** PHRASE If you are **under** someone's **thumb**, you are under their control, or very heavily influenced by them. ▢ *I cannot tell you what pain I feel when I see how much my mother is under my father's thumb.* **4** **green thumb** → see **green** **5** **rule of thumb** → see **rule**

thumb|nail /θʌmneɪl/ (thumbnails) also **thumb-nail** **1** N-COUNT Your **thumbnail** is the nail on your thumb. **2** ADJ [ADJ n] A **thumbnail** sketch or account is a very short description of an event, idea, or plan which gives only the main details. **3** N-COUNT In computing, a **thumbnail** is a very small picture, which you can expand by clicking on it. [COMPUTING] ▢ *Click on the thumbnails to view larger, more legible images.*

thumb|print /θʌmprɪnt/ (thumbprints) also **thumb print** **1** N-COUNT A **thumbprint** is a mark made by a person's thumb which shows the pattern of lines on its surface. **2** N-COUNT If you say that something such as a project has someone's **thumbprint** on it, you mean that it has features that make it obvious that they have been involved with it. ▢ *It's got your thumbprint all over it.*

thumb|screw /θʌmskruː/ (thumbscrews) also **thumb screw** **1** N-COUNT A **thumbscrew** is an object that was used in the past to torture people by crushing their thumbs. **2** N-COUNT If someone puts the **thumbscrews** on you, they start to put you under extreme pressure in order to force you to do something.

thumbs down also **thumbs-down** N-SING If someone gives a plan, idea, or suggestion **the thumbs-down**, they do not approve of it and refuse to accept it. [INFORMAL]

thumbs-up also **thumbs up** **1** N-SING A **thumbs-up** or a **thumbs-up sign** is a sign that you make by raising your thumb to show someone that you agree with someone, that you are happy with an idea or situation, or that everything is all right. ▢ *She checked the hall, then gave the others a thumbs-up.* **2** N-SING [the N] If you give a plan, idea, or suggestion **the thumbs-up**, you indicate that you approve of it and are willing to accept it. [INFORMAL] ▢ *The financial markets have given the thumbs up to the new policy.*

thumb|tack /θʌmtæk/ (thumbtacks) N-COUNT A **thumbtack** is a short pin with a broad flat top which is used for fastening papers or pictures to a board, wall, or other surface. [AM]

in BRIT, use **drawing pin**

thump /θʌmp/ (thumps, thumping, thumped) **1** V-T/V-I If you **thump** something, you hit it hard, usually with your fist. ▢ *He thumped my shoulder affectionately, nearly knocking me over.* ▢ *I heard you thumping on the door.* • N-COUNT **Thump** is also a noun. ▢ *He felt a thump on his shoulder.* **2** V-T If you **thump** someone, you attack them and hit them with your fist. [INFORMAL] ▢ *Don't say it serves me right or I'll thump you.* **3** V-T/V-I If you **thump** something somewhere or if it **thumps** there, it makes a loud, dull sound by hitting something else. ▢ *Their teacher thumped her pen on her book.* • N-COUNT **Thump** is also a noun. ▢ *There was a loud thump as the horse crashed into the van.* **4** V-I When your heart **thumps**, it beats strongly and quickly, usually because you are afraid or excited. ▢ *My heart was thumping wildly but I didn't let my face show any emotion.*

thun|der /θʌndər/ (thunders, thundering, thundered) **1** N-UNCOUNT **Thunder** is the loud noise that you hear from the sky after a flash of lightning, especially during a storm. ▢ *There was thunder and lightning, and torrential rain.* **2** V-I When it **thunders**, a loud noise comes from the sky after a flash of lightning ▢ *The day was heavy and still. It would probably thunder later.* **3** N-UNCOUNT The **thunder of** something that is moving or making a sound is the loud deep noise it makes. ▢ *The thunder of the sea on the rocks seemed to blank out other thoughts.* **4** V-I If something or someone **thunders** somewhere, they move there quickly and with a lot of noise. ▢ *The horses thundered across the valley floor.*

thunder|bolt /θʌndərboʊlt/ (thunderbolts) N-COUNT A **thunderbolt** is a flash of lightning, accompanied by thunder, which strikes something such as a building or a tree.

thunder|clap /θʌndərklæp/ (thunderclaps) N-COUNT A **thunderclap** is a short loud noise that you hear in the sky just after you see a flash of lightning.

thunder|cloud /θʌndərklaʊd/ (thunderclouds) N-COUNT A **thundercloud** is a large dark cloud that is likely to produce thunder and lightning.

thunder|head /θʌndərhɛd/ (thunderheads) N-COUNT A **thunderhead** is the top part of a thundercloud.

thun|der|ous /θʌndərəs/ ADJ If you describe a noise as **thunderous**, you mean that it is very loud and deep. ▢ *The audience responded with thunderous applause.*

thunder|storm /θʌndərstɔːrm/ (thunderstorms) N-COUNT A **thunderstorm** is a storm with thunder and lightning and a lot of heavy rain.

thunder|struck /θʌndərstrʌk/ ADJ [usu v-link ADJ] If you say that someone is **thunderstruck**, you mean that they are extremely surprised or shocked.

thun|dery /θʌndəri/ ADJ When the weather is **thundery**, there is a lot of thunder, or there are heavy clouds which make you think that there will be thunder soon. ▢ *Heavy thundery rain fell throughout Thursday.*

Thurs.

The spelling **Thur.** is also used.

Thurs. is a written abbreviation for **Thursday**. [mainly BRIT]

Thurs|day ♦♦♦ /θɜːrzdeɪ, -di/ (Thursdays) N-VAR **Thursday** is the day after Wednesday and before Friday. ▢ *On Thursday Barrett invited me for a drink.* ▢ *We go and do the weekly shopping every Thursday morning.*

thus ♦♦◊ /ðʌs/ **1** ADV [ADV with cl/group] You use **thus** to show that what you are about to mention is the result of something else that you have just mentioned. [FORMAL] ▢ *Neither of them thought of turning on the news. Thus Caroline didn't hear of John's death until Peter telephoned.* **2** ADV If you say that something is **thus** or happens **thus** you mean that it is, or happens, as you have just described or as you are just about to describe. [FORMAL] ❑ *Joanna was pouring the wine. While she was thus engaged, Charles sat on one of the bar-stools.*

SYNONYMS

thus
ADV **1**
consequently: *Relations between the two companies had, consequently, never been close.*
therefore: *Muscle cells need lots of fuel, and therefore burn lots of calories.*
so: *I was an only child, and so had no experience of large families.*
hence: *The Socialist Party was profoundly divided, and hence very weak.*

---

thwack /θwæk/ (**thwacks**) N-COUNT; SOUND A **thwack** is a sound made when two solid objects hit each other hard. ❑ *I listened to the thwack of the metal balls.* ❑ *Then the woodcutter let his ax fly – Thwack! Everyone heard it.*

thwart /θwɔːrt/ (**thwarts, thwarting, thwarted**) V-T If you **thwart** someone or **thwart** their plans, you prevent them from doing or getting what they want. ❑ *The security forces were doing all they could to thwart terrorists.*

thy /ðaɪ/ DET **Thy** is an old-fashioned, poetic, or religious word for 'your' when you are talking to one person. ❑ *Honor thy father and thy mother.*

thyme /taɪm/ N-UNCOUNT **Thyme** is a type of herb used in cooking.

thy|roid /θaɪrɔɪd/ (**thyroids**) N-COUNT Your **thyroid** or your **thyroid gland** is a gland in your neck that produces chemicals which control the way your body grows and functions.

thy|self /ðaɪsɛlf/ PRON **Thyself** is an old-fashioned, poetic, or religious word for 'yourself' when you are talking to only one person. ❑ *Love thy neighbor as thyself.*

ti|ara /tiɑːrə/ (**tiaras**) N-COUNT A **tiara** is a metal band shaped like half a circle and decorated with jewels that girls or women wear on their heads.

Ti|bet|an /tɪbɛtən/ (**Tibetans**) **1** ADJ **Tibetan** means belonging or relating to Tibet, or to its people, language, or culture. **2** N-COUNT A **Tibetan** is a Tibetan citizen or a person of Tibetan origin. **3** N-COUNT **Tibetan** is a language spoken by people who live in Tibet.

tibia /tɪbiə/ (**tibias**) **1** N-COUNT Your **tibia** is the inner bone of the two bones in the lower part of your leg. [MEDICAL] **2** → See also color supplement

tic /tɪk/ (**tics**) N-COUNT If someone has a **tic**, a part of their face or body keeps making a small uncontrollable movement, for example, because they are tired or have a nervous illness. ❑ *...people with nervous tics.*

tick /tɪk/ (**ticks, ticking, ticked**) **1** V-I When a clock or watch **ticks**, it makes a regular series of short sounds as it works. ❑ *A wind-up clock ticked busily from the kitchen counter.* • PHRASAL VERB **Tick away** means the same as **tick**. ❑ *A grandfather clock ticked away in a corner.* • **tick|ing** N-UNCOUNT ❑ *...the endless ticking of clocks.* **2** N-COUNT The **tick** of a clock or watch is the series of short sounds it makes when it is working, or one of those sounds. ❑ *He sat listening to the tick of the grandfather clock.* **3** N-COUNT A **tick** is a written mark like a V: ✓. It is used to show that something is correct or has been selected or dealt with. [BRIT]

in AM, use **check**

4 N-COUNT A **tick** is a small creature which lives on the bodies of people or animals and uses their blood as food. ❑ *The company produces chemicals that destroy ticks and mites.* **5** V-T If you **tick** something that is written on a piece of paper, you put a tick next to it. [BRIT]

in AM, use **check**

▶ **tick off** **1** PHRASAL VERB If you **tick off** items on a list, you write a tick or other mark next to them, in order to show that they have been dealt with. [BRIT]

in AM, usually use **check off**

2 PHRASAL VERB If you say that someone or something **ticks** you **off**, you mean that they annoy you. [AM, INFORMAL] ❑ *I can't lay blame anywhere and that ticks me off.*

tick|er /tɪkər/ (**tickers**) **1** N-COUNT A **ticker** is a machine that records information such as stock exchange prices, either electronically or on ticker tape. ❑ *They look at the stock ticker to see where the stock price is.* ❑ *AT&T's ticker symbol on the New York Stock Exchange will remain T.* **2** N-COUNT Your **ticker** is your heart. [INFORMAL, OLD-FASHIONED]

tick|er tape N-UNCOUNT [oft N n] **Ticker tape** consists of long narrow strips of paper on which information such as stock exchange prices is printed by a machine. In American cities, people sometimes throw ticker tape or other paper from high windows as a way of celebrating and honoring someone in public. ❑ *A half million people watched the troops march in New York's ticker tape parade.*

tick|et ✦✦◇ /tɪkɪt/ (**tickets**) **1** N-COUNT [also by n] A **ticket** is a small, official piece of paper or card which shows that you have paid to enter a place such as a theater or a sports stadium, or shows that you have paid for a trip. ❑ *He had a ticket for a flight on Friday.* ❑ *...two tickets for the game.* **2** N-COUNT A **ticket** is an official piece of paper which orders you to pay a fine or to appear in court because you have committed a driving or parking offense. ❑ *Slow down or you'll get a ticket.* **3** N-COUNT A **ticket** for a game of chance such as a raffle or a lottery is a piece of paper with a number on it. If the number on your ticket matches the number chosen, you win a prize. ❑ *She bought a lottery ticket and won more than $33 million.* **4** → see also **season ticket**

tick|et|ing /tɪkɪtɪŋ/ N-UNCOUNT [oft N n] **Ticketing** is the act or activity of selling tickets. ❑ *...automatic ticketing machines.*

ticket|less /tɪkɪtlɪs/ **1** ADJ Someone who is **ticketless** does not have a ticket for a particular event such as a concert or a sports game. ❑ *The band begged ticketless fans to stay away.* **2** ADJ A **ticketless** system is a way of buying something, such as a seat on an aircraft, without being given a ticket. ❑ *...a ticketless reservation system.*

tick|le /tɪkəl/ (**tickles, tickling, tickled**) **1** V-T When you **tickle** someone, you move your fingers lightly over a sensitive part of their body, often in order to make them laugh. ❑ *I was tickling him, and he was laughing and giggling.* **2** V-T/V-I If something **tickles** you or **tickles**, it causes an irritating feeling by lightly touching a part of your body. ❑ *...a yellow hat with a great feather that tickled her ear.*

tick|lish /tɪklɪʃ/ **1** ADJ [usu ADJ n] A **ticklish** problem, situation, or task is difficult and needs to be dealt with carefully. ❑ *So car makers are faced with the ticklish problem of how to project products at new buyers.* **2** ADJ Someone who is **ticklish** is sensitive to being tickled, and laughs as soon as you tickle them. ❑ *This massage method is not recommended for anyone who is very ticklish.*

tic-tac-toe /tɪktæktoʊ/ also **tick-tack-toe** N-UNCOUNT **Tic-tac-toe** is a game in which two players take turns in drawing either an 'O' or an 'X' in one square of a grid consisting of nine squares. The winner is the first player to get three of the same symbols in a row. [AM] ❑ *...a game of tic-tac-toe.*

tid|al /taɪdəl/ ADJ **Tidal** means relating to or produced by tides. ❑ *The tidal stream or current gradually decreases in the shallows.*

tid|al wave (**tidal waves**) N-COUNT A **tidal wave** is a very large wave, often caused by an earthquake, that flows onto the land and destroys things. ❑ *A massive tidal wave swept the ship up and away.*

tid|bit /tɪdbɪt/ (**tidbits**)

in BRIT, use **titbit**

1 N-COUNT You can refer to a small piece of information about someone's private affairs as a **tidbit**, especially when it is interesting and shocking. **2** N-COUNT A **tidbit** is a small piece of food.

tiddly|wink /tɪdəliwɪŋk/ (**tiddlywinks**) **1** N-UNCOUNT **Tiddlywinks** is a game in which the players try to make small round pieces of plastic jump into a container, by pressing their edges with a larger piece of plastic. **2** N-COUNT **Tiddlywinks** are the small round piece of plastic used in the game of tiddlywinks.

tide ♦♢♢ /taɪd/ (tides) **1** N-COUNT The **tide** is the regular change in the level of the ocean on the beach. You say the tide is in when water reaches a high point on the land or out when the water leaves the land. ❑ *The tide was at its highest.* ❑ *The tide was going out, and the sand was smooth and glittering.* **2** N-COUNT A **tide** is a current in the sea that is caused by the regular and continuous movement of large areas of water toward and away from the shore. ❑ *Roman vessels used to sail with the tide from Boulogne to Richborough.* **3** N-SING The **tide of** opinion, for example, is what the majority of people think at a particular time. ❑ *The tide of opinion seems overwhelmingly in his favor.*

SYNONYMS

tide
NOUN **2**
current: *The couple were swept away by the strong current.*
flow: *It works only in the veins, where the blood flow is slower.*

---

tid|ings /ˈtaɪdɪŋz/ N-PLURAL [usu adj N, oft N of n] You can use **tidings** to refer to news that someone tells you. [FORMAL, OLD-FASHIONED] ❑ *He hated to be the bearer of bad tidings.*

tidy /ˈtaɪdi/ (tidier, tidiest, tidies, tidying, tidied) **1** ADJ Someone who is **tidy** likes everything to be neat and arranged in an organized way. [mainly BRIT]
- in AM, use **neat**

● **tidi|ness** N-UNCOUNT ❑ *I'm very impressed by your tidiness and order.* **2** ADJ Something that is **tidy** is neat and is arranged in an organized way. [mainly BRIT]
- in AM, use **neat**

● **tidi|ly** /ˈtaɪdɪli/ ADV ❑ *...books and magazines stacked tidily on shelves.* ● **tidi|ness** N-UNCOUNT ❑ *Employees are expected to maintain a high standard of tidiness in their dress and appearance.* **3** V-T When you **tidy** a place such as a room or closet, you make it neat by putting things in their proper places. [mainly BRIT]
- in AM, use **clean**

▶ **tidy away** PHRASAL VERB When you **tidy** something **away**, you put it in something else so that it is not in the way. [mainly BRIT]
- in AM, use **put away**

▶ **tidy up** PHRASAL VERB When you **tidy up** or **tidy** a place **up**, you put things back in their proper places so that everything is neat. [mainly BRIT]
- in AM, use **clean up**

tie ♦♦♢ /taɪ/ (ties, tying, tied)
→ Please look at meaning **12** to see if the expression you are looking for is shown under another headword.

1 V-T If you **tie** two things together or **tie** them, you fasten them together with a knot. ❑ *He tied the ends of the plastic bag together.* **2** V-T If you **tie** something or someone in a particular place or position, you put them there and fasten them using rope or string. ❑ *He had tied the dog to one of the trees near the canal.* **3** V-T If you **tie** a piece of string or cloth around something or **tie** something with a piece of string or cloth, you put the piece of string or cloth around it and fasten the ends together. ❑ *She tied her scarf over her head.* ❑ *Roll the meat and tie it with string.* **4** V-T If you **tie** a knot or bow in something or **tie** something in a knot or bow, you fasten the ends together. ❑ *He took a short length of rope and swiftly tied a slip knot.* ❑ *She tied a knot in a cherry stem.* **5** V-T/V-I When you **tie** something or when something **ties**, you close or fasten it using a bow or knot. ❑ *He pulled on his heavy suede shoes and tied the laces.* ❑ *...a long white thing around his neck that tied in front in a floppy bow.* **6** N-COUNT A **tie** is a long narrow piece of cloth that is worn around the neck under a shirt collar and tied in a knot at the front. Ties are worn mainly by men. ❑ *Jason had taken off his jacket and loosened his tie.* **7** V-T [usu passive] If one thing **is tied** to another or two things **are tied**, the two things have a close connection or link. ❑ *Their cancers are not so clearly tied to radiation exposure.* **8** V-T [usu passive] If you **are tied** to a particular place or situation, you are forced to accept it and cannot change it. ❑ *They had children and were consequently tied to the school vacations.* **9** N-COUNT [usu pl, oft N prep] **Ties** are the connections you have with people or a place. ❑ *Quebec has always had particularly close ties to France.* **10** V-RECIP If two people **tie** in a competition or game or if they **tie** with each other, they have the same number of points or the same degree of success. ❑ *Ronan Rafferty had tied with Frank Nobilo.* ● N-COUNT **Tie** is also a noun. ❑ *The first game ended in a tie.* **11** N-COUNT In sports, a **tie** is a match that is part of a competition. The losers leave the competition and the winners go on to the next round. [BRIT] ❑ *They'll meet the winners of the first round tie.* **12 your hands are tied** → see **hand** ①

▶ **tie down** PHRASAL VERB A person or thing that **ties** you **down** restricts your freedom in some way. ❑ *We'd agreed from the beginning not to tie each other down.* ❑ *He didn't want a family because he didn't want to be tied down.*

▶ **tie up** **1** PHRASAL VERB When you **tie** something **up**, you fasten string or rope around it so that it is firm or secure. ❑ *He tied up the bag and took it outside.* **2** PHRASAL VERB If someone **ties** another person **up**, they fasten ropes around them so that they cannot move or escape. ❑ *Masked robbers broke in, tied him up, and made off with $8,000.* **3** PHRASAL VERB If you **tie** an animal **up**, you fasten it to a fixed object with a piece of rope so that it cannot run away. ❑ *Would you go and tie your horse up please?*

tie-breaker (tie-breakers) also **tie-break** **1** N-COUNT A **tie-breaker** is an extra game which is played in a tennis match when the score in a set is 6-6. The player who wins the **tie-breaker** wins the set. **2** N-COUNT A **tie-breaker** is an extra question or round that decides the winner of a competition or game when two or more people have the same score at the end.

tied up ADJ [v-link ADJ] If someone or something is **tied up**, they are busy or being used, with the result that they are not available for anything else. [INFORMAL] ❑ *He's tied up with his new book. He's working hard, you know.*

tie-dye (tie-dyes, tie-dyeing, tie-dyed) **1** V-T [usu passive] If a piece of cloth or a garment **is tie-dyed**, it is tied in knots and then put into dye, so that some parts become more deeply colored than others. ❑ *He wore a T-shirt that had been tie-dyed in bright colors.* ❑ *I bought a great tie-dyed silk scarf.* **2** N-VAR [usu N n] A **tie-dye** is a garment or piece of cloth that has been tie-dyed. ❑ *They wore tie-dyes and ponchos.* ❑ *...a hideous tie-dye shirt.*

tie-pin (tie-pins) also **tiepin** N-COUNT A **tie-pin** is a small ornamental pin that is used to pin a person's tie to their shirt.

tier /tɪər/ (tiers) **1** N-COUNT A **tier** is a row or layer of something that has other layers above or below it. ❑ *...the auditorium with the tiers of seats around and above it.* ● COMB IN ADJ **Tier** is also a combining form. ❑ *...a three-tier wedding cake.* **2** N-COUNT A **tier** is a level in an organization or system. ❑ *Islanders have campaigned for the abolition of one of the three tiers of municipal power on the island.* ● COMB IN ADJ **Tier** is also a combining form. ❑ *...the possibility of a two-tier system of universities.*

tie tack (tie tacks) N-COUNT A **tie tack** is the same as a **tie-pin**. [AM]

tie-up (tie-ups) **1** N-COUNT A **tie-up** or a **traffic tie-up** is a long line of vehicles that cannot move forward because there is too much traffic, or because the road is blocked by something. [AM] ❑ *In some cities this morning, there were traffic tie-ups up to 40 miles long.*
- in BRIT, use **traffic jam**

2 N-COUNT [oft N between pl-n, N with n] A **tie-up** between two organizations is a business connection that has been arranged between them. ❑ *...joint ventures and tie-ups for mutual benefit.*

tiff /tɪf/ (tiffs) N-COUNT A **tiff** is a small unimportant quarrel, especially between two close friends or between people in a romantic relationship.

ti|ger /ˈtaɪɡər/ (tigers) N-COUNT A **tiger** is a large fierce animal belonging to the cat family. Tigers are orange with black stripes.

tight ♦♢♢ /taɪt/ (tighter, tightest) **1** ADJ **Tight** clothes or shoes are small and fit closely to your body. ❑ *She walked off the plane in*

tighten

a miniskirt and tight top. • **tight|ly** ADV [ADV with v] ◻ *He buttoned his collar tightly round his thick neck.* **2** ADV [ADV after v] If you hold someone or something **tight**, you hold them firmly and securely. ◻ *She just fell into my arms, clutching me tight for a moment.* ◻ *Just hold tight to my hand and follow along.* • ADJ **Tight** is also an adjective. ◻ *As he and Hannah passed through the gate he kept a tight hold of her arm.* • **tight|ly** ADV [ADV after v] ◻ *She climbed back into bed and wrapped her arms tightly around her body.* **3** ADJ **Tight** controls or rules are very strict. ◻ *The measures include tight control of media coverage.* ◻ *The government was prepared to keep a tight hold on public sector pay rises.* • **tight|ly** ADV ◻ *The internal media was tightly controlled by the government during the war.* **4** ADV Something that is shut **tight** is shut very firmly. ◻ *The baby lay on his back with his eyes closed tight.* ◻ *I keep the flour and sugar in individual jars, sealed tight with their glass lids.* • **tight|ly** ADV ◻ *Pemberton frowned and closed his eyes tightly.* **5** ADJ Skin, cloth, or string that is **tight** is stretched or pulled so that it is smooth or straight. ◻ *My skin feels tight and lacking in moisture.* • **tight|ly** ADV [ADV with v] ◻ *Her sallow skin was drawn tightly across the bones of her face.* **6** ADJ **Tight** is used to describe a group of things or an amount of something that is closely packed together. ◻ *She curled up in a tight ball, with her knees tucked up at her chin.* • ADV **Tight** is also an adverb. ◻ *The people sleep on army cots packed tight, end to end.* • **tight|ly** ADV ◻ *Many animals travel in tightly packed trucks and are deprived of food, water and rest.* **7** ADJ If a part of your body is **tight**, it feels uncomfortable and painful, for example, because you are sick, anxious, or angry. ◻ *It is better to stretch the tight muscles first.* **8** ADJ A **tight** group of people is one whose members are closely linked by beliefs, feelings, or interests. ◻ *We're a tight group, so we do keep in touch.* **9** ADJ A **tight** bend or corner is one that changes direction very quickly so that you cannot see very far around it. ◻ *They collided on a tight bend and both cars were extensively damaged.* **10** ADJ A **tight** schedule or budget allows very little time or money for unexpected events or expenses. ◻ *It's difficult to cram everything into a tight schedule .* ◻ *Emma is on a tight budget for clothes.* **11** → see also **airtight** **12** **to keep a tight rein on** → see **rein** **13** **to sit tight** → see **sit**

tight|en /taɪtᵊn/ (**tightens, tightening, tightened**) **1** V-T/V-I If you **tighten** your grip on something, or if your grip **tightens**, you hold the thing more firmly or securely. ◻ *Luke answered by tightening his grip on her shoulder.* ◻ *Her arms tightened about his neck in gratitude.* **2** V-T/V-I If you **tighten** a rope or chain, or if it **tightens**, it is stretched or pulled hard until it is straight. ◻ *The anchorman flung his whole weight back, tightening the rope.* **3** V-T/V-I If a government or organization **tightens** its grip on a group of people or an activity, or if its grip **tightens**, it begins to have more control over it. ◻ *He knows he has considerable support for his plans to tighten his grip on the machinery of central government.* **4** V-T When you **tighten** a screw, nut, or other device, you turn it or move it so that it is more firmly in place or holds something more firmly. ◻ *I used my thumbnail to tighten the screw on my lamp.* • PHRASAL VERB **Tighten up** means the same as **tighten**. ◻ *It's important to tighten up the wheels properly, otherwise they vibrate loose and fall off.* **5** V-I If a part of your body **tightens**, the muscles in it become tense and stiff, for example, because you are angry or afraid. ◻ *Sofia's throat had tightened and she couldn't speak.* **6** V-T If someone in authority **tightens** a rule, a policy, or a system, they make it stricter or more efficient. ◻ *The United States plans to tighten the economic sanctions currently in place.* • PHRASAL VERB **Tighten up** means the same as **tighten**. ◻ *Until this week, every attempt to tighten up the law had failed.* **7** **to tighten your belt** → see **belt**

tight-fisted ADJ If you describe someone as **tight-fisted**, you disapprove of them because they are unwilling to spend money. [DISAPPROVAL] ◻ *He had the reputation of being one of the most tight-fisted and demanding of employers.*

tight-lipped **1** ADJ [oft ADJ about n/wh] If you describe someone as **tight-lipped**, you mean that they are unwilling to give any information about something. ◻ *Military officials are still tight-lipped about whether or when their forces will launch a ground offensive.* **2** ADJ Someone who is **tight-lipped** has their lips pressed tightly together, especially because they are angry or disapproving. ◻ *He was sitting at the other end of the table, tight-lipped and angry.*

tight|rope /taɪtroʊp/ (**tightropes**) **1** N-COUNT A **tightrope** is a tightly stretched piece of rope on which someone balances and performs tricks in a circus. **2** N-COUNT [usu sing] You can use **tightrope** in expressions such as **walk a tightrope** and **live on a tightrope** to indicate that someone is in a difficult situation and has to be very careful about what they say or do. ◻ *The movie tries to walk a tightrope between drama and comedy but fails at both.*

tights /taɪts/ **1** N-PLURAL [also *a pair of* N] **Tights** are a piece of clothing, worn by women and girls. They are usually made of nylon and cover the hips, legs, and feet. [mainly BRIT]

in AM, also use **pantyhose**

2 N-PLURAL [also *a pair of* N] **Tights** are a piece of tight clothing, usually worn by dancers, acrobats, or people in exercise classes, and covering the hips and legs but not the feet.

ti|gress /taɪgrɪs/ (**tigresses**) N-COUNT A **tigress** is a female tiger.

til|de /tɪldə/ (**tildes**) N-COUNT A **tilde** is a symbol that is written over the letter 'n' in Spanish (ñ) and the letters 'o' (õ) and 'a' (ã) in Portuguese to indicate the way in which they should be pronounced.

tile /taɪl/ (**tiles**) **1** N-VAR **Tiles** are flat, square pieces of baked clay, carpet, cork, or other substance, which are fixed as a covering onto a floor or wall. ◻ *Amy's shoes squeaked on the tiles as she walked down the corridor.* **2** N-VAR **Tiles** are flat pieces of baked clay which are used for covering roofs. ◻ *...a fine building, with a neat little porch and ornamental tiles on the roof.*

til|ing /taɪlɪŋ/ **1** N-UNCOUNT You can refer to a surface that is covered by tiles as **tiling**. ◻ *The kitchen had beautiful black tiling, countertops, and cupboards.* **2** → see also **tile**

till ♦◇◇ /tɪl/ (**tills**) **1** PREP In spoken English and informal written English, **till** is often used instead of **until**. ◻ *They had to wait till Monday to phone the bank.* • CONJ **Till** is also a conjunction. ◻ *I hadn't left home till I was nineteen.* **2** N-COUNT A **till** is the drawer of a cash register, where the money is kept. [AM] ◻ *He checked the register. There was money in the till.* **3** N-COUNT In a store or other place of business, a **till** is a counter or cash register where money is kept, and where customers pay for what they have bought. [BRIT]

in AM, use **cash register**

till|er /tɪlər/ (**tillers**) N-COUNT The **tiller** of a boat is a handle that is fixed to the rudder. It is used to turn the rudder, which then steers the boat.

tilt /tɪlt/ (**tilts, tilting, tilted**) **1** V-T/V-I If you **tilt** an object or if it **tilts**, it moves into a sloping position with one end or side higher than the other. ◻ *She tilted the mirror and began to comb her hair.* ◻ *Leonard tilted his chair back on two legs and stretched his long body.* **2** V-T If you **tilt** part of your body, usually your head, you move it slightly upward or to one side. ◻ *Mari tilted her head back so that she could look at him.* ◻ *His wife tilted his head to the side and inspected the wound.* • N-COUNT **Tilt** is also a noun. ◻ *He opened the rear door for me with an apologetic tilt of his head.* **3** N-COUNT The **tilt** of something is the fact that it tilts or slopes, or the angle at which it tilts or slopes. ◻ *...calculations based on our understanding of the tilt of the Earth's axis.* **4** V-I If a person or thing **tilts** toward a particular opinion or if something **tilts** them toward it, they change slightly so that they become more in agreement with that opinion or position. ◻ *Political will might finally tilt toward some sort of national health plan.*

tim|ber /tɪmbər/ N-UNCOUNT **Timber** is wood that is used for building houses and making furniture. You can also refer to trees that are grown for this purpose as **timber**. ◻ *These Michigan woods have been exploited for timber since the Great Fire of Chicago.*

tim|bered /tɪmbərd/ **1** ADJ [usu ADJ n] A **timbered** building has a wooden frame or wooden beams showing on the outside. **2** → see also **half-timbered**

tim|ber yard → see **lumberyard**

tim|bre /tæmbər/ (**timbres**) N-COUNT [usu sing, oft N *of* n] The **timbre** of someone's voice or of a musical instrument is the particular quality of sound that it has. [TECHNICAL] ◻ *His voice had a deep timbre.* ◻ *The timbre of the violin is far richer than that of the mouth organ.*

TIME

① NOUN USES
② VERB USES
③ PHRASES: GROUP 1
④ PHRASES: GROUP 2
⑤ PHRASES: GROUP 3

① **time** ♦♦♦ /taɪm/ (times) **1** N-UNCOUNT **Time** is what we measure in minutes, hours, days, and years. ❑ ...*a two-week period of time.* ❑ *Time passed, and still Ma did not appear.* **2** N-SING You use **time** to ask or talk about a specific point in the day, which can be stated in hours and minutes and is shown on clocks. ❑ *"What time is it?"—"Eight o'clock."* ❑ *He asked me the time.* **3** N-COUNT The **time** when something happens is the point in the day when it happens or is supposed to happen. ❑ *Departure times are 08.15 from Baltimore, and 10.15 from Newark.* **4** N-UNCOUNT You use **time** to refer to the system of expressing time and counting hours that is used in a particular part of the world. ❑ *The incident happened just after ten o'clock local time.* **5** N-UNCOUNT [also *a* N] You use **time** to refer to the period that you spend doing something or when something has been happening. ❑ *Adam spent a lot of time in his grandfather's office.* ❑ *He wouldn't have the time or money to take care of me.* ❑ *Listen to me, I haven't got much time.* ❑ *It's obvious that you need more time to think.* **6** N-SING If you say that something has been happening for **a time**, you mean that it has been happening for a fairly long period of time. ❑ *He was also for a time an art critic.* ❑ *He stayed for quite a time.* **7** N-COUNT You use **time** to refer to a period of time or a point in time, when you are describing what is happening then. For example, if something happened **at** a particular **time**, that is when it happened. If it happens **at all times**, it always happens. ❑ *We were in the same college, which was male-only at that time.* ❑ *By this time he was thirty.* ❑ *It was a time of terrible uncertainty.* **8** N-COUNT You use **time** or **times** to talk about a particular period in history or in your life. ❑ *They were hard times and his parents had been struggling to raise their family.* ❑ *We'll be alone together, just like old times.* **9** N-PLURAL You can use **the times** to refer to the present time and to modern fashions, tastes, and developments. For example, if you say that someone **keeps up with the times**, you mean they are fashionable or aware of modern developments. If you say they are **behind the times**, you mean they are unfashionable or not aware of them. ❑ *This approach is now seriously out of step with the times.* **10** N-COUNT When you describe the **time** that you had on a particular occasion or during a particular part of your life, you are describing the sort of experience that you had then. ❑ *Sarah and I had a great time while the kids were away.* **11** N-SING Your **time** is the amount of time that you have to live, or to do a particular thing. ❑ *Now that Martin has begun to suffer the effects of AIDS, he says his time is running out.* **12** N-UNCOUNT If you say it is **time for** something, **time** to do something, or **time** you did something, you mean that this thing ought to happen or be done now. ❑ *Opinion polls indicated a feeling among the public that it was time for a change.* ❑ *It was time for him to go to work.* **13** N-COUNT When you talk about a **time** when something happens, you are referring to a specific occasion when it happens. ❑ *Every time she travels on the bus it's delayed by at least three hours.* **14** N-COUNT You use **time** after numbers to say how often something happens. ❑ *It was her job to make tea three times a day.* **15** N-PLURAL You use **times** after numbers when comparing one thing to another and saying, for example, how much bigger, smaller, better, or worse it is. ❑ *Its profits are rising four times faster than the average company.* **16** CONJ You use **times** to show multiplication. Three times five is 3x5. ❑ *Four times six is 24.* **17** N-COUNT Someone's **time** in a race is the amount of time it takes them to finish the race. ❑ *He was over a second faster than his previous best time.*

USAGE

time

1 **Time** is usually an uncountable noun, so don't use 'a' with it. Don't say, for example, 'I don't have a time to go shopping.' Say 'I don't have **time** to go shopping.' *Do you have* **time** *for a coffee?*

2 You don't usually use 'time' when you are saying how long something takes or lasts. Don't say, for example, 'Each song lasts ten minutes' time.' Say 'Each song lasts ten minutes.' *The whole process takes* **twenty-five years**.

VOCABULARY IN CONTEXT

Time

Time flies, people say. We also talk about **wasting time** and **killing time**, but the fact is, we don't really do either of these. There are 24 hours in every day, and seven days in every week, and this doesn't change whatever we do and however we choose to **spend our time**. Very busy people talk about being "crunched for time," and often resent those who are not; indeed, there's a slight sting in remarking that some people have too much time on their hands. For centuries, writers and artists have had a **fascination** with time. Its **constancy** delights and confounds because no one can harness the ever-moving sands of time. Many have explored themes of **time travel**, particularly with regard to regrets. What if we could **turn the clock back**? Would we do things differently? But no one can turn back time, so the best we can do is live in the present and look toward the future.

② **time** ♦♦♦ /taɪm/ (times, timing, timed) **1** V-T If you **time** something for a particular hour, day, or period, you plan or decide to do it or cause it to happen at this time. ❑ *He timed the election to coincide with new measures to boost the economy.* ❑ *I timed our visit for March 7.* **2** V-T If you **time** an action or activity, you measure how long someone takes to do it or how long it lasts. ❑ *A radar gun timed the speed of the baseball.* **3** → see also **timing**

③ **time** ♦♦♦ /taɪm/ (times) **1** PHRASE If you say it is **about time** that something was done, you are saying in an emphatic way that it should happen or be done now, and really should have happened or been done sooner. [EMPHASIS] ❑ *It's about time a few movie makers with original ideas were given a chance.* **2** PHRASE If you do something **ahead of time**, you do it before a particular event or before you need to, in order to be well prepared. ❑ *Find out ahead of time what regulations apply to your situation.* **3** PHRASE If someone is **ahead of** their **time** or **before** their **time**, they have new ideas a long time before other people start to think in the same way. ❑ *She was ahead of her time in employing recovering addicts.* **4** PHRASE If something happens or is done **all the time**, it happens or is done continually. ❑ *We can't be together all the time.* **5** PHRASE You say **at a time** after an amount to say how many things or how much of something is involved in one action, place, or group. ❑ *Beat in the eggs, one at a time.* **6** PHRASE If something could happen **at any time**, it is possible that it will happen very soon, though nobody can predict exactly when. ❑ *Conditions are still very tense and the fighting could escalate at any time.* **7** PHRASE If you say that something was the case **at one time**, you mean that it was the case during a particular period in the past. ❑ *At one time 400 men, women and children lived in the village.* **8** PHRASE If two or more things exist, happen, or are true **at the same time**, they exist, happen, or are true together although they seem to contradict each other. ❑ *I was afraid of her, but at the same time I really liked her.* **9** PHRASE **At the same time** is used to introduce a statement that slightly changes or contradicts the previous statement. ❑ *I don't think I set out to come up with a different sound for each CD. At the same time, I do have a sense of what is right for the moment.* **10** PHRASE You use **at times** to say that something happens or is true on some occasions or at some moments. ❑ *The debate was highly emotional at times.* **11** PHRASE If you say that something will be the

time case **for all time**, you mean that it will always be the case. ☐ *He promised to love her for all time.* **12** PHRASE If something is the case or will happen **for the time being**, it is the case or will happen now, but only until something else becomes possible or happens. ☐ *For the time being, however, immunotherapy is still in its experimental stages.* **13** PHRASE If you do something **from time to time**, you do it occasionally but not regularly. ☐ *Her daughters visited him from time to time when he was bedridden.*

④ **time** ♦♦♦ /taɪm/ **1** PHRASE If you say that something is the case **half the time** you mean that it often is the case. [INFORMAL] ☐ *Half the time, I don't have the slightest idea what he's talking about.* **2** PHRASE If you are **in time** for a particular event, you are not too late for it. ☐ *I arrived just in time for my flight to Hawaii.* **3** PHRASE If you say that something will happen **in time** or **given time**, you mean that it will happen eventually, when a lot of time has passed. ☐ *He would sort out his own problems, in time.* **4** PHRASE If you are playing, singing, or dancing **in time** with a piece of music, you are following the rhythm and speed of the music correctly. If you are **out of time** with it, you are not following the rhythm and speed of the music correctly. ☐ *Her body swayed in time with the music.* **5** PHRASE If you say that something will happen, for example, **in a week's time** or **in two years' time**, you mean that it will happen a week from now or two years from now. ☐ *Presidential elections are due to be held in ten days' time.* **6** PHRASE If you arrive somewhere **in good time**, you arrive early so that there is time to spare before a particular event. ☐ *We got there in good time for the opening ceremony.* **7** PHRASE If something happens **in no time** or **in next to no time**, it happens almost immediately or very quickly. ☐ *He's going to be just fine. At his age he'll heal in no time.* **8** PHRASE If you **keep time** when playing or singing music, you follow or play the beat, without going too fast or too slowly. ☐ *As he sang he kept time on a small drum.* **9** PHRASE When you talk about how well a watch or clock **keeps time**, you are talking about how accurately it measures time. ☐ *Some pulsars keep time better than the Earth's most accurate clocks.* **10** PHRASE If you **make time** for a particular activity or person, you arrange to have some free time so that you can do the activity or spend time with the person. ☐ *Before leaving the city, be sure to make time for a shopping trip.* **11** PHRASE If you say that you **made good time** on a trip, you mean that it did not take you very long compared to the length of time you expected it to take. ☐ *They had left early in the morning, on quiet roads, and made good time.* **12** PHRASE If someone is **making up for lost time**, they are doing something actively and with enthusiasm because they have not had the opportunity to do it before or when they were younger. ☐ *Five years older than the majority of officers of his same rank, he was determined to make up for lost time.* **13** PHRASE If you say that something happens or is the case **nine times out of ten** or **ninety-nine times out of a hundred**, you mean that it happens on nearly every occasion or is almost always the case. ☐ *When they want something, nine times out of ten they get it.*

⑤ **time** ♦♦♦ /taɪm/ (**times**)
→ Please look at meaning **13** to see if the expression you are looking for is shown under another headword.
1 PHRASE If you say that someone or something is, for example, the best writer **of all time**, or the most successful movie **of all time**, you mean that they are the best or most successful that there has ever been. ☐ *"Monopoly" is one of the best-selling games of all time.* **2** PHRASE If you are **on time**, you are not late. ☐ *Don't worry, she'll be on time.* **3** PHRASE If you say that it is **only a matter of time** or **only a question of time** before something happens, you mean that it cannot be avoided and will definitely happen at some future date. ☐ *It now seems only a matter of time before they resign.* **4** PHRASE If you do something to **pass the time** you do it because you have some time available and not because you really want to do it. ☐ *Without particular interest and just to pass the time, I read a story.* **5** PHRASE If you say that something will **take time**, you mean that it will take a long time. ☐ *Change will come, but it will take time.* **6** PHRASE If you **take** your **time** doing something, you do it slowly and do not hurry. ☐ *"Take your time," Ted told him. "I'm in no hurry."* **7** PHRASE If a child can **tell the time**, they are able to find out what the time is by looking at a clock or watch. ☐ *My four-year-old daughter cannot quite tell the time.* **8** PHRASE If something happens **time after time**, it happens in a similar way on many occasions. ☐ *Burns had escaped from jail time after*

time. **9** PHRASE If you say that **time flies**, you mean that it seems to pass very quickly. ☐ *Time flies when you're having fun.* **10** PHRASE If you say there is **no time to lose** or **no time to be lost**, you mean you must hurry as fast as you can to do something. ☐ *He rushed home, realizing there was no time to lose.* **11** PHRASE If you say that **time will tell** whether something is true or correct, you mean that it will not be known until some time in the future whether it is true or correct. ☐ *Only time will tell whether Broughton's optimism is justified.* **12** PHRASE If you **waste no time** in doing something, you take the opportunity to do it immediately or quickly. ☐ *Tom wasted no time in telling me why he had come.* **13 time and again** → see **again**

time and mo|tion N-UNCOUNT [usu N n] A **time and motion** study is a study of the way that people do a particular job, or the way they work in a particular place in order to discover the most efficient and safe methods of working.

time bomb (**time bombs**) also **time-bomb** **1** N-COUNT A **time bomb** is a bomb with a mechanism that causes it to explode at a particular time. **2** N-COUNT [oft adj N] If you describe something as a **time bomb**, you mean that it is likely to have a serious effect on a person or situation at a later date, especially if you think it will cause a lot of damage. ☐ *Unemployment is building up into a social time bomb across the industrialized world.*

time-consuming also **time consuming** **1** ADJ If something is **time-consuming**, it takes a lot of time. ☐ *It's just very time consuming to get such a large quantity of data.* **2** → See feature box at **leisure**

time frame (**time frames**) N-COUNT The **time frame** of an event is the length of time during which it happens or develops. [FORMAL] ☐ *The time frame within which all this occurred was from September 2004 to March 2005.*

time-honored

in BRIT, use **time-honoured**

ADJ [ADJ n] A **time-honored** tradition or way of doing something is one that has been used and respected for a very long time. ☐ *Raising the money is done in the usual time-honored ways – college events, garage sales, and the like.*

time|keep|er /ˈtaɪmkiːpər/ (**timekeepers**) also **time-keeper** N-COUNT A **timekeeper** is a person or an instrument that records or checks the time.

time|keep|ing /ˈtaɪmkiːpɪŋ/ N-UNCOUNT **Timekeeping** is the process or activity of timing an event or series of events. ☐ *Who did the timekeeping?*

time lag (**time lags**) also **time-lag** N-COUNT [usu sing, oft N between pl-n] A **time lag** is a fairly long interval of time between one event and another related event that happens after it. ☐ *There is a time-lag between theoretical research and practical applications.*

time|less /ˈtaɪmləs/ **1** ADJ If you describe something as **timeless**, you mean that it is so good or beautiful that it cannot be affected by changes in society or fashion. ☐ *There is a timeless quality to his best work.* **2** → See feature box at **fashion**

time lim|it (**time limits**) N-COUNT A **time limit** is a date before which a particular task must be completed. ☐ *We have extended the time limit for claims until July 30.*

time|line /ˈtaɪmlaɪn/ (**timelines**) also **time line** **1** N-COUNT A **timeline** is a visual representation of a sequence of events, especially historical events. ☐ *The timeline shows important events from the Earth's creation to the present day.* **2** N-COUNT A **timeline** is the length of time that a project is expected to take. [BUSINESS] ☐ *Use your deadlines to establish the timeline for your research plan.*

time|ly /ˈtaɪmli/ (**timelier, timeliest**) ADJ If you describe an event as **timely**, it happens exactly at the moment when it is most useful, effective, or relevant. [APPROVAL] ☐ *The recent outbreaks of cholera are a timely reminder that this disease is still a serious health hazard.*

time man|age|ment N-UNCOUNT **Time management** is the process of deciding on the order in which you will do tasks, and making sure that they are done on schedule. [BUSINESS]

time out (**time outs**) also **time-out** **1** N-VAR In basketball, football, ice hockey, and some other sports, when a team calls a **time out**, they call a stop to the game for a few minutes in order to rest and discuss how they are going to play. ❏ *With 22.2 seconds to go before halftime, Brown wanted to call a time-out.* ◨ N-UNCOUNT [oft N *from* n, N *to-*inf] If you take **time out** from a job or activity, you have a break from it and do something different instead. ❏ *He took time out from campaigning to accompany his mother to dinner.*

time|piece /taɪmpis/ (**timepieces**) also **time piece** N-COUNT A **timepiece** is a clock, watch, or other device that measures and shows time. [OLD-FASHIONED]

tim|er /taɪmər/ (**timers**) ◧ N-COUNT A **timer** is a small device that can be set to ring in a certain number of minutes, usually to remind you to do something. ❏ *Put the chicken in the oven when the timer goes off.* ◨ N-COUNT A **timer** is a device that measures time, especially one that is part of a machine and causes it to start or stop working at specific times. ❏ *...electronic timers that automatically switch on the lights when it gets dark.* ◪ → see also **egg timer**

time|scale /taɪmskeɪl/ (**timescales**) also **time scale** N-COUNT The **timescale** of an event is the length of time during which it happens or develops. ❏ *The likelihood is that these companies now will show excellent profits on a two-year timescale.*

time-share (**time-shares**) also **time share** N-VAR If you have a **time-share**, you have the right to use a particular property as vacation accommodations for a specific amount of time each year. ❏ *Other prizes include hotel discounts and a time-share at a resort in Palm Springs.*

time sig|na|ture (**time signatures**) N-COUNT The **time signature** of a piece of music consists of two numbers written at the beginning that show how many beats there are in each bar.

time slot (**time slots**) N-COUNT A television or radio program's **time slot** is the time when it is broadcast. ❏ *90 percent of listeners stayed with the program when it changed its time slot.*

time switch (**time switches**) N-COUNT A **time switch** is a device that causes a machine to start or stop working at specific times.

time|table /taɪmteɪbəl/ (**timetables**) ◧ N-COUNT A **timetable** is a plan of the times when particular events will take place. ❏ *The timetable was hopelessly optimistic.* ◨ N-COUNT A **timetable** is a list of the times when trains, boats, buses, or airplanes are supposed to arrive at or leave from a particular place. [mainly BRIT]

| in AM, usually use **schedule** |

◪ N-COUNT In a school or college, a **timetable** is a list that shows the times in the week at which particular subjects are taught. You can also refer to the range of subjects that a student learns or the classes that a teacher teaches as their **timetable**. [BRIT]

| in AM, usually use **class schedule** |

time tri|al (**time trials**) N-COUNT In cycling and some other sports, a **time trial** is a contest in which competitors race along a course individually and their time is recorded, instead of racing directly against each other.

time wast|er (**time wasters**) also **time-waster** N-COUNT If you say that someone or something is a **time waster**, you mean that they cause you to spend a lot of time doing something that is unnecessary or does not produce any benefit. [DISAPPROVAL] ❏ *Surfing the internet is fun, but it's also a time waster.*

time|worn /taɪmwɔrn/ ADJ Something that is **timeworn** is old or has been used a lot over a long period of time. ❏ *Even in the dim light the equipment looked old and timeworn.*

time zone (**time zones**) N-COUNT A **time zone** is one of the areas into which the world is divided according to what time it is there. For example, the Pacific time zone is two hours behind the Central time zone which is one hour behind the Eastern time zone.

tim|id /tɪmɪd/ ADJ **Timid** people are shy, nervous, and lack courage or confidence in themselves. ❏ *A timid child, Isabella had learned obedience at an early age.* ● **ti|mid|ity** /tɪmɪdɪti/ N-UNCOUNT ❏ *She doesn't ridicule my timidity.* ● **tim|id|ly** ADV ❏ *The little boy stepped forward timidly and shook Leo's hand.*

tim|ing /taɪmɪŋ/ ◧ N-UNCOUNT **Timing** is the skill or action of judging the right moment in a situation or activity at which to do something. ❏ *His photo is a wonderful happy moment caught with perfect timing.* ◨ N-UNCOUNT **Timing** is used to refer to the time at which something happens or is planned to happen, or to the length of time that something takes. ❏ *They had concerns about the timing of the report.* ◪ → see also **time** ①

tim|or|ous /tɪmərəs/ ◧ ADJ If you describe someone as **timorous**, you mean that they are frightened and nervous of other people and situations. [LITERARY] ❏ *He is a reclusive, timorous creature.* ◨ ADJ If you describe someone's actions or decisions as **timorous**, you are criticizing them for being too cautious or weak, because the person is not very confident and is worried about the possible consequences of their actions. [DISAPPROVAL] ❏ *Some delegates believe the final declaration is likely to be too timorous.*

tim|pa|ni /tɪmpəni/ N-PLURAL **Timpani** are large drums that are played in an orchestra.

tin /tɪn/ (**tins**) ◧ N-UNCOUNT **Tin** is a soft silvery-white metal. ❏ *...a factory that turns scrap metal into tin cans.* ◨ N-COUNT A **tin** is a metal container with a lid in which things such as cookies, cakes, or tobacco can be kept. ❏ *Store the cookies in an airtight tin.* ◪ N-COUNT You can use **tin** to refer to a tin and its contents, or to the contents only. ❏ *...a tin of paint.* ◩ N-COUNT A **tin** is a metal container which is filled with food and sealed in order to preserve the food for long periods of time. [mainly BRIT] ◫ N-COUNT You can use **tin** to refer to a tin and its contents, or to the contents only. [mainly BRIT]

| in AM, usually use **can** |

◬ N-COUNT A baking **tin** is a metal container used for baking things such as cakes and bread in an oven. [BRIT]

| in AM, use **pan** |

◭ to have a **tin ear** → see **ear** ◮ → See feature box at **recycle**; See also color supplement

tinc|ture /tɪŋktʃər/ (**tinctures**) N-VAR [oft N *of* n] A **tincture** is a medicine consisting of alcohol and a small amount of a drug, herb, or medicine. ❏ *...a few drops of tincture of valerian.*

tin|der /tɪndər/ N-UNCOUNT **Tinder** consists of small pieces of something dry, especially wood or grass, that burns easily and can be used for lighting a fire.

tinder|box /tɪndərbɒks/ (**tinderboxes**) also **tinder box** N-COUNT [usu sing] If you say that a situation is a **tinderbox**, you mean that it is very tense and something dangerous or bad is likely to happen very soon.

tine /taɪn/ (**tines**) N-COUNT The **tines** of something such as a fork are the long pointed parts.

tin|foil /tɪnfɔɪl/ also **tin foil** N-UNCOUNT **Tinfoil** consists of shiny metal in the form of a thin sheet which is used for wrapping food.

tinge /tɪndʒ/ (**tinges**) N-COUNT A **tinge** of a color, feeling, or quality is a small amount of it. ❏ *His skin had an unhealthy grayish tinge.*

tinged /tɪndʒd/ ◧ ADJ If something is **tinged** with a particular color, it has a small amount of that color in it. ❏ *His dark hair was just tinged with gray.* ◨ ADJ If something is **tinged with** a particular feeling or quality, it has or shows a small amount of that feeling or quality. ❏ *Her homecoming was tinged with sadness.*

tin|gle /tɪŋɡəl/ (**tingles, tingling, tingled**) ◧ V-I When a part of your body **tingles**, you have a slight stinging feeling there. ❏ *The backs of his thighs tingled.* ● **tin|gling** N-UNCOUNT ❏ *Its effects on the nervous system include weakness, paralysis, and tingling in the hands and feet.* ◨ V-I If you **tingle** with a feeling such as excitement, you feel it very strongly. ❏ *She tingled with excitement.* ● N-COUNT **Tingle** is also a noun. ❏ *I felt a sudden tingle of excitement.*

tin|gly /tɪŋɡli/ (**tinglier, tingliest**) ◧ ADJ If something makes your body feel **tingly**, it gives you a slight stinging feeling. ❏ *These lotions tend to give the skin a tingly sensation.* ◨ ADJ If something pleasant or exciting makes you feel **tingly**, it gives you a pleasant warm feeling. ❏ *He had a way of sounding so sincere. It made me warm and tingly.*

tink|er /tɪŋkər/ (tinkers, tinkering, tinkered) V-I If you **tinker with** something, you make some small changes to it, in an attempt to improve it or repair it. ❑ *Instead of the country admitting its error, it just tinkered with the problem.*

tin|kle /tɪŋkəl/ (tinkles, tinkling, tinkled) **1** V-I If something **tinkles**, it makes a clear, high-pitched, ringing noise, especially as small parts of it strike a surface. ❑ *A fresh cascade of splintered glass tinkled to the floor.* ❑ *We strolled past tinkling fountains and perfumed gardens.* • N-COUNT [usu sing] **Tinkle** is also a noun. ❑ *...a tinkle of broken glass.* **2** V-T/V-I If a bell **tinkles** or if you **tinkle** it, it makes a quiet ringing noise as you shake it. ❑ *An old-fashioned bell tinkled as he pushed open the door.* ❑ *The teacher tinkled her desk bell and they all sat down again.* • N-COUNT [usu sing] **Tinkle** is also a noun. ❑ *...the tinkle of goat bells.* **3** V-I If someone **tinkles**, they urinate. [INFORMAL] ❑ *Take me to the potty. I need to tinkle.* • N-COUNT **Tinkle** is also a noun. ❑ *She needed a tinkle.*

tinned /tɪnd/ ADJ **Tinned** food is food that has been preserved by being sealed in a tin. [mainly BRIT]

in AM, usually use **canned**

tin|ny /tɪni/ (tinnier, tinniest) **1** ADJ If you describe a sound as **tinny**, you mean that it has an irritating, high-pitched quality. ❑ *He could hear the tinny sound of a radio playing a pop song.* **2** ADJ If you use **tinny** to describe something such as a cheap car, you mean that it is made of thin metal and is of poor quality. ❑ *It is one of the cheapest cars on the market, with tinny bodywork.*

tin open|er [BRIT] → see **can opener**

tin|pot /tɪnpɒt/ also **tin-pot** ADJ [ADJ n] You can use **tinpot** to describe a leader, country, or government that you consider to be unimportant and inferior to most others. [DISAPPROVAL] ❑ *...a tinpot dictator.*

tin|sel /tɪnsəl/ N-UNCOUNT **Tinsel** consists of small strips of shiny paper attached to long pieces of thread. People use tinsel as a decoration at Christmas.

Tin|sel|town /tɪnsəltaʊn/ N-PROPER People sometimes refer to Hollywood as **Tinseltown**, especially when they want to show that they disapprove of it or when they are making fun of it.

tint /tɪnt/ (tints, tinting, tinted) **1** N-COUNT A **tint** is a small amount of color. ❑ *Its large leaves often show a delicate purple tint.* **2** V-T [usu passive] If something is **tinted**, it has a small amount of a particular color or dye in it. ❑ *Eyebrows can be tinted with the same dye.*

tin whis|tle (tin whistles) N-COUNT A **tin whistle** is a simple musical instrument in the shape of a metal pipe with holes. Tin whistles make a high sound and are often used in folk music, for example, Irish music.

tiny ✦✧✧ /taɪni/ (tinier, tiniest) ADJ Something or someone that is **tiny** is extremely small. ❑ *The living room is tiny.* ❑ *Though she was tiny, she had a very loud voice.*

SUFFIX
-tion
forms nouns that refer to a state or process, or to an instance of that process. *For example, the* **protection** *of something is the act of protecting it.*

tip ✦✧✧ /tɪp/ (tips, tipping, tipped) **1** N-COUNT The **tip** of something long and narrow is the end of it. ❑ *The sleeves covered his hands to the tips of his fingers.* **2** V-T/V-I If you tip an object or part of your body or if it **tips**, it moves into a sloping position with one end or side higher than the other. ❑ *He leaned away from her, and she had to tip her head back to see him.* **3** V-T If you **tip** something somewhere, you pour it there. ❑ *Tip the vegetables into a bowl.* **4** V-T If you **tip** someone such as a waiter in a restaurant, you give them some money in order to thank them for their services. ❑ *We usually tip 18-20%.* **5** N-COUNT If you give a **tip** to someone such as a waiter in a restaurant, you give them some money to thank them for their services. ❑ *I gave the barber a tip.* **6** N-COUNT A **tip** is a useful piece of advice. ❑ *It shows how to prepare a resume, and gives tips on applying for jobs.* **7** N-COUNT A **tip** is the same as a **dump** or a **garbage dump**. [BRIT] **8** PHRASE If you say that a problem is **the tip of the iceberg**, you mean that it is one small part of a much larger problem. ❑ *Unless we're all a lot more careful, the people who have died so far will be just the tip of the iceberg.* **9** PHRASE If something **tips the scales** or **tips the balance**, it gives someone a slight advantage. ❑ *Today's slightly shorter race could well help to tip the scales in her favor.*

▶ **tip off** PHRASAL VERB If someone **tips** you **off**, they give you information about something that has happened or is going to happen. ❑ *Greg tipped police off about a drunk driver.*

▶ **tip over** PHRASAL VERB If you **tip** something **over** or if it **tips over**, it falls over or turns over. ❑ *He tipped the table over in front of him.* ❑ *Don't tip over that glass.*

COLLOCATIONS
tip
NOUN **6**
noun + **tip**: insider, style, travel
adjective + **tip**: handy, hot, top, useful
verb + **tip**: offer, provide, share

tip-off (tip-offs) N-COUNT A **tip-off** is a piece of information or a warning that you give to someone, often privately or secretly. ❑ *The man was arrested at his home after a tip-off to police from a member of the public.*

-tipped /-tɪpt/ COMB IN ADJ **-tipped** combines with nouns to form adjectives that describe something as having a tip made of a particular substance or covered with a particular material. ❑ *In his hand, he carried a gold-tipped cane.* ❑ *...poison-tipped arrows.*

tip|ple /tɪpəl/ (tipples) N-COUNT [usu supp N] A person's **tipple** is the alcoholic drink that they usually drink. [mainly BRIT, INFORMAL] ❑ *My favorite tipple is a glass of port.*

tip|ster /tɪpstər/ (tipsters) N-COUNT A **tipster** is someone who tells you, usually in exchange for money, which horses they think will win particular races, so that you can bet money on the horses.

tip|sy /tɪpsi/ (tipsier, tipsiest) ADJ If someone is **tipsy**, they are slightly drunk. ❑ *I'm feeling a little tipsy.*

tip|toe /tɪptoʊ/ (tiptoes, tiptoeing, tiptoed) **1** V-I If you **tiptoe** somewhere, you walk there very quietly without putting your heels on the floor when you walk. ❑ *She slipped out of bed and tiptoed to the window.* **2** PHRASE If you do something **on tiptoe** or **on tiptoes**, you do it standing or walking on the front part of your foot, without putting your heels on the ground. ❑ *She leaned her bike against the stone wall and stood on tiptoe to peer over it.*

tip|top /tɪptɒp/ ADJ [usu ADJ n] You can use **tiptop** to indicate that something is extremely good. [INFORMAL, OLD-FASHIONED] ❑ *Her hair was thick, glossy and in tiptop condition.*

ti|rade /taɪreɪd/ (tirades) N-COUNT A **tirade** is a long angry speech in which someone criticizes a person or thing. ❑ *She launched into a tirade against the policies that ruined her business.*

tire /taɪər/ (tires, tiring, tired) **1** V-T/V-I If something **tires** you or you **tire**, you feel that you have used a lot of energy and you want to rest or sleep. ❑ *If driving tires you, take the train.* **2** V-I [no passive] If you **tire of** something, you no longer wish to do it, because you have become bored of it or unhappy with it. ❑ *He felt he would never tire of listening to her stories.* **3** N-COUNT A **tire** is a thick piece of rubber which is fitted onto the wheels of vehicles such as cars, buses, and bicycles.

in BRIT, use **tyre**

4 → See also color supplement

tired ✦✧✧ /taɪərd/ **1** ADJ If you are **tired**, you feel that you want to rest or sleep. ❑ *Michael is tired and he has to rest after his long trip.* • **tired|ness** N-UNCOUNT ❑ *He had to cancel some engagements because of tiredness.* **2** ADJ You can describe a part of your body as **tired** if it looks or feels as if you need to rest it or to sleep. ❑ *Cucumber is good for soothing tired eyes.* **3** ADJ [v-link ADJ of n/-ing] If you are **tired of** something, you do not want it to continue because you are bored of it or unhappy with it. ❑ *I am tired of all the speculation.*

SYNONYMS
tired
ADJ **1**
exhausted: *She was too exhausted and distressed to talk about the tragedy.*
weary: *Rachel looked pale and weary.*
drained: *United left the pitch looking stunned and drained.*
worn out: *Before the race, he is fine. But afterwards, he is worn out.*

tire|less /taɪərlɪs/ ADJ If you describe someone or their efforts as **tireless**, you approve of the fact that they put a lot of hard work into something, and refuse to give up or take a rest. [APPROVAL] ☐ ...Mother Teresa's tireless efforts to help the poor. • **tire|less|ly** ADV [ADV with v] ☐ He worked tirelessly for the cause of health and safety.

tire|some /taɪərsəm/ ADJ If you describe someone or something as **tiresome**, you mean that you find them irritating or boring. ☐ ...the tiresome man next door.

tir|ing /taɪərɪŋ/ ADJ If you describe something as **tiring**, you mean that it makes you tired so that you want to rest or sleep. ☐ It had been a long and tiring day.

'tis /tɪz/ also **tis** In the past, 'it is' was sometimes written as '**tis**. [OLD-FASHIONED] ☐ 'Tis bitter cold.

tis|sue ♦◇◇ /tɪʃuː/ (**tissues**) **1** N-UNCOUNT [also N in pl] In animals and plants, **tissue** consists of cells that are similar to each other in appearance and that have the same function. ☐ As we age we lose muscle tissue. **2** N-UNCOUNT **Tissue paper** is thin paper that is used for wrapping things that are easily damaged, such as objects made of glass or china. ☐ ...a small package wrapped in tissue paper. **3** N-COUNT A **tissue** is a piece of thin soft paper that you use to blow your nose. ☐ ...a box of tissues.

─── **COLLOCATIONS** ───
tissue
NOUN **1**
noun + **tissue**: brain, breast, muscle, scar; animal, plant
adjective + **tissue**: cancerous, damaged, healthy; connective, fatty, ovarian, soft
verb + **tissue**: regenerate, repair; destroy, remove

tit /tɪt/ (**tits**) **1** N-COUNT [usu pl] A woman's **tits** are her breasts. [INFORMAL, VULGAR] **2** N-COUNT A **tit** is a small European or North American bird that eats insects and seeds. There are several kinds of **tit**. **3** → see also **blue tit**

ti|tan /taɪtᵊn/ (**titans**) N-COUNT [usu N n, N of n] If you describe someone as a **titan** of a particular field, you mean that they are very important and powerful or successful in that field. ☐ ...the country's two richest business titans.

ti|tan|ic /taɪtænɪk/ ADJ [usu ADJ n] If you describe something as **titanic**, you mean that it is very big or important, and usually that it involves very powerful forces. ☐ The world had witnessed a titanic struggle between two visions of the future.

ti|ta|nium /taɪteɪniəm/ **1** N-UNCOUNT **Titanium** is a light strong white metal. **2** → See also color supplement

tit|bit /tɪtbɪt/ → see **tidbit**

tit-for-tat ADJ [usu ADJ n] A **tit-for-tat** action is one where someone takes revenge on another person for what they have done by doing something similar to them. ☐ The two countries have each expelled another diplomat following a round of tit-for-tat expulsions.

tithe /taɪð/ (**tithes**) N-COUNT A **tithe** is a fixed amount of money or goods that is given regularly in order to support a church, a priest, or a charity.

tit|il|late /tɪtᵊleɪt/ (**titillates, titillating, titillated**) V-T If something **titillates** someone, it pleases and excites them, especially in a sexual way. ☐ The pictures were not meant to titillate audiences. • **tit|il|lat|ing** ADJ ☐ ...deliberately titillating lyrics.

ti|tle ♦♦◇ /taɪtᵊl/ (**titles, titling, titled**) **1** N-COUNT The **title** of a book, play, movie, or piece of music is its name. ☐ "Patience and Sarah" was first published in 1969 under the title "A Place for Us." **2** V-T When a writer, composer, or artist **titles** a work, they give it a name. ☐ Pirandello titled his play "Six Characters in Search of an Author." ☐ The single is titled "White Love." **3** N-COUNT Publishers and booksellers often refer to books or magazines as **titles**. ☐ The magazine has become the biggest publisher of new poetry, with 50 new titles a year. **4** N-COUNT Someone's **title** is a word such as 'Mr,' 'Mrs,' or 'Doctor,' that is used before their own name in order to show their status or profession. ☐ Please fill in your name and title. **5** N-COUNT Someone's **title** is a name that describes their job or status in an organization. ☐ He was given the title of assistant manager. **6** N-COUNT If a person or team wins a particular **title**, they win a sports competition that is held regularly. Usually a person keeps a title until someone else defeats them. ☐ He became Jamaica's first Olympic gold medalist when he won the 400 meter title in 1948. **7** N-COUNT In Britain, and some other countries, a person's **title** is a word such as 'Sir,' 'Lord,' or 'Lady' that is used in front of their name, or a phrase that is used instead of their name, and indicates that they have a high rank in society. ☐ Her husband was also honored with his title "Sir Denis."

ti|tled ♦◇◇ /taɪtᵊld/ ADJ In Britain, someone who is **titled** has a title such as 'Lord,' 'Lady,' 'Sir,' or 'Princess' before their name, showing that they have a high rank in society. ☐ Her mother was a titled lady.

title|holder /taɪtᵊlhoʊldər/ (**titleholders**) also **title-holder** N-COUNT The **titleholder** is the person who most recently won a sports competition that is held regularly. ☐ Kasparov became the youngest world titleholder at 22.

ti|tle role (**title roles**) N-COUNT [the N] The **title role** in a play or movie is the role referred to in the name of the play or movie. ☐ Will Smith played the title role in "Ali."

ti|tle track (**title tracks**) N-COUNT [usu sing] The **title track** on a CD, record, or tape is a song or piece of music that has the same title as the CD, record, or tape. ☐ They come from Tuam, a place they refer to on the title track of their album, "All the Way From Tuam."

ti|tlist /taɪtᵊlɪst/ (**titlists**) N-COUNT The **titlist** is the person who most recently won a sports competition that is held regularly. [AM] ☐ ...the defending Stanley Cup titlists.

in BRIT, use **titleholder**

tit|ter /tɪtər/ (**titters, tittering, tittered**) V-I If someone **titters**, they give a short nervous laugh, especially when they are embarrassed about something. ☐ Mention sex therapy and most people will titter in embarrassment. • N-COUNT **Titter** is also a noun. ☐ Mollie gave an uneasy little titter. • **tit|ter|ing** N-UNCOUNT ☐ There was nervous tittering in the studio audience.

tittle-tattle /tɪtᵊl tætᵊl/ N-UNCOUNT If you refer to something that a group of people talk about as **tittle-tattle**, you mean that you disapprove of it because it is not important, and there is no real evidence that it is true. [DISAPPROVAL] ☐ ...tittle-tattle about the private lives of celebrities.

titu|lar /tɪtʃələr/ ADJ [ADJ n] A **titular** job or position has a name that makes it seem important, although the person who has it is not really powerful. ☐ He is titular head, and merely signs laws occasionally.

tiz|zy /tɪzi/ PHRASE If you get **in a tizzy** or **into a tizzy**, you get excited, worried, or nervous about something, especially something that is not important. [INFORMAL] ☐ He was in a complete tizzy, muttering and swearing. ☐ Older veterans have been sent into a tizzy by the idea of female fighter pilots.

TL;DR /tiː el diː ɑːr/ (**TL;DRs**) also **tl;dr** N-COUNT A **TL;DR** is a summary of the main points in something such as an online post or an article. **TL;DR** is an abbreviation for 'too long; didn't read.' ☐ It could launch into a long impassioned defense of its stance, but really the tl;dr is: 'Hahaha, don't be stupid.'

TLC /tiː el siː/ N-UNCOUNT If someone or something needs some **TLC**, they need to be treated in a kind and caring way. **TLC** is an abbreviation for 'tender loving care.' [INFORMAL] ☐ "She's badly in need of some TLC," said one colleague. ☐ Plants with small, yellow leaves will need some TLC.

TM /tiː em/ TM is a written abbreviation for **trademark**.

TNT /tiː en tiː/ N-UNCOUNT **TNT** is a powerful explosive substance. **TNT** is an abbreviation for 'trinitrotoluene.'

─── **TO** ───
① PREPOSITION AND ADVERB USES
② USED BEFORE THE BASE FORM OF A VERB

① **to** ♦♦♦

Usually pronounced /tə/ before a consonant and /tu/ before a vowel, but pronounced /tuː/ when you are emphasizing it.

In addition to the uses shown below, **to** is used in phrasal verbs such as 'see to' and 'come to.' It is also used with some verbs that have two objects in order to introduce the second object.

to

1 PREP You use **to** when indicating the place that someone or something visits, moves toward, or points at. ☐ *Two friends and I drove to Florida during spring break.* ☐ *She went to the window and looked out.* **2** PREP If you go **to** an event, you go where it is taking place. ☐ *We went to a party at the Kurt's house.* ☐ *He came to dinner.* **3** PREP If something is attached **to** something larger or fixed to it, the two things are joined together. ☐ *There was a piece of cloth tied to the dog's collar.* **4** PREP You use **to** when indicating the position of something. For example, if something is **to** your left, it is nearer your left side than your right side. ☐ *Hemingway's studio is to the right.* **5** PREP [v n PREP n] When you give something **to** someone, they receive it. ☐ *He picked up the knife and gave it to me.* **6** PREP [adj/n PREP n] You use **to** to indicate who or what an action or a feeling is directed toward. ☐ *Marcus has been really mean to me today.* ☐ *...troops loyal to the government.* **7** PREP [adj/n PREP n] **To** can show who is affected by something. ☐ *He is a witty man, and an inspiration to all of us.* **8** PREP If you say something **to** someone, you want that person to listen and understand what you are saying. ☐ *I will explain to them that I can't pay them.* **9** PREP You use **to** when showing someone's reaction to something or their feelings about a situation or event. For example, if you say that something happens **to** someone's surprise you mean that they are surprised when it happens. ☐ *To his surprise, the bedroom door was locked.* **10** PREP **To** can show whose opinion is being stated. ☐ *It was clear to me that he respected his boss.* **11** PREP You use **to** when indicating what something or someone is becoming, or the state or situation that they are progressing toward. ☐ *The shouts changed to laughter.* ☐ *...an old ranch house that has been converted to a nature center.* **12** PREP [n PREP n] **To** can be used as a way of introducing the person or organization you are employed by. ☐ *He worked as a dresser to a famous theater actor.* **13** PREP **To** can show a span of time. ☐ *From 1977 to 1985 the United States gross national product grew 21 percent.* **14** PREP [from n PREP n] You use **to** to show two extreme examples of something. ☐ *I read everything from fiction to history.* **15** PREP [from n PREP n] If someone goes from place **to** place or from job **to** job, they go to several places, or work in several jobs, and spend only a short time in each one. ☐ *Larry and Andy had drifted from place to place, working at this and that.* **16** PHRASE If someone moves **to and fro**, they move repeatedly from one place to another and back again, or from side to side. ☐ *She stood up and began to pace to and fro.* **17** PREP [num/n PREP num] You use **to** when you are stating a time less than thirty minutes before an hour. For example, if it is 'five **to** eight,' it is five minutes before eight o'clock. ☐ *At twenty to six I was waiting by the entrance to the station.* **18** PREP You use **to** when giving ratios and rates. ☐ *...engines that can run at 60 miles to the gallon.* **19** PREP You use **to** when indicating that two things happen at the same time. For example, if something is done **to** music, it is done at the same time as music is being played. ☐ *Romeo left the stage, to enthusiastic applause.* **20** CONVENTION If you say 'There's nothing to it,' 'There's not much to it,' or 'That's all there is to it,' you are emphasizing how simple you think something is. [EMPHASIS] ☐ *"There is nothing to it," those I asked about it told me.* **21** → see also **according to** **22** → see also **too** ①

② **to** ✦✦✦

Pronounced /tə/ before a consonant and /tu/ before a vowel.

1 PREP You use **to** before the base form of a verb to form the to-infinitive. You use the to-infinitive after certain verbs, nouns, and adjectives, and after words such as 'how,' 'which,' and 'where.' ☐ *The management wanted to know what I was doing there.* ☐ *She told the family of her decision to resign.* **2** PREP You use **to** before the base form of a verb to indicate the purpose or intention of an action. ☐ *...using the experience of big companies to help small businesses.* **3** PREP You use **to** before the base form of a verb when you are commenting on a statement that you are making, for example, when saying that you are being honest or brief, or that you are summing up or giving an example. ☐ *I'm disappointed, to be honest.* **4** PREP You use **to** before the base form of a verb when indicating what situation follows a particular action. ☐ *From the garden you walk down to discover a large and beautiful lake.* **5** You use **to** with 'too' and 'enough' in expressions like **too much to** and **old enough to**; see **too** ① and **enough**.

toad /toʊd/ (**toads**) N-COUNT A **toad** is a creature which is similar to a frog but which has a drier skin and spends less time in water.

toad|stool /toʊdstul/ (**toadstools**) N-COUNT A **toadstool** is a mushroom that you cannot eat because it is poisonous.

toady /toʊdi/ (**toadies, toadying, toadied**) **1** N-COUNT If you refer to someone as a **toady**, you disapprove of them because they flatter or are nice to an important or powerful person in the hope of getting some advantage from them. [DISAPPROVAL] **2** V-I If you say that someone **is toadying** to an important or powerful person, you disapprove of them because they are flattering or being pleasant toward that person in the hope of getting some advantage from them. [DISAPPROVAL] ☐ *They came backstage afterward, cooing and toadying to him.*

toast /toʊst/ (**toasts, toasting, toasted**) **1** N-UNCOUNT **Toast** is bread which has been cut into slices and made brown and crisp by cooking at a high temperature. ☐ *...a piece of toast.* **2** V-T When you **toast** something such as bread, you cook it at a high temperature so that it becomes brown and crisp. ☐ *Toast the bread lightly on both sides.* **3** N-COUNT When you drink a **toast** to someone or something, you drink some wine or another alcoholic drink as a symbolic gesture, in order to show your appreciation of them or to wish them success. ☐ *Eleanor and I drank a toast to the bride and groom.* **4** V-T When you **toast** someone or something, you drink a toast to them. ☐ *We all toasted his health.*

toast|er /toʊstər/ (**toasters**) **1** N-COUNT A **toaster** is a piece of electric equipment used to toast bread. **2** → See feature box at **household**

toast|master /toʊstmæstər/ (**toastmasters**) N-COUNT At a special ceremony or formal dinner, the **toastmaster** is the person who proposes toasts and introduces the speakers.

toast rack (**toast racks**) N-COUNT A **toast rack** is an object that is designed to hold pieces of toast in an upright position and separate from each other, ready for people to eat.

toasty /toʊsti/ (**toastier, toastiest**) ADJ If something is **toasty**, it is comfortably warm. [INFORMAL] ☐ *The heat of the fire keeps things toasty.*

to|bac|co /təbækoʊ/ (**tobaccos**) **1** N-MASS **Tobacco** is dried leaves which people smoke in pipes, cigars, and cigarettes. You can also refer to pipes, cigars, and cigarettes as a whole as **tobacco**. ☐ *Try to do without tobacco and alcohol.* **2** N-UNCOUNT **Tobacco** is the plant from which tobacco is obtained. ☐ *...Cuba's tobacco crop.*

to|bac|co|nist /təbækənɪst/ (**tobacconists**) N-COUNT [oft the N] A **tobacconist** or a **tobacconist's** is a store that sells things such as tobacco, cigarettes, and cigars.

to|bog|gan /təbɒgən/ (**toboggans**) N-COUNT A **toboggan** is a light wooden board with a curved front, used for traveling down hills on snow or ice.

toc|ca|ta /təkɑtə/ (**toccatas**) N-COUNT [oft in names] A **toccata** is a fast piece of music for the piano, organ, or other keyboard instrument.

to|day ✦✦✦ /tədeɪ/ **1** ADV [ADV with cl] You use **today** to refer to this day on which you are speaking or writing. ☐ *How are you feeling today?* • N-UNCOUNT **Today** is also a noun. ☐ *Today is Friday, September 14th.* **2** → see also **yesterday, tomorrow** **3** ADV You can refer to the present period of history as **today**. ☐ *The United States is in a serious recession today.* • N-UNCOUNT **Today** is also a noun. ☐ *In today's America, health care is one of the very biggest businesses.*

USAGE

today
Don't use 'today' in front of **morning, afternoon,** or **evening**. Instead, use **this**. *His plane left this morning.*

tod|dle /tɒdᵊl/ (**toddles, toddling, toddled**) V-I When a child **toddles**, it walks unsteadily with short, quick steps. ☐ *...once your baby starts toddling.* ☐ *She fell while toddling around.*

tod|dler /tɒdlər/ (**toddlers**) N-COUNT A **toddler** is a young child who has only just learned to walk or who still walks unsteadily with short, quick steps. ☐ *I had a toddler at home and two other children at school.*

tod|dy /tɒdi/ (toddies) N-VAR [usu supp N] A **toddy** is a drink that is made by adding hot water and sugar to a strong alcoholic drink such as whiskey, rum, or brandy. ❑ ...*a hot toddy.*

to-do /tə duː/ N-SING When there is a **to-do**, people are very excited, confused, or angry about something. [INFORMAL]

toe /toʊ/ (toes) **1** N-COUNT Your **toes** are the five movable parts at the end of each foot. ❑ *She wiggled her toes against the packed sand.* **2** PHRASE If you say that someone or something **keeps** you **on** your **toes**, you mean that they cause you to remain alert and ready for anything that might happen. ❑ *His fiery campaign rhetoric has kept opposition parties on their toes for months.*

toe|cap /toʊkæp/ (toecaps) also **toe-cap** N-COUNT A **toecap** is a piece of leather or metal which is fitted over the end of a shoe or boot in order to protect or strengthen it.

TOEFL /toʊfᵊl/ N-PROPER **TOEFL** is an English language examination which is often taken by foreign students who want to study at universities in English-speaking countries. TOEFL is an abbreviation of 'Test of English as a Foreign Language.'

toe|hold /toʊhoʊld/ (toeholds) also **toe-hold** N-COUNT [usu sing, usu N in/on n] If you have a **toehold** in a situation, you have managed to gain an uncertain position or a small amount of power in it, which you hope will give you the opportunity to get a better or more powerful position. ❑ *The firm's agreement with one of their biggest competitors gave them a toehold in South East Asia.*

toe|nail /toʊneɪl/ (toenails) N-COUNT Your **toenails** are the thin hard areas at the end of each of your toes.

tof|fee /tɒfi/ (toffees) **1** N-VAR **Toffee** or **English toffee** is a hard brown candy made with butter and sugar. **2** N-VAR **Toffee** is a sticky candy that is very chewy. It is made by boiling sugar and butter together with water. [BRIT]

> in AM, use **taffy**

to|fu /toʊfuː/ N-UNCOUNT **Tofu** is a soft white or brown food made from soybeans. ❑ ...*alternative foods like tofu, couscous, and hummus.*

tog /tɒg/ (togs) N-PLURAL **Togs** are clothes, especially ones for a particular purpose. [INFORMAL] ❑ *The photograph showed him wearing football togs.*

toga /toʊgə/ (togas) N-COUNT A **toga** is a piece of clothing which was worn by the ancient Romans.

to|geth|er ♦♦♦ /təgɛðər/

> In addition to the uses shown below, **together** is used in phrasal verbs such as 'piece together,' 'pull together,' and 'sleep together.'

1 ADV If people do something **together**, they do it with each other. ❑ *We went on long bicycle rides together.* ❑ *He and I worked together on a book.* **2** ADV [ADV after v] If things are joined **together**, they are joined with each other so that they touch or form one whole. ❑ *Mix the ingredients together thoroughly.* **3** ADV [ADV after v] If things or people are situated **together**, they are in the same place and very near to each other. ❑ *The trees grew close together.* ❑ *Ginette and I gathered our things together.* **4** ADV [ADV after v] If a group of people are held or kept **together**, they are united with each other in some way. ❑ *He has done a lot to keep the family together.* • ADJ [v-link ADJ] **Together** is also an adjective. ❑ *We are together in the way we're looking at this situation.* **5** ADJ If two people are **together**, they are married or having a sexual relationship with each other. ❑ *We were together for five years.* **6** ADV [ADV after v] If two things happen or are done **together**, they happen or are done at the same time. ❑ *Three horses crossed the finish line together.* **7** ADV You use **together** when you are adding two or more amounts or things to each other in order to consider a total amount or effect. ❑ *Together we earn $60,000 per year.* **8** PHRASE If you say that two things **go together**, or that one thing **goes together** with another, you mean that they go well with each other or cannot be separated from each other. ❑ *I can see that some colors go together and some don't.* **9** PHRASE You use **together with** to mention someone or something else that is also involved in an action or situation. ❑ *Every month we'll deliver the very best articles, together with the latest fashion and beauty news.* **10 to get your act together** → see **act 11 to put your heads together** → see **head** ③

to|geth|er|ness /təgɛðərnɪs/ N-UNCOUNT **Togetherness** is a happy feeling of affection and closeness to other people, especially your friends and family. ❑ *Nothing can ever take the place of real love and family togetherness.*

tog|gle /tɒgᵊl/ (toggles, toggling, toggled) **1** N-COUNT A **toggle** is a small piece of wood or plastic which is sewn to something such as a coat or bag, and which is pushed through a loop or hole to fasten it. **2** V-I On computers and some other machines, if you **toggle** between two functions, you use a part of the machine that allows you to switch from one function to the other one. ❑ *You can toggle between them and the normal icons by selecting View Options.* ❑ *He toggled the com to talk to air traffic control.* • N-COUNT [oft N n] **Toggle** is also a noun. ❑ *Zimmer reached down on his console and flipped a toggle switch.*

toil /tɔɪl/ (toils, toiling, toiled) V-T/V-I When people **toil**, they work very hard doing unpleasant or tiring tasks. [LITERARY] ❑ *People who toiled in dim, dank factories were too exhausted to enjoy their family life.* ❑ *Workers toiled long hours.* • PHRASAL VERB **Toil away** means the same as **toil**. ❑ *He doesn't spend every minute toiling away at his desk.*

toi|let /tɔɪlɪt/ (toilets) **1** N-COUNT A **toilet** is a large bowl with a seat, or a platform with a hole, which is connected to a water system and which you use when you want to get rid of urine or feces from your body. ❑ *She made Tina flush the pills down the toilet.* **2** N-COUNT A **toilet** is a room in a house or public building that contains a toilet. [mainly BRIT]

> in AM, usually use **bathroom**

3 PHRASE You can say that someone **goes to the toilet** to mean that they get rid of waste substances from their body, especially when you want to avoid using words that you think may offend people. [mainly BRIT]

> in AM, usually use **go to the bathroom**

toi|let pa|per also **toilet tissue** N-UNCOUNT **Toilet paper** is thin soft paper that people use to clean themselves after they have gotten rid of urine or feces from their body.

toi|let|ries /tɔɪlətriz/ N-PLURAL **Toiletries** are things that you use when washing or taking care of your body, for example, soap and toothpaste.

toi|let roll (toilet rolls) N-VAR A **toilet roll** is a long narrow strip of toilet paper that is wound around a small cardboard tube. [BRIT]

toi|let|ry bag (toiletry bags) N-COUNT A **toiletry bag** is a small bag in which you keep things such as soap, a washcloth, and a toothbrush when you are traveling.

toi|let tissue → see **toilet paper**

toi|let trained ADJ If a child is **toilet trained**, he or she has learned to use the toilet.

toi|let train|ing N-UNCOUNT **Toilet training** is the process of teaching a child to use the toilet.

toi|let wa|ter (toilet waters) N-MASS **Toilet water** is fairly weak and inexpensive perfume.

to-ing and fro-ing N-UNCOUNT If you say that there is a lot of **to-ing and fro-ing**, you mean that the same actions or movements or the same arguments are being repeated many times. ❑ *After some to-ing and fro-ing, Elsie and the children moved back to Louisiana.*

to|ken /toʊkən/ (tokens) **1** ADJ [ADJ n] You use **token** to describe things or actions which are small or unimportant but are meant to show particular intentions or feelings which may not be sincere. ❑ *The announcement was welcomed as a step in the right direction, but was widely seen as a token gesture.* **2** N-COUNT A **token** is a round flat piece of metal or plastic that is sometimes used instead of money. ❑ ...*slot-machine tokens.* **3** N-COUNT A **token** is a piece of paper or card that can be exchanged for goods, either in a particular store or as part of a special offer. [BRIT]

> in AM, use **coupon**

4 PHRASE You use **by the same token** to introduce a statement that you think is true for the same reasons that were given for a previous statement. ❑ *If you give up exercise, your muscles shrink and fat increases. By the same token, if you expend more energy you will lose fat.*

to|ken|ism /tóukənɪzəm/ N-UNCOUNT If you refer to an action as **tokenism**, you disapprove of it because you think it is just done for effect, in order to show a particular intention or to impress a particular type of person. [DISAPPROVAL] ☐ *Is his promotion evidence of the minorities' advance, or mere tokenism?*

told /tould/ **1** **Told** is the past tense and past participle of **tell**. **2** PHRASE You can use **all told** to introduce or follow a summary, general statement, or total. ☐ *All told there were 104 people on the payroll.*

tol|er|able /tɒlərəbəl/ ADJ If you describe something as **tolerable**, you mean that you can bear it, even though it is unpleasant or painful. ☐ *Our living conditions are tolerable, but I can't wait to leave.* • **tol|er|ably** /tɒlərəbli/ ADV ☐ *Their captors treated them tolerably well.*

tol|er|ance /tɒlərəns/ **1** N-UNCOUNT **Tolerance** is the quality of allowing other people to say and do what they like, even if you do not agree with or approve of it. [APPROVAL] ☐ *...his tolerance and understanding of diverse human nature.* **2** N-UNCOUNT **Tolerance** is the ability to bear something painful or unpleasant. ☐ *There is lowered pain tolerance, lowered resistance to infection.*

tol|er|ant /tɒlərənt/ **1** ADJ If you describe someone as **tolerant**, you approve of the fact that they allow other people to say and do as they like and that they are willing to accept different races, religions, and lifestyles. [APPROVAL] ☐ *They need to be tolerant of different points of view.* **2** ADJ [v-link ADJ of n] If a plant, animal, or machine is **tolerant of** particular conditions or types of treatment, it is able to bear them without being damaged or hurt. ☐ *...plants which are more tolerant of dry conditions.*

tol|er|ate /tɒləreɪt/ (tolerates, tolerating, tolerated) **1** V-T If you **tolerate** a situation or person, you accept them although you do not particularly like them. ☐ *She can no longer tolerate the position that she's in.* **2** V-T If you can **tolerate** something bad or painful, you are able to bear it. ☐ *The ability to tolerate pain varies from person to person.*

toll /toul/ (tolls, tolling, tolled) **1** V-T/V-I When a bell **tolls** or when someone **tolls** it, it rings slowly and repeatedly, often as a sign that someone has died. ☐ *Church bells tolled and black flags fluttered.* **2** N-COUNT A **toll** is a sum of money that you have to pay in order to use a particular bridge or road. ☐ *You can pay a toll to drive on Pike's Peak Highway or relax and take the Pike's Peak Cog Railway.* **3** N-COUNT [N n] A **toll** road or **toll** bridge is a road or bridge that you have to pay to use. ☐ *Most people who drive the toll roads don't use them every day.* **4** N-COUNT A **toll** is a total number of deaths, accidents, or disasters that occur in a particular period of time. [JOURNALISM] ☐ *There are fears that the casualty toll may be higher.* **5** → see also **death toll** **6** PHRASE If you say that something **takes its toll** or **takes a heavy toll**, you mean that it has a bad effect or causes a lot of suffering. ☐ *Winter takes its toll on your health.*

toll-free ADJ [usu ADJ n] A **toll-free** telephone number is one which you can dial without having to pay for the call. [AM]

in BRIT, use **Freefone**

• ADV [ADV after v] **Toll-free** is also an adverb. ☐ *Call our customer service staff toll-free.*

toll pla|za (toll plazas) N-COUNT A **toll plaza** is the entrance to a toll road or toll bridge. [AM] ☐ *When the new highway segment opens, motorists will pay $2.75 at its toll plaza.*

toll|way /toulweɪ/ (tollways) N-COUNT A **tollway** is a road that you have to pay to use. [AM] ☐ *I abandoned the New York tollway south of Albany in search of roads less costly.*

tom /tɒm/ (toms) N-COUNT A **tom** is a male cat.

toma|hawk /tɒməhɔːk/ (tomahawks) N-COUNT A **tomahawk** is a small light ax that was used by Native American peoples.

to|ma|to /təmeɪtoʊ/ (tomatoes) N-VAR **Tomatoes** are soft, red fruit that you can eat raw in salads or cooked as a vegetable.

tomb /tuːm/ (tombs) N-COUNT A **tomb** is a grave, especially one that is above ground and that usually has a sculpture or other decoration on it. ☐ *...the continuing excavation of the emperor's tomb.*

tom|boy /tɒmbɔɪ/ (tomboys) N-COUNT If you say that a girl is a **tomboy**, you mean she likes doing things that are traditionally considered to be things that boys enjoy.

tomb|stone /tuːmstoʊn/ (tombstones) N-COUNT A **tombstone** is a large stone with words carved into it, which is placed on a grave.

tomb|ston|ing /tuːmstoʊnɪŋ/ N-UNCOUNT **Tombstoning** is the activity of jumping off high cliffs into water. ☐ *Tombstoning has claimed four lives already this summer.*

tom cat (tomcats) also **tomcat** N-COUNT A **tom cat** is a male cat.

tome /toʊm/ (tomes) **1** N-COUNT A **tome** is a very large, heavy book. [FORMAL] **2** → See feature box at **book**

tom|fool|ery /tɒmfuːləri/ N-UNCOUNT **Tomfoolery** is playful behavior, usually of a silly, noisy, or rough kind. [OLD-FASHIONED] ☐ *Were you serious, or was that a bit of tomfoolery?*

to|mor|row ✦✧ /təmɒroʊ/ (tomorrows) **1** ADV [ADV with cl] You use **tomorrow** to refer to the day after today. ☐ *Bye, see you tomorrow.* • N-UNCOUNT **Tomorrow** is also a noun. ☐ *What's on your agenda for tomorrow?* **2** ADV [ADV with cl] You can refer to the future, especially the near future, as **tomorrow**. ☐ *What is education going to look like tomorrow?* • N-UNCOUNT [also N in pl] **Tomorrow** is also a noun. ☐ *...tomorrow's computer industry.*

tom-tom (tom-toms) N-COUNT A **tom-tom** is a tall narrow drum that is usually played with the hands.

ton ✦ /tʌn/ (tons) **1** N-COUNT A **ton** is a unit of weight that is equal to 2,000 pounds. ☐ *Hundreds of tons of oil spilled into the ocean.* **2** N-COUNT A **ton** is the same as a **tonne** or **metric ton**, which is 1,000 kilograms. [BRIT]

to|nal /toʊnəl/ ADJ [usu ADJ n] **Tonal** means relating to the qualities or pitch of a sound or to the tonality of a piece of music. ☐ *There is little tonal variety in his voice.* ☐ *...tonal music.*

to|nal|ity /toʊnælɪti/ (tonalities) N-VAR **Tonality** is the presence of a musical key in a piece of music. [TECHNICAL]

tone ✦✧ /toʊn/ (tones, toning, toned) **1** N-COUNT The **tone** of a sound is its particular quality. ☐ *Cross could hear him speaking in low tones to Sarah.* **2** N-COUNT Someone's **tone** is a quality in their voice which shows what they are feeling or thinking. ☐ *I still didn't like his tone of voice; he sounded angry and accusing.* **3** N-SING [also in N] The **tone** of a speech or piece of writing is its style and the opinions or ideas expressed in it. ☐ *The tone of the letter was very friendly.* **4** N-SING The **tone** of a place or an event is its general atmosphere. ☐ *There were no stores that would lower the tone of the area.* **5** N-UNCOUNT The **tone** of someone's body, especially their muscles, is its degree of firmness and strength. ☐ *...stretch exercises that improve muscle tone.* **6** V-T/V-I Something that **tones** your body makes it firm and strong. ☐ *This movement lengthens your spine and tones the spinal nerves.* ☐ *Try these toning exercises before you start the day.* • PHRASAL VERB **Tone up** means the same as **tone**. ☐ *Exercise tones up your body.* **7** N-VAR A **tone** is one of the lighter, darker, or brighter shades of the same color. ☐ *Each brick also varies slightly in tone, texture and size.* **8** N-SING A **tone** is one of the sounds that you hear when you are using a telephone, for example, the sound that tells you that a number is busy, or no longer exists. ☐ *I can't get a dial tone on this phone.*

▶ **tone down** **1** PHRASAL VERB If you **tone down** something that you have written or said, you make it less forceful, severe, or offensive. ☐ *The fiery right-wing leader toned down his militant statements after the meeting.* **2** PHRASAL VERB If you **tone down** a color or a flavor, you make it less bright or strong. ☐ *He was asked to tone down the spices and garlic in his recipes.*

-toned /-toʊnd/ COMB IN ADJ **-toned** combines with adjectives to indicate that something has a particular kind of tone. ☐ *...soft, pastel-toned drawings.*

tone-deaf ADJ If you say that someone is **tone-deaf**, you mean that they cannot sing in tune or recognize different musical notes.

tone|less /toʊnlɪs/ ADJ A **toneless** voice is dull and does not express any feeling. [WRITTEN] • **tone|less|ly** ADV [ADV after v] ☐ *"That's most kind of him," Eleanor said tonelessly.*

ton|er /toʊnər/ (toners) **1** N-MASS A **toner** is a substance which you can put on your skin, for example, to clean it or make it less oily. **2** N-MASS **Toner** is a substance that you put in a photocopier or laser printer in order to produce an image on paper.

tongs /tɒŋz/ **1** N-PLURAL [also *a pair of* N] **Tongs** are a tool that you use to grip and pick up objects that you do not want to touch. They consist of two long narrow pieces of metal joined together at one end. **2** **hammer and tongs** → see **hammer**

tongue /tʌŋ/ (tongues) **1** N-COUNT Your **tongue** is the soft movable part inside your mouth which you use for tasting, eating, and speaking. ❏ *I walked over to the mirror and stuck my tongue out.* **2** N-COUNT You can use **tongue** to refer to the kind of things that a person says. ❏ *She had a nasty tongue.* **3** N-COUNT A **tongue** is a language. [LITERARY] ❏ *The French feel passionately about their native tongue.* **4** PHRASE A **tongue-in-cheek** remark or attitude is not serious, although it may seem to be. ❏ *...a lighthearted, tongue-in-cheek approach.* **5** **to bite your tongue** → see **bite**

tongue de|pres|sor /tʌŋ dɪprɛsər/ (tongue depressors) N-COUNT A **tongue depressor** is a medical instrument that is used to press a patient's tongue down so that their mouth or throat can be examined more easily. [MEDICAL] ❏ *Dr. Avery took the tongue depressor out of Rae's mouth.*

tongue-in-cheek → see **tongue**

tongue-lashing (tongue-lashings) also **tongue lashing** N-COUNT If someone gives you a **tongue-lashing**, they shout at you or criticize you in a very forceful way. [INFORMAL] ❏ *After a cruel tongue lashing, he threw the girl out of the group.*

tongue-tied ADJ [usu v-link ADJ] If someone is **tongue-tied**, they are unable to say anything because they feel shy or nervous. ❏ *In their presence I became self-conscious and tongue-tied.*

tongue-twister (tongue-twisters) also **tongue twister** N-COUNT A **tongue-twister** is a sentence or expression which is very difficult to say correctly, especially when you try to say it quickly. An example of a tongue-twister is 'Red leather, yellow leather.'

ton|ic /tɒnɪk/ (tonics) **1** N-MASS **Tonic** or **tonic water** is a colorless carbonated drink that has a slightly bitter flavor and is often mixed with alcoholic drinks, especially gin. ❏ *Keeler sipped at his gin and tonic.* **2** N-MASS A **tonic** is a medicine that makes you feel stronger, healthier, and less tired. ❏ *People are spending twice as much on health tonics as they were five years ago.*

to|night ✦✧ /tənaɪt/ ADV **Tonight** is used to refer to the evening of today or the night that follows today. ❏ *I'm at home tonight.* ❏ *Tonight he proved what a great player he was.* • N-UNCOUNT **Tonight** is also a noun. ❏ *Tonight is the opening night of the opera.*

ton|nage /tʌnɪdʒ/ (tonnages) **1** N-VAR The **tonnage** of a ship is its size or the amount of space that it has inside it for cargo. [TECHNICAL] **2** N-VAR **Tonnage** is the total number of tons that something weighs, or the total amount that there is of it.

tonne /tʌn/ (tonnes) **1** N-COUNT A **tonne** is a metric unit of weight that is equal to 1,000 kilograms. [BRIT]

in AM, use **metric ton**

2 → see also **ton**

ton|sil|li|tis /tɒnsɪlaɪtɪs/ N-UNCOUNT **Tonsillitis** is a painful swelling of your tonsils caused by an infection.

ton|sils /tɒnsəlz/

The form **tonsil** is used as a modifier.

N-PLURAL Your **tonsils** are the two small soft lumps in your throat at the back of your mouth.

tony /toʊni/ (tonier, toniest) ADJ GRADED; ADV If you describe something as **tony**, you mean it is stylish and sophisticated. [AM] ❏ *...a tony dance club in Manhattan.*

TOO
① ADDING SOMETHING OR RESPONDING
② INDICATING EXCESS

① **too** ✦✦✦ /tu/ **1** ADV [cl/group ADV] You use **too** after mentioning another person, thing, or aspect that a previous statement applies to or includes. ❏ *"Nice to talk to you."—"Nice to talk to you too."* ❏ *"I've got a great feeling about it."—"Me too."* **2** ADV [cl/group ADV] You use **too** after adding a piece of information or a comment to a statement, in order to emphasize that it is surprising or important. [EMPHASIS] ❏ *We did learn to read, and quickly too.*

② **too** ✦✦✦ /tu/
→ Please look at meaning **4** to see if the expression you are looking for is shown under another headword.

1 ADV You use **too** in order to indicate that there is a greater amount or degree of something than is desirable, necessary, or acceptable. ❏ *Leather jeans that are too big will make you look larger.* ❏ *I'm turning up the heat, it's too cold.* **2** ADV [with brd-neg, ADV adj] You use **too** with a negative to make what you are saying sound less forceful or more polite or cautious. [VAGUENESS] ❏ *I wasn't too happy with what I'd written so far.* **3** PHRASE You use **all too** or **only too** to emphasize that something happens to a greater extent or degree than is good or desirable. [EMPHASIS] ❏ *She remembered it all too well.* **4** **none too** → see **none**

took /tʊk/ **Took** is the past tense of **take** ①.

tool ✦✧ /tul/ (tools) **1** N-COUNT A **tool** is any instrument or simple piece of equipment that you hold in your hands and use to do a particular kind of work. For example, spades, hammers, and knives are all tools. ❏ *I find the best tool for the purpose is a pair of shears.* **2** N-COUNT You can refer to anything that you use for a particular purpose as a particular type of **tool**. ❏ *Writing is a good tool for expressing feelings.* **3** → See also color supplement

---
COLLOCATIONS

tool
NOUN **2**
noun + **tool**: bargaining, management, marketing, propaganda; software
adjective + **tool**: diagnostic, educational, online; effective, powerful, useful

---

tool|bar /tulbɑr/ (toolbars) N-COUNT A **toolbar** is a narrow strip across a computer screen containing pictures, called icons, which represent different computer functions. When you want to use a particular function, you move the cursor onto its icon using a mouse and click. Compare **taskbar**. [COMPUTING]

tool box (tool boxes) N-COUNT A **tool box** is a metal or plastic box which contains general tools that you need at home, for example, to do repairs in your house or car.

tool kit (tool kits) N-COUNT A **tool kit** is a special set of tools that are kept together and that are often used for a particular purpose.

toot /tut/ (toots, tooting, tooted) V-T/V-I If someone **toots** their car horn or if a car horn **toots**, it produces a short sound or series of sounds. ❏ *People set off fireworks and tooted their car horns.* ❏ *Car horns toot as cyclists dart precariously through the traffic.* • N-SING **Toot** is also a noun. ❏ *The driver gave me a wave and a toot.*

tooth ✦✧ /tuθ/ (teeth) **1** N-COUNT Your **teeth** are the hard white objects in your mouth, which you use for biting and chewing. ❏ *She had very pretty straight teeth.* **2** N-PLURAL The **teeth** of something such as a comb, saw, cog, or zipper are the parts that stick out in a row on its edge. ❏ *The front cog has 44 teeth.* **3** PHRASE If you have a **sweet tooth**, you like sweet food very much. ❏ *Add more honey if you have a sweet tooth.* **4** **to grit your teeth** → see **grit** **5** **kick in the teeth** → see **kick**

tooth|ache /tuθeɪk/ N-SING A **toothache** is a pain in one of your teeth.

tooth|brush /tuθbrʌʃ/ (toothbrushes) N-COUNT A **toothbrush** is a small brush that you use for cleaning your teeth.

tooth de|cay N-UNCOUNT If you have **tooth decay**, one or more of your teeth has become decayed.

tooth fairy (tooth fairies) N-COUNT [usu the N in sing] The **tooth fairy** is an imaginary creature. A child whose tooth comes out is told that if they put it under their pillow, the tooth fairy will take it away while they are sleeping and leave a coin in its place. ❏ *It has vanished as surely as one's belief in Santa Claus or the tooth fairy.*

tooth|less /tuθlɪs/ **1** ADJ [usu ADJ n] You use **toothless** to describe a person or their smile when they have no teeth. **2** ADJ If you describe something such as an official group or a law as **toothless**, you mean it has no real power and is not effective. ❏ *In his view, the commission remains a toothless and ineffectual body.*

tooth|paste /tu:θpeɪst/ (toothpastes) N-MASS **Toothpaste** is a thick substance which you put on your toothbrush and use to clean your teeth. ☐ *Shaving supplies, toothpaste, and soap were found inside.*

tooth|pick /tu:θpɪk/ (toothpicks) N-COUNT A **toothpick** is a small stick which you use to remove food from between your teeth.

tooth|some /tu:θsəm/ ADJ If you describe food as **toothsome**, you mean that it tastes very good. ☐ *...the toothsome honey-sweetened gingerbread.*

toothy /tu:θi/ (toothier, toothiest) ADJ [ADJ n] A **toothy** smile is one in which a person shows a lot of teeth.

too|tle /tu:t°l/ (tootles, tootling, tootled) **1** V-I If you **tootle** somewhere, you travel or go there without rushing or without any particular aim. [INFORMAL] ☐ *I'm sure Ted is tootling down the motorway at this very moment.* **2** V-T/V-I If you **tootle** a tune on an instrument, you play it quietly, without concentrating or taking it seriously. [INFORMAL] ☐ *McCann tootled a tune on the piano.* ☐ *There was a little wooden flute in there. I tootled on it and passed it around.*

TOP
① NOUN AND ADJECTIVE USES
② VERB AND PHRASAL VERBS
③ PHRASES
---

① **top** ♦♦♦ /tɒp/ (tops) **1** N-COUNT The **top** of something is its highest point or part. ☐ *I waited at the top of the stairs.* ☐ *...the picture at the top of the page.* • ADJ [ADJ n] **Top** is also an adjective. ☐ *...the top corner of the newspaper.* **2** ADJ [ADJ n] The **top** thing or layer in a series of things or layers is the highest one. ☐ *I can't reach the top shelf.* **3** N-COUNT The **top** of something such as a bottle, jar, or tube is a cap, lid, or other device that fits or screws onto one end of it. ☐ *...the plastic tops from soda bottles.* **4** N-SING The **top** of a street, garden, bed, or table is the end of it that is farthest away from where you usually enter it or from where you are. [BRIT]

in AM, use **end**

5 N-COUNT A **top** is a piece of clothing that you wear on the upper half of your body, for example, a blouse or shirt. [INFORMAL] ☐ *Look at my new top.* **6** ADJ [ADJ n] You can use **top** to indicate that something or someone is at the highest level of a scale or measurement. ☐ *The vehicles have a top speed of 80 miles per hour.* **7** N-SING The **top** of an organization or career structure is the highest level in it. ☐ *We started from the bottom and we had to work our way up to the top.* ☐ *...his dramatic rise to the top of the military hierarchy.* • ADJ [ADJ n] **Top** is also an adjective. ☐ *I need to have the top people in this company pull together.* **8** ADJ [ADJ n] You can use **top** to describe the most important or famous people or things in a particular area of work or activity. ☐ *So you want to be a top model.* **9** N-SING If someone is **at the top** of, for example, a table or league or is **the top** of the table or league, their performance is better than that of all the other people involved. ☐ *...the golfer at the top of the leaderboard.* • ADJ **Top** is also an adjective. ☐ *He was the top student in physics.* **10** ADJ You can use **top** to indicate that something is the first thing you are going to do, because you consider it to be the most important. ☐ *Cleaning up the water supply is their top priority.* **11** ADJ [ADJ n] You can use **top** to indicate that someone does a particular thing more times than anyone else or that something is chosen more times than anything else. ☐ *Jamillah Lang was Colorado's top scorer.*

② **top** ♦♦♦ /tɒp/ (tops, topping, topped) V-T To **top** a list means to be mentioned or chosen more times than anyone or anything else. [JOURNALISM] ☐ *It was the first time in years that a Japanese manufacturer had not topped the list for imported vehicles.*

▶ **top out** PHRASAL VERB If something such as a price **tops out** at a particular amount, that is the highest amount that it reaches. [AM] ☐ *The stock topped out at more than $25.* ☐ *Last Friday was a warm day, topping out at 85 degrees.*

▶ **top up** PHRASAL VERB If you **top** something **up**, you make it full again when part of it has been used. [mainly BRIT] ☐ *We topped up the water tanks.*

③ **top** ♦♦♦ /tɒp/ (tops) **1** PHRASE If you say that you clean or examine something **from top to bottom**, you are emphasizing that you do it completely and thoroughly.
[EMPHASIS] ☐ *She would clean the house from top to bottom.* **2** PHRASE You can use **from top to toe** to emphasize that the whole of someone's body is covered or dressed in a particular thing or type of clothing. [mainly BRIT, EMPHASIS] ☐ *They were sensibly dressed from top to toe in rain gear.* **3** PHRASE When something **gets on top of** you, it makes you feel unhappy or depressed because it is very difficult or worrying, or because it involves more work than you can manage. ☐ *Things have been getting on top of me lately.* **4** PHRASE If you **are on top of** or **get on top of** something that you are doing, you are dealing with it successfully. ☐ *...the government's inability to get on top of the situation.* **5** PHRASE If you say something **off the top of** your **head**, you say it without thinking about it much before you speak, especially because you do not have enough time. ☐ *It was the best I could think of off the top of my head.* **6** PHRASE If one thing is **on top** of another, it is placed over it or on its highest part. ☐ *He was sound asleep on top of the covers.* **7** PHRASE You can use **on top** or **on top of** to indicate that a particular problem exists in addition to a number of other problems. ☐ *A stepfamily usually faces all the problems that a so-called normal family has, with a set of additional problems on top.* **8** PHRASE You say that someone is **on top** when they have reached the most important position in an organization or business. ☐ *In such a fast-changing business, it's hard to stay on top.* **9** PHRASE If you say that you feel **on top of the world**, you are emphasizing that you feel extremely happy and healthy. [EMPHASIS] ☐ *Two months before she gave birth to Jason she left work feeling on top of the world.* **10** PHRASE [V PHR, PHR N] If someone pays **top dollar** for something, they pay the highest possible price for it. [INFORMAL] ☐ *People will always pay top dollar for something exclusive.* **11** PHRASE If one thing is **over the top** of another, it is placed over it so that it is completely covering it. ☐ *I placed a sheet of plastic over the top of the container.* **12** PHRASE You describe something as **over the top** when you think that it is exaggerated, and therefore unacceptable. [mainly BRIT, INFORMAL] ☐ *The special effects are a bit over the top but I enjoyed it.* **13** PHRASE If you say something **at the top of** your **voice**, you say it very loudly. ☐ *"Stephen, come back!" shouted Marcia at the top of her voice.*

to|paz /toʊpæz/ (topazes) **1** N-VAR A **topaz** is a precious stone which is usually yellowish-brown in color. **2** → See also color supplement

top brass N-SING-COLL [also no det] In the army or in other organizations, the **top brass** are the people in the highest positions. [INFORMAL] ☐ *...a reshuffle of the army's top brass.*

top-class also **top class** ADJ **Top-class** means among the finest of its kind. ☐ *We think he'll turn into a top-class player.*

top|coat /tɒpkoʊt/ (topcoats) also **top coat** **1** N-COUNT A **topcoat** is a coat that you wear over your other clothes. **2** N-VAR A **topcoat** is the final layer of paint or varnish that is put on something. **Topcoat** is the type of paint or varnish that you use for the final layer. Compare **undercoat**.

top dog (top dogs) N-COUNT If a person or organization is **top dog**, they are the most successful or powerful one in a particular group. [INFORMAL] ☐ *Reynolds has never concealed his ambition to be the top dog.*

top dollar → see top dollar ③

top-down ADJ [usu ADJ n] In a **top-down** organization, all the important decisions are made by the most senior people in the organization. ☐ *...the traditional top-down authoritarian company.* ☐ *He complains that the underlying approach is top-down and involves the government dictating the rules.*

top-drawer ADJ [usu ADJ n] If you describe someone or something as **top-drawer**, you are saying, often in a humorous way, that they have a high social standing or are of very good quality.

top-end ADJ **Top-end** products are expensive and of extremely high quality. [BUSINESS] ☐ *...top-end camcorders.*

top hat (top hats) **1** N-COUNT A **top hat** is a tall hat with a narrow brim. Top hats are considered old-fashioned now, but are sometimes worn by dancers and performers. **2** → See also color supplement

top-heavy **1** ADJ Something that is **top-heavy** is larger or heavier at the top than at the bottom, and might therefore fall over. ☐ *...top-heavy flowers such as sunflowers.* **2** ADJ If you describe a business or other organization as **top-heavy**, you mean that it has too many senior managers in relation to the number of junior managers or workers. [DISAPPROVAL] ❑ ...top-heavy bureaucratic structures.

to|pi|ary /toʊpiɛri/ N-UNCOUNT **Topiary** is the art of cutting trees and bushes into different shapes, for example, into the shapes of birds or animals.

top|ic /tɒpɪk/ (topics) N-COUNT A **topic** is a particular subject that you discuss, study, or write about. ❑ *The weather is a constant topic of conversation in Alaska.*

topi|cal /tɒpɪkəl/ ADJ **Topical** is used to describe something that concerns or relates to events that are happening at the present time. ❑ *The newscast covers topical events and entertainment.*

top|knot /tɒpnɒt/ (topknots) N-COUNT If someone has their hair in a **topknot**, the hair is arranged in a small neat bun or knot on top of their head.

top|less /tɒplɪs/ ADJ If a woman is **topless**, she does not wear anything to cover her breasts. ❑ *I wouldn't sunbathe topless if I thought I might offend anyone.*

top-level ADJ [ADJ n] A **top-level** discussion or activity is one that involves the people with the greatest amount of power and authority in an organization or country. ❑ *...a top-level meeting of American generals at the Pentagon.*

top|most /tɒpmoʊst/ ADJ [ADJ n] The **topmost** thing in a number of things is the one that is highest or nearest the top. ❑ *...the topmost branches of a gigantic oak tree.*

top-notch also **top notch** ADJ If you describe someone or something as **top-notch**, you mean that they are of a very high standard or quality. [INFORMAL]

topo|graphi|cal /tɒpəgræfɪkəl/ ADJ [usu ADJ n] A **topographical** survey or map relates to or shows the physical features of an area of land, for example, its hills, valleys, and rivers.

to|pog|ra|phy /təpɒgrəfi/ (topographies) **1** N-UNCOUNT **Topography** is the study and description of the physical features of an area, for example, its hills, valleys, or rivers, or the representation of these features on maps. **2** N-COUNT [usu sing, with poss] The **topography** of a particular area is its physical shape, including its hills, valleys, and rivers. ❑ *The topography of the river's basin has changed significantly since the floods.*

top|ping /tɒpɪŋ/ (toppings) **1** N-MASS A **topping** is food, such as whipped cream or cheese, that is poured or put on top of other food in order to decorate it or add to its flavor. **2** → see also **top** ② → See feature box at **cooking**

top|ple /tɒpəl/ (topples, toppling, toppled) **1** V-T/V-I If someone or something **topples** somewhere or if you **topple** them, they become unsteady or unstable and fall over. ❑ *He just released his hold and toppled slowly backwards.* • PHRASAL VERB **Topple over** means the same as **topple**. ❑ *The tree is so badly damaged they are worried it might topple over.* **2** V-T To **topple** a government or leader, especially one that is not elected by the people, means to cause them to lose power. [JOURNALISM] ❑ *...the revolution which toppled the regime.*

top-ranked ADJ [ADJ n] A **top-ranked** athlete or team is the most successful player or team in a particular sport. [JOURNALISM]

top-ranking ADJ [ADJ n] A **top-ranking** person is someone who has a very high rank or status in a particular organisation or field of activity. ❑ *...top-ranking military officials.*

top-rated ADJ [ADJ n] A **top-rated** show or service is the most successful or highly regarded of its kind. [JOURNALISM] ❑ *...the top-rated American television series.*

top round N-UNCOUNT **Top round** is a cut of beef that is from the upper part of the cow's leg. It is usually cooked by roasting or stewing. [AM]

in BRIT, use **topside**

top se|cret ADJ **Top secret** information or activity is intended to be kept completely secret, for example, in order to prevent a country's enemies from finding out about it. ❑ *The top secret documents had to do with the most advanced military equipment.*

top shelf ADJ **Top-shelf** things or people are of a very high standard or quality. [AM] ❑ *...top-shelf hotel resorts.* ❑ *The selection of bottled beverages is distinctly top-shelf.*

top|side /tɒpsaɪd/ (topsides) **1** ADV [ADV after v] On a ship, if you go **topside**, you go up onto the top deck. [TECHNICAL] ❑ *He left the control station and went topside.* **2** N-COUNT [usu pl] The **topside** or **topsides** of a ship or boat are the top deck or the parts which you can see above the water. [TECHNICAL] **3** N-UNCOUNT → see **top round**

top|soil /tɒpsɔɪl/ N-UNCOUNT **Topsoil** is the layer of soil nearest the surface of the ground.

top|spin /tɒpspɪn/ N-UNCOUNT In sports such as tennis, **topspin** is the way that a ball spins rapidly when you hit it in a certain way. ❑ *Sabatini used her exaggerated topspin to good effect.* ❑ *He put a lot more topspin on his backhand.*

topsy-turvy /tɒpsi tɜrvi/ ADJ Something that is **topsy-turvy** is in a confused or disorganized state. [INFORMAL] ❑ *The world has turned topsy-turvy in my lifetime.*

To|rah /tɔrə/ N-PROPER [the N] In the Jewish religion, the **Torah** is the first five books of the Old Testament of the Bible, regarded collectively. ❑ *...the first school for the study of the Torah.*

torch /tɔrtʃ/ (torches) **1** N-COUNT A **torch** is a long stick with burning material at one end, used to provide light or to set things on fire. ❑ *The shepherd followed, carrying a torch to light his way.* **2** N-COUNT A **torch** is a device that produces a hot flame and is used for tasks such as cutting or joining pieces of metal. ❑ *The gang worked for up to ten hours with acetylene torches to open the vault.* **3** N-COUNT A **torch** is a small electric light which is powered by batteries and which you can carry in your hand. [BRIT]

in AM, use **flashlight**

4 → See feature box at **Olympic Games**

torch|light /tɔrtʃlaɪt/ N-UNCOUNT [oft by N, N n] If you do something by **torchlight**, you do it using the light that is produced by a torch or torches. ❑ *Surgeons are performing operations in tents by torchlight.*

torch song (torch songs) N-COUNT A **torch song** is a sentimental popular song about love. [OLD-FASHIONED]

tore /tɔr/ **Tore** is the past tense of **tear** ①.

tor|ment (torments, tormenting, tormented)

The noun is pronounced /tɔrmɛnt/. The verb is pronounced /tɔrmɛnt/.

1 N-UNCOUNT **Torment** is extreme suffering, usually mental suffering. ❑ *After years of turmoil and torment, she is finally at peace.* **2** N-COUNT A **torment** is something that causes extreme suffering, usually mental suffering. ❑ *Sooner or later most writers end up making books about the torments of being a writer.* **3** V-T If something **torments** you, it causes you extreme mental suffering. ❑ *At times the memories returned to torment her.*

tor|men|tor /tɔrmɛntər/ (tormentors) N-COUNT [usu poss N] Someone's **tormentor** is a person who deliberately causes them physical or mental pain. ❑ *...cases where women subjected to years of brutality lose control and kill their tormentors.*

torn /tɔrn/ **1 Torn** is the past participle of **tear** ①. **2** ADJ If you are **torn** between two or more things, you cannot decide which to choose, and so you feel anxious or troubled. ❑ *Robb is torn between becoming a doctor and a career in athletics.*

tor|na|do /tɔrneɪdoʊ/ (tornadoes or tornados) N-COUNT A **tornado** is a violent wind storm consisting of a tall column of air which spins around very fast and causes a lot of damage.

tor|pe|do /tɔrpidoʊ/ (torpedoes, torpedoing, torpedoed) **1** N-COUNT A **torpedo** is a bomb that is shaped like a tube and that travels under water. **2** V-T [usu passive] If a ship is **torpedoed**, it is hit, and usually sunk, by a torpedo or torpedoes. ❑ *More than a thousand people died when the Lusitania was torpedoed.*

tor|pid /tɔrpɪd/ ADJ If you are **torpid**, you are mentally or physically inactive, especially because you are feeling lazy or sleepy. [FORMAL]

tor|por /tɔrpər/ N-UNCOUNT [also a N] **Torpor** is the state of being completely inactive mentally or physically, for example, because of illness or laziness. [FORMAL] ❑ *He had slumped into a state of torpor from which nothing could rouse him.* ❑ *The sick person gradually falls into a torpor.*

torque /tɔrk/ N-UNCOUNT **Torque** is a force that causes something to spin around a central point such as an axle. [TECHNICAL]

tor|rent /tɔrənt/ (torrents) **1** N-COUNT A **torrent** is a lot of water falling or flowing rapidly or violently. ❑ *Torrents of water gushed into the reservoir.* **2** N-COUNT A **torrent** of abuse or questions is a lot of abuse or questions directed continuously at someone. ❑ *He turned around and directed a torrent of abuse at me.*

tor|ren|tial /tɔrɛnʃəl/ ADJ **Torrential** rain pours down very rapidly and in great quantities. ❑ *The storms and torrential rain caused traffic chaos across the country.*

tor|rid /tɔrɪd/ **1** ADJ [usu ADJ n] **Torrid** weather is extremely hot and dry. [LITERARY] ❑ *...the torrid heat of a Arizona summer.* **2** ADJ [usu ADJ n] A **torrid** relationship or incident involves very strong emotions connected with love and sex. ❑ *She began a torrid love affair with a theatrical designer.*

tor|sion /tɔrʃən/ N-UNCOUNT **Torsion** is a twisting effect on something such as a piece of metal or an organ of the body. [TECHNICAL]

tor|so /tɔrsoʊ/ (torsos) N-COUNT Your **torso** is the main part of your body, and does not include your head, arms, and legs. [FORMAL] ❑ *The man had the bulky upper torso of a weightlifter.*

tort /tɔrt/ (torts) N-VAR A **tort** is something that you do or fail to do which harms someone else and for which you can be sued for damages. [LEGAL]

tor|til|la /tɔrtiyə/ (tortillas) N-VAR A **tortilla** is a piece of thin flat bread that first came from Mexico, and is made from corn, or wheat.

tor|til|la chip (tortilla chips) N-COUNT [usu pl] **Tortilla chips** is another name for **corn chips**.

tor|toise /tɔrtəs/ (tortoises) N-COUNT A **tortoise** is a slow-moving animal with a shell into which it can pull its head and legs for protection.

tortoise|shell /tɔrtəsʃɛl/ **1** N-UNCOUNT **Tortoiseshell** is the hard shell of a kind of sea turtle. It is brown and yellow in color and is often polished and used to make jewelry and ornaments. **2** ADJ [usu ADJ n] **Tortoiseshell** means made of tortoiseshell or made of a material which resembles tortoiseshell. ❑ *He wears huge spectacles with thick tortoiseshell frames.*

tor|tu|ous /tɔrtʃuəs/ **1** ADJ A **tortuous** road is full of bends and twists. ❑ *The only road access is a tortuous mountain route.* **2** ADJ A **tortuous** process or piece of writing is very long and complicated. ❑ *...these long and tortuous negotiations aimed at ending the conflict.*

tor|ture /tɔrtʃər/ (tortures, torturing, tortured) **1** V-T If someone **is tortured**, another person deliberately causes them terrible pain over a period of time, in order to punish them or to make them reveal information. ❑ *Despite being tortured she proclaimed her innocence.* • N-VAR **Torture** is also a noun. ❑ *...alleged cases of torture and murder by the security forces.* **2** V-T To **torture** someone means to cause them to suffer mental pain or anxiety. ❑ *He would not torture her further by trying to argue with her.*

tor|tur|er /tɔrtʃərər/ (torturers) N-COUNT A **torturer** is someone who tortures people.

tor|tur|ous /tɔrtʃərəs/ ADJ Something that is **torturous** is extremely painful and causes great suffering. ❑ *This is a torturous, agonizing way to kill someone.*

toss /tɔs/ (tosses, tossing, tossed) **1** V-T If you **toss** something somewhere, you throw it there lightly, often in a careless way. ❑ *Just toss it in the trash.* **2** V-T If you **toss** your head or **toss** your hair, you move your head backward, quickly and suddenly, often as a way of expressing an emotion such as anger or contempt. ❑ *"I'm sure I don't know." Deb tossed her head.* • N-COUNT **Toss** is also a noun. ❑ *With a toss of his head and a few hard gulps, Bob finished the last of his beer.* **3** V-T In sports and informal situations, if you decide something by **tossing** a coin, you spin a coin into the air and guess which side of the coin will face upward when it lands. ❑ *We tossed a coin to decide who would go out and buy the bagels.* • N-COUNT **Toss** is also a noun. ❑ *It would be better to decide it on the toss of a coin.* **4** PHRASE If you **toss and turn**, you keep moving around in bed and cannot sleep, for example, because you are sick or worried. ❑ *I try to go back to sleep and toss and turn for a while.*

toss-up (toss-ups) N-COUNT If you say that it is a **toss-up** whether one thing will happen or another thing will happen, you mean that either result seems equally likely. ❑ *It's a toss-up whether oil prices will go up or down over the days ahead.*

tot /tɒt/ (tots, totting, totted) **1** N-COUNT A **tot** is a very young child. [INFORMAL] **2** N-COUNT [usu N of n] A **tot** is a small amount of a strong alcoholic drink such as brandy. [mainly BRIT]

in AM, use **shot**

▶ **tot up** PHRASAL VERB To **tot up** a total or a list of numbers means to add up several numbers in order to reach a total. [BRIT] ❑ *I finally sat down to tot up the full extent of my debt.*

to|tal ✦✦✦ /toʊtəl/ (totals, totaling or totalling, totaled or totalled) **1** N-COUNT A **total** is the number that you get when you add several numbers together or when you count how many things there are in a group. ❑ *The companies have a total of 1,776 employees.* **2** ADJ [ADJ n] The **total** number or cost of something is the number or cost that you get when you add together or count all the parts in it. ❑ *They said that the total number of cows dying from BSE would be twenty thousand.* **3** PHRASE If there are a number of things **in total**, there are that number when you count or add them all together. ❑ *I was with my husband for eight years in total.* **4** V-T If several numbers or things **total** a certain figure, that figure is the total of all the numbers or all the things. ❑ *The unit's exports will total $85 million this year.* **5** V-T If someone **totals** a vehicle, they are in a serious accident and the vehicle is so badly damaged that it is not worth repairing. [AM, INFORMAL] ❑ *Buddy totaled his car.* **6** ADJ You can use **total** to emphasize that something is as great in extent, degree, or amount as it possibly can be. [EMPHASIS] ❑ *You were a total failure if you hadn't married by the time you were about twenty-three.* • **to|tal|ly** ADV ❑ *Young people want something totally different from the old ways.*

to|tali|tar|ian /toʊtælɪtɛəriən/ ADJ A **totalitarian** political system is one in which there is only one political party which controls everything and does not allow any opposition parties. [DISAPPROVAL] ❑ *...a brutal totalitarian regime.*

to|tali|tari|an|ism /toʊtælɪtɛəriənɪzəm/ N-UNCOUNT **Totalitarianism** is the ideas, principles, and practices of totalitarian political systems.

to|tal|ity /toʊtælɪti/ N-UNCOUNT [oft N of n, in its/their N] The **totality** of something is the whole of it. [FORMAL] ❑ *...a process of social, economic and political change which involves the totality of human experience.*

to|tal qual|ity man|age|ment N-UNCOUNT **Total quality management** is a set of management principles aimed at improving performance throughout a company, especially by involving employees in decision-making. The abbreviation **TQM** is also used. [BUSINESS] ❑ *He is a firm believer in total quality management.*

tote /toʊt/ (totes, toting, toted) **1** V-T To **tote** something, especially a gun, means to carry it with you. [JOURNALISM] ❑ *The demonstrators fled when soldiers toting machine guns advanced on the crowd.* • **-toting** COMB IN ADJ ❑ *They are too frightened to speak out against the gun-toting thugs.* **2** N-COUNT A **tote** is a sturdy bag that you use to carry things. ❑ *...a canvas tote full of books.*

tote bag (tote bags) N-COUNT A **tote bag** is a large strong bag. ❑ *She was carrying a Gucci tote bag.*

to|tem /toʊtəm/ (totems) **1** N-COUNT In some societies, a family's **totem** is the particular animal, plant, or natural object which they regard as a special symbol and which they believe has spiritual significance. **2** N-COUNT [oft N of n] Something that is a **totem** of another thing is a symbol of it. [WRITTEN] ❑ *This opera is one of the cultural totems of Western civilization.*

to|tem pole (totem poles) N-COUNT A **totem pole** is a long wooden pole with symbols and pictures carved and painted on it. Totem poles are made by some Native American peoples and placed outside their homes.

tot|ter /tɒtər/ (totters, tottering, tottered) V-I If someone **totters** somewhere, they walk there in an unsteady way, for example, because they are drunk. ❑ *She came tottering in in her mother's high heels.*

tou|can /tˈuːkæn/ (toucans) N-COUNT A **toucan** is a South American bird with a very large brightly-colored beak.

TOUCH
① VERB AND NOUN USES
② PHRASES AND PHRASAL VERBS

① **touch** ◆◇◇ /tʌtʃ/ (touches, touching, touched) **1** V-T/V-I If you **touch** something, you put your hand onto it in order to feel it or to make contact with it. ◻ *Her tiny hands gently touched my face.* ◻ *Don't touch!* • N-COUNT **Touch** is also a noun. ◻ *Sometimes even a light touch on the face is enough to trigger off this pain.* **2** V-RECIP If two things **are touching**, if one thing **touches** another, or if you **touch** two things, their surfaces come into contact with each other. ◻ *Their knees were touching.* ◻ *A cyclist crashed when he touched wheels with another rider.* **3** N-UNCOUNT Your sense of **touch** is your ability to tell what something is like when you feel it with your hands. ◻ *The evidence suggests that our sense of touch is programmed to diminish with age.* **4** V-T To **touch** something means to strike it, usually quite gently. ◻ *He scored the first time he touched the ball.* **5** V-T [usu passive, with brd-neg] If something **has** not **been touched**, nobody has dealt with it or taken care of it. ◻ *When John began to restore the house in the 1960s, nothing had been touched for 40 years.* **6** V-T [with brd-neg] If you say that you did not **touch** someone or something, you are emphasizing that you did not attack, harm or destroy them, especially when you have been accused of doing so. [EMPHASIS] ◻ *Pearce remained adamant, saying "I didn't touch him."* **7** V-T [no passive, with brd-neg] You say that you never **touch** something or that you have not **touched** something for a long time to emphasize that you never use it, or you have not used it for a long time. [EMPHASIS] ◻ *He doesn't drink much and doesn't touch drugs.* **8** V-I If you **touch on** a particular subject or problem, you mention it or write briefly about it. ◻ *The film touches on these issues, but only superficially.* **9** V-T If something **touches** you, it affects you in some way for a short time. ◻ *...a guilt that in some sense touches everyone.* **10** V-T If something that someone says or does **touches** you, it affects you emotionally, often because you see that they are suffering a lot or that they are being very kind. ◻ *It has touched me deeply to see how these people live.* • **touched** ADJ [v-link ADJ] ◻ *I was touched to find that he regards me as engaging.* **11** N-COUNT [supp N] A **touch** is a detail which is added to something to improve it. ◻ *They called the event "a tribute to heroes," which was a nice touch.* **12** N-SING If someone has a particular kind of **touch**, they have a particular way of doing something. ◻ *The dishes he produces all have a personal touch.* **13** QUANT [QUANT of n-uncount] A **touch of** something is a very small amount of it. ◻ *She thought she just had a touch of the flu.* **14** → see also **touching**

② **touch** ◆◇◇ /tʌtʃ/ (touches, touching, touched)
→ Please look at meanings **6** and **7** to see if the expression you are looking for is shown under another headword.
1 PHRASE You use **at the touch of** in expressions such as **at the touch of a button** and **at the touch of a key** to indicate that something is possible by simply touching a switch or one of the keys of a keyboard. ◻ *Staff will be able to trace calls at the touch of a button.* **2** PHRASE If you **get in touch** with someone, you contact them by writing to them or telephoning them. If you are, keep, or stay **in touch** with them, you write, phone, or visit each other regularly. ◻ *I will get in touch with my lawyer about this.* **3** PHRASE If you are **in touch** with a subject or situation, or if someone keeps you **in touch** with it, you know the latest news or information about it. If you are **out of touch** with it, you do not know the latest news or information about it. ◻ *...keeping the unemployed in touch with the job market.* **4** PHRASE If you **lose touch** with someone, you gradually stop writing, telephoning, or visiting them. ◻ *In my job one tends to lose touch with friends.* **5** PHRASE If you **lose touch** with something, you no longer have the latest news or information about it. ◻ *Their leaders have lost touch with what is happening in the country.* **6** **the finishing touch** → see **finish**
7 touch wood → see **wood**
▶ **touch down** PHRASAL VERB When an aircraft **touches down**, it lands. ◻ *The space shuttle touched down yesterday.*
▶ **touch off** PHRASAL VERB If something **touches off** a situation or series of events, it causes it to start happening. ◻ *The lightning could touch off wildfires in Eastern Washington.*
▶ **touch up** PHRASAL VERB If you **touch** something **up**, you improve its appearance by covering up small marks with paint or another substance. ◻ *...editing tools to help people touch up photos.* ◻ *The painting has yellowed but the gallery has resisted pressure to touch it up.*

touch|down /tˈʌtʃdaʊn/ (touchdowns) **1** N-VAR **Touchdown** is the landing of an aircraft or spacecraft. ◻ *The astronauts are preparing for touchdown tomorrow morning.* **2** N-COUNT In football and rugby, a **touchdown** is when a team scores points by taking the ball over the opposition's goal line. **3** → See feature box at **travel**

tou|ché /tuːʃˈeɪ/ CONVENTION You say **touché** when you want to admit that the other person in an argument has won a point, usually with a short and witty remark.

touch|ing /tˈʌtʃɪŋ/ **1** ADJ If something is **touching**, it causes feelings of sadness or sympathy. ◻ *Her story is the touching tale of a woman who stood by her life partner, through thick and thin.* **2** → see also **touch** ①, **touch** ②

touch|less /tˈʌtʃlɪs/ ADJ A **touchless** device is controlled by movements or sounds and does not require the user to touch a keypad or screen. [COMPUTING] ◻ *The phone has a touchless display and is controlled by voice.*

touch|pad /tˈʌtʃpæd/ (touchpads) **1** N-COUNT A **touchpad** is a flat pad on some computers that you slide your finger over in order to move the cursor. [COMPUTING] **2** → See also color supplement

touch|screen /tˈʌtʃskriːn/ (touchscreens) also **touch-screen**
1 N-COUNT A **touchscreen** is a computer screen that allows the user to give commands to the computer by touching parts of the screen rather than by using a keyboard or mouse. [COMPUTING] ◻ *...touchscreen voting machines.* **2** → See feature box at **technology**

touch-sen|si|tive ADJ **Touch-sensitive** equipment is operated by the user touching it. [COMPUTING] ◻ *The touch-sensitive controls are easy to operate.*

touch|stone /tˈʌtʃstoʊn/ (touchstones) N-COUNT [usu N of/for n] If you use one thing as a **touchstone** of another, you use it as a test or standard by which you judge the second thing. ◻ *Job security has become the touchstone of a good job for many employees.*

touch-tone ADJ [ADJ n] A **touch-tone** telephone has numbered buttons that make different sounds when you press them. Some automatic telephone services can only be used with this kind of telephone.

touchy /tˈʌtʃi/ (touchier, touchiest) ADJ If you describe someone as **touchy**, you mean that they are easily upset, offended, or irritated. [DISAPPROVAL] ◻ *She is very touchy about her past.*

touchy-feely /tˈʌtʃi fˈiːli/ ADJ If you describe something as **touchy-feely**, you mean that it involves people expressing emotions such as love and affection openly in a way which you find embarrassing and silly. [DISAPPROVAL] ◻ *...a touchy-feely song about making your life worth living.*

tough ◆◆◇ /tʌf/ (tougher, toughest) **1** ADJ A **tough** person is strong and determined, and can tolerate difficulty or suffering. ◻ *She built up a reputation as being a tough, but fair businesswoman.* • **tough|ness** N-UNCOUNT ◻ *Ms. Potter has won a reputation for toughness and determination on her way to the top.* **2** ADJ If you describe someone as **tough**, you mean that they are rough and violent. ◻ *He had shot three people dead earning himself a reputation as a tough guy.* **3** ADJ A **tough** place or area is considered to have a lot of crime and violence. ◻ *She doesn't seem cut out for this tough neighborhood.* **4** ADJ A **tough** way of life or period of time is difficult or full of suffering. ◻ *She had a pretty tough childhood.* **5** ADJ A **tough** task or problem is difficult to do or solve. ◻ *It was a very tough decision but we feel we made the right one.* **6** ADJ **Tough** policies or actions are strict and firm. ◻ *He is known for taking a tough line on security.* **7** ADJ A **tough** substance is strong, and difficult to break, cut, or tear. ◻ *In industry, diamond can form a tough, non-corrosive coating for tools.* **8** ADJ **Tough** meat is difficult to cut and chew. ◻ *The steak was tough and the peas were like bullets.*

tough cookie (tough cookies) N-COUNT If you describe someone as a **tough cookie**, you mean that they are unemotional and are not easily hurt by what people say or do.

tough|en /tʌfᵊn/ (toughens, toughening, toughened) **1** V-T If you **toughen** something or if it **toughens**, you make it stronger so that it will not break easily. ❏ *Months of walking barefoot had toughened his feet.* **2** V-T If a person, institution, or law **toughens** its policies, regulations, or punishments, it makes them firmer or stricter. ❏ *Talks are under way to toughen trade restrictions.* • PHRASAL VERB **Toughen up** means the same as **toughen**. ❏ *The new law toughens up penalties for those that misuse guns.* **3** V-T If an experience **toughens** you, it makes you stronger and more independent in character. ❏ *They believe that participating in fights toughens boys and shows them how to be men.* • PHRASAL VERB **Toughen up** means the same as **toughen**. ❏ *He thinks boxing is good for kids, that it toughens them up.*

tough love N-UNCOUNT **Tough love** is the practice of being very strict with a relative or friend who has an addiction or other problem in order to help them overcome the problem. ❏ *She relied on tough love and her parenting instincts to help him quit drinking.*

tou|pee /tupeɪ/ (toupees) N-COUNT A **toupee** is a piece of artificial hair worn by a man to cover a patch on his head where he has lost his hair.

tour ♦♦◊ /tʊər/ (tours, touring, toured) **1** N-COUNT A **tour** is an organized trip that people such as musicians, politicians, or theater companies go on to several different places, stopping to meet people or perform. ❏ *The band is currently on a two-month tour of Europe.* • PHRASE When people are traveling on a tour, you can say that they are **on tour**. ❏ *The band will be going on tour.* **2** V-T/V-I When people such as musicians, politicians, or theater companies **tour**, they go on a tour, for example, in order to perform or to meet people. ❏ *A few years ago they toured the country with a roadshow.* **3** N-COUNT A **tour** is a trip during which you visit several places that interest you. ❏ *It was week five of my tour of the major cities of Europe.* **4** N-COUNT A **tour** is a short trip that you make around a place, for example, around a historical building, so that you can look at it. ❏ *...a guided tour.* **5** V-T If you **tour** a place, you go on a trip or journey around it. ❏ *You can also tour the site on bicycle.*

tour de force /tʊər də fɔrs/ (tours de force) N-COUNT [usu sing] If you call something such as a performance, speech, or production a **tour de force**, you are emphasizing that it is extremely good or extremely well done or made. [EMPHASIS] ❏ *Stevenson's deeply felt performance is a tour-de-force.*

Tourette's syn|drome /tʊrɛts sɪndroʊm/ also **Tourette's** N-UNCOUNT **Tourette's syndrome** is a brain disorder that causes the person who has it to make sudden uncontrolled movements and sometimes swear and spit. ❏ *He has Tourette's syndrome.*

tour guide (tour guides) **1** N-COUNT A **tour guide** is a person employed by a travel company to assist people who are on vacation. ❏ *There is a tour guide throughout the trip who will organize optional dinners and sightseeing.* **2** N-COUNT A **tour guide** is someone who shows tourists around places such as museums or cities. ❏ *...an old tour guide at the temple.*

tour|ism /tʊərɪzəm/ N-UNCOUNT **Tourism** is the business of providing services for people on vacation, for example, hotels, restaurants, and trips. ❏ *Tourism is vital for the economy.*

tour|ist ♦◊◊ /tʊərɪst/ (tourists) N-COUNT A **tourist** is a person who is visiting a place for pleasure and interest, especially when they are on vacation. ❏ *...a tourist attraction.*

SYNONYMS

tourist
NOUN
traveler: *Many air travelers suffer puffy ankles and feet during long flights.*
sightseer: *...busloads of sightseers.*
globe-trotter: *He's a globe-trotter.*

tour|isty /tʊərɪsti/ ADJ If you describe a place as **touristy**, you do not like it because it is full of tourists or full of things for tourists to buy and do. [INFORMAL, DISAPPROVAL] ❏ *Visit some of the less touristy islands.*

VOCABULARY IN CONTEXT

Tourism

Budget travel is no longer only for students and **backpackers**. There's a certain glamour attached to the raw experience of **traveling on a shoestring**. Even supermodels have been seen flying on a well-known British **no-frills airline**. **Trekking** through the jungle with a local guide to some **off-the-beaten-track** temple is a lot more exciting for some travelers than a week by the pool at a luxury all-inclusive **resort**. **Budget airlines** don't always offer the cheapest deals, though, especially if you get hit with unexpected charges for **excess baggage**. In **peak season**, there are only a few seats at low prices, although if you can travel on a weekday in **low season**, prices can be so low you only pay the taxes. These airlines are notorious for delays and **overbooking** but, if you know your rights, you can sometimes get compensation or even complimentary tickets or **hotel stays**.

tour|na|ment ♦◊◊ /tʊərnəmənt, tɜr-/ (tournaments) **1** N-COUNT A **tournament** is a sports competition in which players who win a match continue to play further matches in the competition until just one person or team is left. ❏ *...the biggest golf tournament to be held in Australia.* **2** → See feature box at **Olympic Games**

SYNONYMS

tournament
NOUN
contest: *Few contests in the history of British boxing have been as thrilling.*
competition: *...a surfing competition.*
game: *He regularly watched our games from the stands.*
match: *He was watching a soccer match.*

tour|ni|quet /tɜrnɪkɪt, tʊər-/ (tourniquets) N-COUNT A **tourniquet** is a strip of cloth that is tied tightly around an injured arm or leg in order to stop it from bleeding or in order to prevent the spread of poison from a snake or spider bite.

tour of duty (tours of duty) N-COUNT A soldier's **tour of duty** is a period of time when the soldier is involved in a particular duty or stationed in a particular place such as a war zone. ❏ *...a Green Beret who served two tours of duty in Vietnam.*

tour op|era|tor (tour operators) N-COUNT A **tour operator** is a company that provides vacations in which your travel and accommodations are booked for you.

tou|sled /taʊzᵊld/ ADJ If you have **tousled** hair, it is messy and looks as if it has not been brushed or combed.

tout /taʊt/ (touts, touting, touted) **1** V-T If someone **touts** something, they try to sell it or convince people that it is good. [DISAPPROVAL] ❏ *...slick television ads touting the candidates.* **2** V-T If someone **touts** tickets, they sell them outside a sports stadium or theater, usually for more than their original value. [BRIT]

in AM, use **scalp**

tow

3 N-COUNT A **tout** is someone who sells things such as tickets unofficially, usually at prices which are higher than the official ones. [BRIT]

☐ in AM, use **scalper**

tow /toʊ/ (**tows, towing, towed**) V-T If one vehicle **tows** another, it pulls it along behind it. ☐ *He had been using the vehicle to tow his work trailer..* ☐ *They threatened to tow away my car.*

to|ward ◆◇◇ /tɔrd/ also **towards**

☐ In addition to the uses shown below, **toward** is used in phrasal verbs such as 'count toward' and 'lean toward.'

1 PREP If you move, look, or point **toward** something or someone, you move, look, or point in their direction. ☐ *They were all moving toward him down the stairs.* ☐ *When he looked toward me, I smiled and waved.* **2** PREP [PREP n/-ing] If things develop **toward** a particular situation, that situation becomes nearer in time or more likely to happen. ☐ *The agreement is a major step toward peace.* **3** PREP If you have a particular attitude **toward** something or someone, you have that attitude when you think about them or deal with them. ☐ *My attitude toward religion has been shaped by this man.* **4** PREP If something happens **toward** a particular time, it happens just before that time. ☐ *There was a forecast of cooler weather toward the end of the week.* **5** PREP If something is **toward** part of a place or thing, it is near that part. ☐ *Gulls are nesting on a small island toward the eastern shore.* **6** PREP If you give money **toward** something, you give it to help pay for that thing. ☐ *Taxes only get part of the way toward a $50 billion deficit.*

tow|el /taʊəl/ (**towels, toweling** or **towelling, toweled** or **towelled**) **1** N-COUNT A **towel** is a piece of thick soft cloth that you use to dry yourself. ☐ *...a bath towel.* ☐ *...a hand towel.* ☐ *...a beach towel.* **2** V-T If you **towel** something or **towel** it dry, you dry it with a towel. ☐ *James came out of his bedroom, toweling his wet hair.* ☐ *I toweled myself dry.* **3** PHRASE If you **throw in the towel**, you stop trying to do something because you realize that you cannot succeed. [INFORMAL] ☐ *It seemed as if the police had thrown in the towel and were abandoning the investigation.*

tow|el|ing /taʊəlɪŋ/

☐ in BRIT, also use **towelling**

N-UNCOUNT [oft N n] **Toweling** is a kind of fairly thick soft cloth that is used especially for making towels. ☐ *...a toweling bathrobe.*

tow|er ◆◇◇ /taʊər/ (**towers, towering, towered**) **1** N-COUNT; N-IN-NAMES A **tower** is a tall, narrow building, that either stands alone or forms part of another building such as a church or castle. ☐ *...an eleventh century castle with 120-foot high towers.* **2** V-I Someone or something that **towers** over surrounding people or things is a lot taller than they are. ☐ *He stood up and towered over her.* **3** N-COUNT A **tower** is a tall structure that is used for sending radio or television signals. ☐ *Troops are still in control of the television and radio tower.* **4** N-COUNT A **tower** is a tall box that contains the main parts of a computer, such as the hard disk and the drives. [COMPUTING] **5** → See also color supplement

tow|er block (**tower blocks**) N-COUNT A **tower block** is a tall building divided into apartments or offices. [BRIT]

☐ in AM, use **high-rise building**

tow|er|ing /taʊərɪŋ/ **1** ADJ [ADJ n] If you describe something such as a mountain or cliff as **towering**, you mean that it is very tall and therefore impressive. [LITERARY] ☐ *...towering cliffs of black granite which rise straight out of the sea.* **2** ADJ [ADJ n] If you describe someone or something as **towering**, you are emphasizing that they are impressive because of their importance, skill, or intensity. [LITERARY, EMPHASIS] ☐ *He remains a towering figure in rock and roll.*

town ◆◆◆ /taʊn/ (**towns**) **1** N-COUNT A **town** is a place with streets and buildings, where people live and work. Towns are larger than neighborhoods and smaller than cities. In informal English, cities are sometimes called towns. ☐ *...the northern California town of Albany.* • N-COUNT You can use **the town** to refer to the people of a town. ☐ *The town takes immense pride in recent achievements.* **2** N-UNCOUNT You use **town** in order to refer to the town where you live. ☐ *He admits he doesn't even know when his brother is in town.* **3** N-UNCOUNT You use **town** in

township

order to refer to the central area of a town where most of the stores and offices are. ☐ *I walked into town.* **4** → see also **downtown, uptown**

VOCABULARY IN CONTEXT

The gentrification of towns

Gentrification is a global phenomenon. From Rio to London, cities around the world are seeing their **run-down** areas gradually transformed into **trendy bohemian quarters**, with **pedestrianized** areas, **bike lanes**, street markets, **hipster cafés**, and **boutique hotels**.

You might think this can only be a good thing. Gentrification brings more money into the **inner city** and reduces the pressure to build housing on the **green belt**. However, because prices rise as people with more money move into an area, families who may have lived there for generations are **displaced**, and it becomes harder and harder for some people to find **affordable housing** within the city.

town coun|cil (**town councils**) N-COUNT-COLL [oft in names] A **town council** is a group of people who have been appointed or elected to govern a town.

town cri|er (**town criers**) N-COUNT In former times, a **town crier** was a man whose job was to walk through the streets of a town shouting out news and official announcements.

town hall (**town halls**) also **Town Hall** N-COUNT A **town hall** is a building or hall used for local government business, usually a building which is the main office of a town council.

town|home /taʊnhoʊm/ (**townhomes**) also **town home** N-COUNT A **townhome** is the same as a **townhouse**. [AM] ☐ *Construction of condominiums and townhomes is down 29.6 percent.*

town|house /taʊnhaʊs/ (**town houses**) also **town house** **1** N-COUNT A **town house** is a tall narrow house in a town or city, usually in a row of similar houses which are connected together. **2** N-COUNT [with poss] The **town house** of a wealthy person is the house that they own in a town or city, rather than another house that they own in the country.

townie /taʊni/ (**townies**) N-COUNT People who live in the countryside sometimes refer to people from a town or city as **townies**. [DISAPPROVAL]

town meet|ing (**town meetings**) N-COUNT A **town meeting** is a meeting held by the residents of a town, or by the people who are eligible to vote in a town. [AM] ☐ *One way to gauge public opinion on the issue is to call a town meeting.*

town plan|ning N-UNCOUNT [oft N n] **Town planning** is the planning and design of all the new buildings, roads, and parks in a place in order to make them attractive and convenient for the people who live there.

towns|folk /taʊnzfoʊk/ N-PLURAL The **townsfolk** of a town or city are the people who live there. [OLD-FASHIONED]

town|ship /taʊnʃɪp/ (**townships**) **1** N-COUNT In the United States and Canada, a **township** is an area of land, especially a part of a county which is organized as a unit of local government. ☐ *...her 20 years of service with the township and county.* **2** N-COUNT In South Africa, a **township** was a town where only black people lived. ☐ *...the South African township of Soweto.*

towns|people /taʊnzpiːpᵊl/ N-PLURAL The **townspeople** of a town or city are the people who live there. ☐ *Food shortages forced many townspeople into the country to grow their own food.*

tow|path /toʊpæθ/ (**towpaths**) N-COUNT A **towpath** is a path along the side of a canal or river, which horses used to walk on when they pulled boats.

tow|rope /toʊroʊp/ (**towropes**) also **tow rope** N-COUNT A **towrope** is a strong rope that is used for pulling vehicles.

tow truck (**tow trucks**) N-COUNT A **tow truck** is a truck which is used to pull broken or damaged cars and other vehicles.

tox|ic /tɒksɪk/ ADJ A **toxic** substance is poisonous. ☐ *...the cost of cleaning up toxic waste.*

toxi|col|ogy /tɒksɪkɒlədʒi/ N-UNCOUNT **Toxicology** is the study of poisons. ● **toxi|co|logi|cal** /tɒksɪkəlɒdʒɪkᵊl/ ADJ [ADJ n] ☐ *There were no adverse toxicological effects.* ● **toxi|colo|gist** (**toxicologists**) N-COUNT ☐ *The toxicologist said we were poisoned by pesticides.*

tox|in /tɒksɪn/ (**toxins**) N-VAR A **toxin** is any poisonous substance produced by bacteria, animals, or plants. ☐ *Tests showed increased levels of toxin in shellfish.*

toy ✦✧✧ /tɔɪ/ (**toys, toying, toyed**) N-COUNT A **toy** is an object that children play with, for example, a doll or a model car. ☐ *He was really too old for children's toys.*
▸ **toy with** ① PHRASAL VERB If you **toy with** an idea, you consider it casually without making any decisions about it. ☐ *He toyed with the idea of going to China.* ② PHRASAL VERB If you **toy with** food or drink, you do not eat or drink it with any enthusiasm, but only take a bite or a little drink from time to time. ☐ *She had no appetite, and merely toyed with the bread and cheese.*

toy|boy /tɔɪbɔɪ/ (**toyboys**) N-COUNT People sometimes refer to someone's lover as their **toyboy** when he is much younger than they are. [HUMOROUS, INFORMAL]

TQM /tiː kjuː em/ N-UNCOUNT **TQM** is a set of management principles aimed at improving performance throughout a company, especially by involving employees in decision-making. **TQM** is an abbreviation for **total quality management**. [BUSINESS] ☐ *One of the main themes of TQM is employee involvement.* ☐ *Under TQM principles the search for quality is continuous.*

trace ✦✧✧ /treɪs/ (**traces, tracing, traced**) ① V-T If you **trace** the origin or development of something, you find out or describe how it started or developed. ☐ *The exhibition traces the history of graphic design in America from the 19th century to the present.* ● PHRASAL VERB **Trace back** means the same as **trace**. ☐ *...Bronx residents who trace their families back to Dutch settlers.* ② V-T If you **trace** someone or something, you find them after looking for them. ☐ *Police are anxious to trace two men seen leaving the house just before 8am.* ③ V-T If you **trace** something such as a pattern or a shape, for example, with your finger or toe, you mark its outline on a surface. ☐ *I traced the course of the river on the map spread out on my briefcase.* ④ V-T If you **trace** a picture, you copy it by covering it with a piece of transparent paper and drawing over the lines underneath. ☐ *She learned to draw by tracing pictures out of old storybooks.* ⑤ N-COUNT A **trace** of something is a very small amount of it. ☐ *Wash them in cold water to remove all traces of sand.* ⑥ PHRASE If you say that someone or something **disappears without a trace**, you mean that they stop existing or stop being successful very suddenly and completely. ☐ *One day he left, disappeared without a trace.*

▬▬▬ SYNONYMS ▬▬▬
trace
VERB ②
find: *The police also found a pistol.*
track down: *She had spent years trying to track down her parents.*
discover: *A few days later, his badly beaten body was discovered on a roadside outside the city.*
unearth: *...unearthing a plot to assassinate the President.*

trace|able /treɪsəbᵊl/ ADJ If one thing is **traceable** to another, there is evidence to suggest that the first thing was caused by or is connected to the second thing. ☐ *The probable cause of his death is traceable to an incident in 1724.*

trace el|ement (**trace elements**) ① N-COUNT A **trace element** is a chemical element such as iron or zinc that occurs in very small amounts in living things and is necessary for normal growth and development. ② N-COUNT A **trace element** is a very small amount of a chemical element that is found in a metal or other substance.

tra|chea /treɪkiə/ (**tracheas** or **tracheae** /treɪkiː/) ① N-COUNT Your **trachea** is your windpipe. [MEDICAL] ② → See also color supplement

trac|ing pa|per N-UNCOUNT **Tracing paper** is transparent paper which you put over a picture so that you can draw over its lines in order to produce a copy of it.

track ✦✦✧ /træk/ (**tracks, tracking, tracked**)
→ Please look at meaning ⓯ to see if the expression you are looking for is shown under another headword.
① N-COUNT A **track** is a rough, unpaved road or path. ☐ *We set off once more, over a rough mountain track.* ② N-COUNT A **track** is a piece of ground, often oval-shaped, that is used for races involving running, cars, bicycles, horses, or dogs called greyhounds. ☐ *...the athletics track.* ③ N-COUNT Railroad **tracks** are the rails that a train travels along. ☐ *A cow stood on the tracks.* ④ N-COUNT A **track** is one of the songs or pieces of music on a CD, record, or tape. ☐ *I only like two of the ten tracks on this CD.* ⑤ N-PLURAL **Tracks** are marks left in the ground by the feet of animals or people. ☐ *The only evidence of pandas was their tracks in the snow.* ⑥ V-T If you **track** animals or people, you try to follow them by looking for the signs that they have left behind, for example, the marks left by their feet. ☐ *He thought he had better track this wolf and see where it lived.* ⑦ V-T To **track** someone or something means to follow their movements by means of a special device, such as a satellite or radar. ☐ *Our radar began tracking the jets.* ⑧ → see also **fast track, racetrack, soundtrack** ⑨ PHRASE If you **keep track of** a situation or a person, you make sure that you have the newest and most accurate information about them all the time. ☐ *With eleven thousand employees, it's very difficult to keep track of them all.* ⑩ PHRASE If you **lose track of** someone or something, you no longer know where they are or what is happening. ☐ *You become so deeply absorbed in an activity that you lose track of time.* ⑪ PHRASE If someone or something is **on track**, they are acting or progressing in a way that is likely to result in success. ☐ *It may take some time to get the economy back on track.* ⑫ PHRASE If you are **on the right track**, you are acting or progressing in a way that is likely to result in success. If you are **on the wrong track**, you are acting or progressing in a way that is likely to result in failure. ☐ *Guests are returning in increasing numbers – a sure sign that we are on the right track.* ⑬ PHRASE If someone or something **stops** you **in your tracks**, or if you **stop dead in your tracks**, you suddenly stop moving because you are very surprised, impressed, or frightened. ☐ *This magnificent church cannot fail to stop you in your tracks.* ⑭ PHRASE If someone or something **stops** a process or activity **in its tracks**, or if it **stops dead in its tracks**, they prevent the process or activity from continuing. ☐ *Francis felt he would like to stop this conversation in its tracks.* ⑮ **off the beaten track** → see **beaten**
▸ **track down** PHRASAL VERB If you **track down** someone or something, you find them, or find information about them, after a difficult or long search. ☐ *She had spent years trying to track down her parents.*

▬▬▬ SYNONYMS ▬▬▬
track
NOUN ①
path: *We followed the path along the clifftops.*
way: *...the well-trodden, 250-mile Pennine Way.*
trail: *He was following a broad trail through the trees.*
pathway: *...a pathway leading towards the nearby river.*

track and field N-UNCOUNT **Track and field** refers to sports that are played or performed on a racetrack and a nearby field, such as running, the high jump, and the javelin. ☐ *...events that range from track and field to soccer, rugby and hockey.*

track|ball /trækbɔːl/ (**trackballs**) also **track ball**, **tracker ball** N-COUNT A **trackball** is a ball on some computers that you turn in order to move the cursor. [COMPUTING]

track|er /trækər/ (**trackers**) N-COUNT A **tracker** is a person or animal that finds other people or animals by following the marks left by their feet and other signs that show where they have been.

track event (track events) N-COUNT A **track event** is a track and field contest which involves running or walking around a racetrack, in contrast to events that involve only jumping or throwing.

track meet (track meets) N-COUNT A **track meet** is an event in which athletes come to a particular place in order to take part in a race or races. [AM] ☐ *A good student, she ran in track meets.*

track|pad /trǽkpæd/ (trackpads) N-COUNT A **trackpad** is a flat pad on some computers that you slide your finger over in order to move the cursor. [COMPUTING] ☐ *...with enhancements like a trackpad instead of a trackball.*

track rec|ord (track records) N-COUNT If you talk about the **track record** of a person, company, or product, you are referring to their past performance, achievements, or failures in it. ☐ *The job needs someone with a good track record in investment.*

track|suit /trǽksut/ (tracksuits) also **track suit** N-COUNT A **tracksuit** is a loose, warm suit consisting of pants and a top which people wear to relax and to do exercise.

tract /trǽkt/ (tracts) **1** N-COUNT [usu N *of* n] A **tract** of land is a very large area of land. ☐ *A vast tract of land is ready for development.* **2** N-COUNT A **tract** is a short article expressing a strong opinion on a religious, moral, or political subject in order to try to influence people's attitudes. ☐ *She produced a feminist tract, "Comments on Birth-Control," in 1930.* **3** N-COUNT [usu supp N] A **tract** is a system of organs and tubes in an animal's or person's body that has a particular function, especially the function of processing a substance in the body. [MEDICAL] ☐ *Foods are broken down in the digestive tract.*

trac|table /trǽktəbəl/ ADJ If you say that a person, problem, or device is **tractable**, you mean that they can be easily controlled or dealt with. [FORMAL] ☐ *...the country's least tractable social problems.*

tract house (tract houses) also **tract home** N-COUNT A **tract house** or a **tract home** is a house that is mass produced by a builder in an area with other houses that have similar floor plans and styles. [AM] ☐ *...a small development of tract houses.*

trac|tion /trǽkʃən/ **1** N-UNCOUNT **Traction** is the grip that something has on the ground, especially the wheels of a vehicle. **2** N-UNCOUNT [usu supp N] **Traction** is a particular form of power that makes a vehicle move. **3** N-UNCOUNT [oft *in* N] **Traction** is a form of medical treatment, in which weights and pulleys are used to gently pull or stretch an injured part of the body for a period of time. You say that a person who is having this treatment is **in traction**. ☐ *Isabelle's legs were in traction for about two and a half weeks.*

trac|tor /trǽktər/ (tractors) **1** N-COUNT A **tractor** is a farm vehicle that is used to pull farm machinery. **2** N-COUNT A **tractor** is a short vehicle with a powerful engine and a driver's cab. It is used to pull a trailer, such as in a tractor-trailer. ☐ *The truck was an 18-wheeler with a white tractor.*

tractor-trailer (tractor-trailers) N-COUNT A **tractor-trailer** is a large truck that is made in two separate sections, a tractor and a trailer, which are joined together by metal bars. [AM] ☐ *Driving a tractor-trailer is not an easy job.*

trade ♦♦♦ /treɪd/ (trades, trading, traded) **1** V-RECIP If someone **trades** one thing for another or if two people **trade** things, they agree to exchange one thing for the other thing [mainly AM] ☐ *They traded land for goods and money.* ☐ *Kids used to trade baseball cards.* • N-COUNT **Trade** is also a noun. ☐ *I am willing to make a trade with you.*

in BRIT, usually use **exchange**

2 V-RECIP If you **trade** places with someone or if the two of you **trade** places, you move into the other person's position or situation, and they move into yours. [mainly AM] ☐ *Mike asked George to trade places with him so he could ride with Tomas.* **3** V-RECIP If two people or groups **trade** something such as blows, insults, or jokes, they hit each other, insult each other, or tell each other jokes. [mainly AM] ☐ *Children would settle disputes by trading punches or insults in the schoolyard.* **4** N-UNCOUNT **Trade** is the activity of buying, selling, or exchanging goods or services between people, companies, or countries. [BUSINESS] ☐ *Texas has a long history of trade with Mexico.* ☐ *...negotiations on a new international trade agreement.* **5** V-I When people, companies, or countries **trade**, they buy, sell, or exchange goods or services between themselves. [BUSINESS] ☐ *They may refuse to trade, even when offered attractive prices.* ☐ *They had years of experience of trading with the West.* • **trad|ing** N-UNCOUNT ☐ *Trading on the stock exchange may be suspended.* **6** N-COUNT A **trade** is a particular area of business or industry. [BUSINESS] ☐ *They've ruined the tourist trade for the next few years.* **7** N-COUNT [oft poss N, also by N] Someone's **trade** is the kind of work that they do, especially when they have been trained to do it over a period of time. [BUSINESS] ☐ *He learned his trade as a diver in the North Sea.* ☐ *Alicia was a jeweler by trade.*

▶ **trade down** PHRASAL VERB If someone **trades down**, they sell something such as their car or house and buy a less expensive one. ☐ *They are selling their five-bedroom house and trading down to a two-bedroom apartment.*

▶ **trade up** PHRASAL VERB If someone **trades up**, they sell something such as their car or their house and buy a more expensive one. ☐ *Gas prices are discouraging small car owners from trading up to SUV's.*

trade as|so|cia|tion (trade associations) N-COUNT A **trade association** is a body representing organizations within the same trade. It aims to protect their collective interests, especially in negotiations with governments and labor unions. ☐ *...one of the two main trade associations for antique dealers.*

trade defi|cit (trade deficits) N-COUNT [usu sing] A **trade deficit** is a situation in which a country imports goods worth more than the value of the goods that it exports. [BUSINESS] ☐ *The US trade deficit grew to just under $30 billion in the third quarter.*

trade fair (trade fairs) N-COUNT A **trade fair** is the same as a trade show.

trade gap (trade gaps) N-COUNT [usu sing] A **trade gap** is the same as a trade deficit. [BUSINESS] ☐ *The trade gap surprised most analysts by shrinking, rather than growing.*

trade-in (trade-ins) N-COUNT [usu sing] A **trade-in** is an arrangement in which someone buys a new car at a reduced price by giving their old one, as well as money, in payment. [BUSINESS] ☐ *...the trade-in value of the car.*

trade|mark /treɪdmɑrk/ (trademarks) also **trade mark** **1** N-COUNT A **trademark** is a name or symbol that a company uses on its products and that cannot legally be used by another company. [BUSINESS] ☐ *She has registered a trademark for a new range of perfumes.* **2** N-COUNT If you say that something is the **trademark** of a particular person or place, you mean that it is characteristic of them or typically associated with them. ☐ *...the spiky punk hairdo that became his trademark.*

trade name (trade names) N-COUNT A **trade name** is the name which manufacturers give to a product or to a range of products. [BUSINESS] ☐ *It's marketed under the trade name "Mirage."*

trade-off (trade-offs) also **tradeoff** N-COUNT A **trade-off** is a situation where you make a compromise between two things, or where you exchange all or part of one thing for another. [JOURNALISM] ☐ *...the trade-off between inflation and unemployment.*

trad|er ♦♢♢ /treɪdər/ (traders) N-COUNT A **trader** is a person whose job is to trade in goods or stocks. [BUSINESS] ☐ *Market traders display an exotic selection of the island's produce.*

trade route (trade routes) N-COUNT A **trade route** is a route, often covering long distances, that is used by traders.

trade se|cret (trade secrets) N-COUNT A **trade secret** is information that is known, used, and kept secret by a particular company, for example, about a method of production or a chemical process. [BUSINESS] ☐ *The nature of the polymer is currently a trade secret.*

trade show (trade shows) N-COUNT A **trade show** is an exhibition where manufacturers show their products to other people in industry and try to get business. [mainly AM] ☐ *Each year, hundreds of candy manufacturers and distributors come to a Chicago trade show.*

in BRIT, usually use **trade fair**

trades|man /treɪdzmən/ (tradesmen) N-COUNT A **tradesman** is a man who is a skilled worker. [BUSINESS] ☐ *...tradesmen such as electricians or plumbers.*

trade sur|plus (trade surpluses) N-COUNT If a country has a **trade surplus**, it exports more than it imports. [BUSINESS] ☐ *The country's trade surplus widened to 16.5 billion dollars.*

trades|woman /treɪdzwʊmən/ (**tradeswomen**) N-COUNT A **tradeswoman** is a woman who is a skilled worker. [BUSINESS]

trade un|ion [mainly BRIT] → see **union, labor union**

trad|ing card (**trading cards**) N-COUNT A **trading card** is one of a set of thin pieces of cardboard with a picture relating to a particular theme, such as baseball or football, printed on it. Collectors buy the cards or trade them with other collectors. [mainly AM] □ *Now collectors can choose trading cards from a variety of sports.*

tra|di|tion ✦✧✧ /trədɪʃən/ (**traditions**) N-VAR A **tradition** is a custom or belief that has existed for a long time. □ *...the rich traditions of Afro-Cuban music and dance.*

tra|di|tion|al ✦✦✧ /trədɪʃənəl/ **1** ADJ **Traditional** customs, beliefs, or methods are ones that have existed for a long time without changing. □ *Traditional teaching methods sometimes only succeeded in putting students off learning.* • **tra|di|tion|al|ly** ADV [ADV with cl/group] □ *Getting a good education is traditionally seen as being a priority in this community.* **2** ADJ A **traditional** organization or person prefers older methods and ideas to modern ones. □ *We're still a traditional school in a lot of ways.* • **tra|di|tion|al|ly** ADV □ *He is loathed by some of the more traditionally minded officers.*

> **SYNONYMS**
> **traditional**
> ADJ **2**
> **old-fashioned:** *There are some traditional farmers left who still make cheese the old-fashioned way.*
> **conventional:** *...a respectable, married woman with conventional opinions.*
> **orthodox:** *Payne gained a reputation for sound, if orthodox, views.*

tra|di|tion|al|ism /trədɪʃənəlɪzəm/ N-UNCOUNT **Traditionalism** is behavior and ideas that support established customs and beliefs, rather than modern ones.

tra|di|tion|al|ist /trədɪʃənəlɪst/ (**traditionalists**) **1** N-COUNT A **traditionalist** is a person who supports the established customs and beliefs of his or her society or group, and does not want to change them. **2** ADJ A **traditionalist** idea, argument, or organization supports the established customs and beliefs of a society or group, rather than modern ones.

tra|duce /trədjuːs/ (**traduces, traducing, traduced**) V-T [usu passive] If someone has **been traduced**, unpleasant and untrue things have deliberately been said about them. [FORMAL] □ *We have been traduced in the press as xenophobic bigots.*

traf|fic ✦✧✧ /træfɪk/ (**traffics, trafficking, trafficked**) **1** N-UNCOUNT [also the N] **Traffic** refers to all the vehicles that are moving along the roads in a particular area. □ *There was heavy traffic on the roads.* □ *Traffic was unusually light for that time of day.* **2** N-UNCOUNT **Traffic** refers to the movement of ships, trains, or aircraft between one place and another. **Traffic** also refers to the people and goods that are being transported. □ *Air traffic had returned to normal.* **3** N-UNCOUNT **Traffic** in something such as drugs or stolen goods is an illegal trade in them. □ *...the widespread traffic in stolen cultural artifacts.* **4** V-I Someone who **traffics** in something such as drugs or stolen goods buys and sells them even though it is illegal to do so. □ *The president said illegal drugs are hurting the entire world and anyone who traffics in them should be brought to justice.* • **traf|fick|ing** N-UNCOUNT □ *He was sentenced to ten years in prison on charges of drug trafficking.* **5** → See feature box at **accident, commute**

> **SYNONYMS**
> **traffic**
> NOUN **1**
> **vehicles:** *There were too many vehicles on the road.*
> **transportation:** *The company will provide transportation.*

traf|fic cir|cle (**traffic circles**) N-COUNT A **traffic circle** is a circular structure in the road at a place where several roads meet. You drive around it until you come to the road that you want. [AM]

> in BRIT, use **roundabout**

traf|fic cone (**traffic cones**) N-COUNT A **traffic cone** is a plastic object with a pointed top that is placed on a road to prevent people from driving or parking there.

traf|fic jam (**traffic jams**) N-COUNT A **traffic jam** is a long line of vehicles that cannot move forward because there is too much traffic, or because the road is blocked by something.

traf|fick|er /træfɪkər/ (**traffickers**) N-COUNT A **trafficker** in particular goods, especially drugs, is a person who illegally buys or sells these goods. □ *They have been arrested as suspected drug traffickers.*

traf|fic light (**traffic lights**) N-COUNT **Traffic lights** are sets of red, yellow, and green lights at the places where roads meet. They control the traffic by signaling red when vehicles have to stop and green when they can go.

trag|edy ✦✧✧ /trædʒɪdi/ (**tragedies**) **1** N-VAR A **tragedy** is an extremely sad event or situation. □ *They have suffered an enormous personal tragedy.* **2** N-VAR **Tragedy** is a type of literature, especially drama, that is serious and sad, and often ends with the death of the main character. □ *The story has elements of tragedy and farce.*

> **SYNONYMS**
> **tragedy**
> NOUN **1**
> **catastrophe:** *From all points of view, war would be a catastrophe.*
> **misfortune:** *He had his full share of misfortune.*
> **disaster:** *Many had lost all in the disaster and were destitute.*

trag|ic /trædʒɪk/ **1** ADJ A **tragic** event or situation is extremely sad, usually because it involves death or suffering. □ *It was just a tragic accident.* □ *...the tragic loss of so many lives.* • **tragi|cal|ly** /trædʒɪkli/ ADV □ *Tragically, she never saw the completed building because she died before it was finished.* **2** ADJ [ADJ n] **Tragic** is used to refer to tragedy as a type of literature. □ *...Shakespeare's tragic hero, Hamlet.* **3** → See feature box at **disaster**

tragi|com|edy /trædʒɪkɒmədi/ (**tragicomedies**) also **tragi-comedy** N-COUNT A **tragicomedy** is a play or other written work that is both sad and amusing.

tragi|com|ic /trædʒɪkɒmɪk/ also **tragi-comic** ADJ Something that is **tragicomic** is both sad and amusing at the same time.

trail ✦✧✧ /treɪl/ (**trails, trailing, trailed**) **1** N-COUNT A **trail** is a rough path across open country or through forests. □ *He was following a trail through the trees.* **2** N-COUNT A **trail** is a route along a series of paths or roads, often one that has been planned and marked out for a particular purpose. □ *...a large area of woodland with hiking and walking trails.* **3** N-COUNT A **trail** is a series of marks or other signs of movement or other activities left by someone or something. □ *Everywhere in the house was a sticky trail of orange juice.* **4** V-T If you **trail** someone or something, you follow them secretly, often by finding the marks or signs that they have left. □ *Two detectives were trailing him.* **5** N-COUNT You can refer to all the places that a politician visits in the period before an election as their campaign **trail**. □ *During a recent speech on the campaign trail, he was interrupted by hecklers.* **6** V-T/V-I If you **trail** something or it **trails**, it hangs down loosely behind you as you move along. □ *She came down the stairs slowly, trailing the coat behind her.* **7** PHRASE If you are **on the trail of** a person or thing, you are trying hard to find them or find out about them. □ *The police were hot on his trail.*

> **COLLOCATIONS**
> **trail**
> NOUN **2**
> noun + **trail**: hiking, nature, walking; forest, mountain
> adjective + **trail**: marked, scenic

trail|blaz|er /treɪlbleɪzər/ (**trailblazers**) N-COUNT A **trailblazer** is a person who is the leader in a particular field, especially a person who does a particular thing before anyone else does. □ *Vita was a trailblazer, a vigorous independent.*

trail|blaz|ing /treɪlbleɪzɪŋ/ ADJ [ADJ n] A **trailblazing** idea, event, or organization is new, exciting, and original. □ *...a trailblazing agreement that could lead to a global ban on nuclear weapons.*

trail|er /treɪlər/ (**trailers**) **1** N-COUNT A **trailer** is a long narrow house made to be delivered to a home site, where it becomes a permanent home. **2** N-COUNT A **trailer** is a temporary vacation home that is pulled by a car to each vacation spot.

> in BRIT, use **caravan**

3 N-COUNT A **trailer** is a container on wheels which is pulled by a car or other vehicle and which is used for transporting large or heavy items. **4** N-COUNT A **trailer** for a movie or television program is a set of short extracts which are shown to advertise it. ❑ ...a misleadingly violent trailer for the movie.

trail|er park (trailer parks) N-COUNT A **trailer park** is an area where people can pay to park their trailers and live in them. [AM]

in BRIT, use **caravan site**

trail|er trash N-UNCOUNT-COLL Some people use **trailer trash** to refer to poor uneducated people who live in trailer parks and who they think are vulgar or worthless. This could cause offense. [AM, INFORMAL, OFFENSIVE, DISAPPROVAL]

trail|er truck (trailer trucks) N-COUNT A **trailer truck** is the same as a **tractor-trailer**. [mainly AM]

in BRIT, usually use **articulated lorry**

TRAIN
① NOUN USES
② VERB USES

① **train** ✦✧ /treɪn/ (trains) **1** N-COUNT [also by N] A **train** is a number of containers on wheels which are all connected together and which are pulled by an engine along a railroad. Trains carry people and goods from one place to another. ❑ The train pulled into a station. ❑ We can catch the early morning train. **2** N-COUNT A **train** of vehicles, people, or animals is a long line of them traveling slowly in the same direction. ❑ In the old days this used to be done with a baggage train of camels. **3** N-COUNT A **train** of thought or a **train** of events is a connected sequence, in which each thought or event seems to occur naturally or logically as a result of the previous one. ❑ He lost his train of thought for a moment, then recovered it.

② **train** ✦✧ /treɪn/ (trains, training, trained) **1** V-T/V-I If someone **trains** you to do something, they teach you the skills that you need in order to do it. If you **train** to do something, you learn the skills that you need in order to do it. ❑ He was training us to be soldiers. ● **-trained** COMB IN ADJ ❑ Michael is a professionally-trained chef. ● **train|er** (trainers) N-COUNT ❑ ...a book for both teachers and teacher trainers. **2** V-T To **train** a natural quality or talent that someone has, for example, their voice or musical ability, means to help them to develop it. ❑ I see my degree as something which will train my mind and improve my chances of getting a job. **3** V-T/V-I If you **train** for a physical activity such as a race or if someone **trains** you for it, you prepare for it by doing particular physical exercises. ❑ Strachan is training for the new season. ● **train|er** N-COUNT ❑ She went to the gym with her personal trainer. **4** V-T If an animal or bird **is trained** to do particular things, it is taught to do them, for example, in order to be able to work for someone or to be a good pet. ❑ Sniffer dogs could be trained to track them down. ● **train|er** N-COUNT ❑ The horse made a winning start for his new trainer. **5** → see also **training**

SYNONYMS
train
VERB ② **1**
teach: She taught Julie to read.
instruct: He instructed family members in nursing techniques.
coach: I had coached the Alliance team for some time.
drill: He drills the choir to a high standard.

trainee /treɪniː/ (trainees) N-COUNT [oft N n] A **trainee** is someone who is employed at a low level in a particular job in order to learn the skills needed for that job. [BUSINESS] ❑ He is a 24-year-old trainee reporter.

train|er /treɪnər/ (trainers) **1** N-COUNT **Trainers** are shoes that people wear, especially for running and other sports. [BRIT]

in AM, use **sneakers**

2 → see also **train** ②

train|ing /treɪnɪŋ/ **1** N-UNCOUNT **Training** is the process of learning the skills that you need for a particular job or activity. [BUSINESS] ❑ He called for much higher spending on education and training. ❑ Kennedy had no formal training as a decorator. **2** N-UNCOUNT **Training** is physical exercise that you do regularly in order to keep fit or to prepare for an activity such as a race. ❑ The emphasis is on developing fitness through exercises and training.

COLLOCATIONS
training
NOUN
1
noun + **training**: management, skills, staff; driver, officer, teacher
adjective + **training**: basic, full, intensive, rigorous; formal, special, vocational; military
verb + **training**: complete, receive, start, undergo; offer, provide; require
2
noun + **training**: fitness, weight
adjective + **training**: physical, pre-season; hard, tough
verb + **training**: begin, resume, start; miss

SYNONYMS
training
NOUN **1**
instruction: Each candidate is given instruction in safety.
practice: She was taking all three of her daughters to basketball practice every day.
schooling: He had little formal schooling.
grounding: The degree provides a thorough grounding in both mathematics and statistics.

train|ing camp (training camps) N-COUNT A **training camp** for soldiers or athletes is an organized period of training at a particular place.

traipse /treɪps/ (traipses, traipsing, traipsed) **1** V-I If you **traipse** somewhere, you go there unwillingly, often because you are tired or unhappy. ❑ If traipsing around shops does not appeal to you, perhaps using a catalog will. **2** V-I If you talk about people **traipsing** somewhere, you mean that they are going there or moving around in a way that annoys someone or gets in their way. [DISAPPROVAL] ❑ You will have to get used to a lot of people traipsing in and out of your home.

trait /treɪt/ (traits) **1** N-COUNT A **trait** is a particular characteristic, quality, or tendency that someone or something has. ❑ The study found that some alcoholics had clear personality traits showing up early in childhood. **2** → See feature box at **genetics**

trai|tor /treɪtər/ (traitors) **1** N-COUNT If you call someone a **traitor**, you mean that they have betrayed beliefs that they used to hold, or that their friends hold, by their words or actions. [DISAPPROVAL] ❑ Some say he's a traitor to the peace movement. **2** N-COUNT If someone is a **traitor**, they betray their country, friends, or a group of which they are a member by helping its enemies, especially during time of war. ❑ ...rumors that there were traitors among us who were sending messages to the enemy.

trai|tor|ous /treɪtərəs/ ADJ A **traitorous** action will betray or bring danger to a country or to the group of people that someone belongs to. ❑ The movement could be labeled as divisive, even traitorous.

tra|jec|tory /trədʒɛktəri/ (trajectories) **1** N-COUNT [with supp] The **trajectory** of a moving object is the path that it follows as it moves. ❑ ...the trajectory of an artillery shell. **2** N-COUNT [with supp] The **trajectory** of something such as a person's career is the course that it follows over time. ❑ ...a relentlessly upward career trajectory.

tram /træm/ (trams) **1** N-COUNT [also by N] A **tram** is a public transportation vehicle, usually powered by electricity from wires above it, which travels along rails laid in the surface of a street. ❑ You can get to the beach easily from the center of town by tram.

in AM, use **streetcar**

2 N-COUNT A **tram** is the same as a **cable car**. [AM]

tram|line /træmlaɪn/ (tramlines) N-COUNT A **tramline** is one of the rails laid in the surface of a road that trams travel along.

tramp /træmp/ (tramps, tramping, tramped) **1** N-COUNT A **tramp** is a person who has no home or job, and very little money. Tramps go from place to place, and get food or money by asking people or by doing casual work. ❑ *Hypothermia is common among tramps sleeping outdoors.* **2** V-T/V-I If you **tramp** somewhere, you walk there slowly and with regular, heavy steps, for a long time. ❑ *They put on their coats and tramped through the falling snow.* **3** N-UNCOUNT The **tramp** of people is the sound of their heavy, regular walking. ❑ *He heard the slow, heavy tramp of feet on the stairs.* **4** N-COUNT **Tramp** is an insulting word for a woman who is thought to have many sexual partners. [mainly AM, OFFENSIVE, DISAPPROVAL] ❑ *He'd think I was a tramp, a cheap slut, and he'd lose all respect for me.*

tram|ple /ˈtræmpəl/ (tramples, trampling, trampled) **1** V-T/V-I To **trample** on someone's rights or values or to **trample** them means to deliberately ignore them. ❑ *They say loggers are destroying rain forests and trampling on the rights of natives.* **2** V-T [usu passive] If someone **is trampled**, they are injured or killed by being stepped on by animals or by other people. ❑ *Many people were trampled in the panic that followed.* **3** V-T/V-I If someone **tramples** something or **tramples** on it, they step heavily and carelessly on it and damage it. ❑ *They don't want people trampling the grass, pitching tents or building fires.*

tram|po|line /ˈtræmpəlin/ (trampolines) N-COUNT A **trampoline** is a piece of equipment on which you jump up and down as a sport. It consists of a large piece of strong cloth held by springs in a frame.

tram|way /ˈtræmweɪ/ (tramways) N-COUNT A **tramway** is a set of rails laid in the surface of a road for trams to travel along.

trance /trɑːns/ (trances) N-COUNT A **trance** is a state of mind in which someone seems to be asleep and to have no conscious control over their thoughts or actions, but in which they can see and hear things and respond to commands given by other people. ❑ *Like a man in a trance, Blake found his way back to his rooms.*

tranche /trɑːnʃ/ (tranches) **1** N-COUNT [usu N *of* n] In economics, a **tranche** of shares in a company, or a **tranche** of a company, is a number of shares in that company. [BUSINESS] ❑ *On February 12th he put up for sale a second tranche of 32 state-owned companies.* **2** N-COUNT [usu N *of* n] A **tranche** of something is a piece, section, or part of it. A **tranche** of things is a group of them. [FORMAL] ❑ *They risk losing the next tranche of funding.*

tran|quil /ˈtræŋkwɪl/ ADJ Something that is **tranquil** is calm and peaceful. ❑ *The tranquil atmosphere of the inn allows guests to feel totally at home.* • **tran|quil|lity** /træŋˈkwɪlɪti/ N-UNCOUNT ❑ *The hotel is a haven of peace and tranquillity.*

tran|quil|ize /ˈtræŋkwɪlaɪz/ (tranquilizes, tranquilizing, tranquilized)

in BRIT, also use **tranquilise**

V-T To **tranquilize** a person or an animal means to make them become calm, sleepy, or unconscious by means of a drug. ❑ *This powerful drug is used to tranquilize patients undergoing surgery.*

tran|quil|iz|er /ˈtræŋkwɪlaɪzər/ (tranquilizers)

in BRIT, also use **tranquiliser**

N-COUNT A **tranquilizer** is a drug that makes people feel calmer or less anxious. Tranquilizers are sometimes used to make people or animals become sleepy or unconscious. ❑ *If a tranquilizer is prescribed, be sure your physician informs you of its possible side effects.*

trans. **trans.** is a written abbreviation for 'translated by.'

PREFIX

trans-
is used to form adjectives which indicate that something involves or enables travel from one side of an area to the other. *For example, a **transcontinental** journey is a journey across a continent.*

trans|act /trænˈzækt/ (transacts, transacting, transacted) V-T If you **transact** business, you enter into a deal with someone, for example, by buying or selling something. [FORMAL] ❑ *This would free them to transact business across state lines.*

trans|ac|tion /trænˈzækʃən/ (transactions) N-COUNT A **transaction** is a piece of business, for example, an act of buying or selling something. [FORMAL, BUSINESS] ❑ *The transaction is completed by payment of the fee.*

trans|at|lan|tic /trænzətˈlæntɪk/ ADJ [ADJ n] **Transatlantic** flights or signals go across the Atlantic Ocean, usually between the United States and Britain. ❑ *Many transatlantic flights land there.*

trans|cend /trænˈsɛnd/ (transcends, transcending, transcended) V-T Something that **transcends** normal limits or boundaries goes beyond them, because it is more significant than them. ❑ *...issues like disaster relief that transcend party loyalty.*

tran|scend|ence /trænˈsɛndəns/ N-UNCOUNT **Transcendence** is the quality of being able to go beyond normal limits or boundaries. ❑ *The Arab-American Society promotes the transcendence of racial and religious differences.*

trans|cend|ent /trænˈsɛndənt/ ADJ Something that is **transcendent** goes beyond normal limits or boundaries, because it is more significant than them. ❑ *...the idea of a transcendent God who stood apart from mankind.*

tran|scen|den|tal /trænsɛnˈdɛntəl/ ADJ [usu ADJ n] **Transcendental** refers to things that lie beyond the practical experience of ordinary people, and cannot be discovered or understood by ordinary reasoning. ❑ *...the transcendental nature of God.*

tran|scen|den|tal medi|ta|tion N-UNCOUNT **Transcendental meditation** is a kind of meditation in which people mentally relax by silently repeating special words over and over again.

trans|con|ti|nen|tal /trænskɒntɪˈnɛntəl/ ADJ [usu ADJ n] A **transcontinental** journey or route goes from one side of a continent to the other. **Transcontinental** usually means from one side of the United States to the other, not including Alaska and Hawaii. ❑ *...in mid-nineteenth-century America, before the transcontinental railroad was built.*

tran|scribe /trænˈskraɪb/ (transcribes, transcribing, transcribed) V-T If you **transcribe** a speech or text, you write or type it out, for example, from notes or from a tape recording. ❑ *She is transcribing, from his dictation, the diaries of Simon Forman.*

tran|script /ˈtrænskrɪpt/ (transcripts) N-COUNT A **transcript** of a conversation or speech is a written text of it, based on a recording or notes. ❑ *A transcript of this PBS program is available through our website, pbs.com.*

tran|scrip|tion /trænˈskrɪpʃən/ (transcriptions) **1** N-UNCOUNT **Transcription** of speech or text is the process of transcribing it. **2** N-COUNT A **transcription** of a conversation or speech is a written text of it, based on a recording or notes.

trans|der|mal /trænzˈdɜːrməl/ ADJ **Transdermal** medicine is absorbed through the skin, for example, by means of a skin patch. ❑ *...a transdermal cream.*

tran|sept /ˈtrænsɛpt/ (transepts) N-COUNT In a cathedral or church, the **transepts** are the parts that project to the north or south of the main part of the building, forming a cross shape with it.

trans|femi|nine /trænzˈfɛmɪnɪn/ ADJ Someone who is **transfeminine** was said to be male when they were born, but identifies as female.

trans|fer (transfers, transferring, transferred)

The verb is pronounced /trænsˈfɜːr/. The noun is pronounced /ˈtrænsfɜːr/.

1 V-T/V-I If you **transfer** something or someone from one place to another, or they **transfer** from one place to another, they go from the first place to the second. ❑ *Transfer the meat to a platter and leave in a warm place.* • N-VAR [oft N *of* n] **Transfer** is also a noun. ❑ *Arrange for the transfer of medical records to your new doctor.* **2** V-T/V-I If something **is transferred**, or **transfers**, from one person or group of people to another, the second person or group gets it instead of the first. ❑ *The decision to transfer the investigation from the police to the district attorney's office is a mutual one.* • N-VAR **Transfer** is also a noun. ❑ *...the transfer of power from the old to the new regimes.* **3** V-T/V-I If you **are transferred**, or if you **transfer**, to a different job or place, the company moves

transferable

you to a different job or you start working in a different part of the same company or organization. ❑ *I was transferred to the book department.* ❑ *I suspect that she is going to be transferred to Fort Meyer.* • N-VAR [oft N to n] **Transfer** is also a noun. ❑ *They will be offered transfers to other locations.* ❑ V-T When information **is transferred** onto a different medium, it is copied from one medium to another. ❑ *Such information is easily transferred onto microfilm.* • N-UNCOUNT **Transfer** is also a noun. ❑ *It can be connected to a PC for the transfer of information.*

COLLOCATIONS

transfer
NOUN ❶
noun + **transfer**: balance, money; luggage, prisoner; heat
verb + **transfer**: arrange, authorize, complete, facilitate
noun + **transfer**: airport, bus
VERB ❶
transfer + noun: asset, fund, money; heat
transfer + adverb: electronically

SYNONYMS

transfer
VERB ❶
move: *She moved the sheaf of papers into position.*
carry: *She carried her son to the car.*
transport: *The troops were transported to Moscow.*
shift: *He stopped, shifting his cane to his left hand.*

---

trans|fer|able /trænsfɜrəbəl/ ADJ If something is **transferable**, it can be passed or moved from one person or organization to another and used by them. ❑ *Use the transferable skills acquired from your previous working background.*

trans|fer|ence /trænsfərəns/ N-UNCOUNT [oft N of n] The **transference** of something such as power, information, or affection from one person or place to another is the action of taking or moving it. ❑ *It is a struggle for a transference of power.*

trans|fig|ure /trænsfɪgyər/ (**transfigures, transfiguring, transfigured**) V-T To **be transfigured** means to be changed into something great or beautiful. [LITERARY] ❑ *They are transfigured by the healing powers of art.* ❑ *The colors of the morning and evening transfigure the trees.*

trans|fix /trænsfɪks/ (**transfixes, transfixing, transfixed**) V-T If you **are transfixed** by something, it captures all of your interest or attention, so that you are unable to think of anything else or unable to act. ❑ *We were all transfixed by the images of the war.* • **trans|fixed** ADJ [v-link ADJ, ADJ after v] ❑ *Her eyes were transfixed with terror.* ❑ *For hours he stood transfixed.*

trans|form ◆◇◇ /trænsfɔrm/ (**transforms, transforming, transformed**) ❶ V-T To **transform** something into something else means to change or convert it into that thing. ❑ *Your metabolic rate is the speed at which your body transforms food into energy.* • **trans|for|ma|tion** /trænsfərmeɪʃən/ (**transformations**) N-VAR ❑ *Norah made plans for the transformation of an attic room into a study.* ❷ V-T To **transform** something or someone means to change them completely and suddenly so that they are much better or more attractive. ❑ *Industrialization transformed the world.* • **trans|for|ma|tion** N-VAR ❑ *In the last five years he's undergone a personal transformation.*

SYNONYMS

transform
VERB
❶
change: *She has now changed into a happy, self-confident woman.*
convert: *The signal will be converted into digital code.*
alter: *Little had altered in the village.*
❷
overhaul: *The study says air traffic control systems must be completely overhauled.*
revamp: *Ricardo Bofill, the Catalan architect, has designed the revamped airport.*
renovate: *The couple spent thousands renovating the house.*

---

trans|form|er /trænsfɔrmər/ (**transformers**) N-COUNT A **transformer** is a piece of electrical equipment which changes a voltage to a higher or lower voltage.

1371

transitional

trans|fu|sion /trænsfyuʒən/ (**transfusions**) N-VAR A **transfusion** is the same as a **blood transfusion**.

trans|gen|der /trænzdʒɛndər/ ADJ Someone who is **transgender** has a gender identity which does not fully correspond to the sex assigned to them at birth. ❑ *...a three-year-project designed to overcome prejudice toward gay, lesbian, bisexual and transgender people.*

trans|gen|ic /trænzdʒɛnɪk/ ADJ [ADJ n] **Transgenic** plants or animals contain genetic material that has been added to them from another species. [TECHNICAL] ❑ *...transgenic sheep that secrete a human protein into their milk.*

trans|gress /trænzgrɛs/ (**transgresses, transgressing, transgressed**) V-T/V-I If someone **transgresses**, they break a moral law or a rule of behavior. ❑ *If a politician transgresses, that is not the fault of the media.* ❑ *It seemed to me that he had transgressed the boundaries of good taste.* • **trans|gres|sion** /trænzgrɛʃən/ (**transgressions**) N-VAR ❑ *Tales of the candidate's alleged past transgressions have begun springing up.*

trans|gres|sive /trænzgrɛsɪv/ ADJ **Transgressive** is used to describe actions that break a moral law or a rule of behavior. [FORMAL] ❑ *To write and publish this poem was a daring, transgressive act.*

trans|gres|sor /trænzgrɛsər/ (**transgressors**) N-COUNT A **transgressor** is someone who has broken a particular rule or law or has done something that is generally considered unacceptable. [FORMAL]

tran|si|ence /trænʃəns/ N-UNCOUNT If you talk about the **transience** of a situation, you mean that it lasts only a short time or is constantly changing. [FORMAL] ❑ *...the superficiality and transience of the club scene.*

tran|si|ent /trænʃənt/ (**transients**) ❶ ADJ **Transient** is used to describe a situation that lasts only a short time or is constantly changing. [FORMAL] ❑ *...the transient nature of high fashion.* ❷ N-COUNT [usu pl] **Transients** are people who stay in a place for only a short time and then move somewhere else. [FORMAL] ❑ *...a dormitory for transients.*

tran|sis|tor /trænzɪstər/ (**transistors**) ❶ N-COUNT A **transistor** is a small electronic part in something such as a television or radio, which controls the flow of electricity. ❷ N-COUNT A **transistor** or a **transistor radio** is a small portable radio. [OLD-FASHIONED]

tran|sit /trænzɪt/ ❶ N-UNCOUNT **Transit** is the carrying of goods or people by vehicle from one place to another. ❑ *During their talks, the two presidents discussed the transit of goods between the two countries.* ❑ *...a transit time of about 42 minutes.* • PHRASE If people or things are **in transit**, they are traveling or being taken from one place to another. ❷ ADJ [ADJ n] A **transit** area is an area where people wait or where goods are kept between different stages of a journey. ❑ *...refugees arriving at the two transit camps.* ❸ N-UNCOUNT A **transit system** is a system for moving people or goods from one place to another, for example, using buses or trains. [AM] ❑ *The president wants to improve the nation's highways and mass transit systems.*

in BRIT, use **transport system**

tran|si|tion ◆◇◇ /trænzɪʃən/ (**transitions, transitioning, transitioned**) ❶ N-VAR **Transition** is the process in which something changes from one state to another. ❑ *The transition from a dictatorship to a multi-party democracy is proving to be difficult.* ❷ V-I If someone **transitions** from one state or activity to another, they move gradually from one to the other. [BUSINESS] ❑ *Most of the discussion was on what needed to be done now as we transitioned from the security issues to the challenging economic issues.*

SYNONYMS

transition
NOUN ❶
change: *In my country, political change is on its way.*
shift: *...a shift in government policy.*
conversion: *...the conversion of disused railroad tracks into bike trails.*

---

tran|si|tion|al /trænzɪʃənəl/ ❶ ADJ [ADJ n] A **transitional** period is one in which things are changing from one state to another. ❑ *...a transitional period following more than a decade of civil war.* ❷ ADJ [ADJ n] **Transitional** is used to describe something

t

that happens or exists during a transitional period. ❏ *The main rebel groups have agreed to join in a meeting to set up a transitional government.*

tran|si|tive /trǽnzɪtɪv/ ADJ A **transitive** verb has a direct object.

tran|si|tiv|ity /trænzɪtɪ́vɪti/ N-UNCOUNT The **transitivity** of a verb is whether or not it is used with a direct object.

tran|si|tory /trǽnzɪtɔri/ ADJ If you say that something is **transitory**, you mean that it lasts only for a short time. ❏ *Most teenage romances are transitory.*

trans|late /trǽnzleɪt/ (translates, translating, translated) **1** V-T/V-I If something said or written **is translated** from one language into another, it is said or written again in the second language. ❏ *Only a small number of her books have been translated into English.* ❏ *The Spanish word "acequia" is translated as "irrigation ditch."* ❏ *The girls waited for Mr. Esch to translate.* • **trans|la|tion** N-UNCOUNT ❏ *The papers have been sent to Saudi Arabia for translation.* **2** V-I If a name, a word, or an expression **translates** as something in a different language, that is what it means in that language. ❏ *His family's Cantonese nickname for him translates as Never Sits Still.* **3** V-T/V-I If one thing **translates** or **is translated** into another, the second happens or is done as a result of the first. ❏ *Reforming the stagnant economy requires harsh measures that would translate into job losses.*

trans|la|tion /trænzleɪ́ʃᵊn/ (translations) **1** N-COUNT [also in N] A **translation** is a piece of writing or speech that has been put into a different language. ❏ *...a translation of the Iliad.* **2** → see also **translate**

trans|la|tor /trǽnzleɪtər/ (translators) N-COUNT A **translator** is a person whose job is translating writing or speech from one language to another.

trans|lu|cent /trænzlúːsᵊnt/ ADJ If a material is **translucent**, some light can pass through it. ❏ *The building is roofed entirely with translucent corrugated plastic.*

trans|mas|cu|line /trænzmǽskyəlɪn/ ADJ Someone who is **transmasculine** was said to be female when they were born, but identifies as male.

trans|mis|sion /trænzmɪ́ʃᵊn/ (transmissions) **1** N-UNCOUNT The **transmission** of something is the passing or sending of it to a different person or place. ❏ *Heterosexual contact is responsible for the bulk of HIV transmission.* **2** N-UNCOUNT The **transmission** of television or radio programs is the broadcasting of them. ❏ *The transmission of the program was brought forward due to its unexpected topicality.* **3** N-COUNT A **transmission** is a broadcast. ❏ *...foreign television transmissions.*

trans|mit /trænzmɪ́t/ (transmits, transmitting, transmitted) **1** V-T/V-I When radio and television programs, computer data, or other electronic messages **are transmitted**, they are sent from one place to another, using wires, radio waves, or satellites. ❏ *The game was transmitted live.* ❏ *This is currently the most efficient way to transmit certain types of data like electronic mail.* **2** V-T If one person or animal **transmits** a disease to another, they have the disease and cause the other person or animal to have it. [FORMAL] ❏ *...mosquitoes that transmit disease to humans.* **3** V-T If an object or substance **transmits** something such as sound or electrical signals, the sound or signals are able to pass through it. ❏ *These thin crystals transmit much of the power.*

trans|mit|ter /trǽnzmɪtər/ (transmitters) N-COUNT A **transmitter** is a piece of equipment that is used for broadcasting television or radio programs. ❏ *...a homemade radio transmitter.*

trans|mute /trænzmyúːt/ (transmutes, transmuting, transmuted) V-T/V-I If something **transmutes** or **is transmuted** into a different form, it is changed into that form. [FORMAL] ❏ *She ceased to think, as anger transmuted into passion.* ❏ *Scientists transmuted matter into pure energy and exploded the first atomic bomb.* • **trans|mu|ta|tion** (transmutations) N-VAR [oft N of n] ❏ *...the transmutation of food into energy.*

trans|na|tion|al /trænznǽʃənᵊl/ (transnationals) **1** ADJ [usu ADJ n] A **transnational** company has branches or owns companies in many different countries. ❏ *...large transnational corporations like those in the pharmaceutical industry.* • N-COUNT **Transnational** is also a noun. ❏ *...pharmaceutical transnationals such as Glaxo-Wellcome.* **2** ADJ Something that is **transnational** extends beyond the borders of a single country. ❏ *...the activities of counterfeiting and piracy, which are transnational in nature.*

tran|som /trǽnsəm/ (transoms) **1** N-COUNT The **transom** of a boat is the surface that forms its stern. ❏ *Her name and port of registration (Jersey) are painted on her transom in navy blue.* **2** N-COUNT A **transom** is a small window above a door or above another window. [AM] ❏ *He glanced up and saw an open transom leading to the locked office next door.*

in BRIT, use **fanlight**

trans|par|en|cy /trænspɛ́rənsi, -pǽr-/ (transparencies) **1** N-COUNT A **transparency** is a small piece of photographic film with a frame around it which can be projected onto a screen so that you can see the picture. ❏ *...transparencies of masterpieces from Lizzie's art collection.* **2** N-UNCOUNT **Transparency** is the quality that an object or substance has when you can see through it. ❏ *Cataracts affect the transparency of the eye's lenses.*

trans|par|ent /trænspɛ́rənt, -pǽr-/ **1** ADJ If an object or substance is **transparent**, you can see through it. ❏ *...a sheet of transparent colored plastic.* **2** ADJ If a situation, system, or activity is **transparent**, it is easily understood or recognized. ❏ *The company has to make its accounts and operations as transparent as possible.* **3** ADJ You use **transparent** to describe a statement or action that is obviously dishonest or wrong, and that you think will not deceive people. If a person is transparent, you can see their true bad motives. ❏ *He thought he could fool people with transparent deceptions.* ❏ *He's so transparent.*

trans|phobe /trǽnzfoʊb/ (transphobes) N-COUNT A **transphobe** is someone who fears or hates transgender people. [DISAPPROVAL] ❏ *They claimed she was a transphobe and should not have been invited to speak.*

trans|pho|bia /trænzfóʊbiə/ N-UNCOUNT **Transphobia** is fear or hatred of transgender people. [DISAPPROVAL] ❏ *They campaign against homophobia and transphobia in sport.*

trans|pho|bic /trænzfóʊbɪk/ ADJ A **transphobic** person or remark shows a fear or hatred of transgender people. [DISAPPROVAL] ❏ *They advise schools on how to deal with transphobic bullying.*

tran|spi|ra|tion /trænspɪreɪ́ʃᵊn/ **1** N-UNCOUNT **Transpiration** is the evaporation of water from a plant's leaves, stem, or flowers. ❏ *Plants release water through their leaves by transpiration.* **2** → See also **color supplement**

tran|spire /trænspaɪ́ər/ (transpires, transpiring, transpired) **1** V-T When it **transpires** that something is the case, people discover that it is the case. [FORMAL] ❏ *It transpired that Kareem had left his driver's license at home.* **2** V-I When something **transpires**, it happens. ❏ *Nothing is known as yet about what transpired at the meeting.*

trans|plant (transplants, transplanting, transplanted)

The noun is pronounced /trǽnsplænt/. The verb is pronounced /trænsplǽnt/.

1 N-VAR A **transplant** is a medical operation in which a part of a person's body is replaced because it is diseased. ❏ *He was recovering from a heart transplant operation.* **2** V-T If doctors **transplant** an organ such as a heart or a kidney, they use it to replace a patient's diseased organ. ❏ *The operation to transplant a kidney is now fairly routine.* **3** V-T To **transplant** a plant, person, or thing means to move them to a different place. ❏ *I have to transplant the begonias.*

trans|pond|er /trænspɒ́ndər/ (transponders) N-COUNT A **transponder** is a type of radio transmitter that transmits signals automatically when it receives particular signals. ❏ *In Singapore, every car is fitted with a digital transponder that triggers automatic tollbooths as it passes.*

trans|port ✦✧ (transports, transporting, transported)

The verb is pronounced /trænspɔ́rt/. The noun is pronounced /trǽnspɔrt/.

1 V-T To **transport** people or goods somewhere is to take them from one place to another in a vehicle. ❏ *They are banned from launching any flights except to transport people.* **2** N-UNCOUNT **Transport** refers to any vehicle that you can travel in or carry goods in. [mainly BRIT]

in AM, usually use **transportation**

3 N-UNCOUNT **Transport** is a system for taking people or goods from one place to another, for example, using buses or trains. [mainly BRIT]

> in AM, usually use **transportation**

4 N-UNCOUNT **Transport** is the activity of taking goods or people from one place to another in a vehicle. [mainly BRIT]

> in AM, usually use **transportation**

trans|por|ta|tion ◆◇ /trænspərteɪʃ³n/ **1** N-UNCOUNT **Transportation** refers to any type of vehicle that you can travel in or carry goods in. [mainly AM] ❏ *The company will provide transportation.*

> in BRIT, usually use **transport**

2 N-UNCOUNT **Transportation** is a system for taking people or goods from one place to another, for example, using buses or trains. [mainly AM] ❏ *Campuses are usually accessible by public transportation.*

> in BRIT, usually use **transport**

3 N-UNCOUNT **Transportation** is the activity of taking goods or people from one place to another in a vehicle. [mainly AM] ❏ *The baggage was being rapidly stowed away for transportation.*

> in BRIT, usually use **transport**

4 → See feature box at **commute**

trans|port|er /trænspɔrtər/ (**transporters**) N-COUNT A **transporter** is a large vehicle or an airplane that is used for carrying very large or heavy objects, for example, cars.

trans|pose /trænspoʊz/ (**transposes, transposing, transposed**) **1** V-T If you **transpose** something from one place or situation to another, you move it there. ❏ *The director transposes the action from sixteenth-century France to post-Civil War America.* • **trans|po|si|tion** /trænspəzɪʃ³n/ (**transpositions**) N-VAR [oft N of n] ❏ *...a transposition of "Macbeth" to third century BC China.* **2** V-T If you **transpose** two things, you reverse them or put them in each other's place. ❏ *Many people inadvertently transpose digits of the ZIP code.* • **trans|po|si|tion** N-VAR [oft N of n] ❏ *...the transposition of the last two letters.*

trans|put|er /trænspyutər/ (**transputers**) N-COUNT A **transputer** is a type of fast powerful microchip. [COMPUTING]

trans|sex|ual /trænsɛkʃuəl/ (**transsexuals**) N-COUNT A **transsexual** is a person who has decided that they want to live as a person of the opposite sex, and so has changed their name and appearance in order to do this. Transsexuals sometimes have an operation to change their sex.

trans|verse /trænzvɜrs/ ADJ [usu ADJ n] **Transverse** is used to describe something that is at right angles to something else.

trans|ves|tism /trænzvɛstɪzəm/ N-UNCOUNT **Transvestism** is the practice of wearing clothes normally worn by a person of the opposite sex, usually for pleasure.

trans|ves|tite /trænzvɛstaɪt/ (**transvestites**) N-COUNT A **transvestite** is someone who enjoys wearing clothes normally worn by people of the opposite sex.

trap ◆◇ /træp/ (**traps, trapping, trapped**) **1** N-COUNT A **trap** is a device which is placed somewhere or a hole which is dug somewhere in order to catch animals or birds. ❏ *Nathan's dog got caught in a trap.* **2** V-T If a person **traps** animals or birds, he or she catches them using traps. ❏ *The locals were encouraged to trap and kill mice to stop the spread of the virus.* **3** N-COUNT A **trap** is a trick that is intended to catch or deceive someone. ❏ *He failed to keep a rendezvous after sensing a police trap.* **4** V-T If you **trap** someone into doing or saying something, you trick them so that they do or say it, although they did not want to. ❏ *Were you just trying to trap her into making some admission?* **5** V-T To **trap** someone, especially a criminal, means to capture them. ❏ *The police knew they had to trap the killer.* **6** N-COUNT A **trap** is an unpleasant situation that you cannot easily escape from. ❏ *The government has found that it's caught in a trap of its own making.* **7** V-T If you **are trapped** somewhere, something falls onto you or blocks your way and prevents you from moving or escaping. ❏ *The train was trapped underground by a fire.* ❏ *The light aircraft then cartwheeled, trapping both men.* **8** V-T When something **traps** gas, water, or energy, it prevents it from escaping. ❏ *Wool traps your body heat, keeping the chill at bay.*

9 → see also **trapped, deathtrap** **10** → See feature box at **global warming**

trap|door (**trapdoors** /træpdɔr/) also **trap door** N-COUNT A **trapdoor** is a small horizontal door in a floor, a ceiling, or on a stage.

tra|peze /trəpiz/ (**trapezes**) N-COUNT A **trapeze** is a bar of wood or metal hanging from two ropes on which people in a circus swing and perform skillful movements.

trapped /træpt/ **1** ADJ If you feel **trapped**, you are in an unpleasant situation in which you lack freedom, and you feel you cannot escape from it. ❏ *...people who think of themselves as trapped in mundane jobs.* **2** → see also **trap**

trap|per /træpər/ (**trappers**) N-COUNT A **trapper** is a person who traps animals, especially for their fur.

trap|pings /træpɪŋz/ N-PLURAL The **trappings** of power, wealth, or a particular job are the extra things, such as decorations and luxury items, that go with it. [DISAPPROVAL] ❏ *The family ruled for several generations and evidently loved the trappings of power.*

trash /træʃ/ **1** N-UNCOUNT [also the N] **Trash** consists of unwanted things or waste material such as used paper, empty containers and bottles, and waste food. [AM] ❏ *The yards are overgrown and cluttered with trash.* ❏ *Would you take out the trash?*

> in BRIT, use **rubbish**

2 N-UNCOUNT If you say that something such as a book, painting, or movie is **trash**, you mean that it is of very bad quality. [INFORMAL] ❏ *Pop music doesn't have to be trash; it can be art.* **3** N-SING **The trash** means the trash can. ❏ *I threw it in the trash.*

trash can (**trash cans**) N-COUNT A **trash can** is a large round container where people put their trash. [AM]

trashed /træʃt/ ADJ If someone is **trashed**, they are very drunk. ❏ *They get trashed and act totally out of character, shouting and swearing.*

trash talk (**trash talks, trash talking, trash talked**) also **trash-talk** V-T/V-I If athletes who are competing against each other **trash talk**, they say unkind things to one another in order to disturb one another's concentration. [AM, INFORMAL, DISAPPROVAL] ❏ *When people trash talk, it can motivate both teams.* ❏ *He has a reputation for trash talking his rivals.* • N-UNCOUNT **Trash talk** is also a noun. ❏ *But all the trash talk was forgotten as he shook the champ's hand at the end.*

trashy /træʃi/ (**trashier, trashiest**) ADJ If you describe something as **trashy**, you think it is of very poor quality. [INFORMAL, DISAPPROVAL] ❏ *I was reading some trashy romance novel.*

trat|to|ria /trɒtəriə/ (**trattorias**) N-COUNT A **trattoria** is an Italian restaurant.

trau|ma /traʊmə, trɔ-/ (**traumas**) N-VAR **Trauma** is a very severe shock or very upsetting experience, which may cause psychological damage. ❏ *I'd been through the trauma of losing a house.*

trau|mat|ic /trəmætɪk/ ADJ A **traumatic** experience is very shocking and upsetting, and may cause psychological damage. ❏ *I suffered a nervous breakdown. It was a traumatic experience.*

trau|ma|tize /traʊmətaɪz, trɔ-/ (**traumatizes, traumatizing, traumatized**)

> in BRIT, also use **traumatise**

V-T If someone **is traumatized** by an event or situation, it shocks or upsets them very much, and may cause them psychological damage. ❏ *My wife was traumatized by the experience.* • **trau|ma|tized** ADJ ❏ *He left her in the middle of the road, shaking and deeply traumatized.*

trav|ail /trəveɪl/ (**travails**) N-VAR [usu pl] You can refer to hard work or difficult problems as **travail**. [LITERARY] ❏ *The team, despite their recent travails, are still in the game.*

trav|el ◆◆ /træv³l/ (**travels, traveling or travelling, traveled or travelled**) **1** V-T/V-I If you **travel**, you go from one place to another, often to a place that is far away. ❏ *You had better travel to Nova Scotia tomorrow.* ❏ *I've been traveling all day.* ❏ *Students often travel hundreds of miles to get here.* **2** N-UNCOUNT **Travel** is the activity of traveling. ❑ *Information on travel in New Zealand is available at the hotel.* ❑ *He detested air travel.* **3** V-T If you **travel** the world, the country, or the area, you go to many different places in the world or in a particular country or area. ❑ *He was a very wealthy man who had traveled the world.* **4** V-I When light or sound from one place reaches another, you say that it **travels** to the other place. ❑ *When sound travels through water, strange things can happen.* **5** V-I When news becomes known by people in different places, you can say that it **travels** to them. ❑ *News of his work traveled all the way to Asia.* **6** N-PLURAL Someone's **travels** are the trips that they make to places a long way from their home. ❑ *He also collects things for the house on his travels abroad.* **7** PHRASE If you **travel light**, you travel without taking much luggage. ❑ *It would be good to be able to travel light, but I end up taking too many clothes.* **8** → See feature box at **time**, **tourism**

VOCABULARY IN CONTEXT

Space travel

Astronauts have to train for years before **manned missions** into space, but there's far more to their training than learning how to pilot the **shuttle**. In actual fact, the **launch** is controlled by computer, though the pilots have to perform safety checks prior to **countdown** and **lift-off**, and the pilot will only take over if the flight is aborted because of technical failure. Likewise, most of the **reentry** is handled by autopilot, but a human commander controls the final minute or so of **touchdown**. The shuttle **accelerates** from 0 to 17,500 miles per hour during the 8.5 minutes it takes to get into **orbit**. This is when the astronauts achieve **weightlessness** and the need for the rest of their extensive training kicks in. Life under the microgravity conditions **aboard** a **spacecraft** means adapting almost every task from eating to washing and sleeping.

trav|el agen|cy (travel agencies) N-COUNT A **travel agency** is a business which makes arrangements for people's vacations and trips.

trav|el agent (travel agents) **1** N-COUNT A **travel agent** or **travel agent's** is a store or office where you can go to arrange a vacation or trip. ❑ *He worked in a travel agent's.* **2** N-COUNT A **travel agent** is a person or business that arranges people's vacations and trips.

trav|el|er ♦◇◇ /trǽvələr/ (travelers) also **traveller** N-COUNT A **traveler** is a person who is on a trip or a person who travels a lot. ❑ *Airline travelers need to be confident that their bookings will be honored.*

COLLOCATIONS

traveler
NOUN
adjective + **traveler**: frequent, seasoned; intrepid; inveterate, keen; discerning, savvy; weary; solo
verb + **traveler**: strand; entice, lure, woo
noun + **traveler**: armchair; business, leisure; air, rail, train; budget

trav|el|er's check (traveler's checks) N-COUNT Traveler's checks are checks that you buy at a bank and take with you when you travel, for example, so that you can exchange them for the currency of the country that you are in.

trav|el|ing /trǽvəlɪŋ/ also **travelling** ADJ [ADJ n] A **traveling** actor or musician, for example, is one who travels around an area or country performing in different places. ❑ *...traveling entertainers.*

trav|el|ing sales|man (traveling salesmen) N-COUNT A **traveling salesman** is the same as a **traveling salesperson**.

trav|el|ing sales|per|son (traveling salespeople) N-COUNT A **traveling salesperson** is a salesperson who travels to different places and meets people in order to sell goods or take orders.

trav|el|ing sales|wo|man (traveling saleswomen) N-COUNT A **traveling saleswoman** is the same as a **traveling salesperson**.

trav|elogue /trǽvəlɒg, -lɔg/ (travelogues) N-COUNT A **travelogue** is a talk, diary, or film about travel or about a particular person's travels.

trav|el sick|ness **1** N-UNCOUNT If someone has **travel sickness**, they feel sick as a result of traveling in a vehicle. **2** → see also **seasick**

trav|erse /trǽvɜrs, trəvɜ́rs/ (traverses, traversing, traversed) V-T If someone or something **traverses** an area of land or water, they go across it. [LITERARY] ❑ *I traversed the narrow pedestrian bridge.*

trav|es|ty /trǽvəsti/ (travesties) N-COUNT If you describe something as a **travesty** of another thing, you mean that it is a very bad representation of that other thing. ❑ *Her research suggests that Smith's reputation today is a travesty of what he really stood for.*

trawl /trɔl/ (trawls, trawling, trawled) **1** V-T/V-I If you **trawl** through a large number of similar things, you search through them looking for something that you want or something that is suitable for a particular purpose. ❑ *A team of officers is trawling through the records of thousands of petty thieves.* ❑ *Petra trawled the aisles of the Europa supermarket.* **2** V-T/V-I When fishermen **trawl** for fish, they pull a wide net behind their ship in order to catch fish. ❑ *They had seen him trawling and therefore knew that there were fish.* ❑ *She would walk on to the beach and watch the night fishermen trawl the shallow waters.*

trawl|er /trɔ́lər/ (trawlers) **1** N-COUNT A **trawler** is a fishing boat that is used for trawling. **2** → See feature box at **boat**; See also color supplement

tray /treɪ/ (trays) N-COUNT A **tray** is a flat piece of wood, plastic, or metal, which usually has raised edges and which is used for carrying things, especially food and drinks.

treach|er|ous /trɛ́tʃərəs/ **1** ADJ If you describe someone as **treacherous**, you mean that they are likely to betray you and cannot be trusted. [DISAPPROVAL] ❑ *He publicly left the party and denounced its treacherous leaders.* **2** ADJ If you say that something is **treacherous**, you mean that it is very dangerous and unpredictable. ❑ *The current of the river is fast flowing and treacherous.*

treach|ery /trɛ́tʃəri/ N-UNCOUNT **Treachery** is behavior or an action in which someone betrays their country or betrays a person who trusts them. ❑ *He was deeply wounded by the treachery of close aides and old friends.*

trea|cle /trík°l/ N-UNCOUNT **Treacle** is a thick, sweet, sticky liquid that is obtained when sugar is processed. It is used in making cakes and desserts such as steamed puddings. [BRIT]

in AM, use **molasses**

tread /trɛd/ (treads, treading, trod, trodden) **1** N-VAR The **tread** of a tire or shoe is the pattern of thin lines cut into its surface that stops it from slipping. ❑ *The fat, broad tires had a good depth of tread.* **2** V-I If you **tread** in a particular way, you walk that way. [LITERARY] ❑ *She trod casually, enjoying the touch of the damp grass on her feet.* **3** V-I If you **tread** carefully, you behave in a careful or cautious way. ❑ *If you are hoping to form a new relationship, tread carefully and slowly to begin with.* **4** V-I If you **tread on** something, you put your foot on it when you are walking or standing. [mainly BRIT]

in AM, usually use **step**

treadle

5 PHRASE If you **tread** a particular **path**, you take a particular course of action or do something in a particular way. ❏ *He continues to tread an unconventional path.* **6** → See feature box at **theater**

trea|dle /trɛdəl/ (treadles) N-COUNT The **treadle** on a spinning wheel or sewing machine is a lever that you operate with your foot in order to turn a wheel in the machine.

tread|mill /trɛdmɪl/ (treadmills) **1** N-COUNT You can refer to a task or a job as a **treadmill** when you have to keep doing it although it is unpleasant and exhausting. ❏ *He exhausted himself on an endless treadmill to pay for rent and food.* **2** N-COUNT A **treadmill** is a piece of equipment, for example, an exercise machine, consisting of a wheel with steps around its edge or a continuous moving belt. The weight of a person or animal walking on it causes the wheel or belt to turn.

trea|son /triːzən/ N-UNCOUNT **Treason** is the crime of betraying your country, for example, by helping its enemies or by trying to remove its government using violence. ❏ *They were tried and found guilty of treason.*

trea|son|able /triːzənəbəl/ ADJ **Treasonable** activities are criminal activities which someone carries out with the intention of helping their country's enemies or removing its government using violence. ❏ *They were brought to trial for treasonable conspiracy.*

treas|ure /trɛʒər/ (treasures, treasuring, treasured) **1** N-UNCOUNT **Treasure** is a collection of valuable old objects such as gold coins and jewels that has been hidden or lost. [LITERARY] ❏ *It was here, the buried treasure, she knew it was.* **2** N-COUNT **Treasures** are valuable objects, especially works of art and items of historical value. ❏ *The house was large and full of art treasures.* **3** V-T If you **treasure** something that you have, you keep it or care for it carefully because it gives you great pleasure and you think it is very special. ❏ *She treasures her memories of those joyous days.* ● N-COUNT **Treasure** is also a noun. ❏ *His greatest treasure is his collection of rock records.* ● **treas|ured** ADJ [ADJ n] ❏ *These books are still among my most treasured possessions.*

treas|ure chest (treasure chests) **1** N-COUNT A **treasure chest** is a box containing treasure. **2** N-COUNT [usu N of n] If you describe something as a **treasure chest** of a particular thing, you mean that it is very good source of that thing. ❏ *This book is a treasure chest of information.*

treas|ur|er /trɛʒərər/ (treasurers) N-COUNT The **treasurer** of a society or organization is the person who is in charge of its finances and keeps its accounts.

treas|ure trove (treasure troves) **1** N-COUNT [usu sing, N of n] If you describe something or someone as a **treasure trove of** a particular thing, you mean that they are a very good or rich source of that thing. ❏ *The dictionary is a vast treasure trove of information.* **2** N-COUNT [usu sing, oft N for n] You can refer to a collection of valuable objects as a **treasure trove**.

treas|ury ✦◇◇ /trɛʒəri/ (treasuries) **1** N-COUNT-COLL In the United States and some other countries, the **Treasury** is the government department that deals with the country's finances. ❏ *...a senior official at the Treasury.* **2** N-PLURAL **Treasuries** are financial bonds that are issued by the United States government in order to raise money. [AM] ❏ *...people who invest in 10- and 20- and 30 year Treasuries.*

treas|ury bill (treasury bills) also **Treasury bill, Treasury Bill** N-COUNT A **treasury bill** is a short-term bond that is issued by the United States government in order to raise money. [AM] ❏ *The Japanese routinely purchase more than a third of U.S. Treasury Bills.*

treat ✦◇◇ /triːt/ (treats, treating, treated) **1** V-T If you **treat** someone or something in a particular way, you behave toward them or deal with them in that way. ❏ *Artie treated most women with indifference.* ❏ *Police say they're treating it as a case of attempted murder.* **2** V-T When a doctor or nurse **treats** a patient or an illness, he or she tries to make the patient well again. ❏ *Doctors treated her with aspirin.* ❏ *The boy was treated for a minor head wound.* **3** V-T If something **is treated** with a particular substance, the substance is put onto or into it in order to clean it, to protect it, or to give it special properties. ❏ *About 70% of the cocoa acreage is treated with insecticide.* **4** V-T If you **treat** someone to something special which they will enjoy, you buy it or arrange it for them. ❏ *She was always treating him to ice cream.* ❏ *Tomorrow I'll treat myself to a day's gardening.* **5** N-COUNT If you give someone a **treat**, you buy or arrange something special for them which they will enjoy. ❏ *Lettie had never yet failed to return from town without some special treat for him.*

SYNONYMS

treat
VERB
1
deal with: *...the way that airlines deal with complaints.*
handle: *You must learn how to handle your feelings.*
2
minister: *For 44 years, he had ministered to the poor, the sick, the neglected, and the deprived.*
cure: *An operation finally cured his shin injury.*
heal: *No doctor has ever healed a broken bone: he or she sets them.*
NOUN **5**
luxury: *A week by the sea is a luxury they can no longer afford.*
indulgence: *The car is one of my few indulgences.*

---

treat|able /triːtəbəl/ ADJ A **treatable** disease is one which can be cured or controlled, usually by the use of drugs. ❏ *This is a treatable condition.* ❏ *Depression is treatable.*

trea|tise /triːtɪs/ (treatises) N-COUNT A **treatise** is a long, formal piece of writing about a particular subject. ❏ *...Locke's Treatise on Civil Government.*

treat|ment ✦◇ /triːtmənt/ (treatments) **1** N-VAR **Treatment** is medical attention given to a sick or injured person or animal. ❏ *Many patients are not getting the medical treatment they need.* ❏ *...a veterinary surgeon who specializes in the treatment of caged birds.* **2** N-UNCOUNT Your **treatment** of someone is the way you behave toward them or deal with them. ❏ *We don't want any special treatment.* **3** N-VAR **Treatment** of something involves putting a particular substance onto or into it, in order to clean it, to protect it, or to give it special properties. ❏ *There should be greater treatment of sewage before it is discharged.* **4** → See feature box at **medicine**

SYNONYMS

treatment
NOUN **1**
medicine: *...herbal medicines.*
remedy: *...natural remedies to help overcome winter infections.*
cure: *There is still no cure for a cold.*
medication: *She stopped taking the prescribed medications.*

---

trea|ty ✦◇ /triːti/ (treaties) **1** N-COUNT A **treaty** is a written agreement between countries in which they agree to do a particular thing or to help each other. ❏ *...negotiations over a treaty on global warming.* **2** → See feature box at **history**

SYNONYMS

treaty
NOUN **1**
agreement: *The two countries signed an agreement to jointly launch satellites.*
pact: *Last month, he signed a new non-aggression pact with Germany.*
contract: *The company won a prestigious contract for work on Europe's tallest building.*

---

tre|ble /trɛbəl/ (trebles, trebling, trebled) **1** N-COUNT On a stereo system or radio, the **treble** is the ability to reproduce the higher musical notes. The **treble** is also the knob which controls this. **2** V-T/V-I If something **trebles** or if you **treble** it, it becomes three times greater in number or amount than it was. [mainly BRIT] ❏ *They will have to pay much more when rents treble in January.*

in AM, use **triple**

3 PREDET If one thing is **treble** the size or amount of another thing, it is three times greater in size or amount. [mainly BRIT, FORMAL]

in AM, use **triple**

tre|ble clef (treble clefs) N-COUNT A **treble clef** is a symbol that you use when writing music in order to show that the notes on the staff are above middle C.

tree /triː/ (trees) N-COUNT A **tree** is a tall plant that has a hard trunk, branches, and leaves. ▫ *I planted those apple trees.*

tree|house /ˈtriːhaʊs/ (treehouses) N-COUNT A **treehouse** is a shelter that is built in a tree, usually for children, to play in. ▫ *I wanted to build a treehouse for my children but I couldn't because of the lack of branches.*

tree|less /ˈtriːlɪs/ ADJ A **treeless** area or place has no trees in it.

tree-lined ADJ [usu ADJ n] A **tree-lined** road or street has trees on both sides. ▫ *...the broad, tree-lined avenues.*

tree|top /ˈtriːtɒp/ (treetops) also **tree tops** N-COUNT [usu pl] The **treetops** are the top branches of the trees.

tree trunk (tree trunks) N-COUNT A **tree trunk** is the wide central part of a tree, from which the branches grow.

trek /trɛk/ (treks, trekking, trekked) ■ V-I If you **trek** somewhere, you go on a journey across difficult country, usually on foot. ▫ *...trekking through the jungles.* • N-COUNT **Trek** is also a noun. ▫ *He is on a trek through the South Gobi desert.* ■ V-I If you **trek** somewhere, you go there heavily and unwillingly, usually because you are tired. ▫ *They trekked from shop to shop in search of white knee-high socks.* ■ → See feature box at **tourism**

trel|lis /ˈtrɛlɪs/ (trellises) N-VAR A **trellis** is a frame which supports climbing plants.

trem|ble /ˈtrɛmbəl/ (trembles, trembling, trembled) ■ V-I If you **tremble**, you shake slightly because you are frightened or cold. ▫ *His mouth became dry, his eyes widened, and he began to tremble all over.* ▫ *Lisa was white and trembling with anger.* • N-SING **Tremble** is also a noun. ▫ *I will never forget the look on the patient's face, the tremble in his hand.* ■ V-I If something **trembles**, it shakes slightly. [LITERARY] ▫ *He felt the earth tremble under him.* ■ V-I If your voice **trembles**, it sounds unsteady and uncertain, usually because you are upset or nervous. [LITERARY] ▫ *His voice trembled, on the verge of tears.* • N-SING **Tremble** is also a noun. ▫ *"Please understand this," she began, a tremble in her voice.*

tre|men|dous /trɪˈmɛndəs/ ■ ADJ You use **tremendous** to emphasize how strong a feeling or quality is, or how large an amount is. [EMPHASIS] ▫ *I felt a tremendous pressure on my chest.* • **tre|men|dous|ly** ADV ▫ *I thought they played tremendously well, didn't you?* ■ ADJ You can describe someone or something as **tremendous** when you think they are very good or very impressive. ▫ *I thought it was absolutely tremendous.*

> **SYNONYMS**
>
> **tremendous**
> ADJ ■
> **great:** *I'll take great care of it.*
> **immense:** *With immense relief, I stopped running.*
> **enormous:** *It was an enormous disappointment.*

tremo|lo /ˈtrɛmələʊ/ N-UNCOUNT [also a N] If someone's singing or speaking voice has a **tremolo** in it, it moves up and down instead of staying on the same note.

trem|or /ˈtrɛmər/ (tremors) ■ N-COUNT A **tremor** is a small earthquake. ▫ *The earthquake sent tremors through the region.* ■ N-COUNT If an event causes a **tremor** in a group or organization, it threatens to make the group or organization less strong or stable. ▫ *News of 160 lay-offs had sent tremors through the community.* ■ N-COUNT A **tremor** is a shaking of your body or voice that you cannot control. ▫ *The old man has a tremor in his hands.*

tremu|lous /ˈtrɛmjʊləs/ ADJ If someone's voice, smile, or actions are **tremulous**, they are unsteady because the person is uncertain, afraid, or upset. [LITERARY] ▫ *She fidgeted in her chair as she took a deep, tremulous breath.* • **tremu|lous|ly** ADV [ADV with v] ▫ *"He was so good to me," she said tremulously.*

trench /trɛntʃ/ (trenches) ■ N-COUNT A **trench** is a long narrow channel that is cut into the ground, for example, in order to lay pipes or get rid of water. ■ N-COUNT A **trench** is a long narrow channel in the ground used by soldiers in order to protect themselves from the enemy. People often refer to the battlegrounds of the First World War in Northern France and Belgium as **the trenches**. ▫ *We fought with them in the trenches.*

trench|ant /ˈtrɛntʃənt/ ADJ You can use **trenchant** to describe something such as a criticism or comment that is very clear, effective, and forceful. [FORMAL] ▫ *He resigned in the face of trenchant criticism of his policies.* ▫ *His comment was trenchant and perceptive.*

trench coat (trench coats) also **trenchcoat** N-COUNT A **trench coat** is a type of raincoat with pockets and a belt. Trench coats are often similar in design to military coats.

trend /trɛnd/ (trends) ■ N-COUNT A **trend** is a change or development toward something new or different. ▫ *This is a growing trend.* ▫ *...a trend toward part-time employment.* ■ N-COUNT To set a **trend** means to do something that becomes accepted or fashionable, and that a lot of other people copy. ▫ *The latest trend is gardening.* ■ → See feature box at **upcycle**

> **SYNONYMS**
>
> **trend**
> NOUN ■
> **inclination:** *He set out to follow his artistic inclinations.*
> **tendency:** *...the government's tendency towards secrecy in recent years.*
> **fashion:** *He stayed at the top, through all changes and fashions in pop music.*
> **craze:** *...the craze for Mutant Ninja Turtles.*
> **fad:** *Hamnett does not believe environmental concern is a passing fad.*

trend|setter /ˈtrɛndsɛtər/ (trendsetters) N-COUNT A **trendsetter** is a person or institution that starts a new fashion or trend.

trendy /ˈtrɛndi/ (trendier, trendiest) ■ ADJ If you say that something or someone is **trendy**, you mean that they are very fashionable and modern. [INFORMAL] ▫ *...a trendy Seattle night club.* ■ → See feature box at **town**

trepi|da|tion /ˌtrɛpɪˈdeɪʃən/ N-UNCOUNT **Trepidation** is fear or anxiety about something that you are going to do or experience. [FORMAL] ▫ *It was with some trepidation that I viewed the prospect of cycling across Uganda.*

tres|pass /ˈtrɛspəs, -pæs/ (trespasses, trespassing, trespassed) V-I If someone **trespasses**, they go onto someone else's land without their permission. ▫ *They were trespassing on private property.* • N-VAR **Trespass** is the act of trespassing. [LEGAL] ▫ *You could be prosecuted for trespass.*

tress /trɛs/ (tresses) N-COUNT [usu pl] A woman's **tresses** are her long flowing hair. [LITERARY]

tres|tle /ˈtrɛsəl/ (trestles) N-COUNT A **trestle** is a wooden or metal structure that is used, for example, as one of the supports for a table. It has two pairs of sloping legs which are joined by a flat piece across the top.

tres|tle ta|ble (trestle tables) N-COUNT A **trestle table** is a table made of a long board that is supported on trestles.

> **PREFIX**
>
> **tri-**
> is used at the beginning of nouns and adjectives that have 'three' as part of their meaning. *For example, a **tripartite** meeting takes place between representatives from three organizations.*

tri|ad /ˈtraɪæd/ (triads)

> The spelling **Triad** is also used for meaning ■.

■ N-COUNT [usu pl, oft N n] The **Triads** were Chinese secret societies in old China that were often associated with organized crime. ■ N-COUNT [oft N of n] A **triad** is a group of three similar things. [FORMAL] ▫ *For the faculty, there exists the triad of responsibilities: teaching, research, and service.*

tri|age /ˈtriːɑːʒ/ N-UNCOUNT [oft N n] **Triage** is the process of quickly examining sick or injured people, for example, after an accident or a battle, so that those who are in the most serious condition can be treated first. [MEDICAL] ▫ *...the triage process.*

tri|al /ˈtraɪəl/ (trials) ■ N-VAR A **trial** is a formal meeting in a law court, at which a judge and jury listen to evidence and decide whether a person is guilty of a crime. ▫ *New evidence showed the police lied at the trial.* ▫ *I have the right to a trial with a jury of my peers.* ■ N-VAR A **trial** is an experiment in which you test something by using it or doing it for a period of time to see how well it works. If something is **on trial**, it is being tested in this way. ▫ *They have been treated with this drug in clinical trials.*

❏ *I took the car out for a trial on the roads.* **3** N-COUNT If you refer to the **trials** of a situation, you mean the unpleasant things that you experience in it. ❏ *...the trials of adolescence.* **4** PHRASE If you do something by **trial and error**, you try several different methods of doing it until you find the method that works best. ❏ *Many drugs were found by trial and error.* **5** PHRASE If someone is **on trial**, they are being tried in a court of law. ❏ *He is currently on trial for drunk driving.* **6** PHRASE If you say that someone or something is **on trial**, you mean that they are in a situation where people are observing them to see whether they succeed or fail. ❏ *The president will be drawn into a damaging battle in which his credentials will be on trial.* **7** PHRASE If someone **stands trial**, they are tried in court for a crime they are accused of. ❏ *He was found to be mentally unfit to stand trial.* **8** → See feature box at **legal**

SYNONYMS

trial
NOUN
1
hearing: *The judge adjourned the hearing until next Tuesday.*
case: *It can be difficult for public figures to win a libel case.*
tribunal: *His case comes before an industrial tribunal in March.*
2
test: *...the banning of nuclear tests.*
experiment: *...a proposed new law on animal experiments.*
pilot: *...a ten-year pilot project backed by the trade and industry department.*

---

tri|al bal|loon (trial balloons) N-COUNT A **trial balloon** is a proposal that you mention or an action that you try in order to find out other people's reactions to it, especially if you think they are likely to oppose it. [mainly AM] ❏ *The petition could be just a trial balloon to test the administration's reaction.*

tri|al run (trial runs) N-COUNT A **trial run** is a first attempt at doing something to make sure you can really do it.

tri|an|gle /traɪæŋgəl/ (triangles) **1** N-COUNT A **triangle** is an object, arrangement, or flat shape with three straight sides and three angles. ❏ *This design is in pastel colors with three rectangles and three triangles.* ❏ *Its outline roughly forms an equilateral triangle.* **2** N-COUNT The **triangle** is a musical instrument that consists of a piece of metal shaped like a triangle. You play it by hitting it with a short metal bar. ❏ *My musical career consisted of playing the triangle in kindergarten.*

tri|an|gu|lar /traɪæŋgyələr/ ADJ Something that is **triangular** is in the shape of a triangle. ❏ *...a triangular roof.*

tri|ath|lete /traɪæθlit/ (triathletes) N-COUNT A **triathlete** is someone who takes part in a triathlon.

tri|ath|lon /traɪæθlɒn/ (triathlons) N-COUNT [usu sing] A **triathlon** is a track and field competition in which each competitor takes part in three events: swimming, cycling, and running.

trib|al /traɪbəl/ ADJ **Tribal** is used to describe things relating to or belonging to tribes and the way that they are organized. ❏ *...tribal warfare.* ❏ *...the Navajo Tribal Council.*

trib|al|ism /traɪbəlɪzəm/ **1** N-UNCOUNT **Tribalism** is the state of existing as a tribe. ❏ *Apartheid used tribalism as the basis of its "divide-and-rule" homeland policies.* **2** N-UNCOUNT You can use **tribalism** to refer to the loyalties that people feel toward particular social groups and to the way these loyalties affect their behavior and their attitudes toward others. [DISAPPROVAL] ❏ *His argument was that multi-party systems encourage tribalism.*

tribe /traɪb/ (tribes) N-COUNT-COLL **Tribe** is sometimes used to refer to a group of people of the same race, language, and customs, especially in a developing country. Some people disapprove of this use. ❏ *...three-hundred members of the Xhosa tribe.*

tribes|man /traɪbzmən/ (tribesmen) N-COUNT A **tribesman** is a man who belongs to a tribe.

tribes|woman /traɪbzwʊmən/ (tribeswomen) N-COUNT A **tribeswoman** is a woman who belongs to a tribe.

tribu|la|tion /trɪbyəleɪʃən/ (tribulations) N-VAR You can refer to the suffering or difficulty that you experience in a particular situation as **tribulations**. [FORMAL] ❏ *...the trials and tribulations of everyday life.*

tri|bu|nal /traɪbyunəl/ (tribunals) N-COUNT-COLL A **tribunal** is a special court or committee that is appointed to deal with particular problems. ❏ *His case comes before an industrial tribunal in March.*

tribu|tary /trɪbyəteri/ (tributaries) N-COUNT [oft N n] A **tributary** is a stream or river that flows into a larger one. ❏ *...the Napo river, a tributary of the Amazon.*

trib|ute /trɪbyut/ (tributes) **1** N-VAR A **tribute** is something that you say, do, or make to show your admiration and respect for someone. ❏ *The song is a tribute to Roy Orbison.* **2** N-SING If one thing is a **tribute** to another, the first thing is the result of the second and shows how good it is. ❏ *His success has been a tribute to hard work, to professionalism.*

trib|ute band (tribute bands) N-COUNT A **tribute band** is a pop group that plays the music and copies the style of another, much more famous pop group. ❏ *...a Beatles tribute band, the Prefab Four.*

trice /traɪs/ PHRASE If someone does something **in a trice**, they do it very quickly. ❏ *He will sew it up in a trice.* ❏ *She was back in a trice.*

tri|ceps /traɪsɛps/ (triceps) N-COUNT Your **triceps** is the muscle in the back part of your upper arm.

trick ✦◇◇ /trɪk/ (tricks, tricking, tricked) **1** N-COUNT A **trick** is an action that is intended to fool or deceive someone. ❏ *We are playing a trick on a man who keeps bothering me.* **2** V-T If someone **tricks** you, they deceive you, often in order to make you do something. ❏ *Stephen is going to be pretty upset when he finds out how you tricked him.* ❏ *His family tricked him into going to Pakistan, and once he was there, they took away his passport.* **3** N-COUNT A **trick** is a clever or skillful action that someone does in order to entertain people. ❏ *...magic tricks.* ❏ *He shows me card tricks.* **4** N-COUNT A **trick** is a clever way of doing something. ❏ *Everything I cooked was a trick of my mother's.* **5** → see also **hat trick** **6** PHRASE If something **does the trick**, it achieves what you wanted. [INFORMAL] ❏ *Sometimes a few choice words will do the trick.* **7** PHRASE If someone tries **every trick in the book**, they try every possible thing that they can think of in order to achieve something. [INFORMAL] ❏ *Companies are using every trick in the book to stay one step in front of their competitors.* **8** PHRASE The **tricks of the trade** are the quick and clever ways of doing something that are known by people who regularly do a particular activity. ❏ *To get you started, we have asked five successful writers to reveal some of the tricks of the trade.*

trick|ery /trɪkəri/ N-UNCOUNT **Trickery** is the use of dishonest methods in order to achieve something.

trick|le /trɪkəl/ (trickles, trickling, trickled) **1** V-T/V-I When a liquid **trickles**, or when you **trickle** it, it flows slowly in a thin stream. ❏ *A tear trickled down the old man's cheek.* • N-COUNT **Trickle** is also a noun. ❏ *There was not so much as a trickle of water.* **2** V-I When people or things **trickle** in a particular direction, they move there slowly in small groups or amounts, rather than all together. ❏ *Some donations are already trickling in.* • N-COUNT **Trickle** is also a noun. ❏ *The flood of cars has now slowed to a trickle.*
▶ **trickle down** PHRASAL VERB If benefits given to people at the top of a society or system **trickle down**, they are eventually passed on to people lower down the society or system. ❏ *...the failure of the prosperity of Las Vegas casinos to trickle down to poor neighborhoods.*

trickle-down ADJ [ADJ n] The **trickle-down** theory is the theory that benefits given to people at the top of a system will eventually be passed on to people lower down the system. For example, if the rich receive tax cuts, they will pass these benefits on to the poor by creating jobs. ❏ *The government is not simply relying on trickle-down economics to tackle poverty.*

trick or treat N-UNCOUNT **Trick or treat** is an activity in which children knock on the doors of houses at Halloween and shout 'trick or treat.' The person who answers the door is expected to give the children candy.

trick ques|tion (trick questions) N-COUNT If someone asks you a **trick question**, they ask you a question which is very difficult to answer, for example, because there is a hidden difficulty or because the answer that seems obvious is not the correct one.

trick|ster /tr_ɪ_kstər/ (tricksters) N-COUNT A **trickster** is a person who deceives or cheats people, often in order to get money from them. [INFORMAL]

tricky /tr_ɪ_ki/ (trickier, trickiest) ADJ If you describe a task or problem as **tricky**, you mean that it is difficult to do or deal with. ❑ *Parking can be tricky downtown.*

tri|col|or /tra_ɪ_kʌlər/ (tricolors)

in BRIT, use **tricolour**

N-COUNT A **tricolor** is a flag which is made up of blocks of three different colors, such as the Mexican flag.

tri|cy|cle /tra_ɪ_sɪkəl/ (tricycles) **1** N-COUNT A **tricycle** is a bike with three wheels, two at the back and one at the front. Tricycles are ridden by young children. **2** → See also color supplement

tried /tra_ɪ_d/ **1** ADJ [ADJ *and* adj] **Tried** is used in the expressions **tried and tested**, **tried and trusted**, and **tried and true**, which describe a product or method that has already been used and has been found to be successful. ❑ *...over 1,000 tried-and-tested recipes.* **2** → see also **try**

tri|fle /tra_ɪ_fəl/ (trifles) **1** PHRASE You can use **a trifle** to mean slightly or to a small extent, especially in order to make something you say seem less extreme. [OLD-FASHIONED, VAGUENESS] ❑ *As a photographer, he'd found both locations just a trifle disappointing.* **2** N-COUNT A **trifle** is something that is considered to have little importance, value, or significance. ❑ *He had no money to spare on trifles.* **3** N-VAR **Trifle** is a cold dessert made of layers of sponge cake, fruit gelatin, fruit, and custard, and usually covered with cream. ❑ *...a bowl of trifle.*

tri|fling /tra_ɪ_flɪŋ/ ADJ [oft *a* ADJ amount] A **trifling** matter is small and unimportant. ❑ *Outside California these difficulties may seem fairly trifling.* ❑ *...a comparatively trifling 360 yards.*

trig|ger ✦◇◇ /tr_ɪ_gər/ (triggers, triggering, triggered) **1** N-COUNT The **trigger** of a gun is a small lever which you pull to fire it. ❑ *A man pointed a gun at them and pulled the trigger.* **2** N-COUNT The **trigger** of a bomb is the device which causes it to explode. ❑ *...trigger devices for nuclear weapons.* **3** V-T To **trigger** a bomb or system means to cause it to work. ❑ *The thieves must have deliberately triggered the alarm and hidden inside the house.* **4** V-T If something **triggers** an event or situation, it causes it to begin to happen or exist. ❑ *...the incident which triggered the outbreak of the First World War.* • PHRASAL VERB **Trigger off** means the same as **trigger**. ❑ *It is still not clear what events triggered off the demonstrations.* **5** N-COUNT If something acts as a **trigger** for another thing such as an illness, event, or situation, the first thing causes the second thing to begin to happen or exist. ❑ *Stress may act as a trigger for these illnesses.* **6** VERB If something **triggers** someone, it causes them to have an extreme reaction of fear, upset, or anger, especially because they remember a traumatic experience. ❑ *Something obviously triggered her because she started screaming.* **7** N-COUNT Someone's **triggers** are things that can cause them to have an extreme reaction of fear, upset, or anger, especially because they remembering a traumatic experience. ❑ *You need to understand what your triggers are, for example loud noises.*

SYNONYMS

trigger
VERB
3
set off: *Any escape, once it's detected, sets off the alarm.*
activate: *Video cameras with night vision can be activated by movement.*
4
bring about: *The only way they can bring about political change is by putting pressure on the country.*
provoke: *His election success has provoked a shocked reaction.*
spark: *What was it that sparked your interest in sailing?*

---

trigger-happy also **trigger happy** ADJ If you describe someone as **trigger-happy**, you disapprove of them because they are too ready and willing to use violence and weapons, especially guns. [INFORMAL, DISAPPROVAL] ❑ *Some of them are a little trigger-happy—they'll shoot at anything that moves.*

trig|ger warn|ing (trigger warnings) N-COUNT A **trigger warning** is a warning before something such as a film or piece of writing that suggests that it may particularly upset some people, especially people who have had a traumatic experience.

trigo|nom|etry /tr_ɪ_gən_ɒ_mɪtri/ N-UNCOUNT **Trigonometry** is the branch of mathematics that is concerned with calculating the angles of triangles or the lengths of their sides.

trike /tra_ɪ_k/ (trikes) N-COUNT A **trike** is a child's **tricycle**. [INFORMAL]

trill /tr_ɪ_l/ (trills, trilling, trilled) **1** V-I If a bird **trills**, it sings with short, high-pitched, repeated notes. ❑ *At one point a bird trilled in the conservatory.* **2** V-T If someone **trills** a sound such as the letter 'r,' they make the sound by tapping the end of their tongue against the inside of their mouth rapidly and repeatedly. [TECHNICAL] ❑ *He also trilled his r's.* **3** N-COUNT A **trill** is the playing of two musical notes repeatedly and quickly one after the other. [TECHNICAL]

tril|lion /tr_ɪ_lyən/ (trillions)

The plural form is **trillion** after a number, or after a word or expression referring to a number, such as 'several' or 'a few.'

1 NUM A **trillion** is 1,000,000,000,000. [AM] ❑ *...a 4 trillion dollar debt.*

in BRIT, use **billion**

2 NUM A **trillion** is 1,000,000,000,000,000,000. [BRIT]

in AM, use **quintillion**

tril|ogy /tr_ɪ_lədʒi/ (trilogies) **1** N-COUNT A **trilogy** is a series of three books, plays, or movies that have the same subject or the same characters. ❑ *...Tolkien's trilogy, The Lord of the Rings.* **2** → See feature box at **book**

trim /tr_ɪ_m/ (trimmer, trimmest, trims, trimming, trimmed) **1** ADJ Something that is **trim** is neat and attractive. ❑ *The neighbors' gardens were trim and neat.* **2** ADJ If you describe someone's figure as **trim**, you mean that it is attractive because there is no extra fat on their body. [APPROVAL] ❑ *The driver was a trim young woman of perhaps thirty.* **3** V-T If you **trim** something, for example, someone's hair, you cut off small amounts of it in order to make it look neater. ❑ *My friend trims my hair every eight weeks.* • N-SING **Trim** is also a noun. ❑ *His hair needed a trim.* **4** V-T If a government or other organization **trims** something such as a plan, policy, or amount, they reduce it slightly in extent or size. ❑ *American companies looked at ways they could trim these costs.* **5** V-T [usu passive] If something such as a piece of clothing **is trimmed** with a type of material or design, it is decorated with it, usually along its edges. ❑ *...jackets, which are then trimmed with crocheted flowers.* **6** N-VAR The **trim** on something such as a piece of clothing is a decoration, for example, along its edges, that is in a different color or material. ❑ *...a white satin scarf with black trim.* **7** → See feature box at **DIY**

tri|ma|ran /tra_ɪ_məræn/ (trimarans) N-COUNT A **trimaran** is a fast sailboat similar to a catamaran, but with three hulls instead of two.

tri|mes|ter /tra_ɪ_m_ɛ_stər/ (trimesters) **1** N-COUNT The first **trimester** of a pregnancy is the first three months of the pregnancy. The second **trimester** is the period from three months to six months, and the third **trimester** is the period from six months to nine months. ❑ *At the end of the first trimester, the fetus is about three inches long.* **2** N-COUNT In colleges and universities in some countries, a **trimester** is one of the three main periods into which the year is divided. ❑ *...the proposed school's trimester calendar.*

trim|ming /tr_ɪ_mɪŋ/ (trimmings) **1** N-VAR The **trimming** on something such as a piece of clothing is the decoration, for example, along its edges, that is in a different color or material. ❑ *...the lace trimming on her satin nightgown.* **2** N-PLURAL **Trimmings** are pieces of something, usually food, which are left over after you have cut what you need. ❑ *Use the pastry trimmings to decorate the pie.*

Trini|ty /tr_ɪ_nɪti/ N-PROPER [*the* N] In the Christian religion, **the Trinity** or **the Holy Trinity** is the union of the Father, the Son, and the Holy Spirit in one God.

trin|ket /tr_ɪ_ŋkɪt/ (trinkets) N-COUNT A **trinket** is a pretty piece of jewelry or small ornament that is inexpensive.

trio /tríːoʊ/ (trios) N-COUNT-COLL A **trio** is a group of three people together, especially musicians or singers, or a group of three things that have something in common. ❑ ...classy American songs from a Texas trio.

trip ✦✧ /trɪp/ (trips, tripping, tripped) **1** N-COUNT A **trip** is a journey that you make to a particular place. ❑ We're taking a trip to Montana. ❑ On Thursday we went out on a day trip. **2** → see also **round trip** **3** V-I If you **trip** when you are walking, you knock your foot against something and fall or nearly fall. ❑ She tripped and fell last night and broke her hip. • PHRASAL VERB **Trip up** means the same as **trip**. ❑ I tripped up and hurt my foot. **4** V-T If you **trip** someone who is walking or running, you put your foot or something else in front of them, so that they knock their own foot against it and fall or nearly fall. ❑ One guy stuck his foot out and tried to trip me. • PHRASAL VERB **Trip up** means the same as **trip**. ❑ He made a sudden dive for Uncle Jim's legs to try to trip him up.

> **COLLOCATIONS**
>
> **trip**
> NOUN **1**
> noun + **trip**: boat, fishing, shopping; business, school; road, return
> adjective + **trip**: long, quick, short; recent, regular; foreign, overseas
> verb + **trip**: book, organize, plan; cancel

tri|par|tite /traɪpɑːrtaɪt/ ADJ [usu ADJ n] You can use **tripartite** to describe something that has three parts or that involves three groups of people. [FORMAL] ❑ ...the tripartite French-Russia-China statement.

tripe /traɪp/ **1** N-UNCOUNT **Tripe** is the stomach of a pig, cow, or ox which is eaten as food. **2** N-UNCOUNT You refer to something that someone has said or written as **tripe** when you think that it is silly and worthless. [INFORMAL] ❑ I've never heard such a load of tripe in all my life.

tri|ple /trɪpəl/ (triples, tripling, tripled) **1** ADJ [ADJ n] **Triple** means consisting of three things or parts. ❑ ...a triple somersault. **2** V-T/V-I If something **triples** or if you **triple** it, it becomes three times as large in size or number. ❑ I got a fantastic new job and my salary tripled. ❑ The exhibition has tripled in size from last year. **3** PREDET [PREDET the n] If something is **triple** the amount or size of another thing, it is three times as large. ❑ The mine reportedly had an accident rate triple the national average.

tri|ple jump N-SING [usu the N] The **triple jump** is a track and field event in which competitors have to jump as far as they can, and are allowed to touch the ground once with each foot in the course of the jump.

tri|plet /trɪplɪt/ (triplets) N-COUNT **Triplets** are three children born at the same time to the same mother. ❑ Guess what? Katinka had triplets–all healthy.

trip|li|cate /trɪplɪkət/ N-UNCOUNT [usu in N] If something written is in **triplicate**, there are three copies of it. ❑ Folders, files, and forms in triplicate were strewn across Emily's desk.

tri|pod /traɪpɒd/ (tripods) **1** N-COUNT A **tripod** is a stand with three legs that is used to support something such as a camera or a telescope. **2** → See feature box at **experiment**

trip|tych /trɪptɪk/ (triptychs) N-COUNT A **triptych** is a painting or a carving on three panels that are usually joined together by hinges.

trip|wire /trɪpwaɪər/ (tripwires) N-COUNT A **tripwire** is a wire stretched just above the ground, which sets off something such as a trap or an explosion if someone touches it.

tri|state /traɪsteɪt/ also **tri-state** ADJ [ADJ n] A **tristate** area is an area consisting of three states, especially the states of New York, New Jersey, and Pennsylvania. [AM] ❑ Amateur skaters from all over the tristate area compete.

trite /traɪt/ ADJ If you say that something such as an idea, remark, or story is **trite**, you mean that it is boring because it has been said or told too many times. ❑ The movie is teeming with obvious and trite ideas.

tri|umph ✦✧ /traɪʌmf/ (triumphs, triumphing, triumphed) **1** N-VAR A **triumph** is a great success or achievement, often one that has been gained with a lot of skill or effort. ❑ The championships proved to be a personal triumph for their coach. **2** N-UNCOUNT **Triumph** is a feeling of great satisfaction and pride resulting from a success or victory. ❑ Her sense of triumph was short-lived. **3** V-I If someone or something **triumphs**, they gain complete success, control, or victory, often after a long or difficult struggle. ❑ All her life, Kelly had stuck with difficult tasks and challenges, and triumphed. **4** → See feature box at **competition, conflict**

> **SYNONYMS**
>
> **triumph**
> NOUN **1**
> **victory:** Union leaders are heading for victory in their battle over workplace rights.
> **success:** ...the success of European business.
> **achievement:** Reaching this agreement so quickly was a great achievement.

tri|um|phal /traɪʌmfəl/ ADJ [usu ADJ n] **Triumphal** is used to describe things that are done or made to celebrate a victory or great success. ❑ He made a triumphal entry into the city.

tri|um|phal|ism /traɪʌmfəlɪzəm/ N-UNCOUNT People sometimes refer to behavior which celebrates a great victory or success as **triumphalism**, especially when this behavior is intended to upset the people they have defeated. ❑ There was a touch of triumphalism about the occasion.

tri|umph|al|ist /traɪʌmfəlɪst/ ADJ [ADJ n] **Triumphalist** behavior is behavior in which politicians or organizations celebrate a victory or a great success, especially when this is intended to upset the people they have defeated. ❑ ...a triumphalist celebration of their supremacy.

tri|um|phant /traɪʌmfənt/ ADJ Someone who is **triumphant** has gained a victory or succeeded in something and feels very happy about it. ❑ The captain's voice was triumphant. • **tri|um|phant|ly** ADV ❑ They marched triumphantly into the capital.

tri|um|vi|rate /traɪʌmvərɪt/ N-SING-COLL [oft N of n] A **triumvirate** is a group of three people who work together, especially when they are in charge of something. [FORMAL] ❑ ...the triumvirate of women who worked together on the TV dramatization of the novel.

trivia /trɪviə/ N-UNCOUNT **Trivia** is unimportant facts or details that are considered to be interesting rather than serious or useful. ❑ The two men chatted about such trivia as their favorite kinds of fast food.

triv|ial /trɪviəl/ ADJ If you describe something as **trivial**, you think that it is unimportant and not serious. ❑ The director tried to wave aside these issues as trivial details that could be settled later.

triv|ial|ity /trɪviælɪti/ (trivialities) N-VAR If you refer to something as a **triviality**, you think that it is unimportant and not serious. ❑ He accused me of making a great fuss about trivialities. ❑ The reporter apologized for the triviality of his question.

triv|ial|ize /trɪviəlaɪz/ (trivializes, trivializing, trivialized)

> in BRIT, also use **trivialise**

V-T If you say that someone **trivializes** something important, you disapprove of them because they make it seem less important, serious, and complex than it is. [DISAPPROVAL] ❑ It never ceases to amaze me how the business world continues to trivialize the world's environmental problems.

trod /trɒd/ **Trod** is the past tense of **tread**.

trod|den /trɒdən/ **Trodden** is the past participle of **tread**.

trog|lo|dyte /trɒglədaɪt/ (troglodytes) **1** N-COUNT A **troglodyte** is someone who lives in a cave. [FORMAL] **2** N-COUNT If you refer to someone as a **troglodyte**, you mean that they are unsophisticated and do not know very much about anything. [DISAPPROVAL] ❑ He dismissed advocates of a completely free market as economic troglodytes with no concern for the social consequences.

troi|ka /trɔɪkə/ (troikas) N-COUNT [usu sing, oft N of n] Journalists sometimes refer to a group of three powerful politicians or states as a **troika**. ❑ ...leader of the troika of past, present and future presidents.

Tro|jan horse (Trojan horses) **1** N-COUNT [usu sing, oft N for/ of n] If you describe a person or thing as a **Trojan horse**, you

troll mean that they are being used to hide someone's true purpose or intentions. [DISAPPROVAL] ❏ *They claim he is being used by the opposition parties as a Trojan horse within the commission.* **2** N-COUNT A **Trojan horse** is a computer program that gets access to a computer or system by appearing to be harmless, but is designed to do something damaging. [COMPUTING]

troll /troʊl/ (**trolls, trolling, trolled**) **1** N-COUNT In Scandinavian mythology, **trolls** are creatures who look like ugly people. They live in caves or on mountains and steal children. **2** V-I If you **troll** somewhere, you go there in a casual and unhurried way. [mainly BRIT, INFORMAL] ❏ *I trolled along to see Michael Frayn's play, "Noises Off."* **3** V-I If you **troll** through papers or files, you look through them in a fairly casual way. [mainly BRIT, INFORMAL] ❏ *Trolling through the files revealed a photograph of me drinking coffee in the office.*

trol|ley /trɒli/ (**trolleys**) **1** N-COUNT A **trolley** or **trolley car** is an electric vehicle for carrying people which travels on rails in the streets of a city or town. [AM] ❏ *He took a northbound trolley on State Street.*

| in BRIT, use **tram** |

2 N-COUNT A **trolley** is an object with wheels that you use to transport heavy things such as shopping or luggage. [BRIT]

| in AM, use **cart** |

3 N-COUNT A **trolley** is a small table on wheels which is used for serving drinks or food. [BRIT]

| in AM, use **cart** |

4 N-COUNT A **trolley** is a bed on wheels for moving patients in a hospital. [BRIT]

| in AM, use **gurney** |

trol|ley bus (**trolley buses**) N-COUNT [also *by* N] A **trolley bus** is a bus that is driven by electric power taken from cables above the street.

trom|bone /trɒmboʊn/ (**trombones**) N-VAR [oft *the* N] A **trombone** is a large musical instrument of the brass family. It consists of two long oval tubes, one of which can be pushed backward and forward to play different notes. ❏ *Her husband had played the trombone in the band for a decade.*

trom|bon|ist /trɒmboʊnɪst/ (**trombonists**) N-COUNT A **trombonist** is someone who plays the trombone.

trompe l'oeil /trɒmp lɔɪ/ (**trompe l'oeils**) **1** N-UNCOUNT [oft N N] **Trompe l'oeil** is a technique used in art in which objects are painted their normal size in a very realistic way, to make people think that the objects are solid and real. ❏ *...a trompe l'oeil painting.* **2** N-COUNT A **trompe l'oeil** is a trompe l'oeil painting.

troop ♦♦◊ /truːp/ (**troops, trooping, trooped**) **1** N-PLURAL **Troops** are soldiers, especially when they are in a large organized group doing a particular task. ❏ *The next phase of the operation will involve the deployment of more than 35,000 troops from a dozen countries.* **2** N-COUNT-COLL A **troop** is a group of soldiers. ❏ *...a troop of American Marines.* **3** N-COUNT A **troop** of people or animals is a group of them. ❏ *The whole troop of men and women wore their hair fairly short.* **4** V-I If people **troop** somewhere, they walk there in a group, often in a sad or tired way. [INFORMAL] ❏ *They all trooped back to the house for a rest.*

troop|er /truːpər/ (**troopers**) **1** N-COUNT In the United States, a **trooper** is a police officer in a state police force. ❏ *Once long ago he had considered becoming a state trooper.* **2** N-COUNT; N-TITLE A **trooper** is a soldier of low rank in the cavalry or in an armored regiment in the army. ❏ *...a trooper from the 7th Cavalry.*

troop|ship /truːpʃɪp/ (**troopships**) also **troop ship** N-COUNT A **troopship** is a ship on which large numbers of soldiers are taken from one place to another.

tro|phy /troʊfi/ (**trophies**) **1** N-COUNT A **trophy** is a prize, for example, a silver cup, that is given to the winner of a competition or race. ❏ *The special trophy for the best rider went to Chris Read.* **2** N-COUNT A **trophy** is something that you keep in order to show that you have done something very difficult. ❏ *His office was lined with animal heads, trophies of his hunting hobby.*

tropi|cal /trɒpɪkəl/ **1** ADJ [ADJ n] **Tropical** means belonging to or typical of the tropics. ❏ *...tropical diseases.* **2** ADJ **Tropical**

trouble weather is hot and damp weather typical of the tropics. ❏ *The cool, sweet milk is just what you need in the tropical heat.* **3** → See feature box at **ecosystem**

Trop|ic of Can|cer /trɒpɪk əv kænsər/ N-PROPER The **Tropic of Cancer** is an imaginary line around the Earth 23° 26′ north of the equator.

Trop|ic of Cap|ri|corn /trɒpɪk əv kæprɪkɔːrn/ N-PROPER The **Tropic of Capricorn** is an imaginary line around the Earth 23° 26′ south of the equator.

trop|ics /trɒpɪks/ N-PLURAL The **tropics** are the parts of the world that lie between two lines of latitude, the tropic of Cancer, north of the equator, and the tropic of Capricorn, south of the equator. ❏ *Being in the tropics meant that insects formed a large part of our life.*

trot /trɒt/ (**trots, trotting, trotted**) **1** V-I If you **trot** somewhere, you move fairly fast at a speed between walking and running, taking small quick steps. ❏ *I trotted down the steps and out to the shed.* • N-SING **Trot** is also a noun. ❏ *He walked briskly, but without breaking into a trot.* **2** V-I When an animal such as a horse **trots**, it moves fairly fast, taking quick small steps. You can also say that the rider of the animal **is trotting**. ❏ *Alan took the reins and the small horse started trotting.* • N-SING **Trot** is also a noun. ❏ *As they started up again, the horse broke into a brisk trot.*

Trot|sky|ist /trɒtskiɪst/ (**Trotskyists**) N-COUNT A **Trotskyist** is someone who supports the revolutionary left-wing ideas of Leon Trotsky.

trou|ba|dour /truːbədɔːr/ (**troubadours**) **1** N-COUNT **Troubadours** were poets and singers who used to travel around and perform for noble families in Italy and France in the twelfth and thirteenth centuries. **2** N-COUNT People sometimes refer to popular singers as **troubadours**, especially when the words of their songs are an important part of their music.

trou|ble ♦♦◊ /trʌbəl/ (**troubles, troubling, troubled**) **1** N-UNCOUNT [oft *in* N, also N *in* pl] You can refer to problems or difficulties as **trouble**. ❏ *I had trouble parking.* ❏ *You've caused us a lot of trouble.* **2** N-SING If you say that one aspect of a situation is the **trouble**, you mean that it is the aspect which is causing problems or making the situation unsatisfactory. ❏ *The trouble is that these restrictions have remained while other things have changed.* **3** N-PLURAL Your **troubles** are the things that you are worried about. ❏ *She tells me her troubles. I tell mine.* **4** N-UNCOUNT If you have kidney **trouble** or back **trouble**, for example, there is something wrong with your kidneys or your back. ❏ *An old bed is the most likely cause of back trouble.* ❏ *Her husband had never before had any heart trouble.* **5** N-UNCOUNT [also N *in* pl] If there is **trouble** somewhere, especially in a public place, there is fighting or rioting there. ❏ *Riot police are being deployed throughout the city to prevent any trouble.* ❏ *Fans who make trouble during the World Cup will be arrested.* **6** N-UNCOUNT If you tell someone that it is no **trouble** to do something for them, you are saying politely that you can or will do it, because it is easy or convenient for you. [POLITENESS] ❏ *It's no trouble at all; on the contrary, it will be a great pleasure to help you.* **7** N-UNCOUNT If you say that a person or animal is no **trouble**, you mean that they are very easy to look after. ❏ *My little grandson is no trouble at all, but his 6-year-old sister is a handful.* **8** V-T If something **troubles** you, it makes you feel worried. ❏ *Is anything troubling you?* • **trou|bling** ADJ ❏ *But most troubling of all was the simple fact that nobody knew what was going on.* **9** V-T If a part of your body **troubles** you, it causes you physical pain or discomfort. ❏ *The ulcer had been troubling her for several years.* **10** V-T If you say that someone does not **trouble** to do something, you are critical of them because they do not do something that they should, and you think that this would require very little effort. [DISAPPROVAL] ❏ *He burps, not troubling to cover his mouth.* **11** V-T You use **trouble** in expressions such as **I'm sorry to trouble you** when you are apologizing to someone for disturbing them in order to ask them something. [FORMULAE] ❏ *I'm sorry to trouble you, but I wondered if by any chance you know where he is.* **12** PHRASE If someone is **in trouble**, they are in a situation in which a person in authority is angry with them or is likely to punish them because they have done something wrong. ❏ *He was in trouble with his teachers.* **13** PHRASE If you **take the trouble** to do something, you do something which requires a small amount of additional effort. ❏ *He did not take the trouble to see the movie before he attacked it.*

COLLOCATIONS

trouble
NOUN
❶
adjective + **trouble**: deep, real, serious; financial, marital
verb + **trouble**: cause, invite, spell, strike
❺
verb + **trouble**: foment, make, spark, stir up; avoid, prevent

---

trou|bled /trʌbəld/ ❶ ADJ Someone who is **troubled** is worried because they have problems. ❏ *Rose sounded deeply troubled.* ❷ ADJ A **troubled** place, situation, organization, or time has many problems or conflicts. ❏ *There is so much we can do to help this troubled country.*

trouble-free ADJ Something that is **trouble-free** does not cause any problems or difficulties. ❏ *The carnival got off to a virtually trouble-free start with the police reporting only one arrest.*

trouble|maker /trʌbəlmeɪkər/ (**troublemakers**) N-COUNT If you refer to someone as a **troublemaker**, you mean that they cause unpleasantness, quarrels, or fights, especially by encouraging people to oppose authority. [DISAPPROVAL] ❏ *The fair coordinator has been given powers to expel suspected troublemakers.*

trouble|shooter /trʌbəlʃuːtər/ (**troubleshooters**) also **trouble-shooter** N-COUNT A **troubleshooter** is a person whose job is to solve major problems or difficulties that occur in a company or government. ❏ *The United Nations dispatched a team of troubleshooters to Somalia today.*

trouble|shooting /trʌbəlʃuːtɪŋ/ N-UNCOUNT **Troubleshooting** is the activity or process of solving major problems or difficulties that occur in a company or government.

trou|ble|some /trʌbəlsəm/ ADJ You use **troublesome** to describe something or someone that causes annoying problems or difficulties. ❏ *He needed surgery to cure a troublesome back injury.*

trou|ble spot (**trouble spots**) also **trouble-spot** N-COUNT A **trouble spot** is a country or an area of a country where there is repeated fighting.

trough /trɒf/ (**troughs**) ❶ N-COUNT A **trough** is a long narrow container from which farm animals drink or eat. ❏ *The old stone cattle trough still sits by the main entrance.* ❷ N-COUNT A **trough** is a low area between two big waves on the sea. ❏ *The boat rolled heavily in the troughs between the waves.* ❸ N-COUNT A **trough** is a low point in a process that has regular high and low points, for example, a period in business when people do not produce as much as usual. ❏ *...recovery from the industry's worst-ever trough in 2001 and 2002.* ❹ N-COUNT A **trough** of low pressure is a long narrow area of low air pressure between two areas of higher pressure. [TECHNICAL] ❏ *The trough of low pressure extends over 1,000 miles.*

trounce /traʊns/ (**trounces, trouncing, trounced**) V-T If you **trounce** someone in a competition or contest, you defeat them easily or by a large score. [INFORMAL] ❏ *The 49ers trounced the Miami Dolphins 38-16.*

troupe /truːp/ (**troupes**) ❶ N-COUNT-COLL A **troupe** is a group of actors, singers, or dancers who work together and often travel around together, performing in different places. ❏ *...troupes of traveling actors.* ❷ → See feature box at **humor**

troup|er /truːpər/ (**troupers**) N-COUNT You can refer to an actor or other performer as a **trouper**, especially when you want to suggest that they have a lot of experience and can deal with difficult situations in a professional way. ❏ *Like the old trouper he is, he timed his entry to perfection.*

trou|sers /traʊzərz/

The form **trouser** is used as a modifier.

N-PLURAL [also *a pair of* N] **Trousers** are a piece of clothing that cover the body from the waist downward, and that cover each leg separately. [FORMAL] ❏ *He was dressed in a shirt, dark trousers and boots.* ❏ *I bought myself a fabulous pair of trousers.*

USAGE

trousers
Don't talk about 'a trousers.' Say **trousers** or **a pair of trousers**. *Claud was wearing a pair of black trousers.*

---

trou|ser suit (**trouser suits**) N-COUNT A **trouser suit** is women's clothing consisting of a pair of trousers and a jacket which are made from the same material. [BRIT]

in AM, use **pantsuit**

trous|seau /truːsoʊ/ (**trousseaux**) N-COUNT A **trousseau** is a collection of clothes and other possessions that a bride brings with her when she gets married. [OLD-FASHIONED]

trout /traʊt/ (**trout** or **trouts**)

The plural can be either **trout** or **trouts**.

N-VAR A **trout** is a fairly large fish that lives in rivers and streams. • N-UNCOUNT **Trout** is this fish eaten as food. ❏ *Grilled trout needs only a squeeze of lemon.*

trove /troʊv/ → see **treasure trove**

trow|el /traʊəl/ (**trowels**) ❶ N-COUNT A **trowel** is a small garden tool which you use for digging small holes or removing weeds. ❷ N-COUNT A **trowel** is a small tool with a flat blade that you use for spreading things such as cement and plaster onto walls and other surfaces. ❸ → See also color supplement

tru|an|cy /truːənsi/ N-UNCOUNT **Truancy** is when children stay away from school without permission.

tru|ant /truːənt/ (**truants**) ❶ N-COUNT A **truant** is a student who stays away from school without permission. ❏ *The parents of persistent truants can be put in jail.* ❷ PHRASE If a student **plays truant**, he or she stays away from school without permission. [BRIT] ❏ *She was getting into trouble over playing truant from school.*

truce /truːs/ (**truces**) N-COUNT A **truce** is an agreement between two people or groups of people to stop fighting or arguing for a short time. ❏ *The fighting of recent days has given way to an uneasy truce between the two sides.*

truck ✦✧ /trʌk/ (**trucks, trucking, trucked**) ❶ N-COUNT A **truck** is a large vehicle that is used to transport goods by road. [mainly AM] ❏ *Now and then they heard the roar of a heavy truck.* ❏ *My dad is a truck driver.*

in BRIT, usually use **lorry**

❷ N-COUNT A **truck** is a vehicle with a large area in the back for carrying things with low sides to make it easy to load and unload. A **truck** is the same as a **pickup**. [mainly AM] ❏ *We can only seat two in the truck.* ❏ *Throw the dogs in the back of the truck.* ❸ N-COUNT A **truck** is an open vehicle used for carrying goods on a railroad. [BRIT]

in AM, use **freight car**

❹ V-T [usu passive] When something or someone **is trucked** somewhere, they are driven there in a truck. [mainly AM] ❏ *The liquor was sold legally and trucked out of the state.*

truck|er /trʌkər/ (**truckers**) N-COUNT A **trucker** is someone who drives a truck as their job. [mainly AM] ❏ *...the type of place where truckers and farmers stopped for coffee and pie.*

in BRIT, use **lorry driver**

truck|ing /trʌkɪŋ/ N-UNCOUNT [usu N n] **Trucking** is the activity of transporting goods from one place to another using trucks. [mainly AM] ❏ *...the deregulation of the trucking industry.*

in BRIT, use **haulage**

truck|load /trʌkloʊd/ (**truckloads**) also **truck load** N-COUNT [usu N of n] A **truckload** of goods or people is the amount of them that a truck can carry. ❏ *Truckloads of food, blankets, and other necessities reached the city.*

truck stop (**truck stops**) N-COUNT A **truck stop** is a place where drivers, especially truck drivers, can stop to rest in their truck or to get something to eat. [mainly AM]

trucu|lent /trʌkyələnt/ ADJ If you say that someone is **truculent**, you mean that they are bad-tempered and aggressive. • **trucu|lence** /trʌkyələns/ N-UNCOUNT ❏ *"What do you want?" she asked with her usual truculence.*

trudge /trʌdʒ/ (**trudges, trudging, trudged**) V-I If you **trudge** somewhere, you walk there slowly and with heavy steps, especially because you are tired or unhappy. ❏ *We had to trudge up the track back to the station.* • N-SING **Trudge** is also a noun. ❏ *We were reluctant to start the long trudge home.*

true ◆◆◇ /truː/ (truer, truest) **1** ADJ If something is **true**, it is based on facts rather than being invented or imagined, and is accurate and reliable. ❑ *Everything I had heard about him was true.* ❑ *He said it was true that a collision had happened.* **2** ADJ [ADJ n] You use **true** to emphasize that a person or thing is sincere or genuine, often in contrast to something that is pretended or hidden. [EMPHASIS] ❑ *I allowed myself to acknowledge my true feelings.* **3** ADJ [ADJ n] If you use **true** to describe something or someone, you approve of them because they have all the characteristics or qualities that such a person or thing typically has. [APPROVAL] ❑ *This country professes to be a true democracy.* ❑ *Maybe one day you'll find true love.* **4** ADJ [v-link ADJ of/for n] If you say that a fact is **true** of a particular person or situation, you mean that it is valid or relevant for them. ❑ *I accept that the romance may have gone out of the marriage, but surely this is true of many couples.* **5** ADJ [v-link ADJ to n] If you are **true to** someone, you remain committed and loyal to them. If you are **true to** an idea or promise, you remain committed to it and continue to act according to it. ❑ *David was true to his wife.* ❑ *India has remained true to democracy.* **6** PHRASE If a dream, wish, or prediction **comes true**, it actually happens. ❑ *Many of his predictions are coming true.* **7** PHRASE If a general statement **holds true** in particular circumstances, or if your previous statement **holds true** in different circumstances, it is true or valid in those circumstances. [FORMAL] ❑ *This law is known to hold true for galaxies at a distance of at least several billion light years.* **8** PHRASE If you say that something seems **too good to be true**, you are suspicious of it because it seems better than you had expected, and you think there may be something wrong with it that you have not noticed. ❑ *On the whole the celebrations were remarkably good-humored and peaceful. It seemed almost too good to be true.* **9 to ring true** → see **ring** ① **10 tried and true** → see **tried**

true-blue also **true blue** ADJ A **true-blue** supporter of something is someone who is very loyal and reliable. [AM, INFORMAL]

truf|fle /trʌfᵊl/ (truffles) **1** N-COUNT A **truffle** is a soft round candy made with chocolate. **2** N-COUNT A **truffle** is a round type of fungus which is expensive and considered very good to eat.

tru|ism /truːɪzəm/ (truisms) N-COUNT A **truism** is a statement that is generally accepted as obviously true and is repeated so often that it has become boring. ❑ *...the truism that nothing succeeds like success.*

tru|ly ◆◇◇ /truːli/ **1** ADV You use **truly** to emphasize that something has all the features or qualities of a particular thing, or is the case to the fullest possible extent. [EMPHASIS] ❑ *...a truly democratic system.* ❑ *Not all doctors truly understand the reproductive cycle.* **2** ADV [ADV adj] You can use **truly** in order to emphasize your description of something. [EMPHASIS] ❑ *...a truly splendid man.* **3** ADV You use **truly** to emphasize that feelings are genuine and sincere. [EMPHASIS] ❑ *Believe me, Susan, I am truly sorry.* **4 well and truly** → see **well** ③ **5** CONVENTION You write **Yours truly** at the end of a formal letter, and before signing your name, to someone you do not know very well. [OLD-FASHIONED] ❑ *Yours truly, Phil Turner.*

trump /trʌmp/ (trumps, trumping, trumped) **1** N-UNCOUNT-COLL In a game of cards, **trumps** is the suit which is chosen to have the highest value in one particular game. ❑ *Hearts are trumps.* **2** N-COUNT In a game of cards, a **trump** is a playing card which belongs to the suit which has been chosen as trumps. ❑ *He played a trump.* **3** V-T If you **trump** what someone has said or done, you beat it by saying or doing something else that seems better. ❑ *The Republicans tried to trump this with their slogan.* **4** PHRASE Your **trump card** is something powerful that you can use or do, which gives you an advantage over someone. ❑ *The administration knows that's their trump card and will keep playing it as long as they can.*

trumped-up ADJ [usu ADJ n] **Trumped-up** charges are untrue, and made up in order to punish someone unfairly.

trum|pet /trʌmpɪt/ (trumpets) N-VAR [oft the N] A **trumpet** is a musical instrument of the brass family which plays comparatively high notes. ❑ *I played the trumpet in the school orchestra.*

trum|pet|er /trʌmpɪtər/ (trumpeters) N-COUNT A **trumpeter** is someone who plays a trumpet.

trun|cat|ed /trʌŋkeɪtɪd/ ADJ [usu ADJ n] A **truncated** version of something is one that has been shortened. ❑ *The review body has produced a truncated version of its annual report.*

trun|cheon /trʌntʃən/ (truncheons) N-COUNT A **truncheon** is a short, thick stick that is carried as a weapon by a police officer. [BRIT]

in AM, use **night stick**

trun|dle /trʌndᵊl/ (trundles, trundling, trundled) **1** V-I If a vehicle **trundles** somewhere, it moves there slowly, often with difficulty or an irregular movement. ❑ *The truck was trundling along the escarpment of the Zambesi valley.* **2** V-T If you **trundle** something somewhere, especially a small, heavy object with wheels, you move or roll it along slowly. ❑ *The old man lifted the wheelbarrow and trundled it away.*

trunk /trʌŋk/ (trunks) **1** N-COUNT The **trunk** of a tree is the large main stem from which the branches grow. ❑ *...the gnarled trunk of a birch tree.* **2** N-COUNT A **trunk** is a large, strong case or box used for storing things or for taking on a trip. ❑ *Maloney unlocked his trunk and took out some coveralls.* **3** N-COUNT An elephant's **trunk** is its very long nose that it uses to lift food and water to its mouth. ❑ *Manfred the elephant reached out with his trunk and gently scooped up the baby.* **4** N-COUNT The **trunk** of a car is a covered space at the back or front in which you put luggage or other things. [AM] ❑ *She opened the trunk of the car and started to take out a bag of groceries.*

in BRIT, use **boot**

5 N-PLURAL **Trunks** are shorts that a man wears when he goes swimming. **6** N-COUNT [usu sing] Your **trunk** is the central part of your body, from your neck to your waist. [FORMAL] ❑ *The leg to be stretched should be positioned behind your trunk with your knee bent.* **7** → See also color supplement

truss /trʌs/ (trusses, trussing, trussed) **1** V-T To **truss** someone means to tie them up very tightly so that they cannot move. [WRITTEN] ❑ *She trussed him quickly with stolen bandage, and gagged his mouth.* • PHRASAL VERB [usu passive] **Truss up** means the same as **truss**. ❑ *She was trussed up with yellow nylon rope.* **2** N-COUNT A **truss** is a special belt with a pad that a person wears when they have a hernia in order to prevent it from getting worse.

▶ **truss up** → see **truss** 1

trust ◆◆◇ /trʌst/ (trusts, trusting, trusted)

→ Please look at meaning **12** to see if the expression you are looking for is shown under another headword.

1 V-T If you **trust** someone, you believe that they are honest and sincere and will not deliberately do anything to harm you. ❑ *"I trust you completely," he said.* **2** N-UNCOUNT Your **trust** in someone is your belief that they are honest and sincere and will not deliberately do anything to harm you. ❑ *He destroyed me and my trust in men.* ❑ *You've betrayed their trust.* **3** V-T If you **trust** someone to do something, you believe that they will do it. ❑ *That's why I must trust you to keep this secret.* **4** V-T If you **trust** someone **with** something important or valuable, you allow them to look after it or deal with it. ❑ *This could make your superiors hesitate to trust you with major responsibilities.* • N-UNCOUNT **Trust** is also a noun. ❑ *She was organizing and running a large household, a position of trust which was generously paid.* **5** V-T If you do not **trust** something, you feel that it is not safe or reliable. ❑ *She nodded, not trusting her own voice.* ❑ *For one thing, he didn't trust his legs to hold him up.* **6** V-T If you **trust** someone's judgment or advice, you believe that it is good or right. ❑ *Jake has raised two incredible kids and I trust his judgement.* **7** V-T If you say you **trust that** something is true, you mean you hope and expect that it is true. [FORMAL] ❑ *I trust you will take the earliest opportunity to make a full apology.* **8** V-I If you **trust in** someone or something, you believe strongly in them, and do not doubt their powers or their good intentions. [FORMAL] ❑ *For a believer, replies to all the questions about life and work are far different because he trusts in God.* **9** N-COUNT [also in N] A **trust** is a financial arrangement in which a group of people or an organization keeps and invests money for someone. [BUSINESS] ❑ *You could also set up a trust so the children can't spend any inheritance until they are a certain age.* **10** N-COUNT A **trust** is a group of people or an organization that has control of an amount of money or property and invests it on behalf of other people or as a charity. [BUSINESS] ❑ *He had set up two charitable trusts.* **11** → see also **unit trust** **12 tried and trusted** → see **tried**

SYNONYMS

trust
NOUN **2**
confidence: *The events have contributed to the lack of confidence in the police.*
belief: *...a belief in personal liberty.*
faith: *She had placed a great deal of faith in Mr Penleigh.*

---

trus|tee /trʌstiː/ (trustees) N-COUNT A **trustee** is someone with legal control of money or property that is kept or invested for another person, company, or organization. [BUSINESS] ❑ *The trustees of your pension fund decide which fund manager will invest some or all of your future income.*

trust fund (trust funds) N-COUNT A **trust fund** is an amount of money or property that someone owns, usually after inheriting it, but which is kept and invested for them. [BUSINESS] ❑ *The money will be placed in a trust fund for her daughter.*

trust|ing /trʌstɪŋ/ ADJ A **trusting** person believes that people are honest and sincere and do not intend to harm him or her. ❑ *She has an open, trusting nature.*

trust|worthy /trʌstwɜːrði/ ADJ A **trustworthy** person is reliable, responsible, and can be trusted completely. ❑ *He is a trustworthy and level-headed leader.*

trusty /trʌsti/ (trustier, trustiest) ADJ [ADJ n] **Trusty** things, animals, or people are reliable and have always worked well in the past. ❑ *She still drives her trusty old Dodge.*

truth ✦✦◇ /truːθ/ (truths) **1** N-UNCOUNT The **truth** about something is all the facts about it, rather than things that are imagined or invented. ❑ *Is it possible to separate truth from fiction?* ❑ *I must tell you the truth about this business.* **2** N-UNCOUNT If you say that there is some **truth** in a statement or story, you mean that it is true, or at least partly true. ❑ *There is no truth in this story.* ❑ *Is there any truth to the rumors?* **3** N-COUNT A **truth** is something that is believed to be true. ❑ *It is an almost universal*

VOCABULARY IN CONTEXT

Truth and lies

How people communicate on social media is the subject of countless academic studies. Apparently many of us present a version of our lives that is quite **untrue**. We project the image we want others to have of us, even if that view is **fake**. It's not that we are all **liars**, but there is a societal pressure to appear accomplished and happy. **White lies** are one thing, but the internet is also the vehicle for a more sinister practice. Cyberbullying is a cruel form of online **gossip** and harassment. Often, **rumors** of a **malicious** nature are spread about the person being targeted. Sometimes very private or digitally-altered photos of the person are shared. These **fraudulent** images and other **untruths** are designed to embarrass the victim. While **slander** is not a crime in many parts of the world, new laws mean that cyberbullies can now be prosecuted.

---

truth that the more we are promoted in a job, the less we actually exercise the skills we initially used to perform it. **4** PHRASE You say **to tell you the truth** or **truth to tell** in order to indicate that you are telling someone something in an open and honest way, without trying to hide anything. ❑ *To tell you the truth, I was afraid to see him.*

truth|ful /truːθfəl/ ADJ If a person or their comments are **truthful**, they are honest and do not tell any lies. ❑ *Most religions teach you to be truthful.* ❑ *We've all learned to be fairly truthful about our personal lives.* • **truth|ful|ly** ADV [ADV with v] ❑ *I answered all their questions truthfully.* • **truth|ful|ness** N-UNCOUNT ❑ *I can say, with absolute truthfulness, that I did my best.*

try ✦✦✦ /traɪ/ (tries, trying, tried)
→ Please look at meanings **10** to **12** to see if the expression you are looking for is shown under another headword.
1 V-T/V-I If you **try** to do something, you want to do it, and you take action which you hope will help you to do it. ❑ *He secretly tried to help her at work.* ❑ *Does it annoy you if others don't seem to try hard enough?* • N-COUNT **Try** is also a noun. ❑ *It wasn't that she'd really expected to get any money out of him; it had just seemed worth a try.* **2** V-T To **try** and do something means to try to do it. [INFORMAL] ❑ *I must try and see him.* **3** V-I If you **try for** something, you make an effort to get it or achieve it. ❑ *My partner and I have been trying for a baby for two years.* **4** V-T If you **try** something new or different, you use it, do it, or experience it in order to discover its qualities or effects. ❑ *It's best not to try a new recipe for the first time on such an important occasion.* • N-COUNT **Try** is also a noun. ❑ *If you're still skeptical about exercising, we can only ask you to trust us and give it a try.* **5** V-T If you **try** a particular place or person, you go to that place or person because you think that they may be able to provide you with what you want. ❑ *Have you tried the local music shops?* **6** V-T If you **try** a door or window, you try to open it. ❑ *Bob tried the door. To his surprise it opened.* **7** V-T When a person **is tried**, he or she has to appear in a law court and is found innocent or guilty after the judge and jury have heard the evidence. When a legal case **is tried**, it is considered in a court of law. ❑ *He suggested that those responsible should be tried for crimes against humanity.* ❑ *Whether he is innocent or guilty is a decision that will be made when the case is tried in court.* **8** N-COUNT In the game of rugby, a **try** is the action of scoring by putting the ball down behind the goal line of the opposing team. ❑ *The French, who led 21-3 at half time, scored eight tries.* **9** → see also **tried, trying** **10 to try your best** → see **best** **11 to try your hand** → see **hand** ① **12 to try someone's patience** → see **patience**
▶ **try on** PHRASAL VERB If you **try on** a piece of clothing, you put it on to see if it fits you or if it looks nice. ❑ *Try on clothing and shoes to make sure they fit.*
▶ **try out** PHRASAL VERB If you **try** something **out**, you test it in order to find out how useful or effective it is or what it is like. ❑ *I wanted to try the boat out next weekend.* ❑ *Some owners wish they could try out the car in a race track.*

try|ing /traɪɪŋ/ **1** ADJ If you describe something or someone as **trying**, you mean that they are difficult to deal with and make you feel impatient or annoyed. ❑ *Support from those closest to you is vital in these trying times.* **2** → see also **try**

try|out /traɪaʊt/ (tryouts) N-COUNT If you give something a **tryout**, you try it or test it to see how useful it is. ❑ *The recycling program gets its first tryout in Idaho.*

tryst /trɪst/ (trysts) N-COUNT A **tryst** is a meeting between lovers in a quiet secret place. [LITERARY]

tsar /zɑːr/ → see **czar**

tsa|ri|na /zɑːriːnə/ → see **czarina**

tsar|ist /zɑːrɪst/ → see **czarist**

tset|se fly /tsɛtsi flaɪ/ (tsetse flies) also **tsetse** N-VAR A **tsetse fly** or a **tsetse** is an African fly that feeds on blood and can cause serious diseases in the people and animals that it bites.

T-shirt (T-shirts) also **tee-shirt** N-COUNT A **T-shirt** is a cotton shirt with no collar or buttons. T-shirts usually have short sleeves.

tsp. (tsps) In recipes, **tsp.** is a written abbreviation for teaspoon.

tsu|na|mi /tsʊnɑːmi/ (tsunamis) **1** N-COUNT A **tsunami** is a very large wave, often caused by an earthquake, that flows onto the land and can cause widespread deaths and destruction. **2** → See feature box at **disaster**

tub /tʌb/ (tubs) **1** N-COUNT A **tub** is the same as a **bathtub**. [AM] □ *She lay back in the tub.* **2** N-COUNT A **tub** is a deep container of any size. □ *He peeled the paper top off a little white tub and poured the cream into his coffee.* **3** N-COUNT You can use **tub** to refer to a tub and its contents, or to the contents only. □ *She would eat four tubs of ice cream in one sitting.*

tuba /tjuːbə/ (tubas) N-VAR [oft the N] A **tuba** is a large musical instrument of the brass family which produces very low notes. It consists of a long metal tube folded around several times with a wide opening at the end.

tub|by /tʌbi/ (tubbier, tubbiest) ADJ If you describe someone as **tubby**, you mean that they are a little fat. [INFORMAL]

tube ♦♢♢ /tjuːb/ (tubes) **1** N-COUNT A **tube** is a long hollow object that is usually round, like a pipe. □ *He is fed by a tube that enters his nose.* **2** N-COUNT A **tube** of something such as paste is a long, thin container which you squeeze in order to force the paste out. □ *I went out today and bought a tube of toothpaste.* **3** N-COUNT Some long, thin, hollow parts in your body are referred to as **tubes**. □ *The lungs are in fact constructed of thousands of tiny tubes.* **4** N-COUNT You can refer to the television as **the tube**. [AM, INFORMAL] □ *The only baseball he saw was on the tube.*

in BRIT, use **the box**

5 N-SING **The Tube** is the underground railway system in London. [BRIT, TRADEMARK] □ *I took the Tube then the train and came straight here.* **6** N-SING **The tube** is the name used for any underground railway system. [BRIT] □ *He travelled by tube.*

― COLLOCATIONS ―
tube
NOUN **1**
noun + **tube**: breathing, feeding; cardboard, metal, plastic, rubber
adjective + **tube**: fluorescent, hollow; flexible, long, narrow, thin
verb + **tube**: connect, insert, remove

tu|ber /tjuːbər/ (tubers) N-COUNT A **tuber** is the swollen underground stem of particular types of plants.

tu|ber|cu|lar /tjuːbɜːrkjələr/ ADJ **Tubercular** means suffering from, relating to, or causing tuberculosis. □ *...tubercular patients.* □ *He died of tubercular meningitis.* □ *...tubercular bacteria.*

tu|ber|cu|lo|sis /tjuːbɜːrkjəloʊsɪs/ N-UNCOUNT **Tuberculosis** is a serious infectious disease that affects someone's lungs and other parts of their body. The abbreviation **TB** is also used.

tube top (tube tops) N-COUNT A **tube top** is a piece of women's clothing that is made of stretchy material and covers her chest but leaves her shoulders bare. [AM]

in BRIT, use **boob tube**

tub|ing /tjuːbɪŋ/ N-UNCOUNT **Tubing** is plastic, rubber, or another material in the shape of a tube. □ *...metres of plastic tubing.*

tubu|lar /tjuːbjələr/ ADJ Something that is **tubular** is long, round, and hollow in shape, like a tube. □ *...a modern table with chrome tubular legs.*

tuck /tʌk/ (tucks, tucking, tucked) **1** V-T If you **tuck** something somewhere, you put it there so that it is safe, comfortable, or neat. □ *He tried to tuck his flapping shirt inside his trousers.* **2** N-COUNT You can use **tuck** to refer to a form of plastic surgery which involves reducing the size of a part of someone's body. □ *She'd undergone 13 operations, including a tummy tuck.*

▶ **tuck away** **1** PHRASAL VERB If you **tuck away** something such as money, you store it in a safe place. □ *The extra income has meant Phillippa can tuck away the rent.* **2** PHRASAL VERB If someone or something **is tucked away**, they are well hidden in a quiet place where very few people go. □ *We were tucked away in a secluded corner of the room.*

▶ **tuck in** **1** PHRASAL VERB If you **tuck in** a piece of material, you keep it in position by placing one edge or end of it behind or under something else. For example, if you **tuck in** your shirt, you place the bottom part of it inside your pants or skirt. **2** PHRASAL VERB If you **tuck** a child **in bed** or **tuck** them **in**, you make them comfortable by straightening the sheets and blankets and pushing the loose ends under the mattress. □ *I read Lili a story and tucked her in.*

tuck|er /tʌkər/ N-UNCOUNT **Tucker** is food. [mainly AUSTRALIAN, INFORMAL] □ *...a man who knows what constitutes decent tucker and how to go about serving it up.*

tuck|ered out /tʌkərd aʊt/ also **tuckered** ADJ If you are **tuckered out** or **tuckered**, you are extremely tired. [mainly AM, INFORMAL]

Tues.

The spelling **Tue.** is also used.

Tues. is a written abbreviation for **Tuesday**.

Tues|day ♦♦♦ /tjuːzdeɪ, -di/ (Tuesdays) N-VAR **Tuesday** is the day after Monday and before Wednesday. □ *He phoned on Tuesday, just before you came.* □ *Talks are likely to start next Tuesday.*

tuft /tʌft/ (tufts) N-COUNT [oft N *of* n] A **tuft** of something such as hair or grass is a small amount of it which is growing together in one place or is held together at the bottom. □ *He had a small tuft of hair on his chin.*

tuft|ed /tʌftɪd/ ADJ Something that is **tufted** has a tuft or tufts on it.

tug /tʌg/ (tugs, tugging, tugged) **1** V-T/V-I If you **tug** something or **tug** at it, you give it a quick and usually strong pull. □ *A little boy came running up and tugged at his sleeve excitedly.* • N-COUNT **Tug** is also a noun. □ *I felt a tug at my sleeve.* **2** N-COUNT A **tug** or a **tug boat** is a small powerful boat which pulls large ships, usually when they come into a port. □ *...a 76,000-ton barge pulled by five tug boats.*

tug-of-war (tugs-of-war) also **tug of war** **1** N-VAR A **tug-of-war** is a sports event in which two teams test their strength by pulling against each other on opposite ends of a rope. **2** N-VAR You can use **tug-of-war** to refer to a situation in which two people or groups both want the same thing and are fairly equally matched in their struggle to get it. □ *...a tug of war over intellectual property rights.*

tui|tion /tjuɪʃən/ **1** N-UNCOUNT You can use **tuition** to refer to the amount of money that you have to pay for being taught at a university, college, or private school. □ *Angela's $7,000 tuition at university this year will be paid for with scholarships.* **2** N-UNCOUNT If you are given **tuition** in a particular subject, you are taught about that subject. [mainly BRIT]

in AM, usually use **instruction**

tu|lip /tjuːlɪp/ (tulips) N-COUNT **Tulips** are flowers that grow in the spring from bulbs, and have oval or pointed petals packed closely together.

― WORD HISTORY ―
tulip
Tulip comes from Turkish *tulbend*, meaning 'turban,' because of the shape of the flowers.

tulle /tjuːl/ N-UNCOUNT **Tulle** is a soft nylon or silk cloth similar to net, that is used for making evening dresses.

tum|ble /tʌmbəl/ (tumbles, tumbling, tumbled) **1** V-I If someone or something **tumbles** somewhere, they fall there with a rolling or bouncing movement. □ *A small boy tumbled off the porch.* • N-COUNT [usu sing] **Tumble** is also a noun. □ *He injured his ribs in a tumble from his horse.* **2** V-I If prices or levels of something **are tumbling**, they are decreasing rapidly. [JOURNALISM] □ *Profit after taxes tumbled by half to $15.8 million.* □ *Share prices continued to tumble today on the Tokyo stock market.* • N-COUNT **Tumble** is also a noun. □ *Oil prices took a tumble yesterday.* **3** V-I If water **tumbles**, it flows quickly over an uneven surface. □ *Waterfalls crash and tumble over rocks.*

tumble|down /tʌmbəldaʊn/ ADJ [usu ADJ n] A **tumbledown** building is in such a bad condition that it is partly falling down or has holes in it.

tum|ble dry|er (tumble dryers) also **tumble drier** N-COUNT A **tumble dryer** is an electric machine which dries washing by turning it over and over and blowing warm air onto it. [mainly BRIT]

in AM, use **dryer**

tum|bler /tʌmblər/ (tumblers) **1** N-COUNT A **tumbler** is a drinking glass with straight sides and no handle or stem. **2** → See also color supplement

tumble|weed /tʌmbᵊlwiːd/ N-UNCOUNT **Tumbleweed** is a plant that grows in desert areas in North America. It breaks off from its roots at the end of its life and then blows around on the ground, looking like a large ball of twigs. [AM]

tum|my /tʌmi/ (tummies) **1** N-COUNT Your **tummy** is the part of the front of your body below your waist. **Tummy** is often used by children or by adults talking to children. ❏ *Your baby's tummy should feel warm, but not hot.* **2** N-COUNT You can use **tummy** to refer to the parts inside your body where food is digested. **Tummy** is often used by children or by adults talking to children. ❏ *I've got a sore tummy.* ❏ *...a tummy ache.*

tu|mor /tuːmər/ (tumors)

in BRIT, use **tumour**

N-COUNT A **tumor** is a mass of diseased or abnormal cells that has grown in a person's or animal's body. ❏ *...a malignant brain tumor.*

tu|mult /tuːmʌlt/ **1** N-SING [also no det, oft N of n] A **tumult** is a state of great confusion or excitement. ❏ *A tumult of feelings inside her fought for supremacy.* ❏ *...the recent tumult in global financial markets.* **2** N-SING [also no det, oft N of n] A **tumult** is a lot of noise made by a crowd of people. ❏ *Round one ends, to a tumult of whistles, screams and shouts!*

tu|mul|tu|ous /tuːmʌltʃuəs/ **1** ADJ A **tumultuous** event or period of time involves many exciting and confusing events or feelings. ❏ *...the tumultuous changes in Eastern Europe.* **2** ADJ A **tumultuous** reaction to something is very noisy, because the people involved are very happy or excited. ❏ *A tumultuous welcome from a 2,000 strong crowd greeted the champion.*

tuna /tuːnə/ (tuna or tunas)

The plural can be either **tuna** or **tunas**.

N-VAR **Tuna** or **tuna fish** are large fish that live in warm seas and are caught for food. ❏ *...a shoal of tuna.* • N-UNCOUNT **Tuna** or **tuna fish** is this fish eaten as food. ❏ *She began opening a can of tuna.*

tun|dra /tʌndrə/ (tundras) **1** N-VAR **Tundra** is one of the large flat areas of land in the north of Europe, Asia, and America. The ground below the top layer of soil is always frozen and no trees grow there. **2** → See feature box at **ecosystem**

tune ✦◇◇ /tuːn/ (tunes, tuning, tuned) **1** N-COUNT A **tune** is a series of musical notes that is pleasant and easy to remember. ❏ *She was humming a merry little tune.* **2** N-COUNT You can refer to a song or a short piece of music as a **tune**. ❏ *She'll also be playing your favorite pop tunes.* **3** V-T When someone **tunes** a musical instrument, they adjust it so that it produces the right notes. ❏ *"We do tune our guitars before we go on," he insisted.* • PHRASAL VERB **Tune up** means the same as **tune**. ❏ *Others were quietly tuning up their instruments.* **4** V-T [usu passive] When an engine or machine is **tuned**, it is adjusted so that it works well. ❏ *Drivers are urged to make sure that car engines are properly tuned.* • PHRASAL VERB **Tune up** means the same as **tune**. ❏ *The shop charges up to $500 to tune up a Porsche.* **5** V-T [usu passive] If your radio or television **is tuned** to a particular channel or broadcasting station, you are listening to or watching the programs being broadcast by that station. ❏ *A small color television was tuned to an afternoon soap opera.* **6** → see also **fine-tune** **7** PHRASE If you say that a person or organization **is calling the tune**, you mean that they are in a position of power or control in a particular situation. ❏ *It is Williams who is calling the tune so far this season.* **8** PHRASE If you say that someone **has changed** their **tune**, you are criticizing them because they have changed their opinion or way of doing things. [DISAPPROVAL] ❏ *You've changed your tune since this morning, haven't you?* **9** PHRASE A person or musical instrument that is **in tune** produces exactly the right notes. A person or musical instrument that is **out of tune** does not produce exactly the right notes. ❏ *It was just an ordinary voice, but he sang in tune.* **10** → See feature box at **music**
▸ **tune in** **1** PHRASAL VERB If you **tune in** to a particular television or radio station or program, you watch or listen to it. ❏ *All over the country, youngsters tune in to Sesame Street every day.* **2** PHRASAL VERB If you **tune in** to something such as your own or other people's feelings, you become aware of them. ❏ *You can start now to tune in to your own physical, social and spiritual needs.*
▸ **tune out** PHRASAL VERB If you **tune out**, you stop listening or paying attention to what is being said. ❏ *Children rapidly tune out if you go beyond them.* ❏ *Rose heard the familiar voice, but tuned out the words.*

tuned in ADJ [usu v-link ADJ to n] If someone is **tuned in** to something, they are aware of it and concentrating on it. ❏ *He's just not tuned in to the child's feelings.*

tune|ful /tuːnfəl/ ADJ A piece of music that is **tuneful** has a pleasant tune.

tune|less /tuːnlɪs/ ADJ [usu ADJ n] **Tuneless** music and voices do not sound pleasant. ❏ *Someone walked by, singing a tuneless song.* • **tune|less|ly** ADV ❏ *My dad whistled tunelessly through his teeth.*

tun|er /tuːnər/ (tuners) N-COUNT [oft supp N] The **tuner** in a radio or television set is the part which you adjust to receive different radio or television signals, so that you can watch or listen to the program that you want.

tung|sten /tʌŋstən/ N-UNCOUNT **Tungsten** is a grayish-white metal.

tu|nic /tuːnɪk/ (tunics) N-COUNT A **tunic** is a long sleeveless garment that is worn on the top part of your body. ❏ *...a cotton tunic.*

tun|ing fork (tuning forks) N-COUNT A **tuning fork** is a small steel instrument which is used to tune instruments by striking it against something to produce a note of fixed musical pitch.

Tu|ni|sian /tuːnɪʒən/ (Tunisians) **1** ADJ **Tunisian** means belonging to or relating to Tunisia, or to its people or culture. **2** N-COUNT A **Tunisian** is a Tunisian citizen, or a person of Tunisian origin.

tun|nel ✦◇◇ /tʌnᵊl/ (tunnels, tunneling, tunneled)

in BRIT, use **tunnelling, tunnelled**

1 N-COUNT A **tunnel** is a long passage which has been made under the ground, usually through a hill or under the sea. ❏ *Boston drivers love the tunnel.* **2** V-I To **tunnel** somewhere means to make a tunnel there. ❏ *The thieves tunneled under all the security devices.*

tun|nel vi|sion **1** N-UNCOUNT If you have **tunnel vision**, you are unable to see things that are not straight in front of you. **2** N-UNCOUNT If you say that someone has **tunnel vision**, you disapprove of them because they are concentrating completely on achieving a particular aim, and do not notice or consider anything else. [DISAPPROVAL]

Tup|per|ware /tʌpərwɛər/ N-UNCOUNT [oft N n] **Tupperware** is a brand name for a range of plastic containers with tight-fitting lids that are used for storing food. [TRADEMARK] ❏ *...a Tupperware box.*

tur|ban /tɜrbən/ (turbans) **1** N-COUNT A **turban** is a long piece of cloth that is wound around the head. It is worn by Sikh men and by some Hindu and Muslim men. **2** → See also color supplement

tur|bine /tɜrbɪn, -baɪn/ (turbines) **1** N-COUNT A **turbine** is a machine or engine which uses a stream of air, gas, water, or steam to turn a wheel and produce power. ❏ *The new ship will be powered by two gas turbines and four diesel engines.* **2** → See also color supplement

turbo /tɜrboʊ/ (turbos) N-COUNT A **turbo** is a fan in the engine of a car or plane that improves its performance by using exhaust gases to blow fuel vapor into the engine.

tur|bo|charged /tɜrboʊtʃɑrdʒd/ also **turbo-charged** ADJ [usu ADJ n] A **turbocharged** engine or vehicle is fitted with a turbo.

tur|bo|prop /tɜrboʊprɒp/ (turboprops) also **turbo-prop** **1** N-COUNT A **turboprop** is a turbine engine that makes an aircraft propeller go around. **2** N-COUNT A **turboprop** is an aircraft with one or more turboprops.

tur|bot /tɜrbət/ (turbot) N-VAR **Turbot** are a type of edible flat fish that live in European seas. • N-UNCOUNT **Turbot** is this fish eaten as food.

tur|bu|lence /tɜrbyələns/ **1** N-UNCOUNT **Turbulence** is a state of confusion and disorganized change. ❏ *The 1960s and early 1970s were a time of change and turbulence.* **2** N-UNCOUNT **Turbulence** is violent and uneven movement within a

tur|bu|lent /tɜrbyələnt/ **1** ADJ A **turbulent** time, place, or relationship is one in which there is a lot of change, confusion, and disorder. ❑ *They had been together for five or six turbulent years of break-ups and reconciliations.* **2** ADJ **Turbulent** water or air contains strong currents which change direction suddenly. ❑ *I had to have a boat that could handle turbulent seas.*

turd /tɜrd/ (**turds**) N-COUNT A **turd** is a lump of feces. [INFORMAL, VULGAR]

tu|reen /tʊrin/ (**tureens**) N-COUNT A **tureen** is a large bowl with a lid from which you can serve soup or vegetables.

turf /tɜrf/ **1** N-UNCOUNT [also the N] **Turf** is short, thick, even grass. ❑ *They shuffled slowly down the turf toward the cliff's edge.* **2** N-UNCOUNT Someone's **turf** is the area which is most familiar to them or where they feel most confident. ❑ *Their turf was St. Louis: its streets, theaters, homes, and parks.*

turf war (**turf wars**) also **turf battle** **1** N-COUNT [oft N between N, N over N] A **turf war** is a struggle between criminals or gangs over who controls a particular area. [mainly JOURNALISM] ❑ *The estate is at the center of a bitter turf war between rival drug gangs.* **2** N-COUNT [oft N between N, N over N] A **turf war** is a struggle between people over who controls a particular activity. [mainly JOURNALISM] ❑ *Both sides say this is more than just a turf war between big and small banks.*

tur|gid /tɜrdʒɪd/ ADJ If you describe something such as a piece of writing or a movie as **turgid**, you think it is too serious and difficult to understand. ❑ *He used to make extremely dull, turgid and frankly awful speeches.*

Turk /tɜrk/ (**Turks**) N-COUNT A **Turk** is a Turkish citizen, or a person of Turkish origin.

tur|key /tɜrki/ (**turkeys**) N-COUNT A **turkey** is a large bird that is kept on a farm for its meat. • N-UNCOUNT **Turkey** is the meat of this bird eaten as food. ❑ *They will sit down to a traditional turkey dinner early this afternoon.*

tur|key shoot (**turkey shoots**) N-COUNT [usu sing: a N] If someone refers to a battle or other conflict as a **turkey shoot**, they mean that one side is so much stronger or better armed than the other one that the weaker side has no chance of winning at all. [AM, INFORMAL] ❑ *Some American pilots described the experience as a turkey shoot.*

Turk|ish /tɜrkɪʃ/ **1** ADJ **Turkish** means belonging or relating to Turkey, or to its people, language, or culture. **2** N-UNCOUNT **Turkish** is the main language spoken in Turkey.

Turk|ish bath (**Turkish baths**) **1** N-COUNT A **Turkish bath** is a type of bath in which you sit in a very hot steamy room, then wash, get a massage, and finally swim or shower in very cold water. **2** N-COUNT A **Turkish bath** is a place where you can have a Turkish bath.

Turk|ish de|light (**Turkish delights**) N-VAR **Turkish delight** is a gelatin-like candy that is covered with powdered sugar or chocolate.

tur|mer|ic /tɜrmərɪk/ N-UNCOUNT **Turmeric** is a yellow spice that is used to flavor food such as curry.

tur|moil /tɜrmɔɪl/ (**turmoils**) N-VAR **Turmoil** is a state of confusion, disorder, uncertainty, or great anxiety. ❑ *...the political turmoil of 1989.*

TURN

① VERB AND NOUN USES
② PHRASES
③ PHRASAL VERBS

---

① **turn** ◆◆◆ /tɜrn/ (**turns, turning, turned**) **1** V-T/V-I When you **turn** or when you **turn** part of your body, you move your body or part of your body so that it is facing in a different or opposite direction. ❑ *He turned abruptly and walked away.* ❑ *He sighed, turning away and surveying the sea.* • PHRASAL VERB **Turn around** means the same as **turn**. ❑ *I felt a tapping on my shoulder and I turned around.* **2** V-T When you **turn** something, you move it so that it is facing in a different or opposite direction, or is in a very different position. ❑ *They turned their telescopes toward other nearby galaxies.* ❑ *She had turned the bedside chair to face the door.* **3** V-T/V-I When something such as a wheel **turns**, or when you **turn** it, it continually moves around in a particular direction. ❑ *As the wheel turned, the potter shaped the clay.* **4** V-T/V-I When you **turn** something such as a key, knob, or switch, or when it **turns**, you hold it and twist your hand, in order to open something or make it start working. ❑ *Turn the key three times to the right.* ❑ *Turn the heat to very low and cook for 20 minutes.* **5** V-T/V-I When you **turn** in a particular direction or **turn** a corner, you change the direction in which you are moving or traveling. ❑ *He turned into the narrow street where he lived.* ❑ *Now turn right to follow West Ferry Road.* • N-COUNT **Turn** is also a noun. ❑ *You can't do a right-hand turn here.* **6** V-I The point where a road, path, or river **turns** is the point where it has a bend or curve in it. ❑ *...the corner where Tenterfield Road turned into the main road.* • N-COUNT **Turn** is also a noun. ❑ *...a sharp turn in the road.* **7** V-I When the tide **turns**, it starts coming in or going out. ❑ *There was not much time before the tide turned.* **8** V-T When you **turn** a page of a book or magazine, you move it so that it is flat against the previous page, and you can read the next page. ❑ *He turned the pages of a file in front of him.* **9** V-T If you **turn** a weapon or an aggressive feeling **on** someone, you point it at them or direct it at them. ❑ *He tried to turn the gun on me.* **10** V-I If you **turn to** a particular page in a book or magazine, you open it at that page. ❑ *To order, turn to page 236.* **11** V-T/V-I If you **turn** your attention or thoughts **to** a particular subject or if you **turn to** it, you start thinking about it or discussing it. ❑ *We turned our attention to the practical matters relating to forming a company.* ❑ *We turn now to our primary question.* **12** V-I If you **turn to** someone, you ask for their help or advice. ❑ *For assistance, they turned to one of the city's most innovative museums.* **13** V-I If you **turn to** a particular activity, job, or way of doing something, you start doing or using it. ❑ *These communities are now turning to recycling as a cheaper alternative to landfills.* **14** V-T/V-I To **turn** or **be turned** into something means to become that thing. ❑ *A prince turns into a frog in this cartoon fairytale.* **15** V-LINK You can use **turn** before an adjective to indicate that something or someone changes by acquiring the quality described by the adjective. ❑ *If the bailiff thinks that things could turn nasty he will enlist the help of the police.* **16** V-LINK If something **turns** a particular color or if something **turns** it a particular color, it becomes that color. ❑ *The sea would turn pale pink and the sky blood red.* **17** V-LINK You can use **turn** to indicate that there is a change to a particular kind of weather. For example, if it **turns** cold, the weather starts being cold. ❑ *If it turns cold, cover the plants.* **18** N-COUNT If a situation or trend takes a particular kind of **turn**, it changes so that it starts developing in a different or opposite way. ❑ *The scandal took a new turn over the weekend.* **19** V-T [no passive] If a business **turns** a profit, it earns more money than it spends. [BUSINESS] ❑ *The firm will be able to pay off its debts and still turn a modest profit.* **20** V-T When someone **turns** a particular age, they pass that age. When it **turns** a particular time, it passes that time. ❑ *It was his ambition to accumulate a million dollars before he turned thirty.* **21** N-SING **Turn** is used in expressions such as **the turn of the century** and **the turn of the year** to refer to a period of time when one century or year is ending and the next one is beginning. ❑ *They fled to South America around the turn of the century.* **22** N-COUNT If it is your **turn** to do something, you now have the duty, chance, or right to do it, when other people have done it before you or will do it after you. ❑ *Tonight it's my turn to cook.* **23** → see also **turning**

② **turn** ◆◆◆ /tɜrn/ (**turns**) **1** PHRASE If there is a particular **turn of events**, a particular series of things happen. ❑ *They were horrified at this unexpected turn of events.* **2** PHRASE If you say that something happens **at every turn**, you are emphasizing that it happens frequently or all the time, usually so that it prevents you from achieving what you want. [EMPHASIS] ❑ *Its operations were hampered at every turn by inadequate numbers of trained staff.* **3** PHRASE If you do someone **a good turn**, you do something that helps or benefits them. ❑ *He did you a good turn by resigning.* **4** PHRASE You use **in turn** to refer to actions or events that are in a sequence one after the other, for example, because one causes the other. ❑ *One of the members of the surgical team leaked the story to a fellow physician who, in turn, confided in a reporter.* **5** PHRASE If each person in a group does something **in turn**, they do it one after the other in a fixed or agreed order. ❑ *There were cheers for each of the women as they spoke in turn.* **6** PHRASE If two or more people **take turns** to do something, they do it one after the other several times, rather than doing it together. ❑ *We took turns driving.* **7** PHRASE If a situation **takes a turn for the worse**, it suddenly becomes worse. If a situation **takes a turn for the better**, it suddenly becomes better. ❑ *Her condition took a sharp turn for the worse.*

③ **turn** ♦♦♦ /tɜrn/ (**turns, turning, turned**)
▶ **turn against** PHRASAL VERB If you **turn against** someone or something, or if you **are turned against** them, you stop supporting them, trusting them, or liking them, and sometimes you work against them. ❑ *A kid I used to be friends with turned against me after being told that I'd been insulting him.*
▶ **turn around** **1** → see **turn** ① 1 **2** PHRASAL VERB If you **turn** something **around**, or if it **turns around**, it is moved so that it faces the opposite direction. ❑ *Bud turned the truck around, and started back for Dalton Pond.* ❑ *He had reached over to turn around a bottle of champagne so that the label didn't show.* **3** PHRASAL VERB If something such as a business or economy **turns around**, or if someone **turns** it **around**, it becomes successful, after being unsuccessful for a period of time. [BUSINESS] ❑ *Turning the company around won't be easy.* ❑ *In his long career, Horton turned around two entire divisions.*
▶ **turn away** **1** PHRASAL VERB If you **turn** someone **away**, you do not allow them to enter your country, home, or other place. ❑ *Turning Cuban boat people away would be an inhumane action.* **2** PHRASAL VERB To **turn away** from something such as a method or an idea means to stop using it or to become different from it. ❑ *Japanese companies have been turning away from production and have moved into real estate.*
▶ **turn back** **1** PHRASAL VERB If you **turn back** or if something **turns** you **back** when you are going somewhere, you change direction and go toward where you started from. ❑ *She turned back toward home.* ❑ *Police attempted to turn back.* **2** PHRASAL VERB [with brd-neg] If you cannot **turn back**, you cannot change your plans and decide not to do something, because the action you have already taken makes it impossible. ❑ *The Senate has now endorsed the bill and can't turn back.* **3** → See feature box at **time**
▶ **turn down** **1** PHRASAL VERB If you **turn down** a person or their request or offer, you refuse their request or offer. ❑ *I thanked him for the offer but turned it down.* **2** PHRASAL VERB When you **turn down** a radio, heater, or other piece of equipment, you reduce the amount of sound or heat being produced, by adjusting the controls. ❑ *He kept turning the central heating down.*
▶ **turn off** **1** PHRASAL VERB If you **turn off** the road or path you are going along, you start going along a different road or path which leads away from it. ❑ *The truck turned off the main road, and went along the gravelly track which led to the farm.* **2** PHRASAL VERB When you **turn off** a piece of equipment or a supply of something, you stop heat, sound, or water from being produced by adjusting the controls. ❑ *The light's a bit too harsh. You can turn it off.* **3** PHRASAL VERB If something **turns** you **off** a particular subject or activity, it makes you have no interest in it. ❑ *What turns teenagers off science?* ❑ *Greed on the part of owners and athletes turns fans off completely.* **4** → see also **turnoff**
▶ **turn on** **1** PHRASAL VERB When you **turn on** a piece of equipment or a supply of something, you cause heat, sound, or water to be produced by adjusting the controls. ❑ *I want to turn on the television.* **2** PHRASAL VERB If someone or something **turns** you **on**, they attract you and make you feel sexually excited. [INFORMAL] ❑ *Physical perfection doesn't tend to turn most people on.* **3** PHRASAL VERB If someone **turns on** you, they suddenly attack you or speak angrily to you. ❑ *Demonstrators turned on police, overturning vehicles and setting fire to them.*
▶ **turn out** **1** PHRASAL VERB If something **turns out** a particular way, it happens in that way or has the result or degree of success indicated. ❑ *I had no idea that it would turn out like this.* ❑ *I was positive things were going to turn out fine.* **2** PHRASAL VERB If something **turns out** to be a particular thing, it is discovered to be that thing. ❑ *Cosgrave's forecast turned out to be completely wrong.* **3** PHRASAL VERB When you **turn out** something such as a light, you move the switch or knob that controls it so that it stops giving out light or heat. ❑ *The janitor comes around to turn the lights out.* **4** → see also **turnout**
▶ **turn over** **1** PHRASAL VERB If you **turn** something **over**, or if it **turns over**, it is moved so that the top part is now facing downward. ❑ *Liz picked up the blue envelope and turned it over curiously.* ❑ *The buggy turned over and Nancy was thrown out.* **2** PHRASAL VERB If you **turn over**, for example, when you are lying in bed, you move your body so that you are lying in a different position. ❑ *Ann turned over in her bed once more.* **3** PHRASAL VERB If you **turn** something **over** in your mind, you think carefully about it. ❑ *Even when she didn't say anything you could see her turning things over in her mind.* **4** PHRASAL VERB If you **turn** something **over** to someone, you give it to them when they ask for it, because they have a right to it. ❑ *I would have to turn the evidence over to the police.* **5** → see also **turnover**
▶ **turn round** [BRIT] → see **turn around**
▶ **turn up** **1** PHRASAL VERB If you say that someone or something **turns up**, you mean that they arrive unexpectedly or after you have been waiting a long time. ❑ *They finally turned up at nearly midnight.* ❑ *Richard had turned up on Christmas Eve with Tony.* **2** PHRASAL VERB If you **turn** something **up** or if it **turns up**, you find, discover, or notice it. ❑ *Investigations have never turned up any evidence.* **3** PHRASAL VERB When you **turn up** a radio, heater, or other piece of equipment, you increase the amount of sound, heat, or power being produced, by adjusting the controls. ❑ *Can you turn up the TV?* ❑ *I turned the volume up.*

> **Turn** is used in a large number of other expressions which are explained under other words in the dictionary. For example, the expression 'turn over a new leaf' is explained at **leaf**.

turn|about /tɜrnəbaʊt/ N-SING [oft N *in* n] A **turnabout** is a complete change in opinion, attitude, or method. [BRIT] ❑ *As her confidence grows you may well see a considerable turnabout in her attitude.*

turn|around /tɜrnəraʊnd/ (**turnarounds**) **1** N-COUNT [oft N *in* n] A **turnaround** is a complete change in opinion, attitude, or method. ❑ *I have personally never done such a complete turnaround in my opinion of a person.* **2** N-COUNT [usu sing, oft N *in* n] A **turnaround** is a sudden improvement, especially in the success of a business or a country's economy. ❑ *The company has been enjoying a turnaround in recent months.* **3** N-VAR The **turnaround** or **turnaround time** of a task is the amount of time that it takes. ❑ *It is possible to produce a result within 34 hours but the standard turnaround is 12 days.* ❑ *The agency should reduce turnaround time by 11 percent.*

turn|coat /tɜrnkoʊt/ (**turncoats**) N-COUNT If you describe someone as a **turncoat**, you think they are disloyal or deceitful, because they have left their party or organization and joined an opposing one. [DISAPPROVAL]

turned out ADJ [adv ADJ] If you are well **turned out** or beautifully **turned out**, you are dressed very nicely. ❑ *...a well-turned-out young man in a black suit.*

turn|ing /tɜrnɪŋ/ (**turnings**) N-COUNT If you take a particular **turning**, you go along a road which leads away from the side of another road. [mainly BRIT]

> in AM, usually use **turn**

turn|ing point (**turning points**) N-COUNT A **turning point** is a time at which an important change takes place which affects the future of a person or thing. ❑ *The vote yesterday appears to mark a turning point in the war.*

tur|nip /tɜrnɪp/ (**turnips**) N-VAR A **turnip** is a round root vegetable with a cream-colored skin.

turn|off /tɜrnɔf/ (**turnoffs**) **1** N-COUNT A **turnoff** is a road leading away from a major road or a highway. **2** N-COUNT [usu sing] Something that is a **turnoff** causes you to lose interest or sexual excitement. [INFORMAL]

turn-on (**turn-ons**) N-COUNT [usu sing] Something or someone that is a **turn-on** is sexually exciting. [INFORMAL]

turn|out /tɜrnaʊt/ (**turnouts**) N-COUNT The **turnout** at an event is the number of people who go to it or take part in it. ❑ *On the big night there was a massive turnout.*

turn|over /tɜrnoʊvər/ (**turnovers**) **1** N-VAR The **turnover** of a company is the value of the goods or services sold during a particular period of time. [BUSINESS] ❑ *The company had a turnover of $3.8 million.* **2** N-VAR The **turnover** of people in an organization or place is the rate at which people leave and are replaced. [BUSINESS] ❑ *Short-term contracts increase staff turnover.* **3** → See feature box at **business**

turn|pike /tɜrnpaɪk/ (turnpikes) N-COUNT A **turnpike** is a road, especially an expressway, which people have to pay to drive on. [mainly AM]

turn sig|nal (turn signals) N-COUNT A car's **turn signals** are the flashing lights that tell you it is going to turn left or right. [AM] ❑ *He flipped his turn signal, and took a left.*

in BRIT, use **indicators**

turn|stile /tɜrnstaɪl/ (turnstiles) N-COUNT A **turnstile** is a mechanical barrier at the entrance to a place such as a museum or a sports arena. Turnstiles have metal arms that you push around as you go through them and enter the building or area.

turn|table /tɜrnteɪbəl/ (turntables) N-COUNT A **turntable** is the flat, round part of a record player on which a record is put when it is played.

turn-up [BRIT] → see **cuff 2**

tur|pen|tine /tɜrpəntaɪn/ N-UNCOUNT **Turpentine** is a colorless strong liquid used, for example, for cleaning paint off brushes.

tur|pi|tude /tɜrpɪtud/ N-UNCOUNT [usu supp N] **Turpitude** is very immoral behavior. [FORMAL]

tur|quoise /tɜrkwɔɪz/ (turquoises) 〓 COLOR **Turquoise** or **turquoise blue** is used to describe things that are of a light greenish-blue color. ❑ *...a clear turquoise sea.* 〓 N-VAR [oft N n] **Turquoise** is a bright blue stone that is often used in jewelry. ❑ *...beautiful silver and turquoise jewelry.* 〓 → See also **color supplement**

tur|ret /tɜrɪt/ (turrets) 〓 N-COUNT A **turret** is a small narrow tower on top of a building or a larger tower. 〓 N-COUNT [oft n N] The **turret** on a tank or warship is the part where the guns are fixed, which can be turned in any direction.

tur|tle /tɜrtəl/ (turtles) 〓 N-COUNT A **turtle** is any reptile that has a thick shell around its body, for example a tortoise or terrapin, and can pull its whole body into its shell. [AM] ❑ *...a pet turtle.* ❑ *...the giant sea turtle.* 〓 → See feature box at **ocean**

tur|tle dove (turtle doves) also **turtle-dove** N-COUNT A **turtle dove** is a type of light-brown dove which makes a soft pleasant sound and which is said to behave in a very affectionate way toward its mate and its young.

turtle|neck /tɜrtəlnɛk/ (turtlenecks) 〓 N-COUNT A **turtleneck** is knit shirt that pulls over your head, with a high neck which folds over. [AM]

in BRIT, use **polo neck**

〓 N-COUNT A **turtleneck** is a knit shirt that pulls over your head, with a short round collar that fits closely around your neck. [BRIT]

in AM, use **mock turtleneck**

tusk /tʌsk/ (tusks) 〓 N-COUNT The **tusks** of an elephant, wild boar, or walrus are its two very long, curved, pointed teeth. 〓 → See feature box at **endanger**

tus|sle /tʌsəl/ (tussles, tussling, tussled) V-RECIP If one person **tussles** with another, or if they **tussle**, they get hold of each other and struggle or fight. ❑ *They ended up ripping down perimeter fencing and tussling with the security staff.* ❑ *He grabbed my microphone and we tussled over that.* • N-COUNT **Tussle** is also a noun. ❑ *Two players were ejected after a tussle on the field.*

tus|sock /tʌsək/ (tussocks) N-COUNT [oft N of n] A **tussock** is a small piece of grass which is much longer and thicker than the grass around it.

tut /tʌt/ (tuts, tutting, tutted) 〓 V-I **Tut** is used in writing to represent the sound that you make with your tongue touching the top of your mouth when you want to indicate disapproval, annoyance, or sympathy. 〓 V-I If you **tut**, you make a sound with your tongue touching the top of your mouth when you want to indicate disapproval, annoyance, or sympathy. ❑ *He tutted and shook his head.* 〓 → see also **tut-tut**

tu|telage /tutɪlɪdʒ/ N-UNCOUNT [usu under N] If one person, group, or country does something **under the tutelage of** another, they do it while they are being taught or guided by them. [FORMAL]

tu|tor /tutər/ (tutors) 〓 N-COUNT A **tutor** is someone who gives private lessons to one student or a very small group of students. ❑ *...a Spanish tutor.* 〓 N-COUNT In some American universities or colleges, a **tutor** is a teacher of the lowest rank.

tu|to|rial /tutɔriəl/ (tutorials) 〓 N-COUNT In a university or college, a **tutorial** is a regular meeting between a tutor or professor and one or several students, for discussion of a subject that is being studied. ❑ *The methods of study include lectures, tutorials, case studies and practical sessions.* 〓 N-COUNT A **tutorial** is part of a book or a computer program which helps you learn something step-by-step without a teacher. ❑ *There is an excellent tutorial section, which carefully walks you through how to play.* 〓 ADJ [ADJ n] **Tutorial** means relating to a tutor or tutors, especially one at a university or college. ❑ *Students may decide to seek tutorial guidance.*

tut-tut (tut-tuts, tut-tutting, tut-tutted) also **tut tut**
〓 CONVENTION **Tut-tut** is used in writing to represent the sound that you make with your tongue touching the top of your mouth when you want to indicate disapproval, annoyance, or sympathy. [FEELINGS] 〓 V-I If you **tut-tut** about something, you express your disapproval of it, especially by making a sound with your tongue touching the top of your mouth. ❑ *We all spent a lot of time tut-tutting about Angie and her lifestyle.* ❑ *The doctor tut-tutted, dismissing my words as excuses.*

tutu /tutu/ (tutus) N-COUNT A **tutu** is a costume worn by female ballet dancers. It has a very short stiff skirt made of many layers of material that sticks out from the waist.

tux /tʌks/ (tuxes) N-COUNT A **tux** is the same as a **tuxedo**. [INFORMAL]

tux|edo /tʌksidoʊ/ (tuxedos) 〓 N-COUNT A **tuxedo** is a suit, usually black, that is worn mainly by men for formal social events. [mainly AM] 〓 N-COUNT A **tuxedo** is a black or white jacket worn mainly by men for formal social events. [mainly AM]

in BRIT, usually use **dinner jacket**

TV ✦✧✧ /ti vi/ (TVs) also **T.V.** N-VAR **TV** means the same as **television**. ❑ *The TV was on.* ❑ *What's on TV?* ❑ *They watch too much TV.*

TV din|ner (TV dinners) N-COUNT A **TV dinner** is a complete meal that is sold in a single container. It can be heated up quickly and eaten from the container it is cooked in.

twad|dle /twɒdəl/ N-UNCOUNT If you refer to something that someone says as **twaddle**, you mean that it is silly or untrue. [INFORMAL, DISAPPROVAL]

twang /twæŋ/ (twangs, twanging, twanged) 〓 V-T/V-I If you **twang** something such as a tight string or elastic band, or if it **twangs**, it makes a fairly loud, ringing sound because it has been pulled and then released. ❑ *...people who sat at the back of class and twanged an elastic band.* ❑ *The song is a fiery mix of twanging guitar with relentless drumming.* ❑ *The fiddle began to twang.* • N-COUNT; SOUND **Twang** is also a noun. ❑ *Something gave a loud discordant twang.* 〓 N-COUNT [usu sing] A **twang** is a quality in someone's way of speaking in which sound seems to be coming through the nose. ❑ *...her broad Australian twang.*

twat /twɒt/ (twats) N-COUNT If someone calls another person a **twat**, they are insulting them and showing that they do not like or respect them. [INFORMAL, OFFENSIVE, VULGAR, DISAPPROVAL]

tweak /twik/ (tweaks, tweaking, tweaked) 〓 V-T If you **tweak** something, especially part of someone's body, you hold it between your finger and thumb and twist it or pull it. ❑ *He tweaked Guy's ear roughly.* 〓 V-T If you **tweak** something such as a system or a design, you improve it by making a slight change. [INFORMAL] ❑ *He expects the system to get even better as the engineers tweak its performance.* • N-COUNT **Tweak** is also a noun. ❑ *The camera has undergone only two minor tweaks since its introduction.*

tweed /twid/ (tweeds) N-MASS **Tweed** is a thick woolen cloth, often woven from different colored threads. ❑ *...a tweed jacket.*

tweedy /twidi/ (tweedier, tweediest) ADJ GRADED; ADJ **Tweedy** clothes are made from tweed.

tweet /twit/ (tweets, tweeting, tweeted) 〓 N-COUNT; SOUND A **tweet** is a short, high-pitched sound made by a small bird.

tweetable

2 V-T/V-I If you **tweet** or **tweet** something, you send a short message on the Twitter website. ❏ *Thousands of people tweeted their disapproval.*

tweet|able /twiːtəbəl/ ADJ A **tweetable** message is suitable for posting on the social media site Twitter, for example because it is short. ❏ *It's difficult to sum up such a complex issue in a tweetable one-liner.*

twee|zers /twiːzərz/ **1** N-PLURAL [oft a pair of N] **Tweezers** are a small tool that you use for tasks such as picking up small objects or pulling out hairs or splinters. Tweezers consist of two strips of metal or plastic joined together at one end. **2** → See feature box at **household**

twelfth ♦♦◇ /twɛlfθ/ (**twelfths**) **1** ORD The **twelfth** item in a series is the one that you count as number twelve. ❏ *...the twelfth anniversary of the April revolution.* **2** FRACTION A **twelfth** is one of twelve equal parts of something. ❏ *She is entitled to a twelfth of the cash.*

twelve ♦♦♦ /twɛlv/ (**twelves**) NUM **Twelve** is the number 12.

twen|ti|eth ♦♦◇ /twɛntiəθ/ (**twentieths**) **1** ORD The **twentieth** item in a series is the one that you count as number twenty. ❏ *...the twentieth century.* **2** FRACTION A **twentieth** is one of twenty equal parts of something. ❏ *A few twentieths of a gram can be critical.*

twen|ty ♦♦♦ /twɛnti/ (**twenties**) **1** NUM **Twenty** is the number 20. **2** N-PLURAL When you talk about the **twenties**, you are referring to numbers between 20 and 29. For example, if you are **in** your **twenties**, you are aged between 20 and 29. If the temperature is **in the twenties**, the temperature is between 20 and 29 degrees. ❏ *They're both in their twenties and both married with children of their own.* **3** N-PLURAL **The twenties** is the decade between 1920 and 1929. ❏ *It was written in the Twenties, but it still really stands out.*

24-7 /twɛntifɔːrsɛvən/ also **twenty-four seven** ADV [ADV after v] If something happens **24-7**, it happens all the time without ever stopping. **24-7** means twenty-four hours a day, seven days a week. [mainly AM, INFORMAL] ❏ *I feel like sleeping 24-7.* • ADJ [ADJ n] **24-7** is also an adjective. ❏ *Now it is a 24-7 radio station that generates $30 million a year in advertising revenue.*

twerk /twɜːrk/ (**twerks**, **twerking**, **twerked**) VERB If someone **twerks**, they dance by bending their knees, sticking their buttocks out and moving or shaking them quickly. ❏ *...a new type of exercise class that promised to teach people to twerk.* • **twerk|ing** N-UNCOUNT ❏ *Her twerking on TV caused a sensation.*

twerp /twɜːrp/ (**twerps**) N-COUNT If you call someone a **twerp**, you are insulting them and saying that they are silly or stupid. [INFORMAL, OFFENSIVE, DISAPPROVAL]

twice ♦♦♦ /twaɪs/ **1** ADV If something happens **twice**, it happens two times, or there are two actions or events of the same kind. ❏ *He visited me twice that fall and called me on the telephone often.* ❏ *The government has twice declined to back the scheme.* **2** ADV [ADV as n] You use **twice** in expressions such as **twice a day** and **twice a week** to indicate that something happens two times in each day or week. ❏ *I phoned twice a day, leaving messages with his wife.* **3** ADV [ADV as adj/adv] If one thing is, for example, **twice as** big as or old as another, the first thing is double the size or age of the second. People sometimes say that one thing is **twice as** good or hard as another when they want to emphasize that the first thing is much better or harder than the second. ❏ *The figure of seventy-million dollars was twice as big as expected.* • PREDET [PREDET the n] **Twice** is also a predeterminer. ❏ *Unemployment here is twice the national average.* **4** PHRASE If you **think twice** about doing something, you consider it again and decide not to do it, or decide to do it differently. ❏ *From now on, think twice before saying stupid things.* **5** **once or twice** → see **once** **6** **twice over** → see **over** ②

twid|dle /twɪdəl/ (**twiddles**, **twiddling**, **twiddled**) V-T/V-I If you **twiddle** something, you twist it or turn it quickly with your fingers. ❏ *He twiddled a knob on the dashboard.* ❏ *She had sat there twiddling nervously with the clasp of her handbag.*

twig /twɪg/ (**twigs**) N-COUNT A **twig** is a very small thin branch that grows out from a main branch of a tree or bush. ❏ *There is the bird, sitting on a twig halfway up the tree.*

twi|light /twaɪlaɪt/ N-UNCOUNT **Twilight** is the time just before night when the daylight has almost gone but when it is not completely dark. ❏ *They returned at twilight.*

twill /twɪl/ N-UNCOUNT **Twill** is cloth, usually cotton, that is woven in a way which produces parallel sloping lines across it.

twin ♦◇◇ /twɪn/ (**twins**) **1** N-COUNT **Twins** are two people who were born at the same time from the same mother. ❏ *Sarah was looking after the twins.* ❏ *I think there are many positive aspects to being a twin.* **2** ADJ [ADJ n] **Twin** is used to describe a pair of things that look the same and are close together. ❏ *...the twin spires of the cathedral.* **3** ADJ [ADJ n] **Twin** is used to describe two things or ideas that are similar or connected in some way. ❏ *...the twin concepts of liberty and equality.*

twin bed (**twin beds**) N-COUNT [usu pl] **Twin beds** are two single beds in one bedroom.

twine /twaɪn/ (**twines**, **twining**, **twined**) **1** N-UNCOUNT **Twine** is strong string used especially in gardening and farming. **2** V-T/V-I If you **twine** one thing around another, or if one thing **twines** around another, the first thing is twisted or wound around the second. ❏ *He had twined his chubby arms around Vincent's neck.* ❏ *These strands of molecules twine around each other to form cable-like structures.*

twinge /twɪndʒ/ (**twinges**) **1** N-COUNT [with supp, usu N of n] A **twinge** is a sudden sharp feeling or emotion, usually an unpleasant one. ❏ *For a moment, Arnold felt a twinge of sympathy for Mr. Wilson.* **2** N-COUNT A **twinge** is a sudden sharp pain. ❏ *He felt a slight twinge in his damaged hamstring.*

twin|kle /twɪŋkəl/ (**twinkles**, **twinkling**, **twinkled**) **1** V-I If a star or a light **twinkles**, it shines with an unsteady light which rapidly and constantly changes from bright to faint. ❏ *At night, lights twinkle in distant cabins across the valleys.* **2** V-I If you say that someone's eyes **twinkle**, you mean that their eyes express good humor or amusement. ❏ *She saw her mother's eyes twinkle with amusement.* • N-SING **Twinkle** is also a noun. ❏ *A kindly twinkle came into her eyes.* **3** → See feature box at **light**

twin|set /twɪnsɛt/ (**twinsets**) also **twin set**, **twin-set** N-COUNT A **twinset** is a set of women's clothing, consisting of a cardigan and sweater of the same color.

twirl /twɜːrl/ (**twirls**, **twirling**, **twirled**) **1** V-T/V-I If you **twirl** something or if it **twirls**, it turns around and around with a smooth, fast movement. ❏ *Bonnie twirled her empty glass in her fingers.* **2** V-I If you **twirl**, you turn around and around quickly, for example, when you are dancing. ❏ *Several hundred people twirl around the ballroom dance floor.*

twist ♦◇◇ /twɪst/ (**twists**, **twisting**, **twisted**)
→ Please look at meanings **9** and **10** to see if the expression you are looking for is shown under another headword.
1 V-T If you **twist** something, you turn it to make a spiral shape, for example, by turning the two ends of it in opposite directions. ❏ *Her hands began to twist the handles of the bag she carried.* **2** V-T/V-I If you **twist** something, especially a part of your body, or if it **twists**, it moves into an unusual, uncomfortable, or bent position, for example, because of being hit or pushed, or because you are upset. ❏ *He twisted her arms behind her back and clipped a pair of handcuffs on her wrists.* ❏ *Sophia's face twisted in perplexity.* **3** V-T/V-I If you **twist** part of your body such as your head or your shoulders, you turn that part while keeping the rest of your body still. ❏ *She twisted her head sideways and looked toward the door.* ❏ *Susan twisted round in her seat until she could see Graham behind her.* **4** V-T If you **twist** a part of your body such as your ankle or wrist, you injure it by turning it too sharply, or in an unusual direction. ❏ *He fell and twisted his ankle.* **5** V-T If you **twist** something, you turn it so that it moves around in a circular direction. ❏ *She was staring down at her hands, twisting the ring on her finger.* • N-COUNT **Twist** is also a noun. ❏ *Just a twist of the handle is all it takes to wring out the mop.* **6** V-I If a road or river **twists**, it has a lot of sudden changes of direction in it. ❏ *The roads twist around hairpin bends.* • N-COUNT [usu pl] **Twist** is also a noun. ❏ *It allows the train to maintain a constant speed through the twists and turns of existing track.* **7** V-T If you say that someone **has twisted** something that you have said, you disapprove of them because they have repeated it in a way that changes its meaning, in order to harm you or benefit themselves. [DISAPPROVAL] ❏ *It's a shame the way the media can twist your words and misrepresent you.* **8** N-COUNT A **twist** in something is an unexpected and significant development. ❏ *The battle of the sexes also took a new*

twist. ◼9 **to twist someone's arm** → see **arm** ① ◼10 **to twist the knife in sb's wound** → see **knife**

twist|ed /twɪstɪd/ ADJ If you describe a person as **twisted**, you dislike them because you think they are bad or mentally unbalanced. [DISAPPROVAL] ❑ ...*a twisted man who shot at the president.*

twist|er /twɪstər/ (**twisters**) N-COUNT A **twister** is the same as a **tornado**. [AM, INFORMAL]

twisty /twɪsti/ (**twistier, twistiest**) ADJ A **twisty** road, track, or river has a lot of sharp bends and corners.

twitch /twɪtʃ/ (**twitches, twitching, twitched**) V-T/V-I If something, especially a part of your body, **twitches** or if you **twitch** it, it makes a little jumping movement. ❑ *When I stood up to her, her right cheek would begin to twitch.* • N-COUNT **Twitch** is also a noun. ❑ *He developed a nervous twitch and began to blink constantly.*

twitchy /twɪtʃi/ (**twitchier, twitchiest**) ADJ If you are **twitchy**, you are behaving in a nervous way that shows you feel anxious and cannot relax. [INFORMAL] ❑ *Afraid of bad publicity, the department had suddenly become very twitchy about journalists.*

twit|ter /twɪtər/ (**twitters, twittering, twittered**) ◼1 V-I When birds **twitter**, they make a lot of short high-pitched sounds. ❑ *There were birds twittering in the eucalyptus trees.* ❑ ...*a tree filled with twittering birds.* • N-UNCOUNT [usu N of n] **Twitter** is also a noun. ❑ *Naomi would waken to the twitter of birds.* ◼2 V-I If you say that someone **is twittering** about something, you mean that they are speaking about silly or unimportant things, usually somewhat fast or in a high-pitched voice. ❑ *They were twittering excitedly about their forthcoming holiday.*

two ✦✦✦ /tu/ (**twos**) ◼1 NUM **Two** is the number 2. ◼2 PHRASE If you say **it takes two** or **it takes two to tango**, you mean that a situation or argument involves two people and they are both therefore responsible for it. ❑ *Divorce is never the fault of one partner; it takes two.* ◼3 PHRASE If you **put two and two together**, you work out the truth about something for yourself, by using the information that is available to you. ❑ *Putting two and two together, I assume that this was the car he used.* ◼4 **to kill two birds with one stone** → see **bird**

two-bit ADJ [ADJ n] You use **two-bit** to describe someone or something that you have no respect for or that you think is inferior. [AM, INFORMAL, DISAPPROVAL] ❑ ...*some two-bit little dictator.* ❑ *That may be two-bit psychology, but it's the only explanation I have.*

two-dimensional also **two dimensional** ◼1 ADJ [usu ADJ n] A **two-dimensional** object or figure is flat rather than solid so that only its length and width can be measured. ❑ ...*new software, which generates both two-dimensional drawings and three-dimensional images.* ◼2 ADJ If you describe fictional characters as **two-dimensional**, you are critical of them because they are very simple and not realistic enough to be taken seriously. [DISAPPROVAL] ❑ *I found the characters very two-dimensional and dull.*

two-faced ADJ If you describe someone as **two-faced**, you are critical of them because they say they do or believe one thing when their behavior or words show that they do not do it or do not believe it. [DISAPPROVAL] ❑ *There's nothing two-faced about him.*

two|fold /tufoʊld/ also **two-fold** ADJ You can use **twofold** to introduce a topic that has two equally important parts. [FORMAL] ❑ *The reason for the interview is twofold: we want to find out what he can tell us, plus we also want to find out what condition he is in.*

two-handed ADJ A **two-handed** blow or catch is done using both hands.

two-horse ADJ [ADJ n] If you describe a contest as a **two-horse** race, you mean that only two of the people or things taking part have any chance of winning. ❑ *The election may not be the traditional two-horse race between the preferred Democrat and Republican party candidates.*

two-percent milk N-UNCOUNT **Two-percent milk** is milk from which half of the cream or fat has been removed. [AM]

in BRIT, use **semi-skimmed milk**

two-piece (**two-pieces**) also **two piece** ◼1 ADJ [ADJ n] You can use **two-piece** to describe something, especially a set of clothing, that is in two parts. ❑ ...*a two-piece bathing suit.* ◼2 N-COUNT A **two-piece** is a suit which consists of a jacket and a skirt or pair of pants. [BRIT, OLD-FASHIONED]

two|some /tusəm/ (**twosomes**) N-COUNT A **twosome** is a group of two people.

two-thirds also **two thirds** QUANT [QUANT of n] **Two-thirds** of something is an amount that is two out of three equal parts of it. ❑ *Two-thirds of householders in this state live in a mortgaged home.* • PRON **Two-thirds** is also a pronoun. ❑ *The United States and Russia hope to conclude a treaty to cut their nuclear arsenals by two-thirds.* • ADV [ADV adj/-ed] **Two-thirds** is also an adverb. ❑ *Do not fill the container more than two-thirds full.* ❑ *A second book has already been commissioned and is two-thirds finished.* • ADJ [ADJ n] **Two-thirds** is also an adjective. ❑ *A two thirds majority is needed to make changes.*

two-way ◼1 ADJ **Two-way** means moving or working in two opposite directions or allowing something to move or work in two opposite directions. ❑ *The bridge is now open to two-way traffic.* ◼2 ADJ [ADJ n] A **two-way** radio can send and receive signals. ❑ *Each squad has a two-way radio to stay in touch.*

ty|coon /taɪkun/ (**tycoons**) N-COUNT A **tycoon** is a person who is successful in business and so has become rich and powerful. ❑ ...*a self-made Irish-American property tycoon.*

tyke /taɪk/ (**tykes**) N-COUNT You can refer to a child, especially a naughty or playful one, as a **tyke** when you want to show affection for them. [INFORMAL, APPROVAL]

Ty|le|nol /taɪlənɒl/ (**Tylenols**) N-VAR [oft N n] **Tylenol** is a mild drug which reduces pain and fever. [AM, TRADEMARK] ❑ ...*a bottle of Tylenol.* ❑ *I took four Tylenol capsules.*

tym|pa|ni /tɪmpəni/ → see **timpani**

TYPE
① SORT OR KIND
② WRITING AND PRINTING

① **type** ✦✦◇ /taɪp/ (**types**) ◼1 N-COUNT A **type** of something is a group of those things that have particular features in common. ❑ ...*several types of lettuce.* ❑ *There are various types of the disease.* ◼2 N-COUNT If you refer to a particular thing or person as a **type** of something more general, you are considering that thing or person as an example of that more general group. ❑ *Have you done this type of work before?* ❑ *Rates of interest for this type of borrowing can be high.* ◼3 N-COUNT If you refer to a person as a particular **type**, you mean that they have that particular appearance, character, or type of behavior. ❑ *It's the first time I, a fair-skinned, freckly type, have sailed in the sun without burning.*

SYNONYMS
type
NOUN ① ◼1
kind: *I'm not the kind of person to get married.*
sort: *What sort of school did you go to?*
variety: *I'm always pleased to try out a new variety.*

② **type** ✦✦◇ /taɪp/ (**types, typing, typed**) ◼1 V-T/V-I If you **type** something, you use a typewriter or computer keyboard to write it. ❑ *I can type your essays for you.* ❑ *I had never really learned to type properly.* ◼2 N-UNCOUNT **Type** is printed text as it appears in a book or newspaper, or the small pieces of metal that are used to create this. ❑ *The correction had already been set in type.* ❑ *I can't read this small type.* ◼3 → see also **typing**

▶ **type in** also **type into** PHRASAL VERB If you **type** information **into** a computer or **type** it **in**, you press keys on the keyboard so that the computer stores or processes the information. ❑ *Officials type each passport number into a computer.* ❑ *You have to type in commands, such as "help" and "print."*

▶ **type up** PHRASAL VERB If you **type up** a text that has been written by hand, you produce a typed copy of it. ❑ *When the first draft was completed, Nichols typed it up.*

type|cast /taɪpkæst/ (**typecasts, typecasting**)

The form **typecast** is used in the present tense and is the past tense and past participle.

V-T [usu passive] If an actor **is typecast**, they play the same type of character in every play or movie that they are in. ❑ *I didn't want to be typecast and I think I've maintained a large variety* in the roles I've played. ◻ African-American actors are still often typecast as entertainers or criminals.

type|face /t<u>ei</u>pfeis/ (**typefaces**) N-COUNT In printing, a **typeface** is a set of alphabetical characters, numbers, and other characters that all have the same design. There are many different typefaces. ◻ ...the ubiquitous Times New Roman typeface.

type|script /t<u>ai</u>pskript/ (**typescripts**) N-VAR A **typescript** is a typed copy of an article or literary work.

type|set /t<u>ai</u>pset/ (**typesets, typesetting, typeset**) V-T [usu pass] When something written **is typeset**, it is arranged and prepared for printing either by hand or by the use of a computer. ◻ The newspaper was being typeset and printed. ◻ I design the layout and send it over, then they typeset it. • **type|set|ter** /t<u>ai</u>psetər/ (**typesetters**) N-COUNT ◻ For a number of years I worked as a typesetter. • **type|set|ting** /t<u>ai</u>pset<u>i</u>ŋ/ N-UNCOUNT ◻ There were errors in typesetting. ◻ ...computerized typesetting systems.

type|writ|er /t<u>ai</u>praitər/ (**typewriters**) N-COUNT A **typewriter** is a machine that was commonly used in the past and which has keys which are pressed in order to print letters, numbers, or other characters onto paper.

type|writ|ten /t<u>ai</u>prit³n/ ADJ A **typewritten** document has been typed on a typewriter or computer keyboard.

ty|phoid /t<u>ai</u>foid/ N-UNCOUNT **Typhoid** or **typhoid fever** is a serious infectious disease that produces fever and diarrhea and can cause death. It is spread by dirty water or food.

ty|phoon /taif<u>u</u>n/ (**typhoons**) N-COUNT A **typhoon** is a very violent tropical storm.

ty|phus /t<u>ai</u>fəs/ N-UNCOUNT **Typhus** is a serious infectious disease that produces spots on the skin, a high fever, and a severe headache.

typi|cal ✦✧✧ /t<u>i</u>pik³l/ ADJ You use **typical** to describe someone or something that shows the most usual characteristics of a particular type of person or thing, and is therefore a good example of that type. ◻ He is everyone's image of a typical cop. **2** ADJ If a particular action or feature is **typical** of someone or something, it shows their usual qualities or characteristics. ◻ This reluctance to move toward a democratic state is typical of totalitarian regimes. **3** ADJ If you say that something is **typical** of a person, situation, or thing, you are criticizing them or complaining about them and saying that they are just as bad or disappointing as you expected them to be. [FEELINGS] ◻ She threw her hands into the air. "That is just typical of you, isn't it?"

typi|cal|ly /t<u>i</u>pikli/ **1** ADV [ADV with cl/group] You use **typically** to say that something usually happens in the way that you are describing. ◻ It typically takes a day or two, depending on size. **2** ADV [ADV adj] You use **typically** to say that something shows all the most usual characteristics of a particular type of person or thing. ◻ Philip paced the floor, a typically nervous expectant father. **3** ADV You use **typically** to indicate that someone has behaved in the way that they normally do. ◻ Typically, the Norwegians were on the mountain two hours before anyone else.

typi|fy /t<u>i</u>pifai/ (**typifies, typifying, typified**) V-T If something or someone **typifies** a situation or type of thing or person, they have all the usual characteristics of it and are a typical example of it. ◻ These two buildings typify the rich extremes of local architecture.

typ|ing /t<u>ai</u>piŋ/ **1** N-UNCOUNT **Typing** is the work or activity of typing something by means of a typewriter or computer keyboard. ◻ I'm taking a typing class. **2** N-UNCOUNT **Typing** is the skill of using a typewriter or keyboard quickly and accurately. ◻ My typing is hideous.

typ|ist /t<u>ai</u>pist/ (**typists**) N-COUNT A **typist** is someone who works in an office typing letters and other documents.

ty|po /t<u>ai</u>pou/ (**typos**) N-COUNT A **typo** is a typographical error. [INFORMAL] ◻ It is now listed in the classifieds, with no typos or misprints.

ty|po|graphi|cal /taipəgr<u>æ</u>fik³l/ ADJ [ADJ n] **Typographical** relates to the way in which printed material is presented. ◻ Because of a typographical error, the town of Longridge was spelt as Longbridge.

ty|pog|ra|phy /taip<u>o</u>grəfi/ N-UNCOUNT **Typography** is the way in which written material is arranged and prepared for printing.

ty|pol|ogy /taip<u>o</u>lədʒi/ (**typologies**) N-COUNT A **typology** is a system for dividing things into different types, especially in science and the social sciences. [FORMAL]

ty|ran|ni|cal /tir<u>æ</u>nik³l/ **1** ADJ If you describe someone as **tyrannical**, you mean that they are severe or unfair toward the people that they have authority over. ◻ She grew up with a drunken mother and a tyrannical father. **2** ADJ If you describe a government or organization as **tyrannical**, you mean that it acts without considering the wishes of its people and treats them cruelly or unfairly. ◻ ...one of the world's most oppressive and tyrannical regimes.

tyr|an|nize /t<u>i</u>rənaiz/ (**tyrannizes, tyrannizing, tyrannized**)

in BRIT, also use **tyrannise**

V-T/V-I If you say that one person **tyrannizes** another, you mean that the first person uses their power over the second person in order to treat them very cruelly and unfairly. ◻ ...fathers who tyrannize their families. ◻ Armed groups use their power to tyrannize over civilians.

tyr|an|ny /t<u>i</u>rəni/ (**tyrannies**) **1** N-VAR A **tyranny** is a cruel, harsh, and unfair government in which a person or small group of people have power over everyone else. ◻ Self-expression and individuality are the greatest weapons against tyranny. **2** N-UNCOUNT If you describe someone's behavior and treatment of others that they have authority over as **tyranny**, you mean that they are severe with them or unfair to them. ◻ I'm the sole victim of Mother's tyranny.

ty|rant /t<u>ai</u>rənt/ (**tyrants**) N-COUNT You can use **tyrant** to refer to someone who treats the people they have authority over in a cruel and unfair way. ◻ ...households where the father was a tyrant.

tyre /t<u>ai</u>ər/ [mainly BRIT] → see **tire**

tyro /t<u>ai</u>rou/ (**tyros**) N-COUNT [oft N n] A **tyro** is a person who is just beginning to learn something or who has very little experience of something. [JOURNALISM] ◻ ...a tyro journalist.

Uu

U also **u** /yu/ (**U's, u's**) N-VAR **U** is the twenty-first letter of the English alphabet.

uber- /ubər-/ COMB IN N-COUNT; COMB IN ADJ **Uber-** combines with nouns and adjectives to form nouns and adjectives that refer to a great or extreme example of something. [JOURNALISM] ❑ *She became the uber-nerd of the tech world.* ❑ *McNally now owns a clutch of uberchic downtown celebrity hang-outs.*

ubiqui|tous /yubɪkwɪtəs/ ADJ If you describe something or someone as **ubiquitous**, you mean that they seem to be everywhere. [FORMAL] ❑ *Sugar is ubiquitous in the diet.*

ubiquity /yubɪkwɪti/ N-UNCOUNT [oft N of n] If you talk about the **ubiquity** of something, you mean that it seems to be everywhere. [FORMAL]

ud|der /ʌdər/ (**udders**) N-COUNT A cow's **udder** is the organ that hangs below its body and produces milk.

UFO /yu ɛf oʊ, yufoʊ/ (**UFOs**) N-COUNT A **UFO** is an object seen in the sky or landing on earth which cannot be identified and which is often believed to be from another planet. **UFO** is an abbreviation for 'unidentified flying object.' ❑ *There has been a surge of UFO sightings in Kansas.*

Ugan|dan /yugændən/ (**Ugandans**) **1** ADJ **Ugandan** means belonging or relating to Uganda or to its people or culture. **2** N-COUNT A **Ugandan** is a Ugandan citizen, or a person of Ugandan origin.

ugh EXCLAM **Ugh** is used in writing to represent the sound that people make if they think something is unpleasant, horrible, or disgusting. ❑ *Ugh – it was horrible.*

ugly /ʌgli/ (**uglier, ugliest**) **1** ADJ If you say that someone or something is **ugly**, you mean that they are very unattractive and unpleasant to look at. ❑ *...an ugly little hat.* • **ug|li|ness** N-UNCOUNT ❑ *Dekkeret found the landscape startling in its ugliness.* **2** ADJ If you refer to an event or situation as **ugly**, you mean that it is very unpleasant, usually because it involves violent or aggressive behavior. ❑ *There have been some ugly scenes.* ❑ *The confrontation turned ugly.* • **ug|li|ness** N-UNCOUNT ❑ *...the ugliness of sexual harassment.* **3 to rear its ugly head** → see **head** ③

Ugly Ameri|can (**Ugly Americans**) also **ugly American** N-COUNT An **Ugly American** is an American who travels to a foreign country and gives the United States a bad reputation by acting in an offensive way. [DISAPPROVAL] ❑ *The term "Ugly American" comes from people traveling with the attitude that people are, or should be, the same everywhere.*

ugly duck|ling (**ugly ducklings**) N-COUNT [usu sing] If you say that someone, especially a child, is an **ugly duckling**, you mean that they are unattractive or awkward now, but will probably develop into an attractive and successful person.

UGV / yu dʒi vi/ (**UGVs**) N-COUNT A **UGV** is a vehicle that does not need a driver but can be controlled remotely or can control itself. **UGV** is an abbreviation for 'unmanned ground vehicle.' ❑ *This UGV has already been deployed in place of troops.*

UHF /yu eɪtʃ ɛf/ N-UNCOUNT [oft n n] **UHF** is a range of radio waves which allows a radio or television receiver to produce a good quality of sound. **UHF** is an abbreviation for 'ultra-high frequency.' ❑ *...Boston UHF channels.*

uh huh ♦◊◊ also **uh-huh** CONVENTION **Uh huh** is used in writing to represent a sound that people make when they are agreeing with you, when they want to show that they understand what you are saying, or when they are answering 'yes' to a question. [INFORMAL] ❑ *"Did she?"—"Uh huh."*

U.K. ♦♦◊ /yu keɪ/ also **UK** N-PROPER [the n] The **U.K.** is England, Wales, Scotland, and Northern Ireland. **U.K.** is an abbreviation for **United Kingdom**.

uku|lele /yukəleɪli/ (**ukuleles**) also **ukelele** N-COUNT A **ukulele** is a small guitar with four strings.

ul|cer /ʌlsər/ (**ulcers**) N-COUNT An **ulcer** is a sore area on the outside or inside of your body which is very painful and may bleed or produce a poisonous substance. ❑ *In addition to headaches, you may develop stomach ulcers as well.*

ul|cer|at|ed /ʌlsəreɪtɪd/ ADJ If a part of someone's body is **ulcerated**, ulcers have developed on it. ❑ *...ulcerated mouths.*

ULEZ / yu el i zi/ (**ULEZs**) N-COUNT A **ULEZ** is an area, especially one in a big city, where most vehicles have to pay to enter and vehicles that produce a lot of pollution have to pay more. **ULEZ** is an abbreviation for 'ultra-low emission zone.'

ul|te|ri|or /ʌltɪəriər/ ADJ [ADJ n] If you say that someone has an **ulterior** motive for doing something, you believe that they have a hidden reason for doing it. ❑ *Sheila had an ulterior motive for trying to help Stan.*

ul|ti|mate ♦◊◊ /ʌltɪmɪt/ **1** ADJ [ADJ n] You use **ultimate** to describe the final result or aim of a long series of events. ❑ *He said it is still not possible to predict the ultimate outcome.* **2** ADJ [ADJ n] You use **ultimate** to describe the original source or cause of something. ❑ *Plants are the ultimate source of all foodstuffs.* **3** ADJ [ADJ n] You use **ultimate** to describe the most important or powerful thing of a particular kind. ❑ *My experience as player, coach and manager has prepared me for this ultimate challenge.* **4** ADJ [ADJ n] You use **ultimate** to describe the most extreme and unpleasant example of a particular thing. ❑ *Bringing back the death penalty would be the ultimate abuse of human rights.* ❑ *Treachery was the ultimate sin.* **5** ADJ [ADJ n] You use **ultimate** to describe the best possible example of a particular thing. ❑ *Experience the ultimate adventure!* **6** PHRASE **The ultimate in** something is the best or most advanced example of it. ❑ *Ballet is the ultimate in human movement.* ❑ *This hotel is the ultimate in luxury.*

SYNONYMS

ultimate
ADJ **1**
final: *Astronauts will make a final attempt today to rescue a communications satellite.*
eventual: *The eventual aim is reunification.*
last: *This is his last chance as Prime Minister.*

---

ul|ti|mate|ly ♦◊◊ /ʌltɪmɪtli/ **1** ADV **Ultimately** means finally, after a long and often complicated series of events. ❑ *Whatever the scientists ultimately conclude, all of their data will immediately be disputed.* **2** ADV [ADV with cl] You use **ultimately** to indicate that what you are saying is the most important point in a discussion. ❑ *Ultimately, Judge Lewin has the final say.*

SYNONYMS

ultimately
ADV
1
finally: *The word was finally given for us to get on board.*
eventually: *The flight eventually took off, six hours late.*
in the end: *I toyed with the idea of calling the police, but in the end, I didn't.*
2
fundamentally: *He can be very charming, but he is fundamentally a bully.*
essentially: *Essentially, vines and grapes need water, heat, and light.*
basically: *Battery charging systems remain basically the same as those in use half a century ago.*
primarily: *Overcrowding is primarily an urban problem.*

ul|ti|ma|tum /ˌʌltɪmeɪtəm/ (ultimatums) N-COUNT An **ultimatum** is a warning to someone that unless they act in a particular way, action will be taken against them. ◻ *They issued an ultimatum to the police to rid the area of racist attackers, or they will take the law into their own hands.*

PREFIX

ultra-
forms adjectives that refer to people and things that possess a quality to a very large degree. For example, an **ultralight** fabric is extremely light.

ultra|ma|rine /ˌʌltrəməriːn/ COLOR **Ultramarine** is used to describe things that are very bright blue in color. ◻ *...an ultramarine sky.*

ultra|son|ic /ˌʌltrəsɒnɪk/ ADJ [usu ADJ n] **Ultrasonic** sounds have very high frequencies, which human beings cannot hear.

ultra|sound /ˌʌltrəsaʊnd/ ◼ N-UNCOUNT **Ultrasound** is sound waves which travel at such a high frequency that they cannot be heard by humans. Ultrasound is used in medicine to get pictures of the inside of people's bodies. ◻ *I had an ultrasound scan to see how the pregnancy was progressing.* ◼ → See feature box at **birth**

ultra|vio|let /ˌʌltrəvaɪəlɪt/ ADJ **Ultraviolet** light or radiation is what causes your skin to become darker in color after you have been in sunlight. In large amounts ultraviolet light is harmful. ◻ *The sun's ultraviolet rays are responsible for both tanning and burning.*

ulu|late /ˈʌlyəleɪt, ˈyuːl-/ (ululates, ululating, ululated) V-I If someone **ululates**, they make quickly repeated loud sounds, often to express sorrow or happiness. [LITERARY] ◻ *In Ancient Arabia, a chorus of women would ululate on the battlefield.*

um **Um** is used in writing to represent a sound that people make when they are hesitating, usually while deciding what they want to say next. ◻ *She felt her face going red. "I'm sorry Rob, it's just that I'm, um, overwhelmed."*

um|ber /ˈʌmbər/ COLOR **Umber** is used to describe things that are yellowish or reddish brown in color. ◻ *...umber paint.*

um|bili|cal cord /ʌmbɪlɪkəl kɔrd/ (umbilical cords) N-COUNT [usu sing] The **umbilical cord** is the tube that connects an unborn baby to its mother, through which it receives oxygen and food.

um|brage /ˈʌmbrɪdʒ/ PHRASE If you say that a person **takes umbrage**, you mean that they are upset or offended by something that someone says or does to them, often without much reason. [FORMAL] ◻ *He takes umbrage against anyone who criticizes him.*

um|brel|la /ʌmbrɛlə/ (umbrellas) ◼ N-COUNT An **umbrella** is an object which you use to protect yourself from the rain or hot sun. It consists of a long stick with a folding frame covered in cloth. ◻ *Harry held an umbrella over Denise.* ◼ N-SING **Umbrella** is used to refer to a single group or description that includes a lot of different organizations or ideas. ◻ *The country's blood banks are under the umbrella of the American Red Cross.*

um|laut /ˈʊmlaʊt/ (umlauts) N-COUNT An **umlaut** is a symbol that is written over vowels in German and some other languages to indicate the way in which they should be pronounced. For example, the word 'für' has an umlaut over the 'u.'

ump /ʌmp/ (umps, umping, umped) N-COUNT An **ump** is the same as an **umpire**. [AM, INFORMAL] ◻ *...the home plate ump changed his call, saying Jedkins had stepped on the plate trying to bunt.* • V-I **Ump** is also a verb. ◻ *"I'll ump," said Jerry.*

um|pire /ˈʌmpaɪər/ (umpires, umpiring, umpired) ◼ N-COUNT An **umpire** is a person whose job is to make sure that a sports contest or game is played fairly and that the rules are not broken. ◻ *The umpire's decision is final.* ◼ V-T/V-I To **umpire** means to be the umpire in a sports contest or game. ◻ *He umpired baseball games.*

ump|teen /ˌʌmptiːn/ DET [DET pl-n] **Umpteen** can be used to refer to an extremely large number of things or people. [INFORMAL, EMPHASIS] ◻ *He was interrupted by applause umpteen times.*

ump|teenth /ˌʌmptiːnθ/ ORD You use **umpteenth** to indicate that an occasion, thing, or person happens or comes after many others. [INFORMAL, EMPHASIS] ◻ *He checked his watch for the umpteenth time.*

PREFIX

un-
can be added to some words to form words that have the opposite meaning. For example, if something is **unacceptable**, it is not acceptable.

U.N. ♦♦◇ /yuː ɛn/ also **UN** N-PROPER The **U.N.** is the same as the **United Nations**. ◻ *...a U.N. peacekeeping mission.*

un|abashed /ˌʌnəbæʃt/ ADJ If you describe someone as **unabashed**, you mean that they are not ashamed, embarrassed, or shy about something, especially when you think most people would be. ◻ *He seems unabashed by his recent defeat.*

un|abat|ed /ˌʌnəbeɪtɪd/ ADJ If something continues **unabated**, it continues without any reduction in intensity or amount. ◻ *The fighting has continued unabated for over 24 hours.*

un|able ♦◇ /ʌneɪbəl/ ADJ [v-link ADJ to-inf] If you are **unable** to do something, it is impossible for you to do it, for example because you do not have the necessary skill or knowledge, or because you do not have enough time or money. ◻ *The military may feel unable to hand over power to a civilian president next year.*

un|abridged /ˌʌnəbrɪdʒd/ ADJ An **unabridged** piece of writing, for example a book or article, is complete and not shortened in any way.

un|ac|cep|table /ˌʌnəksɛptəbəl/ ◼ ADJ If you describe something as **unacceptable**, you strongly disapprove of it or object to it and feel that it should not be allowed to continue. ◻ *It is totally unacceptable for children to swear.* ◼ → See feature box at **review**

un|ac|com|pa|nied /ˌʌnəkʌmpənid/ ◼ ADJ If someone is **unaccompanied**, they are alone. ◻ *Many of those unaccompanied children are orphans.* ◼ ADJ [ADJ n] **Unaccompanied** baggage or goods are being sent or transported separately from their owner. ◻ *Unaccompanied bags are either searched or removed.* ◼ ADJ [ADJ n, ADJ after v] An **unaccompanied** voice or instrument sings or plays alone, with no other instruments playing at the same time. ◻ *...an unaccompanied flute.*

un|ac|count|able /ˌʌnəkaʊntəbəl/ ◼ ADJ [usu ADJ n] Something that is **unaccountable** does not seem to have any sensible explanation. ◻ *For some unaccountable reason, it struck me as extremely funny.* • **un|ac|count|ably** /ˌʌnəkaʊntəbli/ ADV ◻ *And then, unaccountably, she giggled.* ◼ ADJ If you describe a person or organization as **unaccountable**, you are critical of them because they are not responsible to anyone for their actions, or do not feel they have to explain their actions to anyone. [DISAPPROVAL] ◻ *Economic policy should not be run by an unaccountable committee of governors of central banks.*

un|ac|count|ed for /ˌʌnəkaʊntɪd fɔr/ ADJ [v-link ADJ] If people or things are **unaccounted for**, you do not know where they are or what has happened to them. ◻ *5,000 American servicemen who fought in Korea are still unaccounted for.*

un|ac|cus|tomed /ˌʌnəkʌstəmd/ ◼ ADJ [v-link ADJ to n/-ing] If you are **unaccustomed to** something, you do not know it very well or have not experienced it very often. [WRITTEN] ◻ *They were unaccustomed to such military setbacks.* ◼ ADJ [ADJ n] If you describe someone's behavior or experiences as **unaccustomed**, you mean that they do not usually behave like this or have experiences of this kind. [WRITTEN] ◻ *He began to comfort me with such unaccustomed gentleness.*

un|ac|knowl|edged /ˌʌnæknɒlɪdʒd/ ◼ ADJ [usu ADJ n] If you describe something or someone as **unacknowledged**, you mean that people ignore their existence or presence, or are not aware of it. ◻ *Unresolved or unacknowledged fears can trigger sleepwalking.* ◼ ADJ If you describe something or someone as **unacknowledged**, you mean that their existence or importance is not recognized officially or publicly. ◻ *This tradition goes totally unacknowledged in official guidebooks.*

un|ac|quaint|ed /ˌʌnəkweɪntɪd/ ADJ [v-link ADJ with n] If you are **unacquainted with** something, you do not know about it or do not have any experience of it. ◻ *I was then totally unacquainted with his poems.*

un|adorned /ˌʌnədɔrnd/ ADJ Something that is **unadorned** is plain, rather than having decoration on it. ◻ *The room is typically simple and unadorned, with white walls and a tiled floor.*

un|adul|ter|at|ed /ʌnədʌltəreɪtɪd/ **1** ADJ Something that is **unadulterated** is completely pure and has had nothing added to it. ❑ *Organic food is unadulterated food produced without artificial chemicals or pesticides.* **2** ADJ [ADJ n] You can also use **unadulterated** to emphasize a particular quality, often a bad quality. [EMPHASIS] ❑ *It was pure, unadulterated hell.*

un|af|fect|ed /ʌnəfɛktɪd/ **1** ADJ [v-link ADJ] If someone or something is **unaffected** by an event or occurrence, they are not changed by it in any way. ❑ *She seemed totally unaffected by what she'd drunk.* **2** ADJ If you describe someone as **unaffected**, you mean that they are natural and genuine in their behavior, and do not act as though they are more important than other people. [APPROVAL] ❑ *...this unaffected, charming couple.*

un|afraid /ʌnəfreɪd/ ADJ If you are **unafraid** to do something, you are confident and not at all nervous about doing it. ❑ *He is a man with a reputation for being tough and unafraid of unpopular decisions.*

un|aid|ed /ʌneɪdɪd/ ADJ If you do something **unaided**, you do it without help from anyone or anything else. ❑ *There have been at least thirteen previous attempts to reach the North Pole unaided.*

un|al|ien|able /ʌneɪlyənəbəl/ → see **inalienable**

un|al|loyed /ʌnəlɔɪd/ ADJ [usu ADJ n] If you describe a feeling such as happiness or relief as **unalloyed**, you are emphasizing that it is a strong feeling and no other feeling is involved. [LITERARY, EMPHASIS] ❑ *...an occasion of unalloyed joy.*

un|al|ter|able /ʌnɔːltərəbəl/ ADJ [usu ADJ n] Something that is **unalterable** cannot be changed. ❑ *...an unalterable fact of life.*

un|al|tered /ʌnɔːltərd/ ADJ Something that remains **unaltered** has not changed or been changed. ❑ *The rest of the apartment had fortunately remained unaltered since that time.*

un|am|bigu|ous /ʌnæmbɪgyuəs/ ADJ If you describe a message or comment as **unambiguous**, you mean that it is clear and cannot be understood wrongly. ❑ *...an election result that sent the party an unambiguous message.* • **un|am|bigu|ous|ly** ADV ❑ *The president said that she had stated the U.S. position very clearly and unambiguously.*

un|am|bi|tious /ʌnæmbɪʃəs/ **1** ADJ An **unambitious** person is not particularly interested in improving their position in life or in being successful, rich, or powerful. **2** ADJ An **unambitious** idea or plan is not very complicated, risky, or new, and is easy to carry out successfully.

un-Ameri|can /ʌnəmɛrɪkən/ **1** ADJ If you describe someone or something as **un-American**, you think that they are not in accordance with American ideals and customs. [DISAPPROVAL] ❑ *He used the same cinematographer, Owen Roizman, to create a dark, intense atmosphere which was very un-American at the time.* **2** ADJ **Un-American** activities are political activities that are considered to be against the interests of the U.S. ❑ *They were called before the House Un-American Activities Committee and blacklisted.*

una|nim|ity /yuːnənɪmɪti/ N-UNCOUNT When there is **unanimity** among a group of people, they all agree about something or all vote for the same thing. ❑ *All decisions would require unanimity.*

unani|mous /yuːnænɪməs/ **1** ADJ When a group of people are **unanimous**, they all agree about something or all vote for the same thing. ❑ *Editors were unanimous in their condemnation of the proposals.* • **unani|mous|ly** ADV [ADV with v] ❑ *The board unanimously approved the project last week.* **2** ADJ A **unanimous** vote, decision, or agreement is one in which all the people involved agree. ❑ *Their decision was unanimous.*

un|an|nounced /ʌnənaʊnst/ ADJ If someone arrives or does something **unannounced**, they do it unexpectedly and without anyone having been told about it beforehand. ❑ *He had just arrived unannounced from South America.*

un|an|swer|able /ʌnænsərəbəl/ **1** ADJ If you describe a question as **unanswerable**, you mean that it has no possible answer or that a particular person cannot possibly answer it. ❑ *They would ask their mother unanswerable questions.* **2** ADJ If you describe a case or argument as **unanswerable**, you think that it is obviously true or correct and that nobody could disagree with it. ❑ *The argument for recruiting McGregor was unanswerable.*

un|an|swered /ʌnænsərd/ ADJ Something such as a question or letter that is **unanswered** has not been answered. ❑ *Some of the most important questions remain unanswered.* ❑ *The report of the judges leaves a lot of unanswered questions.*

un|ap|peal|ing /ʌnəpiːlɪŋ/ ADJ If you describe someone or something as **unappealing**, you find them unpleasant and unattractive. ❑ *The hat is an unappealing shade of green.*

un|ap|pe|tiz|ing /ʌnæpɪtaɪzɪŋ/

in BRIT, also use **unappetising**

ADJ If you describe food as **unappetizing**, you think it will be unpleasant to eat because of its appearance. ❑ *...cold and unappetizing chicken.*

un|ap|proach|able /ʌnəproʊtʃəbəl/ ADJ If you describe someone as **unapproachable**, you mean that they seem to be difficult to talk to and not very friendly.

un|ar|gu|able /ʌnɑːrgyuəbəl/ ADJ If you describe a statement or opinion as **unarguable**, you think that it is obviously true or correct and that nobody could disagree with it. ❑ *He is making the unarguable point that our desires and preferences have a social component.* • **un|ar|gu|ably** /ʌnɑːrgyuəbli/ ADV ❑ *He is unarguably an outstanding man.*

un|armed /ʌnɑːrmd/ ADJ If a person or vehicle is **unarmed**, they are not carrying any weapons. ❑ *The soldiers concerned were unarmed at the time.* • ADV [ADV after v] **Unarmed** is also an adverb. ❑ *He says he walks inside the prison without guards, unarmed.*

un|ashamed /ʌnəʃeɪmd/ ADJ If you describe someone's behavior or attitude as **unashamed**, you mean that they are open and honest about things that other people might find embarrassing or shocking. ❑ *I grinned at him in unashamed delight.* • **un|asham|ed|ly** /ʌnəʃeɪmɪdli/ ADV ❑ *He was unashamedly proud of his working-class roots*

un|asked /ʌnæskt/ **1** ADJ An **unasked** question is one that has not been asked, although people are wondering what the answer is. ❑ *She was undernourished, an observation that prompted yet another unasked question.* **2** ADJ [ADJ after v] If someone says or does something **unasked**, they say or do it without being asked to do it. ❑ *His advice, offered to her unasked, was to stay home and make the best of things.*

un|as|sail|able /ʌnəseɪləbəl/ ADJ If you describe something or someone as **unassailable**, you mean that nothing can alter, destroy, or challenge them. ❑ *Our seemingly unassailable lead in specialty manufacturing has dwindled.*

un|as|sist|ed /ʌnəsɪstɪd/ ADJ [ADJ after v, ADJ n] If you do something **unassisted**, you do it on your own and no one helps you. ❑ *At other times, he'd force her to walk totally unassisted.*

un|as|sum|ing /ʌnəsuːmɪŋ/ ADJ If you describe a person or their behavior as **unassuming**, you approve of them because they are quiet and do not try to appear important. [APPROVAL] ❑ *He's a man of few words, very polite and unassuming.*

un|at|tached /ʌnətætʃt/ ADJ Someone who is **unattached** is not married or does not have a girlfriend or boyfriend. ❑ *I knew only two or three unattached men.*

un|at|tain|able /ʌnəteɪnəbəl/ ADJ If you say that something is **unattainable**, you mean that it cannot be achieved or is not available. ❑ *There are those who argue that true independent advice is unattainable.*

un|at|tend|ed /ʌnətɛndɪd/ ADJ When people or things are left **unattended**, they are not being watched or taken care of. ❑ *Never leave young children unattended near any pool or water tank.* ❑ *An unattended backpack was found in a garbage pail.*

un|at|trac|tive /ʌnətræktɪv/ **1** ADJ **Unattractive** people and things are unpleasant in appearance. ❑ *I felt lonely and unattractive.* ❑ *...an unattractive shade of orange.* **2** ADJ If you describe something as **unattractive**, you mean that people do not like it and do not want to be involved with it. ❑ *The market is still unattractive to many insurers.*

un|author|ized /ʌnɔːθəraɪzd/

in BRIT, also use **unauthorised**

ADJ If something is **unauthorized**, it has been produced or is happening without official permission. ❑ *...a new unauthorized biography of the Russian president.* ❑ *It has also been made quite clear that the trip was unauthorized.*

un|avail|able /ʌnəveɪləbəl/ ADJ When things or people are **unavailable**, you cannot obtain them, meet them, or talk to them. ☐ *Mr. Hicks is out of the country and so unavailable for comment.*

un|avail|ing /ʌnəveɪlɪŋ/ ADJ An **unavailing** attempt to do something does not succeed. ☐ *Efforts to reach the people proved unavailing.*

un|avoid|able /ʌnəvɔɪdəbəl/ ADJ If something is **unavoidable**, it cannot be avoided or prevented. ☐ *Managers said the job losses were unavoidable.*

un|aware /ʌnəweər/ ADJ [v-link ADJ] If you are **unaware** of something, you do not know about it. ☐ *Many people are unaware of just how much food and drink they consume.*

un|awares /ʌnəweərz/ PHRASE If something **catches** you **unawares** or **takes** you **unawares**, it happens when you are not expecting it. ☐ *Investors and currency dealers were caught completely unawares by the bank's action.*

un|bal|ance /ʌnbæləns/ (**unbalances, unbalancing, unbalanced**) **1** V-T If something **unbalances** a relationship, system, or group, it disturbs or upsets it so that it is no longer successful or functioning properly. ☐ *Tax cuts may unbalance the budget.* **2** V-T To **unbalance** something means to make it unsteady and likely to tip over. ☐ *The driver said the load may have shifted and unbalanced the truck.*

un|bal|anced /ʌnbælənst/ **1** ADJ If you describe someone as **unbalanced**, you mean that they appear disturbed and upset or they are behaving in a strange way. ☐ *I knew how unbalanced Paula had been since my uncle Peter died.* **2** ADJ If you describe something such as a report or argument as **unbalanced**, you think that it is unfair or inaccurate because it emphasizes some things and ignores others. ☐ *UN officials argued that the report was unbalanced.*

un|bear|able /ʌnbeərəbəl/ ADJ If you describe something as **unbearable**, you mean that it is so unpleasant, painful, or upsetting that you feel unable to accept it or deal with it. ☐ *War has made life almost unbearable for the civilians remaining in the capital.* • **un|bear|ably** /ʌnbeərəbli/ ADV ☐ *By the evening it had become unbearably hot.*

un|beat|able /ʌnbiːtəbəl/ **1** ADJ If you describe something as **unbeatable**, you mean that it is the best thing of its kind. [EMPHASIS] ☐ *These resorts remain unbeatable in terms of price.* **2** ADJ In a game or competition, if you describe a person or team as **unbeatable**, you mean that they win so often, or perform so well that they are unlikely to be beaten by anyone. ☐ *With two more days of competition to go China is in an unbeatable position.*

un|beat|en /ʌnbiːtən/ ADJ In sports, if a person or their performance is **unbeaten**, nobody else has performed well enough to beat them. ☐ *He's unbeaten in 20 fights.*

un|be|com|ing /ʌnbɪkʌmɪŋ/ **1** ADJ If you describe things such as clothes as **unbecoming**, you mean that they look unattractive. [OLD-FASHIONED] **2** ADJ If you describe a person's behavior or remarks as **unbecoming**, you mean that they are shocking and unsuitable for that person. [FORMAL] ☐ *Austin displayed conduct unbecoming of an officer and a gentleman.*

un|be|knownst /ʌnbɪnoʊnst/

The form **unbeknown** /ʌnbɪnoʊn/ is also used,

PHRASE If something happens **unbeknownst to** you or **unbeknown to** you, you do not know about it. ☐ *I am appalled that children can mount up debts unbeknownst to their parents.* ☐ *Unbeknownst to her father, she began taking dancing lessons.*

un|be|liev|able /ʌnbɪliːvəbəl/ **1** ADJ If you say that something is **unbelievable**, you are emphasizing that it is very good, impressive, intense, or extreme. [EMPHASIS] ☐ *His guitar solos are just unbelievable.* ☐ *The pressure they put us under was unbelievable.* • **un|be|liev|ably** /ʌnbɪliːvəbli/ ADV [ADV with cl/ group] ☐ *It was unbelievably dramatic as lightning crackled all around the van.* ☐ *Our car was still going unbelievably well.* **2** ADJ You can use **unbelievable** to emphasize that you think something is very bad or shocking. [EMPHASIS] ☐ *I find it unbelievable that people can accept this sort of behavior.* • **un|be|liev|ably** ADV [ADV with cl/group] ☐ *What you did was unbelievably stupid.* **3** ADJ If an idea or statement is **unbelievable**, it seems so unlikely to be true that you cannot believe it. ☐ *I still find this story both fascinating and unbelievable.* • **un|be|liev|ably** ADV [ADV with cl/group] ☐ *Lainey was, unbelievably, pregnant again.*

un|be|liev|er /ʌnbɪliːvər/ (**unbelievers**) N-COUNT People who do not believe in a particular religion are sometimes referred to as **unbelievers**.

un|be|liev|ing /ʌnbɪliːvɪŋ/ ADJ If you describe someone as **unbelieving**, you mean that they do not believe something that they have been told. ☐ *He looked at me with unbelieving eyes.*

un|bend /ʌnbend/ (**unbends, unbending, unbent**) V-I If someone **unbends**, their attitude becomes less strict than it was. ☐ *In her dying days the old queen unbent a little.*

un|bend|ing /ʌnbendɪŋ/ ADJ If you describe a person or their behavior as **unbending**, you mean that they have very strict beliefs and attitudes, which they are unwilling to change. ☐ *He was rigid and unbending.*

un|bi|ased /ʌnbaɪəst/ also **unbiassed** ADJ If you describe someone or something as **unbiased**, you mean they are fair and not likely to support one particular person or group involved in something. ☐ *There is no clear and unbiased information available for consumers.*

un|bid|den /ʌnbɪdən/ ADJ If something happens **unbidden**, it happens without you expecting or wanting it to happen. [LITERARY] ☐ *The name came unbidden to Eric's mind – Albert Wong.*

un|bind /ʌnbaɪnd/ (**unbinds, unbinding, unbound**) V-T If you **unbind** something or someone, you take off a piece of cloth, string, or rope that has been tied around them. ☐ *She unbound her hair and let it flow loose in the wind.*

un|blem|ished /ʌnblemɪʃt/ **1** ADJ [usu ADJ n] If you describe something such as someone's record, reputation, or character as **unblemished**, you mean it has not been harmed or spoiled. ☐ *...Lee's unblemished reputation as a man of honor and principle.* **2** ADJ [usu ADJ n] If you describe something as **unblemished**, you mean that it has no marks or holes on its surface. ☐ *Be sure to select firm, unblemished fruit.*

un|blink|ing /ʌnblɪŋkɪŋ/ ADJ If you describe someone's eyes or expression as **unblinking**, you mean that they are looking steadily at something without blinking. [LITERARY] ☐ *He stared into Leo's unblinking eyes.* • **un|blink|ing|ly** ADV [usu ADV after v] ☐ *She looked at him unblinkingly.*

un|born /ʌnbɔːrn/ ADJ An **unborn** child has not yet been born and is still inside its mother's uterus. ☐ *...her unborn baby.* • N-PLURAL **The unborn** are children who are not born yet. ☐ *...a law that protects the lives of pregnant women and the unborn.*

un|bound /ʌnbaʊnd/ **Unbound** is the past tense and past participle of **unbind**.

un|bound|ed /ʌnbaʊndɪd/ ADJ If you describe something as **unbounded**, you mean that it has, or seems to have, no limits. ☐ *He was a strong leader with unbounded optimism.*

un|break|able /ʌnbreɪkəbəl/ **1** ADJ **Unbreakable** objects cannot be broken, usually because they are made of a very strong material. ☐ *Tableware for outdoor use should ideally be unbreakable.* **2** ADJ An **unbreakable** rule or limit must be obeyed. ☐ *One unbreakable rule in our school is that no child can be tested without written parental permission.*

un|bridge|able /ʌnbrɪdʒəbəl/ ADJ An **unbridgeable** gap or divide between two sides in an argument is so great that the two sides seem unlikely ever to agree. [JOURNALISM] ☐ *...the so-called unbridgeable gap between the world of humans and that of chimpanzees.*

un|bri|dled /ʌnbraɪdəld/ ADJ [usu ADJ n] If you describe behavior or feelings as **unbridled**, you mean that they are not controlled or limited in any way. ☐ *...a tale of lust and unbridled passion.*

un|bro|ken /ʌnbroʊkən/ ADJ If something is **unbroken**, it is continuous or complete and has not been interrupted or broken. ☐ *...an unbroken string of victories.* ☐ *We've had ten days of almost unbroken sunshine.*

un|buck|le /ʌnbʌkəl/ (**unbuckles, unbuckling, unbuckled**) V-T If you **unbuckle** something such as a belt or a shoe, you undo the buckle fastening it. ☐ *He unbuckled his seat belt.*

un|bur|den /ʌnbɜːrdən/ (**unburdens, unburdening, unburdened**) V-T If you **unburden** yourself or your problems to someone, you tell them about something which you have been secretly worrying about. ❏ *He listened to his parents unburden themselves in therapy.*

un|but|ton /ʌnbʌtᵊn/ (**unbuttons, unbuttoning, unbuttoned**) V-T If you **unbutton** an item of clothing, you undo the buttons fastening it. ❏ *She had begun to unbutton her blouse.*

un|called for /ʌnkɔld fɔr/ ADJ If you describe a remark or criticism as **uncalled for**, you mean that it should not have been made, because it was unkind or unfair. ❏ *I'm sorry. That was uncalled for.*

un|can|ny /ʌnkæni/ (**uncannier, uncanniest**) ADJ If you describe something as **uncanny**, you mean that it is strange and difficult to explain. ❏ *She bears an uncanny resemblance to the new president.* • **un|can|ni|ly** /ʌnkænɪli/ ADV ❏ *They have uncannily similar voices.*

un|cared for /ʌnkɛərd fɔr/ ADJ [usu v-link ADJ] If you describe people or animals as **uncared for**, you mean that they have not been taken care of properly and as a result are hungry, dirty, or ill. ❏ *...people who feel unwanted, unloved, and uncared for.*

un|caring /ʌnkɛərɪŋ/ ADJ If you describe someone as **uncaring**, you are critical of them for not caring about other people, especially people who are in a bad situation. [DISAPPROVAL] ❏ *It portrays him as cold and uncaring.*

un|ceas|ing /ʌnsisɪŋ/ ADJ [usu ADJ n] If you describe something as **unceasing**, you are emphasizing that it continues without stopping. [EMPHASIS] ❏ *...his unceasing labors.* • **un|ceas|ing|ly** ADV [ADV with v] ❏ *Paul talked unceasingly from dawn to dusk.*

un|cer|emo|ni|ous|ly /ʌnsɛrɪmoʊniəsli/ ADV [ADV with v] If someone or something is removed, left, or put somewhere **unceremoniously**, this is done in a sudden or rude way that shows they are not thought to be important. ❏ *She was unceremoniously dumped to be replaced by a leader who could win the election.*

un|cer|tain /ʌnsɜrtᵊn/ **1** ADJ If you are **uncertain** about something, you do not know what you should do, what is going to happen, or what the truth is about something. ❏ *He was uncertain about his brother's intentions.* ❏ *They were uncertain of the total value of the transaction.* • **un|cer|tain|ly** ADV ❏ *He entered the hallway and stood uncertainly.* **2** ADJ If something is **uncertain**, it is not known or definite. ❏ *How much practical help they can give us is uncertain.* ❏ *It's uncertain whether they will accept the plan.* **3** PHRASE If you say that someone tells a person something **in no uncertain terms**, you are emphasizing that they say it strongly and clearly so that there is no doubt about what they mean. [EMPHASIS] ❏ *She told him in no uncertain terms to go away.*

un|cer|tain|ty /ʌnsɜrtᵊnti/ (**uncertainties**) N-VAR **Uncertainty** is a state of doubt about the future or about what is the right thing to do. ❏ *...a period of political uncertainty.*

un|chal|lenged /ʌntʃælɪndʒd/ **1** ADJ When something goes **unchallenged** or is **unchallenged**, people accept it without asking questions about whether it is right or wrong. ❏ *These views have not gone unchallenged.* ❏ *His integrity was unchallenged.* **2** ADJ If you say that someone's position of authority is **unchallenged**, you mean that it is strong and no one tries to replace them. ❏ *He is the unchallenged leader of the chess club.*

un|change|able /ʌntʃeɪndʒəbᵊl/ ADJ Something that is **unchangeable** cannot be changed at all. ❏ *The doctrine is unchangeable.*

un|changed /ʌntʃeɪndʒd/ ADJ If something is **unchanged**, it has stayed the same for a particular period of time. ❏ *For many years prices have remained virtually unchanged.*

un|chang|ing /ʌntʃeɪndʒɪŋ/ ADJ Something that is **unchanging** always stays the same. ❏ *...eternal and unchanging truths.*

un|char|ac|ter|is|tic /ʌnkærɪktərɪstɪk/ ADJ If you describe something as **uncharacteristic** of someone, you mean that it is not typical of them. ❏ *It was uncharacteristic of her father to disappear like this.* • **un|char|ac|ter|is|ti|cal|ly** /ʌnkærɪktərɪstɪkli/ ADV ❏ *Owen has been uncharacteristically silent.*

un|chari|table /ʌntʃærɪtəbᵊl/ ADJ If you describe someone's remarks, thoughts, or behavior as **uncharitable**, you think they are being unkind or unfair to someone. ❏ *This was an uncharitable assessment of the reasons for the failure.*

un|chart|ed /ʌntʃɑrtɪd/ ADJ [usu ADJ n] If you describe a situation, experience, or activity as **uncharted** territory or waters, you mean that it is new or unfamiliar. ❏ *Carter's fourth album definitely moves into uncharted territory.*

un|checked /ʌntʃɛkt/ ADJ If something harmful or undesirable is left **unchecked**, nobody controls it or prevents it from growing or developing. ❏ *If left unchecked, weeds will flourish.* ❏ *...a world in which brutality and lawlessness are allowed to go unchecked.*

un|civi|lized /ʌnsɪvɪlaɪzd/

in BRIT, also use **uncivilised**

1 ADJ If you describe someone's behavior as **uncivilized**, you find it unacceptable, for example because it is very cruel or very rude. [DISAPPROVAL] ❏ *I think any sport involving harm to animals is barbaric and uncivilized.* **2** → See feature box at **polite**

un|claimed /ʌnkleɪmd/ ADJ If something is **unclaimed**, nobody has claimed it or said that it belongs to them. ❏ *Her luggage remained unclaimed at departures.*

un|clas|si|fied /ʌnklæsɪfaɪd/ ADJ If information or a document is **unclassified**, it is not secret and is available to the general public.

un|cle ♦♦◊ /ʌŋkᵊl/ (**uncles**) N-FAMILY; N-TITLE Someone's **uncle** is the brother of their mother or father, or the husband of their aunt. ❏ *My uncle was the mayor of Memphis.* ❏ *An email from Uncle Fred arrived.*

un|clean /ʌnklin/ **1** ADJ Something that is **unclean** is dirty and likely to cause disease. ❏ *...the Western attitude to insects as being dirty and unclean.* **2** ADJ If you describe someone or something as **unclean**, you consider them to be spiritually or morally bad. ❏ *They felt as though they had done something discreditable and unclean.*

un|clear /ʌnklɪər/ **1** ADJ If something is **unclear**, it is not known or not certain. ❏ *It is unclear how much popular support they have among the island's population.* ❏ *Just what the soldier was doing there is unclear.* **2** ADJ [v-link ADJ] If you are **unclear** about something, you do not understand it well or are not sure about it. ❏ *He is still unclear about his own future.*

Uncle Sam /ʌŋkᵊl sæm/ N-PROPER Some people refer to the United States of America or its government as **Uncle Sam**. [JOURNALISM] ❏ *They are ready to defend themselves against Uncle Sam's imperialist policies.*

Uncle Tom /ʌŋkᵊl tɒm/ (**Uncle Toms**) N-COUNT In the past, some Black people used **Uncle Tom** to refer to a Black man when they disapproved of him because he was too respectful or friendly toward White people. [OFFENSIVE, DISAPPROVAL] ❏ *For Blacks to compromise means they risk being called Uncle Toms by their co-workers.*

un|clothed /ʌnkloʊðd/ ADJ If someone is **unclothed**, they are not wearing any clothes. [FORMAL] ❏ *He learned how to draw the unclothed human frame.*

un|clut|tered /ʌnklʌtərd/ ADJ If you describe something as **uncluttered**, you mean that it is simple and does not contain or consist of a lot of unnecessary things. ❏ *If you keep a room uncluttered it makes it seem lighter and bigger.*

un|coil /ʌnkɔɪl/ (**uncoils, uncoiling, uncoiled**) V-T/V-I If something **uncoils** or if you **uncoil** it, it becomes straight after it has been wound or curled up. If someone who is curled up **uncoils**, they move so that their body becomes straight. ❏ *He uncoiled the hose and gave them a thorough drenching.*

un|combed /ʌnkoʊmd/ ADJ If someone's hair is **uncombed**, it is messy because it has not been brushed or combed.

un|com|fort|able /ʌnkʌmftəbᵊl, -kʌmfərtə-/ **1** ADJ If you are **uncomfortable**, you are slightly worried or embarrassed, and not relaxed and confident. ❏ *The request for money made them feel uncomfortable.* ❏ *If you are uncomfortable with your therapist, you must discuss it.* • **un|com|fort|ably** /ʌnkʌmftəbli, -kʌmfərtə-/ ADV ❏ *Sandy leaned across the table, his face uncomfortably close to Brad's.* ❏ *I became uncomfortably aware that the people at the next table were watching me.* **2** ADJ Something that is **uncomfortable** makes you feel slight pain or physical discomfort when you experience it or use it. ❏ *Wigs are hot and uncomfortable to wear* constantly. ❏ *The ride back to the center of the town was hot and uncomfortable.* • **un|com|fort|ably** ADV [ADV adj] ❏ *The water was uncomfortably cold.* **3** ADJ If you are **uncomfortable**, you are not physically content and relaxed, and feel slight pain or discomfort. ❏ *I sometimes feel uncomfortable after eating in the evening.* • **un|com|fort|ably** ADV ❏ *He felt uncomfortably hot.*

un|com|mit|ted /ʌnkəmɪtɪd/ **1** ADJ If you are **uncommitted**, you have not yet decided to support a particular idea, belief, group, or person, or you are unwilling to show your support. ❏ *The allegiance of uncommitted voters will be crucial.* ❏ *I was still uncommitted to the venture when we reached Kanpur.* • N-PLURAL [the N] **The uncommitted** are people who are uncommitted. ❏ *It was the uncommitted that the candidates needed to reach.* **2** ADJ If resources are **uncommitted**, it has not yet been decided what to use them for. ❏ *...$32.3m of uncommitted loans.*

un|com|mon /ʌnkɒmən/ ADJ If you describe something as **uncommon**, you mean that it does not happen often or is not often seen. ❏ *Fortunately, cancer of the breast in young women is uncommon.*

un|com|mu|ni|ca|tive /ʌnkəmyuːnɪkeɪtɪv, -kətɪv/ ADJ If you describe someone as **uncommunicative**, you are critical of them because they do not talk to other people very much and are unwilling to express opinions or give information. [DISAPPROVAL] ❏ *My daughter is very difficult, uncommunicative and moody.*

un|com|plain|ing /ʌnkəmpleɪnɪŋ/ ADJ If you describe someone as **uncomplaining**, you approve of them because they do difficult or unpleasant things and do not complain about them. [APPROVAL] ❏ *He was a cheerful and uncomplaining travel companion.*

un|com|pli|cat|ed /ʌnkɒmplɪkeɪtɪd/ ADJ If you describe someone or something as **uncomplicated**, you approve of them because they are easy to deal with or understand. [APPROVAL] ❏ *She is a beautiful, uncomplicated girl.*

un|com|pre|hend|ing /ʌnkɒmprɪhɛndɪŋ/ ADJ If you describe someone as **uncomprehending**, you mean that they do not understand what is happening or what someone has said. ❏ *He gave the bottle a long, uncomprehending look.*

un|com|pro|mis|ing /ʌnkɒmprəmaɪzɪŋ/ **1** ADJ If you describe someone as **uncompromising**, you mean that they are determined not to change their opinions or aims in any way. ❏ *Voters have elected an uncompromising nationalist as their new president.* **2** ADJ If you describe something as **uncompromising**, you mean that it does not attempt to make something that is shocking or unpleasant any more acceptable to people. ❏ *...a movie of uncompromising brutality.*

un|con|cealed /ʌnkənsiːld/ ADJ [usu ADJ n] An **unconcealed** emotion is one that someone has made no attempt to hide. ❏ *His message was received with unconcealed anger.*

un|con|cern /ʌnkənsɜːrn/ N-UNCOUNT A person's **unconcern** is their lack of interest in or anxiety about something, often something that most people would be concerned about. ❏ *She'd mentioned it casually once, surprising him by her unconcern.*

un|con|cerned /ʌnkənsɜːrnd/ ADJ If a person is **unconcerned** about something, usually something that most people would care about, they are not interested in it or worried about it. ❏ *Paul was unconcerned about what he had done.*

un|con|di|tion|al /ʌnkəndɪʃənəl/ ADJ If you describe something as **unconditional**, you mean that the person doing or giving it does not require anything to be done by other people in exchange. ❏ *Children need unconditional love from their parents.* • **un|con|di|tion|al|ly** ADV [ADV with v] ❏ *The hostages were released unconditionally.*

un|con|firmed /ʌnkənfɜːrmd/ ADJ If a report or a rumor is **unconfirmed**, there is no definite proof as to whether it is true or not. ❏ *There are unconfirmed reports of several small villages buried by mudslides.*

un|con|gen|ial /ʌnkəndʒiːnyəl/ ADJ If you describe a person or place as **uncongenial**, you mean that they are unfriendly and unpleasant. ❏ *He continued to find the Simpsons uncongenial bores.*

un|con|nect|ed /ʌnkənɛktɪd/ ADJ If one thing is **unconnected** with another or the two things are **unconnected**, the things are not related to each other in any way. ❏ *She had personal problems unconnected with her marriage.*

un|con|scion|able /ʌnkɒnʃənəbəl/ ADJ If you describe something as **unconscionable**, you mean that the person responsible for it ought to be ashamed of it, especially because its effects are so great or severe. [LITERARY] ❏ *It's unconscionable for the government to do anything for a man who admits to smuggling cocaine into the United States.*

un|con|scious /ʌnkɒnʃəs/ **1** ADJ Someone who is **unconscious** is in a state similar to sleep, usually as the result of a serious injury or a lack of oxygen. ❏ *By the time the ambulance arrived he was unconscious.* • **un|con|scious|ness** N-UNCOUNT ❏ *He knew that he might soon lapse into unconsciousness.* **2** ADJ [v-link ADJ of n] If you are **unconscious** of something, you are unaware of it. ❏ *He himself seemed totally unconscious of his failure.* • **un|con|scious|ly** ADV ❏ *"I was very unsure of myself after the divorce," she says, unconsciously sweeping back the curls from her forehead.* **3** ADJ If feelings or attitudes are **unconscious**, you are not aware that you have them, but they show in the way that you behave. ❏ *...my unconscious ambivalence about becoming a mother.* • **un|con|scious|ly** ADV ❏ *Many women whose fathers left home unconsciously expect to be betrayed by their own mates.*

un|con|sid|ered /ʌnkənsɪdərd/ **1** ADJ [usu ADJ n] An **unconsidered** act or opinion has not been carefully planned or thought about in advance. ❏ *...unconsidered, hasty decisions.* **2** ADJ [usu ADJ n] If a person or thing is described as **unconsidered**, they are not noticed or taken into account by anyone. ❏ *I did notice a couple of unconsidered aspects.*

un|con|sti|tu|tion|al /ʌnkɒnstɪtjuːʃənəl/ ADJ If something is **unconstitutional**, it breaks the rules of a constitution. ❏ *Lincoln decided that seceding from the Union was unconstitutional.* • **un|con|sti|tu|tion|al|ly** ADV [ADV with v] ❏ *They claimed that he acted unconstitutionally when he banned their party.* • **un|con|sti|tu|tion|al|ity** /ʌnkɒnstɪtjuːʃənælɪti/ N-UNCOUNT ❏ *...the unconstitutionality of such legislation.*

un|con|trol|lable /ʌnkəntroʊləbəl/ **1** ADJ If you describe a feeling or physical action as **uncontrollable**, you mean that you cannot control it or prevent yourself from feeling or doing it. ❏ *It had been a time of almost uncontrollable excitement.* ❏ *William was seized with uncontrollable rage.* • **un|con|trol|lably** /ʌnkəntroʊləbli/ ADV ❏ *I started shaking uncontrollably and began to cry.* **2** ADJ If you describe a person as **uncontrollable**, you mean that their behavior is bad and that nobody can make them behave more sensibly. ❏ *Mark was withdrawn and uncontrollable.* **3** ADJ If you describe a situation or series of events as **uncontrollable**, you believe that nothing can be done to control them or to prevent things from getting worse. ❏ *If political problems are not resolved, the situation may become uncontrollable.*

un|con|trolled /ʌnkəntroʊld/ **1** ADJ If you describe someone's behavior as **uncontrolled**, you mean they appear unable to stop it or to make it less extreme. ❏ *His uncontrolled behavior disturbed the entire class.* **2** ADJ If a situation or activity is **uncontrolled**, no one is controlling it or preventing it from continuing or growing. ❏ *...the central bank's uncontrolled printing of money.*

un|con|ven|tion|al /ʌnkənvɛnʃənəl/ **1** ADJ If you describe a person or their attitude or behavior as **unconventional**, you mean that they do not behave in the same way as most other people in their society. ❏ *They are seen as being unconventional geniuses.* ❏ *He was known for his unconventional behavior.* **2** ADJ An **unconventional** way of doing something is not the usual way of doing it, and may be surprising. ❏ *The vaccine had been produced by an unconventional technique.* ❏ *Despite his unconventional methods, he has inspired students more than anyone else.*

un|con|vinced /ʌnkənvɪnst/ ADJ If you are **unconvinced** that something is true or right, you are not at all certain that it is true or right. ❏ *Consumers seem unconvinced that the recession is over.*

un|con|vinc|ing /ʌnkənvɪnsɪŋ/ **1** ADJ If you describe something such as an argument or explanation as **unconvincing**, you find it difficult to believe because it does not seem real. ❏ *Mr. Patel phoned the university for an explanation, and he was given the usual unconvincing excuses.* • **un|con|vinc|ing|ly** ADV [ADV with v] ❏ *"It's not that I don't believe you, Meg," Jack said, unconvincingly.* **2** ADJ If you describe a story or a character in a story as **unconvincing**, you think they do not seem likely or real. ❏ *...an unconvincing love story.*

un|cooked /ʌnkʊkt/ ADJ **Uncooked** food has not yet been cooked.

un|cool /ʌnkul/ ADJ [oft v-link ADJ] If you say that a person, thing, or activity is **uncool**, you disapprove of them because they are not fashionable, sophisticated, or attractive. [INFORMAL, DISAPPROVAL] ❏ *People are very laid-back about spotting celebrities here - nobody wants to look uncool by pointing and shouting.*

un|co|opera|tive /ʌnkoʊɒpərətɪv/ ADJ [usu v-link ADJ] If you describe someone as **uncooperative**, you mean that they make no effort at all to help other people or to make other people's lives easier. ❏ *She became uncooperative: unwilling to do her homework or help with any household chores.*

un|co|ordi|nat|ed /ʌnkoʊɔrd^əneɪtɪd/

in BRIT, also use **unco-ordinated**

1 ADJ If you describe someone as **uncoordinated** you mean that their movements are not smooth or controlled. ❏ *They were unsteady on their feet and rather uncoordinated.* **2** ADJ If you describe actions or plans as **uncoordinated**, you mean they are not well-organized. ❏ *Government action has been half-hearted and uncoordinated.*

un|cork /ʌnkɔrk/ (**uncorks**, **uncorking**, **uncorked**) V-T When you **uncork** a bottle, you open it by pulling the cork out of it. ❏ *Steve uncorked bottles of champagne to toast the achievement.*

un|cor|robo|rat|ed /ʌnkərɒbəreɪtɪd/ ADJ [usu ADJ n] An **uncorroborated** statement or claim is not supported by any evidence or information. ❏ *Uncorroborated confessions should no longer be accepted by courts.*

un|count|able noun /ʌnkaʊntəb^əl naʊn/ (**uncountable nouns**) N-COUNT An **uncountable noun** is a noun such as 'gold,' 'information,' or 'furniture' which has only one form and can be used without a determiner.

un|count noun /ʌnkaʊnt naʊn/ (**uncount nouns**) N-COUNT An **uncount noun** is the same as an **uncountable noun**.

un|cou|ple /ʌnkʌp^əl/ (**uncouples**, **uncoupling**, **uncoupled**) **1** V-T If two vehicles or pieces of equipment **are uncoupled**, they have been unfastened and are no longer joined together. ❏ *They uncoupled the passenger cars from the train engine.* **2** V-T If two things that were connected or combined **are uncoupled**, they have been separated from each other. ❏ *The government uncoupled the peso from the dollar yesterday for the first time in 11 years.*

un|couth /ʌnkuθ/ ADJ If you describe a person as **uncouth**, you mean that their behavior is vulgar, noisy, and unpleasant. [DISAPPROVAL]

un|cov|er /ʌnkʌvər/ (**uncovers**, **uncovering**, **uncovered**) **1** V-T If you **uncover** something, especially something that has been kept secret, you discover or find out about it. ❏ *Auditors said they had uncovered evidence of fraud.* **2** V-T To **uncover** something means to remove something that is covering it. ❏ *When the seedlings sprout, uncover the tray.*

un|cov|ered /ʌnkʌvərd/ ADJ Something that is left **uncovered** does not have anything covering it. ❏ *Minor cuts and scrapes can usually be left uncovered to heal by themselves.*

un|criti|cal /ʌnkrɪtɪk^əl/ ADJ If you describe a person or their behavior as **uncritical**, you mean that they do not judge whether someone or something is good or bad, or right or wrong, before supporting or believing them. ❏ *...the conventional notion of many people as uncritical purchasers of heavily advertised products.* ● **un|criti|cal|ly** /ʌnkrɪtɪkli/ ADV ❏ *The Supreme Court often has uncritically accepted military judgments.*

unc|tu|ous /ʌŋktʃuəs/ **1** ADJ If you describe someone as **unctuous**, you are critical of them because they seem to be full of praise, kindness, or interest, but are obviously insincere. [FORMAL, DISAPPROVAL] ❏ *...the kind of unctuous tone that I've heard often at diplomatic parties.* **2** ADJ If you describe food or drink as **unctuous**, you mean that it is creamy or oily. [FORMAL]

un|cul|ti|vat|ed /ʌnkʌltɪveɪtɪd/ ADJ If land is **uncultivated**, there are no crops growing on it. ❏ *...the flat, largely uncultivated plains.*

un|cul|tured /ʌnkʌltʃərd/ ADJ If you describe someone as **uncultured**, you are critical of them because they do not seem to know much about art, literature, and other cultural topics. [DISAPPROVAL]

un|cut /ʌnkʌt/ **1** ADJ Something that is **uncut** has not been cut. ❏ *...a patch of uncut grass.* ❏ *Trees were to be left uncut, roads unpaved.* **2** ADJ [usu ADJ n] An **uncut** book, play, or movie has not had parts removed. ❏ *We saw the uncut version of "Caligula" when we were in Europe.* **3** ADJ [usu ADJ n] **Uncut** diamonds and other precious stones have not been cut into a regular shape.

un|dam|aged /ʌndæmɪdʒd/ ADJ Something that is **undamaged** has not been damaged or spoiled in any way. ❏ *The Korean ship was apparently undamaged.*

un|dat|ed /ʌndeɪtɪd/ ADJ Something that is **undated** does not have a date written on it. ❏ *In each packet there are batches of letters, most of which are undated.*

un|daunt|ed /ʌndɔntɪd/ ADJ If you are **undaunted**, you are not at all afraid or worried about dealing with something, especially something that would frighten or worry most people. ❏ *Undaunted by the scale of the job, Lesley set about planning how each room should look.*

un|de|cid|ed /ʌndɪsaɪdɪd/ ADJ If someone is **undecided**, they cannot decide about something or have not yet decided about it. ❏ *After college she was still undecided as to what career she wanted to pursue.*

un|de|feat|ed /ʌndɪfitɪd/ ADJ If an athlete or team is **undefeated**, nobody has beaten them over a particular period of time. ❏ *She was undefeated for 13 years.*

un|de|mand|ing /ʌndɪmɑndɪŋ/ **1** ADJ [usu ADJ n] If you describe something such as a job as **undemanding**, you mean that it does not require you to work very hard or to think a great deal about it. ❏ *Over a tenth of the population have secure, undemanding jobs.* **2** ADJ If you describe someone as **undemanding**, you mean they are easy to be with and do not ask other people to do a great deal for them. ❏ *...an undemanding companion.*

un|demo|crat|ic /ʌndɛməkrætɪk/ ADJ A system, process, or decision that is **undemocratic** is one that is controlled or made by one person or a small number of people, rather than by all the people involved. ❏ *...the undemocratic rule of the former political establishment.* ❏ *Opponents denounced the law as undemocratic and unconstitutional.*

un|de|mon|stra|tive /ʌndɪmɒnstrətɪv/ ADJ Someone who is **undemonstrative** does not often show affection. ❏ *...an undemonstrative man of few words and even fewer emotional outbursts.*

un|de|ni|able /ʌndɪnaɪəb^əl/ ADJ If you say that something is **undeniable**, you mean that it is definitely true. ❏ *Her charm is undeniable.* ● **un|de|ni|ably** /ʌndɪnaɪəbli/ ADV ❏ *Bringing up a baby is undeniably hard work.*

un|der ♦♦♦ /ʌndər/

In addition to the uses shown below, **under** is also used in phrasal verbs such as 'go under' and 'knuckle under.'

1 PREP If a person or thing is **under** something, they are at a lower level than that thing, and may be covered or hidden by it. ❏ *They found a labyrinth of tunnels under the ground.* ❏ *...swimming in the pool or lying under an umbrella.* ❏ *A path runs under the trees.* **2** PREP In a place such as an ocean, river, or swimming pool, if someone or something is **under** the water, they are fully in the water and covered by it. ❏ *She held her breath for three minutes under the water.* ● ADV [ADV after v] **Under** is also an adverb. ❏ *He took a deep breath before he went under.* **3** PREP If you go **under** something, you move from one side to the other of something that is at a higher level than you. ❏ *He went under a brick arch.* **4** PREP Something that is **under** a layer of something, especially clothing, is covered by that layer. ❏ *I was wearing two sweaters under the green army jacket.* ❏ *...a faded striped shirt under a knit sweater.* **5** PREP You can use **under** before a noun to indicate that a person or thing is being affected by something or is going through a particular process. ❏ *...fishermen whose livelihoods are under threat.* ❏ *Firemen said they had the blaze under control.* **6** PREP If something happens **under** particular circumstances or conditions, it happens when those circumstances or conditions exist. ❏ *His best friend died under questionable circumstances.* ❏ *Under normal conditions, only about 20 to 40 percent of vitamin E is absorbed.* **7** PREP If something happens **under** a law, agreement, or system, it happens because that law, agreement, or system says that it should happen. ❏ *Under law, your employer has the right to hire a temporary* worker to replace you. ❑ *Under the new regulations, one in five cars may need repairs costing as much as $120.* **8** PREP If something happens **under** a particular person or government, it happens when that person or government is in power. ❑ *There would be no new taxes under his leadership.* ❑ *...the realities of life under a brutal dictatorship.* **9** PREP If you study or work **under** a particular person, that person teaches you or tells you what to do. ❑ *Kiefer was just one of the artists who had studied under Beuys in the early Sixties.* ❑ *General Lewis Hyde had served under General Mitchell.* **10** PREP If you do something **under** a particular name, you use that name instead of your real name. ❑ *Were any of your books published under the name Amanda Fairchild?* **11** PREP You use **under** to say which section of a list, book, or system something is in. ❑ *The "General Diseases of the Eye" study is filed under E.* **12** PREP [PREP amount] If something or someone is **under** a particular age or amount, they are less than that age or amount. ❑ *...jobs for those under 65.* ❑ *Nearly half of mothers with children under five have a job.* • ADV [amount and ADV] **Under** is also an adverb. ❑ *...free or subsidized health insurance for children 13 and under.* **13 under wraps** → see **wrap**

---PREFIX---

under-
forms words that refer to an amount or value being too low or not enough. *For example, if someone is **underweight**, their weight is lower than it should be.*

---

under|achieve /ˌʌndərəˈtʃiv/ (underachieves, underachieving, underachieved) V-I If someone **underachieves** in something such as schoolwork or a job, they do not perform as well as they could. ❑ *Some people might think I've underachieved in my job.* • **under|achiev|er** (underachievers) N-COUNT ❑ *He just wanted people to stop calling him disadvantaged, an underachiever.*

under|age /ˌʌndərˈeɪdʒ/ also **under age** **1** ADJ A person who is **underage** is legally too young to do something, for example to drink alcohol, have sex, or vote. ❑ *Underage youths can often obtain alcohol from their older friends.* **2** ADJ [ADJ n] **Underage** activities such as drinking or smoking are carried out by people who are legally too young to do them. ❑ *...his efforts to stop underage drinking and drug abuse.*

under|arm /ˈʌndərɑrm/ (underarms) **1** ADJ [ADJ n] **Underarm** means in or for the areas under your arms, where they are joined to your body. ❑ *...underarm deodorants.* • N-COUNT [usu pl] **Underarm** is also a noun. ❑ *Wash the feet, underarms and body surface using a soap.* **2** ADJ [ADJ n] You use **underarm** to describe actions, such as throwing a ball, in which you do not raise your arm above your shoulder. [BRIT] ❑ *...an underarm throw.* • ADV [ADV after v] **Underarm** is also an adverb. ❑ *Practice throwing a ball underarm.*

in AM, use **underhand**

under|belly /ˈʌndərbɛli/ (underbellies) **1** N-COUNT The **underbelly** of something is the part of it that can be most easily attacked or criticized. ❑ *I know where his soft underbelly is, and that's his material possessions.* **2** N-COUNT The **underbelly** of an animal or a vehicle is the underneath part of it. ❑ *The missiles emerge from the underbelly of the transport plane.*

under|brush /ˈʌndərbrʌʃ/ N-UNCOUNT **Underbrush** consists of bushes and plants growing close together under the trees in a forest. [AM] ❑ *...the cool underbrush of the rain forest.*

in BRIT, use **undergrowth**

under|carriage /ˈʌndərkærɪdʒ/ (undercarriages) **1** N-COUNT The **undercarriage** of an airplane is the part, including the wheels, which supports the airplane when it is on the ground and when it is landing or taking off. [mainly BRIT]

in AM, use **landing gear**

2 → See also color supplement

under|class /ˈʌndərklæs/ (underclasses) N-COUNT [usu sing] A country's **underclass** consists of those members of its population who are poor, and who have little chance of improving their situation. ❑ *Two of the basic problems of the inner-city underclass are inadequate housing and lack of jobs.*

under|clothes /ˈʌndərkloʊz, -kloʊðz/ N-PLURAL Your **underclothes** are the items of clothing that you wear next to your skin and under your other clothes. ❑ *...from multi-patterned sweaters to attractive underclothes.*

under|cloth|ing /ˈʌndərkloʊðɪŋ/ N-UNCOUNT **Underclothing** is the same as **underclothes**. ❑ *...a common brand of men's underclothing.*

under|coat /ˈʌndərkoʊt/ (undercoats) N-VAR An **undercoat** is a covering of paint or varnish put onto a surface as a base for a final covering of paint or varnish. Compare **topcoat**.

under|cov|er /ˌʌndərˈkʌvər/ ADJ **Undercover** work involves secretly obtaining information for the government or the police. ❑ *...an undercover operation designed to catch drug smugglers.* ❑ *...undercover FBI agents.* • ADV [ADV after v] **Undercover** is also an adverb. ❑ *Swanson persuaded Hubley to work undercover to capture the killer.*

under|cur|rent /ˈʌndərkɜrənt/ (undercurrents) **1** N-COUNT If there is an **undercurrent** of a feeling, you are hardly aware of the feeling, but it influences the way you think or behave. ❑ *...the strong undercurrent of pro-business sentiment in Congress.* **2** N-COUNT An **undercurrent** is a strong current of water that is moving below the surface current and in a different direction to it. ❑ *Karen tried to swim after him but the strong undercurrent swept them apart.*

under|cut /ˌʌndərˈkʌt/ (undercuts, undercutting)

The form **undercut** is used in the present tense and is also the past tense and past participle.

V-T If you **undercut** someone or **undercut** their prices, you sell a product more cheaply than they do. [BUSINESS] ❑ *Subsidies allow growers to undercut competitors and depress world prices.* ❑ *...promises to undercut air fares on some routes by 40 percent.*

under|de|vel|oped /ˌʌndərdɪˈvɛləpt/ ADJ An **underdeveloped** country or region does not have modern industries and usually has a low standard of living. Some people dislike this term and prefer to use **developing**. ❑ *Underdeveloped countries should be assisted by allowing them access to modern technology.*

under|dog /ˈʌndərdɔg/ (underdogs) N-COUNT The **underdog** in a competition or situation is the person who seems least likely to succeed or win. ❑ *Most of the crowd were cheering for the underdog to win just this one time.*

under|done /ˌʌndərˈdʌn/ ADJ **Underdone** food has been cooked for less time than necessary, and so is not pleasant to eat. ❑ *The second batch of bread came out underdone.*

under|em|ployed /ˌʌndərɪmˈplɔɪd/ ADJ If someone is **underemployed**, they have not got enough work to do, or their work does not make full use of their skills or abilities.

under|es|ti|mate /ˌʌndərˈɛstɪmeɪt/ (underestimates, underestimating, underestimated) **1** V-T If you **underestimate** something, you do not realize how large or great it is or will be. ❑ *None of us should ever underestimate the degree of difficulty women continue to face in career advancement.* **2** V-T If you **underestimate** someone, you do not realize what they are capable of doing. ❑ *I think a lot of people still underestimate him.*

under|ex|posed /ˌʌndərɪkˈspoʊzd/ ADJ If a photograph is **underexposed**, it is darker than it should be because the film was not exposed to enough light.

under|fed /ˌʌndərˈfɛd/ ADJ People who are **underfed** do not get enough food to eat. ❑ *Kate still looks pale and underfed.*

under|fi|nanced /ˌʌndərfaɪˈnænst/ ADJ [usu v link ADJ] **Underfinanced** means the same as **underfunded**. ❑ *From the beginning, the project was underfinanced.*

under|foot /ˌʌndərˈfʊt/ **1** ADV [ADV after v, n ADV] You describe something as being **underfoot** when you are standing or walking on it. ❑ *...a room, high and square with carpet underfoot and tapestries on the walls.* ❑ *It was still wet underfoot.* **2** ADV [ADV after v] If you trample or crush something **underfoot**, you spoil or destroy it by stepping on it. ❑ *Morgan dropped his cigarette and crushed it underfoot.*

under|fund|ed /ˌʌndərˈfʌndɪd/ ADJ An organization or institution that is **underfunded** does not have enough money to spend, and so it cannot function properly. ❑ *For years we have argued that the FDA is underfunded.*

under|gar|ment /ˈʌndərgɑrmənt/ (undergarments) N-COUNT [usu pl] **Undergarments** are items of clothing that you wear next to your skin and under your other clothes. [OLD-FASHIONED]

under|go /ʌndərgoʊ/ (undergoes, undergoing, underwent, undergone) V-T If you **undergo** something necessary or unpleasant, it happens to you. ❑ *New recruits have been undergoing training in recent weeks.*

under|grad /ʌndərgræd/ (undergrads) N-COUNT An **undergrad** is a student at a university or college who is studying for a bachelor's or associate's degree. [INFORMAL]

under|gradu|ate /ʌndərgrædʒuɪt/ (undergraduates) **1** N-COUNT An **undergraduate** is a student at a university or college who is studying for a bachelor's or associate's degree. ❑ *Economics undergraduates are probably the brightest in the university.* **2** → See feature box at **university**

under|ground ✦✦✦

> The adverb is pronounced /ʌndərgraʊnd/. The noun and adjective are pronounced /ʌndərgraʊnd/.

1 ADV [ADV after v] Something that is **underground** is below the surface of the ground. ❑ *Solid low-level waste will be disposed of deep underground.* • ADJ [ADJ n] **Underground** is also an adjective. ❑ *...an underground parking garage for 2,100 vehicles.* **2** N-SING [the N, also by N] The **underground** in a city is the railroad system in which electric trains travel below the ground in tunnels. [BRIT]

| in AM, use **subway** |

3 ADJ [ADJ n] **Underground** groups and activities are secret because their purpose is to oppose the government and they are illegal. ❑ *...the underground resistance movement.* **4** ADV [ADV after v] If you go **underground**, you hide from the authorities or the police because your political ideas or activities are illegal. ❑ *After the violent clashes of 1981 they either went underground or left the country.* **5** → See feature box at **water**

under|growth /ʌndərgroʊθ/ also **underbrush** N-UNCOUNT **Undergrowth** consists of bushes and plants growing together under the trees in a forest. ❑ *...plunging through the undergrowth.*

under|hand /ʌndərhænd/ also **underhanded** /ʌndərhændəd/ **1** ADJ [usu ADJ n] If an action is **underhand** or if it is done in an **underhand** way, it is done secretly and dishonestly. [DISAPPROVAL] ❑ *...underhand financial deals.* ❑ *...a list of the underhanded ways in which their influence operates in the United States.* **2** ADJ [ADJ n] You use **underhand** or **underhanded** to described actions, such as throwing a ball, in which you do not raise your arm above your shoulder. [AM] ❑ *...an underhand pitch.* • ADV [ADV after v] **Underhand** is also an adverb. ❑ *In softball, pitches are tossed underhand.*

| in BRIT, use **underarm** |

under|lay /ʌndərleɪ/ **Underlay** is the past tense of **underlie**.

under|lie /ʌndərlaɪ/ (underlies, underlying, underlay, underlain) **1** V-T If something **underlies** a feeling or a situation, it is the cause or basis of it. ❑ *Try to figure out what feeling underlies your anger.* **2** → see also **underlying**

under|line /ʌndərlaɪn/ (underlines, underlining, underlined) **1** V-T If one thing, for example an action or an event, **underlines** another, it draws attention to it and emphasizes its importance. ❑ *The report underlined his concern that standards were at risk.* ❑ *This incident underlines the danger of traveling in the border area.* **2** V-T If you **underline** something such as a word or a sentence, you draw a line underneath it in order to make people notice it or to give it extra importance. ❑ *Underline the following that apply to you.*

under|ling /ʌndərlɪŋ/ (underlings) N-COUNT You refer to someone as an **underling** when they are inferior in rank or status to someone else and take orders from them. You use this word to show that you do not respect someone. [DISAPPROVAL] ❑ *...underlings who do the dirty work.*

under|ly|ing /ʌndərlaɪɪŋ/ **1** ADJ [ADJ n] The **underlying** features of an object, event, or situation are not obvious, and it may be difficult to discover or reveal them. ❑ *To stop a problem you have to understand its underlying causes.* **2** ADJ [ADJ n] You describe something as **underlying** when it is below the surface of something else. ❑ *...hills with the hard underlying rock poking through the turf.* **3** → see also **underlie**

under|manned /ʌndərmænd/ ADJ [usu v-link ADJ] If an organization is **undermanned**, it does not have enough employees to function properly. ❑ *In some stores we were undermanned and customer service was suffering.*

under|mine ✦◇◇ /ʌndərmaɪn/ (undermines, undermining, undermined) **1** V-T If you **undermine** something such as a feeling or a system, you make it less strong or less secure than it was before, often by a gradual process or by repeated efforts. ❑ *Offering advice on each and every problem will undermine her feeling of being adult.* **2** V-T If you **undermine** someone or **undermine** their position or authority, you make their authority or position less secure, often by indirect methods. ❑ *She undermined him and destroyed his confidence in his own talent.* **3** V-T If you **undermine** someone's efforts or **undermine** their chances of achieving something, you behave in a way that makes them less likely to succeed. ❑ *The continued fighting threatens to undermine efforts to negotiate an agreement.*

under|neath /ʌndərniθ/ **1** PREP If one thing is **underneath** another, it is directly under it, and may be covered or hidden by it. ❑ *The device exploded underneath a van.* ❑ *...using dogs to locate people trapped underneath collapsed buildings.* • ADV **Underneath** is also an adverb. ❑ *He has on his jeans and a long-sleeved blue denim shirt with a white T-shirt underneath.* ❑ *The shooting-range is lit from underneath by rows of ruby-red light fixtures.* **2** ADV The part of something which is **underneath** is the part which normally touches the ground or faces toward the ground. ❑ *Check the actual construction of the chair by looking underneath.* ❑ *The sand martin is a brown bird with white underneath.* • N-SING **Underneath** is also a noun. ❑ *Now I know what the underneath of a car looks like.* **3** ADV [ADV with cl] You use **underneath** when talking about feelings and emotions that people do not show in their behavior. ❑ *He was as violent as Nick underneath.* • PREP **Underneath** is also a preposition. ❑ *Underneath his outgoing behavior Luke was shy.*

under|nour|ished /ʌndərnɜrɪʃt/ ADJ [usu v-link ADJ] If someone is **undernourished**, they are weak and unhealthy because they have not been eating enough food or the right kind of food. ❑ *...undernourished children.*

under|nour|ish|ment /ʌndərnɜrɪʃmənt/ N-UNCOUNT If someone is suffering from **undernourishment**, they have poor health because they are not eating enough food or are eating the wrong kind of food.

under|paid /ʌndərpeɪd/ ADJ People who are **underpaid** are not paid enough money for the job that they do. ❑ *Women are frequently underpaid for the work that they do.*

under|pants /ʌndərpænts/ N-PLURAL [also a pair of N] **Underpants** are a piece of underwear which have two holes to put your legs through and elastic around the top to hold them up around your waist or hips. ❑ *Half of men admit that their underpants are their oldest item of clothing.*

under|pass /ʌndərpæs/ (underpasses) N-COUNT An **underpass** is a road or path that goes underneath a railroad or another road. ❑ *The underpass was closed through flooding.*

under|per|form /ʌndərpərfɔrm/ also **under-perform** (underperforms, underperforming, underperformed) V-T/V-I If someone **underperforms** in something such as a sports contest, or if one thing **underperforms** another thing, they do not perform as well as they could, or they perform less well than the other thing. ❑ *Our offense has underperformed all year.* ❑ *Smaller companies' stocks generally have underperformed larger ones in the past several years.* • **under|per|form|er** /ʌndərpərfɔrmər/ N-COUNT ❑ *The retail sector has been a significant underperformer.* • **under|per|for|mance** /ʌndərpərfɔrməns/ N-UNCOUNT ❑ *...one reason for the underperformance of European stock markets.*

under|pin /ʌndərpɪn/ (underpins, underpinning, underpinned) V-T If one thing **underpins** another, it helps the other thing to continue or succeed by supporting and strengthening it. ❑ *...mystical themes that underpin all religions.* • **under|pin|ning** (underpinnings) N-VAR ❑ *...the economic underpinning of ancient Mexican society.*

under|play /ʌndərpleɪ/ (underplays, underplaying, underplayed) V-T If you **underplay** something, you make it seem less important than it really is. [mainly BRIT] ❑ *We often underplay the skills we have.*

| in AM, usually use **play down** |

under|popu|lat|ed /ʌndərpɒpyəleɪtɪd/ ADJ You describe a country or region as **underpopulated** when it could support a much larger population than it has. ❑ *Many of the islands are mainly wild and underpopulated.*

under|privi|leged /ˌʌndərprɪvɪlɪdʒd, -prɪvlɪdʒd/ ADJ [usu ADJ n] **Underprivileged** people have less money and fewer possessions and opportunities than other people in their society. ❑ *...helping underprivileged children to learn to read.* • N-PLURAL [the N] **The underprivileged** are people who are underprivileged. ❑ *...government plans to make more jobs available to the underprivileged.*

under|rate /ˌʌndərreɪt/ (underrates, underrating, underrated) V-T If you **underrate** someone or something, you do not recognize how intelligent, important, or significant they are. ❑ *We women have a lot of good business skills, although we tend to underrate ourselves.* • **under|rat|ed** ADJ ❑ *He is a very underrated poet.*

under|score /ˌʌndərskɔr/ (underscores, underscoring, underscored) **1** V-T If something such as an action or an event **underscores** another, it draws attention to the other thing and emphasizes its importance. [mainly AM] ❑ *The Labor Department figures underscore the shaky state of the economic recovery.*

> in BRIT, usually use **underline**

2 V-T If you **underscore** something such as a word or a sentence, you draw a line underneath it in order to make people notice it or give it extra importance. [mainly AM] ❑ *He heavily underscored his note to Shelley.*

> in BRIT, usually use **underline**

under|sea /ˌʌndərsi/ ADJ [ADJ n] **Undersea** things or activities exist or happen below the surface of the sea. ❑ *...an undersea pipeline running to Europe.*

under|sec|re|tary /ˌʌndərsɛkrətɛri/ (undersecretaries) also **under-secretary** N-COUNT An **undersecretary** is a senior official with an important post in a government department. ❑ *...Under-Secretary of State Reginald Bartholomew.*

under|shirt /ˌʌndərʃɜrt/ (undershirts) N-COUNT An **undershirt** is a piece of clothing that you wear on the top half of your body next to your skin and under your regular shirt, in order to keep warm. [AM] ❑ *He put on a pair of boxer shorts and an undershirt.*

> in BRIT, use **vest**

under|side /ˌʌndərsaɪd/ (undersides) N-COUNT The **underside** of something is the part of it which normally faces toward the ground. ❑ *...the underside of the car.*

under|signed /ˌʌndərsaɪnd/ ADJ [ADJ n] On a legal document, the **undersigned** people are the ones who have signed their names at the bottom of the document. [LEGAL] ❑ *The undersigned buyers agree to pay a 5,000 dollar deposit.* • N-PLURAL [the N] **The undersigned** are the people who have signed a legal document. ❑ *...we the undersigned, all prominent doctors in our fields.*

under|sized /ˌʌndərsaɪzd/ ADJ [usu ADJ n] **Undersized** people or things are smaller than usual, or smaller than they should be. ❑ *...undersized and underweight babies.*

under|spend /ˌʌndərspɛnd/ (underspends, underspending, underspent) V-I If an organization or country **underspends**, it spends less money than it plans to or less money than it can afford. [BUSINESS] ❑ *...a country that underspends on health and overspends on statisticians.* • N-COUNT **Underspend** is also a noun. ❑ *There has been an underspend in the department's budget.*

under|staffed /ˌʌndərstæft/ ADJ [usu v-link ADJ] If an organization is **understaffed**, it does not have enough employees to do its work properly. ❑ *Many institutions offering child care are understaffed and underequipped.*

under|staff|ing /ˌʌndərstæfɪŋ/ N-UNCOUNT **Understaffing** is a situation in which an organization does not have enough employees to do its work properly. ❑ *Understaffing and overcrowding led to an increase in prison violence.*

under|stand ✦✦✦ /ˌʌndərstænd/ (understands, understanding, understood) **1** V-T [no cont] If you **understand** someone or understand what they are saying, you know what they mean. ❑ *I think you heard and also understand me.* ❑ *I don't understand what you are talking about.* **2** V-T [no cont] If you **understand** a language, you know what someone is saying when they are speaking that language. ❑ *I couldn't read or understand a word of Yiddish, so I asked him to translate.* **3** V-T [no cont] To **understand** someone means to know how they feel and why they behave in the way that they do. ❑ *It would be nice to have someone who really understood me, a friend.* ❑ *Trish had not exactly understood his feelings.* **4** V-T [no cont] You say that you **understand** something when you know why or how it happens. ❑ *They are too young to understand what is going on.* ❑ *She didn't understand why the TV was kept out of reach of the patients.* **5** V-T [no cont] If you **understand** that something is the case, you think it is true because you have heard or read that it is. You can say that something **is understood** to be the case to mean that people generally think it is true. ❑ *We understand that she's in the studio recording her second album.* ❑ *As I understand it, she has a house in the city.* ❑ *The management is understood to be very unwilling to agree to this request.*

under|stand|able /ˌʌndərstændəbəl/ **1** ADJ If you describe someone's behavior or feelings as **understandable**, you think that they have reacted to a situation in a natural way or in the way you would expect. ❑ *His unhappiness was understandable.* • **under|stand|ably** /ˌʌndərstændəbli/ ADV ❑ *Officials are understandably nervous about the tense situation in the neighborhood.* **2** ADJ If you say that something such as a statement or theory is **understandable**, you mean that people can easily understand it. ❑ *Roger Neuberg writes in a simple and understandable way.*

under|stand|ing ✦◇◇ /ˌʌndərstændɪŋ/ (understandings) **1** N-VAR If you have an **understanding of** something, you know how it works or know what it means. ❑ *They have to have a basic understanding of computers in order to use the advanced technology.* **2** ADJ If you are **understanding** toward someone, you are kind and forgiving. ❑ *Her boss, who was very understanding, gave her time off.* **3** N-UNCOUNT If you show **understanding**, you show that you realize how someone feels or why they did something, and are not hostile toward them. ❑ *We would like to thank them for their patience and understanding.* **4** N-UNCOUNT If there is **understanding** between people, they are friendly toward each other and trust each other. ❑ *There was complete understanding between Wilson and myself.* **5** N-COUNT An **understanding** is an informal agreement about something. ❑ *We had not set a date for marriage but there was an understanding between us.* **6** N-SING If you say that it is your **understanding** that something is the case, you mean that you believe it to be the case because you have heard or read that it is. ❑ *It is my understanding that the meeting is Thursday.* **7** PHRASE If you agree to do something **on the understanding that** something else will be done, you do it because you have been told that the other thing will definitely be done. ❑ *Poverty forced her to surrender him to foster families, but only on the understanding that she could eventually regain custody.*

under|state /ˌʌndərsteɪt/ (understates, understating, understated) V-T If you **understate** something, you describe it in a way that suggests that it is less important or serious than it really is. ❑ *The government chooses deliberately to understate the increase in prices.*

under|stat|ed /ˌʌndərsteɪtɪd/ ADJ [ADJ n] If you describe a style, color, or effect as **understated**, you mean that it is simple and plain, and does not attract attention to itself. ❑ *I have always liked understated clothes.*

under|state|ment /ˌʌndərsteɪtmənt/ (understatements) **1** N-COUNT If you say that a statement is an **understatement**, you mean that it does not fully express the extent to which something is true. ❑ *To say I'm disappointed is an understatement.* **2** N-UNCOUNT **Understatement** is the practice of suggesting that things have much less of a particular quality than they really have. ❑ *...typical British understatement.* **3** → See feature box at **review**

under|stood /ˌʌndərstʊd/ **Understood** is the past tense and past participle of **understand**.

under|study /ˌʌndərstʌdi/ (understudies) N-COUNT An actor's **understudy** is the person who has learned their part in a play and can act the part if the actor is ill. ❑ *He was an understudy to Charlie Chaplin on a tour of the U.S.*

under|take /ˌʌndərteɪk/ (undertakes, undertaking, undertook, undertaken) **1** V-T When you **undertake** a task or job, you start doing it and accept responsibility for it. ❑ *She undertook the task of monitoring the elections.* **2** V-T If you

undertake to do something, you promise that you will do it. ❑ *He undertook to edit the text himself.*

under|tak|er /ˈʌndərteɪkər/ (**undertakers**) N-COUNT An **undertaker** is a person whose job is to deal with the bodies of people who have died and to arrange funerals. ❑ *An undertaker had already taken the body to be embalmed.*

under|tak|ing /ˈʌndərteɪkɪŋ/ (**undertakings**) N-COUNT An **undertaking** is a task or job, especially a large or difficult one. ❑ *Organizing the show has been a massive undertaking.*

under|tone /ˈʌndərtoʊn/ (**undertones**) **1** N-COUNT [in N] If you say something in an **undertone**, you say it very quietly. ❑ *"What d'you think?" she asked in an undertone.* **2** N-COUNT [with supp] If something has **undertones** of a particular kind, it suggests ideas or attitudes of this kind without expressing them directly. ❑ *...a witty, racy story with surprisingly serious undertones.*

under|took /ˈʌndərtʊk/ **Undertook** is the past tense of **undertake**.

under|tow /ˈʌndərtoʊ/ (**undertows**) **1** N-COUNT [usu with supp] If there is an **undertow** of a feeling, that feeling exists in such a weak form that you are hardly aware of it, but it influences the way you think or behave. ❑ *...an undertow of sadness.* **2** N-COUNT An **undertow** is a strong current of water that is moving below the surface current and in a different direction to it.

under|used /ˈʌndəryuzd/ also **under-used** ADJ Something useful that is **underused** is not used as much for people's benefit as it could be. ❑ *Currently many schools' sports grounds are grossly underused.*

under|uti|lized /ˈʌndəryutɪlaɪzd/

| in BRIT, also use **underutilised** |

ADJ [usu ADJ n] **Underutilized** is a more formal word for **underused**. ❑ *They had to sell off 10 percent of all underutilized farmland.*

under|value /ˈʌndərvælyu/ (**undervalues, undervaluing, undervalued**) V-T If you **undervalue** something or someone, you fail to recognize how valuable or important they are. ❑ *We must never undervalue freedom.*

under|wa|ter /ˈʌndərwɔtər/ **1** ADV Something that exists or happens **underwater** exists or happens below the surface of the ocean, a river, or a lake. ❑ *...giant submarines able to travel at high speeds underwater.* ● ADJ [ADJ n] **Underwater** is also an adjective. ❑ *...underwater exploration.* ❑ *...underwater fishing with harpoons.* **2** ADJ [ADJ n] **Underwater** devices are specially made so that they can work in water. ❑ *...underwater camera equipment.*

under|way /ˈʌndərweɪ/ ADJ [v-link ADJ] If an activity is **underway**, it has already started. If an activity gets **underway**, it starts. ❑ *An investigation is underway to find out how the disaster happened.* ❑ *It was a cold evening, winter well underway.*

under|wear /ˈʌndərwɛər/ N-UNCOUNT **Underwear** is items of clothing that you wear next to your skin and under your other clothes. ❑ *For Christmas my brother and I got new underwear, one toy and one book.*

under|weight /ˈʌndəweɪt/ ADJ [usu v-link ADJ] If someone is **underweight**, they are too thin, and therefore not healthy. ❑ *Nearly a third of the children were severely underweight.*

under|went /ˈʌndərwɛnt/ **Underwent** is the past tense of **undergo**.

under|whelmed /ˈʌndərwɛlmd/ ADJ If you are **underwhelmed** by something, you are not impressed or excited by it. [INFORMAL] ❑ *I was distinctly underwhelmed by the quality of the wines.*

under|whelm|ing /ˈʌndərwɛlmɪŋ/ ADJ If you use **underwhelming** to describe the response or reaction to something, you mean that people were not very impressed or excited by it. [INFORMAL] ❑ *...the distinctly underwhelming response to their second album.*

under|world /ˈʌndərwɜrld/ N-SING The **underworld** in a city is the organized crime and the people who are involved in it. ❑ *...an underworld of gangs, drugs and violence* ❑ *Some claim that she still has connections to the criminal underworld.*

under|write /ˈʌndərraɪt/ (**underwrites, underwriting, underwrote, underwritten**) V-T If an institution or company **underwrites** an activity or **underwrites** the cost of it, they agree to provide any money that is needed to cover losses or buy special equipment, often for an agreed-upon fee. [BUSINESS] ❑ *The government will have to create a special agency to underwrite small business loans.*

under|writ|er /ˈʌndərraɪtər/ (**underwriters**) **1** N-COUNT An **underwriter** is someone whose job involves agreeing to provide money for a particular activity or to pay for any losses. [BUSINESS] ❑ *If the market will not buy the shares, the underwriter buys them.* **2** N-COUNT An **underwriter** is someone whose job is to judge the risks involved in certain activities and decide how much to charge for insurance. [BUSINESS] ❑ *AIG is an organization of insurance underwriters.*

un|de|served /ˌʌndɪzˈzɜrvd/ ADJ If you describe something such as a reaction, treatment, or result as **undeserved**, you mean that the person who experiences it has not earned it and should not really have it. ❑ *Douglas has an undeserved reputation for being dull and dry.*

un|de|sir|able /ˌʌndɪzaɪərəbəl/ ADJ If you describe something or someone as **undesirable**, you think they will have harmful effects. ❑ *Inflation is considered to be undesirable because of its adverse effects on income distribution.*

un|de|tect|ed /ˌʌndɪtɛktɪd/ ADJ If you are **undetected** or if you do something **undetected**, people do not find out where you are or what you are doing. ❑ *The spy ring had a fifth member as yet still undetected.* ❑ *They managed to get away from the coast undetected.*

un|de|vel|oped /ˌʌndɪvɛləpt/ ADJ [usu ADJ n] An **undeveloped** country or region does not have modern industries and usually has a low standard of living. ❑ *The big losers will be the undeveloped countries, especially in sub-Saharan Africa.* **2** ADJ **Undeveloped** land has not been built on or used for activities such as mining and farming. ❑ *Vast tracts of the country are wild and undeveloped.*

un|did /ʌnˈdɪd/ **Undid** is the past tense of **undo**.

un|dies /ˈʌndiz/ N-PLURAL [oft poss N] You can refer to underwear for women or girls as their **undies**. [INFORMAL]

un|dig|ni|fied /ʌnˈdɪɡnɪfaɪd/ ADJ If you describe someone's actions as **undignified**, you mean they are foolish or embarrassing. ❑ *It is sad to see a county confine its activities to undignified public bickering.*

un|di|lut|ed /ˌʌndaɪˈlutɪd/ **1** ADJ [usu ADJ n] If you describe someone's feelings or characteristics as **undiluted**, you are emphasizing that they are very strong and not mixed with any other feeling or quality. ❑ *I will look back at this one with undiluted pleasure.* **2** ADJ A liquid that is **undiluted** has not been made weak by mixing it with water.

un|dip|lo|mat|ic /ˌʌndɪpləˈmætɪk/ ADJ If someone is described as **undiplomatic**, they say or do things that offend people, usually not on purpose. ❑ *He could be the most undiplomatic man ever to hold such a post.* ● **un|dip|lo|mati|cal|ly** ADV [ADV with v] ❑ *The former US ambassador to Ireland has behaved most undiplomatically by describing his two years in Dublin as "very, very boring."*

un|dis|ci|plined /ʌnˈdɪsɪplɪnd/ ADJ If you describe someone as **undisciplined**, you mean that they behave badly or in a disorganized way. ❑ *...a noisy and undisciplined group of students.*

un|dis|closed /ˌʌndɪsˈkloʊzd/ ADJ **Undisclosed** information is not revealed to the public. ❑ *The company has been sold for an undisclosed amount.*

un|dis|cov|ered /ˌʌndɪsˈkʌvərd/ ADJ Something that is **undiscovered** has not been discovered or noticed. ❑ *The name Vulcan was given to the undiscovered planet.*

un|dis|crimi|nat|ing /ˌʌndɪsˈkrɪmɪneɪtɪŋ/ **1** ADJ Someone who is **undiscriminating** is not able to judge which things are of good quality and therefore does not make good choices. [DISAPPROVAL] ❑ *These are shows aimed at the undiscriminating viewer.* **2** ADJ If something such as an action or policy is described as **undiscriminating**, it does not make careful distinctions between people or things. [DISAPPROVAL] ❑ *Her parents were determined to do something to help other victims of this undiscriminating disease.*

un|dis|guised /ˌʌndɪsˈɡaɪzd/ ADJ [usu ADJ n] If you describe someone's feelings as **undisguised**, you mean that they show them openly and do not make any attempt to hide them. ❑ *Hean looked down at Bauer in undisguised disgust.*

un|dis|mayed /ˌʌndɪsˈmeɪd/ ADJ [v-link ADJ] If you say that someone is **undismayed** by something unpleasant or unexpected, you mean that they do not feel any fear, worry, or sadness about it. [FORMAL] ❑ *He was undismayed by the prospect of failure.*

un|dis|put|ed /ˌʌndɪsˈpjuːtɪd/ **1** ADJ If you describe a fact or opinion as **undisputed**, you are trying to persuade someone that it is generally accepted as true or correct. ❑ *...an undisputed fact.* ❑ *...his undisputed genius.* **2** ADJ If you describe someone as the **undisputed** leader or champion, you mean that everyone accepts their position as leader or champion. ❑ *She won 20 tournaments, and was the undisputed world champion.* ❑ *At 78 years of age, he's still undisputed leader of his country.*

un|dis|tin|guished /ˌʌndɪsˈtɪŋɡwɪʃt/ ADJ If you describe someone or something as **undistinguished**, you mean they are not attractive, interesting, or successful. ❑ *...his short and undistinguished career as an art student.*

un|dis|turbed /ˌʌndɪsˈtɜːbd/ **1** ADJ Something that remains **undisturbed** is not touched, moved, or used by anyone. ❑ *The desk looked undisturbed.* **2** ADJ A place that is **undisturbed** is peaceful and has not been affected by changes that have happened in other places. ❑ *It was one of the most peaceful and undisturbed places she had found.* **3** ADJ If you are **undisturbed** in something that you are doing, you are able to continue doing it and are not affected by something that is happening. ❑ *I can spend the whole day undisturbed at the warehouse.* ❑ *There was a small restaurant on Sullivan Street where we could talk undisturbed.* **4** ADJ If someone is **undisturbed** by something, it does not affect, bother, or upset them. ❑ *Victoria was strangely undisturbed by this symptom, even though her husband and family were frightened.*

un|di|vid|ed /ˌʌndɪˈvaɪdɪd/ **1** ADJ [usu ADJ n] If you give someone or something your **undivided** attention, you concentrate on them fully and do not think about anything else. ❑ *Eldest children are the only ones to have experienced the undivided attention of their parents.* **2** ADJ [usu ADJ n] **Undivided** feelings are ones that are very strong and not mixed with other feelings. ❑ *The paintings she produced in those months won undivided admiration.* **3** ADJ An **undivided** country or organization is one that is not separated into smaller parts or groups. ❑ *Mandela said, "We want a united, undivided South Africa."*

undo /ʌnˈduː/ (undoes, undoing, undid, undone) **1** V-T If you **undo** something that is closed, tied, or held together, or if you **undo** the thing holding it, you loosen or remove the thing holding it. ❑ *I managed secretly to undo a corner of the parcel.* ❑ *I undid the bottom two buttons of my yellow and gray shirt.* **2** V-T To **undo** something that has been done means to reverse its effect. ❑ *A heavy-handed approach from the police could undo that good impression.* ❑ *She knew it would be difficult to undo the damage that had been done.* **3** → see also **undoing**

un|do|ing /ʌnˈduːɪŋ/ N-SING If something is someone's **undoing**, it is the cause of their failure. ❑ *His lack of experience may prove to be his undoing.*

un|done /ʌnˈdʌn/ **1** ADJ [ADJ after v] Work that is **undone** has not yet been done. ❑ *He left nothing undone that needed attention.* **2** → see also **undo**

un|doubt|ed /ʌnˈdaʊtɪd/ ADJ You can use **undoubted** to emphasize that something exists or is true. [EMPHASIS] ❑ *The event was an undoubted success.* ❑ *...a man of your undoubted ability.* ● **un|doubt|ed|ly** ADV ❑ *Undoubtedly, political and economic factors have played their part.*

un|dreamed of /ʌnˈdriːmd ʌv/

in BRIT, sometimes in AM, also use **undreamt of**

ADJ If you describe something as **undreamed of**, you are emphasizing that it is much better, worse, or more unusual than you thought was possible. [EMPHASIS] ❑ *This new design will offer undreamed of levels of comfort, safety and speed.*

un|dress /ʌnˈdrɛs/ (undresses, undressing, undressed) V-T/V-I When you **undress** or **undress** someone, you take off your clothes or someone else's clothes. ❑ *She went out, leaving Rachel to undress and take a shower.*

un|dressed /ʌnˈdrɛst/ ADJ If you are **undressed**, you are wearing no clothes or your underwear or pajamas. If you get **undressed**, you take off your clothes. ❑ *Fifteen minutes later he was undressed and in bed.*

un|due /ʌnˈdjuː/ ADJ [ADJ n] If you describe something bad as **undue**, you mean that it is greater or more extreme than you think is reasonable or appropriate. ❑ *This would help the families to survive the drought without undue suffering.* ❑ *It is unrealistic to put undue pressure on ourselves by saying we are the best.*

un|du|late /ˈʌndʒəleɪt/ (undulates, undulating, undulated) V-I Something that **undulates** has gentle curves or slopes, or moves gently and slowly up and down or from side to side in an attractive manner. [LITERARY] ❑ *As we travel south, the countryside begins to undulate as the rolling hills sweep down to the riverbanks.* ● **un|du|lat|ing** ADJ ❑ *...gently undulating hills.*

un|du|ly /ʌnˈdjuːli/ ADV If you say that something does not happen or is not done **unduly**, you mean that it does not happen or is not done to an excessive or unnecessary extent. ❑ *"But you're not unduly worried about doing this report?"—"No."* ❑ *This will achieve greater security without unduly burdening the consumers or the economy.*

un|dy|ing /ʌnˈdaɪɪŋ/ ADJ [usu ADJ n] If you refer to someone's **undying** feelings, you mean that the feelings are very strong and are unlikely to change. [LITERARY] ❑ *Dianne declared her undying love for Sam.*

un|earned in|come /ʌnɜːrnd ˈɪnkʌm/ N-UNCOUNT **Unearned income** is money that people gain from interest or profit from property or investment, rather than money that they earn from a job. [BUSINESS] ❑ *Your IRA deduction cannot be taken from unearned income.*

un|earth /ʌnˈɜːθ/ (unearths, unearthing, unearthed) **1** V-T If someone **unearths** facts or evidence, they discover them with difficulty. ❑ *Researchers have unearthed documents from the 1600s.* ❑ *Other financial scandals are out there waiting to be unearthed.* **2** V-T If someone **unearths** something that is buried, they find it by digging in the ground. ❑ *Fossil hunters have unearthed the bones of an elephant believed to be 500,000 years old.* ❑ *More human remains have been unearthed in the north.* **3** V-T If you say that someone **has unearthed** something, you mean that they have found it after it had been hidden or lost for some time. ❑ *From somewhere, he had unearthed a black silk suit.* ❑ *Today I unearthed a copy of "90 Minutes" and had a chuckle at your article.*

un|earth|ly /ʌnˈɜːθli/ **1** ADJ [usu ADJ n] You use **unearthly** to describe something that seems very strange and unnatural. ❑ *For a few seconds we watched the unearthly lights on the water.* ❑ *The sound was so serene that it seemed unearthly.* **2** ADJ [ADJ n] If you refer to a time as an **unearthly** hour, you are emphasizing that it is very early in the morning. [EMPHASIS] ❑ *They arranged to meet in Riverside Park at the unearthly hour of seven in the morning.* **3** ADJ [usu ADJ n] An **unearthly** noise is unpleasant because it sounds frightening and unnatural. ❑ *She heard the sirens scream their unearthly wail.*

un|ease /ʌnˈiːz/ **1** N-UNCOUNT If you have a feeling of **unease**, you feel anxious or afraid, because you think that something is wrong. ❑ *Sensing my unease about the afternoon ahead, he told me, "These men are pretty easy to talk to."* ❑ *We left with a deep sense of unease, because we knew something was being hidden from us.* **2** N-UNCOUNT If you say that there is **unease** in a situation, you mean that people are dissatisfied or angry, but have not yet started to take any action. ❑ *He faces growing unease among the Democrats about the likelihood of war.* ❑ *...the depth of public unease about the economy.*

un|easy /ʌnˈiːzi/ (uneasier, uneasiest) **1** ADJ If you are **uneasy**, you feel anxious, afraid, or embarrassed, because you think that something is wrong or that there is danger. ❑ *He said nothing but gave me a sly grin that made me feel terribly uneasy.* ❑ *He looked uneasy and refused to answer questions.* ● **un|easi|ly** /ʌnˈiːzɪli/ ADV ❑ *Meg shifted uneasily on her chair.* ● **un|easi|ness** N-UNCOUNT ❑ *With a small degree of uneasiness, he pushed it open and stuck his head inside.* **2** ADJ If you are **uneasy** about doing something, you are not sure that it is correct or wise. ▫ *Richard was uneasy about how best to approach his elderly mother.* • **un|easi|ness** N-UNCOUNT ▫ *I felt a certain uneasiness about meeting her again.* **3** ADJ If you describe a situation or relationship as **uneasy**, you mean that the situation is not settled and may not last. [JOURNALISM] ▫ *An uneasy calm has settled over Los Angeles.* ▫ *There is an uneasy relationship between us and the politicians.* • **un|easi|ly** ADV ▫ *...a country whose component parts fit uneasily together.*

un|eco|nom|ic /ʌnɛkənɒmɪk, -ik-/ **1** ADJ If you describe something such as an industry or business as **uneconomic**, you mean that it does not produce enough profit. [BUSINESS] ▫ *...the closure of uneconomic factories.* **2** ADJ [v-link ADJ] If you say that an action or plan is **uneconomic**, you think it will cost a lot of money and not be successful or not be worth the expense. ▫ *It would be uneconomic to try and repair it.*

un|eco|nomi|cal /ʌnɛkənɒmɪkəl, -ik-/ ADJ If you say that an action, a method, or a product is **uneconomical**, you mean that it does not make a profit. [BUSINESS] ▫ *It would be uneconomical to send a brand new book..*

un|edu|cat|ed /ʌnɛdʒʊkeɪtɪd/ ADJ Someone who is **uneducated** has not received much education. ▫ *Though an uneducated man, Charlie was not a stupid one.* • N-PLURAL [the N] **The uneducated** are people who are uneducated. ▫ *The poor and uneducated did worst under these reforms.*

un|emo|tion|al /ʌnɪmoʊʃənəl/ ADJ If you describe someone as **unemotional**, you mean that they do not show any feelings. ▫ *At first I kept cool and unemotional, then I began to cry.* • **un|emo|tion|al|ly** ADV [ADV after v] ▫ *McKinnon looked at him unemotionally.*

un|em|ploya|ble /ʌnɪmplɔɪəbəl/ ADJ Someone who is **unemployable** does not have a job and is unlikely to get a job, because they do not have the skills or abilities that an employer might want. ▫ *He freely admits he is unemployable and will probably never find a job.*

un|em|ployed /ʌnɪmplɔɪd/ ADJ Someone who is **unemployed** does not have a job. ▫ *The problem is millions of people are unemployed.* ▫ *This workshop helps young unemployed people.* • N-PLURAL **The unemployed** are people who are unemployed. ▫ *We want to create jobs for the unemployed.*

un|em|ploy|ment ♦⬨⬨ /ʌnɪmplɔɪmənt/ **1** N-UNCOUNT **Unemployment** is the fact that people who want jobs cannot get them. ▫ *The state's unemployment rate rose slightly to 7.1 percent last month.* **2** N-UNCOUNT **Unemployment** is the same as **unemployment compensation**. [AM] ▫ *He worked most of the year. Now he's getting unemployment.* **3** → See feature box at **work**

un|em|ploy|ment ben|efit (**unemployment benefits**) N-VAR [also N in pl] **Unemployment benefit** is money that some people receive from the state when they do not have a job and are unable to find one. ▫ *That year, more than three million were receiving unemployment benefits.* ▫ *Unemployment benefits are directly related to previous earnings.*

un|em|ploy|ment com|pen|sa|tion N-UNCOUNT **Unemployment compensation** is money that some people receive from the state, usually for a limited time after losing a job, when they do not have a job and are unable to find one. [AM] ▫ *He has to get by on unemployment compensation.*

un|em|ploy|ment line (**unemployment lines**) **1** N-COUNT When people talk about the **unemployment line**, they are talking about the state of being unemployed, especially when saying how many people are unemployed. [AM] ▫ *Many white-collar workers, like stockbrokers and investment bankers, find themselves in the unemployment lines.*

in BRIT, use **dole queue**

2 → See feature box at **work**

un|end|ing /ʌnɛndɪŋ/ ADJ [usu ADJ n] If you describe something as **unending**, you mean that it continues without stopping for a very long time. ▫ *...the country's seemingly unending cycle of political violence.*

un|en|dur|able /ʌnɪndʊərəbəl/ ADJ If you describe a bad situation as **unendurable**, you mean that it is so extremely unpleasant that you have to end it. [FORMAL] ▫ *Isaac had found the work unendurable and walked out of the job.*

un|en|vi|able /ʌnɛnviəbəl/ ADJ [usu ADJ n] If you describe a situation or task as **unenviable**, you mean that nobody would enjoy dealing with it because it is very difficult, dangerous, or unpleasant. ▫ *She had the unenviable task of making the first few phone calls.*

un|equal /ʌnikwəl/ **1** ADJ [usu ADJ n] An **unequal** system or situation is unfair because it gives more power or privileges to one person or group of people than to others. ▫ *This country still had a deeply oppressive, unequal and divisive political system.* • **un|equal|ly** ADV ▫ *The victims were treated unequally.* **2** ADJ [v-link ADJ to n] If someone is **unequal to** a task they have to do, they do not have the abilities needed to do it well. [FORMAL] ▫ *He felt unequal to the job and wished there were someone he could go to for advice.* **3** ADJ **Unequal** means being different in size, strength, or amount. ▫ *The Egyptians probably measured their day in twenty-four hours of unequal length.*

un|equaled /ʌnikwəld/

in BRIT, sometimes in AM, use **unequalled**

ADJ If you describe something as **unequaled**, you mean that it is greater, better, or more extreme than anything else of the same kind. ▫ *This record figure was unequaled for 13 years.*

un|equivo|cal /ʌnɪkwɪvəkəl/ ADJ If you describe someone's attitude as **unequivocal**, you mean that it is completely clear and very firm. [FORMAL] ▫ *...Richardson's unequivocal commitment to fair play.* • **un|equivo|cal|ly** /ʌnɪkwɪvəkli/ ADV ▫ *He stated unequivocally that the forces were ready to go to war.*

un|err|ing /ʌnɜːrɪŋ, -ɛrɪŋ/ ADJ [usu ADJ n] If you describe someone's judgment or ability as **unerring**, you mean that they are always correct and never mistaken. ▫ *She has an unerring instinct for people's weak spots.* • **un|err|ing|ly** ADV [ADV with v, ADV adj] ▫ *It was wonderful to watch her fingers moving deftly and unerringly.*

un|escort|ed /ʌnɪskɔːrtɪd/ ADJ If someone or something is **unescorted**, they are not protected or supervised. ▫ *Unescorted children are not allowed beyond this point.*

un|ethi|cal /ʌnɛθɪkəl/ ADJ Behavior that is **unethical** is wrong and unacceptable according to rules or beliefs about morality. ▫ *It's simply unethical to promote and advertise such a dangerous product.* ▫ *I thought it was unethical for doctors to operate upon their families.*

un|even /ʌniːvən/ **1** ADJ An **uneven** surface or edge is not smooth, flat, or straight. ▫ *He staggered on the uneven surface.* ▫ *The pathways were uneven, broken and dangerous.* **2** ADJ Something that is **uneven** is not regular or consistent. ▫ *He could hear that her breathing was uneven.* **3** ADJ An **uneven** system or situation is unfairly arranged or organized. ▫ *Some of the victims are complaining loudly about the uneven distribution of emergency aid.* **4** → See feature box at **snow**

un|event|ful /ʌnɪvɛntfəl/ ADJ If you describe a period of time as **uneventful**, you mean that nothing interesting, exciting, or important happened during it. ▫ *The return trip was uneventful, the car running perfectly.*

un|ex|cep|tion|able /ʌnɪksɛpʃənəbəl/ ADJ If you describe someone or something as **unexceptionable**, you mean that they are unlikely to be criticized or objected to, but are not new or exciting, and may have some hidden bad qualities. [FORMAL] ▫ *The candidate was quite unexceptionable, a well-known travel writer and TV personality.* ▫ *The school's unexceptionable purpose is to involve parents more closely in the education of their children.*

un|ex|cep|tion|al /ʌnɪksɛpʃənəl/ ADJ If you describe something as **unexceptional**, you mean that it is ordinary, not very interesting, and often disappointing. ▫ *Since then, Michael has lived an unexceptional life.*

un|ex|cit|ing /ʌnɪksaɪtɪŋ/ ADJ If you describe someone or something as **unexciting**, you think they are rather boring, and not likely to shock or surprise you in any way. ▫ *He is regarded as very capable but unexciting.* ▫ *It was a methodical, unexciting chore.*

un|ex|pec|ted ♦⬨⬨ /ʌnɪkspɛktɪd/ ADJ If an event or someone's behavior is **unexpected**, it surprises you because you did not think that it was likely to happen. ▫ *His death was totally unexpected.* ▫ *He made a brief, unexpected appearance at the office.* • **un|ex|pect|ed|ly** ADV ▫ *Moss had clamped an unexpectedly strong grip on his arm.*

> **SYNONYMS**
>
> **unexpected**
> ADJ
> **unforeseen:** Call regularly to check that no unforeseen problems have arisen.
> **surprise:** Baxter arrived here this afternoon, on a surprise visit.
> **sudden:** He had been deeply affected by the sudden death of his father-in-law.

un|ex|plained /ˌʌnɪksplˈeɪnd/ ADJ If you describe something as **unexplained**, you mean that the reason for it or cause of it is unclear or is not known. ❑ An unexplained death is difficult to come to terms with. ❑ The city's water supply has been cut for unexplained reasons.

un|fail|ing /ʌnfˈeɪlɪŋ/ ADJ [usu ADJ n] If you describe someone's good qualities or behavior as **unfailing**, you mean that they never change. ❑ He had the unfailing care and support of Erica, his wife. ● **un|fail|ing|ly** ADV ❑ He was unfailingly polite to customers.

un|fair ♦◇◇ /ʌnfˈɛər/ ADJ An **unfair** action or situation is not right or fair. ❑ She was awarded $5,000 in compensation for unfair dismissal. ❑ It was unfair that he should suffer so much. ● **un|fair|ly** ADV ❑ He unfairly blamed Frances for the failure.

un|fair dis|mis|sal N-UNCOUNT If an employee claims **unfair dismissal**, they begin a legal action against their employer in which they claim that they were dismissed from their job unfairly. [BUSINESS] ❑ His former chauffeur is claiming unfair dismissal on the grounds of racial discrimination.

un|faith|ful /ʌnfˈeɪθfəl/ ADJ If someone is **unfaithful** to their partner or to the person they are married to, they have a sexual relationship with someone else. ❑ James had been unfaithful to Christine for the entire four years they'd been together.

un|fa|mil|iar /ˌʌnfəmˈɪljər/ **1** ADJ If something is **unfamiliar** to you, you know nothing or very little about it, because you have not seen or experienced it before. ❑ She grew many wonderful plants that were unfamiliar to me. **2** ADJ [v-link ADJ with n] If you are **unfamiliar with** something, you know nothing or very little about it. ❑ She speaks no Japanese and is unfamiliar with Japanese culture.

un|fash|ion|able /ʌnfˈæʃənəbəl/ ADJ If something is **unfashionable**, it is not approved of or done by most people because it is out of style. ❑ Wearing fur has become unfashionable.

un|fas|ten /ʌnfˈæsən/ (unfastens, unfastening, unfastened) V-T If you **unfasten** something that is closed, tied, or held together, or if you **unfasten** the thing holding it, you loosen or remove the thing holding it. ❑ When Ted was six we decided that he needed to know how to fasten and unfasten his seat belt.

un|fath|om|able /ʌnfˈæðəməbəl/ **1** ADJ If you describe something as **unfathomable**, you mean that it cannot be understood or explained, usually because it is very strange or complicated. ❑ For some unfathomable reason, there are no stairs where there should be. **2** ADJ If you use **unfathomable** to describe a person or the expression on their face, you mean that you cannot tell what they are thinking or what they intend to do. [LITERARY] ❑ ...a strange, unfathomable and unpredictable individual.

un|fa|vor|able /ʌnfˈeɪvərəbəl/

> in BRIT, use **unfavourable**

1 ADJ **Unfavorable** conditions or circumstances cause problems for you and reduce your chances of success. ❑ The decision to delay the launch stems from unfavorable weather conditions. ❑ The whole international economic situation is very unfavorable for the countries in the south. **2** ADJ If you have an **unfavorable** reaction to something, you do not like it. ❑ The president is drawing unfavorable comments on his new forest policy. ❑ ...views unfavorable to the capitalist system. ● **un|fa|vor|ably** /ʌnfˈeɪvərəbli/ ADV [ADV after v] ❑ Other medications or foods may react unfavorably with it. **3** ADJ [ADJ n] If you make an **unfavorable** comparison between two things, you say that one thing seems worse than the other. ❑ I didn't expect unfavorable comparisons between my sons and their friends. ● **un|fa|vor|ably** ADV [ADV with v] ❑ Tax rates compare unfavorably with the less heavy-handed North American agreement.

un|fea|sible /ʌnfˈiːzəbəl/ ADJ If you say that something is **unfeasible**, you mean that you do not think it can be done, made, or achieved. ❑ The weather made it unfeasible to be outdoors.

un|feel|ing /ʌnfˈiːlɪŋ/ ADJ If you describe someone as **unfeeling**, you are criticizing them for their lack of kindness or sympathy for other people. [WRITTEN, DISAPPROVAL] ❑ He was branded an unfeeling bully.

un|fet|tered /ʌnfˈɛtərd/ ADJ If you describe something as **unfettered**, you mean that it is not controlled or limited by anyone or anything. [FORMAL] ❑ ...unfettered free trade.

un|fin|ished /ʌnfˈɪnɪʃt/ ADJ If you describe something such as a work of art or a piece of work as **unfinished**, you mean that it is not complete, for example because it was abandoned or there was no time to complete it. ❑ ...Jane Austen's unfinished novel. ❑ The cathedral was eventually completed in 1490, though the Gothic facade remains unfinished.

un|fit /ʌnfˈɪt/ **1** ADJ If you are **unfit**, your body is not in good condition because you have not been getting regular exercise. ❑ Many children are so unfit they are unable to do even basic exercises. **2** ADJ If someone is **unfit** for something, he or she is unable to do it because of injury or illness. ❑ He had a third examination and was declared unfit for duty. **3** ADJ If you say that someone or something is **unfit** for a particular purpose or job, you are criticizing them because they are not good enough for that purpose or job. [DISAPPROVAL] ❑ Existing houses are becoming totally unfit for human habitation. ❑ They were utterly unfit to govern.

un|flag|ging /ʌnflˈæɡɪŋ/ ADJ If you describe something such as support, effort, or enthusiasm as **unflagging**, you mean that it does not stop or get less as time passes. [APPROVAL] ❑ He was sustained by the unflagging support of his family.

un|flap|pable /ʌnflˈæpəbəl/ ADJ Someone who is **unflappable** is always calm and never panics or gets upset or angry.

un|flat|ter|ing /ʌnflˈætərɪŋ/ ADJ If you describe something as **unflattering**, you mean that it makes a person or thing seem less attractive than they really are. ❑ He depicted the town's respectable families in an unflattering light.

un|flinch|ing /ʌnflˈɪntʃɪŋ/ ADJ You can use **unflinching** in expressions such as **unflinching honesty** and **unflinching support** to indicate that a good quality which someone has is strong and steady, and never weakens. ❑ ...the armed forces, all of whom had pledged their unflinching support and loyalty to the government. ● **un|flinch|ing|ly** ADV ❑ They were unflinchingly loyal to their friends.

un|fo|cused /ʌnfˈoʊkəst/ also **unfocussed** **1** ADJ If someone's eyes are **unfocused**, they are open, but not looking at anything. ❑ Her eyes were unfocused, as if she were staring inside at her memories of the day. **2** ADJ If you describe someone's feelings or plans as **unfocused**, you are criticizing them because they do not seem to be clearly formed or have any clear purpose. [DISAPPROVAL] ❑ But for now, she is in the grip of a blind, unfocused anger.

un|fold /ʌnfˈoʊld/ (unfolds, unfolding, unfolded) **1** V-I If a situation **unfolds**, it develops and becomes known or understood. ❑ The outcome depends on conditions as well as how events unfold. **2** V-T/V-I If a story **unfolds** or if someone **unfolds** it, it is told to someone else. ❑ Don's story unfolded as the cruise got under way. **3** V-T/V-I If someone **unfolds** something which has been folded or if it **unfolds**, it is opened out and becomes flat. ❑ He quickly unfolded the blankets and spread them on the mattress.

un|fol|low /ʌnfˈɒloʊ/ (unfollows, unfollowing, unfollowed) VERB If you **unfollow** someone, you choose to stop seeing messages and pictures that they post on a social media website. ❑ The first step in erasing him from her life was to unfollow him on Instagram. ❑ If you don't like my tweets, just unfollow me.

un|fore|see|able /ˌʌnfɔrsˈiːəbəl/ ADJ An **unforeseeable** problem or unpleasant event is one which you did not expect and could not have predicted. ❑ This is such an unforeseeable situation that anything could happen.

un|fore|seen /ˌʌnfɔrsˈiːn/ ADJ If something that has happened was **unforeseen**, it was not expected to happen or known about beforehand. ❑ Radiation may damage cells in a way that was previously unforeseen. ❑ Unfortunately, due to unforeseen circumstances, this year's show has been canceled.

un|for|get|table /ˌʌnfərɡˈɛtəbəl/ ADJ If you describe something as **unforgettable**, you mean that it is, for example, extremely beautiful, enjoyable, or unusual, so that you remember it for a long time. You can also refer to extremely unpleasant things as **unforgettable**. ❑ *A visit to the museum is an unforgettable experience.* ❑ *...the outdoor activities that will make your vacation unforgettable.*

un|for|giv|able /ˌʌnfərgɪvəbəl/ ADJ If you say that something is **unforgivable**, you mean that it is very bad, cruel, or socially unacceptable. ❑ *These people are animals and what they did was unforgivable.*

un|for|giv|ing /ˌʌnfərgɪvɪŋ/ **1** ADJ If you describe someone as **unforgiving**, you mean that they are unwilling to forgive other people. [FORMAL] ❑ *He was an unforgiving man who never forgot a slight.* **2** ADJ If you describe a situation or activity as **unforgiving**, you mean that it causes a lot of people to experience great difficulty or failure, even people who deserve to succeed. ❑ *Business is a competitive activity. It is very fierce and very unforgiving.*

un|formed /ˌʌnfɔrmd/ ADJ If you describe someone or something as **unformed**, you mean that they are in an early stage of development and not fully formed or matured. [FORMAL] ❑ *The market for which they are competing is still unformed.*

un|for|tu|nate /ˌʌnfɔrtʃənɪt/ (**unfortunates**) **1** ADJ If you describe someone as **unfortunate**, you mean that something unpleasant or unlucky has happened to them. You can also describe the unpleasant things that happen to them as **unfortunate**. ❑ *Some unfortunate person passing below could all too easily be seriously injured.* ❑ *Apparently he had been unfortunate enough to fall victim to a gang of thugs.* **2** ADJ If you describe something that has happened as **unfortunate**, you think that it is inappropriate, embarrassing, awkward, or undesirable. ❑ *It is unfortunate that your flight was canceled.* ❑ *...the unfortunate incident of the upside-down Canadian flag.* **3** ADJ You can describe someone as **unfortunate** when they are poor or have a difficult life. ❑ *Every year we have fundraisers to raise money for unfortunate people.* • N-COUNT An **unfortunate** is someone who is unfortunate. ❑ *Dorothy was another of life's unfortunates.*

un|for|tu|nate|ly ✦✦✧ /ˌʌnfɔrtʃənɪtli/ ADV You can use **unfortunately** to introduce or refer to a statement when you consider that it is sad or disappointing, or when you want to express regret. [FEELINGS] ❑ *Unfortunately, my time is limited.* ❑ *Unfortunately for him, his title brought obligations as well as privileges.*

---SYNONYMS---

unfortunately
ADV
sadly: *Sadly, bamboo plants die after flowering.*
unluckily: *Unluckily for him, the fraud officers were watching this flight, too.*
regrettably: *The incidents are regrettably true.*

---

un|found|ed /ˌʌnfaʊndɪd/ ADJ If you describe a rumor, belief, or feeling as **unfounded**, you mean that it is wrong and is not based on facts or evidence. ❑ *Unfounded rumors of accounting problems hit stocks of other companies.* ❑ *The allegations were totally unfounded.*

un|friend /ˌʌnfrɛnd/ (**unfriends, unfriending, unfriended**) VERB If you **unfriend** someone, you stop being their friend on a social media website. ❑ *My 16-year-old has now unfriended me.*

un|friend|ly /ˌʌnfrɛndli/ (**unfriendlier, unfriendliest**) ADJ If you describe a person, organization, or their behavior as **unfriendly**, you mean that they behave toward you in an unkind or slightly hostile way. ❑ *Some people were unfriendly to the new recruit.* ❑ *People always complain that the big banks and big companies are unfriendly and unhelpful.*

-unfriendly /-ˌʌnfrɛndli/ COMB IN ADJ **-unfriendly** combines with nouns, and sometimes adverbs, to form adjectives which describe something which is bad for a particular thing. ❑ *It's couched in such very user-unfriendly terminology.*

un|ful|filled /ˌʌnfʊlfɪld/ **1** ADJ If you use **unfulfilled** to describe something such as a promise, ambition, or need, you mean that what was promised, hoped for, or needed has not happened. ❑ *Do you have any unfulfilled ambitions?* ❑ *...angry at unfulfilled promises of jobs and decent housing.* **2** ADJ If you describe someone as **unfulfilled**, you mean that they feel dissatisfied with life or with what they have done. ❑ *You must let go of the idea that to be single is to be unhappy and unfulfilled.*

un|fun|ny /ˌʌnfʌni/ (**unfunnier, unfunniest**) ADJ If you describe something or someone as **unfunny**, you mean that they do not make you laugh, although this was their intention or purpose. ❑ *We became increasingly fed up with his unfunny comments.*

un|furl /ˌʌnfɜrl/ (**unfurls, unfurling, unfurled**) **1** V-T/V-I If you **unfurl** something rolled or folded such as an umbrella, sail, or flag, you open it, so that it is spread out. You can also say that it **unfurls**. ❑ *Once outside the inner breakwater, we began to unfurl all the sails.* **2** V-I If you say that events, stories, or scenes **unfurl** before you, you mean that you are aware of them or can see them as they happen or develop. ❑ *The dramatic changes in Europe continue to unfurl.*

un|fur|nished /ˌʌnfɜrnɪʃt/ ADJ If you rent an **unfurnished** house or apartment, no furniture is provided by the owner.

un|gain|ly /ˌʌngeɪnli/ ADJ If you describe a person, animal, or vehicle as **ungainly**, you mean that they look awkward or clumsy, often because they are big. [FORMAL] ❑ *Paul swam in his ungainly way to the side of the pool.*

un|gen|er|ous /ˌʌndʒɛnərəs/ **1** ADJ If you describe someone's remarks, thoughts, or actions as **ungenerous**, you mean that they are unfair or unkind. [FORMAL] ❑ *This was a typically ungenerous response.* **2** ADJ You can use **ungenerous** when you are describing a person or organization that is unwilling to give much money to other people. [FORMAL]

un|glued /ˌʌnglud/ **1** PHRASE If someone **comes unglued**, they become very upset and emotional, and perhaps confused or mentally ill. [mainly AM, INFORMAL] ❑ *If she hears what you're saying, she's going to come unglued.* **2** PHRASE To **come unglued** means to fail. [mainly AM, INFORMAL] ❑ *Their marriage finally came unglued.*

> in BRIT, usually use **come unstuck**

3 PHRASE If something **comes unglued**, it becomes separated from the thing that it was attached to. ❑ *I wear my old shoes every day. One sole has come unglued.*

un|god|ly /ˌʌngɒdli/ **1** ADJ If you describe someone or something as **ungodly**, you mean that they are morally bad or are opposed to religion. **2** ADJ [ADJ n] If you refer to a time as an **ungodly** hour, you are emphasizing that it is very early in the morning. [EMPHASIS] ❑ *...at the ungodly hour of 4:00 a.m.* **3** ADJ [ADJ n] If you refer to the amount or volume of something as **ungodly**, you mean that it is excessive or unreasonable. ❑ *...a power struggle of ungodly proportions.*

un|gov|ern|able /ˌʌngʌvərnəbəl/ **1** ADJ [usu v-link ADJ] If you describe a country or region as **ungovernable**, you mean that it seems impossible to control or govern it effectively, for example, because of violence or conflict among the population. ❑ *The country has become virtually ungovernable.* **2** ADJ [usu ADJ n] If you describe feelings as **ungovernable**, you mean that they are so strong that they cannot be controlled. ❑ *He was filled with an ungovernable rage.*

un|gra|cious /ˌʌngreɪʃəs/ ADJ If you describe a person or their behavior as **ungracious**, you mean that they are not polite or friendly in their speech or behavior. [FORMAL] ❑ *She thought my expression of indifference was ungracious and offensive.*

un|gram|mati|cal /ˌʌngrəmætɪkəl/ ADJ If someone's language is **ungrammatical**, it is not considered correct because it does not obey the rules of grammar. ❑ *Native speakers can distinguish between grammatical and ungrammatical sentences even when they have never heard particular combinations before.* • **un|gram|mati|cal|ly** ADV [ADV after v] ❑ *She talked ungrammatically but fluently.*

un|grate|ful /ˌʌngreɪtfəl/ ADJ If you describe someone as **ungrateful**, you are criticizing them for not showing thanks or for being unkind to someone who has helped them or done them a favor. [DISAPPROVAL] ❑ *I thought it was ungrateful of her.*

un|guard|ed /ˌʌngɑrdɪd/ **1** ADJ If something is **unguarded**, nobody is protecting it or looking after it. ❑ *I should not leave my briefcase and camera bag unguarded.* **2** ADJ [usu ADJ n] If you do or say something in an **unguarded** moment, you do or say it carelessly and without thinking, especially when it is something that you did not want anyone to see or know. ❑ *The photographers managed to capture Jane in an unguarded moment.*

un|ham|pered /ʌnhæmpərd/ ADJ If you are **unhampered** by a problem or obstacle, you are free from it, and so you are able to do what you want to. [WRITTEN] ❑ ...her belief that things go best if businesspeople are allowed to make money unhampered by any kind of regulations.

un|hap|pi|ly /ʌnhæpɪli/ ADV [ADV with cl] You use **unhappily** to introduce or refer to a statement when you consider it to be sad and wish that it were different. ❑ On May 23rd, unhappily, the little boy died. ❑ Unhappily the facts do not wholly bear out the theory.

un|hap|py ♦◇◇ /ʌnhæpi/ (**unhappier**, **unhappiest**) **1** ADJ If you are **unhappy**, you are sad and depressed. ❑ Her marriage is in trouble and she is desperately unhappy. ❑ He was a shy, sometimes unhappy man. ● **un|hap|pi|ly** ADV ❑ "I don't have your imagination," Kevin said unhappily. ● **un|hap|pi|ness** N-UNCOUNT ❑ There was a lot of unhappiness in my adolescence. **2** ADJ [v-link ADJ] If you are **unhappy** about something, you are not pleased about it or not satisfied with it. ❑ He has been unhappy with his son's political leanings. ❑ College students are unhappy with their school bookstores. ● **un|hap|pi|ness** N-UNCOUNT ❑ He has, by submitting his resignation, signaled his unhappiness with the government's decision. **3** ADJ [ADJ n] An **unhappy** situation or choice is not satisfactory or desirable. ❑ It is our hope that this unhappy chapter in the history of relations between our two countries will soon be closed. ❑ The legislation represents in itself an unhappy compromise.

SYNONYMS

unhappy
ADJ **1**
sad: I'd grown fond of our little house and felt sad to leave it.
depressed: He seemed somewhat depressed.
miserable: She went to bed, miserable and humiliated.
gloomy: Miller is gloomy about the fate of the serious playwright in America.

---

un|harmed /ʌnhɑrmd/ ADJ [ADJ after v, v-link ADJ] If someone or something is **unharmed** after an accident or violent incident, they are not hurt or damaged in any way. ❑ They both escaped unharmed.

un|healthy /ʌnhɛlθi/ (**unhealthier**, **unhealthiest**) **1** ADJ Something that is **unhealthy** is likely to cause illness or bad health. ❑ Avoid unhealthy foods such as hamburgers and fries. **2** ADJ If you are **unhealthy**, you are sick or not in good physical condition. ❑ ...a pale, unhealthy looking man. **3** ADJ An **unhealthy** economy or company is financially weak and unsuccessful. ❑ If you have an unhealthy economy, the poor will get hurt worst because they are the most vulnerable. **4** ADJ If you describe someone's behavior or interests as **unhealthy**, you do not consider them to be normal and think they may involve mental problems. ❑ Frank has developed an unhealthy relationship with these people.

un|heard /ʌnhɜrd/ **1** ADJ If you say that a person or their words go **unheard**, you are expressing criticism because someone refuses to pay attention to what is said or take it into consideration. [WRITTEN, DISAPPROVAL] ❑ His impassioned pleas went unheard. **2** ADJ If you describe spoken comments or pieces of music as **unheard**, you mean that most people are not familiar with them because they have not been expressed or performed in public. ❑ ...a country where social criticism was largely unheard until this year. **3** ADJ [usu v-link ADJ] If someone's words or cries go **unheard**, nobody can hear them, or a particular person cannot hear them. [WRITTEN] ❑ Her cries for help went unheard due to the blaring music over the loudspeaker.

un|heard of /ʌnhɜrd ʌv/ ADJ [v-link ADJ] An event or situation that is **unheard of** never happens. ❑ Riots are almost unheard of in Japan.

un|heed|ed /ʌnhidɪd/ ADJ If you say that something such as a warning or danger goes **unheeded**, you mean that it has not been taken seriously or dealt with. [WRITTEN] ❑ The advice of experts went unheeded.

un|help|ful /ʌnhɛlpfəl/ ADJ If you say that someone or something is **unhelpful**, you mean that they do not help you or improve a situation, and may even make things worse. ❑ The criticism is both unfair and unhelpful.

un|her|ald|ed /ʌnhɛrəldɪd/ **1** ADJ [usu ADJ n] If you describe an artist or athlete as **unheralded**, you mean that people have not recognized their talent or ability. [JOURNALISM] ❑ They are inviting talented but unheralded movie-makers to submit examples of their work. **2** ADJ If you describe something that happens as **unheralded**, you mean that you did not expect it, because nobody mentioned it beforehand. [WRITTEN] ❑ ...Sandi's unheralded arrival on her doorstep.

un|hesi|tat|ing|ly /ʌnhɛzɪteɪtɪŋli/ ADV If you say that someone does something **unhesitatingly**, you mean that they do it immediately and confidently, without any doubt or anxiety. ❑ I would unhesitatingly choose the latter option.

un|hinge /ʌnhɪndʒ/ (**unhinges**, **unhinging**, **unhinged**) V-T If you say that an experience **has unhinged** someone, you mean that it has affected them so deeply that they have become mentally ill. ❑ The stress of war temporarily unhinged him.

un|hinged /ʌnhɪndʒd/ ADJ If you say that someone **comes** or **becomes unhinged**, you mean that they begin to behave in an uncontrolled or unreasonable way. [DISAPPROVAL] ❑ Robert De Niro plays an obsessed Boston Red Sox fan who becomes unhinged after he loses his job.

un|hip /ʌnhɪp/ ADJ If you describe someone or something as **unhip**, you mean that they are not at all fashionable or modern. [INFORMAL] ❑ ...two rather stiff, unhip, middle-aged men.

un|ho|ly /ʌnhoʊli/ **1** ADJ [ADJ n] You use **unholy** to emphasize how unreasonable or unpleasant you think something is. [EMPHASIS] ❑ The economy is still an unholy mess. **2** ADJ [ADJ n] If you refer to two or more people or groups working together as an **unholy** alliance, you mean that this arrangement is unusual because the people usually oppose each other. [DISAPPROVAL] ❑ Art shouldn't enter an unholy alliance with business. **3** ADJ [usu ADJ n] If you describe something as **unholy**, you mean that it is wicked or bad. ❑ "This ought to be fun," he told Alex, eyes gleaming with an almost unholy relish.

un|hook /ʌnhʊk/ (**unhooks**, **unhooking**, **unhooked**) **1** V-T If you **unhook** a piece of clothing that is fastened with hooks, you undo the hooks. ❑ She unhooked her dress. **2** V-T If you **unhook** something that is held in place by hooks, you open it or remove it by undoing the hooks. ❑ Chris unhooked the shutters and went out on the balcony.

un|hur|ried /ʌnhɜrid, -hʌr-/ ADJ If you describe something as **unhurried**, you approve of it because it is relaxed and slow, and is not rushed or anxious. [APPROVAL] ❑ ...an unhurried pace of life.

un|hurt /ʌnhɜrt/ ADJ [ADJ after v, v-link ADJ] If someone who has been attacked, or involved in an accident, is **unhurt**, they are not injured. ❑ The driver escaped unhurt, but a pedestrian was injured.

un|hy|gien|ic /ʌnhaɪdʒiɛnɪk, -dʒɛnɪk/ ADJ If you describe something as **unhygienic**, you mean that it is dirty and likely to cause infection or disease. ❑ Parts of the shop were very dirty, unhygienic, and an ideal breeding ground for bacteria.

uni|corn /yunɪkɔrn/ (**unicorns**) N-COUNT In stories and legends, a **unicorn** is an imaginary animal that looks like a white horse and has a horn growing from its forehead.

un|iden|ti|fi|able /ʌnaɪdɛntɪfaɪəbəl/ ADJ If something or someone is **unidentifiable**, you are not able to say exactly what it is or who they are. ❑ ...unidentifiable howling noises. ❑ All the bodies were totally unidentifiable.

un|iden|ti|fied ♦◇◇ /ʌnaɪdɛntɪfaɪd/ **1** ADJ If you describe someone or something as **unidentified**, you mean that nobody knows who or what they are. ❑ He was shot this morning by unidentified intruders at his house. **2** ADJ If you use **unidentified** to describe people, groups, and organizations, you do not want to give their names. [JOURNALISM] ❑ His claims were based on the comments of anonymous and unidentified sources.

uni|fi|ca|tion /yunɪfɪkeɪʃən/ N-UNCOUNT **Unification** is the process by which two or more countries join together and become one country. ❑ ...the process of European unification.

uni|form ♦◇◇ /yunɪfɔrm/ (**uniforms**) **1** N-VAR A **uniform** is a special set of clothes which some people, for example soldiers or the police, wear to work in and which some children wear in school. ❑ The police wear dark blue uniforms. ❑ Felipe was in uniform for the parade. **2** ADJ If something is **uniform**, it does not vary, but is even and regular throughout. ❑ Cut down between the bones so that all the chops are of uniform size. ❑ All flowing water, though it appears to be uniform, is actually divided into extensive inner surfaces, or layers, moving against one another. • **uni|form|ity** /yunɪfˈɔrmɪti/ N-UNCOUNT ❑ ...the caramel that was used to maintain uniformity of color in the brandy. • **uni|form|ly** ADV ❑ Beyond the windows, a November midday was uniformly gray. **❸** ADJ If you describe a number of things as **uniform**, you mean that they are all the same. ❑ Along each wall stretched uniform green metal filing cabinets. • **uni|form|ity** N-UNCOUNT ❑ ...the dull uniformity of the houses. • **uni|form|ly** ADV ❑ They are all about twenty years old, serious, smart, a bit conventional perhaps, but uniformly pleasant.

SYNONYMS

uniform
ADJ
❷
consistent: ...his consistent support of free trade.
even: How important is it to have an even temperature when you're working?
unvarying: ...her unvarying refusal to make public appearances.
regular: ...regular rows of wooden huts.
❸
alike: We looked very alike.
similar: ...a group of similar pictures.
identical: Nearly all the houses were identical.

uni|formed /yunɪfˈɔrmd/ ADJ If you use **uniformed** to describe someone who does a particular job, you mean that they are wearing a uniform. ❑ ...uniformed police officers.

uni|form|ity /yunɪfˈɔrmɪti/ **❶** N-UNCOUNT If there is **uniformity** in something such as a system, organization, or group of countries, the same rules, ideas, or methods are applied in all parts of it. ❑ He argues that we need statewide uniformity. **❷** → see also **uniform**

uni|fy /yunɪfaɪ/ (unifies, unifying, unified) V-T/V-I If someone **unifies** different parts or things, or if the things or parts **unify**, they are brought together to form one thing. ❑ He pledged to unify the city's political factions. ❑ ...constitutional reforms designed to unify the country. • **uni|fied** ADJ ❑ ...a unified system of taxation.

uni|lat|er|al /yunɪlætərəl/ ADJ A **unilateral** decision is made by only one of the groups, organizations, or countries that are involved in a particular situation, without the agreement of the others. ❑ ...unilateral nuclear disarmament.

uni|lat|er|al|ism /yunɪlætərəlɪzəm/ **❶** N-UNCOUNT **Unilateralism** is the belief that one country should get rid of all its own nuclear weapons, without waiting for other countries to do the same. **❷** N-UNCOUNT **Unilateralism** is used to refer to a policy in which one country or group involved in a situation takes a decision or action on its own, without the agreement of the other countries or groups involved. ❑ ...the recent history of American aggressive unilateralism on trade.

un|im|agi|nable /ʌnɪmædʒɪnəbəl/ ADJ If you describe something as **unimaginable**, you are emphasizing that it is difficult to imagine or understand well, because it is not part of people's normal experience. [EMPHASIS] ❑ The scale of the fighting is almost unimaginable. • **un|im|agi|nably** /ʌnɪmædʒɪnəbli/ ADV [ADV adj] ❑ Conditions in prisons out there are unimaginably bad.

un|im|agi|na|tive /ʌnɪmædʒɪnətɪv/ **❶** ADJ If you describe someone as **unimaginative**, you are criticizing them because they do not think of new methods or things to do. [DISAPPROVAL] ❑ Her second husband was a steady, unimaginative, corporate lawyer. **❷** ADJ [usu ADJ n] If you describe something as **unimaginative**, you mean that it is boring or unattractive because very little imagination or effort has been used on it. [DISAPPROVAL] ❑ ...unimaginative food.

un|im|paired /ʌnɪmpɛərd/ ADJ If something is **unimpaired** after something bad or unpleasant has happened to it, it is not damaged or made worse. [FORMAL] ❑ His health and vigor were unimpaired by a stroke.

un|im|peach|able /ʌnɪmpiːtʃəbəl/ ADJ If you describe someone as **unimpeachable**, you mean that they are completely honest and reliable. [FORMAL] ❑ He said all five were men of unimpeachable character.

un|im|ped|ed /ʌnɪmpiːdɪd/ ADJ If something moves or happens **unimpeded**, it continues without being stopped or interrupted by anything. [FORMAL] ❑ She could drive unimpeded by slow-moving traffic.

un|im|por|tant /ʌnɪmpɔrtənt/ ADJ If you describe something or someone as **unimportant**, you mean that they do not have much influence, effect, or value, and are therefore not worth serious consideration. ❑ When they had married, six years before, the difference in their ages had seemed unimportant.

un|im|pressed /ʌnɪmprɛst/ ADJ [v-link ADJ] If you are **unimpressed** by something or someone, you do not think they are very good, intelligent, or useful. ❑ He was also very unimpressed by his teachers.

un|im|pres|sive /ʌnɪmprɛsɪv/ ADJ If you describe someone or something as **unimpressive**, you mean they appear very ordinary, without any special or exciting qualities. ❑ Dewey was an unimpressive, rather dull lecturer.

un|in|forma|tive /ʌnɪnfɔrmətɪv/ ADJ Something that is **uninformative** does not give you enough useful information. ❑ It was a singularly uninformative document.

un|in|formed /ʌnɪnfɔrmd/ ADJ If you describe someone as **uninformed**, you mean that they have very little knowledge or information about a particular situation or subject. ❑ He could not complain that he was uninformed about the true nature of the regime.

un|in|hab|it|able /ʌnɪnhæbɪtəbəl/ ADJ If a place is **uninhabitable**, it is impossible for people to live there, for example because it is dangerous or unhealthy. ❑ As parts of the world become uninhabitable, millions of people will try to migrate to more hospitable areas.

un|in|hab|it|ed /ʌnɪnhæbɪtɪd/ ADJ An **uninhabited** place is one where nobody lives. ❑ ...an uninhabited island in the North Pacific. ❑ The area is largely uninhabited.

un|in|hib|it|ed /ʌnɪnhɪbɪtɪd/ ADJ If you describe a person or their behavior as **uninhibited**, you mean that they express their opinions and feelings openly, and behave as they want to, without worrying what other people think. ❑ ...a bold and uninhibited entertainer. ❑ The dancing is uninhibited and as frenzied as an aerobics class.

un|ini|ti|at|ed /ʌnɪnɪʃieɪtɪd/ N-PLURAL [the N] You can refer to people who have no knowledge or experience of a particular subject or activity as the **uninitiated**. ❑ For the uninitiated, Western Swing is a fusion of jazz, rhythm and blues, rock and roll, and country music. • ADJ **Uninitiated** is also an adjective. ❑ For those uninitiated in scientific ocean drilling, the previous record was a little over 4 km.

un|in|jured /ʌnɪndʒərd/ ADJ [ADJ after v, v-link ADJ] If someone is **uninjured** after an accident or attack, they are not hurt, even though you would expect them to be. ❑ The man's wife, a passenger in the van, was uninjured in the accident.

un|in|spired /ʌnɪnspaɪərd/ ADJ If you describe something or someone as **uninspired**, you are criticizing them because they do not seem to have any original or exciting qualities. [DISAPPROVAL] ❑ The script was singularly uninspired.

un|in|spir|ing /ʌnɪnspaɪərɪŋ/ ADJ If you describe something or someone as **uninspiring**, you are criticizing them because they have no special or exciting qualities, and make you feel bored. [DISAPPROVAL] ❑ The house had a tiny kitchen with an uninspiring view.

un|in|stall /ʌnɪnstɔl/ (uninstalls, uninstalling, uninstalled) V-T If you **uninstall** a computer program, you remove it permanently from your computer. [COMPUTING] ❑ If you don't like the program, just uninstall it and forget it.

un|in|tel|li|gent /ʌnɪntɛlɪdʒənt/ ADJ If you describe a person as **unintelligent**, you mean that they are stupid, or do not show any sensible ideas or thoughts. ❑ He believes him to be a weak and unintelligent man. ❑ He certainly was not unintelligent.

un|in|tel|li|gible /ʌnɪntɛlɪdʒɪbəl/ ADJ **Unintelligible** language is impossible to understand, for example because it is not written or pronounced clearly, or because its meaning is confused or complicated. ❑ He muttered something unintelligible.

un|in|tend|ed /ʌnɪntɛndɪd/ ADJ **Unintended** results were not planned to happen, although they happened. ❑ ...the unintended consequences of human action.

un|in|ten|tion|al /ʌnɪntɛnʃənəl/ ADJ Something that is **unintentional** is not done deliberately, but happens by accident. ❑ Perhaps he had slightly misled them, but it was quite

unintentional. • **un|in|ten|tion|al|ly** ADV ❑ ...an overblown and unintentionally funny adaptation of "Dracula."

un|in|ter|est|ed /ʌnɪntərestɪd, -trɪstɪd/ ADJ If you are uninterested in something or someone, you do not want to know any more about them, because you think they have no special or exciting qualities. ❑ I was so uninterested in the result that I didn't even bother to look at it.

un|in|ter|est|ing /ʌnɪntərestɪŋ, -trɪstɪŋ/ ADJ If you describe something or someone as uninteresting, you mean they have no special or exciting qualities. ❑ Their media have earned the reputation for being rather dull and uninteresting.

un|in|ter|rupt|ed /ʌnɪntərʌptɪd/ **1** ADJ If something is uninterrupted, it is continuous and has no breaks or interruptions in it. ❑ This enables the healing process to continue uninterrupted. ❑ His hearing remained good, so that his contact with the world was uninterrupted. **2** ADJ An uninterrupted view of something is a clear view of it, without any obstacles in the way. ❑ Diners can enjoy an uninterrupted view of the gardens.

un|in|vit|ed /ʌnɪnvaɪtɪd/ ADJ If someone does something or goes somewhere uninvited, they do it or go there without being asked, often when their action or presence is not wanted. ❑ He came uninvited to one of Stein's parties.

un|ion ♦♦♦ /yunyən/ (unions) **1** N-COUNT A union is a workers' organization which represents its members and which tries to improve things such as their working conditions and pay. ❑ Do all teachers have a right to join a union? **2** N-UNCOUNT When the union of two or more things occurs, they are joined together and become one thing. ❑ In 1918 the Romanian majority in this former czarist province voted for union with Romania. **3** N-SING When two or more things, for example countries or organizations, have been joined together to form one thing, you can refer to them as a union. ❑ Tanzania is a union of the states of Tanganyika and Zanzibar.

SYNONYMS

union
NOUN
2
unification: ...the process of general European unification.
combination: ...the combination of science and art.
integration: They see progress towards integration.
3
alliance: The two parties were still too much apart to form an alliance.
league: ...the League of Nations.
association: ...the Association of British Travel Agents.
coalition: Since June, the country has had a coalition government.

---

un|ion|ism /yunyənɪzəm/ N-UNCOUNT Unionism is any set of political principles based on the idea that two or more political or national units should be joined or remain together, for example that Quebec should remain part of Canada. • **un|ion|ist** (unionists) N-COUNT ❑ ...traditional unionists fearful of home rule.

un|ioni|za|tion /yunyənɪzeɪʃən/

in BRIT, also use **unionisation**

N-UNCOUNT The unionization of workers or industries is the process of workers becoming members of labor unions. ❑ Increasing unionization led to demands for higher wages and shorter hours.

un|ion|ized /yunyənaɪzd/

in BRIT, also use **unionised**

ADJ Unionized workers belong to labor unions. If a company or place is unionized, most of the workers there belong to labor unions.

Un|ion Jack (Union Jacks) N-COUNT [usu sing, oft the N] The Union Jack is the national flag of the United Kingdom. It consists of a blue background with red and white crosses on it.

un|ion suit (union suits) N-COUNT A union suit is a piece of underwear, worn by men or boys, that covers the body and legs. [AM]

unique ♦♦◊ /yunik/ **1** ADJ Something that is unique is the only one of its kind. ❑ Each person's signature is unique. • **unique|ly** ADV ❑ Because of the extreme cold, the Antarctic is a uniquely fragile environment. • **unique|ness** N-UNCOUNT ❑ ...the uniqueness of China's own experience. **2** ADJ You can use unique to describe things that you admire because they are very unusual and special. [APPROVAL] ❑ She was a woman of unique talent and determination. • **unique|ly** ADV ❑ There'll never be a shortage of people who consider themselves uniquely qualified to be president of the United States. **3** ADJ [v-link ADJ to n] If something is unique to one thing, person, group, or place, it concerns or belongs only to that thing, person, group, or place. ❑ No one knows for sure why adolescence is unique to humans. • **unique|ly** ADV [ADV adj] ❑ The problem isn't uniquely American.

uni|sex /yunɪseks/ ADJ Unisex is used to describe things, usually clothes or places, which are designed for use by both men and women rather than by only one sex. ❑ ...the classic unisex hair salon.

uni|son /yunɪsən, -zən/ **1** PHRASE If two or more people do something in unison, they do it together at the same time. ❑ Every morning the kids say the Pledge of Allegiance in unison. **2** PHRASE If people or organizations act in unison, they act the same way because they agree with each other or because they want to achieve the same goals. ❑ The international community is ready to work in unison against him.

unit ♦♦◊ /yunɪt/ (units) **1** N-COUNT If you consider something as a unit, you consider it as a single, complete thing. ❑ Agriculture was based in the past on the family as a unit. **2** N-COUNT A unit is a group of people who work together at a specific job, often in a particular place. ❑ ...the environmental research unit. **3** N-COUNT A unit is a group within an armed force or police force, whose members fight or work together or carry out a particular task. ❑ ...a firefighting unit. **4** N-COUNT A unit is a small machine which has a particular function, often part of a larger machine. ❑ The unit plugs into any TV set. **5** N-COUNT A unit of measurement is a fixed standard quantity, length, or weight that is used for measuring things. The quart, the inch, and the ounce are all units. **6** N-COUNT A unit is one of the parts that a textbook is divided into. ❑ Unit V of this book explains those errors in detail and shows you ways to correct them.

Uni|tar|ian /yunɪtɛəriən/ (Unitarians) **1** N-COUNT Unitarians are Christians who reject the idea of the Trinity and believe that God is a single being. ❑ They were Unitarians. **2** ADJ Unitarian means relating to the religious beliefs or practices of Unitarians. ❑ ...a Unitarian minister.

uni|tary /yunɪteri/ ADJ [ADJ n] A unitary country or organization is one in which two or more areas or groups have joined together, have the same aims, and are controlled by a single government. ❑ ...a call for the creation of a single unitary state.

unit cost (unit costs) N-COUNT Unit cost is the amount of money that it costs a company to produce one article. [BUSINESS] ❑ They hope to reduce unit costs through extra sales.

unite /yunaɪt/ (unites, uniting, united) V-T/V-I If a group of people or things unite or if something unites them, they join together and act as a group. ❑ We need to unite against terrorism.

unit|ed ♦♦◊ /yunaɪtɪd/ **1** ADJ When people are united about something, they agree about it and act together. ❑ They are united by their love of soccer. **2** ADJ United is used to describe a country which has been formed from two or more states or countries. ❑ ...the first elections to be held in a united Germany for fifty-eight years.

Unit|ed King|dom ♦◊◊ N-PROPER [the N] The United Kingdom is the official name for the country consisting of Great Britain and Northern Ireland.

Unit|ed Na|tions ♦♦◊ N-PROPER [the N] The United Nations is an organization which most countries belong to. Its role is to encourage international peace, cooperation, and friendship.

Unit|ed States N-PROPER [the N] The United States of America is the official name for the country in North America that consists of fifty states and the District of Columbia. It is bordered by Canada in the north and Mexico in the south. The form United States is also used.

unit sales N-PLURAL Unit sales refers to the number of individual items that a company sells. [BUSINESS] ❑ Unit sales of T-shirts increased 6%.

unit trust (unit trusts) N-COUNT Unit trust means the same as mutual fund. [BRIT, BUSINESS]

unity /yúnɪti/ **1** N-UNCOUNT **Unity** is the state of different areas or groups being joined together to form a single country or organization. ❑ *We have to act to preserve the unity of this nation.* **2** N-UNCOUNT When there is **unity**, people are in agreement and act together for a particular purpose. ❑ *...a renewed unity of purpose.* ❑ *Speakers at the rally expressed sentiments of unity.*

Univ also **Univ. Univ** is a written abbreviation for **University** which is used especially in the names of universities. ❑ *...the Wharton School, Univ. of Pennsylvania.*

uni|ver|sal /yúnɪvɜrsəl/ **1** ADJ Something that is **universal** relates to everyone in the world or everyone in a particular group or society. ❑ *The insurance industry has produced its own proposals for universal health care.* ❑ *The desire to look attractive is universal.* **2** ADJ Something that is **universal** affects or relates to every part of the world or the universe. ❑ *...universal diseases.*

uni|ver|sal bank (universal banks) N-COUNT A **universal bank** is a bank that offers both banking and stockbroking services to its clients. [BUSINESS] ❑ *...universal banks offering a wide range of services.*

uni|ver|sal|ly /yúnɪvɜrsəli/ **1** ADV If something is **universally** believed or accepted, it is believed or accepted by everyone with no disagreement. ❑ *...a universally accepted point of view.* **2** ADV If something is **universally** true, it is true everywhere in the world or in all situations. ❑ *The disadvantage is that it is not universally available.*

uni|verse /yúnɪvɜrs/ (universes) **1** N-COUNT The **universe** is the whole of space and all the stars, planets, and other forms of matter and energy in it. ❑ *Einstein's equations showed the universe to be expanding.* **2** N-COUNT If you talk about someone's **universe**, you are referring to the whole of their experience or an important part of it. ❑ *Good writers suck in what they see of the world, re-creating their own universe on the page.*

VOCABULARY IN CONTEXT

University education

The leap to **tertiary education** is an enormous one. First, college applications can be daunting, requiring the prospective student to pore over one **prospectus** after another trying to choose between various **undergraduate courses**. Then there is the anxiety of **conditional offers** contingent on exam results. Assuming you're accepted into the program you want, relocating is often necessary, and many students haven't lived away from home before. Some get a place in the **residence halls**; others move into shared accommodations. Then there's the matter of **college fees** and **student loans** for those who don't receive a **grant** or financial support from their families. Suddenly, young people are faced with a completely new **academic** system. Before they really know their **faculty** members, they must submit **course work** in a format that's new to them. And now they're responsible for getting themselves to **lectures**, **seminars**, and **recitations**, too. It's certainly an exciting time, but adjusting to university life can be quite overwhelming at first.

---

uni|ver|sity /yúnɪvɜrsɪti/ (universities) N-VAR; N-IN-NAMES A **university** is an institution where students study for degrees and where academic research is done. ❑ *Offenbacker earned an education degree at the University of Washington and taught elementary school.* ❑ *She goes to Duke University.*

un|just /ʌndʒʌ́st/ ADJ If you describe an action, system, or law as **unjust**, you think that it treats a person or group badly in a way that they do not deserve. ❑ *The attack on Charles was unjust.* • **un|just|ly** ADV ❑ *She was unjustly accused of stealing money, and then fired.*

un|jus|ti|fi|able /ʌndʒʌ́stɪfaɪəbəl, ʌndʒʌstɪfaɪəbəl/ ADJ If you describe an action, especially one that harms someone, as **unjustifiable**, you mean there is no good reason for it. ❑ *Using these missiles to down civilian aircraft is simply immoral and totally unjustifiable.* • **un|jus|ti|fi|ably** ADV ❑ *The press invade people's privacy unfairly and unjustifiably every day.*

un|jus|ti|fied /ʌndʒʌ́stɪfaɪd/ ADJ If you describe a belief or action as **unjustified**, you think that there is no good reason for having it or doing it. ❑ *Your report last week was unfair. It was based upon wholly unfounded and totally unjustified allegations.*

un|kempt /ʌnkɛ́mpt/ ADJ If you describe something or someone as **unkempt**, you mean that they are dirty, and not taken care of or kept neat. ❑ *His hair was unkempt and filthy.*

un|kind /ʌnkáɪnd/ (unkinder, unkindest) **1** ADJ If someone is **unkind**, they behave in an unpleasant, unfriendly, or slightly cruel way. You can also describe someone's words or actions as **unkind**. ❑ *All last summer he'd been unkind to her.* ❑ *No one has an unkind word to say about him.* • **un|kind|ly** ADV ❑ *Several viewers commented unkindly on her costumes.* • **un|kind|ness** N-UNCOUNT ❑ *He realized the unkindness of the remark and immediately regretted having hurt her with it.* **2** ADJ If you describe something bad that happens to someone as **unkind**, you mean that they do not deserve it. [WRITTEN] ❑ *The weather was unkind to those pipers who played in the morning.*

un|know|able /ʌnnóʊəbəl/ ADJ If you describe something as **unknowable**, you mean that it is impossible for human beings to know anything about it. [WRITTEN] ❑ *The specific impact of the greenhouse effect is unknowable.*

un|know|ing /ʌnnóʊɪŋ/ ADJ [usu ADJ n] If you describe a person as **unknowing**, you mean that they are not aware of what is happening or of what they are doing. ❑ *Some governments have been victims and perhaps unknowing accomplices in the bank's activities.*

un|know|ing|ly /ʌnnóʊɪŋli/ ADV If someone does something **unknowingly**, they do it without being aware of it. ❑ *The firm says it unknowingly published incorrect statistics.*

un|known /ʌnnóʊn/ (unknowns) **1** ADJ If something is **unknown** to you, you have no knowledge of it. ❑ *An unknown number of demonstrators were arrested.* ❑ *The motive for the killing is unknown.* • N-COUNT An **unknown** is something that is unknown. ❑ *The length of the war is one of the biggest unknowns.* **2** ADJ An **unknown** person is someone whose name you do not know or whose character you do not know anything about. ❑ *...the tomb of the unknown soldier.* **3** ADJ An **unknown** person is not famous or publicly recognized. ❑ *He was an unknown writer.* • N-COUNT An **unknown** is a person who is unknown. ❑ *Within a short space of time a group of complete unknowns had established a wholly original form of humor.* **4** ADJ If you say that a particular problem or situation is **unknown**, you mean that it never occurs. ❑ *A hundred years ago coronary heart disease was virtually unknown in America.* **5** N-SING The **unknown** refers generally to things or places that people do not know about or understand. ❑ *Ignorance of people brings fear, fear of the unknown.*

un|law|ful /ʌnlɔ́fəl/ ADJ If something is **unlawful**, the law does not allow you to do it. [FORMAL] ❑ *...employees who believe their dismissal was unlawful.* • **un|law|ful|ly** ADV [ADV with v] ❑ *The government acted unlawfully in imposing the restrictions.*

un|law|ful kill|ing (unlawful killings) N-VAR **Unlawful killing** is used to refer to crimes which involve one person killing another. [LEGAL]

un|lead|ed /ʌnlɛ́dɪd/ ADJ **Unleaded** fuel contains a smaller amount of lead than most fuels so that it produces fewer harmful substances when it is burned. ❑ *He filled up his Toyota with regular unleaded gas.* • N-UNCOUNT **Unleaded** is also a noun. ❑ *All its V8 engines will run happily on unleaded.*

un|learn /ʌnlɜrn/ (unlearns, unlearning, unlearned) V-T If you **unlearn** something that you have learned, you try to forget it or ignore it, often because it is wrong or it is having a bad influence on you. ❑ *They learn new roles and unlearn old ones.*

un|leash /ʌnliʃ/ (unleashes, unleashing, unleashed) V-T If you say that someone or something **unleashes** a powerful force, feeling, activity, or group, you mean that they suddenly start it or send it somewhere. ❑ *The announcement unleashed a storm of protest from the public.* ❑ *The officers were still reluctant to unleash their troops in pursuit of a defeated enemy.*

un|leav|ened /ʌnlɛvənd/ ADJ [usu ADJ n] **Unleavened** bread or dough is made without any yeast.

un|less ✦✧ /ʌnlɛs/ CONJ You use **unless** to introduce the only circumstances in which an event you are mentioning will not take place or in which a statement you are making is not true. ❑ *Unless you are trying to lose weight to please yourself, it's going to be tough to keep your motivation level high.* ❑ *We cannot understand disease unless we understand the person who has the disease.*

un|li|censed /ʌnlaɪsənst/ **1** ADJ If you are **unlicensed**, you do not have official permission from the government or from the authorities to do something. ❑ *...unscrupulous, and usually unlicensed investment managers who regularly target wealthy widows.* **2** ADJ If something that you own or use is **unlicensed**, you do not have official permission to own it or use it. ❑ *He went out with an unlicensed shotgun to look for the intruders.* **3** ADJ If a place such as a bar or restaurant is **unlicensed**, it does not have a license to sell alcoholic drinks. **4** ADJ If something such as an activity or product is **unlicensed**, it takes place or is produced without official permission. ❑ *Unlicensed steroids are being disguised as herbal medicines.*

un|like ✦✧ /ʌnlaɪk/ **1** PREP If one thing is **unlike** another thing, the two things have different qualities or characteristics from each other. ❑ *This was a foreign country, so unlike San Jose.* **2** PREP You can use **unlike** to contrast two people, things, or situations, and show how they are different. ❑ *Unlike aerobics, walking entails no expensive fees for classes or clubs.* **3** PREP If you describe something that a particular person has done as being **unlike** them, you mean that you are surprised by it because it is not typical of their character or normal behavior. ❑ *It was so unlike him to say something like that, with such intensity, that I was astonished.*

un|like|ly ✦✧ /ʌnlaɪkli/ (unlikeliest) ADJ If you say that something is **unlikely** to happen or **unlikely** to be true, you believe that it will not happen or that it is not true, although you are not completely sure. ❑ *A military coup seems unlikely.* ❑ *As with many technological revolutions, you are unlikely to be aware of it.*

un|lim|it|ed /ʌnlɪmɪtɪd/ ADJ If there is an **unlimited** quantity of something, you can have as much or as many of that thing as you want. ❑ *An unlimited number of copies can still be made from the original.* ❑ *You'll also have unlimited access to the swimming pool.*

un|list|ed /ʌnlɪstɪd/ **1** ADJ If a person or their telephone number is **unlisted**, the number is not listed in the telephone book, and the telephone company will refuse to give it to people who ask for it. [mainly AM] ❑ *Mr. Marra, whose New York telephone number is unlisted, could not be contacted yesterday.*

in BRIT, usually use **ex-directory**

2 ADJ An **unlisted** company or **unlisted** stock is not listed officially on a stock exchange. [BUSINESS] ❑ *Its shares are traded on the Unlisted Securities Market.*

un|lis|ten|able /ʌnlɪsənəbəl/ ADJ If you describe music as **unlistenable**, you mean that is very poor in quality. [DISAPPROVAL] ❑ *The early stuff is mostly unlistenable.*

un|lit /ʌnlɪt/ **1** ADJ An **unlit** fire or cigarette has not been made to start burning. **2** ADJ An **unlit** street or building is dark because there are no lights switched on in it.

un|load /ʌnloʊd/ (unloads, unloading, unloaded) V-T If you **unload** goods from a vehicle, or you **unload** a vehicle, you remove the goods from the vehicle, usually after they have been transported from one place to another. ❑ *Unload everything from the boat and clean it thoroughly.*

un|lock /ʌnlɒk/ (unlocks, unlocking, unlocked) **1** V-T If you **unlock** something such as a door, a room, or a container that has a lock, you open it using a key. ❑ *He unlocked the car and threw the coat on to the back seat.* **2** V-T If you **unlock** the potential or the secrets of something or someone, you release them. ❑ *The point of the competition is to encourage all people to unlock their hidden potential.*

un|lov|able /ʌnlʌvəbəl/ ADJ If someone is **unlovable**, they are not likely to be loved by anyone, because they do not have any attractive qualities.

un|loved /ʌnlʌvd/ ADJ If someone feels **unloved**, they feel that nobody loves them. ❑ *I think she feels wounded and unloved at the moment.*

un|love|ly /ʌnlʌvli/ (unlovelier, unloveliest) ADJ If you describe something as **unlovely**, you mean that it is unattractive or unpleasant in some way. [WRITTEN] ❑ *She found a small, inexpensive motel on the outskirts of the town; it was barren and unlovely.*

un|lov|ing /ʌnlʌvɪŋ/ ADJ If you describe a person as **unloving**, you believe that they do not love, or show love to, the people they ought to love. ❑ *The overworked, overextended parent may be seen as unloving, but may simply be exhausted.*

un|lucki|ly /ʌnlʌkɪli/ ADV You use **unluckily** as a comment on something bad or unpleasant that happens to someone, in order to suggest sympathy for them or that it was not their fault. ❑ *Unluckily for him, the officers were watching this flight too.*

un|lucky /ʌnlʌki/ (unluckier, unluckiest) **1** ADJ If someone is **unlucky**, they have bad luck. ❑ *You certainly were unlucky to get that horrible illness.* **2** ADJ You can use **unlucky** to describe unpleasant things which happen to someone, especially when you feel that the person does not deserve them. ❑ *...Argentina's unlucky defeat by Ireland.* **3** ADJ **Unlucky** is used to describe something that is thought to cause bad luck. ❑ *Some people think it is unlucky to walk under a ladder.*

un|made /ʌnmeɪd/ ADJ An **unmade** bed has not had the sheets and covers neatly arranged after it was last slept in.

un|man|age|able /ʌnmænɪdʒəbəl/ **1** ADJ If you describe something as **unmanageable**, you mean that it is difficult to use, deal with, or control. ❑ *People were visiting the house every day, sometimes in unmanageable numbers.* **2** ADJ If you describe someone, especially a young person, as **unmanageable**, you mean that they behave in an unacceptable way and are difficult to control. ❑ *The signs are that indulged children tend to become unmanageable when they reach their teens.*

un|man|ly /ʌnmænli/ ADJ [usu v-link ADJ] If you describe a boy's or man's behavior as **unmanly**, you are critical of the fact that they are behaving in a way that you think is inappropriate for a man. [DISAPPROVAL] ❑ *Your partner can feel the loss as acutely as you, but may feel that it is unmanly to cry.*

un|manned /ʌnmænd/ **1** ADJ [usu ADJ n] **Unmanned** vehicles such as spacecraft do not have any people in them and operate automatically or are controlled from a distance. ❑ *...a special unmanned spacecraft.* **2** ADJ If a place is **unmanned**, there is nobody working there. ❑ *Unmanned post offices meant millions of letters went unsorted.*

un|marked /ʌnmɑrkt/ **1** ADJ Something that is **unmarked** has no marks on it. ❑ *Her shoes are still white and unmarked.* **2** ADJ Something that is **unmarked** has no marking on it which identifies what it is or whose it is. ❑ *He had seen them come out and get into the unmarked police car.*

un|mar|ried /ʌnmærɪd/ ADJ Someone who is **unmarried** is not married.

un|mask /ʌnmæsk/ (unmasks, unmasking, unmasked) V-T If you **unmask** someone or something bad, you show or make known their true nature or character, when they had previously been thought to be good. ❑ *Elliott unmasked and confronted the master spy and traitor Kim Philby.*

un|matched /ʌnmætʃt/ ADJ If you describe something as **unmatched**, you are emphasizing that it is better or greater than all other things of the same kind. [EMPHASIS] ❑ *...a landscape of unmatched beauty.*

un|men|tion|able /ʌnmɛnʃənəbəl/ ADJ If you describe something as **unmentionable**, you mean that it is too embarrassing or unpleasant to talk about. ❑ *Has he got some unmentionable disease?*

un|mer|ci|ful|ly /ʌnmɜrsɪfəli/ ADV If you do something unmercifully, you do it a lot, showing no pity. ❑ *Uncle Sebastian used to tease Mother and Daddy unmercifully that all they could produce was girls.*

un|met /ʌnmɛt/ ADJ Unmet needs or demands are not satisfied. ❑ *...the unmet demand for quality family planning services.*

un|me|tered /ʌnmitərd/ ADJ An unmetered service for something such as water supply is one that allows you to use as much as you want for a basic cost, instead of paying for the amount you use. ❑ *Clients are not charged by the minute but given unmetered access to the Internet for a fixed fee.*

un|mis|tak|able /ʌnmɪsteɪkəbəl/ also unmistakeable ADJ If you describe something as unmistakable, you mean that it is so obvious that it cannot be mistaken for anything else. ❑ *He didn't give his name, but the voice was unmistakable.* ● **un|mis|tak|ably** /ʌnmɪsteɪkəbli/ ADV ❑ *It's still unmistakably a Minnelli movie.* ❑ *...an unmistakably American accent.*

un|miti|gat|ed /ʌnmɪtɪgeɪtɪd/ ADJ [ADJ n] You use unmitigated to emphasize that a bad situation or quality is totally bad. [EMPHASIS] ❑ *Last year's cotton crop was an unmitigated disaster.*

un|mo|lest|ed /ʌnməlɛstɪd/ ADJ If someone does something unmolested, they do it without being stopped or interfered with. ❑ *Like many fugitives, he lived in Argentina unmolested for many years.*

un|moved /ʌnmuvd/ ADJ [v-link ADJ] If you are unmoved by something, you are not emotionally affected by it. ❑ *Mr. Bird remained unmoved by the corruption allegations.*

un|mu|si|cal /ʌnmyuzɪkəl/ **1** ADJ An unmusical sound is unpleasant to listen to. ❑ *Lainey had a terrible voice, unmusical and sharp.* **2** ADJ An unmusical person cannot play or appreciate music. ❑ *They're completely unmusical.*

un|mute /ʌnmyut/ (unmutes, unmuting, unmuted) VERB If you unmute someone or something, you make them able to be heard again after they have been on mute.

un|named /ʌnneɪmd/ **1** ADJ Unnamed people or things are talked about but their names are not mentioned. ❑ *Perot accused unnamed U.S. officials of covering up the facts.* **2** ADJ Unnamed things have not been given a name. ❑ *...unnamed comets and asteroids.*

un|natu|ral /ʌnnætʃərəl/ **1** ADJ If you describe something as unnatural, you mean that it is strange and often frightening, because it is different from what you normally expect. ❑ *The aircraft rose with unnatural speed on takeoff.* ● **un|natu|ral|ly** ADV [ADV adj] ❑ *The house was unnaturally silent.* **2** ADJ Behavior that is unnatural seems artificial and not normal or genuine. ❑ *She gave him a bright, determined smile which seemed unnatural.* ● **un|natu|ral|ly** ADV [ADV with v] ❑ *Try to avoid shouting or speaking unnaturally.*

un|natu|ral|ly /ʌnnætʃərəli/ **1** PHRASE You can use **not unnaturally** to indicate that the situation you are describing is exactly as you would expect in the circumstances. ❑ *The result, not unnaturally, was that he became more tense and increasingly frustrated.* **2** → see also **unnatural**

un|nec|es|sary /ʌnnɛsəsɛri/ ADJ If you describe something as unnecessary, you mean that it is not needed or does not have to be done. ❑ *The slaughter of whales is unnecessary and inhuman.* ● **un|nec|es|sari|ly** /ʌnnɛsəsɛrɪli/ ADV ❑ *I didn't want to upset my husband or my daughter unnecessarily.*

un|nerve /ʌnnɜrv/ (unnerves, unnerving, unnerved) V-T If you say that something unnerves you, you mean that it worries or troubles you. ❑ *The news about Dermot had unnerved me.*

un|nerv|ing /ʌnnɜrvɪŋ/ ADJ If you describe something as unnerving, you mean that it makes you feel worried or uncomfortable. ❑ *It is very unnerving to find out that someone you see every day is carrying a potentially deadly virus.*

un|no|ticed /ʌnnoʊtɪst/ ADJ If something happens or passes unnoticed, it is not seen or noticed by anyone. ❑ *I tried to slip up the stairs unnoticed.*

un|ob|served /ʌnəbzɜrvd/ ADJ If you do something unobserved, you do it without being seen by other people. ❑ *Looking around to make sure he was unobserved, he slipped through the door.*

un|ob|tain|able /ʌnəbteɪnəbəl/ ADJ If something or someone is unobtainable, you cannot get them. ❑ *Fish was unobtainable in certain sections of Tokyo.*

un|ob|tru|sive /ʌnəbtrusɪv/ ADJ If you describe something or someone as unobtrusive, you mean that they are not easily noticed or do not draw attention to themselves. [FORMAL] ❑ *The coffee table is glass, to be as unobtrusive as possible.* ● **un|ob|tru|sive|ly** ADV ❑ *They slipped away unobtrusively.*

un|oc|cu|pied /ʌnɒkyupaɪd/ ADJ If a building is unoccupied, there is nobody in it. ❑ *The house was unoccupied at the time of the explosion.*

un|of|fi|cial /ʌnəfɪʃəl/ ADJ An unofficial action or statement is not organized or approved by a person or group in authority. ❑ *Staff voted to continue an unofficial strike in support of seven colleagues who were dismissed last week.* ● **un|of|fi|cial|ly** ADV ❑ *Some workers are legally employed, but the majority work unofficially with neither health insurance nor wage security.*

un|opened /ʌnoʊpənd/ ADJ If something is unopened, it has not been opened yet. ❑ *...unopened bottles of olive oil.* ❑ *The letter lay unopened on the table.* ❑ *Catherine put all the envelopes aside unopened.*

un|op|posed /ʌnəpoʊzd/ ADJ In something such as an election or a war, if someone is unopposed, there are no opponents competing or fighting against them. ❑ *Mark Johnston was running unopposed for mayor in Saco, Maine.*

un|or|gan|ized /ʌnɔrgənaɪzd/

in BRIT, also use **unorganised**

1 ADJ If you describe an activity or a group of people as unorganized, you mean that things are not planned or being done in a structured way. ❑ *Supporters complained that the White House seemed unorganized and without a communications strategy.* **2** → see also **disorganized**

un|ortho|dox /ʌnɔrθədɒks/ ADJ If you describe someone's behavior, beliefs, or customs as unorthodox, you mean that they are different from what is generally accepted. ❑ *The reality-based show followed the unorthodox lives of Ozzy, his wife Sharon, daughter Kelly, and son Jack.*

un|pack /ʌnpæk/ (unpacks, unpacking, unpacked) V-T/V-I When you unpack a suitcase, box, or similar container, or you unpack the things inside it, you take the things out of the container. ❑ *He unpacked his bag.*

un|paid /ʌnpeɪd/ **1** ADJ [ADJ n] If you do unpaid work or are an unpaid worker, you do a job without receiving any money for it. ❑ *Even unpaid work for charity is better than nothing.* **2** ADJ Unpaid taxes or bills, for example, are taxes or bills which have not been paid yet. ❑ *...millions of dollars in unpaid taxes.*

un|pal|at|able /ʌnpælɪtəbəl/ **1** ADJ If you describe an idea as unpalatable, you mean that you find it unpleasant and difficult to accept. ❑ *It was only then that I began to learn the unpalatable truth about John.* **2** ADJ If you describe food as unpalatable, you mean that it is so unpleasant that you can hardly eat it. ❑ *...a lump of dry, unpalatable cheese.*

un|par|al|leled /ʌnpærəlɛld/ ADJ If you describe something as unparalleled, you are emphasizing that it is, for example, bigger, better, or worse than anything else of its kind, or anything that has happened before. [EMPHASIS] ❑ *...a period of unparalleled economic growth.*

un|par|don|able /ʌnpɑrdənəbəl/ ADJ If you say that someone's behavior is unpardonable, you mean that it is very wrong or offensive, and completely unacceptable. ❑ *...an unpardonable lack of discipline.*

un|pick /ʌnpɪk/ (unpicks, unpicking, unpicked) V-T If you unpick a piece of sewing, you remove the stitches from it. ❑ *You can always unpick the hems on the dungarees if you don't like them.*

un|pleas|ant /ʌnplɛzənt/ **1** ADJ If something is unpleasant, it gives you bad feelings, for example by making you feel upset or uncomfortable. ❑ *The symptoms can be uncomfortable, unpleasant and serious.* ❑ *The vacuum has an unpleasant smell.* ● **un|pleas|ant|ly** ADV ❑ *The water moved around the body, unpleasantly thick and brown.* ❑ *The smell was unpleasantly strong.* **2** ADJ An unpleasant person is very unfriendly and rude. ❑ *She thought he was an unpleasant man.* ● **un|pleas|ant|ly** ADV ❑ *Melissa laughed unpleasantly.*

un|plug /ʌnplʌg/ (unplugs, unplugging, unplugged) V-T If you **unplug** an electrical device or telephone, you pull a wire out of an outlet so that it stops working. ❑ *Whenever there's a storm, I unplug my computer.*

un|plugged /ʌnplʌgd/ ADJ [ADJ after v, ADJ n] If a pop group or musician performs **unplugged**, they perform without any electric instruments. [JOURNALISM] ❑ *Do you remember when everyone went unplugged and acoustic?*

un|pol|lut|ed /ʌnpəlutɪd/ ADJ Something that is **unpolluted** is free from pollution.

un|popu|lar /ʌnpɒpyʊlər/ ADJ If something or someone is **unpopular**, most people do not like them. ❑ *It was a painful and unpopular decision.* ❑ *In high school, I was very unpopular, and I did encounter a little prejudice.* • **un|popu|lar|ity** /ʌnpɒpyələrɪti/ N-UNCOUNT ❑ *...his unpopularity among his colleagues.*

un|prec|edent|ed /ʌnprɛsɪdɛntɪd/ **1** ADJ If something is **unprecedented**, it has never happened before. ❑ *Such a move is rare, but not unprecedented.* **2** ADJ If you describe something as **unprecedented**, you are emphasizing that it is very great in quality, amount, or scale. [EMPHASIS] ❑ *The mission has been hailed as an unprecedented success.*

un|pre|dict|able /ʌnprɪdɪktəbəl/ **1** ADJ If you describe someone or something as **unpredictable**, you mean that you cannot tell what they are going to do or how they are going to behave. ❑ *He is utterly unpredictable.* • **un|pre|dict|abil|ity** /ʌnprɪdɪktəbɪlɪti/ N-UNCOUNT [oft with poss] ❑ *...the unpredictability of the weather.* **2** → See feature box at **commute**

un|pre|pared /ʌnprɪpɛərd/ **1** ADJ If you are **unprepared** for something, you are not ready for it, and you are therefore surprised or at a disadvantage when it happens. ❑ *I was totally unprepared for the announcement on the next day.* ❑ *Faculty members complain that their students are unprepared to do college-level work.* **2** ADJ [v-link ADJ to-inf] If you are **unprepared** to do something, you are not willing to do it. ❑ *They are unprepared to accept the real reasons for their domestic and foreign situation.*

un|pre|pos|sess|ing /ʌnpripəzɛsɪŋ/ ADJ If you describe someone or something as **unprepossessing**, you mean that they look rather plain or ordinary, although they may have good or special qualities that are hidden. [FORMAL] ❑ *We found the tastiest tapas in the most unprepossessing bars.*

un|pre|ten|tious /ʌnprɪtɛnʃəs/ ADJ If you describe a place, person, or thing as **unpretentious**, you approve of them because they are simple in appearance or character, rather than sophisticated or luxurious. [APPROVAL] ❑ *The Tides Inn is both comfortable and unpretentious.*

un|prin|ci|pled /ʌnprɪnsɪpəld/ ADJ If you describe a person or their actions as **unprincipled**, you are criticizing them for their lack of moral principles and because they do things which are immoral or dishonest. [DISAPPROVAL] ❑ *It is a market where people can be very unprincipled and unpleasant.*

un|print|able /ʌnprɪntəbəl/ ADJ If you describe something that someone has said or done as **unprintable**, you mean that it is so vulgar or shocking that you do not want to say exactly what it was. ❑ *Her reply was unprintable.*

un|pro|duc|tive /ʌnprədʌktɪv/ ADJ Something that is **unproductive** does not produce any good results. ❑ *Research workers are well aware that much of their time and effort is unproductive.*

un|pro|fes|sion|al /ʌnprəfɛʃənəl/ ADJ If you use **unprofessional** to describe someone's behavior at work, you are criticizing them for not behaving according to the standards that are expected of a person in their profession. [DISAPPROVAL] ❑ *He was fired for unprofessional conduct.*

un|prof|it|able /ʌnprɒfɪtəbəl/ **1** ADJ An industry, company, or product that is **unprofitable** does not make any profit or does not make enough profit. [BUSINESS] ❑ *...unprofitable, badly-run industries.* **2** ADJ **Unprofitable** activities or efforts do not produce any useful or helpful results. ❑ *...an endless, unprofitable argument.*

un|prom|is|ing /ʌnprɒmɪsɪŋ/ ADJ If you describe something as **unpromising**, you think that it is unlikely to be successful or produce anything good in the future. ❑ *In fact, his business career had distinctly unpromising beginnings.*

un|pro|nounce|able /ʌnprənaʊnsəbəl/ ADJ An **unpronounceable** word or name is too difficult to say.

un|pro|tect|ed /ʌnprətɛktɪd/ **1** ADJ An **unprotected** person or place is not watched over or defended, and so they may be harmed or attacked. ❑ *The landing beaches would be unprotected.* **2** ADJ If something is **unprotected**, it is not covered or treated with anything, and so it may easily be damaged. ❑ *Exposure of unprotected skin to the sun carries the risk of developing skin cancer.* **3** ADJ [ADJ n] If two people have **unprotected** sex, they do not use a condom when they have sex. ❑ *...the dangers of unprotected sex.*

un|prov|en /ʌnpruvən/ also **unproved** ADJ If something is **unproven**, it has not definitely been proved to be true. ❑ *There are a lot of unproven allegations flying around.*

un|pro|voked /ʌnprəvoʊkt/ ADJ If someone makes an **unprovoked** attack, they attack someone who has not tried to harm them in any way.

un|pub|lished /ʌnpʌblɪʃt/ ADJ An **unpublished** book, letter, or report has never been published. An **unpublished** writer has never had his or her work published. ❑ *Much of his writing remains unpublished.*

un|pun|ished /ʌnpʌnɪʃt/ ADJ If a criminal or crime goes **unpunished**, the criminal is not punished. ❑ *Persistent criminals who have gone unpunished by the courts have been dealt with by local people.*

un|quali|fied /ʌnkwɒlɪfaɪd/ **1** ADJ If you are **unqualified**, you do not have any qualifications, or you do not have the right qualifications for a particular job. ❑ *She was unqualified for the job.* **2** ADJ **Unqualified** means total or unlimited. [EMPHASIS] ❑ *The event was an unqualified success.*

un|ques|tion|able /ʌnkwɛstʃənəbəl/ ADJ If you describe something as **unquestionable**, you are emphasizing that it is so obviously true or real that nobody can doubt it. [EMPHASIS] ❑ *He inspires affection and respect as a man of unquestionable integrity.* • **un|ques|tion|ably** /ʌnkwɛstʃənəbli/ ADV [ADV with cl/group] ❑ *They have seen the change as unquestionably beneficial to the country.*

un|ques|tioned /ʌnkwɛstʃənd/ **1** ADJ You use **unquestioned** to emphasize that something is so obvious, real, or great that nobody can doubt it or disagree with it. [EMPHASIS] ❑ *His commitment has been unquestioned.* **2** ADJ If something or someone is **unquestioned**, they are accepted by everyone, without anyone doubting or disagreeing. ❑ *He was established as the unquestioned leader of the team.* **3** ADJ [ADJ n] If you describe someone's belief or attitude as **unquestioned**, you are emphasizing that they accept something without any doubt or disagreement. [EMPHASIS] ❑ *People are forced to give unquestioned obedience to authority.*

un|ques|tion|ing /ʌnkwɛstʃənɪŋ/ ADJ [usu ADJ n] If you describe a person or their beliefs as **unquestioning**, you are emphasizing that they accept something without any doubt or disagreement. [EMPHASIS] ❑ *Isabella had been taught unquestioning obedience.* • **un|ques|tion|ing|ly** ADV [ADV with v] ❑ *She supported him unquestioningly.*

un|quote /ʌnkwoʊt/ PHRASE You can say **quote** before and **unquote** after a word or phrase, or **quote, unquote** before or after it, to show that you are quoting someone or that you do not believe that a word or phrase used by others is accurate. [SPOKEN] ❑ *The New York Times called it quote "a stupid idea" unquote.*

un|rav|el /ʌnrævəl/ (unravels, unraveling or unravelling, unraveled or unravelled) **1** V-T/V-I If you **unravel** something that is knotted, woven, or knitted, or if it **unravels**, it becomes one straight piece again or separates into its different threads. ❑ *He could unravel a knot that others wouldn't even attempt.* **2** V-T/V-I If you **unravel** a mystery or puzzle, or it **unravels**, it gradually becomes clearer until you can work out the answer to it. ❑ *A young mother has flown to Iceland to unravel the mystery of her husband's disappearance.*

un|read /ʌnrɛd/ ADJ If a book or other piece of writing is **unread**, you or other people have not read it, for example because it is boring or because you have no time. ❑ *All his unpublished writing should be destroyed unread.*

un|read|able /ʌnridəbəl/ **1** ADJ If you use **unreadable** to describe a book or other piece of writing, you are criticizing it because it is very boring, complicated, or difficult to understand. [DISAPPROVAL] ❑ *For some this is the greatest novel in the world. For others it is unreadable.* **2** ADJ [usu v-link ADJ] If a piece of writing is **unreadable**, it is impossible to read because the letters are unclear, especially because it has been damaged in some way. ❑ ...*if contracts are unreadable because of the microscopic print.* **3** ADJ If someone's face or expression is **unreadable**, it is impossible to tell what they are thinking or feeling. [LITERARY] ❑ *He looked back at the woman for approval, but her face was unreadable.*

un|real /ʌnrɪəl/ **1** ADJ [v-link ADJ] If you say that a situation is **unreal**, you mean that it is so strange that you find it difficult to believe it is happening. ❑ *Then we won our next 10 games, which remains a record. It was unreal.* ● **un|re|al|ity** /ʌnriæliti/ N-UNCOUNT ❑ *To his surprise he didn't feel too weak. Light-headed certainly, and with a sense of unreality, but able to walk.* **2** ADJ If you use **unreal** to describe something, you are critical of it because you think that it is not like, or not related to, things you expect to find in the real world. [DISAPPROVAL] ❑ *Almost all fictional detectives are unreal.*

un|re|al|is|tic /ʌnriəlɪstɪk/ ADJ If you say that someone is being **unrealistic**, you mean that they do not recognize the truth about a situation, especially about the difficulties involved in something they want to achieve. ❑ *There are many who feel that the players are being completely unrealistic in their demands.* ❑ *It would be unrealistic to expect such a process ever to be completed.*

un|rea|son|able /ʌnriːzənəbəl/ **1** ADJ If you say that someone is being **unreasonable**, you mean that they are behaving in a way that is not fair or sensible. ❑ *The strikers were being unreasonable in their demands, having rejected the deal two weeks ago.* ❑ *It was her unreasonable behavior with a Texan playboy which broke up her marriage.* ● **un|rea|son|ably** /ʌnriːzənəbli/ ADV ❑ *We unreasonably expect near perfect behavior from our children.* **2** ADJ An **unreasonable** decision, action, price, or amount seems unfair and difficult to justify. ❑ *...unreasonable increases in the price of gas.* ● **un|rea|son|ably** ADV ❑ *The banks' charges are unreasonably high.*

un|rea|son|ing /ʌnriːzənɪŋ/ ADJ [ADJ n] **Unreasoning** feelings or actions are not logical, sensible, or controlled. [LITERARY] ❑ *At this moment of success I found only an unreasoning sense of futility.*

un|rec|og|niz|able /ʌnrɛkəɡnaɪzəbəl, -naɪz-/

> in BRIT, also use **unrecognisable**

ADJ [oft ADJ to n] If someone or something is **unrecognizable**, they have become impossible to recognize or identify, for example because they have been greatly changed or damaged. ❑ *Today that same hotel is almost unrecognizable.*

un|rec|og|nized /ʌnrɛkəɡnaɪzd/

> in BRIT, also use **unrecognised**

1 ADJ [ADJ after v, v-link ADJ] If someone does something **unrecognized**, nobody knows or recognizes them while they do it. ❑ *The politician's face had appeared on too many news programs for him to go unrecognized.* **2** ADJ If something is **unrecognized**, people are not aware of it. ❑ *There is the possibility that hypothermia can go unrecognized.* **3** ADJ If you or your achievements or qualities are **unrecognized**, you have not been properly appreciated or acknowledged by other people for what you have done. ❑ *Hard work and talent so often go unrecognized and unrewarded.* **4** ADJ [usu ADJ n] An **unrecognized** meeting, agreement, or political party is not formally acknowledged as legal or valid by the authorities.

un|re|con|struct|ed /ʌnriːkənstrʌktɪd/ ADJ [usu ADJ n] If you describe systems, beliefs, policies, or people as **unreconstructed**, you are critical of them because they have not changed at all, in spite of new ideas and circumstances. [DISAPPROVAL] ❑ *...unreconstructed bigots who oppose all progressive social change.*

un|re|cord|ed /ʌnrɪkɔːrdɪd/ ADJ You use **unrecorded** to describe something that has not been written down or recorded officially, especially when it should have been. ❑ *...this fascinating piece of Newfoundland's unrecorded history.*

un|re|fined /ʌnrɪfaɪnd/ ADJ [usu ADJ n] An **unrefined** food or other substance is in its natural state and has not been processed. ❑ *Unrefined carbohydrates include brown rice and other grains.*

un|re|hearsed /ʌnrɪhɜːrst/ ADJ **Unrehearsed** activities or performances have not been prepared, planned, or practiced beforehand. ❑ *In fact, the recordings were mostly unrehearsed improvisations.*

un|re|lat|ed /ʌnrɪleɪtɪd/ **1** ADJ If one thing is **unrelated** to another, there is no connection between them. You can also say that two things are **unrelated**. ❑ *My line of work is entirely unrelated to politics.* **2** ADJ If one person is **unrelated** to another, they are not members of the same family. You can also say that two people are **unrelated**. [WRITTEN] ❑ *Jimmy is adopted and thus unrelated to Beth by blood.*

un|re|lent|ing /ʌnrɪlɛntɪŋ/ **1** ADJ If you describe someone's behavior as **unrelenting**, you mean that they are continuing to do something in a very determined way, often without caring whether they hurt or embarrass other people. ❑ *She established her authority with unrelenting thoroughness.* **2** ADJ If you describe something unpleasant as **unrelenting**, you mean that it continues without stopping. ❑ *...an unrelenting downpour of rain.*

un|re|li|able /ʌnrɪlaɪəbəl/ ADJ If you describe a person, machine, or method as **unreliable**, you mean that you cannot trust them. ❑ *Diplomats can be a notoriously unreliable and misleading source of information.* ❑ *His judgment was unreliable.*

un|re|lieved /ʌnrɪliːvd/ ADJ [oft ADJ by n] If you describe something unpleasant as **unrelieved**, you mean that it is very severe and is not replaced by anything better, even for a short time. ❑ *...unrelieved misery.* ❑ *The sun baked down on the concrete, unrelieved by any breeze.*

un|re|mark|able /ʌnrɪmɑːrkəbəl/ ADJ If you describe someone or something as **unremarkable**, you mean that they are very ordinary, without many exciting, original, or attractive qualities. ❑ *...a tall, lean man, with an unremarkable face.*

un|re|marked /ʌnrɪmɑːrkt/ ADJ If something happens or goes **unremarked**, people say nothing about it, because they consider it normal or do not notice it. [FORMAL] ❑ *His departure, in fact, went almost unremarked.*

un|re|mit|ting /ʌnrɪmɪtɪŋ/ ADJ [usu ADJ n] Something that is **unremitting** continues without stopping or becoming less intense. [FORMAL] ❑ *I was sent to boarding school, where I spent six years of unremitting misery.* ❑ *He watched her with unremitting attention.* ● **un|re|mit|ting|ly** ADV ❑ *The weather was unremittingly awful.*

un|re|pent|ant /ʌnrɪpɛntənt/ ADJ If you are **unrepentant**, you are not ashamed of your beliefs or actions. ❑ *Pamela was unrepentant about her strong language and abrasive remarks.*

un|rep|re|senta|tive /ʌnrɛprɪzɛntətɪv/ ADJ [oft ADJ of n] If you describe a group of people as **unrepresentative**, you mean that their views are not typical of the community or society to which they belong. ❑ *The president denounced the demonstrators as unrepresentative of the people.*

un|rep|re|sent|ed /ʌnrɛprɪzɛntɪd/ ADJ If you are **unrepresented** in something such as a legislature, law court, or meeting, there is nobody there speaking or acting for you, for example to give your opinions or instructions. ❑ *...groups who feel they've been officially unrecognized or unrepresented in international councils.*

un|re|quit|ed /ʌnrɪkwaɪtɪd/ ADJ If you have **unrequited** love for someone, you have romantic feelings for them, but they do not feel the same about you. [LITERARY] ❑ *...his unrequited love for a married woman.*

un|re|served /ʌnrɪzɜːrvd/ ADJ [usu ADJ n] An **unreserved** opinion or statement is one that expresses a feeling or opinion completely and without any doubts. ❑ *Charles displays unreserved admiration for his grandfather.* ❑ *Jones' lawyers are seeking an unreserved apology from the newspaper.* ● **un|re|serv|ed|ly** /ʌnrɪzɜːrvɪdli/ ADV [ADV with v] ❑ *We apologize unreservedly for any incorrect behavior by Mr. Taylor.*

un|re|solved /ʌnrɪzɒlvd/ ADJ If a problem or difficulty is **unresolved**, no satisfactory solution has been found to it. ❑ *The murder remains unresolved.*

un|re|spon|sive /ʌnrɪspɒnsɪv/ **1** ADJ [oft ADJ to n] An **unresponsive** person does not react or pay enough attention to something, for example to an urgent situation or to people's needs. [FORMAL] ❑ *He was totally unresponsive to the needs of the majority of the population.* **2** ADJ If a person or their body is **unresponsive**, they do not react physically in a normal way, or do not make any movements. [FORMAL] ❑ *I found her in a coma, totally unresponsive.*

un|rest /ʌnrɛst/ N-UNCOUNT If there is **unrest** in a particular place or society, people are expressing anger and dissatisfaction about something, often by demonstrating or rioting. [JOURNALISM] ❑ *The real danger is civil unrest in the east of the country.*

un|re|strained /ʌnrɪstreɪnd/ ADJ If you describe someone's behavior as **unrestrained**, you mean that it is extreme or intense, for example because they are expressing their feelings strongly or loudly. ❑ *There was unrestrained joy on the faces of the people.*

un|re|strict|ed /ʌnrɪstrɪktɪd/ **1** ADJ If an activity is **unrestricted**, you are free to do it in the way that you want, without being limited by any rules. ❑ *Freedom to pursue extracurricular activities is totally unrestricted.* **2** ADJ If you have an **unrestricted** view of something, you can see it fully and clearly, because there is nothing in the way. ❑ *Nearly all seats have an unrestricted view.*

un|re|ward|ed /ʌnrɪwɔrdɪd/ ADJ You can say that someone goes **unrewarded**, or that their activities go **unrewarded**, when their achievements are not rewarded or acknowledged. ❑ *Success in many societies often goes unrewarded.*

un|re|ward|ing /ʌnrɪwɔrdɪŋ/ ADJ If you describe an activity as **unrewarding**, you mean that it does not give you any feelings of achievement or pleasure. ❑ *...dirty and unrewarding work.*

un|ripe /ʌnraɪp/ ADJ **Unripe** fruit or vegetables are not yet ready to eat.

un|ri|valed /ʌnraɪvᵊld/

in BRIT, use **unrivalled**

ADJ If you describe something as **unrivaled**, you are emphasizing that it is better than anything else of the same kind. [EMPHASIS] ❑ *He acquired unrivaled knowledge of party affairs.*

un|roll /ʌnroʊl/ (unrolls, unrolling, unrolled) V-T/V-I If you **unroll** something such as a sheet of paper or cloth, or if it **unrolls**, it opens up and becomes flat when it was previously rolled in a cylindrical shape. ❑ *I unrolled my sleeping bag on the floor as usual.*

un|ruf|fled /ʌnrʌfᵊld/ ADJ If you describe someone as **unruffled**, you mean that they are calm and do not seem to be affected by surprising or frightening events.

un|ru|ly /ʌnruli/ (unrulier, unruliest) **1** ADJ If you describe people, especially children, as **unruly**, you mean that they behave badly and are difficult to control. ❑ *...unruly behavior.* **2** ADJ **Unruly** hair is difficult to keep tidy. ❑ *The man had remarkably black, unruly hair.*

un|safe /ʌnseɪf/ **1** ADJ If a building, machine, activity, or area is **unsafe**, it is dangerous. ❑ *Critics claim the trucks are unsafe.* **2** ADJ [v-link ADJ] If you are **unsafe**, you are in danger of being harmed. ❑ *In the larger neighborhood, I felt very unsafe.*

un|said /ʌnsɛd/ ADJ If something is **left unsaid** or **goes unsaid** in a particular situation, it is not said, although you might have expected it to be said. ❑ *Some things, Donald, are better left unsaid.*

un|sal|able /ʌnseɪləbᵊl/

in BRIT, sometimes in AM, use **unsaleable**

ADJ If something is **unsalable**, it cannot be sold because nobody wants to buy it. ❑ *The food is edible, yet often unsalable because of incorrect labeling or damaged packaging.*

un|sani|tary /ʌnsænɪtɛri/ ADJ Something that is **unsanitary** is dirty and unhealthy, so that you may catch a disease from it. ❑ *...diseases caused by unsanitary conditions.* ❑ *Discharge of raw sewage into the sea is unsanitary and unsafe.*

un|sat|is|fac|tory /ʌnsætɪsfæktəri/ **1** ADJ If you describe something as **unsatisfactory**, you mean that it is not as good as it should be, and cannot be considered acceptable. ❑ *He asked a few more questions, to which he received unsatisfactory answers.* **2** → See feature box at **review**

un|sat|is|fied /ʌnsætɪsfaɪd/ **1** ADJ If you are **unsatisfied** with something, you are disappointed because you have not gotten what you hoped to get. ❑ *The game ended a few hours too early, leaving players and spectators unsatisfied.* **2** ADJ [usu ADJ n] If a need or demand is **unsatisfied**, it is not dealt with. ❑ *There is a great, unsatisfied demand for fresh milk in this area.*

un|sat|is|fy|ing /ʌnsætɪsfaɪɪŋ/ ADJ If you find something **unsatisfying**, you do not get any satisfaction from it. ❑ *Rose says so far the marriage has been unsatisfying.*

un|sa|vory /ʌnseɪvəri/

in BRIT, use **unsavoury**

ADJ If you describe a person, place, or thing as **unsavory**, you mean that you find them unpleasant or morally unacceptable. [DISAPPROVAL] ❑ *Police officers meet more unsavory characters in a week than most of us do in a lifetime.*

un|scathed /ʌnskeɪðd/ ADJ [ADJ after v, v-link ADJ] If you are **unscathed** after a dangerous experience, you have not been injured or harmed by it. ❑ *Tony emerged unscathed apart from a severely bruised finger.* ❑ *East Los Angeles was left relatively unscathed by the riots.*

un|sched|uled /ʌnskɛdʒuld/ ADJ [usu ADJ n] An **unscheduled** event was not planned to happen, but happens unexpectedly or because someone changes their plans at a late stage. ❑ *...an unscheduled meeting with Robin Cook.* ❑ *The ship made an unscheduled stop at Hawaii.*

un|schooled /ʌnskuld/ ADJ An **unschooled** person has had no formal education. [LITERARY] ❑ *...unskilled work done by unschooled people.*

un|sci|en|tif|ic /ʌnsaɪəntɪfɪk/ ADJ Research or treatment that is **unscientific** is not likely to be good because it is not based on facts or is not done in the proper way. ❑ *No member of the team was medically qualified and its methods were considered totally unscientific.*

un|scram|ble /ʌnskræmbᵊl/ (unscrambles, unscrambling, unscrambled) V-T To **unscramble** things that are in a state of confusion or disorder means to arrange them so that they can be understood or seen clearly. ❑ *All you have to do to win is unscramble the words here to find four names of birds.*

un|screw /ʌnskru/ (unscrews, unscrewing, unscrewed) **1** V-T/V-I If you **unscrew** something such as a lid, or if it **unscrews**, you keep turning it until you can remove it. ❑ *She unscrewed the cap of her water bottle and gave him a drink.* **2** V-T If you **unscrew** something such as a sign or mirror which is fastened to something by screws, you remove it by taking out the screws. ❑ *He unscrewed the back of the telephone and started connecting it to the cable.*

un|script|ed /ʌnskrɪptɪd/ ADJ [usu ADJ n] An **unscripted** talk or speech is made without detailed preparation, rather than being read out. ❑ *...unscripted radio programs.*

un|scru|pu|lous /ʌnskrupyələs/ ADJ If you describe a person as **unscrupulous**, you are critical of the fact that they are prepared to act in a dishonest or immoral way in order to get what they want. [DISAPPROVAL] ❑ *These kids are being exploited by very unscrupulous people.*

un|sea|son|ably /ʌnsizənəbli/ ADV [ADV adj] **Unseasonably** warm, cold, or mild weather is warmer, colder, or milder than it usually is at the time of year. ❑ *...a spell of unseasonably warm weather.*

un|seat /ʌnsit/ (unseats, unseating, unseated) V-T When people try to **unseat** a person who is in an important job or position, they try to remove him or her from that job or position. ❑ *It is still not clear who was behind Sunday's attempt to unseat the president.*

un|secured /ʌnsɪkyʊərd/ **1** ADJ **Unsecured** is used to describe loans or debts that are not guaranteed by a particular asset such as a person's home. [BUSINESS] ❑ *Sam received an unsecured loan of $282,000.* **2** → See feature box at **finance**

un|seed|ed /ʌnsidɪd/ ADJ In tennis and badminton competitions, an **unseeded** player is someone who has not been ranked among the top 16 players by the competition's organizers. ❑ *Venus was the first unseeded woman in history to reach the final round.*

un|see|ing /ʌnsiɪŋ/ ADJ If you describe a person or their eyes as **unseeing**, you mean that they are not looking at anything, or not noticing something, although their eyes are open. [LITERARY] ❑ *Max was staring at the wood paneling with unseeing eyes.*

un|seem|ly /ʌnsimli/ ADJ If you say that someone's behavior is **unseemly**, you disapprove of it because it is not polite or not suitable for a particular situation or occasion. [LITERARY, DISAPPROVAL] ❑ *It would be unseemly for judges to receive pay increases when others are having to tighten their belts.*

un|seen /ʌnsi̱ːn/ **1** ADJ If you describe something as **unseen**, you mean that it has not been seen for a long time. ❑ *...a spectacular ballroom, unseen by the public for over 30 years.* **2** ADJ [ADJ n, ADJ after v] You can use **unseen** to describe things which people cannot see. ❑ *For me, a performance is in front of a microphone, over the radio, to an unseen audience.*

un|self|ish /ʌnse̱lfɪʃ/ ADJ If you describe someone as **unselfish**, you approve of the fact that they regard other people's wishes and interests as more important than their own. [APPROVAL] ❑ *She started to get a reputation as an unselfish girl with a heart of gold.* ❑ *As a player he was unselfish, a true team man.* ● **un|self|ish|ly** ADV [ADV with v] ❑ *She has loyally and unselfishly spent every day at her husband's side.* ● **un|self|ish|ness** N-UNCOUNT ❑ *...acts of unselfishness and care.*

un|sen|ti|men|tal /ʌnse̱ntɪme̱ntəl/ ADJ If you describe someone as **unsentimental**, you mean that they do not allow emotions like pity or affection to interfere with their work or decisions. ❑ *She was a practical, unsentimental woman.*

un|set|tle /ʌnse̱tᵊl/ (**unsettles, unsettling, unsettled**) V-T If something **unsettles** you, it makes you feel rather worried or uncertain. ❑ *The presence of the two police officers unsettled her.*

un|set|tled /ʌnse̱tᵊld/ **1** ADJ In an **unsettled** situation, there is a lot of uncertainty about what will happen. ❑ *The developments leave the airline with several problems, including an unsettled labor situation.* **2** ADJ [v-link ADJ] If you are **unsettled**, you cannot concentrate on anything because you are worried. ❑ *To tell the truth, I'm a bit unsettled tonight.* **3** ADJ An **unsettled** argument or dispute has not yet been resolved. ❑ *They were in the process of resolving all the unsettled issues.* **4** ADJ **Unsettled** weather is unpredictable and changes a lot. ❑ *Despite the unsettled weather, we had a marvelous weekend.*

un|set|tling /ʌnse̱tᵊlɪŋ/ ADJ If you describe something as **unsettling**, you mean that it makes you feel worried or uncertain. ❑ *Phil had several unsettling dreams every night.*

un|shad|ed /ʌnʃe̱ɪdɪd/ ADJ [ADJ n] An **unshaded** light or light bulb has no shade fitted to it.

un|shak|able /ʌnʃe̱ɪkəbᵊl/ also **unshakeable** ADJ [usu ADJ n] If you describe someone's beliefs as **unshakable**, you are emphasizing that they are so strong that they cannot be destroyed or altered. [EMPHASIS] ❑ *She had an unshakable faith in human goodness and natural honesty.*

un|shak|en /ʌnʃe̱ɪkən/ **1** ADJ [usu v-link ADJ] If your beliefs are **unshaken**, you still have those beliefs, although they have been attacked or challenged. ❑ *His faith that men such as the Reverend John Leale tried to do their best is unshaken.* **2** ADJ [usu v-link ADJ] If you are **unshaken** by something, you are not emotionally affected by it. ❑ *Mona remains unshaken by her ordeal and is matter-of-fact about her courage.*

un|shav|en /ʌnʃe̱ɪvᵊn/ ADJ If a man is **unshaven**, he has not shaved recently and there are short hairs on his face or chin.

un|sight|ly /ʌnsa̱ɪtli/ ADJ If you describe something as **unsightly**, you mean that it is ugly. ❑ *...an unsightly pile of garbage right in front of the restaurant.*

un|signed /ʌnsa̱ɪnd/ **1** ADJ An **unsigned** document does not have anyone's signature on it. **2** ADJ [usu ADJ n] An **unsigned** band has not signed a contract with a company to produce CDs.

un|skilled /ʌnski̱ld/ **1** ADJ People who are **unskilled** do not have any special training for a job. ❑ *He worked as an unskilled laborer.* **2** ADJ **Unskilled** work does not require any special training. ❑ *In the U.S., minorities and immigrants have generally gone into low-paid, unskilled jobs.*

un|smil|ing /ʌnsma̱ɪlɪŋ/ ADJ An **unsmiling** person is not smiling, and looks serious or unfriendly. [LITERARY] ❑ *He was unsmiling and silent.*

un|so|ciable /ʌnso̱ʊʃəbᵊl/ ADJ Someone who is **unsociable** does not like talking to other people and tries to avoid meeting them. ❑ *My marriage has broken up. It has made me reclusive and unsociable.*

un|sold /ʌnso̱ʊld/ ADJ **Unsold** goods have been available for people to buy but nobody has bought them. ❑ *...piles of unsold books.*

un|so|lic|it|ed /ʌnsəlɪ̱sɪtɪd/ ADJ Something that is **unsolicited** has been given without being asked for and may not have been wanted. ❑ *She's always full of unsolicited advice.*

un|solved /ʌnsɒ̱lvd/ ADJ An **unsolved** mystery or problem has never been solved. ❑ *...America's unsolved problems of poverty and racism.*

un|so|phis|ti|cat|ed /ʌnsəfɪ̱stɪkeɪtɪd/ **1** ADJ **Unsophisticated** people do not have a wide range of experience or knowledge and have simple tastes. ❑ *It was music which unsophisticated audiences enjoyed listening to.* **2** ADJ An **unsophisticated** method or device is very simple and often not very effective. ❑ *...an unsophisticated alarm system.*

un|sound /ʌnsa̱ʊnd/ **1** ADJ [usu v-link ADJ] If a conclusion or method is **unsound**, it is based on ideas that are wrong. ❑ *The national tests were educationally unsound.* **2** ADJ If something or someone is **unsound**, they are unreliable. ❑ *No sensible person would put his money in a bank he knew to be unsound.* **3** ADJ If you say that something is **unsound** in some way, you mean that it is damaging in that way or to the thing mentioned. ❑ *The project is environmentally unsound.* **4** ADJ [usu v-link ADJ] If a building or other structure is **unsound**, it is in poor condition and is likely to collapse. ❑ *The church was structurally unsound.*

un|speak|able /ʌnspi̱ːkəbᵊl/ ADJ If you describe something as **unspeakable**, you are emphasizing that it is extremely unpleasant. [EMPHASIS] ❑ *...the unspeakable horrors of chemical weapons.* ❑ *The pain is unspeakable.* ● **un|speak|ably** /ʌnspi̱ːkəbli/ ADV ❑ *The novel was unspeakably boring.*

un|speci|fied /ʌnspe̱sɪfaɪd/ ADJ You say that something is **unspecified** when you are not told exactly what it is. ❑ *The company said that an unspecified number of people were offered jobs.*

un|spec|tacu|lar /ʌnspektæ̱kjələr/ ADJ If you describe something as **unspectacular**, you mean that it is rather dull and not remarkable in any way. ❑ *His progress at school had been unspectacular compared to his brother's.*

un|spoiled /ʌnspɔ̱ɪld/

in BRIT, also use **unspoilt**

ADJ If you describe a place as **unspoiled**, you think it is beautiful because it has not been changed or built on for a long time. ❑ *The port is quiet and unspoiled.*

un|spo|ken /ʌnspo̱ʊkən/ **1** ADJ If your thoughts, wishes, or feelings are **unspoken**, you do not speak about them. ❑ *His face was expressionless, but Alex felt the unspoken criticism.* **2** ADJ [ADJ n] When there is an **unspoken** agreement or understanding between people, their behavior shows that they agree about something or understand it, even though they have never spoken about it. ❑ *There was an unspoken agreement that he and Viv would look after the frail old couple.*

un|sport|ing /ʌnspɔ̱ːtɪŋ/ ADJ [mainly BRIT] → see **unsportsmanlike**

un|sports|man|like /ʌnspɔ̱ːtsmənlaɪk/ ADJ **Unsportsmanlike** behavior is behavior that is rude, aggressive, or unfair, especially during a game. [mainly AM] ❑ *He was ejected for unsportsmanlike conduct.*

un|sta|ble /ʌnste̱ɪbᵊl/ **1** ADJ You can describe something as **unstable** if it is likely to change suddenly, especially if this creates difficulty or danger. ❑ *The situation is unstable and potentially dangerous.* **2** ADJ **Unstable** objects are likely to move or fall. ❑ *Both clay and sandstone are unstable rock formations.* **3** ADJ If people are **unstable**, their emotions and behavior keep changing because their minds are disturbed or upset. ❑ *He was emotionally unstable.*

un|stat|ed /ʌnste̱ɪtɪd/ ADJ You say that something is **unstated** when it has not been expressed in words. ❑ *The implication was plain, if left unstated.*

un|steady /ʌnste̱di/ **1** ADJ If you are **unsteady**, you have difficulty doing something, for example walking, because you cannot completely control your legs or your body. ❑ *The boy was very unsteady and had staggered around when he got up.* ● **un|steadi|ly** /ʌnste̱dᵊli/ ADV [ADV with v] ❑ *She pulled herself unsteadily from the bed to the dresser.* **2** ADJ If you describe something as **unsteady**, you mean that it is not regular or stable, but unreliable or unpredictable. ❑ *His voice was unsteady and only just audible.* **3** ADJ **Unsteady** objects are not held, attached, or balanced securely. ❑ *...a slightly unsteady table.*

un|stick /ʌnstɪk/ (**unsticks, unsticking, unstuck**) **1** V-T/V-I If you **unstick** something or if it **unsticks**, it becomes separated from the thing that it was stuck to. ❑ *Mike shook his head, to unstick his hair from his sweating forehead.* **2** → see also **unstuck**

un|stint|ing /ʌnstɪntɪŋ/ ADJ [usu ADJ n] **Unstinting** help, care, or praise is great in amount or degree and is given generously. ❑ *...her unstinting charity work.*

un|stop|pable /ʌnstɒpəbəl/ ADJ Something that is **unstoppable** cannot be prevented from continuing or developing. ❑ *The progress of science is unstoppable.*

un|stressed /ʌnstrɛst/ ADJ If a word or syllable is **unstressed**, it is pronounced without emphasis. [TECHNICAL] ❑ *...the unstressed syllable of words like "above," "surround" or "arrive."*

un|struc|tured /ʌnstrʌktʃərd/ ADJ Something such as a meeting, interview, or activity that is **unstructured** is not organized in a complete or detailed way. ❑ *Our aim was that these meetings be unstructured and informal.*

un|stuck /ʌnstʌk/ **1** PHRASE If something **comes unstuck**, it becomes separated from the thing that it was attached to. ❑ *The brown vinyl covering all the horizontal surfaces is coming unstuck in several places.* **2** PHRASE To **come unstuck** means the same as to **come unglued.** [mainly BRIT, INFORMAL] **3** → see also **unstick**

un|sub|scribe /ʌnsəbskraɪb/ (**unsubscribes, unsubscribing, unsubscribed**) V-I If you **unsubscribe** from an online service, you send a message saying that you no longer wish to receive that service. [COMPUTING] ❑ *Go to the website today and you can unsubscribe online.*

un|sub|stan|ti|at|ed /ʌnsəbstænʃieɪtɪd/ ADJ A claim, accusation, or story that is **unsubstantiated** has not been proven to be valid or true. ❑ *I do object to their claim, which I find totally unsubstantiated.*

un|suc|cess|ful /ʌnsəksɛsfəl/ **1** ADJ Something that is **unsuccessful** does not achieve what it was intended to achieve. ❑ *His efforts were unsuccessful.* ❑ *...a second unsuccessful operation on his knee.* • **un|suc|cess|ful|ly** ADV [ADV with v] ❑ *He has been trying unsuccessfully to sell the business in one piece since early last year.* **2** ADJ Someone who is **unsuccessful** does not achieve what they intended to achieve, especially in their career. ❑ *The difference between successful and unsuccessful people is that successful people put into practice the things they learn.*

un|suit|able /ʌnsutəbəl/ ADJ Someone or something that is **unsuitable** for a particular purpose or situation does not have the right qualities for it. ❑ *Amy's shoes were unsuitable for walking any distance.*

un|suit|ed /ʌnsutɪd/ **1** ADJ [oft ADJ to n/-ing] If someone or something is **unsuited** to a particular job, situation, or place, they do not have the right qualities or characteristics for it. ❑ *He's totally unsuited to the job.* **2** ADJ [oft ADJ to n] If two people are **unsuited** to each other, they have different personalities or interests, and so are unlikely to have a successful relationship. ❑ *By the end of that first year, I knew how totally unsuited we were to each other.*

un|sul|lied /ʌnsʌlid/ ADJ If something is **unsullied**, it has not been spoiled or made less pure by the addition of something unpleasant or unacceptable. [LITERARY] ❑ *She had the combined talents of toughness, intellect, experience and unsullied reputation.*

un|sung /ʌnsʌŋ/ ADJ **Unsung** is used to describe people, things, or places that are not appreciated or praised, although you think they deserve to be. ❑ *They are among the unsung heroes of our time.*

un|sup|port|ed /ʌnsəpɔrtɪd/ **1** ADJ If a statement or theory is **unsupported**, there is no evidence which proves that it is true or correct. ❑ *It was a theory unsupported by evidence.* **2** ADJ [usu ADJ n] An **unsupported** person does not have anyone to provide them with money and the things they need. ❑ *Unsupported mothers are one of the fastest-growing groups of welfare claimants.* **3** ADJ [usu ADJ n] An **unsupported** building or person is not being physically supported or held up by anything. ❑ *...the vast unsupported wall of the Ajuda Palace in Lisbon.* ❑ *...the child's first unsupported step.*

un|sure /ʌnʃʊər/ **1** ADJ If you are **unsure** of yourself, you lack confidence. ❑ *The evening show was terrible, with hesitant unsure performances from all.* **2** ADJ [v-link ADJ] If you are **unsure** about something, you feel uncertain about it. ❑ *Fifty-two percent were unsure about the idea.*

un|sur|passed /ʌnsərpæst/ ADJ If you describe something as **unsurpassed**, you are emphasizing that it is better or greater than anything else of its kind. [EMPHASIS] ❑ *...a man whom they believe possesses unsurpassed wisdom and power.*

un|sur|pris|ing /ʌnsərpraɪzɪŋ/ ADJ If something is **unsurprising**, you are not surprised by it because you would expect it to happen or be like it is. ❑ *His choice was unsurprising.* • **un|sur|pris|ing|ly** ADV ❑ *Unsurprisingly, not everyone agrees that things are better.*

un|sus|pect|ed /ʌnsəspɛktɪd/ ADJ [usu ADJ n] If you describe something as **unsuspected**, you mean that people do not realize it or are not aware of it. ❑ *A surprising number of ailments are caused by unsuspected environmental factors.*

un|sus|pect|ing /ʌnsəspɛktɪŋ/ ADJ You can use **unsuspecting** to describe someone who is not at all aware of something that is happening or going to happen. ❑ *She threw a surprise party for her unsuspecting husband.*

un|sweet|ened /ʌnswitənd/ ADJ [usu ADJ n] **Unsweetened** food or drink does not have any sugar or other sweet substance added to it.

un|swerv|ing /ʌnswɜrvɪŋ/ ADJ [usu ADJ n] If you describe someone's attitude, feeling, or way of behaving as **unswerving**, you mean that it is strong and firm and does not weaken or change. ❑ *...her unswerving belief in her father's innocence.*

un|sym|pa|thet|ic /ʌnsɪmpəθɛtɪk/ **1** ADJ If someone is **unsympathetic**, they are not kind or helpful to a person in difficulties. ❑ *Her husband was unsympathetic and she felt she had no one to turn to.* **2** ADJ An **unsympathetic** person is unpleasant and difficult to like. ❑ *...a very unsympathetic main character.* **3** ADJ [v-link ADJ to n] If you are **unsympathetic to** a particular idea or aim, you are not willing to support it. ❑ *I'm highly unsympathetic to what you are trying to achieve.*

un|tamed /ʌnteɪmd/ ADJ An **untamed** area or place is in its original or natural state and has not been changed or affected by people. [LITERARY] ❑ *...the wild, untamed undergrowth.*

un|tan|gle /ʌntæŋgəl/ (**untangles, untangling, untangled**) **1** V-T If you **untangle** something that is knotted or has become twisted around something, you undo the knots in it or free it. ❑ *He was found desperately trying to untangle several reels of film.* **2** V-T If you **untangle** a confused or complicated situation, you make the different things involved clear, or put the situation right. ❑ *Lawyers and accountants began trying to untangle the complex affairs of the bank.*

un|tapped /ʌntæpt/ ADJ [usu ADJ n] An **untapped** supply or source of something has not yet been used. ❑ *Mongolia, although poor, has considerable untapped resources of oil and minerals.*

un|ten|able /ʌntɛnəbəl/ ADJ An argument, theory, or position that is **untenable** cannot be defended successfully against criticism or attack. ❑ *This argument is untenable from an intellectual, moral and practical standpoint.*

un|test|ed /ʌntɛstɪd/ **1** ADJ If something or someone is **untested**, they have not yet been tried out or have not yet experienced a particular situation, so you do not know what they will be like. ❑ *The Egyptian Army remained an untested force.* **2** ADJ [usu ADJ n] If you describe something such as a drug or chemical as **untested**, you mean that it has not been subject to scientific tests to find out if it is safe to use. ❑ *...the dangers of giving untested drugs to people.*

un|think|able /ʌnθɪŋkəbəl/ ADJ If you say that something is **unthinkable**, you are emphasizing that it cannot possibly be accepted or imagined as a possibility. [EMPHASIS] ❑ *Her strong Catholic beliefs made abortion unthinkable.* • N-SING [the N] **The unthinkable** is something that is unthinkable. ❑ *Teresa Zapata told her family the unthinkable; she was going to work in the United States.*

un|think|ing /ʌnθɪŋkɪŋ/ ADJ If you say that someone is **unthinking**, you are critical of them because you consider that they do not think carefully about the effects of their behavior. [DISAPPROVAL] ❑ *He doesn't say those silly things that* unthinking people say. • **un|think|ing|ly** ADV [usu ADV with v, also ADV adj] ◻ *Many motor accidents are the result of unthinkingly mixing speed and alcohol.*

un|ti|dy /ʌntaɪdi/ [mainly BRIT] (untidier, untidiest) → see **messy**

un|tie /ʌntaɪ/ (unties, untying, untied) **1** V-T If you **untie** something that is tied to another thing or if you **untie** two things that are tied together, you remove the string or rope that holds them or that has been tied around them. ◻ *Nicholas untied the boat from her mooring.* ◻ *Just untie my hands.* **2** V-T If you **untie** something such as string or rope, you undo it so that there is no knot or so that it is no longer tying something. ◻ *She hurriedly untied the ropes binding her ankles.* **3** V-T When you **untie** your shoelaces or your shoes, you loosen or undo the laces of your shoes. ◻ *She untied the laces on one of her sneakers.*

un|til ♦♦♦ /ʌntɪl/ **1** PREP [PREP n/prep] If something happens **until** a particular time, it happens during the period before that time and stops at that time. ◻ *Until 2004, she lived in Canada.* • CONJ **Until** is also a conjunction. ◻ *I waited until it got dark.* **2** PREP [PREP after neg] You use **until** with a negative to emphasize the moment in time after which the rest of your statement becomes true, or the condition which would make it true. ◻ *The traffic laws don't take effect until the end of the year.* • CONJ **Until** is also a conjunction. ◻ *The government said that it has suspended all aid to Haiti until that country's legitimate government is restored.* **3 up until** → see **up** ②

USAGE

until

1 You only use **until** or **till** when you are talking about time. Don't use these words to talk about position. Don't say, for example, '~~She walked until the post office.~~' You say 'She walked **as far as** the post office.' *They drove as far as the Cantabrian mountains.*
2 Don't use 'until' or 'till' to say that something will have happened before a particular time. Don't say, for example, '~~The work will be finished until four o'clock.~~' You say 'The work will be finished **by** four o'clock.' *Total sales will reach 1 million by 2022.*

---

un|time|ly /ʌntaɪmli/ **1** ADJ [usu ADJ n] If you describe an event as **untimely**, you mean that it happened earlier than it should, or sooner than you expected. ◻ *His mother's untimely death had a catastrophic effect on him.* **2** ADJ You can describe something as **untimely** if it happens at an unsuitable time. ◻ *Bowden issued an apology for his mindless and untimely remark.*

un|tir|ing /ʌntaɪərɪŋ/ ADJ [usu ADJ n] If you describe a person or their efforts as **untiring**, you approve of them because they continue what they are doing without slowing down or stopping. [APPROVAL] ◻ *...an untiring fighter for justice, democracy and tolerance.*

un|tit|led /ʌntaɪt³ld/ ADJ If something such as a book, movie, or song is **untitled**, it does not have a title. ◻ *The full-length feature, as yet untitled, will include interviews plus footage of their live gigs.*

unto /ʌntu/ **1** PREP **Unto** was used to indicate that something was done or given to someone. [LITERARY] ◻ *And he said unto him, "Who is my neighbor?"* **2** PREP **Unto** was used to indicate that something continued until a particular time. [LITERARY] ◻ *Be ye faithful unto the end.* **3** PREP If you say that something is, for example, a world **unto** itself or a place **unto** itself, you mean that it has special qualities that it does not share with other, similar things, and so it should be treated or understood differently from those other things. ◻ *Southern Pennsylvania is still a world unto itself.* ◻ *The army's always been a society unto itself.*

un|told /ʌntoʊld/ **1** ADJ [ADJ n] You can use **untold** to emphasize how bad or unpleasant something is. [EMPHASIS] ◻ *Landmines have caused untold misery to thousands of innocent people.* **2** ADJ [ADJ n] You can use **untold** to emphasize that an amount or quantity is very large, especially when you are not sure how large it is. [EMPHASIS] ◻ *...the nation's untold millions of anglers.*

un|touch|able /ʌntʌtʃəb³l/ (untouchables) **1** ADJ If you say that someone is **untouchable**, you mean that they cannot be affected or punished in any way. ◻ *I want to make it clear,* however, that no one is untouchable in this investigation. • N-COUNT An **untouchable** is someone who is untouchable. ◻ *...an anti-corruption squad nicknamed the "Untouchables."* **2** ADJ If you describe someone, especially an athlete or entertainer, as **untouchable**, you are emphasizing that they are better than anyone else in what they do. [EMPHASIS] ◻ *A lot of the players began to feel they were untouchable.* **3** N-COUNT Some people refer to Hindus of the lowest social rank as **untouchables**. [OFFENSIVE] ◻ *He was born an untouchable in a very poor village in south India.*

un|touched /ʌntʌtʃt/ **1** ADJ [v-link ADJ, ADJ after v] Something that is **untouched** by something else is not affected by it. ◻ *Asian airlines remain untouched by the deregulation that has swept the U.S.* **2** ADJ [v-link ADJ, ADJ after v] If something is **untouched**, it is not damaged in any way, although it has been in a situation where it could easily have been damaged. ◻ *Michael pointed out to me that in all the rubble, there was one building that remained untouched.* **3** ADJ An **untouched** area or place is thought to be beautiful because it is still in its original state and has not been changed or damaged in any way. ◻ *Ducie is one of the world's last untouched islands.* **4** ADJ If food or drink is **untouched**, none of it has been eaten or drunk. ◻ *The coffee was untouched, the toast was cold.*

un|to|ward /ʌntɔrd/ ADJ If you say that something **untoward** happens, you mean that something happens that is unexpected and causes difficulties. [FORMAL] ◻ *The surveyor's report didn't highlight anything untoward.*

un|trace|able /ʌntreɪsəb³l/ ADJ If someone or something is **untraceable**, it is impossible to find them. ◻ *...a world where electronic crime is untraceable.*

un|trained /ʌntreɪnd/ ADJ Someone who is **untrained** has not been taught the skills that they need for a particular job, activity, or situation. ◻ *It is nonsense to say we have untrained staff dealing with emergencies.*

un|tram|meled /ʌntræm³ld/

in BRIT, sometimes in AM, use **untrammelled**

ADJ [oft ADJ by n] Someone who is **untrammeled** is able to act freely in the way they want to, rather than being restricted by something. [LITERARY] ◻ *It was the only place where the royal family could really relax and lead an untrammeled domestic life.* ◻ *She thought of herself as a free woman, untrammeled by family relationships.*

un|treat|ed /ʌntritɪd/ **1** ADJ If an injury or illness is left **untreated**, it is not given medical treatment. ◻ *If left untreated, the condition may become chronic.* **2** ADJ **Untreated** materials, water, or chemicals are harmful and have not been made safe. ◻ *...the dumping of nuclear waste and untreated sewage.* **3** ADJ **Untreated** materials are in their natural or original state, often before being prepared for use in a particular process. ◻ *All the bedding is made of simple, untreated cotton.*

un|tried /ʌntraɪd/ ADJ If someone or something is **untried**, they have not yet experienced certain situations or have not yet been tried out, so you do not know what they will be like. ◻ *He was young and untried, with no reputation of his own.*

un|trou|bled /ʌntrʌb³ld/ ADJ If you are **untroubled** by something, you are not affected or worried by it. ◻ *She is untroubled by the fact that she didn't win.*

un|true /ʌntru/ **1** ADJ If a statement or idea is **untrue**, it is false and not based on facts. ◻ *The allegations were completely untrue.* ◻ *It was untrue to say that all political prisoners have been released.* **2** → See feature box at **truth**

un|trust|wor|thy /ʌntrʌstwɜrði/ ADJ If you say that someone is **untrustworthy**, you think they are unreliable and cannot be trusted. ◻ *I think he is shallow, vain and untrustworthy.*

un|truth /ʌntruθ/ (untruths /ʌntruðz/) **1** N-VAR An **untruth** is a lie. [FORMAL] ◻ *Wall Street has been aware of the Internet's power in spreading malicious untruths.* **2** → See feature box at **truth**

un|truth|ful /ʌntruθfʊl/ ADJ If someone is **untruthful** or if they say **untruthful** things, they are dishonest and say things that they know are not true. ◻ *Some people may be tempted to give untruthful answers.*

un|tu|tored /ʌntutərd/ ADJ If someone is **untutored**, they have not been formally trained to do something, although they may be quite skilled at it. [FORMAL] ❑ *This untutored mathematician had an obsession with numbers.*

un|typi|cal /ʌntɪpɪkəl/ ADJ [usu v-link ADJ] If someone or something is **untypical** of a particular type of person or thing, they are not a good example of the way that type of person or thing normally is. People sometimes say something is **not untypical** when they mean that it is quite normal. ❑ *She was in many respects untypical of the screenwriting trade.* • **un|typi|cal|ly** /ʌntɪpɪkli/ ADV ❑ *Untypically for a man in that situation he became interested in Buddhism.*

un|us|able /ʌnyuːzəbəl/ ADJ Something that is **unusable** is not in a good enough state or condition to be used. ❑ *Bombing had made roads and railways unusable.*

un|used

Pronounced /ʌnyuːzd/ for meaning 1, and /ʌnyuːst/ for meaning 2.

1 ADJ Something that is **unused** has not been used or is not being used at the moment. ❑ *...unused containers of food.* **2** ADJ [v-link ADJ *to* n] If you are **unused to** something, you have not often done it or experienced it before, so it feels unusual and unfamiliar to you. ❑ *My mother was entirely unused to such hard work.*

un|usual ♦◇◇ /ʌnyuːʒuəl/ **1** ADJ If something is **unusual**, it does not happen very often or you do not see it or hear it very often. ❑ *They have replanted many areas with rare and unusual plants.* **2** ADJ If you describe someone as **unusual**, you think that they are interesting and different from other people. ❑ *He was an unusual man with great business talents.*

un|usu|al|ly /ʌnyuːʒuəli/ **1** ADV [ADV adj] You use **unusually** to emphasize that someone or something has more of a particular quality than is usual. [EMPHASIS] ❑ *He was an unusually complex man.* **2** ADV You can use **unusually** to suggest that something is not what normally happens. ❑ *Unusually, for an experienced politician, he isn't a very good public speaker.*

un|ut|ter|able /ʌnʌtərəbəl/ ADJ [ADJ n] You can use **unutterable** to emphasize that something, especially a bad quality, is great in degree or intensity. [WRITTEN, EMPHASIS] ❑ *...unutterable rubbish.* • **un|ut|ter|ably** /ʌnʌtərəbli/ ADV ❑ *I suddenly felt unutterably depressed.*

un|vary|ing /ʌnvɛəriɪŋ/ ADJ [usu ADJ n] If you describe something as **unvarying**, you mean that it stays the same and never changes. ❑ *...her unvarying refusal to make public appearances.*

un|veil /ʌnveɪl/ (unveils, unveiling, unveiled) **1** V-T If someone formally **unveils** something such as a new statue or painting, they draw back the curtain which is covering it. ❑ *...a ceremony to unveil a monument to the victims.* **2** V-T If you **unveil** a plan, new product, or some other thing that has been kept secret, you introduce it to the public. ❑ *Mr. Werner unveiled his new strategy this week.*

un|want|ed /ʌnwɒntɪd/ ADJ If you say that something or someone is **unwanted**, you mean that you do not want them, or that nobody wants them. ❑ *...the misery of unwanted pregnancies.* ❑ *She felt unwanted.*

un|war|rant|ed /ʌnwɔːrəntɪd/ ADJ If you describe something as **unwarranted**, you are critical of it because there is no need or reason for it. [FORMAL, DISAPPROVAL] ❑ *Any attempt to discuss the issue of human rights was rejected as an unwarranted interference in the country's internal affairs.*

un|wary /ʌnwɛəri/ ADJ [usu ADJ n] If you describe someone as **unwary**, you mean that they are not cautious or experienced and are therefore likely to be harmed or deceived. [FORMAL] ❑ *With its quicksands the river usually drowns a few unwary visitors every season.* • N-SING [the N] **The unwary** are people who are unwary. ❑ *Specialist subjects are full of pitfalls for the unwary.*

un|washed /ʌnwɒʃt/ **1** ADJ **Unwashed** people or objects are dirty and need to be washed. ❑ *Leftover food and unwashed dishes cover the dirty counters.* **2** PHRASE **The unwashed** or **the great unwashed** is a way of referring to poor or ordinary people. [HUMOROUS] ❑ *By viewing great art, the great unwashed would become civilized.*

un|wa|ver|ing /ʌnweɪvərɪŋ/ ADJ If you describe a feeling or attitude as **unwavering**, you mean that it is strong and firm and does not weaken. ❑ *She has been encouraged by the unwavering support of her family.*

un|wel|come /ʌnwɛlkəm/ **1** ADJ An **unwelcome** experience is one that you do not like and did not want. ❑ *The mayor delivered the unwelcome news that city employees may have to take unpaid time off.* **2** ADJ If you say that a visitor is **unwelcome**, you mean that you did not want them to come. ❑ *...an unwelcome guest.*

un|wel|com|ing /ʌnwɛlkəmɪŋ/ **1** ADJ If someone is **unwelcoming**, or if they behave in an **unwelcoming** way, they are unfriendly or hostile when you visit or approach them. [DISAPPROVAL] ❑ *His manner was cold and unwelcoming.* **2** ADJ If you describe a place as **unwelcoming**, you mean that it looks unattractive or difficult to live or work in. ❑ *My room was cold and unwelcoming.*

un|well /ʌnwɛl/ ADJ [v-link ADJ] If you are **unwell**, you are sick. ❑ *Their grandmother was feeling unwell and had to stay at home.*

un|whole|some /ʌnhoʊlsəm/ **1** ADJ **Unwholesome** food or drink is not healthy or good for you. ❑ *The fish were unwholesome and old.* **2** ADJ If you describe someone's feelings or behavior as **unwholesome**, you are critical of them because they are unpleasant or unnatural. [DISAPPROVAL] ❑ *My yearning to be rich was an insane, unwholesome desire.*

un|wieldy /ʌnwiːldi/ **1** ADJ If you describe an object as **unwieldy**, you mean that it is difficult to move or carry because it is so big or heavy. ❑ *They came panting up to his door with their unwieldy baggage.* **2** ADJ If you describe a system as **unwieldy**, you mean that it does not work very well as a result of it being too large or badly organized. ❑ *His company has to deal with unwieldy Russian bureaucracy.*

un|will|ing /ʌnwɪlɪŋ/ **1** ADJ If you are **unwilling** to do something, you do not want to do it and will not agree to do it. ❑ *Initially the government was unwilling to accept the defeat.* • **un|will|ing|ness** N-UNCOUNT ❑ *...their unwillingness to accept responsibility for mistakes.* **2** ADJ You can use **unwilling** to describe someone who does not really want to do the thing they are doing. ❑ *A youthful teacher, he finds himself an unwilling participant in school politics.* • **un|will|ing|ly** ADV ❑ *He accepted his orders very unwillingly.*

un|wind /ʌnwaɪnd/ (unwinds, unwinding, unwound) **1** V-I When you **unwind**, you relax after you have done something that makes you tense or tired. ❑ *It helps them to unwind after a busy day at work.* **2** V-T/V-I If you **unwind** a length of something that is wrapped around something else or around itself, you loosen it and make it straight. You can also say that it **unwinds**. ❑ *One of them unwound a length of rope from around his waist.*

un|wise /ʌnwaɪz/ ADJ If you describe something as **unwise**, you think that it is foolish and likely to lead to a bad result. ❑ *It would be unwise to expect too much.* ❑ *I think this is extremely unwise.* • **un|wise|ly** ADV ❑ *She accepted that she had acted unwisely.*

un|wit|ting /ʌnwɪtɪŋ/ ADJ If you describe a person or their actions as **unwitting**, you mean that the person does something or is involved in something without realizing it. ❑ *We were unwitting collaborators in his plan.* • **un|wit|ting|ly** ADV ❑ *He was unwittingly caught up in the confrontation.*

un|woman|ly /ʌnwʊmənli/ ADJ If you describe a girl's or woman's behavior as **unwomanly**, you are critical of the fact that they are behaving in a way that you think is inappropriate for a woman. [DISAPPROVAL] ❑ *Society contrived to terrorize women with the threat that certain behavior is unnatural and unwomanly.*

un|work|able /ʌnwɜːrkəbəl/ ADJ If a plan, law, or system is **unworkable**, it cannot be successful. ❑ *There is the strong possibility that such cooperation will prove unworkable.*

un|world|ly /ʌnwɜːrldli/ **1** ADJ If you describe someone as **unworldly**, you mean that they have not experienced many things in their life and do not know what sort of things usually happen to other people during their lives. ❑ *She was so young, so unworldly.* **2** ADJ If you describe someone as **unworldly**, you mean that they are not interested in having a lot of money or possessions. ❑ *Kitty's family was unworldly, unimpressed by power or money.*

un|wor|thy /ʌnwɜːrði/ (unworthier, unworthiest) ADJ If a person or thing is **unworthy** of something good, they do not deserve it. ❏ *You may feel unworthy of the attention and help people offer you.*

un|wound /ʌnwaʊnd/ **Unwound** is the past tense and past participle of **unwind**.

un|wrap /ʌnræp/ (unwraps, unwrapping, unwrapped) V-T When you **unwrap** something, you take off the paper, plastic, or other covering that is around it. ❏ *I untied the bow and unwrapped the small box.*

un|writ|ten /ʌnrɪtᵊn/ **1** ADJ Something such as a book that is **unwritten** has not been printed or written down. ❏ *Universal has agreed to pay $5 million for her next, as yet unwritten, novel.* **2** ADJ An **unwritten** rule, law, or agreement is one that is understood and accepted by everyone, although it may not have been formally or officially established. ❏ *They obey the one unwritten rule that binds them all – no talking.* **3** → See feature box at **polite**

un|yield|ing /ʌnyiːldɪŋ/ **1** ADJ You describe someone as **unyielding** when they have very strong, fixed ideas about something and are unlikely to change their mind. [WRITTEN] ❏ *The authorities proved unyielding on one crucial demand.* **2** ADJ If a barrier or surface is **unyielding**, it is very solid or hard. [LITERARY] ❏ *...the troopers, who had to build roads through those unyielding mountains.*

un|zip /ʌnzɪp/ (unzips, unzipping, unzipped) **1** V-T/V-I When you **unzip** something which is fastened by a zipper or when it **unzips**, you open it by pulling open the zipper. ❏ *James unzipped his bag.* **2** V-T To **unzip** a computer file means to open a file that has been compressed. [COMPUTING] ❏ *Unzip the icons into a subdirectory.*

UP

① PREPOSITION, ADVERB, AND ADJECTIVE USES
② USED IN COMBINATION AS A PREPOSITION
③ VERB USES

---

① **up** ✦✦✦

The preposition is pronounced /ʌp/. The adverb and adjective are pronounced /ʌp/.

Up is often used with verbs of movement such as 'jump' and 'pull', and also in phrasal verbs such as 'give up' and 'wash up.'

→ Please look at meaning **16** to see if the expression you are looking for is shown under another headword.

1 PREP If a person or thing goes **up** something such as a slope, ladder, or chimney, they move away from the ground or to a higher position. ❏ *They were climbing up a narrow mountain road.* ❏ *I ran up the stairs and saw Alison lying at the top.* • ADV **Up** is also an adverb. ❏ *Finally, after an hour, I went up to Jeremy's room.* ❏ *Intense balls of flame rose up into the sky.* **2** PREP If a person or thing is **up** something such as a ladder or a mountain, they are near the top of it. ❏ *He was up a ladder sawing off the tops of his apple trees.* • ADV [ADV after v] **Up** is also an adverb. ❏ *...a research station perched 4,000 meters up on the lip of the crater.* **3** ADV [ADV after v] You use **up** to indicate that you are looking or facing in a direction that is away from the ground or toward a higher level. ❏ *Keep your head up, and look around you from time to time.* **4** ADV [ADV after v] If someone stands **up**, they move so that they are standing. ❏ *He stood up and went to the window.* **5** PREP [V PREP n] If you go or look **up** something such as a road or river, you go or look along it. If you are **up** a road or river, you are somewhere along it. ❏ *A line of tanks came up the road from the city.* ❏ *We leaned on the wooden rail of the bridge and looked up the river.* **6** ADV If you are traveling to a particular place, you can say that you are going **up** to that place, especially if it is going toward the north or to a higher level of land. If you are already in such a place, you can say that you are **up** there. [mainly SPOKEN] ❏ *I'll be up to see you tomorrow.* ❏ *He was living up North.* **7** ADV If you go **up** to something or someone, you move to the place where they are and stop there. ❏ *The girl ran the rest of the way across the street and up to the car.* ❏ *On the way out a boy of about ten came up on roller skates.* **8** ADV If an amount of something goes **up**, it increases. If an amount of something is **up**, it has increased and is at a higher level than it was. ❏ *The total budget went up almost $300 million.* ❏ *Tourism is up, jobs are up, individual income is up.* **9** ADJ [v-link ADJ] If you are **up**, you are not in bed. ❏ *Are you sure you should be up?* ❏ *These days they were up at the crack of dawn.* **10** ADJ [v-link ADJ] If a period of time is **up**, it has come to an end. ❏ *The moment the half-hour was up, Brooks rose.* **11** ADJ [v-link ADJ] If a computer or computer system is **up**, it is working. Compare **down**. ❏ *The new system is up and ready to run.* **12** PHRASE If someone who has been in bed for some time, for example because they have been sick, is **up and about**, they are now out of bed and living their normal life. ❏ *How are you Lennox? Good to see you up and about.* **13** PHRASE If you say that **something is up**, you mean that something is wrong or that something worrying is happening. [INFORMAL] ❏ *What is it then? Something's up, isn't it?* **14** PHRASE If you say to someone '**What's up?**' or if you tell them **what's up**, you are asking them or telling them what is wrong or what is worrying them. [INFORMAL] ❏ *"What's up?" I said to him.—"Just tired," he answered.* **15** PHRASE If you move **up and down** somewhere, you move there repeatedly in one direction and then in the opposite direction. ❏ *I used to jump up and down to keep warm.* ❏ *I strolled up and down thoughtfully before calling a taxi.* **16 up in arms** → see **arm** ②

② **up** ✦✦✦ /ʌp/

→ Please look at meaning **9** to see if the expression you are looking for is shown under another headword.

1 PHRASE If you feel **up to** doing something, you are well enough to do it. ❏ *Those patients who were up to it could move to the adjacent pool.* ❏ *His fellow directors were not up to running the business without him.* **2** PHRASE To be **up to** something means to be secretly doing something that you should not be doing. [INFORMAL] ❏ *Why did you need a room unless you were up to something?* ❏ *They must have known what their father was up to.* **3** PHRASE If you say that it is **up to** someone to do something, you mean that it is their responsibility to do it. ❏ *It was up to him to make it right, no matter how long it took.* ❏ *I'm sure I'd have spotted him if it had been up to me.* **4** PHRASE **Up until** or **up to** are used to indicate the latest time at which something can happen, or the end of the period of time that you are referring to. ❏ *Please feel free to call me any time up until 9:30 at night.* **5** PHRASE You use **up to** to say how large something can be or what level it has reached. ❏ *Up to twenty thousand students paid between five and six thousand dollars.* **6** PHRASE If someone or something is **up for** election, review, or discussion, they are about to be considered. ❏ *A third of the Senate and the entire House are up for re-election.* **7** PHRASE If you are **up for** something, you are willing or eager to do it. [INFORMAL] ❏ *I'm starved. Who's up for pizza?* **8** PHRASE If you are **up against** something, you have a very difficult situation or problem to deal with. ❏ *The chairwoman is up against the greatest challenge to her position.* **9 up to par** → see **par**

③ **up** /ʌp/ (ups, upping, upped) **1** V-T If you **up** something such as the amount of money you are offering for something, you increase it. ❏ *He upped his offer for the company.* ❏ *Drug stores upped sales by 63 percent.* **2** V-I If you **up** and leave a place, you go away from it, often suddenly or unexpectedly. ❏ *One day he just upped and left.*

up-and-com|ing ADJ [ADJ n] **Up-and-coming** people are likely to be successful in the future. ❏ *...his readiness to share the limelight with young, up-and-coming stars.*

up|beat /ʌpbiːt/ **1** ADJ If people or their opinions are **upbeat**, they are cheerful and hopeful about a situation. [INFORMAL] ❏ *The Defense Secretary gave an upbeat assessment of the war so far.* ❏ *Neil's colleagues said he was actually in a joking, upbeat mood in spite of the bad news.* **2** → See feature box at **music**

up|braid /ʌpbreɪd/ (upbraids, upbraiding, upbraided) V-T If you **upbraid** someone, you tell them that they have done something wrong and criticize them for doing it. [FORMAL] ❏ *His mother summoned him, upbraided him, wept and prayed.*

up|bring|ing /ʌpbrɪŋɪŋ/ N-UNCOUNT Your **upbringing** is the way that your parents treat you and the things that they teach you when you are growing up. ❏ *Martin's upbringing shaped his whole life.*

up|chuck /ʌptʃʌk/ (upchucks, upchucking, upchucked) V-I
If you **upchuck**, food and drink comes back up from your stomach and out through your mouth. [AM, INFORMAL]

up|com|ing /ʌpkʌmɪŋ/ ADJ [ADJ n] **Upcoming** events will happen in the near future. ❑ *We'll face a tough fight in the upcoming election.*

up|country /ʌpkʌntri/ ADJ [ADJ n] **Upcountry** places are toward the middle or north of a large country, usually in the countryside. ❑ *...a collection of upcountry hamlets.* • ADV [be ADV, ADV after v] **Upcountry** is also an adverb. ❑ *I hired a car to take us upcountry.*

up|cy|cle /ʌpsaɪkᵊl/ (upcycles, upcycling, upcycled) V-T If you **upcycle** things that have already been used, such as pieces of furniture, you create an object of even greater value or use.

VOCABULARY IN CONTEXT

Upcycling: something old, something new

Upcycling refers to the ultramodern **trend** of giving a **dated** piece of furniture a new **lease of life** by turning it into something else or using it in a different way. At the simplest level, you might buy a **dilapidated** old chair in an **antiques** shop, re-paint and re-upholster it, and produce something right **up-to-the-minute**. But many upcyclers would do something much more **innovative** with that **period piece**. For example, a jam jar could become a light fitting, or a **vintage** sewing machine stand could become a table. It's all about being creative and seeing an old object in a **novel** way.

up|date /ʌpdeɪt/ (updates, updating, updated)

The verb is pronounced /ʌpdeɪt/. The noun is pronounced /ʌpdeɪt/.

1 V-T/V-I If you **update** something, you make it more modern, usually by adding new parts to it or giving new information. ❑ *He was back in the office, updating the work schedule on the computer.* ❑ *Airlines would prefer to update rather than retrain crews.* **2** N-COUNT An **update** is a news item containing the latest information about a particular situation. ❑ *She had heard the newsflash on a TV channel's news update.* ❑ *...a weather update.* **3** V-T If you **update** someone **on** a situation, you tell them the latest developments in that situation. ❑ *We'll update you on the day's top news stories.*

up|end /ʌpɛnd/ (upends, upending, upended) V-T If you **upend** something, you turn it upside down. ❑ *He upended the beer, and swallowed.*

up front also **up-front** **1** ADJ If you are **up front** about something, you act openly or publicly so that people know what you are doing or what you believe. [INFORMAL] ❑ *You can't help being biased so you may as well be up front about it.* **2** ADV [ADV after v] If a payment is made **up front**, it is made in advance and openly, so that the person being paid can see that the money is there. ❑ *Some companies charge a fee up front, but we don't think that's right.* • ADJ [ADJ n] **Up front** is also an adjective. ❑ *The eleven percent loan has no up-front costs.*

up|grade /ʌpgreɪd, -greɪd/ (upgrades, upgrading, upgraded) **1** V-T [usu passive] If equipment or services are **upgraded**, they are improved or made more efficient. ❑ *Helicopters have been upgraded and modernized.* ❑ *Medical facilities are being reorganized and upgraded.* • N-COUNT **Upgrade** is also a noun. ❑ *...equipment which needs expensive upgrades.* **2** V-T [usu passive] If someone **is upgraded**, their job or status is changed so that they become more important or receive more money. ❑ *He was upgraded to security guard.* **3** V-T/V-I If you **upgrade** or **are upgraded**, you change something such as your plane ticket or your hotel room to one that is more expensive. ❑ *His family was upgraded from economy to business class.*

up|heav|al /ʌphiːvᵊl/ (upheavals) **1** N-COUNT An **upheaval** is a big change which causes a lot of trouble, confusion, and worry. ❑ *Algeria has been going through political upheaval for the past two months.* **2** → See feature box at **challenge**

up|held /ʌphɛld/ **Upheld** is the past tense and past participle of **uphold**.

up|hill /ʌphɪl/ **1** ADV If something or someone is **uphill** or is moving **uphill**, they are near the top of a hill or are going up a slope. ❑ *He had been running uphill a long way.* ❑ *The man was no more than ten yards away and slightly uphill.* • ADJ **Uphill** is also an adjective. ❑ *...a long, uphill journey.* **2** ADJ [ADJ n] If you refer to something as an **uphill** battle or an **uphill** struggle, you mean that it requires a lot of effort and determination, but it should be possible to achieve it. ❑ *It had been an uphill battle to achieve what she had wanted.*

up|hold /ʌphoʊld/ (upholds, upholding, upheld) **1** V-T If you **uphold** something such as a law, a principle, or a decision, you support and maintain it. ❑ *Our policy has been to uphold the law.* ❑ *It is the responsibility of every government to uphold certain basic principles.* **2** V-T If a court of law **upholds** a legal decision that has already been made, it decides that it was the correct decision. ❑ *The State Supreme Court upheld the Superior Court judge's decision.*

up|hold|er /ʌphoʊldər/ (upholders) N-COUNT An **upholder** of a particular tradition or system is someone who believes strongly in it and will support it when it is threatened. [FORMAL] ❑ *...upholders of the traditional family unit.*

up|hol|stered /ʌphoʊlstərd, əpoʊl-/ ADJ [oft ADJ in n] **Upholstered** chairs and seats have a soft covering that makes them comfortable to sit on. ❑ *All of their furniture was upholstered in flowery materials.*

up|hol|ster|er /ʌphoʊlstərər, əpoʊl-/ (upholsterers) N-COUNT An **upholsterer** is someone whose job is to make and fit the soft covering on chairs and seats.

up|hol|stery /ʌphoʊlstəri, əpoʊl-/ N-UNCOUNT **Upholstery** is the soft covering on chairs and seats that makes them more comfortable to sit on. ❑ *...white leather upholstery.*

up|keep /ʌpkiːp/ **1** N-UNCOUNT The **upkeep** of a building or place is the work of keeping it in good condition. ❑ *The money will be used for the upkeep of the park.* **2** N-UNCOUNT The **upkeep** of a group of people or services is the process of providing them with the things that they need. ❑ *He offered to pay $250 a month toward his son's upkeep.*

up|land /ʌplənd, -lænd/ (uplands) **1** ADJ [ADJ n] **Upland** places are situated on high land. ❑ *...San Marino, the tiny upland republic.* **2** N-PLURAL **Uplands** are areas of high land. ❑ *...a deep valley ringed by green uplands.*

up|lift (uplifts, uplifting, uplifted)

The verb is pronounced /ʌplɪft/. The noun is pronounced /ʌplɪft/.

1 V-T If something **uplifts** people, it helps them to have a better life, for example by making them feel happy or by improving their social conditions. [LITERARY] ❑ *We need a little something to help sometimes, to uplift us and make us feel better.* • N-VAR **Uplift** is also a noun. ❑ *This victory was a massive uplift for us.* **2** N-COUNT [usu sing, oft N in n] In economics, an **uplift** in something such as the price of shares is an increase in their value. [BUSINESS] ❑ *...an uplift in the stock market.*

up|lift|ed /ʌplɪftɪd/ **1** ADJ [usu ADJ n] If people's faces or arms are **uplifted**, they are pointing them upward or are holding them up. [LITERARY] ❑ *The men support the ballerinas, who pose with their uplifted arms.* **2** ADJ [v-link ADJ] If something makes you feel **uplifted**, it makes you feel very cheerful and happy. ❑ *...people whose presence left you feeling uplifted, happy and full of energy.*

up|lift|ing /ʌplɪftɪŋ/ ADJ You describe something as **uplifting** when it makes you feel very cheerful and happy. ❑ ...*a charming and uplifting love story.*

up|load /ʌploʊd/ (**uploads, uploading, uploaded**) V-T If you **upload** data, you transfer it from a disk to your computer or from your computer to another computer. [COMPUTING] ❑ *All you need to do is upload the files on to your web space.*

up|market /ʌpmɑrkɪt/ also **up-market** ADJ **Upmarket** products or services are expensive, of good quality, and intended to appeal to people with money and education. [mainly BRIT]

in AM, usually use **upscale**

upon ♦♦◊ /əpɒn/

In addition to the uses shown below, **upon** is used in phrasal verbs such as 'come upon' and 'look upon,' and after some other verbs such as 'decide' and 'depend.'

1 PREP If one thing is **upon** another, it is on it. [LITERARY] ❑ *He set the tray upon the table.* ❑ *He bent forward and laid a kiss softly upon her forehead.* **2** PREP [PREP -ing/n] You use **upon** when mentioning an event that is followed immediately by another event. [FORMAL] ❑ *The door on the left, upon entering the church, leads to the Crypt of St. Issac.* **3** PREP [n PREP n] You use **upon** between two occurrences of the same noun in order to say that there are large numbers of the thing mentioned. ❑ *Row upon row of women surged forwards.* **4** PREP [PREP pron] If an event is **upon** you, it is just about to happen. [LITERARY] ❑ *The long-threatened storm was upon us.* ❑ *The wedding season is upon us.*

up|per ♦◊◊ /ʌpər/ **1** ADJ [ADJ n, the ADJ] You use **upper** to describe something that is above something else. ❑ *There is a good restaurant on the upper floor.* **2** ADJ [ADJ n] You use **upper** to describe the higher part of something. ❑ *...the upper part of the foot.* ❑ *...the muscles of the upper back and chest.* **3** PHRASE If you have **the upper hand** in a situation, you have an advantage over other people involved, for example because you have more power or success. ❑ *The home team was beginning to gain the upper hand.* **4** → See feature box at **global warming**

upper|case /ʌpərkeɪs/ also **upper case** ADJ **Uppercase** letters are capital letters. ❑ *Most schools teach children lowercase letters first, and uppercase letters later.* • N-UNCOUNT **Uppercase** is also a noun. ❑ *They should use uppercase.*

up|per class (**upper classes**) also **upper-class** N-COUNT-COLL The **upper class** or the **upper classes** are the group of people in a society who own the most property and have the highest social status, and who may not need to work for money. ❑ *...goods specifically designed to appeal to the tastes of the upper class.* • ADJ **Upper class** is also an adjective. ❑ *All of them came from wealthy, upper class families.*

upper|class|man /ʌpərklæsmən/ (**upperclassmen**) N-COUNT An **upperclassman** is a junior or senior student in an American high school, college, or university. [AM]

upper|class|woman /ʌpərklæswʊmən/ (**upperclasswomen**) N-COUNT An **upperclasswoman** is a junior or senior student in a high school, college, or university. [AM]

up|per crust also **upper-crust** N-SING-COLL The **upper crust** are the upper classes. [INFORMAL] ❑ *...the kind of lifestyle of the privileged upper crust.* • ADJ [ADJ n] **Upper crust** is also an adjective. ❑ *Sergeant Parrott normally spoke with an upper-crust accent.*

upper|cut /ʌpərkʌt/ (**uppercuts**) N-COUNT An **uppercut** is a type of punch used in boxing. It is a hard upward blow to the chin.

Up|per House (**Upper Houses**) **1** N-PROPER In the United States, the **Upper House** is the **Senate**. ❑ *Two Senators represent each state in the Upper House.* **2** N-PROPER In Britain, the **Upper House** is the **House of Lords**. **3** N-COUNT; N-PROPER In other countries where the parliament or legislature is divided into two groups of members, the **Upper House** is the more senior of these groups, although it may not be more powerful. ❑ *...elections for the Upper House of Japan's parliament, the Diet.*

up|per lip (**upper lips**) **1** N-COUNT [usu sing] Your **upper lip** is the part of your face between your mouth and your nose. ❑ *The beginnings of a mustache showed on his upper lip.* **2** N-COUNT Your **upper lip** is the higher of your two lips. ❑ *His upper lip was flat, but the lower one sagged.*

upper|most /ʌpərmoʊst/ **1** ADJ [usu ADJ n] The **uppermost** part of something is the part that is higher than the rest of it. The **uppermost** thing is the highest one of a group of things. ❑ *John was on the uppermost floor of the three-story gatehouse.* • ADV **Uppermost** is also an adverb. ❑ *Lift the fish and carefully place it on a large board, flat side uppermost.* **2** ADJ [usu v-link ADJ] If something is **uppermost** in a particular situation, it is the most important thing in that situation. ❑ *The economy appears to be uppermost in people's minds.*

up|pi|ty /ʌpɪti/ ADJ If you say that someone is **uppity**, you mean that they are behaving as if they were very important and you do not think that they are important. [INFORMAL, DISAPPROVAL] ❑ *If you just tried to show normal dignity, you were viewed as uppity.*

up|raised /ʌpreɪzd/ ADJ If your hand or an object is **upraised**, you are holding it up in the air. ❑ *Mr. Grummage silenced my objections with an upraised hand.*

up|right /ʌpraɪt/ (**uprights**) **1** ADJ If you are sitting or standing **upright**, you are sitting or standing with your back straight, rather than bending or lying down. ❑ *Helen sat upright in her chair.* ❑ *He moved into an upright position.* **2** ADJ [ADJ n] An **upright** vacuum cleaner or freezer is tall rather than wide. **3** ADJ An **upright** chair has a straight back and no arms. ❑ *He was sitting on an upright chair beside his bed, reading.* **4** N-COUNT You can refer to vertical posts or the vertical parts of an object as **uprights**. ❑ *...the uprights of a canopy bed.* **5** ADJ You can describe people as **upright** when they are careful to follow acceptable rules of behavior and behave in a moral way. ❑ *...a very upright, trustworthy man.*

up|right pia|no (**upright pianos**) N-COUNT An **upright piano** is a piano in which the strings are arranged vertically, rather than horizontally as they are in a grand piano.

up|ris|ing /ʌpraɪzɪŋ/ (**uprisings**) N-COUNT When there is an **uprising**, a group of people start fighting against the people who are in power in their country, because they want to bring about a political change. ❑ *...an uprising against the government.*

up|river /ʌprɪvər/ also **up-river** ADV Something that is moving **upriver** is moving toward the source of a river, from a point down the river. Something that is **upriver** is toward the source of a river. ❑ *Heavy goods could be brought upriver in barges.* • ADJ [ADJ n] **Upriver** is also an adjective. ❑ *...an upriver trip in Central Africa.*

up|roar /ʌprɔr/ **1** N-UNCOUNT [also a N, oft in N] If there is **uproar**, there is a lot of shouting and noise because people are very angry or upset about something. ❑ *The announcement caused an uproar in the crowd.* **2** N-UNCOUNT [also a N] You can also use **uproar** to refer to a lot of public criticism and debate about something that has made people angry. ❑ *The town is in an uproar over the dispute.*

up|roari|ous /ʌprɔriəs/ ADJ When events or people are **uproarious**, they make people laugh in a very noisy way. [LITERARY] ❑ *He had spent several uproarious evenings at the Embassy Club.* • **up|roari|ous|ly** ADV ❑ *Bob laughed uproariously.*

up|root /ʌprut/ (**uproots, uprooting, uprooted**) **1** V-T If you **uproot** yourself or if you **are uprooted**, you leave, or are made to leave, a place where you have lived for a long time. ❑ *...the trauma of uprooting themselves from their homes.* ❑ *He had no wish to uproot Dena from her present home.* **2** V-T If someone **uproots** a tree or plant, or if the wind **uproots** it, it is pulled out of the ground. ❑ *They had been forced to uproot their vines and plant wheat.* ❑ *...fallen trees which have been uprooted by the storm.*

up|scale /ʌpskeɪl/ ADJ [usu ADJ n] **Upscale** is used to describe products or services that are expensive, of good quality, and intended to appeal to people with a lot of money and education. [AM] ❑ *...upscale department-store chains such as Bloomingdale's and Saks Fifth Avenue.* • ADV [ADV after v] **Upscale** is also an adverb. ❑ *T-shirts, the epitome of American casualness, have moved upscale.*

in BRIT, use **upmarket**

up|set ♦◊◊ (**upsets, upsetting, upset**)

The verb and adjective are pronounced /ʌpsɛt/. The noun is pronounced /ʌpsɛt/.

1 ADJ If you are **upset**, you are unhappy or disappointed because something bad has happened to you. ❏ *After she died I felt very, very upset.* ❏ *Marta looked upset.* • N-COUNT **Upset** is also a noun. ❏ *...stress and other emotional upsets.* **2** V-T If something **upsets** you, it makes you feel worried or unhappy. ❏ *The whole incident had upset me and my fiancée terribly.* ❏ *She warned me not to say anything to upset him.* • **up|set|ting** ADJ ❏ *Childhood sickness can be upsetting for children and parents alike.* **3** V-T If events **upset** something such as a procedure or a state of affairs, they cause it to go wrong. ❏ *Political problems could upset agreements between Moscow and Kabul.* • N-COUNT **Upset** is also a noun. ❏ *Markets are very sensitive to any upsets in the Japanese economic machine.* **4** V-T If you **upset** an object, you accidentally knock or push it over so that it scatters over a large area. ❏ *Don't upset the piles of sheets under the box.* **5** N-COUNT A stomach **upset** is a slight sickness in your stomach caused by an infection or by something that you have eaten. ❏ *Paul was unwell last night with a stomach upset.* • ADJ [ADJ n] **Upset** is also an adjective. ❏ *Larry has an upset stomach.* **6** to **upset the applecart** → see **applecart**

up|shot /ʌpʃɒt/ N-SING The **upshot** of a series of events or discussions is the final result of them, usually a surprising result. ❏ *The upshot is that we have lots of good but not very happy employees.*

up|side down /ʌpsaɪd daʊn/ also **upside-down** ADV If something is or has been turned **upside down**, it has been turned around so that the part that is usually lowest is above the part that is usually highest. ❏ *The painting was hung upside down.* • ADJ **Upside down** is also an adjective. ❏ *...chandeliers that resemble upside-down wedding cakes.*

up|size /ʌpsaɪz/ (**upsizes, upsizing, upsized**) VERB If you **upsize**, or **upsize** your home, you move to a larger house. ❏ *If you can't upsize, extend.* ❏ *How does a young couple upsize their home as children enter the picture?*

up|stage /ʌpsteɪdʒ/ (**upstages, upstaging, upstaged**) V-T If someone **upstages** you, they draw attention away from you by being more attractive or interesting. ❏ *He had a younger brother who always publicly upstaged him.*

up|stairs /ʌpstɛərz/ **1** ADV [ADV after v] If you go **upstairs** in a building, you go up a staircase toward a higher floor. ❏ *He went upstairs and changed into clean clothes.* **2** ADV If something or someone is **upstairs** in a building, they are on a floor that is higher than the ground floor. ❏ *The restaurant is upstairs and consists of a large, open room.* **3** ADJ [ADJ n] An **upstairs** room or object is situated on a floor of a building that is higher than the ground floor. ❏ *Marsani moved into the upstairs apartment.* **4** N-SING The **upstairs** of a building is the floor or floors that are higher than the ground floor. ❏ *Together we went through the upstairs.*

up|stand|ing /ʌpstændɪŋ/ ADJ [usu ADJ n] **Upstanding** people behave in a morally acceptable way. [FORMAL] ❏ *You look like a nice upstanding young man.*

up|start /ʌpstɑrt/ (**upstarts**) N-COUNT You can refer to someone as an **upstart** when they behave as if they are important, but you think that they are too new in a place or job to be treated as important. [DISAPPROVAL] ❏ *Many prefer a familiar authority figure to a young upstart.*

up|state /ʌpsteɪt/ ADJ [ADJ n] **Upstate** means belonging or relating to the parts of a state that are furthest to the north or furthest from the main city. [mainly AM] ❏ *...an idyllic village in upstate New York.* • ADV [ADV after v, n ADV] **Upstate** is also an adverb. ❏ *These buses will carry families upstate to visit relatives in prison.*

up|stream /ʌpstriːm/ ADV Something that is moving **upstream** is moving toward the source of a river against the current, from a point further down the river. Something that is **upstream** is toward the source of a river. ❏ *Salmon manage to swim upstream to lay their eggs.* ❏ *...the river police, whose headquarters are just upstream of the Ile St. Louis.* • ADJ [ADJ n] **Upstream** is also an adjective. ❏ *We'll go to the upstream side of that big rock.*

up|surge /ʌpsɜrdʒ/ N-SING If there is an **upsurge** in something, there is a sudden, large increase in it. ❏ *...the upsurge in oil prices.*

up|swing /ʌpswɪŋ/ (**upswings**) N-COUNT [usu sing, oft N in n, on the N] An **upswing** is a sudden improvement in something such as an economy, or an increase in an amount or level. ❏ *...an upswing in the economy.*

up|take /ʌpteɪk/ **1** N-SING [usu with supp] A person's **uptake** of something is the amount of it that they take in or absorb. [TECHNICAL] ❏ *The drug increases the number of red cells in the blood, enhancing oxygen uptake by 10 percent.* **2** PHRASE [V-link PHR] You say that someone is **quick on the uptake** when they understand things quickly. You say that someone is **slow on the uptake** when they have difficulty understanding simple or obvious things. ❏ *She is not an intellectual, but is quick on the uptake.*

up-tempo also **uptempo** ADJ [usu ADJ n] An **up-tempo** piece of music has a fast beat. ❏ *...an up-tempo arrangement of "Some Enchanted Evening."*

up|thread /ʌpθrɛd/ ADV Something that has been written **upthread** is written higher up in a series of messages. [COMPUTING] ❏ *I think someone already commented on that upthread somewhere.*

up|tick /ʌptɪk/ (**upticks**) N-COUNT [usu sing] If there is an **uptick** in something, it increases. ❏ *The worst that might happen is an uptick in inflation.*

up|tight /ʌptaɪt/ ADJ Someone who is **uptight** is tense, nervous, or annoyed about something and so is difficult to be with. [INFORMAL] ❏ *Penny never got uptight about exams.*

up-to-date also **up to date** **1** ADJ If something is **up-to-date**, it is the newest thing of its kind. ❏ *...the most up-to-date information available on foods today.* ❏ *Web services are always up-to-date and available.* **2** ADJ If you are **up-to-date** about something, you have the latest information about it. ❏ *We'll keep you up to date with any news.*

up-to the-minute also **up to the minute** **1** ADJ [usu ADJ n] **Up-to-the-minute** information is the latest information that you can get about something. ❏ *...24 hours a day up-to-the-minute instant news.* **2** → See feature box at **fashion**, **upcycle**

up|town /ʌptaʊn/ ADV [ADV after v] If you go **uptown**, or go to a place **uptown**, you go away from the center of a city or town toward the edge. **Uptown** sometimes refers to a part of the city other than the main business district. [mainly AM] ❏ *He rode uptown and made his way to Bob's apartment.* ❏ *Susan continued to live uptown.* • ADJ [ADJ n] **Uptown** is also an adjective. ❏ *...uptown clubs.* ❏ *...a small uptown radio station.*

up|trend /ʌptrɛnd/ N-SING An **uptrend** is a general improvement in something such as a market or the economy. ❏ *The shares have been in a strong uptrend.*

up|turn /ʌptɜrn/ (**upturns**) N-COUNT If there is an **upturn** in the economy or in a company or industry, it improves or becomes more successful. [BUSINESS] ❏ *They do not expect an upturn in the economy until the end of the year.*

up|turned /ʌptɜrnd/ **1** ADJ [usu ADJ n] Something that is **upturned** points upward. ❏ *...his eyes closed and his palms upturned.* **2** ADJ [usu ADJ n] Something that is **upturned** is upside down. ❏ *...upturned buckets.*

up|ward /ʌpwərd/

The form **upwards** is also used for the adverb.

1 ADJ [ADJ n] An **upward** movement or look is directed toward a higher place or a higher level. ❏ *She started once again on the steep upward climb.* ❏ *She gave him a quick, upward look, then lowered her eyes.* **2** ADJ [ADJ n] If you refer to an **upward** trend or an **upward** spiral, you mean that something is increasing in quantity or price. ❏ *...the Army's concern that the upward trend in the numbers avoiding military service may continue.* **3** ADV If someone moves or looks **upward**, they move or look up toward a higher place. ❏ *They climbed upward along the steep cliffs surrounding the village.* ❏ *"There," said Jack, pointing upwards.* **4** ADV [ADV after v] If an amount or rate moves **upward**, it increases. ❏ *...with prices soon heading upward in stores.* ❏ *Unemployment will continue upward for much of this year.* **5** PHRASE A quantity that is **upwards of** a particular number is more than that number. ❏ *It costs upwards of $40,000 a year to keep some prisoners in prison.*

up|ward|ly mo|bile ADJ If you describe someone as **upwardly mobile**, you mean that they are moving, have moved, or are trying to move to a higher social position. ❏ *The party has been unable to attract upwardly mobile voters.*

• N-PLURAL [the N] The **upwardly mobile** are people who are upwardly mobile. ☐ ...*the large houses of the upwardly mobile with their double garages and array of cars.*

up|wards /ʌpwərdz/ → see **upward**

up|wind /ʌpwɪnd/ ADV If something moves **upwind**, it moves in the opposite direction to the wind. If something is **upwind**, the wind is blowing away from it. ☐ ...*riding a bike upwind.* • ADJ [ADJ n] **Upwind** is also an adjective. ☐ ...*big trees at the forest's upwind edge.*

ura|nium /yʊreɪniəm/ N-UNCOUNT **Uranium** is a naturally occurring radioactive metal that is used to produce nuclear energy and weapons.

ur|ban ♦◇◇ /ɜrbən/ **1** ADJ **Urban** means belonging to, or relating to, a city or town. ☐ *For a small state it has a large urban population.* ☐ *Most urban areas are close to a park.* **2** → See feature box at **garden**

SYNONYMS

urban
ADJ
civic: ...*the businesspeople and civic leaders of Manchester.*
metropolitan: ...*the metropolitan district of Miami.*
municipal: ...*the municipal library.*

VOCABULARY IN CONTEXT

Urban issues

The 'broken windows' theory suggests that **antisocial behavior**, and even more serious crimes, may be reduced or prevented by **maintaining** and **monitoring urban** environments and dealing immediately with smaller issues, such as **graffiti**, **littering**, and **vandalism**. The name of the theory comes from the idea that a building with a few broken windows may encourage people to break more windows or even break into the building and become **squatters**. In this way a **respectable** neighborhood can gradually **degenerate** into a **slum**.

This theory led to a zero tolerance approach to **petty crimes** in New York City in the 80s and 90s, which some feel may have contributed to the general drop in the crime rate in recent years.

ur|bane /ɜrbeɪn/ ADJ Someone who is **urbane** is polite and appears comfortable in social situations. ☐ *She describes him as urbane and charming.* ☐ *In conversation, he was suave and urbane.* • **ur|ban|ity** /ɜrbænɪti/ N-UNCOUNT ☐ *Fearey had all the charm and urbanity of the trained diplomat.*

ur|bani|za|tion /ɜrbənɪzeɪʃən/
in BRIT, also use **urbanisation**
N-UNCOUNT **Urbanization** is the process of creating cities or towns in country areas.

ur|ban|ized /ɜrbənaɪzd/
in BRIT, also use **urbanised**
1 ADJ [usu ADJ n] An **urbanized** country or area has many buildings and a lot of industry and business. ☐ *Zambia is Black Africa's most urbanized country.* **2** ADJ An **urbanized** population consists of people who live and work in a city or town.

ur|ban myth (urban myths) also **urban legend** N-COUNT An **urban myth** is a strange or surprising story which many people believe, but which is not actually true. ☐ *Contrary to one of the many urban myths, he doesn't have his shoes hand-made.*

ur|chin /ɜrtʃɪn/ (urchins) **1** N-COUNT An **urchin** is a young child who is dirty and poorly dressed. [OLD-FASHIONED] ☐ *We were in the bazaar with all the little urchins watching us.* **2** → see also **sea urchin**

Urdu /ʊərdu, ɜr-/ N-UNCOUNT **Urdu** is an official language of Pakistan. Urdu is also spoken in India.

urge ♦♦◇ /ɜrdʒ/ (urges, urging, urged) **1** V-T If you **urge** someone to do something, you try hard to persuade them to do it. ☐ *They urged Congress to approve plans for their reform program.* **2** V-T If you **urge** someone somewhere, you make them go there by touching them or talking to them. ☐ *He slipped his arm around her waist and urged her away from the window.* **3** V-T If you **urge** a course of action, you strongly advise that it should be taken. ☐ *He urged restraint on the security forces.* **4** N-COUNT If you have an **urge** to do or have something, you have a strong wish to do or have it. ☐ *He had an urge to open a shop of his own.*

ur|gent ♦◇◇ /ɜrdʒənt/ **1** ADJ If something is **urgent**, it needs to be dealt with as soon as possible. ☐ *There is an urgent need for food and water.* • **ur|gen|cy** N-UNCOUNT ☐ *The urgency of finding a cure attracted some of the best minds in medical science.* • **ur|gent|ly** ADV [ADV with v] ☐ *Red Cross officials said they urgently needed bread and water.* **2** ADJ If you speak in an **urgent** way, you show that you are anxious for people to notice something or to do something. ☐ *His voice was low and urgent.* • **ur|gen|cy** N-UNCOUNT ☐ *She was surprised at the urgency in his voice.* • **ur|gent|ly** ADV [ADV with v] ☐ *They hastened to greet him and asked urgently, "Did you find it?"*

uri|nal /yʊərɪnəl/ (urinals) N-COUNT A **urinal** is a bowl fixed to the wall of a men's public toilet for men to urinate in.

uri|nary /yʊərɪneri/ ADJ [ADJ n] **Urinary** means belonging to or related to the parts of a person's body through which urine flows. [MEDICAL] ☐ ...*urinary tract infections.*

uri|nate /yʊərɪneɪt/ (urinates, urinating, urinated) V-I When someone **urinates**, they get rid of urine from their body.

urine /yʊərɪn/ N-UNCOUNT **Urine** is the liquid that you get rid of from your body when you go to the toilet. ☐ *The doctor took a urine sample and a blood sample.*

URL /yu ɑr ɛl/ (URLs) N-COUNT A **URL** is an address that shows where a particular page can be found on the World Wide Web. **URL** is an abbreviation for 'Uniform Resource Locator.' [COMPUTING] ☐ *The travel company recently changed its URL.*

urn /ɜrn/ (urns) **1** N-COUNT An **urn** is a container in which a dead person's ashes are kept. ☐ ...*a funeral urn.* **2** N-COUNT An **urn** is a metal container used for making a large quantity of tea or coffee and keeping it hot. ☐ ...*the ten gallon coffee urn.*

us ♦♦♦ /əs, STRONG ʌs/

Us is the first person plural pronoun. **Us** is used as the object of a verb or a preposition.

1 PRON-PLURAL [V PRON, prep PRON] A speaker or writer uses **us** to refer both to himself or herself and to one or more other people. You can use **us** before a noun to make it clear which group of people you are referring to. ☐ *Neither of us forgot about it.* ☐ *Heather went to the kitchen to get drinks for us.* ☐ *They don't like us much.* **2** PRON-PLURAL [V PRON, prep PRON] **Us** is sometimes used to refer to people in general. ☐ *All of us will struggle fairly hard to survive if we are in danger.* **3** PRON-PLURAL [V PRON, prep PRON] A speaker or writer may use **us** instead of 'me' in order to include the audience or reader in what they are saying. [mainly FORMAL] ☐ *This brings us to the second question I asked.*

USAGE

us
In standard English, don't use 'us' as the object of a sentence when **we** is the subject. Don't say, for example, 'We bought us some drinks.' You say 'We bought **ourselves** some drinks.' *After the meeting, we introduced ourselves.*

U.S. ◆◆◆ /yu ɛs/ also **US** N-PROPER [the N, N n] The **U.S.** is an abbreviation for the **United States**. ❑ *The first time I saw TV was when I arrived in the U.S. in 1956.* ❑ *He inherited 10,000 U.S. dollars.*

U.S.A. ◆◇◇ /yu ɛs eɪ/ also **USA** N-PROPER [the N] The **U.S.A.** is an abbreviation for the **United States of America**.

us|able /yuzəbəl/ ADJ If something is **usable**, it is in a good enough state or condition to be used. ❑ *It's been reported that no usable fingerprints were found at the scene.*

USAF /yu ɛs eɪ ɛf/ also **U.S.A.F.** N-PROPER [usu the N] **USAF** is an abbreviation for 'United States Air Force.'

us|age /yusɪdʒ/ (**usages**) **1** N-UNCOUNT **Usage** is the way in which words are actually used in particular contexts, especially with regard to their meanings. ❑ *He was a stickler for the correct usage of English.* **2** N-COUNT A **usage** is a meaning that a word has or a way in which it can be used. ❑ *It's very definitely a usage which has come over to Britain from America.* **3** N-UNCOUNT **Usage** is the degree to which something is used or the way in which it is used. ❑ *Parts of the motor were out because of constant usage.*

USB /yu ɛs bi/ (**USBs**) **1** N-COUNT A **USB** or **USB port** on a computer is a place where you can attach another piece of equipment, for example a printer. **USB** is an abbreviation for 'Universal Serial Bus.' [COMPUTING] ❑ *The device plugs into one of the laptop's USB ports.* **2** → See feature box at **computer**

USB stick (**USB sticks**) **1** N-COUNT A **USB stick** is a small object for storing digital information that you can connect to the USB part of a computer or other device. [COMPUTING] ❑ *My history lectures are saved as PowerPoint files on a USB stick.* **2** → See also color supplement

---
USE
① VERB USES
② NOUN USES
---

① **use** ◆◆◆ /yuz/ (**uses, using, used**) **1** V-T If you **use** something, you do something with it in order to do a job or to achieve a particular result or effect. ❑ *Trim off the excess pastry using a sharp knife.* ❑ *The U.S. has used ships to bring most of its heavy material, like tanks, to the region.* **2** V-T If you **use** a supply of something, you finish it so that none of it is left. ❑ *You used all the ice cubes and didn't put the ice trays back.* • PHRASAL VERB **Use up** means the same as **use**. ❑ *It isn't animals who use up the world's resources.* **3** V-T If someone **uses** drugs, they take drugs regularly, especially illegal ones. ❑ *He denied he had used drugs.* **4** V-T You can say that someone **uses** the toilet or bathroom as a polite way of saying that they go to the toilet. [POLITENESS] ❑ *Wash your hands after using the bathroom.* **5** V-T If you **use** a particular word or expression, you say or write it, because it has the meaning that you want to express. ❑ *The judge liked using the word "wicked" of people he had sent to jail.* **6** V-T If you **use** a particular name, you call yourself by that name, especially when it is not the name that you usually call yourself. ❑ *Now I use a false name if I'm meeting people for the first time.* **7** V-T If you say that someone **uses** people, you disapprove of them because they make others do things for them in order to benefit or gain some advantage from it, and not because they care about the other people. [DISAPPROVAL] ❑ *Why do I have the feeling I'm being used again?* **8** • see also **used** ①

② **use** ◆◆◇ /yus/ (**uses**) **1** N-UNCOUNT [also a N, usu N of n] Your **use** of something is the action or fact of your using it. ❑ *The treatment does not involve the use of any artificial drugs.* ❑ *...research into gene therapy and its use in treating certain conditions.* **2** N-SING If you have **a use for** something, you need it or can find something to do with it. ❑ *You will no longer have a use for the magazines.* **3** N-VAR If something has a particular **use**, it is intended for a particular purpose. ❑ *Infrared detectors have many uses.* ❑ *It's an interesting scientific phenomenon, but of no practical use whatever.* ❑ *The report outlined possible uses for the new weapon.* **4** N-UNCOUNT [also the N, usu N of n] If you have the **use of** something, you have the permission or ability to use it. ❑ *She will have the use of the car one night a week.* ❑ *...young people who at some point in the past have lost the use of their limbs.* **5** N-COUNT A **use** of a word is a particular meaning that it has or a particular way in which it can be used. ❑ *There are new uses of words coming in and old uses dying out.* **6** N-UNCOUNT Your **use** of a particular name is the fact of your calling yourself by it. ❑ *Police have been hampered by Mr. Urquhart's use of bogus names.* **7** PHRASE If something is **for the use of** a particular person or group of people, it is for that person or group to use. ❑ *The facilities are there for the use of guests.* **8** PHRASE If you say that being something or knowing someone **has its uses**, you mean that it makes it possible for you to do what you otherwise would not be able to do. [INFORMAL] ❑ *It wasn't a life she particularly enjoyed, but it had its uses.* **9** PHRASE If something such as a technique, building, or machine is **in use**, it is used regularly by people. If it has gone **out of use**, it is no longer used regularly by people. ❑ *...the methods of making champagne which are still in use today.* **10** PHRASE If you **make use of** something, you do something with it in order to do a job or achieve a particular result or effect. [WRITTEN] ❑ *Few found jobs in which they could make use of their new skills.* **11** PHRASE If you say **it's no use**, you mean that you have failed to do something and realize that it is useless to continue trying because it is impossible. ❑ *It's no use. Let's hang up and try for a better line.* **12** PHRASE If something or someone is **of use**, they are useful. If they are **no use**, they are not at all useful. ❑ *The contents of this booklet should be of use to all students.*

USED
① MODAL USES AND PHRASES
② ADJECTIVE USES
---

① **used** ◆◆◇ /yust/ **1** PHRASE If something **used to** be done or **used to** be the case, it was done regularly in the past or was the case in the past. ❑ *People used to come and visit him every day.* ❑ *He used to be one of my professors.* **2** PHRASE If something **did not use to** be done, **used to not be done** or **used not to** be done, it was not done in the past. ❑ *Borrowing used to not be recommended.* ❑ *At some point kids start doing things they didn't use to do. They get more independent.* **3** PHRASE If you **are used to** something, you are familiar with it because you have done it or experienced it many times before. ❑ *I'm used to having my sleep interrupted.* **4** PHRASE If you **get used to** something or someone, you become familiar with it or get to know them, so that you no longer feel that the thing or person is unusual or surprising. ❑ *This is how we do things here. You'll soon get used to it.* ❑ *You quickly get used to using the brakes.*

② **used** /yuzd/ **1** ADJ A **used** object is dirty or spoiled because it has been used, and usually needs to be thrown away or washed. ❑ *...a used cotton ball stained with makeup.* **2** ADJ A **used** car has already had one or more owners. ❑ *Would you buy a used car from this man?*

use|ful ◆◆◇ /yusfəl/ **1** ADJ If something is **useful**, you can use it to do something or to help you in some way. ❑ *The pressure cooker is very useful for people who go out all day.* ❑ *Hypnotherapy can be useful in helping you give up smoking.* • **use|ful|ly** ADV [ADV with v] ❑ *...the problems to which computers could be usefully applied.* • **use|ful|ness** N-UNCOUNT ❑ *His interest lay in the usefulness of his work, rather than in any personal credit.* **2** PHRASE If an object or skill **comes in useful**, it can help you achieve something in a particular situation. ❑ *Extra blank paper will probably come in useful.*

SYNONYMS

useful
ADJ **1**
helpful: *The following information may be helpful to readers.*
effective: *Simple antibiotics are effective against this organism.*
valuable: *The experience was very valuable.*
beneficial: *...vitamins which are beneficial to our health.*
worthwhile: *The President's trip to Washington this week seems to have been worthwhile.*
---

use|less /yuslɪs/ **1** ADJ If something is **useless**, you cannot use it. ❑ *He realized that their money was useless in this country.* **2** ADJ If something is **useless**, it does not achieve anything helpful or good. ❑ *She knew it was useless to protest.* **3** ADJ If you say that someone or something is **useless**, you mean that they are no good at all. ❑ *Their education system is useless.* **4** ADJ If someone feels **useless**, they feel bad because they are unable to help someone or achieve anything. ❑ *She sits at home all day, watching TV and feeling useless.*

Use|net /yuznɛt/ N-UNCOUNT **Usenet** is a computer network that links newsgroups on the internet. [COMPUTING]

user ♦♦◊ /yuzər/ (**users**) N-COUNT A **user** is a person or thing that uses something such as a place, facility, product, or machine. ◻ *Beach users have complained that the bikes are noisy.* ◻ *...a regular user of the subway.*

user-friendly ADJ If you describe something such as a machine or system as **user-friendly**, you mean that it is well designed and easy to use. ◻ *This is an entirely computer-operated system which is very user-friendly.*

user group (**user groups**) N-COUNT A **user group** is a group of people with the same interests, who use a particular product or service. ◻ *...the Stanford-Palo Alto Area PC User Group.*

user|name /yuzərneɪm/ (**usernames**) N-COUNT Your **username** is the name that you use when accessing a particular computer, program, website, or service. ◻ *I typed in my username and password, and the screen was just blank.*

ush|er /ʌʃər/ (**ushers, ushering, ushered**) ◼ V-T If you **usher** someone somewhere, you show them where they should go by going with them. [FORMAL] ◻ *I ushered him into the office.* ◼ N-COUNT An **usher** is a person who shows people where to sit, for example at a wedding or at a concert. ◻ *He did part-time work as an usher in a theater.*

USMC /yu ɛs ɛm si/ also **U.S.M.C.** N-PROPER [usu the N] **USMC** is an abbreviation for 'United States Marine Corps.'

USN /yu ɛs ɛn/ also **U.S.N.** N-PROPER [usu the N] **USN** is an abbreviation for 'United States Navy.'

USP /yu ɛs pi/ (**USPs**) N-COUNT The **USP** of a product or service is a particular feature of it which can be used in advertising to show how it is different from, and better than, other similar products or services. **USP** is an abbreviation for 'Unique Selling Point.' [BUSINESS] ◻ *With Volvo, safety was always the USP.*

usu. **usu.** is a written abbreviation for **usually**.

usu|al ♦♦◊ /yuʒuəl/ ◼ ADJ **Usual** is used to describe what happens or what is done most often in a particular situation. ◻ *It is a neighborhood beset by all the usual inner-city problems.* ◻ *After lunch there was a little more clearing up to do than usual.* • N-SING **Usual** is also a noun. ◻ *The stout barman in a bow tie presented himself to take their order. "Good morning, sir. The usual?"* ◼ PHRASE You use **as usual** to indicate that you are describing something that normally happens or that is normally the case. ◻ *As usual there will be the local and regional elections on June the twelfth.* ◼ PHRASE If something happens **as usual**, it happens in the way that it normally does, especially when other things have changed. ◻ *Surgery was scheduled, but life went on as usual.* ◼ **business as usual** → see **business**

usu|al|ly ♦♦◊ /yuʒuəli/ ◼ ADV If something usually happens, it is the thing that most often happens in a particular situation. ◻ *The best information about hotels usually comes from friends and acquaintances who have been there.* ◻ *Usually, the work is boring.* ◼ PHRASE You use **more than usually** to show that something shows even more of a particular quality than it normally does. ◻ *She felt more than usually hungry after her excursion.*

SYNONYMS

usually
ADV ◼
normally: *Social progress is normally a matter of struggles and conflicts.*
generally: *I generally say and feel too much about these issues.*
commonly: *Parsley is probably the most commonly used of all herbs.*

---

usurp /yusɜrp, -zɜrp/ (**usurps, usurping, usurped**) V-T If you say that someone **usurps** a job, role, title, or position, they take it from someone when they have no right to do this. [FORMAL] ◻ *Did she usurp his place in his mother's heart?*

usurp|er /yusɜrpər, -zɜrp-/ (**usurpers**) N-COUNT A **usurper** is someone who takes another person's title or position when they have no right to. [FORMAL]

usu|ry /yuʒəri/ N-UNCOUNT **Usury** is the practice of lending money at a high rate of interest. [DISAPPROVAL]

ute /yut/ (**utes**) N-COUNT A **ute** is a vehicle that is designed to travel over rough ground. **Ute** is an abbreviation for **utility vehicle**. [AUSTRALIAN, INFORMAL]

uten|sil /yutɛnsəl/ (**utensils**) ◼ N-COUNT **Utensils** are tools or objects that you use in order to help you to cook, serve food, or eat. ◻ *...utensils such as bowls, steamers and frying pans.* ◼ → See also color supplement

u|ter|ine /yutərɪn/ ADJ **Uterine** means relating to the uterus of a woman or a female mammal. [MEDICAL]

uter|us /yutərəs/ (**uteruses**) N-COUNT The **uterus** of a woman or a female mammal is the part of her body where babies develop. [MEDICAL] ◻ *...an ultrasound scan of the uterus.*

utili|tar|ian /yutɪlɪtɛəriən/ (**utilitarians**) ◼ ADJ **Utilitarian** objects and buildings are designed to be useful rather than attractive. ◻ *Bruce's office is utilitarian and unglamorous.* ◼ ADJ **Utilitarian** means based on the idea that the morally correct course of action is the one that produces benefit for the greatest number of people. [TECHNICAL] ◻ *It was James Mill who was the best publicist for utilitarian ideas on government.* • N-COUNT A **utilitarian** is someone with utilitarian views. ◻ *One of the greatest utilitarians was Claude Helvetius.*

utili|tari|an|ism /yutɪlɪtɛəriənɪzəm/ N-UNCOUNT **Utilitarianism** is the idea that the morally correct course of action is the one that produces benefit for the greatest number of people. [TECHNICAL]

util|ity /yutɪlɪti/ (**utilities**) N-COUNT A **utility** is an important service such as water, electricity, or gas that is provided for everyone, and that everyone pays for. ◻ *...public utilities such as gas, electricity and phones.*

util|ity pole (**utility poles**) ◼ N-COUNT A **utility pole** is a tall pole with telephone or electrical wires attached to it. [AM] ◻ *During some lightning storms, a bolt can send a 500-volt spike through the nearest utility pole.* ◼ → see also **telephone pole**

util|ity room (**utility rooms**) N-COUNT A **utility room** is a room in a house which is usually connected to the kitchen and which contains things such as a washing machine, sink, and cleaning equipment.

util|ity ve|hi|cle (**utility vehicles**) N-COUNT A **utility vehicle** is a vehicle that is designed to travel over rough ground. [AUSTRALIAN]

uti|lize /yutɪlaɪz/ (**utilizes, utilizing, utilized**)

in BRIT, also use **utilise**

V-T If you **utilize** something, you use it. [FORMAL] ◻ *Sound engineers utilize a range of techniques to enhance the quality of the recordings.* • **uti|li|za|tion** /yutɪlɪzeɪʃən/ N-UNCOUNT ◻ *...the utilization of human resources.*

ut|most /ʌtmoʊst/ ◼ ADJ [ADJ n] You can use **utmost** to emphasize the importance or seriousness of something or to emphasize the way that it is done. [EMPHASIS] ◻ *It is a matter of the utmost urgency to find out what has happened to these people.* ◻ *Security matters are treated with the utmost seriousness.* ◼ N-SING If you say that you are doing your **utmost** to do something, you are emphasizing that you are trying as hard as you can to do it. [EMPHASIS] ◻ *He would have done his utmost to help her.*

uto|pia /yutoʊpiə/ (**utopias**) N-VAR If you refer to an imaginary situation as a **utopia**, you mean that it is one in which society is perfect and everyone is happy. ◻ *We weren't out to design a contemporary utopia.*

uto|pian /yutoʊpiən/ ◼ ADJ If you describe a plan or idea as **utopian**, you are criticizing it because it is unrealistic and shows a belief that things can be improved much more than is possible. [DISAPPROVAL] ◻ *He was pursuing a utopian dream of world prosperity.* ◼ ADJ **Utopian** is used to describe political or religious philosophies which claim that it is possible to build a new and perfect society in which everyone is happy. [FORMAL] ◻ *His was a utopian vision of nature in its purest form.*

ut|ter /ʌtər/ (**utters, uttering, uttered**) ◼ V-T If someone **utters** sounds or words, they say them. [LITERARY] ◻ *He uttered a snorting laugh.* ◼ ADJ [ADJ n] You use **utter** to emphasize that something is great in extent, degree, or amount. [EMPHASIS] ◻ *This, of course, is utter nonsense.* ◻ *...this utter lack of responsibility.*

ut|ter|ance /ʌtərəns/ (utterances) N-COUNT Someone's **utterances** are the things that they say. [FORMAL] ❑ *These two utterances communicate the same message.*

ut|ter|ly /ʌtərli/ ADV You use **utterly** to emphasize that something is very great in extent, degree, or amount. [EMPHASIS] ❑ *China is utterly different.* ❑ *The new laws coming in are utterly ridiculous.*

U-turn (U-turns) **1** N-COUNT If you make a **U-turn** when you are driving or riding a bicycle, you turn in a half circle in one movement, so that you are then going in the opposite direction. ❑ *Dave made a U-turn on North Main and drove back to Depot Street.* **2** N-COUNT If you describe a change in someone's policy, plans, or actions as a **U-turn**, you mean that it is a complete change. [DISAPPROVAL] ❑ *He's doing a U-turn and forecasting 1% growth this year after earlier predicting a 2% drop.*

Vv

V also **v** /viː/ (**V's**, **v's**) N-VAR **V** is the twenty-second letter of the English alphabet.

v. v. is a written abbreviation for **versus**.

VA /viː eɪ/ N-PROPER [the N] In the United States, the **VA** is a government organization that provides assistance to people who have served in the armed forces. **VA** is an abbreviation for 'Veterans Administration.' ❑ *The VA hospital needs renovation.*

va|can|cy /veɪkənsi/ (**vacancies**) **1** N-COUNT A **vacancy** is a job or position that has not been filled. ❑ *Most vacancies are at the senior level, requiring appropriate qualifications.* **2** N-COUNT If there are **vacancies** at a building such as a hotel, some of the rooms are available to rent. ❑ *This year hotels that usually are jammed had vacancies all summer.*

va|cant /veɪkənt/ **1** ADJ If something is **vacant**, it is not being used by anyone. ❑ *Halfway down the bus was a vacant seat.* **2** ADJ If a job or position is **vacant**, no one is doing it or in it at present, and people can apply for it. ❑ *The position of chairperson has been vacant for some time.* **3** ADJ A **vacant** look or expression is one that suggests that someone does not understand something or that they are not thinking about anything in particular. ❑ *She had a kind of vacant look on her face.* ● **va|cant|ly** ADV [ADV after v] ❑ *He looked vacantly out of the window.*

va|cant lot (**vacant lots**) N-COUNT A **vacant lot** is a small area of land in a city or town that is not occupied or not being used. [AM] ❑ *...the vacant lot at the corner of 31st and Thompson Streets.*

va|cate /veɪkeɪt/ (**vacates**, **vacating**, **vacated**) V-T If you **vacate** a place or a job, you leave it or give it up, making it available for other people. [FORMAL] ❑ *He quickly vacated the gym after the workout.*

va|ca|tion /veɪkeɪʃən/ (**vacations**, **vacationing**, **vacationed**) **1** N-COUNT [also on/from N] A **vacation** is a period of time during which you relax and enjoy yourself away from home. [AM] ❑ *They planned a late summer vacation in Europe.*

> in BRIT, use **holiday**

2 N-COUNT A **vacation** is a period of the year when schools, universities, and colleges are officially closed. ❑ *During his summer vacation he visited Russia.* **3** N-UNCOUNT If you have a particular number of days' or weeks' **vacation**, you do not have to go to work for that number of days or weeks. [AM] ❑ *The French get five to six weeks' vacation a year.*

> in BRIT, use **holiday**

4 V-I If you **are vacationing** in a place away from home, you are on vacation there. [AM] ❑ *Myles vacationed in Jamaica.*

> in BRIT, use **holiday**

COLLOCATIONS

vacation
NOUN **1**
noun + **vacation**: family, school, summer; beach, ski
adjective + **vacation**: all-inclusive, luxury
verb + **vacation**: go on, take; spend

va|ca|tion|er /veɪkeɪʃənər/ (**vacationers**) N-COUNT [usu pl] **Vacationers** are people who are on vacation in a particular place. [mainly AM] ❑ *Camping, biking, hiking and swimming are all available for the vacationer.*

> in BRIT, usually use **holidaymaker**

vac|ci|nate /væksɪneɪt/ (**vaccinates**, **vaccinating**, **vaccinated**) V-T [usu passive] If a person or animal **is vaccinated**, they are given a vaccine, usually by injection, to prevent them from getting a disease. ❑ *Dogs must be vaccinated against distemper.* ❑ *Have you had your child vaccinated against whooping cough?* ● **vac|ci|na|tion** /væksɪneɪʃən/ (**vaccinations**) N-VAR ❑ *Anyone who wants to avoid the flu should consider getting a vaccination.*

vac|cine /væksiːn/ (**vaccines**) N-MASS A **vaccine** is a substance containing a harmless form of the germs that cause a particular disease. It is given to people, usually by injection, to prevent them from getting that disease. ❑ *Anti-malarial vaccines are now undergoing trials.*

vac|il|late /væsɪleɪt/ (**vacillates**, **vacillating**, **vacillated**) V-I If you **vacillate** between two alternatives or choices, you keep changing your mind. [FORMAL] ❑ *She vacillates between studying economics and languages.* ❑ *We cannot vacillate on the question of the party's leadership.*

va|cu|ity /vækyuːɪti, və-/ N-UNCOUNT [usu with poss] If you refer to the **vacuity** of something or someone, you are critical of them because they lack intelligent thought or ideas. [FORMAL, DISAPPROVAL] ❑ *His vacuity was a handicap in these debates.* ❑ *...a campaign notable for its intellectual vacuity and personal nastiness.*

vacu|ous /vækyuəs/ ADJ If you describe a person or their comments as **vacuous**, you are critical of them because they lack intelligent thought or ideas. [DISAPPROVAL] ❑ *Models are not always as vacuous as they are made out to be.*

vacuum /vækyum, -yuəm/ (**vacuums**, **vacuuming**, **vacuumed**) **1** N-COUNT If someone or something creates a **vacuum**, they leave a place or position that then needs to be filled by another person or thing. ❑ *His presence should fill the power vacuum that has been developing over the past few days.* **2** PHRASE If something is done **in a vacuum**, it is not affected by any outside influences or information. ❑ *Moral values cannot be taught in a vacuum.* **3** N-COUNT A **vacuum** is a space that contains no air or other gas. ❑ *Wind is a current of air caused by a vacuum caused by hot air rising.* **4** N-COUNT A **vacuum** is the same as a **vacuum cleaner**. **5** V-T/V-I If you **vacuum** something, you clean it using a vacuum cleaner. ❑ *I vacuumed the carpets today.* ❑ *It's important to vacuum regularly.* **6** → See feature box at **housework**

vacuum bot|tle (**vacuum bottles**) N-COUNT A **vacuum bottle** is a container that is used to keep hot drinks hot or cold drinks cold. It has two silvery glass walls with a vacuum between them. [AM]

> in BRIT, use **vacuum flask**

vacuum clean|er (**vacuum cleaners**) N-COUNT A **vacuum cleaner** or a **vacuum** is an electric machine that sucks up dust and dirt from carpets.

vacuum flask (**vacuum flasks**) N-COUNT A **vacuum flask** is the same as a **vacuum bottle**.

vacuum-packed ADJ Food that is **vacuum-packed** is packed in a bag from which most of the air has been removed, in order to keep the food fresh.

vaga|bond /vægəbɒnd/ (**vagabonds**) N-COUNT A **vagabond** is someone who wanders from place to place and has no home or job. [OLD-FASHIONED]

va|gary /veɪgəri/ (**vagaries**) N-COUNT [usu pl, usu N of n] **Vagaries** are unexpected and unpredictable changes in a situation or in someone's behavior that you have no control over. [FORMAL] ❑ *...the perplexing vagaries of politics.*

va|gi|na /vədʒaɪnə/ (vaginas) N-COUNT A woman's **vagina** is the passage connecting her outer sex organs to her uterus.

vagi|nal /vædʒɪnəl/ ADJ [ADJ n] **Vaginal** means relating to or involving the vagina. ☐ *The creams have been used to reduce vaginal infections.*

va|gran|cy /veɪɡrənsi/ N-UNCOUNT **Vagrancy** is a way of life in which someone moves a lot from place to place because they have no permanent home or job, and have to ask for or steal things in order to live. ☐ *Vagrancy and begging have become commonplace in the city.*

va|grant /veɪɡrənt/ (vagrants) N-COUNT A **vagrant** is someone who moves a lot from place to place because they have no permanent home or job, and have to ask for or steal things in order to live. ☐ *He lived on the street as a vagrant.*

vague /veɪɡ/ (vaguer, vaguest) **1** ADJ If something written or spoken is **vague**, it does not explain or express things clearly. ☐ *A lot of the talk was apparently vague and general.* ☐ *The description was pretty vague.* • **vague|ly** ADV ☐ *"I'm not sure," Liz said vaguely.* **2** ADJ If you have a **vague** memory or idea of something, the memory or idea is not clear. ☐ *They have only a vague idea of the amount of water available.* • **vague|ly** ADV [ADV with v] ☐ *Judith could vaguely remember her mother lying on the sofa.* **3** ADJ If you are **vague** about something, you deliberately do not tell people much about it. ☐ *He was vague, however, about just what U.S. forces might actually do.* **4** ADJ If something such as a feeling is **vague**, you experience it only slightly. ☐ *He was conscious of that vague feeling of irritation again.* **5** ADJ A **vague** shape or outline is not clear and is therefore not easy to see. ☐ *The bus was a vague shape in the distance.*

vague|ly /veɪɡli/ **1** ADV [ADV adj] **Vaguely** means to some degree but not to a very large degree. ☐ *The voice on the line was vaguely familiar, but Crook couldn't place it at first.* **2** → see also **vague**

vain /veɪn/ (vainer, vainest) **1** ADJ [ADJ n] A **vain** attempt or action is one that fails to achieve what was intended. ☐ *The drafting committee worked through the night in a vain attempt to finish on schedule.* • **vain|ly** ADV [ADV with v] ☐ *He hunted vainly through his pockets for a piece of paper.* **2** ADJ If you describe a hope that something will happen as a **vain** hope, you mean that there is no chance of it happening. ☐ *He married his fourth wife, Susan, in the vain hope that she would improve his health.* • **vain|ly** ADV [ADV with v] ☐ *He then set out for Virginia for what he vainly hoped would be a peaceful retirement.* **3** ADJ If you describe someone as **vain**, you are critical of their extreme pride in their own beauty, intelligence, or other good qualities. [DISAPPROVAL] ☐ *He wasn't so vain as to think he was smarter than his boss.* **4** PHRASE If you do something **in vain**, you do not succeed in achieving what you intend. ☐ *He stopped at the door, waiting in vain for her to acknowledge his presence.* **5** PHRASE If you say that something such as someone's death, suffering, or effort was **in vain**, you mean that it was useless because it did not achieve anything. ☐ *He wants the world to know his son did not die in vain.*

vain|glo|ri|ous /veɪnɡlɔːriəs/ ADJ [ADJ n] If you describe someone as **vainglorious**, you are critical of them because they are very proud of what they have done and boast a lot about it. [LITERARY, DISAPPROVAL]

val|ance /væləns/ (valances) **1** N-COUNT A **valance** is a long narrow piece of wood or fabric attached to the top of a window for decoration and to hide the curtain rail. [AM]

in BRIT, use **pelmet**

2 N-COUNT A **valance** is a piece of cloth that hangs down over the sides of a bed in order to make it look nice.

vale /veɪl/ (vales) N-COUNT [oft in names] A **vale** is a valley. [LITERARY] ☐ *...a small vale, sheltering under mist-shrouded hills.*

vale|dic|to|ri|an /vælədɪktɔːriən/ (valedictorians) N-COUNT A **valedictorian** is the student who has the highest grade point average in their class when they graduate from high school or college, and who gives a speech at their graduation ceremony. [AM]

vale|dic|tory /vælədɪktəri/ (valedictories) **1** ADJ [usu ADJ n] A **valedictory** speech, letter, or performance is one that is intended as a way of saying goodbye when someone leaves another person, a place, or a job. [FORMAL] ☐ *...Ms Walker, making her valedictory address after two years as chairwoman.* **2** N-COUNT [oft N n] A **valedictory** is a speech that is given by the student with the highest marks in their class at their graduation ceremony. [AM]

val|en|tine /væləntaɪn/ (valentines) N-COUNT A **valentine** or a **valentine card** is a greeting card that you send to someone who you are in love with or are attracted to on Valentine's Day, the 14th of February.

val|et /væleɪ, vælei, -lɪt/ (valets, valeting, valeted) **1** N-COUNT A **valet** is a male servant who looks after his employer by doing things such as caring for his clothes and cooking for him. **2** V-T If someone **valets** a vehicle, they are paid to clean it thoroughly inside and out. [BRIT]

in AM, use **detail**

val|et park|ing N-UNCOUNT **Valet parking** is a service that operates at places such as hotels and restaurants, in which customers' cars are parked by an attendant. ☐ *Admission is $30. Valet parking will be available.*

val|iant /vælyənt/ ADJ A **valiant** action is very brave and determined, though it may lead to failure or defeat. ☐ *Despite valiant efforts by the finance minister, inflation rose to 36%.* • **val|iant|ly** ADV [ADV with v] ☐ *He suffered further heart attacks and strokes, all of which he fought valiantly.*

val|id /vælɪd/ **1** ADJ A **valid** argument, comment, or idea is based on sensible reasoning. ☐ *They put forward many valid reasons for not exporting.* • **va|lid|ity** /vəlɪdɪti/ N-UNCOUNT ☐ *The editorial says this argument has lost much of its validity.* **2** ADJ Something that is **valid** is important or serious enough to make it worth saying or doing. ☐ *Most designers share the unspoken belief that fashion is a valid form of visual art.* • **va|lid|ity** N-UNCOUNT ☐ *...the validity of making children wear bicycle helmets.* **3** ADJ If a ticket or other document is **valid**, it can be used and will be accepted by people in authority. ☐ *All tickets are valid for two months.* **4** → see also **validity** **5** → See feature box at **research**

vali|date /vælɪdeɪt/ (validates, validating, validated) **1** V-T To **validate** something such as a claim or statement means to prove or confirm that it is true or correct. [FORMAL] ☐ *This discovery seems to validate the claims of popular astrology.* • **vali|da|tion** /vælɪdeɪʃən/ (validations) N-VAR ☐ *When we want validation for our decisions we often turn to friends for advice and approval.* **2** V-T To **validate** a person, state, or system means to prove or confirm that they are valuable or worthwhile. ☐ *The Academy Awards appear to validate his career.* • **vali|da|tion** N-VAR ☐ *I think the film is a validation of our lifestyle.*

va|lid|ity /vəlɪdɪti/ **1** N-UNCOUNT The **validity** of something such as a result or a piece of information is whether it can be trusted or believed. ☐ *Shocked by the results of the elections, they now want to challenge the validity of the vote.* ☐ *Some people, of course, denied the validity of any such claim.* **2** → see also **valid**

Va|lium /væliəm/ (Valium)

Valium is both the singular and the plural form.

N-VAR **Valium** is a drug given to people to calm their nerves when they are very depressed or upset. [TRADEMARK] ☐ *Do you have any Valium?*

val|ley ♦◇◇ /væli/ (valleys) N-COUNT; N-IN-NAMES A **valley** is a low stretch of land between hills, especially one that has a river flowing through it. ☐ *...a wooded valley set against the backdrop of Monte Rosa.*

val|or /vælər/

in BRIT, use **valour**

N-UNCOUNT **Valor** is great bravery, especially in battle. [LITERARY]

valu|able ♦◇◇ /vælyuəbəl/ **1** ADJ If you describe something or someone as **valuable**, you mean that they are very useful and helpful. ☐ *Many of our teachers also have valuable academic links with Heidelberg University.* **2** ADJ **Valuable** objects are objects that are worth a lot of money. ☐ *Just because a camera is old does not mean it is valuable.*

valu|ables /vælyuəbəlz/ N-PLURAL **Valuables** are things that you own that are worth a lot of money, especially small objects such as jewelry. ☐ *Leave your valuables in the hotel safe behind the reception desk.*

valua|tion /vælyueɪʃᵊn/ (valuations) N-VAR A **valuation** is a judgment that someone makes about how much money something is worth. ◻ *Valuation lies at the heart of all takeovers.*

value ✦✦✦ /vælyu/ (values, valuing, valued) **1** N-UNCOUNT [also a N] The **value** of something such as a quality, attitude, or method is its importance or usefulness. If you place a particular **value** on something, that is the importance or usefulness you think it has. ◻ *The value of this work experience should not be underestimated.* • PHRASE If something is **of value**, it is useful or important. If it is **of no value**, it has no usefulness or importance. ◻ *This weekend course will be of value to everyone interested in the Pilgrim Route.* **2** V-T If you **value** something or someone, you think that they are important and you appreciate them. ◻ *I value the opinion of my husband and we agree on most things.* **3** N-VAR The **value** of something is how much money it is worth. ◻ *The value of his investment has risen by more than $50,000.* • PHRASE If something is **of value**, it is worth a lot of money. If it is **of no value**, it is worth very little money. ◻ *...a brooch that is really of no value.* **4** V-T When experts **value** something, they decide how much money it is worth. ◻ *The school board valued the property at $130,000.* ◻ *I asked him to have my jewelry valued.* **5** N-UNCOUNT You use **value** in certain expressions to say whether something is worth the money that it costs. For example, if something is **good value**, or if you get **good value** for your money when you buy something, then it is worth the money that it costs. ◻ *We believe that is good value for money for our customers.* **6** N-PLURAL The **values** of a person or group are the moral principles and beliefs that they think are important. ◻ *The countries of South Asia also share many common values.* **7** N-UNCOUNT **Value** is used after another noun when mentioning an important or noticeable feature about something. ◻ *The script has lost all of its shock value over the intervening 24 years.*

> **SYNONYMS**
> **value**
> NOUN **1**
> **importance:** *We have always stressed the importance of economic reform.*
> **usefulness:** *His interest lay in the usefulness of his work, rather than in any personal credit.*
> **benefit:** *For maximum benefit, use your treatment every day.*
> **merit:** *The argument seemed to have considerable merit.*
> **advantage:** *A good crowd will be a definite advantage to me and the rest of the team.*

value judg|ment (value judgments) N-COUNT If you make a **value judgment** about something, you form an opinion about it based on your principles and beliefs and not on facts that can be checked or proved. ◻ *Social scientists have grown extremely unwilling to make value judgments about cultures.*

value|less /vælyulɪs/ ADJ If you describe something as **valueless**, you mean that it is not at all useful. ◻ *Such attitudes are valueless unless they reflect inner cognition and certainty.* ◻ *...commercially valueless trees.*

valu|er /vælyuər/ (valuers) N-COUNT A **valuer** is the same as an **appraiser**. [BRIT]

value sys|tem (value systems) N-COUNT The **value system** of a group of people is the set of beliefs and attitudes that they all share.

valve /vælv/ (valves) N-COUNT A **valve** is a device attached to a pipe or a tube that controls the flow of air or liquid through the pipe or tube.

vamp /væmp/ (vamps) N-COUNT If you describe a woman as a **vamp**, you mean that she uses her sexual attractiveness to get what she wants. [OLD-FASHIONED, DISAPPROVAL]

vam|pire /væmpaɪər/ (vampires) N-COUNT A **vampire** is a creature in legends and horror stories. Vampires are said to come out of graves at night and suck the blood of living people.

vam|pire bat (vampire bats) N-COUNT A **vampire bat** is a bat from South America that feeds by sucking the blood of other animals.

van ✦◇◇ /væn/ (vans) N-COUNT A **van** is a small or medium-sized road vehicle with one row of seats at the front and a space for carrying goods behind.

van|dal /vændᵊl/ (vandals) N-COUNT A **vandal** is someone who deliberately damages things, especially public property. ◻ *The street lights were out, smashed by vandals.*

van|dal|ism /vændᵊlɪzəm/ N-UNCOUNT **Vandalism** is the deliberate damaging of things, especially public property. ◻ *...a 13-year-old boy whose crime file includes violence, theft, vandalism and bullying.* **2** → See feature box at **urban**

van|dal|ize /vændᵊlaɪz/ (vandalizes, vandalizing, vandalized)

> in BRIT, also use **vandalise**

V-T If something such as a building or part of a building **is vandalized** by someone, it is damaged on purpose. ◻ *The walls had been horribly vandalized with spray paint.*

vane /veɪn/ (vanes) **1** N-COUNT A **vane** is a flat blade that pushes or is pushed by wind or water, and forms part of a machine such as a fan, a windmill, or a ship's propeller. **2** → see also **weather vane**

van|guard /vænɡɑrd/ N-SING If someone is **in the vanguard** of something such as a revolution or an area of research, they are involved in the most advanced part of it. You can also refer to the people themselves as **the vanguard**. ◻ *Students and intellectuals have been in the vanguard of revolutionary change in China.*

va|nil|la /vənɪlə/ N-UNCOUNT **Vanilla** is a flavoring used in ice cream and other sweet food. ◻ *I added a dollop of vanilla ice cream to the pie.*

van|ish /vænɪʃ/ (vanishes, vanishing, vanished) **1** V-I If someone or something **vanishes**, they disappear suddenly or in a way that cannot be explained. ◻ *He just vanished and was never seen again.* ◻ *Anne vanished from outside her home last Wednesday.* **2** V-I If something such as a species of animal or a tradition **vanishes**, it stops existing. ◻ *Many of these species have vanished or are facing extinction.*

van|ish|ing point (vanishing points) **1** N-COUNT [usu sing] The **vanishing point** is the point in the distance where parallel lines seem to meet. ◻ *The highway stretched out ahead of me until it narrowed to a vanishing point some miles away.* **2** N-UNCOUNT If you say that something has reached **vanishing point**, you mean it has become very small or unimportant. ◻ *By 1973, this gap had narrowed almost to vanishing point.*

van|ity /vænɪti/ N-UNCOUNT If you refer to someone's **vanity**, you are critical of them because they take great pride in their appearance or abilities. [DISAPPROVAL] ◻ *Men who use steroids are often motivated by sheer vanity.*

van|quish /væŋkwɪʃ/ (vanquishes, vanquishing, vanquished) V-T To **vanquish** someone means to defeat them completely in a battle or a competition. [LITERARY] ◻ *A happy ending is only possible because the hero has first vanquished the dragons.*

van|tage point /væntɪdʒ pɔɪnt/ (vantage points) **1** N-COUNT A **vantage point** is a place from which you can see a lot of things. ◻ *From a concealed vantage point, he saw a car arrive.* **2** N-COUNT If you view a situation from a particular **vantage point**, you have a clear understanding of it because of the particular period of time you are in. ◻ *From today's vantage point, the 1987 crash seems just a blip in the upward progress of the market.*

vape /veɪp/ (vapes, vaping, vaped) V-I If you **vape**, you inhale vapor from an electronic cigarette.

vap|id /væpɪd/ ADJ If you describe someone or something as **vapid**, you are critical of them because they are dull and uninteresting. [DISAPPROVAL] ◻ *We idolize vapid celebrities.* ◻ *She made a vapid comment about the weather.*

vap|ing /veɪpɪŋ/ N-UNCOUNT **Vaping** is the act or habit of breathing in a flavored steam containing nicotine from a special device. ◻ *Vaping can be a really effective way to quit smoking.*

va|por /veɪpər/ (vapors)

> in BRIT, use **vapour**

N-VAR **Vapor** consists of tiny drops of water or other liquids in the air, that appear as mist. ◻ *...water vapor.*

va|por|ize /veɪpəraɪz/ (vaporizes, vaporizing, vaporized)

> in BRIT, also use **vaporise**

V-T/V-I If a liquid or solid **vaporizes** or if you **vaporize** it, it

vaporizer

changes into vapor or gas. ❑ *The benzene vaporized and formed a huge cloud of gas.* ❑ *The blast may have vaporized the meteorite.*

va|por|iz|er /veɪpəraɪzər/ (**vaporizers**)

in BRIT, also use **vaporiser**

N-COUNT A **vaporizer** is a device that produces steam or that converts liquid medicine into vapor so that it can be inhaled. ❑ *Vaporizers for use in hospitals should be electric.*

in BRIT, also use **vaporiser**

va|por trail (**vapor trails**)

in BRIT, use **vapour trail**

N-COUNT A **vapor trail** is a white line of water vapor left in the sky by an airplane, a rocket, or a missile.

vari|able /vɛəriəbᵊl/ (**variables**) ◼ ADJ Something that is **variable** changes quite often, and there usually seems to be no fixed pattern to these changes. ❑ *The potassium content of foodstuffs is very variable.* • **vari|abil|ity** /vɛəriəbɪlɪti/ N-UNCOUNT ❑ *There's a great deal of variability between individuals.* ◼ N-COUNT A **variable** is a factor that can change in quality, quantity, or size, that you have to take into account in a situation. ❑ *Decisions could be made on the basis of price, delivery dates, after-sales service or any other variable.*

vari|ance /vɛəriəns/ PHRASE If one thing is **at variance** with another, the two things seem to contradict each other. [FORMAL] ❑ *Many of his statements were at variance with the facts.*

vari|ant /vɛəriənt/ (**variants**) N-COUNT A **variant** of a particular thing is something that has a different form from that thing, although it is related to it. ❑ *The quagga was a strikingly beautiful variant of the zebra.*

vari|ation /vɛərieɪʃᵊn/ (**variations**) ◼ N-COUNT A **variation** on something is the same thing presented in a slightly different form. ❑ *This delicious variation on an omelette is quick and easy to prepare.* ◼ N-VAR A **variation** is a change or slight difference in a level, amount, or quantity. ❑ *The survey found a wide variation in the prices charged for canteen food.* ◼ → See feature box at **genetics**

vari|cose vein /værɪkoʊs veɪn/ (**varicose veins**) N-COUNT [usu pl] **Varicose veins** are swollen and painful veins in a person's legs, that sometimes require a medical operation.

var|ied /vɛərid/ ◼ ADJ Something that is **varied** consists of things of different types, sizes, or qualities. ❑ *It is essential that your diet is varied and balanced.* ◼ → see also **vary**

varie|gat|ed /vɛəriəgeɪtɪd, vɛərə-/ ◼ ADJ [usu ADJ n] A **variegated** leaf or plant has different colors on it. [TECHNICAL] ❑ *The leaves are a variegated red.* ◼ ADJ Something that is **variegated** consists of many different parts or types. [FORMAL] ❑ *...our variegated dialects.*

va|ri|ety ◆◇◇ /vəraɪɪti/ (**varieties**) ◼ N-UNCOUNT If something has **variety**, it consists of things that are different from each other. ❑ *Susan's idea of freedom was to have variety in her life style.* ◼ N-SING A **variety** of things is a number of different kinds or examples of the same thing. ❑ *West Hampstead has a variety of good stores and supermarkets.* ❑ *The island offers such a wide variety of scenery and wildlife.* ◼ N-COUNT A **variety** of something is a type of it. ❑ *I'm always pleased to try out a new variety.*

va|ri|ety store (**variety stores**) N-COUNT A **variety store** is a store that sells a wide range of small, inexpensive items. [AM] ❑ *...a small variety store in the city of Oshawa.*

vari|ous ◆◇◇ /vɛəriəs/ ◼ ADJ If you say that there are **various** things, you mean there are several different things of the type mentioned. ❑ *His plan is to spread the capital between various building society accounts.* ◼ ADJ If a number of things are described as **various**, they are very different from one another. ❑ *The methods are many and various.*

vari|ous|ly /vɛəriəsli/ ADV You can use **variously** to introduce a number of different ways that something can be described. ❑ *...the crowds, which were variously estimated at two to several thousand.*

var|mint /vɑrmɪnt/ (**varmints**) N-COUNT A **varmint** is an animal that annoys you or causes problems. [AM, INFORMAL, DISAPPROVAL] ❑ *...the prairie dog, which the state regards as a varmint that should be hunted without limit.*

Vatican

var|nish /vɑrnɪʃ/ (**varnishes, varnishing, varnished**) ◼ N-MASS **Varnish** is an oily liquid that is painted onto wood or other material to give it a hard, clear, shiny surface. ❑ *The varnish comes in six natural wood shades.* ◼ V-T If you **varnish** something, you paint it with varnish. ❑ *Varnish the table with two or three coats of water-based varnish.*

var|sity /vɑrsɪti/ (**varsities**) N-VAR [oft N n] The **varsity** is the main or first team for a particular sport at a high school, college, or university. [AM] ❑ *She has been in the playoffs every year since she made the varsity.* ❑ *They played on varsity two years ago.*

vary ◆◇◇ /vɛəri/ (**varies, varying, varied**) ◼ V-I If things **vary**, they are different from each other in size, amount, or degree. ❑ *As they're handmade, each one varies slightly.* ❑ *The text varies from the earlier versions.* ◼ V-T/V-I If something **varies** or if you **vary** it, it becomes different or changed. ❑ *The cost of the alcohol duty varies according to the amount of wine in the bottle.* ◼ → see also **varied**

SYNONYMS

vary
VERB ◼
differ: *The story he told police differed from the one he told his mother.*
diverge: *His interests increasingly diverged from those of his colleagues.*
contrast with: *Johnson's easy charm contrasted sharply with the moody behavior of his boss.*
◼
change: *A changing world has put pressures on the corporation.*
transform: *Your metabolic rate is the speed at which your body transforms food into energy.*
alter: *Little had altered in the village.*

---

vas|cu|lar /væskyələr/ ADJ [ADJ n] **Vascular** is used to describe the channels and veins through which fluids pass in the bodies of animals and plants. [TECHNICAL] ❑ *...the oldest known vascular plants.* ❑ *...vascular diseases of the legs.*

vase /veɪs, vɑz/ (**vases**) N-COUNT A **vase** is a jar, usually made of glass or pottery, used for holding cut flowers or as an ornament. ❑ *...a vase of red roses.*

vas|ec|to|my /vəsɛktəmi, væ-/ (**vasectomies**) N-VAR A **vasectomy** is a surgical operation in which the tube that carries sperm to a man's penis is cut, usually as a means of contraception.

Vas|eline /væsəlin/ N-UNCOUNT **Vaseline** is a soft clear jelly made from petroleum, that is used to protect the skin and for other purposes. [TRADEMARK]

vas|sal /væsᵊl/ (**vassals**) ◼ N-COUNT In feudal society, a **vassal** was a man who gave military service to a lord, in return for which he was protected by the lord and received land to live on. ◼ N-COUNT [usu sing] If you say that one country is a **vassal** of another, you mean that it is controlled by it. [WRITTEN, DISAPPROVAL] ❑ *Opponents of the treaty argue that monetary union will turn France into a vassal of Germany.*

vast ◆◇◇ /væst/ (**vaster, vastest**) ◼ ADJ Something that is **vast** is extremely large. ❑ *...those farmers who own vast stretches of land.* ◼ → See feature box at **disaster, water**

SYNONYMS

vast
ADJ ◼
huge: *...a tiny, little woman with huge, black glasses.*
massive: *...a massive steamboat.*
enormous: *The main bedroom is enormous.*
immense: *...an immense cloud of smoke.*

---

vast|ly /væstli/ ADV **Vastly** means to an extremely great degree or extent. ❑ *The jury has heard two vastly different accounts.*

vat /væt/ (**vats**) N-COUNT A **vat** is a large barrel or tank in which liquids can be stored.

VAT ◆◇◇ /viː eɪ tiː, væt/ N-UNCOUNT **VAT** is a tax that is added to the price of goods or services. **VAT** is an abbreviation for 'value added tax.' [BRIT]

Vati|can /vætɪkən/ N-PROPER **The Vatican** is the city state in Rome ruled by the pope that is the center of the Roman

Catholic Church. You can also use **the Vatican** to refer to the pope or his officials. ❑ *The president had an audience with the pope in the Vatican.*

vau|de|ville /vɔ́dvɪl, vóʊdə-/ N-UNCOUNT **Vaudeville** is a type of entertainment consisting of short acts such as comedy, singing, and dancing. Vaudeville was especially popular in the early part of the twentieth century. [mainly AM]

in BRIT, usually use **music hall**

vault /vɔlt/ (vaults, vaulting, vaulted) **1** N-COUNT A **vault** is a secure room where money and other valuable things can be kept safely. ❑ *Most of the money was in storage in bank vaults.* **2** N-COUNT A **vault** is a room underneath a church or in a cemetery where people are buried, usually the members of a single family. ❑ *He ordered that Matilda's body should be buried in the family vault.* **3** V-T/V-I If you **vault** something or **vault** over it, you jump quickly onto or over it, especially by putting a hand on top of it to help you balance while you jump. ❑ *He could easily vault the wall.*

vaunt|ed /vɔ́ntɪd/ ADJ [usu ADJ n] If you describe something as **vaunted** or **much vaunted**, you mean that people praise it more than it deserves. [FORMAL] ❑ *Simpson's much vaunted discoveries are in fact commonplace in modern sociology.*

vb vb is a written abbreviation for **verb**.

VC /víː síː/ (**VCs**) N-COUNT VC is an abbreviation for 'vice chairman.'

VCR /víː siː ɑ́r/ (**VCRs**) N-COUNT A **VCR** is a machine that was used in the past to record television programs or movies onto videotapes, so that they could be played back and watched later on a television set. VCR is an abbreviation for 'video cassette recorder.' ❑ *Because many of us no longer own VCRs, camcorders are quickly becoming outdated.*

VD /víː díː/ N-UNCOUNT **VD** is used to refer to diseases such as syphilis and gonorrhea that are passed on by sexual intercourse. VD is an abbreviation for **venereal disease**. [OLD-FASHIONED]

VDT /víː diː tíː/ (**VDTs**) N-COUNT **VDT** is an abbreviation for 'video display terminal.' [mainly AM]

-'ve /-əv, -v/ **'ve** is the usual spoken form of 'have,' especially when 'have' is an auxiliary verb. It is added to the end of the pronoun that is the subject of the verb. For example, 'you have' can be shortened to 'you've.'

veal /viːl/ N-UNCOUNT **Veal** is meat from a calf. ❑ *...a veal cutlet.*

vec|tor /véktər/ (**vectors**) **1** N-COUNT A **vector** is a variable quantity, such as force, that has size and direction. [TECHNICAL] **2** N-COUNT A **vector** is an insect or other organism that causes a disease by carrying a germ or parasite from one person or animal to another. [MEDICAL]

veep /víːp/ (**veeps**) N-COUNT A **veep** is a vice president, especially the vice-president of the United States. [AM, INFORMAL]

veer /víər/ (**veers, veering, veered**) **1** V-I If something **veers** in a certain direction, it suddenly moves in that direction. ❑ *The plane veered off the runway and crashed through the perimeter fence.* **2** V-I If someone or something **veers** in a certain direction, they change their position or direction in a particular situation. ❑ *He is unlikely to veer from his boss's strongly held views.*

veg /vɛdʒ/ (**veg**) N-VAR **Veg** is an abbreviation for **vegetables**. [mainly BRIT, INFORMAL]

in AM, usually use **veggies**

ve|gan /víːɡən/ (**vegans**) ADJ Someone who is **vegan** never eats meat or any animal products such as milk, butter, or cheese. ❑ *The menu changes weekly and usually includes a vegan option.* • N-COUNT A **vegan** is someone who is vegan. ❑ *...vegetarians and vegans.*

veg|eta|ble ♦◇◇ /vɛ́dʒtəbəl, vɛ́dʒɪ-/ (**vegetables**) **1** N-COUNT **Vegetables** are plants such as cabbages, potatoes, and onions that you can cook and eat. ❑ *A good general diet should include plenty of fresh vegetables.* **2** ADJ **Vegetable** matter comes from plants. [FORMAL] ❑ *...compounds of animal, vegetable or mineral origin.* **3** N-COUNT [usu sing] If someone refers to a brain-damaged person as a **vegetable**, they mean that the person cannot move, think, or speak. [INFORMAL, OFFENSIVE]

COLLOCATIONS

vegetable
NOUN **1**
noun + **vegetable**: root, salad, stir-fry; spring, winter
adjective + **vegetable**: green, leafy, mixed, seasonal; fresh, frozen, organic; pickled, roasted, steamed
vegetable + be + adjective: soft, tender
verb + **vegetable**: grow, plant; chop, eat, cook, wash

---

veg|etar|ian /vɛdʒɪtɛ́əriən/ (**vegetarians**) **1** ADJ Someone who is **vegetarian** never eats meat or fish. ❑ *Yasmin sticks to a strict vegetarian diet.* • N-COUNT A **vegetarian** is someone who is vegetarian. ❑ *...a special menu for vegetarians.* **2** ADJ **Vegetarian** food does not contain any meat or fish. ❑ *...vegetarian lasagnes.*

veg|etari|an|ism /vɛdʒɪtɛ́əriənɪzəm/ N-UNCOUNT If someone practices **vegetarianism**, they never eat meat or fish.

veg|etate /vɛ́dʒɪteɪt/ (**vegetates, vegetating, vegetated**) V-I If someone **vegetates**, they spend their time doing boring or worthless things. ❑ *He spends all his free time at home vegetating in front of the TV.*

veg|etat|ed /vɛ́dʒɪteɪtɪd/ ADJ [usu adv ADJ] If an area is **vegetated**, it is covered with plants and trees. [FORMAL]

veg|eta|tion /vɛdʒɪteɪʃən/ **1** N-UNCOUNT Plants, trees, and flowers can be referred to as **vegetation**. [FORMAL] ❑ *The inn has a garden of semi-tropical vegetation.* **2** → See feature box at **ecosystem**

veg|eta|tive /vɛ́dʒɪteɪtɪv/ ADJ [usu ADJ n] If someone is in a **vegetative** state, they are unable to move, think, or speak, and their condition is not likely to improve. [MEDICAL] ❑ *She was in what was described as a vegetative state.*

veg|gie /vɛ́dʒi/ (**veggies**) **1** N-COUNT [usu pl] **Veggies** are plants such as cabbages, potatoes, and onions that you can cook and eat. **Veggies** is an abbreviation for **vegetables**. [mainly AM, INFORMAL] ❑ *...well-balanced meals of fresh fruit and veggies, chicken, fish, pasta, and no red meat.*

in BRIT, usually use **veg**

2 ADJ **Veggie** means the same as **vegetarian**. [INFORMAL] ❑ *You can cook a cheap veggie chilli in 15 minutes.* • N-COUNT A **veggie** is someone who is vegetarian.

veg|gie|burg|er /vɛ́dʒibɜrɡər/ (**veggieburgers**) also **veggie burger** N-COUNT **Veggieburgers** are flat round cakes of food made from vegetables mixed with flour and flavorings. You broil or fry them.

ve|he|ment /víːəmənt/ ADJ If a person or their actions or comments are **vehement**, the person has very strong feelings or opinions and expresses them forcefully. ❑ *She suddenly became very vehement and agitated, jumping around and shouting.* • **ve|he|mence** N-UNCOUNT ❑ *He spoke more loudly and with more vehemence than he had intended.* • **ve|he|ment|ly** ADV ❑ *Krabbe has always vehemently denied stealing the car.*

ve|hi|cle ♦◇◇ /víːɪkəl/ (**vehicles**) **1** N-COUNT A **vehicle** is a machine with an engine, such as a bus, car, or truck, that carries people or things from place to place. ❑ *...a vehicle that was somewhere between a tractor and a truck.* **2** N-COUNT You can use **vehicle** to refer to something that you use in order to achieve a particular purpose. ❑ *Her art became a vehicle for her political beliefs.*

ve|hicu|lar /vihíkyələr/ ADJ [usu ADJ n] **Vehicular** is used to describe something that relates to vehicles and traffic. [FORMAL] ❑ *...vehicular traffic.* ❑ *There is no vehicular access.*

veil /veɪl/ (**veils**) **1** N-COUNT A **veil** is a piece of thin soft cloth that women sometimes wear over their heads and that can also cover their face. ❑ *She's got long fair hair but she's got a veil over it.* **2** N-COUNT You can refer to something that hides or partly hides a situation or activity as a **veil**. ❑ *The country is ridding itself of its disgraced prime minister in a veil of secrecy.* **3** N-COUNT You can refer to something that you can partly see through, such as a mist, as a **veil**. [LITERARY] ❑ *The eruption has left a thin veil of dust in the upper atmosphere.*

veiled /veɪld/ **1** ADJ [ADJ n] A **veiled** comment is expressed in a disguised form rather than directly and openly. ❑ *He made only a veiled reference to international concerns over human rights issues.* **2** ADJ A woman or girl who is **veiled** is wearing a veil. ❑ *A veiled woman gave me a kindly smile.*

vein /veɪn/ (veins) **1** N-COUNT Your **veins** are the thin tubes in your body through which your blood flows toward your heart. Compare **artery**. ❑ *Many veins are found just under the skin.* **2** N-COUNT Something that is written or spoken in a particular **vein** is written or spoken in that style or mood. ❑ *It is one of his finest works in a lighter vein.* **3** N-COUNT A **vein** of a particular quality is evidence of that quality that someone often shows in their behavior or work. ❑ *A rich vein of humor runs through the book.* **4** N-COUNT The **veins** on a leaf are the thin lines on it. ❑ *...the serrated edges and veins of the feathery leaves.*

veined /veɪnd/ **1** ADJ **Veined** skin has a lot of veins showing through it. ❑ *Helen's hands were thin and veined.* **2** ADJ Something that is **veined** has a pattern or coloring like that of veins showing through skin. ❑ *...a bronze ashtray shaped like a veined leaf.*

Vel|cro /vɛlkroʊ/ N-UNCOUNT [oft N n] **Velcro** is a material consisting of two strips of nylon fabric that you press together to close things such as pockets and bags. [TRADEMARK]

veldt /vɛlt, fɛlt/ also **veld** N-SING [usu the N] The **veldt** is a high area of flat grassy land with very few trees in southern Africa.

vel|lum /vɛləm/ N-UNCOUNT **Vellum** is strong paper of good quality for writing on.

ve|loc|ity /vəlɒsɪti/ (velocities) N-VAR **Velocity** is the speed at which something moves in a particular direction. [TECHNICAL] ❑ *...the velocities at which the stars orbit.*

ve|lour /vəlʊər/ N-UNCOUNT [usu N n] **Velour** is a silk or cotton fabric similar to velvet. ❑ *...a gold Mercedes with red velour seats.*

vel|vet /vɛlvɪt/ (velvets) N-MASS **Velvet** is soft material made from cotton, silk, or nylon, that has a thick layer of short cut threads on one side. ❑ *...a charcoal-gray overcoat with a velvet collar.*

vel|vet|een /vɛlvɪtin/ N-UNCOUNT [usu N n] **Velveteen** is a soft fabric that looks and feels like velvet and is sometimes used as a cheaper alternative to velvet. ❑ *...a black velveteen coat.* ❑ *...loose blouses of bright-colored velveteen.*

vel|vety /vɛlviti/ ADJ If you describe something as **velvety**, you mean that it is pleasantly soft to touch and has the appearance or quality of velvet. ❑ *The grass grew thick and velvety.*

ve|nal /vin°l/ ADJ If you describe someone as **venal**, you disapprove of them because they are prepared to do almost anything in return for money, even things that are dishonest or immoral. [DISAPPROVAL] ❑ *He is corrupt and thoroughly venal.* ❑ *...venal politicians.*

ven|det|ta /vɛndɛtə/ (vendettas) N-VAR If one person has a **vendetta** against another, the first person wants revenge for something the second person did to them in the past. ❑ *The vice president said the cartoonist has a personal vendetta against him.*

vend|ing ma|chine /vɛndɪŋ məʃin/ (vending machines) N-COUNT A **vending machine** is a machine from which you can get things such as cigarettes, chocolate, or coffee by putting in money and pressing a button.

ven|dor /vɛndər/ (vendors) **1** N-COUNT A **vendor** is someone who sells things such as newspapers, cigarettes, or food from a small stall or cart. ❑ *...ice cream vendors.* **2** N-COUNT A **vendor** is a company or person that sells a product or service, especially one who sells to other companies that sell to the public. [LEGAL] ❑ *They only act as agents for other vendors in this field.* **3** → See feature box at **service**

ve|neer /vɪnɪər/ (veneers) **1** N-SING If you refer to the pleasant way that someone or something appears as a **veneer**, you are critical of them because you believe that their true, hidden nature is not good. [DISAPPROVAL] ❑ *He was able to fool the world with his veneer of education.* **2** N-VAR **Veneer** is a thin layer of wood or plastic that is used to improve the appearance of something. ❑ *The wood was cut into large sheets of veneer.* ❑ *It's also available in beech with oak veneer.*

ven|er|able /vɛnərəb°l/ **1** ADJ A **venerable** person deserves respect because they are old and wise. ❑ *Her Chinese friends referred to the empress as their venerable ancestor.* **2** ADJ Something that is **venerable** is impressive because it is old or important historically. ❑ *May Day has become a venerable institution.*

ven|er|ate /vɛnəreɪt/ (venerates, venerating, venerated) V-T If you **venerate** someone, you value them or feel great respect for them. [FORMAL] ❑ *My father venerated General Eisenhower.* ● **ven|er|at|ed** ADJ ❑ *Jerusalem is Christianity's most venerated place.* ● **ven|era|tion** N-UNCOUNT ❑ *Churchill was held in near veneration during his lifetime.*

ve|nereal dis|ease /vɪnɪəriəl dɪziz/ (venereal diseases) N-VAR **Venereal disease** is used to refer to diseases such as syphilis and gonorrhea that are passed on by sexual intercourse. The abbreviation **VD** is also used. [OLD-FASHIONED]

Ve|netian blind /vənifən blaɪnd/ (Venetian blinds) N-COUNT A **Venetian blind** is a window blind made of thin horizontal strips that can be adjusted to let in more or less light.

venge|ance /vɛndʒəns/ **1** N-UNCOUNT **Vengeance** is the act of killing, injuring, or harming someone because they have harmed you. ❑ *He swore vengeance on everyone involved in the murder.* **2** PHRASE If you say that something happens **with a vengeance**, you are emphasizing that it happens to a much greater extent than was expected. [EMPHASIS] ❑ *It began to rain again with a vengeance.*

venge|ful /vɛndʒfəl/ ADJ If you describe someone as **vengeful**, you are critical of them because they feel a great desire for revenge. [DISAPPROVAL] ❑ *He was stabbed to death by his vengeful wife.*

veni|son /vɛnɪsən, -zən/ N-UNCOUNT **Venison** is the meat of a deer. ❑ *They had a wonderful lunch of salmon salad and roast venison.*

ven|om /vɛnəm/ (venoms) **1** N-UNCOUNT You can use **venom** to refer to someone's feelings of great bitterness and anger toward someone. ❑ *He reserved particular venom for critics of his foreign policy.* **2** N-MASS The **venom** of a creature such as a snake or spider is the poison that it puts into your body when it bites or stings you. ❑ *...snake handlers who grow immune to snake venom.*

ven|om|ous /vɛnəməs/ **1** ADJ If you describe a person or their behavior as **venomous**, you mean that they show great bitterness and anger toward someone. ❑ *...his terrifying and venomous Aunt Bridget.* **2** ADJ A **venomous** snake, spider, or other creature uses poison to attack other creatures. ❑ *He had been bitten by a venomous snake.*

ve|nous /vinəs/ ADJ [ADJ n] **Venous** is used to describe something that is related to veins. [MEDICAL] ❑ *...venous blood.*

vent /vɛnt/ (vents, venting, vented) **1** N-COUNT A **vent** is a hole in something through which air can come in and smoke, gas, or smells can go out. ❑ *A lot of steam escaped from the vent at the front of the machine.* **2** V-T If you **vent** your feelings, you express your feelings forcefully. ❑ *She telephoned her best friend to vent her frustration.* **3** PHRASE If you **give vent to** your feelings, you express them forcefully. [FORMAL] ❑ *She gave vent to her anger and jealousy.* **4** → See also color supplement

ven|ti|late /vɛnt°leɪt/ (ventilates, ventilating, ventilated) V-T If you **ventilate** a room or building, you allow fresh air to get into it. ❑ *Ventilate the room properly when stripping paint.* ● **ven|ti|la|tion** /vɛnt°leɪʃ°n/ N-UNCOUNT ❑ *The only ventilation comes from tiny sliding windows.*

ven|ti|la|tor /vɛnt°leɪtər/ (ventilators) **1** N-COUNT A **ventilator** is a machine that helps people breathe when they cannot breathe naturally, for example, because they are very ill or have been seriously injured. **2** N-COUNT A **ventilator** is a device that lets fresh air into a room or building and lets old or dirty air out.

ven|tri|cle /vɛntrɪk°l/ (ventricles) **1** N-COUNT A **ventricle** is a part of the heart that pumps blood to the arteries. [MEDICAL] **2** → See also color supplement

ven|trilo|quist /vɛntrɪləkwɪst/ (ventriloquists) N-COUNT A **ventriloquist** is someone who can speak without moving their lips and who entertains people by making their words appear to be spoken by a puppet.

ven|ture ♦◇◇ /vɛntʃər/ (ventures, venturing, ventured) **1** N-COUNT A **venture** is a project or activity that is new, exciting, and difficult because it involves the risk of failure. ❑ *...a Russian-American joint venture.* **2** V-I If you **venture** somewhere, you go somewhere that might be dangerous. [LITERARY] ❑ *People are afraid to venture out for fear of sniper attacks.* **3** V-T If you **venture** a question or statement, you say it in an uncertain way because you are afraid it might be stupid or wrong. [WRITTEN] ❑ *"So you're Leo's girlfriend?" he ventured.*

□ He ventured that plants draw part of their nourishment from the air. ◼ V-T If you **venture** to do something that requires courage or is risky, you do it. □ "Don't ask," he said, whenever Ginny ventured to raise the subject. ◼ V-I If you **venture into** an activity, you do something that involves the risk of failure because it is new and different. □ He enjoyed little success when he ventured into business.

ven|ture capi|tal N-UNCOUNT **Venture capital** is capital that is invested in projects that have a high risk of failure, but that will bring large profits if they are successful. [BUSINESS] □ Successful venture capital investment is a lot harder than it sometimes looks.

ven|ture capi|tal|ist (venture capitalists) ◼ N-COUNT A **venture capitalist** is someone who makes money by investing in high risk projects. [BUSINESS] ◼ → See feature box at **business**

ven|ture|some /vɛntʃərsəm/ ADJ If you describe someone as **venturesome**, you mean that they are willing to take risks and try out new things. [FORMAL] □ ...the venturesome graduate who is determined to succeed.

venue ✦◇◇ /vɛnyu/ (venues) N-COUNT The **venue** for an event or activity is the place where it will happen. □ The International Convention Centre is the venue for a three-day arts festival.

ve|rac|ity /vəræsɪti/ N-UNCOUNT **Veracity** is the quality of being true or the habit of telling the truth. [FORMAL] □ We have total confidence in the veracity of our research.

ve|ran|da /vərændə/ (verandas) also **verandah** N-COUNT A **veranda** is a roofed platform along the outside of a house. □ They had their coffee and tea on the veranda.

verb /vɜrb/ (verbs) ◼ N-COUNT A **verb** is a word such as 'sing,' 'feel,' or 'die' that is used with a subject to say what someone or something does or what happens to them, or to give information about them. ◼ → see also **phrasal verb**

ver|bal /vɜrbəl/ ◼ ADJ You use **verbal** to indicate that something is expressed in speech rather than in writing or action. □ They were jostled and subjected to a torrent of verbal abuse. • **ver|bal|ly** ADV □ Many teachers have been threatened and verbally abused by students. ◼ ADJ [ADJ n] You use **verbal** to indicate that something is connected with words and the use of words. □ The test has scores for verbal skills, mathematical skills, and abstract reasoning skills. ◼ ADJ In grammar, **verbal** means relating to a verb. □ ...a verbal noun. ◼ → See feature box at **debate**

ver|bal|ize /vɜrbəlaɪz/ (verbalizes, verbalizing, verbalized)

in BRIT, also use **verbalise**

V-T If you **verbalize** your feelings, thoughts, or ideas, you express them in words. [FORMAL] □ ...his inability to verbalize his feelings.

ver|ba|tim /vərbeɪtɪm/ ADV [ADV after v] If you repeat something **verbatim**, you say it exactly the same words as were used originally. □ The president's speeches are regularly reproduced verbatim in the state-run newspapers. • ADJ [ADJ n] **Verbatim** is also an adjective. □ I was treated to a verbatim report of every conversation she's taken part in over the past week.

ver|bi|age /vɜrbiɪdʒ/ N-UNCOUNT If you refer to someone's speech or writing as **verbiage**, you are critical of them because they use too many words, and this makes their speech or writing difficult to understand. [FORMAL, DISAPPROVAL] □ Stripped of their pretentious verbiage, his statements come dangerously close to inviting racial hatred.

ver|bose /vɜrboʊs/ ADJ If you describe a person or a piece of writing as **verbose**, you are critical of them because they use more words than are necessary, and so make you feel bored or annoyed. [FORMAL, DISAPPROVAL] □ ...verbose politicians. □ His writing is difficult and often verbose.

verb phrase (verb phrases) N-COUNT A **verb phrase** or **verbal phrase** consists of a verb, or of a main verb following a modal or one or more auxiliaries. Examples are 'walked,' 'can see,' and 'had been waiting.'

ver|dant /vɜrdənt/ ADJ If you describe a place as **verdant**, you mean that it is covered with green grass, trees, and plants. [LITERARY] □ ...a small verdant garden with a glorious view out over Paris.

ver|dict ✦◇◇ /vɜrdɪkt/ (verdicts) ◼ N-COUNT In a court of law, the **verdict** is the decision that is given by the jury or judge at the end of a trial. □ The jury returned a unanimous guilty verdict. ◼ N-COUNT Someone's **verdict** on something is their opinion of it, after thinking about it or investigating it. □ The doctor's verdict was that he was entirely healthy.

---SYNONYMS---

verdict
NOUN ◼
decision: A decision was taken to discipline Marshall.
finding: The government hopes the court will announce its findings before the end of the month.
judgment: The industry was awaiting a judgment from the European Court.

---

ver|di|gris /vɜrdɪgrɪs, -grɪs/ N-UNCOUNT **Verdigris** is a greenish-blue substance that forms on the metals copper, brass, and bronze after they have been left in wet or damp conditions.

verge /vɜrdʒ/ (verges, verging, verged) ◼ PHRASE If you are **on the verge of** something, you are going to do it very soon or it is likely to happen or begin very soon. □ The country was on the verge of becoming prosperous and successful. ◼ N-COUNT The **verge** of a road is a narrow piece of ground by the side of a road, which is usually covered with grass or flowers. [BRIT]

in AM, use **shoulder**

▶ **verge on** PHRASAL VERB If someone or something **verges on** a particular state or quality, they are almost the same as that state or quality. □ ...a fury that verged on madness.

veri|fi|able /vɛrɪfaɪəbəl/ ADJ Something that is **verifiable** can be proved to be true or genuine. □ This is not a romantic notion but verifiable fact.

veri|fy /vɛrɪfaɪ/ (verifies, verifying, verified) ◼ V-T If you **verify** something, you check that it is true by careful examination or investigation. □ I verified the source from which I had that information. • **veri|fi|ca|tion** /vɛrɪfɪkeɪʃən/ N-UNCOUNT □ All charges against her are dropped pending the verification of her story. ◼ V-T [no cont] If you **verify** something, you state or confirm that it is true. □ The government has not verified any of those reports.

veri|ly /vɛrɪli/ ADV **Verily** is an old-fashioned or religious word meaning 'truly.' It is used to emphasize a statement or opinion. [EMPHASIS] □ Verily I say unto you, that one of you shall betray me.

veri|si|mili|tude /vɛrɪsɪmɪlɪtud/ N-UNCOUNT **Verisimilitude** is the quality of seeming to be true or real. [FORMAL] □ At the required level of visual verisimilitude, computer animation is extremely costly.

veri|table /vɛrɪtəbəl/ ADJ You can use **veritable** to emphasize the size, amount, or nature of something. [EMPHASIS] □ ...a veritable feast of pre-game entertainment.

ver|ity /vɛrɪti/ (verities) N-COUNT [usu pl, usu with supp] The **verities** of something are all the things that are believed to be true about it. [FORMAL] □ ...some verities of human nature.

ver|mil|lion /vərmɪlyən/ COLOR **Vermilion** is used to describe things that are bright orange-red in color. [LITERARY] □ ...her vermilion lip gloss. ◼ The furniture on it is glossy vermilion.

ver|min /vɜrmɪn/ N-PLURAL **Vermin** are small animals such as rats and mice which cause problems to humans by carrying disease and damaging crops or food.

ver|mouth /vərmuθ/ (vermouths) N-MASS **Vermouth** is a strong alcoholic drink made from red or white wine flavored with herbs.

ver|nacu|lar /vərnækyələr/ (vernaculars) N-COUNT The **vernacular** is the language or dialect that is most widely spoken by ordinary people in a region or country. □ ...books or plays written in the vernacular.

ver|sa|tile /vɜrsətəl/ ◼ ADJ If you say that a person is **versatile**, you approve of them because they have many different skills. [APPROVAL] □ He had been one of the game's most versatile athletes. • **ver|sa|til|ity** /vɜrsətɪlɪti/ N-UNCOUNT □ She stands out for her incredible versatility as an actor. ◼ ADJ A tool, machine, or material that is **versatile** can be used for many different purposes. □ Never before has computing been so versatile. • **ver|sa|til|ity** N-UNCOUNT □ Velvet as a fabric is not known for its versatility.

verse /vɜrs/ (verses) ◼ N-UNCOUNT **Verse** is writing arranged in lines that have rhythm and that often rhyme at the end.

❏ I have been moved to write a few lines of verse. **2** N-COUNT A **verse** is one of the parts into which a poem, a song, or a chapter of the Bible or the Koran is divided. ❏ This verse describes three signs of spring.

versed /vɜrst/ ADJ [v-link ADJ] If you are **versed in** or **well versed in** something, you know a lot about it. ❏ Page is well versed in many styles of jazz.

ver|sion ♦♦◊ /vɜrʒən/ (versions) **1** N-COUNT A **version** of something is a particular form of it in which some details are different from earlier or later forms. ❏ ...an updated version of his bestselling book. ❏ Ludo is a version of an ancient Indian racing game. **2** N-COUNT Someone's **version** of an event is their own description of it, especially when it is different from other people's. ❏ Some former hostages contradicted the official version of events.

ver|sus /vɜrsəs/ **1** PREP You use **versus** to indicate that two figures, ideas, or choices are opposed. ❏ ...an income of €9.9 million in the first quarter versus €8.5 million in the prior year. **2** PREP **Versus** is used to indicate that two teams or people are competing against each other in a sports event. ❏ Italy versus Japan is turning out to be a surprisingly well matched competition. **3** PREP **Versus** is used in a court of law to indicate that two people or organizations are involved in a law suit. The abbreviation **v** is also used. ❏ That case became known as Healey versus Jones.

ver|te|bra /vɜrtɪbrə/ (vertebrae /vɜrtɪbreɪ, -bri/) N-COUNT **Vertebrae** are the small circular bones that form the spine of a human being or animal.

ver|te|brate /vɜrtɪbrɪt/ (vertebrates) N-COUNT [oft N n] A **vertebrate** is a creature that has a spine. Mammals, birds, reptiles, and fish are vertebrates.

ver|ti|cal /vɜrtɪkəl/ ADJ Something that is **vertical** stands or points straight up. ❏ The climber inched up a vertical wall of rock. ● **ver|ti|cal|ly** ADV [ADV after v] ❏ Cut each bulb in half vertically.

ver|ti|cal gar|den (vertical gardens) N-COUNT A **vertical garden** is a garden created by growing plants in a layer of soil on the surface of a wall.

ver|tigi|nous /vɜrtɪdʒɪnəs/ ADJ [usu ADJ n] A **vertiginous** cliff or mountain is very high and steep. [LITERARY]

ver|ti|go /vɜrtɪgoʊ/ N-UNCOUNT If you get **vertigo** when you look down from a high place, you feel unsteady and sick.

verve /vɜrv/ N-UNCOUNT **Verve** is lively and forceful enthusiasm. [WRITTEN] ❏ He looked for the dramatic, like the sunset in this painting, and painted it with great verve.

very ♦♦♦ /vɛri/ **1** ADV [ADV adj/adv] **Very** is used to give emphasis to an adjective or adverb. [EMPHASIS] ❏ The problem and the answer are very simple. ❏ I'm very sorry. ❏ They are getting the hang of it very quickly. **2** PHRASE **Not very** is used with an adjective or adverb to say that something is not at all true, or that it is true only to a small degree. ❏ She's not very impressed with them. ❏ "How well do you know her?"—"Not very." **3** ADV [ADV superl] You use **very** to give emphasis to a superlative adjective or adverb. For example, if you say that something is **the very best**, you are emphasizing that it is the best. [EMPHASIS] ❏ They will be helped by the very latest in navigation aids. ❏ I am feeling in the very best of spirits. **4** ADJ [ADJ n] You use **very** with certain nouns in order to specify an extreme position or extreme point in time. [EMPHASIS] ❏ At the very back of the yard was a wooden shack. ❏ I turned to the very end of the book, to read the final words. **5** ADJ [ADJ n] You use **very** with nouns to emphasize that something is exactly the right one or exactly the same one. [EMPHASIS] ❏ Everybody says he is the very man for the case. **6** ADJ [ADJ n] You use **very** with nouns to emphasize the importance or seriousness of what you are saying. [EMPHASIS] ❏ At one stage his very life was in danger. ❏ History is taking place before your very eyes. **7** PHRASE The expression **very much so** is an emphatic way of answering 'yes' to something or saying that it is true or correct. [EMPHASIS] ❏ "Are you enjoying your vacation?"—"Very much so." **8** CONVENTION **Very well** is used to say that you agree to do something or you accept someone's answer, even though you might not be completely satisfied with it. [FORMULAE] ❏ "We need proof, sir." Another pause. Then, "Very well." **9** PHRASE If you say that you **cannot very well** do something, you mean that it would not be right or possible to do it. ❏ I said yes. I can't very well say no under the circumstances.

> USAGE
>
> **very**
>
> **1** Don't use 'very' to say that something happens because someone or something has a quality to an unusually large extent. Don't say, for example, 'He looked very funny that we couldn't help laughing.' You say 'He looked **so** funny that we couldn't help laughing.' We were **so** angry that we asked to see the manager.
>
> **2** Don't use 'very' with comparatives. Don't say, for example, 'Tom was very quicker than I was.' Say 'Tom was **much** quicker than I was' or 'Tom was **a lot** quicker than I was.' It is **a lot colder** than yesterday. It is a **much better** picture than the other one.
>
> **3** Don't say that someone is 'very awake' or 'very asleep,' or that two things are 'very apart.' Say that they are **wide awake**, **fast asleep**, or **far apart**. He was **wide awake** all night. Chris is still **fast asleep** in the other bed.

ves|pers /vɛspərz/ N-UNCOUNT In some Christian churches, **vespers** is a service in the evening.

ves|sel ♦◊◊ /vɛsəl/ (vessels) **1** N-COUNT A **vessel** is a ship or large boat. [FORMAL] ❏ ...a New Zealand navy vessel. **2** → see also **blood vessel**

vest /vɛst/ (vests) **1** N-COUNT A **vest** is a sleeveless piece of clothing with buttons that people usually wear over a shirt. [AM]

in BRIT, use **waistcoat**

2 N-COUNT A **vest** is a piece of underwear that you can wear on the top half of your body in order to keep warm. [BRIT]

in AM, use **undershirt**

vest|ed in|ter|est (vested interests) N-VAR If you have a **vested interest** in something, you have a very strong reason for acting in a particular way, for example, to protect your money, power, or reputation. ❏ The administration has no vested interest in proving public schools good or bad.

ves|ti|bule /vɛstɪbyul/ (vestibules) N-COUNT A **vestibule** is an enclosed area between the outside door of a building and the inside door. [FORMAL]

ves|tige /vɛstɪdʒ/ (vestiges) N-COUNT A **vestige** of something is a very small part that still remains of something that was once much larger or more important. [FORMAL] ❏ We represent the last vestige of what made this nation great – hard work.

ves|tig|ial /vɛstɪdʒiəl, -dʒəl/ ADJ [usu ADJ n] **Vestigial** is used to describe the small amounts of something that still remain of a larger or more important thing. [FORMAL] ❏ ...vestigial pagan practices and symbols inside Christian churches.

vest|ments /vɛstmənts/ N-PLURAL **Vestments** are the special clothes worn by priests during church ceremonies.

ves|try /vɛstri/ (vestries) N-COUNT A **vestry** is a room in a church that the clergy use as an office or to change into their ceremonial clothes for church services.

vet /vɛt/ (vets, vetting, vetted) **1** N-COUNT A **vet** is someone who is qualified to treat sick or injured animals. **Vet** is an abbreviation for **veterinarian**. [INFORMAL] ❏ She's at the vet, with her dog, right now. **2** N-COUNT A **vet** is someone who has served in the armed forces of their country, especially during a war. **vet** is an abbreviation for **veteran**. [AM, INFORMAL] ❏ The New England Shelter in Boston will serve Christmas dinner for 200 vets. **3** V-T [usu passive] If someone **is vetted**, they are investigated fully before being given a particular job, role, or position, especially one that involves military or political secrets. [mainly BRIT] ❏ She was secretly vetted before she ever undertook any work for me. ● **vet|ting** N-UNCOUNT ❏ The government is to make major changes to the procedure for carrying out security vetting.

vetch /vɛtʃ/ (vetches) N-MASS **Vetch** is a family of wild plants. Some types of vetch are sometimes grown as a crop.

vet|er|an ♦◊◊ /vɛtərən/ (veterans) **1** N-COUNT A **veteran** is someone who has served in the armed forces of their country, especially during a war. ❏ They approved a $1.1 billion package of pay increases for the veterans of the Persian Gulf War. **2** N-COUNT You use **veteran** to refer to someone who has been involved in a particular activity for a long time. ❏ ...the veteran critic and professor of cinema studies at New York University.

> **COLLOCATIONS**
>
> **veteran**
> NOUN
> **1**
> noun + **veteran**: army, combat, navy, war
> adjective + **veteran**: wounded; retired
> **2**
> noun + **veteran**: industry; comedy, screen, showbiz, theater
> adjective + **veteran**: grizzled, seasoned

Vet|er|ans Day N-UNCOUNT In the United States, **Veterans Day** is November 11, when people honor those who have served or are serving in the armed forces.

vet|eri|nar|ian /vɛtərɪnɛəriən/ (**veterinarians**) N-COUNT A **veterinarian** is a person who is qualified to treat sick or injured animals. [mainly AM]

vet|eri|nary /vɛtərənɛri/ ADJ [ADJ n] **Veterinary** is used to describe the work of a person whose job is to treat sick or injured animals, or to describe the medical treatment of animals. ❑ *It was decided that our veterinary screening of horses at events should be continued.*

vet|eri|nary sur|geon (**veterinary surgeons**) N-COUNT A **veterinary surgeon** is someone who is qualified to treat sick or injured animals. [BRIT, FORMAL]

> in AM, use **veterinarian**

veto /viːtoʊ/ (**vetoes, vetoing, vetoed**) **1** V-T If someone in authority **vetoes** something, they forbid it, or stop it from being put into action. ❑ *The president vetoed the economic package passed by Congress.* • N-COUNT **Veto** is also a noun. ❑ *They need 12 votes to override his veto.* **2** N-UNCOUNT **Veto** is the right that someone in authority has to forbid something. ❑ *...the president's power of veto.*

vex /vɛks/ (**vexes, vexing, vexed**) **1** V-T If someone or something **vexes** you, they make you feel annoyed, puzzled, and frustrated. ❑ *It vexed me to think of others gossiping behind my back.* • **vexed** ADJ ❑ *Exporters, farmers and industrialists alike are vexed and blame the government.* • **vex|ing** ADJ ❑ *There remains, however, another and more vexing problem.* **2** → see also **vexed**

vexa|tion /vɛkseɪʃən/ (**vexations**) N-UNCOUNT [also N in pl] **Vexation** is a feeling of being annoyed, puzzled, and frustrated. [FORMAL] ❑ *He kicked the broken machine in vexation.*

vexed /vɛkst/ **1** ADJ A **vexed** problem or question is very difficult and causes people a lot of trouble. ❑ *Ministers have begun work on the vexed issue of economic union.* **2** → see also **vex**

VHF /viː eɪtʃ ɛf/ N-UNCOUNT [oft N n] **VHF** is used to refer to a range of frequencies that is often used for transmitting radio broadcasts in stereo. **VHF** is an abbreviation for 'very high frequency.'

via ♦◇◇ /vaɪə, viːə/ **1** PREP If you go somewhere **via** a particular place, you go through that place on the way to your destination. ❑ *We drove via Lovech to the old Danube town of Ruse.* **2** PREP If you do something **via** a particular means or person, you do it by making use of that means or person. ❑ *The technology to allow relief workers to contact the outside world via satellite already exists.*

> **SYNONYMS**
>
> **via**
> PREP
> **1**
> **through:** *The main path continues through a tunnel of trees.*
> **by:** *Daddy called and asked me to drop by his office.*
> **2**
> **by means of:** *This is a two-year course taught by means of lectures and seminars.*
> **through:** *The thought of someone suffering through a mistake of mine makes me shiver.*
> **by:** *The all-female yacht crew made history by becoming the first to sail round the world.*

vi|able /vaɪəbəl/ ADJ Something that is **viable** is capable of doing what it is intended to do. ❑ *Cash alone will not make Eastern Europe's banks viable.* • **vi|abil|ity** /vaɪəbɪlɪti/ N-UNCOUNT ❑ *...the shaky financial viability of the nuclear industry.*

via|duct /vaɪədʌkt/ (**viaducts**) N-COUNT A **viaduct** is a long, high bridge that carries a road or a railroad across a valley.

Vi|ag|ra /vaɪægrə/ N-UNCOUNT **Viagra** is a drug that is given to men to help them to have sexual intercourse. [TRADEMARK]

vial /vaɪəl/ (**vials**) N-COUNT A **vial** is a very small bottle that is used to hold something such as perfume or medicine. [FORMAL]

vibe /vaɪb/ (**vibes**) N-COUNT **Vibes** are the good or bad atmosphere that you sense with a person or in a place. [INFORMAL] ❑ *Sorry, Chris, but I have bad vibes about this guy.*

vi|brant /vaɪbrənt/ **1** ADJ Someone or something that is **vibrant** is full of life, energy, and enthusiasm. ❑ *Tom felt himself being drawn toward her vibrant personality.* ❑ *...Shakespeare's vibrant language.* • **vi|bran|cy** /vaɪbrənsi/ N-UNCOUNT ❑ *She was a woman with extraordinary vibrancy and extraordinary knowledge.* **2** ADJ **Vibrant** colors are very bright and clear. ❑ *Horizon blue, corn yellow and pistachio green are just three of the vibrant colors in this range.* • **vi|brant|ly** ADV [ADV adj] ❑ *...a selection of vibrantly colored French cast-iron saucepans.*

vi|bra|phone /vaɪbrəfoʊn/ (**vibraphones**) N-COUNT A **vibraphone** is an electronic musical instrument that consists of a set of metal bars in a frame. When you hit the bars, they produce ringing notes that last for some time.

vi|brate /vaɪbreɪt/ (**vibrates, vibrating, vibrated**) V-T/V-I If something **vibrates** or if you **vibrate** it, it shakes with repeated small, quick movements. ❑ *The ground shook and the cliffs seemed to vibrate.* • **vi|bra|tion** /vaɪbreɪʃən/ (**vibrations**) N-VAR ❑ *The vibrations of the vehicles rattled the store windows.*

vi|bra|to /vɪbrɑːtoʊ/ (**vibratos**) N-VAR **Vibrato** is a rapidly repeated slight change in the pitch of a musical note. Singers and musicians use vibrato to make the music sound more emotional. ❑ *I encourage oboe and clarinet players to use plenty of vibrato.*

vi|bra|tor /vaɪbreɪtər/ (**vibrators**) N-COUNT A **vibrator** is an electric device that vibrates. It is used in massage to reduce pain, or to give sexual pleasure.

vic|ar /vɪkər/ (**vicars**) N-COUNT; N-VOC A **vicar** is a priest who is in charge of a chapel that is associated with a parish church in the Episcopal Church in the United States. [AM]

vi|cari|ous /vaɪkɛəriəs/ ADJ [ADJ n] A **vicarious** pleasure or feeling is experienced by watching, listening to, or reading about other people doing something, rather than by doing it yourself. ❑ *She invents fantasy lives for her own vicarious pleasure.* • **vi|cari|ous|ly** ADV [usu ADV with v] ❑ *...a father who lived vicariously through his sons' success.*

vice ♦◇◇ /vaɪs/ (**vices**) **1** N-COUNT A **vice** is a habit that is regarded as a weakness in someone's character, but not usually as a serious fault. ❑ *His only vice is to get drunk on champagne after concluding a successful piece of business.* **2** N-UNCOUNT **Vice** refers to criminal activities, especially those connected with pornography or prostitution. ❑ *He said those responsible for offences connected with vice, gaming and drugs should be deported on conviction.* **3** N-COUNT A **vice** is a tool with a pair of parts that hold an object tightly while you do work on it. [BRIT]

> in AM, use **vise**

> **PREFIX**
>
> **vice-**
> is used before a rank or title to indicate that someone is next in importance to the person who holds the rank or title mentioned. *For example, the **vice-president** of a country is a senior political leader who has a position that is immediately below that of the president.*

vice-chancellor (**vice-chancellors**) also **vice chancellor** **1** N-COUNT In an American university, the **vice-chancellor** is the person next in rank below the chancellor, who acts as the chancellor's deputy or substitute. **2** N-COUNT In a British university, the **vice-chancellor** is the person in charge of academic and administrative matters.

vice|roy /vaɪsrɔɪ/ (**viceroys**) N-COUNT In former times, a **viceroy** was the person who ruled a colony on behalf of the king, queen, or government.

vice squad (**vice squads**) N-COUNT [usu the N in sing, N n] The **vice squad** is the section of a police force that deals with crime relating to pornography, prostitution, and gambling. ❑ *...ten vice-squad officers.*

vice ver|sa /vaɪsə vɜrsə, vaɪs/ PHRASE **Vice versa** is used to indicate that the reverse of what you have said is true. For example, 'people can perform some tasks better than machines can and vice versa' means that machines can perform some tasks better than people can. ❏ *They want to send students from low-income homes into more affluent neighborhoods and vice versa.*

vi|cin|ity /vɪsɪnɪti/ N-SING If something is **in the vicinity** of a particular place, it is near it. [FORMAL] ❏ *There were a hundred or so hotels in the vicinity of the station.*

vi|cious /vɪʃəs/ **1** ADJ A **vicious** person or a **vicious** blow is violent and cruel. ❏ *He was a cruel and vicious man.* ❏ *He suffered a vicious attack by a gang of White youths.* • **vi|cious|ly** ADV ❏ *She had been viciously attacked with a hammer.* • **vi|cious|ness** N-UNCOUNT ❏ *...the intensity and viciousness of these attacks.* **2** ADJ A **vicious** remark is cruel and intended to upset someone. ❏ *It is a deliberate, nasty and vicious attack on a young man's character.* • **vi|cious|ly** ADV [ADV with v] ❏ *"He deserved to die," said Penelope viciously.*

vi|cious cir|cle (vicious circles) also **vicious cycle** N-COUNT A **vicious circle** is a problem or difficult situation that has the effect of creating new problems that then cause the original problem or situation to occur again. ❏ *The more pesticides are used, the more resistant the insects become so the more pesticides have to be used. It's a vicious circle.*

vi|cis|si|tudes /vɪsɪsɪtudz/ N-PLURAL [oft N of n] You use **vicissitudes** to refer to changes, especially unpleasant ones, that happen to someone or something at different times in their life or development. [FORMAL] ❏ *Whatever the vicissitudes of her past life, Jill now seems to have come through.*

vic|tim ♦♦◊ /vɪktəm/ (victims) **1** N-COUNT A **victim** is someone who has been hurt or killed. ❏ *Statistically our chances of being the victims of violent crime are remote.* **2** N-COUNT A **victim** is someone who has suffered as a result of someone else's actions or beliefs, or as a result of unpleasant circumstances. ❏ *He was a victim of racial prejudice.* ❏ *He described himself and Altman as victims rather than participants in the scandal.* **3** → See feature box at **legal**

vic|tim|ize ♦◊◊ /vɪktəmaɪz/ (victimizes, victimizing, victimized)

in BRIT, also use **victimise**

V-T If someone **is victimized**, they are deliberately treated unfairly. ❏ *He felt the students had been victimized because they'd voiced opposition to the government.* • **vic|timi|za|tion** /vɪktəmɪzeɪʃən/ N-UNCOUNT ❏ *...society's cruel victimization of many women.*

vic|tim|less /vɪktəmlɪs/ ADJ [usu ADJ n] A **victimless** crime is a crime that is considered to be less serious than other crimes because nobody suffers directly as a result of it. [JOURNALISM] ❏ *...the so-called victimless crime of prostitution.*

vic|tim sup|port N-UNCOUNT **Victim support** is the giving of help and advice to people who are victims of crime. ❏ *When the attack took place, there were no victim support programs.*

vic|tor /vɪktər/ (victors) N-COUNT The **victor** in a battle or contest is the person who wins. [LITERARY] ❏ *Oliver Townsend and co-driver Kirk Lee eventually emerged as victors after five different cars had led the event.*

Vic|to|rian /vɪktɔriən/ (Victorians) **1** ADJ **Victorian** means belonging to, connected with, or typical of Britain in the middle and last parts of the 19th century, when Victoria was Queen. ❏ *We have a lovely old Victorian house.* ❏ *...a Victorian-style family portrait.* **2** ADJ You can use **Victorian** to describe people who have old-fashioned attitudes, especially about good behavior and morals. ❏ *Victorian values are much misunderstood.* **3** N-COUNT The **Victorians** were the British people who lived in the time of Queen Victoria. ❏ *The Victorians were the last people to invest properly in the railways.*

Vic|to|ri|ana /vɪktɔriænə, -ɑnə/ N-UNCOUNT **Interesting** or valuable objects made in the time of Queen Victoria are sometimes referred to as **Victoriana**.

vic|to|ri|ous /vɪktɔriəs/ ADJ You use **victorious** to describe someone who has won a victory in a struggle, war, or competition. ❏ *In 1978 he played for the victorious Argentinian side in the World Cup.*

vic|to|ry ♦♦◊ /vɪktəri, vɪktri/ (victories) **1** N-VAR A **victory** is a success in a struggle, war, or competition. ❏ *Union leaders are heading for victory in their battle over workplace rights.* **2** PHRASE If you say that someone has won a **moral victory**, you mean that although they have officially lost a contest or dispute, they have succeeded in showing they are right about something. ❏ *She said her party had won a moral victory.* **3** → See feature box at **competition, conflict**

video ♦♦◊ /vɪdioʊ/ (videos, videoing, videoed) **1** N-COUNT A **video** is a movie or television program recorded digitally (or in the past on tape) for people to watch on a television set. ❏ *...sports and exercise videos.* **2** N-UNCOUNT **Video** is the system of recording movies and events digitally (or in the past on tape). ❏ *She has watched the race on video.* ❏ *...manufacturers of audio and video equipment.* **3** N-COUNT A **video** is a machine that you can use to record television programs and play videotapes on a television set. [mainly BRIT]

in AM, usually use **VCR**

4 V-T If you **video** a television program or event, you record it digitally or (in the past) on tape, so that you can watch it later. [mainly BRIT]

in AM, usually use **tape**

video ar|cade (video arcades) N-COUNT A **video arcade** is a place where you can play video games on machines which work when you put money in them. ❏ *Many are concerned about the violent content of some computer games, especially those seen in video arcades.*

video cam|era (video cameras) N-COUNT A **video camera** is a camera that you use to record something that is happening so that you can watch it later.

video-con|fer|ence (video-conferences) also **videoconference** N-COUNT A **video-conference** is a meeting that takes place using video conferencing. [BUSINESS] ❏ *It is now possible to hold a video conference in real time on a cellphone.*

video con|fer|enc|ing /vɪdioʊ kɒnfrənsɪŋ/ also **video-conferencing, videoconferencing** N-UNCOUNT **Video conferencing** is a system that enables people in various places around the world to have a meeting by seeing and hearing each other on a screen. [BUSINESS] ❏ *We also hope to use video conferencing to train and supervise staff.*

video dia|ry (video diaries) N-COUNT A **video diary** is a movie that someone makes of the things that happen to them over a period of time, recorded using a video camera.

video game (video games) N-COUNT A **video game** is an electronic or computerized game that you play on your television or on a computer screen.

video re|cord|er (video recorders) N-COUNT A **video recorder** or a **video cassette recorder** is the same as a **VCR**.

video|tape /vɪdioʊteɪp/ (videotapes) also **video tape** **1** N-UNCOUNT **Videotape** is magnetic tape that is used to record moving pictures and sounds to be shown on television. ❏ *...the use of videotape in criminal court rooms.* **2** N-COUNT A **videotape** is the same as a **video cassette**.

vie /vaɪ/ (vies, vying, vied) V-RECIP If one person or thing **is vying** with another for something, the people or things are competing for it. [FORMAL] ❏ *California is vying with other states to capture a piece of the growing communications market.* ❏ *The two are vying for the support of New York voters.*

view ♦♦♦ /vyu/ (views, viewing, viewed) **1** N-COUNT Your **views on** something are the beliefs or opinions that you have about it, for example, whether you think it is good, bad, right, or wrong. ❏ *Chris and I usually have similar views on politics and bureaucracy.* ❏ *You should also make your views known to your congressperson.* **2** N-SING Your **view** of a particular subject is the way that you understand and think about it. ❏ *The whole point was to get away from just one specific view of religion.* **3** V-T If you **view** something in a particular way, you think of it in that way. ❏ *First-generation Americans view the United States as a land of golden opportunity.* ❏ *Abigail's mother Linda views her daughter's talent with a mixture of pride and worry.* **4** N-COUNT The **view** from a window or high place is everything that can be seen from that place, especially when it is considered to be beautiful. ❏ *The view from our window was one of beautiful green countryside.* **5** N-SING If you have a **view** of something, you can see it. ❑ *He stood up to get a better view of the blackboard.* **◨** N-UNCOUNT You use **view** in expressions to do with being able to see something. For example, if something is **in view**, you can see it. If something is **in full view of everyone**, everyone can see it. ❑ *She was lying there in full view of anyone who walked by.* **◨** V-T If you **view** something, you look at it for a particular purpose. [FORMAL] ❑ *They came back to view the house again.* **◨** V-T If you **view** a television program, video, or movie, you watch it. [FORMAL] ❑ *We have viewed the video recording of the incident.* **◨** N-SING **View** refers to the way in which a piece of text or graphics is displayed on a computer screen. [COMPUTING] ❑ *To see the current document in full-page view, click the Page Zoom Full button.* **◰** PHRASE You use **in my view** when you want to indicate that you are stating a personal opinion, that other people might not agree with. ❑ *In my view things won't change.* **◱** PHRASE You use **in view of** when you are taking into consideration facts that have just been mentioned or are just about to be mentioned. ❑ *In view of the fact that Hobson was not a trained economist his achievements were remarkable.* **◲** PHRASE If something such as a work of art is **on view**, it is shown in public for people to look at. ❑ *A significant exhibition of contemporary sculpture will be on view at the Portland Gallery.* **◳** PHRASE If you do something **with a view to** doing something else, you do it because you hope it will result in that other thing being done. ❑ *He has called a meeting of all parties tomorrow, with a view to forming a national reconciliation government.*

view|er /vyu̱ər/ (**viewers**) **◨** N-COUNT **Viewers** are people who watch television, or who are watching a particular program on television. ❑ *These programs are each watched by around 19 million viewers every week.* **◨** N-COUNT A **viewer** is someone who is looking carefully at a picture or other interesting object. ❑ *...the relationship between the art object and the viewer.*

view|finder /vyu̱faɪndər/ (**viewfinders**) N-COUNT A **viewfinder** is a small square of glass in a camera that you look through in order to see what you are going to photograph.

view|point /vyu̱pɔɪnt/ (**viewpoints**) **◨** N-COUNT Someone's **viewpoint** is the way that they think about things in general, or the way they think about a particular thing. ❑ *The novel is shown from the girl's viewpoint.* **◨** N-COUNT A **viewpoint** is a place from which you can get a good view of something. ❑ *You have to know where to stand for a good viewpoint.*

vig|il /vɪ̱dʒɪl/ (**vigils**) N-COUNT A **vigil** is a period of time when people remain quietly in a place, especially at night, for example, because they are praying or are making a political protest. ❑ *Protesters are holding a twenty-four-hour vigil outside the socialist party headquarters.* • PHRASE If someone **keeps a vigil** or **keeps vigil** somewhere, they remain there quietly for a period of time, especially at night, for example, because they are praying or are making a political protest.

vigi|lant /vɪ̱dʒɪlənt/ ADJ Someone who is **vigilant** gives careful attention to a particular problem or situation and concentrates on noticing any danger or trouble that there might be. ❑ *He warned the public to be vigilant and report anything suspicious.* • **vigi|lance** N-UNCOUNT ❑ *Constant vigilance is needed to combat this evil.*

vigi|lan|te /vɪ̱dʒɪlænti/ (**vigilantes**) N-COUNT **Vigilantes** are people who organize themselves into an unofficial group to protect their community and to catch and punish criminals. ❑ *The vigilantes dragged the men out.*

vi|gnette /vɪnye̱t/ (**vignettes**) N-COUNT [oft N *of* n] A **vignette** is a short description, picture, or piece of acting that expresses very clearly and neatly the typical characteristics of the thing that it represents. [FORMAL] ❑ *The book is an excellent vignette of some of the major debates in science.*

vig|or /vɪ̱gər/

in BRIT, use **vigour**

N-UNCOUNT **Vigor** is physical or mental energy and enthusiasm. ❑ *He has approached his job with renewed vigor.*

vig|or|ous /vɪ̱gərəs/ **◨** ADJ **Vigorous** physical activities involve using a lot of energy, usually to do short and repeated actions. ❑ *Very vigorous exercise can increase the risk of heart attacks.* • **vig|or|ous|ly** ADV [ADV after v] ❑ *He shook his head vigorously.* **◨** ADJ A **vigorous** person does things with great energy and enthusiasm. A **vigorous** campaign or activity is done with great energy and enthusiasm. ❑ *She was a strong and vigorous politician.* • **vig|or|ous|ly** ADV [ADV with v] ❑ *The police vigorously denied that excessive force had been used.*

vig|our /vɪ̱gər/ [mainly BRIT] → see **vigor**

Vi|king /va̱ɪkɪŋ/ (**Vikings**) N-COUNT The **Vikings** were people who sailed from Scandinavia and attacked villages in most parts of northwestern Europe from the 8th to the 11th centuries.

vile /va̱ɪl/ (**viler**, **vilest**) ADJ If you say that someone or something is **vile**, you mean that they are very unpleasant. ❑ *The weather was consistently vile.*

vili|fy /vɪ̱lɪfaɪ/ (**vilifies**, **vilifying**, **vilified**) V-T If you **are vilified** by someone, they say or write very unpleasant things about you, so that people will have a low opinion of you. [FORMAL] ❑ *The agency has been vilified by some doctors for being unnecessarily slow to approve life-saving drugs.* ❑ *He was vilified, hounded, and forced into exile by the FBI.* • **vili|fi|ca|tion** /vɪ̱lɪfɪkeɪʃən/ N-UNCOUNT ❑ *Conchita did not deserve the vilification she had been subjected to.*

vil|la /vɪ̱lə/ (**villas**) **◨** N-COUNT A **villa** is a fairly large house, especially one in a hot country or a resort. ❑ *He lives in a secluded five-bedroom luxury villa.* **◨** → See also color supplement

vil|lage ✦✦◇ /vɪ̱lɪdʒ/ (**villages**) N-COUNT A **village** consists of a group of houses, together with other buildings such as a church and a school, in a country area. ❑ *He lives quietly in the country in a village near Lahti.*

vil|lag|er /vɪ̱lɪdʒər/ (**villagers**) N-COUNT [usu pl] You refer to the people who live in a village, especially the people who have lived there for most or all of their lives, as the **villagers**. ❑ *Soon the villagers couldn't afford to buy food for themselves.*

vil|lain /vɪ̱lən/ (**villains**) **◨** N-COUNT A **villain** is someone who deliberately harms other people or breaks the law in order to get what he or she wants. ❑ *I left the room, feeling like a villain and a murderer.* **◨** N-COUNT The **villain** in a novel, movie, or play is the main bad character. ❑ *He also played a villain opposite Sylvester Stallone in Demolition Man (1992).*

vil|lain|ous /vɪ̱lənəs/ ADJ [usu ADJ n] A **villainous** person is very bad and willing to harm other people or break the law in order to get what he or she wants. ❑ *He was branded by the press as "villainous" and "diabolical."*

vil|lainy /vɪ̱ləni/ N-UNCOUNT **Villainy** is very bad or criminal behavior. [FORMAL] ❑ *They justify villainy in the name of high ideals.*

vinai|grette /vɪnɪgre̱t/ (**vinaigrettes**) N-MASS **Vinaigrette** is a dressing made by mixing oil, vinegar, salt, pepper, and herbs, that is put on salad.

vin|di|cate /vɪ̱ndɪkeɪt/ (**vindicates**, **vindicating**, **vindicated**) V-T If a person or their decisions, actions, or ideas are **vindicated**, they are proved to be correct, after people have said that they were wrong. [FORMAL] ❑ *The director said he had been vindicated by the experts' report.* • **vin|di|ca|tion** /vɪ̱ndɪkeɪʃən/ N-UNCOUNT [also a N, usu N *of* n] ❑ *He called the success a vindication of his party's free-market economic policy.*

vin|dic|tive /vɪndɪ̱ktɪv/ ADJ If you say that someone is **vindictive**, you are critical of them because they deliberately try to upset or cause trouble for someone who they think has done them harm. [DISAPPROVAL] ❑ *...a vindictive woman desperate for revenge against the man who loved and left her.* • **vin|dic|tive|ness** N-UNCOUNT ❑ *...a dishonest person who is operating completely out of vindictiveness.*

vine /va̱ɪn/ (**vines**) N-VAR A **vine** is a plant that grows up or over things, especially one that produces grapes. ❑ *Every square meter of soil was used, mainly for olives, vines, and almonds.*

vin|egar /vɪ̱nɪgər/ (**vinegars**) N-MASS **Vinegar** is a sharp-tasting liquid, usually made from sour wine or malt, that is used in cooking to make things such as salad dressing.

vin|egary /vɪ̱nɪgəri/ ADJ If something has a **vinegary** taste or smell, it tastes or smells of vinegar. ❑ *The salads taste too vinegary.*

vine|yard /vɪ̱nyərd/ (**vineyards**) N-COUNT A **vineyard** is an area of land where grape vines are grown in order to produce wine. You can also use **vineyard** to refer to the set of buildings in which the wine is produced.

vin|tage /vɪ̱ntɪdʒ/ (**vintages**) **◨** N-COUNT The **vintage** of a good quality wine is the year and place that it was made before being stored to improve it. You can also use **vintage** to refer to the wine that was made in a certain year. ❑ *This wine is from one of the two best vintages of the decade in this region.* **2** ADJ [ADJ n] **Vintage** wine is good quality wine that has been stored for several years in order to improve its quality. ❑ *If you can buy only one case at auction, it should be vintage port.* **3** ADJ [ADJ n] **Vintage** cars or airplanes are old but are admired because they are considered to be the best of their kind. ❑ *The museum will have a permanent exhibition of 60 vintage and racing cars.* **4** ADJ **Vintage** clothing and furniture is old or secondhand, but usually of good quality. ❑ *...collectors of vintage clothing.* **5** → See feature box at **upcycle**

vint|ner /vɪntnər/ (**vintners**) **1** N-COUNT A **vintner** is someone whose job is to buy and sell wine. [FORMAL] **2** N-COUNT A **vintner** is someone who grows grapes and makes wine. [FORMAL]

vi|nyl /vaɪnɪl/ (**vinyls**) **1** N-MASS **Vinyl** is a strong plastic used for making things such as floor coverings and furniture. ❑ *...a modern vinyl floor covering.* **2** N-UNCOUNT You can use **vinyl** to refer to records, especially in contrast to compact discs. ❑ *This compilation was first issued on vinyl in 1984.*

viol /vaɪəl/ (**viols**) N-VAR [oft the N] **Viols** are a family of musical instruments that are made of wood and have six strings. You play the viol with a bow while sitting down.

vio|la /vioʊlə/ (**violas**) N-VAR A **viola** is a musical instrument with four strings that is played with a bow. It is like a violin, but is slightly larger and can play lower notes. ❑ *She also played the viola in some amateur orchestras.*

vio|late ✦✧✧ /vaɪəleɪt/ (**violates, violating, violated**) **1** V-T If someone **violates** an agreement, law, or promise, they break it. [FORMAL] ❑ *They went to prison because they violated the law.* • **vio|la|tion** /vaɪəleɪʃən/ (**violations**) N-VAR ❑ *To deprive the boy of his education is a violation of state law.* **2** V-T If you **violate** someone's privacy or peace, you disturb it. [FORMAL] ❑ *These men were violating her family's privacy.* **3** V-T If someone **violates** a special place such as a grave, they damage it or treat it with disrespect. ❑ *Detectives are still searching for those who violated the graveyard.* • **vio|la|tion** N-UNCOUNT ❑ *The violation of the graves is not the first such incident.*

SYNONYMS

violate
VERB **1**
break: *We didn't know we were breaking the law.*
infringe: *The jury ruled that he had infringed no rules.*
disobey: *He urged the soldiers to disobey orders if asked to fire on civilian targets.*
breach: *The newspaper breached the code of conduct on privacy.*
contravene: *He said the article did not contravene the industry's code of conduct.*

vio|lence ✦✦✧ /vaɪələns/ **1** N-UNCOUNT **Violence** is behavior that is intended to hurt, injure, or kill people. ❑ *Twenty people were killed in the violence.* ❑ *...domestic violence between husband and wife.* **2** N-UNCOUNT If you do or say something with **violence**, you use a lot of force and energy in doing or saying it, often because you are angry. [LITERARY] ❑ *The violence in her tone gave Tyler a shock.*

SYNONYMS

violence
NOUN **1**
brutality: *Her experience of men was of domination and brutality.*
savagery: *...the sheer savagery of war.*
terrorism: *They were accused of terrorism.*
force: *He used brute force to take control.*

vio|lent ✦✦✧ /vaɪələnt/ **1** ADJ If someone is **violent**, or if they do something that is **violent**, they use physical force or weapons to hurt, injure, or kill other people. ❑ *A quarter of current inmates have committed violent crimes.* ❑ *...violent anti government demonstrations.* • **vio|lent|ly** ADV [ADV with v] ❑ *Some opposition activists have been violently attacked.* **2** ADJ A **violent** event happens suddenly and with great force. ❑ *A violent impact hurtled her forward.* • **vio|lent|ly** ADV [ADV with v] ❑ *A nearby volcano erupted violently, sending out a hail of molten rock and boiling mud.* **3** ADJ If you describe something as **violent**, you mean that it is said, done, or felt very strongly. ❑ *Violent opposition to the plan continues.* ❑ *He had violent stomach pains.* • **vio|lent|ly** ADV ❑ *He was violently scolded.* **4** ADJ A **violent** death is painful and unexpected, usually because the person who dies has been murdered. ❑ *...an innocent man who had met a violent death.* • **vio|lent|ly** ADV [ADV with v] ❑ *...a girl who had died violently nine years earlier.* **5** ADJ A **violent** movie or television program contains a lot of scenes that show violence. ❑ *It was the most violent movie that I have ever seen.* **6** → See feature box at **crime**

SYNONYMS

violent
ADJ
1
bloodthirsty: *They were savage and bloodthirsty.*
brutal: *He was the victim of a very brutal murder.*
vicious: *He suffered a vicious attack by a gang of White youths.*
savage: *This was a savage attack on a defenseless young girl.*
aggressive: *Some children are much more aggressive than others.*
2
devastating: *The city of Ormac took the full force of the winds and devastating floods.*
raging: *The field trip involved crossing a raging torrent.*
wild: *The wild weather did not deter some people from swimming in the sea.*

vio|let /vaɪəlɪt/ (**violets**) **1** N-COUNT A **violet** is a small plant that has purple or white flowers in the spring. **2** COLOR Something that is **violet** is a bluish-purple color. ❑ *The light was beginning to drain from a violet sky.* **3** PHRASE If you say that someone is no **shrinking violet**, you mean that they are not at all shy. ❑ *When it comes to expressing himself he is no shrinking violet.*

vio|lin /vaɪəlɪn/ (**violins**) N-VAR A **violin** is a musical instrument. Violins are made of wood and have four strings. You play the violin by holding it under your chin and moving a bow across the strings. ❑ *Lizzie used to play the violin.*

vio|lin|ist /vaɪəlɪnɪst/ (**violinists**) N-COUNT A **violinist** is someone who plays the violin. ❑ *Rose's father was a talented violinist.*

VIP /viː aɪ piː/ (**VIPs**) N-COUNT A **VIP** is someone who is given better treatment than ordinary people because they are famous, influential, or important. **VIP** is an abbreviation for 'very important person.' ❑ *At another bar, there is a seated area for VIPs..*

vi|per /vaɪpər/ (**vipers**) N-COUNT A **viper** is a small poisonous snake found mainly in Europe.

vi|ral /vaɪrəl/ **1** ADJ A **viral** disease or infection is caused by a virus. ❑ *...a 65-year-old patient suffering from severe viral pneumonia.* **2** PHRASE If a video, image, or story **goes viral**, it spreads quickly and widely on the internet through social media and email. ❑ *Their amazing video of the project has now gone viral with millions of views.* **3** → See feature box at **illness**

vi|ral load (**viral loads**) N-COUNT The **viral load** of someone who is infected with a disease is the amount of virus they carry. ❑ *Within two days, you see a huge decline in viral load.*

vi|ral mar|ket|ing N-UNCOUNT **Viral marketing** is a method of marketing in which people are encouraged to share information about a company's products on the Internet. ❑ *The company opted for viral marketing instead of expensive branding.* ❑ *...a viral marketing campaign.*

vir|gin /vɜrdʒɪn/ (**virgins**) **1** N-COUNT A **virgin** is someone who has never had sex. ❑ *I was a virgin until I was thirty years old.* **2** ADJ You use **virgin** to describe something such as land that has never been used or spoiled. ❑ *Within 40 years there will be no virgin forest left.* **3** PHRASE If you say that a situation is **virgin territory**, you mean that you have no experience of it and it is completely new for you. ❑ *The World Cup is virgin territory for Ecuador.* **4** N-COUNT You can use **virgin** to describe someone who has never done or used a particular thing before. ❑ *Until he appeared in "In the Line of Fire" Malkovich had been an action-movie virgin.*

vir|gin|al /vɜrdʒɪnᵊl/ **1** ADJ If you describe someone as **virginal**, you mean that they look young and innocent, as if they have had no experience of sex. ❑ *Somehow she'd always been a child in his mind, pure and virginal.* **2** ADJ Something that is

virginal looks new and clean, as if it has not been used or spoiled. ❑ ...abandoning worn-out land to cultivate virginal pasture.

vir|gin|ity /vərdʒɪnɪti/ N-UNCOUNT **Virginity** is the state of never having had sex. ❑ Some girls want to give up their virginity just to be rebellious. • PHRASE When you **lose** your **virginity**, you have sex for the first time. ❑ She lost her virginity when she was 20.

Vir|go /vɜrgoʊ/ (**Virgos**) **1** N-UNCOUNT **Virgo** is one of the twelve signs of the zodiac. Its symbol is a young woman. People who are born approximately between the 23rd of August and the 22nd of September come under this sign. **2** N-COUNT A **Virgo** is a person whose sign of the zodiac is Virgo.

vir|ile /vɪrᵊl/ ADJ If you describe a man as **virile**, you mean that he has the qualities that a man is traditionally expected to have, such as strength and sexual energy. ❑ He wanted his sons to become strong, virile, and athletic like himself. • **vi|ril|ity** /vɪrɪlɪti/ N-UNCOUNT ❑ Children are also considered proof of a man's virility.

vir|tual /vɜrtʃuəl/ **1** ADJ [ADJ n] You can use **virtual** to indicate that something is so nearly true that for most purposes it can be regarded as true. ❑ Argentina came to a virtual standstill while the game was being played. **2** ADJ [ADJ n] **Virtual** objects and activities are generated by a computer to simulate real objects and activities. [COMPUTING] ❑ Up to four players can compete in a virtual world of role playing. • **vir|tu|al|ity** /vɜrtʃuælɪti/ N-UNCOUNT ❑ People speculate about virtuality systems, but we're already working on it. **3** → See feature box at **learning**

vir|tual as|sis|tant (**virtual assistants**) **1** N-COUNT A **virtual assistant** is a wireless electronic device that can respond to spoken commands, for example by giving information. [COMPUTING] ❑ The voice-controlled virtual assistant makes searching easier. **2** N-COUNT A **virtual assistant** is someone who works for another person or a company as an assistant, from their own house or from a separate office using the internet. ❑ Many small business entrepreneurs use virtual assistants who offer secretarial services remotely.

vir|tu|al|ly ♦◇◇ /vɜrtʃuəli/ ADV [ADV with group] You can use **virtually** to indicate that something is so nearly true that for most purposes it can be regarded as true. ❑ Virtually all cooking was done over coal-fired ranges.

SYNONYMS

virtually
ADV
practically: He'd known the old man practically all his life.
almost: He was almost as tall as Pete, but skinnier.
nearly: Several times Thorne nearly fell.

---

vir|tual memo|ry N-UNCOUNT **Virtual memory** is a computing technique in which you increase the size of a computer's memory by arranging or storing the data in it in a different way. [COMPUTING]

vir|tual re|al|ity N-UNCOUNT **Virtual reality** is an environment that is produced by a computer and seems very like reality to the person experiencing it. [COMPUTING] ❑ One day virtual reality will revolutionize the entertainment industry.

vir|tual stor|age N-UNCOUNT **Virtual storage** is the same as **virtual memory**. [COMPUTING]

vir|tue /vɜrtʃu/ (**virtues**) **1** N-UNCOUNT **Virtue** is thinking and doing what is right and avoiding what is wrong. ❑ Virtue is not confined to those who follow a faith. **2** N-COUNT A **virtue** is a good quality or way of behaving. ❑ His virtue is patience. **3** N-COUNT The **virtue** of something is an advantage or benefit that it has, especially in comparison with something else. ❑ There was no virtue in returning to Calvi the way I had come. **4** PHRASE You use **by virtue of** to explain why something happens or is true. [FORMAL] ❑ The article stuck in my mind by virtue of one detail.

vir|tu|os|ity /vɜrtʃuɒsɪti/ N-UNCOUNT [oft with poss] The **virtuosity** of someone such as an artist or athlete is their great skill. ❑ At that time, his virtuosity on the trumpet had no parallel in jazz.

vir|tuo|so /vɜrtʃuoʊsoʊ/ (**virtuosos** or **virtuosi** /vɜrtʃuoʊsi/) **1** N-COUNT A **virtuoso** is someone who is extremely good at something, especially at playing a musical instrument. ❑ ...one of the nation's leading violin virtuosos. **2** ADJ [ADJ n] A **virtuoso** performance or display shows great skill. ❑ The game was a triumph; the team gave a virtuoso performance.

vir|tu|ous /vɜrtʃuəs/ **1** ADJ A **virtuous** person behaves in a moral and correct way. ❑ Louis was shown as an intelligent, courageous and virtuous family man. **2** ADJ If you describe someone as **virtuous**, you mean that they have done what they ought to do and feel very pleased with themselves, perhaps too pleased. ❑ I cleaned the apartment, which left me feeling virtuous. • **vir|tu|ous|ly** ADV ❑ "I've already done that," said Ronnie virtuously.

vir|tu|ous cir|cle N-SING If you describe a situation as a **virtuous circle**, you mean that once one good thing starts happening, other good things happen, which cause the first thing to continue happening. ❑ Exercise creates its own virtuous circle. You feel so good you want to continue. ❑ ...a virtuous circle of investment and growth.

viru|lence /vɪryələns/ **1** N-UNCOUNT [oft N of n] **Virulence** is great bitterness and hostility. [FORMAL] ❑ The virulence of the café owner's anger had appalled her. **2** N-UNCOUNT The **virulence** of a disease or poison is its ability to harm or kill people or animals. ❑ Medical authorities were baffled, both as to its causes and its virulence.

viru|lent /vɪryələnt/ **1** ADJ **Virulent** feelings or actions are extremely bitter and hostile. [FORMAL] ❑ Now he faces virulent attacks from the Italian media. • **viru|lent|ly** ADV ❑ The talk was virulently hostile to the leadership. **2** ADJ A **virulent** disease or poison is extremely powerful and dangerous. ❑ A very virulent form of the disease appeared in Belgium.

vi|rus ♦◇◇ /vaɪrəs/ (**viruses**) **1** N-COUNT A **virus** is a kind of germ that can cause disease. ❑ There are many different strains of flu virus. **2** N-COUNT In computer technology, a **virus** is a program that introduces itself into a system, altering or destroying the information stored in the system. [COMPUTING] ❑ Hackers are said to have started a computer virus. **3** → See feature box at **email**

visa /vizə/ (**visas**) N-COUNT A **visa** is an official document, or a stamp put in your passport, that allows you to enter or leave a particular country. ❑ His visitor's visa expired. ❑ ...an exit visa.

vis|age /vɪzɪdʒ/ (**visages**) N-COUNT [oft with poss] Someone's **visage** is their face. [LITERARY] ❑ ...his milky-white innocent visage.

vis-à-vis /vizavi/ PREP You use **vis-à-vis** when you are considering a relationship or comparison between two things or quantities. [FORMAL] ❑ Each currency is given a value vis-à-vis the other currencies.

vis|cera /vɪsərə/ N-PLURAL **Viscera** are the large organs inside the body, such as the heart, liver, and stomach. [MEDICAL]

vis|cer|al /vɪsərəl/ ADJ [usu ADJ n] **Visceral** feelings are feelings that you feel very deeply and find it difficult to control or ignore, and that are not the result of thought. [LITERARY] ❑ ...the sheer visceral joy of being alive.

vis|cose /vɪskoʊs/ N-UNCOUNT [oft N n] **Viscose** is a smooth artificial fabric. ❑ ...a black viscose floral dress.

vis|cos|ity /vɪskɒsɪti/ N-UNCOUNT [oft N of n] **Viscosity** is the quality that some liquids have of being thick and sticky. ❑ ...the viscosity of the paint.

vis|count /vaɪkaʊnt/ (**viscounts**) N-COUNT; N-TITLE A **viscount** is a British nobleman who is below an earl and above a baron in rank. ❑ ...a biography of Viscount Mourne.

vis|count|ess /vaɪkaʊntɪs/ (**viscountesses**) N-COUNT; N-TITLE A **viscountess** is the wife of a viscount or a woman who holds the same position as a viscount.

vis|cous /vɪskəs/ ADJ A **viscous** liquid is thick and sticky. ❑ ...dark, viscous blood.

vise /vaɪs/ (**vises**) **1** N-COUNT A **vise** is a tool with a pair of parts that hold an object tightly while you do work on it. [AM]

in BRIT, use **vice**

2 → See also color supplement

vis|ibil|ity /vɪzɪbɪlɪti/ **1** N-UNCOUNT **Visibility** means how far or how clearly you can see in particular weather conditions. ❑ Visibility was poor. **2** N-UNCOUNT If you refer to the **visibility** of something such as a situation or problem, you mean how much it is seen or noticed by other people. ❑ The plight of the Kurds gained global visibility.

vis|ible /vɪzɪbəl/ **1** ADJ If something is **visible**, it can be seen. ◻ *The warning lights were clearly visible.* **2** ADJ You use **visible** to describe something or someone that people notice or recognize. ◻ *The most visible sign of the intensity of the crisis is unemployment.* • **vis|ibly** /vɪzɪbli/ ADV ◻ *The Russians were visibly wavering.*

SYNONYMS

visible
ADJ **1**
perceptible: *Pasternak gave him a barely perceptible smile.*
noticeable: *It is noticeable that women are often just as competitive as men.*
observable: *Mars is too faint and too low in the sky to be observable.*

---

vi|sion /vɪʒən/ (visions) **1** N-COUNT Your **vision** of a future situation or society is what you imagine or hope it would be like, if things were very different from the way they are now. ◻ *I have a vision of a society that is free of exploitation and injustice.* ◻ *That's my vision of how the world could be.* **2** N-COUNT If you have a **vision** of someone in a particular situation, you imagine them in that situation, for example because you are worried that it might happen, or hope that it will happen. ◻ *He had a vision of Cheryl, slumped on a plastic chair in the waiting room.* **3** N-COUNT A **vision** is the experience of seeing something that other people cannot see, for example in a religious experience or as a result of taking drugs. ◻ *It was on June 24, 1981 that young villagers first reported seeing the Virgin Mary in a vision.* **4** N-UNCOUNT Your **vision** is your ability to see clearly with your eyes. ◻ *It causes blindness or serious loss of vision.* **5** N-COUNT Your **vision** is everything that you can see from a particular place or position. ◻ *Jane blocked Craig's vision and he could see nothing.* **6** → *See feature box at* **eyesight**

SYNONYMS

vision
NOUN **1**
idea: *My idea of physical perfection is to be very slender.*
dream: *My dream is to have a house in the country.*
fantasy: *...fantasies of romance and true love.*

---

vi|sion|ary /vɪʒəneri/ (visionaries) **1** N-COUNT If you refer to someone as a **visionary**, you mean that they have strong, original ideas about how things might be different in the future, especially about how things might be improved. ◻ *An entrepreneur is more than just a risk taker. He is a visionary.* **2** ADJ You use **visionary** to describe the strong, original ideas of a visionary. ◻ *...the visionary architecture of Etienne Boullée.*

vis|it /vɪzɪt/ (visits, visiting, visited) **1** V-T/V-I If you **visit** someone, you go to see them and spend time with them. ◻ *He wanted to visit his brother in Worcester.* ◻ *In the evenings, friends would visit.* • N-COUNT **Visit** is also a noun. ◻ *Helen had recently paid him a visit.* **2** V-T/V-I If you **visit** a place, you go there for a short time. ◻ *He'll be visiting four cities including Cagliari in Sardinia.* ◻ *...a visiting family from Texas.* • N-COUNT **Visit** is also a noun. ◻ *...the pope's visit to Canada.* **3** V-T If you **visit** a website, you look at it. [COMPUTING] ◻ *For details visit our website at www.harpercollins.com.* **4** V-T If you **visit** a professional person such as a doctor or lawyer, you go and see them in order to get professional advice. If they **visit** you, they come to see you in order to give you professional advice. ◻ *If necessary the patient can then visit his doctor for further advice.* • N-COUNT **Visit** is also a noun. ◻ *You may have regular home visits from a neonatal nurse.*
▶ **visit with** PHRASAL VERB If you **visit with** someone, you go to see them and spend time talking with them. [AM] ◻ *I visited with him in San Francisco.*

SYNONYMS

visit
VERB **1**
call on: *Sofia was intending to call on Miss Kitts.*
stop by: *I'll stop by to see Leigh before going home.*
look up: *She looked up some friends of bygone years.*

---

vis|ita|tion /vɪzɪteɪʃən/ (visitations) **1** N-COUNT A **visitation** is an event in which God or another nonhuman being seems to appear to someone or contact them. ◻ *The young people have claimed almost daily visitations from the Virgin Mary.* **2** N-COUNT People sometimes refer humorously to a visit from someone, especially from someone in authority, as a **visitation**. ◻ *They had another visitation from Essex police.* **3** N-UNCOUNT [usu with supp] **Visitation** is the act of officially visiting someone. [FORMAL] ◻ *House-to-house visitation has been carried on, under the regulations of the General Board of Health.*

vis|ita|tion rights N-PLURAL If a parent who is divorced and does not live with their child has **visitation rights**, they officially have the right to spend time with their child. ◻ *He was not given any visitation rights by the divorce court.*

vis|it|ing hours N-PLURAL In an institution such as a hospital or prison, **visiting hours** are the times during which people from outside the institution are officially allowed to visit people who are staying at the institution. ◻ *Visiting hours were over.*

vis|it|ing pro|fes|sor (visiting professors) N-COUNT A **visiting professor** is a professor at a college or university who is invited to teach at another college or university for a short period such as one term or one year. ◻ *In addition, he served as a visiting professor at several American universities.*

visi|tor /vɪzɪtər/ (visitors) N-COUNT A **visitor** is someone who is visiting a person or place. ◻ *The other day we had some visitors from Switzerland.*

vi|sor /vaɪzər/ (visors) **1** N-COUNT A **visor** is a movable part of a helmet that can be pulled down to protect a person's eyes or face. ◻ *He pulled on a battered old crash helmet with a scratched visor.* **2** N-COUNT The **visor** of a cap is the part at the front that sticks out over your eyes. [AM] ◻ *His eyes were shaded by the visor of his cap.*

in BRIT, use **peak**

3 N-COUNT [usu n n] A **visor** is a piece of plastic or other material attached to the top of the windshield inside a car, that can be turned down to protect the driver's eyes from bright sunshine.

vis|ta /vɪstə/ (vistas) N-COUNT A **vista** is a view from a particular place, especially a beautiful view from a high place. [WRITTEN] ◻ *From my bedroom window I looked out on a crowded vista of hills and rooftops.*

vis|ual /vɪʒuəl/ (visuals) **1** ADJ **Visual** means relating to sight, or to things that you can see. ◻ *...the graphic visual depiction of violence.* • **visu|al|ly** ADV ◻ *The colors we see visually affect us.* **2** N-COUNT A **visual** is something such as a picture, diagram, or piece of film that is used to show or explain something. ◻ *Remember you want your visuals to reinforce your message, not detract from what you are saying.* **3** → *See feature box at* **fine art**

vis|ual aid (visual aids) N-COUNT **Visual aids** are things that you can look at, such as a film, model, map, or slides, to help you understand something or to remember information.

visu|al|ize /vɪʒuəlaɪz/ (visualizes, visualizing, visualized)

in BRIT, also use **visualise**

V-T If you **visualize** something, you imagine what it is like by forming a mental picture of it. ◻ *Susan visualized her wedding day and saw herself walking down the aisle on her father's arm.* ◻ *He could not visualize her as old.*

vi|tal /vaɪtəl/ ADJ If you say that something is **vital**, you mean that it is necessary or very important. ◻ *The port is vital to supply relief to millions of drought victims.* ◻ *It is vital that parents give children clear and consistent messages about drugs.* • **vi|tal|ly** ADV ◻ *Lesley's career in the church is vitally important to her.*

vi|tal|ity /vaɪtælɪti/ N-UNCOUNT If you say that someone or something has **vitality**, you mean that they have great energy and liveliness. ◻ *Without continued learning, graduates will lose their intellectual vitality.*

vi|tal signs also **vitals** N-PLURAL A person's **vital signs** or **vitals** are the things such as their pulse, blood pressure, and temperature that show that they are alive. ◻ *A doctor checked her vital signs.* ◻ *...the chart which showed his current vitals.*

vi|tal sta|tis|tics **1** N-PLURAL [usu with poss] The **vital statistics** of a population are statistics such as the number of births, deaths, or marriages that take place in it. **2** N-PLURAL [usu with poss] Someone's **vital statistics**, especially a woman's, are the measurements of their body at certain points, for example, at their chest, waist, and hips. [OLD-FASHIONED, INFORMAL]

vita|min ♦◇◇ /vaɪtəmɪn/ (vitamins) N-COUNT **Vitamins** are substances that you need in order to remain healthy, which are found in food or can be eaten in the form of pills. ☐ *Lack of vitamin D is another factor to consider.*

vi|ti|ate /vɪʃieɪt/ (vitiates, vitiating, vitiated) V-T If something is **vitiated**, its effectiveness is spoiled or weakened. [FORMAL] ☐ *Strategic policy during the War was vitiated because of a sharp division between easterners and westerners.* ☐ *But this does not vitiate his scholarship.*

vit|re|ous /vɪtriəs/ ADJ [usu ADJ n] **Vitreous** means made of glass or resembling glass. [TECHNICAL]

vit|ri|ol /vɪtriəl/ N-UNCOUNT If you refer to what someone says or writes as **vitriol**, you disapprove of it because it is full of bitterness and hate, and so causes a lot of distress and pain. [DISAPPROVAL] ☐ *The vitriol he hurled at members of the press knew no bounds.*

vit|ri|ol|ic /vɪtriɒlɪk/ ADJ [usu ADJ n] If you describe someone's language or behavior as **vitriolic**, you disapprove of it because it is full of bitterness and hate, and so causes a lot of distress and pain. [DISAPPROVAL] ☐ *There was a vicious and vitriolic attack on him in one of the Sunday newspapers two weeks ago.*

vitro /vɪtroʊ/ → see **in vitro**

vi|tu|pera|tion /vaɪtupəreɪʃən/ N-UNCOUNT **Vituperation** is language that is full of hate, anger, or insults. [FORMAL]

vi|tu|pera|tive /vaɪtupərətɪv/ ADJ [ADJ n] **Vituperative** remarks are full of hate, anger, or insults. [FORMAL] ☐ *He is often the victim of vituperative remarks concerning his wealth.* ☐ *...one of journalism's most vituperative critics.*

vi|va|cious /vɪveɪʃəs/ ADJ If you describe someone, usually a woman, as **vivacious**, you mean that they are lively, exciting, and attractive. [WRITTEN, APPROVAL] ☐ *She's beautiful, vivacious, and charming.*

vi|vac|ity /vɪvæsɪti/ N-UNCOUNT If you say that someone has **vivacity**, you mean that they are lively, exciting, and attractive. [WRITTEN, APPROVAL]

viv|id /vɪvɪd/ **1** ADJ If you describe memories and descriptions as **vivid**, you mean that they are very clear and detailed. ☐ *People of my generation who lived through World War II have vivid memories of confusion and incompetence.* • **viv|id|ly** ADV ☐ *I can vividly remember the feeling of panic.* **2** ADJ Something that is **vivid** is very bright in color. ☐ *...a vivid blue sky.* • **viv|id|ly** ADV [ADV -ed/adj] ☐ *...vividly colored birds.*

vivi|sec|tion /vɪvɪsɛkʃən/ N-UNCOUNT **Vivisection** is the practice of using live animals for scientific experiments. ☐ *...a fierce opponent of vivisection.*

vix|en /vɪksən/ (vixens) N-COUNT A **vixen** is a female fox.

viz. viz. is used in written English to introduce a list of specific items or examples. ☐ *The school offers two modules in Teaching English as a Foreign Language, viz. Principles and Methods of Language Teaching and Applied Linguistics.*

vlog /vlɒg/ (vlogs) N-COUNT A **vlog** is a set of videos that someone regularly posts on the internet in which they record their thoughts or experiences or talk about a subject. ☐ *He has his own lifestyle vlog.* • **vlog|ger** (vloggers) N-COUNT ☐ *She is a very popular lifestyle vlogger.* • **vlog|ging** N-UNCOUNT ☐ *He is a YouTube vlogging sensation.*

V-neck (V-necks) N-COUNT [oft N n] A **V-neck** or a **V-neck** sweater is a sweater with a neck that is in the shape of the letter V.

vo|cabu|lary /voʊkæbyəlɛri/ (vocabularies) **1** N-VAR Your **vocabulary** is the total number of words you know in a particular language. ☐ *His speech is immature, his vocabulary limited.* **2** N-SING The **vocabulary** of a language is all the words in it. ☐ *...a new word in the German vocabulary.* **3** N-VAR The **vocabulary** of a subject is the group of words that are typically used when discussing it. ☐ *...the vocabulary of natural science.*

vo|cal /voʊkəl/ **1** ADJ You say that people are **vocal** when they speak forcefully about something that they feel strongly about. ☐ *He has been very vocal in his displeasure over the results.* **2** ADJ [ADJ n] **Vocal** means involving the use of the human voice, especially in singing. ☐ *...a wider range of vocal styles.*

vo|cal cords also **vocal chords** N-PLURAL Your **vocal cords** are the part of your throat that vibrates when you speak.

vo|cal|ist /voʊkəlɪst/ (vocalists) N-COUNT A **vocalist** is a singer who sings with a group. ☐ *He and Carla Torgerson take turns as the band's lead vocalist.*

vo|cal|ize /voʊkəlaɪz/ (vocalizes, vocalizing, vocalized)

in BRIT, also use **vocalise**

1 V-T If you **vocalize** a feeling or an idea, you express it in words. ☐ *Archbishop Hunthausen also vocalized his beliefs that women should be more active in the church.* **2** V-T/V-I When you **vocalize** a sound, you use your voice to make it, especially by singing it. ☐ *In India and Bali students learn to vocalize music before ever picking up instruments.*

vo|cals /voʊkəlz/ N-PLURAL In a pop song, the **vocals** are the singing, in contrast to the playing of instruments. ☐ *Johnson now sings backing vocals for Mica Paris.*

vo|ca|tion /voʊkeɪʃən/ (vocations) **1** N-VAR If you have a **vocation**, you have a strong feeling that you are especially suited to do a particular job or to fulfill a particular role in life, especially one that involves helping other people. ☐ *It could well be that he has a real vocation.* **2** N-VAR If you refer to your job or profession as your **vocation**, you feel that you are particularly suited to it. ☐ *Her vocation is her work as a neurosurgeon.*

vo|ca|tion|al /voʊkeɪʃənəl/ ADJ **Vocational** training and skills are the training and skills needed for a particular job or profession. ☐ *...a course designed to provide vocational training in engineering.*

voca|tive /vɒkətɪv/ (vocatives) N-COUNT A **vocative** is a word such as 'darling' or 'sir' that is used to address someone or attract their attention. [TECHNICAL]

vo|cif|er|ous /voʊsɪfərəs/ ADJ If you describe someone as **vociferous**, you mean that they speak with great energy and determination, because they want their views to be heard. ☐ *He was a vociferous opponent of Conservatism.* • **vo|cif|er|ous|ly** ADV ☐ *He vociferously opposed the state of emergency imposed by the government.*

vod|ka /vɒdkə/ (vodkas) N-MASS **Vodka** is a strong, clear, alcoholic drink.

vogue /voʊg/ **1** N-SING If there is a **vogue** for something, it is very popular and fashionable. ☐ *Despite the vogue for so-called health teas, there is no evidence that they are any healthier.* **2** PHRASE If something is **in vogue**, it is very popular and fashionable. If it comes **into vogue**, it becomes very popular and fashionable. ☐ *Pale colors are much more in vogue than autumnal bronzes and coppers.*

voice ♦♦◇ /vɔɪs/ (voices, voicing, voiced) **1** N-COUNT When someone speaks or sings, you hear their **voice**. ☐ *Miriam's voice was strangely calm.* ☐ *"The police are here," she said in a low voice.* **2** N-COUNT Someone's **voice** is their opinion on a particular topic and what they say about it. ☐ *What does one do when a government simply refuses to listen to the voice of the opposition?* **3** V-T If you **voice** something such as an opinion or an emotion, you say what you think or feel. ☐ *Some scientists have voiced concern that the disease could be passed on to humans.* **4** PHRASE If you **give voice to** an opinion, a need, or a desire, you express it aloud. ☐ *...a community radio run by the Catholic Church that gave voice to the protests of the slum-dwellers.* **5** PHRASE If someone tells you to **keep** your **voice down**, they are asking you to speak more quietly. ☐ *Keep your voice down, for goodness sake.* **6** PHRASE If you **lose** your **voice**, you cannot speak for a while because of an illness. ☐ *I had to be careful not to get a sore throat and lose my voice.* **7** PHRASE If you **raise** your **voice**, you speak more loudly. If you **lower** your **voice**, you speak more quietly. ☐ *He raised his voice for the benefit of the other two women.* **8** PHRASE If you say something **at the top of your voice**, you say it as loudly as possible. [EMPHASIS] ☐ *"Damn!" he yelled at the top of his voice.*

voice box (voice boxes) N-COUNT Your **voice box** is the top part of the tube that leads from your throat to your lungs, that contains your vocal cords.

voiced /vɔɪst/ ADJ A **voiced** speech sound is one that is produced with vibration of the vocal cords. [TECHNICAL]

voice|less /vɔɪslɪs/ ADJ A **voiceless** speech sound is one that is produced without vibration of the vocal cords. [TECHNICAL]

voice mail ▪ N-UNCOUNT **Voice mail** is a system of sending messages over the telephone. Calls are answered by a machine that connects you to the person you want to leave a message for, and they can listen to their messages later. ❑ *He was on a call, so I left a message on his voice mail.* ▪ → See feature box at **telephone**

voice note (**voice notes**) N-COUNT A **voice note** is a reminder or note created by speaking into an electronic device. [COMPUTING] ❑ *I was recording voice notes on my phone as I got ready.*

voice-over (**voice-overs**) also **voiceover** N-COUNT The **voice-over** of a movie, television program, or advertisement consists of words spoken by someone who is not seen. ❑ *89% of advertisements had a male voice-over.*

void /vɔɪd/ (**voids, voiding, voided**) ▪ N-COUNT If you describe a situation or a feeling as a **void**, you mean that it seems empty because there is nothing interesting or worthwhile about it. ❑ *His death has left a void in the entertainment world that can never be filled.* ▪ N-COUNT You can describe a large or frightening space as a **void**. ❑ *He stared into the dark void where the battle had been fought.* ▪ ADJ [v-link ADJ] Something that is **void** or **null and void** is officially considered to have no value or authority. ❑ *The original elections were declared void by the former military ruler.* ▪ ADJ [v-link ADJ of n] If you are **void of** something, you do not have any of it. [FORMAL] ❑ *He rose, his face void of emotion as he walked toward the door.* ▪ V-T To **void** something means to officially say that it is not valid. [FORMAL] ❑ *The Supreme Court threw out the confession and voided his conviction for murder.*

voile /vɔɪl/ N-UNCOUNT [oft N n] **Voile** is thin material that is used for making women's clothing, for example, dresses, blouses, and scarves.

vol. ♦◇◇ (**vols**) **Vol.** is used as a written abbreviation for **volume** when you are referring to one or more books in a series of books.

volatile /vɒlətəl/ ▪ ADJ A situation that is **volatile** is likely to change suddenly and unexpectedly. ❑ *There have been riots before and the situation is volatile.* ▪ ADJ If someone is **volatile**, their mood often changes quickly. ❑ *He accompanied the volatile actress to Hollywood the following year.* ▪ ADJ A **volatile** liquid or substance is one that will quickly change into a gas. [TECHNICAL] ❑ *The blast occurred when volatile chemicals exploded.*

volcanic /vɒlkænɪk/ ADJ **Volcanic** means coming from or created by volcanoes. ❑ *Over 200 people have been killed by volcanic eruptions.*

volcano /vɒlkeɪnoʊ/ (**volcanoes**) N-COUNT A **volcano** is a mountain from which hot melted rock, gas, steam, and ash from inside the earth sometimes burst. ❑ *The volcano erupted last year killing about 600 people.*

vole /voʊl/ (**voles**) N-COUNT A **vole** is a small animal that looks like a mouse but has very small ears and a short tail. Voles usually live in fields or near rivers.

volition /voʊlɪʃən, və-/ ▪ N-UNCOUNT Your **volition** is the power you have to decide something for yourself. [FORMAL] ❑ *We like to think that everything we do and everything we think is a product of our volition.* ▪ PHRASE [PHR after v] If you do something of your **own volition**, you do it because you have decided for yourself that you will do it and not because someone else has told you to do it. [FORMAL] ❑ *Makin said Mr. Coombes had gone to the police of his own volition.*

volley /vɒli/ (**volleys, volleying, volleyed**) ▪ V-T/V-I In sports, if someone **volleys** the ball or if they **volley**, they hit the ball before it touches the ground. ❑ *He volleyed the ball spectacularly into the far corner of the net.* • N-COUNT **Volley** is also a noun. ❑ *She hit most of the winning volleys.* ▪ N-COUNT A **volley** of gunfire is a lot of bullets that travel through the air at the same time. ❑ *It's still not known how many died in the volleys of gunfire.*

volleyball /vɒlibɔl/ N-UNCOUNT **Volleyball** is a game in which two teams hit a large ball with their hands back and forth over a high net. If you allow the ball to touch the ground, the other team wins a point.

volt /voʊlt/ (**volts**) N-COUNT A **volt** is a unit used to measure the force of an electric current.

voltage /voʊltɪdʒ/ (**voltages**) N-VAR The **voltage** of an electrical current is its force measured in volts. ❑ *The systems are getting smaller and using lower voltages.*

volte-face /vɒltfɑs/ (**volte-faces**) N-COUNT [usu sing] If you say that someone's behavior is a **volte-face**, you mean that they have changed their opinion or decision completely, so that it is the opposite of what it was before. [mainly BRIT, FORMAL]

in AM, usually use **about face**

voluble /vɒlyəbəl/ ADJ If you say that someone is **voluble**, you mean that they talk a lot with great energy and enthusiasm. [FORMAL] ❑ *She was voluble with excitement.* • *Bert is a voluble, gregarious man.* • **volubly** /vɒlyəbli/ ADV [ADV with v] ❑ *In the next booth he could see an elderly lady, talking volubly.*

volume ♦♦◇ /vɒlyum/ (**volumes**) ▪ N-COUNT The **volume** of something is the amount of it that there is. ❑ *Senior officials will be discussing how the volume of sales might be reduced.* ▪ N-COUNT The **volume** of an object is the amount of space that it contains or occupies. ❑ *When egg whites are beaten they can rise to seven or eight times their original volume.* ▪ N-COUNT A **volume** is one book in a series of books. ❑ *...the first volume of his autobiography.* ▪ N-COUNT A **volume** is a collection of several issues of a magazine, for example, all the issues for one year. ❑ *...bound volumes of the magazine.* ▪ N-UNCOUNT The **volume** of a radio, television, or sound system is the loudness of the sound it produces. ❑ *He turned down the volume.* ▪ PHRASE If something such as an action **speaks volumes** about a person or thing, it gives you a lot of information about them. ❑ *What you wear speaks volumes about you.*

SYNONYMS

volume
NOUN ▪
amount: *He needs that amount of money to survive.*
quantity: *...a small quantity of water.*
size: *Iraq itself has oil reserves second in size only to Saudi Arabia's.*

voluminous /vəlumɪnəs/ ADJ [usu ADJ n] Something that is **voluminous** is very large or contains a lot of things. [FORMAL] ❑ *The FBI kept a voluminous file on Pablo Picasso.*

voluntary ♦◇◇ /vɒləntɛri/ ▪ ADJ **Voluntary** actions or activities are done because someone chooses to do them and not because they have been forced to do them. ❑ *Attention is drawn to a special voluntary course in Commercial French.* • **voluntarily** /vɒləntɛrɪli/ ADV [ADV with v] ❑ *I would never leave here voluntarily.* ▪ ADJ **Voluntary** work is done by people who are not paid for it, but who do it because they want to do it. ❑ *In her spare time she does voluntary work.* ▪ ADJ [ADJ n] A **voluntary** organization is controlled and organized by the people who have chosen to work for it, often without being paid, rather than receiving help or money from the government. ❑ *Some voluntary organizations run workshops for people with disabilities.*

SYNONYMS

voluntary
ADJ ▪
optional: *A vacation isn't an optional extra. In this stressful, frantic world, it's a must.*
discretionary: *Magistrates were given wider discretionary powers.*

volunteer ♦◇◇ /vɒləntɪər/ (**volunteers, volunteering, volunteered**) ▪ N-COUNT A **volunteer** is someone who does work without being paid for it, because they want to do it. ❑ *She now helps in a local school as a volunteer three days a week.* ▪ N-COUNT A **volunteer** is someone who offers to do a particular task or job without being forced to do it. ❑ *Right. What I want now is two volunteers to come down to the front.* ▪ V-I If you **volunteer** to do something, you offer to do it without being forced to do it. ❑ *Aunt Mary volunteered to clean up the kitchen.* ❑ *He volunteered for the army in 1939.* ▪ V-T If you **volunteer** information, you tell someone something without being asked. [FORMAL] ❑ *The room was quiet, no one volunteered any further information.* ❑ *"They were both great supporters of Franco," Ryle volunteered.* ▪ N-COUNT A **volunteer** is someone who chooses to join the armed forces, especially during a war, as opposed to someone who is forced to join by law. ❑ *They fought as volunteers with the Afghan guerrillas.*

voluptuous /vəlʌptʃuəs/ ADJ If you describe a woman as **voluptuous**, you mean that she has large breasts and hips

vomit ... and is considered attractive in a sexual way. □ ...*a voluptuous, well-rounded lady with glossy black hair.*

vom|it /vɒmɪt/ (vomits, vomiting, vomited) **1** V-T/V-I If you **vomit**, food and drink comes back up from your stomach and out through your mouth. □ *Any product made from cow's milk made him vomit.* □ *She began to vomit blood a few days before she died.* **2** N-UNCOUNT **Vomit** is partly digested food and drink that has come back up from someone's stomach and out through their mouth. □ *Zimmer slipped and nearly fell on a pool of vomit.* **3** → See feature box at **illness**

voo|doo /vuːduː/ N-UNCOUNT **Voodoo** is a form of religion involving magic that is practiced by some people in the West Indies, especially Haiti.

vo|ra|cious /vɔːreɪʃəs/ ADJ If you describe a person, or their appetite for something, as **voracious**, you mean that they want a lot of something. [LITERARY] □ *Joseph Smith was a voracious book collector.* □ *All otters have a voracious appetite.*

vor|tex /vɔːrteks/ (vortexes or vortices /vɔːrtɪsiːz/) **1** N-COUNT A **vortex** is a mass of wind or water that spins around so fast that it pulls objects down into its empty center. □ *The polar vortex is a system of wintertime winds.* **2** N-COUNT [usu sing, with supp] If you refer to a situation as a **vortex**, you mean that you are being forced into it without being able to prevent it. □ *When marriages break down children are swept into the vortex of their parents' embittered emotions.*

vote /voʊt/ (votes, voting, voted) **1** N-COUNT A **vote** is a choice made by a particular person or group in a meeting or an election. □ *He walked to the local polling place to cast his vote.* □ *Mr. Reynolds was re-elected by 102 votes to 60.* **2** N-COUNT A **vote** is an occasion when a group of people make a decision by each person indicating his or her choice. The choice that most people support is accepted by the group. □ *Why do you think we should have a vote on that?* **3** N-SING The **vote** is the total number of votes or voters in an election, or the number of votes received or cast by a particular group. □ *Opposition parties won about fifty-five percent of the vote.* **4** N-SING If you have the **vote** in an election, or have a **vote** in a meeting, you have the legal right to indicate your choice. □ *Before that, women did not have a vote at all.* **5** V-T/V-I When you **vote**, you indicate your choice officially at a meeting or in an election, for example, by raising your hand or writing on a piece of paper. □ *Two-thirds of the national electorate had the chance to vote in these elections.* □ *Nearly two-thirds of this group voted for Buchanan.* □ *The residents of Leningrad voted to restore the city's original name of St. Petersburg.* • **vot|ing** N-UNCOUNT □ *Voting began about two hours ago.* **6** V-T If you **vote** a particular political party or leader, or **vote** yes or no, you make that choice with the vote that you have. □ *52.5% of those questioned said they'd vote Republican.* **7** V-T If people **vote** someone a particular title, they choose that person to have that title. □ *His class voted him the man "who had done the most for Yale."* **8** PHRASE If you **vote with** your **feet**, you show that you do not support something by leaving the place where it is happening or leaving the organization that is supporting it. □ *Thousands of citizens are already voting with their feet, and leaving the country.* **9** PHRASE If you say, for example, '**I vote** that we go' or '**I vote** we stay,' you are suggesting that you should go or stay. [INFORMAL] □ *I vote that we all go to Houston immediately.* **10** PHRASE **One man one vote** or **one person one vote** is a system of voting in which every person in a group or country has the right to cast their vote, and in which each individual's vote is counted and has equal value. □ *Mr. Gould called for a move toward "one man one vote."* **11** → See feature box at **politics**

---SYNONYMS---

vote
NOUN **1**
poll: *Polls show that the European treaty has gained support in Denmark.*
election: *...the first fully-free elections for more than fifty years.*
ballot: *The result of the ballot will not be known for two weeks.*
referendum: *Estonia said it too planned to hold a referendum on independence.*

---

vote of con|fi|dence (votes of confidence) **1** N-COUNT [usu sing] A **vote of confidence** is a vote in which members of a group are asked to indicate that they still support the person or group in power, usually the government. □ *The Indian prime minister, V.P. Singh, lost a vote of confidence in the Indian parliament.* **2** N-COUNT [usu sing] A **vote of confidence** is something that you say or do that shows that you approve of or support a person or a group. □ *The ten-year deal is a vote of confidence in coal-fired power stations.*

vote of no con|fi|dence (votes of no confidence) N-COUNT [usu sing] A **vote of no confidence** is a vote in which members of a group are asked to indicate that they do not support the person or group in power, usually the government. □ *The opposition has called for a vote of no confidence in the government.*

vote of thanks (votes of thanks) N-COUNT A **vote of thanks** is an official speech in which the speaker formally thanks a person for doing something. □ *I would like to propose a vote of thanks to our host.*

vot|er /voʊtər/ (voters) N-COUNT **Voters** are people who have the legal right to vote in elections, or people who are voting in a particular election. □ *The turnout was at least 62 percent of registered voters.*

vouch /vaʊtʃ/ (vouches, vouching, vouched)
▶ **vouch for 1** PHRASAL VERB If you say that you can or will **vouch for** someone, you mean that you can guarantee their good behavior. □ *Kim's mother agreed to vouch for Maria and get her a job.* **2** PHRASAL VERB If you say that you can **vouch for** something, you mean that you have evidence from your own personal experience that it is true or correct. □ *He cannot vouch for the accuracy of the story.*

vouch|er /vaʊtʃər/ (vouchers) N-COUNT A **voucher** is a ticket or piece of paper that can be used instead of money to pay for something. □ *The winners will each receive a voucher for a pair of movie tickets.*

vouch|safe /vaʊtʃseɪf/ (vouchsafes, vouchsafing, vouchsafed) V-T If you **are vouchsafed** something or it **is vouchsafed** to you, you are given or granted it. [FORMAL] □ *As we approached the summit we were vouchsafed a rare vision.* □ *Eric gritted his teeth and vouchsafed them a few more drops of brandy.* □ *"He drives like a madman," was all the information he vouchsafed.*

vow /vaʊ/ (vows, vowing, vowed) **1** V-T If you **vow** to do something, you make a serious promise or decision that you will do it. □ *While many models vow to go back to college, few do.* □ *I solemnly vowed that someday I would return to live in Europe.* **2** N-COUNT A **vow** is a serious promise or decision to do a particular thing. □ *I made a silent vow to be more careful in the future.* **3** N-COUNT **Vows** are a particular set of serious promises, such as the promises two people make when they are getting married. □ *I took my marriage vows and kept them.*

vow|el /vaʊəl/ (vowels) N-COUNT A **vowel** is a sound such as the ones represented in writing by the letters 'a,' 'e,' 'i,' 'o,' or 'u', which you pronounce with your mouth open, allowing the air to flow through it. Compare **consonant**. □ *... words containing the five vowels in order.*

voy|age /vɔɪɪdʒ/ (voyages) N-COUNT A **voyage** is a long journey on a ship or in a spacecraft. □ *He aims to follow Columbus's voyage to the West Indies.*

vo|yeur /vwaɪyɜːr, vɔɪ-/ (voyeurs) **1** N-COUNT A **voyeur** is someone who gets sexual pleasure from secretly watching other people having sex or taking their clothes off. **2** N-COUNT If you describe someone as a **voyeur**, you disapprove of them because you think they enjoy watching other people's suffering or problems. [DISAPPROVAL] □ *The media has made unfeeling voyeurs of all of us.*

vo|yeur|ism /vwaɪyɜːrɪzəm, vɔɪ-, vɔɪɜːrɪzəm/ **1** N-UNCOUNT **Voyeurism** is the practice of getting sexual pleasure by secretly watching other people having sex or taking their clothes off. **2** N-UNCOUNT If you describe someone's behavior as **voyeurism**, you disapprove of them because you think they enjoy watching other people's suffering or problems. [DISAPPROVAL] □ *Many people are disgusted by the voyeurism of live media coverage of the conflict.*

vo|yeur|is|tic /vwaɪyərɪstɪk, vɔɪ-/ **1** ADJ **Voyeuristic** behavior involves getting sexual pleasure from secretly watching other people having sex or taking their clothes off. **2** ADJ If you describe someone's behavior as **voyeuristic**, you disapprove of them because you think they enjoy watching other people's suffering or problems. [DISAPPROVAL] □ *We as a society are growing more commercial and voyeuristic all the time.*

vs. vs. is a written abbreviation for **versus**. ❑ *We were watching the Yankees vs. the Red Sox.*

vul|gar /vʌ́lgər/ **1** ADJ If you describe something as **vulgar**, you think it is in bad taste or of poor artistic quality. [DISAPPROVAL] ❑ *I think it's a very vulgar house.* • **vul|gar|ity** /vʌlgǽrɪti/ N-UNCOUNT ❑ *I hate the vulgarity of the bright colors in this room.* **2** ADJ If you describe pictures, gestures, or remarks as **vulgar**, you dislike them because they refer to sex or parts of the body in an offensive way that you find unpleasant. [DISAPPROVAL] ❑ *The women laughed coarsely at the comedian's vulgar jokes.* • **vul|gar|ity** N-UNCOUNT ❑ *Charles was a complete gentleman, incapable of rudeness or vulgarity.* **3** ADJ If you describe a person or their behavior as **vulgar**, you mean that they lack taste or behave offensively. [DISAPPROVAL] ❑ *He was a vulgar old man, but he never swore in front of a woman.* • **vul|gar|ity** N-UNCOUNT ❑ *It's his vulgarity that I can't take.*

vul|ner|able ♦◇◇ /vʌ́lnərəbəl/ **1** ADJ Someone who is **vulnerable** is weak and without protection, with the result that they are easily hurt physically or emotionally. ❑ *Old people can often be particularly vulnerable members of our society.* • **vul|ner|abil|ity** /vʌlnərəbɪ́lɪti/ (**vulnerabilities**) N-VAR ❑ *David accepts his own vulnerability.* **2** ADJ If a person, animal, or plant is **vulnerable** to a disease, they are more likely to get it than other people, animals, or plants. ❑ *People with high blood pressure are especially vulnerable to diabetes.* • **vul|ner|abil|ity** N-UNCOUNT ❑ *Taking long-term courses of certain medicines may increase vulnerability to infection.* **3** ADJ Something that is **vulnerable** can be easily harmed or affected by something bad. ❑ *Their tanks would be vulnerable to attack from the air.* • **vul|ner|abil|ity** N-UNCOUNT ❑ *...anxieties about the country's vulnerability to invasion.* **4** → See feature box at **poverty**

vul|ture /vʌ́ltʃər/ (**vultures**) **1** N-COUNT A **vulture** is a large bird that eats the flesh of dead animals. **2** N-COUNT If you describe a person as a **vulture**, you disapprove of them because you think they are trying to gain from another person's troubles. [JOURNALISM, DISAPPROVAL] ❑ *With no buyer in sight for the company as a whole, the vultures started to circle.*

vul|va /vʌ́lvə/ (**vulvas**) N-COUNT The **vulva** is the outer part of a woman's sexual organs.

vy|ing /vaɪɪŋ/ **Vying** is the present participle of **vie**.

Ww

W also **w** /dʌbəlyu/ (**W's**, **w's**) N-VAR W is the twenty-third letter of the English alphabet.

wacko /wækoʊ/ ADJ If you say that someone is **wacko**, you are saying in an unkind way that they are strange and eccentric. [INFORMAL, DISAPPROVAL] ❑ *Lampley was obviously completely wacko.*

wacky /wæki/ (**wackier**, **wackiest**) also **whacky** ADJ If you describe something or someone as **wacky**, you mean that they are eccentric, unusual, and often funny. [INFORMAL] ❑ *...a wacky new television comedy series.*

wad /wɒd/ (**wads**) N-COUNT A **wad** of something such as paper or cloth is a tight bundle or ball of it. ❑ *...a wad of banknotes.*

wad|ding /wɒdɪŋ/ N-UNCOUNT **Wadding** is soft material that is put around things to protect them, for example, in packing.

wad|dle /wɒdəl/ (**waddles**, **waddling**, **waddled**) V-I To **waddle** somewhere means to walk there with short, quick steps, swinging slightly from side to side. A person or animal that waddles usually has short legs and a fat body. ❑ *McGinnis pushed himself laboriously out of the chair and waddled to the window.*

wade /weɪd/ (**wades**, **wading**, **waded**) **1** V-I If you **wade** through something that makes it difficult to walk, usually water or mud, you walk through it. ❑ *Her mother came to find them, wading across a river to reach them.* **2** V-I To **wade through** a lot of documents or pieces of information means to spend a lot of time and effort reading them or dealing with them. ❑ *It has taken a long time to wade through the "incredible volume" of evidence.*
▶ **wade in** also **wade into** PHRASAL VERB If someone **wades in** or **wades into** something, they get involved in a very determined and forceful way, often without thinking enough about the consequences of their actions. ❑ *They don't just listen sympathetically, they wade in with remarks like, "If I were you..."*

wad|er /weɪdər/ (**waders**) **1** N-COUNT A **wader** is a bird with long legs and a long neck, that lives near water and feeds on fish. There are several different kinds of waders. **2** N-COUNT [usu pl] **Waders** are long rubber boots that cover all of the legs and are worn by fishermen when they are standing in water. **3** → See also color supplement

wadi /wɒdi/ (**wadis**) N-COUNT A **wadi** is a river in North Africa or Arabia which is dry except in the rainy season. [TECHNICAL]

wad|ing pool (**wading pools**) N-COUNT A **wading pool** is a shallow artificial pool for children to play in. [AM]

in BRIT, use **paddling pool**

wa|fer /weɪfər/ (**wafers**) N-COUNT A **wafer** is a thin crisp cookie that is usually eaten with ice cream.

wafer-thin ADJ [ADJ n, v-link ADJ] **Wafer-thin** means extremely thin and flat. ❑ *Cut the fennel into wafer-thin slices.*

waf|fle /wɒfəl/ (**waffles**, **waffling**, **waffled**) V-I If someone **waffles** on an issue or question, they cannot decide what to do or what their opinion is about it. [AM] ❑ *He has waffled on abortion and gay rights.*

waft /wɒft, wæft/ (**wafts**, **wafting**, **wafted**) V-T/V-I If sounds or smells **waft** through the air, or if something such as a light wind **wafts** them, they move gently through the air. ❑ *The scent of climbing roses wafts through the window.*

wag /wæg/ (**wags**, **wagging**, **wagged**) **1** V-T When a dog **wags** its tail, it repeatedly waves its tail from side to side. ❑ *The dog was biting, growling and wagging its tail.* **2** V-T If you **wag** your finger, you shake it repeatedly and quickly from side to side, usually because you are annoyed with someone. ❑ *He wagged a disapproving finger.*

wage ✦✧✧ /weɪdʒ/ (**wages**, **waging**, **waged**) **1** N-COUNT Someone's **wages** are the amount of money that is regularly paid to them for the work that they do. ❑ *His wages have gone up.* **2** V-T If a person, group, or country **wages** a campaign or a war, they start it and continue it over a period of time. ❑ *The government, along with the three factions that had been waging a civil war, signed a peace agreement.*

COLLOCATIONS

wage
NOUN **1**
adjective + **wage**: average, minimum, weekly; decent, high, low
verb + **wage**: earn, receive; pay, raise, set

SYNONYMS

wage
NOUN **1**
pay: *...their complaints about their pay and conditions.*
earnings: *Average weekly earnings rose by 1.5% in July.*
remuneration: *$31,000 is a generous remuneration.*
income: *Over a third of their income comes from comedy videos.*

---

wage pack|et (**wage packets**) N-COUNT People's wages can be referred to as their **wage packet**. [mainly BRIT]

in AM, usually use **paycheck**

wa|ger /weɪdʒər/ (**wagers**, **wagering**, **wagered**) V-T/V-I If you **wager** on the result of a horse race, baseball game, or other event, you give someone a sum of money which they give you back with extra money if the result is what you predicted, or which they keep if it is not. [JOURNALISM] ❑ *Just because people wagered on the Yankees did not mean that they liked them.* ❑ *They wagered a lot of money on the race.* • N-COUNT **Wager** is also a noun. ❑ *There have been various wagers on certain candidates since the senator announced his retirement.*

wag|gle /wægəl/ (**waggles**, **waggling**, **waggled**) V-T/V-I If you **waggle** something, or if something **waggles**, it moves up and down or from side to side with short quick movements. ❑ *He was waggling his toes in his socks.* ❑ *...puppet animals with eyes that move and ears that waggle.*

wag|on /wægən/ (**wagons**) **1** N-COUNT A **wagon** is a strong vehicle with four wheels, usually pulled by horses or oxen and used for carrying heavy loads. **2** N-COUNT A **wagon** is a large container on wheels which is pulled by a train. [BRIT]

in AM, use **freight car**

wag|on train (**wagon trains**) N-COUNT A **wagon train** is a line of horses and wagons, especially one that formerly carried supplies or settlers. [AM] ❑ *150 years ago, wagon trains left from Lanham, Nebraska, bound for Oregon and California.*

wag|tail /wægteɪl/ (**wagtails**) N-COUNT A **wagtail** is a type of small bird that moves its tail quickly up and down as it walks.

wah-wah /wɑ wɑ/ N-UNCOUNT [usu N n] In music, **wah-wah** is used to describe the sound produced by covering and uncovering the open end of a brass instrument. This sound

waif /weɪf/ (waifs) N-COUNT If you refer to a child or young woman as a waif, you mean that they are very thin and look as if they have nowhere to live. ❑ *The dirty-faced waif was only five or six years old.*

wail /weɪl/ (wails, wailing, wailed) **1** V-I If someone wails, they make long, loud, high-pitched cries which express sorrow or pain. ❑ *The women began to wail in mourning.* • N-COUNT Wail is also a noun. ❑ *Wails of grief were heard as visitors filed past the site of the disaster.* **2** V-T If you wail something, you say it in a loud, high-pitched voice that shows that you are unhappy or in pain. ❑ *"Now look what you've done!" Shirley wailed.* **3** V-I If something such as a siren or an alarm wails, it makes a long, loud, high-pitched sound. ❑ *Police cars, their sirens wailing, accompanied the trucks.* • N-UNCOUNT Wail is also a noun. ❑ *The wail of the bagpipe could be heard in the distance.*

waist /weɪst/ (waists) **1** N-COUNT Your waist is the middle part of your body where it narrows slightly above your hips. ❑ *Ricky kept his arm around her waist.* **2** N-COUNT The waist of a garment such as a dress, coat, or pair of pants is the part of it which covers the middle part of your body. ❑ *She tucked her thumbs into the waist of her trousers.*

waist|band /weɪstbænd/ (waistbands) N-COUNT A waistband is a narrow piece of material that is sewn onto a pair of pants, a skirt, or other item of clothing at the waist in order to strengthen it.

waist|coat /weɪstkoʊt, wɛskət/ (waistcoats) N-COUNT A waistcoat is a sleeveless piece of clothing with buttons that people usually wear over a shirt. [BRIT]

in AM, use **vest**

waist|line /weɪstlaɪn/ (waistlines) **1** N-COUNT [oft poss N] Your waistline is your waist measurement. ❑ *A passion for cooking does not necessarily have to be bad for your waistline.* **2** N-COUNT The waistline of a piece of clothing is the place where the upper and lower parts are sewn together, which is near your waist when you wear it.

wait ✦✦✦ /weɪt/ (waits, waiting, waited) **1** V-T/V-I [no passive] When you wait for something or someone, you spend some time doing very little, because you cannot act until that thing happens or that person arrives. ❑ *I walk to a street corner and wait for the school bus.* ❑ *I waited to see how she responded.* ❑ *We had to wait a week before we got the results.* • N-UNCOUNT ❑ *The waiting became almost unbearable.* **2** N-COUNT A wait is a period of time in which you do very little, before something happens or before you can do something. ❑ *...the four-hour wait for the organizers to declare the result.* **3** V-T/V-I [usu cont] If something is waiting for you, it is ready for you to use, have, or do. ❑ *There'll be a car waiting for you.* ❑ *When we came home we had a meal waiting for us.* ❑ *He had a car waiting to take him back to the office.* **4** V-I [no cont] If you say that something can wait, you mean that it is not important or urgent and so you will deal with it or do it later. ❑ *I want to talk to you, but it can wait.* **5** V-I [only imper] You can use wait when you are trying to make someone feel excited, or to encourage or threaten them. ❑ *If you think this all sounds very exciting, just wait until you read the book.* **6** V-T [only imper] Wait is used in expressions such as wait a minute, wait a second, and wait a moment to interrupt someone when they are speaking, for example, because you object to what they are saying or because you want them to repeat something. [SPOKEN] ❑ *"Wait a minute!" he broke in. "This is not giving her a fair hearing!"* **7** V-I If an employee waits on you, for example, in a restaurant or hotel, they take orders from you and bring you what you want. ❑ *There were plenty of servants to wait on her.* **8** PHRASE If you say that you can't wait to do something or can hardly wait to do it, you are emphasizing that you are very excited and eager to do it. [SPOKEN, EMPHASIS] ❑ *We can't wait to get started* **9** PHRASE If you tell someone to wait and see, you tell them that they must be patient or that they must not worry about what is going to happen in the future because they have no control over it. ❑ *We'll have to wait and see what happens.*

▶ **wait around** PHRASAL VERB If you wait around, you stay in the same place, usually doing very little, because you cannot act before something happens or before someone arrives. ❑ *The attacker may have been waiting around for an opportunity to strike.* ❑ *I waited around to speak to the doctor.*

▶ **wait up** PHRASAL VERB If you wait up, you deliberately do not go to bed, especially because you are expecting someone to return home late at night. ❑ *I hope he doesn't expect you to wait up for him.*

wait|er /weɪtər/ (waiters) N-COUNT A waiter is someone, especially a man, who works in a restaurant, serving people food and drink.

wait|ing game (waiting games) N-COUNT [usu sing] If you play a waiting game, you deal with a situation by deliberately doing nothing, because you believe you will gain an advantage by acting later, or because you are waiting to see how other people are going to act. ❑ *He's playing a waiting game. He'll hang on as long as possible until the pressure is off.*

wait|ing list (waiting lists) N-COUNT A waiting list is a list of people who have asked for something that cannot be given to them immediately, such as medical treatment, housing, or training, and who must therefore wait until it is available. ❑ *There were 20,000 people on the waiting list for a home.*

wait|ing room (waiting rooms) N-COUNT A waiting room is a room in a place such as a train station or a clinic, where people can sit down while they wait.

wait|ress /weɪtrɪs/ (waitresses) N-COUNT A waitress is a woman who works in a restaurant, serving people food and drink.

wait|staff /weɪtstæf/ N-COUNT-COLL Waitstaff are waiters or waitresses. [AM] ❑ *The white-jacketed waitstaff are there when you need them.*

waive /weɪv/ (waives, waiving, waived) **1** V-T If you waive your right to something, such as legal representation, you choose not to have it or do it. ❑ *He pleaded guilty to the murders of three boys and waived his right to appeal.* **2** V-T If someone waives a rule, they say that people do not have to obey it in a particular situation. ❑ *The art gallery waives admission charges on Sundays.*

waiv|er /weɪvər/ (waivers) N-COUNT A waiver is when a person, government, or organization agrees to give up a right or says that people do not have to obey a particular rule or law. ❑ *...a waiver of constitutional rights.*

wake ✦◇◇ /weɪk/ (wakes, waking, woke or waked, woken) **1** V-T/V-I When you wake or when someone or something wakes you, you become conscious again after being asleep. ❑ *It was cold and dark when I woke at 6:30.* ❑ *She went upstairs to wake Milton.* • PHRASAL VERB Wake up means the same as wake. ❑ *One morning I woke up and felt something was wrong.* **2** N-COUNT [usu sing, with poss] The wake of a boat or other object moving in the water is the track of waves it makes behind it as it moves through the water. ❑ *Dolphins sometimes play in the wake of the boats.* **3** N-COUNT A wake is a gathering or social event that is held before or after someone's funeral. ❑ *A funeral wake was in progress.* **4** PHRASE If one thing follows in the wake of another, it happens after the other thing is over, often as a result of it. ❑ *The governor has enjoyed a huge surge in the polls in the wake of last week's convention.*

▶ **wake up** **1** PHRASAL VERB If something such as an activity wakes you up, it makes you more alert and ready to do things after you have been lazy or inactive. ❑ *A cool shower wakes up the body and boosts circulation* **2** → see also wake 1

wake|ful /weɪkfəl/ ADJ Someone who is wakeful finds it difficult to get to sleep and wakes up very often when they should be sleeping. • **wake|ful|ness** N-UNCOUNT ❑ *It is never a good idea to take sleeping pills regularly for this kind of wakefulness.*

wak|en /weɪkən/ (wakens, wakening, wakened) V-T/V-I When you waken, or when someone or something wakens you, you wake from sleep [LITERARY] ❑ *The noise outside wakened her.* • PHRASAL VERB Waken up means the same as waken.

wake-up call (wake-up calls) **1** N-COUNT A wake-up call is a telephone call that you can arrange through an operator or at a hotel to make sure that you wake up at a particular time. ❑ *I book a wake-up call for 4:45 a.m.* **2** N-COUNT If you describe something bad that happens as a wake-up call, you mean

walk that it acts as a warning that action needs to be taken to prevent something even worse from happening. ▫ *He urged her to treat the arrest as a wake-up call.*

walk ◆◆◆ /wɔk/ (walks, walking, walked) **1** V-T/V-I When you **walk**, you move forward by putting one foot in front of the other in a regular way. ▫ *Rosanna and Forbes walked in silence.* ▫ *We walked into the foyer.* ▫ *I walked a few steps toward the fence.* **2** N-COUNT A **walk** is a trip that you make by walking, usually for pleasure. ▫ *I went for a walk.* **3** N-SING A **walk** of a particular distance is the distance that a person has to walk to get somewhere. ▫ *It was only a three-mile walk to Kabul from there.* **4** N-COUNT A **walk** is a route suitable for walking along for pleasure. ▫ *...a 2-mile coastal walk.* **5** N-SING A **walk** is a paved pathway. ▫ *She started up the walk toward the front door.* **6** N-SING A **walk** is the action of walking rather than running. ▫ *She slowed to a steady walk.* **7** N-SING Someone's **walk** is the way that they walk. ▫ *George, despite his great height and gangling walk, was a great dancer.* **8** V-T If you **walk** someone somewhere, you walk there with them in order to show politeness or to make sure that they get there safely. ▫ *She walked me to my car.* **9 to walk tall** → see **tall**

▶ **walk away** PHRASAL VERB If you **walk away** from a problem or a difficult situation, you do nothing about it or do not face any bad consequences from it. ▫ *The most appropriate strategy may simply be to walk away from the problem.*

▶ **walk away with** PHRASAL VERB If you **walk away with** something such as a prize, you win it or get it very easily. [JOURNALISM] ▫ *Enter our competition and you could walk away with $10,000.*

▶ **walk into** PHRASAL VERB If you **walk into** an unpleasant situation, you become involved in it without expecting to, especially because you have been careless. ▫ *He's walking into a situation that he absolutely can't control.*

▶ **walk off with** PHRASAL VERB If you **walk off with** something such as a prize, you win it or get it very easily. [JOURNALISM] ▫ *We'd like nothing better than to see him walk off with the big prize.*

▶ **walk out** **1** PHRASAL VERB If you **walk out** of a meeting, a performance, or an unpleasant situation, you leave it suddenly, usually in order to show that you are angry or bored. ▫ *Several dozen councillors walked out of the meeting in protest.* **2** PHRASAL VERB If someone **walks out** on their family or their partner, they leave them suddenly and go to live somewhere else. ▫ *Her husband walked out on her.* **3** PHRASAL VERB If workers **walk out**, they stop doing their work for a period of time, usually in order to try to get better pay or conditions for themselves. ▫ *The miners were furious and threatened to walk out.*

SYNONYMS

walk
VERB **1**
stride: *He turned abruptly and strode off down the corridor.*
wander: *They wandered off in the direction of the nearest store.*
stroll: *Afterwards, we strolled back and settled down with the newspapers.*
march: *He marched into the kitchen without knocking.*

---

walk|er /wɔkər/ (walkers) **1** N-COUNT A **walker** is a person who walks, especially in the countryside for pleasure or in order to keep healthy. **2** N-COUNT [oft supp N] A **walker** is a special kind of frame designed to help babies or people with a disability to walk. ▫ *She eventually used a cane, then a walker, and finally was confined to the house.*

walkie-talkie /wɔki tɔki/ (walkie-talkies) N-COUNT A **walkie-talkie** is a small portable radio that you can talk into and hear messages through so that you can communicate with someone far away.

walk-in (walk-ins) **1** ADJ [ADJ n] A **walk-in** closet or wardrobe is a closet or wardrobe that is large enough for someone to walk into. ▫ *Upstairs, the master bedroom has a walk-in closet.* **2** ADJ [ADJ n] A **walk-in** clinic or medical center is one where you can get medical attention without making an appointment. ▫ *Should blood tests be made more accessible to the public, such as through walk-in clinics in shopping malls?* • N-COUNT **Walk-in** is also a noun. ▫ *They told him they didn't take walk-ins and shooed him away.*

walk|ing /wɔkɪŋ/ N-UNCOUNT **Walking** is the activity of taking walks for exercise or pleasure, especially in the country. ▫ *Recently I've started to do a lot of walking and cycling.*

walk|ing stick (walking sticks) **1** N-COUNT A **walking stick** is a long wooden stick which a person can lean on while walking. **2** N-COUNT A **walking stick** is an insect with a long body and thin legs. It looks like a small stick. [AM]

in BRIT, use **stick insect**

walk of life (walks of life) N-COUNT The **walk of life** that you come from is the position that you have in society and the kind of job you have. ▫ *One of the greatest pleasures of this job is meeting people from all walks of life.*

walk-on ADJ [ADJ n] A **walk-on** part in a play or movie is a very small part that usually does not involve any speaking. ▫ *...fifteen nonspeaking, walk-on parts.*

walk|out /wɔkaʊt/ (walkouts) **1** N-COUNT A **walkout** is a strike. ▫ *But union leaders are holding off on calling the walkout while talks are showing progress.* **2** N-COUNT If there is a **walkout** during a meeting, some or all of the people attending it leave in order to show their disapproval of something that has happened at the meeting. ▫ *The commission's proceedings have been wrecked by tantrums and walkouts.*

walk|over /wɔkoʊvər/ (walkovers) N-COUNT [usu sing] If you say that a competition or contest is a **walkover**, you mean that it is won very easily. [mainly BRIT]

in AM, usually use **cakewalk**

walk-up (walk-ups) N-COUNT A **walk-up** is a tall apartment building that has no elevator. You can also refer to an apartment in such a building as a **walk-up**. [AM] ▫ *She lives in a tiny fifth floor walk-up in New York's East Village.*

walk|way /wɔkweɪ/ (walkways) N-COUNT A **walkway** is a passage or path for people to walk along. Walkways are often raised above the ground. ▫ *...a new concrete walkway between two rows of apartment blocks.*

wall ◆◆◆ /wɔl/ (walls) **1** N-COUNT A **wall** is one of the vertical sides of a building or room. ▫ *Kathryn leaned against the wall of the church.* ▫ *The bedroom walls would be papered with chintz.* **2** N-COUNT A **wall** is a long narrow vertical structure made of stone or brick that surrounds or divides an area of land. ▫ *He sat on the wall in the sun.* **3** N-COUNT The **wall** of something that is hollow is its side. ▫ *He ran his fingers along the inside walls of the box.* **4** → see also **off-the-wall** **5** PHRASE If you say that something or someone **is driving** you **up the wall**, you are emphasizing that they annoy and irritate you. [INFORMAL, EMPHASIS] ▫ *The heat is driving me up the wall.*

wal|la|by /wɒləbi/ (wallabies) N-COUNT A **wallaby** is an animal similar to a small kangaroo. Wallabies live in Australia and New Guinea.

wall|covering /wɔlkʌvərɪŋ/ (wallcoverings) also **wall covering** N-VAR A **wallcovering** is a material such as wallpaper that is used to decorate the walls on the inside of a building.

walled /wɔld/ ADJ If an area of land or a city is **walled**, it is surrounded or enclosed by a wall. ▫ *The city was walled and built upon a rock.*

wal|let /wɒlɪt/ (wallets) N-COUNT A **wallet** is a small flat folded case, usually made of leather or plastic, in which you can keep money and credit cards.

wall|flower /wɔlflaʊər/ (wallflowers) **1** N-COUNT A **wallflower** is a plant that is grown in gardens and has sweet-smelling yellow, red, orange, or purple flowers. **2** N-COUNT If you say that someone is a **wallflower**, you mean that they are shy and do not get involved in dancing or talking to people at social events.

wal|lop /wɒləp/ (wallops, walloping, walloped) V-T If you **wallop** someone or something, you hit them very hard, often causing a dull sound. [INFORMAL] ▫ *Once, she walloped me over the head with a frying pan.* • N-COUNT; SOUND [usu sing] **Wallop** is also a noun. ▫ *With one brutal wallop, Leticia flattened him.*

wal|low /wɒloʊ/ (wallows, wallowing, wallowed) **1** V-I If you say that someone **is wallowing in** an unpleasant situation, you are criticizing them for being deliberately unhappy. [DISAPPROVAL] ▫ *His tired mind continued to wallow in self-pity.*

wallpaper 1449 **war**

2 V-I If a person or animal **wallows** in water or mud, they lie or roll about in it slowly for pleasure. ❑ *Never have I had such a good excuse for wallowing in deep warm baths.*

wall|paper /wɔ:lpeɪpər/ (**wallpapers, wallpapering, wallpapered**) **1** N-MASS **Wallpaper** is thick colored or patterned paper that is used for covering and decorating the walls of rooms. ❑ *...the wallpaper in the bedroom.* **2** V-T If someone **wallpapers** a room, they cover the walls with wallpaper. ❑ *We were going to wallpaper that room anyway.* **3** N-UNCOUNT **Wallpaper** is the background on a computer screen. [COMPUTING] ❑ *...preinstalled wallpaper images.* **4** → See feature box at **DIY**

Wall Street ♦◇◇ N-PROPER **Wall Street** is a street in New York where the Stock Exchange and financial businesses are located. **Wall Street** is often used to refer to the financial business carried out there and to the people who work there. [BUSINESS] ❑ *On Wall Street, stocks closed at their second highest level today.*

wall-to-wall **1** ADJ [usu ADJ n] A **wall-to-wall** carpet covers the floor of a room completely. **2** ADJ [usu ADJ n] You can use **wall-to-wall** to describe something that fills or seems to fill all the available space. ❑ *...television's wall-to-wall election coverage.*

wal|nut /wɔ:lnʌt, -nət/ (**walnuts**) **1** N-VAR **Walnuts** are edible nuts that have a wrinkled shape and a hard round shell that is light brown in color. ❑ *...chopped walnuts.* **2** → See also color supplement

wal|rus /wɔ:lrəs/ (**walruses**) N-COUNT A **walrus** is a large, fat animal which lives in the sea. It has two long teeth called tusks that point downward.

waltz /wɔ:lts, wɒls/ (**waltzes, waltzing, waltzed**) **1** N-COUNT; N-IN-NAMES A **waltz** is a piece of music with a rhythm of three beats in each bar, which people can dance to. ❑ *...Tchaikovsky's "Waltz of the Flowers".* **2** N-COUNT A **waltz** is a dance in which two people hold each other and move around the floor doing special steps in time to waltz music. ❑ *Arthur Murray taught the foxtrot, the tango and the waltz.* **3** V-RECIP If you **waltz** with someone, you dance a waltz with them. ❑ *"Waltz with me," he said, taking her hand.*

wan /wɒn/ (**wanner, wannest**) ADJ If you describe someone as **wan**, you mean that they look pale and tired. [LITERARY] ❑ *He looked wan and tired.*

wand /wɒnd/ (**wands**) **1** N-COUNT A **wand** is the same as a magic **wand**. ❑ *You can't simply wave a wand and get rid of nuclear weapons.* **2** N-COUNT A **wand** is a metal-detecting device shaped like a baton. ❑ *Visitors can expect to be searched with a metal-detecting wand.*

wan|der /wɒndər/ (**wanders, wandering, wandered**) **1** V-T/V-I If you **wander** in a place, you walk around there in a casual way, often without intending to go in any particular direction. ❑ *When he got bored he wandered around the fair.* ❑ *They wandered off in the direction of the nearest store.* ❑ *People wandered the streets aimlessly.* • N-SING **Wander** is also a noun. ❑ *A wander around any market will reveal stalls piled high with vegetables.* **2** V-I If a person or animal **wanders** from a place where they are supposed to stay, they move away from the place without going in a particular direction. ❑ *Because Mother is afraid we'll get lost, we aren't allowed to wander far.* **3** V-I If your mind **wanders** or your thoughts **wander**, you stop concentrating on something and start thinking about other things. ❑ *His mind would wander, and he would lose track of what he was doing.* **4** V-I If your eyes **wander**, you stop looking at one thing and start looking around at other things. ❑ *His eyes wandered restlessly around the room.*

wan|der|er /wɒndərər/ (**wanderers**) N-COUNT A **wanderer** is a person who travels around rather than settling in one place.

wan|der|ing /wɒndərɪŋ/ ADJ [ADJ n] **Wandering** is used to describe people who travel around rather than staying in one place for a long time. [LITERARY] ❑ *...a band of wandering musicians.*

wan|der|ings /wɒndərɪŋz/ N-PLURAL [usu with poss] Someone's **wanderings** are travels that they make from place to place without staying in one place for a long time. ❑ *On his wanderings he's picked up Spanish, Italian, French and a smattering of Russian.*

wan|der|lust /wɒndərlʌst/ N-UNCOUNT Someone who has **wanderlust** has a strong desire to travel. ❑ *His wanderlust would not allow him to stay long in one spot.*

wane /weɪn/ (**wanes, waning, waned**) V-I If something **wanes**, it becomes gradually weaker or less, often so that it eventually disappears. ❑ *While his interest in these sports began to wane, a passion for lacrosse developed.*

wan|gle /wæŋɡəl/ (**wangles, wangling, wangled**) V-T If you **wangle** something that you want, you manage to get it by being clever or persuading someone. [INFORMAL] ❑ *We managed to wangle a few days' leave.* ❑ *He had wangled his way into the country without a visa.* ❑ *I asked the captain to wangle us three tickets to Athens.* ❑ *A friend at the New York office had wangled the tickets for him.*

wan|na /wɒnə/ **Wanna** is used in written English to represent the words 'want to' when they are pronounced informally. ❑ *I wanna be married to you. Do you wanna be married to me?*

wanna|be /wɒnəbi/ (**wannabes**) also **wannabee** N-COUNT [usu n N, N n] If you call someone a **wannabe**, you are saying in an unkind way that they are trying very hard to be like another person or group of people. [INFORMAL, DISAPPROVAL] ❑ *The latest competition drew more than 100,000 pop star wannabes to auditions in seven cities.*

want ♦♦♦ /wɒnt/ (**wants, wanting, wanted**) **1** V-T [no cont, no passive] If you **want** something, you feel a desire or a need for it. ❑ *I want a drink.* ❑ *People wanted to know who this talented designer was.* ❑ *They began to want their father to be the same as other daddies.* ❑ *They didn't want people staring at them as they sat on the lawn, so they put up high walls.* **2** V-T [no cont, no passive] You can say that you **want** to say something to indicate that you are about to say it. ❑ *I want to say how delighted I am that you're having a baby.* **3** V-T [no cont, no passive] If you say to someone that you **want** something, or ask them if they **want** to do it, you are firmly telling them what you want or what you want them to do. ❑ *I want an explanation from you, Jeremy.* ❑ *Do you want to tell me what all this is about?* **4** V-T [no cont, no passive] If you tell someone that they **want** to do a particular thing, you are advising them to do it. [INFORMAL] ❑ *You want to be very careful not to have a man like Crevecoeur for an enemy.* **5** V-T [usu passive] If someone **is wanted** by the police, the police are searching for them because they are thought to have committed a crime. ❑ *He was wanted for the murder of a judge.* • **want|ed** ADJ [ADJ n] ❑ *He is one of the most wanted criminals in Europe.* **6** N-PLURAL Your **wants** are the things that you want. ❑ *She couldn't lift a spoon without a servant anticipating her wants and getting it for her.* **7** PHRASE If you do something **for want of** something else, you do it because the other thing is not available or not possible. ❑ *The factories shut down for want of fuel and materials.*

want ad (**want ads**) N-COUNT [usu pl] The **want ads** in a newspaper or magazine are small advertisements, usually offering things for sale or offering jobs. [mainly AM]

want|ing /wɒntɪŋ/ ADJ [v-link ADJ] If you find something or someone **wanting**, they are not of as high a standard as you think they should be. ❑ *He analyzed his game and found it wanting.*

wan|ton /wɒntən/ **1** ADJ [usu ADJ n] A **wanton** action deliberately causes harm, damage, or waste without having any reason to. ❑ *...this unnecessary and wanton destruction of our environment.* **2** ADJ If someone describes a woman as **wanton**, they disapprove of her because she clearly enjoys sex or has sex with a lot of men. [DISAPPROVAL, OLD-FASHIONED] ❑ *...the idea that only wanton women have sexual passions.*

WAP /wæp/ N-UNCOUNT **WAP** is a system that allows devices such as cellphones to connect to the internet. **WAP** is an abbreviation for **Wireless Application Protocol**. ❑ *...a WAP phone.*

war ♦♦♦ /wɔ:r/ (**wars**) **1** N-VAR A **war** is a period of fighting or conflict between countries or states. ❑ *He spent part of the war in the National Guard.* ❑ *...matters of war and peace.* **2** N-VAR **War** is intense economic competition between countries or organizations. ❑ *The most important thing is to reach an agreement and to avoid a trade war.* **3** N-VAR If you make **war** on someone or something that you are opposed to, you do things to stop them from succeeding. ❑ *She has been involved in the war against organized crime.* **4** → see also **civil war, warring** **5** PHRASE If a

warble

country **goes to war**, it starts fighting a war. ❏ *Do you think this crisis can be settled without going to war?*

war|ble /wɔ̱rbəl/ (warbles, warbling, warbled) **1** V-T/V-I When a bird **warbles**, it sings pleasantly. ❏ *The bird continued to warble.* ❏ *...birds warbling a morning chorus.* **2** V-T/V-I If someone **warbles**, they sing in a high-pitched, rather unsteady voice. ❏ *She warbled as she worked.* ❏ *...singers warbling "Over the Rainbow."*

war|bler /wɔ̱rblər/ (warblers) N-COUNT [usu supp N] **Warblers** are a family of small birds that have a pleasant song.

war chest (war chests) N-COUNT A **war chest** is a fund to finance a project such as a political campaign. ❏ *Governor Caperton has the largest campaign war chest.*

ward /wɔ̱rd/ (wards, warding, warded) N-COUNT A **ward** is a room in a hospital which has beds for many people, often people who need similar treatment. ❏ *They transferred her to the psychiatric ward.*

▶ **ward off** PHRASAL VERB To **ward off** a danger or illness means to prevent it from affecting you or harming you. ❏ *She may have put up a fight to try to ward off her assailant.*

war|den /wɔ̱rdən/ (wardens) **1** N-COUNT A **warden** is a person who is responsible for a particular place or thing, and for making sure that the laws or regulations that relate to it are obeyed. ❏ *He was a warden at the local parish church.* **2** N-COUNT The **warden** of a prison is the person in charge of it. [AM] ❏ *A new warden took over the prison.*

in BRIT, use **governor**

war|der /wɔ̱rdər/ (warders) N-COUNT A **warder** is someone who works in a prison supervising the prisoners. [BRIT]

in AM, use **guard**

ward|robe /wɔ̱rdroʊb/ (wardrobes) **1** N-COUNT Someone's **wardrobe** is the total collection of clothes that they have. ❏ *Her wardrobe consists primarily of huge cashmere sweaters and tiny Italian sandals.* **2** N-COUNT A **wardrobe** is a tall closet or cabinet in which you can hang your clothes.

-ware /-wɛər/ COMB IN N-UNCOUNT **-ware** combines with nouns to refer to objects that are made of a particular material or that are used for a particular purpose in the home. ❏ *...boxes of cheap glassware.*

ware|house /wɛ̱ərhaʊs/ (warehouses) N-COUNT A **warehouse** is a large building where raw materials or manufactured goods are stored until they are exported to other countries or distributed to stores to be sold.

ware|house club (warehouse clubs) N-COUNT A **warehouse club** is a large store that sells goods at reduced prices to people who pay each year to become members of it.

ware|hous|ing /wɛ̱ərhaʊzɪŋ/ N-UNCOUNT **Warehousing** is the act or process of storing large quantities of goods so that they can be sold or used at a later date. ❏ *All donations go toward the cost of warehousing.*

wares /wɛ̱ərz/ N-PLURAL A person's or a company's **wares** are the things that they are selling. ❏ *Many companies are choosing to display their wares online.*

war|fare /wɔ̱rfɛər/ **1** N-UNCOUNT **Warfare** is the activity of fighting a war. ❏ *...the threat of chemical warfare.* **2** N-UNCOUNT **Warfare** is sometimes used to refer to any violent struggle or conflict. ❏ *Much of the violence is related to drugs and gang warfare.*

war game (war games) **1** N-COUNT [usu pl] **War games** are military exercises that are carried out for the purpose of training, and that are designed to imitate a real war as closely as possible. **2** N-COUNT A **war game** is a game in which model soldiers are used to recreate battles that happened in the past. War games can also be played on computers.

war|head /wɔ̱rhɛd/ (warheads) N-COUNT A **warhead** is the front part of a bomb or missile where the explosives are carried. ❏ *...nuclear warheads.*

war|horse /wɔ̱rhɔrs/ (warhorses) also **war-horse** N-COUNT You can refer to someone such as an old soldier or politician who is still active and aggressive as a **warhorse**.

war|like /wɔ̱rlaɪk/ ADJ [usu ADJ n] **Warlike** people seem aggressive and eager to start a war. ❏ *The Scythians were a fiercely warlike people.*

war|lord /wɔ̱rlɔrd/ (warlords) N-COUNT If you describe a leader of a country or organization as a **warlord**, you are critical of them because they have achieved power by behaving in an aggressive and violent way. [DISAPPROVAL] ❏ *He had been a dictator and a warlord who had oppressed and degraded the people of the South.* ❏ *...a drug warlord.*

warm ✦✦◇ /wɔ̱rm/ (warmer, warmest, warms, warming, warmed) **1** ADJ Something that is **warm** has some heat but not enough to be hot. ❏ *Wheat is grown in places which have cold winters and warm, dry summers.* ❏ *Because it was warm, David wore only a white cotton shirt.* **2** ADJ **Warm** clothes and blankets are made of a material such as wool that protects you from the cold. ❏ *They have been forced to sleep in the open without food or warm clothing.* • **warm|ly** ADV ❏ *Remember to wrap up warmly on cold days.* **3** ADJ **Warm** colors have red or yellow in them rather than blue or green, and make you feel comfortable and relaxed. ❏ *The basement hallway is painted a warm yellow.* **4** ADJ A **warm** person is friendly and shows a lot of affection or enthusiasm in their behavior. ❏ *She was a warm and loving mother.* • **warm|ly** ADV [ADV with v] ❏ *New members are warmly welcomed.* **5** V-T If you **warm** a part of your body or if something hot **warms** it, it stops feeling cold and starts to feel hotter. ❏ *The sun had come out to warm his back.* **6** V-I If you **warm to** a person or an idea, you become fonder of the person or more interested in the idea. ❏ *Those who got to know him better warmed to his openness and honesty.*

▶ **warm up** **1** PHRASAL VERB If you **warm** something **up** or if it **warms up**, it gets hotter. ❏ *He blew on his hands to warm them up.* ❏ *All that she would have to do was warm up the pudding.* **2** PHRASAL VERB If you **warm up** for an event such as a race, you prepare yourself for it by doing exercises or by practicing just before it starts. ❏ *In an hour the drivers will be warming up for the main event.* **3** PHRASAL VERB When a machine or engine **warms up** or someone **warms** it **up**, it becomes ready for use a little while after being switched on or started. ❏ *He waited for his car to warm up.*

warm-blooded ADJ A **warm-blooded** animal, such as a bird or a mammal, has a fairly high body temperature that does not change much and is not affected by the surrounding temperature.

warm-down (warm-downs) N-COUNT [usu sing] A **warm-down** is a series of special exercises that you do after a physical activity to help relax your muscles and joints.

warmed-over **1** ADJ [usu ADJ n] **Warmed-over** food has become cold and has been heated up. [AM] ❏ *...warmed-over soup.* **2** ADJ [usu ADJ n] A **warmed-over** idea or product is one that is presented a second time without anything significantly new having been added to it. [mainly AM, DISAPPROVAL] ❏ *...warmed-over versions of products that hit the market long ago.*

warm-hearted ADJ A **warm-hearted** person is friendly and affectionate.

war|monger /wɔ̱rmʌŋgər, -mɒŋgər/ (warmongers) N-COUNT If you describe a politician or leader as a **warmonger**, you disapprove of them because you think they are encouraging people to start or join a war. [DISAPPROVAL]

warmth /wɔ̱rmθ/ **1** N-UNCOUNT The **warmth** of something is the heat that it has or produces. ❏ *She went further into the room, drawn by the warmth of the fire.* **2** N-UNCOUNT The **warmth** of something such as a garment or blanket is the protection that it gives you against the cold. ❏ *The blanket will provide additional warmth and comfort in bed.*

warm-up (warm-ups) N-COUNT A **warm-up** is something that prepares you for an activity or event, usually because it is a short practice or example of what the activity or event will involve. ❏ *The exercises can be fun and a good warm-up for the latter part of the program.*

warn ✦✦◇ /wɔ̱rn/ (warns, warning, warned) **1** V-T/V-I If you **warn** someone about something such as a possible danger or problem, you tell them about it so that they are aware of it. ❏ *When I had my first baby friends warned me that children were expensive.* ❏ *They warned him of the dangers of sailing alone.* ❏ *He warned of a possibility of a new terrorist attack.* **2** V-T/V-I If you **warn** someone not to do something, you advise them not to do it so that they can avoid possible danger or punishment. ❏ *Mrs. Blount warned me not to interfere.* ❏ *"Don't do anything yet," he warned. "Too risky."*

warn|ing ✦◇◇ /wɔrnɪŋ/ (warnings) **1** N-COUNT A **warning** is something said or written to tell people of a possible danger, problem, or other unpleasant thing that might happen. ❑ *The minister gave a warning that if war broke out, it would be catastrophic.* ❑ *He was killed because he ignored a warning to put stronger cords on his parachute.* **2** N-VAR A **warning** is an advance notice of something that will happen, often something unpleasant or dangerous. ❑ *The soldiers opened fire without warning.* **3** ADJ [ADJ n] **Warning** actions or signs give a warning. ❑ *She ignored the warning signals and did not check the patient's medical notes.*

COLLOCATIONS

warning
NOUN **1**
noun + **warning**: health, safety; flood, travel, weather; government
adjective + **warning**: dire, stark, stern; repeated
verb + **warning**: give, issue, sound; heed, ignore

SYNONYMS

warning
NOUN **1**
threat: *He may be forced to carry out his threat to resign.*
caution: *There was a note of caution for the Treasury in the figures.*
alarm: *The other man rang the alarm bell.*
alert: *Due to a security alert, this train will not be stopping at Oxford Circus.*
omen: *Her appearance at this moment is an omen of disaster.*

---

war of nerves N-SING A **war of nerves** is a conflict in which the opposing sides try to make each other feel less confident. ❑ *...the continuing war of nerves between the army and the leadership.*

warp /wɔrp/ (warps, warping, warped) V-T/V-I If something **warps** or **is warped**, it becomes damaged by bending or curving, often because of the effect of heat or water. ❑ *Left out in the heat of the sun, tapes easily warp or get stuck in their cases.*

war paint also **warpaint** N-UNCOUNT **War paint** is the paint that some groups of people used to decorate their faces and bodies before they fought a battle.

war|path /wɔrpæθ/ PHRASE If you say that someone is or has gone **on the warpath**, you mean that they are angry and getting ready for a fight or conflict. [INFORMAL] ❑ *I had warned the children that daddy was on the warpath.*

war|plane /wɔrpleɪn/ (warplanes) N-COUNT A **warplane** is an aircraft that is designed for fighting, for example, to attack other aircraft or to drop bombs.

war|rant /wɔrənt/ (warrants, warranting, warranted) **1** V-T If something **warrants** a particular action, it makes the action seem necessary or appropriate for the circumstances. ❑ *The allegations are serious enough to warrant an investigation.* **2** N-COUNT [oft N for n, also by N] A **warrant** is a legal document that allows someone to do something, especially one that is signed by a judge or magistrate and gives the police permission to arrest someone or search their house. ❑ *Police confirmed that they had issued a warrant for his arrest.*

war|rant of|fic|er (warrant officers) N-COUNT A **warrant officer** is a person in the navy who is above the rank of petty officer and below the rank of ensign.

war|ran|ty /wɔrənti/ (warranties) **1** N-COUNT [also under N] A **warranty** is a written promise by a company that, if you find a fault in something they have sold you within a certain time, they will repair it or replace it free of charge. ❑ *...a twelve-month warranty.* **2** → See feature box at **service**

war|ren /wɔrən/ (warrens) **1** N-COUNT [oft n N] A **warren** is a group of holes in the ground connected by tunnels that rabbits live in. **2** N-COUNT If you describe a building or an area of a city as a **warren**, you mean that there are many narrow passages or streets. ❑ *...a warren of narrow streets.*

war|ring /wɔrɪŋ/ ADJ [ADJ n] **Warring** is used to describe groups of people who are involved in a conflict or quarrel with each other. ❑ *An official said the warring factions have not yet turned in all their heavy weapons.*

war|ri|or /wɔriər/ (warriors) N-COUNT A **warrior** is a fighter or soldier, especially one in former times who was very brave and experienced in fighting. ❑ *...the tale of Bima, the great warrior of Indonesian folklore.*

war|ship /wɔrʃɪp/ (warships) N-COUNT A **warship** is a ship with guns that is used for fighting in wars.

wart /wɔrt/ (warts) N-COUNT A **wart** is a small lump that grows on your skin.

wart|hog /wɔrthɔg/ (warthogs) N-COUNT A **warthog** is a wild pig with two large teeth that curve upward at the sides of its mouth. Warthogs live in Africa.

war|time /wɔrtaɪm/ N-UNCOUNT **Wartime** is a period of time when a war is being fought. ❑ *The government will commandeer ships only in wartime.*

war wid|ow (war widows) N-COUNT A **war widow** is a woman whose husband was killed while he was in the armed forces during a war.

wary /wɛəri/ (warier, wariest) ADJ If you are **wary** of something or someone, you are cautious because you do not know much about them and you believe they may be dangerous or cause problems. ❑ *People did not teach their children to be wary of strangers.* ● **wari|ly** /wɛərɪli/ ADV *She studied me warily, as if I might turn violent.*

was /wəz, STRONG wɑz, wʌz/ **Was** is the first and third person singular of the past tense of **be** ①.

wash ✦◇◇ /wɒʃ/ (washes, washing, washed) **1** V-T If you **wash** something, you clean it using water and usually a substance such as soap or detergent. ❑ *We did odd jobs like farm work and washing dishes.* ❑ *It took a long time to wash the mud out of his hair.* **2** V-T/V-I If you **wash** or if you **wash** part of your body, especially your hands and face, you clean part of your body using soap and water. ❑ *They looked as if they hadn't washed in days.* ❑ *She washed her face with cold water.* **3** V-I /V-I If a sea or river **washes** somewhere, it flows there gently. You can also say that something carried by a sea or river **washes** or **is washed** somewhere. ❑ *The sea washed against the shore.* **4** V-I If a feeling **washes** over you, you suddenly feel it very strongly and cannot control it. [WRITTEN] ❑ *A wave of self-consciousness can wash over her when someone new enters the room.* **5** → see also **washing** **6** PHRASE If you say that something such as an item of clothing **is in the wash**, you mean that it is being washed, is waiting to be washed, or has just been washed and should therefore not be worn or used. [INFORMAL] ❑ *Your jeans are in the wash.* **7 to wash your hands of something** → see **hand** ①

▶ **wash away** PHRASAL VERB If rain or floods **wash away** something, they destroy it and carry it away. ❑ *Flood waters washed away one of the main bridges in Pusan.*

▶ **wash down** **1** PHRASAL VERB If you **wash** something, especially food, **down** with a drink, you drink the drink after eating the food, especially to make the food easier to swallow or digest. ❑ *He took two aspirin immediately and washed them down with three cups of water.* **2** PHRASAL VERB If you **wash down** an object, you wash it all, from top to bottom. ❑ *The prisoner started to wash down the walls of his cell.*

▶ **wash up** **1** PHRASAL VERB If you **wash up**, you clean part of your body with soap and water, especially your hands and face. ❑ *He headed to the bathroom to wash up.* **2** PHRASAL VERB If something **is washed up** on a piece of land, it is carried by a river or sea and left there. ❑ *Thousands of herring and crab are washed up on the beaches during every storm.* **3** PHRASAL VERB If you **wash up**, you wash the plates, cups, flatware, and pans that have been used for cooking and eating a meal. [BRIT]

in AM, use **wash the dishes**

wash|able /wɒʃəbəl/ ADJ **Washable** clothes or materials can be washed in water without being damaged. ❑ *Choose washable curtains.*

wash|cloth /wɒʃklɒθ/ (washcloths) N-COUNT A **washcloth** is a small cloth that you use for washing yourself. [AM]

in BRIT, use **flannel**

washed-out also **washed out** **1** ADJ [usu ADJ n] **Washed-out** colors are very pale. ❑ *He stared at me out of those washed-out blue eyes.* **2** ADJ [usu v-link ADJ] If someone looks **washed-out**, they look very tired and lacking in energy. ❑ *She looked washed out and listless.*

washed-up also **washed up** ADJ If you say that someone is washed-up, you mean that their career or success has ended. [INFORMAL] ❑ *He's all washed up, but he still yells at everyone.*

wash|er /wɒʃər/ (washers) **1** N-COUNT A **washer** is a thin flat ring of metal or rubber that is placed over a bolt before the nut is screwed on. **2** N-COUNT A **washer** is the same as a **washing machine**. [INFORMAL] **3** → See also color supplement

wash|ing /wɒʃɪŋ/ N-UNCOUNT **Washing** is a collection of clothes, sheets, and other things that are waiting to be washed, are being washed, or have just been washed. ❑ *...plastic bags full of dirty washing.*

wash|ing ma|chine (washing machines) N-COUNT A **washing machine** is a machine that you use to wash clothes in.

wash|out /wɒʃaʊt/ (washouts) N-COUNT If an event or plan is a **washout**, it fails completely. [INFORMAL] ❑ *The mission was a washout.*

wash|rag /wɒʃræg/ (washrags) N-COUNT A **washrag** is the same as a **washcloth**. [AM]

wash|room /wɒʃrʊm/ (washrooms) N-COUNT A **washroom** is a room with toilets and washing facilities, situated in a large building such as a factory or an office.

wash|stand /wɒʃstænd/ (washstands) N-COUNT A **washstand** is a piece of furniture designed to hold a bowl for washing your hands and face in, which was used in former times before sinks with faucets.

wasn't /wʌzᵊnt, wɒz-/ **Wasn't** is the usual spoken form of 'was not.'

wasp /wɒsp/ (wasps) N-COUNT A **wasp** is an insect with wings and yellow and black stripes across its body. Wasps have a painful sting like a bee but do not produce honey.

WASP /wɒsp/ (WASPs) N-COUNT [also N n] **WASP** is used to refer to the people in American society whose ancestors came from northern Europe, especially England, and who were formerly considered to have a lot of power and influence. WASP is an abbreviation for 'White Anglo-Saxon Protestant.' [AM, DISAPPROVAL] ❑ *...a WASP with a Yale degree.*

wasp|ish /wɒspɪʃ/ ADJ A **waspish** remark or sense of humor is sharp and critical.

wast|age /weɪstɪdʒ/ N-UNCOUNT **Wastage** of something is the act of wasting it or the amount of it that is wasted. ❑ *There was a lot of wastage and many wrong decisions were hastily taken.*

waste ✦✦◇ /weɪst/ (wastes, wasting, wasted) **1** V-T If you **waste** something such as time, money, or energy, you use too much of it doing something that is not important or necessary, or is unlikely to succeed. ❑ *There could be many reasons and he was not going to waste time speculating on them.* ❑ *I resolved not to waste money on a hotel.* • N-SING **Waste** is also a noun. ❑ *It is a waste of time going to the doctor with most mild complaints.* **2** N-UNCOUNT **Waste** is the use of money or other resources on things that do not need it. ❑ *The packets are measured to reduce waste.* **3** N-UNCOUNT [also N in pl] **Waste** is material that has been used and is no longer wanted, for example, because the valuable or useful part of it has been taken out. ❑ *Congress passed a law that regulates the disposal of waste.* ❑ *...the dangers posed by toxic waste.* **4** V-T If you **waste** an opportunity for something, you do not take advantage of it when it is available. ❑ *Let's not waste an opportunity to see the children.* **5** ADJ **Waste** land is land, especially in or near a city, that is not used or taken care of by anyone, and so is covered by wild plants and garbage. [BRIT]

in AM, use **vacant land**

6 PHRASE If something **goes to waste**, it remains unused or has to be thrown away. ❑ *So much of his enormous effort and talent will go to waste if we are forced to drop one hour of the film.* **7 to waste no time** → see **time** ⑤ **8** → See feature box at **recycle**, **time**

▶ **waste away** PHRASAL VERB If someone **wastes away**, they become extremely thin or weak because they are ill or worried and they are not eating properly. ❑ *Persons dying from cancer grow thin and visibly waste away.*

COLLOCATIONS

waste
NOUN
2
verb + **waste**: eliminate, reduce; hate
3
noun + **waste**: food, household
adjective + **waste**: hazardous, nuclear, radioactive, toxic; domestic, industrial
verb + **waste**: dispose of, dump; recycle
VERB **1**
waste + noun: effort, energy, money, time

---

waste|basket /weɪstbæskɪt/ (wastebaskets) N-COUNT A **wastebasket** is the same as a **wastepaper basket**. [AM]

wast|ed /weɪstɪd/ **1** ADJ A **wasted** action is one that is unnecessary. ❑ *I'm sorry you had a wasted journey.* **2** ADJ Someone who is **wasted** is very tired and weak, often because of an illness. ❑ *They look too wasted to care about much.*

waste|ful /weɪstfəl/ ADJ Action that is **wasteful** uses too much of something valuable such as time, money, or energy. ❑ *This kind of training is ineffective, and wasteful of scarce resources.*

waste|land /weɪstlænd/ (wastelands) **1** N-VAR A **wasteland** is an area of land on which not much can grow or which has been spoiled in some way. ❑ *The pollution has already turned vast areas into a wasteland.* **2** N-COUNT If you refer to a place, situation, or period in time as a **wasteland**, you are criticizing it because you think there is nothing interesting or exciting in it. [DISAPPROVAL] ❑ *...the cultural wasteland of the dictator's repressive rule*

waste|paper bas|ket (wastepaper baskets) N-COUNT A **wastepaper basket** is a container for garbage, especially paper, that is usually placed on the floor in the corner of a room or next to a desk.

wast|ing /weɪstɪŋ/ **1** ADJ [ADJ n] A **wasting** disease is one that makes you gradually become thinner and weaker. **2** → See feature box at **time**

wast|rel /weɪstrəl/ (wastrels) N-COUNT If you describe someone as a **wastrel**, you mean that they are lazy and spend their time and money on foolish things. [LITERARY]

WATCH
① LOOKING AND PAYING ATTENTION
② INSTRUMENT THAT TELLS THE TIME

---

① **watch** ✦✦✦ /wɒtʃ/ (watches, watching, watched)
→ Please look at meaning **10** to see if the expression you are looking for is shown under another headword.

1 V-T/V-I If you **watch** someone or something, you look at them, usually for a period of time, and pay attention to what is happening. ❑ *The man was standing in his doorway watching him.* ❑ *He seems to enjoy watching me work.* ❑ *Here, now watch how I cut this, OK?* ❑ *He watched as the Yankees rallied for a second comeback victory.* **2** V-T If you **watch** something on television or an event such as a sports contest, you spend time looking at it, especially when you see it from the beginning to the end. ❑ *I'd stayed up late to watch the movie.* **3** V-T/V-I If you **watch** a situation or event, you pay attention to it or you are aware of it, but you do not influence it. ❑ *Human rights groups have been closely watching the case.* ❑ *He watched as nine people were swept into the crevasse.* **4** V-T If you **watch** people, especially children or animals, you are responsible for them, and make sure that they are not in danger. ❑ *Parents can't be expected to watch their children 24 hours a day.* **5** V-T If you tell someone to **watch** a particular person or thing, you are warning them to be careful that the person or thing does not get out of control or do something unpleasant. ❑ *You really ought to watch these quiet types.* **6** PHRASE If someone **keeps watch**, they look and listen all the time, while other people are asleep or doing something else, so that they can warn them of danger or an attack. ❑ *Jose, as usual, had climbed a tree to keep watch.* **7** PHRASE If you **keep watch** on events or a situation, you pay attention to what is happening, so that you can take action at the right moment. ❑ *U.S. officials have been keeping close watch on the situation.* **8** PHRASE You say '**watch it**' in order to warn

watch

someone to be careful, especially when you want to threaten them about what will happen if they are not careful. ❏ "Now watch it, Patsy," the sergeant told her. **9** PHRASE If someone is being kept **under watch**, they are being guarded or observed all the time. ❏ Doctors confirmed how serious Josephine's condition was, and she is still being kept under watch. **10** PHRASE You say to someone '**you watch**' or '**just watch**' when you are predicting that something will happen, and you are very confident that it will happen as you say. ❏ You watch. Things will get worse before they get better. **11 to watch your step** → see **step**

▶ **watch for** also **watch out for** PHRASAL VERB If you **watch for** something or **watch out for** it, you pay attention so that you notice it, either because you do not want to miss it or because you want to avoid it. ❏ We'll be watching for any developments.

▶ **watch out** PHRASAL VERB If you tell someone to **watch out**, you are warning them to be careful, because something unpleasant might happen to them or they might get into difficulties. ❏ You have to watch out because there are land mines all over the place.

▶ **watch out for** → see **watch for**

═══ SYNONYMS ═══

watch
VERB ① **1**
look: She turned to look at him.
see: I saw a man making his way towards me.
peer: He watched the customs official peer into the driver's window.
stare: Tamara stared at him in disbelief, shaking her head.

② **watch** ✦✧ /wɒtʃ/ (**watches**) **1** N-COUNT A **watch** is a small clock that you wear on a strap on your wrist, or on a chain. **2** → See also color supplement

watch|dog /wɒtʃdɒg/ (**watchdogs**) **1** N-COUNT A **watchdog** is a person or committee whose job is to make sure that companies do not act illegally or irresponsibly. ❏ ...an anticrime watchdog group funded by New York businesses. **2** N-COUNT A **watchdog** is a fierce dog that has been specially trained to protect a particular place. [mainly AM]

-watcher /-wɒtʃər/ (**-watchers**) COMB IN N-COUNT **-watcher** combines with nouns to form other nouns that refer to people who are interested in a group of animals or people, and who study them closely. ❏ The birdwatchers crept about in the bushes. ❏ ...a veteran Vatican-watcher who wrote a biography of the pope.

watch|ful /wɒtʃfəl/ ADJ Someone who is **watchful** notices everything that is happening. ❏ The best thing is to be watchful and see the family doctor for any change in your normal health.

-watching /-wɒtʃɪŋ/ COMB IN N-UNCOUNT **-watching** combines with nouns to form other nouns that refer to the activity of looking at a group of animals or people and studying them because they interest you. ❏ Whale-watching has become a growth leisure industry. ❏ He is said to have invented the sport of celebrity-watching.

watch|man /wɒtʃmən/ (**watchmen**) **1** N-COUNT A **watchman** is a person whose job is to guard a building or area. **2** → see also **night watchman**

watch|tower /wɒtʃtaʊər/ (**watchtowers**) N-COUNT A **watchtower** is a high building that gives a person a good view of the area around the place that they are guarding.

watch|word /wɒtʃwɜrd/ (**watchwords**) N-COUNT Someone's **watchword** is a word or phrase that sums up their attitude or approach to a particular subject or to things in general. ❏ Caution has been one of Mr. Allan's watchwords.

wa|ter ✦✦✦ /wɔtər/ (**waters, watering, watered**) **1** N-UNCOUNT **Water** is a clear thin liquid that has no color or taste when it is pure. It falls from clouds as rain and enters rivers and seas. All animals and people need water in order to live. ❏ Get me a glass of water. ❏ ...the sound of water hammering on the metal roof. **2** N-PLURAL You use **waters** to refer to a large area of sea, especially the area of sea that is near to a country and that is regarded as belonging to it. ❏ The ship will remain outside Chinese territorial waters. **3** V-T If you **water** plants, you pour water over them in order to help them to grow. ❏ He went out to water the plants. **4** V-I If your eyes **water**, tears build up in them because they are hurting or because you are upset. ❏ His eyes watered from cigarette smoke. **5** V-I If you say that your mouth **is watering**, you mean that you can smell or see some nice food

that makes you want to eat it. ❏ ...cookies to make your mouth water. **6** PHRASE If you say that an event or incident is **water under the bridge**, you mean that it has happened and cannot now be changed, so there is no point in worrying about it anymore. ❏ He was relieved his time in jail was over and regarded it as water under the bridge. **7** PHRASE If you are **in deep water**, you are in a difficult or awkward situation. ❏ You certainly seem to be in deep water. **8** PHRASE If an argument or theory does not **hold water**, it does not seem to be reasonable or be in accordance with the facts. ❏ This argument simply cannot hold water in Europe. **9** PHRASE If you are **in hot water**, you are in trouble. [INFORMAL] ❏ The company has already been in hot water over high prices this year. **10** PHRASE If you **pour cold water on** an idea or suggestion, you show that you have a low opinion of it. ❏ University economists pour cold water on the idea that the economic recovery has begun. **11** PHRASE If you **test the water** or **test the waters**, you try to find out what reaction an action or idea will get before you do it or tell it to people. ❏ You should be cautious when getting involved and test the water before committing yourself. **12 like water off a duck's back** → see **duck** **13 to take to something like a duck to water** → see **duck**

▶ **water down** **1** PHRASAL VERB If you **water down** a substance, such as food or drink, you add water to it to make it weaker. ❏ You can water down a glass of wine and make it last twice as long. **2** PHRASAL VERB If something such as a proposal, speech, or statement **is watered down**, it is made much weaker and less forceful, or less likely to make people angry. ❏ Proposed legislation affecting bird-keepers has been watered down.

═══ VOCABULARY IN CONTEXT ═══

Bodies of water

Our planet Earth is sometimes known as 'the blue planet' because, seen from space, its **vast** bodies of water make it appear blue. Water is found in **abundance** all over the planet, from the **oceans** and **seas** that cover 70% of its surface to **water vapor** in the atmosphere and the vast **underground** network of **aquifers**. As a habitat, bodies of water both above and below the ground offer a **diverse range** of conditions to both **aquatic plants** and animals. In fact, much of the plant and animal life found in water **ecosystems** is as yet undiscovered. **Rivers** and **lakes** are homes to **freshwater** fish, amphibians, and invertebrates, such as trout, frogs, and water boatmen. But aquatic ecosystems provide habitats for many **terrestrial organisms**, too. The **lower course** of a river and its **estuary**, where it joins the ocean, is often populated by aquatic birds such as spoonbills, which search for worms or snails under rocks and in the shallow **reedy marshes**.

water|bed /wɔtərbɛd/ (**waterbeds**) also **water bed** N-COUNT A **waterbed** is a bed that consists of a plastic case filled with water.

wa|ter bird (**water birds**) N-COUNT A **water bird** is a bird that swims or walks in water, especially lakes and rivers. There are many kinds of water bird.

water|borne /wɔtərbɔrn/ also **water-borne** **1** ADJ [ADJ n] A **waterborne** disease or infection is one that people can catch from infected water. **2** ADJ [ADJ n] Something that is **waterborne** travels or is transported on water. ◻ ...*a waterborne safari down the Nile.* ◻ *Environmental pressures are strengthening the case for waterborne freight.*

wa|ter bot|tle (water bottles) **1** N-COUNT A **water bottle** is a small container for carrying water to drink. **2** → see also **hot-water bottle 3** → See also color supplement

wa|ter buf|fa|lo (water buffaloes or water buffalo) N-COUNT A **water buffalo** is an animal like a large cow with long horns that curve upward. In some countries water buffalo are kept for their milk and are used to pull plows.

wa|ter can|non (water cannons or water cannon) N-COUNT A **water cannon** is a machine that shoots out a large, powerful stream of water. It is used by police to break up crowds of people who are protesting or fighting.

wa|ter chest|nut (water chestnuts) N-COUNT A **water chestnut** is the thick bottom part of the stem of a plant that grows in China. It is used in Chinese cooking.

water|color /wɔtərkʌlər/ (watercolors)

in BRIT, use **watercolour**

1 N-VAR **Watercolors** are colored paints, used for painting pictures, which you apply with a wet brush or dissolve in water first. ◻ *Oil paints can be replaced with watercolors.* **2** N-COUNT A **watercolor** is a picture that has been painted with watercolors. ◻ *...a lovely watercolor by J. M. W. Turner.* **3** → See feature box at **fine art**

wa|ter cool|er (water coolers) **1** N-COUNT A **water cooler** is a machine that dispenses drinking water, especially in an office. **2** N-SING **Water cooler** is used in expressions that refer to the informal conversations that people have in their office or workplace. ◻ *The movie makes for great conversation at the water cooler.*

water|course /wɔtərkɔrs/ (watercourses) also **water course** N-COUNT A **watercourse** is a stream or river, or the channel that it flows along. [FORMAL]

water|cress /wɔtərkrɛs/ N-UNCOUNT **Watercress** is a small plant with white flowers that grows in streams and pools. Its leaves have a sharp taste and are eaten raw in salads.

watered-down also **watered down** **1** ADJ If you describe something such as a proposal, speech, or statement as **watered-down**, you mean that it is weaker or less forceful than its original form. ◻ *The mayor introduced a watered-down version of the proposals.* **2** → see also **water down**

water|fall /wɔtərfɔl/ (waterfalls) N-COUNT A **waterfall** is a place where water flows over the edge of a steep, high cliff in hills or mountains, and falls into a pool below. ◻ ...*Angel Falls, the world's highest waterfall.*

wa|ter fea|ture (water features) N-COUNT A **water feature** is something such as an artificial pond or waterfall, usually in a garden.

water|fowl /wɔtərfaʊl/ (waterfowl) N-COUNT **Waterfowl** are birds that swim in water, especially ducks, geese, and swans.

water|front /wɔtərfrʌnt/ (waterfronts) N-COUNT A **waterfront** is a street or piece of land next to an area of water, such as a harbor or the sea. ◻ *They went for a stroll along the waterfront.*

Water|gate /wɔtərgeɪt/ N-PROPER **Watergate** is used to refer to the events that surrounded the break-in at the Watergate building in Washington, D.C., during the U.S. presidential election campaign of 1972, and the impeachment and resignation of President Richard Nixon as a result of his role in the incident. ◻ ...*the Watergate scandal.*

wa|ter hole (water holes) also **waterhole** N-COUNT In a desert or other dry area, a **water hole** is a pool of water where animals can drink.

wa|ter|ing can (watering cans) N-COUNT A **watering can** is a container with a long spout that is used to water plants.

wa|ter|ing hole (watering holes) N-COUNT You can refer to a bar where people go to drink and meet their friends as a **watering hole**. ◻ *I was in my favorite watering hole, waiting for the game to start.*

wa|ter jump (water jumps) N-COUNT A **water jump** is a fence with a pool of water on the far side of it, which people or horses jump over as part of a race or competition.

wa|ter lily (water lilies) also **waterlily** N-COUNT A **water lily** is a plant with large flat leaves and colorful flowers that floats on the surface of lakes and rivers.

water|line /wɔtərlaɪn/ (waterlines) also **water line** N-COUNT [usu sing] The **waterline** is a line, either real or imaginary, on the side of a ship representing the level the water reaches when the ship is at sea. ◻ *Ray painted below the waterline with a special anti-rust paint.*

water|logged /wɔtərlɔgd/ ADJ Something such as soil or land that is **waterlogged** is so wet that it cannot absorb any more water, so that a layer of water remains on its surface. ◻ *Most evacuees began returning to waterlogged homes Sunday.*

wa|ter main (water mains) N-COUNT A **water main** is a very large underground pipe used for supplying water to houses and factories.

water|mark /wɔtərmɑrk/ (watermarks) **1** N-COUNT A **watermark** is a design that is put into paper when it is made, and that you can only see if you hold the paper up to the light. Paper money often has a watermark, to make it harder to copy illegally. **2** → see also **high-water mark**

wa|ter mead|ow (water meadows) N-COUNT [usu pl] **Water meadows** are wet fields of grass near a river, which are often flooded.

water|melon /wɔtərmɛlən/ (watermelons) N-VAR A **watermelon** is a large, heavy fruit with green skin, pink flesh, and black seeds.

water|mill /wɔtərmɪl/ (watermills) also **water mill** N-COUNT A **watermill** is a mill powered by a water wheel.

wa|ter pis|tol (water pistols) N-COUNT A **water pistol** is a small toy gun that shoots out water.

wa|ter polo N-UNCOUNT **Water polo** is a game played in a swimming pool in which two teams of swimmers try to score goals with a ball.

water|proof /wɔtərpruf/ ADJ Something that is **waterproof** does not let water pass through it. ◻ *Take waterproof clothing – Oregon weather is unpredictable.*

water-resistant ADJ Something that is **water-resistant** does not allow water to pass through it easily, or is not easily damaged by water. ◻ *Microfiber fabrics are both water-resistant and windproof.*

water|shed /wɔtərʃɛd/ (watersheds) N-COUNT If something such as an event is a **watershed** in the history or development of something, it is very important because it represents the beginning of a new stage in it. ◻ *The election of Mary Robinson in 1990 was a watershed in Irish politics.*

water|side /wɔtərsaɪd/ N-SING [oft N n] The **waterside** is the area beside a stretch of water such as a river or lake. ◻ *Her garden stretches down to the waterside.*

water-ski (water-skis, water-skiing, water-skied) also **waterski** V-I If you **water-ski**, you stand on skis in the water while being pulled along by a boat. ◻ *The staff will be happy to help arrange for you to swim, sail, or water-ski.* • **water-skiing** N-UNCOUNT ◻ *He offered to teach them water-skiing.*

water-soluble also **water soluble** ADJ Something that is **water-soluble** dissolves in water. ◻ *Vitamin C is water soluble.* ◻ ...*oat bran and other water-soluble fibers.*

wa|ter sup|ply (water supplies) N-COUNT The **water supply** in an area is the water that is collected and passed through pipes to buildings for people to use. ◻ *The town is without electricity and the water supply has been cut off.*

wa|ter ta|ble (water tables) N-COUNT [usu the N] The **water table** is the level below the surface of the ground where water can be found. ◻ *Environmentalists say that diverting water from the river will lower the water table and dry out wells.*

water|tight /wɔtərtaɪt/ also **water-tight** **1** ADJ Something that is **watertight** does not allow water to pass through it, for example, because it is tightly sealed. ◻ *The flask is completely watertight, even when laid on its side.* **2** ADJ A **watertight** case, argument, or agreement is one that has been so carefully put together that nobody will be able to find a fault in it. [mainly BRIT]

in AM, usually use **airtight**

wa|ter tow|er (water towers) N-COUNT A **water tower** is a large tank of water placed on a high metal structure so that water can be supplied at a steady pressure to surrounding buildings.

water|way /wɔ̱tərweɪ/ (waterways) N-COUNT A **waterway** is a canal, river, or narrow channel of sea which ships or boats can sail along. ❑ *There are more than 400 miles of waterways to explore in the area.*

waterwheel /wɔ̱tərwil/ (waterwheels) also **water wheel** N-COUNT A **waterwheel** is a large wheel that is turned by water flowing through it. Waterwheels are used to provide power to drive machinery.

wa|ter wings N-PLURAL **Water wings** are plastic rings filled with air that people who are learning to swim wear on their upper arms to help them float. ❑ *...kids in their little water wings.*

water|works /wɔ̱tərwɜrks/ (waterworks) N-COUNT A **waterworks** is a building where a supply of water is stored and cleaned before being distributed to the public.

wa|tery /wɔ̱təri/ **1** ADJ Something that is **watery** is weak or pale. ❑ *A watery light began to show through the branches.* **2** ADJ If you describe food or drink as **watery**, you dislike it because it contains too much water, or has no flavor. [DISAPPROVAL] ❑ *...a bowl of watery soup.* **3** ADJ Something that is **watery** contains, resembles, or consists of water. ❑ *There was a watery discharge from her ear.*

watt /wɒt/ (watts) N-COUNT A **watt** is a unit of measurement of electrical power. ❑ *Use a 3 amp fuse for equipment up to 720 watts.*

watt|age /wɒtɪdʒ/ N-UNCOUNT The **wattage** of a piece of electrical equipment is the amount of electrical power that it produces or uses, expressed in watts.

wat|tle /wɒtəl/ N-UNCOUNT **Wattle** is a framework made by weaving thin sticks through thick sticks to make fences and walls. [BRIT]

wave ✦✧ /weɪv/ (waves, waving, waved) **1** V-T/V-I If you **wave** or **wave** your hand, you move your hand from side to side in the air, usually in order to say hello or goodbye to someone. ❑ *Jessica caught sight of Lois and waved to her.* ❑ *He grinned, waved, and said, "Hi!"* • N-COUNT **Wave** is also a noun. ❑ *Steve stopped him with a wave of the hand.* **2** V-T If you **wave** someone away or **wave** them on, you make a movement with your hand to indicate that they should move in a particular direction. ❑ *Leshka waved him away with a show of irritation.* ❑ *He waited for a policeman to stop the traffic and wave the people on.* **3** V-T If you **wave** something, you hold it up and move it rapidly from side to side. ❑ *Hospital staff were outside to welcome him, waving flags and applauding.* **4** V-I If something **waves**, it moves gently from side to side or up and down. ❑ *...grass and flowers waving in the wind.* **5** N-COUNT A **wave** is a raised mass of water on the surface of water, especially the sea, which is caused by the wind or by tides making the surface of the water rise and fall. ❑ *...the sound of the waves breaking on the shore.* **6** N-COUNT If someone's hair has **waves**, it curves slightly instead of being straight. ❑ *Her blue eyes shone and caught the light, and so did the platinum waves in her hair.* **7** N-COUNT A **wave** is a sudden increase in heat or energy that spreads out from an earthquake or explosion. ❑ *The shock waves of the earthquake were felt in Teheran.* **8** N-COUNT **Waves** are the form in which things such as sound, light, and radio signals travel. ❑ *Regular repeating actions such as sound waves, light waves, or radio waves have a certain frequency, or number of waves per second.* **9** N-COUNT If you refer to a **wave** of a particular feeling, you mean that it increases quickly and becomes very intense, and then often decreases again. ❑ *She felt a wave of panic, but forced herself to leave the room calmly.* **10** N-COUNT A **wave** is a sudden increase in a particular activity or type of behavior, especially an undesirable or unpleasant one. ❑ *...the current wave of violence.* ❑ *A vaccine may help in warding off a second wave of the pandemic next year.* **11** → see also **new wave**, **tidal wave**

wave|band /weɪvbænd/ (wavebands) N-COUNT A **waveband** is a group of radio waves of similar length that are used for particular types of radio communication.

wave|length /weɪvlɛŋθ/ (wavelengths) **1** N-COUNT A **wavelength** is the distance between a part of a wave of energy such as light or sound and the next similar part. ❑ *Sunlight consists of different wavelengths of radiation.* **2** N-COUNT A **wavelength** is the size of radio wave that a particular radio station uses to broadcast its programs. ❑ *She found the wavelength of their broadcasts, and left the radio tuned to their station.* **3** PHRASE If two people are **on the same wavelength**, they find it easy to understand each other and they tend to agree, because they share similar interests or opinions. ❑ *We could complete each other's sentences because we were on the same wavelength.*

wave|let /weɪvlɪt/ (wavelets) N-COUNT [usu pl] **Wavelets** are small waves on the surface of a sea or lake. [LITERARY]

wa|ver /weɪvər/ (wavers, wavering, wavered) **1** V-I If you **waver**, you cannot decide about something or you consider changing your mind about something. ❑ *Some military commanders wavered over whether to support the coup.* **2** V-I If something **wavers**, it shakes with very slight movements or changes. ❑ *The shadows of the dancers wavered continually.*

wavy /weɪvi/ (wavier, waviest) **1** ADJ **Wavy** hair is not straight or curly, but curves slightly. ❑ *She had short, wavy brown hair.* **2** ADJ A **wavy** line has a series of regular curves along it. ❑ *The boxes were decorated with a wavy gold line.*

wax /wæks/ (waxes, waxing, waxed) **1** N-MASS **Wax** is a solid, slightly shiny substance made of fat or oil that is used to make candles and polish. It melts when it is heated. ❑ *There were colored candles which had spread pools of wax on the furniture.* **2** → see also **beeswax** **3** V-T If you **wax** a surface, you put a thin layer of wax onto it, especially in order to polish it. ❑ *We'd have long talks while she helped me wax the floor.* **4** N-UNCOUNT **Wax** is the sticky yellow substance found in your ears. ❑ *Use a Q-Tip to remove the wax from your ears.* **5** V-T If you have a part of your body **waxed**, for example your legs, you have the hair removed from the area by having wax put on it and then pulled off quickly. ❑ *She has just had her legs waxed at the local beauty parlor.*

waxed pa|per N-UNCOUNT **Waxed paper** is the same as **wax paper**.

wax|en /wæksən/ ADJ A **waxen** face is very pale and looks very unhealthy. [LITERARY]

wax pa|per N-UNCOUNT **Wax paper** is paper that has been covered with a thin layer of wax. It is used mainly in cooking or to wrap food. [AM]

wax|work /wæksw3rk/ (waxworks) **1** N-COUNT A **waxwork** is a model of a person, especially a famous person, made out of wax. **2** N-COUNT A **waxworks** is a place where waxworks are displayed for the public to look at. **Waxworks** is both the singular and the plural form.

waxy /wæksi/ (waxier, waxiest) ADJ [usu ADJ n] Something that is **waxy** looks or feels like wax. ❑ *Choose small waxy potatoes for the salad.* ❑ *...the waxy coating on the insect's body.*

WAY
① NOUN AND ADVERB USES
② PHRASES: GROUP 1
③ PHRASES: GROUP 2
④ PHRASES: GROUP 3
⑤ PHRASES: GROUP 4
---

① **way** ✦✦✦ /weɪ/ (ways) **1** N-COUNT If you refer to a **way** of doing something, you are referring to how you can do it, for example, the action you can take or the method you can use to achieve it. ❑ *Freezing isn't a bad way of preserving food.* ❑ *I worked myself into a frenzy plotting ways to make him jealous.* ❑ *There just might be a way.* **2** N-COUNT If you talk about the **way** someone does something, you are talking about the qualities their action has. ❑ *She smiled in a friendly way.* ❑ *He had a strange way of talking.* **3** N-COUNT If a general statement or description is true in a particular **way**, this is the form of it that is true in a particular case. ❑ *Computerized reservation systems help airline profits in several ways.* ❑ *She was afraid in a way that was quite new to her.* **4** N-COUNT You use **way** in expressions such as **in some ways**, **in many ways**, and **in every way** to indicate the degree or extent to which a statement is true. ❑ *In some ways, the official opening is a formality.* **5** N-PLURAL The **ways** of a particular person or group of people are their customs or their usual behavior. ❑ *He denounces people who urge him to alter his ways.* ❑ *She began to study the ways of the Native Americans.* **6** N-SING If you refer to someone's **way**, you are referring to their usual or preferred type of behavior. ❏ *She is now divorced and, in her usual resourceful way, has started her own business.* **7** N-COUNT You use **way** to refer to one particular opinion or interpretation of something, when others are possible. ❏ *I suppose that's one way of looking at it.* ❏ *With most of her lyrics, however, there are several different ways of interpreting the words.* **8** N-COUNT You use **way** when mentioning one of a number of possible, alternative results or decisions. ❏ *There is no indication which way the vote could go.* **9** N-SING The **way** you feel about something is your attitude to it or your opinion about it. ❏ *I'm so sorry – I had no idea you felt that way.* **10** N-SING If you mention the **way** that something happens, you are mentioning the fact that it happens. ❏ *I hate the way he manipulates people.* **11** N-SING You use **way** in expressions such as **push your way, work your way**, or **eat your way**, followed by a prepositional phrase or adverb, in order to indicate movement, progress, or force as well as the action described by the verb. ❏ *She thrust her way into the crowd.* **12** N-COUNT The **way** somewhere consists of the different places that you go through or the route that you take in order to get there. ❏ *Does anybody know the way to the bathroom?* ❏ *I'm afraid I can't remember the way.* **13** N-SING If you go or look a particular **way**, you go or look in that direction. ❏ *As he strode into the kitchen, he passed Pop coming the other way.* ❏ *They paused at the top of the stairs, doubtful as to which way to go next.* **14** N-SING You can refer to the direction you are traveling in as your **way**. [SPOKEN] ❏ *She would say she was going my way and offer me a lift.* **15** N-SING If you lose your **way**, you take a wrong or unfamiliar route, so that you do not know how to get to the place that you want to go to. If you find your **way**, you manage to get to the place that you want to go to. ❏ *The men lost their way in a sandstorm and crossed the border by mistake.* **16** N-COUNT You talk about people going their different **ways** in order to say that their lives develop differently and they have less contact with each other. ❏ *It wasn't until we each went our separate ways that I began to learn how to do things for myself.* **17** N-SING If something comes your **way**, you get it or receive it. ❏ *Take advantage of the opportunities coming your way in a couple of months.* **18** N-SING You use **way** in expressions such as **the right way up** and **the other way around** to refer to one of two or more possible positions or arrangements that something can have. ❏ *Books have a right and a wrong way up.* **19** ADV [ADV adv/prep] You can use **way** to emphasize, for example, that something is a great distance away or is very much below or above a particular level or amount. [EMPHASIS] ❏ *Way down in the valley to the west is the town of Freiburg.* ❏ *You've waited way too long.* **20** N-PLURAL If you split something a number of **ways**, you divide it into a number of different parts or quantities, usually fairly equal in size. ❏ *The region was split three ways, between Greece, Serbia and Bulgaria.* • COMB IN ADJ [ADJ n] **Way** is also a combining form. ❏ *...a simple three-way division.* **21** N-SING **Way** is used in expressions such as **a long way, a little way**, and **quite a way**, to say how far away something is or how far you have traveled. ❏ *Some of them live in places quite a long way from here.* ❏ *A little way further down the lane we passed the driveway to a house.* **22** N-SING **Way** is used in expressions such as **a long way, a little way**, and **quite a way**, to say how far away in time something is. ❏ *Success is still a long way off.* **23** N-SING You use **way** in expressions such as **all the way, most of the way** and **half the way** to refer to the extent to which an action has been completed. ❏ *He had unscrewed the caps most of the way.*

② **way** ♦♦♦ /weɪ/ (ways) **1** PHRASE You use **all the way** to emphasize how long a distance is. [EMPHASIS] ❏ *He had to walk all the way home.* **2** PHRASE You can use **all the way** to emphasize that your remark applies to every part of a situation, activity, or period of time. [EMPHASIS] ❏ *Having started a revolution we must go all the way.* **3** PHRASE If someone says that you **can't have it both ways**, they are telling you that you have to choose between two things and cannot do or have them both. ❏ *Countries cannot have it both ways: the cost of a cleaner environment may sometimes be fewer jobs in dirty industries.* **4** PHRASE You say **by the way** when you add something to what you are saying, especially something that you have just thought of. [SPOKEN] ❏ *The name Latifah, by the way, means "delicate".* **5** PHRASE If you **clear the way, open the way**, or **prepare the way** for something, you create an opportunity for it to happen. ❏ *The talks are meant to clear the way for formal negotiations on a new constitution.* **6** PHRASE If you say that someone takes **the easy way out**, you disapprove of them because they do what is easiest for them in a difficult situation, rather than dealing with it properly. [DISAPPROVAL] ❏ *As soon as things got difficult he took the easy way out.* **7** PHRASE You use **either way** in order to introduce a statement that is true in each of the two possible or alternative cases that you have just mentioned. ❏ *The sea may rise or the land may fall; either way the sand dunes will be gone in a short time.* **8** PHRASE If you say that a particular type of action or development is **the way forward**, you approve of it because it is likely to lead to success. [APPROVAL] ❏ *...people who genuinely believe that anarchy is the way forward.* **9** PHRASE If someone **gets** their **way** or **has** their **way**, nobody stops them from doing what they want to do. You can also say that someone **gets** their **own way** or **has** their **own way**. ❏ *She is very good at using her charm to get her way.* **10** PHRASE If one thing **gives way to** another, the first thing is replaced by the second. ❏ *First he had been numb. Then the numbness gave way to anger.* **11** PHRASE If an object that is supporting something **gives way**, it breaks or collapses, so that it can no longer support that thing. ❏ *The hook in the ceiling had given way and the lamp had fallen blazing on to the table.*

③ **way** ♦♦♦ /weɪ/ (ways) **1** PHRASE You use **in no way** or **not in any way** to emphasize that a statement is not at all true. [EMPHASIS] ❏ *In no way am I going to adopt any of his methods.* **2** PHRASE If you say that something is true **in a way**, you mean that although it is not completely true, it is true to a limited extent or in certain respects. You use **in a way** to reduce the force of a statement. [VAGUENESS] ❏ *In a way, I suppose I'm frightened of failing.* **3** PHRASE If you say that someone **gets in the way** or **is in the way**, you are annoyed because their presence or their actions stop you from doing something properly. ❏ *"We wouldn't get in the way," Suzanne promised. "We'd just stand quietly in a corner."* **4** PHRASE To **get in the way** of something means to make it difficult for it to happen, continue, or be appreciated properly. ❏ *She had a job which never got in the way of her leisure interests.* **5** PHRASE If you **know** your **way around** a particular subject, system, or job, you know all the procedures and facts about it. ❏ *He knows his way around the intricate maze of patent law.* **6** PHRASE If you **lead the way** along a particular route, you go along it in front of someone in order to show them where to go. ❏ *She grabbed his suitcase and led the way.* **7** PHRASE If a person or group **leads the way** in a particular activity, they are the first person or group to do it or they make the most new developments in it. ❏ *Samsung has led the way in research and development in this area.* **8** PHRASE If you say that someone or something **has come a long way**, you mean that they have developed, progressed, or become very successful. ❏ *He has come a long way since the days he could only afford one meal a day.* **9** PHRASE If you say that something is **a long way from** being true, you are emphasizing that it is definitely not true. [EMPHASIS] ❏ *She is a long way from being the richest person in Florida.* **10** PHRASE If you say that something **goes a long way** toward doing a particular thing, you mean that it is an important factor in achieving that thing. ❏ *Being respectful and courteous goes a long way toward building a relationship.*

④ **way** ♦♦♦ /weɪ/ (ways) **1** PHRASE If you say that someone has **lost** their **way**, you are criticizing them because they do not have any good ideas anymore, or seem to have become unsure about what to do. [DISAPPROVAL] ❏ *Why has the White House lost its way on tax and budget policy?* **2** PHRASE When you **make** your **way** somewhere, you walk or travel there. ❏ *He made his way to the marketplace.* **3** PHRASE If one person or thing **makes way** for another, the first is replaced by the second. ❏ *He said he was prepared to make way for younger people in the party.* **4** PHRASE If you say **there's no way** that something will happen, you are emphasizing that you think it will definitely not happen. [EMPHASIS] ❏ *There was absolutely no way that we were going to be able to retrieve it.* **5** PHRASE You can say **no way** as an emphatic way of saying no. [INFORMAL, EMPHASIS] ❏ *Mike, no way am I playing cards with you for money.* **6** PHRASE If you **are on** your **way**, you have started your trip somewhere. ❏ *He has been allowed to leave the country and is on his way to Hawaii.* **7** PHRASE If something happens **on the way** or **along the way**, it happens during the course of a particular event or process. ❏ *You may have to learn a few new skills along the way.* **8** PHRASE If you are **on** your **way** or **well on** your **way** to something, you have made so much progress that you are almost certain to achieve that thing. ❏ *I am now out of the hospital and well on the way to recovery.* **9** PHRASE If something is **on the way**, it will arrive soon. ❏ *The forecasters say more snow is on the way.* **10** PHRASE You can use **one way or another** or **one way or the other** when you want to say that something definitely happens, but without giving any details about how it happens. [VAGUENESS] ❏ *You know pretty well everyone here, one way or the other.* **11** PHRASE You use **one way or the other** or **one way or another** to refer to two possible decisions or conclusions that have previously been mentioned, without stating which one is reached or preferred. ❏ *We've got to make our decision one way or the other.*

⑤ **way** ✦✦✦ /weɪ/ (ways) **1** PHRASE You use **the other way around** to refer to the opposite of what you have just said. ❏ *You'd think you were the one who did me the favor, and not the other way around.* **2** PHRASE If something or someone is **on the way out** or **on** their **way out**, they are likely to disappear or to be replaced very soon. ❏ *There are encouraging signs that cold war attitudes are on the way out.* **3** PHRASE If you **go out of** your **way** to do something, for example, to help someone, you make a special effort to do it. ❏ *He was very kind to me and seemed to go out of his way to help me.* **4** PHRASE If you **keep out of** someone's **way** or **stay out of** their **way**, you avoid them or do not get involved with them. ❏ *I'd kept out of his way as much as I could.* **5** PHRASE When something is **out of the way**, it has finished or you have dealt with it, so that it is no longer a problem or needs no more time spent on it. ❏ *The plan has to remain confidential at least until the local elections are out of the way.* **6** PHRASE If you **go** your **own way**, you do what you want rather than what everyone else does or expects. ❏ *In school I was a loner. I went my own way.* **7** PHRASE You use **in the same way** to introduce a situation that you are comparing with one that you have just mentioned, because there is a strong similarity between them. ❏ *There is no reason why an aircraft designer should also be a good pilot. In the same way, a good pilot can be a bad driver.* **8** PHRASE You can use **that way** and **this way** to refer to a statement or comment that you have just made. ❏ *We have a beautiful city and we pray it stays that way.* **9** PHRASE You can use **that way** or **this way** to refer to an action or situation that you have just mentioned, when you go on to mention the likely consequence or effect of it. ❏ *Keep the soil moist. That way, the seedling will flourish.* **10** → see also **underway**

-way /-weɪ/ **1** COMB IN ADJ **-way** combines with numbers to form adjectives that describe a means of communication that functions or takes place between the stated number of people. ❏ *...a two-way radio.* ❏ *Features include caller ID and three-way calling.* **2** → see also **one-way, two-way**

way|lay /weɪleɪ/ (waylays, waylaying, waylaid) V-T If someone **waylays** you, they stop you when you are going somewhere, for example, in order to talk to you, to steal something from you, or to attack you. ❏ *The trucks are being waylaid by bandits.* ❏ *I'm sorry, Nick, I got waylaid.*

way of life (ways of life) **1** N-COUNT A **way of life** is the behavior and habits that are typical of a particular person or group, or that are chosen by them. ❏ *Mining activities have totally disrupted the traditional way of life of the Yanomami Indians.* **2** N-COUNT If you describe a particular activity as a **way of life** for someone, you mean that it has become a very important and regular thing in their life, rather than something they do or experience occasionally. ❏ *She likes traveling so much it's become a way of life for her.*

way-out ADJ If you describe someone or something as **way-out**, you are critical of them because they are very unusual, often in a way that is very modern or fashionable. [INFORMAL, DISAPPROVAL] ❏ *They will not allow your more way-out ideas to pass unchallenged.*

way|side /weɪsaɪd/ (waysides) **1** N-COUNT [usu the N in sing] The **wayside** is the side of the road. [LITERARY] **2** PHRASE If a person or plan **falls by the wayside**, they fail or stop before they complete what they set out to do. ❏ *Amateurs fall by the wayside when the going gets tough.*

way sta|tion (way stations) **1** N-COUNT A **way station** is a place where people stop to eat and rest when they are on a long trip. **2** N-COUNT A **way station** is a small station between two large stations on a railroad. [AM]

way|ward /weɪwərd/ ADJ If you describe a person or their behavior as **wayward**, you mean that they behave in a selfish, bad, or unpredictable way, and are difficult to control. ❏ *...wayward children with a history of severe emotional problems.*

we ✦✦✦ /wi, STRONG wiː/

> **We** is the first person plural pronoun. **We** is used as the subject of a verb.

1 PRON-PLURAL A speaker or writer uses **we** to refer both to himself or herself and to one or more other people as a group. You can use **we** before a noun to make it clear which group of people you are referring to. ❏ *We both swore we'd be friends ever after.* ❏ *We ordered another bottle of champagne.* **2** PRON-PLURAL **We** is sometimes used to refer to people in general. ❏ *We need to take care of our bodies.* **3** PRON-PLURAL A speaker or writer may use **we** instead of 'I' in order to include the audience or reader in what they are saying, especially when discussing how a talk or book is organized. [FORMAL] ❏ *We will now consider the raw materials from which the body derives energy.*

weak ✦✦✧ /wiːk/ (weaker, weakest) **1** ADJ If someone is **weak**, they are not healthy or do not have good muscles, so that they cannot move quickly or carry heavy things. ❏ *I was too weak to move or think or speak.* • **weak|ly** ADV [ADV with v] ❏ *"I'm all right," Max said weakly, but his breathing came in jagged gasps.* • **weak|ness** N-UNCOUNT ❏ *Symptoms of anemia include weakness, fatigue and iron deficiency.* **2** ADJ If someone has an organ or sense that is **weak**, it is not very effective or powerful, or is likely to fail. ❏ *She tired easily and had a weak heart.* **3** ADJ If you describe someone as **weak**, you mean that they are not very confident or determined, so that they are often frightened or worried, or easily influenced by other people. ❏ *He was a nice doctor, but a weak man who wasn't going to stick his neck out.* • **weak|ness** N-UNCOUNT ❏ *Many people felt that admitting to stress was a sign of weakness.* **4** ADJ If you describe someone's voice or smile as **weak**, you mean that it not very loud or big, suggesting that the person lacks confidence, enthusiasm, or physical strength. ❏ *His weak voice was almost inaudible.* • **weak|ly** ADV [ADV after v] ❏ *He smiled weakly at reporters.* **5** ADJ If an object or surface is **weak**, it breaks easily and cannot support a lot of weight or resist a lot of strain. ❏ *The owner said the bird may have escaped through a weak spot in the aviary.* **6** ADV A **weak** physical force does not have much power or intensity. ❏ *The molecules in regular liquids are held together by relatively weak bonds.* ❏ *Strong winds can turn boats when the tide is weak.* • **weak|ly** ADV ❏ *The mineral is weakly magnetic.* **7** ADJ If individuals or groups are **weak**, they do not have any power or influence. ❏ *The council was too weak to do anything about it.* • N-PLURAL **The weak** are people who are weak. ❏ *He voiced his solidarity with the weak and defenseless.* • **weak|ness** N-UNCOUNT ❏ *It made me feel patronized, in a position of weakness.* **8** ADJ A **weak** government or leader does not have much control, and is not prepared or able to act firmly or severely. ❏ *The changes come after mounting criticism that the government is weak and indecisive.* • **weak|ly** ADV ❏ *...the weakly-led movement for reform.* • **weak|ness** N-UNCOUNT ❏ *Officials fear that he might interpret the emphasis on diplomacy as a sign of weakness.* **9** ADJ If you describe something such a country's currency, economy, industry, or government as **weak**, you mean that it is not successful, and may be likely to fail or collapse. ❏ *The weak dollar means American goods are relative bargains for foreigners.* • **weak|ness** N-UNCOUNT ❏ *The weakness of his regime is showing more and more.* **10** ADJ If something such as an argument or case is **weak**, it is not convincing or there is little evidence to support it. ❏ *Do you think the prosecution made any particular errors, or did they just have a weak case?* • **weak|ly** ADV [ADV before v] ❏ *The president listened to that statement and responded rather weakly.* • **weak|ness** (weaknesses) N-VAR ❏ *Critical thinking requires that you examine the weaknesses of any argument.* **11** ADJ A **weak** drink, chemical, or drug contains very little of a particular substance, for example, because a lot of water has been added to it. ❏ *Grace poured a cup of weak tea.* **12** ADJ Your **weak** points are the qualities or talents you do not possess, or the things you are not very good at. ❏ *Geography was my weak subject.* • **weak|ness** N-VAR ❏ *His only weakness is his temperament.* **13** → see also **weakness**

weak|en ✦✧✧ /wiːkən/ (weakens, weakening, weakened) **1** V-T/V-I If you **weaken** something or if it **weakens**, it becomes less strong or less powerful. ☐ *The recession has weakened so many businesses that many can no longer survive.* ☐ *Family structures are weakening and breaking up.* **2** V-T/V-I If your resolve **weakens** or if something **weakens** it, you become less determined or less certain about taking a particular course of action that you had previously decided to take. ☐ *I looked at the list and felt my resolve weakening.* ☐ *Jennie weakened, and finally relented.* **3** V-T If something **weakens** you, it causes you to lose some of your physical strength. ☐ *Malnutrition obviously weakens the patient.* **4** V-T If something **weakens** an object, it does something to it that causes it to become less firm and more likely to break. ☐ *A bomb blast had weakened an area of brick on the back wall.*

weak-kneed ADJ If you describe someone as **weak-kneed**, you mean that they are unable or unwilling to do anything because they are influenced by a strong emotion such as fear. [INFORMAL] ☐ *He would need all his authority to keep the weak-kneed volunteers from bolting.*

weak|ling /wi̱klɪŋ/ (**weaklings**) N-COUNT If you describe a person or an animal as a **weakling**, you mean that they are physically weak. [DISAPPROVAL] ☐ *You were never a ninety-eight pound weakling.*

weak|ness /wi̱knɪs/ (**weaknesses**) **1** N-COUNT If you have a **weakness** for something, you like it very much, although this is perhaps surprising or undesirable. ☐ *Stephen himself had a weakness for cats.* **2** → see also **weak**

weal /wi̱l/ (**weals**) N-COUNT A **weal** is a swelling made on someone's skin by a blow, especially from something sharp or thin such as a sword or whip.

wealth ✦✧✧ /we̱lθ/ **1** N-UNCOUNT **Wealth** is the possession of a large amount of money, property, or other valuable things. You can also refer to a particular person's money or property as their **wealth**. ☐ *Economic reform has brought relative wealth to peasant farmers.* **2** N-SING [a N of n] If you say that someone or something has **a wealth of** good qualities or things, you are emphasizing that they have a very large number or amount of them. [FORMAL, EMPHASIS] ☐ *Their websites contain a wealth of information on the topic.* ☐ *The city boasts a wealth of beautiful churches.*

wealthy /we̱lθi/ (**wealthier, wealthiest**) ADJ Someone who is **wealthy** has a large amount of money, property, or valuable possessions. ☐ *...a wealthy international businessman.* • N-PLURAL **The wealthy** are people who are wealthy. ☐ *The best education should not be available only to the wealthy.*

wean /wi̱n/ (**weans, weaning, weaned**) **1** V-T When a baby or baby animal **is weaned**, its mother stops feeding it milk and starts giving it other food, especially solid food. ☐ *When would be the best time to start weaning my baby?* **2** V-T If you **wean** someone off a habit or something they like, you gradually make them stop doing it or liking it, especially when you think it is bad for them. ☐ *You are given capsules or pills with small quantities of nicotine to wean you from the habit.*

weap|on ✦✧✧ /we̱pən/ (**weapons**) N-COUNT A **weapon** is an object such as a gun, a knife, or a missile, which is used to kill or hurt people in a fight or a war. ☐ *...nuclear weapons.*

weap|on|ize /we̱pənaɪz/ (**weaponizes, weaponizing, weaponized**)

[in BRIT, also use **weaponise**]

V-T If a substance or material **is weaponized**, it is used as a weapon or made into a weapon. If an area **is weaponized**, it is used as a location for weapons. ☐ *They were close to weaponizing ricin – a lethal plant toxin.* ☐ *...the plan to weaponize outer space.*

wea|pon|ry /we̱pənri/ N-UNCOUNT **Weaponry** is all the weapons that a group or country has or that are available to it. ☐ *...rich nations, armed with superior weaponry.*

weapons-grade ADJ [ADJ n] **Weapons-grade** substances such as uranium or plutonium are of a quality that makes them suitable for use in the manufacture of nuclear weapons. ☐ *...equipment which can produce weapons-grade uranium.*

weap|ons of mass de|struc|tion N-PLURAL **Weapons of mass destruction** are biological, chemical, or nuclear weapons. The abbreviation **WMD** is often used.

wear ✦✧✧ /we̱ər/ (**wears, wearing, wore, worn**) **1** V-T When you **wear** something such as clothes, shoes, or jewelry, you have them on your body or on part of your body. ☐ *He was wearing a brown uniform.* ☐ *I sometimes wear contact lenses.* **2** V-T If you **wear** your hair or beard in a particular way, you have it cut or styled in that way. ☐ *She wore her hair in a long braid.* **3** N-UNCOUNT You use **wear** to refer to clothes that are suitable for a certain time or place. For example, **evening wear** is clothes suitable for the evening. ☐ *The shop stocks an extensive range of beach wear.* **4** N-UNCOUNT **Wear** is the amount or type of use that something has over a period of time. ☐ *You'll get more wear out of a hat if you choose one in a neutral color.* **5** N-UNCOUNT **Wear** is the damage or change that is caused by something being used a lot or for a long time. ☐ *...a large, well-upholstered armchair which showed signs of wear.* **6** V-I If something **wears**, it becomes thinner or weaker because it is constantly being used over a long period of time. ☐ *The stone steps, dating back to 1855, are beginning to wear.* **7** V-I You can use **wear** to talk about how well something lasts over a period of time. For example, if something **wears well**, it still seems quite new or useful after a long time or a lot of use. ☐ *Ten years on, the original concept was wearing well.*

▶ **wear away** PHRASAL VERB If you **wear** something **away** or if it **wears away**, it becomes thin and eventually disappears because it is used a lot or rubbed a lot. ☐ *I had a saddle with springs sticking out, which wore away the seat of my pants.*

▶ **wear down** **1** PHRASAL VERB If you **wear** something **down** or if it **wears down**, it becomes flatter or smoother as a result of constantly rubbing against something else. ☐ *Pipe smokers sometimes wear down the tips of their teeth where they grip their pipes.* ☐ *The heels on his shoes had worn down.* **2** PHRASAL VERB If you **wear** someone **down**, you make them gradually weaker or less determined until they eventually do what you want. ☐ *None can match your sheer will-power and persistence in wearing down the opposition.* ☐ *They hoped the waiting and the uncertainty would wear down my resistance.*

▶ **wear off** PHRASAL VERB If a drug, sensation, or feeling **wears off**, it disappears slowly until it no longer exists or has any effect. ☐ *For many the philosophy was merely a fashion, and the novelty soon wore off.*

▶ **wear out** **1** PHRASAL VERB When something **wears out** or when you **wear** it **out**, it is used so much that it becomes thin or weak and unable to be used anymore. ☐ *Every time she consulted her watch, she wondered if the batteries were wearing out.* ☐ *Horses used for long-distance riding tend to wear their shoes out more quickly.* **2** PHRASAL VERB If something **wears** you **out**, it makes you feel extremely tired. [INFORMAL] ☐ *The past few days had really worn him out.* ☐ *The young people run around kicking a ball, wearing themselves out.* **3** → see also **worn out**

wear|able /we̱ərəbəl/ **1** ADJ **Wearable** clothes are practical, comfortable, and suitable for ordinary people to wear, rather than being very unusual or extreme. ☐ *His clothes are comfortable and wearable.* **2** ADJ A **wearable** electronic device is designed to be worn on the body. ☐ *...wearable technology.* **3** → See feature box at **technology**

wear and tear /we̱ər ən te̱ər/ N-UNCOUNT **Wear and tear** is the damage or change that is caused to something when it is being used normally. ☐ *...the problem of wear and tear on the equipment in the harsh desert conditions.*

wear|er /we̱ərər/ (**wearers**) N-COUNT [oft N of n, n N] You use **wearer** to indicate that someone is wearing a certain thing on a particular occasion or that they often wear a certain thing. ☐ *These suits are designed to protect the wearer from cold shock as they enter the water.* ☐ *The mascara is suitable for contact lens wearers.*

wear|ing /we̱ərɪŋ/ ADJ [usu v-link ADJ] If you say that a situation or activity is **wearing**, you mean that it requires a lot of energy and makes you feel mentally or physically tired. ☐ *She finds the continual confrontation very wearing.*

wea|ri|some /wɪ̱ərisəm/ ADJ If you describe something as **wearisome**, you mean that it is very tiring and boring or frustrating. [FORMAL] ☐ *...a long and wearisome journey.* ☐ *Day after wearisome day the routine continued.*

wea|ry /wɪ̱əri/ (**wearier, weariest**) **1** ADJ If you are **weary**, you are very tired. ☐ *Rachel looked pale and weary.* • **wea|ri|ly** /wɪ̱ərɪli/ ADV [ADV after v] ☐ *I sighed wearily.* ☐ *He trudged wearily down Arthur Street.* **2** ADJ [v-link ADJ of n/-ing] If you are **weary of** something, you have become tired of it and have lost your enthusiasm for it. ❏ *They're getting awfully weary of this silly war.* • **wea|ri|ly** ADV [usu ADV after v, also ADV adj] ❏ *'I'm not Mrs Reynolds,' she said wearily.* ❏ *Measures like these sound wearily familiar.*

wea|sel /wiːz³l/ (**weasels**) N-COUNT A **weasel** is a small wild animal with a long thin body, a tail, short legs, and reddish-brown fur.

weath|er ✦✦◇ /wɛðər/ (**weathers, weathering, weathered**) **1** N-UNCOUNT The **weather** is the condition of the atmosphere in one area at a particular time, for example, if it is raining, hot, or windy. ❏ *The weather was bad.* ❏ *I like cold weather.* **2** V-T/V-I If something such as wood or rock **weathers** or is **weathered**, it changes color or shape as a result of the wind, sun, rain, or cold. ❏ *Unpainted wooden furniture weathers to a gray color.* **3** V-T If you **weather** a difficult time or a difficult situation, you survive it and are able to continue normally after it has passed or ended. ❏ *The company has weathered the recession.* **4** PHRASE If you say that you are **under the weather**, you mean that you feel slightly ill. ❏ *I was still feeling a bit under the weather.*

USAGE

weather
Weather is an uncountable noun. Don't use 'a' with it. Don't say, for example, 'We are expecting a bad weather.' Say 'We are expecting **bad weather**.' *They completed the climb despite appalling weather.*

VOCABULARY IN CONTEXT

Wet and dry weather

Do you know where the wettest and driest places on Earth are? Ireland, with its seemingly constant **drizzle** might **spring to mind**. But you may be surprised to find out that the wettest place on Earth is actually in northern India. Mawsynram, in the state of Meghalaya, India, has the highest **global annual rainfall**, according to the Guinness Book of Records. The geography of the area, which lies on a **plateau** near to the Bay of Bengal, means that **moisture** from the nearby sea **condenses** into **thick clouds**, causing **constant downpours**. To find the driest place on Earth, we must travel to the Atacama Desert in the province of Arica, Chile. Annual rainfall in Atacama is less than 1mm per year, and in some areas it hasn't rained for more than 500 years! But although **droughts** are common, you would be wrong to assume that there are always beautiful **blue skies** there. In fact, **humidity** is very high, and the skies are often **overcast**.

weather-beaten also **weatherbeaten** **1** ADJ [usu ADJ n] If your face or skin is **weather-beaten**, it is rough with deep lines because you have spent a lot of time outside in bad weather. ❏ *...a stout man with a ruddy, weather-beaten face.* **2** ADJ Something that is **weather beaten** is rough and slightly damaged after being outside for a long time. ❏ *They would look out through the cracks of their weather-beaten door.*

weath|er fore|cast (**weather forecasts**) N-COUNT A **weather forecast** is a statement saying what the weather will be like the next day or for the next few days.

weath|er fore|cast|er (**weather forecasters**) N-COUNT A **weather forecaster** is a person whose job is to study weather conditions and make reports predicting what the weather will be like for the next few days.

weath|er|ize /wɛðəraɪz/ (**weatherizes, weatherizing, weatherized**) V-T If you **weatherize** something such as a house, you protect it from the effects of the weather, for example, by insulating it. [AM] ❏ *...a one-week project to repair and weatherize family homes for elderly, low-income and disabled people.*

weather|man /wɛðərmæn/ (**weathermen**) N-COUNT A **weatherman** is a man who presents weather forecasts on television or radio.

weather|proof /wɛðərpruːf/ ADJ Something that is **weatherproof** is made of material that protects it from the weather or keeps out wind and rain. ❏ *Use a weatherproof case to carry your camera and lenses around in.*

weath|er sta|tion (**weather stations**) N-COUNT A **weather station** is a place where facts about the weather are recorded and studied.

weath|er vane (**weather vanes**) N-COUNT A **weather vane** is a metal object on the roof of a building that turns around as the wind blows. It is used to show the direction of the wind.

weave /wiːv/ (**weaves, weaving, wove, woven**)

The form **weaved** is used for the past tense and past participle for meaning **3**.

1 V-T/V-I If you **weave** cloth or a carpet, you make it by crossing threads over and under each other using a frame or machine called a loom. ❏ *They would spin and weave cloth, cook and attend to the domestic side of life.* ❏ *She sat at her loom and continued to weave.* • **wo|ven** ADJ ❏ *...woven cotton fabrics.* • **weav|ing** N-UNCOUNT ❏ *When I studied weaving, I became intrigued with natural dyes.* **2** V-T If you **weave** something such as a basket, you make it by crossing long plant stems or fibers over and under each other. ❏ *Jenny weaves baskets from willow she grows herself.* • **wo|ven** ADJ ❏ *The floors are covered with woven straw mats.* **3** V-T/V-I If you **weave** your way somewhere, you move between and around things as you go there. ❏ *The cars then weaved in and out of traffic at top speed.* ❏ *He weaved around the tables to where she sat with Bob.* **4** → See feature box at **sewing**

weav|er /wiːvər/ (**weavers**) N-COUNT A **weaver** is a person who weaves cloth, carpets, or baskets.

web ✦✦✦ /wɛb/ (**webs**) **1** N-PROPER [oft N n] The **Web** is a computer system that links documents and pictures into a database that is stored in computers in many different parts of the world and that people everywhere can use. It is also referred to as the **World Wide Web**. [COMPUTING] ❏ *The handbook is available on the Web.* ❏ *She recommended the service on her Web journal after trying it out.* **2** N-COUNT A **web** is a complicated pattern of connections or relationships, sometimes considered as an obstacle or a danger. ❏ *He's forced to untangle a complex web of financial dealings.* **3** N-COUNT A **web** is the thin net made by a spider from a sticky substance that it produces in its body. ❏ *...the spider's web in the window.*

webbed /wɛbd/ ADJ [ADJ n] **Webbed** feet or toes have a piece of skin between the toes. Water birds such as ducks have webbed feet.

web|bing /wɛbɪŋ/ N-UNCOUNT **Webbing** is strong material which is woven in strips and used to make belts or straps, or used in seats to support the springs.

web|cam /wɛbkæm/ (**webcams**) also **Webcam** N-COUNT A **webcam** is a video camera that takes pictures that can be viewed on a website. The pictures are often of something that is happening while you watch. [COMPUTING]

web|cast /wɛbkæst/ (**webcasts**) also **Webcast** N-COUNT A **webcast** is an event such as a musical performance that you can listen to or watch on the internet. [COMPUTING] ❏ *...a Webcast of the Saturday and Sunday concerts.*

web con|fer|ence (**web conferences**) N-COUNT A **web conference** is a meeting in which people in different places can communicate with each other by logging onto a website. ❏ *The scope for misunderstanding is enormous if you rely entirely on email and web conferences.*

web con|fer|enc|ing N-UNCOUNT **Web conferencing** is communication between people in different places who have

web de|vel|op|ment N-UNCOUNT **Web development** is the process of creating and maintaining websites. ◻ *In web development you'll often hear the phrase 'standing on the shoulders of giants.'* ◻ *...a web development company.*

web|i|nar /wɛbɪnɑr/ (**webinars**) N-COUNT A **webinar** is an interactive seminar conducted over the internet. [COMPUTING]

web|log /wɛblɒg/ (**weblogs**) N-COUNT A **weblog** is a website containing a diary or journal on a particular subject. [COMPUTING] ◻ *...a weblog devoted to good writing about New York.*
• **web|log|ger** /wɛblɒgər/ (**webloggers**) N-COUNT ◻ *...friction between print journalists and webloggers in the United States.*
• **web|log|ging** /wɛblɒgɪŋ/ N-UNCOUNT ◻ *New easy-to-use software has led to an explosion in weblogging.*

web|master /wɛbmæstər, -mɑst-/ (**webmasters**) also **Webmaster** N-COUNT [usu sing] A **webmaster** is someone who is in charge of a website, especially someone who does that as their job. [COMPUTING]

web page (**web pages**) also **Web page** N-COUNT A **web page** is a set of data or information that is designed to be viewed as part of a website. [COMPUTING] ◻ *The company also has a Web page for small businesses and a hotline.*

web|site ✦✧ /wɛbsaɪt/ (**websites**) also **Web site, web site** N-COUNT A **website** is a set of data and information about a particular subject that is available on the internet. [COMPUTING] ◻ *...a website devoted to hip-hop music.*

web|zine /wɛbzin/ (**webzines**) N-COUNT A **webzine** is a website that contains the kind of articles, pictures, and advertisements that you would find in a magazine. [COMPUTING] ◻ *The Dismal Scientist, a webzine dedicated to economic news, is fun.*

wed /wɛd/ (**weds, wedded**)

The form **wed** is used in the present tense and is the past tense. The past participle can be either **wed** or **wedded**.

V-RECIP [no cont] If one person **weds** another or if two people **wed** or **are wed**, they get married. [OLD-FASHIONED, JOURNALISM] ◻ *In 1952 she wed film director Roger Vadim.*

Wed.

The spelling **Weds.** is also used.

Wed. is a written abbreviation for **Wednesday**.

we'd /wɪd, STRONG wid/ **1** **We'd** is the usual spoken form of 'we had,' especially when 'had' is an auxiliary verb. ◻ *Come on, George, we'd better get back now.* **2** **We'd** is the usual spoken form of 'we would.' ◻ *If we smoked, we'd light a cigarette and let her try it out.*

wed|ded /wɛdɪd/ **1** ADJ [v-link ADJ to n] If you are **wedded to** something such as an idea, you support it so strongly or like it so much that you are unable to give it up. [FORMAL] ◻ *Conservationists are mostly wedded to preserving diversity in nature.* **2** ADJ [ADJ n] **Wedded** means the same as **married**. [FORMAL] ◻ *He proposed she become his lawfully wedded wife.*

wed|ding ✦✧ /wɛdɪŋ/ (**weddings**) N-COUNT A **wedding** is a marriage ceremony and the party or special meal that often takes place after the ceremony. ◻ *Many couples still want a traditional wedding.* ◻ *...the couple's 22nd wedding anniversary.*

wed|ding band (**wedding bands**) N-COUNT A **wedding band** is the same as a **wedding ring**.

wed|ding cake (**wedding cakes**) N-VAR A **wedding cake** is a large cake, usually decorated with frosting, that is served at a wedding reception.

wed|ding dress (**wedding dresses**) N-COUNT A **wedding dress** is a special dress that a woman wears at her wedding.

wed|ding ring (**wedding rings**) N-COUNT A **wedding ring** is a ring given to you by your husband or wife at your wedding.

wedge /wɛdʒ/ (**wedges, wedging, wedged**) **1** V-T If you **wedge** something, you force it to remain in a particular position by holding it there tightly or by sticking something next to it to prevent it from moving. ◻ *I shut the shed door and wedged it with a log of wood.* **2** V-T If you **wedge** something somewhere, you fit it there tightly. ◻ *Wedge the plug into the hole.* **3** N-COUNT A **wedge** of something such as fruit or cheese is a piece of it that has a thick triangular shape. ◻ *Serve with a wedge of lime.*

wed|lock /wɛdlɒk/ **1** N-UNCOUNT **Wedlock** is the state of being married. [OLD-FASHIONED] **2** PHRASE [PHR after v] If a baby is born **in wedlock**, it is born while its parents are married. If it is born **out of wedlock**, it is born at a time when its parents are not married. [FORMAL]

Wednes|day ✦✦✦ /wɛnzdeɪ, -di/ (**Wednesdays**) N-VAR **Wednesday** is the day after Tuesday and before Thursday. ◻ *Come and have supper with us on Wednesday, if you're free.* ◻ *Did you happen to see her leave last Wednesday?*

wee /wi/ (**weer, weest**) ADJ [ADJ n] **Wee** means small in size or extent. [mainly SCOTTISH, INFORMAL] ◻ *He just needs to calm down a wee bit.*

weed /wid/ (**weeds, weeding, weeded**) **1** N-COUNT A **weed** is a wild plant that grows in gardens or fields of crops and prevents the plants that you want from growing properly. ◻ *With repeated applications of weedkiller, the weeds were overcome.* **2** V-T/V-I If you **weed** an area, you remove the weeds from it. ◻ *Caspar was weeding the garden.* ◻ *Try not to walk on the flowerbeds while weeding.* **3** → See feature box at **garden**
▶ **weed out** PHRASAL VERB If you **weed out** things or people that are useless or unwanted in a group, you find them and get rid of them. ◻ *He is eager to weed out the many applicants he believes may be frauds.*

weed|killer /widkɪlər/ (**weedkillers**) N-MASS **Weedkiller** is a substance you put on your garden or lawn to kill weeds.

weedy /widi/ (**weedier, weediest**) **1** ADJ [usu ADJ n] A **weedy** place is full of weeds. ◻ *We pulled into the weedy parking lot.* **2** ADJ If you describe someone as **weedy**, you are criticizing them because they are thin and physically weak. [INFORMAL, DISAPPROVAL]

week ✦✦✦ /wik/ (**weeks**) **1** N-COUNT A **week** is a period of seven days. Some people consider that a week starts on Monday and ends on Sunday. ◻ *I had a letter from my mother last week.* ◻ *This has been on my mind all week.* **2** N-COUNT A **week** is a period of about seven days. ◻ *Her mother stayed for another two weeks.* ◻ *Only 12 weeks ago he underwent major heart transplant surgery.* **3** N-COUNT Your working **week** is the hours that you spend at work during a week. ◻ *It is not unusual for women to work a 50-hour week.* **4** N-SING **The week** is the part of the week that does not include Saturday and Sunday. ◻ *...the hard work of looking after the children during the week.* **5** N-COUNT You use **week** in expressions such as 'a week last Monday,' 'a week ago this Tuesday,' and 'a week ago yesterday' to mean exactly one week before the day that you mention. ◻ *"That's the time you weren't well, wasn't it?"—"Yes, that's right, that was a week ago last Monday."*

week|day /wikdeɪ/ (**weekdays**) N-COUNT A **weekday** is any of the days of the week except Saturday and Sunday. ◻ *If you want to avoid the crowds, it's best to come on a weekday.*

week|end ✦✦✧ /wikɛnd/ (**weekends**) **1** N-COUNT A **weekend** is Saturday and Sunday. ◻ *She had agreed to have dinner with him in town the following weekend.* **2** → See feature box at **press**

week|end|er /wikɛndər/ (**weekenders**) N-COUNT [usu pl] A **weekender** is someone who goes to a place or lives at a place only on weekends. ◻ *Weekenders from Manhattan enjoy restaurants in the Hudson River Valley.*

week|ly ✦✦✧ /wikli/ (**weeklies**) **1** ADJ [ADJ n] A **weekly** event or publication happens or appears once a week or every week. ◻ *Each course comprises 10–12 informal weekly meetings.* ◻ *We go and do the weekly shopping every Thursday.* • ADV [ADV after v] **Weekly** is also an adverb. ◻ *The group meets weekly.* **2** ADJ [ADJ n] **Weekly** quantities or rates relate to a period of one week. ◻ *Of course, in addition to my weekly pay, I got a lot of tips.* **3** N-COUNT A **weekly** is a newspaper or magazine that is published once a week. ◻ *Two of the four national daily papers are to become weeklies.*

week|night /wiknaɪt/ (**weeknights**) N-COUNT [oft N n] A **weeknight** is the evening or night of a weekday. ◻ *...the half-hour weeknight show.*

wee|nie /wini/ (**weenies**) **1** N-COUNT If you call someone a **weenie**, you are criticizing them for being afraid. [AM, INFORMAL, DISAPPROVAL] ◻ *He's such a weenie that he cares more about what other people think than about me.* **2** N-COUNT A man's **weenie** is his penis. [AM, INFORMAL] **3** → see **wiener**

weep /wip/ (**weeps, weeping, wept**) V-T/V-I If someone **weeps**, they cry. [LITERARY] ◻ *She wanted to laugh and weep all at once.*

❑ *The weeping family hugged and comforted each other.* ❑ *She wept tears of joy.*

weep|ing wil|low (weeping willows) N-COUNT A **weeping willow** is a type of willow tree. It has long thin branches that hang down to the ground.

weepy /wiːpi/ (weepier, weepiest, weepies) **1** ADJ Someone who is **weepy** is sad and likely to cry easily. ❑ *I suddenly felt very weepy.* ❑ *...weepy moods.* **2** N-COUNT A **weepy** is a movie or a story which is sentimental and makes you cry. [BRIT, INFORMAL]

in AM, use **tear jerker**

wee|vil /wiːvəl/ (weevils) N-COUNT A **weevil** is a small insect that feeds on grain and seeds, and destroys crops.

weft /wɛft/ N-SING [usu the N] In weaving, the **weft** of a piece of cloth is the threads that are passed sideways across the other threads.

weigh ♦⟨⟩ /weɪ/ (weighs, weighing, weighed) **1** V-T [no cont] If someone or something **weighs** a particular amount, this amount is how heavy they are. ❑ *It weighs nearly 27 kilos (about 60 pounds).* ❑ *This little ball of gold weighs a quarter of an ounce.* **2** V-T If you **weigh** something or someone, you measure how heavy they are. ❑ *The scales can be used to weigh other items such as parcels.* **3** V-T If you **weigh** the facts about a situation, you consider them very carefully before you make a decision, especially by comparing the various facts involved. ❑ *She weighed her options.* ❑ *He is weighing the possibility of filing criminal charges against the doctor.*
▶ **weigh down** PHRASAL VERB If something that you are wearing or carrying **weighs** you **down**, it stops you moving easily by making you heavier. ❑ *He wrenched off his sneakers. If he had to swim, he didn't want anything weighing him down.*

---SYNONYMS---

weigh
VERB **3**
consider: *You do have to consider the feelings of those around you.*
study: *I invite every citizen to carefully study the document.*
examine: *I have given the matter much thought, examining all the possible alternatives.*
contemplate: *For a time, he contemplated a career as an army medical doctor.*

---

weigh-in (weigh-ins) N-COUNT [usu sing] When there is a **weigh-in** on the day of a boxing match, each competitor is weighed to check their weight before the match. ❑ *The weigh-in proceeded with Jones checking in at a fully dressed 193 pounds.*

weight ♦♦⟨⟩ /weɪt/ (weights, weighting, weighted) **1** N-VAR The **weight** of a person or thing is how heavy they are, measured in units such as kilograms, pounds, or tons. ❑ *What is your height and weight?* • PHRASE If someone **loses weight**, they become lighter. If they **gain weight** or **put on weight**, they become heavier. ❑ *I'm lucky really as I never put on weight.* ❑ *The boy appeared anxious, had lost weight and was not sleeping well.* **2** N-UNCOUNT A person's or thing's **weight** is the fact that they are very heavy. ❑ *His weight was harming his health.* **3** N-SING If you move your **weight**, you change position so that most of the pressure of your body is on a particular part of your body. ❑ *He shifted his weight from one foot to the other.* **4** N-COUNT **Weights** are objects that weigh a known amount and that people lift as a form of exercise. ❑ *I was in the gym lifting weights.* **5** N-COUNT **Weights** are metal objects that weigh a known amount and that are used on a set of scales to weigh other things. **6** N-COUNT You can refer to a heavy object as a **weight**, especially when you have to lift it. ❑ *Straining to lift heavy weights can lead to a rise in blood pressure.* **7** V-T If you **weight** something, you make it heavier by adding something to it, for example, in order to stop it from moving easily. ❑ *It can be sewn into curtain hems to weight the curtain and so allow it to hang better.* **8** N-VAR If something is given a particular **weight**, it is given a particular value according to how important or significant it is. ❑ *The scientists involved put different weight on the conclusions of different models.* **9** N-UNCOUNT If someone or something gives **weight** to what a person says, thinks, or does, they emphasize its significance. ❑ *The fact that he is gone has given more weight to fears that he may try to launch a civil war.* **10** N-UNCOUNT If you give weight to someone or something **weight**, you

consider them to be very important or influential in a particular situation. ❑ *Consumers generally place more weight on negative information than on the positive when deciding what to buy.* **11** → see also **weighting** **12** PHRASE If a person or their opinion **carries weight**, they are respected and are able to influence people. ❑ *The newly-elected Senator already carries considerable weight in Washington.* **13** PHRASE If you say that someone or something is **worth** their **weight in gold**, you are emphasizing that they are so useful, helpful, or valuable that you feel you could not manage without them. [EMPHASIS] ❑ *Any successful manager is worth their weight in gold.* **14** PHRASE If you **pull** your **weight**, you work as hard as everyone else who is involved in the same task or activity. ❑ *He accused the team of not pulling their weight.* **15 a weight off your mind** → see **mind** ①

---COLLOCATIONS---

weight
NOUN **1**
noun + **weight**: body, birth; target
adjective + **weight**: healthy, ideal, normal; considerable, excess, extra
verb + **weight**: bear, carry; gain, lose, reduce, shed; maintain

---

weight|ed /weɪtɪd/ ADJ A system that is **weighted** in favor of a particular person or group is organized so that this person or group has an advantage. ❑ *The current electoral law is still heavily weighted in favor of the ruling party.*

weight|ing /weɪtɪŋ/ (weightings) N-COUNT A **weighting** is a value given to something according to how important or significant it is. ❑ *...an index formed of equal weightings of three statistics.*

weight|less /weɪtləs/ **1** ADJ Something that is **weightless** weighs nothing or seems to weigh nothing. ❑ *Photons have no mass – they are weightless.* **2** ADJ A person or object is **weightless** when they are in space and the Earth's gravity does not affect them, so that they float around. ❑ *Helen described life in a weightless environment during her period in space.* **3** → See feature box at **travel**

weight|lifter /weɪtlɪftər/ (weightlifters) N-COUNT A **weightlifter** is a person who does weightlifting.

weight|lifting /weɪtlɪftɪŋ/ N-UNCOUNT **Weightlifting** is a sport in which the competitor who can lift the heaviest weight wins.

weight train|ing N-UNCOUNT **Weight training** is a kind of physical exercise in which people lift or push heavy weights with their arms and legs in order to strengthen their muscles. ❑ *I used to do weight training years ago.*

weighty /weɪti/ (weightier, weightiest) ADJ If you describe something such as an issue or a decision as **weighty**, you mean that it is serious or important. [FORMAL] ❑ *Surely such weighty matters merit a higher level of debate?*

weir /wɪər/ (weirs) N-COUNT A **weir** is a low barrier built across a river in order to control or direct the flow of water.

weird /wɪərd/ (weirder, weirdest) ADJ If you describe something or someone as **weird**, you mean that they are strange. [INFORMAL] ❑ *That first day was weird.* ❑ *Drugs can make you do all kinds of weird things.*

weir|do /wɪərdoʊ/ (weirdos) N-COUNT If you describe someone as a **weirdo**, you disapprove of them because they behave in an unusual way that you find difficult to understand or accept. [INFORMAL, mainly SPOKEN, DISAPPROVAL]

welch /wɛlʃ/ → see **welsh**

wel|come ♦♦⟨⟩ /wɛlkəm/ (welcomes, welcoming, welcomed) **1** V-T If you **welcome** someone, you greet them in a friendly way when they arrive somewhere. ❑ *Several people came by to welcome me.* ❑ *She was there to welcome him home from war.* ❑ *...a welcoming speech.* • N-COUNT **Welcome** is also a noun. ❑ *There would be a fantastic welcome awaiting him back here.* **2** CONVENTION You use **welcome** in expressions such as **welcome home**, **welcome to Boston**, and **welcome back** when you are greeting someone who has just arrived somewhere. [FORMULAE] ❑ *Welcome to Washington.* **3** V-T If you **welcome** an action, decision, or situation, you approve of it and are pleased that it has occurred. ❑ *She welcomed this move but said that overall the changes didn't go far enough.* • N-COUNT **Welcome** is

welcoming

also a noun. ❑ *Environmental groups have given a guarded welcome to the prime minister's proposal.* **4** ADJ If you describe something as **welcome**, you mean that people wanted it and are happy that it has occurred. ❑ *Any progress in reducing chemical weapons is welcome.* **5** V-T If you say that you **welcome** certain people or actions, you are inviting and encouraging people to do something, for example, to come to a particular place. ❑ *We would welcome your views about the survey.* **6** ADJ If you say that someone is **welcome** in a particular place, you are encouraging them to go there by telling them that they will be liked and accepted. ❑ *New members are always welcome.* **7** ADJ [v-link ADJ] If you tell someone that they are **welcome** to do something, you are encouraging them to do it by telling them that they are allowed to do it. ❑ *You are welcome to visit the hospital at any time.* **8** ADJ [v-link ADJ to n] If you say that someone is **welcome** to something, you mean that you do not want it yourself because you do not like it and you are very willing for them to have it. ❑ *If they want to take this on, they are welcome to as far as I'm concerned.* **9** → see also **welcoming** **10** PHRASE If you **make** someone **welcome** or **make** them **feel welcome**, you make them feel happy and accepted in a new place. ❑ *Here are six Mexican hotels where children are made to feel welcome.* **11** PHRASE If you say that someone **outstays** their **welcome** or **overstays** their **welcome**, you mean that they stay somewhere longer than they are wanted or expected to. ❑ *After the kindness that had been shown to him, he didn't want to outstay his welcome.* **12** CONVENTION You say '**You're welcome**' to someone who has thanked you for something in order to acknowledge their thanks in a polite way. [FORMULAE] ❑ *"Thank you for the information."—"You're welcome."*

wel|com|ing /wɛlkəmɪŋ/ ADJ If someone is **welcoming** or if they behave in a **welcoming** way, they are friendly to you when you arrive somewhere, so that you feel happy and accepted. ❑ *When we arrived at her house Susan was very welcoming.*

weld /wɛld/ (**welds**, **welding**, **welded**) V-T/V-I To **weld** one piece of metal to another means to join them by heating the edges and putting them together so that they cool and harden into one piece. ❑ *It's possible to weld stainless steel to ordinary steel.* ❑ *Where did you learn to weld?*

weld|er /wɛldər/ (**welders**) N-COUNT A **welder** is a person whose job is welding metal.

wel|fare ♦◇◇ /wɛlfɛər/ **1** N-UNCOUNT The **welfare** of a person or group is their health, comfort, and happiness. ❑ *I do not think he is considering Emma's welfare.* **2** ADJ **Welfare** services are provided to help with people's living conditions and financial problems. ❑ *Child welfare services are well established and comprehensive.* **3** N-UNCOUNT **Welfare** is money that is paid by the government to people who are unemployed, poor, or sick. ❑ *States such as Michigan are making deep cuts in welfare.*

SYNONYMS

welfare
NOUN **1**
well-being: *I'm concerned for her well-being.*
good: *Furlaud urged him to resign for the good of the country.*
interests: *Did those directors act in the best interests of their club?*
health: *If you don't look after your health, no one else will.*
happiness: *I think mostly she was looking for happiness.*

wel|fare state N-SING In some countries, the **welfare state** is a system in which the government provides free social services such as health and education and gives money to people when they are unable to work, because they are old, unemployed, or sick. ❑ *...the future of the welfare state.*

WELL
① DISCOURSE USES
② ADVERB USES
③ PHRASES
④ ADJECTIVE USE
⑤ NOUN USES
⑥ VERB USES

① **well** ♦♦♦ /wɛl/

Well is used mainly in spoken English.

→ Please look at meaning ❾ to see if the expression you are looking for is shown under another headword.

well

1 ADV [ADV cl] You say **well** to indicate that you are about to say something. ❑ *Well, it's a pleasure to meet you.* **2** ADV [ADV cl] You say **well** just before or after you pause, especially to give yourself time to think about what you are going to say. ❑ *Look, I'm really sorry I woke you, and, well, I just wanted to tell you I was all right.* **3** ADV [ADV cl/group] You say **well** when you are correcting something that you have just said. ❑ *The comet is going to come back in 2061 and we are all going to be dead, well, our offspring are, anyway.* **4** ADV [ADV cl] You say **well** to express your doubt about something that someone has said. [FEELINGS] ❑ *"But finance is far more serious."—"Well I don't know really."* **5** EXCLAM You say **well** to express your surprise or anger at something that someone has just said or done. [FEELINGS] ❑ *She beamed at Patty. "Well! That was a bit of unexpected excitement."* **6** CONVENTION You say **well** to indicate that you are waiting for someone to say something and often to express your irritation with them. [FEELINGS] ❑ *"Well?" asked Barry, "What does it tell us?" "Well, why don't you ask me?" he said finally.* **7** CONVENTION You use **well** to indicate that you are amused by something you have heard or seen, and often to introduce a comment on it. [FEELINGS] ❑ *Well, well, well. How quickly things change.* **8** CONVENTION You say **oh well** to indicate that you accept a situation or that someone else should accept it, even though you or they are not very happy about it, because it is not too bad and cannot be changed. [FEELINGS] ❑ *Oh well, it could be worse.* ❑ *"I called her and she said no."—"Oh well."* **9 very well** → see **very**

② **well** ♦♦♦ /wɛl/ (**better**, **best**) **1** ADV [ADV after v] If you do something **well**, you do it to a high standard or to a great extent. ❑ *It's important that we play well at home.* ❑ *He speaks English better than I do.* **2** ADV [ADV after v] If you do something **well**, you do it thoroughly and completely. ❑ *Mix all the ingredients well.* **3** ADV [ADV after v] If you speak or think **well** of someone, you say or think favorable things about them. ❑ *"He speaks well of you."—"I'm glad to hear that."* **4** COMB IN ADJ **Well** is used in front of past participles to indicate that something is done to a high standard or to a great extent. ❑ *Helen is a very well-known novelist in Australia.* ❑ *People live longer nowadays, and they are better educated.* **5** ADV You use **well** to ask or talk about the extent or standard of something. ❑ *How well do you remember your mother, Franzi?* ❑ *He wasn't dressed any better than me.* **6** ADV [ADV prep] You use **well** in front of a prepositional phrase to emphasize it. For example, if you say that one thing happened **well before** another, you mean that it happened a long time before it. [EMPHASIS] ❑ *Franklin did not turn up until well after midnight.* ❑ *...a war in which well over a million people died.* **7** ADV [ADV adj] You use **well** before certain adjectives to emphasize them. [EMPHASIS] ❑ *She has a close group of friends who are very well aware of what she has suffered.* **8** ADV You use **well** after adverbs such as 'perfectly,' 'jolly,' or 'damn' in order to emphasize an opinion or the truth of what you are saying. [EMPHASIS] ❑ *You know perfectly well I can't be blamed for the failure of that mission.* **9** ADV [modal ADV] You use **well** after verbs such as 'may' and 'could' when you are saying what you think is likely to happen. [EMPHASIS] ❑ *Ours could well be the last generation for which moviegoing has a sense of magic.*

③ **well** ♦♦♦ /wɛl/

→ Please look at meanings ❼ and ❽ to see if the expression you are looking for is shown under another headword.

1 PHRASE You use **as well** when mentioning something that happens in the same way as something else already mentioned, or that should be considered at the same time as that thing. ❑ *It is most often diagnosed in women in their thirties and forties, although I've seen it in many younger women, as well.* **2** PHRASE You use **as well as** when you want to mention another item connected with the subject you are discussing. ❑ *The movie will appeal to adults as well as children.* **3** PHRASE If you say that something that has happened **is just as well**, you mean that it is fortunate that it happened in the way it did. ❑ *Blue asbestos is far less common in buildings, which is just as well because it's more dangerous than white asbestos.* **4** PHRASE If you say that something, usually something bad, **might as well** be true or **may as well** be true, you mean that the situation is the same or almost the same as if it were true. ❑ *The couple might as well have been strangers.* **5** PHRASE If you say that you **might as well** do something, or that you **may as well** do it, you mean that you will do it although you do not have a strong desire to do it and may even feel slightly unwilling to do it. ❏ *If I've got to go somewhere I may as well just go to Tulsa.* ❏ *Anyway, you're here; you might as well stay.* **6** PHRASE If you say that something is **well and truly** finished, gone, or done, you are emphasizing that it is completely finished or gone, or thoroughly done. [mainly BRIT, EMPHASIS] ❏ *The war is well and truly over.* **7 all very well** → see all ③ **8 to know full well** → see full ②

④ **well** ♦♦♦ /wɛl/ ADJ If you are **well**, you are healthy and not ill. ❏ *I'm not very well today, I can't come in.*

⑤ **well** /wɛl/ (wells) **1** N-COUNT A **well** is a hole in the ground from which a supply of water is extracted. ❏ *I had to fetch water from the well.* **2** N-COUNT A **well** is an oil well. ❏ *About 650 wells are on fire.*

⑥ **well** /wɛl/ (wells, welling, welled) V-I If liquids **well**, they come to the surface and form a pool. ❏ *Tears welled in her eyes.*
• PHRASAL VERB **Well up** means the same as **well**. ❏ *Tears welled up in Anni's eyes.*

we'll /wɪl, STRONG wil/ **We'll** is the usual spoken form of 'we shall' or 'we will.' ❏ *Whatever you want to chat about, we'll do it tonight.*

well-adjusted also **well adjusted** ADJ A **well-adjusted** person has a mature personality and can control their emotions and deal with problems without becoming anxious. ❏ *...a happy, loving and well adjusted family.*

well ad|vised also **well-advised** ADJ [v-link ADJ to-inf] If someone says that you would be **well advised** to do a particular thing, they are advising you to do it. ❏ *She would have been well advised to have settled this out of court.*

well-appointed ADJ A **well-appointed** room or building has furniture or equipment of a high standard. [FORMAL]

well-balanced 1 ADJ If you describe someone as **well-balanced**, you mean that they are sensible and do not have many emotional problems. ❏ *...a fun-loving, well-balanced individual.* **2** ADJ If you describe something that is made up of several parts as **well-balanced**, you mean that the way that the different parts are put together is good, because there is not too much or too little of any one part. ❏ *...a well-balanced diet.*

well-behaved ADJ If you describe someone, especially a child, as **well-behaved**, you mean that they behave in a way that adults generally like and think is correct. ❏ *...well-behaved little boys.*

well-being N-UNCOUNT Someone's **well-being** is their health and happiness. ❏ *Singing can create a sense of well-being.*

well-born also wellborn ADJ Someone who is **well-born** belongs to an upper-class family.

well-bred ADJ A **well-bred** person is very polite and has good manners. ❏ *She was too well-bred to want to hurt the little boy's feelings.*

well-brought-up ADJ If you say that someone, especially a child, is **well-brought-up**, you mean that they are very polite because they have been taught good manners.

well-built ADJ A **well-built** person has quite a big body and quite large muscles. ❏ *Mitchell is well-built, of medium height, with a dark complexion.*

well-connected ADJ Someone who is **well-connected** has important or influential relatives or friends. ❏ *Mr. Guber and Mr. Peters aren't universally loved in Hollywood but they are well-connected.*

well-defined ADJ Something that is **well-defined** is clear and precise and therefore easy to recognize or understand. ❏ *Today's pawnbrokers operate within well-defined financial regulations.*

well-dis|posed ADJ [usu ADJ to/toward n] If you are **well-disposed** to a person, plan, or activity, you are likely to agree with them or support them. ❏ *They are likely to be well disposed to an offer of a separate peace deal.* ❏ *He felt well-disposed toward her.*

well done 1 CONVENTION You say **Well done** to indicate that you are pleased that someone has done something good. [FEELINGS] ❏ *"Daddy! I came second in history!"—"Well done, sweetheart!"* **2** ADJ If something that you have cooked, especially meat, is **well done**, it has been cooked thoroughly. ❏ *Allow an extra 10-15 min if you prefer lamb well done.*

well-dressed ADJ Someone who is **well-dressed** is wearing fashionable or elegant clothes. ❏ *She's always well-dressed.*

well-earned ADJ [usu ADJ n] You can use **well-earned** to indicate that you think something is deserved, usually because the person who gets it has been working very hard. ❏ *Take a well-earned rest and go out and enjoy yourself.* ❏ *...his well-earned win in Sunday's race.*

well-endowed 1 ADJ A woman who is **well-endowed** has large breasts. A man who is **well-endowed** has a large penis. ❏ *I spotted a well-endowed girl in the audience wearing a tight white T-shirt.* ❏ *...the chalk figure of a well-endowed warrior.* **2** ADJ A **well-endowed** organization has a lot of money or resources. ❏ *In a large, well-endowed school, the opportunities for laboratory work are likely to be greater.*

well-established ADJ If you say that something is **well-established**, you mean that it has been in existence for a long time and is successful. ❏ *The university has a well-established tradition of welcoming postgraduate students from overseas.*

well-fed ADJ If you say that someone is **well-fed**, you mean that they get good food regularly. ❏ *...his well-fed children.*

well-founded ADJ If you say that a report, opinion, or feeling is **well-founded**, you mean that it is based on facts and can therefore be justified. ❏ *If the reports are well-founded, the incident could seriously aggravate relations between the two nations.*

well-groomed ADJ A **well-groomed** person is very neat and clean, and looks as if they have taken care over their appearance.

well-heeled ADJ Someone who is **well-heeled** is wealthy.

well-hung ADJ A man who is **well-hung** has a large penis. [HUMOROUS]

well-informed (better-informed) ADJ If you say that someone is **well-informed**, you mean that they know a lot about many different subjects or about one particular subject. ❏ *...a lending library to encourage members to become as well-informed as possible.*

wel|ling|ton /wɛlɪŋtən/ (wellingtons) N-COUNT [usu pl] **Wellingtons** or **wellington boots** are long rubber boots which you wear to keep your feet dry. [mainly BRIT]

well-intentioned also **well intentioned** ADJ If you say that a person or their actions are **well-intentioned**, you mean that they intend to be helpful or kind but they are unsuccessful or cause problems. ❏ *He is well-intentioned but a poor administrator.*

well-kept 1 ADJ A **well-kept** building, street, yard, or other place is always neat and clean because it is taken good care of. ❏ *...her small well-kept apartment.* **2** ADJ [usu ADJ n] A **well-kept** secret has not been told or made known to anyone, or has been told or made known to only a small number of people.

well-known ♦◊◊ **1** ADJ A **well-known** person or thing is known about by a lot of people and is therefore famous or familiar. If someone is **well-known** for a particular activity, a lot of people know about them because of their involvement with that activity. ❏ *Hubbard was well known for his work in the field of drug rehabilitation.* **2** ADJ A **well-known** fact is a fact that is known by people in general. ❏ *It is well-known that bamboo shoots are a panda's staple diet.*

SYNONYMS

well-known
ADJ **1**
famous: *...England's most famous landscape artist, John Constable.*
celebrated: *He was soon one of the most celebrated young painters in England.*
renowned: *...Sir William Crookes, the renowned chemist.*

well-mannered ADJ Someone who is **well-mannered** is polite and has good manners.

well-meaning ADJ If you say that a person or their actions are **well-meaning**, you mean that they intend to be helpful or kind but they are unsuccessful or cause problems. ❏ *He is a well-meaning but ineffectual leader.*

well-meant ADJ A **well-meant** decision, action, or comment is intended to be helpful or kind but is unsuccessful or causes problems. ❑ *Any decision taken by them now, however well-meant, could complicate the peace process.* ❑ *...a well-meant experiment gone wrong.*

well|ness /wɛlnəs/ N-UNCOUNT Your **wellness** is how healthy you are, and how well and happy you feel.

well-nigh ADV [ADV adj] **Well-nigh** means almost, but not completely or exactly. ❑ *Finding a rug that's just the color, size and price you want can be well-nigh impossible.*

well-off ADJ Someone who is **well-off** is rich enough to be able to do and buy most of the things that they want. [INFORMAL] ❑ *My grandparents were quite well-off.*

well-oiled ADJ [ADJ n] Journalists sometimes refer to a system or organization that is operating very efficiently as a **well-oiled** machine. ❑ *...a well-oiled publicity machine.*

well-paid ADJ If you say that a person or their job is **well-paid**, you mean that they receive a lot of money for the work that they do. ❑ *Kate was well-paid and enjoyed her job.*

well-preserved **1** ADJ If you describe a middle-aged or older person as **well-preserved**, you mean that they look good for their age. [HUMOROUS] ❑ *He is a well-preserved 50-year-old.* **2** ADJ A **well-preserved** object or building does not show any signs of its age. ❑ *...well-preserved fossils.*

well-read /wɛl rɛd/ ADJ A **well-read** person has read a lot of books and has learned a lot from them. ❑ *He was clever, well-read and interested in the arts.*

well-rounded **1** ADJ You describe someone as **well-rounded** when you are expressing approval of them because they have a personality which is fully developed in all aspects. [APPROVAL] ❑ *Liberal arts learning helps you become a well-educated, well-rounded person - someone who's interested in the world and interesting to others.* **2** ADJ If you describe something that is made up of several parts as **well-rounded**, you mean that the way that the different parts are put together is good, because there is not too much or too little of any one part. [APPROVAL] ❑ *The wine list is well-rounded and modestly priced.* ❑ *The girls were given a well-rounded education in science, literature, language, and history.*

well-spoken ADJ A **well-spoken** person speaks in a polite, correct way and uses language intelligently. ❑ *I remember her as a quiet, hard-working and well-spoken girl.*

well-thumbed ADJ A book or magazine that is **well-thumbed** is creased and marked because it has been read so often.

well-timed ADJ A **well-timed** action or comment is done or made at the most appropriate or suitable time. ❑ *He built the company through a string of well-timed acquisitions.* ❑ *One well-timed word from you will be all it needs.*

well-to-do ADJ A **well-to-do** person is rich enough to be able to do and buy most of the things that they want. ❑ *...a well-to-do family of diamond cutters.*

well-traveled ADJ A **well-traveled** person has traveled a lot in foreign countries.

well-tried ADJ A **well-tried** treatment, product, or method is one that has been used many times before and so is known to work well or to be successful. ❑ *There are a number of well-tried remedies which are perfectly safe to take.*

well-trodden **1** ADJ [usu ADJ n] A **well-trodden** path is used regularly by a large number of people, and therefore looks worn and is easy to see. ❑ *He made his way along a well-trodden path toward the shed.* **2** ADJ [usu ADJ n] You can use **well-trodden**, especially in expressions such as **a well-trodden path** and **well-trodden ground**, to indicate that a plan or course of action has been tried by a lot of people and so the result of it is easy to predict. ❑ *Political power has long been a well-trodden path to personal wealth.* ❑ *These working parties will be going over well-trodden ground.*

well-versed ADJ [usu v-link ADJ in n] If someone is **well-versed** in a particular subject, they know a lot about it. ❑ *Page is well-versed in many styles of jazz.*

well-wisher (well-wishers) N-COUNT **Well-wishers** are people who hope that a particular person or thing will be successful, and who show this by their behavior. ❑ *The main street was lined with well-wishers.*

well-worn **1** ADJ A **well-worn** expression, remark, or idea has been used so often that it no longer seems to have much meaning or to be interesting. ❑ *To use a well-worn cliche, it is packed with information.* **2** ADJ A **well-worn** object or piece of clothing has been worn or used so frequently that it looks rather old or damaged. ❑ *...well-worn brown shoes.*

welsh /wɛlʃ/ (welshes, welshing, welshed) V-I If someone **welshes** on a deal or an agreement, they do not do the things they promised to do as part of that deal or agreement. [INFORMAL] ❑ *He welshed on his agreement with the team that he would play for them in February.*

Welsh **1** ADJ **Welsh** means belonging or relating to Wales, or to its people, language, or culture. • N-PLURAL [usu the N] The **Welsh** are the people of Wales. **2** N-UNCOUNT **Welsh** is the language that is spoken in some parts of Wales.

Welsh|man /wɛlʃmən/ (Welshmen) N-COUNT A **Welshman** is a man who was born in Wales and considers himself to be Welsh.

Welsh|woman /wɛlʃwʊmən/ (Welshwomen) N-COUNT A **Welshwoman** is a woman who was born in Wales and considers herself to be Welsh.

welt /wɛlt/ (welts) N-COUNT A **welt** is a mark made on someone's skin, usually by a blow from something such as a whip or sword.

wel|ter /wɛltər/ QUANT A **welter of** something is a large quantity of it which occurs suddenly or in a confusing way. [WRITTEN] ❑ *...patients with a welter of confusing symptoms.* ❑ *...the welter of publicity that followed his engagement.*

wench /wɛntʃ/ (wenches) N-COUNT A **wench** was a girl or young woman in the past who worked as a servant or served people food or drink.

wend /wɛnd/ (wends, wending, wended) PHRASE [usu PHR prep/adv] If you **wend** your **way** in a particular direction, you walk, especially slowly, casually, or carefully, in that direction. [LITERARY] ❑ *Sleepy-eyed commuters were wending their way to work.*

went /wɛnt/ **Went** is the past tense of **go** ①.

wept /wɛpt/ **Wept** is the past tense and past participle of **weep**.

were /wər, STRONG wɜr/ **1** **Were** is the plural and the second person singular of the past tense of **be** ①. **2** **Were** is sometimes used instead of 'was' in certain structures, for example, in conditional clauses or after the verb 'wish.' [FORMAL] ❑ *He told a diplomat that he might withdraw if he were allowed to keep part of a disputed oil field.* **3 as it were** → see **as** ①

we're /wɪər/ **We're** is the usual spoken form of 'we are.' ❑ *I'm married, but we're separated.*

weren't /wɜrnt, wɜrənt/ **Weren't** is the usual spoken form of 'were not.'

were|wolf /wɛərwʊlf/ (werewolves) N-COUNT In stories and movies, a **werewolf** is a person who changes into a wolf.

west ♦♦♦ /wɛst/ also **West** **1** N-UNCOUNT [also the N] The **west** is the direction you look toward in the evening in order to see the sun set. ❑ *I pushed on toward Flagstaff, a hundred miles to the west.* **2** N-SING The **west** of a place, country, or region is the part of it which is in the west. ❑ *Many of the buildings in the west of the city are on fire.* **3** ADV [ADV after v] If you go **west**, you travel toward the west. ❑ *We are going west to California.* **4** ADV Something that is **west** of a place is positioned to the west of it. ❑ *Penryn is about 60 miles west of Philadelphia.* **5** ADJ [ADJ n] The **west** part of a place, country, or region is the part which is toward the west. ❑ *...a small island off the west coast of South Korea.* **6** ADJ [ADJ n] **West** is used in the names of some countries, states, and regions in the west of a larger area. ❑ *Mark has been working in West Africa for about six months.* ❑ *...his West Hollywood home.* **7** ADJ [ADJ n] A **west** wind blows from the west. ❑ *...the warm west wind.* **8** N-SING The **West** is used to refer to the United States, Canada, and the countries of Western, Northern, and Southern Europe. ❑ *...relations between Iran and the West.* **9** → See also color supplement

west|bound /wɛstbaʊnd/ ADJ [ADJ n] **Westbound** roads or vehicles lead to the west or are traveling toward the west. ❑ *Traffic is slow on westbound I-80.* ❑ *...the last westbound train to leave Chicago.*

west|er|ly /wɛstərli/ **1** ADJ A **westerly** point, area, or direction is to the west or toward the west. ❑ ...Finisterre, Spain's most westerly point. **2** ADJ A **westerly** wind blows from the west. ❑ ...a prevailing westerly wind.

west|ern ♦♦◊ /wɛstərn/ (**westerns**) also **Western 1** ADJ [ADJ n] **Western** means in or from the west of a region, state, or country. ❑ ...hand-made rugs from Western and Central Asia. **2** ADJ **Western** is used to describe things, people, ideas, or ways of life that come from or are associated with the United States, Canada, and the countries of Western, Northern, and Southern Europe. ❑ Mexico had the support of the big western governments. **3** N-COUNT A **western** is a book or movie about life in the western United States and territories in the nineteenth century, especially the lives of cowboys. ❑ John Agar starred in westerns, war films and low-budget science fiction pictures.

west|ern|er /wɛstərnər/ (**westerners**) also **Westerner** N-COUNT A **westerner** is a person who was born in or lives in the United States, Canada, or Western, Northern, or Southern Europe. ❑ It's the first time a Westerner has been convicted for a drug-related offense in recent years in China.

west|erni|za|tion /wɛstərnɪzeɪʃən/

in BRIT, also use **westernisation**

N-UNCOUNT The **westernization** of a country, place, or person is the process of their adopting ideas and behavior that are typical of Europe and North America, rather than preserving the ideas and behavior traditional in their culture. ❑ ...fundamentalists unhappy with the westernization of Afghan culture.

west|ern|ized /wɛstərnaɪzd/

in BRIT, also use **westernised**

ADJ A **westernized** country, place, or person has adopted ideas and behavior typical of Europe and North America, rather than preserving the ideas and behavior that are traditional in their culture. ❑ Rapid urbanization brings with it a more westernized and generally more sugary diet.

west|ern|most /wɛstərnmoʊst/ ADJ [usu ADJ n] The **westernmost** part of an area or the **westernmost** place is the one that is farthest toward the west. ❑ ...the westernmost province of North Sudan.

West Ger|man (**West Germans**) **1** ADJ **West German** means belonging or relating to the part of Germany that was known as the Federal Republic of Germany before the two parts of Germany were united in 1990. **West German** also means belonging or relating to the people or culture of this part of Germany. **2** N-COUNT A **West German** is someone who was a citizen of the Federal Republic of Germany, or a person of West German origin.

West In|dian (**West Indians**) **1** ADJ **West Indian** means belonging or relating to the West Indies, or to its people or culture. **2** N-COUNT A **West Indian** is a citizen of the West Indies or a person of West Indian origin.

west|ward /wɛstwərd/

The form **westwards** is also used.

ADV **Westward** or **westwards** means toward the west. ❑ He sailed westward from Palos de la Frontera. • ADJ [ADJ n] **Westward** is also an adjective. ❑ ...the one-hour westward flight over the Andes to Lima.

wet ♦♦◊ /wɛt/ (**wetter, wettest, wets, wetting, wet** or **wetted**) **1** ADJ If something is **wet**, it is covered in water, rain, sweat, tears, or another liquid. ❑ He toweled his wet hair. ❑ I lowered myself to the water's edge, getting my feet wet. **2** V-T To **wet** something means to get water or some other liquid over it. ❑ When assembling the pie, wet the edges where the two crusts join. **3** ADJ If the weather is **wet**, it is raining. ❑ If the weather is wet or cold choose an indoor activity. • N-SING **The wet** is used to mean wet weather. ❑ They had come in from the cold and the wet. **4** ADJ If something such as paint, ink, or cement is **wet**, it is not yet dry or solid. ❑ ...leaves dipped in wet paint then pressed on white paper. **5** V-T If people, especially children, **wet** their beds or clothes or **wet** themselves, they urinate in their beds or in their clothes because they cannot stop themselves. ❑ A quarter of 4-year-olds frequently wet the bed.

SYNONYMS

wet
ADJ **1**
damp: Her hair was still damp.
moist: The soil is reasonably moist after the September rain.
soaked: My tent got soaked last night in the storm.

wet|back /wɛtbæk/ (**wetbacks**) N-COUNT **Wetback** is sometimes used to refer to a Mexican or a Mexican-American who has entered the United States illegally in order to work or live there. [AM, INFORMAL, OFFENSIVE]

wet bar (**wet bars**) N-COUNT A **wet bar** in a home or a hotel room is a bar for serving alcoholic drinks that also contains a sink. ❑ Some rooms also have fireplaces, whirlpool baths and wet bars.

wet blan|ket (**wet blankets**) N-COUNT If you say that someone is a **wet blanket**, you are criticizing them because they refuse to join other people in an enjoyable activity or because they want to stop other people from enjoying themselves. [INFORMAL, DISAPPROVAL]

wet dream (**wet dreams**) N-COUNT If a man has a **wet dream**, he has a dream about sex that causes him to have an orgasm while he is asleep.

wet|land /wɛtlænd/ (**wetlands**) N-VAR A **wetland** is an area of very wet, muddy land with wild plants growing in it. You can also refer to an area like this as **wetlands**. ❑ ...a plan that aims to protect the wilderness of the wetlands.

wet mar|ket (**wet markets**) N-COUNT A **wet market** is a market, especially in East Asia, at which live and dead animals of different species are sold to be eaten. ❑ At a wet market in Shanghai, all the chickens had been removed.

wet nurse (**wet nurses**) also **wet-nurse** N-COUNT In former times, a **wet nurse** was a woman who was paid to breast-feed another woman's baby.

wet suit (**wet suits**) also **wetsuit** N-COUNT A **wet suit** is a close-fitting rubber suit that an underwater swimmer wears in order to keep their body warm.

we've /wɪv, STRONG wiv/ **We've** is the usual spoken form of 'we have', especially when 'have' is an auxiliary verb. ❑ It's the first time we've been to the cinema together as a family.

wfh also **WFH** **wfh** is the written abbreviation for 'work from home' or 'working from home.' ❑ I'm WFH because of the strike.

whack /wæk/ (**whacks, whacking, whacked**) **1** V-T If you **whack** someone or something, you hit them hard. [INFORMAL] ❑ You really have to whack the ball. • N-COUNT; SOUND **Whack** is also a noun. ❑ He gave the donkey a whack across the back with his stick. **2** PHRASE [PHR after v, oft v-link PHR] If something is **out of whack**, it is not working properly, often because its natural balance has been upset. [mainly AM, INFORMAL] ❑ The ecosystem will be thrown out of whack.

whacky /wæki/ → see **wacky**

whale /weɪl/ (**whales**) **1** N-COUNT **Whales** are very large mammals that live in the sea. **2** PHRASE If you say that someone **is having a whale of a time**, you mean that they are enjoying themselves very much. [INFORMAL] ❑ I had a whale of a time in Fargo. **3** → See feature box at **animal**

whal|er /weɪlər/ (**whalers**) **1** N-COUNT A **whaler** is a ship used in hunting whales. **2** N-COUNT A **whaler** is someone who works on a ship used in hunting whales.

whal|ing /weɪlɪŋ/ N-UNCOUNT **Whaling** is the activity of hunting and killing whales. ❑ ...a ban on commercial whaling.

wham /wæm/ EXCLAM You use **wham** to indicate that something happens suddenly or forcefully. [INFORMAL] ❑ Then I met someone and wham, bam, I was completely in love.

wham|my /wæmi/ N-SING [adj N] **Whammy** is used in expressions such as **double whammy** and **triple whammy** to indicate that two or three unpleasant or difficult situations occur at the same time, or occur one after the other. [mainly JOURNALISM] ❑ We have a double whammy: inflation coupled with recession.

wharf /wɔrf/ (**wharves** or **wharfs**) N-COUNT A **wharf** is a platform by a river or the sea where ships can be tied up.

what ♦♦♦ /wʌt, wɒt/

Usually pronounced /wɒt/ for meanings **2, 4** and **5**.

1 QUEST You use **what** in questions when you ask for specific information about something that you do not know. ❏ *What do you want?* ❏ *What did she tell you, anyway?* ❏ *"Has something happened?"—"It certainly has."—"What?"* ❏ DET **What** is also a determiner. ❏ *What time is it?* ❏ *What crimes are the defendants being charged with?* ❏ *"The heater works."—"What heater?"* **2** CONJ You use **what** after certain words, especially verbs and adjectives, when you are referring to a situation that is unknown or has not been specified. ❏ *You can imagine what it would be like driving a car into a brick wall at 30 miles an hour.* ❏ *I want to know what happened to Norman.* • DET **What** is also a determiner. ❏ *I didn't know what college I wanted to go to.* ❏ *I didn't know what else to say.* **3** CONJ You use **what** at the beginning of a clause in structures where you are changing the order of the information to give special emphasis to something. [EMPHASIS] ❏ *What precisely triggered off yesterday's riot is still unclear.* ❏ *What I wanted, more than anything, was a few days' rest.* **4** CONJ You use **what** in expressions such as **what is called** and **what amounts to** when you are giving a description of something. ❏ *She had been in what doctors described as an irreversible vegetative state for five years.* **5** CONJ You use **what** to indicate that you are talking about the whole of an amount that is available to you. ❏ *He drinks what is left in his glass as if it were water.* • DET **What** is also a determiner. ❏ *They had used what money they had.* **6** CONVENTION You say '**What?**' to tell someone who has indicated that they want to speak to you that you have heard them and are inviting them to continue. [SPOKEN, FORMULAE] ❏ *"Dad?"—"What?"—"Can I have the car tonight?"* **7** CONVENTION You say '**What?**' when you ask someone to repeat the thing that they have just said because you did not hear or understand it properly. '**What?**' is more informal and less polite than expressions such as '**Pardon?**' and '**Excuse me?**' [SPOKEN, FORMULAE] ❏ *"They could paint this place," she said. "What?" he asked.* **8** CONVENTION You say '**What**' to express surprise. [FEELINGS] ❏ *"Adolphus Kelling, I arrest you on a charge of trafficking in narcotics."—"What?"* **9** PREDET You use **what** in exclamations to emphasize an opinion or reaction. [EMPHASIS] ❏ *What a horrible thing to do.* • DET **What** is also a determiner. ❏ *What pretty hair she has, nice and thick.* **10** ADV [ADV n] You use **what** to indicate that you are making a guess about something such as an amount or value. ❏ *It's, what, eleven years or more since he's seen her.* **11** CONVENTION You say **guess what** or **do you know what** to introduce a piece of information that is surprising, that is not generally known, or that you want to emphasize. ❏ *Guess what? I'm going to dinner at Mrs. Chang's tonight.* **12** PHRASE In conversation, you say **or what?** after a question as a way of stating an opinion forcefully and showing that you expect other people to agree. [EMPHASIS] ❏ *Look at that moon. Is that beautiful or what?* **13** CONVENTION You say **so what?** or **what of it?** to indicate that the previous remark seems unimportant, uninteresting, or irrelevant to you. [FEELINGS] ❏ *"What if there is no kerosene this winter?" said Al.—"So what?" she said. "We still have electricity."* ❏ *"You're talking to yourself."—"Well, what of it?"* **14** PHRASE You say '**Tell you what**' to introduce a suggestion or offer. ❏ *Tell you what, let's stay here another day.* **15** PHRASE You use **what about** at the beginning of a question when you make a suggestion, offer, or request. ❏ *What about going out with me tomorrow?* **16** PHRASE You use **what about** or **what of** when you introduce a new topic or a point that seems relevant to a previous remark. ❏ *Now you've talked about work on daffodils, what about other commercially important flowers, like roses?* **17** PHRASE You say **what about** a particular person or thing when you ask someone to explain why they have asked you about that person or thing. ❏ *"This thing with the Corbett woman."—"Oh, yeah. What about her?"* **18** PHRASE You say **what if** at the beginning of a question when you ask about the consequences of something happening, especially something undesirable. ❏ *What if this doesn't work out?* **19 what's more** → see **more**

USAGE

what
Don't use 'what' when you are asking about one of a small number of people or things. For example, if someone has hurt their finger, don't say to them '~~What finger have you hurt?~~' Say '**Which** finger have you hurt?' '*Go down that road.*' – '**Which** one?'

what|ev|er ◆◆◇ /wɒtɛvər, wɒt-/ **1** CONJ You use **whatever** to refer to anything or everything of a particular type. ❏ *Franklin was free to do pretty much whatever he pleased.* ❏ *When you're older I think you're better equipped mentally to cope with whatever happens.* • DET **Whatever** is also a determiner. ❏ *Whatever doubts he might have had about Ingrid were all over now.* **2** CONJ You use **whatever** to say that something is the case in all circumstances. ❏ *We shall love you whatever happens, Diana.* ❏ *She runs on average about 15 miles a day every day, whatever the circumstances, whatever the weather.* **3** ADV [with brd-neg, n ADV] You use **whatever** after a noun group in order to emphasize a negative statement. [EMPHASIS] ❏ *There is no evidence whatever that competition in broadcasting has ever reduced costs.* **4** QUEST You use **whatever** to ask in an emphatic way about something which you are very surprised about. [EMPHASIS] ❏ *Whatever can you mean?* **5** CONJ You use **whatever** when you are indicating that you do not know the precise identity, meaning, or value of the thing just mentioned. [VAGUENESS] ❏ *I thought that my upbringing was "normal," whatever that is.* **6** PHRASE You use **or whatever** to refer generally to something else of the same kind as the thing or things that you have just mentioned. [INFORMAL] ❏ *They're always protesting about something or saving the trees or whatever.* **7** PHRASE You say **whatever** you **do** when giving advice or warning someone about something. [EMPHASIS] ❏ *Whatever you do, don't ask for a pay increase.*

what|not /wɒtnɒt, wɒt-/ PHRASE [cl/group PHR] People sometimes say '**and whatnot**' or '**or whatnot**' after mentioning one or more things, to refer in a vague way to other things which are similar. [INFORMAL, SPOKEN, VAGUENESS] ❏ *The women were there in their jeans and T-shirts and whatnot.* ❏ *The council can send messages or letters or whatnot in Spanish to their constituents.*

what's /wɒts, wɒts/ **What's** is the usual spoken form of 'what is' or 'what has,' especially when 'has' is an auxiliary verb.

whats|her|name /wɒtsərneɪm, wɒts-/ also **whatsername** PRON You say **whatshername** instead of a woman's name when you cannot remember it or are trying to remember it. [SPOKEN] ❏ *That's the thing that whatshername gave me.*

whats|his|name /wɒtsɪzneɪm, wɒts-/ also **whatsisname** PRON You say **whatshisname** instead of a man's name when you cannot remember it or are trying to remember it. [SPOKEN] ❏ *Look, there's...oh, you know...it's whatsisname.*

whats|it /wɒtsɪt, wɒts-/ (**whatsits**) N-VAR You use **whatsit** instead of a noun or name which you cannot remember or which you do not want to say because it is rude. [SPOKEN] ❏ *We wanted to be here early in case the whatsit, maintenance supervisor had forgotten to deal with it.*

what|so|ev|er /wɒtsoʊɛvər, wɒt-/ ADV You use **whatsoever** after a noun group in order to emphasize a negative statement. [EMPHASIS] ❏ *My school did nothing whatsoever in the way of athletics.*

wheat /wiːt/ (**wheats**) N-MASS **Wheat** is a cereal crop grown for food. **Wheat** is also used to refer to the grain of this crop, which is usually ground into flour and used to make bread. ❏ *...farmers growing wheat, corn, or other crops.*

wheat|germ /wiːtdʒɜːrm/ also **wheat germ** N-UNCOUNT **Wheatgerm** is the middle part of a grain of wheat which is rich in vitamins and is often added to other food.

whee|dle /wiːdəl/ (**wheedles, wheedling, wheedled**) V-T/V-I If you say that someone **wheedles**, you mean that they try to persuade someone to do or give them what they want, for example, by saying nice things that they do not mean. [DISAPPROVAL] ❏ *Cross decided to beg and wheedle a bit.* ❏ *He managed to wheedle his way into the offices.*

wheel ◆◇◇ /wiːl/ (**wheels, wheeling, wheeled**) **1** N-COUNT The **wheels** of a vehicle are the circular objects that are attached underneath it and that enable it to move along the ground. ❏ *The car wheels spun and slipped on some oil on the road.* **2** N-COUNT A **wheel** is a circular object that forms a part of a machine, usually a moving part. ❏ *The wheels are usually fairly large.* **3** N-COUNT The **wheel** of a car or other vehicle is the circular object that is used to steer it. **The wheel** is used in expressions to talk about who is driving a vehicle. For example, if someone is **at the wheel** or **behind the wheel** of a car, they are driving it. ❏ *My co-pilot suddenly grabbed the wheel.* ❏ *Curtis got behind the wheel and they started back toward the cottage.* **4** V-T If you **wheel** an object that has wheels somewhere, you push it along. ❏ *He wheeled his bike into the alley at the side of the house.* **5** N-PLURAL People talk about **the wheels of** an organization or system to mean the way in which it operates. ❏ *He knows the wheels of administration turn slowly.* **6** → see also **steering wheel 7** → See also color supplement

wheel and deal (**wheels and deals**, **wheeling and dealing**, **wheeled and dealed**) V-I If you say that someone **wheels and deals**, you mean that they use a lot of different methods and contacts to achieve what they want in business or politics, often in a way which you consider dishonest. ❏ *He still wheels and deals around the globe.* • **wheel|ing and deal|ing** N-UNCOUNT ❏ *He hates the wheeling and dealing associated with conventional political life.*

wheel|barrow /wˈɪlbærəʊ/ (**wheelbarrows**) **1** N-COUNT A **wheelbarrow** is a small open cart with one wheel and handles that is used for carrying things, for example, in the garden. ❏ *Next to her is a wheelbarrow full of flowers for planting.* **2** → See also color supplement

wheel|base /wˈɪlbeɪs/ (**wheelbases**) N-COUNT [usu sing] The **wheelbase** of a car or other vehicle is the distance between its front and back wheels.

wheel|chair /wˈɪltʃɛər/ (**wheelchairs**) N-COUNT A **wheelchair** is a chair with wheels that you use in order to move around in if you cannot walk properly, for example, because you are sick, or have a disability.

wheel clamp (**wheel clamps**, **wheel clamping**, **wheel clamped**) **1** N-COUNT A **wheel clamp** is a large metal device which is fitted to the wheel of an illegally parked car or other vehicle in order to prevent it from being driven away. The driver has to pay to have the clamp removed. [BRIT]

in AM, use **boot**

2 V-T If a car **is wheel clamped**, a wheel clamp is fixed to one of its wheels so that it cannot be driven away.

wheeler-dealer (**wheeler-dealers**) N-COUNT If you refer to someone, especially in business or politics, as a **wheeler-dealer**, you disapprove of the way that they try to succeed or to get what they want, often by dishonest or unfair methods. [DISAPPROVAL] ❏ ...*a pact with a smooth-talking wheeler-dealer named Mr. Cox.*

wheel|house /wˈɪlhaʊs/ (**wheelhouses**) N-COUNT A **wheelhouse** is a small room or shelter on a ship or boat, where the wheel used for steering the boat is situated.

wheel|wright /wˈɪlraɪt/ (**wheelwrights**) N-COUNT A **wheelwright** is someone who makes and repairs wooden wheels and other wooden things such as carts, carriages, and gates.

wheeze /wiːz/ (**wheezes**, **wheezing**, **wheezed**) V-I If someone **wheezes**, they breathe with difficulty and make a whistling sound. ❏ *He had serious problems with his chest and wheezed and coughed all the time.*

wheezy /wˈiːzi/ (**wheezier**, **wheeziest**) ADJ A **wheezy** cough or laugh comes from someone who has difficulty breathing, so it makes a whistling sound.

whelk /wɛlk/ (**whelks**) N-COUNT A **whelk** is a creature like a snail that is found in the sea near the shore. Whelks have hard shells, and soft bodies that can be eaten.

whelp /wɛlp/ (**whelps**) N-COUNT A **whelp** is a young animal, especially a young dog or wolf. [OLD-FASHIONED]

when ♦♦♦ /wɛn/ **1** QUEST You use **when** to ask questions about the time at which things happen. ❏ *When are you going home?* ❏ *When did you get married?* **2** CONJ If something happens **when** something else is happening, the two things are happening at the same time. ❏ *When eating a whole cooked fish, you should never turn it over to get at the flesh on the other side.* **3** CONJ You use **when** to introduce a clause in which you mention something that happens at some point during an activity, event, or situation. ❏ *When I met the Gills, I had been gardening for nearly ten years.* **4** CONJ You use **when** to introduce a clause where you mention the circumstances under which the event in the main clause happened or will happen.

❏ *When he brought Imelda her drink she gave him a genuine, sweet smile of thanks.* **5** CONJ You use **when** after certain words, especially verbs and adjectives, to introduce a clause where you mention the time at which something happens. ❏ *I asked him when he'd be back to pick me up.* **6** PRON-REL You use **when** to introduce a clause that specifies or refers to the time at which something happens. ❏ *He could remember a time when he had worked like that himself.* **7** CONJ You use **when** to introduce the reason for an opinion, comment, or question. ❏ *How can I love myself when I look like this?* **8** CONJ You use **when** in order to introduce a fact or comment which makes the other part of the sentence rather surprising or unlikely. ❏ *Our mothers sat us down to read and paint, when all we really wanted to do was to make a mess.*

whence /wɛns/ QUEST **Whence** means from where. [LITERARY] ❏ *No one ordered him back whence he came.*

when|ever ♦◊◊ /wɛnˈɛvər/ **1** CONJ You use **whenever** to refer to any time or every time that something happens or is true. ❏ *Whenever I talked to him, he seemed like a pretty regular guy.* ❏ *You can stay at my cottage in the country whenever you like.* **2** CONJ You use **whenever** to refer to a time that you do not know or are not sure about. ❏ *He married Miss Vancouver in 1963, or whenever it was.*

where ♦♦♦ /wɛər/

Usually pronounced /wɛər/ for meanings **2** and **3**.

1 QUEST You use **where** to ask questions about the place something or someone is in, or is coming from or going to. ❏ *Where did you meet him?* ❏ *Where's Anna?* **2** CONJ You use **where** after certain words, especially verbs and adjectives, to introduce a clause in which you mention the place in which something or someone is situated or happens. ❏ *People began looking across to see where the noise was coming from.* ❏ *He knew where Henry Carter had gone.* • PRON-REL **Where** is also a relative pronoun. ❏ *The area where the explosion occurred was closed off by police.* **3** QUEST You use **where** to ask questions about a situation, a stage in something, or an aspect of something. ❏ *If they get their way, where will it stop?* **4** CONJ You use **where** after certain words, especially verbs and adjectives, to introduce a clause in which you mention a situation, a stage in something, or an aspect of something. ❏ *It's not hard to see where she got her feelings about herself.* ❏ *She had a feeling she already knew where this conversation was going to lead.* • PRON-REL **Where** is also a relative pronoun. ❏ *The government is at a stage where it is willing to talk to almost anyone.*

where|abouts

Pronounced /wˈɛərəbaʊts/ for meaning **1**, and /wɛərəbˈaʊts/ for meaning **2**.

1 N-SING-COLL If you refer to the **whereabouts** of a particular person or thing, you mean the place where that person or thing may be found. ❏ *The police are anxious to hear from anyone who may know the whereabouts of the firearms.* **2** QUEST You use **whereabouts** in questions when you are asking precisely where something is. ❏ *"Whereabouts in France?"—"Normandy," I said.* ❏ *Whereabouts are you living?*

where|as ♦◊◊ /wɛərˈæz/ CONJ You use **whereas** to introduce a comment that contrasts with what is said in the main clause. ❏ *Benefits are linked to inflation, whereas they should be linked to the cost of living.*

where|by /wɛərbˈaɪ/ PRON-REL A system of action **whereby** something happens is one that makes that thing happen. [FORMAL] ❏ *The company operates an arrangement whereby employees may select any 8-hour period between 6 a.m. and 8 p.m. to go to work.*

where|fores /wˈɛərfɔːrz/ PHRASE [usu PHR of n] The whys and wherefores of something are the reasons for it. ❏ *Even successful bosses need to be queried about the whys and wherefores of their actions.*

where|in /wɛərˈɪn/ **1** PRON **Wherein** means in which place or thing. [FORMAL, LITERARY or OLD-FASHIONED] ❏ ...*a riding school wherein we could learn the art of horsemanship.* **2** QUEST **Wherein** means in which part or respect. [FORMAL] ❏ *Wherein lies the truth?*

where|upon /wɛərəpˈɒn/ CONJ You use **whereupon** to say that one thing happens immediately after another thing, and usually as a result of it. [FORMAL] ❏ *Mr. Jones refused to talk to them except in the company of his legal colleagues, whereupon the police officers departed.*

wher|ever /wɛrɛvər/ **1** CONJ You use **wherever** to indicate that something happens or is true in any place or situation. ❑ *Some people enjoy themselves wherever they are.* **2** CONJ You use **wherever** when you indicate that you do not know where a person or place is. ❑ *I'd like to leave as soon as possible and join my children, wherever they are.* **3** QUEST You use **wherever** in questions as an emphatic form of 'where,' usually when you are surprised about something. [EMPHASIS] ❑ *Wherever did you get that idea?*

where|with|al /wɛrwɪðɔl, -wɪθ-/ N-SING If you have **the wherewithal** for something, you have the means, especially the money, that you need for it. ❑ *Some of the companies illegally sent the wherewithal for making chemical weapons.*

whet /wɛt/ (whets, whetting, whetted) PHRASE If someone or something **whets** your **appetite** for a particular thing, they increase your desire to have it or know about it, especially by giving you an idea of what it is like. ❑ *A really good catalogue can also whet customers' appetites for merchandise.*

wheth|er ♦♦♦ /wɛðər/ **1** CONJ You use **whether** when you are talking about a choice or doubt between two or more alternatives. ❑ *To this day, it's unclear whether he shot himself or was murdered.* ❑ *Whether it turns out to be a good idea or a bad idea, we'll find out.* **2** CONJ You use **whether** to say that something is true in any of the circumstances that you mention. ❑ *This happens whether the children are in two-parent or one-parent families.* ❑ *Whether they say it aloud or not, most people expect their partners to be faithful.*

whet|stone /wɛtstoʊn/ (whetstones) N-COUNT [usu sing] A **whetstone** is a stone used for sharpening knives or other tools that have a blade.

whew /hyu/ EXCLAM **Whew** is used in writing to represent a sound that you make when you breathe out quickly, for example, because you are very hot, very relieved, or very surprised. [FEELINGS] ❑ *"Whew," he said. "It's hot."*

whey /weɪ/ N-UNCOUNT **Whey** is the watery part of sour milk that is separated from the thick part called curds when you are making cheese.

which ♦♦♦ /wɪtʃ/

Usually pronounced /wɪtʃ/ for meanings **2, 3** and **4**.

1 QUEST You use **which** in questions when there are two or more possible answers or alternatives. ❑ *"You go down that passageway over there."—"Which one?"* ❑ *Which vitamin supplements are good for you?* **2** DET You use **which** to refer to a choice between two or more possible answers or alternatives. ❑ *I wanted to know which school it was you went to.* ❑ *I can't remember which teachers I had.* • CONJ **Which** is also a conjunction. ❑ *In her panic she couldn't remember which was Mr. Grainger's cabin.* **3** PRON-REL You use **which** at the beginning of a relative clause when specifying the thing that you are talking about. In such clauses, **which** has the same meaning as **that**. ❑ *Soldiers opened fire on a car which failed to stop at an army checkpoint.* **4** PRON-REL You use **which** to refer back to an idea or situation expressed in a previous sentence or sentences, especially when you want to give your opinion about it. ❑ *They ran out of drink. Which actually didn't bother me because I wasn't drinking.* • DET **Which** is also a determiner. ❑ *The chances are you haven't fully decided what you want from your career at the moment, in which case you're definitely not cut out to be a boss yet!* **5** PHRASE If you cannot tell the difference between two things, you can say that you do not know **which is which**. ❑ *They all look so alike to me that I'm never sure which is which.*

which|ever /wɪtʃɛvər/ **1** DET You use **whichever** in order to indicate that it does not matter which of the possible alternatives happens or is chosen. ❑ *Whichever way you look at it, nuclear power is the energy of the future.* • CONJ **Whichever** is also a conjunction. ❑ *If you are unhappy with anything you have bought from us, we will gladly exchange your purchase, or refund your money, whichever you prefer.* **2** DET You use **whichever** to specify which of a number of possibilities is the right one or the one you mean. ❑ *Learning to relax by whichever method suits you best is a positive way of contributing to your overall good health.* • CONJ **Whichever** is also a conjunction. ❑ *He has been extraordinarily fortunate or clever, whichever is the right word.*

whiff /wɪf/ (whiffs) N-COUNT If there is a **whiff** of a particular smell, you smell it only slightly or only for a brief period of time, for example, as you walk past someone or something. ❑ *He caught a whiff of her perfume.*

Whig /wɪg/ (Whigs) **1** N-COUNT In the American Revolution, a **Whig** was an American who supported the revolution against the British. [AM] **2** N-COUNT A **Whig** was a member of an American political party in the 19th century that wanted to limit the powers of the president. [AM]

WHILE
① CONJUNCTION USES
② NOUN AND VERB USES
---

① **while** ♦♦♦ /waɪl/

Usually pronounced /waɪl/ for meaning **4**.

in BRIT, also use **whilst**

1 CONJ If something happens **while** something else is happening, the two things are happening at the same time. ❑ *They were grinning and watching while one man laughed and poured beer over the head of another.* ❑ *I sat on the chair to unwrap the package while he stood behind me.* **2** CONJ If something happens **while** something else happens, the first thing happens at some point during the time that the second thing is happening. ❑ *The two ministers have yet to meet, but may do so while in New York.* **3** CONJ You use **while** at the beginning of a clause to introduce information that contrasts with information in the main clause. ❑ *The first two services are free, while the third costs $35.00.* **4** CONJ You use **while**, before making a statement, in order to introduce information that partly conflicts with your statement. ❑ *While the news, so far, has been good, there may be days ahead when it is bad.*

SYNONYMS

while
CONJ ① **3**
though: *He's charming, though not particularly attractive in a physical sense.*
although: *Although the shooting has stopped for now, the destruction left behind is enormous.*
despite the fact that: *She criticized the film despite the fact that she hadn't seen it.*
---

② **while** ♦♦◇ /waɪl/ (whiles, whiling, whiled)

→ Please look at meanings **3** and **4** to see if the expression you are looking for is shown under another headword.

1 N-SING A **while** is a period of time. ❑ *They walked on in silence for a while.* ❑ *He was married a little while ago.* **2** PHRASE You use **all the while** in order to say that something happens continually or that it happens throughout the time when something else is happening. ❑ *All the while the people at the next table watched me eat.* **3** once in a while → see **once** **4** worth your while → see **worth**
▶ **while away** PHRASAL VERB If you **while away** the time in a particular way, you spend time in that way, because you are waiting for something else to happen, or because you have nothing else to do. ❑ *Craig had been whiling away his spare time in our basement.*

whilst ♦◇◇ /waɪlst/ CONJ **Whilst** means the same as the conjunction **while**. [mainly BRIT]

whim /wɪm/ (whims) N-VAR A **whim** is a wish to do or have something that seems to have no serious reason or purpose behind it, and often occurs suddenly. ❑ *We decided, more or less on a whim, to sail to Morocco.*

whim|per /wɪmpər/ (whimpers, whimpering, whimpered) V-I If someone **whimpers**, they make quiet unhappy or frightened sounds, as if they are about to start crying. ❑ *She lay at the bottom of the stairs, whimpering in pain.* • N-COUNT **Whimper** is also a noun. ❑ *David's crying subsided to a whimper.*

whim|si|cal /wɪmzɪkᵊl/ ADJ A **whimsical** person or idea is unusual, playful, and unpredictable, rather than serious and practical. ❑ *McGrath remembers his offbeat sense of humor, his whimsical side.*

whim|sy /wɪmzi/ also **whimsey** N-UNCOUNT **Whimsy** is behavior that is unusual, playful, and unpredictable, rather than having any serious reason or purpose behind it.

whine /waɪn/ (whines, whining, whined) **1** V-I If something or someone **whines**, they make a long, high-pitched noise,

whinny /wɪni/ (whinnies, whinnying, whinnied) V-I When a horse **whinnies**, it makes a series of high-pitched sounds, usually not very loudly. ❑ *The girl's horse whinnied.* • N-COUNT **Whinny** is also a noun. ❑ *With a terrified whinny the horse bolted.*

whip ◆◇◇ /wɪp/ (whips, whipping, whipped) **1** N-COUNT A **whip** is a long thin piece of material such as leather or rope, fastened to a stiff handle. It is used for hitting people or animals. **2** V-T If someone **whips** a person or animal, they beat them or hit them with a whip or something like a whip. ❑ *Eye-witnesses claimed Mr. Melton whipped the horse up to 16 times.* • **whip|ping** (whippings) N-COUNT ❑ *He threatened to give her a whipping.* **3** V-T If someone **whips** something out or **whips** it off, they take it out or take it off very quickly and suddenly. ❑ *Bob whipped out his notebook.* ❑ *Players were whipping their shirts off.* **4** V-T When you **whip** something liquid such as cream or an egg, you stir it very fast until it is thick or stiff. ❑ *Whip the cream until thick.* ❑ *Whip the eggs, oils and honey together.* **5** V-T If you **whip** people **into** an emotional state, you deliberately cause and encourage them to be in that state. ❑ *He could whip a crowd into hysteria.*

▶ **whip up** PHRASAL VERB If someone **whips up** an emotion, especially a dangerous one such as hatred, or if they **whip** people **up** into an emotional state, they deliberately cause and encourage people to feel that emotion. ❑ *He accused politicians of whipping up antiforeign sentiments in order to win right-wing votes.*

whip|lash /wɪplæʃ/ **1** N-UNCOUNT **Whiplash** is a neck injury caused by the head suddenly moving forward and then back again, for example, in a car accident. ❑ *His wife suffered whiplash and shock.* **2** → See feature box at **accident**

whip|per|snap|per /wɪpərsnæpər/ (whippersnappers) N-COUNT If you refer to a young person as a **whippersnapper**, you disapprove of them because you think that they are behaving more confidently than they should. [INFORMAL, OLD-FASHIONED, DISAPPROVAL]

whip|pet /wɪpɪt/ (whippets) N-COUNT A **whippet** is a small thin dog with long legs. Some whippets are used for racing.

whip|ping boy (whipping boys) N-COUNT If someone or something is a **whipping boy** for a particular situation, they get all the blame for it. ❑ *He has become a convenient whipping boy for the failures of the old regime.*

whip|ping cream N-UNCOUNT **Whipping cream** is cream that becomes stiff when it is stirred very fast.

whip|poor|will /wɪpərwɪl/ (whippoorwills) N-COUNT A **whippoorwill** is a North American bird that is active at night and has a call that sounds like 'whip poor will.'

whir /wɜr/ (whirs, whirring, whirred) also **whirr** V-I When something such as a machine or an insect's wing **whirs**, it makes a series of low sounds so quickly that they seem like one continuous sound. ❑ *The camera whirred and clicked.* • N-COUNT; SOUND **Whir** is also a noun. ❑ *He could hear the whir of a vacuum cleaner.*

whirl /wɜrl/ (whirls, whirling, whirled) **1** V-T/V-I If something or someone **whirls** around or if you **whirl** them around, they move around or turn around very quickly. ❑ *Not receiving an answer, she whirled around.* ❑ *He was whirling Anne around the floor.* • N-COUNT **Whirl** is also a noun. ❑ *...the barely audible whirl of wheels.* **2** N-COUNT You can refer to a lot of intense activity as a **whirl** of activity. ❑ *In half an hour's whirl of activity she does it all.* **3** PHRASE If you decide to **give** an activity **a whirl**, you do it even though it is something that you have never tried before. [INFORMAL] ❑ *Why not give acupuncture a whirl?*

whirl|pool /wɜrlpul/ (whirlpools) N-COUNT A **whirlpool** is a small area in a river or the sea where the water is moving quickly around and around, so that objects floating near it are pulled into its center.

whirl|wind /wɜrlwɪnd/ (whirlwinds) **1** N-COUNT A **whirlwind** is a tall column of air that spins around and around very quickly and moves across the land or sea. **2** N-COUNT You can describe a situation in which a lot of things happen very quickly and are very difficult for someone to control as a **whirlwind**. ❑ *I had been running around southern California in a whirlwind of activity.* **3** ADJ [ADJ n] A **whirlwind** event or action happens or is done much more quickly than normal. ❑ *He got married after a whirlwind romance.*

whirr /wɜr/ → see **whir**

whisk /wɪsk/ (whisks, whisking, whisked) **1** V-T If you **whisk** someone or something somewhere, you take them or move them there quickly. ❑ *He whisked her across the dance floor.* **2** V-T If you **whisk** something such as eggs or cream, you stir it very fast, often with an electric device, so that it becomes full of small bubbles. ❑ *Just before serving, whisk the cream.* **3** N-COUNT A **whisk** is a kitchen tool used for whisking eggs or cream. ❑ *Using a whisk, mix the yolks and sugar to a smooth paste.* **4** → See also color supplement

whisk|er /wɪskər/ (whiskers) **1** N-COUNT The **whiskers** of an animal such as a cat or a mouse are the long stiff hairs that grow near its mouth. **2** N-PLURAL You can refer to the hair on a man's face, especially on the sides of his face, as his **whiskers**. ❑ *...wild, savage-looking fellows, with large whiskers and dirty faces.*

whisk|ery /wɪskəri/ ADJ If you describe someone as **whiskery**, you mean that they have lots of stiff little hairs on their face. ❑ *...a whiskery old man.*

whis|key /wɪski/ (whiskeys) N-MASS **Whiskey** is a strong alcoholic drink made, especially in the United States and Ireland, from grain such as barley or rye. ❑ *...a tumbler with about an inch of whiskey in it.* • N-COUNT A **whiskey** is a glass of whiskey. ❑ *Stark took two whiskeys from a tray.*

whis|ky /wɪski/ (whiskies) N-MASS **Whisky** is whiskey that is made especially in Scotland and Canada. • N-COUNT A **whisky** is a glass of whisky.

WORD HISTORY

whisky
The word **whisky** comes from Scottish Gaelic *uisge beatha*, meaning 'water of life.'

---

whis|per ◆◇◇ /wɪspər/ (whispers, whispering, whispered) **1** V-T/V-I When you **whisper**, you say something very quietly, using your breath rather than your throat, so that only one person can hear you. ❑ *"Keep your voice down," I whispered.* ❑ *She sat on Rossi's knee as he whispered in her ear.* ❑ *He whispered the message to David.* • N-COUNT **Whisper** is also a noun. ❑ *Men were talking in whispers in every office.* **2** → See feature box at **onomatopoeia**

whis|per|er /wɪspərər/ (whisperers) N-COUNT You can use **whisperer** to refer to someone who is extremely good at teaching a particular skill or subject, or taming and controlling a particular animal. ❑ *You didn't need to be a dog whisperer to know what Fido was thinking.* ❑ *The former president has given them so many tips that he has been dubbed 'the campaign whisperer.'*

whist /wɪst/ N-UNCOUNT **Whist** is a card game in which people play in pairs against each other.

whis|tle /wɪsəl/ (whistles, whistling, whistled) **1** V-T/V-I When you **whistle** or when you **whistle** a tune, you make a series of musical notes by forcing your breath out between your lips, or your teeth. ❑ *He whistled and sang snatches of songs.* ❑ *He was whistling softly to himself.* **2** V-I When someone **whistles**, they make a sound by forcing their breath out between their lips or their teeth. People sometimes whistle when they are surprised, or to call a dog, to get someone's attention, or to show that they are impressed. ❑ *He whistled, surprised but not shocked.* ❑ *Jenkins whistled through his teeth, impressed at last.* • N-COUNT **Whistle** is also a noun. ❑ *Jackson gave a low whistle.* **3** V-I If something such as a train or a kettle **whistles**, it makes a loud, high sound. ❑ *Somewhere a train whistled.* **4** V-I If something such as the wind or a bullet **whistles** somewhere, it moves there, making a loud, high sound. ❑ *The wind was whistling through the building.* **5** N-COUNT A **whistle** is a loud sound produced by air or steam being forced through a small opening, or by something moving quickly through the air. ❑ *...the whistle of the wind.* ❑ *...a shrill* whistle from the boiling kettle. **6** N-COUNT A **whistle** is a small metal tube that you blow into in order to produce a loud sound and attract someone's attention. ❏ *On the platform, the guard blew his whistle.* **7** PHRASE If you **blow the whistle** on someone, or on something secret or illegal, you tell another person, especially a person in authority, what is happening. ❏ *Companies should protect employees who blow the whistle on dishonest workmates and work practices.* **8** PHRASE If you describe something as **clean as a whistle**, you mean that it is completely clean. ❏ *The kitchen was clean as a whistle.*

whistle-blower (whistle-blowers) also **whistleblower** N-COUNT A **whistle-blower** is someone who finds out that the organization they work for is doing something immoral or illegal and tells the authorities or the public about it. [JOURNALISM] ❏ *An FBI whistle-blower testified to Congress about problems in the agency.*

whistle-blowing also **whistleblowing** N-UNCOUNT **Whistle-blowing** is the act of telling the authorities or the public that the organization you work for is doing something immoral or illegal. ❏ *It took internal whistle-blowing and investigative journalism to uncover the rot.*

whistle-stop ADJ [ADJ n] If someone, especially a politician, goes on a **whistle-stop** tour, they visit a lot of different places in a short time.

whit /wɪt/ PHRASE You say **not a whit** or **not one whit** to emphasize that something is not the case at all. [mainly FORMAL or OLD-FASHIONED, EMPHASIS] ❏ *He cared not a whit for the social, political or moral aspects of literature.*

white ♦♦♦ /waɪt/ (whiter, whitest, whites) **1** COLOR Something that is **white** is the color of snow or milk. ❏ *He had nice square white teeth.* ❏ *Issa's white beach hat gleamed in the harsh lights.* **2** ADJ A **White** person has a pale skin and belongs to a race of European origin. ❏ *Working with White people hasn't been a problem for me or for them.* • N-COUNT **Whites** are White people. **3** ADJ **White** wine is pale yellow in color. ❏ *Gregory poured another glass of white wine and went back to his bedroom.* **4** ADJ [ADJ n] **White** blood cells are the cells in your blood your body uses to fight infection. ❏ *...an AIDS drug that helps restore a patient's white blood cells.* **5** N-VAR The **white** of an egg is the transparent liquid that surrounds the yellow part called the yolk. ❏ *As soon as the whites of the eggs have set, remove the cover.* **6** N-COUNT The **white** of someone's eye is the white part that surrounds the colored part called the iris. ❏ *Susanne stared at me, the whites of her eyes gleaming in the streetlight.*

white|board /waɪtbɔːd/ (whiteboards) N-COUNT A **whiteboard** is a shiny white board on which people draw or write using special pens. Whiteboards are often used for teaching or giving talks.

white Christ|mas (white Christmases) N-COUNT A **white Christmas** is a Christmas when it snows.

white-collar also **white collar** **1** ADJ [ADJ n] **White-collar** workers work in offices rather than doing physical work such as making things in factories or building things. ❏ *White-collar workers now work longer hours.* **2** ADJ [ADJ n] **White-collar** crime is committed by people who work in offices, and involves stealing money secretly from companies or the government, or getting money in an illegal way. ❏ *...a New York lawyer who specializes in white-collar crime.* **3** → See feature box at **prison**

white el|ephant (white elephants) N-COUNT If you describe something as a **white elephant**, you mean that it is a waste of money because it is completely useless. [DISAPPROVAL] ❏ *The venture has been widely dismissed as a $264 million white elephant.*

white goods N-PLURAL People in business sometimes refer to refrigerators, washing machines, and other large pieces of electrical household equipment as **white goods**. ❏ *...the third largest manufacturer of white goods in the South.*

white-haired ADJ Someone who is **white-haired** has white hair, usually because they are old.

White|hall ♦◇◇ /waɪtɔːl/ N-PROPER **Whitehall** is the name of a street in London in which there are many government offices. **Whitehall** also means the British government itself. ❏ *Whitehall said that it hoped to get the change through by the end of June.*

white-hot ADJ If something is **white-hot**, it is extremely hot. ❏ *It is important to get the coals white-hot before you start.*

White House ♦◇◇ N-PROPER **The White House** is the official home in Washington DC of the president of the United States. You can also use **the White House** to refer to the president of the United States and his or her officials. ❏ *He drove to the White House.* ❏ *The White House has not participated in any talks.*

white knight (white knights) N-COUNT A **white knight** is a person or an organization that rescues a company from difficulties such as financial problems or an unwelcome takeover bid. [BUSINESS] ❏ *...a white-knight bid.*

white-knuck|le **1** ADJ [ADJ n] In an amusement park, a **white-knuckle** ride is any large machine that people ride on which is very exciting but also frightening. ❏ *...white-knuckle rides such as the rollercoaster.* **2** ADJ [ADJ n] A **white-knuckle** experience is something that you find very exciting but also very frightening. ❏ *He gets you to your destination without turning the trip into a white-knuckle experience.*

white lie (white lies) **1** N-COUNT If you refer to an untrue statement as a **white lie**, you mean that it is made to avoid hurting someone's feelings or to avoid trouble, and not for an evil purpose. **2** → See feature box at **truth**

white light N-UNCOUNT **White light** is light such as sunlight that contains all the colors of the visible spectrum in roughly equal amounts. [TECHNICAL]

white meat (white meats) N-UNCOUNT [also N in pl] **White meat** is meat such as chicken and pork, which is pale in color after it has been cooked.

whit|en /waɪtᵊn/ (whitens, whitening, whitened) V-T/V-I When something **whitens** or when you **whiten** it, it becomes whiter or paler in color. ❏ *Her knuckles whiten as she clenches her hands harder.* ❏ *...toothpastes that whiten teeth.*

white noise N-UNCOUNT **White noise** is a continuous 'sh' sound, caused by many frequencies of equal intensity. ❏ *They were made to listen to white noise, such as static of the sort you might pick up between radio stations.*

White Pages N-PLURAL **White Pages** is used to refer to the section of a telephone directory that lists names and telephone numbers in alphabetical order. Compare **Yellow Pages**. [AM]

White Pa|per (White Papers) N-COUNT In Britain, Australia, Canada, and some other countries, a **White Paper** is an official report which describes the policy of the Government on a particular subject.

white pep|per N-UNCOUNT **White pepper** is pepper made from the dried insides of the fruits of the pepper plant.

white sauce (white sauces) N-MASS **White sauce** is a thick white sauce made from milk, flour, and butter. Meat, fish, or vegetables are often cooked in or served in white sauce.

white spir|it N-UNCOUNT **White spirit** is a colorless liquid that is made from petroleum and is used, for example, to make paint thinner or to clean surfaces. [BRIT]

in AM, use **turpentine**

White trash N-UNCOUNT-COLL Some people use **White trash** to refer to poor White people who they think are worthless. [AM, OFFENSIVE, DISAPPROVAL] ❏ *...a place peopled by illiterate poor White trash.*

white|wash /waɪtwɒʃ/ (whitewashes, whitewashing, whitewashed) **1** N-UNCOUNT **Whitewash** is a mixture of lime or chalk and water that is used for painting walls white. **2** V-T If a wall or building **has been whitewashed**, it has been painted white with whitewash. ❏ *The walls had been whitewashed.* **3** V-T If you say that people **whitewash** something, you are accusing them of hiding the unpleasant facts or truth about it in order to make it acceptable. [DISAPPROVAL] ❏ *The administration is whitewashing the regime's actions.*

white-water raft|ing N-UNCOUNT **White-water rafting** is the activity of riding on a raft over rough, dangerous parts of a fast-flowing river.

whith|er /wɪðər/ QUEST **Whither** means to where. [LITERARY] ❏ *They knew not whither they went.*

whit|ing /waɪtɪŋ/ (whitings or whiting) N-VAR A **whiting** is a black and silver fish that lives in the sea. • N-UNCOUNT **Whiting** is this fish eaten as food. ❏ *He ordered stuffed whiting.*

whit|ish /ˈwaɪtɪʃ/ COLOR **Whitish** means very pale and almost white in color. ❑ ...a whitish dust.

Whit|sun /ˈwɪtsən/ N-UNCOUNT **Whitsun** is the same as Pentecost. [mainly BRIT]

Whit Sun|day N-UNCOUNT **Whit Sunday** is the same as Pentecost.

whit|tle /ˈwɪtəl/ (whittles, whittling, whittled) V-T If you **whittle** something from a piece of wood, you carve it by cutting pieces off the wood with a knife. ❑ He whittled a new handle for his ax.

▶ **whittle away** PHRASAL VERB To **whittle away** something or **whittle away** at it means to gradually make it smaller, weaker, or less effective. ❑ ...the plight of monkeys and other primates as people whittle away their habitat.

whiz /wɪz/ (whizzes, whizzing, whizzed) also **whizz** ◼ V-I If something **whizzes** somewhere, it moves there very fast. [INFORMAL] ❑ They heard bullets continue to whiz over their heads. ◼ N-COUNT If you are a **whiz** at something, you are very good at it. [INFORMAL] ❑ Simon's a whiz at card games.

whiz-kid (whiz-kids) also **whiz kid** N-COUNT [usu with supp] If you refer to a young person as a **whiz-kid**, you mean that they have achieved success at a young age because they are very clever and very good at something, especially making money. [INFORMAL] ❑ ...a computer whiz-kid. ❑ ...a whiz-kid physics student.

whizzy /ˈwɪzi/ (whizzier, whizziest) ADJ GRADED; ADJ **Whizzy** is used to describe products and activities that are new, exciting, and based on the latest technology. [INFORMAL] ❑ Japanese camera makers continually introduce whizzy new electronic models.

who ◆◆◆ /huː/

Usually pronounced /huː/ for meanings 2 and 3.

Who is used as the subject or object of a verb. See entries at **whom** and **whose**.

◼ QUEST You use **who** in questions when you ask about the name or identity of a person or group of people. ❑ Who's there? ❑ Who is the least popular man around here? ❑ "You reminded me of somebody."—"Who?" ◼ CONJ You use **who** after certain words, especially verbs and adjectives, to introduce a clause where you talk about the identity of a person or a group of people. ❑ Police have not been able to find out who was responsible for the forgeries. ❑ I went over to start up a conversation, asking her who she knew at the party. ◼ PRON-REL You use **who** at the beginning of a relative clause when specifying the person or group of people you are talking about or when giving more information about them. ❑ There are those who eat out for a special occasion, or treat themselves.

WHO /ˌdʌbəlju eɪtʃ ˈoʊ/ N-PROPER **WHO** is an abbreviation for World Health Organization. ❑ About half of all smokers are killed by their addiction, WHO reported.

whoa /woʊ/ ◼ EXCLAM **Whoa** is a command that you give to a horse to slow down or stop. ◼ EXCLAM You can say **whoa** to someone who is talking to you, to indicate that you think they are talking too fast or assuming things that may not be true. [INFORMAL] ❑ Slow down! Whoa!

who'd /hʊd, huːd/ ◼ **Who'd** is the usual spoken form of 'who had,' especially when 'had' is an auxiliary verb. ◼ **Who'd** is a spoken form of 'who would.'

who|dun|it /huːˈdʌnɪt/ (whodunits) also **whodunnit** N-COUNT A **whodunit** is a novel, movie, or play about a murder that does not tell you who the murderer is until the end. [INFORMAL]

who|ever /huːˈevər/ ◼ CONJ You use **whoever** to refer to someone when their identity is not yet known. ❑ Whoever did this will sooner or later be caught and will be punished. ❑ Whoever wins the election is going to have a tough job getting the economy back on its feet. ◼ CONJ You use **whoever** to indicate that the actual identity of the person who does something will not affect a situation. ❑ You can have whoever you like to visit you. ◼ QUEST You use **whoever** in questions as an emphatic way of saying 'who,' usually when you are surprised about something. [EMPHASIS] ❑ Whoever thought up that joke?

whole ◆◆◆ /hoʊl/ (wholes) ◼ QUANT [QUANT of def-n] If you refer to **the whole of** something, you mean all of it. ❑ He has said he will make an apology to the whole of Asia for his country's past behavior. ❑ I was cold throughout the whole of my body. • ADJ [ADJ n] **Whole** is also an adjective. ❑ We spent the whole summer in Italy that year. ◼ N-COUNT A **whole** is a single thing that contains several different parts. ❑ An atom itself is a complete whole, with its electrons, protons and neutrons and other elements. ◼ ADJ [v-link ADJ, v n ADJ] If something is **whole**, it is in one piece and is not broken or damaged. ❑ I struck the glass with my fist with all my might; yet it remained whole. ◼ ADV [ADV adj] You use **whole** to emphasize what you are saying. [INFORMAL, EMPHASIS] ❑ It was like seeing a whole different side of somebody. • ADJ [ADJ n] **Whole** is also an adjective. ❑ That saved me a whole bunch of money. ◼ PHRASE If you refer to something **as a whole**, you are referring to it generally and as a single unit. ❑ He described the move as a victory for the people of South Africa as a whole. ◼ PHRASE You use **on the whole** to indicate that what you are saying is true in general but may not be true in every case, or that you are giving a general opinion or summary of something. ❑ On the whole, people miss the opportunity to enjoy leisure.

▶ **SYNONYMS** ◀

whole
ADJ ◼
entire: He had spent his entire life in China as a doctor.
total: The total cost of the project would be more than $240 million.
complete: A complete city block was burned to the ground.
full: ...a full tank of gas.

whole|grains /ˈhoʊlɡreɪnz/ also **whole grains**

The forms **wholegrain** and **whole-grain** are used as modifiers.

N-PLURAL **Wholegrains** are the grains of cereals such as wheat and corn that have not been processed. ❑ Fruits, vegetables, and wholegrains are rich in potassium. ❑ ...crusty wholegrain bread.

whole|hearted /ˌhoʊlˈhɑːrtɪd/ ADJ If you support or agree to something in a **wholehearted** way, you support or agree to it enthusiastically and completely. [EMPHASIS] ❑ The governor deserves our wholehearted support for having taken a step in this direction. • **whole|hearted|ly** ADV ❑ That's exactly right. I agree wholeheartedly with you.

whole|meal /ˈhoʊlmiːl/ ADJ **Wholemeal** means the same as **wholewheat**

whole|ness /ˈhoʊlnɪs/ N-UNCOUNT **Wholeness** is the quality of being complete or a single unit and not broken or divided into parts. ❑ ...the need for wholeness and harmony in mind, body and spirit.

whole note (whole notes) N-COUNT A **whole note** is a musical note that has a time value equal to two half notes. [AM]

in BRIT, use **semibreve**

whole num|ber (whole numbers) N-COUNT A **whole number** is an exact number such as 1, 7, and 24, as opposed to a number with fractions or decimals.

whole|sale /ˈhoʊlseɪl/ ◼ N-UNCOUNT **Wholesale** is the activity of buying and selling goods in large quantities and therefore at cheaper prices, usually to stores who then sell them to the public. Compare **retail**. [BUSINESS] ❑ Warehouse clubs allow members to buy goods at wholesale prices. ◼ ADV [ADV after v] If something is sold **wholesale**, it is sold in large quantities and at cheaper prices, usually to stores. [BUSINESS] ❑ The fabrics are sold wholesale to retailers, fashion houses, and other manufacturers. ◼ ADJ [ADJ n] You use **wholesale** to describe the destruction, removal, or changing of something when it affects a very large number of things or people. [EMPHASIS] ❑ They are only doing what is necessary to prevent wholesale destruction of vegetation.

whole|sal|er /ˈhoʊlseɪlər/ (wholesalers) N-COUNT A **wholesaler** is a person whose business is buying large quantities of goods and selling them in smaller amounts, for example, to stores. [BUSINESS] ❑ Under state law, bar owners must buy their liquor from wholesalers.

whole|sal|ing /ˈhoʊlseɪlɪŋ/ N-UNCOUNT **Wholesaling** is the activity of buying or selling goods in large amounts, especially in order to sell them in stores or supermarkets. Compare **retailing**. [BUSINESS] ❑ *The business thrived and he turned to wholesaling.*

whole|some /hoʊlsəm/ ◼ ADJ If you describe something as **wholesome**, you approve of it because you think it is likely to have a positive influence on people's behavior or mental state, especially because it does not involve anything sexually immoral. [APPROVAL] ❑ *The Foundation aims to promote wholesome family entertainment.* ◻ ADJ If you describe food as **wholesome**, you approve of it because you think it is good for your health. [APPROVAL] ❑ *...fresh, wholesome ingredients.*

whole|wheat /hoʊlwiːt/ also **whole wheat** ◼ ADJ [usu ADJ n] **Wholewheat** flour is made from the complete grain of the wheat plant, including the outer part. **Wholewheat** bread or pasta is made from wholewheat flour. ❑ *...vegetables with wholewheat noodles.* ◻ N-UNCOUNT **Wholewheat** means wholewheat bread or wholewheat flour. ❑ *...a chicken salad sandwich on whole wheat.*

who'll /huːl, hʊl/ **Who'll** is a spoken form of 'who will' or 'who shall.'

whol|ly /hoʊlli/ ADV You use **wholly** to emphasize the extent or degree to which something is the case. [EMPHASIS] ❑ *While the two are only days apart in age they seem to belong to wholly different generations.*

wholly-owned sub|sidi|ary (wholly-owned subsidiaries) N-COUNT A **wholly-owned subsidiary** is a company whose shares are all owned by another company. [BUSINESS] ❑ *The Boston-owned software company became a wholly-owned subsidiary of IBM.*

whom ♦♦◊ /huːm/

Whom is used in formal or written English instead of 'who' when it is the object of a verb or preposition.

◼ QUEST You use **whom** in questions when you ask about the name or identity of a person or group of people. ❑ *"I want to send a telegram."—"Fine, to whom?"* ❑ *Whom did he expect to answer his phone?* ◻ CONJ You use **whom** after certain words, especially verbs and adjectives, to introduce a clause where you talk about the name or identity of a person or a group of people. ❑ *He asked whom I'd told about his having been away.* ◻ PRON-REL You use **whom** at the beginning of a relative clause when specifying the person or group of people you are talking about or when giving more information about them. ❑ *One writer in whom I had taken an interest was Immanuel Velikovsky.*

whom|ever /huːmɛvər/ CONJ **Whomever** is a formal word for **whoever** when it is the object of a verb or preposition.

whoop /huːp/ (whoops, whooping, whooped) V-I If you **whoop**, you shout loudly in a very happy or excited way. [WRITTEN] ❑ *She whoops with delight at a promise of money.* • N-COUNT **Whoop** is also a noun. ❑ *Scattered groans and whoops broke out in the crowd.*

whoo|pee /wʊpi/ EXCLAM People sometimes shout **whoopee** when they are very happy or excited. [INFORMAL, FEELINGS] ❑ *I can have a week at home in my own bed before I have to leave for New York. Whoopee!*

whoop|ing cough /huːpɪŋ kɔf/ N-UNCOUNT **Whooping cough** is a serious infectious disease that causes people to cough and make a loud noise when they breathe in.

whoops /wʊps/ EXCLAM You say **whoops** to indicate that there has been a slight accident or mistake, or to apologize to someone for it. [INFORMAL, FEELINGS] ❑ *Whoops, that was a mistake.* ❑ *Whoops, it's past 11, I'd better be off home.*

whoosh /wʊʃ, wuːʃ/ (whooshes, whooshing, whooshed) ◼ EXCLAM People sometimes say 'whoosh' when they are emphasizing the fact that something happens very suddenly or very fast. [EMPHASIS] ❑ *Then came the riders amid even louder cheers and whoosh! It was all over.* ◻ V-I If something **whooshes** somewhere, it moves there quickly or suddenly. [INFORMAL] ❑ *Kites whooshed above the beach at intervals.*

whop|per /wɒpər/ (whoppers) ◼ N-COUNT If you describe a lie as a **whopper**, you mean that it is very far from the truth. [INFORMAL] ❑ *...the biggest whopper the president told.* ◻ N-COUNT If you refer to something as a **whopper**, you mean that it is an unusually large example of the thing mentioned. [INFORMAL] ❑ *As comets go, it is a whopper.*

whop|ping /wɒpɪŋ/ ADJ [ADJ n] If you describe an amount as **whopping**, you are emphasizing that it is large. [INFORMAL, EMPHASIS] ❑ *The Russian leader won a whopping 89.9 percent yes vote.*

whore /hɔr/ (whores) N-COUNT **Whore** is an insulting word for a woman who has sex with a lot of different people. [OFFENSIVE, DISAPPROVAL]

who're /huər, hʊər/ **Who're** is a spoken form of 'who are.' ❑ *I've got loads of friends who're unemployed.*

whore|house /hɔrhaʊs/ (whorehouses) N-COUNT A **whorehouse** is the same as a **brothel**.

whorl /wɜrl, wɔrl/ (whorls) N-COUNT A **whorl** is a spiral shape, such as the pattern on the tips of your fingers. [LITERARY] ❑ *He stared at the whorls and lines of her fingertips.* ❑ *...dense whorls of red-purple flowers.*

who's /huːz, hʊz/ **Who's** is the usual spoken form of 'who is' or 'who has,' especially when 'has' is an auxiliary verb.

──────── USAGE ────────

who's
Who is and who has are sometimes contracted and pronounced /huːz/. When you write down what someone says, you can write 'who is' or 'who has' as **who's**. Don't write them as 'whose.' *'Edward drove me here.'*—'**Who's** Edward?' *...an American author **who's** moved to London.*

whose ♦♦♦ /huːz/

Usually pronounced /huz/ for meanings 2 and 3.

◼ PRON-REL You use **whose** at the beginning of a relative clause where you mention something that belongs to or is associated with the person or thing mentioned in the previous clause. ❑ *I saw a man shouting at a driver whose car was blocking the street.* ❑ *...a speedboat, whose fifteen-strong crew claimed to belong to China's navy.* ◻ QUEST You use **whose** in questions to ask about the person or thing that something belongs to or is associated with. ❑ *"Whose is this?"—"It's mine."* ❑ *"It wasn't your fault, John."—"Whose, then?"* ❑ *Whose car were they in?* ❑ *Whose daughter is she?* ◻ DET You use **whose** after certain words, especially verbs and adjectives, to introduce a clause where you talk about the person or thing that something belongs to or is associated with. ❑ *I'm wondering whose mother she is then.* ❑ *I can't remember whose idea it was.* • CONJ **Whose** is also a conjunction. ❑ *I wondered whose the coat was.*

who|so|ever /huːsoʊɛvər/ CONJ **Whosoever** means the same as **whoever**. [LITERARY, OLD-FASHIONED] ❑ *They can transfer or share the contract with whosoever they choose.*

who've /huːv, hʊv/ **Who've** is the usual spoken form of 'who have,' especially when 'have' is an auxiliary verb.

why ♦♦♦ /waɪ/

The conjunction and the pronoun are usually pronounced /waɪ/.

◼ QUEST You use **why** in questions when you ask about the reasons for something. ❑ *Why hasn't he brought the whiskey?* ❑ *Why didn't he stop me?* ◻ CONJ You use **why** at the beginning of a clause in which you talk about the reasons for something. ❑ *He still could not throw any further light on why the elevator could have become jammed.* ❑ *Experts wonder why the U.S. government is not taking similarly strong actions against AIDS in this country.* • ADV **Why** is also an adverb. ❑ *I don't know why.* ❑ *It's obvious why.* ◻ PRON-REL You use **why** to introduce a relative clause after the word 'reason.' ❑ *There's a reason why women don't read this stuff; it's not funny.* • ADV [n ADV] **Why** is also an adverb. ❑ *He confirmed that the city had been closed to foreigners, but gave no reason why.* ◻ QUEST You use **why** with 'not' in questions in order to introduce a suggestion. ❑ *Why not give Charmaine a call?* ◻ QUEST You use **why** with 'not' in questions in order to express your annoyance or anger. [FEELINGS] ❑ *Why don't you look where you're going?* ◻ CONVENTION You say **why not** in order to agree with what someone has suggested. [FORMULAE] ❑ *"Want to spend the afternoon with me?"—"Why not?"* ◻ EXCLAM People say '**Why!**' at the beginning of a sentence when they are surprised, shocked, or angry. [mainly AM, FEELINGS] ❑ *Why, hello, Tom.*

Wic|ca /wɪkə/ N-PROPER **Wicca** is a pagan religion that practices witchcraft.

wick /wɪk/ (wicks) **1** N-COUNT The **wick** of a candle is the piece of string in it that burns when it is lit. **2** N-COUNT The **wick** of an oil lamp or cigarette lighter is the part that supplies the fuel to the flame when it is lit.

wick|ed /wɪkɪd/ ADJ You use **wicked** to describe someone or something that is very bad and deliberately harmful to people. ❑ *She described the shooting as a wicked attack.*

wick|er /wɪkər/ N-UNCOUNT [usu N n] **Wicker** is long thin sticks, stems, or reeds that have been woven together to make things such as baskets and furniture. ❑ *...a wicker basket.*

wicker|work /wɪkərwɜrk/ N-UNCOUNT [usu N n] **Wickerwork** is the same as **wicker**.

wick|et ♦◇◇ /wɪkɪt/ (wickets) **1** N-COUNT In cricket, a **wicket** is a set of three upright sticks with two small sticks on top of them at which the ball is bowled. **2** N-COUNT In cricket, a **wicket** is the area of grass in between the two wickets on the field. **3** N-COUNT In cricket, when a **wicket** falls or is taken, a batsman is out. ❑ *Matthew Hoggard took three wickets in six balls.*

wide ♦♦♦ /waɪd/ (wider, widest) **1** ADJ Something that is **wide** measures a large distance from one side or edge to the other. ❑ *All worktops should be wide enough to allow plenty of space for food preparation.* **2** ADJ If you open or spread something **wide**, you open or spread it as far as possible or to the fullest extent. ❑ *"It was huge," he announced, spreading his arms wide.* **3** ADJ You use **wide** to talk or ask about how much something measures from one side or edge to the other. ❑ *...a corridor of land four miles wide.* ❑ *The road is only one lane wide.* **4** ADJ You use **wide** to describe something that includes a large number of different things or people. ❑ *The brochure offers a wide choice of hotels, apartments and vacation homes.* • **wide|ly** ADV ❑ *He published widely in scientific journals.* **5** ADJ You use **wide** to say that something is found, believed, known, or supported by many people or throughout a large area. ❑ *The case has attracted wide publicity.* • **wide|ly** ADV [ADV with v] ❑ *At present, no widely approved vaccine exists for malaria.* **6** ADJ A **wide** difference or gap between two things, ideas, or qualities is a large difference or gap. ❑ *Research shows a wide difference in tastes around the country.* • **wide|ly** ADV ❑ *The treatment regime may vary widely depending on the type of injury.* **7** ADJ [ADJ n] **Wider** is used to describe something that relates to the most important or general parts of a situation, rather than to the smaller parts or to details. ❑ *He emphasized the wider issue of superpower cooperation.* **8** → see also **wide awake 9 wide of the mark** → see **mark 10 wide open** → see **open** ④ **11** → See feature box at **relationship**

-wide /-waɪd/ COMB IN ADJ **-wide** combines with nouns to form adjectives that indicate that something exists or happens throughout the place or area that the noun refers to. ❑ *...a statewide program for homeless people.* ❑ *Is the problem one that's industry-wide?* • COMB IN ADV **-wide** also combines to form adverbs. ❑ *Unfilled positions number several million countrywide.*

wide-angle lens (wide-angle lenses) N-COUNT A **wide-angle lens** is a lens that allows you to photograph a wider view than a normal lens.

wide awake ADJ [usu v link ADJ] If you are **wide awake**, you are completely awake. ❑ *I could not relax and still felt wide awake.*

wide-eyed ADJ [usu ADJ n] If you describe someone as **wide-eyed**, you mean that they are inexperienced and innocent, and may be easily impressed. ❑ *This generation has lost a lot of its wide-eyed innocence.*

wid|en /waɪdᵊn/ (widens, widening, widened) **1** V-T/V-I If you **widen** something or if it **widens**, it becomes greater in measurement from one side or edge to the other. ❑ *He had an operation last year to widen a heart artery.* **2** V-T/V-I If you **widen** something or if it **widens**, it becomes greater in range or it affects a larger number of people or things. ❑ *U.S. prosecutors have widened a securities-fraud investigation.* **3** V-T/V-I If a difference or gap **widens** or if something **widens** it, it becomes greater. ❑ *Wage differences in the two areas are widening.*

wide-ranging ADJ If you describe something as **wide-ranging**, you mean it deals with or affects a great variety of different things. ❑ *...a package of wide-ranging economic reforms.*

wide|screen /waɪdskrin/ ADJ A **widescreen** television has a screen that is wide in relation to its height.

wide|spread ♦◇◇ /waɪdsprɛd/ ADJ Something that is **widespread** exists or happens over a large area, or to a great extent. ❑ *There is widespread support for the new proposals.*

widg|et /wɪdʒɪt/ (widgets) N-COUNT You can refer to any small device as a **widget** when you do not know exactly what it is or how it works. [INFORMAL] ❑ *The secret is a little widget in the can.*

wid|ow /wɪdoʊ/ (widows) N-COUNT A **widow** is a woman whose spouse has died and who has not married again. ❑ *She became a widow a year ago.*

wid|owed /wɪdoʊd/ V-T PASSIVE If someone **is widowed**, their spouse has died. ❑ *More and more young men are widowed by cancer.*

wid|ow|er /wɪdoʊər/ (widowers) N-COUNT A **widower** is a man whose spouse has died and who has not married again. ❑ *He is a widower and lives in Durango.*

wid|ow|hood /wɪdoʊhʊd/ N-UNCOUNT **Widowhood** is the state of being a widow or widower, or the period of time during which someone is a widow or widower. ❑ *Nothing can prepare you for the shock and grief of widowhood.*

width /wɪdθ, wɪtθ/ (widths) N-VAR The **width** of something is the distance it measures from one side or edge to the other. ❑ *Measure the full width of the window.* ❑ *The road was reduced to 18 ft in width by adding parking bays.*

wield /wild/ (wields, wielding, wielded) **1** V-T If you **wield** a weapon, tool, or piece of equipment, you carry and use it. ❑ *He was attacked by a man wielding a knife.* **2** V-T If someone **wields** power, they have it and are able to use it. ❑ *She is still in charge officially, but wields little power at the company.*

wie|ner /winər/ (wieners) also **weenie, wienie** N-COUNT **Wieners** are sausages made from smoked beef or pork. [AM]

wie|ner schnit|zel /vinər ʃnɪtzᵊl/ (wiener schnitzels) also **Wiener schnitzel** N-VAR **Wiener schnitzel** is a dish consisting of a slice of veal which is coated in egg and breadcrumbs, then fried. ❑ *On the menu is wiener schnitzel and potato salad.*

wife ♦♦♦ /waɪf/ (wives) N-COUNT Someone's **wife** is the woman they are married to. ❑ *He married his wife Jane 37 years ago.*

COLLOCATIONS

wife
NOUN
adjective + **wife**: beloved, dear, loving; first, former, future, second; estranged
verb + **wife**: marry, meet; leave

---

wife|ly /waɪfli/ ADJ [usu ADJ n] **Wifely** is used to describe things that are supposed to be typical of a good wife. [FORMAL] ❑ *Performing her so-called wifely functions was hardly a priority for her.* ❑ *...the ideology of wifely duty.*

Wi-Fi also **wi-fi** /waɪfaɪ/ N-UNCOUNT **Wi-Fi** is a system of using the internet without being connected with a wire. [COMPUTING] ❑ *There is free Wi-Fi throughout the hotel.* ❑ *You can send data to the printer wirelessly over your wi-fi network.*

wig /wɪg/ (wigs) N-COUNT A **wig** is a covering of false hair that you wear on your head, for example, because you have little hair of your own or because you want to cover up your own hair. ❑ *Jo wore a long wig that made her look very sexy.*

wig|gle /wɪgᵊl/ (wiggles, wiggling, wiggled) V-T/V-I If you **wiggle** something or if it **wiggles**, it moves up and down or from side to side in small quick movements. ❑ *She wiggled her finger.* • N-COUNT **Wiggle** is also a noun. ❑ *...a wiggle of the hips.*

wig|wam /wɪgwɑm/ (wigwams) N-COUNT A **wigwam** is a Native American tent, similar to a tepee.

wi|ki /wɪki/ (wikis) N-COUNT A **wiki** is a website that allows anyone visiting it to change or add to the material in it. ❑ *...wiki technology.* ❑ *Most wikis are collaborative websites.*

wild ♦♦◇ /waɪld/ (wilds, wilder, wildest) **1** ADJ **Wild** animals or plants live or grow in natural surroundings and are not taken care of by people. ❑ *We saw two more wild cats creeping toward us in the darkness.* **2** ADJ **Wild** land is natural and is not used by people. ❑ *...a wild area of woods and lakes.* **3** N-PLURAL The **wilds** of a place are the natural areas that are far away from cities and towns. ❑ *They went canoeing in the wilds of Canada.* **4** ADJ **Wild** is used to describe the weather or the sea when it is stormy. ❑ *The wild weather did not deter some people from taking an unseasonable dip in the sea.* **5** ADJ **Wild** behavior is uncontrolled, excited, or energetic. ❑ *The children are wild with joy.* ❑ *As George himself came on stage they went wild.* • **wild|ly** ADV

[ADV with v] As she finished each song, the crowd clapped wildly. **6** ADJ If you describe someone or their behavior as **wild**, you mean that they behave in a very uncontrolled way. The house is in a mess after a wild party. • **wild|ly** ADV [ADV with v] Five people were injured as Reynolds slashed out wildly with a kitchen knife. **7** ADJ [ADJ n] A **wild** idea is unusual or extreme. A wild guess is one that you make without much thought. Browning's prediction is no better than a wild guess. • **wild|ly** ADV "Thirteen?" he guessed wildly. **8** → see also **wildly 9** PHRASE Animals that live **in the wild** live in a free and natural state and are not taken care of by people. Fewer than a thousand giant pandas still live in the wild. **10 beyond your wildest dreams** → see **dream 11 in your wildest dreams** → see **dream**

SYNONYMS

wild
ADJ **1**
savage: ...a savage dog, lunging at the end of a chain.
untamed: ...the wild, untamed undergrowth.
feral: ...feral cats.

---

wild boar (wild boar or wild boars) N-COUNT A **wild boar** is a large fierce pig that has two long curved teeth and a hairy body, and lives in forests.

wild card (wild cards) also **wildcard 1** N-COUNT If you refer to someone or something as a **wild card** in a particular situation, you mean that they cause uncertainty because you do not know how they will behave. The wild card in the picture is eastern Europe. **2** N-COUNT A **wildcard** is a symbol such as * or ? used in some computing commands or searches in order to represent any character or range of characters. [COMPUTING] **3** N-COUNT In card games, if a particular card is named as a **wild card**, the player who holds it may give it any value he chooses. Look. I have a straight of 3, 4, 6, 7 and the wild card for the 5.

wild|cat /waɪldkæt/ (wildcats) **1** N-COUNT A **wildcat** is a fierce cat that lives especially in mountains and forests. A giant wildcat is being hunted after 58 lambs were butchered. **2** ADJ [ADJ n] A **wildcat** strike happens suddenly, as a result of a decision by a group of workers, and is not officially approved by a labor union. Frustration, anger and desperation have led to a series of wildcat strikes.

wil|de|beest /wɪldɪbiːst, vɪl-/ (wildebeest) N-COUNT A **wildebeest** is a large African antelope that has a hairy tail, short curved horns, and long hair under its neck. Wildebeest usually live in large groups.

wil|der|ness /wɪldərnɪs/ (wildernesses) N-COUNT A **wilderness** is a desert or other area of natural land which is not used by people. ...the icy Canadian wilderness.

wild|fire /waɪldfaɪər/ (wildfires) **1** N-COUNT A **wildfire** is a fire that starts, usually by itself, in a wild area such as a forest, and spreads rapidly, causing great damage. ...a wildfire in Montana that's already burned thousands of acres of rich grassland. **2** PHRASE If something, especially news or a rumor, **spreads like wildfire**, it spreads extremely quickly. These stories are spreading like wildfire through the city.

wild|flow|er /waɪldflaʊər/ (wildflowers) also **wild flower** N-COUNT **Wildflowers** are flowers that grow naturally in the countryside, rather than being grown by people in gardens.

wild|fowl /waɪldfaʊl/ N-PLURAL **Wildfowl** are birds such as ducks, swans, and geese that live close to lakes or rivers.

wild goose chase (wild goose chases) also **wild-goose chase** N-COUNT [usu on n] If you are on a **wild goose chase**, you waste a lot of time searching for something that you have little chance of finding, because you have been given incorrect information. Harry wondered if Potts had deliberately sent him on a wild goose chase.

wild|life /waɪldlaɪf/ N-UNCOUNT You can use **wildlife** to refer to the animals and other living things that live in the wild. People were concerned that pets or wildlife could be affected by the pesticides.

wild|ly /waɪldli/ **1** ADV You use **wildly** to emphasize the degree, amount, or intensity of something. [EMPHASIS] Here again, the community and police have wildly different stories of what happened. **2** → see also **wild**

wild rice (wild rices) N-MASS **Wild rice** is the edible grain from a type of tall grass that grows in North America. ...the lakes where the wild rice grows.

Wild West N-SING [the N] **The Wild West** is used to refer to the western part of the United States during the time when Europeans were first settling there.

wiles /waɪlz/ N-PLURAL [usu supp N, N of n] **Wiles** are clever tricks that people use to persuade other people to do something. He was seduced by the wiles of a woman.

WILL
① MODAL VERB USES
② WANTING SOMETHING TO HAPPEN
---

① **will** ♦♦♦ /wɪl/

Will is a modal verb. It is used with the base form of a verb. In spoken English and informal written English, the form **won't** is often used in negative statements.

1 MODAL You use **will** to indicate that you hope, think, or have evidence that something is going to happen or be the case in the future. I'm sure we will find a wide variety of choices available in school cafeterias. Will you ever feel at home here? The ship will not be ready for a month. **2** MODAL You use **will** in order to make statements about official arrangements in the future. The show will be open to the public at 2 pm; admission will be $5. **3** MODAL You use **will** in order to make promises and threats about what is going to happen or be the case in the future. I'll call you tonight. Price quotes on selected product categories will be sent on request. **4** MODAL You use **will** to indicate someone's intention to do something. I will say no more on these matters, important though they are. In this section we will describe common myths about cigarettes, alcohol, and marijuana. "Dinner's ready."—"Thanks, Carrie, but we'll have a drink first." Will you be remaining in the city? **5** MODAL You use **will** in questions in order to make polite invitations or offers. [POLITENESS] Will you stay for supper? Will you join me for a drink? **6** MODAL You use **will** in questions in order to ask or tell someone to do something. Will you drive me home? Will you listen again, Andrew? **7** MODAL You use **will** to say that someone is willing to do something. You use **will not** or **won't** to indicate that someone refuses to do something. All right, I'll forgive you. **8** → see also **willing 9** MODAL You use **will** to say that a person or thing is able to do something in the future. How the country will defend itself in the future has become increasingly important. **10** MODAL You use **will** to indicate that an action usually happens in the particular way mentioned. The thicker the material, the less susceptible the garment will be to wet conditions. **11** MODAL You use **will** in the main clause of some 'if' and 'unless' sentences to indicate something that you consider to be fairly likely to happen. If you overcook the meat it will be dry. **12** MODAL You use **will** to say that someone insists on behaving or doing something in a particular way and you cannot change them. You emphasize **will** when you use it in this way. He will leave his socks lying all over the place and it drives me crazy. **13** MODAL You use **will have** with a past participle when you are saying that you are fairly certain that something will be true by a particular time in the future. As many as ten-million children will have been infected with the virus by the end of the decade. **14** MODAL You use **will have** with a past participle to indicate that you are fairly sure that something is the case. Jack will have been very upset by all this.

② **will** ♦♦◊ /wɪl/ (wills, willing, willed) **1** N-VAR **Will** is the determination to do something. He was said to have lost his will to live. **2** → see also **free will 3** N-SING If something is the **will** of a person or group of people with authority, they want it to happen. He has submitted himself to the will of God. **4** V-T If you **will** something to happen, you try to make it happen by using mental effort rather than physical effort. I looked at the telephone, willing it to ring. **5** N-COUNT A **will** is a document in which you declare what you want to happen to your money and property when you die. Attached to his will was a letter he had written to his wife just days before his death. **6** PHRASE If something is done **against** your **will**, it is done even though you do not want it to be done. No doubt he was forced to leave his family against his will.

will|ful /wɪlfəl/ **1** ADJ [ADJ n] If you describe actions or attitudes as **willful**, you are critical of them because they are done or expressed deliberately, especially with the intention of causing someone harm. The sergeant faces a lesser charge of willful neglect of duty. **2** ADJ If you describe someone as **willful**, you mean that they are determined to do what they want to do, even if it is not sensible. ❏ *Molly was at times impatient and willful.*

will|ing ♦♦◊ /wɪlɪŋ/ **1** ADJ [v-link ADJ to-inf] If someone is **willing** to do something, they are fairly happy about doing it and will do it if they are asked or required to do it. ❏ *There are, of course, questions which she will not be willing to answer.* **2** ADJ **Willing** is used to describe someone who does something fairly enthusiastically and because they want to do it rather than because they are forced to do it. ❏ *Have the party on a Saturday, when you can get your partner and other willing adults to help.* **3** God willing → see god

will-o'-the-wisp /wɪl ə ðə wɪsp/ (will-o'-the-wisps) N-COUNT [usu sing] You can refer to someone or something that keeps disappearing or that is impossible to catch or reach as a **will-o'-the-wisp**.

wil|low /wɪloʊ/ (willows) N-COUNT A **willow** or a **willow tree** is a type of tree with long branches and long narrow leaves that grows near water.

wil|lowy /wɪloʊi/ **1** ADJ A person who is **willowy** is tall, thin, and graceful. **2** → See feature box at **appearance**

will|power /wɪlpaʊər/ also **will-power, will power** N-UNCOUNT **Willpower** is a very strong determination to do something. ❏ *He came in for help after his attempts to stop smoking by willpower alone failed.*

willy-nilly /wɪli nɪli/ also **willy nilly** **1** ADV If something happens to you **willy-nilly**, it happens whether you like it or not. ❏ *These men who were thrown together willy-nilly by the Army had nothing in common.* **2** ADV If someone does something **willy-nilly**, they do it in a careless and disorganized way, without planning it in advance. ❏ *Clerks bundled papers into files willy-nilly.*

wilt /wɪlt/ (wilts, wilting, wilted) V-I If a plant **wilts**, it gradually bends downward and becomes weak because it needs more water or is dying. ❏ *The roses wilted the next day.*

wily /waɪli/ (wilier, wiliest) ADJ If you describe someone or their behavior as **wily**, you mean that they are clever at achieving what they want, especially by tricking people. ❏ *This is a wily politician.*

wimp /wɪmp/ (wimps) N-COUNT If you call someone a **wimp**, you disapprove of them because they lack confidence or determination, or because they are often afraid of things. [INFORMAL, DISAPPROVAL] ❏ *I was a wimp, because I had spent my life being bullied by my Dad.*

wimp|ish /wɪmpɪʃ/ ADJ **Wimpish** means the same as **wimpy**. [INFORMAL, DISAPPROVAL]

wimpy /wɪmpi/ (wimpier, wimpiest) ADJ If you describe a person or their behavior as **wimpy**, you disapprove of them because they are weak and seem to lack confidence or determination. [INFORMAL, DISAPPROVAL] ❏ *...a wimpy unpopular schoolboy.* ❏ *This portrays her as wimpy, but she has a very strong character.*

win ♦♦♦ /wɪn/ (wins, winning, won) **1** V-T/V-I If you **win** something such as a competition, battle, or argument, you defeat those people you are competing or fighting against, or you do better than everyone else involved. ❏ *He does not have any realistic chance of winning the election.* ❏ *The top four teams all won.* • N-COUNT **Win** is also a noun. ❏ *The voters gave a narrow win to Vargas Llosa.* **2** V-T If something **wins** you something such as an election, competition, battle, or argument, it causes you to defeat the people competing with you or fighting you, or to do better than everyone else involved. ❏ *The Democrats had found a message that could win them the White House.* **3** V-T If you **win** something such as a prize or medal, you get it because you have defeated everyone else in something such as an election, competition, battle, or argument, or have done very well in it. ❏ *Trent Dimas won gold in the final men's gymnastic event.* **4** V-T If you **win** something that you want or need, you succeed in getting it. ❏ *...moves to win the support of the poor.*

in BRIT, also use **win round**

5 → see also **winning** **6** to win hands down → see hand ①
▶ **win over** PHRASAL VERB If you **win** someone **over**, you persuade them to support you or agree with you. ❏ *He has won over a significant number of the left-wing deputies.*

wince /wɪns/ (winces, wincing, winced) V-I If you **wince**, the muscles of your face tighten suddenly because you have felt a pain or because you have just seen, heard, or remembered something unpleasant. ❏ *Every time he put any weight on his left leg he winced in pain.*

winch /wɪntʃ/ (winches, winching, winched) **1** N-COUNT A **winch** is a machine that is used to lift heavy objects or people who need to be rescued. It consists of a cylinder around which a rope or chain is wound. **2** V-T If you **winch** an object or person somewhere, you lift or lower them using a winch. ❏ *He would attach a cable around the chassis of the car and winch it up on to the canal bank.*

WIND

① AIR
② TURNING OR WRAPPING

---

① **wind** ♦♦◊ /wɪnd/ (winds, winding, winded) **1** N-VAR A **wind** is a current of air that is moving across the earth's surface. ❏ *There was a strong wind blowing.* **2** N-COUNT Journalists often refer to a trend or factor that influences events as a **wind** of a particular kind. ❏ *The winds of change are blowing across the country.* **3** V-T If you **are winded** by something such as a blow, the air is suddenly knocked out of your lungs so that you have difficulty breathing for a short time. ❏ *He was winded and shaken.* **4** PHRASE If someone **breaks wind**, they release gas from their intestines through their anus. ❏ *If I break wind at dinner, should I say "Pardon," or pretend nothing has happened?* **5** PHRASE If you **get wind of** something, you hear about it, especially when someone else did not want you to know about it. [INFORMAL] ❏ *I don't want the public, and especially not the press, to get wind of it at this stage.* **6** → See feature box at **hot, storm**

SYNONYMS

wind
NOUN ① **1**
breeze: *...a cool, summer breeze.*
gust: *A gust of wind drove down the valley.*
draft: *On a cold day, there can be quite a draft from the letterbox.*

---

② **wind** ♦♦◊ /waɪnd/ (winds, winding, wound) **1** V-T/V-I If a road, river, or line of people **winds** in a particular direction, it goes in that direction with a lot of bends or twists in it. ❏ *Quiet mountain roads wind through groves of bamboo and cedar.* ❏ *...a narrow winding road.* ❏ *We wound our way southeast.* **2** V-T When you **wind** something flexible around something else, you wrap it around it several times. ❏ *The horse jumped forward and around her, winding the rope around her waist.* **3** V-T When you **wind** a mechanical device, for example, a watch or a clock, you turn a knob, key, or handle on it several times in order to make it operate. ❏ *I still hadn't wound my watch so I didn't know the time.* • PHRASAL VERB **Wind up** means the same as **wind**. ❏ *I wound up the watch and listened to it tick.* **4** V-T To **wind** a tape or film **back** or **forward** means to make it move toward its starting or ending position. ❏ *The camcorder winds the tape back or forward at high speed.*

▶ **wind down** **1** PHRASAL VERB When you **wind down** something such as the window of a car, you make it move downward by turning a handle. ❏ *Glass motioned to him to wind down the window.* **2** PHRASAL VERB If you **wind down**, you relax after doing something that has made you feel tired or tense [INFORMAL] ❏ *I regularly go for a run to wind down.* **3** PHRASAL VERB If someone **winds down** a business or activity, or if it **winds down**, they gradually reduce the amount of work that is done or the number of people that are involved, usually before closing or stopping it completely. ❏ *Aid workers have begun winding down their operation.*

▶ **wind up** **1** PHRASAL VERB When you **wind up** an activity, you finish it or stop doing it. ❏ *The president is about to wind up his visit to Somalia.* **2** PHRASAL VERB When you **wind up** something such as the window of a car, you make it move upward by turning a handle. ❏ *He started winding the window up but I grabbed the door and opened it.* **3** → see also **wind** ② **3, wound up**

wind|bag /wɪndbæg/ (windbags) N-COUNT If you call someone a **windbag**, you are saying in a fairly rude way that you think they talk a lot in a boring way. [INFORMAL, DISAPPROVAL]

wind|blown /wɪndbloʊn/ **1** ADJ You can use **windblown** to indicate that something has been blown from one place to another by the wind. ❏ *Silt and windblown soil buried the site even deeper.* **2** ADJ If something such as someone's hair is **windblown**, it is untidy because it has been blown about by the wind.

wind|break /wɪndbreɪk/ (**windbreaks**) N-COUNT A **windbreak** is something such as a line of trees or a fence that gives protection against the wind.

Wind|breaker /wɪndbreɪkər/ (**Windbreakers**) N-COUNT A **Windbreaker** is a jacket that resists the wind and fits closely at the waist and wrists. [mainly AM, TRADEMARK]

wind chill fac|tor also **wind-chill factor, windchill factor** N-SING A **wind chill factor** is a measure of the cooling effect of the wind on the temperature of the air. ❏ *Gusty winds combined with a minus 40 temperature created a wind-chill factor of 80 degrees below zero.*

wind|fall /wɪndfɔl/ (**windfalls**) N-COUNT A **windfall** is a sum of money that you receive unexpectedly or by luck, for example, if you win a lottery. ❏ *…the man who received a $250,000 windfall after a banking error.* ❏ *…windfall profits.*

wind farm /wɪnd fɑrm/ (**wind farms**) N-COUNT A **wind farm** is a place where windmills are used to convert the power of the wind into electricity.

wind in|stru|ment /wɪnd ɪnstrəmənt/ (**wind instruments**) N-COUNT A **wind instrument** is a musical instrument that you blow into in order to produce sounds, such as a flute, a clarinet, or a recorder.

wind|lass /wɪndləs/ (**windlasses**) N-COUNT A **windlass** is a mechanical device for lifting heavy objects, which uses a motor to pull a rope or chain around a cylinder.

wind|less /wɪndlɪs/ ADJ If the air is **windless**, or if it is a **windless** day, it is very calm and still.

wind|mill /wɪndmɪl/ (**windmills**) N-COUNT A **windmill** is a building with long pieces of wood on the outside that turn around as the wind blows and provide energy for a machine that crushes grain. A **windmill** is also a similar structure that uses the power of the wind to pump water or make electricity.

win|dow ♦♦◊ /wɪndoʊ/ (**windows**) **1** N-COUNT A **window** is a space in the wall of a building or in the side of a vehicle, which has glass in it so that light can come in and you can see out. ❏ *He stood at the window, moodily staring out.* ❏ *The room felt very hot and she wondered why someone did not open a window.* **2** N-COUNT A **window** is a glass-covered opening above a counter, for example, in a bank, post office, train station, or museum, which the person serving you sits behind. ❏ *The woman at the ticket window told me that the admission fee was $17.50.* **3** N-COUNT On a computer screen, a **window** is one of the work areas that the screen can be divided into. [COMPUTING] ❏ *Yahoo! Pager puts a small window on your screen containing a list of your "friends."* **4** PHRASE If you say that something such as a plan or a particular way of thinking or behaving **has gone out of the window** or **is out the window**, you mean that it has disappeared completely. ❏ *By now all logic had gone out of the window.*

win|dow box (**window boxes**) N-COUNT A **window box** is a long narrow container on a shelf at the bottom of a window and is used for growing plants.

win|dow dress|ing also **window-dressing** **1** N-UNCOUNT **Window dressing** is the skill of arranging objects attractively in a window, especially a store window, or the way in which they are arranged. **2** N-UNCOUNT If you refer to something as **window dressing**, you are critical of it because it is done in order to create a good impression and to prevent people from realizing the real or more unpleasant nature of someone's activities. [DISAPPROVAL] ❏ *The measures seem to be mere window dressing that won't solve the problem.*

win|dow frame (**window frames**) N-COUNT A **window frame** is a frame around the edges of a window, which glass fits into.

window|pane /wɪndoʊpeɪn/ (**windowpanes**) also **window pane** N-COUNT A **windowpane** is a piece of glass in the window of a building.

win|dow seat (**window seats**) **1** N-COUNT A **window seat** is a seat attached to the wall underneath a window in a room. **2** N-COUNT On a train, bus, or airplane, a **window seat** is a seat next to a window.

win|dow shade (**window shades**) N-COUNT A **window shade** is a piece of stiff cloth or heavy paper that you can pull down over a window as a covering. [AM]

in BRIT, use **blind**

win|dow shop|ping also **window-shopping** **1** N-UNCOUNT If you do some **window shopping**, you spend time looking at the merchandise in the windows of stores without intending to buy anything. **2** → See feature box at **leisure**

window|sill /wɪndoʊsɪl/ (**windowsills**) also **window sill** N-COUNT A **windowsill** is a shelf along the bottom of a window, either inside or outside a building.

wind|pipe /wɪndpaɪp/ (**windpipes**) N-COUNT Your **windpipe** is the tube in your body that carries air into your lungs when you breathe.

wind|shield /wɪndʃild/ (**windshields**) **1** N-COUNT The **windshield** of a car or other vehicle is the glass window at the front through which the driver looks. [AM]

in BRIT, use **windscreen**

2 → See also color supplement

wind|shield wip|er (**windshield wipers**) **1** N-COUNT A **windshield wiper** is a device that wipes rain from a vehicle's windshield. [AM] **2** → See also color supplement

wind|sock /wɪndsɒk/ (**windsocks**) also **wind sock** N-COUNT A **windsock** is a device, consisting of a tube of cloth mounted on a pole, that is used at airports and airfields to indicate the direction and force of the wind. ❏ *The hangar had a windsock on the roof.*

wind|surf /wɪndsɜrf/ (**windsurfs, windsurfing, windsurfed**) V-I If you **windsurf**, you take part in windsurfing. ❏ *Many people teach themselves to windsurf.* ❏ *In "Toxic II," the hero windsurfs to Japan.*

wind|surf|er /wɪndsɜrfər/ (**windsurfers**) **1** N-COUNT A **windsurfer** is a long narrow board with a sail attached to it. You stand on a windsurfer in the sea or on a lake and are blown along by the wind. **2** N-COUNT A **windsurfer** is a person who rides on a windsurfer.

wind|surf|ing /wɪndsɜrfɪŋ/ N-UNCOUNT **Windsurfing** is a sport in which you move along the surface of the sea or a lake on a long narrow board with a sail on it.

wind|swept /wɪndswɛpt/ ADJ A **windswept** place has no shelter and is not protected against strong winds. ❏ *…the remote and windswept hillside.*

wind tun|nel /wɪnd tʌnᵊl/ (**wind tunnels**) N-COUNT A **wind tunnel** is a room or passage through which air can be made to flow at controlled speeds. Wind tunnels are used to test new equipment or machinery, especially cars and airplanes.

wind|up /waɪndʌp/ ADJ [ADJ n] A **windup** device is a mechanical device with a handle or key that you turn several times before you use it in order to make it work. ❏ *…an old-fashioned windup gramophone.*

wind|ward /wɪndwərd/ ADJ [ADJ n] **Windward** is used to describe the side of something, especially a ship, which is facing the wind. ❏ *…the windward side of the quarterdeck.*

windy /wɪndi/ (**windier, windiest**) ADJ If it is **windy**, the wind is blowing a lot. ❏ *It was windy and Jake felt cold.*

wine ♦♦◊ /waɪn/ (**wines**) N-MASS **Wine** is an alcoholic drink made from grapes. You can also refer to alcoholic drinks made from other fruits or vegetables as **wine**. ❏ *…a bottle of white wine.*

wine bar (**wine bars**) N-COUNT A **wine bar** is a place where people can buy and drink wine, and sometimes eat food as well.

wine glass (**wine glasses**) **1** N-COUNT A **wine glass** is a glass, usually with a narrow stem, which you use for drinking wine. **2** → See also color supplement

win|ery /waɪnəri/ (**wineries**) N-COUNT A **winery** is a place where wine is made. [AM]

wing ♦♦◊ /wɪŋ/ (**wings**) **1** N-COUNT The **wings** of a bird or insect are the two parts of its body that it uses for flying.

❑ *The bird flapped its wings furiously.* **2** N-COUNT The **wings** of an airplane are the long flat parts sticking out of its side which support it while it is flying. ❑ *The plane made one pass, dipped its wings, then circled back.* **3** N-COUNT A **wing** of a building is a part of it that sticks out from the main part. ❑ *We were given an office in the empty west wing.* **4** N-COUNT A **wing** of an organization, especially a political organization, is a group within it which has a particular function or particular beliefs. ❑ *...the military wing of the African National Congress.* **5** → see also **left-wing**, **right-wing** **6** N-PLURAL In a theater, **the wings** are the sides of the stage that are hidden from the audience by curtains or scenery. ❑ *Most nights I watched the start of the play from the wings.* **7** PHRASE If you say that someone is waiting **in the wings**, you mean that they are ready and waiting for an opportunity to take action. ❑ *There are now more than 20 big companies waiting in the wings to take over some of its business.* **8** PHRASE If you **spread your wings**, you do something new and somewhat difficult or move to a new place, because you feel more confident in your abilities than you used to and you want to gain wider experience. ❑ *I led a very confined life in my village so I suppose that I wanted to spread my wings.* **9** PHRASE If you **take** someone **under your wing**, you look after them, help them, and protect them. ❑ *Her boss took her under his wing after fully realizing her potential.* **10** → See also color supplement

wing|back /wɪŋbæk/ (**wingbacks**) N-COUNT In soccer, a **wingback** is a defender who also takes part in attacking play.

wing com|mand|er (**wing commanders**) N-COUNT; N-TITLE A **wing commander** is a senior officer in the British air force. ❑ *...Wing Commander Christopher Moran.*

winged /wɪŋd/ ADJ A **winged** insect or other creature has wings. ❑ *Flycatchers feed primarily on winged insects.*

wing|er /wɪŋər/ (**wingers**) N-COUNT In a game such as soccer or hockey, a **winger** is an attacking player who plays mainly on the far left or the far right side of the field.

wing mir|ror (**wing mirrors**) [BRIT] → see **side-view mirror**

wing|span /wɪŋspæn/ (**wingspans**) N-COUNT [usu sing, usu with supp] The **wingspan** of a bird, insect, or airplane is the distance from the end of one wing to the end of the other wing. ❑ *...a glider with an 18-foot wingspan.*

wing|tip /wɪŋtɪp/ (**wingtips**) **1** N-COUNT The **wingtips** of an aircraft are the ends of its wings. ❑ *The Tornado was about thirty feet from Mace's right wingtip.* **2** N-COUNT [usu pl] **Wingtips** are formal men's shoes with laces and a pattern in the shape of a wing on the toe. [AM] ❑ *...a pair of well-polished brown wingtips.*

wink /wɪŋk/ (**winks, winking, winked**) **1** V-I When you **wink** at someone, you look toward them and close one eye very briefly, usually as a signal that something is a joke or a secret. ❑ *Brian winked at his bride-to-be.* • N-COUNT **Wink** is also a noun. ❑ *I gave her a wink.* **2** PHRASE If you say that you **did not sleep a wink** or **did not get a wink of sleep**, you mean that you tried to go to sleep but could not. [INFORMAL] ❑ *I didn't get a wink of sleep on the flight.*

win|kle /wɪŋkəl/ (**winkles**) N-COUNT **Winkles** are small sea snails that can be eaten. [BRIT]

in AM, use **periwinkles**

win|ner ♦♦◇ /wɪnər/ (**winners**) N-COUNT The **winner** of a prize, race, or competition is the person, animal, or thing that wins it. ❑ *She will present the trophies to the award winners.*

win|ning ♦◇◇ /wɪnɪŋ/ **1** ADJ [ADJ n] You can use **winning** to describe a person or thing that wins something such as a competition, game, or election. ❑ *...the winning lotto ticket.* **2** ADJ [ADJ n] You can use **winning** to describe actions or qualities that please other people and make them feel friendly toward you. ❑ *She gave him another of her winning smiles.* **3** → see also **win**

SYNONYMS

winning
ADJ **1**
victorious: *In 1978, he played for the victorious Argentinian side in the World Cup.*
triumphant: *Duncan and his triumphant soldiers celebrate their military victory.*
successful: *I am looking forward to a long and successful partnership with him.*

---

win|ning|est /wɪnɪŋɪst/ ADJ [ADJ n] The **winningest** person or team is the person or team that has won most often. [AM, INFORMAL] ❑ *...the winningest football team in the state of Texas.*

win|nings /wɪnɪŋz/ N-PLURAL You can use **winnings** to refer to the money that someone wins in a competition or by gambling. ❑ *I have come to collect my winnings.*

win|now /wɪnoʊ/ (**winnows, winnowing, winnowed**) V-T If you **winnow** a group of things or people, you reduce its size by separating the ones that are useful or relevant from the ones that are not. [LITERARY] ❑ *Administration officials have winnowed the list of candidates to three.*
▶ **winnow out** PHRASAL VERB If you **winnow out** part of a group of things or people, you identify the part that is not useful or relevant and the part that is. [WRITTEN] ❑ *The committee will need to winnow out the nonsense and produce more practical proposals if it is to achieve results.* ❑ *Time has winnowed out certain of the essays as superior.*

wino /waɪnoʊ/ (**winos**) N-COUNT Some people refer to alcoholics, especially homeless ones, as **winos**. [INFORMAL]

win|some /wɪnsəm/ ADJ If you describe a person or their actions or behavior as **winsome**, you mean that they are attractive and charming. ❑ *She gave him her best winsome smile.*

win|ter ♦◇◇ /wɪntər/ (**winters**) N-VAR **Winter** is the season between fall and spring. In the winter the weather is usually cold. ❑ *In winter the nights are long and cold.* ❑ *...the late winter of 1941.*

win|ter sports N-PLURAL **Winter sports** are sports that take place on ice or snow such as skating and skiing.

winter|time /wɪntərtaɪm/ also **winter time** N-UNCOUNT **Wintertime** is the period of time during which winter lasts.

win|try /wɪntri/ (**wintrier, wintriest**) ADJ [usu ADJ n] **Wintry** weather is cold and has features that are typical of winter. ❑ *Wintry weather continues to sweep across Colorado.* ❑ *...a dark wintry day.*

win-win ADJ [ADJ n] A **win-win** situation is certain to bring good results, sometimes for two people or groups. ❑ *It is surprising that it has taken people so long to take advantage of what is a win-win opportunity.*

wipe ♦◇◇ /waɪp/ (**wipes, wiping, wiped**) **1** V-T If you **wipe** something, you rub its surface to remove dirt or liquid from it. ❑ *I'll just wipe the table.* ❑ *When he had finished washing he began to wipe the basin clean.* • N-COUNT **Wipe** is also a noun. ❑ *Tomorrow I'm going to give the toys a good wipe as some seem a bit greasy.* **2** V-T If you **wipe** dirt or liquid from something, you remove it by using a cloth or your hand. ❑ *Gleb wiped the sweat from his face.* **3** N-COUNT A **wipe** is a small moist cloth for cleaning things and is designed to be used only once. ❑ *...antiseptic wipes.*
▶ **wipe out** PHRASAL VERB To **wipe out** something such as a place or a group of people or animals means to destroy them completely. ❑ *Experts say if the island is not protected, the spill could wipe out the gulf's turtle population.*

wip|er /waɪpər/ (**wipers**) N-COUNT A **wiper** is a device that wipes rain from a vehicle's windshield.

wire ♦◇◇ /waɪər/ (**wires, wiring, wired**) **1** N-VAR A **wire** is a long thin piece of metal that is used to fasten things or to carry electric current. ❑ *...fine copper wire.* **2** N-COUNT A **wire** is a cable that carries power or signals from one place to another. ❑ *I ripped out the telephone wire that ran through to his office.* **3** V-T If you **wire** something such as a building or piece of equipment, you put wires inside it so that electricity or signals can pass into or through it. ❑ *...learning to wire and plumb the house herself.* ❑ *Each of the homes has a security system and is wired for cable television.* • PHRASAL VERB **Wire up** means the same as **wire**. ❑ *Wire the thermometers up to trigger off an alarm bell if the temperature drops.* **4** PHRASE If something goes **to the wire**, it continues until the last possible moment. [mainly JOURNALISM] ❑ *Negotiators again worked right down to the wire to reach an agreement.* **5** → see also **barbed wire** **6** → See feature box at **experiment**

wired /waɪərd/ **1** ADJ [usu v-link ADJ] If someone is **wired**, they are tense, nervous, and unable to relax. [mainly AM, INFORMAL] ❑ *Tonight he is manic, wired and uptight.* **2** ADJ A computer, organization, or person that is **wired** has the equipment that is necessary to use the internet. [INFORMAL] ❑ *Once more people are wired, the potential to change the mainstream* media will be huge. **3** ADJ [usu ADJ n] **Wired** is used to describe material or clothing that has wires sewn into it in order to keep it stiff. ❑ ...*a length of wired ribbon*.

wire|less ◆◇◇ /waɪərlɪs/ **1** ADJ **Wireless** technology uses radio waves rather than electricity and therefore does not require any wires. ❑ ...*the fast-growing wireless communication market*. **2** → See feature box at **computer**

Wire|less Ap|pli|ca|tion Proto|col → see **WAP**

wire|tap /waɪərtæp/ (**wiretaps, wiretapping, wiretapped**) V-T If someone **wiretaps** your telephone, they attach a special device to the line so that they can secretly listen to your conversations. [AM] ❑ *The coach said his club had wiretapped the hotel room of a player during a road trip*. • N-COUNT **Wiretap** is also a noun. ❑ ...*tapes of telephone conversations that can have been obtained only by illegal wiretaps*. • **wire|tapping** N-UNCOUNT ❑ ...*allegations of wiretapping*.

wir|ing /waɪərɪŋ/ N-UNCOUNT The **wiring** in a building or machine is the system of wires that supply electricity to the different parts of it. ❑ *Faulty wiring is the major cause of house fires*.

wiry /waɪəri/ (**wirier, wiriest**) **1** ADJ Someone who is **wiry** is somewhat thin but is also strong. ❑ *His body is wiry and athletic*. **2** ADJ Something such as hair or grass that is **wiry** is stiff and rough to touch. ❑ *Her wiry hair was pushed up on top of her head in an untidy bun*.

wis|dom /wɪzdəm/ **1** N-UNCOUNT **Wisdom** is the ability to use your experience and knowledge in order to make sensible decisions or judgments. ❑ ...*the patience and wisdom that comes from old age*. **2** N-SING If you talk about **the wisdom of** a particular decision or action, you are talking about how sensible it is. ❑ *Many Lithuanians have expressed doubts about the wisdom of the decision*.

wis|dom tooth (**wisdom teeth**) **1** N-COUNT Your **wisdom teeth** are the four large teeth at the back of your mouth that usually grow much later than your other teeth. **2** → See also color supplement

wise ◆◇◇ /waɪz/ (**wiser, wisest**) **1** ADJ A **wise** person is able to use their experience and knowledge in order to make sensible decisions and judgments. ❑ *She has the air of a wise woman*. • **wise|ly** ADV [ADV with v] ❑ *The three of us stood around the machine nodding wisely*. **2** ADJ A **wise** action or decision is sensible. ❑ *It's never wise to withhold evidence*. ❑ *She had made a very wise decision*. • **wise|ly** ADV ❑ *They've invested their money wisely*.

-wise /-waɪz/ **1** COMB IN ADV [ADV with cl] **-wise** is added to nouns to form adverbs indicating that something is the case when considering the particular thing mentioned. ❑ *Career-wise, this illness couldn't have come at a worse time*. ❑ *It was a much better day weather-wise*. **2** COMB IN ADV [ADV after v] **-wise** is added to nouns to form adverbs indicating that something goes in a particular direction or is in a particular position. ❑ *She walked clockwise around the circle*.

wise|crack /waɪzkræk/ (**wisecracks**) N-COUNT A **wisecrack** is a clever remark that is intended to be amusing, but is often unkind.

wise|crack|ing /waɪzkrækɪŋ/ ADJ [usu ADJ n] You can use **wisecracking** to describe someone who keeps making wisecracks. ❑ ...*a wisecracking private eye*.

wise guy (**wise guys**) also **wiseguy** **1** N-COUNT If you say that someone is a **wise guy**, you dislike the fact that they think they are very clever and always have an answer for everything. [INFORMAL, DISAPPROVAL] **2** N-COUNT A **wise guy** is a member of the Mafia. [mainly AM, INFORMAL]

wish ◆◆◇ /wɪʃ/ (**wishes, wishing, wished**) **1** N-COUNT A **wish** is a desire or strong feeling that you want to have something or do something. ❑ *She was sincere and genuine in her wish to make amends for the past*. ❑ *The decision was made against the wishes of the party leader*. **2** V-T/V-I If you **wish** to do something or to have it done for you, you want to do it or have it done. [FORMAL] ❑ *If you wish to go away for the weekend, our office will be delighted to make hotel reservations*. ❑ *We can dress as we wish now*. **3** V-T [no cont] If you **wish** something were true, you would like it to be true, even though you know that it is impossible or unlikely. ❑ *I wish I could do that*. ❑ *Pa, I wish you wouldn't shout*. **4** V-I If you **wish for** something, you express the desire for that thing silently to yourself. In fairy tales, when a person wishes for something, the thing they wish for often happens by magic. ❑ *Be careful what you wish for. You might get it!* • N-COUNT **Wish** is also a noun. ❑ *The custom is for people to try and eat 12 grapes as the clock strikes midnight. Those who are successful can make a wish*. **5** V-T [no cont, with brd-neg] If you say that you would not **wish** a particular thing **on** someone, you mean that the thing is so unpleasant that you would not want them to be forced to experience it. ❑ *It's a horrid experience and I wouldn't wish it on my worst enemy*. **6** V-T If you **wish** someone something such as luck or happiness, you express the hope that they will be lucky or happy. ❑ *I wish you both a good trip*. **7** N-PLURAL If you express your good **wishes** toward someone, you are politely expressing your friendly feelings toward them and your hope that they will be successful or happy. [POLITENESS] ❑ *I found George's story very sad. Please give him my best wishes*.

▬▬▬ SYNONYMS ▬▬▬

wish
NOUN **1**
desire: *I had a strong desire to help and care for people*.
longing: *Imelda spoke of her longing to return home*.
aspiration: ...*the needs and aspirations of our students*.
urge: *He had an urge to open a store of his own*.
need: *Charles has never felt the need to compete with anyone*.

▬▬▬ USAGE ▬▬▬

wish
Don't use 'wish' with a clause to say that you hope something good will happen to someone. Don't say, for example, 'I wish you'll have a nice time in Finland.' Say '**I hope you'll have** a nice time in Finland' or '**I hope you have** a nice time in Finland.' *I hope you like this village*.

wish|bone /wɪʃboʊn/ (**wishbones**) N-COUNT A **wishbone** is a V-shaped bone in chickens, turkeys, and other birds.

wish|ful think|ing N-UNCOUNT If you say that an idea, wish, or hope is **wishful thinking**, you mean that it has failed to come true or is unlikely to come true. ❑ *It is wishful thinking to expect deeper change under his leadership*.

wish list (**wish lists**) N-COUNT [oft with poss] If you refer to someone's **wish list**, you mean all the things which they would like to happen or be given, although these things may be unlikely. [INFORMAL] ❑ ...*one special toy that tops the wish list of every child*.

wishy-washy /wɪʃi wɒʃi/ ADJ If you say that someone is **wishy-washy**, you are critical of them because their ideas are not firm or clear. [INFORMAL, DISAPPROVAL] ❑ *If there's anything I can't stand it's an indecisive, wishy-washy customer*.

wisp /wɪsp/ (**wisps**) **1** N-COUNT [usu N of n] A **wisp** of hair is a small, thin, bunch of it. ❑ *She smoothed away a wisp of hair from her eyes*. **2** N-COUNT [usu N of n] A **wisp** of something such as smoke or cloud is an amount of it in a long thin shape. ❑ *A thin wisp of smoke straggled up through the trees*.

wispy /wɪspi/ (**wispier, wispiest**) **1** ADJ If someone has **wispy** hair, their hair does not grow thickly on their head. **2** ADJ [usu ADJ n] A **wispy** cloud is thin or faint.

wis|te|ria /wɪstɪəriə/ N-UNCOUNT **Wisteria** is a type of climbing plant that has pale purple or white flowers.

wist|ful /wɪstfəl/ ADJ Someone who is **wistful** is sad because they want something and know that they cannot have it. ❑ *I can't help feeling slightly wistful about the perks I'm giving up*. • **wist|ful|ly** ADV [usu ADV with v, also ADV adj] ❑ *'I wish I had a little brother,' said Daphne wistfully*.

wit /wɪt/ (**wits**) **1** N-UNCOUNT **Wit** is the ability to use words or ideas in an amusing, clever, and imaginative way. ❑ *Boulding was known for his biting wit*. **2** N-SING If you say that someone has **the wit** to do something, you mean that they have the intelligence and understanding to make the right decision or take the right action in a particular situation. ❑ *The information is there and waiting to be accessed by anyone with the wit to use it*. **3** N-PLURAL You can refer to your ability to think quickly and effectively in a difficult situation as your **wits**. ❑ *She has used her wits to progress to the position she holds today*. **4** N-PLURAL You can use **wits** in expressions such as **frighten someone out of their wits** and **scare the wits out of** someone to emphasize that a person or thing worries or frightens someone very much. [EMPHASIS] ❑ *You scared us out of our wits. We heard you had an accident.*

witch /wɪtʃ/ (**witches**) **1** N-COUNT In fairy tales, a **witch** is a woman, usually an old woman, who has evil magic powers. Witches often wear a pointed black hat. **2** N-COUNT A **witch** is someone who claims to have magic powers and to be able to use them for good or bad purposes.

witch|craft /wɪtʃkræft/ N-UNCOUNT **Witchcraft** is the use of magic powers, especially evil ones. ❑ *This week Sabrina uses witchcraft to overcome her fear of giving a speech.*

witch doc|tor (**witch doctors**) also **witch-doctor** N-COUNT A **witch doctor** is a person in some societies who is thought to have magic powers that can be used to heal people.

witch ha|zel N-UNCOUNT **Witch hazel** is a liquid that you put on your skin if it is sore or damaged, in order to help it to heal.

witch-hunt (**witch-hunts**) N-COUNT A **witch-hunt** is an attempt to find and punish a particular group of people who are being blamed for something, often simply because of their opinions and not because they have actually done anything wrong. [DISAPPROVAL] ❑ *...Senator Joe McCarthy, who led the witch-hunt against alleged communists in the 1950s.*

witchy /wɪtʃi/ also **witch-like** ADJ A **witchy** person looks or behaves like a witch. **Witchy** things are associated with witches. ❑ *My great-grandmother was old and witchy looking.*

WITH
① IN THE SAME PLACE AT THE SAME TIME
② OTHER USES: METHODS, FEATURES, QUALITIES

① **with** ♦♦♦ /wɪð, wɪθ/ **1** PREP If one person is **with** another, they are together in one place. ❑ *With her were her son and daughter-in-law.* **2** PREP If something is put **with** or is **with** something else, they are used at the same time. ❑ *Serve hot, with pasta or rice and French beans.* **3** PREP If you do something **with** someone else, you both do it together or are both involved in it. ❑ *Parents will be given reports on their child's progress and the right to discuss it with a teacher.*

② **with** ♦♦♦ /wɪð, wɪθ/

Pronounced /wɪð/ for meanings **17** and **18**.

1 PREP If you fight, argue, or compete **with** someone, you oppose them. ❑ *About a thousand students fought with riot police in the capital.* **2** PREP If you do something **with** a particular tool, object, or substance, you do it using that tool, object, or substance. ❑ *Remove the meat with a fork and divide it among four plates.* ❑ *Pack the fruits and nuts into the jars and cover with brandy.* **3** PREP If someone stands or goes somewhere **with** something, they are carrying it. ❑ *A young woman came in with a cup of coffee.* **4** PREP Someone or something **with** a particular feature or possession has that feature or possession. ❑ *He was in his early forties, tall and blond with bright blue eyes.* **5** PREP Someone **with** an illness has that illness. ❑ *I spent a week in bed with flu.* **6** PREP If something is filled or covered **with** a substance or **with** things, it has that substance or those things in it or on it. ❑ *His legs were caked with dried mud.* **7** PREP [adj/n PREP n] If you are, for example, pleased or annoyed **with** someone or something, you have that feeling toward them. ❑ *He was still a little angry with her.* **8** PREP You use **with** to indicate what a state, quality, or action relates to, involves, or affects. ❑ *Our aim is to allow student teachers to become familiar with the classroom.* ❑ *He still has a serious problem with money.* **9** PREP You use **with** when indicating the way that something is done or the feeling that a person has when they do something. ❑ *...teaching her to read music with skill and sensitivity.* **10** PREP You use **with** when indicating a sound or gesture that is made when something is done, or an expression that a person has on their face when they do something. ❑ *With a sigh, she leant back and closed her eyes.* **11** PREP You use **with** to indicate the feeling that makes someone have a particular appearance or type of behavior. ❑ *Gil was white and trembling with anger.* **12** PREP [PREP n prep/-ing] You use **with** when mentioning the position or appearance of a person or thing at the time that they do something, or what someone else is doing at that time. ❑ *Joanne stood with her hands on the sink, staring out the window.* **13** PREP You use **with** to introduce a current situation that is a factor affecting another situation. ❑ *With all the night school courses available, there is no excuse for not getting some sort of training.* **14** PREP You use **with** when making a comparison or contrast between the situations of different people or things. ❑ *We're not like them. It's different with us.* **15** PREP [v PREP n] If something increases or decreases with a particular factor, it changes as that factor changes. ❑ *The risk of developing heart disease increases with the number of cigarettes smoked.* **16** PREP If something moves **with** a wind or current, it moves in the same direction as the wind or current. ❑ *...a piece of driftwood carried down with the current.* **17** PREP [v-link PREP n] If someone says that they are **with** you, they mean that they understand what you are saying. [INFORMAL] ❑ *Yes, I know who you mean. Yes, now I'm with you.* **18** PREP [v-link PREP n] If someone says that they are **with** you, they mean that they support or approve of what you are doing. ❑ *"I'm with you all the way."—"Thank you."* **19** → see also **with it**

In addition to the uses shown here, **with** is used after some verbs, nouns and adjectives in order to introduce extra information. **With** is also used in most reciprocal verbs, such as 'agree' or 'fight,' and in some phrasal verbs, such as 'deal with' and 'dispense with.'

with|draw ♦♦◇ /wɪðdrɔː, wɪθ-/ (**withdraws, withdrawing, withdrew, withdrawn**) **1** V-T If you **withdraw** something from a place, you remove it or take it away. [FORMAL] ❑ *He reached into his pocket and withdrew a sheet of notepaper.* **2** V-T/V-I When groups of people such as troops **withdraw** or when someone **withdraws** them, they leave the place where they are fighting or where they are based and return nearer home. ❑ *He stated that all foreign forces would withdraw as soon as the crisis ended.* ❑ *The United States has announced it is to withdraw forty-thousand troops from Western Europe in the next year.* **3** V-T If you **withdraw** money from a bank account, you take it out of that account. ❑ *Open a savings account that does not charge ridiculous fees to withdraw money.* **4** V-I If you **withdraw** from an activity or organization, you stop taking part in it. ❑ *The African National Congress threatened to withdraw from the talks.*

SYNONYMS
withdraw
VERB **1**
remove: *He went to the refrigerator and removed a bottle of juice.*
take away: *They're going to take my citizenship away.*
extract: *He extracted a small notebook from his hip pocket.*
pull out: *We try not to pull out patients' teeth unnecessarily.*

with|draw|al ♦♦◇ /wɪðdrɔːəl, wɪθ-/ (**withdrawals**) **1** N-VAR The **withdrawal** of something is the act or process of removing it, or ending it. [FORMAL] ❑ *If you experience any unusual symptoms after withdrawal of the treatment then contact your doctor.* **2** N-UNCOUNT Someone's **withdrawal** from an activity or an organization is their decision to stop taking part in it. ❑ *...his withdrawal from government in 1946.* **3** N-COUNT A **withdrawal** is an amount of money that you take from your bank account. ❑ *I went to the machine to make the withdrawal and it told me to see someone inside the bank.* **4** N-UNCOUNT **Withdrawal** is the period during which someone feels ill after they have stopped taking a drug they were addicted to. ❑ *Withdrawal from heroin is actually like a severe attack of gastric flu.*

SYNONYMS
withdrawal
NOUN **1**
removal: *Parliament had decided that his removal from power was illegal.*
termination: *...a dispute which led to the abrupt termination of trade.*
cancellation: *...a march by groups calling for cancellation of Third World debt.*

with|draw|al symp|toms N-PLURAL When someone has **withdrawal symptoms**, they feel ill after they have stopped taking a drug which they were addicted to.

with|drawn /wɪðdrɔːn, wɪθ-/ **1 Withdrawn** is the past participle of **withdraw**. **2** ADJ [v-link ADJ] Someone who is

withdrawn is very quiet, and does not want to talk to other people. ❑ *Her husband had become withdrawn and moody.*

with|drew /wɪðdru, wɪθ-/ **Withdrew** is the past tense of **withdraw**.

with|er /wɪðər/ (withers, withering, withered) **1** V-I If someone or something **withers**, they become very weak. ❑ *When he went into retirement, he visibly withered.* • PHRASAL VERB **Wither away** means the same as **wither**. ❑ *To see my body literally wither away before my eyes was exasperating.* **2** V-I If a flower or plant **withers**, it dries up and dies. ❑ *The flowers in Isabel's room had withered.*

with|ered /wɪðərd/ ADJ If you describe a person or a part of their body as **withered**, you mean that they are thin and their skin looks old. ❑ *Diana grasped his face in her withered hands.*

with|er|ing /wɪðərɪŋ/ ADJ [usu ADJ n] A **withering** look or remark is very critical, and is intended to make someone feel ashamed or stupid. ❑ *Deborah Jane's mother gave her a withering look.*

with|hold /wɪðhoʊld, wɪθ-/ (withholds, withholding, withheld /wɪðhɛld, wɪθ-/) V-T If you **withhold** something that someone wants, you do not let them have it. [FORMAL] ❑ *Police withheld the dead boy's name yesterday until relatives could be told.*

with|hold|ing tax (withholding taxes) N-VAR A **withholding tax** is an amount of money that is taken in advance from someone's income, in order to pay some of the tax they will owe. [mainly AM, BUSINESS]

with|in ♦♦♦ /wɪðɪn, wɪθ-/ **1** PREP If something is **within** a place, area, or object, it is inside it or surrounded by it. [FORMAL] ❑ *Clients are entertained within private dining rooms.* • ADV **Within** is also an adverb. ❑ *A small voice called from within. "Yes, just coming."* **2** PREP Something that happens or exists **within** a society, organization, or system, happens or exists inside it. ❑ *...the spirit of self-sacrifice within an army.* • ADV **Within** is also an adverb. ❑ *The real dangers to these rebels came from within.* **3** PREP If something is **within** a particular limit or set of rules, it does not go beyond it or is not more than what is allowed. ❑ *Troops have agreed to stay within specific boundaries to avoid confrontations.* **4** PREP If you are **within** a particular distance of a place, you are less than that distance from it. ❑ *The man was within a few feet of him.* **5** PREP [PREP amount] **Within** a particular length of time means before that length of time has passed. ❑ *About 40% of all students entering as freshmen graduate within 4 years.* **6** PREP If something is **within sight**, **within earshot**, or **within reach**, you can see it, hear it, or reach it. ❑ *His twenty-five-foot boat was moored within sight of his house.* **7 within reason** → see **reason**

with it also **with-it** **1** ADJ If you say that someone is **with it**, you mean that they are fashionable or know about new things, especially in culture. [INFORMAL, OLD-FASHIONED] **2** ADJ [v-link ADJ, usu with brd-neg] If someone is not **with it**, they do not feel alert and therefore fail to understand things. [INFORMAL] ❑ *She wasn't really with it. She hadn't taken in the practical consequences.*

with|out ♦♦♦ /wɪðaʊt, wɪθ-/

In addition to the uses shown below, **without** is used in the phrasal verbs 'do without,' 'go without,' and 'reckon without.'

1 PREP You use **without** to indicate that someone or something does not have or use the thing mentioned. ❑ *I don't like myself without a beard.* ❑ *She wore a brown shirt pressed without a wrinkle.* **2** PREP [PREP n/-ing] If one thing happens **without** another thing, or if you do something **without** doing something else, the second thing does not happen or occur. ❑ *He was offered a generous pension provided he left without a fuss.* ❑ *They worked without a break until about eight in the evening.* **3** PREP If you do something **without** a particular feeling, you do not have that feeling when you do it. ❑ *Janet Magnusson watched his approach without enthusiasm.* **4** PREP If you do something **without** someone else, they are not in the same place as you are or are not involved in the same action as you. ❑ *I told Franklin he would have to start dinner without me.*

with|stand /wɪðstænd, wɪθ-/ (withstands, withstanding, withstood /wɪðstʊd, wɪθ-/) V-T If something or someone **withstands** a force or action, they survive it or do not give in to it. [FORMAL] ❑ *...armored vehicles designed to withstand chemical attack.*

wit|less /wɪtlɪs/ ADJ If you describe something or someone as **witless**, you mean that they are very foolish or stupid. [DISAPPROVAL] ❑ *...a witless, nasty piece of journalism.*

wit|ness ♦◊◊ /wɪtnɪs/ (witnesses, witnessing, witnessed) **1** N-COUNT A **witness** to an event such as an accident or crime is a person who saw it. ❑ *Witnesses to the crash say they saw an explosion just before the disaster.* **2** V-T If you **witness** something, you see it happen. ❑ *Anyone who witnessed the attack should call the police.* **3** N-COUNT A **witness** is someone who appears in a court of law to say what they know about a crime or other event. ❑ *In the next three or four days, eleven witnesses will be called to testify.* **4** N-COUNT A **witness** is someone who writes their name on a document that you have signed, to confirm that it really is your signature. ❑ *The codicil must first be signed and dated by you in the presence of two witnesses.* **5** V-T If someone **witnesses** your signature on a document, they write their name after it, to confirm that it really is your signature. ❑ *Ask a friend, (not your spouse), to witness your signature.* **6** V-T If you say that a place, period of time, or person **witnessed** a particular event or change, you mean that it happened in that place, during that period of time, or while that person was alive. ❑ *India has witnessed many political changes in recent years.*

> **COLLOCATIONS**
>
> **witness**
> NOUN **3**
> noun + **witness**: defense, prosecution
> adjective + **witness**: credible, reliable, unreliable; expert, key
> verb + **witness**: call, summon; cross-examine, interview, question
> VERB **2**
> **witness** + noun: accident, event, incident
> **witness** + adverb: first-hand

wit|ness stand N-SING [the N] The **witness stand** in a court of law is the place where people stand when they are giving evidence. [AM]

in BRIT, use **witness box**

wit|ti|cism /wɪtɪsɪzəm/ (witticisms) N-COUNT A **witticism** is a witty remark or joke. [FORMAL]

wit|ting|ly /wɪtɪŋli/ ADV If you do something **wittingly**, you are fully aware of what you are doing and what its consequences will be. [FORMAL] ❑ *When she had an affair with her friend's husband, she wittingly set off a chain of crises.*

wit|ty /wɪti/ (wittier, wittiest) **1** ADJ Someone or something that is **witty** is amusing in a clever way. ❑ *His plays were very good, very witty.* **2** → See feature box at **humor**

wives /waɪvz/ **Wives** is the plural of **wife**.

wiz|ard /wɪzərd/ (wizards) **1** N-COUNT In legends and fairy tales, a **wizard** is a man who has magic powers. **2** N-COUNT If you admire someone because they are very good at doing a particular thing, you can say that they are a **wizard**. [APPROVAL] ❑ *...a financial wizard.* **3** N-COUNT A **wizard** is a computer program that guides you through the stages of a particular task. [COMPUTING] ❑ *Wizards and templates can help you create brochures, calendars, and Web pages.*

wiz|ard|ry /wɪzərdri/ N-UNCOUNT You can refer to a very clever achievement or piece of work as **wizardry**, especially when you do not understand how it is done. ❑ *...a piece of technical wizardry.*

wiz|ened /wɪzənd/ ADJ A **wizened** person is old and has a lot of lines on their skin. [FORMAL] ❑ *...a little wizened old fellow with no teeth.*

wk (wks) **wk** is a written abbreviation for **week**.

WMD /dʌbəlyu ɛm di/ N-PLURAL **WMD** is an abbreviation for **weapons of mass destruction**.

wob|ble /wɒbəl/ (wobbles, wobbling, wobbled) V-I If something or someone **wobbles**, they make small movements from side to side, for example, because they are unsteady. ❑ *Some of the tables wobble.* • N-VAR **Wobble** is also a noun. ❑ *We might look for a tiny wobble in the position of a star.*

wob|bly /wɒbli/ (wobblier, wobbliest) ADJ Something that is **wobbly** moves unsteadily from side to side. ❑ *I was sitting on a wobbly plastic chair.* ❑ *...a wobbly green dessert.*

woe /woʊ/ N-UNCOUNT **Woe** is great sadness. [LITERARY] ☐ *He listened to my tale of woe.*

woe|be|gone /woʊbɪɡɔn/ ADJ Someone who is **woebegone** is very sad. [WRITTEN] ☐ *She sniffed and looked woebegone.*

woe|ful /woʊfəl/ **1** ADJ If someone or something is **woeful**, they are very sad. ☐ *...a woeful ballad.* • **woe|ful|ly** ADV [ADV with v] ☐ *He said woefully: "I love my country, but it does not give a damn about me."* **2** ADJ You can use **woeful** to emphasize that something is very bad or undesirable. [JOURNALISM, EMPHASIS] ☐ *...the woeful state of the economy.* • **woe|ful|ly** ADV ☐ *Public expenditure on the arts is woefully inadequate.*

wok /wɒk/ (woks) N-COUNT A **wok** is a large bowl-shaped pan used for Chinese-style cooking.

woke /woʊk/ **1** **Woke** is the past tense of **wake**. **2** ADJ GRADED; ADJ Someone who is **woke** is very aware of social and political unfairness. [INFORMAL]

wok|en /woʊkən/ **Woken** is the past participle of **wake**.

wolf /wʊlf/ (wolves, wolfs, wolfing, wolfed) **1** N-COUNT A **wolf** is a wild animal that looks like a large dog. **2** V-T If someone **wolfs** their food, they eat it all very quickly and greedily. [INFORMAL] ☐ *Hotels were full of rich people wolfing expensive meals.* • PHRASAL VERB **Wolf down** means the same as **wolf**. ☐ *He wolfed down the rest of the biscuit and cheese.*

wolf|hound /wʊlfhaʊnd/ (wolfhounds) N-COUNT A **wolfhound** is a type of very large dog.

wolf-whistle (wolf-whistles, wolf-whistling, wolf-whistled) also **wolf whistle** V-I If someone **wolf-whistles**, they make a whistling sound with a short rising note and a longer falling note. Some people wolf-whistle to show that they find someone attractive. ☐ *They wolf-whistled at me, and I was so embarrassed I tripped up.* • N-COUNT **Wolf whistle** is also a noun. ☐ *Her dancing brought loud cheers, wolf whistles and applause.*

wolves /wʊlvz/ **Wolves** is the plural of **wolf**.

wom|an ◆◆◆ /wʊmən/ (women) **1** N-COUNT A **woman** is an adult female human being. ☐ *...a young Lithuanian woman named Dayva.* ☐ *...men and women over 75 years old.* **2** N-UNCOUNT You can refer to women in general as **woman**. ☐ *...the oppression of woman.* **3** N-COUNT If you say that a woman is, for example, a gambling **woman** or an outdoors **woman**, you mean that she likes to gambling or outdoor activities. ☐ *She is an avid outdoors woman.* ☐ *I'm too old to have a dog now. I'm a cat woman.* **4** N-COUNT If you say that a woman is, for example, a Harvard **woman**, you mean that she went to that university. **5** N-COUNT If you refer to a particular company's or organization's **woman**, you mean a woman who works for or represents that company or organization. [JOURNALISM] ☐ *She was a senior CNN woman.* **6** N-SING Some people refer to a person's wife, lover, or girlfriend as their **woman**. [INFORMAL] **7** → see also **career woman** **8** PHRASE If you say that a woman is **woman enough** to do something, you mean that she has the necessary courage or ability to do it. ☐ *She is woman enough to maintain her own identity.* **9** PHRASE If you say that a woman is her **own woman**, you approve of the fact that she makes her decisions and her plans herself, and does not depend on other people. [APPROVAL] ☐ *Though they remain close, she is very much her own woman.* **10** PHRASE If you say that a group of women are, do, or think something **to a woman**, you are emphasizing that every one of them is, does, or thinks that thing. [EMPHASIS]

USAGE
woman
It is more polite to call someone an **old lady** or an **elderly lady**, rather than an 'old woman.' *There's an old lady who rides a bike around town.*

-woman /-wʊmən/ COMB IN ADJ [ADJ n] **-woman** combines with numbers to indicate that something involves the number of women mentioned. ☐ *...a seven-woman team.*

wom|an|hood /wʊmənhʊd/ **1** N-UNCOUNT **Womanhood** is the state of being a woman rather than a girl, or the period of a woman's adult life. ☐ *Not everyone sees pregnancy as a natural part of womanhood.* **2** N-UNCOUNT You can refer to women in general or the women of a particular country or community as **womanhood**. ☐ *She symbolized for me the best of Indian womanhood.*

wom|an|iz|er /wʊmənaɪzər/ (womanizers)
in BRIT, also use **womaniser**
N-COUNT If you describe a man as a **womanizer**, you disapprove of him because he likes to have many short sexual relationships with women. [DISAPPROVAL]

wom|an|iz|ing /wʊmənaɪzɪŋ/
in BRIT, also use **womanising**
1 N-UNCOUNT If you talk about a man's **womanizing**, you disapprove of him because he likes to have many short sexual relationships with women. [DISAPPROVAL] **2** ADJ [ADJ n] A **womanizing** man likes to have many short sexual relationships with women. [DISAPPROVAL]

wom|an|kind /wʊmənkaɪnd/ N-UNCOUNT You can refer to all women as **womankind** when considering them as a group. [FORMAL]

wom|an|ly /wʊmənli/ ADJ People describe a woman's behavior, character, or appearance as **womanly** when they like it because they think it is typical of, or suitable for, a woman rather than a man or girl. [APPROVAL] ☐ *She had a classical, womanly shape.* ☐ *...womanly tenderness.*

woman-to-woman also **woman to woman** ADJ [ADJ n] If you talk about a **woman-to-woman** conversation, you are talking about an honest and open discussion between two women. • ADV [ADV after v] **Woman to woman** is also an adverb. ☐ *Maybe she would talk to her mother one day, woman to woman.*

womb /wuːm/ (wombs) N-COUNT A woman's **womb** is the part inside her body where a baby grows before it is born. ☐ *...the development of the fetus in the womb.*

wom|bat /wɒmbæt/ (wombats) N-COUNT A **wombat** is a type of furry animal that has very short legs and eats plants. Wombats are found in Australia.

wom|en /wɪmɪn/ **Women** is the plural of **woman**.

women|folk /wɪmɪnfoʊk/ N-PLURAL [oft poss n] Some people refer to the women of a particular community as its **womenfolk**, especially when the community is ruled or organized by men. [OLD-FASHIONED or INFORMAL] ☐ *Men never notice anything in a house run by their womenfolk.*

wom|en's group (women's groups) N-COUNT A **women's group** is a group of women who meet regularly, usually to have discussions or to organize campaigns.

Wom|en's Lib N-UNCOUNT **Women's Lib** is the same as **Women's Liberation**. [INFORMAL, OLD-FASHIONED]

Wom|en's Lib|era|tion N-UNCOUNT [oft N n] **Women's Liberation** is the belief and aim that women should have the same rights and opportunities in society as men. [OLD-FASHIONED]

wom|en's move|ment N-SING [usu the N] You use the **women's movement** to refer to groups of people and organizations who believe that women should have the same rights and opportunities in society as men.

wom|en's room (women's rooms) N-COUNT [usu the N in sing] The **women's room** is a toilet for women in a public building. [mainly AM]

wom|en's shel|ter (women's shelters) N-COUNT A **women's shelter** is a place where women can go for safety and protection, for example, if they feel threatened by violence. [mainly AM] ☐ *One women's shelter in Dallas turns away 3,000 women every year.*

won /wʌn/ **Won** is the past tense and past participle of **win**.

won|der ◆◆◇ /wʌndər/ (wonders, wondering, wondered) **1** V-T/V-I If you **wonder** about something, you think about it, either because it interests you and you want to know more about it, or because you are worried or suspicious about it. ☐ *I wondered what that noise was.* ☐ *"He claims to be her father," said Max. "We've been wondering about him."* **2** V-T/V-I If you **wonder** at something, you are very surprised about it or think about it in a very surprised way. ☐ *I could only wonder at how far this woman had come.* ☐ *I wonder you don't feel it too.* **3** N-SING If you say that it is a **wonder** that something happened, you mean that it is very surprising and unexpected. ☐ *It's a wonder that it took almost ten years.* **4** N-UNCOUNT **Wonder** is a feeling of great surprise and pleasure that you have, for example, when you see something that is very beautiful, or when something happens that you thought was impossible. ❑ *"That's right!" Bobby exclaimed in wonder. "How did you remember that?"* **5** N-COUNT A **wonder** is something that causes people to feel great surprise or admiration. ❑ *...a lecture on the wonders of space and space exploration.* **6** ADJ [ADJ n] If you refer, for example, to a young man as a **wonder** boy, or to a new product as a **wonder** drug, you mean that they are believed by many people to be very good or very effective. ❑ *Mickelson was hailed as the wonder boy of American golf.* **7** PHRASE You can say '**I wonder**' if you want to be very polite when you are asking someone to do something, or when you are asking them for their opinion or for information. [POLITENESS] ❑ *I was just wondering if you could help me.* **8** PHRASE If you say '**no wonder**,' '**little wonder**,' or '**small wonder**,' you mean that something is not surprising. ❑ *No wonder my brother wasn't feeling well.* **9** PHRASE You can say '**No wonder**' when you find out the reason for something that has been puzzling you for some time. ❑ *Brad was Jane's brother! No wonder he reminded me so much of her!* **10** PHRASE If you say that a person or thing **works wonders** or **does wonders**, you mean that they have a very good effect on something. ❑ *A few moments of relaxation can work wonders.*

COLLOCATIONS

wonder
NOUN **5**
adjective + **wonder**: architectural, natural; one-hit
verb + **wonder**: discover, experience, explore; perform

---

won|der|ful ✦✦◇ /wʌndərfəl/ ADJ If you describe something or someone as **wonderful**, you think they are extremely good. ❑ *The cold, misty air felt wonderful on his face.* ❑ *It's wonderful to see you.* • **won|der|ful|ly** ADV ❑ *It's a system that works wonderfully well.*

wonder|land /wʌndərlænd/ N-UNCOUNT **Wonderland** is an imaginary world that exists in fairy tales.

won|der|ment /wʌndərmənt/ N-UNCOUNT [oft *in* n] **Wonderment** is a feeling of great surprise and pleasure. [LITERARY] ❑ *His big blue eyes opened wide in wonderment.*

won|drous /wʌndrəs/ ADJ [usu ADJ n] If you describe something as **wondrous**, you mean it is strange and beautiful or impressive. [LITERARY] ❑ *We were driven across this wondrous vast land of lakes and forests.*

wont /wɒnt/ **1** ADJ [v-link ADJ to-inf] If someone is **wont** to do something, they often or regularly do it. [WRITTEN] ❑ *Both have committed their indiscretions, as human beings are wont to do.* **2** PHRASE If someone does a particular thing **as is** their **wont**, they do that thing often or regularly. [WRITTEN] ❑ *Paul woke early, as was his wont.*

won't /woʊnt/ **Won't** is the usual spoken form of 'will not.' ❑ *The space shuttle won't lift off the launch pad until Sunday at the earliest.*

woo /wuː/ (**woos, wooing, wooed**) V-T If you **woo** people, you try to encourage them to help you, support you, or vote for you, for example, by promising them things which they would like. ❑ *They wooed customers by offering low interest rates.*

wood ✦✦◇ /wʊd/ (**woods**) **1** N-MASS **Wood** is the material that forms the trunks and branches of trees. ❑ *Their dishes were made of wood.* ❑ *There was a smell of damp wood and machine oil.* **2** N-COUNT A **wood** or **woods** is a fairly large area of trees growing near each other. ❑ *After dinner Alice slipped away for a walk in the woods with Artie.* **3** PHRASE If something or someone is **not out of the woods** yet, they are still having difficulties or problems. [INFORMAL] ❑ *The nation's economy is not out of the woods yet.* **4** CONVENTION You can say '**knock on wood**' to indicate that you hope to have good luck in something you are doing, usually after saying that you have been lucky with it so far. ❑ *I got it all taken care of, knock on wood.*

wood-burning stove (**wood-burning stoves**) N-COUNT A **wood-burning stove** is the same as a **wood stove**.

wood carv|ing (**wood carvings**) N-VAR A **wood carving** is a decorative piece of wood that has been carved in an artistic way.

wood|chip /wʊdtʃɪp/ (**woodchips**) N-VAR **Woodchips** are very small pieces of wood, usually made from waste wood, which are used in processes such as making paper. ❑ *...the domestic market for woodchips.*

wood|chuck /wʊdtʃʌk/ (**woodchucks**) N-COUNT A **woodchuck** is a type of small animal with reddish brown fur that is found in North America. [AM] ❑ *We once watched a red fox attacking a woodchuck.*

wood|cock /wʊdkɒk/ (**woodcocks** or **woodcock**) N-COUNT A **woodcock** is a small brown bird with a long beak. **Woodcock** are sometimes shot for sport or food.

wood|cutter /wʊdkʌtər/ (**woodcutters**) N-COUNT A **woodcutter** is someone who cuts down trees or who chops wood as their job. [OLD-FASHIONED]

wood|ed /wʊdɪd/ ADJ A **wooded** area is covered in trees. ❑ *...a wooded valley.*

wood|en ✦◇◇ /wʊdən/ ADJ [ADJ n] **Wooden** objects are made of wood. ❑ *...the shop's bare brick walls and faded wooden floorboards.*

wood|en spoon (**wooden spoons**) N-COUNT A **wooden spoon** is a spoon made of wood and used in cooking.

wood|land /wʊdlənd/ (**woodlands**) **1** N-VAR **Woodland** is land with a lot of trees. ❑ *...an area of dense woodland.* **2** → See feature box at **ecosystem**

wood|louse /wʊdlaʊs/ (**woodlice** /wʊdlaɪs/) N-COUNT A **woodlouse** is a very small gray creature with a hard body and fourteen legs. **Woodlice** live in damp places.

wood|man /wʊdmən/ → see **woodsman**

wood|pecker /wʊdpɛkər/ (**woodpeckers**) N-COUNT A **woodpecker** is a type of bird with a long sharp beak. **Woodpeckers** use their beaks to make holes in tree trunks.

wood|pile /wʊdpaɪl/ (**woodpiles**) N-COUNT [usu sing] A **woodpile** is a pile of wood that is intended to be burned on a fire as fuel.

wood pulp N-UNCOUNT **Wood pulp** is wood that has been cut up into small pieces and crushed. **Wood pulp** is used to make paper.

wood|shed /wʊdʃɛd/ (**woodsheds**) N-COUNT A **woodshed** is a small building used for storing wood for a fire.

woods|man /wʊdzmən/ (**woodsmen**) also **woodman** N-COUNT A **woodsman** is a person who cuts down trees for timber, or a person who lives in a wood. [AM] ❑ *Like trained and skillful woodsmen, they approached without a sound.* ❑ *...the sound of a woodman's ax.*

wood stove (**wood stoves**) also **woodstove** N-COUNT A **wood stove** is a device that burns wood in order to heat a room or house.

wood|wind /wʊdwɪnd/ (**woodwinds**) N-VAR [oft N n] **Woodwind** instruments are musical instruments such as flutes, clarinets, and recorders that you play by blowing into them.

wood|work /wʊdwɜːrk/ **1** N-UNCOUNT You can refer to the doors and other wooden parts of a house as the **woodwork**. ❑ *I love the living room, with its dark woodwork, oriental rugs, and chunky furniture.* **2** N-UNCOUNT **Woodwork** is the activity or skill of making things out of wood. ❑ *I have done woodwork for many years.* **3** → See feature box at **DIY**

wood|worm /wʊdwɜːrm/ (**woodworms** or **woodworm**) **1** N-COUNT **Woodworm** are very small creatures which make holes in wood by eating it. **2** N-UNCOUNT **Woodworm** is damage caused to wood, especially to the wooden parts of a house or to furniture, by woodworm making holes in the wood. ❑ *...treating the ground floor of a house for woodworm.*

woody /wʊdi/ (**woodier, woodiest**) **1** ADJ [usu ADJ n] **Woody** plants have very hard stems. ❑ *Care must be taken when trimming around woody plants like shrubs and trees.* **2** ADJ [usu ADJ n] A **woody** area has a lot of trees in it. ❑ *...the wet and woody Vosges mountains.*

woof /wʊf/ **1** N-SING; SOUND **Woof** is the sound that a dog makes when it barks. [INFORMAL] ❑ *She started going "woof woof."* **2** → See feature box at **onomatopoeia**

wool /wʊl/ (**wools**) **1** N-UNCOUNT **Wool** is the hair that grows on sheep and on some other animals. ❑ *A new invention means sheep do not have to be sheared – the wool just falls off.* **2** N-MASS **Wool** is a material made from animal's wool that is used to make things such as clothes, blankets, and carpets. ❑ *...a wool overcoat.*

wool|en /wʊlən/

in BRIT, use **woollen**

ADJ **Woolen** clothes or materials are made from wool or from a mixture of wool and artificial fibers. ❑ ...*thick woolen socks.*

wool|ly /wʊli/ (**woollier, woolliest**) also **wooly** ADJ Something that is **woolly** is made of wool or looks like wool. ❑ *She wore this woolly hat with pompoms.*

woozy /wuzi/ (**woozier, wooziest**) ADJ [usu v-link ADJ] If you feel **woozy**, you feel slightly weak and unsteady and cannot think clearly. [INFORMAL] ❑ *The fumes made them woozy.*

WORD
① NOUN AND VERB USES
② PHRASES

① **word** ♦♦♦ /wɜrd/ (**words, wording, worded**) **1** N-COUNT A **word** is a single unit of language that can be represented in writing or speech. In English, a word has a space on either side of it when it is written. ❑ *The words stood out clearly on the page.* ❑ *The word "ginseng" comes from the Chinese word "Shen-seng."* **2** N-PLURAL Someone's **words** are what they say or write. ❑ *I was devastated when her words came true.* **3** N-PLURAL The **words** of a song consist of the text that is sung, in contrast to the music that is played. ❑ *Can you hear the words on the album?* **4** N-SING If you have **a word** with someone, you have a short conversation with them. [SPOKEN] ❑ *I think it's time you had a word with him.* **5** N-COUNT If you offer someone **a word of** something such as warning, advice, or praise, you warn, advise, or praise them. ❑ *A word of warning. Don't stick too precisely to what it says in the book.* **6** N-SING If you say that someone does not hear, understand, or say **a word**, you are emphasizing that they hear, understand, or say nothing at all. [EMPHASIS] ❑ *I can't understand a word she says.* **7** N-UNCOUNT If there is **word** of something, people receive news or information about it. ❑ *There is no word from the authorities on the reported attack.* **8** N-SING If you give your **word**, you make a sincere promise to someone. ❑ *...an adult who gave his word the boy would be supervised.* **9** N-SING If someone gives **the word** to do something, they give an order to do it. ❑ *I want nothing said about this until I give the word.* **10** V-T To **word** something in a particular way means to choose or use particular words to express it. ❑ *If I had written the letter, I might have worded it differently.* • **-worded** COMB IN ADJ ❑ *...a strongly-worded statement.* **11** → see also **wording**

② **word** ♦♦♦ /wɜrd/ (**words**)

→ Please look at meaning **10** to see if the expression you are looking for is shown under another headword.

1 PHRASE If you say that people consider something to be **a dirty word**, you mean that they disapprove of it. ❑ *So many people think feminism is a dirty word.* **2** PHRASE If you do something **from the word go**, you do it from the very beginning of a period of time or situation. ❑ *It's essential you make the right decisions from the word go.* **3** PHRASE You can use **in** their **words** or **in** their **own words** to indicate that you are reporting what someone said using the exact words that they used. ❑ *Even the Assistant Secretary of State had to admit that previous policy did not, in his words, produce results.* **4** PHRASE If someone has **the last word** or **the final word** in a discussion, argument, or disagreement, they are the one who wins it or who makes the final decision. ❑ *She does like to have the last word in any discussion.* **5** PHRASE If news or information passes **by word of mouth**, people tell it to each other rather than it being printed in written form. ❑ *The story has been passed down by word of mouth.* **6** PHRASE You say **in other words** in order to introduce a different, and usually simpler, explanation or interpretation of something that has just been said. ❑ *...coronary heart disease, in other words, heart attacks and strokes.* **7** PHRASE If you say something **in** your **own words**, you express it in your own way, without copying or repeating someone else's description. ❑ *Now tell us in your own words about the events of Saturday.* **8** PHRASE If you say to someone '**take my word for it**,' you mean that they should believe you because you are telling the truth. ❑ *You'll buy nothing but trouble if you buy that house, take my word for it.* **9** PHRASE If you repeat something **word for word**, you repeat it exactly as it was originally said or written. ❑ *I don't try to memorize speeches word for word.* **10 the operative word** → see **operative**

-word /-wɜrd/ (**-words**) COMB IN N-COUNT You can use **-word** after a letter of the alphabet to refer politely or humorously to a word beginning with that letter that people find offensive or are embarrassed to use. ❑ *It was the first show to use the F-word and show nudity on stage.* ❑ *Politicians began to use the dreaded R-word: recession.*

word class (**word classes**) N-COUNT A **word class** is a group of words that have the same basic behavior such as nouns, adjectives, or verbs.

word|ing /wɜrdɪŋ/ N-UNCOUNT The **wording** of a piece of writing or a speech are the words used in it, especially when these are chosen to have a particular effect. ❑ *The two sides failed to agree on the wording of a final report.*

word|less /wɜrdlɪs/ **1** ADJ You say that someone is **wordless** when they do not say anything, especially at a time when they are expected to say something. [LITERARY] ❑ *She stared back, now wordless.* ❑ *Here and there, husbands sit in wordless despair.* • **word|less|ly** ADV [ADV with v] ❑ *Garcia downed his food wordlessly, his attention far away.* **2** ADJ [usu ADJ n] If someone makes a **wordless** sound, they make a sound that does not seem to contain any words. [LITERARY] ❑ *...a wordless chant.* ❑ *He shrieked a long, wordless cry.*

word|play /wɜrdpleɪ/ also **word play** N-UNCOUNT **Wordplay** involves making jokes by using the meanings of words in an amusing or clever way.

word pro|cess|ing also **word-processing** N-UNCOUNT **Word processing** is the work or skill of producing printed documents using a computer. [COMPUTING] ❑ *Many temp agencies offer word processing courses to those with rusty office skills.*

word pro|ces|sor (**word processors**) N-COUNT A **word processor** is a computer program or a computer which is used to produce printed documents. [COMPUTING]

word wrap|ping N-UNCOUNT In computing, **word wrapping** is a process by which a word that comes at the end of a line is automatically moved onto a new line in order to keep the text within the margins. [COMPUTING]

wordy /wɜrdi/ (**wordier, wordiest**) ADJ If you describe a person's speech or something that they write as **wordy**, you disapprove of the fact that they use too many words, especially words which are very long, formal, or literary. [DISAPPROVAL] ❑ *The chapter is mostly wordy rhetoric.*

wore /wɔr/ **Wore** is the past tense of **wear**.

WORK
① VERB USES AND PHRASES
② NOUN USES AND PHRASES
③ PHRASAL VERBS

① **work** ♦♦♦ /wɜrk/ (**works, working, worked**) **1** V-I People who **work** have a job, usually one which they are paid to do. ❑ *I started working in a recording studio.* ❑ *He worked as a teacher for 50 years.* ❑ *I want to work, I don't want to be on welfare.* **2** V-T/V-I When you **work**, you do the things that you are paid or required to do in your job. ❑ *I can't talk to you right now – I'm working.* ❑ *He was working at his desk.* ❑ *They work forty hours a week.* **3** V-I When you **work**, you spend time and effort doing a task that needs to be done or trying to achieve something. ❑ *Linda spends all her time working on the garden.* ❑ *The government expressed hope that all the sides will work toward a political solution.* **4** V-I If someone **is working on** a particular subject or question, they are studying or researching it. ❑ *Professor Bonnet has been working for many years on molecules of this type.* **5** V-I If you **work** with a person or a group of people, you spend time and effort trying to help them in some way. ❑ *She spent a period of time working with people dying of cancer.* **6** V-I If a machine or piece of equipment **works**, it operates and performs a particular function. ❑ *The pump doesn't work and we have no running water.* **7** V-I If an idea, system, or way of doing something **works**, it is successful, effective, or satisfactory. ❑ *95 percent of these diets do not work.* **8** V-I If a drug or medicine **works**, it produces a particular physical effect. ❑ *I wake up at 6 a.m. as the sleeping pill doesn't work for more than nine hours.* **9** V-I If your mind or brain **is working**, you are thinking about something or trying to solve a problem. ❑ *My mind was working frantically, running over the events of the evening.* **10** V-I If you **work on** an assumption or idea, you act as if it were true or base other ideas on it, until

work

you have more information. ❑ *We are working on the assumption that it was a gas explosion.* **11** V-T If you **work** someone, you make them spend time and effort doing a particular activity or job. ❑ *They're working me too hard. I'm too old for this.* **12** V-T When people **work** the land, they do all the tasks involved in growing crops. ❑ *Farmers worked the fertile valleys.* **13** V-T If you **work** a machine or piece of equipment, you use or control it. ❑ *If he refused to work the machine, someone else would just do it.* **14** V-I If something **works** into a particular state or condition, it gradually moves so that it is in that state or condition. ❑ *It's important to put a lock washer on that last nut, or it can work loose.* **15** → see also **working** **16** PHRASE If you **work** your **way** somewhere, you move or progress there slowly, and with a lot of effort or work. ❑ *Rescuers were still working their way toward the trapped men.*

VOCABULARY IN CONTEXT

Getting and losing work

Most of us will spend more than 40 years working, so it's worth finding a role that brings **job satisfaction**. But how do we know what's right for us? These days it seems unfair to make students choose their subjects and chart their **career path** so young. But a couple of generations ago it was normal to start a job and work for the same company for life. You **worked your way up**, going from **promotion** to promotion, paying into the company **pension scheme**, and **retiring** in your early 60s. Those days of **job security** are gone. We still have to **earn a living**, but in uncertain economic times, it's harder to **hold down a job**. This has meant that changing **professions** has become the norm. Transferable skills enable us to **find employment** more readily, and to avoid the **unemployment line**. Whether people **hand in their notice** or **are laid off**, there's an increased trend of job-hopping these days.

② **work** ♦♦♦ /wɜrk/ (works) **1** N-UNCOUNT People who have **work** or who are **in work** have a job, usually one which they are paid to do. ❑ *Fewer and fewer people are in work.* ❑ *I was out of work at the time.* **2** N-UNCOUNT Your **work** consists of the things you are paid or required to do in your job. ❑ *We're supposed to be running a business here. I've got work to do.* ❑ *I used to take work home, but I don't do it any more.* **3** N-UNCOUNT **Work** is tasks that need to be done or things that need to be achieved. ❑ *There was a lot of work to do on their house.* **4** N-UNCOUNT **Work** is the place where you do your job. ❑ *Many people travel to work by car.* **5** N-UNCOUNT **Work** is something that you produce as a result of an activity or as a result of doing your job. ❑ *It can help to have an impartial third party look over your work.* **6** N-COUNT A **work** is something such as a painting, book, or piece of music produced by an artist, writer, or composer. ❑ *In my opinion, this is Rembrandt's greatest work.* **7** N-UNCOUNT Someone's **work** is the study or research that they have done on a particular subject or question. ❑ *Their work shows that one-year-olds are much more likely to have allergies if either parent smokes.* **8** N-UNCOUNT **Work** with a particular person or a group of people is time and effort spent trying to help them in some way. ❑ *She became involved in social and relief work among the refugees.*

worked up

9 N-COUNT-COLL A **works** is a place where something is manufactured or where an industrial process is carried out. **Works** is used to refer to one or to more than one of these places. ❑ *...the steelworks in Gary, Indiana.* **10** N-PLURAL **Works** are activities such as digging the ground or building on a large scale. ❑ *...six years of disruptive building works, road construction and urban development.* **11** PHRASE If someone is **at work** they are doing their job or are busy doing a particular activity. ❑ *The salvage teams are already hard at work trying to deal with the spilled oil.* **12** PHRASE If a force or process is **at work**, it is having a particular influence or effect. ❑ *It is important to understand the powerful economic and social forces at work behind our own actions.* **13** PHRASE If you **put** someone **to work** or **set** them **to work**, you give them a job or task to do. ❑ *By stimulating the economy, we're going to put people to work.* **14** PHRASE If you **get to work**, go **to work**, or **set to work** on a job, task, or problem, you start doing it or dealing with it. ❑ *He promised to get to work on the state's massive deficit.*

③ **work** ♦♦♦ /wɜrk/ (works, working, worked)
▸ **work off** PHRASAL VERB If you **work off** energy, stress, or anger, you get rid of it by doing something that requires a lot of physical effort. ❑ *Cleaning my kitchen really works off frustration if I've had a fight with someone.*
▸ **work out** **1** PHRASAL VERB If you **work out** a solution to a problem or mystery, you manage to find the solution by thinking or talking about it. ❑ *Negotiators are due to meet later today to work out a compromise.* ❑ *It took me some time to work out what was causing this.* **2** PHRASAL VERB If you **work out** the answer to a mathematical problem, you calculate it. ❑ *It is proving hard to work out the value of bankrupt companies' assets.* **3** PHRASAL VERB If something **works out** at a particular amount, it is calculated to be that amount after all the facts and figures have been considered. ❑ *The price per pound works out at $3.20.* **4** PHRASAL VERB If a situation **works out** well or **works out**, it happens or progresses in a satisfactory way. ❑ *Things just didn't work out as planned.* ❑ *The deal just isn't working out the way we were promised.* **5** PHRASAL VERB If a process **works** itself **out**, it reaches a conclusion or satisfactory end. ❑ *People involved in it think it's a nightmare, but I'm sure it will work itself out.* **6** PHRASAL VERB If you **work out**, you do physical exercises in order to make your body fit and strong. ❑ *Work out at a gym or swim twice a week.* **7** → see also **workout**
▸ **work up** **1** PHRASAL VERB If you **work** yourself **up**, you make yourself feel very upset or angry about something. ❑ *She worked herself up into a bit of a state.* **2** → see also **worked up** **3** PHRASAL VERB If you **work up** the enthusiasm or courage to do something, you succeed in making yourself feel it. ❑ *Your creative talents can also be put to good use, if you can work up the energy.* **4** PHRASAL VERB If you **work up** a sweat or an appetite, you make yourself sweaty or hungry by doing exercise or hard work. ❑ *Even if you are not prepared to work up a sweat three times a week, any activity is better than none.*

work|able /wɜrkəbəl/ ADJ A **workable** idea or system is realistic and practical, and likely to be effective. ❑ *Investors can simply pay cash, but this isn't a workable solution in most cases.*

worka|day /wɜrkədeɪ/ ADJ [usu ADJ n] **Workaday** means ordinary and not especially interesting or unusual. ❑ *Enough of fantasy, the workaday world awaited him.*

worka|hol|ic /wɜrkəhɒlɪk/ (workaholics) N-COUNT A **workaholic** is a person who works most of the time and finds it difficult to stop working in order to do other things. [INFORMAL] ❑ *Eighteen percent of 30-year-olds claim they are workaholics.*

work|bench /wɜrkbentʃ/ (workbenches) N-COUNT A **workbench** is a heavy wooden table on which people use tools such as a hammer and nails to make or repair things.

work|book /wɜrkbʊk/ (workbooks) N-COUNT A **workbook** is a book to help you learn a particular subject that has questions in it with spaces for the answers. ❑ *Just do one more exercise in this workbook.*

work|day /wɜrkdeɪ/ (workdays) also **work day** **1** N-COUNT A **workday** is the amount of time during a day that you spend doing your job. [mainly AM] ❑ *His workday starts at 3:30 a.m. and lasts 12 hours.* **2** N-COUNT A **workday** is a day on which people go to work. ❑ *What's he doing home on a workday?*

worked up ADJ [v-link ADJ] If someone is **worked up**, they are angry or upset. ❑ *Steve shouted at her. He was really worked up now.*

work|er ♦♦♦ /wɜrkər/ (**workers**) **1** N-COUNT A particular kind of **worker** does the kind of work mentioned. ❏ *She ate her sandwich alongside several other office workers taking their break.* **2** N-COUNT **Workers** are people who are employed in industry or business and who are not managers. ❏ *Wages have been frozen and workers laid off.* **3** N-COUNT You can use **worker** to say how well or badly someone works. ❏ *He is a hard worker and a skilled gardener.* **4** → see also **social worker**

SYNONYMS

worker
NOUN **2**
employee: *He is an employee of Fuji Bank.*
hand: *He now works as a farm hand.*
laborer: *Her husband had been a farm laborer.*
workman: *Millson saw the workman, Terry, descending the ladder.*

work|fare /wɜrkfɛər/ N-UNCOUNT **Workfare** is a government program in which unemployed people have to do community work or learn new skills in order to receive welfare benefits.

work|force /wɜrkfɔrs/ (**workforces**) **1** N-COUNT The **workforce** is the total number of people in a country or region who are physically able to do a job and are available for work. ❏ *...a country where half the workforce is unemployed.* **2** N-COUNT The **workforce** is the total number of people who are employed by a particular company. ❏ *...an employer of a very large workforce.*

work|horse /wɜrkhɔrs/ (**workhorses**) **1** N-COUNT A **workhorse** is a horse which is used to do a job, for example, to pull a plow. **2** N-COUNT [usu with supp] If you describe a person or a machine as a **workhorse**, you mean that they can be relied upon to do a large amount of work, especially work that is dull or routine. ❏ *For years the Apple II had been the workhorse in schools across America.* ❏ *My husband never paid any attention to me. I was just a workhorse bringing up three children.*

work|ing ♦♦♦ /wɜrkɪŋ/ (**workings**) **1** ADJ [ADJ n] **Working** people have jobs that they are paid to do. ❏ *Like working*

VOCABULARY IN CONTEXT

Working conditions

Decent **working conditions** are important for all **employees**, whether they have **full-time** or **part-time contracts**. Broadly, working conditions are the conditions under which a person works, such as the physical working environment, health and safety standards, and the **amenities** available to workers. In most developed countries, there are **labor laws** on working conditions, which **employers** must observe. Set up in 1919, the International Labor Organization (ILO) supports almost 200 countries worldwide. It helps governments, employers, and workers' representatives to set **labor standards**, develop policies, and promote good working conditions. These typically pertain to regulating hours of work, **remuneration**, and **recognition** of a decent work-life balance for employees. Working hours can cover a variety of arrangements, including **shift work**, **flextime**, and **overtime**. The ILO also helps countries to formulate legislation for **minimum wage** rates as well as to set up provisions for paternity and **maternity leave**.

women anywhere, Asian women are buying convenience foods. **2** ADJ [ADJ n] **Working** people are ordinary people who do not have professional or very highly paid jobs. ❏ *The needs and opinions of ordinary working people were ignored.* **3** ADJ [ADJ n] Your **working** life is the period of your life in which you have a job or are of a suitable age to have a job. ❏ *He started his working life as a truck driver.* **4** ADJ [ADJ n] The **working** population of an area consists of all the people in that area who have a job or who are of a suitable age to have a job. ❏ *Almost 13 percent of the working population is already unemployed.* **5** ADJ [ADJ n] **Working** conditions or practices are ones that you have in your job. ❏ *The strikers are demanding higher pay and better working conditions.* **6** ADJ [ADJ n] A **working** farm or business exists to do normal work and make a profit, not only for tourists or as someone's hobby. ❏ *...a vacation spent on a working farm.* **7** ADJ [ADJ n] The **working** parts of a machine are the parts that move and operate the machine, in contrast to the outer case or container in which they are enclosed. ❏ *The reel comes complete with a set of spares for all the working parts.* **8** ADJ [ADJ n] A **working** knowledge or majority is not very great, but is enough to be useful. ❏ *This book was designed in order to provide a working knowledge of finance and accounts.* **9** N-PLURAL The **workings** of a piece of equipment, an organization, or a system are the ways in which it operates and the processes which are involved in it. ❏ *Neural networks are computer systems which mimic the workings of the brain.* **10 in working order** → see **order** ③

work|ing cap|i|tal N-UNCOUNT **Working capital** is money available for use immediately, rather than money invested in land or equipment. [BUSINESS] ❏ *He borrowed a further $1.5 m from conventional sources to provide working capital.*

work|ing class (**working classes**) N-COUNT-COLL The **working class** or the **working classes** are the group of people in a society who do not own much property, who have low social status, and who do jobs that involve using physical skills rather than intellectual skills. ❏ *A quarter of the working class voted for him.* • ADJ **Working class** is also an adjective. ❏ *...a self-educated man from a working class background.*

work|ing day (**working days**) **1** ADJ [ADJ n] A **working** day is the amount of time during a normal day that you spend doing your job. [mainly BRIT]

> in AM, usually use **workday**

2 ADJ [ADJ n] A **working** day is a day on which people go to work. [BRIT]

> in AM, use **workday**

work|ing girl (**working girls**) **1** N-COUNT A **working girl** is a woman who has a paid job. ❏ *...a working girl living from paycheck to paycheck.* **2** N-COUNT A **working girl** is a prostitute. [INFORMAL] ❏ *Are we ready to make prostitution legal to protect working girls and their rights?*

work|ing group (**working groups**) N-COUNT-COLL A **working group** is a committee formed to investigate a particular situation or problem and to produce a report containing its opinions and suggestions. ❏ *There will be a working group on international issues.*

work|ing par|ty (**working parties**) N-COUNT-COLL A **working party** is the same as a **select committee**. [mainly BRIT] ❏ *They set up a working party to look into the issue.*

work|ing stiff (**working stiffs**) N-COUNT A **working stiff** is a person who has an ordinary job that is not well-paid. [AM, INFORMAL] ❏ *Most of the politicians are sensibly out of town, but the poor working stiffs hardly get away at all.*

work|ing week (**working weeks**) N-COUNT A **working week** is the amount of time during a normal week that you spend doing your job. [mainly BRIT]

> in AM, usually use **workweek**

work in pro|gress N-SING A **work in progress** is something that has not been completed or perfected. ❏ *Sample pages from a work in progress.*

work|load /wɜrkloʊd/ (**workloads**) N-COUNT The **workload** of a person or organization is the amount of work that has to be done by them. ❏ *You need someone to bounce ideas off and share your workload.*

work|man /wɜrkmən/ (**workmen**) N-COUNT A **workman** is a man who works with his hands, for example, building or

workmanlike

repairing houses or roads. ▫ *In University Square workmen are building a steel fence.*

work|man|like /wɜrkmənlaɪk/ ADJ If you describe something as **workmanlike**, you mean that it has been done well and sensibly, but not in a particularly imaginative or original way. ▫ *Really it's a workmanlike conference rather than a dramatic one.* ▫ *The script was workmanlike at best.*

work|man|ship /wɜrkmənʃɪp/ N-UNCOUNT **Workmanship** is the skill with which something is made and which affects the appearance and quality of the finished object. ▫ *The problem may be due to poor workmanship.*

work|mate /wɜrkmeɪt/ (**workmates**) N-COUNT Your **workmates** are the people you work with. [mainly BRIT, INFORMAL]

work of art (**works of art**) N-COUNT A **work of art** is a painting or piece of sculpture of high quality. ▫ *...a collection of works of art of international significance.*

work|out /wɜrkaʊt/ (**workouts**) N-COUNT A **workout** is a period of physical exercise or training. ▫ *Give your upper body a workout by using handweights.*

work|place /wɜrkpleɪs/ (**workplaces**) also **work place** N-COUNT Your **workplace** is the place where you work. ▫ *...the difficulties facing women in the workplace.*

work|room /wɜrkrum/ (**workrooms**) N-COUNT A person's **workroom** is a room where they work, especially when their work involves making things.

work|sheet /wɜrkʃit/ (**worksheets**) N-COUNT A **worksheet** is a specially prepared page of exercises designed to improve your knowledge or understanding of a particular subject. ▫ *Complete this worksheet before you decide on the model you want.*

work|shop /wɜrkʃɒp/ (**workshops**) ◼ N-COUNT A **workshop** is a period of discussion or practical work on a particular subject in which a group of people share their knowledge or experience. ▫ *Trumpeter Marcus Belgrave ran a jazz workshop for young artists.* ◼ N-COUNT A **workshop** is a building that contains tools or machinery for making or repairing things, especially using wood or metal. ▫ *...a modestly equipped workshop.*

work|station /wɜrksteɪʃən/ (**workstations**) also **work station** N-COUNT A **workstation** is a screen and keyboard that are part of an office computer system. ▫ *Or you can set up databases on any number of servers and access them from particular workstations.*

work|up /wɜrkʌp/ (**workups**) N-COUNT A **workup** is a detailed medical examination of a patient. [AM] ▫ *Her husband's health is excellent, according to a full medical workup just completed.*

work|week /wɜrkwik/ (**workweeks**) N-COUNT A **workweek** is the amount of time during a normal week that you spend doing your job. [mainly AM] ▫ *The union had sought a wage increase, a shorter workweek.*

world ✦✦✦ /wɜrld/ (**worlds**)
→ Please look at meanings ◼ to ◼ to see if the expression you are looking for is shown under another headword.
◼ N-SING **The world** is the planet that we live on. ▫ *The satellite enables us to calculate their precise location anywhere in the world.*
◼ N-SING **The world** refers to all the people who live on this planet, and our societies, institutions, and ways of life. ▫ *The world was, and remains, shocked.* ▫ *He wants to show the world that anyone can learn to be an ambassador.* ◼ ADJ [ADJ n] You can use **world** to describe someone or something that is one of the most important or significant of its kind on earth. ▫ *China has once again emerged as a world power.* ◼ N-SING You can use **world** in expressions such as **the Arab world**, **the Western world**, and **the ancient world** to refer to a particular group of countries or a particular period in history. ▫ *Athens had strong ties to the Arab world.* ◼ N-COUNT Someone's **world** is the life they lead, the people they have contact with, and the things they experience. ▫ *His world seemed so different from mine.* ◼ N-SING You can use **world** to refer to a particular field of activity, and the people involved in it. ▫ *The publishing world had certainly never seen an event quite like this.* ◼ N-SING You can use **world** to refer to a particular group of living things, for example, **the animal world**, **the plant world**, and **the insect world**. ▫ *When it comes to dodging disaster, the champions of the insect world have to be cockroaches.* ◼ → see also **real world**, **Third World** ◼ PHRASE If you say that someone has **the best of both worlds**, you mean that they have only the benefits of two things and none of the disadvantages. ▫ *Her living room provides the best of both worlds, with an office at one end and comfortable sofas at the other.* ◼ PHRASE If you say that something **has done** someone **a world of good**, you mean that it has made them feel better or improved their life. [INFORMAL] ▫ *Just sit for a while and relax. It will do you a world of good.* ◼ PHRASE You can use **in the world** in expressions such as **what in the world** and **who in the world** to emphasize a question, especially when expressing surprise or anger. [EMPHASIS] ▫ *What in the world is he doing?* ◼ PHRASE You can use **in an ideal world** or **in a perfect world** when you are talking about things that you would like to happen, although you realize that they are not likely to happen. ▫ *In an ideal world Karen Stevens says she would love to stay at home with her two-and-a-half-year-old son.* ◼ PHRASE You can use **the outside world** to refer to all the people who do not live in a particular place or who are not involved in a particular situation. ▫ *For many, the post office is the only link with the outside world.* ◼ **not be the end of the world** → see **end** ① ◼ **the world is your oyster** → see **oyster** ◼ **on top of the world** → see **top** ③ ◼ → See feature box at **Olympic Games**

world-class ADJ A **world-class** athlete, performer, or organization is one of the best in the world. [JOURNALISM] ▫ *He was determined to become a world-class player.*

world-famous ADJ Someone or something that is **world-famous** is known about by people all over the world. ▫ *...the world-famous Hollywood Bowl.*

World Health Or|gani|za|tion N-PROPER [the N] The **World Health Organization** is an organization within the United Nations that is responsible for helping governments to improve their health services. The abbreviation **WHO** is also used. ▫ *The World Health Organization says a cholera epidemic in Peru could spread throughout Latin America.*

world lead|er (**world leaders**) ◼ N-COUNT A **world leader** is someone who is the leader of a country, especially an economically powerful country. ◼ N-COUNT A **world leader** is a product, company, organization, or person that is a **world leader** is the most successful or advanced one in a particular area of activity. [JOURNALISM] ▫ *They were world leaders in their field.*

world|ly /wɜrldli/ (**worldlier**, **worldliest**) ◼ ADJ Someone who is **worldly** is experienced and knows about the practical and social aspects of life. ▫ *He was different from anyone I had known, very worldly, everything that Duane was not.* ◼ ADJ [ADJ n] You can refer to someone's possessions as their **worldly** goods or possessions. [LITERARY] ▫ *...a man who had given up all his worldly goods.*

worldly-wise ADJ If you describe someone as **worldly-wise**, you mean they are experienced and know about the practical or social aspects of life, and are not easily shocked or impressed.

World Trade Or|gani|za|tion N-PROPER The **World Trade Organization** is an international organization that encourages and regulates trade between its member states. The abbreviation **WTO** is also used. ▫ *... institutions such as the World Bank and the World Trade Organization.*

world view (**world views**) also **world-view** N-COUNT A person's **world view** is the way they see and understand the world, especially regarding issues such as politics, philosophy, and religion. ▫ *...their Christian world view.*

world war ✦◇◇ (**world wars**) N-VAR A **world war** is a war that involves countries all over the world. ▫ *He had been through two world wars.*

world-weary ADJ A **world-weary** person no longer feels excited or enthusiastic about anything.

world|wide ✦◇◇ /wɜrldwaɪd/ ADV If something exists or happens **worldwide**, it exists or happens throughout the world. ▫ *His books have sold more than 20 million copies worldwide.* • ADJ **Worldwide** is also an adjective. ▫ *Today, doctors are fearing a worldwide epidemic.*

SYNONYMS

worldwide
ADJ
global: *...a global ban on nuclear testing.*
international: *...emergency aid from the international community.*
universal: *The desire to look attractive is universal.*

World Wide Web N-PROPER The **World Wide Web** is a computer system that links documents and pictures into a

worm /wɜrm/ (worms, worming, wormed) **1** N-COUNT A **worm** is a small animal with a long thin body, no bones, and no legs. **2** V-T If you say that someone **is worming** their **way** to success, or **is worming** their **way** into someone else's affection, you disapprove of the way that they are gradually making someone trust them or like them, often in order to deceive them or gain some advantage. [DISAPPROVAL] ❑ *She never misses a chance to worm her way into the public's hearts.* **3** N-COUNT A **worm** is a computer program that contains a virus which duplicates itself many times in a network. [COMPUTING] ❑ *...a new computer worm that disables security software.* **4** PHRASE If you say that someone is opening **a can of worms**, you are warning them that they are planning to do or talk about something that is much more complicated, unpleasant, or difficult than they realize and that might be better left alone. ❑ *Introducing this legislation would be like opening a can of worms.*

worm|hole /wɜrmhoʊl/ (wormholes) N-COUNT In physics, a **wormhole** is a tunnel in space that is believed to connect different parts of the universe. [TECHNICAL] ❑ *...the story of an astronaut who is sucked through a wormhole into the other side of the universe.*

worm|wood /wɜrmwʊd/ N-UNCOUNT **Wormwood** is a plant that has a very bitter taste and is used in making medicines and alcoholic drinks.

worn /wɔrn/ **1 Worn** is the past participle of **wear**. **2** ADJ **Worn** is used to describe something that is damaged or thin because it is old and has been used a lot. ❑ *Worn rugs increase the danger of tripping.* **3** ADJ [v-link ADJ] If someone looks **worn**, they look tired and old. ❑ *She was looking very haggard and worn.*

worn out also **worn-out** **1** ADJ Something that is **worn out** is so old, damaged, or thin from use that it cannot be used anymore. ❑ *Car buyers tend to replace worn-out tires with the same brand.* **2** ADJ Someone who is **worn out** is extremely tired after hard work or a difficult or unpleasant experience. ❑ *Before the race, he is fine. But afterwards he is worn out.*

wor|ried ✦✧✧ /wɜrid/ ADJ When you are **worried**, you are unhappy because you keep thinking about problems that you have or about unpleasant things that might happen in the future. ❑ *He seemed very worried.*

wor|ri|er /wɜriər/ (worriers) N-COUNT If you describe someone as a **worrier**, you mean that they spend a lot of time thinking about problems that they have or unpleasant things that might happen.

wor|ri|some /wɜrisəm/ ADJ Something that is **worrisome** causes people to worry. [mainly AM] ❑ *It's Houston's injury that is now the most worrisome.*

in BRIT, usually use **worrying**

wor|ry ✦✦✧ /wɜri/ (worries, worrying, worried) **1** V-T/V-I If you **worry**, you keep thinking about problems that you have or about unpleasant things that might happen. ❑ *Don't worry, your luggage will come on afterwards by taxi.* ❑ *I worry about her constantly.* **2** V-T If someone or something **worries** you, they make you anxious because you keep thinking about problems or unpleasant things that might be connected with them. ❑ *I'm still in the early days of my recovery and that worries me.* **3** V-T [oft with neg] If someone or something does not **worry** you, you do not dislike them or you are not annoyed by them. [SPOKEN] ❑ *The cold doesn't worry me.* **4** N-UNCOUNT **Worry** is the state or feeling of anxiety and unhappiness caused by the problems that you have or by thinking about unpleasant things that might happen. ❑ *Modern American life is full of worry: the job, the kids, money, the stock market.* **5** N-COUNT A **worry** is a problem that you keep thinking about and that makes you unhappy. ❑ *My main worry was that Madeleine Johnson would still be there.*

wor|ry|ing /wɜriɪŋ/ ADJ If something is **worrying**, it causes people to worry. [mainly BRIT]

in AM, usually use **worrisome**

wor|ry|wart /wɜriwɔrt/ (worrywarts) N-COUNT If you refer to someone as a **worrywart**, you mean that they worry too much or worry about things that they should not worry about. [INFORMAL, DISAPPROVAL] ❑ *Some worrywarts have predicted that if the scientists actually do create a new universe, it might destroy the existing one.*

worse /wɜrs/ **1 Worse** is the comparative of **bad**. **2 Worse** is the comparative of **badly**. **3** PHRASE If a situation changes **for the worse**, it becomes more unpleasant or more difficult. ❑ *The grandparents sigh and say how things have changed for the worse.*

wors|en /wɜrsən/ (worsens, worsening, worsened) V-T/V-I If a bad situation **worsens** or if something **worsens** it, it becomes more difficult, unpleasant, or unacceptable. ❑ *The security forces had to intervene to prevent the situation worsening.*

wor|ship /wɜrʃɪp/ (worships, worshiping, worshiped)

in BRIT, sometimes in AM, use **worshipping, worshipped**

1 V-T/V-I If you **worship** a god, you show your respect to the god, for example, by saying prayers. ❑ *...disputes over ways of life and ways of worshiping God.* ❑ *He prefers to worship in his own home.* • N-UNCOUNT **Worship** is also a noun. ❑ *...the worship of the ancient Roman gods.* • **wor|ship|er** (worshipers) N-COUNT ❑ *She burst into tears and loud sobs that disturbed the other worshipers.* **2** V-T If you **worship** someone or something, you love them or admire them very much. ❑ *She had worshiped him for years.*

wor|ship|ful /wɜrʃɪpfəl/ ADJ [ADJ n] If someone has a **worshipful** attitude to a person or thing, they show great respect and admiration for them. ❑ *...Franklin's almost worshipful imitation of his cousin.*

worst /wɜrst/ **1 Worst** is the superlative of **bad**. **2 Worst** is the superlative of **badly**. **3** N-SING **The worst** is the most unpleasant or unfavorable thing that could happen or does happen. ❑ *Though home safety has much improved, miners' families still fear the worst.* **4 Worst** is used to form the superlative of compound adjectives beginning with 'bad' and 'badly.' For example, the superlative of 'badly-affected' is 'worst-affected.' ❑ *The worst-affected areas were in Jefferson Parish.* **5** PHRASE You say **worst of all** to indicate that what you are about to mention is the most unpleasant or has the most disadvantages out of all the things you are mentioning. ❑ *The people most closely affected are the passengers who were injured and, worst of all, those who lost relatives.* **6** PHRASE You use **at worst** or **at the worst** to indicate that you are mentioning the worst thing that might happen in a situation. ❑ *At best Nella would be an invalid; at worst she would die.* **7** PHRASE When someone is **at their worst**, they are as unpleasant, bad, or unsuccessful as it is possible for them to be. ❑ *This was their mother at her worst. Her voice was strident, she was ready to be angry at anyone.* **8** PHRASE You use **if worst comes to worst** or **if the worst comes to the worst** to say what you might do if a situation develops in the most unfavorable way possible. ❑ *If worst comes to worst, Europe could withstand a trade war.*

worst-case ADJ [ADJ n] The **worst-case** scenario is the worst possible thing that could happen in a particular situation. ❑ *The worst-case scenario is an aircraft will crash if a bird destroys an engine.* ❑ *Even in a worst-case situation the United States would have been able to retaliate.*

wor|sted /wʊstɪd, wɜr-/ (worsteds) N-MASS **Worsted** is a kind of woolen cloth.

worth ✦✦✧ /wɜrθ/ **1** V-T [v-link **worth** amount] If something is **worth** a particular amount of money, it can be sold for that amount or is considered to have that value. ❑ *A local jeweler says the pearl is worth at least $500.* ❑ *His mother inherited a business worth 15,000 dollars a year.* **2** COMB IN QUANT [QUANT of n] **Worth** combines with amounts of money, so that when you talk about a particular amount of money's **worth** of something, you mean the quantity of it that you can buy for that amount of money. ❑ *I went and bought about six dollars' worth of potato chips.* • PRON **Worth** is also a pronoun. ❑ *Gold reserves had fallen to less than $3 billion worth.* **3** COMB IN QUANT [QUANT of n] **Worth** combines with time expressions, so you can use **worth** with when you are saying how long an amount of something will last. For example, a week's **worth of** food is the amount of food that will last you for a week. ❑ *You've got three years' worth of research money to do what you want with.* • PRON **Worth** is also a pronoun. ❑ *There's really not very much food down there. About two*

worthless — wrangler

weeks' worth. **4** V-T [v-link worth -ing] If you say that something is **worth** having, you mean that it is pleasant or useful, and therefore a good thing to have. ❑ He's decided to get a look at the house and see if it might be worth buying. ❑ Most things worth having never come easy. **5** V-T [v-link worth n/-ing] If something is **worth** a particular action, or if an action is **worth** doing, it is considered to be important enough for that action. ❑ I am spending a lot of money and time on this boat, but is it worth it? ❑ This restaurant is well worth a visit. **6** PHRASE If an action or activity is **worth** someone's **while**, it will be helpful, useful, or enjoyable for them if they do it, even though it requires some effort. ❑ It might be worth your while to go to court and ask for the agreement to be changed. **7 worth your weight in gold** → see **weight**

worth|less /wɜrθlɪs/ **1** ADJ Something that is **worthless** is of no real value or use. ❑ The guarantee could be worthless if the store goes out of business. ❑ Training is worthless unless there is proof that it works. **2** ADJ Someone who is described as **worthless** is considered to have no good qualities or skills. ❑ You feel you really are completely worthless and unlovable.

worth|while /wɜrθwaɪl/ ADJ If something is **worthwhile**, it is enjoyable or useful, and worth the time, money, or effort that is spent on it. ❑ The president's trip to Washington this week seems to have been worthwhile.

wor|thy /wɜrði/ (worthier, worthiest) ADJ If a person or thing is **worthy** of something, they deserve it because they have the qualities or abilities required. [FORMAL] ❑ The bank might think you're worthy of a loan.

-worthy /-wɜrði/ **1** COMB IN ADJ **-worthy** can be added to words to form adjectives that indicate that someone or something deserves a particular thing or action. For example, if a remark or person is **quote-worthy**, they are worth quoting. ❑ You may see yourself as useless, incompetent and blameworthy. **2** → see also **airworthy, creditworthy, newsworthy, noteworthy, praiseworthy, roadworthy, seaworthy, trustworthy**

would ◆◆◆ /wəd, STRONG wʊd/

> Would is a modal verb. It is usually used with the base form of a verb. In spoken English, **would** is often abbreviated to **'d**.

1 MODAL You use **would** when you are saying what someone believed, hoped, or expected to happen or be the case. ❑ No one believed the soldiers stationed at the border would actually open fire. ❑ Would he always be like this? **2** MODAL You use **would** when saying what someone intended to do. ❑ The statement added that although there were a number of differing views, these would be discussed by both sides. **3** MODAL You use **would** when you are referring to the result or effect of a possible situation. ❑ Ordinarily it would be fun to be taken to fabulous restaurants. ❑ It would be wrong to suggest that police officers were not annoyed by acts of indecency. **4** MODAL You use **would**, or **would have** with a past participle, to indicate that you are assuming or guessing that something is true, because you have good reasons for thinking it. ❑ You wouldn't know him. ❑ His fans would already be familiar with Caroline. **5** MODAL You use **would** in the main clause of some 'if' and 'unless' sentences to indicate something you consider to be fairly unlikely to happen. ❑ If only I could get some sleep, I would be able to cope. **6** MODAL You use **would** to say that someone was willing to do something. You use **would not** to indicate that they refused to do something. ❑ They said they would give the police their full cooperation. ❑ He wouldn't say where he had picked up the information. **7** MODAL You use **would not** to indicate that something did not happen, often in spite of a lot of effort. ❑ He kicked, pushed, and hurled his shoulder at the door. It wouldn't open. **8** MODAL You use **would**, especially with 'like,' 'love,' and 'wish,' when saying that someone wants to do or have a particular thing or wants a particular thing to happen. ❑ She asked me what I would like to do and mentioned a particular job. ❑ Ideally, she would love to become pregnant again. **9 would rather** → see **rather** **10** MODAL You use **would** with 'if' clauses in questions when you are asking for permission to do something. ❑ Do you think it would be all right if I smoked? **11** MODAL You use **would**, usually in questions with 'like,' when you are making a polite offer or invitation. [POLITENESS]

❑ Would you like a drink? ❑ Would you like to stay? **12** MODAL You use **would**, usually in questions, when you are politely asking someone to do something. [POLITENESS] ❑ Would you do me a favor and get rid of this letter I've just received? ❑ Would you come in here a moment, please? **13** MODAL You say that someone **would** do something when it is typical of them and you are critical of it. You emphasize the word **would** when you use it in this way. [DISAPPROVAL] ❑ Well, you would say that: you're a man. **14** MODAL You use **would**, or sometimes **would have** with a past participle, when you are expressing your opinion about something or seeing if people agree with you, especially when you are uncertain about what you are saying. [VAGUENESS] ❑ I think you'd agree he's a very respected columnist. ❑ I would have thought he was too old to do that job. **15** MODAL You use **I would** when you are giving someone advice in an informal way. ❑ If I were you I would simply ring your friend's doorbell and ask for your bike back. **16** MODAL You use **you would** in negative sentences with verbs such as 'guess' and 'know' when you want to say that something is not obvious, especially something surprising. ❑ Chris is so full of artistic temperament you'd never think she was the daughter of a banker. **17** MODAL You use **would have** with a past participle when you are saying what was likely to have happened by a particular time. ❑ Within ten weeks of the introduction, 34 million people would have been reached by our television commercials. **18** MODAL You use **would have** with a past participle when you are referring to the result or effect of a possible event in the past. ❑ My daughter would have been 17 this week if she had lived. **19** MODAL If you say that someone **would have** liked or preferred something, you mean that they wanted to do it or have it but were unable to. ❑ I would have liked a life in politics.

would-be ADJ [ADJ n] You can use **would-be** to describe someone who wants or attempts to do a particular thing. For example, a **would-be** writer is someone who wants to be a writer. ❑ ...a book that provides encouragement for would-be writers who cannot get their novel into print.

wouldn't /wʊdᵊnt/ **Wouldn't** is the usual spoken form of 'would not.' ❑ They wouldn't allow me to smoke.

would've /wʊdəv/ **Would've** is a spoken form of 'would have,' when 'have' is an auxiliary verb. ❑ I knew deep down that my mom would've loved one of us to go to college.

WOUND
① VERB FORM OF WIND
② INJURY
---

① **wound** /waʊnd/ **Wound** is the past tense and past participle of **wind** → see **wind** ②

② **wound** ◆◆◇ /wund/ (wounds, wounding, wounded) **1** N-COUNT A **wound** is damage to part of your body, especially a cut or a hole in your flesh, which is caused by a gun, knife, or other weapon. ❑ The wound is healing nicely and the patient is healthy. **2** V-T If a weapon or something sharp **wounds** you, it damages your body. ❑ A bomb exploded in a hotel, killing six people and wounding another five. • N-PLURAL **The wounded** are people who are wounded. ❑ Hospitals said they could not cope with the wounded. **3** V-T If you **are wounded** by what someone says or does, your feelings are deeply hurt. ❑ He was deeply wounded by his son's comments.

wound up /waʊnd ʌp/ ADJ If someone is **wound up**, they are very tense and nervous or angry. ❑ "My caddie got so wound up I had to calm him down," Lancaster said.

wove /woʊv/ **Wove** is the past tense of **weave**.

wo|ven /woʊvᵊn/ **Woven** is a past participle of **weave**.

wow /waʊ/ EXCLAM You can say **'wow'** when you are very impressed, surprised, or pleased. [INFORMAL, FEELINGS] ❑ I thought, "Wow, what a good idea!"

wraith /reɪθ/ (wraiths) N-COUNT A **wraith** is a ghost. [LITERARY] ❑ That child flits about like a wraith.

wran|gle /ræŋgᵊl/ (wrangles, wrangling, wrangled) V-RECIP If you say that someone **is wrangling** with someone over a question or issue, you mean that they have been arguing angrily for a long time about it. ❑ The two sides have spent most of their time wrangling over procedural problems.

wran|gler /ræŋglər/ (wranglers) N-COUNT A **wrangler** is a cowboy who works with cattle and horses. [AM]

wrap ◆◇◇ /ræp/ (wraps, wrapping, wrapped) **1** V-T When you **wrap** something, you fold paper or cloth tightly around it to cover it completely, for example, in order to protect it or so that you can give it to someone as a present. ❑ *Harry had carefully bought and wrapped presents for Mark to give the children.* • PHRASAL VERB **Wrap up** means the same as **wrap**. ❑ *Diana is taking the opportunity to wrap up the family presents.* **2** V-T When you **wrap** something such as a piece of paper or cloth around another thing, you put it around it. ❑ *She wrapped a handkerchief around her bleeding palm in an effort to protect it.* **3** → see also **wrapping 4** PHRASE If you keep something **under wraps**, you keep it secret, often until you are ready to announce it at some time in the future. ❑ *The bids were submitted in May and were kept under wraps until October.* **5** → See feature box at **hot**
▶ **wrap up 1** PHRASAL VERB If you **wrap up**, you put warm clothes on. ❑ *She wrapped up in her mother's red shawl.* ❑ *Kids just love being able to romp around in the fresh air without having to wrap up warm.* **2** PHRASAL VERB If you **wrap up** something such as a job or an agreement, you complete it in a satisfactory way. ❑ *NATO defense ministers wrap up their meeting in Brussels today.*
3 → see also **wrap 1, wrapped up**

wrapped up ADJ [v-link ADJ in/with n] If someone is **wrapped up** in a particular person or thing, they spend nearly all their time thinking about them, so that they forget about other things that may be important. ❑ *He's too serious and dedicated, wrapped up in his career.*

wrap|per /ræpər/ (wrappers) N-COUNT A **wrapper** is a piece of paper, plastic, or thin metal that covers and protects something that you buy, especially food. ❑ *I emptied the candy wrappers from the ashtray.*

wrap|ping /ræpɪŋ/ (wrappings) N-VAR **Wrapping** is something such as paper or plastic that is used to cover and protect something. ❑ *Nick asked for the tile to be delivered in waterproof wrapping.*

wrap|ping pa|per (wrapping papers) N-MASS **Wrapping paper** is special paper used for wrapping presents. ❑ *Foil wrapping paper is beautiful but difficult to use.*

wrath /ræθ/ N-UNCOUNT **Wrath** means the same as anger. [LITERARY] ❑ *He incurred the wrath of the authorities in speaking out against government injustices.*

wreak /riːk/ (wreaks, wreaking, wreaked)

> Some people use the form **wrought** as the past tense and past participle of **wreak**, but many people consider this to be wrong.

V-T Something or someone that **wreaks** havoc or destruction causes a great amount of disorder or damage. [LITERARY, JOURNALISM] ❑ *Violent storms wreaked havoc on the French Riviera, leaving three people dead and dozens injured.*

wreath /riːθ/ (wreaths) **1** N-COUNT A **wreath** is an arrangement of flowers and leaves in the shape of a circle, which you put on a grave or by a statue to show that you remember a person who has died or people who have died. ❑ *The coffin lying before the altar was bare, except for a single wreath of white roses.* **2** N-COUNT A **wreath** is a circle of leaves that some people hang somewhere in their house or on the front door as decoration. ❑ *A Christmas wreath exclaiming PEACE ON EARTH hangs on the restaurant door.*

wreathe /riːð/ (wreathes, wreathing, wreathed) **1** V-T If something **is wreathed** in smoke or mist, it is surrounded by it. [LITERARY] ❑ *The ship was wreathed in smoke.* ❑ *Fog wreathes the temples.* **2** V-T [usu passive] If something **is wreathed** with flowers or leaves, it has a circle or chain of flowers or leaves put around it. ❑ *Its huge columns were wreathed with laurel and magnolia.*

wreck /rɛk/ (wrecks, wrecking, wrecked) **1** V-T To **wreck** something means to completely destroy or ruin it. ❑ *He wrecked the garden.* ❑ *His life has been wrecked by the tragedy.* **2** N-COUNT A **wreck** is something such as a ship, car, plane, or building that has been destroyed, usually in an accident. ❑ *...the wreck of a sailing ship.* ❑ *The car was a total wreck.* **3** N-COUNT A **wreck** is an accident in which a moving vehicle hits something and is damaged or destroyed. [mainly AM] ❑ *He was killed in a car wreck.*

in BRIT, usually use **crash**

4 N-COUNT If you say that someone is a **wreck**, you mean that they are very exhausted or unhealthy. [INFORMAL] ❑ *You look a wreck.*

wreck|age /rɛkɪdʒ/ N-UNCOUNT [also the N] When something such as a plane, car, or building has been destroyed, you can refer to what remains as **wreckage** or **the wreckage**. ❑ *Mark was dragged from the burning wreckage of his car just before it exploded.*

wreck|er /rɛkər/ (wreckers) **1** N-COUNT A **wrecker** is a motor vehicle that pulls broken or damaged vehicles to a place where they can be repaired or broken up, for example, after an accident. [mainly AM] **2** N-COUNT **Wreckers** are people whose job involves destroying old, unwanted, or damaged buildings. [mainly AM]

wren /rɛn/ (wrens) N-COUNT A **wren** is a very small brown bird. There are several kinds of wren.

wrench /rɛntʃ/ (wrenches, wrenching, wrenched) **1** V-T If you **wrench** something that is fixed in a particular position, you pull or twist it violently, in order to move or remove it. ❑ *He felt two men wrench the suitcase from his hand.* **2** V-T If you **wrench** yourself free from someone who is holding you, you get away from them by suddenly twisting the part of your body that is being held. ❑ *She wrenched herself from his grasp.* ❑ *He wrenched his arm free.* **3** N-COUNT A **wrench** is a metal tool used for tightening or loosening metal nuts of different sizes. **4** → see also **monkey wrench 5** V-T If you **wrench** your neck, you hurt it by pulling or twisting it in an unusual way. ❑ *She was involved in a car accident and she wrenched her neck.* **6** PHRASE If someone **throws a wrench** or **throws a monkey wrench** into a process, they prevent something happening smoothly by deliberately causing a problem. [AM] ❑ *The decision will throw a monkey wrench into our efforts to develop a national broadband policy.* **7** → See also color supplement

wrest /rɛst/ (wrests, wresting, wrested) **1** V-T If you **wrest** something from someone else, you take it from them, especially when this is difficult or illegal. [LITERARY, JOURNALISM] ❑ *For the past year he has been trying to wrest control from the central government.* ❑ *The men had returned to wrest back power.* **2** V-T If you **wrest** something from someone who is holding it, you take it from them by pulling or twisting it violently. [LITERARY] ❑ *He wrested the suitcase from the chauffeur.* ❑ *He was attacked by a security man who tried to wrest away a gas cartridge.*

wres|tle /rɛsəl/ (wrestles, wrestling, wrestled) **1** V-I When you **wrestle** with a difficult problem, you try to deal with it. ❑ *Delegates wrestled with the problems of violence and sanctions.* **2** V-I If you **wrestle** with someone, you fight them by forcing them into painful positions or throwing them to the ground, rather than by hitting them. Some people wrestle as a sport. ❑ *They taught me to wrestle.* **3** V-T If you **wrestle** a person or thing somewhere, you move them there using a lot of force, for example, by twisting a part of someone's body into a painful position. ❑ *We had to physically wrestle the child from the man's arms.* **4** → see also **wrestling**

wres|tler /rɛslər/ (wrestlers) N-COUNT A **wrestler** is someone who wrestles as a sport.

wres|tling /rɛslɪŋ/ N-UNCOUNT **Wrestling** is a sport in which two people wrestle and try to throw each other to the ground. ❑ *...a championship wrestling match.*

wretch /rɛtʃ/ (wretches) **1** N-COUNT You can refer to someone as a **wretch** when you feel sorry for them because they are unhappy or unfortunate. [LITERARY] ❑ *Before the poor wretch had time to speak, he was shot.* **2** N-COUNT You can refer to someone as a **wretch** when you think that they are wicked or if they have done something you are angry about. [LITERARY, DISAPPROVAL] ❑ *Oh, what have you done, you wretch!*

wretch|ed /rɛtʃɪd/ **1** ADJ [ADJ n] You use **wretched** to describe someone or something that you dislike or feel angry with. [INFORMAL, FEELINGS] ❑ *Wretched woman, he thought, why the hell can't she wait?* **2** ADJ Someone who feels **wretched** feels very unhappy. [FORMAL] ❑ *I feel really confused and wretched.*

wrig|gle /rɪgəl/ (wriggles, wriggling, wriggled) V-T/V-I If you **wriggle** or **wriggle** part of your body, you twist and turn with quick movements, for example, because you are uncomfortable. ❑ *The babies are wriggling on their tummies.*

▶ **wriggle out of** PHRASAL VERB If you say that someone has **wriggled out of** doing something, you disapprove of the fact that they have managed to avoid doing it, although they should have done it. [DISAPPROVAL] ❑ *He's wriggled out of doing the dishes again.*

wring /rɪŋ/ (wrings, wringing, wrung) **1** V-T If you **wring** something out of someone, you manage to make them give it to you even though they do not want to. ❑ *Buyers use different ruses to wring free credit out of their suppliers.* **2** PHRASE If someone **wrings** their **hands**, they hold them together and twist and turn them, usually because they are very worried or upset about something. You can also say that someone is **wringing** their **hands** when they are expressing sorrow that a situation is so bad but are saying that they are unable to change it. ❑ *We can't simply stand by wringing our hands. We have to do something.*

▶ **wring out** PHRASAL VERB When you **wring out** a wet cloth or a wet piece of clothing, you squeeze the water out of it by twisting it strongly. ❑ *He turned away to wring out the wet shirt.*

wring|er /rɪŋər/ PHRASE If you say that someone **has been put through the wringer** or **has gone through the wringer**, you mean that they have suffered a very difficult or unpleasant experience. [INFORMAL]

wrin|kle /rɪŋkəl/ (wrinkles, wrinkling, wrinkled) **1** N-COUNT **Wrinkles** are lines that form on someone's face as they grow old. ❑ *His face was covered with wrinkles.* **2** V-T/V-I When someone's skin **wrinkles** or when something **wrinkles** it, lines start to form in it because the skin is getting old or damaged. ❑ *The skin on her cheeks and around her eyes was beginning to wrinkle.* ● **wrin|kled** ADJ ❑ *I did indeed look older and more wrinkled than ever.* **3** N-COUNT A **wrinkle** is a raised fold in a piece of cloth or paper that spoils its appearance. ❑ *Ben brushed smooth a wrinkle in his pants.* **4** V-T/V-I If cloth **wrinkles**, or if someone or something **wrinkles** it, it gets folds or lines in it. ❑ *Her stockings wrinkled at the ankles.* ● **wrin|kled** ADJ ❑ *His suit was wrinkled and he looked very tired.* **5** V-T/V-I When you **wrinkle** your nose or forehead, or when it **wrinkles**, you tighten the muscles in your face so that the skin folds. ❑ *Donna wrinkled her nose at her daughter.*

wrin|kly /rɪŋkli/ ADJ [usu ADJ n] A **wrinkly** surface has a lot of wrinkles on it. ❑ *...wrinkly cotton and wool stockings.*

wrist /rɪst/ (wrists) N-COUNT Your **wrist** is the part of your body between your hand and your arm that bends when you move your hand. ❑ *He broke his wrist climbing rocks for a cigarette ad.*

wrist|watch /rɪstwɒtʃ/ (wristwatches) N-COUNT A **wristwatch** is a watch with a strap that you wear around your wrist.

writ /rɪt/ (writs) N-COUNT A **writ** is a legal document that orders a person to do a particular thing. ❑ *He issued a writ against one of his accusers.*

write ✦✦✦ /raɪt/ (writes, writing, wrote, written) **1** V-T/V-I When you **write**, you use something such as a pen or pencil to produce words, letters, or numbers. ❑ *Simply write your name and address on a postcard and send it to us.* ❑ *They were still trying to teach her to read and write.* **2** V-T If you **write** something such as a book, a poem, or a piece of music, you create it and record it on paper or perhaps on a computer. ❑ *I had written quite a lot of orchestral music in my student days.* ❑ *Thereafter she wrote articles for papers and magazines in Paris.* **3** V-I Someone who **writes** creates books, stories, or articles, usually for publication. ❑ *Jay wanted to write.* **4** V-T/V-I When you **write** someone or to someone or **write** them a letter, you give them information, ask them something, or express your feelings in a letter. ❑ *Apparently she had written to her aunt in Holland asking for advice.* ❑ *She had written him a note a couple of weeks earlier.* ❑ *I wrote a letter to the car rental agency, explaining what had happened.* **5 nothing to write home about →** see **home** ① **6** V-T When someone **writes** something such as a check, receipt, or prescription, they put the necessary information on it and usually sign it. ❑ *Snape wrote a receipt with a gold fountain pen.* **7** V-I If you **write** to a computer or a disk, you record data on it. [COMPUTING] ❑ *You should write-protect all disks that you do not usually need to write to.* **8 →** see also **writing, written 9 →** See feature box at **accident, research**

▶ **write back** PHRASAL VERB If you **write back** to someone who has sent you a letter, you write them a letter in reply. ❑ *Macmillan wrote back saying that he could certainly help.*

▶ **write down** PHRASAL VERB When you **write** something **down**, you record it on a piece of paper using a pen or pencil. ❑ *On the morning before starting a diet, write down your starting weight.*

▶ **write in** PHRASAL VERB If you **write in** to an organization, you send them a letter. ❑ *What's the point in writing in when you only print half the letter anyway?*

▶ **write into** PHRASAL VERB If a rule or detail **is written into** a contract, law, or agreement, it is included in it when the contract, law, or agreement is made. ❑ *They insisted that a guaranteed supply of Chinese food was written into their contracts.*

▶ **write off 1** PHRASAL VERB If someone **writes off** a debt or an amount of money that has been spent on a project, they accept that they are never going to get the money back. [BUSINESS] ❑ *It was the president who persuaded the West to write off Polish debts.* **2** PHRASAL VERB If you **write** someone or something **off**, you decide that they are unimportant or useless and that they are not worth further serious attention. ❑ *He is fed up with people writing him off because of his age.* ❑ *His critics write him off as too cautious to succeed.* **3** PHRASAL VERB If you **write off** a plan or project, you accept that it is not going to be successful and do not continue with it. ❑ *We decided to write off the rest of the day and go shopping.* **4** PHRASAL VERB If you **write off** something such as a living expense, you deduct it from your taxes. ❑ *Teachers are still entitled to write off business expenses.* **5** PHRASAL VERB If you **write off** to a company or organization, you send them a letter, usually asking for something. [BRIT] **6 →** see also **write-off**

▶ **write out 1** PHRASAL VERB When you **write out** something fairly long such as a report or a list, you write it on paper. ❑ *We had to write out a list of ten jobs we'd like to do.* **2** PHRASAL VERB If a character in a drama series **is written out**, he or she is taken out of the series. ❑ *Terry's character has been written out of the show.*

▶ **write up** PHRASAL VERB If you **write up** something that has been done or said, you record it on paper in a neat and complete form, usually using notes that you have made. ❑ *He wrote up his visit in a report of over 600 pages.*

write-in (write-ins) N-COUNT [also N n] A **write-in** is a vote that you make by writing the candidate's name on the ballot. ❑ *When Republican write-ins were included, Johnson's margin of victory was only 330 votes.*

write-off (write-offs) **1** N-SING If you describe a plan or period of time as a **write-off**, you mean that it has been a failure and you have achieved nothing. [INFORMAL] ❑ *Today was really a write-off for me.* **2** N-COUNT A **write-off** is something, such as a living expense, that can be deducted from your taxes. ❑ *She got a nice $20,000 tax write-off for 2004.*

writ|er ✦✦ /raɪtər/ (writers) **1** N-COUNT A **writer** is a person who writes books, stories, or articles as a job. ❑ *Turner is a writer and critic.* ❑ *...detective stories by American writers.* **2** N-COUNT The **writer** of a particular article, report, letter, or story is the person who wrote it. ❑ *No one is to see the document without the permission of the writer of the report.*

SYNONYMS

writer
NOUN **1**
author: *...Jill Phillips, author of the book 'Give Your Child Music.'*
novelist: *...a romantic novelist.*
columnist: *...the gossip columnists' favorite target.*
hack: *...tabloid hacks, always eager to find victims in order to sell newspapers.*

COLLOCATIONS

writer
NOUN **1**
noun + **writer**: comedy, crime, food, travel; woman
adjective + **writer**: aspiring, prolific; freelance

---

write-up (write-ups) N-COUNT [usu with supp] A **write-up** is an article in a newspaper or magazine, in which someone gives their opinion of something such as a movie, restaurant, or new product. ❑ *The show received a good write-up.* ❑ *The guide book contains a short write-up of each hotel.*

writhe /raɪð/ (writhes, writhing, writhed) V-I If you **writhe**, your body twists and turns violently backward and forward, usually because you are in great pain or discomfort. ❑ *He was writhing in agony.*

writ|ing ✦✧✧ /raɪtɪŋ/ ❶ N-UNCOUNT **Writing** is something that has been written or printed. ❑ *If you have a complaint about your vacation, please inform us in writing.* ❷ N-UNCOUNT You can refer to any piece of written work as **writing**, especially when you are considering the style of language used in it. ❑ *The writing is brutally tough and savagely humorous.* ❸ N-UNCOUNT **Writing** is the activity of writing, especially of writing books for money. ❑ *She had begun to be a little bored with novel writing.* ❹ N-UNCOUNT Your **writing** is the way that you write with a pen or pencil, which can usually be recognized as belonging to you. ❑ *It was a little difficult to read your writing.*

writ|ing desk (writing desks) N-COUNT A **writing desk** is a piece of furniture with drawers, an area for keeping writing materials, and a surface on which you can rest your paper while writing.

writ|ing pa|per (writing papers) N-MASS **Writing paper** is paper for writing letters on. It is usually of good, smooth quality.

writ|ten ✦✧✧ /rɪtᵊn/ ❶ **Written** is the past participle of **write**. ❷ ADJ A **written** test or piece of work is one that involves writing rather than doing something practical or giving spoken answers. ❑ *...knowledge that can be assessed in a short written test.* ❸ ADJ [ADJ n] A **written** agreement, rule, or law has been officially written down. ❑ *The newspaper broke a written agreement not to sell certain photographs.*

writ|ten word N-SING [usu the N] You use **the written word** to refer to language expressed in writing, especially when contrasted with speech or with other forms of expression such as painting or film. ❑ *Even in the 18th century scholars continued to give primacy to the written word.*

wrong ✦✧✧ /rɒŋ/ (wrongs)
→ Please look at meanings ⓭ and ⓮ to see if the expression you are looking for is shown under another headword.
❶ ADJ [v-link ADJ] If you say there is something **wrong**, you mean there is something unsatisfactory about the situation, person, or thing you are talking about. ❑ *Pain is the body's way of telling us that something is wrong.* ❑ *Nobody seemed to notice anything wrong.* ❑ *What's wrong with him?* ❷ ADJ If you choose the **wrong** thing, person, or method, you make a mistake and do not choose the one that you really want. ❑ *He went to the wrong house.* ❑ *The wrong man had been punished.* • ADV [ADV after v] **Wrong** is also an adverb. ❑ *You've done it wrong.* ❸ ADJ [ADJ n] If something such as a decision, choice, or action is the **wrong** one, it is not the best or most suitable one. ❑ *I really made the wrong decision there.* ❑ *The wrong choice of job might limit your chances of success.* ❹ ADJ If something is **wrong**, it is incorrect and not in accordance with the facts. ❑ *How do you know that this explanation is wrong?* ❑ *...a clock which showed the wrong time.* • ADV [ADV after v] **Wrong** is also an adverb. ❑ *I must have added it up wrong, then.* ❑ *It looks like it's spelled wrong.* • **wrong|ly** ADV [ADV with v] ❑ *A child was wrongly diagnosed as having a bone tumor.* ❺ ADJ [v-link ADJ] If something is **wrong** or **goes wrong** with a machine or piece of equipment, it stops working properly. ❑ *We think there's something wrong with the computer.* ❻ ADJ [v-link ADJ] If you are **wrong** about something, what you say or think about it is not correct. ❑ *I was wrong about it being a casual meeting.* ❑ *I'm sure you've got it wrong. Kate isn't like that.* ❼ ADJ [ADJ to-inf] If you think that someone was **wrong** to do something, you think that they should not have done it because it was bad or immoral. ❑ *She was wrong to leave her child alone.* • N-UNCOUNT **Wrong** is also a noun. ❑ *...a man who believes that he has done no wrong.* ❽ ADJ [v link ADJ] **Wrong** is used to refer to activities or actions that are considered to be morally bad and unacceptable.

❑ *Is it wrong to try to save the life of someone you love?* ❑ *We don't consider we did anything wrong.* • N-UNCOUNT **Wrong** is also a noun. ❑ *Johnson didn't seem to be able to tell the difference between right and wrong.* ❾ N-COUNT A **wrong** is an unfair or immoral action. ❑ *No matter how difficult it might be, she had to right the terrible wrong she'd done to him.* ❿ ADJ [ADJ n] You use **wrong** to describe something that is not thought to be socially acceptable or desirable. ❑ *If you went to the wrong school, you won't get the job.* ⓫ PHRASE If a situation **goes wrong**, it stops progressing in the way that you expected or intended, and becomes much worse. ❑ *We should investigate what happened, what went wrong.* ⓬ PHRASE If someone who is involved in an argument or dispute has behaved in a way which is morally or legally wrong, you can say that they are **in the wrong**. ❑ *He didn't press charges because he was in the wrong.* ⓭ **to get off on the wrong foot** → see **foot** ① ⓮ **to get hold of the wrong end of the stick** → see **stick** ①

wrong|doer /rɒŋduər/ (wrongdoers) N-COUNT A **wrongdoer** is a person who does things that are immoral or illegal. [JOURNALISM]

wrong|doing /rɒŋduɪŋ/ (wrongdoings) N-VAR **Wrongdoing** is behavior that is illegal or immoral. ❑ *The city attorney's office hasn't found any evidence of criminal wrongdoing.*

wrong|ful /rɒŋfᵊl/ ADJ A **wrongful** act is one that is illegal, immoral, or unjust. ❑ *He is on hunger strike in protest at what he claims is his wrongful conviction for murder.* • **wrong|ful|ly** ADV [ADV with v] ❑ *The criminal justice system is in need of urgent reform to prevent more people being wrongfully imprisoned.*

wrong|headed /rɒŋhɛdɪd/ ADJ If you describe someone as **wrongheaded**, you mean that although they act in a determined way, their actions and ideas are based on wrong judgments. ❑ *He told them exactly how wrongheaded they were.*

wrote /roʊt/ **Wrote** is the past tense of **write**.

wrought /rɔt/ V-T [only past] If something has **wrought** a change, it has made it happen. [LITERARY, JOURNALISM] ❑ *Nuclear weapons have wrought a revolution in international relations.*

wrought iron also **wrought-iron** N-UNCOUNT **Wrought iron** is a type of iron that is easily formed into shapes and is used especially for making gates, fences, and furniture.

wrung /rʌŋ/ **Wrung** is the past tense and past participle of **wring**.

wry /raɪ/ (wrier or wryer, wriest or wryest) ❶ ADJ If someone has a **wry** expression, it shows that they find a bad situation or a change in a situation slightly amusing. ❑ *Matthew allowed himself a wry smile.* ❷ ADJ A **wry** remark or piece of writing refers to a bad situation or a change in a situation in an amusing way. ❑ *There is a wry sense of humor in his work.*

wt. also **wt** **wt.** is a written abbreviation for **weight**.

WTO /dʌbᵊlyu ti oʊ/ N-PROPER **WTO** is an abbreviation for 'World Trade Organization'. ❑ *The world desperately needs an effective WTO.*

wuss /wʊs/ (wusses) N-COUNT If you call someone a **wuss**, you are criticizing them for being afraid. [INFORMAL, DISAPPROVAL] ❑ *"I confess to being a big wuss," she admitted.*

WWW /dʌbᵊlyu dʌbᵊlyu dʌbᵊlyu/ **WWW** is an abbreviation for **World Wide Web**. It appears at the beginning of website addresses in the form www. [COMPUTING] ❑ *Check our website at www.harpercollins.com.*

WYSIWYG /wɪziwɪg/ **WYSIWYG** is used to refer to a computer screen display that exactly matches the way that a document will appear when it is printed. **WYSIWYG** is an abbreviation for 'what you see is what you get.' [COMPUTING] ❑ *WYSIWYG editing makes your word processing smoother and more flexible.*

Xx

X also **x** /ɛks/ (**X's, x's**) N-VAR **X** is the twenty-fourth letter of the English alphabet.

X chro|mo|some (**X chromosomes**) N-COUNT An **X chromosome** is one of an identical pair of chromosomes found in a woman's cells, or one of a nonidentical pair found in a man's cells. X chromosomes are associated with female characteristics. Compare **Y chromosome**.

xeno|pho|bia /zɛnəfoʊbiə/ N-UNCOUNT **Xenophobia** is strong and unreasonable dislike or fear of people from other countries. [FORMAL] ❑ ...a just and tolerant society which rejects xenophobia and racism.

WORD HISTORY

xenophobia
Xenophobia comes from the Greek words *xenos*, meaning 'stranger,' and *phobos*, meaning 'fear.'

---

xeno|pho|bic /zɛnəfoʊbɪk/ ADJ If you describe someone as **xenophobic**, you disapprove of them because they show strong dislike or fear of people from other countries. [FORMAL, DISAPPROVAL] ❑ *Service in the armed forces gave many Americans a less xenophobic view of the world.*

Xer|ox /zɪərɒks/ (**Xeroxes, Xeroxing, Xeroxed**) ◼ N-COUNT A **Xerox** is a machine that can make copies of pieces of paper which have writing or other marks on them. [TRADEMARK] ❑ *The rooms are crammed with humming Xerox machines.* ◼ N-COUNT A **Xerox** is a copy of something written or printed on a piece of paper, which has been made using a Xerox machine. ❑ *I got a Xerox of the lyrics, handed them out, and then we had the rehearsals.* ◼ V-T If you **Xerox** a document, you make a copy of it using a Xerox machine. ❑ *I should have simply Xeroxed this sheet for you.*

Xmas Xmas is used in informal written English to represent the word Christmas. ❑ *It would be nice to have my Dad home for Xmas.*

X-rated ADJ [usu ADJ n] An **X-rated** movie or video contains sexual scenes that are considered suitable only for adults. ❑ *...the endless bad sex scenes in many X-rated movies.*

X-ray (**X-rays, X-raying, X-rayed**) also **x-ray** ◼ N-COUNT **X-rays** are a type of radiation that can pass through most solid materials. X-rays are used by doctors to examine the bones or organs inside your body and are also used at airports to see inside people's luggage. ◼ N-COUNT An **X-ray** is a picture made by sending X-rays through something, usually someone's body. ❑ *She was advised to have an abdominal X-ray.* ◼ V-T If someone or something **is X-rayed**, an X-ray picture is taken of them. ❑ *All hand baggage would be X-rayed.*

xy|lo|phone /zaɪləfoʊn/ (**xylophones**) N-COUNT [oft the N] A **xylophone** is a musical instrument that consists of a row of wooden bars of different lengths. You play the xylophone by hitting the bars with special hammers.

Yy

Y also **y** /waɪ/ (**Y's, y's**) N-VAR **Y** is the twenty-fifth letter of the English alphabet.

SUFFIX

-y
1 forms adjectives that mean that something is like something else. *For example, if something looks silky, it looks like silk, although it is not actually silk.*
2 also forms adjectives that indicate that something is full of something else or covered in it. *For example, if something is dirty, it is covered with dirt.*

yacht ✦✧ /yɒt/ (**yachts**) **1** N-COUNT A **yacht** is a large boat with sails or a motor, used for racing or pleasure trips. ❏ *His 36 ft yacht sank suddenly last summer.* **2** → See also color supplement

yacht|ing /yɒtɪŋ/ N-UNCOUNT **Yachting** is the sport or activity of sailing a yacht. ❏ *...the joys of yachting.*

yachts|man /yɒtsmən/ (**yachtsmen**) N-COUNT A **yachtsman** is a man who sails a yacht.

yachts|woman /yɒtswʊmən/ (**yachtswomen**) N-COUNT A **yachtswoman** is a woman who sails a yacht.

yad|da /yɑdə/ also **yada** CONVENTION You use **yadda yadda yadda** or **yadda, yadda, yadda** to refer to something that is said or written without giving the actual words, because you think that they are boring or unimportant. [AM, INFORMAL] ❏ *Oh, I know, I know, it's meant to be so tragic – poor woman, trapped in a loveless marriage, yadda yadda yadda.*

ya|hoo (**yahoos**)

Pronounced /yɑhu/ for meaning 1, and /yɑhu/ for meaning 2.

1 EXCLAM People sometimes shout **yahoo!** when they are very happy or excited about something. **2** N-COUNT You can refer to people as **yahoos** when you disapprove of them because they behave in a noisy or stupid way. [INFORMAL, DISAPPROVAL]

yak /yæk/ (**yaks** or **yak**) N-COUNT A **yak** is a type of cattle that has long hair and long horns. Yaks live mainly in the Himalayan mountains and in Tibet.

y'all PRON In the Southern United States, people use **y'all** when addressing a two or more people. **Y'all** is an informal way of saying 'you all.' [AM, INFORMAL] ❏ *This here'll take a minute. Y'all just talk amongst yourselves.*

yam /yæm/ (**yams**) **1** N-VAR A **yam** is a root vegetable like a potato with orange flesh that grows in tropical regions. **2** N-VAR **Yams** are the same as **sweet potatoes**. [AM]

yang /yæŋ/ N-UNCOUNT In Chinese philosophy, **yang** is one of the two opposing principles whose interaction is believed to influence everything in the universe. **Yang** is positive, bright, and masculine while **yin** is negative, dark, and feminine. ❏ *...a perfect balance of yin and yang.* ❏ *Moving from spring to winter, active yang is inevitably followed by dormant yin.*

yank /yæŋk/ (**yanks, yanking, yanked**) V-T/V-I If you **yank** someone or something somewhere, you pull them there suddenly and with a lot of force ❏ *She yanked open the drawer.* ❏ *She couldn't open the door no matter how hard she yanked.* • N-COUNT **Yank** is also a noun. ❏ *Grabbing his ponytail, Shirley gave it a yank.*

Yank (**Yanks**) N-COUNT Some people refer to people from the United States of America as **Yanks**. This use could cause offense. [INFORMAL]

Yan|kee /yæŋki/ (**Yankees**) **1** N-COUNT A **Yankee** is a person from a northern or northeastern state of the United States. [mainly AM] **2** N-COUNT Some speakers of British English refer to anyone from the United States as a **Yankee**. This use could cause offense. [INFORMAL]

yap /yæp/ (**yaps, yapping, yapped**) V-I If a small dog **yaps**, it makes short loud sounds in an excited way. ❏ *The little dog yapped frantically.*

yard ✦✧ /yɑrd/ (**yards**) **1** N-COUNT A **yard** is a unit of length equal to thirty-six inches or approximately 91.4 centimeters. ❏ *The incident took place about 500 yards from where he was standing.* ❏ *...a long narrow strip of linen two or three yards long.* **2** N-COUNT A **yard** is a flat area of concrete or stone that is next to a building and often has a wall around it. ❏ *I saw him standing in the yard.* **3** N-COUNT You can refer to a large open area where a particular type of work is done as a **yard**. ❏ *...a rail yard.* **4** N-COUNT A **yard** is a piece of land next to someone's house, with grass and plants growing in it. [AM] ❏ *He dug a hole in our yard on Edgerton Avenue to plant a maple tree when I was born.*

in BRIT, use **garden**

yard|age /yɑrdɪdʒ/ **1** N-UNCOUNT **Yardage** is a measurement of the length or distance of something, expressed in yards. ❏ *Vijay Singh says the course will not play as long as the yardage indicates.* **2** N-UNCOUNT In a game of football, **yardage** is the number of yards that a team or player manages to move the ball forward toward their opponent's end zone. **Yardage** is measured by lines that cross the field every five yards. ❏ *The Chiefs nearly doubled the Ravens in total yardage and time of possession.*

-yard line (**-yard lines**) N-COUNT [after num] In football, a team's **5-yard line**, or **10-yard line**, and so on, is a line painted across the field and numbered, that marks the distance from the goal line.

yard sale (**yard sales**) N-COUNT A **yard sale** is a sale where people sell things they no longer want from a table outside their house. [AM]

yard|stick /yɑrdstɪk/ (**yardsticks**) N-COUNT If you use someone or something as a **yardstick**, you use them as a standard for comparison when you are judging other people or things. ❏ *The book gives a yardstick for measuring assets.*

yarn /yɑrn/ (**yarns**) N-MASS **Yarn** is thread used for knitting or making cloth. ❏ *She still spins the yarn and knits sweaters for her family.*

yaw /yɔ/ (**yaws, yawing, yawed**) V-I If an aircraft or a ship **yaws**, it turns to one side so that it changes the direction in which it is moving. [TECHNICAL] ❏ *As the plane climbed to 370 feet, it started yawing.* ❏ *He spun the steering-wheel so that we yawed from side to side.*

yawn /yɔn/ (**yawns, yawning, yawned**) V-I If you **yawn**, you open your mouth very wide and breathe in more air than usual, often when you are tired or when you are not interested in something. ❏ *She yawned, and stretched lazily.* • N-COUNT **Yawn** is also a noun. ❏ *Rosanna stifled a huge yawn.*

Y chro|mo|some (**Y chromosomes**) N-COUNT A **Y chromosome** is the chromosome in a man's cells which will produce a male baby if it joins with a female's X chromosome. Y chromosomes are associated with male characteristics. Compare **X chromosome**.

yd. (**yds.**) **yd.** is a written abbreviation for **yard**. ❏ *The entrance is on the left 200 yds. further on up the road.*

ye /yi/ **1** PRON **Ye** is an old-fashioned, poetic, or religious word for **you** when you are talking to more than one person. ▫ *Abandon hope all ye who enter here.* **2** DET **Ye** is sometimes used in imitation of an old written form of the word 'the.' ▫ *...Ye Olde Tea Shoppe.*

yea /yeɪ/ **1** CONVENTION **Yea** is an old-fashioned, poetic, or religious word for 'yes.' **2** CONVENTION **Yea** is sometimes used to mean 'yes' when people are talking about voting for or agreeing to do something. ▫ *The yeas are 52 and the nays are 49; the nomination is hereby confirmed.*

yeah ♦♦♦ /yɛə/ **1** CONVENTION **Yeah** means yes. [INFORMAL, SPOKEN] ▫ *"Bring us something to drink."—"Yeah, yeah."* **2** → see also **yes**

year ♦♦♦ /yɪər/ (**years**) **1** N-COUNT A **year** is a period of twelve months or 365 or 366 days, beginning on the first of January and ending on the thirty-first of December. ▫ *The year was 1840.* ▫ *We had an election last year.* **2** → see also **leap year** **3** N-COUNT A **year** is any period of twelve months. ▫ *The museums attract more than two and a half million visitors a year.* ▫ *She's done quite a bit of work this past year.* **4** N-COUNT **Year** is used to refer to the age of a person. For example, if someone or something is twenty **years** old or twenty **years** of age, they have lived or existed for twenty years. ▫ *He's 58 years old.* ▫ *I've been in trouble since I was eleven years of age.* **5** N-COUNT A school **year** or academic **year** is the period of time in each twelve months when schools or colleges are open and students are studying there. The school year starts in August or September. ▫ *...the 2014/15 academic year.* **6** N-COUNT A financial or business **year** is an exact period of twelve months which businesses or institutions use as a basis for organizing their finances. [BUSINESS] ▫ *He announced big tax increases for the next two financial years.* **7** N-PLURAL You can use **years** to emphasize that you are referring to a long time. [EMPHASIS] ▫ *I haven't laughed so much in years.* **8** → see also **calendar year, fiscal year** **9** PHRASE If something happens **year after year**, it happens regularly every year. ▫ *Regulars return year after year.* **10** PHRASE If something changes **year by year**, it changes gradually each year. ▫ *This problem has increased year by year.* **11** PHRASE If you say something happens **all year round** or **all the year round**, it happens continually throughout the year. ▫ *Town gardens are ideal because they produce flowers nearly all year round.*

USAGE

year
When you use **year** to talk about age, you must use **old** after it. Don't say, for example, ~~'She is now seventy-four years.'~~ Say 'She is now **seventy-four years old**.'

---

year|book /yɪərbʊk/ (**yearbooks**) N-COUNT A **yearbook** is a book that is published once a year and that contains information about the events and achievements of the previous year, usually concerning a particular place or organization. ▫ *...a college yearbook for 1955.*

year|ling /yɪərlɪŋ/ (**yearlings**) N-COUNT A **yearling** is a racehorse or a deer that is one year old. ▫ *The horse sold for $20,000 as a yearling.*

year-long ADJ [ADJ n] **Year-long** is used to describe something that lasts for a year. ▫ *She is taking a year-long course in English.*

year|ly /yɪərli/ **1** ADJ [ADJ n] A **yearly** event happens once a year or every year. ▫ *The two sisters looked forward to their yearly meetings.* ● ADV [ADV after v] **Yearly** is also an adverb. ▫ *Clients normally pay fees in advance, monthly, quarterly, or yearly.* **2** ADJ [ADJ n] You use **yearly** to describe something such as an amount that relates to a period of one year. ▫ *In Holland, the government sets a yearly budget for health care.* ● ADV [ADV after v] **Yearly** is also an adverb. ▫ *Novello says college students will spend $4.2 billion yearly on alcoholic beverages.*

yearn /yɜrn/ (**yearns, yearning, yearned**) V-T/V-I If someone **yearns** for something that they are unlikely to get, they want it very much. ▫ *He yearned for freedom.* ▫ *I yearned to be an actor.*

yearn|ing /yɜrnɪŋ/ (**yearnings**) N-VAR [oft N for n, N to-inf] A **yearning** for something is a very strong desire for it. ▫ *He spoke of his yearning for another child.* ▫ *He always had a yearning to be a schoolteacher.*

-year-old /-yɪər-oʊld/ (**-year-olds**) COMB IN ADJ [ADJ n] **-year-old** combines with numbers to describe the age of people or things. ▫ *She has a six-year-old daughter.* ● COMB IN N-COUNT **-year-old** also combines to form nouns. ▫ *Snow Puppies is a ski school for 3- to 6-year-olds.*

year-round ADJ [ADJ n] **Year-round** is used to describe something that happens, exists, or is done throughout the year. ▫ *Cuba has a tropical climate with year-round sunshine.* ● ADV [ADV with cl] **Year-round** is also an adverb. ▫ *They work 7 days a week year-round.*

yeast /yist/ N-MASS **Yeast** is a kind of fungus which is used to make bread rise, and in making alcoholic drinks such as beer.

yeasty /yisti/ (**yeastier, yeastiest**) ADJ Something that is **yeasty** tastes or smells strongly of yeast.

yell /yɛl/ (**yells, yelling, yelled**) **1** V-T/V-I If you **yell**, you shout loudly, usually because you are excited, angry, or in pain. ▫ *"Eva!" he yelled.* ▫ *I'm sorry I yelled at you last night.* ● PHRASAL VERB **Yell out** means the same as **yell**. ▫ *"Are you coming or not?" they yelled out after him.* **2** N-COUNT A **yell** is a loud shout given by someone who is afraid or in pain. ▫ *Something brushed past Bob's face and he let out a yell.*

yel|low ♦♦♦ /yɛloʊ/ (**yellows**) COLOR Something that is **yellow** is the color of lemons, butter, or the middle part of an egg. ▫ *The walls have been painted bright yellow.*

yel|low card (**yellow cards**) N-COUNT In soccer, if a player is shown the **yellow card**, the referee holds up a yellow card to indicate that the player has broken the rules, and that if they do so again, they will be ordered to leave the field. ▫ *The striker was then shown a yellow card for dissent.*

yel|low fe|ver N-UNCOUNT **Yellow fever** is a serious infectious disease that people can catch in tropical countries.

yel|low|ish /yɛloʊɪʃ/ ADJ Something that is **yellowish** is slightly yellow in color. ▫ *...a small yellowish cauliflower.*

Yel|low Pages N-UNCOUNT [also a N] **Yellow Pages** is a book that contains advertisements and telephone numbers for businesses and organizations in a particular area, grouped according to the type of business they do. Compare **White Pages**. [TRADEMARK]

yel|lowy /yɛloʊi/ ADJ Something that is **yellowy** is slightly yellow in color. ● COMB IN COLOR **Yellowy** is also a combining form. ▫ *...black ink, fading now to a yellowy brown.*

yelp /yɛlp/ (**yelps, yelping, yelped**) V-I If a person or dog **yelps**, they give a sudden short cry, often because of fear or pain. ▫ *Her dog yelped and came to heel.* ● N-COUNT [oft N of n] **Yelp** is also a noun. ▫ *I had to bite back a yelp of surprise.*

Yem|eni /yɛməni/ (**Yemenis**) **1** ADJ **Yemeni** means belonging or relating to Yemen, or to its people or culture. **2** N-COUNT A **Yemeni** is a Yemeni citizen, or a person of Yemeni origin.

yen ♦◊◊ /yɛn/ (**yen**)

Yen is both the singular and the plural form.

N-COUNT The **yen** is the unit of currency used in Japan. ▫ *She's got a part-time job for which she earns 2,000 yen a month.* ● N-SING The **yen** is also used to refer to the Japanese currency system. ▫ *...sterling's devaluation against the dollar and the yen.*

yeo|man /yoʊmən/ (**yeomen**) N-COUNT In former times, a **yeoman** was a man who was free and not a servant, and who owned and worked on his own land.

yep /yɛp/ CONVENTION **Yep** means yes. [INFORMAL, SPOKEN] ▫ *"Did you like it?"—"Yep."*

yes ♦♦♦ /yɛs/

In informal English, **yes** is often pronounced in a casual way that is usually written as **yeah**.

1 CONVENTION You use **yes** to give a positive response to a question. ▫ *"Are you a friend of Nick's?"—"Yes."* ▫ *"You actually wrote it down, didn't you?"—"Yes."* **2** CONVENTION You use **yes** to accept an offer or request, or to give permission. ▫ *"More wine?"—"Yes please."* ▫ *"Will you take me there?"—"Yes, I will."* **3** CONVENTION You use **yes** to tell someone that what they have said is correct. ▫ *"Well, I suppose it is based on the old lunar months, isn't it?"—"Yes, that's right."* **4** CONVENTION You use **yes** to show that you are ready or willing to speak to the person who wants to speak to you, for example when you are answering a telephone or a knock at your door. ▫ *He pushed a button on the intercom. "Yes?" came a voice.* **5** CONVENTION You use **yes** to indicate that you agree with, accept, or understand what the previous speaker has said. ◻ *"A lot of people find it very difficult indeed to give up smoking."—"Oh yes. I used to smoke three packs a day."* ◨ CONVENTION You use **yes** to encourage someone to continue speaking. ◻ *"I remembered something funny today."—"Yes?"* ◨ CONVENTION You use **yes**, usually followed by 'but,' as a polite way of introducing what you want to say when you disagree with something the previous speaker has just said. [POLITENESS] ◻ *"She is entitled to her personal allowance, which is three thousand dollars of income."—"Yes, but she doesn't earn any money."* ◨ CONVENTION You use **yes** to say that a negative statement or question that the previous speaker has made is wrong or untrue. ◻ *"That is not possible," she said.—"Oh, yes, it is!" Mrs. Gruen insisted.* ◨ CONVENTION You can use **yes** to suggest that you do not believe or agree with what the previous speaker has said, especially when you want to express your annoyance about it. [FEELINGS] ◻ *"There was no way to stop it."—"Oh yeah? Well, here's something else you won't be able to stop."* ◨ CONVENTION You use **yes** to indicate that you had forgotten something and have just remembered it. ◻ *What was I going to say? Oh yeah, we've finally got our second computer.* ◨ CONVENTION You use **yes** to emphasize and confirm a statement that you are making. [EMPHASIS] ◻ *He collected the $10,000 first prize. Yes, $10,000.* ◨ CONVENTION You say **yes and no** in reply to a question when you cannot give a definite answer, because in some ways the answer is yes and in other ways the answer is no. [VAGUENESS] ◻ *"Was it strange for you, going back after such a long absence?"—"Yes and no."*

USAGE

yes

◨ Don't say 'yes' if you want to agree with a negative question. For example, if someone says 'Aren't you going out this evening?,' say '**No**, I'm not.' Don't say '~~Yes, I'm not.~~' *'Didn't you get a dictionary from him?' - '**No**, I didn't.'*
◨ Similarly, don't say 'yes' if you want to agree with a negative statement. For example, if someone says 'He doesn't want to come,' say '**No**, he doesn't.' Don't say '~~Yes, he doesn't.~~' *'That isn't true.' - '**No**, it isn't.'*

yes-man (yes-men) N-COUNT If you describe a man as a **yes-man**, you dislike the fact that he seems always to agree with people who have authority over him, in order to gain favor. [DISAPPROVAL]

yes|ter|day ✦✦✦ /yɛstərdeɪ, -di/ (**yesterdays**) ◨ ADV [ADV with cl] You use **yesterday** to refer to the day before today. ◻ *She left yesterday.* • N-UNCOUNT **Yesterday** is also a noun. ◻ *In yesterday's games, Switzerland beat the United States two to one.* ◨ N-UNCOUNT [also N in pl] You can refer to the past, especially the recent past, as **yesterday**. ◻ *The worker of today is different from the worker of yesterday.*

yes|ter|year /yɛstəryɪər/ N-UNCOUNT You use **yesteryear** to refer to the past, often a period in the past with a set of values or a way of life that no longer exists. [LITERARY] ◻ *The modern-day sex symbol has now taken the place of the old-fashioned hero of yesteryear.*

yes-woman (yes-women) N-COUNT If you describe a woman as a **yes-woman**, you dislike the fact that she seems always to agree with people who have authority over her, in order to gain favor. [DISAPPROVAL]

yet ✦✦✦ /yɛt/ ◨ ADV You use **yet** in negative statements to indicate that something has not happened up to the present time, although it probably will happen. You can also use **yet** in questions to ask if something has happened up to the present time. ◻ *They haven't finished yet.* ◻ *No decision has yet been made.* ◻ *She hasn't yet set a date for her marriage.* ◨ ADV You use **yet** with a negative statement when you are talking about the past, to report something that was not the case then, although it became the case later. ◻ *There was so much that Sam didn't know yet.* ◨ ADV [with brd-neg, ADV with v] If you say that something should not or cannot be done **yet**, you mean that it should not or cannot be done now, although it will have to be done at a later time. ◻ *Don't get up yet.* ◻ *The hostages cannot go home just yet.* ◨ ADV You use **yet** after a superlative to indicate, for example, that something is the worst or the best of its kind up to the present time. ◻ *This is the network's worst idea yet.* ◻ *Her latest novel is her best yet.* ◨ ADV [ADV before v] You use **yet** to say that there is still a possibility that something will happen. ◻ *Like the best stories, this one may yet have a happy ending.* ◨ ADV [N ADV] You can use **yet** after expressions that refer to a period of time, when you want to say how much longer a situation will continue for. ◻ *Unemployment will go on rising for some time yet.* ◻ *Nothing will happen for a few years yet.* ◨ ADV [ADV to-inf] If you say that you have **yet** to do something, you mean that you have never done it, especially when this is surprising or bad. ◻ *She has yet to spend a Christmas with her husband.* ◨ CONJ You can use **yet** to introduce a fact that is rather surprising after the previous fact you have just mentioned. ◻ *I don't eat much, yet I am a size 16.* ◨ ADV You can use **yet** to emphasize a word, especially when you are saying that something is surprising because it is more extreme than previous things of its kind, or a further case of them. [EMPHASIS] ◻ *I saw yet another doctor.* ◻ *They would criticize me, or worse yet, pay me no attention.* ◨ PHRASE You use **as yet** with negative statements to describe a situation that has existed up until the present time. [FORMAL] ◻ *As yet it is not known whether the crash was the result of an accident.*

yew /yu/ (**yews**) N-VAR A **yew** or a **yew tree** is an evergreen tree. It has sharp flat needles and red berries. • N-UNCOUNT **Yew** is the wood of this tree.

Yid|dish /yɪdɪʃ/ N-UNCOUNT **Yiddish** is a language which comes mainly from German and is spoken by many Jewish people of European origin.

yield ✦◇◇ /yild/ (**yields, yielding, yielded**) ◨ V-I If you **yield** to someone or something, you stop resisting them. [FORMAL] ◻ *Carmen yielded to general pressure and grudgingly took the child to a specialist.* ◨ V-T If you **yield** something that you have control of or responsibility for, you allow someone else to have control or responsibility for it. [FORMAL] ◻ *He may yield control.* ◨ V-I If a moving person or a vehicle **yields**, they slow down in order to allow other people or vehicles to pass in front of them. [AM] ◻ *When entering a trail or starting a descent, yield to other skiers.* ◻ *...examples of common signs like No Smoking and Yield.* ◨ V-I If something **yields**, it breaks or moves position because force or pressure has been put on it. ◻ *He reached the massive door of the barn and pushed. It yielded.* ◨ V-T If an area of land **yields** a particular amount of a crop, this is the amount that is produced. You can also say that a number of animals **yield** a particular amount of meat. ◻ *Last year 400,000 acres of land yielded a crop worth $1.75 billion.* ◨ N-COUNT A **yield** is the amount of food produced on an area of land or by a number of animals. ◻ *...improving the yield of the crop.* ◨ V-T If a tax or investment **yields** an amount of money or profit, this money or profit is obtained from it. [BUSINESS] ◻ *It yielded a profit of at least $36 million.* ◨ N-COUNT A **yield** is the amount of money or profit produced by an investment. [BUSINESS] ◻ *...a yield of 4%.* ◻ *The high yields available on the dividend shares made them attractive to private investors.* ◨ V-T If something **yields** a result or piece of information, it produces it. ◻ *This research has been in progress since 1961 and has yielded a great number of positive results.*

COLLOCATIONS

yield
NOUN
◨
noun + **yield**: crop, grain, milk
adjective + **yield**: good, poor
verb + **yield**: boost, increase, produce
◨
noun + **yield**: bond, dividend, gilt
adjective + **yield**: attractive, high, low; average, gross, net, prospective

SYNONYMS

yield
VERB
◨
give in: *Officials say they won't give in to the workers' demands.*
submit: *If I submitted to their demands, they would not press the allegations.*
surrender: *General Martin Bonnet called on the rebels to surrender.*
succumb: *Don't succumb to the temptation.*
◨
relinquish: *He does not intend to relinquish power.*
hand over: *They handed over their financial affairs to another body.*
surrender: *Nadja had to surrender all rights to her property.*
cede: *The General had promised to cede power by January.*

yield|ing /yildɪŋ/ ADJ A **yielding** surface or object is quite soft and will move or bend rather than staying stiff if you put pressure on it. ❏ ...*the yielding ground.* ❏ ...*the soft yielding cushions.*

yin /yɪn/ also **ying** /yɪŋ/ N-UNCOUNT In Chinese philosophy, **yin** is one of the two opposing principles whose interaction is believed to influence everything in the universe. **Yin** is negative, dark, and feminine, while **yang** is positive, bright, and masculine. ❏ ...*a perfect balance of yin and yang.* ❏ ...*a silver chain with a ying-yang symbol.*

yip /yɪp/ (**yips, yipping, yipped**) V-I If a dog or other animal **yips**, it gives a sudden short cry, often because of fear or pain. [mainly AM] ❏ *Far up the west rim of the canyon, a coyote yipped twice.* • N-COUNT [oft N of n] **Yip** is also a noun. ❏ ...*a yip of pain.*

yip|pee /yɪpi/ EXCLAM People sometimes shout **yippee** when they are very pleased or excited.

YMCA /waɪ ɛm si eɪ/ (**YMCAs**) N-COUNT [usu the N in sing] The **YMCA** is a place where people can play sports, take classes, or stay cheaply. It is run by the YMCA organization. **YMCA** is an abbreviation for 'Young Men's Christian Association.'

yo /yoʊ/ CONVENTION People sometimes say **yo** to greet other people or to get their attention. [INFORMAL, SPOKEN] ❏ *Yo, Carl, great outfit man!*

yo|del /yoʊdᵊl/ (**yodels, yodeling** or **yodelling, yodeled** or **yodelled**) V-I When someone **yodels**, they sing normal notes with very high quick notes in between. ❏ *You haven't lived till you've learned how to yodel at a tea dance in a mountain hut!* • **yo|del|ing** N-UNCOUNT ❏ *Switzerland isn't all cow bells and yodeling, you know.*

yoga /yoʊgə/ N-UNCOUNT **Yoga** is a type of exercise in which you move your body into various positions in order to become more fit or flexible, to improve your breathing, and to relax your mind. ❏ *I do yoga twice a week.*

yo|ghurt /yoʊgərt/ → see yogurt

yogi /yoʊgi/ (**yogis**) N-COUNT A **yogi** is a person who has spent many years practicing the philosophy of yoga, and is considered to have reached an advanced spiritual state.

yo|gurt /yoʊgərt/ (**yogurts**) also **yoghurt** N-VAR **Yogurt** is a food in the form of a thick, slightly sour liquid that is made by adding bacteria to milk. A **yogurt** is a small container of yogurt.

yoke /yoʊk/ (**yokes, yoking, yoked**) ◼ N-SING [usu N of n, adj N] If you say that people are under the **yoke** of a bad thing or person, you mean they are forced to live in a difficult or unhappy state because of that thing or person. [LITERARY] ❏ *People are still suffering under the yoke of slavery.* ◼ N-COUNT A **yoke** is a long piece of wood tied across the necks of two animals such as oxen, in order to make them walk close together when they are pulling a plow. ◼ V-T If two or more people or things **are yoked** together, they are forced to be closely linked with each other. ❏ *The introduction attempts to yoke the pieces together.* ❏ *The Auto Pact yoked Ontario into the United States economy.* ❏ *Farmers and politicians are yoked by money and votes.*

yo|kel /yoʊkᵊl/ (**yokels**) N-COUNT If you refer to someone as a **yokel**, you think they are uneducated and stupid because they come from the countryside. [DISAPPROVAL]

yolk /yoʊk/ (**yolks**) N-VAR The **yolk** of an egg is the yellow part in the middle. ❏ *Only the yolk contains cholesterol.*

YOLO /yoʊloʊ/ **YOLO** is the written and sometimes spoken abbreviation for 'you only live once,' used to say that people should do exciting things and enjoy life. [INFORMAL]

Yom Kip|pur /yɒm kɪpʊər/ N-UNCOUNT **Yom Kippur** is the religious holiday when Jewish people do not eat, but say prayers asking to be forgiven for the things they have done wrong. It is in September or October.

yon /yɒn/ ◼ DET **Yon** is an old-fashioned or dialect word for 'that' or 'those.' ❏ *Don't let yon dog nod off.* ◼ **hither and yon** → see **hither**

yon|der /yɒndər/ ADV [ADV with v] **Yonder** is an old-fashioned or dialect word for 'over there.' ❏ *Now look yonder, just beyond the wooden post there.*

yore /yɔr/ PHRASE [n PHR, than PHR] **Of yore** is used to refer to a period of time in the past. [LITERARY, JOURNALISM] ❏ *The images provoked strong surges of nostalgia for the days of yore.*

York|shire pud|ding /yɔrkʃər pʊdɪŋ/ (**Yorkshire puddings**) N-VAR **Yorkshire pudding** is a British food made by baking a thick liquid mixture of flour, milk, and eggs. It is often eaten with roast beef.

you ♦♦♦ /yu/

> **You** is the second person pronoun. **You** can refer to one or more people and is used as the subject of a verb or the object of a verb or preposition.

◼ PRON A speaker or writer uses **you** to refer to the person or people that they are talking or writing to. It is possible to use **you** before a noun to make it clear which group of people you are talking to. ❏ *When I saw you across the room I knew I'd met you before.* ❏ *You two seem very different to me.* ◼ PRON In spoken English and informal written English, **you** is sometimes used to refer to people in general. ❏ *Getting good results gives you confidence.* ❏ *In those days you did what you were told.*

you'd /yud/ ◼ **You'd** is the usual spoken form of 'you had,' when 'had' is an auxiliary verb. ❏ *I think you'd better tell us why you're asking these questions.* ◼ **You'd** is the usual spoken form of 'you would.' ❏ *With your hair and your beautiful skin, you'd look good in red and amber bright colors.*

you'll /yul/ **You'll** is the usual spoken form of 'you will.' ❏ *Promise me you'll take very special care of yourself.*

young ♦♦♦ /yʌŋ/ (**younger** /yʌŋgər/, **youngest** /yʌŋgɪst/) ◼ ADJ A **young** person, animal, or plant has not lived or existed for very long and is not yet mature. ❏ ...*sex information written for young people.* ❏ *I crossed the hill, and found myself in a field of young barley.* • N-PLURAL **The young** are people who are young. ❏ *The association is advising pregnant women, the very young and the elderly to avoid such foods.* ◼ ADJ [ADJ n] You use **young** to describe a time when a person or thing was young. ❏ *In her younger days my mother had been a successful saleswoman.* ◼ ADJ Someone who is **young** in appearance or behavior looks or behaves as if they are young. ❏ *I was twenty-three, I suppose, and young for my age.* ◼ N-PLURAL The **young** of an animal are its babies. ❏ *The hen may not be able to feed its young.*

young gun (**young guns**) N-COUNT [oft plural] You can use **young guns** to talk about people, especially young men, who have lots of energy and talent, and are becoming very successful. [JOURNALISM] ❏ *He may have been eclipsed by the young guns, but his films are still very popular.*

young|ish /yʌŋɪʃ/ ADJ A **youngish** person is fairly young. ❏ ...*a smart, dark-haired, youngish man.*

young|ster ♦◇◇ /yʌŋstər/ (**youngsters**) N-COUNT Young people, especially children, are sometimes referred to as **youngsters**. ❏ *Other youngsters are not so lucky.*

SYNONYMS

youngster
NOUN
adolescent: *Young adolescents are happiest with small groups of close friends.*
youth: ...*gangs of youths who broke windows and looted shops.*
teenager: *As a teenager, he attended Tulse Hill Senior High School.*
juvenile: *The number of juveniles in the general population has fallen.*

---

your ♦♦♦ /yɔr, yʊər/

> **Your** is the second person possessive determiner. **Your** can refer to one or more people.

◼ DET A speaker or writer uses **your** to indicate that something belongs or relates to the person or people that they are talking or writing to. ❏ *Emma, I trust your opinion a great deal.* ❏ *I left all of your messages on your desk.* ◼ DET In spoken English and informal written English, **your** is sometimes used to indicate that something belongs to or relates to people in general. ❏ *Painkillers are very useful in small amounts to bring your temperature down.* ◼ DET In spoken English, a speaker sometimes uses **your** before an adjective such as 'typical' or 'normal' to indicate that the thing referred to is a typical example of its type. ❏ *This isn't your typical economics class.*

you're /yɔr, yʊər/ **You're** is the usual spoken form of 'you are.' ❏ *Go to him, tell him you're sorry.*

yours ✦✧ /yɔrz, yʊərz/

Yours is the second person possessive pronoun. Yours can refer to one or more people.

1 PRON-POSS A speaker or writer uses **yours** to refer to something that belongs or relates to the person or people that they are talking or writing to. ❑ *I'll take my coat upstairs. Shall I take yours, Roberta?* ❑ *I believe Paul was a friend of yours.*
2 CONVENTION People write **yours**, **yours sincerely**, **sincerely yours**, or **yours truly** at the end of a letter before they sign their name. ❑ *With best regards, Yours, George.*

your|self ✦✦✧ /yɔrsɛlf, yʊər-/ (**yourselves**)

Yourself is the second person reflexive pronoun.

1 PRON-REFL [V PRON, prep PRON] A speaker or writer uses **yourself** to refer to the person that they are talking or writing to. **Yourself** is used when the object of a verb or preposition refers to the same person as the subject of the verb. ❑ *Have the courage to be honest with yourself and about yourself.* ❑ *Your baby depends on you to look after yourself properly while you are pregnant.*
2 PRON-REFL-EMPH You use **yourself** to emphasize the person that you are referring to. [EMPHASIS] ❑ *You can't convince others if you yourself aren't convinced.* **3** PRON-REFL-EMPH [V PRON, prep PRON] You use **yourself** instead of 'you' for emphasis or in order to be more polite when 'you' is the object of a verb or preposition. [POLITENESS] ❑ *A wealthy man like yourself is bound to make an enemy or two along the way.* **4** **by yourself** → see **by** ①

youth ✦✦✧ /yuθ/ (**youths** /yuðz/) **1** N-UNCOUNT Someone's **youth** is the period of their life during which they are a child, before they are a fully mature adult. ❑ *In my youth my ambition had been to be an inventor.* **2** N-UNCOUNT **Youth** is the quality or state of being young. ❑ *The team is now a good mixture of experience and youth.* **3** N-COUNT Journalists often refer to young men as **youths**, especially when they are reporting that the young men have caused trouble. ❑ *A 17-year-old youth was arrested yesterday.* **4** N-PLURAL The **youth** are young people considered as a group. ❑ *He represents the opinions of the youth of today.*

youth|ful /yuθfəl/ ADJ Someone who is **youthful** behaves as if they are young or younger than they really are. ❑ *I'm a very youthful 50.* ❑ *...youthful enthusiasm and high spirits.*

youth hos|tel (**youth hostels**) N-COUNT A **youth hostel** is a place where people can stay cheaply when they are traveling.

you've /yuv/ **You've** is the usual spoken form of 'you have,' when 'have' is an auxiliary verb. ❑ *You've got to see it to believe it.*

yowl /yaʊl/ (**yowls, yowling, yowled**) V-I If a person or an animal **yowls**, they make a long loud cry, especially because they are sad or in pain. ❑ *The dog began to yowl.* • N-COUNT **Yowl** is also a noun. ❑ *Patsy could hardly be heard above the baby's yowls.* • **yowl|ing** N-UNCOUNT ❑ *I couldn't stand that yowling.*

yo-yo (**yo-yos**) N-COUNT A **yo-yo** is a toy made of a round piece of wood or plastic attached to a piece of string. You play with the yo-yo by letting it rise and fall on the string. ❑ *...a competition to find the boy or girl who could do the most tricks with a yo-yo.*

yr. (**yrs.**) **yr.** is a written abbreviation for **year**. ❑ *Their imaginations are quite something for 2 yr. olds.*

yuan /yuɑn/ (**yuan**) N-COUNT The **yuan** is the unit of money used in the People's Republic of China. ❑ *For most events, tickets cost one, two or three yuan.* • N-SING [the N] **The yuan** is also used to refer to the Chinese currency system. ❑ *The yuan recovered a little and closed up against the dollar.*

yuck /yʌk/ also **yuk** EXCLAM Some people say '**yuck**' when they think something is very unpleasant or disgusting. [INFORMAL] ❑ *"It's corned beef and cabbage," said Malone. "Yuck," said Maureen.*

yucky /yʌki/ (**yuckier, yuckiest**) ADJ If you describe a food or other substance as **yucky**, you mean that it disgusts you. [INFORMAL, DISAPPROVAL] ❑ *She says it tastes yucky, so nurses add sweetener to make it go down easier.* ❑ *...yucky cigar smoke.*

Yu|go|slav /yugəslɑv/ (**Yugoslavs**) ADJ **Yugoslav** means belonging or relating to the former Yugoslavia, or to its people or culture. • N-COUNT A **Yugoslav** was a Yugoslav citizen, or a person of Yugoslav origin.

Yu|go|sla|vian /yugəslɑviən/ ADJ **Yugoslavian** means the same as **Yugoslav**.

Yule /yul/ N-UNCOUNT **Yule** is an old-fashioned word for Christmas.

Yule|tide /yultaɪd/ N-UNCOUNT [oft N n] **Yuletide** is the period of several days around and including Christmas Day. ❑ *...ideas for Yuletide food, drink and decorations.*

yum /yʌm/ EXCLAM People sometimes say '**yum**' or '**yum yum**' to show that they think something tastes or smells very good. [INFORMAL]

yum|my /yʌmi/ (**yummier, yummiest**) ADJ **Yummy** food tastes very good. [INFORMAL] ❑ *I'll bet they have yummy ice cream.* ❑ *It smells yummy.*

yup|pie /yʌpi/ (**yuppies**) N-COUNT **Yuppie** is a term that was used to describe a young person who had a well-paid job and liked to show that they had a lot of money by buying expensive things and living in an expensive way. [DISAPPROVAL] ❑ *The Porsche 911 reminds me of the worst parts of the yuppie era.*

YWCA /waɪ dʌbᵊlyu si eɪ/ (**YWCAs**) N-COUNT [usu the N in sing] The **YWCA** is a service organization for women. **YWCA** is an abbreviation for 'Young Women's Christian Association.'

Zz

Z also **z** /ziː/ (**Z's, z's**) N-VAR Z is the twenty-sixth and last letter of the English alphabet.

zany /zeɪni/ (**zanier, zaniest**) ADJ [usu ADJ n] Zany humor or a zany person is strange or eccentric in an amusing way. [INFORMAL] ❑ ...the zany humor of the Marx Brothers.

zap /zæp/ (**zaps, zapping, zapped**) ◼ V-T To zap someone or something means to kill, destroy, or hit them, for example, with a gun or in a computer game. [INFORMAL] ❑ A guard zapped him with the stun gun. ◼ V-T To zap something such as a computer file or document means to delete it from the computer memory or to clear it from the screen. [INFORMAL, COMPUTING] ❑ Most IT companies zap millions of spam mails a day from their servers

zap|per /zæpər/ (**zappers**) N-COUNT A zapper is a small device that you use to control a television, video, or stereo from a distance. [INFORMAL]

zeal /ziːl/ N-UNCOUNT Zeal is great enthusiasm, especially in connection with work, religion, or politics. ❑ ...his zeal for teaching.

zeal|ot /zɛlət/ (**zealots**) N-COUNT If you describe someone as a zealot, you think that their views and actions are very extreme, especially in following a particular political or religious belief. [DISAPPROVAL] ❑ He was forceful, but by no means a zealot.

zeal|ous /zɛləs/ ADJ Someone who is zealous spends a lot of time or energy in supporting something that they believe in very strongly, especially a political or religious ideal. ❑ She was a zealous worker for charity.

zeb|ra /ziːbrə/ (**zebras** or **zebra**) N-COUNT A zebra is an African wild horse that has black and white stripes.

zeit|geist /tsaɪtgaɪst, zaɪt-/ N-SING The zeitgeist of a particular place during a particular period in history is the attitudes and ideas that are generally common there at that time, especially the attitudes and ideas shown in literature, philosophy, and politics. ❑ He has caught the zeitgeist of life in the 1960s very well indeed.

Zen /zɛn/ N-UNCOUNT Zen or Zen Buddhism is a form of the Buddhist religion that concentrates on meditation rather than on studying religious writings.

zen|ith /ziːnɪθ/ N-SING The zenith of something is the time when it is most successful or powerful. ❑ His career is now at its zenith.

zeph|yr /zɛfər/ (**zephyrs**) N-COUNT A zephyr is a gentle breeze. [LITERARY] ❑ There was silence now except for the distant sea, a slight zephyr stirring the trees.

zero /zɪəroʊ/ (**zeros** or **zeroes**) ◼ NUM Zero is the number 0. ❑ Visibility at the city's airport came down to zero, bringing air traffic to a standstill. ◼ N-UNCOUNT Zero is a temperature of 0°. It is freezing point on the centigrade and Celsius scales, and 32° below freezing point on the Fahrenheit scale. ❑ It's a sunny late winter day, just a few degrees above zero. ◼ ADJ You can use zero to say that there is none at all of the thing mentioned. ❑ This new ministry was being created with zero assets and zero liabilities.

SYNONYMS

zero
NOUN ◼
naught: Sales rose by naught point four per cent last month.
nothing: Homes in this corner of Mantua that once went for $350,000 are now worth nothing.
nil: His chance of winning is nil.

zero-emission ADJ [ADJ n] A zero-emission vehicle does not produce any dangerous gases. ❑ ...zero-emission electric cars.

zero-sum game N-SING If you refer to a situation as a zero-sum game, you mean that if one person gains an advantage from it, someone else involved must suffer an equivalent disadvantage. ❑ They believe they're playing a zero-sum game, where both must compete for the same resources.

zero tol|er|ance ◼ N-UNCOUNT If a government or organization has a policy of zero tolerance of a particular type of behavior or activity, they will not tolerate it at all. ❑ They have a policy of zero tolerance for sexual harassment. ◼ → See feature box at urban

zest /zɛst/ ◼ N-UNCOUNT [also a N, oft N for n] Zest is a feeling of pleasure and enthusiasm. ❑ He has a zest for life and a quick intellect. ◼ N-UNCOUNT Zest is a quality in an activity or situation which you find exciting. ❑ Live interviews add zest and a touch of the unexpected to any piece of research.

zig|zag /zɪgzæg/ (**zigzags, zigzagging, zigzagged**) also **zig-zag** ◼ N-COUNT A zigzag is a line that has a series of angles in it like a continuous series of Ws. ❑ They staggered in a zigzag across the road. ◼ V-T/V-I If you zigzag, you move forward by going at an angle first to one side then to the other. ❑ I zigzagged down a labyrinth of alleys. ❑ He zigzagged his way across the field.

zilch /zɪltʃ/ PRON Zilch means nothing. [INFORMAL] ❑ At the moment these shares are worth zilch.

zil|lion /zɪlyən/ (**zillions**) NUM If you talk about a zillion people or things, you are emphasizing that there is an extremely large number of them. [INFORMAL, EMPHASIS] ❑ It's been a zillion years since I've seen her.

zinc /zɪŋk/ ◼ N-UNCOUNT Zinc is a bluish-white metal which is used to make other metals such as brass, or to cover other metals such as iron to stop rust from forming. ◼ → See also color supplement

zine /ziːn/ (**zines**) N-COUNT A zine is a magazine about a particular subject, written by people who are interested in that subject rather than by professional journalists.

zing /zɪŋ/ N-UNCOUNT [also a N] If you refer to the zing in someone or something, you mean the quality that makes them lively or interesting. [INFORMAL] ❑ He just lacked that extra zing. ❑ There's nothing like fresh basil to put a zing into a tomato sauce.

zing|er /zɪŋər/ (**zingers**) N-COUNT A zinger is a witty remark, or something that is lively, interesting, amusing, or impressive. [AM, INFORMAL] ❑ I love listening to my friends talk and laugh, throwing in a zinger of my own now and again.

Zi|on|ism /zaɪənɪzəm/ N-UNCOUNT Zionism is a movement which was originally concerned with establishing a political and religious state in Palestine for Jewish people, and is now concerned with the development of Israel.

Zi|on|ist /zaɪənɪst/ (**Zionists**) ◼ N-COUNT A Zionist is someone who believes in Zionism. ❑ He was an ardent Zionist. ◼ ADJ [usu ADJ n] Zionist means relating to Zionism. ❑ ...the Zionist movement.

zip /zɪp/ (**zips, zipping, zipped**) ◼ V-T When you zip something, you fasten it using a zipper. ❑ She zipped her jeans. ◼ V-T To zip a computer file means to compress it so that it needs less space for storage on disk and can be transmitted more quickly. [COMPUTING] ❑ If you zipped the files first, they did not become read-only when written to the CD. ◼ N-COUNT A zip or zip fastener is the same as a zipper. [mainly BRIT] ❑ He pulled the zip of his leather jacket down slightly.

▶ **zip up** ◼ PHRASAL VERB If you zip up something such as a piece of clothing or if it zips up, you are able to fasten it using its zipper. ❑ He zipped up his jeans. ◼ PHRASAL VERB To zip up a

zip code computer file means to compress it so that it needs less space for storage on disk and can be transmitted more quickly. [COMPUTING] ❏ *These files have been zipped up to take up less disk space so they take less time to download.*

zip code (zip codes) also **ZIP code** N-COUNT Your **zip code** is a short sequence of letters and numbers at the end of your address, which helps the post office to sort the mail. [AM] ❏ *Type your street address and zip code.*

in BRIT, use **postcode**

zip disk (zip disks) N-COUNT A **zip disk** is a removable computer disk that is capable of storing great amounts of data. [COMPUTING] ❏ *Zip disks could be used to store the equivalent of three music CDs.*

zip drive (zip drives) N-COUNT A **zip drive** is a piece of computer equipment that reads and writes to zip disks. [COMPUTING] ❏ *Zip drives help people to organize their important information.*

zip file (zip files) N-COUNT A **zip file** is a computer file containing data that has been compressed. [COMPUTING] ❏ *When you download the font it may be in a compressed format, such as a zip file.*

zip|per /zɪpər/ (zippers) N-COUNT A **zipper** is a device used to open and close parts of clothes and bags. It consists of two rows of metal or plastic teeth which separate or fasten together as you pull a small handle along them. [mainly AM] ❏ *...the metal zipper on his jacket.*

in BRIT, usually use **zip**

zip tie (zip ties) N-COUNT A **zip tie** is a long narrow piece of plastic that can be tied around separate things to hold them together. ❏ *Use a small zip tie to secure it permanently to the nozzle.*

zit /zɪt/ (zits) N-COUNT **Zits** are pimples on someone's skin, especially a young person's. [INFORMAL]

zith|er /zɪθər, zɪð-/ (zithers) N-COUNT A **zither** is a musical instrument that consists of two sets of strings stretched over a flat box. You play the zither by pulling the strings with both hands.

zo|di|ac /zoʊdiæk/ N-SING The **zodiac** is a diagram used by astrologers to represent the positions of the planets and stars. It is divided into twelve sections, each of which has its own name and symbol. The zodiac is used to try to calculate the influence of the planets on people's lives. ❏ *...the twelve signs of the zodiac.*

zom|bie /zɒmbi/ (zombies) **1** N-COUNT You can describe someone as a **zombie** if their face or behavior shows no feeling, understanding, or interest in what is going on around them. ❏ *Without sleep you will become a zombie at work.* **2** N-COUNT In horror stories and some religions, a **zombie** is a dead person who has been brought back to life.

WORD HISTORY
zombie
Zombie comes from an African word *zumbi*, meaning 'good-luck charm.'

zone /zoʊn/ (zones, zoning, zoned) **1** N-COUNT A **zone** is an area that has particular features or characteristics. ❏ *Many people have stayed behind in the potential war zone.* ❏ *The area has been declared a disaster zone.* **2** V-T [usu passive] If an area of land **is zoned**, it is formally set aside for a particular purpose. ❏ *The land was not zoned for commercial purposes.* • **zon|ing** N-UNCOUNT ❏ *...the use of zoning to preserve agricultural land.*
▶ **zone out** PHRASAL VERB If you **zone out**, you stop being aware of what is happening around you, either because you are relaxed or because you are bored. ❏ *When I'm on the train, I put on my headphones and zone out.*

SYNONYMS
zone
NOUN **1**
area: *Local authorities have been responsible for the running of schools in their areas.*
region: *...Barcelona, capital of the autonomous region of Catalonia.*
sector: *Officers were going to retake sectors of the city.*
district: *I drove around the business district.*

zonked /zɒŋkt/ ADJ If someone is **zonked** or **zonked out**, they are not capable of doing anything because they are very tired, drunk, or drugged. [INFORMAL]

zoo /zu/ (zoos) N-COUNT; N-IN-NAMES A **zoo** is a park where live animals are kept so that people can look at them. ❏ *He took his son Christopher to the zoo.*

zo|ol|ogy /zoʊɒlədʒi/ N-UNCOUNT **Zoology** is the scientific study of animals.

zoom /zum/ (zooms, zooming, zoomed) V-I If you **zoom** somewhere, you go there very quickly. [INFORMAL] ❏ *We zoomed through the gallery.*
▶ **zoom in** PHRASAL VERB If a camera **zooms in** on something that is being filmed or photographed, it gives a close-up picture of it. ❏ *...a tracking system which can follow a burglar around a building and zoom in on his face.*

zoom lens (zoom lenses) N-COUNT A **zoom lens** is a camera lens that allows you to make the details larger or smaller while always keeping the picture clear.

zuc|chi|ni /zukini/ (zucchini or zucchinis) N-VAR **Zucchini** are long thin vegetables with a dark green skin. [mainly AM]

in BRIT, usually use **courgette**

Zulu /zulu/ (Zulus) **1** N-COUNT A **Zulu** is a member of a race of Black people who live in Southern Africa. **2** N-UNCOUNT **Zulu** is the language spoken by Zulus and also by many other Black South Africans.

Zum|ba /zumbə/ N-UNCOUNT **Zumba** is an exercise program that uses Latin-American music and dance steps. [TRADEMARK] ❏ *Zumba turns 10 styles of Latin dancing into an innovative, energetic workout.*

zy|gote /zaɪgoʊt/ (zygotes) N-COUNT A **zygote** is an egg that has been fertilized by sperm, and which could develop into an embryo.

APPENDICES

Style and Usage

Writing style guide	1505
Special information	1520
Language in use	1524

Writing style guide

Introduction

This section covers such areas as writing plain English, avoiding ambiguity, and writing with the appropriate level of formality. There are numerous examples showing how the guidance given can be put into practice.

What is good style?

When people write with good style, their writing is clear, interesting, elegant, and appropriate for their audience.

The best style to use will vary according to the type of document you are writing: the kind of original, descriptive writing you would use for a creative piece would not be appropriate for a factual report.

There are many aspects to writing with good style, which are discussed in this section.

However, one simple rule applies to all your work: **avoid repeating words.**

Whatever you are writing, it will sound dull and clumsy if you use the same words over and over again. If you read your work aloud, you will notice when you have done this.

Too much repetition	Better ...
Team A discovered ..., Team B discovered ..., Team C discovered ...	Team A discovered ..., Team B found ..., Team C's results showed ...

Sometimes the easiest way to avoid repetition is simply to replace one of the words with a pronoun:

Too much repetition	Better ...
We intend to invite all our friends and ask each friend to bring some food.	We intend to invite all our friends and ask each of them to bring some food.

Writing in sentences

Sentences are the building blocks of our texts. The length of your sentences will depend on who you are writing for, but very long sentences can be confusing, while very short sentences can sound childish. If your sentence is longer than about 15–20 words, see if you can divide it.

Do not try to run lots of sentence parts together using commas. This is a common mistake, and can be confusing.

Writing style guide

Look at the following:

> First, we went to the Tower of London, which was fantastic, our tour guide was excellent, and we saw the crown jewels, later we had our picnic on a lawn near the ravens.

This sentence would be much better using dashes and splitting it into separate sentences, like this:

> First, we went to the Tower of London, which was fantastic – our tour guide was excellent. We saw the crown jewels, and later, we had our picnic on a lawn near the ravens.

However, make sure you use commas where they are needed, as they can help the reader understand your sentences better.

For instance, they are needed if a subordinate clause (less important part of a sentence) comes before the main clause, e.g.:

> If the train is late, call me from the station.

They are also needed for adding small pieces of information about someone or something in your sentence, e.g.:

> My sister, who is a vet, has three children.

Tip for success

Try reading your work aloud. If your sentences work well, it will be easy to read. See where you make natural pauses, and think about whether you need to add commas.

Using plain English

It is important to write in plain English. Plain English is easier to write, and certainly easier to understand. This does not mean that you need to write in baby-talk, but try to follow these rules:

- **Avoid unnecessary jargon.** Don't talk about 'interfacing' with someone when you mean 'communicating' with them, or simply 'talking' to them. Don't say 'design solution' – it's just a design.

Of course, there are times when technical and specialist terms *are* appropriate. If you are writing a science essay, you must use the correct terminology. As always, think of your reader.

- **Avoid unnecessary formality.** Ask yourself if there is a simpler word or phrase that would be appropriate for your reader.

very formal	simpler ...
prior to	before
in excess of	more than
in the vicinity of	near

Writing style guide

- **Try to use active verbs instead of nouns.** This will make your sentences sound less complex and formal.

noun form	active verb form
give encouragement to	encourage
ensure the completion of	complete
make provision for	provide

> **Tip for success**
> In more formal contexts such as academic writing, the use of noun structures is much more common.

Active or passive verbs?

It is usually better to use active verbs in your writing because the structure is simpler. Passives can sound rather formal. Compare these two sentences, for example:

> New recycling methods have been introduced by the committee. (passive)
> The committee has introduced new recycling methods. (active)

However, the passive can be useful in certain cases. For instance, you may use the passive if you do not want to appear to be blaming or criticizing someone:

> You have not paid the money. (active and accusing)
> The money has not been paid. (passive and more neutral)

You may also want to use the passive if you do not want your reader to blame you:

> I'm sorry to report that I have lost your documents. (active and admitting fault)
> I'm sorry to report that your documents have been lost. (passive and implying that it may have been someone else's fault)

The passive is also used when you do not know who carried out an action or it is irrelevant who carried out the action. This will often happen in academic writing in which the slightly more formal style is appropriate:

> The results were analyzed in the laboratory.
> The buildings were knocked down in 1989.

Avoiding clichés

A cliché is a word or phrase that has been used too often. If you use clichés, your writing will be boring. When readers see them, they may lose interest and miss your main message. They may think that if your writing is not original, your ideas cannot be original either.

You may find that clichés slip into the first draft of your writing – after all, it is because they are so well-known and come so easily to mind that they have become clichés.

Writing style guide

Read through your document and try to identify any phrases that seem to fit into this category. If English is not your first language, it may be difficult to do this. In this case, it may be a good idea to ask a native English speaker for advice.

Then, ask yourself: what does this phrase actually mean? It may not really have much meaning at all, in which case you can probably delete it. Examples of this sort of cliché are:

> *at the end of the day*
> *at this moment in time*
> *with all due respect*

Or, it may be that the phrase has been used so much that it has lost all its power, and may well annoy your reader. Examples of this sort of cliché are:

> *moving the goalposts*
> *reinvent the wheel*
> *the best thing since sliced bread*

Sometimes a simple **combination of adjective and noun** can be so overused that it becomes a cliché, e.g.:

> *roaring fire*
> *vice-like grip*
> *long-lost friend*

This does not mean that such combinations should never be used, but try not to use too many obvious combinations, and choose something more original if you can.

One area of language where it is very easy to fall into the trap of using a cliché is the **simile**. More information on **similes** can be found on page 1755.

Look at the following similes:

> *as cold as ice*
> *as fresh as a daisy*

They are so overused that they are not powerful descriptions. Now, look at the following similes, all found in real writing:

> *as cold as a Siberian winter*
> *as cold as a statue of stone*
> *as fresh as green shoots in the morning*
> *as fresh as a big, green, shiny cucumber*

Of course, imaginative similes like these are not suitable for all types of writing. In formal writing, it is probably best to avoid similes altogether. In more creative writing, you should aim to be descriptive and original, but your similes should fit into the overall style of the text.

Avoiding redundancy (unnecessary words)

It is very easy to use more words than you need, but too many words will make your writing less effective and may annoy your readers.

Compare the following:

> *Jack and I are of the same opinion on this matter.*
> *Jack and I agree.*

> *Due to the fact that the train was delayed, we were late for the concert.*
> *We were late for the concert because the train was delayed.*

- **Avoid 'empty' words and phrases** that do not add meaning to your sentences, e.g., *in terms of*, *the fact of the matter*.

- **Avoid saying the same things twice**. This is known as **tautology**. Consider the following:

9 a.m. in the morning	a.m. means 'in the morning' – choose one or the other
re-examine again	just say 're-examine' – the 'again' is expressed in the prefix 're-'
my personal opinion	if it's your opinion, it's personal – you don't need to say so
mutual cooperation	you can't cooperate on your own, so it must be mutual

- **Avoid adding illogical extra words**. Consider the following:

in actual fact	if it's a fact, it must be 'actual' – just say 'in fact'
very unique	something unique is the *only* one of its kind – there are no degrees of uniqueness
added bonus	a bonus is something that you get in addition to something else – there is no need to also say 'added'

Avoiding ambiguity

Ambiguity is when something could possibly be understood in more than one way. It is an easy trap to fall into because *you* know what you mean when you write, but try to put yourself in the reader's place and make sure there is no room for doubt.

Be careful with **words that have more than one meaning**. Often the context will be enough to make it clear which meaning is intended. If you write that you are going to the bank, nobody is likely to think you are going to a river bank. However, consider the following:

> *My teacher is really funny.*
> (Is the teacher humorous or strange?)

> *The food was very hot.*
> (Was it a high temperature, or was it spicy?)

Make it clear whether you are using words and phrases in a **literal or figurative** sense:

> *He was in debt to his friend.*
> (Did he owe his friend money or simply feel grateful?)

Writing style guide

There was a chasm between us.
(Was there a hole in the ground or a big difference of opinion?)

Use pronouns carefully to make sure it is clear who or what they refer to:

Rosie had an argument with Sarah, and she started crying.
(Who cried, Rosie or Sarah?)

I couldn't attach the nest boxes to the posts in the garden because they weren't strong enough.
(Was it the posts or the nest boxes that weren't strong?)

Check the structure of your sentence to make sure it is clear how the parts relate to each other. Compare the following:

We talked about bullying at work.
(Ambiguous – were we at work or not?)

We talked about the issue of workplace bullying.
At work, we talked about bullying.

They told us about the murder at 11 o'clock.
(Ambiguous – did the murder happen at 11 o'clock?)

At 11 o'clock, they told us about the murder.
They told us about the murder that occurred at 11 o'clock.

Make sure it is clear what **your adjectives are describing**:

a large woman's handbag
(Is it the woman or the handbag that is large?)

a formal English test
(Is the test formal, or is it a test of formal English?)

Be clear about **the purpose of your writing**. Imagine you are an employee receiving an email from your boss that includes the following:

It would be a good idea for all staff to take at least 30 minutes for lunch.

It would not be clear whether your boss is saying that you *must* take a 30 minute break or simply that it would be a nice thing if possible.

Register

The word *register* refers to aspects of language such as how formal or informal it is. Compare the following:

They furnished us with the requisite implements. (very formal)
They gave us the necessary tools. (neutral)
They let us have the gear we needed. (informal)

You should match the register of your language to the type of writing you are doing. Using the wrong register can make your writing sound odd and can even cause offense.

Writing style guide

Register can often be shown by the choice of words or phrases:

formal	neutral	informal
wax lyrical	speak enthusiastically	go on about
of one's own volition	voluntarily	on your own
in the ascendancy	becoming successful	on the up

This dictionary marks words which are formal or informal, so you can check if you are not sure. Many idioms and phrasal verbs are either informal or slightly informal, so take care to use them appropriately.

Informal language is fine for personal letters, emails, texts, etc., but for most forms of writing, a neutral or slightly formal style is more appropriate. Remember, though, that formal does not mean pompous. Do not use very formal language to try to impress – it is more important to present your ideas clearly.

> **Tip for success**
> Do not use different registers within the same piece of writing.

Sometimes, words and phrases with a particular register are needed for specific types of writing. For instance, **legal documents** often contain extremely formal language, such as '*hereafter*' or Latin words such as '*ex gratia*', which would be out of place in most other types of writing.

Similarly, some types of writing need to use very specific **technical terms**. For example, a document for medical professionals might use a word such as '*renal*' instead of saying '*related to the kidneys*' because this word will be understood by its readers. In scientific documents, the use of technical terms can be necessary to avoid any ambiguity.

At the other end of the scale, **literary or poetic language** such as '*lovelorn*', '*flaxen*', or '*beauteous*' may be appropriate in some types of creative writing.

A variety of register labels are included in the dictionary to show where the use of a word is usually restricted to a particular subject or style of language.

Your choice of **grammar** and the way you **structure** your sentences can also affect register. Compare the following:

> the man to whom I gave my ticket
> the man I gave my ticket to

In the first example, the use of '*whom*' gives a formal feel to the sentence. In the second sentence, the preposition is used at the end. In the past, this was considered incorrect, but it is now widely accepted, and would be appropriate for any but the most formal of documents.

It is sometimes considered appropriate to use contractions (e.g., *don't, he'd, wouldn't*) in formal writing because they make the text sound less formal.

Writing style guide

Tone

The tone of your writing expresses your **attitude** towards the reader, and it is important to be careful about this.

For instance, if you are writing to complain about a product or service, you need to come across as being assertive and clear about the facts. You must decide for yourself whether to be rude or threatening, too – but if you are, make sure it is on purpose and not because of a poor choice of words!

It can be useful to **imagine that you are talking to your reader**. What sort of tone do you want to take? For example, this might be:

chatty	authoritative	sincere	sympathetic
grateful	serious	assertive	humorous
persuasive	practical	unfriendly	offended
efficient	angry		

If you **think about what you want to achieve** with your writing, it will help you decide what tone to take. For example, when writing a letter to accept a job, the tone should probably be friendly yet professional and show that you are pleased to have been chosen.

It is important to use language that is the **right level of difficulty** for your reader. If you use difficult words, you may sound as if you are showing off, but using very simple language may seem patronizing to the reader.

An important issue that influences tone is the **relationship of the writer to the reader**. For instance, a suggestion for changes to working practices might have a very different tone coming from a junior employee than if it comes from a senior manager.

You should always take into account **how well you know the person** who will read your document. If you do not know them at all, you must be aware that they may be offended by a tone that is too familiar, for instance by being too informal, or by expressing views that they may not share. Humor can also be difficult – if your readers do not know you, they may be unsure whether you are joking or not.

Compare the following letters:

> Dear Emma,
>
> Tom told me you broke your leg skiing – after I'd stopped laughing, it occurred to me that you must be a bit fed up, so I'm sending you these chocolates to cheer you up. See you when (if ???) you can walk again,
>
> Lizzie x

> Dear Emma,
>
> I'm so sorry to hear about your skiing accident. Your mother told me you are likely to be in a cast for several weeks, and I know how hard that will be for you. Do take good care of yourself, and I hope to hear some better news of you soon.
>
> With love from,
>
> Aunty Bea

In the first letter, the tone is chatty and humorous, and while it might make Emma smile, if her injury is serious she might be offended that her friend is joking about it. However, if Lizzie is a very close friend, she will probably have judged the tone of the note appropriately. The second letter is much more sincere and serious, and the tone shows that the writer is really concerned about Emma.

If you are angry about something, it can be very easy to let it show, sometimes without intending to. For example, look at this email:

> Thanks for your offer of database training, but I really don't feel it's necessary, and I wouldn't want to distract you from your work, which is already behind schedule.

The tone of the email makes it clear that the writer was offended by the offer of help and takes revenge by implying that the person offering help cannot manage their own work.

This may be what the writer intends, but if they would prefer to keep a good relationship with their colleague, something like the following would be better:

> Thanks for the offer of database training, but I think I've managed to come to grips with it now, and I wouldn't want to take up your time unnecessarily as I know you are very busy.

> **Key point to remember**
> The tone you choose is up to you, but if your writing does express your attitudes, make sure this is what you intended.

Emphasis

We use emphasis to draw a reader's attention to the points which are most important. There are several ways of doing this:

- **Order within the document**. It is usual to start with the most important points.
- **Order within a sentence or paragraph**. The first part of the sentence will be seen as the most important. Compare the following:

    > A thorough safety assessment is needed urgently, following a number of accidents on site.
    > Following a number of accidents on site, a thorough safety assessment is needed urgently.

Writing style guide

In the first example, the fact that the safety assessment is needed is emphasized by coming first in the sentence. In the second example, the fact that there have been some accidents comes across as the more important point.

- **A summary of main points**. This can be done either at the beginning or the end of a document, and could take the form of ordinary text or a list. For example, a detailed report might start with a section on 'key findings' or 'key recommendations' – simply a list of the main points the author wishes to make.

- **Amount of text**. The more important a point, the more space you are likely to use discussing it. If you add too much detail about minor points, readers may be confused about what is most important.

- **Blank space around a key phrase or sentence**. This is a rather dramatic way of emphasizing one key point:

    The evidence led to one clear conclusion:
    He did not kill his wife.

- **Typeface**. It is very simple to highlight words and phrases by using different forms of typefaces such as **bold**, *italics* or underlining. Italics are probably the most commonly used:

    Please note that students should not bring cell phones to school *at any time*.
    Make sure you take *all* your belongings with you.

Fonts can also be made larger or smaller for emphasis, or a different color may be used to make certain parts of a document stand out.

- **Repetition**. Repetition can be used in several ways to emphasize points. You could make a point and then repeat it immediately, using phrases such as:

    In other words ...
    Put more simply ...

This is a useful way to stress the point you are making and also to explain it in a different way so that you can be certain that your readers will understand it.

If you are writing a long document, you may want to repeat certain points throughout it, using phrases such as:

   This demonstrates yet again ...
   Again we see ...

Repetition can also be a useful stylistic device, in writing as well as in speech. You might repeat a word, a phrase, or part of a phrase:

   They said local businesses would close – not true. They claimed jobs would be lost – not true. They claimed traffic would increase – not true.

- **Headings**. Headings can be used to reinforce the main point that will be made in the parts they refer to.

Writing style guide

- **Sudden change of style**. If readers are surprised by a sudden change of style, they may pay more attention to what is being said. One example would be to use a very short, snappy sentence after one or more longer, more flowing sentences:

    Architects and engineers had assured officials and residents that the techniques used in constructing the bridge would ensure that it remained solid during an earthquake. It did not.

- **Emphatic words and phrases**. These can highlight the most important points, e.g.:

    Our priority now is ...
    The crucial advantage that this scheme offers is ...

In a similar way, sentence adverbs such as *'crucially'* or *'above all'* signal the importance of what follows, as do adjectives such as *'urgent'*, *'vital'*, or *'essential'*.

- **Punctuation**. The most obvious way to emphasize a sentence is to end it with an exclamation point:

    We won over a thousand dollars!

Be careful with exclamation points, though. It is fine to use them in informal letters, emails, etc., but do not use them too often. It is not usually appropriate to use them in more formal writing.

Structuring a sentence with a dash or a colon can also emphasize part of it. See, for example, how the second of these two sentences has more emphasis:

Critics described his performance as terrible.
Critics had one word for his performance: terrible.

Avoiding offense

The simple rule for avoiding offense is this:

Treat everyone equally in your writing, regardless of age, gender, race, sexual orientation, or physical difference.

Always make sure that you are **aware of current customs and values**. For instance, do not assume that couples, even married couples, consist of a man and a woman: same-sex marriages are legal and common in many countries.

Check that the terms you use for sensitive issues, such as race and disability, are the **modern, accepted terms**, and not old-fashioned terms that might be considered offensive. This dictionary uses register labels to show words that might be considered offensive or old-fashioned.

Race and religion

It goes without saying that offensive racial or religious insults or stereotypes should never be used.

Writing style guide

However, it can sometimes be easy to display discrimination without meaning to, simply because of our cultural background. Make sure you follow these general rules:

- **Only mention race or religion if it is relevant to your writing.** If you mention someone's race or religion, ask yourself if you would have mentioned it if it was the same as yours.

- **Make sure you use accepted modern terms**, not old-fashioned ones which many now consider offensive. For instance, a term such as *Red Indian* belongs only in cowboy movies – for all other writing, use *Native American*. Similarly, the term *African-American* is the preferred description for Black Americans of African origin.

- **Be aware of different cultures.** For instance, don't assume that everyone celebrates Christmas, or that July and August are always the hottest months of the year.

When writing about people whose parents or ancestors are from different races, a common and widely-accepted term is *mixed-race*. *Dual-heritage*, with its more positive connotations, is also becoming widely used. If you are in doubt about any terms connected with race or religion, check in the dictionary where register labels will show you if a word needs to be avoided or used with care.

Gender inclusivity

Here are some rules for avoiding sexism and making your writing gender inclusive.

- **Use job titles that are gender neutral.** For example, use *police officer* rather than *policeman*; *chair* or *chairperson* instead of *chairman*.

- **Avoid the suffix -ess on jobs.** Words like *authoress* and *poetess* are very old-fashioned and patronizing, and should not be used. It is best to avoid the *-ess* suffix for jobs altogether: while the word *actress* is still used, many women in the profession prefer *actor*.

- **Do not mention a person's gender if it is not relevant.** It is usually best to avoid terms such as *male nurse* or *female doctor*.

- **Do not make assumptions about the gender of people in a particular profession.** Do not write things like *businessmen and their wives*.

- **Avoid stereotypes of roles and characteristics.** It's not necessarily Mom who cooks the dinner and Dad who fixes the car.

- **Avoid using masculine pronouns.** Sentences such as *Each traveler must present his documents* sound old-fashioned and sexist. Most people now consider it acceptable to use the pronoun *their* in such cases: *Each traveler must present their documents*.

- **Use people's correct pronouns.** Many people state their pronouns, e.g., *she/her, they/their*. If you know someone's pronouns, use them correctly.

- **If you write to someone whose gender you do not know, do not begin your letter** *Dear Sir/s*. You could use *Dear Sir/Madam* in very formal situations, or choose another form of address altogether, e.g., *Dear Friends/Dear Supporters*.

Writing style guide

Disability

When writing about illness and disability, there are several points to bear in mind:

- **Be sure to use current, accepted terms**. Use *bipolar disorder* rather than *manic depression*, for example. Check the register labels in the dictionary if you are not sure.
- **Do not describe someone only by their illness**. Remember that they are a person first of all, so say *someone with epilepsy* rather than *an epileptic*.
- **Try not to portray someone with a disability as a victim**. Avoid words like *victim*, *afflicted with*, *suffering from*. Say *a wheelchair user* rather than *wheelchair-bound*.
- **Do not refer to people without a disability as** *normal*. Say *non-disabled* or *able-bodied* instead.

Increasing your vocabulary

The best way to increase your vocabulary is to **read a lot**. As you read, notice the words that are being used.

If you find a word you do not know, you will sometimes be able to get a good idea of its meaning from the other words around it. If not, **look it up in the dictionary**. It is not always a good idea to look up every new word as you find it because it can be distracting, but you could **underline or highlight** some of the words and look them up at the end.

It can be useful to **keep a vocabulary notebook**, to record new words you have learned. You can arrange the words in whatever way is best for you: by alphabetical order or by subject.

Try to develop an interest in words, and ask yourself questions about them. For instance, you can widen your vocabulary by learning **words in groups**. If you know that *canine* means 'relating to dogs', see if you know the word meaning 'relating to cats' (*feline*) or 'relating to cows' (*bovine*). Similarly, if you know that *carnivorous* means 'meat-eating', do you know the word for 'plant-eating' (*herbivorous*) or for creatures that eat anything (*omnivorous*)?

Notice the context that words are in. You can often make your writing more elegant by choosing which words go together, such as the interesting verbs with the common nouns in these examples:

> ***abandon*** *an attempt*
> ***draw*** *to a close*
> ***adopt*** *a method*

The Collocation feature boxes which are shown throughout the dictionary will help you to learn some common words that often occur together.

Word games such as **crossword puzzles** can help to develop an interest in words and can introduce words you did not know before.

Writing style guide

Terms used in writing English

The following are important terms that refer to different styles of writing and types of words and phrases. You need to know them for studying literature, and also to be aware of them for use in your own writing.

Alliteration

Alliteration is the use of the same letter or sound (especially consonants) at the beginning of two or more words that are close together in a sentence:

> droplets of dew at dawn

Antonyms

An antonym is a word with an opposite meaning. *Legal* and *illegal* are antonyms, as are *mature* and *immature*.

Assonance

Assonance is the repetition of sounds (especially vowel sounds) in two or more words that are close together in a sentence:

> I laughed, but my heart was torn apart.

Euphemism

A euphemism is a word or phrase that is used to avoid talking directly about something that is embarrassing, upsetting, or offensive.

Euphemisms can be used in personal writing to show tact to your reader. For instance, in a letter of sympathy, some people prefer to use the euphemism *passed away* rather than *died*. Euphemisms can be used to avoid embarrassment to readers who are uncomfortable with words connected with sex or bodily functions.

Euphemisms are sometimes used in quite formal writing in order to disguise deliberately an unpleasant truth. For instance, a company press release might talk about *restructuring* or *reorganizing* rather than *sacking staff*. In war, the terms *collateral damage* or *friendly fire* sound much less terrible than the reality of what they describe.

There is no place for euphemism in scientific or technical writing.

Figurative language

Figurative language is where an extra, more imaginative meaning comes from a literal meaning. For instance, the literal meaning of the word *chasm* is 'a large hole in the ground', whereas the figurative meaning refers to a fundamental difference of opinion between people.

Writing style guide

Idioms

Idioms are phrases such as *give someone a hand* and *be over the moon*, where the meaning is not the same as the literal meaning of all the words in the phrase.

Metaphor

Metaphor is the use of a particular word or phrase – usually a concrete noun – to describe the characteristics of something else. For instance we might say *She has a heart of ice*, meaning that she shows no sympathy or emotion.

Proverbs

Proverbs are short sentences that many people know, often expressing advice, or something that many people believe to be true. Examples of proverbs are *Marry in haste, repent at leisure* and *Many hands make light work*.

Similes

Similes are phrases like *as dull as dishwater* or *sing like an angel*, which compare one thing to another. The difference between a simile and a metaphor is that similes say that something is *like* something else, whereas a metaphor says something *is* something else.

Synonyms

Synonyms are words with the same or similar meanings. For instance, *clever* is a synonym of *intelligent*. However, it is important to note that words with similar meanings often have subtle differences in register or tone. *Purchase* is more formal than *buy*, for instance, while *slim* is a much more positive description than *skinny*.

The Synonym feature boxes which are shown throughout the dictionary will help you to learn some useful synonyms of frequent words.

Special information

Abbreviations

It can sometimes be difficult to decide when to use periods in abbreviations. In British English, it is becoming more common to use abbreviations without periods, while in American English, they are used more often. In both varieties of English, there are some forms of abbreviation where it is more common to use periods than others.

In some cases, you may make your decision based on the need to avoid ambiguity, e.g., *a.m.* rather than *am*. Make sure that you treat each form consistently throughout your text.

You must be certain that your readers will understand any abbreviations you use. It is safe to use widely understood abbreviations like *IRS* or *AAA*, though even in these cases, if your audience is not American, you may need to add an explanation. However, less common abbreviations could puzzle your readers, so it is best either to avoid them, or to put the full form in parentheses the first time you use them.

There are a few abbreviations which are so much more widely used than their full forms that it is not necessary to give the full forms at all. Examples of these are *DNA* and *TNT*.

Abbreviations formed from the first letter of all the words can be spelled with or without periods, though it is now more common in British and American English to omit them:

> BBC (British Broadcasting Company)
> FBI (Federal Bureau of Investigation)

Abbreviations formed from the first part of a word are more likely to use periods:

> Prof. (Professor)
> Oct. (October)

Abbreviations formed from the first and last letters of a word usually have a period in American English:

> Mr. (mister)
> Dr. (doctor)

Abbreviations formed from Latin words often use periods:

> e.g. (exempli gratia = for example)
> i.e. (id est = that is to say)
> etc. (et cetera = the other things)

Abbreviations for metric scientific measurements are often formed from the first letter of each of the parts of a compound word. They do not use periods, and never add an *s* to form their plurals:

> kg (**ki**logram or **ki**lograms)
> ml (**m**illi**l**iter or **m**illi**l**iters)

Special information

Abbreviations for imperial measurements are often very irregular, and often do have periods. They typically do not add *s* in the plural:

> *oz.* (*ounce or ounces*) Comes from the Italian word *onza*
> *lb.* (*pound or pounds*, in weight) Comes from the Latin word *libra*

Acronyms

Acronyms are words formed from the first letters of several words or from parts of words. The difference between acronyms and other abbreviations is that acronyms are pronounced as words themselves, rather than as individual letters:

> *NATO* (*North Atlantic Treaty Organization*)
> *GUI* (*graphical user interface*)

Acronyms are not usually written with periods. In fact, many acronyms make a journey from being abbreviations to becoming words in their own right. For example, an acronym such as *AIDS* (*acquired immune deficiency/immunodeficiency syndrome*) has become so widely used, that it is sometimes written *Aids*.

Other words have completed the journey – nobody really thinks of words like *laser* (*light amplification by stimulated emission of radiation*) or *scuba* (*self-contained underwater breathing apparatus*) as being abbreviations at all.

Numbers

Numbers can be written using figures or letters:

> 1   *one*
> 350   *three hundred and fifty*
> 1,299 *one thousand, two hundred and ninety-nine*

Note that we put a comma or a space between each group of three figures, counting from the right:

> 3,490
> 2 350 100

In mathematical and scientific writing, numbers are always written as figures. In general writing, you can use words or figures:

> *480 coulombs is equivalent to 0.005 faradays.*
> *About two hundred people attended the meeting.*
> *We'll need 50 chairs.*

It is quite common to use words for numbers less than 10, and figures for larger numbers. Whatever you decide, be consistent throughout your writing.

However, if you have two numbers together, you may use a combination to avoid confusion:

> *Three 5-year-olds were hurt in a traffic accident near Tulsa.*

Special information

Very large numbers in the millions, billions, or even higher are usually written like this:

> 40 million
> 3 billion

Notice that there is no s on the end of *million* and *billion*.

When there has been more than one king or queen with the same name, their name is followed by an ordinal number, usually written in Roman numerals:

> Henry VIII (Henry the eighth)
> Elizabeth II (Elizabeth the second)

> **Tip for success**
> Take care with spelling the number *forty* – there is no *u* in it.

Dates

There are several accepted ways of writing dates:

> June 11, 1961
> 6/11/1961
> 6/11/61
> 6.11.61

The style you choose will depend on what you are writing – the longer style is suitable for essays, polite letters, or other formal writing, while the shorter styles are used in quick emails, filling out forms, etc.

Note that in American English, we usually order dates: month – day – year. In British English, it is more common to order them: day – month – year:

> 11 June, 1961
> 30/6/2018

If you are writing about centuries, the most common style is:

> During the 15th century …

Remember that the name of the century is always the number above the beginning of the years in it, so for instance 1492 is in the 15th century, and 1997 is in the 20th century.

When we are writing about history, the abbreviations C.E. (of the Common Era) and B.C.E. (Before the Common Era) are used for dates before and after the date when Jesus Christ is believed to have been born. C.E. and B.C.E. have replaced the terms A.D. (Anno Domini) and B.C. (Before Christ) which many people now prefer to avoid.

A.H. means 'year 1' in the Muslim calendar. It is the equivalent of C.E. 622.

Special information

Foreign words and phrases

There are many words in English that come from other languages originally, but then become so absorbed into English that we do not think of them as being foreign any more. Examples are *bazaar* from Persian, *karate* from Japanese, and *intelligentsia* from Russian. These words are used in just the same way as any other English words.

However, for a word or phrase that is self-consciously foreign, *italics* are often used:

> The same complaint was repeated *ad nauseam*.
> (Latin = until we were sickened)

> *Entre nous*, his finances are in a perilous state.
> (French = between ourselves)

> Her writings displayed a bleak *Weltanschauung*.
> (German = view of life and the world)

Sometimes it can be difficult to decide if a word has entered mainstream English. If you are unsure whether or not to use italics, consider whether your reader is likely to think of the word or phrase as being part of 'normal' English.

For instance, if you know a lot about yoga, terms such as *chi* (vital energy) and *chakra* (one of the points of physical or spiritual energy) will probably be well known to you. If you are writing for an audience which is also knowledgeable about yoga, you can probably use them without italics and without explanation. However, if your writing is for a general audience, it is best to use italics to indicate that these are words of foreign origin (Chinese and Sanskrit), and also to explain them, at least the first time they are used.

Many foreign words and phrases will only be suitable in very formal or intellectual forms of writing.

Language in use

Introduction

This section contains typical examples of written and spoken language that will be useful for many common situations. It covers both everyday activities such as telephoning and writing letters, and functions such as expressing certainty or giving advice. The part of the sentence that is written in **bold** type illustrates a common structure that can be used in a range of different situations.

Using the phone

You should get the number from International Directory Assistance.
You omit the '0' when dialing England from Germany.
How do I make an outside call?/What do I dial for an outside line?
What is the area code for Cleveland?
You can dial the number direct.
Hold the line.
The line is busy [AM]/engaged [BRIT].

When someone answers

Could I please have extension 516?/Can you please give me extension 516?
Is this Mr. Lambert's number?
Could I speak to Mr. Swinton, please?/I'd like to speak to Mr. Swinton, please./
   Is Mr. Swinton there, please?
Could you put me through to Dr. Henderson, please?
Who's calling?
I'll try again later.
I'll call back in half an hour.
Could I leave my number for her to call me back?
Would you ask him to call me when he gets back?

When a company answers

Queen's Hotel, can I help you?
Who's calling, please?
Who should I say is calling?
I am connecting you now./I'm putting you through now.
I have a call from Tokyo for Mrs. Thomas.
I have Miss Trotter on the line for you.
Sorry to keep you waiting.
There's no reply.

Language in use

STYLE AND USAGE

Answering the phone

Hello, this is Anne speaking.
Speaking!
Would you like to leave a message?
Can I take a message for him?
Please speak after the tone.

Having difficulty

I can't get through.
We were cut off.
I must have dialed the wrong number.
I got the wrong extension.
This is a very bad line.
I'm sorry, you're breaking up.
I don't have a very good signal here.

Suggestions

Making suggestions

You might like to think it over before giving me your decision.
You could help me clean out my office, **if you don't mind**.
We could stop off in Venice for a day or two, **if you like**.
If I were you, I'd go.
If you ask me, you'd better take some extra cash.

Less certain

I suggest that you go to bed and try to sleep.
In these circumstances, **it might be better to** wait.
It might be a good idea to warn her about this.
Perhaps you should take up running.
If I may make a suggestion, a longer hemline might suit you better.

As a question

I was thinking of going for a drink later. **How about it**?
What would you say to a trip up to the mountains next week?
Would you like to stay in Paris for a couple of nights?
What you need is a change of scene. **Why not** go on a cruise?
Have you ever thought of starting up a magazine of your own?

Language in use

Asking for suggestions

Do you have any idea how I should go about it?
I've no idea what to call our new puppy: do you have any suggestions?
I wonder if you could suggest where we might go for a few days?

Advice

Asking for advice

What would you do if you were me?
Do you think I ought to tell the truth if he asks me where I've been?
Should I exercise in the morning or at night?
What would you advise me to do under the circumstances?
I'd like or I'd appreciate your advice on individual retirement accounts.

Giving advice

It might be a good idea to seek professional advice.
It might be better to think the whole thing over before taking any decisions.
Do be sure to read the small print before you sign anything.
Try to avoid upsetting her; she'll only make your life miserable.
Whatever you do, don't forget your appointment.
If you ask me, you'd better take some extra cash.
If you want my advice, you should steer well clear of them.
If I were you, I'd be thinking about moving on.
I'd be very careful not to commit myself at this stage.
I think you ought to or should seek professional advice.
My advice would be to have nothing to do with them.

Giving a warning

I should warn you that he's not an easy customer to deal with.
Take care not to lose the vaccination certificate.
Watch you don't trip over your shoelaces.
I'd think twice about sharing an apartment with him.

Offers

I would be delighted to help out, if I may.
Do let me know if I can help in any way.
If we can be of any further assistance, please do not hesitate to contact us.
Could I give you a hand with your luggage?
Would you like me to find out more about it for you?
Is there anything I can do to help?
May I or Can I offer you a drink?

Language in use

Requests

Please would you drop by on your way home?
Could you please try to keep the noise down while I'm studying?
Would you mind look**ing** after Hannah for a couple of hours tomorrow?
I would be grateful if you could increase my credit limit to $5,000.
We would ask you not to use the phone for long-distance calls.
You are requested to park at the rear of the building.
We look forward to receiv**ing** confirmation of your order within 14 days.

Less direct

I would rather you didn't breathe a word to anyone about this.
I would appreciate it if you could let me have copies of the best photos.
I hope you don't mind if I borrow your bike.
You won't forget to lock up before you leave, **will you**?

Comparisons

Objective comparisons

The streets are narrow **compared with** those in the new town.
The apartment was small **in comparison with** those on the ground floor.
In contrast to the opulence of the Kirov, the Northern Ballet is a modest company.
Only 30% of women had individual retirement accounts **as opposed to** 60% of men.
Unlike other loan repayments, those to the IMF cannot simply be rescheduled.

Positive comparisons

Orwell was, indeed, **far superior to** him intellectually.
Emma was astute beyond her years and **in a class of her own**.

Negative comparisons

My old chair **was nowhere near as** comfortable **as** my new one.
The opposition **is no match for** the government, which has a massive majority.
Commercially-made ice cream **is far inferior to** the home-made variety.

Comparable

The new computerized system costs **much the same as** a more conventional one.
When it comes to performance, **there's not much to choose between** them.
He is an amateur but he **is on a par with** professional players.
The immune system **can be likened** or **compared to** a complicated electronic network.
There was a close resemblance between her **and** her son.
You can take the train or the bus to get there – **it's six of one and half a dozen of the other**.

Language in use

Incomparable

You cannot compare a small local library **with** a large city one.
There's no comparison between the sort of photos I take **and** those a professional could give you.
Home-made clothes **just cannot compare with** store-bought ones.
We might be twins, but **we have nothing in common**.

Opinions

Asking for opinions

What do you think of the new Managing Director?
What is your opinion on climate change?
What are your thoughts on the way forward?
How do you see the next stage developing?

Giving one's opinion

In my opinion, eight years as President is quite enough for anyone.
We're prepared to prosecute the company, which **to my mind** has committed a criminal offense.
From my point of view, activities like these should not be illegal.
As I see it, everything depended on Karlov being permitted to go to Finland.
Personally, I believe the best way to change a government is through the electoral process.
It seems to me that the successful designer leads the public.
I'm convinced that we all need a new vision of the future.
I daresay there are so many names that you get them mixed up once in a while.
As far as I'm concerned, Barnes had it coming to him.
If you ask me, there's something a bit strange going on.

Not expressing an opinion

It could be seen as a triumph for capitalism, but **it depends on your point of view**.
It's hard or **difficult to say whether** she has benefited from the treatment or not.
I'd prefer not to comment on operational decisions taken by the service in the past.
I'd rather not commit myself at this stage.
I know nothing about fine wine.

Language in use

Likes and dislikes

Asking for preferences

Would you like to visit the castle while you are here?
How would you feel about Simon join**ing** us?
What's your favorite movie?
Which of the two proposed options **do you prefer**?
We could either go to Rome or stay in Florence – **which would you rather do**?

Expressing likes

I'm crazy about garden**ing**.
I'm very fond of white geraniums.
I really enjoy a game of basketball after work.
I've always had a soft spot for Thomas.

Expressing dislikes

Acting **isn't really my thing** – I'm better at singing.
Sitting for hours in traffic jams **is not my idea of** fun.
The idea of walking home at 10 or 11 o'clock at night **doesn't appeal to me**.
I've lost interest in the idea of cycl**ing** round Holland.
I can't stand *or* **bear** the thought of seeing him.
What I hate most is waiting in lines at the grocery store.

Expressing a preference

I'd prefer to *or* **I'd rather** wait until I have enough money to go by plane.
I like the blue curtains **better than** the red ones.
I prefer red wine **to** white wine.

Expressing no preference

It makes no difference whether you have money or not, we won't judge you on your wealth.
It doesn't matter which method you choose to use.
It's all the same to me whether he comes **or** not.
I really don't care what you tell her as long as you tell her something.
I don't mind at all – let's do whatever is easiest.

Plans and intentions

Asking about intentions

Will you take the job?
What do you intend to do?
Did you mean to tell him about it, or did it just slip out?
Do you have anyone in mind for the job?

Language in use

Expressing intentions

I'm thinking of retiring next year.
I'm hoping to see her when I'm in Paris.
I studied history, with a view to becoming a politician.
We bought the land in order to farm it.
We plan to move or We are planning on moving next year.

More definite

I am going to sell the car as soon as possible.
I intend to put the house on the market.
I have made up my mind to or I have decided to go to Japan.
I have set my sights on recapturing the title.

Expressing a lack of intention

I don't mean to offend you, but I think you're wrong.
I don't intend to pay unless he completes the job.
We are not thinking of taking on more work.
I have no intention of accepting the offer.

Expressing wishes

I'd like to see the Sistine Chapel some day.
I want to work abroad when I leave college.
I'm interested in developing the business.
I'm dying to leave home.
I insist on speaking to the manager.

Expressing a lack of desire

I would prefer not to or I would rather not have to speak to her about this.
I don't want to take the credit for something I didn't do.
I have no wish or desire to become rich and famous.
I refuse to be patronized by the likes of her.

Permission

Asking for permission

Can I or Could I borrow your car this afternoon?
Are we allowed to say what we're up to?
Would it be all right if I arrived on Monday instead of Tuesday?
Would it be possible for us to leave the car in your garage?
We leave tomorrow. Is that all right by you?
Do you mind if I come to the meeting next week?

Language in use

Giving permission

You can have anything you want.
You are allowed to visit the museum by prior arrangement.
It's all right by me if you want to skip the Cathedral visit.
I've nothing against her going there with us.
I do not mind if my letter is forwarded to the person concerned.
By all means charge a reasonable consultation fee.

Refusing permission

You can't or **You mustn't** go anywhere near the research lab.
You're not allowed to leave the ship.
I don't want you to see that man again.
I'd rather you didn't give them my name.
I couldn't possibly allow you to pay for all this.
Smoking **is not permitted** at any time.

Obligation

Expressing an obligation

You've got to or **You have to** be back before midnight.
You must have an address in Prague before you can apply for the job.
You need to have a valid passport if you want to leave the country.
He was forced to ask his family for a loan.
Companies **are not always obliged** to offer consumers their money back.
A degree **is indispensable** for future entrants to the profession.
It is essential to know what the career options are before choosing a course of study.
Wearing a seat belt **is compulsory**.
We have no alternative but to fight.
Three passport photos **are required**.

Asking whether one has to do something

Do I have to or **Have I got to** be home by midnight?
Do we have to or **Do we need to** book in advance?
Is it necessary to go into so much detail?
Should I call the police?
Am I supposed to fill out this form?

Expressing that one doesn't have to do something

You don't have to or **You needn't** go there if you don't want to.
You are not obliged to or **You are under no obligation to** invite him.
It is not compulsory to have a letter of acceptance, but it helps.
The Council **does not expect you to** pay all of your bill at once.

Language in use

Expressing that something is not allowed

You are not allowed to take the exam more than three times.
You mustn't show this document to any unauthorized person.
You're not supposed to use this room unless you are a club member.
Smoking **is prohibited** or **not allowed** in the dining room.
It is forbidden to bring cameras into the gallery.

Agreement

Agreeing with views

I agree with you on this point.
We are in complete agreement on this.
I think **we see eye to eye** on this issue.
You're quite right in point**ing** at distribution as the main problem.
It's true that you had the original idea.
I'm all for encourag**ing** a youth section in clubs such as ours.
I couldn't agree with you more.
I am delighted to endorse your campaign.

Agreeing with suggestions

This certainly **seems to be the right way to go about it**.
I will certainly back such a scheme.
It makes sense to enlist help.
It's a great idea.
Cruise control? **I like the sound of that**.
Going for lunch **sounds good to me**!
I'll go along with Ted's proposal.
This is exactly what I had in mind.
Thank you for sending the draft agenda; **I like the look of it**.
We are all very enthusiastic about or **very interested in** his latest set of proposals.
I will certainly give it my backing.
Any game which is as clearly enjoyable as this **meets with my approval**.

Less direct

This solution **is acceptable** to us.
This is a proposal which **deserves our support**.

Agreeing to requests

Of course **I'll be happy to** organize it for you.
I'll do as you suggest and send him the documents.
There's no problem with getting tickets for him.
We would be delighted to cooperate with you in this enterprise.

Language in use

STYLE AND USAGE

Agreeing with an idea

You're quite right to wait before making such an important decision.
I entirely approve of the idea.
I'd certainly go along with that!
I'm very much in favor of that sort of thing.

Agreeing with how something is done

I think very highly of the people who have been leading thus far.
I have a very high regard for the work of the District Attorney.
I certainly admire his courage in telling her what he thought of her.
I must congratulate you on the way you handled the situation.
I appreciate their help.

Disagreement

Disagreeing with something

There must be some mistake – **it can't possibly** cost as much as that.
I'm afraid **he is quite wrong** If he has told you that.
The article **is mistaken in** claiming that it is a waste of public money.
I cannot agree with you on this point.
We must agree to differ on this one.

More definite

I totally disagree with the previous two callers.
I cannot support you on this matter.
Surely you can't believe that he'd do such a thing?

Refusing suggestions

More definite

I'm against this idea.
It is not feasible to change the schedule at this late stage.
This **is not a viable alternative**.
Cutting the budget **is the wrong approach**.

Less direct

I'm not sure about this idea.
I don't think much of this idea.
This doesn't seem to be the right way of dealing with the problem.

Language in use

Refusing requests

More definite

It is **quite out of the question** for the time being.
I won't agree to any plan that involves your brother.
I refuse point blank to have anything to do with this affair.

Less direct

I am afraid I must refuse.
I cannot possibly comply with this request.
I wouldn't dream of doing a thing like that.
I'm sorry but **I just can't** do it.

Objection

This **doesn't seem to be the right way of** going about it.
I don't think much of what this government has done so far.
I can't say I'm pleased about what has happened.
They **should not have refused to** give her the money.

More definite

I'm fed up with having to wait so long.
I've had (just) about enough of this whole thing.
I can't bear or **stand** people who are rude.
How dare he say that!
He was quite wrong to repeat what I said about her.

Certainty, probability, possibility, ability

Certainty

She was bound to discover that you and I had talked.
It is inevitable that they will get to know of our meeting.
I'm positive (that) it was your mother I saw.
I made sure that no one was listening to us.
From all the evidence, **it is clear that** they were planning to escape.
There is no doubt that the talks will be long and difficult.
I can assure you that I have had nothing to do with any dishonest trading.
British universities are **undeniably** good, but they are not turning out enough top scientists.
One thing is certain: the party is far from united.
It is (quite) certain that no amount of aid will solve the long-term problems of the people.
It cannot be denied that there are similarities between the two approaches.

Language in use

Probability

It is **quite likely that** you will get withdrawal symptoms at first.
There is a good chance that they will agree to the deal.
It seems **highly likely that** he saw everything that happened.
You will **very probably** be met at the airport.
The child's hearing will, **in all probability**, be severely affected.
The chances or **the odds are that** he will play it safe.
He **must** know of the painting's existence.
The talks **could very well** spill over into tomorrow.
The package **should** reach you by Saturday.
It wouldn't surprise me if he was working for the Americans.

Possibility

The situation **could** change from day to day.
It is possible that psychological factors play some unknown role in the healing process.
It may be that the contract will have to be amended.
There is a small or **outside chance that** your body could reject the implants.

Expressing ability

Our Design and Print Service **can** supply envelopes and package your existing literature.
Applicants **must be able to** speak English.
He **is qualified** to teach physics.

Doubt, improbability, impossibility, inability

Doubt

I doubt if he knows where it came from.
No-one can say for sure how any child will develop.
It's all up in the air until we see the figures.
We won't know for certain until next week.
I'm not convinced that you can really teach people who don't want to learn.
We are still in the dark about where the letter came from.
How long this muddle can last **is anyone's guess**.
It is doubtful whether anyone would be brave enough to demonstrate publicly.
It remains to be seen whether the security forces will try to intervene.
I have a few reservations about the book.
This raises the whole question of when people should retire.
I find it hard to believe that there is no link between screen violence and violence on the streets.
Her claim to have been the first to discover the phenomenon **lacks credibility**.
Nevertheless, **I remain unconvinced by** his arguments.
Many do not believe that water contains anything dangerous. Sadly, **this is far from the truth**.

Language in use

Improbability

It is very doubtful whether or **doubtful that** the expedition will reach the summit.
In the unlikely event that the room was bugged, the music would drown out their conversation.

Impossibility

There can be no changes in the schedule.
I couldn't possibly invite George and not his wife.
The report **rules out any possibility of** exceptions.
There is no question of us get**ting** this finished on time.

Inability

I can't drive, I'm afraid.
I don't know how to use a scanner.
The army **has been unable to** suppress the violence in the area.
He simply **couldn't cope with** the stresses of family life.
I'm not in a position to say how much substance there is in the reports.
It's impossible for me to describe the confusion of the scene.

Explanations

Prepositions and conjunctions

The reason that we admire him is that he knows what he is doing.
I am in favor of civil disobedience **on** moral **grounds**.
The students were arrested **because of** suspected dissident activities.
He could not come **on account of** his illness.
They are facing higher costs **owing to** rising inflation.
He passed all his exams **as a result of** his hard work.
The full effects will be delayed **due to** factors beyond our control.
Thanks to their generosity, the charity can afford to buy new equipment.
Both companies became profitable again **by means of** severe cost-cutting.
Their defense of family values has acquired a poignancy **in view of** their inability to have children.
In the face of this continued disagreement, the parties have asked for the polling to be postponed.
It is unclear why they went on strike, **given that** negotiations were under way.
As he had been up since 4 a.m., he was very tired.
International intervention was appropriate **since** tensions were running high.
The serious dangers to your health **caused by** cigarettes are now better understood.
This lack of recognition **was at the root of** the dispute.
This unrest **dates from** colonial times.

Language in use

Apologies

Apologies

I'm really sorry but we won't be able to come on Saturday.
I must apologize for what happened.
I owe you an apology; I didn't think you knew what you were talking about.
Please forgive me for behav**ing** so badly.
Please accept our apologies if this has caused you any inconvenience.

Admitting responsibility

I admit I overreacted, but someone needed to speak out.
I have no excuse for what happened.
It is my fault that our marriage is on the rocks.
The government **is not entirely to blame for** the crisis.
I should never have let him rush out of the house in anger.
If only I hadn't lost the keys.
I made a stupid mistake.

With regret

I'm very upset about her decision to move on to new challenges.
It's a shame that the press gives so little coverage to these events.
I feel awful about saying this, but you really ought to spend more time with your children.
It's a pity that my profession can make a lot of money out of the misfortunes of others.
It is unfortunate that the matter should have come to a head just now.
We regret to inform you that the position of editor has now been filled.

By way of explanation

I didn't do it on purpose, it just happened.
I didn't mean to upset you.
I know this hurt you, but **I had no choice**.
I had nothing to do with the placing of any advertisement.

Job applications

Useful structures

In reply to your advertisement for a trainee manager, **I would be grateful if you would send me further details of** the job.
I wish to apply for the position of bilingual correspondent, as advertised in this week's *Euronews*.
I am writing to ask if there is any possibility of work in your company.

Language in use

Work experience

I have three years' **experience of** office work.
As well as speaking fluent English, **I have a working knowledge of** German.
As you will see from my résumé, I have worked in Belgium before.
My current salary is ... per annum.

Motivation

I would like to make better use of my languages.
I am eager to work in public relations.

Ending the letter

I am available for an interview at any time.
Please do not hesitate to contact me for further information.
Please do not contact my current employers.

References

Would you mind if I gave your name as a reference?
Ms. Lee has given us your name as a reference. **We would be grateful if you would let us know whether you would recommend her for this position**.
Your reply will be treated in the strictest confidence.
He has worked for me for four years, and **I can recommend him for the position**.

Accepting or rejecting an offer

Thank you for your letter of March 20. **I will be pleased to attend an interview** on Thursday, April 7, at 10 a.m.
I would like to confirm my acceptance of the position of marketing executive.
Having given your offer careful thought, **I regret that I am unable to accept**.

Business letters

Providing information

In response to your inquiry of March 8, **we have the pleasure in enclosing** full details of our vacation packages, **together with** our price list.
Thank you for inquiry about our products. **I enclose** a price list.

Asking for information

I am writing to ask whether you have in stock a book entitled ...
Please send me your latest price list.

Language in use

Orders

We would like to place an order for the following items.
Please find enclosed our order no. 3011.
Thank you for your order of May 3.
We regret that the goods you ordered are temporarily out of stock.
Please allow 28 days for delivery.

Deliveries

Our delivery time is 60 days from receipt of order.
We await confirmation of your order.
We confirm that the goods were dispatched on September 4.
We cannot accept responsibility for goods damaged in transit.

Complaints

We have not yet received the items we ordered.
Unfortunately, the goods were damaged in transit.
If the goods are not received by October 20, we will have to cancel our order.

Payment

The total amount outstanding is ...
Full payment is due within 14 working days from receipt of goods.
We enclose a check for ... in settlement of your invoice number 2003L/58.
The mistake was due to an accounting error, and we enclose a credit voucher for the sum involved.

General correspondence

Starting the letter

To someone you know well

Dear Grace
Dear Mom and Dad
Thank you or Thanks for your letter which came yesterday.
It was nice to hear from you.

To a company or organization

Dear Mr. Brown
Dear Mrs. Hughes
Dear Mr. and Mrs. Boyle
Dear Miss Roberts
Dear Ms. Jones
Dear Dr. Armstrong

Language in use

Ending the letter

To someone you know well
With love from
All the best
Say hello to Martin **for me**.
Give my love to Daniel and Laura.

To a company or organization
Sincerely
Sincerely yours
Yours truly
Kind regards
I look forward to hearing from you.
If you require any further information, please do not hesitate to contact me.

Making travel plans

Booking a room

Please send me details of your prices.
Please let me know if you have one single room for October 3.
I would like to book a double room.
We expect to arrive in the early evening.
I am afraid (that) I must cancel the reservation for the week beginning September 5.

Saying thanks

Thanks for the lovely book which arrived today.
I can't thank you enough for finding my watch.
(Would you) please thank him from me.
We greatly appreciated your support during our recent difficulties.

Good wishes

Special occasions

I hope you have a terrific vacation.
Best wishes for your wedding anniversary.

Christmas and New Year

Merry Christmas and a Happy New Year
With Season's Greetings

Language in use

STYLE AND USAGE

Birthday

All our love and best wishes on your birthday.
Many happy returns!

Get well soon

Sorry (to hear) you're ill – **get well soon**.
Wishing you a **speedy recovery**.

Good luck

Good luck on your driving test.
Sorry to hear you didn't get the job – **better luck next time**.
We all wish you the best of luck in your new job.

Congratulations

You're expecting a baby? **Congratulations**!
You've finished the job already? **Well done**!
Congratulations and best wishes on your engagement.

Invitations

Invitations to a celebration

We are having a dinner party next Saturday **and would be delighted if** you both could come.
Would you be free for lunch next Tuesday?
Perhaps we could meet for coffee sometime next week?

Accepting an invitation

Yes, I'd love to meet up with you tomorrow
Thank you for your invitation to dinner. **I'm looking forward to it** very much.

Declining an invitation

I'd love to come, but I'm afraid I'm already going out that night.
I wish I could come, but unfortunately I have something else on.
Unfortunately, I will not be able to accept.

Not committing

I'm not sure what I'm doing that night, but I'll let you know later.
It all depends on whether I can get a babysitter.

Language in use

Writing an argument

Giving evidence

Introducing a subject

Let us begin with an examination of the social aspects of this.
It is a well-known fact that computer screens can cause headaches.
First of all, let us consider the advantages of urban life.
It is often the case that early interests lead to a career.
I would like to start with a very sweeping statement which can easily be challenged.
Let us look at what self-respect in your job actually means.
The idea *or* **concept of** getting rich has universal appeal.
There are a number of issues on which we disagree.

Setting out the issue

Retail sales rose sharply last month. This **could be taken to mean that** inflationary pressures remain strong.
In such circumstances, **it might well be prudent** to diversify your investments.
It is probably the case that class sizes are increasing.
Most people **might reasonably assume that** their insurance would cover them in case of an accident.
With this beautiful weather, **you could be forgiven for thinking that** you were abroad.

Generalizing

People who work outside the home **tend to believe that** parenting is an easy option.
Many gardeners **have a tendency to** treat plants like humans.
For the (vast) majority of people, the internet is indispensable.
For most of us, housework is a necessary but boring task.

Making more specific claims

The impact of sciences, and economics **in particular**, was extremely significant.
More specifically, he accused the company of discrimination.

Limiting the scope of the argument

In the first section, I will pursue the question of whether the argument is valid.
I will then deal with the question of whether the evidence is conclusive.
In this chapter, **I will confine myself to** a consideration of therapeutic methods.
Let us now consider how the company is run.
Let us now look at the best responses to this question.

Language in use

Singling out issues

The main issue under discussion is how the party should re-define itself.
A second, related problem is that business ethics has mostly concerned itself with theorizing.
An important aspect of their policy is equal opportunities for all.
Finally, there is the argument that watching too much television may stunt a child's imagination.

Raising questions

This is a question which **merits close(r) examination**.
The accident **has raised fundamental questions about** safety at the plant.
This raises once again the question of the public's right to know.
This poses the question of whether these measures are really helping people.

Offering analysis

It is interesting to consider why this scheme has been so successful.
We are often faced with the choice between our sense of duty **and** our own personal inclinations.
It is reasonable to assume that rising prices will to some extent kill off demand.

Supporting an argument

An argument in support of this approach **is that** it produces results.
In support of his theory, Dr. Gold notes that most oil contains helium-3.
The second reason for advocating this course of action **is that** it benefits the community at large.
The third reason for looking to the future **is that** investors need a successful market.
The fundamental reason for this contradiction seems to me quite simple.

Putting forward a counterargument

Disputing or criticizing

In fact, the idea is somewhat misleading.
I will show that his position is, in fact, **untenable**.
It is claimed, however, that a change of policy is not essential.
This need not mean that we are destined to suffer forever. **Indeed, the opposite may be true**.
On the other hand, there are more important factors that should be taken into consideration.
That **may well be true, but** I find it difficult to believe.
Reform **is all very well, but** it is pointless if the rules are not enforced.
Studies have shown that **his idea does not hold water**.
Their claim to be innocent **does not stand up to** scrutiny.
Another approach may be to develop better treatment plans.
Another way to reduce failure is to improve vocational education.

Language in use

Pulling together the evidence

On balance, making money honestly is more profitable than making it dishonestly.
Since such vitamins are more expensive, **one has to weigh the pros and cons**.
The benefits of partnership certainly **outweigh the disadvantages**.
The fact of the matter is that in a free society you can't turn every home into a fortress.
Although this operation sounds dangerous, **in fact** it is extremely safe.
When all is said and done, it must be acknowledged that this approach cannot solve our problems.

Summing up

This shows how sticking to this theory on crime is at best a matter of reasoned choice.
To recap or **To sum up** or **To summarize, (we may conclude that)** there are two possible solutions to this problem.
Habermas's argument, **in a nutshell**, is as follows.
The key to the whole argument is a single extraordinary paragraph.
To conclude this section on social media, it should play a key role in any marketing strategy.

Drawing conclusions

From all this, it follows that it is impossible to extend security measures to all potential targets.
This **leads to the logical conclusion that** those who work hard should be rewarded.
There is only one logical conclusion we can reach.
We must conclude that there is no solution to the problem of defining crime.
In conclusion, there can be no easy way of preventing conflict.
This only goes to show that good employees are hard to find.
I will listen to her advice, but **at the end of the day**, it is my decision.
Ultimately, we must do our utmost to make our cities safer places.

Building up

In addition, the author does not really empathize with his hero.
Also, there is the question of language.
This is only part of the picture; **added to this are** fears that a major price increase would cause riots.
Furthermore, ozone is, like carbon dioxide, a greenhouse gas.

Comparisons

Compared with the city, our village is quiet and peaceful.
In comparison with the other apartments in the building, theirs is small and cramped.
On the one hand, there is no longer a threat. **On the other (hand)**, the positive changes could have negative side effects.
Similarly, a good historian is not obsessed with dates.
There will be a change in the way we are regarded by our partners, and, **by the same token**, the way we regard them.
There is a fundamental difference between adequate nutrition **and** optimum nutrition.

Language in use

STYLE AND USAGE

Bringing together individual elements

First of all or **First**, I would like to outline the benefits of the system.
In music we are concerned **first and foremost** with the practical application of sounds.
In the first place, the objectives of privatization were contradictory.
In the second place or **Second**, it might be simpler to develop chemical or even nuclear warheads for a large shell than for a missile.
Finally, there is the argument that watching too much television may stunt a child's imagination.

Emphasizing the point

Nowadays, there is clearly less stigma attached to unmarried mothers.
There can be no doubt about his guilt; **the facts speak for themselves**.
Few will argue with the principle that such a fund should be set up.
Hyams **supports this claim** by looking at sentences produced by young children learning the language.
The most important thing is to reach agreement from all sides.
It would be impossible to exaggerate the importance of these two volumes in the development of gospel music.
It should be stressed that people cannot contract this condition from their pets.

Expressing a personal opinion

In my opinion, the government is underestimating the scale of the problem.
Personally, I think that education should be free for all children.
In my view, it only perpetuates the very problem that it sets out to address.
For my part, I cannot agree with the leadership on this question.
Although the author argues the case for patriotism, **I feel that** he does not do it with any great personal conviction.
I believe that people understand that there is no quick fix for economic problems.
It seems to me that we have a political problem that needs to be solved at a political level.

Expressing others' opinions

He claims that intelligence is conditioned by upbringing.
The communiqué **states that** some form of nuclear deterrent will be needed for the foreseeable future.
According to the report, poverty creates a climate favorable to violence.

Giving examples

To take another example, thousands of people have been condemned to a life of poverty.
Let us consider, **for example** or **for instance**, the problems faced by immigrants.
Just consider, **by way of illustration**, the difference in amounts accumulated if interest is paid monthly.
A case in point is the decision to lift the ban on contacts with the republic.

Grammar

General grammar guide	1549
Business English grammar	1567
Academic English grammar	1577

General grammar guide

Introduction

This section gives you the basic rules you need to know about English grammar. In addition, it draws attention to common mistakes and shows you how to avoid them.

Main verbs

Verbs are words that allow us to talk about activities, processes, states of being, and states of mind. You may have heard verbs referred to as 'doing words':

>This basket **holds** quite a lot.
>John **was reading** Katherine's essay.
>Anirban **is preparing** a talk for next week's class.
>Eleni **feels** much happier now.
>I **forgot** that it was your birthday.
>Paul **owned** several old motorcycles.

A **verb phrase** can be a single word or a group of associated words:

>he walks
>he is walking
>he had walked
>he can walk
>he has been walking
>he might have been walking

Transitive verbs are verbs which have to have an object:

>*like*: She likes cheese. (You can't say just *She likes*.)
>*describe*: He described the house. (You can't say just *He described*.)

Intransitive verbs do not have an object:

>*sneeze*: I sneezed loudly. (You can't *sneeze something*.)
>*complain*: He's always complaining. (You can't *complain something*.)

Many verbs can be transitive or intransitive:

>Sales levels **have increased**. (intransitive)
>We **have increased our spending** on training. (transitive)

>The fog made it difficult **to see**. (intransitive)
>The fog made it difficult **to see the mountains**. (transitive)

The **infinitive** form of the verb is the basic form that you would look up in a dictionary. For instance, if you wanted to look up the verb in this sentence:

>She **had encountered** many problems.

You would look up the infinitive, *encounter*, not *encountered*.

General grammar guide

In different situations, the infinitive is used with or without *to*. Without *to*, it is called the **bare infinitive**:

> The child was too small **to reach** the switch.
> I'm sorry **to hear** your news.
> I don't know how **to do** it.
> You must **lock** the door.

Auxiliary verbs

Auxiliary verbs are used with main verbs in order to allow us to talk about different periods of time and to form questions and negatives.

Be and *have* are the **primary auxiliaries**. A primary auxiliary is used to construct compound tenses.

Be is used to make present continuous and past continuous tenses and for the passive:

> I **am working**.
> We **were** all **wondering** about that.
> Martin **was arrested** and held overnight.

Have is used to make present perfect and past perfect tenses:

> Sasha **has finished** fixing the car.
> Amanda **had** already **eaten** when we arrived.

Do is the **supporting auxiliary**. It is used in forming negatives, questions, and emphatic statements:

> I **do not like** sausages at all.
> **Do you like** shrimp?
> You **do like** shrimp, **don't you**?

Modal verbs

Modal verbs are used before other verbs to express ideas such as ability, possibility, and necessity.

The main modal verbs in English are:

can	could	may	might	must
ought	should	will	would	

Modal verbs are different from other verbs because they do not change their form:

> I **can** ride a horse.
> She **can** ride a horse.

General grammar guide

In speech and informal writing, the modal verb will is often shortened to 'll (e.g., I'll, they'll) and the modal verb would is often shortened to 'd (e.g., I'd, they'd).

Negatives of modal verbs are formed like this:

Modal verb	Negative	Short form
can	cannot	can't
could	could not	couldn't
may	may not	(mayn't is formal and very rare)
might	might not	mightn't
must	must not	mustn't
ought (to)	ought not to	oughtn't to
should	should not	shouldn't
will	will not	won't
would	would not	wouldn't

Phrasal verbs

A **phrasal verb** is a type of verb that is created when a main verb is combined with either:

an adverb:

| take off | give in | blow up | break in |

a preposition:

| get at (*someone*) | pick on (*weaker children*) |

or an adverb + preposition:

| put up with (*insults*) | get out of (*doing something*) |

Often the meaning has nothing to do with the literal meaning of the verb or the particle (the adverb or preposition).

Nouns

A **noun** is a word that labels a person, a thing, or an idea.

Proper nouns are the names of people, places, or things, and start with capital letters:

John Lennon   China   Mount Fuji   Thursday

1551

General grammar guide

Common nouns are all the other nouns that refer to things. They can be divided into the following groups:

Abstract nouns. These refer to things that you cannot see or touch:

> honesty   anger   idea   time

Concrete nouns are things you can see or touch:

> dog   teacher   stone   sugar

A concrete noun may refer to a living thing (animate noun) or a physical object (inanimate noun).

Collective nouns refer to collections of people or animals:

> a herd of cows   a swarm of bees

Compound nouns are nouns made from two or more words. Some are written as one word, some as two words, and some with a hyphen:

> teapot   washing machine   break-in

Check in the dictionary if you are not sure.

Countable and uncountable nouns

Countable nouns refer to things that we can count: *one cat, two cats, seventeen cats*, and so on. They have singular and plural forms, which are shown by the spelling. They must be used with a determiner if they are singular:

> **Dogs** ran wild in the streets.
> The **dog** is loose again.

> Fetch a **chair** for Sumit, will you?
> We've bought six new **chairs**.

Uncountable nouns refer to things that we cannot count:

> Sadia asked me for some **advice**.
> Anna gave us some more **information** about her work.
> **Homework** occupied much of Sonia's evening.
> Our **knowledge** of outer space is increasing daily.

Uncountable nouns do not usually have a plural form. They are followed by a singular verb. They are not normally used with the indefinite article. (You cannot talk about *an advice* or *a money*.)

Mass nouns refer to substances that can be divided or measured but not counted. They do not usually have an indefinite article in front:

> **Meat** is usually more expensive than cheese.
> **Sugar** is quite cheap.

Mass nouns only take a plural in special cases, for instance when they refer to a particular type or types of the substance, or when they refer to a single serving of the substance:

>Ros brought out a tempting selection of French **cheeses**.
>The principal **sugars** are glucose, sucrose, and fructose.
>Two **teas**, please.

Pronouns

A **pronoun** is a word that is used instead of a noun phrase or a noun. We use pronouns when we do not want to repeat the same noun in a sentence or paragraph:

>Gary saw Sue, so **he** asked **her** to help **him**.
>Costas was hungry, so **he** stopped at a burger bar.

There are seven different types of pronoun, classified according to their meaning and use.

Personal pronouns can be used as subject or object in a clause:

>**He** gave **her** a box of chocolates.
>**We** saw **them** both on Friday.
>**I** can see **you**!

Reflexive pronouns are used when the action of a verb is performed on the subject by the subject. They are obligatory with certain verbs:

>The puppy entangled **itself** in the leash.
>I've just cut **myself** on a piece of glass.

Reflexive pronouns are also used for emphasis:

>Never mind. I'll do it **myself**.
>The professor **himself** did not know the answer.

Possessive pronouns indicate ownership:

>Give it back, it's **mine**.
>Perhaps it really is **theirs** after all.

Demonstrative pronouns indicate items that are near to or far from us:

>**This** is Betty's, and **that** is Peter's.
>**These** are nice. Where did you find **them**?

Relative pronouns are used to link a modifying clause (the part of a sentence that gives more information about a word or phrase) to a noun phrase or to a clause:

>I don't know **what** you mean.
>That's the girl **who** always comes first.

General grammar guide

Interrogative pronouns are used to ask a question about the noun phrase they stand in for:

> **What** would you like for lunch?
> **Which** is the fresh milk?
> **Who** was responsible?

Indefinite pronouns are used for a broad range of reference when it is not necessary or not possible to use a personal pronoun:

> **Everyone** had a compass and a whistle.
> **Neither** wanted to give in and apologize.
> **Much** needs to be done.

Personal pronouns have subject forms (*I, you, he, she, it, we, they*) and object forms (*me, you, him, her, us, them*). It can sometimes be difficult to decide which to use, especially when you need to use two pronouns or a personal noun and a personal pronoun together. Here are some rules:

- If they are the joint subject of the verb, the subject form of the pronouns must be used:

    > Jerry and **I** are going to paint the house ourselves.
    > He and **I** are going to paint it.
    > Melanie and **I** are going shopping.

- If they are the joint object of the verb, the object form of the pronouns must be used:

    > They decided to help Jane and **me**.
    > I want to give **you** and **him** a present.

- The object form of pronouns must be used after prepositions:

    > Between **you** and **me**, I don't like this place.
    > Wasn't that kind of **him**?

You should follow the rules above, but in some situations the rules on subject and object pronouns are changing. In the following situations, it is now considered acceptable to use object pronouns, and using subject pronouns sounds extremely formal or old-fashioned:

- after the verb *be*.

    > I saw at once that it was **her**.
    > I saw at once that it was **she**.   = formal/old-fashioned

- after *than* in comparison with *be*.

    > Sylvia is cleverer than **me**.
    > Sylvia is cleverer than **I**.   = formal/old-fashioned

General grammar guide

Adjectives

An **adjective** gives more information about a noun. Adjectives help us describe or pick out which particular thing among many is being referred to. Adjectives are sometimes called 'describing words':

> a man   a **tall** man
> their TV   their **new, wide-screen** TV
> the cat   the **fat, black-and-white** cat

When there is more than one adjective, commas are often used between them, though it is common to see lists of adjectives without commas, too. It is possible to use several adjectives at once, but in practice more than four is uncommon:

> a **happy, young, blonde, German** girl
> **beautiful old English thatched** cottages

The comparative form of an adjective is used to compare two people, things, or states:

> Anna is **taller than** Mary, but Mary is **older**.

The superlative form is used for more than two people, things, or states, where one of them has more of a quality than all the others:

> That is **the smallest** camera I have ever seen.

There are two ways in which the comparative and superlative forms of adjectives are formed:

- You add -er (comparative) or -est (superlative) to the adjective. Adjectives with one syllable usually take these endings:

adjective	comparative	superlative
bright	brighter	the brightest
long	longer	the longest
sharp	sharper	the sharpest

If the word already ends in -e, the -e must be left off. If a word ends in -y, it usually takes -er or -est, and the -y changes to -i:

adjective	comparative	superlative
wise	wiser	the wisest
pretty	prettier	the prettiest
weary	wearier	the weariest

General grammar guide

- You add the word *more* or *most* in front of the adjective. Adjectives with three syllables or more use *more* or *most* in front of them:

adjective	comparative	superlative
fortunate	more fortunate	the most fortunate
relevant	more relevant	the most relevant

- Adjectives formed from participles (forms of verbs) use *more* or *most* as well:

adjective	comparative	superlative
provoking	more provoking	the most provoking
enthralled	more enthralled	the most enthralled

- Adjectives with two syllables (including those that already end in *-er*) can follow either pattern or sometimes both patterns. If you are doubtful about a two-syllable adjective, use the *more/most* pattern:

adjective	comparative	superlative
shallow	shallower or more shallow	the shallowest or the most shallow
polite	politer or more polite	the politest or the most polite

- A small group of irregular adjectives have quite different forms for the comparative and superlative forms:

adjective	comparative	superlative
good	better	the best
bad	worse	the worst
far	further / farther	the furthest / the farthest

Remember that in formal English *more* or *-er* should be used to compare two people, things, or states. It is common to see the superlative in sentences such as:

> Tom and Sam are both twelve, but Tom is **tallest**.
> Which of the two sisters is **most beautiful**?

However, in more formal writing, it is safer to use the comparative:

> Tom and Sam are both twelve, but Tom is **taller**.
> Which of the two sisters is **more beautiful**?

General grammar guide

- To indicate the opposite of both the *-er/-est* and the *more/most* forms of comparison, *less* or *least* is always used:

adjective	comparative	superlative
sharp	less sharp	the least sharp
fortunate	less fortunate	the least fortunate
interesting	less interesting	the least interesting
involved	less involved	the least involved

Adverbs

Adverbs can sometimes be difficult to identify because the term 'adverb' covers several quite different types of words. However, the basic characteristic of an adverb is that it gives information about the way that an action is carried out or when and where it takes place.

Most adverbs are formed by adding *-ly* to the end of the related adjective:

    slow → slowly
    clever → cleverly
    annual → annually

Words which end in *-ble* drop the *-e* before *-ly* is added. So do the words *true* and *due*:

    sensible → sensibly
    suitable → suitably
    true → truly
    due → duly

Adjectives that end in *-y* change to *-i* before adding *-ly*, unless, like *sly* or *dry*, they have only one syllable:

    happy → happily
    greedy → greedily
    sly → slyly

Some adverbs keep the same spelling as the adjective to which they are related. It is often difficult to tell at first whether the word is an adjective or an adverb. The general rule is to look at the other words which it occurs with. If it comes before a noun it is probably an adjective:

    a **short** way   a **late** meeting
    a **long** pause   an **early** lecture

If it relates to a verb or an adjective it is probably an adverb:

    The lesson was cut **short**.   We met **late** at night.
    Don't stay **long**.   He came in **early**.

General grammar guide

Sentence adverbs are used at the beginning of sentences or clauses. They can be adverbs ending in *-ly* or other adverbs, e.g., *nevertheless, however*:

> **Foolishly**, I gave him my address.
> **Actually**, I don't mind.
> **Nevertheless**, we must give him an answer.

Adverbs of degree are words like *rather, quite, too*, and *almost*, and they come before adjectives or other adverbs:

> She seems **rather** nice
> Angus is a **very** good tennis player.
> She began to cry, **quite** loudly.

Some **adverbs of place** have the same spelling as prepositions. However, these adverbs do not have an object, and are often found at the end of a sentence or clause:

> He rushed **in**.
> She hurried **over**.
> The two friends fell **out**.

Just like adjectives, some adverbs have comparative and superlative forms. These are usually formed with *more* and *most*:

> Could you speak **more slowly**, please?
> Mrs. Kay's class behaved **(the) most sensibly**.

To indicate the opposite of comparatives and superlatives, *less* and *least* are used:

> I checked her work a bit **less thoroughly** this time.
> This product worked **(the) least effectively**.

Note the adverb forms of *good* and *bad*:

adjective	adverb	comparative adverb	superlative adverb
good	well	better	the best
bad	badly	worse	the worst

Determiners

A **determiner** is used to point more precisely to the person, thing, or idea that is being talked about. Determiners make the reference of nouns more specific. If I say *this car* it is clear that I mean a particular car which is near me. If I change it to *my car* I am saying something quite specific about ownership.

Determiners include:

- The **indefinite article** (*a*) and the **definite article** (*the*).

General grammar guide

- Words known as **demonstratives**, that show where something is, especially in relation to the speaker or writer: *this, that, these, those*.
- Words known as **possessives**, that show who or what something belongs to: *my, your, his, her, its, our, their*.
- Words known as **quantifiers**, that show the amount of something: *some, any, few, enough, much*.
- **Cardinal numbers** (*one, two, three,* etc.) and **ordinal numbers** (*first, second, third,* etc.)
- Words known as **distributives**: *each, every, either, neither*.
- Words known as **exclamatives**, that are used in exclamations: *what, such*.

Prepositions

A **preposition** is one of a small but very common group of words that relate different items to each other. Most English prepositions have a number of meanings that are particular to each preposition.

Simple prepositions consist of one word, e.g., *in, on, under*. **Complex prepositions** consist of more than one word, e.g., *due to, together with, on top of, in spite of, out of*.

The list below shows all the common simple prepositions. Some words can be either prepositions or adverbs, depending on how they are used and what they combine with. A preposition needs an object, rather like a transitive verb. The words in *italics* are the prepositions that can also be used as adverbs.

aboard	atop	for	*over*	to
about	bar	from	*past*	towards
above	*before*	in	pending	*under*
across	*behind*	*inside*	per	*underneath*
after	*below*	*into*	pro	until
against	*beneath*	like	re	unto
along	*beside*	*near*	regarding	*up*
alongside	between	of	*round*	upon
amid	*beyond*	*off*	since	via
among	*by*	*on*	than	with
around	despite	*onto*	*through*	*within*
as	*down*	*opposite*	*throughout*	*without*
at	during	*outside*	till	

In modern English, it is usually considered acceptable to end a sentence with a preposition, though in very formal written English, you may want to avoid it:

> That's the girl we were talking **about**. (= acceptable for most forms of writing)
> That is the girl about whom we were talking. (= very formal)

General grammar guide

Conjunctions

A **conjunction** joins two or more nouns or clauses to each other. Conjunctions are sometimes called 'joining words':

> I went to the shop **and** bought some bread.
> I bought some bread, **but** I forgot to get the milk.

In most formal writing, it is not considered good style to start a sentence with a conjunction. However, in more creative styles of writing, this is sometimes done for effect:

> I did not expect him to give me any financial support. **Or** any support at all, come to that.

Tenses

Verb forms use tense to show the time of what you are writing about, in other words whether it is in the past, the present, or the future:

> Jessica **works** in the post office.
> Laurence **worked** in the post office over the Christmas holidays.

There are two types of tenses in English:

- **Simple tenses** consist of a single word.
- **Compound tenses** are formed using the present or past forms of auxiliary verbs with another verb ending in -*ing* or -*ed*.

These are the tenses in English, showing the forms of the verb 'to play':

Tense	Form	Examples
Present Simple	I/we/you/they play he/she/it plays	I go to college in London. Manuela sings in a choir.
Past Simple	I/we/you/they played he/she/it played	I cooked a meal. He saw a tiger.
Future Simple	I/we/you/they will play he/she/it will play	We will give you the money. Louis will phone you later.
Present Perfect	I/we/you/they have played he/she/it has played	I have ordered a new sofa. This illness has ruined my life.
Past Perfect	I/we/you/they had played he/she/it had played	They had noticed a strange smell. She had visited Paris before.
Future Perfect	I/we/you/they will have played he/she/it will have played	We will have finished before dark. Gerry will have done his work by then.

General grammar guide

Present Continuous	I am playing we/you/they are playing he/she/it is playing	I am waiting for Jack. She is finishing her meal.
Past Continuous	I was playing we/you/they were playing he/she/it was playing	We were trying to see the queen. The water was splashing all over the floor.
Future Continuous	I/we/you/they will be playing he/she/it will be playing	Our choir will be performing in the cathedral. Mom will be worrying about us.
Present Perfect Continuous	I/we/you/they have been playing he/she/it has been playing	We have been trying to phone you all morning. The snow has been falling all night.
Past Perfect Continuous	I/we/you/they had been playing he/she/it had been playing	The children had been using my computer. Anna had been sitting there all day.
Future Perfect Continuous	I/we/you/they will have been playing he/she/it will have been playing	I will have been working on the project for over a year. On Sunday, we will have been living here for 10 years.

Regular and irregular verbs

Regular verbs form their past tenses with -ed:

> She wait**ed** for me.
> I look**ed** but I couldn't see her.

However, there are many common verbs that form their past tenses in a different way. Many of these have a different form for their simple past tenses and their compound past tenses. If you are not sure of the past form of a verb, check in the dictionary: the irregular ones will be shown.

Some examples of common verbs with irregular past forms are:

> become → became → become
> blow → blew → blown
> cost → cost → cost
> go → went → been
> leave → left → left
> swim → swam → swum
> take → took → taken

General grammar guide

Subject, object, and indirect object

The **subject** of a sentence is the person or thing that does the verb. The subject can be a noun, a noun phrase, or a pronoun:

> **Adam** played the piano.
> **The man in the red coat** asked me some questions.
> **Her car** broke down.
> **They** forgot to buy the milk.

All sentences must have a subject.

The **object** of a sentence usually comes after the verb. It can also be a noun, a noun phrase, or a pronoun.

> I spilled **the milk**.
> She saw **a large, black bird**.
> We were able to fix **the broken shelf**.
> I couldn't find **it**.

Not all sentences have an object:

> She was riding. (no object)
> She was riding **a horse**. (with object)
>
> Erica was writing. (no object)
> Erica was writing **a letter**. (with object)

Some verbs also have another sort of object, called an **indirect object**. An indirect object names who or what something is done to or for. It is usually needed with verbs like *give*, *find*, and *owe*:

> Mike owes **Tom** five dollars.
> Naveen gave **me** a box of chocolates.
> Susan bought **her rabbit** some more food.

Agreement

Agreement means making sure that all the words and phrases in a sentence have the correct form in relation to one another.

Subject/verb agreement

The form of the verb must be the correct one to go with the subject:

> The house **is** very large. (singular subject, singular verb)
> The star**s are** very bright. (plural subject, plural verb)

In very long sentences, it can be easy to make a mistake, especially if the verb is a long way from the subject.

General grammar guide

If two singular subjects are joined by *and*, they need a plural verb:

> Parminder and Amandeep **are going** on vacation.
> The table and the desk **need** polishing.

However, if the two things joined with *and* are thought of as one thing, a singular verb is used:

> Spaghetti and meatballs **is** my favorite meal.
> Bed and breakfast **is** the cheapest form of accommodation.

If the subject has *each*, *every*, or *no* before it, the verb should be singular, and the same is true for *any* before a singular subject:

> Every seat **was** taken already.
> Each vase **holds** four or five roses.

Speech

There are two ways of writing about what someone said:

- In **direct speech**, we repeat the actual words used:

  > "There is nothing we can do about it," Mona said.

- In **reported speech** (also called **indirect speech**), we make the words part of our own sentence, usually using a verb such as *say*, *announce*, or *explain*:

  > Mona said that there was nothing we could do about it.

Direct speech

Direct speech is common in novels and other writing where the actual words of speakers are quoted. The reporting verb (e.g., *say*, *announce*, *explain*) may come before the words that were spoken, or after them, or at a natural pause inside the reported sentence:

> **Mona said**, "There is nothing we can do about it."
> "There is nothing we can do about it," **Mona said**.
> "It's no good," **Mona said**, "There's nothing we can do about it."

The words spoken must be written inside quotation marks. They can be single (' ') or double (" "). In British English, single quotation marks are usually used.

The words spoken always begin with a capital letter as long as the sentence is not divided by a reporting verb. The comma comes inside the quotation marks:

> "**G**ive her a chance," Jamie begged.
> "**T**here is," Mona said, "nothing we can do about it."

If the words spoken are a question or an exclamation, there is no comma but a question mark or an exclamation point, which comes inside the quotation marks:

> "Why did you do it?" she asked.
> "Oh, mind your own business!" he snapped.

General grammar guide

The subject and reporting verb can be used in either order:

> "There is nothing we can do about it," **Mona said**.
> "There is nothing we can do about it," **said Mona**.

> **Tip for success**
> If you are writing a long stretch of direct speech between two characters, it is not always necessary to use reporting verbs each time. As long as it is clear which character is speaking, you can just start a new line within new quotation marks each time a different character speaks.

Reported speech

When you use reported speech, the words put into the reported clause do not exactly match the words actually spoken. For example, you will need to change pronouns, words like *here* and *there*, or the tense of the sentence:

> I believe **you**.
> She said that she believed **us**.
>
> I've been **here** before.
> He said that he had been **there** before.
>
> **I've done** the housework.
> He said **he had done** the housework.

Reported speech always has two clauses: the **reported clause** which contains the words that were spoken, usually in a slightly different form, and the **main clause** which contains the reporting verb. The main clause usually comes first:

> **Katie told me** that Marie is going to resign.
> **Sara asked** whether Hardeep was feeling better.

If the reported clause is a statement, the main clause is linked to the reported clause by *that*:

> Monique said **that** her favorite actor was Ben Whishaw.
> John replied **that** he preferred Scarlett Johansson.

The linking word *that* can be left out after most reporting verbs except those that mean 'answer':

> She told me **(that)** she was going to leave.
> I replied **that** I was very sorry to hear that.

If the reported clause is a question, the main verb will be a question word such as *ask, inquire, wonder, query*. The link between the main clause will be *if* or *whether*:

> She asked me **if** I was comfortable.
> He inquired **whether** the changes had been made.

General grammar guide

Reported clauses can also be used to express what someone is thinking as well as what is actually spoken:

> Hussain **wondered** whether *the concert would be sold out*.
> Charlotte **thought** that *she had better go and see her family*.

> **Key point to remember**
> Speech in a reported clause is not separated from the reporting verb by a comma, is not enclosed in quotation marks, and does not begin with a capital letter unless it is a proper noun. Reported questions are not followed by question marks.

Questions

There are three main ways of making questions in English:

- With a **question word**, such as *who*, *why*, or *how*:

    Who *won the race?*
    Which *team was it?*

- With an **auxiliary verb** (*do*, *have*, or *be*):

    Do *your children like sports?*
    Have *you seen her latest movie?*

- With a modal verb, such as *can* or *may*:

    Can *Mahmoud come, too?*
    May *I see the letter?*

Occasionally, we express sentences by our tone of voice, but this would only be appropriate for written English if you are writing direct speech:

> *"**She's left her job?** I thought she was happy there."*

Negative forms of questions almost always use contractions:

> **Doesn't** *he like talking about his childhood?*
> **Can't** *Peter have one, too?*

If the full *not* form is used, it comes immediately after the subject. The full form is very formal:

> *Does he* **not** *like talking about his childhood?*
> *Can Peter* **not** *have one, too?*

Questions should always have a question mark at the end, even if they are headings. The only time that a question does not have a question mark is if it is written in reported speech:

> *Do you like cats?*
> *He asked me if I liked cats.*

General grammar guide

Sentence tags

Sentence tags look like short questions and are used at the end of sentences. They are sometimes called **question tags**, but many sentences ending with a tag are not real questions.

They are usually used to check that the listener or reader agrees with what the speaker or writer has said. Sentence tags are used very commonly in speech and in informal writing, but rarely in formal written English.

If you need to write them, either in a piece of informal writing, or if you are quoting direct speech, remember that they have a comma before them, and a question mark at the end:

> *You've seen the program, haven't you?*
> *Well, we can't jump over it, can we?*
> *You aren't listening, are you?*

Business English grammar

Introduction

There are certain areas of life and activity where particular features of language are found more frequently than in other areas. For example, doctors and engineers commonly use very specific vocabulary in their work-related communication.

Apart from specialized vocabulary, there are also grammatical patterns that occur more frequently in particular contexts. This section looks at forms that are common in the field of business and commerce. Examples of how language is used are organized into four areas:

- Networking
- Negotiating
- Presenting
- Meetings

In many cases, of course, the language that is described can be used in more than one of these topic areas.

Networking

Making social and business arrangements

The dialogue below is an example of the type of conversation that might take place between two people who want to make an arrangement to meet at a later time.

A   Do you want to meet up for lunch sometime next week?
B   Yes. That would be nice. We can talk about the FCL deal. I'm not in on Monday. **I'm going to work** from home. **How about** next Tuesday?
A   Let's see. No, I can't. **I'm taking** some clients to the riverside development. **What about** Wednesday?
B   **I'm going** to Germany on Wednesday. My flight **leaves** around six so I don't need to leave until after lunch. Is that okay?
A   Fine. **Let's** meet at one.

You can use the **present continuous** to talk about future arrangements that you would put in an appointment book. Normally, these arrangements involve other people:

> **We're having** a meeting to discuss the proposal next Tuesday.
> The people from ILC **are coming** for lunch at two.

When future arrangements are not firm plans, but it is your intention that they will happen, you use *be going to* followed by an infinitive:

> **I'm going to have** an early night because I'm tired.
> We'll have some time after the meeting, so **we're going to explore** the old part of the city.

Business English grammar

You use the **present simple** to talk about events in schedules such as transportation timetables or conference programs:

> Our flight **leaves** at six and **gets in** at eight.
> The morning plenary session **starts** at nine-thirty.

There are several ways in which you can make suggestions about what you and someone else should do.

- You can use *Let* followed by *us* shortened to *Let's*:

  > **Let's** have a break and go for a coffee.
  > **Let's** stay in contact.

- You can use a question beginning with *Should we*:

  > **Should we** meet outside the restaurant?
  > **Should we** reward ourselves with a little lunch?

- You can use a question beginning with *Why don't we*:

  > **Why don't we** have a working breakfast in the hotel?
  > **Why don't we** stay an extra day?

- You can use a question beginning with *What about* or *How about* in front of a noun phrase:

  > **How about** a drink after the meeting?
  > **How about** next Sunday?
  > **What about** March 20th?

Asking for and confirming information

To form the different types of commonly used questions in English, you can use a variety of structures, where the word order and the use of auxiliaries can be confusing. The dialogue below is a phone call which might take place between two people where details of an order are discussed.

A   Hello. I'm phoning about an order. The order number is 28443AB.
B   **When did you place the order**, please?
A   Last week.
B   Sorry. **What was the order number again**?
A   28443AB.
B   Oh yes, it was for some switcher units, **wasn't it**?
A   That's right. Can you tell me if it's been processed yet?
B   Yes. They were out of stock but we got some in yesterday. **Didn't you get an email?**
A   Uh, no. **Haven't they been sent yet**?
B   They went this morning.
A   So **do you have any idea when we can expect delivery**?
B   They should be with you tomorrow.
A   OK. Thanks.

Business English grammar

When you are using the present simple or past simple form of *be*, you simply put the verb at the beginning of the clause, followed by the subject:

Are you with me so far?
Is Simon up to the job?
Were they at the meeting?

When the verb is not *be*, you need to use an auxiliary verb (or *do*, *does*, or *did*), followed by the subject and then the main verb:

Is he staying here tonight?
Do you work in a team?
Did they want to talk to me?
Will they accept that?
Have you got the figures with you?

If there is more than one auxiliary verb, the first auxiliary comes at the beginning of the clause, followed by the subject and then other auxiliaries and the main verb:

Has the problem been reported?
Have they been waiting long?

If you are using the present simple or past simple form of *be*, the verb goes after the *wh-* word and in front of the subject:

How **was** your meeting?
Where **is** the customer?
So where **were** your auditors during all of this?

If you are using the present simple or the past simple of any verb except *be*, you put *do*, *does*, or *did* in front of the subject:

Which department **did you want**?
Who **do you work** for?
How **did she make** the decision?
What **does he** really **think** about the deal?

When a *wh-* word is the subject of a verb, or when it forms part of the subject, the word order is the same as in an affirmative clause:

Who invited you?
What happened earlier?
Which bid won?

You can use indirect questions like *Can you tell me*, *Could you tell me*, *Do you know*, and *Do you have any idea* in order to be more polite.

For *yes/no* questions, you use *if* or *whether* followed by a clause with affirmative word order:

Can you tell me **if he got my message**?
Do you know **whether the units have arrived**?

Business English grammar

For *wh-* questions, you use a *wh-* word followed by a clause with affirmative word order:

> Could you tell me **what you have planned today**?
> Have you any idea **what it would cost**?

You can ask for confirmation that something is true by making a statement, and then adding a **question tag** such as *isn't it?* or *doesn't she?*:

> They work on Saturdays, **don't they?**
> You can park there, **can't you?**

You can use a negative question to express surprise at a situation:

> **Didn't you arrange** to meet them at the airport?
> **Wasn't** the meeting at nine?
> **Haven't you finished** yet?

Talking about experience

You use the **present simple** to talk about permanent facts and routines:

> We **offer** a wide range of services for the bio industry.
> Every week, Susan **drives** to Edmonton for a meeting with the factory manager.
> The first thing we **do** is a site survey.

You use the **present continuous** to talk about current situations when you want to emphasize that they are temporary or in progress at the time of speaking:

> We **are updating** our flight rules to adapt to the new scenario.
> Users **are looking** at other ways of financing IT projects.
> He**'s staying** there as the guest of our Taiwan-based supplier.

If you want to talk about a situation or an event that happened at a particular time in the past which is finished, you use the **past simple**. Time expressions like *last week* and *a year ago*, which refer to finished time periods in the past, can be used to make the time reference clear:

> Ballmer **flew** to California last week and **proposed** the merger.
> After Harvard, he **studied** at Oxford University.
> Ms. Caridi previously **worked** in the legal department at Lehman Brothers.

You use the **past continuous** to emphasize an action in progress or to give the background context for events:

> The company **was losing** money, so he decided to sell.
> The plant **was making** a profit of $250,000 a year and the market **was growing** steadily.

The **present perfect simple** can be used to talk about:

- experiences, without stating a specific time
- events and situations that started in the past and continue up to the present
- events and situations that have an immediate effect on the present.

Business English grammar

You cannot use time expressions like *yesterday*, *last year*, or *at Christmas* with the present perfect simple:

> Yes, I**'ve bumped** into him a number of times.
> We**'ve met** with all the major shareholders.
> Spending **has risen** steadily since the beginning of the year.
> **Have** you **brought** the report with you?

You use the **present perfect continuous**:

- when you want to talk about situations that started in the past, that may or may not be completed, but that you see as temporary
- when you want to emphasize duration:

> We **have been looking** for a European partner for some time.
> The company **has been working** hard to reduce its overhead.

If you want to show that one event happened before another in the past, you can use the **past perfect**:

> When people left the meeting, they were more enthusiastic than when they **had arrived**.
> Before the negotiations started, they **had decided** to give employees a 4% raise.

Negotiating

Making and modifying proposals

You can use **comparatives** to show that you are prepared to negotiate on a particular point:

> We need a **more flexible** arrangement.
> I'm looking for a figure **closer** to three dollars a unit.
> Would you be **happier** with a fixed rate?

You can use the modals *would*, *could*, *may*, and *might* to make your message less direct:

> We **might** be able drop the price.
> **Could** we look at that side of your proposal later?
> **Would** you consider reducing discounts?

The modals *could*, *may*, and *might* are also used to say that a particular result or situation is possible:

> There **may** be a slight delay.
> Yes, that **might** be possible.
> Yes, I **can** see that this **could** have great potential.

Business English grammar

You can use **conditional** sentences to discuss options and explore possibilities in a hypothetical way:

> **If you could give us exclusivity**, we can settle this now.
> The discount could be bigger **if you increased the quantity**.
> **If I drop the price**, do we have a deal?
> **Unless you can show a little flexibility**, we might as well call it a day.

Rejecting ideas and proposals

To distance yourself from an opinion, and therefore sound less direct, you can use the **passive** form of a reporting verb with *it* as the *impersonal subject*:

> **It is assumed that** share prices will rise as a result of the operation.
> **It was agreed that** the details would remain confidential.

You can use an adverbial such as *a little*, *a bit*, or *rather* to make a negative message seem less strong:

> That sounds **a little** expensive.
> They may be **a bit late**, I'm afraid.
> Unfortunately, we were **rather** disappointed with the quality of the last delivery.

Expressions like *not very*, *not totally*, *not completely*, and *not entirely* followed by a positive adjective sound more diplomatic than using a negative adjective:

> We are**n't totally** convinced by the idea of using overnight shipping.
> I would**n't** be **very** happy with that arrangement.
> You do**n't** seem **absolutely** certain about that.

The **past continuous** can be used to make a statement more indirect in order to be polite:

> We **were expecting** to hear a new proposal today.
> I **was aiming** to establish a framework for further discussion.
> We **were hoping** to reach agreement about this before we go.

Presenting

Describing change

You can use the **present perfect simple** to talk about events or situations that are still important in the present:

> The Nasdaq Index **has strengthened** further since this morning.
> We **have made** changes based on your concerns and feedback.

To talk about change that is still in progress at the present moment, you can use the **present continuous**:

> The economy **is growing**, but if we look closer, there are some worrying trends.
> In the country's major cities, the quality of life **is improving**.

Business English grammar

Making predictions

You can use *will* when you are certain about a situation in the future:

> The cuts **will** certainly have a negative effect on the economy.
> I believe this attitude **will** soon become the norm.

You can also use *be going to* instead of *will* to make predictions:

> She predicts that earnings **are going to** come down sharply.
> We are trying to decide whether the economy **is going to** go into a recession.

If you want to make a negative prediction, it sounds more polite to introduce an affirmative clause with a phrase like *I don't think* than to use a negative clause:

> **I don't think** this will go down well with the union.
> **I don't think** it's going to be a great success.

You can use *could*, *may*, or *might* to say that it is possible that something will happen:

> These economic issues **could** cause huge problems for the rest of Europe.
> New technology **might** be able to halve the amount of water we use.
> The market **may** eventually accomplish what environmentalists want.

You use *be likely* followed by a *to*-infinitive to say something will probably happen:

> Emerging economies **are likely to face** continuing problems.

You use *be bound* followed by a *to*-infinitive to say strongly that something is certain to happen in the future:

> The pressure on margins **is bound to make** success difficult.

Contrasts and comparisons

You use **conjunctions** like *while*, *although*, *in spite of*, and *despite* to contrast one idea with another:

> Until now, only 8,000 people have registered with the site, **although** the company said the number is still increasing.
> **In spite of** the crisis, sales are actually up on last year.
> Retail sales are plummeting, **while** consumer prices are rising.

Whereas is more formal:

> In France there was a small improvement, **whereas** there was no change in Germany.

You can use an adjective with either *-er* added to the end (*cheaper*, *older*) or *more* placed in front of the adjective (*more expensive*, *more interesting*), followed by *than*:

> The chip is **more economical than** a dedicated system.
> Kondex is **bigger than** Gartex in terms of sales.

Business English grammar

You can also use *not as ... as* or *not so ... as* to compare things:

> Our factories are still **not as efficient as** the car plants in Japan.
> Traditional forms of advertising are **not as effective as** they used to be.

You can use *much*, *a lot*, or *far* in front of comparative adjective forms to emphasize a big difference:

> Manufacturers are **much more cautious** than before about investment plans.
> The job provides her with a **far greater** challenge than ordinary office work would.

You can use *slightly*, *a bit*, or *a little* to emphasize small differences:

> The first-quarter increase was **slightly higher** at 1.2%.
> If anything, employees working from home were **a little more productive** than those in the office.

To emphasize small differences with the *not as ... as* structure you can add *quite*:

> But by other measures, oil is **not quite as expensive as** it seems.

Linking ideas

You can show what sort of connection there is between one sentence and another by using sentence connectors. In a presentation, these connectors prepare the listener for what is coming next.

Connectors such as *on top of that* and *at the same time* can be used to add strength to your argument. In writing, or in more formal situations, you can use *moreover* or *furthermore*:

> The financial crisis continues. **On top of that**, exceptional weather has devastated crops.
> Unemployment has grown rapidly. **At the same time**, there is low demand for existing skills.
> Experts predict that the downturn will be less severe than expected. **Furthermore**, banks plan to lend more freely in the next three months.

You use connectors like *however*, *on the other hand*, or *nevertheless* when you want to give another point of view:

> If you want job security, this is not the position for you. **On the other hand**, the salary is good.
> There was a fall in sales last month. **However**, revenue from digital products rose by nearly 20% in the first half.
> It is necessary for foreign currency traders to think quickly and accurately. **Nevertheless**, mistakes do occasionally occur.

When you want to show that the fact or situation you are mentioning is a result of what you have just referred to, you can begin your statement using a connector like *so* or *as a result*. If you want to sound more formal you can use *consequently* or *therefore*:

Business English grammar

Another 3,100 jobs were lost last year, **so** people no longer trust the company. We lost sight of what our customers wanted. **As a result**, sales slumped. Confidence is still low. **Consequently**, firms are not willing to make new investments.

Distancing yourself

You use the **passive** when you want to focus on actions, views, and decisions, rather than on the people responsible for them. It is frequently used in reports, and it is more common in written English:

> In 2006, 18.3 % of the world's electricity **was produced** using renewable sources.
> When materials **were coated** in the substance, the plating remained stable at room temperature.

The passive is often used to describe processes with adjuncts like *first*, *second*, *then*, and *finally* to indicate order:

> **First**, the raw data **is collated** in tables. It **is then prepared** for processing. **Finally**, the data model **is produced**.

Meetings

Interrupting

When you are participating in a meeting you can use *can I* and *could I* to interrupt politely. *Could* is more polite than *can*:

> **Can I** ask a question here?
> **Could I** just interrupt here for a minute?

Making suggestions

Can and *could* are also used for making suggestions:

> **Could** we maybe develop a new payment system?
> **Can** we ask Network Solutions to help?

To sound more persuasive you can use a negative question:

> **Couldn't we** ask them to come in for a demonstration?
> **Can't we** do this later?

You can also use *Let's* and *Why don't we* to make suggestions:

> **Let's** call it a day.
> **Why don't we** move on to the next point on the agenda?

Business English grammar

Making requests

You can use *Can you* or *Could you* to ask someone to do something. *Could* is more polite than *can*:

> **Can you** summarize the main points, please?
> **Could you** explain that again?

The phrase *Would you mind* followed by the *-ing* form is also used to make polite requests:

> **Would you mind** go**ing** back to the previous graphic?
> **Would you mind** just wait**ing** a minute while I answer that?

Various conditional sentences can also be used in questions to direct a meeting in a polite way:

> **Would it be all right if** we go over that again?
> **Is it okay if** we leave this till later?
> **Do you mind if** we start with a few introductions, please?
> **Would you mind if** I investigate this a little further?

Disagreeing politely

If you want to disagree with someone without offending them, you can use an expression of agreement followed by *but*:

> Well, **I agree up to a point, but** I see it slightly differently.
> **I see what you mean, but** I still don't think it's possible.
> **I take your point about the costs, but** we could still do it.

If you want to contradict somebody, or say something that other people may disagree with, you can avoid sounding rude by using a reporting verb such as *I think* (or *I don't think*) or *I believe* (or *I don't believe*):

> **I think** it's time we stopped.
> **I don't think** that's actually the case.
> **I don't believe** we committed ourselves to maintaining the price.

You can avoid sounding absolutely certain of your information by using the verbs *seem* or *appear*:

> This **seems to be** the only possible solution to the problem.
> It **appears that** the cost of the new system would be minimal.

Academic English grammar

Introduction

When you write or speak in academic contexts, it is important to:

- be clear about what you want to say
- connect and sequence your message
- establish your relationship with the reader appropriately.

The language you choose is related to the purpose of your text. This will vary according to (i) the form in which your message will be presented and (ii) your audience.

A **lecture** or **seminar** presents information and points out areas of disagreement. A lecture is often certain in tone, but it raises questions that can be explored.

A seminar is an occasion where views are presented and discussed. The speaker often uses *you* and *we*.

An **essay** or **assignment** brings together and discusses information. A **dissertation** or a **journal article** investigates a topic. These texts are formal, and the tone is generally impersonal.

A **textbook** presents information for teaching and reference: it tells the reader what is known, and its tone suggests certainty.

Being clear about what you want to say: noun and verb phrases

The aim of academic speech and writing is to communicate a message precisely, and without using too many words. In order to achieve this, speakers and writers concentrate information mainly in **noun** and **verb phrases**.

Research involves investigating or analyzing a subject. This means that nouns and verbs used in academic texts often relate to processes and concepts.

Nominalization

Verbs are often **nominalized** (= made into nouns) in order to focus the reader on a concept or idea instead of the action. For example:

Verb	Noun
demonstrate	demonstration
discover	discovery
measure	measurement
assess	assessment
assist	assistance
maintain	maintenance

Academic English grammar

Note how using nouns instead of verbs in the examples below changes the focus of the sentence, and makes it sound more academic:

> In 1898, Marie and Pierre Curie announced their **discovery** of a new element.
> After an initial **measurement** of the patient's blood glucose, they are given 50g of soluble lactose to drink.
> They base their **assessment** of risk on available scientific evidence.
> The **maintenance** of blood pressure is achieved less rapidly as we age.

The noun phrase (1): Premodifying noun phrases

Premodification allows you to concentrate a lot of information in the noun phrase. You can build the noun phrase in the following ways:

- noun + noun (+ noun)

    ...a food preservation process.

- adverb + -ed participle + noun + noun (+ noun)

    ...a recently developed food preservation process.

    ...strongly motivated history students.

    ...a well-organized advertising campaign.

- -ed adjectives

Some -ed adjectives carry the meaning of something that has already been completed:

> ...finalized plans. (= plans that have been agreed)
>
> ...a previously exhibited work of art. (= a work of art that has been shown previously)
>
> ...a closed case. (= a case belonging to the group of cases that have been solved)
>
> ...a recently completed project. (= a project that has recently been finished)

- adverb + -ed participle + adjective + noun + noun (+ noun)

    ...a recently developed cost-effective food preservation process.

    ...a newly discovered major oil field.

- -ing adjectives

-ing adjectives are used for describing an effect or a process, or a state that continues over a period of time:

> ...changes which may well bring diminishing returns.
> ...measures to control the rising cost of living.

Academic English grammar

Using more than four premodifiers makes the noun phrase difficult to understand, especially when this consists only of nouns. For example:

>...the school team game playing area.

In this case, it would be better to use a prepositional phrase (see prepositional phrases below):

>...playing areas for school team games.

The noun phrase (2): Postmodifying noun phrases

When you need to be more precise about the noun phrase, or to give the reader more information, you can use a **relative clause**, a **participle** or **infinitive clause**, or a **prepositional phrase**.

To identify a subject clearly, you use a **defining relative clause** introduced by a **relative pronoun**. The most common relative pronoun in academic English is *which*:

>A magnet is a device **which strongly attracts certain metals**.

The relative clause is often reduced in academic writing. You can reduce the relative clause in the following ways:

- leaving out the relative pronoun (when the defining relative clause refers to the object of the sentence):

   >The hard drive was erased because of the confidential information (which) **it contained**.

- using a **participle clause**

Participle clauses reduce the relative clause to either an *-ing* participle or an *-ed* participle:

>...one of the hundreds of internet entrepreneurs (who are) **launching startups in Palo Alto**.
>They recommend four to twelve doses (which are) **given a few days apart**.

Other common verbs that are used to reduce the relative clause are *use, base, cause, make,* and *concern*.

- using an **infinitive clause**

Infinitive clauses are less frequent than participle clauses. An infinitive clause often suggests that it is important to do something:

>**A problem to watch for** is loosening of the joints at the top of the legs.
>(instead of *A problem which you should watch for is...*)

>There are some basic psychological principles **to bear in mind**.
>(instead of *There are some basic psychological principles which you should bear in mind*.)

Academic English grammar

- replacing the relative clause with a **prepositional phrase**

When a relative clause contains *have*, you can reduce it to a prepositional phrase using *with*:

> Parliament is a national governing body **with the highest level of legislative power**.
> (instead of ...*a national governing body which has the highest level*...)

When a relative clause contains *is* + preposition, you can reduce it to a simple prepositional phrase:

> A second central concept (which is) **at the core of much developmental research is**...

- adding an identifying noun phrase

You can give further information about a person or thing by using a noun phrase that describes or identifies them or it:

> The Mariana Trench, **11,034m at its deepest point**, is deeper than the height of Mount Everest.
> A quicker alternative, **a simple search program**, makes it easier to search the corpus.

This is common when you are introducing or defining acronyms, abbreviations, or technical terms:

> The Scientific Advisory Committee on Nutrition **(SACN)** has issued a draft report.

A **non-defining relative clause** is not needed to identify the person, thing, or group you are talking about; instead, it gives the reader more information about the subject, or it evaluates or comments on the subject:

> Dark matter, **which may be invisible for many reasons**, has become increasingly important.

The verb phrase

In general, academic English is less concerned with events, and more concerned with what has been learned from the event. Therefore, the focus of the sentence moves away from the verb phrase to the noun phrase. Verbs are often nominalized (= made into nouns) – see **Nominalization** on page 1813.

The range of tenses used in academic English is more restricted than in everyday English: simple forms of verbs are used more frequently; continuous forms, the past perfect, and the future perfect are used less often.

The tense you use shows your attitude and other people's attitude to the subject. For example, it shows whether a piece of research or an idea is still generally accepted or not.

The **present simple** is commonly used in the following ways:

- to refer to something that you believe is still valid:

> The two theories **are known** as 'ridge push' versus 'slab pull' respectively.

Academic English grammar

- to state continuing objectives:

    The aim **is** to direct the energy of the radiation to kill the cancerous cells.

- to describe general principles or laws:

    When water **freezes**, it **expands**.

- to explain or discuss data or results:

    The results **show** that only a portion of world trade **is affected**.

- to make reference to or relate events in literary works, films, etc.:

    Shakespeare, in King Lear, **emphasizes** the social causes of madness.

The **present perfect** is commonly used in the following ways:

- to review research:

    There is a vast literature looking at development issues, the main elements of which **have been reviewed** here.

- to make a general statement about the state of research activity in a given area:

    Little research **has been done** on microscopic plastics.

- to summarize a text:

    In light of the evidence that **has been reviewed** thus far in this book...

The **past simple** is commonly used in the following ways:

- to indicate that something happened or was true at a particular time in the past, and that it may be less valid today:

    The almost universal view **was** that the liver **was** the main organ in the blood system.

- to describe samples and procedures:

    A full study **was conducted** with a sample of managers from the U.K. head office.

- to report findings:

    Their research **showed** that over half of all cancer cases could be prevented.

Will is used to state your intention:

   This study **will examine** the effects of depression.

Will often occurs with an adverb such as *often* or *probably*, because academic writers must avoid suggesting that their personal ideas and theories are facts:

   The desert regions **will probably become** more extensive.
   Changes in practice **will often be** the result of a long political process.

Academic English grammar

Linking verbs are used for describing a situation or a quality, and so they occur frequently in academic English. Linking verbs that are commonly used in academic English are *be*, *become*, *look*, *remain*, *seem*, *appear*, *prove*, and *represent*:

> At first glance, the system **seems** overwhelmingly complex.
> Scientists fear that some viruses may **prove** challenging to deal with.
> The source of the information must **remain** anonymous.

Common complements include:

- nouns:

> The results of this experiment **remain a secret**.
> Their decision **represents a turnaround**.

- adjectives:

> The patients **appeared** to be **immune** to the HIV virus.
> Predictions for next year **look** increasingly **uncertain**.

- object complements:

You can put a noun or adjective complement after the object of some transitive verbs. This complement describes the object, and is called an **object complement**:

> They cannot **keep** the options of both politics and terrorism **open**.
> Television scored significantly higher amongst those who **found** politics **interesting**.
> Some analysts do not **consider** it a **virus**.

Ordering and connecting your message

There are several ways of using language to hold your whole message together and to give it meaning. The first step is to arrange content into a recognizable pattern. When you are planning a piece of work or a talk, you can use the following pattern to sequence your ideas:

describe a situation → outline any problems → suggest a solution → provide an evaluation

The following sections describe techniques for ensuring that your writing or speech holds together well, and that both your intention and your message are clear:

- using grammatical structures and vocabulary to 'signpost' your intention
- referring back and referring forward
- providing connectors to hold sections together.

Using grammatical structures and vocabulary to 'signpost' your intention

There are several ways in which you can use grammatical structures and vocabulary within a section of text to express the following ideas:

- the arrangement of events in time
- procedure (= how something is done)

Academic English grammar

- cause and effect
- comparison and contrast
- advantages and disadvantages.

If you want to show that one thing happened soon after the other, you can use a finite verb in the main clause, and an *-ing* participle in the subordinate clause:

> They **headed** rapidly for the Channel ports, **showing** their passports at the barriers.

You can also indicate the order in which things happened using ordinals and adverbs such as *first, then, later*, etc.:

> **Later**, in December 1989, the committee decided ...

You can use the same structure – a finite verb in the main clause, and an *-ing* participle in the subordinate clause – to show how something is done:

> Researchers **determined** the size of each machine, **taking** into account the properties of the material.

The same structure can be used to show that one thing happened as a result of another:

> Many of the men **returned** home, **causing** local unemployment.

Note that you can also indicate cause and effect in a main clause using a verb such as *cause, lead to*, or *result in*, or a noun such as *effect, result*, or *outcome*:

> The consumption of an excessive amount of sugar can **cause** obesity.
> The **effect** of the famine in 1921–22 was devastating.

You can compare and contrast information in the following ways:

- using a sentence connector:

> **Conversely**, the effect of intravenous administration of the drug is immediate.
> **By contrast**, the more recent publication is more straightforward.

- using a comparative adverb:

> Owner-controlled companies performed **better** than those subject to management control.

- using a verb:

> The aim of this report is to **compare** and **contrast** these two business structures.
> We **will compare** our own findings with those of Mortimore et al., (1988).
> These findings **contrast** strongly with those from other tests.

You can provide an evaluation leading to a conclusion in the following ways:

- using an adjective:

> This method of production is **preferable**.

Academic English grammar

- using a verb:

    Consumers **prefer** our products for their quality and finish.

- using a noun:

    This type of surgery has the **advantage** that no abdominal incision is needed.

- using an adverbial clause of reason or purpose:

    This type of organization should be much smaller **since it will not need employees concerned with line management**.
    You must take as much care as possible **in order to avoid accidents**.

Referring back and referring forward

The most common way of making a text hold together is to refer back to something that you have mentioned earlier, by using pronouns, demonstratives, determiners, and adjectives. It is also common to refer forward, particularly in longer texts.

This and *those* are common in academic contexts:

   ...they had commissioned a specific piece of research. **This** came somewhat late.
   There were, however, wide differences of opinion about party chances. Some of **those** differences...

Note that the demonstrative is often linked with a noun referring to:

- spoken events:

    That's a good question.

- ideas:

    This view is also held by Rey and Stiglitz (1988).

- actions and events:

    During **this** process, cracks appeared in the limestone.
    This situation continued for almost two decades.

- pieces of writing:

    As **this** research has shown, customer brand loyalty is very hard to achieve.

You use *such* as a **determiner** and **predeterminer** to refer back:

   They generally agree on which aspects of police work they like and dislike. **Such** a consensus was originally explained as...

   The report highlights the high level of overcrowding in some prisons. In **such** circumstances...

Academic English grammar

Other words and expressions used for referring back are *previous*, *above*, and *the former ... the latter*:

> The **previous** arguments have pointed to two ways in which the system might be improved.
> What is said **above** gives the background to what follows.
> The French have two words for citizenship: 'citoyenneté' and 'civisme', **the former** describing the status, **the latter**, attitude and behavior.

To refer forward to sections of the text, you can use:

- *following* as an adjective, or *the following*, to refer to texts, ideas, and pieces of writing:

    > The **following** passage summarizes Schmidt's views:...
    > Symptoms of the condition may include any of **the following**: chest pains, headache, difficulty breathing, and joint pain.

- the adverb *below*, normally after nouns referring to texts and pieces of writing:

    > The trade blockade with India, described **below**, resulted in severe energy shortages.

Sentence connectors show the relationship between two sentences, clauses, or sections of text. The following are particularly common in academic speech and writing:

function	sentence connectors
indicating a further argument	additionally, in addition, also, furthermore, moreover
indicating a similar situation	again, equally, likewise, similarly
indicating contrast	alternatively, in contrast, conversely, even so, however, nevertheless, nonetheless, on the contrary, on the other hand, although
indicating cause	accordingly, as a result, as a consequence, consequently, hence, thereby, therefore, thus
indicating purpose	in order to, so that, lest

The style of your message

Once you have decided on your message, you need to formulate it so that you can achieve the effect you are aiming for. Common ways of presenting information are described below.

Distancing

Present your text using an impersonal voice. This allows you to focus on the issues rather than on the people involved. The structures below are especially useful for avoiding *I*.

- You can remove focus from people by using impersonal *it*:

    > **It** is almost an occupational hazard accepted by virologists.

Academic English grammar

- Use impersonal *it* and a passive form of a reporting verb if your message is an opinion held by an unspecified group of people:

    It is widely **believed** that this substance is harmful.
    It is acknowledged that resources are unevenly distributed.

- Note that you can also use a reporting verb in the passive, followed by a *to*-infinitive:

    This substance **is believed to be** harmful.
    UVB and UVA **are** both **reported to cause** skin cancer.

When you want to say that something exists, or you want to introduce something new, use *there* as a subject:

There are several claims to be considered in relation to this perspective.
There are no fewer than thirteen different species of otters.

In a conclusion or an example, do not write *I have discovered...*. Instead, put a word such as *findings* or *results* in subject position:

These **findings** suggest that there are two different processing methods.
The **results** show that this problem is widespread.

You can use the passive without *by* to describe procedures when the performer of the action does not need to be specified:

The tissue sample **was removed, analyzed, and stored**.
The engine **was retested** after the malfunction.

Note that it is important not to overuse the passive, as it can make your writing difficult to read.

Use verbs such as *continue*, *decrease*, and *increase* to describe events that involve a change of state:

The situation **continues** to be a cause for concern.
The rate of change **slowed** in the second half of the year.

The result of a change of state can be shown in a subordinate clause beginning with an *-ing* form:

Prices rose, **leading to a fall in demand**.
Appetite is lessened, **resulting in weight loss and dietary problems**.

Reporting

An important aspect of academic speaking and writing involves reporting (or citing) the work of other academics.

Citations can be used to explain the basis of your work, to support and illustrate your arguments, or to contrast your ideas with other writers' theories.

Academic English grammar

However, do not be tempted to include too many quotations. You are the author, and your ideas and analysis are the most important part of your writing. Your writing should not rely too heavily on quotations – they should be there to support your work but not to form the main part of it.

Make sure that any quotations you do add are there for a good reason – do not put them in simply to make your document longer. Too many quotations can interrupt the flow of your writing and make the text seem cluttered.

Remember that there is a big difference between quoting and **plagiarizing**, which means using the work of others as if it were your own. Even if you use different words rather than quoting directly, if you are using someone else's ideas, you should say so.

Always make sure your quotations are **accurate**. If you have found your quotation as a quotation in someone else's work, you should go back to the original source, if possible, to check it.

It is **not necessary to use whole sentences** in quotes – in fact it is usually best to use only the parts that are relevant to your argument. However, if you take a sentence out of a paragraph, or a word or phrase out of a sentence, make sure that you do not change the author or speaker's intended meaning.

If you use a quote, you must always **explain why you have used it** and what you think its importance is. This can be done very simply. For example, If the quotation clearly backs up a point you have just made, you could use a phrase like:

> As x says ...

Other quotations may need more **analysis and explanation**. You cannot assume that your reader will draw the same conclusions from a quotation as you do, so you must make it very clear what you think its significance is. You might start your next sentence with phrases such as:

> This shows that ...
> [The author] is clearly of the opinion that ...
> Put more simply, this means ...

It is often useful to give a **context** for your quotation, for example by explaining when and where it was written or spoken, or the situation the writer or speaker was in.

How to show quotations

For long quotations (around 60 words or more), it is common to use a separate paragraph, indented slightly from the rest of the text and often using a slightly smaller font.

Shorter quotations are usually shown as part of a sentence:

> Greenshaw argued that "the upper classes are not capable of compassion."
> She described the children as "motivated and alert."

Quotations can also follow an introductory clause, using a colon or a comma before the quotation marks:

> Charles made a pronouncement: "There will be no more discussion on this matter."
> Oscar Wilde once said, "Always forgive your enemies; nothing annoys them so much."

Academic English grammar

If you are quoting lines of poetry, it is usual to show the ends of lines with /:

> As an unperfect actor on the stage,/Who with his fear is put beside his part

If you want to **omit part of a quotation**, you can use [...]:

> She described the play as "racist in a way that was typical of that time, and deeply upsetting."
> She described the play as "racist [...] and deeply upsetting."

If you want to add something to a quotation (for example, to clarify a point for the reader), you use square brackets:

> Giving evidence, then he said, "I went round to his house with Al [Albert Flynn, brother of the accused]."

If a quotation contains an error, for instance of spelling or grammar, or if it contains something that is surprising, shocking, or offensive, and you want to stress that this is *really* what the person said or wrote, use [sic], which is Latin for *thus*:

> Clarke wrote that he "could of [sic] done it."
> (This should be *could have done it.*")

Quoting or paraphrasing?

While direct quotations are common in academic writing, the reported information should usually be summarized in your own words. This is called **paraphrasing**.

The following reporting verbs are commonly used in academic English to introduce cited material.

These verbs indicate the type of activity reported:

If the activity is:	research-related	mental	verbal
Use:	measure	think	state
	calculate	believe	write
	estimate	consider	define
	find	focus on	challenge
	obtain		

> Nuttall and Gipps (1982) **estimate** that the direct cost of the APU was £800,000 per year.
> Collins and Ellis (2001) also **challenge** the traditional concept of the individual.

Note that the verbs that you use will depend on your academic discipline. Research-related verbs are more common in technical and scientific writing; mental and verbal activity verbs are more common in the humanities and social sciences.

Academic English grammar

These verbs indicate your attitude to the reported material:

If you think it is:	valid	not valid	neutral
Use:	show	fail to	discuss
	establish	overlook	respond
	demonstrate	ignore	comment
			suggest

> Wenger's data **show** that 43 percent of elderly people named as a confidant someone they had known for at least 50 years.
> This evidence **fails to** acknowledge the importance of the children's diet.

These verbs indicate the cited author's attitude to the material:

If the author is:	positive	negative	neutral	tentative
Use:	argue	refute	state	suggest
	maintain	object	write	believe
	see	challenge	discuss	imply
	hold		comment	allude to

> Both Smith and Goodman (2000) **maintain** that skilled adult reading is far from error-free.
> Bly **argues** that the process of initiation into adulthood is easier for women than for men.

Note that verbs that indicate attitude are more commonly used in the humanities and the social sciences.

Think about the purpose of your quotations. For example, in an essay on literature, it may be necessary to have a lot of quotations so that you can discuss and analyze the actual language of the author. For a science essay, it may be more appropriate to paraphrase most of the ideas you discuss.

If you do paraphrase, you must still make it clear whose work you are using. Make sure that your paraphrase does not change the meaning of the original in any way – if you want to add your own comments, or disagree with it, you must make it clear which are your ideas and which are the ideas of the person you are paraphrasing.

Referencing quotations

If you use a quotation, you should always say who the speaker or author is, and – if at all possible – what the source was.

This can be done **within the text**, using your own words to introduce the quotation:

> As Juliet says in Shakespeare's Romeo and Juliet, "Parting is such sweet sorrow."
> In a speech during his visit to Berlin in 1963, U.S. President John F. Kennedy famously said,

Academic English grammar

"Ich bin ein Berliner."

In **academic writing**, it is usual to refer to a footnote or a bibliography (list of books you used) to reference a quotation. Styles for this can vary, so it is a good idea to ask your teacher if there is a recommended style. A common way would be to show the author and the date of the publication in brackets in the main text; then show the whole source in the bibliography.

In the text:

> As Prof Williams points out: "There is a measurable difference between the amount people claim to eat and the amount they actually eat." (Williams, 2007, p.25)

In the bibliography:

> Williams, J. (2007) *The Causes of Obesity*. Newtown: Newtown University Press

If you use a **quotation from a website**, you must reference it in a similar way. Again, there are different styles for this, but a common way would be:

> Author, A (date) *Title of article or web page*. Available at: article.com. Accessed on 04/17/2015

Expressing degrees of certainty

When you are formulating your message, you need to consider how strongly you want to make your claim. Different structures express different degrees of certainty, and allow you to establish a position that you can defend if you are criticized.

For example, it is possible to defend the following statement:

> Certain researchers have attempted to show that some underprivileged children cannot engage in play.

The following would be less easy to defend:

> Researchers have shown that underprivileged children cannot engage in play.

You can use the following adverbs when the available information is not precise:

quantity	frequency	degree	limitation
roughly	often	rather	predominantly
approximately	frequently	quite	mostly
around	occasionally	somewhat	partly
	seldom		partially
	rarely		

> Increased risk of infection is **predominantly** linked to poor sanitation.

You can use more cautious language when you think that other people may disagree with your statement, or when you want to express uncertainty about whether or not a proposition is true. This may be because you really are uncertain, or because you want to create opportunities for readers to decide for themselves.

The following lists show distancing structures that are commonly used for making statements sound more cautious:

modal verbs	semi-auxiliary verbs	adverbs	prepositional phrases	adjectives
could	seem	possibly	in some respects	uncertain
might	appear	seemingly	in a sense	possible
may		arguably	in most cases	
can		likely	in general	
		apparently	in principle	
		evidently		
		generally		
		normally		
		typically		

There is, **arguably**, a common thread in all these positions.
As will be seen later, current models are inadequate **in some respects**.

Note that if you express too much uncertainty, or if you repeatedly show that you are not sure if something is true, your message will have less worth, and it will be difficult to interpret.

Emphasizing

In general English, you can use strong words to emphasize a point. In academic English, you often show emphasis by changing the normal word order of a statement.

Subordinate clauses normally occur in first position in academic texts. The **main clause** carries the new or most important information.

You can use the following structures to show that something important is going to be announced at the end of the sentence:

- **nominal relative clauses**:

    What is now required is a systematic investigation of the data.

- **prefacing structures**:

    The question we now need to consider is whether the dosage should be reduced.

- **split sentences**:

    It was this declaration which triggered the events that followed.

Glossary of Grammatical Terms

Glossary of grammatical terms

abstract noun a noun used to describe a concept such as a quality, an idea, or an experience rather than something physical or concrete; e.g., *joy, size, language*. Compare with **concrete noun**.

active used for describing verb phrases such as *gives*, and *has made*, where the subject is the person or thing doing the action or responsible for the action. Compare with **passive**.

adjective a word used to tell you more about a person or thing, such as its appearance, color, size, or other qualities; e.g., *...a pretty blue dress*.

adjective clause another name for **relative clause**.

adverb a word that gives more information about when, how, where, or in what circumstances something happens; e.g., *quickly, now*. There are several different kinds of adverb; adverbs of degree, manner, place, time, duration, and frequency. There are also **focusing adverbs**.

adverbial a word or combination of words added to a clause to give more information about time, place, or manner. See also **sentence adverbial** and **sentence connector**.

adverb of degree an adverb indicating the amount or extent of a feeling or quality; e.g., *extremely*.

adverb/adverbial of duration an adverb or adverbial indicating how long something lasts; e.g., *briefly, for a long time*

adverb/adverbial of frequency an adverb or adverbial indicating how often something happens; e.g., *often, once a week*.

adverb of manner an adverb indicating the way in which something happens or is done; e.g., *carefully*.

adverb of place an adverb that gives more information about position or direction; e.g., *Move closer*.

adverb particle an adverb used as part of a phrasal verb; e.g., *hide out, sit up, turn round*.

affirmative not containing a negative word. Also called **positive**.

agent another name for **performer**.

agreement the relationship between a subject and its verb, or between a number or determiner and its noun; e.g., *I look/she looks... one bell/three bells*. Also called **concord**.

apostrophe s an ending ('s) added to a noun to mark possession; e.g., *...Harriet's daughter... the professor's husband... the Managing Director's secretary*.

article see **definite article, indefinite article**.

aspect the use of verb forms to show whether an action is continuing, repeated, or finished.

attributive used for describing the position of adjectives when they are used in front of a noun. Compare with **predicative**.

auxiliary verb one of the verbs *be, have*, and *do* when they are used with a main verb to make verb forms, negatives, questions, and so on. Also called **auxiliary**. Modals are also auxiliary verbs.

bare infinitive another name for **infinitive without *to***.

base form the form of a verb that has no letters added to the end and is not a past form; e.g., *walk, go, have, be*. The base form is the form you look up in a dictionary.

broad negative one of a small group of adverbs including *barely* and *seldom* which are used to make a statement almost negative; e.g., *I barely knew her*.

cardinal number a number used for counting; e.g., *one, seven, nineteen*.

classifying adjective an adjective used to identify something as being of a particular type; e.g., *Indian, wooden, mental*. They do not have comparatives or superlatives. Compare with **qualitative adjective**.

Glossary of grammatical terms

clause a group of words containing a verb. See also **main clause** and **subordinate clause**.

clause of manner a subordinate clause that describes the way in which something is done, usually introduced with *as* or *like*; e.g., *She talks like her mother used to*.

collective noun a noun that refers to a group of people or things; e.g., *committee, team*.

color adjective an adjective referring to a color; e.g., *red, blue, scarlet*.

common noun a noun used to refer to a person, thing, or substance; e.g., *sailor, computer, glass*. Compare with **proper noun**.

comparative an adjective or adverb with *-er* on the end or *more* in front of it; e.g., *friendlier, more important, more carefully*.

complement a noun phrase or adjective that comes after a linking verb such as *be*, and gives more information about the subject or object of the clause; e.g., *She is a teacher, She is tired, They made her chairperson*.

complex preposition a preposition that consists of more than one word; e.g., *in spite of, due to*.

complex sentence a sentence consisting of two or more main clauses linked by a subordinating conjunction; e.g., *We went inside when it started to rain*.

compound a combination of two or more words functioning as a unit. For example, *self-centered* and *free-style* are compound adjectives, *bus stop* and *state of affairs* are compound nouns, and *dry-clean* and *roller skate* are compound verbs.

compound sentence a sentence consisting of two or more main clauses linked by a coordinating conjunction; e.g., *They picked her up and took her into the house*.

compound tense a tense that uses an auxiliary verb with another verb ending in *-ing* or *-ed*; e.g., *I have lived here for over ten years*.

concessive clause a subordinate clause, usually introduced by *although* or *while*, that contrasts with a main clause; e.g., *Although I like her, I find her hard to talk to*.

concord another name for **agreement**.

concrete noun a noun that refers to something we can touch or see; e.g., *table, dress, flower*. Compare with **abstract noun**.

conditional clause a subordinate clause usually starting with *if*. The event described in the main clause depends on the condition described in the subordinate clause; e.g., *If it rains, we'll go to the movies... They would be rich if they had taken my advice*.

conjunction a word linking together two clauses, phrases, or words. There are two types of conjunctions – **coordinating conjunctions**, which link parts of a sentence of the same grammatical type (*and, but, or*), and **subordinating conjunctions**, which begin subordinate clauses (*although, when*).

continuous a verb form that contains a form of the verb *be* and an *-ing* participle; e.g., *She was laughing...They had been playing tennis*. Also called **progressive**.

contraction a shortened form in which an auxiliary verb and *not*, or a subject and an auxiliary verb, are joined together and function as one word; e.g., *aren't, she's*.

coordinate clause a clause that is connected to another clause with a coordinating conjunction such as *and* or *but*; e.g., *He fell and broke his leg*.

coordinating conjunction a word such as *and, but*, or *or* which joins together two clauses, phrases, or words of the same grammatical type.

copula a name sometimes used to refer to the verb *be*. In this grammar, the term **linking verb** is used.

count noun a noun that can be singular or plural; e.g., *dog/dogs, lemon/lemons, foot/feet*. Also called **countable noun**.

declarative a clause in the declarative form has the subject followed by the verb. Most

Glossary of grammatical terms

statements are made in the declarative form. Also called **indicative**.

defining non-finite clause a participle clause that is placed after a noun phrase to identify the person or thing you are talking about; e.g., ...*the girl wearing the red hat*.

defining relative clause a relative clause that identifies the person or thing that is being talked about; e.g., *I wrote down everything that she said*. Compare with **non-defining relative clause**.

definite article the determiner *the*.

definite determiner one of a group of determiners including *the*, *that*, and *your* which you use when the person you are speaking to understands which person or thing you are talking about; e.g., *the old man*, *my ideas*.

delexical verb a verb that has very little meaning in itself and is used with an object that carries the main meaning of the structure. *Give*, *have*, and *take* are commonly used as delexical verbs; e.g., *She gave a small cry... I've had a coffee*.

demonstrative one of the words *this*, *that*, *these*, and *those* used in front of a noun; e.g., ...*this woman... that tree*. They are also used as pronouns; e.g., *That looks nice... This is fun*.

dependent clause another name for **subordinate clause**.

determiner one of a group of words including *the*, *a*, *some*, and *my* which are used at the beginning of a noun phrase.

direct object a noun phrase referring to a person or thing affected by an action, in a sentence with an active verb; e.g., *She wrote her name... I shut the windows*.

direct speech speech reported in the words actually spoken by someone, without any changes in tense, person, and so on.

ditransitive verb a verb such as *give*, *take*, or *sell* which can have both an indirect and a direct object; e.g., *She gave me a kiss*.

dynamic verb a verb such as *run*, *give*, or *slice* which describes an action. Compare with **stative verb**.

-ed adjective an adjective that ends in *-ed*, and usually has the same form as the *-ed* participle of a verb, or is formed by adding *-ed* to a noun; e.g., *a worried look... skilled workers*. Adjectives that do not end in *-ed* but have the same forms as irregular *-ed* participles are also called *-ed* adjectives; e.g., *a broken bone*.

-ed participle a verb form such as *walked* or *played*, which is used to make perfect forms and passives, or in some cases an adjective. Irregular participles such as *given* and *broken* are also called *-ed* participles because they behave like regular *-ed* participles. Also called **past participle**.

ellipsis when you leave out words because they are obvious from the context.

emphasizing adjective an adjective such as *complete*, *utter*, or *total* which stresses how strongly you feel about something; e.g., *I feel a complete fool*.

ergative verb a verb that can be either transitive or intransitive in the same meaning. To use the verb intransitively, you use the object of the transitive verb as the subject of the intransitive verb; e.g., *He grows flowers in his garden... Flowers grew in his garden*.

exclamation a word or sentence spoken suddenly and loudly in order to express surprise, anger, and so on; e.g., *Oh gosh!*

exclamative determiner a determiner that is used in an exclamation; e.g., *What a beautiful day!*

finite a finite verb is inflected according to person or tense rather than being an infinitive or a participle.

first person see **person**.

focusing adverb a sentence adverb that indicates the most relevant thing involved; e.g., *only*, *mainly*, *especially*.

future the use of *will* with the base form of the verb to refer to future events; e.g., *She will come tomorrow*.

future continuous the use of *will be* and an *-ing* participle to refer to future events;

Glossary of grammatical terms

e.g., She *will be going* soon. Also called **future progressive**.

future perfect the use of *will have* and an *-ed* participle to refer to future events; e.g., I *will have finished* tomorrow.

future perfect continuous the use of *will* with *have been* and an *-ing* participle to refer to future events; e.g., I *will have been walking* for three hours by then. Also called **future perfect progressive**.

gender a grammatical term referring to the difference between masculine and feminine words such as *he* and *she*.

generic pronoun one of a group of pronouns including *you* and *they* which are used to refer to people in general.

gerund another name for *-ing* **noun**.

gradable a gradable adjective can be used with a word such as *very* to say that the person or thing referred to has more or less of a quality; e.g., *very boring*, *less helpful*.

idiom a group of two or more words with a meaning that cannot be understood by taking the meaning of each individual word; e.g., *to kick the bucket, to run wild*.

***if*-clause** a **conditional clause**; or a clause used to report a *yes/no*-question.

imperative a clause in the imperative has the base form of the verb without a subject, e.g., *Come here... Take two tablets every four hours... Enjoy yourself*.

impersonal *it* *it* is an impersonal subject when it is used to introduce a fact, or when it is used in a split sentence; e.g., *It's raining... It was you who asked*.

indefinite article the determiners *a* and *an*.

indefinite determiner one of a group of determiners including *a*, *many*, and *several* which you use to refer to someone or something of a particular type, without saying which person or thing you mean; e.g., *an* old man, *several* suggestions.

indefinite place adverb one of a group of adverbs including *anywhere* and *somewhere* which are used to indicate position or location in a general or vague way.

indefinite pronoun one of a group of pronouns including *someone* and *anything* which are used to refer to a person or thing in a general way.

indicative another name for **declarative**.

indirect object a second object used with a transitive verb to indicate who or what benefits from an action, or gets something as a result of it; e.g., She gave *me* a rose.

indirect question a way of asking a question that makes it sound more polite; e.g., *Can you tell me where the bank is?* instead of *Where is the bank?*

indirect speech another name for **reported speech**.

infinitive the base form of a verb. It is often used with *to* in front of it; e.g., *(to) take, (to) see, (to) bring*.

infinitive without *to* the infinitive form without *to* in front of it, used with modals and certain other verbs; e.g., *You must go... Let me think*.

inflection the variation in the form of a word to show differences in tense, number, case, and degree.

***-ing* adjective** an adjective that has the same form as the *-ing* participle of a verb; e.g., ... a *smiling* face... a *winning* streak.

***-ing* noun** a noun that has the same form as the *-ing* participle of a verb; e.g., *Swimming* is good for you.

***-ing* participle** a verb form ending in *-ing* that is used to make verb forms, and as an adjective. Also called **present participle**.

interjection another name for **exclamation**.

interrogative a clause in the interrogative form has part or all of the verb phrase in front of the subject. Most questions are asked in the interrogative form.

interrogative adverb one of the adverbs *how, when, where*, and *why* when they are used to ask questions.

Glossary of grammatical terms

interrogative pronoun one of the pronouns *who*, *whose*, *whom*, *what*, and *which* when they are used to ask questions.

intransitive verb a verb that is used to talk about an action or event that only involves the subject and so does not have an object; e.g., *She arrived... I was yawning*.

inversion changing the word order in a sentence, especially changing the order of the subject and the verb.

irregular not following the normal rules for inflection. An irregular verb has a past form and/or *-ed* participle that is formed in a different way from the regular ending.

lexical verb another name for **main verb**.

linking verb a verb that links the subject and complement of a clause; e.g., *be*, *become*, *seem*, *appear*. Also sometimes called **copula**.

main clause a clause that is not dependent on, or is not part of, another clause.

main verb any verb that is not an auxiliary verb. Also called **lexical verb**.

mass noun (in this grammar) a noun that is usually an uncountable noun, but that can be used as a countable noun when it refers to quantities or types of something; e.g., *...two sugars... cough medicines*.

measurement noun a noun that refers to a unit of size, volume, weight, speed, temperature, etc.; e.g., *mile*, *liter*, *degree*.

modal an auxiliary verb that is used with a main verb to indicate a particular attitude, such as possibility, obligation, prediction, or deduction; e.g., *can*, *could*, *may*, *might*. Also called **modal auxiliary** or **modal verb**.

modifier a word or group of words that come in front of a noun; e.g., *...a beautiful sunny day... ...a psychology conference*.

negative used for describing a sentence that uses a word like *not*, *never*, or *no one* to indicate the absence or opposite of something, or to say that something is not the case; e.g., *I don't know you... I'll never forget*.

negative word a word such as *never* and *not* which expresses a negative meaning.

nominalize to change a verb or an adjective into a noun.

nominal relative clause a subordinate clause that functions as a noun and often begins with *what* or *whatever*; e.g., *What he said was true*.

nominal *that*-clause a subordinate clause that functions as a noun and begins with *that*; e.g., *He showed that it was true*.

non-defining relative clause a relative clause that gives more information about someone or something, but that is not needed to identify them; e.g., *That's Mary, who was at university with me*. Compare with **defining relative clause**.

non-finite the non-finite forms of a verb are the infinitive and participle forms; e.g., *to take*, *taking*, *taken*.

noun a word that refers to people, things, and abstract ideas such as feelings and qualities; e.g., *woman*, *Harry*, *guilt*.

noun modifier a noun used in front of another noun, as if it were an adjective; e.g., *...a car door... steel wool*.

noun phrase a group of words that acts as the subject, complement, or object of a clause, or as the object of a preposition.

number the way in which differences between singular and plural are shown; e.g., *flower/flowers*, *that/those*. See also **cardinal number** and **ordinal number**.

object a noun phrase that refers to a person or thing, other than the subject, which is involved in or affected by the action of a verb. See also **direct object** and **indirect object**. Prepositions are also followed by objects.

object complement a word that is used to describe the object of a clause and that occurs with verbs such as *make* and *find*; e.g., *It made me tired... I found her asleep*.

Glossary of grammatical terms

ordinal number a number that is used to indicate where something comes in an order or sequence; e.g., *first, fifth, tenth, hundredth*.

participle a verb form used for making different tenses. See **-ed participle** and **-ing participle** for more details.

partitive a word that gives information about the amount of a particular thing; e.g., *pint, loaf, portion*.

passive verb forms such as *was given, were taken, had been made*, where the subject is the person or thing that is affected by the action. Compare with **active**.

past continuous the use of *was* or *were* with an *-ing* participle, usually to refer to past events; e.g., They *were worrying* about it yesterday. Also called **past progressive**.

past form the form of a verb, often ending in *-ed*, that is used for the past simple.

past participle another name for **-ed participle**.

past perfect the use of *had* with an *-ed* participle to refer to past events; e.g., She *had finished*.

past perfect continuous the use of *had been* with an *-ing* participle to refer to past events; e.g., He *had been waiting* for hours. Also called **past perfect progressive**.

past simple the use of the past form of a verb to refer to past events; e.g., They *waited*... It *fell* over.

past tense a tense used to describe actions or events that took place in the past. See **tense** for more details.

perfect form a verb form with *have* and an *-ed* participle; e.g., I *have met* him... We *had won*.

performative verb a verb that states explicitly what action the speaker is performing when he or she uses it; e.g., *apologize, resign, promise*.

performer the person or thing that is responsible for the action expressed by the verb; e.g., *Mark* phoned ... Our dinner was eaten by *the dog*.

person a term used to refer to the three classes of people who are involved in something that is said. They are the **first person** (the person speaking or writing), the **second person** (the person being addressed), and the **third person** (the people or things that are being talked about).

personal pronoun one of a group of pronouns including *I, you,* and *me* which are used to refer back to the people or things you are talking about.

phrasal verb a combination of a verb and an adverb and/or a preposition, which have a single meaning; e.g., *back down, hand over, look after, look forward to*.

phrase a set of words that is smaller than a clause, and that is based around a particular word class: for example, a verb phrase is based around a main verb, and can also contain auxiliary verbs. See also **noun phrase**, **verb phrase**, and **prepositional phrase**. Phrase is also sometimes used to refer to any group of words.

plural the form used to refer to more than one person or thing; e.g., *dogs, women*.

plural noun a noun that is only used in the plural form; e.g., *trousers, scissors, vermin*.

positive another name for **affirmative**.

possessive a structure used to show possession; e.g., *your, Jerry's, mine*.

possessive determiner a determiner such as *my, your,* and *their*. Also called **possessive adjective**.

possessive pronoun one of the words *mine, yours, hers, his, its, ours,* and *theirs*.

postdeterminer a small group of adjectives used after a determiner and in front of other adjectives; e.g., *certain, remaining*.

predeterminer a word that comes in front of a determiner; e.g., *all* the boys... *double* the trouble... *such* a mess.

predicative used for describing the position of adjectives when they are used following a noun or after a linking verb such as *be*. Compare with **attributive**.

Glossary of grammatical terms

premodifier a word, especially an adjective or a noun, that comes before a noun to add information about it; e.g., *All the nicest people were there*.

preposition a word such as *by*, *with*, or *from*, which is usually followed by a noun phrase or an *-ing* form.

prepositional phrase a structure consisting of a preposition and its object; e.g., *on the table, by the sea*.

present continuous the use of the present simple of the verb *be* with an *-ing* participle to refer to present events; e.g., *Things are improving*. Also called **present progressive**.

present participle another name for *-ing* **participle**.

present perfect the use of the present simple of *have* with an *-ed* participle to refer to past events that exist in the present; e.g., *She has loved him for ten years*.

present perfect continuous the use of *have been* and *has been* with an *-ing* participle to refer to past events that exist in the present; e.g., *We have been sitting here for hours*. Also called **present perfect progressive**.

present simple the use of the base form or the *s* form of a verb, usually to refer to present events; e.g., *I like bananas... My sister hates them*.

present tense a tense used to describe events taking place in the present, or situations that exist in the present.

primary auxiliary *be* and *have* when they are used as auxiliary verbs; e.g., *He is looking for you*.

progressive another name for **continuous**.

pronoun a word used instead of a noun, when you do not want to name someone or something directly; e.g., *it, you, none*.

proper noun a noun that refers to a particular person, place, or institution; e.g., *Anna, Boston, Christmas*. Compare with **common noun**.

purpose clause a subordinate clause, usually introduced by *in order to*, or *so that*; e.g., *I came here in order to ask you out to dinner*.

qualifier any word, phrase, or clause that comes after a noun phrase, and gives extra information to expand its meaning; e.g., *a book with a blue cover ...the shop on the corner*.

qualitative adjective an adjective that is used to indicate a quality, and is gradable; e.g., *funny, intelligent, small*. Compare with **classifying adjective**.

quantifier a word that shows the amount of something; e.g., *some, none*.

quantity expression a phrase ending in *of* that allows you to refer to a quantity of something without being precise about the exact amount; e.g., *some of, a lot of, a little bit of*.

question a structure that typically has the verb in front of the subject and that is used to ask someone about something; e.g., *Have you responded?* Also called **interrogative**.

question tag a structure or word that is used at the end of a statement in order to form a question. Also called **sentence tag**.

reason clause a subordinate clause, usually introduced by *because, since*, or *as*; e.g., *Since you're here, we'll start*.

reciprocal pronoun the pronouns *each other* and *one another*, used to show that two or more people do or feel the same thing; e.g., *They loved each other*.

reciprocal verb a verb that describes an action that involves people affecting each other in the same way with the same action; e.g., *They met in the street... He met her yesterday*.

reflexive pronoun a pronoun ending in *-self*, such as *myself* or *themselves*, which is used as the object of a verb when the person affected by an action is the same as the person doing it.

reflexive verb a verb that is typically used with a reflexive pronoun; e.g., *enjoy yourself, pride yourself on*.

Glossary of grammatical terms

regular verb a verb that follows the normal rules of formation; e.g., *look, start, help*.

relative clause a subordinate clause that gives more information about someone or something mentioned in the main clause. See also **defining relative clause** and **non-defining relative clause**.

relative pronoun a *wh*-word such as *who* or *which*, used to introduce a relative clause; e.g., *...the girl who was carrying the bag*.

reported clause the part of a reporting structure that describes what someone has said; e.g., *She said that I couldn't see her*.

reported question a question that is reported using a reporting structure rather than the exact words used by the speaker.

reported speech speech that is reported using a reporting structure rather than the exact words used by the speaker. Also called **indirect speech**.

reporting clause a clause that contains a reporting verb, which is used to introduce what someone has said; e.g., *They asked if I could come*.

reporting structure a structure that reports what someone has said by using a reported clause rather than repeating their exact words; e.g., *She told me she'd be late*.

reporting verb a verb that describes what people say or think; e.g., *suggest, say, wonder*.

result clause a subordinate clause introduced by *so that* which gives the result of something; e.g., *The house was severely damaged so that it is now uninhabitable*.

rhetorical question a question that you use in order to make a comment rather than to obtain information; e.g., *Oh, isn't it silly?*

second person see **person**.

semi-modal the verbs *dare*, *need*, and *used to* which behave rather like modals.

sentence a group of words that express a statement, question, or command. A sentence usually has a verb and a subject, and may consist of one clause, or two or more clauses. A sentence in writing has a capital letter at the beginning and a period, question mark, or exclamation point at the end.

sentence adverbial an adverbial that applies to the whole clause, rather than to part of it; e.g., *We possibly have to wait and see*. See also **sentence connector**.

sentence connector a sentence adverbial used to introduce a comment or reinforce what is said; e.g., *moreover, besides*.

sentence tag a structure or word that is used at the end of a statement in order to form a question. Also called **question tag**.

s form the base form of a verb with *s* on the end, used in the present simple.

simple sentence a sentence that contains only one clause.

singular the form used to refer to or talk about one person or thing; e.g., *dog, woman*. Compare with **plural**.

singular noun a noun typically used in the singular form; e.g., *sun, business*.

split infinitive the placing of a word between *to* and the base form of a verb; e.g., *...to boldly go where no man has gone before*.

split sentence a sentence in which emphasis is given to either the subject or the object by using a structure beginning with *it*, *what*, or *all*; e.g., *It's a hammer we need... What we need is a hammer*.

stative verb a verb that describes a state; e.g., *be, live, know*. Compare with **dynamic verb**.

subject a noun phrase that usually comes before a verb, and agrees with the verb in person and number. In active sentences, the subject usually refers to the person or thing that does the action expressed by the verb; e.g., *We were going shopping*.

subjunctive a verb form that is used in some languages to express attitudes

Glossary of grammatical terms

such as wishing, hoping, and doubting. The subjunctive is not very common in English, and is used mainly in conditional clauses such as *If I were you*...

submodifying adverb an adverb that is used in front of an adjective or another adverb in order to strengthen or weaken its meaning; e.g., ...*very interesting*... *quite quickly*.

subordinate clause a clause that begins with a subordinating conjunction such as *because* or *while* and which must be used with a main clause.

subordinating conjunction a conjunction that begins a subordinate clause.

substitution the special use of pronouns and other words to replace part or all of a clause; e.g., "*Are you going to the party?*" – "*I hope so.*"

superlative an adjective or adverb with *-est* on the end or *most* in front of it; e.g., *thinnest, quickest, most wisely*.

supporting auxiliary *do* when it is used an an auxiliary verb to form questions, negatives, and emphatic statements; e.g., *Do you like carrots?*

tense the verb form that shows whether you are referring to the past or the present.

that-clause a clause starting with *that* which is used mainly when reporting what someone has said; e.g., *She said that she'd clean up for me*. *That* can be omitted when the clause is used after a reporting verb.

third person see **person**.

time adverbial an adverbial that gives more information about when something happens; e.g., *I saw her yesterday*.

time clause a subordinate clause that indicates the time of an event; e.g., *I'll phone you when I get back*.

title a word used before a person's name to show their position or status; e.g., *Mrs., Dr., Queen*.

to-infinitive the base form of a verb preceded by *to*; e.g., *to go, to have, to jump*.

transitive verb a verb used to talk about an action or event that involves more than one person or thing, and so is followed by an object; e.g., *She's wasting her money*.

uncount noun a noun that refers to a general kind of thing rather than to an individual item, and so has only one form; e.g., *money, furniture, intelligence*. Also called **uncountable noun**.

verb a word used with a subject to say what someone or something does, or what happens to them; e.g., *sing, spill, die*.

verb phrase a main verb, or a main verb preceded by one or more auxiliary verbs, which combines with a subject to say what someone or something does, or what happens to them; e.g., *I'll show them*... *She's been sick*.

vocative a word used when speaking to someone, just as if it were their name; e.g., *darling, madam*.

wh-clause a clause starting with a *wh*-word.

wh-question a question that expects an answer giving a particular person, place, thing, amount, and so on, rather than just *yes* or *no*.

wh-word one of a group of words starting with *wh*-, such as *what, when*, or *who*, which are used in *wh*-questions. *How* is also called a *wh*-word because it behaves like the other *wh*-words.

whether-clause a clause used to report a *yes/no*-question; e.g., *I asked her whether she'd seen him*.

yes/no-question a question that can be answered simply with either *yes* or *no*; e.g., *Would you like some more tea?*

Word Lists

Frequent words   1607

Academic Word List   1620

Frequent words

This is a list of the 3,000 most frequent words in the Collins Corpus.

a
abandon
abandoned
ability
able
abortion
about
above
abroad
absence
absolute
absolutely
abuse
academic
accept
acceptable
accepted
access
accident
accompany
accord
according to
account
accurate
accuse
achieve
achievement
acid
acknowledge
acquire
acquisition
acre
across
act
action
active
activist
activity
actor
actress
actual
actually
ad
add
addition
additional

address
adequate
adjust
administration
admire
admit
adopt
adult
advance
advanced
advantage
advertise
advice
advise
adviser
advocate
affair
affect
afford
afraid
after
afternoon
afterward
again
against
age
agency
agenda
agent
aggressive
ago
agree
agreement
agricultural
agriculture
ah
ahead
aid
aim
air
air force
aircraft
airline
airport
alarm
album

alcohol
alert
alive
all
all right
allegation
alleged
alliance
allied
allow
ally
almost
alone
along
alongside
already
also
alter
alternative
although
altogether
always
amateur
amazing
ambassador
ambition
amendment
amid
among
amount
analysis
analyst
ancient
and
anger
angle
angry
animal
anniversary
announce
announcement
annual
another
answer
antique
anxiety

anxious
any
anybody
anymore
anyone
anything
anyway
anywhere
apart
apartment
apparent
apparently
appeal
appear
appearance
apple
application
apply
appoint
appointment
appreciate
approach
appropriate
approval
approve
April
area
aren't
argue
argument
arise
arm
armed
armed forces
army
around
arrange
arrangement
arrest
arrival
arrive
art
article
artist
as
Asian

aside
ask
aspect
assault
assembly
assess
assessment
asset
assist
assistance
assistant
associate
associated
association
assume
assumption
assured
at
athlete
atmosphere
attach
attack
attempt
attend
attention
attitude
attorney
attract
attractive
auction
audience
audio
August
aunt
author
authority
auto
automatic
autumn
available
avenue
average
avoid
await
award
aware

WORD LISTS

Frequent words

away	beer	bone	businessman	ceasefire
awful	before	book	busy	celebrate
baby	begin	boom	but	celebration
back	beginning	boost	butter	cell
background	behalf	boot	button	center
backing	behave	border	buy	central
bad	behavior	bore	buyer	century
badly	behind	born	by	ceremony
bag	being	borrow	bye	certain
bake	belief	boss	cabinet	certainly
balance	believe	both	cable	chain
ball	bell	bother	cake	chair
ballot	belong	bottle	call	chairman
ban	below	bottom	calm	challenge
band	belt	bound	camera	chamber
bank	bend	bowl	camp	champion
banker	beneath	box	campaign	championship
banking	benefit	boy	can	chance
bar	beside	brain	cancel	chancellor
bare	besides	branch	cancer	change
barely	best	brand	candidate	channel
bargain	bet	brave	cap	chaos
barrel	better	bread	capable	chapter
barrier	between	break	capacity	character
base	beyond	breakfast	capital	characteristic
baseball	bid	breast	captain	charge
based	big	breath	caption	charity
basic	bike	breathe	capture	chart
basically	bill	breed	car	charter
basis	billion	bridge	carbon	chase
basketball	bird	brief	card	chat
bass	birth	bright	care	cheap
bat	birthday	brilliant	career	check
bath	bit	bring	careful	cheer
bathroom	bite	broad	Caribbean	cheese
battle	bitter	broadcast	caring	chemical
bay	black	broadcasting	carrier	chest
be	blame	broker	carry	chicken
beach	blast	brother	case	chief
bean	blind	brown	cash	child
bear	block	brush	cast	childhood
bearing	blood	budget	castle	chip
beat	bloody	build	casualty	chocolate
beaten	blow	building	cat	choice
beating	blue	bunch	catch	choose
beautiful	board	burden	category	chop
beauty	boat	burn	Catholic	Christian
because	body	burst	cause	Christmas
become	boil	bury	cautious	church
bed	bomb	bus	cave	cigarette
bedroom	bond	business	cease	cinema

WORD LISTS

Frequent words

circle	comfortable	confidence	cool	crop
circuit	coming	confident	cooperate	cross
circumstance	command	confirm	cope	crowd
cite	commander	conflict	copy	crown
citizen	comment	confront	core	crucial
city	commentator	confrontation	corner	cruise
civil	commerce	Congress	corporate	cry
civil war	commercial	congressional	corporation	crystal
civilian	commission	connection	correct	cue
claim	commissioner	conscious	correspondent	cultural
clash	commit	consciousness	corruption	culture
class	commitment	consequence	'cos	cup
classic	committee	conservative	cost	cure
classical	common	consider	cottage	curious
clean	communicate	considerable	cotton	currency
clear	communication	consideration	cough	current
clever	communist	considering	could	curtain
client	community	consist	council	customer
climate	company	consistent	counsel	cut
climb	compare	constant	count	cutting
clinic	compared	constitution	counter	cycle
clock	comparison	constitutional	counterpart	dad
close	compensation	construction	country	daily
clothes	compete	consult	countryside	damage
clothing	competition	consultant	county	dance
cloud	competitive	consumer	coup	dancing
club	competitor	contact	couple	danger
coach	complain	contain	courage	dangerous
coal	complaint	contemporary	course	dare
coalition	complete	content	court	dark
coast	complex	contest	cousin	data
coat	complicated	context	cover	date
code	component	continent	coverage	daughter
coffee	comprehensive	continue	cow	day
cold	compromise	contract	crack	dead
collapse	computer	contrast	craft	deadline
colleague	concede	contribute	crash	deal
collect	concentrate	contribution	crazy	dealer
collection	concentration	control	cream	dear
collective	concept	controversial	create	death
college	concern	controversy	creative	debate
colonel	concerned	convention	credit	debt
color	concert	conventional	crew	debut
colored	concession	conversation	cricket	decade
column	conclude	convert	crime	December
combat	conclusion	convict	criminal	decide
combination	concrete	conviction	crisis	decision
combine	condemn	convince	critic	deck
come	condition	convinced	critical	declaration
comedy	conduct	cook	criticism	declare
comfort	conference	cooking	criticize	decline

WORD LISTS

Frequent words

decorate
deep
defeat
defend
defense
deficit
define
definitely
definition
degree
delay
delegate
delegation
deliberate
delight
delighted
deliver
delivery
demand
democracy
democrat
democratic
demonstrate
demonstration
demonstrator
deny
department
departure
depend
deposit
depression
depth
deputy
describe
description
desert
deserve
design
designer
desire
desk
desperate
despite
destroy
destruction
detail
detailed
detective
determine
determined
develop

development
device
dialogue
diary
didn't
die
diet
difference
different
difficult
difficulty
dig
digital
dinner
diplomat
diplomatic
direct
direction
director
dirty
disappear
disappointed
disaster
discipline
discount
discover
discovery
discuss
discussion
disease
dish
dismiss
display
dispute
distance
distribution
district
divide
dividend
division
divorce
do
doctor
document
doesn't
dog
dollar
domestic
dominate
done
door

double
doubt
down
downtown
dozen
draft
drag
drain
drama
dramatic
draw
dream
dress
dressed
drift
drink
drive
driver
drop
drug
drum
dry
due
dump
during
dust
duty
each
eager
ear
earlier
early
earn
earnings
earth
ease
easily
east
eastern
easy
eat
echo
economic
economics
economist
economy
edge
edit
edition
editor
editorial

education
educational
effect
effective
efficient
effort
egg
eight
eighteen
eighteenth
eighth
eightieth
eighty
either
elderly
elect
election
electoral
electric
electricity
electronic
elegant
element
eleven
eleventh
eliminate
else
elsewhere
embassy
emerge
emergency
emotion
emotional
emphasis
emphasize
empire
employ
employee
employer
employment
empty
enable
encounter
encourage
end
enemy
energy
enforcement
engage
engine
engineer

engineering
English
enhance
enjoy
enormous
enough
ensure
enter
enterprise
entertain
entertainment
enthusiasm
entire
entirely
entitle
entrance
entry
environment
environmental
equal
equally
equipment
equity
equivalent
era
error
escape
especially
essential
essentially
establish
establishment
estate
estimate
ethnic
European
even
evening
event
eventually
ever
every
everybody
everyone
everything
everywhere
evidence
evil
exact
exactly
examination

Frequent words

examine	fact	fight	foreigner	gang
example	faction	fighter	forest	gap
excellent	factor	figure	forget	garden
except	factory	file	form	gas
exception	fade	fill	formal	gate
excerpt	fail	film	former	gather
excess	failure	final	formula	gay
exchange	fair	finally	forth	gear
exchange rate	fairly	finance	fortieth	gene
exciting	faith	financial	fortune	general
excuse	fall	find	forty	general election
execute	false	fine	forward	generally
executive	familiar	finger	found	generate
exercise	family	finish	foundation	generation
exhaust	famous	fire	founder	generous
exhibition	fan	firm	four	gentle
exile	fancy	first	fourteen	gentleman
exist	fantasy	fiscal	fourteenth	genuine
existence	far	fish	fourth	gesture
existing	fare	fishing	frame	get
expand	farm	fit	fraud	giant
expansion	farmer	five	free	gift
expect	fashion	fix	freedom	girl
expectation	fast	fixed	freeze	give
expense	fat	flag	frequent	given
expensive	fate	flash	fresh	glad
experience	father	flat	Friday	glance
experiment	fault	flavor	friend	glass
expert	favor	flee	friendly	global
explain	favorite	fleet	friendship	go
explanation	fear	flexible	from	goal
explode	feature	flight	front	god
exploit	February	float	fruit	going
explore	federal	flood	frustrate	gold
explosion	federation	floor	fry	golden
export	fee	flow	fuel	golf
expose	feed	flower	fulfill	gone
exposure	feel	fly	full	good
express	feeling	focus	fully	goods
expression	fellow	fold	fun	got
extend	female	folk	function	govern
extensive	fence	follow	fund	government
extent	festival	following	fundamental	governor
extra	few	food	funding	grab
extraordinary	field	fool	funny	grade
extreme	fierce	foot	furniture	gradually
extremely	fifteen	football	further	graduate
eye	fifteenth	for	future	grain
fabric	fifth	force	gain	grand
face	fiftieth	forecast	gallery	grant
facility	fifty	foreign	game	grass

WORD LISTS

Frequent words

grave	helicopter	huge	income	interesting
gray	hell	human	increase	interim
great	hello	human rights	increasingly	interior
green	help	humor	incredible	internal
grip	her	hundred	indeed	international
gross	here	hundredth	independence	Internet
ground	hero	hunt	independent	intervention
group	herself	hunter	index	interview
grow	hi	hurt	indicate	into
growth	hide	husband	indication	introduce
guarantee	high	I	individual	invasion
guard	high school	ice	industrial	invest
guerrilla	highlight	idea	industry	investigate
guess	highly	ideal	inevitable	investment
guest	highway	identify	infect	investor
guide	hill	identity	infection	invitation
guilty	him	if	inflation	invite
guitar	himself	ignore	influence	involve
gun	hint	ill	inform	involved
guy	hip	illegal	information	involvement
habit	hire	illness	ingredient	iron
hair	his	illustrate	initial	Islam
half	historic	illustration	initially	Islamic
hall	historical	image	initiative	island
halt	history	imagination	injured	issue
hand	hit	imagine	injury	IT
handle	hold	immediate	inner	it
hang	holder	immediately	innocent	item
happen	hole	immigrant	inquiry	its
happy	holiday	immigration	inside	itself
harbor	holy	immune	insist	jacket
hard	home	impact	inspect	jail
hardly	homeless	implement	inspector	January
harm	homosexual	implication	install	jazz
hat	honest	imply	instance	jersey
hate	honor	import	instant	Jesus
have	hook	importance	instead	jet
he	hope	important	institute	Jew
head	horror	impose	institution	Jewish
headline	horse	impossible	instruction	job
headquarters	hospital	impress	instrument	join
heal	host	impression	insurance	joint
health	hostage	impressive	integrate	joke
healthy	hot	improve	intellectual	journal
hear	hotel	improvement	intelligence	journalist
hearing	hour	in	intelligent	journey
heart	house	inch	intend	joy
heat	household	incident	intense	judge
heaven	housing	include	intention	judgment
heavy	how	included	interest	juice
height	however	including	interested	July

Frequent words

jump	lawyer	literature	manner	mere
June	lay	little	manufacture	merely
junior	layer	live	manufacturer	merger
jury	lead	live-in	many	mess
just	leader	living	map	message
justice	leadership	load	March	metal
justify	leading	loan	march	method
keen	leaf	lobby	margin	metre
keep	league	local	marine	middle
key	leak	local authority	mark	middle class
kick	lean	location	marked	Middle East
kid	leap	lock	market	midnight
kill	learn	long	marketing	might
killer	lease	long-term	marriage	mild
killing	least	long-time	married	mile
kilometer	leather	look	marry	militant
kind	leave	loose	mask	military
king	lecture	lord	mass	milk
kiss	left	lose	massive	mill
kitchen	leg	loss	master	million
knee	legal	lost	match	millionth
knife	legislation	lot	mate	mind
knock	lend	loud	material	mine
know	length	love	matter	miner
know-how	lens	lovely	maximum	minimum
knowledge	lesbian	lover	May	minister
label	less	low	may	ministry
labor	lesson	lower	maybe	minor
laboratory	let	luck	mayor	minority
lack	let's	lucky	me	minute
lad	letter	lunch	meal	mirror
lady	level	luxury	mean	Miss
lake	liberal	machine	meaning	miss
land	liberate	mad	means	missile
landscape	liberty	made-up	meanwhile	missing
lane	library	magazine	measure	mission
language	license	magic	meat	mistake
lap	lie	mail	mechanism	mix
large	life	main	medal	mixed
largely	lift	mainly	media	mixture
last	light	maintain	medical	mobile
late	like	major	medicine	model
later	likely	majority	medium	moderate
latest	limit	make	meet	modern
Latin	limited	maker	meeting	modest
latter	line	make-up	member	mom
laugh	link	male	membership	moment
laughter	lip	man	memory	Monday
launch	list	manage	mental	monetary
law	listen	management	mention	money
lawsuit	literary	manager	merchant	monitor

WORD LISTS

Frequent words

month	near	note	onto	package
monthly	nearby	noted	open	pact
mood	nearly	nothing	opening	page
moon	neat	notice	opera	pain
moral	necessarily	notion	operate	painful
more	necessary	novel	operation	paint
moreover	neck	November	operator	painting
morning	need	now	opinion	pair
mortgage	negative	nowhere	opponent	palace
most	negotiate	nuclear	opportunity	pale
mostly	negotiation	number	oppose	pan
mother	neighbor	numerous	opposed	panel
motion	neighborhood	nurse	opposite	panic
motivate	neither	object	opposition	paper
motor	nerve	objective	opt	parent
mount	nervous	observe	optimistic	park
mountain	net	observer	option	parliament
mouth	network	obtain	or	parliamentary
move	never	obvious	orange	part
movement	nevertheless	obviously	order	participate
movie	new	occasion	ordinary	particular
Mr.	newly	occasional	organization	particularly
Mrs.	news	occupation	organize	partly
Ms.	news agency	occupy	organized	partner
much	newscaster	occur	organizer	partnership
mum	newspaper	ocean	origin	party
murder	next	o'clock	original	pass
muscle	nice	October	originally	passage
museum	night	odd	other	passenger
music	nightmare	of	otherwise	passion
musical	nine	of course	ought	past
musician	nineteen	off	our	path
Muslim	nineteenth	offense	ourselves	patient
must	ninetieth	offensive	out	pattern
mutual	ninety	offer	outcome	pause
my	ninth	offering	outline	pay
myself	no	office	output	payment
mystery	no one	officer	outside	peace
myth	nobody	official	outstanding	peaceful
name	nod	often	over	peak
narrow	noise	oh	overall	peer
nation	none	oil	overcome	peg
national	nor	okay	overnight	pen
nationalist	normal	old	overseas	penalty
native	normally	Olympic	overwhelming	penny
natural	north	on	owe	pension
naturally	northeast	once	own	people
nature	northern	one	owner	pepper
naval	northwest	one's	ownership	per
navy	nose	online	pace	percent
Nazi	not	only	pack	percentage

Frequent words

perfect
perfectly
perform
performance
perhaps
period
permanent
permission
permit
person
personal
personality
personally
personnel
perspective
persuade
pet
phase
philosophy
phone
photo
photograph
photographer
phrase
physical
pick
pickup
picture
piece
pile
pill
pilot
pin
pink
pipe
pit
pitch
place
plain
plan
plane
planet
planning
plant
plastic
plate
platform
play
player
playoff
pleasant

please
pleased
pleasure
pledge
plenty
plot
plunge
plus
pocket
poem
poet
poetry
point
point of view
pole
police
policeman
police officer
policy
political
politician
politics
poll
pollution
pool
poor
pop
popular
population
port
portrait
pose
position
positive
possibility
possible
possibly
post
pot
potato
potential
pound
pour
poverty
power
powerful
pp.
practical
practice
praise
precisely

predict
prefer
pregnancy
pregnant
premier
premium
preparation
prepare
prepared
presence
present
preserve
presidency
president
presidential
press
pressure
presumably
pretty
prevent
previous
previously
price
pride
priest
primary
prime
prime minister
prince
princess
principal
principle
print
prior
priority
prison
prisoner
private
privatize
prize
probably
problem
procedure
proceed
process
produce
producer
product
production
profession
professional

professor
profile
profit
program
progress
project
prominent
promise
promote
promotion
prompt
proof
proper
properly
property
proportion
proposal
propose
prosecution
prospect
protect
protection
protein
protest
proud
prove
provide
province
provision
provoke
psychological
pub
public
publication
publicity
publish
publisher
publishing
pull
pump
punch
pupil
purchase
pure
purple
purpose
pursue
push
put
qualified
qualify

quality
quantity
quarter
queen
question
quick
quiet
quite
quote
race
racial
racing
radical
radio
rage
raid
rail
railroad
rain
raise
rally
range
rank
rape
rapid
rare
rarely
rate
rather
rating
raw
ray
reach
react
reaction
read
reader
reading
ready
real
real estate
reality
realize
really
rear
reason
reasonable
rebel
recall
receive
recent

WORD LISTS

1615

Frequent words

recently
recession
reckon
recognition
recognize
recommend
recommendation
record
recording
recover
recovery
recruit
red
reduce
reduction
reel
refer
reference
referendum
reflect
reform
refugee
refuse
regard
regime
region
regional
register
regret
regular
regulation
regulator
reject
relate
related
relation
relationship
relative
relatively
relax
release
reliable
relief
religion
religious
reluctant
rely
remain
remaining
remark
remarkable

remember
remind
remote
remove
renew
rent
repair
repeat
replace
replacement
reply
report
reporter
reporting
represent
representative
republic
republican
reputation
request
require
requirement
rescue
research
reserve
resident
resign
resignation
resist
resistance
resolution
resolve
resort
resource
respect
respond
response
responsibility
responsible
rest
restaurant
restore
restriction
result
resume
retail
retain
retire
retirement
retreat
return

reveal
revenue
reverse
review
revolution
revolutionary
reward
rhythm
rice
rich
rid
ride
rider
right
right-wing
ring
riot
rise
risk
rival
river
road
rock
rocket
role
roll
Roman
romantic
roof
room
root
rose
rough
round
route
routine
row
royal
rugby
ruin
rule
ruling
rumor
run
runner
running
rural
rush
sack
sacrifice
sad

safe
safety
sail
saint
sake
salary
sale
salt
same
sample
sanction
sand
satellite
satisfied
Saturday
sauce
save
saving
say
scale
scandal
scene
schedule
scheme
school
science
scientific
scientist
score
scream
screen
script
sea
seal
search
season
seat
second
secret
secretary
secretary-general
Secretary of State
section
sector
secure
security
Security Council
see
seed
seek
seem

segment
seize
select
selection
self
sell
Senate
senator
send
senior
sense
sensible
sensitive
sentence
separate
September
series
serious
seriously
servant
serve
service
session
set
settle
settlement
setup
seven
seventeen
seventeenth
seventh
seventieth
seventy
several
severe
sex
sexual
shade
shadow
shake
shall
shame
shape
shaped
share
shareholder
sharp
she
shed
sheet
shell

WORD LISTS

1616

Frequent words

shelter	skill	source	state	stupid
shift	skin	south	State Department	style
ship	sky	southeast	statement	subject
shirt	sleep	southern	station	subsequent
shock	slice	southwest	statistic	subsidy
shoe	slide	space	status	substance
shoot	slight	spare	stay	substantial
shop	slightly	spark	steady	substitute
shopping	slim	speak	steal	succeed
shore	slip	speaker	steam	success
short	slow	speaking	steel	successful
shortage	small	special	stem	such
shortly	smart	specialist	step	sudden
short-term	smash	specialize	sterling	suddenly
shot	smell	species	stick	suffer
should	smile	specific	still	sufficient
shoulder	smoke	specifically	stimulate	sugar
shout	smoking	spectacular	stir	suggest
show	smooth	speculate	stock	suggestion
shut	snap	speech	stock exchange	suicide
sick	snow	speed	stock market	suit
side	so	spell	stomach	suitable
sigh	so-called	spend	stone	sum
sight	soccer	spin	stop	summer
sign	social	spirit	store	summit
signal	socialist	spiritual	storm	sun
significant	society	spite	story	Sunday
silence	soft	split	straight	super
silent	software	spokesman	strain	superb
silver	soil	spokeswoman	strange	superior
similar	soldier	sponsor	strategic	supply
simple	solicitor	sport	strategy	support
simply	solid	spot	stream	supporter
since	solution	spray	street	suppose
sing	solve	spread	strength	supposed
singer	some	spring	strengthen	supreme
single	somebody	spur	stress	sure
sink	somehow	squad	stretch	surely
sir	someone	square	strict	surface
sister	something	squeeze	strike	surgery
sit	sometimes	stable	striking	surplus
site	somewhat	stadium	string	surprise
situation	somewhere	staff	strip	surprised
six	son	stage	stroke	surprising
sixteen	song	stake	strong	surrender
sixteenth	soon	stamp	structure	surround
sixth	sophisticated	stand	struggle	survey
sixtieth	sorry	standard	student	survival
sixty	sort	star	studio	survive
size	soul	stare	study	suspect
ski	sound	start	stuff	suspend

WORD LISTS

Frequent words

suspicion
sustain
sweep
sweet
swim
swing
switch
symbol
sympathy
symptom
system
table
tackle
tactic
tail
take
takeover
tale
talent
talk
tall
tank
tap
tape
target
task
taste
tax
tea
teach
teacher
teaching
team
tear
technical
technique
technology
teenager
telephone
television
tell
temperature
temple
temporary
ten
tend
tendency
tennis
tension
tenth
term

terrible
territory
terror
terrorism
terrorist
test
testing
text
than
thank
that
the
theater
their
them
theme
themselves
then
theory
therapy
there
therefore
these
they
thick
thin
thing
think
thinking
third
Third World
thirteen
thirteenth
thirtieth
thirty
this
thorough
those
though
thought
thousand
threat
threaten
threatening
three
throat
through
throughout
throw
Thursday
thus

ticket
tide
tie
tight
till
time
tiny
tip
tired
tissue
title
to
today
together
tomorrow
ton
tone
tonight
too
tool
tooth
top
torture
total
touch
tough
tour
tourist
tournament
toward
tower
town
toy
trace
track
trade
trader
tradition
traditional
traffic
tragedy
trail
train
transaction
transfer
transform
transition
transport
transportation
trap
travel

traveler
treasury
treat
treatment
treaty
tree
tremendous
trend
trial
trick
trigger
trip
triumph
troop
trouble
truck
true
truly
trust
truth
try
tube
Tuesday
tune
tunnel
turn
TV
twelfth
twelve
twentieth
twenty
twice
twin
twist
two
type
typical
ultimate
ultimately
U.N.
unable
uncle
under
underground
undermine
understand
understanding
unemployment
unexpected
unfair
unfortunately

unhappy
unidentified
uniform
union
unique
unit
united
United Nations
unity
universe
university
unknown
unless
unlike
unlikely
until
unusual
up
upon
upper
upset
urban
urge
urgent
us
use
used
useful
user
usual
usually
valley
valuable
value
van
variety
various
vary
vast
vegetable
vehicle
venture
venue
verdict
version
very
vessel
veteran
via
vice
victim

Frequent words

victimize
victory
video
view
village
violate
violence
violent
virtually
virus
visible
vision
visit
visitor
vital
vitamin
voice
volume
voluntary
volunteer
vote
voter
vulnerable
wage
wait
wake
walk
wall
Wall Street
want
war
warm
warn
warning
wash
waste
watch
water
wave
way
we
weak
weaken
wealth
weapon
wear
weather
web
website
wedding
Wednesday
week
weekend
weekly
weigh
weight
welcome
welfare
well
well-known
west
western
wet
what
whatever
wheel
when
whenever
where
whereas
whether
which
while
whilst
whip
whisper
white
White House
who
whole
whom
whose
why
wicket
wide
widespread
wife
wild
will
willing
win
wind
window
wine
wing
winner
winning
winter
wipe
wire
wireless
wise
wish
with
withdraw
withdrawal
within
without
witness
woman
wonder
wonderful
wood
wooden
word
work
worker
working
world
world war
worldwide
worried
worry
worth
would
wound
wrap
write
writer
writing
written
wrong
yacht
yard
yeah
year
yellow
yen
yes
yesterday
yet
yield
you
young
youngster
your
yours
yourself
youth
zone

Academic Word List

This list contains the headwords of the families in the Academic Word List. The numbers indicate the sublist of the Academic Word List, with sublist 1 containing the most frequent words, sublist 2 the next most frequent, and so on. For example, *abandon* and its family members are in sublist 8. The Academic Word List was created by Averil Coxhead and you can find out more about it here: www.victoria.ac.nz/lals/resources/academicwordlist

Word	Sublist	Word	Sublist	Word	Sublist
abandon	8	assign	6	commit	4
abstract	6	assist	2	commodity	8
academy	5	assume	1	communicate	4
access	4	assure	9	community	2
accommodate	9	attach	6	compatible	9
accompany	8	attain	9	compensate	3
accumulate	8	attitude	4	compile	10
accurate	6	attribute	4	complement	8
achieve	2	author	6	complex	2
acknowledge	6	authority	1	component	3
acquire	2	automate	8	compound	5
adapt	7	available	1	comprehensive	7
adequate	4	aware	5	comprise	7
adjacent	10	behalf	9	compute	2
adjust	5	benefit	1	conceive	10
administrate	2	bias	8	concentrate	4
adult	7	bond	6	concept	1
advocate	7	brief	6	conclude	2
affect	2	bulk	9	concurrent	9
aggregate	6	capable	6	conduct	2
aid	7	capacity	5	confer	4
albeit	10	category	2	confine	9
allocate	6	cease	9	confirm	7
alter	5	challenge	5	conflict	5
alternative	3	channel	7	conform	8
ambiguous	8	chapter	2	consent	3
amend	5	chart	8	consequent	2
analogy	9	chemical	7	considerable	3
analyze	1	circumstance	3	consist	1
annual	4	cite	6	constant	3
anticipate	9	civil	4	constitute	1
apparent	4	clarify	8	constrain	3
append	8	classic	7	construct	2
appreciate	8	clause	5	consult	5
approach	1	code	4	consume	2
appropriate	2	coherent	9	contact	5
approximate	4	coincide	9	contemporary	8
arbitrary	8	collapse	10	context	1
area	1	colleague	10	contract	1
aspect	2	commence	9	contradict	8
assemble	10	comment	3	contrary	7
assess	1	commission	2	contrast	4

Academic Word List

contribute	3	domestic	4	fee	6
controversy	9	dominate	3	file	7
convene	3	draft	5	final	2
converse	9	drama	8	finance	1
convert	7	duration	9	finite	7
convince	10	dynamic	7	flexible	6
cooperate	6	economy	1	fluctuate	8
coordinate	3	edit	6	focus	2
core	3	element	2	format	9
corporate	3	eliminate	7	formula	1
correspond	3	emerge	4	forthcoming	10
couple	7	emphasis	3	foundation	7
create	1	empirical	7	found	9
credit	2	enable	5	framework	3
criteria	3	encounter	10	function	1
crucial	8	energy	5	fund	3
culture	2	enforce	5	fundamental	5
currency	8	enhance	6	furthermore	6
cycle	4	enormous	10	gender	6
data	1	ensure	3	generate	5
debate	4	entity	5	generation	5
decade	7	environment	1	globe	7
decline	5	equate	2	goal	4
deduce	3	equip	7	grade	7
define	1	equivalent	5	grant	4
definite	7	erode	9	guarantee	7
demonstrate	3	error	4	guideline	8
denote	8	establish	1	hence	4
deny	7	estate	6	hierarchy	7
depress	10	estimate	1	highlight	8
derive	1	ethic	9	hypothesis	4
design	2	ethnic	4	identical	7
despite	4	evaluate	2	identify	1
detect	8	eventual	8	ideology	7
deviate	8	evident	1	ignorance	6
device	9	evolve	5	illustrate	3
devote	9	exceed	6	image	5
differentiate	7	exclude	3	immigrate	3
dimension	4	exhibit	8	impact	2
diminish	9	expand	5	implement	4
discrete	5	expert	6	implicate	4
discriminate	6	explicit	6	implicit	8
displace	8	exploit	8	imply	3
display	6	export	1	impose	4
dispose	7	expose	5	incentive	6
distinct	2	external	5	incidence	6
distort	9	extract	7	incline	10
distribute	1	facilitate	5	income	1
diverse	6	factor	1	incorporate	6
document	3	feature	2	index	6
domain	6	federal	6	indicate	1

Academic Word List

Word		Word		Word	
individual	1	locate	3	overlap	9
induce	8	logic	5	overseas	6
inevitable	8	maintain	2	panel	10
infer	7	major	1	paradigm	7
infrastructure	8	manipulate	8	paragraph	8
inherent	9	manual	9	parallel	4
inhibit	6	margin	5	parameter	4
initial	3	mature	9	participate	2
initiate	6	maximize	3	partner	3
injure	2	mechanism	4	passive	9
innovate	7	media	7	perceive	2
input	6	mediate	9	percent	1
insert	7	medical	5	period	1
insight	9	medium	9	persist	10
inspect	8	mental	5	perspective	5
instance	3	method	1	phase	4
institute	2	migrate	6	phenomenon	7
instruct	6	military	9	philosophy	3
integral	9	minimal	9	physical	3
integrate	4	minimize	8	plus	8
integrity	10	minimum	6	policy	1
intelligence	6	ministry	6	portion	9
intense	8	minor	3	pose	10
interact	3	mode	7	positive	2
intermediate	9	modify	5	potential	2
internal	4	monitor	5	practitioner	8
interpret	1	motive	6	precede	6
interval	6	mutual	9	precise	5
intervene	7	negate	3	predict	4
intrinsic	10	network	5	predominant	8
invest	2	neutral	6	preliminary	9
investigate	4	nevertheless	6	presume	6
invoke	10	nonetheless	10	previous	2
involve	1	norm	9	primary	2
isolate	7	normal	2	prime	5
issue	1	notion	5	principal	4
item	2	notwithstanding	10	principle	1
job	4	nuclear	8	prior	4
journal	2	objective	5	priority	7
justify	3	obtain	2	proceed	1
label	4	obvious	4	process	1
labor	1	occupy	4	professional	4
layer	3	occur	1	prohibit	7
lecture	6	odd	10	project	4
legal	1	offset	8	promote	4
legislate	1	ongoing	10	proportion	3
levy	10	option	4	prospect	8
liberal	5	orient	5	protocol	9
license	5	outcome	3	psychology	5
likewise	10	output	4	publication	7
link	3	overall	4	publish	3

Academic Word List

purchase	2	section	1	team	9
pursue	5	sector	1	technical	3
qualitative	9	secure	2	technique	3
quote	7	seek	2	technology	3
radical	8	select	2	temporary	9
random	8	sequence	3	tense	8
range	2	series	4	terminate	8
ratio	5	sex	3	text	2
rational	6	shift	3	theme	8
react	3	significant	1	theory	1
recover	6	similar	1	thereby	8
refine	9	simulate	7	thesis	7
regime	4	site	2	topic	7
region	2	so-called	10	trace	6
register	3	sole	7	tradition	2
regulate	2	somewhat	7	transfer	2
reinforce	8	source	1	transform	6
reject	5	specific	1	transit	5
relax	9	specify	3	transmit	7
release	7	sphere	9	transport	6
relevant	2	stable	5	trend	5
reluctance	10	statistic	4	trigger	9
rely	3	status	4	ultimate	7
remove	3	straightforward	10	undergo	10
require	1	strategy	2	underlie	6
research	1	stress	4	undertake	4
reside	2	structure	1	uniform	8
resolve	4	style	5	unify	9
resource	2	submit	7	unique	7
respond	1	subordinate	9	utilize	6
restore	8	subsequent	4	valid	3
restrain	9	subsidy	6	vary	1
restrict	2	substitute	5	vehicle	8
retain	4	successor	7	version	5
reveal	6	sufficient	3	via	8
revenue	5	sum	4	violate	9
reverse	7	summary	4	virtual	8
revise	8	supplement	9	visible	7
revolution	9	survey	2	vision	9
rigid	9	survive	7	visual	8
role	1	suspend	9	volume	3
route	9	sustain	5	voluntary	7
scenario	9	symbol	5	welfare	5
schedule	8	tape	6	whereas	5
scheme	3	target	5	whereby	10
scope	6	task	3	widespread	8

Credits

Credits

Illustrations:

Visual Dictionary supplement

PAGE	CREDIT
11	(flower) BlueRingMedia
12	(compass points) attaphong; (continents) Cienpies Design; (greenhouse effect) Daulon
13	(volcano) Natsmith1; (water cycle) Anna L. e Marina Durant
14	(digestive system) Christos Georghiou; (ear) Alexander_P; (eye) Tefi
15	(heart) BlueRingMedia; (organs) ksenvitaln; (respiratory system) Pawel Graczyk
16	(skeleton) GraphicsRF; (teeth) udaix

Photographs:

All images from Shutterstock.com.